Encyclopædia
of
Religion and Ethics

Encyclopædia of Religion and Ethics

EDITED BY

JAMES HASTINGS

WITH THE ASSISTANCE OF

JOHN A. SELBIE, M.A., D.D.

PROFESSOR OF OLD TESTAMENT LANGUAGE AND LITERATURE IN THE UNITED FREE CHURCH COLLEGE, ABERDEEN

AND

LOUIS H. GRAY, M.A., Ph.D.

SOMETIME FELLOW IN INDO-IRANIAN LANGUAGES IN COLUMBIA UNIVERSITY, NEW YORK

VOLUME XI

SACRIFICE—SUDRA

EDINBURGH: T. & T. CLARK, 38 GEORGE STREET

NEW YORK: CHARLES SCRIBNER'S SONS, 153–157 FIFTH AVENUE

1920

Printed by Morrison & Gibb Limited

FOR

T. & T. CLARK, EDINBURGH

LONDON: SIMPKIN, MARSHALL, HAMILTON, KENT, AND CO. LIMITED

NEW YORK: CHARLES SCRIBNER'S SONS

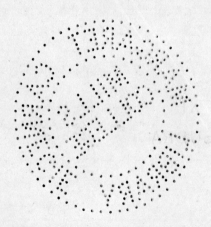

AUTHORS OF ARTICLES IN THIS VOLUME

BELSON (JOSHUA), M.A., D.Lit. (London).
Rabbi, Cardiff; author of *Immanence of God in Rabbinical Literature, Jewish Mysticism, Maimonides on the Jewish Creed.*
Saints and Martyrs (Jewish), **Shammai, Slavery** (Jewish).

ABRAHAMS (ISRAEL), M.A. (Lond. and Camb.), D.D. (Heb. Union Coll., Cincin.).
Reader in Talmudic and Rabbinic Literature in the University of Cambridge; formerly Senior Tutor in the Jews' College, London; editor of the *Jewish Quarterly Review*, 1888–1908.
Sanhedrin, Sects (Jewish).

AGATE (LEONARD DENDY), M.A. (Camb. and Manchester).
Late Curate of Warton, Carnforth; author of *Luther and the Reformation.*
Slavery (Christian).

ALEXANDER (ARCHIBALD BROWNING DRYSDALE), M.A., D.D. (Glas.).
Minister of the United Free Church at Langbank; formerly Lecturer on Ethics and present Assessor to Chair of Ethics and Practical Theology in the United Free Church College, Glasgow; author of *A Short History of Philosophy*, and other works.
Seven Deadly Sins, Seven Virtues.

ALEXANDER (HARTLEY BURR), Ph.D.
Professor of Philosophy in the University of Nebraska; author of vol. x. (*North American*) of *The Mythology of All Races* (1916).
Secret Societies (American), **Sin** (American), **Soul** (Primitive).

AMES (EDWARD SCRIBNER), B.D., Ph.D.
Associate Professor of Philosophy in the University of Chicago; Minister of Hyde Park Church of Disciples, Chicago; author of *The Psychology of Religious Experience*, and other works.
Shame.

ANWYL (Sir EDWARD), M.A. (Oxon.).
Late Professor of Welsh and Comparative Philology, and Dean of the Faculty of Arts, in the University College of Wales, Aberystwyth; author of *Celtic Religion.*
Sacrifice (Celtic).

ARMITAGE-SMITH (GEORGE), D.Lit., M.A.
Principal of Birkbeck College, London, 1896–1918; Dean of the Faculty of Economics in the University of London, 1904–08; Fellow of the Royal Statistical Society; Member of Council of the Royal Economic Society; Lecturer on Economics and Mental Science at Birkbeck College; author of *The Citizen of England* (1895); *The Free Trade Movement* (1898); *Principles and Methods of Taxation* (1906), and other works.
Strikes.

ARNOLD (EDWARD VERNON), Litt.D.
Professor of Latin in the University College of North Wales.
Stoics.

ARNOLD (THOMAS WALKER), C.I.E., Litt.D., M.A.
Professor of Arabic, University of London, University College; author of *The Preaching of Islam*; English editor of *The Encyclopædia of Islām.*
Saints and Martyrs (Muhammadan in India).

ASTON (WILLIAM GEORGE), M.A., D.Litt., C.M.G.
Late Japanese Secretary of H.M. Legation, Tokyo; author of *History of Japanese Literature, Shinto.*
Shinto.

BAIKIE (JAMES).
Fellow of the Royal Astronomical Society; Minister of the United Free Church at Edinburgh; author of *Lands and Peoples of the Bible* (1914).
Sphinx.

BALCH (ALFRED ERNEST), M.A. (Lond.).
Wesleyan Minister; Member of the Probationers' Board of Examiners, Examiner in Literature and Philosophy; author of *An Introduction to the Study of Christian Ethics*, and other works.
Self-sacrifice.

BALL (JAMES DYER), I.S.O., M.R.A.S., M. Ch. Br. R.A.S.
Late of the Hongkong Civil Service; author of *Things Chinese, The Chinese at Home*, and other works; Director L.M.S.
Sin (Chinese).

BARNS (THOMAS), M.A. (Oxon.).
Vicar of Hilderstone, Staffordshire.
Shrove-tide.

BARTON (GEORGE AARON), A.M., Ph.D., LL.D.
Professor of Biblical Literature and Semitic Languages in Bryn Mawr College, Pennsylvania; author of *A Sketch of Semitic Origins*, 'Ecclesiastes' in the *International Critical Commentary*, *The Origin and Development of Babylonian Writing*, *Archæology and the Bible*.
Saints and Martyrs (Semitic and Egyptian), **Salutations, Semites, Sodomy, Soul** (Semitic and Egyptian), **Stones** (Semitic).

BENNETT (WILLIAM HENRY), M.A. (Lond.), D.D. (Aberd.), Litt.D. (Camb.).
Principal of Lancashire College, Manchester; sometime Fellow of St. John's College, Cambridge; author of *The Religion of the Post-Exilic Prophets*, and other works.
Shewbread, Sin (Hebrew and Jewish).

BLACKMAN (AYLWARD MANLEY), D.Litt.
Late Laycock Student of Egyptology at Worcester College, Oxford; Oxford University Nubian Research Scholar, 1910; formerly Scholar of Queen's College.
Salvation (Egyptian), **Sin** (Egyptian).

DE BOER (TJITZE), Philos. Dr.
Professor of Philosophy in the University of Amsterdam.
Soul (Muslim).

BOOTH (W. BRAMWELL).
General of the Salvation Army.
Salvation Army.

BOX (GEORGE HERBERT), M.A., D.D.
Professor of Hebrew and Old Testament Exegesis, King's College, London; Hon. Canon of St. Albans; author of *The Book of Isaiah translated in accordance with the results of Modern Criticism* (1908), *The Ezra Apocalypse* (1912), *The Virgin Birth of Jesus* (1916), *The Gospel according to St. Matthew*, revised ed. ('Century Bible,' 1920).
Sadducees.

BURNET (JOHN), F.B.A., M.A. (Oxon.), LL.D. (Edin.), Ph.D. (Prague).
Professor of Greek in the United College of St. Salvator and St. Leonard, St. Andrews; Hon. Fellow of Merton College, Oxford; author of *Early Greek Philosophy* (1892); editor of *Platonis Opera* (1899–1907), and other works.
Sceptics, Socrates, Soul (Greek).

BURNS (CECIL DELISLE), M.A. (Camb.).
Author of *Political Ideals*, *The Morality of Nations*, *The World of States*, *Greek Ideals*, *International Politics*.
State.

CABATON (ANTOINE).
Professeur à l'École des Langues orientales vivantes et à l'École Coloniale, Paris; Ancien Membre de l'École Française d'Extrême-Orient.
Siam.

CALDWELL (WILLIAM), M.A., D.Sc.
Sir William Macdonald Professor of Philosophy in McGill University, Montreal.
Self-respect.

CAMPBELL (LEWIS), LL.D.
Late Professor of Greek in the University of St. Andrews; author of *Religion in Greek Literature*, and other works.
Sophocles.

CASARTELLI (LOUIS CHARLES), M.A. (Lond.), D.D. and D.Litt. Or. (Louvain), M.R.A.S.
Bishop of Salford; Lecturer on Iranian Languages and Literature in the University of Manchester; formerly Professor of Zend and Pahlavi in the University of Louvain.
Saints and Martyrs (Iranian), **Salvation** (Iranian), **Sasanians, Sin** (Iranian), **Soul** (Iranian), **State of the Dead** (Iranian).

CASE (SHIRLEY JACKSON), M.A., Ph.D., D.D.
Professor of Early Church History and New Testament Interpretation in the University of Chicago; managing editor of the *American Journal of Theology*; author of *The Historicity of Jesus*, *The Evolution of Early Christianity*, *The Millennial Hope*, *The Revelation of John*.
Second Adventism.

CLOW (WILLIAM MACCALLUM), M.A., D.D.
Professor of Christian Ethics and Practical Training in the United Free Church College, Glasgow.
Socinianism.

COATS (ROBERT HAY), M.A., B.D. (Glas.), B.A. (Oxon.).
Minister of the Baptist Church at Handsworth, Birmingham; author of *Types of English Piety*, *The Realm of Prayer*.
Sanctification.

COWAN (HENRY), M.A. (Edin.), D.D. (Aberd.), D.Th. (Gen.), D.C.L. (Dunelm).
Professor of Church History in the University of Aberdeen; Senior Preacher of the University Chapel; author of *The Influence of the Scottish Church in Christendom*, *John Knox*, *Landmarks of Church History*.
Stigmata.

CRAIGIE (WILLIAM ALEXANDER), M.A. (Oxon.), M.A., LL.D. (St. Andrews).
Rawlinson and Bosworth Professor of Anglo-Saxon in the University of Oxford; Fellow of Oriel College; co-editor of the *Oxford English Dictionary*.
State of the Dead (Teutonic).

CROOKE (WILLIAM), B.A., D.Sc.
Ex-Scholar of Trinity College, Dublin; Fellow of the Royal Anthropological Institute; President of the Anthropological Section of the British Association, 1910; President of the Folklore Society, 1911–12; late of the Bengal Civil Service.
Sagar, Saints and Martyrs (Indian), **St. Thomas's Mount, Sakhi Sarwar, Saliva, Sannyasi, Sansi, Santal, Sarasvati, Savaras, Sects** (Hindu), **Seringapatam, Serpent-worship** (Indian), **Sind, Somnath, Stones** (Indian), **Sudra.**

CZAPLICKA (MARIE ANTOINETTE), F.R.A.I., F.R.G.S.
Somerville College and Lady Margaret Hall, Oxford; Mianowski Travelling Scholar, Warsaw; Diplomée in Anthropology, Oxford; Mary Ewart Lecturer in Ethnology to the Committee of Anthropology, University of Oxford; author of *Aboriginal Siberia*, *My Siberian Year*.
Samoyed, Siberia, Slavs.

DAVIDS (T. W. RHYS), LL.D., Ph.D., D.Sc., F.B.A.
Formerly Professor of Comparative Religion, Manchester; President of the Pāli Text Society; author of *Buddhism* (1878), *Questions of King Milinda* (1890–94), *American Lectures on Buddhism* (1896), *Buddhist India* (1902), *Early Buddhism* (1908), *Dialogues of the Buddha* (1899, 1910).
Sects (Buddhist), **Sin** (Buddhist).

DAVIDS (MRS. RHYS), M.A.
Formerly Lecturer on Indian Philosophy in the University of Manchester; Fellow of University College, London; author of *Buddhist Psychological Ethics* (1900), *Psalms of the Early Buddhists* (1909, 1913), *Buddhism* (1912), *Buddhist Psychology* (1914), *Kindred Sayings* (1917), and other works.
Sacrifice (Buddhist), **Salvation** (Buddhist), **Samadhi, Sasana, Self** (Buddhist), **Sin** (Buddhist), **Soul** (Buddhist).

DAVIDSON (WILLIAM LESLIE), M.A., LL.D.
Professor of Logic and Metaphysics in the University of Aberdeen; author of *The Logic of Definition, Theism as Grounded in Human Nature, The Stoic Creed, Political Thought in England: the Utilitarians from Bentham to J. S. Mill.*
Scottish Philosophy.

DAVIES (HENRY), B.D., Ph.D. (Yale).
Rector of Christ Church, Easton, Maryland, U.S.A.
Sentiment.

EDWARDS (EDWARD), B.A. (Wales and Cantab.), M.R.A.S.
Member of the Board of Archæology and the Board of Oriental Studies, and Examiner in Persian to the University of London; Assistant in the Department of Oriental Printed Books and Manuscripts in the British Museum.
Sacrifice (Iranian), **Sects** (Zoroastrian).

EHRHARDT (CHRISTIAN EUGÈNE).
Professeur honoraire de l'Université de Paris; Professeur à la Faculté de Théologie protestante de l'Université de Strasbourg.
Solidarity.

ELLIOT (HUGH).
Editor of the *Annual Register*; author of *Modern Science and the Illusions of Professor Bergson* (1912), *Herbert Spencer* (1917), and other works.
Spencer (Herbert).

FARNELL (LEWIS RICHARD), M.A., D.Litt. (Oxford), Hon. D.Litt. (Geneva and Dublin), Hon. LL.D. (St. Andrews), F.R.A.S., F.B.A.
Rector of Exeter College, Oxford; University Lecturer in Classical Archæology; formerly Hibbert Lecturer and Wilde Lecturer in Natural and Comparative Religion; author of *The Cults of the Greek States* (1896–1909), *The Evolution of Religion* (1905), *Higher Aspects of Greek Religion* (1911), *Greece and Babylon* (1911).
Sacrifice (Greek).

FARQUHAR (JOHN NICOL), M.A., D.Litt. (Oxon.).
Literary Secretary of the Young Men's Christian Association in India; author of *Gita and Gospel, A Primer of Hinduism, The Crown of Hinduism, Modern Religious Movements in India.*
Sadharana Brahma Samaj, Soul (Hindu).

FIGGIS (J. NEVILLE), D.D.
Late of the Community of the Resurrection, Mirfield; Hon. Fellow of St. Catharine's College, Cambridge; author of *Hopes for English Religion*, and other works.
Societas Perfecta.

FLEET (JOHN FAITHFULL), C.I.E.
Late Epigraphist to the Government of India, and Commissioner of Customs in the Bombay Presidency; author of *Pali Sanskrit and Old Canarese Transcriptions*, and other works.
Saka Era.

FOAKES-JACKSON (FREDERICK JOHN), D.D.
Fellow of Jesus College, Cambridge, and Hon. Canon of Peterborough Cathedral; Briggs Graduate Professor of Christian Institutions at Union Theological Seminary, New York; author of *The History of the Christian Church to A.D. 461, A Bible History of the Hebrews*, and other works; co-editor of *Christian Origins.*
Semi-Arianism.

FOUCART (GEORGE B.).
Directeur de l'Institut Français d'Archéologie Orientale du Caire; Professeur d'Histoire des Religions à l'Université d'Aix-Marseille; Ancien Inspecteur en chef du Service des Antiquités de l'Égypte; auteur de *Histoire des Religions et Méthode Comparative*² (1912).
Sky and Sky-gods; Storm, Storm-gods.

FOWLER (WILLIAM WARDE), M.A., Hon. D.Litt. (Manchester), Hon. LL.D. (Edin.).
Fellow and Late Subrector of Lincoln College, Oxford; Gifford Lecturer in Edinburgh University (1909–10).
Soul (Roman).

FRANKS (ROBERT SLEIGHTHOLME), M.A., D.Litt.
Principal of the Western College, Bristol; author of *The New Testament Doctrines of Man, Sin, and Salvation* (1908), *A History of the Doctrine of the Work of Christ* (1918).
Satisfaction.

FRAZER (ROBERT WATSON), LL.B., C.E., I.C.S. (retired).
Lecturer in Tamil and Telugu, University College, London; formerly Principal Librarian, London Institution; author of *A Literary History of India, Indian Thought Past and Present.*
Saivism, Sati.

FULFORD (HENRY WILLIAM), M.A.
Fellow of Clare College, Cambridge, and Rector of Crowmarsh, Oxon.
Schism.

FYFFE (DAVID), M.A. (Edin.).
Minister of the Presbyterian Church at Newcastle; Lecturer at Armstrong College, Newcastle; author of *Essential Beliefs of Christianity.*
Spirituality.

GARBE (RICHARD), Ph.D.
Professor des Sanskrit und der allgemeinen Religionsgeschichte an der Universität zu Tübingen.
Sankhya.

GARDNER (ALICE), F.R.Hist.S.
Lecturer and Associate of Newnham College, Cambridge; author of *Julian, Philosopher and Emperor; Theodore of Studium.*
Self-consciousness.

GARDNER (EDMUND G.), M.A., Litt.D.
Barlow Lecturer on Dante, University College, London; author of *Dante's Ten Heavens, Dukes and Poets in Ferrara, Saint Catherine of Siena, Dante and the Mystics.*
Savonarola.

GARDNER (PERCY), Litt.D., LL.D., F.S.A.
Professor of Classical Archæology in the University of Oxford; Vice-President of the Hellenic Society; author of *Exploratio Evangelica* (1899), *Principles of Greek Art* (1913), and other works.
Stones (Greek and Roman).

GARVIE (ALFRED ERNEST), M.A. (Oxford), D.D. (Glas.).
Principal of New College, London; author of *The Ritschlian Theology, Studies in the Inner Life of Jesus, Studies of Paul and his Gospel*, and other works.
Sovereignty (Divine).

GASTER (MOSES), Ph.D.
Chief Rabbi, Spanish and Portuguese Congregations, London; formerly President of the Folklore Society; Vice-President of the Royal Asiatic Society.
Sacrifice (Jewish).

GEDEN (ALFRED S.), M.A. (Oxon.), D.D. (Aberd.).
Formerly Professor of Old Testament Languages and Literature and of Comparative Religion in the Wesleyan College, Richmond, Surrey; author of *Studies in the Religions of the East, Introduction to the Hebrew Bible, Comparative Religion*; translator of Deussen's *Philosophy of the Upanishads.*
Salvation (Hindu).

GHATE (VINAYAK SAKHARAM), M.A. (Bombay), B.A. (Camb.), Docteur-ès-Lettres (Paris).
Late Professor of Sanskrit in Elphinstone College, Bombay; author of *Lectures on Rigveda, Le Vedānta, étude sur les Brahmasūtras et leurs cinq commentaires.*
Sankaracharya.

GILBERTSON (ALBERT NICOLAY), M.A. (Minn.), S.T.M. (Harvard), Ph.D. (Clark).
Rector of St. Luke's Church, Malden, Mass.; formerly Fellow and Lecturer in Anthropology, Clark University, and Instructor in Anthropology, University of Minnesota.
Slavery (Primitive).

GRASS (KARL KONRAD), Dr.Theol.
Formerly Professor of New Testament Exegesis in the Imperatorskij Jurjevskij University, Dorpat, Esthonian Republic; Counsellor of State.
Sects (Russian).

GRIERSON (Sir GEORGE ABRAHAM), K.C.I.E., Ph.D. (Halle), D.Litt. (Dublin), I.C.S. (retired).
Fellow of the British Academy; Honorary Member of the American Oriental Society; Honorary Fellow of the Asiatic Society of Bengal; Foreign Associate Member of the Société Asiatique de Paris; Hon. Secretary of the Royal Asiatic Society; Superintendent of the Linguistic Survey of India.
Sadhs, Sadhan-Panthis, Sadhu, Sakhi-Bhavas, Satnamis, Saurapatas, Senapanthis, Shins, Siva-Narayanis.

GUIDI (IGNAZIO).
Senatore del Regno, Rome.
Seven Sleepers.

HALDANE (ELIZABETH SANDERSON), C.H., LL.D.
Author of *The Life of James Ferrier* (1899), *Life of Descartes* (1905); joint-translator of *Hegel's History of Philosophy* (1892), and *The Philosophical Works of Descartes* (1911–12).
Schopenhauer.

HALL (GEORGE NOEL LANKESTER), M.A.
Vice-Principal of Ely Theological College; formerly Scholar of St. John's College, Cambridge.
Simon Magus.

HALL (H. R.), M.A., D.Litt., F.S.A.
Assistant-Keeper of Egyptian and Assyrian Antiquities in the British Museum.
Scarabs.

HAMILTON-GRIERSON (Sir PHILIP JAMES, Kt.), B.A., LL.D.
Fellow of the Society of Scottish Antiquaries; Fellow of the Royal Anthropological Institute; Solicitor for Scotland to the Board of Inland Revenue.
Strangers.

HARRIS (CHARLES), D.D. (Oxon.).
Rector of Colwall; Examining Chaplain to the Bishop of Llandaff; formerly Lecturer in Theology, St. David's College, Lampeter.
State of the Dead (Christian).

HARRISON (JANE ELLEN), LL.D. (Aberd.), D.Litt. (Durham).
Staff Lecturer and sometime Fellow of Newnham College, Cambridge; author of *The Religion of Ancient Greece* (1905), *Prolegomena to the Study of Greek Religion* (1907), *Themis: a Study of the Social Origins of Greek Religion* (1912).
Satyrs, Silenoi.

HARTLAND (EDWIN SIDNEY), LL.D., F.S.A.
President of the Folklore Society, 1899; President of the Anthropological Section of the British Association, 1906; President of Section I (Religions of the Lower Culture) at the Oxford International Congress for the History of Religions, 1908; author of *The Legend of Perseus, Primitive Paternity, Ritual and Belief.*
Satanism, Sin-eating, Stones (Introductory and Primitive).

HICKS (ROBERT DREW), M.A.
Fellow and formerly Classical Lecturer of Trinity College, Cambridge.
Sophists.

HOBHOUSE (LEONARD TRELAWNY), M.A. (Oxon.), D.Litt. (Durham), LL.D. (St. Andrews).
Martin White Professor of Sociology in the University of London; author of *Mind in Evolution, Morals in Evolution*, and other works.
Sociology.

HOERNLÉ (REINHOLD FRIEDRICH ALFRED), M.A., B.Sc. (Oxon.).
Professor of Philosophy, Armstrong College, in the University of Durham.
Solipsism.

HOPE (JOHN MAURICE VAIZEY), M.A. (Cantab. et Oxon.).
Lecturer, in Moral Philosophy, of Clare College; sometime Scholar of Trinity College, Cambridge; late Fellow of St. Augustine's College, Canterbury.
Slander.

HOPKINS (EDWARD WASHBURN), Ph.D., LL.D.
Professor of Sanskrit and Comparative Philology in Yale University; former President of the American Oriental Society; author of *The Religions of India, The Great Epic of India, India Old and New, Epic Mythology.*
Soma.

HOYLE (RICHARD BIRCH), A.T.S.
Ward Scholar and Davies Semitic Prizeman in Regent's Park College, London.
Spirit (Holy).

HYAMSON (ALBERT MONTEFIORE), F.R.Hist.S.
Corresponding Member of the American Jewish Historical Society; Member of Council of the Jewish Historical Society of England; author of *A History of the Jews in England.*
Sambatyon.

HYSLOP (JAMES HERVEY), Ph.D., LL.D.
Secretary of the American Society for Psychical Research; formerly Professor of Logic and Ethics in Columbia University.
Sense, Sensibility, Spontaneity.

JAMES (EDWIN OLIVER), B.Sc., B.Litt. (Oxon.), F.C.S. (Lond.).
Vicar of St. Peter's, Limehouse; Fellow of the Royal Anthropological Institute; Member of Council of the Folklore Society; Secretary of the Anthropological Section of the British Association; author of *Primitive Ritual and Belief, An Introduction to Anthropology*, and other works.
Sacrifice (Introductory and Primitive), **Sieve, Smoking, Staff.**

JOLLY (JULIUS), Ph.D. (Munich), Hon. M.D. (Göttingen), Hon. D.Litt. (Oxford).
Ord. Professor of Sanskrit and Comparative Philology in the University of Würzburg; formerly Tagore Professor of Law in the University of Calcutta; Geheimer Hofrat.
Slavery (Hindu), **Stupa.**

JONES (EMILY ELIZABETH CONSTANCE), Hon. D.Litt. (Wales).
Formerly Mistress of Girton College, Cambridge; Member of Council of Bristol University; author of *Primer of Logic, A New Law of Thought*, and other works.
Sidgwick (Henry).

JONES (RUFUS M.), M.A., D.Litt.
Professor of Philosophy in Haverford College, Haverford, Pennsylvania; author of *Social Law in the Spiritual World* (1904), *Studies in Mystical Religion* (1909), *Spiritual Reformers* (1914), *The Inner Life* (1916).
Seekers, Silence.

JOSEPH (MORRIS).
Senior Minister of the West London Synagogue; author of *Judaism as Creed and Life* (1910).
Salvation (Jewish).

KEITH (ARTHUR BERRIEDALE), D.C.L., D.Litt.
Barrister-at-Law; Regius Professor of Sanskrit and Comparative Philology in the University of Edinburgh.
Sin (Hindu), **State of the Dead** (Hindu).

KELLETT (ERNEST EDWARD), M.A.
Assistant Master at the Leys School, Cambridge; formerly Scholar of Wadham College, Oxford.
Spinoza.

KILPATRICK (THOMAS B.), M.A., B.D., D.D.
Professor of Systematic Theology in Knox College, Toronto; author of the articles 'Conscience' and 'Philosophy' in the *Dictionary of the Bible*, and of 'Character of Christ' and 'Incarnation' in the *Dictionary of Christ and the Gospels.*
Salvation (Christian), **Soteriology.**

LANCHESTER (HENRY CRAVEN ORD), M.A.
Rector of Framlingham with Saxtead; sometime Fellow of Pembroke College, Cambridge.
Sibylline Oracles.

LANGDON (STEPHEN HERBERT), M.A., B.D., Ph.D.
Professor of Assyriology and Comparative Semitic Philology in the University of Oxford; Member of Council of the Royal Asiatic Society; author of *Neo-Babylonian Royal Inscriptions* (V.A.B. vol. iv.), *Sumerian and Babylonian Psalms, A Sumerian Grammar, Babylonian Liturgies.*
Sin (Babylonian).

LAWLOR (HUGH JACKSON), D.D., Litt.D.
Beresford Professor of Ecclesiastical History in the University of Dublin; Canon and Precentor of St. Patrick's Cathedral, Dublin; Sub-Dean of the Chapel Royal, Dublin.
Samosatenism.

LAWSON (ALEXANDER), M.A., B.D., D.D.
Formerly Berry Professor of English Literature in the University of St. Andrews.
Solemn League and Covenant.

LINDSAY (JAMES), M.A., B.Sc., D.D., F.R.S.L., F.R.S.E., F.G.S., M.R.A.S.
Author of *A Philosophical System of Theistic Idealism, Studies in European Philosophy, Recent Advances in Theistic Philosophy of Religion, The Fundamental Problems of Metaphysics.*
Substance.

MACALISTER (ROBERT ALEXANDER STEWART), Litt.D., F.S.A.
Professor of Celtic Archæology in University College, Dublin; formerly Director of Excavations of the Palestine Exploration Fund; author of *A History of Civilization in Palestine* (1912), *The Excavation of Gezer* (1912).
Sacrifice (Semitic), **Stone Monuments** (Rude).

MACCULLOCH (JOHN ARNOTT), Hon. D.D. (St. Andrews).
Rector of St. Saviour's, Bridge of Allan; Hon. Canon of the Cathedral of the Holy Spirit, Cumbrae; Examiner in Comparative Religion and Philosophy of Religion, Victoria University, Manchester; Examining Chaplain to the Bishop of St. Andrews; author of *The Religion of the Ancient Celts.*
Sacrifice (Celtic), **Secret Societies** (Introductory, Melanesian and Polynesian), **Serpent-worship** (Introductory and Primitive), **Shamanism, Shoes and Sandals, Sin** (Celtic), **State of the Dead** (Primitive and Savage).

McIntyre (James Lewis), M.A. (Edin. and Oxon.), D.Sc. (Edin.).
Anderson Lecturer in Comparative Psychology to the University of Aberdeen; Lecturer in Psychology, Logic, and Ethics to the Aberdeen Provincial Committee for the Training of Teachers; formerly Examiner in Philosophy to the Universities of Edinburgh and London; author of *Giordano Bruno* (1903).
Subconsciousness.

Mackean (Walter George).
Of the Scottish Universities' Mission in Sikkim.
Sikkim.

Mackintosh (Hugh Ross), M.A., D.Phil. (Edin.), D.D. (Edin.).
Professor of Systematic Theology in New College, Edinburgh; author of *The Doctrine of the Person of Jesus Christ* (1912), *Immortality and the Future* (1915), *The Originality of the Christian Message* (1920).
Sin (Christian).

Maclagan (P. J.), M.A., D.Phil.
Foreign Mission Secretary of the Presbyterian Church of England; formerly of the English Presbyterian Mission, Swatow.
Saints and Martyrs (Chinese).

Maclean (Arthur John), D.D. (Camb.), Hon. D.D. (Glas.).
Bishop of Moray, Ross, and Caithness; author of *Dictionary and Grammar of Vernacular Syriac, Ancient Church Orders*, and other works; editor of *East Syrian Liturgies.*
Simony, Stations.

Mair (Alexander William), M.A. (Aberd. and Camb.), Litt.D. (Aberd.).
Sometime Fellow of Gonville and Caius College, Cambridge; Professor of Greek in the University of Edinburgh; editor of *Hesiod.*
Sin (Greek).

Major (Henry Dewsbury Alves), M.A., B.D. (Oxon.).
Principal of Ripon Hall, Oxford.
Subordination.

Malinowski (Boris), Ph.D. (Cracow), D.Sc. (London).
Robert Mond Travelling Student, University of London; author of *The Family among the Australian Aborigines.*
Spirit Children.

Malter (Henry), Ph.D. (Heidelberg).
Professor of Rabbinical Literature, Dropsie College, Philadelphia.
Se'adiah.

Margoliouth (David Samuel), M.A., D.Litt., F.B.A.
Fellow of New College, and Laudian Professor of Arabic in the University of Oxford; author of *Mohammed and the Rise of Islam, Mohammedanism, The Early Development of Mohammedanism.*
Sanusi.

Martin (Hugh), M.A. (Glas.).
Assistant Secretary of the Student Christian Movement of Great Britain and Ireland; author of *The Meaning of the Old Testament, According to St. Luke.*
Student Christian Movement.

Masterman (Ernest W. G.), M.D., F.R.C.S., F.R.G.S.
Hon. Secretary of the Palestine Exploration Fund.
Saints and Martyrs (Syrian).

Mellone (Sydney H.), M.A. (Lond.), D.Sc. (Edin.).
Principal of the Unitarian Home Missionary College, Manchester; Lecturer in the History of Christian Doctrine in the University of Manchester; author of *Studies in Philosophical Criticism, Eternal Life Here and Hereafter*, and other works.
Scholasticism.

Mellor (Stanley Alfred), B.A. (Oxon.), Ph.D. (Harvard).
Minister of Hope Street Church, Liverpool.
Socialism.

Minns (Ellis Hovell), Litt.D.
Fellow and Librarian of Pembroke College, Cambridge; University Lecturer in Palæography; author of *Scythians and Greeks.*
Scythians.

Moffatt (James), D.D., D.Litt., Hon. M.A. (Oxon.).
Professor of Church History in the United Free Church College, Glasgow; author of *Critical Introduction to New Testament Literature*, and other works.
Scribes.

Moore-Willson (Mrs. Minnie).
Author of *The Seminoles of Florida, The Least Known Wilderness of America.*
Seminoles.

Moulton (Warren J.), M.A., D.D.
Hayes Professor of New Testament Language and Literature in the Theological Seminary, Bangor, Maine.
Samaritans.

Mullinger (J. Bass), Litt.D. (Camb.).
Late University Lecturer in History; formerly University Lecturer and Librarian of St. John's College, Cambridge.
Speronistæ.

Orr (James), M.A., D.D.
Late Professor of Systematic Theology and Apologetics in the United Free Church College, Glasgow; author of *The Christian View of God and the World, David Hume* in the 'Epoch Makers' series.
Sublapsarianism.

Ottley (Robert Laurence), D.D.
Regius Professor of Pastoral Theology, and Canon of Christ Church, Oxford; author of *The Doctrine of the Incarnation* (1895), *Aspects of the Old Testament* (1905), and other works.
Self-culture, Sobriety.

Paton (Lewis Bayles), Ph.D., D.D.
Nettleton Professor of Old Testament Exegesis and Criticism, and Instructor in Assyrian, in Hartford Theological Seminary; formerly Director of the American School of Archæology in Jerusalem; author of *The Early History of Syria and Palestine, Jerusalem in Bible Times, The Early Religion of Israel,* 'Esther' in the *International Critical Commentary.*
Sanchuniathon.

PATTON (WALTER MELVILLE), M.A., Ph.D., D.D.
Professor of Biblical Literature and History of Religion, and Director of the Library, Carleton College, Northfield, Minnesota.
Saints and Martyrs (Muhammadan), **Shī'ahs.**

PEARSON (A. C.), M.A., Litt.D.
Professor of Greek in the University of Liverpool; editor of *Fragments of Sophocles*, Euripides' *Helena*, *Heraclidæ*, and *Phœnissæ*, *Zeno and Cleanthes: Fragments.*
Seneca, Styx.

PETRIE (WILLIAM MATTHEW FLINDERS), D.C.L. (Oxon.), LL.D. (Edin. and Aberd.), Litt.D. (Camb.).
Fellow of the Royal Society and of the British Academy; Edwards Professor of Egyptology in the University of London.
Soul-house.

PHILLIPS (DAVID), B.A. (Wales), M.A. (Cantab.).
Professor of the Philosophy and History of Religion in the Theological College, Bala, North Wales.
Self-assertion and Self-subjection, Self-satisfaction.

PHILLPOTTS (BERTHA SURTEES), O.B.E., M.A., Litt.D. (Dublin), F.R.Hist.Soc.
Principal of Westfield College (University of London); Fellow of the Royal Society of Northern Antiquaries (Copenhagen); formerly Librarian of Girton College, Cambridge, and Lady Carlisle Research Fellow of Somerville College, Oxford; author of *Kindred and Clan: A Study in the Sociology of the Teutonic Races* (1913); *The Elder Edda and Ancient Scandinavian Drama* (1920).
Soul (Teutonic).

PINCHES (THEOPHILUS GOLDRIDGE), LL.D. (Glas.), M.R.A.S.
Lecturer in Assyrian at University College, London, and at the Institute of Archæology, Liverpool; Hon. Member of the Société Asiatique.
Salvation (Assyro-Babylonian).

POUSSIN (LOUIS DE LA VALLÉE), Docteur en philosophie et lettres (Liége), en langues orientales (Louvain).
Professor de sanscrit à l'Université de Gand; Membre de l'Académie royale de Belgique; Hibbert Lecturer (1916); Membre de la R.A.S. et de la Société Asiatique; Membre correspondant de l'Académie impériale de Petrograd; Correspondant de l'Ecole Française d'Extrême-Orient.
Sammitiyas, Sautrantikas, Scepticism (Buddhist).

PRICE (JULIUS JOSEPH), B.A., M.A., Ph.D.
Rabbi, New Jersey; editor of Yemenite MSS of Pesaḥim, Megilla and Mo'ed Kaṭon.
Shekinah.

PRINCE (JOHN DYNELEY), B.A., Ph.D.
Professor of Semitic Languages in Columbia University, N.Y.; Member of the New Jersey Legislature; Advisory Commissioner on Crime and Dependency for New Jersey; Speaker of New Jersey House; President of New Jersey Senate; Acting-Governor of New Jersey.
Scapegoat (Semitic).

PUNNETT (REGINALD CRUNDALL), M.A., F.R.S.
Arthur Balfour Professor of Genetics in the University of Cambridge; author of *Mendelism.*
Sex.

REES (THOMAS), M.A. (Lond.), B.A. (Oxon.).
Principal and Professor of Theology at the Bala-Bangor Independent College, Bangor, N. Wales; author of *The Holy Spirit in Thought and Experience*, and other works.
Sensationalism.

REID (JAMES SMITH), M.A., LL.D., Litt.D.
Fellow and late Tutor of Gonville and Caius College, Cambridge; Professor of Ancient History in the University of Cambridge; editor of the *Academica* and other works of Cicero; author of *Municipalities of the Roman Empire.*
Sacrilege (Greek and Roman), **Sin** (Roman), **State of the Dead** (Greek and Roman).

REVON (MICHEL), LL.D., D.Litt.
Professor of History of the Civilization of the Far East in the University of Paris; formerly Professor of Law in the Imperial University of Tokyo and Legal Adviser to the Japanese Government; author of *Le Shinntoïsme.*
Sacrifice (Japanese), **Saints and Martyrs** (Japanese), **Sin** (Japanese).

RICE (B. LEWIS), C.I.E.
Formerly Director of Archæological Researches, Mysore, and Director of Public Instruction in Mysore and Coorg; Hon. Fellow of the University of Madras; author of *Mysore*, *Bibliotheca Carnatica*, *Epigraphia Carnatica.*
Smartas.

RICHARD (TIMOTHY), D.D., Litt.D.
Late General Secretary of the Christian Literature Society for China; author of *The New Testament of Higher Buddhism*, and other works.
Sects (Chinese).

RILEY (I. WOODBRIDGE), M.A., Ph.D.
Professor of Philosophy in Vassar College, Poughkeepsie, New York; author of *American Philosophy: the Early Schools*, and other works.
Saints (Latter-Day).

RIVERS (W. H. R.), M.A., M.D., F.R.S., F.R.C.P.
Fellow of St. John's College, Cambridge; President of the Anthropological Section of the British Association, 1911; author of *The Todas*, *History of Melanesian Society*, *Kinship and Social Organisation.*
Ships and Boats, Solomon Islands.

ROBINSON (HENRY WHEELER), M.A. (Oxon. and Edin.).
Principal and Professor of Systematic Theology and Hebrew in Regent's Park (Baptist) College, London; author of 'Hebrew Psychology in relation to Pauline Anthropology' in *Mansfield College Essays*, *The Christian Doctrine of Man*, *The Religious Ideas of the Old Testament.*
Skin, Soul (Christian).

ROGERS (ROBERT WILLIAM), M.A., Ph.D., LL.D., S.T.D., Hon. Litt.D. (Dublin).
Professor in Drew Theological Seminary, Madison, New Jersey; Lecturer in Columbia University Summer Sessions; author of *History of Babylonia and Assyria, Religion of Babylonia and Assyria, Cuneiform Parallels to the Old Testament, The Recovery of the Ancient Orient, History and Literature of the Hebrew People.*
State of the Dead (Babylonian).

ROSE (HORACE ARTHUR), I.C.S. (retired).
Superintendent of Ethnography, Panjab, 1901–1906; author of *A Glossary of Punjab Tribes and Castes*, and other works.
Shahids, Sikhs.

SCHILLER (FERDINAND CANNING SCOTT), M.A., D.Sc. (Oxon.).
Fellow and Senior Tutor of Corpus Christi College, Oxford; author of *Riddles of the Sphinx* (new ed. 1910), *Humanism* (1903, new ed. 1912), *Studies in Humanism* (1907, 1912), *Plato or Protagoras?* (1908), *Formal Logic* (1912), etc.
Spiritism, Spiritualism.

SCHMIDT (NATHANIEL), M.A.
Professor of Semitic Languages and Literatures in Cornell University; sometime Director of the American School of Archæology in Jerusalem; author of *The Prophet of Nazareth, The Messages of the Poets.*
Sects (Samaritan).

SELBIE (WILLIAM BOOTHBY), M.A. (Oxon.), Hon. D.D. (Glas.).
Principal of Mansfield College, Oxford.
Schleiermacher, Subjectivism and Subjectivity.

SELIGMAN (CHARLES G.), M.D., F.R.S., F.R.C.P.
Professor of Ethnology in the University of London; President of the Anthropological Section of the British Association, 1915; author of *The Melanesians of British New Guinea*; joint-author of *The Veddas.*
Shilluk.

SELL (EDWARD), B.D., D.D., M.R.A.S.
Fellow of the University of Madras; Hon. Canon of St. George's Cathedral, Madras; Secretary of the Church Missionary Society, Madras; author of *The Faith of Islam, The Historical Development of the Qur'ān, The Life of Muḥammad, The Religious Orders of Islam.*
Salvation (Muslim), **Sin** (Muslim).

SHOREY (PAUL), Ph.D., LL.D., Litt.D.
Professor and Head of the Department of Greek in the University of Chicago; Roosevelt Professor at the University of Berlin, 1913; Member of the American Institute of Arts and Letters; Fellow of the American Academy of Arts and Letters.
Sirens.

SKINNER (ALANSON BUCK).
Member of the Scientific Staff of the Museum of the American Indian Heye Foundation; formerly Assistant Curator of the Department of Ethnology of the American Museum of Natural History, New York.
Siouans.

SMITH (VINCENT ARTHUR), M.A., Litt.D.
Late of the Indian Civil Service (retired); author of *Asoka* in 'Rulers of India,' *Early History of India, A History of Fine Art in India and Ceylon, Akbar the Great Mogul, Oxford History of India.*
Sarnath.

STARBUCK (EDWIN DILLER), Ph.D.
Professor of Philosophy in the State University of Iowa; author of *The Psychology of Religion.*
Self-expression.

STEAD (FRANCIS HERBERT), M.A. (Glas.).
Warden of the Robert Browning Settlement, Walworth, London.
Settlements.

STOKES (GEORGE J.), M.A. (Trinity College, Dublin).
Of Lincoln's Inn, Barrister-at-Law; Professor of Philosophy and Jurisprudence in University College, Cork, National University of Ireland.
Space.

STROMBERG (A. BARON VON).
Dorpat.
Sects (Russian).

SWANTON (JOHN REED), Ph.D.
Ethnologist in the Bureau of American Ethnology, Smithsonian Institution, Washington, D.C.; President of the Anthropological Society of Washington, 1916.
Salish.

TAKAKUSU (JYUN), M.A., D.Litt. (Oxford), Dr. Phil. (Leipzig).
Professor of Sanskrit in the University of Tokyo.
Sarvastivadins.

TALBOT (NEVILLE STUART), M.C., M.A., D.D. (Oxon.).
Bishop of Pretoria.
Student Christian Movement.

TENNANT (FREDERICK ROBERT), D.D., B.Sc.
Fellow and Lecturer of Trinity College, Cambridge.
Self-realization.

THOMAS (EDWARD JOSEPH), M.A. (St. And. and Camb.), B.A. (Lond.).
Under-Librarian of Cambridge University; editor of *Buddhist Scriptures*; joint-editor of *Mahāniddesa* and *Jātaka Tales.*
Saints and Martyrs (Buddhist), **Sariputta, State of the Dead** (Buddhist).

THOMAS (NORTHCOTE WHITRIDGE).
Élève diplômé de l'École pratique des Hautes Études; Corresponding Member of the Société d'Anthropologie de Paris; Member of Council of the Folklore Society; author of *Thought Transference, Kinship Organization and Group Marriage in Australia.*
Secret Societies (African).

THOMSON (J. ARTHUR), M.A., LL.D.
Regius Professor of Natural History in the University of Aberdeen; author of *The Study of Animal Life, The Science of Life, Heredity, The Bible of Nature, Darwinism and Human Life, Outlines of Zoology, The Biology of the Seasons, Introduction to Science, The Wonder of Life.*
Science, Struggle for Existence.

THURSTON (HERBERT), B.A., S.J.
Joint-editor of the Westminster Library for Priests and Students; author of *Life of St. Hugh of Lincoln, The Holy Year of Jubilee, The Stations of the Cross.*
Saints and Martyrs (Christian).

VOLLERS (KARL), Dr. phil.
Ehemals Professor der Semitischen Sprachen an der Universität, und Direktor des Grossherzogl. Munzkabinets zu Jena.
Ash-Sha'rani.

WADDELL (L. AUSTINE), C.B., C.I.E., LL.D., F.L.S., F.R.A.I., M.R.A.S., M.F.L.S., M.S.B.A., Lt.-Colonel I.M.S. (retired).
Formerly Professor of Tibetan in University College, London; Hon. Correspondent of the Archæological Survey of India; author of *The Buddhism of Tibet, Lhasa and its Mysteries.*
State of the Dead (Tibetan).

WALPOLE (GEORGE HENRY SOMERSET), M.A. (Camb.), Hon. D.D. (Edin.).
Bishop of Edinburgh.
Sponsors.

WATERHOUSE (ERIC STRICKLAND), M.A., B.D. (Lond.).
Lecturer in Philosophy at the Wesleyan College, Richmond; author of *Modern Theories of Religion, The Psychology of the Christian Life*, and other works.
Secularism.

WATKINS (CHARLES H.), M.A., D.Theol.
Principal of Carmichael College, Rangpur, Bengal.
Self-righteousness.

WEIR (THOMAS HUNTER), B.D., M.R.A.S.
Lecturer in Arabic in the University of Glasgow; formerly Examiner in Hebrew and Aramaic in the University of London.
Sacrifice (Muhammadan).

WELSFORD (ENID ELDER HANCOCK).
Fellow of Newnham College, Cambridge.
Serpent-worship (Teutonic and Balto-Slavic).

WHITLEY (WILLIAM THOMAS), M.A., LL.D., F.R.Hist.S., F.T.S.
Honorary Secretary and editor of the Baptist Historical Society; Member of the American Historical Association; author of *Roman Catholic and Protestant Bibles, Missionary Achievement*; editor of *A Baptist Bibliography, The Works of John Smyth.*
Sects (Christian), **Southcottians.**

WHITTUCK (CHARLES AUGUSTUS), M.A. (Oxon).
Vicar of St. Mary-the-Virgin, Oxford; late Fellow of Brasenose College, Oxford; author of *The Church of England and Recent Religious Thought.*
Self-love.

WILDE (NORMAN), Ph.D.
Professor of Philosophy in the University of Minnesota.
Self-preservation.

WOOD (IRVING FRANCIS), Ph.D., D.D.
Professor of Biblical Literature and Comparative Religion in Smith College, Northampton, Mass.
State of the Dead (Hebrew, Muhammadan).

WOODHOUSE (WILLIAM J.), M.A.
Professor of Greek in the University of Sydney, New South Wales.
Scapegoat (Greek), **Slavery** (Greek, Roman).

WORKMAN (HERBERT B.), M.A., D.Lit.
Principal of Westminster Training College; Member of the Board of Studies in the Faculty of Theology, London University; author of *The Dawn of the Reformation, The Letters of John Hus, Persecution in the Early Church*, and *Christian Thought to the Reformation.*
Stedingers.

YOUNGERT (SVEN GUSTAF), Ph.D., D.D.
Professor of Philosophy and Greek New Testament Exegesis at Augustana College and Theological Seminary, Rock Island, Ill.
Sacrifice (Teutonic), **Salvation** (Teutonic), **Sin** (Teutonic).

CROSS-REFERENCES

In addition to the cross-references throughout the volume, the following list of minor references may be useful:

Topic.	Title of Article.
Saho	Hamites and East Africa.
Santa Claus	Abbot of Unreason.
Sappho	Love (Greek).
Sarabaitæ	Monasticism.
Saturnalia	Festivals and Fasts (Roman).
Scandinavia	Teutons.
Scourging	Crimes and Punishments.
Sectarianism	Schism.
Seduction	Crimes and Punishments.
Self-abasement	Abasement.
Self-absorption	Concentration, Samadhi.
Self-determination	Libertarianism.
Self-development	Self-culture.
Self-renunciation	Renunciation.
Self-sufficiency	Self-satisfaction.
Selungs	Burma.
Semikah	Ordination (Jewish).
Sensation	Development (Mental), Intellect, Sense.
Septuagint	Bible.
Sepulchre	Tomb.
Sermon	Preaching.
Sethians	Gnosticism.
Seventh-Day Adventists	Second Adventism.
Severians	Encratites.
Sewaras	Kaṛā Liṅgīs.
Shangalas	Abyssinia.
Shingrawa	Burma.
Sibokoism	Totemism.
Sidama	Hamites and East Africa.
Signs	Prodigies and Portents, Symbolism.
Singing	Music.
Singpho	Burma.
Sinlessness	Jesus Christ, Sin.
Sin (Original)	Original Sin.
Sisterhood	Religious Orders, Pusey.
Sittars	Śaivism.
Smell	Nose.
Sneezing	Nose.
Social Contract	Government.
Society	Sociology.
Society of Friends	Friends, Society of.
Son of God	Jesus Christ.
Son of Man	Jesus Christ.
Sons and Daughters	Family.
Sorrow	Suffering.
Special Gods	Momentary Gods.
Spells	Charms and Amulets.
Spiritual Gifts	Charismata.
Śrāddha	Ancestor-worship (Indian).
Sravakas	Pratyekabuddha.
Stage	Drama.
Subliminal Self	Subconsciousness.
Submission	Abrenuntio, Obedience, Passivity.
Substitution	Expiation and Atonement.
Subterranean Gods	Underworld.

LISTS OF ABBREVIATIONS

I. General

A.H. = Anno Hijrae (A.D. 622).
Ak. = Akkadian.
Alex. = Alexandrian.
Amer. = American.
Apoc. = Apocalypse, Apocalyptic.
Apocr. = Apocrypha.
Aq. = Aquila.
Arab. = Arabic.
Aram. = Aramaic.
Arm. = Armenian.
Ary. = Aryan.
As. = Asiatic.
Assyr. = Assyrian.
AT = Altes Testament.
AV = Authorized Version.
AVm = Authorized Version margin.
A.Y. = Anno Yazdagird (A.D. 639).
Bab. = Babylonian.
c. = *circa*, about.
Can. = Canaanite.
cf. = compare.
ct. = contrast.
D = Deuteronomist.
E = Elohist.
edd. = editions or editors.
Egyp. = Egyptian.
Eng. = English.
Eth. = Ethiopic.
EV, EVV = English Version, Versions.
f. = and following verse or page.
ff. = and following verses or pages.
Fr. = French.
Germ. = German.
Gr. = Greek.
H = Law of Holiness.
Heb. = Hebrew.
Hel. = Hellenistic.
Hex. = Hexateuch.
Himy. = Himyaritic.
Ir. = Irish.
Iran. = Iranian.
Isr. = Israelite.
J = Jahwist.
J″ = Jehovah.
Jerus. = Jerusalem.
Jos. = Josephus.
LXX = Septuagint.
Min. = Minæan.
MSS = Manuscripts.
MT = Massoretic Text.
n. = note.
NT = New Testament.
Onk. = Onkelos.
OT = Old Testament.
P = Priestly Narrative.
Pal. = Palestine, Palestinian.
Pent. = Pentateuch.
Pers. = Persian.
Phil. = Philistine.
Phœn. = Phœnician.
Pr. Bk. = Prayer Book.
R = Redactor.
Rom. = Roman.
RV = Revised Version.
RVm = Revised Version margin.
Sab. = Sabæan.
Sam. = Samaritan.
Sem. = Semitic.
Sept. = Septuagint.
Sin. = Sinaitic.
Skr. = Sanskrit.
Symm. = Symmachus.
Syr. = Syriac.
t. (following a number) = times.
Talm. = Talmud.
Targ. = Targum.
Theod. = Theodotion.
TR = Textus Receptus, Received Text.
tr. = translated or translation.
VSS = Versions.
Vulg., Vg. = Vulgate.
WH = Westcott and Hort's text.

II. Books of the Bible

Old Testament.

Gn = Genesis.
Ex = Exodus.
Lv = Leviticus.
Nu = Numbers.
Dt = Deuteronomy.
Jos = Joshua.
Jg = Judges.
Ru = Ruth.
1 S, 2 S = 1 and 2 Samuel.
1 K, 2 K = 1 and 2 Kings.
1 Ch, 2 Ch = 1 and 2 Chronicles.
Ezr = Ezra.
Neh = Nehemiah.
Est = Esther.
Job.
Ps = Psalms.
Pr = Proverbs.
Ec = Ecclesiastes.
Ca = Canticles.
Is = Isaiah.
Jer = Jeremiah.
La = Lamentations.
Ezk = Ezekiel.
Dn = Daniel.
Hos = Hosea.
Jl = Joel.
Am = Amos.
Ob = Obadiah.
Jon = Jonah.
Mic = Micah.
Nah = Nahum.
Hab = Habakkuk.
Zeph = Zephaniah.
Hag = Haggai.
Zec = Zechariah.
Mal = Malachi.

Apocrypha.

1 Es, 2 Es = 1 and 2 Esdras.
To = Tobit.
Jth = Judith.
Ad. Est = Additions to Esther.
Wis = Wisdom.
Sir = Sirach or Ecclesiasticus.
Bar = Baruch.
Three = Song of the Three Children.
Sus = Susanna.
Bel = Bel and the Dragon.
Pr. Man = Prayer of Manasses.
1 Mac, 2 Mac = 1 and 2 Maccabees.

New Testament.

Mt = Matthew.
Mk = Mark.
Lk = Luke.
Jn = John.
Ac = Acts.
Ro = Romans.
1 Co, 2 Co = 1 and 2 Corinthians.
Gal = Galatians.
Eph = Ephesians.
Ph = Philippians.
Col = Colossians.
1 Th, 2 Th = 1 and 2 Thessalonians.
1 Ti, 2 Ti = 1 and 2 Timothy.
Tit = Titus.
Philem = Philemon.
He = Hebrews.
Ja = James.
1 P, 2 P = 1 and 2 Peter.
1 Jn, 2 Jn, 3 Jn = 1, 2, and 3 John.
Jude.
Rev = Revelation.

III. For the Literature

1. The following authors' names, when unaccompanied by the title of a book, stand for the works in the list below.

Baethgen = *Beiträge zur sem. Religionsgesch.*, 1888.
Baldwin = *Dict. of Philosophy and Psychology*, 3 vols. 1901–05.
Barth = *Nominalbildung in den sem. Sprachen*, 2 vols. 1889, 1891 ([2]1894).
Benzinger = *Heb. Archäologie*, 1894.
Brockelmann = *Gesch. d. arab. Litteratur*, 2 vols. 1897–1902.
Bruns-Sachau = *Syr.-Röm. Rechtsbuch aus dem fünften Jahrhundert*, 1880.
Budge = *Gods of the Egyptians*, 2 vols. 1903.
Daremberg-Saglio = *Dict. des ant. grec. et rom.*, 1886–90.
De la Saussaye = *Lehrbuch der Religionsgesch.*[3], 1905.
Denzinger = *Enchiridion Symbolorum*[11], Freiburg im Br., 1911.
Deussen = *Die Philos. d. Upanishads*, 1899 [Eng. tr., 1906].
Doughty = *Arabia Deserta*, 2 vols. 1888.
Grimm = *Deutsche Mythologie*[4], 3 vols. 1875–78, Eng. tr. *Teutonic Mythology*, 4 vols. 1882–88.
Hamburger = *Realencyclopädie für Bibel u. Talmud*, i. 1870 ([2]1892), ii. 1883, suppl. 1886, 1891 f., 1897.
Holder = *Altceltischer Sprachschatz*, 1891 ff.
Holtzmann-Zöpffel = *Lexicon f. Theol. u. Kirchenwesen*[2], 1895.
Howitt = *Native Tribes of S.E. Australia*, 1904.
Jubainville = *Cours de Litt. celtique*, i.–xii., 1883 ff.
Lagrange = *Études sur les religions sémitiques*[2], 1904.
Lane = *An Arabic-English Lexicon*, 1863 ff.
Lang = *Myth, Ritual, and Religion*[2], 2 vols. 1899.
Lepsius = *Denkmäler aus Aegypten u. Aethiopien*, 1849–60.
Lichtenberger = *Encyc. des sciences religieuses*, 1876.
Lidzbarski = *Handbuch der nordsem. Epigraphik*, 1898.
McCurdy = *History, Prophecy, and the Monuments*, 2 vols. 1894–96.
Muir = *Orig. Sanskrit Texts*, 1858–72.
Muss-Arnolt = *A Concise Dict. of the Assyrian Language*, 1894 ff.
Nowack = *Lehrbuch d. heb. Archäologie*, 2 vols. 1894.
Pauly-Wissowa = *Realencyc. der classischen Altertumswissenschaft*, 1894 ff.
Perrot-Chipiez = *Hist. de l'art dans l'antiquité*, 1881 ff.
Preller = *Römische Mythologie*, 1858.
Réville = *Religion des peuples non-civilisés*, 1883.
Riehm = *Handwörterbuch d. bibl. Altertums*[2], 1893–94.
Robinson = *Biblical Researches in Palestine*[2], 1856.
Roscher = *Lex. d. gr. u. röm. Mythologie*, 1884 ff.
Schaff-Herzog = *The New Schaff-Herzog Encyclopedia of Religious Knowledge*, 1908 ff.
Schenkel = *Bibel-Lexicon*, 5 vols. 1869–75.
Schürer = *GJV*[3], 3 vols. 1898–1901 [*HJP*, 5 vols. 1890 ff.].
Schwally = *Leben nach dem Tode*, 1892.
Siegfried-Stade = *Heb. Wörterbuch zum AT*, 1893.
Smend = *Lehrbuch der alttest. Religionsgesch.*[2], 1899.
Smith (G. A.) = *Historical Geography of the Holy Land*[4], 1897.
Smith (W. R.) = *Religion of the Semites*[2], 1894.
Spencer (H.) = *Principles of Sociology*[3], 1885–96.
Spencer-Gillen[a] = *Native Tribes of Central Australia*, 1899.
Spencer-Gillen[b] = *Northern Tribes of Central Australia*, 1904.
Swete = *The OT in Greek*, 3 vols. 1893 ff.
Tylor (E. B.) = *Primitive Culture*[3], 1891 [[4]1903].
Ueberweg = *Hist. of Philosophy*, Eng. tr., 2 vols. 1872–74.
Weber = *Jüdische Theologie auf Grund des Talmud u. verwandten Schriften*[2], 1897.
Wiedemann = *Die Religion der alten Aegypter*, 1890 [Eng. tr., revised, *Religion of the Anc. Egyptians*, 1897].
Wilkinson = *Manners and Customs of the Ancient Egyptians*, 3 vols. 1878.
Zunz = *Die gottesdienstlichen Vorträge der Juden*[2], 1892.

2. Periodicals, Dictionaries, Encyclopædias, and other standard works frequently cited.

AA = Archiv für Anthropologie.
AAOJ = American Antiquarian and Oriental Journal.
ABAW = Abhandlungen d. Berliner Akad. d. Wissenschaften.
AE = Archiv für Ethnographie.
AEG = Assyr. and Eng. Glossary (Johns Hopkins University).
AGG = Abhandlungen der Göttinger Gesellschaft der Wissenschaften.
AGPh = Archiv für Geschichte der Philosophie.
AHR = American Historical Review.
AHT = Ancient Hebrew Tradition (Hommel).
AJPh = American Journal of Philology.
AJPs = American Journal of Psychology.
AJRPE = American Journal of Religious Psychology and Education.
AJSL = American Journal of Semitic Languages and Literature.
AJTh = American Journal of Theology.
AMG = Annales du Musée Guimet.
APES = American Palestine Exploration Society.
APF = Archiv für Papyrusforschung.
AR = Anthropological Review.
ARW = Archiv für Religionswissenschaft.
AS = Acta Sanctorum (Bollandus).
ASG = Abhandlungen der Sächsischen Gesellschaft der Wissenschaften.
ASoc = L'Année Sociologique.
ASWI = Archæological Survey of W. India.
AZ = Allgemeine Zeitung.
BAG = Beiträge zur alten Geschichte.
BASS = Beiträge zur Assyriologie u. sem. Sprachwissenschaft (edd. Delitzsch and Haupt).
BCH = Bulletin de Correspondance Hellénique.
BE = Bureau of Ethnology.
BG = Bombay Gazetteer.
BJ = Bellum Judaicum (Josephus).
BL = Bampton Lectures.
BLE = Bulletin de Littérature Ecclésiastique.
BOR = Bab. and Oriental Record.
BS = Bibliotheca Sacra.
BSA = Annual of the British School at Athens.
BSAA = Bulletin de la Soc. archéologique à Alexandrie.
BSAL = Bulletin de la Soc. d'Anthropologie de Lyon.
BSAP = Bulletin de la Soc. d'Anthropologie, etc., Paris.
BSG = Bulletin de la Soc. de Géographie.
BTS = Buddhist Text Society.
BW = Biblical World.
BZ = Biblische Zeitschrift.

CAIBL = Comptes rendus de l'Académie des Inscriptions et Belles-Lettres.
CBTS = Calcutta Buddhist Text Society.
CE = Catholic Encyclopædia.
CF = Childhood of Fiction (MacCulloch).
CGS = Cults of the Greek States (Farnell).
CI = Census of India.
CIA = Corpus Inscrip. Atticarum.
CIE = Corpus Inscrip. Etruscarum.
CIG = Corpus Inscrip. Græcarum.
CIL = Corpus Inscrip. Latinarum.
CIS = Corpus Inscrip. Semiticarum.
COT = Cuneiform Inscriptions and the OT [Eng. tr. of KAT^2; see below].
CR = Contemporary Review.
CeR = Celtic Review.
ClR = Classical Review.
CQR = Church Quarterly Review.
CSEL = Corpus Script. Eccles. Latinorum.
DAC = Dict. of the Apostolic Church.
DACL = Dict. d'Archéologie chrétienne et de Liturgie (Cabrol).
DB = Dict. of the Bible.
DCA = Dict. of Christian Antiquities (Smith-Cheetham).
DCB = Dict. of Christian Biography (Smith-Wace).
DCG = Dict. of Christ and the Gospels.
DI = Dict. of Islam (Hughes).
DNB = Dict. of National Biography.
DPhP = Dict. of Philosophy and Psychology.
DWAW = Denkschriften der Wiener Akad. der Wissenschaften.
EBi = Encyclopædia Biblica.
EBr = Encyclopædia Britannica.
EEFM = Egyp. Explor. Fund Memoirs.
EI = Encyclopaedia of Islām.
ERE = The present work.
Exp = Expositor.
ExpT = Expository Times.
FHG = Fragmenta Historicorum Græcorum (coll. C. Müller, Paris, 1885).
FL = Folklore.
FLJ = Folklore Journal.
FLR = Folklore Record.
GA = Gazette Archéologique.
GB = Golden Bough (Frazer).
GGA = Göttingische Gelehrte Anzeigen.
GGN = Göttingische Gelehrte Nachrichten (Nachrichten der königl. Gesellschaft der Wissenschaften zu Göttingen).
GIAP = Grundriss d. Indo-Arischen Philologie.
GIrP = Grundriss d. Iranischen Philologie.
GJV = Geschichte des jüdischen Volkes.
GVI = Geschichte des Volkes Israel.
HAI = Handbook of American Indians.
HDB = Hastings' Dict. of the Bible.
HE = Historia Ecclesiastica.
HGHL = Historical Geography of the Holy Land (G. A. Smith).
HI = History of Israel.
HJ = Hibbert Journal.
HJP = History of the Jewish People.
HL = Hibbert Lectures.
HN = Historia Naturalis (Pliny).
HWB = Handwörterbuch.
IA = Indian Antiquary.
ICC = International Critical Commentary.
ICO = International Congress of Orientalists.
ICR = Indian Census Report.
IG = Inscrip. Græcæ (publ. under auspices of Berlin Academy, 1873 ff.).
IGA = Inscrip. Græcæ Antiquissimæ.
IGI = Imperial Gazetteer of India² (1885); new edition (1908–09).
IJE = International Journal of Ethics.
ITL = International Theological Library.
JA = Journal Asiatique.
JAFL = Journal of American Folklore.
JAI = Journal of the Anthropological Institute.
JAOS = Journal of the American Oriental Society.
JASB = Journal of the Anthropological Society of Bombay.
JASBe = Journ. of As. Soc. of Bengal.
JBL = Journal of Biblical Literature.
JBTS = Journal of the Buddhist Text Society.
JD = Journal des Débats.
JDTh = Jahrbücher f. deutsche Theologie.
JE = Jewish Encyclopedia.
JGOS = Journal of the German Oriental Society.
JHC = Johns Hopkins University Circulars.
JHS = Journal of Hellenic Studies.
JLZ = Jenäer Litteraturzeitung.
JPh = Journal of Philology.
JPTh = Jahrbücher für protestantische Theologie.
JPTS = Journal of the Pāli Text Society.
JQR = Jewish Quarterly Review.
JRAI = Journal of the Royal Anthropological Institute.
JRAS = Journal of the Royal Asiatic Society.
JRASBo = Journal of the Royal Asiatic Society, Bombay branch.
JRASC = Journal of the Royal Asiatic Society, Ceylon branch.
JRASK = Journal of the Royal Asiatic Society, Korean branch.
JRGS = Journal of the Royal Geographical Society.
JRS = Journal of Roman Studies.
JThSt = Journal of Theological Studies.
KAT^2 = Die Keilinschriften und das AT^2 (Schrader), 1883.
KAT^3 = Zimmern-Winckler's ed. of the preceding (really a totally distinct work), 1903.
KB or *KIB* = Keilinschriftliche Bibliothek (Schrader), 1889 ff.
KGF = Keilinschriften und die Geschichtsforschung, 1878.
LCBl = Literarisches Centralblatt.
LOPh = Literaturblatt für Oriental. Philologie.
LOT = Introduction to Literature of OT (Driver).
LP = Legend of Perseus (Hartland).
LSSt = Leipziger sem. Studien.
M = Mélusine.
MAIBL = Mémoires de l'Acad. des Inscriptions et Belles-Lettres.
MBAW = Monatsbericht d. Berliner Akad. d. Wissenschaften.
MGH = Monumenta Germaniæ Historica (Pertz).
MGJV = Mittheilungen der Gesellschaft für jüdische Volkskunde.
MGWJ = Monatsschrift für Geschichte und Wissenschaft des Judentums.
MI = Origin and Development of the Moral Ideas (Westermarck).
MNDPV = Mittheilungen u. Nachrichten des deutschen Palästina-Vereins.
MR = Methodist Review.
MVG = Mittheilungen der vorderasiatischen Gesellschaft.
MWJ = Magazin für die Wissenschaft des Judentums.
NBAC = Nuovo Bullettino di Archeologia Cristiana.
NC = Nineteenth Century.
NHWB = Neuhebräisches Wörterbuch.
NINQ = North Indian Notes and Queries.
NKZ = Neue kirchliche Zeitschrift.
NQ = Notes and Queries.
NR = Native Races of the Pacific States (Bancroft).
NTZG = Neutestamentliche Zeitgeschichte.
OED = Oxford English Dictionary.
OLZ = Orientalische Litteraturzeitung.
OS = Onomastica Sacra.
OTJC = Old Testament in the Jewish Church (W. R. Smith).
OTP = Oriental Translation Fund Publications.
PAOS = Proceedings of American Oriental Society.

PASB = Proceedings of the Anthropological Soc. of Bombay.
PB = Polychrome Bible (English).
PBE = Publications of the Bureau of Ethnology.
PC = Primitive Culture (Tylor).
PEFM = Palestine Exploration Fund Quarterly Memoirs.
PEFSt = Palestine Exploration Fund Statement.
PG = Patrologia Græca (Migne).
PJB = Preussische Jahrbücher.
PL = Patrologia Latina (Migne).
PNQ = Punjab Notes and Queries.
PR = Popular Religion and Folklore of N. India (Crooke).
PRE[3] = Prot. Realencyclopädie (Herzog–Hauck).
PRR = Presbyterian and Reformed Review.
PRS = Proceedings of the Royal Society.
PRSE = Proceedings Royal Soc. of Edinburgh.
PSBA = Proceedings of the Society of Biblical Archæology.
PTS = Pāli Text Society.
RA = Revue Archéologique.
RAnth = Revue d'Anthropologie.
RAS = Royal Asiatic Society.
RAssyr = Revue d'Assyriologie.
RB = Revue Biblique.
RBEW = Reports of the Bureau of Ethnology (Washington).
RC = Revue Critique.
RCel = Revue Celtique.
RCh = Revue Chrétienne.
RDM = Revue des Deux Mondes.
RE = Realencyclopädie.
REG = Revue des Études Grecques.
REg = Revue Égyptologique.
REJ = Revue des Études Juives.
REth = Revue d'Ethnographie.
RGG = Die Religion in Geschichte und Gegenwart.
RHLR = Revue d'Histoire et de Littérature religieuses.
RHR = Revue de l'Histoire des Religions.
RMM = Revue du monde musulman.
RN = Revue Numismatique.
RP = Records of the Past.
RPh = Revue Philosophique.
RQ = Römische Quartalschrift.
RS = Revue sémitique d'Épigraphie et d'Hist. ancienne.
RSA = Recueil de la Soc. archéologique.
RSI = Reports of the Smithsonian Institution.
RTAP = Recueil de Travaux rélatifs à l'Archéologie et à la Philologie.
RTP = Revue des traditions populaires.
RThPh = Revue de Théologie et de Philosophie.
RTr = Recueil de Travaux.
RVV = Religionsgeschichtliche Versuche und Vorarbeitungen.
RWB = Realwörterbuch.
SBAW = Sitzungsberichte d. Berliner Akademie d. Wissenschaften.
SBB = Sacred Books of the Buddhists.
SBE = Sacred Books of the East.
SBOT = Sacred Books of the OT (Hebrew).
SDB = Single-vol. Dict. of the Bible (Hastings).
SK = Studien und Kritiken.
SMA = Sitzungsberichte d. Münchener Akademie.
SSGW = Sitzungsberichte d. Kgl. Sächs. Gesellsch. d. Wissenschaften.
SWAW = Sitzungsberichte d. Wiener Akademie d. Wissenschaften.
TAPA = Transactions of American Philological Association.
TASJ = Transactions of the Asiatic Soc. of Japan.
TC = Tribes and Castes.
TES = Transactions of Ethnological Society.
ThLZ = Theologische Litteraturzeitung.
ThT = Theol. Tijdschrift.
TRHS = Transactions of Royal Historical Society.
TRSE = Transactions of Royal Soc. of Edinburgh.
TS = Texts and Studies.
TSBA = Transactions of the Soc. of Biblical Archæology.
TU = Texte und Untersuchungen.
WAI = Western Asiatic Inscriptions.
WZKM = Wiener Zeitschrift f. Kunde des Morgenlandes.
ZA = Zeitschrift für Assyriologie.
ZÄ = Zeitschrift für ägyp. Sprache u. Altertumswissenschaft.
ZATW = Zeitschrift für die alttest. Wissenschaft.
ZCK = Zeitschrift für christliche Kunst.
ZCP = Zeitschrift für celtische Philologie.
ZDA = Zeitschrift für deutsches Altertum.
ZDMG = Zeitschrift der deutschen morgenländischen Gesellschaft.
ZDPV = Zeitschrift des deutschen Palästina-Vereins.
ZE = Zeitschrift für Ethnologie.
ZKF = Zeitschrift für Keilschriftforschung.
ZKG = Zeitschrift für Kirchengeschichte.
ZKT = Zeitschrift für kathol. Theologie.
ZKWL = Zeitschrift für kirchl. Wissenschaft und kirchl. Leben.
ZM = Zeitschrift für die Mythologie.
ZNTW = Zeitschrift für die neutest. Wissenschaft.
ZPhP = Zeitschrift für Philosophie und Pädagogik.
ZTK = Zeitschrift für Theologie und Kirche.
ZVK = Zeitschrift für Volkskunde.
ZVRW = Zeitschrift für vergleichende Rechtswissenschaft.
ZWT = Zeitschrift für wissenschaftliche Theologie.

[A small superior number designates the particular edition of the work referred to, as *KAT*[2], *LOT*[6], etc.]

ENCYCLOPÆDIA
OF
RELIGION AND ETHICS

S

SACRIFICE.

SACRIFICE (Introductory and Primitive).—Sacrifice (Lat. *sacrificium; sacer*, 'holy,' and *facere*, 'to make') may be defined generally as a rite in the course of which something is forfeited or destroyed, its object being to establish relations between a source of spiritual strength and one in need of such strength, for the benefit of the latter. This relationship may be one of communion, *i.e.* one by which strength is conceived to be imparted to man (communal type); or, conversely, it may be one whereby a human weakness is held to be withdrawn and neutralized (piacular type). An instance of the first type occurs whenever the victim is consumed in a sacred meal, of the second whenever it is treated as unclean and cast away to beasts of prey.

1. Origin.—It was not until the spirit of historical inquiry had come to pervade the study of religion, during the latter part of the last century, that scientific theories regarding the origin and significance of sacrifice were put forward by anthropologists. Hitherto the institution had been usually regarded as of divine appointment, since from Gn 4$^{3-5}$ and He 11^{4} it appears that the divine authority sanctioned Abel's offering, and considered it, by faith, more acceptable than that of Cain. It need not, however, follow on theological grounds that the ordinance is of divine origin because it is said that by faith Abel's offering to Jahweh was a more excellent sacrifice than that of Cain. For the Jahwistic writer treats sacrifice as a natural institution, an instinctive mode of worship, while the Priestly creation-document ignores the existence of the rite altogether. But such a theory of the origin of sacrifice hardly harmonizes with the present tendency of historical theology or of the science of religions. To-day the divine origin of religious institutions is sought in the ever-developing minds of men rather than in sacred tradition.

(*a*) *E. B. Tylor.*—As soon as it became apparent that sacrifice involved a natural desire on the part of man to establish a bond between himself and that which he conceived to be sacred, the way was opened for scientific investigation of the rite. E. B. Tylor was the first to enter the field with the hypothesis that sacrifice was originally a gift offered to supernatural beings to secure their favour or minimize their hostility. As this purpose gradually became transformed in the mind of the sacrificers, the dominant note became that of homage, which again passed into that of renunciation.[1]

Herbert Spencer was of much the same opinion. The origin of sacrifice, he says, is to be found in the custom of leaving food and drink at the graves of the dead, and as the ancestral spirits rose to divine rank the refreshments placed for the dead developed into sacrifices.[2] Now the conception of sacrifice as a gift to the deity is very wide-spread, especially among people in a relatively advanced state of culture. 'Gifts,' says Hesiod, 'prevail upon gods and reverend kings.' Offerings to

[1] *PC*[5], London, 1913, ii. 375 f.
[2] *Principles of Sociology*[3], London, 1885, i. 277 ff.

sacred trees, etc., are common in parts of Africa.[1] Sacrificial gifts are often offered to appease the soul of the victim after a successful head-hunting expedition or similar escapade;[2] and the numerous examples of the oblation of the firstfruits (*q.v.*) come under the same category.[3] The Hebrew term for sacrifice (*minḥah*, 'gift') is used of both bloody and unbloody offerings, though from the time of Ezekiel (6th cent. B.C.) onwards it became a technical term for cereal offerings (Gn $4^{3f.}$, Lv 2). To this class too belongs the unction of sacred stones (menhirs, etc.) to the deity in the *maṣṣēbhāh* (*q.v.*). Oblations of fruits, etc., were also presented to local *numina* by being deposited within the sacred precincts or thrown into sacred wells. Likewise the holocaust, or whole burnt-offering, that plays so important a part in the sacrificial system of the Priestly narrative in the OT can scarcely be regarded otherwise than as an offering of food—a gift—since it was all assigned to the deity. According to Robertson Smith, this type of sacrifice was evolved from the original sacramental meal by the discontinuance of the use of totemic conceptions, and the recourse to human victims to renew the bond between the worshippers and the worshipped. The eating of human flesh became in time repugnant to the mind of man, and the human victim was therefore offered as a holocaust. In process of time an animal came to be substituted for a human victim, and the whole burnt-offering resulted.[4] Thus he makes the holocaust a late derivative of an earlier rite in which the eating of flesh and drinking of blood played an important part[5]—a theory largely based on late Arabic practice.

(*b*) *W. Robertson Smith.*—Robertson Smith's encyclopædia article on 'Sacrifice'[6] marks a new departure in the history of religion. In his paper on 'Animal Worship and Animal Tribes,' in *The Journal of Philology*,[7] after discussing the question of totemism on the strength of the evidence furnished by J. F. McLennan in the *Fortnightly Review*,[8] he proceeded to make totemic cult the basis of sacrifice. In 1889 (two years after J. G. Frazer's encyclopædia article on 'Totemism'[9] had appeared) he published the well-known lectures on *The Religion of the Semites*, in which, while he again suggested a totemic basis for Semitic religion, he was careful to add:

'It is one thing to say that the phenomena of Semitic religion carry us back to totemism, and another thing to say that they are all to be explained from totemism.'[10]

Nevertheless, he held that the conclusion that the Semites did pass through a totemic stage can be avoided only by supposing them to be an exception to the universal rule. He proceeded to restate his theory in order to overcome the difficulty resulting from his view that the god became identified with the animal or plant kind by the blood-bond—a custom which he now regarded as relatively late. On the new hypothesis he considered the god, the victim, and the totemic group to belong to the same kin. The original totem is female, and therefore descent 'follows the distaff' in primitive society. With the introduction of patrilineal descent the totem became male. Sacrifice in the first instance is, he thinks, a communion established by a bond of kinship.

1 A. B. Ellis, *The Ewe-speaking Peoples of the Slave Coast of W. Africa*, London, 1890, p. 49 ff.; H. H. Johnston, *The Uganda Protectorate*, London, 1890, ii. 832; GB^3, pt. i., *The Magic Art*, do. 1911, ii. 30.
2 GB^3, pt. ii., *Taboo and the Perils of the Soul*, London, 1911, p. 166.
3 *Ib.*, pt. v., *Spirits of the Corn and of the Wild*, London, 1912, ii. 117.
4 *The Religion of the Semites*², London, 1894, pp. 353–387.
5 *Ib.* p. 312 ff.
6 EBr^9 xxi. 132 ff.
7 ix. [1880] 95 ff.
8 vi. [1869] 407 ff. and 532 ff., vii. [1870] 194 ff.
9 EBr^9 xxiii. 467 ff.
10 *Rel. Sem.*² p. 139.

In these lectures he developed his theory of the 'theanthropic' animal, at once god and kinsman, as the originating cause of sacrifice of the communal type.[1] He considered Frazer to have proved the existence of annual totem sacraments involving actual communion in the flesh and blood of the sacred animal.[2]

This view distinguishes (1) honorific, (2) piacular, and (3) mystical or sacramental offerings. His leading conception is the distinction between the view of sacrifice as a gift to the deity—the worshipper laying upon the altar the offerings of the firstfruits of the harvest as a tribute to the god—and the view that regards it as a sacramental ritualistic act whereby the worshippers pass into actual communion with the god by partaking of food and drink in which the deity is immanent. In the *Religion of the Semites* Robertson Smith appears to confuse the two distinguishable aspects of sacrificial communion—the mystic and the non-mystic. The kinship of man with the divinity celebrated by sharing in a common meal, or in any other non-mystic manner, is by no means the same thing as a sacramental communion in the deeper and truly mystic sense, in which the deity and man enter into vital relationship by the latter partaking of divine food (see artt. COMMUNION WITH DEITY).

In support of his view that an expiatory function may attach to the sharing of animal flesh, Robertson Smith quotes numerous examples (such as the shedding of blood and offering of hair) in which there is no death of a victim and no idea of penal satisfaction given to the deity. In the Hebrew ritual he lays special stress on the *zebhaḥ*, *i.e.* the ordinary festal sacrifices, vows, and free-will offerings, of which the deity's share was the blood and the fat of the intestines, the rest of the carcass, after payment of certain dues to the priest, being left to the worshipper for a social feast. This he contrasts with the offerings wholly given to the god, likening the distinction to that between animal and vegetable offerings, the latter not being conciliatory. This hypothesis, however, takes no account of the holocaust and the piaculum, expiatory sacrifices in which there is no communal eating. To obviate this difficulty, Robertson Smith propounds the theory of the derivation of these from an earlier rite in which the sacrificial meal played an important part.

(*c*) *F. B. Jevons.*—Jevons, in his *Introduction to the History of Religion*,[3] derives inspiration directly from Robertson Smith's theory, basing his investigations on the assumption that a totemic system was the earliest form of society. He supposes totemism to have originated in a covenant or alliance between a human society and what the savage conceives as an animal clan organized on the same lines as his own. At this stage, he says, 'man imagines all things, animate or inanimate, to think and act and feel like himself.'[4] But apparently he forgets that the savage, like the child, realizes that some things are not alive. The primitive mind attributes *mana* (*q.v.*) only to those things that act abnormally or that present a strange or uncanny appearance. Jevons then argues that, since savages take up a blood-feud against an animal species, therefore they may establish an alliance with them.[5] Exactly how this alliance comes thereupon to be reinterpreted as a real flesh and blood union between man and beast is a point over which he passes lightly. Presumably he would say that it was by a natural extension of the initiation rite, whereby a youth is anointed with tribal blood and so becomes infused with a new life which is the common life of the

1 *Rel. Sem.*² p. 409.
2 *Ib.* p. 405.
3 London, 1896, p. 96 ff.
4 *Ib.* p. 99.
5 *Ib.* p. 100.

clan. In this way the society becomes a religious community, since each initiated member participates in the divine essence of its totem. In due course the animal is advanced to the status of a sort of superman—a hypothetical father of the human group.[1]

The blood-covenant established, the rite of sacrifice and the subsequent communion, he supposes, arose as the natural corollary from the savage principle that the blood is the life. The obvious procedure, if the 'real presence' of the totem—the sacred ally of the people—be desired, is to shed its blood. In such a sacrificial rite the essential feature is that the worshipper should partake of the sacred animal so that its supernatural qualities may be absorbed and evil influences expelled.

On this hypothesis the offering of an animal as a gift to a superhuman being is the result of the domestication of animals, the victim, which was originally itself sacred, having degenerated into a mere food animal, now held inferior to a stone hewn into the likeness of a human god, assumed to possess anthropomorphic qualities.[2] Thus arose the custom of sacrifice to non-totemic deities—the normal manner of approaching any god.[3]

(*d*) *Salomon Reinach.*—Reinach, in *Cultes, Mythes, et Religions*,[4] also professedly adopts the theory of Robertson Smith. With Jevons he thinks that the evolutionary processes which fused the communion type of sacrifice with that of the later sacrifice by gift were agriculture and the domestication of animals, dispelling the mystery surrounding the different forms of plant and animal life. Thus little by little the idea of a divinity hedging certain species of animals faded away, and man began to create the godhead in his own likeness. Yet there remained a tradition of animals sacrificed and eaten by the community. Therefore both sacrifice and banquet were retained in the belief that the god—anthropomorphic now—smelt the blood and inhaled the smoke of the burnt-offering. To provide him with a representative, a priest assisted at the ceremony, until in the end he and his ritual completely dwarfed the part which was played by the body of the faithful, and, while the sacrifice and banquet still survived, their significance was wholly inverted.[5]

(*e*) *L. Marillier.*—Some anthropologists, however, refuse to regard the theory of totemic sacrifice as primitive. Marillier, *e.g.*, argues that an original bond of union between the god and the kin eliminates the need for sacrificial rites, and therefore makes initiation ceremonies superfluous.[6] On the other hand, if the common meal was the only bond between the god and the kin, it does not appear that the god is a totem.

(*f*) *H. Hubert and M. Mauss.*—Hubert and Mauss think that the evidence of Semitic types of sacrifice may be only fragmentary, and in any case there is no proof that they are primitive. They hold that the numerous forms of sacrifice cannot be reduced to 'the unity of a single arbitrarily chosen principle.'[7] In view of the paucity of accurate accounts of early ritual, they reject the 'genealogical' or evolutionary method, and devote themselves to an analysis of the ancient Hindu and Hebrew sacrificial ritual. Thus they arrive at the following 'definition of type':

> 'Sacrifice is a religious act, which, by the consecration of a victim, modifies the state of the moral person who performs it, or of certain objects in which this person is interested.'[8]

Like Robertson Smith, they think that sacrifice establishes a union between the human and the divine. This is effected by the intermediation of a victim destroyed in the rite, and eaten by the worshippers or by the priests. But the victim must be ceremonially prepared for the rite, and freed from tabu after the ceremony has been performed. It must be remembered, however, that the rituals chosen by Hubert and Mauss for analysis are by no means primitive, and therefore can hardly be said to represent fairly the essential nature of sacrifice in the earliest cults of undeveloped peoples.

(*g*) *E. Westermarck.*—Westermarck takes the view that 'the idea that supernatural beings have human appetites and human wants' led to the practice of sacrificial gifts being offered to them by men. 'If such offerings fail them, they may even suffer want and become feeble and powerless.' Thus 'in early religion the most common motive is undoubtedly a desire to avert evils.'[1] The practice of human sacrifice, according to this writer, is based on the idea of the substitution of a victim for other individuals whose lives are in danger, which in course of time led to the offering of animals instead of men.[2]

(*h*) *J. G. Frazer.*—Frazer, in the first edition of *The Golden Bough*, says that the central idea of his essay—'the conception of the slain god'—is derived directly from his friend, Robertson Smith. In the second edition, however, he virtually contradicts this statement, maintaining that he never assented to Robertson Smith's theory. This change of opinion was apparently due to the fact that Frazer, on further investigating the subject in the production of his work *Totemism and Exogamy*, came to lay more stress on the social side of totemism, whereas Robertson Smith throughout emphasized its religious aspect. Furthermore, to follow Robertson Smith meant destroying his newly-formulated stratigraphical distinction between magic and religion. There could not, on this hypothesis, be any sacramentalism, *i.e.* something religious, in an age of magic. Therefore what on the face of it appears to him to be sacramental communion is for him simply a magical rite. It is difficult to understand how he reconciles this view with the fact that, in the highest and purest form of religion that the world has so far known, sacramental union with the Deity is the essential feature. To avoid deriving the slain god from the sacrifice of totemic animals, or from any operation of vegetation magic, Frazer is forced to find the origin of the rite in the slaying of the king. But, if the slain god is to be identified with the slain king, the king must first be proved divine. Thus he argues that, since kings and chiefs are tabu, they must therefore be sacred, in the sense that they are possessed by a god or a spirit. The numerous examples quoted do not, however, cover the whole field of primitive religion. Moreover, by his own definition of tabu as negative magic,[3] he divides sacred things into two classes—those that are divine and those that are not divine. Now kings are divine because they are tabu; and tabu is merely a 'negative magic.' Once more we are faced with the problem of how to derive the religious from the non-religious.

It is somewhat surprising that Frazer should have abandoned his original theory just at the moment when most remarkable evidence in favour of the mystical union between the totem or 'theanthropic' animal and the totemite was forthcoming from Australia, on the authority of Spencer and Gillen.

2. The Australian totemic rites.—By the performance of sacred ceremonies known as *intichiuma*

1 *Ib.* p. 108. 2 *Ib.* pp. 135, 139.
3 *Ib.* p. 230. 4 Paris, 1905–12, i. 103.
5 *Ib.* p. 104. 6 *RHR* xxxvi. [1897] 243.
7 'Essai sur le sacrifice,' *L'Année sociologique*, ii. [1899].
8 *Ib.*

1 *MI*, London, 1908, ii. 611 ff.; cf. Gn 28[20ff.]
2 *MI* i. 469 ff. 3 *GB*[3], pt. i., *The Magic Art*, i. 111.

it appears that the Arunta endeavour to secure the multiplication of some particular animal or plant, and actually enter into sacramental relations with the totem. After the performance of *intichiuma* at Emily Gap (a place specially associated with the mythical Alcheringa ancestors and the totems) the witchetty grub is tabu to the members of the totem, and must on no account be eaten by them till it is abundant.[1] The Purula and Kumara classes may eat it at any time, provided it be cooked in camp. After *intichiuma*, when the totem is plentiful, large supplies are gathered, brought into camp, cooked, and stored away in bark vessels called *pitchi*. In due course—at the period analogous to harvest-time among agricultural people—they are taken to the *ungunja*, or men's camp, where all the men assemble. The leader grinds up the contents of the *pitchi* between two stones. Then he and the other men of the totem eat a little and distribute what remains to those who do not belong to the totem. He repeats the operation with a *pitchi* from his own store. The witchetty grub totem may then eat sparingly of the grub.[2]

Similar rites take place in other totems in Central Australia, differing, of course, in detail, but everywhere made up of the same essential elements.[3]

Among the Undiara Kangaroo, *e.g.*, when an *intichiuma* ceremony is to be performed, the men proceed to the foot of a hill on the slope of which two blocks of stone project, one above the other. One of these stones is supposed to represent a male, the other a female, kangaroo. The headman of the totem clan and a man who is in the relation of mother's uncle to him climb up to a rocky ledge, supposed to be haunted by the spirits of ancestral kangaroos, and paint it with stripes of red and white to indicate the red fur and white bones of the kangaroo. When this is done, a certain number of young men sit on the top of the ledge, while the men below sing of the increase of the kangaroos. Blood-letting follows. 'The young men open veins in their arms and allow the blood to stream out on to, and over, the edge of the sacred ceremonial stone which represents the spot where a celebrated kangaroo of the Alcheringa went down into the earth, its spirit part remaining in the stone which arose to mark the place.'[4]

After the rite has been duly performed, the young men go and hunt the kangaroo, bringing their spoils back to the camp. Here the old men, with the *alatunja* in the midst, eat a little of the flesh of the animal and anoint with the fat the bodies of those who took part in the *intichiuma*, after which the meat is divided among all the men assembled. The men then decorate themselves with totemic designs, and the night is spent in singing songs relating to the exploits of the Alcheringa men. When this has been done, the animal may be eaten sparingly.[5]

When men of the emu totem desire to perform *intichiuma* ceremonies, several of the men open veins in their arms and allow the blood to stream on the ground till it is saturated. When the serum has coagulated, they trace designs in it in white, yellow, and black, representing the different parts of the body of an emu. Several men of the totem then dress themselves to resemble emus and imitate the manners and customs of the bird. They fasten *churinga* on their heads to represent the neck of the emu, and chant a song to the emu constructed in the blood. They think that this act has the effect of preventing the totem from disappearing, by quickening the embryos of the new generation.[6]

In the Unjiamba or Hakea-flower totem an *intichiuma* ceremony is performed by the men of the Bulthara and Panunga classes at a shallow, oval-shaped pit, by the side of which grows an ancient *hakea*-tree. In the centre of the depression is a small projecting and much worn block of stone, which is supposed to represent a mass of *hakea*-flowers. After the pit has been swept and songs sung inviting the tree to flower much and the blossoms to be full of honey, a young man is told to open a vein in his arm and allow the blood to sprinkle on the stone till it is covered. This done, the ceremony is complete. The stone is regarded as a *churinga*, and the spot is forbidden to women, children, and the uninitiated.[7] In other words, the ceremony has established a blood-bond between the totem and the totemites, and the place of the rite is rendered sacred and therefore tabu.

Spencer and Gillen, in a paper contributed to the *Journal of the Anthropological Institute*, say that for the totemite 'the one essential feature (of the ceremonies) is the necessity of identifying himself closely with his totem.'[1] That is to say, by opening a vein in his arm upon the kangaroo rocks, or eating the flesh of the sacred animal, or having its fat—a substance which with the Australian ranks equally with the blood as regards potency—rubbed on his body, the totemite establishes a union of a sacramental nature with the totem. True, the present-day native explanation of the ceremonies is that they drive out in all directions the spirits of the kangaroos, etc., and so increase the number of the animals.[2] But is this the only purpose of the rites? To prevent the totems from vanishing from the land, an alliance, in the nature of a blood-covenant, is made with the animal species by means of a solemn sacrificial meal. The blood rite, therefore, has a twofold efficacy. It is with the communion aspect that we are here concerned. The slain kangaroo closely resembles a sacrificial victim, although it can hardly be described as a 'mediator' between man and the sacred species, exactly in the sense suggested by Robertson Smith in his theory of the 'theanthropic' animal. The *mana* concentrated in the victim (especially in its blood) goes out and gives strength to the communicant, neutralizing his infirmities by drawing them into itself. In this way, rather than as an intermediary between God and man, the totem may be regarded as a victim.

Another difference between the Australian and more advanced forms of sacrifice lies in the fact that the animal in this case is naturally sacred, while ordinarily it acquires this character during the rite. But a mystic sacramental union between the totem and the totemite is none the less established by the *intichiuma* ceremony. A man of the witchetty grub or emu totem believes himself to be a witchetty grub or an emu. In order to keep this quality, he assimilates the flesh of the creature, that he may dwell in the totem and the totem in him. The solemn preparations show with what reverential awe these sacramental meals are regarded by the natives. The fasts, the *churinga*, the totemic decorations, the sacred rocks and designs, all testify to the sacred atmosphere surrounding the mysteries.[3] In the blood ceremonies we see exemplified not only the means whereby a blood-covenant is made with the totem, but also the psychological concept that in later cults develops into the sacrificial shedding of the blood of bulls and goats. As the Arunta sprinkle the sacred rocks or the totemic design with blood, so, in the more advanced religions, the priest offers upon the altar the blood of the sacrificial victim (Ex 29^{10-14}, Lv 9^{8-11}).

3. The primitive conception of sacrifice.—E. Durkheim maintains that both the essential forms of evolved sacrifice—the act of oblation and the act of communion—are found in germinal form in the *intichiuma* rites. The only difference, he thinks, is that in the later offerings the two acts in the *intichiuma* are parts of one undivided rite, while in the Australian ceremonies they are separated.[4] But, apart from the evidence of Strehlow that the hymn which is sung at the *intichiuma* of the kangaroo describes the offering of a morsel of kangaroo-fat to make the fat of the kangaroos increase,[5] the act of oblation can hardly be said to form a part of the Australian totemic rites. Apart from this instance, and from offerings to the dead consisting of stone hatchets, clubs, water, and in modern times matches,[6] there

[1] Spencer-Gillen[a], pp. 170–179; cf. E. O. James, *Primitive Ritual and Belief*, London, 1917, p. 120 ff.
[2] Spencer-Gillen[a], p. 203.
[3] *Ib.* p. 295 ff.; Spencer-Gillen[b], pp. 294, 296; J. D. Woods, *Native Tribes of S. Australia*, Adelaide, 1879, p. 187.
[4] Spencer-Gillen[a], p. 462.
[5] *Ib.* p. 204.
[6] *Ib.* p. 181.
[7] *Ib.* p. 184 f.

[1] *JAI* xxviii. [1899] 278.
[2] Spencer-Gillen[a], p. 206; C. Strehlow, *ZE* iii. [1871] 7, 12, ver. 7.
[3] E. Durkheim, *Les Formes élémentaires de la vie religieuse*, Paris, 1912, p. 484.
[4] *Ib.*
[5] *ZE* iii. 12, ver. 7.
[6] Howitt, p. 465.

is no evidence of gift-sacrifice in Australia. If, as we suggest, the *intichiuma* be regarded as the earliest form of sacrifice, it seems that the rite automatically involves the union of the totem and the totemite through the communication to the latter of the *mana* resident in the former (especially in the blood and its sacred flesh). The effect of this sacramental union is the neutralization or expulsion of the evil in man, by contact (as distinct from contract) with his supernatural ally. It is only when animistic and theistic conceptions arise that offerings of food are made to divine beings to secure their favour or to minimize their hostility. True, the Australian has a very real belief in tribal All-Fathers, but only as remote anthropomorphic beings in need of nothing that man can give. Therefore they are not the recipients of sacrificial gifts. Consequently we contend that, in what R. R. Marett calls the 'pre-animistic' type of religion,[1] the earliest attempts at sacrifice were means whereby the worshippers were placed in physical contact, after a sacramental manner, with their totem. But, it may be asked, do the Australians really represent a truly primitive people? Have they not had countless generations in which to evolve social and religious institutions? In order to answer these not unreasonable objections to a hypothesis founded on evidence from Australia, a brief survey must be made of the archæological facts which we have at our disposal.

4. Primeval sacrificial rites.—Within recent years numerous paintings and engravings of animals together with other designs have been discovered on the walls of palæolithic caverns in France and Spain,[2] having, it is supposed, magico-religious significance. If these caves were not 'pre-historic sanctuaries,'[3] why should palæolithic man draw outlines of animals and fish in the dark recesses of a mountain? Surely, if he were gratifying his æsthetic tastes, he would have chosen a place open to the light of day, where he and his companions might enjoy the fruits of their labours. It therefore seems much more reasonable to regard such caves as Niaux and Gargas as sacred spots where primeval mysteries were duly celebrated, and which had to be approached with solemn and esoteric rites. In the latter rock-shelter curious interlacings and arabesques have been made, either with the fingers or with some pointed instrument, in the gluey clay of the walls and roof of the cave. These have been described as imitations of the scratches left by the claws of the cave-bear, perhaps a totem of these particular Aurignacians.[4] In support of this view may be mentioned the numerous deep striæ on the walls of the cave of Font-de-Gaume. On the floor of this cavern a great many bones of the cave-bear have been found, as well as striæ corresponding to the rows of claws on the bear's foot, and the red outline drawing of the animal at the end of the gallery. Of course, this is slender evidence upon which to base the assumption that palæolithic man was given to totemism, but, taken in conjunction with the cave-paintings representing animals and designs similar to the totemic decorations of the Central Australians at Emily Gap, and the incised figures painted over with vermilion on the totemic grave-posts used by the American Indians, it makes it highly probable that these primeval inhabitants of Europe were acquainted with this primitive mode of social and religious organization. Moreover, the dots and bands in red and black ochre with which the pebbles found by E. Piette at Mas d'Azil are decorated correspond to the designs on the Australian *churinga*, while the so-called *bâtons de commandement* may have played their part in primeval totemic ceremonies.[1] But, even if these palæolithic paintings had no totemic significance, it can hardly be denied that they were used for magico-religious purposes.

[1] *The Threshold of Religion*², London, 1914, p. xxi.

[2] Cf. art. ART, 'Note on the Use of Painting in Primitive Religion,' vol. i. p. 821 ff.; E. A. Parkyn, *An Introd. to the Study of Prehistoric Art*, London, 1915, pp. 19–131.

[3] Marett, pp. 203–220.

[4] *L'Anthropologie*, xxi. [1910] 139, 142; cf. Marett, p. 217.

It is well known that the modern savage frequently depicts the image of a creature in order to obtain magical power over the real animal. F. H. Cushing describes the images of totems carved out of stone by the Zuñi Indians, with a flint arrow bound to the 'fetiche.'[2] Likewise among the Ojibwa Indians the medicine-man makes a drawing of the animal to be hunted and paints the heart in vermilion, drawing a line from it to the mouth, along which magic is supposed to pass at his incantation.[3] Now, in the pre-historic caverns at Niaux and Font-de-Gaume bisons are represented with arrows painted in their sides, and, in the former, there is a curious design showing a wounded bison surrounded by marks which have been likened to boomerangs. Such drawings are inexplicable except as a means whereby these ancient hunters endeavoured to procure success in the chase.

It has been noticed that among the Central Australians, in order to cause a multiplication of the totem, *intichiuma* ceremonies were held in places in which the sacred animal is symbolically represented on rocks, or, in the case of the emu totem, on the ground. Since palæolithic man, like his modern representative the Australian, was a hunter, depending on the chase for his subsistence, the conclusion seems inevitable that he too performed sacred ceremonies in the dark recesses of his 'sanctuaries' for the same purpose. Of course, it is not suggested that the totemic cult of modern aborigines is in any way identical with that of primeval man, but, judging from the numerous similarities between the two cultures, the Arunta rites appear to represent the nearest approach to the totemic mysteries celebrated by palæolithic man at Gargas, Niaux, and similar sites. If this is so, the rudimentary conceptions of sacrifice set forth in *intichiuma* ceremonies formed part of magico-religious cult at least as early as the Aurignacian culture-period in Western Europe.

5. Ideas connected with sacrifice.—(*a*) *Communion.*—Jevons is of the opinion that 'the core of worship is communion.'[4] This conception, if it is used in the wide sense of contact, is, as we have seen, the fundamental principle underlying the most rudimentary forms of sacrifice. Wherever totemism is found, a union with the sacred species is effected by physical assimilation of the supernatural qualities of the divine animal or plant. A typical instance is the well-known sacramental eating of the bear among the Ainus.[5] The Ainus, like many other primitive people, also eat sacramentally the new crops.[6]

In New Caledonia the eating of the first yams of the season is a solemn ceremony in which the women take no part.

> Seven or eight yams are dug up with the greatest precaution, wrapped in leaves, and carried before the great wooden images, rudely carved in human form. The yams are then cooked in special pots by boys, and eaten by them. The pots are afterwards buried, and the chief addresses the crowd, praying the images to give them a good crop of yams every year. The new yams are then dressed and eaten.[7]

[1] *L'Anthropologie*, xiv. [1903] 357; cf. M. Bernardin, *Revue savoisienne*, Feb. 1876; Spencer-Gillen^a, p. 128; cf. art. STAFF.

[2] *2 RBEW* [1883], pp. 9–43.

[3] W. J. Hoffman, *7 RBEW* [1891], pp. 221–223.

[4] *Introd. to Hist. of Religion*, p. 225.

[5] A full description is given in art. AINUS, vol. i. p. 249 f.

[6] See art. AINUS, vol. i. p. 248^b.

[7] *GB*³, pt. v., *Spirits of the Corn and of the Wild*, ii. 53.

The inherent tendency, the yearning of the feeble human soul to reach out towards and make itself part of the divine nature, which finds its satisfaction in the Christian Eucharist, is even more clearly set forth in the sacrificial ritual of the native tribes of America. The most notable and instructive example is the custom observed among the Aztecs of sacramentally eating bread as the body of the god Huitzilopochtli or Vitzilipaztli.

In addition to the holding of a feast at which the people ate their god sacramentally in the outward and visible shape of bread and grain,[1] they entered into a closer union by fortifying dough with human blood. A youth was chosen and named for the god. For months the person doomed to play the fatal part of divinity was treated with divine honour, and permitted to taste all the joys of the world to which he was soon to bid farewell. At the expiration of the set time he was slain on the altar and his fresh blood was mixed with dough, which was divided among the worshippers and eaten.[2] Thus they became partakers of the divine nature.

Savages sometimes seek to enter into communion with the dead by eating part of the body of the deceased or by holding a feast as part of the funeral rites. Sometimes the flesh provided at the banquets is that of the dead man himself, as in the case of the Dieri.[3] More frequently animal victims, whose blood and soul the dead man has consumed, are slain and their flesh is eaten by the survivors to establish a sacramental union with the deceased. The Nicobar Islanders hold a feast at the grave 'in the presence of the dead' after a funeral,[4] and in Melanesia the chief mourner takes a piece of fowl and of yam and calls the names of those who have recently died in the place saying, 'This is for you.'[5]

Robertson Smith explains the mutilation of the bodies or garments of the living as constituting a bond of union between them and the dead.[6] It seems reasonable to suppose that by causing their blood to flow over the corpse or grave a 'covenant in blood' is established; conversely, other primitive people daub themselves with the blood, etc., of their kinsman, and thus incorporate in themselves a portion of the dead. For the same reason bones, hands, locks of hair, and the like are retained by survivors. Likewise, savages often endeavour to form a covenant with their dead enemies by establishing a blood-brotherhood with them.

Thus, 'when an Arawak Indian of British Guiana has murdered another, he repairs on the third night to the grave of his victim, and pressing a pointed stick through the corpse he licks off and swallows any blood that he finds adhering to the stick.'[7] If this were not done, it is believed that the murderer would go mad and die.

Sometimes it is thought sufficient merely to anoint the communicant with the blood or oil exuded from the body of the deceased.[8]

Parallel with these rites is another mourning rite—that of cutting or tearing the hair and burying it with the body or dedicating it at the grave. In the case of certain tribes in Central Australia the hair is burnt instead of dedicated.[9] The object of these rites, as with the blood ceremonies, is seemingly to form a bond of union with the dead, so as to prevent his inflicting any harm on the survivors. It may be that hair is thrown on the corpse for the same reason.

(*b*) *Conciliation*.—Although the most common motive in early conceptions of sacrifice is undoubtedly a desire to enter into sacramental relations with a source of spiritual strength, and thereby to obtain *mana*, yet the wish to avert, neutralize, or expel evil is by no means an uncommon source of sacrificial offerings among primitive people. The savage is very susceptible to apprehensions of danger from supernatural powers, and, although there is no proof that fear was the cause of the earliest attempts at sacrifice, yet in the course of the development of the rite, the idea of 'conciliation' soon arose. Thus the 'piacular,' or propitiatory, offering of an atoning nature came into force. The 'gods' were thought to be displeased with men, and in consequence a sacrifice had to be offered to avert their supposed anger or indignation. In very primitive cult offerings were made to anything that was considered to be dangerous—rocks, glaciers, earthquakes, diseases, death, and so forth, or even curiously shaped stones, fish, animals, trees, etc.[1] In S.E. Australia, when a man of another clan entered a certain tract of country, he had to propitiate the local spirits by performing such rites.[2] On building or entering a new house or canoe, starting on a war or trade expedition, and, as has been seen, at the time of sowing or reaping the new crops, sacrifices were made to bring 'luck' and the 'blessing of heaven' on the venture. Parallel to these rites is the offering of the first-born of man and beast.[3] When sin is regarded as contagious and capable of transmission, a sacrificial victim is used as a scapegoat.[4] Such a vicarious sacrifice, however, is expiatory only in the sense that the death of the victim expiates the guilt of the actual offender.

(*c*) *Honorific offerings*. — Another aspect of more developed sacrifice is the free-will offering in grateful recognition of the goodness and beneficence of the deity. Although the desire of primitive man to show his thankfulness to the higher powers is secondary to the communal and piacular conception, it is by no means unknown in early cult. The offerings of firstfruits and many other gift-sacrifices conceived of as an honorarium rather than a bribe come under this division.

'When certain natives of Eastern Central Africa, after they have prayed for a successful hunting expedition, return home laden with venison and ivory, they know that they are indebted to "their old relative" for their good fortune, and give him a thank-offering.'[5]

The 'eucharistic' conception of sacrifice—*i.e.* one free from the desire to secure material benefits in the future (cf. Gn 28[20ff.])—is seldom found in really primitive cult.

In the higher religions the ethical notions of self-sacrifice and the oblation of a contrite heart develop conceptions involving intelligent self-unification with God through prayer, penitence, and abstinence. Such ideas, however, are entirely absent from primitive cult. In the rudimentary form of the rite the communion-theory is adequate to cover most of the facts if it be construed on liberal lines, remembering that the primitive mind is more concerned with getting into contact with his supernatural ally than in entering into elaborate and solemn contracts with him. What he needs is *mana* both to join himself on to his source of strength and to neutralize and expel the evil in and about him. The *intichiuma* rite is a means of attaining this end, since the *mana* concentrated in the victim goes out and gives strength to the communicant, drawing into itself his infirmities. With the rise of animistic and theistic beliefs,

1 *GB*³, pt. v., *Spirits of the Corn and of the Wild*, ii. 86 ff.
2 B. de Sahagun, *Hist. générale des choses de la Nouvelle-Espagne*, French tr., Paris, 1880, p. 203 f.
3 Howitt, p. 449.
4 *AE* vi. [1893] 25.
5 R. H. Codrington, *The Melanesians*, Oxford, 1891, p. 284.
6 *Rel. Sem*². p. 336.
7 *GB*³, pt. v., *Spirits of the Corn and of the Wild*, ii. 154.
8 Howitt, p. 467.
9 Spencer-Gillen^b, pp. 507, 520.

1 *GB*³, pt. i., *The Magic Art*, ii. 15, pt. v., *Spirits of the Corn and of the Wild*, ii. 291.
2 Howitt, p. 403.
3 *GB*³, pt. iii., *The Dying God*, London, 1911, p. 179 ff.; R. Brough Smyth, *The Aborigines of Victoria*, Melbourne, 1878, ii. 311; Ex 13²⁻¹⁵, Nu 18¹⁵ᶠ·, Gn 22¹⁻¹³; cf. Mic 6⁷; *MI* i. 458; artt. FIRST-BORN.
4 *GB*³, pt. vi., *The Scapegoat*, London, 1913; cf. Lv 16²¹ artt. EXPIATION AND ATONEMENT, PROPITIATION, SCAPEGOAT.
5 *MI* ii. 615

gifts, honorific offerings, and the whole complex system of developed sacrificial ritual are gradually added to the original rite.

LITERATURE.—Sources are cited in the footnotes.

E. O. JAMES.

SACRIFICE (Buddhist). — The attitude of Buddhism towards every kind of external sacrificial ritual was one of uncompromising dissent. It judged such ritual (1) to be the futile expression of misdirected outlay and effort, and (2) in some of its forms to involve cruelty. And (3) the kind of benefits hoped for from the rites was not sufficiently, as we should say, spiritual. References to this opposition, however, are far to seek in its ancient literature, and we are tempted to infer that such sacrificial feasts as involved the taking of life or much elaborate ceremonial were not of periodical occurrence, and indeed were rare events. It is only in the tending of a consecrated fire, and in oblations made through that fire, not apparently to the deceased Vedic god Agni, but to 'great Brahmā,' that any continuity of sacrificial observance appears. Had sacrifices of animals been of frequent occurrence, it is probable that the canonical accounts of the Buddha's deeds and words would have contained more frequent records of protest publicly made. As it is, no such public protest is to be found in any of these books. There does not in fact appear to have been any sacrificial ceremonial made at stated intervals by a hierarchy acting for the people and for the people's welfare. Such sacrificial ceremonies could be arranged by the powerful and wealthy, but they were held on behalf of some individual, and not by or for the community. Thus the king of Kosala, the Pasenadi, is recorded as commanding a great animal sacrifice, explained in the commentary as advised by his chaplains to avert personal evil threatened in a dream.[1] The *seṭṭhi*, or leading millionaire merchant of Rājagaha, was supposed, on one occasion, by his brother-in-law, Anāthapiṇḍika, to be preparing 'a great sacrifice,' so absorbed did he appear to his visitor.[2] In the *Kūṭadanta Suttanta* an eminent Brāhman abbot is represented as preparing a great animal sacrifice, concerning the complicated procedure of which he consults the Buddha's wisdom.[3] This, as the translator points out, is a deliberate fiction full of ironical humour, since to ask such advice is 'the last thing a Brahmin of position would do.'[4] Other allusions to 'great sacrifices' (*mahā yañña*) may be found in the *Jātaka* stories, and are of course no less deliberate fictions,[5] especially the story of the king consenting to sacrifice all his family.[6] It is only on the occasion of the king of Kosala's great sacrifice just mentioned that we meet with any expressly uttered protest against such a ceremony. Even here the protest is made, not to king or people, but to the disciples who bring the news to the *vihāra* (or grove 'settlement'). It is only in the commentary, and in that of the *Jātaka*,[7] that we read of the utterance being promptly reported to the king and of his countermanding the ceremony. And the terms of the protest are so general as to suggest with some force that verses and *sutta* were a piece of ancient editorial work carried out with very scanty material. They may be found in the writer's translation of *Saṃyutta*, i.[8] The verses ran thus:

> 'The sacrifices called the Horse, the Man,
> The Peg-thrown Site, the Drink of Victory,
> The Bolts Withdrawn, and all the mighty fuss:—
> These are not rites that bring a rich result.
> Where divers goats and sheep and kine are slain,
> Never to such a rite as that repair
> The noble seers who walk the perfect way.
> But rites where is no slaughter nor no fuss,
> Are offerings meet, bequests perpetual,
> Where never goats and sheep and kine are slain.
> To such a sacrifice as this repair
> The noble seers who walk the perfect way.
> These are the rites entailing great results.
> These to the celebrant are blest, not cursed.
> Th' oblation runneth o'er; the gods are pleased.'

This is not so much a reasoned argument against such rites as a categorical impeachment of 'much ado about nothing,' of ineffective activity, coupled with an implicit contempt for acts and beliefs that could no longer appeal to men of lofty mind. Herein, as Rhys Davids writes, the early Buddhists evidently took up and carried on to complete victory the growing feeling of intelligence and humaneness to which the seal is set in that Rock Edict of King Aśoka which begins: 'No animal may be slaughtered for sacrifice.'

> 'Isolated instances of such sacrifices are known even down to the Muhammadan invasion. But the battle was really won by the Buddhists and their allies,' especially, as is probable, by the Nigaṇṭhas or Jains, with their central tenet of *ahiṃsā*, or 'non-injury.' 'And the combined ridicule and earnestness of the Kūṭadanta Suttanta will have had its share in bringing about the victory.'[1]

The sacrifice stories, moreover, in the *Jātakas*, especially the extraordinarily outspoken sarcasm of Bhūridatta's verses, in the *Jātaka* of that name,[2] will have helped later to consummate that victory, appealing, as they must have done, to popular audiences who, instead of rising in shocked wrath to stone a blaspheming narrator, sat and listened with the amused appreciation of the enfranchised.

More pointed than the above-cited protest is the rebuke against the futility of oblation by fire, which is put, with felicitous irony, into the mouth not of a teacher, but of the divine object himself. It occurs in the same book.[3] A Brāhmanee, whose son is a pervert—in other words, a young *arahant* in the Buddha's order—is a habitual sacrificer to Brahmā. Her son approaches her house on his round for alms. Brahmā appears to her and utters a eulogy of the son as the more fitting recipient of the food which she is wasting:

> 'Far hence, O brahminee, is Brahmā's world,
> To whom thou servest offerings alway.
> And Brahmā feedeth not on food like that.
> What babblest thou unwitting of the way,
> O brahminee, unto the Brahmā world?
> Lo here! this Brahmadeva, son of thine,
> A man who ne'er will see another world,
> A man who past the gods hath won his way;
> . . . .
> Meet for oblations from both gods and men,
> . . . .
> Let him enjoy the choice meats thou hast served.'

Our second point, that in the 'great sacrifice' the slaughter of life was reprehensible, appears, in the *Suttas*, in the doctrine of the four classes of individuals—those, namely, who (1) torment themselves, (2) torment others, (3) torment both self and others, (4) torment neither. Of these the first practise austerities; the second include butchers, trappers, fishermen, brigands, etc.; the third include kings or mighty priests who, on some such occasion as the opening of a new mote-hall, hold a sacrifice with great ritual, with the slaughter of many cattle, goats, and rams, with wood-cutting and grass-strewing, and with much bullying and hustling of servants and slaves, working in fear of chastisement.[4] This point as to cruelty is much more eloquently expressed in the *Bhūridatta*,[5] in the address uttered by the *bodhisatta* (Buddha-to-be) on the futility of sacrifices practised by Brāh-

---

1 *Saṃyutta*, i. 76. 2 *Vinaya Texts*, *SBE* xx. [1885] 180.
3 *Dialogues of the Buddha*, tr. T. W. Rhys Davids, Oxford, 1899, i. 173.
4 P. 163. 5 *E.g.*, vol. iii. nos. 314, 433.
6 Vol. vi. no. 542. 7 Vol. iii. no. 314.
8 *The Book of Kindred Sayings*, *PTS*, 1917, p. 102.

1 *Dialogues*, *loc. cit.* 2 Tr. vi. 109–112.
3 *Saṃyutta*, i. 139 f., tr. 176 f.
4 *Majjhima*, i. 342 f.; *Aṅguttara*, ii. 205.
5 *Jātaka*, vol. vi. no. 543.

mans, and on the abuses to which those practices led:

'If he who kills is counted innocent,

. . . .

Let Brahmins Brahmins kill. . . .
We see no cattle asking to be slain
That they a new and better life may gain.
Rather they go unwilling to their death,
And in vain struggles yield their latest breath.
To veil the post, the victim and the blow,
The Brahmins let their choicest rhetoric flow.

. . . .

These cruel cheats, as ignorant as vile,
Weave their long frauds the simple to beguile.'

The sympathy with animal suffering betrayed here is essential to the view that spoke, in its religious terms, not of 'all men' only, but of 'all beings' or 'creatures' (*sabbe sattā, bhūtā*) as objects for compassion. And this standpoint would of itself, without other reasons, rule all blood-sacrifice out of court as monstrous.

The third point, as to the low aspirations which the sacrificial rites were intended to further, is best illustrated by the words ascribed to a notable early convert, Kassapa of Uruvelā. His conversion is recorded in a series of legends.[1] The Buddha invites him to make public confession of his faith:

'What hast thou seen, thou of Uruvelā,
That thou, preacher and votary austere,
Hast left the Fire? I ask thee, Kassapa,
The cause of this. Why is thy sacrifice
Of holy fire bereft of all thy care?'

To this Kassapa replies:

'The sacrifices speak to us of things
We see and hear, yea, taste, of men's desires
And women. I have learnt to say of things
That bring rebirth, "Lo! it is canker." Hence
No more delight I take in sacrifice
Nor in oblation.'

He then tells what he has 'seen.' Kassapa might well have made out a better case for the loftier-minded among celebrants, without violating the truth. From the standpoint of Buddhist saintship, however, such loftier aspirations as the prayer so to live as to be reborn in Brahmā's heaven were but a palliative, and not the real 'escape.' The contrast is shown in Kassapa's verses preserved in the anthology:

'Once well content with sacrifice, 'bove all
Concerned within these worlds[2] once more to live,
Now have I set myself to extirpate
All passion, all ill will, illusion too.'[3]

The transformation and spiritualization of the two aspects of sacrifice—as symbol and as self-devotion—are emphasized by Buddhism much as they were by Hebrew psalmist and prophet. The stations in the road to the good life—the perfect lay life and the perfect religious life—are, in the *Kūṭadanta Suttanta*,[4] set forth as so many degrees of 'sacrifice' (*yañña*). Elsewhere the inwardness of the right sacrificial celebration is dwelt upon:

'I lay no wood, brahmin, for fires on altars.
Only within burneth the fire I kindle.
Ever my fire burns; ever tense and ardent
I, Arahant, work out the life that's holy.
. . . . the heart's the altar,
The fire thereon, this is man's self well tamèd.'[5]

And of such fire-tending no class could hold a monopoly:

'Ask not of birth. Ask of the course of conduct.
From any sticks verily fire doth take birth.
The steadfast seer, though his descent be lowly,
To intellect's aristocrats is lifted,
By noble shame all that is evil curbing.'[6]

As to the surrender of self or property in the right sacrifice, the votary of the religious life in leaving the world had surrendered his all; to the layman not so sacrificing it was left to offer often

[1] *Vinaya Texts*, *SBE* xiii. [1881] 118–139.
[2] 'These worlds' includes every sphere, terrestrial or celestial, of life.
[3] *Psalms of the Brethren*, ed. C. A. F. Rhys Davids, *PTS*, 1909–13, ccx.; cf. also his brother's verses, cciii.
[4] Referred to above (*Dialogues*, i. 173 f.).
[5] *Saṃyutta*, i. 169. [6] *Ib.* p. 167.

and gladly of his goods to these sons and daughters of the homeless life. By thus sowing his harvest in that 'field of supreme merit,' he maintained the high religious standard in his community, and the means of hearing good doctrine, and he also lived in faith of reaping a crop of happiness in both the near and the distant future.[1]

LITERATURE.—The literary references are given in the article. T. W. Rhys Davids, *Buddhist India*, London, 1903, pp. 240 f., 248 f., 294, should also be consulted.

C. A. F. RHYS DAVIDS.

SACRIFICE (Celtic).[2]—**1. Evidence of ancient writers.**—As has already been pointed out in art. COMMUNION WITH DEITY (Celtic), statements are made by Cæsar and other writers of antiquity that the Celts offered human sacrifices. Cæsar[3] says that in Gaul men who were suffering from serious illness, or who were in the midst of war or any other great danger, would sacrifice or promise to sacrifice human victims, in the belief that the majesty of the gods could be appeased only when a life was given for a life. He also refers to the burning of human sacrifices enclosed in huge wicker images (*simulacra*). In the first instance the victims chosen for such a fate were such criminals as brigands and thieves, but, in default of such criminals, innocent victims would be sacrificed. Lucan[4] speaks of human sacrifices as being offered among the Gauls to the gods Hesus, Taranis, and Teutates; and his statement is repeated by Lactantius, who says: 'Hesum atque Teutatem humano cruore placabant.'[5] Diodorus Siculus,[6] following Posidonius, refers to the quinquennial sacrifice of evil-doers (κακούργους) by impalement. He further states that captives taken in battle, as well as certain animals similarly captured, were by some tribes sacrificed by burning or otherwise.

In one passage[7] Diodorus speaks of a certain general as having sacrificed to the gods the handsomest of the youths. Tacitus[8] speaks of the Britons as thinking it right to offer up the blood of captives, and Plutarch[9] mentions the human sacrifices of the Gauls, which they considered, he says, of all sacrifices the most perfect (τελεωτάτην θυσίαν). Athenæus,[10] too, refers to the Gaulish sacrifice of prisoners of war in the case of a defeat. According to Pliny,[11] the human sacrifices of Gaul were suppressed by Tiberius, but, according to Mela,[12] a vestige of the ancient practice remained in the cutting off of a portion of the flesh of those condemned to death. The notes on Lucan called 'Commenta Lucani Usener' say that Hesus, whom the commentator identifies with Mars, was appeased by the hanging of a man in a tree, until his limbs wasted away, while, in another passage, he identifies Hesus with Mercury, and says that he is worshipped by merchants. With Mercury he also identifies Teutates, and states that he was appeased by thrusting a man head-foremost into a full vat, and keeping him in that position until he was drowned. Taranis he identifies with Jupiter, and says that he used to be appeased with human beings, but that he was now content with cattle. How far the commentator was speaking from knowledge it is impossible to say. According to Suetonius,[13] it was Claudius (not Tiberius) who completely abolished druidism, after Augustus had prohibited Roman citizens from taking any part in its rites. In Pausanias[14] we are told that the Gauls under Combutis and Orestorios put to death the whole male population of Callieas, and then drank the blood and tasted the flesh of the slain. A passage from Procopius[15] also speaks of the Celts as especially prizing the sacrifice of their first prisoner of war; the form which the sacrifice took, according to him, was that of hanging the victim from a tree, throwing him amid thorns, or putting him to death in some other horrible fashion.

2. Expiation and atonement as explanations of earlier practices.—In view of the evidence of Cæsar and others, it would be useless to deny that the Celts offered up human victims; and certainly, in Cæsar's time, as in the time of Posidonius, who was the chief authority of Strabo and Diodorus, the human sacrifices that were offered, whether

[1] Cf., *e.g.*, *Saṃyutta*, p. 97, tr. p. 123 ff.
[2] Cf. throughout artt. CELTS and COMMUNION WITH DEITY (Celtic).
[3] *De Bell. Gall.* vi. 16. [4] *Pharsal.* i. 444 ff.
[5] *Div. Inst.* i. 21. [6] v. 32. [7] v. 31.
[8] *Ann.* xiv. 30. [9] *De Superstit.* 13, p. 171 B.
[10] ii. 51. [11] *HN* xxx. 4.
[12] iii. 2. 18. [13] *Claud.* 25.
[14] x. 22. [15] *De Bell. Goth.* ii. 15.

quinquennially or otherwise, seem distinctly to have had a religious sanction, and to have then been regarded as piacular. It is, however, worth considering whether the practice of ridding society of superfluous members may not have been, in its origin, independent of religious considerations, and based rather upon the co-operation of instincts of antipathy to the unfit with a state of economic pressure. The religious sanction and interpretation of the practice may well be later than the practice itself, and it is not improbable that religious and ethical development helped to mitigate the custom and to lead to the substitution of animal for human victims. It is clear from the testimony of ancient writers that the Celts of antiquity were characterized by two well-marked traits: (1) a remarkable indifference to human life in themselves and in others, and (2) an intense and scrupulous regard for religious observance.[1] With their indifference to life was closely connected their belief in its duration after death. Under the conditions of Celtic life, children must have grown up with a most vivid sense of the uncertainty of existence. Fathers, according to Cæsar,[2] had the power of life and death over their own wives and children, and the practice of sons not appearing in their father's presence[3] until they reached manhood may have originated in a judicious concealment by the mothers of the boys from the sight of their fathers, lest the head of the household should decide to reduce the number of his children. In battle, too, it was considered improper for the attendants of a chieftain to survive him, and the institution of the *soldurii*[4] probably constitutes, on the highest plane in the Celtic community, a practice of non-survival on the part of dependents which was originally doubtless more compulsory than voluntary. The wanderings of the Celts in antiquity speak of intense economic pressure; and, in times of famine, or in districts where the supply of food was inadequate, it is in the highest degree probable that the stronger elements in the community would not hesitate to eliminate the weaker or those whose continued existence increased rather than lessened the burden of the community. It was probably this economic pressure, combined with the idea that the dead had the same wants as the living, that caused the wives and servants of a dead man to accept death voluntarily on his decease, or the attendants of a king to be willing not to survive him. When brought face to face with sheer necessity and economic conditions which threaten society with extinction, human nature, in its crude state, is capable of great harshness in order to ensure its own preservation; and the human sacrifices of the Celts, as well as of other races, probably owe their origin to economic rather than religious ideas. The strain of living had probably much to do with the proverbial ferocity of the ancient Celts. In normal times it is not improbable that the better placed Celts came, by adjustment to their environment, to be relieved from the continuous necessity of weeding out the community; but times of abnormal stress would arise, and recourse would be had to the ancient practice of eliminating the unfit, and its employment would probably now take a double form. On the one hand, it might be adopted as a measure partly of economic, partly of religious, necessity in the actual period of exceptional stress, or it might be adopted in anticipation of a threatened calamity. Its character as a solemn and deliberate act of the whole community, in relation to events which were beyond man's control, would ensure its interpretation in current religious terms. In course of time some effort would be made to bring the practice into relation also to the needs of primitive jurisprudence, and, as Cæsar[1] states was the case in Gaul, the victims offered would, as far as possible, be those who deserved punishment for their conduct. As in all ancient customs, there would be a tendency to continue human sacrifice, especially when the idea of the necessity of appeasing angered gods and of restoring communion with them had become firmly implanted in the mind of the community; but the relief of economic pressure, through the improvement of tillage and the like, would in most cases tend to humaner practices. There would ensue, *e.g.*, a reduction in the number of victims, and a substitution for human victims of animals, while the sacrifice would tend to change its character, from being viewed as an act of expiation or atonement to becoming mainly a remedial or medicinal rite. Thus, a practice which originally arose in the main from a real or supposed economic necessity might, at different stages in its history, receive a different interpretation. The interpretation need not necessarily be religious, but at a certain stage the practice in question and the domain of religious thought would be so closely connected that a practice of remote and non-religious origin would receive a religious interpretation, just as at a still later stage its interpretation as a charm might be purely remedial or medicinal.

The idea that the gods were specially in need of human victims before they could be appeased could have arisen only in the days of a belief in humanized deities, while there is abundant evidence from the names of Celtic deities that they were originally far from being exclusively or mainly human. The practice of human sacrifice belongs, as its wide-spread traces show, to a far deeper layer of mankind's history than the development of anthropomorphic deities; and the conclusion appears inevitable that the practice existed long before its explanation as a piacular sacrifice, whether private or public, especially pleasing to anthropomorphic deities, could have arisen.

Among the Celts, as among other races, the practice in question would appear to have become associated with certain periods of the year and with certain agricultural operations. The association of the form of sacrificial death with a tree, or with thorns, or with wicker-work images, appears to point to its connexion at an earlier epoch in its history with some of the main events of the agricultural year. And economic stress in the case of man, as in the case of cattle, would be more acutely felt at certain periods than at others, and might then lead to drastic action. Certain times of the year, too, more than others, would make clear who were the worthless members of the community. Hindrances to vegetable growth would suggest the desirability of promoting it by a clearance of such human elements as were deemed likely to check it. The Celtic year began in the beginning of November, while its second half began in the beginning of May; and, as these periods became more and more fixed, the clearances, by burning and otherwise, which took place in them might include some human elements. The Beltane fires, which continued in Scotland well into the 18th cent., clearly suggest in some of their features[2] that originally they included the burning of human victims.

3. General survivals in folk-custom and folk-lore.—Through the diligent researches of members

[1] As shown by the statement of Diodorus (v. 27) that, in spite of the fondness of the Celts for money, gold could be left unguarded among the inland Celts in temples and on consecrated ground without the slightest risk of its being touched. Cæsar (vi. 16) bears witness to the intense hold which religious scruple had upon the Celts, and the allusions to the practice of consulting soothsayers and others as to the future, even in early Christian centuries, show the strength of their old beliefs. See A. Holder, *Altcelt. Sprachschatz*, Leipzig, 1891–1913, *s.v.* 'Caragus.'

[2] vi. 19.

[3] *Ib.* vi. 18.

[4] Mentioned in Nicolaus Damasc. *Hist.* frag. 86, p. 79 D, in Athenæus, vi. 54, p. 249 A–B. Here they are called σιλοδούροι, and an instance is given of 600 men who, in return for the privilege of ruling with their king and wearing the same raiment, vowed to die with him, whether he fell in battle or was carried off by disease, and no one was known to have broken the vow. Cæsar (iii. 22) calls them *soldurii*.

[1] vi. 16.

[2] See *GB*[3], pt. vii., *Balder the Beautiful*, London, 1913, i. 146 ff.

of the Folk-Lore Society and others into the folk-lore of Celtic countries various traces of sacrifices have been discovered which bear the impress of the stage when such sacrifices were interpreted through conceptions of expiation and atonement and through the closely allied conception of purification.

Rhŷs[1] mentions a tradition at St. John's in the Isle of Man that witches were at one time punished by being set to roll down the steep side of the mountain in spiked barrels. He also tells[2] of the burning of a calf by a farmer to secure luck after he had lost a number of his cattle. The same author quotes R. N. Worth's *History of Devonshire* (London, 1886) as saying: 'Living animals have been burnt alive in sacrifice within memory to avert the loss of other stock. The burial of three puppies "brandise-wise" in a field is supposed to rid it of weeds.'[3] He also records[4] an account given by an old woman of the burning of a sheep in Andreas parish in the Isle of Man on Old May-day, but he was not satisfied that the narrator heard the burning spoken of, when it occurred, as a sacrifice. We are told again[5] of a cattle-dealer in Ireland who was familiar with the practice of driving cattle through fire or between fires on May-day. Cormac is quoted[6] as explaining that 'Belltaine (May-day) was so called from the "lucky fire" or the "two fires" which the druids of Erin used to make on that day with great incantations.' It is significant that Cormac makes no reference to sacrifice either of sheep or of human beings. In the old Welsh poem called the *Gododin* there is a reference to the lowering of a sacrifice upon a bonfire, 'Aberth am goelcerth a discynnyn.'[7] In *FL* vi. [1895] 164 an account is given by John Abercromby (on the authority of a MS by Malcolm MacPhail, formerly schoolmaster in Lewis and afterwards Free Church minister in Argyllshire) of the practice of 'sacrifice to procure good fishing.' This practice of sacrificing a sheep or goat at the commencement of the herring-fishing season was employed on the west side of Lewis. The oldest fisherman in the district was selected to perform the ceremony on the very edge of the sea, 'so that any of the blood that might be spilt would fall into the water.' The blood of the animal was collected with scrupulous care in a boat's bailer. When the blood had ceased to flow, the old fisherman waded into the water and poured it out to the ruler of the deep. The body of the victim was cut up into portions sufficient to give one to each of the paupers of the district. This ceremony appears to have been performed once with due solemnity within the last ninety years. There is an account (p. 165) from the same MacPhail MS of an invocation and offering to Shoni (or Sonidh) for sea-ware (*i.e.* sea-weed), with which it was the custom to manure the fields. The offering on this occasion took the form, not of the sacrifice of a living creature, but of a libation of malt liquor. There is also a description of this practice by M. Martin.[8] In *FL* vi. 167[9] there is an account of the sacrifice of a black cock to cure epilepsy. The black cock had to be one hatched in March, and was 'buried alive, with clippings of the patient's hair and nails, at the very spot where the sufferer had had his first attack.' The same article contains an account of the sacrifice of a black cock on account of disease in cattle. About ninety years ago, according to the same article, a black sheep was flayed alive, and the skin, while still warm, was placed over the diseased limbs of a person suffering from rheumatism, with a view to their cure. About the same period, too,[10] it was the practice, on the first night when cattle were brought home and housed for the winter, to carry fire around them three times in the direction of the sun. Whether this was a vestige of any sacrificial practice it is difficult to say. In *FL* ii. [1891] 20 there is an account of a vestige of sacrifice at Whitsuntide in the parish of King's Teignton, Devonshire, where a lamb was killed and roasted whole in the middle of the village, for the purpose, it is said, of obtaining water. The lamb was decorated with garlands, and the roasted flesh was given to the poor. The same article speaks of the similar roasting of a whole ram lamb at Holne, on one of the spurs of Dartmoor, in a field called 'the Ploy Field,' in the centre of which is a *menhir* 6 or 7 ft. high. In *FL* iv. [1893] 498 ff., in a valuable article on the sanctuary of Mourie, there is a quotation from the records of the Presbytery of Dingwall for 5th Sept. 1656, referring to the 'abhominable and heathenishe practices' of the people of 'Appilcross,' who used to sacrifice bulls at a certain time on 25th August. It was decided 'that quhosoever sall be found to commit such abhominations, especiallie Sacrifices of any kynd, or at any tyme, sall publickly appear and be rebuked.' There is a similar reference in another minute of 9th Sept. 1656 to 'the sacrificing of beasts' at Gairloch as well as to the 'pouring of milk upon hills as oblationes.' In *FL* x. [1899] 118 there is an account by Leland L. Duncan of the survival in Ireland of the sacrifice at the building of a house at Kiltubbrid, Co. Leitrim. When the ground for the house had been measured out, a sod was turned at each of the four corners. The four sods would be left for two or three nights to see if the house were on a fairy 'walk,' in which case they would surely be found replaced, and another site would have to be found. If nothing occurred, a hen or some small animal would be killed, and the blood allowed to drip into the four holes, after which the building of the house might proceed. According to N. W. Thomas,[1] there was a custom in Wales at the end of the 18th cent.[2] of throwing a victim down a precipice, whenever a murrain broke out among the cattle.

Frazer[3] refers to the practice of burning, at Lesneven in Lower Brittany on Ash Wednesday, a straw man covered with rags, after he had been promenaded round the town. This practice is strikingly similar to that at Massilia (whether Greek or Celtic) mentioned by Servius (see art. COMMUNION WITH DEITY [Celtic], 3). With this custom Frazer compares the English practice of burning Jack o' Lent. In *GB*³, pt. v., *Spirits of the Corn and of the Wild*, London, 1912, ii. 322 f., there is a reference to an ancient rite of sacrifice that occurred in the Highlands of Scotland and in St. Kilda, described by John Ramsay, laird of Ochtertyre.[4] Here, however, there may be rather a vestige of totemistic communion, as in the passage quoted in C. Elton, *Origins of English History*², London, 1890, p. 411. In the case of the later vestiges of sacrifice the interpretation given when the sacrifice is medicinal is that of transference of the evil from the sufferer to another living creature. In *GB*³, pt. vi., *The Scapegoat*, London, 1913, p. 52, there is an interesting account of a practice, once in existence in the village of Llandegla in Denbighshire, where a fowl of the same sex as the sufferer was used to heal the falling sickness, by having the disease transferred to it. As late as 1855[5] the old parish clerk of Llandegla remembered the practice.

4. Survivals at bonfires.—Perhaps the clearest traces of sacrifices, which were doubtless at one time represented as piacular, are to be found in the case of the Beltane fires of Scotland and Ireland, and of the bonfires of other Celtic countries. The fullest description of the Scottish bonfires is that given by Ramsay of Ochtertyre, the patron of Burns and the friend of Sir Walter Scott. A selection of his voluminous MSS has been published in *Scotland and Scotsmen of the Eighteenth Century*. In *GB*³, pt. vii., *Balder the Beautiful*, i. 147 ff., there are quotations from this work that give an excellent account of the Beltane fires, which appear to have marked the commencement of the second half of the Celtic year in the beginning of May. There are traces in these of the ceremony of choosing a victim on behalf of the community, and also of the ceremony of burning human and animal victims for the public benefit. The choosing of a victim was probably the original object of the Beltane cake, which was divided into a number of pieces and distributed among the company. There was, however, one particular piece the obtaining of which gave the person to whose lot it fell the name of *cailleach beal-tine*, 'the Beltane *carline*,' a term of great reproach (i. 148). When this person was known, part of the company took hold of him and pretended to put him into the fire, but, through the interposition of the majority, he was rescued. In some places the person in question was laid flat on the ground, and there was then a pretence of quartering him. Afterwards the person so treated was pelted with egg-shells, and bore his opprobrious name for a whole year, during which time it was the custom to regard him as no longer living. In the parish of Callander the Beltane customs were in vogue towards the end of the 18th century (i. 150). There, again, a portion of the cake was marked out from the rest, being blackened with charcoal. The person who drew it was regarded as the devoted person, and had to leap three times through the flames.[6]

In some countries, as in Brittany, the chief bonfires were lit at the summer solstice, and somewhat similar customs prevailed there; *e.g.*, in Upper Brittany people leap over the glowing

1 *Celtic Folklore: Welsh and Manx*, Oxford, 1901, i. 296.
2 i. 306. 3 i. 339. 4 i. 307.
5 i. 309. 6 i. 310.
7 T. Stephens, *The Gododin of Aneurin Gwawdrydd*, London, 1881, pp. 124–126.
8 *A Description of the Western Islands of Scotland*, London, 1673, reprinted in Pinkerton's *Voyages and Travels*, do. 1808–14, iii. 583.
9 Cf. also *FL* xiv. [1903] 370 10 *FL* vi. 170.

1 *FL* xvii. [1906] 276, 'The Scape-Goat in European Folklore.'
2 Mentioned by W. Owen [Pughe], *Heroic Elegies of Llywarch-Hen*, London, 1792, p. xxxi.
3 *GB*³, pt. iii., *The Dying God*, London, 1911, p. 229 f.
4 *Scotland and Scotsmen in the Eighteenth Century*, ed. A. Allardyce, Edinburgh and London, 1888, ii. 438 ff.
5 J. Brand, *Observations on Popular Antiquities*³, ed. W. C. Hazlitt, London, 1870, ii. 375.
6 James Robertson (parish minister of Callander), in John Sinclair's *Statistical Account of Scotland*, Edinburgh, 1791–99, xi. 620 ff.

embers of the bonfires.[1] 'In many parishes of Brittany the priest used to go in procession with the crucifix and kindle the bonfire with his own hands; and farmers were wont to drive their flocks and herds through the fire, in order to preserve them from sickness till midsummer of the following year.'[2] There is a reference[3] to bonfires in Ireland in 1782, in which it is said that the people danced round the fires, and, at the close, went through the fire, and the whole was conducted with religious solemnity. In *FLR* iv. [1881] 97 there is a statement by G. H. Kinahan that, in Munster and Connaught, it is said that a bone must always be burnt in the fire.

There are also some traces of sacrifice in the case of the Hallowe'en (31st Oct.) bonfires of Scotland, which were most common in the Perthshire Highlands. The Hallowe'en fires are described by Ramsay.[4]

James Robertson[5] speaks of the practice of carefully collecting the ashes into the form of a circle, and putting in a stone, 'near the circumference, for every person of the several families interested in the bonfire. Next morning, if any of these stones was found to be displaced or injured, the people made sure that the person represented by it was *fey* or devoted, and that he could not live twelve months from that day.' Frazer[6] states that, in the case of the Hallowe'en fires in some districts of the north-east of Scotland, such as Buchan, each of the youths present at the bonfire would lay himself on the ground as near to the fire as he could without being burnt, and, while so lying, would allow the smoke to roll over him. The others ran through the smoke and leapt over their prostrate companion. According to a MS of the traveller Thomas Pennant,[7] it was the custom in N. Wales for each person present at the Coel Certh, or bonfire kindled on All Saints' Eve, to throw a marked white stone into the fire and for these stones to be examined next morning. If any person's stone was missing, he was regarded as doomed to die before he saw another All Saints' Eve. Rhŷs[8] refers to the Welsh superstition which held that the *Hwch ddu gota* ('the short black sow') would take the man who was hindmost of those who ran away after throwing their stones into the fire.

5. Sacrifice and substitution.—In view of the foregoing accounts it appears probable that, in Celtic as in other countries, ideas of expiation and atonement once played their part in religious thought, but certain of the harsher practices of the Celts, such as human sacrifices, probably did not originate from these ideas, but were older and came to be interpreted through them, and it may well be that the ideas of expiation and atonement were helpful in diminishing the number of victims, and in gradually changing their character, through the development of the idea of the substitution of one type of victim for another. The real motive for the human sacrifices was probably, in the main, real or supposed economic pressure, and there are some traces in folk-lore of such a practice as the dispatch of an aged parent by his able-bodied son.

Cf. art. by G. L. Gomme, in *FL* i. [1890] 197 ff., containing the outline of 'A Highland Folk-tale,' collected by J. F. Campbell, after the publication of his *Popular Tales of the West Highlands* (Edinburgh, 1862). John Aubrey also refers to an English 'countrie-story' of 'the holy mawle, which (they fancy) hung behind the church dore, which, when the father was seaventie, the sonne might fetch to knock his father in the head, as effœte, & of no more use.'[9]

It may well be, too, that the human clearances from which human sacrifices may have originated were not at first regular institutions, but, like wars, arose when necessity seemed to require. Among the ancient Celts and races similarly situated the risk of a death by violence, whether in war or otherwise, was probably viewed with as little normal perturbation as the risk of death through illness, and the possibility of having to die when an occasion for human sacrifice arose was accepted as a matter of course. All the writers of antiquity who speak of the Celts refer to their remarkable fearlessness and indifference to death. Much of the ferocity which ancient writers attribute to them was probably also due to the high tension produced by the strain of living and by preoccupation with the constant problem of procuring food for their vigorous and prolific communities.

See also artt. COMMUNION WITH DEITY (Celtic), 4, CELTS, xiii. 2, and SIN-EATING.

LITERATURE.—This has been sufficiently indicated in the course of the article.

E. ANWYL.

6. Human sacrifice among the Irish Celts.—The existence of human sacrifice among the Irish Celts has been denied by E. O'Curry and P. W. Joyce.[1] But, as O'Curry's editor, W. K. Sullivan, says—

'As the Gauls, Germans, and Slavonians practised human sacrifice, it is very improbable that the Irish had not a custom which seems to have been universal among all the other European branches of the Aryans.'[2]

The practice certainly existed among the British Celts down to A.D. 77,[3] and among the Gauls, the latter of whom were rather more civilized than the Goidels of Ireland. Hence there seems no good reason for this denial, especially as the evidence of certain passages in the Irish MSS points to it. This is the more remarkable as pagan rites are apt to be glossed over by the Christian scribes who handed down or recomposed the tales and myths of an earlier age. In the cult of Cromm Cruaich the Irish are said to have given a third of their healthy issue for the milk and corn which they asked of the god.[4] The *Dindšenchas* also says that 'the firstlings of every issue and the chief scions of every clan' were offered to this god.[5] Joyce compares the *Dindšenchas* notice of the custom with the mythical tales contained in it, and says that the one is as incredible as the other, forgetting that the myths were credible to the pagan Irish. The archaic evidences of ritual in the *Dindšenchas* may certainly be regarded as credible. An exaggerated memory of human sacrifice either among the Celts or among a pre-Celtic people in Ireland is found in the mythico-historic account of the peopling of the land. To the Fomorians—a group of gods who may have been evil divinities of the Celts, or perhaps the gods of the aborigines regarded by the incoming Celts as hostile to themselves—the Nemedians are said to have given in tribute two-thirds of their children born throughout the year and two-thirds of the year's supply of milk and corn.[6] The Fomorians are here regarded as an actual race; but there is no doubt that they were supernatural beings, and that tribute here means sacrifice, exaggerated though it may be. St. Patrick is said to have preached against 'the slaying of milch cows and yoke oxen and the burning of the first-born progeny' at the fair of Taillte.[7] 'First-born progeny' may here refer to children.

Human sacrifices to remove plague—the equivalent of the Gaulish sacrifice for health mentioned by Cæsar — are mentioned in the metrical *Dindšenchas.*

'During the Trena of Taillte, at sunrise
I twice invoked Mac Erc
The three plagues to remove
From Erin, though it be a woman's command.
Their hostages were brought out;
The drowning of the bonds of the violated treaties,
Immolating the son of Aedh Slane
To Mac Erc—it was not a cause of shame.'[8]

Through the obscurity of these lines may be discerned a memory of sacrifice, the offering of

[1] P. Sébillot, *Coutumes populaires de la Haute-Bretagne*, Paris, 1886, pp. 192–195.
[2] *GB*[3], pt. vii., *Balder the Beautiful*, i. 184 f. [3] *Ib.* i. 202.
[4] ii. 437 ff. [5] In *Statist. Acc. of Scotland*, xi. 621 ff.
[6] *GB*[3], pt. vii., *Balder the Beautiful*, i. 233.
[7] Quoted by Brand, i. 389 ff.
[8] *Celtic Heathendom*[3], London and Edinburgh, 1898, p. 575 ff.
[9] *Remaines of Gentilisme and Judaisme, 1686–87*, London, 1881, p. 19.

[1] E. O'Curry, *Manners and Customs of the Ancient Irish*, London, 1873, ii. 222; P. W. Joyce, *Social History of Ancient Ireland*, do. 1903, vol. i. ch. ix.
[2] O'Curry, i., Introd. p. cccxxxiii.
[3] Pliny, *HN* xxx. 4. 13; cf. Dio Cass. lxii. 6; Tac. *Ann.* xiv. 30.
[4] *Book of Leinster*, p. 213*b*.
[5] *Rennes Dindšenchas*, text and tr. by W. Stokes, *RCel*, xvi. [1895] 35.
[6] *Book of Leinster*, p. 7*a*. [7] O'Curry, i. p. dcxli.
[8] *Ib.* i. p. dcxl, ii. 222.

hostages and of a captive prince to dispel blight and disease. Myth also refers to the necessary offering of the son of a sinless couple and the sprinkling of his blood on the doorposts and over the land of Tara during a time of blight, caused by the marriage of Conn, king of Erin, to Becuma, a goddess banished from the gods' land because of her sin with the son of the god Manannan. The son of the sinless couple was the son of a queen of the divine land. But, when he was about to be slain, his mother appeared with a cow and recommended that it should be slain in his stead.[1] The memory of human sacrifice and of its commutation for an animal offering is obvious here, in spite of its being enshrined in this curious mythical story.

Traditions of the human foundation sacrifice[2] are also found among both the Irish and the British Celts. In one case the legend has become attached to the account of the founding of the monastery of Iona, but must first have been told in some other connexion.

St. Columba is reported to have said to his monks: 'It is good for us that our roots should go under the earth here; it is permitted that one of you should go under the clay of this island to hallow it.' St. Oran agreed to do this, and the church was built over the grave. As a reward he went straight to heaven.[3] Perhaps the story was connected with Oran because he was the first to be buried in the churchyard which still bears his name. But it is evident that memory of the old pagan rite suggested that it must have been used at the founding of Columba's monastery. This is clear, because in another version a different reason is given for Oran's death. He was buried alive as a judgment and through Columba's curse because after a visit to the other world he denied the current beliefs about it.[4]

The ritual aspect of the foundation sacrifice is more evident in the story of the building of Vortigern's castle on Snowdon, told by Nennius. The building materials disappeared as soon as they were brought together. Vortigern's 'wise men' (probably druids) informed him that he must find a child born without a father and put him to death, sprinkling with his blood the ground where the castle was to stand.[5] The child Embreis or Ambrose escaped by showing the real cause of the trouble; in Geoffrey's *History* he is Merlin, of Arthurian fame. The foundation of the palace of Emain Macha was also laid with a human victim, as was that of a stone fort mentioned in the *Book of Lecan*, under which 'groaning hostages' were enclosed.[6] Similar legends are attached to many buildings all over the Celtic area.

For the sacrifice of human victims at funerals see art. CELTS, vol. iii. p. 302[b].

J. A. MACCULLOCH.

SACRIFICE (Greek).—**1. Theistic significance of the rite.**—In order to obtain a clear understanding and definition of sacrifice, in accordance with its signification for the Hellenic peoples within the Hellenic period, we must interpret it in the terms of the word θυσία; and, as this word had always a 'theistic' intention, always denoting a certain act performed in relation to a certain deity or semi-divine personality, we must not apply it to those acts of ceremony or ritual which might bear an outward resemblance to an ordinary act of sacrifice, but bore no direct reference to any deity, being performed solely as acts of automatic or magical efficacy. For research into the primitive origins of sacrifice impresses on us the fact that much that on the higher plane of religion is done in honour of the god is performed on the lower plane without any such intention. This is particularly the case in what is often loosely called 'blood-offering.' Finding clear evidence in a story recorded by Pausanias[1] of the survival of a ritual at Haliartos in Bœotia of shedding human blood over a dry land in order to obtain water, we must not interpret this as a blood-sacrifice to the earth-goddess, though it could easily have developed into that; but, accepting the simple account as it stands, we must regard it as a magical rite, dictated by the belief common to so many primitive peoples in the automatic magical efficacy of blood. Again, when the people of Methana, near Troizen, carried round their vineyards the dismembered limbs of a cock to preserve the fruit from the baneful effects of a certain wind,[2] this act, as Pausanias presents it, may be best called pre-animistic magic; not a word in his account authorizes us to call it a sacrifice to a wind-god. It may be that later Greek authors applied the term θυσία to an act of ritual that originally had not, perhaps never came to have, any such religious character. But the application of the word proves that the author himself attached a theistic significance to the rite. On the other hand, it is clear that not every kind of offering to a deity was called a θυσία, which must be distinguished from mere ἀναθήματα, such as the dedication of a statue, or the spoils of war, or a woven garment. Only the ceremonial oblation of animals, vegetables, fruits, or liquids—blood, wine, milk, water, honey, oil—is normally described as a θυσία. It was not always necessary that these should be brought up to or laid upon an altar. A more primitive ritual, belonging to a less developed stage of anthropomorphism, appears in a passage of the *Iliad*[3] describing the Trojan sacrifice to the river Skamandros; not only were bulls offered to him in the usual way, but horses were thrown alive into the water; and the fashion survived in the historic period, for we hear of horses and bulls being thrown into the sea to Poseidon,[4] of the Rhodians sinking a four-horsed chariot into the waters for the service of Helios.[5] That such acts were regarded as 'sacrifices' in the proper sense is proved by a ritual law preserved in an inscription of Mykonos ordaining a sacrifice of a ram and lambs to the river-god, Acheloos, of which some are to be 'slaughtered' by the altar, some 'cast into the river,' the same word being used for both acts.[6] Other ceremonies therefore of the same type—the oblation of barley-cakes to Ge,[7] which were thrown down into a chasm at Athens, the throwing down of pigs to Demeter and Kore into their μέγαρα, or underground vaults[8]—may also be described as θυσίαι.

But normally, and in nearly all the public as well as the private services of religion, the altar was the essential requisite for the sacrifice; and from the first the word θύειν would imply some kind of altar or table for holding the fire, if the theory that derives it from a root meaning 'to smoke' or 'to burn' is certain. At any rate, the ideas of greatest interest attaching to the Greek sacrifice will be found to arise from its association with the altar, which gives a special sanctity to the victim and the participants.

2. Communion-feast theory.—Before we consider the different types of Greek sacrifice, it is convenient to raise the question whether they can be all interpreted from one single point of view. To explain sacrifice in general as a gift to the god seemed to some ancient writers, and has seemed to

[1] *Book of Fermoy*, p. 89 f., ed. and tr. in *Ériu*, iii. [1907] 150 f.
[2] See art. FOUNDATION, vol. vi. p. 113.
[3] Adamnan, *Vita S. Columbæ*, ed. W. Reeves, 1874, p. 288.
[4] From a local tradition given in A. Carmichael, *Carmina Gadelica*, Edinburgh, 1900, ii. 317.
[5] Nennius, *Hist. Britonum*, ch. 40.
[6] W. Stokes, *Three Irish Glossaries*, London, 1862, p. xli; O'Curry, ii. 9.

[1] IX. xxxiii. 4. [2] II. xxxiv. 2. [3] xxi. 130–132.
[4] Athenæus, p. 261 D; Serv. on Verg. *Georg.* i. 13.
[5] Festus, *s.v.* 'October equus.'
[6] Dittenberger, *Sylloge*[2], 615, 35.
[7] Paus. I. xviii. 7; cf. Theophr. *de Plant. Hist.* IX. viii. 7.
[8] At Athens in the Thesmophoria (Clem. Alex. *Protr.* p. 14 P; Lucian, schol. in *Rhein. Mus.* xxv. [1870] 548); at Potniai (Paus. IX. viii. 1).

many moderns, a satisfactory account of it. But a new theory has been brought into vogue, chiefly through the insight and researches of Robertson Smith,[1] which interprets ancient sacrifice, Greek as well as Semitic, as a communion-feast with the divinity, in which the god and his people 'become of one flesh' by partaking in common of the flesh of the victim, the animal being regarded as in some degree divine, as having the divine spirit incarnate in it. And that writer himself and some of his followers drew the corollary that, where the view of the sacrifice as a gift or mere bribe to the god prevailed, that was a later degeneracy of religion, possible only when the sense of communion had faded from the ceremony. This theory needs much modification to bring it into harmony with modern knowledge and research. It was disfigured by immature ideas concerning totemism; and modern anthropology disproves that part of it which asserts the gift-sacrifice to be invariably due to a later degeneracy. Nevertheless, it retains its value as a guide to our researches into ancient sacrifice. And, if we find two types of sacrifice—one that may be called the gift type, one the sacramental or communion type—we need not for our present purpose discuss the question whether the one arose from the other; for both are certainly older than the beginnings of the Hellenic period.

It is obvious that no sacramental character, none of the ideas associated with a communion-feast, was likely to attach to those primitive acts of oblation mentioned above, offered without an altar—the throwing of the animal victim or cakes into the water or a chasm of the earth; these must have been regarded as gifts given to please, placate, or stimulate the divine powers of earth and water.

3. Bloodless offerings. — Turning now to the much larger question of the altar-sacrifice, we are confronted at once with the important distinction, familiar to us through the story of Cain and Abel, between the bloodless offering and the blood-offering—a distinction that runs all through Greek ritual. Upon certain altars a severe local law might prevail that no blood could be shed, but only harmless cereals, vegetables, fruit, and 'sober' liquids might be offered. The most conspicuous examples are the so-called 'pure' altar of Apollo in Delos,[2] καθαρός specially connoting purity from contact with blood, and the altar of Zeus Ὕπατος,[3] 'the Highest,' in Athens. As all blood-offerings required fire, to convey the flesh of the victim in fragrance to the divine participant, bloodless offerings might be sometimes called ἄπυρα when they consisted of fruits and liquids for which no fire was required. Thus we hear of ἄπυρα ἱερά being prescribed by an immemorial law of ritual in the shrine of Athene at Lindos;[4] nor does it appear that such offerings as cakes, which required fire for the baking, needed an altar-fire for their offering, as they were in most cases merely laid on the altar;[5] yet a fire might be maintained, even when the offerings were bloodless, for the sake of the incense thrown into it.

Cereal and vegetable offerings and fruits, as vital elements of human nourishment, were natural oblations to the deities of vegetative growth and fertility, and most of the Hellenic divinities included this among their other functions; they were natural therefore and common in the cults of Demeter and her daughter, of the Earth-Mother, of the Great Mother of the Gods, and of Dionysos, and are found even in the ritual of Poseidon and Herakles. Yet all of these admitted and accepted, except in certain shrines, the blood-offering as well; therefore, whatever philosophers of the later period might assert about the higher refinement and spirituality of the bloodless oblation, no Greek divinity down to the end of paganism could be regarded as championing any such dogma. The worship of Athene at Lindos, for some local reason that we cannot trace, might proscribe the animal victim; but elsewhere Athene delighted in it as did Zeus and the 'pure' Apollo. In fact the divergences of Greek ritual in this respect are not to be explained by the operation of any high moral idea.[1]

Such oblations were made at various times throughout the year according to the ritual calendars of the Greek states, and in accordance with the religious needs of early agrarian society. The various festivals of Demeter in Attica range throughout the agricultural year; and in one of them at least—the Haloa, or festival of the threshing-floor—we are explicitly informed that the animal victim was forbidden. The most critical time was the beginning of harvest, when all the Greek states, we may affirm with confidence, offered ἀπαρχαί, or firstfruits, of field and vintage to the protecting deities of tilth, orchard, and vineyard.

Are we to regard this class of sacrificial offerings as a pure gift to the divinity? Gifts in some sense they certainly were; and there is no evidence that the bloodless offerings of the altar were ever consumed by the worshippers in the ordinary public cults as a sacramental meal or for purposes of sacramental communion with the deity. If they were eaten by the people as 'blessed bread,' some feeling of communion might have arisen; for we may trace faint survivals of the primitive belief that Demeter was incarnate in the corn;[2] and some of these sacrificial cakes were shaped so as to bear the insignia of the divinity—*e.g.*, cakes offered to Apollo in the form of lyre or bow or arrows[3]—whereby the essence of the divinity might be attracted into them. But we are fairly certain that such offerings laid on the altar were never eaten by the worshipper, though an unscrupulous priest might surreptitiously purloin them.[4]

On the other hand, in the ritual of the Greek mysteries—Eleusinian, Samothracian, and those of Attis-Kybele—we have some evidence, mainly indeed doubtful, that the votaries attained to a sense of communion with the divinity by eating holy bread or drinking some preparation from cereals,[5] and on a vase in Naples we have probably an actual representation of the administration to the *μύσται* of the sacred cup containing the *κυκεών*, or the mixture of the barley-meal, which the goddess was believed to have drunk in her sorrow. But it does not appear that the *κυκεών* had ever been hallowed on the altar in any form of sacrifice, or that the communicant was ever penetrated with any mystic idea that it contained the divine substance of the goddess.

We must believe, then, that the average Greek offered these bloodless oblations to his divinities as pure gifts, partly to secure their blessing and favour for the year to come, partly as a thank-

1 See especially his *Religion of the Semites*², London, 1894, p. 269 ff.

2 Diog. Laert. VIII. i. 13; Macrob. III. vi. 2; Clem. Alex. *Strom.* p. 848 P.

3 Paus. I. xxvi. 5.

4 Pind. *Ol.* vii. 48; Diod. Sic. v. 56.

5 See Aristoph. *Plut.* 661 and schol.; the only exception perhaps was the ὄμπναι, sacrificial cakes burnt in the altar-fire, according to Kallimachos, schol. Nikand. *Alex.* l. 450.

1 Occasionally the character of the deity might explain the type of offering regarded as appropriate; *e.g.*, only the blood-offering was considered acceptable to Ares (*Anth. Pal.* vi. 324).

2 See *CGS* iii. 33 f.

3 Steph. Byz., *s.v.* Πάταρα.

4 See the humorous passage, Aristoph. *Plut.* 676–681. The harvest-offerings laid before the image of Demeter at Mykalessos remained fresh for a year (Paus. IX. xix. 5).

5 *CGS* iii. 195, 240 f.: 'Sacrificial Communion in Greek Religion,' in *HJ* ii. 317.

offering for the blessings of the past year. But in respect of the ἀπαρχαί, of the firstfruits of the harvest and vintage, another motive, belonging to a different order of ideas, may be discerned or surmised. On the day called the Pithoigia, 'the opening of the wine-casks'—the first day of the Attic Anthesteria, when the new wine was ready for drinking—the citizens bore a mixture of the sweet wine to Dionysos 'in the marshes' before they ventured to drink themselves.[1] We may regard this as a religious rite instituted for the purpose of removing the tabu from the new vintage; and, as there is abundant evidence of the belief that a religious sanctity conserves and fences round the growths of the field before they are fit for the use of man, we may suppose that the ἀπαρχαί of corn had originally this significance. The most conspicuous example of these was the ἀπαρχαί sent from a great part of the Greek world to the goddesses at Eleusis; but a detailed inscription of the 5th cent. reveals that they came to be regarded as mere tributes or thank-offerings, and a certain residue of them were sold in the market, the price being devoted to the purchase of ἀναθήματα.[2]

4. Blood-sacrifices and the gift theory.—The blood-sacrifices have now to be considered, and it is to these rather than to those of the former type that certain ideas which may be called mystic will be found to attach. Before considering any general theory about them, one must review the facts. The first question is whether any general principle is discoverable governing the choice of animals. The choice was certainly a wide one, including all domesticated animals, all edible birds, even fish, and all the wild beasts of the chase. The domesticated animals are nearly always those that form the ordinary food of man. The only exceptions were dogs occasionally offered to Hekate, Ares, and Eileithyia,[3] horses offered to Helios and Poseidon,[4] and asses to Apollo and the winds;[5] we have a record of the sacrifice of an elephant offered by one of the Ptolemies on a single occasion, which excited so much popular disapproval that it was not repeated.

Apart from these few exceptions, the facts at first sight seem to be sufficiently explained by the gift theory, namely, that the meat-offerings were tributes paid to the deity for favours received in the past or expected in the future, or to deprecate his anger. And such a rite reveals the working of the primitive idea that the deity is not of his own nature immortal and self-existing, but is dependent like mortals on continual nourishment for his continual existence—an idea plainly enough expressed in Egyptian, Babylonian, and Vedic religions. It is true that in no articulate Greek utterance, nowhere in the earliest literature, is the belief bluntly proclaimed that the divinity would perish if not fed by the sacrifices, and later thinkers scoffed at the view that the gods needed them in any sense. But we cannot avoid supposing that such an idea, however inarticulate, was in the background of the popular religious consciousness; and, in spite of the refining influence of more cultured thought, the popular faith must have long prevailed that the deities in some way actually ate of the flesh of the victim and always delighted in it. Hence arose at some indeterminate date such divine epithets as Αἰγοφάγος, 'goat-eater,' Ταυροφάγος, 'bull-eater,' of Hera[6] and Dionysos,[7] derived from the victims offered. Also, in a well-known passage in the *Iliad*, Zeus himself admits that he owes great consideration to Hektor in

1 *CGS* v. 214 f.
2 Dittenberger[2], 20, ll. 10–12; see *The Year's Work in Classical Studies, 1914*, London, 1915, p. 114 f.
3 *CGS* ii. 707 n.
4 See above, § 1.
5 *CIG* 1688; *CGS* iv. 100; *Et. Mag.*, *s.v.* Ἀνεμύτας.
6 Paus. III. xv. 9.
7 Schol. Aristoph. *Ran.* 360.

return for his many offerings.[1] This is the fundamental view of the gift theory.

But, when we look more closely into the facts, whether in regard to the choice of victims or in regard to the actual forms of the sacrifice itself, the more we find that this theory, even if always true to some extent, is seriously inadequate. If the sacrifice were regarded merely as a gift to provide the divinity with food, why should the rule obtain on the whole that the god prefers the male victim, the goddess the female?[2] Why should it have been supposed that a maiden heifer should be more acceptable as food to a maiden goddess?[3] Why should the horns of the ox be elaborately decked with gold, its neck in later times with wreaths, and why should the rule have been generally insisted on that the victims should be καθαρά and ὁλόκληρα, pure and unblemished?[4] Certainly the primitive mind applies certain ideas of sympathetic magic to the choice of food; and we can explain, in reference to them, why a pregnant sow should be offered to the earth-goddess to stimulate her fertility,[5] why entire male victims, ἔνορχα, should be chosen as sacrificial food by specially virile divinities such as Ares, Poseidon, the river-gods, and certain heroes, and why a cock should be an appropriate offering to the war-god, to quicken his fighting powers. But the simple food theory, whether assisted or not by ideas of magical working, would not explain why black animals should be offered to the dark powers below the earth, called 'chthonian,' and to the gods of storm, and animals of bright hue to celestial powers, the Olympians, and the deities of brightness.[6] Such a choice would be dictated by the idea that there should be some resemblance or affinity between the animal of sacrifice and the divinity. And later writers of classical antiquity were evidently aware of this prevalent feeling; we find such pronouncements as that bulls were offered to Selene because the horns of the animal resemble the horns of the moon,[7] and a general axiom that 'victims are offered because of some similitude' to the deity.[8] The author of this phrase impairs its value by adding to it the words 'or because of some contrariety,' which is explained by his later statement, 'victims are offered which are detrimental to the deity'—'immolantur quae obsunt.'[9] This was doubtless suggested by such facts as that the goat was commonly offered to Dionysos, and the goat was injurious to vines. But we are certain that this view is false, and that it was utterly repugnant to ancient Hellenic thought and feeling that an animal should be chosen for sacrifice which was naturally detrimental or hostile to the divinity. On the contrary, evidence can be given establishing a mysterious connexion or sympathy between the victim and the divine power to whom it is consecrated on the altar, and it is this that compels us, in certain forms of sacrifice, to regard the gift theory as inadequate.

5. Sanctity of the altar.—It is now necessary to consider those forms for which the earliest evidence is afforded by certain passages in the Homeric poems. By combining some of them we can present a typical Homeric sacrifice, as offered by a tribe or a group of men.

1 *Il.* xxiv. 64 ff.
2 To this rule, formulated by Arnobius (*adv. Gent.* vii. 19), the exceptions are very numerous (some shrines were indifferent as to the sex of the victim—*e.g.*, at Thasos [Roehl, *Ins. Græc. Ant.*, Berlin, 1882, no. 379]); but on the whole it prevailed.
3 *Il.* vi. 275.
4 Aristot. frag. 108 (Athenæus, 674 f.); for curious exception to this rule see Æl. *Nat. An.* xii. 34.
5 Prott-Ziehen, *Leges Sacræ*, 26.
6 Serv. on Verg. *Æn.* iii. 18; Aristoph. *Ran.* 847.
7 Lact. *Div. Inst.* i. 21.
8 Serv. on Verg. *Georg.* ii. 380.
9 *Ib. Æn.* iii. 18.

The victim, one or many, was brought near the altar; holy water, barley-stalks in a basket, and a vessel for catching the blood were held in readiness; the sacrificers purified themselves with the holy water and formally raised up in their hands the barley-stalks, which had been sanctified by some preliminary rite; then the chief officiator—the king or chieftain or, more rarely, the priest—cut off some of the victim's hair and threw it into the fire, at the same time or immediately afterwards uttering the prayer to the deity for blessing or special aid. At this point the sacrificers 'threw forward the shredded barley (or barley-stalks)'; the victim, if a powerful one like an ox or a bull, whose struggles would be embarrassing, was smitten with an axe in such a way as to render it impotent; then, if women were present, they raised the ὀλολυγή, which was an auspicious appeal to the deity by name to grace the ritual with his or her presence;[1] the animal, if the oblation was to the Olympians, was lifted off the ground, its head drawn back so that its face was turned to the sky, and its throat cut; the blood was probably caught in the sacred vessel, though we do not know for what purpose; the dismembering of the carcass began, the thighs were cut away and wrapped in fat, and, with portions of meat cut probably from every part of the victim, were placed on the altar and roasted, while a libation of wine was poured over them. While these were roasting, the worshippers ceremonially partook of the inward parts—σπλάγχνα—which had been cooked; then the other parts of the victim were cut up and roasted on spits and provided a common feast for the sacrificers; the feast was followed by a wine-drinking, inaugurated by a libation to the deities, and in certain cases the rite might close with religious dance and singing.[2] There is much here that needs skilled interpretation. Homer is not an expounder of ritual; much of his account is stereotyped and has the quality of shorthand. One point of importance is obvious: the victim is not a gift to the gods for their own exclusive use; only that portion of it belongs to them which is burnt on the altar; the rest serves as a feast for the people, in which they may be supposed to be feasting with their divinity; so that the typical Homeric sacrifice may best be described, not as a tribute or bribe, but rather as a communal meal in which the people strengthened their sense of fellowship with the god or goddess. But is there any trace of the idea that the victim is in itself divine? Nowhere in the Homeric poems is there any hint of such a character attaching to it before it has been brought into touch with the altar. But we may discern in part of the ritual the intention to sanctify the animal, to fill it with the divine spirit; and, as the altar was the centre to which the divine spirit was attracted, this aim would be effected by establishing a *rapport* between the deity represented by the altar and the victim. Such might well have been the intention of throwing its hair into the altar-fire before the immolation, for by a well-known law the sanctification of the part means the sanctification of the whole. There is reason for thinking that this was also the intention and use of the οὐλόχυται, though careful consideration is needed before arriving at any definite view of these. The acts expressed by οὐλοχύτας ἀνέλοντο and οὐλοχύτας προβάλοντο belong to the initial part called ἀπάρχεσθαι, which preceded the central act of sacrifice and of which the purpose was the sanctification of the victim and the worshippers. A comparison of many later authorities suggests the following interpretation:[1] the barley-stalks are first placed on the altar, and thus become charged with its spirit, as does everything that touches it; they are then solemnly taken up and 'thrown forward' so as to strike the victim or touch it on the forehead, whereby the holy spirit passes into it. When, elsewhere, the Achæans have no barley at hand, they use leaves,[2] and we know that in later ages leaves were strewn on altars. There is no hint that barley or any other cereal had this mystic power, independently of contact with the altar. Thus charged, the victim is no longer, as it had been hitherto, a merely secular beast, but becomes holy flesh, and those who partake of it are filled with the divine spirit and enter into mystic fellowship with their deity, however faintly this may have been realized by the poet and his contemporaries. This idea will also explain the ceremonial tasting of the σπλάγχνα before the communal feast begins; and it is in the Homeric evidence concerning this part of the whole rite that the sacramental concept emerges most clearly.[3]

Such is the general type of sacrifice familiar to Homer, from which we must carefully distinguish another that we may call the oath-sacrifice; this, which was known to Homer and the later periods, presents special characteristics and will be discussed below. The communal sacrificial feast, which has been described above and which may be interpreted as a ceremony in which the worshippers feasted with the deity and feasted on flesh into which the divine spirit had temporarily entered, was a genial institution, containing potential germs of advanced religion. It may have inspired Hesiod with his vision of a golden age, 'when immortal gods and mortal men had fellowship in the banquet and sat together.'[4] And, although in the later periods the sense of inner fellowship and mystic union with the divine may have waxed dim, the forms of it certainly survived. The later literature gives us abundant testimony that the altar continued to be the radiating centre of sanctity for the whole sacrifice. The οὐλαί, barley-stalks or meal, continued to be strewn on the altar and used for the sanctification of the victim and even perhaps the bystanders; the χέρνιψ, or holy water, was sanctified by a brand from the altar being dipped in it; the κανâ, or baskets containing cereals, were sanctified by being taken in solemn procession round the altar; and, thus charged, they sanctified the sacrificial knife which was carried in them.[5] Connected thus by more than one link with the centre of sanctity, the victim became temporarily a sacrosanct beast, and the eating of its flesh might be felt in some degree to be a sacrament. The belief that a part of the personality of the deity might be thus incarnated for a time in the victim explains many of the old rules concerning the choice of animals: the maiden goddess might prefer a maiden victim, the bright deities a bright-haired victim.

6. Bouphonia ritual.—This view of the sacrifice emerges clearly in the ritual of the Bouphonia at Athens and in the legends concerning it, upon which much has been written in the way of con-

[1] This has been wrongly interpreted as a cry of sorrow, also as a cry to avert evil spirits (*e.g.*, G. G. A. Murray, *The Rise of the Greek Epic*², Oxford, 1911, p. 87); in no passage in Greek literature is ὀλολυγή or its cognates a sorrowful cry (the two examples quoted in Liddell and Scott, *s.v.*, are false); it is generally joyful, always auspicious.

[2] The two most complete passages from which this description is taken are *Il.* i. 447–474, and *Od.* iii. 440–463; cf. *Od.* iii. 5, *Il.* ix. 220.

[1] The most important references are schol. Hom. *Od.* iii. 441, 445, schol. *Il.* i. 449; schol. Aristoph. *Eq.* 1167; Eustath. *Il.* i. 449; Aristoph. *Pax*, 961; for modern theory see Ziehen, in *Hermes*, xxxvii. [1902] 391; and Stengel, *Opferbräuche der Griechen*.

[2] *Od.* xii. 357.

[3] See art. Greek Religion, vol. vi. p. 398.

[4] Frag. 82 (Rzach).

[5] Athenæus, pp. 297 D, 409 B; Aristoph. *Pax*, 948–960, *Lysistr.* 1129; Eur. *Elect.* 800–814 (full account of 5th cent. sacrifice); cf. *Iph. Aul.* 955, 1111, 1471, 1540; Herod. i. 160.

troversy and theorizing.[1] The sacred character of the ox in this ceremony is shown in strange and impressive ways: he dedicates himself to the god by voluntarily approaching the altar and eating the corn upon it; the priest who slays him flees into feigned exile, a solemn trial is held for his murder, and the axe of sacrifice is adjudged guilty and cast into the sea. All partake of his flesh, and a simulated resurrection of the ox is enacted by sewing his hide together, filling it with hay, and yoking it to the plough. This ox has been interpreted by Robertson Smith as a totem-animal, and the name 'theanthropic' has been applied to him; but the theory of totemism breaks down here when critically examined, and the name 'theanthropic' has no right to be applied to any sacrificial beast in Greece; some were regarded temporarily as divine, but none as at once divine and human. There is much more to be said for Frazer's theory that this ox is the vegetation-spirit; but the theory is not essential to explain the facts. What emerges clearly from the records of the ritual and the legends is that the ox has no innate and independent sanctity of his own; this quality enters into him only after his contact with the altar, whereto he is called by the god; henceforth he is charged with the god's spirit, and the slaying of him is felt to be an awful deed, though necessary; and the eating of his flesh is felt to be a sacrament, whereby the Cretan stranger who in the legend performs the ceremony becomes of one flesh with the citizens and is admitted to citizenship. The feigned resurrection may be an apology to the spirit of the ox. Similar ideas are discernible in the ritual of Zeus Sosipolis of Magnesia, as attested by a famous inscription of the latter part of the 3rd cent. B.C.[2] At the beginning of the agricultural year the finest bull that could be procured was solemnly dedicated to Zeus, 'the Saviour of the City,' in a ceremony called the *ἀνάδειξις*; we are not told, but we may suppose, that the consecration took place by the altar of the god; towards the close of the year, when the harvest was ripe, the bull, having been treated with great reverence and care all through the months, was led in a solemn procession and sacrificed to Zeus, and his flesh was distributed among those who took part in the procession. There is no reason to suppose that the bull possessed any independent sanctity previous to his dedication; but by that ceremony the spirit of Zeus, who was undoubtedly a god of fertility in Magnesia, became temporarily incarnate in the bull, and those who ate the sacrificial meat would be put in communion with him; if they ate it in a communal meal round the altar, the concluding act of the ritual would be exactly parallel to the old Homeric sacrificial feast. And that this was a common practice in the State sacrifices is indicated by such not infrequent formulæ as *οὐκ ἀποφορά*, or *δαινύσθων αὐτοῦ*, 'let not the flesh be taken away' (from the neighbourhood of the altar), 'let them banquet there' (around the altar)[3]—rules which show that the flesh was considered too holy to be removed with safety into private dwellings, and that the full virtue of the sacrifice could be maintained only if the worshippers ate the sacred flesh in the presence of their deity.[4]

Moreover, the mystic power that the animal acquired from the altar and through the sacrifice remained after its death. Its blood might be used for cathartic purposes, and specially and chiefly for washing the altar-steps,[1] probably a post-Homeric ceremony. The *ὅσιοι*, the 'holy' priests of Delphi, acquired their holiness from the victim that had been sacrificed to Apollo and was called *ὁσιωτήρ*,[2] 'he who makes holy,' because the beast communicated holiness to the official, probably by means of some ritual contact. Also the skin of the sacrificial animal might long retain mystic power: the *Διὸς κώδιον*, the skin of the ram offered to Zeus Meilichios at Athens, was employed in the purification of homicides;[3] the consultants of the prophetic hero, Kalchas, slept on the fleece of the black ram that had been offered to him;[4] the *αἰγίς* of Athene, probably nothing more than the skin of the goat yearly offered to her on the Acropolis at Athens, was taken round by the priestess to bless newly-married couples with.[5] But these are exceptional cases; ordinarily the sacrificial skins—so great was their number in the Greek States and especially in Athens—formed a valuable revenue from which the priest sometimes got his dues and the State an appreciable return.

We no longer hear of the ceremonial or sacramental eating of the *σπλάγχνα* by the worshippers, and we have some evidence that these might be given to the priest or sacrificer for his private profit or burned on the altar as the deities' portion;[6] but they evidently retained here and there a certain mystic value, for sometimes they were separately placed on the knees of the idol,[7] and in the narrative of Herodotus the Spartan prince who desired to extract from his mother a solemn attestation sacrificed and placed in her hands the *σπλάγχνα* of the victim as she swore.[8] We may say, then, that the belief remained vivid down through the later periods that the divine spirit was specially infused into these parts; and it was therefore these that were of chief avail in the post-Homeric ritual of divination.

7. Incarnation of deity in certain animals.—In the cases hitherto dealt with it appears that the sacrificial animal obtains his temporarily divine character merely through contact with the altar. But we are able to discover traces in ritual legend of the primitive belief that the deity habitually incarnated himself or herself in some favourite animal—*e.g.*, Apollo in the wolf,[9] Artemis in the bear;[10] and that such holy animals might occasionally be offered—an act of ritual which might evolve the conception that the deity actually died in the sacrifice. Most of such legends are vague and difficult to interpret with certainty, and, though the bear which contained the spirit of Artemis and the wolf that incarnated Apollo might at times have been sacrificed, we are not told that this was for the purpose of a sacramental feast; and no higher Hellenic divinity was supposed to die in and through the sacrifice. It is only when the Thracian Dionysos is admitted into Greece that such ideas can be traced in the legend and ritual, especially in the Mænad and Bacchic 'omophagies,' or rendings of the bull or goat, and the drinking of its hot blood, which was the very spirit or substance of the god.[11]

[1] Paus. I. xxiv. 4; Porph. *de Abst.* II. xxix. 30 (from Theophrastos); *CGS* i. 56 f., 88–92; Robertson Smith, *Rel. Sem.*², p. 304 ff.; *GB*³, pt. v., *Spirits of the Corn and of the Wild*, London, 1912, ii. 5–9; Nilsson, *Griechische Feste*, p. 14.

[2] O. Kern, *Die Inschr. von Magnesia am Maeander*, Berlin, 1900, no. 98; Nilsson, p. 26.

[3] See examples in Ada Thomsen, 'Der Trug des Prometheus,' *ARW* xii. [1909] 467.

[4] That this type of sacrifice and this view of it were rife in later paganism is proved by St. Paul's phrase, *τραπέζης δαιμονίων μετέχειν* (1 Co 10[21]).

[1] *αἱμάσσειν τοὺς βωμούς* (schol. Hom. *Od.* iii. 444); Pollux, i. 27; Stengel, *Opferbräuche der Griechen*, p. 19.

[2] Plut. *Quæst. Græc.* 9.

[3] Suidas, p. 1404, *Διὸς κώδιον*; Eustath. pp. 1935–1938.

[4] Strabo, p. 284.

[5] Varro, *de Re Rustica*, I. ii. 19; Suidas, *s.v.* *Αἰγίς*.

[6] See Dittenberger², 371; *Athen. Mitt.* xiii. 166; Athenæus p. 661 A; Stengel, *Jahrb. des kais. deut. arch. Inst.* ix. [1894 114.

[7] *BCH*, 1913, p. 195; Aristoph. *Birds*, 518.

[8] vi. 67 f.

[9] *CGS* iv. 113–123.

[10] *Ib.* ii. 434–438.

[11] *Ib.* v. 164–181.

Originally these were no acts of sacrifice, but acts of wild ecstatic communion, enacted without fire or altar. But in a more civilized Hellenic form they survived in a unique ritual practised down to a late period in Tenedos. The citizens selected a pregnant cow and treated it with great respect until the calf was born; the latter they dressed up in buskins—part of the human equipment of Dionysos—and sacrificed it to the god, but pelted the sacrificer with stones and drove him into exile for a time.[1] Here both animals are semi-divine, not through any contact with the altar; but the preference of the god for and his immanence in the new-born calf are quaintly and picturesquely displayed; therefore by those who devoured its flesh—and we must suppose that this was the intention of the sacrifice—the idea of sacramental communion must have been vividly realized.

8. Underworld sacrifices. — There is another type of Greek sacrifice, essentially distinct from the above, wherein none of the worshippers partook of the food, but all was made over to the divine or semi-divine power. The simplest forms of it, where the gift was offered directly without an altar, have been already considered. In other cases the victim was wholly burned on the altar, and no sacrificial meal was allowed (ὁλοκαύματα).[2] We find this rule most frequently, though not exclusively, in the ritual associated with the lower world, the cults of the chthonian deities, heroes, and souls of the dead. In these cases the blood was usually poured down through an opening into the βόθρος, the grave or the earth-hollow,[3] and the flesh of the victim was wholly consumed in the altar fire. The underlying motive was, no doubt, the desire to avoid communion with the lower world lest its contagion should blast the living; hence ὁλοκαύματα were offered to the Eumenides,[4] to Zeus Meilichios,[5] and usually to the heroes.[6] The words ἐνάγισμα, ἐναγίζειν, specially used for sacrifices to the last, express the tabu put upon the food-offering, and point to the same feeling, which would also explain why only the most abandoned vagrant would venture to taste the offerings placed for Hekate, the ghost-goddess, at the cross-roads.[7] Nevertheless, it is interesting to note that this fear of the contagion of death did not so far possess the imagination of the later Greeks (more sensitive as they were in this respect than was the Homeric world) as to prevent their desire at times to enter into communion with the kindly powers of the lower world by means of a sacrificial feast of the Homeric type. An inscription records a sacrifice at Mykonos to 'Zeus of the under world' and 'Ge of the under world,' in which a communion-meal was held round the altar and only citizens could partake;[8] and a similar rite occurred in the cult of the θεοὶ Μειλίχιοι, undoubtedly chthonian gods in Lokris.[9] We have more than one example of communion-feasts with heroes;[10] and in the private grave-ritual there is clear evidence of a family meal taken with the departed spirit.[11]

On the other hand, in the case of the ἀποτρόπαιοι θυσίαι, sacrifices to avert evils and to assuage the wrath of δαίμονες, vaguely conceived powers of revenge and pestilence, it was an absolute rule that the offerings must not be tasted and even that the officiator must purify himself after the ceremony before returning to the society of men;[1] and the victim chosen for these rites of 'aversion' or 'riddance' was often an animal unfit for human food, such as the dog.[2] Akin to the 'apotropæic' rites are the 'cathartic,' those intended to purify from stain, and especially the stain of bloodshed. Much of the latter ritual does not concern sacrifice at all; but, when it was performed at an altar, as was sometimes the case,[3] it is probable that a purificatory victim was sacrificed upon it. Any thought of a sacrificial meal would be repugnant here; but the animal's blood or skin would be used in the purification; the blood of the pig, the familiar animal of the lower-world powers, was specially effective in the case of homicide;[4] and we hear of the 'fleece of god,' the skin of the ram offered to Zeus Meilichios, being used for the same purpose.[5] In these instances the person to be purified is brought into spiritual contact, through the immanent sanctity of the sacrificial animal, with the offended divine powers. Therefore, though there is no question of a sacrificial meal, we must reckon with the possibility that the idea of divine communion underlies some of the ritual of Greek κάθαρσις.

9. The oath sacrifice.—Again, in the type of ritual which may be called the oath-sacrifice, if the ratification of the oath was accompanied by the slaying of an animal, the flesh was never eaten, but was either buried or cast into the sea. The flesh was tabued, because the slaying was the enacting of a conditional curse against oneself.[6] The animal was consecrated to a divinity only in order that the divine power might be present at the oath-taking; and those swearing put themselves into communion with the deity by touching a portion of the victim;[7] this contact ensured dangerous consequences in the event of perjury. The gift-theory of sacrifice has no meaning here.

10. 'Sober' and wine offerings. — Another special distinction in Greek sacrifices is between those that were called 'sober' (νηφάλια) offerings of, or with, non-intoxicant liquids and those that were accompanied with wine. The scholiast on Sophokles[8] declares that the former were offered to Mnemosyne, the Muses, Eos, Helios, Selene, the Nymphs, Aphrodite Ourania; we have other evidence that enables us to add to this list Zeus Γεωργός, the god of agriculture, the Eumenides, the child-god Sosipolis of Elis, the winds, and in some cults Poseidon and even Dionysos.[9] Merely looking at the variety of this list of names, we see that no single explanation will apply to all of them. The cheerless powers of the dark world might refuse wine, yet it was offered generally to the dead and to the heroes.[10] Nor can we suppose that the rule arose in a period before the introduction of wine;[11] for these cults are by no means all among the most ancient. In some centres of worship the rule might be explained by the date of the

1 Æl. *Nat. An.* xii. 34.

2 Cf. the name καυτός for the purificatory pig burned at Kos (W. R. Paton and E. L. Hicks, *The Inscriptions of Cos*, Oxford, 1891, no. 37).

3 Hom. *Od.* x. 517; Porph. *de Antro Nymph.* 6; Lucian, *Char.* 22.

4 Æsch. *Eum.* 106; schol. Soph. *Œd. Col.* 39.

5 Xen. *Anab.* VII. viii. 3 f.

6 The proper word to designate the altar of the hero was ἐσχάρα. The sacrifice to him took place towards evening, to the Olympians in the forenoon (Diog. Laert. viii. 1, p. 33; schol. Apoll. Rhod. i. 587).

7 Demosth. *in Konon*, § 39.

8 Dittenberger², 615, l. 25.

9 Paus. x. xxxviii. 8.

10 *Ib.* x. iv. 10, v. xiii. 2.

11 *E.g.* the περίδειπνον (Artemid. *Oneirok.* v. 82).

1 Porphyr. *de Abst.* ii. 44; cf. E. Littré, *Œuvres complètes d'Hippocrate*, Paris, 1839–61, vi. 362.

2 Plut. *Quæst. Rom.* iii. p. 290 D.

3 *E.g.* Paus. I. xxxvii. 4.

4 See art. PURIFICATION (Greek); cf. Athenæus, p. 410 A–B (quoting from Doritheos).

5 Above, p. 16.

6 Cf. Hom. *Il.* iii. 103, xix. 267.

7 Æsch. *Sept.* 45; Demosth. κ. Ἀριστοκράτ., § 68; Hom. *Il.* iii. 274. Plato, *Kritias*, p. 120 A, imagines a form of oath-taking among his citizens of Atlantis which may be called an ordeal by communion; those who swear drink the blood of the bull sacrificed to Poseidon.

8 *Œd. Col.* 109.

9 See *CGS* v. 199 f.

10 Plut. *Quæst. Rom.* p. 270 B; Hom. *Od.* x. 517; Lucian, *Charon*, 22.

11 J. E. Harrison, *Prolegomena to the Study of Greek Religion*, Cambridge, 1903, pp. 90–94.

sacrifice, occurring at a time of the year when no wine was forthcoming.

11. Human sacrifice.—The most striking phenomenon in the history of Greek sacrifice, namely, the offering of a human victim, which survived either as a real or as a simulated act of ritual down to the late period of paganism, is treated separately in art. HUMAN SACRIFICE (Greek), and in art. GREEK RELIGION, § 14. Nearly all the recorded types stand in profound contrast to the cheerful Homeric conception of θυσία; they exclude the idea of a sacramental communion or a sacrificial meal. Only in the legends of Zeus Lykaios and King Lykaon, who sacrifices his own son and feasts on his flesh with Zeus, we may recognize the reflex of a primitive cannibalistic sacrament, in which the tribe feast on human flesh supposed to incarnate a divine life;[1] and, if this interpretation of half-incoherent legend is precarious, we can safely apply it to the legends of the rending asunder, σπαραγμός, of the human victim in old Dionysiac ritual.

Some of the legends concerning human sacrifice bear the print of savage religious conception: we have a glimpse of deities, especially the earth-powers, craving human blood; in others we discern a more advanced idea, but still belonging to barbaric ethics, that an angry and vindictive deity demands a life by way of vengeance for sin committed.[2] But what is of much more interest and peculiar value in Greek mythology is the early emergence of the belief that the high deity is merciful and hated such oblations and himself provided the substitute of the ram. In a legend concerning Tyndareus and Helen we have an exact parallel to the story of Abraham and Isaac, in one of Idomeneus to the story of Jephthah and his daughter, except that the Greek myth ends more mercifully.[3] From an early period the higher conscience of Hellas, the most merciful in antiquity, revolted from the cruel rite; in time of great panic and peril it might be practised on an alien as late as the 5th cent.; in most centres of cult it was abolished as a regular ordinance or converted into a sham; here and there where it survived—and we hear of it surviving till the period of Hadrian—it was moralized by the selection of a criminal as the victim.

12. Conclusion.—The current Greek view of all sacrifice was that it was a gift to the gods.[4] Apart from the inadequacy of this as an account of the popular ritual, its moral weakness was felt by the more refined natures; and a higher theory and ethical view concerning sacrifice emerge in Greek literature and philosophy. To some, as to Euripides and Theophrastos, 'the sacrifice without fire of all fruits of earth poured forth in abundance on the altar' appeared more acceptable to a merciful deity than the blood-offering of an animal victim.[5] Even the Delphic oracle was supposed to encourage the idea that the simplest offering of the poor man with righteousness was more acceptable than the lavish hecatombs of the rich.[6] 'Know well that when one sacrifices to the gods in piety one wins salvation though the sacrifice be little' is a sentence preserved from a lost play of Euripides.[7] One of the last writers of Greek paganism who deal with the subject, Iamblichus, in his book *de Mysteriis*,[8] rejects altogether the theory that sacrifice is a gift that could bribe God, but justifies it as a symbol of friendship between the mortal and the deity. But neither he nor any other Greek theorist appears cognizant of the idea of sacramental communion.

The types and forms of Greek sacrifice here sketched present a general resemblance to those prevalent among the older leading peoples of ancient civilization. But they also show certain characteristics that mark the Hellenic spirit. The ritual belongs on the whole to real religion of the genial character proper to the Greek State and family. There is little or no magic in it, little debasing superstition: the sacrifice did not compel the deity or control the course of nature; nor did the sanctity that attached to it so stupefy the public sense that the sacrifice itself could come to be deified or that the priest who administered it could attain a detrimental degree of divine prestige. In fact in his attitude towards ritual we mark as clearly as elsewhere the characteristic difference of the Greek from the Indian and the ancient Egyptian.

LITERATURE.—See the references given in notes and also: P. Stengel, *Die griechischen Kultusaltertümer*, in Iwan von Müller's *Handbuch der klassischen Altertumswissenschaft*, v. iii., Munich, 1898, and *Opferbräuche der Griechen*, Leipzig, 1910; H. von Fritze, *Die Rauchopfer bei den Griechen*, Berlin, 1894; M. P. Nilsson, *Griechische Feste*, Leipzig, 1906; A. Thomsen, 'Der Trug des Prometheus,' in *ARW* xii. [1909] 460 ff.; L. R. Farnell, 'Sacrificial Communion in Greek Religion,' *HJ* ii. [1903–04] 306 ff., 'Magic and Religion in Early Hellenic Society,' *ARW* xvii. [1914] 17 ff. Epigraphic material mainly in W. Dittenberger, *Sylloge Inscriptionum Græcarum*², Leipzig, 1901, ii.; and I. de Prott and L. Ziehen, *Leges Græcorum sacræ*, do. 1896–1906.

L. R. FARNELL.

[1] *CGS* i. 41 f.

[2] There is no evidence for J. C. Lawson's suggestions (*Modern Greek Folk-lore and Ancient Greek Religion*, Cambridge, 1910, pp. 339, 350) that the human victim in Greece was ever offered as the spouse of the divinity or was ever intended as a messenger to convey the prayers of the living.

[3] See art. GREEK RELIGION, vol. vi. pp. 401, 416; Serv. on Verg. *Æn.* iii. 121.

[4] Plato, *Euthyphro*, p. 14 C: τὸ θύειν δωρεῖσθαί ἐστι τοῖς θεοῖς.

[5] Eur. frag. 904; Porph. *de Abst.* ii. 29.

[6] *CGS* iv. 210.

[7] Stob. *Flor.* (Meineke, iv. 264).

[8] V. 9.

SACRIFICE (Iranian).

1. Prevalence in early Īrān.—Even in the earliest times the Iranians were accustomed to bring offerings and sacrifices to complete and render more acceptable and effective their worship of the gods. It was certainly a feature of the united or Aryan period. Evidence of this is afforded by a comparison of the sacrificial terminology and usages as found in the Vedas and in the Avesta. Resemblances in procedure and identity as to certain elements are so manifest that only a common practice during the Indo-Iranian period sufficiently accounts for them. Notably is this the case in respect of *haoma* (Skr. *soma*), the sacred 'death-averting' beverage,[1] and the *baresma*, or *barsom*,[2] twigs which have always[3] been, and remain to this day, essential elements in all Parsi sacrificial rites.

2. Animal sacrifices.—There is no reason to suppose that the vegetable kingdom supplied all the ritual requirements of the early Iranian worshippers. Not only do we find that their Indian fellow-Aryans extensively employed animals for sacrifices in Vedic times, which, it must be admitted, in view of their absence from early Avestan ritual, does not of itself constitute a sufficient proof of their use by the contemporary Iranians; but this, taken in conjunction with the testimony of Herodotus,[4] which, as we have seen,[5] has reference to the practices of a date anterior to his own, leaves little doubt that animals formed in early times important, and possibly the principal, elements in Iranian sacrifices. The references in the *Yashts*[6] to heroes such as Vishtaspa as having extensively practised animal sacrifice indicate the existence of a tradition that the custom was of great antiquity in Īrān.

[1] See art. HAOMA.

[2] See art. BARSOM.

[3] *Haoma* at least must be excepted for the duration and in the area of Zarathushtra's public ministry. Owing to its intoxicating character, it is strongly condemned in the *Gāthas* (see *Ys.* xlviii. 10; cf. also xxxii. 14). Even the *Yasna haptanhaiti*, which is later than the *Gāthas*, contains no allusion to *haoma*.

[4] i. 132.

[5] Art. GOD (Iranian), vol. vi. p. 290.

[6] *Yt.* v. 21, 25, 29, 33, 37, 108, etc.

3. Zarathushtra and animal sacrifice.—Just as *haoma*-sacrifice conflicted with the distinctly ethical character of the prophet's reform, so also did animal-sacrifice conflict with the highly spiritual conception of God to which he attained. We are prepared, therefore, to learn that under his influence the practice was discontinued,[1] and the emphasis on ritual generally was greatly reduced.[2] Plutarch was undoubtedly right when he said[3] that Zarathushtra taught the Persians to sacrifice to Ahura Mazda 'vows and thanksgivings.' Even Anāhita, who, according to the *Yashts*, was honoured by all her other devotees with 100 stallions, 1000 oxen, and 10,000 sheep, was invoked by Zarathushtra with no animal gift.[4] But after the death of the prophet—how long we cannot say—and with the return of the old nature-worship, the custom of sacrificing animals returned, just as did the practice of preparing and drinking the *haoma*-juice at the service.

4. Animal sacrifice and the dualism of later Mazdaism.—The revival of the custom, however, did not take place without encountering and overcoming more than one difficulty. In addition to the spiritual and religious opposition to animal sacrifices which was part of the inheritance bequeathed to his successors by Zarathushtra, the dualism of the later Mazdaism, whether inherent in the prophet's teaching or only due to a wrong and inconsequential development by the Magi, presented a cosmological problem which had to be solved before animal-sacrifice could be reinstated in the Mazdæan ritual as it existed in pre-Zarathushtrian days. All life, with perhaps the exception of that of a few noxious creatures, belonged to the kingdom of Mazda, and death to that of Ahriman. Hence to bring about the death of even a sacrificial animal seemed to limit the kingdom of the good and to extend that of evil. As to the manner in which the Persians surmounted this difficulty, Strabo's remark[5] may have much significance when he says that the deity claimed the soul of the victim. The principle of life, therefore, as it left the animal, was regarded as returning to its original source in Mazda, and the kingdom of death was deprived of the prize that seemed to have come so near its grasp. And the use to which the flesh of the animal was put (see below) also served to assist the sacrificer's belief that the whole animal was made to serve divine ends.

5. Animal sacrifices in the later Avesta.—When we come to the period of the *Yashts* and later portions of the Avesta, the sacrifice of animals and other living creatures is fully restored. The victims used were chiefly horses, camels, oxen, asses, deer, and birds. But it is to be noted that these sacrifices were offered almost exclusively, not to Ahura Mazda or the *amesha spentas*, but to the *yazatas*, or angels. Anāhita's acceptable offerings have already been mentioned. Mithra was invoked with cattle and birds, together with *haoma* and libations.[6] In the liturgy the *yazatas* are invited to the sacrificial feast singly or in groups.[7] Different portions of the slaughtered animal were assigned and dedicated to various divinities. The Pahlavi *Shāyast lā-Shāyast*[8] supplies what seems to be an exhaustive list of these assignments. Ahura Mazda has assigned to *haoma*, *e.g.*, the jawbone, the tongue, and the left eye of the victim, or, according to a later tradition, the whole head.

6. Persian kings and animal sacrifices.—The sacrificial practices of the Achæmenian kings, as described by Greek writers, seem to have been on a very large scale,[1] and uninfluenced by the reform of Zarathushtra. But it can hardly be claimed that these kings represented the orthodox Mazdaism of their age. Moreover, where the Greek historians have exceeded the limits of the bare objective facts and sought to supply the motive and significance of Persian religious customs, it does not follow that their interpretations were always right. They would naturally be for the most part in terms of Greek usages. When Herodotus,[2] therefore, records that Xerxes offered 1000 oxen as a sacrifice to Athene of Ilium, it may signify only that the beasts were consecrated to the deity, to whom they were regarded as sacred, before being killed for human consumption; while the deity named would probably be the Greek counterpart of the Persian god actually honoured. Xenophon[3] says that at the feasts of kings consecrated flesh had to be used. The same was true of the Sasanian kings. And, when Elisæus says that Yazdagird II. caused a large number of white bulls and fine rams to be offered in recognition of his victory, it is very probably to be understood that the animals were consecrated to the deity and then employed to make a great commemorative feast for the victory.

7. Method of sacrificing animals.—The victim was led to a clean or consecrated spot, which, as Herodotus says, was frequently on the summit of a high mountain;[4] and, after the deity in whose honour the sacrifice was made had been invoked and his favour and blessing implored on behalf of the king and the whole Persian people, the animal was slain, according to Strabo,[5] not by the use of a knife to pour out the blood, but by striking with a log of wood or pestle. Under no circumstances was the offering burnt, although Strabo[6] records that sometimes a little of the caul was thrown upon the fire, but only to make the fire burn more brightly. The slaughtered animal was then taken limb from limb—whether by the sacrificer, as suggested by Herodotus,[7] or by the Magus, as Strabo states.[8] The flesh was seethed and placed on a carpet of tender herbage, 'preferably clover,' says Herodotus.[9] The Magus then sang his theogony or hymn of praise to the deity, whose presence was always symbolized by the fire which was the invariable concomitant of such sacrifices.[10] When the flesh had remained a little longer on its vegetable altar, it was taken away and used for human consumption partly by the bringer of the offering and partly by the Magus.[11] The somewhat modified form of procedure employed in their sacrifices to water, as given by Strabo, has already been detailed under ALTAR (Persian), vol. i. p. 346.

8. Sacrifices and offerings other than those of animals in Zoroastrianism.—Prominent as we have found the place of animals at the sacrifices to have been in pre-Zarathushtrian and late Avestan times as well as in the usages of the Persian kings, nevertheless the impression received from the Avesta as a whole is that throughout its history, excepting the Gāthic period, the centre of the Mazdayasnian ritual was the preparation and offering of *haoma*; and the greater part of the gifts brought and spread out by the *bihdīnān* for the divinities and departed spirits was derived from the vegetable world. It is true, as M. N. Dhalla says,[12] that 'up to the middle of the last

1 See J. H. Moulton, *Early Zoroastrianism*, London, 1913, p. 395, note 1.
2 See art. PRIEST (Iranian), vol. x. p. 319.
3 *De Is. et Osir.* 46.
4 *Yt.* v. 104.
5 xv. iii. 13.
6 *Yt.* x. 119.
7 *Ys.* i. 19, ii. 18; *Yt.* xi. 17.
8 xi. 4.

1 Athenæus (iv. 10) states that the Persian kings brought 1000 cattle, horses, and asses every day for sacrifice.
2 vii. 43.
3 *Cyr.* VIII. iii. 9 ff.
4 See art. ALTAR (Persian), vol. i. p. 346.
5 xv. iii. 15.
6 *Loc. cit.*
7 i. 132.
8 *Loc. cit.*
9 *Loc. cit.*
10 See art. ALTAR (Persian).
11 See Herod. and Strabo, *locc. citt.*
12 *Zoroastrian Theology*, New York, 1914, p. 355.

century the priest consecrated the fresh tongue, the jaw, and the left eye of the sacrificial animal to the angel Hom'; and that 'it was similarly the practice until very recently with the officiating priest to slaughter a goat with his own hands on the third day after the death of a person, and to dedicate the fat to the fire on the dawn of the fourth day.' Still at the great *yasna* ceremony to-day the only real vestige of animal-sacrifice[1] consists of three, five, or seven hairs of a white bull (*varasa*), tied together by a metal ring, generally of gold, and placed in a cup and deposited, with other sacrificial objects, on the *takht i ālāt*, or low stone table, in front of the chief officiating priest.

The other principal elements in the sacrifices were, and still are to-day, a twig of the pomegranate (*hadhānaēpata*, often called simply *urvara*, or 'plant'), which is pounded in a mortar and forms one of the ingredients of *parahaoma*, or juice of *haoma*, fresh milk (*gāush jīvya*), butter (*gāush hudhāo*), *zaothra*, or consecrated water, *darūn* or *draona*[2] (a sacrificial wafer), and fruit and flowers, together with incense and sandal-wood for the fire.

The method of the presentation of these offerings and their place in the ceremonies will be more fully and fittingly described in art. WORSHIP (Iranian). Here it may be explained that the officiating priest, after announcing the sacrifice that he is about to make and invoking the divinities whom he wishes to honour, takes up the *barsom*, sprinkles it with holy water or with milk, and repeats the invocations. He then consecrates the offerings of milk, fruit, and viands, together with the wood and perfumes for the fire. After a prayer to Ahura Mazda and the other divinities there follows the presentation of the offering.[3] Then the *mobed*, as the representative of the divinities invoked, partakes of the offerings. These, however, are really only preparatory, and to be followed now by the principal offering of *haoma* or, rather, *parahaoma—i.e.* the prepared juice of the plant. After the praises of the sacred beverage have been celebrated,[4] the *mobed* and his assistant priest drink some of it, and what remains is poured on the fire altar.

In early times, as appears from *Visparad*, iii., there were present on this occasion representatives of all the classes of Mazdayasnians. The priest closes the *yasna* ceremony by renewing the offering and invoking this time the *fravashis*, or spirits of the departed faithful. The *haoma* is twice prepared during the whole service, corresponding, as Haug says,[5] to the morning and mid-day libation of the Brāhmans. There was no evening libation among the Parsis; for this, it was held, would benefit only the *daēvas*.[6]

In addition to the great *yasna* ceremonies, at which all the offerings are present, there are at least two lesser ceremonies which may be and are held independently of the *yasna* service, and at which some of the subsidiary offerings of the *yasna* became the principal sacrifices. The first is the *darūn* ceremony. It is with this offering

1 Unless we reckon the viands prepared from meat, which are apparently still in use.

2 The *darūn* is a flat cake of about the size of the palm of the hand, made of wheaten flour and water with a little melted butter, and fried. The *darūn* is not mentioned under its specific name in the Avesta, but is included under the more general term, *myazda*, which is employed to designate consumable offerings either individually or collectively. While originally and etymologically meaning 'meat' or 'flesh,' *myazda* at the present day seems to be applied to fruits and flowers such as are used at the *Srôsh darūn*.

3 *Ys.* vii.

4 *Ib.* ix.-xi.

5 *Essays on the Sacred Language, Writings, and Religion of the Parsis*⁴, ed. E. W. West, London, 1907, p. 282 f.

6 *Ib.* p. 283; see also Dhalla, p. 139; Moulton, p. 129 f.; cf. *Vend.* vii. 79; *Yt.* v. 94.

that the young Parsi is initiated[1] into the circle of believers. The *amesha spentas* and Sraosha are honoured with the *darūn*, which is always held also at the *Gahanbārs*.[2] In addition to the plain *darūn* wafers, two of which are used at the ceremony, two others are necessary in which three rows of three dents or cuts, *i.e.* nine in all, are made with the finger-nail before frying, while repeating the words *humata, hukhta, hvarshta* thrice, one word for each of the nine cuts. This dented cake is called *frasast*. The four wafers are placed on the *takht i ālāt*, the two *frasasts* being on the right and the plain *darūns* on the left. On one *frasast* is placed a twig of pomegranate, and a little butter as a rule accompanies the *darūn*, and between them, according to Haug,[3] is placed an egg. After the formulæ prescribed for the service[4] have been recited, into which the name of the angel or *fravashi* in whose honour the sacrifice is made is introduced, the priests and those present partake of the cakes.

The other important secondary ceremony is the *afrīngān*. This again is in honour of a *yazata* or of the spirit of a deceased person. Special prayers called *afrīngān* are recited by the priests. The following is a Parsi description of this ceremony.

'The prayers are recited on a carpet spread on the floor on which are placed, either in a metallic tray or in plantain leaves, the choicest and most fragrant flowers of the season, while glasses are filled with fresh milk, pure water, wine and sherbet. These prayers are recited with the object either of expressing remembrance of the souls of the dear departed or of invoking the aid of some guardian angel.'[5]

9. The Mazdayasnian conception of the purpose and significance of sacrifice.—Certain aspects of the procedure followed by the Persians at their sacrificial ceremonies, as described by Herodotus and Strabo, are highly suggestive of the meaning of early Iranian sacrifices. The custom of laying the flesh of the victim on attractive herbage and allowing it to remain for a while upon its vegetable altar before it was removed and employed (as no doubt it was) for human consumption must signify that it was offered as food to the gods. Before the time of Strabo, however, the Persians had advanced in their conception of the nature of their divinities and believed that the gods needed only the soul of the animal. Originally the idea at the root of this custom was undoubtedly similar to that underlying the phenomenon of the 'shew-bread' (*q.v.*) among the Hebrews.[6] The manner in which some of the *yazatas* are represented as soliciting the offerings of their devotees also suggests that they thought these gods needed strengthening and encouraging as well as honouring and invoking, and consequently more abundant blessings would result to their worshippers.

In the Avesta the offerings and sacrifices are not frequently brought into relation to sin. In *Vendīdād*, xviii. 70-76, however, the man who has had relations with the *dashtān* woman atones for his sin with many sacrifices, including that of supplying the carcasses of some noxious creatures. The Pahlavi literature, on the other hand, contains several allusions to the vicarious or atoning character of the sacrifices. The *darūn* offering, *e.g.*, is regarded as a sufficient atonement for a class of transgression called *tanāpūhar*.[7] If the *barsom* twigs were used, they possessed the virtue of raising the atoning value of the offering tenfold.

Plutarch attributes still another motive to some Zarathushtrian oblations; for, while the Persians offered vows and thanksgiving to Ormazd, they

1 The whole ceremony is called *gītī khirīd*.

2 See art. FESTIVALS AND FASTS (Iranian).

3 P. 407.

4 *Ys.* iii.-vii., xxiii. f., xxviii.

5 Dosābhāi Framjee Karaka, *Hist. of the Parsis*, London, 1884, ii. 171.

6 Cf. Moulton, p. 394, note 4.

7 See *Shāyast lā-Shāyast*, viii. 20; cf. also i. 1, xvi. 6; *Dātistān i Dīnīk*, lxxii. 11, lxxviii. 19.

brought other offerings to Ahriman for averting evil.[1] There is, however, much improbability in this statement, inasmuch as it involves a direct contradiction of the fundamental doctrine of Mazdaism, that the evil one was not to be propitiated, but strenuously opposed.[2] If Plutarch was describing an actual phenomenon, it was observable only in a degenerate or counterfeit Mazdaism.

LITERATURE.—In addition to the works already referred to in the article, the following may be consulted: F. Spiegel, *Erânische Alterthumskunde*, Leipzig, 1871–78, iii. 559–596; C. de Harlez, *Avesta, traduit du texte zend*, Liége, 1875–78, vol. ii. p. 15 ff.; A. Rapp, 'Die Religion und Sitte der Perser,' *ZDMG* xx. [1866] 77–94; J. Darmesteter, *Le Zend Avesta*, Paris, 1892–93, i., Introd. iii. pp. lxv–lxix (*AMG* xxi.); Spiegel, *Zend-Avesta*, Vienna, 1853–58, ii., Einleitung, ch. iv. pp. 62–83; J. H. Moulton, *The Treasure of the Magi*, Oxford, 1917, ch. iv.

E. EDWARDS.

SACRIFICE (Japanese). — **1. Importance of sacrifice in Shintō.**—When we consider that the primitive Japanese had a very practical mind, and that their dealings with the gods were more frequently of the character of a bargain than of mystic adoration,[3] we are not surprised to find that offerings occupied a particularly important place in their religion—so much so that, in the curious account of a solemn sacrifice offered by the first legendary emperor, Jimmu Tennō, the food-offering is personified, and even deified, under the name of Idzu-uka no me.[4] Sacrifice appears also at other important parts of the mythological account—*e.g.*, when the gods themselves reveal to the empress Jingō the special offerings which will permit her to cross the sea and conquer Korea.[5] But it is particularly in the worship that the importance of offerings may be best gauged. The eclipse-legend,[6] which gives the divine prototype of the Shintō cult, shows the gods hanging strings of jewels on the highest branches of a huge *sakaki* (*Cleyera japonica*), a mirror on its middle branches, and pieces of cloth on its lowest branches. These primitive offerings were afterwards increased, and by the time of the ancient rituals they formed long imposing lists—in fact, the evolution of the offerings presented or promised to the gods occupies the greater part of the text.[7] Moreover, not only are those offerings prepared with the greatest care, in order to avoid all pollution, but they are often duplicated, so that at least one portion of the things offered may escape possible blemish, which would forfeit the whole magical effect expected; *e.g.*, the rice for the coronation feast (*Oho-nihe*) was brought from two different provinces and preserved for the time being in two separate buildings; the first portion was called *yuki* ('religious purity'), and the second *suki* ('subsidiary'). Lastly, the deification which we noticed in the story of Jimmu becomes generalized in the worship: the mirror or the sword, which was at first a simple offering, comes to be regarded as implying the real presence of the god, and finally as being the god himself or at least one of his material incarnations (*shintai*, 'body of the god').

2. Psychological basis.—It is a question whether Shintō offerings are made with the idea that they may supply, in some mysterious manner, the physical needs of the god or the spirit of a dead person, or whether they are merely symbolical. W. G. Aston supported the latter theory, but he was building mainly on considerations derived from observation of the sentiments of a modern European, *i.e.* of a man who, like Montaigne and St. Augustine before him, thinks, *e.g.*, that the funerary rites are a consolation for the living rather than a help to the dead.[1] In agreement with the majority of those who have studied comparative religion, the present writer thinks rather that the state of mind of uncivilized man was as a rule much more commonplace; and it is certain that the ancient Japanese, in particular, took a very material view of things. If the learned theologian, Hirata, in the 19th cent., did not hesitate to claim that food-offerings lose their savour in a manner inexplicable by natural causes, this crude conception must have been all the more strong among the primitive Shintōists. The question has been discussed in art. ANCESTOR-WORSHIP AND CULT OF THE DEAD (Japanese), vol. i. p. 457ᵃ; and the reasons stated there with regard to offerings to the dead apply equally to offerings to the gods, conceived by men in their own image.

3. The reason for offerings.—Offerings are made often with a general intention of propitiation, but often also as a distinct reward for services rendered by the gods or expected from them in the future. The offerings were then one of the terms of a kind of mutual contract concluded between the gods and men.[2] The result was that these offerings were sometimes of a conditional character.[3] There were also expiatory sacrifices (*aga-mono*, 'things of ransom') for cleansing the faithful from any ritual impurity. The most famous example of these—showing also their mythical origin—is the removal of the hair and nails of Susa-no-wo.[4]

4. Recipients of offerings.—The offerings were made sometimes to the spirits of the dead, sometimes to the gods.[5] Between the offerings to the dead and the offerings to the gods, we may mention as a natural transition the offerings to the *manes* of emperors or other deified personages. The offerings to the gods properly so called, *i.e.* especially to the powers of nature, were sometimes made to one or several individual gods, sometimes to a collective category of gods, and sometimes to all the gods;[6] *e.g.*, the offerings of the *Toshigohi no Matsuri*[7] were made to the deities of the 3,132 official temples, *i.e.* to all the deities in a mass.

5. The sacrificers.—Originally the offerings were undoubtedly individual, and they evidently remained so in many cases, as the accompaniment of the prayers of each worshipper. But for various reasons (the increased price of certain of the things offered, the necessity of preparing the offerings with particular care in order to avoid all ritual pollution, etc.) they naturally tended to assume a collective character. This tendency was further developed by the progressive concentration of all the powers, religious as well as political, in the hands of the emperor, who from that time officiated in name of all his people. When a subject accompanied the emperor, he had not the right to make his offering to the gods himself; his personality disappeared somehow, and was included in that of his sovereign.[8] That is why the emperor Jimmu Tennō (see above) personally performed the sacrifice. But, the very concentration of powers having later involved their division, the Mikado entrusted his religious functions to the care of various hereditary sacerdotal colleges; and, just as the *nakatomi*

[1] *De Is. et Osir.* 46. [2] Cf. Moulton, pp. 128 f., 399, note 8.
[3] See art. MAGIC (Japanese).
[4] Text cited in art. COMMUNION WITH DEITY (Japanese), vol. iii. p. 775ᵃ.
[5] See art. POSSESSION (Japanese), vol. x. p. 131ᵇ.
[6] Cf. art. NATURE (Japanese), vol. ix. p. 235ᵃ.
[7] See, *e.g.*, the text of the 3rd *norito* in art. PRAYER (Japanese), vol. x. p. 191ᵃ.

[1] *Shinto*, London, 1905, pp. 59 f., 210 f.
[2] For typical examples of those bargains see art. MAGIC (Japanese).
[3] See, *e.g.*, *ib.* vol. viii. pp. 296ᵇ, 297ᵃ, and cf. art. PRAYER (Japanese), vol. x. p. 191ᵃ.
[4] See *Kojiki*², tr. B. H. Chamberlain, Tokyo, 1906, p. 70.
[5] The offerings to the dead are discussed in art. ANCESTOR-WORSHIP AND CULT OF THE DEAD (Japanese).
[6] See art. MAGIC (Japanese), *passim*.
[7] *Ib.* vol. viii. p. 296ᵇ.
[8] See M. Revon, *Anthologie de la littérature japonaise*³, Paris, 1918, p. 109.

were specially commissioned to pray in place of him,[1] so the *imibe*, or *imbe* ('abstaining priests'), had the special duty of preparing the offerings. Their very name (*imi* expresses the idea of abstinence) comes from the care with which they had to avoid all cause of impurity during the preparation. Moreover, by their mythical origin they were connected with the god Futo-dama, whose name may be translated 'great gift or offering,' and whose rôle in the eclipse-myth agrees with this presentation of offerings. Historically they were probably the successors of the 'abstainer' of primitive Japan,[2] with the single difference that, while, like him, observing ritual purity, they were not obliged to abstain from eating meat or approaching women except during the few days before a religious festival, and that, far from not being able to wash themselves or comb their hair, they had always to attend carefully to their personal cleanliness. Their part in connexion with offerings in the chief Shintō festivals is prescribed in the ancient rituals; they officiated especially at the *Toshigohi no Matsuri* (*norito* 1),[3] at the *Ohotono-Hogahi* (*norito* 8),[4] and at the *Oho-nihe* (*norito* 14).[5] There are also other priests, inferior to them, the *hafuri*, or *hōri*, whose name (from the verb *hoburu*, or *hafuru*, 'to slaughter,' 'to throw away') denotes that they were originally sacrificers; in fact, the *Nihongi* mentions, in the year 642, a sacrifice of horses and cattle directed by them to obtain rain. The *oho-hafuri* ('great *hafuri*'), the legendary descendant and high-priest of the god Take-mina-gata at Suwa, still superintends sacrifices of deer, whose heads are offered to his divine ancestor.

6. Objects sacrificed. — The most interesting question in this respect is that of the human sacrifices of primitive Japan.[6] For these human victims others were substituted, either animal victims[7] or effigies of baked earth or even metal.[8] Slaves were also offered to the temples.[9]

Besides those ancient human sacrifices and their more modern substitutes, we find offered to the gods all the things that man regards as useful or even merely pleasing to them—in the first place, the things corresponding to the three primordial needs of food, clothing, and habitation, and then things corresponding to secondary requirements.

i. OFFERINGS CORRESPONDING TO THE THREE ESSENTIAL NEEDS.—(*a*) *Offerings of food.*—In the sacrifice of Jimmu Tennō, mentioned above, the only offerings were of food. Indeed the offering of the things most necessary for life, viz. food and drink, is the most ancient form of sacrifice. It is also the most important; more than once, therefore, in the titles of the rituals connected with the chief Shintō festivals the word *nihe* ('food-offering') appears, beginning with the *Oho-nihe* ('great food-offering'), the most solemn of these festivals. Those food-offerings include all the chief elements of Japanese feeding: as food and drink of mineral origin, salt and water; as food of vegetable origin, rice in its different forms (in the ear and in grain, hulled and in husk), and also in rice-cakes, then various kinds of pulse and fruits, especially edible sea-weed, and, as drink, *sake*, also made from rice; of animal origin, on the one hand, fish of all kinds, especially the favourite of the Japanese, *tai* (a kind of gold-bream), on the other hand, game, either with hair (deer, boars, and hares) or feathered (pheasants, wild ducks, and other birds). The ritual quoted in art. PRAYER (Japanese), vol. x. p. 191[a], gives a good example of the catalogue of foods generally offered.

(*b*) *Offerings of clothing.*—As the clothing of the primitive Japanese was made mainly of hemp (*asa*) and *yufu* (the fibre of the inner bark of the paper mulberry-tree), these are the materials, raw or woven, that figured in the ancient offerings. Silk, which was of comparatively recent importation at the time when the rituals were drawn up, had only a secondary place in them. As a rule, a certain weight of fibre (of hemp or mulberry-bark) or a certain number of pieces of cloth made from these materials was offered; and it was only natural that woven stuffs, which were the money of the period, should take the place of other articles more perishable, such as food, or more difficult to procure. The *awo-nigi-te* ('soft blue articles') and the *shira-nigi-te* ('soft white articles') which, in the eclipse-myth, the gods hung on the low branches of the sacred tree were respectively hemp and *yufu*. These are the *nusa* ('offerings'), the prototype of the later offerings. They afterwards took the more conventional form of the *oho-nusa* ('great offering'), consisting of two sticks set up side by side, the one of *sakaki*, the other of bamboo, from the top of which hung fibres of hemp and strips of paper, the latter representing the bark of the mulberry from which it was made.[1] This manner of supporting religious offerings was most natural, because, even in everyday life, Japanese politeness demanded that an inferior should offer anything to a superior only at a respectful distance, from the end of the branch of a tree.[2] With this may be connected the *tama-gushi* (probable meaning 'gift-skewer'), branches of *sakaki* or bamboo, with tufts of *yufu*, which formed a simpler way of presenting the *nusa*.[3] Still later the *oho-nusa* were generally displaced by the *gohei*, made of a single stick from which hung strips of white paper, cut at right angles. This is the emblem seen at the present day in all the Shintō temples; and, having lost its primitive signification of substitute for the ancient cloth-offerings, it is now regarded by the worshippers as a symbolical representation of divinity, or even as the temporary dwelling-place of the deity himself, who, at certain festivals, by the mere pronunciation of the formula called *kami-oroshi* ('bringing down the god'), descends into it, and remains in it during the whole ceremony.[4] One more form of *nusa* deserves mention, less important and still more simple, the *ko-nusa* ('little offerings') or *kiri-nusa* ('cut offerings'), consisting of paper with raw *sakaki* or hemp leaves mixed with rice; these are the portable *nusa*, which the traveller took with him in a small bag (*nusa-bukuro*, 'offering-bag') for the religious offerings which he might have to make during his journey.[5]

Such was the evolution of the important offerings of cloth, from the primitive *nusa* of mythology to the modern *gohei*. Besides these typical and general offerings, other articles of clothing were offered to the gods—sometimes skins of bears, boars, deer, or cattle, sometimes bright-coloured materials or even made-up garments.[6] But these are secondary offerings and of a somewhat exceptional kind.

Along with clothing mention must be made of adornment—that accessary which was so important among primitive races that in their eyes it often surpassed clothing itself. Now, in contrast to the modern Japanese, who (even the women), with a few rare exceptions introduced by

1 See art. PRAYER (Japanese), vol. x. p. 189[b].
2 See art. ASCETICISM (Japanese), vol. ii. p. 96[a].
3 See art. MAGIC (Japanese), vol. viii. p. 296[b].
4 *Ib.* p. 297[a].
5 *Ib.* p. 298[b].
6 See artt. HUMAN SACRIFICE (Japanese and Korean) and ANCESTOR-WORSHIP AND CULT OF THE DEAD (Japanese).
7 See art. HUMAN SACRIFICE (Japanese and Korean), vol. vi. p. 856[a].
8 *Ib.* p. 857[a].
9 *Ib.*

1 Cf. the sceptre, with tufts of wool, of the Homeric age.
2 See Revon, p. 168.
3 Cf. the wool-crowned olive-branches of the suppliants of Greek tragedy.
4 Cf. art. POSSESSION (Japanese), vol. x. p. 132[a].
5 See Revon, p. 347.
6 See art. PRAYER (Japanese), vol. x. p. 191[a].

imitation of Europeans, regard our use of jewels as barbarous, the primitive Japanese willingly covered themselves with head-ornaments, necklets, and armlets, the beads of which, some round, some tube-shaped (*kuda-tama*) or comma-shaped (*maga-tama*), and made of various stones, otherwise of no great value (chalcedony, jasper, chrysoprase, serpentine, crystal, etc.), are found in the excavations of the oldest native tombs. The celestial gods had a divine jeweller among them, whom we meet in the eclipse-legend, the god Toyo-tama ('rich jewel'), the legendary ancestor of the corporation of imperial jewellers; and in the mythology reference is continually being made to the jewels of the gods, which are mentioned even in the most important stories.[1] We gather therefore that jewels play a comparatively large part in the Shintō ceremonies and that they sometimes figure among the religious offerings.[2]

(c) *Offerings of habitation.*—Just as the gods desire offerings of food (*nihe*) and clothing (*nusa*), so they desire offerings of dwelling-places; and the word *miya*, applied to Shintō temples, means nothing else than 'august house'; *miya* also denotes a palace. Another word for temple, *araka*, seems likewise to signify 'dwelling-place.' In the mythology we often find the gods requesting the raising of a temple to them 'to make them rest well.' To the present writer it seems probable that the meaning of the word *yashiro*, 'house-representative,' also used to denote Shintō temples, refers specially to the rite which consisted in fixing the boundaries of an open place on the ground[3] for the time being consecrated as the god's place of abode during a ceremony—just as, even at the present day, a small enclosure of this kind (*himorogi*) is reserved for the purification which precedes every great Shintō festival—but that this substitution of a temporary residence for a real building represents merely a later simplification of the more ancient, very material, conception of the *miya*.

This *miya*, being intended as the dwelling-place of the god, does not require to be very large; and it is not calculated to hold a vast assembly; it is only in the precincts of large temples that there is, among other secondary buildings, an oratory (*haiden*) meant for the imperial envoy who may occasionally come there; as a rule, the worshipper who passes a Shintō temple simply stops at the outside, says a short prayer, and goes on. This explains the fact that to-day in the Japanese empire there are close on 200,000 Shintō temples. The smallest temples (*hokora*) can be carried about on a cart; the largest, such as those of Ise, are of quite modest proportions, and of a very simple structure, which purposely intends to represent only an architectural enlargement of the ancestral thatched cottage. In the 10th cent., of 3,132 officially recognized temples only 492 were classed as important enough to have offerings deposited on an altar; in the other 2,640 they were simply laid on the ground; with still greater reason the innumerable small temples dotted over the whole surface of the country were only very slim buildings, where the offerings were as humble as the worshippers. We must mention, lastly, the modest domestic altar (*kami-dana*, 'god-shelf') in each house, devoted principally to the cult of the family ancestors, who are thought to dwell there—at least during certain festivals.

In this dwelling-place the gods required furniture. And the furniture was as simple as that of Japanese houses, which includes hardly any of the pieces of furniture considered essential in our too complicated modern civilization. The most important piece was perhaps the *makura*, the native wood-pillow, for the sleep of the god—the pillow which, in certain cases, was regarded as so much impregnated with his divinity that it was made a *shintai*. The same thing happened not only with the metal mirrors which, originally simple offerings, were readily deified (*e.g.*, that of the sun-goddess of Ise), but also—a much more curious thing at first sight—with simple articles of pottery, which were naturally offered to the gods as to the ancestors,[1] and which ended by being worshipped as 'god-bodies.' We may conclude, therefore, that those objects of furniture, having, as it were, become fixtures on account of their purpose and their connexion with the dwelling-place, have gradually, by long contact with the deity dwelling there, assumed that permanent and precious character which leads to their deification.

ii. OFFERINGS CORRESPONDING TO SECONDARY NEEDS.—One of the most important of the secondary requirements is locomotion. Therefore, just as living horses, for which horses of baked earth were afterwards substituted, were buried in the tombs of the Mikados and princes,[2] so offerings were made to the gods of living horses, preferably white (the colour of the sun), which were left at liberty in the precincts of the temple; for these also there were afterwards substituted at first wooden effigies (in certain processions men represented the horses of the gods by mounting *koma-gata*, 'hobby-horses,' or by carrying attached to their chest a wooden horse's head), and then painted horses. The last phase of the evolution led to the construction of special buildings called *emadō*, 'horse-picture-galleries,' collections of *ex-votos* which may be seen in the precincts of some of the large temples. Lastly, the gods also have their carriage, the *mikoshi*, which, on the contrary, presents a sumptuous appearance; on religious feast-days the worshippers carry the *shintai* in this *mikoshi* on their shoulders.

A people essentially agricultural, as the Japanese seem to have been originally, whose Mikado himself occasionally set the example of ceremonially digging the earth, and among whom every year at Kasuga the young girls called *miko* ('august children') might be seen solemnly planting rice with their pure hands, was necessarily inclined to suppose that the gods devoted themselves to agriculture. And, as a matter of fact, the mythology, beginning with the great stories about the sun-goddess (the crimes committed by Susa-no-wo against her cultivations), shows that it was really one of the chief occupations of the deities on the Plain of the High Heavens. It was natural, therefore, that offerings of this kind should be made to those deities; and agricultural implements, reels for winding yarn, etc., figure in certain lists of offerings.

Another important requirement in a warlike country like primitive Japan was weapons for war. The mythology abounds in stories of marvellous swords—*e.g.*, the famous Kusa-nagi-no-tachi ('the herb-quelling great sword') which Susa-no-wo found in the body of the monster of Koshi,[3] which reappears later in the legend of Yamato-dake,[4] and which is worshipped at Atsuta as one of the three insignia of the imperial power. The majority of those swords must originally have been offerings, which gradually became *shintai* and even gods—

[1] See, *e.g.*, art. COSMOGONY AND COSMOLOGY (Japanese), vol. iv. p. 164a.

[2] See art. MAGIC (Japanese), vol. viii. p. 297a, *norito* 8, p. 298b, *norito* 15, p. 299a, *norito* 25, p. 299b, *norito* 27.

[3] Cf. the Roman *templum*.

[1] See art. ANCESTOR-WORSHIP AND CULT OF THE DEAD (Japanese), vol. i. p. 457a.

[2] See art. HUMAN SACRIFICE (Japanese and Korean), vol. vi. p. 856b.

[3] See *ib.* vol. vi. p. 855b.

[4] See art. HEROES AND HERO-GODS (Japanese), vol. vi. p. 663b.

e.g., the war-gods Take-mika-dzuchi and Futsu-nushi. In the 10th cent. offerings of wooden swords were already substituted for real weapons, and these have continued to the present day.[1] Other weapons, both offensive and defensive, were also offered — lances, bows and arrows, and shields.[2]

Lastly, even the need of entertainment, which was logically attributed to gods as to men, gave rise to appropriate offerings. Each important temple possessed a platform for the performance of sacred dances (*kagura*), the name of which is written with two Chinese characters meaning 'pleasure of the god.' Those pantomimes, whose mythical origin is found in the dance, before the cavern of the sun-goddess, of the goddess Uzume, the ancestor of the Sarume ('monkey-women'), the religious dancers of the court, were performed in the chief temples, to the accompaniment of flutes and castanets, by the *miko*, who thus represented the great episodes of the sacred story. The present writer was once present at the *kagura* in an old temple of Nara, and noticed to what an extent this dance of priestesses has, after all those centuries, scrupulously observed to this day the antique gestures and symbolical attitudes as we find them in the most ancient monuments of Japanese art. By a curious turn of events those primitive pantomimes, at first intended to charm the Shintō gods, later, after various developments, became the *nō*, or lyrical drama, generally composed by the bonzes or in any case under Buddhist inspiration, and thus greatly helped in the propaganda of the foreign religion. A fact which proves clearly that those artistic dances were at heart real offerings is that the rituals themselves, as the eclipse-legend shows, were, in the same way, regarded as charming the gods by the harmonious beauty of their language and the grandeur of their solemn declamation. Artistic pleasure, like literary pleasure, was regarded as a requirement of the gods which men must satisfy.

Besides these æsthetic enjoyments of a general kind, other more specified offerings might be made to the gods with the same intention of amusing them, as the texts clearly show; *e.g.*, to keep away the deities who send plagues, the Japanese gave them 'as things to play with, beads.'[3]

7. Fate of the offerings.—The offerings, once made, had various fates. The food-offerings were usually consumed—as, *e.g.*, after the emperor Jimmu's sacrifice. At the festival of firstfruits (*Nihiname*) the emperor tasted the new rice which had just been offered to the gods;[4] the priests followed his example, and even the simple worshippers might do the same. So also at the festival of Kasuga[5] the participants proceeded solemnly to eat the offerings in a dining-hall, while the servants of the imperial stables, who had had charge of the horses offered to the gods, were given a drink of the sacred *sake*. Even to-day pilgrims to the temples of Ise eat the rice of the offerings, which they buy from the priests. At the festival of the god of Suwa, mentioned before, while the heads of the seventy-five sacrificed deer are presented as offerings, the flesh is eaten by the priests, and the worshippers may also take a share of it, on condition that they obtain from the priests chopsticks which will allow them to do so without contamination. On the other hand, offerings of a valuable and durable kind, such as mirrors and swords, remained in the temple, where they were not placed on the altar, but were locked in the treasury; there they remained permanently, as *shimpō*, 'divine treasures,' later on often becoming *shintai* or even gods. The same thing happened in the case of the sixty white, red, and green jewels of the 27th ritual.[1]

Between those two extremes of ephemeral and permanent offerings there were offerings of a durable kind but not so precious—*e.g.*, bells or pottery—which were presented and then taken away to be presented again, so that the same objects were always used, just as to-day at Buddhist funerals, when birds are set at liberty, the undertakers make arrangements to capture them again immediately after the ceremony in order to use them on the next occasion.

The *aga-mono*, expiatory offerings to which were magically attached the impurities from which the worshippers wanted to be cleansed, were removed and thrown into the river.[2]

8. Buddhist offerings.—As Buddhist offerings have no special characteristic in Japan, they require no treatment here. We mention them merely to point out, by way of contrast, that the only original religion of the Japanese, viz. the ancient official Shintō, knew nothing of burnt incense, lighted candles, flowers on the altar—in a word, the characteristic Buddhist offerings. As regards offerings of flowers, we may mention that, at certain Buddhist festivals which require lotus flowers, but which fall at a period of the year when the lotus (or, more correctly, the *Nelumbium*, which is the lotus of Japan) is not in bloom, the equally pure magnolia flowers are used.

LITERATURE.—This is cited throughout the article.

M. REVON.

SACRIFICE (Jewish).—The destruction of the Temple in Jerusalem wrought a profound change in the religious life of the Jews. The entire divine service had come to a standstill. The priests and Levites had lost their position and occupation, and to the Israelite the very centre of worship had been destroyed. The sacrifices, among other things, had ceased. But divine ordinances cannot be abrogated. They are merely temporarily suspended until the time comes when they can again be enacted. A time will come when a new Jerusalem and a new Temple will be built up again. This conviction lives deep down in the hearts of the Jews, who look forward to the realization of the divine prophecies and with that the restoration of the ancient worship. This was the hope of Ezekiel, who in the midst of the Babylonian exile not only foretold the return, but went so far as to draw the picture of the future Temple. In the Talmudic literature there is a treatise called *Middôth*, *i.e.* the measurements of the pre-Herodian Temple—as the present writer has shown elsewhere[3]—and not of the Herodian described by Josephus. The preservation of this detailed description of the Temple is due not to any antiquarian interest, but to the desire to keep alive for the future the architectural details of the last Temple. It is to serve as a guide for the reconstruction. In *4 Ezra* and other apocalyptic writings, and especially in Revelation, we have the picture of the heavenly Jerusalem which will descend from on high at the consummation of the appointed time, and within it the heavenly Temple. Similar descriptions can be found in other eschatological writings, all testifying to the belief that the destruction of the Temple was only a temporary event. The service has been suspended for a while, to be taken up again at the proper time. The Jewish sages maintain the principle of the everlasting value of the ordinances of the Law,

1 See art. MAGIC (Japanese), vol. viii. p. 298a, *norito* 11.
2 *Ib.* p. 299a, *norito* 25. 3 *Ib.* p. 299a, *norito* 25.
4 See art. COMMUNION WITH DEITY (Japanese).
5 See art. MAGIC (Japanese), vol. viii. p. 296b

1 See art. MAGIC (Japanese), vol. viii. p. 299b.
2 *Ib.* p. 297b, *norito* 10, and p. 298, *norito* 11.
3 *RThPh* x. [1914–15] 21–31.

though they do not go so far as the author of the book of *Jubilees*. According to the latter, the patriarchs already had kept them; nay, they were written on the tablets of heaven and kept by the angels, although, according to the legend,[1] Moses heard the angel recite the *shᵉmaʻ* (Dt 6^{1-10}) and therefore he instituted it afterwards as part of the daily service. The fact that the Jews considered that the service in the Temple with the sacrifice was merely temporarily suspended, owing to the impossibility of carrying it out, is shown also by the compilation of many treatises in the Mishnāh forming the section *Ḳoddashim, i.e.* things connected with the sanctuary, in which minute details are preserved as to the services, sacrifices, offerings, etc., in the Temple; and the belief in the re-establishment of the sacrifice is found repeatedly referred to in the Jewish prayers recited in the daily service and on festival occasions. Thus in the *ʻamidah*, which every observant Jew is expected to repeat three times daily, he prays:

'Mayest thou bring back the sacrifice to thy holy house, and the fire offerings as well as their prayers receive with favour.'

This is also the preamble in the *musaf ʻamidah* on Sabbath, new moon, and festivals, etc., before the recital of the corresponding portion of the Bible (see below), when it is said:

'May it be thy will, O Lord our God, and the God of our fathers, that thou mayest bring us up with joy to our country, and there we will perform before thee all the obligatory sacrifices, the permanent ones according to their order and the additional ones according to the law.'

This formula varies but slightly and it is retained in every such prayer.[2]

This constant prayer for the re-establishment of sacrifice has been a bone of contention between the Reform Jews and the Conservative Jews. The former contend that they can no longer pray for the re-establishment of sacrifices. Æsthetical considerations of no real value are put forward to explain this position. But the vast majority of Jews have retained the ancient formula together with the undying hope of the revival of a national life in the land of their fathers according to divine promise. In this hope all the Jewish sects unite—the Rabbanites as well as the Ḳaraites, and the Falashas no less than the Samaritans, who, however, pray in a different form for the removal of the *Fanutha* (the turning away) and the return of the *Rachutha* (the divine favour), and the restoration of the service on their holy Mt. Gerizim. It must be pointed out at the same time that the Jewish sages are alive to the great difficulties which will have to be overcome before the sacrifices can be renewed, for they acknowledge those difficulties to be insurmountable unless removed by superhuman intervention. The *kōhănîm* (priests) are all defiled by the touch of dead bodies, of which defilement they cannot now purify themselves in the absence of the ashes of the red heifer. They have also intermarried to such an extent that the purity of their descent has in many cases become doubtful. The prophet Elijah then will segregate the right from the wrong and will purify those to be set aside as fit for the service.[3] Thus the practicability of restoring sacrifices is made to depend on the re-appearance of the prophet Elijah, whose coming before the great day is the last message of the last prophet (Mal $4^{5f.}$). It is relegated to a distant future, but the obligatory character of the sacrifices is not thereby affected. It was therefore necessary to establish temporary substitutes for the actual sacrifice. The sacrifices themselves varied in character. There were the early morning and afternoon sacrifices; there were additional sacrifices at new moon and festivals. These were collective sacrifices brought in the name and by the means of the entire nation. There were, besides, individual sacrifices—sin-offerings, thank-offerings, etc. Some were of a propitiatory nature; others were expiatory sacrifices. It is necessary to bear in mind this multifarious character of the sacrifices in the Temple if a correct description is to be given of the manner in which the Jews kept up the ordinances of the sacrifices and perpetuated them without Temple and priests. They spiritualized the sacrifice. The prophets had paved the way for this spiritualization. They already hinted at acceptable substitutes for the animal sacrifice. It is the sacrifice of self that they preach—the offering of the heart and of the soul, the outpourings of the broken heart, of the meek mind, which are accepted of the Lord, 'the sacrifice of the lips instead of the calves' (Hos 14^2), the meditations of the heart (Ps 19^{14}).

Whatever interpretation of the origin and meaning of sacrifice be given—and the interpretations are many and contradictory—the primitive stage had already been passed when, in the religious evolution of Israel, sacrifices took their place. Sacrifice represented then a free-will offering to God of what is best in man—an act of exaltation by which man, purified through this voluntary act of self-abnegation, draws nearer to God. He has either atoned thereby for his sin or given public expression of his thankfulness for the inexhaustible mercy of God. He may also expiate in his death, though not as a vicarious atonement, the guilt of others. The sacrifice of life, of health, and of wealth now takes the place of the sacrifice in the Temple of oxen and rams, or, rather, the substitutes are prayer, self-chastisement, and almsgiving. Traces of the ancient form of animal sacrifice still survive, however, on rare occasions and among Jewish sects.

(1) Foremost among those new substitutes for sacrifice stands *prayer*—the sacrifice of the lips. Prayer has taken the place of the service altogether, but here we shall consider only that part of the prayer which is exclusively regarded as the substitute for the sacrifice. The prayers are ordained to take place at the time when sacrifices were brought in the Temple; but, whilst the patriarchs are credited with having established the evening, morning, and afternoon prayer,[1] these were later to take the place of the sacrifice. Daniel prayed three times (Dn 6^{10} 9^4).

The practices in the second Temple paved the way for the substitution of prayers for sacrifices. There were the daily sacrifices which were brought in the name of the whole nation, and for which the shekel contributed by every Jew was used. Now, the nation could not all be present on the occasion of the offering, and thus a rota of deputies was established which, by tradition, was carried back to the time of David. The country was divided into twenty-four sections;[2] and out of each of these sections representatives, consisting of priests, Levites, and Israelites living in that section, went up to Jerusalem and were present, or 'stood by,' on the occasion of the sacrifices (hence the name *maʻamad*, pl. *maʻamadôth*). Thus the whole nation was practically represented by such delegates throughout the year; but, while the delegation was standing by in Jerusalem, the priests, Levites, and Israelites left at home gathered in their assemblies (synagogues) and, as it were, united with their brethren in Jerusalem. On that occasion they recited portions of the first chapter of Genesis in addition to the general benedictions and prayers, such as the *shᵉmaʻ*, and probably they also recited hymns, whilst their brethren

[1] *Tanḥûmā* in Vaetḥanan and in Deut. *Rab. ib.*; and also *Tanya Rab.*, ed. S. Horwitz, Warsaw, 1897, p. 16.

[2] M. Gaster, *Sephardic Prayer-Book*, London, 1901–06, i. 117.

[3] See *Mechilta*, ed. M. B. J. Friedmann, Vienna, 1870, fol. 51 to Ex $16^{32f.}$.

[1] *Gen. Rab.* 68.

[2] *Taʻănîth*, iv. 2.

in Jerusalem did likewise. If it were not for the *ma'amadôth*, the world would not exist.[1] No doubt on that occasion, while the *ma'amadôth* were present at the sacrifice, the corresponding passages from the Law concerning the institution of this sacrifice were recited in the synagogues in the provinces. Thus the first step was taken to represent sacrifice by prayer and recitation. This was afterwards enlarged upon when the Temple was destroyed and the possibility of bringing sacrifices had come to an end.

It has already been observed that the revival of the sacrifice is earnestly prayed for. But this alone does not suffice. The chapter of the corresponding portion in the Bible in which the Law commands the bringing of the sacrifice was to be publicly recited. Here we have to divide it in accordance with the Jewish form of liturgy: there are (1) a private devotion, which, however, does not materially differ from the public, especially on week-days; (2) the public worship of week-days, in which no lessons of the Bible, or practically none, are recited; and (3) the Sabbath, new moon, and festivals, in which, in addition to the special prayer, lessons from the scroll of the Law are also recited. The substitution, therefore, of corresponding portions had to be adjusted to these varying forms of the Liturgy. On week-days reference is made to the 'perpetual sacrifice' morning and evening, and the few verses of the Bible containing this commandment are recited in the early part of the prayers and hymns called *b^erākhôth* or *z^emirôth*. On the special days (Sabbath, new moon, and festivals), when in the Temple an additional sacrifice was brought (*musaf*), an additional portion is added, and in the additional (*musaf*) *'amidah* the same verses are again repeated. The introductory formula runs thus, and it contains practically the whole basis for the substitution of prayer for sacrifice according to Jewish tradition:

'Sovereign of the universe! thou didst command us to offer the daily sacrifice in its appointed time and that the priests should officiate in their service and the Levites at their stand and the Israelites by their delegates. But, at present, on account of our sins, the temple is laid waste, and the daily sacrifice hath ceased; for we have neither an officiating priest, nor a Levite at his stand, nor an Israelite as delegate. But thou hast said that the prayers of our lips shall be as the offering of bulls (Hos 14[2]). Therefore let it be thy will, O Lord our God, and the God of our fathers, that the prayers of our lips may be accounted, accepted, and esteemed before thee, as if we had offered the daily sacrifice at its appointed time, and had been represented by our delegation.'[2]

On the Day of Atonement the central portion of the *musaf* service contains a minute and elaborate description of the sacrifices offered in the course of the service performed by the high-priest on that day in the Temple in Jerusalem. Thus far concerning the daily prayer incumbent upon every Israelite, whether in public or in private devotion. In addition to those portions included in the prayer, and possibly of a higher antiquity, are the lessons read at the public service. These are read from the scrolls on Sabbaths, new moon, and festivals. On these occasions such sections of the Law are read as refer to specific festivals, such as Passover, Tabernacles, etc. They are read from one scroll independently of the weekly lesson on the Sabbath and the special lesson containing the institution of these festivals. On the new moon they form the only lesson, which is read from a single scroll brought out on that day. Of special significance in this connexion is the lesson read from the first scroll on the second day of the New Year. It is Gn 22, containing the story of the sacrifice of Isaac. This is embellished by a legend of the Rabbis in which it is stated that, for the sake of Abraham's compliance with the divine command of offering up Isaac, God would accept hereafter sacrifices of animals as an atonement for the people's sin. When Abraham asked, 'What will happen if they will no longer be able to bring such sacrifices?', God replied, 'Let them recite it before me, and it will be for me like unto the sacrifice.'[1] This view, then, that prayers, and above all the recital of the portions dealing with sacrifices, are the proper substitute for sacrifice, is often repeated in passages in the Talmud—*e.g.*, *B^erākh.* 15*a* and *b*, 33*a*; *Sukk.* 45*a*; *Ta'ăn.* 26*a*–27*b*; *M^eg.* 31*a*; *Midr. Psalm*, ed. S. Buber, p. 54; *Yalk.* to Ps 90, ii. § 533 and i. § 77; *Midr. Rab.* ch. 18 (end), ch. 30, § 3; *P^esiktā*, ed. Buber, fol. 102*b*; *Ruth Rab.* to ch. 3.[2]

'Behold the one who is asked to "offer up" prayers for the community is invited to do so by using the word "Kerab," which means both "draw near" and "offer up" a sacrifice, for prayers are like sacrifices.'[2] 'To prepare thyself for prayer is like building an altar for bringing a sacrifice.'[3]

The substitution of recital of portions of the Law for sacrifices seems to go back to a very ancient time—the time of the *ma'amadôth* before the destruction of the Temple. It is therefore not surprising to find the same practice among the Samaritans. In their prayers, as already remarked, they also invoke God's blessing and pray for the restoration of the ancient sacrifices, which are considered by them also as only temporarily suspended until the advent of the Taheb. They also have similar lessons, which they read on special days, on the eve of Sabbath, and on festivals; and they insert in their prayers corresponding portions of the Law describing either the institution or the sacrifice set aside for special occasions.[4] Moreover, they also have the term 'addition,' which they, curiously enough, spell *mozef*, not *musaf*; and they form from it a verb which they write *yozef*, 'to add.' They also introduce into their prayers verses from the Bible applicable to the significance of the day, which they group together to form an anthology, *catef*, thus substituting the recital of verses and of whole sections of the Bible for the sacrifices no longer to be offered in their Temple, which has been destroyed. Unfortunately A. E. Cowley did not realize the importance either of these *catefs* or of the Biblical lessons, and has omitted them from his *Samaritan Liturgy*,[5] and has thereby rendered reference to the peculiar form of the *catef* found in the rubric unintelligible. For their sacrifice of the Paschal lamb see below. The same principle is also followed by the Ķaraites, who in a way approximate to the practice of the Samaritans by accumulating Biblical verses of similar contents into collects in which the name of the festival forms, as it were, a kind of catch-word.

(2) *Study of the Law* in general is also considered an equivalent substitute for sacrifice, and the study of the chapters dealing with the various forms of sacrifice—peace-offerings, sin-offerings, thank-offerings—or the chapters containing the description of the sacrifice is considered of the highest merit. Studying the portion of thank-offering is like bringing it.[6] It is even put into the mouth of God that it is as acceptable to Him as the sacrifice of old in the Temple. The sin of Eli cannot be atoned by sacrifice, but only by the study of the Law.[7] And this has been extended to the study or recital of those portions in Rabbinical literature which contain references to the sacrifices in the Temple, such as *Zebaḥim*, 5; then the description of the incense[8] and the order of service arranged by Abbaye;[9] also *Lev. Rab.* ad Lv 1[11]; *Kolbo*, ch. ii.; *Siddur Rashi*, fol. 4.

(3) The same principle applies to the substitution of *fasting* for sacrifice: 'To fast is to bring a

[1] *B.T. Ta'ănîth*, 26*a*–27*b*.
[2] Gaster, *Prayer-Book*, i. 11.

[1] *Ta'ăn.* 12*a*, 27; *M^eg.* 31*a*.
[2] Jer. *B^erākh.* iv. 17.
[3] *B^erākh.* 46*b*.
[4] See Codex Gaster, 829.
[5] London, 1906.
[6] *Menaḥoth*, 110*a*.
[7] *Rōsh. Hash.* 18*a*.
[8] *Keritôth*, 6*a*.
[9] *Yômā*, 33*a*; see Gaster, *Prayer-Book*, i. 11 f.

sacrifice.'[1] And joined with it is almsgiving. In each case this means sacrifice of substance, both spiritual and material.

Fasting can be either individual or general, for propitiatory purposes (to avert impending evil) or for an expiatory reason (to atone for sin committed and to avert the dreaded consequences). The real object, however, in all cases is not to obtain God's favour, as it were, by a bribe, but to give outward expression to the mortification caused by sin and backsliding, in contrition of heart, self-chastisement, self-abnegation, and meekness, and to appeal to God's mercy and forgiveness. The result expected from self-denial and charitable deeds was inner purification and approach to God, from whom man had departed by forsaking His ways or breaking His commands. The great prototype, of course, is the Day of Atonement, but during the Temple period it was accompanied also by sacrifice, and on that day (see above) the recital forms part of the service. Now only the fasting remains, and it is considered as an equivalent for the sacrifice on every other occasion. In the prayer accompanying the individual fast as well as in those used on public occasions of fasting the words used by Rabbi Simeon[2] find their place:

'Therefore, O Lord! with thy abundant mercy answer me at this time and hour and let the diminution of my fat and blood, which hath by this day's fast been diminished, be accounted and favourably accepted before thee as the fat of the sacrifice laid on thine altar; that it may atone for what I have sinned, trespassed and transgressed against thee, whether accidentally or by choice; through ignorance or presumption; knowingly or unknowingly.'[3]

The same sentiments run through all the propitiatory and expiatory prayers connected with fasting. The Talmud has many examples of men who fasted a number of days and continued to fast even for years in order to avert impending evil—*e.g.*, Rabbi Ṣadoḳ, who fasted 40 years to avert the impending doom of Jerusalem,[4] and Rabbi Ḥanina, who fasted to avert misfortune from an individual.[5] A well-known fast is that of Adam, who fasted 130 years to expiate his sin.[6] These men, as it were, sacrificed themselves for the benefit of others and hoped to win thereby the favour of God, just as if they had brought sacrifices to the altar.

In a way self-mortification is considered a substitute for sacrifice, inasmuch as man offers himself up entirely to the service of God. It is a minor form of martyrdom, not free from selfish motives. Judaism has not looked with favour upon asceticism, celibacy, and self-mortification. The institution of the Nazirite, however, is recognized by the Law, but the Nazirite was expected, on the conclusion of his period, to bring an offering, which, as is explained by the sages in the Talmud, was a kind of expiation for the sin of self-mortification. Fasting is described as almost equivalent to sin;[7] it is almost like committing suicide.[8] It is not the fasting that brings the desired result, but repentance and almsgiving;[9] for fasting must lead to charity.[10] But the institution, as such, was a kind of self-sacrifice. Both men and women were allowed to take the vow of abstinence. In the Rabbinical literature a whole treatise has been preserved (*Mishnāh Nazir*) in which all the details connected with the Nazirite, as observed during the Temple period, are minutely described. It is there[11] said among other things that the Nazirite can be only in Palestine, and that Queen Helena of Adiabene had observed the vows of a Nazirite for seven years, and, on coming to Jerusalem to bring her offerings, was told that she had to keep the vows for seven years more, inasmuch as she could not take them outside of Palestine. But after the destruction of the Temple, when the cutting off of the hair and the other sacrifice brought at the conclusion of the period of the vow could no longer be observed, the practice of living as a Nazirite seems to have still persisted. A few men are known in Jewish history as Nazirites, and to one, Isaac Nazir, the origin of the later phase in the development of the Ḳabbālā is ascribed. He is the reputed first teacher of the new doctrine which was afterwards propagated by R. Abraham ben David. Otherwise very few examples are known.

The whole principle of celibacy and seclusion was unnatural to Judaism. Among the Samaritans there are also parallels to the practice of Naziriteship. In the Samaritan version of the Susanna legend[1] the two wicked old men who bring the false accusation against an innocent young woman are described as Nazirites, and the young woman herself, who was the daughter of a high-priest, was also a Nazirite; and in the present writer's Codex 1170 there has been preserved a very curious prayer, which, according to Samaritan tradition, was the one offered up by the Nazirite when taking the vow. The practice of Naziriteship seems to continue among the Falashas of Abyssinia. See also art. NAZIRITES.

(4) The highest form of sacrifice is for the *glorification of the name of God*, or for the *expiation of sin*. Although Judaism does not encourage self-sacrifice or even asceticism, yet the principle is laid down that a Jew should offer himself up as a sacrifice for his principles and convictions rather than commit the three cardinal sins—idolatry, immorality, and murder.[2] The sentence often appears, 'May my death be accepted as a sacrifice before the Lord, as an atonement for my sins.'[3] The Rabbis say that death is a sin-offering; *i.e.*, it atones for sin as a sin-offering. And it is only in the light of this conception that the remarkable law which is mentioned in Nu 35^{25-28} may be explained. It is there stated that one guilty of manslaughter who has found safety in the city of refuge must dwell there until the death of the high-priest, after which he is free to return to his own home unmolested. The connexion between the death of the high-priest and the freedom thereby accorded to the man guilty of murder can be explained if the death of the high-priest is regarded as an atonement for all the sins and sinners of his time. To this the statement in the Talmud, 'the death of the high-priest is an atonement,' seems to point.[4] In fact it is said that the righteous man dies for the sin of his generation. He is, as it were, the victim and the sacrifice of atonement for the sins of his generation. One sage is reputed to have offered himself up as an atonement sacrifice for R. Ḥanina and his children.[5] The death of the pious atones or purifies like the sprinkling of the ashes of the red heifer.[6] Another saying is, 'May I be an atonement for my daughter Kuza!'[7] When the son of R. Simeon ben Sheṭaḥ was falsely accused and condemned to death, he said, 'May my death not be an atonement for my sins if I am guilty!'[8] Moses' grave was facing Beth-peor in order that by his death he might atone for the sins of the Israelites committed at that place.[9] Moreover, the souls of the pious are, according to a saying in the Midrāsh, recorded also in the Jewish burial service,[10] offered up as a sacrifice to God on the heavenly altar by

[1] *Berākh.* 33*a*. [2] *Ib.* 17*a*.
[3] Gaster, *Prayer-Book*, i. 174. [4] *Giṭṭin*, 56*b*.
[5] *Bābā Meṣī'ā*, 33*a*.
[6] *Book of Adam and Eve*, and *'Erūbin*, 18*b*.
[7] *Ta'ănith*, 8*b*. [8] *Sanh.* 105*a*.
[9] *Berākh.* 6*a*; *Ta'ănith*, 8*b*, 17*a*.
[10] *Berākh.* 6*b*. [11] Ch. iii.

[1] Discovered and published by the present writer in the *International Journal of Apocrypha*, July 1913.
[2] Jer. *Ḥagīgāh*, ch. i. [3] *Berākh.* 60*a*.
[4] Jer. *Yōmā*, vii.; *Makkōth*, 11*b*.
[5] *Sukk.* 20*a*. [6] *Mo'ed Ḳaṭan*, 28*a*.
[7] *Yebamōth*, 70*a* [8] *Sanh.* 44*b*.
[9] *Sōṭāh*, 14*a*. [10] Gaster, *Prayer-Book*, i. 197.

the archangel Michael, who is described as offering up sacrifices and prayers before that great altar in heaven.[1] The sinners respond from hell shortly before the advent of the Messiah and thus obtain their liberation.[2]

(5) Another substitute for sacrifice is *charity*, which, however, has not been considered to be an equivalent to sacrifice in the full sense of the word. The giving of alms, the support of the poor, the succour of the sick, and every assistance that is given to those who have succumbed to the trials of the world are meritorious acts in themselves, but are not to be regarded as equal to the sacrifices offered in the Temple. Nevertheless the giving of alms is regarded by the sages as almost equivalent to sacrifices. So we are told in the Talmud that he who gives alms to the scholar is like one who brings a sacrifice.[3] Or, again, a man's table is like the altar of the Temple: on it he brings a sacrifice.[4] The charity performed by the Gentiles is like a sacrifice brought by the Jews.[5] The giving of charity is like the sacrifice of atonement,[6] and in the *Chapters of R. Eliezer*[7] it is said, 'More beloved is to me the service of loving-kindness than sacrifice.' Fasting and prayer, especially when they are of an expiatory character, are expected at the same time to be supplemented by liberal gifts to the poor—a kind of sacrifice of atonement for wrong done, and even for evil thoughts, which have mastered men's minds for a while (see above). In later times a symbolical meaning has been added to the eighteen pieces given to charity (for חי, whose numerical value is 18, means also 'life'). The underlying idea is that of ransom of oneself, as in the five pieces of silver given to the *kôhēn* as a ransom for the first-born male child (Nu 18[16]).[8] This is also a substitute for sacrifice, as is the other Biblical ordinance of the ransom of an animal unfit for sacrifice (Ex 13[13]).

(6) Another substitute for sacrifice may be mentioned here, although the author of the *Shûlḥān 'Ărûkh*, R. Joseph Ḳaro,[9] strongly condemns it and calls it a stupid practice. It is the practice of *offering up a white cock or hen as a ransom* (sacrifice) on the eve of the Day of Atonement. The bird is afterwards slaughtered according to the Law and is given away as a gift to the poor.[10] Curiously enough, the present writer has learnt from the Samaritans that, whenever they kill an animal or a fowl during the ten penitential days—*i.e.* from the 1st to the 10th of Tishri, from New Year to the Day of Atonement—in addition to the usual blessing, they repeat the following three words: לכפר ולכפר יכפר, 'to atone, and to atone, he shall atone.'[11] These are evidently taken as sin-offerings preparatory to the Day of Atonement; on it, through fasting and prayer, the great atonement is made for obtaining God's forgiveness for the spiritual and moral sins committed during the year.

(7) It remains now to refer to practices of *sacrifice outside of Jerusalem*, probably going back to the time of the second Temple. It must remain an open question whether in the temple of Onias in Egypt real animal sacrifices were brought, especially sin-offerings. Though the results at which Flinders Petrie[12] has arrived could be fairly accepted, the finding of burnt animals' bones on the spot identified by him with the ancient temple of Onias may still be explained in a different manner. It is well known that, in addition to the sacrifice brought into the Temple, there was the offering of the Paschal lamb initiated in Egypt and then continued in the desert long before the Temple existed. That being the case, the sacrifice of the Paschal lamb may also have been brought outside the Temple and after the destruction of the Temple. It may be, therefore, that the bones found in the Onias temple are the remains, not of the regular service, but of these Paschal sacrifices, which were believed to be independent of the Temple in Jerusalem and could be offered anywhere. The sacrifice of the Paschal lamb seems to have been a persistent independent feature in pre- and post-Biblical Judaism. Sacrifice seems to be referred to as part of the service in the temple of Yeb in Assuan, described in the Elephantine papyri. In the letters of the people addressed to Sanballat and to the high-priest in Jerusalem they complain of the cessation of various sacrifices. It will be noticed that in his reply the high-priest refers only to the incense- and meal-offerings, avoiding mention of the animal-sacrifice, which, from the point of view of the Temple in Jerusalem, could not well be sanctioned outside its precincts. The *ostrakon* published by Sayce[1] and commented upon by Daiches,[2] in which reference is made to preparation for the Passover, seems to refer to the preparation of the Paschal lamb, though the lamb is not mentioned, but the name 'Pascha' may refer to the lamb in addition to the flour for the cake. This is the same use of the word *pascha* or 'passover' for the lamb as in Mt 26[7], Mk 14[2], Lk 22[7. 8. 11]. A certain Theodosius in Rome took the liberty of eating on the first night of Passover the young kid slaughtered and prepared in accordance with the prescription for the Paschal lamb, and the patriarch (R. Gamliel) tolerated it, as he wrote, out of personal consideration for this Theodosius. Better known than these facts is the continual sacrifice of the Paschal lamb by the Samaritans on Mt. Gerizim. It has often been described by outsiders, and even photographed.[3]

We may mention here also the continuation of sacrifice by the Falashas in Abyssinia, but it is doubtful whether they sacrifice animals or merely make incense- and meal-offerings like those referred to in the papyri of Assuan. They seem to offer them up on special occasions, especially at the new moon. In the same connexion reference must be made to the peculiar form of the ancient synagogue, now destroyed, and once possessed by the Chinese Jews in Kai-Fong-Fu, of which a tracing has been preserved. Although some of the books of the liturgy, taken from these Jews by the missionaries more than a century and a half ago and now lying at Lincoln's Inn, agree in the main with the other Jewish Prayer Books hitherto known, they show a strong Persian influence. They have evidently travelled *via* Persia to the interior of China, as also have their ancient scrolls and books of the Law. Still the structure of that synagogue resembles very closely the inner structure of the Temple in Jerusalem, and in the very centre of it stands what appears to be an altar. Whilst real animal sacrifices are not likely to have been brought there, still incense-offerings and perhaps meal-offerings may have been brought, in

[1] *Hagîgāh*, 12*b*; cf. *Zebaḥim*, 62*a*.
[2] *Ôtiot de R. Aḳiba*, letter *shin*.
[3] *Berākh.* 10*a*.
[4] *Ib.* 55*a*.
[5] *Bābā Bathrā*, 10*b*.
[6] *Ib.*
[7] Friedländer's tr., London, 1916, p. 276.
[8] For the ceremony see Gaster, *Prayer-Book*, i. 181.
[9] See art. QARO.
[10] See *Abodat Yisrael*, ed. S. Baer, Rödelheim, 1868, p. 409 f.; and *Siddur Hegyon Leb.*, ed. L. Landshuth and H. Edelmann, Königsberg, 1845, p. 482 f.
[11] Gaster, Codex 1170, p. 343.
[12] *Hyksos and Israelite Cities*, London, 1906.

[1] *PSBA*, 1911, 183 f., [1912] 212.
[2] *Ib.* [1912] 17–23.
[3] A full description of the method of procedure and of the manner in which it is prepared and divided according to Samaritan law is found in Gaster, Cod. 872, fol. 129 ff., and there, as well as in some of the MS Prayer Books for the festival of Passover, a rough illustration is given of the vessels used and of the manner in which they are disposed (so in Gaster, Cod. 1120, fol. 55 f.).

accordance with the example of the Chinese worship. Unfortunately no detailed description of their mode of worship has been preserved, but from the Prayer Books just mentioned we may conclude that in general outline their worship was identical with that of the rest of the Jews.

Finally, reference must be made here to the letter which Joseph the king of the Khazars had sent to the Jewish vizier in Spain, Ḥisdai Aben Chiprut (middle of the 10th century).[1] In this letter he informs R. Ḥisdai that he has built in his capital a temple according to the model of that in Jerusalem, and among the vessels in that temple he mentions the table, the candlestick, and the altar. Whether he meant here the altar for the sacrifices or the golden altar for burning the incense remains obscure. In any case, the idea of bringing some sort of sacrifice could not have been absent from his mind. But, though there are these scattered reminiscences among sectarians and remote isolated communities, the only generally recognized substitutes for the sacrifices offered up in the Temple are the recital of the Biblical lessons and of the passages containing the institution of the sacrifices for daily services and for other occasional services such as Sabbaths, new moons, festivals, etc., accompanied by prayers, fasting, and charity.

LITERATURE.—The literature is given in the article. The subject has not been dealt with anywhere else.

M. GASTER.

SACRIFICE (Muhammadan).—**1. Meaning of sacrifice among the Arabs.**—As there are, properly speaking, no temples and no priesthood in Islām, so there is no sacrifice in the ordinary acceptation of the term. The sense of sin and the need for an atonement are even more strongly felt by the pious Muslim than by us, but they are not brought into connexion with the shedding of blood, whether of animals or of human beings. Thus in the Qur'ān the atonement (*kaffārah*, a Hebrew word) for the sin of deliberate perjury is not a sacrifice, but the feeding or clothing of ten poor folk, or the freeing of a Muslim slave, or, if these are beyond the culprit's means, then a fast of three days (v. 91). In v. 96, it is true, the penalty for killing game while in pilgrim garb is the slaying of some domestic animal of equal value (*e.g.*, a sheep for an antelope, a pigeon for a partridge), which is to be brought as an offering (*hady*) to the Ka'bah, but even here the purpose is not to make propitiation for sin, but simply to prevent the delinquent from being a gainer by his breach of the law. And so it is the alternative penalty of feeding the poor or fasting that is called an atonement. The expiation of sin in Islām rests entirely on the repentance of the sinner and the forgiving and merciful nature of God, to which must be added, in the popular religion, the intercession of Muhammad. The fact that the worst sinner in order to be saved has merely to declare himself a Muslim cuts the ground from under the feet of any theory of an atoning sacrifice. To be a follower of the Prophet is to be forgiven ; not to be such is the unpardoned crime.

The idea, again, which is said (perhaps in error) to have lain at the foundation of sacrifice among the Hebrews and other ancient peoples—that the Deity was an invisible guest at the sacrificial meal and that His share was the blood, the smoke, or the smell—would have been as repugnant to the Muslims as it is to common sense. The vicarious element in sacrifice also is excluded by the Muslims' strong sense of justice and of fate. With the idea, on the other hand, that the virtue of the pious might in effect be imputed to the wicked they were not unfamiliar. Muhammad was asked by one of his wives: 'Can we perish as long as amongst us are the pious?' He replied: 'Yes, if wickedness be great.' The one devout Umayyad Khalīfah 'Umar II. († A.H. 101, A.D. 720) also said: 'It used to be said: "God will not punish the many for the fault of the few," but if the wickedness be done openly, they deserve all to perish.'

2. Influence of climate.—Even if the pagan Arabs had held any of these theories of sacrifice, they would have been prevented from putting them into practice by the same cause which has led to the discontinuance of sacrifice among the Hebrews, namely, their poverty. Animal sacrifice could arise and continue only in a country rich in pasture, in which a sheep or even a camel could be easily spared ; but in Arabia, if we leave out of account the south-west corner, the whole population outside the towns has always been in a chronic state of semi-starvation. So poor were the Arabs that up to the time of Muhammad they were in the habit of burying their female infants, nominally for fear lest they should, by capture or otherwise, bring dishonour upon the tribe to which they belonged, but in reality because they had not the means of supporting them. The ordinary food of the desert Arab consisted of dates and the milk of his camels when available, and, when his inveterate hospitality did lead him to the lavish slaughter of his beasts, every particle that could be eaten was consumed, if not by himself and his guests, by the destitute women and children who hung about his tent, so that not much was left for the dogs. The only occasion on which there is waste of animal food in Arabia is at the great slaughter of beasts in the valley of Minā at the annual pilgrimage, and that is from sheer inability to consume or carry it away.

3. Motives of sacrifice.—The motives which underlie the very faint shadow of sacrifice as it was practised by the people of Arabia, and through them by the Muhammadan nations today, are different from those which actuated the more happily situated northern Semites or the races of Europe.

(*a*) Perhaps the most radical of all was the instinctive belief of the Semitic peoples in the sacredness of blood. Hence every slaughter of an animal, by the shedding of its blood, is an act of religion. Accordingly the same word is used in the Semitic languages for 'to slaughter' and 'to sacrifice' (Heb. *zābhaḥ*), and the Muslim always pronounces the name of God as he strikes the animal. A second motive for sacrifice among the Arabs was the natural belief of man that he can get something on which he has set his heart by surrendering something which he already possesses, or which he values less. Hence sacrifice is very commonly the fulfilment of a vow. Muhammad's grandfather vowed that, if he became the father of ten sons, he would offer up one of them as a sacrifice; and, when his wish was realized, he expiated his vow by a sacrifice of camels instead. A third commonly occurring motive is the natural inclination of men, when they have done anything of which their conscience disapproves, or which is against the tribal ethics, to punish themselves by a self-inflicted penalty. This motive is called *jazā'*, 'compensation'; and an example of it is the case mentioned above of the person who kills game while on pilgrimage. Connected with this motive and complementary to it is the instinctive impulse of any one who has met with a piece of good fortune to do some act of kindness to those who have not had the same fortune. An instance of this is the sacrifice of a sheep after the birth of a child, referred to below and named *'aqīqah*. But in all these cases there is no real sacrifice in the

[1] Reprinted by J. Buxtorf, jun., in his ed. of the *Cuzari*, Basel, 1660, and also in an Eng. tr., *Miscellany of Hebrew Literature*, London, 1872, p. 107.

ritualistic sense. The sacrifice is really simply a feast, in which, as a rule, the poor share. No portion of the victim is supposed to be consumed by the Deity, nor is there any religious mystery inherent in the rite. The beast is killed just as it might be killed in the hunting-field, except for the fact that the blood is not eaten, but the idea that the blood is the portion of the Deity would be entirely abhorrent to a Muslim.

(*b*) The great day of sacrifice in Islām is one of the days of the annual pilgrimage, the 10th of the twelfth month (Dhu'l-Ḥijjah). The motive in this case is not any of those mentioned above, but is purely historical and commemorative, as were, from one point of view, the feasts of ancient Israel. According to the prevalent belief, it was not Isaac but Ishmael that Abraham was commanded to offer up in sacrifice. The story given in the Qur'ān is as follows:

'And We [God] gave him [Abraham] good tidings of a gentle son. Then when he was old enough to work along with him, he said to him, "My son, I am seeing in sleep that I am to sacrifice [*dhabaḥ*] thee: therefore consider what thou thinkest we should do." He said: "My father, do what thou art commanded: thou shalt find me, please God, one of the patient." So when they thus submitted themselves, and he had laid him with his forehead on the ground, We called to him, "Abraham! Thou hast believed the vision. Thus do We compensate those who do right. This is a clear trial," and We redeemed him with a mighty sacrifice [*dhibḥ*].'[1]

It will be seen that the Qur'ān does not specify either Ishmael or Isaac, but the fact that it goes on to mention the latter is taken to mean that here the former is intended. The place of the intended sacrifice is commonly believed to have been the valley of Minā, a few hours' journey to the east of Mecca, and the ram which became the substitute is said to have come down from Mt. Thabīr, which abuts on the valley. It is this event that is commemorated on the occasion of the annual pilgrimage. On the 8th of Dhu'l-Ḥijjah the pilgrims remove from Mecca to Minā, where they spend the night. Early on the 9th they go in haste to Mt. 'Arafāt, where they hear the sermon, returning the same evening to Muzdalifah between 'Arafāt and Minā; and, after a night spent in devotion, the morning of the 10th finds them back again at Minā. There they slay the victims which they have brought with them, and, their purpose thus accomplished, they shave their heads. What they cannot eat of the victims they either carry away or give to the poor. Even so, however, the waste of only too precious food every year is enormous. But the point to be noted for our present purpose is that the whole ceremony is purely commemorative. It is the keeping up of an old national custom. It is not the sacrifice that redeems the pious Muslim from his sins, but the visitation of the House of God in Mecca.

4. All taking of animal life sacrificial.—As there is no proper sacrificial ritual in Islām, so the words now employed in a semi-religious sense originally meant to slaughter in the ordinary everyday usage, or else they are words borrowed from other faiths, in which sacrifice was a truly religious act. Any ritual slaughtering that there might be in Islām is founded, not on any innovations introduced by Muhammad, but merely on the primitive human instinct which feels a natural repugnance to the shedding of blood. The Muhammadans generally hold the belief that the spirit escapes through the wound that is the cause of death. Thus a man who dies a natural death is said in Arabic to die 'the death of his nose'; *i.e.*, his spirit goes out at his nostrils. It may have been a superstitious dread of the vengeance of this spirit that originated the custom of making every act of slaughtering an animal an act of religion, which

[1] xxxvii. 99 ff.

put, as it were, the responsibility upon God, by always invoking His name. This would be the case all the more among the Hebrews, since the animals killed among them for food were mostly animals of considerable size. We do not read in the OT of domestic fowls being used for food, but the Muslim kills a cock in just the same way as he kills a sheep, and with the same formality; *i.e.*, he faces in the direction of Mecca and says, 'In the name of God,' as he cuts its throat.

5. Mode of slaughter.—Islām is a religion without mystery and therefore without sacraments. Consequently it is not possible to draw a distinction between sacrificing an animal and simply slaughtering it for food. There is no difference at this point between the religious and the secular. In the case of the Hebrews, although they use the same word to denote sacrificing and killing for food, it is possible to say when it is used in the one sense and when in the other. But it is a mistake to suppose that this difference exists in orthodox Islām. With the Hebrews, as with many other ancient nations, sacrifices were consumed in whole or in part upon the altar; but in Islām there is no altar. The Muslim slays his 'sacrifice' exactly as the Jew kills beasts for the market; the one act is as religious as the other. The legal mode of slaughter, whether merely for food, when it is called *dhakāt*, or for 'sacrifice,' when it is called *dhabḥ*, is, except in the case of camels, by cutting the throat. In *dhakāt* the knife must sever the windpipe and gullet, but the school of Mālik say the gullet and the veins of the neck; others say the two jugular veins, or one of the jugular veins. The same remarks apply to *dhabḥ*.[1] These rules are based upon those of the Jews.

6. Technical terms.—(*a*) *Naḥr*.—The noun denotes the upper part of the chest where the windpipe begins, which is the spot where a camel is stabbed for slaughter. The infinitive *naḥr* denotes the act of stabbing a camel in this place in order to kill it. In this respect it is distinguished from *dhabḥ*, which means slaughtering an animal by cutting its throat. The two are also different in that the former is a pure Arabic word, whereas the latter represents the Heb. *zebhaḥ*, 'slaughtering' or 'sacrificing.' Perhaps it is due to its pagan connotation that the former occurs once only in the Qur'ān (cviii. 2); 'We [God] have given the Kauthar: then pray to thy Lord and slaughter.' Kauthar is explained as the name of a river in Paradise, but this is the usual explanation given of the unknown vocables in the Qur'ān. Perhaps it is nothing else than the Heb. *kosher*, 'lawful,' used of meat killed in the legal manner. As all blood is sacred, so all slaughtering of beasts partakes of a semi-religious character; but the 10th of Dhu'l-Ḥijjah is named esp. *yaum an-naḥr*, 'the day of slaughter.' On it the great pilgrimage culminates in the slaying of the victims (*hady*) at Minā near Mecca in imitation of the sacrifice of Ishmael there. On the same day all over the Muslim world sheep are killed in the principal towns. In Tangier the sheep is carried in great haste from the slaughtering-place at the top of the town through the principal street down to the great mosque. If it is still alive when it arrives there, it is considered a good omen for the coming year. On the same day sheep are killed in every household that can afford it, and the flesh is shared with the poor.

(*b*) *Hady*.—This word is properly the inf. of the verb *hadā*, 'to lead (or bring),' esp. to bring a gift or offering (*hadīyah*), consisting of a camel, cow, sheep, or goat, to the Ka'bah at Mecca for sacrifice or slaughter. It occurs in Qur'ān, ii. 196, v. 96, xlviii. 25; and in v. 2, 98 the garlands (*qalā'id*) hung upon the victim to mark it as sacred are also mentioned. *Hady* is used specifically of offering a sacrificial gift, but *hadīyah* is the general word for 'anything which is taken without any stipulation for service rendered.'[2] The rules for the *hady* and the traditions regarding it, *i.e.* the practice of Muhammad and the first Muslims, as they are given in the oldest collection of traditions available, the *Muwaṭṭa'* of Mālik ibn Anas († A.H. 179, A.D. 795), are as follows:

Those who could afford to do so usually offered one head of large cattle (called a *badna*), a camel, a cow, or a bull, but 'Abdallah, son of Khalīfah 'Umar I., usually sacrificed two *badna* at every visit to Mecca, and there was no limit to the number which might be offered. It was not thought right to ride the victim on the journey to Mecca, but Muhammad permitted this to be done. The Arab's humanity, however, did

[1] Muḥammad 'Alī at-Tahānawī, *Kitāb Kashshāf Iṣṭilāḥāt al-Funūn*, i. 511.

[2] Jurjānī, *Ta'rīfāt*, ed. G. Flügel, Leipzig, 1845, p. 277.

not always let him take advantage of the indulgence. Similarly, it was not thought proper to drink the milk of the she-camel destined for sacrifice, except under necessity. If the she-camel should calve on the journey, her calf might be carried, if necessary, upon the back of the dam, and it was sacrificed along with her. The victim was 'garlanded' and 'marked.' The garland did not consist of flowers, which were, of course, not to be found. In the times of 'ignorance' before Islām the pagan Arabs used bark from the trees of the sacred territory of Mecca. Thereafter any object served. 'Abdallah ibn 'Umar, mentioned above, used to hang a pair of worn-out sandals on it, facing the *qiblah* as he did so. The 'mark' was an incision made with a fleam or lancet on one side of the camel's hump, sufficient to draw blood. 'Abdallah used in addition to cover the sacrifice with fine, white Egyptian linen or other saddle-cloth (*jull*), which, when done with, he presented to the Ka'bah, or, if it should have already been 'clothed,' gave away in charity. According to this 'Abdallah also, the camel should be not less than five full years old, and other animals in their third year at least. Another of the early Muslims used to bid his son 'not to offer to God any beast which he would be ashamed to offer to his most honoured friend, for God is the noblest of the noble, and the worthiest of those for whom choice is made.' Should a camel break down on the road through fatigue, Muhammad ordered it to be slaughtered, its garland to be dipped in its blood, and its flesh to be eaten. If the offering was purely voluntary, it was then regarded as accomplished; otherwise—if, *e.g.*, it was in fulfilment of a vow—the offerer must find another victim. If any one missed the pilgrimage, *i.e.* failed, whether through losing his way or through miscalculating the days, to be present at Minā on the day of sacrifice, 'Umar required him to offer another victim the next year. If he had not the wherewithal, he must fast three days during the pilgrimage, and seven on his return home.[1] This verse mentions the sacrifice of 'what is convenient' as an atonement for not duly performing the pilgrimage. The phrase is generally taken to mean a sheep or goat. The sacrifice which is a penalty for killing game during the pilgrimage or a similar offence must be offered in Mecca;[2] but, if it take the form of fasting or of alms, this may be accomplished in whatever place the penitent may choose. As originally signifying 'a gift,' these terms may be compared to the Hebrew *minḥah*.

(*c*) *Nusuk, nusk*, and *nasīkah* are all used of a victim offered in sacrifice. In the Qur'ān the pilgrim who through sickness cannot shave his head (in token of having performed all the ceremonies and fulfilled his vow) must pay a ransom or forfeit by fasting or giving alms or sacrificing a sheep (*nusuk*).[3] The other forms of the word do not occur in the Qur'ān. In later times the word came to mean asceticism, and already in the Qur'ān *nusuk* is used in the sense of worship generally,[4] and *mansak* means a religious ceremony, and *nasaka* to practise these ceremonies or rites.[5] The root meaning of the word appears to be to wash or cleanse—*e.g.*, a garment. *Nasīkah* is synonymous with *dhabīḥah*. The terms are probably derived from the Heb. *nesekh*, a libation of oil often joined with the meal-offering (Nu $28^{7ff.}$ etc.).

(*d*) *'Aqīqah*.—This is the hair which covers the head of a new-born infant, and which the Muslims shave off on the seventh day after birth. Herodotus[6] mentions a similar custom in Egypt. The occasion is celebrated by the slaughter of a ram or a goat, the flesh of which is cooked and distributed to the poor. This victim is also named *'aqīqah*. The practice is not mentioned in the Qur'ān, but Mālik ibn Anas states that Muhammad, being asked about it, replied that he did not like it; Mālik adds that he only meant that he did not like the name, not the thing, as the word means a beast having its throat slit right across, and so was considered ill-omened. It is related in a tradition that Fāṭimah weighed the *'aqīqah* of each of Muhammad's grandsons, Ḥasan and Ḥuṣain, and gave the weight in silver in alms; and this became a recognized custom. One of the early Muslims permitted the substitution of a bird for a sheep,[7] but this was not approved, and the practice is one sheep for each child, whether a boy or a girl. Moreover, the sheep must be without blemish—not blind, emaciated, sick, or having a broken horn—nor may any of its flesh or its skin be sold. The blood also must not be allowed to touch the child.

(*e*) *Ḍaḥīyah*.—The victim slaughtered on the morning (*ḍuḥa*) of the 10th of Dhu'l-Ḥijjah is so named from the hour at which the sacrifice takes place. The word has various forms, in both singular and plural. The collective is *'aḍhā*, from which the day is named *yaum al-'aḍḥā*, 'the day of the victim'; also *'īd al-'aḍḥā*, 'festival of the victims.' These words do not occur in the Qur'ān. The regulations laid down in the *Muwaṭṭa'*[8] are identical with or supplementary to those for the sacrifice under its other names. Muhammad, asked what was to be avoided in the *ḍaḥīyah*, replied: 'Four things: the lame whose limping is visible, the evidently blind, the evidently diseased, and what is so starved as to have no fat.' To these must be added that it be of the proper age (see above, [*b*]). Hence 'Abdallah ibn 'Umar sacrificed any victim that was of the right age and without blemish; and this is the principle approved by Mālik.

In the great pilgrimage no one may slay his sacrifice before the *imām*, or leader of the pilgrimage, has slain his; still less may he slay it at an earlier hour of the day. In either case Muhammad ordered the offender to sacrifice a fresh victim, even if he could not find one that had attained the prescribed age. Muhammad on one occasion forbade the eating of the *ḍaḥīyah* after three days. It was pointed out to him that the people were in the habit of melting the fat and preserving it in skins. He replied that he had said what he did only for the behoof of certain Arabs of the desert who had been driven by drought into the town; and he gave full permission to preserve and store the meat of the sacrifice. Opinions are divided as to whether it is allowable for a number of pilgrims to take shares in a sacrifice. On the one hand, it is related that al-Ḥudaibiyah, when Muhammad was prevented from entering Mecca and sacrificed on the spot the victims which he had brought with him, seven of his followers went shares in each camel or each head of cattle. Hence the Shāfi'ites and Ḥanbalites hold that partnership in a sacrifice is legitimate. Mālik, on the other hand, maintains the preferable doctrine that, whilst people of the same family may sacrifice for the family, for those who are not so connected to contribute towards the purchase of the beast and then share in its flesh is a thing 'to be hated.' Sometimes a child still unborn was made a partner.

(*f*) *Qorbān*.—This is simply the Hebrew word taken over into Arabic. It occurs three times in the Qur'ān—iii. 179, where it is put into the mouth of the Jews; v. 30, in the story of Cain and Abel; and xlvi. 27, where, however, it means 'a *near* associate,' from the verb which in Arabic, as in Hebrew, means 'to bring near' or 'to sacrifice.' No doubt it is borrowed from the Hebrew. Lane[1] mentions a tradition, 'Prayer is the offering of every pious man,' meaning that it is what brings him near to God.

7. Arab and Hebrew sacrifice compared.—In conclusion it may be of interest to note some of the points of contrast between Arab and Hebrew ideas about sacrifice. The most important is that the idea of an atonement scarcely, if at all, enters into Arab sacrifice. Even when the offerer is regarded as having forfeited his life, as in the case of the pilgrim who breaks his *iḥrām*, he is ransomed not by the act of slaying a victim, but by the act of benevolence in distributing the portions to the poor. There is, again, no holocaust in Muhammadan sacrifice; the victims are slain to be eaten; only the blood is rejected, but it is so whether the slaughtering has any religious import or not. There is no libation, no meal-, wave-, or heave-offering in Islām; the sacrifice is always a beast or bird which is killed. With the Hebrews the beast sacrificed was a male; with the more open-handed Arabs it was often a female. With the Arabs the sacrifice was shared, not with the priests—an unknown class among them—but with the poor. With them also the only sacrifice of a communal character, if any can be considered such, is the annual sacrifice of the Great Feast. The rich man's offering with them is the camel, an animal held unclean by the Hebrews. Among the latter every sacrifice, and even every implement, was salted; on the other hand, preserving the flesh for future use was not allowed. Partnership in a sacrifice, except between members of a family, is (by the Mālikite school) forbidden in Islām. All these differences point to the fact that with the Hebrews sacrifice was a really ritualistic act of worship, whilst it was not so among the Muslims.

LITERATURE.—Muḥammad 'Alī at-Tahānawi, *Kitāb Kashshāf Iṣṭilāḥāt al-Funūn* ('Dictionary of Technical Terms'), ed. W. N. Lees and others, Calcutta, 1854–62, *s.vv.*; Al-Bukhārī, *Les Traditions islamiques, traduites de l'arabe, avec notes et index*, ed. O. Houdas and W. Marçais, Paris, 1903 ff., index; Mālik ibn Anas, *Al-Muwaṭṭa'*, any ed., contents; E. W. Lane, *The Thousand and One Nights*, London, 1883, introd., note 1, ch. i., note 16, iii. 63, iv. 24, v. 40, vi. 11; R. F. Burton, *Personal Narrative of a Pilgrimage to El-Medinah and Meccah*, do. 1855–56, iii. 302 ff.; E. Westermarck, 'The Popular Ritual of the Great Feast in Morocco,' *FL* xxii. [1911] 131–182.

T. H. WEIR.

SACRIFICE (Semitic).—In this section we consider the subject of sacrifice among the following peoples—Egyptians, Babylonians, Assyrians, Aramæan and Arab tribes (ancient and modern), Hebrews, Phœnicians and Carthaginians, and Abyssinians. On the propriety of including (with reservations) the Egyptians in the foregoing list see the beginning of art. HUMAN SACRIFICE (Semitic).

1 *Qur'ān*, ii. 196. 2 v. 96. 3 ii. 196. 4 vi. 163.
5 xxii. 66. 6 ii. 65. 7 Cf. Lv 12^8.
8 P. 186 ff. (ed. Delhi, 1307 A.H.).

1 *Arab.-Eng. Lex.*, 1863–93, *s.v.*

1. Occasion of sacrifice.—One of the most satisfactory classifications of sacrifices available is that which divides them into (*a*) periodic, and (*b*) non-periodic or occasional. To the former belong sacrifices on feast-days recurrent at certain seasons or days of the year; to the latter belong sacrifices offered on particular occasions, as at the birth of a son, the foundation of a building, the initiation of some military or other enterprise, etc.

(*a*) Periodic sacrifices may be daily, monthly, or seasonal. In Egypt part of the daily temple services consisted in clothing and decorating a figure of the deity, and then setting before it an offering of food—bread, geese, beef, wine, and water. These, after standing a while before the god, were most probably appropriated by the priests (cf. the story of Bel and the Dragon). The dead were supposed to partake of this daily banquet.[1] At certain great feasts—*e.g.*, the anniversaries of the birthday of the god, or of his mighty deeds—there were increased offerings, which the worshippers shared in a common feast.

In the fully developed sacrificial liturgy of the Hebrews we read of a variety of periodic sacrifices—the daily burnt-offering (Nu 28³); the weekly offering on the Sabbath, double in number of the daily offerings (28⁹); the monthly sacrifice, at the new moon (28¹¹); and certain annual sacrifices, as the Passover (full moon of first month), the day of the firstfruits, the beginning of the second half of the year (first day of seventh month), and the full moon of the seventh month (28¹⁶–29⁴⁰).

In Arab heathendom the annual sacrifices of the month Rajab must be mentioned; this was perhaps the most important ceremonial event of the pre-Muhammadan religion.

Examples of periodic sacrifice might be multiplied from the other branches of the Semitic world, but these will suffice. It is obvious that they all depend on the motions or phenomena of the heavenly bodies (sun, moon, the planet Venus, etc.), or on the annual recurrence of seed-time and harvest, or on the increase of flocks. They are such as would naturally arise in the regular unbroken existence of a pastoral or an agricultural community.

(*b*) Non-periodic sacrifices are more of a personal nature. They take place on the occasions which break the monotony of the existence of such a community, or of individual members thereof. The birth and circumcision of a son; the foundation of a house; the beginning of a military or other enterprise, and its successful conclusion—all these are events celebrated by a sacrifice. Moreover, by sacrifice an individual seeks to obtain some desired boon from the gods—the health of a sick relative, purification from the sense or consequence of sin, and the like. A few examples may be cited in illustration.

(1) *Birth.*—Among the Arabs 'the child must be taken on a pilgrimage to the shrine to which the sheik of the tribe belongs. The minister of the shrine sacrifices for them near the threshold. The child is anointed on his forehead, or on his nose, with a mark of the blood of the victim.'[2] The Hebrews do not appear to have had a special sacrifice to celebrate a birth, but the first-born son had to be redeemed (Ex 13¹³ 34²⁰) with a money payment of five shekels.

(2) *Children.*—The modern Arabs offer sacrifices for a child (especially a son), if there is any fear that it may not live. It is also customary to offer sacrifices at circumcisions. In sacrificing for a child care must be taken (according to Curtiss)[3] not to break one of the animal's bones, lest a similar injury be inflicted on the child.

(3) *Foundation of a building.*—A tablet given by Zimmern[4] apparently records a sacrifice at a new house. In various Palestinian excavations traces of foundation-offerings of one kind or another have been found.[1] Among the modern Arabs a sheep is sacrificed when a new building is begun.

(4) *Inauguration of a king.*—In Egypt the king began his reign with a sacrifice to Min, the god of fertility, in the presence of the statues of his ancestors. 'A priest presents him with the royal sickle, with which he cuts a sheaf of corn; he then strews it before the white bull, symbolizing the offering of the first-fruits of his reign. He then offers incense before the statue of the god, while the priest recites from the mysterious books of the "dances of Min."'[2] Cf. the inauguration of Saul (1 S 10⁸).

(5) *Dedication or consecration of a building.*—Ashurnaṣirpāl dedicated the temple of Ninib in Calah with prayer and offerings,[3] as did Solomon the Temple of Jahweh at Jerusalem (1 K 8).

(6) *As a sin-offering.*—Curtiss[4] quotes 'a devout Muslim, of good sense but unlettered,' as saying that 'sacrifice would cover sin.' He likewise quotes from Burton a statement that the victim at the Mecca pilgrimage is sacrificed 'as a confession that the offender deems himself worthy of death.' The sin-offering occupies a conspicuous place in Hebrew ritual (Lv 4²²ff. etc.), as does the analogous purification-offering from various forms of uncleanness (Lv 14, 15, Nu 19). The Babylonians likewise had purification-sacrifices for a house after sickness.[5]

(7) *Sickness.*—In Babylon, according to a ritual tablet printed by Jastrow,[6] a lamb was to be sacrificed near a sick man, the body of the animal being opened and its inwards torn out—possibly with the idea of tearing out the malady by sympathetic magic. Sacrifices at exorcism of demons and at the purification of a house may also be mentioned here.

(8) *Death and funeral ceremonies.*—Offerings of the mourners' own hair and blood to the dead are forbidden to the Hebrews (Lv 19²⁸), but were nevertheless practised (Jer 16⁶). W. R. Smith[7] and Curtiss[8] note similar customs among the Arabs. The latter cites a peasant informant as telling him that 'when a man comes to die he appoints some one as executor to sacrifice some animal. It is preferable for a man to offer the sacrifice during his life. . . . He rides the animal across the narrow way on the day of judgment.' Another informant told him that 'only the Arabs [*i.e.* the Bedawin] offer sacrifice for the dead';[9] but Curtiss questions the accuracy of this statement. The sacrifice for the dead is not eaten in a feast, like other Arab sacrifices, but is given to the poor.[10]

(9) *Sacrifice of spoil captured in war.*—This, according to Diodorus Siculus,[11] was a custom of the Carthaginians; and it is indicated for the Hebrews by 1 S 14³⁴ 15¹⁵; cf. also David's laying up of Goliath's sword. A similar instance is cited from Arab heathendom by Wellhausen.[12]

The above must suffice as a selection of the occasions on which non-periodic sacrifices were offered among the Semitic tribes. A full list, with a properly marshalled series of illustrative examples, would fill a large volume. It may be said in short that there was hardly any possible event in the individual or communal life that was not marked by a sacrifice among one or more of the Semitic peoples.

2. The persons and materials involved.—The persons involved, in a complete sacrificial ritual, are four in number—either four individuals or four communities. These are (1) the person or persons offering the sacrifice; (2) the person or persons for whose benefit the sacrifice is offered; (3) the intermediary or priest, who receives the sacrifice from the person offering and disposes of it according to the rubrics governing the ritual; and (4) the person to whom the sacrifice is offered. On occasion these four may be reduced to three, (1) and (2) being identical, or even to two, (1), (2), and (3) being identical; but as a rule the interposition of a priest between the person offering and the recipient is considered desirable, as he by his ordination and consecration is supposed to be more familiar with the unseen world, and by his special knowledge is able to avoid ritual mistakes. Among the Hebrews the Passover sacrifice was the only one that could be offered without the mediation of a priest.

The person or persons offering the sacrifice may be any member of the tribe or any group of fellow-

[1] A. Erman, *Handbook of Egyptian Religion*, tr. A. S. Griffith, London, 1907, p. 46 f.
[2] Curtiss, *Primitive Semitic Religion To-day*, p. 201.
[3] P. 178.
[4] *Beiträge zur Kenntnis der bab. Religion*, pp. 147–149.

[1] See R. A. S. Macalister, *The Excavation of Gezer*, London, 1912, ii. 426–437.
[2] Erman, *Life in Ancient Egypt*, tr. H. M. Tirard, London, 1894, p. 66.
[3] Jastrow, *Rel. Babyloniens und Assyriens*, i. 225.
[4] P. 211.
[5] Jastrow, *Religious Belief in Bab. and Assyr.* p. 318.
[6] *Rel. Bab. und Assyr.* i. 350.
[7] *Religion of the Semites*², p. 323.
[8] P. 178.
[9] P. 179.
[10] *Ib.*
[11] xx. 65
[12] *Reste arab. Heidentums*², p. 112.

tribesmen (a family, clan, gild, secret society, etc.). Foreigners are as a rule excluded from participation in the presentation of offerings (Lv 22^{25}); and the priest must be chosen by some special sign (*e.g.*, heredity, as among the Hebrews) and set apart for his calling by ordination. The recipient of the sacrifice is as a rule a deity; but sacrifices, as we have just seen, may be offered to the dead, and may even be claimed as a mark of divinity by a king during his lifetime.[1]

The materials involved (*i.e.* the object offered in sacrifice) can be grouped into a number of different classes. The object sacrificed is a kind of intermediary whereby the worshipper comes into contact with the divinity. Such contact as a rule is of this indirect kind; but there are cases when the worshipper offers a part or characteristic of himself, in which the contact is more direct—*e.g.*, the numerous offerings of blood or of hair, and sacrifices of manhood or of female chastity.[2] More commonly, however, the offering consists of some object not a part of the offerer, though selected from his property; and in the vast majority of cases it is an animal. Vegetable offerings are also made, especially of the firstfruits of the field or of the trees; but mineral offerings are rare except as a simple *ex voto* donation or as a concomitant of animal or vegetable offerings (especially salt).

The animal kingdom is divided by every tribe into beasts which may, and beasts which may not, be sacrificed. According to the totemistic theory of the origin of sacrifice (see below), the totem-animals would in the beginning be the normal, if not the only admissible, victims; and W. R. Smith saw relics of totemism in the sacrifices of swine, dogs, and mice reproved by the second Isaiah.[3] The sacrifice of the totem-animal had already in pre-historic times given place to the practice of sacrificing the animals normally used as food, especially of the cow and sheep kind. Besides these the Hebrews admitted sacrifice of goats, turtle-doves, and pigeons. Fish, though eaten, was not sacrificed, nor were wild beasts. The Arabs added to these permissible animals the camel[4] and gazelle (as a miserly substitute for a sheep).[5] The same animals—cow, sheep, goat, and fawn—as well as some kind of domestic bird (cock and hen?) are enumerated on the Marseilles and Carthaginian sacrificial tablets.[6] The Babylonians added fish and cream[7] to the list. Human sacrifice is discussed under its own heading and need not be referred to here.

The vegetable offerings were those of the ordinary harvest produce, and need not be specially enumerated. Dates and other fruits were offered in Babylon. The burning of aromatic gums (see art. INCENSE) calls for passing notice here; it is found in sacrificial worship among all the Semitic peoples[8] except, apparently, the Arabs.[9] Wine-libations and the use of oils (like the holy ointment of which the prescription will be found in Ex $30^{23ff.}$) also belong to this category. These also are not found among the Arabs. Milk is the normal Arab drink-offering.[10] There is some inconsistency in the Hebrew documents as to the use of leaven in the sacrifice. It is forbidden in Ex 23^{18} and Lv 2^{11}; the latter passage also excludes honey. On the other hand, it is enjoined in Lv 7^{13} 23^{17}, with which passages Am 4^{5} may be compared. Probably W. R. Smith is right in associating with the prohibition of leaven the precautions taken to prevent any of the meat of the sacrifice being left over; similar precautions are found in the Arab rites, and are evidently designed to prevent the sacred flesh from putrefying.

Among minerals we need refer only to salt (Lv 2^{13}). David's libation of water (2 S 23^{16}) is an exceptional and special case, not indicating any rule. The gifts of gold from which Aaron made the calf (Ex 32^{2}) hardly come under the head of sacrificial material. The total or partial destruction of the object sacrificed distinguishes a sacrifice from an *ex voto*.

3. The purpose of sacrifice.—It may be taken that in all cases the purpose of sacrifice is to secure a benefit, but the benefit may be for the donor, for the recipient, or for a third party.

The majority of sacrifices are for the benefit of the donor (whether an individual or a community) or of some third party. Such are the primitive communal sacrifices, in which the god and his worshippers partake of a common meal. Here the meal preserves the fatherhood of the tribal deity from suffering eclipse owing to neglect or transgression on the part of the tribe, and thus keeps the deity on friendly relations with his children. The offerings of firstfruits belong to the same category: the bounty of the tribal god is acknowledged by the gift and by that form of gratitude manifested which has been cynically defined as 'a lively sense of favours to come.'

Such is, primarily, the purpose of the seasonal sacrifices. The deity is periodically fed by the gifts of his children, and thus is kept continually favourable towards them. But the non-periodic sacrifices are likewise meant to secure a favour of one kind or another. Special sacrifices, when the deity is for any reason supposed to be angry with his people, or cathartic or piacular sacrifices, designed to win for the offerer a deliverance from disease or from sin or its consequences, fall under the same category.

The only sacrifices in which the recipient is directly benefited, without a necessary reflexion of the benefit on the donor, are sacrifices made to the dead or offerings deposited in the tomb. As the latter not infrequently consist of human beings or animals put to death, to provide the dead with servants or assistants in the future life, these may fairly be included among sacrifices; as is well known, even inanimate objects are often broken, to liberate their spiritual essence; and excavation in Palestine and elsewhere has shown that this is the case in the Semitic world as well as elsewhere. Food offerings are also given, perhaps, as E. S. Hartland has ingeniously suggested,[1] that the shade may not be compelled by hunger to eat of the food in the other world, and so be obliged to remain there for ever, in accordance with an ancient and wide-spread belief. In Egypt offerings to the dead were often endowed, an attendant being paid to keep the tomb in order and supplied with relays of gifts. In special cases, from an early time, the endowment was granted by the king himself, and the prayer 'Let the king give an offering' begins almost every funerary inscription in Egypt.[2] The specific purpose of the various kinds of Semitic sacrifice can, however, be more conveniently considered in connexion with the ritual observed, to which we now turn.

4. The method of sacrifice.—(*a*) *The place.*—Sacrifice must be offered at an appointed holy place. The killing of a sacrificeable animal else-

1 As by Gudea; see Jastrow, *Rel. Bab. und Assyr.* i. 170.
2 See Lucian, *de Dea Syria, passim.*
3 *Rel. Sem.*[2] p. 290 ff.; on the occasional use of certain other animals—deer, stags, wild asses, quails—see additional Note F in the same work.
4 Wellhausen, p. 114, etc.; *Qur'ān*, xxii. 38.
5 Wellhausen, p. 115.
6 *CIS* i. 165–170; *RHR* lxix. 70, and references there.
7 Jastrow, *Rel. Bab. und Assyr.* i. 59.
8 *Ib.* i. 385, etc.; Erman, *Life in Ancient Egypt*, p. 507; Lv 10^{1}, etc.
9 Wellhausen, p. 114.
10 *Ib.*

1 *The Science of Fairy Tales*, London, 1891, p. 47.
2 Erman, *Handbook of Egyp. Rel.* p. 123 f.

where is a murder, to be expiated as such (Lv 17^{3-5}). Even in patriarchal times, as a rule, sacrifice takes place on a spot hallowed by a theophany (Gn 28^{17}); it is probably indeed a mere accident when specific mention of the theophany is omitted (4^{3-7} 8^{20}). Moses cannot allow his followers to sacrifice to their Lord in Egypt; he must conduct them to a place 'three days' journey into the wilderness' for the purpose (Ex 3^{18}). The 'camp' of the wandering Israelites, owing to the presence of the Ark, is *ipso facto* a holy place, and therefore anything that defiles, such as the burning of the sin-offering (29^{14}), the bodies of the sacrilegious Nadab and Abihu (Lv 10^4), a leper (13^{46}), the execution of a criminal (24^{14}), must not profane the sacred precinct. The same ideas are to be traced among the Arab tribes.[1]

(*b*) *The altar.*—This has already been described,[2] so that few words are necessary here. The necessity for the altar arose from two requirements—the need of something visible and tangible to which to apply a gift supposed to be made to a physically invisible and intangible deity, and the need of something to prevent the sacrilege of the holy blood falling on the level earth.[3] For this purpose a heap of stones (such as, we may presume, the altar that Abraham built [Gn 13^{18}]), a bank or mound of earth consecrated for the purpose (Ex 20^{24}), or a large stone (1 S 14^{33}) would serve. According to the Book of the Covenant, a stone altar was not to be profaned with the touch of new-fangled metal tools (Ex 20^{25}), though doubtless this rule was not universally observed—*e.g.*, by Ahaz (2 K 16^{10}). An altar, however, is not absolutely necessary; Gideon (Jg 6^{20}) offers his sacrifice on a rock (which may, however, have been an altar-like mass or boss of rock). The altar of Elijah (1 K 18) was apparently a cairn of stones surrounded by a circle of twelve monoliths outside which was a trench; it is the most completely described 'high place' altar mentioned in Hebrew history.

Among the Arabs the sacred stone (*nuṣb*) served the purpose of an altar. It was, however, more than an altar; rather was it a representation of the divinity, sometimes indeed hewn into a form to represent him.[4] A curious series of rock-cuttings found some years ago at Petra[5] may perhaps be a late Aramæan or Nabatæan place of sacrifice, as has been supposed. But the rocks of Palestine are cut about in all sorts of ways, with quarries, wine-presses, tombs, etc.; and, unless evidence were found confirming the explanation of these Petra cuttings as a kind of sanctuary, it would be rash to build very much upon them. For Egyptian altars, and the few facts known about altars of the other Semitic peoples, reference may be made to the artt. ALTAR.

(*c*) *The ritual.*—This naturally varied according to the character of the sacrifice. In the primitive communal sacrifice the animal was slaughtered, usually by having its throat cut (with an antique form of knife),[6] and the blood was allowed to fall over the altar-stones. This was the share of the deity, and its application to the sacred stone was equivalent to feeding the deity upon it. In the official Hebrew legislation sacrifice could be offered only by those of the house of Levi; but in the earlier history Jethro (Ex 18^{12}) and Balaam (Nu $23^{1ff.}$) offer sacrifices to Jahweh. The flesh of the animal was divided among the worshippers and eaten by them; thus they shared in the meal with their deity. Such a sacrifice is known in the Hebrew Scriptures as זֶבַח or שֶׁלֶם, translated 'sacrifice' and 'peace-offering'[1] respectively in the RV. The etymology on which the latter translation is based is not absolutely certain.[2] The former word, like the modern Arabic ذبح, includes the slaying of animals for food, after such an action had ceased to have any special sacrificial significance. The occasions for such a sacrifice, besides the periodic feasts, were numerous—any time of rejoicing, such as the end of a successful war (1 S 11^{15}), the cessation of a pestilence (2 S 24^{25}), and a family gathering (1 S 20^6). A preliminary sanctification was obligatory on the worshippers, with lustrations, continence, and change of garments (Ex 19^{10-14}). When the animal was slaughtered, the blood and the fat—the portion assigned to the divinity—were consumed on the altar, and the rest was divided between the priests and the worshippers. Hophni and Phinehas in their greed seized more than their share, before the portion meant for the deity had been set aside (1 S 2^{12-14}). With the offering was unleavened bread. The flesh was boiled—Hophni and Phinehas offended the people's religious feelings by requiring it to be roasted. Similarly, Curtiss tells us,[3] 'the ministers of some [modern Arab] shrines are inclined to frown upon the custom of preparing the sacrificial meal away from the shrine.'

On occasions when the joyful feast of the שֶׁלֶם was inappropriate the proper sacrifice was the עֹלָה.[4] In times of war, doubt, or difficulty the animal was slain beside the altar and there wholly consumed. The sacrificers did not in this case partake of it; the whole was, as it were, volatilized and placed at the service of the deity.

While in Hebrew and Arab theory the animal thus offered seems to have been regarded as a tribute, Babylonia preserves for us an older stage of the development which may well be totemistic in origin. Here the idea of tribute is secondary. The primary purpose of sacrifice, so far as the sacrificers are concerned, is divination, especially by markings upon the animal's liver (interpreted as modern charlatans interpret the markings on the human hand). This form of divination is referred to in Ezk 21^{21}. The sacrificed animal seems to have been considered as having partaken of the divine nature, just as an animal whose flesh has been eaten by a man enters his organism and henceforth partakes of his nature; the various parts of its organism are therefore essentially the corresponding parts of the divinity, in tangible form; and on them are impressed signs of the divine foreknowledge. This is conspicuously the case of the liver, which is regarded as the seat of the soul.[5]

The treatment of offerings other than animal victims (cereals, meal, etc.) was presumably similar to that of animal victims. Under the Levitical code part was consumed by the altar-fire, and the other part was at the disposal of the priests (Lv 6^{14-16}). Under the Levitical régime a sacred fire (perhaps kept burning perpetually from a flame supposed to have been miraculously kindled) was used for these ritual purposes. To use other fire was sacrilege (Lv 10). The Arabs, on the other hand, scarcely offered fire-sacrifices at all.

1 W. R. Smith^2, pp. 115–118.
2 See art. ALTAR (Semitic), vol. i. p. 350.
3 See Jevons, *Introd. to the Hist. of Religion*, p. 131.
4 Wellhausen, p. 101 f.
5 See, for references, *ERE* i. 351.
6 Wellhausen, p. 115.

1 A more general term for gift or offering is מִנְחָה, which in the later books denotes more specifically offerings of cereals. The general term in the later books is קָרְבָּן. אִשֶּׁה is a 'fire-offering.'
2 See W. R. Smith^2, p. 237.
3 P. 171, n. 5.
4 The עֹלָה seems, properly speaking, to have originally meant the part of a sacrifice burnt. A 'whole burnt-offering,' in which the entire animal is burnt, was כָּלִיל (Nowack, *Archäologie*, ii. 215).
5 See Jastrow, *Rel. Belief in Bab. and Assyr.* p. 147 ff.; also his *Rel. Bab. und Assyr.*, *passim*, esp. ii. 213 ff.

'The altar,' says Wellhausen,[1] 'is not a hearth: no fire burns on it.' After mentioning a few doubtful exceptions, he adds: 'The normal Arab rite of animal sacrifice consists simply in smearing the blood on the sacred stone, or pouring it into the *ghabghab*' (the receptacle for this offering).

Among the Babylonians, however, fire was essential to sacrifice: by fire the offering was brought to the presence of the gods, and fire symbolized the intermediation between the worshipper and the divinity. Owing to this fact the fire-god Girru-Nusku (a conflation of two ancient fire- or solar-deities) was present at every sacrifice.[2]

For a discussion of some of the minutiæ of Hebrew sacrificial ritual, such as the ceremony of 'waving' and 'heaving' the portions set aside for the priests, reference should be made to special works on Hebrew archæology (such as that of Nowack or of Benzinger) or to the standard commentaries on the legislative parts of the Pentateuch. We must, however, note some peculiar rites which do not fall under the foregoing heads.

(*a*) The first of these is the rite of the *scapegoat* (Lv $16^{8.\ 10.\ 26}$). In this very primitive rite, on the great Day of Atonement, two goats were brought to the sanctuary. One was slain, and the other, after confession of the people's sin had been made over it, was turned loose in the wilderness 'for Azazel' (AV 'for a scapegoat,' a translation based on an analysis of the name now deemed untenable). Whatever Azazel (*q.v.*) may have been—a question to which no certain answer can be given—the sacrifice evidently belongs to a well-known group of purificatory rites in which uncleanness is transferred to another man or animal. A precisely similar rite, with birds, was performed at the purification of a leper—one of two birds being sacrificed, the other, after being sprinkled with the blood, wherewith the leper also was sprinkled, being set free (Lv $14^{1ff.}$; cf. also v.$^{51ff.}$). The whole subject has been studied by J. G. Frazer in *GB*^{3}, pt. vi., *The Scapegoat*, London, 1913. See, further, art. SCAPEGOAT (Semitic).

(*β*) Another form of sacrifice involving the liberation of an animal is recorded from Arabia in which a camel, stallion, etc., being dedicated to some deity, is allowed to go free and can never again be used.[3] The milk of such a dedicated animal could be used only by the poor and by guests.[4]

(*γ*) *Libations.* — David's water libation has already been mentioned as an exceptional case.

'The libation, which holds quite a secondary place in the more advanced Semitic rituals, and is generally a mere accessory to a fire offering, has great prominence among the Arabs, to whom sacrifices by fire were practically unknown, except in the case of human sacrifice.'[5]

Smith cites libations of blood and milk. He might have added coffee, of which among the modern Arabs libations are poured at feasts in honour of a being called Shaikh Shādli.[6] A libation, presumably of wine and oil, was poured by Jacob on the stone at Bethel (Gn 35^{14}); and elsewhere throughout the OT we find passages which indicate that among the Hebrews wine was the proper material for 'drink-offerings,' and a regular accompaniment of animal-sacrifice—*e.g.*, Ex 29^{40}, Lv $23^{13.\ 18.\ 37}$, Nu 15^{5}, Dt 32^{38}. From these we learn that $\frac{1}{4}$ *hin* (about 3 pints) of wine was the proper drink-offering to accompany a lamb, $\frac{1}{3}$ *hin* (2 quarts) of wine a ram, and $\frac{1}{2}$ *hin* (3 quarts) of wine a bullock. Drink-offerings of blood are condemned in Ps 16^{4} as heathenish, but on the other hand a wine-offering to the deity Meni is referred to in Is 65^{11}. The actual ritual is nowhere described, but presumably the libation was poured over or beside the altar. The heathenish rites of the Israelite women, who worshipped the 'Queen of Heaven' (*q.v.*) with 'cakes' (כַּוָּן, *i.e.* probably terra-cotta plaques stamped with the likeness of the divinity, such as have come to light in large numbers in Palestine), included libations as an essential element, though the material is not specified (Jer 19^{13} 32^{29} $44^{17ff.}$). The water poured annually into a cleft in the temple at Hierapolis[1] was probably not a libation, but a rain-making or fertilizing charm.

It is not quite correct to speak of libations as occupying 'quite a secondary place in the more advanced Semitic rituals.' Certainly in Mesopotamia they are abundantly referred to as an essential concomitant of the burnt-offering. The material is not often specified; a libation of some drink prepared from a cereal is mentioned in a tablet given by Jastrow.[2]

(*δ*) *Lectisternia.*—The table of shewbread was the Hebrew equivalent of the lectisternia, a table laden with food being set before the god. The name of this offering would perhaps be better and more intelligibly translated 'bread of the presence' (of Jahweh). The custom of laying up food before the god is wide-spread, and was no doubt adopted into the official Priestly Code from earlier pre-Pentateuchal rites. We have already seen illustrations from Egypt, and have referred to the tale of Bel and the Dragon. In the earlier rites the consumption of the food by the priests of the temple was probably secret, and arranged to keep up among the uninitiated the fiction that the god himself partook of the banquet. In the Hebrew rite, however, the food was openly the perquisite of the priests, and in the earlier times could even be given by them to laymen (1 S 21). The same or a similar rite was observed by heathenish Israelites: Is 65^{11} speaks of people 'preparing a table for Gad,' doubtless a god.

(*ε*) *The Passover*, though ostensibly a memorial feast commemorative of the Exodus, is probably one of the most primitive of the religious rites which Hebrew ritual preserved, belonging in fact, like the sheep-shearing festival of 1 S 25, to the time when the ancestors of the Hebrews were nomad shepherds. The special characteristics of the Passover are (1) that it took place in spring, at the time of the vernal equinox (Ex 13^{4}, Dt 16^{1}); (2) that the victim was a lamb or a kid (Ex 12^{5}), a male in its first year; (3) that, unlike the other sacrifices, this was a domestic celebration, the lamb being sacrificed by the head of the house, not at any special sanctuary, and not by any special religious functionary (Ex 12, though this is modified in the Deuteronomic legislation [$16^{2.\ 6.\ 7}$]); (4) that the entire lamb was to be roasted, not boiled as in other sacrifices (see above), and eaten by the household in haste (two households individually too small to dispose of a whole victim being allowed to combine), all properly initiated Israelites attached to the household being admitted, as well as any foreigners naturalized by the rite of circumcision, though all uncircumcised foreigners were excluded (Ex 12^{43-51}); (5) that, when the animal was slaughtered, the blood was smeared on the door-posts and lintels of the house. The feast was followed by a period of a week in which no leavened bread was to be used; but it seems to be a doubtful point whether this was an intrinsic part of the Passover ceremony or whether the proximity of the two ceremonies in the calendar is not merely accidental. The events said to be commemorated by the Passover were (i.) the last of the Egyptian plagues, when the first-born in the land of Egypt was smitten except in those houses on which the paschal blood was smeared; (ii.) the hasty departure of the people from the land. The original

[1] P. 116.
[2] Jastrow, *Rel. Bab. und Assyr.* i. 297, 486.
[3] Wellhausen, p. 112 ff.
[4] *Ib.* p. 113.
[5] W. R. Smith^{2}, p. 229.
[6] Curtiss, p. 183; see also J. E. Hanauer, *Folk-lore of the Holy Land*, London, 1907, p. 293.

[1] Lucian, *de Dea Syria*, 13.
[2] *Rel. Bab. und Assyr.* i. 448.

celebration is, however, probably much older, and the connexion with the Exodus only secondary and ætiological. Wellhausen[1] and J. Müller[2] see in the sacrifice a survival of an ancient pastoral feast, when the firstfruits of the flock were sacrificed (as in the sacrifice of Abel [Gn 4^4]). The 'sacrifice in the wilderness,' which was the ostensible motive of the Exodus, was, in fact, the Passover; and the king of Egypt, by preventing this, roused the wrath of Jahweh, who in punishment took to Himself the first-born of Egypt. The domestic nature of the rite certainly favours its origin among a simple and primitive pastoral organization; but the peculiar details of the rite—the rapid devouring of the whole animal and the smearing of the doorway with the blood—show that it is in its nature something more than a mere offering of *primitiæ*. With regard to the former, we are irresistibly reminded of the famous Arab camel-sacrifice described by Nilus, to which frequent reference is made by W. R. Smith[3] and by the writers who follow him; and the analogy suggests that the haste with which the animal was to be eaten was primarily inspired by a similar cause—a ceremonial requirement that it should be disposed of before some (astronomical?) occurrence had taken place. The door-post rites indicate that the ceremony belonged to the numerous blood and threshold covenants (on which see the works of Trumbull). The sedulous avoidance of the chance putrefaction in any form, to which allusion has already been made, is specially to be noticed in the Passover rite.

(ζ) *The red heifer sacrifice.*—This singular rite is described in Nu 19. A red cow (note the sex, which is the opposite to that of most sacrificial victims) which was without blemish and had never been used in a yoke was to be taken 'without the camp'—*i.e.* outside the temple hill—by a subordinate priest (the high-priest could not risk the contamination of the rite). A second official slaughtered the animal, and the first priest dipped his finger seven times in the blood, sprinkling it 'towards the tabernacle.' A pyre having been erected, the body of the heifer was to be placed upon it and reduced wholly to ashes, sweet-smelling woods being thrown on the fire during the ceremony. A third official was to gather the ashes of the heifer and of the pyre together and deposit them 'without the camp' in a clean place, where they were to be preserved. The three officials involved in the rite were made unclean, *i.e.* tabu, by the ceremony till the evening, when by washing they recovered their normal condition. The ashes thus obtained and preserved were to be used in lustrations necessitated by the uncleanness involved by contact with a dead body or any part thereof (such as a bone), some of the ashes being placed in a vessel and having running water poured over them, which was then sprinkled with hyssop on the person or thing requiring to be cleansed. The rite, though the description of it is preserved in a comparatively late document, is probably in its origin of very great antiquity. The red colour of the cow, and the scarlet cloth burnt on the pyre with the aromatic woods, suggest the colour of blood; the aromatic woods are also probably connected with primitive ideas of the cathartic value of odours such as they produce.[4]

Analogous with this rite, but to be carefully distinguished from it, is the sacrifice of a heifer in Dt $21^{1ff.}$ as an expiation for an unexplained murder. Here the village nearest to the spot where the murdered body was discovered had to provide a heifer (colour not specified) which, like the red heifer, had never been brought under a yoke. The village elders were to lead the animal to 'a rough valley' and there to break its neck, probably by precipitating it over a high rock. Over the body the elders were then to take an oath of compurgation.[1]

5. Origin of sacrifice among the Semites.—It may be taken as a universal rule that no trustworthy account of the origin of sacrifice, or of specific sacrifices, is to be gleaned from those who themselves perform the ceremonies. In every case they give us ætiological myths of other than historic interest. Thus it is necessary in considering the development, and especially the origin, of sacrifice among any people to apply the comparative method and to draw our conclusions from a large number of related examples. In an article like the present it is not possible to give more than the conclusions, with references which will enable the reader to follow out for himself the premisses and arguments of the authors quoted.

E. B. Tylor[2] was the first to endeavour to give a scientific explanation of sacrifice. He regarded the rite as simply the offering of a gift or bribe to a divinity, precisely analogous to the gift or bribe that might be offered to an Oriental potentate, and for analogous reasons—to secure favour or to avert anger. As the gods recede from man, the gift becomes more and more an act of homage and self-abnegation. This theory, as Hubert and Mauss well say,[3] describes rather the moral development of the rite than its actual machinery, and, while it doubtless contains an element of truth, is little more than a restatement, in definite scientific language, of the vague pre-scientific ætiological myths.

W. R. Smith[4] showed that the problem was much more complicated, and involved a variety of elements. His work, though in certain minor details proved open to criticism, has stood as the foundation of all subsequent study of the subject. Beginning with totemism, which J. F. McLennan had (a short time previous to the first publication of this book) brought to the notice of anthropologists, he formulated a theory which may be thus briefly summarized. In the primitive nomadic life the solidarity and unity of the clan is an essential feature. Its members are bound by a tie of common blood with one another and with the god, their father. The domestic animals of the tribe to some extent share in this community, at least inasmuch as they are the tribal guests, and have the privilege of adoption conferred on human strangers by the mere fact of guesthood. When the god is angry, his favour can be restored by an act of communion between him and his worshippers; and the victim is the non-human member of the clan (*i.e.* the totem). When the nomad ceases from his wandering life and becomes an agriculturist, his relation with the god alters. The god is no longer a father, but a king or proprietor, from whose hand the worshipper receives his land as a tenant. The sacrifice is now not so much a communion as a tribute. The god is fed (both in the earlier and in the later theories) first by leaving portions of the flesh by the sacred stone; afterwards (as less materialistic ideas of the nature of deity develop) by pouring out the life-bearing blood on the earth as his portion, which, as it sinks and disappears, can more readily be supposed to be absorbed by the Deity than the solid flesh; and finally by burning the victim, which thus becomes volatilized and, as it were,

[1] *Prolegomena zur Gesch. Israels*^{6}, Berlin, 1905, pp. 82–94.
[2] *Kritischer Versuch über den Ursprung und die geschichtliche Entwicklung des Pesach- und Mazzothfestes*, Bonn, 1883, esp. p. 69.
[3] Pp. 281 ff., 381 f.
[4] See art. INCENSE.

[1] For the peculiar method of slaughtering the animal whereby effusion of blood was avoided see W. R. Smith^2, pp. 371, 419.
[2] *PC*^{4} ii. ch. xviii. p. 362.
[3] *L'Année sociologique*, ii. 30.
[4] *Rel. Sem.*^{2}, *passim*, esp. lects. vi.–xi.

etherialized by the smoke. The deity is thus satisfied by the 'sweet savour' of the offering. The temper of a master is more doubtful than that of a father, so that the worshippers are uncertain whether he is satisfied. In the stress of calamity human victims are offered, and finally victims counted unclean and therefore exceptionally sacrosanct. W. R. Smith seems to have been the first to insist on the importance of distinguishing three types of sacrifice: the communion form, in which the god and his people were commensals; the piacular form, an expiation for sin—essentially substitutionary in character, the [totem] animal being slain as a substitute for the guilty tribesman; and the mystical form, in which the god himself, in bodily form, is supposed to be slain by his worshippers and ceremonially eaten by them.

A covenant-sacrifice is the most obvious illustration of the communion-nature of the rite. When two men (as Jacob and Laban) made a covenant, they held a common meal on an altar (Gn 31[46]). When Abraham and the deity made a covenant, victims were divided, and God, typified by a torch, passed between them (Gn 15). When Moses made a covenant with God on behalf of the people, he poured half the blood of the victims on the altar and sprinkled the people with the other half (Ex 24[4-8]).

That offerings are regarded as literally the food of the gods is illustrated by numerous texts. In one of the Babylonian penitential hymns, as restored from a fragmentary tablet by Jastrow, the sinner confesses to having eaten and drunk unknowingly of the food and drink of his goddess, and also to having eaten what was unclean (*i.e.* tabu) to her; and Tabi-utul-Bel, king in Nippur, speaks of troubles having fallen upon him 'as though he had eaten of his god's food, and neglected to bring drink to his goddess.'[1] Another tablet speaks of offerings as 'the pure heavenly food.'[2]

Frazer[3] founds his work on the foregoing conclusions, but in some points carries it farther. Especially with regard to the last-named point, he infers from the comparison of an enormous number of related rites from all parts of the world that the ceremonial god-slaying is intended to prevent the god from being overborne by old age.

These theories have not gone unchallenged. L. Marillier doubts the essential postulate on which they are based, that an animal-god is necessarily a totem-god; and Hubert and Mauss question the essential connexion between the communal meal at the god's table and the more complex form of sacrifice.[4] M. J. Lagrange,[5] following Smend,[6] objects to Smith's theory, while doing full justice to the value of his masterly work, that totemism is assumed rather than proved for the Semitic tribes, and substitutes for his view of the origin of sacrifice among these people the theory that sacrifice is essentially an act, not of consecration, but of de-consecration. Starting from animism, whereby the savage sees a spirit in everything, he argues that, if a savage wished to make use of anything—say, an animal whose flesh he desired to eat—the presence of the spirit would make it tabu. By sacrifice the savage desecrates the desired object; by leaving a part of it (*e.g.*, the blood) as the share of the spirit he hopes to obtain the rest for himself. By offering the firstfruits of his flocks and his crops, and even of his own family, he earns the right to secure the remainder of the produce to his own use. The newly-planted tree (Lv 19[23]) remains 'uncircumcised' (*i.e.* tabu) for three years; its fruit for the fourth year is given to the deity; from the fifth year onwards it may be freely used. The sacrifice of the firstfruits was probably the beginning of animal-sacrifice. Lagrange holds that, while animals might have entered into totemistic relationship with a human clan, they could hardly be supposed to have similar relations to gods, and that to regard every immolation as a sacred act is not the same as to abstain from all immolation except when one is definitely intending to engage in an act of worship; moreover, that to admit the whole clan to a share in the feast does not mean that no slaughter can take place without the consent of the whole clan.

Curtiss, as a result of his researches in modern Palestine, was led to dissent from the theories of the origin of sacrifice usually associated with the name of W. R. Smith. According to his view, the essential point was not the gift or the eating of the sacrificial animal, but the effusion of its blood, the substitutionary idea being in his belief the prevalent and the original essence of the rite.[1] Thus, a sheep is slain at the foundation of a house because every new house requires a life; the life of the sheep redeems that of an occupant of the house. A sheep slain on behalf of a sick person, likewise, is a substitute whereby the life of the patient is redeemed. The blood is placed on the door-post and lintels of the shrine 'perhaps to remind the saint of the blood of the victim that has been slain.' The fallacy that the East is 'immovable,' however, vitiates some of these deductions. It is true that very primitive rites and beliefs survive among the modern Arabs; but they do not necessarily survive in their primitive form, or with primitive ideas attached to them. On the contrary, they have been modified profoundly by the leavening influence of Islām. Moreover, Curtiss takes no account of the bloodless sacrifices or those in which the effusion of blood is carefully avoided.[2]

LITERATURE.—i. *GENERAL.*—For brevity only the later works are named; references to older books will be found in the bibliographies in *HDB*, *EBi*, *EBr*[11], *s.v.* 'Sacrifice'; H. C. Trumbull, *The Blood Covenant*, London, 1887; W. R. Smith, *Lectures on the Religion of the Semites*, do. 1889, reprint of 2nd ed., 1907; L. Marillier, 'La Place du totémisme dans l'évolution religieuse,' *RHR* xxxvi. [1897] 208, and subsequent numbers; Trumbull, *The Threshold Covenant*, Edinburgh, 1892; P. Sartori, 'Ueber das Bauopfer,' *ZE* xxx. [1898] 1; F. B. Jevons, *An Introd. to the Hist. of Religion*, London, 1896; H. Hubert and M. Mauss, 'Essai sur la nature et la fonction du sacrifice,' *L'Année sociologique*, ii. [1897–98] 29–138; G. A. Wilken, *Eene nieuwe theorie over den oorsprong der offers*, in *Verspreide Geschriften*, Hague, 1912 ff., iv. 157.

ii. *EGYPT.*—The works of Erman mentioned in the article; E. Naville, *The Old Egyptian Faith*, London, 1909, p. 295 ff.

iii. *BABYLONIA AND ASSYRIA.*—H. Zimmern, *Beiträge zur Kenntnis der babylonischen Religion*, Leipzig, 1901; E. Schrader, *Die Keilinschriften und das Alte Testament*[3], Berlin, 1903, esp. p. 594 ff.; M. Jastrow, Jr., *Die Religion Babyloniens und Assyriens*, 2 vols., Giessen, 1905–12, *Aspects of Religious Belief and Practice in Babylonia and Assyria*, New York, 1911.

iv. *ARAB AND ARAMÆAN TRIBES.*—J. Wellhausen, *Reste arabischen Heidentums*[2], Berlin, 1897; S. I. Curtiss, *Primitive Semitic Religion To-day*, London, 1902.

v. *HEBREWS.*—The standard commentaries on the books of the Pentateuch and the prophets (esp. Ezekiel); also G. F. Moore, art. 'Sacrifice,' in *EBi*, and E. G. Hirsch, art. 'Sacrifice,' in *JE* (very useful for late Jewish belief and practice). See also W. Nowack, *Lehrbuch der hebräischen Archäologie*, Freiburg i. B., 1894; R. Smend, *Lehrbuch der alttestamentlichen Religionsgeschichte*, do. 1893; K. Marti, *Gesch. der israelitischen Religion*, Strassburg, 1907; I. Benzinger, *Hebräische Archäologie*, Freiburg i. B., 1894, [2]rewritten, Tübingen, 1907; S. A. Cook, 'The Significance of the Elephantine Papyri for the Hist. of Hebrew Religion,' *AJTh* xix. [1915] 346; O. Schmitz, *Die Opferanschauung des späteren Judentums und die Opferaussagen des Neuen Testaments*, Tübingen, 1910.

vi. *PHŒNICIANS AND CARTHAGINIANS.* — F. C. Movers, *Untersuchungen über die Religion und die Gottheiten der Phönizier*, Bonn, 1841; R. Dussaud, 'Les Tarifs sacrificiels carthaginois et leurs rapports avec le lévitique,' *RHR* lxix. [1914] 70; P. D. Chantepie de la Saussaye, *Lehrbuch der Religionsgeschichte*[2], Freiburg i. B., 1897, i. 237.

[1] Jastrow, *Rel. Bab. und Assyr.* ii. 102, 126.
[2] *Ib.* ii. 93, n. 8.
[3] *GB*[3], *passim.*
[4] For the references see the bibliography at the end.
[5] *Études sur les religions sémitiques*, Paris, 1905, ch. vii.
[6] *Lehrbuch der alttest. Religionsgeschichte*, p. 123 ff.

[1] See esp. p. 224 ff.
[2] On which see W. R. Smith[2], p. 418.

vii. *SOUTHERN SEMITES (ABYSSINIANS).*—No satisfactory literature; but, owing to their close connexion with the Yemenite Arabs, there was probably a close community of belief and religious practice between them. See L. J. Morié, *Hist. de l'Éthiopie*, Paris, 1904, ii.

R. A. S. MACALISTER.

SACRIFICE (Teutonic).—For our knowledge of the ancient Teuton religion we are almost entirely dependent on Icelandic sources, as in Iceland there was a great literary activity in the 12th and 13th centuries, when several prominent men collected whatever of ancient oral or written tradition had come down to their own time in poetry or prose. In other Teutonic countries we find only occasional references to the religious rites of heathen times, though a great many names occur in Scandinavia, Germany, and England signifying religious customs and reminding of ancient rites. Often such names as Frey, Thor, Odin, Baldr, and a few others are prefixed to mounds, hills, groves, springs, etc., indicating that those places formerly were dedicated to the divinities mentioned. In Sweden there is a great number of such places.[1] It is difficult, however, to decide whether a given rite or legend which is mentioned only in the Icelandic literature was really peculiar to that country alone or to the North generally, or whether it was once the common property of all Teutonic peoples.[2] In many cases we shall have to leave this matter undecided or be satisfied with probabilities. Yet it is well understood that long before those public religious festivals were instituted of which Snorra Sturlason, Saxo Grammaticus, Adam of Bremen, and others write there had been sacrifices offered by the Teuton tribes to their gods, and that long before priests were set apart among the northern Teutons sacrifices were made by the people themselves, either for the sake of the offerer alone or in a representative way for his family or tribe. Everybody felt himself in duty bound to some particular god or gods, and this duty was most religiously observed. As the gods were many and of several kinds, so must those services, sacrifices, and offerings have been. Minor things such as fruit, bread, fowl, prepared foods, trinkets, and even money were offered and brought to holy springs, bogs, lakes, and hills, where they were dedicated and turned over to the god of the place with such formalities as were considered proper. One of these demanded scrupulous cleanliness[3]—a cleanliness which in certain cases required that the sacrificer should approach the god in a naked state.

For how many generations and to what extent these individual offerings were carried on it may be difficult to determine, but all indications agree that some gods were sacrificially worshipped in Sweden at a very remote period. Montelius holds that Frey was worshipped there for at least two thousand years before the Christian era.

With the advancing civilization arising from conditions of more settled habits and of larger tribal and political unifications, together, in some countries at least, with a more generally recognized order of sacred persons or priests, certain periods for public sacrificial festivals were decided upon and observed, at first by the vicinity mostly and then by the entire realm. Thus there were three yearly sacrificial festivals—in autumn, midwinter, and spring. These festivals assembled and unified the people and served to foster the idea of their mutual social union as of divine character. Participation in these sacrificial feasts and meals made peace between the rival races.[4]

Some of these feasts were in a special sense connected with the memory of the dead. This

[1] Hyltén-Cavallius, *Wärend och Wirdarna*, i. 2 f.
[2] *EBr*[11] xxvi. 683.
[3] Herrmann, *Nordische Mythologie*, p. 451.
[4] *Yngl. Saga*, 24.

was the case with the midwinter festival—the greatest feast and family reunion of the Teutons—when the departed and disembodied spirits returned to their own, and, mingling with them, gave them cheer and encouragement, or proffered warnings of impending danger. At this season the gods themselves also showed special favours, helping in every way and keeping off the evil spirits, so that entire peace and goodwill might prevail. A general peace applying to the entire festival period was also declared by the king himself, so that no wrong could be done then. Under the shield of this peace the sacrifices with the attendant banquet were prepared, deliberations were held, sentence was passed, and commerce conducted, for which reason *thing*, the old name of these conventions, stands for sacrifice, banquet, diet, assize, and fair.[1] Upon the general celebrations of these great festivals at Upsala was founded the right of the Svear, or Swedes, to give a sovereign to the whole realm, for the Upsala king was the guardian of the holy altar.[2]

Frey, or Froe, was the northern god of fertility and peace. He was the patron god of Sweden and was worshipped as the god of plenty. According to Adam of Bremen, his worship was of the phallic order, and as such gave rise to very popular gatherings and religious feasts; as we have already seen, Montelius considers that the worship of Frey was current in Sweden at least two thousand years before Christ. Saxo has the following:

> 'Also Frey, the regent of the gods, took his abode not far from Upsala, where he exchanged for a ghastly and infamous sin-offering the old custom of prayer and sacrifice, which had been in use for so many ages and generations. For he paid to the gods abominable offerings by beginning to slaughter human victims.'[3]

The Frey-period is contemporary with that of Odin in Sweden, but there it begins much earlier. No doubt, human sacrifices occurred also during the régime of Frey at Upsala. At a later period we know that human victims were sacrificed to the name of that god. Ibn Fadhlan, the Arabian geographer, reports in 921 that he had been present at an immolation among Teuton varings on the Volga, when a young girl was sacrificed according to the funeral rite of Frey.[4] Thus the same religious customs prevailed wherever the Teutons happened to live. It is also known that religious festivals similar to those at Upsala were held in other countries, but the Upsala ones became better known, being more fully described in Icelandic and northern literature. From most of these sources it is inferred that Odin established them. Indeed, it is said that, when taking possession of the land, he erected a temple there and sacrificed after the manner of the Asæ. To him people paid tribute, that he might be propitious to them and give them good harvest. Snorra Sturlason says:

> 'Odin made laws for his country, laws which formerly obtained among the Æsir. At the beginning of winter sacrifices should be made for a good year, in the midwinter for good crop, and in the spring for victory in intended campaigns. Tribute was given to him "for every nose" the country over, in order that he should protect the people in times of war and grant to them a good year.'[5]

In the *Saga of Hakon the Good* we have the following full description of one of these religious festivals:

> 'It was an old custom that when there was to be sacrifice all the bonders should come to the spot where the temple stood, and bring with them all that they required while the festival of the sacrifice lasted. To this festival all the men brought ale with them. All kinds of cattle, as well as horses, were slaughtered, and all the blood that came from them was called *hlaut*, and

[1] E. G. Geijer, *Hist. of the Swedes*, tr. J. H. Turner, London [1845?], p. 31.
[2] *Yngl. Saga*, 24. [3] i. 186.
[4] Frähn, *Ibn-Fozlan's und anderer Araber Berichte über die Russen älterer Zeit*; Thomsen, *Ryska Rikets grundläggning genom Skandinaverne.*
[5] *Yngl. Saga*, 8.

the vessels in which it was collected were called *hlaut*-vessels. *Hlaut*-vessels were made, like sprinkling brushes, with which the whole of the altars and the temple walls, both outside and inside, were sprinkled. The people were also sprinkled with the blood, and the flesh was boiled into savoury meat for those present. The fire was in the middle of the floor of the temple, and over it hung the kettles. The full goblets were handed across the fire, and he who made the feast, and was chief, blessed all the full goblets, and the meat of the sacrifice. First Odin's goblet was emptied for victory and power to the king, and thereafter Njord's and Freyja's goblets for peace and a good season. Then it was the custom of many to empty the Bragi-goblet, and then the guests emptied the goblet, called the "remembrance-goblet," to the memory of departed friends.'

After this description of the feast itself Snorra continues:

'Sigurd, the earl, was an open-handed man, who did what was very much celebrated, for he made a great sacrifice-festival at Hlader, of which he paid all the expenses. Kormak Ogmundson sings of it in his ballad of Sigurd:

"Of cup or platter need has none
The guests who seek the generous one,—
Sigurd the Generous, who can trace
His lineage from the giant race . . .
He loves the gods,—his liberal hand
Scatters his sword's gains o'er the land."'[1]

Following chapters of this saga (17–19) are of special interest in regard to the Teutonic sacrifices, as they treat of the Frosta-thing, King Hakon's sacrifice, and the sacrifice at More.

Bloody sacrifices were always made by the priests, or the chiefs who acted as priests, usually at the beginning and the close of the great public festivals. All the people of the realm, or as many as could be present, were in close attendance at the rite and were blessed. Expiatory sacrifices were held once in every nine years at Upsala and at Lethra in Sealand, at which a great number of animals and human victims were offered.[2] At the beginning of wars and other great undertakings, such as the election of kings and leaders for great battles, great and imposing sacrifices were made.

All animals were offered according to prescribed forms, which were well known to the people and because of which they all could understand and take part. If occasion required, as in times of famine and great danger from enemies, human sacrifices were made, the victims ranging from innocent children up to the king himself, who was offered because his was the most precious life in the whole land and therefore a most valuable gift to bring the gods for reconciliation. Among the Goths, the Saxons, the Langobards, and other Teutonic tribes it was also common to present prisoners of war as sacrifices to the god who had given the victory. Jordanes tells us that in some cases such prisoners were immolated by the Teutons. In later writers we read that such captives were hung to the branches of the trees in the sacred grove, and sometimes they were decapitated or slaughtered, 'not for vengeance but as a thank-offering.' To 'inscribe the bloody eagle' on the back of the conquered enemy was an inhuman mode of vengeance sometimes practised by the vikings, and may be considered as a sacrificial act, as it was done in the name and to the honour of the war-god.[3]

Several authors hold that it was not uncommon to sacrifice a thrall or some other person whose life could be taken without cause, when a great journey was to be undertaken or some decisive matter attended to. The offerer smeared his own body with the blood of the victim and then considered himself well protected. Other shocking cruelties were performed in the name of Teutonic religion, as when in a certain year of poor harvest it was agreed that there would never more be a good year until a boy from one of the foremost families had been sacrificed to Odin.[4]

[1] Ch. 16. [2] Adam Brem. iv. 27.
[3] See E. H. Meyer, *Germ. Myth.* p. 200; also G. Storm, in *Norsk Historisk Tidskrift*, ii. 436.
[4] *Herv. Saga*, 9.

Capital punishments of sacramental nature were of common occurrence. They were made in the first place as an expiation of sin and then as a thank-offering for the restored condition of favour with the divinity. Cowards and infamous people were sometimes sunk in some fen or bog—*e.g.*, in the great pool of Upsala.[1] According to Odin's own command, traitors must be hanged.[2] In *Starkad's Saga* it is said that in times of divine wrath the hanging of the king would bring great reconciliation, if the victim was pierced through with a spear as a sacrifice to Odin. Common malefactors had their backs broken, just as Thor broke the neck of Greip and Gjalp. In old age men were sometimes thrust down from steep rocks, so as to bring them sooner to their god.[3]

Thus with its decline the heathen religion became more and more cruel and savage. Indeed, it is said in the appendix of the old law of Gothland that 'they then sacrificed to the heathen gods their sons and daughters and their cattle with meat and drink.' But this was in an age 'when men yet believed in groves and mounds, in holy places and palings.'[4] It is probable that the unbelief as regards the old religion was a greater cause of the cruelties of the viking age than the belief itself. Adam of Bremen writes that about that time a Christian traveller had related that he had seen seventy-two dead bodies of immolated men and animals hanging in the grove of the temple at Upsala, which shone with gold and had the images of Odin, Thor, and Frey set up in the interior. In German countries the Teuton religion had ceased to exercise any power long before that time, while in other parts of Europe, as in the Baltic provinces, it may have had its devotees for yet a few generations.

LITERATURE.—*The Poetic* or *Sæmundar Edda*, crit. ed. S. Bugge, Christiania, 1867, tr. Benjamin Thorpe, London, 1866, literal tr. in G. Vigfusson and F. Y. Powell, *Corpus Poeticum Boreale*, 2 vols., Oxford, 1883; *Snorra Edda*, ed. Copenhagen, 1848–87, partially tr. L. A. Blackwell, in *Northern Antiquities*, London, 1847, tr. R. B. Anderson, *The Younger Edda*, Chicago, 1880; **Snorra Sturlason**, *Heimskringla*, Eng. tr. Samuel Laing, in the Norrœna Library, 3 vols., London, 1844, also ed. R. B. Anderson, New York, 1907; **Saxo Grammaticus**, *Danish Hist.*, bks. i.–ix., tr. O. Elton, London, 1894; **Tacitus**, *Germania*; *The Fall of the Nibelungers* (the *Nibelungenlied*), tr. W. N. Lettsom, London, 1850, New York, 1901; **Jordanes**, *de Or. Act. Get.*, ed. C. A. Closs, Freiburg i. Br., 1882; **E. H. Meyer**, *Völuspa*, Berlin, 1889 (this work has a good list of references to sources of literature and books of reference); **W. Mannhardt**, *Der Baumkultus der Germanen und ihrer Nachbarstämme*, Berlin, 1875; **H. Pfannenschmid**, *Germanische Erntfeste*, Hanover, 1878; **U. Jahn**, *Die deutschen Opfergebräuche*, Breslau, 1884; **H. M. Chadwick**, *The Cult of Othin*, London, 1879; **H. Gering**, 'Die Edda,' in K. Müllenhoff, *Deutsche Altertumskunde*, vol. v., Berlin, 1892; **E. H. Meyer**, *Germanische Mythologie*, do. 1891; **P. Herrmann**, *Nordische Mythologie*, Leipzig, 1903; **P. D. Chantepie de la Saussaye**, *The Religion of the Teutons*, Eng. tr., Boston and London, 1902; **S. Bugge**, *Studier over de nordiske Gude- og Heltesagns Oprindelse*, i.–ii., Christiania, 1881–89, Germ. tr. by O. Brenner, Munich, 1889, Eng. tr. of vol. ii. by W. H. Schofield, *The Home of the Eddic Poems*, London, 1899; **A. V. Rydberg**, *Undersökningar i germanisk Mythologi*, i.–ii., Stockholm, 1886–89, Eng. tr. of vol. i. by R. B. Anderson, *Teutonic Mythology*, London, 1889, and in the Norrœna Library, 3 vols., New York, 1906; **G. O. Hyltén-Cavallius**, *Wärend och Wirdarna*, 2 vols., Stockholm, 1863; **H. Reuterdahl**, *Svenska Kyrkans Historia*, vol. i., Lund, 1838; **H. Petersen**, *Om Nordboernes Gudedyrkelse og Gudetro i Hedenold*, Copenhagen, 1876; **H. Schück**, 'Svensk gudatro under hednatiden,' in *Finsk Tidskrift*, 1889, *Studier i Nordisk Literatur- och Religionshistoria*, Stockholm, 1903–04; **C. P. Tiele**, *Kompendium der Religionsgeschichte*³, tr. N. Söderblom, Breslau, 1903; **J. G. Frazer**, *GB*³, 12 vols., London, 1907–15; **E. Westermarck**, *MI*, do. 1906–08 (esp. vol. i. for human sacrifice); **C. M. Frähn**, *Ibn-Fozlan's und anderer Araber Berichte über die Russen älterer Zeit*, Petrograd, 1823; **C. Thomsen**, *Ryska Rikets grundläggning genom Skandinaverne*, Copenhagen, 1882. (The report of Fadhlan is, in its bearing on the Frey-ritual, given in full in H Schück, *Studier i Nordisk Literatur- och Religionshistoria*, pt. ii. pp. 288–295.)

S. G. YOUNGERT.

[1] Adam Brem. iv. 26. [2] *Yngl. Saga*, 6 f.
[3] Strabo, vii. 2–3; see also art. OLD AGE (Teutonic).
[4] Geijer, *Hist. of the Swedes*, ch. ii. p. 32.

SACRIFICE (Human).—See HUMAN SACRIFICE.

SACRILEGE.—See TABU, CRIMES AND PUNISHMENTS (Primitive and Savage).

SACRILEGE (Greek and Roman).—When the Greek term ἱεροσυλία and the Latin *sacrilegium* were used by lawyers of the classical periods, they implied, like the corresponding phrases in modern systems of law, the removal from sacred places of property dedicated to sacred uses. Sacrilege was a form of theft, distinguished from other forms only by the nature of the objects affected. But in the later forms of ancient law, and still more in popular usage, the idea of sacrilege was stretched far beyond these limits. There was a natural tendency to regard as cognate, and as deserving the same punishment, many other offences which could be viewed as outrages on the dignity of gods, or of beings raised above the ordinary human level, especially autocratic rulers and the spirits of the dead.

I. *GREEK*.—**1. Temples.**—In Athens the strict definition of the crime of sacrilege made it consist in the robbery of movable property dedicated to a divinity from his temple and not from the sacred precincts outside it (Syrianus, *ad Hermog.* iv. 497, ed. C. Walz, Stuttgart, 1833). A crime against the protecting gods of the State was a crime against the State itself, and hence in all periods the conceptions of sacrilege and treason lay very near together. One and the same Athenian statute punished both these iniquities (Xenophon, *Hellenica*, I. vii. 22). Ancient Greek writers treat both, along with murder, as the most heinous breaches of law (Plato, *Laws*, 854, and elsewhere; Antiphon, *de Herodis cæde*, 10). In Athens the capital penalty was assigned to the sacrilegious, and it was accompanied by a confiscation of property and a prohibition against the burial of the offender in Attic ground. But execution was not a special mark of reprobation, since it was allotted to smaller crimes, when regarded as directed against the nation, the procedure being that called γραφή. Even the common thief could be so treated, and especially the stealer of clothes, the cutpurse, the burglar, and the kidnapper (Xen. *Memorabilia*, I. ii. 62). And in all these cases the amount of the property involved was immaterial (Isocrates, *c. Lochitem*, 6). Such was the theory of the Athenian law; in practice it was not always carried out with strict severity. Stealing from the precincts of a temple or appropriating money belonging to the temple was often dealt with as ordinary theft. Apparently there was a form of charge for 'appropriating sacred property' (κλοπὴ ἱερῶν χρημάτων), which led to less stringent procedure than was assigned for sacrilege. In many directions we find extensions of the idea of ἱεροσυλία. Demosthenes (*c. Timocratem*, 120) qualifies as sacrilege the withholding of tithes due to a temple. In Greek inscriptions the endeavour to protect property given over to sacred uses is carried further. At Iasos an inscribed column set forth the rights of certain priests, and any one who made away with the pillar or even damaged the inscription was to be treated as ἱερόσυλος (W. Dittenberger, *Sylloge Inscriptionum Græcarum*, Leipzig, 1898–1901, no. 602). At Teos in Asia Minor there was a benefaction for the education of boys and girls, and he who embezzled the funds was to suffer the penalties inflicted by the laws on the sacrilegious. The offender was also to be held accursed, like the offender against early Roman laws on whom the doom was pronounced, 'Sacer esto' (*ib.* no. 513). At Dyme in the Peloponnese stealing sacred treasure and coining it entailed death (*ib.* no. 513). In the island of Syros offences against the festival of Demeter were sacrilegious (*ib.* no. 680).

There was in Athens a form of prosecution for ἀσέβεια ('impiety'), which to some extent overlapped that for ἱεροσυλία, but it included a much wider range of crimes against the dignity of beings and possessions under divine protection. Polybius (xxxvii. 1) describes this impiety as directed against gods, parents, and the dead. The mutilation of the Hermæ in Athens, which occurred about the time when the expedition against Sicily started in 415 B.C., is a famous example of this class of wrong, which included contempt for the gods of the city, violation of the mysteries of Eleusis, and similar errors. To injure sacred olives in Attica entailed banishment and confiscation.

2. Asylum.—A very important kind of impiety recognized all over Hellas, and specially characteristic of the Hellenic peoples as opposed to those of Italy and the barbaric West generally, was the violation of the right of asylum. To drag away suppliants who had committed themselves to the protection of an altar or the precincts of a temple was an enormity. In wars between Greeks a shrine was deemed inviolable (ἄσυλον) (Thucydides, iv. 97). In general persons who had been condemned by a regular court or had undergone deprivation of civic privilege (ἀτιμία) had no right to the protection of the god. The Spartans, however, held even these to be immune if they sought asylum (Polybius, iv. 35). There is a complaint in the *Ion* of Euripides that the inviolable sanctuary protects the unjust and the just alike (line 1315). The Hellenic theory that all sacred places should afford a refuge to suppliants was of course often rudely broken through in practice. For such impiety there was ordinarily no secular penalty. The divine being was left to avenge these wrongs, which he oftentimes did through human instruments. A curse would lie upon the offender and his progeny. Great families could be made to suffer politically for the sins of their ancestry.

Megacles, the head of the great Athenian family of the Alcmæonidæ, in 612 B.C. treacherously slew Cylon, who had attempted to make himself despot in Athens, and his followers, when they had shielded themselves in the temple of Athene on the Acropolis, and had surrendered on a promise that their lives should be spared. The religious blight that lay on the house was repeatedly exploited for political purposes in the two centuries that followed. At the beginning of the Peloponnesian war Sparta demanded that the Alcmæonidæ should be expelled from Attica. This was a blow aimed at Pericles, who was an Alcmæonid on his mother's side. He parried the attack by calling attention to the impious stain (ἄγος) that rested on Sparta for having torn away Helots from the very sacred sanctuary of Poseidon at Cape Tænarus. The Spartans themselves believed that the great earthquakes at Sparta in 464 B.C. came as a punishment inflicted by Poseidon himself, the 'earthshaking' god.

Sometimes it seems to have been thought that the divine vengeance might be escaped if the refugee were done to death without shedding of blood.

Thus the Spartan king Pausanias, who had commanded against the Persians, was walled in at the temple of Athene Chalkioikos, and perished of hunger.

Sometimes a suppliant was forced to surrender by the application of fire. On the other hand, there are not wanting remarkable examples of the protection afforded by the holy precincts.

In 445 B.C. another king of Sparta, Pleistoanax, fell under suspicion of having been in collusion with the enemy, and was condemned to pay a heavy fine. He took shelter in the sacred enclosure (τέμενος) which surrounded the temple of Zeus Lykaios at Megalopolis, and there lived for nineteen years (Thuc. v. 16). His son Pausanias had a similar fate. Being convicted of treason, he fled to the shrine of Athene Alea at Tegea and lived out his life in her domain.

The right of sanctuary accorded in lands to which Hellenic culture extended was important to slaves, and was one of many influences which rendered slavery on the Eastern side of the ancient world less grievous than on the Western. In Athens the temple of Theseus was a notable refuge, and in Laconia that of Poseidon at Cape Tænarus. The tricky slave who, after committing some misdeed, seated himself on an altar and jeered at his owner was a common figure in the later Greek comedy. The scene is to be found on a number of ancient works of art, and has been transferred by Plautus from Greek originals to his *Rudens* and *Mostellaria*. Sometimes the priest of a shrine would arbitrate between the slave and his master; of this we have an illustration in an inscription from the temple of Apollo Karneios at Andania in Messenia (Dittenberger, no. 653, line 81 ff.). Athenian law permitted a slave who had taken sanctuary owing to cruel treatment to demand that he should be sold to another master.

As time went on, this right of asylum, having been widely extended in barbarian regions which fell under Hellenic influence, naturally became less effective, and conceptions of the inviolability of sacred places became confused. In Attica, so far as the free citizens were concerned, the privilege of sanctuary seems to have died out, because a burgess who had been condemned in a court was held to have no right of access to sacred places. The Acropolis of Athens, which had sheltered Cylon, protected no conspirators in the later time. Among Greeks generally the degree of respect in which consecrated buildings and ground were held varied greatly. Sometimes the sanctity of a consecrated spot was recognized only by the inhabitants of the country in which it was situated. In other instances there was wider, and only in a few universal, recognition. In the case of fugitives from foreign countries extradition was to some extent practised. The evidence of coins and inscriptions, as well as literature, shows that a very great number of towns in Asia Minor claimed inviolability, not only for their temples with the precincts, but for a wider area and sometimes for the whole territory of the city. Naturally there was a great desire to obtain from dynasts and free communities a formal acquiescence in these claims. Alexander and his successors often responded to appeals in such matters. Sometimes ancient privilege was definitely enlarged. Mithridates increased the extent of the holy enclosure of Artemis at Ephesus. The Romans followed the earlier precedents. L. Scipio bestowed like favour on Magnesia after his victory there; and Sulla, Julius Cæsar, Mark Antony, Augustus, and other Romans took similar action in a number of cases. Inscriptions record extraordinary activity on the part of commonwealths desirous of obtaining admission of the sanctity of their temples and the land round them; *e.g.*, we have a remarkable list of towns which confirmed the inviolability of the temple of Hecate at Stratonice (Dittenberger, *Orientis Græcæ Inscr.*, Leipzig, 1903-05, no. 441). A record of places entitled to be regarded as inviolable seems to have been kept at Delphi (*ib.* no. 228). Often the compact had only a political value, and the title 'inviolate' (ἄσυλος) was a mere compliment. So—to take one example from many —the Ætolians contracted to treat as holy the temple of Athene Nikephoros at Pergamon, as a mark of respect for the king. Agreements of the sort frequently have reference to the establishment of games and festivals connected with temples. It was an attraction to visitors to know that the sanctity of the territory to which they were to travel was generally admitted.

Such compliments were often purely personal—*i.e.*, the inviolability was conferred on individuals as a distinction. We have a very long series of inscriptions of this kind, many of them interesting. That great and wide-spread gild, the company of Dionysiac artists, passed for inviolable throughout the Greek world.

The Greek right of asylum, as claimed by temples in Asia Minor, became a trouble to the Roman government. At the sanctuaries were wont to assemble throngs of insolvent debtors, criminals of all sorts, slaves, and every class of refugee. The injury to local administration came to be so serious that in the reign of Tiberius a great inquisition was held into the privileges which were asserted. As Tacitus drily remarked, a god would shield the scoundrelisms of mankind as though they belonged to his own ritual (*Ann.* iii. 60). The senate grew weary of the innumerable claims and authorized the consuls to deal with them, referring to the body only doubtful cases. The list of *asyla* was obviously cut down with severity. See art. ASYLUM.

3. Tombs.—There is little information concerning protection for the sanctity of tombs in the age of Greek independence. But the sepulchral monument was very commonly regarded as a kind of shrine. The 'tomb-breaker' (τυμβώρυχος) was punished as impious by public indictment under Athenian law, and generally in the Greek States. By permission of authority pecuniary penalties for violation were also created, and sometimes set forth on tombs, recoverable in court by any common prosecutor. The crime of injuring sepulchres was sometimes brought under the head of sacrilege (ἱεροσυλία) and sometimes under that of impiety (ἀσέβεια). (See Mommsen, *Röm. Strafrecht*, p. 821, n. 2.)

II. *ROMAN*. — In some important respects sacrilege and impiety were treated differently on the Eastern and the Western sides of the ancient world.

1. Temples.—In the Roman law of the republican and early imperial times *sacrilegium* was defined as robbery of movable objects dedicated to a divinity in his own house (Cicero, *de Leg.* ii. 22). Theoretically this offence could be committed only against Roman civic gods, for each commonwealth would punish crimes committed against its special divinities. The extension of protection to non-Roman shrines by the Roman government was a matter of favour. But the public mind at Rome was early shocked by outrages upon temples committed by Romans in allied and even in hostile States.

Thus Fulvius Flaccus, who pillaged the temple of Juno at the Lacinian promontory soon after the Hannibalic war, and Pleminius, the violator of temples in S. Italy during the war, and Fulvius Nobilior, who plundered Ambracia a little later, were reprobated by opinion, and expiation was in such cases sometimes made by the government.

The robbery by Q. Servilius Cæpio and his accomplices in 104 B.C. of the gold deposited in the temple of Apollo in Tolosa was punished by a Roman court as an offence against the Roman treasury, into which booty taken from an enemy ought to be paid. But the public belief was that the god sent to a miserable death all who had stained their hands by the outrage (Aul. Gell. III. ix. 7). In the late Republic the feeling of Roman officials about such matters had become gravely corrupted. But the popular estimate remained the same. In the strict interpretation of the Roman lawyers a man was not sacrilegious unless he stole from the holy place something which had been so dedicated as to become the actual property of the god. For full sanctity dedication by public authority was necessary. In doubtful cases the *pontifices* decided. Cicero indeed declared that what was entrusted to the god's keeping was in the same case (*de Leg.* ii. 22). This was a very important matter, since the temples served often the purpose of the modern banks, and the officials made money for the divinity by lending the capital deposited with them. The question seems to have been in dispute until it was authoritatively decided by the emperor Severus that robbery of this kind was not sacrilege, but theft (*Digest.* xlviii. 13. 6. 5). In some respects the privileges of a temple depended on what was called the *lex templi*, which was laid down for the regulation of all matters connected with it. The law of the temple of Diana on the Aventine hill in Rome seems often to have served as a model. (See H. Dessau, *Inscriptiones Latinæ*, Berlin, 1892–1906, nos. 112 and 4907.)

It seems clear that the law drew a distinction between dedicated objects and money belonging to a temple. Theft of this *pecunia sacra* was classed as *peculatus*, *i.e.* appropriation of moneys belonging to the State. There was a single statute (*lex Iulia*) dealing with the two offences of *peculatus* and *sacrilegium* (*Digest.* xlviii. 13). The distinction between sacred and national property was often not drawn (cf. *CIL* i. 185, 6: 'aut sacrum aut poublicom').

Instances are not wanting of an appropriation of sacred treasures by the government in times of crisis. Thus, *e.g.*, Sulla in 82 B.C. melted down the gold and silver possessions of the temples in order to provide pay for his soldiers (Val. Max. VII. vi. 4).

The Roman tradition was that in very early days the secular punishment of sacrilege was death. In the historic age it was pecuniary until a *lex Iulia* passed either by Cæsar or by Augustus added the penalty of exile. In the imperial period the personal suffering that might be inflicted was more severe. In the reign of the emperor Tiberius the form of exile called *deportatio* was introduced (Quintilian, III. x. 1). In accordance with the general custom which was established by the end of the 2nd cent. A.D., lighter chastisement was imposed on the rigidly defined class of the 'more honourable' (*honestiores*) than on the others, the 'more humble' (*humiliores*). Ulpian (early in the 3rd cent.) stated that in his time many had been condemned to the arena, to perish by the wild beasts, or to be burned alive or crucified (*Digest.* xlviii. 13. 4. 2). Theft from shrines privately consecrated was regarded as 'more than theft (*furtum*) and less than sacrilege' (*ib.* xlviii. 13. 9. 1).

Corresponding to the form of prosecution for ἀσέβεια in Attic law, there was an indictment for injuring religion (*crimen læsæ religionis*) in Rome, and the line between this and sacrilege tended to be loosely drawn. The tendency was stimulated by the partial divinization of the living emperor; and this cause also helped to confuse the distinction between treason (*maiestas*) and sacrilege and the contempt of religion. Tacitus (*Ann.* iii. 24) blames Augustus for inflicting death or exile on the paramours of his daughter Iulia and her daughter Iulia. He qualified their fault 'by the serious title of injured religious usage (*læsarum religionum*) and treason (*violatæ maiestatis*).' This is an early example of the elasticity of the criminal law in all matters that could be described by any stretch as affecting the sacred person of the emperor. Ulpian, early in the 3rd cent., described treason as *quasi sacrilegium.* His lawyer's conscience would hardly allow him to identify completely the two offences. But popular usage had already obliterated the distinction. Tertullian spoke of the Christians being charged with *sacrilegium* (*Apol.* 2). The *Acta* of the martyrdom of Symphorianus (A.D. 179) indicate him as guilty of *maiestatis sacrilegium*—a curious expression (T. Ruinart, *Acta primorum martyrum*, Paris, 1689, p. 129). The refusal to take an oath by the genius of the emperor was sufficient ground for the indictment (Tert. *Apol.* 32). The emperor Constans II. treated coining as sacrilegious, and the definition was extended even to less serious crimes. A great variety of infringements of imperial edicts could be so treated. In this connexion it may be noted that even after the acceptance of Christianity the rulers and all that appertained to them retained in official language the quality of 'sacred' and 'divine.'

After the time of Constantine very many offences against Christianity and the orthodox beliefs and the property and privileges of the Church and clergy were regarded in the light of sacrilege. An imperial edict of the year 380 stamps as sacrilegious 'those who either by ignorance confuse religious law or by carelessness outrage it and scorn it' (*Cod. Justin.* ix. 29. 1). This appears to have been at first directed against bishops on the eastern side of the empire who were lukewarm in repressing heresy.

2. Tombs.—In the view of the Romans, which spread throughout the West, a tomb was a shrine dedicated to the spirit of the dead. Inscriptions not uncommonly present the two denotations as alternatives. The emperor Gordian, in the 3rd cent., treated the violation of a place of burial as *crimen læsæ religionis* (Cod. ix. 19. 1); and Julian, with some exaggeration, declared that the 'ancestors' of the Romans had looked upon the crime as *sacrilegium.* He assimilated the penalties of the two offences (*ib.* ix. 19. 4). In popular usage this view had long been adopted (*CIL* vi. 10120). For a long time, however, wrongs done to monuments and places of sepulture had been vindicated by pecuniary damages, which parties legally interested could recover by the aid of the *prætor urbanus.* Only gradually did *sepulcri violatio* come to be regarded as in the full sense a public crime. In innumerable extant inscriptions from tombs of the imperial age mention is made of particular sums of money which an offender may be compelled to pay. It appears that in Rome the authority of the *pontifices* was required to render the penalty effective, while, outside, permission was required from the municipal authorities. At first the fines, which might be sued for by any prosecutor, went in Rome into the coffers of the *pontifices* and Vestal Virgins, and elsewhere into the municipal treasuries. Condemnation in such a case, though not regarded as strictly criminal, carried with it the disabilities which were connoted by the term *infamia.* It seems probable that general statutes prescribed maxima which might be exacted. These maxima were not the same in all the quarters of the empire.

About the middle of the 2nd cent. A.D. the crime of desecrating tombs had evidently become very prevalent, and fresh means were sought of protecting them from attack. The custom was introduced of devoting part of the fines to the senatorial treasury (*ærarium*) or the imperial exchequer (*fiscus*), which before long became the sole public treasury. Sometimes a share remained for the local municipal exchequer (Mommsen, pp. 812–815, with notes). The destruction of tombs to provide material for new buildings became, in spite of these fines, increasingly common, and Christianity even stimulated the process. Criminal punishment, which in the age of Cæsar had been possible only where violence had been used (under the *lex Iulia de vi privata*), was extended to all instances of the offence, and the punishments became more and more severe. The methods of protection afforded to sepulchres by fines became common in Italy and all over the eastern side of the empire, in the Græcized lands of the East, but did not spread generally over the West.

3. Asylum.—The right of asylum attached to

temples, which was of immemorial antiquity among the Greeks, was not an indigenous Roman or Italic institution. It finds a place in the fable of the foundation of Rome by Romulus; but that is only an example of Greek imagination playing on the darkness of pre-historic times; and no Latin term could be discovered which was the equivalent of ἄσυλον. In the desire to support the ancient tale, scholars have ransacked the records of Roman religion to find a divinity whose shrine might conceivably have possessed the right of sanctuary, but in vain. When Dionysius of Halicarnassus (iv. 26) spoke of the temple of Diana on the Aventine as sacred and inviolable, he perhaps had a hazy recollection of its long connexion with the plebeian tribunes, whose persons were sacrosanct. Only when Julius Cæsar was deified a temple was founded which was possessed of the privilege of asylum (Dio Cass. xlvii. 19). As the persons of the emperors were in a way above human level, the custom grew of taking refuge at an imperial statue. It became a public nuisance and caused trouble to the senate (Tac. *Ann.* iii. 36, 60, iv. 67; Suet. *Tib.* 53). Soldiers in the camp sought protection from the imperial effigy in the camp shrine (Tac. *Ann.* xii. 17). Slaves who fled to the temples of the gods and the statues of the emperors had to be restrained. Often they were warned off by inscriptions. But Antoninus Pius laid down that, if it were found that their masters had treated them intolerably, they might claim, as they could under old Attic law, to be sold to other masters (Gaius, i. 53).

LITERATURE.—Information is to be found on these matters in works on Greek and Roman antiquities, of which the following may be mentioned: H. E. Meier and G. F. Schömann, *Der attische Process*², 2 vols., Berlin, 1883–87; C. F. Hermann, *Lehrbuch der griechischen Antiquitäten*, 3 vols., Heidelberg, 1841–52; Pauly-Wissowa, esp. *s.vv.* 'Asylon' and 'Hierosulias Graphē (ἱεροσυλίας γραφή)'; Daremberg-Saglio, *s.vv.* 'Asylum,' 'Hierosulia,' and 'Sacrilegium' (where references will be found to special monographs); T. Mommsen, *Römisches Strafrecht*, Leipzig, 1899 (which includes much information about later Greek usage).

J. S. REID.

SADDHARMA-PUṆḌARĪKA.—See LOTUS OF THE TRUE LAW.

SADDUCEES.—As usually understood, 'Sadducees' is the name of a party which was engaged in controversy and conflict with the Pharisees down to the destruction of Jerusalem and the Temple in A.D. 70 and even later. Did this party stand for positions distinctively and genuinely religious? Did it represent the old conservative scribism, which had within it a large priestly element? Or was it primarily political in character? These questions have been raised by recent criticism, and it is necessary at the outset to face the issues opened up by them.

1. The Sadducees primarily an ecclesiastical party.—G. Hölscher, in an important monograph,[1] has argued that the Sadducees are to be regarded not as an organized party, with definite and positive beliefs, but as 'the lax, the scoffers who make merry over the strict religious practice of the pious, as the infidels and godless.' They represented a tendency which favoured Græco-Roman culture and enlightenment, and which was influential among the rich and high-class Jews, especially those who had relations with the Roman government. The attitude of the Sadducees towards religious questions was purely negative, being fundamentally determined by political and cultural considerations. They were not recruited, as is commonly supposed, from the priestly nobility of Jerusalem, but included the rich merchants, officials, and others. The Sadducees were thus not a religious party at all, but simply a body of people loosely bound together by a common interest to maintain the existing *régime*. The name is explained as meaning 'Zadokites,'[1] and was given to them by their opponents, the Pharisees, who borrowed it from an earlier age, the period of Antiochus Epiphanes, when the descendants of Zadok, who then filled the high-priestly office, identified themselves with Hellenism in its most dangerous forms. It could thus, according to Hölscher, be used appropriately at a later time to brand with ignominy similar tendencies which would appear to the Pharisees to be godless and unpatriotic.

This theory seems to have been suggested by the later unhistorical use of the term 'Sadducee' as an equivalent of 'free-thinker' or 'Epicurean.' In the later Rabbinical literature 'Sadducee' is often used in this loose way. But in the earlier sources, Josephus and the NT, Sadduceeism appears to be combined with certain definite religious positions of a conservative kind. And this is, no doubt, historical.

It may be assumed, then, that the Sadducees represented the old priestly party of which the earlier Sōpherîm were largely composed; that they inherited the cautious and conservative orthodoxy of which the book of Ecclesiasticus is probably an excellent expression; and that the division between the two elements which became the opposed parties of Sadducees and Pharisees did not occur till the Maccabæan period.

2. Name and antecedent.—The best explanation of the name is that already assumed above and first proposed by A. Geiger, viz. that 'Sadducees' (Gr. Σαδδουκαῖοι) means 'Zadokites'; and the Heb. צרוקי (point צְדוּקִי) is an adjective meaning an adherent of the בְּנֵי צָדוֹק.[2] The 'sons of Zadok' were the members of the priestly family who traced their descent back to Zadok, head of the priesthood in the days of David and Solomon (cf. 1 K 1^{34} 2^{35}). They were singled out by Ezekiel (44^{10-15}) as worthy to be entrusted with supreme authority in the Temple; and in fact members of this family formed the Temple-hierarchy down to the time of Ben Sira, who, in the psalm preserved in the Hebrew text of Sir 51^{12}—if it be genuine, as it almost certainly is—gives thanks to 'Him that chooseth the sons of Zadok to be priests.' At a later time the 'sons of Zadok' (*i.e.* the priestly aristocracy) succumbed to the seductive influence of Hellenism (especially in the time of the Seleucidæ). It is possible that at this period the name 'Sadducee' was coined by the 'pious' (the Ḥasîdîm) as a term of reproach for those who followed the degenerate priestly aristocracy, and that, when these ceased to hold the office of high-priest, which was usurped by the Hasmonæan princes, the party name was retained for the adherents of the old high-priestly families among the priests. On the other hand, it is not certain that the designation 'Zadokite' (צְדוּקִי) was actually given by opponents in the first place. It may well have been the title assumed by the conservative element in the priesthood who, after the disappearance of the old Zadokite high-priests, may have wished, under the altered conditions that grew up in the 2nd cent. B.C., to perpetuate the traditions of an earlier time. It is clear, as we shall see, that the Sadducæan party did stand for an older religious tradition and practice; and the most reasonable hypothesis is that it consisted essentially of the priestly party which upheld conservative priestly traditions. The later high-priests were no doubt, as a rule, adherents of this party. It is unfortunate that we have no statement of the Sadducæan position from

1 *Der Sadduzäismus*, Leipzig, 1906.

1 *I.e.* בְּנֵי צָדוֹק.

2 A philological objection has been urged on the ground of the double ד (δ); but this may be explained as compensatory.

themselves,[1] unless the 'Zadokite' work discovered and published by S. Schechter represents, as is possible, the views of a section of this party. The result is that their religious positions have been placed before us only by opponents. No doubt the Sadducees appeared to their Pharisaic opponents often to take up positions inimical to the 'truth.' It is easy to understand how, in the bitterness engendered by conflict, the very name of 'Sadducee' came to be identified, in Pharisaic circles, with 'infidel.' R. Leszynsky,[2] who accepts the connexion of the name 'Sadducees' with 'the sons of Zadok,' finds also a cardinal difference of principle between them and their Pharisaic opponents on the question of the Messianic hope. Whereas the latter held fast to the old popular expectation of a Davidic Messiah, the Sadducees, he contends, maintained that the kingship was vested in the priestly line. For them the Pentateuch was decisive on this point. True, the Pharisees could appeal to Gn 49^{10} ('The sceptre shall not depart from Judah, nor the ruler's staff from between his feet'); but other passages could be cited from the Tôrāh which could be held to override the Messianic interpretation of this passage. Had not Aaron and his tribe been specially chosen by God, and had not God concluded an eternal covenant with Phinehas? But the strongest proof-text was found in Ex 19^6 'And ye shall be unto me a kingdom of priests, and an holy nation.' It might be inferred from this declaration that the priests were also destined to possess the kingdom, and not a family of the tribe of Judah. That a controversy was in fact focused on this text is a not improbable inference from the phenomena of the ancient versions, where particular pains seem to have been taken to exclude the possibility of such an interpretation as the assumed Sadducæan one. Thus the Palestinian Targum renders the verse: 'And before Me you shall be crowned kings, and sanctified priests, and a holy people.'[3] There was also the precedent of the priest-king Melchizedek (Gn $14^{18ff.}$), to which the Hasmonæan priest-kings undoubtedly appealed when they assumed the title of 'priest of God most High,'[4] and which was cited also by the writer of Ps 110^4, which many scholars think was originally written in honour of Simon Maccabæus. The ascription of this Psalm to 'David' is doubtless due to Pharisaic influence. Leszynsky thinks that Pss 89 and 132 are Pharisaic protests against this Sadducæan doctrine. It is easy to see how the assumption of the priestly and regal dignity in one person by the Maccabæan princes, who themselves belonged to one of the most distinguished priestly families, would appeal to those who held the view just referred to, while it would excite the bitter hostility of the Pharisees, as in fact it did. Doubtless it was due to this hostility that both John Hyrcanus and Alexander Jannæus found it expedient to recommend an arrangement of the succession which would separate the two offices.[5]

The name 'Melchizedek,' which may be interpreted to mean 'true king,' would also suggest a significant reference to 'Sadducee.' Its latter element 'zedek' is strikingly suggestive of 'Zadok,' and it almost inevitably brings to mind the idea that Melchizedek is really equivalent to 'Zadok-king,' or 'Sadducæan-king.' For the history of the division between the two parties see art. PHARISEES, §§ 1, 3.

3. Doctrinal beliefs and principles.—The Rabbinical literature contains many references to points of controversy between the Sadducees and Pharisees, which it will be impossible to enumerate fully and discuss here. It will suffice to point out and endeavour to estimate the significance of the fundamental points of difference.

When Josephus depicts the Sadducees as representing nobility, power, and wealth, and as engrossed in political affairs and interests,[1] all that this need mean is that the high-priest and his *entourage* were members of the Sadducæan party. It need not mean that the ideals of this party were purely worldly and political. Nor because a high-priest was a Sadducee does it follow that he was necessarily destitute of religious convictions. The numerous points of controversy between the Pharisees and Sadducees all proceed from radical divergence of principles.[2]

The most important of these was the position taken up with regard to the written Law (the Pentateuch). Both parties assigned supremacy to the Law. But, whereas the Pharisees supplemented the written Law by the oral tradition, and placed this on an equality with the Mosaic Tôrāh, the Sadducees refused to accept any ordinance as having Scriptural authority unless it was based directly upon the written Tôrāh. They also claimed, as priests, on the authority of Dt $17^{8ff.}$, the legal power to decree and revoke ordinances from time to time of a temporary character. This position has been well stated by J. Z. Lauterbach:[3]

> 'Considering themselves as interpreters of the Law, like their fathers, they could see no reason for departing from the rules and methods, or losing the privileges of their fathers. Like their fathers, they held that there was only one law of absolute authority, and this was the Law of Moses as contained in the Pentateuch, which the people of the time of Ezra had sworn to keep and obey. . . . The priestly group and their followers, who formed the Sadducean party, did not . . . differ at all from the former priestly teachers, their ancestors, the Soferim, in their attitude towards the Law. They accepted and followed, strictly, the simple, sound interpretations of the Soferim, based upon the plain sense of the words of the Law. They rightly assumed that, as a code of laws, the Torah is clear, distinct, and unambiguous in expression, that every commandment or law is stated in plain and simple words, easily understood by men for whom the laws and commandments are intended. . . . The Sadducees held that "the Torah speaks in human language," a principle which was retained long after even among the Pharisees by the representatives of the older Halakah, which has many points in common with the teachings of the Sadducees. . . . They would not devise ingenious methods to explain away a written law, or give it a new meaning not warranted by the plain sense of the words. They also held in reverence the unwritten laws and traditional customs and usages of which, as priests, they were in possession. They observed them in most cases in the same manner as their fathers had done.'

It is probably a mistake to say that they 'rejected' the prophetic and other Scriptures outside the Pentateuch. Their attitude towards these books is well expressed by a sentence quoted by C. Taylor in his edition of the *Pirqe Ābhôth*, Excursus iii.:

> 'And therefore I say that the Prophets and Hagiographa are called words of Qabbalah [*i.e.* mere tradition], because they were received by διαδοχή [succession], . . . and by no means are they equal to the five books, which are all precepts and ordinances.'[4]

Whereas the Pharisees would harmonize an apparent contradiction between the Tôrāh and the prophets by exegetical devices which might conform both to a part of the oral law, the Sadducees did not hesitate to reject outright doctrines and practices which could not be based primarily on the written Law.[5] An interesting example may be cited to illustrate these points.

[1] No doubt Sirach represents the older orthodoxy inherited by the Sadducees; but the Sadducæan party is later.
[2] *Die Sadduzäer*, Berlin, 1912, p. 95 ff.
[3] See R. H. Charles, *The Book of Jubilees*, London, 1902, p. 116, for a full list of the passages, and add 2 Mac 2^{17}.
[4] Jos. *Ant.* XVI. vi. 2.
[5] Cf. Jos. *Ant.* XIII. xi. 1, xv. 5.

[1] *Ant.* XVIII. i. 4.
[2] This is denied by M. H. Segal in 'Pharisees and Sadducees,' in *Exp*, 8th ser., vol. xiii. [1917] 81 ff. Segal maintains that the Sadducees had no religious principles, but were solely interested in securing political power. His arguments are unconvincing.
[3] In *Studies in Jewish Literature issued in Honour of Prof. Kaufmann Kohler*, London, 1913, p. 182 ff.
[4] *Sayings of the Fathers*[2], Cambridge, 1897, p. 114.
[5] Cf. Jos. *Ant.* XIII. x. 6.

A certain Jacob of Kefar Nibburaya (A.D. 4th cent.) taught in Tyre certain practices which were regarded by R. Ḥaggai as heterodox. The rabbi summoned the delinquent before him, and asked him to justify himself. Jacob quoted passages from the Law (Nu 1^{18} and Gn 17^{12}). The rabbi declared that his teaching was wrong, and justified his view of its erroneousness by quoting a passage from the Hagiographa, viz. Ezr 10^{3}. Jacob was consequently condemned to be flogged. 'What!' he exclaimed, 'will you have me flogged on the strength of mere Ḳabbalah?'[1]

We have already seen that the Sadducees rejected the Messianic doctrine of the Pharisees, which looked for a Davidic Messiah, because they considered that the prophetic teaching on this subject was in conflict with that of the Tôrāh. They further rejected the Pharisaic doctrine of the resurrection of the body, on the same ground.[2] It should be noted that both in the Talmudic and in the NT passages just cited the question in debate is not, 'Is there a resurrection or not?' but rather, 'How can the resurrection be proved from the Tôrāh?' According to Ac 23^{8}, the Sadducees also denied the existence of angels and spirits. This can hardly mean, however, a mere denial of the reality of such existences, for it is obvious that the Pentateuch contains many narratives which affirm the activity and appearance of angels. The statement may possibly mean that they did not accept the developed and elaborated angelology and demonology—in which angels and demons were graded and assigned special names and functions—that had grown up in the Persian period under Persian and Babylonian influence. In matters of binding rule and law (Halākhāh) the Sadducees were, as we should expect, apt to press the literal and plain meaning of the letter of the Tôrāh. The most notorious example of this is their insistence on the literal interpretation of the law of retaliation: 'An eye for an eye, a tooth for a tooth' (Ex 21^{24}).[3] Another instance is their famous controversy with the Pharisees over the method of reckoning Pentecost. They contended that the seven weeks from the offering of the 'omer' (first barley sheaf) to Pentecost should be counted as Lv $23^{15f.}$ directs, 'from the morrow after the Sabbath,' 'Sabbath' being interpreted as the Saturday which fell in Passover week, with the consequence that Pentecost would always fall on a Sunday, whereas the Pharisees reckoned from the day immediately following the Passover (reckoned as a 'Sabbath'). Here, as generally, the Sadducæan rule undoubtedly conformed to ancient practice.[4] It was naturally within the Temple precincts that Sadducæan influence was strongest and most firmly entrenched. While the Pharisees were supreme outside the Temple, and even made their power felt within it for at least a century before A.D. 70—it must always be remembered that there were many Pharisaic priests—yet they did not secure absolute power in the Temple itself till about A.D. 50 to 60. Thus the Sadducees claimed that the high-priest's burnt-offering should be provided at his own expense, in accordance with Nu 28^{4} (where the singular is used), whereas the Pharisees insisted that the sacrifice was a national one, and should be provided out of the Temple treasury. Against the Pharisees they laid great stress on the high degree of purity of those who officiated at the preparation of the ashes of the red heifer,[5] and they extended the power of contamination to indirect as well as to direct contact.[1] On the other hand, they refused to accept the Pharisaic view that the scrolls of Holy Scripture 'defile the hands' like any holy vessel.[2] They also refused to countenance the ingenious method devised by the Pharisees for evading the strict Sabbath law, known as *'Erūb*. They opposed the popular festivity of the water-drawing, and its associated processions, which took place at the Feast of Tabernacles. In all these cases they were faithful to their fundamental principle—that what could not be proved by the letter of the written Tôrāh was not to be made of binding obligation.

Reference has been made to the fact that the Sadducees, when they found it necessary to develop or innovate on the letter of the Law in order to meet the needs of the time, issued decrees or decisions on their own authority, as provided by the Law itself (Dt $17^{8ff.}$). But these 'decrees' were never put on a level with the letter of the Law; and they could be modified or abrogated as circumstances dictated. The evidence for the existence of such a 'Book of Decrees' (or legal decisions) is contained in the *Mᵉgillāth Ta'ănîth*,[3] iv., where under date of the 14th of Tammuz this 'book' (ספר גזירתא) is stated to have been finally abrogated (by the victory of the Pharisees over the Sadducees). The 'book' is explained by the glossator to mean the Sadducæan code of laws, or rather, it is probable, a collection of case-law. Instances are given of the harsh interpretation of Biblical law on which the Sadducees proceeded, and the day when this code was finally abrogated is marked as a festival.

With the destruction of the Temple in A.D. 70 the power of the Sadducees, which had already been seriously impaired, still further declined. Though their influence was still apparent in various ways, and was later perpetuated, it would seem, by the Ḳaraites, their organized force as a party vanished with the Temple and the cultus.

4. The vitality and influence of Sadduceeism.—That Sadduceeism stood for something more than mere negations is evident from the persistence with which it waged its age-long conflict with Pharisaism. It even impressed itself, to some extent, on the latter, and we can see its influence especially in the conservative element among the Pharisees represented by the school of Shammai.[4] If, as is generally conceded, the book of Ben Sira represents the standpoint of the primitive Zaddukim, it is clear that Sadduceeism inherited a positive, though conservative, theology. The attitude of Ben Sira, in this connexion, to the books of the Bible outside the Law is interesting. He quotes freely from all parts of the Hebrew Scriptures to illustrate his themes, though he would, of course, not found any doctrine on a book outside the Tôrāh, nor uphold such unless it could be proved from the Pentateuch.[5] We must also be on our guard against identifying Sadduceeism as a whole with the small body of the Temple hierarchy. Doubtless the high-priest and his immediate circle were (up to quite the last years of the existence of the Temple) members of the Sadducæan party. But the worldly and political character of this small section must not be imputed to the party as a whole. It must be remembered

1 See *Qoheleth rabbāh*, vii. 23. The rabbi evidently felt the force of this appeal, for he immediately cited a further proof from the Law itself (Dt 7^{3}), whereupon Jacob gracefully submitted.

2 Cf. T.B. *Sanh.* 90*b*; Mk 12^{18}.

3 Cf. T.B. *Bābhā Qamma*, 84*a*; Mt 5^{38}.

4 Another old view interpreted 'Sabbath' as = 'festival-week' in this passage (*i.e.* Nisan 15–21); its 'morrow' would then be Nisan 22; see the writer's Introd. to *The Book of Jubilees*, London, 1917, p. xviii.

5 *Parah*, iii. 7.

1 *Yad*, iv. 7. 2 *Yad*, iv. 6.

3 The *Mᵉgillāth Ta'ănîth*, in its original form, is written in Aramaic, and was probably compiled within the first decade of the Christian era. It enumerates 35 eventful days which were to be kept as joyful festivals, and which were reminders of glorious events in the life of the nation.

4 After the destruction of the Temple the most consistent Shammaite was Eliezer b. Hyrḳanos (end of 1st-beginning of 2nd cent.). R. Jose the Galilæan (early 2nd cent.) maintained in his Halākhāh older conservative tradition.

5 1 Mac may also be a Sadducæan work, the companion book of 2 Mac being a Pharisaic counterblast.

that the gulf between the aristocratic priests and the main body of the priests was almost as marked as that between the conflicting parties. Doubtless among the priests generally there were many pious Sadducees as well as Pharisees. Nor must the possibility be lost sight of that there may have been different circles or schools of Sadducees, just as there were among the Pharisees—a possibility which recent discussion and research have made increasingly probable.

The whole question of Sadduceeism may be said to have entered on a new phase, owing to the remarkable discovery by Schechter of documents emanating from a Zadokite sect.[1] It is true that the exact value of this writing has not yet been finally settled, some scholars (*e.g.*, A. Büchler) impugning its early character; but, on the whole, its importance and genuineness as an early production, written before the destruction of the Temple in A.D. 70, have been vindicated by critical discussion.[2] Not only Schechter, but Lévi, Leszynsky, Charles, G. Margoliouth, and Kohler believe the writing to be of early origin. Leszynsky, in his discussion of the Zadokite Fragments, has no difficulty in demonstrating its Sadducæan affinities, which are found especially in the rejection of Pharisaic tradition and in the recognition of the written Tôrāh as the only law-book. There are, however, two striking developments which, at first sight, are surprising in a Sadducæan document. A system of exegesis is adopted which is remarkably like that of the Pharisees. But, as Leszynsky remarks, we were already aware that Pharisaic methods of interpreting Scripture had a vogue in the later period (1st Christian cent.) far beyond the boundaries of Pharisaism proper. Both Jesus and Paul, the enemies of Pharisaic tradition, were ready, on occasion, to adopt Pharisaic methods of exegesis. The second striking development is the recognition of the sacred character of the prophetic writings. But here, again, it is unnecessary to suppose that all sections of Sadducees refused to recognize the sacred character of all books outside the Pentateuch. It may be true that certain sects of Sadducees did so, agreeing in this respect with the Samaritans. The Zadokite Fragments reveal striking features, which point to a Sadducæan origin. The glorification of the priesthood and the corresponding depreciation of the royal Davidic house, already apparent in Sirach (45 f.), are even more pronounced in this work.

'David is accused of ignorance of the Law (vii. 5). The title "king" (מלך) is replaced by that of "prince" (נשיא [vii. 4]). In ix. 7 the passage from Am 9[11], which promises the setting up of "the tabernacle of David that is fallen," is explained in such a way that all reference to David is got rid of; for "the king" is said to denote "the Congregation," and "the tabernacle of the king" to denote "the books of the Law."'[3]

This work has a Messianic expectation of its own. It looks forward to the advent of a Messiah 'from Aaron and from Israel.' In other words, it expects a priestly Messiah. From v.[6] it also appears that the author believed in immortality.

We have here, then, the Messianic manifesto of a party or section of the Sadducees, which may have differed from the main body in its acceptance of a Messianic hope and a doctrine of immortality (not resurrection of the body). Kohler regards it as a manifesto setting forth the claims of the Messiah of the Dositheau sect (Samaritan). But this is improbable.[1] According to pseudo-Tertullian,[2] Dositheus was the first to deny the Prophets, whereas the Fragments put them almost on an equality with the Law.

After our previous discussion we are prepared to discover, with Leszynsky, a Sadducæan element in certain apocryphal and pseudepigraphical books. These are the *Book of Jubilees*, the *Testaments of the Twelve Patriarchs*, the *Book of Enoch* (with the exception of the similitudes), and the *Assumption of Moses*. It is also noteworthy that Jesus seems to have sided with the Sadducees against the Pharisees on certain points. He, it is true, upheld the resurrection doctrine of the Pharisees against the Sadducees. But He certainly agreed with the latter in their main contention, viz. the rejection of the Pharisaic traditional law.

It may be said that recent investigation and discussion have revealed Sadduceeism in a new light, as an active, energetic movement, full of life, variety, and vital developments.

LITERATURE.—To the literature cited in the body of the art. and at the end of the art. PHARISEES add K. Kohler, art. 'Sadducees,' in *JE*; G. H. Box, in *Exp*, 8th ser., xv. [1918] 401 ff., xvi. [1918] 55 ff.; and A. Büchler, *Das grosse Synedrion in Jerusalem*, Vienna, 1902. Büchler's art. impugning the early character of the 'Zadokite Fragments' was published in *JQR*, new ser., iii. [1913] 429–485, and Schechter's rejoinder, *ib.* iv. [1914] 449–474.

G. H. BOX.

SĀDHS.—The Sādhs are a unitarian sect of N. India, founded in 1543 by Bīrbhān, of Bijēsar, near Nārnaul in the S.E. Panjāb. The sect may be looked upon as an offshoot of the Raī Dāsīs (*q.v.*), Bīrbhān having claimed to be inspired by Ūdhō, or Uddhava, Dāsa, who was a pupil of Raī Dāsa; but, like Kabīr, they have wandered rather far from the Vaiṣṇava teaching of Rāmānanda, Raī Dāsa's master. Regarding the origin of the name, see art. SĀDHU. The Sādhs call upon God under the name Satnām, said to mean 'the True Name,' and among themselves employ Satnāmī as the name of the sect. The name Satnāmī (*q.v.*) is, however, also applied to at least two other sects.

The Sādhs are found in the United Provinces and in the Panjāb. Their principal seats are at Āgrā, Jaipur, Farrukhābād, and Mirzāpur in the former, and in the Districts of Delhi and Rohtak, close to Nārnaul, in the latter. Their number has not been accurately recorded, but probably amounts to between two and three thousand.

The following summary of the facts about this sect is given by Crooke:

'Adults are required to wear a white dress: and ornament and the use of rich apparel of every kind are prohibited. They never wear a cap, but use instead a turban of a peculiar shape. They are enjoined by their religion never to tell a lie and never to take an oath. They are in the same way prohibited from using any kind of intoxicant or any article which borders upon luxury. Wine, opium, *gānja*, *bhang*, betel and tobacco are abominations to them. They have an intense respect for animal life, which extends to even the smallest insect, and the use of any kind of animal food is strictly denounced. They will salute no one but the Divine principle, which they term Sat or "The Truth"; and when they meet a European or any superior they salute merely by raising the hands to the level of the breast. They detest idolatry and all outward forms of religious belief. They are very reticent about their beliefs, and it is only with the greatest difficulty that it has been possible to obtain a copy, which is probably incomplete, of the book of religious songs (*bāni*) which embody the principles of their faith. All controversy or argument on religious matters with strangers to the sect is reprobated. Their religious books, known as *pōthī*, are written in *Bhāshā*, or ordinary Hindi, and are not the work of any single author, but contain a number of songs, many of which are taken from the writings of Nānak and Kabīr. These books are read almost daily in their chapel or meeting-house, which is known as *jumlaghar*, or "house of assembly," or *chauki*, "station." The service takes place in the evening, when all members of the sect, male and female, attend. This is their only form of worship.'[3]

The substance of these *pōthīs* is contained in a tract called *Ādi Upadēś*, or 'First Precepts,' which

[1] *Documents of Jewish Sectaries*, vol. i., *Fragments of a Zadokite Work*, Cambridge, 1910.

[2] See esp. Israel Lévi in *REJ* lxi. [1911] 161–205; Leszynsky, *ib.* p. 142 ff.; Charles, 'The Fragments of a Zadokite Work,' in *Apocrypha and Pseudepigrapha of the Old Testament*, Oxford, 1913, ii. 785–834; K. Kohler, 'Dositheus, the Samaritan Heresiarch,' in *AJTh* xv. [1911] 404–435.

[3] Charles, *Apoc. and Pseud. of OT*, ii. 796. It is significant that in T.B. *Sanh.* 100*b* 'the books of the Sadducees and the Book of Ben Sira' are classed together.

[1] We should hardly expect such a manifesto to be written in Biblical Hebrew.

[2] *Adv. omnes Hær.* i.

[3] *Tribes and Castes*, iv. 245.

includes the twelve *hukms*, or commandments of the sect. Put summarily,[1] these are:

(1) There is only one God. Worship thou Him. (2) Be modest. Adhere to thine own creed. Mix not with those of other faith. (3) Lie not. Speak not evil of any. Employ the tongue only for the praise of God. Steal not. Look not at improper things. (4) Listen not to evil discourse, nor to music or singing except of hymns. (5) Covet not. God is the Giver of all. (6) Declare thyself a Sādh, but engage not in controversy. (7) Wear white garments, and no ornaments or sectarian distinctions. (8) Avoid intoxicants, perfumes, tobacco. Bow not down to idols or to men. (9) Kill not. Take not by force. (10) A man may have only one wife, and a woman only one husband. The woman to be obedient to the man, and to eat his leavings. (11) Wear not a mendicant's garb, nor beg for alms. (12) Be not superstitious as to days, times, seasons, or omens. Seek only the will of God.

Raī Dāsa was a contemporary of Kabīr (*q.v.*), and his fellow-disciple. The teaching of the latter was strongly unitarian, and at the same time borrowed freely from the Christian Scriptures. It is evident that the unitarian doctrines of the Sādhs were borrowed, with the traces of Christianity evident in the above, either from Kabīr or from his successor Nānak (*q.v.*). In other respects, such as cosmogony, and the belief in transmigration and in *mukti* (final release), the doctrines of the Sādhs do not differ from those of other Vaiṣṇava Hindus.

The Sādhs, under the name of Satnāmīs, appear to have been the heroes of the revolt of Hindu devotees against Aurangzīb in 1672. The leaders were mendicant Satnāmīs, who were nicknamed by the people 'Muṇḍiyās,' or 'Shavelings,' from their habit of shaving the body clean of all hair. Ḫāfī Ḫān, a contemporary, who gives the fullest account of this rising, describes them in the following terms:

'There were four or five thousand of these, who were householders in the *parganas* of Nārnaul and Mēwāt. These men dress like devotees, but they nevertheless carry on agriculture and trade, though their trade is on a small scale. In the way of their religion they have dignified themselves with the title of "Good name," this being the meaning of *Sat-nām*. They are not allowed to acquire wealth in any but a lawful calling. If any one attempts to wrong or oppress them by force, or by exercise of authority, they will not endure it. Many of them have weapons and arms.'[2]

This description, together with their connexion with Nārnaul, would be sufficient to identify them with the Sādhs, were it not for another and contradictory account given by Īśwara-dāsa Nāgara, the Hindu historian, also a contemporary:

'The Satnāmīs are extremely filthy and wicked. In their rules they make no distinction between Hindūs and Musalmāns, and eat pigs and other unclean animals. If a dog is served up before them, they do not show any disgust at it. In sin and immorality they see no blame.'[3]

This, however, is evidently written by a bigoted Hindu, and, in the light of Ḫāfī Ḫān's remarks, it may be considered as a false and libellous attack on a Hindu heresy which acknowledged no caste and refused to worship the customary Hindu deities.

Owing to oppression exercised by Aurangzīb's revenue officials, and led by an old prophetess who promised them invulnerability against the emperor's weapons, they rose in arms. Most of the royal troops were at the time engaged in S. India, and for a space the revolters had considerable success, defeating small local bodies of soldiers. Magical powers were soon attributed to them, and discontented landholders of the neighbourhood adhered to their cause. The revolt had acquired most serious proportions, and the rebels had sacked Nārnaul and other towns and had approached Delhi, when Aurangzīb sent against them a large force, protected by rival spells to counteract their magic. There was a bloody and obstinate battle, in which several thousands of the Satnāmīs were slain and the rest put to flight. This terminated the revolt.

LITERATURE.—The principal authorities, on which the foregoing account has been based, are H. H. Wilson, *Sketch of the Religious Sects of the Hindus*, London, 1861, p. 352 ff., and W. Crooke, *Tribes and Castes of the North-Western Provinces and Oudh*, Calcutta, 1896, iv. 245 ff. Wilson gives some earlier authorities not quoted here. Crooke's account is especially full and valuable, and the reader is referred to it for further particulars. Cf. also *PNQ* i. [1883–84] 1033; *NINQ* i. [1891–92] 790, ii. [1892–93] 429; and D. C. J. Ibbetson, *Outlines of Panjāb Ethnography*, Calcutta, 1883, § 521.

For the Satnāmī revolt see Sāki Musta'idd Ḫān, in H. M. Elliot, *Hist. of India as told by its own Historians*, London, 1867–77, vii. 185 f., and Ḫāfī Ḫān, *ib.* p. 294 ff.; N. Manucci, *Storia do Mogor*, tr. W. Irvine, do. 1907, ii. 167 ff.; Jadunāth Sarkār, 'Satnamis and Sikhs: 17th Century,' in *The Modern Review*, xix. [Calcutta, 1916] 385.

G. A. GRIERSON.

SADHAN-PANTHĪS.—The Sadhan-panthīs, a petty Vaiṣṇava sect of Benares, founded by Sadhan, a butcher, who is said to have lived there in the 17th cent., are really nothing more than a group of men of the despised butcher caste, who would not be received as members by any respectable Vaiṣṇava community, and therefore formed a sect for themselves. So far as is known, they have no distinctive tenets, professing to follow the ordinary Ramāwat doctrines (see art. RĀMĀNANDĪS).

In order to lend respectability to their founder, they assert that, although he sold meat, he never slaughtered animals, but purchased it ready slain. For weighing his wares he had a marvellous *śālagrāma* stone, which became any weight that was for the time required, from the smallest to the greatest. This was given to him by a wandering ascetic, and he worshipped it so devoutly that Viṣṇu was propitiated, and conferred upon him all his desires. When on a pilgrimage, a Brāhmaṇa woman fell in love with him, and, misinterpreting his rejection of her advances, murdered her husband. When Sadhan still refused to have anything to do with her, she burnt herself on her husband's funeral pyre. Sadhan thereupon remarked, 'No one knows the ways of woman; she kills her husband and becomes a *satī*,' which has passed into a proverb, and has been adopted as the tag for a popular folk-tale current in many parts of India.[1]

LITERATURE.—H. H. Wilson, *Sketch of the Religious Sects of the Hindus*, London, 1861, p. 181, where the sect is called 'Sadhaná Panthis'; M. A. Sherring, *Hindu Tribes and Castes in Benares*, Calcutta, Bombay, and London, 1872–81, i. 266.

G. A. GRIERSON.

SĀDHĀRAṆA BRĀHMA SAMĀJ.—When Keshab Chandra Sen married his daughter to the Mahārājā of Kuch Bihār in 1877, the majority of the members of his society, the Brāhma Samāj of India, rose in opposition and tried to depose him from the leadership.[2] Failing to do this, they left the Samāj, and, after consulting with the various Brāhma Samājes throughout the country, formed a new society, the Sādhāraṇa Brāhma Samāj. The word *sādhāraṇa* means 'general,' and corresponds to the broad, democratic character of the new society and its organization. The chief desire of the leaders was to continue the theistic teaching, social service, and philanthropy which had been Keshab's own programme when the Brāhma Samāj of India was founded; but they were also determined to have no autocratic leadership such as Keshab's rule had developed into.

The Sādhārana Samāj has had no outstanding leader, and its history is a story of quiet steady growth without any remarkable events. It is now the one solid and influential section of the Brāhma

[1] They are very diffuse, and contain much repetition. Full translations are given by Wilson, *Religious Sects of the Hindus*, p. 354 f., and Crooke, iv. 248 f.

[2] *Ap.* Elliot, *Hist. of India*, vii. 294.

[3] Quoted by Jadunāth Sarkār, 'Satnamis and Sikhs,' in *The Modern Review*, xix. 385.

[1] See, *e.g.*, G. A. Grierson, *Hātim's Songs and Stories*, London, 1919, story iii.

[2] See art. BRĀHMA SAMĀJ, §§ 5–7.

movement; for the old and conservative Ādi Samāj has little vigour left, Keshab's New Dispensation Samāj is rendered impotent through divisions and quarrelling, and even the Prārthanā Samāj of Bombay shows little power to make progress. The Calcutta Samāj with its group of buildings in Cornwallis Street is by far the strongest of the Sādhāran societies, but there are many smaller bodies scattered over India. The governing organization is in Calcutta.

The work is carried on by a large general committee representative of all the local Samājes, and an executive committee. The actual workers are of three types—missionaries, unordained workers, and lay volunteers. There are eight ordained missionaries, and on them falls the heavy work of general supervision and of touring and preaching throughout India. The nine unordained workers are all grouped under the Sādhan Āśram, or Training Institute, in Calcutta, but there are branches in three other towns. In the Sevak Mandali, or Lay Workers' Union, there are fifty members.

Besides the ministerial work required in Calcutta and in the 47 affiliated Samājes, and the missionary propaganda, the most interesting feature of the work is the Brāhma Mission on the Khāsi Hills, where Brāhma unitarianism is being offered to uncultured hill-people, and various educational and philanthropic activities are carried on.

The propaganda of the Samāj seems to be most successful at present in the Telugu field and in Travancore.

The Samāj publishes a weekly in English called *The Indian Messenger* and a fortnightly in Bengali called *Tattvakaumudī*. East Bengal publishes a vernacular monthly called the *Sevaka*, while the *Brahmabādī* appears at Barisal, the *Brahmaprachāraka* in Lahore, and the *Dharmasādhanī* in Coconada. The Samāj in Madras publishes an English weekly, *Humanity*.

There is some reason for asking whether the Samāj is not nearing a crisis in its history. For many years the progressives have been able to keep what may be called the Hinduizing party within the Samāj well in check, but there are signs that the latter section is rapidly growing in power. The change is traceable in large measure to the increasing vigour and boldness of the various movements within Hinduism for its full defence and re-organization; but it has also been considerably hastened by the teaching and influence of Rabindra Nath Tagore. So far as one can see, the reactionaries have not yet agreed on a definite policy, but their teaching and opinions would unquestionably tend to check aggressive theism in favour of the more general atmosphere of the higher Hinduism. If this party should gain the upper hand, the Samāj will clearly be in grave peril.

The following, taken from the Report for 1910, is the official statement of the principles of the Sādhārana Samāj:

'(1) There is only one God who is the Creator, Preserver and Saviour of this world. He is spirit; He is infinite in power, wisdom, love, justice and holiness; He is omnipresent, eternal and blissful.

(2) The human soul is immortal, and capable of infinite progress, and is responsible to God for its doings.

(3) God is to be worshipped in spirit and in truth. Divine worship is necessary for attaining true felicity and salvation.

(4) To love God and to carry out His will in all the concerns of life constitute true worship.

(5) Prayer and dependence on God and a constant realization of His presence are the means of attaining spiritual growth.

(6) No created object is to be worshipped as God, nor is any person or book to be considered as infallible and as the sole means of salvation; but truth is to be reverently accepted from all scriptures and from the teaching of all persons without distinction of creed or country.

(7) The Fatherhood of God and the Brotherhood of man and kindness to all living beings are the essence of true religion.

(8) God rewards virtue, and punishes sin. His punishments are remedial and not eternal.

(9) Cessation from sin accompanied by sincere repentance is the only atonement for it; and union with God in wisdom, goodness and holiness is true salvation.'

LITERATURE.—Sivanath Sastri, *Hist. of the Brahmo Samaj*, Calcutta, 1911–12, ii. 119 ff., *Mission of the Brahmo Samaj*, do. 1910; J. N. Farquhar, *Modern Religious Movements in India*, New York, 1915, pp. 54 f., 70 ff.

J. N. FARQUHAR.

SĀDHU.

SĀDHU.—*Sādhu* is a Sanskrit word literally meaning 'straight,' and hence 'pure,' 'holy.' In modern India it is commonly applied, as an equivalent to 'saintlike,' to any respected Hindu saint or devotee. In the Hindī language the final *u* is commonly dropped, and the resultant word Sādh (*q.v.*) is also used to connote a certain sect.

G. A. GRIERSON.

SĀGAR, SAUGOR.

SĀGAR, SAUGOR. — This island, at the mouth of the Hugli, Bengal (lat. 21° 36′ N.; long. 88° 2′ E.), is famous for its annual bathing fair held in January. It lasts for three days and is attended by a multitude of pilgrims from all parts of India, who visit the place to wash away their sins. Before British rule was established in Bengal, it was believed that suicide in the Ganges was a means of obtaining immediate beatification.

At this place, according to W. Ward, 'it is accounted an auspicious sign if the person is speedily seized by a shark, or an alligator; but his future happiness is supposed to be very doubtful if he should remain long in the water before he is drowned. The British Government, for some years past, has sent a guard of sepoys to prevent persons from murdering themselves and their children at this junction of the Ganges with the sea, at the annual festivals held in this place.' The same writer adds that in 1805 he saw a Brāhman woman 'dripping with wet and shivering with cold, who had just been prevented from drowning herself, and during my continuance there I heard of several mothers who had been prevented from drowning their children.'[1]

The island derives its name from Sagara, whose story is told in the *Vishṇu Purāṇa*.[2]

He was of the solar race, king of Ayodhya. He performed the Aśvamedha or horse-sacrifice; but, guarded though it was by his sixty thousand sons, the horse was carried off to Pātāla, the nether world. Sagara ordered his sons to recover it, and, digging their way down, they found Kapila, the sage, engaged in meditation. They accused him of the theft, and the enraged saint, looking upon them, reduced them to ashes by means of the sacred flame which issued from his body. Anśumat found their ashes, and begged Kapila to pardon them and restore them to heaven. He promised that the grandson of Anśumat should accomplish this by bringing down the river of heaven. When Sagara heard this, he completed his sacrifice, and called the chasm which his sons had dug Sāgara, the ocean. Bhagīratha, grandson of Anśumat, by the force of his austerities brought down the Ganges from heaven, and its waters cleansed the sons of Sagara, and their spirits became fitted for the death rites and for admission to heaven, or Svarga.

Sagara was possibly a historical personage, who warred with the Śakas, Yavanas, Kāmbojas, Pāradas, and Pahlavas, northern tribes who invaded India.[3] At the temple of Kapila on the island pilgrims write their names on the walls, or hang a piece of earth or bark on a banyan-tree close by, with a promise of an offering if the boon prayed for be granted.[4]

LITERATURE.—H. H. Wilson, *Essays and Lectures chiefly on the Religion of the Hindus*, London, 1862, ii. 164 ff.; *IGI* xxi. [1908] 366; W. J. Wilkins, *Modern Hinduism*, London, 1887, p. 255 ff.; T. Bowrey, *A Geographical Account of the Countries round the Bay of Bengal, 1669–79* (Hakluyt Society Publications), do. 1905, p. 202 f.

W. CROOKE.

SAGHALIEN.

SAGHALIEN.—See AINUS, GILYAKS.

1 *View of the Hist., Lit., and Relig. of the Hindoos*, Serampore, 1815, ii. 314. For religious suicide in India see Crooke, *PR*² i. 256, ii. 169; Rājendralāla Mitra, *The Indo-Aryans*, London, 1881, i. 70; and for offering first-born children to the Ganges *NINQ* iv. [1894–95] 187.

2 ed. H. H. Wilson, London, 1840, p. 373 ff.

3 V. A. Smith, *The Early Hist. of India*², Oxford, 1908, p. 190.

4 H. H. Wilson, *Essays*, ii. 169; cf. *FL* iv. [1893] 458.

SAINTS AND MARTYRS.

SAINTS AND MARTYRS (Buddhist).—The popular notion of the saint, as a being of eminent holiness, and especially as one of the immediate disciples of the Master, holds a prominent place in early Buddhism. The term is used occasionally as a technical translation of *arhat* (*q.v.*), but this does not correspond exactly with the usual idea of the saints of history. These are rather the apostles of Buddhism (*anubuddha*, 'minor Buddhas') or 'Buddha-sons,' such as Ānanda the favourite disciple, who did not win *arhat*-ship till after Buddha's death; Asita, the Simeon of Buddhism; the two chief disciples, Sāriputta and Moggallāna; or Anāthapiṇḍika and Visākhā, the great lay disciples.

1. Saints in the Buddha legend.—Starting from the historical nucleus of the Buddha and his first followers, the records of saints form an integral part of the Buddha legend. This account is a growth, and, though traces of combination, accretion, and systematization have been pointed out in it,[1] it has not yet been sufficiently analyzed to make it possible to treat it otherwise than as legend.

The legends in their earliest attainable form are doubtless the separate stories that occur in the various parts of the *Suttas*, but some which we should naturally expect to find there are omitted. In the *Majjhima*, no. 26, Buddha tells how he left his weeping parents, removed his hair and beard, put on the yellow robe, and went out to a homeless life; how, after following two teachers, he left them in disgust, went to Uruvelā, attained enlightenment, and was persuaded by Brahmā to preach the Doctrine; how he thought of first doing so to his former teachers, but, on being told by certain divinities that they were dead, went to his five former disciples, and preached to them. In this account nothing is said of his seeing the four omens that induced him to leave the world, of the flight from his palace with Chhanna, of the food given by Sujātā under the *bodhi*-tree, or of his first two lay converts.

Part of this occurs in the *Vinaya*,[2] but, besides showing variations of detail, it differs from the *Sutta* account in the addition of incidents to the story and a continuation of further legends. It is here that some of the chief legends of the saints occur. Beginning with the first events after the enlightenment, it inserts the story of the conversion of the two laymen, Tapussa and Bhallika, recounts the conversion of the five disciples, and continues with the stories of the conversion of Yasa, his parents, and his companions, and of the three Kassapas, the visit of King Bimbisāra, the conversion of the two chief disciples, Sāriputta and Moggallāna, of Upāli, and the admission of Buddha's son Rāhula to the order. The whole forms a quasi-historical sequence, and, apart from the extremely composite *Mahāparinibbāna Sutta*,[3] an account of the last few months of Buddha's life, it is the nearest approach in the Scriptures to a connected Buddha legend. Several stories prominent in later accounts occur in the *Sutta Nipāta*—Bimbisāra's visit to Buddha at the time of his renunciation, Māra's temptation (which is here represented as before the enlightenment), and the visit of the sage Asita, or Kāladevala, to the infant Buddha.

[1] H. Oldenberg, *Buddha, his Life, his Doctrine, his Order*, Eng. tr., London, 1882, Excursus 2, p. 411 ff.
[2] *Mahāvagga*, i. ff.
[3] *Dīgha*, no. 16

2. Development of the legends.—These *Sutta* accounts, with perhaps the *Vinaya* tales as a second stratum, form the basis of the legends of saints. The *Suttas* themselves, however, reveal different stages, and show evidence of systematization. In the *Mahāpadāna Sutta*[1] a list of the seven Buddhas is given. Not only has the historical Buddha a chief attendant, two chief disciples, a certain *bodhi*-tree, and so on, but all the Buddhas have the same. In the *Buddhavaṃsa*, also a canonical text, the list of Buddhas is increased to 25 (besides three whose history is not given), and to their common characteristics are added two chief female disciples, and four chief lay attendants, two men and two women. In the case of the historical Buddha, these disciples and attendants are among the foremost saints.

There is here the possibility that certain features in the story of Gautama Buddha are due to the adoption of legends originally relating to previous Buddhas, but nothing as to the historical existence of these can be affirmed. Fausböll indeed made the extraordinary statement[2] that one of them (Kanakamuni; Pāli Koṇāgamana) was a real historical person, because a *stūpa* was erected to him, and Aśoka worshipped before it and restored it. But the legend of previous Buddhas was an established belief certainly before the time of Aśoka, and the *stūpa* to Kanakamuni merely illustrates the existence of this belief. The historicity of the person commemorated is quite another matter.

Further systematization is shown in the *Aṅguttara*, i. 24 ff., where a list of 80 of the chief disciples is given, divided into the usual four classes of monks, nuns, laymen, and laywomen. Each has a special epithet descriptive of the feature in which he or she was eminent. But the most comprehensive list occurs in the *Thera-* and *Therīgāthā*. Most of these are said in the commentary to have won complete knowledge (*aññā*), or to have attained *arhat*-ship. There are 259 possible names of monks, and over 70 of nuns, many of whom are otherwise unknown, but both lists contain the prominent disciples of the *Suttas*. The history of each is given in Dhammapāla's commentary.[3] Cf. artt. ĀNANDA, DEVADATTA, MOGGALLĀNA, SĀRIPUTTA.

3. Extra-canonical legends.—The chief later development of the Buddha legend is the *Nidānakathā*, the introduction to the *Jātaka*, the author of which in various places refers for his authorities to the *Vinaya* and *Suttas*, as well as to the 'commentary' (*Aṭṭhakathā*) and 'other commentaries.' The commentary mentioned is probably the *Mahāaṭṭhakathā*, or Great Commentary, a work which Siṅhalese tradition says was fixed at the first

[1] *Dīgha*, no. 14.
[2] *The Jātaka with its Commentary*, ed. V. Fausböll, tr. T. W. Rhys Davids, London, 1877–91, vol. vii. 'Index to the *Jātaka*,' p. xi.
[3] Translated in C. A. F. Rhys Davids' *Psalms of the Early Buddhists.*

Council, and introduced by Mahinda with the Scriptures into Ceylon.[1] Whatever its actual form and origin, it is no doubt mainly from this that the extra-canonical legends have come. Many are found in the existing commentaries on the *Jātaka* and *Dhammapada*.

4. Influence of Brāhman legends.—In the case of two saints Windisch derives features of their legends from Brāhman sources.[2] The *Mahāvastu*[3] gives a description of Moggallāna's visit to the hells and heavens. Evidently, says Windisch, the account in the *Mahābhārata*[4] of his pious ancestor Mudgala, or Maudgalya, who obtains the favour of going to heaven with his body, has been transferred to Moggallāna. But the question of transference is more complicated than this. The late account in the *Mahāvastu* goes back to earlier Pāli versions that do not mention Moggallāna. In *Jātaka* 541 a visit to the hells and heavens with their description is told of King Nimi, and in *Jātaka* 530 a similar description occurs which has several verses in common with the *Mahāvastu* account.[5] That there has been a borrowing of legends is probable, but it is not possible to say that this borrowing is direct,[6] and Moggallāna does not owe his individuality to Brāhmanism. Windisch grants that he is an historical character.

The other instance is Asita, or Kāladevala, the sage who visited the infant Gautama. In this case it is probable that Buddhism has adopted the name of a character well known in Brāhman legend. He is said in the commentary on *Sutta Nipāta* 679 to have been *purohita*, or family priest, to Suddhodana's father, but there is no trace of the Buddhist legend in Brāhmanism.

5. Saints in the Mahāyāna.—In the Mahāyāna schools the legendary basis is much the same, but further developed. Some entirely new saints in the line of patriarchs appear, such as Upagupta, who came from the bottom of the sea to prevent Māra from disturbing a sacrifice celebrated by Aśoka,[7] and Asaṅga, who in the 5th cent. A.D. went up to the Tusita heaven and received the doctrine of the Void as a new revelation from Maitreya.[8] But, though the disciples remain as interlocutors in the *Suttas*, their importance as a religious and devotional factor is overshadowed by the growth of *bodhisattva*-worship and of new Buddhas. See artt. BODHISATTVA, ĀDIBUDDHA, AMITĀYUS, ASAṄGA, AVALOKITEŚVARA, MAÑJUŚRĪ.

6. Saint-worship. — The worship of Buddhas and their apostles consists in the honour done to them, their relics, or other memorials. The worship confers merit, and consists in reverent salutation, adornment of the shrines with garlands and unguents, and a ceremonial procession round.[9] The most general term for a memorial is *chetiya*, usually divided into bodily relics (*sārīrika*), objects that have served the use of a Buddha (*paribhogika*), and shrines or memorials (*uddesika*).[10] The *chetiyas* include sacred localities, trees, and commemorative buildings, cairns, or *stūpas*, which may also contain relics.

1 *Mahāvaṃsa*, xxxiii. 100.
2 'Brahmanischer Einfluss im Buddhismus,' *Aufsätze Ernst Kuhn gewidmet*, Breslau, 1916, p. 1 ff.
3 i. 4 ff.
4 iii., Adhyāya 259 and 260; cf. J. Muir, *Orig. Sanskrit Texts*, London, 1858–72, v. 324.
5 *Jātaka*, v. 266; *Mahāvastu*, i. 9.
6 O. Franke, 'Jātaka-Mahābhārata-Parallelen,' *Vienna Or. Journ.* xx. [1906] 317 ff.
7 C. Duroiselle, 'Upagutta et Māra,' *Bull. de l'École française de l'Extrême-Orient*, jan.–juin, 1904; *Divyāvadāna*, p. 356 ff.; another version in Tāranātha, *Gesch. des Buddhismus in Indien*, tr. A. Schiefner, Petrograd, 1869, p. 18.
8 S. Lévi, Introd. to *Mahāyāna-sūtrālaṃkāra*, Paris, 1911, p. 2.
9 *Kathāvatthu*, xiii. 2.
10 *Jātaka*, iv. 228; *Bodhivaṃsa*, p. 59.

In the *Mahāparinibbāna Sutta*[1] the Buddha gives a list of four classes of persons who are worthy to have a *stūpa* erected to them—a Buddha, a *pratyekabuddha*, a disciple of the Master, and a universal king. This indicates Buddhist belief at the time of the composition of this *Sutta*, and the account of Fa-Hian[2] in the 5th cent. shows its full development. He found in India *stūpas* to the Buddha, previous Buddhas, and to such saints as Ānanda, Sāriputta, Moggallāna, and Mahāpajāpatī Gotamī. The development of the idea of the patron saint is also shown in the nuns making offerings at Ānanda's shrine, because it was he who persuaded Buddha to admit nuns to the order. Similarly the patron saint of the novices was Rāhula.[3]

Pilgrimages to places memorable in the life of a Buddha are also recommended in the same *Sutta*,[4] and Buddha prophesies:

> 'There will come believing monks and nuns, laymen and laywomen, and say, "Here the Tathāgata was born," "Here the Tathāgata became supreme Buddha with highest supreme enlightenment," "Here the Tathāgata began to turn the highest Wheel of the Doctrine," and "Here the Tathāgata attained Nirvāṇa with the Nirvāṇa that leaves no element behind." And all they who die while making pilgrimages to *chetiyas* shall, with the dissolution of the body after death, be born in the happy world of heaven.'[5]

References to pre-Buddhistic *chetiyas* are common in the Scriptures, and there is no doubt that *chetiya*-worship is merely a continuation of a general Hindu custom. It is referred to several times in the *Vinaya* as being an established practice.[6] See art. CHAITYA.

7. Martyrs.—The martyrs of a religion usually arise from persecution, but it is unnecessary to discuss here the question of Buddhist persecutions, as none is recorded in the Scriptures, and the later accounts of Brāhman and Jain hostility have not given rise to a martyrology. Among the early saints extra-canonical records mention the murder of Moggallāna as due to the enmity of the Jains, who hired robbers to kill him, because he was able to go to heaven and find out how the disciples of Buddha went to heaven and those of the naked ascetics to hell.[7]

The real martyrology of Buddhism is the *Jātaka* commentary, which records the sufferings and repeated death of the *bodhisattva* and his disciples, especially in exhibiting the virtues of patience and self-sacrifice. In *Jātaka* 313 the *bodhisattva* as an ascetic preaches the Doctrine to the royal *harīm*, and is tortured and cut to pieces by the king. In several the persecution is due to the jealousy of Devadatta, a motive which is already found in the Scriptures. The *bodhisattva* suffers for the sake of the *Dharma*, but, except in the case of the legends of Jains, it cannot be said that the persecution is due specially to anti-Buddhistic hostility; nor is there any definite historical evidence for the supposed Brāhmanical persecutions, which were once supposed to have exterminated Buddhism in India.[8]

The Mahāyāna teaching degenerates into the most grotesque and gruesome tales of suffering (often self-inflicted) for the sake of the *Dharma*. They are imaginative developments, due to the idea of acquiring merit in repeated births for the

1 *Dīgha*, ii. 142; *Dialogues of the Buddha*, ii. 156.
2 See art. YUAN CHWANG.
3 *A Record of Buddhist Kingdoms*, tr. J. Legge, Oxford, 1886, pp. 44–46.
4 *Dīgha*, ii. 140; *Dialogues*, ii. 153.
5 *Dīgha*, ii. 141; *Dialogues*, ii. 153.
6 *Nissaggiya*, xxx. 2; *Pāchittiya*, lxxxii. 2.
7 *Jātaka*, v. 125 ff., tr. p. 62 ff.; *Dhammapada Comm.* iii. 65; R. S. Hardy, *A Manual of Budhism*², London, 1890, p. 349 ff.
8 See H. H. Wilson, 'On Buddha and Buddhism,' *JRAS* xvi. [1856] 229 ff.; R. S. Hardy, *The Legends and Theories of the Buddhists*, London, 1886, p. 205; T. W. Rhys Davids, 'Persecution of the Buddhists in India,' *JPTS* [1896] 87 ff.; V. A. Smith, *The Early History of India*³, Oxford, 1914, p. 202.

sake of becoming a *bodhisattva*, rather than compositions having any relation to history or legend.

LITERATURE.—References to the sources are given throughout. See also C. A. F. Rhys Davids, Introductions to *Psalms of the Early Buddhists*, 2 vols., London, 1909–13; E. Müller, Introduction to *Paramatthadipanī*, pt. v., *Commentary on the Therigāthā*, do. 1893; Mabel Bode, 'Women Leaders of the Buddhist Reformation,' *JRAS*, 1893, p. 517 ff.; K. F. Köppen, *Die Religion des Buddha*, i., Berlin, 1857.

EDWARD J. THOMAS.

SAINTS AND MARTYRS (Chinese).—The word *sêng*, which has been adopted in Chinese Christian literature as the translation of 'holy,' hardly suggests that relation to the divine which is connoted by the English word. It lays stress rather on the idea of perfect realization of human nature, and at least as much on the intellectual as on the moral side, whence it is also often translated 'sage.' Of those of the Confucian school who are reckoned as entitled to be called *sèng jên*, 'holy men,' 'sages,' Confucius (*q.v.*) is the latest and most famous. The doctrine which he transmitted and taught is the 'holy teaching.'

The other teachings in China—Taoism and Buddhism—have also those in whom their ideal of human nature or conduct received embodiment.

E.g., the *Shên Sien Thung Kàm* gives 'a series of biographical sketches for the most part legendary and fabulous, of upwards of 800 saints, sages and divinities selected chiefly from the ranks of Taoism but some Buddhist characters are also admitted into the number.'[1]

The Christian Church in China, as elsewhere, is proving itself to be the nursery of that type of character which is entitled in the Christian sense to be called 'holy.'[2]

It has been said that in the biographical records of the Chinese we find 'extraordinarily few instances of religious fanaticism, bigotry, and persecution; still fewer, if any, examples of men and women who have suffered for their faith, when mere verbal recantation would have saved them from a dreaded fate.'[3] The supremacy of right even over life itself is, however, recognized: 'I desire life and I desire right; if I cannot keep both together, I will give up life and choose right';[4] and in China there have never been lacking those who have been willing to lay down their lives for an idea to the truth and worth of which they thus witnessed; nor, as during the Boxer troubles, have there been lacking martyrs in the full Christian sense of that term.

P. J. MACLAGAN.

SAINTS AND MARTYRS (Christian).—**I. Dogmatic teaching.**—The Roman Church, together with the Oriental Churches, and notably the Orthodox Eastern Church in all its branches, considers the doctrine of the veneration of saints to be an integral part of Catholic tradition. Both by Greeks and by Latins this teaching is held to follow from the conception of the Church's unity. In the *Longer Orthodox Catechism* of Philaret,[5] *e.g.*, we have the following questions and answers:

'262. Q. Is there likewise unity between the Church on earth and the Church in heaven?

A. Doubtless there is, both by their common relation to one Head, our Lord Jesus Christ, and by mutual communion with one another.

263. Q. What means of communion has the Church on earth with the Church in heaven?

A. The prayer of faith and love. The faithful who belong to the Church militant upon earth, in offering their prayers to God, call at the same time to their aid the saints who belong to the Church in heaven; and these, standing on the highest steps of approach to God, by their prayers and intercessions purify, strengthen, and offer before God the prayers of the faithful living upon earth, and by the will of God work graciously and beneficently upon them, either by invisible virtue, or by distinct apparitions, and in divers other ways.'

[1] A. Wylie, *Notes on Chinese Literature*, London, 1867, p. 178.
[2] *E.g.*, Mrs. Howard Taylor, *Pastor Hsi*, London, 1904; C. Campbell Brown, *A Chinese St. Francis*, do. 1912.
[3] H. A. Giles, *Confucianism and its Rivals*, London, 1915, p. 1.
[4] Mencius, VI. ii. 10. 1.
[5] See *ERE* vi. 432[b].

The *Catechism* then goes on to declare that the rule of the Church upon earth to invoke in prayer the saints of the Church in heaven is grounded upon 'a holy tradition, the principle of which is to be seen also in holy Scripture,' and it appeals to 1 Ch 29^{18}, where David cried out in prayer, 'O Lord, the God of Abraham, of Isaac, and of Israel, our fathers,' 'exactly,' we are told, 'as now the Orthodox Church calls upon Christ our true God, by the prayers of His most pure Mother and all His saints.' Scripture is further appealed to as supplying warrant for the mediatory prayer of the saints in heaven (Rev $8^{3f.}$), for the fact of beneficent apparitions of saints from heaven (Mt $27^{52f.}$), and for the belief that the saints after their departure work miracles through certain earthly means (2 K 13^{21} and Ac 19^{12}). Moreover, all these points of ecclesiastical tradition are illustrated and enforced by testimonies cited from the great Greek Fathers.

Not less clearly defined is the belief of the Roman Church formulated in a decree of the Council of Trent and summarized in these words of the Creed of Pope Pius IV.:

'In like manner I hold that the saints reigning with God are to be venerated and invoked, and that they offer prayers to God for us, and that their relics are to be venerated.'

Although no anathemas are attached to the canon drafted by the Council itself, the Fathers declared that those who deny the lawfulness of invoking the saints 'hold an impious opinion' (*impie sentire*); on the other hand, the affirmative portion of the canon is couched in studiously moderate language:

'The saints reigning with Christ offer their prayers to God on behalf of men, moreover it is good and useful to invoke them as suppliants and to have recourse to their prayers, support, and help, in order to obtain benefits from God through His Son, Jesus Christ our Lord, who is our only Redeemer and Saviour.'[1]

The Council also goes on to say:

'The holy bodies of holy martyrs, and of others now living with Christ—which bodies were the living members of Christ and the temple of the Holy Ghost (1 Co 3^{16}), and which are by Him to be raised unto eternal life, and to be glorified—are to be venerated by the faithful, through which bodies many benefits are bestowed by God on men.'[2]

Finally, we have this very careful statement of the Catholic teaching with reference to the use of images:

'Moreover, that the images of Christ, of the Virgin Mother of God, and of the other saints, are to be had and retained particularly in churches, and that due honour and veneration are to be given them; not that any divinity or virtue is believed to be in them, on account of which they are to be worshipped; or that anything is to be asked of them; or that trust is to be reposed in images, as was of old done by the Gentiles, who placed their hope in idols; but because the honour which is shown them is referred to the prototypes which those images represent; in such wise that by the images which we kiss, and before which we uncover the head, and prostrate ourselves, we adore Christ, and we venerate the saints, whose similitudes they bear; as, by the decrees of Councils, and especially of the second Synod of Nicæa, has been defined against the opponents of images.'[3]

Similar limitations are emphasized in the authoritative *Roman Catechism*, issued in accordance with the Tridentine decrees. It is there pointed out in detail that there is a wide difference between the prayers addressed to God and those addressed to the saints:

'We ask God to grant blessings, we ask the saints to be our advocates. To God we say: "Have mercy on us"; to the saints we commonly say: "Pray for us"; and if at times we ask the saints also to have mercy on us, it is in a different sense. We beg of them, as they are pitiful, to take compassion on us and to interpose in our behalf.'[4]

In the 22nd of the Thirty-nine Articles the Church of England, following the example set in the *Augsburg Confession* and other dogmatic pronouncements of the Reformers, condemns

'the Romish doctrine concerning Purgatory, Pardons, Worshipping and Adoration, as well of Images as of Reliques, and also invocation of Saints' as 'a fond thing vainly invented, and grounded upon no warranty of Scripture, but rather repugnant to the Word of God.'

[1] Sess. xxv. [2] *Ib.* [3] *Ib.*
[4] *Roman Catechism*, Eng. tr., Dublin, 1829, p. 466 f.

It has been maintained by many, and notably in recent years by Bishop John Wordsworth of Salisbury, that the 'Romish doctrine' here rejected was the official teaching of the Church of Rome as formulated by the scholastic theologians and the Council of Trent. The admission, indeed, is made that the decree of the Council quoted above was passed only in Dec. 1563, some months after the Article in question had been accepted by both Houses of Convocation; but, on the other hand, as Wordsworth[1] contended, there are references both to purgatory and to the veneration of saints in the decree of the 22nd Session, passed on 17th Sept. 1562. In reply to this, Darwell Stone[2] and others have urged with reason that in the earlier Tridentine canon there is no proper reference to the *invocation* of saints or to relics, images, and pardons. Hence they consider themselves still free to hold that by the 'Romish doctrine' referred to was meant, not the official teaching of Roman authority, but the extravagances of an extreme section. Further, some evidence has been quoted to show that the phrase 'invocation of saints' was used to denote addresses to the saints similar in wording to the adoration which we render to God, and 'formal and absolute prayers tendered to saints, as distinguished from requests for the prayers of the saints.' According to this view, the Articles, both in connexion with the veneration of saints and in dealing with sundry other controverted points, were deliberately framed with a purpose of comprehension rather than exclusion. Consequently the Church of England, it is maintained, only condemned the extreme practices and ways of thought in which the saints, being called upon to grant favours which are in the power of God alone, had been given a prominence in devotion which was derogatory to the divine honour. Thus the question was left open whether the clergy might express approval of the practice of invoking the saints in the limited sense of seeking from them the help of their prayers.[3] Undoubtedly many Anglican theologians of the 17th cent. seemed to adopt this view, and the extreme iconoclasm of men like Hooper and Latimer soon gave place to the academic speculations of the Caroline divines. Bishop W. Forbes of Edinburgh, whose *Considerationes modestæ . . . de . . . invocatione sanctorum* was published posthumously in 1658, approximated closely to the Roman and Orthodox position. In one chapter[4] he defends the proposition that the simple invoking of or appealing to the angels and saints to pray to God with us and for us is not to be reprobated as either useless or unlawful. Still even the most advanced of the High Church party in England were hardly prepared to go as far as this. In 1716 proposals were made by the non-juring bishops, who called themselves 'the Catholic Remnant of the British Churches,' for a concordat with the Orthodox Eastern Churches. Among matters recognized as 'the five Points of present Disagreement' we find the two following heads:

'Though they [the Remnant] call the Mother of our Lord Blessed, and magnify the Grace of God which so highly exalted her, they were afraid of giving the glory of God to a creature, or to run to any extreme by unduly blessing or magnifying her.

As to angels and saints, they were jealous of detracting in the least from the Mediation of Jesus Christ, and therefore could not use a direct Invocation to any of them, the Blessed Virgin herself not excepted.'

The four Oriental patriarchs, in reply, appeal to the distinction which had been recognized even in the West from the time of St. Augustine onwards, and which both the Roman and the Orthodox Church still emphasize.

[1] *The Invocation of Saints and the Twenty-second Article*, London, 1908, and in *The Guardian*, 26th May, 2nd June, 21st July, 1909.

[2] *The Invocation of Saints*[3], p. 39 ff.

[3] Stone, p. 49.

[4] Pt. ii. ch. 3.

'The Greeks,' say the patriarchs, 'know how to make a distinction in worship, and they give that of Latria to God only, and that of Dulia to the holy Apostles, martyrs and righteous and godly Fathers, honouring them as faithful servants and true friends of God. They worship our Lady, the Virgin Mother of God with Hyperdulia, not as God, but as the θεοτόκος and Mother of God; not with Latria—God forbid, that would be blasphemy; God alone they worship with Latria—but they make her their intercessor with Him for post-baptismal sin, and hope through her to receive remission from Him.'

The patriarchs then go on to make it clear that, upon this head and in the matter of the invocation of saints, their position is unalterable. Indeed the tone of their reply to the English bishops is not conciliatory:

'Set yourselves free from the heavy bondage and the captivity of prejudice, and submit yourselves to those true doctrines which have been received from the beginning and the traditions of the holy fathers and are not opposed to the Holy Scriptures.'[1]

Of late years among a certain school of Russian theologians there has been a tendency, probably fostered by Anglican influences, to discover a distinction between the Orthodox and the Roman point of view as to the relations of the Church militant and the Church triumphant. 'The Easterns,' W. J. Birkbeck[2] insists, 'when they think of the Church, think more of it as a whole than is the custom in the West.' They are familiar with the conception of St. John Chrysostom,[3] who speaks of the body of Christ as 'the faithful from all parts of the world, who are, have been, and shall be.' Mutual intercessions are, it is said, at once the expression and condition of that faith and love which constitute the organism of the Church. Birkbeck writes:

'One of the most solemn thoughts that I have met with in conversing with Russians is, that not only is each one of us assisted by the prayers of the Blessed Virgin and of all saints, but that the saints themselves, and even the glorious and ever-blessed Mother of God, were assisted by the prayers, foreknown to God, of every member of the Church that has lived, or ever will live upon earth.'[4]

But this seems after all to differ very little from the conception of the communion of saints which will be found presented at large in the *Roman Catechism* and elaborated in such a work as that of J. P. Kirsch, *Die Lehre von der Gemeinschaft der Heiligen im christlichen Altertum.* On the other hand, a greater familiarity with the teaching and practice of the Eastern Churches seems to have done something towards modifying the intransigeance of official Anglicanism in this matter of saint-worship. During the Church Congress held at Southampton in 1913 the bishop of London (A. F. Winnington Ingram), who not so long before had visited Russia, preached a sermon on the invocation of saints. After weighing the arguments for and against and rejecting any direct form of invocation, such as 'Saint Andrew, pray for us,' etc., he approved the practice of 'comprecation,' which has been defined as praying to God to receive benefit by means of the prayers of the saints.

'We recognize,' he said, 'the fellowship of the saints in our praise. . . . Why should we not have in the new supplement to the Prayer-Book some form of comprecation which shall recognize more fully their fellowship in prayer?'

2. History.—It is admitted without dispute that the veneration of saints had its starting-point in the veneration of the martyrs who suffered death for the Christian faith. The word 'martyr,' of course, means witness, but already in the NT we have indications of a tendency to use this term as a label, even if not yet exactly to limit it to those who sealed their testimony with their blood. 'Ye shall be my witnesses,' we read in Ac 1^8 (cf.

[1] See A. H. Hore, *Eighteen Centuries of the Orthodox Greek Church*, London, 1899, pp. 597–605, who summarizes the documents published by G. Williams in his *Orthodox Church of the East in the 18th Century*.

[2] A. Riley, *Birkbeck and the Russian Church*, p. 237.

[3] *In Epist. ad Ephes.* hom. x. 1 (*PG* lxii. 75).

[4] Riley, *Birkbeck and the Russian Church*, pp. 237, 345.

Lk 21[13], Jn 15[27], Mt 10[18]) and in Rev 17[6] 'I saw the woman drunken with the blood of the saints, and with the blood of the martyrs (RVm witnesses) of Jesus.' The same document, for which, in the opinion of the present writer, no later date can be assigned than A.D. 96, describes 'underneath the altar the souls of them that had been slain for the word of God, and for the testimony (μαρτυρίαν) which they held. . . . And there was given them to each one a white robe,' etc. (Rev 6[9. 11]). Similarly 'I saw thrones . . . and the souls of them that had been beheaded for the testimony of Jesus' (Rev 20[4]). We do not wish to pronounce too positively, but this looks very like a beginning of cultus, and the evidence becomes unmistakable in the account of the martyrdom of St. Polycarp in the middle of the 2nd century. The pagans and Jews of Smyrna wished the saint's body to be reduced to ashes, 'lest they [the Christians] should abandon the crucified one and begin to worship this man.' The Christians of Smyrna indignantly repudiate the insinuation that they could ever renounce 'the Christ who suffered for the salvation of the whole world,' and they continue :

'For Him, being the Son of God, we adore, but the martyrs, as disciples and imitators of the Lord, we cherish as they deserve for their matchless affection towards their King and teacher. . . . And so we afterwards took up his bones, which are more valuable than precious stones and finer than refined gold, and laid them in a suitable place, where the Lord will permit us to gather ourselves together, as we are able, in gladness and joy and to celebrate the birthday of his martyrdom (τὴν τοῦ μαρτυρίου αὐτοῦ ἡμέραν γενέθλιον) for the commemoration of those who have already fought in the contest and for the training and preparation of those that shall do so hereafter.'[1]

These passages are important as bearing witness not only to the dignity of martyrdom and to the sense of joy and triumph associated with it, but also to the idea of a sacrifice over the martyr's remains, and of an annual commemoration in his honour to be maintained in future years. This 'birthday,' the γενέθλιος (ἡμέρα) or *natale*, was afterwards to become a very conspicuous feature in the calendars and martyrologies. No doubt paganism among both Greeks and Romans had long before been familiar with the yearly commemoration of the illustrious dead ; but, while in the case of the emperors and other famous men it was literally their birthday that was kept in remembrance, the Christian martyr was honoured on the anniversary of his death. The dignity of the martyrs was emphasized in many other ways. Tertullian, Origen, Clement of Alexandria, and Cyprian proclaim it in glowing language.[2] Already in the *Pastor* of Hermas[3] the martyrs are represented as wearing crowns ; Hippolytus,[4] Dionysius of Alexandria,[5] and Tertullian[6] describe them as fellow-judges with Christ, seated beside Him on thrones. The most laudatory epithets—*e.g.* μακάριος, σεμνός, θεῖος, *benedictus*, *beatus*, etc. — are applied to them. On the other hand, we find an intense desire for martyrdom, regarded as a privilege and a trust, manifested by such confessors of the faith as the apostolic Ignatius of Antioch, the nonagenarian Pothinus of Lyons, the boy Origen, the scholarly bishop Cyprian, the mothers of young children like Perpetua and Felicitas, the tender maiden Blandina, with many others of whom authentic records are preserved. Frequently the idea is made prominent that it is Christ Himself who is present and who suffers in the person of the martyr.[7] As a natural consequence, the greatest veneration was shown to the martyrs by the faithful during the period of their incarceration, and, as the letters of St. Cyprian in particular allow us to see, their standing in the Church was altogether exceptional—so much so that their mediation was accepted as decisive when it was exercised in favour of those who sought reconciliation after falling away from the faith. No doubt there were abuses. The Novatianist heresy[1] was an indirect result of a too rigoristic view of the discipline which ought to be followed in such cases. On the other hand, it became a commonplace among the writers of the 3rd cent. to hold that the giving of one's life for Christ, the baptism of blood, was the equivalent of sacramental baptism in its effect of completely remitting sin and rendering the sufferer worthy of immediate admission to the joys of paradise. The passages in Tertullian, Cyprian, and other writers of that age which bear witness to this belief are very numerous.[2] In the contemporary *Acts of the Scillitan Martyrs* (A.D. 180) Nartzalus cries out, when sentence is pronounced, 'Hodie martyres in caelis sumus. Deo gratias.' Further, the martyr's lot while he remained alive was in every way a privileged one. A reflected lustre shone upon his family and even upon the town in which he resided,[3] and he himself, while awaiting in prison the hour of the supreme sacrifice, was an object of solicitude and veneration to all his fellow-Christians. The long passage which stands at the beginning of the 5th book of the *Apostolical Constitutions* probably reflects a much older tradition, and it is in any case very striking :

'If any Christian, on account of the name of Christ, and love and faith towards God, be condemned by the ungodly to the games, to the beasts, or to the mines, do ye not overlook him ; but send to him from your labour and your very sweat for his sustenance, and for a bribe to the soldiers, that he may be eased and taken care of . . . for he that is condemned for the name of the Lord God is an holy martyr, a brother of the Lord, the son of the Most High, a receptacle of the Holy Spirit . . . by being vouchsafed the incorruptible crown, and the testimony of Christ's sufferings and the fellowship of His blood, to be made conformable to the death of Christ for the adoption of children.'

Lucian in his *de Morte Peregrini* satirizes the attentions lavished upon those who suffered for the Christian faith. Moreover, the confessors who, after bearing testimony in bonds, escaped the final ordeal were regarded as the *élite* of the faithful, and their steadfastness in the hour of trial became a sort of title to the episcopal office.[4] In the primitive Church Order, which Schermann has conveniently labelled *ET* (*ecclesiastica traditio*), and which he would trace back to the inspiration of St. Clement of Rome, the martyr (*i.e.* one who has suffered torment for the name of Christ) is described as already possessing the dignity of the priesthood without ordination. Hands are to be laid upon him only when he is to be promoted to the episcopate.[5] Despite the attitude of veneration to which these facts bear witness, we have no satisfactory evidence of any general practice of cultus before the middle of the 3rd century. The origins of this cultus are no doubt to be found in the funeral rites which the Christians, in accordance with the customs of the pagan society in which they lived, paid to their honoured dead. Even in the case of those who had suffered capital punishment, Roman practice usually conceded to the relatives of the deceased the free disposal of their remains. For the most part, therefore, the martyrs, like their fellow-believers, were buried with such observances as everyday usage prescribed, so far at any rate as these rites involved no direct recognition

[1] *Letter of the Smyrnæans*, xvii. f.
[2] See, *e.g.*, the extracts given at length in J. P. Kirsch, *Gemeinschaft der Heiligen*, Eng. tr., pt. ii. ch. 3, p. 73 ff.
[3] *Simil.* viii. 3, 6.
[4] *In Dan.* ii. 37, ed. G. N. Bonwetsch and H. Achelis, i. 112.
[5] *Ap.* Eusebius, *HE* vi. xlii.
[6] *De Resurr. carnis*, 43, and *de Anima*, 55.
[7] Delehaye, *Les Origines du culte des martyrs*, p. 11 ff.

[1] See art. NOVATIANISTS.
[2] See H. Achelis, *Das Christentum in den ersten drei Jahrhunderten*, Leipzig, 1912, ii. 340, 439.
[3] See Delehaye, pp. 12–28.
[4] See Eus. *HE* iii. xx. 6, vi. viii. 7, etc.
[5] See T. Schermann, *Ein Weiherituale*, Munich, 1913, p. 31, and *Die allgemeine Kirchenordnung*, Paderborn, 1914–16, p. 51

of polytheism or pagan superstition. For the sacrifices to the gods was substituted the Eucharistic oblation; the banquets offered to the dead at the tomb were replaced by the Christian love-feast,[1] and the same intervals between the celebrations were observed—3rd day, 9th day, 30th day (which in later centuries became the 'month's mind'), and anniversary. It was no doubt from these elements that the cultus of the Christian martyr took its point of departure. All are agreed that, where the existence of a sepulchral chamber or mausoleum rendered it possible, the Eucharist was celebrated at the grave side, and at this not merely the family but the whole Christian community seems to have assisted. There has, however, been some difference of opinion regarding the manner in which these rites were carried out. F. Wieland,[2] in opposition to the traditional view, holds that 'the breaking of bread' was not originally conceived of as a sacrifice in any proper sense, and that even in the case of martyrs the tomb itself, in the pre-Constantinian period, was not treated as an altar. But the question is mainly one of the date of the development of this sacrificial conception. It certainly did establish itself before long, as J. Wilpert[3] and others have shown. During the ages of persecution the faithful, anxious to live as inconspicuously as possible among their fellow-citizens, very probably emphasized unduly the feature of the funeral banquet, which was common to all, pagans and Christians alike. In the case of the pagans these banquets (*cenæ*) were meals offered to the *manes* of the departed; for the Christian community they were love-feasts which, on the one hand, provided charitably for the needs of the poor, and, on the other, veiled the true nature of the Eucharistic oblation, celebrated as a memorial of the Last Supper. In time the love-feasts led to abuses and were to a large extent suppressed, but the celebration of the liturgy still brought these little assemblies of the faithful together beside the graves of the honoured dead. It was inevitable that this solemn rite, though offered in the same forms at the tomb of the martyr and at that of the ordinary Christian, should in the former case soon assume a different colour in the eyes of the worshippers. Though the liturgy from the earliest times, as still in the East to-day, offered the sacrifice to God *for* (ὑπέρ) the holy apostles and the martyrs, as well as for all the faithful who have fallen asleep, the note of triumph soon came to prevail, whenever the Church paid honour to her champions.

The *Oratio Constantini* tells us how 'the martyr's death is followed by hymns and psalms and songs of praise to the all-seeing God, and a sacrifice is offered in memory of such men, a blameless, innocuous sacrifice.'[4]

Cyril of Jerusalem in the middle of the 4th cent. draws a clear distinction between the commemoration in the liturgy of 'patriarchs, prophets, apostles and martyrs, that by their prayers and mediation God may receive our petitions,' and, on the other hand, the appeal made in behalf of 'the holy fathers and bishops and all those who have fallen asleep,' whose souls, says Cyril, we are assured will be benefited by the offering of this most holy sacrifice.[5] Half a century later we find both Chrysostom[6] and Augustine explaining the commemoration of the martyrs in the liturgy in much the same sense. Their names are recited, says the latter, but they are not prayed for;[7] and in another place he urges that, when the sacrifice of the altar and alms are offered for all Christians departed, 'it is a sacrifice of thanksgiving for the perfect and a propitiation for those whose virtue is incomplete.'[1] At this date, the close of the 4th cent., we find all the great orators of the Church both in the East and in the West preaching panegyrics of the holy martyrs before vast audiences assembled to pay respect to these champions of the faith on their festivals, and at such reunions the celebration of the liturgy formed the central feature. It is true that, as St. Augustine and others expressly pointed out, the sacrifice was offered to God, and in no sense *to* the saint himself, but it was none the less a supreme recognition of the martyr's dignity and formed the germ from which the whole calendar of saints' days ultimately developed.

It is at this period also that we find the practice of the invocation of saints firmly established in every part of the Church. Prayers and appeals to the dead, as many inscriptions on pagan tombstones prove, were by no means unfamiliar to the heathen of Greece and Rome. But, as P. Dörfler[2] has recently pointed out, we find running through all these appeals a certain element of fear. The *manes* of the dead were asked to spare. They were conceived of as resenting neglect and as rewarding dutiful service. 'O manes parcite, ni parcetis, credite mi, nemo referet solemnia vobis' may be taken as a more or less typical example of the tone commonly prevalent. In Christian sepulchral inscriptions of the early centuries we also often find an appeal to the dead—even to those who were not martyrs—but the spirit is notably different. What the survivors ask of their dead is remembrance and sometimes prayer—*e.g.*, 'Marine im et mentem . . . nos . . . habeto' or 'Pete pro parentes tuos.'[3] Naturally enough, such an attitude towards the dead must have paved the way for the more formal invocation of those who had laid down their lives for Christ. Once it was generally admitted, as even pagans like Æschylus[4] and Plato[5] seemed ready to admit, that those who had passed into the next world might have knowledge of human needs and desires, it was inevitable that Christians who already made a practice of commending themselves to the prayers of the martyrs in prison should renew their appeal when the martyrs' triumph was completed by death. Hence, as early as the time of Hippolytus and Origen we find unmistakable traces of a belief in the power of the holy dead to intercede for those on earth.[6] The rude inscriptions and *graffiti* in the Catacombs, which, however, it is unfortunately very hard to date, may be appealed to as supplying similar evidence from the 3rd cent. onwards—*e.g.*, 'Domina Bassilla commandamus tibi Crescentinus et Micina filia nostra Crescen . . . que vixit men. x et dies . . .' (the title 'Domina' given to the martyr is an indication of early date); 'Sancte Laurenti suscepta habeto anim[am eius]'; 'Salba me Domne Crescentione meam luce.'[7] As appears in many of these ungrammatical memorials, it is the martyr's protection that is asked, and often for quite young children. Hence it seems probable that the prevalent atmosphere of paganism exercised some vague influence upon Christian feeling, especially in the case of the ruder populace. The strongly marked desire to be buried near the martyrs is no doubt to be attributed to a similar hope of protection. It was a matter not so much of logic as of a deep and primitive instinct—the

1 See art. AGAPE.
2 *Mensa und Confessio*, Munich, 1906, *Altar und Altargrabe*, Leipzig, 1912.
3 *Fractio Panis*, Freiburg i. B., 1895.
4 Cf. Delehaye, p. 50.
5 *Cat. Myst.* xxiii. 9.
6 *In Acta Apost.* xxi. 4 (*PG* lx. 170).
7 *Sermo* clix. 1 (*PL* xxxviii. 868).

1 *Enchiridion*, n. 110; *PL* xl. 283.
2 *Die Anfänge der Heiligenverehrung*, Munich, 1913.
3 See many examples in O. Marucchi, *Christian Epigraphy*, Eng. tr., Cambridge, 1912, pp. 151–156.
4 *Choeph.* 129–141, 476–478.
5 *Sympos.* 23.
6 See examples in Delehaye, p. 131 f.
7 Marucchi, nos. 125, 124, 473, etc.

same which in pagan times had led to the development of hero-worship.[1] Even for Christians the passage to another world was fearsome. It was felt that help might be looked for from those who had made the journey in triumph and whose acceptance with God was assured. Burial in proximity to the martyrs was itself a form of commendation, a tacit request for their intercession.

Be this as it may, the direct invocation of the holy dead had become by the latter half of the 4th cent. a received practice among Christians in both East and West. St. Basil († 379), St. Gregory of Nazianzus († 390), St. Ambrose († 397), not to speak of St. Chrysostom, St. Jerome, and St. Augustine, all furnish evidence which shows that in their time the practice of praying to the martyrs was already firmly established. St. Gregory of Nazianzus, *e.g.*, not only tells the story of a girl who in the hour of danger called upon the Blessed Virgin for aid, but himself in his sermon on St. Cyprian unequivocally invokes the martyr.[2] St. Ambrose writes :

'Martyres obsecrandi . . . possunt pro peccatis rogare nostris, qui proprio sanguine, etiam si qua habuerunt peccata, laverunt . . . non erubescamus eos intercessores nostrae infirmitatis adhibere,' etc.[3]

In St. John Chrysostom evidence of what may be called active devotion to the martyrs meets us at every turn.[4] But perhaps no better illustration can be found of the attitude of the devout laity than an incident from the newly recovered *Life of St. Melania the Younger*. Living in Rome in the year 403, she, owing to her self-imposed vigils on the eve of the feast of St. Lawrence, gave birth prematurely to a child and her life was in imminent danger. Thereupon her husband, rushing off to the shrine of St. Lawrence ('festinus perrexit ad S. martyrem'), prostrated himself before the tomb beneath the altar and with tears and lamentations begged God to spare the mother (ἐβόα πρὸς Κύριον περὶ τῆς ζωῆς αὐτῆς). Both the Greek and Latin redactions of the *Life* clearly show that, though the martyr's intercession was invoked, it was to God, the master of life and death, that the ultimate appeal was directed. Similarly Melania, just before her death at Jerusalem in 438, asked to be carried to the shrine of the martyrs. Then she called upon them as '*athletes* of the Lord' and asked them to have pity upon her, their unworthy servant, who had always venerated their relics, adding :

'O ye, who have always free speech with God that loves mankind, be my intercessors (πρεσβεύσατε) with Him that He may receive my soul in peace.'[5]

It is just this παρρησία, attributed to the martyrs, that is put forward again and again in patristic writers as the motive for having recourse to their help.[6]

Undoubtedly one of the causes which contributed most powerfully to the rapid extension of the veneration of martyrs was the multiplication of shrines and saints' days, due to the Oriental practice of translating and dividing relics. It was beside the tomb of the martyr and upon his *dies natalis*, or anniversary, that his aid was primarily invoked. In the West the old Roman idea of the sacredness and inviolability of the tomb persisted for many hundred years. Even Gregory the Great, upon whom Harnack lays the blame of 'systematizing that resort to saints and relics which had already existed for a long time,' still firmly refused at the end of the 6th cent. to allow the resting-places of the great Christian heroes of Rome to be in any way disturbed. In a famous letter addressed to the empress Constantina, he point-blank refused her request to allow the head of St. Paul or some other portion of his body to be transported to Constantinople.[1] It was not, he declared, the Roman custom to allow any but representative relics, the *brandea* or *sanctuaria*, *i.e.* cloths which had been lowered into the tombs, to be given to applicants, however illustrious. Nearly a century earlier, in 519, the legates of Pope Hormisdas had maintained the same attitude in regard to a request of the emperor Justinian. The Oriental custom, however, was different, and the Greeks were not content with the legal fiction of *brandea*. Thus, as early as 351–354 we have definite record of the translation to Daphne, a suburb of Antioch, of the body of the martyr St. Babylas, and this was followed by many other translations. Still more fraught with the possibilities of future abuse were the dismemberment of the bodies of martyrs and the division of objects connected with them. This aspect of the question of relics (*q.v.*) is only touched upon here to explain the multiplication of centres of cultus and also the multiplication of feasts, for the translation commonly entailed the observance of a perpetual anniversary. The miraculous effects attributed to these relics, wonders which were attested by St. Hilary, St. Ambrose, St. Augustine, and all the great Christian teachers of that age,[2] must undoubtedly have accounted for much in the abnormally rapid development of the cultus of the martyrs.

So far we have taken no account of any saints but those who within the knowledge of all men had given their lives for the faith. As early, however, as the time of St. Cyprian we find in that writer constant references to a class of *confessores*, and, though Lucius has asserted that Cyprian's use of the term is loose and confused, his consistency has of late been successfully vindicated. J. Ernst[3] shows that in Cyprian's idea the martyrs *par excellence* are those who have actually laid down their lives for Christ, but that he also extends this term to all who have suffered grievous torment for the faith. On the other hand, the confessor is one who has borne testimony to his belief at some cost to himself—*e.g.*, by imprisonment or exile. All martyrs are therefore of necessity confessors ; but, where the terms are contrasted, the confessor, as opposed to the martyr, is one who has not been put to the test of grievous bodily torment. Still Cyprian's language clearly suggests that, while the martyr's dignity is pre-eminent, the confessor in many cases is worthy to stand beside him and must also be highly honoured. 'A man *has* suffered,' he urges rather rhetorically, 'all that he was willing to suffer.'[4] This was in substance the principle in virtue of which a second category of saints gradually came to be recognized. In point of historical development, however, the process was greatly assisted by the practice of according a special commemoration in the liturgy to deceased bishops and of keeping locally a formal record of their anniversaries. Cyril of Jerusalem (*c.* 349), as pointed out above, indicates the classes of those no longer living for whom prayer is made in the liturgy. The first consists of 'patriarchs, prophets, apostles, martyrs'—and it is worth noting that St. Hilary[5] names just these four groups in the same order ; the second class is that of the 'holy fathers and bishops who have fallen asleep before.' Now this distinction is in noteworthy accord with

1 Cf. *ERE* vi. 652 ff. 2 *Orat.* xxiv. 11 (*PG* xxxv. 1181).
3 *De Viduis*, 9 (*PL* xvi. 251).
4 See, *e.g.*, Kirsch, *Gemeinschaft*, pt. iii. ch. 4, Eng. tr., p. 216 ff.
5 See M. Rampolla, *S. Melania Giuniore*, Rome, 1905, pp. 6, 45, 81.
6 See, for a summary of some of this evidence, Stone[3], pp. 9–38, and Kirsch, pt. iii. ch. 4, Eng. tr., p. 212 ff.

1 See *Regesta*, iv. 30, ed. Ewald, *MGH* i. [1891] 264 f.
2 See Delehaye, pp. 139–157.
3 In *Historisches Jahrbuch*, xxxiv. [1913] 328–353 ; and cf., still more recently, R. Reitzenstein, *Die Bezeichnung Märtyrer* (*GGN*, Phil.-Hist. Klasse, 1916, p. 417 ff.).
4 'Qui se tormentis et morti sub oculis Dei obtulit, passus est quidquid pati voluit, non enim ipse tormentis sed tormenta ipsi defuerunt' (*Ep.* xii., ed. Hartel, p. 503).
5 *Tractatus in Ps.* 146, ed. Zingerle, p. 851.

the data supplied by the famous *Chronography* of Philocalus[1] (A.D. 354). In this are preserved two separate documents of the Roman Church, one originally drafted in 332, which, under the heading 'Depositio episcoporum,' furnishes a record of the anniversaries of the bishops of Rome with their names and places of interment, the other, a separate list, headed 'Depositio martyrum,' giving similar information regarding the Roman martyrs. Be it noted in passing that even in 354 this Roman 'Depositio martyrum' had been augmented by two African anniversaries (those of St. Cyprian and of Perpetua with Felicitas) and also by another entry described as 'natale Petri de cathedra,' now known as the Feast of St. Peter's Chair. In these two short lists, thus gradually amplified and eventually blended into one, we may recognize the first rude outlines of the elaborate *calendaria* and *martyrologia* which came to play so prominent a part in the hagiographical developments of the Middle Ages. Other important Churches besides that of Rome kept similar lists of the anniversaries of their martyrs and of their bishops. In the 4th and even in the 5th cent. it appears that on account of the exalted dignity of the martyrs the two sets of records were still kept separate, and the traces of this distinction, as Delehaye has pointed out,[2] survived to a later period in the prayers of the *Leonine Sacramentary.* But before long the two lists, as might be expected, were fused into one document. From certain details in the Syriac *martyrologium* of 411 it has been inferred that this had already occurred at Antioch before that date. But the fusion is more conspicuous in the ancient calendar of Carthage, compiled apparently about 525. Here the commemorations of African martyrs and of a number of bishops of Carthage who were not martyrs stand side by side, together with other entries not of local origin. This process of equalizing confessors and martyrs seems to have begun soon after the restoration of peace to the Church. It was realized that holy ascetics like St. Anthony the hermit, or devoted bishops like St. Meletius of Antioch, not to speak of Chrysostom and Athanasius, suffered more in a lifetime of courageous endurance than if they had actually shed their blood for Christ. Further, a sort of middle term was found in the patriarchs and prophets of the OT, who, as pointed out above, were already grouped in the liturgy with the apostles and martyrs. The miracles attributed to some apostolic preachers like Gregory Thaumaturgus († 274), and the cult of relics, which, *e.g.*, in the case of the hermit Hilarion, though he was no martyr, led to the translation of his remains almost immediately after his death, brought about rapid developments. Hence we may fairly consider such a panegyric as that of St. Gregory of Nyssa upon Ephraem Syrus, which was spoken seemingly upon his anniversary and which ends with a direct invocation, to be evidence that the cultus of confessors was already established. Still the recognition of a definite category of 'saints,' in such sort that the word ἅγιος or *sanctus* was no longer a descriptive epithet but the formal style of a class of specially venerated champions of the faith, cannot be said to have yet taken root. The monograph of Delehaye[3] discusses in detail the development of the word *sanctus* and shows that even the epitaphs of Pope Damasus († 384) supply no example of the technical significance which finally attached to it.[4] It is not until the next century that the use of such a phrase as 'Sanctus Athanasius' can be taken by itself as any evidence of cultus.

When we go on to ask what elements entered into that conception of a 'saint' which gradually grew up in the early Church and has lasted until our own day, we have to distinguish between a genuine claim to saintship and one which is to some extent only ostensible and illusory. The genuine claim rests upon local cultus initiated by the clergy and people who had personal knowledge of the saint's martyrdom or of his heroic virtue. His name and anniversary were entered in the local *martyrologium.* His feast was kept by a synaxis, at which a panegyric was delivered and the liturgy was celebrated. His *Acta* were collected and preserved, and, when possible, the tomb enclosing his remains was honoured by the erection over it of an altar and a church. There are cases —*e.g.*, that of St. Polycarp—in which we have evidence of all these things. There are other instances in which they can be inferred with little risk of error; but at a later date, when the martyrologies were no longer local and had enlarged their scope, it must be admitted that many names were added to the roll of saints without adequate investigation and upon quite insufficient data. Delehaye has pointed out numerous examples of these 'literary canonizations,' as he has called them.[1] An old-world story familiar to modern readers as that of Faust was at one time attached to the name of a mythical St. Cyprian of Antioch; the gruesome tale of Œdipus seems responsible for the evolution of a St. Albanus and other imaginary personages; while the well-known legend of Buddha re-appears in Christian hagiography under the guise of the *Acta* of Saints Barlaam and Joasaph. In very few, however, of the more extreme cases can it be pretended that there was any real cultus of the supposed saint. On the other hand, there are a number of instances in which a perfectly legitimate cultus, contemporaneous with the saint's death, has afterwards become surcharged with all sorts of legendary excrescences, often preposterous in themselves, and quite inconsistent with the facts of history. The stories recounted in the apocryphal *Acta* of St. Thomas, or in those of his fellow-apostles, or of Thecla, St. Paul's reputed convert, do not constitute a valid disproof of their title to veneration. In the case of St. Procopius, again, who was undoubtedly an authentic martyr, the character of the saint was in time completely transformed. In reality Procopius was a studious ascetic; in legend he becomes a warrior-saint, the hero of incredible adventures.[2] A similar extravagance pervades all the *Lives* of St. George, the 'megalo-martyr,' although, according to Delehaye,[3] we know no more that is authentic about him than the bare fact of his existence. The same process, of course, went on in secular history. For mediæval readers the personality of Alexander the Great or of Charlemagne became quite unrecognizable owing to the myths which by a sort of magnetic attraction attached themselves to all such famous names. Moreover, even where no doubt can be felt as to the existence and the holiness of the person venerated, it is not always possible to explain how the cultus first arose. Often enough its chief developments were associated with the discovery of relics of doubtful authenticity, or with the occurrence of cures believed to be miraculous. The information given by St. Augustine regarding the marvels wrought by the relics of St. Stephen at Uzalum throws an

[1] See art. CALENDAR (Christian), § I.
[2] P. 114.
[3] In *Analecta Bollandiana*, xxviii. [1909] 145-200.
[4] Curiously enough, however, in the *Amherst Papyrus*, described by B. P. Grenfell and A. S. Hunt (*Amherst Papyri*, London, 1900, pt. i. pp. 23-28), which may be dated with Harnack between A.D. 250 and 350, the word ἅγιοι occurs three times in the sense of the blessed in heaven.

[1] For a classification of the various forms of literary canonization see Delehaye, *Legends of the Saints*, Eng. tr., p. 113 ff.
[2] See Delehaye, *Les Légendes grecques des saints militaires*, pp. 77-89.
[3] *Ib.* p. 70.

interesting light on the spread of popular devotion to the saints in quite early times.[1] It has been maintained,[2] on the ground of a passage of Optatus of Milevis which condemns the veneration of the relics of one who was a martyr but 'necdum vindicatus,'[3] that some process of official inquiry and canonization (*vindicatio*) existed even at this early date; but such a conclusion, as O. Marucchi has shown,[4] is not borne out by the facts adduced to support it. Although the attempt may sometimes have been made to preserve the 'proconsular acts,' *i.e.* the official record of the trial and condemnation of certain martyrs, very little material of this kind has come down to us, and even less seems to have been known (*c.* 380) to so devoted a student of their history as Pope Damasus.[5] As a result, legend and historical fact have in many cases become hopelessly confused. Though the primitive local martyrologies were no doubt trustworthy as to the very simple data they enshrined, consisting probably of little more than the name, the day of the anniversary, and the place of burial, the case is quite otherwise when we come to the later compilations formed by the unskilful combination of lists and materials derived from many different churches.

The most famous among these is the document falsely ascribed to St. Jerome and known as the *Martyrologium Hieronymianum.* This was probably first compiled in Italy, and then revised and added to in Gaul at the end of the 6th century. Among the sources used we may recognize (1) a general martyrology probably written in Greek at Nicomedia and embracing the churches of the East, (2) the local martyrology of Rome, (3) a general martyrology of Africa, (4) a general martyrology of Italy, (5) some literary sources, including Eusebius. Unfortunately the text has reached us in a very corrupt state. From the nature of the case, the document consists of little else than lists of names arranged according to the days of each month, and these names have constantly been misplaced, miswritten, and confused.

The Venerable Bede seems to have been the originator of a new type of *martyrologium*, in which the number of entries was much reduced but brief historical details were added concerning the saints who were commemorated. It was only in 1908 that Bede's true text was isolated from subsequent accretions by the researches of H. Quentin.[6] The importance of Bede's work lay especially in this, that he had several mediæval imitators, the best known being Ado and Usuard, and that mainly from the work of the last-named the present quasi-official Roman martyrology, which is read in choir as part of the liturgical office, was compiled by Cardinal Baronius at the end of the 16th century. It need hardly be pointed out that, although the name suggests a roll of 'martyrs,' all these martyrologies without exception included many 'confessors.' The earliest document in which this fusion is found is possibly the fragment of a Thracian Gothic calendar in the Ulfilas codex.

We can touch but briefly upon the later developments of Christian hagiology. It seems probable that the more emotional manifestations of devotion to the Madonna and the saints are traceable ultimately to East Syrian influences. E. Lucius[7] has rightly called attention to the extremely romantic spirit conspicuous in the writings of St. Ephraem and his school. From Syria this movement in some strange fashion made itself felt apparently in Spain, and by this channel was carried to Ireland, whence it spread to Britain and the Continent.[8] Certain it is, in any case, that the devotional atmosphere of such a writer as Cynewulf in the 8th cent. differs hardly at all from that of St. Bernard or Jacopone da Todi many hundred years later. But, however it came about, this attitude of mind and sense of personal relation to the saints exercised a wide influence upon many aspects of life. The system of patrons, shrines, pilgrimages, gilds, etc., reacted in a thousand ways upon art, literature, trade, and social economics generally. Despite many abuses and blunders, even the most rigid censor will find it difficult to maintain that the influence thus exercised was entirely evil. The origins of the practice of choosing saints for patrons may be traced back to the time of Dionysius of Alexandria († 265), who bears witness to the custom prevalent among Christians of giving to their children the names of Peter or Paul or John, and assigns motives for such a choice.[1] Chrysostom and especially Theodoret[2] furnish further evidence to the same effect. In the Middle Ages the selection of patrons was often determined by the most grotesque of reasons. St. Barbara, who was believed to secure for her clients the boon of receiving the sacraments before death, was invoked especially in thunderstorms, and became the patroness of all the more dangerous trades, notably miners, tilers, masons, and those who had to do with firearms. Similarly the association of St. Clare with sufferers from sore eyes, as also with glass-workers and laundresses, seems to have been dictated by no better reason than the fact that her name (Clara) suggested transparency and whiteness. Examples of this kind of extravagance were undoubtedly very numerous.

In Celtic lands confusion has been caused by native writers who frequently use the term *sanctus* of those consecrated to a religious life independently of personal holiness.

The title of the Celtic saint, says Willis-Bund,[3] 'rested on the fact that he was either the member of a certain family or of a certain monastery,' and he goes on to declare that 'a Celtic saint was never the person whom a Celt invoked in prayer. . . . No churches were dedicated to him. . . . No shrine containing his relics was set apart for the adoration of the faithful.'

Even if this statement be from any point of view correct, its general import is certainly misleading. The Celtic Church venerated apostles, martyrs, and ascetics exactly as the other Churches did. One of the earliest texts of the Litany of the Saints is that of the Stowe Missal,[4] where it appears as part of the priest's ordinary preparation for Mass. The *Félire* of Oengus, the earliest of the four extant Irish martyrologies, and many similar Celtic documents are extravagant in their invocation of, and their expressions of veneration for, 'Christ's kingfolk' (*rigrad Christ*), *i.e.* the saints. The whole truth seems to be that in some Celtic countries the word 'saint' was used of all men dedicated to God—the celebrated communion hymn, '*Sancti* venite, Christi corpus sumite,' is plainly addressed to a community—and that in Wales certain clans or families were regarded as a sort of priestly caste of whom it was expected that they should furnish recruits for the ascetic life. No doubt abuses followed. It was clearly undesirable that a 'saint' should establish a claim in perpetuity to a particular church merely by proving his nearness of kin to the founder and by fasting for forty days on the site;[5] but there is no reason to suppose that the Celts did not distinguish between this official sanctity and true holiness of life, and, though Druidical traditions may have familiarized the people with the idea of a hereditary priestly caste, there is little direct evidence, beyond the existence of the genealogies, to prove that the

1 See Delehaye, *Culte*, pp. 148–158.
2 *E.g.*, by G. B. de Rossi, *Roma sotterranea*, Rome, 1903, ii. 61.
3 *De Schismate Donatistarum*, i. 16 (*PL* x. 917).
4 *Nuovo Bullettino di Arch. Crist.* xv. [1909] 40 ff.
5 See Delehaye, *Legends of the Saints*, Eng. tr., pp. 73, 111.
6 *Les Martyrologes historiques du Moyen Age.*
7 *Anfänge des Heiligenkults*, p. 441 ff.
8 See Edmund Bishop, *Liturgica Historica*, Oxford, 1918, pp. 162, 178 ff.

1 See Eus. *HE* VII. xxv. 14.
2 *Græc. affect. Curatio*, viii. (*PG* lxxxiii. 1033).
3 *Celtic Church of Wales*, p. 415.
4 See E. Bishop, *Liturgica Historica*, p. 137 ff.
5 See Baring-Gould and Fisher, *Lives of the British Saints*, i. 3.

system was acquiesced in without protest. There is no indication of any such element among the Culdees,[1] and in Ireland Whitley Stokes[2] denies that even the pagan Druids 'constituted a hierarchy or a separate caste.' Further, if certain patriotic Celts have professed to count their national saints by thousands, this does not show that the conditions in Wales or Ireland differed from the rest of the Christian world, but only that they have taken advantage of a simple ambiguity of language. In truth, terms of respect seem particularly liable to such misinterpretation. The phrase 'Your Holiness' (*Sanctitas vestra*) was everywhere of common occurrence in the Middle Ages, and was addressed to ordinary bishops. It is now part of the official style of the Roman pontiff, but of course does not imply that the pope is deserving of liturgical cultus. Similarly the word 'venerable' is used at the present day in three different senses. An Anglican, *e.g.*, may speak of 'the Venerable Archdeacon Wilberforce,' a Roman Catholic of 'the Venerable Father Southwell,' or an agnostic of 'the venerable author of the *Origin of Species*.' In the first case the word is a title of courtesy; in the second it designates one who has reached a particular stage in the process of canonization; in the third it expresses the writer's belief that Darwin was a scientist worthy of reverence.

The reproach has constantly been made against the veneration of saints, as it was practised in the Christian Church from the 4th cent. onwards, that it differed little either in its essence or in its manifestations from the pagan worship of gods and heroes.

Harnack, *e.g.*, while admitting the early date of this development, describes it as 'polytheism in the fullest sense of the word,' and declares elsewhere that 'the saints took the place of the local deities, their festivals were substituted for the old provincial services of the gods.'[3]

Many other writers have emphasized the same objection in various forms, from the scholarly and temperate treatise of E. Lucius, *Die Anfänge des Heiligenkults*, to such highly polemical works as *Les Saints, successeurs des Dieux* of 'P. Saintyves' or the *Orpheus* of Salomon Reinach. A number of monographs have also been written to deal with separate cases and to prove that this or that deity has passed into Christian hagiography under some more or less unfamiliar designation. Thus E. Maas and H. Usener have identified St. Pelagia with Aphrodite; Rendel Harris sees a replica of the Dioscuri in nearly all such pairs of saints as Gervase and Protase or Cosmas and Damian; A. von Gutschmidt maintains that St. George is no other than Mithras, and so forth. The matter can be touched on only very briefly here, but it seems worth while to lay stress on the following points:

(1) The object of cultus, in the beginning, as we have shown, was undoubtedly a historical personage, whose cruel death or ascetical life was well known to those who paid reverence to his memory and invoked his aid by prayer. It is incredible that, in the beginning of things at any rate, those who honoured the martyr for the very fact that he was willing to lay down his life rather than sacrifice to Jupiter or pay unlawful honour to the deified emperors should themselves have elevated him into an object of worship and a rival to the true God. The evidence of such a case as that of St. Melania, quoted above—and many others might be added—proves clearly that by all Christians of education and intelligence the saint was honoured only subordinately and relatively. He was in no true sense worshipped. The charge of virtual polytheism was urged against the Christians by such antagonists as Julian the Apostate, Vigilantius, and Faustus. On their side the apologists—Jerome, Augustine, Theodoret, Maximus of Turin, and many more—invariably replied that λατρεία was paid to God alone:

'Colimus martyres eo cultu dilectionis et societatis . . . Cultu, quae Graece λατρεία dicitur, . . . nec colimus, nec colendum docemus, nisi unum Deum.'[1]

'We do not worship the saints . . . but we venerate them as men of God.'[2]

(2) The almost ineradicable tendency among the rude and uneducated to cling to their primitive customs led beyond doubt to a certain amount of compromise in matters which were not judged to be distinctively pagan. It was the advice of St. Gregory Thaumaturgus, of St. Augustine, and of St. Gregory the Great that an attempt should be made to Christianize their popular observances, if not absolutely evil in themselves, rather than to extirpate them. If a particular day had been kept as a holiday, let it be transformed into a Christian festival; if there had been resort to a particular site for superstitious purposes, let some worthier object of pilgrimage be substituted; if certain practices connected with funerals, weddings, or other ceremonial occasions had established themselves firmly in the hearts of the people, let them be given a Christian colouring or significance. Certainly there was much danger of grave abuses resulting from such condescensions, but also it may be doubted whether a too rigid attitude would not have frustrated the work of conversion altogether, if we take into account ingrained habits of the mass of the people. There is more force than some would be disposed to admit in a remark of F. C. Conybeare:

'Perhaps we ought to be grateful to the Catholic Church in Latin countries for having established cults so respectable as those of the Virgin and the saints, for it is certain that, in default of them, the Latin peasant would relapse into a fetichism as old as the hills around him. You can turn Spanish and Italian peasants into anticlericals, but you seldom turn them into Rationalists. They may give up Christianity, but they only believe all the more firmly in the evil eye and in all the debasing practices which attend the belief.'[3]

(3) While the ceremonial of Christianity and that of paganism include many identical elements—*e.g.*, the use of ablutions, lights, incense, prostrations, unctions, linen vestures, *ex votos*, etc.—it would be rash to conclude that in all cases, or even in any case, the Church was guilty of conscious imitation. In such external rites the range of choice is limited. Moreover, an act which has become familiar from its being frequently practised or witnessed soon seems to be a natural and spontaneous expression of inward feeling, and men lose the sense that it belongs distinctively to one cult rather than another. Even with regard to such a matter as incubation (*q.v.*) it must not be forgotten that the Christian vigils, which probably grew out of the primitive celebration of Easter Eve, familiarized men with the idea of spending the night in the church. On the other hand, as Delehaye points out,[4] it would be foolish to deny the existence of this and other survivals of paganism in isolated cases.

Lastly, it may fairly be said that the attempted identification of saints with pagan heroes and deities has been much more commonly a matter of guesswork than of scientific method. The unsatisfactory character of the proofs adduced has often been pointed out in the reviews of such works appearing in the *Analecta Bollandiana*, a periodical specially devoted to hagiographical research and criticism. In any case it cannot be

[1] W. F. Skene, *Celtic Scotland*², Edinburgh, 1886-90, ii. 226-277.
[2] *Tripartite Life* (Rolls Series), London, 1887, i. p. clix.
[3] *Lehrbuch der Dogmengeschichte*⁴, Tübingen, 1909-10, ii. 442, 471-490.

[1] Augustine, *c. Faustum*, xx. 21.
[2] Theodoret, *Græc. affect. Curatio*, viii. (*PG* lxxxiii. 1032).
[3] *Myth, Magic, and Morals*, London, 1909, p. 360.
[4] *Legends of the Saints*, ch. vi.

contested that the identifications to which different scholars have been led are often widely divergent.

LITERATURE.—i. *HISTORY.*—H. Delehaye, *Les Origines du culte des martyrs*, Brussels, 1912, *Les Légendes hagiographiques*[2], do. 1906, Eng. tr., London, 1907, *Les Légendes grecques des saints militaires*, Paris, 1909, 'Sanctus' in *Analecta Bollandiana*, xxviii. [1909] 145–200, and many other articles in the same review; E. Lucius, *Die Anfänge des Heiligenkults*, Tübingen, 1904; P. Dörfler, *Die Anfänge der Heiligenverehrung*, Munich, 1913; W. Hellmanns, *Wertschätzung des Martyriums*, Breslau, 1912; R. Reitzenstein, *Die Bezeichnung Märtyrer* (*GGN*, Phil.-Hist. Klasse, 1916, pp. 417–467); P. Allard, art. 'Martyre,' in A. d'Alès, *Dict. apologétique de la foi catholique*[4], iii. [1918] 331–491, *Dix Leçons sur le martyre*[5], Paris, 1913; A. Harnack, *Die Mission und Ausbreitung des Christenthums in den ersten drei Jahrhunderten*[2], 2 vols., Leipzig, 1906; W. M. Ramsay, *The Church in the Roman Empire before A.D. 170*[5], London, 1897; G. N. Bonwetsch, 'Heilige und Heiligenverehrung,' in *PRE*[3]; E. Vacandard, *Etudes de Critique et d'histoire religieuse*, 3rd ser., Paris, 1912; P. Saintyves (E. Nourry), *Les Saints, successeurs des Dieux*, do. 1907; M. von Wulf, *Ueber Heilige und Heiligenverehrung*, Leipzig, 1910; H. Usener, *Vorträge und Aufsätze*, do. 1907, *Legenden der heiligen Pelagia*, Bonn, 1879; O. Weinreich, *Antike Heilungswunder*, Giessen, 1909; G. Rabeau, *Le Culte des saints dans l'Afrique chrétienne*, Paris, 1903; J. Rendel Harris, *The Cult of the Heavenly Twins*, Cambridge, 1906.

ii. *DOGMA.*—J. P. Kirsch, *Die Lehre von der Gemeinschaft der Heiligen im christlichen Altertum*, Mayence, 1900, Eng. tr., Edinburgh, 1910; A. Tanquerey, *Synopsis Theologicæ Dogmaticæ*[12], Tournai, 1909, i. 616 ff.; N. Wiseman, *Lectures on Principal Doctrines and Practices of the Catholic Church*[2], London, 1844, lect. xiii.; Darwell Stone, *The Invocation of Saints*[3], do. 1909; H. F. Stewart, *Doctrina Romanensium de Invocatione Sanctorum*, do. 1897; H. R. Percival, *The Invocation of Saints treated Theologically and Historically*, do. 1896; G. Williams, *The Orthodox Church of the East in the 18th Century*, do. 1868; W. Palmer, *Dissertations on Subjects relating to the 'Orthodox Eastern Catholic' Communion*, do. 1853; W. J. Birkbeck, *Russia and the English Church*, i., do. 1895; A. Riley, *Birkbeck and the Russian Church, containing Essays and Articles by the late W. J. Birkbeck*, do. 1917.

iii. *MISCELLANEOUS.*—G. B. de Rossi and L. Duchesne, *Les Sources du Martyrologe hieronymien*, Rome, 1885; *Martyrologium hieronymianum*, in *AS*, Nov., II. i., Brussels, 1894, pp. 1–195; H. Achelis, *Die Martyrologien: ihre Geschichte und ihr Wert*, Berlin, 1900; H. Delehaye, 'Le Témoignage des Martyrologes,' in *Analecta Bollandiana*, xxvi. [1907] 78 ff.; A. Urbain, *Ein Martyrologium der christlichen Gemeinde zu Rom*, Leipzig, 1901; H. Quentin, *Les Martyrologes historiques du Moyen Âge*, Paris, 1908; J. W. Willis-Bund, *The Celtic Church of Wales*, London, 1897, ch. ix.; S. Baring-Gould and J. Fisher, *The Lives of the British Saints*, 4 vols., do. 1906–14.

H. THURSTON.

SAINTS AND MARTYRS (Indian).

SAINTS AND MARTYRS (Indian).—The study of Indian hagiology is of exceptional difficulty; the number of personages worshipped or venerated is enormous, and a voluminous cycle of legend has been collected round them. The reason of this abundance of saints lies in the fact that Hindu and Muhammadan society is broken up into numerous groups. Thus there are tribal and caste saints, and the founders of sects and religious orders are usually credited with miraculous powers which lead to their veneration or worship. There is, again, no controlling organization, no prescribed system of canonization, such as that of the Roman curia; and any tribe, caste, order, or village is at liberty to confer the honour of saintship on any worthy at its own discretion. It has been the rule in India from the earliest times that each village worships its own local gods—godlings of fertility, who promote the happiness of the community, and repel famine, pestilence, and other misfortunes which are believed to be caused by the action of foreign and necessarily hostile spirits. These deities, under Musalmān influence, are often superseded or absorbed by the local saint who performs the same functions as his predecessor.

1. Powers ascribed to living saints.—The worship or reverence paid to deceased worthies of this class depends on the popular reputation of the living saint. This has been well described by H. B. Edwardes from his experience of the N.W. Frontier:

'For him [the Bannūchī] the whistle of the far-thrown bullet, or the nearer sheen of his enemy's shumsheer [shamshīr, 'a sword'] has no terrors; blood was simply a red fluid, and to remove a neighbour's head at the shoulder as easy as cutting cucumbers. But to be cursed in Arabic, or anything that sounded like it; to be told that the blessed Prophet had put a black mark against his soul, for not giving his best field to one of the Prophet's own posterity; to have the saliva of a disappointed saint left in anger on his door-post; or to behold a Hajee [Ḥājī], who had gone three times to Mecca, deliberately sit down and enchant his camels with the itch, and his sheep with the rot; these were things which made the dagger drop out of the hand of the awe-stricken savage, his knees to knock together, his liver to turn to water, and his parched tongue to be scarce able to articulate a full and complete concession of the blasphemous demand.'[1]

From this point of view it is clearly advisable that each village, caste, or tribe should be provided with a saintly protector.

'The Afrīdī Paṭhāns of Tīrāh had shame in the sight of their brethren, in that their territory was blessed with no holy shrine at which they might worship, and that they had to be beholden to the saints of their neighbours when they wished for divine aid. Smarting under a sense of incompleteness, they induced by generous offers a saint of the most notorious piety to take up his abode amongst them. They then made quite sure of his staying with them by cutting his throat, they buried him honourably, they built over his bones a splendid shrine at which they might worship him and implore his aid and intercession in their behalf, and thus they purged themselves of their reproach.'[2]

2. Buddhist, Jain, and Hindu saints.—The three great religions of India—Buddhism, Jainism, Hinduism—recognize to a less or greater extent the reverence or worship of saints.

(*a*) *Buddhist.*—In its orthodox form Buddhism does not admit saint-worship; but in its later developments, such as the Mahāyāna, we find it recognized. In the Indian cave-temples images of Buddha are associated with those of *bodhisattvas*, or saints who in the next birth become Buddhas. *Stūpas* were erected to contain not only the relics of Buddha, but also those of the *sthaviras* or *theras*, elders of the faith; images of Padmapāni and Mañjuṣrī are specially associated with those of Buddha, and at Junnar there is an altar (*toraṇa*) on which relics of Buddha or of Buddhist saints were placed.[3] The saints of Lamaist or Tibetan Buddhism are both Indian and Tibetan, with a few from China and Mongolia. Of the Indian saints the chief are the leading disciples of Buddha, and the sixteen *sthavira*, or chief apostles or missionaries.[4]

(*b*) *Jain.*—In Jain hagiology 63 persons, including 24 *tīrthaṅkaras*, or perfected saints, are regarded as 'pre-eminently spiritual.' 'These are not all "saints," *i.e. sādhus*, but spiritually great souls.'[5] In W. India each Jain temple contains an image of the *tīrthaṅkara* who was most popular with the person or persons who erected the temple; these images are placed in shrines fixed on raised seats, and are called *mūlnāyak*, or 'chief leaders.'[6] Luard reports that in Central India Jains revere the *tīrthaṅkaras*, but do not worship them, regarding them as models and mediators, but not in themselves objects of worship; the *ṣrāvaks*, 'hearers,' at first are taught to worship them, but, as they rise in knowledge and religious standing, they cease to do so; *gurus* or *yatis* look on the *tīrthaṅkaras* as only examples to be followed.[7]

(*c*) *Hindu.*—The chief Hindu saint is Gorakhnāth.[8] One account describes him as flitting round the earth with a train of nine *nāths*, 'lords,' and 84 *siddhs* (Skr. *siddha*, 'perfected,' 'versed in magical arts,' 'sanctified by penance and austerities'). These *siddhs* are, properly speaking, saints of exceptional purity of life who have attained to a semi-divine existence; but in the eyes of the vulgar

[1] *A Year on the Punjab Frontier*, London, 1851, i. 83 f.
[2] D. C. J. Ibbetson, *Outlines of Punjab Ethnography*, Calcutta, 1883, p. 144.
[3] J. Fergusson and J. Burgess, *The Cave Temples of India*, London, 1880, pp. 172, 177, 239, 255, 298, 354, 357, 371.
[4] L. A. Waddell, *The Buddhism of Tibet*, London, 1895, p. 376 ff.
[5] Jagmanderlal Jaini, *Outlines of Jainism*, Cambridge, 1916 pp. 5, 129 ff.
[6] *BG* ix. pt. i. [1901] 111.
[7] *ICR, 1901*, xiii., *Central Provinces*, pt. i. 67.
[8] *ERE* vi. 328 ff.

they seem to be little more than demons who have gained their power from Gorakhnāth. In the hilly parts of the Panjāb, where they are especially reverenced, they are often worshipped in the form of stones and the like, the distinctive emblem of their votaries being a silver *siṅgī*, a cylindrical ornament worn on a thread round the neck.[1] The Ghirth tribe erect a small shrine or a pillar bearing a relief in stone of the feet of the *siddh*; he is worshipped every morning like the other house gods, or at least on Sunday. The Gaddī tribe offer a sack, a stick of rosewood, a crutch, sandals, and a thick cake of bread to him, regarding him as a wandering ascetic.[2]

Another class of Hindu saints is that of the *bhagats*, or sect leaders, of whom the most important are Kabīr (*q.v.*) with his successors, Rāmānand, said to be the founder of the *bhagats*, and Nāmdeo, the cotton-printer, who has become the patron saint of the Chhimbas, or dyers of the Panjāb.[3] The saint Gūgā or Guggā is of another type. He is also known as Zāhir Pīr, which is usually taken to mean 'the saint apparent'; but Harikishan Kaul[4] says that the proper form of the word is Zahriā, 'poisonous,' because while in his cradle he sucked the head of a snake. He is regarded as an incarnation of Nāga Rāja, the snake-king, and there seems good reason to believe that he is a snake-godling turned into a saint.[5]

3. Saint-worship on the N.W. Frontier.—Saint-worship in its most primitive form appears among the savage Musalmān tribes of the N.W. Frontier.

'Nowhere are saints held in greater worship than in the Brāhūī country. A place without a shrine is a place to be avoided; a shrineless road is wearisome, unlucky, unsafe. Happily there are very few of either. For the typical shrines of the Brāhūī country are not the domed shrines one sees in Las Bela and the Kachhi and occasionally in Jhalawān, but rough piles of stones, strewn about almost at random, often surrounded by a low wall. They can be descried from afar by the rags and tatters that flutter from the collection of poles stuck up over them. Though a shrine is often the actual grave of some saint, almost anything seems to serve as an excuse. One shrine may mark the spot where the saint disappeared below the earth; another the spot where he performed some miracle; another, more humble in origin, but none the less worshipful for that, the spot where he said his prayers. Hither come all who are in need, sickness, or any other adversity, to entreat the saint for the fulfilment of their desires, vowing to sacrifice this or that in return—the barren woman to pray for children, the sick to pray for health, the traveller for a safe return from his travels, the hunter for luck in the chase. Hard by most shrines of high reverence there are sacrificial altars, where the attendants preside at the sacrifice and receive a set portion of the flesh as their wage before it is distributed in alms. . . . Some shrines there are in which largish stones, polished and, to all seeming, chiselled with devoted care, occupy the place of honour in the niche towards which the worshippers direct their prayers. In a certain Chāgai shrine there stands a stone, about two feet high, with a flat base and a rounded, bullet-shaped head, too lifelike, it would seem, to be other than the conscious work of men's hands. It is hard to avoid the conclusion that in this far-off shrine the pious Musalmān is bowing his head all unwittingly before a *lingam*, an ancient relic of pre-Islamic times.'[6] 'The belief of the Hindus in Muhammadan saints is nearly as great as that of the Muhammadans themselves. Pilgrimages are made by the Hindus to the shrines of the various Musalmān Pīrs, who are believed to have power to cure diseases, give children, and perform all kinds of miracles. One of the most favourite places of pilgrimage is Shāh Bilāwal on the Windhar river near Sonmiāni in Las Bela. The Hindus have gone so far as to name the stream which passes the shrine of Shāh Bilāwal the Ganges, and the ashes of the dead are thrown into its water.'[7]

4. The orthodox Muhammadan saints.—The orthodox saints of Islām in India form a heterogeneous group. Among the titles applied to them are *pīr*, 'old,' 'reverend'; *walī*, 'one who is very near';[1] *quṭb*, 'axis,' 'pivot,' the highest degree of sanctity among Muslim saints; *ghauṣ*, 'one to whom we can cry for help'; *buzurg*, 'high'; *zāhid*, 'abstinent,' 'ascetic'; *'ābid*, 'a worshipper [of God]'; *sālik*, 'a traveller,' a Ṣūfī term; *faqīr*, 'one who is poor in the sight of God'; *shaikh*, *mīr*, *miyāñ*, 'chief,' 'master.'[2] See art. SAINTS AND MARTYRS (Muhammadan in India).

5. Martyrs.—The Arabic word for 'martyr' used in India is *shahīd*, 'one who is present as a witness,' the perfect martyr (*ash-shahīdu' l-kāmil*) being one who has been killed in a *jihād*, or religious war.[3] The sites of battles with Hindus or other 'infidels' are known as 'treasuries of martyrs' (*ganj-i-shahīdān*). It is remarkable that many of these shrines are visited by Hindus, who have themselves adopted the cult, as among the Hindu and Sikh Jāṭs of the Panjāb, whose tribal shrine (*jaṭherā*) sometimes commemorates an ancestor who was a martyr, the spot being marked by a mound of earth or a masonry shrine, round which the bridegroom walks and bows his head at his wedding.[4] Sūr Sadi, a Chibh Rājput, died by a violent death in the reign of Aurangzīb, and is venerated as a martyr. The Muhammadan branch of the sept offer the scalp-locks of their children at his tomb, and, until this rite is performed, the child is not considered to be a true Chibh, and his mother is not allowed to eat meat.[5]

LITERATURE.—See the literature quoted in the article.

W. CROOKE.

1 *ICR, 1891*, xix., *Punjab*, pt. i. 114 f.
2 H. A. Rose, *A Glossary of the Tribes and Castes of the Punjab and N.W. Frontier Province*, ii., Lahore, 1911–14, ii. 294, 268.
3 *Ib.* ii. 417, 166; *ICR, 1911*, xiv., *Punjab*, pt. i. 122; R. C. Temple, *Legends of the Punjāb*, Bombay, 1884–85, ii. 52, 99. A full account of these worthies will be found in H. H. Wilson, *Essays and Lectures on the Religion of the Hindus*, i., London, 1861; G. A. Grierson, 'Modern Vernacular Literature of Hindustan,' *JASB*, pt. i. [1888].
4 *ICR, 1911*, xiv., *Punjab*, pt. i. 121.
5 Ibbetson, p. 115; Temple, i. 121, iii. 261.
6 *ICR, 1911*, iv., *Baluchistan*, p. 62 f.
7 *Ib., 1901*, v. p. 47.

1 'Are not, verily, friends (*auliyā*, pl. of *walī*) of God they on whom is no fear?' (*Qur'ān*, x. 63).
2 Hughes, *DI*, *s.vv.*
3 *Qur'ān*, ii. 155: 'Count not those who are killed in the way of God as dead, but living with the Lord.'
4 Rose, ii. 371.
5 *Ib.* ii. 169; for offerings of hair at tombs see *GB*³, pt. i., *The Magic Art*, London, 1911, i. 31: 'If the sacrifice of hair, especially at puberty, is sometimes intended to strengthen the divine beings to whom it is offered by feeding or fertilising them, we can the better understand . . . the common practice of offering hair to the shadowy dead.'

SAINTS AND MARTYRS (Iranian).

1. Introductory.—The idea of 'saints' and 'saintship' will of course differ greatly in various religious systems. Whilst all will involve blamelessness of character and life and, generally at least, beneficence to others, in some there will be also combined the ideas of asceticism, or intensity of devotion, and even absorption in the Divinity, often with the addition of extraordinary supernatural powers, such as the gifts of miracle-working and prophecy. The Indian religions afford many illustrations of these ideas. Perhaps a more general formula would be that of the most perfect conformity in life and conduct to the ideals and precepts of the particular faith to which the saint belongs and of which he is looked upon as a hero or model. The Zoroastrian idea of saintship is simple and easily defined. At no era of its development has the idea of asceticism ever entered into the concept.[6] As M. N. Dhalla writes, speaking of the Gāthic theology:

'The Zoroastrian saint is more a saint in action than in thought. He is the one whose mission for the advancement of the world is to live in society and to minister to the wants and grievances of the less fortunate of mankind. He is not the recluse who assumes the tonsure, dons the ash-coloured robe, and besmears his face. The Zoroastrian saint does not sacrifice for the self-centred self, he sacrifices for others. The ascetic that selfishly seeks his own personal salvation, without contributing his mite to the general uplift of humanity and the regeneration of society, as well as the redemption of the universe, is not so much the beloved of Ormazd as is the active saint who lives in the world of joy and sorrow, without separating himself from the world of activity. . . . The true devotee of religion does not withdraw from the company of men in seeking the blessed company of Ormazd.'[7]

6 See art. CELIBACY (Iranian).
7 *Zoroastrian Theology*, New York, 1914, p. 15.

All this is practically true of the Mazdean religion throughout its history and in all its stages. It is the characteristic difference between Mazdeism and all forms of Hinduism, with its *yōgis*, *sannyāsis*, or *faqīrs*. But, more than this, Dhalla's last sentence hints at the absence of another element, which has led J. H. Moulton, in his posthumous work, to say :

'One who loves and reveres Zarathushtra confesses with keen reluctance that saintship seems less easy to find in his community than in some religions which are far inferior in the apprehension of Truth. The reader will have realized ere this that with all its grandeur and purity Zoroastrianism as a whole has a certain coldness.'[1]

In other words, there is lacking, as above remarked, the element of personal 'devotion' to the Deity, so conspicuous not only in India but also, *e.g.*, in the Ṣūfīs of Persia. As Moulton puts it, 'Love is not the power that inspires the Gathas. The very word is practically absent from them.'[2]

The Avestan word that corresponds to our 'saint' is *ashavan* (*aśavan*, pl. *aśaono*), a derivative of the substantive *asha* (*aśa*), whether used as an abstract term signifying 'righteousness,' 'holiness'—the Old Persian *arta*, so common as an element in proper names, corresponding etymologically with the Skr. *ṛta*, 'established order,' 'divine law,' 'truth,' 'right,' and the Latin *ritus*—or as the name of the archangel or genius Asha, the personification of these ideas, originally conceived as an attribute of Ahura Mazda 'within the hypostasis of deity.'[3] *Ashavan* is strictly opposed to *dregvant*, the latter indicating a follower of Angra Mainyu, the spirit of evil, and his *daevas*, the former an adherent of Ahura Mazda, the supreme deity, and his 'good law.'[4] In this sense, then, it may be used in general of all good Zoroastrians, like 'saints' in the NT. But it also indicates specially the chief and most illustrious members of the Faith, and of course, κατ' ἐξοχήν, Zarathushtra himself.[5] Among those to whom the title of *ashavan* is specifically given in the Avesta we find such heroes of the Faith as Frashaostra, Jamāsp, Vīshtāspa (the Prophet's royal patron), Hvōvi (the Prophet's wife).

2. Cult of the saints.—Under this heading must come the special homage paid to those enigmatical beings, the *fravashis* of the holy ones.[6] Among the *Yashts* there is a very long 'litany of the saints,' the *Farvardīn Yasht*,[7] devoted to these personages—at least 336 in number—which Darmesteter likens to 'a Homer's catalogue.'[8] The last 27 are the names of female saints, either married or 'holy maids,' headed by Zarathushtra's wife Hvōvi and his three daughters. The great bulk of the names in the catalogue are quite unknown; some are of mythical personages; a considerable number are of the Prophet's patrons and chief disciples, headed by his own name. Like the other *Yashts*, this 'litany' is of comparatively late date, so we are not surprised to find here and there certain miraculous powers attributed to some of the saints. But it is more interesting to note that it not only embraces 'the first man,' Gayo Meretan, and winds up with Saoshyant, the future Saviour, who is to come at the end of the world, but includes also a number of those personages called *paoiryō-ṭkaēsha*, 'men of the Old Law,' who were believed to have worshipped Ahura Mazda and held his religion even before the coming of Zarathushtra, and who may be strictly compared to the Patriarchs of the OT before the Mosaic dispensation. To each name of the litany is attached the verb *yazamaide*, 'we worship (or venerate).'

[1] *The Treasure of the Magi*, London, 1917, p. 194 f.
[2] *Ib.* p. 195. [3] *Ib.* p. 24. [4] See art. ORMAZD.
[5] *Passim*, in both *Gāthās* and Later Avesta—once even without his name (*Yt.* xii. 1, 'the Saint').
[6] See art. FRAVASHI. [7] *Yt.* xiii.
[8] *SBE* xxiii. [1883] 179.

In the later Pahlavi, or so-called 'patristic,' literature the term *arta*, exactly corresponding to the Old Persian, as opposed to the Zend or Avestan form, is used as an epithet like our 'saint,' applied once at least to Zaratûsht (Zarathushtra) himself, and especially to Vīrāf, the Mazdean Dante, whose famous visit to hell and heaven is the subject matter of the *Artā-i Vīrāf Nāmak*,[1] which may be exactly translated 'the Book of Saint Vīrāf.'[2]

3. Martyrs.—Strictly speaking, a martyr is one who lays down his life in the cause of his religion or faith. There is a fairly unanimous tradition that the prophet Zarathushtra himself ended his life in this manner with 80 of his priests. The whole story is gone into with great wealth of detail and careful weighing of evidence by A. V. Williams Jackson in his life of the Prophet.[3] Briefly summed up, it comes to this :

During the last twenty years of Zarathushtra's life there were waged 'holy wars' between the Iranian king Vīshtāspa, the Prophet's convert—who has been styled the Constantine or the Ethelbert of his religion—and the Turanian Arejataspa, or Arjasp, the great enemy of the Faith. A dispute about tribute is said to have been the pretext of the Turanian invasions: 'the actual ground for difficulty, however, seems to have been the religious difference; for Vīshtāsp's adoption of the new Faith really lies at the basis of the trouble.'[4] The tradition is that it was during the second invasion, in all probability 583 B.C., that Zarathushtra with the other priests was massacred whilst at worship in the fire-temple (according to some at Balkh), and 'the fire was quenched with their blood.' The Greek legend about the Prophet's death by lightning seems to be quite apocryphal.

The celebrated 'magophonia,' or slaughter of the Magi, under the Achæmenid monarch Darius (521 B.C.) can hardly be reckoned in this category of martyrdoms; for it is by no means certain that these 'Magi' were really Zoroastrians, whilst, on the other hand, the bloody execution was a political measure rather than a religious persecution. Alexander the Great, after his overthrow of the Persian monarchy, though he was always referred to in subsequent Mazdean literature as 'the accursed Alexander' (*gajastak Alaksagdar*) and credited with the wanton destruction by fire of the greater part of the original Avesta, adopted a policy of conciliation with the Persians, and no religious persecution or martyrdom marked his reign. But the Arab conquest (A.D. 641) brought with it violent persecution of the Mazdean religion and real martyrdom for the few unhappy adherents of the national Faith who refused to adopt the creed of Islām, or did not succeed in making their escape from Persia, like the small band of 'Pilgrim Fathers,' the forbears of the modern Parsis of India. The great majority of the people seem to have been thus forcibly 'converted' to Muhammadanism—it is said at the rate of 100,000 a day[5]—so that the number of those who laid down their lives instead of apostatizing must have been relatively small, and no record of them seems to have been kept.[6]

LITERATURE.—See the ordinary translations and commentaries of the Avesta, and the writings of Dhalla, Moulton, and Williams Jackson as quoted in the footnotes.

L. C. CASARTELLI.

SAINTS AND MARTYRS (Japanese).—The true national religion of Japan, *i.e.* Shintō, knows neither saints nor martyrs. The absence of martyrs is easily explained. A martyr, in the proper sense of the word, is a man who suffers torture and even death to testify to the truth of his religious faith. Now, at the dawn of Japanese history we find Shintō firmly established as an official religion, its

[1] Ed. M. Haug and E. W. West, *The Book of Arda-Viraf*, Bombay, 1872.
[2] See the present writer's 'The Persian Dante,' in *The Dastur Hoshang Memorial Volume*, Bombay, 1913; and J. J. Modi, *Dante Papers*, do. 1914.
[3] *Zoroaster*, New York, 1901, pp. 102–132.
[4] Jackson, p. 106.
[5] D. F. Karaka, *Hist. of the Parsis*, London, 1884, i. 23.
[6] Cf. art. PERSECUTION (Muhammadan).

origin lost in legend; later, when Buddhism was introduced, its triumphal progress, largely due to the eclecticism of the Japanese, entailed no persecution of the partisans of the ancient worship. If we take the word 'martyr' in the broader sense of a man who suffers death for any noble cause—for the defence of a particular idea or of a political opinion — we find innumerable examples in the history of a heroic people like the Japanese, even in modern times; but these are not martyrs in the normal sense, the sense in which we speak of Christian martyrs.

As regards saints, their non-appearance in Shintō is simply due to their confusion with the gods. An expression which appears continually in Japanese literature is 'the *kami* and the *hotoke*,' 'the gods [of Shintō] and the saints [of Buddhism],' meaning the whole spiritual world of the two religions. Whilst Buddhism has practically no gods, but simply saints, Shintō has, properly speaking, no saints, but only gods. It does not, like Buddhism, reserve its admiration exclusively for men who, by their wisdom and intelligence, usually through several successive existences, have finally reached the perfection of Buddhas. Nor has it, like Christianity, a special category for the souls of the faithful who, sustained by divine grace, have died in the observance of certain religious virtues, have earned fame by miracles, and been assigned a place in paradise by their living adorers. In Shintō those who would be called saints by Buddhists or Christians are enrolled directly in the ranks of the deities, with the same rights as nature-powers or ancestors famed for achievements, services, useful discoveries, or other merits equally unconnected with sanctity. This conception appears very natural when we remember the extremely vague and relative character of the Japanese *kami*. See art. HEROES AND HERO-GODS (Japanese).

MICHEL REVON.

SAINTS AND MARTYRS (Jewish).—Judaism has its martyrs and its martyrologies, its saints and its specialized teachings on saintliness; but the position held by these in the Synagogue and its liturgy is far less prominent than that held in the Christian Church by the parallel literature. The Jew understood the word 'saint' (*ḳădôsh*, *ḥăsîd*, or *tsăddîḳ*) in quite a different sense. He was never made an object of religious worship, whether in life or in death; and the Christian idea of the canonization of saints on account of their eminently pious and pure lives is quite foreign to Jewish theology, which has nothing analogous to the *Acta Martyrum* and the *Acta Sanctorum* of the older Church. Whilst the Christian Church celebrated the anniversaries of the deaths of its saints by the intensely mystic formulæ connected with the sacrifice of the Mass, the Synagogue looked upon the heroes of the faith as Jews who had fulfilled the Law with heart, soul, and might, and who, if the necessity arose, would have undergone torture and death rather than infringe its commands. Many of these saints certainly did lay down their lives for the Law, but their claim to sainthood is based not upon the fact of their martyrdom but upon the exemplary Jewish life which they led. Nevertheless, the Synagogue perpetuated the memory of these martyred saints in a prayer commencing 'Āb Hā-rāḥămîm' ('Father of Mercies'), which was, and still is at this day, recited in all places of worship on the last days of festivals, on the Day of Atonement, and on the Sabbaths preceding the feast of Pentecost and the 9th of Ab (the anniversary of the destruction of Jerusalem).

But there was another way — one partaking rather of a religio-secular character—in which the memories of saints and martyrs were kept from fading. The custom arose among the Jews of mediæval Europe of compiling necrologies. MS lists which, originally known as *Sĕfĕr Hă-Zikrōnōth* (*i.e.* 'Book of Records'), afterwards became generally known as 'Memor-Books' (Germ. *Memorbuch*) were made of the names of martyrs and of the localities in which they met their fate. These 'Memor-Books' were possessed by many a mediæval synagogue, and the contents were read out to the congregation during service on holy days and on the Day of Atonement. The 'Memor-Books' bore some resemblance to the necrologies, calendars, and martyrologies of the Roman Catholic Church —but only in form; in matter they are essentially and characteristically Jewish. The object of the compilation seems to have been not so much that of inciting to prayer on behalf of the dead—a practice by no means over-prominent in Jewish worship—as that of preserving for future generations the inner history of local communities. The names recorded in these lists—the earliest extant specimen being the *Memor Book of Nüremberg*, begun in 1296 by a scribe, Isaac ben Samuel of Meiningen, and presented to the community of Nüremberg at the dedication of one of its synagogues in 1296—are principally, though by no means entirely, those of Jews distinguished for their great Talmudic learning or for their admirable qualities as philanthropists or communal workers. The entire book, in which numerous entries were made after 1296, was edited by S. Salfeld[1] in 1896–98, and contains, besides poems (in Hebrew) and prayers for the heroes who sleep their last sleep, an elaborate martyrology which is introduced by a summary of the persecutions suffered by the Jews of France and Germany from 1096 (the year of the First Crusade) till 1298, the names of the martyrs between 1096 and 1349, and a list of towns and villages in which abundant martyrdoms took place at the time of the Black Death (1348–49). It is of this blood-stained period of Jewish history, stretching down to the 17th cent., that Graetz says:

> 'The persecutions and massacres of the Jews increased with frightful rapidity and intensity, and only alternated with inhuman decrees issued both by the Church and by the State, the aim and purport of all of which were to humiliate the Jews, to mark them with conspicuous brands, and to drive them to suicide. . . . It mattered little to the Jews whether they lived under proper government or under anarchy, for they suffered under the one no less than under the other.'[2]

The mediæval Jewish communities which suffered the greatest numbers of martyrdoms were those of Worms (1096 and 1349), Cologne (1096), Mayence (1096 and 1349), Blois (1171), Nüremberg (1298), Troyes (1288), Navarre (1328), Augsburg (1349), and Erfurt (1349). According to Zunz,[3] the communities of Cologne, Worms, Mayence, and a few other cities in the Rhine district observed fast-days in memory of the saints and martyrs who perished 'for the Sanctification of the Name' during the First Crusade (1096).

Mention must here be made of one exceptionally striking martyrology to be found in the Midrashic literature and known as the מדרש עשרה הרוני מלכות ('the Midrash of the Ten Martyrs') or מדרש אלה אזכרה ('the Midrash beginning with the words, "These do I remember"'). There are four extant versions of this, each differing from the others in various points of detail.[4] The work is a product of the Gaonic period of Rabbinic literature and is a curious embellishment of the narratives given in many passages of the Babylonian Talmud and the

[1] *Das Martyrologium des Nürnberger Memorbuches*, Berlin, 1898.
[2] *Hist. of the Jews*, Eng. tr., London, 1891–92, iii. 630 f.
[3] *Die Monatstage des Kalenderjahres*, Berlin, 1872, pp. 40–58.
[4] See A. Jellinek, *Bet ha-Midrasch*², Leipzig and Vienna, 1853–77, i. 64, vi. 19.

early Palestinian Midrashim[1] of how ten great and saintly teachers of the Law suffered martyrdom in the reign of Hadrian for having, in defiance of an imperial edict, founded schools for the study of the *Tôrāh*. The ten martyrdoms are represented as having taken place on one and the same day, which is contrary to the Talmudic view. This was most probably done with the intention of heightening the effect on the reader. These ten martyrs were all of them 'saints' in the real Jewish sense of that term—men of exceptional learning in the Law and of spotless conduct, whose single-minded, self-sacrificing zeal in the cause of the propagation of the *Tôrāh* among the masses showed itself in a readiness to accept torture and death rather than a life in which the Law of God had no place. The most famous of the ten is 'Aqiba ben Joseph (A.D. 50–130), whose last moments are invested by the Rabbinic recorders with an ultra-heroic fortitude.

Amidst his excruciating agonies he recited the *Shema* with a peaceful smile on his face. Asked by the executioner whether he was not a sorcerer, seeing that he appeared to feel no pain, 'Aqiba replied: 'I am no sorcerer, but am overcome with joy at the thought that the opportunity has at last been given me of carrying out the Deuteronomic precept, "And thou shalt love the Lord thy God with all thy heart, and with all thy soul, and with all thy might."' He expired with the word 'One' (*i.e.* confession of the Divine Unity) on his lips.

The deaths of several of the remaining nine martyrs are ornamented with highly-coloured details which are purely legendary. It has ever been, and still is to-day, the custom of the Synagogue to recite the martyrdom of these ten sainted Rabbis in a special *seliḥah* (*i.e.* prayer for forgiveness) on the Day of Atonement. The *seliḥah* is a poem based on the above-mentioned 'Midrash of the Ten Martyrs.' Another poetic form of it appears in the *Kīnah*, commencing with the words 'Cedars of Lebanon,' recited in all orthodox synagogues on the 9th of Ab.

It remains now to state more explicitly what, in the Jewish view, constitutes the quality of saintliness and the title to the dignity of sainthood. As has already been said, one need not have undergone martyrdom in order to be regarded as a saint; and the fact that many among the latter order became martyrs is but one of the accidents of history. M. H. Luzzatto has aptly characterized the Jewish standpoint thus:

'Whosoever loveth God the Creator with a true love will not think that he has acquitted himself of this duty of love by merely following out the religious rules which are practised by Jews generally. He will rather resemble the loving son who carries out the father's wish to an extent far beyond what the father expects of him—and all for the purpose of causing him additional pleasure.'[2]

In other words, saintliness is a higher stage of religious loyalty transcending all idea of law or rule. The Talmud expresses it thus:

'Sanctify thyself even in that which is permitted to thee.'[3]

Such is the saintliness which in the Talmud and all the Jewish mediæval theology is termed *ḥăsīdūth*. The doer of it (*i.e.* the *ḥăsīd*) does not wait for a distinct commandment. His service of God is prompted and sustained by his own inner instincts untrammelled by any instruction from without. One possession, however, is indispensable to him—learning. The saint must be a man of learning; and only a man of learning can be a saint.[4] The Mishnāh speaks ironically of the 'illiterate saint,' stigmatizing him as belonging to those undesirables 'who turn the universe into a chaos';[5] and the Talmud describes such an 'illiterate saint' as 'one who would see a woman drown without giving her a helping hand because of the rule forbidding a man to look upon a woman.'[6]

[1] See, *e.g.*, T.B. *'Abōdāh Zārāh*, 17*b*, 18*a*; *Ber.* 61*b*; *Sanh.* 14*a*; *Lam. Rabbāh*, ii. 2.
[2] See *Messīlat Yeshārīm*, Amsterdam, 1740, ch. xviii.
[3] T.B. *Yebāmōth*, 20*a*.
[4] Cf. *Mishnāh Abōth*, ii. 6.
[5] *Mishnāh Sôṭāh*, v. 2.
[6] T.B. *Sôṭāh*, 21*b*.

Besides the saints mentioned in the early part of this article as having undergone martyrdom, the following who were not martyrs stand out prominently: Hillel the Elder (30 B.C.–A.D. 10), who at his death was eulogized as 'the saint, the meek, the disciple of Ezra';[1] R. Hūna and R. Ḥisda (4th cent. A.D.), whose prayers for rain were very efficacious;[2] Mar Zūtra (4th cent. A.D.), who, when finding it necessary to rebuke a disciple and put him under the ban (*ḥĕrem*), would first exercise these inflictions on himself and then on the disciple.[3] The typical Jewish saint of the Middle Ages is R. Judah ben Samuel Hă Ḥăsīd of Regensburg († 1217), who wrote, in Hebrew, a famous ethical work (*Ṣĕfĕr Ḥăsīdīm*) which contains various original and quaint maxims relating to this order. The mediæval *ḥăsīd* was usually saint and mystic combined. Superior holiness, independence of 'law,' and a partial withdrawal from things earthly brought about a state of communion with the divine which is the prime incentive to the mystic life.

LITERATURE.—In addition to the literature already alluded to ee A. Neubauer, 'Le Memorbuch de Mayence,' in *REJ* iv. [1887] 1 ff.; H. Graetz, *Gesch. der Juden*, Leipzig, 1866–78, iv. 161 ff.; S. Schechter, *Some Aspects of Rabbinic Theology*, London, 1909, pp. 199–218; *JE*, *s.vv.* 'Martyrology,' 'Martyrs, the Ten,' 'Saint and Saintliness.'

J. ABELSON.

SAINTS AND MARTYRS (Muhammadan).

—**1. Relation of the two terms.**—The saints of Islām are commonly regarded as martyrs, but the latter term is of wider application than the word 'saint.' Those who die in the 'holy war' (*jihād*) are martyrs, but not necessarily saints.

2. General prevalence of the veneration of saints.—Every neighbourhood in the Muslim world has its patron saint and in addition recognizes the claims of saints elsewhere. There are also saints who belong to the universal community of believers rather than to the special shrines where they are honoured. To this class belong the Prophet, the first three *khalīfahs*, 'Alī, his two sons, the Khidr, the greatest of the OT worthies, and possibly some others.

3. Names.—The common Arabic term for a saint is *walī*; for a martyr it is *shahīd*. The former implies more precisely one who is near, a friend (*i.e.* of God); it is usually applied to living saints, but is very generally employed of the dead. The term is also used regularly in a secondary sense for the tombs of the saints. *Shahīd* is, primarily, one who gives testimony as an eye-witness, then one who seals his testimony with his blood (commonly employed in the plural *shuhadā* of those who are killed fighting the battles of Islām). The living saint, particularly, is spoken of as the *shaikh*, in the same honorific way as we make use of 'elder,' though with more intensive meaning. *Zāhid* has a special reference to the ascetic self-denial of the eminently pious. *Sā'iḥ* has in view rather the hermit saint who retires from the common life to dwell in the desert. The Ṣūfī is a member of the mystical movement called in Islām Ṣūfiism (*q.v.*). The Ṣūfī may be a saint, but the term does not necessarily declare that he is.

4. Attitude of Islām towards saint-worship.—(*a*) *Sunnīs.*—Since the days of al-Ghazālī (12th cent. A.D.) the Sunnite branch of Islām (excepting the Hanbalite school) has given its approval to the cult of the saints. The orthodox teachers claim that what is accorded the saint is not worship. Nor is there any thought of the saint having power in himself to answer prayer. The Qur'ān and the Sunnah recognize intercession on the part of those favoured by Allāh, and the orthodox Sunnīs say that there is no cult of saints beyond the permissible seeking of their help as mediators

[1] T.B. *Sôṭāh*, 48*b*.
[2] See T.B. *Ta'ănīth*, 22*a*, *b*.
[3] T.B. *Mô'ēd Kāṭān*, 17*a*.

with God. The more intelligent may approach Allāh in this orthodox way, but the vast majority of unthinking Muslims regard the *walī* as being a proper object of worship and in himself the source of blessing. The Bedawīn and the Kabyle tribes of N. Africa, with the *fellaḥīn* of Egypt and Syria, may employ phrases which seem to imply an orthodox attitude, but in reality the saint is a far more real God to them than Allāh is. If the orthodox teachers of the Sunnīs were not compelled to accept the facts of the situation, they would see that the general practice of Islām as to the saints was a violation of the Qur'ān and the Sunnah. It imperils the unique deity of Allāh and leads directly to *shirk*, the 'association' of other objects with Him in worship. It sets aside the authority of the Prophet in adopting a basis of religion which is in conflict with the primary sources sanctioned by him.

(*b*) *Shī'ahs*—The Shī'ahs are enthusiastic worshippers of the saints, and their writers especially have been responsible for the production of martyrologies and other literature relating to them. Persia has been the home of Muslim mysticism. It is the native soil of the Ṣūfī movement, and within Ṣūfīism there is provided a prescribed discipline for saintship. The whole Shī'ah movement is one which gathers round the idea of a 'Holy Family,' and most of all about the sufferings of the 'People of the House,' as the family of 'Alī and the Prophet's daughter Faṭima were styled. In the 'People of the House' (*Ahlu 'l-Bait*) there has been found a conspicuous invitation calling their followers to saintship, and in the spiritual atmosphere charged with emotion excited by their pains and sacrifices there has been a powerful stimulus to imitation. The Ṣūfīs have gone beyond loyalty to recognized authority as understood by the Shī'ah. Their ideal is a life in which law and authority have no place and the notion of obedience is excluded. For this reason the orthodox Shī'ahs are jealously suspicious of the professors of saintship among the Ṣūfīs. The saints of the Shī'ah provinces have very often based their claims upon alleged descent from the holy *imāms*: they are *sayyids*, nobility. They are in parts so numerous that their number has become a subject of innocent jesting. The Persians, as well as the Berbers of N. Africa, are more favourable to women saints than are the Arabs.

(*c*) *Hanbalites.*—The Hanbalites find no room for the cult of the saints. They hold that it is contrary to the Qur'ān and the Sunnah. To this the other Sunnites, who are favourable to the cult, answer that it is supported by the Consensus of Islām through hundreds of years. The Hanbalites do not deny the authority of the Consensus (*Ijmā'*), but claim that *Ijmā'*, properly understood, embraces only the agreed opinion of the first age of Islām. The Consensus of the Companions of the Prophet condemns the offering of worship to any but Allāh, and this, added to the voice of the other great authorities, Qur'ān and Tradition, is deemed to be decisive against the practice. The Hanbalite school has made its influence felt at different times. 'Umār II., at a date earlier than the foundation of the school, had refused to face the grave of the Prophet towards Mecca, lest it should become a shrine where prayer would be offered to the Prophet along with Allāh. Ibn Taimīyya, a Hanbalite, in the 14th cent. A.D. wrote against the veneration of the *walīs*, including the cult of the Prophet's tomb at Medīna. The latter had become part of the prescriptions for the *hajj* and had come under Hanbalite censure as *bid'a*, 'innovation.' Earnestly as Ibn Taimīyya set himself to oppose the popular favour shown to the saints, he accomplished little and brought persecution upon himself. He died in prison in A.D. 1328, and by a certain irony of fate came to be regarded as a saint by those who accepted his views. The Hanbalites kept alive his principles until, at the end of the 18th cent., the iconoclastic Wahhābī crusade again sought to make them effective by the destruction of tombs and shrines throughout Arabia and the adjacent lands. Not even the most venerable shrines, such as the tombs of the Prophet and the earliest *khalīfahs* at Medīna, and the shrines of the great martyrs of the Shī'ahs—'Alī, Ḥusain, and the *imām* Riḍā—were spared. The Wahhābī desolation was brought to an end when Muhammad 'Alī's forces finally overcame the Wahhābī army in 1818. Since that time the Wahhābīs have been indeed represented by the Wahhābī State in central Arabia, by groups of extreme Hanbalites in the eastern part of Arabia, and by a few sectaries in India; but the attempt to check saint-worship has been a failure, nor will it ever succeed as long as Islām continues to be what it has been for 900 years past.

5. The conception of saintship in Islām.—The saint is one who is near to God, a 'friend of God.' In Islām, as in less advanced religions, this has no necessary ethical implication. It does imply the indwelling and inspiration of 'divinity.' The saint has a supernatural quality by reason of which he (or she) is held to be above criticism and by some is thought to be invulnerable against attack on either body or soul. It is this quality that explains the superhuman knowledge and power of the saint and makes him the source of either miraculous blessing or terrible and mysterious curses.

This 'light of the saint' is said by the orthodox to come to him as a gift of God through the mediation of the Prophet. The miracles (*karamāt*) are a grace from Allāh with which He honours His servant. The orthodox will not allow that the saint is by nature more than human nature commonly suggests. What is beyond that is endowment. In the thought of the Muslim peasantry and the Bedawīn of the desert there is only one conception, namely, that the saint is of a divine nature and can by reason of his inherent capacity do acts that lie properly within the power of God and know things knowable only to a god. It has been truly said that, in spite of their profession of Islām, the ignorant populations in many Muslim lands have but slight spiritual relations in religious thought and feeling with any god other than the *walī*. Allāh is at most a name, without power to stir interest in those who use it, and without effect in moulding their purposes.

In the case of each individual saint there was a time when he began to be esteemed a saint. Those about him took note of certain characteristic features. He was a man whose thought was filled with God, who lived in God, and whose acts were moved by God. He was judged to be a man who had renounced desire and had become completely passive, a vessel for divine inspiration, a receptacle for a deposit of divine qualities and influences. To the soul thus prepared there come such thoughts and impulses as are proper to a life secluded, shut off from the avenues of ordinary human experience, and shut in to a purely self-occupied experience which is saturated by a ruling religious motive. The impression made by a man of such a mode of life would be infallibly that of a man 'possessed' by divine influences. Such a mysterious human being easily fancied himself the recipient of divine communications or one appointed to undertake marvels. His proofs were subjective and were not easily disputed by others. Many of the saints have been eccentrics, defectives, or idiots (not insane). Such persons have been thought to be saints because they, too, have become emptied receptacles which Allāh was to fill and use. Their pure souls have been taken up to heaven, and what has remained of them was esteemed a most meet and fitting vessel of inspiration. As long as this class of persons was typical of what a saint should be, the lesser peculiarities, begotten of mere habitual introspection and negation of self, procured a reputation for sanctity in proportion to their extravagance.

While many who have achieved saintship did not renounce the world and separate themselves from their fellow-men, the surest path to saintship was found in poverty and a contempt of the world. Thus it comes about that the typical garb of the saint is that of the beggar and his habit of life is that which answers to his garb. Poverty and sanctity are so far synonymous that the most effective counterfeit of the saint is the *faqīr*, or beggar—a term which still serves to indicate the saint, but is also all too commonly made to denote beggars who, being such and nothing more, would pass for saints.

The contempt for the world led a fair proportion of the saints to a hermit life in the desert or, in the case of the Ṣūfīs, to a cloister life under the direction of a *murshid*, or spiritual director, often in a *zāwiyah*, or community house. Scorn of the world also finds expression in another way. The saint spurns the esteem of men, deeming it a temptation to a divided devotion, and provokes with careful deliberation their ill-will. In this way he is the more inevitably set apart unto God. With this traditional attitude, it is easy to understand that in the early days of the khalifate the 'saints' were in many cases opposed to the government of their time and were found allied with seditious movements and conspiracies. For one or other party in a quarrel to obtain the support of some powerful *shaikh* was sure to bring many to that side. The saints as a matter of course were generally of the revolutionary party; but they were not always so. The illustrious martyr, the *imām* Riḍā, was bought at a great price to support the policy of the *khalīfah* al-Mamun, and many of the most influential of the *shaikhs* of Morocco in the 16th cent. A.D. were supporters of the reigning rulers. The earliest of the Safawid kings of Persia in the 16th cent. were themselves saints and enjoyed the spontaneous support of the *shaikhs* of their time. In fact, the saints of the modern period of history have been loyal to the powers that be and have been held in esteem by them.

One of the cherished evidences of saintship is the inspired dream or the ecstatic vision in which the Prophet, one of the *imāms*, or one of the greater saints appears to one who is thus shown to be in the favour of heaven. The nature of the communication granted is not as important as the vision itself.

There is no disapproval of the warlike character in a saint. It has always been to the glory of the Prophet that he was a man of war; and, among his successors, the holy martyrs 'Alī and Ḥusain acquired an added lustre of saintliness from the fact that they were men of proved martial quality. In the hagiologies the warlike deeds of the saints find a large place. There is found also allusion to carrying a saint's dead body into battle to ensure victory.

According to the accepted view, the *walīs* form an invisible order with ascending dignities and ranks. At the head is the leading saint of the age, who bears the title *quṭb* (literally 'pole,' 'axis'). Under him are deputies, commonly reckoned to be three in number, and in Egypt designated by the respective names, *nakīb*, *nagīb*, and *badīl*. He has his favourite abodes on earth, one of which is the roof of the Ka'bah in Mecca and another the Bab-az-Zuwailah (or Bab al-Mutawallī) in Cairo. It is his custom to appear in some familiar disguise among men, and to reveal his presence at times by the performance of some mysterious and uncanny act which, despite unpromising appearances, often turns out to be really beneficent in its purpose. Among the saints of Morocco two or three are said to have attained the rank of *quṭb*, but there is reason to suppose that this refers rather to the perfect stage of the Ṣūfī *tarīqah*, or discipline.

The pains and death of the *walīs*, especially of such as had been the victims of persecution, were deemed to have a merit not needed on their own account by beings of such sanctity. Such merit therefore is supposed to be available for those who seek the intercession and help of the saint. It is both prudent and pious to entrust one's soul to such an one as the *walī*, whether for this life or for the life to come. It is from this kind of motive that Muslims in all parts of Islām desire that their bodies should rest under the shadow of some *walī* (here used in the secondary sense of the tomb of a *walī*). The presence of the tomb of Ḥusain at Kerbela, that of 'Alī at Nejef, and that of the *imām* Riḍā at Meshed have caused the bodies of thousands of persons to be brought to these places for burial, sometimes from a great distance. In Syria[1] the *walīs* (tombs of the saints) stand frequently in the midst of a number of humbler graves which have gathered about them as time has passed. The dead rest in peace under the protection of the *walī*.

While it would be admitted to have occurred only in very rare cases, the teaching of Islām is that the gifts of a saint may be withdrawn by Allāh for mortal sin or for infidelity.

6. Origins of the cult of saints.—It is in the essential nature of Islām that it should call for a renunciation of the world and a committal of oneself to God. Consistently, therefore, the Prophet himself, on entering upon his preaching mission, gave up secular ambitions (*dunya*) and urged his hearers to do the same. In contrast to the motive of later saintship, Muhammad's motive in demanding renunciation of the world was not to meet the requirements of a profession, but to glorify Allāh and save men's souls. The term which came to be applied to such an ascetic withdrawal from the world as Muhammad at first contemplated is *zuhd*. It implies an ideal which the opportunities and temptations of power soon thrust out of his thought, and as long as his followers were occupied with the lust and sweets of military conquest it remained neglected. There are traditions dealing with the Prophet's Medīnan period which echo even positive disapproval of the ascetic life. Shortly after Muhammad's death the pious life seemed to have found its best type in men diligent in religious duties while at the same time efficiently pursuing the aims of their earthly vocation. It was inevitable that a religious revolution like Islām, in its period of reconstruction following the early conquests, should revert to its original ideal. The ascetic life claimed many followers and in the early days of the Umayyad *khalīfahs* they were described by a special name, *'ubbad* (='religious' in the French sense of the word). This term implies a life with two distinctive aspects: (1) exclusive occupation with God (*tawakkul*); (2) worship in prayer, recitation of the Qur'ān, and meditation (*dhikr*).

About the close of the 1st cent. of the Hegira men began to write about the marks and rules of the saintly life, and devotees began to be regarded as divinely inspired. There was furnished a motive to turn true saintliness into a professional

[1] Cf. art. SAINTS AND MARTYRS (Syrian).

calling. For this the suggestion was conveniently at hand in the presence of Christian monks and hermits within the Muslim domain. Abstinence, poverty, and reproach became the badge of sanctity, and the rough woollen garb (*ṣūf*) of the beggar and criminal was chosen to advertise saintship as a vocation. The Ṣūfī movement took its start from this unorganized pursuit of what was now conventionally recognized as a holy life. Ṣūfīism originated in Persia, but before it took its rise the profession of the saint was already as widespread as Islām itself.

It has been intimated that the earlier saints of Islām were men engaged in the public affairs of their time. With the growing ascendancy of the Turks in the eastern khalifate, the devotees were gradually eliminated from positions of influence, but meanwhile the Ṣūfī life had become more popular, and the number of those who adopted it gradually increased. The movement was carried into Africa and Syria, and wherever it went it produced its own type of saints—a type which exaggerated the features of the earlier devotees and intensified the interest in the mystic aspects of religion. The later saints of Islām have probably all felt the influence of the Ṣūfī spirit and practice, though even among the Shī'ahs the extreme type of Ṣūfī is condemned; in Egypt they are under the supervision of the Shaikh al-Bakrī. The Safawid dynasty had its origin in a line of Ṣūfī saints, and in its early days (1502 onwards) there were fairly good relations between official Shī'ism and Ṣūfīism.

7. Cult of the saints.—The living saint is resorted to for the purpose of securing his advice or his decision in a legal dispute, to obtain his opinion as to the success of private or public undertakings, to ask his intercession on behalf of the sick, or to seek the gift of a child, especially a son. His active help may be requested and given for various purposes, inasmuch as nothing is too difficult for his miraculous powers. The removal of some blight or plague from field or flock, the healing of human ailments, the confounding of enemies, are all within the province and gift of the *shaikh*. Those whom he serves are only too glad to provide for him the means of living. His interposition is beneficent to those who ask it with honest purpose, but to those who oppose him or act dishonestly his supernatural power works in awful and mysterious punishment. The supernatural element in the saint is an extremely jealous and resentful power, very like the divinities of primitive monolatrous communities. There is a natural awe before one on whom has descended the 'light of inspiration'; in his immediate vicinity marvels happen; men do not presume to treat him familiarly; only the profane would venture to dispute his purposes, and only the recklessly wicked would dare to inflict persecution upon him. Physical contact with a saint, whether with or without his knowledge, may draw from him a supernatural effluence for healing or blessing, and objects that have been in close relation to his person may operate for good or harm without his being present.

The dead saint is in the nearer presence of God, and, according to a principle found widely in primitive religions, is more fully charged with supernatural influence than he was during his lifetime. He is now a *walī* in a more potent sense, one in whom the divine is more intimately at home and more readily active. Many more persons now resort to him, and much greater pains are taken to gain access to him and to do him honour. Men assume towards him the same worshipful attitude as they assume towards God, and freely think of him as one who can secure to them all the blessings for which men usually ask God. For the unreflecting worshipper the approach to the saint seeks no Higher Being beyond him, and rests fully satisfied in his sufficiency. The cultivation of the *walī* is a truly religious practice which often takes the place of the worship of Allāh. The phrases of orthodoxy and the Qur'ān are echoed in the liturgy of the saints, but they are used by ignorant and humble worshippers as magical formulas to predispose the saint favourably. Nevertheless, Muslim authority has taken the *walī* cult under its protection, and one may say that the real power of Islām over its lower classes lies in its promotion of saint-worship on the one hand and in the emotional atmosphere created by Ṣūfīism on the other. It is to the credit of al-Ghazālī that he found a way to retain these more vital forms of religious life as elements of Islām wherewith to counteract the effects of its unappealing dogmatism and institutionalism.

The local centre of the saint's influence after his death is his tomb. From that centre a tutelary benefit extends over the neighbouring community, of which he is the patron spirit. Beyond that his magical influence may reach as far as a prosaic peasant imagination may deem it strong enough to go, possibly to a radius of fifteen miles from the tomb. But the virtue of a *walī* may be carried to any distance by his relics. The most cherished of these is his ragged robe, which falls to the successor nominated by himself. It is especially infected by the supernatural quality of its one-time owner.

One leaves one's prayer with a saint at his shrine together with a vow to be fulfilled when the answer is received. Meanwhile the act of petition truly performed has been an act of faith in a power believed to be divine, and the petitioner goes away comforted by the reaction of his own faith—a blessing of no little moment. Occasionally prayers are written and left in faith at the grave of the saint.

8. Tombs of the saints: walīs.—These are of common occurrence in all parts of the Muhammadan world. Every little village has its *walī*. As a rule they are placed in a conspicuous position and are readily recognized by the domed roof of the building containing the grave. The dome (*ḳubbah*) is whitewashed, care being taken in every well-regulated community that some individual or family shall assume responsibility to give it a new coat when needed.

In poor and out-of-the-way places the tomb, sometimes called *ḳubbah* as well as *walī*, may be only a rude, frail structure of sticks, perhaps open above to the sky. In some cases a natural cave has been chosen as the shrine because of ancient religious or demonic associations. Sometimes the location of *walīs* has been determined by a lingering tradition from an earlier pagan or Jewish sanctuary. Again there are cases where, in the lack of a historical saint, the name of the place itself becomes the text for a saint's legend, which then becomes attached to the spot and makes out of it a *walī*, or saint's tomb. In settled communities the *walī* comprises a plot of ground, the front part of which constitutes a court, possibly 20 ft. square, and generally surrounded by a wall. Beyond this is the tomb proper (*ḳubbah*), which is often a low building 15 to 20 ft. square. Within the *ḳubbah* is the grave, which may be a somewhat elaborate structure, or again may be only a plain cenotaph. There may be grated windows, a grating overhead, and a grated door. The door-posts, the lintel, and the threshold or door-step play an important part in the blood ritual of the saint's cult. The grave is covered with a cloth, sometimes green, sometimes white.

Within the *ḳubbah* are found offerings of many kinds which have been left with the saint, though edible offerings, where they are left at the shrine, are perquisites of the *shaikh*, or ministrant. In some of the *walīs* there have been found great numbers of jars and other pieces of pottery, many of which have been broken in honour of the saint. Attached to the gratings of the *ḳubbah* or placed upon the grave are articles of apparel or rags torn from them. Those who thus leave in contact with the *walī* articles which have been associated closely with their persons are supposed to be under his care and to share in the blessing of his efficacious influence. The neighbouring tree or grove of the saint is his property and a part of the shrine. To the tree of the *walī* rags and articles of clothing are likewise attached, and with a similar motive.

In the court of the *walī* there is sometimes found a spring forming a pool or fountain. It may be a mineral spring, possibly a hot spring, in which case it is connected with the healing powers of the *shaikh*, and to drink or bathe, as the case may be, will cure disease, remove sterility, or restore the mentally deranged, provided the good offices of the saint can be secured.

The area of the *walī* affords asylum from blood revenge and places animals or other property which may in any way come within the sacred limits under the protection of the saint; the animal or article becomes his property for the time being. In various parts of Syria farming implements are found lying about the tomb of a *walī*; there is no likelihood of their ever being disturbed or appropriated, as the curse of the saint is thought to rest upon the violator of his tomb. In spite of this feeling that the saint will fully guard his own rights, there is also a lively jealousy on the part of the saint's worshippers in certain cases, and intrusion upon the sanctity of a shrine may be violently punished by them. This E. H. Palmer[1] proved on the occasion of his visit to the famous tomb of Nebī Harīn, in the Sinaitic peninsula. The Benē-Ma'azeh, who are the special followers of the saint, angrily resented the visit which they supposed he had made to the shrine, and serious trouble was narrowly averted.

The *shaikh*, or ministrant, as a rule lives in the neighbouring village or town. The office generally descends in a given family, and in some cases not merely one member is set aside as *shaikh*, but the several males of the family are designated to act. The function of the *shaikh* is to direct worshippers as to their duties, to supervise the offering of votive sacrifices, and to receive the portion of the saint, which is quarter of a sheep or goat, together with the hide, or a relatively smaller share if the victim be a larger animal, such as a cow or camel. The *shaikh* may be called upon to furnish what is lacking to a sacrificial meal, if the number of participants be too large for the offerer's portion of his sacrifice. The offerer may ask or buy from the ministrant the additional provision which he requires.

The sacrificial victim is regularly a male animal at least six months old. It is slaughtered by the offerer, usually at the door-step of the *ḳubbah*. It is thrown upon its left side and made to face towards Mecca, and is killed in this position. The blood is applied to the door-posts of the tomb and sometimes to the lintel. In a number of instances the victim is slaughtered upon the roof of the *ḳubbah* in such a position that its blood flows down over the lintel of the door-opening. Very often, instead of the blood being smeared, the hand of the offerer is dipped in the sacrificial blood and imprinted upon the door-posts. In the case of a child who has been the subject of a vow the blood is applied to the forehead and the tip of the nose or to the latter only.

Where the offerer is too poor to afford anything more, it is permissible to bring to the saint a fowl. In the case of inability to bring the victim, or to have present at the shrine those who should take part in the feast, permission may be given to conduct the ceremonies at home and bring the price of the *shaikh's* part to the *walī*.

Most of the offerings are votive in character. A visit is made to the saint's tomb with the object of obtaining his help in order to secure some desired end. The petition is presented with due observance of the required ritual, and with it a vow is made contingent upon the fulfilment of the petition. When the prayer has been fulfilled, the vow is due. It may be a vow calling for an offering made once for all, or it may call for a yearly offering. If the vow be not paid, the saint is supposed to visit dire temporal misfortune on the recreant worshipper; notwithstanding this, unpaid vows are regularly collected in some places by a person appointed for the purpose.

The feast which is enjoyed by the worshipper and his friends is not a commensal feast in which the divinity makes one with other guests at the table, nor is there any notion of the victim being itself sacred or divine. The view is that the *walī*, out of what has become his property by the gift of the offerer, spreads a feast for his guests and they, as they share the feast, rejoice before him. The victim is made ready, not by roasting, but by boiling.

The occasional worship represented by the visits of those who have vows to make and petitions to present, or who wish to pay a vow, contains also an element of honorific worship. The motive is not wholly self-centred. The ritual expresses reverence and adoration such as belong to religious worship, and the desire is to celebrate the greatness of the saint and give him his meed of respect. The recitation of the Qur'ān, the repetition of the formulas, the feast, are *for* the saint in the sense of being for his advantage. They are *to* him in the sense of being a tribute of worship. The offering of the blood has a special motive; in many instances it is a *keffārah*, which may be understood to be a means of removing sin; in other more numerous instances it is a *fedū*, which may be taken to imply a propitiatory offering or a ransom.

The individual or family visits to the *walī* are properly described by the term *ziyārah*, though less frequently the term *ḥajj* is employed. The latter term in strictness belongs to the Meccan pilgrimage. The *ziyārah* is more especially applied to the annual pilgrimage which is observed in connexion with the greater number of shrines. These annual pilgrimages are occasions when the whole community, men, women, and children, takes part, and, in the case of some famous saints, people from far and near also participate. This is to be observed at the annual feast of Nebī Mūsā, east of the Dead Sea. There are reported to have been as many as 15,000 present at the annual celebration of this *walī*. The great days at Meshed, Nejef, and Kerbela are occasions for the whole Shī'ah world. At some of the shrines Jews and Christians are present to do honour to one who has often had a longer record of respect with them than among the Muslims. The participation on the part of non-Muslims is confined for the most part to saints who were Jewish or Christian before they were Muslim. At very many *walīs* the intermingling of outsiders and Muhammadans is not allowed. As Palmer[1] described the annual *ziyārah* at Nebī Sāleh, it included a procession round the *ḳubbah*, a visit to the grave, the sacrifices, and the common festival meal. Outside of these prescribed obligations, the time was occupied by merry-making and apparently love-making, by games

[1] *The Desert of the Exodus*, New York, 1872, p. 364 ff.

[1] *Op. cit.* p. 218 f.

and contests of various kinds. The annual feast of the saint is regularly fixed on the traditional day of his birth, the *maulid* of the *walī*.

Other feasts are held at many shrines. In some cases the month day of the saint is kept.

Such saints as al-Khidr, the Quṭb, 'Alī, Ḥusain, and Ḥasan, and even St. George (Mar Jirjis, *mar* =*walī* in Syria), are deemed ubiquitous, though they have their local shrines and local community of worshippers. The same may be said of some of the Shī'ah *imāms*, especially 'the Hidden *imām*.'

The Metāwileh and the Nuṣairīyah of Syria have an exaggerated reverence for saints. The latter should not be regarded, however, as Muslims. The Isma'ilīyah, wherever they are found, have developed extreme views likewise.

9. Efficacy of the cult.—It is firmly believed that miraculous answers are granted to the petitions presented to the saints, and it may be allowed that instances of child-bearing have followed such prayers. For these the most satisfactory explanation is that mental suggestion has been powerful enough to effect a desired physiological change. It is the belief of the *walī*-worshippers that, in cases of barrenness, conception, if it occurs, is to be attributed to the saint. It is said that this belief leads the *shaikhs* in charge of some shrines to actual cohabitation with women who come seeking the gift of a child from the saint. It has not been shown that this occurs often.

The relics of the saint are often preserved in connexion with the tomb and have in themselves efficacy for blessing. The merits of the saint have atoning value with God and constitute a ground of confidence in the efficacy of his intercession. To the merits of the *walī* the devotions of those who worship at his grave add increase continually. But, as intimated above, for most of those who come the idea of the saint as a mediator is not uppermost. He is looked upon by them as in himself an original source of help and blessing.

The effect of the *walī*-cult has been to foster superstition and belief in magic among the ignorant classes of Islām. It has, nevertheless, served to bind more firmly to the Muslim faith those who are its votaries. For centuries the orthodox leaders of Islām have endorsed the cult and allowed it to develop as it would. They have supported it with contributions and recognized continually and officially the gifts of private individuals for the maintenance of the local and national shrines of the saints.

LITERATURE.—S. I. Curtiss, *Primitive Semitic Religion To-day*, New York and London, 1902; T. H. Weir, *The Shaikhs of Morocco in the 16th Century*, London, 1904; E. W. Lane, *Manners and Customs of the Modern Egyptians*[5], do. 1860; P. M. Sykes, *The Glory of the Shia World*, do. 1910; J. Malcolm, *Hist. of Persia*, do. 1815, ii.; I. Goldziher, *Mohammed and Islam*, New Haven, 1917; *EBr*[9], *s.v.* 'Mohammedanism'; D. S. Margoliouth, *The Early Development of Mohammedanism* (*HL*), London, 1914; C. Snouck Hurgronje, *Mohammedanism*, do. 1916; L. Rinn, *Marabouts et Khouan*, Paris, 1885; T. P. Hughes, *DI*, *s.v.* 'Saints'; J. P. Brown, *The Dervishes*, London, 1868; F. J. Bliss, *The Religions of Modern Syria and Palestine*, Edinburgh, 1912.

WALTER M. PATTON.

SAINTS AND MARTYRS (Muhammadan in India).—The hagiology of Muslim India is as abundant and diversified as that of any other part of the Muhammadan world, and in many respects this rich development is probably due to the Hindu influences with which Islām in that country has been surrounded. As in all hagiographic literature, we find not only that historical personages have been canonized, but that legends have grown up around names for which there is no authentic record, and the cult of local saints can often be shown to be the survival of an earlier faith which has passed on into Islām under another guise.

1. Chishtī saints.—Among the saints of whom there are ample historical records there are certain outstanding figures whose influence upon the religious history of Muslim India has been considerable, especially those belonging to religious orders, such as the Chishtī, the Suhrawardī, the Qādirī, the Shaṭṭārī, and the Naqshbandī. Each of these religious orders originated outside India, but enjoyed a considerable vogue in that country; the first was introduced by Khwājah Mu'īn al-Dīn Chishtī, a native of Sīstān, who migrated to India and reached Dihlī in the year (1193) in which the troops of Muḥammad Ghōrī captured that city; later he settled in Ājmēr, where he attracted to himself a large number of disciples; he died at Ājmēr in 1236, and his tomb still attracts thousands of pilgrims. In the same year died another saint of the Chishtī order, Khwājah Quṭb al-Dīn Bakhtiyār Kākī, who was born in Farghāna and spent a wandering life visiting holy men in Baghdād and other places; when he came to India, Iltutmish wished to make him *shaikh al-Islām*, but the saint refused this high office; he spent the last years of his life in intimate friendship with Mu'īn al-Dīn Chishtī, whom he predeceased by a few months; he was buried at Dihlī near the great minaret, the Quṭb Mīnār, which is called after his name. Among his disciples was Shaikh Farīd al-Dīn Shakarganj, who died in 1265 and was buried at Pākpattan, midway between Multān and Lahore, where his shrine is visited by a large number of devotees and is still in charge of one of the descendants of the saint. He had two famous disciples, each of whom has given his name to a separate branch of the Chishtī order, his nephew Shaikh 'Alī Ṣābir († 1291), and Niẓām al-Dīn Awliyā, who was recognized by Farīd al-Dīn as his *khalīfah* ('successor') when he was only twenty years of age; he established a *khānqāh* (convent of dervishes) in the neighbourhood of Dihlī and exercised a great influence over the court and the men of letters who were attracted to the capital; he died in 1325 and his grave has been a place of pilgrimage ever since. One of his disciples, Sayyid Burhān al-Dīn, is one of the most famous saints of the Deccan, and is buried in Rawẓah (in the Ḥaidarābād State), where also is the tomb of his equally famous successor, Zain al-Dīn Dā'ūd († 1370). Niẓām al-Dīn's spiritual successor was Nāṣir al-Dīn Maḥmūd († 1356), known as Chirāgh-i-Dihlī ('the lamp of Dihlī'), whose tomb is also visited by many of the faithful. One of his disciples, Muḥammad Gīsūdārāz (*i.e.* 'with long curls'), migrated to the Deccan, where he and his descendants enjoyed the liberal patronage of the Bahmanī Sultans, and a magnificent tomb was erected in Gulbarga over his remains when he died in 1422; for persons who are unable to undertake the journey to Arabia a pilgrimage to his tomb is said to be attended with the same benefit as performing the pilgrimage to Mecca. The renown of these saints gave a great impulse to the spread of the Chishtī order, which in succeeding centuries produced a large number of saints, among whom two are of special importance—Shaikh Salīm Chishtī († 1572), in whose house the emperor Jahāngīr was born, an event which prompted his father, Akbar, to build the wonderful city of Fatḥpūr-Sīkrī in the vicinity of the saint's hermitage; and Khwājah Nūr Muḥammad, known as Qibla-i-'Ālam († 1791), whose influence led to a wide extension of the Chishtī order in the Panjāb and Sindh.

2. Suhrawardī saints.—The Suhrawardī order was introduced into India by disciples of the founder of the order, Shihāb al-Dīn Suhrawardī, who taught in Baghdād; one of these, Shaikh Jalāl al-Dīn Tabrīzī († 1244), made his way to Bengal, where a shrine, to which is attached a rich endowment, was erected in his honour; another, Bahā al-Dīn Zakarīyā († 1266), settled in Multān, in the neighbourhood of which he had been born, and his tomb, which he is said to have built during his lifetime, is one of the few great monuments of Indian architecture of this period. One of his disciples, Jalāl al-Dīn Surkhpōsh († 1291), a Sayyid from Bukhārā, settled in Ucch (in the present Bahāwalpūr State) and was the progenitor of a long line of saints, and his descendants still guard the shrine of their great ancestor; but his fame is outshone by that of his grandson and successor, Sayyid Jalāl, known as Makhdūm-i-Jahāniyān ('served by all mankind'), who is said to have made the pilgrimage to Mecca 36 times and to have performed innumerable miracles. One of his grandsons, Burhān al-Dīn († 1453), known as Quṭb-i-'Ālam ('the pole-star of the world'), settled in Gujarāt, as did his son, Muḥammad Shāh 'Ālam († 1475), who played an important part in the political and religious life of his time.

3. Qādirī saints.—The Qādirī order has had a considerable extension in India, as in most other parts of the Muslim world; though the founder, 'Abd al-Qādir al-Jīlānī ([*q.v.*] † 1166), never visited India, shrines erected in his honour are common, in some of which relics of him are venerated; *e.g.*, his tooth-brush is said to have taken root in Ludhiāna and to have grown into a tree, near which an annual fair is held, which is attended by 40,000 to 50,000 persons. The festival of his death is widely celebrated in India on the eleventh day of the month Rabī' II., with reading of the Qur'ān, offering of prayers, and the reciting of the 99 names of the saint;[1] at times of plague or cholera processions are held in his honour, and childless parents vow to dedicate to him any son or daughter that may be born to them through his intercession. The Qādirī order was introduced into India by Sayyid Muḥammad, known as Bandagī Muḥammad Ghawth, a native of Aleppo, who migrated to India and settled in Ucch in 1482, and died there 35 years later; many of his descendants were also saints and workers of miracles, and his tomb at Ucch is still kept up by members of his family, who preserve there some precious relics, such as a footprint of the Prophet, a turban of 'Abd al-Qādir al-Jīlānī, etc. Among the numerous saints of the Qādirī order mention may be made of Shaikh Mīr Muḥammad, known as Miyān Mīr, who died at Lahore in 1635—he was the spiritual preceptor of Prince Dārā Shikōh, and his tomb is still held in reverence—and of Tāj al-Dīn († 1698), one of the descendants of 'Abd al-Qādir al-Jīlānī, whose tomb is at Aurangābād.

4. Shaṭṭārī saints.—The Shaṭṭārī order has also produced a number of saints—*e.g.*, Muḥammad Ghawth, who counted the emperor Humāyūn among his disciples; when he died in 1562, Akbar built a magnificent tomb in his honour at Gwalior; one of his disciples, Wajīh al-Dīn Gujarātī, a man of great learning and considerable literary activity († 1589), is buried at Aḥmadābād. Another saint of the same order, Shāh Pīr († 1632), is buried at Meerut in a mausoleum erected by Nūr Jahān, wife of the emperor Jahāngīr.

5. Naqshbandī saints.—The Naqshbandī order did not attain such a vogue in India as the others mentioned above; it was introduced there by Shaikh Aḥmad al-Fārūqī, who died at Sirhind in 1625, and there are several other shrines of saints of this order in India, notably that of Shāh Musāfir († 1698) at Aurangābād.

It is not possible here to enumerate all the religious orders of Muslim India, or the hundreds of saints that have arisen within them or outside. Of those already mentioned there is some historical record, but in many instances it is difficult to disentangle historical fact from a mass of superincumbent legend.

6. Missionaries and miracle-workers. — Many of the Muhammadan saints played an important part in the promulgation of Islām in India; *e.g.*, Mu'īn al-Dīn Chishtī is said to have received a call to preach Islām to the unbelievers in India while on a pilgrimage to Medīna, when the Prophet appeared to him in a dream and bade him spread the faith in that country; he is said to have converted 700 persons in Dihlī on his way to Ajmēr, and when he settled in the latter city the number of his converts increased rapidly. Makhdūm-i-Jahāniyān is said to have converted several of the tribes in the Panjāb, and both Bahā al-Dīn Zakarīyā and Farīd al-Dīn Shakarganj were successful in their missionary work in this part of India. Sayyid Nathar Shāh († 1039) was the pioneer of Islām in S. India, and his tomb in Trichinopoly is still a place of pilgrimage; a later saint, Shāh al-Ḥamīd, who died in Nagore, carried out successful missionary tours in this part of India and finally settled in Nagore, where he is buried. A number of saints are famous for the conversions which they effected in the Deccan; among them is Muḥammad Gīsūdarāz, mentioned above. The success of their propaganda is often attributed to miraculous powers.

E.g., Jalāl al-Dīn Tabrīzī is said to have converted a Hindu milkman to Islām merely by a look. Ḥasan Kabīr al-Dīn, one of the saints of Ucch, is said to have had a like miraculous power, and it is told of him that once when he was sick he called in a Hindu physician, who refused to come, fearing that the saint might convert him by a mere glance, but sent word that he would examine his urine; and, as soon as he looked at it, he at once accepted Islām. Imām Shāh of Pīrāna, who worked in Gujarāt in the latter half of the 15th cent., converted a large body of Hindu cultivators by bringing about a fall of rain after two seasons of scarcity; on another occasion, meeting a band of Hindu pilgrims passing through Pīrāna on their way to Benares, he offered to take them there; they agreed and in a moment were in the holy city, where they bathed in the Ganges and paid their vows; they then awoke to find themselves still in Pīrāna and adopted the faith of the saint who could perform such a miracle. A similar story is told of Ḥasan Kabīr al-Dīn, who saw a number of Hindu pilgrims passing through Ucch on their way to the Ganges; he offered to show them both of the holy rivers, the Ganges and the Jamna, flowing at that very spot, if they would renounce their false religion; certain definite marks of identification were agreed upon whereby the rivers might be recognized, and next morning they saw the Ganges and the Jamna flowing parallel to one another, and having all the marks of identification that had been asked for; whereupon all the pilgrims embraced Islām.

7. Ascetic practices. — Several of the saints referred to above spent many years in wandering, making frequent pilgrimages to Mecca, or visiting contemporary saints and the tombs of departed saints. Miyān Ḥātim of Sambhal († 1562) spent ten years roaming about, bareheaded and barefooted, in the waste country about Sambhal and Amroha, never sleeping on a bed. Muḥammad Ghawth († 1562) spent twelve years among the hills north of the Ganges, practising severe austerities, feeding on the leaves of trees, and sleeping in caves. Al-Badāōnī gives interesting details of the ascetic practices of the saints who were his contemporaries. Of Shaikh Burhān († 1563) he writes:

'For nearly fifty years (before his death) he had abstained from fleshmeat and from most other articles of food and drink, contenting himself with a little milk and some sweetmeats; and at the end of his life he abstained also from drinking water, so that to outward appearance he was an incorporated spiritual form, supernaturally illuminated. He had a very small and dark cell in which he constantly sat, engaged in reciting God's praises and in meditation and contemplation.'[1]

Al-Badāōnī describes also the state of ecstasy or religious trance which was a frequent experience in the religious life of these saints. Of Miyān Ḥātim he says:

'He was a man who took a keen pleasure in contemplating

[1] For an account of this festival see Jaffur Shurreef, *Qanoon-e-Islam*, ch. xviii.

[1] *Muntakhabu-t-tawārīkh*, tr. T. W. Haig, iii. 10.

God and whom the singing of God's praises threw into an ecstasy of delight, and ever, as he spoke and smiled, the name of God was on his tongue. In his last years the intoxication of joy which he experienced in his love of God so overpowered him that to listen but for a short space to the chanting of God's praises placed him beside himself.'[1]

The saints belonging to the various religious orders spent much of their time in the devotions peculiar to the order (the so-called *dhikr*), which consisted of continued repetitions of the name of God, of the creed, etc., and in instructing their disciples in the due performance of these devotions and in the practice of meditation. These religious exercises were sometimes (especially among the members of the Chishtī and Suhrawardī orders) accompanied by religious songs and dances, and many anecdotes are recorded of the intense religious fervour excited on such occasions. Of Shaikh Badr al-Dīn (a contemporary of Farīd al-Dīn Shakarganj) it was said:

'In his old age when he was unable to move, the sound of a hymn would excite him to ecstasy and he would dance like a youth. When asked how it was that the Shaikh could dance notwithstanding his decrepitude he replied: "Where is the Shaikh? It is Love that dances."'[2]

8. Unorthodox saints.—A clear distinction is drawn in India between (*a*) the above-mentioned religious orders, which are *ba-shar'*, *i.e.* in accordance with the ordinances of the Muslim law—the adherents of which, and the devotees of the saints belonging to them, are for the most part orthodox Muhammadans and comprise persons of culture and education—and (*b*) the *be-shar'* orders, the members of which often do not submit their lives to the customary rules of the religious law of Islām; the devotees of their saints are mostly to be found among the uneducated sections of the Muhammadan population and among those Hindus who worship Muhammadan saints. It is seldom possible to find any historical foundation for the legends of these saints, which are filled with wild and fantastic stories; it is, *e.g.*, doubtful whether there was ever such a person as Shāh Mādār, whose shrine is at Makanpūr, about 40 miles from Cawnpore; according to the legend, he was a converted Jew, born at Aleppo in the middle of the 11th cent.; he made his way to India and expelled a demon named Makan Deo from the spot where he himself is now venerated; he is believed to be still alive within his tomb. His devotees are said to be secure against snakes and scorpions and to have power to cure those who have suffered injury from them. The *faqīrs* who are termed Mādārī, after the name of their patron saint, are wandering mendicants or jugglers and do not observe the ordinary Muslim prayers, and are consequently regarded with disfavour by the orthodox. His cult has a wide extension in Muhammadan India and a large number of pilgrims visit his tomb.[3] There is equal uncertainty as to the historicity of Sakhī Sarwar, a famous worker of miracles, who has been variously assigned to the 12th or 13th cent.; after many wanderings he settled down in Nigāha, at the edge of the Sulaimān mountains, where his shrine is visited by a large number of pilgrims, Hindu and Sikh as well as Muhammadan; but other shrines of this saint are found elsewhere and almost every village in the Central Panjāb contains one.[4] Among the *be-shar'* orders are reckoned the followers of Mūsā Suhāg, who lived at the close of the 15th cent.; his prayers for rain are said to have delivered the country from a threatened famine; he dressed in women's clothes as a symbol that he was devoted to God as a wife to her husband, and the members of his order still dress like women and are celibate. Near his tomb at Aḥmadābād is a tree the branches of which are covered with glass bangles, thrown by persons who pay their vows to the saint; if the bangles stay in the tree, they believe that their petition will be granted. Among the ignorant Muhammadans there is a quintet of saints who enjoy an extensive popularity; these are the Pāñch Pīr, 'five saints,' who are worshipped by illiterate persons throughout the greater part of Muslim India, as well as by large numbers of Hindus. They are fully treated in art. PANCHPIRIYĀ. One of the saints who is often reckoned among the Pāñch Pīr is Khwājah Khiẓr, a saint who is known all over the Muhammadan world and is commonly identified with the nameless companion of Moses in the Qur'ān;[1] he is worshipped in India as the protector of travellers and especially of seamen and boatmen and of all whose occupation is connected with water in any form; *e.g.*, a goat is sacrificed to him when a new well is sunk, and in Bengal his annual festival is celebrated by setting afloat on a river at sunset little rafts of plantain stems or small paper boats, carrying a light.

Veneration is also commonly paid to giant saints, the so-called *naugaza*, or saints nine yards high, whose tombs are of this length; often no knowledge is claimed of the name of the saint, or he may be described merely as a *shahīd* ('martyr'); in some cases an impossible attempt is made to identify the *naugaza* with one of the Companions of the Prophet; *e.g.*, such an antiquity is claimed for the giant saint, Muḥammad Ibrāhīm, whose tomb is at Jalna, in the Ḥaidarābād State. The *naugaza* at Fīrōzpūr, in the Panjāb, is identified with Ja'far al-Ṣādiq, sixth *imām*, who died at Medīna in 765.

9. Famous shrines.—The worship of saints is severely reprobated by many Muhammadans, notably by the Wahhābīs; and those of the educated classes who do resort to their shrines maintain that the saints are only asked to intercede with God; but there is no doubt that among the lower classes prayers are directly addressed to the saint and the desired result is believed to lie within his power. Devotees may resort to the shrines of the saints on any occasion of need; but there are certain saints who are especially prayed to for particular temporal blessings. A large number are believed to grant the petitions of childless women, and others effect the cure of special diseases; *e.g.*, lepers resort to the tomb of Shāh Sufaid, in the Jhelum District, or that of Dā'ūd Jahāniyān, in Muzaffargarh; Mīrān Nau Bahār, a disciple of Farīd al-Dīn Shakarganj, cures hysterical fits; a cock should be offered at the tomb of Shaikh Saddū, in Amroha, for the cure of mental ailments. Niẓām al-Dīn († 1705), whose tomb is at Lahore, is famous for curing warts; dust from the shrine of Pīr Bukhārī in Quetta is a specific for venereal diseases; in the Hazāra country persons suffering from neuralgia make a pilgrimage to a shrine at Jatti Pind, those troubled with coughs to the shrine of 'Abdul Wahhāb Ghāzī at Qāziān. The litigant appeals to Shāh Mīnā († 1478), in Lucknow, for help in legal difficulties, or to Manṣūr Pīr, at Gaya. In Lahore the oilmen frequent the tomb of Hassū Tēlī, the blacksmiths that of Shaikh Mūsā, the dyers that of 'Alī Rangrēz. In Bengal Pīr Badar of Chittagong is the guardian saint of sailors, while the boatmen on the Chināb and the Indus invoke Bahā al-Dīn Zakarīyā as their patron saint in times of difficulty. Owners of barren cows pay vows at the tomb of Khākī Ṣaḥāba or of Mūsā Nawāb in the Bahāwalpūr Territory. Shēr Shāh of Multān is the protector of persecuted lovers. To Shāh Daula

[1] *Muntakhabu-t-tawārīkh*, iii. 3.

[2] Abu'l Fazl, *Ā'īn-i-Akbarī*, tr. H. S. Jarrett, iii. 368.

[3] W. Crooke, *The Tribes and Castes of the N.W. Provinces and Oudh*, Calcutta, 1896, iii. 397 ff.

[4] H. G. Raverty, 'Account of a Visit to the Shrine of Sakhi Sarwar,' *JASB* xxiv. [1855] 239 ff.; M. Macauliffe, 'The Fair at Sakhi Sarwar,' *Calcutta Review*, lx. [1875] 78 ff.

[1] xviii. 64–81.

of Gujrāt in the Panjāb parents dedicate microcephalic children. Students make offerings of sugar at the tombs of Shāh Laṭīf Qādirī or of Amīr Ḥasan Sanjarī († 1337) in the Aurangābād District (Ḥaidarābād State), in the hope of improving their memories. The shrine of Shāh Daula used to be frequented every Friday by dancing-girls, and they also look upon Tānsēn, the famous musician of Akbar, as their patron saint. The worship of Shaikh Saddū is in Bengal almost entirely confined to Muhammadan prostitutes, but there are several other saints for whom they have a predilection. Persons possessed by spirits are cured at the shrine of Mīrān Sayyid 'Alī in N. Gujarāt, and several other saints are invoked by persons so afflicted.

There are some shrines into which women are not admitted, such as that of Jatī Abdāl ('Abdāl the chaste ascetic'), a servant of Prince Dārā Shikōh, in the Multān District; some, on the other hand, are especially frequented by women—*e.g.*, the grave of Sulṭān Aḥmad Qattāl, who was born at Ucch in 1542 and, after many years of wandering, during which he visited the holy cities of Islām, settled down in Jalālpūr (in the District of Multān), where he died in 1631; a large fair is held near his tomb every Friday in the month of Chet (March–April), during which evil spirits are exorcized from women who are believed to be troubled by *jinns*; the tomb of Zain al-Dīn Biyābānī († 1503), at Fukrābād (Ḥaidarābād State), is also especially frequented by women.

There are also a certain number of shrines of women saints, particularly in Baluchistān; *e.g.*, that of Bībī Nāhzan (near Kalāt), who sank into the earth together with her maid when they were persecuted by some infidels, is visited by persons who have been bitten by mad dogs, and those who pay a fixed contribution to the shrine secure immunity from cholera; persons bitten by mad dogs also resort to the tomb of Bībī Nāzo, a Sayyid lady of Mastung; in the Loralai District a virgin saint, named Haro Ana, guards the Wanēchīs (a section of the Tarīn Afghāns) from the incursions of their enemies; in the neighbouring Marri country (at the southern end of the Sulaimān Range) there are also the shrines of several female saints. In the Panjāb, in the District of Multān, is the tomb of a woman named Māī Sapūran, who has given her name to the village where she lies buried; she was a disciple of a saint named 'Abdul Ḥakīm, who died in 1732; she was able to spread her prayer-carpet on the waters of the river Ravi and kneel for prayer upon it, and could cure the bites of mad dogs. At Fīrōzpūr, in the same province, an annual fair is held in honour of a woman saint, named Māī Amīrān Ṣāḥiba.

10. Offerings and festivals.—To win the favour of some saints, certain specific offerings have to be presented. To Sālār Mas'ūd at Bahraich a long embroidered flag is offered. Khājūria Pīr, whose tomb is at Ambala, must be given a white cock in full plumage and a plateful of sugar and cardamoms, to effect a cure of the palsy. Bahā al-Dīn, a Bukhārī Sayyid, a boy-saint who died at the age of five, is propitiated by the gift of a clay horse, and these toy horses are stacked up round his tomb in thousands. Childless women offer toy cradles at the shrine of Quṭb Nikka, in Baluchistān. Small horses made of cotton cloth, stuffed with sawdust, are hung up in the tomb of Shāh 'Ālam († 1475), near Aḥmadābād. But the usual offerings are of sweetmeats or some kind of food, and a goat or a fowl on special occasions.

The annual festival held in commemoration of a Muslim saint in India is called *'urs* (*i.e.* 'nuptials,' as signifying the union of the saint with God) and usually takes place on the date of his death. The day before the *'urs* is in some parts of the country called the *sandal*, because pots containing sandal-wood paste are carried in procession through the streets and deposited at the shrine for the use of the votaries. The festivities sometimes last for several days and are attended by a large concourse of persons; at Ajmēr, *e.g.*, the celebration of the *'urs* of Mu'īn al-Dīn Chishtī is continued for six days, and in some years as many as 25,000 persons, from all parts of India, have taken part in it; in the courtyard of the shrine are two enormous copper boilers fitted into solid masonry, the larger one capable of holding 5400 lbs. of rice, the other about half as much; these are filled with a mixture of rice, milk, honey, etc., and the contents, when thoroughly cooked, are distributed among the pilgrims. From 50,000 to 60,000 persons are said to attend the *'urs* of Farīd al-Dīn Shakarganj, who is reported to have declared that whosoever should pass through his shrine on the anniversary of his death would gain a place in paradise; the silver entrance-door through which the pilgrims struggle is known as the Gate of Paradise. The annual festival of 'Alā al-Dīn Ṣābir, at Pīrān Kaliar (in the Sahāranpūr District), is attended by 40,000 pilgrims, while as many as 100,000 flock to the tomb of Sālār Mas'ūd at Bahraich.

Some of the tombs of Muslim saints in India are stately, magnificent buildings and are counted among the finest monuments of Muhammadan architecture in the country, having been erected by emperors, sultans, or wealthy devotees. Some shrines also receive gifts from Hindus; *e.g.*, a railing of solid silver was given to the shrine of Mīrān Sayyid 'Alī in N. Gujarāt by a Gaikwar of Baroda. Many of these tombs, on the other hand, are plain, unpretentious buildings, or may even have nothing to distinguish them from the graves of ordinary men.

Besides the tomb of a saint there is often a subsidiary memorial of him to mark the place where he kept a *chillā*, or fast of 40 days, and invocations are offered to him here also. In the Deccan there are about 360 *chillās* sacred to the memory of Dāwal Shāh Walī, the son of one of the nobles of Maḥmūd Bīgarah (1459–1511), who travelled about extensively on proselytizing missions.

11. Upkeep.—Several of the greater shrines of Muhammadan saints have large endowments or have attached to them landed property, from which a considerable income is derived. If the original saint was a historical personage, this religious endowment is generally in the hands of one of his descendants, who is styled the *sajjāda-nishīn* (lit. 'sitting on the prayer-carpet'); the office is generally hereditary, or in default of issue descends to a successor nominated by the childless *sajjāda-nishīn*; he has a number of *murīds* (disciples or followers), some of whom live at a distance, and an agent of the *sajjāda-nishīn* goes round among them at intervals to collect contributions. Other shrines depend merely on casual contributions. At the shrine of Sakhī Sarwar the pilgrims enter into a regular contract with the spirit of the saint, and written promises of future payment are inscribed on the walls, on condition of the fulfilment of certain petitions.

12. Outstanding examples of saint-worship.—In no part of India has the worship of saints attained so rich a development as in the Paṭhān country in the north-west and among the Brahūīs in Baluchistān. Almost every village has its patron saint, who is credited with the possession of miraculous powers of healing or protection; some are said to have produced the spring from which the village obtains its water; others are canonized ancestors. In the Brahūī country a place without a shrine is held to be a place that should be avoided, and the Paṭhāns carry their reverence for shrines to such an extent that in Bhangikhel (in the Mianwali District, Panjāb) a Sayyid is said to have been murdered and buried, in order to supply the deficiency of a sacred tomb in the neighbourhood.[1]

A similar story is told of the Afrīdī Paṭhāns of Tīrāh, who 'had shame in the sight of their brethren, in that their territory was blessed with no holy shrine at which they might worship, and that they had to be beholden to the saints of their neighbours when they wished for divine aid. Smarting under a sense of incompleteness, they induced by generous offers a saint of the most notorious piety to take up his abode amongst them. They then made quite sure of his staying with them by cutting his throat, they buried him honourably, they built over his bones a splendid shrine at which they might worship him and implore his aid and intercession in their behalf, and thus they purged themselves of their reproach.'[2]

13. Muslim saints and Hindu cults.—In many instances there is no doubt that the shrine of a Muslim saint marks the site of some local cult which was practised on the spot long before the introduction of Islām. Such a survival has frequently occurred in the Buddhist shrines in the Gandhāra country (in the north-west of India) and to an enormous extent in the case of Hindu sacred places in Kashmir; *e.g.*, the tomb of Bāmadīn Ṣāḥib, which is a popular place of pilgrimage for Muhammadans in Kashmir, has been identified with an ancient Hindu temple built by Bhīma Sahi, the last Hindu king of Kabul († 1026); the saint is now said to have been a Hindu ascetic, who bore the name of Bhūma Sādhī before his conversion to Islām; a pious Hindu monarch is thus transformed into a Muhammadan saint, and a legend formed to bring the local cult into harmony with the new faith.[3] In like manner many Muhammadan shrines in Kashmir mark the site of a *tīrtha*, or place of pilgrimage, in the Hindu period. In India proper the origin of the local cult is often more difficult to ascertain, but it is significant that the tomb of Sālār Mas'ūd is said to occupy the site of a former temple of the sun, and the mosque of Shaikh Saddū, at Amroha, was also originally a temple. The Pāñch Pīr are undoubtedly reminiscent of the Pāṇḍavas, the five hero brothers of the *Mahābhārata*, and it is significant that the shrine of Sakhī Sarwar (in the Dera Ghāzī Khān District) contains, besides the tombs of the saint and his wife, a shrine dedicated to Bābā Nānak and a temple to Viṣṇu, and that Hindus believe that Shāh Mādār is an incarnation of Lakṣmana, the brother of the god Rāma. The influence of Hinduism on a Muhammadan religious order is strikingly exemplified in the case of the shrine of Ṣādiq Nihang, in the Jhang District (Panjāb); the *faqīrs* in charge of the shrine keep up a number of Hindu practices; *e.g.*, the superior of the order remains celibate[4] and a disciple succeeds him, in contrast to the usual practice at a Muhammadan shrine, where the succession passes from father to son; a fire is kept alight day and night, and once a year a large loaf of bread is cooked at this fire and distributed to all present. These are Hindu customs, but there is no doubt about the Muslim orthodoxy of the superior and the other *faqīrs*. In a similar manner there is little doubt that Bābā Ratan, whose shrine is at Bhatinda in the Patiala State, is a Hindu Yōgī who has been adopted into the Muhammadan calendar of saints.[5]

The process of canonization continues to the present day, and new saints are from time to time included in the calendar; *e.g.*, at Mōtīhāri in Bengal a *pīr*, named Patukī Sā'īn, who died between 1860 and 1870, is worshipped as possessed of miraculous power and is invoked by litigants.

[1] *Census of India, 1911*, vol. xiv., *Punjab*, Calcutta, 1913, pt. i. p. 172.

[2] *Report of the Census of the Punjab, 1881*, Calcutta, 1883, i. 144.

[3] Kalhaṇa, *Rājataraṅgiṇī*, tr. M. A. Stein, London, 1900, i. 249.

[4] The *sajjāda-nishīn* of the tomb of Shauq Ilāhī, in the Bahāwalpūr State, is also always celibate.

[5] *Journal of the Panjab Historical Society*, Calcutta, 1913, vol. ii. no. 2.

14. Martyrs' graves. — The term *shahīd* ('martyr') is given a wide interpretation in Muslim India; primarily it commonly means one who has died while fighting in defence of the faith, but nineteen other ways of attaining the glory of martyrdom are enumerated—*e.g.*, dying in the act of reciting the Qur'ān or while praying; being murdered by robbers or struck by lightning; being drowned, or killed by falling into a dry well, etc.[1] In the case of many of the graves that are pointed out as being graves of *shahīds* there is no record or even tradition as to how the martyr met his fate; but in others he is said to have died in battle with the Hindus. The most famous of these is Sālār Mas'ūd, the nephew of Sulṭān Maḥmūd of Ghaznī, who is believed to have performed prodigies of valour in his conflicts with the Hindus and to have been slain by them in battle in 1033 and buried at Bahraich in Oudh, where his *shādī* ('wedding') is annually celebrated in the month of Jeṭh (May–June); he is commonly known as Ghāzī Miyān, and his festival is celebrated throughout India.

In S. India a famous martyr is Sayyid Ibrāhīm Shahīd, who put himself at the head of an invading force and waged war against the Pandyan kingdom; after a brief period of success he was put to death by the heir to the Pandyan throne, towards the close of the 12th cent.; he is buried at Ervadi and is revered as a saint. To the same period belongs a martyr named Sayyid Ni'mat Ullāh Shahīd, whose tomb is at Hānsī, a town in the Hisār District of the Panjāb; he is said to have been present at the battle of Thanesar in 1192, when Muḥammad Ghōrī laid the foundation of the subjugation of N. India by his defeat of the Rājpūt army; the festival held at his tomb is called 'the feast of lances.' A mound with a mosque about three miles from the same town, Hānsī, is styled Shahīd Ganj, because 150,000 Muhammadans are said to have perished there. Many of the *naugaza*, or saints nine yards long, mentioned above are stated to have been *shahīds*.

A *shahīd* who was not slain in battle with the infidels is Shādnā Shahīd, who was killed by his own mother; she had brought an accusation of unchastity against Bahā al-Dīn Zakarīyā, and her infant son, who was then only ten months old, gave miraculous evidence on behalf of the saint, like the child in the cradle who exculpated Joseph when he was accused by Potiphar's wife;[2] Bahā al-Dīn restored the child to life, and he became the faithful attendant of the saint until he died a natural death, and a shrine was erected over his grave near the Dihlī gate of the city of Multān. A famous *shahīd* of Bengal, Shāh Ismā'īl Ghāzī, is said to have come from Mecca to fight against the infidels in India, and, after performing great feats of valour in Bengal, was put to death in 1474 by order of the Muhammadan sultan, who listened to the slanders of one of his Hindu officers who falsely accused Ismā'īl of plotting to set up an independent kingdom. There are four shrines erected to his honour in Rangpūr, one over his body and another over his head, and they are famous resorts for pilgrims and enjoy a considerable revenue. Pīr Bālāwal Shāh, who is said to have been a contemporary of the emperor Akbar and is buried at Fīrōzpūr (Panjāb), became a *shahīd* by being put to death by a man who had been robbed; he mistook the saint for a thief, as the actual thieves had put some of their plunder as a pious offering under the saint's pillow while he was asleep.

Among the *shahīds* is reckoned 'Alā al-Dīn, a

[1] Shurreef, *Qanoon-e-Islam*, ch. xii. *fin.*

[2] *Qur'ān*, xii. 26.

grandson of the great saint of the Deccan, Burhān al-Dīn († 1331); he is said, when returning from a pilgrimage to the tombs of the saints of Gulbarga, to have met a Hindu goddess, whom he destroyed; a band of demons then made their appearance, and in fighting with them he suffered martyrdom.

A number of martyrs are commemorated at Karnāl in the eastern Panjāb; the legend is that a Brāhman girl was abducted by a rājā, and a saint named Asthān Sayyid Maḥmūd led a large force of Muhammadans and rescued the maiden, but not before 500 of his followers had lost their lives. Each one of them was honoured as a *shahīd*, and small tombs were erected over them, at which lamps are kindled every Thursday; but the number of shrines is now considerably in excess of the 500, as every remarkable object in the neighbourhood (such as a milestone, etc.) has been turned into one. Similarly, the tombs of three brothers, known collectively as Jetha-Bhutta (after the names of two of them), are venerated as the graves of martyrs and receive a grant from the Bahāwalpūr Government; they are said to have been appealed to by a woman who had been robbed, and in their attempt to recover her property from the robbers they were killed and thus attained the glory of martyrdom. Lāl Sohanra, one of the disciples of Bahā al-Dīn Zakarīyā, also became a *shahīd*, when helping some persons against a gang of robbers in Sindh.

LITERATURE.—For the original Persian sources see *EI*, *s.v.* 'India,' § 5. Among such works as have been translated into English may be mentioned Abu'l-Fazl, *Ā'īn-i-Akbarī*, tr. H. S. Jarrett, Calcutta, 1873–94, iii. 349–375; al-Badāōnī, *Muntakhabu-t-tawārīkh*, tr. T. W. Haig, do. 1899, iii.; Jaffur Shurreef, *Qanoon-e-Islam, or the Customs of the Mussulmans of India*, tr. G. A. Herklots, London, 1832, ²Madras, 1863, reprinted 1895; R. C. Temple, *The Legends of the Panjab*, Bombay, 1884–1901. The official publications of the Government of India—*e.g.*, those of the Ethnological Survey, Census Reports, and Gazetteers—contain a mass of information; but otherwise the subject has received little attention from European writers; some account of Muslim saints is to be found in J. H. Garcin de Tassy, *Mémoire sur les particularités de la religion musulmane dans l'Inde*³, Paris, 1874, pp. 380–403; H. A. Rose, *A Glossary of the Tribes and Castes of the Punjab*, Lahore, 1911 ff., i. 529 ff.; A. J. O'Brien, 'The Mohammedan Saints of the Indus Valley,' *JAI* xli. [1911] 509–520.

T. W. ARNOLD.

SAINTS AND MARTYRS (Semitic and Egyptian).—The word 'saint,' as we apply it to individuals among the Babylonians and Egyptians, must necessarily have a connotation different from that which it bears in Christianity. It could not indicate sanctity of an ethical quality; rather it denotes the heroes, tales of whose lives and deeds embodied the qualities which men then regarded as desirable. These heroes might be real men, half-legendary individuals, or wholly mythical; so long as their memories were cherished as examples of desirable forms of life, attained by the possession of crude sanctity or qualities that linked them with the gods, they occupied the place filled in the Christian religion by saints.

I. *BABYLONIAN*.—The earliest heroes of this type in Babylonia were half-mythical kings. A tablet in the University Museum in Philadelphia contains a list of these.[1] They were the following:

'Galumum, who ruled 900 (?) years,
Zugagib, 840 (?) years,
Aripi (or Ademe), 720 years,
Etana, the shepherd, who ascended to heaven, 635 years,
Pilikam, 350 years,
Enmenunna, 611 years,
Melan-Kish, 900 years,
Barsalnunna, 1200 years,
Meszamu, . . . years,
Meskingashir, 325 years,
Enmeirgan, 420 years,
Lugalbanda, the shepherd, 1200 years,
Dumuzi, 100 years,
Gilgamesh, 126 years.'

Dumuzi, of this list, is a god. Etana and Gilgamesh were heroes about whose names legends and myths were collected. They will be treated more fully below. Each of these beings, whether real or mythical, was believed to possess a quality that enabled him to live and rule for hundreds of years. The early Babylonians yearned for long life.[1] Probably they did not clearly distinguish in thought between 'holiness' and 'divinity.' Power to live and rule as long as these kings are said to have done constituted them at least saints, as we believe the Babylonians conceived the equivalent of sainthood.

As time passed, the unique quality of these or similar monarchs so impressed the imagination of the Babylonians that the length of their reigns was greatly extended. Berossos, a Babylonian priest who died about 260 B.C., compiled a list of kings who lived and reigned before the Flood, attributing to them much longer reigns. His list is as follows:

'Alorus, who reigned 36,000 years,
Alaparos, 10,800 years,
Amēlon, 46,800 years,
Ammenon, 43,200 years,
Megalaros, 64,800 years,
Daonos, or Daos, 36,000 years,
Euedorachos, 64,800 years,
Amempsinos, 36,000 years,
Otiartes, 28,800 years,
Xisouthros, 64,800 years.'

Poebel thinks that these kings are different from those mentioned above;[2] the present writer believes that most of them are corruptions of the list first mentioned.[3] In either case they were believed by Babylonians to have possessed in such a degree that quality which among them corresponded to saintliness that they were permitted to survive to these extraordinary ages. Long life was not the only way in which the Babylonians thought that saintliness manifested itself.

1. Mythical saints.—About the names of certain individuals, partly contained within the first of the above lists and partly outside of it, legends and myths gathered, attracted by the heroic quality believed to reside in the individual.

(1) *Etana*, who is said in the tablet of long-lived kings to have been a shepherd and to have gone to heaven, is the hero of various tales. These are woven into a story, which seems to have existed in various recensions, and of which large fragments, though not all, have been recovered. The outline of the story is as follows:[4]

The Igigi, or spirits of heaven, were hostile to a certain city that seems to have been deserted by its patron deity or deities. Confusion and anarchy existed; productivity ceased on earth: the gods were deaf to appeals or were powerless to intervene. The Anunaki, or spirits of earth, held a council, and Enlil and Ishtar were chosen to come to its rescue. A king, who is designated a shepherd, and so may have been Etana, was put in power by Ishtar. An eagle and a serpent allied themselves to carry on the work of destruction, and defied Shamash, the god of justice and order. They went with their young into the mountain to seek food. Each found some and shared it with the young, but the eagle could not resist the temptation to consume the young of the serpent. The serpent thereupon appealed to Shamash, who advised him to conceal himself in the carcass of a wild bull and, when the eagle swooped down upon it, to seize him and tear him in pieces. The ruse succeeded. The serpent tore the wings and feathers of the eagle and left him to die in a hole in the mountains. The eagle then appealed to Shamash, promising eternal obedience for his aid. At the same time Etana appealed to Shamash to show him the plant of birth to bring fertility to his sheep. This plant grew in the very hollow in the mountains into which the eagle had been cast. Shamash told Etana of this, and one of the young of the eagle guided him to the spot. The eagle

[1] The tablet is published by A. Poebel, *Publications of the Babylonian Section of the Museum of the University of Pennsylvania*, Philadelphia, 1914, vol. v. *Historical and Grammatical Texts*, no. 2; it is translated by him, *ib.* vol. iv. *Historical Texts*, p. 73 f.; also by G. A. Barton, *Archæology and the Bible*, Philadelphia, 1916, p. 264 f.

[1] See art. OLD AGE (Semitic). [2] iv. 85 f.
[3] Cf. Barton, *Archæology and the Bible*, p. 270 f., and *JBL* xxxiv. [1915] 6 f.
[4] Cf. Jastrow's reconstruction in *JAOS* xxx. [1910] 123 f., which is in the main followed here.

appealed to Etana to release him and promised to fly with him to the dwelling of the gods. We are not told (owing to a break in the text) whether Etana obtained the plant of birth, but on the back of the eagle he flew upward to the gate of Anu, Enlil, and Ea, *i.e.* to the ecliptic. A break in the text deprives us of what occurred there. From there, at the instance of the eagle, they started to fly to the place where Ishtar dwelt. After flying for six hours, they began a precipitous descent, whether through failure of the eagle's strength or through Ishtar's displeasure is not clear. For six hours they fell through space to the ground. The close of the story is missing, but it is clear that the purpose of the flight failed. Etana had striven for immortality, as other heroes did, but had failed.

(2) *Gilgamesh* is the hero of a well-known epic[1] in twelve tablets or cantos. The composite story represents the powers and limitations of a saintly hero, according to a crude idea of saintliness. He could do mighty deeds, rule, oppress, build, fight enemies, kill extraordinary bulls, voyage to the isles of the blessed, but was powerless in the face of the mystery of death. That dark mystery baffled all, even Gilgamesh.

(3) *Engidu*[2] (*Enki-du*) has been described in treating of Gilgamesh.[3] He represents the wild uncivilized man of the steppe. He consorted with animals, was clothed with hair, ate grass with gazelles, drank at the streams with cattle, his heart was pleased with the living things in the streams. From this life he was enticed to the city by a *hierodoulos.* She cast aside her garments, exposed her charms, let him glut his passion, and led him in her thrall to civilization. For a time he was half satisfied, but his restless heart ultimately took him back to the animals and the steppe. His friendship with Gilgamesh continued; he joined with him in raiding Humbaba and in fighting the bull, but death ended his career.

Engidu, the heroic wild man, was believed to be created by a goddess. His marvellous powers were said to be due to sanctity of the rude sort believed in by early men. His story has been thought to embody in myth the civilizing influence of woman and family life.

(4) *Adapa* was another Babylonian hero about whom saintly myths collected.[4] He represented to the Babylonians something of the same story as that concerning Adam in Gn 3. Like Adam he obtained knowledge; like Adam too he missed immortality through the jealousy of a god.

(5) *Utnapishtim* (called in Sumerian *Ziugiddu*, and in later time *Atrakhasis*) was the Babylonian hero of the Deluge. From the different versions of the Deluge now extant we know that the legend concerning him was of gradual growth.[5] In its final form the story runs that Utnapishtim, warned by the god Ea of a coming deluge, built a ship and collected in it all that he had as well as all forms of life. The flood came, drowned all others in the lands, while he and his ship survived. The ship grounded on Mt. Nizir, as the water subsided. Utnapishtim built an altar, and offered sacrifice to the hungry gods. Bel then made Utnapishtim and his wife immortal. In its later form the story has become an episode in the Gilgamesh epic. A hero who could achieve such things fulfilled the Babylonian ideals of a saint.

(6) *Ishum*, a man of the city Dûr-ilu, was another hero about whom legends of familiarity with deity have clustered. The fragmentary text[6] which tells us of him opens with an account of how the god Urra was inflicting various plagues upon

[1] For an account of this poem see *ERE* vi. 643[a]; for translations of the epic cf. P. Jensen in *KB* vi. [1900] 116 ff., and A. Ungnad's *Das Gilgamesch-Epos.*

[2] Our knowledge of Engidu is derived from the Gilgamesh epic.

[3] See *ERE* vi. 643[a]. [4] *Ib.* p. 644[a].

[5] For the different accounts cf. Barton, *Archæology and the Bible*, pt. ii. chs. vi. vii.

[6] Cf. O. Weber, *Literatur der Babylonier und Assyrier*, p. 104 ff., and, for the text, Jensen in *KB* vi. 56 ff., and Ungnad in H. Gressmann, *Altoriental. Texte und Bilder zum AT*, Tübingen, 1909, p. 71 ff.

Babylonia. Ishum boldly complained to the god, saying:

'The Babylonians are as birds
And thou hast become their catcher,
With the net thou subduest, catchest, destroyest them.'

In a long address Ishum recounted the sufferings of Babylon, of Nippur, and of Dûr-ilu; he accused Urra of destroying the righteous and the wicked alike. In reply Urra said to Ishum in part:

'The Sea-land the Sea-land,
Mesopotamia Mesopotamia,
The Assyrians the Assyrian,
The Elamites the Elamite,
The Kassites the Kassite,
The Kuthæans the Kuthæan,
The Lulubites the Lulubite,
One land another, one house another, one man another,
Brother shall not spare brother; they shall kill one another,
And thereupon the Accadian shall raise himself up;
They are all struck down, together thrown to the ground.'

The text then goes on to relate how Ishum fulfilled the destiny thus pointed out to him and overran these lands.

(7) *Takku* (read by Langdon *Tagtug*) was a Babylonian hero, whose nature is not yet fully determined. It is possible that he was a deified king, but, in the opinion of the present writer, probably an agricultural deity.[1] Whatever his origin, he was regarded as a sort of representative or patron of humanity. Enki (Ea) revealed to him the secrets of agriculture, in order that he might be able to take advantage of the irrigating waters that Enki had created. This made the goddess Ninkharsag, the spouse of Enlil of Nippur, jealous of him, and in the name of Enki she uttered a curse against him denying him immortality. Enlil thereupon placated her by promising that her name along with Enlil's should be invoked at Nippur. After this, apparently to compensate Takku for the loss of immortality (some lines are broken from the text at this point), the medicinal properties of several herbs were revealed to Takku.[2] In another text, containing an account of the creation,[3] Takku appears as the creator of land and water, to whom many shrines were dedicated. He appears to have been a Babylonian saint, but, in the judgment of the present writer, a purely mythological one.

(8) *Enmeduranki* was the name of another hero, believed in later generations to have been a king of Agadé or Sippar. He was reverenced as the discoverer of the art of forecasting events by pouring oil on water.[4]

(9) *Tabu-utul-Bêl*,[5] or *Laluralim*,[6] was another hero, who has been designated a Babylonian Job. He is said to have been a king of Nippur, and a meticulously righteous man, who omitted no known religious or ethical duty. Like Job, he was overtaken with a torturing sickness, which called forth from him a sorrowful lament. At last he found a magician who drove away the sickness and relieved him of his affliction. The tale of his sufferings and deliverance was calculated to make the Babylonians believe that magic was more potent than righteousness.

2. Historical saints. — In addition to these mythical or semi-mythical saints, a number of Babylonian kings must be placed among the heroes who in the estimation of their countrymen attained a similar distinction.

[1] See *AJTh* xxi. [1917] 596 ff.

[2] Stephen Langdon's interpretation is quite different, but Jastrow's and J. D. Prince's agree closely with that of the present writer. For full references to the literature see *AJTh* xxi. 576.

[3] Cf. Barton, *Miscellaneous Babylonian Inscriptions*, i., New Haven, 1918, no. 8, and *AJTh* xxi. 592 f.

[4] Mentioned in H. Zimmern, *Ritualtafeln für den Wahrsager*, Leipzig, 1900, no. 24 ff.

[5] For the poem cf. Barton, *Archæology and the Bible*[2], Philadelphia, 1917, p. 392 ff.

[6] Cf. H. C. Rawlinson, *WAI* v. 44, 17 b.

(1) *Sargon* of Agadé, who about 2800 B.C. founded the dynasty of Agadé and Kish, was the first of these. So great was his success as a military leader and ruler that a legend of his birth was treasured down to the time of Ashurbanipal (668–626 B.C.).[1] According to this legend, Sargon was begotten by an unknown father and brought forth in secret. His mother, apparently ashamed of him, placed him in a basket of reeds lined with bitumen and set him afloat on the Euphrates. The water carried him to Akki, the irrigator, who adopted him and reared him as his son. The goddess Ishtar became his patron and made him ruler of the people.

Sargon practised liver-divination, and, if he did not introduce it into Babylonia, he made it so popular that it was ever afterwards practised. In the time of Urkagina, thirty years before Sargon, the favourite method of divination at Lagash had been by means of oil on water. The markings on livers consulted by Sargon before each great undertaking were recorded and became the basis of the science of liver-divination in subsequent centuries.[2] If one could obtain the same omen as the mighty Sargon had beheld before accomplishing some successful deed, one felt sure of success.

(2) *Rimush*, who was perhaps Sargon's immediate successor, was during his lifetime regarded as a god. What the cause was that led his subjects to accord him this honour we do not know, but it was, no doubt, the possession of qualities that passed among them for saintliness.

(3) *Naram-Sin*, of the same dynasty, whose reign of 44 years began about 2700 B.C., was also regarded as a god while he lived.[3] We know that he was a successful warrior and a great builder, but why he more than many others should have been accorded this honour we do not know.

(4) *Shargalisharri* was Naram-Sin's successor. His name is once preceded by the determinative for deity in one of his own inscriptions.[4] He probably inherited the honour from his predecessor.

(5) *Gudea*, the great Patesi of Lagash about 2500 B.C., was also deified. He appears as a god in certain proper names, such as Gin-dGudea and Lù-dGudea. Probably this occurred in his lifetime, though the names in question come from the dynasty of Ur.

(6) *Dungi*, of the dynasty of Ur, who ruled 2429–2371 B.C., was the next king, so far as we know, to be deified during his lifetime. While he was still living, men in his service bore such names as:

Lù-dDun-gi, 'man of the god Dungi'; dDun-gi-ḫê-gál, 'the god Dungi makes abundance'; dDun-gi-ra-kalam-ma, 'for the god Dungi is the land'; dDun-gi-kalam-ma-ḫi-li-bi, 'the god Dungi—the land is his delight'; dDun-gi-à-uru, 'the god Dungi is the reward of the slave'; dDun-gi-ki-ḫar-šag, 'with the god Dungi is great favour'; Ka-dDun-gi-ib-ta-ê, 'the word of the god Dungi has gone forth'; dDun-gi-a-du-kalam-ma, 'the god Dungi is the counsellor of the land'; Ama-dDun-gi-e-dUr-ru, 'the mother of the god Dungi is the goddess Urru'; dDun-gi-ú-nam-ti, 'the god Dungi is the food of life';[5] and Tab-dDun-gi-dNannar, 'the twin of the god Dungi is the god Nannar.'[6]

A hymn,[7] apparently addressed to him while he lived, contained the most fulsome praise. Some of its lines are:

> 'Wise ruler, hero, come!
> Give rest to the land!
> A faithful hero, a sun-god, who art just,
> At the head with sceptre thou standest.
> O exalted lion, the fat of life thou eatest.
> O ox, mighty wild ox, O ram great to bless,
> Thy word breaks the mountain—holy and just.
> . . . . . .
> Enlil,
> The faithful lady, Ninlil,
> Whom he loves in his heart,
> O my king, are like thee.
> . . . . . .
> O mountain of fate, the firm bow of Nannar
> For the land thou carriest
> To fight in gladness.
> . . . . . .
> Enlil below thou art!'

(7) *Bur-Sin*, *Gimil-Sin*, and *Ibi-Sin*, three successors of Dungi, were also accounted divine. Their names are regularly written preceded by determinatives for deity. A fragmentary hymn[1] addressed to Ibi-Sin, apparently while he lived, contains the following:

> 'Food and drink abundantly thou . . .
> For the people as protector thou . . .
> My king, known of Nannar, exalted one of Enlil,
> Ibi-Sin, in exalted power thou art alone!'

The names of other kings are at times found preceded by the determinative for deity—*e.g.*, Ur-Ninib, Irraimiti, Zanbia, Ishbiurra, Idin-Dagan, Ishmi-Dagan, Libit-Ishtar, Itirpisha, Damiqilu-shu, Ibiq-Adad, Nur-Adad, Warad-Sin, Rim-Sin, and Ḫammurabi.[2] All these were deified for the same reason.

It may be said that the Babylonian conception of saintliness was the successful exercise of the will to power. Often it was believed to be exhibited in the form of political power, but often, too, in unusual deeds of other kinds.

Only one possible trace in Babylonian lore of anything that could be called martyrdom is known to the present writer. That is the myth preserved by Berossos[3] that Oannes cut off his own head and mingled his blood with the dust to create man. As Oannes is but another name for the god Ea, this cannot be called martyrdom as the term is ordinarily understood.

II. *EGYPTIAN*. — The Egyptian conception of sainthood was of the same semi-primitive, heroic character as that in Babylonia, though it manifested itself in some respects in a different way. In Babylonia some kings were considered divine; in Egypt all kings were so considered. The cause that led to this is shrouded in the mystery that conceals all things pre-historic, but it was probably the primitive way of recognizing that one who could gain control over his fellows possessed rare ability. Such ability was regarded as an especial attribute of divinity. Some Egyptian kings, such as Mena, Khufu, and Thothmes III., possessed unusual ability. The divinity of many of the kings was, however, purely traditional.

More illuminating than the saintship of Egyptian kings is the study of the type of heroes about whose names Egyptian traditions clustered. These reveal at once the likeness and the difference between the Babylonian and the Egyptian conceptions. The likeness consists in the heroic quality that passed among both peoples as saintliness, the difference in the fact that intellectual power attracted the Egyptians quite as much as brute force, and apparently to a somewhat greater degree than it did the Babylonians. This will become evident as we glance at some of the Egyptian heroes and note their qualities.

(1) *Imhotep* was a vizier of King Zoser of the IIIrd dynasty. He was famed for his priestly wisdom, his knowledge of magic, his reputation for making wise proverbs, his knowledge of medicine, and his ability as an architect. So great

[1] Cf. Barton, *Archæology and the Bible*, p. 310 f.

[2] Cf. H. Radau, *Early Babylonian History*, New York, 1900, p. 157 ff. His name is uniformly written with the determinative for deity.

[3] See Barton, *Sumerian Business and Administrative Documents from the Earliest Times to the Dynasty of Agade*, Philadelphia, 1915, no. 25.

[4] See H. V. Hilprecht, *Old Babylonian Inscriptions*, Philadelphia, 1896, no. 2.

[5] See Barton, *Haverford Library Collection of Cuneiform Tablets*, Philadelphia, 1905–14, pt. ii. pl. 53, no. 10, and *JAOS* xxxvii. 162 ff.

[6] Barton, *Haverford Library Collection*, pt. i. pl. 12, no. 52, line 9.

[7] Barton, *Miscellaneous Babylonian Inscriptions*, no. 3.

[1] Barton, *Miscellaneous Babylonian Inscriptions*, no. 7.

[2] Cf., for references, *JAOS* xxxvi. 365 ff.

[3] Cf. I. P. Cory, *The Ancient Fragments*, London, 1828, p. 23 f.

was his reputation that he became the patron spirit of later scribes, who regularly poured out to him a libation from their water-jar before beginning their work. Centuries later people sang his proverbs, and twenty-five hundred years later he had become a god of medicine. The Greeks called him Imouthes, and regarded him as the equivalent of their own Asklepios. A temple was erected to him near the Serapeum at Memphis, and numerous statues of him have been found.[1]

(2) *Other magicians* were also reverenced, and tales concerning them circulated in later centuries.[2] One of these, *Ubaaner*, lived under Khufu of the IVth dynasty, the builder of the Great Pyramid. He is said to have made a wax crocodile, which, when thrown into the water, became a living crocodile and devoured a lover of Ubaaner's wife. Another was *Tchatchamānkh*, who flourished in the time of Seneferu, who reigned between Zoser and Khufu. When a bracelet was lost in a lake, he is said to have made the water in one half of it stand upon that of the other half, so that the bracelet could be seen upon the dry bottom. Still another, *Teta*, is said to have lived in the reign of Khufu and was believed to have power to restore life to dead animals. A fourth magician, *Ruttetet*, is said to have foretold to King Khufu the birth of three sons of the god Rē who should overthrow the IVth dynasty—a prophecy that was believed to have been fulfilled by the establishment of the Vth dynasty.

(3) *Ptahhotep* was an Egyptian sage who is said to have lived during the Vth dynasty, about 2600 B.C. To him later ages attributed a body of 'precepts' that are certainly as old as 2000 B.C. and perhaps older.[3] These 'precepts' are designed to guide Egyptians to the way of happily and successfully living in the social *ensemble*. They form an ethical code of a remarkably high order. If Ptahhotep was their author, he is worthy of being compared to Confucius.

(4) *Ipuwer* was another Egyptian sage who lived before 2000 B.C. and whose name later centuries reverenced for his wisdom. Certain 'admonitions,' said to have been uttered in the presence of the king, are attributed to him.[4] In these 'admonitions' the imperfections of the social order of the time are arraigned, and it is predicted that an ideal king will arise and establish justice.

(5) *Hunanep*, the 'eloquent peasant,' was a 'saint' of a different character.[5] Whether he was a real person or only a character in a story may perhaps be open to question. When one considers the concreteness of ancient thinking and writing, the probability is that he was a real character who lived in the feudal age before 2000 B.C. He is the hero of the story of *The Eloquent Peasant*, whose pleading for the rights of the poor so delighted a local governor that he purposely referred his case to the king, so that the king might have the pleasure of listening to one so eloquent. The speeches of Hunanep embody social ideals that were long cherished in Egypt.

(6) *Bata* was an Egyptian hero of a somewhat different sort, since he was apparently in part a real character, though his story has attracted to itself a number of mythical elements. He is the righteous younger brother in the Egyptian *Tale of Two Brothers*, who, like Joseph, was faithful, underwent temptation without yielding, was falsely accused, but, unlike Joseph, escaped punishment.[1] How he went to the Lebanon and became a tree, became an animal and returned to Egypt, became a shrub planted by his brother's door, etc., are mythical elements, derived perhaps from some form of the Osiris myth. The integrity of Bata himself is a close approach to saintliness in its later sense. Whether it was this or the mythical elements that made the tale popular with the Egyptians it is difficult now to tell.

These heroic figures, whose memory and writings were treasured by the Egyptians, indicate that the people of Egypt reverenced the social virtues. Had we only the Babylonian heroic stories as evidence, we should say that the Babylonians fell behind the Egyptians in this respect. The code of Ḥammurabi is proof, however, that such an inference would be wrong. Social qualities were as strongly developed among them as among the Egyptians, though the evidence for it is not found in the tales concerning their heroes.

III. *JEWISH*.—See art. SAINTS AND MARTYRS (Jewish).

IV. *ABYSSINIAN*.—With the exception of a few inscriptions, all our sources of information concerning Abyssinia relate to the Christian period of its history. The country was Christianized in the 4th cent. from Egypt, so that the Abyssinian Church is an offshoot of the Coptic Church. In the Abyssinian liturgy prayers are offered for the patriarch of Alexandria as archpope.[2] Abyssinian Christianity has, therefore, a general Christian inheritance, a specific Egyptian inheritance, and a native element. The native element is partly from pre-Christian Abyssinian heathenism, on which Christianity was grafted, and partly a development within the Abyssinian Church itself. Abyssinian saints are accordingly derived from all these sources.

1. **Catholic saints,** or saints recognized by the Church Catholic, are numerous in Abyssinia. There is, of course, the Virgin Mary, Stephen the protomartyr,[3] Zacharias the priest, John the Baptist, Matthew, Mark, Luke, and John, Peter, Andrew, James and John, Philip, Bartholomew, Thomas, Matthew, Thaddeus, Nathaniel, James the son of Alpheus, and Matthias ; also James the brother of Jesus, Paul, Timothy, Silas, Barnabas, Titus, Philemon, Clement. In addition to these, the 72 disciples of Lk 10, the 500 companions of 1 Co 15[6], and the 318 Orthodox are also counted as saints, the merits of whom are invoked in the liturgy.[4] In the thought of the people some of these are more important than others. The Virgin Mary naturally holds an important place. Next to her is St. John, to whom many places are sacred. On his festival firstfruits are offered, and people bathe—a rare thing in Abyssinia ![5] On his day also a sheep is led around people who are supposed to be possessed of the devil.[6] St. Stephen is also fairly popular. There are several churches called after him.

The archangels Michael, Gabriel, Raphael, and Suriel are also made saints. Michael and Gabriel are among the most popular. Abraham, Isaac, Jacob, and Jonah are counted saints, as are the four living creatures, the four-and-twenty elders, and the 144,000 of the book of Revelation. St. George, conqueror of the dragon, has also a place.[7]

[1] Cf. J. H. Breasted, *Hist. of Egypt*[2], p. 112 f.
[2] See E. A. W. Budge, *The Literature of the Ancient Egyptians*, p. 25 ff.
[3] Cf. Breasted, *Development of Religion and Thought in Ancient Egypt*, p. 231 ff., and Barton, *Archæology and the Bible*, p. 409 f.
[4] Breasted, *Development of Religion and Thought*, p. 204 f. ; Barton, *Archæology and the Bible*, p. 421 f. ; A. H. Gardiner, *The Admonitions of an Egyptian Sage*.
[5] Cf. F. Vogelsang and A. H. Gardiner, *Die Klagen des Bauern*, and Barton, *Archæology and the Bible*, p. 418 f.

[1] Cf. W. M. F. Petrie, *Egyptian Tales*, 2nd ser., p. 36 ff., and Barton, *Archæology and the Bible*, p. 300 ff.
[2] F. E. Brightman, *Liturgies Eastern and Western*, p. 228, and S. A. B. Mercer, *The Ethiopic Liturgy*, p. 343.
[3] Cf. I. Guidi, *Annales Iohannis I.*, in *Corpus Script. Christ. Orient.* (*Script. Æthiop.*, 2nd ser., vol. v.), Leipzig, 1903, pp. 22, 46.
[4] Cf. Brightman, p. 228 f., and Mercer, p. 350.
[5] M. Parkyns, *Life in Abyssinia*, ii. 66 f.
[6] *Ib.* p. 81.
[7] *Ib.* p. 78.

A St. Ewostatewos, who is called the Just,[1] is probably no other than St. Eustathius, bishop of Antioch (A.D. 324–331), a determined foe of the Arians.

2. Saints of Egyptian origin include St. Athanasius and St. Cyril, who are also recognized by the Church Catholic. Less clear is the identity of SS. Mercury, Basilides, Claudius, Mennas, Manādelēwos, Philotheus, Mermehnām, Kirkōs, Victor, Abli, and Esderos; but they are of Egyptian or Roman origin.[2] Maximus and Demetrius are called 'our holy Roman fathers.'[3] Antony, Besōi, John Kamā, Pachomius, Barsūmās, Sīnōdā, Besnedā, and Būlā are saints of the Coptic Church,[4] and were introduced from Egypt. All these were imported into Abyssinia and naturalized there.

3. Native Abyssinian saints were of three classes. (*a*) There were native heathen deities, worshipped on hill-tops, that were taken over and christened as Christian saints. Five of the most important churches in Abyssinia had apparently been heathen shrines, and to this day the heathen idea of sanctuary attaches to them. Such are the churches at Axum, Adowa, Waldeba, Gundi-gundi, Debra-Damot, and Debra-Abaī.[5] A number of the most sacred churches are situated on hill-tops and surrounded by groves. Doubtless they are ancient Semitic high-places. Two on isolated peaks near Axum contain the shrines of saints. One is that of Abbalicanos, said to have been the confessor of Queen Candace, the other that of a certain Abbapantalian who is supposed to have been so holy that the place is one 'of great devotion amongst them.'[6] Three others near Axum are said to be the residences or burial-places of saints and are regarded as very holy. One, the Hallelujah Monastery, is on a high hill surrounded by trees. It is said to have been given its name because a holy man who dwelt there when the monastery was first built claimed that at night he heard the angels in heaven singing 'Hallelujah.' Another was named for Abbagarima, who, it was said, left his kingdom in Greece and spent his life near Axum doing penance, and who is believed still to work miracles. The third, also on a hill, is named for St. John,[7] a very favourite saint in Abyssinia. A fountain, believed to have healing properties, near the plain of Gobe is also named for St. John. It is, no doubt, an old Semitic sacred spring.[8] Another sacred cave, the sanctity of which doubtless dates from heathen times, contained in the 16th cent. a church named Imbra Christus. Here, it was believed, a holy king named Abraham was buried. There are numerous St. Johns, just as in Europe there are different Virgin Marys at different shrines, and at least some of these are heathen deities baptized with Christian names. Abuna Aragawy, the saint of the celebrated monastery of Debra-Damot, is said to have been a missionary sent to the country by Athanasius. He gained access to the inaccessible height on which the monastery stands by clinging to the tail of a boa-constrictor, which pulled him up.[9] The caves about are full of snakes, and the boa that helped the saint up the hill is believed by some to be still alive there. The place was, no doubt, the site of ancient serpent-worship before the introduction of Christianity.

(*b*) Other native Abyssinian saints have developed out of their dead kings. Just as many a Muslim *walī* is inhabited by a dead *shaikh*, so a number of Abyssinian shrines are believed to be the resting-places of departed monarchs. St. Theodore, the patron saint of Rohabaita, is believed to be a great worker of miracles.[1] Perhaps he is very old; but, if so, he is now confused with King Theodore I., who reigned 1409–12, and who is believed to have been a great worker of miracles. It is expected that another king will arise in his name, restore the Holy Sepulchre to the Cross, and make Ethiopia the first of the nations.[2] Other saintly kings were Lalibela and Abraham.[3]

(*c*) Less exalted holy men have, as elsewhere, developed into saints. Alvares tells of an *ichee*, or monk, who was very holy, was thought to work miracles, and at whose tomb a monastery was built.[4] One of the most noteworthy of this class of saints is Takla Hāymānōt,[5] who was the patron saint of King Menelik.[6] His life and actions are believed to have been an exact copy of those of Christ, even to the fact that his father was a carpenter named Joseph and his mother was named Mary.[7] Gabro Menfos Kuddos ('slave of the Holy Spirit') is believed to have been a saint from his birth.[8] On his festal day everybody eats vetch-peas which have been made to sprout by soaking them in water for three days. Portions of these peas are sent as presents to friends and neighbours.[9]

Abyssinian saints are numberless.[10] Those named are but examples of the different classes. Saints are held in the highest reverence, often being preferred to the Deity Himself. One who would not hesitate to invoke the name of God in witness to a falsehood cannot be persuaded so to invoke the name of his patron saint. Beggars who vainly ask alms for the sake of God obtain them if they ask for the sake of the Virgin Mary or Takla Hāymānōt.[11]

It is a common custom to vow to one's patron saint the sacrifice of a bullock or sheep on his festal day, in order to secure his favour and protection for the rest of the year. Each family has its patron saint, who is handed down from father to son. On the festal day of this saint each family according to its means entertains its friends with some sort of merry-making. The saints most popular as patrons are St. Michael, the Virgin Mary, St. John the Baptist, Takla Hāymānōt, and Gabro Menfos Kuddos.[12]

Numerous stories, mostly of a trivial and childish character, are told of Abyssinian saints.

An example of these is the story told above of Abuna Aragawy and the boa-constrictor. Of Gabro Menfos Kuddos it is said that as soon as he was born he stood up. When three days old he bowed thrice, saying in a distinct voice: 'Glory be to the Father and to the Son and to the Holy Ghost.' He never tasted his mother's milk; through his whole life he never tasted food or drink. Once, when praying on a mountain, he fell over a precipice 200 ft. high. Two angels immediately spread their wings to support him, but he declined their assistance, and, trusting in God, was unhurt. Another time, while ascending a mountain, he was worn out with fatigue, and the Holy Spirit came and helped him up. After a very long life God sent Azazel, the angel of death, to take him, but he refused to die, saying that, as he had neither eaten nor drunk all his life, he could not die. Then all the saints in paradise came, one by one, to try to persuade him to leave the world and go to paradise. The first to come was St. John the Baptist, who said to him: 'I have

1 Cf. Guidi, pp. 39, 40, 48.

2 This is clear from a comparison of the Abyssinian prayer of intercession (Brightman, p. 230; Mercer, p. 369) with the similar prayer in the Coptic liturgy (Brightman, p. 169).

3 Brightman, p. 230; cf. p. 169.

4 Most of their names are corruptions of Coptic names; cf. Brightman, p. 230, and Mercer, p. 369 f., with Brightman, p. 169. Some, such as Sīnōdā, who do not appear in the Coptic liturgy, are known from Ethiopic translations of Coptic works to have been introduced into Abyssinia from Egypt; cf. *ZDMG* lxvii. [1913] 187 ff.

5 Cf. J. C. Hotten, *Abyssinia and its People*, London, 1868, p. 48 f., and Parkyns, p. 185 f.

6 F. Alvares, *The Portuguese Embassy to Abyssinia*, Eng. tr., p. 86.

7 *Ib.* p. 88 ff.

8 Parkyns, i. 241 ff.

9 *Ib.* ii. 86.

1 Parkyns, i. 265 f.

2 J. T. Bent, *The Sacred City of the Ethiopians*, London, 1893, p. 156.

3 Alvares, p. 130.

4 *Ib.* p. 161.

5 Guidi, pp. 9, 25, 39, 48.

6 Mercer, p 359.

7 Parkyns, ii. 86.

8 *Ib.* p. 85 f.

9 *Ib.* p. 65.

10 *Ib.* p. 84.

11 *Ib.*

12 *Ib.* p. 70 f.

gone the way of all flesh, notwithstanding all my privations and sufferings.' To this Gabro replied: 'Yes; but *you* could not fast even forty days, but fed on locusts and wild honey.' Thus he replied to all the saints, and even at last to the Virgin and to our Saviour. Nevertheless his life was at last taken from him, since the decrees of the Almighty must be obeyed. Then the elements fell to disputing as to what should be done with his body. The earth refused to receive it, since he had never partaken of her produce; the water refused, because he had never drunk a drop of it; fire had equally strong objections. So the saint was restored to life and taken up alive to heaven. Notwithstanding this, his tomb is shown at Zukwala in Shoa.[1] It is told of other saints that they plucked out their eyes and cast them before vultures, and that they rode on lions.[2]

Lives of saints, filled with such stories, are written in large numbers and circulated throughout Abyssinia.

Martyrs play no large part in Abyssinian thought. The intercessory prayer of their liturgy intercedes for Stephen the proto-martyr, for 'all the martyrs,' for the 'holy abba Nob, virgin and singular martyr, Eleazar . . . and all the martyrs,' for 'holy abba Moses,' and for the 49 martyrs.[3] Although the abba Nob does not appear in the liturgy of the Coptic Jacobites,[4] it is probable that he too is an Egyptian martyr. Martyrdom appears to have formed no important part of the experience of Abyssinian Christians, and their attention to it is accordingly not great. It is an exotic in their midst.

LITERATURE.—Arno Poebel, *Historical Texts (Publications of the Babylonian Section of the Museum of the University of Pennsylvania*, vol. iv.), Philadelphia, 1914, pp. 73–140; P. Jensen, *Assyrisch-babylon. Mythen und Epen*, in E. Schrader's *Keilinschriftliche Bibliothek*, vi., Berlin, 1900, *passim*; A. Ungnad, *Das Gilgamesch-Epos*, Göttingen, 1911; P. Dhorme, *Choix de textes religieux assyro-babyloniens*, Paris, 1907, *passim*; M. Jastrow, *Die Religion Babyloniens und Assyriens*, Giessen, 1905–12, ii., *passim*, and in *JAOS* xxx. [1910] 101–120; O. Weber, *Die Literatur der Babylonier und Assyrier*, Leipzig, 1907, *passim*; G. A. Barton, *Archæology and the Bible*[2], Philadelphia, 1917, pt. ii., *passim*, and in *JBL* xxxiv. [1915] 1–9, *JAOS* xxxvii. [1917] 23–49, 162 f., *AJTh* xxi. [1917] 576–597; J. H. Breasted, *Hist. of Egypt*[2], New York, 1909, p. 112 f., *Development of Religion and Thought in Ancient Egypt*, do. 1912, *passim*; E. A. W. Budge, *The Literature of the Ancient Egyptians*, London, 1914, ch. iii.; F. Vogelsang and A. H. Gardiner, *Die Klagen des Bauern*, Leipzig, 1908; A. H. Gardiner, *The Admonitions of an Egyptian Sage*, do. 1909; W. M. F. Petrie, *Egyptian Tales*, 2nd ser., London, 1895; F. E. Brightman, *Liturgies Eastern and Western*, Oxford, 1896, i. 228–231; S. A. B. Mercer, *The Ethiopic Liturgy*, Milwaukee and London, 1915, pp. 350 ff., 369 ff.; F. Alvares, *The Portuguese Embassy to Abyssinia during the Years 1520–1527*, tr. and ed. Lord Stanley of Alderley, Hakluyt Society Publications, vol. lxiv., London, 1881, pp. 86–90; M. Parkyns, *Life in Abyssinia*, London, 1853, New York, 1854, vol. ii. ch. xxxi.

GEORGE A. BARTON.

SAINTS AND MARTYRS (Syrian).—

1. Introduction. — Although to the superficial observer the religions of the modern inhabitants of Palestine and Syria may be classified with apparent exactitude under a number of well-recognized divisions—Christianity, Judaism, Muhammadanism, Druse, etc.—and these religions again may be divided into a great variety of sects, each, with fanatic devotion, holding to very definite and characteristic doctrines and ritual, yet such a classification by no means covers the whole ground. When the peoples of these lands are more closely studied—particularly the *fellaḥīn*, or villagers, and the *bedu*, or nomads—it will be found that under the outward profession of adherence to orthodox creeds lies a substratum of more primitive belief, common, in varying degrees, to all the religions, and reaching far deeper into the heart of things than all the outward forms. This is broadly true of Christian and Jew, of orthodox (Sunnite) Muslim and Metāwileh (Shī'ite), of Druse and Nāṣiriyyah. This primitive faith includes an animistic belief in *jinn* and *ghūl*, a common faith in various spirit agencies as causing misfortune, illness, and death, a profound dread of the 'evil eye' which leads to the almost universal use of charms, similar customs with regard to vows and their fulfilment, a belief in the efficacy of sacrificial rites, and a universal respect paid to dead saints and heroes. For the great majority of the native inhabitants of the land, in all but the largest towns, these items of belief have for long ages made up substantially their real religion; and even the average town-dwellers, though making more intelligent and sincere profession of their nominal faith, have a fundamental regard for those more primitive beliefs, as is constantly demonstrated by their reversion to them in times of moral stress. The importance of these beliefs to the proper understanding of all the higher developments of Semitic religion is unquestionable. The cult of saints and heroes, though, on the one hand, inextricably mixed with the other primitive beliefs enumerated above and, on the other hand, shading off into the orthodox professions, presents many features of great interest and importance.

2. The shrines.—It may be said that a certain degree of superstitious reverence is given to all tombs, and still more to all cemeteries, as they are viewed as places charged with potential spiritual forces. Some special historical association or some supposed manifestation of supernatural influence is usually necessary to call out the devotion of the inhabitants of an extended area to any special site. The shrines which to-day enjoy an acknowledged reputation may be classified very roughly into three groups: (*a*) the village *maḳām*, (*b*) the *walī*, and (*c*) the universally visited shrines, such as Nabī Mūsa, Nabī Rūbīn, etc., at which annual festivals are held.

(*a*) *The maḳām.*[1]—In practically every village in the land may be found a *maḳām* (lit. a 'place of standing') dedicated to some dead worthy and sometimes covering his actual grave. This is looked upon as the shrine of the guardian-spirit of the neighbourhood. It is usually a small square building surmounted by a whitewashed cupola (hence the not infrequent name of such a shrine, *ḳubbah*, 'dome'); it is commonly shaded by one or more trees—*e.g.*, oak, terebinth, carob, or *sidr*—which themselves partake of the sacredness of the shrine. Sometimes the building may cover a cenotaph only; sometimes there may be nothing but a bare floor with a few straw mats, but almost always there is a *miḥrab* pointing the pious Muslim to Mecca. In other cases the building itself has long ago perished, and is now represented by the mere foundations of four walls or by an irregular pile of stones, shaded, it may be, by a sacred tree. With the *bedu* in particular the shrine is commonly a tomb often little better than an ordinary grave. But, whether conspicuous or not, the spot is 'holy' and under the protection of a spirit, or *walī*, usually called *shaikh* or *nabī* (lit. 'prophet'), less commonly *saidna* ('our lord') or *ḥājj* ('pilgrim'). In the case of a building no one dare enter without using some such expression as *Dastūr ya mubārak*, 'By your leave, O blessed one!' Goods left under the protection of the spirit of the shrine are never touched. Such spots, whether actual buildings or even lonely graves, are commonly seen surrounded by bundles of wood, ploughs, and other instruments of husbandry, left to the care of the *walī* till the owner comes to claim them, while sometimes less valuable things—*e.g.*, old rusty knives, worthless coins, etc.—are left as offerings. The stones of the shrine and even the twigs from the neighbouring trees are sacred and must on no account be taken for use, though a fragment may be removed as a charm. Many stories are told of the mis-

[1] Parkyns, p. 85 f.

[2] Cf. C. W. Isenberg and J. L. Krapf, *Journals . . . detailing their Proceedings in the Kingdom of Shoa*, London, 1843, p. 161.

[3] Cf. Brightman, p. 230, and Mercer, p. 369 f.

[4] Brightman, p. 169.

[1] This Arab word appears to be the exact equivalent of the Heb. מקומות of Dt 12[2].

fortunes befalling the impious who removed wood or stone for his own use.

(*b*) *The walī.*—In addition to the *maḳām* a more sacred class of shrine is found on the tops of many hills or hidden within isolated sacred groves. Through the length and breadth of Palestine the tops of lofty hills are crowned with these buildings, sometimes with conspicuous, whitewashed cupolas, sometimes marked only from a distance by a great tree, and sometimes, through neglect, reduced to four ruined walls—but always revered. Such a place is popularly known as a *walī*[1] (lit. 'protector'), a name applied strictly to the saint himself; sometimes the name *ḳubbah*, 'dome,' is given if such a structure crowns the building; and occasionally we find the name *mazār*, 'place of visitation,' a term which might be applied to most of these shrines, for to any one of them pilgrimages may be made, and sometimes a man, particularly one from a distant land, will make a round of all the best known *walīs* in succession. Many of these shrines have annual feast-days, when they are specially visited by the pious. They are all dedicated to some more or less powerful saint. There is no sharp line of division between the village *maḳām* and the more potent *walī*, but the latter is a spot specially honoured by some supposed powerful manifestation of supernatural influence —*e.g.*, some strange occurrence at the time of burial, the bearers being dragged apparently against their will away from the proposed place of burial to an unexpected spot, where alone the body of the *walī* consents to be interred; an answered prayer or a portentous dream; or an exhibition of vengeful power upon one who slighted the place. The influence of *walīs* is, however, usually friendly in contrast to the malevolent freaks of the *jinn*. Any tomb or any village *maḳām* may become worthy to rank as a *walī*, if credited with active supernatural powers to an unusual degree. These lonely shrines are usually under the guardianship of the neighbouring village *shaikh* or of a special 'holy man' or dervish, who lives on the offerings of the faithful and often becomes credited with much of the influence of the *walī* himself. Although the tops of hills are favourite sites, they are by no means the only ones. All along the deep cleft of the Jordan Valley there are such buildings, many of them not improbably the tombs of Arab warriors who perished in the conquest of Palestine during the first enthusiastic outburst of Islām.

(*c*) *The greater shrines.*—In the front rank of importance are a few shrines, venerated all over the land, which are each visited at a special annual feast (*maulid*) by thousands of people. In the case of some of them the duties of guardianship belong to certain families and are hereditary; considerable property has become attached to such resorts, and the hereditary guardians, besides keeping the buildings in repair, use part of these endowments for their own support, and with part provide contributions in food (sheep, rice, butter, etc.) to the annual festivities.

3. The cult of the walī.—The spiritual personalities inhabiting all these varieties of shrines are conceived of as very active and powerful. Their influence extends a varying distance from the neighbourhood of the 'holy' place—in the case of the village *maḳām* probably not farther than the boundaries of the village property, but very much wider in the case of the most important *walīs*. To offend a *walī* would appear to be more dreaded than to offend God Himself. Certainly a vow made at a shrine in the name of the *walī* is more binding than one made in the name of God or on the sacred books. Many a man has perjured his oath made under the latter circumstance, trusting, as some of them have openly said, to the mercy of the All-Compassionate; but he dare not offend the *walī*, whose vengeance knows no compassion and is sure. Hence all over the land these places are used for the public taking of oaths. Of these the following are common.

(*a*) *The oath of purgation or innocence.*—The accusing parties take the accused to the shrine, and, if he takes solemn oath in the name of the *walī* that he has not committed the crime of which he is accused, he is acknowledged to be innocent. Any one wishing to bind a *fellah* or a *bedawī* by a serious oath can assure himself by insisting on his swearing at a *maḳām* of repute. Rather than perjure himself at such awful risk, many a man has quietly made restitution of stolen goods. To the *walī* Shaikh Aḥmad at Felujah, near Gaza, the people come from all parts of the country to take an oath of purgation, after which they receive a certificate from the attendant of the shrine sealed by the village *mukhtār*. The possession of such a document is considered sure evidence of innocence.

(*b*) *The vow of the incense* (*nidhr al bakhūr*) is also a common vow at a *walī*. The person making such a vow visits the *maḳām*, kisses it, recites the *fatḥah*,[1] and then utters some such prayer as the following:

'I make a vow in order that the sick one should recover (or the absent one return in safety). I present thee with this incense, oh my Lord! Oh my Lord, accept this vow for God the highest.'

He then places a small piece of metal or a sherd of pottery before the *maḳām* and burns some incense in it. He also very commonly lights a small pottery hand-lamp, and, before leaving, he again kisses the sacred spot. Around all important shrines will be found fragments of pottery or metal marked by the burning incense and sometimes lamps also.

(*c*) *The vow of the veil.*—A similar vow is the *nidhr al istar*, 'vow of the veil (or covering),' which may be made instead of the former or in association with it. A person wishing to make a solemn vow brings a piece of green calico or linen about a yard and a half long, which he affixes to the pillar at the head of the tomb with the same ceremony and with words similar to those quoted above, except that he says, 'I bring thee this veil,' etc.

(*d*) *The vow of pilgrimage.*—A more ceremonious vow is made by richer people on special occasions —*e.g.*, in petitioning for the restoration to health of a beloved one or for the birth of a son. This is the *nidhr az ziyārah*, 'vow of pilgrimage.' The details vary in different localities. In parts of Galilee the custom is as follows:

The man and his nearer relatives and friends, men, women, and children, dressed in their best, make a solemn procession to the shrine. In front walks the head of the family, accompanied by the men; then (when a son is to be petitioned for) there is often a young man or boy on horseback, who is named the *arīs*, 'bridegroom'; behind him come the maidens walking two or three together; and in the rear the married women. Such a *ziyārah*, or pilgrimage, may last two or (if the distance is considerable) three days. On arriving at the shrine, the man kisses the tomb, recites the *fatḥah*, and makes his vow somewhat as follows: 'Oh my lord, I have a vow to make and have come to visit thee. If God gives us a son, I will bring thee a beast for sacrifice and a sack of rice.' After he has again kissed the spot, a feast is held. On the second day they celebrate what is called a *fantasīyah* (*i.e.* dancing and games) at the spot. On the last day the man who has vowed lays at the foot of the tomb, in the presence of the *arīs*, a small money-offering, which is kept by the caretaker, if there be such, or is given to the poor, if there is no regular custodian. It is not always necessary to make this ceremonial visit when making the vow; the man may simply look towards the distant shrine and raise a *mashhad*[2] (a pile of small stones) to witness his oath. But, when the prayer has been granted, a pilgrimage

[1] Much less commonly *walīyah* (female *walī*) is used, the traditions connecting the shrine with a woman.

[1] The opening verses of the Qur'ān.

[2] The *marqemah*, 'heap of stones,' of Pr 26[8] (RV).

must be made with banners and beating of the tom-tom (*tubl*); the devoted sheep and other food are eaten by the whole party, parts of the banquet being reserved for the caretaker.

(*e*) *Various offerings.*—The *bedu* of Moab, before going on a warlike expedition, sacrifice sheep at a tomb or *walī* to bring success. If there is sickness among the flocks, they may be driven to the *walī* for cure, or one of the flock may be sacrificed. A sick person may sometimes sleep at a sacred tomb to obtain healing, and on such occasions the saint himself, usually as a venerable man, appears in a vision or a dream and brings health and encouragement. In attending these places for prayer or vows, sometimes the worshippers sprinkle on their faces and necks some of the dust from the neighbourhood, and sometimes they carry away a portion of this or of the surrounding herbage as a charm; the earth from Mecca is sold in this way all over Syria. Among the *bedu* of Moab the first milk taken in the spring, the first butter made, the earliest wheat or lentils, and the first-born of the flock are presented to the *walī*, and are there either given to the guardian of the shrine or to the poor in the name of the *walī* or, in the case of milk or butter, simply poured out on the ground. When an animal is sacrificed at such a spot, some of the blood is poured on the tomb, and, if there is a building, some is commonly sprinkled on the lintel and sideposts of the door. In the case of tombs attended by a class of people slightly more educated, it is common to find written petitions to the dead saint thrust into the tomb or into parts of the building connected with it. This is specially noticeable in connexion with the well-known Mosque of the Patriarchs at Hebron. Many of the more important shrines have annual feasts connected with them attended by multitudes, some of which are referred to below.

4. The personalities honoured at the shrines.—These are various. Some are connected with Biblical traditions, some with the history of Islām, but a considerable number are known to be of no great antiquity. A few of the tombs are those of persons who were known in life by many still living. As will be seen, greatness or goodness in this life is by no means necessary to make a man a much-respected *walī* after death.

Among the shrines in the front rank of importance, which have each an annual feast (*maulid*) attended by thousands of people, are Nabī Mūsa, the tomb of Moses, according to Muslim tradition, in the Jordan Valley between Jerusalem and the Dead Sea; Nabī Rūbīn, identified in tradition with the son of Jacob, south of Jaffa; and Nabī Sālih, in the peninsula of Sinai, in memory of an unknown pious man. The annual festival of Nabī Mūsa is held for a week at Easter,[1] that of Nabī Rūbīn for ten days in September, and that of Nabī Sālih for three days in June. Thousands of Muslim pilgrims from all over the country attend these gatherings; at Nabī Rūbīn Christians as well as Muslims assemble. Another shrine of Nabī Sālih near Ramleh also attracts many Muslim pilgrims in the spring.

The building called Nabī Daūd, the reputed tomb of King David, and the shrine of al-Khudr (Elijah) on Mt. Carmel are held in equal veneration by Muslims, Christians, and Jews. The former is specially visited by Muslim women and also by the Yemen Jews annually at their New Year. The annual feast of the latter is attended by members of all these religions. Nabī Sha'ib, the reputed tomb of the father of Jethro, near Hattīn, and Nabī Safa, near Rashiyah, are both held in the highest honour by the Druses.

It is impossible to enumerate more than a small percentage of the hundreds of shrines which are held in reverence. The traditional tomb of Aaron on Mt. Hor, that of Joseph at Nāblus (venerated equally by Muslims, Samaritans, Jews, and Christians), the tombs of Abraham, Isaac, and Jacob and their wives at Hebron, and the tomb of Rachel on the road to Bethlehem (specially honoured by the Jews) are some of the best known; but there are few notable early OT characters whose memory is not preserved in this way, and some have several sanctuaries.

The saints, however, are by no means limited to Bible characters; some are historical personages whose true history has in many cases been long lost in myth. Thus the tomb of the *imām* 'Alī ibn 'Ala Ta'lib, the son-in-law of Muhammad, and that of Bellah ibn Rubāb—both at Jericho—are now supposed by many to be those of Joshua and his servant. A revered shrine is the *makām* of Saidna 'Alī ibn 'Alam, north of Jaffa, the tomb of a warrior who bravely defended Arsūf against the Christians in Crusading times.

A number of shrines are dedicated to the 'forty martyrs,' but who these individuals were it is impossible to ascertain. In Hebron a ruin is shown called Deir al-Arba'in, said to be dedicated to the forty witnesses of the transaction whereby Abraham acquired his property in Hebron.[1] At Safed there is a mosque called Jama' al-Arba'in. On Mt. Carmel there is a splendid grove of evergreen oaks known as Shajaret al-Arba'in, 'the trees of the forty,' or, as the Christians say, 'of the forty martyrs.' Under these trees there is a *mihrāb* and there appear to be traces of an ancient altar. The *fellahīn* of the district believe that the spirits of the saints hold an annual festival here, but the date of the anniversary is secret. To take the smallest branch, even of the dead twigs, from this sacred grove is sure to bring disaster upon the aggressor. At Ramleh also the white mosque is dedicated to the Arba' in Ghazāwi, 'forty victors,' and there are several other such places.

Many of the shrines are dedicated to *shaikhs*, *nabīs*, etc., whose names are obviously apocryphal—*e.g.*, the *walī* of Shaikh Nabī Billān, near Nāblus, is certainly so called from *billān*, a common shrub which from its quantity gives its name to the mountain and neighbouring valley. It is common, too, to put Nabī before the name of a village or town when naming the adjoining *makām*. Some of the names are very curious. At Safed the most sacred *makām*, at which judicial oaths are regularly made, is that of Shaikh Abu Kamīs, lit. 'the old man of the shirt,' a name given to the tomb because it is that of a dervish who was peculiar in having that garment only. On Carmel the Kabr al-Majdūbi, 'the tomb of the idiot,' is revered; and farther south we find the 'tomb of the madman.' In Moab there is a Walī Khanzīr, *i.e.* 'the *walī* of the pig,' which by local tradition actually covers the head of a wild boar. Yet it is much respected.[2]

It is by no means necessary that the man buried at the tomb should have lived very long; indeed some *walīs* belong to people who have died within living memory. Nor need he have been in any way a pious follower of religion or morals. The revered tomb of Abu Ghōsh between Jerusalem and Jaffa covers the remains of a cut-throat bandit who plundered the whole district in the middle of last century. Near Safed there is a shrine on the eastern extremity of Jabal Kana'an dedicated to Shaikh Hadīd, a man who was well known to many of the present residents of Safed. When the

[1] Beginning on the Friday before the Greek Good Friday.

[1] The tale is told in J. E. Hanauer, *Folk-lore of the Holy Land*, p. 30 f.

[2] See also the story of 'Ayr in Hanauer, *Tales Told in Palestine*, p. 165 f.

old man died and his body was being carried to burial, the bearers professed that they were dragged by supernatural influence beyond the ordinary cemetery (a common indication of the sanctity of a dead person) and over two miles of rough stony ground until the corpse came to rest at this lone spot overlooking the Jordan Valley. Although so modern a *walī*, the *shaikh's* tomb is much reverenced, as is shown by the following recent incident.

A few years ago some Jews were anxious to buy the part of the mountain on which this shrine stands—a proposal much resented by the more fanatic Muslims. At this juncture one of the *shaikhs* of Ṣafed declared that Shaikh Hadīd had appeared to him in a dream and had told him that he was against this proposed transaction and had recorded his wishes on a paper which would be found sticking in a certain part of his tomb. The ignorant people, unsuspicious of any fraud, went to the spot and found there a paper bearing many threats in Arabic of the evils which would fall on the town if its inhabitants allowed so impious a sale. Needless to say, this stopped all further negotiations.

The saints of many of these shrines are little more than names, and nothing is really known of them; yet their influence is great. When the saint is credited with having belonged to one of the four orders[1] of dervishes, the colours of the different orders are frequently tied to some part of the tomb.

Common as are these shrines and sacred groves in Palestine, they are even more plentiful and influential in the Lebanon mountains; and Palgrave and other travellers witness that similar holy places occur in the deserts of Arabia.[2]

5. Christian and Jewish shrines.—Christian and Jewish tombs and shrines have a similar cult. By far the greater proportion of the peasantry of Palestine are Muslims—of various sects—but among the Christian *fellaḥīn* in a similar state of culture practically the same ideas prevail as regards saints and heroes. In many of the towns and villages the Christians have a more intelligent view of their religion, and their customs merge into adoration of the ordinary Christian saints;[3] but, among the more ignorant, considerable numbers pay reverence to exactly the same shrines as the Muslims and follow identical customs. Famous *walīs* are visited by parties of Christians for the payment of vows. One example, among many known instances, must suffice here: there is a ruined *walī* overhung by an old *sidr*-tree on the northern shore of the Lake of Galilee near Tell 'Oraimah called Shaikh 'Alī as-Sayyād which is considered by the neighbouring *bedu* a very powerful *walī*; till quite recently a number of Christians at Ramah used to come annually and sacrifice a sheep and hold a day's feast at this *walī*.

The Christians hold an annual festival at the reputed cave of Elijah at the foot of Mt. Carmel; it is a Muslim shrine, guarded by hereditary Muslim custodians, but it is also held in high repute by Jews and Christians. At the Convent of Elijah on Mt. Carmel an annual feast is held on 20th July, which is attended by thousands of Christians as well as by Muslims, Jews, and Druses. Many sheep are sacrificed on such occasions.

Among the Oriental Jews the cult of sacred tombs and the worship of saints—under the name of rabbis—are very prominent. The sacredness of three of the four 'Holy Cities' of the Jews depends almost entirely upon the tombs in their neighbourhood. Thus Hebron contains the tombs of the Patriarchs; Tiberias is the site of the reputed tombs of Maimonides, Rabbi Meir Baal Nes, and Rabbi 'Aqība. Rabbi Meir is one in whose name an oath is more binding than one by God or any of the Patriarchs; his tomb is credited with wonder-working powers, and every spring a great festival is held there in his honour, to which hundreds of Jewish pilgrims come from all parts of the Orient. The celebration is similar to the older feast held at the tomb of Rabbi Simeon ben Yoḥai near Ṣafed. Near this town are many tombs to which great virtues are ascribed—*e.g.*, the tomb of Benāt Ya'qūb, belonging to the Muslims, and the tomb of Hoshea ben Ba'ari, which are visited in times of drought as spots favourable to prayers for rain. For similar reasons the tomb of Khune Amagdol, near Far'am, a village near Ṣafed, is a place of pilgrimage; this rabbi is said to have slept for seventy years, and, according to the Talmud, he was in his lifetime a successful intercessor for rain. At Merōn, a village to the west of Ṣafed, are the reputed tombs of several great rabbis. Those of Hillel and his disciples and of Rabbi Shammai are shown, but the most important is the tomb of Rabbi Simeon ben Yoḥai, the reputed author of the *Zôhār*. Over this tomb and that of his son, Eleazar, is erected a large synagogue with adjoining courtyard and lodgings somewhat similar in appearance to the buildings at Nabī Mūsa. The whitewashed domes make it conspicuous from afar, and the customs connected with it are quite comparable with those associated with Nabī Mūsa. Here in May—on the 33rd of 'Omar[1] and succeeding day—an extraordinary festival is held which seems to preserve many elements of paganism.

Jews assemble from all parts of the country—indeed, even from distant lands. On the afternoon of the first day the *Tôrāh* is carried in grand procession from Ṣafed. After sunset the place becomes packed with people, who gradually work themselves up into frenzied excitement, dancing wildly in the courtyard, chanting in Hebrew, throwing about lighted matches and fireworks, and eating and drinking. At length, when darkness has fully gathered, a series of bonfires are lit, made of garments saturated in olive oil. For the privilege of lighting the first fire, which is kindled in memory of Rabbi Simeon ben Yoḥai himself, a heavy price is paid, and until recent years costly garments and jewellery were cast into the blaze. The other fires are kindled successively in honour of Rabbi Eleazar and two other worthies. While the fires are blazing, the Jews, with linked hands, dance frantically round the flames, shouting and singing, while those of a quieter disposition engage in muttered devotions. On this occasion many vows are fulfilled; thus fathers who have made a vow to do so dance for hours, each with a little child of his own perched upon his shoulder; others buy the holy oil for the bonfires before ignition, paying a considerable sum for a small quantity, considering it endowed with supernatural virtues. On the second day of the feast little boys are brought to the neighbouring tomb of Yuhannan ha-sandalar to have the first beginnings of their side-locks (*peyūt*) trimmed in his honour.

A very similar gathering, though considerably quieter, is held twice a year in the spring at the reputed tomb (wrongly, as a Latin inscription found there proves) of Shaddek Shim'on (Simeon the Just) in the upper part of the Valley of Jehoshaphat, north-east of Jerusalem. On the 50th day after the Passover, and also for some days before the feast of Tabernacles, the Jews pour out of the city to the neighbourhood of this tomb. The majority make little more than a picnic, but the pious burn candles and recite psalms within the cave-tomb itself.[2]

6. Al-Khudr. — Besides the saints with local shrines there are two personages who belong to a category by themselves. The first of these is al-Khudr, 'the green (or ever-living) one,' confused by Muslims and Jews with Elijah or with Phinehas, the son of Aaron (Ex 6^{25}, Nu 25^{7} 31^{6}, Jos 22^{13} etc.), and by Christians with St. George. The shrines of this saint are not tombs, because he did not die; for this reason indeed his influence is looked upon

[1] The distinguishing colours of the four orders are as follows: Sulṭān 'Abd al-Ḳadir, white; Sayyad 'Abd al-Bedāwi, red; Rafa'i, green and red; Dusuki, white with a red stripe at the edge. The colours of all four orders are found on some tombs.

[2] Opposition to these shrines is one of the great tenets of the Waḥhabis of Arabia.

[3] See art. SAINTS AND MARTYRS (Christian).

[1] This is traditionally the day of his death, yet the feast is called 'Hillula' ('wedding') of Simeon ben Yoḥai.

[2] For a fuller account of the Jewish places of pilgrimage in Palestine see *JE*, *s.v.* 'Pilgrimage'; and cf. art. PILGRIMAGE (Hebrew and Jewish).

as peculiarly potent. The village of al-Khudr, between Bethlehem and Hebron, is a small Muslim village in the midst of which is the Convent of St. George, where Muslims and Christians pay their vows and bring their sick friends, lunatics in particular, for healing. When attending the place to pay a vow, the *fellaḥīn* (usually Muslims) are permitted to sacrifice animals in the courtyard of the convent, and they hand over to the priest a share of the meat. The church is full of the offerings of those who have vowed in time of need, and the very chain to which the unfortunate lunatics are fixed is credited with miraculous powers. A somewhat similar institution to this is Mar Jirius on the Nicophorea, near the Jaffa Gate, Jerusalem; and there are three other churches dedicated to this saint in the city. Before pictures of Mar Jirius (St. George) the native Christians make vows and burn incense, and they have many tales of how al-Khudr, or St. George, appeared on a white horse to help one who called upon him in difficulty or danger. Of the many shrines to al-Khudr all over the land the most famous, besides those mentioned, are the Church of St. George at Lydda, where by tradition St. George was buried; the ruined church of Mar Jirius at Ṭaiyibah, north of Jerusalem, about which a curious folk-lore tale is told;[1] the great Convent of Elijah on Mt. Carmel; the above-mentioned cave of Elijah at the foot of Carmel; and the synagogue dedicated to Elijah at Jobar, near Damascus. The last by tradition marks the spot where Elijah anointed Elisha to be a prophet, and at the back of the building is an underground chamber where by tradition Elijah was fed by the ravens. In this chamber, as in the cave at the foot of Carmel, sick folk, especially lunatics, are shut up in order to obtain health and healing.

This identification of Elijah and St. George under the name of al-Khudr is very curious, and it is suggestive, too, that the feast of St. George, held, according to the Arabic calendar, on 26th April, is called 'the feast of the spring,' which makes everything green — al-Khudr from some aspects appears to be a deity of the spring and of vegetation, but his identification with Elijah and St. George is inexplicable.

7. Shaikh ash-Shadhilly.—Another mysterious personage is Shaikh ash-Shadhilly, the supposed inventor of coffee, to whom libations of coffee are made whenever that beverage is drunk in public assembly, and in whose name coffee is sometimes poured out before the feet of a bride as she leaves her parents' home. Oaths are made in his name; he is a true *walī*.

8. The bearing of the cult of saint- and hero-worship upon other Semitic religious customs.—When the essence of the cult of *walī*-worship is examined, it will be found that among the majority of the ignorant the saint is looked upon as the one from whom the favour is actually asked; he is the being who is obeyed and dreaded; vows to him must be kept because his activity is great and his power of vengeance is sure. He is a much more active force, whether as guardian or as persecutor, than a far-off, unchanging God or even a personal devil. It is hardly necessary to say that all this is quite contrary to the orthodox religions, emphatically so as regards Islām; the better-educated religious leaders know and confess this, though they have practically to bow to it.

It is the same contest as has been going on in these lands for millenniums. Josiah fought against these local shrines (2 K $23^{8.13}$) just as any reforming Muslim would have to do to-day. In Arabia the very spots which once were idol-shrines are now *walīs* with very similar cult, and this may be said of many of the more important shrines in Palestine and Syria.

The whole cult merges into many kindred ideas. On the one hand, it is difficult to draw a hard and fast line between this worship at tombs of *walīs* and *shaikhs* and the whole cult of worship of the dead, feasting at tombs, etc.; and, on the other hand, the visits to these shrines are identical with what the orthodox Muslim does when he makes the *ḥajj* to Mecca — which was a pre-Islāmic heathen shrine—or the orthodox Oriental Christian when he makes the annual pilgrimage to the Holy Sepulchre and other 'holy' places.

Another closely allied subject is the cult of sacred stones, caves, springs, and trees, all looked upon by the *fellaḥīn* as inhabited by some supernatural being and likewise as objects of special reverence and worship. Many of these are quite unconnected with any historical or mythological personage. The people burn incense at these spots and make their vows in the same way as at the tomb. Some such spots are credited with healing virtues; others are believed to be beneficial for sterility. The belief in the incarnation of the deity in certain historical or living personages, which is found in the Druse, Nāṣirīyyah, and Bābite faiths, though closely connected with the present subject, is one which is dealt with elsewhere.[1]

LITERATURE.—E. W. Lane, *Manners and Customs of the Modern Egyptians*, London, 1836, ch. x.; W. R. Smith, *The Religion of the Semites*², London, 1894; C. R. Conder, 'Moslem Makams,' in *PEFM*, vol. iv. 'Special Papers,' pp. 258–273; C. Clermont Ganneau, 'The Arabs in Palestine,' *ib.* pp. 315–330; S. I. Curtiss, *Primitive Semitic Religion To-day*, New York and London, 1902; J. E. Hanauer, *Folk-lore of the Holy Land*, London, 1907, *Tales Told in Palestine*, Cincinnati, 1904; A. J. Jaussen, *Coutumes des Arabes au pays de Moab*, Paris, 1908; Lydia Einsler, 'Mar Elias, el Chadr und Mar Dschirjis,' *ZDPV* xvii. [1894] 42–55, 65–74; E. W. G. Masterman and R. A. S. Macalister, 'Tales of Welys and Dervishes,' *PEFSt*, 1915, 1916, 1917; E. von Mülinen, *Beiträge zur Kenntnis des Carmels*, Leipzig, 1908.

E. W. G. MASTERMAN.

SAINTS, LATTER-DAY.—The Church of Jesus Christ of Latter-Day Saints, commonly called Mormons, an American sect, claims to number over 300,000 adherents, whose capital is Salt Lake City, Utah.

I. *DOCTRINES AND ORGANIZATION.*—**1. The creed.**—According to the present official handbook, the religion of the Latter-Day Saints consists of doctrines, commandments, ordinances, and rites revealed from God to the present age. The first principle is faith in God and in Jesus Christ; the next is repentance from all sin; then follows baptism for the remission of sin, as a preparation for the gift of the Holy Ghost, bestowed by the laying on of hands. Obedience to these principles is necessary for membership in the Church of Jesus Christ of Latter-Day Saints. Faith in God is the beginning of religion, and confers spiritual gifts such as healings, miracles, tongues, the interpretation of tongues, discernment, visions, dreams, prophecy, and revelation. Authority to administer in the name of the Deity must of necessity come from God. This involves revelation. There having been no communication with heaven for hundreds of years, the world was without divine authority to administer gospel ordinances until Joseph Smith came. By John the Baptist he was ordained to the lesser or Aaronic priesthood, and by Peter, James, and John to the higher or Melchizedek priesthood, receiving the holy apostleship and the keys of the kingdom with power to seal on earth so that it might be sealed in heaven. The religion of the Latter-Day Saints is progressive. It cannot be defined in a written creed. It is added to by the revelations of God as the capacities of the Saints enlarge and the needs of the Church increase. Every member of the Church is entitled

[1] See Hanauer, *Folk-lore of the Holy Land*, p. 52 ff.

[1] See artt. SECTS (Christian), (Muslim), BĀB, BĀBĪS.

to the blessings of divine communion and revelation for his or her own comfort and guidance. Revelations for the whole Church are given only through its President, who is its earthly head and holds the keys of the kingdom. Among the later revelations to the Church are the doctrines of baptism for the dead and of celestial marriage. As there was no authority among men to administer the ordinances of the gospel from the days of the early apostles, or shortly after, to the time of the restoration of the priesthood to Joseph Smith the Prophet, all the baptisms during the intervening period were void. The friends of the dead, however, are permitted to take their names and be baptized in their stead, the ceremony being duly witnessed and recorded on earth and accepted and ratified in heaven. Other ordinances may also be admitted by proxy, the living on behalf of the dead.[1]

In the above declaration three principles are of significance: (*a*) continued revelation and primitive 'gifts,' (*b*) baptism for the dead, and (*c*) 'celestial' marriage or authorized polygamy. Of these principles the first was obviously borrowed from the Restorationists, a local sect, contemporary with the founding of Mormonism. The second was a retro-active application of the Roman Catholic doctrine of Purgatory. The third was more than a logical variation upon the doctrines of other religious bodies.

(*a*) *Continued revelation and primitive 'gifts.'*—The first principle is set forth by the chief Mormon theologian, Parley P. Pratt, as follows:

'Theology is the science of communication, or of correspondence between God, angels, spirits, and men, by means of visions, dreams, interpretations, conversations, inspirations, or the spirit of prophecy and revelation; it is the science by which worlds are organized, sustained and directed and the elements controlled; it is the science of knowledge, and the key and power thereof, by which the heavens are opened, and lawful access is obtained to the treasures of wisdom and intelligence—inexhaustible, infinite, embracing the past, the present, and the future; it is the science of life, endless and eternal, by which the living are changed or translated, and the dead raised; it is the science of faith, reformation, and remission of sins, whereby a fallen race of mortals may be justified, cleansed, and restored to the communion and fellowship of that Holy Spirit which is the light of the world, and of every intelligence therein; it is the science of spiritual gifts by which the blind see, the deaf hear, the lame walk, the sick are healed, and demons are expelled from the human system.'[2]

(*b*) *Baptism for the dead.*—The second principle means that some living believer shall be baptized as proxy for some one of the dead. This doctrine, whereby 'the hearts of the children are turned to the fathers,' is thus expounded by J. E. Talmage:

'The redemption of the dead will be effected in strict accordance with the law of God, which is written in justice and framed in mercy. It is alike impossible for any spirit, in the flesh or disembodied, to obtain even the promise of eternal glory, except on condition of obedience to the laws and ordinances of the gospel. And, as baptism is essential to the salvation of the living, it is likewise indispensable to the redemption of the dead. . . . The necessity of vicarious work is here shown—the living laboring in behalf of the dead; the children doing for their progenitors what is beyond the power of the latter to do for themselves.'[3]

(*c*) *Celestial marriage.*—The practice of 'spiritual wifehood' started early in the Latter-Day Church. The doctrine was an afterthought promulgated in defence of what was plain polygamy. In the last year of the life of Joseph Smith, jr., founder of Mormonism, there came the notorious *Revelation on the Eternity of the Marriage Covenant, including Plurality of Wives. Given through Joseph, the Seer, in Nauvoo, Hancock County, Illinois, July 12th, 1843.* The salient parts of this revelation are as follows:

'Verily, thus saith the Lord unto you, my servant Joseph, that inasmuch as you have inquired of my hand, to know and understand wherein I, the Lord, justified my servants Abraham, Isaac and Jacob; as also Moses, David and Solomon, my servants, as touching the principle and doctrine of their having many wives and concubines:

Behold! and lo, I am the Lord thy God, and will answer thee as touching this matter:

Therefore, prepare thy heart to receive and obey the instructions which I am about to give unto you; for all those who have this law revealed unto them must obey the same;

For behold! I reveal unto you a new and an everlasting covenant; and if ye abide not that covenant, then are ye damned; for no one can reject this covenant, and be permitted to enter into my glory;

For all who will have a blessing at my hands, shall abide the law which was appointed for that blessing, and the conditions thereof, as were instituted from before the foundation of the world:

And as pertaining to the new and everlasting covenant, it was instituted for the fullness of my glory; and he that receiveth a fullness thereof, must and shall abide the law, or he shall be damned, saith the Lord God.

And verily I say unto you, that the conditions of this law are these:—All covenants, contracts, bonds, obligations, oaths, vows, performances, connections, associations, or expectations that are not made, and entered into, and sealed, by the Holy Spirit of promise, of him who is anointed, both as well for time and for all eternity, and that too most holy, by revelation and commandment through the medium of mine anointed, whom I have appointed on the earth to hold this power (and I have appointed unto my servant Joseph to hold this power in the last days, and there is never but one on the earth at a time, on whom this power and the keys of this Priesthood are conferred), are of no efficacy, virtue or force, in and after the resurrection from the dead; for all contracts that are not made unto this end, have an end when men are dead. . . .

As pertaining to the law of the Priesthood: If any man espouse a virgin, and desire to espouse another, and the first give her consent; and if he espouse the second, and they are virgins, and have vowed to no other man, then is he justified; he cannot commit adultery, for they are given unto him; for he cannot commit adultery with that that belongeth unto him and to no one else;

And if he have ten virgins given unto him by this law, he cannot commit adultery, for they belong to him, and they are given unto him, therefore is he justified.'[1]

Although this document was not officially promulgated until 1852, when Smith was dead and his followers were safe in Salt Lake Valley, its authenticity is provable from its similarity in style to the other sacred books of the Mormons. As to this series, there was a kind of gross philosophic basis to the doctrine of 'celestial' marriage. This doctrine is perhaps remotely attributable to the notions of an obscure sect, the German Pietists of Pennsylvania, followers of Tauler and other mediæval mystics. Dwelling in the same State in which the early writings of Joseph Smith were excogitated, they likewise taught a doctrine of the 'spiritual' union of the male and female. It may be paradoxical to assert that Mormonism was made in Germany, yet Conrad Beissel, head of the Ephrata community, initiated in the doctrine of the heavenly *Sophia*, may have been the fount and origin of the esoteric teachings of the Latter-Day Saints. Then, too, Sidney Rigdon, or that 'German peddler' who at one time influenced Smith, may easily have served as the vehicle of transmission for these perverted notions of a cosmic dualism. Be that as it may, precisely what the Prophet himself taught on the 'mysteries of the kingdom' is unknowable, since part of his testimony in Rigdon's trial was declared unprintable. Nevertheless, the system of Mormon metaphysics, justifying plurality of wives, is to be gathered from the writings of the two Pratts.

According to Orson Pratt, called 'the Gauge of Philosophy,' 'celestial marriage opens the way for all women who wish to marry to fill the measure of their creation. . . . It shows how the innumerable creations of God (*i.e.* this world and other planets) may be peopled with intelligences. . . . Woman without man and man without woman cannot be saved. The larger a progeny a man has, the greater will be the fullness of his eternal glory.'[2]

Such was the first promulgation and vindication of the doctrine of 'spiritual wifehood' in the early

[1] Cf. *The Book of Doctrine and Covenants of the Church of Latter-Day Saints*, Kirtland, Ohio, 1833, sect. 20.
[2] *Key to the Science of Theology*, Liverpool, 1855, p. 15 f.
[3] *Articles of Faith*, Salt Lake City, 1899, p. 152.

[1] *Doctrine and Covenants*, sect. 132.
[2] *Treatise on the Regeneration and Eternal Duration of Matter*, 1840.

days of the Church. The present official handbook contains this account of the matter:

'Celestial marriage is marriage unto all eternity. According to the revelation on this subject all the marriages entered into without divine authority are dissolved by death. Celestial marriage is entered into by those who have obeyed the gospel and become the sons and daughters of God by adoption. The woman is given to the man and they become one flesh. That which is thus sealed on earth is sealed in heaven, and is as valid as though performed in person by the Deity. If a wife thus sealed to her husband should precede him in death, it would be his privilege to wed another. The second wife, or third, if the second should die, would be sealed to him in the same manner as the first. They would all be his equally. In the resurrection he would have three wives, with their children, belonging to him in the everlasting covenant. The revelation on celestial marriage declares that if given to man in the everlasting covenant in the way appointed to God, he is not under condemnation, but is justified in receiving more wives than one. They are sealed to him and become his, and he cannot commit adultery with them because they are his and his alone. None of them are concubines or mistresses, or mere ministers of lust. Celestial marriage in its fullness is ordained of God. It is an establishment of religion. It is ecclesiastical in its nature and government. It is, therefore, outside the domain of constitutional law. Being within the pale of the Church, its free exercise cannot of right be prohibited.'

2. Organization.—The Mormon hierarchy is complicated. Joseph Smith and Oliver Cowdery were the first two elders and apostles in the Church. Smith, who bore the title of 'Prophet, Seer, and Revelator,' stood at the head of the Melchizedek priesthood, of which three presiding high-priests, chosen by the body, form a quorum of the Presidency of the Church. The President of the Church and his two counsellors form the First Presidency, and the three together represent the Trinity. The Twelve Apostles form a quorum equal in authority and power to the three Presidents previously mentioned. The Twelve are a travelling presiding High Council, under the direction of the Presidency of the Church, to build up the Church and regulate its affairs in all nations. The Seventies are also called to preach the gospel and form a quorum equal in authority to that of the Twelve. The Seventy Elders have seven presidents to preside over them, chosen out of the number of the Seventy. In addition to these the officers of the Melchizedek priesthood are high-priests and elders. The officers of the Aaronic or lesser priesthood are priests, teachers, and deacons. There are twenty-one 'Stakes of Zion' in Utah. Over each stake there is a presidency consisting of a president and two counsellors, who are high-priests. This presidency bears the same relation to the stake that the First Presidency bears to the whole Church. A high council in each stake, consisting of twelve members, who are also high-priests, acts for the stake as the travelling presiding High Council acts for the Church in all the world. It is the province of the high-priests to preside, while the special calling of the Seventy is to travel and preach the gospel and build up the Church.

The Mormon system of proselytizing is simple. Twice each year, at the annual and semi-annual conferences held in Salt Lake City, a number of the faithful elders of the Church are selected by the authorities and 'called' by the assembled Saints to visit the home or the foreign field. They travel at their own charges. Each mission is presided over by some elder selected by the general authorities of the Church, and the minor divisions of branches and conferences have their proper officers. The Utah missionaries remain in their fields of labour from two to four years and until released by competent authority to return home. Mormon missionaries have gone to Canada, Mexico, the Antilles, Brazil, Peru, Great Britain, Germany, Switzerland, France, Italy, Denmark, Sweden, Norway, Iceland, Finland, S. Africa, India, the East Indies, China, Australia, New Zealand, the Society Islands, and the Hawaiian Islands. The Church has an organization known as the Perpetual Emigration Fund Company, which makes advances of money to assist the faithful to Utah and adjoining districts.

II. *History.*—**1. The founder of Mormonism.**—The growth of the Church of Latter-Day Saints in both beliefs and structure is most clearly portrayed in the history of its founder.

Joseph Smith was born at Sharon, Windsor County, Vermont, in Dec. 1805. There are three views concerning his personality—the orthodox, the popular, and the critical. The first makes him 'God's vicegerent, a prophet of Jehovah, a seer and a martyr: Every Mormon, if true to his faith, believed as freely in his holy character as they did that God existed.'[1] The second view makes him a visionary, a fanatic, an impostor, and a libertine. The third view is a compromise; taking both the accounts of early Church narrators and the contemporary adverse descriptions, it attempts to explain the conviction of his followers that their leader was the medium of supernatural communication, and the belief of his neighbours and contemporaries that his character was marked by abnormal peculiarities. The naturalistic explanation further depends upon a study of heredity and environment. According to suppressed sources, particularly the *Biographical Sketches* of the Prophet's mother, his paternal grandfather, Asael Smith, was a man of distorted views on religion, while his maternal grandfather, Solomon Mack, an infirm beggar, was highly credulous, believing, like Joseph's mother, in cures by faith and in dreams as warnings from heaven. The career of the father, Joseph Smith, was that of a wanderer; failing as a farmer, a store-keeper, and a root-digger in Vermont and New Hampshire, he assumed a land claim in Ontario County, New York, in 1815. Like his son, he believed in witchcraft and demon-possession. In his autobiography Smith declared that these were the reports of evil-disposed and designing persons. At the least they disclose three traits inherited by the youthful seer—his illiteracy, his restlessness, and his credulity. Furthermore, the ancestral characteristics may be interpreted from a pathological standpoint, for there was much to be transmitted in the way of erratic tendencies. On the maternal side Joseph's grandfather was subject to 'falling fits,' consequent upon a severe wound to his head. This was received about a year before the birth of the Prophet's mother, Lucy Mack, who was in turn liable to mental hallucinations, such as hearing supernal voices and seeing luminous faces. On the paternal side Joseph's grandfather, Asael, nicknamed, for a bodily deformity, 'Crook-necked Smith,' is spoken of,[2] at the age of eighty-six, as 'just recovering from a severe fit,' and of a 'weak mind.' Granting that these were merely the symptoms of senility and not transmissible qualities, Asael's son was nevertheless the victim of decided neural instability, being at times 'much excited upon the subject of religion.'[3] If to this aberrant history of his progenitors be added the fact that 'fits' have reappeared in the fifth generation, some grave neuropathic disturbance, such as epilepsy, is to be surmised as the most likely cause of the Prophet's abnormalities. In particular, his phantasms may be considered as the epileptic reduplications not only of the 'lights' seen by his 'imagining but agitated' maternal grandfather, but also of the 'visions' of his own father, the last of which was 'received' in 1819. His own peculiar psychic experiences the Latter-Day seer was wont to liken to those of St. Paul; they may be more appropriately compared to those of Muhammad, whose

[1] *Times and Seasons*, v. 856.
[2] Lucy Smith, *Biographical Sketches*, p. 154 f.
[3] *Times and Seasons*, v. 173.

career as prophet-statesman is to be similarly interpreted by means of the formulæ of modern psychology.[1]

The 'conversion' of Joseph Smith took place near Palmyra, New York, in 1820—in a region infested by fanatic sects and at a period marked by excessive revivalism. Of this affair Smith in his maturity gave the following account:

'Some time in the second year after our removal to Manchester, there was in the place where we lived an unusual excitement on the subject of religion. . . . I was at this time in my fifteenth year. . . . During this time of great excitement, my mind was called up to serious reflection and great uneasiness; but though my feelings were deep and often pungent, still I kept myself aloof from all those parties, though I attended their several meetings as often as occasion would permit. . . .

It was on the morning of a beautiful clear day, early in the spring of eighteen hundred and twenty. It was the first time in my life that I had made such an attempt, for amidst all my anxieties I had never as yet made the attempt to pray vocally.

After I had retired into the place where I had previously designed to go, having looked around me and finding myself alone, I kneeled down and began to offer up the desires of my heart to God. I had scarcely done so, when immediately I was seized upon by some power which entirely overcame me, and had such astonishing influence over me as to bind my tongue so that I could not speak. Thick darkness gathered around me, and it seemed to me for a time as if I were doomed to sudden destruction. But, exerting all my powers to call upon God to deliver me out of the power of this enemy which had seized upon me, and at the very moment when I was ready to sink into despair and abandon myself to destruction, not to an imaginary ruin, but to the power of some actual being from the unseen world, who had such a marvellous power as I had never before felt in any being, just at this moment of great alarm, I saw a pillar of light exactly over my head, above the brightness of the Sun, which descended gradually until it fell upon me. It no sooner appeared than I found myself delivered from the enemy which held me bound. When the light rested upon me, I saw two personages whose brightness and glory defy all description, standing above me in the air. One of them spake unto me. . . . When I came to myself again I found myself lying on my back, looking up into heaven.'[2]

The second of the 'visions of Joseph' took place on 21st Sept. 1823, when the heavenly messenger disclosed the hiding-place of the gold plates upon which the *Book of Mormon* was asserted to be engraved. There was a series of seven visions in all, extending over as many years, and variously characterized by epileptic symptoms, such as dazzling colour sensations, dizziness, coma, vacuity, and bodily bruises. This explanation of the 'visits of the angels' to their leader is, of course, repudiated by the orthodox Saints, as is the report that the Prophet's wife asserted that she never believed in what her husband called his apparitions or revelations, as she thought him labouring under a diseased mind. Nevertheless, psychological method goes far to explain not only Smith's visions but his more pretentious activities in 'translating' the *Book of Mormon*. Connected with his abnormal trances is the so-called 'transcription of the gold plates.' Having dug for fabled treasures among Indian mounds on the western frontier, Joseph Smith found a 'peek-stone,' which became the later 'Urim and Thummim' whereby 'Joseph the Seer translated the reformed Egyptian of the plates of Nephi.' Recent inspection of the original 'transcription,' with its crude superscription 'Caractors,' and its partial back-handed autographs, shows it to be nothing but the automatic scrawl of the self-hypnotized crystal-gazer. And Smith's peculiar method of giving 'revelations' bears out this hypothesis of a subconscious activity. Hidden behind a blanket and throwing himself into a condition of reverie by gazing into his 'interpreters,' he dictated to his scribes communications of supposedly supernatural origin. Of these writings the first was the *Book of Mormon*, begun in Sept. 1827, at Manchester, New York, continued at Harmony, Pennsylvania, and finished at Fayette, New York, in June 1829. The original MS has disappeared; there remains only a duplicate made by Smith's principal scribe, the schoolmaster Oliver Cowdery. This Cowdery copy is of value as containing the author's preface with its original erasures and its misspellings, solecisms, and improprieties. The first edition also presents this illuminating title page:

'The *Book of Mormon*, an Account written by the Hand of Mormon, upon plates taken from the plates of Nephi. Wherefore it is an abridgment of the record of the people of Nephi; and also of the Lamanites, who are a remnant of the House of Israel; and also to Jew and Gentile; written by way of commandment, and also by the spirit of Prophecy and of Revelation. Written, and sealed up, and hid up unto the Lord, that they might not be destroyed; to come forth by the gift and power of God unto the interpretation thereof; sealed by the hand of Moroni, and hid up unto the Lord, to come forth in due time by the way of Gentile; the interpretation thereof by the gift of God. An abridgment taken from the Book of Ether. Also, which is a Record of the people of Jared; which were scattered at the time the Lord confounded the language of the people when they were building a tower to get to Heaven; which is to shew unto the remnant of the House of Israel how great things the Lord hath done for their fathers; and that they may know the covenants of the Lord, that they are not cast off forever; and also to the convincing of the Jew and Gentile that Jesus is the Christ, the Eternal God, manifesting Himself unto all nations. And now if there be fault, it be the mistake of men; wherefore condemn not the things of God, that ye may be found spotless at the judgment-seat of Christ. By Joseph Smith, junior, Author and Proprietor, Palmyra, printed by E. B. Grandin, for the author, 1830.'

The fifteen books of this 'Sacred History of Ancient America from the Earliest Ages after the Flood to the Beginning of the Fifth Century of the Christian Era' Smith himself thus summarized:

'We are informed by these records that America, in ancient times, has been inhabited by two distinct races of people. The first were called Jaredites, and came directly from the Tower of Babel. The second race came directly from the city of Jerusalem, about six hundred years before Christ. They were principally Israelites, of the descendants of Joseph. The Jaredites were destroyed, about the time that the Israelites came from Jerusalem, who succeeded them in the inhabitance of the country. The principal nation of the second race fell in battle towards the close of the fourth century. The remnant are the *Indians*, who now inhabit this country. This book also tells us that our Saviour made His appearance upon this continent after His resurrection; that He planted the gospel here in all its fulness and richness, and power, and blessing; that they had apostles, prophets, pastors, teachers, evangelists; the same order, the same priesthood, the same ordinances, gifts, powers, and blessing, as was enjoyed on the Eastern continent; that the people were cut off in consequence of their transgressions; that the last of their prophets who existed among them was commanded to write an abridgment of their prophecies, history, etc., and to hide it up in the earth, and that it should come forth and be united with the Bible, for the accomplishment of the purposes of God in the last days.'[1]

As a product of abnormal mentality, this 'account of the aborigines of America' has been recently described as made up of fantastic explorations of the imagination, assumptions of narrative, incidents, and style apparently foreign to the subject's normal intelligence, the invention of fictitious names, persons, places, and things—incidents and details which may be traced to the authentic experiences of the subject, but experiences which may have been subconsciously realized, and are certainly recorded while in an abnormal state of dissociation.[2] Here again is furnished a mediating position between the orthodox view, which holds the *Book of Mormon* to be the authentic Word of God, vouchsafed through verbal inspiration, and the hostile view, which considers it a rank imposture—a blending of petty information, gross anachronisms, and the muddled superstitions of the rural mind. Rather does the critical view hold that the work contains some details of historic interest, since there appear in it, in Scriptural paraphrase, references to the agitations of the day against Romanism, Deism, and Freemasonry, besides references to Swedenborgianism with its three heavens, and to the 'Washingtonian' movement for total abstinence. The current theory that the Indians were the lost ten tribes of Israel

[1] D. S. Margoliouth, *Mohammed and the Rise of Islam*, New York and London, 1905, p. vii f.

[2] *Pearl of Great Price*, p. 84 ff.

[1] Smith's art. 'Mormonism,' in I. D. Rupp, *He Pasa Ekklesia: An Original Hist. of the Religious Denominations of the United States*, Philadelphia, 1844, p. 4.

[2] J. Jastrow, in the *Psychological Review*, Jan. 1903, p. 70.

is also embodied. But, while the Nephites in their actions were the modern Redmen in disguise, in their mental habits they more closely resembled the local sectarians. Thus the speech of Nephi contains quotations from the *Westminster Confession of Faith*, and the speech of Lehi the heretical tenets charged against the Presbytery of Geneva, New York, in whose bounds Joseph himself lived. The book is also interspersed with the catch-words of the Methodist camp-meeting exhorter, its last section, in fact, being a palpable imitation of a Methodist book of discipline.

Such higher criticism of the most sacred book of the Latter-Day Saints is apparently unacceptable to their apologists; yet it might be of service to them, since it goes far to render untenable the chief contention against the authenticity of the work. This is, in a word, that the ideas in the book were not within the mental horizon of a youth who described himself as 'a rough stone, desiring the learning of heaven alone.'[1] But this ignores the more popular sources of information open to Smith. His Calvinism need not have been derived even from the *New England Primer*, nor his arguments on Deism from Thomas Paine's *Age of Reason*, since the backwoods pulpit and tavern gossip supplied the notions in question. Hence, if the internal evidence makes the *Book of Mormon* indigenous, the external evidence is equally against the supposition of a foreign authorship as presented in the ordinary Spaulding-Rigdon theory. This is, briefly, that a romance of pre-historic America, written in Ohio in 1812 by a Congregational minister, Solomon Spaulding, was the 'source, root, and inspiration' by which Smith's associate, Sidney Rigdon, concocted the scheme of a Golden Bible. The recovery in 1885 of the purported original of Spaulding's 'Manuscript Story' has been to the Saints conclusive proof of its non-connexion with the *Book of Mormon*, for there is no real resemblance between the two. The theory is further invalidated by the fact that it is impossible to show how, when, or through whom Smith could have obtained one of the two copies of the Spaulding MS.

The founder of Mormonism entered upon the second phase in his career, that of 'Prophet, Seer, and Revelator,' with the publication of the next instrument in the Mormon canon, the *Book of Commandments*. This, like its enlargement, the *Book of Doctrine and Covenants*, contains 'revelations to Joseph Smith, Junior, for the building up of the kingdom of God in the last days.' These oracular utterances range from an interpretation of the Ancient of Days to predictions of the Second Advent. Their reception as authentic vaticinations among Smith's first adherents is to be explained by the credulity of his audience and the religious primitiveness of the times. The local relish for the predictive and oracular is manifest by the success of other founders of occult sects in those parts. Jemima Wilkinson prophesied at Crooked Lake; at Rochester William Miller predicted the end of the world; and the Fox sisters started spiritualism only ten miles from Smith's home. Moreover, the return of apostolic gifts was hoped for by the local Quakers, Primitive Baptists, and Restorationists. Upon this prepared soil the Latter-Day Prophet now assumed the additional rôle of exorcist.

When Newel Knight, an early convert, was 'attacked by the power of Satan, and after he had thus suffered for a time,' narrates Smith,[2] 'I succeeded in getting hold of him by the hand, when almost immediately he spoke to me, and with very great earnestness required of me that I should cast the devil out of him. . . . I rebuked the devil and commanded him in the name of Jesus Christ to depart from him.' And so 'at the first conference of the Church,' continues Knight,[1] 'many prophesied, others had the heavens opened to their view, which tended to confirm our faith in Joseph Smith being the instrument in the hands of God, to restore the priesthood again to man on earth, and to set up the Kingdom of God.'

[1] G. Q. Cannon, *Life of Joseph Smith the Prophet*, Salt Lake City, 1888, p. 496.
[2] Newel Knight, *Journal*, Salt Lake City, 1883, p. 50.

As in the case of the 'Three Witnesses' to the *Book of Mormon*, Smith here appears to have exerted a partially hypnotic influence over his followers. As by mental suggestion he had induced a veritable hallucination in which his closest disciples thought they saw the 'gold plates,' so now he exerted this influence upon a wider circle of adherents, and induced in them an absolute confidence in his powers as exorcist and faith-healer. In these new activities it has been claimed that the Mormon leader achieved his successes by borrowing the principles and methods of kindred pseudo-scientific cults which swept over the country. But it was too early in the century for him to be acquainted either with the French animal magnetism or with its American variety, the so-called electro-biology.

Hence it is more logical to suppose that his knowledge of hypnotic possibilities was inadvertently discovered, and that his attempts to bring about ecstatic trances, speaking with tongues, and healing by prayer were connected with belief in the restoration of apostolic gifts, such as was promulgated by the two Campbells in Scotland and in America. But, although the practice of hypnotic suggestion was empirical, it was none the less successful. It is true that during the revival meetings of the Mormons in Ohio the trances and prostrations led to uncontrollable spasms and convulsions, yet subsequently the Prophet brought about some actual cures. While Smith, with his accustomed opportunism, attributed his failures to the creeping in of false spirits, and his successes to the restoration of the priesthood again to man on earth, both are rather to be attributed to the unstable neurotic condition of the young body of believers. On the one hand, the people looked on the Kirtland frenzy as a 'sign,' and were loath to abandon such strange 'handling by the spirits'; on the other hand, their mental suggestibility was highly conducive to 'divine' healing and to 'miraculous' cures. And so the casting out of devils led to the casting out of diseases. As in the case of the Irvingites and of the Oneida Community of Perfectionists, veritable therapeutic results were obtained in the sphere of non-organic troubles. Laying on of hands did not cure cholera, nor prayer brain-fever, but psychic suggestion alleviated a case of rheumatism, and a sort of collective hypnosis toned up the systems of the fever-ridden Saints on the banks of the Mississippi.

That Joseph Smith in all his activities as 'Prophet, Seer, and Revelator,' occultist, exorcist, and faith-healer, was the real master of Mormondom is borne out by a number of accounts of him in the height of his power. The view that, along with his impressive manner in making the healing suggestion, there was 'an expression peculiar to himself, which the eye was never weary of beholding,'[2] is obviously due to the false perspective of emotional excitement. Yet the descriptions of non-Mormon eye-witnesses imply that there was something remarkably forceful in the man. One of these described him as maintaining a grave demeanour;[3] another as of indomitable perseverance, strange and striking views, and great influence over enemies and followers alike;[4] a third as a man of commanding appearance leaving an

[1] Newel Knight, *Journal*, p. 52 f.
[2] P. P. Pratt, *Autobiography*, Chicago, 1888, p. 47.
[3] J. S. Buckingham, *The Eastern and Western States of America*, London, 1841, iii. 193.
[4] P. H. Burnett, *Recollections and Opinions of an old Pioneer*, New York, 1880, p. 66.

impression of rugged power. To the last portrait, however, its author, Josiah Quincy, added the qualification that, while Smith gave the impression of kingly power, his talk was garnished with forcible vulgarisms; and, while he had a statesmanlike prevision in advocating the buying of slaves, eleven years before Emerson advocated that scheme, yet with it all he betrayed unexampled absurdities in showing off his museum containing Egyptian mummies and the autograph of Moses.

'The man mingled Utopian fallacies with his shrewd suggestions. He talked as from a strong mind utterly unenlightened by the teachings of history.'[1]

While the success of Mormonism is chiefly attributable to the personality of its founder, there was another leader among the Latter-Day Saints who had much to do in shaping both the character of the movement and the character of the man. In striking contrast to Joseph Smith, the illiterate son of an ignorant father, was Sidney Rigdon, an ex-Baptist preacher, who was in actuality something of a Biblical scholar and in reputation held to be learned in history and literature. In comparing the two men, a friend of both said that Rigdon did not possess the native intellect of Smith and lacked his determined will.[2] But we may add that what Rigdon lacked in strength of character he made up in breadth of ideas. For one thing, he was acquainted with some of the socialistic notions of that day. While an adherent of Alexander Campbell, who had attacked Robert Owen in a notorious debate in Cincinnati, Rigdon had indirectly obtained from the father of English socialism those communistic notions which he utilized in his branch of the Disciples' Church in Ohio. This collectivist community, made up of a score of families, Smith took over upon his arrival at Kirtland. But, in thus borrowing through Rigdon what were remotely the ideas of Fourier, Smith, of course, gave credit neither to their foreign originator nor to their native intermediary. In a characteristic passage he said that, because Rigdon's church at Kirtland 'had all things in common, the idea arose that this was the case with the Church of Jesus Christ.' He added that the plan of 'common stock' which had existed in what was called 'the family . . . was readily abandoned for the more perfect law of the Lord.' To this explanation was added a special revelation of Feb. 1831:

'Behold, thou shalt consecrate all thy properties which thou hast to impart unto me with a covenant and a deed which cannot be broken . . . And it shall come to pass, that the bishop of my church, after that he has received the properties of my church, that it cannot be taken from the church, he shall appoint every man a steward over his own property, or that which he has received, inasmuch as is sufficient for himself and family; and the residue shall be kept to administer to him who has not, that every man may receive accordingly as he stands in need: and the residue shall be kept in my storehouse, to administer to the poor and needy, as shall be appointed by the elders of the church and the bishop; and for the purpose of purchasing lands, and the building up of the New Jerusalem, which is hereafter to be revealed.'[3]

With the advent of Rigdon, Smith's activities took a turn more comprehensible but less successful than were his occult performances. The eloquent ex-Campbellite minister was at first received as a messenger 'sent to prepare the way'; in a dozen years he was thrown off by the prophet as 'a millstone on his back.' Smith had hitherto confined himself to vague predictions of a good time coming. But, when definite financial schemes were added to millennial promises, the bubble burst. The story of the Smith-Rigdon business enterprises is a story of continued misfortune. It includes the failure of a general store at Hiram, of the paper City of Zion at Kirtland, of the church sawmill, of the church tannery, and of a $40,000 temple, upon which was left a debt of nearly half its value. But before the crash in the Kirtland Safety Society Anti-Banking Company, for the altering of whose notes Secretary Rigdon and Treasurer Smith were forced to flee to Missouri, the Prophet had put a typical religious veneer upon his utopian projects. In 1833 he 'dedicated to the Lord' the printing-office of the *Latter-Day Saints' Messenger and Advocate*. In 1834 he organized the First High Council of the Church of Christ, with himself, Rigdon, and Williams as the first Presidency. In 1835 he chose the Twelve Apostles, among whom were Brigham Young, 'the Lion of the Lord,' Parley Pratt, 'the Archer of Paradise,' and Lyman Wight, 'the Wild Ram of the Mountains.' In 1836 Smith instituted the several quorums, or executive bodies of the Church—first the Presidency, then the Twelve, and the Seventy, also the counsellors of Kirtland and Zion. In 1837 he set apart apostles Kimball and Hyde to go on a mission to Great Britain, the first foreign mission of the Church. This mission appealed strongly to English weaver, Welsh farmer, and Scotch miner, by holding out the promise to each convert of owning his own farm in the land of Missouri, where 'the Lord had been raining down manna in profusion.'

While the outward success of Mormonism abroad is not to be attributed so much to the imaginative Smith as to practical emissaries like Brigham Young, the internal dissensions at home are to be laid at the former's door. In 1832, as a prophet of woe urging the Saints to sell all that they had and flee from the wrath to come, Smith brought the mob upon himself and Rigdon, and the two were tarred and feathered by 'a banditti of blacklegs, religious bigots, and cut-throats.' In the great apostasy of 1836 the Church lost some of its pillars. The Three Witnesses to the *Book of Mormon* were soon cut off. In the bull of excommunication David Whitmer, the anti-polygamist, was compared to Balaam's ass; Martin Harris was called a negro with a white skin; while 'all the dissenters,' said the Prophet, 'are so far beneath my contempt, that to notice any of them would be too great a sacrifice for a gentleman to make.'[1] Again, when the town of Independence, Missouri, was declared the new City of Zion, the converts poured in from the Middle Atlantic States and Canada with such rapidity that the non-Mormons were somewhat alarmed. And the ill-advised printing of the *Book of Commandments*, with its revelations to the Saints calling Missouri 'the land of your inheritance, which is now the land of your enemies,' led to acts of hostility from the citizens of Jackson County. The burning of barns and the shooting into Mormon houses at night were followed by demands for the removal of the Mormons from the county within a reasonable time, and for the prohibition of future Mormon settlement therein.

The history of the events which led up to the 'martyrdom'[2] of Joseph Smith is a tangled tale in which both sides are implicated. Border ruffians were doubtless responsible for the speedy destruction of the Church printing-office, and for the tarring and feathering of Bishop Partridge, yet the Saints themselves were not without fault. Their agreement to depart within eight months was written, as they alleged, 'supposing that before the time arrived the mob would see their error and stop the violence.' Such reasoning may justly be ascribed to the Mormon leader's mental duplicity, which led to further untoward results. While, until 1838, the town of Far West was materially prosperous and on good terms with

[1] Josiah Quincy, *Figures of the Past*, Boston, 1883, pp. 376–379.
[2] Burnett, p. 67. [3] *Book of Commandments*, ch. 44.

[1] *Elders' Journal*, July 1837.
[2] Cf. L. O. Littlefield, *The Martyrs; Joseph and Hyrum Smith*, Salt Lake City, 1882, chs. vi.–viii.

its neighbours, upon the Prophet's arrival there arose dissensions within and without. The Presidency was deposed on a charge of misappropriating trust funds, and Oliver Cowdery was expelled for counterfeiting. With the later defection of the Twelve, and of Orson Hyde, one of the original apostles, there came the establishing of an organization named the Danite Band, and known popularly as 'the Avenging Angels.' Bound to secrecy by blood oaths, obeying every behest of the Church against property and life, this Western variety of Thugs owed its origin to Smith's revelation of 6th Aug. 1833:

> 'Thine enemy is in thine hands, and if thou reward him according to his works thou art justified; if he has sought thy life, and thy life is endangered by him, thine enemy is in thine hands and thou art justified.'

For the agitations of those days Smith was not entirely responsible. While it was upon his suggestion that the organization of the 'Fur Company' let loose foraging bands over the country, yet the beginning of civil strife in Missouri dates from Rigdon's 'salt sermon,' a Fourth of July oration of 1838, in which there was officially predicted a war of extermination between Saints and Gentiles. Then followed the killing of the Danite leader, 'Fear Not' Patten, the defeat of the Missouri Captain Bogart, and the retaliation upon the Mormons in the infamous Hawn's Mill massacre. On 27th Oct. the governor issued orders that the Mormons must be treated as enemies, and must be exterminated or driven from the State, and there ensued a determined campaign against them. The final terms of surrender, offered at Far West by General Lucas, included the payment of debts and the expulsion from the State of all the Latter-Day Saints except the leaders, who were subject to prosecution. In the trial of Joseph and Hyrum Smith, Rigdon, and others, at Liberty, testimony was given that the members of the Danite Band considered themselves as much bound to obey the heads of the Church as to obey God, and that Smith advised his followers to spoil the Gentiles. Smith was confined in Liberty gaol until April 1839, but in vain.

The Mormon leader now employed politics to alleviate persecution, but with what proved to be fatal results. Mass meetings were called in the Eastern cities to express sympathy with the Mormons as oppressed by the enemies of the freedom of religious opinion. Moreover, through the promise of obtaining the votes of the Saints, the Illinois legislature granted charters for the new Mormon capital, the city of Nauvoo, and for the Nauvoo Legion, a militia organization which the Prophet held up as an instrument to 'warn the lawless not to be precipitate in any interference in our affairs.'[1] As the military head of a theocratic Church, 'General' Smith's high ambitions now seem to have turned his head. Confounding State and Church, and relying upon the implicit devotion of his followers, he not only defied the local authorities, but made preposterous claims upon the Federal Government. Indicted as the instigator of the plot to assassinate Governor Boggs of Missouri, whom he had called 'knave, butcher, and murderer,' he was released by his own municipal court. Inflated by his power in controlling the votes of the faithful, and exasperated both by the civil suits against himself and by the property losses sustained by his adherents, he called on President Van Buren, with a claim on the public treasury amounting to $1,383,044. 55¼. Having failed to obtain redress from Congress, Smith penned a letter of inquiry to the opposition, and asked the Whig candidate: 'What will be your rule of action relative to us as a people, should fortune favor your ascension to the chief magistracy?' Henry Clay's answer being noncommittal, Smith called him a black-leg, and became a candidate for the Presidency himself.

[1] Cf. *Revised Laws of the Nauvoo Legion*, Nauvoo, 1844.

The irritating effects of the Prophet's public activities were now increased by the discovery of his equally illicit private practices. That he was in some degree involved in polygamy is probable from a variety of evidence. The introduction of spiritual wifeism was indeed fathered upon the older men like Rigdon, Hurlbut, and Bennett, yet as early as 1833 the Prophet began to 'unfold the mysteries of the kingdom,' and within a decade the Saints in the city of Nauvoo expressed the wish to have the privilege of enjoying their 'peculiarities' unmolested. Besides various revelations concerning this and that 'handmaid,' and concerning care in guarding against 'evils which may arise from accounts given of women,' outward proof of the teaching of the plurality of wives is found in the supersession of the monogamous *Book of Commandments* by the polygamous *Book of Doctrine and Covenants*, and of its practice in such virulent persecutions as caused the expulsion of 15,000 Saints from Missouri.

Discussion now arose within the Mormon community itself. Three of the more intelligent men —R. D. Foster and William and Wilson Law—published a journal called the *Expositor*. This advocated 'disobedience to political revelations' and sought to 'explode the vicious principles of Joseph Smith.' Of this journal there was but one number. This condemned not only the plurality of wives but also the Church appropriation of property without accounting and the preaching of the doctrine of plural gods. Smith's order for the destruction of the *Expositor* press under the plea of martial law increased the excitement among non-Mormons to such an extent that on 22nd June the Prophet and a small number of followers started to flee to the Rocky Mountains. Governor Ford now promised to protect Smith, and the latter surrendered himself to the authorities. Charged with treason in levying war against the State, Smith and his brother Hyrum were shut up in Carthage gaol. Through the governor's bad judgment in appointing as guard the Carthage Grays, who were the confessed enemies of the Smiths, and through evident collusion with a band of disguised assailants, the Prophet and his brother were assassinated on 27th June 1844.

2. The Schismatics and Brigham Young.—The rival claimants to the prophetic successorship were J. J. Strang, Smith's own son, and Brigham Young. The 'Strangites' disappeared when their leader was killed in 1856 because of his practice of polygamy. The 'Young Josephites,' however, founded in 1852 the Re-organized Church of Jesus Christ of Latter-Day Saints, which still exists under the presidency of Joseph Smith, 3rd. It claims to be the continuation of the original Church of Latter-Day Saints, and has been recognized as such by the courts. It maintains that the doctrines of plurality and community of wives are heresies. The headquarters of the Church is at Lamoni, Iowa. It has a publishing-house, and issues two weekly papers (*Zion's Hope*, for Sunday schools, and the *Saints' Herald*, a general religious weekly and the official organ), a monthly magazine (*Autumn Leaves*) for young people, and books and tracts. It maintains Graceland College and a home for the aged poor. There is another establishment at Independence, Mo., with a printing-press, whence are issued *Zion's Ensign*, a weekly paper, books, and tracts. The Church has about 45,000 members.

Of the three claimants Brigham Young was the logical successor of the Prophet. He had joined the Latter-Day Saints in 1832, had been sent as missionary to tour Canada, had returned to Ohio with a band of adherents, and in 1834 went with the 'Army of Zion' to Missouri as one of the 'Captains of Tens.' Appointed one of the original quorum of Twelve, Young helped Smith to flee to Missouri in 1838. For these services Young was left President of the Twelve upon Smith's assassination.

3. The Mormon Hegira. — Smith's brutal murder did not soften the hearts of the enemies of the Mormons. In 1845 they repealed the Nauvoo charter, and Young made plans to go far west. A small group of Saints was sent ahead to spy out good locations in California and Oregon. Through an accidental meeting with some trappers, the Great Salt Lake Valley was chosen as a final resting-place. Then began the remarkable flight of the Mormon tribe. Under Young's leadership their organization was most effective. This was given in the form of a revelation:

'The Word and Will of the Lord, given through President Brigham Young, at the Winter Quarters of the Camp of Israel, Omaha Nation, West Bank of Missouri River, near Council Bluffs, January 14, 1847.

The word and will of the Lord concerning the Camp of Israel in their journeyings to the West; let all the people of the Church of Jesus Christ of Latter-Day Saints, and those who journey with them, be organized into companies, with a covenant and promise to keep all the commandments and statutes of the Lord our God; let the companies be organized with captains of hundreds, captains of fifties, and captains of tens, with a president and his two counselors at their head, under the direction of the Twelve Apostles; and this shall be our covenant, that we will walk in all the ordinances of the Lord; let each company provide themselves with all the teams, wagons, provisions, clothing, and other necessaries for the journey that they can; when the companies are organized, let them go to with their might, to prepare for those who are to tarry; let each company with their captains and presidents decide how many can go next spring; then choose out a sufficient number of able-bodied and expert men, to take teams, seeds, and farming utensils, to go as pioneers to prepare for putting in spring crops; let each company bear an equal proportion, according to the dividend of their property, in taking the poor, the widows, the fatherless, and the families of those who have gone into the army, that the cries of the widow and the fatherless come not up into the ears of the Lord against this people; let each company prepare houses; and fields for raising grain, for those who are to remain behind this season, and this is the will of the Lord concerning his people; let every man use all his influence and property to remove this people to the place where the Lord shall locate a Stake of Zion.'[1]

The versatility of the American pioneer was displayed in the establishment of way-stations, with various repair-shops and with a flour-mill built by Young himself. The largest company, which started from Elk Horn River on 4th July, included 1553 persons, with 566 wagons. By 1848 all the Mormons had crossed the plains, except a few left on the Missouri as forwarding agents for emigrants from the Eastern States and Europe.

4. The settlement in Salt Lake.—Despite the poor crops and great sufferings of the first winter in Utah, glowing accounts of the new Zion were sent abroad. The English immigration included men of varied professions and trades, for Young proposed to start cotton-mills and woollen- and glass-factories. Since there were no manufactured goods to be obtained nearer than 1000 miles, the Mormon leader sought to create a self-sustaining State, but the accounts of 1852 showed a deficit, in spite of an attempt to retrench expenses by giving less help to immigrants coming across the Great Plains. But the economic salvation of the Mormon State arose less from the financial ability of the leaders than from the money spent in Utah by the Forty-Niners hastening to the California gold-fields, and from the building of the Pacific Railroad. Young's dictatorship over the new State of Deseret was based on both personal and religious grounds. His people knew him as 'hard-working' Brigham Young; they also believed that his word was the word of God. His power being further increased by the issue of paper money and the tithing system, there now arose a veritable despotism with such means of espionage as the School of the Prophets and Church Confessors (to visit the families of the Saints).

[1] *Doctrine and Covenants*, sect. 136.

By 1856 great discontent arose, but the disaffected were weeded out in the so-called 'Reformation.' Young now instigated the murder of William R. Parrish, who attempted to apostatize, organized 400 'Wolf Hunters' to prevent such rare escapes out of the valley as that of Frederick Loba and his wife, and instituted blood atonement, as exemplified in the throat-cutting of Rosmos Anderson, who wished to marry his step-daughter, contrary to the wishes of the ward bishop.

Such were the means used for keeping Zion pure within. From without the irruption of the Gentiles was prevented by such cases of frightfulness as the murder of the Akin party in 1857 by 'Brigham's Destroying Angel,' Bill Hickman, and the Mountain Meadows massacre of a party of Gentiles from Arkansas and Missouri who were passing through Utah on their way to S. California. For this the Mormon Bishop Lee was executed by the Federal Government twenty years later.[1]

5. Relations to the Federal Government.—The Mormons who sought to found a State within a State were long neglected by the authorities at Washington. This was due in large measure to the approach of the Civil War and the ignorance of officialdom as to the practices and principles of the Latter-Day Saints. Thus, when Young flouted a federal judge and threatened vengeance for infringement upon his personal rights because of the appointment of another governor, President Buchanan declared that there was no longer any government in Utah but Brigham Young. Moreover, General Scott's expedition to punish the leaders charged with adultery was rendered ineffective by President Buchanan's pardon, while President Lincoln had his hands so tied by the war between North and South that he was unable to back up Colonel Connor's plans to keep Young in subjection. It took another generation before the heads of the Church unwillingly exchanged polygamy for statehood.

6. Anti-polygamy legislation. — Federal legislation against plural marriage began with the Morrill bill of 1860, which was ineffective, as the severest penalty was that for bigamy. The Cullom bill of 1869 was opposed by the Mormon delegate to Congress, who claimed that the United States constitution guaranteed essential principles of religious faith, and that pluralism was one of these principles, so far as the Saints were concerned. The root of the matter was not reached until 1879, when President Hayes declared that polygamy could be suppressed only by taking away the political power of the sect. This eventuated in the Edmunds bill of 1882, which disfranchised polygamists and forbade their holding federal offices. Within two years 1200 persons were deprived of their right to vote, and within eight years 468 persons were convicted of polygamy or unlawful cohabitation. In 1890 the courts declared the ecclesiastical property confiscated because the Mormon Church was an organized rebellion. Hereupon Young's successor, President Wilford Woodruff, advised his followers to 'refrain from contracting any marriage forbidden by the law of the land.'

In 1893 the federal authorities declared an amnesty for all offenders who could prove that they had not broken the law since 1890. The un-

[1] Cf. *Mormonism Unveiled; or the Life and Confessions of John D. Lee*, St. Louis, 1892.

seating of Congressman Roberts, six years later, led to the official declaration from the Latter-Day Saints that they 'form not a rival power as against the Union, but an apostolic ministry to it, and their political gospel is State rights and self-government.' Since obtaining statehood in 1896, the Mormons have been more circumspect in their conduct, the State constitution of Utah expressly forbidding polygamy. Anti-Mormons, however, still claim that it is even yet practised in the remote rural districts, and that plural wives, old and new, are clandestinely supported by the wealthy Church leaders. Charges have also been recently made that the practices of the parents have been imitated by the younger generation.[1] The defence of the doctrine of plural marriage, in theory at least, is still attempted.

'The truth of the matter,' says one of the most recent apologists, 'is that the Mormon estimate of this institution makes it an actual means of grace, an eminent instrument for the salvation of souls. Just as they hold most strenuously to the doctrine of salvation of the dead by means of proxy baptism, just so, with the belief in pre-existence, as already explained, they consider it an act of eminent piety to provide for the birth of a human soul under the fullness of Gospel influences. That the birth of as many souls as possible under such conditions will hasten the redemption of humanity, and of the world, is an evident corollary to the high importance attached to life on earth in the teachings of the Mormon system. In this aspect of the matter, it is easy to see how that parenthood could be made to assume the aspect of a high virtue, involving that a person who had brought many souls into life was entitled to honor, as an instrument in God's hands in the grand work of populating the world with a race, whose leading attribute is the possession of the Divine Spirit. Because, however, the child-bearing capacity of the average woman is limited, it is evident that the only available means by which a worthy man could multiply his offspring would be by taking to himself a plurality of wives.'[2]

LITERATURE.—The four chief collections of *Mormoniana* in America are: the Church Archives at Salt Lake City; Government publications at Washington; the Berrian Collection, New York Public Library, rich in first editions and rare publications of the early Church; and the collection of the State Historical Society of Wisconsin, at Madison, which includes the unique private collection of A. T. Schroeder, late of Salt Lake City.

i. *MORMON PERIODICALS.*—*Deseret News*, Salt Lake City, 1852–87; *Elders' Journal*, Kirtland, Ohio, and Far West, Missouri, 1837–39; *Evening and Morning Star*, Independence Missouri, and Kirtland, Ohio, 1832–34; *Journal of Discourses* (by Brigham Young and the Church leaders), Liverpool, 1854–86; *Latter-Day Saints' Messenger and Advocate*, Kirtland, Ohio, 1834–37; *Latter-Day Saints' Millennial Star*, Liverpool, 1840 ff.; *The Times and Seasons*, Nauvoo, Illinois, 1839–45, vol. iii. ed. Joseph Smith; early files suppressed by Brigham Young.

ii. *PRO-MORMON WORKS.*—H. H. Bancroft, *Hist. of the Pacific States*, vol. xxi., 'Utah, 1540–1886,' San Francisco, 1889; *Handbook of Reference to the Hist., Chronology, Religion and Country of the Latter-Day Saints*, Salt Lake City, 1884; B. H. Roberts, *Defence of the Faith and the Saints*, do. 1907; Joseph Smith, Jr., *A Book of Commandments for the Government of the Church of Christ*, Zion, Jackson County, Missouri, 1833 (exceedingly rare); *Salt Lake City Tribune*, reprint, 1884; *Book of Mormon*, Palmyra, New York, 1830, 2nd ed. (equally rare), Kirtland, Ohio, 1835; *The Pearl of Great Price* (selections from the writings of Smith), Liverpool, 1851, and Salt Lake City, 1891; Lucy Smith, *Biographical Sketches of Joseph Smith and his Progenitors for many Generations*, Liverpool, 1853, and Plano, Illinois, 1880 (by the mother of the prophet, suppressed by Brigham Young); Joseph Smith (3rd) and Heman C. Smith, *A Hist. of the Church of Jesus Christ of Latter-Day Saints*, Lamoni, Iowa, 1901 (from the standpoint of the Reorganized Church); Charles Thompson, *Evidences in Proof of the 'Book of Mormon,'* Batavia, New York, 1841 (suppressed by Brigham Young); E. W. Tullidge, *Hist. of Salt Lake City*, Salt Lake City, 1886 (the work of a reformer, but censored by the Church); R. C. Webb, *The Real Mormonism*, New York, 1916 (the ablest modern apologetic); David Whitmer, *An Address to All Believers in Christ*, Richmond, Missouri, 1887 (written by a primitive non-polygamous Mormon).

iii. *ANTI-MORMON WORKS.*—B. G. Ferris, *Utah and the Mormons*, New York, 1854; J. W. Gunnison, *The Mormons*, Philadelphia, 1856 (description of early life in Utah by an army officer); E. D. Howe, *Mormonism Unveiled*, Painesville, Ohio, 1834 (the earliest first-hand information against Smith; very rare); John Hyde, Jr., *Mormonism: its Leaders and Designs*, New York, 1857 (the confessions of an apostate); T. B. H. Stenhouse, *The Rocky Mountain Saints*, London, 1870 (a vivid portrayal by an able ex-Mormon); Pomeroy Tucker, *Origin, Rise and Progress of Mormonism*, New York, 1867 (the exposé of a fellow-townsman of Smith).

iv. *CRITICAL WORKS.*—W. A. Linn, *The Story of the Mormons*, New York, 1902 (the most complete and exhaustive history of Mormonism); I. Woodbridge Riley, *The Founder of Mormonism: a Psychological Study of Joseph Smith, Jr.*, New York, 1902, London, 1903 (with bibliography); *Utah Commission* (Government Reports under the Edmunds Law, Washington); Eduard Meyer, *Ursprung und Gesch. der Mormonen, mit Exkursen über die Anfänge des Islâms und des Christentums*, Halle, 1912.

I. WOODBRIDGE RILEY.

[1] Cf. W. M. Gallichan, *Woman under Polygamy*, New York, 1915, Preface.

[2] Robert C. Webb, *The Real Mormonism*, p. 240.

ST. THOMAS'S MOUNT.—St. Thomas's Mount, a town in the Chingleput District of Madras, lat. 13° N., long. 80° 12′ E., is known to the natives as Parangīmalai, 'hill of the Franks.' The connexion of St. Thomas with this place has been much disputed. G. M. Rae writes:

'The view which seems on the whole most consistent with all the facts of the case is, that the local or South Indian tradition concerning St. Thomas is an example of that curious phenomenon commonly described under the name of the migration of traditions. Not St. Thomas, but only the tradition, migrated to Southern India. . . . We shall find proof that St. Thomas is described as giving his services to the cause of Gospel propagation in a locality far removed from Southern India, and that he lived and laboured, died and was buried, in that remote locality [Caramene, or Caramana, the modern Kermān in E. Persia; but, if not at Calama, the town mentioned by Nearchus, on the seaboard of Gedrosia], so that not only is no opportunity left for a visit to Southern India, but the probability of it is excluded.'[1]

On the summit of the hill stands the curious old Portuguese Church of the Expectation of the Blessed Virgin. At this place, in A.D. 1547, while the foundations of a chapel or hermitage were being dug, there was found a slab of dark granite, one face of which was decorated with a cross in bas-relief of the Greek type, with floriated ornament at all the ends. At the top of the upright shaft is figured a bird like a dove, with its wings expanded, supposed to represent the Holy Spirit. On the slab is an inscription which was interpreted by an unscrupulous Brāhman to set forth the story of the Incarnation and of the spread of Christianity through the world by the agency of the twelve apostles—how one of the apostles came to Mailāpur (Tamil Mayillāpur, 'peacock city'), a place about three miles S.S.W. of the city of Madras, with a pilgrim's staff in his hands, and how St. Thomas died by the hands of a Brāhman, and his blood formed a cross.[2] A similar cross found at Cottayam in N. Travancore is attributed by A. C. Burnell[3] to the 7th or 8th cent. A.D., and the inscription may be interpreted to mean: 'In punishment by the cross (was) the suffering of this one; He who is the true Christ, and God above, and Guide ever pure.'

According to Rae, the Cottayam inscription 'sets forth a view of the person of Christ characteristic of Indian Nestorianism; for in no other theological literature, so far as I am aware, will the notion be found which this inscription seems intended to convey. The first or shorter part speaks of the suffering Saviour, "who," continues the second part, "is the true Messiah, and God above and Holy Ghost." Nothing can be inferred from the order in which the persons of the Trinity are here named, being the same as in the Apostolic benediction; but the second clause of the inscription seems intended to give expression to a doctrinal belief entertained in olden time among the Syrian Christians in Southern India, and often quoted from those books of theirs which were condemned as heretical by the Synod of Diamper (1599 A.D.). The doctrine was to the effect that in the Christ each of the persons of the Trinity was incarnate. . . . The doctrine is peculiar—the Godhead, not the Logos only, being incarnate. It seems intelligible on Nestorian premises, but its genesis historically is probably impossible to trace.'[4]

Rae goes on to show that the symbol of the peacock, said to be connected with St. Thomas, is probably of S. Indian origin.

LITERATURE.—C. D. Macleane, *Manual of the Administration of the Madras Presidency*, iii. [1893] 778; G. M. Rae, *The Syrian Church in India*, Edinburgh, 1892, p. 29 ff.; S. Mateer, *The Land of Charity*, London, 1871, p. 236 ff.; *Census of India, 1901*, vol. xv. *Madras*, pt. i. p. 43 f.; *IGI* xxi. 387 ff.

W. CROOKE.

[1] *The Syrian Church in India*, p. 24 f.

[2] H. Yule, *Book of Marco Polo*, London, 1871, ii. 293 f.; Rae, pp. 19, 119 f.

[3] *IA* iii. [1874] 308 ff.

[4] *The Syrian Church in India*, p. 29.

ŚAIVISM.—In orthodox Hinduism the religious instructor (*guru*) bestows consecration (*dīkṣa*) on his disciple by informing him of the name of the deity to be worshipped. The name of the deity is given to the disciple in the root-formula (*mūla-mantra*).

'If the mūla-mantra contains the name of Vāsudeva or Nārāyaṇa, he is a Vaiṣṇava, if it contains the name of Śiva he is a Śaiva, if the name of the mūla-mantra is Durgā, Kālī, Tārā, or Tripura-Sundari he is a Śakta. The initiated Hindu may be personally free from sectarian narrowness, still he must be classed as a sectary.'[1]

In Śaiva temples and in Śaiva households the deity Śiva is honoured and worshipped as Śiva-Rudra, 'the auspicious Rudra.' In early Vedic times the deity Rudra was a personification, in vague and uncertain anthropomorphic form, of the destructive powers of nature, of the storms, of the lightning and forest-fires.[2] In *Rigveda*, I. cxiv. 8, Rudra was invoked so that he might become auspicious and benign:

'Do not out of thy anger injure our children and descendants, our people, our cattle, our houses, and do not kill our men. We invoke thee always with offerings.'

In the *Śata-Rudrīya* the deity Rudra is invoked by the one hundred names by which he is still invoked by all devout worshippers of Śiva-Rudra. He is invoked[3] as a haunter of the mountains (*girīśa*), and as lying on a mountain. He is blue-necked and of red countenance like a thunder-cloud edged with the red gleam of the lightning. He has braided hair (*kadarpin*) and wears a hide (*kṛttin vasānaḥ*). He is invoked as lord of the forest and of burglars, the cheat and the swindler, as the dweller with Yama, the god of the dead, yet as a physician bearing healing herbs. He is the bearer of a drum, the wearer of the triple thread, the lord of cattle (*paśunām-pati*), dread and destructive like a fierce wild beast. He is prayed to so that he may become auspicious, and be Śaṅkara, or beneficent, be Sambhu, or benign, and he is lauded as Śiva, or auspicious.[4] The name Śiva becomes the distinctive term for Rudra in the later *Vājasaneyi Saṁhita* and in the *Atharvaveda* and *Aitarēya* and *Saṁkhyāyana Brāhmaṇas*. For all Śaivas the deity Śiva-Rudra is the one great god, the Mahādeva and Maheśvara and the ruler, Īśāna. In the non-sectarian *Svētaśvatara Upaniṣad* the deity Rudra-Śiva is declared to be known through love and faith (*bhāva*), so that it has been said:

This *Upaniṣad* 'stands at the door of the Bhakti school and pours its loving adoration on Rudra-Śiva instead of on Vāsudeva-Kṛṣṇa as the Bhagavad Gīta did in later times when Bhakti doctrine was in full swing.'[5]

The *Upaniṣad* lauds Rudra-Śiva as a deity to be worshipped by all Aryans who were acquainted with Vedic ritual and Vedic traditions. It is permeated with Vedantic and Sāṅkhya teachings and inculcates a mystic knowledge of the divine through meditation and Yōgic practices. The *Śata-Rudrīya* rendered homage to many Rudras as *gaṇa-patis*, or leaders or lords of tribes and hosts. It paid homage to the worshippers of the Rudras, to the non-Vedic potters, carpenters, smiths, cart-makers, and to the Niṣādas, or forest tribes. It paid homage to Rudra as Bhava, the eternal and the creator, as Śarva, the destroyer or arrow-wielder. In the *Śatapatha Brāhmaṇa*[6] Agni is declared to be the gentle name of Rudra whom the Eastern people call Śarva and the Bāhikas Bhava and Paśunām-pati, lord of cattle. All these names, except Agni, are said to be ungentle.[1] In the *Atharvaveda*[2] Rudra is besought to free his worshippers from unlucky omens:

'May shrieking female demons with dishevelled hair go far from us.'

In the *Atharvaveda* also the gods are said to have made Mahādeva the deliverer from the upper region, Rudra from the lower, Ugra from the southern, Bhava from the eastern, and Īśāna from all intermediate regions. It also describes Bhava and Śarva as *bhūta-patis*, 'lords of *bhutas* (evil spirits)'; and the inclusion of such deities of outlying folk of feverish tracts under the name of Śiva-Rudra or Agni is indicated by invoking Rudra in the words:

'Reverence be to him whose consumption, whose cough, whose bolt assails some one like the neighing of a stallion.'[3]

In the *Bhāgavata Purāṇa*,[4] which follows the epic tradition,[5] the story is told of how Dakṣa gave his daughter Umā in marriage to Śiva, how Śiva neglected to bow down in respect before the Vedic rites, and how he was thereupon cursed by Dakṣa. Śiva is described in the story as an impure and proud demolisher of rites, as roaming about in cemeteries attended by hosts of ghosts and spirits, as like a madman, naked, with dishevelled hair, as laughing and weeping, as smeared with ashes from funeral pyres, as wearing a garland of dead men's skulls, pretending to be Śiva ('auspicious') but being in reality Aśiva ('inauspicious'), as insane and the lord of *bhūtas*. Śiva was cursed by Dakṣa as being the lowest of the gods, as Bhava, as unworthy of receiving any homage or offering along with the Vedic deities Indra and Viṣṇu. The Purāṇic account illustrates the mode of transition from a period of religion based on Vedic traditions and Brāhmanic supremacy to a period when it became necessary to recognize the worship of the demoniacal gods and deified heroes by the outlying non-Aryan Niṣādas and Dravidians, who were not allowed to study the Vedas or to perform the Vedic rites. The local shrines, with their associated worship of deified heroes and their appeasing of ghosts and evil-working spirits of the dead by human and blood sacrifices and magic spells, were scattered throughout the villages of India, where the aboriginal primitive ritual was ministered by local sorcerers and priests. As these local shrines became more renowned, they grew in wealth and importance, and became endowed by local chieftains and landowners. The shrines became temples wherein the aboriginal deities were raised to new honour and rank as manifestations or servants of Śiva and Viṣṇu, or of their *śaktis* (female consorts). From the beginning of the 5th cent. of our era, when Brāhmanism was passing into Hinduism,[6] all the gods and deified heroes of India were given Purāṇic legends until 'myriads of gods connected one way or another with the Vedic and Epic deities appear and vanish in the kaleidoscopic panorama of the Hindu pantheon.'[7]

Under Brāhmanic guidance the deities of the villagers become Śiva ('auspicious'), and their goddesses become identified with Kālī or Bhavāni, the wife, or female energy, of Śiva. Under Brāhmanic guidance human sacrifices are gradually abandoned, and in most southern temples blood sacrifices are displaced by offerings of incense and flowers. The rites once lay in the hands of the aboriginal village priests.

'But the transition to Hinduism took place when they were celebrated under Brāhmanic auspices. As in all districts and

1 Ramaprasad Chanda, *Indo-Aryan Races*, Rajshahi, 1916, p. 144.
2 Cf. art. BRĀHMANISM.
3 A. B. Keith, *Taittirīya Saṁhita* [Harvard Oriental Ser. xviii. xix.], Cambridge, Mass., 1914, pt. ii. p. 353.
4 Cf. Muir, *Orig. Sanskrit Texts*[2], iv. 328.
5 R. G. Bhandarkar, *Vaiṣṇavism, Saivism and minor Religious Systems* (=*GIAP* III. vi.), Strassburg, 1913; cf., however, art. BHAKTI-MĀRGA and G. A. Grierson, *JRAS*, 1907, p. 494.
6 I. vii. 3. 8.

1 *Agnir iti eva śāntam.*
2 XI. ii. 11.
3 *Atharvaveda*, XI. ii. 22.
4 IV. ii. 7.
5 Cf. Muir[2], iv. 373 ff.
6 Cf. art. HINDUISM.
7 Note received from M. Srinivasa Aiyangar.

sects of India, the really important point was not the character of the god, the doctrine, or the ceremony, but the admission that the right to worship, teach and officiate resided in the Brāhmans.'[1]

In some well-known temples in S. India the ancient blood rites and drunken orgies are permitted to be revived yearly as a compromise with the aboriginal worshippers, whose primitive shrines were annexed by Brāhman priests acting under the protection of local chieftains, who in return for their patronage and countenance obtained rank as Kṣatriyas with spurious pedigrees. Dubois[2] mentions cases where out-caste pariahs still act as priests in Hindu temples, and others in which the village out-castes have the prior right to enter the sanctuary of the temple and make offerings to the gods, and the Brāhmans do not begin till they have ended. The *Sthala Māhātmya* (local record) of the now ruined temple at Sri Sailam (the Holy Mount) describes its dedication to Mallikārjuna, and how in the 4th cent. B.C. the daughter of the Maurya Chandra Gupta was so full of love for the deity that she presented jasmine flowers (*mallikā*) daily at the shrine.

It is also recorded that the Buddhist Nāgārjuna 'summoned Bhikshus or devotees to reside in it and stored it with all the Buddhist canonical books and their commentaries.'[3]

Brāhmanism gained the temple on the decay of Buddhism and dedicated it to the worship of Śiva and his *śakti*, Mādhavi or Brahma-rambhā. It is, however, the only temple in the south where all castes and creeds, both men and women, can join in the worship. In the 14th cent. there were evidently human sacrifices, for an inscription of that period records:

'Hosts of Koṅgu heroes highly excited under religious fervour cut off their heads and tongues as offerings and obtained a brilliant body of blessed limbs. The next moment they shine with three eyes, five faces and five tongues and become the eight embodied Śiva.'[4]

The annual festival now held to the god and goddess lasts from February to the end of May, at which period the Brāhman head of the Pushpagiri Maṭha at Cudapah officiates. At other times a Śaiva mendicant attends to the temple and deity, while the jungle Chenchus do service. Here the transition is clear from the worship of a primitive forest deity by human sacrifices to the settling of Buddhists, who in turn were ousted by Brāhmans, who brought the aboriginal deity into Hinduism under the form of Śiva. At the Śaiva temple at Tiruvottīyūr inscriptions of the 13th cent. record that a ritual was then in vogue in the temple which included animal sacrifices and their surrounding saturnalia of horrors, and at the present day animal sacrifices are made yearly to the goddess and intoxicating drink is offered to her.

'Orgiastic rites are observed and the terrible and all swallowing spirit is believed to be appeased.'[5]

At Tiruvottīyūr, as at the temple at Melkote in Mysore, the aboriginal object of worship was an ant-hill, abode of the cobra or *nāga*-snake. The prevailing animism of the village folk of S. India has always incited them to worship objects which they imagine to be the abode of some personal agency or power.

It is reported that in 1904 two little boys watching cattle in the fields of a village near Ellore imagined that they heard a noise of trumpets resounding from an ant-hill. The news spread, and the place became a place of pilgrimage. 'Every Sunday as many as 5000 people, men and women, assembled before the ant-hill, and might be seen prostrate on their faces, rapt in adoration.'[6]

[1] Charles Eliot, *JRAS*, 1910, p. 1158.
[2] Cf. *Hindu Manners and Customs*[3], Eng. tr., Oxford, 1906, p. 583.
[3] See *Epig. Report*, Madras, 1915, p. 91.
[4] Cf. H. Krishna Sastri, *S. Indian Images of Gods and Goddesses*, Madras, 1916, p. 161 note.
[5] *Epig. Report*, Madras, 1912, p. 67.
[6] H. Whitehead, *The Village Gods of South India*, London and Calcutta, 1916, p. 15.

With few exceptions all the village deities of S. India are goddesses, wandering spirits of the dead, goddesses of famine, plague, and pestilence, all of whom are appeased by sacrifices and offerings of sheep, goats, fowls, buffaloes, and pigs.

The explanation of the fact that these evil spirits are goddesses is 'in all probability simply that the feminine characteristics of the Dravidians are such as to make their ghosts more feared than those of men.'[1]

These local goddesses are often considered to be wives of Śiva.

'A favourite method of attaching a Dravidian goddess to the Hindu pantheon is by a marriage with Śiva or some one of his incarnations.'[2]

The fact that Śaktism, or the worship of cosmic power personified as a female, has not developed into a special cult in Tamil-land, as it did in Bengal, has been held to militate against the theory that the worship of tribal goddesses was based on a matriarchal state of society.[3]

Instances are numerous where the deities worshipped are merely images representing local saints or recent heroes.

Many Śaiva temples of S. India are now being renovated by Nāttukottai Cettis, and it has been recorded that they 'have often found human bones and ashes at some depth below the floor on which the sacred image stands, thus indicating that the original shrine was erected over the relics of some saint or important person.'[4] One record, of the 9th cent. A.D., at Solapuram, N. Arcot, states that the Ganga King Rājāditya caused to be built a temple to Iśvara Śiva on the spot where his father had been buried. Another inscription records that a shrine was built over or near the burial-ground of the Chola King Aditya I. An inscription found in the Cholesvara temple at Melpadi states that, at the end of the 10th cent. A.D., Rājarāja I. 'had been pleased to build the temple of Arinjiśvara as a burial place for the lord who died at Arrūr.'[5] It has been suggested that 'the cell-like proportions of the shrine chamber of a typical South Indian temple may be traced to the Dravidian cell tomb or Dolmen.'[6]

Instances are known where dolmens have actually been transformed into Śiva shrines by placing in them the typical symbol of the deity.[7]

In S. India the typical Hindu temples were endowed and enlarged from the 10th to the 12th centuries, under the Chola kings, and in Bengal from the 9th to the 12th centuries, under the Pāla dynasties. The origin of the worship of Śiva, as symbolized in the chief temples of the early Pallava, Pāndya, and Chola dynasties by the *liṅga*, has been explained as follows:

The *liṅga* 'resembled the tomb stone, or Vīrakals which used to be set on the graves of Dravidian warriors and sometimes worshipped. Some of the Śaiva temples are even believed to be the graves of Siddhas, or Saints.'[8]

Purāṇic Hinduism, which arose during the period of the revival of Hindu rule and tradition under the Guptas of Kanauj, from the 4th and 5th centuries, absorbed the prevailing Mahāyāna Buddhist idol-worship. The Buddhist worship of the burial-mound, or votive *stūpa*, has also been held to have been absorbed into Hinduism in the form of the worship of the *liṅga* by Śaivas.[9]

Śiva is not only worshipped under the form of Ardhanārīśa,[10] but is symbolized everywhere by the bull Nandi and by the phallic male and female emblems, the *liṅga* and the *yōni*. The two earliest known representations of the *liṅga* are said to date from about the 1st cent. B.C.; one from Bhiṭa is now in the Lucknow Museum, the other

[1] W. T. Elmore, *Dravidian Gods in Modern Hinduism*, New York, 1915, p. 146.
[2] *Ib.* p. 84.
[3] See Chanda, p. 156 f.
[4] *Annual Report, Arch. Dep. S. Circle*, Madras, 1915-16, p. 29.
[5] *S. Indian Inscriptions*, ed. and tr. E. Hultzsch, Madras, 1900-03, vol. iii. pt. i. p. 26 f.
[6] *Annual Report, Arch. Dep. S. Circle*, 1915-16, p. 35.
[7] *Ib.* p. 29.
[8] Private note from M. Srinivasa Aiyangar, dated July 1916.
[9] Cf. E. B. Havell, *The Ideals of Indian Art*, London, 1911, p. 87.
[10] Cf. art. HINDUISM, vol. vi. p. 702[a].

was recently discovered[1] at Gudimallam in N. Arcot.

'Although they are realistically phallic, it is claimed that 'there is nothing to be ashamed of; the two great Generative Principles of the Universe, Śiva and Śakti, or Puruṣa and Prakṛti, the father and mother of all creations, the energy and matter of the physical scientist, are symbolized briefly in the form of the liṅga and yōni. For the past two thousand years at least, the Hindus, males and females, have been offering worship to this symbol of the Great Architect of the Universe, without in the least adverting to or feeling conscious of the so-called obscenity of this pure symbol of the fatherhood and motherhood of the supreme deity; to them it is a symbol and nothing more.'[2]

The stronghold of those worshippers of Śiva who venerate the deity in the form of the *liṅga* and who are known as Liṅgayats (*q.v.*) is in S. Bombay, Belgaum, Bijāpur, and Dhānvār, while of the 3,000,000 Liṅgayats classed as such in the *Indian Census Report* of 1911 only a little over one-tenth are to be found in the Madras Presidency. The stronghold of the Śaktas, or worshippers of the Śakti aspect of Śiva, is in Bengal, where the majority of Brāhmans, Kayasthas, and Vaidyas are Śāktas, who are also spread throughout N. Bihār, Gujarāt, and in the Marāthā countries.[3] The worship of the *śakti*, or female energy, of Śiva is inculcated in *Tantras* chiefly devoted to the goddess known as Ānanda-bhairavi, Tripura Sundarī, and Lalita, the worship known as the Chakrapujā being centred chiefly in mystic circles, representing in some cases the material object worshipped through pictures, though in other cases the living material object is worshipped. Śiva is thus considered subsidiary to his *śakti*, and the ideal is that motherhood is the chief element in creation. The Śāktas base their doctrines on the assumption that through Śiva and Śakti there is a drop, Bindu, formed which develops into a female element Nāda (sound), containing in itself the names of all things to be created. With Bindu and Nāda are associated male and female elements so that the substance—*kāmakalā*—is formed from which creation ensues.

Rāmānuja, in the 12th cent., states[4] that there were two extreme sects of worshippers of Śiva, known as the Kāpālikas and Kālāmukhas, who held fanciful theories of reality, all of which are opposed to the *Vedas*. The Kāpālikas are those who hope to reach *nirvāṇa* by meditation and who know the meaning of the six marks (*mudrās*) —the necklace, the gold ornament, the earring, the head-jewel, the ashes, and the sacred thread. There seems to have been but slight difference recognized between the Kāpālikas and Kālāmukhas, whose chief temple was at Śrīśaila, the Holy Mount. Rāmānuja describes the Kālāmukhas as using a skull as a drinking-vessel, smearing themselves with the ashes of a dead body, eating human flesh, holding a club, setting up a wine-jar as a site for offerings to the deity. Both Mādhava[5] and Ānandagiri described Śaṅkara as having controversies with the Kāpālikas—at Ujjayini according to the commentators—where Śiva, as Bhairava, was worshipped with human sacrifices and wine libations. Śaṅkara, in the 8th cent., in his commentary on the *Vedānta Sūtras*,[6] states that the Śaivas, or Maheśvaras, held that Paśupati, or Śiva, was 'the Lord' and the 'operative cause' of the creation of the world. They believed that Śiva taught five categories, viz. *kārya* (effect), *kāraṇa* (cause), *yōga* (union), *viddhi* (ritual), *duḥkhānta* (the end of pain and final deliverance, so that the bonds of the soul [*paśu*] might be severed). Mādhava, in the latter half of the 14th cent., in his *Sarva-darśana-saṅgraha*, described three Śaiva systems — the Nakulīśa-Paśupatas,[1] the Śaiva system, and the Pratyabhijña, or recognitive system. In his account of the Nakulīśa-Pāśupatas he states that they teach the five topics mentioned by Śaṅkara as the tenets of the worshippers of Paśupati, viz. *kārya, kāraṇa, yōga, viddhi*, and *duḥkhānta*, as taught in a work entitled the *Pañchādhyāyi* or *Pañchārtha-vidyā*. The name Lakulin means one who bears a club (*lakula*), and, according to the Purāṇic account,[2] Śiva, by his Yōga powers, entered into a dead body at a cemetery and became incarnate as Lakulī at Kalyāvarōhana or Kārōhana, in the Laṭa country at Baroda. The system as taught by Lakulī, probably the author of the *Pañchādhyāyi*[3] in the 1st cent. A.D., was the main system from which later Śaiva systems arose. This main system, according to Mādhava, aimed at union or conjunction of the soul with Śiva—a mystic union to be reached by pious mutterings, meditation, and the cessation of all action, so that a state of mere feeling (*saṁvid*) is attained. By Yōgic practices the ascetic (*siddha*) gains miraculous powers of assuming various shapes and forms and of receiving messages from the dead. The religious emotions are to be excited by song and dance, by laughter, by simulating the acts and gestures of one in love, by speaking wildly, by wearing ashes and flowers from the images in the temples, and by loud uttering of a sacred sound, *hum*, like the sound *vaṣaṭ*, an imitation of a sound ascribed to a bull. The nature of the *viddhi*, or rules of conduct, of the Kālāmukhas, which appears to have been identical with that of the Nakulīśa-paśupatas, may be judged from the following statement:

'It appears quite probable that this viddhi of the paśupatas is responsible for the origin and existence of obscene sculptures in Hindu temples.'[4]

Mādhava describes the Pratyabhijña, or recognitive, system of teaching as follows:

'There being a God whose omnipotence is learned from accredited legendaries, from accepted revelation, and from argumentation, there arises in relation to my presented personal self the cognition that I am that very God—in virtue of the recollection of the powers of that God.'[5]

This system was expounded in Kashmir by Abhinava Gupta at the beginning of the 11th cent. (A.D. 993–1015) in his commentaries—the *Pratyabhijña-vimarṣiṇi* and *Paramārtha-sāra*—which he wrote on the *Śiva-dṛṣṭi* of the *siddha* Somānanda, from whom he was fourth in succession. The *Śiva-dṛṣṭi*, which set forth the metaphysical doctrines of Kashmir Śaivism is now lost, but an epitome was composed by Utpāla, the pupil of Abhinava Gupta, in 190 *anuṣṭubh* verses known as the *Pratyabhijña sūtras*. The system described by Mādhava under the name of the Śaiva system corresponds to the Śaiva Siddhānta system of Tamil-land and has been described as 'a dualistic system fundamentally different from the monistic philosophy which constitutes Kashmir Shaivaism.'[6] The same authority further describes this Śaiva system as 'plain and unvarnished dualism or even pluralism.'[7] The Kashmir and Tamil schools of Śaivism, which arose out of the extreme schools of the Nakulīśa-paśupatas, were both faced by the difficulties inherent in teaching what they both describe as the highest mysticism—an absorption of the soul into a universal unconscious Soul of the universe, which often ends in nothing—and at

1 Gopinatha Rao, *Elements of Hindu Iconography*, London, 1915, vol. i. pt. i. p. 65.
2 *Ib.* p. 69; cf. also G. Jouveau-Dubreuil, *Archéologie du Sud de l'Inde*, Paris, 1914, ii. 11.
3 Chanda, p. 143.
4 *Vedānta-sūtras*, II. ii. 36.
5 *Śaṅkara-dig-vijaya*, xv. 1–28.
6 II. ii. 37.

1 Cf. art. HINDUISM.
2 *Vāyu*, xxi. 205–212; *Liṅga*, xxiv. 124–133.
3 Cf. Bhandarkar, *JRASBo* xxii. [1910] 151 ff., and J. F. Fleet, *JRAS*, 1907, p. 419 ff.
4 Gopinatha Rao, vol. ii. pt. i. p. 23.
5 *Sarva-Darśana-Sangraha*, tr. E. B. Cowell and A. E. Gough, London, 1894, p. 131.
6 J. C. Chatterji, *Kaśhmir Shaivaism*, Srinagar, 1914, p. 20, note 1.
7 Cf. L. D. Barnett, tr. of *Paramārthā-sāra*, in *JRAS*, 1910.

the same time the realization of a personal revealed God. The revelation of Śiva, according to Āgamic teachings, was uttered from the divine voice of the five faces of the deity, representing his *chit*, *ānanda*, *ichchhā*, *jñāna*, and *kriyā* aspects (intelligence, bliss, will, knowledge, creation) called Iśāna, Tat-puruṣa, Sadyōjaṭa, Aghora, and Vāma. Here the revelation rests on the dualism, but in Kashmir in the 9th cent. the sage Vasugupta declared a new revelation, as expounded by his pupil Kallaṭa, in the *Spanda-sūtras*, or *kārikas*, teaching the *advaita*, or non-dualism, of the Kashmir system or Trika (the Pati-paśu-pāśam). In this Spanda school the soul gains knowledge through intense Yōgic contemplation, whereby the vision of Parama-Śiva ('highest Śiva') as Supreme Soul of the universe is realized and the individual soul is absorbed in a mystic trance of peace and quietism. In the Pratyabhijña school the soul by its own intuition, trained under the instruction of a *guru*, recognizes itself as God and so rests in mystic bliss of oneness with God. The sectarian *Upaniṣads*, which treat of the nature of Śiva, in many instances teach this spiritual monism. The Saiva *Kaivalya Upaniṣad* says of Śiva:

'He is Brahmā, he is Śiva, he is Indra, he is undecaying, supreme, self-resplendent, he is Viṣṇu, he is breath, he is the spirit, the supreme Lord, he is all that has been or that shall be eternal.'

The *Atharvaśiras* also teaches that Rudra is Śiva 'who evolves, creates and sustains all worlds. The *Nīla-Rudra Upaniṣad* says of the soul:

'I formed of earth (Pṛthivi-mayaḥ) beheld descending from the sky, that blue-necked Rudra.'

In the *Pañcha-brahma Upaniṣad*, 20, we read:

'In this city of Brahman (body) there is, O Sage, a small lotus-like house. In the centre of it there is a subtle ether. He is Śiva, Sad-chid-ānanda. He should be sought after by those desirous for salvation.'

In order to explain the true nature of Śiva and his manifestations throughout the universe, Śaivism essays a metaphysical analysis of objective reality through its 'thatnesses,' or *tattvas*. These *tattvas* transcend all physical notions of reality, but are believed capable of being realized through the long trained thought of Eastern sages.

To realize them the means are said to be 'self-culture, mental, moral, spiritual and even physical, which constitutes what is called Yoga, in the true sense of the word, which enables a Spirit to shake off the very limitations that make of the real experiencer such a limited entity and to rise to those regions of experience which the highest Tattvas are. Those who train themselves by this method of Yoga, and who are called Yogins, can and do realize the Tattvas by direct experience as clearly as, indeed more clearly than, we perceive the physical and sense objects.'[1]

The primary *tattvas* are 36 in number, and the highest *tattva* is that of the spiritual essence, or 'thatness,' of Śiva, existing alone before the manifestation of a universe. Śiva manifests in the universe through his grace in order that the *paśu*, the flock of souls, may gain knowledge of their oneness with the Supreme Soul and so find rest from transmigrations through which they are doomed to pass by their ignorance and resulting actions. The manifestation of the universe is analyzed, through the *tattvas*, in Kashmir Śaivism in the same way as it is in the Śaiva school of S. India,[2] where the Parama Brahman, or Śiva, manifests regions (*bhuvanas*) for the souls, through a *śakti* associated with a metaphysical conception of abstract matter termed pure *māyā* or *suddha māyā*. This pure *māyā* is also termed *kuṭali*, *kuṇḍalinī*, and sometimes *vindu* and even *śakti*; and its first manifestation is *nātam* or *vāc*—the subtle basis of the 'sound' or 'word' which precedes the beginning of all things. From the Śiva-Śakti *tattva* arises the Sadā Śiva *tattva*, or the eternal aspect of Śiva, also termed Sādākhya, in which the *śaktis*, or energies of *jñāna* (wisdom) and *kriyā* (action or creation), are in equilibrium. In the term Sādākhya

[1] Chatterji, p. 162. [2] Cf. art. DRAVIDIANS (South India).

the first glimmer of a physical conception arises from amid the vague metaphysical speculations of the Śaiva systems both of Kashmir and of S. India. In the southern school[1] the workings of Śiva and *śakti* are figuratively illustrated by the analogy of the reproductive organism of a lotus, where the stamens of the lotus are compared to the lord, the Sadā Śiva, and the pistil to the Śakti-*tattva*, while above the *śakti* is seated the supreme Śiva. The same system teaches[2] that the subtlest form of matter, the imperceptible *māyā*, is the product of Bindu, or Vindu, which means a seed, a drop, or a point. In Yōga teachings Bindu was the centre of a mystic wheel (*chakra*), of which there are supposed to be six in the body as dynamic tattvic centres, the principal of which, the *mūlādhāra*, or chief region, is described as like a red lotus of four petals situated in the lower part of the body near the spinal cord.[3] By concentrating the mind on these *chakras*, or force centres, in the body, the Yōgi, ever since Vedic times, has hoped to obtain absolute knowledge, and to discover the mysteries of creation, in the psychic energy of the *kuṇḍalini*. In the Hatha Yōga, and the higher Yōga, the Rāja Yōga, the *kuṇḍalini* is described as the highest *śakti*. It is supposed to be coiled up like a serpent (*kuṇḍali*) nine inches from the middle of the body, and is covered by a membranous covering. In the Yōga system the terms *kuṭali*, *kuṇḍalini*, *śakti*, *īśvarī*, *bindu*, or *vindu*, are thus used to signify the seat and source of creative energy in man and are then applied to mean the creative force, or *śakti*, of the creator.[4]

In the Śaiva systems of Kashmir and S. India the Sādākhya *tattva* or Sadā-Śiva *tattva* is the beginning of the development of the manifest world from the energy of the Śiva-Śakti *tattva*. The term Sādākhya implies the beginning of the being (*sat*) of a real manifest world free from Yōgic mysticism and metaphysical speculations or dogmas.

Although the Sādākhya *tattva* is a stepping-stone towards a reality,[5] it is held to be 'just the beginning of activity—of just the first stirring of life—and therefore the thought or feeling of the Ideal Universe at this stage is only a dim one, like a faint and indistinct picture of a long-forgotten scene which is beginning to reform itself in one's memory and is still in the background of consciousness.'[6]

Hence creation is described as a process where from the Sadā Śiva *tattva* arises the Mahēśvara *tattva*, or principle of obscuring (*tirobhava*) true knowledge from the soul until it has eaten the fruits of its *karma*. Thence springs the pure *tattva* of wisdom, the *suddhā vidyā tattva*, known as Rudra, the source of destruction and regeneration, which *suddhā vidyā* further develops as Brahmā the creator and Viṣṇu the preserver of the universe.

From *suddhā vidyā* arise through impure *māyā* the five *tattvas* of limited experiences—those of (1) *kālam*, 'time'; (2) *niyati*, 'order' or 'necessity,' through which *karma* acts on its fate or destiny; thence (3) *kalā*, 'learning' or 'continency,' the *tattva* of the faculty which enables man to experience perceptions; then (4) *vidyā*, 'knowledge,' for the intellectual power of the soul; from *vidyā* arises (5) *rāgam*, 'desire,' and thence *puruṣa*, or limited individual spirit or man, with a five-fold clothing or body, the *pañcha-kanchuka* of *kālam*,

[1] *Śiva-jñāna-Siddhiyar*, ix. 9. [2] *Ib.* i. 12.

[3] Cf. A. Avalon, *Tantra of the Great Liberation*, London, 1913, p. lvii, also *Gospel of Sri Rama Krishna*, Madras, 1912, p. 85, note: 'The Muladhara is the first lotus with four petals in which the Yogi meditates upon Siva and Sakti (God personal and impersonal) as manifest in their glory. It is the root of the Sushumna in the spinal cord.'

[4] Cf. Swātmarām Swāmi, *Hatha Yōga pradīpika*, Bombay, 1893, p. 44.

[5] Cf. *Sādākhyāyām-bhavam yatas prabhriti Sad itiprakhyā*, quoted in Chatterji, p. 67. (The derivation from Sā-dākshya by Western authorities is clearly erroneous.)

[6] Chatterji, p. 67.

niyati, *kalā*, *rāgam*, and *vidyā*. From the *tattva kalā* arises *prakṛti*, undeveloped matter, with the three *guṇas* of *sattva*, *rajas*, *tamas*, 'goodness,' 'passion,' 'darkness,' in equilibrium. Thence ensue *tattvas* of the *buddhi*, 'intellect,' of *manas*, 'mind,' of *ahamkāram*, 'individuality,' of *chitta*, 'will,' with the *tattvas* of the five organs of sense, of the five organs of action, and five subtle elements of sound, touch, form, taste, smell, and of ether, air, fire, water, and earth.

The Kashmir school of thought is based on the belief that 'concentration of thought can be practised to absolute perfection and that when perfected, by its means alone, everything can be known and realized by direct experience.'[1]

The system teaches that through a knowledge of the *tattvas* the soul can realize God, as identical with the individual soul, as pure unconscious soul of the universe.

The Tamil Śaivas of S. India base their knowledge of Śiva on twelve Sanskrit *sūtras* forming a portion of the *Vidyā* section of the *Raurava Āgama* which were expounded at the beginning of the 13th cent. by the Veḷḷāla, Meykaṇḍa Devar, 'the divine Seer of Truth,' in his *Śiva-jñāna-bodham*, 'Instruction in the knowledge of Truth.' The Śaiva *Āgamas*[2] are each divided into four parts of *Charyā*, *Kriyā*, *Yōga*, and *Vidyā*. The chief Śaiva *Āgamas* are 28 in number, and are held to contain a direct revelation from Śiva for all classes, even Śudras and women, who were competent to receive *dīkṣā*, or consecration from a *gurū*, and to follow the path to salvation. The Śaiva sage Tiru Mūlar, who has been ascribed to the 9th cent. A.D., says in his *Tiru Mantiram*:

'The Vedas and the Āgamas are both true and both are the word of God. The first is a general treatise and the latter a special one. When examined and where difference is perceived between the Vedānta and Siddhānta they will perceive no difference.'[3]

The distinction between the *Vedas* and *Āgamas* was not only a religious but also a racial distinction. Brāhman Śaivas still adhere to the Vedic ritual, as they hold that the *Vedas* and *Vedānta* were a special revelation for all Aryan people. All Śudras, and consequently most of the Dravidians and people who resided outside the Aryan pale, were excluded from even hearing the sacred sound of the *Vedas*, and accordingly they, with all women and those of mixed castes, were excluded from Vedic religious ceremonies and from salvation. Brāhmans who were Śaiva worshipped Śiva according to the Vedic ritual; but, as the Dravidian population of S. India was in the majority, the claim was early raised that both *Vedas* and *Āgamas*, or *Tantras*, were of equal authority in ritual and ceremony. Śrikaṇṭha Śivāchārya, held by Tamil Śaivas to have lived before the 9th cent., wrote a commentary based on Āgamic teachings, in which he held that there was no difference between the *Vedas* and *Āgamas*.[4] He declared that the *Vedas* may properly be called Śiva *Āgamas* as having been revealed by, or come down (*āgama*) from, Śiva.

'Accordingly Śiva Āgama is two-fold, one being intended for the three higher castes, the other being intended for all. The Vedas are intended for people of the three classes, and the other for all.'[5]

It was not until the 17th cent. that the Śaiva teacher Appaya Dīkshitar (1552–1624) endeavoured to unite the two streams of belief and salvation which flowed from Aryan Vedic and non-Aryan Āgamic sources. Appaya Dīkshitar was intellectually swayed—as all southern Śaivas are—by the spiritual singularism of the *māyā* doctrines of Śaṅkara, but he would gladly have accepted a personal deity such as the Nārāyaṇa of the school of the Vaiṣṇava Āchārya Rāmānuja. He begins his *Siddhānta-lēśa*, an exposition of the teachings of Śaṅkara, with this statement:

'Just as the Ganges springs from the feet of Viṣṇu and gains many a land and flourishes, so the wise words which flowed from the fair lotus lips of Śaṅkara have divided a thousand-fold as they reach teachers among whom arise differences as to the nature of God and of the soul's bondage, all of which teachings are intended as stepping-stones to the true knowledge that Brahman is One only, without a Second.'[1]

The S. Indian Tamil school of Śaivism, known as the 'pure' (or Śuddha) Śaiva Siddhānta, in its ultimate teachings, has always contended against a non-dualism, or *advaita*, wherein the soul loses its identity through final absorption into an unconscious soul of the universe—into *Brahman*, 'One only, without a second.' It has also striven to free itself from the *māyā* teachings of Śaṅkara and to approach an ideal where the soul in final salvation

'retains its individual consciousness, remains for evermore in separate existence, sharing the blessedness and wisdom of the Supreme, but unmingled with his essence. In fact the doctrine held by Śaivas on this point is hardly to be distinguished from Christian teachings.'[2]

The Śaiva Siddhānta in Tamil-land rests for its primary dogmas on the exposition by Meykaṇḍa, in the 13th cent., of the twelve Sanskrit stanzas from the *Raurava Āgama*. The *Āgamas* have been ascribed to a period somewhere between the 5th and 8th centuries of our era, and the development of Tantric worship has been ascribed to a period before Nāgārjuna (*c.* A.D. 200).[3] The *Uttara Kāraṇa Āgama* refers to the persecution of the Jains by Tiru-Jñāna Sambandhar, held to have taken place in the 7th cent.; and other *Āgamas* direct that the hymns of the earlier Śaiva saints, Appar and Sundara, should be recited during the temple services. The *Āgamas* are referred to frequently in the hymns of the Śaiva saint, Māṇikka Vāchakar, who has been assigned to about the 9th century.[4] Down to the present day non-Aryan Śaivas adopt the Āgamic teachings and ritual, while the Aryan Śaivas retain the Vedic ritual, although Vaidik, or Smārta, Brāhmans may be found worshipping the *liṅga* in the Śaiva temple. The Āgamic ritual and teachings were current long before the time of Meykaṇḍa in the 13th century. The Chola sovereign Rājarāja (A.D. 985–1014), who built the Bṛhadīśvara temple at Tanjore, is recorded to have appointed Brāhman priests from the Ārya, Madhya, and Gauḍa countries to act as teachers and priests in the temple. Rajēndra Chola, shortly afterwards, in the first quarter of the 11th cent., is recorded in Āgamanta works to have brought Brāhman Śaiva teachers to the south from the Amardaka Maṭha on the banks of the Godavari with the following result:

'An impetus was given to the spread of Śaivaism and a very large number of original works belonging to the Āgamanta school of Saivaism was written.'[5]

The early Śaiva saints had, from the 5th to the 11th century, sung of their faith in Śiva and of his grace, whereby he had revealed himself to them as ideal love and bliss. These Śaiva saints were 63 in number, and their hymns were sung in 274 Śaiva temples[6] still held sacred as having been visited by these saints. The most renowned of the temples had been built and endowed by Pallava and Chola kings on the sites of previous and primitive shrines. The Śaiva saints believed in

[1] Cf. Chatterji, *The Hindu Realism*, Allahābād, 1912, p. 143 f.
[2] Cf. Shanmukha Sundara M., *Sakala-āgama-sāra-saṅgraham*, Madras, 1900, who published separate *Āgamas* with Tamil commentaries.
[3] Cf. Tamil ed. of M. V. Viśvanātha Pillai, Madras, 1912, p. 406, no. 2397.
[4] *Na vayam Veda Śivāgamayor bhedam paśyāmah.*
[5] Bhāshya on II. ii. 38; *Siddhānta Dīpika*, ii. 267.

[1] Tr. by A. Venis, in *The Pandit*, nos. 21, 22, and 23, Benares.
[2] G. U. Pope, *The Tiruvāçagam*, Oxford, 1900, p. lxv; cf. art. DRAVIDIANS (South India).
[3] See A. Avalon, *Principles of Tantra*, London, 1914, p. lix.
[4] See L. D. Barnett and G. U. Pope, *Tamil Books in the British Museum*, London, 1909, p. v, for many references to the date of the saint.
[5] Gopinatha Rao, vol. ii. pt. i. p. 4.
[6] See V. T. Subramanya Pillai, *Śiva-sthala-manjari*, Madras, 1905, pp. 1–7.

the revelation that their inward eye had gained of the divine, and the Śaiva sages who succeeded them placed this mystic knowledge of God as the foundation of all their efforts to reason out their beliefs and faiths. The Śaiva Siddhānta, which they formulated, is therefore closer akin to a mystic phase of religious belief than it is to a philosophic school of reasoning from the known to the unknown. The sages strove in their chief, fourteen Śiva Siddhānta, *Sūtras* to steer clear of a mysticism wherein the self vanishes with the absorption of the soul and all personality into a *Brahman* as the unconscious Soul of the universe. Still Tamil Śaivas style their system as follows:

'Mysticism of the highest quality as its bed-rock is formed of the twenty-eight divine Āgamas of spiritually supernal order.'[1]

The *Siddhānta* teaches that the soul is eternal, formless, all-pervasive (*vibhu*), and that its all-pervading nature (*vyāpaka*) leads it to become one with what it dwells in for the time being, with the material or the divine. The original sin, the *pāva-mūlam*, of the soul is an eternal ignorance which reduces the soul to the condition of *āṇava* (from *aṇu*, 'atom'), so that it cannot attain to its true all-pervading nature freed from the material body. The soul, by assimilating itself to the material, which is without intelligence and unknowing, the product of elemental matter (*māyā*), has desires and delusions which draw it into actions (*karma*), good and evil. Through its *āṇava* it tends to be drawn away from the feet of the Lord. Its true intuitions tend to urge it to free itself from its material surroundings and to seek rest and support in the absolute true and real, the ideal love and bliss—the ideal which has set Śiva as supreme god of Tamil-land.

The soul can know nothing of itself. It is not pure knowledge (*chit*), like the Lord; for the soul and its surroundings of *karma*, *māyā*, and *āṇava* are unintelligent. How then, it is asked, can the soul gain knowledge of the divine? The answer is that knowledge can be gained only through the free grace of the Lord, and the soul becomes 'intelligent or unintelligent according as divine irradiation is given or withheld.'[2] The authoritative *Śiva-jñāna-Siddhiyar* of Aruṇandi Śiva Āchārya, a pupil of Meykaṇḍa, says of Śiva:

'If you contemplate Him as beyond contemplation, even this gives no benefit as it is a mere fiction. If you contemplate Him as yourself, this also is a fiction. The only way to know Him is by understanding Him through his Arul, or Grace.'[3]

The same idea of final salvation flowing from the grace of Śiva was set forth by Umāpati, a Śaiva sage of the 14th cent., in his *Tiru-Aruḷ-payan* ('Fruit of Divine Grace') in the words:

'Where the search ends there is the abode of the Lord.'

LITERATURE.—See the authorities given in the course of the art., and especially artt. BRĀHMANISM, HINDUISM, and DRAVIDIANS (South India).

R. W. FRAZER.

1 *Siddhānta Dīpika*, x. 476.

2 Umāpati, *Tiru-Aruḷ-payan*, tr. J. M. Nallaswami Pillai, Madras, 1896, iv. 37.

3 vi. 7.

ŚAKA ERA.

—The Śaka era is one of many reckonings which are or have been in use in India, and has the special interest of being the most important of them. It is treated as running from either of two points in March, A.D. 78—as a solar reckoning, from the Hindu vernal equinox, and, as a luni-solar reckoning, from the first day of the bright fortnight of the Hindu month Chaitra.

In N. India, *i.e.* in those parts which lie to the north of the rivers Narbadā and Mahānadī, the chief reckoning is the Vikrama or Samvat era, known in an early stage as the time or reckoning of the Mālava people, the starting-point of which, as fixed in mediæval times, is, from one point of view, the earlier one, the first day of the bright fortnight at Kārttika, in September, 58 B.C., and, from another point of view, the same day of Chaitra in March of the same year. The Śaka era is the chief reckoning of S. India, though, in fact, it had its origin in western parts of N. India; it prevails, however, to a certain extent in N. India too, and in Kashmīr, Nēpāl, and Assam. Like the Vikrama era, it is in use for historical, calendrical, and all general purposes. But it is also an astronomers' reckoning, which the Vikrama era never has been.

The first Indian astronomical reckoning was the Kaliyuga era; this was devised by the Hindu astronomers about A.D. 400, and was laid out so as to start from an assumed general conjunction of the sun, moon, and the planets, at the conventional Hindu vernal equinox in February 3102 B.C. The Kaliyuga era has always been more or less in use for astronomy from the time of its invention, and to a small extent for other purposes also. But about A.D. 500 the Śaka era was taken up by the Hindu astronomers as a second reckoning, for laying down more recent epochs for some of their calculative purposes, and was fitted by them to the exact solar and luni-solar starting-points mentioned above; they used it to such an extent that it soon very largely superseded the Kaliyuga reckoning; and it is, in fact, owing to its adoption by them, and to their use of it for calendrical as well as calculative purposes, that it gradually acquired its wide prevalence, extending not only throughout India but also across the sea to Cambodia, Java, and Ceylon.

The Kaliyuga era is a purely artificial reckoning, invented by the astronomers. Not so, however, the Vikrama and Śaka eras. These have actually existed from 58 B.C. and A.D. 78 respectively, and had their origins in historical events which happened in those years, the Śaka era owing its birth to an irruption of foreigners, who invaded India from the west, established themselves and acquired dominion in India, and founded this reckoning there, and who, whether they were or were not actually Śakas, *i.e.* Scythians, were recalled as Śakas in later times.

In its earliest stages the reckoning of A.D. 78, like other Indian eras, ran on for a long time without a name, its years being simply quoted by their numbers as 'the year so-and-so,' and in this way it is found used in inscriptions and on coins from soon after its foundation down to nearly A.D. 400. The earliest inscriptional instance of the connexion of the name of the Śakas with the reckoning is found in a record of A.D. 578, after which time it was habitual; the connexion, however, is carried back to A.D. 505 by an astronomical date. The era also became known as the era of Śālivāhana; but this name for it was of late invention, the earliest known certain instance of the use of it being found in an inscription of A.D. 1354; it was applied to the Śaka era in imitation of the association of the name of Vikrama with the northern era, which dates from some time in the 9th or 10th century A.D. The popular belief, shown, *e.g.*, in the introductory passages of some of the *Pañchāngs*, or Hindu almanacs, is that the Vikrama era was founded by a King Vikrama reigning in 58 B.C. at Ujjain in Mālwā, and that the Śaka era was founded by a King Śālivāhana reigning A.D. 78 at Pratishṭhāna, which is the modern Paiṭhaṇ, on the Gōdāvarī, in the Nizam's territory; this, however, is fiction, without any real basis.

LITERATURE.—For more details about the Śaka, Vikrama, and Kaliyuga eras, with an account of the other reckonings and the Hindu calendar, see the present writer's art. 'Hindu Chronology,' in *EBr*[11] xiii. 491–501; see also R. Sewell and S. B. Dikshit, *The Indian Calendar*, London, 1896.

J. F. FLEET.

SAKHĪBHĀVAS.—The Sakhībhāvas are a branch of the Rādhāvallabhīs (*q.v*), small in number and of little importance. They carry to extremes the worship of Rādhā, Kṛṣṇa's mistress, whom they look upon as his *śakti*, or energic power. The men assume the character of Rādhā's *sakhīs*, or girl friends, and, to enforce the idea of the change of sex, assume female garb, with all women's manners and customs, even pretending to be subject to the catamenia. Their aim is to be accepted as genuine *sakhīs* in a future life, and thus to enjoy a share of Kṛṣṇa's favours. They are of ill repute, and do not show themselves much in public. According to Wilson, they are to be found in Jaipur and Benares and also in Bengal. Some of them also are wandering mendicants. They appear to have been numerous in the 17th century.

LITERATURE.—H. H. Wilson, *Sketch of the Religious Sects of the Hindus*, London, 1861, p. 177; A. Barth, *The Religions of India*, Eng. tr., do. 1882, p. 236; M. A. Sherring, *Hindu Tribes and Castes in Benares*, Calcutta, Bombay, and London, 1872–81, i. 264; R. G. Bhandarkar, 'Vaiṣṇavism, Śaivism, and Minor Religious Systems,' *GIAP* III. vi. [1913] 86.

G. A. GRIERSON.

SAKHĪ SARWAR.—Sakhi Sarwar, or Nigāhā, is a famous Muhammadan shrine in the Derā Ghazī Khān District of the Panjāb (lat. 29° 59′ N.; long. 70° 18′ E.), situated on the high bank of a hill stream in the Dāman-i-Koh, or flanks of the Sulaimān range, in arid jungle scenery.

The place takes its name from the saint Sakhī Sarwar, or 'generous leader,' also known as Lakhdātā, 'giver of lakhs,' Lālanwālā, 'he of the rubies,' or Rohiānwālā, 'he of the hills.' He is generally known by the title of Sulṭān, 'lord.' His real name was Sayyid Aḥmad, but his exact date is unknown, tradition varying from the 12th to the 16th cent. A.D. His life is a mass of legends, describing the miracles which he worked. Within the enclosure of his shrine are to be seen the tomb of the saint, of his lady known as Bībī Rāē, and that of a *jinn*, or demon, whom he overcame. The place is visited by sick people, who, as a proof of their recovery, hang small ornamented pillows on the walls, or, when cured of ophthalmia, offer, in performance of a vow, eyes made of gold or silver.[1] Other persons vow to shave the hair of an expected child at the shrine and to present its weight in gold or silver. Some childless people vow their first child to the saint, and on its birth take it to the shrine with a cord round its neck. Sacred pigeons, fed from the proceeds of an endowment, are attached to the shrine. The marks of the finger of 'Alī, son-in-law of the Prophet, and the print of his foot are shown to visitors. Diseases, like hysteria, which are supposed to be the result of spirit action are said to be cured here. Huge cakes are offered at the tomb, on receipt of which the priests read the benediction (*darūd*), return a portion of the offering, and keep the remainder for themselves.[2] Many shrines of the saint are found in other parts of the Province. A favourite method of sacrificing to him is to place dough on a piece of ground on which a large fire has been previously lighted, and to distribute it when it is baked. He is also worshipped by the rite of sleeping on the ground instead of on a bed—a primitive ascetic rite.[3] The followers of the saint are known as Sulṭānī, and have special priests called Barhai, or Bharai.[4] Rose[5] traces a connexion between them and the Yogīs (*q.v.*). The cult, again, is associated with that of the earth-god, Bhairoṅ, and Bhāī Pherū, the *numen* of the whirlwinds common in the Panjāb. There is also a tradition of a criminal leaping over a rock near the shrine, which may be associated with a fertility cult.[1]

Rose further states that at pilgrimages 'blankets of black, the colour of Śiva, are worn. In the east of the Punjāb, at least, the cult of Sakhī Sarwar is peculiarly favoured by women, which is consistent with its connection with Bhairava, the earth being the emblem of fertility, and this again is in accord with the somewhat Paphian rites observed at the shrine itself. Further, the theory that the worship is really one of the earth-god would account for its being essentially the cult of the Jāṭ peasantry.'[2]

It therefore seems probable that the place may have been for ages the seat of the cult of the earth-god and of the powers of fertility and that this was taken over by Buddhism and Hinduism, and finally connected with a modern Muhammadan saint—an interesting example of that fusion of cults which is at the basis of so much in modern Hinduism.

LITERATURE.—*Census of India, 1891*, vol. xix., *Punjab*, pt. i. p. 132 ff., Calcutta, 1892, *1901*, vol. xvii., *Punjab*, pt. i. p. 133, do. 1902; M. A. Macauliffe, *The Sikh Religion*, Oxford, 1909, iii. 7, 419, iv. 147 n., 339; W. Crooke, *PR*²i. 208 ff.; A. O'Brien, 'The Mohammedan Saints of the W. Punjab,' *JRAI* xli. [1911] 519 f.; *IGI* xxi. 390; E. D. Maclagan, *Census Report, Panjab, 1891*, pt. i., Calcutta, 1892, p. 134 ff. (*Census of India Reports*, vol. xix.).

W. CROOKE.

SĀKTAS.—See HINDUISM, vol. vi. p. 705 f.

ŚĀKYAMUNI.—See BUDDHA, BODHISATTVA, ĀDIBUDDHA.

SALISH.—The Salish peoples lived in the four adjacent States of Washington, Idaho, Montana, and Oregon. A marked distinction existed between the coast Salish west of the Cascade range and the Salish of the interior. The social organization of both was very loose, the various tribes having little unity in spite of the existence of a head or premier chief for each. The coast Salish possessed three castes, but clans and gentes were replaced by village communities in which descent was usually patrilineal, although a man might also become a chief among his mother's people. In the interior, however, personal ability counted for more than descent in determining leadership, whether in war, in peace, or in religious ceremonials. The interior tribes also depended far more on the chase than did those of the coast, who were principally fish-eaters.

I. *COAST SALISH.*—**1. Supernatural beings.**—Among most of the coast Salish 'the Great Transformer,' called usually by some variant of the word Käls, was the highest object of worship, though the Nanaimo, while recognizing him, paid higher regard to the sun. Käls was similar in character to Raven[3] and Mink of the northern tribes, but, since he was also the highest deity, he was not such an utter charlatan. C. Hill-Tout[4] mentions a 'sky chief,' addressed by the Halkomelem tribe as 'parent,' 'father,' or 'creator,' but does not state whether he was identical with Käls.

A multitude of lesser potencies furnished individual helpers, or *sulia*, with which each person was provided among the more southerly tribes. Nearer the Kwakiutl, however, they were obtained only by prominent men such as shamans, warriors, hunters, and chiefs. Among most of the lower Fraser tribes the chief was also a tribal high-priest, without whom no religious ceremony or observance could be performed; in other words, he was the leader in national religious observances.

2. Shamanism.—The shamans were of three

[1] Cf. the offerings at the shrine of Æsculapius (J. G. Frazer, *Pausanias*, London, 1898, iii. 248 ff.; J. E. Harrison, *Prolegomena to the Study of Greek Religion*, Cambridge, 1903, p. 345).
[2] M. A. Macauliffe, *The Sikh Religion*, iii. 419.
[3] Cf. the Selloi (Homer, *Il.* xvi. 234 f.); *Census of India, 1901*, vol. xvii. pt. i. p. 118 f.; *FL* xix. [1908] 68.
[4] D. C. J. Ibbetson, *Punjab Ethnography*, Calcutta, 1883, p. 227.
[5] *Census of India, 1901*, vol. xvii. pt. i. p. 133.

[1] Cf. *GB*³, pt. vi., *The Scapegoat*, London, 1913, p. 196 f.
[2] *Census of India, 1901*, vol. xvii. pt. i. p. 133.
[3] See art. HAIDA, vol. vi. p. 473.
[4] *Report of the British Association for the Advancement of Science*, 1902, p. 410.

kinds: (1) the shamans proper, called *skelam* ('to heal,' 'to make well') by some of the Fraser tribes, cured internal diseases produced by witchcraft, the absence of the soul, etc., and employed the usual methods; (2) the *olia*, or soothsayer, besides interpreting dreams, visions, omens, and portents, healed external injuries and took care of the bodies of the dead; he alone might prepare a body for burial and protect a person from the evil influence of ghosts, of which all the Salish were extremely afraid; (3) the *seuwel*, or wizards, who might be men or women, instead of being universally abhorred as among most tribes, were recognized as a regular class. They were employed to injure people, and they did this by washing their hands in water at sun-down and repeating the victim's name, or by repeating formulæ over some of his belongings. They were also engaged by the relatives of a deceased person to hold converse with the ghost and adjure it never to come back to trouble the living. After a person had died, they were employed to drive away sickness. Corresponding to this class among the Songish were the *sioua* women, who were acquainted with herbs and performed the functions of midwives.

3. The dead.—The stories told of the world of the dead were obtained from the first class of shamans and differed little from those found elsewhere. The salmon-feast, celebrated by all these tribes when the great salmon-run began, was the only one of importance outside of the winter potlatches, and partook somewhat of a religious character.

II. *BELLACOOLA.*—The Bellacoola, an isolated Salish group on Bentinck arm and Dean inlet, were unlike all the others in having evolved a mythology of considerable system and originality.[1] They postulated five different worlds, two of which were above and two below the plane of this earth. In the highest realm, called Atsaaktl, resided an old woman called Kamaits, Tsi sisnaahitl ('our woman'), or Eku yakimtotlsitl ('afraid of nothing'). This world was believed to be a treeless plain over which a wind continually blew towards Kamaits's house, situated in the far east; but near the house it was calm. In front stood a post in the shape of a monster whose mouth formed the door, and near it was gravel of three colours, blue, black, and white. Behind the house was a salt-water pond in which Kamaits bathed. In the same pond lived a snake, or fish, prominent in Bellacoola mythology, called the *sisiutl*.

In the centre of the lower heaven, Sonh, stood the House of Myths (Nusmeta), also known as 'the-house-where-man-was-created,' 'the-house-from-which-people-came-down,' or 'the-house-to-which-people-go.' This was ruled by Senh, the sun, also called 'our father,' or 'sacred one.' He was the only deity to whom the Bellacoola prayed, for they did not pray to Kamaits. Indeed, Kamaits does not appear prominently in the religious thought of the nation except for the war which she waged in primitive times with the mountains and her final victory over them. A second deity, who lived in the back part of the House of Myths, and who was of almost equal importance with Senh, was Atlkuntam. The two together might be called the rulers of mankind. Near the fire was an old man called Snutlkulhals, who formerly ruled over the house, but had given up his place in favour of those two deities. Besides those three there were a number of inferior beings, many of whom had to do solely with the *kusiut* ceremony. Of the others, one gave a child its individual features; another, a female deity, rocked infants and the young of animals before sending them down into the world; a third was 'the mother of flowers'; and there were two beings whose function it was to determine when a person was to die. Still others acted as messengers for the superior deities. Raven was said by some to have his abode in this house, and to him was attributed the invention of the salmon-weir and of the ceremonial whistles and the institution of the ceremonies themselves. The beings concerned particularly with the *kusiut* were nine brothers and a sister. There were special deities to initiate shamans and one whose office was to protect mountain-goat hunters. We also find a belief in the thunder-bird. In a room in the back part of the House of Myths resided several deities who initiated the cannibal dancer and other novices. Along the course pursued by the sun, which is represented as a celestial bridge, were stationed several additional beings, and twenty-four were guardians of the sky, which they fed with fire-wood continually. Where the sun set was a post supporting the sky and preventing the sun from falling into the lower world. Our world was supposed to be an island in the ocean, held up by a giant who sat in the far east with legs apart. The earth was fastened by two ropes to a long stone bar held in his hands, and, when he got tired and moved his hands, there was an earthquake. If he moved the earth westward, people had epidemics; if eastward, sickness disappeared. In the sea dwelt a being who swallowed and gave forth the water of the ocean twice every day. Salmon were supposed to come from a land in the far west. The world nearest beneath us was described as the country of the ghosts and lay along the sandy banks of the river. Winter in their country was our summer, and their summer was our winter; their night was our day, and their day our night. There was a dancing-house in that country, where the *kusiut* was performed, and the ghosts entered it through the smoke-hole by means of a rope-ladder. They were not allowed to return directly to our earth by this ladder to be reborn, but might ascend another to the lower heaven and be sent down from there by the deities. Those who enjoyed staying in the ghost country descended to the lowest world of all, whence there was no return. From the world above were sent down the ancestors of each of the Bellacoola village communities.

III. *THOMPSON RIVER TRIBES.*—Thanks to the researches of Boas, Teit, and Hill-Tout, our knowledge of the religion of the Ntlakyapamuk, or Thompson River Indians, is much more ample than that of any other of the interior Salish tribes, but the rites and beliefs of all were nearly the same.

1. Cosmological beliefs. — According to Teit, the Thompson River Indians believed the world to be square with its corners directed towards the cardinal points, and Lytton, where Coyote's son reached the earth, was its centre. Round the edges were lakes, over which clouds and mists hovered. The earth rose towards the north, and that was why it was colder there. Cold winds were caused every time people far in the north left their houses, and warm winds by people far in the south. Formerly the northern and southern people waged war with each other, exposing the earth to alternate periods of extreme heat and extreme cold, but their wars were ended by the marriage of the daughter of the chief of the south to the son of the chief of the north. Thunder was caused by a huge bird like a grouse. It shot arrows by using its wings as a bow, and their rebound in the air produced the noise. Fog or mist was described as the steam of the earth rising

[1] The Bellacoola information is all taken from Boas, 'The Mythology of the Bella Coola Indians,' in *Memoirs of the Jesup North Pacific Expedition*, vol. i. pt. ii. [1898].

when it was heated, or was said to be caused by Coyote turning over. Lakes and ponds originated at the time of a deluge, which also swept the fish into them. Fire and water were in the possession of certain animals, from which they were liberated. By the Upper Thompsons rain and snow were said to be made by the 'Old Man' scratching his back or urinating, but the Lower Thompsons ascribed their production to a female deity. The sun and moon were formerly men, and the reason why the latter is less bright is that his sister Hare or Frog sits continually on his face. Haloes about the sun and moon were their respective 'houses.' Stars were described as transformed people or as roots growing in the upper world, though special tales were told of the Pleiades and the stars of the Great Dipper. The Milky Way was called 'the trail of the stars,' 'what has been emptied on the trail of the stars,' or 'the tracks of the dead.' The rainbow was formerly a friend of the thunder, which was in the habit of painting its face frequently with bright colours.

2. Supernatural beings. — All sorts of 'land mysteries' and 'water mysteries' were prayed to. Those that might in any way be considered tribal deities were the sun, the dawn, the rain, tops of mountains, certain lakes, the spirit of sweat-bathing, and perhaps also the Old Man, who was said to live on the tops of high mountains, and in former days sent the Old Coyote, the principal Ntlakyapamuk transformer, to set the world in order. There were also three brothers, called Koaktlka, and another individual, who acted as transformers. The three brothers were finally changed into stone, while Old Coyote retreated to his house of ice. After that the Old Man himself travelled throughout the world. He thus appears to have occupied an elevated position in native mythology, but little attention was actually paid to him in daily life. The leading objects of regard were the sun and the dawn, the latter being frequently invoked by boys and girls during their puberty ceremonials. The spirit of sweat-bathing naturally derived his importance from the prominent place which sweat-bathing occupied in the acquirement of guardian-spirits. Each person, male or female, whether a shaman or not, possessed a guardian-spirit which differed somewhat for a shaman, warrior, hunter, fisherman, gambler, runner, etc., but all were otherwise much alike and resembled the personal *manitus* found elsewhere in N. America. A very few shamans inherited guardian-spirits which had been especially powerful, but most were acquired by a longer or shorter course of sweat-bathing, fasting, abstinence from women, and isolation in the mountains. Dwarfs and giants were believed in by the Upper Thompson Indians, the latter being supposed to inhabit the Okinagan country, and there was a race of pale, ghost-like people who sometimes pursued lonely travellers. They were different from ghosts only in one particular—they could not be deterred from pursuit by turning out of the trail.

3. The dead.—The land of souls was thought to be beneath, towards sunset, and was approached over a dimly-lit trail, which finally descended a gentle slope and came to a stream spanned by a single log. Just before this another trail joined it, used by shamans as a short cut when pursuing a soul that had been carried off. At either end of the log bridge was a guardian, who sent back souls whose time had not yet come. Another stood at the entrance of the land of souls. From the bridge the trail rose gradually, and it began to grow light again. At the top of the ascent was an immense pile of clothing, where the souls left everything that they had worn in this world. Further on the trail ended at the door of a great lodge, made of hard white material similar to limestone. This door was narrow, but at the opposite or western end was a wider one opening into the soul country. In the lodge there was always some one to welcome the new-comer, and generally his departed friends gathered there to receive him when they learned that he was coming. The land of the souls was a most delightful country, full of berries and flowers; the air was pleasant and still; and it was always light and warm. Some said that the souls went naked without appearing to notice it, but others supposed that they wore clothes such as they had had on earth. There is another story describing the journey to the land of souls which makes it lead to a lake on which one must paddle for days in a dim atmosphere. A notion existed that animals also have worlds situated under ground; when many went back there, they became scarce on our earth.

Each soul had a shadow or ghost, which remained behind after death, visiting for four days the persons and places formerly frequented by the dead man, after which it generally haunted the place where the body was buried. These ghosts plotted to take away souls from living persons, and were consequently much feared. Suicides did not go to the abode of souls, but became 'lost,' or ceased to exist. The souls of those who were drowned perished entirely, or continued to dwell in the water, or followed the waters to a land beyond them which shamans could not reach. Some said that the souls of those who had led good lives reached the spirit country much more quickly, but in general moral character seems to have affected their future very slightly. The soul of a dead child might return in one of the same sex born soon afterwards, but otherwise rebirth was not believed in. It was thought that the souls would continue in the country of the dead until the Old Man and Coyote came again. These would be preceded by messengers and would bring the souls with them. Christians were believed to go to the land of souls over a different trail from that used by others.

4. Shamanism and witchcraft.—The doings of shamans and wizards, although interesting, present few features not found in other parts of the continent. It was believed that they could harm a person wearing an article of clothing of Indian make more easily than one who was dressed like a white man. Shamans were greatly feared on account of their power of bewitching; but, if it was thought that they had injured or caused the death of any one, they were sometimes killed, though ordinarily failure to cure simply made it necessary to return the fee. Occasionally they were called in to treat horses or dogs if these were highly valued.

5. Prophets.—As elsewhere in America, prophets made their appearance every now and then, generally claiming some message from the spirit-world, and they drew large followings for a time, the Indians gathering from all quarters to see and hear them. They foretold such affairs of general interest as epidemics and the coming of the Whites with the consequent changes in customs and manners. See art. PROPHECY (American).

6. Tabus, etc.—There were numerous tabus and certain ceremonies when the firstfruits, roots, etc., came. When the first tobacco was gathered, the inhabitants of each lodge went through a special ceremony, and there were larger festivals for feasting, dancing, and praying participated in by each neighbourhood.

LITERATURE.—The Salish have been treated by F. Boas in report v. 'On the North-Western Tribes of Canada,' in *Report of the British Association for the Advancement of Science*, 1889, p. 801 ff., report vi., *ib.* 1890, p. 562 ff., report vii., *ib.* 1891, p. 408 ff., and report x., *ib.* 1895, p. 523 ff., and by C. Hill-Tout, 'On the Ethnological Survey of Canada,' in *Rep. Brit. Assoc. for Adv. of Science*, 1899, p. 500 ff., 1900, p. 472 ff., and 1902, p. 355 ff., and in *JAI* xxxiv. [1904] 20-91. Besides having report vii. 'On the N.W. Tribes of Canada' devoted to them, the Bellacoola have been the subject of a special paper by Boas, in *Memoirs of the Amer. Mus. of Nat. Hist.*, *Jesup North Pacific Expedition*, vol. i. pt. ii. [1898], 'The Mythology of the Bella Coola Indians.' The interior Salish have been discussed by Boas in report vi. 'On the N.W. Tribes of Canada,' and by Hill-Tout, 'On the Ethnological Survey of Canada,' 1899, but most thoroughly by J. Teit and F. Boas, 'The Thompson Indians of British Columbia,' in *Memoirs of Amer. Mus. of Nat. Hist.*, *Jesup N. Pacific Expedition*, vol. i. pt. iv. [1900], and by Teit in vol. ii. pts. v. and vii. of the same series. The myths of the Thompson River Indians have been treated by Teit in the *Memoirs of the American Folk-lore Society*, vi. [1898]. The material on the Salish of Washington and Oregon leaves much to be desired. We are dependent principally on G. Gibbs, 'The Tribes of Western Washington and North-Western Oregon' (*Contributions to N. American Ethnology*, vol. i., Washington, 1877), in J. W. Powell's *Survey of the Rocky Mountain Region*, and M. Eells, 'The Twana, Chemakum and Klallam Indians of Washington Territory,' in the *Report of the Smithsonian Institution* for 1887, pt. i., Washington, 1889, p. 605; also see Boas in *JAFL* xi. [1898] 23 ff., 133 ff., and 'Kathlanet Texts,' *Bull* 26, *BE*, Washington, 1901; and *Globus*, lxiii. [1893] 154 ff., 172 ff., 190 ff.

JOHN R. SWANTON.

SALIVA.—In the folk-beliefs of most backward races and among the less intelligent classes in civilized communities many superstitious beliefs are associated with this bodily secretion.

According to J. E. Crombie, this has been explained as follows:

'At one time the life of a man must have been generally believed to have been bound up in his saliva; just as it can be shown that the life of a man has been very generally believed to have been bound up in his blood . . . therefore the spitting rite is a parallel to the blood rite.'[1]

This theory has been extended by E. S. Hartland:

'The transfer of saliva is more than a gift of a portion of the spitter's life. It is a gift of a portion of himself, which is thus put into the power of the recipient as a pledge of goodwill. Nay, it is a bodily union with the recipient, such as can be effected by a blood-covenant. Possibly, as Mr. Crombie suggests, it is, where an interchange of saliva occurs, a form of blood-covenant consequent upon milder manners. . . . Rather it seems to be a more evanescent and less solemn, though still emphatic, form, intended only for temporary purposes.'[2]

To this it may be added that the effect of the transfer of saliva depends upon the intention of the spitter. It is often the result of a kindly intention, that of associating the personality of the spitter with the person on whom it is discharged; where the intent is hostile, it implies reprobation, abhorrence, or contempt. The exact purport of some of the beliefs and usages quoted below is vague and uncertain; but most of the cases may be explained on the principles already stated.

1. Saliva as a part of the personality. — This often appears in popular belief and usage; *e.g.*, English slang 'spit'=a facsimile—'He's the very spit of his father or mother'; French, 'C'est son père tout craché';[3] 'Ce'estoit luy tout craché.'[4] In the folk-tales saliva is often represented as speaking, warning the hero or heroine of approaching danger, and so on.[5] Among practices to obtain children Hartland quotes the case of a gypsy woman drinking the water in which her husband has spat.

'What is the meaning of the expression "He is the very spit of his father" current not only in England, but also, according to the learned Liebrecht, in France, Italy, and Portugal, and alluded to by Voltaire and La Fontaine, if it point not back to a similar, perhaps a more repulsive ceremony formerly practised by the folk all over Western Europe?'[6]

1 *The International Folk-lore Congress, 1891: Papers and Transactions*, p. 251.
2 *LP* ii. 260.
3 A. Barrère and C. G. Leland, *A Dict. of Slang, Jargon, and Cant*, London, 1897, ii. 273.
4 R. Cotgrave, *French and Eng. Dict.*, London, 1650, *s.v.* 'Crache.'
5 M. R. Cox, *Cinderella*, London, 1893, pp. 428, 518; J. A. MacCulloch, *CF*, do. 1905, pp. 171, 193, 197.
6 *Primitive Paternity*, London, 1909, i. 70.

2. Saliva causing conception.—The belief that saliva, as part of the personality, may cause conception is common in the lower culture.

In the *Popol Vuh* the demi-god Hunhun Ahpu spits into the hand of the princess Xquiq, and she finds herself pregnant.[1] According to the Hindu legend, Agni spat upon the waters, and three personages, Ekata, Dvita, and Trita, were born.[2] The Chapotās of Bengal profess to be descended from a man who sprang from some betel-leaf which Siva, after chewing it, spat out.[3] In the Teutonic myth Qvasir, at the making of a covenant between the Aesir and the Vanir, was formed out of their spittle, and in the Edda the spittle of the waves was shaped by the gods into a man.[4] In the Garo creation legend Nostu spits upon the lilies and grass in the water, and the land is formed.[5] In Egyptian mythology Isis gathers up the spittle which falls from Ra, and from earth and the spittle forms a snake.[6] In parts of England the fertilization of the turkey and the capercailzie is caused by the same means.[7] Many similar beliefs are collected by Hartland.[8]

3. Black magic worked through saliva.—The belief that magic may be worked to the injury of the owner by the acquisition of a piece of his clothing, hair, nail-parings, or other personal relics is common in the lower culture, and extends to saliva.[9]

'Every part of a man's body is regarded by primitive science as impregnated with his properties; but such parts are especially so considered which themselves are held to have a special connection with the life and soul.'[10]

In S. India saliva is placed in a coco-nut, which is pierced with twenty-one nails, buried, and a fowl sacrificed, for purposes of black magic.[11] In Polynesia sorcerers 'secure something connected with the body of the object of vengeance; the parings of the nails, a lock of the hair, the saliva from the mouth, or other secretions from the body.'[12] Spittle, like hair, is *tapu* in New Zealand.[13] Among the Columbians spittle is collected and given to a magician, who charms away the owner's life.[14] Hence this substance is carefully guarded.

'The use of the portable spittoon by the Sandwich Island chiefs, in which the saliva was carefully deposited, carried by a confidential servant, and buried every morning . . . originated in their dread of sorcery.'[15]

In Hawaii a chief of high rank held the office of spittoon-bearer to the king.[16] Among the Burmese and Shans the disposal of the saliva and water in which clothes have been washed is superintended with anxious care to avoid witchcraft.[17]

4. Spitting on oneself.—Hence spitting on oneself, clothes, or other personal articles enforces the influence of the personality on such things, and produces union or communion with them.

In Theocritus the maiden who rejects a rough country lover spits in her breast as a protective (τρὶς εἰς ἑὸν ἔπτυσε κόλπον).[18]

'Hunc puer, hunc iuvenis turba circumterit arcta;
Despuit in molles et sibi quisque sinus.'[19]

The Cherokee brave, on the eve of battle, chewed a charmed root and spat the juice on his body to protect himself from bullets.[20] In Lesbos, if a person admires a child, the mother spits three times in her bosom.[21] In Germany, if a person happens to spit on himself, he will hear some news; in Jamaica it means that some one is saying something untrue about him.[22]

5. Union promoted by spitting on another.—The belief that, by dropping saliva on a person or thing, union may be created, or immunity from sorcery,

1 H. H. Bancroft, *NR* iii. [New York, 1875] 478.
2 *SBE* xlii. [1897] 521.
3 *Census of India, 1901*, Calcutta, 1902, vol. vi., *Bengal*, pt. i. p. 405.
4 J. Grimm, *Teutonic Mythology*, Eng. tr., London, 1882, i. 319; G. Vigfusson and F. Y. Powell, *Corpus Poeticum Boreale*, Oxford, 1883, i. 464.
5 A. Playfair, *The Garos*, London, 1909, p. 84.
6 *GB*³, pt. ii., *Taboo and the Perils of the Soul*, London, 1911, p. 387.
7 *FL* viii. [1897] 375 f.
8 *Primitive Paternity*, i. 12, 18, 19, 68, 73 f.
9 J. G. Frazer, *The Belief in Immortality*, London, 1913, i. 413 f.
10 A. E. Crawley, *The Mystic Rose*, London, 1902, p. 104.
11 E. Thurston, *Ethnog. Notes on S. India*, Madras, 1906, p. 328; cf. Westermarck, *MI* i. 589 f.
12 W. Ellis, *Polynesian Researches*, London, 1830, ii. 228.
13 E. Tregear, 'The Maoris,' *JAI* xix. [1890] 123.
14 Bancroft, *NR* i. 171 n.
15 Ellis, ii. 229.
16 *FL* vi. [1895] 73.
17 *Gazetteer of Upper Burma*, Rangoon, 1900, pt. i. vol. ii. p. 37.
18 *Idyll.* xx. 11; cf. vi. 39.
19 Tibullus, *Eleg.* I. ii. 95 f.; cf. Theophrastus, *Charact.* (*de Superst.*) xvi.
20 J. Mooney, 7 *RBEW* (1891), p. 389.
21 W. H. D. Rouse, 'Folklore Firstfruits from Lesbos,' *FL* vii. [1896] 148.
22 Grimm, iv. 1795; *FL* xvi. [1905] 76.

witchcraft, or the evil eye secured, is common. The idea appears in many different forms.

(*a*) *Spitting as a form of salutation or greeting.*—

'The Wa-chaga share with the Masai . . . a curious habit of *spitting* on things or people as a compliment or sign of gratitude. I remember one man . . . was so pleased at my safe return that he took my hand in his and spat repeatedly at the sky, saying constantly "Erua icha!"—"God is good!."'[1] 'The old lady's farewell of me was peculiar; she took my hand in her two, turned it palm upwards, and spat on it . . . the doctor [Nassau] . . . says the spitting is accidental, a by-product [of the performance which the natives call *bata*, and which consisted in blowing a blessing].'[2] On the Lower Congo, 'in saying good-bye to each other, they pretend to spit on the forehead and hands of the departing one, and on some grass which, after being spat upon, they stick in the hair of the beloved one leaving them. This is to bring good luck and keep away evil spirits.'[3] In Yucatan 'the highest mark of respect was to place the right hand, anointed with spittle, on the ground, and then to rub it over the heart.'[4] Among the Masai spitting is a sign of welcome; women spit on their palms and shake hands with a visitor.[5]

(*b*) ***On receiving the handsel or first coin in the day, or a gift.***—

''Tis a common use in London, and perhaps over great part of England, for Apple-woemen, Oyster-woemen &c. & some Butchers, to spit on the money wch they first recieve in the morning, wch they call good handsell.'[6] The custom is common in Great Britain and Ireland.[7] In E. Africa people spit on a gift for good luck.[8] 'An Atlas Berber . . . spat on the coin which I gave him . . . and my native friends told me that he did so for fear lest the coin, owing to some sorcery on my part, should not only itself return to me, but at the same time take with it all the money with which it had been in contact in his bag.'[9]

(*c*) *Lustration of children with saliva.*—The usual explanation of this custom is that it is intended to ward off the spells of witches or fairies or to counteract the evil eye.

Hartland regards this as 'only a specialisation of a more general intention. The evidence points to the meaning of the ceremony as a welcome into the world, an acknowledgment of kindred, a desire to express those friendly feelings which in archaic times none but a kinsman could entertain, whatever flattering words might be spoken.'[10]

In Cork, immediately after birth, the child is sometimes spat on by the father, and in Wicklow they spit on a child for luck the first day it is brought out after birth; at Innisbofin, when old women meet a baby out with its nurse, they spit on the ground all round it in a circle, to keep fairies from it.[11] In modern Greece a visitor's first greeting to a baby is to spit on it.[12]

A special case is that of the use of saliva in the baptismal rite of the Roman Catholic Church. 'The priest exorcises the child; anoints his ears and nostrils with spittle—after our Lord's example, who thus cured the deaf and dumb man—and asks him in three separate interrogations whether he renounces Satan, all his works, and all his pomps.'[13]

In modern Greece 'at a baptism . . . the priest opens the service by exorcising all evil spirits and influences from the four corners of the room by swinging his censer, but the midwife, who usually knows something of magic, or one of the godparents, accompanies him and makes assurance doubly sure by spitting in each suspected nook.'[14]

1 H. H. Johnston, 'The People of E. Equatorial Africa,' *JAI* xv. [1886] 11.
2 M. H. Kingsley, *Travels in W. Africa*, London, 1897, pp. 288, 453.
3 J. H. Weeks, 'Some Customs of the Lower Congo People,' *FL* xx. [1909] 470.
4 Bancroft, *NR* ii. 635.
5 J. Bland-Sutton, *Man and Beast in E. Ethiopia*, London, 1911, p. 98; J. Thomson, *Through Masai Land*, do. 1887, p. 166; H. H. Johnston, *The Uganda Protectorate*, do. 1902, ii. 833; S. L. Hinde, *The Last of the Masai*, do. 1901, p. 47 f.; for the Dinka custom see *ERE* iv. 712.
6 J. Aubrey, *Remaines of Gentilisme and Judaisme* [1686–87], ed. J. Britten, London, 1881, pp. 80, 231.
7 *NQ*, 4th ser., vi. [1870] 339 f., 5th ser., viii. [1877] 46; J. Brand, *Observations on Popular Antiquities*, London, 1849, iii. 262; J. Nicholson, *Folk-lore of E. Yorkshire*, do. 1890, p. 82.
8 Mrs. French-Sheldon, 'Customs among the Natives of E. Africa,' *JAI* xxi. [1892] 383.
9 Westermarck, *MI* i. 594; cf. L. Decle, *Three Years in Savage Africa*, London, 1898, p. 77, for the Barotse: 'When they do not want a thing touched they spit on straws and stick them all about the object.'
10 *LP* ii. 263.
11 A. C. Haddon, 'A Batch of Irish Folk-lore,' *FL* iv. [1893] 357 f., 361.
12 *Ib.* v. [1894] 339; cf. Tylor, *PC*² ii. 441.
13 W. E. Addis and T. Arnold, *A Catholic Dict.*⁶, London, 1893, p. 72; *ERE* ii. 372 f., 400.
14 J. C. Lawson, *Modern Greek Folklore and Ancient Greek Religion*, Cambridge, 1910, p. 15 f.

(*d*) *Procuring communion with sacred objects by means of saliva.*—In many places communion with sacred objects is procured by spitting upon them.

In Guatemala at small chapels along the road the passer-by halted, gathered a handful of herbs, rubbed his legs with them, spat reverently upon them, and with a prayer placed them upon the altar with a small stone and an offering of pepper, salt, or cacao, which no one dared to touch.[1]

In Korea 'my coolies occasionally added a few stones to the heaps of more than usual importance even by the wayside, bowing before them and expectorating on them.'[2] In the practice of folk-medicine in Borneo 'the sorcerer then takes the image from the boat and instructs it what to say to the spirit on behalf of the patient; after abusing the image and enforcing on his mind the necessity of remembering the lesson, by way of indelibly fixing it on his memory, he winds up by spitting sirih juice in its face.'[3] 'The Basutos worship a big block of granite, dance round it on one leg, and at the same time spit on it.'[4]

At Brighton there is a stone wall in which is a crystal, called by schoolboys 'the holy stone'; it used to be the custom for every boy who passed this stone to spit on it for luck.'[5]

Sometimes the spitting seems to be a form of coercion of the *numen* in the sacred object:

'In the Tamil districts, if a temple car does not move from its position when an attempt is made to drag it, a lot of people, who are allowed to get intoxicated, are given toddy mixed with castor-oil. Some of this they spit out upon the wheels of the car, which cannot stand defilement, and proceeds to move.'[6]

The idea of communion is perhaps shown when in Japan pilgrims to Buddhist shrines chew strips of paper into pellets and spit them out at the images of guardian deities; if the pellet sticks, the prayer will be heard; if not, the prayer will not be heard.[7]

(*e*) *Spitting as an asseveration or as a bond of union.*—

Among the Bechuanas, 'when it thunders every one trembles; if there are several together, one asks the other with uneasiness, Is there any one amongst us who devours the wealth of others? All then spit on the ground saying, We do not devour the wealth of others.'[8] When in the 18th cent. English tenants combined against their landlords, 'it is usual with them to assemble round a great Stone, upon which they are to spit, believing this practice (joyn'd with a promise of what they will do, and stand to) to be as sacred and binding as if they had taken a publick oath.'[9]

Spitting, again, is a means of transmitting magical powers.

In Baluchistan the holy man who is able to charm away locusts passes on the charm to his successor by spitting into his mouth; the man thus initiated goes mad, but this passes off and leaves wonderful power.[10]

6. Spitting as a mark of contempt or hatred.—Here the intent is changed, and the object is to exhibit enmity or aversion.

Spitting in the face was common among the Jews.[11] Among the Greeks we have the phrase of Sophocles, πτύσας προσώπῳ.[12] Compare with this Shakespeare's:

'I do defy him, and I spit at him;
Call him a slanderous coward and a villain.'[13]

'As she spit in his face, so she defied him.'[14]

'The fanatic nigger, spitting in disgust on the ground, declared that this made matters worse, and that he believed me not only to be a Kafir (infidel), but also a spy.'[15]

When a girl in S. Africa is found not to be a virgin, the women spit on her pudenda.[16] Among the Fellaḥin of Palestine, if a man marries a widow, unless she needs protection, the men

1 Bancroft, *NR* ii. 738, iii. 481.
2 W. Gowland, 'Dolmens and other Antiquities of Korea,' *JAI* xxiv. [1894–95] 329.
3 H. Ling Roth, *The Natives of Sarawak and British N. Borneo*, London, 1896, i. 284.
4 T. Hahn, *Tsuni-Goam*, London, 1881, p. 91.
5 *NQ*, 5th ser., iv. [1875] 495.
6 Thurston, *Ethnog. Notes*, p. 296.
7 B. H. Chamberlain, 'Minor Japanese Religious Practices,' *JAI* xxii. [1893] 357.
8 T. Arbousset and F. Daumas, *Narr. of an Exploratory Tour to the N.E. of the Colony of the Cape of Good Hope*, Eng. tr., London, 1852, p. 322 f., quoted in Westermarck, *MI* ii. 60.
9 E. Laurence, *The Duty of a Steward to his Lord*, London, 1727, quoted in *NQ*, 4th ser., x. [1872] 312.
10 *Census of India, 1911*, vol. iv., *Baluchistan*, i. 67 f.
11 Nu 12¹⁴, Job 30¹⁰, Mt 26⁶⁷, Lk 18³²; cf. Gal 4¹⁴.
12 *Ant.* 1232. 13 *Richard II.*, act. i. sc. i. l. 60 f.
14 *Measure for Measure*, act. ii. sc. i. l. 86.
15 M. Parkyns, *Life in Abyssinia*, London, 1853, ii. 379.
16 J. Macdonald, 'Manners, Customs, Superstitions and Religions of S. African Tribes,' *JAI* xx. [1891] 118.

spit on her face as she goes to her new home.[1] If a Hebrew refused to perform his legal duties towards his sister-in-law, she was directed to spit in his face, saying: 'So shall it be done unto the man that doth not build up his brother's house';[2] and, if a widow repudiates the levirate, she takes off her sandal and spits on the ground.[3] In Scotland, when two boys quarrelled, and one wet the buttons of the other with his saliva, this was a challenge to fight or be dubbed a coward; when children try to solve a puzzle, the usual way of acknowledging defeat is to spit on the ground.[4]

Hence spitting becomes an embodied curse.[5]

When a Zulu is doing magic, while he is eating 'he spits in different directions, especially in the direction of those he hates, or who are at enmity with him, and whom he thus, as it were, defies, fully believing that he is surrounding himself with a preserving influence against their machinations and power, and at the same time exerting an influence injurious to them.'[6]

7. Saliva of various kinds.—There are numerous varieties of saliva in folk-belief.

(*a*) *Saliva of gods.*—

Of Marduk, the god of Babylon, it is said, 'the spittle of life is thine,' probably in allusion to its magical qualities.[7] The spittle of the Teutonic gods had mighty virtues.[8] Tchim-paz or Chkai, the god of the Mordvins, spat on the waters, and his spittle grew into a mountain.[9]

'The modern Icelanders relate that Christ, while walking with Peter along the seashore, spat into the sea, and from his spittle a stone-grig developed. Peter also spat, and his saliva turned into a female stone-grig. Both these are excellent eating. The Devil, who was not far behind, saw this, and also spat into the sea. But his spittle changed into a jellyfish, which is fit for nothing.'[10]

(*b*) *Saliva of holy men.*—The spittle of holy men has manifold virtues.

Vaiṣṇavas in S. India regard a piece of food which a *guru* has masticated and the water with which he has rinsed out his mouth as sacred, and swallow them with avidity.[11] In Madras a Mādiga woman spits on the assembled people, who believe that the spittle removes pollution because she is an impersonation of the goddess Mātangi.[12]

The Quissama of Angola 'practise the fine old recipe that Mr. Hamilton has remarked to be so much in vogue among the Kaffir medicine men, *i.e.*, that, in cases where medicine has been administered, in order to give it proper efficacy, the doctor spits his saliva down the patient's throat.'[13] In Borneo the natives 'brought portions of cooked rice on leaves, and begged the Englishmen to spit into them. After which they ate them up, thinking they should be the better for it.'[14]

At the sacrifice of the Meriah victim of the Kandhs (*q.v.*), who was regarded as semi-divine, while he was being taken in procession, some persons solicited a drop of his saliva and anointed their heads with it.[15]

(*c*) *Saliva poisonous.*—Some saliva is regarded as poisonous.

According to Socrates, a man ejects saliva because it is injurious to keep it in his system.[16] The famous Maḥmūd Begaḍā of Gujarāt was, it is said, nourished on poison, and by chewing certain fruits he could discharge saliva so poisonous that any one touching it died.[17] In the Malay Peninsula the Kenaboi have such an evil reputation that any one treading on their spittle is believed to suffer from boils and blains.[18] The spittle of a witch—*e.g.*, among the Babylonians—is naturally poisonous.[19] So also is the saliva of various animals—the lizard, the snake, the rukh in the East; in Ireland, if a weasel spits in milk, those who drink it suffer from gripes.[20]

1 Mrs. H. H. Spoer (A. Goodrich Freer), 'Marriage Customs of the Bedu and Fellaḥin,' *FL* xxi. [1910] 275.
2 Dt 25⁹. 3 *ERE* v. 56.
4 J. Napier, *Folk-Lore or Superstitious Beliefs in the W. of Scotland*, Paisley, 1879, p. 101.
5 Westermarck, *MI* i. 255, 589, ii. 209.
6 H. Callaway, *Nursery Tales, Traditions, and Histories of the Zulus*, Natal and London, 1868, i. 163 n.
7 L. R. Farnell, *Greece and Babylon*, Edinburgh, 1911, p. 176.
8 Grimm³, iv. 1377.
9 F. Max Müller, *Contributions to the Science of Mythology*, London, 1897, ii. 250 f.
10 *FL* iii. [1892] 325.
11 J. A. Dubois, *Hindu Manners*³, Eng. tr., Oxford, 1906, p. 132.
12 Thurston, *Castes and Tribes of S. India*, Madras, 1909, iv. 295.
13 F. G. H. Price, 'A Description of the Quissama Tribes,' *JAI* i. [1872] 192.
14 Ling Roth, i. 241.
15 J. Campbell, *Thirteen Years' Service among the Wild Tribes of Khondistan*, London, 1864, p. 112.
16 Xenophon, *Mem.* I. ii. 54.
17 L. di Varthema, *Travels in Egypt, Syria, etc.*, Eng. tr., London, 1863, p. 110; *BG*, vol. i. pt. i. [1896] p. 248 f. note.
18 W. W. Skeat and C. O. Blagden, *Pagan Races of the Malay Peninsula*, London, 1906, i. 67 n.
19 *HDB* v. 554.
20 *BG*, vol. ix. pt. i. [1901] p. 380; Somadeva, *Kathāsaritsāgara*, Calcutta, 1884, ii. 296; H. M. Elliot, *The Hist. of India*, London, 1867–77, ii. 203; *FL* xxii. [1911] 452.

(*d*) *Saliva medicinal.*—Some saliva is curative. The virtues of fasting spittle are widely recognized.

In Scotland its prophylactic properties are famous,[1] as also in Arabia,[2] and in Madagascar.[3] Pliny gives many prescriptions of this kind. Beneath the tongue of a mad dog is a slimy saliva which, taken in drink, prevents hydrophobia; the foam from a horse's mouth is useful in ear disease, in chafing caused by riding, and in diseases of the uterus.[4] Serpent's slime and foam form the *anguinum*, or snake-egg, which has magical powers.[5] A dry white moss grows on stones near streams; if one of these stones, with the addition of human saliva, is rubbed against another, it cures ring-worm when rubbed on the part affected, with the spell, 'Cantharides begone, a wild wolf seeks thy blood!'[6] Some people used to rub their own spittle with the finger behind the ear to relieve disquietude of mind.[7] Sometimes the cure was effected by transference, as when a person suffering from cough spat into the mouth of a small frog and gained relief.[8] A sort of lizard in Malabar is believed to suck the blood of children by looking at them; as soon as people catch sight of the creature, they apply saliva to the child's navel, from which it is supposed that the poisoned blood is thus extracted.[9] As a cure for gout, in Italy, a small boy, while fasting, is made to spit thrice on the affected limb, to repeat a charm, and to spit behind him thrice for three successive mornings.[10] In the Greek Islands thrush (*afta*) in a child is cured by the mother showing the sore to the evening stars, spitting on it, and saying: 'This evening stars and *afta*, tomorrow no stars and no *afta*.'[11] In the Panjāb a clan of Arorās can cure hydrophobia by spitting on a little earth and applying it to the bite.[12] A gentleman travelling by train in Germany was asked to spit in the face of a man suffering from a fit.[13] Magyars believe that styes on the eye can be cured by some one spitting on them.[14] In Lesbos, to cure a wasp sting spit four times on the place, do this thrice, and say πίθι, 'drink.'[15] In Ireland it is believed that pricking of the foot ('pins and needles') is relieved by wetting the popliteal space with saliva.[16]

8. Protective powers of saliva.—The use of saliva is valuable against fascination and ill-luck generally.

(*a*) *Against fascination.*—Spitting is a common mode of repelling the evil eye.

In Greece saliva obtained from a person who is suspected of having unintentionally over-looked a child is mixed with water, and the patient is made to drink it; or the incautious person is asked to spit in the child's face.[17] In Scotland spitting three times in a person's face, turning a live coal in the fire, and exclaiming, 'The Lord be with us!' protects from the evil eye.[18] When making a protective necklace in the Malay Peninsula, the maker recites a charm and spits twice on the necklace.[19] Overpraise—'fore-speaking,' as it is called in Scotland—is dangerous. In Russia, if a person praises a baby without the precautionary ejaculation, 'God save the mark!' the nurse spits in the person's face.[20]

(*b*) *Against unlucky animals, things, etc.*—

In Aetolia, when travellers meet an unlucky animal, they spit three times before continuing the journey.[21] In Macedonia a certain insect which enters houses in summer is supposed to bring fever, and people spit three times when it appears.[22] In Great Britain and Ireland the sight of a single magpie is ominous, and in Cheshire people spit on the ground and make a cross with the foot to drive away ill luck.[23] The Irish, when they see a caterpillar creeping, spit three times on it, lest it may come to the house and sleep with the person who has seen it; they do the same on meeting a stoat in the morning.[24] In Central India people spit three times on seeing a falling star.[25] In Italy, when a hare is released as a scape-animal, to remove disease, the officiant must spit three times behind it, and must not look back or leave the house for three-quarters of an hour.[26] In Kumaun, in order to stop a hail-storm, people spit on the stones as they fall, or sprinkle on them some drops of blood from the body of a noted magician.[27] It is a common practice to spit on a witch

1 Napier, p. 98 f.
2 S. M. Zwemer, *Arabia, the Cradle of Islam*, Edinburgh, 1900, p. 282.
3 *FLR* ii. [1879] 36 f.
4 *HN* xxix. 32, xxviii. 48, 61, 77. 5 *Ib.* xxix. 12.
6 *Ib.* xxvii. 75. 7 *Ib.* xxviii. 5. 8 *Ib.* xxxii. 29.
9 Thurston, *Omens and Superstitions of S. India*, London, 1912, p. 98.
10 C. G. Leland, *Etruscan Roman Remains*, London, 1892, p. 297.
11 J. T. Bent, *The Cyclades*, London, 1885, p. 436.
12 H. A. Rose, *Glossary of Tribes and Castes*, Lahore, 1911, ii. 19.
13 *FL* xxi. 388. 14 *FLJ* i. [1883] 359; cf. Grimm, iv. 1789.
15 *FL* vii. 143. 16 *Ib.* v. 283.
17 G. F. Abbott, *Macedonian Folk-lore*, Cambridge, 1903, p. 143; cf. Persius, *Sat.* ii. 30 ff.; Petronius, 131; R. Rodd, *Customs and Lore of Modern Greece*, London, 1892, p. 161 f.
18 Napier, p. 39.
19 Skeat-Blagden, i. 153. 20 Grimm, iii. 1102.
21 Lawson, p. 307. 22 Abbott, p. 110.
23 *NQ*, 4th ser., xii. [1873] 327.
24 *Ib.* p. 469; *FL* xxii. [1911] 452. 25 *NINQ* ii. 184.
26 Leland, p. 259 f. 27 *NINQ* iii. 135.

or sorcerer, or, as a protective, to get the witch to spit on her supposed victim.[1] Muḥammad, in order to make a bad dream harmless, used to spit three times over the left shoulder—a habit still prevailing in Egypt.[2] In the Ægean Islands, when dough is being kneaded by a woman, if another woman chances to arrive, she must spit on the ground to charm away the evil of her presence; otherwise she will 'carry away the bread with her.'[3] In Shetland, when a sick person describes his ailment, the listener is apt to have the disease conveyed to himself, unless he spits covertly.[4]

Among the Kikuyu of E. Africa 'if a man hears that a near relative is very ill he makes a point of going to see him, and takes the precaution of getting him to spit ceremonially on his hand and rub his visitor on his navel. If a man goes to see his sick father or mother he takes a piece of mutton fat, and the sick parent ceremonially spits on it, and the visitor rubs the saliva covered piece of fat on his navel.'[5]

The same procedure takes place on hearing unlucky names.

In parts of Wales it was the custom to spit when the name of the Devil was mentioned, and at the prayer in the Litany 'to beat down Satan under our feet.'[6] In Greece, if children are sent to draw water, they must spit three times into the spring before they dip their pitchers, to escape the Nereids; in ford rites the traveller spits in the water before crossing or when crossing haunted water.[7]

Muḥammad ordained: 'There is a demon called Khinzab, who casts doubt into prayer; when you are aware of it, take protection with God, and spit over your left arm three times. . . . When you stand up to prayer, spit not in front because you are then in God's presence; neither spit on your right hand, because an angel is there; spit therefore on your left side, or under your feet, and throw earth over it.'[8]

The evil influence of seeing the moon through glass or through the bough of a tree is broken by taking a piece of money from the pocket and spitting on each side of the coin.

In Clare, when the new moon is seen for the first time, people turn thrice sunwards, bowing and spitting at each turn.[9]

Spitting thus becomes a symbolical purification from the effects of tabu.

In Japan 'in the Izanagi myth a God of the Spittle (Haya-tama no wo) is the result of that deity's spitting during the ceremony of divorce. The "spittle" deity is here associated with another God, who is styled a God of Purification. A commentator on this passage says that "at the present day spitting is essential in the purification ceremony." The ritual, however, does not mention it. Another writer adds that "this is the reason why at the present day people spit when they see anything impure." In the myth of Susa no wo spittle is mentioned along with the nails of the fingers and toes and nose-mucus among the materials for expiatory offerings. When Hohodemi is recommended to "spit thrice" before giving back the lost fish-hook to his brother, a magical effect is probably intended, such as to convey to him any impurity which may have become attached to his own person. Rinsing the mouth as a purifying ceremony before pronouncing an oath is mentioned in the *Nihongi* [ii. 96].'[10]

9. Reinforcing the powers of spittle.—The efficacy of the saliva is increased by spitting out certain substances with it.

At the Lemuria the Roman house-father laid the ghosts by spitting out black beans as he walked, saying, 'With these I redeem me and mine.'[11] In Melanesia a charm for stopping rain is to chew ginger, which is then expectorated in a fine spray; the same process, with appropriate words, is used to propitiate or avert any possibly dangerous influence, as, *e.g.*, that of a stranger; Government parties and camps are charmed by a man walking round them and spraying chewed ginger from his mouth.'[12] When the Shans are building a house, they chew betel-nut and spit it into each hole dug for a post, to expel evil spirits; to expel disease the Malay medicine-man, with a charm, ejects chewed betel-leaf on the patient's person, and, when taking omens for agriculture, the farmer chews betel, repeats charms, and spits it out in the direction of the cardinal points.[1] At meals the Hausas always spit out some of the kola-nut on the ground as an offering.[2]

To relieve evil dreams the Zulu medicine-man prescribes: 'When you dream of him, take this medicine and chew it; then take a stone or a piece of firewood, and spit on it the spittle which is in your mouth when you dream of him, mixed with this medicine . . . and throw it behind your back without looking.'[3]

10. The use of saliva in magic.—This assumes many forms which may be explained on the principles already stated.

In N. India, at cotton-picking, women spit out parched rice as a magical mode of improving the produce.[4] In a Vedic charm to appease wrath the person takes a stone, spits round it while reciting a charm, and lays an arrow on a bow while standing in the shadow of the wrathful one.[5] Natives of Australia of the Irriakura [a certain bulb] totem, before eating the tubers, rub them in their hands, and, putting them in their mouths, blow them out again in all directions, obviously to increase the crop.[6] In W. Africa the owner of a portable charm, in the morning, before speaking to any one, wets his finger with saliva, draws it over the amulet, and then down his forehead, saying: 'May every man, woman, and child do good to me.'[7] In Shetland the fishermen spit into the mouth of the last caught cod, 'and the consequence, they say, is that it will be followed by a fish equally large or larger.'[8] In India it is believed that buffalo's saliva, if applied to the soles of the feet, causes sleep, possibly because the animal is sluggish.[9]

'The Galelareese think that when your teeth are being filed you should keep spitting on a pebble, for this establishes a homeopathic connexion between you and the pebble, by virtue of which your teeth will henceforth be as hard and durable as a stone.'[10]

11. Toleration and horror of saliva.—Among some people saliva, preferably that of women, is not regarded with abhorrence.

In some of the Polynesian islands the kava root is chewed by old women in a ceremonial way and distributed at feasts.[11] Among some American Indian tribes cassava root is chewed by young women and the liquor drunk.[12] It is believed that the Kafir beer is made in the same way.[13]

But among people, like the Hindus, who are subject to rigid tabus of food and drinking it is regarded with disgust.

Dubois remarks that 'their strong aversion to wind instruments of music' is due to 'their insurmountable horror of saliva. They would look on a man who spat upon the floor as quite destitute of good manners. Spittoons are to be found in every house; but should none be provided and any one require to spit he would have to go outside.'[14]

The danger of treading on saliva is as old as the days of Manu,[15] and has been perpetuated in the custom which prevailed among some menial tribes in Bombay, Madras, and the Central Provinces up to quite recent times, of requiring them to carry spitting-pots hung round their necks in order to avoid danger to travellers.[16] Spitting on a man of high caste is a serious offence in India. 'They who spat upon the Brāhmaṇa . . . sit in the middle of a pool of blood, chewing hair.'[17] If a low caste man spits on a superior, the king shall cause his lips to be cut off.[18] After spitting, a Brāhman has to sip water.[19]

In Ceylon 'the most dreaded of all punishments under the Kandyan dynasty was to hand over the lady of a high caste offender to the Rodiyas [degraded menials]; and the mode of her adoption was by the Rodiya taking betel from his own mouth and placing it in hers, after which till death her degradation was indelible.'[20]

Buddhist monks in Burma may not spit on green grass or in fresh water.[21] The ancient Persians never defiled a river with

---

1 Hartland, *LP* ii. 272 f.; Grimm, iii. 1102 f.
2 *NINQ* i. 120; E. W. Lane, *The Modern Egyptians*⁵, London, 1871, i. 330.
3 *FL* xviii. [1907] 330.
4 *County Folk-lore*, III., *Orkney and Shetland Islands*, London, 1903, p. 159.
5 C. W. Hobley, 'Kikuyu and Kamba Religious Beliefs and Customs,' *JRAI* xli. [1911] 429.
6 *NQ*, 4th ser., viii. [1871] 547, 11th ser., iii. [1911] 148.
7 Lawson, p. 160; *FL* xxi. [1910] 159; Grimm, iii. 1102 f.
8 Muḥammad ibn 'Abd Allah, *Mishcat-ul-Masabih*, tr. A. N. Mathews, Calcutta, 1809–10, i. 24, 150.
9 *NQ*, 4th ser., xi. [1873] 141; *FL* xxii. 54.
10 W. G. Aston, *Shinto*, London, 1905, p. 260 f.; cf. p. 114.
11 Ovid, *Fasti*, v. 429 ff.; W. W. Fowler, *The Roman Festivals*, London, 1899, p. 109.
12 C. G. Seligmann, *The Melanesians of British New Guinea*, London, 1910, p. 735; cf. pp. 85, 287.

---

1 Mrs. Leslie Milne, *Shans at Home*, London, 1910, p. 101; Skeat-Blagden, i. 366.
2 A. J. N. Tremearne, *The Tailed Head-hunters of Nigeria*, London, 1912, p. 247.
3 H. Callaway, *The Religious System of the Amazulu*, London, 1870, p. 160.
4 Crooke, *PR*² ii. 306.
5 *SBE* xlii. 479.
6 J. G. Frazer, *Totemism and Exogamy*, London, 1910, i. 110 f.
7 *FL* xxii. 397.
8 *County Folk-lore*, III., *Orkney and Shetland Islands*, p. 166.
9 *PNQ* iii. 26.
10 *GB*³, pt. i., *The Magic Art*, London, 1911, i. 157.
11 *JAI* xxvii. [1898] 424 f.
12 H. A. Wickham, 'Notes on the Soumoo or Woolwa Indians,' *JAI* xxiv. [1895] 203; Bancroft, *NR* i. 739.
13 E. S. Hartland, 'Travel Notes in S. Africa,' *FL* xvii. [1906] 481.
14 *Hindu Manners*³, p. 183.
15 *Laws*, iv. 132.
16 *BG* ix. pt. i. [1901] p. 341, xx. [1884] 176; Thurston, *Castes and Tribes*, i. 44, iii. 428; *Eth. Surv. Central Provinces*, ix. [Allahabad, 1911] 97.
17 *SBE* xlii. 171.
18 Manu, *Laws*, viii. 282.
19 *Ib.* v. 145.
20 J. Tennent, *Ceylon*, London, 1860, ii. 189.
21 Shway Yoe, *The Burman*, London, 1882, i. 147.

the secretions of their bodies, and Deioces forbade any one to spit in the royal presence; the term *hikhra*, 'impurity,' was applied to bodily refuse or excretions from men or dogs, including saliva.[1] In India to spit in the direction of the tomb of a saint excites his wrath; and, in China, if any one dares to spit towards the north, he outrages the gods and profanes their presence.[2] The prohibition against spitting on fire is very common. In Scotland some evil is likely to befall those who do so.[3] Negroes in Jamaica believe that spitting in the fire causes the saliva to dry up.[4] On the Lower Congo, if a person spits in the fire, his blood will become thin, his hair turn reddish, and dropsy of the stomach will follow.[5] The Yezidis never spit in the fire.[6]

'Even the breath of man or his spittle is sufficient to desecrate it [the Iranian sacred fire]. Therefore even the priest before the fire-altar must perform his ceremonies and recite his prayers with his mouth covered.'[7] 'A decent man will not spit or eject any impurity in front of the moon, fire, the sun, water, wind, or any respectable person.'[8]

LITERATURE.—E. S. Hartland, *The Legend of Perseus*, London, 1894-96, ii. 258 ff.; J. E. Crombie, 'The Saliva Superstition,' *The International Folk-lore Congress, 1891: Papers and Transactions*, London, 1892, p. 249 ff.; J. Tuchman, 'La Fascination,' *Mélusine*, Paris, 1878- , vols. i., ii., v., vi., viii., ix.; C. de Mensignac, *Recherches ethnographiques sur la salive et le crachat*, Bordeaux, 1892. The classical references have been collected and discussed by F. W. Nicholson, *Harvard Studies in Classical Philology*, viii. [Boston, 1897] 23 ff.

W. CROOKE.

SALT.—See METALS AND MINERALS, vol. viii. p. 591 f.

SALUTATIONS.—Salutations have in all parts of the world been an index of ethics and frequently have had religious significance. They vary from the elaborate ceremonies by which savages of different tribes prove to one another, when they approach, that they have no hostile intent, to the informal greetings with which modern civilized man accosts a comrade.

1. Australian savages probably preserve better than other peoples savage customs in their purest form.

'They have a very strict code of etiquette and distinct terms, implying strong disapproval, which they apply to any member of the tribe who does not observe this. Visits are frequently made, either by individuals or by parties of men and women, to friendly groups of natives living in distant parts. If it be only one man who is paying a visit he will often, in the first place, make a series of smokes so as to inform those to whose camp he is coming that some one is approaching.'[9] The fact that he thus makes his approach known proves that he has no hostile intention. 'Coming within sight of the camp he does not at first go close up to it, but sits down in silence. Apparently no one takes the slightest notice of him, and etiquette forbids him from moving without being invited to do so. After perhaps an hour or two one of the older men will walk over to him and quietly seat himself on the ground beside the stranger. If the latter be the bearer of any message, or of any credentials, he will hand these over, and then perhaps the old man will embrace him and invite him to come into the camp, where he goes to the *ungunja* (men's camp) and joins the men. Very likely he will be provided with a temporary wife during his visit, who will of course belong to the special group with which it is lawful for him to have marital relations.'[10]

Spencer and Gillen[11] describe what actually took place when a party of some thirty Arunta men visited a group of Alice Springs people.

The Arunta group, each wearing two curiously flaked sticks on his head, with a tuft of eagle-hawk feathers in his waist, and armed with boomerang and spears, sat down about half a mile away from the Alice Springs camp. After a time they were invited to come up. They did so on the run, holding their spears aloft. Some of the older Alice Springs women came out to meet them, gesticulating, yelling, and dancing wildly before them. They were received in a small flat among some hills. As they approached the spot some Alice Springs men stood on the tops of the surrounding hillocks, their bodies being sharply outlined against the sky, waving their spears. As soon as the visitors had reached the open flat, they were joined by a number of local men. All then formed into a series of lines four deep and marched round and round the place, led by the chief man of the visitors. This march was accompanied by a considerable amount of excitement, and soon the whole camp—men, women, and children—were assembled at the spot. When this preliminary dance was over, the visitors sat down on the level space and the Alice Springs people grouped themselves on the rocks at one side. The head man of the visiting party then collected all the flaked sticks and handed them over to the head man of the Alice Springs group. This indicated that the visitors came with no hostile intent. A fire was then made and the sticks were burned.

Danger of hostile attack had not yet passed, for after a short pause members of the Alice Springs group began, one after another, to taunt individual visitors with various delinquencies. One was accused of not having mourned properly for his father-in-law, an Alice Springs man; another was challenged to fight for having killed the brother of an Alice Springs man, while a visitor accused a local man of not having cleared out of camp according to custom when his father-in-law died. He should have remained away until the grass was green upon the father-in-law's grave. These and other taunts led to individual scuffles. A general *mêlée* followed, during which every one seemed to be accusing every one else; the women ran in and out among the men, all of whom were talking or yelling at the top of their voices, while spears and boomerangs were raised ready to be thrown. After about three-quarters of an hour the men separated and camped apart. During the next day the relations of the two camps were strained, but by the third day harmony was restored.

The same authorities also relate[1] the ceremonies by which the Warramunga tribe welcomed a party of men from the Walpari tribe.

The visitors sent a messenger ahead to give warning of their approach, and about mid-day six Warramunga men went out to meet them, taking food and water with them. Here they remained until late in the afternoon. Then the local people assembled on a specially cleared space of ground a quarter of a mile from the main camp. They were divided into three groups—a central group of men and two side groups of women. They all stood except two of the principal men, who squatted on the ground. The group of women that came from the territory nearest to the Walpari, peculiarly decorated with white spots running down their breasts and across their shoulders, moved backwards and forwards with arms extended as if beckoning to the strangers to come on. A few local men had meanwhile joined the strangers, and now approached with them in single file. The leader carried a spear, but with the point turned towards the ground; each of the others carried a spear, but grasped it near the head, to show that he had no hostile intent. As they approached, they performed a series of evolutions in the form of a huge S. At the close of each evolution they grouped themselves about the leader for a minute or two, shouting '*Wah! wah!*' The group of women that had beckoned to them answered with the same cry. Finally, at a signal from one of the local men, they approached the Warramunga people. The women who had answered their cry fell in behind them and performed the last evolution with them. The women then returned to their place, and the visitors sat down on the ground. They had their backs to the Warramunga men and were about five yards from them. After a silence of two or three minutes the women who had taken part in the evolution, at a signal from the same old man, threw food at the visitors. The strangers caught it, and the women returned to their places while the visitors ate the food. The Warramunga men, with the exception of three officials, then withdrew. These officials gave the visitors more food, apologizing for the smallness of the quantity. After the repast was over, the visitors were led to camp. In the evening a dance was performed in honour of their arrival.

These Australian customs indicate, perhaps, the kind of elaborate etiquette by which in savage days men everywhere approached strangers. Since the establishment of settled civilized society forms of salutation have been greatly simplified. These forms naturally vary almost endlessly in different parts of the world. To describe all the variations would demand a volume. It may be noted in general that among equals salutations tend to become brief and simple, while salutations to sovereigns by their subjects, or to persons of higher rank by those of lower rank, retain much elaborate ceremoniousness.

2. Civilized equals, as a rule, greet one another briefly and simply, though naturally the salutation to a friend who has been long absent, or to an equal to whom one is introduced for the first time, is more elaborate and formal than the greeting given to a comrade with whom one associates daily. Greetings of the last-mentioned type assume many

1 Herod. i. 139, 99; M. Haug, *Essays on the Sacred Language, Writings, and Religion of the Parsis*, London, 1907, p. 325 n.

2 R. K. Douglas, *Confucianism and Taoism*, London, 1877, p. 268.

3 Napier, p. 37. 4 *FL* xv. [1904] 211. 5 *Ib.* xx. 476.

6 A. H. Layard, *Nineveh and its Remains*, London, 1849, i. 301.

7 W. Geiger, *Civilization of the E. Irānians*, Eng. tr., London, 1885-86, i. 10.

8 *Vishnu Purana*, ed. H. H. Wilson, London, 1840, p. 311; cf. Manu, *Laws*, iv. 52.

9 Spencer-Gillen, *The Northern Tribes of Central Australia*, p. 569.

10 *Ib.* p. 570. 11 *Ib.* p. 570 ff.

1 Spencer-Gillen, *The Northern Tribes of Central Australia*, p. 576 ff.

forms. The ancient Greeks said, Χαῖρε!, 'Be glad!', 'Be joyful!' The Romans said, '*Salve!*', 'Be well!', 'Be in good health,' or, more formally, '*Salvere jubeo*,' 'I bid you be well.' The idea underlying this Roman salutation underlies that of many modern peoples, though in different countries the reference to the health of one's friends is expressed in different ways. Thus in English one says, 'How are you?', 'How do you do?', or 'I hope you are well?' The French say, '*Comment vous portez-vous?*', 'How do you carry yourself?', and the Germans, '*Wie befinden Sie sich?*', 'How do you find yourself?' Similarly the Arabic '*Salaam aleika*,' 'Peace be unto thee!', includes the idea of a wish for the health of the one saluted, as did the Hebrew '*Shalom*,' 'Peace!' Both, however, included much more, as will be noted below.

In common intercourse still less formal greetings are generally employed. Thus in English we say, 'Good morning!' (Old English, 'Good morrow!'), 'Good day!', or 'Good evening!' The Germans say, '*Guten Morgen!*', the French, '*Bon jour!*', the Italians, '*Buono giorno!*' The Arabs of the Levant similarly say, '*Naharak saïd!*', 'May your day be happy!'. All these imply the wish that the one saluted may have a happy day or evening. Possibly the original meaning was, 'May God give you a good day!' In Occidental lands one replies to such a greeting by simply repeating it, but in the Levant politeness demands that the response shall add something to the original wish. Thus, when a friend says, '*Naharak saïd!*', it is polite to reply, '*Naharak saïd wa mubarrak!*', 'May your day be happy and blessed!' In Japan the greetings among equals are similarly brief. Thus in the morning one says to a friend, '*Ohayo!*', literally, 'Honourably early!'; later one says, '*Konnichiwa!*', literally, 'To-day!'; and in the evening the greeting is '*Oyasuminasai!*', 'Honourably rest!' In like manner in China one says, '*Tso shan!*', literally, 'Early time!', which is equivalent to 'Good morning!', and '*Tso tau!*', 'Early rest!', for 'Good night!' The Japanese also have a greeting which makes inquiry for one's health—'*Ikagadesuka?*', 'How is it?' In Occidental countries the more formal salutations addressed to friends who have been long absent or to persons to whom one is introduced for the first time are not as a rule crystallized into such set phrases as those that have just been considered. They express the pleasure of the speaker at seeing a friend again or at making the acquaintance of the stranger: 'I am glad to see you again!', 'I am glad to meet you!', or 'I am delighted to see you!' The Japanese, when introduced to a stranger, say, '*Hajimeete omeni kakaiimusu!*', literally, 'See you for the first time!' A young person meeting an older person says, '*Doka yoroshiku!*', 'Please in your favour!' The Chinese have a form of salutation, '*Yat yat pat kiu ue sam tsau hai!*', literally, 'One day not see like three falls!', equivalent to 'If I do not see you for a day, it is like three years!'.

In the Occident, when one receives a call, the greetings are soon over and the time is passed in conversation upon other topics, but in Syria the greetings and inquiries for the guest's health and that of his family last for some time, and during the call the conversation will often be interrupted by saying the greetings and making the inquiries all over again. Among equals the salutations at parting are as a rule brief and informal. The Greeks employed at times the same phrase as in greeting, Χαῖρε! at others Ἔρρωσθε! 'Be strengthened!'. The Romans said, '*Vale!*', or '*Valeas!*', 'Be well!', 'Be strong!' Akin to this is the English 'Farewell!', meaning, 'May it go well with you!', or 'May you prosper!' More frequently 'Good-bye' is employed. This is believed by many to be a corruption of 'God be with you!'. If this be the correct etymology, it has a religious colouring. Probably a similar thought underlay the German '*Auf Wiedersehen!*' and the French '*Au revoir!*' Of similar import was the Hebrew parting salutation, 'Go in peace!' (1 S 20^{42}), and the modern Arabic '*Ma'salameh*,' 'With peace!' The Chinese say, '*Maan maan haang*,' 'Slowly, slowly walk!', or '*Tsing wooi*,' 'Please return!' The Japanese say, '*Sayōnara*,' 'If it must be so!'

Along with the words which are uttered in formal and impressive salutations there are often physical contacts. These vary with different countries and with the degree of intimacy between the persons concerned. In civilized countries the most common and universal form of contact is 'shaking hands.' The persons performing the salutation grasp each other by the right hand and gently shake or press the hand thus grasped. The cordiality of the salutation may be graded by the vigour or listlessness of the pressure. Another method of expressing cordial salutation frequent among relatives and intimate friends is kissing (*q.v.*), sometimes on the cheek, or, in cases of great intimacy, on the mouth. In some countries kissing is largely confined to greetings between women. In Syria men as well as women kiss one another, often on both cheeks. Sometimes men will grasp one another by the shoulders and, without kissing, place the head first over one shoulder and then over the other. Perhaps this is the modern survival of 'falling on the neck' (Gn 33^4 45^{14}). Still another method of physical contact is 'touching noses.' This is employed among various savage peoples, as, *e.g.*, the Melanesians.[1]

Even when there is no physical contact, any salutation which is at all formal is accompanied by a bow or an inclination of the head. This is almost universal in modern civilized society, and in some parts of the world the custom is very ancient. Confucius is said by his disciples to have bowed forward when saluting one who was in mourning.[2] In Syria a bow is often accompanied by a sweeping motion of the right hand towards the ground. At other times the hand is made to touch one's breast, lips, and forehead.

In some countries there is a strict etiquette concerning salutations.

> 'Among modern Moslems one riding should first salute one on foot; one who passes by should first salute a person standing or sitting; a small party those of a large party; a young person should be first saluted by the aged. One who enters a house should first salute the people of that house.'[3]
>
> Similarly among the Tikopia of Melanesia[4] 'a man who wishes to pass another who is sitting down will call out as he approaches: "*O mata, mata*," meaning "eye," and if the answer comes "*Poi, erau*," "Yes, all right," he goes by. If there are two or more people sitting down, he will say, "*Oto mata*," and will be answered as before. Several men going together ask leave to pass in the same way. A man walks upright, but a woman who is passing bends down slightly with her hands between her thighs. If a man went by without the proper greeting, it would be supposed that he was angry and he would have to return and sit down near those whom he had passed. If he explained that this behaviour had been due to carelessness, he would be called a fool and his apologies would be accepted. . . . When a man goes to visit another at his house, he calls out the name of the occupant at some distance, and if the latter is at home, the visitor is invited to enter. If there is no answer, the visitor will wait for a time and then go away. Only near relatives may enter a house without invitation. Similarly in the Levant a Moslem on approaching the house of a neighbour gives a peculiar call in order that the women may retire to their own apartments before he enters.'

It is not possible to trace in detail the customs of salutation among all peoples within the compass of an article. Certain forms of etiquette are observed throughout the world. Among the peasantry of

1 See W. H. R. Rivers, *The Hist. of Melanesian Society*, i. 305.

2 *Analects*, bk. x. ch. xvi. 2 f.

3 E. W. Rice, *Orientalisms in Bible Lands*, p. 79.

4 Rivers, p. 324 f.

Palestine, *e.g.*, one says to a guest, '*Fût*,' 'Enter,' '*Foddel!*', 'Welcome!', '*Marḥabâ!*', 'Welcome!', or '*Mîyet marḥabâ!*', 'A hundred welcomes!' One familiarly asks, '*Kaif ḥalak?*', 'How are you?' The reply is, '*Ḥumdillah*,' 'Praise God!', *i.e.* 'Praise God I am well,' the full form of the phrase being '*Ḥumdillah salaameh*.' In the early morning one greets another with '*Ṣubaḥkum b'l-khair!*', 'May your morning be in good [fortune]!', to which the reply is, '*Yâ ṣubaḥ el-khair*,' 'Oh, the morning is good!' At evening the greeting is '*Mesaikum b'l-khair!*', and the response, '*Mesâ el-khair!*' At night it is '*Lailtak saideh!*', 'May your night be happy!'[1]

3. To monarchs. — Superiors and especially monarchs are in all countries saluted with much greater formality than equals. In the countries around the eastern end of the Mediterranean it was customary in ancient times to prostrate oneself before a monarch. Thus Araunah, the Jebusite, bowed himself before David with his face to the ground (2 S 24^{20}). Not only the foreigner, but Nathan, David's frequent adviser, did likewise (1 K 1^{23}), and even David's favourite wife, Bathsheba ($1^{16, 31}$). Such homage was not, however, confined to kings, but was also accorded to prophets (see 2 K 2^{15} 4^{37}). Its motive was probably the belief that in both kings and prophets a superhuman spirit dwelt. Physicians are still often thus saluted at hospitals in the Levant.[2] Perhaps this is in part an earnest way of proffering a request for healing, just as Esther is said to have fallen on her face before Ahasuerus (Xerxes) when she wished to make a particularly urgent request (Est 8^{3}). Where such customs prevailed, it was natural that conquered princes should fall on their faces and kiss the feet of their conquerors. The act was at once an expression of homage and an appeal for mercy. Assyrian kings say again and again in their annals that such-and-such a king came and kissed their feet, and the Black Obelisk of Shalmaneser III. pictures Sua, king of Gilzan, and Jehu, king of Israel, in the act of doing this.

Similar customs are found in many other parts of the world. Thus among the Melanesians a visitor who visits a chief in his house kneels at the door and moves towards the chief on his hands and knees. When he reaches him, they touch noses in the customary manner, and the visitor withdraws a pace or two, and sits down cross-legged. No other position is allowed in the presence of the chief. When the interview is finished, the visitor asks permission to go, and leaves on his hands and knees in a similar manner, without turning his back to the chief. If a man wishes to pass a chief out of doors, he will say, '*O mata pa*' (*mata*, 'eye'; *pa*, 'father'). The chief will reply, '*Elau! saere, opoi!*', 'All right! Walk, yes,' and the man will go by on hands and knees as when approaching him.[3]

In India similarly deep obeisance has always been performed before a sovereign. Thus we read in the *Rāmāyaṇa*:

> 'And with greetings and obeisance spake their message calm and bold,
> Softly fell their gentle accents as their happy tale they told.
> Greetings to thee, mighty monarch!'[4]

According to the *Sakuntala* of Kalidasa, the Shakespeare of India, it was customary for subjects on approaching a king to shout, 'May the king be victorious!', 'O king, be victorious!', or 'May our sovereign be victorious!'[5]

In like manner in less effusive China the customs, as we learn from the *Analects* of Confucius, were not radically different. When Confucius entered the gate of the palace of the prince, it was with body somewhat bent forward, almost as though he could not be admitted. When passing the throne, his look would change somewhat; he would turn aside and make a sort of obeisance, and the words that he spoke seemed as though he were deficient in utterance.[1]

At modern European courts the ceremonial, though less demonstrative than that among many of the ancients, nevertheless emphasizes in a variety of ways that the sovereign is not an ordinary mortal and must be much more ceremoniously saluted. The climax of salutations to royal personages is found in the public ceremonies of welcome which are prepared for them when they pay visits to cities on public occasions or return from victories or long absences. A fine literary description of such a welcoming salute is found in the *Rāmāyaṇa*, in the passage which tells of Rāma's return to Ayodhya:

> 'Elephants in golden trappings thousand chiefs and nobles bore,
> Chariot cars and gallant chargers speeding by Sarayu's shore,
>
> And the serried troops of battle marched with colours rich and brave,
> Proudly o'er the gay procession did Ayodhya's banners wave.
>
> In their stately gilded litters royal dames and damsels came,
> Queen Kausalya first and foremost, Queen Sumitra rich in fame,
>
> Pious priest and learned Brahman, chief of guild from near and far,
> Noble chief and stately courtier with the wreath and water jar.
>
> . . . .
>
> Stately march of gallant chargers and the roll of battle car,
> Heavy tread of royal tuskers and the beat of drum of war.
>
> . . . .
>
> Women with their loving greetings, children with their joyous cry,
> Tottering age and lisping infant hailed the righteous chief and high.
>
> Bharat lifted up his glances unto Rama from afar,
> Unto Sita, unto Lakhsman, seated on the Pushpa car,
>
> And he wafted high his greetings and he poured his pious lay,
> As one wafts the pious *mantra* to the rising God of Day!'[2]

Mutatis mutandis, similar scenes of salutation have occurred in all civilized countries. They have been accorded not to kings alone, but to presidents, generals, governors, and distinguished visitors. Salutations given in different cities and countries to visiting delegations since the Great War began, such as the French delegation to the United States of America in May 1917, although they lacked the peculiar colour imparted by the native Indian bent as well as the religious flavour of that accorded to Rāma, in spontaneous heartiness and general interest resembled that described in the epic.

4. In letters.—Salutations in letters exhibit much the same variation as other greetings, though they have some peculiarities of their own. Among the ancient Romans the salutation in a letter was reduced to a designation of the person addressed and of the writer of the letter. Thus a letter of Cicero, selected at random, begins: '*Cicero Attico S.*,'[3] the '*S.*' standing for *socio*, 'colleague.' A letter of Pliny selected in the same way begins: '*C. Plinius Hispullæ suæ S.*'[4] This dignified brevity corresponds to the French form, in which after the name of the person addressed a simple '*Monsieur*' or '*Madame*' is placed. In very

[1] Cf. E. Grant, *The Peasantry of Palestine*, p. 161 f.
[2] Cf. Rice, p. 78. [3] Rivers, p. 305.
[4] Cf. R. C. Dutt, *The Ramayana and the Mahabharata condensed into English Verse*, p. 7.
[5] See the ed. published by T. Holme, London, 1902, pp. 43 and 76.

[1] *Analects*, bk. x. chs. 1–4. [2] Dutt, p. 167 f.
[3] See *M. T. Ciceronis Epistolæ*, ed. J. Billerbeck, Hanover, 1836, i., *Ep.* lx.
[4] Pliny, *Epistularum Libri Novem*, ed. H. Keil, Leipzig, 1876, p. 161.

formal letters in English the name is followed by a simple 'Sir' or 'Madam,' but it is far more common to prefix to the 'Sir' or 'Madam' a conventional 'Dear.' Similarly the Germans in beginning a letter place after the name of the person addressed '*Mein Herr*,' literally 'My lord,' though *Herr* has been attenuated till it means simply 'gentleman.' In ancient Babylonia it was customary to insert after the address a sentence of good wishes. Thus in a letter selected at random from the time of the Ist dynasty of Babylon (*c.* 2000 B.C.) we find the following beginning:

'To Manatum speak, saying: Yamsi-Shamash says: "May Shamash and Marduk make thee to live!"'[1]

Then the business follows. Most of the letters from the time of the Neo-Babylonian and early Persian empires (*c.* 550–450 B.C.) are somewhat more elaborate. An equal is addressed as 'brother,' a priest as 'father.' Thus a letter taken at random begins:

'Letter from Nabu-zira-ibni to Rimut, his brother. May Bel and Nabu grant peace unto my brother.'

Another runs:

'Letter from Nabu-zira-ibashshi to the lady Sikkû, my sister. May Bel and Nabu grant peace and life unto my sister.'

Still another:

'Letter from Nabu-suma-ibni unto the priest of Sippar, my father. May Bel and Nabu grant peace and life unto my father.'[2]

A somewhat similar form of letter was widely employed in the Levant for centuries. A letter written from Egypt in 172 B.C. begins:

'Isias to her brother, greeting: If you are well and other things happen as you wish, it would be in accordance with my constant prayer to the gods. I too am in good health, and so is the boy: and all at home make constant remembrance of you.'[3]

In the letters of Paul to the Thessalonians we have the same elements expanded. The salutation is longer; the prayer is made more prominent; and the assertion that the recipients of the letter are constantly borne in mind is more emphatic. Still another letter from Egypt may be cited to show the frequent recurrence of the religious element in such salutations:

'Ammonios to his sister Tachnumi, much greeting: Before all things I pray that you may be in good health, and each day I make the act of worship for you.'[4]

The classical Arabic form of greeting in a letter is given in the story of Bilkis, in the letter which Solomon is said to have written the Sabæan queen:

'From the servant of Allah, Solomon son of David, to Bilkis queen of Saba. In the name of Allah, the Merciful, the Gracious! Peace upon all those who follow the right guidance! As to what follows'[5] (then follows the business in hand).

Epistolary salutations present an endless variety. The above are but a few examples.

As in the case of oral greetings, the salutations in letters addressed to monarchs are more elaborate and tend to greater adulation. The following is typical of the beginnings of letters addressed to Assyrian kings of the Sargonid dynasty:

'To the king my lord, thy servant Ishtar-iddin-apla, chief of the astronomers of Arbela, makes report to the king, my lord. May Nabu, Marduk, and Ishtar of Arbela be gracious to the king, my lord.'[6]

There are many variations in detail. The climax of adulatory addresses to sovereigns is reached in the letters sent by Syrian vassals and officials in the 14th cent. B.C. to their overlord, the king of Egypt. One of these runs:

'Rib-Adda sends to his lord, the king of countries, the great king, the king of battle. May Ba'alat of Gebal give power to the king, my lord. At the feet of my lord, my sun-god, seven times and seven times I fall!' (then the business which called forth the letter is taken up).[1]

In all monarchical countries letters to the sovereign are of course begun in a more formal way than letters to one's equals, though in Occidental countries and in modern times such adulation as was expressed to the kings of Egypt is lacking. The correspondence of one monarch with another (unless they are of close kin, as in modern Europe) has probably always been attended with greater formality than that between private persons. The El-Amarna letters afford us glimpses of the earliest royal international correspondence of which we know. Kings greeted one another as follows:

'To Kadashman-Kharbe king of Karduniash (Babylon), my brother, speak saying: Nimmuria (Amenophis III.), the great king, king of Egypt, thy brother. With me there is peace (or health). With thee may there be peace (or health); to thy house, to thy wife, to thy sons, to thy princes, to thy horses, to thy chariots, in the midst of thy lands may there be peace (or health)!'[2]

The salutations of the Babylonian king and the king of Mitanni to the king of Egypt are variations of this formula.

The salutations at the conclusions of letters differ greatly in different countries and with different individuals. Letters written in ancient Babylonia and Assyria contained no salutation at the end; when the business part was completed, the epistle broke off abruptly. The Romans at the close of a letter wrote a simple '*Vale!*' At the end of many letters written in κοινῇ Greek salutations are sent by the writer to friends of the recipient or members of his family. The term employed is ἀσπάζομαι, 'I welcome,' 'I greet,' 'I salute.'[3] It is employed in the Gospels, where the disciples are bidden to salute the house which they entered (Mt 10^{12}). Similar greetings expressed by the same word are found in the Epistles of Paul (see, *e.g.*, Ro $16^{3ff.}$, 1 Co $16^{19f.}$). In addition to such greetings Greek letters usually concluded with a farewell expressed by some form of the verb ῥώννυμι, 'I strengthen,' 'I make strong.' Thus the letter sent by the Church at Jerusalem to the Christians of Antioch, Syria, and Cilicia (Ac 15^{23-29}) ends with a simple ἔρρωσθε, 'Farewell.' Later Christian usage expanded this. Thus Ignatius concludes his letter to Polycarp with ἔρρωσθε ἐν τῷ Κυρίῳ, 'Farewell in the Lord.' In the papyri the formula is often expanded as ἐρρῶσθαι σε εὔχομαι, 'I pray that you may be strong,'[4] ἐρρῶσθαι σοι εὔχομαι πολλοῖς χρόνοις, 'It be strengthened to you I pray many times.'[5] The Japanese write, '*Oomni gotaisetsuni*,' 'Take care of your honourable body.' In the Occident such salutations have shrunk to an expression of 'good wishes,' 'kind regards,' an assurance of the writer's '*sentiments très distingués*,' or some equivalent formula. Often this is accompanied by a 'Good-bye,' '*Au revoir*,' or '*Auf Wiedersehen*.'

5. The religious element is prominent in many of the salutations which have been noted above. All those which call upon God or some god to bless or to give health breathe a religious atmosphere. This atmosphere is wide-spread; it is found in some degree in most parts of the world, though it is much more prominent among some peoples than among others. There is very little, if any, of it in Japanese salutations. One such Chinese salutation is known to the writer: '*Poo shat tsunk fok fai ko tseung tai*,' 'The gods bless you and make you grow very fast.' In Spain, when one wishes to deny

[1] Cf. A. Ungnad, *Babylonische Briefe aus der Zeit der Hammurapi-Dynastie*, Leipzig, 1914, no. 175.
[2] Cf. R. C. Thompson, *Late Babylonian Letters*, London, 1906, p. 123.
[3] Cf. *Exp.*, 5th ser., viii. [1898] 164. [4] *Ib.* p. 166.
[5] Cf. R. Brünnow, *Chrestomathie aus arabischen Prosaschriftstellern*, Berlin, 1895, p. 8.
[6] From F. Delitzsch, *Assyrische Lesestücke*[5], Leipzig, 1912, p. 92.

[1] From O. Schroeder, *Die Thontafeln von El-Amarna*, no. 56, in *Vorderasiatische Schriftdenkmäler*, xi., Leipzig, 1914.
[2] Cf. J. A. Knudtzon, *Die El-Amarna Tafeln*, Leipzig, 1912, no. 1.
[3] Cf., *e.g.*, B. P. Grenfell and A. S. Hunt, *The Oxyrhynchus Papyri*, London, 1898–1914, x. no. 1296.
[4] *Ib.* viii. no. 1160. [5] *Ib.* no. 1158.

a beggar, he says, 'Pardon brother!' or 'May God relieve you!' The beggar answers, 'Go, your worships, with God; another time it will be.'

Certain religions, such as early Christianity and Muhammadanism, introduced new elements into salutations or gave new emphasis to old ones. The influence of early Christianity upon salutations is patent to one who compares early Christian letters with other letters of the time. This difference is most manifest in letters addressed to groups of people or to churches. Thus in the Epistles of Paul the ordinary χαίρειν is displaced by the benediction: 'Grace to you, and peace, from God our Father and the Lord Jesus Christ' (Ro 1^{7}; cf. also 1 Co 1^{3}, 2 Co 1^{2}, Gal 1^{3}, Eph 1^{2}, Ph 1^{2}, Col 1^{2}). Similarly in place of the farewell ἔρρωσθε he employed a benediction. It varies in different Epistles more than the greeting at the beginning does, but nearly always contains the phrase, 'The grace of our Lord Jesus Christ be with you.'

The letters of Ignatius of Antioch contain a variety of salutations. Like Paul, he introduces considerable theology into his descriptions of the churches addressed, but his actual salutations are much more varied than those of Paul.

Thus to the Smyrnæans he employs πλεῖστα χαίρειν, 'Much greeting'; to the Trallians he says, 'Whom I greet in the fullness in the apostolic manner and pray for much joy' (εὔχομαι πλεῖστα χαίρειν); to the Magnesians, 'In whom [viz. Jesus Christ] may you have much joy' (πλεῖστα χαίρειν ὑμᾶς εἴη); but to the Philadelphians, 'Whom I greet (ἀσπάζομαι) in the blood of Jesus Christ, which is an eternal and abiding joy.'

His final salutations also differ from those in heathen letters of the time.

Thus to the Smyrnæans he says, 'Farewell [or be strong—ἔρρωσθε] in the grace of God'; to the Philadelphians, 'Farewell in Jesus Christ, our common hope'; to the Magnesians, 'Farewell in divine unity, possessing no party spirit, which is Jesus Christ'; to the Trallians, 'Farewell in Jesus Christ, being in subjection to the bishop as to the commandment, likewise also to the presbyter; and each of you love one another with undivided heart. My spirit sanctifies itself for you, not only now, but when I attain to God (for I am still in danger), but faithful is the Father in Jesus Christ to fulfil my desire and yours; in whom may we be found blameless!'

As time passed, this exuberance of Christian greeting in some degree subsided, but still Christian epistolary greeting retained a character of its own. The letters of Augustine, *e.g.*, begin with the salutation '*In Domino salutem.*' As in the letters of Paul and Ignatius of Antioch, many adjectives and sometimes some theology are introduced into the description of the person addressed, but, however much of this there may be, the real address usually concludes with the salutation '*In Domino salutem.*' The parting salutations of the letters of Augustine are exceedingly varied. Sometimes they end with a benediction, sometimes with a simple '*Amen*,'[1] sometimes with a salutation such as: '*Saluto et pignus pacis, quod Domino Deo nostro adjuvante feliciter accepisti ea dilectione qua debeo*';[2] at times they conclude abruptly without salutation.

Again passing over several centuries and taking the letters of Bernard of Clairvaux as an example, we find numerous instances where there is reversion to the old Roman form. Thus one letter begins, '*Bernardus abbas Claræ-Vallis, Romano suo, quod suo*';[3] another, '*Thomæ dilecto filio, Bernardus, quod filio.*'[4] At other times he recurs to the formula of Augustine, '*In Domino salutem*';[5] still again he varies this with such phrases as '*Salutem plurimam dicit.*'[1] Formal salutations at the end of the letter he usually omits.

[1] Cf. *PL* xxxiii. 1013.
[2] *Ib.* 1020.
[3] Cf. *ib.* clxxxii. 240.
[4] *Ib.* 242.
[5] *Ib.* 225.

It is clear from these examples that for a time at least Christianity imparted a religious flavour peculiarly its own to epistolary salutations. Indeed, in circles that are particularly pious some attempts are still made to retain something of this flavour. Such writers begin letters 'Dear brother' and conclude them with 'Yours in the Lord' or a similar phrase.

The colouring that Muhammadanism imparted to epistolary salutations has been already indicated by the quotation made from the story of Bilkis (above, § 4). Islām has, however, imparted a religious significance to one old Semitic greeting, '*Salaameh alaik!*', 'Peace (or health) be to you!', to which the proper reply is, '*Wa alaik salaameh!*', 'And to you be peace!' This is regarded as a proper greeting among believers, but it is thought not quite right to say it to foreigners. When one meets Bedū or Muslims from the desert, who seldom come in contact with foreigners, one may, even though a Christian, receive this greeting, but in the towns, where the inhabitants are sophisticated, one will be saluted with '*Naharak saïd!*' or some phrase to which no religious interpretation could possibly attach. When the Bedū meet one another, they often employ the salutation '*Gawwāk!*', an abbreviation of '*Gawwāk Allah!*', 'May Allah give you strength!' Sometimes the invocation of peace is varied thus: '*Allah yusallimak!*', 'Allah preserve you in peace!'[2]

6. National characteristics are often strikingly manifest in salutations. One needs only to glance at the difference between a list of Japanese salutations and a similar list of those employed in the Levant to be convinced of this. The Japanese greetings are non-religious and self-restrained; they are polite but dignified. Those of the Levant often exhibit great religiosity and servility. Perhaps it is not quite accurate to call these national characteristics, as they are in the Levant confined to no one nation; in this region race has mingled with race as in a great melting-pot until the forms of salutation have in some degree become those of a region rather than a nation. It has been said that the characteristics of Western peoples are also revealed by their greetings. Thus the French '*Comment vous portez-vous?*' betrays the French feeling for artistic effect. The German '*Wie befinden Sie sich?*' is prompted by the Teutonic tendency to introspection; one wishes to know what his neighbour discovers when he turns his outer consciousness in upon his Ego. The English and American 'How do you do?' reveals the social bent towards work and activity; the standard of wellbeing is efficient work.

LITERATURE.—B. Spencer and F. J. Gillen, *The Northern Tribes of Central Australia*, London, 1904, ch. xix.; W. H. R. Rivers, *The Hist. of Melanesian Society*, Cambridge, 1914, i. 305 ff., 324 f.; E. Grant, *The Peasantry of Palestine*, Boston, 1907, pp. 160–165; A. Jaussen, *Coutumes des Arabes au pays de Moab*, Paris, 1908, p. 279 ff.; E. W. Rice, *Orientalisms in Bible Lands*, Philadelphia, 1910, chs. xi. xii.; R. C. Dutt, *The Ramayana and Mahabharata condensed into English Verse*, in 'Everyman's Library,' London and New York, 1910, pp. 166–168; *The Analects of Confucius*, bk. x. (e.g., *Chinese Literature*, London and New York, 1900, in 'Literature of the Orient' series, ed. E. Wilson).

GEORGE A. BARTON.

[1] Cf. *PL* clxxxii. 228.
[2] See A. Jaussen, *Coutumes des Arabes au pays de Moab*, p. 279 f.

SALVATION.

SALVATION (Assyro-Babylonian).—Notwithstanding all the inscriptions of a religious nature left by the Assyro-Babylonians, there are few which show any really spiritual conception of the future life in which the people believed, and the state of existence therein. The belief which they had in heaven and hell ('the land of No-return') was a very different one[1] from that of Christian theology, though the latter is based upon the teaching of the Hebrews (who were likewise Semites) among whom Christianity had its origin. In one thing, however, the creed of the Babylonians and our own are in agreement — the necessity for salvation from the pains of hell. Their conception of that place, however, differed considerably from the views which Christians hold. The hell of the Babylonians was apparently not a place of fire and brimstone, in which the unrighteous were tormented, but simply a domain of ignominious existence, 'where dust was their nourishment, and their food mud.' Both creeds, however, have felt the necessity of salvation from this undesirable abode, whatever its torments and its miseries may have been conceived to be.

The Babylonians, therefore, like the Christians, found a belief in the existence of a 'merciful God' needful, the deity in question being Merodach,[2] though the adjective (*rêminû*) could probably be applied to other divinities of their pantheon. In both cases the right to accord salvation was based upon self-sacrifice; but, unlike Christ, Merodach did not submit to anything resembling the death of the Cross—his self-sacrifice was the conflict waged by him[3] on behalf of Creation as a whole, and the shedding of his blood[4] in order that mankind might come into being.

It is doubtful whether the Babylonians held the dogma of original sin. That some isolated sect may have believed in this is not only possible, but probable. In this connexion it is to be noted that the Babylonians seem to have thought that the sin or misdeed which brought upon a man the anger of the gods might possibly have been an involuntary one. He might, without knowing, have eaten of some forbidden thing or have trampled upon some sacred object. And not only might the sin have been committed unawares, but the deity sinned against might be one whom he did not know. These involuntary sins, with others which were not so, were expiated by punishment in this world; hence the need of litanies and prayers to excite the divine being's commiseration and pardon, so that the sin that a man had sinned might turn to good, and the misdeed that he had committed might be carried away by the wind. No second expiation, in all probability, was in such a case regarded as being necessary; and it may likewise be supposed that, if a man had already been saved from the effects of his sins in this world, no saving power needed to be invoked on his behalf in the world to come.

Another aspect of the question of salvation and divine disfavour, however, is to be found in the final tablet of the Gilgameš legend, which gives descriptions of the two states of happiness and misery, and regards the two differing treatments accorded to the dead (in this case a warrior) as being due to the consideration whether the departed had received due burial or not.[1] But there was apparently something more than this—he had to die the death of the [? righteous], or the like. The happy warrior, who had fallen in battle, supported by his father and mother and attended by his wife, reposed in the resting-place of [? the just], pure (holy) water was given him to drink, and the food which he ate was probably of the same sacred nature.

The above is followed by the second picture. The spirit (*êdimmu*) of him whose corpse had been thrown down on the plain reposed not in the earth. Apparently it remained, in this case, without a caretaker, and was compelled to subsist on the leavings of the dish and the remains of the food which was thrown into the street (? in the great city of the under world, presided over by Ereš-ki-gal and Nergal, her spouse). It is clear that the spirits of the departed, saved and unsaved, needed nourishment, like their contemporaries and descendants who still inhabited the earth.

These details seem to have been given by the spirit of Enkidu (Êa-bani) to his old friend and master, Gilgameš, when the former was allowed to visit earth again and communicate what he had seen in the regions below. But the ideal of existence is that announced by Ut-napištim in the Flood-story which forms the 11th tablet of that same series. In this[2] the Babylonian Noah states that he intended, on account of the hatred of Enlil, the 'older Bêl,' in whose territory he could no longer dwell, to descend to the Abyss, the abode of Êa (Oannes) his lord, where he would henceforth constantly dwell. This view of the life beyond the grave seems to have been that generally accepted by the Sumero-Akkadians of Babylonia during the final centuries of the 3rd millennium B.C., and probably later. When a man died, it was said that his god took him to himself, and we may therefore suppose that there were as many heavens or abodes of bliss as there were great gods in the Babylonian pantheon. Every good man (*i.e.* every man after his god's own heart) was regarded as going and dwelling evermore with the deity whom he had worshipped and served faithfully during his lifetime. Each god thus became a saviour, and had for his faithful servants his own special salvation—even Nergal, the king of the under world, in whose abode the hero Etana[3] seems finally to have dwelt.

The word for 'salvation' in Semitic Akkadian (Babylonian), when found, will probably be some form of *êzēbu*, 'to escape.' For 'to save' the Shaphel (or Shuphul) was used, as in Aramaic: *Aššur-šêziba(n)ni*, 'Aššur, save me'; *Nabû-šêzib-(anni)*, 'Nebo, save (me),' etc., also *Mušêzib-Marduk*, 'Merodach is a saviour,' etc., with such feminines as *Mušêzibtum*, 'She who saves,' in which a goddess's name is understood. [*Êṭēr*]*a gamāl û šûzubu tîdi*, 'Thou knowest (how to) protect, spare, and save (O Šamaš)'; *Yâti Nabû-na'id šar Bâbîli*

1 See *ERE* ii. 316. 2 *Ib.* ii. 311 f.
3 *Ib.* iv. 129, vi. 644.
4 T. G. Pinches, *The OT in the Light of Hist. Records*3, p. 28.

1 *ERE* ii. 316. 2 Pinches3, p. 102.
3 *ERE* ii. 315a.

ina ḫiṭu ilûti-ka rabîti šûzibanni-ma balāṭa ûmu rûqûti ana širikti šurkam, 'As for me, Nabonidus, king of Babylon, save me (O Sin), from sin against thy great divinity, and give (me), as a gift, to live to remote days.' Thus prays the learned restorer of the temple of the moon at Mugheir (Ur of the Chaldees), the restorer of many temples, of divers gods, thus becoming a candidate with many deities for the reward of salvation in their heavenly abodes.

LITERATURE.—Friedrich Delitzsch, *Assyrisches Handwörterbuch*, Leipzig, 1896, p. 35*a*; T. G. Pinches, *The OT in the Light of the Historical Records and Legends of Assyria and Babylonia*,[3] London, 1908, pp. 49–52, *The Religion of Babylonia and Assyria*, do. 1906, p. 120 ff.

T. G. PINCHES.

SALVATION (Buddhist). — As meaning (1) well-being won and held against disaster, (2) assurance and realization of blissful security hereafter, salvation is a structural idea in Buddhism no less than in other religions. The facts of suffering and of death wherever there is life, the possibility of escape *from all three* for all living things —these are corner-stones of Buddhist doctrine. But the question of ultimate safety is developed in accordance with the evolutionary and non-animistic standpoint of that doctrine.

The word 'salvation' has its counterpart in the terms *su-v-atthi* or *sotthi* and *sotthibhāva* ('well-being,' 'health,' *salus*, 'safe,' and 'safety'), and *khema*, or *yogakkhema*, 'security,' 'salvation.' See, *e.g.*, the refrain:

> *Etena saccena suvatthi hotu!*
> 'By this truth salvation may there be!'

in the *Rătănă-sutta* of the *Sutta-Nipāta* and *Khuddaka-pāṭha*; and in the *Mangala-sutta* of the same works:

> 'They who such things have done are nowhere worsted. Everywhere they go to salvation' (or 'walk in safety,' *sotthiṃ gacchanti*),

where 'salvation' and 'safety' refer to present and future. Or, again, the frequent references in the anthologies of the Canon, such as:

> 'O would that I who hourly waste might change
> For that which ne'er decays—who ever burn
> Might change for that cool bliss, e'en for the peace
> That passeth all, safety beyond compare!
> . . . . . Make thee
> Adept in the path to sure salvation leading.
> . . . . .
> Yea, to the mighty haven doth it wend;
> High peace it brings and bliss lies at the end.'[1]

In these verses 'safety,' 'salvation,' 'haven' are all equivalents of [*yogak*] *khema*. And the two terms are combined in a *sutta* of the *Aṅguttara-Nikāya*,[2] where a layman asks Ānanda the Elder whether there is any one thing (or doctrine, *dhamma*) where (*sic*) an earnest devoted member of the order could win emancipation, or eradicate the *āsavas*,[3] or win ultimate *yogakkhema*. Ānanda replies in terms of mental training of eleven stages. The layman exclaims that, whereas, if he were in a burning house, one door would suffice 'to make himself safe (*sotthiṃ*),' he had now learnt of eleven doors to the 'ambrosial'[4] whereby safety was attainable.

To these terms should be added that of 'refuge' (lit. 'resort,' *saraṇa*). To confess that he 'takes refuge in the Buddha, the Norm, the Order' is the first step of every Buddhist layman or *religieux* in the path to salvation.[5] And the *Sutta* literature abounds in similar figures illustrating life as perilous and pointing to the pressing need of seeking salvation.

Coming from terms to meaning, we find that salvation in Buddhism is, ultimately, escape from *dukkha*, *i.e.* from suffering, pain, misery, sorrow, proximately, from the lusts, enmity, and stupidity that inevitably entail suffering, however much they may induce transient delights or satisfaction. These causes of *dukkha* are constantly represented as dangerous, not because, as a body of 'sin,' they set man at enmity with a deity, but because they hold him in bondage to misery now or hereafter. Thus 'salvation,' for a Buddhist, is a state of sentient existence conceived as freed from *dukkha*. Nor is the sentient, conceived as thus freed in a future life, considered as a saved 'soul' or detached entity. Salvation as fruition is the pleasanter environment in some heaven, the happier mental processes set going afresh in a suitable celestial mind-and-body, which are the resultants of previous mental activity. But such salvation is relative only. In a celestial rebirth *dukkha* is driven far away, for the chief sorrow is decay, disease, death, and the gods (*i.e.* the communities of happily reborn persons) live well and long. But eventually death comes again, for life is, in its essence, growth followed by decay. And the only final salvation is to end life, either as *arhat* on earth or as a god in some immaterial heaven. Of the ultimate destiny of those who accomplish the final going out, or *parinibbāna*, as of flame in water, the scriptures speak in solemn triumph, but do not speculate. Neither the words nor the concepts of life apply.

> 'Nowhere is measure for one gone to oblivion,
> That whereby we speak of him—that exists no longer.
> Wholly cut off are all forms of our knowing,
> Cut off the channels of speech, every one.'[1]
>
> 'Whose range is in the Void and th' Unmarked
> And Liberty: as flight of birds in air
> So hard is it to track the trail of him.'[2]
>
> 'Set free from bonds, happy and void of longing
> Him gods and men, here on this earth or yonder
> Or in the heavens, in every sphere of being
> Seeking they seek vainly, they will not find him.'[3]

LITERATURE.—C. A. F. Rhys Davids, *Buddhism* (Home University Library), London, 1912, ch. vii. The texts and translations quoted in the art. are published by the Pāli Text Society. On the subject of assurance of salvation and the grounds thereof see S. Z. Aung and C. A. F. Rhys Davids, *Points of Controversy* (the *Kathāvatthu*), London, 1915, pp. 177, 185, 383.

C. A. F. RHYS DAVIDS.

SALVATION (Christian).—This article does not intrude into the domain of exegetical or doctrinal theology. It attempts to follow, through the history of Israel and through the period covered by the NT, the experience of salvation. The point of view from which it has been written, as well as the conclusion which it seeks to establish, is the unity and continuity of the experience, as well as its vital and growing quality.

I. *THE EXPERIENCE OF SALVATION IN THE HISTORY OF ISRAEL*.—**1. Its interpreters.**—An older method of study went to the OT to discover what it had to say of all topics which theology had defined, and particularly how its utterances anticipated and illustrated conclusions at which dogmatic had arrived. Such a method was, no doubt, mechanical, and inevitably missed the vividness and fullness with which the OT presents the great varieties of religion. But it did grasp one fact of first-rate importance, viz. the unity of the OT as a statement of the salvation experienced in Israel and set forth by its great religious teachers. Its error lay in its conception of unity as bare logical identity, to which the actual increases brought by

[1] C. A. F. Rhys Davids, *Psalms of the Early Buddhists*, 2 vols., London, 1910–13, ii. verses 32, 415, 422.
[2] v. 342 f.
[3] The poisons of sense-desires, renewed life, opinions or error, and nescience.
[4] *Amata*, lit. the 'not-dead,' 'immortal,' a word equivalent to 'salvation,' but implying not safety so much as 'the divine,' or 'bliss,' and, in its first intention, like ἀμβροσία, a heavenly elixir.
[5] *Khuddaka-pāṭha*, i.; *Vinaya Texts*, i. (*SBE* xiii.) 115.

[1] *Sutta-Nipāta*, verse 1075.
[2] *Psalms of the Early Buddhists*, ii.; *Psalms of the Brethren*, verse 92.
[3] C. A. F. Rhys Davids, *Kindred Sayings*, London, 1917, i. 32.

the discipline of centuries are indifferent and irrelevant. It ought to be possible to conserve the truth of this older view without being misled by its rigid and abstract scheme.

The historical and critical method of study has established what the least technically trained mind never failed to discover, viz. that the OT is a history, the history of a salvation, which had very rude and even crude beginnings, which grew in ethical quality and religious meaning, till it was ready under the quickening force of new influences to enter upon a further historic development, of which the NT is the literary record and the whole subsequent history of man the rich and varied consequence. It is literal fact that the salvation which, in the Christian gospel, has penetrated to the confines of the world, and is producing profound and revolutionary changes among all races of men, had its historic origin in the experience of a group of tribes which entered Palestine from the desert and occupied it in the name of Jahweh, their God.

It is in this experience, and in this only, that the significance and value of Israel for the moral progress of mankind consist. The point of interest does not lie in the customs prevalent in Israel, which differed little from those of surrounding peoples; or in the details of legislation, which may have been copied from the laws of nations somewhat higher in the scale of material civilization; or in the apparatus of worship, which, in the earlier periods at any rate, had little in it that was unique or distinctive; or even in the ideas entertained by Hebrews regarding creation, cosmogony, or similar subjects, which seem to have been drawn from the common stock of Semitic reflexion upon the mysteries of the universe. Our valuation of Israel's history depends entirely on its whole scope, and on the tendency manifested in its whole development. An observer of its earlier stages would have found nothing to indicate its future course. He would have noted merely one more Semitic people, and would have predicted no more than an ordinary political career, including possibly a period of imperial expansion, followed by swift decay and complete extinction. In one sense, indeed, such a prediction, made so easily and so confidently, would have been sound and accurate. Israel showed no more political genius than its neighbours and rivals, and shared in the disasters that overtook the Oriental world. All this estimate and prediction, however, would have been superficial, and would have missed the heart of Israel's historic value. Beneath the casing of customs and culture and philosophical opinion, apart from, and deeper than, the surface movements that led through calamity to ruin, there was a life of the spirit, for which it is no more than plain justice to claim absolute uniqueness. It could not have been predicted from the phenomena attendant upon Israel's origin, it could not have been inferred from any qualities displayed by Israel at any stage of its career, that, as the ages rolled by, there would have been developed a conscience singularly enlightened and sensitive, clear to discern everlasting moral verities, and drastic in self-analysis and self-condemnation, together with an extraordinary power of moral recovery, and a conviction, deeper even than the sense of sin and failure, of the presence and action, in all the long tragedy of Israel's political destruction, of a purpose at once omnipotent and redemptive. Yet this is precisely what did happen; and this is the pre-Christian stage of that salvation which, through the Christian Church, has become the permanent possession of the race and is gradually being communicated to the whole world.

The history of such a salvation was, as we have said, unpredictable from the standpoint of its beginning. It was also unnoticed by the vast majority of those who took part in its onward movement. Even very sophisticated and self-conscious people are not continually reflecting upon the lives they are leading day by day. They act for the most part automatically; other incidents of life flow by in a kind of dream. Conceive, then, how few, in an age long previous to the intense subjectivism which is our inheritance, were capable of estimating the nature of the forces which moved in their national history or of discovering their direction. The multitudes of men and women which made up the Israel of these early times were no more intelligent or introspective than the modern *fellahīn* who till the same fields where their remote ancestors carried on a scarcely less primitive agriculture. At the same time, two points are to be noted. First, these simple and unknowing souls were experiencing, to the extent of their capacity, the salvation of which they had such dim and shallow apprehension. They lived by things of which they could give no adequate account. He who toiled in vineyard or wheatfield and brought his offering to Jahweh, and, if need were, died in defence of his wife and children, was 'being saved,' and was proving a living link in the chain which binds the dim apprehensions of primitive times to the richer and clearer experiences of the Christian believer. Second, not all in Israel, even in the very early stages of its advance, were thus spiritually unawakened. In the history of Israel, as in all history, we have to reckon with personality. That there should arise in any nation at any time a man who is able to lift himself above the stream of incident and event in which most of his contemporaries are submerged, and to grasp the significance of a history which to most other men is blind or misleading, is very wonderful. All attempts to explain such a man fail. This wonder stands out in the history of Israel, not to be missed or explained away. The prophets understood: that is their greatness. In the mirror of their consciousness we discern the meaning of Israel's history. They are not students of the history, painfully piecing together its chronicles, and precariously drawing deductions. Nor are they makers of the history in the sense in which monarchs and conquerors make or mar the fortunes of men. Their function, in reference to their nation, is more intimate, and their influence more profound and far-reaching. Their experience is that of the people to whom they belong, with all the difference that lies between consciousness and unconsciousness, between clear sight and purblind vision, and with the yet wider difference between subjection to an unknown purpose and devotion to a purpose recognized with deep intuition and accepted, with entire consecration, as the vocation of life. Their salvation is the salvation of Israel. They, like the humblest of their fellow-countrymen, are being educated and trained in the moral life. Salvation means for them, as for others, a moral discipline. In them, however, in virtue not so much of greater religious susceptibility as of greater willingness to obey a higher guidance, the salvation proceeds at a swifter rate and reaches nobler results.

As we read the story of their inner life, we see what no observer could have predicted — the intended issue of Israel's history. Not to create a State or Empire, but to make men like these, is the teleology of Israel's strange and infinitely tragic career. This is the salvation of which Israel was meant to be the recipient and the exponent—the creation of just such a character related in this manner to God, marked by such communion with

Him, and showing in life and conduct the ethical fruit of such divine fellowship. The prophets were themselves 'saved' with a salvation which is not static, but dynamic, and exerts upon and through its recipients a moral energy which is inexhaustible. Their salvation, accordingly, is not merely a high degree of that which was common to all Israelites. It becomes, in their experience of it, the condition under which salvation is possible as an experience for all. Being saved themselves, they become the saviours of those whose life they share, as being with them members of Israel.

They have a message to deliver to their fellows. They have much moral and religious truth to communicate. Their duty was, as one of their titles signifies, to interpret for the ignorant and unenlightened the divine principles immanent in the history of Israel. But the supreme service that they rendered to their people was the life they lived. By it they illustrated the meaning of the divine salvation, and proved its reality. By it, moreover, they mediated that salvation to their people. Salvation became, in the life and ministry of these men, a fact of the moral order. Through them and their actions and sufferings God was approaching Israel, in the energy of His redeeming purpose. To cleave to them, to obey their counsels, and to breathe their spirit was salvation for the whole body of the people, or, failing a national obedience, for such circles as might permit the prophetic spirit to permeate and govern them. Such is the fact of salvation, as it presents itself in the history of Israel and in that interpretation of the history, given by prophetic men, which we find in the OT. It is an experience which rises from rudimentary forms towards great spiritual fullness, and contains the promise and the potency of yet greater experience, still to come.

2. Its source.—The salvation which was an experience in Israel originated in the act of God. No doubt, Israel might be saved at any given moment of need by human instrumentality. But the instinct of Israel always passed beyond the human agent to the real doer, who was Jahweh Himself, 'who himself saveth you out of all your calamities and your distresses' (1 S 10^{19}). To prefer the human to the divine Saviour is practical apostasy. The creed of Israel is, in brief, 'Jahweh saves'; and their creed is not the work of philosophers, the product of speculation, but the immediate deliverance of an experience, too real and too great to be susceptible of any other explanation than this, that it is the direct, though not unmediated, operation of God Himself.

The OT as a whole is no more than illustration and exposition of this primary conviction. In its most rudimentary form this creed contains the germs of the whole subsequent religious development. Two elements of special importance lie hidden in Israel's earliest confession of faith.

(*a*) *The nature of God.*—God is conceived as a Power, who does things. To pass from the *Upaniṣads* to the Prophets is to leave one universe of religious thought for another, wholly different in fundamental conceptions. In the one God is substance, in the other He is power. In the one He is, and all being is merged in Him. In the other He acts, and is the source of all the energy that is needed for His purposes. It may be that some higher synthesis of these widely contrasted ideas of the divine nature is possible; but no attempt to harmonize them must ignore their difference. To say '*Brahman-atmān*,' and to say 'Jahweh saves,' represent two worlds of experience, which cannot be inhabited together. Indian thought is, necessarily, without history, and does no more than confront the illusory manifold of the world's life with the sublime monotony of its assertion that all being is one. Hebrew experience is essentially historic, and is the product of an immanent energy, moving towards a goal, which the rarer minds alone, and they only dimly, can discern in the distant future.

A curious contrast may be observed between the ancient Hebrew cultivator and the toiler in the wide Gangetic plain. The former is not nearly so intellectual or reflective as the latter. He holds no metaphysical theory about the constitution of the world. He is simpler and cruder in his ideas, and stands much nearer the primitive animism. Yet he entertains an idea, and he uses a term, which are destined to carry his successors towards experiences incomparably richer than his and yet genetically connected with them. The idea is that God is one who exerts power, and the term is 'the Spirit of God.' From the beginning of Israel's history, so far as we know it, the Hebrew mind discerned the operation of God in the world, and yet never proceeded to a philosophical theory of the relation of God to the world. Its ideas had little philosophic breadth, but great experimental intensity. The powers that control the history of Israel are God's; and, wherever these powers are seen in action, they are identified with the Spirit of God. God—God acting in the world—God acting by His Spirit: this is the primitive, simple, yet far-reaching Hebrew doctrine of God.

(*b*) *The character of God.*—In 'Jahweh saves' the emphasis passes from the one term to the other. Jahweh is known as Saviour of Israel. God loves Israel, and will save Israel out of all his distresses. What that saving action might involve—what exertions on God's part, and what discipline on man's—what issues it might have for the people, and what form it might assume lay within the unknown future. But the abiding conviction was that God's action would be saving, that His settled purpose was redemptive, and that He would not cease His dealing with Israel till the deliverance was complete. Here we touch the earliest Hebrew thought of God: He is one who loves and saves. Whatever His love and His people's need require, He will do. Whatever He does is the expression of His love for His people, and is meant for the furtherance of their salvation. It would be ridiculous to attribute to the early mind of Israel exalted conceptions of the moral character of God and rich religious experience of salvation. But it would be equally unhistorical to deny, even to the tribes that broke in from the desert to occupy the hills and valleys of Palestine, the conviction that they were living under the direction and inspira- of a Saviour-God.

History itself, becoming articulate in the prophets, would unfold the meaning of salvation, and would bring home to the awakening religious consciousness what are the real evils from which men are suffering, and what God is willing to do for their deliverance. But, whatever befalls the people of Israel, whether judgments smite them or mercies crown them, they are being 'saved'; God is making His salvation known; God is revealing Himself. Students of the OT are apt to be disastrously doctrinaire in their methods, whether their conclusions are conservative or advanced. The interest of the OT lies not in opinions which may or may not be supported by proof texts, but in the picture which it presents of a nation in the hands of God. Israel does not consist in pupils being instructed in theological lore; it is a community of men and women who, collectively and individually, are being saved, with a salvation which is, fundamentally, a moral experience. Of that experience, and of those in those far-off days subjected to it, the members of the Christian Church are the heirs and the successors. The history of Israel is not closed. It is continued in the history of mankind. The religion of Israel is not superseded. It remains, man's only religion. The theology of Israel is not an anachronism. It is the abiding truth of God.

3. Its warrant.—Salvation in Israel is an experience of the present, and contains a prophecy of the future. But it is securely grounded in the past, and derives therefrom its confidence and its strength. 'Behind the people's national life lay the consciousness of redemption as much as it lies behind the life of the Christian.'[1] The point of interest is not the outward form which the deed of redemption assumed. It is certain that some visitor (let us suppose) from the Farther East would have sent to the court which he represented a very different account of the incidents connected with the deliverance from Egypt from that which the prophetic historian gives in Exodus. Such differences do not impugn the historicity of the event itself, and in no way invalidate its significance for the conscience and intelligence of Israel. In this event the religion of Israel is born. Upon this event the salvation of Israel is established. In the experience which Israel then passed through God became known to His people; not, be it noted, by a formula, but by a personal name, which gathered to itself epithets descriptive of personal qualities. When we ask how the primitive mind would most naturally express the relation towards God into which the experience of deliverance had introduced the redeemed people, one form at once suggests itself, viz. a 'covenant.' It is true that most of the great 'covenant' passages belong to an age far later than that of the exodus—*e.g.*, Lv 26^{44}, Ezk 16^{60}. But this is no evidence against the primitive character of the thought and no proof of the unhistoric nature of the narrative, which describes the institu-

[1] A. B. Davidson, *s.v.* 'God,' in *HDB* ii. 202^b.

tion of the covenant as following immediately upon the national deliverance. The very fact of the redemption creates the covenant relationship. The God who saves does, in the very act, pledge Himself to persevere in one line of action towards the people whom He has redeemed. Salvation was undertaken on His initiative. It becomes the goal of His action. He is vitally concerned with reaching it. His movement towards it is the only reliable revelation of His nature, and forms the ever-renewed proof of His being. In every time of strain and doubt the disciplined mind of Israel goes back to the covenant into which God entered of His own free motion, and cleaves, even amid sorest trial, to the faithfulness which will not suffer Him to forget His obligations. In like manner, the people who are the subjects of God's redeeming action stand pledged to carry out the divine purpose in saving them, as it is gradually disclosed to them. Salvation is their privilege. It is also their vocation. The scope of the privilege and the nature of the vocation are alike disclosed only through long ages, in which the self-consciousness of the nation became explicit and the national ideal became clear and full. But the most glorious utterances of the most inspired prophet turn back upon the earliest experiences of mutual pledges between Jahweh and Israel, and present the fulfilment of what was germinal therein (cf. Dt 26^{16-19}).

It is impossible, in describing the covenant relation between Jahweh and Israel, to avoid using terms which imply personality on both sides. God is intensely personal and has all the qualities by which men recognize a personal as distinguished from an impersonal force. Israel also is personal, viewed in its national and corporate existence—in this sense at least that it is susceptible of a moral discipline and is being led to a spiritual consummation, in both of which every individual Israelite has his part as a member of a living whole. God and Israel, accordingly, confront one another, God viewing Israel as the object of His love, and Israel gradually recognizing God for what He is and discerning more clearly His demands and purposes.

The relationship between these two, therefore, is wholly personal. God knows Israel in its weakness, its need, and its possibilities, and bends Himself to make of Israel what He will. Israel makes progressive discovery of God, gaining insight into His character and beginning to discern His aim.

> 'All Israel's history is filled with this reciprocal knowledge, rising up from strength to strength, till One came who knew the Father, and whom the Father knew in fulness.'[1]

Knowledge of God, in fact, is one of the Biblical synonyms for salvation; and in this lies the uniqueness of the Bible among all the 'Sacred Books of the East.' It is not a disquisition; it is the record of an experience, gained in actual fellowship with God.

4. Its verification and exploration.—It belongs to the essence of religious experience that it can never be immobile. In the life of the spirit there is no stable equilibrium. The intense interest belonging to Israel's history lies in the double movement discernible throughout its whole course. On the one hand, there is a constant downward tendency, a ceaseless misunderstanding of God and misinterpretation of His salvation. On the other hand, there is an upward movement, towards a discovery of God and a realization of His purposes. This movement, though it be the true life of Israel, does not proceed by steady uninterrupted progress, nor does it include within its scope even the majority of the people. It is marked by revivals. It is concentrated in unique personalities. It extends to circles who are but dimly discernible and whose exact numbers cannot be calculated. The details of this experimental verification and exploration of the divine salvation are of thrilling interest. They have their parallels and analogies in all religions and in the discipline of every separate soul.

The history of religious experience in Israel has never been written; and still less has a history of religious experience as such been attempted. Perhaps such books, condensing the spiritual progress of mankind, could never be composed with any hope of accuracy. The value of the OT literature is that it presents a touchstone, by which we may evaluate religion anywhere and note its progress in races or individuals. That touchstone is the ethical element in the conception of God. Where it is seen that God is righteous and requires righteousness, there the higher life of man ripens towards noble fruit; the divine salvation opens to vision and appropriation that are in fact boundless; and communion with God is not an occasional ecstasy, but a reality of the daily life and its continual delight. The use of this ethical standpoint, in reviewing religious life in general, establishes this conclusion, viz. that progress in the discovery of salvation is always accompanied by disillusion, and often by the utmost sorrow and pain. The form of salvation breaks, as advance is made; and salvation itself has to be sought in some deeper region, where the soul shall find itself more perfectly at home.

The OT records are full of this strange commingling of victory and defeat, of despair and exultation. The form which salvation at first assumes is national and political. It is identical with the integrity and independence of the Hebrew nationality. Its great events are deliverances from national peril. Its scope and contents consist in peace and plenty, and the abundance and security of those possessions are the normal conditions of happy and prosperous living. Precisely at this point lay the testing of Israel's moral sense; and here emerges the tragedy of Israel's history. Will Israel discover no more in Jahweh than Moab in Chemosh? Will Israel explore the farther reaches of salvation or be satisfied with external satisfactions and external deliverances?

The history gives a sad and terrible answer to these questions. The 'Israel' which we name as such, for purposes of comparison with 'Egypt' or 'Assyria,' failed in moral discernment, and was not merely destroyed politically, but deprived of place and function in the moral development of mankind. At the same time, there was another 'Israel,' the true Israel, consisting of those persons, whose numbers are unknown and whose experiences are largely unrecorded, who were being taught another conception of God and were making proof of another kind of salvation. Their existence and the continuity of their religious experience are facts absolutely certain, and of transcendent importance for the vindication of revelation and the upward movement of humanity. While the political fabric of Israel's existence lasted, they testified that the condition of its permanence was obedience to the moral will of Israel's God, that God would save those who yielded Him this obedience, and that, should disaster threaten, such obedience would secure the divine salvation. Those OT writings which belong to the period of national independence develop the idea of righteousness into its social applications, and connect it vitally with the presence of God and the enjoyment of His favour. We have before us the picture of a community of which God is at once the Head and the indwelling life. Every member of this organism is related to every other, through

[1] A. B. Davidson, *The Theology of the OT*, Edinburgh, 1904, p. 78.

the relation in which all stand to the unseen King. In their fulfilment of their mutual obligations, they are glorifying God and are pursuing a path of moral education in which conscience will be enlightened, the will trained, and faith strengthened.

Israel is the microcosm of salvation, the prefigurement of a redeemed and perfected humanity.

'J" chose a nation, because His idea of mankind, of which He will be God, is that of a social organism. It is this organism of which He is God. But though the relation might seem to be with the ideal unity, it operated in disposing all the parts making up the unity rightly to one another. And in this way each individual felt J" to be his God.'[1]

This conception of a religious organism and a social salvation is the contribution of pre-Exilic Israel to the spiritual progress of the race. Any experience, Christian or other, which omits it is to that extent impoverished, and is condemned from the point of view of a full salvation.

The time came, however, when the national form of existence, which had conveyed and conserved the divine salvation, became too narrow and limited for the experience which had been made possible within it. Whether the transition to a fuller salvation could have been made without the tragedy of Israel's destruction as a political institution is a fruitless problem. We may dream of a people learning to distinguish between form and content, discovering that the essence of salvation was separable from the outward framework of the State, and passing onward to a knowledge of God, so deep and intimate that it ceased to be a national perquisite and was fitted to the needs and destined for the reception of all men everywhere.

In point of fact, however, the political 'Israel' did not rise to this thought of God, and so failed in its historic mission. It did not 'lose' its life, and therefore did not 'save' it. It perished as a nation, and did not survive as a community of the Spirit. The inner Israel, which did know God and was testing His power to save, suffered intensely at the hands of its politically-minded fellow-citizens. Its affirmation of an ethically conditioned salvation seemed, at one period, to be the dream of an impossible patriotism, and, at another, to be treason against the State and impiety against a God whose very existence was bound up with that of His people. Then, when the worst happened, and the political Israel passed amid unknown agonies to its doom, those very persons who were proving in their own souls the permanence of a moral union with God shared the sorrows of those whose ignorance and disobedience had made that judgment inevitable, and felt their griefs the more intensely that they discerned the nature and guilt of the sin which was thus receiving its due reward.

Thus the older form of salvation was broken up and a new experience of God's saving help was born, amid such confusion and pain as have made the Exile the symbol of the utmost desolation that the human soul can bear.

The transition was accomplished in anguish—an anguish which, ideally, need not have been. Yet through the agony the new fact came gloriously into being, a salvation in which the living God grasped and mastered and held the soul, when all the lesser values of life were discredited, and all its earthly treasures dispersed for ever. Salvation, in this era of national disintegration, is concentrated in the experience of individuals, of whom Jeremiah and Ezekiel stand out as examples. The State is gone; but God remains; and His presence is salvation. The religious experience of such men forms at once the goal of Israel's past and the starting-point of Israel's future.

The secret of Israel is its relation to God. Its salvation rests on the 'covenant' between God and His people. And now the covenant is passing to a new stage of experimental verification and new ranges of discovery. Its subjects are human souls, taken out of the broken forms of national life and dealt with in their bare humanity, with its needs and possibilities; and its experiences lie within the compass of a divine fellowship, realized with an intensity and tenderness unknown hitherto. It is a 'new covenant,' and yet its source is the changeless love of God; its guarantee is His steadfast purpose of mercy; and its issue is the understanding of His unchangeable will of righteousness and profound surrender to it. This is the imperishable gain of the Exile. Salvation is a relation of the human soul to God, a fellowship of man with God, enduring through the dissolution of forms of life, which had seemed inseparable from well-being, and dependent only on man's entire subjection to divine holy will and unwavering confidence in divine power and faithfulness. This individual salvation is the complement to the social salvation of the pre-Exilic period. Israel has made the experiment for humanity. A social salvation that is not rooted in a personal covenant with God is imperfect and insecure.

The history of Israel, however, is not closed with the Exile; nor is its contribution to the religious experience of mankind exhausted. There follow the strange and disappointing centuries which intervene between the Exile and Israel's new birth in Christianity. We observe with impatience and regret that the vision of a new religious life, individual, subjective, free, and rich, is clouded over by the intervention of another external framework. It is not now a political fabric that in part conceals, and in part conveys, the new salvation. It is something more unfamiliar, and even less pleasing, to modern eyes—a system of ceremonial law, laid with iron rigidity upon souls which had caught the sight and even tasted the joys of the liberty of the spirit. If it was difficult to imagine the religious life of the national period, it is still more difficult to figure to ourselves the possibility of any noble, joyous, and progressive life lived under the yoke of the law. Yet the patent and amazing fact is that such a life was lived by a community which accepted every jot and tittle of the law as of divine enactment, and set itself resolutely to the laborious task of complete fulfilment.

In short, we have to revise our first rough estimate of the ceremonial law, and to distinguish between law and legalism.

We can well imagine that a discipline of law was needed for a religious consciousness which had been formed in the intense and individualizing experiences of the Exile. There is danger of subjectivism and mysticism, with their incapacity for educative or evangelistic work. There is need of training in the ethical and religious meanings and issues of a life lived in thoroughgoing submission to the will of a holy God. The sequence with which we are familiar in the inner life—after conversion, sanctification—is wrought out in the life of Israel: after the Exile, the return to Palestine and the scheme of 'a holy people in a holy land.' We are conscious of a change of atmosphere when we compare the post-Exilic 'Church' with the pre-Exilic 'nation.' The priest is a much less inspiring personality than the prophet. The social salvation of the earlier period seems more ethically fruitful, and more capable of modern applications, than the religious experience shaped and limited by a legal dispensation. Yet this judgment is certainly incomplete and misleading. Conceive the inner life of this people as depicted in the Psalter. Follow the narrative of their conflicts with heathen elements surviving among themselves and their splendid resistance to a tyranny which would have destroyed their very soul. How easily they might have perished, absorbed into surrounding populations, and losing all religious function in the history of the race! And, instead of this doom, the divine saving power is manifest in their life; and they verify the salvation of God by a demonstration absolutely conclusive, and explore its riches in a manner which has made their devotional literature the nourishment of the soul of man in every age and clime. The sense of sin as an infinite injury to God and man, the exercise of faith which throws itself absolutely on God and owes its standing to His sovereign grace, the joy of reconciliation and forgiveness, the

[1] A. B. Davidson, *s.v.* 'Prophecy,' in *HDB* iv. 120.

converse of the soul with God, progress in moral achievement through lowliest obedience—these elements of a full salvation were being wrought into the experience of men and women, to form permanent features in the redemption of man. With such a treasure they could not afford to part. Persecution might break upon them, but its bitterness did not lessen their assurance of salvation. Rather did the things that they suffered unlock the stores of divine help. The fire not only tried and purified them, but it revealed a Presence with them, which, in its radiance and its sustaining comfort, was their salvation and their song. The OT ought not to have closed with Malachi; it ought to have culminated in the books of the Maccabees.

At the same time, these blessed experiences were enclosed, as it were, in a rigid framework of precept. Israel was still in the hands of a Pædagogue, and the time of liberty was not yet. The defects of law are manifest. It is a burden, not an inspiration. It suggests a false inference, viz. that men are saved by their observance of precepts, not by their inward relation to the Source of all truth and right, by works, not by faith. It begets a misconception of God, exaggerating His transcendence, neglecting His knowableness and accessibility, forgetting the affinity of man with God and the susceptibility of human nature for divine fellowship. It creates a spirit of bigotry and exclusiveness, and makes those who are the subjects of divine salvation not the saviours of men, but their tyrants.

These defects had not belonged to the great days of Israel's religion, when the prophets were its evangelists and its examples. But they were rife in the days when the priest and the scribe dominated the spirit of the people.

It became increasingly evident, accordingly, that the end was not yet. The salvation of men lay still in the future. Not till the shell of law was broken, even as the older shell of nationality had been broken, could the human spirit enter on the treasure of grace reserved for it in the intention of Him who is the Saviour of men. In this legal period the true evangelical succession belongs to those who, penetrated by the sense of need, waited for the consolation of Israel.

Once more the easily neglected fact of 'the Remnant' stands out as the most remarkable and the most influential element in the history of Israel. Once more the unifying principle in the history of divine salvation becomes apparent, binding the far-off Hebrew tribes breaking into Palestine in the power of a recent deliverance with the disciplined souls who poured forth in the Psalms their confessions and aspirations, and with all, in every age, who have made the supreme discovery that, in the stress of life, the human spirit cannot stay itself upon any form, political, ritual, or intellectual, but only upon God, obeyed and trusted to the last limit of a surrendered will.

5. Its instruments and mediators.—As long as the religion of Israel is living, *i.e.* as long as men are conscious of redeeming forces operating in their lives, God is known to be acting directly for and within His people. His presence and His power are both immediate. It is only when the last and most decadent state of religion in Israel is reached that God is conceived of as remote, and a cosmological and metaphysical machinery has to be invented to connect Him with His world and provide channels for the course of His operations. In that age such an OT concept as 'the Spirit of God,' which was meant to express God's presence to and in the world without identifying Him with it, has been changed to mean a kind of being intermediate between God and the world. It may be said, broadly, for all religion and all theology that only when the sense of the divine salvation has become feeble and empty is such an artificial conception of God's relation to the world and human history tolerable to the intelligence; attractive to the heart that pants after the living God it never can be. The divine salvation in Israel, accordingly, is always God's own immediate work. It does not follow that it operates magically or without means and instruments. The idea of mediation runs deep through the OT.[1] But it stands in no manner of opposition to the immediacy of God's presence and working. It has no reference to the supposed necessity of an intermediate being to cross the chasm between infinite and finite. It belongs to a totally different universe of thought. It means that the divine salvation, being the salvation of man, must find in man its adequate organ. God and man are by nature so close together that nothing that is not perfectly human is needed, or can be permitted, to intervene between them. Man needs to be saved. Only God can save him; and God can save man only by man.

This is the message of Israel's religion. Its history is the history of saviours, *i.e.* of organs and instruments of the divine salvation, human all of them, each with some special aspect of the great work to do, each with special aptitude and fitness. In each it is the Spirit of God, *i.e.* God Himself in power, who operates. In each the saviour is not the man, but God, choosing, preparing, finding, in the man, the adequate organ for His saving work, and so, also, for the revelation of His being and character. As we turn the pages of the record, we note that, in every age, men needed, and God provided, saviours. We observe the suddenness of their appearance and the spontaneity of their ministry. There is nothing stereotyped or predictable in their service. There is clearly-marked immediacy in their personal experience and strongly-defined originality in their service. Yet there is equally observable a profound unity connecting them; so that, from whatever grade they come (peasant or prince), to whatever age they belong (pre-Exilic, Exilic, or post-Exilic), whatever their precise commission may be (that of warrior, statesman, priest, or prophet), they form one company and toil at one task. They are the agents of one salvation, which originates in the counsels of a righteous God, consists in moral oneness with Him, and is secure in His power and goodness. The mediation of salvation in the OT is not confined, however, to the individual saviours, to whose actions more or less full allusion is made. A broad generalization arises out of the history. Thoughts begin to shape themselves which rise beyond the confines of the history. It becomes apparent, *e.g.*, that the full salvation of Israel cannot be achieved by the sporadic endeavours of any individual members of Israel. The double conception of Israel, noticed before, receives now a special and crowning application. Not only is 'the Remnant,' the inner, the true 'Israel,' the subject of the divine salvation; it is also the mediator of that salvation to the political 'Israel,' whose ignorance of God's real character and mind was plunging it into ruin. Not only so; but, when the political Israel perishes, the true Israel survives, not in weakened, but in heightened, power and nobler function. It is called to mediate salvation to nations that know not God, to be the instrument of a salvation which shall include mankind. There is no doctrinaire universalism in those writings which thus exalt the function of Israel. They are not operating with abstract conceptions and deductive logic. They are interpreting the experience of a people and of disciplined souls within it.

Thus there arose, says Davidson, 'the great conception of "the servant of the Lord." The phrase expresses the highest generalization on the meaning of Israel in the religious life of mankind—Israel is the Servant of J″ to the nations to bring to them the knowledge of God.'[1]

When we ponder the work of mediation, we perceive that it necessarily involved two sides or aspects, and that, therefore, those who laboured at it must necessarily have possessed a twofold qualification. On the one side, God must be made known to man—not in a theoretic manner, and not through a magical phrase, but in His character as a living God, engaged in carrying forward His purposes for His people. On the other, men must be led into a condition of moral harmony with the will of God, not as mere acceptance of a code, but as loyal surrender to a personal and gracious authority.

The servants of God through whose activities and experiences this double work is done have

[1] Though the word μεσίτης occurs only once in LXX (Job 9[33]); see art. MEDIATION.

[1] *HDB* iv. 122.

plainly a double relationship—to God, on the one hand, and to the people, on the other. They are God's agents and representatives. They also act on behalf of the people and represent them. This is true of them all, princes and statesmen and warriors, as well as prophets and priests; true also of the company, or inner circle, which constituted the true Israel. To discharge their functions, accordingly, their sympathy must include both God and man. They must be at one with God, knowing His mind and receiving communications from Him. They must be at one with the people, not as being mere political nationalists, but as discerning, realizing, and seeking to further the true purpose of the nation's existence and the real trend of its history. Technical distinctions ought not to hide from us that which underlies separate stereotyped manner or office, viz. a life actually lived, in which God is moving towards man, and man is rising towards God. In the religious experience of such servants the divine salvation becomes a power available for all who range themselves with them in their faith and obedience. In this sense, while they are being saved themselves, they become saviours of their people. They are the organic centre of the redeemed community. In them God is present as saving power. The degree of their consciousness or the outward form of their work does not alter the reality of their divine vocation. They serve, in the measure of their loyalty and in the sphere of their operation, as meeting-points for God and man. Mediation is accomplished, not by cultus or dogma, but by life.

This life, moreover, as the problem of salvation deepened in the course of Israel's history, necessarily became harder and more marked by suffering. A soldier or statesman in Israel, if he was a genuine servant of Jahweh, had hard work to do and much suffering to undergo, and his labour and pain were the condition of the people's salvation. Yet he might not penetrate to the heart of God's concern for Israel or to the depths of Israel's need. He might not, accordingly, load himself with the whole burden created by the people's ignorance and sin. Suppose, however, a different case. Suppose a patriotic Israelite, clearly discerning the mistaken optimism of the 'false prophets,' *i.e.* the political nationalists; feeling in his inmost soul the demands made as well by the love as by the holiness of God, and the failure on Israel's part to respond by a changed mind and a morally renewed life; reading aright the story of Israel's past, and foreseeing nothing but multiplied disaster and ultimate ruin as the issue of present materialism and corruption. It is plain that he will suffer, as none other in Israel save those like-minded with himself can suffer. The afflictions of his people, coming on them as the fruit of their doings, are his afflictions, though he deserve them not; and in his case they are intensified a thousandfold by his sense of the guilt of which they are the exposure and the judgment. It is true, the guilt is not his, and his sufferings are not his punishment. But, if any one should imagine that on that account the suffering is less, or that the sufferer is able to throw off the pain, he cannot know the passionate heart of one who knows and loves both God and his fellow-countrymen. There is no sorrow like the sorrow of the soul which is consciously and voluntarily identified with God in His holiness and man in his need.

This is the sorrow that sounds, as one long cry of anguish, through the life of Jeremiah. It was the sorrow also of others, unrecorded, who are, however, grouped around the central figures in the tragedy of Israel's judgment, a dim and piteous remnant of the nation that had so fearfully missed its way. This sorrow, the experience of living souls in Israel, lasted through the centuries, and is the most significant fact in the history of Israel. The prophetic minds which surveyed and interpreted that history could not miss this significance. Such sorrow has atoning value. Sin makes a breach with God. The life of the innocent Servant of the Lord, freely and consciously given, amid unknown grief and pain, for a guilty nation, is an expiation for guilt, and effects the reconciliation of God and man. Language borrowed from the ritual of sacrificial worship is applied with enriched meaning to the sorrows of the Servant: 'God hath laid on him the iniquity of us all. . . . He bears the sin of many, he makes intercession for the transgressors' (Is 53[6. 12]). The theological implications of such a view of the sufferings of the Servant will necessarily be of the highest importance for thought. The important point is that the sufferings actually endured by servants of God in Israel, or by Israel as the Servant, have value for God and have a saving efficacy for men. Yet not merely as the pain of individuals, standing apart from God. If this were the meaning, we would have a reversion to a heathen view of God and of sacrifice, as though a man offered his pain to God and God were placated thereby. God in Israel is not thus separated from His servants. Their pain is His. 'In all their affliction he is afflicted' (Is 63[9]). At the heart of the religion of Israel there is pain, divine pain. This is the everlasting rock on which the divine salvation rests; and this is the power which, exerted upon the hearts of men, leads them to a new vision of God and wakens in them deep compunction and relenting towards Him. No religion which ever linked man with God has been without some sight of this principle of redemptive suffering. But in the religion of Israel it finds rich and adequate expression, and becomes the chief and proximate source of the Christian message of salvation, as proclaimed and illustrated in NT Scriptures.

As we ponder the conception of the Suffering Servant and note how the NT reverts to it in its fullest interpretation of the Person and Work of Christ, we are apt to ask what becomes of it in the intervening period. It is incredible that it should have disappeared for hundreds of years, and then have owed its re-emergence to the genius of the apostle Paul, who used it to replace the primitive religion of Jesus by a Christianity of which he was practically the inventor. Two points here are of importance.

(1) The true succession in religion does not run through books, or systems of thought, or ceremonial practices. It is to be traced in actual experience; or else its existence evaporates into scholastic theology or magic ritual. The succession in Israel is manifest, and belongs, not to any officials, but to the souls which, through national and personal discipline, were led into an apprehension of God far other than theoretic and a service greater than political or intellectual. The existence of such servants and sufferers is not in any doubt in the centuries immediately preceding the rise of Christianity. They form, in part, the martyr-age of the religion of Israel; and, where no names stand pre-eminent, there is an unmistakable company of those that 'wait for the consolation' of Israel. In them the calling of the true Israel, the Servant of the Lord, is continued. Out of the heart of their experience there shall arise the final redemption of man.

(2) But, further, it would seem that the absence from Palestinian Jewish literature of the idea of the redemptive value of the suffering of the righteous is due to Pharisaism, which, in its just quarrel with the later Maccabees, sought to obliterate almost the very memory of the deeds and sufferings of the great founders of the family. Where the influence of Pharisaism is not felt, these sufferings are remembered and are interpreted in the spirit of Is 53.

'In Second but more especially in Fourth Maccabees we have the only clear survivals in the later Jewish literature of that doctrine of vicarious suffering, atonement, or reconciliation of the Divine favour by the blood of heroes willingly offered for the nation, which appears so clearly in the doctrine of the Suffering Servant of Deutero-Isaiah, and thereafter seems obliterated from synagogue teaching, awakening again to a world-wide significance only in the Christian doctrine of the Cross.'[1]

Pharisaism had no use for the doctrine; but it formed a vital part of the religion of the common people, who believed, unintelligently and crudely perhaps, but passionately, that the sufferings of

[1] B. W. Bacon, in *HJ* xv. [1917] 268.

the righteous did have atoning value, and annually in the Feast of Renewal celebrated the memory of such martyred yet triumphant servants of God. Thus the main stream of Israel's religion passes through the ages and is ushered at last into the great ocean of the Christian salvation.

6. Its consummation.—Salvation, in the widest, most formal conception of it, is throughout the OT a life completely determined by the sovereign will of God. The content of this idea grows richer as God is construed with an ever-increasing moral and spiritual discernment. Gradually it becomes identical with knowledge of God and fellowship with Him, implying at the same time removal of all barriers to those blessed experiences. But the religion of Israel is never individualistic and mystical, though it is intensely personal and intimate. It could never rest content with a *merely* individual religious life; or, rather, it kept true to its deeply social and historic character. Salvation cannot be consummated, even for the individual, without the environment of a redeemed community, and, indeed, a redeemed world. Cosmology has no interest *per se* for the OT or, we may add, for the NT. But the religious mind of Israel demands the complete penetration of the whole sphere of human life by the sovereign will of God. Till that be accomplished salvation is incomplete. Out of this demand apocalyptic is born. Faith grasps ever more firmly the thought of the divine supremacy. At the same time, it sees ever more clearly that the utmost efforts, even of the most devoted servants of God, cannot vindicate this supremacy, under the existing circumstances of human life. Nothing earthly, no human society or institution can perfectly express the glory of God. Even nature itself in some sense fails to do so. And, as terrible and prolonged experience shows, there are evil forces running rampant among men and occupying the very air around them which baffle the wit and overwhelm the power of man. Very early, therefore, faith rises above the level of human enterprise and fastens upon divine intervention, as essential to final salvation. In doing so faith strikes upon a radical incapacity of the human understanding. It is not possible to express in terms of time and space that which is, in the very idea of it, above both. Apocalyptic is, therefore, necessarily and essentially symbolical. Its truth is the supremacy and omnipotence and faithfulness of God—in short, the central message of the OT, viz. that Jahweh saves. Its religious value is hope, sustaining, comforting, strengthening, especially in dark times of oppression and persecution and apparent disaster. Its vehicle is picture and symbol, whose use and value lie wholly in their vivid presentation to the mind of that which no picture or symbol can adequately represent. Take the symbol apart from the religious truth, and it becomes crass, foolish, mischievous. Take apocalyptic away from prophecy, and it becomes mere mythology. This, however, is very likely to happen when faith decays; and it is precisely what did happen in the later stages of Israel's religion, and, we may add, has happened again and again in the religious life of mankind. Indeed, when we note the amount of apocalyptic in the later literature of Israel, and note how its figures are drawn from the mythologies of the nations around, we are apt to think that this kind of thing, materialistic and semi-pagan, was the whole religion of the Jews, or at least constituted their main religious pabulum. But such a view would certainly be an exaggeration. Within the circles which formed the religious core of the nation, 'the circles in which Christianity arose,'[1] the great thoughts of prophecy regarding redemption are still dominant. Apocalyptic did, indeed, make definite some of these thoughts, notably the personality of Him in whom Jahweh would visit His people and achieve His salvation; and it did carry forward the religious mind towards questions which the OT canonical writings did not settle, particularly the problem of death and immortality; and in general it did fulfil its proper function of inspiring hope and courage. Educated in faith, quickened in hope, patient in prolonged delay, the true Israel, undeluded by political fantasies, and unintoxicated by mythical imaginings, waited for its 'consolation' with gaze fixed heavenwards for the breaking of the day.

II. *SALVATION AS AN EXPERIENCE WITHIN THE TIMES OF THE NT.*—The Christian creed and the Christian Church can be understood only through the experience of which they are, respectively, the intellectual and the institutional forms. It may be doubted whether Biblical Theology, Church History, and History of Dogma have always borne in mind that they were dealing, not with intellectual conceptions or institutional forms *per se*, but with these as the outcome and vesture of an actual religious experience, which is, in a large measure, different from, and, in respect of value, much greater than, the forms in which it was clothed and through which it, in part, expressed itself. Certain it is that the point of view of experience must be carefully adhered to, if the birth and permanence of the Christian community are to be understood; and those studies, now happily increasing, which seek to depict the experience which lies behind creed and culture bring new light and life to the more rigidly intellectual disciplines. It may happen that 'advanced' views will have to endure correction, as well as those that are 'conservative.' Our hope must be that the result will be a new valuation of redeeming forces, a new emphasis on vital truths, and a new discernment of continuity amid change and unity amid variety.

1. Jesus and His disciples.—The fact presented to our view in the Synoptic Gospels is a religious experience, possessed by a group of persons, gathered round the central figure of Jesus of Nazareth.

In seeking to realize what that experience was, all the difficulties beset us which belong to the problem of life. If Christianity were a mosaic of ideas and practices, the work of understanding it though toilsome would be comparatively simple. But Christianity is, primarily and ultimately, life; and to penetrate to its secret needs more than tabulation and classification of details. This, at least, is true, that life begets life. There were religious life and experience in Israel before Jesus gathered His disciples about Him. It is certain that neither to His consciousness nor to theirs did the life and experience which they possessed present themselves as marking a breach with the past. They did rejoice in what they regarded as development, or even transition, into a new region of saving powers. But they would have rejected with horror the suggestion that they were founding a new religion, or were abandoning the highway of salvation, trodden by patriot and martyr, saint and seer, of Israel's lineage. Their conviction expresses the literal truth, and we may accept their estimate as the clue to the facts regarding them. They represent the element which is continuous in the history of Israel from the very earliest times. Their religion is the religion of the prophets. Jesus Himself and, with one or two exceptions, the young men who were attracted to Him or were summoned by Him to His side belonged to that inner heart of Israel which in every age had beat true to God and had consciously received the com-

[1] Cf. G. A. Smith, *Jerusalem*, London, 1907–08, ii. 539 ff.

munications of His mind and will. They inherited the fruits of that discipline of spirit which is the real history of Israel, and which lies behind and apart from political changes and varying forms of thought. The religious gains of that history may be summed up in two words—possession and expectation. The devotional literature on which the souls of the contemporaries of Jesus were nourished bears witness to a real knowledge of God, certifying itself in a definite moral character. The men and women who gathered round Jesus were not legalists. They were oppressed by legalism, administered by bigots. But their religion was not law; and it seems certain that the experience of Paul was not the path by which the primitive believers ordinarily entered the Christian Church. To believe in a living God, to know the effects of His saving power, to love Him with heart and soul and mind, to obey Him with more than formal rectitude—these elements of a deep and true religion were found in the aspirations and, in a measure, in the spiritual attainments of those who came to hail Jesus as Lord. Yet none of them was satisfied with the position that He had reached, or recognized in it the end of God's dealing with His people. The Kingdom of God had not come; and nothing in the state of Israel or the world could be right till there came a direct, manifest, and supernatural intervention of divine power and glory. This expectation centred in the figure of the King-Messiah. In endeavouring to reproduce the mind of those who became disciples of Jesus we must do justice to the religious quality of this expectation. It is true that it was at once apocalyptic and political. They could not conceive of divine intervention in any other form than that of which the deliverance from Egypt was the classical example. Another deliverer was to secure the emancipation of Israel and to establish Jewish supremacy. As nationalist, as particularist, this was the form of their hope. And yet it would be gross misunderstanding to suppose that their expectation had no other contents. They shared with all Israel the Baptist's summons to repentance. For them the coming of the Kingdom was poised upon a religious preparation; and its arrival was to be accompanied by a perfecting of religious knowledge, as well as by national triumph.

By both these influences—their actual religious life and their Messianic hope—they were attracted to Jesus. This is the twofold explanation of the Christian movement, as we find it in the first group of disciples, and as we trace it afterwards throughout the Hellenic world. Christianity was borne into both Jewish and Hellenic circles on a wave of Messianism; but it had power and permanence only as a religious experience; and it is in its religious qualities that we must seek for its essence.

When we watch the cinematographic pictures in the Synoptic Gospels, and seek to comprehend the life behind the stories, the following notes and characteristics cannot be missed.

(*a*) *The experience was intensely individual.*—It is difficult to remember, when reading the Synoptic Gospels, that we are watching the beginning of a great world movement, which gave rise, in its development, to vast intellectual systems and huge ecclesiastical apparatus. In these stories we seem to be concerned only with a man among other men. And, indeed, this is precisely where the point of interest does lie. Let apocalyptic lie over. Let Christology wait. Meantime, see what one Man made of other men. The beginning of Christianity was not a 'mass movement.' It was personal contact of individuals with Jesus and, later, of individuals with other single souls. The Gospels are largely made up of 'cases.' The details of the narrative, the outward form of recorded events, are of subordinate value. The heart of the situation lies in the souls with whom Jesus dealt, His handling of them, and the stamp He put upon them. Sometimes the need which confronted Jesus was mainly physical; and He met it in quick compassion with a word of power. Sometimes the need was definitely and keenly religious, and then His compassion was yet more tender, and His power more wonderful (Lk 7^{36-50} 19^{1-10} 23^{39-43}). Sometimes the case was harder than that of conscious need—a condition of moral torpor—and this He provoked into action by a summons and a challenge (Mk 2^{13-15}, Lk $5^{27f.}$). Often He had to deal with an unawakened conscience and a spiritual self-sufficiency which was impervious to criticism, and then He spared no sternness of rebuke that might pierce the harness of conceit (Lk 7^{40}, Mt 23^{13}). Where He found an open mind and an unprejudiced judgment, He was frank to acknowledge the honest and good heart and eager to win a full surrender to the claim of God (Mk 12^{28-34}).

The moral state which moved Him to most severe criticism and most sorely tried His good will was that of a divided heart; and here His demand for absolute surrender was inexorable (Lk 9^{57-62}, Mk 10^{17-22}). The cases recorded in the first chapter of the Fourth Gospel (vv.$^{34-51}$) are too thoroughly human to be dismissed as unhistorical. They are at least typical of the manner in which disciples attached themselves to Jesus. They came by way of the Messianic expectation, and they cast their thoughts into Messianic forms; but the roots of their conviction run deep into the soil of a personal experience. The Messianic form might break, or be changed out of knowledge, but the attachment would remain and be ready to find for itself more adequate expression. These stories give the real origins of Christianity. Forms of thought, inherited from Jewish tradition, or intruded from Oriental religions or from Hellenic speculation, do not afford the clue. The clue is the universal demand of the human spirit, welling up in real human hearts and met by a living human voice.

(*b*) *The experience was, fundamentally, a process of education.*—A book which marked an epoch in the study of the Gospels bears the title, *The Training of the Twelve*, but the idea of training for a vocation might be extended beyond the Twelve to all disciples. Jesus is characteristically Hebrew in His conception of religion. He is not misled by intellectualism or subdued by emotionalism. He is living in the region of redemptive forces which operated in the long history of Israel, and He desires to have every man whom He summons to be subjected to these forces, to be mastered and made by them, and to become their living vehicle. His deepest equation for 'salvation' is 'life'—not a state, but an energy, working now as a dynamic in the world of men, and finding its triumph in a universe remade. His 'message of the Kingdom' was not a phrase to be learned in a few moments of memory-work and then repeated with fanatic reiteration or deadly monotony. Entrance into the Kingdom is not accomplished by cold assent or spasmodic feeling. The Kingdom is a great determining and fertilizing idea, or world of ideas, a realm of facts and forces, of motives and ideals, into which men could enter only *sub persona infantis*, whose wealth is open only to the poor in spirit, amid whose impulses and influences men might live and grow to a wonderful maturity of knowledge, character, and power. In one sense, men were already in the Kingdom and the Kingdom was in them. In another sense, they were to be prepared for the Kingdom and were to be at once its heralds and its servants. It is both *Gabe* and

Aufgabe. When we ponder the fact, than which none in the gospel narrative is more certain, that Jesus occupied Himself mainly in the making and training of men, we are growingly convinced that both the 'liberal Jesus' picture and the 'apocalyptic dreamer' picture are out of focus. If either of these was accurate, we would need to say that His methods did not correspond with His aims, and we would need to explain the success of the movement which bears His name by attributing it to some other than Himself. He could have no central place in the Christian religion.

How, then, did Jesus train men for the Kingdom of God? The answer is: By making them sharers in His own thought of God. Yet there is nothing doctrinaire in this. He gives no new definition of God, though He does use a new name for God—new, at least, in His use of it. He stands deep within the OT religion, and is Himself the fulfilment of the highest spiritual type which the OT records supply, viz. the believing man, the man who knows God, deriving His knowledge, on the one hand, from God's self-communications in revealing words and deeds and, on the other, from the activity of his own soul in prayer and meditation, in deep discernment and lowly obedience. The God of Jesus is the God of the OT, apprehended, not through the medium of Jewish forms of thought, but directly with the unveiled face of a Hebrew prophet. He knows God; He sees God; He hears God speaking. And it is into His own acquaintance with God that He seeks to lead His disciples. He will be satisfied if He can give them the guiding principle by which they will be led into a life-long exploration of the divine nature and a continuous application of the divine mind to all the emergencies of their life in the world. In that case the cause which He has at heart will be secure. They will be fit persons to preach the gospel, to bear witness to Him, and to prepare for the coming of the Kingdom. In the nature of the case, accordingly, the educative process to which Jesus submitted His disciples could not follow the conventional forms of school theology. He trained His disciples mainly in two ways.

(1) He trained them by admitting them to a share in His own experience, whether of action or of suffering. In Mk 3^{14} we have the reason of His appointment of the Twelve, viz. to 'be with Him.' The stories illustrate the meaning. They watched Him at His work; they underwent a slow and largely unconscious revolution in their thoughts of the Kingdom of God and of the salvation of men. They heard Him speak to the people, and they were profoundly disturbed. Not that there was any obscurity in the words of Jesus. They were simple, lowly, and persuasive. But the disciples differed from probably the majority of the hearers of Jesus in not being satisfied with the mere charm of His teaching. They were constantly being thrown into amazement and perplexity. Their distress of mind, indeed, is evidence that their Master's method was proving successful. They were learning, very slowly indeed, but surely, to think, to apprehend, to discover, and to possess. Their fathers' God was being interpreted for them by Jesus; and they began to understand what human life might be under such divine governance, and what their vocation was as servants of such a redeeming purpose. Their being 'with Him,' however, meant far more than seeing or hearing. It meant what was indefinable, and indescribable in any memoirs, their entrance into the secret of His personality, and that secret was His life in God. They heard Him pray. They felt the thrill of His exultation (Lk 10^{21}). Three of them, at least, felt beneath them the unplumbed depth of His sorrow (Mk 14^{32-34}). No human beings were ever nearer God than these men who had been with Jesus from the beginning (Jn 15^{27}). What they carried out of that companionship was Christianity. Lessons, however, are not learned by looking on. They require the supplement of, at least, tentative effort.

(2) This, accordingly, was the second aspect of Jesus' training of His disciples. He sent them forth to preach (Mk 3^{14}). Such tentative efforts at evangelism must have been very crude, and could have had little success. Yet in them the disciples were exploring the divine resources, and Jesus recognized in their achievements the operation of the divine omnipotence and the presage of the triumph of the Kingdom (Lk 10^{17-20}). More broadly and more deeply He impressed upon them the necessity of a living experience as the condition of growing knowledge. He is leading them into new regions of unexplored truth. They must, therefore, literally come after Him, putting their feet down in His very footsteps. He is introducing them to new values. To appreciate them, they must be willing to forgo every other advantage. He is opening to them a new life. To obtain it, they must die. The surrender value of the Kingdom is life itself (Mk 9^{42-50}, Mt 16^{24-26}, Lk 14^{25-35}). This, then, is what we behold in the Gospels—men in process of being made.

> 'The greatest miracle in history seems to me the transformation that Jesus effected in those men. Everything else in Christian or secular history, compared to it, seems easy and explicable; and it was achieved by the love of Jesus.'[1]

The Gospels explain Christianity. To go outside of them is to pick up a great deal of information, and to throw light on many points in the history of the Christian movement; but the Gospels contain the only authentic and valid explanation of how Christianity got under way, and of what it essentially is. It began as an experience created by Jesus of Nazareth, and that is what it is at this day.

(*c*) *The experience may be characterized as a paradox.*—(1) It has the note of immediacy. Jesus is concerned with the condition of men, as it directly presents itself to His penetrating insight, and He seeks to produce an immediate effect within their life and character.

(*a*) Thus, the need and peril of men are interpreted by Him in the light of their present moral state; and His main effort is to direct men to an apprehension of their inward condition as the source of their real danger. The distinction of righteous and unrighteous, of those who were sure of their place in the Kingdom and those who had no such hope, had been externalized and falsified beyond endurance by a mind which understood God so well as to have pity on man. To be formally correct in opinion and conduct, while permitting the soul to be devastated by moral evil; to allow evil desires to occupy the imagination, even though they find no concrete expression; to be legally just, without one generous impulse overflowing in unconscious grace of helpfulness; above all, to have no decision of character, and to allow the cause of God to remain unchosen and unserved—these are real grounds of exclusion from the Kingdom and its salvation. Moral evil, clothing itself in actions which the perpetrators themselves know to be wrong, is, of course, absolutely inconsistent with a place in the Realm of God. On this Jesus did not need to insist. What He emphasized was rather, first, the ruinous effects of sin within the life; and, second, the attitude of God towards those who were thus hopelessly lost.

The yearning of God over sinful, suffering Israel which utters its passion through a Hosea or a Jeremiah finds new and more compassionate voice

[1] T. R. Glover, *The Jesus of History*, London, 1917, p. 88 f.

in Jesus of Nazareth. The old religion of Israel, never forgotten, though sorely travestied by its professional exponents, came to life again through the ministry of Jesus, and surrounded those who were its objects with a more inexorable holiness and a more tender pity.

(β) If the need which Jesus uncovered so relentlessly and so mercifully was thus immediate, so also was the salvation which He promised. It was, as it has been happily described, 'a thoroughly effective salvation.' It was not to take effect at an unknown date, amid scenes of apocalyptic splendour, but right now, in the moment in which sin was actually ruining human life. This immediate salvation shines in a twofold light. It is forgiveness by God, and it is sonship towards God; and these two are one. The one Jesus announces directly, positively, absolutely, in full view of the action of legalism in at once banishing the soul from the Realm of God and enclosing it in the paralysis of despair. He never argues the matter. He has authority to forgive sins, and He exercises it royally. He understands God. He has caught the simplicities of an old-time experience: 'There is forgiveness with thee'; and He echoes it in His pronouncement: 'Thy sins are forgiven.' To imagine that Jesus, and those to whom He gave such assurance, were thinking only of a future when they would find themselves denizens of a glittering region of Jewish supremacy is to misread the simplest records of the human heart. God in His love, man in his need, Jesus speaking for God and bringing God near—these are the abiding three in the Christian salvation; and their relations to one another are never more vividly presented than in the stories of forgiven sinners told in the Gospels. The other view of salvation, viz. sonship, cannot, in the nature of the case, be thus condensed into a sentence. It is the translation into human life of Jesus' conception of God. The 'Jahweh' of the OT, Redeemer, Saviour, Father, of His people, is 'the Father' of Jesus' faith and preaching. Words, even Jesus' words, cannot exhaust the fullness of this Fatherhood. The Father loves and saves; He cares and keeps. The world is under the Father's governance; and His omnipotence is available for all the ends of His love. Into such a region of fatherly control and filial confidence the disciples of Jesus enter in company with their Master. To say that it was an unfamiliar region, and that their steps in it were slow and stumbling, that they but dimly apprehended the mind of God, often burdened themselves with needless anxieties and ridiculous scruples, and often behaved in an unfilial and unbrotherly manner, is only to repeat what we have noted—that they were in process of training, a training, however, which was conducted within the circle of divine saving power and, in essence, was their salvation. No doubt, Jesus had much to communicate before He could set forth His whole thought of God, and so demonstrate it that it would waken in sinful hearts a perfect conviction and a victorious faith.

Still it remains true that, in the company of Jesus, as He lived and taught, salvation, both as deliverance from sin and as enjoyment of God, was a fact of human experience—a fact, in respect of range and degree, new in the history of the human spirit, type and norm of Christian salvation as such, a religious standard of absolute and universal validity.

(2) It had, besides the note of immediacy, the contrasted note of imperfection and expectation. The difference between these two notes is one of emphasis on Jesus' part, and of appreciation on the part of the disciples. It is remarkable that each receives such ample recognition in the Synoptic narratives. Either by itself might have formed the organizing idea in a constructive theory of Jesus' message and mission. In point of fact, both are present, and there is no theoretic synthesis of them. The centre of unity must lie in Jesus' dynamic conception of the Reign of God. God is working for the salvation of men. Age after age He has been present in redeeming power. In every age men have had experience of this 'plenteous redemption.' Yet no age has seen the completion of the divine history. Always men have been waiting for that consummation which will mean that God's power is operating in unhindered freedom throughout the whole creation. Jesus was conscious that that power was operating in His ministry. The healing of disease, the expulsion of demons, the forgiveness of sins, the unfailing providence of the Heavenly Father, the development of the filial character, the reproduction of the Father's 'perfection,' meant for Him the presence of the Kingdom; and for those who partook of such benefits they meant aspects and proofs of the great salvation. Yet the highest range of such blessed experiences did not amount in sum to the whole salvation; and the Kingdom had not come, though its influence, as a dynamic both in the inner man and in the outer world, was making itself plainly felt. Jesus' gaze throughout His whole mission is fixed on the future. He is as convinced as any of the prophets that the present is not the end, that, beyond any present achievement of divine power, there is a goal when the divine movement shall be complete and the Kingdom shall have come. Teleology and eschatology are essential to Jesus' conception of God and His relation to the world. But Jesus' occupation with the future never led Him to belittle the present. He did not despise this world and man's life in it; and His directions as to conduct are not merely temporary rules for a mode of existence which stands in no living relation to the Messianic Kingdom. The end is certain; and, when confronted by doubt or outrageous denial, He asserted His own amazing claims and His own sublime faith. Yet He never represents the Kingdom as coming with the inevitableness of bare omnipotent decree. For Him, as for the Hebrew prophets, the coming of the Kingdom is ethically conditioned. It is the goal of God's saving work, and that goal cannot be reached apart from man's attitude to the Kingdom. The Kingdom is God's, and the power is wholly His, and the glory shall be His alone. Nevertheless, the Kingdom is an end for man, to be served by man, with complete inward identification of will with the will of God.

This service of the Kingdom takes two forms. On the one hand, with reference to the world, it is a ministry of help to be carried out to the last limit of life itself. On the other hand, with reference to God, it is fulfilled in intercessory prayer. In prayer, especially in intercessory prayer, there is more than submission to the divine will. There is such an entrance into the will of God as gives to it scope and freedom and enables God to carry out His purpose with a fullness and swiftness which, apart from such prayer, would be impossible (Mt $9^{37f.}$, Mk 11^{22-25}, Lk 11^{5-13} 18^{1-8}). The actual word for 'hope' does not appear in the recorded teaching of Jesus. The explanation is probably His desire to differentiate His gospel of the Kingdom from the excited anticipations or fatalistic passivity which were the natural result of popular apocalyptic. In any case, His strong assurance of the coming of the Kingdom is blent with His deep insight into the conditions of its coming.

It comes through service. The certainty of its coming quickens the present ministry of those who expect a share in it. Those whom Jesus called were being prepared for the Kingdom. But their preparation was not a tedious interval, to be hurried through, that the joys of the Kingdom might the sooner be possessed. It was itself result and proof of the imminence of the Kingdom, and was conducted under the present control of spiritual powers resident in the Kingdom. The disciple band is the community of the Kingdom. Its members are in possession of the privileges of the Kingdom. The OT oracle of the New Covenant is fulfilled in their experience. Their sins are forgiven. God is their God, and they are His people. His law is not a burden, but is within, the standard of their character and the delight of their souls. They know God in His Fatherhood, and commit themselves to the omnipotence of His love. They thrill with the sense that the redemption of Israel is proceeding before their eyes, and they answer joyfully the call to prepare the way for its consummation. These brief months of discipleship, before the Cross had thrown its shadow on their souls, were the springtime of Christianity. The Christian salvation is there, in bloom and promise. The Kingdom of God has come, as a possession, and is sure to come, as an inheritance.

The teaching of Jesus is an exultant 'Lift up your hearts!' The company of disciples makes response, 'We lift them up unto the Lord.'

(*d*) *The experience is the creation of Jesus.*—This aspect of the experience of the disciples carries us beyond what is observable in any company that ever surrounded any human leader of a school or founder of a religion. It is not that they ever paid Him, consciously and expressly, divine honours. Disciples of other masters have been led to regard their teachers as in some sense divine. The disciples of Jesus, however, were too thoroughgoing in their monotheism to dream of regarding Him as a second God or as a demi-god. It is the more remarkable to observe, therefore, that the religious experience of the disciples is the creation of Jesus. In its origin and development it is bound up with the Person and Presence of their Master. He pervades it as an immediate possession, and His figure stands at the goal of its consummation.

Take any element of their religious life, and Jesus is inseparable from it, in a sense and degree which wholly differentiates their relation to Him from that of pupil to teacher. *He created in them the sense of sin.* What legalism could not produce, what the thunders of the Baptist's threatenings could not effect, the personality of Jesus wrought for them and in them. To hear Him as He re-valued legal estimates of right and wrong was not to listen to a wise Teacher merely, but to look into a stainless soul, moving in unshadowed light, and wielding absolute moral authority. Even the general hearers felt this: 'for he taught them as one having authority, and not as the scribes' (Mt 7^{29}). How much more those to whom He unveiled the inmost secrets of the moral life, forcing them to face the infinite standard of divine purity and love (Mt $6^{14f.}$ $18^{15\text{-}35}$), and turning them back on themselves with a correspondingly absolute demand (Mt $18^{1ff.}$ $19^{10\text{-}12.\ 24\text{-}26}$, Mk $9^{41\text{-}49}$). Yet even such hearing was not enough. They might have stood out against it. More penetrating and illumining was the sight of sin which they got, standing by, when Jesus laid bare the festering sores of some human soul. They were gazing through His eyes into the moral abyss that yawns beneath the surface of respectable society and underlies the most decorous existence. Nay, more: they could not fail to note that sinners whom law had failed to convince broke down in godly sorrow under the spell of Jesus' holy yet tender influence. Above all, they were themselves in the same condemnation, and even in a deeper self-judgment, subjected as they were to a more constant and more searching discipline. Whatever occasions the prominence given to Peter in the Synoptic narrative, there is no doubt that the references form a human document of profound psychological interest, and of first-rate historic importance.

We see the thing happening: conviction of sin wrought by the personality of Jesus; a character displayed and a character re-made. Whatever the world knows of sin—and apart from knowledge of sin the knowledge of salvation is worthless—it owes to Jesus of Nazareth, as He stamped it deep in the hearts of these men.

He won from them trust in Himself as Saviour. We would, indeed, have been entitled to suspect the narrative had we found resounding titles adorning it and a theory of their Master's Person and Work detailed therein. What we do find is much more impressive: a company of men and women, gathered round one Man, and finding Him to be for them the means and assurance of divine salvation, the source of their confidence towards God, the warrant of their standing in His Kingdom, a fountain of life and joy, the object of a hope that rose above the earth. They were moving up and down in the Realm of God, with Jesus as Instructor and Guide, Shepherd and Friend. They were themselves the community of the Kingdom (Lk 12^{32}), the new Temple, of which their Master is the Builder, Maker, and Lord (Mt $16^{18f.}$). The most sacred thing in the aspirations of humanity is theirs; and they owe it to Jesus. They heard Him pray. He taught them to pray. He introduced them to God. He brought God to them. This they had because Jesus gave it to them, and without Him it would not have been possible, and as a dream (Mt $6^{9\text{-}13}$ $7^{7\text{-}11}$). To Jesus, accordingly, they surrendered themselves with an absoluteness which must have been the degradation and enslavement, if it had not been the emancipation and perfecting, of their manhood (Mt $4^{18\text{-}22}$ 19^{27} $5^{10\text{-}12}$ $10^{32f.}$). Words like these open a view into the consciousness of Jesus which carries with it amazing inferences as to His person. But they also reveal the consciousness of the disciples, created through intercourse with Jesus, rising towards Him, under the constraint of His holiness and love, in the spontaneity of a free and full surrender. This is not learning a lesson in religion. It is religion itself, and its centre is Jesus. They had, in their vocabulary, only one name to give Him (Mt 16^{16}), and this title of Messiah carried with it to their imagination much that had to be unlearned and laid aside. None the less, it summed up for them what they believed of God's redemptive work in the history of His people; and their application of it to Jesus was not the result of ingenious exegesis, but the expression of an attitude towards Him that was, in essence, religious trust (Mt 16^{17}). We are a long way from Jn $1^{12\text{-}18}$; but that statement contains no more than this experience, of which it is only the expression in the terms suggested by the educative processes of a generation.

'For those who attached themselves to Him, Jesus became Messiah *and more*. And . . . the experience of "the more" was also latent in the consciousness of the disciples, waiting to be quickened by [an] . . . event, and developed by a future experience.'[1]

(*e*) *Estimate.*—In seeking to estimate the salvation value of this experience of the disciples of Jesus, we cannot fail to be impressed by its superiority to anything that contemporary religion in Palestine could supply. To vindicate its superiority, it is enough to say that it was the religion of Israel, in all the highest qualities manifest in the post-Exilic stage of its history. Here we have the piety of the Psalter, with its sense of sin and of the holiness of God, its realization of forgiveness, and its possession of the divine favour; and, at the same time, the alertness and certainty of moral judgment begotten of centuries of discipline and education under Law and Prophets; together with the hope which never failed the old religion, and was never brighter or more confident than in those disciples of the Nazarene.

We have all these things, with an added intensity and assurance, which differentiate the experience of the disciples from the type of spiritual life of which theirs was the consequence and the flower. The difference is felt in the whole narrative. It is the difference which their Master made. It is the difference of a new era in the religious history of mankind (Lk $10^{23f.}$). And it is needless to say that the religion of the disciples knows nothing of the gleam of legalism; while, with all its mistaken Messianism, it is free from craze or frenzy. It is salvation in the concrete, communion with God, and deliverance from fear. We are not surprised, accordingly, to find that it has the note of joy,

[1] C. A. Scott, *s.v.* 'Christ, Christology,' in *DAC* i. 183b.

heard in the OT fitfully like songs in the night, but now full-throated and exuberant, like the joy of 'children of the bride-chamber' (Mt 9[15]). A. B. Bruce has a chapter on 'the joy of the Jesus-circle,'[1] which he analyzes as 'the joy of *love*, the joy of *fresh inspiration*, and the joy of *liberty*.' It is the 'shining morning face' of the young Church of Christ, never seen again in history, yet very lovely in the time of its continuance, 'while the Bridegroom was with them.'

The very beauty of this phase of religious life, however, reminds us that it was, in the nature of the case, vague, inadequate, and unstable. These features, of course, with the dangers which threatened, were quite hidden from the minds of the disciples themselves. To them the matter seemed definite enough, and they were confident in its permanence. They had in the current Messianism a form of thought into which they easily ran all their experiences. Their Master was the Messiah. He would inaugurate and preside over the coming Reign of God. True, they were learning a great deal about God and His Kingdom which was inconsistent with popular Messianism. But they were not critically minded; and the growing spiritual content did not lead them, as yet, even to modify the general thought form.

In one respect this uncriticalness of theirs seriously misled them. It rendered them incapable of assimilating one profound element in OT religion, namely, the place which suffering had to play in the divine salvation. The function of the great sufferers of Israel's past was too deeply printed in the history, the prophecies, and the psalms of Israel's sacred writings to be ignored by any whose souls were fed by these inspired records. The idea of a suffering remnant, of heroes and martyrs, nay, of a martyr nation, lay at the very core of the nation's faith. Even cynicism could make use of such a conception to excuse its selfishness and cruelty (Jn 11[49f.]). The disciples could have dared and borne anything for such a Master, passing on His way to a throne (Mk 10[38f.]). They were even prepared (or thought they were) to perish with Him in His failure (14[31]). But that suffering should be the lot of the Messianic King Himself was unthinkable (Mk 8[29. 32]). Cross-bearing might be the law of discipleship (Lk 14[27]); but it could never apply to Him, who was to approve and reward His servants. The redemptive value of the suffering of righteous servants of the Lord had not perished out of the religious consciousness of Israel, even under the blight of legalism, and was destined to a splendid revival. But never, within the OT canon or out of it, had a synthesis been made of the Suffering Servant and the Messianic King. Never had it been discerned that His were the sufferings that were to redeem Israel and inaugurate the Kingdom.

That synthesis took place in the consciousness of Jesus. To Him 'Son of Man' = 'Messiah' = 'Suffering Servant'; and He sees that by the path of suffering, at once divinely appointed and freely chosen, and by none other, can the purpose of God be fulfilled and salvation won (Mk 8[31] 9[12] 10[45] 14[22-24]). But teaching, warning, and prediction fell unheeded on ears stopped by theological commonplaces. Between them and their Master a rift opened, which, in His death, widened to a great gulf. Refusing to catch His meaning, they missed the element of sorrow borne and victory won which was needed to give their experience depth and permanence and to enable their faith to bear undismayed the fact of the Crucifixion.

It is an absolutely safe historical judgment that no development of the religion of Israel could take place till the synthesis referred to had been made. Without the combination of the two elements which lay side by side within it, viz. Messianic sovereignty and vicarious suffering, the religion of Israel could not have survived. In point of fact, it has not survived, apart from this combination. Christianity is the religion of Israel, thought through in its ideal unity, and grasped in the reality of a great experience.

The salvation value of the experience of the disciples, prior to the Crucifixion, depended on their being able to rise experimentally to the height of this great synthesis. If they are not able to do so, then, the Messiahship of the Master being disproved, as suffering would disprove it, the experience itself would vanish with the form with which, unhappily, they had identified it. Three things are needed ere they can move to a higher plane of religious attainment: (i.) a death, which shall shatter their false Messianism; (ii.) a victory, which shall restore to them all of which they deemed the death had robbed them; (iii.) the abiding presence of Jesus, which shall reproduce in undreamed of power and joy their life with Him in Galilee.

2. The Apostolic Church.—(*a*) *The creation of the Church.*—The movement inaugurated by Jesus of Nazareth seemed, both to its enemies and to its adherents (Lk 24[21]), to have been brought to a close by His death. In point of fact, after a few weeks during which it had disappeared from observation, it is seen to be in action, with renewed energies, equipped with new instrumentalities, and manifesting unconquerable hope. A community exists, consisting of the original disciples, united, as they had been before His death, by common allegiance to Jesus, and living the same kind of life which they had formerly owed to His presence with them; and to this community accessions are constantly being made, as they had formerly been, by the spell of His personality. The creation, more properly the reconstitution, of the Church of Christ is due to three vital facts.

(1) The first is a fact of religious experience, appreciable only by its subjects, though its outward manifestation fell under common observation; viz. that Jesus is present in power in the company of those who believe in Him. This is the meaning of Pentecost (Ac 2[33]), as well as of all those gifts and powers and fruits which occupy so large a space in the records and are always referred to the Spirit of God. They mean that Jesus is operating in full saving power in the lives of His disciples. They are simply Jesus at work now, as once He worked in the days of His flesh. To say that the Spirit is present, or that Jesus is present in the Spirit, is to say the same thing (Ro 8[9], 2 Co 3[17], 1 Co 6[17]). It is certain that the Church would not have come into existence to cultivate a hero's memory or perpetuate the cult of a demi-god. It was essentially the community of the Spirit; and that meant the spiritual presence of Jesus. This was as true on the day of Pentecost as it has ever been in the ages of the Church's ripest spirituality and clearest thought, though in the first stages of its experience the operations of the Spirit were little understood, and the quality and reach of the saving power of Christ had only begun to be appreciated.

(2) The second is a fact of history, which, however, derives its significance from, while at the same time supplying the necessary basis to, the experience of the day of Pentecost. Only One whom the power of God had raised to a position of sovereignty in the realm of redeeming forces could 'pour' on His disciples what was seen and heard that day and has been repeated in every age of the Church's history and in the life of every believer. The resurrection of Jesus, accordingly, stands behind the gift of the Spirit, and, along with that gift, forms the foundation of the Church of Christ. These two were never separate in the apprehension of the Church, and together they establish the Messiahship of Jesus. Jesus is enthroned; and the Spirit has come (Ac 2[32f.]). Therefore, Jesus is the Messiah (2[36]). The attendant circumstances of the Resurrection and the Pentecostal gift cannot now be straightened out into a formally consistent

[1] *The Galilean Gospel*, Edinburgh, 1882, ch. xii.

narrative. But the two facts themselves establish the redemptive supremacy of Jesus. They explain the existence of the Christian Church; and nothing else does. And they form the bridge, at once historical and experimental, by which the experience of salvation passed over from the confines of Palestine to occupy the wide world of humanity and become the inheritance of mankind.

(3) The third is the fact, terrible in its cruel actuality, of the Cross. It is a strange testimony to the place which Jesus occupied in the Church's faith, and a curious comment on the narrowness of intellectual processes, that this fact had in later ages to be insisted on in its crassness and horror. To the primitive disciples, however, precisely its literalness was its preciousness. By one stroke it destroyed the Messianism which hid from them their Master's Messiahship. In one revealing act it did for them what even their Master's words had failed to do, and brought together what their dogmatic had held apart—the glory of King Messiah and the suffering of the Servant of the Lord. It gave to their growing apprehension the whole world of truth and power, which lay in suffering. What had been missing in their experience before the Crucifixion, the lack of which had doomed to evanescence its highest joys, has been supplied. Through death, inflicted by 'wicked hands,' but appointed by divine redeeming will, Jesus enters on His kingly position. The Kingdom of God is no longer an object to be anticipated, but a power already victorious over the utmost that sin can do. God is not planning salvation; He has effected it, and will make it effective to all who will receive it. 'Christ died for our sins' (1 Co 15[3]). This is the gospel which Paul 'received.' It is the absolutely primitive faith of the Christian Church. Without it the Church could not have existed. Only such a transmutation of death into victory could have brought the Church into being. The death of Jesus meant either utter and absolute defeat or the fulfilment and interpretation of Is 53. There was no interval of time—not a day or an hour—in which a Christianity existed which did not centre in the Cross. There was never a movement of Christian faith which did not converge on Jesus, Servant of the Lord, suffering and victorious. Anselm did not invent the Atonement, nor did Paul, though they and countless others have sought for theories of it. Suffering needs no key. It is its own interpreter. The religion of Israel had its sanctuary in pain, the suffering of God; and Christianity began its career with this in its heart—'Christ died for our sins.'

(*b*) *The Christian message of salvation.*—The religion of Israel had always been presented as a gospel. The prophets preached Jahweh as the Redeemer of His people—not an idea, not a remote and careless Deity, but a living being, animated by a gracious purpose and seeking its consummation through toil and pain, opposed by enemies, hindered by His servants, but sure to triumph in a day of mercy and of judgment, for the dawning of which expectant and penitent souls waited in deepest silence. The apostles had no other message, though, as it came from their disciplined and instructed hearts, it had a richer content and a more confident note. Their proclamation still concerned the redeeming power of God. They declared, regarding it, that in Jesus its operation was complete. He is its Agent and Mediator. Through Him, suffering and victorious, it enters afresh the lives of men—of His own selected people, and, as they soon discover to their unspeakable amazement, of all men everywhere who will believingly submit themselves to Jesus. It works with an effective salvation, redeeming men from the evils that had all their lifetime oppressed them, and placing them under the emancipating influences of the Reign of God, constituting them also heirs of the Kingdom, when, in the hands of the Crucified and Exalted Lord, it shall be established in complete and unquestioned dominion. All this they summed up in a word, which needed the interpretation which they gave it, yet did carry with it the answer to the demand of the heart of Israel, and, indeed, to the religious demands of the human spirit amid all the races of the earth. Jesus is the Christ. Through Him God works savingly. He is the Saving Power of God to all who accept Him.

The proposition, 'Jesus is the Christ,' is not an opinion, however true, which may be held by a sect or by an individual, like any other tenet which intellect might devise and bigotry retain. It is the utterance of an experience, the experience of actual salvation as a power in personal life. It receives from that experience its warrant and proof, its illustration and interpretation. Above all, it is the outcome of an irresistible impulse, to propagate the experience and to bring all men within the scope of the divine salvation. Nothing in the history of the Christian Church is more impressive than the fact that its birth hour is the beginning of its evangelism. The subjects of salvation are its instruments. The disciples remembered how their Master had not kept them always 'with Him,' much as they needed His presence, but had 'despatched them to preach, with the power of casting out demons' (Mk 3[14]). And now the same thing is happening under more wonderful conditions. He is with them in power, and He is sending them out on the same errand of mercy. His very voice is in their ears with 'majestic instancy,' saying, 'Go to all the world and preach the gospel to every creation' (16[15]). There is nothing formal about it, no clank of machinery. The world, and all the men and women in it, are under bondage. Jesus saves. They knew it by experience; and, therefore, they spoke. They could not help themselves. 'Not for a single day did they cease to teach and preach the gospel of Jesus the Christ in the temple and at home' (Ac 5[42]). And on journeys of business or flight they did the same thing (8[4]).

It follows that we need not look in the records for any exact reproduction of the mission preaching of the early Church, which must have been marked by the widest variety and must have included every kind of simple and unstudied testimony as well as more formal addresses. A theory can be put into swaddling bands, an experience never. We can see, however, what elements belonged to the message and gave it driving power.

(1) Stories about Jesus.—If any part of the NT gives us the 'mission preaching' of the primitive Church, it is the Synoptic Gospels. Many of the narratives bear traces, according to Denney, of being 'sermon notes.' In any case, they provide what the preacher needed. He claimed that Jesus was the Messiah, and that in Him the power of God wrought savingly. Being challenged, he replied not by argument, but by instances. He gave case after case of Jesus' power to heal and save; and so the Gospels are full of miracles wrought on the bodies and souls of men. He quoted sayings of Jesus, which showed His deep spiritual-mindedness, a knowledge of God greater than that of sage and prophet; and so the Gospels contain teachings of Jesus, though they never present Him merely as a teacher. Above all, he conveyed the impression made by Jesus on those who knew Him; and so the Gospels contain a portrait of Christ at once in His deep humanity and in that quality which, without separating from men, lifts Him out of the class of the 'lost' and sinful and makes it possible for Him to bring near to them the divine salvation. We constantly think of the Gospels as written up, or down, to some theological theory. In point of fact, they are the gospel, as told by individual Christians, in all sorts of places, to all sorts of audiences, told in tale after tale, on a roof-top, by the wayside at the noon hour, round the camp fire, in synagogue or market-place. What the preacher sought to accumulate on the minds of his hearers was simply this: 'If there is to be a Messiah, He is certainly Jesus; not what we had expected; but certainly Jesus is He.'

(2) The word of the Cross.—There were audiences among whom the story of the death of the Christ might seem to bring the missionary's office to an end; for some would think it 'sheer folly' and others would be outraged by such an insult to national and religious feeling. Yet the preacher had no option. He might leave to teachers more learned than he—a Paul or an Apollos—the task of supplying an intellectual solution

of the problem raised by the Cross. But the Cross itself was no problem; it was an integral part of the gospel—the gospel which he and all Christians 'received.' It was simply the redeeming love of God, which, in all ages of Israel's history, had been burdened by the sins of His people, in its last and final act of sin-bearing. Accordingly, even the least lettered preachers told the story of Jesus, with the shadow in it mounting steadily towards the blackness of Calvary. It has been, curiously, maintained that the Gospels sink beneath the level of the primitive gospel which the first disciples 'received' by ignoring the connexion between the death of Jesus and the sins from which He redeemed His people, leaving us no more than a benign and singularly endowed Teacher. The Gospels would thus represent a lapse towards legalism. The absence from the Gospels of such a construction of the Atonement as we get, *e.g.*, in Ro 3 may, however, be much more simply explained.

The early missionaries, whose 'sermon notes' we are supposing the Gospels to be, had no theory, and needed none. But they had a story to tell, and they told it with utter artlessness and consummate skill. They let their hearers feel the weight of sorrow which their Master carried in an intensity of love and pity which divided Him from those whom He sought to save, while it drew Him to them in great nearness of spirit (Mt 11$^{28ff.}$ 8^{17}). They told how, once and again, the anguish of His soul broke into tears as He contemplated a woe which He alone understood. They told how, in suggested figure or dark and pregnant saying, He had indicated something of what lay upon His heart; and how He had even definitely predicted a grief so intolerable that it paralyzed their intelligence. Finally, they told the story of the last hours, with such fullness and selection of detail as make them, not an impressive tragedy, but the fulfilment of a purpose, the crowning issue of self-dedication. The narrative is given without one pause of theological explanation, but not without prophetic consciousness.

Simple as they are, these missionaries have been bred on the prophetic writings, and have been instructed by the event to lift into the light the element by which they had been baffled, and to bind together the suffering of the Servant with Messiah's saving work. Their very language echoes strains from the songs of the Servant.[1] They had no theory of the Atonement; but their identification of their Master with the Messiah and with the Servant of the Lord was intentional and was complete. This identification was the very nerve of their gospel. The sorrow of the Redeemer, which is the very sorrow of God (Ac 20^{28}), is set in such relation to the sin of man that it constitutes deliverance from the evils that sin has wrought. The religion of Israel is that of a living God pledged to redemption. In Is 53 the pledge is made in most solemn articulation. In the Cross of Christ it is fulfilled with divine completeness. This is the gospel which the first converts 'received' and which they 'passed on,' not in the language of Romans or Hebrews, but in that of the Synoptic Gospels, as that repeats and illustrates the language of Isaiah (Ac 8$^{28-33}$).

(3) **The resurrection of Jesus.**—The heart of the Church's message was redemption. The preaching contained nothing that was not relevant to this mighty fact of the moral world. To prove and illustrate this, the stories of Jesus' ministry were told. He had been, in the experience of His own disciples and of all who trusted Him, the redeeming power of God. The story of the Cross grounds this redemption in suffering, and matches the world's sin with the Redeemer's pain, blood-shedding and sin-remission standing together in the history of God's redeeming acts (Mk 14^{24}, Mt 26^{28}). Here is a claim of transcendent magnitude; the divine redemption is now in action; the divine salvation is now guaranteed. But it is liable to utter rejection, if He in whose name it is made is dead and gone. Death, that complex fact of the physical and moral world, if it be the final act of Jesus' life, does indeed end all. There can be no talk of redemption or salvation, none of a Redeemer and Lord, if there be no more operative in the world the redeeming forces concentrated in Jesus and inseparable from His personality. On this point the missionaries were competent to speak. Their evidence reached the point at issue and established the twofold fact: Jesus lives; Jesus reigns. The first part of the evidence deals with the conquest of death and the continuity between Him whom they had known in the flesh and the glorified being who now reveals Himself to them. He has not changed, nor has His function altered; He still takes command and opens to them the powers and privileges of the Kingdom. The second part of the evidence, accordingly, is the life of the redeemed in the actual experience of reconciliation and forgiveness, of moral power and spiritual joy. This witness is primitive. It is found articulated in such a record as 1 Co 15$^{3-11.\ 12-19}$. It is repeated in every disciple, as such, who is a living witness to the power of the living Christ. 'The primary testimony of the disciples to Jesus was their testimony to His resurrection: except as Risen and Exalted they never preached Jesus at all.'[2] What they preached was not a bare physical fact; and what it meant was not the apotheosis of Jesus, who now takes His place as a 'cult god,' comparable to Serapis or Mithras in the ethnic faiths. It was the crowning act of God's long labour of redemption. It was the victory of Jahweh, the Redeemer of Israel. It meant that the power of God to save, as it had worked through Jesus of Nazareth and had been embodied in Him, now operates in Him, whom it has raised from the dead, in unhindered omnipotence, throughout the whole universe of man's life and discipline. Jesus had always wrought His redeeming works in His Father's name and power. Now, by the Resurrection, He exerts that same power, unrestrained by the limitations of the flesh and the conditions of His earthly ministry, in sovereign freedom and exultant victory. They could remember strange moods and words of His, in which the sense of power and victory found expression—*e.g.*, Lk 10$^{17-24}$. Already Jesus had been living in the new age, when Satan should be overthrown (v.^{18}), and the supreme authority vested in the Son (v.^{22}) should be vindicated to the 'simple-minded,' who were already in a position of privilege for which prophets and kings had longed in vain.

And now the new day, the day of the Resurrection, has dawned. The Crucified is King. This is the message: 'So let all the house of Israel understand beyond a doubt that God has made him both Lord and Christ, this very Jesus whom you have crucified' (Ac 2^{36}). The supremacy of Jesus is an integral part of the Church's faith and the Church's proclamation. The question is not as to the title Kyrios; and no vital element of the faith would be affected by proof that it came into use only after Christianity had been 'carried from the soil of Judaism to that of Hellenism.'[1] The real question is as to the function of Jesus in the divine salvation and His place in the Church's faith and witness. This problem was raised, and was settled, on 'the soil of Judaism,' or, rather, within the religion of Israel, by the revelation which, beginning in the life experiences of the prophets and like-minded souls in Israel, culminated in Jesus. It is the question whether the divine action was carried out in Him, and is now being carried on by Him. This question has been answered by the Resurrection. By the Resurrection Jesus is set in a place apart in relation both to God, the only Saviour of men, and to sinful men, needing deliverance. In this place and function the primitive missionaries preached Him. Whatever words they used, even if 'Kyrios' never fell from their lips, they bear witness to His resurrection and to His supremacy; and this is essential Christianity, whatever phrases, in any age, may be used to express the meaning.

(4) **The return of Jesus.**—The Church's message of salvation is now, in one sense, complete. Jesus in His exaltation is God's final and glorious organ of salvation. The Reign of God has entered on its triumph. Salvation is being made effective in the lives of believers, and the company of the disciples is being increased daily by the addition of the 'saved' (Ac 2^{47}). In Jesus, therefore, in His earthly ministry and in His exaltation to Heaven, the disciples were beholding the culmination of the history whose former periods had been marked by God's redemptive dealings with His people Israel; and this they were proclaiming with an exultant confidence, which every new manifestation of saving power made more strong and joyful. The culmination itself, however, is a period, not a point of time. The Resurrection is the beginning of that period, and contains the warrant of its progress, but it is not itself the end.

Contemporaneous with the new age of divine victory there is the old age, in which powers of evil still rage and men are still held in bondage and in misery. The Christian missionaries are confronted, both in Judaism and in the Gentile world, with a vast mass of wretchedness and despair, caused by forces of evil, to which, whether seated in human nature or occupying a place in a supersensuous region, men have yielded, and from which they have sought deliverance in vain. To such a world the message proclaimed (i.) the absolute supremacy of the Exalted Christ over every possible force of evil; (ii.) His return, when 'the end' appointed by God shall have come, in final judgment of all evil, and the salvation of His people. The Parousia, accordingly, is part of the message. It derives its whole value, however, from that which is the heart and core of the message, viz. that the Kingdom has come, Jesus is supreme, salvation is a present experience. It is vain, therefore, either to rule eschatology out of primitive Christianity or to make it the whole of Christianity. The so-called 'consistent eschatology' is too easy. It breaks upon the data. God's redeeming action, in the hands of Him who is the only and altogether adequate organ of this saving power, will be completed in a definite, recognizable, and most glorious intervention. We can understand the powerful effect of this part of the message, how weighty an argument it was for repentance on the part of those who had belonged to the evil age (Ac 3$^{19-24}$); what a mighty source of comfort to those harassed and oppressed by world powers (1 Th 4^{18}, Ph 4^{5}); and what a steadying influence to those who were labouring in the service of the Kingdom (1 Co 15^{58}). We can imagine also how the Christian hope would shine into the darkness of the world beyond the confines of Israel, where the same sense of an evil age and the same longing for a new dispensation were deep-seated and universal.

When the message was proclaimed, there was possible for the hearer only one of two attitudes. Either he might believe what was told him, viz. that Jesus was the power of God for salvation, or he might reject it. The nature of the former attitude, moreover, is defined by the burden of the message. It is an attitude, or act, of the soul in reference, not to a proposition, but to a personal

[1] For instances see H. A. A. Kennedy, in *ExpT* xix. [1907–08] 346 ff., 394 ff., 442 ff., 487 ff.

[2] J. Denney, *Jesus and the Gospel*[4], London, 1913, p. 107.

[1] W. Morgan, *The Religion and Theology of Paul*, Edinburgh, 1917, p. 47.

power. It carries with it the recognition of that power as now operative in Jesus, the confidence that it is capable of effecting salvation and that nothing is beyond its scope, and the trustful commitment of the soul to Jesus as the active power of God and the bearer of the divine salvation. It is, accordingly, very much more than intellectual assent. It is, even in its most rudimentary stages, a religious experience with the promise and potency of rich moral development. It is the condition of man's realization of the divine salvation, and is the human counterpart of divine power.

The whole of God's redemptive action centres in Jesus the Christ. The whole of man's response to the divine appeal is centred in faith. The object of this faith is always God in His saving power; but it is never truly and adequately exercised apart from Him in whom that power is operative. The range and action of that faith ought to be as wide as the love of God, which has all His power at its disposal. The Christian life itself is simply a training in the exercise of faith. The ministry of Jesus supplied the evangelists with ample illustration of the nature and operation of faith.[1]

Their own daily experience added new instances, and made more definite their conception of faith (Ac 3[16] 16[31]). Faith may vary widely, from the crudest 'miracle faith' to the most articulate and educated apprehension. But its value never varies. It is the turning of the soul to Jesus; and in that act the divine salvation enters human life, and begins its beneficent and far-reaching operation.

(c) *Salvation within the Church.*—Christ is 'the power of God' (1 Co 1[24]). The gospel is 'God's saving power' (Ro 1[16]). Salvation consists in the effects wrought by God's power in the lives of those who submit themselves trustfully to Christ, meeting 'point by point'[2] the ultimate and universal needs of man. Christian faith is belief in the willingness and power of God to deal thus effectively with man's whole case, as he stands in the midst of the world, to the uttermost of his need, to the utmost of his capacity.

Christianity, accordingly, can be understood only through 'human documents,' which, when sympathetically read, become 'human sacraments.'[3] These documents are open to our view in the NT. A great deal of the material consists in life stories, in character studies, exhibiting the entrance of divine power into human life through the point of contact established by faith in Christ. Even where names and incidents do not occur, we are aware of many persons thus 'saved,' gathered into small communities at various places in the great world, and all together forming a brotherhood, sharing a common experience, aiding one another in religious faith, and ministering to one another's need to the utmost of gifts and resources. For such persons the various NT writings were composed, in a familiar and occasional manner, according as exigencies required and love prompted. And they were composed, it is also to be particularly noted, by persons who, however gifted naturally or specially endowed by the divine spirit, belonged to the same class as those for and to whom they wrote. They wrote out of the fullness of that very experience which belonged to their readers as well as, though it might be not in the same degree as, themselves. There is, therefore, nothing *ab extra* in the NT as regards its content. It is experimental through and through. Forms of thought may be picked up here or there; but one thing underlies all forms, and that is the experience of God's saving power as it meets man in Christ and the message. It is quite possible to turn over the leaves of the NT and to say, 'Lo this is Oriental, this is Hellenic, this is Roman, and the bulk is Jewish!' But to conclude that, therefore, Christianity is a mosaic of bits picked up, or a window formed of pieces of glass stained by the imaginations of men, is wholly to miss our way. Such a mosaic, or rose-window, of religion might be very beautiful, but it would bear no analogy to Christianity, which in its very origin and in its inmost being is life, is power, is Christ. This point of view, securely established as it is by modern scientific method, has, without doubt, great apologetic value.[1] But it is not a pronouncement in favour of any system of theology which may claim to be orthodox. Rather does it give an earnest warning against the idea that finality can be attained in the work of theological reconstruction; and it suggests that the task of theology is the interpretation of the ever-living experience of the Church, including the criticism of those forms of thought in which that experience has been clothed by the growing apprehension of disciplined Christian intelligence.

1 *E.g.*, Mk 5[34-36] 10[52] 2[1-12], Mt 8[5-13] 9[29] 15[28], Lk 7[50], Mt 13[58], Mk 6[6] 4[40].

2 Cf. W. P. Paterson, *The Rule of Faith*, London, 1912, p. 179.

3 P. T. Forsyth, *The Principle of Authority*, London, n.d. [1913], p. 23 f.

When we turn to the NT, to discern what needs of men are met and what blessings are gained in the great salvation, it cannot be with any expectation of making an analysis or enumeration that could conceivably be complete. For one thing, human need is endlessly varied amid the innumerable experiences that make up the sum of human life. For another, growth and development culturally and morally are registered by increasing sense of need. But, more particularly, the greatest needs are not felt till there be a revelation of God to the soul. The religious attitude of the human spirit to God is not, 'Here is a list of my needs; now satisfy them,' but, 'I need Thee,' and the divine response is at the same time the revelation of need and the answer of love.

This, then, is what we find in the NT—a voyage of discovery, an exploration at once of human life and of the divine resources. Those who make the journey report continually new 'finds,' new experiences, new possessions, new prospects. Their language rings with wonder, joy, and praise. One explorer testifies to his friends, as the considered result of his own experience: 'My God shall fulfil every need of yours according to his riches in glory in Christ Jesus' (Ph 4[19]).

Although, however, the acceptance of the gospel brings with it wealth that is 'fathomless' (Eph 3[8]) and therefore incalculable, it is possible, contrasting the world to which the bearers of the message belonged with that to which they were introduced through faith, to catch some definite aspects of their experience and to begin to understand what Christianity meant for them.

(1) **Darkness.**—The Gentile world was steeped in darkness. It is true that God was never without His witness; and it is true that He does not deal with men according to the abstractness and hardness of human judgment, but according to His own individual knowledge of them (Ac 10[35]). None the less, a gross darkness did cover the nations, and such light as they had only renders less excusable their misunderstanding of the divine nature and character (Ro 1[20f.]). The Jewish world is in a different condition, and Jews are in a position of immensely superior privilege—if only they had availed themselves of it (2[17-24]). None the less, the ripest and most intelligent adherent of the religion of Israel is still waiting for the light of the knowledge of God. He has not the key to the Scriptures, and is liable to think of God and His ways with men in a manner that mistakes and dishonours Him (Mt 16[23]). But He has in Christ made Himself known. That which had been partially disclosed in the progress of Israel's redemption has been gathered into one act. He has sent His Son into the world. God is known, as in Israel, so now in Christ. The darkness is past. The true light is shining. To accept Jesus, preached as Christ, is to pass out of shadows into marvellous light. Conceive the ideas of God entertained in Judaism—how remote and unapproachable! Think of the gods of the Gentiles—how foolish and helpless, how, often, monstrous, capricious, and

1 Cf. T. R. Glover, *The Christian Tradition and its Verification*, London, 1913.

unclean! Then imagine the effect of being led through faith in Jesus to know God in His holy character and in the triumph of His love! It is impossible to mark the contrast too widely (1 Co 12^{2}, 1 Th 1^{9}, Ph 3^{8}, Jn 14^{9} 17^{3}). Even when, in the effort of philosophic thought, the idea of God had been purified and exalted, the end of the religious quest was still unreached; and the missionary of Christ had to proclaim a God, ethical and gracious, dealing with the world in mercy and in judgment (Ac 17$^{23ff. 30f.}$). Knowledge of God, accordingly, gained through historic deeds and a historic character, is salvation.

(2) **Sin.**—The world to which all men, Jews as well as Gentiles, belonged was a world of sin. The deepest problems of the religious heart were relief from guilt, the remission of sins, and reconciliation to God, whom conscience reckoned hostile. The question is not really debatable. The gospel is preached in view of an undeniable situation. Sin? 'Christ died for our sins.' The salvation offered is forgiveness, reconciliation; and the offer is amply verified in the experience. We are so accustomed to go to the NT for theories of atonement that we are apt not to lay the emphasis on the primary fact portrayed in the NT, viz. a life lived without the over-hanging sense of guilt and condemnation. To accept the divine mercy extended in a Christ who died and was now enthroned in power is to pass into a new world. The writings make the contrast vivid; and always the emphasis lies on the immediacy of the experience: instead of guilt, pardon; instead of enmity, reconciliation; instead of despair, peace and joyful confidence. There is nothing abstract, doctrinaire, intellectualist. All is concrete, living, personal. To believe in Jesus, the Christ, was to gain in the moment what all religions sought and none had to offer, not even Judaism. What Jesus gave in the days of His flesh (Mk 2^{10}, Mt 11^{28}) He gives now in the day of His accomplished sovereignty. 'In him we enjoy our redemption, that is, the forgiveness of sins' (Col 1^{14}). This is not theory. It is life, and salvation.

(3) **Human life.**—In the world, where men dwell in alienation from God, human life has not its proper value and human beings have not secured to them their true rank. It is true that theoretical affirmations of the independence and worth of the individual were common in an age when the steam-roller of empire had crushed national and civic freedom. It is true that the Jews claimed to be a spiritual *élite*, and to stand high in the favour of God; but a claim to spiritual rank grounded on ethnic descent defeats itself. All theory, however, broke on the hard facts of the social condition of the Roman world, where the dignity and security of man depended on accidents of birth and fortune. But the situation is absolutely changed for those who have seen and received God in Christ. It is impossible to put this too strongly, if we are to enter into the heart of primitive Christianity. Had Christ been 'a god' or 'a demi-god,' belief in Him would have left the chasms that yawned between man and man uncrossed. But, if God, Creator and Redeemer, be so present in Christ that He manifests and fulfils His gracious will towards sinful men, there is simply no room left for distinctions of grade in humanity.

Man is admitted to the divine. He has gained, in the act of faith, a rank compared with which the decorations of the world are paltry and unreal. This sense of human dignity was profoundly marked in all the teaching of Jesus; and now it belongs to the consciousness of all who believe in Him as the living organ of the divine salvation. Take the highest rank known on earth, rank that carried with it the most sacred privilege and the holiest religious function—kingship and priesthood; that belonged to the humblest believer in Jesus, the slave-girl equally with the Roman noble (Rev 1$^{5f.}$). More profoundly still, consider a standing which belonged in the religion of Israel to the Messianic King, or to the privileged people as a whole. Note how this position of sonship towards God belonged to Jesus, and received in His person an interpretation beyond anything that the highest reach of Hebrew religious aspiration had conceived. Then note what happens in the act of faith in Jesus as Christ. Entrance is made into that very standing of filial relationship to God. It is simple matter of fact that to be receptive of, and to be laid hold of by, the saving power of God in Christ makes a man, not a servant, but a son, not a doorkeeper, but a child in the Father's house. This is Jesus' assurance to His disciples, so confident and comprehensive that the Christian Church even yet grasps it too timidly. But it is typical and essential Christianity. It is not the thin and jejune dogma of a vague and philosophic theism. It is a fact in the lives of those who have made the transition from one universe to another through faith in Christ. 'Children of God! That is what we are' (1 Jn 3^{1}). This is not a guarded inference. It is an actual experience. This is what 'salvation' means for a Christian.

(4) **Corruption.**—The world into which Christianity entered was morally corrupt. Salvation, operative as a force in that world, meant moral transformation (1 Co 6$^{9-11}$). It is not necessary to exaggerate. Even Paul, who dips his brush in darkest colours (Ro 1$^{21-32}$), is ready to recognize higher elements in the society to which he bore his message. But the terrible facts of moral decay and impotence are patent. The heart of mankind was aware that the remedy lay not with itself. The demand was for a 'Saviour,' and no religion had any chance of winning adherents which did not present a method of 'salvation.' Historically, Christianity ranks as one of these religions. Its historic warrant lies simply in the fact that it did what it professed to do. It did not, of course, profess to make, on the instant, morally perfect beings. But it did claim that persons submitting themselves to Jesus were, in that act of soul, lifted out of the region of moral decay and death, and were placed in a new world and made subjects of healing and transforming agencies which contained the promise and potency of a result nothing less than divine perfection.

And the actual healings, the progressive transformations, verified the claim. Whatever may be thought of Jn 4^{42} as the authentic record of an incident in the life of Jesus, it is the exact and reliable account of an experience which included, not only the dwellers in a remote Samaritan town, but all men everywhere who made experiment in the saving power of God in Christ. The method of the Church was the method of Jesus (Mk 2^{17}). The success of the Church was the success of Jesus, multiplied by all the difference between a ministry accomplished in the limitations of the body and one achieved in the unhindered exercise of sovereign power (Jn 5^{36} 14$^{12f.}$). Jesus Himself was profoundly aware that a new world of moral and religious powers was coming into being with Himself (Lk 16^{16}, Mt 11^{11}), and those who enter it become new, as if they had—as indeed they really had—begun life over again (Mt 18^{3}). And this sense of newness pervades the NT (2 Co 5^{17}, Gal 6^{15}, Eph 4^{24}, Ro 12^{2}, Tit 3$^{4f.}$, Ro 6^{4}). Christians live and move in a 'new sphere of life,' and no symbol is too strong to suggest the wonder of the change—creation, resurrection, or birth. But no physical analogy or metaphysical explanation affects the fact, which is a moral experience, the possibility of which lies in the power of God, and the responsibility for which lies in man's act of repentance and faith. Even as Jesus wrought a moral miracle in His training of His disciples when He was with them, so does He now continue the same operation, through the discipline of life, till He has gained an even more marvellous result. He puts His stamp on them. They are transformed into His likeness. Salvation is none other than this process.

(5) **Bondage.**—The world lying outside the moral universe, where the holy love of God is dominant through the exalted Saviour, lies in bondage. The philosophic Greek mind construed this through a physical or metaphysical dualism of form and matter. Men, unhappily, are immersed in a material element and are wholly subdued by it. The mind of Israel is not obsessed by such metaphysical abstractions. It knows nothing of metaphysical dualism, and sees in man a unity of matter and spirit, of body and soul, within the sphere of personal life. The religion of Israel, developing through ages of moral education, has reached an analysis of man's condition at once darker and more hopeful than the Greek. The dualism is not between two substances or elements of which man is the combination, but between man in his self-will and God in His holy sovereignty. Sin, therefore, is worse than a misfortune or cruel destiny, of which even great criminals are the helpless and hapless instruments. It is an act of man, which, thrown back upon his own nature and on human society, has produced anarchy and confusion, disorganization and enslavement. To escape from this bondage, the Gentile world had its philosophies and moralities, its popular faiths, and its mystery-religions. The Jews had their Law, magnificently superior in moral quality to anything that the rest of the world could provide. It was, however, at its best, a conspicuous failure, and left men, indeed, in a double bondage—bondage to a code, without the faintest degree of freedom from the tyranny of sin. Here the Christian message intervened and, in a word, emancipated the human spirit for ever. The saving power of God, the power that has met and vanquished sin, is ever active and accessible in Jesus, the living Lord. To accept Jesus as Saviour and Lord is, in that act, to receive the power of God into the springs of life, and to be forthwith under its enabling influence. This power is designated the Spirit, the term which the religion of Israel reserved for God in His indwelling and inworking, in the sphere of human life and on behalf of men. To be a Christian is to believe in Jesus the Christ *and* to receive the Spirit. To believe in Jesus as the Christ, without having received the Spirit, is not yet to be a Christian (Ac 19$^{1-7}$). To believe in and seek to possess the power of God, without repentance and faith in Christ, is to be miserably self-deceived and hideously guilty (8$^{18-24}$). Here is a moral principle of boundless applicability. Its range of action could not be discerned at first. Dangers threaten its application. But from the beginning 'the reception of the Spirit is the whole of Christianity.'[1]

Christianity is the religion of the Spirit. The Church is the community of the Spirit. Legalism, magic, externalism of every sort is condemned from the outset. Without the Spirit there is no salvation. The possession of the Spirit gives the Christian salvation the notes of power (Eph 3$^{14-20}$), freedom (2 Co 3^{17}), and joy (Lk 10^{21}, Ro 14^{17}).

(6) **Fear of demons.**—It is impossible to contemplate the ancient world without observing one feature which it shares with all lands which at the present time are under control of animism—the wide-spread fear of demons. Whatever psychologists or members of the Society for Psychical Research may make of the phenomena, the fear itself is beyond all question. Illustrations abound; and we are to conceive to ourselves a state of mind according to which the supersensuous region, the 'air,' is inhabited by malignant beings seeking the destruction of men in body and in soul. Beings well-disposed towards man no doubt exist and give their aid; but the battle is sore, and the issue is undecided, and the fear remains. The Christian missionaries, like Jesus Himself, shared the belief in the existence of such evil powers, and admitted the helplessness of man in conflict with them. But the message declared that the power of God, almighty in its holiness and love, is now effective in the person of the conquering Christ, to beat back the worst assaults of such enemies and ultimately to banish

[1] J. Denney, *s.v.* 'Holy Spirit,' in *DCG* i. 738.

them from the universe of God. This is the claim of Jesus (Mt 12^{28}); and the claim is verified by the cases of cure (Mk $1^{32ff.}$). The power of victory resides in the message, and is exercised by those who proclaim it (Mk 3^{15} 16^{17}). The NT is steeped in the conviction of the reality and fearful workings of these evil spirits, and in the triumphant assurance that they cannot harm those who have taken refuge with the power of God, which acts through the uplifted Lord by faith in Him (2 P 2^4, Rev 9^{20}, 2 Ti 1^7, 1 Jn 4^6, Ja 2^{19} 3^{15}, Ac 5^{16} 8^7 $16^{16\text{-}40}$). The apostle Paul moves in this region of thought, and contemplates with awe and triumph the havoc wrought by these evil powers and their overwhelming defeat by the sovereign power of God in Christ (Eph 2^2 6^{12}, Ph 2^{10}, 1 Co 2^8, Col 1^{13} $2^{14f.}$, Gal $4^{8ff.}$, Ro $8^{38f.}$). The point of interest is to be found, of course, not in the alleged reality of these evil beings (a question which, be it noted in passing, has been reopened by the discovery of the 'subconscious'), but in the reality of the fear, and in its expulsion by the conviction of the sole supremacy of that God who, through Jesus, has revealed Himself as the only Redeemer. To the men of that day salvation carried with it deliverance from demons, and to animists of the present day it means the same thing. Missionary records echo the NT sense of immense relief, and the confident security, which is like an awakening out of nightmare.

(7) **Fear of death.**—A yet more intimate and personal fear possessed the world, apart from the influence that streamed from the resurrection of Jesus—the fear of death. The human heart reacted passionately against this inevitable end of human aspirations and endeavour and enjoyment. And in the age in which Christianity entered on the scene of human hopes and fears the demand for assurance of immortality was loud and insistent. It was met by philosophical arguments and by the promises of the mystery-religions. But the fear and the doubt brooded over mankind. Those who were trained in the religion of Israel were in a different position. Apocalyptic conceptions might help (Dn 12^2), and might issue in a dogma of 'resurrection at the last day.' But such a belief was scarcely a deliverance from the gloom of separation from the sphere of life and love. The real line of hope lay in the faith which apprehended God as Redeemer. In this, after the terrible discipline of the Exile, the religion of Israel culminated. The individual human being who commits himself to God possesses a salvation which is not limited to time and space. 'God is not the God of the dead, but of the living' (Lk 20^{38}). Such a faith, however, needs to be grounded in an act of God, which meets the fact of death once for all, and for ever changes its significance.

The hope of immortality cannot stand apart from the triumph of redeeming love. When that triumph takes place, hope becomes certainty, being, indeed, simply the register of the inner quality of redemption. Salvation from sin is salvation from death, because the enthroned Lord has the whole power of God at His disposal, and none of the powers of the earth or of the air can make head against Him (Ro $8^{38f.}$). Hence, the message met this profound need of man, not with a speculation, but with a fact: 'Christ is risen.' Questions remain regarding the attendant circumstances of man's future life; but they do not touch the central fact of the resurrection of Christ, which carries everything with it and without which nothing remains (1 Co $15^{13f.\ 16f.\ 20}$). Much of Paul's arguing may slip over us, but, as he meets the conjoined evil of sin and death with the double fact of the Cross and the Resurrection of Christ, he is on the secure ground of history and experience; and on that ground the whole primitive Church stands with him.

Salvation, therefore, means deliverance from the thraldom of a life-long fear of death (He $2^{14f.}$). It means, too, a change in the very nature of death, so that it becomes comparable to the sleep which precedes the daily resurrection to life and action (1 Co 15^{18}). It means, even more, a transfiguration in the experience of dying, which is no longer a fate, but an opportunity and condition of realizing what the power of God in Christ can do for a mortal man (1 Co 3^{22}). The defeat of death lies in the moral sphere, and is already absolute. The physical counterpart of that victory belongs to the consummation of salvation, when the period ushered in by the Resurrection shall be crowned by the return of the Lord. Then in a transition which, in the nature of the case, is unimaginable death shall be 'swallowed up in victory' (1 Co 15^{54}). But this anticipation is not a hope thrown into the unknown; it is the sure and certain issue of a salvation which is a present experience.

(8) **Sensitiveness to suffering.**—The world which saw the Roman Empire erect itself above shattered cities and states and an artificial society plant itself upon varied masses of enslaved humanity could not but be full of pain. And the rise of an intense individualism was necessarily accompanied by a developed sensitiveness to suffering. Obviously, here was a need in which body and soul cried for relief and the heart of tortured humanity imperiously demanded comfort. It was slow in coming and miserably inadequate to cope with the extent or the depth of human distress. In the Hellenic-Roman world a noble effort was made to bid defiance to pain and take refuge in the inwardness of the true Good. The defect of this view is the irrelevance of pain. Pain is not conquered till it is seen to have a meaning, in relation to the realization of the highest good of mankind. The wise and devout had much to say of the disciplinary value of suffering and sorrow, and cultivated the hope of another world, which would make amends for the griefs of this one. Yet, apart from the fact that such a literature of consolation, eloquent and tender though it was, did not reach beyond the *élite* of cultured sufferers and had no message for the dumb pain of the unknown multitude, it missed the point. A Providence which does not take pain into itself can scarcely be a Deity to which the sorrow-laden will take their case. Accordingly, myths of a divine suffering had a wonderful attraction for a world in pain. But they were too unsubstantial, too remote from the bitterness of the woman, the slave, the prisoner, the bereaved, the tormented, to constitute a world-remedy.

Within the discipline of Israel a thought was growing which might seem to have little of hope in it, and yet did contain the secret of consolation. The problem before the exercised soul of Israel was pure pain—not pain demanded by guilt, but the pain of the guiltless, suffering in a world in which moral considerations are confounded and the wicked flourish, while the righteous are cast down. The customary consolations are offered: that the triumphing of the wicked is short, that judgment is sure though delayed, that suffering is disciplinary, that God is the true good of man, and that this good, being inward, spiritual, and permanent, outweighs the evils of life—and all are of no avail. None of them goes to the root of the matter or stays the revolt of the soul. But there was a suffering in Israel which had in it redemptive value—the suffering of those Servants of God who held office under Him as mediators of His redeeming purpose, whose vocation (it came to be seen) was fulfilled in suffering, a suffering, not inflicted by a God who stood outside in untouched bliss, but appointed by God in pursuit of His gracious design, and in some sense shared in by Himself. And this suffering of God is seen in Jesus, identified in the faith of the disciples as the Suffering Servant of the Lord. The message of salvation to a suffering world does not come down upon it from a region of empyrean bliss, but enters it through the door of sympathy, and speaks to it of a divine experience of pain, and comforts it, from within, from a sanctuary of sorrow. Jesus is prepared for His saving office through pain (He 2^{10} $5^{8f.}$). Thus, and thus only, is He enabled to offer 'eternal salvation,' and to 'save to the uttermost' of man's need. Corresponding to human suffering is the suffering of the Christ of God. The Christian preachers did not unfold a theodicy. They laid bare the heart of God. From the point of view of faith in the Servant of the Lord, suffering and victorious, the fact of pain is met, not theoretically, but experimentally.

In the first place, it appears as the thing which ought not to be in the universe where love is supreme. It belongs essentially to this world, where the love of God has still to win its practical lordship. Jesus healed disease and relieved suffering as part of His redemptive work; and the Church continued His task, bringing to bear the resources of God which were available to faith both in direct healings (1 Co 12^9) and in a ceaseless ministry of comfort (2 Co $1^{3f.}$).

Not merely, however, is pain met by the counter-remedy of divine power; it is taken up into the redemptive operation of God, and is thus transmuted into blessing. It is not endured apart from Christ, nor is He separated from it. Those who preceded Him in time were caught in the tide of suffering, whose waves submerged the soul of Jesus (He 11^{26}). And those who follow Him do so by the way of the Cross, and share His pain, as He does theirs; and in their case, as in His, the suffering is an element in the salvation (Ro 8^{17}, Ph 3^{10}). A sorrow shared with the Man of Sorrows is a sorrow healed. Never had there been such sufferers as the disciples of Jesus, and never souls so glad (2 Co 4^8). In the experience of the sufferers pain acts as it did in Jesus, who was perfected by suffering, though in the case of disciples pain had a relation to personal sin which it had not in His case (He $12^{7\text{-}11}$). Nay, the pain of Christians, borne as part of their witness to the world, reproduces the very sufferings of Christ (2 Co 1^5), and continues them on behalf of the Church (Col 1^{24}). Nevertheless, the pain remains as pain, glorified though it be (1 P $4^{13f.}$). The NT is superhuman, but not inhuman. It does not glorify pain as such, and the Christian experience of pain was not touched with fanaticism. Pain belongs to that period of time in which the Kingdom of God has not yet come in fullness; and the brevity of the trial is frankly appealed to as an element of encouragement (1 P 1^6, Ro 8^{18}, 2 Co $4^{17f.}$). From a world where pain is inevitable the suffering Church lifted its eyes to that other world where 'there shall be no more death, neither sorrow, nor crying, neither shall there be any more pain' (Rev 21^4). Meantime, the life-story of believers is included in the redeeming purpose of God, which is no matter of doubt, because it has triumphed in Christ. Providence (*q.v.*) in the NT was not a Stoic theorem; it was an inference from redemption achieved in Christ (Ro 8^{28}). Pain, therefore, in Christian experience is not merely defeated; it is transfigured. Christians are not merely stern and magnificent bearers of pain, they are 'more than conquerors' over it (8^{37}); they are saved in it and by it, out of it and over it.

(9) **Moral evil.**—Passing from separate evils belonging to the present period, we note in it one comprehensive quality. This world is under the control of moral evil; it stands condemned by the holiness of God; and it is reserved for His final judgment. A modern revision of Christianity may reverse this estimate of the world, and take an optimistic view of the forces evident in it. But it is indisputable that the gloomier view was universal in the century in which Christianity was born. It was entertained by reflective minds everywhere. The Christian preachers had scarcely anything to add to its darkness, though they construed it through a more ethical conception of God and a more austere idea of His holiness. Proof that this was the Christian view of the world lies broadcast through the

NT, and may be collected under the heads of αἰών, κόσμος, and γενεά. In relation to this world, therefore, salvation, which means, as we have seen, so much positively in Christian experience, takes on a strongly negative quality. To be saved is to be saved out of this world and from the 'wrath' which is about to break upon it. It is the purpose of Messiah's coming to save men from this evil world (Gal 1^{4}, 1 Th 1^{10}). This salvation rests upon, and is guaranteed by, His atoning death (Ro 5^{9}).

From the very beginning the message warns and pleads in view of this coming doom (Ac 2^{40}; cf. Mt 3^{7}). Christians are 'refugees' (He 6^{18}), who, in another metaphor, are anchored to the hope which is as immovable as 'the inner Presence within the veil.' This negative attitude to the world has to be made good by a continual rupture of all ties which could bind a man to that which he has forsaken. Sins are to be broken off (Col $3^{3.5}$, Ro $6^{11f.}$, 1 P $4^{1f.}$). Even things not sinful must be renounced if they threaten the integrity of a disciple's devotion to the Kingdom. The strenuousness of the Master's words was not forgotten (Lk $9^{57.62}$ $14^{25f.}$), and is echoed by those who know His mind (1 Co $9^{25ff.}$).

Yet salvation, while thus consisting in deliverance from this world, and carrying with it a negative relation to the world, is not in itself negative. It is essentially positive and dynamic. It is intensely individual, but it is not individualistic, and does not terminate in the escape of the solitary soul. It is a gift; but it is the impartation of divine power, of which the 'saved' are at once the subjects and the organs. Hence it is also a task, and is possessed only in fulfilment of vocation. The disciple band, accompanying the Master, trained by Him and sent forth on errands of mercy, remains type and norm of the Christian Church in the primitive times, and, we may surely add, in every period of its history. The task is set by the gift. The gift is God's redeeming love in Jesus, who lived, and died, and rose again. It is received in faith, and operates inexhaustibly through the experience of a lifetime, and, after this life, will continue towards issues of inconceivable glory and joy. Being received, it rises in the individual as a fountain of energy corresponding to its own nature. Received as redeeming love, it acts through the saved, as redeeming love for those whom Jesus died to redeem. There is a uniqueness and absoluteness in the Person and Work of Christ, from which Christian faith has never wavered; but this did not hinder recognition of the moral congruousness of the Church's task with that of its Lord, or the sense of obligation to continue the operation of redeeming love towards the world. To separate the service of love from the experience of love is to cut the nerve of Christian faith. The service is twofold: (i.) confession of Jesus as Lord (Ro 10^{9}, Mt 10^{32}), witness-bearing to the fact and power of His resurrection (Ac 1^{8} 2^{32}); evangelism, a ministry of reconciliation which is the very action of God towards men between whom and God there exists a state of enmity (2 Co 5^{18}–6^{1}); (ii.) the activities of love in sympathy and help. Love is essentially social. Its bent is towards an organism. The primitive Christians had no social theory; but they were a society. They had no stereotyped programme; but they acted on an inspiration of compassion, and sought to gather into their living body the very Body of Christ, the *disiecta membra* of the dissolving fabric of contemporary civilization. This is what we see in the NT—love in action, having in it the very quality of the divine mercy, seeking the worst, despairing of none, integrating all into the organic unity of the society which is created by Christ and lives in Him. Salvation, accordingly, is social or it is nothing. It is the organization of mankind under the rule of redeeming love.

(10) **Doom of the world.**—Finally, salvation within the Church, whether viewed as the possession of the 'good things' which the Heavenly Father delights to bestow on His children or as escape from a world which is 'not of the Father' and is doomed to destruction, is not complete in an experience which is measurable by time. There is no hope for this world. Its doom is irrevocable. The only hope for mankind is the replacing of this order by another, in which other powers bear sway and other relations prevail. Salvation belongs to that other order, and comes when that order shall supervene upon this. This is the paradox of the Kingdom of God. It is, and it is to be. Salvation, in like manner, is both immediate as a fact and future as a hope. It is impossible to miss this futuristic note of the Christianity of the NT, however great may be our prejudice against it, or however carefully we may exclude it from our own type of religion. The 'saved' of the times of the NT are looking for a 'salvation' yet to come, ensured to them by the faithfulness of God, certified by the earnest of the Spirit (2 Co 1^{22} 5^{5}) and by incalculable riches of Christ (Eph $2^{7f.}$). Sometimes the future seems, as it were, in process, and the 'saved' are 'being saved' (1 Co 1^{18} 15^{2}, 2 Co 2^{15}). Oftener it is regarded as about to be ushered in, in a day or an event, whose date cannot be fixed, but which stands imminent to the faith and awe of believers (Ro 13^{11}, 1 Co 3^{15}, Ph 1^{28}, 1 Th 5^{8}, 2 Th 2^{13}, He 1^{14} $2^{3.10}$ 5^{9} 6^{9} 9^{28}, 1 P $1^{5.9}$). It is obvious that there was much in this Christian attitude to this world and outlook towards a world to come which resembled the views and estimates entertained by non-Christians. There is, however, one radical and characteristic difference, viz. that the Greek was operating, if we may use the phrase, with the category of substance, the Christian with that of power. The Greek thought of matter, from which he desired to be free. The Christian, trained in the OT, thought of moral evil working through the lower nature but not identical with it; and from this evil he knew he could be delivered only by the act of God. Already he knew by experience the efficacy of that power; and he expected a day of its complete vindication, in salvation and in judgment.

The 19th cent. mind, accustomed to speak of a 'Christian civilization,' and hearing vaguely of 'evolution,' resented this position, and preferred an optimistic view of the world, as being in a condition of progressive improvement. Probably the Great War will modify, if not reverse, this general estimate, and may lead back to the primitive Christian attitude and outlook. In any case, neither optimism nor meliorism represents the primitive Christian attitude. At the same time, that attitude will be utterly misconceived, if it is stated as a pessimism, with the practical result of leaving the world to grow worse and worse, and even being satisfied that it should do so. Salvation certainly is perfected in the Parousia. But this does not mean that the Kingdom of God is non-existent or impotent, or that its subjects are to stand by as idle spectators of the world's tragedy. The rule of God is real, living, and almighty. It is in the hands of the King Messiah. He is at work in the world. Its evil powers are already broken. He has overcome the world. In the interval which lasts till His return He is in conflict with the world powers. That divine warfare is waged above man, in a manner and by means beyond human calculation; so that believers have constantly to look on, while the Angel of the Lord works wondrously. But it is not waged wholly apart from man. The believer is also a participator in this great conflict. His faith is a factor in the victory. It has three lines of operation: (i.) direct action with reference to the world, in witness-bearing and in Christian ministry, both of these being a vindication of the sovereignty of Christ, leading to the winning of men to His allegiance; (ii.) waiting, watching, looking out for the coming Kingdom, and hastening towards it; devout men in the primitive Church are the direct successors of those who waited for the consolation of Israel, and they continue the waiting attitude, which is the essential piety of Israel, from the Exile onwards (Is 40^{31}, Ps $62^{1.5}$ $130^{5f.}$, Mk $13^{33f.35.37}$, Mt $24^{42f.}$ 25^{13}, Lk 21^{36}, 1 Co 1^{7} 16^{13}, 1 Th 1^{10}, 1 P 1^{13}, Ja 5^{7}, Rev 3^{3} 16^{15}, 2 P 3^{12}); such waiting is very far from passivity; it is itself issue and proof of the powers of the Kingdom, and is a condition of its arrival; (iii.) as the accompaniment of waiting, prayer. The NT practice of prayer is controlled by the thought of the Kingdom. Its typical aspiration is for the coming of the Kingdom (Mt 6^{10}). Its requests are directed to all things which carry out the designs of the Kingdom, and are granted, as they are preferred, in the name of Christ (Jn $14^{13f.}$). Above all, prayer, especially in its intercessory form, is work done for the Kingdom, and conditions the coming of the Kingdom. The Kingdom will not come to an unwatchful and prayerless Church. In this, as in other forms of service, the power is God's; and prayer means the presence and operation of God, and, therefore, is sure of its answer (Ro $8^{26f.}$, He 7^{25}, Jn $16^{23.26f.}$).

The coming of the Kingdom, accordingly, with the realization of salvation is 'at hand.' Jesus will return 'very soon' (Rev 22^{20}). The unseen world, eternal and divine, impends over this doomed and transient world, and may break through into it at any moment. And yet its arrival is not a bare event, poised on nothing in human life and history. Some of the conditions of its coming lie within the divine vision only; and therefore the mind of men and angels, as of Messiah Himself in the days of His earthly manifestation, contains no means for determining the date. Others lie within the reach of man, and are summed up in faith, with its exercises of loving service, watchfulness, and prayer. Salvation, in its beginning, continuance, and consummation, as gift, and task, and heritage, is relative to faith, and apart from faith is impossible as an experience. Hence the NT closes, not with a prediction, but with a prayer, 'Amen, Lord Jesus, Come.'

(*d*) *Defensive statement of the Christian salvation.*—The Christian message of salvation is not addressed to the intellect as a 'faculty,' and does not terminate in the construction of an intellectual system. It comes as a living word, instinct with life and power, and evokes an experience in which the whole man participates, and brings salvation as an invincible spiritual dynamic. If the NT thus escapes intellectualism, however, it is equally removed from emotionalism, and its insistence on experience does not mean surrender to the caprices of subjectivity. It never attempts to separate life and thought. The experience grows towards 'knowledge,' a discernment of the realities of God's character and purpose, of the values and powers of human life, of man's state and need, as well as his destiny and perfection. Such 'knowledge' is a 'gift' of the Spirit (1 Co 12^{8}). But it is for the use of the Church at large, and its diffusion and increase are an object of prayer (Ph 1^{9}, Eph $1^{17ff.}$). By such knowledge the experience of salvation is interpreted and made aware of itself, and grows clear-eyed and strong. Such an interpretation is the necessary task of the Church throughout all the periods of its history. Gathered into succinct expression as the voice of the Church, it forms creeds and symbols. Developed systematically, it forms a body of doctrine, growing through criticism to fuller and more concrete statement. Theology is properly soteriology, 'the science of realised redemption.'[1] In the NT, however, the interpretation has not yet taken the form of articulated creed or systematized doctrine. Rather we have in it the work of men, who had the gift of knowledge, setting forth, as occasion served and the needs of the Church required, aspects of the great salvation, and bringing before the minds of Christians the necessary implications and issues of the faith by which they lived. There is no speculation *in vacuo*. Everything said is practical in aim and is relevant to the actual condition of believers. The concern of the writer is always salvation, as message and as experience. Full details belong to the discipline of exegetical and Biblical theology. Here it will be enough to indicate the points at which danger threatened the Church's treasure of salvation within the times covered by the NT literature, and the character of the defensive statement made of the Christian experience.

(1) *Misuse of the Christian hope.*—Eschatology has been, in all ages, the happy hunting-ground for religious cranks. The primitive Church did not escape the presence of such pests. If we suppose the bare idea of the Parousia to take possession of the mind, without any deep insight into the nature of God's redeeming power, or any experimental acquaintance with His salvation, the effect will be inevitable; and there will be persons wandering about in idleness, spinning endless yarns out of their own brains, and sponging on their neighbours for the necessaries of existence. This was met on the part of the leaders of the Christian movement by a strong emphasis on the value of the present, as affording the sphere of moral discipline and the opportunity of loving service. It mattered not how short the interval before the Parousia might be; the immediate duty of living under the direction of God's holy will remains unaffected. The certainty of the Return gives great comfort and encouragement in the discipline of life, and adds great urgency to the vocation of the Christian. But there is a conspicuous absence of luscious description of the delights of heaven, and there is a resolute insistence upon the performance of common duties (1 Th $4^{11f.}$ 5^{14}, 2 Th $2^{1f.}$ 3^{9-12}). There is no withdrawal of the hope. A Church, or a soul, in 'the great tribulation' could not tolerate that. But there is balance and proportion in statement and conspicuous ethical sanity.

(2) *Perversion of the gift of the Spirit.*—The idea of the Spirit of God has a long history, and is bound up with the idea of salvation. As the latter deepens in moral and religious quality, the former grows in purity and is more and more removed from physical or psychical excitement. Yet there are obvious dangers connected with the possession of the Spirit, which are marked in almost every 'revival.' It is accompanied by intensity and fervour, which are very apt to take crude, offensive, or even unethical forms. The Christian movement did not escape this peril. To believe in Jesus was to receive the Spirit and to become the subject of its special operations. Some of these implied psychical disturbance and the manifestation of supernormal experiences and powers. Inevitably these attracted attention, and captivated the imaginations of minds untrained in the Christian life. The whole Christian movement was in danger of being assimilated to popular animism, especially in those lands where statelier and colder religions were already being replaced by more fervid and even frenzied types. The apostle Paul understood the danger as none of the other leaders could, and it is the great achievement of his career that he met it fully, and beat back an evil which would have made the Christian salvation a mockery. He did not deny the value of ecstatic phenomena. Intense experiences in the crisis of the soul's inner history may be expected, are to be counted a privilege, and are not to be condemned or repressed (1 Co 14^{18}, 2 Co 12^{1-5}, 1 Th 5^{19}). But they are not the only or the chief gifts of the Spirit. They occur among many others (1 Co $12^{4-11.\ 28-31}$, Ro 12^{6-8}, Eph 4^{11}). They must submit themselves to one obvious test, viz. value for edification and ministry. Submitted to this test, they sink to the bottom of the scale (1 Co 14^{19}). The apostle has a broader treatment of the question. He carries out the process begun within the OT, and lifts into full view the moral and religious value of the Spirit. He interprets it through Jesus (Ro 8^{9}, 2 Co $3^{3.\ 17f.}$). This, indeed, is the ultimate valuation of the Spirit as the power of the Christian salvation; for Paul fully believes in demonic powers which are hostile to man and to the Redeemer of men (1 Co 12^{3}). The ecstatic phenomena, though prized, fall out of notice, as he fills the idea of the Spirit with the meaning of salvation, as wrought by the living Lord within the higher life of man.

(3) *Lowering the level of the salvation experience from grace to legalism.*—Here we have a danger, the exact opposite of that which we have just noticed, though often in fact connected with it. An immature Christian has been delivered from the present 'world' or 'age' with its dominant powers of evil. The historic events of the Cross and the Resurrection stand behind him as the guarantees of his deliverance. But how is he to live, and order his doings, in this new world into which he has entered? The intoxicating sense of emancipation carries him on for a while; but, as it subsides, what is to take its place? The nearest, most familiar, answer is to be found in rules and statutes. Let him govern himself by these, and all will be well. The gospel itself, to one in this state of mind, is a new law, embodying the old law, with additions of its own. Salvation, it seems, while made possible by an event now past, has still to be won, and appears as a recompense for a steadfast adhesion to law and a requisite number of 'works.' Thus legalism follows hard upon the gospel. This peril appears within the times of the NT; but it is a familiar phenomenon in the mission field to-day. In another way the danger of legalism threatened. Suppose the intoxicating sense of liberty to be cultivated, and its most intense and bizarre expressions to be prized as notes of a high degree of spirituality, while sheer immorality threatens the unstable soul, how shall this evil be met? A direct and obvious answer is: Cut out the liberty itself, and put this soul, that is not fit for freedom, into the shackles of law. Let the Church administer salvation under a code, apportioning it according to the measure of obedience. The tendency to legalism, accordingly, is entirely natural, and yet it is plain that it subverts Christianity in its inmost essence. Legalism, in point of fact, is not religion at all. Certainly it is not the religion of the OT. Law in the OT presupposes grace. The *Psalmi Paulini*, born in the midst of a law-observing Church, stand an imperishable witness against legalism. Ezekiel, the parent of the later systematized law in Israel, is no legalist.

'In his sketch of the ideal sanctuary of the future, a great moral change in the people, brought about by the Spirit of Jahveh, is presupposed. The nation, in whose midst Jahveh

[1] P. T. Forsyth, *The Person and Place of Jesus Christ*, London, 1909, p. 216.

deigns to dwell, is a nation prepared for His indwelling by a thorough regeneration of heart and life. . . . Ezekiel's conception of holiness is rooted in a profound conviction of the evil of sin, and in a keen sense of the necessity of personal faith and repentance for acceptance with God.'[1]

When the religion of Israel culminated in the Person and Work of the Redeemer, it certainly was not to sink its adherents to a lower stage than had been known in the OT. The new stage of the religion of redemption is inaugurated not by a mere event of the past, but by an abiding event, if it may be so described. Resurrection and Pentecost go together. The Redeemer is not dead and relegated to a distant throne. He is living, as Spirit, in His Church. He, by the Spirit, is present and operative in all believers. He is everything to them, standard and strength, guidance and power.

The answer to the practical problem, 'How shall the believer conduct himself in the new world?' is met, as the first demand for salvation is met, by the appeal for faith. Trust the living Lord; receive the Spirit of Jesus. Live by the Spirit; be guided by the Spirit (Gal 5^{25}). No doubt there are dangers in such a course (5^{13}). But they are to be met, not by a faint-hearted compromise with legalism, but by the interpretation of the Spirit through the historic Lord, whose *alter ego* the Spirit is—an interpretation which is gathered up into love, that very love which is the essence of God and the motive of the Redeemer's sacrifice (Eph 5^{2}). To a clear eye legalism and the gospel of God stand as contradictions (Gal 5^{2}). Legalism is bondage and shuts the soul into that old world where 'elemental spirits' vaunt themselves against God's redeeming power (4^{1-9}). No compromise is possible ($2^{3f.}$). What is at stake is salvation itself. If legalism triumphs, the labour and suffering of God have been of no avail. He has been defeated. He can do no more. We can understand Paul's passion as he fronted the Judaizers. He saved Christianity as the religion of the Spirit.

(4) *Changing the nature of salvation from the power of God to magic.*—Amid the welter of religions which in the first century of our era were offering 'salvation' to a needy world there was one general conception and one prevalent method. The conception is union with the divine; the method is rite and ceremony, acting magically. The details are curious, but the interest lies in the ruling idea that it is possible by an external act to be united with some superior being or substance, and so be saved from a world which, being material, is inherently evil. The problem, the idea, and the machinery all belong to a far lower level of religious experience than that occupied in common by the religion of Israel and by Christianity. It is true that these 'mystery-religions' were a notable evidence of the world-wide sense of need and did form a *preparatio evangelica* which might truly be regarded as inspired by God. A skilful missionary, therefore, would not enter the lists against them in arid controversy. He would use everything in them which he could transmute into Christian uses. But on two points he could make no compromise: (i.) the nature of faith as the 'universal coefficient of all spiritual blessing' (Ro 1^{17});[2] (ii.) the ethical quality belonging to the Spirit of God and to the life in salvation. Paul is conspicuous for his sympathetic appreciation of all elements, even in heathenism, which have affinities with the religion of redemption. But his conceptions of faith and of the Spirit are rooted in the religion of Israel, and are determined through the Person of Christ, as God's agent in redemption, and the source of salvation to all who believe.

[1] R. L. Ottley, *The Religion of Israel*, Cambridge, 1905, p. 118.

[2] J. V. Bartlet, in art. BAPTISM (New Testament), vol. ii. p. 377^{b}.

'The evidence,' says H. A. A. Kennedy, 'makes it wholly superfluous to seek for the explanation of Paul's use of any of these terms in Hellenistic Mystery-Religion. What we do learn from the parallels is the ability of many of his readers to catch the meaning of a more or less technical terminology, due not merely to a course of instruction in the Old Testament, but to their acquaintance with a religious vocabulary already current among the Mystery-associations.'[1]

There is only one 'saving' institution in Christianity, and that is the gospel (Ro $1^{16f.}$, 1 Co 1^{18}). Any rite tolerable in the Christian cultus derives its value from the measure in which it sets forth the gospel, and the 'coefficient' of any blessing that it conveys is only and always faith.

(5) *Depriving Christ of His unique function and supreme place in the divine salvation.*—This danger threatened as soon as Christianity entered the region where Greek thought formed the intellectual atmosphere of educated men. The general scheme, developed in various forms of Gnosticism (*q.v.*), and later systematized as Neo-Platonism (*q.v.*), runs on lines such as these: (i.) the idea of God as the indeterminate, a Being above the categories of human thought, and wholly removed from contact with matter; (ii.) the metaphysical and cosmological problem, arising from this dualism of God and the world, viz. how to cross the gulf separating the two—a problem two-sided, how the ineffable perfection of God can conceivably be connected with the material world and how man can rise out of the material to the divine; (iii.) the speculative problem solved by subordinationism, the invention of intermediate beings to account for the existence of the material world; (iv.) the religious problem, solved in three stages—morality, legal and ascetic; contemplation, knowledge; ecstasy, the vision of God, and metaphysical absorption in Him. At this last point philosophical thought joined hands with the mystery-religions.

Such a scheme might readily make room for Christianity, by accommodating Christ with a place, possibly even the first place, amid the crowd of intermediaries, and by giving a Christian tone to asceticism and contemplation, and by transforming the Christian symbols of baptism and the Lord's Supper into 'mysteries.' This subtle danger belongs mainly to a period subsequent to that covered by the NT and, indeed, proved too strong for the early Church, producing that amalgam of historic Christianity with Hellenism and the mystery-religions which we know as Catholicism.

Within the NT itself, however, lies the answer to this peril, and to the NT every revival of Christianity owes its standard and inspiration. It is to be carefully observed, at the same time, wherein the nerve of the answer lies. It does not lie in NT Christology, if by that is meant an intellectual system, woven by St. Paul and crowned by St. John, and reproduced by professional theologians in their various elaborations. It is to be sought in the experience of salvation, which underlies all theory and is registered, particularly, in Christology. For OT and NT alike salvation is not a scheme; it is an action. God is the only Saviour. He acts directly. There are no lists of subordinate beings who should form links between the divine and the human. There is no metaphysical obstacle to His approach to man and to His operation on man's behalf. The history of redemption is the history of such approach and such operation. Its climax is Jesus the Christ. In Jesus God works out to its glorious consummation the salvation of men. There is no other agent of the divine salvation. 'There is no salvation by any one else, nor even a second name under heaven appointed for us men and our salvation' (Ac 4^{12}). Far less is there an array of mythological figures, gorgeous or

[1] *St. Paul and the Mystery-Religions*, p. 198.

grotesque, to help men across the gulf to God. This is historic Christianity, the only Christianity which has a right to the name. Again, however, it is to be repeated that what is primitive and normative for our conception of essential Christianity is the experience of salvation through acceptance of Jesus as Saviour, and not a Christology in the systematized form which we know as Pauline or Johannine. The experience is vital and developing. The Christology keeps pace with it as the registration of its values. The salvation is never construed cosmologically. It is always interpreted, through the sense of sin, as forgiveness and possession of the Spirit (Ac 2^{38} 3^{26} 10^{43}). And, whatever rank is ascribed to Jesus, it is His alone.

'Jesus had in the earliest preaching and the earliest faith of Christians that solitary and incommunicable place which the Church assigns Him still.'[1]

From this starting-point the life and thought of the Church move forward together. There is a growing experience of salvation as a present possession, element after element in the great fact of salvation being appropriate to the manifold needs of humanity. There is a corresponding growth in the conception of Christ, a more and more adoring view of Him in His sole sufficiency for salvation, whatever its dimensions and content may be. Various types of Christology are to be found in the NT, but they are not mutually exclusive. The distinctions between them are to be found 'in the aspects of religious experience which are respectively emphasized.'[2]

Some of these Christologies are 'higher' than others, because they recognize wider reaches of Christ's saving function, not because they have left the ground of experience and have entered the region of speculation. It is true, they use freely the terminology of the educated world of the day, and sometimes deliberately adopt the catch-words of current systems. But they never force Christ and Christian experience into these intellectual formulæ, and they never commit the grotesque mistake, fatally committed by later theology, of imagining that they have explained Christ. Their aim is practical and defensive throughout. They reply to cloudy and pretentious schemes by claiming for Jesus all that they have guessed or imagined, and have distributed among vague divinities. What words are these—'Lord,' 'Logos,' 'Image,' 'Fullness'? They all belong to Jesus. He is Lord of all. He is the Word of God. He is the image of the invisible God. In Him dwells the Fullness. But, though the phrases be borrowed, their content is derived from what the Church knows of Jesus, the only Redeemer. Over against all these elaborate and baseless systems, and high above the frenzied efforts of the mystery-religions, there stands the figure of Jesus, the historic Jesus, the exalted Saviour. All that God is is seen in Him. All that God does is done through Him. God is in Him reconciling the world to Himself. Instead of asceticism, or so-called knowledge, or ecstasy, there is but one condition of salvation—the faith that throws itself on the divine mercy, as it reaches men in the depths of their need through Jesus. This is the answer of the NT to the peril of Gnosticism, Docetism, subordinationism, and mysticism, in every shape and form, earlier or later.

(6) Reviewing the experience whose history we have sought to trace, we name, in conclusion, one or two of its abiding features. (i.) Its unity and continuity. It begins deep in the religion of Israel; it culminates in the NT; it moves onwards through the ages; it lives to-day throughout the wide world; and into it multitudes of every race

[1] Denney, *Jesus and the Gospel*[4], p. 17.
[2] Scott, *s.v.* 'Christ, Christology' in *DAC*.

and culture are continually entering. But fundamentally it is one thing—the action of the Redeeming God, whose nature is love, who moves, through judgment and mercy, to the victory of His saving purpose; and corresponding to this action is the answer of the human heart in trust and devotion. There is no other Christianity than this. (ii.) The place of Jesus in it. The action of God centres in Him. The character of God is disclosed in Him. In Him God enters human life, and through Him communicates Himself to man. The action of faith, in like manner, centres in Him, meets God in Him, knows God as revealed in Him. In Him man enters divine life, and through Him believes in God, worships and serves God, and returns to God the natural gifts which He Himself has imparted. This supremacy of Jesus is essential to Christianity. Wherever and by whomsoever this supremacy is practically acknowledged, there is essential Christianity, even if it be inarticulate. (iii.) Its expansion, intensively and extensively. It is measureless as the love of God, which is a shoreless, unfathomable ocean, covering the deeps of human need, surrounding, comprehending, and satisfying the capacities and dreams of man. Hence, it manifests itself in endless variety from generation to generation and from soul to soul. It cannot be run into a mould or stereotyped in a formula. Even within the NT the emphasis varies from the crudest expectation of the Parousia to the wealth of a present union with the living Lord. And always there is the sense of a beyond, uplifting the soul, revealing its necessities, and leading to unknown reaches of attainment. (iv.) It rises out of depths which cannot be plumbed by the logic of the mere understanding. Yet it constantly seeks conscious expression. It is not doctrine; yet a doctrine of salvation is a necessity for those who are 'being saved.' It is needed for their own sakes, that their experience may be strong and deep, able to resist disintegration and perversion; and for the world's sake, that the message of salvation may be clear and powerful. The formulation of such a doctrine, however, can never be complete or final. It is the task of a living Church, continuous and expanding, as the experience of which it is the vital interpretation.

LITERATURE.—In addition to the articles in *HDB*, *SDB*, *DCG*, and *DAC*, see D. S. Adam, *Cardinal Elements of the Christian Faith*, London, 1911; W. Beyschlag, *New Testament Theology*, Edinburgh, 1895; J. S. Candlish, *The Christian Salvation*, do. 1899; J. Estlin Carpenter, in *Studies in Theology*, London, 1903; J. Denney, *The Christian Doctrine of Reconciliation*, do. 1917; A. Dorner, in *Beiträge zur Weiterentwicklung der christlichen Religion*, Munich, 1905; W. P. Du Bose, *Soteriology of the New Testament*, New York, 1892; F. von Hügel, *Eternal Life*, Edinburgh, 1912; H. A. A. Kennedy, *St. Paul and the Mystery-Religions*, London, 1913; E. Ménégoz, *Le Péché et la rédemption d'après St. Paul*, Paris, 1882; A. Ritschl, *Die christliche Lehre von der Rechtfertigung und Versöhnung*[3], 3 vols., Bonn, 1888–89, Eng. tr. of vol. i., Edinburgh, 1872, of vol. iii., do. 1905; J. Rivière, *Le Dogme de la rédemption*, Paris, 1905; G. B. Stevens, *The Christian Doctrine of Salvation*, New York, 1905, *The Theology of the New Testament*, Edinburgh, 1899; A. Titius, *Die neutestamentliche Lehre von der Seligkeit*, 4 parts, Freiburg, 1895–1900; K. W. Zeigler, *Die Versöhnung mit Gott: Bekenntnisse und Erkenntniswege*, Tübingen, 1902; C. A. Scott, *Dominus Noster*, London, 1918.

T. B. KILPATRICK.

SALVATION (Egyptian).—1. Conceptions of posthumous happiness.

—The Egyptian conceptions of posthumous happiness are confused and conflicting. The blessed dead, we are told, dwell in heaven as the intimate companions of the sun-god.[1] It is said of him 'who has reached (the existence yonder) without wrongdoing' that 'he shall continue yonder like a god, stepping forward

[1] A. Erman, *Gespräch eines Lebensmüden mit seiner Seele*, Berlin, 1896, lines 142–147, *A Handbook of Egyptian Religion*, Eng. tr., London, 1907, p. 89; J. H. Breasted, *Development of Religion and Thought in Ancient Egypt*, New York and London, 1912, p. 118 ff.

boldly like the Lords of Eternity.'[1] The *bai* of such an one 'shall abide beside the Lord of All, his name shall be good in the mouth of the living.'[2] A righteous dead person, we are also informed, has his place in the Hall before the great god (Osiris),[3] or he is clothed in fine linen and is near Osiris.[4] Again, he may dwell in the Field of Earu, or Field of Offerings, the great city, the possessor of winds, where he is a mighty one (*sakhem*) and a blessed one (*ikh*) and where he ploughs, reaps, eats, drinks, copulates, and does all that is done on earth.[5]

A great official of the XVIIIth dynasty expresses his desire for a happy life after death in the following terms:

'May the memory of me remain on earth, may my soul live with the Lord of Eternity. The keepers of the doors, the guardians of the portals of the Tēi shall not drive it back when it comes forth at the summons of the oblationer in my Tomb of the necropolis. May it [my soul] abound in bread, may it overflow with beer, and may it drink the water upon the eddy of the stream. May I enter in and come forth like the blessed who have done what their gods praise. May my name be good among men in the years to come, and may they give me praises at the two seasons by the favour of the city god.'[6]

2. The means of attaining posthumous happiness.—(*a*) *The virtuous life.*—The idea that the deceased's happiness depended upon his obtaining a favourable verdict at the posthumous trial is already found in inscriptions of the Old Kingdom.[7] To obtain such a verdict, a man must have been righteous during his life on earth.[8]

Osiris himself did not attain to his position of king and judge of the dead until he had undergone trial before the judicial council of gods at Heliopolis and had by them been proclaimed 'justified' or 'righteous (true) of voice.'[9]

(*b*) *Identification with Osiris.*—Side by side with the view that the happiness of the dead depended upon how their life on earth had been spent existed the idea that they could attain bliss hereafter through identification with Osiris. Originally only the dead Pharaoh was identified with Osiris, who appears in the *Pyramid Texts* as the prototype of all dead Pharaohs, the dead Pharaoh *par excellence*. This identification ensured to the deceased Pharaoh the same renewed and glorified existence as that of the god. As Osiris lives, he also will live; as Osiris dies not, he will not die; as Osiris was not destroyed, he will not be destroyed.[10] The gods do for the deceased Pharaoh what in the first instance they did for Osiris. Nut, the mother of Osiris, gives the dead Piōpi his head, unites for him his bones, puts together his limbs for him, and places his heart in his body.[11] Isis and Nephthys may also perform this service for him and make his eyes to shine in his head.[12] Again, he is washed and embalmed by Anubis[13] and revivified by Horus.[14] As the representative or successor of Osiris, the departed is said to be a blessed one or spirit (*ikh*), and to be mighty as a god. His soul (*bai*) is within him and his power (*sakhem*) behind him.[15] Finally, the dead Pharaoh must appear before the judicial council of the gods, by whom, like Osiris, he is pronounced 'justified,' 'righteous

1 A. H. Gardiner, *Journ. of Egyptian Archæology*, i. [1914] 27, § 13.
2 K. Sethe, *Urkunden des ägyptischen Altertums*, iv. [Leipzig, 1905–09] 62, line 6 f.
3 E. Naville, *Das ägyptische Todtenbuch der xviii. bis xx. Dynastie*, 2 vols., Berlin, 1886 (hereafter referred to as *Tdb.*), ch. 99, line 38.
4 F. Ll. Griffith, *Stories of the High Priests of Memphis*, Oxford, 1900, p. 48 f.
5 *Tdb.* ch. 110 (Einleitung), lines 1–3.
6 Sethe, *Urkunden*, iv. 430.
7 See art. RIGHTEOUSNESS (Egyptian), §§ 5, 9 (1), (i.)–(iv.).
8 *Ib.*
9 Breasted, p. 34 ff.; art. RIGHTEOUSNESS (Egyptian), § 7.
10 K. Sethe, *Die altägyp. Pyramidentexte*, Leipzig, 1908–10 (hereafter cited as *Pyr.*), § 167.
11 *Ib.* § 834 f.
12 *Ib.* § 1981.
13 *Ib.* § 1122 *c*, 1364 f., 1995 f.; Breasted, p. 27.
14 Breasted, pp. 31–33.
15 *Pyr.* § 752; Breasted, p. 162.

of voice,'[1] thanks to the pleading of Thōth, who also made Osiris to triumph over his enemies.[2] He can now enter upon a glorified existence—according to one conception, in heaven, or, according to another, in the West.[3] After the VIth dynasty every dead person was identified with Osiris, and the custom then arose of appending to the deceased's name the Osirian epithet 'justified.' The tendency, therefore, was to regard the deceased as righteous or 'justified,' not on his own merits, but, owing to his identification with Osiris, his personality and acts becoming merged in those of his righteous and justified prototype.[4] This is apparent in the following passages, which depict the dead in the rôle of the accused and justified Osiris:

'He [the dead Unis identified with Osiris] is justified by what he hath done. . . . The Two Rights have held the legal hearing. Shu was witness. The Two Rights have ordained that the thrones of Geb belong to him, that he should raise himself up for that which he desired, that his limbs which were in concealment should be joined together, that he should unite with those who are in Nun, and that he should put an end to the words in Heliopolis.'[5]

'Atum, father of the gods, is satisfied, Shu and Tefnut are satisfied, Geb and Nut are satisfied, Osiris and Isis are satisfied, Sēth and Nephthys are satisfied . . . with that great and mighty utterance that came out of the mouth of Thōth in favour of Osiris, treasurer of life, seal-bearer of the gods. Anubis who reckons the hearts, he reckons the Osiris Piōpi from among the gods who belong to the earth unto the gods who are in heaven.'[6]

'O Thōth, who justified Osiris against his enemies, justify NN. against his enemies even as thou didst justify Osiris against his enemies before the judicial council . . . in Heliopolis.'[7]

It should here be noted that a deceased person was identified with Osiris only in his earlier rôle of a dead god-king who had been killed and revivified, and who finally had triumphed over his accusing enemies at the trial before the judicial council in Heliopolis. The deceased is always clearly differentiated from Osiris in his later rôle of judge of the dead.[8]

For the various ceremonies and spells through the performance or by the repetition of which a person, during his life or after death, was identified or associated with Osiris, or was rendered righteous or accounted as such, and so obtained justification and posthumous bliss, see art. RIGHTEOUSNESS (Egyptian), § 10.

LITERATURE.—See the works cited in the footnotes.

AYLWARD M. BLACKMAN.

SALVATION (Hindu).—The Sanskrit term for 'deliverance' or 'salvation' is *mukti* or *mokṣa* (*q.v.*). Derived from the root *muc'*, it signified in the first instance 'deliverance' or 'release' in general from pains and penalties of any kind. In all systems, however, of Hindu philosophical and religious thought *mukti*, or *mokṣa*, has become the technical and specialized expression to denote that deliverance from bondage to the world and its fetters which is the desired and ideal end of the Hindu religious life. Hindu aspiration and longing centre always in *mukti*, in deliverance in one way or another from the weariness and bondage universally associated with temporal existence.

The *mukta*, therefore, is one who is emancipated from all that detracts from fullness of life, who has been discharged from the cramped and fettered conditions of earthly existence, and has entered upon a state of endless freedom and felicity. The sects differ in their interpretation of the conditions and character of the state itself and the means and methods of its attainment. Ultimately, however, Hindu religious thought always formu-

1 *Pyr.* § 316 f.
2 *Ib.* § 1522 f.; *Tdb.* chs. 18–20.
3 Erman, *Handbook*, p. 96 f.; Breasted, p. 159 ff.
4 See art. RIGHTEOUSNESS (Egyptian), § 10.
5 *Pyr.* § 316 ff.; Breasted, p. 34.
6 *Pyr.* § 1521 ff.; Breasted, p. 35.
7 *Tdb.* ch. xviii. line 1 f.; cf. chs. xix., xx.
8 See also Breasted, p. 164.

lates 'salvation' in terms of release from bondage to the present evil world to a further unworldly existence, which is not subject to change or liable to distress and harm.

Both terms are employed in the literature in a more general sense. Thus *dāsatvamukti* is release from servitude,[1] *śāpamukti* or *mokṣa* is release from an anathema or curse,[2] and the *śāpamukta* is one who has been thus set free. *Praśnamokṣa* is the answer to or resolution of a question.[3] The words are also used with an active connotation; e.g., *ṛiṇamukti* or *mokṣa* is the discharge of an obligation or debt. Technically also *muktimārga* or *mokṣamārga* is the path or way of emancipation.

1. Essential character and principles. — In Hindu thought and teaching, therefore, 'salvation' is essentially the solution of intercourse with the material world, with the universe created and visible; it is emancipation from bondage to matter with all that this involves of pain and penalty, and entrance into a haven of rest and peace for ever untroubled by the afflictions and sorrows that attend upon all earthly conditions. There underlies the doctrine, therefore, that deep-rooted conviction of the essential poverty and wretchedness of earthly existence which is so characteristic of every variety of Eastern thought. Throughout the long history of Indian speculation in all its modifications and varieties and in all the sects this conception has retained a leading place, that true freedom and happiness are not attainable here, under the dominance and constraint of earthly passions and privations; only by and through deliverance from every earthly fetter is salvation secure. In the many varieties of religious teaching the goal is ever the same, although the means prescribed for its attainment vary greatly. By the more or less complete suppression of the desires and faculties of the body, by mechanical devices, ascetic or other, for controlling the bodily passions, partial satisfaction is given to the longing for emancipation even in the course of this present life. The final goal, however, is unchanged and unchangeable, and demands the severance of the last earthly tie. This doctrine of salvation by release from earthly bonds is one of the most enduring of Hindu dogmas, because based on the deep underlying presuppositions of Indian thought.

It is further and almost of necessity allied to the equally widely held doctrine of transmigration. Salvation and rest are not attainable, in most instances at least, at once and immediately when the dissolution of the bodily frame supervenes upon death. Through a series of 'recurrent deaths' and rebirths into a new existence upon earth, when the varied fruits of merit and demerit have been fully and finally gathered, and action with its resultant effects is nullified, when *karma* ceases, only then may the goal be reached. The vista of these renewed lives, with their dreary and indefinite sameness of misery, has driven many a man to despair. To hasten their progress is all that in most instances he can hope to do; and the end, whether near or far, often appears so uncertain as to be hardly worth the struggle and endurance necessary for its attainment.

2. History and development of the doctrine.— The most definite statements with regard to the nature and character of *mukti* are to be found in the *Upaniṣad* literature, and in the commentaries of Śaṅkara and Rāmānuja (*qq.v.*) on the *Vedānta Sūtras.*[4] These thinkers expound, with an insight and conviction that have rarely, if ever, been excelled, its philosophical content and import. The religious aspect of *mukti* and its value for the individual soul are set forth in works of a more definitely religious character and aim, especially in the *Bhagavad-Gītā* (*q.v.*), and in the popular religious literature of the sects. It is the teaching of the last, rehearsed in the ears of the people and enforced in the schools, that has made the meaning and worth of *mukti* a possession of all the Indian peoples, or at least of that overwhelming proportion of them which has come within the range and influence of Hindu thought. The difference between the two—the philosophical and the religious and popular—may be broadly stated as the difference between salvation by knowledge and salvation by faith. Moreover, in India philosophical theory is in practice always modified and coloured by religious emotion and need; and the creeds and conclusions of religion are rarely, if ever, separated from the principles and doctrines of a generally accepted metaphysic.

In the early literature of the Vedic hymns deliverance is by favour of the gods. The prayers and aspirations of the worshippers are for the most part concerned with the obtaining of earthly good, and their aim and outlook are limited to the present life. The benefits sought are those conducive to temporal well-being and enjoyment, nor is there any apparent consciousness of a need for deliverance, except in so far as it is deliverance from the adverse conditions of the present earthly existence. By the *ṛṣis* and poets, therefore, of this early age 'salvation,' so far as it was a subject of thought at all, was conceived in material, not spiritual, terms, and meant rescue from the pains and penalties of a troubled life to a state of existence more abundantly endowed with earthly goods. The future beyond the grave was not illuminated by a hope which made the present life seem valueless in comparison, nor, on the other hand, did it bear any sure deterrent prospect for the evil-doer. The desire and expectation of good for the most part found their satisfaction in worldly and material advantage. To a future existence after death, with its alternative of felicity or suffering, conditioned by righteous or unjust dealing here, little if any thought was given.

It is in the *Upaniṣads* and the philosophical systems based upon them that the Hindu conception of *mukti* is most fully worked out and expounded. Their leading thought was essentially idealistic, and the only knowledge worthy of the name was in what way and under what conditions release (*mukti*) might be gained from the woes of an earthly life. This teaching, expounded with little order or system in the *Upaniṣad* treatises themselves, was later systematized in the Vedānta under the influence and guidance of Śaṅkara, and became the dominant conception of Hindu religious thought. Its only serious rival on the philosophical side, as an ordered theory of human life and destiny, was found in the Sāṅkhya (*q.v.*); and here the difference lay rather in the means by which salvation was to be sought and attained than in the nature of the salvation itself. Invariably the end in view was escape from the world. A more profound distinction separated the philosophic doctrine of the Vedānta from the spiritual aspirations and faith of the great popular religions. In the latter a formal profession of belief and acceptance of dogma was quickened by strong emotion and a fervent longing for personal and individual communion with the deity. The adherent of the *bhakti-mārga* (*q.v.*), as he pursued a different road from that of the pure Vedāntist or the convinced and life-long ascetic, so sought and won a goal, the nature of which, although it might be and was expressed in similar terms, was interpreted in an entirely different spirit. From the philosophical point of view, however, the Vedāntic doctrine has remained dominant, and has been almost universally accepted in India; and has thus, apart from external influences, Christian or other, determined and controlled the form of the

[1] *Kathās.* xxviii. 171. [2] *Ib.* xxxiv. 139. [3] *Ib.* v. 53.
[4] See also artt. UPANIṢADS and MOKṢA.

eschatological thought of the great majority of Hindus.

It is not a little remarkable that no direct proof of a doctrine so comprehensive, and so intimately affecting the future state and destiny of man, appears ever to have been attempted, or the want of it to have been deplored. It is dogmatically asserted, with many repetitions and in slightly varying forms; and the contrary teaching is declared untenable, sometimes with the semblance of an attempt at logical or scientific refutation. Full and frequent exposition of the doctrine is also offered; but this always assumes a dogmatic form, and no light is thrown upon its historical development or upon the steps by which the conclusions formulated have been reached. Nor is any direct connexion made with earlier forms of belief as suggested or traced in the Vedic hymns and elsewhere. The doctrine appears complete, thought out in all its relations, and is adopted and enforced as the one tenable and sufficient view of the character and destiny of the human soul.

3. Methods of attainment of salvation.—Indian writers on *mokṣa* almost invariably seek to illuminate their subject by an illustration or an analogy; and these, far more than a rigid or logical proof, make appeal to their readers' sympathies and command their assent. The statements made, however, with regard to *mukti* converge upon the same point of view and express essentially the same thought. The principal authorities in the ancient philosophical literature besides the *Upaniṣads* are the *Vedānta Sūtras*, with the commentaries or expositions thereon, and the *Bhagavad-Gītā*, together with other chapters or treatises of the same tendency contained in the *Mahābhārata* (*q.v.*). The *Bhagavad-Gītā* in particular has for its leading motive the duty or propriety of so ordering present conduct as to secure future and abiding felicity, redemption from the evils of this world in submission to the will and leading of the supreme Lord. This redemption is set forth negatively and positively. A few out of many references that might be given will sufficiently indicate the character of the Indian teaching.

(1) *Mukti* is negatively release from the restraints of the body to a condition of bodiless existence, which is thenceforth unchanging and eternal.[1] The *mukta*, therefore, is not subject to rebirth or death.[2]

(2) The passions of desire and self-love, of craving for earthly objects, have ceased to exercise him; he has attained to rest of soul, and no longer fears.[3]

(3) The *mukta* is no more bound and bewildered by *avidyā* (ignorance), or fretted by consciousness of earthly things.[4]

Mokṣa or *mukti* is at times described metaphorically as a fruit, to be plucked and enjoyed.[5] Other metaphors are employed, as that of dreams, etc.[6]

False views also are combated—*e.g.*, that *mukti* may be obtained through sleep.[7] It is argued that this would imply a return to earthly conditions, but *mukti* is eternal.

Positively, however, and in its fullest expression, *mukti* is union with the supreme Brahman. This is the highest goal, the true life, when all the shadows have passed away, a blissful eternal rest untouched by sorrow and untroubled by fear. To describe this state figurative expressions are freely employed; it is perfect knowledge, supreme felicity, unrestrained freedom. The central thought, however, the background and support of all metaphor, is always that of oneness with Brahman. There is nothing beyond this to be coveted or experienced.

He whose mind is restrained attains emancipation in union with him;[8] *mokṣa* is oneness with Brahman, and is eternal;[9] release is the intuition of the highest Self consequent on the destruction of ignorance;[1] the individual soul is Brahman, or has itself in Brahman.[2]

[1] Cf. *Vedānta Sūtras*, I. i. 4, IV. i. 15. [2] *Bhag.-Gītā*, ii. 3.
[3] *Anug.* xiii. 27; *Bhag.-Gītā*, ii. 59, iii. 17, xviii. 1 ff.; *Maitr. Brāh. Up.* vi. 25.
[4] *Vedānta Sūtras*, I. i. 1, ii. 12, II. i. 15, iii. 19.
[5] *Ib.* IV. iv. 1. [6] *Ib.* IV. iv. 13 f.
[7] *Ib.* III. ii. 10, IV. iv. 17.
[8] *Inst. of Viṣṇu*, xcvii. 14; *Vedānta Sūtras*, I. i. 4.
[9] *Vedānta Sūtras*, I. i. 13, ii. 12.

Indian writers further expound and discuss many ways by which the one end may be reached, some negative, enjoining the disuse or destruction of modes of action and thought which cloud the insight and understanding, and hinder devotion; and some positive, which aim at quickening faith and fortifying the motives or qualities that hasten its attainment. The goal in prospect, however, is always the same; it is *yoga* in the widest acceptation of the term, the severance of all earthly bonds in permanent union with the one and only Lord. In the philosophical idealism of the Vedānta this union is represented as in fact already existent; it is not a hardly-won achievement, a goal to be reached by endeavour, neither is it in the strict sense a union at all. *Mukti* is the lifting of the veil of ignorance, which conceals from the soul the truth that it is and always has been one with Brahman. Where there is only one and not another, there can be no union, no coming together of two parties. In the realization of this identity *mokṣa* consists, and the road thereto lies not through something done or accomplished, but through knowledge and the removal of the delusive cloud of ignorance.

There are, however, to the Vedāntist himself subsidiary and less secure methods by which the desired end may be attained, some more ready and effectual than others, but all wearisome and difficult to the soul compared with the direct way of revelation and knowledge. The more noteworthy of these urge the abandonment of all action, thereby to break the bonds of *karma* and secure the cessation of all attachment or desire. Works performed without desire (*tṛṣṇā*, 'thirst') are valueless, and do not forge fresh links in the otherwise endless unrolling chain of *karma*.[3]

A second and much-frequented path lies through renunciation (*q.v.*), the voluntary setting aside of the cares and claims of the world, and adoption of a life of entire devotion to spiritual aims and thoughts, either as a *brahmachārin*, or a hermit in the recesses of the forest, or in other ways.[4] Such ascetic devotion and self-denial are means of very considerable efficacy for the attainment of redemption, and are often commended as an honourable and sure, if long and exacting, way to success;[5] perfection is by renunciation.[6] Not seldom this is set forth polemically; the exact performance of the Vedic ritual and the study of Vedic books are no real means to salvation.[7] It is allowed, however, that these, and especially sacrifice to the gods, are in a less degree efficient for securing deliverance.[8]

By concentration of thought also and meditation (*samādhi* [*q.v.*]) the soul is led to Brahman and achieves its deliverance from bondage to the world;[9] a man should practise meditation until he is free;[10] *samādhi* is the condition of release from worldly fetters.[11]

The perfect way, the path chosen by the wise, which supersedes all other ways, is through knowledge.

[1] *Vedānta Sūtras*, II. i. 14. [2] *Ib.* III. ii. 37–40, iv. 52.
[3] Cf. *Vedānta Sūtras*, III. i. 9, IV. i. 13, 15, not clinging to works; *Bhag.-Gītā*, xvii. 30, without expectation of fruit; *Sanats.* iv. 17.
[4] *Bhag.-Gītā*, vi. 14, viii. 11 *et al.*; *Sanats.* iv. 17.
[5] *Bhag.-Gītā*, vi. 13, 42, xvi. 1–7, xviii. 49.
[6] *Anug.* iv. 1 ff.; *Inst. of Viṣṇu, passim*; *Maitr.* vi. 20, through the serenity of the thought he kills all actions . . . and obtains imperishable bliss.
[7] E.g., *Bhag.-Gītā*, ii. 42 ff., iv. 28 ff.; *Anug.* xix. 7; *Vedānta Sūtras*, I. i. 4.
[8] *Bhag.-Gita*, xvii. 30.
[9] *Ib.* viii. 10; *Vedānta Sūtras*, I. i. 1.
[10] *Vedānta Sūtras*, II. iii. 38. [11] *Ib.* iii. 40; Manu, iv. 258.

Śvet. i. 11, when that god [Brahman] is known . . . birth and death cease; *ib.* ii. 15, he who sees the real nature of Brahman . . . is freed from all fetters; *ib.* vi. 12–15, the wise who perceive him . . . theirs is eternal happiness . . . they pass over death; *Bhag.-Gītā*, iv. 18, the man of understanding attains by knowledge to the everlasting glory; *Vedānta Sūtras*, I. i. 3 f., release follows upon the knowledge of Brahman; iv. 22, etc.; I. i. 1, the cognition of Brahman is that which effects final release.

In the later and more popular religious literature the chief exponent of these conflicting views of redemption is Kṛṣṇa in the *Bhagavad-Gītā*. There are put into his mouth strong and urgent appeals for devotion, self-consecration to the one divine Lord, that in union with him deliverance and rest may be found; and, on the other hand, doctrinal expositions of the Vedāntic theory of redemption through knowledge alone, delivered with apparently as urgent and sincere conviction as though no other means of salvation existed or were conceivable. Both doctrines seem to be recognized as orthodox, and equally effective for salvation.

Historically also it is through the *Bhagavad-Gītā* and the popular poems of the *Rāmāyaṇa* (*q.v.*) that these thoughts and conceptions of final deliverance have permeated the minds of the Indian peoples, and become a constant part of their accepted philosophy of life. It is with reason that the *Bhagavad-Gītā* has been termed the New Testament of all thoughtful Hindus. Similar teaching has everywhere been popularized and enforced in the vernacular songs and epics, recited in the village assemblies, and taught in the village schools. Philosophically at least Hindu thought is remarkably consentient and harmonious with regard to the ultimate destiny of the soul delivered from the bondage of evil.

4. **Nature of final mukti.**—The protagonists of the two great schools of Hindu eschatological belief as it concerns the nature and means of ultimate redemption are Śaṅkara, to whom the elaboration and completion of idealistic Vedāntic doctrine are due, and Rāmānuja, the champion of an intimate and personal theism. These two influential teachers in their commentaries on the *Vedānta Sūtras* interpreted the same text in entirely different ways;[1] and the controversy between them turned mainly upon the question of the character and quality of redemption, and the means by which it was to be attained. The philosophical and religious thought of India has been practically determined upon these lines, upon the basis of what may be termed idealistic and theistic teaching respectively, by these leaders and the disciples who followed them. To Śaṅkara, the exponent of the strictest Vedānta, redemption, which was only loosely and inaccurately described as union with Brahman, was not something to be achieved or won, a step forward in a progressive gain or accretion; it was not a new fact, superadded upon the existing facts of experience and life. It was in the fullest sense a revelation, an opening of the eyes, an awakened consciousness of a real fact which had always been there, but veiled from the mind by apathy and ignorance. *Mukti*, therefore, was arrived at through knowledge, the sweeping aside of the delusive veil of *avidyā*. It was not an actual addition to the sum of human possessions and enjoyments, a new fact breaking forth where nothing had been before, but the removal of a barrier and the entering into the secure realization of a permanent and inalienable truth. It is not easy to formulate the Vedāntic conception of *mukti* without employing categories and terms that inevitably suggest personality and its assumed qualities or attributes. To the consistent Vedāntist 'personality' was meaningless; the term had no force, and conveyed no idea that was capable of being contained within the four corners of his scheme of philosophy. 'I am thou,' 'thou art that' (*i.e.* Brahman), *tat tvam asi*; Brahman and the individual soul of man (*ātman*) were one and the same, and neither was an individual at all in any ordinary or intelligible sense of the word. *Mokṣa*, or *mukti*, was essentially the apprehension of this fact.

[1] See *SBE* xxxiv. [1890], xxxviii. [1896], xlviii. [1904], where the respective commentaries are translated and elucidated.

There were thus two chief methods of attainment or lines of approach—the ideal or metaphysical, by the way of knowledge, and the theistic and practical, by the way of *bhakti*, faith and love; in each case the end was the same, *mukti*, deliverance from this evil world, achieved not within it by redemption from sin, but by passing beyond it, so as to be no longer within its bounds or subject to its control. It was in this regard that the so-called popular religions, which were all theistic, found themselves in strongest contrast to the metaphysics of the Vedānta. For the most part the belief of the popular faiths has accepted the interpretation of Rāmānuja, and while honouring Śaṅkara has found his doctrine too abstract and uninspiring to satisfy the needs of daily life. Union with Brahman was still the end, the *terminus ad quem*; but it was defined as a goal to be reached by endeavour, not a present and persistent fact to be realized; and the consummated union was such as did not imply the loss of individual self-consciousness or life. In neither case, therefore, was there 'absorption,' in any real or interpretable meaning of the word. That could not be 'absorbed' which was already one with the divine. And in the belief of the adherents of Rāmānuja, or of any one of the numerous successors who accepted his teaching, the soul, when it entered into the bliss of union with its Lord, was not effaced or 'absorbed' in an unconscious identity, but maintained its self-knowledge and capacity, and enjoyed the fruit of its faith and endeavour in unending felicity. With varying degrees of apprehension and detail the religious thought of the Hindus, apart from the bare and unfruitful philosophical theory, holds on to this view of future deliverance, and craves a union with the divine, the essential element of which is not the cessation or destruction of consciousness and personality, but their maintenance, purification, and exaltation.

Practically, therefore, by the Hindus as a whole, both of the north and of the south, the stress is laid upon *bhakti*, not upon any abstract doctrine of the Vedānta. The latter is accepted for argumentative or controversial purposes by those—and they are numerous in India—who have an interest in these things. The real faith as regards the future, upon which a man falls back in circumstances of distress or need, is not an intellectual conclusion of abstract reasoning, but an emotional impulse and conviction of the heart. Apart from the influence of modern sceptical thought, which in India has been neither penetrating nor far-reaching, the belief of the great majority of the Hindu people is neither atheist nor agnostic, but represents a sure and convinced theism.

The third and admittedly subordinate and inferior method was that of works (*karma-mārga*, *karma-kāṇḍa*). For those who were incapable of proceeding by the way of faith or knowledge the less sure way of works was open, and by sacrifice and toil, energy and perseverance, they might finally attain salvation (*mukti*). It was consistently maintained, however, that this was a secondary, tedious, and not always effective road to the end in view. By some its efficacy was altogether denied. Others assigned to it a preliminary or introductory place in the scheme of redemption, claiming that it afforded guidance at the beginning of the journey, but could not conduct to the goal. For this the enlightenment of knowledge or faith was needed. The weary traveller and seeker after rest must add to his works a further achievement of thought or will, and according to the school to whose teaching he lent his ear must trust or know. His future then was secure, and *mukti* already virtually won.

How far these doctrines and theories exercised a really practical influence upon the lives of the theorists or of those whom they taught it is not easy to determine. Probably they always remained to a considerable extent theoretical, accepted like the Vedānta teaching as a whole as a matter of belief, but modifying little the course of daily habit and life. Certainly throughout Indian history, as far as it is possible to trace the hopes and ideas of the great majority of the people, it has been present, not future, deliverance that has occupied their thoughts. *Mukti* has been negative, from the oppressive fear and malign power of the demons, not positive, to a future state of felicity; and immediate deliverance from the grasp of the jealous and ever-present evil powers was that for which men sacrificed and prayed. Demonolatry, sorcery, magic, and the countless charms upon which the common people rested their faith must at all times as now have craved and demanded a deliverance that should be at once effective, not with promise for the future only, but with performance in the present. The nature-worship of both earlier and more recent times has regard to immediate and sensible needs, and pays little heed to the possibilities of a remote future.

In the modern reform movements—the Brāhma Samāj, Sadhāraṇa Samāj (*qq.v.*), and others—the conception of deliverance or salvation, as formulated in the Indian classics, has been modified by Christian influence. The Ārya Samāj (*q.v.*), indeed, stands apart. It is strongly imitative, but consciously and intentionally anti-Christian, and to an even greater extent anti-foreign. The general type of belief and doctrine maintained by the earlier reformers, as by those of preceding centuries, was confessedly eclectic. In regard to the doctrine of *mukti* the ancient Indian faith which found expression in the *Bhagavad-Gītā*, and the teaching of the NT, more especially the words and example of Christ Himself, were combined in a profession of faith which, except in the denial of the divinity of our Lord, was hardly distinguishable from Christian formulas. Practically, however, the tendency was always, as in more recent periods in the West, to lay stress on present duty and service, on an altruism which accentuated the need of immediate physical relief, and to ignore the prospects and conditions of the future, at least so far as they might be supposed to serve as incentives to action in the present. In this service and in devotion to the wellbeing of their fellow-men the Ārya Samāj have led the way. Theoretically, however, the purpose of all was the same, viz. to secure for man union with the divine. With Vedāntic thought they were at variance, in that salvation, whatever its terms, was to them a matter of future attainment, not of immediate intellectual recognition of an existing fact. Thus conceived and defined, *mukti*, as a consciously desired goal, came to be more remote and shadowy, as the urgency of present need increased. The doctrine of the abiding felicity of the future in union with God was indeed maintained as a hope, passionately clung to by the more mystical and devout souls; but for the most part men sought the satisfaction of their religious cravings in the discharge of present duty as it appeared to be set before them within the circle of their sect or caste, or in rarer cases as determined by the appeal of the suffering or need of their fellow-men.

The reformers also accepted and emphasized the ancient Hindu belief, practically universal in spite of philosophical dogma, in the permanence of the individual life. The doctrine of absorption, regarded as implying future and final unconsciousness and the cessation of individual being, although theoretically maintained, has never effectively modified or controlled Hindu faith. Partly under the influence of Christianity it was now set aside in favour of a redemption which was definite, personal, and abiding. The future promised a felicity with God, in which the individual according to his merits would or might have a conscious and abiding part.

5. Comparison with other faiths.—The Hindu doctrine, in what it teaches, in the facts of experience which it ignores, and in the difficulties of reason and thought over which it lightly passes, challenges comparison with the teaching of other faiths, especially with Christianity and with some forms of Buddhism. With both these creeds Hinduism in the days of its greatest plasticity and receptiveness was in long and intimate contact; and it would have been strange if no traces of the mutual intercourse remained. The inference may be accepted; but sufficient evidence is not available to indicate with certainty the doctrines or elements of belief derived from a foreign source. The fundamental thought of *bhakti*, with regard to which the claim of Christian indebtedness has been more often and confidently made than with regard to any other Hindu doctrine or practice, is certainly of Indian origin, and served as a religious motive in India long before Christianity entered the country. In its development and progress it may have owed much to Christian teaching and example. From the first, however, salvation through *bhakti* has laid greater stress upon emotion, upon feeling, and the play of the affections, than Christianity, at least in its more restrained and orthodox forms, has done. The duty or claims of faith and works, when recognized at all, have been relegated to an altogether subordinate position.

The relation of the *mukti* doctrine to Buddhism is more uncertain. It is indeed only with the Mahāyāna teaching that comparison is profitable, or mutual accommodation of doctrine through mutual intercourse may seem to have been possible. For in the Hīnayāna the thought of salvation won as the reward of individual insight and achievement, through and in the monastic career alone, is in every respect by way of contrast to the Hindu; even if the same end is sought, the method and means by which deliverance is to be gained are entirely divergent. Of the Mahāyāna doctrine it might not unfairly be said that together with the *bhakti* teaching of Hinduism it is more nearly akin to Christian principle and thought on this subject than any of the other faiths of the world. The difference is to be found rather in the stress laid upon different aspects or elements of the doctrine than in the general or essential character of the respective teaching. The Mahāyāna doctrine emphasizes the necessity and omnipotence of faith to a degree that is strange to Hindu thought. By mere faith in Amida the greatest sinner is delivered from the power and penalty of his sins, and secures entrance into the heaven of eternal bliss. The Indian affinities of this doctrine cannot be questioned. But in its evolution as a doctrine of faith and trust in a living and personal Saviour it has gone far beyond any indigenous teaching of the land whence it came. It is difficult to resist the impression that, where there is so much in common between the *bhakti-mārga* and the Christian and Mahāyāna creeds, there have been also mutual intercourse and discussion that have led to the adoption of elements of belief, perhaps on more sides than one.

In two respects, however, the contrast between the doctrines taught by these three systems is sufficiently great, between Christianity on the one hand, and Hinduism and Mahāyāna Buddhism on the other, to be worthy of notice. Christianity emphasizes and has always emphasized the necessity of moral reformation and effort, if salvation is to be attained; it is by the grace of God, but by grace which co-operates with human endeavour. The element of strain and search on man's part is not wholly absent from this form of Buddhism or from the teaching of Hindu preachers and reformers; but it has, as it were, never taken effect. The ordinary and orthodox attitude is that of passivity, in which the part played by the man himself is reduced to the vanishing point; and there is an entire lack of moral urgency or impulse, or of any conception of need of moral regeneration of character. This may well be deemed the most important and far-reaching distinction. It is not, however, confined to this one doctrine. It underlies all the thought of East and West, and of Christianity as estimating and encountering rival systems and creeds. The doctrine of salvation in Hinduism is essentially colourless as regards any ethical requirement or necessity.

In another respect also neither Hinduism nor Buddhism has made any approximation to the Christian belief. The Hindu doctrine in particular relegates the attainment of salvation to a distant and uncertain future. It has not formulated, and on its premisses it was hardly possible that it should formulate, a doctrine of present and immediate deliverance from the strain and distress of life, or from the thraldom of evil. Only at the close of a series of rebirths and travail in this world is deliverance achieved. Then, when the power of *karma* is exhausted, and no more fruit of deeds remains to be gathered, the end is reached as it were automatically, *mukti* is the attained and inevitable goal. But the way is hard and long, and not all have the courage and good fortune to persevere through successive births, and by zeal and devotion and good works to hasten the desired end.[1] Salvation is from the power and grip of *karma* to a union with the divine, when there will be no further rebirth to the servitude and misery of a life on earth—or, as the Hindu teaching would prefer to express it, no more 'recurrent death' (*punarmṛityu*)—but in its place a changeless passionless immortality (*amṛitatvam*).

A reminder, however, must be given in conclusion that among the millions who call themselves Hindus it is hardly possible to assert a definitely consistent or unified belief on any theme. Hinduism is almost the last system in the world to possess a clear-cut and stable doctrine. Modifications due to temperament, education, and environment will be found on every hand. Essentially the doctrines above described may be said to represent the convictions of all thoughtful Hindus, and to form the basis of all formulated creed or belief with regard to relief from the burden of the present and final salvation. Moreover, in their application to the hard realities of daily life, and in practical realization of their force and efficacy as a rule or motive of conduct, there will be, as might be expected, almost infinite variation in individual instances. To the majority of the people ultimate *mukti* is a thing too remote to be a controlling factor in their thoughts or lives. At the best it is a theory to which they render a more or less convinced and intellectual assent. The prospect and possibilities of the immediate future make sufficient demands upon their thought and care. To the successive æons of a more distant future and a *saṁsāra* which holds them in its relentless grasp they pay little practical heed.

LITERATURE.—Reference is made to the subject of *mukti* in all books on Hindu religion or philosophy, but no special treatise is available. Cf. P. Deussen, *The Philosophy of the Upanishads*, tr. A. S. Geden, Edinburgh, 1906; R. W. Frazer, *Indian Thought, Past and Present*, London, 1915; A. Barth, *The Religions of India*[3], tr. J. Wood, do. 1891; N. Macnicol, *Indian Theism*, Oxford, 1915. For the *bhakti* doctrine see esp. art. BHAKTI-MĀRGA.

A. S. GEDEN.

SALVATION (Iranian).—The idea of 'salvation' may be considered in reference either to the individual or to the community, or indeed to the whole race. In the former acceptance there is nothing in the Avestan system to correspond to the Indian concept of liberation from a succession of rebirths by final extinction or absorption, as not only in Buddhism, but also in other Hindu systems. The Mazdean ideal is quite simple and singularly like the Christian—the delivery from evil, moral and physical, in this life and the securing of eternal happiness in a conscious individual life of bliss after death. Man is helped to the attainment of this consummation by the revelation of the Good Law of Ahura Mazda and is invited to choose between the service of the supreme deity and that of his enemy, Angra Mainyu, the spirit of evil. Man is endowed with free will and thus has the power and responsibility of the choice. By good thoughts, good words, and good deeds (*humata, hūkhta, hvarshta*), a constantly repeated formula, he acquires merits during his lifetime here and thereby takes his share in the perennial warfare between the good and evil spirits. If he yields to the seductions of evil and indulges in evil thoughts, evil words, and evil deeds (*duzhmata, duzhūkhta, duzhvarshta*), he becomes an enemy of Ahura Mazda and a follower of the *druj*, acquiring demerits for the future. After death there occurs what has been termed a 'spiritual book-keeping'—the soul of the deceased has to face a judgment before the three spirits, Mithra, Rashnu, and Sraosha (personifications of truth, justice, and obedience), and this takes the form of a 'weighing' of merits and demerits.[1] The preponderance of good or evil merits determines the safe passage of the 'Chinvat Bridge' ('the Bridge of Separation'), and the entrance of the soul into Ahura Mazda's heaven, Garō-nmāna—in other words, its eternal salvation. It would appear that we have here a somewhat awkward syncretism of two concepts—that of a regular trial by weighing (as in Egypt) and that of a mythological bridge-test, afterwards borrowed in the Muhammadan Al-Sīrat. In any case the soul's salvation and eternal bliss are worked out by its conduct here below in obedience to the Good Law of Ahura as revealed by his prophet Zarathushtra. There is, of course, no idea at all corresponding to the Christian idea of atonement, or the apprehension of the merits of a Saviour, as is found even in some forms of Buddhism. The post-Avestan doctrine is substantially the same, but more precise views are set forth in the Pahlavi treatises on the subject of merit (*kerfak*), and at least in one treatise there is mention of a treasury (*ganj*) of merits accruing from divine worship, which is placed in the hands of the *yazads*, or celestial spirits, who can confer it on the souls of the just.[2] Spiegel thinks that this concept is of Semitic origin. On the whole, then, the Mazdean doctrine is that each man works out his own salvation, though under the guidance of divine revelation and with the powerful spiritual aids of Ahura Mazda and his hierarchy of spirits, and of the teachings and examples of Zarathushtra and his followers.

When we turn to the question of the salvation of the world, or of humanity at large, we are met with the figure of a future saviour or saviours to come at the end of the world. The word 'Saoshyant' (Pahlavi Soshyōs or Soshyāns) is the future participle of the verb *su* or *sav*, 'to benefit,' 'do good,' 'save,' which is temptingly reminiscent of the Greek verb σάω, whose future participle σώσοντ- is practically identical in form. Now this word can be used both as a common noun and in the plural as well as in the singular: thus in the *Gāthās* Zoroaster and his fellow-workers are denominated *saoshyantō*, 'saviours.' But, used as a proper noun in the Later Avesta and in Pahlavi literature, it indicates specifically the three last great prophets, who are to be miraculously born of the seed of Zarathushtra,[3] and who are to reign

1 Cf. Mt 7[14], στενὴ ἡ πύλη καὶ τεθλιμμένη ἡ ὁδὸς ἡ ἀπάγουσα εἰς τὴν ζωήν, which some have thought to be an echo of Buddhist teaching.

1 For a fuller discussion of the whole scene see J. H. Moulton, *Early Zoroastrianism*, London, 1913, pp. 164–177.

2 *Shāyast lā-Shāyast*, viii. 4, in *SBE* v. [1880].

3 An ingenious attempt to 'rationalize' the grotesque story of the manner of these miraculous conceptions and births as

each at the end of a millennium (counting from the end of the millennium of Zarathushtra himself). They are named respectively Ukhshyat-ereta, (Pahl. Hōshedar), Ukhshyat-nemah (Pahl. Hōshedarmāh), and Astvat-ereta, who is κατ' ἐξοχήν the Saoshyant or 'Messiah' to whom Mazdeans still look forward (the title Sōshyōs alone has survived in Pahlavi, with no individual name). It is this last saviour who is to preside, according to the detailed accounts of the Pahlavi *Bahman-Yasht* and the *Būndahishn*,[1] at the resurrection of the dead and the regeneration of mankind (*tanū-i pasīn*, the Avestan *frasho-kereti*), followed by the great flood of molten metal, which is not only to destroy but to purify the creation. It is he, too, who is to prepare, after a great sacrifice of the mystic ox, the ambrosia (*hūsh*) which is to render mankind immortal. According to some authorities, this ἀποκατάστασις is to extend even to hell and the wicked therein :

'Praise to Him, the merciful Lord who maketh the final Retribution, and who at the end shall deliver even the wicked from Hell and restore the whole creation in purity.'[2]

As to the end of the evil spirit, Ahriman (Angra Mainyu) himself, the Pahlavi theologians are not in agreement. Some seem to have believed in his total annihilation. The Muhammadan treatise *Ulamā-i Islam*[3] quotes five different opinions concerning the final end of evil.

LITERATURE.—The ordinary translations of the Avesta and treatises on Mazdeism by F. Spiegel (*Eranische Alterthumskunde*, 3 vols., Leipzig, 1871–78, *Die arische Periode*, do. 1881); C. de Harlez (*Des Origines du Zoroastrisme*, Paris, 1879); A. V. Williams Jackson ('Die iranische Religion,' in *GIrP* ii. [1904] 612 ff.); N. Söderblom (*La Vie future d'après le Mazdéisme*, tr. J. de Coussanges, Paris, 1901); J. H. Moulton, (*The Treasure of the Magi*, London, 1917); M. N. Dhalla (*Zoroastrian Theology*, New York, 1914). For Pahlavi (Sasanian) theology specially see L. C. Casartelli, *La Philosophie religieuse du Mazdéisme sous les Sassanides*, Louvain, 1884, Eng. tr. *The Philosophy of the Mazdayasnian Religion under the Sassanids*, by Firoz Jamaspji Dastur, Bombay, 1889.

L. C. CASARTELLI.

SALVATION (Jewish).—I. *SIGNIFICATION OF THE TERM.*—Judaism has no equivalent for 'salvation' used theologically, unless we are to see a very rare example of such usage in the phrase *teshu'ah ve-hazalah* in Maimonides' *Yād*.[4] Redemption from sin here, and deliverance from its consequences hereafter, is an idea which occupies a large place in Jewish theology; but there is no word that succinctly and exactly expresses either side of it, certainly no word that expresses it in its entirety. The Rabbinical writers know such a phrase as *nekiyuth meavon*, or, more briefly, *nekiyuth* ('purification from sin' or 'purification'). For the second aspect of the idea there is no word or phrase. The sacramentalism attaching to the English term is foreign to Jewish thought. Redemption, according to Judaism, is no mysterious or supernatural process, but essentially simple and straightforward. The divine grace plays a certain part in it, but the chief part, by common consent, is performed by the man himself. In the case of sin—and all men are sinners in various degree—expiation by repentance and suffering is the condition precedent to acceptance by God; and, if that essential condition is satisfied, forgiveness and reconciliation follow as a matter of course. No superhuman ally is needed by the atoning soul. The forces in the sinner's own breast suffice. If they are marshalled in their full strength, they are all-powerful; if they are insufficiently used, or not used at all, nothing avails. The divine grace is freely given, not to supersede, but to aid and crown the sinner's repentance. Salvation, then, is a simpler affair for the Jew than it is for the Christian—simpler because less recondite; but it is less simple, too, in the sense of being less automatic. The Jew trusts to the reformed life as the one trustworthy means of making his peace with God and his conscience. At one of the most impressive moments in the service on the New Year Festival and on the Day of Atonement—the most solemn occasions in the Jewish year—there comes the characteristic cry, 'Repentance, prayer, and righteousness avert the evil decree.' For the Jew contrition, supplication, and, more important still, the contrite life suffice for salvation. Thus it is that the word itself seems somewhat strange to the Jewish mind. The Jew does not anxiously ask himself, 'Am I saved?', as though the matter called for profound heart-searchings. They are superfluous, seeing that, as the means of salvation are obvious and within a man's own control, there can be no doubt about his spiritual state either one way or the other. Rather he will ask himself, 'Am I worthy? Am I genuinely penitent?' Moreover, salvation, in its eschatological sense of deliverance from punishment or assurance of eternal life hereafter, means less to the Jew than to some others. This is because the hereafter generally bulks less in his thoughts. Not, however, because his belief in futurity is less strong, but because it is less dominant. The next world fills a smaller space in his mind because of the larger space occupied by this world. He has his work to do here—work at once mundane and heavenly—and this immediate duty keeps him from thinking mainly about the hereafter. He divides his attention equally between both worlds. This life, with all its strenuous, health-giving activities, is good—good in itself and also in its quality as a preparation for the life to come.[1] It is, according to Rabbinic doctrine, man's one sure chance of justifying himself, of redeeming himself, in God's sight. So he must take this life and make it as good as he can. If he is to be 'saved' hereafter, he must save himself here—save himself by living the worldly life in worthy fashion, by interpreting it in terms of the divine, and energetically giving effect to the interpretation. Thus it is that, while the idea of salvation is in the thoughts and heart of the Jew, the word is never on his lips. He believes in a blissful realm 'beyond these voices,' but he knows that his one hope of entering it lies in his helping to win from those voices their underlying music, to found a Kingdom of God on earth. This is his immediate business and, therefore, his chief concern and preoccupation.

1. In OT.—The word 'salvation,' however, occurs frequently in the English version of the OT. The Hebrew terms so translated are *yesha'*, *yeshuah*, and *teshu'ah*. Like the English word, these terms have various meanings. They, and the verbal forms connected with them, stand for 'help,' for deliverance from distress or peril of some kind, particularly from enemies (Ps 18^{2} 34^{6}, Is 33^{2}, Jer 14^{8}, 1 S 4^{3}); they are also used to denote rescue from death (Ps 6^{5} 68^{20}) and from sin (Ezk 36^{29}, Ps 51^{14}). The deliverance is sometimes wrought by earthly means (Ps 33^{17} 'An horse is a vain thing for safety'; cf. Pr. 21^{31}), more frequently by superhuman agencies. The Hebrew terms further stand for victory (1 S 14^{45}, 2 S 19^{2} 23^{10}, 2 K 5^{1}; probably the cry rendered 'Save now' in Ps 118^{25} should be rendered 'Give victory'; it voiced the presentiment of the Maccabæan

allegories of the teachings of the Prophet concerning *humata*, *hūkhta*, and *hvarshta* (see above) by a Parsi scholar, Aerpat Meherjibhai Palanji Madan (*Actes du douzième Congrès international des Orientalistes, Rome, 1899*, Florence, 1901, i. 213–224), does not seem to have met with any acceptance either from his co-religionists or from Western scholars.

[1] Both translated by E. W. West in *SBE* v.

[2] *Dīnkarṭ*, ed. Peshotan, Bombay, 1874–1917, ii. ch. 81, § 6.

[3] Tr. J. A. Vullers, *Fragmente über die Religion des Zoroaster*, Bonn, 1831, p. 67.

[4] *Ḥilc. Teshūbāh*, iii. 4.

[1] See art. LIFE AND DEATH (Jewish).

triumph). They variously connote the victory (*a*) of God (Is $45^{22ff.}$ $51^{6.\ 8}$), (*β*) of Israel, his redemption from captivity, the fulfilment of his mission and the conquest of the Gentiles (Is 45^{17} 49^{8} 60^{18}, Ps 14^{7} $98^{1ff.}$), and (*γ*) of God and Israel together (Is $60^{10ff.}$). In Second Isaiah, indeed, the two are identical. The salvation of Israel is always a vindication of God, the redemption of the elect people always the redemption of the divine promise (cf. $51^{4ff.}$ $56^{1ff.}$). Nor is the promised salvation limited to Israel; it extends to 'the ends of the earth'; but knowledge of the true God, submission to Him, a confession of His kingdom and righteousness, are the conditions precedent (Is $45^{22ff.}$). Thus the Hebrew terms acquire not only a universalistic, but also a spiritual significance. In Is 56 God's 'salvation' is declared to be near, and among its manifestations is the union of 'the strangers' to the Lord. They are to minister unto Him, to love His name, and to be His servants; them He will bring to His holy mountain and make joyful in His house of prayer, which is to be called a house of prayer for all peoples. The worship of the true God, with the inner regeneration which it betokens, is an element of the redemption itself as well as its essential preliminary. And prominent among the instruments of that redemption is Israel; the radiance of His own life is to light the path of regeneration for others: 'I will also give thee for a light to the Gentiles, that thou mayest be my salvation unto the end of the earth' (49^{6}). The Hebrew terms are also used eschatologically. Is 25^{8}, which describes God as 'swallowing up death for ever (or in victory),' is possibly a reference to the Resurrection (the next chapter plainly alludes to it)—certainly a formulation of the doctrine of last things. The word used to characterize this miraculous event is 'salvation': 'And it shall be said in that day, Lo, this is our God; we have waited for him, and he will save us . . . we will be glad and rejoice in his salvation' (v.^{9}). But the dividing line between the worldly and the spiritual salvation is necessarily faint and indefinite. God's salvation, just because it is His, must, from the very facts of the case, touch the spirit, though outwardly and directly it affects the temporal life. It implies a recognition of God, homage to Him as the Redeemer; it implies a deepened faith and a changed heart. And this higher connotation of the term is not restricted to eschatological passages; it is to be met with in utterances dealing with the present world-order. Thus one Psalmist (Ps 25^{5}) can pray: 'Lead me in thy truth, and teach me: for thou art the God of my salvation; on thee do I wait all the day.' Another can cry: 'Mine eyes fail for thy salvation, and for thy righteous word' (119^{123}). In these passages salvation almost certainly means the higher deliverance which is wrought by the illumination of the spirit and the invigoration of the will. In other words, men are helped and saved through the divine truth; they are saved from themselves and for God (cf. Ps $27^{9f.}$).

2. In Apocrypha and Pseudepigrapha.—In the Apocryphal and Pseudepigraphical writings the usage corresponds in most of its variations with that in the OT (cf. Wis 16^{7}, Jth 9^{11}, 1 Mac 4^{30}). But the eschatological signification becomes more pronounced. Thus in *Enoch* the repentant sinners are saved, delivered from punishment, 'in those days,' *i.e.* at the Last Judgment (50^{3}; cf. *4 Ezr.* 6^{25} $7^{66.\ 131}$ 9^{7}, where the just are saved 'either because of their works or their faith'; *Ps. Sol.* 18^{6}).

3. In Talmudic literature.—In the Talmudic literature deliverance, or salvation, is one of the boons associated with the Messianic order. The Messiah is specifically styled *Gō'ēl*, the 'Redeemer' or 'Saviour.'[1] He was to save not only Israel but humanity.

'The Messiah,' says J. Klausner,[2] 'was to be both king and saviour. He was not only to overthrow the enemies of the Jewish people, to restore the kingdom, and to rebuild the Temple, but also to set free all mankind from idolatry, to proclaim the glory of the one God throughout the world, and to destroy sin out of the earth.'

The Talmudic connotations of the term may be conveniently gathered from the Prayer Book, in which the equivalent word for 'salvation' denotes deliverance from earthly ills, but more often is used eschatologically. In one paragraph of the *'Amīdhah* (the prayer recited 'standing,' sometimes called the 'Eighteen Blessings') the salvation asked for is health;[3] but in another paragraph it expresses the belief in the Resurrection,[4] and in yet another the Messianic hope.[5] In at least one instance it seems to have a spiritual connotation; on Sabbaths and festivals a prayer[6] is offered for such higher blessings as sanctification through the Commandment (*mitzvah*) and the inner purity of sincere service, and with these there is associated the further boon of joy in the divine 'salvation,' to which the context warrants us in attaching a spiritual significance. The hope of salvation in the Messianic time expresses itself with especial force and clearness in certain services of the Synagogue. One example is the service held on Saturday night at the close of the Sabbath; it includes a string of Prophetic utterances containing the promise of national redemption—*e.g.*, Is $12^{2f.}$: 'Behold, God is my salvation; I will trust, and not be afraid. . . . Therefore with joy shall ye draw water out of the wells of salvation.' And the climax of the service is reached in the rite of *habhdālāh*,[7] which is a thanksgiving for the 'separation' of the Sabbath from the workaday week and of Israel from the Gentiles. The rite is introduced, at private worship, by other Messianic verses from the OT, and also by a prayer for the coming of Elijah the precursor (see Mal 4^{5}). The cup of wine used in the ceremony is styled 'the cup of salvation' (see Ps 116^{13}). At least equally notable is the fact that a special day, the seventh day of the Feast of Tabernacles, has been set apart by the Synagogue in honour, so to speak, of the idea of salvation. On that festival, as the Mishnāh records,[8] a circuit of the altar in the Temple was made daily to the sound of the trumpet (*shōphār*), the worshippers carrying their palms and repeating the cry, 'Save now, I beseech thee,' in Ps 118^{25}. The cry in the Hebrew original is *Hoshiāh-nā*, which was abbreviated into *Hosha'nā* (the 'Hosanna' of Mt 21^{9}). On the seventh day there were seven circuits, and hence the day came to be known as *Hosha'nā Rabbāh*, 'the Great Hosannā.' The salvation asked for seems to have been, specifically, the salvation of the soil from drought—the season in which the Tabernacles falls being that of the autumn rains, of which the willow of the brook bound up with the palm (cf. Lv 23^{40}), and on this occasion decking the altar, was regarded as the symbol. In course of time an extended significance was given to the Great Hosanna Day. The circuits were taken over by the Synagogue from the Temple, and in the accompanying prayers (called *hosha'noth* from *hosanna*, their refrain) other boons besides rain, the general fertility of the earth, and the physical well-being of man and beast, were asked for—Israel's final ingathering, *e.g.*, the advent of the Messiah, and the restoration of Jerusalem; and they were asked for all the

1 Midr. *Rabbāh* to Ru 2^{14}; cf. *The Authorised Daily Prayer Book*[9], London, 1914, p. 44; the usage is based on Is 59^{20}.

2 *Die messianischen Vorstellungen des jüdischen Volkes im Zeitalter der Tannaiten*, Berlin, 1904.

3 *Authorised Daily Prayer Book*[9], p. 47.

4 *Ib.* p. 45.

5 P. 49; cf. p. 282.

6 P. 117.

7 See *Berākhôth*, 33*a*.

8 *Sukkāh*, iv. 5

more passionately because the land was lost and the people scattered. The Great Hosanna (originally only the 'Seventh Day of the Willow,' as the Talmud styles it) had meanwhile, probably because Tabernacles was regarded as a Day of Judgment for the Fruits,[1] become a day of penitence, a faint reminiscence and revival of the recent Day of Atonement, and a supplementary and final effort after reconciliation with God. The additional boon of the divine forgiveness and salvation was accordingly added to the blessings invoked, and the following prayer, with others of a like tenor, was included in the service: 'O God, like sheep we all have gone astray. From out Thy book wipe not our name away. Save! O Save!'[2] The penitential character of the day (especially emphasized in the Spanish liturgy) is recognizable in all the orthodox Prayer Books. At the final point of the service the palm is laid aside, but the willow is retained, the worshipper beating off its leaves to the cry, 'A voice bringeth good tidings' (cf. Is 52^{7}), and then follows a prayer for the Messianic redemption, and for the spiritual 'waters that satisfy the thirsty soul' (cf. Ps 107^{9}).

Thus salvation, attaining its highest and most personal significance, becomes a synonym for redemption from sin and its consequences. As was to be expected, the term is used largely in this sense in the liturgy for the Day of Atonement, the day of the divine salvation.[3] There the cry is for spiritual redemption, for escape from the effects and the very bondage of sin, for the creation of the new and the higher man: 'We have done wickedly, therefore we are not saved; but do Thou put it into our hearts to forsake the way of wickedness, and hasten our salvation.'[4] The utterance is typical. The worshipper's renunciation of the way of wickedness, his restoration to the divine fellowship, constitute his salvation, and the divine help is to hasten it.

II. *ATTAINMENT OF SALVATION.*—Understanding 'salvation' to mean moral and spiritual redemption here or hereafter, let us now consider how, and by whom, it may be attained according to Jewish teaching.

1. OT teaching.—In the OT and the Apocrypha the chief, practically the sole, way to divine acceptance lies through obedience and, in the case of sin, through repentance: 'What doth the Lord thy God require of thee, but to fear the Lord thy God, to walk in all his ways, and to love him, and to serve the Lord thy God with all thy heart and with all thy soul'; and, further, 'The Lord shall scatter you among the nations . . . and there ye shall serve gods, the work of men's hands . . . But if from thence thou shalt seek the Lord thy God, thou shalt find him, if thou seek him with all thy heart and with all thy soul' (Dt 10^{12} $4^{27ff.}$). These typical utterances might be multiplied indefinitely. Here and there we come upon pregnant sentences briefly summarizing the essentials of the acceptable life. There is, *e.g.*, Ps 15, with its list of prerequisites for him who would abide in God's tabernacle, dwell in His holy hill. The catalogue is almost exclusively ethical; it includes such virtues as truthfulness and sincerity, the avoidance of detraction and usury, and of wrongdoing generally to one's neighbour. Micah (6^{8}) has a yet shorter formula: 'What doth the Lord require of thee, but to do justly, and to love mercy, and to walk humbly with thy God?' These utterances are sublime because of their very simplicity. Beside them the tangled schemes of salvation propounded by later theologians seem forced and artificial. Equally simple are the prescriptions for achieving redemption from sin. Nothing is finer, or more characteristic of the Prophetic teaching on this point, than the exhortation of Hosea ($14^{1f.}$): 'O Israel, return unto the Lord thy God; for thou hast fallen by thine iniquity. Take with you words, and return unto the Lord: say unto him, Take away all iniquity, and accept that which is good (in us)'; upon which follows (v.$^{4f.}$) the saving promise: 'I will heal their backsliding, I will love them freely. . . . I will be as the dew unto Israel.' But the repentance must be whole-hearted, not merely lip service or outward show. God refuses to hear the man whose hands are stained with blood, and the sinner must rend his heart and not his garments if he is really to turn unto God (Is 1^{15}, Jl 2^{13}).

2. Apocrypha.—The OT is echoed by the Apocrypha. The one way of salvation is service, obedience to the Commandment or the Law (God 'hath mercy on them that accept the Law, and that diligently seek after his statutes' [Sir 18^{14}, according to Kautzsch's reading; cf. 35^{16} Eng. RV and *4 Ezr.* $7^{72f.}$ $9^{32ff.}$]). Repentance, too, must be real, finding its expression in amendment: 'Return unto the Lord, and forsake the sin' (Sir 17^{25}). Sometimes faith is postulated as the avenue to acceptance (cf. *4 Ezr.* 9^{7}), but exceptionally; the chief stress is laid upon works. In an utterance reproduced by the Talmud[1] Ben Sira says ($34^{25f.}$): 'He that washeth himself after touching a dead body, and toucheth it again, what profit hath he in his washing? Even so a man fasting for his sins, and going again, and doing the same; who will listen to his prayer?' In like manner, according to Wis 1^{1} $5^{2ff.}$, the divine criterion of human merit is 'righteousness,' *i.e.* morality touched by religion, which, in the case of the Jew, becomes obedience to the law or the 'discipline.' They that 'take their fill of lawlessness are consumed'; they are 'amazed at the marvel of God's salvation' wrought for the righteous, who 'live for ever and receive the diadem of beauty from the Lord's hand' ($5^{2.7.15f.}$). And righteousness is to know God and to love men (12^{19} 15^{3}). But even for the sinner there is acceptance if he repents, and God so accepts him because He loves all His creatures and cannot hate any of them: 'Thou sparest all things, because they are thine . . . for thine incorruptible spirit is in all things' (11^{26} 12^{1}; cf. Ps 119^{94}). The thought that man is God's handiwork, akin to Him, moreover, through the soul, moves the divine heart to compassion and forgiveness (cf. Is $64^{8f.}$). The *Psalms of Solomon*, though a product of a different school of religious thought, contain similar doctrine: 'Faithful is the Lord to them that love him in truth, to them that walk in the righteousness of his commandments, in the law which he commanded us that we might live'; and the singer praises God for having accepted his repentance, for having saved him and not appointed him for destruction with sinners ($14^{1f.}$ 16^{5}). In *4 Ezra* God declares that 'few shall be saved'; but Ezra invokes the divine rectitude and goodness as a plea for mercy towards 'them that have no store of good works' ($8^{1.3.36}$). Thus the Commandment, or the Law, takes high rank in the Apocrypha among the essentials of the acceptable life. It is the Law that nerves the Maccabees for their desperate and glorious conflict with the Greeks (1 Mac 2^{27} etc.).

3. Talmud and Midrash.—(*a*) *The Law.*—The Law enjoys no less estimation in the Talmud and the Midrashim. The *Tôrāh* is the one 'way of life' here and hereafter,[2] the corrective to the

[1] Cf. *Mishnāh R. Hashānāh*, i. 2.
[2] *Service of the Synagogue*, iv., *Tabernacles*, ed. Davis and Adler, London, 1908, p. 178.
[3] Cf. Midr. *Tehillim* to Ps 27^{1}.
[4] *Service of the Synagogue*, ii., *Atonement Eve*, London, 1904, p. 46.

[1] *Ta'ănîth*, 16*a*.
[2] *Shab.* 30*a*, Midr. *Rabbāh* to Lv 23^{24}; Philo (*de Vita Mosis*,

evil impulse, the antidote to sin, the source and the guarantee of all moral and spiritual good.[1] In a striking passage the Rabbis, commenting on the words (Jer 16[11]), 'They have forsaken me and have not kept my law,' picture God as saying, 'Would that they had forsaken Me, but kept My Law!' But how is it possible to keep the Law while forsaking God? The answer is that, if they had occupied themselves with the Law, it would have led them back to God.[2] The study of the *Tôrāh* is a saving influence—the idea fills a large place in the Rabbinic doctrine. The Mishnāh[3] gives a catalogue of good actions of which the usufruct is secured in this world, but which are stored up by way of capital, or substance, for enjoyment in the world to come—*e.g.*, filial reverence, visiting the sick, dowering the bride, and peacemaking—and it ends by adding that 'the study of the Law is equal to them all.' What does the phrase mean? Does it mean study only? Was the man of evil life who pondered the *Tôrāh* (*i.e.* the whole body of religious lore) day and night automatically guaranteed salvation according to the Rabbinic teaching? The entire Talmud and its allied literature refute the notion. Again and again with '*Tôrāh*' the phrase 'good deeds' is joined, to show that religious study and meditation are not enough, that the guarantee of salvation, though it may be obtained through them, is something higher, something essentially independent of them, and is to be looked for in the obedient and devout life. The final aim of knowledge (*i.e.* of the Law), say the Rabbis, is repentance and good deeds, and God is described as saying, 'Keep my *Tôrāh* in thy heart, but let the fear of me also be before thine eyes; guard thy life from all sin, and purify thyself from all iniquity. Then I will be with thee.'[4] And, still more plainly and trenchantly, the Rabbis say: 'He that studies *Tôrāh* without practising it—better for him if he had never been born.'[5] Weber[6] cites some of these passages, but implies, in spite of them, that the Rabbinical conception of salvation is essentially mechanical. The Psalmists, he remembers, also have high praise for the Law (cf. esp. Ps 119), but on their lips the Law means something more than the written word, something wider and higher. For the Rabbis, on the contrary, the *Tôrāh* is Law pure and simple, and as such they extol it. The distinction is false, as will have been seen. Sometimes, it is true, the *Tôrāh*, or even the study of the *Tôrāh*, stands alone in Talmud and Midrash as the *summum bonum*, as containing all the promise and potency of salvation. But that the thought underlying such utterances is larger than the literal meaning is proved by the quotations just given, and by the spirit of the Talmudic doctrine generally. And this repeated insistence upon the importance of the Law becomes intelligible when it is remembered that, for the Rabbis, the *Tôrāh*, used in the wider sense above indicated, contained all the knowledge and the inspiration needed by the Jew for attaining to the good life. Through study of the Word, and of the teachings which provide its explanation and complement, that saving knowledge and inspiration could most certainly be acquired; but they were useless unless they were translated into action. The very phrase 'to study the Law' was often used in a larger sense, and included obedience to it; and every morning the devout Jew prays for help in his endeavour to understand the *Tôrāh* and lovingly to fulfil it.[7] The ardour of the Jewish fathers for the *Tôrāh* was no more mechanical, and no less worthy, than is the zeal of the good Christian who diligently searches the Scriptures for the guidance and illumination which are essential to right living. Unquestionably part of the charm of the *Tôrāh* for the Jew was, and is, the very fact of its being law, though not in the mechanical sense imagined by Weber. For the Jew the *Tôrāh* is law understood as the supreme commandment, and also as discipline. It contains definite, concrete rules, which it is his greatest delight to perform, seeing that they have come from God. 'The joy of the Commandment (*mitzvah*)' is a familiar Rabbinic expression,[1] and the joy was not only real, but also spiritual, springing not from the consciousness of a merely automatic obedience, but from the thought of being at one, through obedience, with the Divine Master. Through the joy of the Commandment, the Talmud explicitly declares,[2] the Divine Presence is brought down and abides; and this joy, a mediæval teacher adds, is even more pleasing to God than the obedience.[3] 'To do the will of the Father in heaven' is an equally familiar phrase of the Rabbis; for that a man should make himself light as an eagle, swift as a hart, strong as a lion.[4] For obedience to the divine commands gives to life all its real meaning and savour. The *Tôrāh*, moreover, was law in the sense of a saving discipline. The Jew saw this, and the thought gladdened him. How low might he not have fallen, to what debasing bondage might he not have been reduced, but for that corrective and exalting influence! He might have been an idolater, a thief, a sensualist—a slave, in short, to his worst self. 'There goes John Bunyan but for the grace of God!'—the saying has its parallel in the utterance of Rabbi Joseph on Pentecost, the Feast of the Law: 'But for this day I might have been some low man in the street.'[5] The *Tôrāh* saved him from that degradation. 'I will walk at liberty,' says the Psalmist (Ps 119[45]), 'for I have sought thy precepts'; and 'He only is free who gives himself to the *Tôrāh*,' taught the Rabbis in their turn.[6] 'They that busy themselves with *Tôrāh* and deeds of love,' they say elsewhere,[7] 'are the masters of their lives; they are free from the yoke of sin, from sorrow, from oppression, from death.' The *Tôrāh* is the guarantee of salvation both here and hereafter. Greater than sacrifice, which procures only earthly life, it secures the heavenly life also.[8] For, when a man passes hence, none of his possessions goes with him, neither silver, nor gold, nor precious stones, but only *Tôrāh* and good works; they alone hearten him and plead for him.[9] In this world, too, their power is tremendous. 'He that accepts one single commandment in perfect faith deserves that the Holy Spirit should rest upon him,'[10] and still more definitely Maimonides declares that to fulfil only one of the 613 precepts of the *Tôrāh* for the love of God is to be worthy of eternal life.[11] In fine, the *Tôrāh*, according to the Rabbinic conception, is at once the base and the crown of the good life. Its acquisition is the seal of the moral and spiritual perfection which has been already attained by the quest of it. This thought is set forth in a striking passage[12] in which various qualifications, covering almost the entire domain of human excellence, are enumerated as

ed. Mangey, ii. 7) speaks of the 'incomparable' Law, and Josephus (*c. Apion.* ii. 22) deems the loss of all material treasures unimportant as long as the 'eternal Law' remains.

1 *Qid.* 30*b*.
2 Jer. *Hagigāh*, 76*c*.
3 *Peah*, i. 1.
4 *Berākhôth*, 17*a*.
5 *Sifra* to Lv 26[3].
6 *Jüdische Theologie*, p. 24.
7 Cf. *Authorised Daily Prayer Book*[9], p. 39f.; for the wide signification of '*Tôrāh*' see Schechter, *Some Aspects of Rabbinic Theology*, p. 117 ff.

1 Cf. *e.g. Shab.* 30*b*.
2 *Ib.*
3 Baḥya ibn Ḥalwah, in *Kad Haqemah*, cited by Schechter, p. 15.
4 *Ābhôth*, v. 23.
5 *Pesāḥîm*, 68*b*.
6 *Boraithā of R. Meir*, 2.
7 '*Abōdāh Zārāh*, 5*b*.
8 *Shab.* 30*a*.
9 *Boraithā of R. Meir*, 9.
10 *Meḥilta* to Ex 15[1].
11 Commentary on Mishn. *Makkôth*, iii. 16; see Schechter, p. 165.
12 *Boraithā of R. Meir*, 6.

essential to that acquisition—moderation in worldly enjoyment, patience, goodness of heart, submission under tribulation, contentment, humility, love to God and man. To possess *Tôrāh* is to be assured of salvation because it guarantees the possession of the high attributes by which salvation is automatically attained.

(*b*) *Faith and belief.*—The Law, then, means practical goodness, but also faith. The sharp distinction between faith and works as the means of salvation is unknown to Judaism. This is easily understood. In a certain sense acceptance by God necessarily presupposes belief in Him. If that belief is lacking—if there is no conviction of God's saving power, no desire for it—then the very idea of salvation is excluded. Used in this sense, faith does, and must, enter into the Rabbinic scheme. 'The just shall live by his faith,' cries Habakkuk (2^{4}), and this utterance a Talmudic sage cites as an epitome of the entire religion.[1] Faith, moreover, is a saving virtue; it is so fine, so courageous, when confronted with the trials and the tragedy of life, as to deserve God's best blessings. It was Abraham's faith that won for him life in this world and in the next.[2] In virtue of faith the Israelites were redeemed from Egypt;[3] they believed in the divine promise of redemption, though their misery 'shrieked against the creed.' But, as has been said, the salvation of God is obviously conditioned by faith in Him. The good life is the one saving force, according to Judaism, and the good life, also according to Judaism, is the God-inspired life. We reach the same conclusion when we think of salvation through repentance. By repentance all the Jewish teachers mean return to God. Judaism knows no other kind; the word for repentance—*tᵉshûbāh*—means 'return.' But to go back to God implies the possession of a God to go back to—in other words, it presupposes belief and faith in Him. Works and faith, then, are inseparably bound up together in Judaism as in every other religion. Works are the substance of the ideal life; faith is its spirit, its driving force. But farther than this it is unnecessary to go. The familiar assertion that, according to Judaism, God judges men by their lives, which are within their own control, and not by their creed, which is not, remains unquestionably true. Attempts have been made in the Jewish domain to embody the essentials of belief in a rigid scheme or formula, and they have been rashly understood as touchstones of the Jew's orthodoxy and even of his fitness for salvation. The Thirteen Articles propounded by Maimonides[4] are the best-known example. But, as all Jewish scholars agree, Maimonides' scheme was never formally accepted by the Synagogue; on the contrary, it was fiercely assailed by many great authorities, some of whom propounded alternative schemes of their own—Abba Mari (13th cent.), with his three creeds, Ḥisdai Kreskas (14th cent.), with fifteen, and Joseph Albo (15th cent.), also with three. On the other hand, Isaac Abravanel (15th cent.) scouted every attempt to frame a dogmatic scheme; every word of the *Tôrāh*, he declared, was a dogma. Nor did Maimonides himself give out his Thirteen Articles in the name of the Synagogue, though it has in a measure fathered them by permitting their inclusion in the liturgy in hymnal form.[5] He had no power to claim general authority for them. They represent his personal opinions only, and in selecting them he probably had an eye to the special religious needs and the theological controversies of his day—a remark which applies to most of the dogmatic schemes put forth by Jewish teachers at various periods. But that Maimonides thoroughly believed in the saving character of his creeds and formulated them only after profound consideration is clear from his own explicit statements.[1]

Of far greater moment is the famous passage in the Mishnāh[2] which runs as follows:

> 'All Israel have a share in the future life. But these have no share in it:—he who says that the dogma of the Resurrection of the Dead is not taught by the *Tôrāh* [or more broadly, according to another reading, 'he who denies the Resurrection of the Dead'], or that the *Tôrāh* has not come from God, and the "Epicurean." Rabbi Aqiba says, he also that reads external [*i.e.* heretical] books, or that uses a Scriptural verse as an incantation in order to heal a wound. Abba Saul says, he also that pronounces the Divine Name (the Tetragrammaton) as it is written.'

The Mishnāh then proceeds to supplement these categories by adding the names of certain notorious transgressors, among them Jeroboam, Ahab, King Manasseh, and Balaam. Rabbi Jehudah, however, puts in a plea for Manasseh. The importance of this passage lies in the fact that it forms part of the Mishnāh, the recognized code of the Rabbinical law, and has consequently, in so far as its uncontentious dicta are concerned, to be regarded as an authoritative utterance of the Synagogue. That it has always possessed this character is certain, and it has shaped not only the belief of orthodoxy, but its practice also. A Jew who denied, *e.g.*, the Scriptural authority of resurrection would be deemed unfit, even to-day, to hold the position either of Rabbi or of religious teacher in a rigidly orthodox congregation. The inclusion of this passage in the Mishnāh has stereotyped orthodox opinion on this particular question beyond the possibility of modification. If it had escaped the Mishnāh, and appeared merely as an *obiter dictum* of the Talmud at large, it might conceivably have gone more or less unregarded. The question arises, however, whether orthodoxy has not invested the passage with a significance which it was never meant to possess. When its various authors declared that this or that person, or category of persons, would have no share in the future life, did they mean the phrase to be taken literally, as a deliberate expression of their opinion that such person or category would be eternally lost? Were they not rather speaking loosely and rhetorically, using the formula, 'these have no share in the future life,' not in its exact eschatological sense, but merely as an arresting way of expressing their opinion of the heinousness of the offences specified? In other words, are we not at liberty to see in the formula one of those exaggerated modes of speech purposely impressive, but literally inexact, which are so dear to the Oriental mind?[3] Other Talmudic passages lend support to this suggestion. According to Jer. *Sanh.* x. 28*a*, among the 'heretical books,' the readers of which, in the opinion of Rabbi Aqiba, will have no share in the future life, are the 'books of Ben Sira.'[4] Now, Ben Sira (Ecclesiasticus), far from being a heretical book in the opinion of the Talmudic doctors generally, is a work which they prize and often cite with approval.[5] How, then, could Aqiba have been speaking literally when he consigned to perdition a man who read it? Anticipating the view of a later generation of teachers,[6] he doubted whether Ecclesiasticus was a 'safe'

[1] *Makkôth*, 24*a*. [2] *Meḥilta* to Ex 14^{31}. [3] *Ib.*

[4] In his commentary on Mishn. *Sanh.* x.; for the Articles see the *Authorised Daily Prayer Book*^{9}, p. 89 f.

[5] Cf. *Authorised Daily Prayer Book*^{9}, p. 2 f.

[1] Cf. his Introduction to Mishn. *Sanh.* x., end; see, on the whole subject, Schechter, *Studies in Judaism*, 1st ser. ch. vi.

[2] *Sanh.* x. 1.

[3] Cf. Mk 3^{29}. This theory is advanced after full consideration of the parallel passage in *R. Hashānāh*, 17*a*, with its circumstantial description of the future fate of these heretics and sinners.

[4] M. Joel, *Blicke in die Religionsgeschichte*, Breslau, 1880, p. 68 ff., tries to show that 'Ben Sira' has been erroneously substituted for some other name.

[5] Cf. *e.g.* *Bābhā Bathrā*, 98*b*; Jer. *Ḥagîgāh*, 77*c*.

[6] See *Sanh.* c. (100) *b*.

book, and he expressed his doubts with a certain rhetorical violence. But more than this he could not possibly have meant. Again, in *Ābhôth de R. Nathan*[1] it is declared that among those who have no share in the future life are the judges of a city. The source of this dictum is to be found in the Talmud.[2] Merely because the troubles that have befallen Israel are there laid at the door of corrupt judges, therefore the judges of a city, without distinction of moral character, are excluded, for all time, from the world to come. Good and bad are classed together indiscriminately. Is it possible to understand such an utterance literally? Yet again they are declared[3] to be eternally lost who profane holy things or despise the religious feasts, and those, again, who put a fellow-man to public shame (the last category is omitted from some variants), and they are lost 'even though they possess *Tôrāh* and good deeds.' These are comparatively venial offences, and yet they are to be visited with eternal perdition. Even so conservative a writer as Bacher does not seem to think that the last-cited statement should be taken seriously; he regards it as embodying the theme of a sermon directed against the sins or heresies of the preacher's time.[4] That all such utterances should be marked by some extravagance of expression is quite intelligible, and that the Rabbis were accustomed to resort to these rhetorical devices is made clear by their language when, instead of denying, they affirm a man's chances of future life. A certain type of persons or actions is declared to merit happiness hereafter for quite inadequate reasons. 'Who,' *e.g.*, the Talmud asks, 'is worthy of the world to come?' And some of the various answers are: he that, at prayer, joins the *'Amīdhah* to the benediction for Israel's deliverance; or he that shows respect to the aged; and he that repeats Ps 145 thrice daily.[5] These exaggerations are the most familiar things in the Talmudic literature. In *Bᵉrākhôth*, 4*b*, it is declared that he who transgresses the injunctions of the sages makes himself liable to the death penalty. But the offence against which these words are intended as a warning is the trivial one of reading the evening *shᵉma'* (Dt 6^4) after midnight. Yet it is admitted that the right time for reading it lasts till dawn, and that the sages only desire to make the proverbial 'fence to the law,' and to keep men from transgression. Is it not clear, then, that this portentous dictum is merely a conscious exaggeration used for this specific purpose, and not a literally intended pronouncement? It is true that this loose and rhetorical use of the eschatological phrase, in both its positive and its negative forms, seems to have become more frequent in the later Talmudic period, but the fact does not exclude the possibility of its having been in vogue in the earlier times from which the Mishnāh in *Sanhedrin* is to be dated. In fact Elazar of Modin, the author of the saying in *Abhôth* above cited, which denies salvation to those who despise the festivals, belongs to those times. This passage, like the Mishnāh in *Sanhedrin*, was doubtless a polemical utterance aimed at theological opponents (mainly the Jewish Christians),[6] such fulminations being the only means of self-defence possessed by the Synagogue. But this very circumstance supports the hypothesis that these expressions were only rhetorical. The invective of rival theologians is notoriously inexact and wild; and, when the Mishnaic sages consigned

[1] Ed. Schechter, Vienna, 1887, p. 108. [2] *Shab.* 139*a*.
[3] By R. Elazar of Modin in *Abhôth*, iii. 11.
[4] *Die Agada der Tannaïten*², Strassburg, 1903, i. 190.
[5] *Berākhôth*, 4*b*; *Bābhā Bathrā*, 10*b*; cf. *Shab.* 118*a*, where those who keep the ordinance of the 'three Sabbath meals' are promised immunity from Gehenna!
[6] See J. Guttmann, in *MGWJ* xlii. [1898] 289 ff.

their opponents to perdition, they may consciously have meant to do no more than imply that the opinions and the acts which they had in mind were a source of danger to the religion.[1]

As an eschatological statement Mishnāh *Sanh.* x. 1 must be deemed ineffective from another point of view also. There was always an obvious antidote to its sting. Maimonides[2] embodies the Mishnaic dictum in his code of Jewish law, as he was bound to do; but he is careful to add that it applies only to offenders who die impenitent. Let the sinner repent, he says, and, though his sin be a denial of the divine existence itself, he will enjoy everlasting life, 'for nothing can stand against repentance.'[3] Elsewhere[4] he seems to affirm that the attainment of moral and spiritual perfection automatically secures eternal bliss for men, the bliss being the perfection itself. Thus, according to the best Jewish teaching, there is hope for the most deep-dyed sinner, even for the worst heretics. The phrase indeed is inadequate; for Judaism has always laid less stress on the revolt of opinion than on the revolt of action. There are teachers, like Moses Mendelssohn, who go so far as to deny that Judaism has any saving truths whatever. Nowhere, said Mendelssohn, does the Bible command men to believe; it commands them to know. Punishment, in the Biblical age, began only at the point where opinion passed over into overt action; up to that point a man might think what he pleased without being chargeable with heresy.

'I recognize,' he says, 'only those as eternal truths which the human mind can comprehend and human powers verify,' and he adds: 'The divine religion brandishes no avenging sword; its power is the divine might of truth.'[5]

It follows that, according to Jewish doctrine, duly considered and properly understood, there is salvation for all. The general declaration of the Mishnāh above quoted, 'All Israel have a share in the future life,' might well stand without the subsequent qualifications.[6] But, as we shall see, for 'all Israel' there might have been substituted 'all men,' if the real heart of Judaism is to be regarded as speaking.

(*c*) *Repentance.*—We are thrown back, then, upon works as the essential condition of salvation. If they fail, there is, as already stated, repentance, *i.e.* return to God, and conversion from the evil life. Thus repentance, which K. Kohler[7] calls 'an exclusively Jewish conception,' is essentially good works; it is a change of temper issuing in the changed, the reformed, life (cf. Is 55^7, Jl 2^{13}, and the OT Prophets, *passim*). The Rabbis emphasize the idea. In the liturgy for New Year and the Day of Atonement, the great festivals of repentance, it is declared that 'penitence, prayer and righteousness (of which charity is the typical example) avert the evil decree.'[8] With repentance good deeds are repeatedly coupled in the

[1] I. Abrahams (*Studies in Pharisaism*, p. 143) characterizes these utterances as 'theoretical metaphysics rather than practical religious teaching.' Cf. Schechter, *Studies*, 1st ser. ch. vi.
[2] *Yād; Hilc. Teshūbāh*, iii. 6 ff.
[3] *Ib.* iii. 14. According to the Rabbis, God created repentance before the world, which could not otherwise have stood; cf. Midr. *Rabbāh* to Gn 1^4; and, as Abrahams (p. 145) acutely points out, though the confession of sins on the Day of Atonement specifies offences theoretically unpardonable, the worshipper adds, 'For all these forgive us, O God of forgiveness.'
[4] Introd. to Mish. *Sanh.* x.
[5] Cf. his *Jerusalem*, Berlin, 1783, Eng. tr., 2 vols., London, 1838, and his letters in M. Kayserling, *Moses Mendelssohn*, Leipzig, 1862; for his views at length see Graetz, *Gesch. der Juden*, Leipzig, 1866–78, ii. 86 ff.
[6] 'The angel that keeps Gehenna,' according to the *Alphabet of R. Akiba* (Introd.), 'has no power over Israel, for he studies and fulfils the *Tôrāh*, and the love of him is for ever in God's heart.'
[7] *Grundriss*, p. 187.
[8] *Service of the Synagogue*, iii., *The Day of Atonement*, London, 1905. The original is in the *Tanḥuma* to Gn 8^{15}; cf. Jer. *Ta'ănîth*, 65*b*; *Sanh.* 28*c*.

Rabbinic literature.[1] 'For him,' declare the Rabbis, 'who saith, "I will sin and repent," repentance availeth not.'[2] Repentance, they also say, 'makes a man a new creature';[3] if it fails to do this, it is nothing. But, when it does achieve this, it is all-powerful; it lifts the sinner to the very throne of God.[4] The sinner is to repent every day; a man's garments should be always white.[5] But, since man is forgetful of his highest interests, there are special days, the 'Ten Days of Repentance,' ear-marked for this duty and particularly favourable for its fulfilment. On those days the Divine Presence dwells among Israel.[6] Beginning with the New Year Festival, the Biblical 'Day of Blowing the Trumpets' (Lv $23^{23ff.}$), they reach their close and climax on the Fast of Atonement, the most solemn celebration of the Jewish year (the observance of the 'Day of Blowing the Trumpets' as the New Year festival is post-Exilic, according to Friedmann;[7] but the distinctive rite of the feast, and its proximity to the Day of Atonement, must have invested it with some of its present solemn and penitential character at an early date; to-day the Prayer Book for the festival shares many of the special features of the liturgy for the Day of Atonement). The traditional solemnity of the Day of Atonement, which extends back to Biblical times (Lv $16^{1ff.}$), its historic associations, the mortification of body and spirit, and the withdrawal from the world, which form part of its observance, make it a peculiarly appropriate opportunity for repentance. It is also a day for the exercise of God's special grace in response to the strenuous effort after reconciliation put forth by a united Israel. It is the day of moral and spiritual salvation *par excellence*. But the sinner must aid its gracious work by his contrition. Three books, say the Rabbis, are opened on New Year's Day—one for the righteous, who are written down for life straightway, another for the wicked, who are irrevocably condemned to die, a third for the 'intermediates,' whose fate, held in abeyance until the Day of Atonement, is determined by the quality of their repentance.[8] According to another view, repentance atones for small sins; but for the expiation of more serious offences the Day of Atonement is also needed.[9] But there are limits even to the Day's great power. Without repentance it is ineffective, and, if the worshipper trusts to it alone to bring him absolution automatically, the Day avails him nothing.[10] Moreover, before the sinner can make his peace with Heaven, he must make it with his brother.[11] Apart from these admirable reservations, the austerities of the Day have an inherent value as an aid to reconciliation. Fasting takes the place of the ancient sin-offering, and the 'affliction of the soul' is an acceptable offering in God's eyes; He will regard the fat and blood lost by the fasting worshipper as though it were laid upon the altar.[12]

(*d*) *Asceticism and tribulation.*—Further, there are certain aids to salvation which, joined to amendment, may increase its effectiveness. Among these are the ascetic life, tribulation, and 'the merit of the fathers.' The first is held in especial favour by the mystical school. Thus Baḥya ibn Pakudah (11th cent.) writes that he

[1] Cf. *e.g.* ***Abhôth***, iv. 17: 'Better an hour of repentance and good deeds in this world than all the life of the world to come.'

[2] Mishn. *Yômā*, viii. 9.

[3] *Pesīqtā Rabbathi*, 169*a*, ed. M. Friedmann, Vienna, 1880; cf. 2 Co 5^{17},

[4] *Yômā*, 86*a*.

[5] *Shab*. 153*a*, in allusion to Ec 9^{8}.

[6] *Pesīqtā R*. 156*b*.

[7] *JQR* i. [1889] 67.

[8] *R. Hashānāh*, 16*b*; later teaching extended the time of grace to the Great Hosannā.

[9] Mishn. *Yômā*, viii. 9.

[10] Tos. *Yômā*, iv. 10; Mishn. *Yômā*, viii. 9.

[11] *Ib*.

[12] Midr. *Tehillim* to Ps 25^{3}; *Berākhôth*, 17*a*. These ideas are woven into the liturgy; cf. *Service of the Synagogue*, iii., *The Day of Atonement*, p. 224 ff.

who prefers death in God's service to life in revolt from Him, poverty to riches for His sake, sickness to health, suffering to well-being, and who submits himself joyfully to the divine decrees, is fitted to receive the beatitude which God, in His love and grace, hath stored up in the future world.[1] But asceticism as a means of reconciliation with God is not the exclusive prescription of any one school. Penances for sin are a familiar feature in Jewish teaching and practice; the Rabbinical writings contain many references to them and even prescribe them in detail, their severity being proportionate to the nature of the offence.[2] Tribulation, too, is an aid to expiation, and opens the way to heaven.[3] To go for long without tribulation is to arouse doubts as to one's certainty of eternal life, to justify a man's fear that he is getting his reward here instead of hereafter.[4] 'If,' say the Rabbis, 'thou desirest life, hope for affliction.'[5] But, if tribulation atones, death, the supreme visitation, necessarily does so. In this respect it is the mightier of the two; it absolves when affliction and repentance together are powerless.[6] Death, say the Rabbis,[7] expiates every sin, blasphemy alone excepted—an utterance which, taken alone, would stretch the scheme of salvation almost to the widest possible limits.

(*e*) *Imputed merit.*—A potent aid to salvation, in the case of Israel, is the merit of the fathers—an idea which has played a larger part in the literature of the Jew than in his life. The excellences of the three patriarchs (those of the matriarchs also, though this idea is far less emphasized), and indeed of all the righteous Israelites of the past, are supposed to be thrown into a common stock for the benefit of their people, collectively and individually, in every age. The salvation which the Jew might possibly not attain in virtue of his own life may be assured to him by the merit of the righteous dead. Even as a living vine is supported by a lifeless prop, and is thereby kept verdant and flourishing, so the living Israel is upheld by the virtues of the fathers who sleep in the dust.[8] 'I am black, but comely,' says Israel with Ca 1^{5}—'black because of my own actions, comely because of the acts of the fathers.'[9] The germ of the idea is Biblical. Moses, interceding for his people, appeals, in arrest of judgment, to the righteousness of the patriarchs, God's 'servants' (Ex 32^{13}; cf. Lv 26^{42}), though the chief stress is laid on God's covenant with them rather than on their virtues. The Rabbis, however, see in Moses' intercession an appeal to ancestral merit, and expound his appeal in the following parable:

There was once a king, with whom his friend deposited a string of ten pearls. The friend died, leaving one daughter, whom the king then married, giving her as a bridal gift a string of ten pearls of his own. In course of time she lost the gift, and the king threatened to divorce her. Her nearest friend interceded on her behalf. 'Why divorce her?', he pleaded, 'hast thou forgotten the pearls which her father deposited with thee? Take them and make good thy loss.' And the king consented. So, when Israel sinned in the matter of the Golden Calf, and God would have cast them off, Moses makes intercession for them. 'Why,' he asks, 'wouldst thou cast off thy people?' 'Because,' God answers, 'they have broken my Ten Commandments.' 'Remember,' Moses answers, 'the ten temptations that Father Abraham withstood, and let them atone for Israel's ten sins.'[10]

This idea of ancestral merit, M. Lazarus rightly says,[11] is specifically Jewish. The merit of the fathers, in Jewish teaching, unlike the Atonement

[1] *Ḥoboth Halebaboth*, ch. iv., ed. M. E. Stern, Vienna, 1856, p. 239; cf. *Reshith Ḥokhmāh* (16th cent.), ch. vi. end. The Introduction to the *Roqeaḥ* (12th cent.), another work of the mystical school, contains similar doctrine.

[2] See the *Hilc. Teshūbāh* appended to the Introduction to the *Roqeaḥ*.

[3] *Berākhôth*, 5*a*; *Yômā*, 86*a*.

[4] *Eraḥin*, 16*b*, 17*a*.

[5] Midr. *Tehillim* to Ps 16^{11}.

[6] *Sifrē* to Nu 15^{31}; *Ḥagigāh*, 9*a*.

[7] *Sifrē, loc. cit.*

[8] Midr. *Rabbāh* to Ex 32^{13}.

[9] *Ib*. to the verse.

[10] *Ib*. to Ex 32^{13}.

[11] *The Ethics of Judaism*, Philadelphia, 1901-02, ii. 289.

in Christianity, does not depend for its efficacy upon the self-immolation of its possessors. The fathers do not deliberately sacrifice themselves for the salvation either of posterity or of their own generation. They may be quite unconscious of the expiatory value of their goodness. What is supposed to happen is a transfer, under God's grace, of that goodness to the credit side of other men's moral account. But, just as probably the belief in the Atonement has seldom weakened any Christian's sense of personal responsibility for his sins, so the thought of imputed virtue has seldom lessened a Jew's desire for personal virtue, or his effort to attain it. The Rabbis make it clear, indeed, that the merit of the fathers is of no avail unless part, at least, of the virtues of the fathers is transmitted with it, and the Jew is expressly warned against saying, 'My father was righteous; I shall be saved for his sake'; Abraham did not save Ishmael.[1] God, moreover, as S. Levy points out,[2] credits the virtues of the fathers to the children as a token of His love; it is an act of divine grace which no man can claim as a right, or count upon as certain to be exercised. On the other hand, the divine grace is operative when ancestral merit is not available,[3] and yet, as we have seen, the good life, equally with the divine grace, is an essential condition of salvation. It is true, then, to say that, great as is the place which the theory of ancestral merit fills in Jewish teaching, its influence upon Jewish conduct has been very small. The Jew has prayed fervently for the exercise of the divine forgiveness on the ground of the virtues of the fathers; but all the time he has felt, and known, that his moral salvation was, in the last resort, mainly, if not exclusively, dependent upon himself.[4]

The 'fathers' whose merit is thus imputed are not exclusively those who lived in the remote past; they may have lived and died recently. The son of a righteous man gets the benefit of his father's rectitude, which directly transmits to him gifts like beauty, wisdom, and longevity, but also aids him indirectly by increasing his worth in the sight of God.[5] These expiatory offices of the righteous may be exercised even during their life-time by their prayers and even by their very existence. Their merit avails to redeem the whole world; their lives may redeem it, and so may their death.[6] The importance attached to this imputed merit is exemplified by the choice of the story of the sacrificial 'binding' of Isaac (Gn $22^{1ff.}$) as the lesson read on the New Year festival. On that day the prayer is offered:

> 'As Abraham overcame his compassion in order implicitly to do thy will, so may thy compassion overcome thine anger against us.'[7]

In some Jewish liturgies, indeed, Gn 22 is set down for recital every day in the course of the morning service. But the Prayer Book is full of the general idea. In the '*Amīdhah*, one of the oldest and most important constituents of the liturgy, God is described as remembering the pious deeds of the patriarchs, and as bringing a redeemer to their children's children;[8] and the passage is typical of many similar utterances. The seven circuits of the synagogue, made by the palm-bearers on the Great Hosannā (see above), are associated with the three patriarchs together with Moses, Aaron, Phinehas, and David, whose virtues are invoked as a plea for the divine salvation.[9]

The doctrine of imputed virtue has still wider implications. The good deeds not only of the righteous but also of the average man are placed to the credit of the general account. The world, say the Rabbis, is made up of righteous men and sinners; it is the divine will that they shall live together in a united society so that the righteous may absolve the sinners. When this happens, God is truly exalted.[1] In like manner Maimonides says that it behoves a man to regard himself as partly innocent and partly guilty, and with himself the world at large. If he does one good deed, he inclines himself and the whole world on the side of merit, and obtains 'salvation' and deliverance for himself and for his fellow-men.[2] According to a beautiful Talmudic idea, if there are no righteous men in a generation, it is saved by the children in the school-house.[3] This vicarious power is not, and should not be, merely automatic. The Jewish moralists exhort their readers to strive after the salvation of others, to seek, by precept and example, 'to lead the sinner gently heavenwards.'[4] As to salvation hereafter, that, too, may be aided by the action of the living. A godly son, by his very godliness, may win eternal rest for his parent.[5] Hence the superstitious idea which ascribes the same effect to the recital of the *Qaddish*[6] by orphans; for the fervent 'Amens' of the righteous deliver sinners from Gehenna.[7] Intercessory prayer for the dead is not unknown to the Synagogue; but no example of a 'fixed' prayer of this kind is to be found during the first ten centuries of the Christian era.[8]

(*f*) *Mediation.* — Here the question of the Jewish attitude to mediation as an aid to redemption presents itself. Salvation through a mediator is not an idea alien to Judaism. Intercessory prayer is a familiar feature in Jewish history, Biblical and post-Biblical. What is alien to Judaism is the idea that salvation is possible through a mediator alone, that it may be automatic, that faith in the mediator may avail without repentance or good works.[9] Equally foreign to Judaism is the idea that invocation may properly be made to the mediator. So to invoke him is to associate divine or semi-divine beings with God, and in effect to limit His power, seeing that He is supposed to need the intercession of others to move His justice or His mercy. It is also to limit the sonship of man, to deprive him of his right of going straight to the Father with his wants and his prayers. It is true that invocations of angels have found a place here and there in the Jewish Prayer Book, though not in the statutory portions of it, but their inclusion has been due chiefly to the influence of the mystics, and representative authority has consistently opposed it.[10] That salvation is of God alone is, it need hardly be said, a reiterated Biblical doctrine (cf. Hos 13^{4}, Dt 32^{39}, Is 12^{2} 43^{11}, Jon 2^{9}, Ps 3^{8} etc.). Hence the idea of the merit of the fathers, as a means of salvation for their descendants, has not gone unchallenged in Judaism. Even some of the

1 Midr. to Ps 46^{2}.
2 *Original Virtue*, p. 23.
3 Midr. *Rabbāh* to Lv 39^{6}.
4 Cf. Schechter, *Aspects*, p. 170.
5 *Eduyôth*, ii. 9; *Yebhāmôth*, 64*a*.
6 *Sukkāh*, 45*a*; *Moëd Qaton*, 28*a*; Eleazar, the martyr of the Maccabæan age, prays when dying that his soul may be accepted in substitution for the souls of his people; cf. 4 Mac 6^{29}.
7 Cf. *Authorised Prayer Book*[9], p. 250.
8 *Ib.* p. 44.
9 Cf. *Derekh Eres Zutā*, i., where the seven are specified as those who made a 'covenant' with God. In some liturgies Joseph is substituted for Phinehas.

1 Midr. *Rabbāh* to Lv 23^{40}.
2 *Hilc. Teshūbāh*, iii. 4.
3 *Shab.* 33*b*. Merit, indeed, may be fully retro-active; the living may be saved by those yet to be born. Thus Noah is said to have owed his deliverance from the Flood to the goodness of his descendants; cf. Midr. *Rabbāh* to Gn 6^{8}.
4 Introduction to the *Roqeaḥ*.
5 *Sanh.* 104*a*; *T. de b. Eliyahū*, ii. 12, end; Abraham bar Ḥiyah (*c.* 1100), however, strenuously rejects the idea; see his *Sepher Hegyon Ha-hephesh*, Leipzig, 1860, p. 32*a*.
6 *Authorised Prayer Book*[9], p. 77.
7 *Yalqūt Shimōni* to Is 26^{2}.
8 Cf. Schechter, *Aspects*, p. 198.
9 On the difference between Judaism and Christianity thus suggested see F. Delitzsch's remark quoted in a footnote in *JQR* xvi. [1904] 212.
10 Cf., *e.g.*, Maimonides' Commentary on *Sanh.* x. 1,

Talmudic Rabbis contested it.[1] According to one opinion, God's grace was extended to the Israelites as a reward for their refusing to rely upon ancestral merit when pleading for pardon.[2] There were Rabbis also who held that the merit of the fathers, operative once, was efficacious no longer, and they busied themselves about the precise date on which it lost its saving force.[3] But all teachers alike maintain that the one external saving power is the divine grace. In the *'Amīdhah* the Jew pleads not only the merits of the fathers, but also God's 'Name,' *i.e.* His reputation, His bond with himself, as a ground for salvation.[4] On the other hand, the theory of imputed virtue has, for its necessary correlative, the idea of imputed sin. The iniquity of the fathers is visited upon the children, especially if the children perpetuate that iniquity.[5] But, as a rule, the transmission of the responsibility for ancestral transgression is limited to the sin of Adam, which brought death into the world and increased liability to suffering. The poison with which the serpent infected Eve was transmitted to her descendants; but the *Tôrāh* is its antidote.[6] Moreover, the transgression of the individual, like his good deeds, may affect the moral and, with it, the material well-being of his generation.[7] But let Israel be united, let them love one another, and their salvation is assured.[8]

(*g*) *Grace.*—Crowning all the means of salvation, and completing their effectiveness, is the divine mercy, which compensates for human deficiencies and supplements human merits. 'Not because of our righteous acts,' so the Jew prays daily, 'do we lay our supplications before Thee, but because of Thine abundant mercies. What are we? What is our piety? What our righteousness?'[9] In like manner, 'He who would purify himself,' say the Rabbis, 'is helped.'[10] 'If,' they also say, 'men have no merits (*i.e.* no sufficient merits), God gives them His grace; can there be greater goodness than this?'[11] The idea inspires the extemporary prayers publicly offered by various sages on days of fasting and humiliation. Thus one cries, 'O King and Father, have mercy upon us for Thine own sake';[12] and another prays, 'If we are bare of good works, deal charitably with us for the sake of the sanctification of Thy name.'[13] And the very words of these prayers, as well as their spirit, have been incorporated into the liturgy. This divine grace or mercy consists in the acceptance of repentance as the sinner's expiation.[14] In a striking passage the Rabbis speak of repentance as 'a bribe,' which God accepts for the salvation of the sinner. But He does so only in this life; at the judgment hereafter He will be swayed by stern justice only.[15]

III. *SALVATION HEREAFTER.*—Thus the complex question arises: What does salvation hereafter mean according to Judaism? What is the future reward of the just? As to the Bible, little can be said on the subject with certainty. The belief in Sheol, the region of the shades or ghosts, prevailed at an early period (cf. Gn 37^{35}), but Sheol seems to have been a colourless, almost a negative, existence, which was regarded with dread. The Psalmists pray to be delivered from it, and apparently to be delivered from it, not for extinction, but for a heavenly life of conscious spiritual beatitude more or less intense (cf. Ps $16^{10f.}$ 17^{15} 49^{15}). But such utterances are probably late, and express Jewish thought as it was moulded by external, notably by Greek, influences. On the other hand, there is the story of the translation of Enoch (Gn 5^{24}), who 'walked with God, and he was not; for God took him.' Does this necessarily mean extinction, a preferable alternative to Sheol, as the reward of the patriarch's righteousness? 'God,' says the Psalmist (Ps 49^{15}), 'will redeem my soul from the power of Sheol; verily he will receive me,' and the Hebrew word for 'receive' is identical with that for 'took' used in the case of Enoch. Does it not seem as though the hope breathed by the poet animated the historian also? At any rate we are entitled to say that, at some period in the Biblical age, the idea, even the conviction, of a spiritual reward for the righteous hereafter was cherished by certain minds in Israel. Parallel with this conviction was the belief in a Messianic era, with which the idea of a resurrection of the dead and a last judgment was closely associated (Is $25^{8f.}$ 26^{19}, Dn $12^{1ff.}$). This belief is elaborated in the Apocrypha, and is stoutly upheld by the Talmud and the Midrashim. The hope in a physical resurrection was reinforced for the Rabbis by the thought of the miraculous revivals accomplished by Biblical prophets,[1] of the germination of the seed sown in the earth,[2] and of the divine justice which, to vindicate itself, must needs judge body and soul together, united as in life.[3] Restricted at first to the righteous, the resurrection came to be regarded as universal (certain individual sinners and categories of sinners being specifically excepted, as above stated), and the dogma has for centuries past retained this character in orthodox Judaism.[4] It is embodied in the Prayer Book in many places, notably in the second benediction of the *'Amīdhah*,[5] in the burial service (where the resurrection is associated with the judgment), and in the ancient prayer, originally intended to be recited privately by the Jew on awaking in the morning, which begins, 'O my God, the soul which Thou gavest me is pure.'[6] The resurrection and the judgment were conceived of as following the advent of the Messianic era, though originally they were supposed to precede it. The dead, aroused by the sound of the trumpet, would rise and be judged; the wicked would be condemned to punishment, temporary or endless, or to extinction (opinion differed on these points), the righteous to everlasting life in paradise. The generic Talmudic name for the future life was *'Olam Habā*, 'the world to come.' It was at first applied indiscriminately to the Messianic era, the resurrection, and the life in paradise. But at an early date (probably in the 1st or 2nd cent. of the Christian era) the application of the term was limited to the last of these three stages —a practice possibly due to the increased emphasis of individual as distinguished from national hopes of salvation which was the natural consequence of the downfall of the Jewish State.[7] Thus we find a Talmudic teacher of the 3rd cent. (Rabbi Joḥanan) declaring that the Biblical prophets only predicted the events of the Messianic age, but, as to the *'Olam Habā*, no eye but God's hath seen it; and yet another (his contemporary Samuel) affirming that the only difference between the present world-order and the Messianic will be the destruc-

[1] Cf. *Sifrē* to Dt 32^{39}. [2] *Shab.* 89*b*.
[3] *Ib.* 55*a*; Jer. *Sanh.* 27*d*; Midr. *Rabbāh* to Lv 39^{6}—all cited by Schechter, *Aspects*, p. 177.
[4] Cf. *Authorised Prayer Book*[9], p. 44; and S. Baer, in his *Seder 'Aboḍat Yisrael*, Rödelheim, 1868, on the passage.
[5] *Sanh.* 27*b*.
[6] Midr. *Rabbāh* to Ec 7^{13}; *'Abhōdāh Zārāh*, 22*b*.
[7] *Qîd.* 40*b*; *Tanḥumā* to Dt 29^{10}.
[8] *Ib.*; Midr. *Rabbāh* to Gn 11^{1}; *T. de b. Eliyahū*, xxviii.
[9] *Authorised Prayer Book*[9], p. 7.
[10] *Yômā*, 38*b*. [11] Midr. *Tehillim* to Ps 72^{1}.
[12] *Ta'ănîth*, 25*b*. [13] Midr. *Tehillim* to Ps 22^{2}.
[14] See Midr. *Tehillim* to Ps 57^{1}.
[15] Midr. *Tehillim* to Ps 17^{5}.

[1] Midr. *Rabbāh* to Lv 27^{4}. [2] *Sanh.* 90*b*.
[3] *Sifrē* to Dt 10^{6}; *Sanh.* 91*a*.
[4] Cf., *e.g.*, M. H. Seligsberg, *S'dë Ḥayim*, Rödelheim, 1845, p. 219.
[5] Cf. *Authorised Prayer Book*[9], p. 44 f.
[6] *Ib.* p. 319, 5.
[7] See *MGWJ* xli. [1897] 392 ff.; the credit for having discovered this change of usage belongs to Abraham Geiger.

tion of despotism which is to mark the latter.[1] At one and the same time, then, the Messianic age was shorn of much of its miraculous character and its joys, and the true, the ideal, *'Olam Habā* relegated to a heavenly realm which it was beyond human power to picture. This sharp differentiation of the two states of existence became the rule. The modern Jew still distinguishes in his prayers between 'the days of the Messiah' and 'the life of the *'Olam Habā*,' asking to see and taste the varying blessedness associated with each of them.[2] Concerning the nature of the heavenly bliss conflicting ideas prevailed. According to some teachers, paradise (*Gan Eden*) was an existence, even a place, of fleshly delights; according to others, its joys were purely spiritual.

'Better a single hour of blissfulness of spirit in the world to come than all the life of this world'; and again, 'The future world is not like this world; there is no eating or drinking there, no bodily pleasures, no strife or jealousy or rancour, but the righteous sit with crowns on their heads nourished by the divine splendour';[3] and Maimonides[4] declares that even the crowns in the latter passage are but a figure of speech.

There were teachers, as we have seen, who deprecated any attempt to depict the happiness of the future world, quoting in their support Is 64[4]: Men have not heard, nor perceived by the ear, neither hath the eye seen what God hath prepared for him that waiteth for him. Maimonides himself seems to have had two minds on this subject. While in his Commentary on the Mishnāh[5] he accepted the dogma of a physical resurrection, and also wrote a special tract to vindicate the sincerity of his belief in it, he ignored it altogether in his *Yād*, and gave an exclusively spiritual interpretation of the future world.[6] But materialistic conceptions of the heavenly life were frankly avowed by certain Jewish teachers in the mediæval period, and it was the task of writers like Maimonides to make war upon their ideas. A like divergence of view prevailed with regard to future punishment. According to some writers—and they formed the majority—there is a veritable Gehenna; 'there is no hell,' say others.[7] Some teach the doctrine of eternal punishment;[8] others deny it, regarding Gehenna as a place of purgatory only.[9] This purgatory lasts twelve months, and its redemptive action is quickened by the intercession of the righteous.[10] Maimonides, in his turn, seems to reject the idea of a hell; the punishment of the evil-doer unworthy of heaven is eternal death, and this death is what is meant by the 'excision' threatened in Gn 17[14] and elsewhere in the Pentateuch.[11] Paradise, on the other hand, according to the Rabbinic teachers, is variously a place fragrant with flowers and resplendent with gold and precious stones, through which flow streams of milk, wine, and honey,[12] but more frequently it is simply a beatific state of being. Maimonides expresses the general view when he says that the reward of the just hereafter is 'bliss.'[13] Joseph Albo, in a fine passage,[14] spiritualizes the punishment as well as the reward. It lies, he says, in the torment of the soul torn by conflicting desires —by its old sinful longings which it can no longer gratify, and by its yearnings after the higher joys which it is not yet pure enough to attain. Agony such as this, he adds, far surpasses all earthly pain.

[1] *Berākhôth*, 34*b*.
[2] Cf. *Authorised Prayer Book*[9], pp. 74 f., 285.
[3] *Ābhôth*, iv. 21; *Berākhôth*, 17*a*.
[4] *Hilc. Teshūbāh*, viii. 2.
[5] To *Sanh.* x. 1.
[6] On the other hand, in his less lofty-minded *Morë* (iii. 27, li. 2) he denies eternal bliss to all but the most gifted souls, whose spiritual endowments automatically guarantee that immortality. This limited outlook was contested by Ḥisdai Kreskas (*Or Adonai*, 2. 6. 1 ff.).
[7] *Nedārîm*, 8*b*.
[8] *R. Hashānāh*, 16*b*.
[9] *Eduyôth*, ii. 10; *Yalqūt Shimōni* to Mal 4[3].
[10] *Ib.*
[11] *Hilc. Teshūbāh*, viii. 1.
[12] *Yalqūt Shimōni* to Gn 2[9].
[13] *Hilc. Teshūbāh*, viii. 1.
[14] *Ikkarîm*, iv. 33.

With the process of time Jewish conceptions of the hereafter have become definitely spiritual. The tendency is to look, when picturing the future life, not to a resurrection of the body, but to the bliss of the soul. The idea of resurrection is sharing the fate of the Messianic hope. Just as the modern Jew pins his faith to a Messianic age rather than to a Messianic person, so he interprets the resurrection wholly in terms of the spirit. For him salvation, both here and hereafter, means life with God—here in the quest of the higher good, hereafter in its full and certain attainment.

IV. *SALVATION OF THE GENTILES.*—Finally, there is the question of the Gentiles' chances of salvation. From an early date the belief in the universality of the divine grace existed among the Jews. The book of Jonah was written to uphold it, and it found support among the Rabbis. According to the Midrash,[1] Adam was warned that on the day he ate of the forbidden fruit he should die; but God, in His grace, interpreted the word 'day' to mean one of His own days, which lasts a thousand years (Ps 90[4]), and, so prolonging Adam's life, saved him from the punishment entailed by his sin. Adam, in this passage, stands for all humanity, and the idea of universal salvation is thus implicit in the legend. The greatest utterance of the Law, say the Talmudic sages, is 'This is the book of the generations of man; in the day that God created man, in the likeness of God made he him' (Gn 5[1]), which proclaims the high lineage of men, all of whom are sons of God. 'Say not, then, O man,' the sages continue, '"I am vile, and my neighbour shall be vile with me." If thou sayest so, know that thou despisest the Divine image in thee and thy neighbour.'[2] Equal, or only inferior, in rank to this verse, according to the Rabbis,[3] is the command (Lv 19[18]), 'Thou shalt love thy neighbour as thyself,' which declares that all men are equal in the sight of God. Consistently, then, the Rabbis see in an early *Tôrāh* (the seven Noachian precepts [*q.v.*], which prohibit idolatry, incest, homicide, blasphemy, robbery, lawlessness, and the eating of living flesh) the means of salvation ordained for the world before the birth of Israel and the revelation at Sinai.[4] In like manner the Talmud points out that the refrain, 'His mercy endureth for ever,' which occurs 26 times in Ps 136, corresponds with the same number of generations that existed before the *Tôrāh* was given, but for whom the divine grace atoned.[5] Even for such deep-dyed sinners as the generation of the Flood God waited in the hope of their repentance.[6] Nor were the Gentiles cut off from salvation after the *Tôrāh* was given; 'deeds of mercy,' declares the Talmud, 'are their sin-offering,' reconciling them with God.[7] The 70 sacrifices offered in the Temple on the Feast of Tabernacles atoned for the 70 nations.[8] A striking utterance on this subject is that of the *Pesiqtā Rabbāthi*,[9] in which God is described as judging the Gentiles mercifully by their own moral standards and equipment, and in the night, when, for the time, they have ceased from evil-doing. For 'God delighteth not in the destruction of the wicked; all men are His creatures, and what potter desireth that his vessels shall be broken?' Equally impressive is the saying, '"Peace, peace," God cries to him that is far off as well as to him that is near: "to every human being that draws nigh unto me in repentance I will come and heal him."'[10]

[1] Midr. *Rabbāh* to Gn 3[8]; *Pesiqtā Rab.*, ed. Friedmann, 167*a*.
[2] Jer. *Nedārîm*, ix. 4; Midr. *Rabbāh* to Gn 5[1].
[3] *Ib.*
[4] *Sanh.* 56*a*.
[5] *P sāḥîm*, 118*a*; *Pesiqtā R.*, ed. Friedmann, 15*b*.
[6] *Sanh.* 108*a*.
[7] *Pesāḥîm*, 118*a*.
[8] *Sukkāh*, 55*b*.
[9] Ed. Friedmann, p. 167*b*.
[10] Midr. *Tehillim* to Ps 120[7]; cf. *Sepher Hegyon Ha-hephesh*, p. 8*a*.

Thus much as to this life. What of the future life? Here a diversity of opinion confronts us. It is exemplified in the controversy[1] between two Rabbis, one of whom denies, while the other affirms, the possibility of eternal salvation for the Gentile. A passage in the Tosefta[2] declares plainly that the righteous among the Gentiles will have a share in the *'Olam Habā*, and the saying recurs four times in Maimonides' codex.[3] Even the Mishnāh in *Sanh.* x. 1, repeatedly quoted in this article, implies the possibility of salvation for others besides the Jew. Since it specifically excludes Balaam from the future life, it would seem to follow that, as a rule, Gentiles are included. This, indeed, is the inference drawn by the Gemara in its comment on the Mishnaic text.[4] Nine, say the Rabbis elsewhere,[5] entered paradise living, among them Enoch, Eliezer, the servant of Abraham, Hiram, Ebed-melech, the Ethiopian (cf. Jer $38^{7ff.}$), and Pharaoh's daughter, none of whom was an Israelite. In a notable passage in the *Yalqūt Shimōni* (to Is 26^2) God is described as having compassion, at the Last Judgment, upon the sinners in Israel and the righteous among the Gentiles, who are left in Gehenna, but who, with the cry of 'Amen,' acknowledge the justice of their sentence. 'It is the evil impulse,' He says, 'that has caused them to sin.' Thereupon He gives the keys of Gehenna to Michael and Gabriel, who bathe and anoint the sinners, heal them of 'the wounds of purgatory,' clothe them in fair raiment, and finally lift them to God.[6] It is also noteworthy that eternal salvation for the Gentile is preached even in times of persecution, and by those who had experienced that persecution in their own person. Thus it is not surprising to find the names of deceased Gentiles of eminence—monarchs, philosophers, and others—followed by pious ejaculations, such as 'Peace be to him!' or 'May paradise be his rest!', which are commonly associated with the mention of departed Jews.[7] In later times Jewish doctrine on this subject became more liberal still. Zunz[8] tells how a Rabbi of the 17th cent., being asked whether Christians could be saved hereafter, answered that 'God must indeed be cruel if He consigns them to perdition, seeing that they are not bound to obey the Jewish Law.' This common-sense view was virtually anticipated by the author of the *Tana de b. Eliyahū*, who exclaims, 'I call Heaven and earth to witness that, whether he be Jew or Gentile, the Divine Spirit rests upon every man if his life be worthy,'[9] and by Ḥisdai Kreskas, who declares that salvation is attained not by subscription to metaphysical dogmas, but solely by love to God fulfilling itself in action. 'That,' he adds, 'is the cardinal truth of Judaism.'[10] This is the view embodied in the latest teaching. Men like Moses Mendelssohn and H. Wessely, conservative in temper though they were, could say:

> 'According to the Talmudic doctrine concerning the future happiness of the righteous, the greater part of existing mankind, acknowledging as it does the principles of Revelation and the Divine Unity, is finally destined to everlasting bliss.'[11]

This view is expressed with especial emphasis and frequency with regard to Christians. They are not idolaters, and, on the other hand, they respect the laws of morality; therefore the denunciations of the Talmud do not apply to them. They are ensured the divine love here and hereafter. They are in every respect on the same level as Jews; 'they are our brothers.'[1] The famous Paris Sanhedrin, convoked by Napoleon I. in 1807, formally reiterated these teachings, and to-day they are fast embedded in the Jewish consciousness. All men, every Jew will now unhesitatingly affirm, are judged by their lives, not by their creed, and all have an equal chance of salvation. Jewish particularism no longer extends to the eschatological domain. On the contrary, since each man's fitness for eternal happiness depends upon his conformity to the standards of conduct imposed upon him by his ethical or spiritual knowledge, it is especially hard for the Jew to enter into the Kingdom of Heaven. 'You only have I known of all the families of the earth: *therefore* I will visit upon you all your iniquities'—the warning of Amos (3^2) still holds good. The election of the Jew does not give him a larger share, or a greater assurance, of the divine grace than it gives to others; it simply increases, in his case, the difficulty of winning it. And, as to the Gentile, let him be true to his own conception of goodness, and he has in that very faithfulness the full guarantee of salvation hereafter.[2] Far from saying 'Only believe and you shall be saved,' modern Judaism says, 'In spite of not believing you shall be saved.' The Jew holds that his theism will one day be the universal religion; but he holds, too, that until that day comes the just God will not reject any of His human children, whatever their theology may be. He could not consistently hold any other view. His religion preaches the fatherhood of God and the brotherhood of man; and, if the sonship binds man to service of the Highest, the fatherhood binds God to forbearance and compassion when the service has been feeble and imperfect. 'I am thine, save me,' cries the Psalmist; the plea is not Jewish merely, but human, and the conviction of its validity comes from the inmost soul of Judaism.

LITERATURE.—I. Abrahams, *Studies in Pharisaism and the Gospels*, Cambridge, 1917; W. Bousset, *Die Religion des Judenthums im NT Zeitalter*², Berlin, 1906; R. H. Charles, *The Apocrypha and Pseudepigrapha of the OT*, 2 vols., Oxford, 1913; I. Elbogen, *Der jüdische Gottesdienst*, Leipzig, 1913; Hamburger, various artt.; J. Holzer, *Zur Gesch. der Dogmenlehre in der jüdischen Relig.-Philosophie des Mittelalters*, Berlin, 1901; M. Joseph, *Judaism as Creed and Life*³, London, 1909; *JE*, various artt.; D. Castelli, 'Future Life in Rabbinic Literature,' in *JQR* i. [1889] 314 ff.; C. G. Montefiore, 'Rabbinic Conceptions of Repentance,' *ib.* xvi. [1904] 209 ff.; J. Abelson, 'Maimonides on the Jewish Creed,' *ib.* xix. [1907] 24 ff.; E. Kautzsch, *Apokryphen und Pseudepigraphen des AT*, 2 vols., Tübingen, 1900; K. Kohler, *Grundriss einer systematischen Theologie des Judenthums*, Leipzig, 1910; S. Levy, *Original Virtue and other Short Studies*, London, 1907; S. Schechter, *Studies in Judaism*, 1st ser., London and Philadelphia, 1896, 2nd ser., do. 1908, *Aspects of Rabbinic Theology*, London, 1909; E. Schürer, *HJP*, Edinburgh, 1890–91, ii.; F. Weber, *Jüdische Theologie*, Leipzig, 1897.

MORRIS JOSEPH.

SALVATION (Muslim).—Immediately after Adam and Eve fell and were banished from 'the place in which they were,' God promised them guidance—a promise which also applies to their descendants:

> 'Guidance shall come to you from me; whoso shall follow my guidance on them shall come no fear, neither shall they be grieved.'[3]

Thus early did God declare that some persons would be saved. Man must be willing to receive this guidance; the wicked cannot receive it.

> 'Many will He mislead and many guide; but none will He mislead thereby except the wicked.'[4] 'God guideth whom He will; and He best knoweth who will yield to guidance.'[5] 'When they went astray, God led their hearts astray, for God guideth not a perverse people.'[6]

[1] In *Sanh.* 105*a*; cf. Midr. *Tehillim* to Ps 9^{17}.
[2] *Sanh.* xiii. 2.
[3] Cf., *e.g.*, *Hilc. Teshūbāh*, iii. 5; cf. also *T. de b. Eliyahū*, ii. 12, where the righteous Gentile is described as enjoying the light which will shine forth for the just both in the Messianic time and in the future world; and by the righteous Gentile is meant he who obeys the seven Noachian precepts; see also ch. xx., end.
[4] Cf. *Sanh.* 105*a*.
[5] *Derekh Eres Zutā*, 1.
[6] Cf. *The Alphabet of R. Akiba*, letter Zain.
[7] Cf. Zunz, *Zur Geschichte und Literatur*, Berlin, 1845, p. 388.
[8] P. 385.
[9] Ch. ix., beginning.
[10] *Or Adonai*, 2. 6. 1.
[11] Zunz, p. 385; cf. the fine passage in S. R. Hirsch's *Nineteen Letters of Ben Uziel*, tr. B. Drachmann, New York, 1899, p. 142 ff.

[1] For the authorities see Hamburger, *s.v.* 'Christian.'
[2] Joseph, *Judaism as Creed and Life*³, pp. 154, 272, 510; C. G. Montefiore, *Liberal Judaism and Hellenism*, London, 1918, p. 122.
[3] *Qur'ān*, ii. 36.
[4] ii. 24.
[5] xxviii. 56.
[6] lxi. 5.

This offer of guidance, which leads to salvation, is made to all.

'The truth is from your Lord; let him then who will believe.'[1] 'This is no other than a warning to all creatures, to him among you who willeth to walk in a straight path: but you shall not will unless as God willeth.'[2]

God then purposes to forgive some men, *i.e.* to give them salvation.

'Thus make we our signs clear to those who consider, and God calleth to the abode of peace (paradise), and He guideth whom He will into the right way.'[3]

This is God's gift to those who believe and obey. They enter into heaven because they have fulfilled certain conditions. It is independent of any moral change in the believer. In emphasizing the idea of forgiveness the Qur'ān seems to lose sight of the fact that man is in a position from which he needs to be redeemed. Thus we read much of guidance and instruction, but little or nothing of redemption. The Qur'ān nowhere teaches that the sinner must be regenerated. According to it, man is not dead in sin; so no new birth of the Spirit is needed; but he must repent.

We shall now see how these ideas are practically worked out in Islām. Though words such as 'mercy' and 'forgiveness' are common, the word for salvation (*najāh*) is only once used in the Qur'ān:

'O my people, how is it that I bid you to salvation, but that ye bid me to the fire?'[4]

The idea which the term *najāh* conveys to the Muslim mind is that of escape from future punishment in hell. *Khalāṣ*, which means 'deliverance,' is also used in the same sense. Thus it is not so much escape from the power of sin in this life as escape from its punishment hereafter that is implied in the term 'salvation.' A mystic might look upon it as release now from ignorance of God's nature—ignorance which prevents the union of the human soul with Him—but even then it is intellectual deliverance, not moral. Muslim theologians explain what may be termed 'the way of salvation' as consisting in submission to the orders concerning the due performance of the five duties of Islām—the recital of the creed, the saying of the five stated daily prayers, fasting (especially in the month of Ramaḍān), the payment of the legal alms, and the pilgrimage to Mecca. He who does these things is in a state of salvation, though whether he will really attain to salvation he cannot say, as it depends ultimately on the arbitrary decree of God concerning him. To ensure merit all these actions must be done with the closest attention to the prescribed ritual. Muhammad is reported to have said regarding the ablutions before prayer:

'My people will be summoned at the day of judgment with foreheads, arms and feet resplendent with the effects of *wuḍū* [legal ablutions].'

The pilgrimage to Mecca is a sure means of salvation. Man is to be saved by his own works. A believer must accept without reserve the dogmas of Islām, especially those concerning the unity of God and the apostleship of Muhammad; and he perfects that faith by good works. A man who neglects good works would not be a perfect believer, but he will find salvation; for no Muslim, however wicked he may be, can be finally lost. If his intellectual belief from the Muslim standpoint is sound, his moral character is quite a secondary matter. No matter what his crimes may have been, after a period of punishment he will attain salvation, *i.e.* release from the punishment of his sin.[5] It will thus be seen that salvation does not necessarily imply a change in the moral nature. All the minute details about ceremonial purification[6] and the tedious ritual connected with the ceremonies for the removal of bodily defilement show that stress is laid on outward purification of the body rather than on moral or spiritual purity. It is true that pious men here and there speak of outward purity as being the shell of inward purity, which is the kernel; but neither the Qur'ān nor the traditions nor the books on law put forward moral purity as the essential thing. The notion rather is fostered that salvation depends on scrupulous attention to the ritual of outward purification. Again, as the joys held out to the Muslim in another life are carnal, they do not tend to elevate the moral nature in this life. Many good Muslims escape this danger by looking upon these statements as figurative expressions denoting spiritual joys. It seems doubtful whether Muhammad so intended them, and certainly his followers, except a very few, do not so understand them.

The Islāmic conception of salvation, then, is entirely legalistic; it is not a moral change in the heart now, leading a man to have power over sin to repress it, but a release in the next world from the punishment of hell, in virtue of certain good acts done in this life. It is not a becoming, but a receiving. If, however, the good deeds fall short, then, provided the intellectual assent to certain dogmas is correct, the release may be postponed, but it will come at last, and so all Muslims will be saved.

LITERATURE.—W. R. W. Gardner, *The Qur'ānic Doctrine of Salvation*, London, Madras, and Colombo, 1914; E. Sell, *The Faith of Islām*³, London, 1907; W. St. Clair Tisdall, *The Path of Life*, London, Madras, and Colombo, 1912; D. B. Macdonald, *Development of Muslim Theology, Jurisprudence, and Constitutional Theory*, London, 1903, App. i., *The Religious Attitude and Life in Islam*, Chicago, 1909, lect. vi.; *DI*.

EDWARD SELL.

SALVATION (Teutonic).—To the ancient Teuton the idea of salvation applied in the first place to the getting rid of those things which to him were absolutely evil. It also meant preservation from such destruction, danger, and calamity as he expected to meet. Salvation thus meant delivery from evil spirits and from anything which they might bring about. Of evil spirits there were a great number and many kinds, such as dwarfs, giants, dragons, and kobolds. Then there were the witches and wizards, the sorcerers and the enchanters, with all their arts and incantations used for the destruction of man. These powers the old Teuton wished to be free from, or, still better, to know how to become independent of. Salvation as a state of happiness was to be achieved only by fight and honest victory, as is abundantly witnessed in the *Nibelungenlied* and in the heroic lays of the Older Edda. How closely the same ideal obtains in regard to salvation in a future existence is seen in such songs as the *Völuspa* and the *Lay of Vafthrudnir*, while in *Hávamál* and in the *Song of the Sun* we observe that no rest or victory of moral order can be had except on the same ground.

The dread of evil, as noticed in all the ancient Teutonic literary remains, was ever at hand, and thus those persons were considered great and real heroes of the people who understood how to combat this evil, whether it was done by craftiness and secret arts, as often in the heroic lays of the Edda, or by valour and strength, as in the Siegfried legends and in the *Beowulf*. The lesson is the same: man had to learn and to dare in order to overcome so as to save or to be saved. Many are the tales of heroes and great men who were either preserved or destroyed in such contest.

Through secret arts man could obtain influence and power even over nature itself, so that he could start storms or still the waves according to his own pleasure. The witches, at least, were expected to be able to do so. Thus all through life men had to be engaged in a constant warfare

[1] xviii. 28. [2] lxxxi. 27–29. [3] x. 6. [4] xl. 44.
[5] See artt. FAITH (Muslim) and SIN (Muslim).
[6] Cf. art. PURIFICATION (Muslim).

with opposing powers, some of which were almost fathomless in strength and cunning. To those who would not fight, and did not dare to conquer, there was no future. They were stranded somewhere and lost. Thus there are hosts of departed spirits who continue as shadows only; they have no individuality. Before such souls will find rest, they will have to be driven about for ages in winds and storms and among the most forsaken places and awful situations; and, if they are saved at all, it must be through some kind of redemption, as they are unable to extricate themselves from their unhappy state.

These and similar ideas are constantly brought to the front in the Teutonic epics, folklore, and sagas, of which even the *Nibelungenlied* and the *Gudrunlied* are eloquent witnesses.

Now, while salvation or deliverance thus far spoken about refers, in the main, to this life, we also meet with ideas of salvation in the world to come, when that which will never die, 'judgment upon each one dead,' shall be pronounced,[1] for that world is reached only through the Hel-way which all men have to go.

Various are the ways to the kingdom of Death, the abode of Hel, whose habitation is Helheim under one of the roots of Yggdrasil. Her realms all must enter, but all will not have the same future. There are those who can proceed to the regions of the blessed Æsir, and those who must go to Niflheim, the place of punishment for the wicked. All must go as they came. The way of all who fell by the sword is sure to lead to Valhall, to which Odin invites those who are slain in battle. Half of that number, however, belong to Freyja, and those she receives in Folkvang, where her beautiful mansion, Sesrumner, stands. Those received by Odin himself are the great champions, or Einherjars—Odin's elect, who now will enjoy themselves more than ever with battles during the day and during the night with feasts which are held in the great refectory of Gladsheim, the palace of the Æsir. Those who had no opportunity to fall in the fight, but who by risting themselves with the spear-point as a dedication to Odin returned their souls to him, are also received by him as his friends and guests.

And there are other ways to the happy regions of the blessed—ways of peaceable virtues, which lead to salvation, though in other parts of the Æsir heaven, as in Vingolf, the mansion of bliss for noble women with the Asynjes themselves, and in Thrudvang, or Thrudheim, which is Thor's abode. Here he receives his own in his magnificent castle, Bilskirner.

Most people who were drowned are received by Ægir's wife, Ran, in her palace, which she holds open for them at the bottom of the sea, and where they are welcomed and offered 'seat and bed.'[2] Hoenir cares for those who die in tender years. Indeed, in Egil Skallagrimson's *Sonatorrek*, 20, we read of still another being called Gauta Spjalli, who in the most tender manner is similarly engaged.

The rest of mankind—workers of the peaceful arts, in the field and at home, men and women who have died during the countless ages of human history, but who did not use the sword—have, it is true, no place assigned to them in the Teutonic heaven, yet are understood to pass on and to be somewhere, anxiously awaiting the final outcome of the great strife which they know is going on.

Warriors by profession are not secured a place with Odin or Freyja, but only those who in the great trial have fought the good fight. This brings out the importance, according to Teutonic evaluation, of having preserved a good name and established a good report while in this life. On this we have the famous 76th and 77th strophes in *Hávamál*, where it says:

> 'Your cattle shall die; your kindred shall die; you yourself shall die; one thing I know which never dies: the fair name of him who has earned it, and the judgment upon each one dead.'

The more complete interpretation of this passage we must leave out here, but no one will venture to dispute that the main idea conveyed is that man can have no greater possession, when going from this world, than a good name, and that nothing can be of more value to him than a reputation established and known for its integrity. That will go with him to the judgment.

When a deceased person who has received good testimony leaves the Thing in the lower realms, he is brought to a home, which has been prepared for him somewhere 'in the green world of the gods.' What he then first of all has to do is to *leita kunnis*, find and visit kinsmen and friends, who have gone before him to their destination.[1] He not only finds those with whom he became personally acquainted on earth, but he may also visit and converse with ancestors from the beginning of time; and he may hear the history of his race—nay, the history of all past generations—told by persons who were eye-witnesses of the things themselves.[2] The ways he travels are *munvegar*,[3] paths of pleasure, where the wonderful regions of Urd's and Mimer's realms lie open before him—the entire past and its history.

Above the courts of the Æsirs and far away from the recesses of Hel there is yet another region of bliss, where that god dwells whom no one is as yet able to mention. His hall is called Gimle, and will become the abode of the righteous after Ragnarok, the final dissolution both of the Æsir world and of the Vanir and the race of men. Then, at 'the twilight of the gods,' the last reckoning shall be taken and judgment pronounced. This judgment all mankind and all the Æsir gods are anxiously waiting for. And it will come. Everything will be tried then, for the long strife between good and evil must finally reach a crisis. There will be a call for a great battle which will take place on the Vigrid fields. To that battle Odin will come, with his Einherjars, together with all the Æsirs; all that is good will meet on one side and all that is evil, cowardly, beastly, gruesome, and wicked will hold together on the other. The fight will be fierce and will end with the combat between the Æsir gods and the sons of Surt. The gods are vanquished; Thor and Jörmungandur, Heimdall and Loki, destroy each other. Odin is swallowed up by the Fenris wolf, which in turn is crushed by Vidar, Odin's son. This is the end of the reign of the Æsir. Then the great and mighty one appears, and he will drive all evil to Niflheim, while the good will be gathered together in the halls of Gimle, the home of eternal bliss. Valhall ceases to be Valhall; Serumner, Vingolf, and Thrudvang are no more; for all is Gimle and happiness and joy.

Gimle, however, is joined with the new-born earth—the earth which has come in place of the former one, as the new-born from the mother. Of this earth and the conditions brought with her we read in *Völuspa* as follows:

> 'She (the Vala) sees arise, for the second time, the earth from the deep, beauteously green, waterfalls descending; the eagle flying over, which in the fell captures fish. The Æsir meet on Ida's plain, and of the mighty earth-encircler speak, and there to memory call their mighty deeds, and the supreme god's ancient lore. There shall the wondrous golden tablets in the grass be found, which in days of old had possessed the ruler of the gods, and Fiölnir's race. Unsown shall the fields bring forth; all evil amended. Baldr shall come; Hödr and Baldr, the heavenly gods, Hropt's[4] glorious dwelling shall

[1] *Hávamál*, 77.
[2] V. Rydberg, *Teutonic Mythology*, Eng. tr., ii. 422.

[1] *Sonatorrek*, 17.
[2] Rydberg, ii. 529.
[3] *Sonatorrek*, 10.
[4] Another name for Odin.

inhabit. Understand you yet or not?—A hall standing than the sun brighter, with gold bedecked, in Gimle: there shall the righteous people dwell, and for evermore happiness enjoy. Then comes the mighty one to the great judgment, the powerful from above, who rules o'er all. He shall dooms pronounce, and strifes allay, holy peace establish which shall ever be.'[1]

We believe that in this description ancient Teutonism and Christian eschatology are blended, at least to some extent, but so far no one has been able to tell which is which. The hope of final salvation is expressed, and in terms which we meet in many other of the literary remains of the Teutons. In the Younger Edda, which was composed from ancient sources by Snorra Sturlason († 1241), we read things similar to those in the *Völuspa*. Some of the ideas there presented appear more ethical and ancient than those in the Older Edda, while their form indicates a later period together with more admixtures of external elements than in the strophes just quoted. He says:

'There will be many abodes, some good and some bad. The best place will be Gimle, in heaven, and all who delight in quaffing good drink will find a great store in the hall called Brimir, which is also in the heaven in the region Okolni. There is also a fair hall of ruddy gold called Sindri, which stands on the mountains of Nida. In those halls righteous and well-minded men shall abide. . . . There will arise out of the seas another earth most lovely and verdant, with pleasant fields where the grain shall grow unsown. Vidar and Vali shall survive; neither the flood nor Surtur's fire shall harm them. They shall dwell on the plain of Ida, where Asgard formerly stood. Thither shall come the sons of Thor, Modi and Magni, bringing with them their Father's mallet Mjolnir. Baldr and Hödr shall also repair thither from their abode in Hel. There shall they sit and converse together, and call to mind their former knowledge and the perils they underwent, and the fight with the wolf Fenris and the Midgard serpent. There too shall they find in the grass those golden tablets which the Æsir once possessed:

> There dwell Vidar and Vali
> In the god's holy seats,
> When slaked Surtur's fire is,
> But Modi and Magni will Mjolnir possess
> And strife put to an end.'

'Thou must know, moreover,' so the prophecy continues, 'that during the conflagration caused by Surtur's fire, a woman named Lif (Life), and a man named Lifthrasir, lie concealed in Hod-Mimir's forest. They shall feed on morning dew, and their descendants shall soon spread over the whole earth. But what thou wilt deem more wonderful is, that the sun shall have brought forth a daughter more lovely than herself, who shall go in the same track formerly trodden by her mother. And now, if thou hast any further questions to ask, I know not who can answer thee, for I never heard tell of any one who could relate what will happen in the other ages of the world. Make, therefore, the best use thou canst of what has been imparted to thee.'[2]

From the *Völuspa* we have learnt that 'the righteous people shall dwell in Gimle for ever and happiness enjoy.' It is the same view as here quoted that we meet in the *Gylfaginning*. And let us note with regard to 'Lif and Lifthrasir,' who had been kept safe in Hod-Mimir's grove even through the terrible Fimbul-winter, which immediately precedes Ragnarok and the final restoration of all things, that they symbolize the ancient Teutonic belief that the life which in time's morning developed out of chaos is not destroyed even by Surtur's flames, but rescues itself, purified, for the coming age of the world. The same human race will live again. It is not a new creation that the Teutonic people waits for as the final salvation, but a complete regeneration of all—a perfect *ἀποκατάστασις τῶν παντῶν*—when even Surtur himself shall be in Gimle, as we read in the Upsala codex of the *Gylfaginning*: 'best er att vera a Gimle medr Surt.'

See also artt. BLEST, ABODE OF THE (Teutonic), STATE OF THE DEAD (Teutonic).

LITERATURE.—*Völuspa*, in *Sæmundar Edda*, crit. ed., S. Bugge, Christiania, 1867; E. H. Meyer, *Völuspa*, Berlin, 1889; Snorra Sturlason, *The Younger Edda*, tr. I. A. Blackwell, Norrœna Society, New York, 1907; V. Rydberg, *Teutonic Mythology*, tr. R. B. Anderson, 3 vols., do. 1906, vol. i.; see also literature to art. SACRIFICE (Teutonic).

S. G. YOUNGERT.

[1] *Völuspa*, 57-64. [2] *Snorra Edda Gylfaginning*, 66 f.

SALVATION ARMY

SALVATION ARMY.—The Salvation Army is a religious organization of international scope which had its beginnings in England in 1865. It may be regarded as having three functions, which are closely interwoven and to be treated as one: it is (1) a mission of Christ's gospel, (2) a religious community, (3) an agency to combat poverty and vice and to further social reform. Its philanthropic and reforming activities have come about as the result of a natural evolution, and have not affected its primary object of militant evangelism, except to strengthen it. The purpose underlying all its activities is to subdue in Christ's name—not merely to teach, but to compel men everywhere to become the disciples of the Son of God.

I. *ORIGIN AND DEVELOPMENT*.—**1. The founder and first General.**—The founder and first General of the Salvation Army was William Booth, who was born at Nottingham in 1829. He was brought up within the Church of England, and to its early influence he attributed the fact that, although subsequently becoming a Methodist minister, he never entirely accepted some of the Nonconformist views of denominationalism.[1] At the age of fifteen, about which time he was converted, he joined the Wesleyan Methodists and, as he said later in life, decided that 'God Almighty should have all there was of William Booth.'[2] Soon afterwards he became the leader of a band of zealous young men whose methods of evangelizing their own town had a curious resemblance, on a small scale, to those adopted by the Salvation Army in later years. They worked among the poorest, utilized in some capacity those who joined them, and anticipated the Army in their aggressiveness, in their meetings for penitents, and even in their small demonstrations of rejoicing. The time was one of unrest in Wesleyan Methodism, and a Reforming element was breaking with the parent body, but the dispute bore chiefly on methods of government, and these did not greatly interest this young disciple. Nevertheless, as the result of a hasty action on the part of his superintendent minister, he became attached to the Reformers. He had already resigned his local preachership, feeling that the pulpit work allotted to him afforded too little scope for his already ardent evangelism. His minister jumped to the conclusion that he was a 'Reformer,' and cut him off from membership. The Reformers thereupon invited him to join them. This he did in 1851, and became a minister of their body at Spalding in Lincolnshire. A prospective Congregational pulpit had been offered to him, but he found himself unable to accept the Calvinistic doctrines set forth in the books recommended him for preparatory study. Although now a member of the Reforming body, he never seems to have championed their cause as against other Methodists; moreover, he saw that their organization had few elements of permanence (most of the Reformers merged themselves a few years later into what became the United Methodist Free Churches), and, after he had given careful study to the Methodist New Connexion system, he offered himself for its ministry and was accepted. The Methodist New Connexion did not differ greatly in doctrine and general usage from the Wesleyan Methodist, from which it had been the first important secession, but its Conference was constituted on a more democratic pattern, and William Booth hoped to obtain a considerable measure of freedom for the exercise of his evangelistic ambitions. He 'travelled' in its circuits until 1861, but his heart was set upon work among the classes altogether

[1] Hulda Friederichs, *The Romance of the Salvation Army*, p. 2 f.
[2] G. S. Railton, *General Booth, by his first Commissioner*, p. iv.

outside the Churches. He had been greatly influenced by C. G. Finney, whose direct and personal manner helped to mould his own style of appeal, while the American evangelist's 'anxious bench' was perhaps the forerunner of the Salvation Army penitent form. William Booth himself and his wife Catherine,[1] who was becoming known as a preacher of considerable power, had remarkable results following upon their revival services. Certain influences in their Connexion, however, had crystallized against all itinerant evangelism, and at the Conference of 1861 considerable opposition was manifested to the proposal which Booth made, that he should be set apart for purely evangelistic work. A suggested compromise whereby he should retain a circuit while giving part of his time to evangelistic campaigns elsewhere he declined as unworkable, and in the end Mr. and Mrs. Booth left the Connexion. They began at once to travel in various parts of the country conducting services, which were often the means of important spiritual awakenings.

2. Beginnings in the East End of London.—Drawn at last to London, partly because of the opportunities for such work which the metropolis presented, and partly from a desire to have a settled home, William Booth 'found his destiny,' as he expressed it, among the outlying masses of the East End. He received an invitation to conduct some services in a tent which had been erected in Whitechapel, the appointed missioner having fallen ill; and, faced by these East End multitudes, he felt, as even he had never felt it before, 'the compassion for souls.' He saw focused there all the problems which arose out of a reckless and godless population, largely untouched by any civilizing or Christianizing influence, and presenting a very Niagara of poverty and vice. He thus describes his experiences:

'When I saw those masses of poor people, so many of them evidently without God or hope in the world, and found that they so readily and eagerly listened to me, following from Open-Air Meeting to tent, and accepting, in many instances, my invitation to kneel at the Saviour's feet there and then, my whole heart went out to them. I walked back to our West-End home and said to my wife:

"O Kate, I have found my destiny! These are the people for whose salvation I have been longing all these years. As I passed by the doors of the flaming gin-palaces to-night I seemed to hear a voice sounding in my ears, 'Where can you go and find such heathen as these, and where is there so great a need for your labours?' And there and then in my soul I offered myself and you and the children up to this great work. Those people shall be our people, and they shall have our God for their God."'[2]

Mrs. Booth's later account of her reply to this announcement is almost as illuminating:

'I remember the emotion that this produced in my soul. I sat gazing into the fire, and the Devil whispered to me, "This means another departure, another start in life!" The question of our support constituted a serious difficulty. Hitherto we had been able to meet our expenses out of the collections which we had made from our more respectable audiences. But it was impossible to suppose that we could do so among the poverty-stricken East-enders—we were afraid even to ask for a collection in such a locality.

Nevertheless, I did not answer discouragingly. After a momentary pause for thought and prayer, I replied, "Well, if you feel you ought to stay, stay. We have trusted the Lord *once* for our support, and we can trust Him *again*!"'

The Mission in the East End, like the Salvation Army into which it grew, was thus in the first instance to the lowest, those whom society regarded as its outcasts, the 'submerged tenth.' In an address to the Wesleyan Conference in 1880 William Booth described himself and his fellow-missioners as 'moral scavengers who netted the very sewers.'[3] 'We want all we can get, but we want the lowest of the low.' Many years afterwards he declared to Cecil Rhodes that he dreamed, day and night, of making new men out of the waste of humanity.

3. Growth of the Christian Mission.—When William Booth began his services in the East End, he had no idea of anything beyond a purely local work. It was with some difficulty that he found a suitable habitation for his Mission, and various places were occupied in turn, some of them the most unlikely, to all appearance, for such an enterprise. But his faith was justified, and by 1875, after ten years of vicissitude, trial, and contumely, the Christian Mission, as it was called, was being carried on at 32 stations, in charge of an equal number of evangelists supported out of its funds. It had extended beyond the borders of East London, to Portsmouth and Chatham among other places, largely as the result of campaigns undertaken by Mrs. Booth. Her work in the provinces prepared the way for the spread of the organization, for in every place which she visited she left a nucleus of people whom she had impressed, so that the Christian Mission had only to enter into possession. What the movement owed during those formative years, and subsequently, to 'the Mother of the Army' it is very difficult to estimate. Catherine Booth was a woman of prophetic vision, commanding eloquence, and rare intellectual power. She was the means of introducing to the Mission a new kind of leader, drawn from a different class of society, who was able to devote to the common cause a cultivated mind as well as a consecrated heart. She also helped to secure the support, or at least the sympathetic toleration, of influential people, including certain friends of all evangelical effort who were too zealous for the end in view to be antagonized by methods which undoubtedly shocked their sense of decorum. Along with her persuasive speech she had a capacity for strategy which stood the new organization in good stead. She shared to the full her husband's hope and courage, and her deeply earnest and spiritual temperament was itself a guarantee that beneath the apparent irreverences attaching to an entirely new type of evangelistic propaganda there was a thoroughly wholesome spirit. The converts of the Mission were soon to be counted by the thousand. Many of them had been reclaimed from the utmost degradation, and their testimony was extremely effective. The immediate use of the converts, to work for the salvation of others as an attestation of their own changed lives, was one of the principles by which the Mission developed. The man who had been saved from some vicious course was found to exercise a remarkable spell over his former associates when he appeared among them as a changed character. Writing on this subject later, General Booth said:

'I found that ordinary working-men in their corduroys and bowler hats could command attention from their own class which was refused point-blank to me with my theological terms and superior knowledge. I found that the slaves of intemperance were accessible to the influence and testimony of a little band of converted drunkards, whose message was a message of hope when mine was only too often one of condemnation. I found that the wild and unruly East-enders, whose highest idea of happiness was too often enshrined in a skittle-alley, or a boxing-booth, or a "penny gaff," could be made to feel that there was, after all, "something in religion" when they found their old acquaintances living clean and yet happy and prosperous lives under its influence.'[1]

4. The name: 'The Salvation Army.'—During the first ten or twelve years William Booth was feeling his way out of the conventionalism which had hitherto fettered the presentation of religion to the lapsed masses. He saw that some more energetic propaganda was needed than was possible through the ordinary churches and chapels with their formality and sombreness. Already he had been freed from many limitations of both thought and outlook, but his early experiences of irregular 'warfare' in the East End compelled him to revise his whole conception of evangelistic effort, in respect of both the form of its popular appeal and

[1] William Booth married Catherine Mumford in 1855.
[2] Railton, p. 56.
[3] *Ib.* p. 77.

[1] Friederichs, Preface by General William Booth, p. 4.

the organization necessary to make that appeal continuous. No more than with George Fox in the 17th cent., or John Wesley in the 18th, had the formation of a new sect been his aim. At first, indeed, he passed on his converts to the various Church organizations around, until he found that in some cases they did not go where they were sent, and that in others, when they did go, they were not welcomed, and in consequence were in danger of lapsing. He drew them therefore into small societies, under the care of appointed leaders, and gradually he perceived that his organization, with its love for the lost and sinful, its spirit of aggression, its definite objective, and its impact upon evil at close quarters, had the elements of an army, waging incessant warfare against the enemy of souls. The idea of a war for the souls of men had abundant Biblical foundation, while Bunyan's *Holy War* could be cited, as well as some of the most sacred hymns of the Church. Although the conception of an army came gradually, the name was the result of a sudden inspiration, some months after a semi-military constitution had actually been decided on. The late Commissioner Railton, in drafting an account of the work, had written: 'It will thus be seen that the Christian Mission is a Volunteer Army,' and William Booth revised the sentence to read: 'The Christian Mission is a *Salvation* Army.'

5. The military constitution.—The adoption of a *quasi*-military system was by no means a mere matter of titles and uniforms; it was not intended as a spectacular demonstration, either to please the adherent or to touch the imagination of the outside public. It corresponded to the conception of a fighting religion. William and Catherine Booth, and now also the small group of kindred spirits whom they had gathered around them, came to see that a military form of government was most likely to secure the authority and discipline which are at the root of all fighting power. Perhaps nothing has been elaborated in the history of mankind which is so effective for bringing instant force to bear upon an objective as a military organization, especially when those who compose it are prompted by a high motive. It is prompt, energetic, decisive, and mobile. It may have the disadvantage of involving a kind of autocracy, but the first General (whose title came about by a process of elimination —he was known at first as General Superintendent) found in practice that what his people wanted was leadership, and that, as long as they were led, the possible evils arising from the concentration of power in the hands of a few individuals little concerned them. The main thing was to secure such a direction of their energies as should tell to the fullest advantage. The Christian Mission had been governed at first on purely paternal lines, all management and control proceeding from its General Superintendent and his immediate assistants. Then it was remodelled on the lines of the representative system of liberal Nonconformity, with conferences and committees; but this entailed obstruction, or at least delay, and at the same time the Mission lost distinctiveness, and was in danger of becoming sectarian. Finally, the committee system was abandoned in favour of this vigorous reorganization into a military body with a 'Council of War' instead of a 'Conference'; and, while this change provoked ridicule in some quarters and resentment in others, especially among religious people, it immediately gave greater cohesion with uniformity and oneness of direction. The inner spirit of the movement all through these early years had been the spirit of war. This was now for the first time recognized. Ranks and titles and military terms came later. No one appreciated better than the founder that organizations are only temporary adjustments to existing conditions, and that what ultimately signifies is the spirit which animates them.[1] Nevertheless, it is claimed that the government of the Army presents in its main features a strong resemblance to the divinely-appointed government of the Jewish nation and church, and bears a certain likeness also to the system which prevailed in the early Gentile churches, so far as can be judged from the NT. This reorganization on a military basis took place in 1878, in which year a deed-poll was executed and registered setting forth the constitution of the Christian Mission (the name of 'The Salvation Army' was endorsed on the deed by memorandum two years later) and declaring it to be a religious society, composed of persons desiring to unite together for the purpose of spreading the gospel, under the direction of a General Superintendent. The work at once went forward and came into touch with a wider public. At the time of its reorganization it was being carried on at 80 stations, each of them the centre of a witnessing community in a town or district, and these became known as 'corps,' with their 'citadels' or 'halls.' Within less than ten years from that date the 1000th British corps was established, and the work had extended internationally in a remarkable way.

6. Openings in other lands.—The progressive extension of the work of the Salvation Army will be best appreciated from the following list (the dates given are those at which the Army flag was unfurled in the respective countries):

England (1865), Scotland (1878), Wales (1879), Ireland (1880), United States (1880), Australia (1880), France (1881), Canada (1882), Sweden (1882), India (1882), Switzerland (1882), S. Africa (1883), Ceylon (1883), New Zealand (1883), Germany (1886), Denmark (1887), Italy (1887), Holland (1887), Norway (1888), S. America (five Republics) (1889), Finland (1889), Belgium (1889), W. Indies (1892), Dutch E. Indies (1894), Iceland (1895), Japan (1895), Korea (1908), Burma (1914), China (1915), Russia (1917).[2]

The openings in many of these countries have come about as a result of the inherent vitality of the movement rather than as part of a deliberate scheme. In the case of the United States the first party of officers was sent out in response to an appeal from a family of Salvationist immigrants who had begun to hold meetings in Philadelphia; immigrants were also the means of planting the Army flag in Australia and New Zealand. Within two years the Army extended from the United States into Canada, and it was also by way of America that the Army gained a footing in Germany. A German-American, having been influenced by the Army in New York to such an extent as to resolve to devote his life to the salvation of the Fatherland, was sent to German Switzerland, there to learn more about the Army's work, and subsequently was commissioned to launch it in Stuttgart. In Sweden the work began with the same apparent casualness through a lady who was influenced at meetings addressed by Bramwell Booth, then Chief of the Staff, on a vacation visit to that country; and from this new centre Norway was in turn occupied, the Army finding in all these northern lands some of its most devoted officers. In Holland the way was prepared by a retired officer of the Dutch army who, having seen something of the work in England, introduced workers from London to Amsterdam. From Holland the work spread to the Dutch E. Indies, where there are now corps, not only of Javanese and Sumatran 'soldiers,' but also of Malay and Chinese, with an extensive and growing social organization. The entrance into India, Japan, and other Eastern

1 *Orders and Regulations for Staff Officers*, London, 1904, Introd. by General William Booth, p. xv.

2 In Russia there had been for some years the nucleus of an organization, but not until after the revolution of 1917, when religious liberty was proclaimed, was the way cleared for the open establishment of the Army.

countries was gained also under circumstances in which very little of human design was perceptible, and so the expansion went on until 63 countries and colonies have been occupied (the latest being Burma and the new republics of Russia and China), and the salvation of Jesus Christ is proclaimed in 40 languages. In all its missionary activities the Salvation Army adheres to the principle of adaptability of method which characterized its beginnings. No means of approach is slighted, if it seems likely to open a way into the mental processes of the people. This is especially illustrated in India, of which country a famous Hindu said that it would accept Christ 'when He stepped out of trousers and shoes.' The Salvation Army officers have not hesitated to do that when it seemed likely to be availing, and to adopt the turban and dhotee. Its first leader in India, Commissioner Frederick Booth-Tucker, was formerly a member of the Indian Civil Service, who was powerfully attracted to the Salvation Army through a chance reading of the English *War Cry*. The organization in the Indian Empire comprises, besides its direct salvation efforts in a thousand places, a whole network of social and educational agencies, including special schemes for reforming the very lowest of the pariah classes. It aims at nothing less than the general leavening of the lump of India with the spirit of the gospel of Jesus.[1]

7. Co-operation with Governments.—One remarkable piece of Army work in India is that which is carried on among the criminal tribes, really an aboriginal remnant. The care of some thousands of these outlaws has been handed over to the Army by the Government, and in 32 settlements (continually increasing) they are now being cared for and taught useful occupations. The native non-Christian press, which at one time urged the expulsion of the Army from India, is now generously appreciative of the efforts in this direction.[2] Various other Governments have given practical expression of their confidence by handing over certain work to the Army and subsidizing it, as, *e.g.*, the work among reformatory boys in Australia and inebriates in New Zealand; and in many colonies the Army has been called into co-operation in the matter of dealing with criminals both before and after their discharge from prison. Holland has done the same, and the Government of the Dutch E. Indies has placed certain of its institutions and hospitals under Army care. Several of the cantonal Governments of Switzerland as well as certain German, Scandinavian, and S. American municipalities subsidize one or other of the Army's agencies; and in nearly every country the recognition of rulers and Governments is forthcoming, by way of special grants and privileges, or (particularly in the case of the United States) by being called into State counsel on problems connected with social relief, or by the personal interest and help of sovereigns and presidents. In some countries the philanthropic side of the work is more appreciated, while in others its purely evangelistic propaganda is regarded as being of the highest value. But the motive of the Army has not altered with the widening of its field and the dispersal of early prejudices; if there has been change, it is in the attitude of those who view it from without.

II. *ORGANIZATION AND POLITY.* — **1. The structure of the Army.**—The General, or, as he is sometimes designated, the Commander-in-Chief, is in control of the entire Army, directing its operations throughout the world, and appointing the commissioners and other leading officers in the several countries. Each General is required under the deed-poll of 1878 (see above, § 5) at once to appoint his successor, which he does under seal, and the name of the person chosen is not divulged until the proper time. When the first General 'laid down his sword' in 1912, he was succeeded, in harmony with this arrangement, by Bramwell Booth, his eldest son, who had been Chief of the Staff for more than 30 years. This does not imply, however, that the office is hereditary, or that the succession belongs to the holder of any particular command. In 1904 means were provided by deed-poll approved and adopted by the International Staff Council of that year for removing from the position any General proved to be unworthy of confidence, and also for the selection of a General by a High Council of the Army called into being for this purpose, on which every territory is to be represented, should the position become vacant through failure to appoint or from any other cause.

For administrative purposes the Army is organized in two main sections, one of which is known as International Headquarters, and the other as territorial commands. International Headquarters, having its seat in London, includes a number of personally directed departments which are concerned with the oversight and management of the entire Army in its world-wide, as distinct from its local, operations. These departments are controlled by responsible officers acting under instructions of the General and his Chief of the Staff. To International Headquarters are also attached a number of commissioners who travel the world in the spiritual interests of the Army and to stimulate missionary enthusiasm at the various bases. Territorial commands are concerned each with the direction of Army affairs in one or other of the geographical areas into which the world-operations of the Army are divided. A territory, which is the command of an officer known as a territorial commissioner, may include a whole country or part of a country, or a group of two or more countries.[1] It is further partitioned into divisions. Each of the divisions consists of a group of local corps, under a divisional commander who maintains the general oversight and control of the affairs of the group. The local corps, together with their auxiliary wards for the working of towns and districts, are the units of the Army. A corps may consist of one society of Salvationists or a number of such societies together; in the latter case they are known as circle corps. Each is under a commanding officer, who may be assisted by a second, or even by two subordinates.

2. Property and finance.—(*a*) *Property.* — The whole of the Army's property is vested in the General for the time being, as trustee, with full power to dispose of it in any way (in harmony with the trusts) which he thinks most likely to promote the objects of the Army. He is required, however, to keep full accounts, and to publish every year an audited balance-sheet. This enables the General to arrange for the holding and administration of the property in harmony with the various legal systems obtaining in the several countries, while still preserving to himself and his successors the supreme direction and control. The object in view in making these arrangements has been threefold: (1) to secure the property for the Army; (2) to prevent any interference in its management which might be alien to Army principles; (3) to retain perfect freedom to use or dispose of the

[1] See Harold Begbie, *The Light of India.*

[2] The *Khalsa Advocate*, devoted to championing the cause of the Sikhs, wrote (1913): 'In the Punjab and United Provinces the work of the Salvation Army has been splendidly successful and the Collectors of these districts have warmly praised their activities and spoken of their marvellous achievements in terms of the highest approbation. The number of criminal classes has rapidly diminished as a result of their beneficial influence.'

[1] At the time of writing they number 23, but this number may be increased at any time.

property for the advance of the work, in any way that changing circumstances may require. In some countries, such as the United States, the Army is incorporated under a special act of legislature which defines and guarantees the position of the board of officers by whom the property is administered. In other cases, as in certain Australian States and in S. Africa, the property is administered under trusts publicly declared, on behalf of the General, by the territorial commissioner for the time being. In yet other cases, owing to the absence of any legal recognition of trusteeship for charities or religious associations, the constitution and machinery of a limited liability company have been set up, with the share capital so divided and controlled that, while the requirements of the laws have been complied with, a paramount voice is assured to the General; this is the case in Germany and Norway. In yet other cases, as, *e.g.*, the W. Indies and some of the S. American States, the respective legislatures have constituted the General a 'corporation sole.'

In these various ways 'it is believed that the character of a trust has been imposed upon the property of the Army which the courts of all countries will recognize, and to which they will, within the limits of their respective jurisdictions, give effect.'[1]

(*b*) *Finance.*—In obtaining funds for its work three guiding principles have actuated the leaders of the Army: (1) to stimulate and require the freewill offerings of its own people, in the belief that, if religion is worth anything at all, it is worth paying for; (2) to expect officers of the Army, working as they do for the souls of the people, to live in a simple and self-denying way, and that not as a matter of economy only, but because it harmonizes with the example of Jesus Christ and the spirit of their endeavours; (3) to ask for and accept support from irreligious people for the purpose of spreading religion among them —'getting supplies from the enemy.' The ideal aimed at in arranging the Army's finance is that each country should support its own work, and also contribute to the extension and maintenance of the Army in other and more needy parts of the world, particularly in non-Christian lands. The Salvation Army is an international organization, and, although it has not advanced in the same degree in this matter in all countries, it is very widely realized that the responsibility for the extension of its work and influence rests as much upon the Salvationists of, *e.g.*, the United States or Holland as upon those of Switzerland or the United Kingdom. This principle of international responsibility is illustrated in the work on the whole field. Nor does this apply only or mainly to money. In India, *e.g.*, officers from the United Kingdom, from half-a-dozen European countries, and from the Americas have been working together;[2] and more recently the missionary contingent which was sent out to China in 1917 was recruited from no fewer than five countries East and West.

Salvation Army finance is divided into national (or territorial) and international categories, and in each territory the finance may again be divided into funds for national and funds for local purposes, the former division holding good in respect of both the evangelistic and the social side of the work. National funds for spiritual work are employed in the general control and extension of the work within a country, and the first charge upon them is the maintenance—necessarily somewhat costly—of the strong driving power at the centre of each command. From this same source contributions are made to new branches and to branches not yet self-supporting, and there are allocations also for such objects as the training of young officers, the assistance of sick and disabled officers and soldiers, and the cost of special campaigns. A somewhat similar system operates in each of the divisions. Local or corps funds are used for the payment of local expenses and for the acquisition and maintenance of buildings. A small proportion of the corps income is remitted to the headquarters of the division, and of this a proportion is remitted in turn to the territorial headquarters. In this way a fair adjustment of local and central claims is secured. The other section of territorial finance—the social fund—is again divided into (1) funds for the maintenance of the social work, including operations among the homeless, the unemployed, the vicious and unfortunate, and support of the hospitals, schools, and reformatories, which form part of the Army's social work; and (2) local funds for social relief.

The funds of International Headquarters, again, are divided into those for spiritual and those for social purposes. The former, which is the major division, is utilized again in the maintenance of the central driving force, and also in the carrying through of evangelistic campaigns, the training of officers, field and staff, the making of grants for new work (outside the British Isles), and the upkeep of the general organization. The sources of income for this fund are (1) donations of the benevolent outside the Army; (2) gifts of those who have benefited by the Army; (3) certain surpluses from territorial or local funds, which from time to time are forwarded voluntarily; (4) contributions raised by the annual Self-denial Fund[1] (half the proceeds of which are remitted to International Headquarters, mainly for work in non-Christian countries); (5) legacies; (6) profits of publications; (7) proceeds of the sale of uniforms, musical instruments, and other incidentals of Army work. The social funds of International Headquarters are provided in much the same way, by gifts from outsiders, the contributions of people who have benefited, a proportion of the Self-denial Fund, and legacies.

The oversight of expenditure is conducted on a very precise system. Every payment is made in the General's name, and theoretically he is the first party to every transaction, but he is assisted by finance councils and expenditure boards, whose business it is to frame estimates and check outgoings. The functions of these bodies, however, are advisory only, and the final approval of all budgets rests with the highest command. A rigid system of account-keeping is in vogue, and the departments and commands are subject to a double audit—one an internal Army audit with its travelling accountants whose business it is to criticize expenditure as well as to attest accuracy and who report directly to International Headquarters, and the other the audit of the central accounts of each country, including those in London, by local public auditors.

3. Officers' commands.—The officers of the Army, who are, in fact, its ministers and who universally testify to having received a definite call of the Holy Spirit to devote themselves to its work, are divided into two classes—staff officers and field officers. All are commissioned either by the General for the time being or in his name; they abandon all secular employments, devote themselves entirely to Army service, and are supported out of its funds.

The staff officers, with the Chief of the Staff at their head, are responsible to the General for the direction of the Army's operations, either internationally or territorially. The highest rank is that of commissioner. Officers of that rank have the direction of departments at International Headquarters, or command the work of the Army in a territory, or are charged with the conduct of some special branch, and are assisted by staff of varying rank.[2] The field officers are mostly in command of local corps. Their ranks vary.[3] It is their business to seek the salvation of the people, to visit, instruct, and advise the soldiers of their corps, to look after the converts, to carry out the weekly programme of meetings, to attend to the organizing side of the work, and generally to represent the Army and exercise an influence for aggressive religion in the neighbourhood. These field officers, unlike the staff officers, who have more the character of fixed points in the Army system, may be likened to an army of manœuvre. They may be required at any time, without reference to their own choice, to transfer their services from one part of the field to another.

The commissioned officers are assisted by local officers, who are soldiers selected for particular work in their own corps, and who give their time without remuneration, many of them following some secular calling. They answer to the lay workers in some of the churches, except that their responsibility is generally carried much further, and correspondingly they are expected to attain, and many of them do attain, a high standard of self-denial, obedience, and spiritual efficiency. They must give evidence of certain spiritual qualifications; they provide and wear their own prescribed uniform; they neither smoke nor drink; and they are covenanted to discharge the duties allotted to them. They are known by various titles,

[1] L. A. Atherley-Jones, 'Legal and financial Aspects of the Salvation Army,' in *Essays and Sketches*, p. 196.

[2] Bramwell Booth, *Servants of All*², London, 1901, p. 120.

[1] The Self-denial Fund originated in 1886, when £4820 was collected; in 1918 the sum raised in the United Kingdom alone was £117,503. The scheme extended to other countries until now at least 70 per cent of the Army's forces all over the world voluntarily join in this yearly self-denying ordinance.

[2] The ranks of staff officers are (in 1918) commissioner (in some countries described as commander or kommandant), colonel, lieutenant-colonel, brigadier, major, staff-captain, and staff-lieutenant.

[3] The ranks of field officers are commandant, adjutant, ensign, captain, lieutenant, and sub-lieutenant.

including sergeant-major, secretary, treasurer, bandmaster, young people's sergeant-major, and quarter-master. These local officers are a great strength to the Army, often constituting a powerful link between the local leaders and the outside population. The junior or young people's section of the corps is, in the main, organized and maintained by the local officers. The children's services, the company meetings, the Young People's Legion, the Corps Cadets' Brigade, the Life-Saving Scouts and Life-Saving Guards, together with other agencies, form a comprehensive system for the salvation and instruction of young people both in childhood and in adolescence.[1]

The Army claims to be a thoroughly democratic body in this respect that the soldier may aspire to any command, and, in fact, all or very nearly all promotion is from the ranks. Candidates for officership, who must be soldiers in good standing, receive a course of instruction (for not less than one year and not more than three) at one or other of the Army's 'Training Garrisons' or colleges. These training institutions, the first of which was opened in London in 1880, have now been established in 22 countries. The training given is not so much scholastic as spiritual and practical, and the cadet learns to do the actual work among the people in which he or she will presently be entirely engaged. Afterwards the 'probationary' is generally appointed in the first instance as lieutenant or sub-lieutenant under a captain of a corps, and continues for a time in the field the studies begun at the training centre. The fitness of officers is judged not alone by their ability to speak, and still less by their erudition, but by the proof that they give of their faith in God, their devotion to their work—above all, by their love of souls.

4. Position of women.—One of the foundation principles of the Salvation Army is that for any position, up to the Generalship itself, women are as eligible as men. Two of the territorial commands at the time of writing—those of the United States and of Denmark—are filled by women, and women are also at the head of many departments, while hundreds of them are in command of local corps. The principle that women have an equal standing with men as publishers of salvation to the world followed as a natural result from the part which women played in the early history of the Army; Catherine Booth was one of those who, long before the birth of the Army, protested strongly against the circumscribed sphere of women's labour in the churches.[2] She had expressed the belief, in letters written before her marriage, that much of the non-success of the gospel was to be attributed to the restrictions imposed upon the Holy Spirit in this particular. The rise of the Quakers—'the Salvationists of the 17th century'—had already opened the door to a female ministry, and Mrs. Booth, who amid obloquy and misrepresentations pioneered the ministry of these sisters of the people and shaped the Salvation Army bonnet, was assisting perhaps the next most striking step in religious history in the spiritual enfranchisement of women. When she died in 1890, the number of women officers of the Salvation Army exceeded 5000, and the godly women who publicly declared the works of Jesus Christ were to be counted by tens of thousands.

5. Orders and Regulations.—The system of the Salvation Army and the principles which govern its warfare are set out in a series of *Orders and Regulations.* Separate volumes have been compiled for different classes of officers according to the nature of their service, and every command and following in the Army has its own *vade mecum.* There are *Orders and Regulations* not only for soldiers in the ranks, but also for the various local officers, field officers, officers engaged in social work, staff officers, and territorial commissioners.[3] The general aim of this comprehensive series is not only to furnish definite instructions in methods of Army service and principles of organization and government, but also to offer counsel from the vast treasury of experience which the first General and those associated with him have accumulated. William Booth first began to issue instructions to his helpers in the form of correspondence, but with

[1] *Orders and Regulations for Local Officers*, London, 1917.
[2] Catherine Booth, *Practical Religion*[3], pp. 133–167.
[3] See 'Literature' at end of article.

the growth of the work this method soon became impracticable, and gradually he came to embody his wishes in sets of printed regulations.[1] It was recognized that no code, however deliberately planned, and however capable the men upon whose practical experience it drew, could suffice as a final rule of faith and practice,[2] but by continual revision and reference to explicit cases these various directions have been made and will continue to be made as useful and particularized as possible. The leaders of the Army have never aimed at anything approaching a compendium of mechanical rules set forth in immutable terms; their aim has been rather to give expression to the demands of a living organism which grows and moves in response to the needs of the world of men for whom it works and to the mind of Christ which those leaders believe it has received of Him.

These regulations make severe demands. Intoxicating liquor is prohibited, severe plainness of dress is enjoined, the wearing of uniform is urged as a witness to salvation, the use of tobacco in the case of officers is required to be given up, and in the case of soldiers, although the renunciation is not compulsory, persistence in the habit is a barrier to promotion, even to the rank of sergeant or bandsman.

In the solemn matters of courtship and marriage the Army takes something more than a parental prerogative. All who are married under the Army flag subscribe to certain *Articles of Marriage*, the purport of which may be gathered from the first of them:

'We do solemnly declare that we have not sought this marriage for the sake of our own happiness and interests only, although we hope these will be furthered thereby; but because we believe that the union will enable us better to please and serve God, and more earnestly and successfully to fight and work in the Salvation Army.'

In their infancy the children of members are dedicated to become future soldiers in the war. The Salvationist conception of domestic duty is perhaps best unfolded in books by William and Catherine Booth.[3]

6. The Salvationist and the State.—The position of the Salvationist with regard to politics and the State is, in general, one of neutrality. It is impressed upon him in his *Orders and Regulations* that, 'although still living in the world, he is not of it,' and has no more business with its politics than with its pleasures. He is enjoined to render obedience to the Government under which he lives for the time being, to respect authority, and to conform, as far as he conscientiously can, to its requirements. While not forbidden under certain circumstances to join in patriotic or local demonstrations, he is reminded that the Salvation Army is a company of men and women of many nationalities who, while rendering to Cæsar the things that are his, acknowledge a higher authority than Cæsar's.[4] The super-national character of the Salvation Army is very well illustrated in the German Salvationist adaptation of Hoffman's patriotic song:

'Jesus, Jesus über alles,
Über alles in der Welt.'

At the same time its attitude to public questions is not necessarily negative. When social reform is to the fore, or any matter which concerns the moral well-being of the community, or the position of the Salvation Army, the Salvationist is at liberty to give his support to parties and organizations which are prepared to further the principles to which he stands committed as a Salvationist, but his support of those parties and organizations ceases with the accomplishment of the immediate object. He is advised even then to concern himself, not with parties, but with measures, and with measures only in so far as they have a direct bearing upon his principles and his work as a Salvation soldier. The same rule holds good in local

[1] The first *Orders and Regulations* was issued in 1878, but certain rules were printed as early as 1874.
[2] *Orders and Regulations for Staff Officers*, Introd. p. xv.
[3] William Booth, *Religion for Every Day*, and *The Training of Children*; Catherine Booth, *Practical Religion*[3].
[4] *Orders and Regulations for Soldiers of the Salvation Army*[5], London, 1907.

politics, while in the case of industrial disputes the Salvation Army still maintains this neutral attitude so far as the merits of the case are concerned, although ready for any opportunity to reconcile the disputants and to alleviate distress.

The Salvation Army in the United Kingdom has at various times assisted in bringing about legislation having a moral purpose; it helped to secure the passage of the Criminal Law Amendment Acts and the Children's Act. It has acted in a like way in other countries, as, *e.g.*, in Japan, where it has been the means of bringing about changes in the laws protecting women. It has helped to win further liberty of speech and opinion both in the United Kingdom and in some Continental countries, where at first it was bitterly persecuted. In the early days of its history in England Acts of Parliament were erroneously evoked, and by-laws were frequently made to prevent open-air meetings. In one year alone more than 600 Salvationists in England, as well as considerable numbers in Sweden, Switzerland, India, and the United States, suffered imprisonment for their action in the open air. The decisions, however, of some local authorities were carried to the higher courts and there reversed; and in many other cases, without taking such a course, the Salvation Army, by a firm though non-provocative attitude, has carried its point and gained toleration and protection for its own street propaganda and that of other bodies. In a wider aspect still the Salvation Army by its work among vast subject populations is rendering a certain amount of imperial service, for it is developing the native power along purely Salvationist and therefore non-insurrectionary lines.

III. *THE SALVATION ARMY AS A SPIRITUAL FORCE.*—**1. 'Articles of War.'**—The simplest exposition of the religion of the Army is to be found in its 'Articles of War,' to which every Salvationist subscribes on enrolment. These 'Articles' number sixteen, half of them mainly doctrinal in character, the other half mainly ethical. They are quoted in full in art. CONFESSIONS, vol. iii. p. 887.

2. The need for conversion. — The doctrinal standards of the Salvation Army are in general those of evangelical Christianity.

'We believe,' wrote William Booth, 'the three creeds of the Church with all our heart. We believe every word of the Commination Service, and we go about denouncing the wrath of God against sinners just as people must who really believe that all these things are true.'[1]

Catherine Booth was equally explicit:

'We have not given up any of the fundamental doctrines of Christianity, such as the fall, the universal call to repentance, justification by faith through Jesus Christ, a life of obedience, and heaven and hell.'[2]

Salvationist theology includes the leading truths which are held by all orthodox communities, and any apparent newness of presentation is due mainly to its concentration upon those few and simple truths which it holds to be vital to salvation. In an interview which the late General afforded one of his journalists on the fiftieth anniversary of his own conversion he expounded his idea of the scheme of salvation in considerable detail. After the elementary truths regarding the work of each Person of the Trinity, he instanced three other doctrines upon which, he said, constant stress was laid at almost every public effort of Salvationists. These concerned the day of judgment, the existence of a real place of punishment, and the existence of 'a glorious heaven where all faithful and victorious soldiers will enjoy unspeakable happiness in companionship with saints, angels, and God.' Beyond these, again, there were certain other truths which had a formative influence upon his mind and, in consequence, upon the doctrinal position of the Army. These had been borne in upon him alike by personal experience, by observation, and by his study of the Bible. One was the division of all men into two classes in their relation to God and eternity—the righteous and the wicked. These answered to the two destinies of heaven and hell which awaited men in the next world. There was nothing clearer than that there is a right side and a wrong in the relations of each individual to

[1] *CR* xlii. [1882] 176.
[2] Catherine Booth, *The Salvation Army in Relation to the Church and State*, p. 30.

the salvation offered by God through the sacrifice of Christ, and that it is within a man's own determination which side he should be on. Change of character can be brought about only by a change of nature, and of this change God is the Author, with the consequence that it is possible to expect and to witness this change even in the worst of characters, where, in the nature of the case, no merely human means, such as good resolutions, even when fortified by ceremonial, can avail. It is God who saves, and therefore no man is beyond the pale of this miracle. At the same time, he could never admit that forfeiture of individual responsibility which seemed to be involved in the extreme Calvinist position. Every man was responsible for his own salvation. It was clear that a man must be empowered to accept or reject the proffered mercy, and that upon his acceptance or rejection depended his eternal destiny, and, further, that this great act of reconciliation with God was a definite transaction, occurring at a given time, on the simple conditions of repentance and faith.

3. Holiness teaching. — The Salvation Army from the beginning had insisted upon the need for definite spiritual development after conversion, or on what it calls a 'full salvation.' In the prominence which it has thus given to the doctrine of entire sanctification it has shown itself in the inheritance of John Wesley, who consistently taught that the same power which pardoned the sinner could purify the heart from evil tendencies and tempers, and it has gone in advance of Wesley in insisting that this perfecting of the heart in love will result in a life of conflict and sacrifice for the salvation of others. Full salvation is not to be introspective merely, but a practical following of Jesus Christ as a living sacrifice; not so much a 'rest of faith' as a 'fighting holiness.'[1] This truth has been placed in the forefront of Salvation Army work, and the 'holiness meeting' is usually a feature of the weekly programme of a corps in every country. The teaching is that the Holy Spirit is able to subdue the whole man—will, thought, feeling, and action—to the law of love and keep him walking according to that law in holiness and righteousness all the days of his life.

This experience is taught as a definite state, first towards sin, and then as to conformity to the known will of God. In a series of *Letters to Salvationists* on this subject William Booth speaks of three conditions in which the soul may be:

'In the first stage the soul is *under* sin—it must sin and sin rules. In the second stage the soul is *over* sin. The yoke of evil is broken. Deliverance as well as pardon has come by Christ. In the third stage, the soul is *without* sin. Then the soul may adopt the words of the Apostle, with a variation, and say, "The very God of peace has sanctified me wholly, and He preserves my whole spirit and soul and body blameless, and He will continue to do so unto the coming of our Lord Jesus Christ. Faithful is He that has called me to this experience of purity, who also will do it."'[2]

The conditions of obtaining this pure heart are (1) obedience in separation from evil, (2) surrender of the soul to the will of God, and (3) faith, which is the committal of the soul to the Sanctifier in full confidence that He will cleanse and keep it from sin.

4. Sacraments.—Conceiving its purpose to be that of calling universal attention to central and vital truths, and making them stand out in the utmost directness before the individual conscience, the Salvation Army has largely avoided the subtleties and intricacies of controversial theology, and this not merely for the sake of peace but for the sake of concentration. The administration of the sacraments was abandoned in 1882, and all ritual which might be supposed to contain some intrinsic

[1] See Samuel L. Brengle, *The Way of Holiness.*
[2] William Booth, *Purity of Heart*, p. 36 f.

or mystic merit was put on one side. The Army has never denied the value of the sacraments in individual cases, and indeed, occasionally, its members have been granted liberty to partake of these ordinances in one or other of the Churches. But the broad fact upon which Salvationism rests is that the sacraments are not necessary to salvation—whether salvation is considered as an act of divine grace or as a holy life.

The present attitude of the Army on this subject is identical in practice with that of the Society of Friends. The Friends, however, arrived at their position by way of the doctrine of the 'inward light,' whereas the Army takes the simple utilitarian ground that these observances introduce complication, that they are open to argument and attack, and that by many who would participate in them they would not be understood, and, most important of all, that they would often obscure the necessity for the vital experience.

5. Salvationizing methods. — With unchangeableness of principle there is combined the utmost flexibility of method. Some features of the Army's assemblies have aroused intense criticism, but a good deal of its procedure which might seem to be extravagant or even irreverent when described at second-hand is not so at all in the actual circumstances of the occasion. Army demonstrativeness, as Catherine Booth once said, is not a putting on, but a letting out. The Salvationist's vision of a rebellious world and of perishing souls seems to justify any and every device, however sharp, striking, or even vulgar, for attracting, for compelling, the attention of the hardened and indifferent to whom his appeal is made. For this reason ordinary religious phraseology is largely laid on one side, and what has been called 'surprise power' or novelty is utilized. The testimony meeting is described as a 'free and easy,' and the response of 'Amen' as a 'volley.' Many Army services are punctuated from first to last with joyous exclamations, clapping of hands, laughter, or tears. The soul-winning propaganda of the Salvation Army, as illustrated in its street marches and in meetings of an unusual type, has sometimes taken the form of almost physical persuasion. Among the people to whom the Salvationist goes he has to compete with a hundred other clamant appeals to eye-gate and ear-gate, and, his object being to win men for the highest good, he sees it necessary to be in his way as vociferous and aggressive as any. Above all things he is to be definite. It is not his business to produce a vague emotion; he is to bring men to a state in which they are convinced of sin and convicted of its guilt and of its awful peril. Mere belief is not enough; there must be an active repentance. Therein lies one chief reason for the penitent form or mercy-seat. This feature of Salvationist public gatherings is a row of seats immediately in front of the platform, at which seekers are invited to kneel in token of their resolution to abandon their sins and to live henceforth to please God. It is a method which the Army defends on the ground that it is conspicuous enough to register a distinct break in a man's life, and does not lend itself to a mere passing impressionism. A further reason for Salvationist enthusiasm is seen in the fact that many of the workers have themselves passed through such inward experiences as to make it unnatural for them to maintain their ordinary reserve when they speak of such things.[1] Many of them also have witnessed remarkable—they often justify the word 'miraculous'—changes occurring in the lives of others, such as those described[1] as having occurred in one London corps, where a group of men known locally as 'the terrible ten' were won for God.

6. Other features of propaganda.—Although the first Army band was not established until 1879, the enthusiasm of the movement found expression in song from the very beginning. It carried a step further the evangelistic singing which had been such a feature of the Methodist revival in the previous century. Soon after the commencement of his work in the East End of London William Booth published *The Christian Mission Hymn-Book*, and later a whole series of *Salvation Army Song Books*, which contained songs[2] in abundance, some of original composition and others gathered from every quarter. These songs were taken up by his people with fervour and spontaneity. Rather to the offence of a good many outsiders, the leaders of the Salvation Army have systematically adapted sacred words to popular tunes on the principle, 'We'll take these songs from the devil; he has no right to a note of music.' But always both rhythm and words were subservient to the Salvationist sentiment. Soon the penetrating melodies, especially those of Salvation Army origin, demanded a more considered musical accompaniment, and bands began to be formed, at first among families or groups of Salvationists, and then as a regular part of each corps, until now, with nearly 30,000 bandsmen and more than 20,000 members of Songsters' Brigades, the Salvation Army, as Samuel Morley once prophesied would be the case, has 'sung its way round the world.' In the jubilant cadences has been found a language in which Salvationists of every tongue can understand one another and tell to all men the joy that is in them. The band (in some countries a guitar combination, but more generally with brass instruments) is a feature of Salvation Army work in every part of the world. The strictest surveillance over the bands, both as to personnel and as to music, is maintained at each territorial headquarters. Bandsmen have their own *Orders and Regulations*, and the part which the instruments can take in the meetings, both in time and in volume, is carefully limited so as to assist the proceedings without monopolizing them.

Another means of propaganda which the Army was quick to appreciate was the printing-press. Within a few months of the organization becoming known as the Salvation Army the first *War Cry* was established to inspire Salvationists, educate them, and bind them together. This, the *Official Gazette* of the Army, has now (1918) some 80 companions, most of them weekly periodicals, issued in more than 20 languages, including several of the languages of Asia and Africa. The combined circulation is more than seven millions, 1¼ millions for each issue, and the total number of readers is estimated at more than seven millions. The selling of these papers by members of the Army is looked upon as offering a precious opportunity of witnessing for Christ. In most territories the name *War Cry*, or its equivalent, is adopted as the title of the official organ—*e.g.*, the *Strijdkreet* of Holland and *Il Grido di Guerre* of Italy; and in addition there are in most countries, as in the United Kingdom, magazines for special departments of the Army's work. By means of explicit instructions and vigilant insight it is ensured that these papers reflect the spirit and polity of the one movement, both in the kind of articles they publish and in the way in which they deal with topics of interest. The power of the

[1] See art. CONVERSION, vol. iv. p. 109b: 'The type of religious experience that seems native to a cultured community is calm and restrained; but the fervours of the Salvation Army and the Methodist meeting are to the psychologist no less natural.'

[1] Harold Begbie, *Broken Earthenware*.
[2] Always 'songs' rather than 'hymns,' following the general custom of the Scriptures.

printed word has also been recognized in the systematic publication of books dealing with phases of Salvation Army thought and experience, and of many volumes of a didactic character by William and Catherine Booth, G. S. Railton, and others.

7. Indirect influences.—The influence of any organization beyond the ranks of its immediate followers is difficult to estimate, but some of the features of the Salvation Army are so marked a departure from ordinary religious life and methods that they could hardly fail to have important reactions in the Christian Churches. In one form or another many of the leading authorities of the religious world have testified that its spirit and example have brought about changes which amount to a revolution in the methods of the Church. Bishop Lightfoot of Durham pointed out one influence of the Army upon his own Church — the Church of England:

'Shall we be satisfied with going on as hitherto, picking up one here and there, gathering together a more or less select congregation, forgetful meanwhile of the Master's command, "Go ye into the highways and hedges and compel them to come in"? The Salvation Army has taught us a higher lesson than this. Whatever may be its faults, it has at least recalled us to this lost ideal of the work of the Church—the universal compulsion of the souls of men.'

Not only has the Salvation Army stimulated a more aggressive evangelism, but it has also suggested methods of presenting religion to the masses upon which in some instances other bodies have admittedly modelled their own propaganda. The idea of a military organization has been taken up in some cases,[1] and in others the influence of the Army has been apparent in various 'forward movements' in Britain. The same leaven has been at work in other lands, as, *e.g.*, in the 'Innere Mission' of Germany, in its counterpart in the Scandinavian countries, and similar home mission movements in the United States and the British colonies. In India a 'Buddhist Salvation Army' concerns itself with the moral uplifting of those whom it seeks to influence. Individual inspirations, though acknowledged by public men of every communion, including Lutherans, Roman Catholics, Jewish rabbis, and priests of the Greek Church, cannot of course be catalogued; but here again there is abundant evidence that in almost every land the indirect influence of the Army has awakened interest in religion or revived a shaken faith or a languishing devotion among many who have not enlisted under its flag. Thousands of ministers, missionaries, and lay workers serving in other Churches took the first step that led to their present vocation as a result of influences set in motion at its meetings or on reading its publications.

IV. *SOCIAL WORK.* — **1. The incentive.** — The revival of evangelical zeal in the second half of the 19th cent. which the Salvation Army undoubtedly greatly helped to produce, and which in turn did much to help forward the Salvation Army, brought with it a further realization of the inter-relationship of moral failures and physical and economical evils.[2] The social conscience of the people was being quickened, and it was revolted by the spectacle of large sections of the people living either on the edge of economic disaster or plunged already into a sea of grinding want, vice, or crime. At the same time, it was seen that the problems to be dealt with required statesmanlike judgment as well as the philanthropic spirit.

[1] *E.g.*, a 'Church Salvation Army' was started at Oxford (1882–85), the title being chosen 'as a tribute to General Booth'; the organization was one of those which were subsequently merged into the Church Army. See Edgar Rowan, *Wilson Carlile and the Church Army*, London, 1905, p. 140.

[2] Gilbert Slater, *The Making of Modern England*, London, 1913.

William Booth had always deeply sympathized with the workless.

'When but a mere child,' he says, 'the degradation and helpless misery of the poor Stockingers of my native town, wandering gaunt and hunger-stricken through the streets, droning out their melancholy ditties, crowding the Union or toiling like galley slaves on relief works for a bare subsistence, kindled in my heart yearnings to help the poor which have continued to this day and which have had a powerful influence on my whole life.'[1]

It is not surprising, therefore, that quite early in its history (1874–78) the Salvation Army had looked with anxious solicitude into the under-world of want and vice, and had stretched out a hand to certain classes of its sad inhabitants. Prison-gate homes and food depots and some scattered efforts on behalf of lost women—the beginnings of the social work which was presently to grow to such world-wide dimensions—were established. But it was not until the middle eighties that the General, greatly moved by the sight of the vagrant and destitute classes, made certain extensive experiments. Then came a more comprehensive scheme, an organized warfare against social evils—at least the worst of them—as a preliminary to evangelizing the outcast with the saving health of religion. It was a deep spiritual sympathy with suffering that led the Salvation Army into its social enterprises, but with this sympathy was linked a keen appreciation of the sufferers' temporal misery and need.

The social work of the Army is not to be regarded as an additional wing to its main structure, or as a sudden afterthought to modify its governing idea. It is a natural development, involving no departure from the principles by which the Army has been actuated from the beginning. It is true that so far as finance is concerned the spiritual and social operations have since the launching of the Darkest England scheme been sharply distinguished, and subscribers must say to which fund their contributions shall go. This is a matter of legal correctness and of administrative convenience.[2] The place of social work in the Army's operations was definitely indicated by William Booth when he wrote:

'In providing for the relief of temporal misery I reckon that I am only making it easy where it is now difficult, and possible where it is now all but impossible, for men and women to find their way to the Cross.'[3]

The Darkest England scheme, therefore, when it was unfolded in 1890, did not break so freshly upon the Salvation Army itself as it did upon the outside public, whom it awakened in an extraordinary degree to the social misery which existed, and to the availability of the Army for coping with at least some part of the problem by virtue of the extent and solidarity of its organization. The details of the proposed scheme were only in sketch, to be altered, abandoned, or added to as experience and advisability determined. The general purpose was to offer in the first place to the workless and destitute a chance of recovery through industry and discipline, the Army providing them with the opportunity and meeting their immediate needs. Industrial reclamation was, of course, only one phase of the problem, and perhaps not the acutest. The vicious and the morally helpless had to be dealt with, special provision had to be made for prisoners on their discharge, for the habitually drunken, for lawless lads, and for fallen or tempted women. At the back of every effort was the hope of the spiritual reformation of the individual. His character must be changed, if his character was in question, before any change in circumstances could greatly avail.

The principles of social work as laid down in *Orders and Regulations for Social Officers* (1915) include the importance of

[1] *In Darkest England and the Way Out*, Preface, p. i.

[2] The Darkest England scheme was declared a separate trust by deed-poll, dated Jan. 1891.

[3] *In Darkest England and the Way Out*, Preface, p. iv.

a change of environment, the provision of useful occupation, the cultivation of a spirit of mutual assistance, discipline, and so on, but first of all 'the salvation of the individual through faith in Jesus Christ,' not, indeed, as a condition of being helped, but as the chief ground of hope for effecting any permanent improvement.

2. Organizations.—The social enterprises of the Salvation Army lend themselves to descriptive detail, but here it will be enough to refer the reader to the published accounts of various aspects of the work.[1] The following enumeration of the social activities of the Army, though the list may not be quite complete, affords some idea of the variety and scope of its efforts for the benefit of the poor and friendless of every land:

(*a*) *For the starving.*—Children's free and farthing breakfasts, midnight soup and bread brigades for the homeless, cheap food depots, special relief funds for cases of special destitution, old clothes depots for slum families, poor men's hotels, cheap grain stores, famine loan fund for the destitute of the East.

(*b*) *For the drunkards.*—Drunkards' brigades, drunkards' advice and home bureaux, homes for inebriates (men and women).

(*c*) *For the paupers.*—Workhouse brigades, salvation guardians of the poor, pauper colonies, pauper transportation, labour bureaux, homes for the aged and for the dying.

(*d*) *For the unemployed.*—Labour bureaux (men and women), industrial homes, labour wood-yards, city salvage brigades, workshops, elevators.

(*e*) *For the homeless.*—Midnight scouts in cities, shelters for men and women, metropoles.

(*f*) *For the criminals.*—Prison visitation, police-court work, prison-gate work, prison corps, probationary policy, correspondence bureaux, ex-criminals' homes, and criminal settlements.

(*g*) *For the daughters of shame.*—Organized visitation of 'walks,' brothels, red-light districts, yoshiwaras, clubs, etc., midnight meetings and marches, receiving homes, industrial homes, factories, 'out of love' funds, service girls' brigades, shepherding brigades, maternity homes, investigation and affiliation departments, mothers' hospitals.

(*h*) *Slum work.*—Visitation, first-aid brigades, district nursing, 'poorest of the poor' aid.

(*i*) *For the sick.*—Visitation, hospitals, dispensaries, village dispensing, leper hospitals, maternity nursing.

(*j*) *For the lost.*—Inquiry and correspondence bureaux, legal assistance.

(*k*) *Preventive and protective work for young girls.*—Servants' homes, city institutes, registries, students' homes, residential clubs.

(*l*) *Anti-suicide bureaux.*—Advice department, loan department.

(*m*) *Land schemes.*—Emigration, home colonization, colonization over the sea, land and farm and irrigation colonies, small holdings

(*n*) *Deep sea brigades.*—Mission boats, lifeboat.

(*o*) *Training colleges.*

(*p*) *Students' homes.*

(*q*) *Working-men's associations.*

(*r*) *Village banks* (agricultural).

LITERATURE.—i. *HISTORICAL AND DESCRIPTIVE.*—**William Booth**, *The General's Letters*, London, 1885, *In Darkest England and the Way Out*, do. 1890, *Sergeant-Major Do-Your-Best, or The Inner Workings of a Salvation Army Corps*, do. 1906; **Catherine Booth**, *The Salvation Army in Relation to the Church and State*, do. 1883; **W. Bramwell Booth**, *Light in Darkest England*, do. 1895, *Social Reparation*, do. 1899, *Friends of the Poor*, do. 1901; **Mary B. Booth**, *With the B.E.F. in France*, do. 1916; **F. de L. Booth-Tucker**, *What the Salvation Army is doing in India and Ceylon*, Simla, 1911; **E. D. Booth-Hellberg**, *Der soziale Zweig der ersten christlichen Kirche*, Berne, 1904; **Charles Booth**, *Life and Labour of the People of London*, 3rd ser., *Religious Influences*, 7 vols., London, 1903; **Margaret Allen**, *Kingdom-Makers in Shelter, Street, and Slum*, do. 1902, *Eastward Bound*, do. 1903; **Harold Begbie**, *Broken Earthenware*, do. 1910, *The Light of India*, do. 1912; **E. R. Brengle**, *The Army Drum*, do. 1909; **L. Brentano**, *Die christlich-soziale Bewegung in England*[2], Leipzig, 1883; **A. Brückner**, *Erweckungsbewegungen*, Hamburg, 1909; **L. Bruyère**, *Les Œuvres philanthropiques de l'Armée du Salut, en 1905*, Paris, 1906; **Josephine Butler**, *The Salvation Army in Switzerland*, London, 1883; **P. A. Clasen**, *Der Salutismus: eine sozialwissenschaftliche Monographie über General Booth und seine Heilsarmee*, Jena, 1913; **L. Colze**, 'Die Heilsarmee und ihre soziale Arbeit,' *Sozialer Fortschritt*, Leipzig, 1905; **Arthur E. Copping**, *Souls in Khaki*, London, 1917; **Mildred Duff**, *Three Coronations*, do. 1901; **Hulda Friederichs**, *The Romance of the Salvation Army*, do. 1908; **H. Fuchs**, *Heilsarmee*, Jena, 1910; **O. Funcke**, *Englische Bilder in deutscher Beleuchtung*[2], Bremen, 1883; **A. de Gasparin**, *Lisez et Jugez: Armée soi-disant du Salut*, Geneva, 1884; **M. Gerhard**, *Der religiose Charakter der Heilsarmee*, Bonn, 1906; **R. Giffen**, *The Progress of the Working Classes*, London, 1884; **H. Rider Haggard**, *Report of the Salvation Army Colonies in the U.S.A. and at Hadleigh, Essex*, do. 1905, *Regeneration*, do. 1910; **Theodor Kolde**, *Die Heilsarmee*[2], Leipzig, 1899, and art. 'Heilsarmee,' in *PRE*[3] vii. 578-593; **Selma Lagerlöf**, *Körkarlen*, Stockholm; **Jack London**, *The People of the Abyss*, London, 1903; **David Lyall**, *Handicapped*, do. 1914; **F. A. MacKenzie**, *Waste Humanity*, do. 1909, *Serving the King's Men*, do. 1918; **Olive C. Malvery**, *Thirteen Nights*, do. 1908, *The Soul Market*, do. 1907; **J. Page**, *The Christianity of the Continent*, do. 1905; **Agnes Palmer**, *The Salvage of Men*, New York, 1913; **J. Pestalozzi**, *Was ist die Heilsarmee?* Halle, 1886; **A. Peyron**, *Réflexions et expériences d'un Salutiste*, Paris, 1895; **G. S. Railton**, *Heathen England and the Salvation Army*, London, 1884, *Twenty-One Years Salvation Army*, do. 1886, *Apostolic Warfare*, do. 1889, *Our War in S. Africa*, do. 1901, *Precipices*, do. 1905, *Day by Day in the Salvation Army*, do. 1910, *Forward against Misery*, do. 1913, *Some Prophecies Fulfilled*, do. 1912, *Jugez l'Armée du Salut*, Paris, 1884; **Erland Richter**, *I Missionären's Spar*, Stockholm, 1915; **W. P. Ryan**, *The Romance of a Motor Mission*, London, 1906; **Annie S. Swan**, *The Outsiders*, do. 1906; **Mrs. Verini**, *Deeds of Love and Courage*, do. 1915, *Worth from Waste*, do. 1916, *Round the Clock*, do. 1917; **A. Schindler**, *Die Gefahren in der Kirche*, Ascona, 1900, *Die evangelische Kirche und die Heilsarmee*[3], do. 1905, *Reich und Arm*, do. 1901, *Die soziale Not unserer Zeit und die Heilsarmee*, do. 1902; **E. Spiller**, *Slums: Erlebnisse in den Schlammvierteln moderner Grossstädte*, Aarau, 1911; **Arnold White**, *Truth about the Salvation Army*, London, 1906, *The Great Idea*, do. 1909; **A. Zimmermann**, *J. Wesley und W. Booth; eine historische Parallele*, Munich, 1907; and miscellaneous publications: *La Vérité à l'égard de l'Armée du Salut*, Paris, 1881; *Le Crime des Salutistes*, do. 1883; *L'Alliance évangélique et la liberté religieuse*, Neuchâtel, 1890; *La Liberté de sauver*, Geneva, 1890; *Rapport du conseil fédéral à l'assemblée fédérale sur les petitions concernant l'armée du salut*, Geneva, 1890; *Lettre à mes concitoyens par Aimé Humbert*, Neuchâtel, 1890; *The Progress of the Salvation Army during the Year*, London, 1891; *Correspondence respecting the Expulsion of certain British Subjects from the Cantons of Geneva and Neuchâtel*, do. 1884; *Essays and Sketches: Papers by Eminent People on Salvation Army Work*, do. 1906; *Salvation Army Year Books*, from 1906 to 1918; *Salvation Army War Despatches*, do. 1906; *Phases of the Work of the Salvation Army*, do. 1911; *The Salvation Army Officer at Work*, do. 1908; *Letters to the Centre*, do. 1912; *L'Armée Salut en France*, Paris, 1911; *Saving and Serving*, London, 1916; *Won*, do. 1916; *Some Aspects of Salvation Army Social Work*, do. 1917; *International Social Addresses*, do. 1914.

ii. *BIOGRAPHICAL.*—**F. de L. Booth-Tucker**, *The Life of Catherine Booth, the Mother of the Salvation Army*, 2 vols., London, 1892, *The Life of Colonel Weerasooriya*, do. 1905, *The Consul: A Sketch of Emma Booth-Tucker*, do. 1904; **C. T. Bateman**, *Everybody's Life of General Booth*, do. 1914; **T. F. G. Coates**, *The Prophet of the Poor: the Life Story of General Booth*, do. 1905; **Mary A. Denison**, *Captain Molly*, Boston, Mass., 1897; **Mildred Duff**, *Hedwig von Haartman*, London, 1905; **John Law**, *Captain Lobe*, do. 1887; **W. E. Oliphant**, *Catherine Booth*, do.; **G. S. Railton**, *General Booth, by his first Commissioner*, do. 1912, *The Salvation Navvy (John Allen)*, do. 1880, *Commissioner Dowdle, the saved Railway Guard*, do. 1902, *Life of Lieut.-Colonel Junker*, do. 1903, *Captain Ted (Edward Irons)*, do. 1880; **W. T. Stead**, *General Booth*, do. 1886, *Mrs. Booth of the Salvation Army*, do. 1900.

iii. *DOCTRINAL AND SPIRITUAL.*—**William Booth**, *Salvation Soldiery*, London, 1879, *The Training of Children*, do. 1884, *Purity of Heart*, do. 1902, *Religion for Every Day*, do. 1902, *Visions*, do. 1906, *The Seven Spirits*, do. 1907; **Catherine Booth**, *Godliness*, do. 1890, *Life and Death*, do. 1890; *Practical Religion*[3], do. 1891, *Popular Christianity*, do. 1887; **W. Bramwell Booth**, *Books that Bless*, do. 1899, *Servants of All*, do. 1900, *Our Master*, do. 1908, *Bible Battle-axes*, do. 1901; **E. R. Brengle**, *What hinders you?* do. 1886; **S. L. Brengle**, *Helps to Holiness*, do. 1903, *Heart-Talks on Holiness*, do. 1905, *The Soul-Winner's Secret*, do. 1905, *The Way of Holiness*, do. 1910; **Eileen Douglas**, *The Fruits of the Spirit*, do. 1909; **T. Henry Howard**, *Standards of Life and Service*, do. 1909; **T. Kitching**, *Forms and Ceremonies*, do. 1910; *The Doctrines of the Salvation Army*, do. 1880; *Faith Healing (Memorandum for Officers)*, do. 1902; *A Ladder to Holiness*, do. 1903; *Holy Living*, do. 1901; *How to be Saved*, do. 1903; *The Salvation Army Directory, Nos. 1 and 2*, do. 1901; *Helps to the Directory*, do. 1902; *Salvation Army Songs*, do. 1900.

iv. *REGULATIONS.*—*The Why and Wherefore of the Rules and Regulations of the Salvation Army*, London, 1900; *Orders and Regulations* for Territorial Commissioners and Chief Secretaries (1904), Divisional Commanders (1904), Staff Officers (1904), Field Officers (1917), Social Officers (1917), Local Officers (1917), Soldiers (1908), the Training of Field Officers (1905).

W. BRAMWELL BOOTH.

[1] *E.g.*, H. Rider Haggard, *Regeneration*; Arnold White, *The Great Idea*; F. A. MacKenzie, *Waste Humanity*; David Lyall, *Handicapped*; see also 'Literature' below.

SAMĀDHI.—The use of this term in Buddhism has been explained briefly in the art. DHYĀNA (Pali *jhāna*). *Samādhi* is a many-sided word, signifying both (1) a complex state or habit of mind and (2) a system of training or culture intended to produce that state or habit. As (2) it forms one of the three bodies of doctrine (*khandhā*) with which all followers of the holy life in Buddhism were to be continually occupied: *sīlak-*

khandha (morals, ethics), *samādhikkhandha*, and *paññākkhandha* (wisdom, insight).

Thus the distinguished Sister Dhammadinnā comprises the Eightfold Path under these three:

Sīla { right speech / „ action / „ livelihood.

Samādhi { right effort / „ mindfulness / „ *samādhi*.

Paññā { right views / „ intention or aspiration.

She is then asked: 'What is *samādhi*? What induces[1] it? What are the requisites for it? What is the culture of it?' She replies: 'It is concentration of mind; the Four Applications of Mindfulness induce it; the Four Supreme Efforts are its requisites; the practice, development, repetition of these things are the culture of it.'[2]

Here we see the twofold import of the term as stated above. Let us consider each of these two in order. Concentration is *chittass' ekaggatā*, that is, one-pointedness of mind, or the power of exclusive single-minded attention. This definition is repeated and elaborated in the *Abhidhamma* analyses, where *samādhi* and concentration are described in similar terms:

'Stability, solidity, absorbed steadfastness of thought which . . . is the absence of distraction, is balance, unperturbed mental procedure, calm, the faculty and power of concentration.'[3]

The commentaries maintained this teaching as handed on by Buddhaghoṣa:

'What is *samādhi*? It is of many aspects and divers modes . . . not to confuse the issues just here, we say it is concentration of good consciousness. In meaning it is the *samādhānaṃ*;—the "thorough-placing-on-to," that is, on one object of consciousness and its concomitants. Its salient mark is balance; its essential property is the expulsion of wavering, its resulting manifestation is impassivity; happy ease is its proximate antecedent.'[4]

The various channels and modes of *samādhi* are then gone into at length, including *jhāna*, whether induced by self-hypnotism or otherwise. The chief of these are subsequently developed in the following ten chapters of *Visuddhi-Magga*. He concludes the chapter in question with a reply to the inquiries: How is *samādhi* to be cultivated? What is the advantage gained by its culture? The former question is also answered in the ten following chapters. In the eleventh the advantage is stated to be fivefold, according to the lower or higher aims and modes of culture in each practiser:—present happiness, insight into things 'as they really have become' (*yathābhūtaṃ*), superknowledge (*abhiññā*),[5] rebirth in the Brahmā heaven, and *Nirvāṇa*.

Coming to the more discriminating psychological analyses of later scholastics—*e.g.*, in the *Compendium of Philosophy* by Anuruddha—we find that, whereas *chittass' ekaggatā* is recognized as a constant factor among the seven factors present in every unit of conscious activity, *samādhi* is reserved for the whole of a given state of mind describable as concentration[6] and is also called 'ecstatic apperception'[7] in states of mystic or jhānic rapture. In other words, the factor in every act of consciousness which we know as 'selection' becomes, when trained and developed, the power and faculty (*indriya*) of *samādhi*.[8]

Thus *samādhi* is no more confined to the highest, most unworldly aims and activities than is 'concentration' in English-speaking culture. Nor is it right to speak of it as the 'sole' or even the chief aim of the Buddhist. It is quite essential as a means. But the aims and ideals which it made possible to realize are reserved by Buddhaghoṣa for the *Paññākkhandha*, the third and last section of the *Visuddhi-Magga*.

[1] *Nimitta*; see *Points of Controversy* (*PTS*), London, 1915, p. 388.

[2] *Majjhima*, i. 301.

[3] *Dhamma-saṅgaṇi*, §§ 11, 15, tr. in C. A. F. Rhys Davids, *A Buddhist Manual of Psychological Ethics*, London, 1900, pp. 13 f., 17.

[4] *Visuddhi-Magga*, ch. iii.; cf. *Atthasālinī*, p. 118, where he cites the figures from the *Questions of King Milinda*, i. 60, comparing *samādhi* to the ridgepole of a roof, binding and crowning the moral consciousness, and to a king as head and nucleus of his armies.

[5] Cf. art. DHYĀNA, § 5 (*c*).

[6] P. 108 f. (f), (g).

[7] *Ib.* p. 129, n. 1.

[8] *Ib.* pp. 54 f., 89, n. 4, 129, n. 1.

LITERATURE.—*A Yogāvacara's Manual*, ed. T. W. Rhys Davids, *PTS*, London, 1896 (the introduction cites a number of passages on *samādhi* from the canon); *A Compendium of Philosophy* (a Pali Manual of approx. 12th cent. A.D.), tr. S. Z. Aung and C. A. F. Rhys Davids, London, 1910, pp. 16, § 5, 53–65, 237, 240.

C. A. F. RHYS DAVIDS.

SAMARITANS.

1. Name.—Those who to-day are called Samaritans are but the last little remnant of a Jewish sect that for centuries has looked upon Mt. Gerizim in Palestine as the one rightful place appointed unto it by God for His worship. Their name has come to its present meaning through several stages of development. First of all it was applied to the once famous capital of the kingdom of Northern Israel. Then, by a natural extension, it was made to include the entire district of which this city was the political head; any dweller within this territory might properly be called a Samaritan. Finally, through NT usage and the practice of early Christian writers, the word came to be limited to adherents of a particular form of faith.[1]

2. Origin.—The origin of the Samaritans is veiled in obscurity. The meagre data at our disposal permit and have received different interpretations. According to the Biblical narrative in 2 K 17–18, their beginning is to be dated from the downfall of the kingdom of Northern Israel in 722 B.C.

Then it was that 'Jahweh removed Israel out of his sight, as he spake by the hand of all his servants the prophets. So Israel was carried away out of their own land to Assyria, unto this day. And the king of Assyria brought men from Babylon, and from Cuthah, and from Avva, and from Hamath and Sepharvaim, and placed them in the cities of Samaria instead of the children of Israel: and they possessed Samaria, and dwelt in the cities thereof' (2 K $17^{23f.}$). Thus it came to pass that Israel was removed and that 'there was none left but the tribe of Judah only' (cf. 2 K 17^{18}).

These diverse imported peoples, settled in the devastated land of Israel, were made by Jewish teachers to be the progenitors of the Samaritans. That such a mixed group should speedily come to resemble Israel closely in customs and manner of worship was said to be due to the fact that they were 'lion converts.' Being menaced by a scourge of savage beasts, they found deliverance by worshipping Jahweh as the God of the land under the guidance of a priest, or priests, who were sent back from among the captive Israelites.[2] Meanwhile they did not abandon their former idolatrous cults,

[1] The city of Samaria is said to have received its name from one Shemer (שֶׁמֶר), who sold to Omri the site on which the city was built (1 K 16^{24}). The term 'Samaritans' (*Shomeronim*, שֹׁמְרֹנִים) is found only once in the OT (2 K 17^{29}). Rabbinical writers frequently allude to their northern neighbours as Cutheans, while Josephus calls them by preference Shechemites. They themselves lay claim to the title 'Israel' or 'the Children of Israel.' They acquiesce, however, in the name Samaritans, giving to it their own interpretation of 'observers' or 'keepers,' namely, of the Law or the Sabbath (*i.e. Shomerim*, שֹׁמְרִים, from שמר).

[2] 'And so it was, at the beginning of their dwelling there, that they feared not the Lord: therefore the Lord sent lions among them, which killed some of them. Wherefore they spake to the king of Assyria, saying, The nations which thou hast carried away, and placed in the cities of Samaria, know not the manner of the God of the land: therefore he hath sent lions among them, and, behold, they slay them, because they know not the manner of the God of the land. Then the king of Assyria commanded, saying, Carry thither one of the priests whom ye brought from thence; and let *them* go and dwell there, and let *him* teach them the manner of the God of the land. So one of the priests whom they had carried away from Samaria came and dwelt in Beth-el, and taught them how they should fear the Lord' (2 K 17^{25-28}). The text fluctuates between the singular and plural in its allusion to the priest or priests. It is probable that the plural should be retained throughout. Josephus (*Ant.* IX. xiv. 3) makes the danger that threatened them to have been a pestilence.

for, while 'they feared Jahweh,' at the same time they 'served their own gods, after the manner of the nations from among whom they had been carried away' (2 K 17^{33}).

Two further OT allusions to the introduction of foreign colonists are found in the book of Ezra. In the first (4^{2}) the Samaritans make request to have part with the returned exiles in rebuilding the Temple at Jerusalem, and urge their claim on the ground that they worship Jahweh as do the Jews, and that they have sacrificed unto Him from the time that they were brought into the land by Esar-haddon, king of Assyria (681–668 B.C.).[1] Further on in the chapter the same people are described as belonging to the 'nations whom the great and noble Osnappar brought over, and set in the city of Samaria, and in the rest of the country beyond the river' (Ezr 4^{10}).[2] Both the latter statements are beset with textual difficulties, but they agree with the account of 2 Kings in emphasizing the alien origin of the Samaritans. Later Jewish tradition perpetuates the same disparaging view and uses by preference the term 'Cuthean' for the people of the north.[3]

The fall of Israel and the deportation of its people are also mentioned in two Assyrian inscriptions. It appears that Shalmaneser IV. (727–722), who began the siege of the city of Samaria, died before its completion, and that accordingly the glory of the conquest was claimed by his successor, Sargon II. (722–705). The latter king says:

> 'At the beginning of my reign, in my first year . . . Samaria I besieged, I captured. 27,290 people from its midst I carried captive. 50 chariots I took there as an addition to my royal force . . . I returned and made more than formerly to dwell. People from lands which my hands had captured I settled in the midst. My officers over them as governors I appointed. Tribute and taxes I imposed upon them after the Assyrian manner.'[4]

The second inscription is of like purport, with an added statement to the effect that those who were left undisturbed in their homes were permitted to retain their possessions.[5] In the royal enumeration of the exiles probably only the heads of families were counted, and consequently the total number of captives may have been much greater; but, even so, this deportation can have affected only a small percentage of the entire population.[6] The capital and the larger towns would doubtless suffer most, whereas the smaller villages of the rural districts would remain largely undisturbed. The concern of the Assyrian conqueror would be to remove the more influential political and religious leaders. Whether there was a further deportation two years later, when Samaria joined in a fruitless uprising against Sargon II., is not stated in the surviving fragments of the inscription which commemorates the event. Accordingly, so far as Assyrian records permit any inference, it appears that the major portion of the Israelites continued to dwell in their own land subject to local Assyrian governors.

[1] Josephus, in reporting this incident, states that the king in question was Shalmaneser IV. (*Ant.* XI. ii. 1; cf. *ICC*, *ad loc.*, and Torrey, *Ezra Studies*, p. 169).

[2] It is probable that the name Osnappar is a corruption, since it is not otherwise known to have been borne by any king or high official. A widely accepted conjecture would substitute Asshurbanipal (668–626 B.C.) on the ground of resemblance and because he alone of the later Assyrian kings would be in a position to deport colonists from Susa and Elam. Others would restore Shalmaneser, a reading that has the support of Lucian's text of the LXX (cf. L. W. Batten, *The Books of Ezra and Nehemiah* [*ICC*], Edinburgh, 1913, p. 172; *HDB* iii. 634; Torrey, p. 169).

[3] Jos. *Ant.* IX. xiv. 3, XI. iv. 3, vii. 2; Schürer, *GJV*³ ii. 15, note 43, for passages in the Mishnāh.

[4] *KAT*³, as tr. by G. A. Barton, *Archæology and the Bible*, Philadelphia, 1916, p. 369.

[5] This at least is the presumable meaning of the passage (*ib.* p. 370).

[6] There is a tradition of much larger deportations from Judah. Sennacherib speaks of devastating 46 fortified towns of Hezekiah, the Judæan, and of leading captive 200,150 'people, small and great, male and female' (*KAT*³, tr. Barton, p. 373).

Such a conclusion receives a measure of confirmation from Biblical data. The Chronicler states that soon after the fall of Samaria King Hezekiah (715 (?)–686 (?) B.C.) sent to all Israel and 'wrote letters also to Ephraim and Manasseh,' inviting them to participate in a great Passover at Jerusalem, with the result that many came from Asher, Manasseh, and Zebulun (2 Ch $30^{1.11}$). This implies the continued presence of Israelites in the north.[1] In the next century the reform of Josiah (639–608 B.C.) purged Bethel of its idolatry and took away 'all the houses also of the high places that were in the cities of Samaria, which the kings of Israel had made to provoke Jahweh to anger' (2 K 23^{15-20}). There is no suggestion in this tradition that these high places differed in any particular from those in the south, or that the cultus was other than that which had been established by the kings of Israel. The Chronicler includes Manasseh, Ephraim, and 'all the remnant of Israel' among those who contributed to the repairs of the Temple in the days of Josiah (2 Ch 34^{9}; cf. 2 K 22^{4}). In the 5th cent. we hear of 80 men who came out of Shechem, Shiloh, and Samaria, bringing offerings to the house of Jahweh. They came in the garb of mourning, doubtless because of the desolation of Jerusalem and the ruin of the Temple (Jer 41^{5}). It seems most natural to suppose that these worshippers were Israelites, and that the former relationship to Jerusalem had not yet been interrupted. To a somewhat later period in the same century belongs the tradition already discussed, that the inhabitants of the north claimed the right to co-operate with the returned exiles in the rebuilding of the Temple (Ezr 4^{2}).

These scattered notices are best understood by supposing that the descendants of the Israelites continued to live on in the land of their fathers and that they are the same people that emerged later as the sect of the Samaritans. The loss of the Ten Tribes would then be due more to vicissitudes suffered at home than to deportations. The whole religious development of the Samaritans requires such an ancestry and would be largely inexplicable without it. Rabbinical enactments appear at times frankly to recognize the true situation. A Talmudic booklet (*Massekheth Kuthim*) dealing with the Samaritans closes as follows:

> 'When shall we receive them? When they give up their faith in Mount Gerizim and acknowledge Jerusalem and the resurrection of the dead. Thenceforth he who robs a Samaritan will be as he who robs an Israelite.'[2]

Anthropology, working independently, has reached the same conclusion. H. M. Huxley gives it as his judgment that the Samaritans 'are to-day the sole, though degenerate, representatives of the ancient Hebrews.'[3]

3. The emergence of the Samaritans as an independent religious community.—As to the time and circumstances of the final rupture between the Jews and the Northern Israelites there are two divergent traditions.

One rests upon a brief allusion in Neh $13^{28f.}$, where it is stated that 'one of the sons of Joiada, the son of Eliashib the high priest, was son in law to Sanballat the Horonite: therefore I chased him from me. Remember them, O my God, because they have defiled the priesthood, and the covenant of the priesthood, and of the Levites.'

The second and more explicit tradition is recounted by Josephus, who tells us that the schism was occasioned by the marriage of Manasseh, a brother of the high priest Jaddua, to an alien wife, namely to Nikaso, the daughter of Sanballat, the Persian governor of Samaria. The elders at Jerusalem and the high priest demanded that the wife should be divorced, or that Manasseh should renounce his sacerdotal rights. Unwilling to accept such an alternative, he sought help from his aged father-

[1] Cf. E. L. Curtis and A. A. Madsen, *The Books of Chronicles* (*ICC*), Edinburgh, 1910, p. 471 ff., and Montgomery, *The Samaritans*, p. 55.

[2] Nutt, *A Samaritan Targum*, p. 172; Montgomery, p. 203. On the whole attitude of Jewish teachers, cf. Montgomery, pp. 165–203.

[3] *JE* x. 676.

in-law, who promised to secure for him the dignity and rights of the high priesthood in connexion with a temple that should be built on Mt. Gerizim. The young priest was likewise assured that he should be Sanballat's successor in temporal power. Ultimately the promised religious privileges were gained under the sanction of Alexander the Great, who had meanwhile defeated the Persians at Issus and conquered Syria. Forthwith the temple was built and regular worship was established at the rival sanctuary.[1] If Josephus can thus record an incident that establishes the legitimacy of the priestly line of the rival temple, it is evident that the tradition must have appeared to him well founded, for he otherwise gives abundant evidence of his hostility towards the Samaritans. It is further stated in his account that Manasseh was joined by many priests and Levites who had alien wives, and also that other disaffected Jews, who from time to time became guilty of breaches of the law at Jerusalem, found refuge with the Shechemites.[2]

These two accounts have this much in common, that each makes mention of the marriage of a member of the Jewish high-priestly family to the daughter of a Sanballat; but in the former instance the priest in question was an unnamed son of Joiada and a grandson of the high priest Eliashib, while in Josephus he is Manasseh, brother of the high priest Jaddua, who was a contemporary of Alexander the Great. Thus the incident would occur, according to Josephus, in 332–331 B.C., or about a century after Nehemiah. Again we note that Nehemiah speaks only of the expulsion of the offender and gives no hint that this act of discipline resulted in the founding of a rival sanctuary on Mt. Gerizim, or in any way affected the Samaritans.[3] Without entering upon a discussion of the problem that is thus presented, it may be said that the date fixed by Josephus for the schism appears to be confirmed by several important facts. First in order is the agreement of the Samaritans with the Jews in accepting the fully revised and developed Pentateuch. Had the separation taken place before the sacred documents assumed their present form, the Samaritan Bible would almost certainly give some evidence of belonging to the earlier period. It is further highly significant that, so far as we can discover, Samaritan worship and ritual from the first conformed closely to Jewish rites and practices—a result that could hardly have been anticipated if Jewish influence had made itself felt only indirectly in the time after Nehemiah. A further reason for the later dating of the Samaritan schism is furnished by the recently discovered Elephantinē temple papyrus. This document, written in 408–407 B.C., gives no suggestion that a state of bitterest enmity existed openly between Jews and Samaritans. On the other hand, the Jewish community of Egypt can appeal with confidence not only to Jerusalem, but also to the political heads of Samaria for assistance. There is no allusion to a religious head of the Samaritans in this connexion, doubtless because as yet none existed.[4]

Whether the final separation between Judæa and Samaria dates from the days of Alexander the Great, or whether it came earlier, we may suppose that it was the culmination of an antagonism that had long existed. Henceforth the enmity was intense, as is made evident by the few manifestations of it that can still be traced in the centuries immediately following and in NT times. During the 3rd cent. we have the testimony of the Chronicler, whose attitude is shown by the way in which he idealizes Rehoboam and his successors, thereby throwing Israel's apostasy into darker relief.[1] He denies to them the right of being regarded as a part of the people of God (2 Ch 13^{9} 25^{7}). As for their successors, the Samaritans, they are idolaters and self-confessed aliens (Ezr $4^{1f.}$). In the opening years of the 2nd cent. Jesus Sirach (*c.* 180 B.C.) voices a like reprobation. For him, too, the Samaritans are a 'no nation,' a foolish (or godless) people that dwell in Shechem ($50^{25f.}$).[2] At the opening of the Christian era the traditional hatred flashed out in deeds of violence,[3] and at all times there existed a dangerous tenseness of feeling (Jn 4^{9} 8^{48}, Lk $9^{52f.}$).

4. Later history.—Of the experiences of the Samaritans in the disturbed period following the death of Alexander we have little reliable information; but that they suffered severely, as the tide of war swept backward and forward through their land, may be accepted as certain. During the troubled years of the 3rd and 2nd centuries B.C. doubtless not a few of them found their way to Egypt as emigrants or captives, and became the nucleus of the colonies that existed later at Alexandria and Cairo.[4] Meanwhile the province of Samaria, by virtue of its geographical position and accessibility, was open to foreign influences. Under the Syrians the city of Samaria continued to be a Gentile centre and the seat of civil administration, as it had been during Persian supremacy. The Samaritans apparently escaped extreme persecution during this early period. This is to be attributed to the fact that they were not disturbed as were the Jews by party factions, and that they held aloof from political movements. However, 2 Mac ($5^{23f.}$ 6^{2}) implies that in the 2nd cent. they were included by Antiochus Epiphanes in the repressive measures employed by him against the Jews.[5] Hellenizing influences may well have served to consolidate them more and more and to

[1] Jos. *Ant.* XI. vii. 2, viii. [2] *Ib.* XI. viii. 2, 7.

[3] In spite of these important differences in detail, it is quite generally believed that both accounts must refer to the same experience. Usually a way out of the difficulty is sought by making Josephus to be in error as to the date. It is assumed that Nehemiah's stringent reform in the matter of marriage must have been the immediate occasion of the violent rupture between Jews and Samaritans. On the other hand, it is coming to be recognized that Josephus is here following an independent source which ought not to be discarded too hastily. It is not easy to discover any valid reason why his narrative may not be essentially correct, barring a few details that may have been borrowed from Nehemiah (cf. C. Steuernagel, *SK* lxxxii. [1909] 5, and *Handkommentar zum AT*, Göttingen, 1900, iii. 276; B. Stade and A. Bertholet, *Bibl. Theol. des AT*, Tübingen, 1905–11, ii. 27 f.). Torrey would hold the Chronicler responsible for our difficulty, on the supposition that he has fashioned the passage in Nehemiah in such a way as to reflect later events (pp. 330 f., 235, 249). It was desired to show thereby how Nehemiah had dealt with a case precisely like that of Manasseh. It is urged by Torrey with much cogency that, if the great patriot Nehemiah had been connected in written tradition with the Samaritan secession, the facts would not have been forgotten in Jerusalem. No more would the name of the high priest in whose time the momentous event occurred have been lost to memory.

[4] The Elephantinē papyrus is an appeal from a military colony of Egyptian Jews and is addressed to Bagoses (Bagohi), the Persian governor of Judæa. The petitioners desire permission, or assistance in gaining permission, to rebuild their temple of Jahweh which had been destroyed by their adversaries three years previously. In the course of the letter we learn that an earlier application has been made to the governor, and that at the same time letters of like purport had been dispatched to the high priest in Jerusalem and to influential Jewish leaders. Since no replies had been received, the request to the governor was renewed, and it was added that an appeal for assistance was likewise being forwarded to Dalajah and Shelemjah, the sons of Sanballat the governor of Samaria (cf. Barton, p. 387 ff.). The papyrus proves that there was a governor named Sanballat who was in office in 407 B.C., and in so far corroborates the narrative of Neh 13^{28}. It is quite possible, however, that a grandson of this man, bearing the same name, may have been in authority at the time of Alexander (this is the view of Torrey, p. 330 f.; cf. also pp. 324 and 315 f., and Steuernagel, *SK* lxxxii. [1909] 4 f.).

[1] Cf. 2 Ch 11 and 1 K 12^{21-24}, 2 Ch 13^{4-12} and 1 K $15^{3.4}$, and see Stade-Bertholet, ii. 75 f.

[2] The authenticity of these verses was questioned by Edersheim, but they are now generally accepted (cf. R. Smend, *Die Weisheit des Jesus Sirach erklärt*, Berlin, 1906, p. 491). Various OT passages have been thought without sufficient reason to contain references of like purport to the Samaritans. Cheyne so interpreted Is 65 and 66^{1-22} (*Jewish Religious Life after the Exile*, New York, 1898, p. 25 f.), but a more probable interpretation can be suggested (cf. Montgomery, p. 70 f.).

[3] Jos. *Ant.* XVIII. ii. 2, XX. vi., *BJ* II. xii. 3; cf. *GJV*³ ii. 17.

[4] Jos. *Ant.* XII. i., XIII. iii. 4.

[5] Josephus charges the Samaritans with a lapse from faith under Antiochus IV.; but this accusation may have been born of Jewish prejudice, since their subsequent history seems to disprove the charge (*Ant.* XII. v. 5).

mark them off from the other inhabitants of the district as a distinct sect. In any event it was during this obscure period that they came to wear the aspect under which we know them in later days.

A new crisis in Samaritan history was brought about by the remarkable rise of the Maccabæan princes of Judæa. These leaders gradually extended their conquests northward until they not only mastered Shechem and Mt. Gerizim, but also captured and destroyed the city of Samaria itself. Once established, the Jewish dominion continued, with one or two possible interruptions, down to the days of Pompey and Roman supremacy (63 B.C.). At the time of the destruction of the temple on Mt. Gerizim by John Hyrcanus in 128 B.C.,[1] we can well believe that the Samaritans were called upon to endure other hardships besides the loss of the place and privileges of worship. Roman dominion must have brought most welcome release from the oppression of their hated Jewish rivals. For a time they once again enjoyed a position of relative religious independence, which was not disturbed when they passed under the rule of Herod and then of Archelaus.

Very little is known of the part played by the Samaritans in the Jewish war of A.D. 66–70. Quite probably they held aloof or acted independently, since they could hardly bring themselves to co-operate with their Jewish adversaries, even though they might have little liking for the tyranny of unprincipled Roman officials.[2] A portion of the sect took part in a fanatical uprising that was quelled by Vespasian with much bloodshed in A.D. 67.[3] In the centuries immediately following the Jewish war there are traditions of measures of repression and persecution under the direction of the Roman authorities;[4] but, through all these trying ordeals, the Samaritans seem to have remained loyal to their faith.

There was a brighter period of considerable material prosperity, as well as of intellectual and religious awakening, in the 4th cent. under the leadership of the national hero Baba Rabba. Marqah, who is honoured by the Samaritans as their greatest theologian, lived somewhat later in the same century.[5] For the most part, however, Samaritan history under the Christian emperors is a tale of disaster. Repeated fanatical outbreaks were forcibly repressed and severest penalties were inflicted. Often these took the form of drastic legal restraint and the abrogation of civil and religious rights. Finally, in A.D. 529 Justinian quelled a formidable uprising with a harshness from which the Samaritans never recovered. Many were killed, others fled, and still others apostatized.

Whether a second Samaritan temple was built after the destruction of the first by John Hyrcanus in 128 B.C. is not certainly known. By some scholars it is supposed that the Romans did permit such a restoration in the 2nd cent. A.D. as a reward for aid given by the Samaritans in suppressing the rebellion of the Jews under Bar Kokhba (A.D. 132–135). This second temple, it is thought, was finally destroyed in A.D. 484.[6]

[1] Jos. *Ant.* XIII. ix. 1, *BJ* I. ii. 6.

[2] The recall and banishment of Pontius Pilate in A.D. 36 was brought about by an unwarranted attack that he had made upon a company of Samaritan pilgrims that had assembled at the call of a false prophet (Jos. *Ant.* XVIII. iv. 1, 2). See also the reference given above to the recall of Cumanus (*ib.* XX. vi., *BJ* II. xii. 1–7).

[3] Jos. *BJ* III. vii. 32.

[4] Cf. Montgomery, p. 89 f.

[5] Cf. Montgomery, p. 294 f.; Cowley, *JE* x. 677.

[6] So Cowley, *JE* x. 672, on the basis of *Chronicon Paschale*, *Chron. Abu'l Fath*, and *Chron. Adler*. On the other hand, Procopius, *de Ædificiis*, v. 7, states that there was no rebuilding of the temple. A temple is depicted upon early coins of Neapolis, but doubtless it is the one built by Hadrian and dedicated to the Most High Jupiter (*GJV*³ i. 651, note 13; cf. Montgomery, p. 91, note 35). The first Christian church on Mt. Gerizim was built in A.D. 484.

Under Muhammadan supremacy the Samaritans had to endure their share of oppression and suffering. Small surviving groups came to be distributed through the larger cities of Palestine. Outside of Nablus, the most important and influential was settled at Damascus.[1] All these communities have long since disappeared, and to-day the sole survivors are found at Nablus, where their numbers have steadily decreased.[2]

5. Religious beliefs.—The faith of the Samaritans was Jewish monotheism, and there is nothing to indicate that it was influenced in any fundamental way by infusions from pagan religions. It has rather every appearance of being an arrested development of Judaism. The Samaritan canon included only the Pentateuch, which was supposed to be the sole source and standard for faith and conduct. The vital spiritual element, which was represented in Judaism by the prophets, was largely lacking. The writings of the prophets of Northern Israel were not received, and would have been lost had they not been kept by the Jews. Modifications in creed came for the most part through a process of accretion under outside influences and not through a living development from within. The dominant trait of Samaritanism was a conservative and tenacious adherence to traditional belief. This characteristic can be traced even in the heretical movements that are treated in art. SECTS (Samaritan).

In doctrinal achievement the Samaritans seem to have reached a climax in the 4th cent. of the Christian era in the work of Marqah. The essential articles of their faith had, however, become fixed earlier during periods of which we have only the most meagre information. Under the Muslims in the 11th cent. there was an epoch of some little literary activity, and still another in the 14th cent., while Phinehas (Finias) was high priest, but neither era seems to have resulted in any material contribution to theology. Declining numbers and the struggle for existence are perhaps largely accountable for this lack of intellectual fruitfulness. At the same time, even under favourable conditions, the Samaritans appear never to have shown any theological originality that was at all comparable to that manifested in Judaism. They were distinguished rather at all times by a rigid, if not turbulent, persistence in their ancestral faith. This darker side is somewhat relieved by the brighter picture of their responsiveness to noble impulses that is presented in the NT.

(*a*) *God.*—The monotheistic confession, 'There is no God but the One' (לית אלה אלא אחד), is an ever-recurring refrain in Samaritan liturgies. It was with this formula, elaborated and adapted in various ways, that they opposed Christian teaching and Gnostic speculation. In all Samaritan literature a constant theme is the unity of God and His absolute holiness and righteousness. He is usually conceived of as spirit, and there are few expressions that suggest His localization. In Marqah there is a tendency towards the hypostatization of the divine attributes, but this cannot be said to be characteristic of Samaritanism. The avoidance of anthropomorphic and anthropopathic expressions is more marked in the Samaritan Targum than in that of the Jews. At times, however, as in the account of the giving of the Law, the Biblical narrative is closely followed, and it is taught that God wrote the Tables with His own hand and gave them to Moses (Ex 31[18]). The disinclination to ascribe to God any form of sensuous activity is prob-

[1] On Samaritan inscriptions that have been found in Damascus, cf. *SWAW* xxxix. [1903] 127 f.; *MNDPV*, 1902, no. 5.

[2] In 1163 Benjamin of Tudela speaks of 1000 still clinging to the sacred mountain, whereas now there are fewer than 200, who live in a special quarter of the city of Nablus.

ably accountable for the failure of the Samaritans to follow the Jews in developing a doctrine of divine fatherhood, since otherwise such a conception would be in accord with their exaltation of His mercy and loving-kindness. The utterance of the ineffable name of Jahweh was avoided by them as by the Jews, but it was written without hesitation.[1]

(*b*) *The Law*.—The one sacred book of the Samaritans was the Pentateuch, which, they believed, embodied the supreme revelation of the divine will. They taught that it was most intimately associated with the being of God, and they accorded it the highest veneration. To-day the surviving Samaritans have one particular roll which they cherish with jealous care, and for which they claim a great antiquity.[2] Their version of the Law differs from the current Hebrew text in numerous details, but variants of real material importance are comparatively few.[3] One instance of particular interest is Dt 27^4 (cf. Jos 8^{30}), where the Samaritan version makes Moses command the building of an altar on Mt. Gerizim, and not on Mt. Ebal, as in the Hebrew. The charge is often made against the Samaritans that they have tampered with the text of the passage[4], but there is even greater likelihood of an alteration of the original reading on the part of the Jews.[5] At the close of the Decalogue in Ex 20^{17} and Dt 5^{21} the present Samaritan text also has an added command to build an altar and offer sacrifices on Mt. Gerizim.

The Samaritans were always extremely punctilious in the observance of the Law. Even their Jewish opponents recognized their excessive zeal regarding certain commandments. Rabbi Simon, the son of Gamaliel, is reported to have said, 'Every command the Samaritans keep, they are more scrupulous in observing than Israel.'[6] The moral side of the Law was emphasized by the Samaritans, and they were less inclined to theoretical speculation regarding its precepts than were the Jews.

(*c*) *Moses*.—Something of the sanctity of the Law itself was made by the Samaritans to attach to Moses, through whom the Law was revealed. He is for them the one incomparable prophet and apostle of God. Their Targum in Dt 34^{10}, by a change of reading, affirms that none shall rise like unto him.[7] None indeed will be needed, for all things were shown to him in the Holy Mount. There appears to be no particular glorification of his death, but the story of his birth was much embellished and at times took a form that implied pre-existence or a unique creation. His efficacy as mediator and intercessor is highly extolled in later liturgies. Doubtless the advances over Jewish tradition in his exaltation are to be attributed in large measure to Christian and Muhammadan influences, but an additional motive may be found in the fact that the Samaritan Bible did not include a prophetic canon. A measure of compensation for this very serious lack was found in thus venerating Moses, not alone as giver of the Law, but also as the full and perfect embodiment of the prophetic ideal. For them the Messiah, the Restorer, was a figure of lesser importance. Abraham likewise did not play the same significant part that was assigned to him in Jewish teaching, and much the same may be said of Aaron, and this too in spite of the dominance of priestly influence among the Samaritans. The patriarchs and early leaders did receive, however, a considerable measure of honour, and there was a doctrine of the merits of the Fathers, as in the case of the Jews.

(*d*) *Mt. Gerizim*.—The claim that Mt. Gerizim was the one rightful centre for the worship of Jahweh continued to be the chief cause of the bitterest strife with the Jews. The issue was clearly stated by the woman of Samaria: 'Our fathers worshipped in this mountain; and ye say, that in Jerusalem is the place where men ought to worship' (Jn 4^{20}). However favourably disposed towards the Samaritans large-minded Jewish teachers might be at times, the claim for the sanctity of Mt. Gerizim always remained an insuperable and divisive dogma.[1] In seeking to substantiate the extravagant claims for this mountain it was possible to point to many sacred associations gathering about its summit and the immediate locality. Abraham, Jacob, and Joshua had worshipped here; the bones of Joseph were buried near at hand; and the Samaritan Scriptures recorded a special command given through Moses to build an altar on this spot.[2] With such a real basis of tradition it was not difficult to devise further sanctions by identifying Gerizim with Bethel, by making it to be the site of the garden of Eden, the place where altars were built by Adam, Seth, and Noah, the spot of Abraham's sacrifice of Isaac, the mountain which was still shadowed by the presence of God, and to which at last the tabernacle was to be restored. Even when its temple had been destroyed, the Samaritans still clung devotedly to its slopes; and, whenever the way was open, they celebrated their chief festivals near the site of their former sanctuary.[3]

(*e*) *The Messiah*.—The expectation of a coming Messiah was doubtless cherished by the Samaritans at an early date, notwithstanding the fact that such a doctrine does not properly fall within the limits of Pentateuchal teachings. While the beginning of the hope is undoubtedly to be attributed to Jewish influence, its later development must have been greatly stimulated by the successive hardships and calamities through which the Samaritans were called to pass. Their Targum is silent on the subject, but we have evidence in Jn 4 for the existence of the belief in definite form in the last Christian century. This testimony is confirmed by the ready response of the Samaritans to the claims of a Messianic pretender in the days of Pontius Pilate.[4] In the 2nd cent. Justin Martyr ascribes Messianic hopes to the Samaritans as well as to the Jews,[5] while in the 4th cent. we have in Marqah testimony to the same fact. The first extended treatment of the subject comes, however, from the 14th cent. and, consequently, after an interval that leaves large opportunity for development; but, even so, the primitive character of the hope is apparent when it is compared with Jewish and Christian views.

The name given by the Samaritans to their Messiah is Taheb, 'Restorer.'[6] His office was to

[1] In reading they substitute for Jahweh 'the Name' (שְׁמָא). The malicious charge that they worshipped a God Ashima (אֲשִׁימָא, 2 K 17^{30}) may possibly have come from this practice (cf. Petermann, *PRE*[1] xiii. 372). Equally false was the claim that the Samaritans had a dove-cult (cf. *ib.*; Montgomery, p. 320 f.). For the great variety of names and titles given to God by the Samaritans, see Montgomery, p. 214 f.

[2] They affirm that it was copied by Abishua, the son of Phinehas, the son of Eleazar, the son of Aaron. This tradition appears first in the 14th cent. (Abu'l Fath), and consequently the MS in question may be somewhat older.

[3] A brief analysis of the Samaritan variants from the Hebrew is given by E. König, *HDB* v. 68–72.

[4] Cf. Montgomery, p. 235.

[5] Cf. Torrey, p. 322 ff.; E. Meyer, *Die Israeliten und ihre Nachbarstämme*, Halle, 1906, p. 545 ff.

[6] Cf. Montgomery, p. 170.

[7] It was held that Dt 18^{15} referred to Joshua alone.

[1] Cf. citation above from *Massekheth Kuthim*, p. 162^b.

[2] Dt 27^4; cf. previous statement and the note regarding the reading.

[3] For a considerable time during the 18th and 19th centuries they were denied all access to the mountain, and the same was doubtless true of earlier periods.

[4] Jos. *Ant.* XVIII. iv. 1–2.

[5] *Apol.* i. 53.

[6] Most probably תהב (תהבה) is derived from the Aramaic root תוב=Heb. שׁוב. For a discussion of the various meanings

bring in for Israel the age of divine favour, and to restore the Tabernacle and its services to Mt. Gerizim. It was expected that he would be of the house of Joseph and that he would live for 110 years. He apparently was not thought of as divine, but ranked in importance below Moses. After his death and burial there was to come a culmination of evil, and, following this, the day of judgment. In due course of time various passages from the Pentateuch were interpreted in such a manner as to support the doctrine of the Taheb.[1]

(*f*) *Angels*.—There are repeated allusions in early Christian writers to Samaritan disbelief in angels.[2] But such statements must be received with caution, since the angelic messengers of the Pentateuch can never have been altogether overlooked. Furthermore, a belief in an order of higher spiritual beings is attested with certainty for the 4th cent. by the first Samaritan literary remains. And this witness is confirmed by their Targum, which often substitutes the mention of an angel for the name of God. Thus it states that man was made in the image of angels, that an angel spake to Moses from the bush, that Enoch was not, for the angels took him. Originally Samaritan teaching on this subject may have been akin to that of the Sadducees, but with the passing years it was doubtless variously modified. It should be added that, while the existence of angels, both good and bad, was an accepted article of belief, these intermediate agents never played the important part with the Samaritans that was assigned to them in later Judaism and Muhammadanism.

(*g*) *Eschatology*.—The Samaritan doctrine of the future is known to us only in its later developments. It is safe to conjecture that the earliest views were identical with those of the least progressive Judaism of the day. There was the expectation of the Great Day of the Lord, a day of vengeance and recompense.[3] Starting with the belief that this was to bring national vindication, they probably advanced, as did the Jews, to the thought of individual reward for the righteous. Such a teaching is found in the 4th cent. in Marqah, who cherishes the hope of the resurrection and the future life. Accordingly, the assertion of early Jewish and Christian writers that the Samaritans were without such a belief is not true for this period, whatever may have been the case earlier. Paradise was usually pictured as a transfigured Gerizim. The wicked, on the other hand, were to be burned with fire. The possibility of repentance after death seems not to have been cut off altogether, at least not for the faithful who may die in their sins, since for such there are prayers of intercession.[4] The Taheb, at his coming, was to usher in a new age of divine favour (*Rachutha*, רחותה or רצון = Arabic *Ridhwan*) and thus bring to an end the present period of God's displeasure (*Fanutha*, פנותה). According to the Samaritans, this had continued from the day when Eli forsook Mt. Gerizim and established a sanctuary at Shiloh, thus inaugurating the schism of the Jews. In general it should be noted that eschatological speculation did not play the important part with the Samaritans that it did with the post-Exilic Jews, especially in their later apocalypses, nor did it ever have the prominent place that it occupies in Muhammadan teaching.

that have been proposed for the name, cf. Cowley, *Exp*, 5th ser., i. 161 ff.; Montgomery, p. 245 ff., and the literature there cited.

1 Cf. Montgomery, p. 247 f.

2 *e.g.*, Epiphanius, *Haer*. ix.

3 יוֹם נָקָם וְשִׁלֵּם (Dt 32[35]). By a change of reading (ליום for לו) this passage was made to support a doctrine of future rewards and punishments. 'Till the Day of Vengeance; till the times when their foot shall slide' (cf. Cowley, *JQR* viii. 569 ff.; Montgomery, p. 240).

4 Cf. Cowley, in *JE* and in *JQR*, *locc. citt.*

(*h*) *Festivals*.—We have no account of the earliest festival observances of the Samaritans, but there is no reason to suppose that there was any radical departure from Jewish practice, not at least in so far as this usage was sanctioned by the Pentateuch (cf. Lv 25). After the destruction of the temple on Mt. Gerizim sacrifices were offered only in connexion with the Passover. For a considerable time the Samaritans have been wont to keep this festival on a little plot of ground which they have been able to acquire some distance below and to the west of the summit of the mountain where their temple once stood. Here they encamp with elaborate equipment and in much comfort for the celebration of the Passover and the feast of unleavened bread. No longer do they fear the enemies that formerly made such a protracted sojourn dangerous. Seven lambs have usually been sacrificed in recent years. After having been offered and dressed with due ceremony, they are roasted for several hours in a heated pit and then are hastily eaten with unleavened bread and bitter herbs. All bones and remnants, together with the utensils that have been used in the service, are straightway burned. Everything is supposed to be done in exact accordance with the requirements of the Law (Ex 12).[1]

The feast of Pentecost was kept as the anniversary of the giving of the Law. The solemn fast of the Day of Atonement was observed with greater strictness than by the Jews. Not even children under seven were exempted from this fast, but only nursing infants. Conversation was forbidden, and from sunrise to sunset the day was spent in fasting, vigil, and the reading of the Pentateuch and the liturgy.[2] In connexion with the major celebrations of the Passover of Unleavened Bread, Pentecost, and Tabernacles, there were sacred processions up Mt. Gerizim whenever this was possible. Special liturgical services, made up largely of citations from the Pentateuch, were elaborated in the course of time for these and for lesser occasions.

The sacredness of the Sabbath seems always to have been rigorously guarded by the Samaritans. They allowed no Sabbath day's journey or kindred exceptions, but remained at home except for attendance at the synagogue. The Law was portioned out for reading at their Sabbath services in such a way as to include the whole Pentateuch during the year.[3]

(*i*) *The priesthood*.—The central importance of the priesthood among the Samaritans is noteworthy. It appears that from earliest times the high priest and those associated with him have dominated the community. It is said that in 1623–24 successors in the line of Aaron died out, and that since that time the office has been filled by those who are sprung from the tribe of Levi, being descended from the house of Uzziel, son of Kohath. In later days, at least, the Samaritan calendar was calculated semi-annually by the high priest for an ensuing period of six months, and was delivered to the people at two assemblies (צִמּוּת) held 60 days before the first of Nisan and the first of Tishri respectively.[4] On these occasions the half-shekel prescribed by the Law (Ex 30[13f.]) was supposed to be paid to the high priest. These payments, together with the tithes, made up the major part of his very slender income.[5]

6. Writings.—(*a*) *Pentateuch*.—The Samaritan Pentateuch was known to early Jewish and Christian writers, but later

1 Among the earlier accounts of the Passover ceremony that by the German Orientalist Petermann is particularly valuable. He was present in 1853, and has recorded his observations in *Reisen im Orient*, Leipzig, 1860, i. 260–292, and in *PRE*[1] xiii. 378 ff. The present writer has described the Passover of 1903 in *JBL* xxii. [1903] pt. ii. 187–194, and in *ZDPV* xvii. [1904] 194. For recent articles of importance see *Palästinajahrbuch*, viii. [Berlin, 1913], ed. G. Dalman.

2 *PRE*[1] xiii. 382.

3 *JQR* vii. 134–140.

4 *PRE*[1] xiii. 382; *JQR* vii. 127.

5 *PRE*[1] xiii. 382.

seems to have been altogether overlooked, until it was rediscovered and brought to the attention of the modern world by Pietro della Valle in 1616. It is written in the Hebrew language and with a script resembling the most ancient Hebrew characters. The urgent need of a critical text is now at last being supplied by the splendid edition of August Freiherr von Gall.[1] There are some indications of the existence of an early Greek version of the Samaritan Pentateuch, but no MSS of such a translation are known to survive.

The paraphrase of the Pentateuch in the vernacular Aramaic known as the Samaritan Targum is doubtless of a very early date, although we have no reliable information as to its beginning. Quite possibly it may go back ultimately to the same traditional oral Aramaic rendering as is represented in the Jewish Targum of Onqelos.[2] Its aim was to reproduce the original Hebrew text with a slavish literalness, and consequently the study of the Targum has not thus far yielded any considerable results for Samaritan teaching. The language of the work is important because it represents the particular form of the Aramaic dialect that was in current use among the Samaritans in the period of their greatest vigour. Their earliest and most important surviving literary productions are written in this language, which, however, differed but little from other dialects of Palestinian Aramaic.[3] An edition of this Targum was begun by Petermann and subsequently completed by C. Vollers.[4]

Under Muslim supremacy, with the passing of the Aramaic vernacular, the Targum was superseded by an Arabic version of the Pentateuch which recent investigators have concluded dates from the 11th century. This, too, is marked by a painstaking adherence to the original Hebrew.

(*b*) *Commentaries*.[5]—Of the expository and controversial literature of the Samaritans very little has survived, and what exists is, for the most part, in MS form. A Midrāshic work of Marqah in Samaritan Aramaic, belonging probably to the 4th cent. A.D., treats of a variety of topics and of Scriptural passages that were of particular interest to the author. Of the later commentaries in Arabic that by Ibrahim ibn Yaqub (15th or 16th cent.) on the first four books of the Pentateuch is the most important.

(*c*) *Liturgies*.—Doubtless the most significant feature of the worship of the Samaritans was always the reading of the Law. To this there came to be added at an early date the use of prayers, hymns, and responses, made up in large measure of Scriptural phrases. The earliest existing collection of such material is the *Defter* ('the Book,' Arab. دَفْتَر, Gr. διφθέρα), which dates from the 4th cent. and consists for the most part of compositions of Marqah and of a certain Amram, who was probably his father.[6] The language is Aramaic, and this dialect continues to be used for liturgical compositions down to the 14th cent., when it is superseded by a decadent form of Hebrew. During the 11th and 12th centuries the *Defter* was extended by the inclusion of later prayers and hymns, and the same thing took place again in the 14th century. In the last-named period the new developments in the liturgy were due to the inspiring influence of Phinehas ben Joseph (1308–63). Special services for the several feasts and fasts were now arranged, and, with various modifications and elaborations, they have continued to be used down to the present time. In all this progress the influence of Jewish teaching and practice is clearly discernible.[7]

(*d*) *Chronicles*.—As historical records the Samaritan Chronicles have little value. They are relatively late, vague, and contradictory, but it is possible that they have preserved at times older sources.[8] An Arabic book of Joshua covering the period from the last days of Moses to the 4th cent. is thought to be a compilation going back to the 13th century.[9] There is a Chronicle called *El-tholideh* (*Et-taulideh*) which was begun by Eleazar ben Amram in the 12th cent. (1149–50), continued by Jacob ben Ishmael, a priest of Damascus, in the 14th cent. (1346–47), and brought down to modern times, probably by Jacob ben Aaron in 1859–60.[10] It is written in Samaritan Hebrew, with an Arabic translation, and covers the period from Adam to the present. Its most valuable feature is the statement of each successive writer regarding the genealogy of the high priests and leading Samaritan families of his day.

[1] Giessen, 1914; three parts, including Gen., Ex., and Lev., have thus far been received in America.
[2] So Cowley, *JE* x. 677. [3] Cf. Kautzsch, *PRE*³ xvii. 438.
[4] *Pentateuchus Samaritanus*, Berlin, 1872–91.
[5] Cf. Cowley, *JE* x. 677 f.; Montgomery, pp. 294–297.
[6] A full collection of liturgical texts, ed. Cowley, was published in two vols. by the Clarendon Press in 1909. The introduction describes the MSS used, and collects the known facts regarding the several authors of liturgical compositions, together with genealogical tables. There is also a glossary of the Aramaic texts and grammatical notes supplementing the treatment of Petermann in his *Brevis Linguæ Samaritanæ Grammatica*, forming pt. iii. of the *Porta Linguarum Orientalium* (Leipzig, 1873).
[7] Cf. Cowley, *The Samaritan Liturgy*, ii. pp. xx–xxv, *JQR* vii. 121 ff.
[8] Cf. Montgomery, p. 308 ff.
[9] T. G. J. Juynboll, *Chronicon Samaritanum . . . cui titulus est Liber Josuæ*, Leyden, 1848; O. T. Crane, *The Samaritan Chronicle or the Book of Joshua*, New York, 1890.
[10] Published by A. Neubauer, in *JA*, 1869, p. 385, and Heidenheim, *Vierteljahrsschrift*, iv. [1871] 347 ff.

The *Chronicle* of Abu'l Fath is one of the fruits of the renaissance of the 14th century. It is written in Arabic and is compiled from earlier sources. The original author brought his account down to the time of Muslim supremacy, and in some MSS there are continuations by later hands.[1]

The *Chronicle Adler*, so named from its publisher, was compiled in Hebrew from earlier sources in 1900.[2]

(*e*) *Letters*.—Finally, mention should be made of the correspondence that has been carried on between the Samaritans and European scholars during the last 300 years. Two letters, one from Shechem and one from a Samaritan in Cairo, were sent to Joseph Scaliger in the year 1589 in response to inquiries previously made by him.[3] In the next century Samaritan letters were received by Robert Huntington, afterwards bishop of Raphoe, and by Hiob Ludolf, the German Orientalist, while in the 19th cent. there was a particularly valuable correspondence with de Sacy. Within the last half century less important letters have been sent, among others to Kautzsch, Cowley, and Montgomery.[4]

LITERATURE.—Many of the more important works have been mentioned throughout the article. A full Samaritan bibliography is given by J. A. Montgomery, *The Samaritans, the Earliest Jewish Sect: their History, Theology and Literature*, Philadelphia, 1907, pp. 322–346; cf. also A. E. Cowley, *EBi* iv. 4264 f., *JE* x. 681; J. H. Petermann, *Reisen im Orient*, Leipzig, 1860, i. 233 ff., 260 ff.; *PRE*¹ xiii. 359–391; J. Mills, *Three Months' Residence at Nablus, and an Account of the Modern Samaritans*, London, 1864; J. W. Nutt, *Fragments of a Samaritan Targum, edited from a Bodleian Manuscript, with an Introd. containing a Sketch of Samaritan Hist., Dogma, and Literature*, do. 1874; M. Heidenheim, in *Deutsche Vierteljahrsschrift für englisch-theologische Forschung und Kritik*, i. [1864]–iv. [1871]; L. Wreschner, *Samaritanische Traditionen mitgeteilt und nach ihrer geschichtl. Entwickelung untersucht*, Berlin, 1888; I. Taglicht, *Die Kuthäer als Beobachter des Gesetzes nach talmudischen Quellen nebst Berücksichtigung der samaritanischen Correspondenz und Liturgie*, Erlangen, 1888; A. E. Cowley, *The Samaritan Liturgy*, 2 vols., Oxford, 1909; *JE*, *EBi*, and *EBr*¹¹, *s.v.* 'Samaritans'; *JQR* vii. [1894] 121 ff., viii. [1896] 562 ff., xvi. [1904] 474 ff.; *Exp*, 5th ser., i. [1895] 161 ff.; E. Kautzsch, *PRE*³, *s.v.* 'Samaritaner'; C. C. Torrey, *Ezra Studies*, Chicago, 1910.

WARREN J. MOULTON.

SAMBATYON (or SABBATION).—The Sambatyon, a mythical river which, according to some narratives, runs on six days and rests on the seventh, and, according to others, runs only every seventh day, is mentioned in several of the mediæval Lost Ten Tribes legends. Its situation varies from Caucasia in the north to Arabia in the south, and from India and even China in the east to Ethiopia in the west. The river, although it had then no mystical or Ten Tribes associations, is first mentioned by Josephus.

'It runs in the middle between Arcea, belonging to Agrippa's kingdom, and Raphanea . . . when it runs, its current is strong, and has plenty of water; after which its springs fail for six days together, and leave its channel dry, as any one may see; after which days it runs on the seventh day as it did before, and as though it had undergone no change at all; it hath also been observed to keep this order perpetually and exactly: whence it is that they call it *the Sabbatic river*, the name being taken from the sacred seventh day among the Jews.'[5]

Pliny[6] also mentions the river, but in his account it runs on six days and rests on the seventh. It was in the latter character that Rabbi Aḳibah referred to it as evidence of the sanctity of the Sabbath.

In the Middle Ages the river was frequently mentioned in the writings of Christians and Arabs as well as of the rabbis, and apparently there was a wide-spread belief in its existence. It was closely interwoven in the legends of Prester John (*q.v.*), and in fact it was practically impossible to accept the authenticity of that potentate without

[1] E. Vilmar, *Abulfathi Annales Samaritani*, Gotha, 1865; R. Payne Smith, *The Samaritan Chronicle of Abu'l Fatah*, in Heidenheim, *Vierteljahrsschrift*, ii. [1866] 303 ff., 431 ff.
[2] E. N. Adler and M. Séligsohn, 'Une nouvelle Chronique samaritaine,' *REJ* xliv. [1902] 188 ff., xlv. [1902] 70 ff., 223 ff., xlvi. [1903] 123 ff., and reprint, Paris, 1903. The text is accompanied by a good French tr., together with notes.
[3] Cf. Petermann, *PRE*¹ xiii. 371.
[4] Some of the earlier letters were published, with tr., in J. G. Eichhorn, *Repertorium für biblische und morgenländische Litteratur*, Leipzig, 1777–86, xiii. 257 ff., 277 ff. Later correspondence is included in *Notices et extraits des manuscrits de la Bibliothèque du Roi*, xii. [1831] 1–235, under the title *Correspondance des Samaritains de Naplouse pendant les années 1808 et suivant*. For additional literature, cf. Montgomery, p. 6 ff.
[5] *BJ* VII. v. 1. [6] *HN* xxxi. 2 (18).

accepting that of the river also. Eldad Hadani, who visited Europe in the 9th cent., coming, as he said, from the Lost Ten Tribes who were settled in Asia, gave the legend renewed and fortified currency in Jewish circles. According to Eldad's account, the river surrounded the Sons of Moses, a tribe of Levites, and separated their territories from the tribes of Dan, Naphtali, Gad, and Asher, who dwelt in the land of Cush. It was full of sand and stones, but had little water.

'The stones make a great noise like the waves of the sea and a stormy wind, so that in the night the noise is heard at a distance of half a day's journey . . . and this river of stone and sand rolls during the six working days and rests on the Sabbath-day. As soon as the Sabbath begins, fire surrounds the river, and the flames remain till the next evening, when the Sabbath ends. Thus no human being can reach the river for a distance of half a mile on either side; the fire consumes all that grows there.'[1]

Prester John places the river in India.

'Know that from the stone-sea flows a river, which comes from Paradise, passing between us and the great country of the mighty Daniel, king of the Jews. This river flows all the week-days, but remains quiet on the Sabbath-day. When full, this river carries a great quantity of precious stones, consequently no one can pass it except on the Sabbath.'[2]

In another account, the letter to the Emperor Frederick, it is stated:

'On one side of our country is a river, on the border of which all kinds of excellent spices are found. Near to it is another river, full of stones, which falls into the ocean which flows between the sea and the Nine Tribes of Israel. This river runs all the week till the Sabbath-day, when it rests; it carries large and small stones to the sea, like a river of water does; consequently the Nine Tribes of Israel cannot pass the river.'[3]

The Italian-Jewish traveller, Obadiah di Bertinoro, writing in 1489, mentioned, on the authority of some Muhammadan traders, that the river was to be found at a distance of fifty days' journey inland from Aden, where it separated the territories of the Children of Moses from other Jewish tribes.

'This river rolls stones all the week-days and rests only during the Sabbath-day; it is therefore impossible for any Jew to go there without profaning the Sabbath.'[4]

Obadiah learnt from another source that Prester John had entirely defeated the Jewish tribes. A few decades earlier, however, a report was current in Jerusalem to the effect that the Sambatyon had dried up and that the Jewish tribes had crossed and had attacked Prester John. Abraham Farissol (1451–1525 ?), the Italian-Jewish scholar and geographer, identified the Sambatyon and also the river of Gozan (2 K 17[6]) with the Ganges, which he believed separated the Indians from the Jews. He placed Prester John also in that region. Abraham Yagel, another Italian-Jewish scholar (16th and 17th centuries), held similar views. Quoting unpublished letters of Maimonides, he said:

'As to your question concerning the Ten Tribes, know ye that their existence is quite certain, and we expect daily their arrival from the dark mountains, the river of Gozan, and the river Sambatyon, places where now they are hidden away. This river flows all the week-days, and rests on the Sabbath. Indeed in the time of my learned and pious grandfather, a bottle was brought filled with the sand of this river, which sand was in movement the six days, and rested on the Sabbath. This is a true fact, for more persons have seen it with their own eyes.'[5]

Yagel mentioned the Sambatyon on several occasions in the course of his writings. He quoted a Christian, named Vincenzo Milano, who said that he had spent twenty-five years as a prisoner of the Turks and in the course of his journeys with them had visited the river.

In his account the river 'is full of water all the week-days, so strong that it rolls along great stones and a quantity of sand, so that no ship dare venture upon it; but on Friday towards sunset, the river rests, and becomes quite dry, so that a child can cross it. It is said that the river is in some places one and a half, three and four miles broad . . . ships which venture on it lose their way; indeed no ship is yet known to have returned safely from this river.'[1]

In the year 1630 a Jerusalem Jew, Rabbi Baruch, is said to have found himself in the neighbourhood of the river and to have been given a letter from the Children of Moses and neighbouring Jewish tribes to be delivered in Jerusalem. There seems no reason to doubt that a letter purporting to come from the Lost Tribes did exist, for there is considerable evidence to that effect, but regarding its authenticity there is much room for doubt. Baruch's account of the Sambatyon agrees with that of Eldad Hadani.

Manasseh ben Israel repeated in his *Hope of Israel* most of the statements that had previously been made regarding the Sambatyon, in whose existence he believed. He added that a book on the subject was written by two Polish Jews in the year 1634, but was at the instigation of the Jesuits ordered by the senate at Breslau to be burnt. Manasseh also tells a story of a glass of Sambatyon sand being mysteriously agitated. He quotes his father as his authority.

'He told me there was an Arabian at Lisbon, who had such an hour-glass: and that every Friday at evening he would walk in the street called the New Street, and show this glass to Jews who counterfeited Christianity and say, "Ye Jews, shut up your shops, for now the Sabbath comes." Another worthy of credit told me of another hour-glass, which he had some years before, before the Port Mysketa. The Cadi, or Judge of that place, saw him by chance passing that way, and asked him what it was. He commanded it to be taken away, rebuking the Mahomedans that, by this, they did confirm the Jewish Sabbath.'[2]

As late as 1847 one hears of the existence of the river Sambatyon, on the authority of the governor of Aden. In that year a messenger from Tiberias arrived at Aden on a journey in search of assistance for the Jews of the Holy Land. The governor is reported to have advised him to visit the great Jewish kingdom some forty days' journey inland from Aden, the discovery of which, he stated, he had reported to London. The discovery of that great and wealthy kingdom, the governor added, had converted him to the belief in the advent of the Messiah and the return of the kingdom to Israel. But Sambatyon was not there. The governor added that there was another Jewish kingdom in China and that there the river Sambatyon was to be found.

LITERATURE.—A. Neubauer, 'Where are the Ten Tribes?' *JQR* i. [1889] *passim*; M. Seligsohn, art. 'Sambation,' in *JE*; I. Abrahams, art. 'Sabbation,' in *EBr*[11]; Manasseh ben Israel, *The Hope of Israel*, Eng. tr., London, 1650; David Kaufmann, 'Le Sambation,' in *REJ* xxii. [1891] 285 ff.

ALBERT M. HYAMSON.

SĀMMITĪYAS.[3]—Details as to the position of this sect in the development of the Buddhist Church are given in the so-called 'genealogies of the sects,' found in the *Kathāvatthu*[4] and in several Tibetan sources.[5] They are conflicting. Two points are ascertained: (1) the Sāṁmitīyas were a branch of the Vātsīputrīyas and were sometimes styled 'Vātsīputrīya-Sāṁmitīyas';[6] (2) they constituted, in the days of Yuan Chwang, one of the most important sections of the Saṅgha.[7] They

1 See Eldad Ha-Dani's *Diary*, printed by A. Jellinek, in *Beth ha-Midrasch*, Leipzig, 1853-78, pt. v. pp. 17–21; also *JQR* i. [1889] 102.

2 *Sammelband* of the Meqiṣa Nirdamim, Berlin, 1889, iii. 14.

3 *Ib.* iii. 19.

4 *Jahrbücher für die Gesch. der Juden und des Judenthums*, iii. [1863] 222.

5 *Sammelband*, iv. 37 f.; and G. Oppert, *Der Presbyter Johannes in Sage und Geschichte*, Berlin, 1864, p. 18.

1 *Sammelband*, iv. 42.

2 *The Hope of Israel*, p. 27.

3 See *Madhyamakavṛtti*, p. 148; *Dīpavaṁsa*, v. 46, has Sammiti; the forms Sammitiya and Sammatīya are also known. The Tibetan *maṅ pos bkur pa*, or *kun gyis bkur pa*, means 'honoured by many,' 'honoured by all'; for Chinese equivalents see Wassilieff, *Buddhismus*, Petrograd, 1860, p. 231.

4 Tr. in S. Z. Aung and C. A. F. Rhys Davids, *Points of Controversy* (*PTS*), London, 1915.

5 Vasumitra, in Wassilieff, *Buddhismus*; Bhavya, in W. W. Rockhill, *Life of the Buddha*, London, 1884; Tāranātha, *Gesch. des Buddhismus in Indien*, Petrograd, 1869, pp. 175, 271. See the summaries of H. Kern, *Hist. du Bouddhisme dans l'Inde*, tr. G. Huet, 2 vols., Paris, 1901, and cf. C. A. F. Rhys Davids, *Points of Controversy*, preface; see also art. SECTS (Buddhist).

6 *Abhidharmakośavyākhyā*, MS Burnouf, fol. 473.

7 See T. Watters, *On Yuan Chwang's Travels in India*, London, 1905, *passim*.

were both a sect and a school; *i.e.*, they had a special rule of discipline—viz. as concerns the undergarment, the girdle, remedies, and beds[1]—and they maintained a number of philosophical tenets. Many of these tenets were admitted by the schools (not sects) of a later age—the Vaibhāṣikas, *e.g.*—and also by some of the old sects.

Of the views of the Sāṁmitīyas[2] the following seem worthy of notice. (1) An *arhat*, *i.e.* a saint already in possession of *nirvāṇa*, a *jīvanmukta* (*q.v.*), can fall away; this opinion was common; its importance has been emphasized and exaggerated by J. P. Minayeff.[3] (2) There is an 'intermediate state' (*antarābhava*); *i.e.*, the dying consciousness creates a shortlived being which finds the right matrix where the dead being is reborn—a view shared by many sects (Vaibhāṣikas, Tāntrikas).[4] (3) As concerns *karman*, (*a*) there is a *paribhogānvaya puṇya* distinct from the *tyāgānvaya puṇya*; *i.e.*, while there is a merit in giving (*tyāga*), there is also a merit accruing to the giver by the use (*bhoga*) which a monk makes of the object given;[5] (*b*) the 'orthodox' strictly understood morality as 'abstaining from (killing, etc.)' (*virati*); but the 'declaration' (*vijñapti*) by which a monk binds himself under the obligation of non-killing, etc., is also a moral act; (*c*) such a *vijñapti* creates the kind of action that is styled *avijñapti*;[6] independently of any further mental action, a man who has 'declared' that he will not kill, etc., goes on accumulating merit.[7] (4) The most important tenet of the Sāṁmitīya creed (and of the Vātsīputrīya creed) is the *pudgalavāda*, the belief in a *pudgala*, a sort of person or soul. Whereas the other tenets of the school are the common property of many sects, the *pudgalavāda* is severely criticized by all the non-Sāṁmitīyas (or non-Vātsīputrīyas) and appears as a form of *satkāyadṛṣṭi* or *śāsvatadṛṣṭi*, belief in permanence, belief in *ātman*—a view obviously condemned by Śākyamuni and the scriptures of every sect without exception.[8]

According to the *Kathāvatthu*, the chief scriptural authorities of the Sāṁmitīyas are a number of texts[9] which point to the existence of some transmigrating entity; the Sanskrit sources, including Uddyotakara,[10] lay the stress of the discussion on the *Bhārahārasūtra*,[11] 'the *sūtra* of the burden-bearer,' which describes the *pudgala* as a 'bearer.' In short, the five *skandhas* (the physical and intellectual 'constituents' of the Ego) are the burden; to desire (*tṛṣṇā*, 'thirst') is to shoulder the burden; to give up desire is to lay down the burden; the bearer is the *pudgala*—*e.g.*, 'this monk, of such a name, of such a family, living on such food, living so many years.' Now, is it not clear that the bearer (*pudgala*) is not the burden (*skandhas*), that there is an Ego independent of the so-called 'constituents' of the Ego? Thus say the Sāṁmitīyas. But the answer is at hand: 'The desire, owing to which the *pudgala* shoulders a new burden at each new birth, is evidently a part of the burden itself.' The simile therefore is not to be understood strictly.

While they maintain that the *pudgala* is different from the *skandhas*, the Sāṁmitīyas admit that the *pudgala* is not non-different from the *skandhas*; technically the *pudgala* is 'indescribable' (*avāchya*); it cannot be described either as different or as non-different from the *skandhas*.[1] A favourite argument is the attitude of Buddha to the so-called 'unsettled question,' Is the living principle or soul (*jīva*) the body or not?[2] Buddha condemns both alternatives; he admits the existence of a *jīva*, but refuses to state the relations of the *jīva* with the body. The 'orthodox' answer is that a thing which cannot be described as different or non-different (*sattvānyatva*) is really no thing. No answer can be given to the question, Are the fruits of the mango-trees in the palace of Milinda sweet or bitter?, because there are no mango-trees in the palace of Milinda.[3] In the same way there is no *pudgala* or soul (*jīva*):[4] its 'undenotability' establishes its non-existence.

The present writer believes that the position of the Sāṁmitīyas is a good and truly Buddhistic one. If we try to state it in plain language, we should say that the relation of the *pudgala* to the *skandhas* is like the relation of the whole (*avayavin*) to its part (*avayava*). The Sāṁmitīyas do not maintain that there is a soul existing *in se* apart from the *skandhas*—just as there is no whole apart from its parts, no cloth apart from its threads—but they say that a man is something more than a collection of *skandhas*: he is a *pudgala*, 'a monk of such name, of such family, living so many years.' All these characters, while they belong to the whole, do not belong to the parts or to the constituents; the whole is made up of parts, but it is lacking neither in unity nor in continuity. The *pudgala* cannot be said to be transitory (*anitya*), like the *skandhas*, since it transmigrates, laying down the burden (*skandhas*), shouldering a new burden; it cannot be said to be permanent (*nitya*), since it is made of transitory constituents. The orthodox say that there are parts (threads), but not a whole (a cloth); that there is a series (*saṁtāna*) of states of consciousness, but not a 'serial entity' (*saṁtānin*); and the orthodox are right so far; but are the Sāṁmitīyas wrong when they choose to style *saṁtānin* the very processus (*saṁtāna*) of states of consciousness?

The only known treatise where the views of the Sāṁmitīyas are explained by themselves is the *Sāṁmitīyaśāstra* or *Sāṁmitīyanikāyaśāstra*, a book translated into Chinese between A.D. 350 and 431.[5] Until it has been studied, we are dependent upon the statements of the 'orthodox.' It is worth while to remark that they recognize that 'the doctrine of *pudgala* has been taught by Buddha.'[6]

LITERATURE.—See the works quoted in the footnotes.

L. DE LA VALLÉE POUSSIN.

---

1 See I-tsing, *A Record of the Buddhist Religion*, tr. J. Takakusu, Oxford, 1896, pp. 7, 66, 140; on the geographical repartition of the sect see preface, p. xxiv.

2 The tables of C. A. F. Rhys Davids (*op. cit.*) are excellent; see also Wassilieff, pp. 252, 257 (*Saṁkrāntivādin*); Rockhill, p. 193; *Madhyamakavṛtti*, p. 148 (a curious theory on the fourteenfold *parivāra*: production of production, etc.).

3 *Recherches sur le bouddhisme*, tr. R. H. Assier de Pompignan, Paris, 1894, ch. ix., 'Les Doctrines hérétiques.' The schools which maintain that an *arhat* may fall agree that he will in any case recover his state before dying (*Abhidharmakośa*, ch. vi.).

4 See L. de la Vallée Poussin, *The Way to Nirvāṇa*, Cambridge, 1917, p. 83, *JA* ii. [1902] 295; *Abhidharmakośa*, ch. iii.

5 See *Madhyamakavṛtti*, p. 309 f., and *Kathāvatthu*, vii. 5.

6 xv. 11.

7 See artt. KARMA and RELIGIOUS ORDERS (Indian); those three opinions are held by the Vaibhāṣikas.

8 Accordingly the Vātsīputrīya-Sāṁmitīyas are styled *antaścharatīrthika*, 'infidels within the church' (*Bodhicharyāvatāra*, ix. 60, *fin.*).

9 *Itivuttaka*, § 24; *Saṁyutta*, iii. 149; *Petavatthu*, iv. 7. 3; *Majjhima*, i. 482; *Aṅguttara*, ii. 97.

10 *Nyāyavārttika*, p. 342.

11 *Saṁyutta*, iii. 25, tr. H. C. Warren, *Buddhism in Translation*, Cambridge, Mass., 1900, p. 159, and E. Burnouf, *Introd. à l'hist. du buddhisme indien*, Paris, 1844, p. 507; see *JA* ii. [1902] 266; *JRAS*, 1901, pp. 308, 573 (notes by the present writer and E. Hardy); also A. Barth, *The Religions of India*, Eng. tr., London, 1882, p. 112; Minayeff, *Recherches*, p. 225.

1 See *Bodhicharyāvatārapañjikā*, ad ix. 60, *fin.*; *Madhyamakavṛtti*, pp. 64, n. 3, 192, 283, n. 4, 529; *Madhyamakāvatāra*, vi. 146; Bhavya, *ap.* Rockhill, p. 194; Vasumitra, *ap.* Wassilieff, p. 252.

2 See art. AGNOSTICISM (Buddhist).

3 From the Northern *Milindapaṇha*, as quoted in *Abhidharmakośabhāṣya*; see S. Lévi, *CAIBL*, 1893, p. 232.

4 *Madhyamakavṛtti*, p. 389 (the five 'things' which do not exist).

5 See B. Nanjio, *Catalogue of the Chinese Translation of the Buddhist Tripiṭaka*, Oxford, 1883, no. 272.

6 See *Madhyamakavṛtti*, pp. 248, 276, 357.

SAMOA.—See POLYNESIA.

SAMOSATENISM.—It was apparently in A.D. 260 that Paul, a native of Samosata and a *protégé* of Zenobia, queen of Palmyra,[1] succeeded Demetrianus as bishop of Antioch. He had the title of *ducenarius*, from which it may be inferred that along with his bishopric he held high office under Odenathus and Zenobia and was probably governor of Antioch. Not long after his elevation to the episcopate his mode of life and his unorthodox teaching began to cause scandal. A contemporary description of him, taken from an encyclical letter of the Synod of Antioch, to which reference will be made below, is still preserved.[2] It may be exaggerated in detail, but it cannot be wholly misleading.

In that document it is asserted that Paul, though in his youth he had been poor, and though he had neither inherited property nor prospered in business, had amassed great wealth by acts of sacrilege (ἱεροσυλιῶν) and by extortion and deceit. He was vain, ostentatious, and fond of notoriety, preferring the title of *ducenarius* to that of bishop, attending to his correspondence as he walked in public, surrounded by his guards, and preceded and followed by crowds. Even in ecclesiastical assemblies (σύνοδοι) he must have his bema and lofty throne and *secretum*, like the rulers of the world; and in his discourses he used violent gesticulations and demanded uproarious applause, as if he were in a theatre. Moreover, he made insulting attacks on the Biblical interpreters of former days, bragging of himself as a sophist. He put a stop to the customary psalms addressed to the Lord Jesus Christ, calling them modern compositions, and had psalms sung to himself by women in the midst of the church on Easter Day. He did not forbid his adulators to describe him, even in his presence, as an angel from heaven—conduct all the more blasphemous because he denied that the Saviour Himself came down from heaven. He had in his household women who at Antioch were called *subintroductæ* (συνείσακτοι), of whom two accompanied him wherever he went. He also connived at similar practices among his clergy, though some had thereby fallen into sin, that he might bind them to himself. And he lived in luxury and surfeiting.

It seems that in Antioch at this period there was a perpetual synod of bishops, priests, and deacons, somewhat resembling the σύνοδος ἐνδημοῦσα of a later date in Constantinople.

That there was a synod in constant session at Antioch seems to be implied by Eus. *HE* VI. xlvi. 3, VII. xxvii. 2. In each of these passages reference is made to 'the synod,' though there is no previous statement that such an assembly had been convened. The synod apparently consisted of such bishops of neighbouring cities and provinces as might be in Antioch, together with a smaller number of priests and deacons.[3] That it was a fluctuating body may be inferred from the words of Eusebius,[4] πάντων οὖν κατὰ καιροὺς διαφόρως καὶ πολλάκις ἐπὶ ταὐτὸ συνιόντων, κτλ. And the inference is supported by the varying numbers of bishops who were present on different occasions. Six wrote a letter to Paul,[5] seventy or eighty voted for his deposition, and between ten and fourteen were responsible for the encyclical epistle which announced it to the Church. These facts give probability to the hypothesis that the epistle was drawn up some time after the condemnation of Paul, when many of those who concurred in it had left Antioch. Further, 'the synod' was actually engaged on the business of Paul for a considerable period. The proceedings against him began before Eusebius, the deacon of Alexandria, became bishop of Laodicea, and lasted till after his death.[6] In his *Chronicle* Eusebius makes the interval between those events five years (273–278). This may be correct, though his dates are too late; there is at any rate no ground for assuming that the episcopate of Eusebius of Laodicea was short. Helenus of Tarsus presided over the synod on two occasions. We may perhaps infer that the bishop of Antioch was not the normal president; for Harnack's explanation that on the first occasion the see was vacant[1] is scarcely tenable: Dionysius of Alexandria seems to have been invited to the synod by the letter in which he was informed that Demetrianus had been elected bishop.[2] In times of special difficulty bishops from distant places were summoned to the assistance of the synod,[3] though the decrees actually ran in the name of the local members.[4] It is clear that Eusebius used the word σύνοδος in this context not only for the council as a permanent body, but also for its frequent meetings.[5] One of these was no doubt the 'final synod'[6]—*i.e.* the meeting at which a final decision was reached—though we need not suppose that it was the last which concerned itself with Paul. As we have seen, the encyclical epistle was probably later.

It was natural that Paul's improprieties should be discussed by this synod; but the irregularity of his conduct was soon overshadowed by the unorthodox teaching attributed to him, with which some of his malpractices had an obvious connexion. Accordingly, about the year 264 the synod called to its aid some eminent bishops, among the rest Firmilian of Cappadocia and Dionysius of Alexandria. Dionysius, now old and infirm, contented himself with writing a letter to the church of Antioch expressing his opinion on the questions at issue. Firmilian attended twice and condemned Paul's doctrine. Through his influence, however, Paul having promised to recant, decisive measures were postponed. But the promise was not fulfilled, and matters at last came to a head. Apparently the fresh proceedings began with the presentation to Paul of a statement of belief by six bishops, with a request that he would inform them whether he assented to it.[7] Subsequently a disputation was held between Paul and a presbyter named Malchion, who was head of the Greek school at Antioch. This disputation was reduced to writing by stenographers. Finally, the synod, including seventy[8] or eighty[9] bishops, deposed and excommunicated Paul and elected Domnus to succeed him in the episcopate. These facts were communicated to the Church throughout the empire in the encyclical already mentioned, which was addressed primarily to the bishops of Rome and Alexandria. It reported the opinions of the heresiarch at considerable length. St. Jerome tells us[10] that it was written by Malchion; and it was certainly based, to a large extent, on the speeches made by him in the course of the disputation. The *Acta Disputationis* and the letter of Dionysius referred to above were enclosed with it.

The principal dates may be determined thus. The epistle of the synod was addressed to Dionysius of Rome and Maximus of Alexandria. It must therefore have been dispatched before the death of the former (26th Dec. 268) had been reported at Antioch. We may assume that the deposition, which was somewhat earlier, took place in 268 at the latest. Eusebius in his *History* wrongly places it under Aurelian; in the *Chronicle* he assigns it to the year 265–266. Paul is unlikely to have been appointed bishop before 260, when Antioch fell into the hands of Odenathus. As his episcopate is said to have lasted eight years,[11] we may therefore infer that it began in 260, and that he was deposed in 268. The proceedings against Paul began before the death of Dionysius of Alexandria (12 Gallienus, the year ending Sept. 265);[12] but the date cannot be fixed more accurately than between 260 and the early part of 265. His expulsion obviously occurred while Aurelian was in Antioch in 272.

Fortunately sayings of Paul are still extant in sufficient number to enable us to reconstruct his system of doctrine in its main lines without having recourse to the unsupported statements of his enemies. It may be summarized as follows.

He held a Monarchianist doctrine of the God-

1 Athan. *Hist. Arian.* 71.
2 Eus. *HE* VII. xxx. 7–14.
3 Eus. *HE* VII. xxviii. 1, xxx. 2; note that at least the first ten of the sixteen named in the latter passage were bishops and at least the last two of lower rank.
4 *Ib.* VII. xxviii. 2.
5 Routh, *Rel. Sac.*[2] iii. 289.
6 *HE* VII. xxxii. 5, 21.

1 *Chronologie*, i. 215.
2 Eus. *HE* VI. xlvi. 3, 4.
3 παρακαλεῖσθαι (*ib.* VI. xlvi. 3, VII. xxvii. 2, xxx. 3); but καλέω of a neighbouring bishop (VII. xxxii. 21). The deacon Eusebius does not seem to have been summoned (VII. xxxii. 5); he may have been sent by Dionysius of Alexandria.
4 *Ib.* VII. xxx. 2.
5 *Ib.* VII. xxviii. 2, xxix. 1; cf. xxx. 9.
6 *Ib.* xxix. 1.
7 Theodoret, *Hær. Fab.* ii. 8; Routh[2], iii. 289 ff.
8 Athan. *de Syn.* 43.
9 Hil. Pict. *de Syn.* 86.
10 *De Vir. Ill.* 71.
11 Harnack, *Chronologie*, i. 95.
12 See C. H. Turner, in *JThSt* i. [1900] 189.

head.[1] He insisted strongly on the unity of God, relying mainly on Dt 6[4]; and he identified the uni-personal God with the Father. But the Word or Wisdom was from eternity (ἀεί) in God, in the same manner as reason (λόγος) is in the heart of man, as an element of his personality. Thus the Word is rightly described as ὁμοούσιος τῷ θεῷ (πατρί), inasmuch as its οὐσία or ὑπόστασις is identical with that of the Father. The Word was begotten of God before the ages and so had a real existence. Though impersonal, it was therefore in a true sense the Son of God. The word was essentially λόγος προφορικός, λόγος ἐνεργός, and therefore attained full existence only in activity. When not active, it may be regarded as dormant in God: it was then not ἐνυπόστατος, almost ἀνύπαρκτος, existed τῷ προορισμῷ; when active, it existed τῇ ὑπάρξει.

The Holy Spirit is not often mentioned by Paul, but always as distinct from the Word. He seems to imply some inferiority of the Word to the Spirit, if he is rightly credited with the pronouncement that the Word had need of the Spirit before it became incarnate;[2] but, on the other hand, Jesus Christ, though begotten of the Spirit, was in no sense divine; it was in virtue of the indwelling Word that he at length 'became God.'

Paul's Christology was Adoptianist.[3] Jesus Christ, begotten of the Holy Ghost and born of the Virgin, was a mere man. But 'the man' was anointed by the Holy Ghost and for that reason was called Christ. (Once,[4] if our texts are correct, Paul said that through the Wisdom he became Christ.) There is no express statement concerning the time or manner of this anointing. But, inasmuch as we are told that Jesus Christ (not merely Jesus) was begotten by the Holy Spirit and born of the Virgin, it may be inferred that it took place at the very moment of conception. Thus Christ was a man like one of us, yet superior to other men in all respects, 'since grace was upon him from the Holy Ghost, and from the promises and from the things that are written' in the Scriptures. So he had a special preparation (κατασκευή), such as was vouchsafed to no other, for the reception of the divine Logos. For the Logos or Wisdom went forth from God and was joined to him. In virtue of his unique preparation, the Logos entered into him, not as into a strange place, but, as it were, coming to its home. It came before his birth, for 'Mary received the Logos.' It had come to others, for Wisdom was in the prophets, and still more in Moses. But it was in Christ in such a manner as it had never been in any other; it took up its abode in him as in a sanctuary; it was in the whole man.[5] Thus dwelling in him, the Logos inspired Christ and through him proclaimed the gospel (Ac 10[36]), as in former times God spoke through the prophets. The Logos was seen in him. By its active indwelling in Christ it attained its true existence; so that it might be said that its being had its beginning from Nazareth. At length it returned to God and resumed its former state in God, as reason is in the heart of man. So Paul seems to explain the significance of the Ascension.

But, though the Logos was in Christ, it did not invest him with divinity. It dwelt in Christ as we dwell in our houses, neither being part of the other. Each retained its own nature. They were not fused together as constituent parts of a single person, having a single essence, though Christ was one with the Logos, and so Son.[6] Christ was a human person, who possessed the Logos as an attribute. As man, in virtue of his nature he suffered; as man, in virtue of the grace bestowed on him by the Holy Spirit, he worked miracles. But, by reason of the indwelling of the Logos, the life of Christ was a continuous progress towards higher things. 'By wisdom he became great.' By the steadfastness of his purpose he was made like to God and remained pure from sin. By contest and labour he conquered the sins of our first parent and established virtue. Finally he became God; *i.e.*, he was united to God in the only way in which unity between persons is possible, by absolute harmony of will. So he attained the title of Redeemer and Saviour of the race. His miracles manifested the harmony of his will with the will of God. Having preserved it inviolable, he is granted the Name which is above every name. His union with God is eternal and will never be dissolved.

Since this deification of Christ seems to have followed by a considerable interval the 'anointing' and the coming of the Logos and to have preceded his contest with sin and the exhibition of his miraculous power, it may probably be connected with the Baptism. It did not entitle Christ to worship as God.[1]

The ultimate source of this theological system has been a subject of dispute. Newman maintained that it was of Jewish origin and was devised in order to secure the favour of Queen Zenobia.[2] But it is improbable that, as Newman assumes and Athanasius states,[3] Zenobia was a Jewess;[4] and the accusation of judaizing which was so often made against Paul, especially by Epiphanius, or the earlier writer whom he followed, may be explained without the aid of this hypothesis. Any teacher who substituted a uni-personal God for the Trinity laid himself open to the charge. The epistle of the Synod of Antioch[5] implies that Paul's doctrine was a modification of that of the heretic Artemas (Artemon). If that be true, the accusation of judaizing must be at least transferred to his spiritual 'father.' It is unfortunate that we know nothing about Artemon except that he was, in the main, a follower of Theodotus the cobbler, that he probably flourished about the middle of the 3rd cent., and that he was apparently still living in 268.[6] But Paul's doctrine of God has striking points of contact with that of Hippolytus, who seems in this matter to have differed little from the Theodotians, while the Christology of Paul approaches closely to that of the earlier Theodotians, and still more to that of the Melchizedekians, a later sect of the same school. Thus the testimony of the epistle is confirmed.[7]

Paul refused to submit to the Synod of Antioch. He continued in possession of the 'house of the church' for four years, protected no doubt by Queen Zenobia and still retaining the office of *ducenarius*, which must have given him formidable means of resisting his opponents. He seems also to have had considerable ecclesiastical support. For Basil the deacon tells us that after his excommunication 'there arose schisms of congregations (λαῶν), revolts of priests, disorder of pastors.'[8] And the epistle of the synod implies as much. It claims indeed to express the unanimous opinion of the assembled ecclesiastics;[9] but it admits[10] the existence of bishops and presbyters of adjacent places — apparently not a few — who 'flattered' Paul, and (as it seems) preached his doctrines. Thus the immediate result of the condemnation of Paul was the formation of his followers into a sect

[1] See art. MONARCHIANISM, vol. viii. p. 779.
[2] *JThSt* xix. 119.
[3] See art. ADOPTIANISM, vol. i. p. 103.
[4] *JThSt* xix. 118, frag. viii.
[5] *Ib.* p. 116.
[6] *Ib.* p. 118, frag. viii.

[1] Eus. *HE* VII. xxx. 10.
[2] *Arians of the Fourth Century*[3], London, 1871, pp. 4 f., 22 f.
[3] *Hist. Arian.* 71.
[4] H. Graetz, *Gesch. der Juden*, Leipzig, 1866–78, iv. 295, 297 f.
[5] Eus. *HE* VII. xxx. 16.
[6] *Ib.* § 17.
[7] See *JThSt* xix. 44; cf. Theodoret, *Hær. Fab.* ii. 4.
[8] Mansi, *Concil.* iv. 1103.
[9] Eus. *HE* VII. xxx. 2; cf. the statement of Eusebius in § 1.
[10] § 10.

outside the Catholic Church. It was evidently for some time a powerful rival of the church in Antioch and its neighbourhood, though its influence was probably not strong outside that district. Its adherents were known later as the Paulianists and were nick-named Samosatites and New Jews by Epiphanius, or the author of his source.

It may be supposed that the synod made attempts to dislodge the heresiarch from the 'house of the church'; and it was probably while this struggle was proceeding that Anatolius, formerly deacon of Alexandria, now co-bishop of Cæsarea, first took part in its deliberations.[1] But whatever efforts were made proved fruitless. At length Antioch was wrested from Zenobia by the emperor Aurelian in 272; and, while he was in the city, in response to a petition of the orthodox he decreed that the house should be given to those to whom the bishops of Italy and Rome should award it.[2]

After this we hear nothing of Paul. He probably died or left Antioch soon afterwards. But the sect did not immediately die out. Its second head was Lucian, one of the most famous Biblical critics and interpreters of the age.[3] This we learn from a letter of Alexander, bishop of Alexandria, written about 315.[4] Lucian, like Paul, was a native of Samosata. He studied at Edessa under Macarius and afterwards settled at Antioch, where he founded a school and was ordained presbyter, probably by Paul. After the deposition of Paul he remained out of the communion of the Church, as Alexander tells us, under three bishops of Antioch. Since the episcopate of Cyril, Paul's third successor in the see, ended in 303,[5] Lucian must have been reconciled to the Church in that year or perhaps a few years earlier. He was a celibate and famed for his ascetic piety. He suffered martyrdom in 312.

Lucian was the real founder of Arianism.[6] Many of the early Arians and Semi-Arians were his pupils, and did not consciously deviate from his teaching. This need not surprise us; for, though on his re-admission to the Church he must have satisfied the ecclesiastical authorities at Antioch of his orthodoxy, it does not follow that he would have been accounted orthodox by the Nicene fathers. Thus Epiphanius[7] charges Lucian and all the Lucianists with denying that the Son of God assumed a soul (ψυχή), 'for they say that he had only flesh.' This doctrine does seem to have been held by Lucian in his later days;[8] but it is also the reiterated statement of the Synod of Antioch.[9]

The connexion of Lucian with the Paulianists, though the only evidence for it is the statement of Alexander, can scarcely be questioned; and it is important. He seems to have taken no prominent part in the proceedings at Antioch up to 268. In the contemporary documents Paul is represented as the only person with whom the synod had to do; in the final debate Malchion and Paul were the only disputants. But it is clear that the argument on both sides turned largely on the interpretation of passages in the Old and New Testaments.[10] It is impossible to doubt that Lucian, the most learned of Paul's adherents and the founder of the new school of Biblical study at Antioch, was in many instances responsible for the glosses which his bishop put upon them. We do not forget Paul's avowed contempt for the commentators of previous generations. But we may go further. Paul, in spite of the fact that he claimed to be a sophist, was not one who might be expected to elaborate a carefully constructed scheme of theology. He was a man of affairs. Moreover, his life and character could have had no attraction for a pious ascetic student like Lucian. It is most difficult to believe that he was Lucian's teacher. The probabilities are much in favour of the supposition that tradition had reversed the relation which subsisted between the two men. It is at least worth suggesting that Lucian was the author of the heresy of which Paul, by reason of his exalted ecclesiastical position, his prominence in civil affairs, and his popular gifts, was in his lifetime esteemed the head and after his death the originator; in other words, that Paul was the disciple of Lucian, not Lucian of Paul.

[1] Eus. *HE* VII. xxxii. 21. [2] *Ib.* VII. xxx. 19.
[3] See art. ANTIOCHENE THEOLOGY, vol. i. p. 584.
[4] *Ap.* Theodoret, *HE* i. 4.
[5] *Passio SS. Quattuor Coronatorum*, auctore Porphyrio, § 6, in *AS*, Nov., vol. iii. p. 769; Eus. *HE* VII. xxxii. 2, 4; cf. Harnack, *Chronologie*, i. 217.
[6] See art. ARIANISM, vol. i. p. 776. [7] *Anc.* 33.
[8] See his *Apologia*, in Routh², iv. 6, ll. 8 f., 19 f.
[9] *JThSt* xix. 116. [10] *Ib.* pp. 26, 115 f.

The Paulianist sect remained in being for some time after the defection of Lucian, though apparently in an enfeebled condition. Canon xix. of the Council of Nicæa regards it as an existing body; but the enactment concerning the treatment of such of its clergy and deaconesses as desired admission to the Church suggests that it was dwindling away. Later in the same century St. Athanasius hints that its members were divided among themselves on important questions.[1] In the 5th cent. evidences of its existence are not numerous. Pope Innocent I. refers to it as a contemporary sect; but he cannot have known much about it, for in direct contradiction of Athanasius[2] he denies that the Paulianists baptized in the three Names.[3] Theodoret[4] classes them with the heresies which had utterly perished, and the very names of which were known only to a few.

Samosatenism cannot be said to have made any considerable contribution to the development of Christian belief. It was an attempt to revivify a system of doctrine which the common sense of the Church had already rejected. It was overwhelmed by the flood of new teaching let loose by its former exponent, Lucian, the martyr of Antioch.

LITERATURE.—Most of the authoritative documents relating to Paul of Samosata may be read in M. J. Routh, *Reliquiæ Sacræ*², Oxford, 1846–48, iii. 285–367. For some which he has omitted see Epiphanius, *adv. Hær.* 65; A. Mai, *Nova Collectio*, Rome, 1825–38, vii. 68 ff.; J. B. Pitra, *Analecta Sacra*, Paris, 1876–88, iv. 183–186, 423–425. The sayings of Paul are collected in *JThSt* xix. [1918] 20–45, 115–120. Accounts of his teaching are given in all works on the history of the Church and of Christian doctrine. See especially I. A. Dorner, *Hist. of the Development of the Doctrine of the Person of Christ*, Eng. tr., Edinburgh, 1861–63, div. i. vol. ii. pp. 10–15; A. Harnack, *Die Überlieferung und Bestand der altchr. Litteratur*, Leipzig, 1893, pp. 520–525, *Die Chronologie*, do. 1897–1904, ii. 135–138, *Hist. of Dogma*³, Eng. tr., London, 1894–99, iii. 38–48. On Lucian see Eusebius, *HE* VIII. xiii. 2, IX. vi. 3; Jerome, *de Vir. Ill.* 77; Pseudo-Athanasius, *Synopsis Scripturæ Sacræ*, 77; Philostorgius, *HE* ii. 12, 13; Suidas, and the material collected by Routh, *Rel. Sac.*² iv. 3–17. See also Harnack, in *PRE*³ xi. 659 ff., and his *Überlieferung und Bestand*, pp. 526–532, *Chronologie*, ii. 138–146; H. B. Swete, *Introd. to the Old Testament in Greek*, Cambridge, 1900, pp. 81–86.

H. J. LAWLOR.

SAMOYED.—I. *ETHNOLOGY.*—**1. Distribution and number.**—Where the coast-line of European Russia is no longer inhabited by Lapps, we find another group of Arctic natives, the Samoyed. Their habitat stretches from the eastern part of the government of Archangel, namely Cheskaya Bay, across the Urals, along the Siberian coast and islands as far east as the Khatonga, between the Yenisei and the Lena. Not all this region, however, is inhabited, the exception being three-quarters of the north-eastern portion of the Taimyr peninsula, which, owing to scarcity of reindeer-moss and of driftwood for fire, is left vacant.

The name 'Samoyed' is perhaps derived from one of the following Russian words: *sam-syebye-yed*, 'self-eater,' 'cannibal' (this derivation is scarcely possible, since cannibalism is not found among the Samoyed); *syryo-yed*, 'raw-eater,' 'raw-meat-eater'; and *sam-odin*, 'alone,' this being the most probable derivation, since 'Samodin' and not 'Samoyed' is the colloquial name for these natives even now. The name 'Samoyed' has also been traced from *Suomi*, the Finnish name for Finland. The Eastern and Taz Samoyed call themselves Nyenach or Khassauo, both words meaning 'man.'

The total number of Samoyed in Europe and

[1] *Orat. adv. Arian.* iv. 30. [2] *Ib.* ii. 43.
[3] *Ep.* xvii. 10. [4] *Hær. Fab.* ii. 11.

Asia is about 20,000. Those living in Asiatic Russia numbered 12,502 in 1897, and about 14,986 in 1911. Among the Asiatic Samoyed the largest group is formed by the people speaking Yurak Samoyed; in 1911 they numbered 7059. The number of Ostyak Samoyed, or Forest Samoyed, was then 6559, and of Yenisei and Avamsk, or Eastern, Samoyed 1376.

The people speaking the Yurak Samoyed language and the Eastern Samoyed live along the Arctic shore and inland in the mossy or rocky *tundra*, the Ostyak Samoyed in the forests (*taiga*) from the Upper Taz and Baikha rivers to the Tym and Ket, and even as far south as the Chulim, where, however, the population is very much mixed and is Turkic in speech. Still farther south, in the Kansk district, along the Kana, there is a small remnant (about 400) of the Kamashints nation, which is supposed to be of Samoyedic race—at least it seems to have been so linguistically, though Turkic is their principal language at present.

Besides the Kamashints, several other tribes of the Upper Yenisei are held by some scientists to be of Samoyedic descent. These doubtful Samoyed are: the Karagass, the Beltir, the Sagai, the Motor, the Soyot, and various tribes called Tuba, in the Altai-Sayan region. At the present time, however, all these tribes are linguistically and ethnologically more Turkic than anything else.

2. Language.—The Samoyed languages belong to the Ural-Altaic linguistic group. Castrén, the first linguist to investigate the Samoyed languages and at the same time one of the greatest authorities on the subject, expressed the opinion that the Samoyed languages have 'no nearer relation in the world than the Finnic stock,'[1] and that in fact they form one linguistic family. According to him, the resemblance lies in the fact that in both Finnic and Samoyedic the process of agglutination has made far more progress than in Mongolic, Tungusic, or even Turkic, and also in the great number of root forms they have in common. He conceived Finno-Samoyedic as forming a bridge between Indo-European and Ural-Altaic.[2] Later Finnish linguists have contradicted Castrén's theory. Thus Finsch,[3] quoting Bergroth, says that, while the Ostyak and the Vogul belong to the Finnic linguistic race, the Samoyed have no place in it, and Ahlqvist expresses the opinion that in vocabulary and grammar Finnic and Samoyedic resemble each other no more closely than do Swedish and Portuguese.[4]

Since the Samoyed languages have been less studied than other Ural-Altaic languages, it is perhaps too soon to define the linguistic relationships of these Northern people. With what knowledge we have at present, Castrén's linguistic classification of the Samoyed dialects[5] still holds good. His linguistic division[6] is as follows:

(1) Yurak Samoyed, spoken in the north, from the White Sea to the Yenisei Valley.

(2) Tavgi Samoyed, also spoken in the north, from the Yenisei to the Khatonga by the Tavgi proper and the Avamsk Samoyed.

(3) Ostyak Samoyed, spoken on the Upper Taz, Upper Ob, along the Yenisei (Yenisei-Samoyed), and along the Kana (Kamashints).

Each of these groups may be subdivided into several sub-groups.

3. Origin.—There are two main theories as to the geographical position of the original home of the Samoyed.

(1) The first is that they came to their present abode from S. Siberia.[7] Thus Fischer saw in the Samoyed and the Ugrian Ostyak remnants of the ancient and powerful Chud of Mid-Siberia. Pallas[8] believed himself to have discovered some remnants of the Samoyed among the Kamashints, Karagass, Koibal, Motor, Arine, and Assan, all living on the Upper Yenisei at the time of his travels. This was contradicted by the traveller who followed him, Stepanoff,[9] who declared that all these people were Turko-Tatars. Castrén was the next to investigate the racial relationship of these tribes; he stated[1] that in his time only the Kamashints remained Samoyed, and that the others were now Turks, but had traditions of having used other languages in the past. From this statement, and the fact that some of the clan names of these people are similar in sound to the clan names of the Northern Samoyed, Castrén carried his linguistic views into the sphere of ethnology and concluded that the Finnic, Samoyedic, and Turkic tribes all originated in Central Asia, moving from there to the Upper Yenisei and the Sayan mountains.[2] Thus Castrén and his followers believe that the majority of the Samoyed migrated northwards from the Sayan mountains along the Yenisei and then spread to the west across the Urals and to the east as far as the river Khatonga. The Samoyed who remained behind and became Mongolized or Turkicized are the present tribes of Soyot, Koibal, and Karagass, together with the group called Tuba, inhabiting the Upper Yenisei region.[3]

(2) The second theory was advocated by P. J. Strahlenberg[4] as early as 1730 and brings the Samoyed and the Siberian Finns from the west. Strahlenberg believes that they migrated from Lapland, and, in the opinion of modern Finnish investigators, the Samoyed came to their present homes from the Ural district, whence they spread north-west, north-east, and southwards.[5] In any case the well-developed reindeer culture of the Samoyed proves that, from whatever region they originally came, they must have been in the Arctic regions for a considerable time. We know also from the Ostyak traditions[6] that, when this tribe came to W. Siberia (not later than the 11th cent.), they found the Samoyed already there.

4. Physical type.—Influenced by Castrén's superficial identification of the Samoyed with the Finnic tribes, too many ethnologists are inclined to see a resemblance between the peoples of these stocks. The first reliable description of the physical characters of the Samoyed was given by A. T. Middendorff,[7] who distinguishes among them two main types—the Mongol type (*e.g.*, the Timansk Samoyed) and the Finnic type (*e.g.*, the Kaninsk Samoyed). For the last ten years the attention of anthropologists (K. I. Goroshchenko, A. A. Ivanowski,[8] and S. I. Rudyenko[9]) has been directed to the resemblance between the Samoyed and the Soyot of the Sayan mountains. But, since the discovery of this resemblance is the result of a comparatively small number of measurements (for some characters the measurements were taken on 20 individuals only), and on the observation of only six anthropological characters (colour of eyes and hair, cephalic index, alveolar index, stature, and length of lower limbs), it is safer to look forward to more exhaustive studies and meanwhile to adopt the classification of Ivanowski,[10] and make of the Samoyed a special anthropological group. This group can be characterized as follows: dark eyes, dark, straight, and coarse hair, yellow-grey skin, short stature with long trunk and short legs, broad heads, long faces, prominent cheek-bones projecting sideways, absence of Mongolian eye-fold, though the eye has usually the Mongolian narrowness and obliquity.

The present writer's anthropological investigation of the Eastern and Taz-Yurak Samoyed compared with the Western Samoyed (from the Urals to the Taz), studied by Rudyenko,[11] seems to show that in all the chief anthropological characters the Eastern and Western Samoyed resemble one another—in fact, are often identical—while the Yurak Samoyed of Taz form a wedge of a slightly different type, taller, with narrower nose, wider forehead, and broader head.

5. Cultural type.—The Samoyed have now one of the most perfect Arctic cultures, namely the reindeer culture. They seem to have conquered

1 M. A. Castrén, *Nordische Reisen und Forschungen*, iv. 82.
2 *Ib.*
3 O. Finsch, *Reise nach West-Sibirien im Jahre 1876*, p. 500.
4 Quoted by S. I. Rudyenko, *Antropologicheskiya Izsledovanya Inorodtsev Syevyero-Zapadnoi Sibiri*, p. 109.
5 Castrén, iv. 83 ff. 6 *Ib.* p. 82.
7 J. E. Fischer, *Sibirische Gesch. von der Entdeckung Sibiriens bis auf die Eroberung dieses Landes durch die russischen Waffen*, pp. 120, 123.
8 *Reise durch verschiedene Provinzen des russischen Reichs*, iii. 304, 373 ff.
9 A. P. Stepanoff, *Yeniseyskaya Gubernya*, pt. ii. pp. 37, 45 ff.

1 Castrén, iv. 83–86. 2 *Ib.* v. 107–122.
3 D. Carruthers, *Unknown Mongolia*, i. 20.
4 *Das nord- und ostliche Teil von Europa und Asien*, pp. 36, 46.
5 Kai Donner, quoted by F. Nansen, *Through Siberia*, p. 92.
6 See art. OSTYAKS.
7 *Putieshestvie na Syevyer i Vostok Sibiri*, ii. 626 f.
8 K. I. Goroshchenko and A. A. Ivanowski, 'Yeniseyskiye Inorodtsy.'
9 S. Rudyenko, *Antropologicheskiya Izsledovanya Inorodtsev Syevyero-Zapadnoi Sibiri*, pp. 108–110.
10 Supplement to his *Nasyelyenye Zyemnovo Shara*, Moscow, 1912.
11 *Op. cit.*

the severe climate and to have developed the appropriate technique, their culture being very little inferior in this respect to that of the Eskimos and Lapps, and decidedly superior to that of the Tungus; hence they are much less capable than the Tungus of accepting European culture and a settled mode of life. Reindeer culture is based on reindeer-breeding,[1] but fishing, hunting, and trapping seem always to be additional aids in the struggle for existence. The Samoyed who live in the sub-Arctic forest regions have far fewer reindeer, and here hunting and fishing may be said to be their chief, sometimes their only, occupations.

All the Samoyed are wanderers, but superficially they may also be called seasonal nomads, as they live along the rivers, lakes, and seashore in summer, and inland, in the *tundra* or the forest, in winter. Some Archangel Samoyed and some Ostyak Samoyed adopt a settled mode of life.

Though reindeer-breeding is an industry which all Northern Europeans and Asiatics practise, there are great differences in method, pointing to the small degree of contact which the present inhabitants of N. Siberia have with one another. Not only do the terms for the reindeer at different stages of its life vary according to the tribe, but we see too, *e.g.*, that the Samoyed never ride their reindeer, which is a favourite mode of progression among the Tungus; that the Samoyed (and Ostyak) drive from the left side of the sledge, while the Tungus (and Yakut) drive from the right, and so on. Whether the Samoyed evolved for themselves the culture under which they now live or adopted it from the former inhabitants of the country, it is clear that they must have been in the Arctic regions for a very long time to have reached their present stage.[2]

II. *RELIGION.*—The Samoyed, like the other natives of N. Asia, and indeed of the Arctic region generally, are shamanists; *i.e.*, their religion is based on animistic beliefs, and all knowledge of religious secrets is in the possession of a shaman. Nominally only a part of the Yurak Samoyed are still pagan; the rest are members of the Russian Orthodox Church.

1. The shaman.—The shaman of the Samoyed of the river Ket must be a man; among the Tavgi Samoyed and the Yurak Samoyed there are often shamanesses. But, although the most successful healing is often achieved by a Yurak Samoyed shamaness, we never find her as a leader of religious ceremonies. This office is reserved for a male shaman. Also, being a woman, she is debarred from offering sacrifices to the domestic gods—a rite which is performed by an elder male member of the family.

In the northern region, far away from the colonists, the shaman's costume is very rich, but among the Ostyak Samoyed of the forest region it is quite plain. This is due to the prohibition of costumes, as well as of shamanistic practices, by the Russian authorities. In a general way, the details of the costume are not unlike those of the costume of the Ostyak shaman;[3] the figure of the ancestor spirit occupies an important place, and the whole universe is represented by various objects embellishing the coat. We find, however, much less iron on the Samoyed shaman's coat than on that of the Ostyak, which, again, has less iron than that of the Yakut and Tungus shamans. The Yurak shamans of the river Taz sometimes have costumes made entirely of skins and furs, reindeer-bone, and mammoth-ivory, but the figure of the sun is usually made of metal.

The shaman is the man who knows the religious secrets and the order of the religious ceremonies. He is an intermediary between the people and the spirits, whose words he interprets. He also acts as an adviser and medicine-man. The office of shaman is often hereditary. The Samoyed call their shaman *tadibey*, and the spirits through which the shaman communicates with the spiritual world *tadebtsy*. The *tadebtsy* act as benevolent or malevolent spirits according to the use which the shaman makes of them.[4] The Yurak Samoyed call the *tadebtsy syaddai* or *syadachi*, and represent them by wooden anthropomorphic figures, which are used in divination in the same way as the divining-ring (*arpa*) is used by the shamans of the Lapps. Among the Ob Samoyed the shaman's spirit is sometimes called *löz*, *lòh*, or *koika*.

[1] See art. PASTORAL PEOPLES.

[2] See artt. OSTYAKS and PASTORAL PEOPLES.

[3] See art. OSTYAKS.

[4] M. A. Czaplicka, *Aboriginal Siberia*, p. 289.

2. Gods and spirits.—The name for the shaman's spirits is collective, but each shaman has his own spirits, who accompany him when he is performing his duties. These may be called the shaman's individual spirits. There are three more kinds of spirits: (1) those common to one family—domestic god-spirits; (2) those common to a local group (probably originally to one clan)—ancestor god-spirits; and (3) those common to all the Samoyed—spirits dwelling in the water, stones, and forests.[1]

The domestic gods are called by the Yurak Samoyed *haha* (*hahe*); sometimes they are represented by roots or stones of unusual shape, sometimes by anthropomorphic figures. Usually each family has at least one male and one female domestic god; they are kept covered on a special sledge, the '*haha*-sledge,' which is not used for any other purpose, and, when the family moves, special '*haha*-reindeer' draw the sledge. Women are not allowed to uncover the '*haha*-sledge' or even to take care of the reindeer. Even a shamaness, who has her shamanistic spirit and propitiates the higher clan-god, is not allowed to take care of the domestic gods. The '*haha*-sledge' usually stands behind the *chum* (tent) on the outer side of the place of honour called *si*, which is occupied only by the eldest male of the family.

Some of the spirits common to all the Samoyed, such as the spirits of the water (usually malicious) and the spirits of the bushes (usually benevolent), have local names; but the collective name for the chief spirit-gods, whether common to one group or to all the Samoyed, is *num* (*nim*, *nga*). Sometimes the word *haha* is used not only for domestic deities, but also as a generic term for 'deity' in the same sense as *num*. *Num* also means the thunder and the sky, or perhaps it would be more correct to say that the thunder, being a voice of Num, is one of his characteristics, and the sky, being the abode of one of the chief *nums* (usually the ancestor *num*), is thus identified with him. Thus the fact that the same word is used for 'deity' and for 'sky' does not necessarily imply that sky-worship is the highest expression of Samoyed religion. In the Yurak Samoyed tales we meet with expressions such as these: 'Num became summer,' 'I sat until Num dawned'; at the same time 'to pray to Num' is a usual expression, but an individual name is then added to the title Num. The lesser spirits dwelling in natural objects are vaguely defined; the highest beings have their own individual characteristics, often anthropomorphic or zoomorphic. If by the term 'highest god' we understand the one to whom sacrifices are most often made, and who is concerned directly or indirectly with human affairs, then in the highest god of almost every locality we can trace the ancestor of the people. Among the national gods and goddesses common to all the Samoyed are those connected with fertility.

The house-ancestor gods are identified with a material object more often than are the nature-gods. Sometimes it is difficult to determine whether a god is to be considered as common to one group only or to all the Samoyed; for, if a small group of Yurak Samoyed lives among the Tavgi Samoyed, it may borrow the gods of the latter, even their ancestral gods.

The chief national gods can travel from one place to another; there are, however, several places, far distant from one another, of which nearly all the Samoyed would have heard as being

[1] The forest-spirit exists among the Ostyak Samoyed of the forest region.

holy, as the dwelling-places of gods. Such a Samoyed Jerusalem is to be found on the island of Waigach, which possesses several important *nums* (also called *haha*), some of which are related to one another. Thus the three-headed old man Wesako-haha, living in the extreme south-west of the island, is supposed to be the husband of Nyebye-haha (Mother-god), who lives in the central part of the island, while their son, Nyu-haha, lives in the extreme north-west. Islavin[1] thinks that the gods (represented by stone figures) residing in three other northern localities, viz. at Minisei, a peak of the Urals, in the Yaumau Peninsula, and at a place about 20 versts from Mesen, are also sons of Wesako-haha and Nyebye-haha.

The highest gods worshipped by the Yurak Samoyed are Numkympoi ('among the stars'), who watches man from above; Yaumau ('land's end'); and Yahammü ('out of the water'). The meaning of the term Yaumau is, strictly speaking, 'land's end,' but it is also sometimes used to mean 'river-source,' since the mouth of the river—which is called by the Samoyed the river-source—is understood to be at the end of the earth. The same word is used for the name of a peninsula to the west of the Gulf of Ob. Yaumau has never shown himself to man, but has sent him his iron staff (a rod, probably of Russian workmanship), which was found in the *tundra*. This staff is kept by the Yurak Samoyed near the Plakhina sand-banks on the Northern Yenisei and is held by them in great veneration. Then there is Yaumau-Haddaku (*haddaku*='grandmother'), goddess of the fishes, who is responsible for good and bad fishing seasons, and who lives at the mouth of the Ob. The outward shapes of Yaumau and Numkympoi are known only to the shamans, who see them in visions and make wooden images of them. These images are not regarded as gods, but only as their representations. The only image which is held to be itself a god is that of Yahammü. It is supposed to have fallen from the sky into a river, whence it was taken by a Yurak Samoyed, and is a stone of sufficiently unusual shape to have attracted the finder's attention. Its size is about that of a child of five, and it closely resembles the figure of a man in a sitting posture, holding the head of some animal by a bridle. This figure is in charge of a great shaman at a spot about 100 versts from the settlement of Tazovskoye, on the river Taz. Since Yahammü has actually 'descended' to men, he is on the whole more esteemed than Yaumau and Numkympoi, though it is the last-named who is always called 'grandfather' and treated as tribal ancestor, while other gods are so addressed only at the moment when sacrifice is being offered to them.

Among the lesser gods is the god-owner of quadrupeds, particularly reindeer. He is called Illibium Parche, and it is said that he needs no sacrifices, for he has reindeer enough, and, besides, he does not help or heal men.

Kai Donner[2] found that along the river Tym the Ostyak Samoyed consider their highest god the 'grandfather of the clan,' who is worshipped under various names, while the Ostyak Samoyed along the river Ket symbolize him by a living bear. The Ostyak Samoyed of Ket believe in the transformation of man into an animal, and *vice versa*. If a man jumps over fallen trees and pronounces certain incantations, he will change into a bear.[3]

Although in a general way we can call the Samoyed polytheists, in practice they are nearer to monotheism. Each Samoyed local group has several gods, but the individual chooses one god, whom he propitiates, while behaving reverently to the others. In the agglutinative language of the Yurak Samoyed there is a special compound expression *Amgenulumhehon*, meaning 'What *num* do you worship?'—a question which people ask one another when they meet for the first time. It often happens that, if one god does not satisfy the needs of the worshipper, he takes up another.

3. Dualism.—Since the Samoyed believe that evil must be overcome with evil, it is not possible to make a clear division of their spirits into good and bad, for an essentially 'good' spirit can, as a shaman's assistant, act either for good or for evil. Both the shaman's spirits and the highest clan or tribal spirits are apt to act for good or evil according to circumstances. There are, however, two classes of spirits which are well-defined in this respect. The *haha*, or domestic gods, may be described as a class of good spirits, for we never hear of malevolent actions being performed by them against any one, and they are well-disposed towards the inhabitants of the tent, whom they protect in a passive way against *illike*. The latter can be defined clearly as a class of bad spirits. The chief of all the *illike* is Chir or Non, who lives in the dark north. Whenever there is a storm with lightning, the Samoyed say that Chir is fighting with one of the *nums*. All the other gods are a combination of good and evil, but are benevolent to the men who carefully perform the required ceremonies. The evil spirits are conceived by some Samoyed as dwelling underground, and by others as in the water, and no representations of them are made. The shaman's spirit assistants, especially those of the great shamans, are more evil than good, but they can be beneficent to the petitioner when they use their evil powers against his and the shaman's enemies. Although images of these spirits are made and kept by each shaman, it is dangerous for any one except the shaman who owns the spirits to look at them. During the shamanistic ceremonies, however, they are shown to the public.

4. Religious ceremonies.—Among the Yurak Samoyed one of the male members of a family will often offer private sacrifices to their domestic god, but to propitiate the higher gods it is necessary to offer the sacrifice through a shaman. The domestic gods are propitiated by sacrifices of small objects or portions of food, but a sacrifice to the higher gods must take the form of a reindeer or a dog. If a private person sacrifices an animal to the domestic or to the clan gods, care must be taken that no blood is shed. The animal must be strangled by means of a rope twisted round its neck, the ends being held by a man on either side of the victim. While the deer is being choked to death, a third man prods it in the side with a goad, the object being to hasten the sacrifice along the road to the god or spirit for whom it is destined. The sacrifice is accompanied by petitions to the *num* whom it is designed to propitiate, that he may vouchsafe help to the worshippers in return for the sacrifice offered. If blood is shed, a shaman is summoned, and the petitioners await his pronouncement anxiously, hoping that he will only enjoin the sacrifice of another reindeer and say that they had chosen a wrong one or that one was not sufficient. For the shaman may say that the fact that blood came from the nostrils or mouth of the deer signifies that the god desires a human victim, and then somebody will die soon. Some unimportant fishing or hunting expeditions may be started with a private sacrifice, but important ones like the salmon-fishing on the Yenisei can never be started without a shaman.

One of the most important ceremonies of the

[1] *Samoyedy, v domashniem i obshchestvennom bytu*, p. 19.
[2] Quoted by Santeri Yacobson, 'Sredi Sibirskikh Samoyedov,' *Sibirskaya Jisn*, no. 96, May 1916.
[3] *Ib.*

Samoyed is the sacrifice to Yaumau-Haddaku, goddess of the fishes.

The finest fish of the first catch of the season is opened and cleaned as for eating. It is then impaled on a stick and planted at the water's edge. The head of the fish is turned towards the water, and a small image of the goddess is placed astride its tail, the idea being that the goddess is riding the fish into the water. The entrails of the fish must be very carefully burnt; for, if any part of it is thrown away (as is usually done with the entrails), it will not reach the goddess, who may then do harm to the community instead of sending good fishing.

But the sacrifices are not necessarily all blood sacrifices. Reindeer may be consecrated to the gods without being actually killed, which means that nobody can make use of them. Children may also be consecrated, which means that they must not marry.

Another of the principal Yurak Samoyed ceremonies is the changing of the sledges on which the images of the gods are kept. This takes place once a year in the spring. The most elaborate performance is that connected with the sledge of the god Yahammü.

A shaman is usually the leader of the ceremony. It is a great privilege to make even one small part of the new sledge. Each man who has a share in the making of it kills a reindeer and smears with its blood the part that he has made. The work on the new sledge is carried on only while the sun is shining, and with the dusk every one retires to the *chum*, where the shaman shamanizes. This shamanizing is not for healing the sick, or any other practical purpose, but for the glory of Yahammü. No women or children may be present while the sledge is being made, or during the placing of the god on the new sledge, but they may take part in the shamanistic performances at night. The god is placed on the sledge so that he faces the south, the region of light and life, while the old sledge is placed behind the other, so that its forepart is turned towards the north, the land of darkness and death. In front of the sanctuary of Yahammü a regular forest of old sledges may be seen.

The Avamsk Samoyed, more strictly than the others, hold a sun-festival when the sun returns in January. It is now held only every second year.

It lasts about nine days and must be timed so that the sun will appear on the sixth day. The shaman shamanizes during all the dark hours of the first six days, and the dance begins on the sixth day, *i.e.* the first day of the sun's appearance. Great freedom is observed between young men and young women, but it does not reach anything like that displayed in the orgiastic spring dances of the Yenisei Ostyak. The shaman takes part in the dance, but on this occasion he lays aside his drum and some of his most important garments. Towards the end of the festival the shaman heals the sick and foretells the future. All the shamanistic performances are held in the 'clean *chum*,' a tent specially erected and made of the skins of young reindeer. This *chum* must not be used for taking meals or for any other purpose than that of shamanizing.

5. The soul.—The Yurak Samoyed, as well as the Yenisei Samoyed, believe that a man possesses three kinds of soul: (1) the soul through which he feels and thinks (the intellectual soul), (2) the soul-life (the physical soul), and (3) the soul accompanying a man outside himself (the shadow-soul). The soul-life is called *iindad*, and the same word is used for breath and also for the vapour which rises from the bodies of men and animals in winter. Thus the Yurak Samoyed say, '*Iindytte ngaidapta*,' 'He let go his soul' ('He sighed'), and they believe that death is caused by the malevolent spirit Illike Nga carrying away a man's *iindad*.

There is no theory as to what happens to the *iindad* of an ordinary man after it is separated from his body; but the *iindad* of a shaman becomes an *iterma*, a spirit more dangerous than benevolent. In spite of the separation of the *iindad* from man and his other souls, the dead are believed to live in their own Land of the Dead in the north and also to have the power of returning to do harm to living men. This belief is shown by the Samoyed custom of moving with their *chums* from the place where a death has occurred and occasionally leaving behind a person at the point of death. Sometimes the body is nailed to the ground during the burial ceremony, and the eyes are as a rule covered with heavy objects. Another custom which may be ascribed to fear of a dead person is that of turning away the head when driving near a tomb. The name of the dead is strictly tabued. The Land of the Dead seems to be at the mouth of a river—the Yenisei among the Yenisei Samoyed, and the Ob among the Yurak. The dead person receives all his belongings to assist him in his other life, which is supposed to be similar to the life that he led on earth. One or more of his personal reindeer are sacrificed, and the antlers are hung on the tomb, which is composed of a wooden box made of driftwood; usually some of the poles of his tent are also used in its construction. The sledges and other objects are usually slightly damaged; for otherwise, say the Samoyed, the dead man will not have the use of them. There is always a reindeer-skin pouch containing valuables, including Russian money—not gold and silver coins, which the Samoyed value highly, but paper money; or even such paper as the wrappers of tobacco-packets, which resemble paper money in colour. Kai Donner[1] says that the Ostyak Samoyed believe the Land of the Dead to be at the mouth of the Ob and ruled over by a woman, who sends death to the Samoyed through her numerous spirit-assistants. She also regulates birth.

6. Totemism.—The social organization, especially the marriage regulations, of the Samoyed have been to a great extent modified or destroyed by contact with colonists. This is shown clearly by the acceptance by the Samoyed of the Russian names given to them at their official baptism, which often leads to their forgetting their own, and also by their acceptance of certain Russian marriage restrictions enforced by Russian law, while they remain true shamanists in the marriage ceremonies. It is therefore difficult to trace their totemism by a study of their exogamy, and it seems doubtful whether a regular relation between the two exists among them. We find clans with plant- and animal-names, but these are by no means exclusive or even in a majority; for alongside of such names we find many others, given to clans for some peculiarity which characterizes their members. Neither in terminology nor in mythology nor in real life do we find any relation between the clan-group named after an animal and the animal itself, such as is found among typical totemists. Thus the clans of the Yurak Samoyed of Obdorsk and Taz include: Horelle, 'bucks'; Nguluchi, 'of the grass'; Lampai, 'the base of the antlers of the buck reindeer'; Maryik, 'the neck of the wild buck reindeer'; Nohoi (Nokhoi), 'of the white fox'; but they have also clans with such names as Yadanye, 'walkers'; Shiallanke, 'runners'; Ngasyedda, 'without feet.'

The tales of the Yenisei Samoyed are rich in names of heroes suggesting totemistic elements: we hear in one tale about a fight between seven *chums* of Grass Fringes (the people of these *chums* would have grass fringes hanging on the back of their winter coats) and seven *chums* of Talnik Fringes (with *talnik*, or dwarf willow, twigs hanging on the back of their winter coats). The power of the first-named comes from their grass fringes, for another hero says to one of them: 'Comrade, how heavy you are; you look very small to me, but you have on your back a grass fringe, one string of which would make a canoe.' There is a hero named White Owl and another named Eagle Buck, but besides these there are heroes called Iron-Cube-Belt, Silver Buttons, Iron Boots, etc. With the exception of the Ostyak Samoyed, the Samoyedic tribes are much more given to ancestor- and hero-worship than to animal-worship. This does not prevent the anthropomorphic gods from having many animal characteristics (*e.g.*, they

[1] *Loc. cit.*

can fly and can change into animals) nor certain animals from having special places assigned to them in the shamanistic mysteries as the shaman's spirit-assistants. As far as is known at present, only the Ostyak Samoyed have any beliefs which can be called totemistic. Itte, the hero of the epic of the Ostyak Samoyed recorded by Kai Donner,[1] had by one of his wives, the daughter of Massul-lözi, 'Forest-Spirit,' a son, 'Bear-Spirit' (Pärgäi-kuorgai lözi or Pärgäi-kuorg, *pärgäi* meaning 'bear-spirit'); from this son the Samoyed of the Ket river derive their descent. For this reason they call themselves Kuorgai-tämder, 'race of bears.'

Along the river Tym, Kai Donner found that the name for the forest spirit is Päryä, which must be the same word as occurs in the form Pärgäi-kuorg (Pärgäi-bear).[2] We can hardly reckon the animal monsters with which this epic is filled as traces of totemism; and even Pärgäi-bear is, after all, the descendant of Itte, a man-hero. It is only among the Ostyak Samoyed of the river Ket that the bear rises to the dignity of an ancestral god. Since, as far as is known, these Samoyed are the only ones who personify their ancestral god in animal form, it may be only a local variation in the method of picturing the ancestor. The worshipping of a tribal ancestor is common to all the Samoyed, and endowing him with the form of a bear may merely indicate his unusual origin, having no reference to totemistic beliefs. Much the same can be said about the shaman's spirit-assistants, which are represented by animal forms, though never identified with animals.

7. Mythology.—Samoyed mythology is extraordinarily rich not only in variety of motives but also in variety of forms. The two chief forms are the tale which is sung, called by the Yurak Samoyed *syodobobs*, and the tale which is told, *uahanoku*. We do not include in Samoyed mythology any songs, whether the shaman's songs, which are more or less alike among all the Northern natives, or the songs, so characteristic of the Northern Samoyed, which are sung at burials and match-makings. Thus the widower will sing at his wife's funeral a song expressing his sorrow and loneliness, while the young wooer will express his affection in song. These ceremonial songs are disappearing from Samoyed life more rapidly than the myths.

The tales of the Yurak Samoyed and Yenisei Samoyed can be divided according to their contents into customary tales and fantastic tales. Both are to a certain extent hero-tales. The customary tales relate various events in the life of the family or the clan, and are usually put into the mouth of the hero or heroine, who relates them in the first person. This device and the wonderfully artistic and realistic descriptions, obtained by the simplest means, make these customary tales a mine of rich material for the study of primitive mentality as well as of social anthropology. They are full of descriptions of hunting and fishing expeditions, marriage- and initiation-ceremonies, tribal law, and various incidents arising out of love affairs; and, though all are related as they really occur, yet, when touched with the characteristic logic of the primitive mind, they receive a mythical colouring. But it is the other kind of tale that really deserves the name of myth—the fantastic hero-tale, which perhaps originated as a customary tale, but from long ages of oral reproduction has received a hyperbolic form. Many details indicate that this type of Samoyed literature is older than the customary tales. The hero is usually a warrior wandering about in search of adventures. At the same time, he often possesses shamanistic power, or at least meets the great shamans, so that the hero-tales are interwoven with religious beliefs. If the hero is a shaman, it is nearly always his struggle with another great shaman that forms the subject of the tale, and in this case the other shaman is very often of Yakut nationality, since the Yakut shamans have a widespread reputation. In a Yenisei Samoyed tale of the great shaman Kuobaldi, he fights the Yakut shaman first on land, then in the sky, and then under the water.

[1] *A Samoyede Epic*, p. 6. [2] *Ib.* p. 9.

Far from disappearing with the decline of native life, the customary myths are actually growing. As to the fantastic tales, alongside of the ancient ones new ones occasionally come into existence even now, after the death of a prominent shaman or hunter; there are no more new legends of warriors, since the Samoyed no longer fight.

Although there are no myths concerned only with gods and spirits, these hero-myths have frequent references to them. There seems to be no type of zoological myth among the Samoyed as there is among the Palaeo-Siberians and among the people belonging to the N. Pacific culture-ring generally; but the heroes can temporarily change into animals, or at least assume animal characteristics, though they never cease to be men. To this class belongs the myth recorded by Kai Donner among the Ostyak Samoyed of the forest region along the rivers Ket and Tym, which he calls 'the Samoyed epic of the hero Itte.'[1] Itte's chief struggles were with the giant man-eater, Pünegusse, whom he at last vanquished. Although forced by foreign evil spirits to leave the Samoyed lands, he is expected to return one day to make the Samoyed rich and happy, just as the return of the hero Alba is looked for by the Yenisei Ostyak.[2]

LITERATURE.—**M. A. Castrén**, *Nordische Reisen und Forschungen*, Germ. tr., Petrograd, 1849–62, iii. 'Vorlesungen über die finnische Mythologie' [1853], vii. 'Grammatik der samojedischen Sprachen' [1854], viii. 'Wörterverzeichnisse aus den samojedischen Sprachen' [1855], iv. 'Ethnologische Vorlesungen über die altaischen Völker' [1857], v. 'Kleinere Schriften' [1862]; **D. Carruthers**, *Unknown Mongolia*, 2 vols., London, 1913; **M. A. Czaplicka**, *Aboriginal Siberia*, Oxford, 1914, 'The Influence of Environment upon the Religious Ideas and Practices of the Aborigines of Northern Asia,' *FL* xxv. [1914] 34 ff., *My Siberian Year*, London, 1916; **Kai Donner**, *A Samoyede Epic* (Extrait du Journ. de la Société finno-ougrienne, xxx. 26), Helsingfors, 1913; **O. Finsch**, *Reise nach West-Sibirien im Jahre 1876*, Berlin, 1879; **J. E. Fischer**, *Sibirische Gesch. von der Entdeckung Sibiriens bis auf die Eroberung dieses Landes durch die russischen Waffen*, Petrograd, 1768; **K. I. Goroshchenko** and **A. A. Ivanowski**, 'Yeniseyskiye Inorodtsy,' *Russ. Anthrop. Journ.* xxv., xxvi. [Moscow, 1907]; **A. A. Ivanowski**, Supplement to *Nasyelenye Zyemnovo Shara*, Moscow, 1912; **V. Islavin**, *Samoyedy, v domashniem i obshchestvennom bytu*, Petrograd, 1847; **M. Krivoshapkine**, *Yeniseyskii Okrug i yevo jisn*, do. 1865; **N. V. Latkine**, 'Yeniseyskaya Gubernya,' *Bull. Siberian Sect. Imp. Geogr. Soc., 1865*, do. 1892; **A. T. Middendorff**, *Putieshestvie na Syevyer i Vostok Sibiri*, do. 1869, ii., *Sibirische Reise*, do. 1848–75, vol. IV. pt. ii.; **A. Montefiore**, 'Notes on the Samoyads of the Great Tundra,' *JAI* xxiv. [1895] 388 f.; **A. Mordvinoff**, 'Inorodtsy, Obitayushchie v Turukhanskom kraye,' *Bull. Imp. Geogr. Soc.* xxviii. pt. ii. [1860] 25–64; **F. Nansen**, *Through Siberia*, London, 1914; **P. S. Pallas**, *Reise durch verschiedene Provinzen des russischen Reichs*, 3 vols., Petrograd, 1771–76, *Travels into Siberia and Tartary*, London, 1788 (=vol. ii. of *The Habitable World described*, ed. John Trusler, 20 vols., London, 1788–97); **I. Pyestoff**, *Zapiski ob Yeniseyskoi Gubernii*, Moscow, 1833; **W. Radloff**, *Aus Sibirien*, 2 vols., Leipzig, 1884; **S. I. Rudyenko**, *Antropologicheskiya Izsledovanya Inorodtsev Syevyero-Zapadnoi Sibiri*, Petrograd, 1914; **S. Sommier**, 'Siriéni, Ostiacchi e Samoiedi dell' Ob,' *Archivio per Antrop.* xvii. [Florence, 1887] fasc. 1, 2; **A. P. Stepanoff**, *Yeniseyskaya Gubernya*, Petrograd, 1835; **P. J. Strahlenberg**, *Das nord- und ostliche Teil von Europa und Asien*, Stockholm, 1730; **N. I. Zograf**, 'Antropologicheskii Ochork Samoyedov,' *Bull. of Soc. of Friends of Natural Science . . . Moscow*, xxxi. [1878–79] suppl. pp. 61–87; for summary of it see *RAnth* ii. [1881] 117–128.

M. A. CZAPLICKA.

SANCHUNIATHON. — A. *HISTORICAL NOTICES.* — Sanchuniathon (Gr. Σαγχουνιάθων, Σαγχωνιάθων, Συνιαίθων) is said by Porphyry[3] to

[1] *A Samoyede Epic*, p. 3 ff.
[2] See artt. OSTYAKS and SHAMANISM.
[3] In Eusebius, *Præp. Evang.*, ed. Gifford, p. 31a.

have been a native of Berytus (Beirūt) who lived before the Trojan war, about the times of Moses and Semiramis, who wrote in the Phœnician language a history of his people and of their religion, based on the records of the cities and the registers of the temples and on records received from a certain Hierombalos (=Jerub-ba'al), priest of the god Ieuo (=Jahweh). This he dedicated to Abibalos=Abi-ba'al, king of Berytus. It was translated into Greek by Philo of Byblos.[1] Philo Byblius[2] says that Sanchuniathon was a man of much learning and curiosity, who searched out a history written by the god Thōth.[3] He also found the secret writings of the *ammouneis* (= *ḥammānim*, 'sacred pillars').[4] The teaching of Thōth was preserved by the seven sons of Ṣuduḳ, the Kabeiroi, and by their brother Asklēpios (= Eshmun). These stories were allegorized by a certain Thabion and handed on to the prophets and to their successors, one of whom was Eisirios, the brother of Chna (Canaan), who was afterwards called Phoinix (Phœnicia).[5] Many generations afterwards a god Sourmoubelos and Thuro, whose name was changed to Eusarthis, brought to light the theology of Thōth.[6] Suidas calls him 'a Tyrian philosopher, who lived about the time of the Trojan war, who translated into Phœnician a work of Hermes (Thōth) concerning the origin of things, who wrote in Phœnician on the institutions of the Tyrians, Egyptian theology, and some other matters.' He is also mentioned by Athenæus,[7] by Eusebius,[8] and by Theodoret.[9]

Sanchuniathon is not named by any Greek writer before Philo; but this is no proof of his non-existence, since a Phœnician author would not be known to Greeks unless he were translated. The references in Athenæus, Porphyry, Eusebius, Theodoret, and Suidas are probably all derived from Philo; but this also proves nothing, since Philo's translation was the only form in which Sanchuniathon was accessible to Greek readers. Sanchuniathon is a genuine Phœnician name, Sankun (or Sakkun)-yaton, 'Sakkun has given.'[10] As far as it goes, this is evidence that he was a real person.

B. *THE TRANSMISSION OF SANCHUNIATHON'S HISTORY.*—The Phœnician original of Sanchuniathon, if it ever existed, has perished, and we know only the reputed Greek translation of Philo Byblius (*q.v.*). In 1836 F. Wagenfeld reported the discovery in Portugal of a MS of Philo.[11] This was soon shown to be a fraud, particularly by F. C. Movers.[12] Philo is known to us only from the citations in Porphyry, Eusebius, Johannes Lydus, and Stephen of Byzantium.

The fragments of Philo have been gathered by J. C. Orelli, *Sanchoniathonis Berytii quæ feruntur Fragmenta* (Leipzig, 1826). This edition is incomplete and uses a defective text of Eusebius. A better ed. is that of C. Müller, *FHG* iii. [1849] 560–576. Here Gaisford's revised text of Eusebius is followed. The bulk of the quotations of Philo are found in Eusebius (*Præp. Evang.* i. 9–10, iv. 16), who uses them in a furious attack on Porphyry to prove that the gods of the heathen are only deified men. Eusebius is ed. by T. Gaisford, *Eusebii Pamphili Evangelicæ Præparationis*, Oxford, 1843; and by E. H. Gifford, 4 vols. in 5, Oxford, 1903 (a more critical ed.). English translations of the fragments of Philo in Eusebius are given by R. Cumberland, *Sanchoniatho's Phœnician History*, London, 1720; I. P. Cory, *The Ancient Fragments*, do. 1826, [2]1832, [3]ed. R. E. Hodges, 1876, and by E. H. Gifford, in vol. iii. of his ed. of the *Præp. Evang.*

1 See also Porphyry, *de Abstin.* ii. 56.
2 In Eus. *Præp. Evang.* p. 31d.
3 Cf. 34a.
4 32b.
5 39c. d.
6 40b.
7 iii. 126.
8 *Præp. Evang.* p. 9, ed. Gifford, 30d.
9 *De Cur. Græc. affect.*, serm. ii.
10 See art. PHŒNICIANS, vol. ix. p. 893, § 4*b*.
11 *Sanchuniathons Urgeschichte der Phönizier*, Hanover, 1836, *Sanchuniathonis histor. Phoen. libros novem*, Bremen, 1837, Germ. tr., Lübeck, 1837.
12 *Jahrb. für Theol. und christ. Philos.* VII. i. 95 f.; see also C. L. Grotefend, *Die Sanchuniathonische Streitfrage*, Hanover, 1836.

C. *CONTENTS AND COMPOSITION.*—The extracts preserved by Eusebius fall into three groups.

1. A cosmogony (i. 10; 33b–34b).—According to this, the beginning of the universe was Dark Air and Chaos dark as Erebus. These correspond to darkness and the Deep (Tĕhôm) in Gn 1^{2} and to Apsu and Ti'āmat of the Babylonian creation story.[1]

From Darkness and Chaos sprang Wind (Pneuma) and Desire (Pothos). With this agrees the statement of Damascius[2] that the Sidonians 'before all things place Chronos and Pothos, and Omichles' (=אם כל איש, 'mother of every man'?). Wind corresponds to the Wind of Elohim in Gn 1^{2}. Desire is not found in the Babylonian or in the Hebrew cosmogony, but appears as Eros, 'love,' in Hesiod[3] and as Pothos in the theology of the Ophites as reported by Epiphanius.[4]

From the union of Wind and Desire Mōt was produced. This Philo defines as 'slime, or putrid water,' which shows that it is an abstract noun formed from the Phœnician and Hebrew word *mô*, or *may*, 'water' (cf. Eth. plu. *māyat*). It corresponds to the waters (*mayim*) of Gn 1^{2} and to Mummu, 'waters,' the offspring of Apsu and Ti'āmat in the Babylonian cosmology.[5] The same idea appears in Egypt.[6] Mōt had the form of an egg (following the textual emendation of Bunsen, Renan, and Baudissin). The conception of a world-egg was known in Egypt,[7] in India,[8] and among the Greeks.[9] No trace of this conception is found in Babylonia, unless it be in the splitting of Ti'āmat and setting up of half as the dome of the sky; but it is suggested in Gn 1^{2} by the statement that the Wind (or Spirit) of Elohim was *mĕraḥepheth* upon the face of the waters. Even if *mĕraḥepheth* does not mean 'brood,' but 'swoop,'[10] still the word is applied only to birds and therefore hints dimly at the idea of the world-egg.

Within Mōt were formed first 'germs of creation,' then 'animals without sensation,' and from the latter grew 'intelligent animals' called *zōphasēmín* (צפי שמין), which Philo correctly translates 'observers of heaven.' The Aramaic form *semin*, instead of Phœnician *samim* (cf. [Sa]mem-roumos, 34d), is to be set to the credit of Eusebius rather than to that of Philo. All these creatures remained motionless within the world-egg until it opened. This is different from the Babylonian and the Hebrew accounts, which know no creation of plants and animals *in posse* before their creation *in esse*.

Mōt then burst forth into light, and sun, and moon, and stars, and the great constellations. As a result of the action of the light, the waters were 'separated' (διεκρίθη) and clouds were formed. This corresponds to the Babylonian narrative of the appearance of Marduk, the god of light, who split the body of Ti'āmat into halves and set up the upper half to form the sky, in which he placed the heavenly bodies. It corresponds also to the Hebrew narrative of God's creation of light and His 'splitting' the waters under the firmament from the waters above the firmament and setting the sun, moon, and stars in the firmament (Gn $1^{3-10.\ 14-19}$). The meeting of the clouds in the sky caused thunder, and on hearing this the animals that had been formed in the world-egg 'woke up and began to move, on land and sea, male and female.' With this corresponds Marduk's creation of plants and animals in the Babylonian story and the appearance of all forms of life at the word of Elohim (Gn 1^{20-22}).

2. The origin of men and their discovery of the arts (i. 34b–36a).—The original pair were 'the wind Kolpía and his wife Báau.' Kolpía=Ḳōl-piāḥ, 'voice of a breath,' which suggests the statement of Gn 2^{7} that Jahweh 'breathed into man the breath of life.' Báau=Bōhû, the primal chaos of Gn 1^{2}; it corresponds also to the 'dust' of Gn 2^{7} into which the breath of Jahweh entered to create man.

The children of Kolpía and Báau were Aiōn, 'lifetime'= Ḥawwa (Eve), 'life,' and Prōtogonos, 'first-born'=Adam (first) 'man'; 'and Aiōn discovered the food obtained from trees,' which corresponds to Eve's plucking of the forbidden fruit.

The children of Prōtogonos and Aiōn were Génos and Geneá. Génos, 'race'=Enosh, 'mankind' (Gn 4^{26}), and Geneá is his female counterpart. They first worshipped the sun, whom they called Beelsámēn, which in the Phœnician language is 'Lord of Heaven' and in Greek Zeus.[11] In like manner Gn 4^{26} says of Enosh that he was the first to call upon the name of Jahweh.

The sons of Génos were Light, Fire, and Flame. 'These discovered fire from rubbing pieces of wood together, and taught the use of it.' This recalls the myth of Prometheus and similar Aryan myths. There is no mention of the discovery of fire in Babylonia or in the narrative of the origin of the arts in Gn 4^{16-22}; still it is implied by Tubal-ḳayin's invention of the forging of metals (Gn 4^{22}). Ḳayin, son of the man (Gn 4^{1}, J), or Ḳeynān, son of man (Gn 5^{9}, P), means 'smith,' and the smith's art is impossible without fire. Ḳayin's sacrifice (Gn $4^{3f.}$) also presupposes the use of fire. The Babylonian

1 For similar Greek conceptions see *ERE* iv. 145–148.
2 *De Prim. Princip.* 125, ed. J. Kopp, Frankfort, 1826, p. 385.
3 *ERE* iv. 146.
4 *Hær.* xv. 5.
5 Cf. Damascius, 125.
6 *ERE* iv. 144, § 1.
7 A. Erman, *A Handbook of Egyp. Religion*, Eng. tr., London, 1907, pp. 26, 81, 157.
8 *ERE* iv. 156 f.
9 *Ib.* p. 148.
10 J. P. Peters, in *JBL* xxxiii. [1914] 81.
11 *ERE* ii. 288, § 8.

fire-god Girru is specially described as the patron of smiths,[1] and Ḳeynān appears as a Sabæan God.[2] It appears probable, therefore, that the original Hebrew legend and other Semitic legends narrated the invention of fire.

From Fire the Giants were born who gave their names to the mountains of Phœnicia. These correspond to the Nephilim, or 'giants' (Gn 6^{4} J, Nu 13^{33} JE), also to the monstrous brood of Ti'âmat in the Babylonian creation-story, and to the Giants and Titans of Greek mythology.[3] To this race belonged [Sa]mēmroumos (Shamîm-rûm), which Philo correctly translates Hupsouranios, 'heaven-high.' He was the first city-builder, and therefore corresponds to Cain, the city-builder, in Gn 4^{17}. He quarrelled with his brother Ousōos. This is the counterpart of Cain's quarrel with Abel, only here the brother's name is Ousōos, the equivalent of 'Ēsau. The two pairs of hostile brothers Cain and Abel and Jacob and Esau have been confused. Ousōos was a hunter who invented garments of skin. This agrees with the characteristics of Esau in Gn $27^{3.11}$. Ousōos originated the use of standing-stones in worship and the pouring of libations of blood upon them. This corresponds to Abel, who first offered bloody sacrifices. After his death he was worshipped as a god. There is abundant evidence that 'Ēsau, 'maker,' was the name of an ancient Canaanite deity.[4]

Sanchuniathon then enumerates six pairs of brothers who were inventors of the arts:

(1) Agreus, 'hunter,' and Halieus, 'fisher'=Phœn. Ṣîd and Dayyōg (Heb. דַּיָּג). Ṣîd is known as a Phœnician god.[5] In character he corresponds to Nimrod, the mighty hunter of Gn 10^{9}.

(2) Chrusor, or Hephaistos, and Zeus Meilichios. Chrusor-Hephaistos=Heb. חָרָשׁ, Phœn. Ḥārōsh, 'smith.'[6] He was 'the discoverer of iron and the method of working it,' and also 'practised incantations and divinations.' This is a play on the two meanings of Ḥārōsh, viz. 'smith' and 'magician.' He is the counterpart of Tubal-ḳayin, or Tubal the smith, the father of every *ḥôrēsh*, or metal-worker (Gn 4^{22}). His brother Meilichios=Malliḥ, 'the sailor,' 'invented the hook, and bait, and line, and raft, and was first of all men to make a voyage.'

(3) Technítēs, 'artificer,' and Gēinos-Autóchthōn, 'earth-born aboriginal.' These invented sun-dried bricks and roofs. Technítēs seems to correspond to Heb. *ḳayin*, 'artificer' (cf. Tubal-ḳayin, Gn 4^{22}), and Gēinos-Autóchthōn to Adam, who was made out of the ground, *adāmā* (Gn 2^{7} 3^{19}).

(4) Agrós, 'country,' and Agrótēs, 'countryman.' Of the latter 'there is a much venerated statue and a shrine drawn by yokes of oxen, and among the people of Byblos he is named pre-eminently the greatest of the gods. From them came farmers and huntsmen.' Agrótēs seems to represent the local *ba'al* of Byblos.[7] Agrós will then be a minor *ba'al* associated with him. This inventor of agriculture corresponds to Cain, the 'tiller of the ground,' who 'brought of the fruit of the ground' (Gn $4^{2f.}$).

(5) Amunos and Magos (both in acc., Amunon and Magon), 'who established villages and sheepfolds.' In 32b Philo speaks of the secret writings of the *ammouneis* hidden in the temples. This seems to refer to the *ḥammānim* (Heb. חַמָּנִים), or steles.[8] In the inscriptions Ḥammōn, or Ammōn, appears as a god in 'Abd-ḥammōn, 'servant of the stele,'[9] or more frequently Ba'l-ḥammōn.[10] Amunos, accordingly, seems to equal the well-known Phœnician god Ba'l-ḥammōn. Magos (in acc. Magon)= Ma'on, who appears as a god in the place-name Ba'al-Ma'on,[11] or Beth-Ba'al-Ma'on;[12] also mentioned in Nu 32^{38}, 1 Ch 5^{8}, Ezk 25^{9}, Jos 13^{17}; perhaps also in the name of the Arabian people Ma'on.

(6) Misor and Ṣuduḳ (משר and צרק), which Philo correctly translates 'straight' and 'just.' They are identical with Mesharu, 'equity,' and Kettu, 'justice,' the children of Shamash, the god of justice in the Babylonian religion.[13] Ṣuduḳ, or Ṣedeḳ, is a well-known Canaanite god.[14] He also appears in S. Arabia[15] and in many OT names compounded with Ẓedeḳ.

(7) From Misor Taautos was born, whom the Egyptians call Thouth, the Alexandrians Thōth, and the Greeks Hermes. He was the inventor of writing. This is clearly the Egyptian god Thōth who has been incorporated into the Phœnician pantheon.[16]

(8) 'From Ṣuduḳ came the Dioscuri, or Kabeiroi, or Corybantes, or Samothraces.'[17] The Kabeiroi (*q.v.*), whose cult spread so far in the Greek world, bore the Semitic name רבירים, 'the mighty,' and were doubtless genuine Phœnician divinities.

This genealogy is composed out of at least three independent traditions. Prōtogonos is the counterpart of Génos and Autóchthōn. Hupsouranios and also Technítēs and Gēinos are the inventors of houses. Ousōos and also Agrós and Agrótēs are the inventors of hunting. Ousōos, Meilichios, and the Kabeiroi are the inventors of boats.

3. The theogony and war of the gods (36a–40d).—The original pair of gods were (1) Elioun, 'high'=Heb. 'Elyōn,[1] and (2) Bērouth, an abbreviation of Ba'alat Bērūth, 'mistress of Beirūt,' or possibly 'mistress of the cypress' (=Aram. בְּרוֹת, Heb. בְּרוֹשׁ, 'who dwelt in the neighbourhood of Byblos').[2] 'Elyon was killed by wild beasts; *i.e.*, he was identical with the Phœnician Adôn, Adonis, 'lord,' the consort of the Ba'alat of Byblos.[3] The children of 'Elyōn were (3) Ouranos, 'sky,' and (4) Gē, 'earth.' Ouranos is Ba'al-Shamim, 'owner of the sky.'[4] He corresponds to the Babylonian Anu, 'the sky,' 'father of the gods.' Earth is named as a Carthaginian goddess in the treaty of Hannibal.[5] A trace of similar conceptions among the Hebrews is found in the formula of Gn 2^{4a}, 'These are the generations [*i.e.* 'offspring'] of the heaven and of the earth.' Similarly in Hesiod Ouranos and Gē are the parents of the Titans and gods.[6]

The children of Ouranos were (5) Ēlos=Ēl, 'god';[7] Philo translates Kronos (*i.e.* Saturn), in imitation of Hesiod,[8] who makes the Titan Kronos the son of Ouranos; he was the builder of the temple and of the city of Byblos; (6) Baitulos= Bēth-ēl, 'abode of deity,' *i.e.* a *maṣṣēbhāh*, or standing-stone inhabited by a god;[9] in *Præp. Evang.* 37d Sanchuniathon expresses the same idea when he says that 'Ouranos devised the *baitulia*, having contrived to put life into stones'; (7) Dagōn,[10] which Philo translates *sitōn*, 'corn' (=Heb. *dāgān*), and says[11] that he discovered corn and the plough and therefore was called Zeus Arotrios, 'Zeus of ploughing'; (8) Atlas (Phœnician equivalent unknown), whom Ēl threw into a deep pit and buried;[12] this deed Hesiod relates of Ouranos in his treatment of his children, which shows that Philo does not borrow this myth from Hesiod; (9) Zeus Demarous=Ba'al Tamar;[13] he and his brother Ēl waged unsuccessful war against (10) Pontos, 'the sea' (=בעל־ימם). The son of Ba'al Tamar was (11) Melcathros, or Hercules, *i.e.* Melḳart, the Ba'al of Tyre.[14] (12) Astarte= 'Ashtart[15] was 'the greatest goddess, who reigned over Phœnicia with Ba'al-Tamar and Hadad; she set the head of a bull on her head as a mark of royalty, and, finding a fallen star, she consecrated it as the holy island of Tyre.' (13) Rhea (=Tanit?) in Hesiod is the wife, not the daughter, of Kronos. (14) To Dione= Baaltis, *i.e.* Ba'alat, 'mistress,' Ēl gave the city of Byblos (Gebal). The Phœnicians say that she is Aphrodite. She is evidently the old Ba'alat of Gebal.[16] (15) Eimarmene, 'fate'=Měnî, 'fate,' a god of the Arabs[17] and of the Nabatæans,[18] is mentioned in Is 65^{11}; perhaps also in the personal name Man(n)asseh, 'Měnî has lifted up.' (16) Hora, 'season'='Ate. Philo has confused the word, עת, 'season,'[19] with עתא, the god 'Ate.[20]

In company with his brothers and sisters, Ēl waged war on his father, the Sky, and eventually succeeded in emasculating him with a sickle, so that his blood stains the waters of one of the rivers of Phœnicia to this day. This is the counterpart of the war of the gods of light and order against the forces of chaos in the Babylonian creation epic and in the OT, and of Zeus's victory over the older gods in Hesiod, where also the sickle and the emasculation appear, only in Hesiod it is the children of Kronos who overthrow him, while here Kronos and his brethren overthrow their father Ouranos. Sanchuniathon adds that the allies of Ēl were called Eloim, *i.e.* Elohim, 'gods.'

The children of Ēl (Kronos) were as follows: (17) Persephone (Phœnician equivalent unknown); (18) Athene='Anath;[21] the equation of 'Anath and Athene is found in bilingual inscriptions; to her was given the kingdom of Attica; (19) Sadidos=Shaddai (Phœn. שר in גר־שר=גרשר, 'client of Shaddai'), whom Ēl slew with the sword; (20) a daughter whose head Ēl cut off; these correspond to the children of Kronos in Hesiod whom their father devoured as soon as they were born; (21) by his sister Astarte, seven daughters, the Titanides, and two sons; (22) Pothos, 'desire,' and (23) Eros, 'love'; by his sister Rhea, seven sons, one of whom was (24) Muth, 'death';[22] (25) by his sister Baaltis, daughters; (26) Kronos (or Ēl) of the same name as his father; (27) Zeus Bēlos (=Bēl, the Babylonian god),[23] the father of (28) Nereus (=Ea?), the father of (29) Pontos (=Ba'al-yammim), the father of (30) Sidon (=Ṣîd)[24] and Poseidon (=Ba'al-Ṣîdōn); (31) by the nymph Anobret='En-'obereth, 'overflowing spring,' or 'En-ḥobereth, 'uniting spring,' he had an only-begotten son called Iedud (Heb. *yědîd*, 'beloved'); in a time of great danger Ēl arrayed this son in royal apparel, prepared an altar, and sacrificed him.[25] It has often been claimed that this

[1] H. C. Rawlinson, *WAI* iv. [1891] 14. 2.
[2] *CIS* iv. no. 8, l. 2.
[3] *ERE* vi. 193.
[4] *Ib.* iii. 183, § 12.
[5] *Ib.* § 14; W. W. Baudissin, *Studien*, i. 16; M. Lidzbarski, *Handbuch der nordsem. Epigraphik*, Berlin, 1898, p. 356.
[6] Lidzbarski, p. 281.
[7] *ERE* ii. 293.
[8] See *ib.* 287, § 5.
[9] Lidzbarski, p. 333.
[10] *Ib.* p. 239.
[11] *Mesha Inscr.* 9.
[12] *Ib.* 30.
[13] H. Zimmern, *Beitr. zur Kenntnis der bab. Rel.*, Leipzig, 1901, p. 90; A. Deimel, *Pantheon Babylonicum*, Rome, 1914, no. 1750; cf. Ps 89^{15}.
[14] *ERE* iii. 183a, § 15.
[15] Baudissin, p. 15.
[16] See *ERE* ix. 894, § 72.
[17] Cf. *Præp. Evang.* 37b.

[1] *ERE* iii. 180, § 13.
[2] On the cypress as the sacred tree of 'Ashtart see Baudissin, pp. 192–198.
[3] *ERE* ii. 118.
[4] *Ib.* p. 288b.
[5] Polyb. vii. 9.
[6] *Theog.* 104 ff.
[7] *ERE* iii. 178, § 1, ix. 889, § 1.
[8] *Theog.* 137.
[9] *ERE* ii. 287, § 5, iii. 186, § 1, ix. 895, § 3.
[10] *Ib.* iv. 386.
[11] *Præp. Evang.* 37d.
[12] *Ib.* 37a.
[13] *ERE* ii. 286b.
[14] *Ib.* ii. 292, ix. 892, § 25.
[15] *Ib.* ii. 115.
[16] *Ib.* ii. 117, 293.
[17] J. Wellhausen, *Reste arab. Heidentums*², Berlin, 1887, p. 25.
[18] J. Euting, *Nabatäische Inschriften*, Berlin, 1885, 2[1. 5].
[19] Lidzbarski, p. 347.
[20] *Ib.* p. 348; see *ERE* ii. 165, 166 end, 168b.
[21] *ERE* iii. 182, § 2.
[22] *Ib.* § 10.
[23] *Ib.* ii. 296–298.
[24] *Ib.* iii. 183, § 14.
[25] Cf. *Præp. Evang.* 156d.

story is based upon the Biblical narrative of Abraham's sacrifice of Isaac, especially because it was found in Sanchuniathon's *History of the Jews*, but there is no evidence of any direct connexion. More probably both stories go back to some common early Canaanite original.

D. *AUTHENTICITY OF THE PHŒNICIAN HISTORY OF SANCHUNIATHON*.—**1. Theory that Eusebius invented the fragments.**—C. A. Lobeck,[1] on the basis of their euhemerism, holds that the reputed extracts from Philo are the invention of Eusebius himself or of another late Christian writer; but this is impossible in view of the strong Semitic flavour of the material. The names of the gods are mainly Phœnician, and the Phœnician words are correctly translated. The extraordinary frequency of καί at the beginning of sentences also indicates translation from a Semitic original. The stories have points of contact with the OT, but are so different that they cannot have been derived from it. In their divergences they have analogies in Babylonia and in other parts of the Semitic world. Neither Eusebius nor any other Christian writer of his period possessed the knowledge of Semitic religion necessary for the composition of these fragments. The genuineness of Eusebius's quotations is proved further by the fact that Johannes Lydus[2] gives an extract from the Phœnician *History* that is not found in Eusebius. This shows that he derived his information directly from Eusebius's source and not from Eusebius himself. In the other passages Lydus agrees closely with Eusebius, which shows that the latter has correctly reported his original.

2. Theory that Eusebius derived the fragments from Porphyry.—Eusebius[3] quotes Porphyry, *Against the Christians*, as an authority in regard to Sanchuniathon. Gifford[4] and others think that this shows that Eusebius derived his quotations of Philo from Porphyry. This is unlikely. Eusebius quotes Porphyry only as witness to the antiquity and credibility of Sanchuniathon. He never mentions him in connexion with the extracts, but names only Philo himself. This shows that he had access to Philo's work directly. Lydus also cites Philo, not Porphyry. Porphyry was a Neo-Platonist and defender of the old gods. He was the last man to approve and quote extensively the euhemeristic legends preserved by Eusebius. Still less is it possible that Porphyry invented the fragments ascribed to Philo. It is true that he was a native of Tyre, but he received a Greek education, was a pupil of Plotinus, and spent most of his life in Rome. It is improbable that he possessed the Semitic knowledge necessary for the composition of these extracts; and, as remarked above, they do not agree with his philosophy.

3. Theory that Philo invented the fragments.—F. C. Movers, in his earliest treatise on the subject, 'Die Unächtheit der Fragmente des Sanchoniathon,'[5] pronounced the extracts given by Eusebius an invention of Philo. The claim to have discovered a work that had been hidden by the priests, which in its turn was based upon secret writings of the *ammouneis*, bore on its face the mark of fraud. Philo was a native of Byblos and knew the names of the Phœnician gods and their popular identification with Greek divinities. He derived the stories which he ascribes to Sanchuniathon from Hesiod and other Greek poets and philosophers. This theory, like the foregoing, does not do justice to the strong Semitic character of the fragments and to their analogies in the OT and in other Semitic literatures.

4. Theory that Philo gathered late Phœnician traditions which he worked over to suit his purposes.—Movers in his later works abandoned the extreme view that he held at first and maintained that Philo used genuine Phœnician traditions, but did not find them already collected by Sanchuniathon. This is the view also of Bunsen, Duncker, von Gutschmid, Baudissin, Wachsmuth, and most of the recent writers. This theory does justice to the Phœnician material found in the fragments, but emphasizes the lateness of the tradition as shown in the following characteristics.

(*a*) *Syncretism of the fragments.*—The Phœnician gods are identified with Egyptian and Greek gods, and the mingling of Egyptian, Hebrew, Persian, and Greek ideas in the legends shows, it is said, that the tradition cannot have arisen before the beginning of the Christian era.

In the case of Egypt the only clear borrowing is Thōth, the scribe of the gods and inventor of writing.[1] Here, however, it may be questioned whether this name, like Hermes, is not merely Philo's translation of some Phœnician god of writing, such as Nabu, the antiquity of whose cult in Canaan is attested.[2] Granted, however, that Thōth is original, Egyptian influence on the religion of Canaan began so early that we do not have to wait for the age of Philo for the introduction of this deity into the Phœnician pantheon.[3]

In relation to the OT there are many similarities in the fragments, but there is no evidence that any of the myths are derived from the OT; on the contrary, they are so independent as to indicate that they are both variants of a primitive Canaanite tradition.

Persian influence is claimed in the reference to Zoroaster the Magian in the *Sacred Collection of Persian Records*.[4] This, however, is given by Philo, not as a quotation from Sanchuniathon, but as a new extract from a different work. The other supposed trace of Persian influence is Magos, 'the Magian,' who with his brother Amunos established villages and sheepfolds.[5] The activity of this personage does not point to a Persian origin; and, as remarked above, it is probable that Magos does not mean 'Magian,' but is merely a transcription of the Phœnician name Ma'on.

Greek influence is shown in the identification of the gods of Phœnicia with Greek divinities, but this may be the work of Philo rather than of his Semitic originals. In most cases Philo gives the Phœnician name alongside of the Greek name, and the former may have been the only one in his sources. Movers claims that the supposed Sanchuniathon derives some of his stories from Greek etymologies; *e.g.*, he states that Persephone, Περσεφόνη, 'died a virgin,' which shows that he derived Persephone from παρθένος and φονή; but this is too far-fetched to be probable. Of Astarte he says that she found a star and consecrated it as the island of Tyre, which shows that he derived 'Ashtart from ἀστήρ; but the connexion of 'Ashtart with the planet Venus can be traced back in Babylonia at least as far as the dynasty of Ḫammurabi.[6] It is even possible that ἀστήρ may be a derivative from 'Ashtar. It is claimed further that the supposed Sanchuniathon depends upon Hesiod in his theogony and war of the gods. Unquestionably Philo knows Hesiod and follows him in translating the names of the Phœnician gods; but, as remarked before, the numerous deviations from Hesiod show that he is not the source of the narrative. Both Hesiod and Sanchuniathon go back to a common Semitic original.

(*b*) *Euhemerism of the fragments.*—The fragments show throughout the effort to explain the gods as men who have been deified after death for the

1 *Aglaophamus*, pp. 1265–1279.
2 *FHG* iii. 571.
3 31a.
4 Eus. *Præp. Evang.* i. 36.
5 *Jahrb. für Theol. und christl. Philos.* VII. i. 51 f.

1 *ERE* v. 246a, vi. 380b.
2 *Ib.* iii. 184, § 6, ix. 894, § 72.
3 *Ib.* iii. 184 f.
4 *Præp. Evang.* 42a.
5 *Ib.* 35d.
6 *ERE* vii. 432, § 13.

services that they have rendered to humanity. This feature cannot be attributed to the translator; it lies in the very substance of the material. This theory of the origin of the gods was first given currency by Euhemerus, a contemporary of Alexander the Great. It gained favour, particularly among the Romans, at the beginning of the Christian era and found a fanatical advocate in Philo; accordingly, it is argued that its presence in these fragments proves their origin in the Greek period.

Against this view it may be argued that so-called euhemerism is far older than Euhemerus even among the Greeks[1] and existed still earlier among the Semites. The work ascribed to Lucian, *de Dea Syria*, which certainly depends throughout on Semitic sources, shows as pronounced euhemerism as do the fragments preserved by Philo. The legends in Gn 1–11, preserved not only by P but also by J, show a similar euhemerism. The names recorded both in J's and in P's list of the descendants of Adam are found elsewhere in the Semitic world as gods, but here they have become men, the discoverers of the arts, just as in Sanchuniathon. It seems, therefore, that this feature characterized already the primitive Canaanite tradition which underlay both Sanchuniathon and the OT.

5. Theory that Philo translated an older Phœnician writer.—Influenced by the foregoing considerations, Ewald, Renan, Tiele, and Spiegel accept the genuineness of the Sanchuniathon fragments and believe that Philo has given us a real, if somewhat free, translation. Ewald dates Sanchuniathon in the pre-Davidic age, Tiele in the Persian period, Renan in the Seleucid. Ewald attempts to prove that Porphyry knew the Phœnician original of Sanchuniathon and did not depend on Philo's translation. Renan argues from the scientific spirit of Philo that he would not have been likely to forge a document. It is impossible to prove the existence of Sanchuniathon, since we have only the testimony of Philo; still it is equally impossible to disprove it, so that critical opinion will probably continue to vacillate between this theory and the preceding one.

LITERATURE.—**C. A. Lobeck**, *Aglaophamus*, Königsberg, 1829, pp. 1265–1279; **F. C. Movers**, 'Die Unächtheit der im Eusebius erhaltenen Fragmente des Sanchoniathon bewiesen,' *Jahrb. für Theol. und christl. Philos.* VII. i. [1836] 51–94; **C. F. Bähr**, art. 'Sanchuniathon,' in Pauly-Wissowa, VI. i. [1852]; **H. Ewald**, 'Abhandlung über die phönikischen Ansichten von der Weltschöpfung und den geschichtlichen Werth Sanchuniathon's,' *AGG* v. [1851–52] 3–68; **E. Renan**, 'Mémoire sur l'origine et le caractère véritable de l'histoire phénicienne qui porte le nom de Sanchoniathon,' *MAIBL* XXIII. ii. [1858] 241–334; **H. Ewald**, review of Renan's art. in *GGA* cxiv. [1859] 1441–1447; **F. Spiegel**, art. 'Sanchuniathon,' in *PRE* xiii. [1860]; **W. W. Baudissin**, 'Ueber den religionsgeschichtlichen Werth der phönicischen Geschichte Sanchuniathon's,' in *Studien zur semitischen Religionsgeschichte*, Leipzig, 1876–78, i. 1 ff.; **F. Lenormant**, *Les Origines de l'histoire*, Paris, 1880, Eng. tr., *The Beginnings of History*, London and New York, 1883; **J. Halévy**, 'Les Principes cosmogoniques phéniciens ΠΟΘΟΣ et ΜΩΤ,' in *Mélanges de critique et d'histoire*, Paris, 1883, pp. 381–388; **O. Gruppe**, *Die griechischen Culte und Mythen in ihren Beziehungen zu den orientalischen Religionen*, Leipzig, 1887, pp. 347-409; **F. Lukas**, *Die Grundbegriffe in den Kosmogonien der alten Völker*, do. 1893, p. 139 ff.; **M. J. Lagrange**, *Études sur les religions sémitiques*², Paris, 1905, pp. 396–437; Baudissin, art. 'Sanchuniathon,' in *PRE*³ xvii. [1906] 452–470 (with full bibliography of the older literature); R. Gottheil, art. 'Sanchoniathon,' in *Johnson's Universal Cyclopedia*, New York, 1895; H. Gressmann, art. 'Sanchuniathon,' in *RGG* v. [Tübingen, 1913] 248; see also the literature under PHILO BYBLIUS, PHŒNICIANS.

LEWIS BAYLES PATON.

SANCTIFICATION.

1. The term in theology.—In general, sanctification is the work of the Holy Spirit of God, in delivering men from the guilt and power of sin, in consecrating them to the service and love of God, and in imparting to them, initially and progressively, the fruits of Christ's redemption and the graces of a holy life.

The term ἁγιάζειν is also applied in the NT to (*a*) the reverent recognition or making known of an already existing sanctity (Mt 6^{9}, 1 P 3^{15}; cf. Nu 20^{12}, Is 8^{13}, Ezk 20^{41}); (*b*) the setting apart of material objects as holy, through their special association with God or with things divine (Mt $23^{17.19}$, 1 Ti 4^{5}; cf. Ex $29^{27.37}$, Lv 27^{16-21})[1]; (*c*) God's consecration of Christ, or Christ's consecration of Himself, to the office and work of the Messiah (Jn 10^{36} 17^{19}; cf. Ex 40^{13}, 2 Ch 5^{11} 30^{17}).

Sanctification is usually the subjective side of salvation (*q.v.*), particularly as viewed in relation to God's purity. That reinstatement of the sinful soul in the divine favour which the term 'justification' describes under the figure of a court of law (with reference to God's righteousness), and which the terms 'adoption' and 'regeneration' describe under the figure of family life (with reference to God's fatherliness), the term 'sanctification' describes in terms of ritual worship (with reference to God's holiness). Just as God's ceremonial purity, in the OT, forbade the near approach of that which was levitically unclean, until its defilement should be purged by the blood of sprinkling, and required that the offering should be withdrawn from profane or common use and dedicated in sacrifice upon the altar, so, in the NT, God's ethical holiness demands that the souls of sinners, who are in themselves unworthy to draw nigh to Him, shall be purged from the defilement of personal sin, sprinkled from an evil conscience through the blood of the everlasting covenant, separated from worldly and profane service, and dedicated to a progressive hallowing in the service and love of God (He 9^{11-13} $10^{10-14.19-22.29}$ 12^{14}, Ro 12^{1}).

2. NT doctrine.—The following points receive emphasis in the NT. (*a*) The whole process is based upon and conditioned by Christ's perfectly achieved holiness, which grounds and guarantees the sanctification of all His followers and is a perpetual life within them, overcoming sin (1 Co 1^{30}, Eph 5^{26}, He 2^{11} $10^{10.12.14}$ 13^{12}; cf. the use of καθαρίζειν, He 1^{3}, 2 P 1^{9}). (*b*) The gift and process of sanctification are primarily traceable to the free grace of the divine consecrating Spirit, normally associated with or taking full effect through baptism (Jn $17^{17.19}$, 1 Co 6^{11}, 1 Th 5^{23}, 2 Th 2^{13}, Ro 15^{16}); yet they also involve, though in a subordinate degree and as a result of the foregoing, the believer's own self-dedication and ethical striving, through faith, strenuous self-discipline, and moral habit (Ac 26^{18}, 1 Th 4^{3-7}, Ro 6^{19-22}, 2 Co 7^{1}, He 12^{14}, 1 Ti 4^{7}; cf. the use of ἁγνίζειν in Ja 4^{8}, 1 P 1^{22}, 1 Jn 3^{3}). These two necessary conditions, of human obedience and divine sprinkling, are brought together in 1 P 1^{2} (cf. Ph 2^{16}). (*c*) Sanctification has no prescribed limits set to it in this earthly life, and it is intended to be finally complete and perfect through the fidelity of God (1 Th 3^{13} 5^{23}, 1 Co $1^{8.9}$, Eph $1^{13.14}$ 3^{16-19}); yet the term 'sanctified' (present participle) is applicable to all who are renewed in Christ Jesus, to whatever degree of holiness they may have attained (Ac 20^{32} 26^{18}, 1 Co 1^{2}, He 10^{14}). Generally, sanctification (ἁγιασμός), as an act or process, begun by God and ever going on 'in Christ,' is distinguished from holiness or sanctity (ἁγιότης [2 Co 1^{12}, He 12^{10}]) and moral purity (ἁγιωσύνη [1 Th 3^{13}, 2 Co 7^{1}]), which are the state and quality respectively. See, further, art. HOLINESS, and *HDB*, *s.v.* 'Sanctification.'

In historically unfolding and developing the NT doctrine of sanctification the Christian Church has concerned itself chiefly with (*a*) the manner in which grace is related to faith in the work of sanctification, and (*b*) the degree to which sanctification may be carried in the present life.

3. Teaching of Augustine.—The Church's thought on the subject flowed first of all into the moulds provided for it by Augustine. His opposi-

[1] *ERE* v. 572.

[1] See art. CONSECRATION.

tion to Pelagianism ([*q.v.*] which represented a strong tendency in prior Catholic piety, especially in the East) led him to insist that the whole process of sanctification has its beginning, middle, and end in the grace of God, freely and spontaneously bestowed, man's co-operating effort being itself a divine gift. Further, his view of original sin, and of human nature as radically corrupted by the Fall, led him to conceive that sanctifying grace as a new supernatural impartation of divine life. Finally, his doctrine of the Church led him to regard that infused energy of grace as operating exclusively within the Church through the sacraments—a view not fully reconciled with his doctrine of predestination and the final perseverance of the elect. Augustine never lost sight of the importance of personal love to Christ as a constituent element of Christian holiness; yet the tendency of his system to take a metaphysical and almost physical view of grace (due to the influence of Neo-Platonism) and the absence from it of any due emphasis on the religious preoccupation of faith with the historic redeeming Christ, revealed in the gospel, as the prime factor in the transformation of the Christian's character, profoundly affected the subsequent theology of the Church in this as in other directions.

Augustine in theory allowed for the possibility of perfect sanctification in this life through the special operation of supernatural, irresistible grace; but he somewhat weakened the admission by affirming that, by the judicial act of God, such entire sanctification had never been achieved. 'See how unexampled among men is an instance of perfect righteousness; but yet it is not impossible. For it might be achieved if there were only applied as much of a favourable will as suffices for so great a work . . . Now the fact that this is not realized, is not owing to any intrinsic impossibility, but to God's judicial act.'[1]

4. Mediæval Catholic developments.—The teaching of Augustine was further developed by Aquinas and systematized into the mediæval doctrines of scholastic Catholicism, which received their dogmatic sanction and final form in the decrees of the Council of Trent. Ordinary human nature being incapable of forsaking sin, or meriting salvation, or truly apprehending God, supernatural grace is imparted, as 'aliquod habituale donum naturae superadditum,'[2] to raise the soul to a new level or higher order of being and so enable it to achieve its heavenly destiny and beatitude of knowing, possessing, and enjoying God. This sanctifying grace is derived in the first instance from the inexhaustible treasury of Christ's merit, at the disposal of the Church, and made available by means of sacraments, which prolong and universalize Christ's incarnate activities as Redeemer. From the divine side, the presence of this sanctifying or sufficient grace within the soul remits original sin, imparts a permanent habit of inherent righteousness, and carries within itself the promise and potency of all perfection. Out of it, as from a divine seed, emerges the tree of spiritual life, which branches out into the three theological and four cardinal virtues and yields ultimately the seven ripe fruits of the Holy Spirit. Only by mortal sin can its operations be neutralized or destroyed, the guilt which is contracted subsequently to baptism being removed by the eucharist in the case of venial sins and by the penitential system of the Church in the case of those that are more serious. From the human side, good works or supernatural acts of faith working through love have merit before God and secure increase of grace on that account; yet no such meritorious works are possible without the continuous assistance of actual, co-operating, or efficacious grace, which supplements the sanctifying grace originally bestowed, and mysteriously inclines the will, by its own effort, to give a free assent to righteousness. The resulting process and goal of holiness are spoken of, not as sanctification (which is already bestowed in God's initial act), but as justification, or the actual making just or righteous, through infused grace leading to final perseverance, of him who was once a sinner but can now stand before the bar of God, deserving eternal life.

'Quae [justificatio] non est sola peccatorum remissio, sed et sanctificatio et renovatio interioris hominis per voluntariam susceptionem gratiae et donorum; unde homo ex injusto fit justus.'[1]

According to Roman Catholic teaching, there is no particular sin which may not be wholly overcome by sanctifying grace, and no commandments of God which are impossible to the justified;[2] but the perfect eradication of all sin in this earthly life implies such a special infusion of assisting grace that it cannot be predicated of any one save of the Blessed Virgin.[3] Nor can any one be so sanctified during this life as to be able to assure himself that he will not fall from grace.[4] 'The Catholic can obtain the forgiveness of his sins only when he abandons them, and in this view the justified man—the man acceptable to God—is identical in every respect with the sanctified.'[5]

5. Reformed doctrine.—The Reformed doctrine of sanctification differed from the mediæval in laying stress on the category of sin and redemption rather than on that of nature and supernature. Grace did not mean to Luther a supernatural essence or virtually impersonal energy, derived from God and mysteriously yet infallibly infused into the soul by means of the sacraments. That view he found linked, in popular practice, to the immoral system of the sale of indulgences for sin. Rather, grace was conceived by him, more religiously, in the light of the teaching of the NT and his own experiences of inward piety, as the free, unmerited favour of God to sinners, in opening His fatherly heart to them in the forgiving love of Christ. This personal divine grace of Christ in the Holy Spirit, mediated primarily through the Word and only secondarily and derivatively through the sacraments, regenerates the soul and spontaneously evokes in us, in accordance with the laws of moral personality, a childlike confidence or trust (*fiducia*), which at once justifies us before God (thus delivering us from the guilt of sin) and through the further gift of the Holy Spirit continuously sanctifies us (delivering us also from the power of sin), so enabling us to produce good works.

'The soul, through faith alone, without works, is, from the Word of God, justified, sanctified, endued with truth, peace, and liberty, and filled full with every good thing, and is truly made the child of God.'[6]

Sanctification was thus conceived by Luther as the necessary corollary or complement of justification, the fulfilling of the law through love, though never in this life could that goal be perfectly attained.

In his view, 'the gospel . . . while it awakens faith, does not limit itself to the task of bestowing upon that faith forgiveness of sins through Christ, and, by assurance of this, pacifying the conscience. It proceeds further to bestow the gift of the Holy Ghost, in order that the soul may exhibit that reciprocity of love towards God which evinces itself in the fulfilling of the law. Although such fulfilment is of course always imperfect, it is still obligatory, because the law is of everlasting obligation.'[7]

The position of Calvinism was very similar, as may be seen from the following statements of the *Westminster Confession* (1647), ch. xiii.:

'(i.) They who are effectually called and regenerated, having a new heart and a new spirit created in them, are further sanctified really and personally, through the virtue of Christ's death and resurrection, by His word and Spirit dwelling in them; the dominion of the whole body of sin is destroyed, and the

1 'On the Spirit and the Letter,' ch. 63, in *Works*, ed. M. Dods, Edinburgh, 1872, iv. 226 f.
2 *Summa Theol.* II. i. qu. cix. art. 1.

1 *Council of Trent*, sess. vi. cap. 7. See, further, art. GRACE.
2 *Ib.* sess. vi. cap. 11. 3 *Ib.* sess. vi. cap. 23.
4 *Ib.* sess. vi. cap. 9, 13.
5 J. A. Moehler, *Symbolism*, tr. J. B. Robertson, London, 1894, p. 116.
6 'On Christian Liberty,' in Luther's *Primary Works*, ed. H. Wace and C. A. Buchheim, London, 1896, p. 110.
7 A. Ritschl, *A Critical Hist. of the Christian Doctrine of Justification and Reconciliation*, tr. J. S. Black, Edinburgh, 1872, p. 171.

several lusts thereof are more and more weakened and mortified, and they are more and more quickened and strengthened in all saving graces, to the practice of true holiness, without which no man shall see the Lord.

(ii.) This sanctification is throughout the whole man, yet imperfect in this life; there abideth still some remnant of corruption in every part: whence ariseth a continual and irreconcilable war; the flesh lusting against the Spirit and the Spirit against the flesh.

(iii.) In which war, although the remaining corruption for a time may much prevail, yet, through the continual supply of strength from the sanctifying Spirit of Christ, the regenerate part doth overcome; and so the saints grow in grace, perfecting holiness in the fear of God.'

6. Pietism, Moravianism, and Methodism.—The Reformers, however, largely because of their preoccupation with the Roman controversy and the doctrine of justification, did not fully develop the doctrine of sanctification; nor did it receive much attention from later Protestant scholasticism. A more experimental interest in the subject came with Pietism, Moravianism, and Methodism (*qq.v.*). Here the emphasis shifted from the ecclesiastical method and discipline of holiness, and all abstract theories and theological conceptions of grace, whether Catholic or Protestant, to a more directly personal, emotional, and evangelical inward communion with Christ Himself, as the Divine Sanctifier and ultimate object of faith, love, and adoration. It was claimed that hourly fellowship with Him, through the Holy Spirit, in the thoughts and activities of ordinary life, ought normally to lead to entire sanctification, an unswerving loyalty, at least, of love and fidelity to God.

In defence of this position it was argued (*a*) that it is the office and work of the Holy Spirit to administer as perfect an atonement inwardly as Christ on the Cross has accomplished for us outwardly; (*b*) that Christ Himself bade His followers be perfect; (*c*) that St. Paul contemplated the complete destruction of sin in the believer even in this life (Ro 6[6. 7. 11. 22]), and that St. John spoke of the continued presence of sin in the truly regenerate as an impossible event (1 Jn 3[9]); (*d*) that the NT repeatedly either prays, promises, or exhorts that men should be 'filled with the Spirit,' 'sanctified wholly,' 'perfected in love,' 'redeemed from all iniquity,' 'purified even as He is pure,' 'filled unto all the fulness of God,' 'presented unblamable before God at Christ's coming'; (*e*) that only a non-Christian (Gnostic or Manichæan) view of human nature can regard sin as necessary, and entire sanctification as impossible, for physical reasons; (*f*) that 'evangelical' perfection, or blamelessness of sincere reaction against all sin, and inward consecration to the rule of love, in reliance upon divine grace, is quite compatible with intellectual mistakes, creaturely limitations, and even moral lapses due to transmitted tendencies to evil or the pressure of a hostile environment; (*g*) that sensitiveness to evil, humility arising out of past sin, vicarious penitence before God, and the corporate confession of the sins of others continue to be the marks of true holiness even among the blessed; (*h*) that the moral and spiritual conditions of entire sanctification cannot be affected by the physical fact of death, but must be the same here as they shall be hereafter.

'The NT gives no ground for supposing that there is such an absolute contrast between the conditions of the heavenly life and those of the Christian life in this world that sin must be entirely alien to the one and inevitable in the other. In the absence of such a contrast, the commands, instructions, and prayers which look to entire sanctification or perfect love carry a certain presumption that the state which these terms define is of possible attainment in this life.'[1]

At the same time, it was recognized that, while such a sincere spiritual fidelity of the soul to its opportunities and ideals might be achieved in this life, no guarantee could be given that it would consistently be maintained. See, further, artt. BACKSLIDING and PERFECTION (Christian).

The revivalist type of piety favoured an experimental and even doctrinal dualism between the soul's imperfect first love in conversion (which might easily cool or become lost) and the 'second blessing' of a perfectly clean heart in sanctification (or the conscious and glad experience of love habitually prevailing in all one's actions). Many, however, thought that this separated justification and sanctification too widely, and claimed that an immediate entrance into full sanctification, *per saltum*, as it were (yet not so as to exclude the progressive enlightenment of the mind and refinement of the conscience), was possible and incumbent upon all Christians. Others went farther and advocated full sanctification in a more absolute sense, denying the possibility of any progressive hallowing of the spiritually loyal will or conscience, as distinct from mere growth out of mental ignorance or mistakes of judgment. See art. HOLINESS, *ad fin.*

7. Kant.—An entirely new approach to the Christian doctrine of sanctification was made necessary by the revolutionary philosophical thinking inaugurated by Kant. Although reared in the atmosphere of Pietism, Kant broke away from the whole dogmatic system of supernatural or 'revealed' religion on which it rested and based the necessity of holiness solely on the nature of the thinking, experiencing, and acting self, and on the categoric claims of the moral law, without any reference to a theology of grace. Man's ethical nature demands, as its supreme good, the union of perfect virtue and perfect happiness. Such a consummation requires God to guarantee it, freedom to realize it, and immortality to perfect it. In this view, sanctification is construed in terms of moral character alone, and all hope of its being in any sense complete during this earthly life is swept away.

'The perfect accordance of the will with the moral law is *holiness*, a perfection of which no rational being of the sensible world is capable at any moment of his existence. Since, nevertheless, it is required as practically necessary, it can only be found in a *progress in infinitum* towards that perfect accordance, and on the principles of pure practical reason it is necessary to assume such a practical progress as the real object of our will.'[1]

8. Schleiermacher.—If Roman Catholicism conceived sanctification institutionally, and Kant ethically, Schleiermacher conceived it mystically and subjectively. Growth in holiness is the progressive domination of the God-consciousness within us over the merely sentient and ever morally defective world-consciousness. This is derived by us historically from the perfect and archetypal God-consciousness of Christ and mediated to us spiritually through the redemptive life-fellowship of the Church. Within that fellowship the Holy Spirit rouses our free, loving surrender to the attractive and formative personality of the Redeemer, who in His turn communicates to us, relatively but in ever-increasing measure, His own supreme blessedness and unclouded consciousness of God.[2] It is noticeable that, whereas Kant's moral and individualistic view of sanctification demanded a personal immortality for its perfecting, Schleiermacher's more emotional and social view looked to the perfecting of sanctification in a fellowship and was consistent in his mind with an almost impersonal pantheism.

9. Ritschl.—Ritschl's doctrine of sanctification was determined by his governing conception of the Kingdom of God. If in the experience of redemption we find ourselves forgiven and regenerate, it is not with a view to our subsequent personal holiness before God, as a Pietist might say, nor yet with a view to our attaining the freedom of perfect moral character, as Kant might say, but rather with a view to the practical fulfilment of our vocation as members of God's kingdom of goodness, righteousness, and love. This inward experience of redemption, begun in our awareness

[1] H. C. Sheldon, *System of Christian Doctrine*, Cincinnati, 1903, p. 468.

[1] *Critique of Practical Reason*[6], ed. T. K. Abbott, London, 1909, p. 218.

[2] *Der christliche Glaube*[3], Berlin, 1836, §§ 88, 100.

of reconciliation with God and restored harmony with the universe through the inner life of Jesus, historically and spiritually mediated to us through the Church, is consummated by the help of God the Holy Spirit. Ritschl, however, conceived the Holy Spirit, not metaphysically as a Person of the Trinity, but religiously and experimentally as 'the power of the complete knowledge of God which is common to believers in Christ,' 'an attribute of the Christian community,' 'the motive-power of the life of all Christians—a life which, as such, is necessarily directed to the common end of the Kingdom of God.'[1] This indwelling spirit of life imparts justification, regeneration, and sanctification primarily to the Church or community of believers and only secondarily to such individual members as personally appropriate these gifts through faith; since 'it is not permissible for any man to determine his relation to the Holy Spirit by observation of himself, in which he isolates himself from all others.'[2] The result is perfection, or 'faith in the Fatherly providence of God, which maintains a right feeling with God through humility, and with the world through patience, and which expresses and confirms itself through prayer . . . with the disposition to obey the moral law and with good action in one's calling.'[3] Ritschl's repudiation of the Augustinian doctrine of original or transmitted sinfulness, and his own teaching that sin is not the violation of an absolute or statutory moral law, but only a relative failure to fulfil one's vocation in the service of the Kingdom and in the active exercise of patience, humility, and prayer, lead naturally to the view that sanctification may quite well be complete, qualitatively if not quantitatively, during the present life.

'The conception of a moral perfection in the Christian life ought on no account to be associated with the idea of a fruitless search for actual sinlessness of conduct in all the details of life. It rather means that our moral achievement or life-work in connection with the Kingdom of God should, however limited in amount, be conceived as possessing the quality of a whole in its own order . . . the realisation of the universal good within the special limited domain of our vocation.'[4]

10. Modern Christian view.—This modern emphasis on social service and moral sacrificial action as integral parts of true holiness is heartily to be welcomed. 'It has been the bane of evangelical Christianity, and often its perdition, to have severed justification in the cross (or religion) from sanctification in the spirit (or ethic).'[5] It is obvious, however, that in the course of our survey we have already travelled far from the original idea of temple-sprinkling and the conditions of approach to a holy God. Viewed in the light of NT teaching, Ritschl's doctrine is defective in three respects. (*a*) His interest in the practical aspects of religion, and his dislike of mysticism led him to conceive sanctification as a moral and social task of mutual loyalty laid upon the community in its dominion over the world, rather than as a religious privilege, training, and aspiration experienced by the individual in his fellowship with God. (*b*) While he dealt suggestively with the moral vocation of Jesus and His influence upon men as the Founder of the Kingdom and humanity's ideal representative before God, he related inadequately the work of Christ to the divine holiness and righteousness in taking away the sin of the world and so providing a moral and spiritual basis for forgiveness and sanctification. (*c*) He minimized the distinctive testimony of the Christian consciousness as to the nature and function of the exalted Christ and the personal work of the Holy Spirit in sanctification.

It has been the work of subsequent theology to endeavour to remedy these defects. A modern Christian view of sanctification is likely to bring the Roman Catholic doctrine of grace objectively given and the Protestant doctrine of grace subjectively realized into closer relation with one another, by means of a more comprehensive and dynamic doctrine of the Holy Spirit, and so to regard justification and sanctification, not as separate and detached experiences, but as complementary aspects of one vital relationship of union with the living Christ. 'The attitude of faith in justification implies the implicit energy of sanctification.'[1] At the present day there is evidence of a revived interest in the more experimental aspects of Christian holiness. The increase in the number of clerical and lay retreats, prayer-circles, fellowships of silence, conventions for the deepening of spiritual life, and the like, shows that the subject of personal sanctification is again taking possession of men's minds. Of the growingly popular Roman Catholic retreats for working men, *e.g.*, it has been written:

'The effects are lasting. The men have had serious instruction, have faced life calmly and sensibly, have deepened their religious spirit. You meet them coming in from thirty leagues round to make a retreat, and you ask them where they are going; they answer: "To sanctify ourselves."'[2]

See, further, artt. HOLINESS, PERFECTION (Christian), and the literature there cited.

LITERATURE.—See the references in the footnotes.

R. H. COATS.

SANCTION.—See REWARDS AND PUNISHMENTS, UTILITARIANISM.

SANCTUARY.—See ASYLUM.

SANDEMANIANS.—See GLASITES.

SANDWICH ISLANDS.—See POLYNESIA.

SANHEDRIN.—A certain reaction seems due against what may be termed historical scepticism as applied to the history of Israel. Uncritical acceptance of so-called traditions needed the severest testing and repudiation; but, when this process tends to an equally uncritical denial of all traditions, it must be the function of a true scientific criticism to redress the balance. In brief, legendary embellishments in an olden narrative do not necessarily destroy the whole trust to be placed in it.[3] This judgment applies with special force to the Jewish 'traditions' as to the communal organization in Judæa. Criticism has been inclined to a catastrophic series, while tradition has posited continuity. Thus the 'Great Synagogue' forms the traditional link between the prophets and the teachers of the type who constituted the Sanhedrin.[4] In the Great Synagogue were included, according to one form of the tradition, the latest of the prophets—Haggai, Zechariah, and Malachi. The activity assigned to the Great Synagogue was clearly meant to represent the completion of the work of Ezra and to account for the internal development during the Persian period, the records of which are so scanty. The functions of the Great Synagogue were taken to be threefold: 'the preservation of the Scriptures, the establishing of the Liturgy, and the foundation of the Oral Law.'[5] Clearly, the 'tradition'

[1] *The Christian Doctrine of Justification and Reconciliation*, tr. H. R. Mackintosh and A. B. Macaulay, Edinburgh, 1900, p. 605.
[2] *Ib.* p. 606. [3] *Ib.* p. 652. [4] *Ib.* pp. 665, 667.
[5] P. T. Forsyth, *The Christian Ethic of War*, London, 1916, p. 86.

[1] H. Wheeler Robinson, *The Christian Doctrine of Man*, Edinburgh, 1911, p. 319.
[2] C. Plater, *Retreats for the People*, London, 1912, p. 157.
[3] Cf. two articles by the present writer on 'The Two Books of the Maccabees,' and 'The Letter of Aristeas,' in *JQR* xiii. [1901] 508 ff. and xiv. [1902] 321 ff.
[4] *Mishnāh Abhôth*, i. (begin.).
[5] S. Krauss, *JQR* x. [1898] 363.

as to the Great Synagogue based itself on the reports contained in Neh 8–10. The returned exiles had to organize the community round the Second Temple as a centre. Hence the leaders constituted an assembly for the purpose. The traditional chronology regarding the date and contemporaneity of the leaders cannot be defended; thus the Tannaitic chronology treats the whole Persian period as extending over only 34 years. Then Alexander the Great appears, and with him ends the Great Synagogue.[1]

Here, however, we are faced by the consideration to which allusion has been made above. As Bacher cautiously concludes, it must be assumed that *some* governing council of a more or less central character existed throughout the Persian period.[2] It is undeniable that a great change had occurred in the standard of conduct and in devotion to the Law between Nehemiah and Mattathias, a period of some two centuries.

'This,' as Krauss points out, 'can only be understood if, during that period, the laws were studied, commented upon, and taught. No high-priests of the class of Joiakim and Eliashib at the time of Ezra, or of Alcimus and Menelaus of the Greek period, would have been able to produce such a signal change in the life of the people. Quite a different class of men must have been at work, who executed and spread the divine teachings with the whole force of religious conviction. Such men were, according to Talmudical information, the men of the Great Synod.'[3]

Nevertheless, Schürer expresses the general conclusion when he asserts that 'the existence of a Jewish γερουσία earlier than the Greek period cannot be proved with any degree of certainty.'[4] It was the work of Hellenism to reorganize the Orient; but, as Schürer concedes, such a council, with tolerably large powers, may date back to the Persian period. The new institution would be not a creation, but a revision. The main difference in the points of view between the Talmudic and the modern conceptions is the position of the priesthood. 'At the *head* of the Jewish commonwealth, and therefore of the γερουσία as well, stood the *hereditary high-priest.*' With the Maccabæan triumph, the chief alteration was the substitution of a new line of high-priests, but throughout the Roman period the high-priest stood at the head of the συνέδριον—a term which, though probably current in this sense in the 2nd cent. B.C., first meets us in the decree of Gabinius, 57 B.C. The power of the Jerusalem Sanhedrin, especially as supreme court of justice, was emphasized by the Roman régime until in A.D. 70 the existing powers of the Sanhedrin were removed, and it became a civil and religious, instead of being a political, body. The Rabbinic tradition regarded the Sanhedrin as an academic court, composed of the teachers of the Law. But it is now recognized 'from the concurrent testimony of Josephus and the New Testament that, till the very last, the head of the sacerdotal aristocracy continued to preside over the Sanhedrin.'[5] On the other hand, Schürer modifies his view by conceding that the growth of Pharisaism must have affected the constitution of the Sanhedrin so that in the Roman period the council was a composite body, consisting most probably of 71 members, among whom were included the Sadducean priestly aristocracy and the Pharisaic lay democracy.[6]

It is not proposed here to enter into the details of the powers and activities of the Sanhedrin, as referred to in the NT or Rabbinic period, beyond remarking that there is a fair consensus of opinion that the accounts of the trial of Jesus are in many respects irreconcilable with what is recorded in Jewish sources as to the legal and regular procedure before the court. But attention must be drawn to the fresh light thrown by recent investigation on another apparently irreconcilable conflict of evidence—the relation of priest to laity in the headship of the Sanhedrin. There is here a bold contradiction between the NT and Josephus on the one side and the Rabbinic records on the other. It has recently been urged that the two sets of documents relate to quite different bodies—that there were in fact two councils: (1) a political Sanhedrin, continuous with the γερουσία, and (2) a religious Sanhedrin of later institution. The two, on this theory, co-existed in the Roman period. The former directed public affairs and administered the criminal law (under the control of the procurator); of this Sanhedrin, mainly sacerdotal and aristocratic, the high-priest was president. The latter was lay and democratic, and almost exclusively Pharisaic. It supervised the religious life, supervised the priesthood, discussed the interpretation of the Law, regulated ritual, and arranged the calendar. At the head of this council was the *nasi*, a Pharisaic teacher.[1] This latter Sanhedrin survived the fall of the city in A.D. 70; at all events an academy of the type was founded at Jabneh and afterwards moved to Tiberias. Such an academy existed in Palestine until the 5th cent. A.D.; to it is due the great development of law and learning contained in the Rabbinic books.

A very curious revival of a Sanhedrin occurred in the year 1807. Napoleon convened this assembly of Jewish notables so as to use its decisions as a basis for his legislation. These decisions concerned chiefly the relations of Jews to the State and upheld the principle that the Jew in modern states is in no way precluded by his religion from identifying himself completely with the national life of the state of which he is a citizen.

LITERATURE.—See the works cited in the footnotes.

I. ABRAHAMS.

ŚAṄKARĀCHĀRYA. — No name is better known in the history of Brāhmanic philosophy than that of Śaṅkarāchārya, and no doctrine has exercised greater influence than his on Hindu thought in general. Traces of its influence are unmistakable even at present, notwithstanding the existence of a number of rival systems of Hindu philosophy, whose main if not sole object was and has been to controvert his doctrine. With all this, it is surprising that very little that is of historical importance is known about the life of this great philosopher and the age in which he lived.

1. Date. — It is now generally accepted that Śaṅkara lived in the latter half of the 8th century. The view which assigned him to the 7th cent., and which was so eloquently propounded by Telang, has been completely refuted by the arguments of K. B. Pathak, who regards A.D. 788 as the year of Śaṅkara's birth, specially depending upon a MS from which he gives an extract in *IA* xi. [1882] 174 ff.[2]

2. Life.—Many legends of miraculous powers and fabulous incidents are associated with Śaṅkara's biography. The two works pretending to

[1] For a good account of Kuenen's view, to the effect that the 'Great Synagogue' was at most a temporary phenomenon of the age of Nehemiah, see J. A. Selbie, in *HDB* iv. 643 f.; the literature on the subject is there given. An excellent survey of the whole question by W. Bacher is to be found in *JE* xi. 640 ff.

[2] Cf. J. Derenbourg, *Essai sur l'histoire et la géographie de la Palestine*, Paris, 1867, ch. ii.

[3] *JQR* x. 349.

[4] *GJV*[4] II. i. 166.

[5] *Ib.* p. 174.

[6] *Ib.* p. 248 f.

[1] The view that there were two councils is admirably developed by A. Büchler, *Das Synhedrion in Jerusalem*, Vienna, 1902. A criticism of the view may be read in G. A. Smith, *Jerusalem*, London, 1907, i. 419 ff. The two councils are, on the other hand, accepted by J. Z. Lauterbach, in *JE* xi. 41 ff.

[2] Further discussion of this question of date will be found in *JRASBo* xvi. [1885] 190, xvii. pt. 2 [1889] 63, xviii. [1894] 1, 147 (and esp. pp. 88, 213 for Pathak's further arguments); *IA* xi. 174, xiii. [1884] 95, xvi. [1887] 41, 160; H. H. Wilson, *Works*, London, 1861–77, i. 198; *Saṅkṣepa-Śaṅkara-vijaya*, ed. Kesnalāla Govindarāma Devāśrayi, Bombay, 1899.

give an account of his life are the *Śaṅkara-dig-vijaya* of Mādhavāchārya and the *Śaṅkara-vijaya* of Ānandagiri. Both these biographers deify their hero, regarding him as an incarnation of the god Śiva for the special purpose of putting an end to Buddhists and dualists, and establishing the Brāhmanical religion and philosophy.

The account of his birth is related differently by the two biographers. According to Mādhavāchārya, in the Kerala country (modern Malabar), in a village named Kālaṭī, there lived a Brāhman named Vidyādhirāja who had a son named Śivaguru. This Śivaguru, after having completed his studies, married. Up to very old age he and his wife had no issue; so they worshipped Śiva, practising severe austerities. Śiva appeared before them in a dream and asked them if they would like to have one son of great merit and knowledge, but of short life, or many sons of the opposite character. The parents chose the former; and at last a son was born to them, when all the constellations were in their most favourable positions.

According to Ānandagiri, Viśvajit and Viśiṣṭā were the parents of Śaṅkara. Viśvajit went into a forest to practise penance, and in his absence Viśiṣṭā, who lived at a place named Chidambarapura (also in Kerala), worshipped Chidambareśvara (name of the local Śivaliṅga). This Śivaliṅga entered into her, and the result was the birth of Śaṅkara. Even at a very early age Śaṅkara was master of all the sciences, and various miraculous exploits are attributed to him. Thus, *e.g.*, he is said to have brought the local river near his house in order to save his mother the trouble of going to a distance for water. So also he is credited with having forced his mother to consent to his becoming a *sannyāsin*, while passing through a river, when a crocodile seized him by the foot and would not leave him, unless he made up his mind to retire from the householder's life. After some time Śaṅkara went to the forest called Govindanātha on the bank of the river Indubhavā (Narmadā, according to the commentator), where he met Govinda and became his pupil. We find the name Govinda in the various colophons in the works of Śaṅkara, who always calls himself 'Śrīmad-govinda-bhagavat-pūjyapāda-śiṣya.' This Govinda is the pupil of Gauḍapādāchārya, who in his turn is supposed to be the pupil of Śuka, the son of Vyāsa, identified with the author of the *Brahma-Sūtras*. Next Śaṅkara, at the command of his *guru*, went to Kāśī and composed the commentary (*bhāṣya*) on the *Brahma-Sūtras*. At Prayāga he met Kumārilabhaṭṭa, the great Mīmāṃsā-writer, who was burning himself as punishment for the sin of having destroyed the family of Sugata, his teacher, and of having discarded Īśvara, out of his zeal for the Mīmāṃsā doctrine of Jaimini.

The next great event in Śaṅkara's life is his visit to Maṇḍanamiśra, a very ardent exponent of Mīmāṃsā at Māhiṣmatī, and his dialectical contest with him, which lasted for several days and at the end of which Maṇḍanamiśra, accepting defeat, became a *sannyāsin* and Śaṅkara's most beloved pupil—afterwards known as Sureśvarāchārya, the writer of a *vārtika* on Śaṅkara's *Bṛhadāraṇyakopaniṣad-bhāṣya*. To be able to answer satisfactorily the questions pertaining to erotics put to him by the wife of Maṇḍanamiśra, Śaṅkara next entered into the dead body of a king named Amaraka and had all the experience of the science in question, a result of which was a poem ascribed to him, called *Amaruśataka*.

Śaṅkara then made a tour through India, refuting all doctrines except that of absolute monism (*kevalādvaita*) by his wonderful power of dialectic. He attracted several zealous and clever pupils—*e.g.*, Padmapāda, Toṭaka, Hastāmalaka, and others. He succeeded in mounting the seat of omniscience (*sarvajña-pīṭha*) in the temple of Śāradā in Kashmīr, while others could not even get through the doors of the temple.

Śaṅkara attended his mother during her last illness; and, when she was dead, the relatives refused to give him fire with which to burn her, since Śaṅkara was a *sannyāsin*. At this Śaṅkara cursed them all, saying that they would be excluded from the study of the Vedas (*veda-bahiṣkṛta*), that no *sannyāsin* would receive alms from them, and that the cemetery would be very near their houses.[1] Śaṅkara died at the early age of thirty-two.

The great object of Śaṅkara's labours was the revival of the system of religion and philosophy taught in the *Upaniṣads*; and for this he wrote many works and carried on dialectical controversies all through India, from Kāmarūpa or Assam in the north-east to Kashmīr and Kalkha in the north-west, and from the Himālayas down to Cape Komorin, and succeeded in putting down the heterodox systems and establishing the doctrine of absolute monism. He established four *maṭhas*, or seats of religion, at the four ends of India—the Śṛṅgerimaṭha on the Śṛṅgeri hills in the south, the Śāradāmaṭha at Dwarka in the west, the Jyotirmaṭha at Badarikāśrama in the north, and the Govardhanamaṭha at Puri in the east. Each of these *maṭhas* has a *sannyāsin* at its head, who bears the title of Śaṅkarāchārya in general, with a proper name of his own, and who exercises only a nominal control over the religious matters in the province.

[1] And such is the case even at present in that part, remarks the author of *Śaṅkara-dig-vijaya*.

3. Works.—The following is a brief notice of the works supposed to be written by Śaṅkara, but about the authorship of some we are not sure:

The best, of course, is (1) his commentary on the *Brahma-Sūtrās*, which, apart from its philosophical value, is a masterpiece as a literary product. Śaṅkara also wrote (2) commentaries on the ten principal *Upaniṣads* and (3) on the *Bhagavad-Gītā*, the two other *prasthānas* of the Vedānta. His main object was to show that the *Upaniṣads* and the *Bhagavad-Gītā* contain no doctrine but absolute monism. There are also his commentaries (4) on the *Viṣṇu-sahasra-nāma* and (5) on the *Sanatsujātīya*, both *prakaraṇas* from the *Mahābhārata*. He also wrote several independent treatises dealing with the principal topics of the Vedānta-doctrine, such as (6) *Viveka-chūḍāmaṇi*, (7) *Upadeśasahasrī*, (8) *Aparokṣānubhūti*, (9) *Ātmabodha*, (10) *Daśa-śloki*, (11) *Mohamudgara*, and many other minor works, such as (12) *stotras* in praise of Viṣṇu, Devi, and other deities.[1]

4. Doctrine.—In Europe by the name Vedānta is generally understood the philosophical doctrine of Śaṅkara; but it is a misunderstanding. There are several philosophical schools which bear the name of Vedānta—*e.g.*, those of Rāmānuja, Vallabha, Madhva, etc., which, however, differ essentially from each other, not only in the theological and practical parts, but even in the metaphysical part properly so called. For this reason the several Vedānta schools have their distinctive significant names also. The name which distinguishes the doctrine of Śaṅkara is 'Kevalādvaita,' or absolute non-duality. This doctrine may be briefly expressed in the well-known line: *Brahma satyaṃ jagan mithyā jīvo Brahmaiva nāparaḥ*, '*Brahman* or the supreme spirit is real; the world is unreal; the individual self is only the supreme self, and no other.' Only intelligence (*chaitanya*), which is without form, without qualities, without any limitations of time, space, or causality, is real; everything else without exception is unreal, phenomenal, erroneously superimposed upon the self-existing, self-refulgent intelligence. Thus the unity of the *Brahman* or the supreme self, according to Śaṅkara, is absolute, without the slightest trace of plurality, which can belong only to the ephemeral and the empirical world; and, if the essence of philosophic thought consists in proceeding from plurality to unity, in finding the one which underlies the many that we see in us and around us, no human conception can go any farther.

(*a*) *Nescience.*—But how can unity be reconciled with the plurality by which we are surrounded and of which we cannot get rid? This question Śaṅkara solves by bringing in the principle of *māyā*, or illusion. Thus his doctrine has always two aspects, esoteric and exoteric, be it in reference to theology, cosmology, or psychology. This is the great merit of Śaṅkara, viz. that he has succeeded in a most satisfactory manner in reconciling the mutually opposed texts of the *Upaniṣads*, which sometimes speak of the unity of the supreme spirit, without attributes, which alone is real and of which one can give only a negative description, but sometimes assert the plurality, the supreme cause being possessed of qualities and capable of controlling from within the world intelligent as well as non-intelligent. The principle of illusion served like a two-edged sword to cut asunder all kinds of opposition. The world around us consists of souls with limited knowledge and of non-intelligent objects; and, if we once admit the existence of a supreme spirit without any limitation, omnipresent, omniscient, how can we explain the creation of souls with limited knowledge and of objects without intelligence, from this omniscient spirit, except as the result of ignorance or

[1] The ed. in 20 vols. of Śaṅkarāchārya's *Works*, published at Śrirangam, 1910 ff., is recommended.

nescience, which, so to speak, puts limitations on the unlimited spirit? And that there exists such ignorance is not only a fact mentioned in the Scripture, but a matter of ordinary experience, as when one has consciousness in the form, 'I am ignorant.' If this consciousness is true, it is a proof of ignorance; if it is not true, it is an even better proof of the same ignorance.

Thus the highest intelligence, which is really without quality, without any limitations, appears to be possessed of qualities, limited in nature, owing to its being conditioned by nescience, which cannot be described as 'being' (*sat*), for it is, as a matter of fact, not real; nor can this nescience be described as 'not being' (*a-sat*), for its effects are incontestable. This nescience consists in erroneously superimposing on something something else that does not exist there, as, *e.g.*, mistaking a rope, which is not a serpent, for a serpent. This nescience manifests itself in various ways and is the cause of all the misery suffered by the soul, though, in its original nature, the soul is nothing but existence, intelligence, and bliss. The most striking and far-reaching example of this is the confusion of the subject with the object, of the knower with the knowable—in fact, of what is real with what is not real or what is only phenomenal.

'It is a matter not requiring any proof,' says Śaṅkara, in the very beginning of his commentary on the *Brahma-Sūtras*, 'that the object and the subject whose respective spheres are the notion of the "Thou" (the Non-Ego) and the "Ego," and which are opposed to each other, as much as darkness and light are, cannot be identified. All the less can their respective attributes be identified. Hence it follows that it is wrong to superimpose upon the subject—whose Self is intelligence, and which has for its sphere the notion of the Ego—the object whose sphere is the notion of the Non-Ego, and the attributes of the object, and vice versâ to superimpose the subject and the attributes of the subject on the object. In spite of this it is on the part of man a natural procedure—which has its cause in wrong knowledge—not to distinguish the two entities (object and subject) and their respective attributes, although they are absolutely distinct, but to superimpose upon each the characteristic nature and the attributes of the other, and thus, coupling the Real and the Unreal, to make use of expressions such as "That am I," "That is mine."'[1]

Śaṅkara gives several definitions of this superimposition (*adhyāsa*), but lays down at last that its essence consists in the apparent presentation of the attributes of one thing in another thing, with which agrees the popular view exemplified by expressions such as 'Mother-of-pearl appears like silver,' 'The moon, although one only, appears as if she were double.'

'This superimposition,' he says further on, 'learned men consider to be Nescience (*avidyā*), and the ascertainment of the true nature of that which is (the Self) by means of the discrimination of that (which is superimposed on the Self), they call knowledge (*vidyā*). There being such knowledge (neither the Self nor the Non-Self) are affected in the least by any blemish or (good) quality produced by their mutual superimposition. This mutual superimposition of the Self and the Non-Self, which is termed Nescience, is the presupposition on which there base all the practical distinctions—those made in ordinary life as well as those laid down by the Veda—between means of knowledge, objects of knowledge (and knowing persons), and all scriptural texts, whether they are concerned with injunctions and prohibitions (of meritorious and non-meritorious actions), or with final release.'[2]

Notwithstanding the fact that the whole objective world is the result of nescience, Śaṅkara allows that this objective world is real for all practical purposes (*vyavahārārtham*). Thus, although the *Brahman* alone has an existence real (*pāramārthika*) in the highest sense of the word, the objective world also has an existence, but with a reality of the second order, or practical (*vyāvahārika*); or we may say that the former represents the metaphysical or esoteric or absolute reality, while the latter represents only the practical or exoteric or relative reality. Thus, esoterically, the *Brahman* alone is real, while the individual souls (*chid*) and the inanimate world (*achid*) are unreal, mere appearance, a mirage. Exoterically, however, the individual souls and the material objects exist for all practical purposes, and, as long as the right knowledge has not arisen, we cannot and must not ignore them.

(*b*) *Theology*. — Even the *Brahman* has, for Śaṅkara, a double character. Esoterically the *Brahman* is knowledge or realization itself, non-qualified, absolutely incapable of change, unknowable, indescribable, absolutely unique, nothing but existence, intelligence, and bliss — the *para* or *nirguṇa Brahma*. Exoterically, however, the *Brahman* is qualified, possessed of an infinite number of auspicious attributes, capable of producing the world from itself and of re-absorbing it into itself; in brief it is Īśvara, or God—the *apara* or *saguṇa Brahma*.

(*c*) *Cosmology*.—The exoteric cosmology, according to the natural but erroneous realism (*avidyā*) in which we are born, considers the world as real and can express its entire dependence on *Brahman* only by the mythical way of a creation of the world by *Brahman*, thus implying a temporal character of this creation. But this is against the 'beginninglessness' of the migration of souls. Śaṅkara, therefore, to reconcile this, teaches that there is not a single creation once for all, but that the world in great periods is created and re-absorbed by *Brahman*, and this succession of creation and re-absorption lasts from eternity, and no creation is the first. This never-ceasing creation is a moral necessity — it is not for God's glorification, not for His particular amusement, not for love of mankind. Thus explains itself the theory of *karma* and of *saṃsāra*, which goes on, as the sprout grows from the seed, which grows from a previous sprout, and so on.

The esoteric cosmology, however, says that all this is a mere representation of the truth. The manifold world is only an illusion (*māyā*), a mirage (*mṛgatṛṣṇikā*), a dream; and the reality is to be attained not by reasoning (*tarka*), but by introspective realization (*anubhava*). If you return from this variegated world to the inmost recesses of your soul, you will become aware of a reality, a timeless, spaceless, changeless reality. The same thing was said by Plato, according to whom this world is a world of shadows and not of realities, and also by Kant, to whom the world is an appearance only, and not the thing-in-itself.

(*d*) *Psychology*. — According to the esoteric psychology, the *jīva*, or the individual soul, is *Brahman*, or the supreme spirit itself, fully and totally possessed of eternity, omnipresence, omniscience, etc., but these divine qualities are hidden in the individual as the fire is hidden in the wood, and will appear only after the final deliverance. *Brahman* itself, which is one and limitless, appears as the *jīva*, limited and multiple, owing to its being conditioned by *māyā*, just as, *e.g.*, ether (*ākāśa*), which is one and all-pervading, is looked upon as so many different ethers limited (*e.g.*, the ether contained by a jar or that contained by a room), the notion of limitedness and multiplicity being due to the conditioning objects, but having nothing to correspond to it in the ether itself. Thus exoterically the individual souls are limited in size and qualities, infinite in number, one for each body, the cause of this concealment of their original divine nature being the external adjuncts which condition them (*upādhi*), such as the mind (*manas*), the sense-organs (*indriyāṇi*), and the vital airs (*prāṇāḥ*) which constitute the subtle body (*sūkṣmaśarīra*). This whole psychological apparatus together with *karma* accompanies the soul in all its ways of migration, without essentially infecting its divine nature. These *upādhis* are of course only part of the phenomenal world, due to the innate *avidyā*.

[1] *SBE* xxxiv. 3 f.

[2] *Ib.* p. 6.

But whence comes this *avidyā*, this primeval cause of ignorance, sin, and misery? No satisfactory answer has been given to this question; or the question itself is inadmissible; for causality goes only as far as the *saṃsāra*, and we do not know anything farther.

(*e*) *Eschatology.*—From the conception of rewards in heaven and punishments in a dark region contained in the hymns of the *Rigveda* there arose the theory of *saṃsāra*, teaching rewards and punishments in the form of a new birth on earth. The Vedānta thus exoterically admits of a threefold division: those who perform good deeds, sacrifices, etc., follow the path of the fathers (*pitṛ-yāṇa*) and are born again; those who worship the qualified *Brahman* or Īśvara follow the path of gods (*deva-yāna*) and are on their way to final deliverance; and those who are evil-doers have a third place (*tṛtīya-sthāna*) reserved for them. Esoterically, however, the only reality is *Brahman* and its knowledge itself is *mokṣa*.

(*f*) *The pramāṇas, or sources of knowledge.*—According to Śaṅkara's system, there are three principal sources of knowledge—*pratyakṣa*, or sensuous perception; *anumāna*, or reasoning; and *śabda*, or word; to which later writers on Śaṅkara's Vedānta have added *upamāna*, or comparison; *arthāpatti*, or implication; and *abhāva*, or negation.[1] Of the three first *śabda* is the most important, while *pratyakṣa* and *anumāna* play only a secondary rôle, especially in the case of ascertaining the truth regarding purely metaphysical and abstract matters like the nature of the cause of the universe, etc. By *śabda* is meant revelation, or *śruti*, represented by the *Samhitās* and *Brāhmaṇas*, which relate to action and form the *Karma-kāṇḍa*, and by the *Upaniṣads*, which relate to knowledge and form the *Jñāna-kāṇḍa*. It would appear curious to most philosophers that revelation could ever claim more than a subordinate place as a source of knowledge; but, if we remember that the highest object of the Vedānta is to prove that there is only one true reality, namely *Brahman*, and that the manifoldness of the visible world is but the result of that nescience which the Vedānta is meant to destroy, it will become easily intelligible why an appeal to the evidence of the senses or to inference would be out of place and almost self-contradictory.[2] Reasoning or speculation (*tarka*) is to be employed, but only when it does not go against the fundamental truths proclaimed by revelation. Thus Śaṅkara says, while commenting on *Sūtra* II. i. 11:

'In matters to be known from Scripture mere reasoning is not to be relied on. . . . As the thoughts of man are altogether unfettered, reasoning which disregards the holy texts and rests on individual opinion only has no proper foundation . . . since we observe that even men of the most undoubted intellectual eminence, such as Kapila, Kaṇāda, and other founders of philosophical schools, have contradicted one another.'[3]

Śaṅkara is naturally taunted by his adversaries with using reason against reasoning. His final position according to Vedānta is that Scripture is the principal source of knowledge with regard to *Brahman*, and that reasoning is allowed only as it is subordinate to and in conformity with Scripture. But in other matters reasoning has its full scope.[4]

(*g*) *The doctrine of karma.*—Individual souls are partially bound by their former acts and are partially free to better or to worsen their lot. So far as they can claim any reality, they date from all eternity and not from the day of their birth on earth. They are clothed in their *upādhis*, or conditioning adjuncts, according to the merit or demerit which they have acquired by their former, though long-forgotten, acts. This doctrine of *karma* (*q.v.*), which has remained to the present day and has leavened the whole of India, furnishes the principal moral element of the Vedānta. The whole world, such as it is, is the result of acts; the character and fate of each man in this life are the result of his acts in this or in a former life; and it entirely depends on his acts here what he will be in the next life. This is the solution of what we venture to call the injustice of God. A man who suffers, and suffers, as it appears to us, unjustly, is only paying off a debt or laying up capital for another life. A man who enjoys health and wealth is made to feel that he is spending more than he has earned, and that he has therefore to make up his debt by new efforts. It cannot be by a divine caprice that one man is born deaf, dumb, or blind, another strong and healthy. It can only be the result of former acts, whether, in this life, the doer of them is aware of them or not. The merit which can be acquired by man is such that he may rise even to the status of a god, though for a time only, for at the end of a *kalpa* even gods like Indra and the rest have to begin their career afresh.

(*h*) *Cause and effect.*—The relation between cause and effect is one of the questions that have engaged the attention of all the schools of philosophy. The Vedāntists in general hold that absolute identity of substance exists between cause and effect (*kārya-kāraṇābheda*). The effect, even before its production, is already existent in the cause; for it is in fact nothing but the cause (*sat-kārya-vāda*). This follows not only from the Scripture, but also from observation.

'The non-difference [of cause and effect],' says Śaṅkara, commenting on *Sutra* II. i. 15, 'is perceived, for instance, in an aggregate of threads, where we do not perceive a thing called "cloth" in addition to the threads, but merely threads running lengthways and crossways. So again, in the threads we perceive finer threads . . . in them again finer threads, and so on. On the ground of this our perception we conclude that the finest parts which we can perceive are ultimately identical with their causes, viz. red, white and black (the colours of fire, water, and earth); those, again, with air, the latter with ether, and ether with Brahman, which is one and without a second.'[1]

But this implies an element of plurality and modification with regard to *Brahman*, while the Scriptures declare *Brahman* to be one, without a second, unchangeable. How can such a *Brahman* be called the material cause (*upādāna*) of the intelligent and non-intelligent world? No such difficulty, however, exists for Śaṅkara, according to whom the whole of the world is unreal, while *Brahman* alone is real. What the rope mistaken for a snake is to the snake, that *Brahman* is to the world. There is no idea of claiming for the rope a real change into a snake, and in the same way no real change can be claimed for *Brahman* when perceived as the world. *Brahman* presents itself as the world, and, apart from *Brahman*, the world would be simply nothing. If, therefore, *Brahman* is called the material cause of the world, this is not meant in the sense in which the clay is the material cause of a jar. *Brahman* is only the real substratum of the apparent and illusory existence of the world. This is what is called the doctrine of *vivarta* ('illusory manifestation') peculiar to Śaṅkara, as opposed to that of *pariṇāma* ('modification') held by the other Vedānta schools and especially by the Sāṅkhya (*q.v.*).

(*i*) *Two kinds of knowledge and mokṣa.*—Corresponding to the twofold distinction of *Brahman*, higher and lower, owing to *māyā* or the two kinds of reality, absolute and relative, there are two kinds of knowledge and two kinds of *mokṣa* resulting therefrom. The higher knowledge consists in the distinction and thereby the freedom of the

[1] See, *e.g.*, Dharmarājādhvarīndra, *Vedānta-paribhāṣā*.

[2] Cf. *SBE* xxxiv. 323 f. Notice that the words *pratyakṣa* and *anumāna*, which ordinarily mean 'sensuous perception' and 'inference,' are used by the author of the *Brahma-Sūtras* in the sense of *śruti*, 'revelation,' and *smṛti*, 'tradition.'

[3] *SBE* xxxiv. 314 f.

[4] *Ib.* p. 315 ff.

[1] *SBE* xxxiv. 331 f.

self from all its *upādhis*. It is the knowledge of the absolute unity of *Brahman*, apart from which nothing really is. The higher *mokṣa*, which arises simultaneously with such a knowledge, consists in the entire absorption of the individual soul into *Brahman*. This does not mean any approach of the individual soul towards *Brahman* or their union, such an idea being impossible where there is absolute identity; it is only a recovery, a restitution, a return, a becoming of the soul of what it has always been, a revival of its true nature.

On the other hand, the lower knowledge consists in the worship, or *upāsanā*, of the lower *Brahman*, or *Brahman* in its phenomenal state, conceived as a personal Lord and Creator, Īśvara. This *upāsanā* is obligatory on all who have not yet reached the highest knowledge. Such worshippers of a personal God are really worshipping *Brahman*, though in its phenomenal aspect, and they are promised as a reward, not only happiness on earth and in heaven, but, by way of preparation, a kind of second-class *mukti* (*krama-mukti*) which gradually leads to the complete deliverance or highest *mukti*.

In this sense it may be truly said that Śaṅkara did not attack or destroy idolatry, though with him it was always symbolism rather than idolatry. It may be easily understood how he condemned all ritualism and *karma* and at the same time defended the worship of popular gods. Idolatry, if understood in the right spirit, is nothing but religious symbolism, and, as such, it can be open to no objection. Symbolism there must be, whether in words or in things. Verbal symbols appeal to the ear and the symbols of things to the eye, and that is all the difference between them. Verbal symbolism is language; and, if this is allowed in religion, why should not also the other? At one stage of its growth idolatry is a necessity of our nature. When the religious spirit is mature, symbols are either given up or suffered to remain from their harmlessness. Thus Śaṅkara allowed idols as symbols of the great Infinite for those who cannot raise themselves to the comprehension of the one, changeless, non-qualified *Brahman*.

(*j*) *The means of mokṣa.*—Knowledge and knowledge alone can lead to *mokṣa*. For *mokṣa* (*q.v.*) is not something to be obtained or produced. It is only a realization of our real nature, of which we can never be really deprived, but of which we have been only forgetful; it is therefore only knowledge that can be the means of *mokṣa*. The performance of actions, however, and the practice of moral virtues are allowed as being preparatory to knowledge. Good works, even merely ceremonial works, if performed from pure motives and without any hope of reward, form an excellent preparation for reaching that highest knowledge which it is the final aim of the Vedānta to impart. It is in this sense that we read:

'Brāhmaṇas seek to know Him by the study of the Veda, by sacrifices, by charitable gifts.'[1]

Thus a person qualified for the study of Vedānta is described as being one who has studied the Vedas and the Vedāntas, who has got a general idea thereof, whose spirit has been entirely purified by the performance of the obligatory, occasional, and expiatory acts and by the avoidance of all interested and forbidden acts, who possesses discrimination between what is eternal and what is not eternal, who is indifferent and without the least attachment to the enjoyment of rewards here or in the next world, who has tranquillity of spirit, self-restraint, quiescence, endurance, concentration of mind, and faith, and who longs to be free. But, when the knowledge of the highest *Brahman* has

[1] *Bṛhadāraṇyaka Upan.* IV. iv. 22 (*SBE* xv. 179).

once been reached, all works, whether good or bad, fall away.

'The fetter of the heart is broken, all doubts are solved, extinguished are all his works, when He has been beheld who is both high and low.'[1]

(*k*) *Tat tvam asi.*—The well-known formula *tat tvam asi* (lit. 'Thou art that'), which asserts the identity of the individual soul and the supreme self, would be interpreted according to Śaṅkara's doctrine thus: *tat* literally means the *Brahman* with omniscience, omnipresence, absence of limitations, etc.; *tvam* literally means the *jīva*, or the individual self, with limited knowledge, powers, etc.; and the copula *asi* signifies the apposition (*sāmānādhikaraṇya*) of these two. Now this is not possible in the full literal sense. So what is inconsistent in the connotations of the two terms is to be rejected and what is consistent is alone to be retained—which is only intelligence (*chaitanya*) pure and simple, indivisible and without attributes, all the rest being only phenomenal and consequently illusory. In other words, the identity of 'thou' and 'that' is not possible, unless one alone is real, and the other unreal. In the same way is to be understood the formula *sarvaṃ khalvidaṃ Brahma* (lit. 'All this is *Brahman*'), which asserts the identity of the world and the supreme spirit.

LITERATURE.—Śaṅkara's Commentary on the *Vedānta-Sūtras*, tr. G. Thibaut, in *SBE* xxxiv. [1890] xxxviii. [1896], tr. P. Deussen, Leipzig, 1887; *Vedānta-sāra*, tr. G. A. Jacob, London, 1881. There are many treatises and manuals in Sanskrit dealing with the system of Śaṅkara, like *Vedānta-paribhāṣā*, *Pañchadaśī*, *Advaita-siddhi*, *Naiṣkarmya-siddhi*, which cannot all be mentioned here. Some of these are translated in the volumes of *The Pandit* and *The Indian Thought*. H. T. Colebrooke, *Essays on the Religion and Philosophy of the Hindus*, new ed., London, 1858; A. E. Gough, *The Philosophy of the Upanishads, and ancient Indian Metaphysics*, do. 1882; F. Max Müller, *The Six Systems of Indian Philosophy*, do. 1899, *Three Lectures on the Vedānta Philosophy*, do. 1894; P. Deussen, *The Philosophy of the Upanishads*, Eng. tr., Edinburgh, 1906, may also be recommended.

V. S. GHATE.

SĀṄKHYA.—*Sāṅkhya* is the title of the oldest system of Indian philosophy, the founder of which was Kapila. Its origin must be sought in a reaction against the idealistic monism of the *Upaniṣads* (*q.v.*), and its rise may be attributed to the same district of India as produced Buddhism. According to the native tradition, the Sāṅkhya is older than Buddha (*c.* 500 B.C.), and was used by him as the basis of his own system. The correctness of this tradition is confirmed by a series of coincidences in doctrinal statement, and is not to be refuted by a reference to the fact that the specific text-books of the Sāṅkhya originate from a much more recent date. The oldest text-book of this system that has come down to us complete belongs to the 5th cent. A.D.

Originally the Sāṅkhya must have taken up a position of direct opposition to the doctrines of the Brāhmans, as is proved *inter alia* by its polemic against their ceremonial. Nevertheless, in the 1st cent. B.C. the Brāhmans began to adopt the doctrines of the Sāṅkhya, and later on it was received into the number of the so-called orthodox systems, after its adherents had acquiesced in a nominal recognition of the infallibility of the sacred scriptures of the Brāhmans. The Sāṅkhya system flourished chiefly in the early centuries of our era; and, if we bear in mind the active relations which at that period existed between India and Alexandria, it is not to be wondered at that the Gnostic systems and Neo-Platonism have been deeply influenced by Sāṅkhyan ideas. Since that time the whole of Indian literature, so far as it touches philosophical thought, beginning with the *Mahābhārata* and the law-book of Manu, especially the literature of the mythological and legendary *Purāṇas*, has been saturated with the doctrines of the Sāṅkhya.

[1] *Muṇḍaka Upan.* II. ii. 11 (*SBE* xv. 37).

The founder of the Sāṅkhya system was a clear and practical thinker of an altogether different class from the authors of the *Upaniṣads*, who, in a lofty and enthusiastic spirit, endeavoured to solve the great riddle of existence. Kapila did not attempt to find unity in everything, but sought to maintain variety. He not only rejected the *Brahman*, the All-Soul, but emphatically denied the existence of God. It is true that he continued to hold the ordinary Indian views to the extent of believing in the transient forms of the popular religion, in gods, demi-gods, and demons, together with heavens and hells; but this popular faith had nothing at all to do with the question of a real eternal God in the theistic sense of an independent creator and ruler of the universe. The denial of a God of this nature is one of the characteristic features of the Sāṅkhya philosophy, and the system is therefore in India described explicitly as atheistic.

The Sāṅkhya system is throughout rationalistic. It recognizes two uncreated substances, existing from all eternity, but differing essentially from one another. These are (1) matter, which Kapila, in opposition to the doctrine of the *Upaniṣads*, regarded not as an illusory appearance, but as something real; and (2) souls, which are conceived not as emanations from the world-soul, but as an *infinite multitude of individual souls*.

The material universe is traced back by a correct philosophical method to a first cause. The Sāṅkhya doctrine proceeds on the principle that the product is none other than the 'material cause' in a definite stage of evolution, and that the preceding stages are to be inferred from that which lies open before us. By this means a first principle was finally reached, which is of the nature of cause only, and not also of product. This is *prakṛti*, primitive matter, from which the universe is evolved in regular course. It further teaches the existence in the entire material universe of three substances (*guṇa*), united in dissimilar and unstable proportions, of which the first (*sattva*) exhibits the qualities of lightness, illumination, and joy; the second (*rajas*), of movement, excitation, and pain; the third (*tamas*), of heaviness, obstruction, and sloth. Hence the conclusion necessarily follows that primitive matter also was composed of these three constituents. Undeveloped primitive matter is the 'state of equilibrium of the three *guṇas*.' As the result of a disturbance, which is not more definitely described, of this condition of equilibrium, the material universe is evolved, first the subtle elements, out of which are formed the psychical organs of living creatures, and, lastly, the gross elements of matter. At the close of a world-period the products return by a reverse movement into the preceding stage of development, and so, finally, into primitive matter. By this process of re-absorption matter regains precisely the same condition in which it had existed in the period before the evolution, and remains in this condition until the time arrives for the development of a new universe. This cycle of evolution, existence, and decay has never had a beginning, and will never have an end.

Unconscious primitive matter then issues from its stable equilibrium and becomes the subject of evolution; and matter during the period of the existence of the universe continually brings forth new products. For this process it becomes necessary to assign some cause. The developments and combinations of inert matter which take place unceasingly would be inexplicable if they were not effected by a spiritual principle. This principle is the collective influence of the innumerable individual souls which—themselves incapable of any activity—contemplate, as spectators from all eternity, the movement of matter. It is not by conscious will that the souls exert an influence on matter, but by their mere presence, which in a purely mechanical way excites matter to activity and development, just as the magnet acts on the iron.

As to the physiological side of the Sāṅkhya system, however great the difference of organization that may exist between living creatures endowed with souls, it is yet one of degree only, not of essence. Every living being, according to the Sāṅkhya doctrine, possesses within the gross material body, which suffers dissolution after death, an inner or subtle body which is formed essentially out of the psychical organs and the senses. This subtle body accompanies the soul in the cycle of existences from one gross body to another. It is, however, not only the basis of metempsychosis and the principle of personal identity in the various existences, but also the vehicle of personality in this life; for in the subtle body all the events and states which we are accustomed to term psychical have their home and origin.

Here we already touch upon the most peculiar part of the Sāṅkhya system, its psychology. It has already been pointed out that the Sāṅkhya professes the most uncompromising dualism conceivable, since it starts from the absolute and essential difference of matter and soul. In one respect only are the two alike—in the absence of beginning and end; but in this likeness is already involved the most important distinction between them; for the soul is eternally unchangeable, while matter is eternally subject to change. The soul is defined as 'pure spirit.' Further description in a positive sense is impossible. Whatever can be asserted of it is of a negative character. The soul is without attributes or qualities, without parts, and therefore imperishable, motionless, absolutely inactive and impassive, unaffected by pleasure or pain or any other emotion, completely indifferent towards all sensations. The soul being conceived in this negative manner, and since changes, according to the Sāṅkhya doctrine, can be effected solely and alone in matter, it is evident that all the states and events also which appear to us to belong to the realm of the psychical—*e.g.*, perception, idea, thought, feeling, will, etc.—belong in reality to the realm of matter. For they imply in fact an alteration, a change.

Mention has previously been made of the psychical organs, because the easily misunderstood expression 'inner organs,' which our authorities use, must be avoided until an explanation of the conception has been given. In the inner organs all those functions and affections take place which we erroneously call psychical. The inner organs are purely physical and material throughout—as material, to use the ordinary example of the Sāṅkhya texts, as pots and other objects of the external world. The Sāṅkhya philosophy assumes three such inner organs, which are closely related to one another. It treats them, however, very frequently as one, and the same course will be adopted in the following paragraphs. This combined material inner organ exactly corresponds, as regards its unspiritual nature and all the functions that the Sāṅkhya doctrine ascribes to it, to the nervous system. This comparison may be made in order to indicate the place of the inner organ in the animal organism, although naturally no teacher of the Sāṅkhya had any conception of the nervous system as it is understood by modern science.

When the inner organ receives the objects presented to it by the external world by means of the senses, it assumes—as is said in the texts—the form of these objects; in other words, an image of the object rises up within us. The most diverse results follow. An impression latent in the inner organ may thereby be aroused, and so the recollection excited of earlier experiences. The images of external objects and recollection may suggest abstract conclusions, but may also call forth affection, aversion, joy, pain, desire, or other emotions. These in turn may excite the will and the determination to act, and may urge them on a definite course. All these numerous processes consist, just as simple perceptions, in changes or modifications of the inner organ, so that at each moment it assumes a different form. This incessant transformation, effected in the inner organ by perception, thought, emotion, and will, is not essentially distinct from the change and variety which are found everywhere in the external world. In the one case as in the other we have to do entirely with material changes, with purely mechanical processes carried on in matter.

What place, however, in a system which maintains such views is to be found for the soul? Strangely enough, former scholars who made exhaustive investigations into the Sāṅkhya system did not succeed in answering this question. They regard the soul in this system as entirely superfluous, and hold that its founder would have shown himself more logical if he had altogether eliminated it. And yet the function of the soul in the household of the individual life is, according to the Sāṅkhya doctrine, of the greatest importance. That the soul by its mere presence excites matter, and therefore the inner organ which belongs to matter, to the path of activity has already been mentioned. Here, however, we are concerned with a much more important office which the soul has to fulfil in the life of the individual. It is true that only figurative expressions are here employed by the original texts; but there is no possibility of mistaking their meaning when they ascribe to the soul the *illumination* of the processes going on in the inner organ. All these processes must indeed remain purely mechanical and unconscious, unless the soul, 'by virtue of its nearness,' illuminates them, *i.e.* brings them to consciousness. The soul remains, on its side, in the most complete passivity, in harmony with its nature, as already described. It is regarded by no means as an illuminating substance; and the texts emphasize the fact that in speaking of the illumination they use a metaphorical expression to explain the process. In the same sense in which the enlightening office of the soul is spoken of, our authorities employ a further illustration which in a similar way is intended to make intelligible the soul's independence of the processes in the inner organ, and its influence on these processes. The Sāṅkhya texts compare the soul with a looking-glass, in which the inner organ is reflected. It is certainly no accident that the Neo-Platonist Plotinus not only compares soul with light, as the Sāṅkhya philosophy does, but also, in order to explain conscious knowledge, makes use of the other comparison of the looking-glass in which the images of objects appear, just as it occurs in the Sāṅkhya texts. This fact supplies one of the arguments in favour of the direct dependence of the Neo-Platonic doctrine on the Sāṅkhya philosophy.

Briefly described, therefore, the relation between soul and inner organ in the Sāṅkhya system is conceived in the following way: from the purely immaterial soul a power that excites consciousness issues and flows forth uninterruptedly, so that no process in the inner organ remains unconscious. If the soul, then, according to the Sāṅkhya doctrine, thus fulfils its office without either doing or suffering anything further, it is scarcely necessary to point out how closely related this view is to certain modern conceptions of the soul which assert the passivity of consciousness.

Like all the Indian philosophical systems (with the exception of materialism), the Sāṅkhya also aims at setting man free from the sufferings of earthly existence. In no other system, however, does the pessimistic view of the universe which lies at the basis of Buddhism find such distinct expression as in the teaching of the Sāṅkhya. All conscious existence is suffering; and even pleasure, which falls to the lot of comparatively few individuals, conceals pain in its womb, and leads infallibly to suffering. Thus pleasure also 'is accounted pain by the wise.'

The connexion of the soul with suffering consists, then, as may be inferred from the preceding, in the soul's bringing to consciousness the pain of which the body, or, more precisely, the inner organ, is the seat. This peculiar relation between soul and suffering or inner organ (which amounts to the same thing) is not essential to the soul; for in that case it would be totally impossible to bring it to an end. The Sāṅkhya regards this connexion as determined solely by 'want of discrimination,' *i.e.* by our failure to recognize the essential distinctness of soul from matter, and especially from the most subtle products of matter, the inner organ and the senses. The cause of this want of discrimination is the disposition innate in man, a fatal inheritance from the last existence, the after-effect of the want of discrimination at that time. Here also, if we look backwards, we arrive at a *regressus in infinitum*, as in the case of the retributive power of action.

As the 'want of discrimination' is the root of all evil according to the Sāṅkhya doctrine, the sole means of deliverance is the 'discriminating knowledge' by virtue of which we discern the absolute difference between soul and matter. When once we have recognized that it is in matter that everything which happens takes place, that the soul, the *ego*, has no part in any movement or change, any suffering or sorrow, and stands aloof from it all, and that the soul is just as little affected by re-birth and death as by the other processes in the inner organ, release is at once attained. For the soul of the wise matter ceases to be active, as the dancer ceases to dance when the spectators are satisfied.

That the life of the emancipated does not forthwith come to an end with the acquisition of knowledge, but still endures for a considerable time, 'as the potter's wheel continues to revolve in consequence of the initial impulse even after the completion of the pot,' is explained in the same way as in the other philosophical systems of the Brāhmans. The present life is the result of works, the seed of which has sprung up before the attainment of the emancipating knowledge. These works must come to full maturity, and for that purpose the continuance of life is necessary, while, on the contrary, the germinating force of those works whose seed has not yet sprung up 'is consumed by knowledge.' When the power of the works that bear fruit in the present life is exhausted, and death overtakes the emancipated man, for him no re-birth is possible.

With the close of the bodily life the soul of the emancipated attains independence. The inner organ connected with it is dissolved, and the subtle body, on which hitherto the wandering through various forms of existence has been dependent, perishes. The soul continues to exist individually in the state of emancipation, *i.e.* of final separation from matter; but it abides in eternal unconsciousness, since, indeed, the material basis necessary for all the processes of knowledge and experience is wanting. Moreover, the remark constantly made in older treatises on the Sāṅkhya philosophy, that the text-books of the system do not describe the state of the soul after its release from earthly existence, is a mere error; for they expressly declare that during life the very same condition is temporarily attained in deep dreamless sleep, in swoons, and in abstraction that reaches the stage of unconsciousness as in emancipation after death. 'The soul therefore abides eternally released from the delusion and suffering of this world, as a seer who no longer sees anything, a glass in which nothing is any longer reflected, as pure untroubled light by which nothing is illuminated.' With these words H. Oldenberg[1] closes his brief exposition of the Sāṅkhya system.

LITERATURE.—R. Garbe, *Die Sāṅkhya-Philosophie*, Leipzig, 1894; cf. also *GIAP* iii. 4 A; A. Barth, *Religions of India*[3], London, 1891; F. Max Müller, *The Six Systems of Indian Philosophy*, London, 1899, ch. vi.; Monier Monier-Williams, *Indian Wisdom*[4], London, 1893: P. Deussen, *Philosophie der Upanishads*, Leipzig, 1899, ch. x. (Eng. tr., Edinburgh, 1905); *Sāṅkhya kārikā*, ed. and tr. Colebrooke and Wilson, Oxford, 1837, reprinted Bombay, 1887; *Sarva-darśana-saṅgraha*, tr. Cowell and Gough, 2nd ed., London, 1894, ch. xiv.

R. GARBE.

SANNYASA.—See RENUNCIATION (Hindu).

SANNYĀSĪ.—**1. Meaning of the name.**—The term Sannyāsī (Skr. *sannyāsin*) is defined as follows:

'One who lays down or deposits; one who abandons or resigns; an ascetic, devotee; especially one who retires from worldly concerns, and is no longer bound to read the *Mantras* and perform sacrifice, but only to read the Āraṇyakas or Upanishads.'[2]

The name is sometimes applied to Vaiṣṇava ascetics, as in the case of the officiants at the Kṛṣṇa temple at Udipi in S. Kanara District, Madras.[3] It is also used to designate the fourth stage (*āśrama*) of the life of an orthodox Brāhman, when he abandons earthly concerns and devotes himself to penance and meditation:

'But having passed the third part of (a man's natural term of) life in the forest, he may live as an ascetic during the fourth part of his existence, after abandoning all attachment to worldly objects. He who after passing from order to order, after offering sacrifice and subduing his senses, becomes tired with (giving) alms and offerings of food, an ascetic, gains bliss after death.'[4]

2. Numbers and distribution.—According to the *Census of India, 1911*,[5] the Sannyāsīs, also known as Swāmi ('lord') or Atīt ([*q.v.*] Skr. *atīta* 'gone by,' 'past,' 'passed away,' 'dead'), numbered 147,016, of whom about half were found in Bihār and Orissa, and, of the remainder, the majority were recorded in the United Provinces and Rājputāna. But the designations and enumeration of the ascetic orders are very uncertain, and, though Sannyāsīs are known in S. India,[6] they do not appear under that name in the census returns.

Monier-Williams writes:

'A Sannyāsī may have been once a married man. But there are Sannyāsīs (such as the late Dayānanda) who have become so without going through the previous stages of Gṛihastha [householder] or Vānaprastha [anchorite]. Equivalent expressions for Sannyāsīs are Parivrājaka [wandering mendicant], Bhikshu [beggar], Daṇḍin [one who carries a staff], and Maskarin [one who carries a cane] (Pāṇini, VI. i. 154); but the term Bhikshu is now applied in Western India to those clerical Brāhmans (as opposed to lay) who perform religious ceremonies and are not engaged in worldly pursuits.'[1]

3. Admission to the order.—As a general rule, the order is open to all Hindus except Śūdras.

'Any Hindu of the three first classes may become a Sannyāsī or Daṇḍī, or, in these degenerate days, a Hindu of any caste may adopt the life and emblems of the order. Such are sometimes met with, as also are Brāhmans, who, without connecting themselves with any community, assume the character of this class of mendicants. These constitute the Daṇḍīs simply so termed, and are regarded as distinct from the primitive members of the order, to whom the appellation of Daśnāmīs [*ERE* vi. 332] is also applied, and who admit none but Brāhmans into their fraternity.'[2]

In the Panjāb the rule is somewhat different.

'Some of the Saniāsīs in order to oppose the Muhammadan invasions, endeavoured to found a militant branch of the Order, but this was opposed by other Saniāsīs on the ground that the Order was spiritual, not secular. The Sangiri Maṭh, however, at last agreed that if Rājputs were admitted into the Order, Saniāsīs might bear arms.[3] All the other Maṭhs concurred. Later on Vaiśyas were also admitted and managed the finances and commissariat of the Order. Lastly, all restrictions were removed, and even men of inferior castes admitted, but they cannot rise to the position to which Brāhmans and Rājputs may rise, and the higher castes never eat food cooked by them, nor may they learn the Vedas. In other words, caste restrictions hold good after admission into the Order.'[4]

They mark their devotion to Śiva in various ways.

They 'not infrequently bear the *Śaiva* mark upon the forehead, smearing it with the *Tripundra*, a triple transverse line made with the *Vibhūti*, or ashes which should be taken from the fire of an *Agnihotra* Brāhman [one who practises the cult of fire], or they may be ashes of burnt cowdung from an oblation offered to the god. They also adopt the initiating *Mantra* of all the *Śaiva* classes, either the five or six syllable Mantra, *Nama Śivāya*, or *Om, Nama Sivāya* ["In the name of Siva!"].'[5]

For the organization of the order see art. GOSĀĪN, vol. vi. p. 332 f.; *Census of India, 1911*, xiv., *Punjab*, pt. i., p. 117 ff.

4. Death rites.—The Sannyāsī death rites are of special interest.

'A dead Sanniāsī is always buried in the sitting attitude of religious meditation with the legs crossed. The grave may be dug with a side receptacle for the corpse so that the earth, on being filled in, does not fall on it. The corpse is bathed and rubbed with ashes and clad in a new reddish-coloured shirt, with a rosary round the neck. The begging-wallet with some flour and pulse is placed in the grave, and also a gourd and staff. Salt is put round the body to preserve it, and an earthen pot is put over the head. Sometimes cocoanuts are broken on the skull, to crack it and give exit to the soul.[6] Perhaps the idea of burial and of preserving the corpse with salt is that the body of an ascetic does not need to be purified by fire from the appetites and passions of the flesh like that of an ordinary Hindu; it is already cleansed of all earthly frailty by his austerities, and the belief may therefore have originally been that such a man would carry his body with him to the afterworld or absorption with the deity. The burial of a Sanniāsī is often accompanied with music and signs of rejoicing. Mr. Oman[7] describes such a funeral in which the corpse was seated in a litter, open on sides so that it could be seen; it was tied to the back of the litter, and garlands of flowers partly covered the body, but could not conceal the hideousness of death as the unconscious head rolled helplessly from side to side with the movement of the litter. The procession was headed by a European brass band and by men carrying censers of incense.'[8]

In the United Provinces the present writer witnessed the funeral of a Sannyāsī, in which the body was carried in a litter in procession to the bank of the Ganges, where it was tied up between four large slabs of stone. This coffin was carried in a boat to the middle of the river and flung into the water amidst the shouts of the mourners.[9]

1 *Buddha*[3], Berlin, 1897, p. 67.
2 M. Monier-Williams, *Skr.-Eng. Dict.*, Oxford, 1872, *s.v.*
3 H. H. Wilson, *Sketch of the Religious Sects of the Hindus*, London, 1861, i. 141; but the same writer (i. 183) remarks: 'Although, however, *Sannyāsīs* and *Vairāgīs*, and other similar denominations are used, and correctly used in a wide acceptation, yet we occasionally do find them limited in meaning, and designating distinct and inimical bodies of men. When this is the case, it may be generally concluded, that the *Sannyāsīs* imply the mendicant followers of Siva, and the Vairāgīs those of Vishnu' (see art. BAIRĀGĪ, vol. ii. p. 337).
4 Manu, *Laws*, vi. 333 f. (*SBE* xxv. [1886] 204 f.).
5 Vol. i. pt. ii. [Calcutta, 1913] p. 222.
6 Thurston, *Castes and Tribes of S. India*, vi. 295.

1 *Brāhmanism and Hindūism*[4], London, 1891, p. 55, note.
2 Wilson, i. 197.
3 This seems to imply that Sannyāsīs were formerly not recruited from Rājpūts. It may be that originally they were recruited only from Brāhmans, as is indeed expressly stated by P. Harikishan Kaul.
4 H. A. Rose, *A Glossary of the Tribes and Castes of the Punjab and N.W. Frontier Province*, iii. 358.
5 Wilson, i. 194 f.
6 The intention is to open the skull suture known as *brahmārandhra*, 'Brahmā's fissure,' or *sushumṇa-nāḍi*, 'blessed suture'; see *PR*[2] i. 238 f.; J. E. Padfield, *The Hindu at Home*, Madras, 1896, p. 249; Thurston, ii. 299.
7 *The Mystics, Ascetics, and Saints of India*, p. 156 f.
8 R. V. Russell, *Tribes and Castes of the Central Provinces*, iii. 158.
9 For the death rites of Sannyāsīs see also J. A. Dubois, *Hindu Manners, Customs, and Ceremonies*[3], Eng. tr., Oxford, 1906, p. 538 ff.; *BG* ix. pt. i. [1901] 49 f., xviii. pt. i. [1885] 562 ff., xxiv. [1886] 145 f.; *PNQ* iv. [1886-87] 5, 177.

5. The militant Sannyāsīs.—The Sannyāsīs from an early period have been known as a turbulent order. In A.D. 1567, when the emperor Akbar arrived at Thānesar in the S.E. Panjāb, he found an assemblage of Yogīs and Sannyāsīs at the site of the great battle of the *Mahābhārata*, Kurukṣetra.

'In consequence of a feud which existed between these two sects, they came to the Emperor, seeking permission to settle it by fighting. The *Sannyāsīs* were between two and three hundred in number, and the *Jogīs*, who only wear rags, were over five hundred. When the adversaries stood ready to begin the fray, by the Emperor's orders some soldiers smeared their bodies with ashes, and went to support the *Sannyāsīs*, who were the weaker party. A fierce fight ensued, and many were killed. The Emperor greatly enjoyed the sight. At length the *Jogīs* were defeated, and the *Sannyāsīs* were victors.'[1]

'The name of Sunnyasee was applied familiarly in Bengal, c. A.D. 1760–75, to a body of banditti claiming to belong to a religious fraternity, who, in the interval between the decay of the imperial authority and the regular establishment of our own, had their headquarters in the forest-tracts at the foot of the Himālaya. From thence they used to issue periodically in large bodies, plundering and levying exactions far and wide, and returning to their asylum when threatened with pursuit.'[2]

LITERATURE.—R. V. Russell, *The Tribes and Castes of the Central Provinces of India*, London, 1916, iii. 150 ff.; W. Crooke, *The Tribes and Castes of the N.W. Provinces and Oudh*, Calcutta, 1896, iv. 273 ff.; E. Thurston, *Castes and Tribes of Southern India*, Madras, 1909, vi. 295 f.; Jogendra Nath Bhattacharya, *Hindu Castes and Sects*, Calcutta, 1896, p. 374 ff.; D. C. J. Ibbetson, *Outlines of Punjab Ethnography*, do. 1883, p. 286; H. A. Rose, *A Glossary of the Tribes and Castes of the Punjab and N.W. Frontier Province*, Lahore, 1911–14, iii. 353 ff.; *Census of India, 1891*, xix., *Punjab and Feudatories*, pt. i.; *Census of India, 1911*, xiv., *Punjab*, pt. i., p. 117 ff.; J. C. Oman, *The Mystics, Ascetics, and Saints of India*², London, 1905, p. 152 ff.

W. CROOKE.

SĀNSĪ, SĀNSIYĀ.—The Sānsī are a gypsy-like Indian tribe, numbering 34,459 at the census of 1911, found chiefly in the Panjāb, United Provinces, Rājputāna, Central Provinces, and Berār.

In occupation, if not in origin, they closely resemble the Bediyā (*q.v.*). They are the vagrants of the Central Panjāb, seldom or never settling in one place. They catch all kinds of wild animals, clean and unclean, and eat carrion. They keep donkeys, sheep, goats, and pigs, work in grass, straw, and reeds, and beg, while their women dance and sing and are prostitutes. They have a curious connexion with the Jāṭs of the Central Panjāb, of whom they are the hereditary bards and genealogists, and even in Rājputāna they call themselves Bhāṭ (*q.v.*). They derive their name from their eponym, Sāṅs Mall of Bharatpur, whom they revere as their *guru*; and they are said to worship his patron saint under the name of Malang Shāh, Malang being the title of an order of *faqīrs*, followers of Jaman Jatī, a disciple of Shāh Madār.[3] In the Panjāb they also worship Gūgā or Guggā Pīr, a saint who was originally a snake-god. They cremate their dead, and after a death they feed their sisters' sons—a survival of mother-right. They are said to worship the sword, and an oath on it is held binding. Their religious beliefs, however, are almost entirely confined to the rites performed at birth, marriage, and death.

In the Eastern Panjāb they call on Rāma morning and evening, and worship Gūgā or Guggā Pīr. They cook rice in honour of the goddess Juālāmukhī (*q.v.*) and Kālikā, the mother-goddess; they perform the usual death rites according to Hindu custom, but in an incomplete manner.[4]

'All Sānsis are said to worship the sword; and so an oath sworn on a *talwār* [the Indian sword] is popularly said to be binding on a Sānsi, but this may be a fiction set going by the Sānsis for their own ends. In Sialkot, however, it is probably true to say that no Sānsi will ever take a false oath on a sword.'[1]

In Bombay the most binding oath is on Gangā, the Ganges, or on Kālikā. The former is taken by raising a pot containing water, salt, charcoal, and millet grains, and swearing to speak the truth; the latter by pouring a little liquor on the ground out of a bottle while affirming.[2]

Their deified ancestors appear to be of a malignant rather than a benignant type. The Sānsī have no clear idea of the fate of the soul after death, but women who die in childbirth are supposed to linger on in this world and torment living beings. Some members of the tribe act as sorcerers and practise an elaborate system of casting out evil spirits.[3] In the United Provinces they have a vague idea of a Creator, and some worship the goddess Devī or Kālī. They are in constant fear of malignant ghosts (*bhūt*) and propitiate the dead by feeding virgin girls of the tribe in their honour. They revere a saint whom they call Miyāṅ, 'Master,' who is said to be king of the snakes.[4] They form one of the most notoriously criminal tribes in India, committing thefts, gang-robberies, and house-breaking. For this purpose parties of them go as far south as the Central Provinces, Bombay, and the Deccan.

LITERATURE.—In addition to the authorities quoted in the footnotes see R. V. Russell, *The Tribes and Castes of the Central Provinces of India*, London, 1916, iv. 485 ff.; M. Kennedy, *Notes on the Criminal Classes in the Bombay Presidency*, Bombay, 1908, p. 245 ff.; E. J. Gunthorpe, *Notes on the Criminal Tribes of Bombay, Berar, and the Central Provinces*, do. 1882, p. 46 ff.; D. C. J. Ibbetson, *Outlines of Punjab Ethnography*, Calcutta, 1883, p. 311.

W. CROOKE.

SANTĀL.—The Santāl are a tribe of the Mundā stock, inhabiting the Santāl Parganas, the southern portion of the Bhāgalpur Division, Bengal, and numbering 2,068,000 at the census of 1911.

1. Name and origin.—H. H. Risley has the following:

'According to Mr. Skrefsrud, the name Santāl is a corruption of Sāontār, and was adopted by the tribe after their sojourn for several generations in the country about Sāont in Midnapur. Before they went to Sāont they are said to have been called Kharwār [*q.v.*], the root of which, *khar*, is a variant of *hor* "man," the name which all Santāls use among themselves. As regards the derivation of the name from Sāont, an obscure village, somewhat off the main line of their recent migrations, it may be observed that Colonel Dalton suggested a doubt whether the name of the place may not have been taken from the tribe, and this view seems to derive some support from the discovery of a small tribe of Sāonts in Sargujā and Keunjhar. The point, however, is not one of great importance. At the present day when a Santāl is asked what caste he belongs to, he will almost invariably reply "Mānjhī" (literally "village headman," one of the commonest titles of the tribe), adding "Santāl Mānhji" if further explanation is demanded of him.'[5]

They seem to be connected with the Hazārībāgh tableland, as they venerate the Dāmodar river, by which its southern face is drained. Their features are of the Negritic type, and their colour varies from very dark brown to almost charcoal black. They speak a singularly elaborate language of the Mundā family.[6]

2. Religion.—The creation legend of the tribe is of the totemistic type, tracing the origin of the tribe to a wild goose that laid two eggs, from which sprang the parents of the race; and many of the names of their septs and sub-septs are derived from those of animals and plants.[7] Skrefsrud traces in the background of their religion a *fainéant* supreme deity, called Thākur, 'Lord,' who troubles

1 Nizāmu-d-din Aḥmad, *Tabakāt-i-Akbarī*, in H. M. Elliot, *Hist. of India as told by its own Historians*, London, 1867–77, v. 318.

2 H. Yule and A. C. Burnell, *Hobson-Jobson: a Glossary of Colloquial Anglo-Indian Words and Phrases*², ed. W. Crooke, London, 1903, p. 871 f., with numerous quotations; T. Pennant, *The View of Hindoostan*, do. 1798, ii. 192.

3 See art. SAINTS AND MARTYRS (Indian).

4 *Census of India, 1911*, vol. xiv. *Punjab*, p. 147.

1 H. A. Rose, *A Glossary of the Tribes and Castes of the Punjab and N.W. Frontier Province*, Lahore, 1911–14, iii. 367.

2 M. Kennedy, *Notes on the Criminal Classes in Bombay Presidency*, p. 248.

3 Rose, iii. 362 ff.

4 W. Crooke, *The Tribes and Castes of the N.W. Provinces and Oudh*, Calcutta, 1896, iv. 277 ff.

5 *The Tribes and Castes of Bengal*, Calcutta, 1891, ii. 224 f.

6 *Census of India, 1901*, Calcutta, 1903, vol. i. pt. i. p. 279 ff.

7 Risley, ii., Appendix, i. 125 ff.

himself little with human affairs; some identify him with the sun, and the Santāls regard him as a good god, worshipping him every fifth or tenth year with a sacrifice of goats. There are six great gods in their pantheon: Marang Buru, the great mountain, the leader of the group, with far-reaching powers by virtue of which he associates both with gods and with demons; Moreko, fire, now a single god, but formerly known in the form of five brothers; Jāir Erā, sister of Moreko, the goddess of the sacred grove (*jāhirthān*), which is preserved inviolate in every village as a home for the deities; Gosāin Erā, a younger sister of Jāir Erā; Parganā, chief of the gods (*bongā*), and in particular master of all witches—a function which causes him to be highly respected; and Mānjhī, the second in command to Parganā, a personage who is supposed to be particularly active in restraining the other gods from doing harm to men. Some of these names, like Gosāin (*q.v.*) and Parganā, 'a barony,' are derived from Hindu sources and suggest some contamination of beliefs since they came into contact with Hindus. All these, the greater gods, have their places in the sacred grove and are worshipped only in public, except Marang Buru, who also ranks as a family god. Besides these, each family has two gods of its own, the *orakbonga*, or household god, and the *abgēbonga*, or secret god. No Santāl will divulge the name of his secret god to any one but his eldest son.

'Men are particularly careful to keep this sacred knowledge from their wives for fear lest they should acquire undue influence with the bongas, become witches, and eat up the family with impunity when the protection of its gods has been withdrawn.'[1]

When sacrifices are offered to the *orakbongas*, the whole family partake of the offerings; but only men may touch the food which has been laid before the *abgēbongas*. Sacrifice is offered once a year, and each man chooses the most convenient time for offering it. There are traditions within recent times of human sacrifices being made to a mountain-god of unknown name.

3. Festivals.—The tribal festivals are especially interesting. The *Sarhūl* or *Bahāpūjā* is held towards the end of March, when the *sāl*-tree (*Shorea robusta*) blossoms.

'Tribal and family sacrifices are held, many victims are slain and eaten by the worshippers, every one entertains their friends, dancing goes on day and night, and the best songs and flute-music are performed. A peculiar feature of this festival is a sort of water-bottle in which men and women throw water at each other until they are completely drenched.'[2]

The most important feast is the *Sohrāī*, or harvest festival, held in November-December; the headman entertains the people, the cattle are anointed with oil and daubed with vermilion, and a share of the rice-beer is given to each animal. Public sacrifices of fowls are offered by the priest in the sacred grove; goats and fowls are sacrificed by private families, and a general Saturnalia of drunkenness and licence prevails; chastity is in abeyance for the time, and all unmarried persons may indulge in promiscuous intercourse, but this licence does not extend to adultery, nor does it sanction intercourse between persons of the same sept, though even this offence, if committed during the *Sohrāī*, is punished less severely than at other times.[3] The agricultural festivals include those at sowing, offering of the firstfruits of millet, sprouting of the rice, and the offering of firstfruits of the winter crop. Bread, parched grain, and molasses are offered to dead relatives in November-December. *Māgh-sim*, the cutting of the jungle grass in January-February, marks the end of the year, when servants receive their wages and fresh engagements are made; the village officials go through the form of resigning their appointments, and all the tenants give notice of throwing up their lands. But after a few days they agree to change their minds, and there is a general carouse of rice-beer. The *sīmabongas*, or boundary gods, are propitiated twice a year with sacrifices of fowls offered at the village boundary. *Jom-sim pūjā* is an offering of two goats, or of a goat and a sheep, to the sun. Every Santāl ought to perform this sacrifice at least once in his life. After a year's interval it is, or ought to be, followed by *kutamdangra*, when a cow is offered to the household gods and an ox to Marang Buru and to the spirits of the dead; the fire-god, Moreko, receives an offering of three goats and many fowls when any calamity, such as a failure of the crops or an outbreak of epidemic disease, occurs.[1]

1 Risley, ii. 232. 2 *Ib.* ii. 233.

3 E. T. Dalton, *Descriptive Ethnology of Bengal*, Calcutta, 1872, p. 213; Risley, ii. 233.

LITERATURE.—Besides the authorities quoted in the art. see F. B. Bradley-Birt, *The Story of an Indian Upland*, London, 1905; E. G. Man, *Sonthalia and the Sonthals*, Calcutta and London, 1867. For the folklore see A. Campbell, *Santal Folk Tales*, Pokhuria, 1891; C. H. Bompas, *Folklore of the Santal Parganas*, London, 1909. For the geography and history of the tribe see W. W. Hunter, *The Annals of Rural Bengal*[7], London, 1897; *IGI* xxii. 60 ff.

W. CROOKE.

SANŪSĪ (fem. or plur. Sanūsiyyah). — **1. History.**—Sanūsī is the name of a religious order founded by Sī Muḥammad ibn Sī 'Ali al-Sanūsī al-Khaṭṭābī al-Ḥasani al-Idrisi al-Muhajiri.[2] His name Idrisi was derived from his supposed ancestor Idris, great-grandson of Ḥasan II., son of Ḥasan the Prophet's grandson; his name Khaṭṭābī refers to the tribe Khaṭāṭibah, to which his family belonged. He was born at Mostaganem in 1806 (or earlier) and migrated with his father to Fez in 1814, where he came under the influence of Shaikh Aḥmad Tijānī, founder of the Tijāniyyah order. In 1829 he went on pilgrimage to Mecca, after having been initiated into numerous orders in Africa and having studied at al-Azhar, where he encountered opposition. In Mecca he attached himself to Sī Aḥmad b. Idris of Fez, head of the Khiḍriyyah order, which had been founded in 1713 by Sī 'Abd al-'Azīz Dabbar. Sī Aḥmad b. Idris taught in Mecca from 1797 to 1833; in the latter year, owing to difficulties with the other religious authorities, he fled to Sobia in the Yemen, whither Sanūsī with other adherents accompanied him. At his death in 1835 the Khiḍri order split into two divisions, headed respectively by Sī Muḥammad Salaḥ Magharani and Sanūsī, who both returned to Mecca, where the latter established the first *zāwiyah* of his new order on the historic Mt. Abū Qubais. He continued to reside there till 1843, when his situation became intolerable owing to the opposition of the rival sect, which was more easily able to win the approval of the established authorities; he therefore, ostensibly in accordance with an injunction from the Prophet to go and found new *zāwiyahs* in other countries, returned to Africa and founded at al-Baiḍa in the Jibāl Akhḍar in the Tripolitaine the institution whence his system began to spread far and wide. Towards 1855, owing to the hostility of Turkish, Egyptian, and Meccan authorities, he transferred his headquarters to Jaghbūb, some days' march to the south-west of his former seat. It was in Baiḍa that his sons, Shaikh Mahdī and Sī Muḥammad Sharīf, were born; and on his death in 1859, as is usual with these orders he was succeeded by them; they were very young at the time, but they were well served by their guardians and instructors, and after a time assumed control, the former as administrator, the latter as spiritual teacher. The latter died in 1895; and in the same year the former secretly transferred his residence to the oasis of Kufra in the Eastern Sahara, where he remained till 1900;

1 Risley, ii. 234.

2 See also art. RELIGIOUS ORDERS (Muslim), § 38.

in 1900 he moved yet farther south to Garu in Dar Gurani of the Wadai region of the Sūdān. In 1902 his followers endeavoured to resist the French attack on Kanam, east of Lake Chad, and their failure caused him to die of chagrin on 30th May of that year. He was succeeded by his brother's son, Aḥmad Sharīf, who again made Kufra his headquarters.

2. The Sanūsī doctrines.—The system advocated by Sanūsī and his followers appears to be a combination of Wahhabism with Ṣūfism (*qq.v.*). It professes to aim at restoring the primitive 'purity' of Islām, as taught in the Qur'ān and the Prophet's *sunnah*; hence it prohibits music, dancing, singing, tobacco, and coffee. On the other hand, like other 'orders,' it prescribes certain forms of devotion; in prayer the arms are crossed on the breast, with the left wrist held by the thumb and forefinger of the right hand. The rosary should be carried in the hand, not hung on the neck. In the *dhikr*, or additional devotions, certain formulæ are to be repeated forty, others a hundred, times.[1] Several other practices are ascribed to them that are at variance with the Maliki practice, which, however, they profess (or professed) to observe; these are enumerated in a polemical treatise directed against them, of which Depont and Coppolani give a French translation.[2] What appears to be the greatest enormity criticized is that the Shaikh Mahdī received visitors only at particular hours and after repeated applications for an audience and habitually absented himself from public prayer, even on the Fridays. His admirers attributed this to his wish to meditate and pray in solitude.

The founder appears to have been unwilling to start an additional order in the style of the many already existing, maintaining that membership of another order was not inconsistent with adherence to his own society; he therefore, in spite of his puritanism, made certain concessions to orders that had adopted practices of which his system ordinarily disapproved—*e.g.*, the dances of the Maulawiyyah, the cries of the Rifā'iyyah, and the swaying of the Qādiriyyah. Certain practices which go farther than these in the direction of producing ecstasy were not tolerated; and indeed the main purpose of Ṣūfī practice—the production by hypnotism of the sense of unity or identity with the Deity—does not appear to have lain within his scope.

On the other hand, what rendered his order specially important was his insistence on a doctrine which orthodox Islām at times maintains, viz. that no Muslim should live in any region where Islām is not the dominant power. Hence, when a Muslim finds himself in a country which fails to answer to that description, it is his duty to emigrate; and the founder of the order sought in the desert of the Sahara that freedom from non-Muslim authority which was wanting in the large portions of Asia and Africa where Christian powers were dominant, and very imperfectly realized in those nominally independent Islāmic empires whose policy was subordinate to European guidance. Moreover, the Shaikh Mahdī was certainly identified by many of his followers, and possibly claimed identity himself, with the 'expected Mahdī,'[3] a fact which would have rendered it impossible for him to subordinate himself to any other sovereign, Islāmic or non-Islāmic.

3. Spread of the order.—The founder, as has been seen, employed his followers, especially those among them who were illiterate, in building *zāwiyahs*. These were then organized on the principle described in the art. DERVISH. In a few years after his arrival at Jibāl Akhḍar it was literally covered with establishments; he then undertook new constructions, first in the rest of the Tripolitaine, then in the south of Tunisia, on the shores of the Sea of Marmora, in Egypt, Arabia, and Central Africa, among the Tawariq, and in the Sūdān. By the end of his life he was practically sovereign of the region bounded by the Mediterranean from Alexandria to Gabes and stretching south to the negro kingdoms. But he also acquired a great following in the Hijaz, where a number of tribes—the Banu Ḥarb, Lam, Ḥarith, Thaqif, and others — accepted Sanūsī as their supreme lord. It is asserted that all the Bedawīn tribes of W. Arabia which had not embraced Wahhabi tenets adopted his; and the movement spread with no less rapidity among the Bedawīn or nomad tribes of the Sinaitic peninsula and Palestine. Before leaving Arabia, in spite of the opposition which drove him thence, he had founded *zāwiyahs* in various places of importance in addition to the original institution on Abū Qubais, viz. Ta'if, Medīna, Badr, Jedda, and Yanbu'. The original presidents of these and their successors are enumerated by Le Chatelier, *Les Confréries musulmanes du Hedjaz*, p. 273 f. In the *Manār* for 1330 (1912), pp. 532-538, there is an enumeration of the *zāwiyahs* belonging to this community to be found between Alexandria and Derna (140 miles N.E. of Benghāzī); the distance is eleven stages for camel-riders, and there are about twice that number of *zāwiyahs*. The inhabitants belong mainly to the Wuld 'Ali, who are without exception members of the order. To each *zāwiyah* (according to this account) about 2000 persons are attached, who complete the Qur'ān once a month in the buildings, which also serve as hospices to travellers in this region; no money is taken from the guests, as the institutions are maintained out of the land which is attached to them. Surplus produce is sent as tribute to the head of the order at Jaghbūb or Kufra. In addition to these, the same writer enumerates many more in the adjoining country. His list exhibits a great advance on that of Depont and Coppolani,[1] which bears date 1897, both in the number of the institutions and in that of their adherents. It has at times been asserted that there are great numbers of secret adherents of the order in Egypt, the Sūdān, and other Islāmic countries, in addition to those who make no concealment of their membership.

4. Reason for the progress of the movement.—Rinn attributes the great success which attended the efforts of the Shaikh Sanūsī largely to his personal qualities; he understood how to organize the community which he had founded and to maintain rigorous discipline; further, he attracted adherents by the boldness of his teaching and the dexterity which he displayed in basing his profound and learned exegesis on the most orthodox conceptions.

> 'Hence it may be said that his moral and intellectual superiority impressed all the Muslims who approached him, since the austerity of his puritanical precepts, his gloomy and taciturn character, his severity towards himself and every one else, were not of a nature to win much sympathy.'[2]

This statement is scarcely borne out by experience in either Eastern or Western revivalism. His influence in Wadai was due to his having purchased a caravan of slaves which the nomads had plundered from the slave-dealers; these he manumitted, had trained at his *zāwiyah* in Jaghbūb, and, some years later, when he believed them to be sufficiently qualified, sent home as missionaries to their native country; from that time the negroes of Wadai regarded themselves as servants of the

1 These are given by Rinn, *Marabouts et Khouan*, p. 503.
2 *Les Confréries religieuses musulmanes*, p. 546 ff.
3 See art. MAHDĪ.

1 P. 569 f. 2 Rinn, p. 491.

Sanūsī institutions, and their Sultan became one of the most faithful followers of the Shaikh Sanūsī.

Of his successor, the Shaikh Mahdī, the organ of reformed Islām speaks in glowing terms, similar to those quoted about his father; and the names of several followers are mentioned who seem to have been men of unusual energy and ability.

Besides these personal qualities, it is probable that the notion of creating an area in which Islām would be undisturbed by any foreign—*i.e.* non-Arabian—influence had great attractions for those who found Turkish rule unsupportable, and who, even if they recognized the blessings which European protection confers, held that they were too dearly purchased by the humiliation of Islām which such an arrangement involves. Further, the principle by which adherence to the new order was made compatible with membership of the older orders was likely to win for the Sanūsī system those whose spiritual needs required some such ritual as the orders enjoin, but who desired some sort of unity between the orders to be effected. We can scarcely be wrong in finding the main cause in the partition of Africa, which, commencing with the French occupation of Algiers, has now rendered the whole continent a European colony.

5. Political activities of the order.—The rise of the order was viewed with alarm by the French in Africa, as also by the Turks; for, although the order abstained from all warlike enterprises, there was a general belief that such were ultimately contemplated, and indeed that the head of the order in his oasis was amassing guns and ammunition for the purpose of starting a *jihad* when the time arrived. It was in this belief that in 1896 a French adventurer, the Marquis de Morès, led a small expedition into the interior of the Sahara with the view of offering his services as military leader to the Shaikh Mahdī at his oasis; he was, however, murdered at Bir Yusuf by the Tawariq before he reached his destination.[1] Nevertheless numerous earlier attempts to employ the supposed force of the Sanūsī chief in the interests of one Power or another had failed; thus in 1872 the Germans endeavoured to approach the Shaikh Mahdī with the view of getting him to preach the *jihad* against the French, but the envoys were not even permitted to enter the Shaikh's presence; the Ottoman Sultan was no more successful when he endeavoured to obtain the help of the Sanūsīs against the Russians in the war of 1876–78; the Italian mission to the Cyrenaica in 1881, the object of which was to form an alliance with the Sanūsīs in order to counterbalance French influence in Tunisia, was a failure; in the same year the Egyptian insurgent Arabi Pasha could gain no help from them; and in 1884 the Shaikh Mahdī not only declined to lend his aid to the Sūdānese Mahdī, but publicly declared him to be a liar and impostor. The principle which was supposed to guide their action was not to attack, but to defend themselves when attacked; and probably the need for armed resistance on their part first materialized in connexion with the French advance in Central Africa early in this century. The first important victory for the French was the capture of the *zāwiyah* of Bir Alali in Kanen, north-east of Lake Chad, in Jan. 1902. After more than eleven years of war the Sanūsīs in 1913 still held six or more important *zāwiyahs*, some of them strongly fortified, in Borku and Tibesti. The capture of these was effected by the Largeau expedition in 1913–14. After severe fighting, Sī Muhammad Sunni, the chief official of the Sanūsīs in these regions, his son Sī Mahdī, and the remnant of the army fled to Kufra. As soon as the European War commenced in 1914 the Sanūsī chief, Sayyid Aḥmad, adopted a threatening attitude towards the Egyptian government, but it was not till Nov. 1915 that he definitely threw in his lot with the Turks and Germans. In that month two English steamers were torpedoed and one Egyptian steamer sunk by fire from a German submarine in Sollum harbour, while three coastguard posts were attacked by Sanūsī forces. The whole number of fighting men in the service of the Sanūsī Shaikh appears to have been under 10,000; he himself displayed no ability of any sort as a commander or fighter, but he had in his employ a Turkish officer of some ability, who had been trained in Germany, named Ja'far. It was necessary to prevent danger from this source assuming serious dimensions, and an expedition was sent against the Sanūsīs first commanded by General Wallace, who was succeeded on 9th Feb. 1916 by General Peyton. The campaign practically terminated in Feb. 1917, and was uniformly successful; from Matruḥ, to which the Sanūsī army had advanced, it was by a series of defeats driven westward, and afterwards southward into the desert. Sollum was taken on 26th Feb. 1916, when Ja'far and his staff were captured, and in Feb. 1917 Sayyid Aḥmad was driven from the Siwa oasis, whither he had fled. It is possible that the disasters brought upon the sect by the part taken by this chief in the War may lead to a decline in its influence and eventually to its extinction.

[1] See Auguste Pavy, *L'Expédition de Morès*, Paris, 1897.

LITERATURE.—L. Rinn, *Marabouts et Khouan: Etude sur l'Islam en Algérie*, Algiers, 1885; A. Le Chatelier, *Les Confréries musulmanes du Hedjaz*, Paris, 1887; O. Depont and X. Coppolani, *Les Confréries religieuses musulmanes*, Algiers, 1897; the Egyptian journal *Manar*, xv. [1912] 532–538; *Geographical Journal*, xlvii. [1916] 129 f.; W. T. Massey, *The Desert Campaigns*, London, 1918.

D. S. MARGOLIOUTH.

SARAPIS.—See GRÆCO-EGYPTIAN RELIGION.

SARASVATĪ

SARASVATĪ (Skr. *saras*, originally perhaps 'flowing water'; *sarasvat*, 'having water,' 'watery,' 'elegant').—In the *Rigveda* there is nothing to show that Sarasvatī is ever anything more than a river-goddess, but we find her in the *Brāhmaṇas* identified with Vāch, 'speech,' and in post-Vedic mythology she has become goddess of eloquence and wisdom, invoked as a muse and regarded as wife of Brahmā.[1]

'The Sarasvatī appears to have been to the early Indians what the Ganges (which is only twice mentioned in the Rigveda) became to their descendants. . . . When once the river had acquired a divine character, it was quite natural that she should be regarded as the patroness of the ceremonies which were celebrated on the margin of her holy waters, and that her direction and blessing should be invoked as essential to their proper performance and success. The connection into which she was thus brought with sacred rites may have led to the further step of imagining her to have an influence on the composition of the hymns which formed so important a part of the proceedings, and of identifying her with Vāch, the goddess of speech.'[2]

The name is at present applied to two rivers in N. and W. India. The first, in the Panjāb, rises in the Sirmūr State and, after disappearing in the sand, emerges once more and joins the Ghaggar in Patiāla territory; the second, rising in the Arāvallī range, falls into the lesser Rann of Cutch. The latter is visited by Hindus, particularly those who have lost their mothers, whose propitiatory rites are performed at Sidhpur. There has been much controversy as to the identity of the river of which the goddess Sarasvatī is the personification.

'The name is identical with that of the Avestan river Haraqaiti in Afghanistan, and it may have been the latter river which was first lauded as the Sarasvatī. But Roth, Grassman, Ludvig, and Zimmer are of opinion that in the Rigveda Sarasvatī usually and originally meant a mighty stream, probably the Indus (Sarasvatī being the sacred and Sindhu the secular name), but that it occasionally designates the small stream in Madhyadeśa [the first mentioned above] to

[1] A. A. Macdonell, *Vedic Mythology*, p. 86 ff.

[2] J. Muir, *Orig. Sanskrit Texts*, v. [1870] 338 ff.

which its name and its sacred character were in later times transferred. Max Müller believes it to be identical with the small river Sarasvatī, which with the Dṛṣadvatī formed the boundaries of the sacred region Brahmāvarta,[1] and which loses itself in the sands of the desert, but in Vedic times reached the sea. According to Oldham, a survey of ancient river-beds affords evidence that the Sarasvatī was originally a tributary of the Sutudrī (the modern Sutlej), and that when the latter left its old bed and joined the Vipāś, the Sarasvatī continued to flow in the old bed of the Sutudrī.'[2]

LITERATURE.—*IGI* xxii. 97; A. A. Macdonell, *Vedic Mythology*, Strassburg, 1897, p. 86 ff.; A. A. Macdonell and A. B. Keith, *Vedic Index of Names and Subjects*, London, 1912, ii. 434 ff.; J. Muir, *Original Sanskrit Texts*,[3] 5 vols., do. 1858–70, *passim*; J. Dowson, *Classical Dict. of Hindu Mythology*, do. 1879, p. 284 f. For the Saraswati Brāhmans, J. Wilson, *Indian Caste*, Bombay, 1877, ii. 124 ff.

W. CROOKE.

SĀRIPUTTA.—Sāriputta was one of the two chief disciples of the Buddha. In Sanskrit works the name occurs as Śāriputra, Śāliputra, Śārisuta, and Śāradvatīputra, *i.e.* 'son of the woman Śārī, Śālī, or Śāradvatī.' He is also called Upatissa (Skr. Upatiṣya), which was probably his personal name, though the commentary on his verses in *Theragāthā*, 981 ff., explains it differently. The story of his conversion is told in art. MOGGALLĀNA. He has the title Dhammasenāpati, 'general of the Dharma,' and in *Sutta-Nipāta*, 557, the Buddha, when asked who is his general, declares that after himself it is Sāriputta who turns the Wheel of the Dharma.[3] It is thus not surprising to find several discourses in the Scriptures as well as whole *suttas* ascribed to him.[4] He is also found as the author of Mahāyāna works.[5] In the list of chief disciples in the *Aṅguttara*[6] he is mentioned as the first of those possessing great insight (*paññā*). An account of his previous existences is given in the commentary on the *Theragāthā*.[7] The commentary on *Jātaka*, i. 391, makes the Buddha, when deciding to pass away, refer to the death of Sāriputta at the village of Nāla in the room in which he was born; but this looks like an accretion, as the account of Buddha's death in the *Mahāparinibbāna Sutta* ignores all reference to Sāriputta, though it does introduce him as a short time previously uttering his *sīhanāda* (lion's roar), his great confession of faith in the Buddha; even this is probably inserted here from other parts of the Scriptures.[8] There are still later accounts of his death, which naturally increase in detail.[9] In the Mahāyānist *Saddharmapuṇḍarīka*[10] he is transformed into a *bodhisattva*, who is to appear as the future Buddha Padmaprabha.

LITERATURE.—The sources are given above.

EDWARD J. THOMAS.

SĀRNĀTH.—Sārnāth is the name applied to an extensive group of Buddhist ruins situated in the Benares District, United Provinces, India, about 3½ miles to the north of Benares city (*q.v.*), in N. lat. 25° 23′, E. long. 83° 2′. The name properly belongs to a Śaiva temple called Sārnāth to the south-east of the prominent Dhamēkh *stūpa*. An annual fair is, or used to be, held close to the temple—a circumstance which caused its name to become well known. The locality seems to have been sacred and the resort of ascetics from very ancient times, even before the days of Gautama Buddha. Its fame is due to the belief that the site includes the Deer-park (Skr. *mṛgadāva*, Pāli *migadāya*) adjoining Ṛṣipattana (Pāli Isipattana), where Buddha, in or about 528 B.C., preached to his first five adherents the 'first sermon,' expounding the 'four noble truths.' The legend and the substance of the sermon may be read in most of the books about Buddhism. The Deer-park, now known as Sārnāth, thus became one of the four principal holy places of Buddhism, the others being Kapilavastu with the Lumbinī garden, Bodh Gayā, and Kuśinagara (*qq.v.*). The sanctity thus acquired naturally resulted in the erection of commemorative monuments, magnificent monasteries, and all the appurtenances of a first-class place of pilgrimage.

The construction of monuments probably began before the close of the 5th cent. B.C., but at present no part of the remains can be assigned with confidence to a date earlier than the middle of the 3rd cent. B.C., in the reign of Aśoka. The Buddhist buildings were destroyed by the Musalmān invaders a little before the close of the 12th cent. of the Christian era. The ruins of Buddhist edifices, so far as yet ascertained, consequently cover a period of about fourteen centuries and a half. A modern Jain temple and many ancient images indicate that the locality is and long has been sacred in the eyes of the Jains, while the existence of the shrine of Sārnāth above mentioned and sundry mediæval sculptures prove that it is venerable also for Brāhmanical Hindus. But the whole interest of the site is connected with the Buddhist legends and remains, which alone need be noticed.

Exploration.—A visit of the Pādshāh Humāyūn to the site is commemorated by an inscription set up by his son Akbar in A.D. 1588, but the Musalmāns neither knew nor cared anything about the local history. Attention to the nature of the ruins was first attracted by excavations conducted in 1794 by a landholder for the sake of building material, which destroyed a *stūpa* and disclosed a relic casket and certain Buddhist images. Jonathan Duncan, then Resident at Benares, recorded a note on the subject. Other persons subsequently made desultory researches, but the first attempt at systematic exploration was made by Cunningham in 1834–36. Kittoe and others, between 1853 and 1865, did some more excavation. Cunningham recorded all information known up to date in his *Archæol. Survey Report* for 1861–62, published as the first vol. of his *Reports* at Simla in 1871. Nothing further of importance was done at the site until 1904–05, when Oertel made interesting discoveries. The work was taken up officially by the Archæological Department in 1907 and has been continued with excellent results. A museum has been built on the site, and a scholarly catalogue of its contents was published in 1914.

The site is divided into two distinct areas by an ancient wall running east and west. The monastery area to the north of that wall was occupied by four monasteries of various ages. The *stūpa* area south of the wall contains the remains of innumerable edifices, small and great. The 'main shrine' (*mūlagandhi kuṭi*) occupied the centre of the western section, and the Aśoka column discovered by Oertel stood to the west of the main shrine. The inscription, fortunately preserved, is classed as a 'minor pillar edict,' and is directed against schismatics. Jagat Singh's *stūpa*, the one dug up in 1794, is to the south of the main shrine. The Dhamēkh (Dharmekṣā) *stūpa*, a memorial of some sacred incident, not a depository for relics, stands in the south-eastern part of the area. It dates from the 5th or 6th cent. in the Gupta period and is adorned with fine decorative designs. It is impossible to enumerate the minor buildings. The principal establishment was known as the 'Monastery of the Wheel of the Law' (*dharmachakra*). Buddhists figured the first preaching of the Master as the 'turning of the wheel of the law.' Aśoka's column, accordingly, was surmounted by a wheel, and the symbol recurs frequently on the sculptures.

About A.D. 300 the leading sect at the locality was the Sarvāstivādin (*q.v.*). A little later the Sāṃmitīya (*q.v.*) sect or school prevailed, and in Hiuen Tsiang's time it had 1500 monks. Both sects were Hīnayāna.

The buildings, from Maurya or pre-Maurya times to the closing years of the 12th cent., were

1 Manu, *Laws*, ii. 17. 2 Macdonell, p. 87 f.
3 Cf. *Aṅguttara*, i. 23 (Ekapuggala).
4 *E.g.*, *Dīgha*, iii. 210, 272; *Majjhima*, i. 13; *Aṅguttara*, ii. 160, etc.
5 H. Kern, *Manual of Indian Buddhism* (*GIAP* III. viii.), Strassburg, 1896, p. 5.
6 i. 23 (Etad-agga).
7 Unpublished, but tr. by C. A. F. Rhys Davids in *Psalms of the Early Buddhists* (*PTS*), London, 1909–13, ii. *Psalms of the Brethren*.
8 Cf. *Dīgha*, ii. 81 with *Dīgha*, iii. 99, *Saṃyutta*, v. 159.
9 Kern, p. 42. 10 iii. 22.

destroyed more than once and frequently rebuilt. The first destruction perhaps occurred in the Hun period (6th century). Restorations are recorded in 1026 and the first half of the 12th century. The end came about 1193 at the hands of Kutb-ud-dīn's fierce Muslims. The traces of more than one burning are clearly visible.

The hundreds of sculptures include the magnificent capital, 7 ft. high, of the Aśoka column, the finest known Maurya composition, and multitudes of excellent works in the 'suave and gracious' Gupta style, some of which rank in the first class of Indian sculpture. In fact, the Sārnāth finds in themselves are almost enough to illustrate adequately a history of Indian sculpture. They are equally important as illustrations of Buddhism, and especially of the development of the Buddha cult and the later worship of minor deities, male and female. Jambhala or Vaiśravana, Vasudhārā, Tārā, Mārīchī, and others are frequently represented. Only one *Jātaka*, that of Kshāntivādin, has been noticed, but many discoveries of all kinds may yet be made.

LITERATURE.—Daya Ram Sahni, *Catalogue of the Museum of Archæology at Sārnāth*, with introd. by J. P. Vogel, plan and full bibliography, Calcutta, 1914 (well illustrated, gives the best general account); A. Cunningham, *Arch. Survey of India Reports*, i. Simla, 1871; *Arch. Survey Annual Reports, for 1904–05, 1906–07, and 1907–08*, Calcutta, 1906–12. The Chinese pilgrim Hiuen Tsiang (Yuan Chwang), in any of the versions, gives a detailed description. See also the other pilgrims, sundry books about Benares (*q.v.*), and a multitude of publications listed in Vogel's bibliography.

VINCENT A. SMITH.

SARVĀSTIVĀDINS.—Sarvāstivāda is one of the eighteen schools of Buddhism[1] and was at one time the most wide-spread and influential of all. As a philosophy, it is a school which holds a realistic view, as the name indicates (*sarva*, 'all'; *asti*, 'exist'; *vāda*, 'saying,' *i.e.* one who maintains that everything, external as well as internal, is real); and it is one of the earliest, if not the earliest, in deviating from the opinions of the orthodox Theravāda school.

In the course of 100 to 200 years after the Buddha's *nirvāṇa*, *i.e.* after the Council of Vaiśālī, the object of which was chiefly to refute the ten theses of the Vajjian *bhikkhus*, the Buddhist Church is said to have split into various schools.[2] We are told in the *Dīpavaṁsa*, v. 47, that the Mahiṁsāsaka (Mahiśāsaka) separated itself from the Theravāda, and from the Mahiṁsāsaka the Sabbatthivāda (=Sarvāstivāda) and the Dhammagutta (=Dharmagupta).

The Mahīśāsaka and the Dharmagupta will subsequently be found as the subdivisions of the school,[3] and we may assume from this fact that these three schools did not differ much in their philosophical opinions. The history of this school, however, begins practically with the Council of Pāṭaliputra under King Aśoka, for it was in that Council (240 B.C.) that Moggaliputta Tissa, the head of the Council, compiled the *Kathāvatthu*[4] to refute the schismatic views current at his time. This work directs only three questions against the Sabbatthivāda: (1) Does every thing exist? (2) Can an *arhat* fall from *arhat*-ship? (3) Is continuation of thought *samādhi*?[5] All these questions would be answered in the affirmative by the Sabbatthivādas, contrary to the opinions of the orthodox school.

1 The enumeration of eighteen schools is official as well as historical. See Takakusu, 'The Abhidharma Literature of the Sarvāstivādins,' *JPTS*, 1905, pp. 67–146.

2 *Dīpavaṁsa*, v. 16–18; *Mahāvaṁsa*, v. 8.

3 See Takakusu, *A Record of the Buddhist Religion as practised in India and the Malay Archipelago (A.D. 671–695) by I-tsing*, Oxford, 1896, p. xxiv.

4 *Points of Controversy*, tr. with commentary by C. A. F. Rhys Davids, London, 1915.

5 C. A. F. Rhys Davids, *Points of Controversy*, i. 6 (p. 84), i. 2 (p. 64), xi. 6 (p. 260), and *JRAS*, 1892, p. 8.

Though it does not seem to have played a very important part at the time of King Aśoka, it must have found a new home in the northernmost regions and flourished vigorously there as the Vaibhāṣikas of Gandhāra and Kaśmīra. The word 'Vaibhāṣika' is derived from *Vibhāṣā* ('Option'), which is the name of a great commentary compiled some time after Kaniṣka's reign to explain the *Jñānaprasthāna* ('Origin of Knowledge') by Kātyāyanīputra, a brilliant philosopher of this school.[1] The commentary receives its name from the fact that different opinions of the leading teachers of the school are carefully recorded, so that the reader may at his own option adopt whatever opinion he feels inclined to.

The *Vibhāṣā* and the *Mahāvibhāṣā* in three Chinese versions were translated in A.D. 383, 427, and 659 respectively,[2] and we have therefore to attribute the compilation to a period prior to the first date and to assume that the period during which this literature was studied must cover those dates. The Sarvāstivādins appear from this work to have been, after their first deviation from the original school, the upholders of a well-organized philosophical system. This is fully borne out by subsequent writers, especially Vasubandhu (*c.* A.D. 420–500)[3] and his powerful opponent Saṅghabhadra, who often refer to and criticize the opinions of the Kaśmīra Vaibhāṣikas as a body of thinkers.[4]

According to Paramārtha (A.D. 499–569), the *Vibhāṣā* was a principal subject of philosophical discussion during the 5th cent., when there was also a great controversy between Buddhist and Sāṅkhya philosophers.[5] The Neo-Vibhāṣanic activity seems practically to have ceased with the conversion of Vasubandhu to the idealistic philosophy, though his work appears to have been still in vogue among Buddhist scholars, Guṇamati, Vasumitra, and Yaśomitra successively compiling a commentary on it.[6]

Śaṅkarāchārya ([*q.v.*] born *c.* A.D. 788), while explaining Bādarāyaṇa's *Vedānta-sūtra*, remembers the Vaibhāṣika school and refutes its doctrine of realism (*sarvāstitvavāda*) along with the other systems of Buddhism, idealism (*vijñānamātratvavāda*) and negativism (*sarvaśūnyatvavāda*).[7]

Vāchaspatimiśra's *Bhāmatī* of the 12th cent. follows Śaṅkarāchārya in giving three schools of Buddhism, classifying the Sarvāstivādins as those of inferior thought (*hīnamati*) against those of middle (*madhyama*, the idealist) and advanced thought (*prakṛṣṭamati*, the negativist).

In the 14th cent. the system is reviewed as one of the four Buddhist schools by Mādhavāchārya.[8] Here it is expressly stated that the Vaibhāṣikas acknowledge the direct perception of external objects (*vāhyārtha-pratyakṣatva*), while the Sautrāntikas (*q.v.*), to whom Vasubandhu himself was

1 Hiuen Tsiang's statement that this commentary was drawn up by 500 *arhats* in the Buddhist Council under King Kaniṣka is very doubtful, because the book relates a miracle which it says occurred *formerly* in the reign of that king; see T. Watters, *On Yuan Chwang's Travels in India, 629–645*, London, 1904–05, i. 277.

2 Bunyio Nanjio, *A Catalogue of the Chinese Translation of the Buddhist Tripiṭaka*, Oxford, 1883, nos. 1299, 1264, 1263.

3 In spite of a grave objection raised by M. Peri and B. Shiio, the present writer still holds A.D. 420–500 to be the safest date for Vasubandhu.

4 Vasubandhu's *Abhidharmakośa* (Nanjio, no. 1267), Saṅghabhadra's *Satyānusāra* (no. 1265) and *Samaya pradīpikā* (no. 1266) often quote the Kaśmīra Vaibhāṣikas. For Yaśomitra's explanation of the name see his *Abhidharmakośavyākhyā*, ch. iii.

5 See Takakusu, 'Paramārtha's Life of Vasubandhu,' *Tong-pao*, July, 1904, pp. 279, 287, 289, and also 'The Date of Vasubandhu,' *JRAS*, Jan. 1905, p. 47.

6 See C. Bendall, *Catalogue of Buddhist Sanskrit MSS in the [Cambridge] University Library*, Cambridge, 1883, add. 1041, p. 26.

7 G. Thibaut, *Vedānta-sūtra*, pt. I. (ii. 2–18), *SBE* xxxiv. [1890] 401.

8 *Sarvadarśana-saṅgraha*, ch. ii.

inclined, hold that external objects merely exist as images and can only be inferred (*vāhyārthānumeyatva*).

Though the existence of the Sarvāstivādins can be traced during more than fifteen centuries of Indian history, yet the exhaustive study of their religious practices was not undertaken till the 7th cent., when I-tsing translated the whole of their Vinaya literature and wrote a treatise on the current practices.[1] The geographical extension described by him is more minute than those of his predecessors. Fa-Hian (A.D. 399–414) says that the Sarvāstivāda was followed in Pāṭaliputra as well as in China in his time.[2] According to Hiuen Tsiang (A.D. 629–645), the school was found chiefly in Kaśgar (Central Asia), Udyāna (Yusefzay, N.W. Frontier), and the neighbouring territories, in Matipura, Kanauj, and a place near Rājagṛha in Mid-India, and also in Persia in the West.[3] I-tsing (A.D. 671–695), himself a Sarvāstivādin, gives a fairly detailed description of this school. The places enumerated by him as belonging to it are the following:

C. India	Magadha, where it is chiefly flourishing.
W. India	Lāṭa (Gujarāt) and Sindhu, where it had a few adherents.
N. India	Almost all belonged to it.
S. India	A few adherents are found.
E. India	Side by side with the other schools.
(Ceylon	No adherents.)
Sumatra, Java, Bali Islands	Almost all belong to it.
Champā (Cochin-China)	A few adherents.
S. China	The south valley of the Yang-tse-kiang, Kwang-tung, and Kwang-si, where it is chiefly flourishing.

The three subdivisions of this school, Dharmagupta, Mahīśāsaka, and Kāśyapīya, are found in Central Asia (Kharachar, *i.e.* Kuche, and Kustana, *i.e.* Khotan) and the N.W. Frontier (Udyāna, *i.e.* Yusefzay); and the Dharmagupta alone is flourishing in E. China and also in W. China (Shen-si).[4]

The Tibetan Buddhism is said to belong to this school, while in Japan a tenet founded on the *Abhidharmakośa* is still studied as the foundation of a philosophical training. This wide-spread school was, according to I-tsing, in possession of a *Tripiṭaka* (sacred books so called) amounting to 300,000 *ślokas*.[5] Whether this statement is to be taken as literally true or not, an examination of the extant Buddhist literature shows clearly that this school had a separate *Vinaya Piṭaka*[6] and also a distinct *Abhidharma Piṭaka*.[7] These are very complete in contents, a counterpart of almost all the Theravāda works being found in them. A striking resemblance between the names of the seven works of the *Abhidharma* of the two schools is so puzzling to the present writer that he has thought it necessary to show clearly that the two sets had no real connexion with each other.[8]

The whole of the *Abhidharma* literature centres on the work *Jñāna-prasthāna* ('Origin of Knowledge') by Kātyāyanīputra. Hiuen Tsiang tells us that he composed this work about 300 years after the Buddha's decease, in a monastery called Tāmasāvana of Cīnabhukti, N. India, in which the traveller himself found 300 brethren of the Sarvāstivādins learning the Hīnayāna doctrine. The work treats of matter (*bhūta*, *bhauta*) and mind (*chitta*, *chaitta*) with all their bearings, giving definitions and classifications when necessary. Among the subjects discussed we find the supramundane state (*lokāgra-dharma*), knowledge (*jñāna*), thought (*chetanā*), meditation (*samādhi*), views (*dṛṣṭi*), person (*pudgala*), form (*rūpa*), elements (*mahābhūta*), bondage (*saṁyojana*), path (*mārga*), action (*karma*), and the like. It is to this work that six authors, either contemporaries or successors, wrote each a supplementary treatise called the *pāda* ('foot'). The six *pādas* take up the subjects again and try to systematize or supplement what is, in their eyes, wanting in their predecessors.

The *Saṅgīti* ('Rehearsal') by Mahākauṣṭhila arranges the subjects in the numerical order, while the *Prakaraṇa* ('Classification') by Vasumitra tries to group the questions under chief heads. The *Vijñāna-kāya* ('Consciousness-body') of Devaśarman, the *Dhātukāya* ('Element-body') of Pūrṇa, the *Dharma-skandha* ('Norm-group') of Śāriputra, and the *Prajñapti* ('World-formation') of Maudgalyāyana treat of a subject each as the title indicates. These constitute the seven official works of the school,[1] but they by no means exhaust all the literature of the Sarvāstivādins.

As is shown in the present writer's 'Analysis,'[2] there are the *Vibhāṣā* (14 fasciculi, no. 1299) and the *Mahāvibhāṣā* (200 fasciculi, nos. 1263, 1264), each being a different translation of a commentary on the *Jñāna-prasthāna* just mentioned. This *Vibhāṣā* is practically an encyclopædia of the Vaibhāṣika philosophy, for it records carefully the often conflicting opinions of various realistic philosophers residing at the two great centres of Kaśmīra and Gandhāra.[3] The bulk of this great commentary and the discrepancy of the opinions expressed in it gradually made the necessity of a concise treatise or a short versification keenly felt. To supply this need there appeared the *Abhidharmakośa* (no. 1269) of Vasubandhu early in the 5th cent.[4] and in opposition to it the two treatises of Saṁghabhadra called the *Satyānusāra* (no. 1265) and the *Samaya-pradīpikā* (no. 1266). Saṁghabhadra represents the orthodox opinion of realism, while Vasubandhu was much inclined towards the Sautrāntic philosophy and introduced some ideas foreign and heretical in the eyes of the orthodox. The brilliant leader of the Neo-Vaibhāṣakas soon proved the founder of the idealistic school. Of all the *Abhidharma* literature we have no original Sanskrit text at present, nor is there any prospect as yet of its being discovered in the remote Himālayan regions. The Chinese translation is, therefore, the sole authority.[5] To compensate for this, we have Yaśomitra's *Abhidharma-kośa-vyākhyā-sphuṭārtha*, a Sanskrit commentary on the *Kośa* of Vasubandhu. This is almost the last work which reflects the activity of the Sarvāstivāda philosophy on Indian soil.

In Japan, however, the *Kośa* doctrine is still

1 See Takakusu, *I-tsing's Record*, p. xxxvii.

2 Fa-Hian, *Record of Buddhistic Kingdoms*, ch. xxxix., ed. J. Legge, Oxford, 1886, p. 99.

3 Hiuen Tsiang mentions some thirteen places as belonging to this school, but the number of its adherents in India proper was not so great as in those of the other schools (see T. W. Rhys Davids, *JRAS*, 1891, p. 420).

4 See Takakusu, *I-tsing's Record*, p. xxiv.

5 A *śloka*=32 syllables.

6 For the list of nineteen works of the *Vinaya* in 189 volumes see Takakusu, *I-tsing's Record*, p. xxxvii.

7 The present writer has analyzed the *Abhidharma* literature of this school in *JPTS*, 1905, pp. 67–146.

8 A question was raised by H. Kern and M. Walleser as to a possible connexion of the Pāli with the Chinese, and the result of an examination was communicated to *JRAS*, 1905, pp. 160–162.

1 That these were authentic classics of the school is seen from Yaśomitra's giving a list of these authors as handed down. See *Abhidharmakośa-vyākhyā Kārikā*, iii. The *Mahāvyutpatti*, §§ 65, 91–96, gives six works and omits *Vijñānakāya*. For Takakusu's list of Sanskrit, Tibetan, and Chinese (transliteration and translation) equivalents see *JPTS*, 1905, p. 75.

2 *JPTS*, 1905, p. 125 f.

3 The text cites the views of at least six schools, viz. Vibhajyavādin (Theravāda), Sautrāntika, Dharmagupta, Mahīśasaka (the two are the subdivisions of the Sarvāstivādins), Vātsīputrīya, and the school which holds the distinction of *chitta* (mind) and *chetanā* (thought). Among the names of philosophers quoted we find Dharmatrāta, Buddhadeva, Ghoṣa, Pārśva, Vasumitra, and Kātyāyanīputra.

4 See p. 198b, n. 3.

5 No text is found in Tibetan. The Tibetan *Dharmaskandha* (*Mdo*, xx. 3, wa 39–46) to which M. Walleser refers (*Die philosoph. Grunde.*, Heidelberg, 1904, p. 18) proved, on comparison, to be an entirely different work (see Takakusu, in *JPTS*, 1905, p. 77).

studied by Buddhist scholars, and a considerable amount of literature is in existence. Among others, we have the two priceless commentaries on the *Kośa* (each 30 vols., being notes of Hiuen Tsiang's lectures) by Fu-kuang and Fa-pao (A.D. 645–664 with Hiuen Tsiang) and two other commentaries of a little later date (each 29 vols.) by Yüan-hui and Tun-lin, all of which were lost in their original home, China.[1] The preservation of these works in the Far East, along with a Turkish commentary found in Central Asia,[2] is a proof of the wide propagation of the Sarvāstivāda school.

As to the religious life and the monastic rules of the school, there are numerous points of interest in which they differ from the orthodox school. These will become clear when all the *Vinaya-piṭakas* (eleven in all) have been examined, and then I-tsing's painstaking *Record* will assert its importance in religious history.[3]

There are some doubtful points as to the name of the school. Sarvāstivāda (Pāli Sabbatthivāda) is the regular name of it. The *Dīpavaṁsa*, v. 47, however, gives Sabbatthavāda, which looks like Sarvārthavāda in Sanskrit, but 'attha' for 'atthi' is probably due to a euphonic change. The oldest Chinese name Sā-p'o-to (Jap. Sat-ba-ta) very probably represents the Pāli Sabbattha.[4] An ingenious suggestion of F. W. Thomas of the India Office Library, that it may represent Sad-vāda in contradistinction to Asadvāda, is very appropriate, if we can only adduce any evidence of the use of such a name in Buddhist literature.[5] When the three minor schools[6] became subordinate to it in the 7th cent., this school seems to have used the name Mūla-sarvāstivāda. A general appellation, comprising the four together, is, according to I-tsing, the Ārya-mūla-sarvāstivāda-nikāya, *i.e.* the 'noble fundamental school which affirms the existence of all.' We have no reason to doubt the accuracy of I-tsing's statement when we have the evidence of the name Sarvāstitva-vāda (which is practically the same as Sarvāstivāda) used by Śaṅkarāchārya and Vāchaspatimiśra.[7] The *Mahāvyutpatti*, § 275, further gives two forms of the name, Ārya-sarvāstivāda and Mūla-sarvāstivāda, in conformity with the names given by I-tsing. In conclusion a summary of the above description of the philosophical and literary activity of the school may be useful:

Sarvāstivādins

Gandhāra Abhidharmikas. Kaśmīra Abhidharmikas
(*Jñāna-prasthāna* and its six *pādas*)

Vaibhāṣika-śāstrins
(*Vibhāṣā* and *Mahāvibhāṣā*)

Neo-Vaibhāṣika śāstrins

Vasubandhu (Sautrāntic) (*Abhidharmakośa* and the *Kārikā*) | Saṅghabhadra (Orthodox) (Satyānusāra and Samaya-pradīpikā)

Fu-kuang and Fa-pao (pupils of Hiuen Tsiang)
(The two great commentators on the *Kośa*)

The other commentators in Sanskrit, Chinese, Turkish, etc.

LITERATURE.—See the works cited in footnotes.

J. TAKAKUSU.

[1] First published in Japan in the Kyoto ed. of the *Tripiṭaka* (Continuation series, cases 84–86).

[2] This work is now being studied by E. D. Ross. It seems to have been translated into Turkish from Chinese.

[3] The present writer is now engaged on publishing *Buddhaghosa's Commentary on the Vinaya, the Samantapāsādikā*, of which a Chinese text exists.

[4] This name Sā-p'o-to is used from the Three Chin dynasty (A.D. 350–431). Watters restored it into a very unlikely form 'Sarvata.' Though phonetically this may fit better than 'Sabbattha,' we cannot assume that such a form as 'Sarvata' has ever existed as a name.

[5] In *JPTS*, 1905, p. 72, the present writer gave *sarvavāda* instead of *sadvāda* by mistake.

[6] See above, p. 199a, n. 1. [7] See above, p. 198b.

SĀSANA.—This term, meaning 'instruction,' 'teaching,' 'injunction,' and etymologically allied to *satthā*, 'teacher,' and *śāstra* (Skr.), 'treatise,' 'didactic compilation,' appears in the earliest books of the Buddhist canon. There it almost invariably means the teaching, doctrine, or evangel of the Buddha.

There is this special touch of similarity with the word 'evangel' (εὐαγγέλιον) that *sāsana* is occasionally employed in the commentaries to mean 'message' or 'news'—*e.g.*, 'the king sent a message, saying' . . .[1]

In such passages as those translated 'the teaching of the Master,'[2] 'the doctrine of the Teacher,'[3] 'Gotama's commandments,'[4] the original is *satthu* or *Gotamassa sāsanaṃ*. And we find it repeatedly used as a co-ordinate and equivalent of *dhamma* and *vinaya*—'doctrine' and 'discipline,' or 'rule': 'this is the Dhamma, this is the Vinaya, this is the Teacher's Teaching.'[5] In fact, in so far as *dhamma* meant formulated doctrine, and *vinaya* meant spiritual discipline, *sāsana* implied both of these. For it connoted essentially 'precept,' 'ordinance,' enjoined by an instructor on a pupil as a rule of life; hence the term for a loyal recluse, *sāsana-karo* (*-karī*, or *-kārako*[6]), 'doer of the *sāsana*'; and hence the frequent refrain of triumph when he realizes that he has graduated in such a course:

> 'And all the Buddha's ordinance is done.'[7]

Occasionally the *sāsana* so obeyed is ascribed to a notable teacher in the order, even though it were to a contemporary of the Buddha—*e.g.*, Sister Paṭāchārā:

> 'THE SISTER: "Do ye the Buddha's *sāsana*" . . .
> The will (*sāsana*) of her who spake, Paṭāchārā,
> The thirty sisters heard and swift obeyed . . .
> . . . . they hailed her blest:
> "Fulfillèd is thy will!"'[8]

Once only is the teaching of one 'outside' the order (*ito bahiddhā*) called his *sāsana*. This was the saintly Sunetta,[9] and he belonged to the dim past.

Gradually the import of the word developed. From meaning the fluid series of personal teachings it came to represent both a body of compiled if unwritten literature (*pariyatti-sāsana*), which was to be committed to memory, and the system of conduct and mental training (*paṭipatti sāsana*), as enumerated in the *Niddesa*.[10] It has been sought to reproduce this organic development in the term by the word 'rule':

> 'But I will in this Rule renounce the world.'[11]
> 'If he the training in the Rule fulfil.'[12]

In its relation to the individual follower's consciousness, it coincides with the word 'religion.' And in historical documents of Buddhism, such as the account of the growth of the seventeen partly divergent schools,[13] and the *Mahāvaṃsa* and *Dīpa-*

[1] *The Jātaka*, ed. V. Fausböll, London, 1877, i. 60, etc., tr. T. W. Rhys Davids, in *Buddhist Birth Stories*, London, 1880, i. 79, 119 f.; cf. *Dhammapada Commentary* (*PTS*), ed. H. C. Norman, Oxford, 1906–14, i. 60.

[2] *Dialogues of the Buddha* (*SBB*), tr. T. W. and C. A. F. Rhys Davids, London, 1910, ii. 135.

[3] *Mahāvagga*, I. vi. 32 (*SBE* xiii. [1881] 98); cf. *Dhammapada*, 183, 185 (*SBE* x.[2] [1898] pt. i. p. 51).

[4] *Sutta-Nipāta*, II. xiv. 19 (*SBE* x.[2] pt. ii. p. 169).

[5] *Aṅguttara Nikāya*, ii. 168, iv. 143, 280.

[6] *Majjhima Nikāya*, i. 129, 234; *Aṅguttara Nikāya*, ii. 26; *Sutta-Nipāta*, 445 (*SBE* x.[2] pt. ii. p. 70).

[7] *Psalms of the Early Buddhists* (*PTS*), London, 1909–13, i. 26, etc., ii. 107, etc.

[8] *Ib.* i. 74; cf. 95, where *anusāsani* ('instructions') is substituted probably *metri causa*.

[9] *Aṅguttara Nikāya*, iv. 104; cf. 136: *ito bahiddhā*.

[10] *Mahā-Niddesa*, 143. This is the canonical commentary on part of the *Sutta-Nipāta*; it is here commenting on the word *sāsana* (precepts) in verse 815 (*SBE* x.[2] pt. ii. p. 151). 'Religion' would have been a better rendering here of *sāsana* than 'precepts.'

[11] *Psalms of the Early Buddhists*, ii. 313; cf. F. Max Müller, *Dhammapada*, 164 (*SBE* x.[2] pt. i. p. 46).

[12] *Kindred Sayings* (*PTS*), London, 1917, i. 246, tr. of *Saṃyutta*, i.

[13] *Points of Controversy* (*PTS*), London, 1915, p. 2, n. 1; see art. SECTS (Buddhist).

vaṃsa, sāsana can rightly be translated 'the faith,' 'religion,' 'the church.'

So H. Oldenberg ('Will exist as long as the Faith'[1]); W. Geiger and M. H. Bode ('Is there a kinsman of Buddha's religion?');[2] S. Z. Aung and C. A. F. Rhys Davids ('Now the Sāsana held on its way as these eighteen early schools').[3]

Such down to the present day is the significance of the term to a Buddhist.

LITERATURE.—See the sources indicated in the footnotes.

C. A. F. RHYS DAVIDS.

SASANIANS. — **I. History.** — The national dynasty which, overthrowing the Arsacid line, ruled in Persia from A.D. 226 to 651 — George Rawlinson's 'Seventh Great Oriental Monarchy' —derives its name from Sasan, father of Papak (otherwise Babek), whose son **Ardashir I.** (same name as Artaxerxes) was the founder of the line of some 28 monarchs who ruled Irān for over four centuries. We are concerned here with this long dynasty only so far as it was connected with the history of the national religion as well as with Christianity. The question whether the great Achæmenian dynasty (559-331 B.C.), which was certainly Mazdean (for its kings proclaim themselves in their famous rock-inscriptions as 'Mazdayasnian'), was also Zoroastrian, as has been held by so many, or whether it professed another form of that cult, is still one of the unsolved riddles of history, in spite of J. H. Moulton's able advocacy of the former solution.[4] The faith of the Parthian or Arsacid dynasty (250 B.C.–A.D. 226) is a subject of considerable obscurity; it was perhaps a debased form of Mazdeism, with a heterogeneous syncretism of alien and pagan cults. Still Zoroastrianism continued to subsist, at least in the more purely Persian parts of the empire, and the fragments of the sacred books which had escaped the (traditional) destruction by Alexander the Great were handed down during the 476 years of the dynasty; probably it was also during this period that the surviving portions of the Avesta were translated into Pahlavi, the daughter and successor of the Old Persian language.[5] Be this as it may, with the Sasanians the Zoroastrian religion, though much altered from the days of the Prophet and his *Gāthās*, mounted the throne of Persia and became the undoubted national faith of a mighty empire. The kings of this line were ardent, and only too frequently intolerant, upholders of the faith. Ardashir himself on his coins styles himself from the beginning 'Mazdayasn,' *i.e.* worshipper of Mazda, like the Achæmenian 'Auramazdiya,' and his successors retained the title. It was under the second king, **Shahpuhr (Sapor) I.**, that Māni, the founder of the subsequently world-wide system of Manichæism (*q.v.*), first came into prominence. By the Persians he was always regarded as a heretic and his religion as a 'heresy' of Mazdeism. He was cruelly put to death by Varahran (Bahram) I. in 272. His execution seems to have been concomitant with an extensive persecution, by the Magian priesthood, not only of Māni's followers, but also of the Christians. The long reign of **Shahpuhr II.** (A.D. 309-380) is of importance in the religious history in that, at least according to the native tradition, the celebrated priest Aderbad Marehspand (Aturpāt-i Maraspandān) completed during it the final redaction and correction of all that remained of the Avesta texts in the form in which we now possess them.[6] To him is also ascribed the compilation of the *Khorda Avesta*, or 'Little Avesta,' being selections from various sacred texts and

[1] Tr. of *Dīpavaṃsa*, London, 1879, p. 135.
[2] Tr. of *Mahāvaṃsa*, London, 1912, p. 42.
[3] *Points of Controversy*, p. 5.
[4] In his *Early Zoroastrianism.*
[5] On the Arsacid religion see Justi in *GIrP* ii. 694.
[6] See K. Geldner, *GIrP* ii. 34 f.; West, *ib.* pp. 94-96.

containing the *Nyayishes*, or 'Litanies,'[1] together with the *Gahs*, *Siroza*, and *Afringān*. Other original compositions in Pahlavi are attributed to him, especially his *Andarj*, or 'Book of Counsel' to his son.[2] Of Aturpāt and his fellow 'diaskeuasts' Geldner says:

'Out of the surviving remains and fragments [of the Avesta] they built up a new Canon. With old materials they erected a new edifice. What materials they found, what they themselves added, how far they reproduced passages literally or recast them, it is impossible to decide.'[3]

Probably we owe to them the division into chapters and verses. West takes a less favourable view of the work of these revisers. Certainly a great deal of the meaning of the sacred texts had been forgotten—many of them are still in a very corrupt state—and we do not exactly know in what script they were preserved; for, strange as it sounds, what is now known as the Zend or Avestan alphabet, in which all existing MSS of the sacred book are written and which is now used in printing, is posterior to and derived from the Pahlavi alphabet, and evolved from the latter possibly as late as the 6th cent. A.D., eked out with vowel characters borrowed from the Greek.

The reign of **Yazdagird II.** (Yazdakart, lit. θεόκτιστος), A.D. 438–457, is noteworthy in the religious history for his violent attempts to force the Mazdean religion upon the Armenians, and after a long religious war Zoroastrianism was imposed upon that nation, amidst bloody episodes, in 456. As a preliminary to this scheme of proselytism must be mentioned the celebrated 'Edict of Mihr Narseh,' the vazir or prime minister, addressed to the Armenian people and preserved to us by the Armenian historians. It is extremely curious in many ways. It begins with the solemn words: 'Ye must know that every one of those who live beneath the sky and hold not the Mazdean religion is deaf and blind and deceived by the demons,' and proceeds to give a summary of that faith, followed by a detailed criticism of the doctrines of Christianity, insisting especially on the absurdity of the divine incarnation, the crucifixion of God, abstinence and celibacy, and so forth. It is surprising to find, however, that the form of Mazdeism which this official edict sets forth is no other than what would be termed the heterodox one of Zervanism, or the reduction of the primitive dualism to the primordial principle or deity Zervan ('Time'), of whom were born in fantastic wise both Ormazd and Ahriman.[4] We must suppose, therefore, that this represents the royal belief at the time. The Christian bishops under the catholicos Joseph drew up a reply to the document. What argumentation failed to effect was, as we have seen, subsequently carried out by ruthless persecution.

The eventful reign of **Kobad (Kavāt) I.** (A.D. 490-531) is remarkable for a most unusual episode in the history of the Zoroastrian faith. This was the rise of the second great 'heresy' in its midst, the extravagant communism of Mazdak (*q.v.*), a Magian priest, whose name is constantly coupled in the Pahlavi writings with that of Māni as a heresiarch in terms of special reprobation. The extraordinary thing is that the king himself fell under the influence of this wildly ultra-socialistic system and became not only a protector but even a proselyte of Mazdak. This led to his deposition in 498 and the substitution of his brother Jamasp. After his restoration Kobad broke with the sect, which was now plotting his overthrow, and inflicted a general massacre upon them. Mazdak himself survived till the next reign, but Chosroes

[1] 'A sort of religious chrestomathy . . . employed in daily use by laymen as well as by priests,' separately ed. and tr. by M. N. Dhalla, New York, 1908.
[2] Tr. C. de Harlez, Louvain, 1887.
[3] P. 35.
[4] See art. PHILOSOPHY (Iranian), § 2.

(Khusrau) I. exterminated the sect, slaughtering the heresiarch with 100,000 of his followers. It will be seen that, whilst Manichæism was a philosophical and theological system, Mazdakism was almost exclusively of a social and economic character, proclaiming communism not only of goods but even of women. Its extension in both Persia and Armenia was at one time very remarkable.

We now come to the most illustrious of all the Sasanian reigns, that of the well-known **Chosroes Anoshervan** (in Pahlavi, Khusrau-i Anōshak-rūbāno, *i.e.* 'the immortal souled'), A.D. 531–579. This was the golden age of the imperial Mazdean religion and of the Pahlavi literature. To it belong most of the many Pahlavi treatises which have been preserved to us and of which by far the fullest and best account is that of E. W. West in *GIrP* ii. 75–129. It is quite evident that the court of this famous monarch was a great centre of intellectual activity. Foreign philosophers and men of science, Indian, Syrian, and Greek, from East and West, met and discussed; whilst even in the national religion itself we know that rival theological and philosophical sects existed side by side, on the evidence of an eye- and ear-witness, Paul the Persian.[1] The king himself seems to have taken a keen personal interest in theological questions. If we may credit a strange tale recorded by the Syriac historian Barhebræus,[2] he summoned on one occasion a Nestorian catholicos ('who had formerly been a magus') and held a brief discussion with him concerning Cyril and Nestorius, apparently trying to persuade him to give up Nestorianism for Christian orthodoxy. It is distressing to learn that, as the royal logic did not convert the unfortunate man, he was incarcerated and subsequently put to death. Several Pahlavi compositions are attributed to Chosroes himself—it is difficult to say with what authority. There is a very interesting Aśoka-like doctrinal proclamation, styled 'The Ten Precepts of the Immortal-souled Khusrau, King of Kings,' embodied in the *Dīnkarṭ*,[3] and translated by the present writer in *The Babylonian and Oriental Record*.[4] More interesting still is the *Andarj-i Khusrau-i Kavātān*, a little treatise first published with some others by Dastur Peshotan at Bombay in 1888. Whether this piece be merely a rhetorical composition of subsequent date, such as Xenophon's dying speech of Cyrus the Great is supposed to be, or whether it be genuinely the last will and testament of the great Sasanian monarch, in any case it is a noble composition of lofty morality and sentiments worthy of a Christian, surpassing in its reverent humility the words put by Xenophon in the mouth of his hero.[5]

'As soon as this life shall be parted from my body,' it begins, 'take this my throne and bear it to Ispahan, and in Ispahan set me up; before the face of the people make ye proclamation, saying: "O men, from doing sin preserve yourselves; and in the working of meritorious deeds be ye active; and the splendour of the world hold ye in contempt. For this is the body of him who yesterday was in the body, and whom men approached with three obeisances; in every place he cultivated purity and the splendour of this world. But to-day on account of his condition of impurity,[6] every one who placeth his hand upon him is thereafter obliged to purify himself by the *bareshnum*, else to the worship of God and the converse of the good they do not admit him. Yesterday on account of the pomp of his sovereignty he gave not his hand to any one: to-day on account of his condition of impurity, no man putteth his hand on him!"'

There follow a number of truly admirable moral and religious precepts addressed to his people; and the conclusion is:

'From before the majesty of Aūharmazd have I come, for the purpose of overthrowing the Evil Spirit am I here; again before the majesty of Aūharmazd must I go; moreover this is required of me—holiness and the actions proper to the wise and the living in union with wisdom and the due ordering of my nature.'

It is of course only natural that all kinds of traditional utterances should gather round the name of so celebrated a ruler, of whom his subjects made not only an Alexander and a Justinian, but also a Solomon. Numerous conversations, shrewd replies, solutions of cases, and messages to foreign monarchs are preserved by Eastern writers, such as the Arab chronicler Tabarī, and at least eighteen letters and speeches are quoted as his in Firdausi's great national epic, the *Shāh-nāmah*. One of these[1] he introduces with the words: 'I have seen in an old book that (Chosroes wrote as follows).'

Whatever be thought of the attribution to the King of Kings himself of participation by word or pen in the active literary and scientific life of his court, it is quite certain that the royal patronage stimulated an extraordinary intellectual activity in the national literature. We are told that he encouraged translations from foreign writers of all kinds, ordering the works of Aristotle and Plato to be rendered into Pahlavi, and that even Homer was similarly translated. Philosophers persecuted by Justinian were received with open arms, as well as Syrian scholars. Indeed it is to this golden age of Persian literature that the Arabs owed their introduction to Greek culture.[2] One important influence of the kind in Sasanian times was that of Greek medicine—an influence, by the way, which goes back to the Achæmenian dynasty (Demokedes, under Darius I.,[3] Ktesias, Apollonides). The Greek Stephanos of Edessa cured Kobad I.[4] It appears that at the same time was begun the compilation of a 'King's Book,' or royal chronicle, to which subsequently Firdausi owed so much of the material for his epic. Probably, too, several of the standard Pahlavi treatises began to take shape at this time. Among these the first rank belongs to the invaluable *Būndahishn* (or *Būndehesh*, lit. 'The Original Creation'), which, though doubtless extended and revised much later, preserves some very ancient material—in some cases old traditions and myths which are even pre-Zoroastrian, such as those referring to the creation and the first men. The very miscellaneous *Dīnkarṭ* ('Acts of Religion'), 'a collection of information regarding the doctrines, customs, traditions, history and literature of the Mazda-worshipping religion'[5]—the most extensive of all Pahlavi works—was certainly completed as a kind of encyclopædia or miscellany several centuries later in Muhammadan times; but it contains a good deal of older material, including

1 See art. PHILOSOPHY (Iranian), § 2.
2 *Chronicon Ecclesiasticum*, ed. Abbeloos and Lamy, Louvain, 1872–77, ii. coll. 91–96.
3 Ed. Darab Peshotan, London and Bombay, 1874–1917, vol. v. ch. 201.
4 iii. [1889].
5 Tr. by the present writer in *BOR* i. [1887].
6 It is well known that in the Mazdean system death, through the operation of the demon Nasu, renders the corpse impure—so held by the Parsis to the present day.

1 J. Mohl, *Le Livre des rois*, Paris, 1876–78, vi. 408.
2 It was at this time that there came from India the famous story *Kalīla va Dimna*, translated into Pahlavi from Sanskrit, and with it the game of chess, the treatise on which, narrating the sending of the game to Khusrau, is still preserved in the little treatise, *Chatrang-nāmak*, published by Peshotan in 1885. From the Persian court both the tale and the now universal game rapidly spread throughout the Western world. On the important subject of Sasanian art see M. Dieulafoy, *L'Art antique de la Perse*, Paris, 1884, and, for the most recent (highly laudatory) appreciation, W. M. Flinders Petrie, *Eastern Exploration Past and Future*, London, 1918, pp. 39–42 ('Of the Sassanian Empire our estimate must be mainly from its political power and its artistic work. The huge rock-cut monuments . . . are of excellent work, equal to good Hellenic carving, and above what Rome could do at that age. The coinage of the Sassanians is quite equal to that of Rome in the third century. We want to know much more of this age, in order to trace the effect of Persian art on the West').
3 Herod. iii. 130.
4 For the relations between Greek (and Indian) medical science and that of Sasanian Persia see E. Haas, *ZDMG* II. xxx., xxxi., A. Müller, *ib.* xxxiv., and the present writer's *Traité de médecine mazdéenne traduit du Pehlevi*, Louvain, 1886.
5 West, *GIrP* ii.

certain 'enclaves,' or short treatises, preserved, like flies in amber, in chapters of the larger compilation. Such a one is the medical tractate referred to in art. DISEASE AND MEDICINE (Persian), as also the *Andarj*, or 'Ten Precepts,' mentioned above. But its chief value is in the preservation of a detailed analysis of the contents of all the 21 *nasks*, or books, of the original Avesta, whose text had long since perished.[1] There seems no reason to doubt that these summaries may faithfully represent the subject-matter of the lost sacred books.

Chosroes II., known as Parvēz, grandson of Chosroes I. (A.D. 590–628), conquered Jerusalem and carried off the True Cross, afterwards restored under the emperor Heraclius. This was the last great king of the Sasanian dynasty. Four years after his death the ill-starred **Yazdagird III.** (A.D. 632–651), the last of his race, acceded and in the last-named year had the unhappiness to witness the final conquest of his kingdom by the Muslim, he himself perishing miserably by the hand of an assassin.

2. Relations with Christianity.—Christianity spread widely and was well organized in the Persian Empire under the Sasanians, especially in its Nestorian form. At the moment of the Musalmān invasion it counted seven metropolitan provinces and 80 bishoprics, stretching from Armenia to India. Not infrequently Christians enjoyed high favour at the court, especially during the great reign of the first Chosroes. Both that mighty monarch and his grandson namesake had Christian wives, the wife of the latter being the beautiful Shirin, renowned in Persian poetry, to whose influence may be largely attributed his proclamation of liberty of conscience and his liberality to the Christian Church. Notwithstanding all this, the history of the dynasty contains records of persecutions as terrible as any in the Church's annals. We have seen that the execution of Māni was the occasion of a massacre not only of his own followers but of Christians also. There were political as well as religious reasons for these persecutions. It is true that the Mazdeism of the time was intolerant on principle. The fourth of the 'Ten Precepts' attributed in the *Andarj* to the great Chosroes runs: 'To destroy with crushing severity the teaching of heretics from out of Irān,' and the eighth: 'To smite, smash up, and overthrow the diabolical, violent, and idolatrous disobedience [to the religion] which may co-exist.' The Pahlavi treatises constantly group together Manichæans, Christians, and Jews among these heretics. There is a great amount of polemical argument in several of these treatises directed against Christian teaching, showing a considerable acquaintance with the books of both the OT and the NT. This is especially the case with the *Shikand-gūmānīk Vijār* ('Doubt-dispelling Explanation'),[2] which actually contains an (incomplete) Pahlavi version of the Lord's Prayer. Very remarkable is a passage in the *Dīnkart*,[3] which is a direct attempt to discredit the teaching concerning the Λόγος in Jn 1.

But there was also, as said above, a strong political motive for many of these persecutions. The Roman emperors, now Christian, from being fierce persecutors, had become the friends and protectors of the Church. And the great Persian Empire, whether under the Arsacids or under the Sasanians, was the lifelong foe of 'the Empire of Rūm.' The Christian religion was looked upon as

1 Tr. West in *SBE* xxxvii. [1892]; Pahlavi text recently published by Darab Peshotan in his fine ed. of the *Dīnkart*, vol. xv. [1916] and vol. xvi. [1917].
2 Tr. West in *SBE* xxiv. [1885] 115 ff.
3 Ed. Peshotan, iii. 130, tr. by present writer in *Philosophie rel. du Mazdéisme*, §§ 59–61.

essentially 'the religion of Rūm.' The natural sympathy of Christians in all lands with the now Christian Empire not unnaturally rendered them suspect to the kings who were the ardent followers and champions of the national 'religion of Īrān.'[1]

The Persian persecutions extended, with various intervals, from the reign of Shahpuhr II. to the 7th century. Their cruelty was often incredible—for excessively cruel punishments were a characteristic of Persian governments in all ages and under all dynasties, so that 'Persian torments' became an epithet of specially dreadful tortures. The most memorable of these persecutions is the one proclaimed in 340, which lasted till Shahpuhr's death. It is unequalled for its duration, its ferocity, and the number of the martyrs, said by some to have been 190,000. In spite of this, it is recorded that apostates were less numerous than during the great persecutions of the pagan Roman emperors. After Shahpuhr's death persecution of the Christians continued, but with less intensity until the reign of Bahram (Varahran) V. (A.D. 420–438), who, at the instigation of the Magian priests, ordered a general persecution, which lasted, with intervals, for thirty years. Under his successor, Yazdagird II., occurred the celebrated massacre of the Christians at Beit-Slokh in 446—said, perhaps with exaggeration, to have claimed 12,000 victims—the beginning of a persecution which may have lasted till 450. Under subsequent monarchs there occurred from time to time cruel treatment of Christians, though by no means on so vast a scale. Even Chosroes I. and Chosroes II. are stated to have made some martyrs.

The *Acta* of these Persian martyrs have received a considerable amount of careful and critical study of late years, and on the whole, with the natural exception of certain unreliable or exaggerated portions, their general credibility has been maintained. To Louis H. Gray belongs the credit of having most carefully worked over these *Acta Martyrum*, as far as they are yet available, in search of fresh material for the study of Mazdean religion of the times.[2] His research has revealed a considerable amount of Zoroastrian religious material.

These writings, he remarks, 'possess one great advantage over the pagan classical sources. They record, in many cases, the experiences and the words of converts to Christianity from Zoroastrianism. . . . What we read here will scarcely coincide with the Pahlavi treatises which date, at least in conception, from this same Sasanid period; but this is only a superficial objection. . . . Our concern is with the religion of the masses, on which a valuable side-light is cast by the Christian *Acts of the Saints*.'[3]

This remark seems to the present writer of great importance.

LITERATURE.—F. Justi, *Gesch. des alten Persiens*, Berlin, 1879; G. Rawlinson, *The Seventh Great Oriental Monarchy*, London, 1876; E. W. West, 'Pahlavi Literature,' in *GIrP* ii. [Strassburg, 1895–1904]; F. Justi, 'Gesch. Irans von den ältesten Zeiten bis zum Ausgang der Sāsāniden,' *ib.*; L. C. Casartelli, *La Philosophie religieuse du Mazdéisme sous les Sassanides*, Louvain, 1884, tr. Firoz Jamaspji, Bombay, 1889. For relations to Christianity and persecutions of Christians see esp. J. Labourt, *Le Christianisme dans l'empire perse sous la dynastie sassanide*, Paris, 1904; a useful condensation in D. Marsiglia, *Il Martirio Cristiano*, Rome, 1913; and special articles as quoted in text.

L. C. CASARTELLI.

SATAN.—See DEMONS AND SPIRITS.

SATANISM.—The worship of the Devil alleged during the two final decades of the 19th cent. to have been carried on in various countries of Europe

1 Christianity is known under various titles in Pahlavi literature, such as *Kēsh-i Mashīh* ('religion of the Messiah'), *Kilisyākīh* (apparently from *Kilisya*=ἐκκλησία), and the obscure name *Tarsāk* (surely no connexion with Tarsus?). Also a 'white demon' (*shēdā-spīh*) is attributed to Christianity.
2 His results are embodied in a valuable paper in the *Journal of the Manchester Egyptian and Oriental Society*, 1913–14, pp. 37–55.
3 *Ib.* p. 39.

and America was stated to have two branches or divisions. One of these, to which the name Satanism is more strictly applicable, was a worship of Satan, the adversary of God and of Christianity, admitting that he is an evil being, a rebel against God, a lost archangel. The worshippers are said to have had recourse to the Devil because they held that God had betrayed the human race; they knowingly entered into alliance with His adversary and worshipped him with rites which were a defiance of the true God. It was a counsel of despair; and we are not surprised to be told that the adherents of this mad cult consisted of 'scattered associations or isolated persons, labouring alone, or with the aid of a few seers, and pursuing a personal aim,' that they were in fact recluses, and that they had no relations with the other and more important group.[1]

The latter group, with which we are mainly concerned, was known under the alternative names of Luciferians and Palladists. They were said to adore Lucifer, the equal and foe of Adonai, or Jahweh. He was in their view the God of light, the good principle, while Adonai was the God of darkness, the evil principle. In short, he was Satan himself. This worship was founded on a dualistic philosophy and was a sort of topsy-turvy Christianity.[2] The name of Palladists is derived from a palladium which they were said to revere, namely the Baphomet, or grotesque idol, the worship of which was one of the articles of accusation against the Knights Templars in the 14th century. It was alleged that the Baphomet was preserved in secret through nearly five centuries after the suppression of the order and ultimately carried by one Isaac Long in 1801, together with the skull of the last Grand Master, the unhappy Jacques du Molay, from Paris to Charleston in the United States of America. These relics were averred to have there become the sacred objects of a society which was a development of Freemasonry. The head of the society, we are told, was one Albert Pike, under whose influence it spread all over the civilized world. The tendencies already at work in his lifetime, but in some measure held in check by him, were left unfettered by his death. His successor, Adriano Lemmi, transferred the supreme direction of the society from Charleston to Rome. The practice of magic blossomed out in its lodges, accompanied by not merely nonsensical but foul, cruel, and obscene rites, culminating in the formal abjuration of Christ and His religion, the apparition of the Devil in person to his votaries, and their organized and periodical worship of him.

Some of these charges were among those brought against the Knights Templars in the year 1307. Charges to the same effect continued to be made against persons accused of witchcraft so long as the witch-trials persisted. Inasmuch as torture was nearly always practised in connexion with legal proceedings for witchcraft, the persecutors of witches could usually extract a confession in the sense they required. By that means they succeeded in securing against their victims a great mass of what they called evidence, which is now altogether discredited by every rational being. What astounds an intelligent reader is to find these ancient accusations, refurbished and mingled with new ones equally improbable, and indeed impossible, brought with an apparently serious purpose against a body of citizens of every civilized country in the last quarter of the 19th century. It behoves therefore to inquire into the circumstances of the 'disclosures' on which the accusations are founded.

[1] J. K. Huysmans, pref. to J. Bois, *Le Satanisme et la magie*, Paris, 1895, p. xvi.
[2] *Ib.*

The evidence for the existence of either Satanists or Palladists consists entirely of the writings of a group of men in Paris. The earlier of these writings seem to have suggested a novel called *Là-bas* (Paris, 1891), by J. K. Huysmans, a literary man of some reputation who had professed materialism and afterwards abandoned it. One of the chief personages of the novel is a certain Canon Docre, a renegade priest whose portrait is alleged to be sketched from a real man then living in Belgium. He acts as the leader of the Satanists and performs the Black Mass, which is of course a horrible and indecent parody of the Roman Catholic rite. In one form or other the Black Mass is a very old story; heretics and witches from the Middle Ages downwards have often been accused of it. Huysmans relates it in detail, sparing nothing. More tangible evidence of the existence of the Satanists and their worship than that of Huysmans in this novel and in his subsequent preface to the book by J. Bois cited above has yet to be produced. At any rate the allegations as to the sect have supplied little more than a background for the hardly less lurid 'revelations' concerning the Palladists.

These were originally undertaken by a young man named Gabriel Jogand, a Provençal, born at Marseilles in 1854. He was educated at a Jesuit college, but, speedily breaking loose from it, led a Bohemian life and attempted to make a livelihood by bitter vituperative attacks upon the Roman Catholic Church and everybody and everything connected with it. For his assaults on religion and libels on individuals he was repeatedly condemned by various French tribunals to fine and imprisonment. In 1881 he became a Freemason; but, as he left the order within the same year in consequence of a quarrel, it is obvious that he did not proceed very far into its mysteries. A man of considerable resource, restless, vain, he was constantly devising something fresh to bring himself before the public and to put into his pocket the money of which he was sorely in need. Suddenly in April 1885 he professed to be 'converted.' He repudiated his old opinions and his old associates. He expressed the deepest contrition. He offered himself to confession at the parish church of St. Merri. After a little suspicion and delay he was accepted and reconciled to the Church. Two years later he went to Rome, where he was solemnly received by the pope, Leo XIII., and his labours against the Freemasons were approved and blessed.

Immediately after his conversion he had begun the publication of a work in four volumes, entitled *Révélations complètes sur la franc-maçonnerie* (Paris, 1886). From this time until 1897 one book and periodical after another poured forth from his pen and those of his co-operators, each of them containing 'revelations' more blood-curdling than its predecessor. They were boomed by the hierarchy and the religious press and greedily bought by the orthodox public in France, Germany, and Italy. In his unconverted years Jogand had adopted 'Léo Taxil' as his pen-name; and he continued to write under this signature. He had many assistants and ecclesiastical backers. Prominent among the latter were Fava, bishop of Grenoble, and Meurin, archbishop of Port Louis in the Mauritius, who distinguished themselves by the virulence of their anti-masonic writings. Meurin, in 1892, issued a book entitled *La Franc-maçonnerie, Synagogue de Satan*, in which he connected Palladism with the Jewish Kabbala and elaborated the mystic value of numbers into proofs of the enemy's diabolical conspiracy. Another assistant (or rather confederate) was a German, C. Hacks, who wrote under the name of Bataille.

Another was Domenico Margiotta, who claimed to have been born in 1858 at Palmi, in Italy, and to have been a Freemason of very high dignity in the order. If we may believe his statements, he was 'converted' and from his former position was able to make very important revelations concerning masonic doings and beliefs. His principal work was published at Paris in 1894, on Adriano Lemmi, whom he alleged to be the supreme head of the Freemasons throughout the world. Even earlier than he, yet another German, Paul Rosen, originally of Berlin, but then in Paris, had published in French a work directed against the Freemasons under the title of *L'Ennemie sociale* (Brussels, 1890). But, valuable as was the help thus lent to him by others (and the enumeration above is not exhaustive), Léo Taxil was by no means dependent upon it. Fertile in his ingenuity, audacious, and cynical, he wrote rapidly and recklessly under the name by which he was known as a writer; and, when tired of that or desirous of creating a new sensation, he freely invented further pseudonyms. These were represented to be the real names of real persons whose adventures were sometimes mysteriously referred to, sometimes given more or less at length. One such was A. M. Ricoux, who pretended to have been a settler for four years in Chile. Under this name Taxil wrote in defence of his own allegation that there were female Freemasons. As Ricoux, he professed to have obtained a code of secret instructions to supreme councils and grand lodges, alleged to have been printed at Charleston in 1891, from which he claimed to have learned that the Supreme Directory of universal Freemasonry was centred in Berlin, with subordinate Directories in Naples, Calcutta, Washington, and Monte Video, a Chief of Political Action in Rome, and a Grand Depositary of Sacred Traditions, the Sovereign Pontiff of Freemasonry, at Charleston, an office then filled by Albert Pike.

Bataille's principal, but not his only, contribution to the revelations was a work which appeared in serial parts entitled *Le Diable au xix*ᵉ *siècle* (Paris, 1893–94). In it he related his travels and adventures among Freemasons in various parts of the world, including India and America, both North and South. In the course of his journeys he met (so he declared) a certain Miss Diana Vaughan, in whose company he visited the Mammoth Cave of Kentucky and was present at a *séance* with Asmodeus in person. Shortly afterwards this lady was more directly introduced to the gaping antimasonic public of Paris as the editor of the *Palladium régénéré et libre*, a periodical represented to be the outcome of a quarrel between herself and other highly-placed authorities of the Palladist organization. Only three numbers, however, appeared. Nominally directed to the advocacy of a reformed Palladism, it was obviously only a step to a further development. When it had served the purpose of an attempt to convince the world of the real objective existence of the Palladist society, Miss Diana Vaughan's conversion to the Roman Catholic Church was announced; and within a month afterwards, in July 1895, she began the publication of her autobiography, under the title of *Mémoires d'une Ex-Palladiste*. It proved quite exciting and supplied pabulum for the faithful during many months of serial publication. She averred herself a descendant of Thomas Vaughan, the twin brother of Henry Vaughan, the Silurist. Thomas Vaughan was always mystical. At one period of his life he was devoted to alchemy, which he appears to have afterwards renounced. Diana Vaughan imputed to him Rosicrucianism, which he distinctly disclaimed; and she related that he was himself the executioner of Archbishop Laud, and that he had steeped a linen cloth in the 'martyr's' blood, and burnt it by way of a sacrifice to the Devil. The Devil thereupon made his appearance and entered into a pact with him. Diana Vaughan sent her 'ancestor' subsequently to America, where he wedded Venus-Astarte, who came down out of heaven and remained with him for eleven days, leaving with him when she reascended a child, the fruit of their union. It need not be said that this is pure nonsense. Thomas Vaughan never was in America, so far as is known from any authentic record. Of the same character is Diana's account of her own birth and early life. She declares that she was early initiated into Palladism, advanced from grade to grade, ultimately appointed grand priestess of Lucifer, and destined to be united in marriage with no less a personage than Asmodeus. Her progress is described in the most melodramatic fashion. It includes of course interviews with Lucifer himself, exchange of affectionate passages with her future bridegroom, Asmodeus, the description of a terrific combat between the hosts of Lucifer and those of Adonai, which she was privileged to witness and describe after the manner of a war-correspondent, and her visit, transported in the arms of Lucifer, to a distant region of the universe in which he was supreme.

With the help of these and other writers, some real, some fictitious, a deluge of 'revelations' was poured forth for about twelve years. Not merely was the rise of Palladism narrated, or rather its development out of the highest grades of Freemasonry under the hands of Albert Pike, with its headquarters at Charleston and its subordinate branches throughout the world, but also the cleavage of the institution into two mutually hostile forces, the one led by Diana Vaughan, the other by Adriano Lemmi. The personal and family history of Diana Vaughan occupies a considerable part of the *Mémoires* with which she enlightened the world. Weird details accompany and complete the story. But they yield in extravagance to Bataille's marvellous travels. He started by being a ship's doctor on the Eastern service. If he may be credited, he was introduced into Freemasonry at Naples and by bribery succeeded in obtaining the highest degree. Armed with this, he penetrated the most secret dens of the order in East and West, one of which he describes as being a Presbyterian chapel at Singapore, where he witnessed the initiation of a Mistress-Templar according to the Palladian rite, that is to say, with revolting obscenity. He attended a lodge in Calcutta, at which Lucifer himself was present, delivered an oration, and accepted a human sacrifice. At Gibraltar he explored caverns in the great rock, which were occupied, so he says, by British criminals condemned to life-servitude. They were engaged in the making of Baphomets and other idols and of various instruments of black magic, including terrible poisons for putting away any one whose destruction was desired. These travels are cast in a form and adorned with particulars both grotesque and gruesome that would not have been out of place in mediæval witch-tales.

Léo Taxil and his co-operators succeeded in imposing, by such means, on a large number of the ecclesiastics and devout laity on the Continent. The 'revelations' were of course denied and denounced as lies by the Freemasons. Demands to produce Miss Diana Vaughan were eluded on the pretext that she was compelled to remain in concealment for the preservation of her life from the attacks of infuriated Freemasons and Palladists. Letters written in her name by (as it afterwards turned out) Léo Taxil's female secretary, and in some cases accompanied by presentation copies of her works, were received by high dignitaries of the

Church and the papal court and were replied to in the most flattering manner. The pope himself, if we may believe Léo Taxil, sent her his apostolic blessing. The bishop of Grenoble repeatedly affirmed his childlike belief in her existence and the sincerity of her conversion. He compared her with Joan of Arc and exhorted her to pray, to labour, to struggle, and even to die on the gallows if necessary; for victory sometimes exacted that price. Such rodomontade was naturally published by the conspirators to augment the faith of those who accepted the 'revelations.'

The excitement caused among credulous people aroused special interest in the Antimasonic Congress which was to be held at Trent in 1896. At the same town that was the scene of the great Council in the 16th cent. it was hoped to give the final blow to Freemasonry and Protestantism. The campaign started by Pope Leo XIII. against Freemasonry had acquired an added impulse by the 'revelations' of Léo Taxil and his confederates. Yet doubts as to the 'revelations' had been expressed in various quarters; and there was an undercurrent of scepticism. Léo Taxil faced the situation with characteristic courage and audacity. He went to Trent, met the Congress, and delivered an impassioned harangue. In answer to demands for information as to Diana Vaughan's existence, history, and conversion, he solemnly affirmed her existence; he declared that he had seen her with his own eyes, but she could not venture from her concealment, threatened as she was every hour by the daggers of the Freemasons. To a confidential committee only would he entrust his proofs. The result was a complete success. Doubters were silenced. Taxil was victorious. The hero of the hour, he was rewarded with enthusiastic and continuous thunders of applause, he was invited to the episcopal palace, where he was received by the bishop, and mingled with the most distinguished representatives of ecclesiastics and nobles from various Roman Catholic states.

But the imposture was now approaching its end. At the close of September Taxil had triumphed at the Congress. Scarcely more than a fortnight later Bataille (Hacks) threw off the mask. He wrote to the *Kölnische Volkszeitung*, expressing his complete contempt for the Roman Catholic religion, and a little later, on 2nd Nov., to the *Univers* at Paris, declaring that *Le Diable au xixe siècle* and Diana Vaughan were *Märchen* (idle tales) and a thorough swindle. Taxil brazened it out a few months longer. At last he announced a meeting at the Geographical Society's rooms, Boulevard St. Germain, Paris, on 19th April 1897, at which Diana Vaughan would make her public appearance. At the meeting he mounted the platform alone. To a crowded assembly he confessed that Palladism and Diana Vaughan were inventions of his own, and that the revelations that had poured forth so lavishly from his press for years were a gigantic fraud, or, in his own euphemism, 'a mystification.' 'I have always loved mystification,' he explained, and impudently went on to express his thanks to the Catholic press and bishops for the splendid help they had given him to organize the finest mystification of all, which was to crown his career.

The rage of his deluded victims was boundless, but impotent. At first they declined to believe his confession; they could not abandon their faith in Diana Vaughan; they distinguished between Taxil's earlier and later 'disclosures'; there must, they said, be substantial facts underlying at least the former. Some of course asserted that they had suspected the truth all along; and their efforts were directed to show that the pope and other high ecclesiastical authorities were not committed to belief in the swindle. But the violence of the denunciations which were naturally heaped upon him did not disturb Léo Taxil. He had doubtless made money; he had achieved notoriety; he had imposed a succession of extravagant lies by the most ingenious methods on his open-mouthed disciples. When the bubble burst, as sooner or later it inevitably would, he retired to write the story of how he had befooled the Catholic world.

The soil had been prepared for the sowing, or the seed scattered by Taxil would not have taken root. During the long twilight of the Middle Ages and later a vast number of legends had accumulated concerning the relations of the spiritual world with humanity, including temptations by evil spirits in corporeal or quasi-corporeal form and leagues entered into by individual men with the Devil himself. These legends had never been repudiated by the Church of Rome. Rather they had been accepted and stamped with authority, seeing that they had been incorporated in monastic chronicles and in the lives and writings of the most eminent saints and teachers, they had been confirmed by confessions wrung from the victims of the witch-prosecutions, recorded solemnly by ecclesiastical and civil courts, as the evidence on which thousands of men and women had been condemned to the most barbarous deaths, and they had been taught as facts without any doubt by the Inquisitor Sprenger, the Jesuit Delrio, and other authors of works on magic and witchcraft. From early ages witchcraft, sexual immorality of the grossest kind, and foul rites, amounting to a rival and obscene religion, had been imputed to heretics and unbelievers. The Church had long been definitely opposed to Freemasonry — an opposition probably arising, first, from jealousy of its secrecy, and, secondly, from its well-known liberalism. Recently Pius IX. had denounced the Freemasons as 'the Synagogue of Satan' and had approved and encouraged a French fraternity, founded under the influence of the Ultramontane party to exterminate them. In 1884, the year before the 'conversion' of Léo Taxil, Leo XIII. by his Encyclical had inveighed against them in no measured terms as guilty of unbridled licence in crime, as regardless of the marriage-bond, as going about to destroy the foundations of law and morality, a sect whose object was to prepare the ruin of mankind; and he had called upon the faithful to unmask and oppose them. He thus practically initiated a new crusade, which he subsequently drove further by a succession of fresh appeals to the ignorance and bigotry of his flock.

Into a soil thus charged with sectarian bitterness and misrepresentation Taxil astutely dropped his seed. Charges of witchcraft and the Black Mass had been made in a sporadic manner during the previous century and a half. They had thus strengthened the traditional attitude of the Roman Church and provided new, if slender, foundations for the popes' battery of denunciation. Taxil's 'revelations' and those of his confederates were eagerly seized by the bigots and speedily spread all over the Continent. No sort of criticism was applied to them. The denials of the Freemasons were treated as negligible. The organization attributed to Freemasons and Palladists was in fact a parody of the real organization of the Jesuits. If the correspondence between the two was observed, the known existence of the Jesuit organization merely served to render credible to the minds of the faithful that of which their opponents were accused. An examination of Taxil's romances shows that they were derived from the old works of the Inquisitors and other writers on witchcraft, supplemented by hints from A. L.

Constant's *Dogme et rituel de la haute magie*[2] (Paris, 1861), written under the pseudonym of Eliphas Lévi, and from the researches of the French Freemason, Ragon. Hacks's yet more extraordinary stories were inspired by Archbishop Meurin's farrago. Diana Vaughan's confessions were founded on those of Taxil and Hacks. If any basis of fact underlay the superstructure of 'mystification,' it was supplied by allegations, widely believed, of the theft without apparent motive of the consecrated host from various churches in France and elsewhere. How far these allegations were true it is impossible to say; no prosecutions are known to have been instituted against any one for the crime. Taxil indeed after the crash was suspected by members of the committee of the Congress of Trent to have contrived such a theft from Notre Dame in Paris in order to provide sensational material for his pen; but the charge was probably mere gossip. So remarkable a hoax has seldom, if ever, been perpetrated; and it could not have succeeded in an environment less dense with ignorance and fanaticism.

LITERATURE.—Besides the works of Huysmans, Taxil, and others mentioned throughout, reference may be made to A. E. Waite, *Devil-worship in France*, London, 1896; A. Lillie, *The Worship of Satan in Modern France, being a Second Editon of 'Modern Mystics and Modern Magic,'* do. 1896, preface; and J. Rieks, *Leo XIII. und der Satanskult*, Berlin, 1897. The two English books named were published before the 'mystification' was confessed.

E. SIDNEY HARTLAND.

SATĪ.—*Satī* is a feminine noun formed from the verbal root *sat*, meaning what is real, true, good, or virtuous. A *satī* therefore signified a woman whom her religion considered as good and virtuous if she sought death on the decease of her husband and was burned along with his corpse. It was not until 1829 that this custom of widow-burning was declared illegal in British India. The Indian penal code enacted that whoever attempts to commit suicide and does any act towards the commission of such offence shall be punishable with imprisonment for a term which may extend to one year. The code further enacted that, if any person commits suicide, whoever abets the commission of such suicide shall be punished with imprisonment which may extend to ten years. Any one who applauds or encourages an act of *satī* is also held by the penal code to have abetted suicide.

Schrader[1] states that Indo-Germanic custom ordained that the wife should die with her husband, and this custom he ascribes to the desire to provide the deceased with what was dear to him during life as well as 'to make the life of the housefather safe on all sides, and to render him an object of perpetual care and anxiety to his family.'[2]

In the *Atharvaveda*[3] the suicide of the widow on the death of her husband is said to be 'her ancient duty'; but, although she ascended the funeral pyre and lay by the side of her husband, she is said to have as her reward 'progeny and property.' Here, as in the *Rigveda*,[4] the widow is made to rise up from the funeral pyre and is led away by a new husband. The *Atharvaveda* declares:

> 'Get up, O Woman, to the world of the living; thou liest by this one who is deceased; come! to him who grasps thy hand, thy second spouse, thou hast now entered into the relation of wife to husband.'[5]

The ancient custom and ancient duty of the widow to burn herself on her husband's death had therefore given place in Vedic India to a second marriage; but in later times[1] the ancient custom was revived under the influence of Brāhmans anxious to obtain command over the property of the widow. In order to give the custom a religious sanction, a passage in the *Rigveda*[2] which directed the widow to rise from her husband's funeral pyre and go forth in front (*agre*) was altered into to go into the fire (*agneḥ*). The result was that, wherever Brāhmanic influences predominated, especially along the Ganges valley, in Bengal and in Oudh, as well as in Rājputāna, widow-burning increased from the 6th cent. onwards, while in outlying districts of the Panjāb it was not commonly practised and was forbidden in most parts of S. India.

A gifted writer and a zealous defender of Hinduism, T. Ramakrishna, of Madras, has forcibly stated the Hindu religious sanction for widow-burning in the words:

> 'If the husband predeceases the wife, she must face a new situation with a courageous heart, and remain to pray day and night for the repose of his soul, or, if unable to bear the pang of separation she wishes to ascend the funeral pyre to be consumed to ashes with her dead husband, her religion allows her to do so.'[3]

On the other hand, Romesh Chunder Dutt referred to *satī* as 'a barbarous custom' and as 'the most cruel of all human institutions.'[4]

LITERATURE.—See especially A. R. Coomaraswamy, 'Sati: a Vindication of Hindu Women,' paper given to Sociological Society, London, 1912.

R. W. FRAZER.

SATISFACTION.—'Satisfaction' is defined by the mediæval Schoolmen as the third part of penance (*q.v.*).

> 'In perfectione autem poenitentiae tria observanda sunt: scilicet, compunctio cordis, confessio oris, satisfactio operis.'[5]

1. History of the idea in the Latin Fathers and in the early Middle Ages.—The introduction into theology of the term 'satisfaction' is due to the quondam Roman jurist Tertullian, who, in describing the relation of man to God, frequently makes use of the word *satisfacere*, which is a term of Roman law belonging especially to the sphere of obligations. Here, in the wider sense of each word, *satisfacere* and *solvere* are equivalents: both refer simply to the discharge of an obligation in any manner whatever. But there is a distinction between *satisfacere* in the narrower sense and *solvere* in the narrower sense: *solvere* is the strict fulfilment of the obligation, *satisfacere* is the discharge of it by some other means than its strict fulfilment, which yet is agreeable to the creditor.

> 'Nam quia id quo quis contentus erat ei praestabatur, satisfieri dictum est.'[6] In this sense it is said: 'Satisfactio pro solutione est.'[7]

Tertullian applies the term *satisfacere* especially to the sphere of penance. In the earliest times it was held by the Christian Church that after baptism, while lighter sins needed only to be confessed to the gracious God,[8] serious sins excluded the offender altogether from the community.[9] But this rigorous practice was soon broken through, and by a public confession of sins even gross sinners were allowed restoration, though at first not more than once. This mitigation is announced by Hermas as a special divine revelation:

> 'The sinner who repents must be received, but not frequently. For there is only one repentance for the servants of God.'[10]

The public confession (ἐξομολόγησις) was in each case associated with visible signs of humiliation, in order to testify to the genuineness of the repent-

[1] *Prehistoric Antiquities of the Aryan Peoples*, Eng. tr., London, 1890, p. 391.
[2] Cf. Cæsar, *de Bell. Gall.* vi. 19.
[3] XVIII. iii. 1.
[4] X. xviii. 8.
[5] XVIII. iii. 2; see *Atharvaveda*, tr. W. D. Whitney and ed. C. R. Lanman (Harvard Oriental Ser., vol. viii.), Cambridge, Mass., 1905.

[1] See Fitz Edward Hall, *JRAS*, new ser., iii. [1866] 183–192.
[2] X. xviii. 7.
[3] *Early Reminiscences*, Madras, 1907 (for private circulation only), p. 71.
[4] *Hist. of Civilization in Ancient India*, Calcutta, 1889–90, i. 110.
[5] Lombard, *Liber Sententiarum*, iv. dist. 16 A.
[6] Justinian, *Digest.* 45. 1. 15. 3.
[7] *Ib.* 46. 3, 52.
[8] Cf. 1 Jn 1[9].
[9] See Loofs, *Dogmengeschichte*[4], p. 205.
[10] *Mand.* IV. i. 8.

ance experienced. Discipline was at first exercised by the community as a whole, but from the 2nd cent. onwards the community was represented in this matter by the bishop. Tertullian now views this penitential humiliation as a satisfaction to God. He regards God as the Roman law viewed an injured person:

'Thou hast offended, but thou canst still be reconciled; thou hast One to whom to make satisfaction, who also is willing to receive it.'[1]

The means of this satisfaction are self-humiliation and voluntary self-denial, above all fasting:

Man is to make satisfaction to God, through the same thing through which he had offended (in Adam's fall).[2] The penitent must 'offer to an offended God self-humiliation (*castigatio*) in food and dress.'[3]

It is important to observe that the idea of satisfaction thus constituted has two sides. (*a*) On the one hand, it touches the notion of merit (*q.v.*), of which it is in fact a sub-species.[4] If merit in general establishes a claim to a reward, where an obligation has been caused by a wrong, the merit that has been acquired can serve as satisfaction, and the reward to which it establishes a claim is from the nature of the case pardon or remission of punishment. The thought in the background is of course that of the power of God to enforce His claim by punishment, if satisfaction is not forthcoming. Tertullian says:

'How foolish and unjust it is to leave penance unperformed and yet to expect pardon for our sins! What is it but to fail to pay the price, and yet to stretch out one's hand for the reward? The Lord has decreed that pardon has to be awarded at this price; He purposes that the remission of punishment shall be bought by this payment of penance.'[5]

(*b*) On the other hand, penitential satisfaction is regarded in a way that brings it nearer to the conception of punishment than to that of merit. Here it appears not as a positive good work, which cancels the liability to punishment, but as a substitute for punishment, of kindred nature, but of different degree. Thus Tertullian says:

'So far as thou hast not spared thyself, so far, believe me, will God spare thee.'[6] 'All these things penance does . . . that it may, by itself pronouncing against the sinner, take the place of God's indignation and by temporal mortification, I will not say, frustrate, but discharge, eternal punishment.'[7] 'Every sin is discharged either by pardon or punishment, pardon as the result of self-chastisement, punishment as the result of condemnation.'[8]

The key-note of this conception of penance is the substitution of temporal for eternal punishment. We may finally observe that, in the above doctrine of Tertullian, satisfaction is not yet a *part* of penance, but the *whole* penance, including the public confession and the accompanying austerities, is viewed as a satisfaction to God.

The Latin Fathers after Tertullian continue, with some developments, the same ideas as to penance and satisfaction which we have found in him. On the one hand, we have passages where penance is regarded as a good work or merit, which avails as a satisfaction for post-baptismal sin. Thus Cyprian says:

'He who has thus made satisfaction to God, will not only deserve the Divine pardon, but also a crown.'[9]

This passage is noteworthy as bringing out the relation between merit and satisfaction which has already been explained—where merit does more than extinguish the debt of sin; it wins a reward besides. In Cyprian, moreover, we see how the notion of the transferability of merit begins to affect penitential satisfaction.

'God can reckon to the penitent . . . whatever the martyrs have asked, or the priests have done, for such persons.'[10]

Yet, because penitential satisfaction was a sign of personal repentance, it could not have been entirely superseded by the merit of others.

1 *De Pœn.* 7. 2 See *de Jejun.* 3. 3 *De Pœn.* 11.
4 Cf. the phrase 'merita poenitentiae' (*de Pœn.* 2).
5 *De Pœn.* 6. 6 *Ib.* 9. 7 *Ib.*
8 *De Pud.* 2. 9 *De Laps.* 36. 10 *Ib.*

Augustine follows in the same strain:

'The life must be amended, and God must be propitiated for past sins by almsgiving. . . . For He has given no one licence to sin, although in pity He blots out sins already committed, if proper satisfaction is not neglected. For the small and light sins of every day, however, . . . the daily prayer of the faithful is sufficient satisfaction.'[1] 'There are many kinds of almsgiving, the doing of which assists in the remission of our sins.'[2]

On the other hand, we have places in the Latin Fathers where penitential satisfaction is viewed as being of the nature of punishment. Thus Augustine says:

'In penance every one must use severity against himself, that, being judged by himself, he may not be judged by the Lord.'[3] 'He who truly repents does nothing but refuse to allow what he has done wrong to remain unpunished.'[4]

So also Gregory the Great writes:

'God cuts away our sins either by our means, or by His own hand, even when He forgives them. For He seeks to wash away from His elect by temporal chastisement the stains of the wickednesses, which He hates to see in them for ever.'[5]

We have next to notice a change in the form of penance which affects the idea of satisfaction. In the East public penance died out after the union of Church and State under Constantine, which made ecclesiastical control of morals more difficult, in so far as a denunciation of mortal sin before a bishop became equivalent to a denunciation of crime to the State. In the West, to alleviate this difficulty, the severity of the ancient penance was modified in the case of secret sins (*peccata occulta*) from complete publicity to the publicity involved merely in belonging to the penitents. Such was the state of affairs at the break-up of the Western Empire. The stormy nature of the times which followed prevented a consistent practice of discipline from being enforced upon the new races who came in to occupy the territory of the Empire. For secret sins public penance fell altogether into disuse. In Ireland and England it was never enforced, though under the Carlovingians it was restored in France for open sins. From the end of the 11th cent. onwards, however, public penance became 'a mere curiosity in the inventory of possible Church procedure against sinners.'[6]

On the other hand, there grew up in the West, at first side by side with public penance and ultimately almost entirely displacing it, a custom of private penance. This was a growth of the monastic spirit and aimed at extending the discipline of the Church over other sins than those which in the ancient Church were regarded as mortal. It was accompanied by an extension of the idea of mortal sin to the roots of sin in the heart. The circumstances of this private penance were confession to a priest and performance of a satisfaction which, as a condition of his absolution, he prescribed in accordance with the character of the sin. It is easy to understand how the pride of races who would not willingly submit to public penance (the outward humiliation of which they regarded as degrading to free men) favoured the extension of this private penance, originally intended for the discipline of the cloister, among the laity also.

In connexion with this newer penitential discipline three things in particular are to be noted:

(1) Penitential discipline was converted into a sacrament, in so far as confession to the priest assumes a continually more important position, and the theory establishes itself that his absolution converts even mortal sins into venial sins, which require to be expiated, not in hell, but in purgatory, unless they are cancelled by the satisfaction appointed by the priest. The pseudo-Augustinian treatise, *de Vera et Falsa Pœnitentia* (11th cent.), says:

'In that [the sinner] of himself speaks to the priest, and overcomes his shame by the fear of an offended God, there

1 *Ench.* 70 f. 2 *Ib.* 72.
3 *Serm.* 351. 7. 4 *Ep.* 153. 6.
5 *Moral.* ix. 34 on Job 9^{28}. 6 Loofs[4], p. 478.

comes about the forgiveness of the crime. For that which was criminal in the doing becomes venial through confession, and even if it is not purged away at once [*i.e.* by satisfaction] nevertheless that becomes venial, which as committed was mortal.'[1]

(2) Penitential satisfaction tends more and more to be regarded as a merit that can be detached from the person and treated upon commercial lines. This change is particularly evidenced by the 'Penitential Books' which were composed (on the basis of the ancient canons of various Church Councils as to penance), first in Ireland, then in England, and finally on the Continent, with a view to assisting the priest in his office as confessor. In the ancient Church it had been allowed that in cases of extraordinary penitence the satisfaction might be diminished. But in the penitential books we find a complete tariff of 'redemptions,' or commutations, by which the fasting of others might be substituted for personal fasting or the more exacting satisfaction of fasting might be redeemed by almsgiving.

(3) Closely connected with the 'redemptions' is a yet more momentous development in regard to penitential satisfaction, viz. that of 'indulgences' (*q.v.*). These were remissions of the temporal punishments which were still owed by those who had received absolution. Their origin is obscure, but it is clear (*a*) that they were in the first place episcopal indulgences, granted to those who made pilgrimage and brought offerings to a particular church on its dedication or other annual festival; (*b*) that they originated in the south of France before A.D. 1050.[2]

2. The mediæval doctrine of penitential satisfaction.—In the 12th cent. penance was definitely included among the seven sacraments by Peter Lombard, whose division of penance into the three parts of contrition, confession, and satisfaction has already been quoted. The mediæval doctrine of penance was, however, finally put into shape by the great Schoolmen of the 13th century. The following account of it, especially as concerns penitential satisfaction, is taken from Thomas Aquinas, *Summa Theologica*; the part which deals with satisfaction in particular is, however, from the 'Supplementum,' which has been added from the author's earlier commentary on the *Sentences* to complete the doctrine of the sacraments, which Thomas left unfinished at his death.

The general basis for the doctrine of satisfaction is to be found in the distinction made[3] between guilt (involving an obligation to eternal punishment) and an obligation to temporal punishment. Mortal sin involves a turning away from the unchangeable good and an inordinate turning to the changeable good. The former demands eternal punishment, the latter temporal punishment. Venial sin is an inordinate turning to the changeable good without a turning from the unchangeable good. Hence it demands only temporal punishment.

Qu. lxxxvii. art. 2 teaches that venial sins may be remitted without the sacrament of penance, though some act of a penitential character is required. But no new infusion of grace is necessary, as venial sin does not constitute a fall from grace. In the case of mortal sins the sacrament of penance is required.

According to qu. xc. art. 2, the *form* of penance is the absolution of the priest; its threefold *matter* consists in contrition, confession, and satisfaction. Contrition and confession, with the absolution of the priest, remove the guilt of sin and the obligation to eternal punishment and lessen the obligation to temporal punishment (in purgatory) to such a degree that it can be expiated by the satisfaction appointed by the priest.[4]

Suppl. qu. xii. deals with satisfaction, 'quoad ejus quidditatem.' According to art. 1, satisfaction is formally an act of virtue, in so far as it implies the idea of the mean, which is the formal essence of virtue. The mean which it implies is that of equality, 'for no satisfaction is said to be made except in accordance with a proportion of equality to somewhat.'

Further light is cast upon the subject by the treatment of the following difficulties:

(1) Satisfaction cannot be an act of virtue, for every act of virtue is meritorious. Satisfaction, however, is not meritorious; for merit is gratuitous, but satisfaction is in respect of debt.

Answer: Although satisfaction is in respect of debt, yet in so far as it is voluntary it is meritorious.

(2) Every act of virtue is voluntary, but satisfaction sometimes is involuntary, as when a man is punished by a judge for an offence.

Answer: In the case of satisfaction through punishment inflicted by a judge the act of virtue is in the judge; where, however (as in penance), a man punishes himself, the act of virtue is in him.

(3) The principal thing in virtue is choice, but satisfaction has to do, not with choice, but with external works.

Answer: The principal thing that makes satisfaction an act of virtue is choice, but the principal thing that differentiates it from other virtues is external works.

According to art. 2, since it is equality on which satisfaction turns, the particular virtue shown in it is justice, and, since the equalization takes place in respect of the debt created by an offence, the particular kind of justice exemplified is vindicative justice.

Art. 3 teaches that satisfaction is not merely compensation for past offences, but is also a preservative from future transgression. This medicinal office of satisfaction is another reason (cf. art. 1) why it is to be regarded as an act of virtue, for nothing can destroy sin except virtue.

Qu. xiii. deals with the possibility of satisfaction. According to art. 1, men cannot in the strict sense satisfy God, but only by means of an equality proportional to their relative positions. As sin is infinite in view of the infinity of the Divine majesty, so satisfaction obtains a certain infinity from the Divine mercy, so far as it is informed by grace, by which what man can do is made acceptable to God. Another form of statement is to say that satisfaction is sufficient by the virtue of the merit of Christ, which is in a certain way infinite; but this practically comes to the same thing, as grace is given through faith in Christ the Mediator. If, however, grace were given otherwise, satisfaction would still be possible.

Art. 2 states that one man can satisfy for another as regards the payment of the debt of sin, if he does it in charity. Such vicarious satisfaction, however, is not a medicine against future sin, except accidentally, so far as it merits for the other the grace which may help him to avoid sin; but this mode of operation is by way of merit rather than of satisfaction.

Qu. xiv. treats of the quality of satisfaction. According to art. 1, it is impossible to satisfy for one sin apart from others, since the removal of the offence is the same thing as reconciliation with God, which cannot take place as long as any hindrances to it remain.

Art. 2 teaches that, for similar reasons, it is impossible for one who has again fallen into sin to satisfy for sins already repented of.

Art. 3 maintains that it is impossible for works of satisfaction done out of grace to receive value from charity afterwards infused.

According to art. 4, works done without charity merit nothing 'de condigno'; by the Divine goodness, however, they merit somewhat 'de congruo,' viz. temporal mercies, a disposition to grace, and the habit of good works.[1]

Finally, art. 5 teaches that works done without charity obtain a mitigation of eternal punishment only in so far as they avoid the sin of omission and also prevent a man from falling farther into sin.

Qu. xv. is entitled, 'De his per quae fit satisfactio.' According to art. 1, satisfaction must be made by works of a penal character, in so far as the equalization demanded by justice in the matter of the offence requires something to be given to the offended party and something to be taken away from the offending party. As regards God, nothing can be given Him, but man can take away from himself by works of a penal character. It is clear also from its medicinal nature that satisfaction must be penal in character. Art. 2 teaches that God's temporal chastisements may become of the nature of satisfaction for us, in so far as they are voluntarily accepted by us.

Finally, according to art. 3, almsgiving, fasting, and prayer are the three forms of works of satisfaction. By them we humiliate ourselves before God, in our goods, our body, and our soul.

In qu. xxv. art. 1 Thomas discusses 'whether anything can be remitted from the punishment of satisfaction by means of indulgences.' His doctrine is that there is in the Church a treasure of merits, consisting both of the merit of Christ, as it exceeds by its infinity its effect in the sacraments, and of the merits of the saints, so far as they superabounded in works of satisfaction for the good of the whole Church. This treasure can then be applied for the good of the individual by the ruler of the Church (*i.e.* the pope), for the remission not merely of penitential satisfaction, but also of punishment in purgatory. According to art. 2, indulgences avail for their published value, if there be authority in the giver, charity in the recipient, and piety in the reason of the granting of the indulgence.

3. The controversy at the Reformation concerning penitential satisfaction. — The Reformation began with Luther's *Ninety-five Theses* of 1517 against indulgences, in which it was argued, among other things, that the repentance of a Christian man should be lifelong, that the pope could not remit any punishment beyond that of penitential satisfaction, and that every truly con-

[1] x. (25).
[2] See Loofs[4], p. 495 f.
[3] *Summa*, III. qu. lxxxvi. art. 4.
[4] Suppl. qu. ix. art. 2.

[1] For the distinction between *meritum de condigno* and *meritum de congruo*, see art. MERIT (Christian), vol. viii. p. 564.

trite Christian has complete remission of both punishment and guilt, without any indulgence.

In his immediately subsequent sermon on indulgence and grace Luther went on to declare that the common division of repentance into contrition, confession, and satisfaction had no foundation either in Scripture or in the Fathers, and that it could not be proved from Scripture that the Divine righteousness required of the sinner any pain or satisfaction, except his true repentance and conversion, with the intention to carry the cross of Christ and do the fitting works (which, however, are not appointed by any). Christian men should not seek indulgence.

A protest against the doctrine of penitential satisfaction thus became a point in the propaganda of the Reformation. It is admirably voiced by Melanchthon in his *Apology for the Augsburg Confession*, in the section 'On Confession and Satisfaction' (art. XII. vi.):

(19) The canonic satisfactions are not necessary by the Divine law for the remission of sins. 'For the opinion concerning faith must be preserved, that by faith we obtain the remission of sins for Christ's sake, and not because of our works either preceding or following.'

(20) The error here is aggravated by the Scholastic definition of satisfaction, viz. that it takes place for the placation of the Divine anger.

(21) Our adversaries, however, admit that satisfactions do not avail for the remission of guilt. But they fable that they are of value for the remission of punishments in purgatory or elsewhere. They teach that in the remission of sin God forgives its guilt and yet, since the Divine justice must punish sin, changes eternal into temporal punishment. They add also that part of this temporal punishment is remitted by the power of the keys; the rest is redeemed by satisfaction.

(22) All this is a fable, recently concocted without the authority of Scripture and the older ecclesiastical writers. The Schoolmen, in fact, mixed up things spiritual and political and imagined that the satisfactions, which were intended for ecclesiastical discipline, availed to appease God.

(34) True repentance is conversion and regeneration, which are followed by good works as their natural fruits.

(35) When Christ says 'Repent,' He speaks of regeneration and its fruits, not of the fictitious satisfactions of the Schoolmen.

(45) Though external works can be done beyond the Divine commandment, it is vain confidence to suppose that they satisfy the Divine law.

(46) True prayers, alms, and fasts are *in* the Divine commandment; what goes beyond it is of human tradition.

(53) The Schoolmen say that it belongs to the Divine justice to punish sin. God punishes it, however, in contrition, which is more truly the punishment of sin than any satisfaction.

The Reformation protest is met in the canons of the Council of Trent by a section 'de Satisfactionis necessitate et fructu' (sess. xiv. cap. viii.). The Catholic argument is briefly as follows:

Of all the parts of penance satisfaction is most attacked by the innovators, who assert that the remission of guilt is always accompanied by the entire remission of punishment. Scripture (Gn 3[10f.], 2 S 12[13f.], Nu 12[14f.] 20[11f.]) and tradition combine to refute the Protestants together with reason, which shows that the Divine justice must make different demands upon those who sin in ignorance before baptism and those who sin against the Holy Ghost after baptism. Besides, penitential satisfactions are a great preservative against further sin, and the Church has always seen in them, if performed with true contrition, a guarantee against the Divine punishment. In them, further, we are conformed to Christ, who made satisfaction for us, and we know that, if we suffer with Him, we shall be also glorified with Him. Nor does our satisfaction take place without the help of Christ, so that we do not glory in ourselves, but in Him, through whom we live, and acquire merit, and make satisfaction. The sacrament of penance, again, is no judgment-seat of wrath, just as no Roman Catholic ever thought that our satisfactions obscured or diminished the virtue of the merit or satisfaction of our Lord Jesus Christ. When innovators make true repentance no more than regeneration, this amounts to taking away satisfaction altogether.

Finally, the *Decretum de indulgentiis* (sess. xxv., 'Continuatio sessionis') maintains that Christ has given to the Church the power of granting indulgences, which power has been in use since the earliest times (Mt 16[19], Jn 20[23]). Indulgences, it is held, are therefore salutary for the Church and not to be done away with; but the power of indulgence is to be applied with moderation, that discipline may not suffer.

LITERATURE.—W. Moeller, *Lehrbuch der Kirchengeschichte*, i.[2], Tübingen, 1902; A. Harnack, *Lehrbuch der Dogmengeschichte*[4], do. 3 vols., 1909–10, Eng. tr. of 3rd ed., 7 vols., London, 1894–99; F. Loofs, *Leitfaden zum Studium der Dogmengeschichte*[4], Halle, 1906; R. Seeberg, *Lehrbuch der Dogmengeschichte*[2], 3 vols., Leipzig, 1908–13; H. Wasserschleben, *Die Bussordnungen der abendländischen Kirche*, Halle, 1851, *Die irische Kanonensammlung*[2], Leipzig, 1885; H. J. Schmitz, *Die Bussbücher und die Bussdisciplin der Kirche*, Mainz, 1883; H. Schultz, 'Der sittliche Begriff des Verdienstes und seine Aufwendung auf das Verständniss des Werkes Christi,' in *SK* lxvii. [1894] 7–50, 245–313, 445–553. See also artt. INDULGENCES, MERIT (Christian).

ROBERT S. FRANKS.

SATNĀMĪS.—The Hindī word *Satnām* is said to mean 'the True Name' or 'the Name of Truth' and, like *Sat*, 'Truth,' has been used by several Hindu reformers to connote the Supreme Deity. *Sat* is usually stated to be a corruption of the Sanskrit *satya*, 'truth,' but this is phonetically impossible. It is most probably derived from *sattwa*, 'true essence,' and hence, as a religious technical term, it connotes the abstract quality of purity and goodness. *Satnām* therefore really means 'He whose name is Purity and Goodness.' At least three religious bodies of N. India have adopted the term 'Satnāmī' as the title of their respective sects. We shall consider them separately.

1. The name 'Satnāmī' is employed among themselves by the sect of Sādhs (*q.v.*). It is probable that it was these Sādhs who were responsible for the Satnāmī revolt against Aurangzīb in 1672.

The Sādhs claim an indirect spiritual descent from Raī Dāsa, but, as is pointed out in the article devoted to them, the important unitarian side of their doctrine is derived rather from the teaching of another of Rāmānanda's disciples—Kabīr.

2. The next sect calling itself Satnāmī was founded by Jag-jīvan Dāsa of Sardaha in the Bārabankī District of the United Provinces. He was born in 1682 and began his religious career as a Kabīrpanthī—indeed, according to some authorities, these Satnāmīs are merely a branch of that faith.[1] In the United Provinces they number about 75,000, but in other parts of India figures have not been recorded for them.

Jag-jīvan Dāsa lived the greater part of his life at Sardaha, gaining reputation and followers by his miracles. He was a Chandēl Ṭhākur by caste, and his four chief disciples were all of high caste—Brāhmaṇas or Ṭhākurs—but, like Kabīr and Nānak, he adapted his teaching to all classes. Among his followers were low-caste Hindus, such as Chamārs (curriers), and he succeeded in establishing some community of thought between himself and Islām. Two at least of his disciples were Musalmāns. The fullest account of his teaching is that contained in the *Oudh Gazetteer* (see Literature); it has been repeatedly copied by subsequent writers.

The Satnāmīs profess to adore the so-called True Name alone, the one God, the Cause and Creator of all things, the *Nirguṇa*, or He who is void of all sensible qualities, without beginning and without end. As in the Vedānta philosophy, worldly existence is illusion, or the work of Māyā, whom they identify with Bhavānī, the consort of Śiva. They recognize the whole Hindu pantheon, and, although they profess to worship but one God, they pay reverence to his manifestations as revealed in incarnations, particularly those of Rāma and Kṛṣṇa. Their moral code enjoins indifference to the world, its pleasures and its pains; devotion to the *guru*, or spiritual guide; clemency and gentleness; rigid adherence to truth; the discharge of all social and religious obligations; and the hope of final absorption into the Supreme. Caste-distinction is not lost on profession, and care is taken not to interfere with caste-prejudices or social customs. Fasts are kept, at least to a partial extent, on Tuesday (the day of Hanumān) and on Sunday (the day of the sun). A good deal of liberality is shown towards local superstitions, especially as regards Rāmachandra and his monkey-ally Hanumān, and the ordinary festivals are regularly observed.

The water in which the *guru's* feet have been washed is drunk only when his caste is equal to or higher than that of the disciple. The distinctive mark of the sect is a black and white twisted thread, generally of silk, worn on the right wrist. It is technically known as *ādū*. The full-blown *mahanth* wears an

[1] Wilson, *Religious Sects of the Hindus*, p. 96.

ādū on each wrist and each ankle.[1] On the forehead is worn a *tilak*, consisting of one black perpendicular streak. The bodies of the dead are buried, not burnt.

The consumption of flesh, certain pulses, and intoxicating liquors is forbidden. It is also forbidden to eat the *brinjal*, or egg-plant. The last prohibition is due to the belief that, by prayer, it is capable of being converted into meat. The legend on which this belief is based will be found in most of the authorities quoted below.

Several works are attributed to Jag-jīvan. The most important, ranking as the sacred book of the sect, is called *Aghavināśa*,[2] 'The Destruction of Sin.' It is in verse and is believed to be inspired. Its contents are miscellaneous stories from the *Purāṇas*, lessons on morals, ethics, divinity, and rules of piety. Most of these are taken from earlier Sanskrit works and translated. Other works attributed to him are the *Jñāna-prakāśa* (dated 1761), the *Mahā-pralaya*, and the *Prathama-grantha*. The last is in the familiar form of a dialogue between Śiva and Pārvatī.

LITERATURE.—H. H. Wilson, *Sketch of the Religious Sects of the Hindus*, London, 1861, p. 356 ff.; *Gazetteer of the Province of Oudh*, Lucknow, 1877, i. 362 ff.; this has formed the basis of all subsequent accounts, such as B. H. Badley, in *IA* viii. [1879] 289 ff.; W. Crooke, *Tribes and Castes of the N.W. Provinces and Oudh*, Calcutta, 1896, iv. 299; H. R. Nevill, *Bara Banki Gazetteer*, Allahabad, 1904, p. 67 ff.

3. Another sect called Satnāmīs is found in Chhattīsgarh in the east of the Central Provinces of India. In 1901 it numbered nearly 400,000 persons, of whom all but 2000 were members of the caste of Chamārs. It originated with Ghāsī Rāma, a Chamār of Bilāspur District, between 1820 and 1830. He apparently got his inspiration from the Satnāmī teaching of the followers of Jag-jīvan Dāsa mentioned above, but the sect claims that it is a branch of the Raī Dāsīs (*q.v.*) founded by Raī Dāsa the Chamār, who was one of the twelve apostles of Rāmānanda.[3] There seems to be no basis for the claim, and so little do these Satnāmīs know about their alleged founder that they miscall him Rōhī Dāsa and themselves Rōhī Dāsīs.

Ghāsī Rāma was originally a poor farm-servant in a village named Girod, then in the Bilāspur, but now in the Raipur District. He took to ascetic practices and became venerated as a saintly man whose miracles quickly gained him fame. He next retired for a season to the forest and emerged with what he called a new revelation for the Chamārs, which was really a repetition of the tenets of Jag-jīvan Dāsa, with a few additions.[4] His teaching included the worship of the name of one solitary supreme God; abstinence from meat, liquor, and certain vegetables including (as in the case of Jag-jīvan's disciples) the *brinjal*; the abolition of idol-worship; and the prohibition of the employment of cows for agriculture and of ploughing after the midday meal. His followers were bidden to cast all idols from their homes, but were permitted to reverence the sun, as representing the Deity, every morning and evening with a pious ejaculation. Caste was abolished, and all men were declared to be socially equal, except the family of Ghāsī Rāma, in which the priesthood of the cult was to remain hereditary.

Since the death of its founder in 1850 this simple faith has become overlaid with much legend and superstition; and aboriginal social rites which, in spite of his teaching, had survived have only lately been abandoned in a few isolated localities, where they are said to be still occasionally practised. One of these was a kind of social prostitution in which a newly-married wife had to submit for one night to the embraces of a number of men of the village whom she named to her husband as her *gurus*, or spiritual guides—a variation of the *jus primæ noctis*, in which the woman selected the men who were to be favoured by her. One important sub-sect has arisen, the schism turning on the question as to whether the use of tobacco is or is not prohibited. The pro-smokers claim that in his later years Ghāsī Rāma withdrew his former prohibition; but, with tobacco, these *chungiās*, as they are called, have also returned to idolatry, and their villages contain stones covered with vermilion, which the true Satnāmīs eschew.

Satnāmīs admit to their ranks all persons except members of the impure castes, such as Dhōbīs (washermen), Ghasiās (grass-cutters), and Mehtars (sweepers), whom they regard as inferior to themselves. They bury their dead and observe mourning for three days. On the third day they have the head shaved, with the exception of the upper lip, which is never touched by the razor.

All over India the Chamārs are one of the lowest and most despised castes, and there can be no doubt that, as in the case of the Raī Dāsīs and similar sects, the success of Ghāsī Rāma's teaching was primarily due to his decree that caste was abolished, and that consequently the Chamār was as good as any other Hindu. It is this that has roused the bitter hostility to the sect on the part of Hindus of the higher castes—a hostility which is repaid with interest by its members. The women now wear nose-rings, an ornament hitherto forbidden to the lower castes, and the Satnāmīs show their contempt for orthodox Hinduism by rudely parodying Hindu sacred festivals. They insist on travelling in the trains in the same compartments with caste Hindus, who are defiled by their touch and against whom they do not hesitate to jostle. This anti-caste feeling has operated in more ways than one. It has created a feeling of independence among a formerly down-trodden people, which, in its basis, is worthy of all commendation; but its assertion has given rise to a bitter class-antagonism. The relations between a Chamār tenant and his Hindu landlord are often seriously strained, one side or other or both being to blame, and many Chamārs have developed into dangerous criminals, restrained only by their cowardice from the worst outrages against person and property.

LITERATURE.—The foundation of all accounts of these Satnāmīs is contained in J. W. Chisholm, *Bilaspur Settlement Report*, Nāgpur, 1861, p. 45 ff. Based on this, in each case with additions and corrections, are the following: *The Central Provinces Gazetteer*, Nāgpur, 1870, pp. 100 ff., 412 ff.; A. E. Nelson, *Gazetteer of the Raipur District*, Bombay, 1909, p. 79 ff.; R. V. Russell, *The Tribes and Castes of the Central Provinces of India*, London, 1916, i. 307. The last-named contains all that is in the preceding works, with some additional information.

G. A. GRIERSON.

SATYRS.—The word 'satyr' conjures up to the modern mind a fabulous creature half-man, half-beast, goat-footed, with pointed ears, shaggy body, a creature mainly malevolent, sportive but always on the verge of licence; unlike the solitary fawn, the Satyr hunts in troops; he is one of the θίασος of Dionysos. The picture is substantially correct, but with one important reservation. In origin the Satyr is not a mere imagined fabulous monster; he is an actually existing ritual mummer. This simple fact explains the whole being and functions of the creature. In the time of Antony it was still the custom for men to dress up and walk in procession as Satyrs.

Plutarch tells us that, when Antony entered Ephesus and was hailed as Dionysos, 'women disguised as Bacchæ and men and boys as Satyroi and Panes marched before him.'[1]

We are apt to explain such figures as men dressed

[1] An *ādū* is, properly speaking, the chain or hobble fastened round an elephant's ankles, when he is tied up.

[2] Misprinted *Aghavinsa* in *IA*, and so in later writings copied therefrom.

[3] See artt. RĀMĀNANDĪS, SĀDHS.

[4] The present writer would suggest that this retirement to the forest really covered a visit to N. India, where he met some Chamār follower of Jag-jīvan and learnt from him the Satnāmī doctrine.

[1] *Ant.* 24.

in imitation of Satyrs. We thereby disguise the simple fact that from these ritual figures the mythological conception of Satyrs or Panes sprang.

The *locus classicus* on the origin and nature of the Satyrs is Strabo, x. 3. He is mainly concerned to discuss the Kouretes (*q.v.*), but incidentally he throws out the priceless indication that a number of other mythological figures—Silenoi, Satyroi, Tityroi, Bacchæ—are of like origin. All these he calls δαίμονες—creatures half-divine, half-human. Their semi-divinity is instantly understood if we realize that they are not unreal monsters, but ritual mummers, real men, yet half-removed from reality, set apart, *i.e.* semi-divinized by their ritual disguise and function.

Once this substantial unity is clearly grasped, the diversity in forms and names need not embarrass us. Each local ritual would have for its δαίμονες its local ritual dress and local name. The disguise was usually half-animal; the worshipper was dressed up as a horse or a bull or a goat. The object of the disguise in animal form has been made abundantly clear by the study of beast-dances among primitive peoples all over the world. They danced as horses or goats or bulls according as they wished to promote the fertility of horse or goat or bull. Hence the ταῦροι, bull-δαίμονες of Ephesos, the τράγοι, goat-δαίμονες of Athens, the ἵπποι, horse-δαίμονες of the Peloponnese.

It is fortunate that in one case we are able from the monumental evidence to say with certainty what particular beast-form attaches to a special name. The horse-δαίμονες, creatures with horses' hoofs and manifest upspringing horse-tails, are Silenoi. This fact is put beyond doubt by inscriptions. On the early black-figured krater of Klitias and Ergotimos, now in the Museo Greco-Etrusco at Florence, three δαίμονες ithyphallic, with horses' ears, tails, and legs, are clearly inscribed 'Silenoi.'[1] It has long been the custom to call the horse-δίαμονες of the Attic vases, who constantly attend Dionysos, 'Satyrs'; accuracy obliges us to substitute the term 'Silenoi.'

It is to be regretted that we have no monumental certainty as to the precise animal-form of the Satyr. But the deficiency is less important than it seems. The particular animal-form is merely, as we saw, a matter of local differentiation springing from particular local circumstances and does not affect the ritual gist of the figure. As to the etymology of the word, again we cannot claim certainty. The most probable suggestion is that of F. Solensen,[2] who holds that both Σά-τυροι and Tί-τυροι are authentic Greek words from the root τῠ, 'to swell,' appearing in τύμβος, ταῦρος, etc. The Satyroi are δαίμονες of the budding, germinating, of plant and animal life; they are fertility figures, and with this their constant ithyphallic character quite agrees. Whatever the original animal-form of the Satyroi, the name came to cover pretty well the whole field of fertility δαίμονες. The cause of the dominance of the Satyr-name is lost to us.

As to the functions of the Satyrs, happily Strabo is explicit—they celebrated 'orgies'—and their relation to Dionysos was the same as that of the Kouretes to Zeus in Crete. Strabo's view is confirmed or rather anticipated by Euripides, whom he quotes.[3] The ritual of Dionysos, son of Semele, is substantially that of the Phrygian Mother; the Kouretes are substantially the same as the Satyroi. The sacred mime that they enact is that of the birth, the rescue, and the initiation of the holy child. With the birth and magic growth of the child are re-enacted and magically reinforced the re-birth and re-growth, the *renouveau*, of the whole animal and vegetable world.

The Satyrs far more than the Kouretes are essentially revellers. The Kouretes are essentially child-rearers, more quiet, more conservative. The rite of the birth and finding and cherishing of the child is, it is now known, only one factor in a wider magical folk-play—a folk-play that is in effect the utterance of the cycle of the life of man and of plants and animals. The play in full was cyclic—a birth, a contest, a death, a resurrection, a triumphant marriage, and again a birth. The whole cycle is preserved to us in the mime observed by R. M. Dawkins[1] at Viza in E. Thrace—the region of Dionysos himself. But it is obvious that in one place or another one feature of a plot so diverse may easily be emphasized in contrast to the rest. Crete and the Kouretes emphasize the birth of the child; the Satyrs emphasize the marriage, κῶμος. The Satyrs are in fact the κῶμος, the festival marriage procession incarnate; their leader is Comus. In the fragments of the recently discovered Satyr-play by Sophocles, the *Ichneutai*, 'Trackers,' the Satyrs, however, attend the birth of the wonder-child Hermes.[2] The Satyr-play lies at the basis not only of tragedy, but first and foremost of comedy—the song of the κῶμος. Whether the Satyr-play becomes tragedy or comedy depends on which point in the drama-cycle one elects to stop at. Tragedy ends with a death, comedy with a marriage.

But—and the point needs emphasis—it must never be forgotten that tragedy and comedy, important though they are to us, are late and purely literary developments. In the history of the ritual folk-mime they are, so to speak, episodic. Among the Greeks the ritual-mime, the Satyr-play, was caught up by men of conspicuous literary genius, Æschylus and Aristophanes, and used by them as the vehicle of tragedy and comedy. So splendid was the final transfiguration that the humble origin was all but lost, and only with difficulty has it been rediscovered by the industry of recent days. But it must always be remembered that tragedy and comedy alike, though especially tragedy, are exceptional phenomena occurring only sporadically and always calling for local and temporal explanation; it is the ritual-mime that is the permanent basic fact.

The reason is clear: the primary intent of the ritual-mime, the Satyr-play, was practical, *i.e.* magical, the object, to secure the fertility of man and flocks and fields. As in the Hymn of the Kouretes, the disguised worshippers 'leap for full years, and leap for fleecy flocks, and leap for fields of fruit and . . . leap for young citizens.'[3] With the decay of magic and the emergence of full-blown Olympians to be approached by prayer and sacrifice rather than compelled by magic, the magical aspect of the Satyrs of course dwindled, and their practical magical dance was misconceived as an idle sport. Even as early as Hesiod the process is well-nigh complete. Hesiod tells of the

> 'worthless, idle race of Satyrs
> And the gods, Kouretes, lovers of sport and dancing.'[4]

But—and this is conclusive for the substantial truth of the view here maintained—when Greek comedy and tragedy, splendid sporadic off-shoots, were dead and gone, the permanent element, the ritual-mime, lived on and lives to-day as a folk-play; and this folk-play is still credited with a faint magical potency; it is played at fixed seasons, mainly Christmas and Easter or Whitsuntide, and

1 A. Furtwängler and K. Reichhold, *Griech. Vasenmalerei*, Munich, 1904–09, i. 58, plates xi., xii.; and see fig. in art. SILENOI.

2 *Indogermanische Forschungen*, xxx. [1912] 31 ff.

3 Strabo, x. 3, p. 468; see J. E. Harrison, *Themis*, p. 39.

1 *JHS* xxvi. 191 ff.

2 See J. E. Harrison, 'Sophocles, *Ichneutæ*,' in *Essays and Studies presented to William Ridgeway*, Cambridge, 1913, p. 136 ff.

3 See 'Hymn of the Kouretes,' *BSA* xv. 359.

4 Frag. cxxix.

played 'for luck.' The players are still disguised as beasts, with horns and beast-skins, and sometimes horses' or bulls' heads. They still enact the fight, the *ἀγών*, of summer and winter, the death, the ritual resurrection, the marriage with its *κῶμος*, its revel rout (Comus). They still bring luck to the house where they enact their ritual-play. Finally, they are still always a band, a *θίασος*, pointing back to the days when the group and not the individual was the begetter of sanctities. We think of Dionysos as 'attended by a band of Satyrs'; it was from the band of Satyrs that Dionysos sprang.

LITERATURE.—For Satyrs in art and literature see **E. Kühnert**, in Roscher, *s.v.* 'Satyroi'; **O. Navarre**, in Daremberg-Saglio, *s.v.* 'Satyres'; **O. Gruppe**, *Griechische Mythologie und Religionsgeschichte*, Munich, 1897–1906, *s.v.* 'Satyroi.'

For origins and relation of Satyroi to Kouretes and other figures and for discussion of Strabo passage, see **J. E. Harrison**, 'Kouretes and Zeus Kouros,' in *BSA* xv. [1908–09] 308–338, and *Themis*, Cambridge, 1912, pp. 1–49. For Satyrs and Satyr-play see **Gilbert Murray**, 'Ritual Forms preserved in Greek Tragedy,' in Excursus to *Themis*, pp. 341–363; **F. M. Cornford**, *The Origin of Attic Comedy*, London, 1914; **A. B. Cook**, *Zeus*, Cambridge, 1914, i. 695–705, where full reference to preceding literature will be found. For survivals of ritual Satyr-mimes see **R. M. Dawkins**, 'The Modern Carnival in Thrace and the Cult of Dionysus,' *JHS* xxvi. [1906] 191; **A. J. B. Wace**, 'North Greek Festivals,' *BSA* xvi. [1909–10] 232; **J. C. Lawson**, *Modern Greek Folk-Lore and Ancient Greek Religion*, Cambridge, 1910, pp. 190–255; **E. K. Chambers**, *The Mediæval Stage*, 2 vols., London, 1903, *passim*; **J. Spens**, *An Essay on Shakespeare's Relation to Tradition*, London, 1916, pp. 35–55. For Indian parallels to Satyrs and Kouretes see **L. von Schröder**, *Mysterium und Mimus im Rigveda*, Leipzig, 1908, *passim*.

J. E. HARRISON.

SAURAPĀTAS, SAURAS, or SAURYAS.—

This is the name of a small sect in Central and Southern India, whose special object of worship is the sun. According to the *Manual of the Administration of the Madras Presidency*,[1] those of the south are all Drāviḍa Brāhmaṇas, form a sub-tribe of that caste, and are very few in number. According to Wilson, they scarcely differ from other Hindus in their general observances. This is to be expected, for the worship of the sun forms a part of every orthodox Hindu's worship. The *tilaka*, or frontal mark, is of red sandal and of a special shape, and the necklace is of crystal. According to the *ICR* for 1901,[2] the *tilaka* of the Sauryas of Central India may be one of three varieties—three straight lines across the forehead, a single perpendicular line, or a double crescent joined by a bar in the middle. Here also 'they are nearly all Brāhmaṇas.'

They do not eat until they have seen the sun; and on every Sunday, and on the day of the sun's entry into a fresh sign of the zodiac, they eat one meal without salt.

For the general history of sun-worship in India see art. SUN, MOON, AND STARS (Hindu). Cf. also art. NATURE (Hindu), vol. ix. p. 230. The forest tribe Sauras (=Savarās) is treated in art. SAVARĀS.

LITERATURE.—**H. H. Wilson**, *Sketch of the Religious Sects of the Hindus*, ed. R. Rost, London, 1861, p. 266, from which much of the above is taken; **R. G. Bhandarkar**, *Vaiṣṇavism, Śaivism and Minor Religious Systems* (=*GIAP* iii. 6), Strassburg, 1913, p. 151ff.

GEORGE A. GRIERSON.

SAUTRĀNTIKAS.—1. Name, scriptural position, and character.

—The philosophers of the Little Vehicle (Hīnayāna [*q.v.*]) were divided into two schools: on the one hand, the Vaibhāṣikas, who accepted the Abhidharma books of the Sarvāstivādins (the seven Abhidharmas) as 'revealed' scripture (*ipsissima verba*), and the commentary on them, *Vibhāṣā*, as the oldest and the most authoritative 'treatise' (*śāstra*); on the other hand, the Sautrāntikas, who considered the seven books simply as 'treatises' (*śāstra*) of human inspiration

1 Madras, 1885–93, iii. 863.
2 Vol. xix., *Central India*, Lucknow, 1902, p. 86.

and therefore liable to error, who maintained that Buddha had not composed treatises dealing with Abhidharma or given indications for the composition of such treatises under his authority (a working hypothesis in Pāli scholasticism),[1] but had taught Abhidharma doctrines in certain *Sūtras* (or *Sūtrāntas*).[2] According to them, these *Sūtras*, the *Arthaviniśchaya*, etc., constitute 'the Basket of Abhidharma.' Hence their name Sautrāntikas, the philosophers who recognize the authority of the *Sūtrāntas* alone.

They are also named Dārṣṭāntikas, 'philosophers who deal with similes' (*dṛṣṭānta*);[3] but there is some reason to believe that the Dārṣṭāntikas are a branch of the Sautrāntikas.

The following gives an accurate idea of the character of the school, and the progress accomplished by Buddhist thought is evident when the Sautrāntikas are compared with the older Pāli or Sanskrit schools:

> The point to be discussed is of importance. Does the eye or the 'consciousness' (or the 'mind') see visible objects? (1) The Mahāsāṃghikas (an old sect and school) adhere to the letter of the scriptural text: 'When he sees an object with the eye . . .' and believe that the eye—the subtle eye, not the eye of the flesh—sees visible objects. (2) The orthodox Pāli school (Vibhajjavādin) maintains that, in this scriptural statement, 'eye' indicates the necessary instrument of vision, as when we say 'wounded by a bow,' when, in fact, the wound is inflicted by an arrow. The eye, they say, being matter, does not see; seeing belongs to 'consciousness' (*vijñāna*).[4] (3) The Vaibhāṣikas agree with the Mahāsāṃghikas: the eye sees, the consciousness or 'discernment' (*vijñāna*) discerns (*vijānāti*); they refute the Pāli point of view (by adducing a new simile, *mañchāḥ krośanti*, 'stalls applaud'). (4) The Sautrāntikas recognize the weight of the scriptural text: 'When he sees an object with the eye . . .' but, by referring to other scriptural evidence, they show that the problem is not well stated: 'What is the use of this discussion? Very much like "chewing space." It has been said by the Lord that, "the eye being given and a visible object also being given, there arises, depending on both, a visual cognition." Therefore such a question as "Who sees?" is not justified, as therein no activity comes into play. These are only correlated phenomena, causes and effect—in fact a blue image resulting from a mechanical process, no seer, no vision. It is said that the eye sees, that the discernment (*vijñāna*) discerns (*vijānāti*)—mere metaphorical phrases which we must not take literally, on which we must not lay stress (*abhiniveśa*), says the Lord.'[5]

2. Sources.[6]—Although the origin of the Sautrāntikas may be traced to the time of the rise of the Vaibhāṣikas—Sautrāntika doctors are quoted in the *Vibhāṣā*[7]—it seems that the Vaibhāṣikas preceded the Sautrāntikas in the systematization of their doctrines. That would explain why the views of the latter are to be found chiefly in commentaries on the books of the former. Vasubandhu, in his *Abhidharmakośa*, 'the scabbard of the Abhidharmas' (meaning the seven Abhidharmas of the Sarvāstivādins),[8] sets out to state the views of the Vaibhāṣikas of Kaṣmīr, but in his *Bhāṣya* (auto-commentary) to the *Kośa* he points out the errors of the Vaibhāṣikas, and these errors are dealt with in the *Vyākhyā* (sub-commentary) of Yaśomitra.[9] A number of doctors, among them

1 See, *e.g.*, Atthasālinī (*PTS*, London, 1897), p. 3.
2 *Abhidharmakośakārikās*, and *Bhāṣya*, Tib. tr., ed. T. de Stcherbatskoi, *Bibl. Buddhica*, xx. [Petrograd, 1917] 7; Tāranātha, *Gesch. des Buddhismus in Indien*, tr. A. Schiefner, do. 1869, p. 56; Tibetan text, do. 1868, p. 56.
3 E. Burnouf, *Introd. à l'histoire du Buddhisme indien*, Paris, 1845, p. 448; W. Wassilieff, *Der Buddhismus*, Petrograd, 1860, p. 274; Tāranātha, tr. Schiefner, p. 274.
4 *Kathāvatthu*, xviii. 9, tr. S. Z. Aung and C. A. F. Rhys Davids, *Points of Controversy*, London, 1915, p. 333.
5 *Abhidharmakośakārikās*, p. 76 f.
6 European sources: H. Kern, *Manual of Indian Buddhism*, Strassburg, 1896, p. 126, *Geschiedenis van het Buddhisme in Indie*, 2 vols., Haarlem, 1882–84, French tr., *Histoire du Bouddhisme dans l'Inde*, Paris, 1903, ii. 395–402; Burnouf, *Introduction*, p. 447; Wassilieff, *Der Buddhismus*, p. 222.
7 See *Abhidharmakośavyākhyā* ad i. 20. On the date of Kumāralabdha see H. Ui, *The Vaiśeṣika Philosophy*, London, 1917, pp. 43, 45.
8 See *Abhidharmakośakārikās*, p. 2.
9 See J. Takakusu, 'On the Abhidharma Literature of the Sarvāstivādins,' *JPTS*, 1904–05, p. 67, and sources quoted; Paramārtha, 'Life of Vasubandhu,' *Tong-pao*, July 1904, pp. 278, 290.

Saṃghabhadra, thought that Vasubandhu had unduly sacrificed the 'orthodox system,' and they wrote purely Vaibhāṣika commentaries to the *Kośa*, refuting the particular views of the Sautrāntikas. These books (*Samayapradipa*, *Nyāyānusāra*) exist only in Chinese translations.

There are a few references to the Sautrāntikas in the *Madhyamakavṛtti*[1] and in Vinītadeva's commentary to the *Nyāyabindu.*[2] Tāranātha gives some information on the history of the school and the activity of its scholars;[3] and so do the Chinese pilgrims.[4] Some Tibetan treatises (*siddhāntas*), especially the *Mañjughoṣa-hāsavajrasiddhānta*, explain at length the position of the Sautrāntikas. These *siddhāntas* are intricate, and Wassilieff, who has summarized them, is not to blame when his statements are obscure.[5] Most fortunately, Brāhmanical and Jain philosophers have paid attention to the theory of the origin of knowledge as stated by the Sautrāntika school, and they furnish us with the best account that we possess. In many cases their evidence is supported from Buddhist sources.[6]

3. Doctrines.—It is not possible to give a systematic account of the doctrines of the Sautrāntikas. On the other hand, a mere list of the points referred to in our authorities would involve the reader in a maze of obscure technicalities. A few remarks will show the variety and the importance of their views.

(1) Thought knows itself, just as a lamp renders itself manifest—a theory (*svasaṃvedana, svasaṃvitti*, 'self-consciousness') which has often been opposed by the Indian philosophers from the days of the *Upaniṣads*, and which is admitted in Buddhism by the Vijñānavādins alone,[7] who have much in common with the Sautrāntikas.

(2) There is no direct perception of exterior objects (*contra* the Vaibhāṣikas); exterior objects are known by inference, not by evidence.

(3) The exterior object really exists (*vastusat*); but it is an open and much debated question whether it possesses a form (*ākāra*) of its own. Some Sautrāntikas believe that 'form' belongs to the object; some maintain that thought 'imposes its own form on the object'; others, again, as the result of a more delicate inquiry, admit a compromise—the semi-realistic theory of the 'two halves of an egg.'

(4) The Sautrāntikas have had a certain share in the development of the atomistic theory. They say that there is no contact (*sparśa*) between atoms; for, as atoms have no parts, contact could not be contact between parts; it would be contact between wholes and therefore would involve identity; a compound of atoms would not be larger than one atom (so far the reasoning of the Vijnānavādins, who deny the existence of matter). But there is 'contiguity' between atoms—literally 'there is no interval' (*nirantaratva*) between them, for matter is impenetrable.[1]

(5) Matter (*rūpa*) is only 'colour' (*varṇa*), not 'shape' or 'figure' (*saṃsthāna*) (*contra* the Vaibhāṣikas).[2]

(6) Everything is painful. Pleasant feeling itself is painful, as it is only attenuated pain.

(7) Destruction has no cause: things are perishable by their very nature; they are not transitory (*anitya*), they are 'momentary' (*kṣaṇika*).[3] Birth or production (*utpāda*) is 'existence after having not existed' (*abhūtvā bhāvaḥ*); neither the past nor the future exists. *Pudgala* ('soul') and space (*ākāśa*) are also mere names.

LITERATURE.—See the sources quoted in the footnotes.

L. DE LA VALLÉE POUSSIN.

1 *Bibl. Buddhica*, iv. [Petrograd, 1913] 61, 263, 281, 413, 444, 488, 523.

2 *Bibl. Indica*, Calcutta, 1908, pp. 34, 40, 59; see also *Saṃtānāntarasiddhi*, Tib. tr., ed. T. de Stcherbatskoi, *Bibl. Buddhica*, xix. [1916].

3 Tāranātha, tr. Schiefner, pp. 56, 58, 78, 271, 274; the Sautrāntikas are often regarded as a branch of the Sarvāstivādins, the second branch being the Mūlasarvāstivādins (W. W. Rockhill, *Life of the Buddha*, London, 1884, p. 186), or as scions of the Tāmraśatiyas.

4 T. Watters, *On Yuan Chwang's Travels in India*, London, 1904–05, i. 210, 245, 318, 322, 326, 374, ii. 225, 286. The four suns of the Sautrāntikas—Kumāralābha (or °labdha), the reputed founder of the school (see Watters, ii. 225, and cf. ii. 286), Dharmatrāta, Buddhadeva, and Srīlābha—are frequently quoted in the *Kośa* literature.

5 Wassilieff, *loc. cit.*; Kern (*Geschiedenis*) has translated a part of the summary of Wassilieff.

6 Mādhavāchārya, *Sarvadarśanasaṃgraha*, ch. ii., tr. A. E. Gough in E. B. Cowell and A. E. Gough, *The Sarva-Darśana-Saṃgraha: Review of the Different Systems of Hindu Philosophy*², London, 1894; tr. L. de la Vallée Poussin, in *Muséon*, new ser., ii. [1901] 56, 187 (notes contain references to Buddhist and Brāhmanical sources); Haribhadra, *Ṣaḍdarśanasamuchchaya*, ed. L. Suali, *Bibl. Indica*, Calcutta, 1905; *Sarvasiddhāntasaṃgraha*, ed. F. W. Thomas and L. de la Vallée Poussin, in *Muséon*, new ser., iii. [1902] 403, and ed. M. Rangāchārya, Madras, 1909, pt. i. p. 9; *Brahmasūtras*, with commentaries, ii. 2, 18; *Sāṃkhyasūtras*, i. 42, v. 77; *Nyāyasūtras*, iv. 2, 35; *Ślokavārttika* (Chowkhambā Sanskrit Series), p. 272.

7 See *Kathāvatthu*, v. 9.

1 See Wassilieff, p. 333; *Abhidharmakośakārikās*, i. 43; *Sarvadarśana*, Fr. tr. n. 77; *Nyāyavārttika*, Calcutta, 1907, p. 518; cf. Ui, p. 26 f., and art. ATOMIC THEORY (Indian).

2 *Abhidharmakośa*, iv.

3 *Madhyamakvṛtti*, p. 281.

SAVARĀS.—The Savarās, Saoras, or Sauras, a forest tribe of India, numbering 582,342 at the census of 1911, are found in largest numbers in Madras, the Central Provinces, the United Provinces of Agra and Oudh, and Bihār and Orissa. The name of the tribe, popularly derived from Skr. *śava*, 'a corpse,' is interpreted by Cunningham to mean 'axe-men,' the axe being the implement characteristic of forest-dwellers. They have been identified with the Śabaras, who were grouped with the Andhras, Pundras, Pulindas, and Mūtibas, 'the most degraded classes of men, the rabble for the most part.'[4] In the United Provinces of Agra and Oudh they are represented by the Soerī, Soirī, or Suirī.[5]

As might have been expected in the case of a tribe dispersed over a large area of forest country, their environment preventing inter-communication between the various groups, there are considerable differences of belief.

In Bengal the members of the tribe in the Bankura District 'have become thoroughly Hinduised, and Brahmans serve them as priests in the worship of the standard gods. These Brahmans are received on equal terms by the *purohits* [family priests] of Bagdis, Koras, Kewats, and other low castes. In Orissa the original faith of the tribe has been less modified by the influence of Hindu usage. The worship of the Brahmanical deities is indeed gaining ground among them, but the elder gods, Thánpati, who dwells in the *thán* or sacred grove of the village, and "Bansuri or Thákuráini, no doubt the same as the blood-thirsty she-devil revered by the Bhuiyás,"[6] still receive offerings of goats or fowls at the hands of the elders of the community, who have not yet been supplanted in their office by the professional Brahman.'[7]

The Soerīs of the United Provinces are worshippers of Śiva, Mahābīr, or Hanumān, the monkey god, Sītalā Māī, the smallpox goddess, and the Pāñchoñ Pīr.[8]

In Madras the tribal beliefs are of a more primitive kind. In the Vizagapatam District they worship Jākarā or Loḍḍlū, the latter being sometimes a generic term for the gods in a body, who have no regular temples, but are symbolized by a stone placed under a big tree. Sacrifices of goats are made to them when the various crops are ripening, and the victim must first eat food offered

4 *Aitareya Brāhmaṇa*, vii. 18, ed. M. Haug, Bombay, 1863, ii. 470; cf. J. Muir, *Orig. Sanskrit Texts*, pt. ii. [1860] p. 381; W. W. Hunter, *Orissa*, London, 1872, i. 175.

5 W. Crooke, *Tribes and Castes of N.W. Provinces and Oudh* iv. 320 ff.

6 E. T. Dalton, *Descriptive Ethnology of Bengal*, Calcutta, 1872, p. 149.

7 H. H. Risley, *Tribes and Castes of Bengal*, ii. 244.

8 See art. PANCHPIRIYĀ.

to it.[1] The hill Savarās fear Jaliā, who in some villages is provided with a home under a small thatched shed, in which are placed images of household implements and requisites as well as figures of men, animals, birds, and the like.[2] F. Fawcett[3] remarks that Jaliā is sometimes male, sometimes female, and very malevolent, going from one village to another and causing death. The god's shrine is provided with all sorts of furniture for his or her use or amusement; goats are killed close by, and the blood is poured on the platform. Among other gods he named Kitung, said to be the creator, who brought the tribe to their present settlements; Rathū, who causes pains in the neck; Dharmabojā or Lankan, 'the one above,' or Ayungang, the sun, who causes all births and is not always benevolent, sometimes bringing sickness; Kannī, who is very malevolent and lives in big trees, those haunted by him never being cut down. Some of these hill deities resemble the spirits of the dead. The same writer adds that the *kadang* is a medium, sometimes a woman, all to the manner born and needing no training, who communicates with the unseen world. Their gradual approximation to Hinduism is shown by the belief that they can gain union with the gods in a future life by worshipping at the Śivarātrī, or 'night festival' of Śiva, at his ancient temple at Mehendragiri. There is no distinct evidence of human sacrifice like that of the Kandhs (*q.v.*); but J. Campbell remarks that they used to participate in the *meriah* rite of the Kandhs, though they did not seem to attach much importance to it and readily promised to discontinue the practice.[4] They have no commemorative sacrifices or feasts, those which are held being intended to appease evil spirits, especially those of the angry dead. They make offerings to the sun at the mango harvest, an offering of food or a small sacrifice when a child is born, and an offering to Sattīvā at the sprouting of the rice crop to secure a good harvest. On this occasion a stake made from a sacred tree is planted in the ground, the top of it is sharpened to a point, on which is impaled a live young pig or chicken, and over the animal an inverted earthen pot daubed over with white rings is placed.[5]

In the Central Provinces they worship the goddess Bhavānī under various names and Dulhā Deo, the young bridegroom who was killed by a tiger.[6] He is believed to dwell in the house kitchen. In other places Būṛhā Deo, or Baḍ Rāul, is worshipped, and, as the tribe becomes Hinduized, he develops into Bhairava, 'the terrible one,' just as farther north the earth-god Bhairon is similarly transformed.[7] Like all secluded tribes, they are notorious for their knowledge of sorcery, and their charms are specially valued by those who have to appease the spirits of persons who have died by violence. In former times, if a member of the family was seriously ill, they were accustomed to set fire to the forest, in the hope that by burning the small animals and insects they might propitiate the angry gods.

LITERATURE.—H. H. Risley, *Tribes and Castes of Bengal*, Calcutta, 1891, ii. 241 ff.; W. Crooke, *Tribes and Castes of N.W. Provinces and Oudh*, do. 1896, iv. 320 ff.; E. Thurston, *Castes and Tribes of S. India*, Madras, 1909, i. 258 ff., vi. 304 ff.; *Census of India, 1901*, vol. xv. pt. i. p. 177, do. *1911*, vol. xii. pt. i. p. 64; *Ethnographic Survey: Central Provinces*, pt. iii., Allahabad, 1907, p. 75 ff.; A. E. Nelson, *Gazetteer of Bilaspur*, do. 1910, i. 91 ff.; L. S. S. O'Malley, *Gazetteer of Sambalpur*, do. 1909, i. 74; E. A. de Brett, *Gazetteer Chhattisgarh Feudatory States*, do. 1909, i. 210; J. N. Bose, *JASB* lix. [1890] 289; T. J. Maltby and G. D. Lemam, *Manual of Ganjam*, Madras, 1882; R. V. Russell, *Tribes and Castes of the Central Provinces of India*, London, 1916, iv. 500 ff.

W. CROOKE.

[1] Cf. the test of the victim by its shivering (*BG* ix. pt. i. [1901] p. 516; J. G. Frazer, *Pausanias*, London, 1898, v. 237, *GB*[3], pt. i., *The Magic Art*, London, 1911, i. 384 f.).

[2] W. Francis, *Gazetteer of Vizagapatam*, Madras, 1907, i. 96.

[3] *JRASBo* i. [1886] 242.

[4] *A Personal Narr. of Thirteen Years' Service amongst the Wild Tribes of Khondistan*, London, 1864, p. 204.

[5] *Ib.* p. 259; for further details of the belief in Madras see E. Thurston, *Castes and Tribes of S. India*, vi. 304 ff.

[6] Cf. Crooke, *PR*[2] i. 119 f.

[7] *Ib.* i. 108.

SAVIOUR.—See SALVATION.

SAVONAROLA.

1. Life.—Although we naturally associate Girolamo Savonarola, the prophet of the Italian Renaissance, with Florence, he was not and never regarded himself as a Florentine. Michele Savonarola, a Paduan scientist and man of letters, had settled at Ferrara in 1440 as physician to the court and professor in the university. His son Niccolò married a Mantuan lady, Elena Bonacossi, by whom he had seven children, the martyr being the third. Girolamo was born on 21st Sept. 1452. The second duke of Ferrara, Ercole d'Este, was making his capital a centre of the learning and splendour of the Renaissance; but the young Savonarola, profoundly conscious of the evils of the time and suffering the pangs of unrequited love, poured out his heart in a canzone, *De ruina mundi* (1472), bewailing the perversion of the world and the corruption of the life which he saw around him. He set forth the same conviction in a small prose essay, *Del Dispregio del Mondo*, invoking the divine intervention. On 24th April 1475 he left his home and entered the Dominican order at Bologna.

'The reason,' he wrote to his father, 'that moves me to enter religion is this: first, the great misery of the world, the iniquities of men, the ravishing, the adultery, the pride, the idolatry, the cruel blasphemies; for the age has come to such a pass that not one is found who acts rightly; wherefore, many times the day, did I sing to myself this verse with tears: *Heu! fuge crudeles terras, fuge litus avarum.*'[1]

In his novice's cell he wrote a second canzone, *De ruina ecclesiæ*, deploring the decay of religious life and the corruption of the Church, praying for power 'to break those great wings' of temporal and spiritual power in the hands of the wicked. He returned to Ferrara to preach the Lent of 1481, but failed to impress his countrymen, and was transferred to the convent of San Marco in Florence. Lorenzo de' Medici was then at the height of his power; his rule, though there was no court and republican appearances were maintained, was a despotism in which even art and letters and festivities became instruments of statecraft for holding the people in contented servitude. The uncouth utterances of the new friar-preacher from the north were at first ignored by the cultured and sophisticated Florentines. Poring over the pages of the Hebrew prophets, himself seeing visions and hearing voices, Savonarola became inspired by the conviction that he was set by God as a watchman in the centre of Italy to warn her peoples and princes of impending doom. He first delivered his message at San Gimignano during the Lent of 1485, and then, with greater power and terrible predictions, in the Lent of 1486 at Brescia. The sensation caused by the latter sermons gained him a better hearing on his return to Florence (whither he was recalled at the instance of Lorenzo de' Medici), when, on the first Sunday of August 1489, preaching on the Apocalypse in San Marco, he repeated his three conclusions: the Church would be scourged, then renovated, and these things would come quickly. In 1491 he was elected prior of San Marco. He stood by the deathbed of Lorenzo de' Medici (April 1492) and, according to the disputed but still generally accepted story, bade him gain remission of his sins by restoring liberty to Florence.

Up to this time Savonarola had based his prophecies on natural reason and the authority of the

[1] Villari and Casanova, *Scelta di prediche e scritti*, p. 419.

Scriptures. He now began to speak openly of his visions and to lay claim to divine revelation. In the same year (1492), on the night of Good Friday, he saw 'per immaginazione' the vision of the two crosses—the black cross of the wrath of God in the midst of Rome, the golden cross of the mercy of God rising up over Jerusalem. In the following Advent (Alexander VI. having been elected pope under scandalous circumstances in August) he had 'un' altra immaginazione,' in which he beheld a hand in heaven wielding a sword, of which the point was turned towards the earth. Throughout 1492, 1493, and 1494 his sermons increased in vigour and fearlessness of utterance, as he denounced the crimes and corruption of prelates and princes, bidding men turn for happiness and salvation to 'the simplicity and life of Christ and of the true Christians.' The prelates, he declared, had not only destroyed the Church of God, but had made a Church after their own fashion—the modern Church, which retained only the splendour of outward ceremonies, a mere show falsely satisfying men, like the festivities and spectacles introduced by secular tyrants. His prophecies of imminent chastisement culminated in the sermon on the Deluge (Gn 6^{17}), delivered in the Duomo on 21st Sept. 1494, heralding the French invasion. The vision of the sword seemed fulfilled, and Savonarola hailed Charles VIII. as the minister of God who should reform the Church and the world. The friar's bearing in the crisis that followed the expulsion of the Medici, the passage of the French through Tuscany to the conquest of Naples, and their precipitous retreat in the following year gave him an almost unlimited power in Florence. Henceforth Savonarola claimed a supernatural sanction for his prophecies and conduct, in the religious and political sphere alike. From the pulpit he directed the reorganization of the Republic with a Greater Council, on the model of the Venetian constitution ('which was given them by God'), and the reformation of life and conduct that transformed the city into a theocratic state with Christ as King. There were bonfires of the 'vanities,' the streets echoed with processional hymns and chants of divine love, the children were organized into bands as the chosen emissaries of this holy time. At Ferrara the duke—with whom Savonarola was in constant communication, and who for a while believed unreservedly in his prophecies—attempted a similar reformation. The prior of San Marco was now the central figure in Italy.

'Tell me,' he cries in one of his sermons, 'ye who contradict, —did you ever in your times see a man preach in one city, and his voice run through all Italy and beyond Italy?'[1]

Savonarola, while always professing absolute submission to the doctrines and decrees of the Church, now came into direct conflict, both spiritually and politically, with the pope. Alexander, who had vainly attempted to silence him or induce him to come to Rome, finally sought to bribe him by the offer of a cardinal's hat. The friar's answer was a terrible course of sermons on Amos and Zechariah, in the Lent of 1496, openly denouncing the corruption of the papacy. He continued in the same strain, preaching on Ruth, Micah, and Ezekiel, during this and the earlier part of the following year. At the same time he was engaged, together with the duke of Ferrara (whose faith, however, was wavering), in an intrigue for the return of Charles VIII., in opposition to the league for the defence of Italy formed by the pope, Venice, and the duke of Milan. In June 1497 Alexander issued a bull of excommunication against him. Savonarola respected the bull until Christmas Day, when he publicly celebrated mass. Disregarding the advice of the Ferrarese ambassador, he followed this up by preaching in the Duomo on Septuagesima Sunday, 1498, declaring that the excommunication was invalid and the pope himself a broken tool. He began to talk of the summoning of a Church council. When the government, threatened with an interdict, forbade him to preach again, he prepared an appeal to the princes of Christendom, urging them to summon this general council and depose the pope as a simoniacal usurper. A preliminary dispatch to France was intercepted by a Milanese agent and forwarded to Rome. The duke of Ferrara had already dissociated himself from the friar's cause. Faced by a hostile government in Florence itself and by the increasing enmity of the populace, Savonarola had now no supporters save a dwindling party of religious enthusiasts. The abortive ordeal by fire (7th April 1498) precipitated the inevitable catastrophe. A Franciscan of Santa Croce challenged him to prove his doctrines by passing unscathed through the fire; Savonarola would perhaps have ignored the matter (as he had done on a previous occasion), but his chief follower, Fra Domenico da Pescia, impetuously accepted. The affair was probably an organized plot, and the fiasco was so contrived as to excite the popular indignation still further against him. San Marco was stormed on the following day (Palm Sunday). The friar and his two companions—Fra Domenico da Pescia and Fra Silvestro Maruffi — were subjected to repeated tortures, and Savonarola's depositions were falsified to make it appear that he confessed 'that he had not received from God the things he preached.' Finally, to conclude the prolonged martyrdom, papal commissioners were invited to Florence, and the three Dominicans were hanged and their bodies burned on 23rd May 1498. Savonarola's calm correction of the phrase of the bishop of Vasona in degrading him ('Separo te ab Ecclesia militante atque triumphante') was long remembered: 'Militante, non triumphante; hoc enim tuum non est.'

The personal character of Savonarola was unquestionably one of heroic sanctity. His letters to his mother and other relatives and his attitude towards women and children testify to his strong family affection and innate tenderness of disposition. A mystic and contemplative by nature, he was impelled to action solely by the spirit of holy zeal and the conviction that a special mission had been assigned to him by God.

'Zeal,' he declares in one of his sermons, 'is nought else than an intense love in the heart of the just man, which does not let him rest, but ever seeks to remove all that he sees to be against the honour of God whom he vehemently loves.'[1]

In his *Dialogus de veritate prophetica* he pathetically describes his reluctance to enter the deep sea in his little boat, finding himself far from shore, yearning to return to his cell:

'All those who have known me intimately from my childhood, know that these things which I do at present are contrary and repugnant to my natural desire.'[2]

His inordinate belief in his visions was due to a nervous and highly-strung temperament, to which must likewise be ascribed his intolerance towards political opponents. This at times marred his otherwise enlightened statesmanship; but nowhere in his career is there a trace of personal arrogance or self-seeking. The Ferrarese ambassador wrote of him, on his first accession to power in Florence: 'He aims at nothing save the good of all, seeking for union and peace.' In religious doctrine and practice he remained to the last a fervent and rigid Roman Catholic of the type of the mediæval saint. As a reformer he is the successor of St. Peter Damian, St. Bernard, Dante, and St.

[1] *Prediche*, ed. Baccini, p. 21 f.

[1] *Sermoni e prediche*, Florence, 1845, p. 555.
[2] *Dialogus, ad init.*

Catherine of Siena, rather than a precursor of Luther.

2. Works.—Savonarola's literary works are closely connected with his utterances from the pulpit.

'His religious treatises, including those in the form of epistles to the faithful, set forth, scientifically and more in order, the same ideas that are found scattered in his sermons.'[1]

Savonarola appears to have usually written his sermons beforehand in Latin, though they were delivered and consequently taken down in Italian. His more important treatises (with the exception of the *Reggimento e governo della città di Firenze*) were first published in Latin and afterwards, for the sake of the unlearned, in the vernacular; only in the case of the *Trionfo della Croce* is the Italian version from his own hand; he more generally relied on the assistance of one or other of his followers, such as the poet Girolamo Benivieni. In his shorter writings he used Italian or Latin according to the nature of the subject and the class of readers to whom they were addressed.

(i.) *Sermons.*—There are 15th or early 16th cent. editions of ten courses of Savonarola's sermons: (*a*) on the First Epistle of St. John (probably delivered in 1491); (*b*) on the Psalm *Quam bonus Deus Israel* (Advent, 1493); (*c*) on the Ark of Noah (mainly Lent, 1494); (*d*) on Haggai (1494–95); (*e*) on the Psalms (1495); (*f*) on Job (Lent, 1495); (*g*) on Amos and Zechariah (Lent, 1496); (*h*) on Ruth and Micah (1496); (*i*) on Ezekiel (1496–97); (*k*) on Exodus (1498). Several sermons were separately printed during the preacher's life. There are modern editions of (*a*) and (*b*), *Sermoni e prediche di F. Girolamo Savonarola* (Florence, 1845, and Prato, 1846), and of (*h*), *Prediche di F. Girolamo Savonarola*, ed. G. Baccini (Florence, 1889). An excellent selection is given by Villari and Casanova. Though the magic of the preacher's personality has passed away, and we are mainly dependent upon reporters (and sometimes upon an intermediate Latin version), enough remains to enable us to realize the terrible quality of Savonarola's eloquence, his apocalyptic fire and religious fervour, his zeal for righteousness, his fearlessness of men, and the profound emotion that these discourses must have stirred in his audience.

Savonarola claims[2] to have preached on four subjects: the truth of the faith, the simplicity of the Christian life as the highest wisdom, the imminence of certain future events, the new government of Florence. Consequently he regards as his most significant works the four in which these matters are set forth in writing: the *Trionfo della Croce*, the *Semplicità della vita cristiana*, the *Dialogus de veritate prophetica*, the *Reggimento e governo della città di Firenze*.

(ii.) The *De veritate Fidei in Dominicæ Crucis triumphum*, or *Trionfo della Croce*, the longest of Savonarola's works, was completed in the summer of 1497. Both the Latin and Italian versions are by himself, the latter not being a literal translation, but the setting forth of the contents of the work in a more popular and less scholastic form. He regarded it as the supreme vindication of his orthodoxy. 'From this book,' he wrote to the pope, 'it will appear manifestly whether I am a sower of heresy or of the Catholic faith.' Starting from a pageant of the triumph of Christ (suggested probably by the carnival *trionfi* of the Florentines), he attempts in four books to show that the Christian faith should be accepted, not only by supernatural revelation, but by the natural light of reason. Mainly Thomist in conception but more modern in form and treatment, it sought to give the Renaissance a volume of Roman Catholic apologetics somewhat analogous to what Aquinas had given the 13th cent. with his *Summa contra Gentiles*.

(iii.) The *De simplicitate Christianæ Vitæ* (1496) was written in Latin and followed by an Italian version by Girolamo Benivieni. Here Savonarola defines the essence of the Christian life as the imitation of the life of Christ and the following of His teaching. Such a life is founded not on imagination or on natural reason alone, but on the grace of God which forms it, and the means by which it is chiefly preserved and increased are the sacraments of Penance and the Eucharist. Divine grace produces simplicity of heart, from which proceeds simplicity in external things, which must, however, be always relative, according to a man's state and position and his duty as a citizen. The end of the Christian life is man's true felicity, which consists in the contemplation and fruition of God. We may regard this work as a kind of scholastic companion to the *De imitatione Christi* of Thomas à Kempis.

(iv.) In 1495 Savonarola published his *Compendium Revelationum*, an account of his principal visions, some of which are related with no small dramatic power, while others read like the mere phantasies of the older mediæval seers. The *Dialogus de veritate prophetica* (1497, after the excommunication) is an apologia, not only for the previous work, but for the writer's whole attitude as a prophet of renovation. Its general purport is that he is convinced that he is neither a deceiver nor himself deceived, but that, over and above what he has derived from the light of reason, from the understanding of the Scriptures, and from the practice of the spiritual life, he has received a direct revelation from God. Among his arguments is the perfectly legitimate one, known to all students of mystical experience: these revelations have given him greater intensity and increased purity in his own spiritual life. Both the *Compendium* and the *Dialogus* appeared first in Latin and were followed by Italian versions not by Savonarola himself.

(v.) The *Trattato circa il reggimento e governo della città di Firenze* was written in Italian, apparently in the latter part of 1497 or (as Villari holds) in the first months of 1498, Savonarola intending to produce a larger work in Latin on the same subject later. It is divided into three parts. In the first he distinguishes between three forms of government: the rule of a single man (*regno*), an oligarchy (*governo degli ottimati*), and a genuine republic of all the people (*governo civile*), the third being the form most suitable for Florence. The second part deals with tyranny, of which the worst is that of a private citizen who has become a tyrant. It includes a striking picture of such a tyrant, an imaginary portrait, but with features manifestly drawn from the darker side of the character of Lorenzo de' Medici. The third part, with great insight and true statesmanship, shows how the new form of republican government in Florence, with its *consiglio grande*, is to be regulated, perfected, and maintained. Such a republic, accompanied by moral reformation and based upon faith in God, will transform the city into an earthly paradise, in which civic liberty and true Christian living will be indissolubly united.

(vi.) *Minor works.*—(*a*) *Poetry.*—The most interesting of Savonarola's poems are the two early canzoni, *De ruina mundi* and *De ruina ecclesiæ*, already mentioned. The imitation of Petrarch, here manifested, becomes devout parody in a few later sonnets and canzoni. Though not by nature a poet, there is true lyrical exaltation in some of his *laude*, hymns sung in procession to replace the profane *canti carnascialeschi* of the Florentines:

[1] Villari and Casanova, *Scelta di prediche e scritti*, p. iv.
[2] *Reggimento . . . della città di Firenze, ad init.*

O anima cieca, *Ben venga amore*, *Jesù sommo conforto*, *Che fai qui core*, and especially that on Christ as King of Florence (*Viva, viva in nostro core, Cristo re duce e signore*).

(*b*) *Philosophical.*—To the early days of Savonarola's priorate at San Marco belong three Latin works: *Compendium philosophiæ naturalis*, *Compendium philosophiæ moralis*, *Compendium logicæ*. Written for the use of friar-students, they are Aristotelian and Thomist in theory and treatment, with occasional traces of Neo-Platonic influence. A little later is the *De divisione, ordine, ac utilitate omnium scientiarum*, with an appended fourth book on the art of poetry. Here he protests against the use of pagan mythology by Christian poets, questions the spiritual utility of religious verse, and draws a curious contrast between the classical poets and the inspired prophets.

(*c*) *Mystical and ascetic.*—A somewhat large number of small religious treatises were composed by Savonarola from 1491 down to a few days before his death. Particularly noteworthy are the *Trattato della orazione mentale* and the *Trattato dell' amore di Jesù Cristo* (both in Italian, 1492); the former inculcates inner worship as more fruitful and more pleasing to God than outward ceremonial; the latter, a work of the highest spirituality, is both practical and mystical, a guide for the devout soul on the mystic way; the examples are usually from the life of the cloister, but they are applicable to all, the book ending in a long series of contemplations moving the soul to the impassioned love of Jesus. Two other tracts (originally in Latin) which also still hold their place in spiritual literature are the commentary on the Lord's Prayer, *Expositio Orationis Dominicæ*, and that on Psalm 79 (80), *Qui regis Israel intende*. The *Solatium itineris mei* (of uncertain date) consists of dialogues between the spirit and the soul, anticipating the matter of the *Trionfo della Croce*. Best known of all (partly from the fact of their having been republished by Luther) are the meditations on the Psalms *Miserere mei Deus* (50–51) and *In te Domine speravi* (30–31), written by Savonarola in prison a few days before his death. The first is purely devotional in treatment, closing in the vision of the future renovation of Zion and the writer's oblation of himself as a victim upon the Cross of Christ. In the second, which was left unfinished, a more personal note is struck; it depicts the struggle between hope and despondency in Savonarola's own soul, ending with the vindication of his revelations as 'divine illuminations' and the utterance of his trust in the Lord and in His name.

No complete collection of Savonarola's letters has yet been edited. Some of them are practically tracts, like those on the exercise of charity and on discretion in prayer, addressed to the friars of his own convent, and the beautiful epistle to the sisters of the third order of St. Dominic. We have also tender letters to his mother and members of his own family, letters of spiritual or political counsel to various persons, and correspondence on affairs of Church and State. Peculiarly interesting among the last is his correspondence with the duke of Ferrara, throwing light not only on the character of the friar himself, but also on that of the conscience-tortured prince whom he addressed, and who besought him 'to be a good ambassador for us in the sight of God.'

LITERATURE.—P. Villari, *La Storia di Girolamo Savonarola e de' suoi tempi*, new ed., 2 vols., Florence, 1887–88, Eng. tr. by Linda Villari, *Life and Times of Savonarola*, 2 vols., London, 1888, 3rd ed. in one vol., 1899; A. Cappelli, *Fra Girolamo Savonarola e notizie intorno al suo tempo*, Modena, 1869; A. Gherardi, *Nuovi documenti e studi intorno a Girolamo Savonarola*², Florence, 1887; P. Luotto, *Il vero Savonarola e il Savonarola di L. Pastor*, do. 1897; P. Villari and E. Casanova, *Scelta di prediche e scritti di Fra Girolamo Savonarola con nuovi documenti intorno alla sua vita*, do. 1898; E. Armstrong, 'Savonarola,' in *The Cambridge Modern History*, i. *The Renaissance*, Cambridge, 1902, pp. 144–189; H. Lucas, *Fra Girolamo Savonarola*², Edinburgh and London, 1906; *Sermoni e prediche di F. Girolamo Savonarola*, Florence, 1845, and Prato, 1846; *Prediche di F. Girolamo Savonarola*, ed. G. Baccini, Florence, 1889; *Il Trionfo della Croce*, ed. Lodovico Ferretti, Siena, 1899; *Trattato circa il reggimento e governo della città di Firenze*, ed. Audin de Rians, Florence, 1847; *Poesie di fra Girolamo Savonarola, tratte dall' autografo*, ed. C. Guasti, do. 1862; E. Perowne, *Savonarola: Meditations on Psalm LI. and Part of Psalm XXXI. in Latin with an English Translation*, London, 1900.

EDMUND G. GARDNER.

SAXONS.—See TEUTONS.

SCAPEGOAT.

Greek (W. J. WOODHOUSE), p. 218.
Semitic (J. D. PRINCE), p. 221.
Teutonic.—See PURIFICATION (Teutonic).

SCAPEGOAT (Greek). — The ideas and the ritual analogous, among the Greeks, to those covered by the term 'scapegoat' are connected chiefly with Athens and the festival of the Thargelia, held on the 6th and 7th of the month Thargelion (May–June).[1] Originally and essentially a festival of thanksgiving for the early harvest, or at any rate agrarian in origin and scope, the Thargelia in historical times included also certain ceremonies of purification and perhaps of expiation, connected with the Pharmakoi (Φαρμακοί)[2] hereafter described. Those ceremonies themselves were perhaps originally agrarian, though their original character had become obscured and in a sense moralized. The two elements, or strains of ritual, whether or not springing from the same agrarian stock, were kept so far distinct as to fall on separate days. On the 6th, after sacrifice of a ram to Demeter Chloe ('of green things') on the Akropolis, the city was 'cleansed' by the procession, expulsion, and perhaps ultimate stoning and burning, of the Pharmakoi; on the 7th cereal offerings of various kinds were brought to Apollo, these θαργήλια, 'firstfruits,' giving their name to the whole series of celebrations.

The earliest connected account of this ritual of cleansing is given by Istros (3rd cent. B.C.). He says:

> 'At Athens they used to lead forth (ἐξῆγον, perhaps a ritual term) two men to be purifications for the city (καθάρσια τῆς πόλεως) at the Thargelia, one for the men, and the other for the women.'[1]

Then he gives a legend of a certain Pharmakos, who, having stolen libation-cups from Apollo's temple, was caught and stoned to death by the

[1] The Thargelia is known only as an Ionian festival; likewise a month Thargelion is not found in the calendars of Dorian or Æolian cities. For a definition of the word see A. Mommsen, *Feste der Stadt Athen*, p. 480. For the dates cf. Plut. *Symp.* viii. 1. 1 f., who says that Plato was born at the time of the Thargelia in Athens, and on the 7th of Thargelion, which was also the birthday of Apollo, according to the Delian legend (Diog. Laert. iii. 2). Sokrates was born on the 6th of Thargelion (the birthday of Artemis), 'when the Athenians purify the city' (*ib.* ii. 44—doubtless alluding to the Pharmakos ceremony).

[2] Φαρμᾱκός in Attic, but φάρμᾰκος in Ionic Greek, as always in Hipponax (cf. frag. *ap.* J. Tzetzes, *Chiliades*, ed. Th. Kiessling, Leipzig, 1826, bk. v. p. 726 f.: φάρμακος ἀχθεὶς ἑπτάκις ῥαπισθείη); see O. Hoffmann, *Die griech. Dialekte*, Göttingen, 1898, iii. 136, 316.

[1] See Harpokrat. *s.v.* Φαρμακός; cf. Hesych. *s.v.* Φαρμακοί· καθαρτήριοι, περικαθαίροντες τὰς πόλεις ἀνὴρ καὶ γυνή, where the last words may be due to misunderstanding. But apparent parallels (*e.g.*, Paus. VII. xix. 2 f.) would suggest that sometimes a woman really may have been among the victims.

'companions of Achilles'; of this the ceremony at the Thargelia was, he says, an 'imitation' (*ἀπομιμήματα*).[1] Hence it would appear that at the Thargelia two unfortunates were actually stoned to death, or that at least a show was made of stoning them, as the concluding act of a ritual procession. An earlier allusion to the Pharmakoi, in the speech, attributed to Lysias, against Andokides for impiety (date, 399 B.C.), contains no direct statement as to their violent death; but this may be due to the speaker's wish to confine himself to ritual terms—which of course may mean much more than they say.[2] Nor is the ultimate fate of the Pharmakoi made any clearer in the account of Helladios (3rd cent. A.D.),[3] who tells us that it was the custom in Athens to lead in procession two Pharmakoi with a view to purification (*πρὸς καθαρμὸν ἀγομένους*), the one intended for the men having a string of black figs about his neck, while the one intended for the women wore white figs; they were also called by the mysterious title *Συβάκχοι*. He adds that this ceremony was meant to ward off plague, and gives a legend of the usual type to account for it.[4]

Only the very latest authorities assert in so many words that the Pharmakoi were slain.[5] Of these latest accounts the most detailed is that given by Tzetzes (A.D. 1150).[6] He says:

'The Pharmakos was a purification of this sort of old. If by God's wrath a visitation fell upon a community—famine or pestilence or other ill—they led forth to sacrifice the ugliest of them all for a cleansing and medicine for the suffering city.[7] And, setting the sacrifice in the fit place, they gave him cheese in his hand, and barley-cake and figs; and, having smitten him seven times on his genitals with squills, wild figs, and other wild things, they finally burned him with fire, with faggots of forest trees, and the ashes they scattered to the sea and the winds, a purification of the suffering city.'

Tzetzes proceeds to quote illustrative extracts from the Iambic poet Hipponax of Ephesos (540 B.C.), who is thus embodied as our earliest authority in our latest. Hipponax writes as he does by way of pointing insult at his enemy Boupalos,[8] expressing the hope that Boupalos may share the fate of a Pharmakos; he is alluding to a familiar ritual in vogue either at Ephesos or at Kolophon. It is quite perverse to say that his phrases are 'all comic or rhetorical curses' invoking 'an obsolete and imaginative punishment' on his victim.[9]

It seems, then, that both in the cities of Ionia and in Athens, at some time or other, there was consummated, either annually or at intervals, a ritual man-slaying of human sacrifice, *i.e.* a public religious rite involving and centring in the taking of human life, apparently by stoning. 'In the history of religion there are many strange contradictions; and the bondage of

1 The term *ἀπομιμήματα* can mean (1) a 'reproduction,' death-scene and all; (2) a 'make-believe' or piece of play-acting. Nothing can fairly be based upon its use here, by asserting the one sense to the exclusion of the other.

2 Lysias, vi. 108: *νῦν οὖν χρὴ νομίζειν τιμωρουμένους καὶ ἀπαλλαττομένους Ἀνδοκίδου τὴν πόλιν καθαίρειν καὶ ἀποδιοπομπεῖσθαι καὶ φαρμακὸν ἀποπέμπειν καὶ ἀλιτηρίου ἀπαλλάττεσθαι, ὡς ἓν τούτων οὗτός ἐστιν.* The speech, though perhaps not by Lysias, is by a contemporary. The passage quoted is described by G. Murray, *Rise of the Greek Epic*², p. 327, as 'comic abuse'!

3 See Phot. *Bibl.* p. 534.

4 Phot. *Bibl.* 279, p. 534, Bekk.: *τὸ δὲ καθάρσιον τοῦτο γοιμικῶν νόσων ἀποτροπιασμὸς ἦν, λαβὸν τὴν ἀρχὴν ἀπὸ Ἀνδρόγεω τοῦ Κρητός, οὗ τεθνηκότος ἐν ταῖς Ἀθήναις παρανόμως τὴν λοιμικὴν ἐνόσησαν οἱ Ἀθηναῖοι νόσον, καὶ ἐκράτει τὸ ἔθος ἀεὶ καθαίρειν τὴν πόλιν τοῖς φαρμακοῖς.*

5 Cf. Suid. ii. 2, p. 1423: *φαρμακοὺς τοὺς δημοσίᾳ τρεφομένους, οἳ ἐκάθαιρον τὰς πόλεις τῷ ἑαυτῶν φόνῳ.*

6 *Chiliad.* v. 726 f.

7 *τῶν πάντων ἀμορφότερον ἦγον ὡς πρὸς θυσίαν | εἰς καθαρμὸν καὶ φάρμακον πόλεως τῆς νοσούσης.* The phrase *ὡς πρὸς θυσίαν* indicates the purpose in the mind; it does not mean 'as if for sacrifice.' During the ceremony a certain special strain was played on the flutes (cf. Hesych. *s.v.* *Κραδίης νόμος· νόμον τινὰ ἐπαυλοῦσι τοῖς ἐκπεμπομένοις φαρμακοῖς, κράδαις καὶ θρίοις ἐπιραβδιζομένοις*).

8 Hipponax, therefore, is the progenitor of the use of the word *φαρμακός* as, like its equivalent *κάθαρμα*, 'offscouring,' a current term of abuse and contempt in Attic Greek; cf. Aristoph. *Ran.* 732: *οἷσιν ἡ πόλις πρὸ τοῦ | οὐδὲ φαρμακοῖσιν εἰκῇ ῥᾳδίως ἐχρήσατ' ἄν*, and *Eq.* 1405. These usages throw no light upon the ritual.

9 Murray, p. 327.

ancient ritual is often stronger than the strongest civilizing instinct of the most progressive race.'[1] It is obvious that the establishment of this as a fact for Athens would gravely affect our general view of Attic culture. To dispute the applicability of the term 'sacrifice' here (as, *e.g.*, Harrison, *Proleg.*² p. 103: 'it was not really a sacrifice in our modern sense at all . . . not a sacrifice in the sense of an offering *made to appease an angry God*') seems to the present writer to be quite beside the mark. Who can say what exactly was the mental attitude of the participants in the ritual? Yet upon that question the definition must ultimately turn. For us the real point is simply this—Was human life annually taken, at Athens, as part of public State ritual? No 'misunderstanding of the gist of the ceremony' (*ib.*) can be invoked to defeat this question of fact or to cloud the issue. Whether the evidence is sufficient in amount and quality to enable us to answer it one way or the other is, of course, an entirely different matter.

That at some time in the history of Attica sacrifice of human victims at the Thargelia was in vogue as an element of the national religious cycle is beyond serious dispute. Whether the practice survived as a periodical rite as late as the 5th cent. B.C. is a question generally answered upon purely subjective grounds by appeal to *a priori* ideas of what is appropriate to Periclean Athens, rather than in the light of the facts of tradition, *i.e.* the extant literary evidence. Consequently, neither this nor the general phenomenon of human sacrifice in Greece at large in historical times is treated very honestly; so that it seems necessary here to review the salient facts.

Recorded instance of the offering of human life in Athens belongs to the time when Epimenides was 'purifying Attica by human blood'[2] after the Kyloneian massacre, and a youth named Kratinos voluntarily gave himself for his country (*ὑπὲρ τῆς θρεψαμένης*); his friend Aristodemos 'also devoted himself to death, and so the calamities of the land were stayed.'[3] Again, just before the battle of Salamis, three Persian prisoners of high rank, nephews of Xerxes himself, were brought to Themistokles, and the prophet Euphrantides 'bade him sacrifice them all to Dionysos Omestes (Cannibal), for so would there be deliverance and victory for Greece. Themistokles was horrified at the prophet's strange and monstrous pronouncement; but, as is generally the case in great crises and times of difficulty, the multitude, pinning its faith to irrational rather than rational methods, invoked the god with one voice, and bringing the captives to the altar insisted upon the sacrifice being consummated as the prophet had directed.'[4]

That 'in the fifth century, such sacrifices, even as a desperate expedient in great danger, revolted Attic feeling, of which we can take Æschylus and Euripides as safe interpreters,'[5] is a dictum somewhat hard to reconcile with the surprising frequency with which Euripides avails himself of just this motive of the bloody sacrifice of a noble youth or maiden—once at least apparently quite gratuitously[6]—and still harder to reconcile with the repeated deliberate and official acts of cold-blooded ferocity which stain the pages of Athenian history during that century.[7] When Plutarch, in his account of the battle of Leuktra, describes the searchings of heart of the leaders of the Theban army (371 B.C.), by reason of the vision of

1 *CGS* iv. 275.

2 Athen. *Deipn.* xiii. 78.

3 Diog. Laert. i. 110 has a somewhat different account: *οἱ δὲ τὴν αἰτίαν εἰπεῖν* (*sc.* Epimenides) *τοῦ λοιμοῦ τὸ Κυλώνειον ἄγος, σημαίνοντα τὴν ἀπαλλαγήν· καὶ διὰ τοῦτο ἀποθανεῖν δύο νεανίας, Κρατῖνον καὶ Κτησίβιον, καὶ λυθῆναι τὴν συμφοράν.* That the sacrifice was voluntary (according to the account given by Athenæus) does not alter its character; theoretically, every victim was supposed to offer itself willingly.

4 Plut. *Themist.* 13, *Arist.* 9, *Pelopid.* 21. This narrative, Plutarch observes, is from Phanias (Phainias) of Lesbos, 'a man not unversed in letters and philosophy.' The general modern attitude towards it is reflected by Grote, who remarks (*Hist. of Greece*, new ed., London, 1884, iv. 479) that 'it is pleasing to find sufficient ground for rejecting it.' The incident is, on the contrary, as well vouched for as almost any detail in Greek history that depends upon purely literary authority. Cf. the burying alive in the Forum Boarium at Rome, after the battle of Cannæ, of a 'Gallus et Galla, Graecus et Graeca' (Livy, xxii. 57), and the sacrifice of 300 prisoners to Zeus Ithomatas by Aristomenes (Clem. Alex. *Protrep.* 36).

5 *CGS* iv. 277.

6 *E.g.*, Makaria (*Herakleid.*); Iphigeneia (*Iph. in Aul.*); Chthonia (*Erechth.*); Polyxena (*Hec.*); Menoikeus (*Phœn.*). It is possible that the sacrifice of Makaria was the poet's own invention, independent of tradition; cf. A. Lang, *The World of Homer*, London, 1910, p. 210: 'This enables him to please an Ionian audience by introducing their favourite incident, the sacrifice of a princess: Attic traditions harp eternally on this un-Homeric horror' (speaking of the poet of the *Cypria*), and p. 211: 'the Ionian author of the *Cypria* cannot deny himself an allusion to human sacrifice'; see also p. 279.

7 *E.g.*, Ægina (Thuc. ii. 27, iv. 57); Skione (*ib.* v. 32); Melos (*ib.* v. 116). The sole example of compunction and mercy, that in regard to Mitylene (*ib.* iii. 36), is dealt with at remarkable length by Thucydides precisely because of its rarity.

Pelopidas, which seemed to point to the sacrifice of an 'auburn virgin' as the price of victory, that will prove nothing for Athens, but at best is evidence only for the culture of Pelopidas himself and certain of his colleagues.[1] In the dialogue *Minos*, attributed to Plato, the speaker declares that human sacrifice is in vogue among barbarians, but is considered 'illegal and unholy' by the Greeks[2]—though he is fain to confess that it still survived on Mt. Lykaion and at Halos in Thessaly.[3] When Æschylus calls human sacrifice *ἄνομος*,[4] or Euripides calls it *οὐχ ὅσιος*,[5] that proves little enough for average Greek sentiment at normal temperature and nothing at all for Greek practice at fever heat. For 'it is a marked feature of the evolution of Greek religion that the lower and more embryonic forms of faith survive through the ages by the side of the higher and more developed.'[6]

It is clear enough that, in the popular conception, the gods were little more than the bestowers of physical and material goods, the guardians of herds, of crops, and of human increase, and that the primary purpose of worship lay in the mere instinct of social preservation. The higher thought which found literary expression moves upon a plane widely removed from the conceptions and religious practices of the people as a whole. In some respects, indeed, the religious history of the time exhibits obvious symptoms of retrogression and a resurgence here and there of what may be called the underlying primeval religious magma; *e.g.*, it is only in the 3rd cent. B.C. that we get the extended use of magic tablets, the so-called *Defixionum Tabellæ*, or leaden plates of spells or curses, by means of which the life of a man's enemy was devoted to destruction by nailing down his name.[7]

We may agree, therefore, with the conclusion that 'such sacrifices may have survived in the Greek world sporadically,[8] or as an expedient in a great crisis, far on into the Hellenistic period,'[9] and even later;[10] but we must repudiate the demand that by one means or another the Athenians must be certificated as having emancipated themselves from such practices a long time in advance of the rest of the Greeks.[11] It is at any rate impossible to pitch upon any particular date as marking the time after which a literal performance of the Pharmakos rite is unthinkable for Athens; certainly such date would not fall within the 5th century B.C. The fate of the six generals who saved Athens at Arginusai (406 B.C.), only to be swept to their doom by the 'burst of mournful and vindictive feeling'[1] following the Apatouria festival, on the part of a people which cried out that it was 'monstrous if the Demos shall not be allowed to do as it likes,' is a measure of what in moments of excitement the Athenian populace was capable of doing.[2]

There is ground for drawing a distinction between what may be called the normal annual ritual of the Pharmakos and exceptional occasions of its use. Neglect or ignorance of this distinction has affected the ancient accounts, as is apparent in the two versions of the scapegoat ritual in use at Massilia (a colony of Phokaia). According to Lactantius, a pauper was induced to 'sell' himself for the purpose, and, having been fed at public cost a full year upon specially selected diet, was, on a great day, conducted through the town and finally stoned to death by the people, outside the walls.[3] The account of Servius, copied from Petronius, represents the ceremony, not as an annual lustration, but as exceptionally used in time of plague.[4] So Tzetzes, whether it be the Athenian rite that he has in mind or only that of the Ionian cities, speaks of it as occasional and as applied in times of plague, famine, or other visitation.[5] Similarly the schol. on Aristoph. *Eq.* 1136 says:

> 'The Athenians used to feed up certain very ill-favoured and worthless creatures, and in time of national calamity—pestilence, I mean, or such like—used to sacrifice them, by way of getting cleansed from the defilement.'[6]

It seems that the divergence here noted may be best explained by supposing that, apart from the regular annual purification, extraordinary occasions of public calamity, especially of plague or famine, may have led to repetitions of the ceremony or to its performance at the due date with special solemnity—that is to say, with a reversion for the nonce to the full primitive savage ritual which in normal times was replaced by a fiction or simulation, as is so frequent in the history of religious practice.[7] Such recrudescence of primitive barbarism is a familiar phenomenon.[8]

1 Plut. *Pelop.* 21; Polyæn. ii. 3. 8. The solution of the dilemma by the apparition of the mare and chestnut filly was, of course, a happy thought on the part of Pelopidas and his prophet Theokritos. The arguments purporting to be those of the Theban war council are an invention of the amiable and humane Plutarch himself (though Murray, p. 331, seems to regard the narrative as an authentic record of what actually passed). The story is rather different in Plut. *Amat. Narr.* 3.

2 See § 315 C: *ἡμῖν μὲν οὐ νόμος ἐστὶν ἀνθρώπους θύειν, ἀλλ' ἀνόσιον . . . καὶ μὴ ὅτι βάρβαροι ἄνθρωποι ἡμῶν ἄλλοις νόμοις χρῶνται, ἀλλὰ καὶ οἱ ἐν τῇ Λυκαίᾳ οὗτοι καὶ οἱ τοῦ Ἀθάμαντος ἔκγονοι οἵας θυσίας θύουσιν Ἕλληνες ὄντες.* Cf. Plut. *Quæst. gr.* 38 (Orchomenos).

3 Cf. Plut. *Quæst. gr.* 39; Paus. VIII. xxxviii. 7: *πολυπραγμονῆσαι δὲ οὔ μοι τὰ ἐς τὴν θυσίαν ἡδὺ ἦν, ἐχέτω δὲ ὡς ἔχει καὶ ὡς ἔσχεν ἐξ ἀρχῆς*—the reluctance of Pausanias to speak of it seems to indicate that the sacrifice was still in vogue in his day (*c.* A.D. 170). For Halos see Herod. vii. 197, where note the expression *καθαρμὸν τῆς χώρης ποιευμένων Ἀχαιῶν ἐκ θεοπροπίου Ἀθάμαντα τὸν Αἰόλου καὶ μελλόντων μινθύειν.* It seems fairly clear (though Farnell [*CGS* i. 94] is doubtful) that this sacrifice, without any pretence, was in vogue in 480 B.C., or at any rate that Herodotus thought so.

4 *Agam.* 158.

5 *Iph. in Taur.* 466.

6 L. R. Farnell, *The Higher Aspects of Greek Religion*, London, 1912, p. 5.

7 For specimens see E. S. Roberts and E. A. Gardner, *Introd. to Greek Epigraphy*, Cambridge, 1887–1905, ii. 520. The oldest and most numerous of these plates come from Attica. The Greek term from these *Diræ* is *κατάδεσμοι.*

8 Unless he is simply copying some older authority, we learn from Ovid that in his time the old rite in all its naked horror was still annually observed at Abdera (a colony of Klazomenai)—*Ibis*, 467: 'Aut te devoveat certis Abdera diebus, | Saxaque devotum grandine plura petant,' on which the schol. says: 'Mos erat in Abdera civitate singulis annis homines immolari pro peccatis civium, sed prius septem diebus excommunicari, ut sic omnium peccata solus haberet.' Cf. Strabo, p. 683 (of a promontory near Kourion in Cyprus): *ἀφ' ἧς ῥίπτουσι τοὺς ἁψαμένους τοῦ βωμοῦ τοῦ Ἀπόλλωνος*—apparently a similar ritual then still in use.

9 *CGS* iv. 277.

10 Cf. Lactant. *de Div. Inst.* i. 21: 'apud Cyprios humanam hostiam Jovi Teucrus immolavit, idque sacrificium posteris tradidit, quod est nuper, Hadriano imperante, sublatum'; and cf. Paus. VIII. xxxviii. 7 (quoted above).

11 Cf. E. Rohde, *Psyche*[4], Tübingen, 1907, ii. 78, note 2: 'Gegen die bestimmten Zeugnisse können Erwägungen allgemeiner Art nichts ausrichten'; cf. Murray, p. 31: 'Practices that to us seem like the scarce credible stories of a remote past were to the fifth-century Athenian possibilities and even dangers.'

1 Grote, vii. 437.

2 Xen. *Hell.* i. 7. 12: *τὸ δὲ πλῆθος ἐβόα δεινὸν εἶναι, εἰ μή τις ἐάσει τὸν δῆμον πράττειν ὃ ἂν βούληται.* Cf. Grote, vii. 449: '"Ces pères de famille sont capables de tout"—the same words, understood in a far more awful sense . . . sum up the moral of this melancholy proceeding at Athens.'

3 Lact. Plac. *Comment. in Stat. Theb.* x. 793: 'Lustrare civitatem humana hostia Gallicus mos est. Nam aliquis de egentissimis proiiciebatur praemiis, ut se ad hoc venderet, qui anno toto publicis sumptibus alebatur purioribus cibis, denique certo et sollemni die per totam civitatem ductus ex urbe extra pomeria saxis occidebatur a populo.'

4 Serv. on Verg. *Æn.* iii. 57: 'Nam Massilienses quotiens pestilentia laborabant, unus se ex pauperibus offerebat alendus anno integro publicis sumptibus et purioribus cibis. Hic postea ornatus verbenis et vestibus sacris circumducebatur per totam civitatem cum execrationibus, ut in ipsum reciderent mala totius civitatis, et sic proiiciebatur (praecipitabatur, *Stephanus*): hoc autem in Petronio lectum est.' The terms *quotiens* and *anno integro* are clearly mutually irreconcilable.

5 *Chiliad.* v. 726 f.: *εἶτ' οὖν λιμὸς εἴτε λοιμὸς εἴτε καὶ βλάβος ἄλλο.*

6 *ἔτρεφον γάρ τινας Ἀθηναῖοι λίαν ἀγεννεῖς καὶ ἀχρήστους, καὶ ἐν καιρῷ συμφορᾶς τινος ἐπελθούσης τῇ πόλει, λοιμοῦ λέγω ἢ τοιούτου τινός, ἔθυον τούτους ἕνεκα τοῦ καθαρθῆναι τοῦ μιάσματος· οὓς καὶ ἐπωνόμαζον καθάρματα.*

7 Cf. Serv. on Verg. *Æn.* ii. 116: 'sciendum in sacris simulata pro veris accipi.'

8 Cf. *CGS* ii. 442: 'Where the view prevailed that the animal took the place of the human life, we can believe that in times of great peril the latter might actually be offered as the more real and acceptable sacrifice'; G. Murray, *Four Stages of Greek Religion*, New York, 1912, p. 52: 'Like most manifestations of early religion, they (the Oracles) throve upon human terror: the more blind the terror the stronger became their hold. In such an atmosphere the lowest and most beastlike elements of humanity tended to come to the front; and religion no doubt as a rule joined with them in drowning the voice of criticism and of civilization, that is, of reason and of mercy. When really frightened the oracle generally fell back on some remedy full of pain and blood.' Cf Plut. *Quæst. gr.* 26: the Ainaines, when they lived in the Cirrhaian plain, stoned their king to death in time of drought, in obedience to an oracle, no doubt that of Delphi.

This would help to explain the peculiarity that the Athenian ceremony is never described as one belonging to a remote prehistoric past, as a piece of barbarism later eradicated, or at least ameliorated, under conditions which formed the matter of a sacred story, such as that told about Artemis Triklaria at Patrai,[1] or Artemis of Brauron, upon which Euripides wrote a play. We could still imagine that such amelioration, as the outcome of a slowly developing sense of humanity and justice, did come about as a matter of use and wont under normal circumstances. It is to be remembered, however, that the Greek communities —and this is true of them not merely in the political sense— were ever in a condition of unstable equilibrium. How easily these old horrors could blaze up afresh is well illustrated by the way in which Apollonios of Tyana hounded on the populace of Ephesos to stone to death an old blear-eyed beggar, making out that he was the embodied plague-demon which vexed the city.[2] Even in Athens in the 5th cent. B.C. it was still possible seriously to propose the expulsion of the foremost man in the State, on account of his descent from one who had been guilty of sacrilege nearly two hundred years previously.[3]

Some have thought to save, as it were, the credit of Athens by imagining that only criminals already condemned to death for their crimes were taken for the fatal rôle of the Pharmakos.[4] For this idea, as applied to Athens, there is not a particle of evidence in the tradition, which insists, characteristically, not upon the moral depravity, but upon the physical deformity, of the victims;[5] they are chosen not for their badness, but for their ugliness.

That in some places a condemned criminal was used as a Pharmakos is very true. Thus in Rhodes annually, on the 6th of their month Metageitnion, a man was sacrificed to Kronos. A criminal who had been publicly condemned to death was reserved for the anniversary of the Kronia. Then he was led outside the gates, in face of the image of Aristoboule, and was filled with wine and so slain.[6] A further development is found at Leukas. From the famous crag Leukatas the Leukadians used annually to hurl a criminal into the sea as a scapegoat. To break his fall, he was fastened about with feathers and live birds, and small boats waited below in order to pick him up, if he survived, and to carry him beyond the frontier. This took place at the time of a sacrifice to Apollo, who had a sanctuary at that spot. This was a mitigation, probably, of an earlier custom of actually drowning the scapegoat.[7] An example of still further developed amelioration of the rite was the ceremony annually performed at Chaironeia both by the chief magistrate at the Town Hall and by each head of a family in his own house, and once duly performed by Plutarch himself, who describes it.[8] It was called the 'expulsion of hunger' (βουλίμου ἐξέλασις), and Plutarch speaks of it as an 'ancestral sacrifice' (θυσία πάτριος). A slave was ceremonially beaten with rods of *agnus castus* and then driven forth with the formula: 'Out with hunger, in with wealth and health.' At Delphi the ritual, recurring every ninth year, which Plutarch characterizes as a 'sacrifice with admixture of purification,'[9] connected with the use of an image or puppet (παιδικὸν εἴδωλον), called after Charila, is an example of the Pharmakos ceremony in its most attenuated form.

1 Paus. VII. xix. 2. 2 Philostr. *Vit. Ap.* iv. 10 f.

3 Thuc. i. 127; cf. Aristoph. *Eq.* 445.

4 Cf. *CGS* ii. 439: 'Two human καθάρματα, being probably criminals, were sacrificed in a sort of religious execution.' This was written in 1896. In 1907 (*ib.* iv. 276) Farnell rightly sees that 'we cannot apologize for them [the contemporaries of Perikles and Demosthenes] by saying that, like the Rhodians, they reserved their worst criminals for this fate and merely condemned to a religious death those who deserved a secular.' See also Harrison, p. 104: 'Civilized Athens had its barathron: why should civilized Athens shrink from annually utilizing two vicious and already condemned criminals to "purify the city"?'

5 Cf. Tzetzes, *Chiliad.* v. 726 f.: τῶν μάντων ἀμορφότερον ἦγον; schol. in Aristoph. *Eq.* 1136: λίαν ἀγεννεῖς καὶ ἀχρήστους; schol. in Aristoph. *Ran.* 733: τοὺς φαύλους καὶ παρὰ τῆς φύσεως ἐπιβουλευομένους, 'victims of nature's malice.' At Massilia the scapegoat, being 'aliquis de egentissimis (unus ex pauperibus),' was clearly not necessarily a condemned criminal.

6 Porphyr. *de Abstin.* ii. 54: ἐθύετο . . . ἄνθρωπος τῷ Κρόνῳ. ὃ δὴ ἐπὶ πολὺ κρατῆσαν ἔθος μετεβλήθη· ἕνα γὰρ τῶν ἐπὶ θανάτῳ δημοσίᾳ κατακριθέντων μέχρι μὲν τῶν Κρονίων συνεῖχον, ἐνστάσης δὲ τῆς ἑορτῆς προαγαγόντες τὸν ἄνθρωπον ἔξω πυλῶν ἄντικρυς τοῦ Ἀριστοβούλης ἕδους, οἴνου ποτίσαντες ἔσφαττον. Aristoboule is probably Artemis. What happened if there was no convenient criminal? Were there Rhodian analogues to the argument used to Athenian juries in order to secure a conviction? (cf. Aristoph. *Eq.* 1359 f.; Lysias, xxvii. 1).

7 Strabo, p. 452: ἦν δὲ καὶ πάτριον τοῖς Λευκαδίοις κατ' ἐνιαυτὸν ἐν τῇ θυσίᾳ τοῦ Ἀπόλλωνος ἀπὸ τῆς σκοπῆς ῥιπτεισθαί τινα τῶν ἐν αἰτίαις ὄντων ἀποτροπῆς χάριν, κτλ. Cf. the custom elsewhere of throwing every year a young man into the sea, with the words, 'Be thou our offscouring' (περίψημα ἡμῶν γενοῦ); see Suid. and Phot. *s.v.* Περίψημα (locality not given). The word περίψημα occurs in 1 Co 4[13]: ὡς περικαθάρματα τοῦ κόσμου ἐγενήθημεν, πάντων περίψημα, where it is rendered 'offscouring' in AV and RV.

8 *Quæst. Conv.* vi. 8.

9 *Quæst. gr.* 12: μεμιγμένην τινὰ καθαρμῷ θυσίαν.

The significance of the Pharmakos ritual was probably not so much that of vicarious piacular sacrifice—of expiation or pardon for the sins of the community at the price of a human life—as the more primitive belief that the Pharmakos was a real sin-carrier, whose death purged the community of its sins and misfortunes by virtue of magical transference in a literal and quasi-mechanical way. Combined with this, however, in the inconsistent and illogical manner characteristic of religious thought and procedure, is a function of the Pharmakos in which he acts as an incarnation of the vegetation-power. Hence he is decked out with fruits of the soil, and chastised with stimulating herbs and branches, and finally put to death in order to impregnate the soil with his magically fructifying ashes.[1] Possibly the sacrifice to Demeter Chloe with which the Thargelia opened at Athens on the 6th of the month indicates that originally the Pharmakos incarnated the primitive earth-goddess, who once demanded human victims in Greece, and to whom the cereal offerings of the Thargelia perhaps belonged before Apollo came on the scene. It has also been suggested that the human victims at the Thargelia more particularly masqueraded as spirits of fig-trees, and that the strings of black and white figs hung about their necks were an imitation of the process of caprification or artificial fertilization of cultivated fig-trees by hanging strips of wild figs among the branches.[2] The ceremony, as regards this detail, was therefore one of imitative magic, to assist the fertilization of the fig-trees.[3]

LITERATURE.—V. Stengel, 'Die angeblichen Menschenopfer bei der Thargelien in Athen,' in *Hermes*, xxii. [1887] 86 f.; J. Toepffer, 'Thargeliengebräuche,' in *Rheinisches Museum*, xliii. [1888] 142 f. (repub. in *Beiträge zur griech. Altertumswiss.*, Berlin, 1897); A. Mommsen, *Feste der Stadt Athen im Altertum*, Leipzig, 1898; M. P. Nilsson, *Griech. Feste von religiöser Bedeutung*, do. 1906; *CGS*, Oxford, 1907, iv.; J. E. Harrison, *Prolegomena to the Study of Greek Religion*², Cambridge, 1908; G. Murray, *The Rise of the Greek Epic*², Oxford, 1911 (Appendix A); *GB*³, pt. vi. *The Scapegoat*, London, 1913; F. Schwenn, *Die Menschenopfer bei den Griechen und Römern* (*RVV*, vol. xv. pt. 3), Giessen, n.d. [1918?].

W. J. WOODHOUSE.

SCAPEGOAT (Semitic).—In the Pentateuch (Lv 16) it is stated that on the day of expiation Aaron, the high-priest, was commanded to enter the sanctuary after purifying himself and putting on the sacred vestments. Two goats were chosen as a sacrifice for sin, a young bullock for a sin-offering, and a ram for a burnt-offering. The two goats were placed before Jahweh at the entrance of the tabernacle. The high-priest cast lots upon the two goats, one lot for Jahweh and the other for the scapegoat, which was allotted to the demon Azazel (*q.v.*). The goat upon which the lot for Jahweh fell was sacrificed at once as a sin-offering along with the bullock and the ram. The high-priest, placing his hands on the head of the living goat, confessed over it all the sins of Israel, which were in this manner transmitted to the animal. A special messenger was deputed to lead away the goat into the desert, where it was abandoned to the demon Azazel. Both the high-priest and the

1 Hence Farnell (*CGS* iv. 281) would explain the ætiological legend given by Istros, of the stealing of Apollo's cups by Pharmakos and his atoning, as an indication that the Pharmakos (perhaps in some of the Ionian cities) was, previous to his immolation, treated as an incarnation of the god and carried his emblems. The story of the ugly Æsop, who was accused of stealing temple treasures at Delphi, and was thrown from the rock Hyampeia (Plut. 557b), will probably be a reflex of the same ritual.

2 'Though it must be confessed,' remarks Frazer, *GB*³, pt. vi. *The Scapegoat*, p. 259, 'that the ancient writers who describe the Greek custom appear to regard it merely as a purification of the city and not at all as a mode of fertilizing fig-trees.'

3 See W. R. Paton, 'The φαρμακοί and the Story of the Fall,' in *RA*, 4th ser., ix. [1907] 55 f.

person whose duty it was to lead away the scapegoat were enjoined to purify themselves after the rite of transmission. It is interesting to note in this connexion that a similar usage was followed with birds at the purification of a leper. If the leprous pustules had disappeared from the patient, the priest took two birds, one of which was killed and its blood poured into a vessel over running water. The patient was sprinkled with the blood of the dead bird. The living bird, however, after being soaked in the blood of the dead bird and in this manner infected with the disease, was set at liberty 'out of the city into the open fields' (Lv 14[53]).

It should be noted in connexion with the symptoms of leprosy that the disappearance of the pustules is very common at the beginning of the malady. The initial hyperæmia tends to diminish and to remain latent until the ultimate attack of the leprous fever—sometimes a year later than the first appearance—when the pustules reappear more violently than in the first stages of the disease. It is probable that this fact was not known to the ancient Hebrews, and that they regarded the frequently long disappearance of the leprous symptoms as the result of the rites just described. The subsequent development of the disease was no doubt looked upon as a fresh attack.

These species of transmission rites were not confined to the Semitic peoples. The western Irish still believe, *e.g.*, that whooping-cough may be diverted by passing the patient three times under the belly of an ass, and that certain fevers may be cured by carrying the patient three times round a special kind of tree. In these instances, of course, the triple repetition is due to the belief in the Trinity, in whose name the act is always done.[1] The disease in each case is thought to be transmitted from the patient to the ass or to the tree. In the same way, children with measles or scarlet fever are often given a kitten to play with, in the belief that the animal will contract the malady and thus remove it from the sufferer.

That sin and disease were closely allied in the minds of the ancient Semites has been fully shown in the artt. GOD (Assyro-Babylonian) and DISEASE AND MEDICINE (Assyro-Babylonian), so that the parallel seems to be perfect between the Semitic ideas of transmission and those of the Celtic Irish. Such a natural primitive conception, however, does not imply any connexion between peoples of such different origin who may have held it.

A highly interesting question as to the existence of a rite similar to that of the scapegoat among the Assyro-Babylonians has been discussed technically by the present writer in several articles.[2]

The following inscription seems to indicate a belief in a species of transmission rite:

'Ea, the king of the abyss, speaks to his son Marduk: Go my son Marduk. The plague has seized the man. Take thou the *máš-ḡul-dub-ba*. Place its head upon his head. Chase the plague from the presence of the king, the son of his god [=the patient]. May his saliva run freely in his mouth. May this king be clean; may he be without spot. The man shall no longer know the plague. May it go forth from his body.'[3]

The expression *máš-ḡul-dub-ba* really means 'the horned animal which alleviates pain' and seems to point to a belief that a living scapegoat was actually employed in very much the same manner as appears in the Hebrew sources. The idea that the *máš-ḡul-dub-ba* was a living animal has been called in question by Fossey,[4] who adduces certain passages which we may now cite.

In Zimmern's *Beiträge zur Kenntnis der bab. Religion*, Leipzig, 1896–1901, p. 122, the following interesting passage appears:

'Then with clean purifications thou shalt purify the king. As soon as thou shalt have finished the purification, thou shalt make them [the patients] go forth out of the door. Then with the *máš-xulduppû*, with the *máš-gibillû*, with the sheep of life, with the copper of strength, with the skin of the great bull, and with seed-corn thou shalt cleanse the palace [=the house].'

Here it will be noted that the patients are brought out of the house and the dwelling is purified by various means, among which the *máš-xulduppû* and the *lu-ti-la*, 'the sheep of life,' or perhaps 'the living sheep,' play the principal part. It is certainly significant to find the *máš*, or animal, of the torch mentioned among these means of purification, as flame was a recognized purifying agent. We are forced to conclude, owing to the presence of the Sumerian word *máš*, 'a horned animal,' that all these words were originally names of certain kinds of horned animals which were primitively used in a ceremony like that of the Hebrew scapegoat. When, therefore, we read the phrase cited above, 'place its head [that of the *máš-ḡul-dub-ba*] on the patient's head,' the conclusion seems unavoidable that this was distinctly a ceremony of transmission. A strikingly analogous passage in IV. Rawl. 26, no. 6, 22 ff. is too significant to be ignored:

'The *uriçu* [a sort of horned animal] has been given for his [the patient's] life; the head of the *uriçu* has been given for the head of the man; the neck of the *uriçu* has been given for the neck of the man; the breast of the *uriçu* has been given for the breast of the man.'

This passage plainly shows that an *uriçu* (probably =*máš*, 'horned animal') might serve vicariously for the life of a man, and the parts of the animal are enumerated one by one with the corresponding parts of the man.

An important point in this connexion is now to be observed. Fossey compared the Sumerian word *máš-ḡul-dub-ba* (=Semitic *máš-xulduppû*) with *giš-xul-dub-ba*, which occurs in another passage, undoubtedly as the name of an implement probably used in a purification ceremony. This *giš-xul-dub-ba* is not the *máš-ḡul-dub-ba*, although it may have been used in the same manner. A flood of light is thrown upon the difficulty by the passage in IV. Rawl. 21, no. 1, 28–28, an inscription giving directions how to avert evil, which reads: 'in order to avert anything evil, the *máš-ḡul-dub-ba* is set up in the door-way.' Here is the key to the whole difficulty. In this passage and in the passage just cited from Zimmern the *máš-ḡul-dub-ba* is an image of the original horned animal which alleviates pain and is probably identical with the *uriçu* whose parts were to correspond with the parts of the patient and whose life was given for the life of the man. Zimmern's 'living sheep' or 'sheep of life' was probably an image of the same sort.

In other words, the appearance of the *máš-ḡul-dub-ba* in Zimmern as a probable implement of purification is merely a development of the original force of the *máš-ḡul-dub-ba* seen in the passage in Haupt, no. 12, p. 30 ff. In the primitive rite the horned animal was a live creature endowed with malevolent powers. It might, however, by the use of the proper incantations, be made to carry away disease. This was done, in the one instance, by driving away the evil influence from the patient and, in the other case, by first bringing it into contact with the patient and then driving it away. It may be supposed that in the course of time the practical difficulty of procuring a live animal for the ceremony gave rise to the use of an image of the original animal which was employed ritually in the manner just indicated. In short, the horned animals were malevolent in so far as they represented disease, but might be turned to a benevolent use by the power of the incantation for their expulsion. Hence the pregnant expression arose, *máš-ḡul-dub-ba*='the horned animal which assuages evil or pain.'

A further instance of transmission among the Babylonians is seen in the following passage:

[1] The usual formula after the invocation is: 'Good-morning to you boar-tree bush, Good-morning to you. I come for to leave the heart-fever with you.'

[2] *JAOS* xxi. [1900] 1–22; *JA*, July 1903, pp. 133–156, with contradictory notes by C. Fossey, the reply to which is published in *AJSL* xx. [1904] 173–181.

[3] Paul Haupt, *Akkadische und Sumerische Keilschrifttexte*, Leipzig, 1881–82, no. 12, lines 34–43.

[4] *JA*, July 1903, p. 143, note 2.

'Place the gazelle which ranges the plain before Shamash [the sun-god]. Give the bow to the king, the son of his god [the patient]. When he shall go forth from the house of purification, let him kill the gazelle before Shamash. When the king draws the bow against the gazelle, may the fatal affliction . . . the impure malady, the sorcery, everything which causes evil, every ailment which at the rising of the sun was in his body go far forth from his body like the flight of the arrow.'[1]

To sum up on this point, the facts relating to the transmission rites among the Assyro-Babylonians are as follows. The inscriptions in Haupt, no. 12, deal most plainly with the destruction and expulsion of certain horned creatures which are equivalent in effect to the evil demons. They are sent forth to an unclean place. Then follows the inscription of the *máš-ǵul-dub-ba*, which is to be sought by Marduk and its head placed against the head of the patient, after which the patient is to recover. Then follows the reverse, describing the bowshot which shoots away into the gazelle the malady of the patient. How are we to conclude otherwise than to suppose that the Babylonians, like the Hebrews, had a well-defined transmission ceremony similar to the Biblical rite described above?

LITERATURE.—See the works cited in the footnotes.

J. DYNELEY PRINCE.

SCARABS.—The scarab is one of the most characteristic productions of ancient Egyptian art, and one of the best-known. Scarabs take much the same place in the art of Egypt as coins do in the art of Greece or as the *netsukè* and the *tsuba* (sword-guard) do in that of Japan. We cannot, it is true, claim exactly the same specialized position for the study of the scarab as we can for that of the coin, but nevertheless the two are analogous. Egypt had no coinage, and her artists found in the fabrication and decoration of the scarab the same scope for the exercise of their ingenuity and felicity of design in 'small art' as the Greek and the modern do in their coin or the Japanese in his *netsukè* and *tsuba*. The scarab has a further, a religious, interest. Its religious signification makes it as important a relic of Egyptian religion as it is of art. And, like the coin, though not to so great an extent, it has a historical value.

Stated simply, the scarab is, properly speaking, a seal made in the form of a certain religious amulet, the figure of the sacred beetle, or *scarabæus*, the *Ateuchus sacer*,[2] as entomologists call it. But by no means every scarab was a seal. It was only during the second period of the development of the scarab that most specimens were intended to be seals as well as amulets. Later it became, as it was originally, almost invariably an amulet only, but still retained in most cases the old seal-base, with its inscription or design like that of a seal. Later still images of the insect pure and simple, without inscription, became common again.

Egyptian seals were not from the beginning made in the form of scarabs. It was not till the beginning of the XIIth dynasty that the fashion became general of having one's seal, in the form of the sacred beetle, strung on a ring, string, or necklace. The oldest Egyptian seals were generally, though not invariably, cylinders, meant to roll over the sealing-clay like their congeners in Babylonia and Assyria. Later, under the VIth dynasty, the 'button-seal,' a form apparently introduced from the Ægean islands and Crete, became popular, and from this was developed the scarab-seal. Actual scarab-beetles had been occasionally buried with the dead as early as the pre-dynastic period.[3] Little uninscribed images of the scarab, usually made of blue glazed steatite or of ivory, had been buried with the dead under or even before the VIth dynasty, and doubtless were worn by the living as amulets. Under the VIth dynasty the seal, in itself in some sort an amulet, since it bore the name of the owner—and all students of simple magic know how magically important his name is in the mind of primitive man[1]—became combined with this particular amulet, at any rate in the case of kings. Under the XIIth dynasty private persons chose to have their seals made in the form of the little scarab-amulet instead of the simple 'button' or rosette. Its form was convenient for the purpose: the oval base on which it stood was well-adapted for seal-design; and the name derived added protection from being inscribed on the sacred object.

1. Popularity of the scarab.—Under the XIIth dynasty most scarab-inscriptions are names and titles, whether royal or private, and the scarabs are real seals, of hard stone or faience, intended for use as such. When no inscription appears, the base is usually adorned with a spiral or other linear design of Ægean origin, often combined with plant motives and very beautiful, which was very soon used as a seal too for ordinary purposes when no name was necessary. These seals were worn by the living and buried with the dead. Towards the end of the Middle Kingdom, however, more purely amuletic scarabs began to appear. They bore designs of religious or semi-religious import, lucky symbols, etc., and one can see that they could be regarded as amulets only, though they were still used on occasion as seals. If amulets pure and simple, it was evident that their material need not always be so durable as that necessary for real seals; so faience and a composition ware became more common than hard stone for their fabrication under the XVIIIth dynasty. This was the time of the great manufacture of the scarab. So far it had been, if not exactly an object *de luxe* intended for the use only of kings and great persons, at any rate not a common object in the possession of everybody. But under the XVIIIth dynasty it was vulgarized. Millions of cheap scarabs were made of blue and green glazed steatite or faience, which any *fellah* could string round his neck and use as a seal, if it did not break in the process. We admire their colours now, when these have survived the centuries, and give high prices for them, but to the XVIIIth dynasty Egyptian they were the commonest objects, and probably of no more value than picture postcards are now. The present writer uses the word advisedly. The scarab was now the picture postcard of the ordinary Egyptian. If he went to some well-known shrine to pray, to some religious fair, or *molid*, as his modern descendant would call it, he brought away his cheap memento, his picture postcard, his 'present from Margate,' in the shape of a scarab. Did he go to Karnak, he took home a scarab with an inscription on it—'Good is the coming to Epetesut'—which may almost literally be translated as 'A present from Karnak.' The virtues of the god of Karnak and Thebes are celebrated on thousands of scarabs: 'Amen is strong to help,' 'Fear not; Amen is near,' and so forth. Nor did Ptaḥ of Memphis yield in popularity to Amen, at any rate in the north; and a little later, under the XIXth dynasty, when Egyptian snobbery exalted the Memphite god, to whom the new northern dynasty was more especially bound to pray, the pilgrim could buy at Memphis as good a scarab, advertising the virtues of Ptaḥ, as he could one advertising Amen at the rival shrines of Thebes. Most of the scarabs that we have were the property of the 'man in the street.' Pos-

[1] *JA*, July 1903, p. 143, lines 14–21.

[2] See art. CHARMS AND AMULETS (Egyptian), vol. iii. p. 432a. Scarabs were often made in the likeness of other allied species, such as *Sc. venerabilis*, and other genera such as *Catharsius*, *Copris*, *Gymnopleurus*, and *Hypselogenia* (Petrie, *Scarabs*, p. 5).

[3] Petrie, p. 2.

[1] See art. NAMES (Primitive).

sessors of fine blue scarabs with the name of Thothmes III. or Rameses II. on them are wont to believe that their treasures were once the property of the kings whose names they bear. What millions they must have possessed! A few of the scarabs in our chief collections may have been (some, from the circumstances of their discovery, are known to have been) actual royal possessions, but the old Egyptian liked to have his king's name on his scarab as much as anything else, just as the modern British person likes to have pictures of the King and Queen in his home. But, just as Queen Victoria's was a name universally venerated, and her portrait appeared among the possessions of high and low, so with the Egyptian was the name of Thothmes III. one to conjure with, and that speaking literally. Its magical virtue was obvious, and so it appeared on scarabs innumerable; it was the most popular of all scarab-inscriptions, and that not only during the king's own long life, but for centuries after his death, so that it is now the commonest of scarab legends. Almost half the royal scarabs in existence are of Thothmes III. and of one or two later kinglets who aped his throne-name 'Men-kheper-ra.' Scarabs bearing this name alone are as many in number as all those bearing the names of all the rest of the kings of Egypt. And Phœnicians, understanding nothing of its meaning, went on putting his name on the imitation scarabs which they made for the Greek and Italian market a thousand years after his death.

2. Decadence and disappearance.—It is impossible to say much more of the popular scarab of the XVIIIth and XIXth dynasties, to recount any of the innumerable variations of inscription and design that are found on them: wishes for children, for a good wife or husband, glorification of gods, scenes of the king, as leader of his people, offering to the gods, and so on *ad infinitum*; the most cursory examination of any good collection in one of our museums will show their infinite variety. One of the most characteristic forms of the later XVIIIth dynasty is a picture postcard pure and simple, or rather a cheap popular medal. Thousands of this peculiar type were no doubt made; now we possess but a few specimens, which are regarded as very valuable varieties. We refer to the large scarabs of Amenhetep III., with their proclamatory inscriptions announcing his marriage with Queen Tii, his slaying of lions and wild bulls, etc. These were issued and were acquired by his loyal subjects just as a popular medal commemorating a royal marriage might be now. But all scarabs were not of course of this popular cast, and we have many beautiful specimens which were undoubtedly made for persons of taste and state, even for the royal household itself. Still, even in the best of them, the old beauty of the true seal-scarabs of the XIIth dynasty has gone, and, when we come to certain cheap scarabs of the XIXth dynasty, which were cast in a mould instead of cut or modelled by hand, we see decadence fully setting in, from which not even the manufacture of some really very pretty specimens by the archaizing artists of the XXVth and XXVIth dynasties can save the scarab. Then the Mediterranean commerce of the 7th and 6th centuries B.C. took the scarab abroad into all lands: Naukratite Greeks made it in its cheapest form, and Phœnicians peddled it to Sardinian savages; the Greek artists took it up and made very beautiful Greek scarabs, with purely Greek intaglio designs, in hard stone, to be used as seals; Etruscans acquired them as part of their borrowed raiment of civilization; like Greek vases, they were 'the proper thing' to possess, and 'all the best people' in Etruria used them. And then, whether because they had become too common and the outer foreigners thought too much of them or not, they suddenly lost their charm for their originators. With the coming of the Persian the seal-scarab absolutely disappears. Under the Ptolemies stone scarabs are still made, but without the characteristic seal-base; they are amulets only, and, as one of the quaint conceits of the beast-worshippers of the Nile, they end grotesquely and pitifully under the Romans. The scarab is practically no longer made at all,[1] and the figure of the *scarabæus* appears only in company with absurd cock-headed demons wearing Roman uniform on Gnostic gems or furnishes a telling image either of reprobation or of comparison to early Christian apologists. For the religious importance of the *scarabæus* was as great as, or greater than, ever, and to this we must now return.

3. Religious importance.—What was the religious idea of the scarab? The scarab-beetle, *Ateuchus sacer*, was the emblem of Khepera or Kheperi, the self-begetting, self-creating sun-god, originally a primeval Nilote deity distinct from the sun-god, Ra, or Rē, of Heliopolis.[2] The name Kheperi means 'he who becomes (or creates),' from the verb *khoper*, 'to become (or create),' written with the scarab hieroglyph. The insect itself was called *khepror*, a form of the same word, which seems to have had also the meaning of 'rolling,' 'the roller.' The peculiar habits of the scarab-beetle seemed (as Apion, quoted by Pliny, said) to the indigenous Nilotes to typify the movement of the sun, which appeared to be rolled across the sky like the ball of dung which the beetle rolled along the ground. The beetle therefore became the emblem of the sun-god holding the solar disk, as the beetle holds his dung-ball. And, further, out of the ball of dung, according to the erroneous popular belief, came the little *scarabæi* when their time came to be born. This is an erroneous idea, because, as the great French naturalist, J. Henri Fabre, has shown,[3] the dung-ball of the scarab-beetle is intended to be his food, and has nothing to do with the pear-shaped ball, never seen above ground, in which the female lays her eggs, thus providing food for the larva when it is hatched. The Egyptians appear to have had no idea of the metamorphosis of the insect, and thought that the scarab issued from the egg as a fully-formed beetle. The fact that the round dung-ball is made only by the male beetle was also not known; there seemed to be no difference between the sexes, and so the scarab was supposed to be male only, and to create his offspring without the intervention of a female. This seemed to typify the idea that the sun-god was self-creating.

'Since it was αὐτογενής, the scarab was also μονογενής, and in Horapollo[4] we find it cited as the symbol of μονογενής. This idea, connected with the fact that the scarab lays only one egg, was taken by Christian writers to allow of the scarab being spoken of as a type of Christ, the "only-begotten" son of God, and we even find Our Lord described as "the good Scarab," or as "God's Scarab."'[5] '*Scarabæus in cruce . . . Bonus Scarabæus qui clamavit e ligno* are phrases used of Our Lord by St. Ambrose in his exposition of St. Luke's Gospel.'[6] 'It may be questioned whether this was not a slight misunderstanding, and whether the word μονογενής means in the case of Our Lord quite the same thing as it does in Horapollo with regard to the scarab; he seems to use it rather in the sense of "born of one sole person," in this case the male scarab, without the intervention of a female.'[7]

The idea of personal resurrection was also associated with the scarab in late times. The old Egyptians had no such idea.

'It was a new life in the Underworld that, they hoped, was assured to the dead man by the placing over his heart of a stone image of the Scarabæus-beetle, type and emblem of life

[1] The latest known is one of Antoninus Pius, in the Louvre.
[2] See art. EGYPTIAN RELIGION, § 39.
[3] *Souvenirs entomologiques*, Paris, 1879–1912, v. 1–85.
[4] i. 10.
[5] Hall, *Catalogue of Egyptian Scarabs*, vol. i. p. xviii.
[6] Budge, *The Mummy*, p. 233, note 1.
[7] Hall, *loc. cit.*

ever renewing itself unaided, as its race seemed to beget itself unaided and to spring in multitude from the revolving ball, fosterer of their life as the revolving sun-ball fostered the life of man. So they prayed that with the help of the Scarab over his heart the dead man might find just judgment in the "Hall of Double Truth," that the Powers of the Underworld might not be hostile to him and that the result of the Weighing of his Heart in the presence of the Guardian of the Balance might be satisfactory. In the latter days of Egypt this hope of just judgment and renewed life in the Underworld seems to have been confused with a foreign idea (perhaps of Indian origin?) of renewed life upon this earth, which in fact was confounded by the Christians with their idea of the resurrection of the actual body at the Last Day.'[1]

4. The heart-scarab. — The heart-scarabs, intended as amulets for the protection of the dead, were usually larger in size than the ordinary seal-scarabs, which were primarily intended as amulets for the living, though, of course, constantly buried with the dead. They were emblems of the protecting power of the living sun. In the under world the sun also shone, the dead sun, Osiris, and it is only on the large heart-scarabs of comparatively late times that his figure appears. On the scarabs of the living he is never seen.

'The supposed relation of the Scarab to the heart of a man does not seem very clear to us. Perhaps the heart, as the seat of life, was regarded as specially connected with the Creator god Khepera and his emblem the Scarab, the symbol of "coming-into-being" and of existence generally. In any case, the Scarab was ritually connected with some of the more important chapters of the Book of the Dead, which were believed to save the life of the dead man in the next world, notably the all-embracing chapter lxiv., which was the quintessence of all the magical protective formulæ. The rubric of this chapter and of chapters xxx. and xxxB. prescribe that it shall be said over a Scarab of basalt or green stone, set in an electrum or gold mount or rim, which shall be placed on the heart of a man, after the ceremony of the "Opening of the Mouth" has been performed. This Heart-Scarab, one side of which was sometimes fashioned in the form of a heart, was usually placed over the place of the heart, on the breast of the mummy.'[2]

Its green colour is probably an allusion to the green dung-ball of the beetle. A typical specimen of an early heart-scarab of this kind is that of King Sebekemsaf, of the XIIIth or XVIIth dynasty (*c.* 1800 B.C.), which is in the British Museum.[3] It is a green jasper scarab, ¾ in. long, with domed back and human face, set in a gold plinth, rounded at one end, and 1⅝ ins. long. The legs of the scarab are represented in relief, splayed out on the surface of the gold plinth. On the base and sides of the latter are beaten in sentences from ch. xxxB. of the *Book of the Dead*:

'To be said over his mouth as an incantation: "My heart of my mother, my heart of my mother, my heart of my existences, may naught stand up to bear witness as an enemy against me before the judges." Made over the king Sebekemsaf, justified.'

In accordance with a superstition peculiar to the Old and Middle Kingdoms, the legs of the bird-hieroglyphs are omitted, so that they should not run away from the amulet and so impair the efficacy of the inscription. The providing of the scarab with a human face is a peculiarity of the Middle Kingdom. This face developed under the XVIIIth dynasty into the negro-head which is seen at the back of many scaraboids of that time.

In later times the heart-*scarabæus*, not unusually made of faience, is often inlaid in various colours. Sometimes the figure of the scarab disappeared altogether, and it became an amulet entirely in the shape of a heart, possibly with a human head, and with, cut upon it, a representation of the *bennu*-bird, the sacred crane of Ra of Heliopolis, which was regarded as 'the soul of Kheperi' after the union of the solar cults. Under the Saites, and even earlier, the heart-scarab was often given detachable wings, fastened with thread, and sometimes we see it in the centre of a pylon-shaped pectoral, placed on the breast of the mummy.

We have already said that at a late period we also meet with a small scarab purely amuletic in character and without inscription of any kind, as it has no base on which to put it. Instead of the base is a small ring for suspension.

'In a very interesting set of amulets in the British Museum, exhibited exactly as they were found, we find that this base-less Scarab was put over the throat of the mummy, while a seal-Scarab with base was placed with a model signet-ring (all are made of faience) below its left shoulder, the shoulder over which the scribe usually carried, slung, his writing materials.'[1]

Monstrous forms of the scarab sometimes occur in late times, purely amuletic and without the seal-base like those just described. An instance is the bull-headed scarab, usually made of hæmatite. This was connected with the moon-god Khons, as Horapollo says.[2] Horapollo speaks of the ordinary scarab of Kheperi as 'having the form of a cat,' and also mentions a single-horned scarab sacred to Thoth. The latter, as Petrie says,[3] is no doubt the long-beaked *Hypselogenia*, its beak being compared with that of the ibis, the sacred bird of Thoth. The present writer does not know of any monstrous ibis-headed or cat-headed scarabs, though the former is by no means inconceivable. It is difficult to see any resemblance between the ordinary *scarabœus* and a cat.

The scarab is often figured in the *Book of the Dead*,[4] and sometimes Kheperi appears there as a beetle-headed man. Gigantic stone *scarabœi* were sometimes set up in the temples. There are two (one of remarkable size, but uninscribed) in the British Museum, and one with a long inscription on its high pedestal was found at Karnak by Georges Legrain. In Gnostic iconography the scarab often appears.

5. Modifications of the scarab.—We thus see how it was that the small amulets representing this very sacred object were early adopted as seals on account of their convenient size and material, as well as their magical power; how the two aspects of the scarab are inextricably intermingled; and how it is difficult to treat apart the scarab-seal and the scarab-amulet, with the result that the pure signet of non-scaraboid form, such as the ring, the button-seal, and the cylinder, appears in a comprehensive catalogue like that of the British Museum collection of seals and scarabs at one end of the scale, with at the other the heart-amulet, which has nothing of the seal (or even sometimes of the scarab, except implicitly) about it. The two are connected by the scarab, in its double capacity as seal and amulet, and by its modifications, such as the 'scaraboid,' with scarab-like form and inscribed base, but with back either plain or cut or impressed in various forms like that of the head of a negro, a cynocephalous ape, and so forth; by the 'cowroid,' which is a cross between a scaraboid and a bead of lentoid shape, originally made in the form of a cowry-shell (but afterwards losing all trace of this original) and inscribed on its flat base in the same way as the scarab; and by the 'plaque,' which has lost all trace of the scaraboid form and is merely a plaque-shaped amulet developed from the flat bead and inscribed in the same manner as the seal-scarabs, usually on both sides.

'Various combinations of the Scaraboid and the Plaque are met with. All these derivatives of the Scarab partake of the nature of beads, as also does the Scarab itself to a great extent, since all are perforated for stringing, and, when worn as amulets, were usually strung with beads on necklaces, etc. . . . When intended not to be strung as a bead, but, as was often the case, to be mounted as the bezel of a signet-ring, the Scarab or Plaque was still always perforated, and was secured to the ring by means of a metal wire passing through the perforation.'[5]

Much light was thrown on the popular use of the scarab as an ornament of the living, strung on

[1] Hall, p. xviii f. [2] *Ib.* p. xix f.
[3] No. 7876; Hall, no. 211.

[1] Hall, p. xx. [2] i. 10. [3] P. 3.
[4] Oddly enough, it was occasionally confused with another beetle, the *'apshait*, which had an unlucky significance.
[5] Hall, p. vii f. There is the exception of the small late uninscribed scarabs with a suspension ring beneath, instead of a perforation (see above, § 4).

necklaces, etc., by the discovery of hundreds of small necklaces of scarabs and beads of faience in the dust-heaps of the temple of Queen Hatshepsut at Deir el-Baḥri, in Western Thebes. They were the poor offerings of the *fellaḥīn* at the shrine of Hathor, which the queen annexed to the great temple which she built in honour of Amen. These, when damaged or broken, or when the shrine became too full of them, were thrown out by the sacristans chiefly into the deserted courts of the ancient funerary temple of King Mentuḥetep close by, used in Hatshepsut's time as a dust-heap, where they were found during the excavations of the Egypt Exploration Fund in 1903–07.[1] Nearly all are of XVIIIth dynasty date, and Deir el-Baḥri has been one of the most fruitful sources of the fine blue scarabs of Hatshepsut's reign that are to be seen in our collections.

6. Material and colouring.—This brings us back to the artistic interest of the scarab. 'As the gem and coin are microcosms of Greek art, so the scarab is a microcosm of the art of Egypt.'[2] On some scarabs we see miniatures, whether good or bad, of the great scenes sculptured on the temple-walls, executed within the compass of an oval space half an inch long. On others cheap and inferior artists produced only the roughest of scenes, the rudest of hieroglyphs.

'To trace the development of the scarab and its ornaments from the elaborately conventionalized scenes of the XIIth dynasty with their beautiful spiral patterns or the finely cut legends of their priestly or official owners, through the fine designs of the XVIIIth dynasty to the delicately glazed pale blue faience amulets of the XXVIth, is one of the most interesting studies in the whole realm of ancient art.'[3]

The first and always the most generally used material for the making of scarab-seals was steatite or steaschist, a grey schistose stone (silicate of magnesium) resembling, but not so soft as, soapstone. This when used for scarabs was usually glazed, generally either blue or green. Faience appears under the XIIth dynasty, and was generally used from the time of the XVIIIth dynasty. Under the XIXth the faience scarabs of the cheapest kind were often cast in moulds, with disastrous effect. A fine deep blue glaze was used under the VIth–XIIth dynasties. A delicate blue glaze at the beginning of the XVIIIth dynasty gave way to the brilliant blue of the reign of Hatshepsut and the beginning of that of Thothmes III. During his reign green became the fashion and persisted under the XIXth, though blue is often found. In later times green was usual, until under the Saites a delicate light-blue glaze took its place. The preservation of the colour is more usual on faience than on steatite scarabs. On the latter it has often disappeared or has turned brown. On faience, when the colour goes, blue usually turns white. A homogeneous hard blue paste, usually light-blue, was also used under the XIIth and XVIIIth dynasties, and a soft paste, also light-blue, was very common under the XXVIth. Hard stones of the finest kinds were used from the XIIth to the XIXth dynasty. Amethyst was the most usual in the earlier period, and the amethyst scarabs of the XIIth dynasty often have a gold plate on the base, on which the inscription was engraved. Usually, however, this plate has disappeared, or was never fixed, so that the scarabs have no inscription, though amethyst scarabs with inscriptions cut directly on the base are not unknown. The beautiful light-blue feldspar was also used at this time, as well as hæmatite, carnelian, green jasper, crystal, quartz (sometimes glazed blue), lapis-lazuli, and obsidian. Under the XVIIIth dynasty carnelian was the favourite stone, though it was used more for cowroids than for scarabs proper. Bright yellow jasper followed at the end of the dynasty, and under the XIXth dynasty red jasper, red feldspar, carnelian, sard, and red stones generally, were in fashion, as also were crystal and chalcedony, and even jade (for heart-scarabs), but less commonly. Malachite and turquoise scarabs are very rare. Under the later dynasties lapis-lazuli supplanted all the others for small scarabs, and granite, diorite, and basalt were all used for the large heart-scarabs, as well as a stone usually called 'green basalt,' which is not a true basalt, and is called by Petrie[1] 'durite.' This was common at all periods for heart-scarabs, but was rarely used for the small scarabs. Metal scarabs are rare, though we may well suppose that they were often made of gold, especially under the XIIth and XVIIIth dynasties; and the splendid find of XIIth dynasty jewellery at Dashur includes golden scarabs splendidly inlaid with lapis, feldspar, and carnelian. Silver is so perishable that a silver scarab would be a great rarity. Bronze scarabs are usually Ptolemaic or Roman, rarely XXth dynasty. Blue glass scarabs are known under the XVIIIth and XIXth dynasties; they are often small and rudely cut, obviously of the cheapest description. Amber scarabs are very rare, but there is one of the Middle Kingdom in the British Museum.[2] The material is very perishable. Wood occurs under the XIIth dynasty, but is very rare. Ivory was also rarely used; the small amuletic scarabs of the VIth dynasty may be mentioned, and larger ones are sometimes found later on: these have usually magical inscriptions.[3]

7. Historical value.—The types of the scarabs of the various periods of the XIIth to the XXVIth dynasty are easily distinguishable. Under the XIIth dynasty a very naturalistic type was in vogue side by side with an oblong conventionalized type, which is the commoner of the two. In this type the legs are merely marked by striations at the sides. Under the XIIIth dynasty larger and more oval scarabs of this type were usual. The wing-cases of this type were often not marked, under both dynasties. At the end of the Middle Kingdom we find the wing-cases often replaced by little serrated lines, like palm-sprigs. At the beginning of the XVIIIth dynasty a purely oval base was usual, and the hinder end of the scarab was sharply raised or hunched up; this is characteristic of the time of Amenḥetep I. Later a naturalistic form, with less oval base and with triangular marks at the corners of the wing-cases, was *de règle*; this is the characteristic form of the reign of Thothmes III. and persisted with variations till the time of the Saites. Under the XIXth dynasty highly arched backs were common, and the legs were often cut free. Aberrant forms with almost pyramidal backs and elaborately cut heads are met with under both the XIIth and the XIXth dynasties, but are rarely found in the intervening period; the XIXth dynasty scarab-cutters seem occasionally to have tried to revive the forms of the Middle Kingdom. Under the Ethiopians (XXVth dynasty) began the archaistic revival of art generally, which went for its models back to the Old and Middle Kingdoms. Scarab-forms of the XIIth dynasty were now commonly imitated, and even their spiral base-designs were occasionally revived. But under the Saites of the XXVIth, though the sculpture of the Old Kingdom was imitated, scarabs of the Old Kingdom could not often be imitated, because there were so few to imitate—those in our museums which bear the names of monarchs of the IVth dynasty, for instance, are

[1] Hall, in E. Naville and H. R. Hall, *The XIth Dynasty Temple at Deir el-Bahari*, London, 1907–13, i. 17, iii. 13.
[2] Hall, *Catalogue of Egyp. Scarabs*, vol. i. p. xxiv.
[3] *Ib.*

[1] P. 8. [2] No. 17,718. [3] Brit. Mus., no. 30,730.

considered by most writers on the subject to be all posthumous.[1] So a typical Saite form was evolved, with a characteristic bulbous abdomen which cannot be mistaken. Names of ancient monarchs were often put on them, as had already been the case under the XIXth dynasty. And that of Thothmes III. is almost as common on scarabs of the XXVIth dynasty as on those of his own time.

This fact is apt to make us doubt the historical value of the scarab. If a scarab bearing the name of Menkaura is probably not, or one bearing that of Thothmes III. is not necessarily, of the time of the king whose name it bears, of what value is it as a means of dating objects with which it may be found? If the name of one king can be imitated on later scarabs, why not that of another? We know, however, that only a limited number of royal names were so imitated, and, when we find that a scarab bearing the name of Thothmes III. is identical in style with one bearing that of his successor, Amenḥetep II., whose name was never imitated later, we know that the Thothmes scarab is of the XVIIIth dynasty. And so in all other cases. All scarabs of unimportant monarchs are contemporary, as are also all scarabs of Akhenaten and the other 'disk-worshippers,' who were regarded by all later Egyptians as abominable heretics, and whose names would never be commemorated. There is really very little uncertainty in the matter. So royal scarabs can be used by archæologists well acquainted with scarab-lore as important evidence of the date of other antiquities with which they may be found. A crucial instance of this is the discovery of scarabs and rings of Amenḥetep III., Queen Tii, and Akhenaten with Mycenæan antiquities in Greece. This was rightly taken to prove the date of these antiquities long before the other confirmatory evidence, which has conclusively shown that the Mycenæans and Minoans were contemporary with XVIIIth dynasty Egypt, was available. At the time of the original discovery the study of scarabs in connexion with other Egyptian antiquities had not progressed so far as it has of late years, and doubt as to the contemporaneity of the scarabs with the monarchs whose names they bore was not altogether unjustified. But the criterion of style settles the matter now, and the possibility of a scarab being older than the antiquities with which it is found can thus be dealt with, and its evidence discounted. In the British Museum there is an obsidian scarab of the XIIIth dynasty which has the name of Shishak (XXIInd dynasty) cut upon it.[2] Its real date is settled by its style, about which there is nothing archaistic. The archaistic scarabs of the XXVth-XXVIth dynasty are distinguishable (though sometimes with difficulty) from those which they imitate. They are most easily identified when they bear inscriptions which must demonstrably be later in date than the Middle Kingdom. Some confusion is caused by the habit of the XXVIth dynasty Egyptians of putting names of imaginary kings on scarabs. Our other knowledge and the suspicious forms of the names themselves enable us to put these on one side as historical evidence. The only really 'historical' scarabs are the great medal-like scarabs of Amenḥetep III., already referred to. But the value of the ordinary scarab as historical evidence is clear. The existence of a Hyksos king, Aapeḥti Nubti, who had been regarded as doubtful and been relegated by Eduard Meyer to the realm of religious fable, has possibly been confirmed by a British Museum scarab[3] bearing his name. Its style is unmistakably of his time, the period just about the beginning of the XVIIIth dynasty. It

[1] Petrie is the only exception (pp. 11 ff., 14 ff.).
[2] No. 30,625; Hall, no. 2405. [3] No. 32,368; Hall, no. 301.

and any typical scarab of Aahmes and Amenḥetep I. are as alike as two peas, both in style of make and in cutting of inscription. There is the possibility that the scarab may belong to Thothmes I., who bore the name Aapeḥti among his titles,[1] but it is equally possible that the scarab is King Nubti's. Then a scarab of Thothmes III., usurped by Hatshepsut, which is in the British Museum,[2] confirms to some extent the view of K. Sethe as to the peculiar succession of these two monarchs.[3] Other analogous instances might be quoted. Indirectly much may be gleaned from scarabs. An interesting sidelight on history is given by the design, common on the remarkable scarabs of the Hyksos period, which shows the conflict between the desert lion and the river crocodile, probably typifying the contest between the Hyksos of the north and the Thebans of the south. The peculiar semi-barbaric designs of the scarabs of the Hyksos seem to have persisted in the north under the XVIIIth dynasty, and the Hyksos types come again into prominence, in a somewhat modified form, under the XIXth dynasty, where the style of the later 'Delta-scarabs' strongly reminds us of that of the Hyksos scarabs, which are often known by the same appellation. This is an interesting confirmation of the view that the Hyksos strain was by no means rooted out of the Delta by the XVIIIth dynasty kings, and that the people of the Delta, when it resumed its importance under the XIXth dynasty, were largely of Hyksos origin. The devotion to the god Set which was professed by the XIXth dynasty kings, and the constant appearance of this deity of the Hyksos, so hated in Upper Egypt two centuries before, on the Tanite or Delta scarabs (often in his Hittite form as Sutekh, with horns and pigtail), are strong confirmation of this view. Ptaḥ, the god of Memphis, is naturally also commemorated on scarabs of this period, when the seat of government was in the north. Ptaḥ was the deity of the Memphites, and the Hyksos Set-Sutekh was the god, not only of the court at Tanis, but of the people of the Delta generally, under the XIXth dynasty. It was only when the Ramessids of the XXth dynasty returned to Thebes that Ptaḥ resumed undivided sway over the north, the worship of Set disappeared, and the Hyksos-Tanite style of scarab went out of fashion. We thus see that the historical value of the scarab is by no means negligible, and that on all counts —religious, historical, and artistic—the little Egyptian seal in the form of the sacred beetle is one of the most interesting objects which antiquity has handed down to us.

LITERATURE.—S. Birch, *Catalogue of the Egyptian Antiquities at Alnwick Castle*, privately printed, 1880, p. 103 ff. (the first considerable catalogue of scarabs); E. A. W. Budge, in *Catalogue of the Hilton Price Collection*, London, 1897, p. 20 ff.; *The Lady Meux Collection of Egyptian Antiquities*, do. 1896, p. 185 ff.; *Catalogue of Egyptian Antiquities* (Harrow School Museum), Harrow, 1887, p. 14 ff.; *Catalogue of the Egyptian Antiquities in the Fitzwilliam Museum*, Cambridge, 1893, p. 87 ff. (all valuable for inscriptions); W. J. Loftie, *An Essay of Scarabs*, London, n.d. [1884] (the first general book on the subject; uncritical, but illustrations good); W. M. F. Petrie, *Historical Scarabs*, do. 1889 (the first comprehensive work on royal scarabs); Budge, *The Mummy*, Cambridge, 1894, p. 231 ff. (valuable on the religious side); G. W. Fraser, *Catalogue of Scarabs*, London, 1900; F. Ll. Griffith, 'A Collection of Historical Scarabs' (The John Ward Collection), *PSBA* xxii. [1900] 305 ff., 386 ff., xxiii. [1901] 19 ff., 79 ff. (good illustrations); John Ward, *The Sacred Beetle*, London, 1902 (republication of the above); P. E. Newberry, *Scarabs: an Introd. to the Study of Egyptian Seals and Signet Rings*², do. 1908 (very valuable for scarabs of the Middle Kingdom), *Scarab-shaped Seals*, do. 1907 (forming a vol. of the *Catalogue Général* of the Cairo Museum); H. R. Hall, *Catalogue of Egyptian Scarabs, etc., in the British Museum*, vol. i. 'Royal Scarabs,' etc., do. 1913; Petrie, *Scarabs and Cylinders with Names*, do. 1917. Two artt. by Mrs. Alice Grenfell, 'Amuletic Scarabs for the Deceased,' and 'The Rarer Scarabs of the New Kingdom,' in *RTr* xxx. [1908] 105 ff., and

[1] Petrie, p. 24. [2] No. 29,232; Hall, no. 550.
[3] For a criticism of this view, however, see Hall, *Ancient History of the Near East*, p. 286.

xxxii. [1910] 113 ff., should also be mentioned, and the art. 'Scarab,' by F. Ll. Griffith, in *EBr*[11] xxiv. 301. [It should be noted as a curious fact that practically nothing has been written on scarabs by any but British archæologists.]

H. R. HALL.

SCEPTICS (σκεπτικοί, ἐφεκτικοί).—In this article the term 'sceptics' is used strictly of the adherents of the doctrine which we know best from Sextus Empiricus (2nd cent. A.D.). There were, of course, sceptical tendencies in Greek philosophy long before his time. Xenophanes was regarded by the later sceptics as almost one of themselves, and with considerable justification. Protagoras (*q.v.*), the real author of the sceptical formula 'no more such than such' (οὐδὲν μᾶλλον τοῖον ἢ τοῖον), prepared the way for scepticism, but he was no sceptic himself, and his chief work was known as *The Truth* (Ἀλήθεια). We must carefully distinguish between real scepticism and disbelief in the trustworthiness of the senses, such as we find in the school of Democritus (*q.v.*) and in that of the Megarics (*q.v.*). Both of these rejected sensation altogether, but both maintained the reality of something inaccessible to sense. A disciple of Democritus, Metrodorus of Chios, said indeed,[1] 'None of us knows anything, not even this, whether we know or do not know,' but he also said,[2] 'All things are which one can think' (ἃ ἄν τις νοήσαι), and he taught the doctrine of atoms and the void. The Megarics held that the senses were deceptive, but they maintained the reality of the Good, which they identified with the Eleatic One. The Academy (*q.v.*) under Arcesilaus and Carneades is often regarded as sceptical, but the genuine sceptics refused to admit that it was. The Academics, they said, were really dogmatists, since they affirmed dogmatically that things were 'incomprehensible' (ἀκατάληπτα), and to assert scepticism dogmatically is to cease to be a sceptic. Moreover, the Academics held that a belief might, for practical purposes, be more or less probable or justifiable (εὔλογον) or more or less convincing (πιθανόν). Sextus[3] even reports a statement that Arcesilaus used scepticism only to test his pupils, and that he communicated the doctrine of Plato to those whom he found fit to receive it. The truth of the matter appears to be that the scepticism of the Academy was primarily a scepticism *ad hoc*, directed against the 'comprehensive impression' (καταληπτικὴ φαντασία) of the Stoics, and in opposing that doctrine Arcesilaus and Carneades were faithful to the teaching of Plato, who held firmly that it was impossible to have scientific knowledge of the world of becoming. The Academic doctrine of probability is also Platonic; for Plato conceived it to be possible to give a 'likely account' (εἰκότα λόγον) even of this world. Neither Arcesilaus nor Carneades wrote anything, and of course their controversies with Zeno and Chrysippus would attract more attention than anything else that they may have taught; but there is no evidence that they felt any inconsistency between their official positions as 'successors' (διάδοχοι) of Plato and their doctrine. Cicero and Plutarch, who represent the best Academic tradition, are quite unconscious of any departure from Platonism on their part. It may be that they became so absorbed in their criticism of the materialistic dogmatism of the Stoics that they let the other side of Platonism fall into the background, but there is no reason to think that their sceptical attitude to the Stoic theory of knowledge would have been disowned by the founder of the Academy. In any case, though the sceptics derived most of their arguments from the Academy, they were quite justified in holding that they were separated from it *toto cœlo*.

1 Frag. 1 (Diels).　　　　　　2 Frag. 2 (Diels).
3 *Pyrrh. Hyp.* i. 234.

The favourite formula of the sceptics was that the wise man would withhold his assent from all opinions and would 'suspend his judgment' (ἐπέχειν), and there is good evidence that this formula is due to Arcesilaus. That created a difficulty for the sceptics, who did not wish to appear indebted to the Academy for anything, and it probably explains the fact that they claimed **Pyrrho of Elis** as their founder and liked to call themselves Pyrrhoneans. Pyrrho belonged to an earlier generation than Arcesilaus, and it was possible to represent the Academy as having borrowed its weapons from him. It is very difficult to accept this account of the matter. Cicero often names Pyrrho, but never as a sceptic. For him he represents the doctrine of apathy (*q.v.*), or insensibility to feeling (ἀπάθεια), and he also tells us that he regarded virtue (ἀρετή) as the highest and even the sole good. He says too, more than once, that the doctrine of Pyrrho had long been extinct, and these things make it necessary for us to examine the alleged scepticism of Pyrrho more closely.

For the originality of Arcesilaus cf. Cicero, *Ac.* ii. 77: 'Nemo umquam superiorum non modo expresserat, sed ne dixerat quidem, posse hominem nihil opinari, nec solum posse, sed ita necesse esse sapienti'; and Diog. Laert. iv. 28: (Ἀρκεσίλαος) πρῶτος ἐπισχὼν τὰς ἀποφάσεις. The present writer was therefore wrong in saying (in art. ACADEMY, § 2) that Arcesilaus 'made use of the weapons provided by scepticism.' The doctrine of ἐποχή is entirely his own. In the *de Finibus*[1] Cicero takes Pyrrho as the type of extreme moral rigorism, more extreme even than that of Ariston of Chios at a later date. He apparently knows nothing of a Pyrrhonean scepticism.

Our difficulties are considerably increased by the fact that Pyrrho, like Arcesilaus, wrote nothing, and we are confined to what we can learn on good authority of his life. According to Diogenes Laertius, the chronologist Apollodorus[2] said that he was originally a painter and had 'heard' Bryson (the Megaric philosopher).[3] Subsequently he attached himself to Anaxarchus (the Democritean) and followed him everywhere, so that he associated with the 'Gymnosophists' and 'Magi' in India. That was, of course, when Anaxarchus went there in the train of Alexander the Great (326 B.C.). The authority for this is Pyrrho's younger contemporary, Antigonus of Carystus, who wrote a special treatise on him and visited Elis shortly after his death to collect information about him. Diogenes Laertius[4] quotes him as follows:

'Antigonus of Carystus in his work on Pyrrho says of him that he was originally a poor painter with no reputation, and that a work of his called *Torchbearers* is preserved in the Gymnasium of Elis, which is fairly good. He used to frequent solitary and desert places, and showed himself only on rare occasions to his people at home. This he did from hearing an Indian reproaching Anaxarchus, saying that he could not teach anything good to any one else, since he himself haunted the courts of kings. He was always in the same disposition, so that, if any one left him when he was still speaking, he finished what he had to say for himself, and yet he had been excitable in youth. Often too he went on a journey without giving notice to any one and wandered about with whomsoever he chanced to meet. And once, when Anaxarchus fell into a pond, he passed on without going to his assistance, and, when some blamed him, Anaxarchus himself commended his indifference and absence of affection (τὸ ἀδιάφορον καὶ ἄστοργον αὑτοῦ). And once, when he was caught talking to himself and asked the reason, he said he was practising to be good. He was not overlooked by any one in their inquiries; for he would speak both at large and in answer to questions, so that even Nausiphanes fell a victim to him in his youth and said one should try to combine Pyrrho's character and one's own theories. He said too that Epicurus admired Pyrrho's way of

1 Cf. ii. 43, iii. 12, iv. 43.
2 F. Jacoby, *Apollodors Chronik*, Berlin, 1902, p. 340.
3 Much confusion has been caused by the apparent statement in Diogenes that Pyrrho 'heard Bryson the son of Stilpo.' The present writer would read καὶ ἤκουσε Βρύσωνος [τοῦ Στίλπωνος, ὡς Ἀλέξανδρος ἐν Διαδοχαῖς εἶ]ρ' Ἀναξάρχου, κτλ. Bryson belonged to the first generation of the Megaric school and is mentioned in Plato's thirteenth Epistle (3600). This dispels the chronological difficulties raised by Zeller. The interpolated extract from Alexander no doubt refers to Timon (see below).
4 ix. 62.

life and constantly asked questions about him. Pyrrho was so honoured by his native city that they appointed him chief priest and gave immunity from taxation to all philosophers on his account.'

This passage has been quoted in full because it is the earliest well-attested instance of Indian influence on Greece, and it reflects with obvious fidelity the astonishment of the good people of Elis on finding that they had produced a saint. We see that those who knew Pyrrho well described him as a sort of Buddhist *arhat*, and that is doubtless how we should regard him. He is not so much a sceptic as an ascetic and a quietist.

As we see from Antigonus, Pyrrho was accustomed to expound his views orally, but they were known to later times only from **Timon of Phlius** (*c.* 322–232 B.C.), whom Sextus[1] calls the prophet of his doctrines. Timon is an interesting figure, and we know a good deal about him, as Antigonus also wrote a life of him, some notices from which have found their way into Diogenes Laertius. He had 'heard' Stilpo,[2] but subsequently attached himself to Pyrrho at Elis. After making a competence as a 'sophist' at Chalcedon, he settled at Athens, where he lived to a great age. His best-known work was the *Silloi*, a mock-heroic poem, in which he satirized the philosophers of the past and those of his own day without mercy, in order to bring out the superiority of Pyrrho to them all. He addresses him thus:[3]

'O aged man, O Pyrrho, how or whence didst thou find a way of escape from the service of the beliefs and empty-mindedness of the sophists, and burst the bonds of all deceit and persuasion? Thou didst not care to inquire whose[4] breezes rule in Hellas, whence and whither each one goes.'

This means that Pyrrho had emancipated himself from the vain subtleties of the Megarics (for they are meant by 'sophists' at this date), and there is probably an allusion to the great popularity of Stilpo. In any case, Timon is particularly severe on the Megarics, though he himself was brought up in their school. But he does not mean that Pyrrho found release in scepticism. This is made quite plain in a passage from his elegiac poem *Indalmoi*:

'This, O Pyrrho, is what my heart is longing to hear, how it is that, while as a man thou livest in such great ease and quiet, without a care and immovably constant, thou dost yet rule alone among men, like the god that ranges over the whole earth in his chariot, displaying the fiery burning circle of his rounded sphere.'[5]

And Pyrrho answers:

'Truly I will tell thee, as it appears to me to be, the word of truth (for I have a straight rule to judge how the nature of the divine and of the good is ever) whence comes for a man the most equable life.'[6]

A sceptic can hardly speak of a 'word of truth' (μῦθον ἀληθείης) or of a 'straight rule' (ὀρθὸς κανών) or of the true 'nature' (φύσις) of the divine and good. Sextus[7] feels the difficulty and gets over it only by putting an unnatural emphasis on the words 'as it appears to me to be' (ὥς μοι καταφαίνεται εἶναι). It is surely clear, however, that Timon is making Pyrrho declare a higher truth of some sort. What this was we may partly infer from a quotation from one of Timon's prose works preserved by Aristocles:[8]

'He himself [Pyrrho] has left nothing in writing, but his disciple Timon says that the man who is to be happy must look to these three things: (1) what is the nature of things, (2) what attitude we should take to them, and (3) what those who take this attitude will gain by it. He says that he declared that things were in an equal degree indifferent and unstable and incapable of being tested. For this reason neither our senses nor our opinions are true or false. So we must not put our trust in them but be free from beliefs and inclinations and unshaken, saying of each thing in turn that it no more is than it is not, or that it both is and is not, or that it neither is nor is not. And those who take this attitude, Timon says, will gain first speechlessness (ἀφασία) and then imperturbability (ἀταραξία).'

Now it is easy to see how this could be regarded as scepticism, and so in fact Aristocles regards it. But that is a superficial view. In the first place, all the apparently sceptical phrases are Democritean and such as Pyrrho might well have learnt from Anaxarchus, the disciple of Metrodorus of Chios; and in particular the appeal to the nature of things (οἷα πέφυκε τὰ πράγματα) is one which a sceptic is debarred from making, though quite in order for a Democritean. It is possible too that the doctrine of imperturbability is Democritean, though the importance given to it by Pyrrho is more Indian than Greek. In the light of that we see that the passage has really much more to do with the supposed good things and bad things of life than with speculative questions, and that it is, in fact, a recommendation of the indifference (ἀδιαφορία) and apathy (ἀπάθεια) towards these which is the only doctrine that Cicero attributes to Pyrrho. The really remarkable thing is that Sextus can quote so little of a definitely sceptical character even from Timon. He refers to a saying, 'That honey is sweet, I do not lay down; that it appears sweet, I admit,' which is sound Democritean doctrine, and to an argument that 'nothing divisible can arise in an indivisible time,' which is plainly Megaric. To appreciate the importance of this argument from silence, we must remember that Timon lived at Athens when the controversy between Arcesilaus and Zeno was in full blast, and that he attacked both of them without mercy. If he had ever said anything about suspense of judgment (ἐποχή), we may be sure that Sextus would have repeated it. The speechlessness (ἀφασία) of which Timon did speak is a different thing. Sextus is quite aware of this, and he explains[1] that the sceptics do not receive the doctrine of ἀφασία in the sense that the nature of things is such as to produce speechlessness (which is just what Timon says it is), but as a mere indication of a temporary condition (πάθος) at the moment when they pronounce the word. Sextus is far too candid a writer to identify the sceptical 'suspense of judgment' with an attitude based on the 'nature of things,' which implies a dogma.

The actual words of Sextus are: Τὴν ἀφασίαν παραλαμβάνομεν οὐχ ὡς πρὸς τὴν φύσιν τοιούτων ὄντων τῶν πραγμάτων ὥστε πάντως ἀφασίαν κινεῖν ἀλλὰ δηλοῦντες ὅτι ἡμεῖς νῦν, ὅτε προφερόμεθα αὐτήν, ἐπὶ τῶνδε τῶν ζητουμένων τοῦτο πεπόνθαμεν.[2]

We have seen that Cicero regarded the philosophy of Pyrrho as extinct, and this is confirmed by Menodotus, who is himself reckoned as one of the leading sceptics before Sextus, and who stated distinctly that Timon had no successors, and that the school (ἀγωγή) lapsed till it was revived by Ptolemy of Cyrene.[3] The writers of *Successions* of course give us a complete list of the successors of Pyrrho down to Sextus, but the names are mere names for us, and there are in any case too few of them to bridge the interval. The first tangible personality we come to is **Ænesidemus**, who is of fundamental importance in the history of scepticism as the author of the 'ten tropes.' According to Aristocles,[4] it was he who revived scepticism at Alexandria, and it is certain that he wrote a work called *Pyrrhonean Discourses* (Πυρρώνειοι λόγοι). This was dedicated, Aristocles tells us,[5] to one L. Tubero, who had been a member of the Academy along with Ænesidemus, who had deserted it on the ground that 'those of the Academy, especially the present, sometimes agree with the Stoic doctrines, and, if the truth must be told, they are

[1] *Adv. Math.* i. 53; ὁ προφήτης τῶν Πύρρωνος λόγων.
[2] See art. MEGARICS. [3] Frag. 48 (Diels).
[4] The MS reading is τίνος, which Cobet wrongly changed to τίνες. Surely there is no reference to meteorology, as Diels says. We may take αὖραι in the sense of 'vogue' or 'popularity.' In the last line read ἑκάστη with Wilamowitz.
[5] Frag. 67 (Diels). [6] Frag. 68 (Diels).
[7] *Adv. Math.* xi. 20.
[8] *Ap.* Eusebius, *Præp. Evang.* xiv. 18.

[1] *Pyrrh. Hyp.* i. 192. [2] *Ib.* 193.
[3] *Ap.* Diog. Laert. ix. 115. [4] *Loc. cit.* [5] *Loc. cit.*

like Stoics fighting with Stoics.' We know that it was Antiochus of Ascalon who introduced Stoicism into the Academy, and it is argued that, as Sextus[1] uses very similar language of Antiochus, Ænesidemus must refer to him too. In that case, as Antiochus died not long after 70 B.C., Ænesidemus must be earlier still. This would make it very difficult to explain Cicero's statement that Pyrrhonism was extinct in his time. It is easier to suppose that the successor of Antiochus, his brother Aristus, continued and even aggravated his eclectic tendencies. Cicero stayed with him at Athens in 51 B.C. and was shocked by the 'topsy-turvy' (*sursum deorsum*) condition of the Academic philosophy in his hands.[2]

Aristocles[3] says that no one paid any more attention to the old sceptics than if they had never been born, and that it was only the other day that 'one Ænesidemus' began to rekindle the rubbish at Alexandria (ἐχθὲς καὶ πρῴην ἐν Ἀλεξανδρείᾳ τῇ κατ' Αἴγυπτον Αἰνησίδημός τις ἀναζωπυρεῖν ἤρξατο τὸν ὕθλον τοῦτον). Aristocles belongs to the 2nd cent. A.D., and his words suggest a fairly recent date. On the other hand, H. von Arnim has found at least eight of the ten tropes in Philo[4] and concludes that Ænesidemus must have been earlier than Philo. That, however, is not quite decisive, since the tropes are mostly to be found already in Cicero's *Academica*,[5] which means that they are crumbs from the table of Carneades and may have been put together before Ænesidemus. The idea that the Academy came to an end with Philo and Antiochus is responsible for a good deal of faulty argument on this subject. We know little about it between that time and the rise of Neo-Platonism, but it still went on without interruption. We cannot, therefore, say at what date Ænesidemus seceded from it.

The *Pyrrhonean Discourses* of Ænesidemus were read by the patriarch Photius in the 9th cent. A.D., and he has left us an analysis of their contents. The first book dealt with the divergence between the sceptics and the Academy, and we see that Ænesidemus definitely laid down that things were incomprehensible either by sense or by thought. That, then, is a complete scepticism and the first of which we have any clear record. The subjects of the remaining books, however, are just those we know to have been treated by Carneades and do not suggest any great originality. We are certainly doing Ænesidemus too much honour if we attribute to him the argument against causation reported by Sextus.[6] In this the noticeable thing is that, while he gives a subtle proof of the impossibility of a corporeal thing being the cause of any thing either corporeal or incorporeal, he simply takes for granted that the incorporeal is not the cause of any thing, since it is intangible (ἀναφὴς φύσις) and cannot act or be acted upon. Now Carneades might assume this in arguing against Chrysippus, who would admit it at once, but it is not a sufficient refutation of all possible theories of causation, as it ought to be. The natural conclusion is that we have here simply an argument of Carneades transcribed from Clitomachus. The arrangement in eight 'tropes' (τρόποι) of the various fallacies into which people fall in dealing with problems of causation[7] is more likely to be the original contribution of Ænesidemus to the subject.

Quite distinct from these are the ten 'tropes' (τρόποι, also called τόποι and λόγοι) with which his name is chiefly associated. These are simply a rather unsystematic list of sceptical commonplaces. They are as follows:

(1) From the divergence of animals (some animals have one sense highly developed, some another); (2) from the divergence of human beings; (3) from the different constructions of the organs of sense; (4) from circumstances (sleep, waking, jaundice, etc.); (5) from positions, distances, and situations (the colours in a dove's neck, the square tower which appears round at a distance, the oar which appears bent in water); (6) from mixtures (we never perceive anything by itself, but always accompanied by light, heat, moisture, etc.); (7) from the quantities and structure of objects (scrapings of horn are white, but horns are black; scrapings of silver are black, but silver is white); (8) from relativity (τὸ πρός τι); (9) from frequency or rarity of occurrence; (10) from laws and customs, mythical arguments, and dogmatic prejudices.

Even in the case of Ænesidemus the sceptic still eludes us. According to Sextus,[1] he was not a true sceptic any more than the Academics; for he regarded 'Pyrrhonism' simply as 'a way to lead us to the philosophy of Heraclitus,' and Sextus more than once speaks of 'Ænesidemus after Heraclitus' (Αἰνησίδημος or οἱ περὶ Αἰνησίδημον καθ' Ἡράκλειτον). Zeller and Diels regard this as impossible. It is suggested that Ænesidemus merely gave an account of the philosophy of Heraclitus or that he really meant to say that the philosophy of Heraclitus was a way to lead us to scepticism. It seems impossible to accept either of these explanations. Sextus must have known perfectly well how the matter stood, and he appears to be making a verbal quotation. If we remember that in the Academy, to which Ænesidemus had belonged, scepticism must always have been regarded, at least officially, as a way to lead us to the philosophy of Plato, it is not hard to understand the point of view. There is a perfectly intelligible sense in which a scepticism like that of Ænesidemus might lead to a philosophy like that of Heraclitus (*q.v.*). The Ephesian himself founded his philosophy on the contradictions of the world of appearance, and it was just on those that Ænesidemus insisted. The Stoics themselves appealed to Heraclitus as their precursor, and they distorted his doctrine accordingly, and Ænesidemus may very well have thought that he understood it better than they did, and that it was better approached from the side of scepticism than from that of dogmatism. If that is the true explanation of his attitude, he was quite right in his view, but Sextus was also quite right in refusing to recognize him as a true sceptic.

The man who really formulated the canons of scepticism—those with which Sextus works—was Agrippa, of whom we know nothing whatever except that he must have lived between the time of Ænesidemus and that of Sextus. His name does not occur in any of the lists. His tropes are on a far higher level than those of Ænesidemus and may be given thus:

1. *The argument from discord* (ὁ ἀπὸ τῆς διαφωνίας). On any point proposed we find, both in life and among philosophers, a divergence from which there is no appeal (ἀνεπίκριτος στάσις). One assertion (φάσις) has no more claim to be accepted than its opposite; for each is a part of the discord (μέρος τῆς διαφωνίας).
2. *The argument from infinite regress* (ὁ ἀπὸ τῆς εἰς ἄπειρον ἐκπτώσεως). If we attempt to demonstrate our assertion, that which is brought forward as a proof itself requires a proof, and that in turn another, and so on *ad infinitum*. As we cannot find a point from which to start, we are reduced to suspense (ἐποχή).
3. *The argument from relativity* (ὁ ἀπὸ τοῦ πρός τι). An object appears such and such relatively to the judging subject and to the things along with which it is observed, but we must suspend our judgment as to what it is relatively to nature (πρὸς τὴν φύσιν).
4. *The argument from hypothesis* (ὁ ἐξ ὑποθέσεως). This is applied when the dogmatists arbitrarily select a point in the infinite regress and take it for granted.
5. *The argument from circular reasoning* (ὁ διάλληλος τρόπος). This is applied when the dogmatists give as proof of a thing something which itself requires to be confirmed by that thing.

To these Sextus[2] adds two tropes formulated by 'the more recent sceptics.' These are:

'Everything is apprehended either from itself or from something else. But (1) that nothing is apprehended from itself is proved by the discord among philosophers with regard to all things sensible and intelligible, from which discord there is no appeal, since we can make use of no criterion sensible or intelligible, because whatever we take is untrustworthy as being subject to discord. So (2) nothing is apprehended from anything else; for, if that from which a thing is apprehended always has to be apprehended from something else, we fall either into the argument in a circle (ὁ διάλληλος τρόπος) or into the infinite regress (ὁ ἄπειρος τρόπος).'

1 *Pyrrh. Hyp.* i. 235.
2 Cic. *ad Att.* v. 10. 4.
3 *Loc. cit.*
4 *Phil. Untersuch.*, Berlin, 1888, pt. xi. p. 56 f.
5 See J. S. Reid's ed., London, 1885, Introd. p. 65 f.
6 *Adv. Math.* ix. 218 ff.
7 Sextus, *Pyrrh. Hyp.* i. 180.

1 Sextus, *Pyrrh. Hyp.* i. 210.
2 *Ib.* i. 178.

Scepticism had at last found its formula, and it was soon to find a singularly competent exponent. The date of **Sextus Empiricus** is quite uncertain. He is mentioned in Diogenes Laertius, but not by Galen, so we may probably refer him to the beginning of the 3rd or the end of the 2nd century A.D. Nor do we know where he lived. From his own works it appears that he was a doctor, and his name suggests that he belonged to the empirical school. On the other hand, he expressly denies[1] that the empirical school of medicine was to be identified with the sceptical philosophy. The sceptic would rather adopt the principles of the methodic school. However that may be, the preservation of his writings (which fill over 750 pages in Bekker's edition) is one of the greatest pieces of good fortune in the general wreck of Hellenistic philosophical literature. That is partly, no doubt, because it has preserved so much of the acute dialectic of the Academy (a point which has not yet been sufficiently attended to), but not altogether so. Sextus is a real personality and a genuine thinker, and he is actually at his best in such parts of his work as are obviously original, above all in his polemic against the grammarians. He mentions 'imperturbability' (ἀταραξία) in a perfunctory way, as he was bound to do, but he himself would not have cared for such a state in the least. He has an active mind and a passion for clearness. The ordinary arguments against scepticism do not touch him at all; for it is an attitude with him, and not a doctrine. He is thoroughly sceptical about scepticism itself. He also makes a strong impression of sincerity and candour, and he has great learning and considerable humour. His works are the only key we have to the real meaning of Hellenistic philosophy.

The books entitled Πυρρωνείων ὑποτυπώσεον ΑΒΓ are the most valuable for our purposes, as they contain an outline of the whole system with historical notices. In the MSS the two other works of Sextus are combined under a common title, Πρὸς μαθημτικούς (*adv. Math.*), which properly belongs only to the books against the teachers of the ἐγκύκλια μαθήματα or liberal arts (=*adv. Math.* i.–vi.), while the treatise against the dogmatists (Πρὸς δογματικούς=*adv. Math.* vii.–xi.) is further subdivided into three sections, Πρὸς λογικούς (two books), Πρὸς φυσικούς (two books), and Πρὸς ἠθικούς (one book).

It is, of course, impossible to give here any idea of the wealth of matter in the works of Sextus; but it is desirable to note two points of interest in his philosophy. In the first place he was faced with the necessity of finding some rule of life. The Academic plan of taking probability as our guide was not open to him; for he is too clear-sighted to admit that a sceptic can regard anything as more probable than anything else. He therefore falls back on the rule that we should follow the usage of the society in which we live (ἡ συνήθεια). There is no more reason to suppose that this usage is wrong than to suppose that it is right; and, that being so, the simplest thing is just to follow it. At the very least that will save us from being ridiculous, as the Stoics were apt to be. They declared things which were shocking to ordinary people to be 'indifferent,' but the sceptic has no more reason to believe them indifferent than not, so he will respect all the conventions. Sextus has a true enthusiasm for this doctrine of conformity, and it gives great value to his discussion of grammar, where it is really applicable. It is not a heroic creed, but it will save a man from the worst excesses. The other point is more immediately connected with his medical profession. Though he refuses to admit that anything can be an 'indicative sign' (ἐνδεικτικὸν σημεῖον) of anything else, he fully admits the existence of the 'reminiscent sign' (ἀναμνηστικὸν σημεῖον). There is, after all, a sort of sequence (ἀκολουθία) in appearances, and it is possible to make observation (τήρησις) of this and to act accordingly. When he is on this subject, he uses language very much like that of positivism (*q.v.*), and it may be questioned if he is always quite faithful to his scepticism. Perhaps, if the matter is pressed home, he is not; but he satisfies himself on the point. We have seen that we are to follow the usage of society in our actions, and, if nature too has ways of its own, we may as well conform to these. Everywhere conformity is the lesson of scepticism.

[1] Sextus, *Pyrrh. Hyp.* i. 236.

LITERATURE.—N. MacColl, *The Greek Sceptics from Pyrrho to Sextus*, London, 1869; V. Brochard, *Les Sceptiques grecs*, Paris, 1887; A. Goedeckemeyer, *Die Gesch. des griech. Skeptizismus*, Leipzig, 1905: see also R. Hirzel, *Untersuchungen zu Cicero's philos. Schriften*, do. 1877–83, iii. 64 f.; P. Natorp, *Forschungen zur Gesch. des Erkenntnissproblems im Alterthum*, Berlin, 1884, p. 63 ff., and the Appendix.

The fragments of Timon of Phlius have been last edited by Diels along with the Life of Diogenes Laertius in *Poetarum Philosophorum Fragmenta*, Berlin, 1901. The most recent edition of Sextus Empiricus is that of Bekker (Berlin, 1842), but a new one by H. Mutschmann was in preparation before the War.

JOHN BURNET.

SCEPTICISM.—See AGNOSTICISM, BELIEF, DOUBT.

SCEPTICISM (Buddhist).—**1. Buddhism a 'rationalism.'**—Buddhism is a 'faith,' since it is ultimately based upon the authoritative word of the Master, the omniscient one; but it is also a 'free thought' or a philosophy, since the Master is not satisfied with a blind adhesion to his word and emphasizes the necessity of personal conviction, of personal inquiry. A Buddhist walks by 'sight' (*darśana*), not by 'faith' (*śraddhā*):

'Now, O monks, are you going to say: "We respect the Master, and out of respect for the Master, we believe this and that"?'—'No, O Lord'—'Is not what you will say to be true, that exactly which you have yourselves, and by yourselves, known, seen, apprehended?'—'Exactly so, O Lord.'[1]

This attitude of the Buddhist mind, which is an early one and may be described as the attitude of 'criticism,' is illustrated by the formula, 'Every thing that is well and truly said is a word of Buddha'—a recast of an earlier formula, 'Every Buddha's word is well said.'[2] The Buddhist philosopher is justified in developing any consequence of the traditional sayings, in evolving any theory—even a quite new one—which 'is' right, in denying the truth of any traditional saying which seems to be wrong. That has been taught by Buddha, not because it is true, but because it is useful.

'That *sūtra* is not a *sūtra* of "an obvious meaning" (*nītārtha*), but of a "meaning to be understood" (*neyārtha*); that has been said with an intention (*saṃdhāya*); for "it is the habit of Buddhas to comply with the world."'[3]

Buddhists, if not from the beginning, at least at a very early stage in the development of their philosophy, have been sceptics as concerns the truth of the obvious meaning of the Buddha's sayings: that only is to be regarded as true which can be proved to be true.

2. Scepticism properly so called.—Scepticism is likely to arise from rationalism, as soon as the philosopher admits that what does not support critical, dialectical inquiry (*vichārāsaha*) cannot be true. Such is the position of the Buddhist philosopher who recognizes in pure reasoning the standard of truth. The later Buddhism states this position very clearly;[4] but early Buddhism also gives evidences of it.

[1] See *Majjhima*, i. 265; cf. i. 71, and *Mahāniddesa*, p. 235; L. de la Vallée Poussin, 'Authority of the Buddhist Āgamas,' *JRAS*, new ser., xxxiv. [1902] 375, *Bouddhisme: Opinions sur l'histoire de la dogmatique*, Paris, 1909, p. 139, *The Way to Nirvāṇa*, Cambridge, 1917, p. 155.

[2] Cf. and ct. *Suttanipāta*, p. 78, and *Sikṣāsamuchchaya* (Bibl. Buddh. i., Petrograd, 1902), p. 15.

[3] See *Mūlamadhyamaka* (Bibl. Buddh. iv., Petrograd, 1913), pp. 41, n. 1, 59 f.

[4] See artt. MADHYAMAKA, MAHĀYĀNA, NIHILISM (Buddhist), PHILOSOPHY (Buddhist).

Early Buddhism[1] denies the existence of a 'doer,' of a permanent self. It does not deny that there is a 'doer' or a self from the experimental or common standpoint (*sammutisachcha*). People at large (*mahatī janatā*) believe that 'thought, mind, or consciousness' is an 'I,' but this belief is the result of the inveterate habit of regarding thought as an 'I'; for, if we examine the notion of a permanent 'I,' we see that such an 'I' would be the master of his sensations. There are perceptions, feelings, states of consciousness; a permanent 'I' cannot be these perceptions, or the place of these perceptions, etc. Later Buddhism criticizes not only the notion of 'I,' but also either the notion of an exterior thing (*bāhya*)—the Vijñānavādins[2]—or all notions—the Mādhyamikas (*q.v.*).

The last-named philosophers have surpassed all Buddhists in dialectical inquiry; they have no tenets of their own; their only aim and task is to show the real or supposed antinomies which destroy all the commonly accepted ideas:[3]

> Who walks? The man who has not begun walking, or the man who has finished walking, or the 'walker' (*gantā*)? Not the walker, since there would be two 'walkings': the walking by reason of which the walker is styled a walker and the walking which is attributed to the walker if one were to say that the walker walks.
>
> Who obtains liberation? The man who is bound or the man who is not bound? Not the former, for he is bound; not the latter, for he is liberated.
>
> The object of knowledge is previous to, or simultaneous with, or posterior to knowledge. The three hypotheses are absurd.
>
> A cause (*pratyaya*) is so called because another thing is produced by reason of it. As long as the 'another thing' is not produced, the so-called cause is not a cause and cannot produce any effect. Seeds do not produce oil, just as sand does not produce oil, because, as long as oil is not produced, seeds, just like sand, are not a cause.
>
> The effect is either existent or non-existent. If it is existent, it does not require a cause; if it is non-existent, thousands of causes cannot do anything to it.
>
> There is a doer because there is a deed; there is a deed because there is a doer. Does the doer exist first and then the deed? or the deed first and then the doer? The existence of both is very much jeopardized.
>
> Knowledge, say the Vijñānavādins, knows both itself and its object, just as a candle renders visible both itself and the non-self. If that were the case, darkness would darken itself as it does darken the non-self, and darkness therefore would not be visible.

Several of the Madhyamaka antinomies look rather sophistical and even childish; some may be worthy of attention. But is the general principle of their inquiry sound? Are facts (*vatthusachcha*) ascertained through the right means of knowledge (*pamāna*) to be rejected because we fail to understand them, to give a satisfactory definition of them (*lakkhaṇasachcha*)? Is the dialectical method the criterion of existence and non-existence? Śaṅkara rightly criticizes this philosophical position, and his remarks are worth considering.[4] But, as a matter of fact, Buddhists do not deny the existence of the things which they regard as logically impossible; they are sceptics as concerns ultimate reality, not as concerns mere existence. In the same way, Śaṅkara himself believes that individual experiences and objects exist without being real; and we may wonder how Śaṅkara, who has stated so clearly the contrast between the two truths, existence and reality, in the *Upaniṣads* and in the Vedānta, could be so slow in discovering his own theories in Buddhism.

LITERATURE.—See the works quoted in the footnotes.

L. DE LA VALLÉE POUSSIN.

[1] See art. HĪNAYĀNA.

[2] See art. PHILOSOPHY (Buddhist), 3 (*b*); *Mūlamadhyamaka*, *passim*, esp. i. 5, 6, 7, 13, ii. 1, vii. 12.

[3] See *Nyāyasūtra*, II. i. 8; and Vasubandhu's *Viṃśakakārikā*, ed. and tr. in *Muséon*, xiii. [1912] 53.

[4] The Buddhist maintains that external things are impossible; for aggregates can be defined neither as different nor as non-different from the atoms, etc. 'This conclusion we rejoin is improper, since the possibility or impossibility of things is to be determined only on the ground of the operation or non-operation of the means of right knowledge; while, on the other hand, the operation and non-operation of the means of right knowledge are not to be made dependent on preconceived possibilities or impossibilities. Possible is whatever is apprehended by perception or some other means of proof; impossible is what is not so apprehended. Now the external things are, according to their nature, apprehended by all the instruments of knowledge; how then can you maintain that they are not possible, on the ground of such idle dilemmas as that about their difference or non-difference from atoms?' (Comm. on *Vedāntasūtra*, II. ii. 28, tr. G. Thibaut, *SBE* xxxiv. [1890] 421).

SCHISM.

1. Meaning of the word.—The word *σχίσμα*, as used in classical Greek, means a 'tear' or 'rent.' Aristotle[1] employs it to denote a cleft or division in a hoof, and Theophrastus[2] to denote a division in a leaf. In the Synoptists it has the same literal meaning. In Mt 9^{16}=Mk 2^{21} it means a rent in a garment. In the Gospel of St. John and 1 Cor. it has a metaphorical sense, signifying in Jn 7^{43} 9^{16} 10^{19} a difference of opinion about our Lord, and in 1 Co 1^{10} $11^{18f.}$ party strife in the Church. In the second of the passages from 1 Cor. it is connected with *αἵρεσις*:

> ἀκούω σχίσματα ἐν ὑμῖν ὑπάρχειν . . . δεῖ γὰρ καὶ αἱρέσεις ἐν ὑμῖν εἶναι· ἵνα οἱ δόκιμοι φανεροὶ γένωνται ἐν ὑμῖν.

Various attempts have been made to distinguish between *σχίσμα* and *αἵρεσις* in this passage,[3] but the two words probably mean much the same.[4] If there is any distinction to be made between them, *αἵρεσις* may imply the formation of a separate society or faction, not merely the holding of views different from those of the majority. In any case the difference is of degree, not of kind.

In the writings of the 'Apostolic' Fathers *σχίσμα* is used in much the same sense as in the passages quoted from 1 Cor., of party strife *within the Church.*[5] On the other hand, *αἵρεσις* has already come to mean 'false belief,' as in Ignatius, *ad Trall.* vi., where, speaking of Docetism, he says:

> ἀλλοτρίας δὲ βοτάνης ἀπέχεσθαι, ἥτις ἐστὶν αἵρεσις.[6]

But differences of opinion in the Church tended to become separation from the Church, especially when the Church began to spread among men of various nationalities and modes of thought. Thus, in course of time, the word *σχίσμα* came to denote a separation from the main body of the Church, not involving the rejection of any of the fundamental doctrines of the faith, while *αἵρεσις* was confined to a denial of one or more of the fundamental doctrines. This use of *σχίσμα* appears first in Irenæus, whose words are:

> 'Ανακρινεῖ δὲ καὶ τοὺς τὰ σχίσματα ἐργαζομένους κενοὺς ὄντας τῆς τοῦ θεοῦ ἀγάπης, καὶ το ἴδιον λυσιτελὲς σκοποῦντας, ἀλλὰ μὴ τὴν ἕνωσιν τῆς ἐκκλησίας· καὶ διὰ μικρὰς καὶ τὰς τυχούσας αἰτίας τὸ μέγα καὶ ἔνδοξον σῶμα τοῦ Χριστοῦ τέμνοντας καὶ διαιροῦντας, καὶ ὅσιν τὸ ἐπ' αὐτοῖς, ἀναιροῦντας . . . Οὐδεμία δὲ τηλικαύτη δύναται πρὸς αὐτῶν κατόρθωσις γενέσθαι· ἡλίκη τοῦ σχίσματός ἐστιν ἡ βλάβη.[7]

Among the Fathers writing in Latin Augustine may be regarded as representative. In his treatise against Faustus he defines schism, as distinct from heresy, in the following terms:

> 'Schisma . . . est eadem opinantem atque eodem ritu colentem quo caeteri solo congregationis delectari discidio.'[8]

Some of the Fathers assert indeed that schism tends to become heresy. Jerome says:

> 'Inter haeresim et schisma hoc esse arbitrantur, quod haeresis perversum dogma habeat; schisma propter episcopalem dissensionem ab Ecclesia separetur. Caeterum nullum schisma non sibi aliquam confingit haeresim.'[9]

[1] *Hist. An.* ii. 1. 26.

[2] *Ph.* III. xi. 1.

[3] *E.g.*, Trench, *NT Synonyms*[8], London, 1876, p. 359.

[4] Theodoret, in his commentary on the passage (J. A. Cramer, *Catenæ Græcorum Patrum in NT*, Oxford, 1844, v. 214), says: Σχίσματα οὐ δογματικὰ λέγει· ἀλλ' ἐκεῖνα τὰ τῆς φιλαρχίας . . . αἱρέσεις τὰς φιλονεικίας λέγει, οὐ τὰς τῶν δογμάτων διαφοράς. Cf. Cyprian, *Test.* iii. 86, 93. In Tit 3^{10} αἱρετικός=σχισματικός. But cf. *Essays on the Early Hist. of the Church and the Ministry*, ed. H. B. Swete, London, 1918, pp. 45, 319.

[5] Clem. *ad Cor. I.* 2^6 49^5 54^2; *Didache*, iv. 3; Barnabas, *Ep.* xix. 12; Hermas, *Sim.* viii. 9.

[6] Cf. *ad Ephes.* vi.

[7] *Adv. Hær.* IV. xxxiii. 7. He is speaking of the 'discipulus spiritalis' of 1 Co 2^{15}.

[8] *C. Faustum*, xx. 3; cf. *c. Crescon.* ii. 3–7, *Quæst. in Matthæum*, xi. 1f.: 'Haeretici falsa credunt . . . schismaticos non fides diversa [facit], sed communionis disrupta societas,' *c. Gaudent.* ii. 9.

[9] *In Epist. ad Titum*, iii. 10.

And Cyprian appears even to identify the two.[1] But on the whole the distinction in meaning between the two words is preserved both by ancient and by more recent writers.[2]

2. The Church and schism.—Cyprian is the first writer to discuss the relation of the Church to schism. He had to combat Novatianism, which, like Montanism and the later Donatism, was a Puritan movement on the part of men impatient of the evils in the Church and dreading the contamination of what they regarded as Catholic laxity.[3] 'Those who tolerate such laxity,' they said, 'cease to be a part of the true Church.'[4] Cyprian's attitude towards schism may be gathered from his letters and especially from his tract *de Unitate Ecclesiæ*.

> 'Deus unus est,' are his words, 'et Christus unus, et una Ecclesia eius, et fides una, et plebs una in solidam corporis unitatem concordiae glutino copulata . . . Quidquid a matrice discesserit, seorsum vivere et spirare non poterit.'[5]

He heaps up metaphors to illustrate the unity of the Church. It is like the unity of the three Persons of the Godhead. He who does not keep this unity does not keep the law of God or the faith of the Father and the Son:

> 'Hanc unitatem qui non tenet, Dei legem non tenet, non tenet Patris et Filii fidem, vitam non tenet, et salutem.'[6]

The schismatic is worse than the apostate. The latter sins and may repent; the former sins daily and glories in his sin. Apostates injure themselves only; the schismatic endangers the souls of very many.[7]

Augustine had to deal with the Donatists (*q.v.*). He takes much the same view of schism as Cyprian had done. The Donatists argued that the Catholics by their laxity had forfeited their baptismal privilege, and that the Donatists alone formed the true Church. To this Augustine replied that the validity of a sacrament does not depend upon the holiness of him who administers it, and that the only feature by which the true Church can be recognized is its catholicity.

> 'Securus iudicat orbis terrarum, bonos non esse qui se dividunt ab orbe terrarum.'[8]

Schismatics like the Donatists should be punished. Those who are outside the Church have not Christ, the head of the Church.

> 'Clamate, si audetis puniantur . . . sceleris sive libidinis facinora seu flagitia; sola sacrilegia volumus a regnantium legibus impunita.'[9] 'Habere autem caput Christum nemo poterit, nisi qui in eius corpore fuerit.'[10]

But he does not go so far as Cyprian, who had maintained that sacraments administered by separatists were invalid.[11] He only asserts that no schismatic can receive them validly, so long as he remains a stranger to that unity in love which is the Catholic Church. And in his general attitude towards schismatics, like Optatus of Milevis, he is more kindly than Cyprian.[12] But schism, in his view, as in that of Cyprian, is a grievous sin.

Schism, then, since it is rebellion against authority, and since it causes a breach in the unity of the Church, was always regarded in early times as a very serious matter. To maintain unimpaired the unity of the Catholic Church was the duty of all good Christians.[1] But how was this unity to be maintained? By means of the sacraments, especially the Eucharist, the *sacramentum unitatis*. And, further, the centre of unity was the bishop. What Ignatius[2] constantly affirmed of particular churches Cyprian transferred to the Church as a whole.

> 'The Episcopate is one,' he says; 'the individual bishops are members of a great brotherhood, bound together in a corporate unity. Bishops form a kind of equal co-partnership.'[3]

This view of the episcopate, however, gradually gave place to another. Quite early in the writings of the Fathers is found the idea that churches founded by the apostles and churches to which they wrote letters were able to say with more certainty than others what the teaching of the apostles really was. Irenæus speaks of Rome and Smyrna as such churches. His words are:

> 'Maximae et antiquissimae, et omnibus cognitae, a gloriosissimis duobus apostolis Petro et Paulo Romae fundatae et constitutae ecclesiae, eam quam habet ab apostolis traditionem . . . indicantes, confundimus omnes eos . . . qui praeterquam oportet colligunt.'[4]

And a little later:

> Καὶ Πολύκαρπος . . . ὑπὸ Ἀποστόλων κατασταθεὶς . . . ἐν τῇ ἐν Σμύρνῃ Ἐκκλησίᾳ, ἐπίσκοπος . . . ἐξῆλθε τοῦ βίου, ταῦτα διδάξας ἀεί, ἃ καὶ παρὰ τῶν Ἀποστόλων ἔμαθεν, ἃ καὶ ἡ Ἐκκλησία παραδίδωσιν, ἃ καὶ μόνα ἐστὶν ἀληθῆ.[5]

Tertullian[6] enumerates Ephesus, Smyrna, Rome, Corinth, Philippi. Fulgentius[7] speaks of Rome, Alexandria, Jerusalem. In all these lists Rome appears. Rome had been the capital of the world, and the bishop of Rome came to occupy a position of exceptional influence, partly because of the orthodoxy of the Roman Church, partly because of the position and history of Rome. The bishop of Rome, in fact, wielded in the Church the same kind of authority as the emperors had wielded in the State. Thus, in course of time, obedience to the Roman pontiff became the test of catholicity. Those who refused to submit to his authority were branded as schismatics. Optatus[8] is perhaps the first of the Fathers to claim for the bishop of Rome universal jurisdiction—a claim which eventually came to be admitted by the Western Church generally. The growth of papal absolutism was indeed slow and was not without its checks—as, *e.g.*, when Gregory the Great repudiated for him-

[1] Cyprian, *Ep.* iii. 3, lii. 1, lxxiii. 2, lxxiv. 11, quoted by Harnack, *Hist. of Dogma*, Eng. tr., London, 1893, ii. 92.

[2] Cf. Hooker, *Ecclesiastical Polity*, v. 68. 6 *ad fin.*: 'Heretics, as touching those points of doctrine wherein they fail, and schismatics, as touching the quarrels for which or the duties wherein they divide themselves from their brethren . . . have all forsaken the true Church of God.'

[3] 'Schism may have what we must call a nobler root [than pride and self-assertion]. It may spring from impatient, undisciplined zeal against evil in the Church' (C. Gore, *Roman Catholic Claims*[9], London, 1905, p. 126).

[4] See art. NOVATIANISTS.

[5] *De Unitate*, 23.

[6] *Ib.* 6.

[7] *De Unit.* 19; E. W. Benson, *Cyprian*, London, 1899, ch. iv.; J. F. Bethune Baker, *Introd. to Early Hist. of Christian Doctrine*, do. 1903, p. 363 ff.; T. A. Lacey, *Unity and Schism*, do. 1917, pp. 34 ff., 168 ff.

[8] *C. Epist. Parmen.* iii. 24 *ad fin.*

[9] *C. Gaudent.* 20, *c. Epist. Parmen.* i. 16, *de Correctione Don.* (=*Epp.* 185) vi.

[10] *De Unit.* 49.

[11] Cf. Basil, *Epist. Canon. I. ad Amphilochium.*

[12] Optatus, *de Schism. Don.* I. iii. 28: 'Sunt sine dubio [Donatistae] fratres, quamvis non boni.' For Optatus see O. R. Vassall-Phillips, *St. Optatus of Milevis*, London, 1917. The Church recognized degrees of schism. The gravity of the schism was in proportion to the degree of separation from the main body (J. Bingham, *Antiquities of the Christian Church*, ed. London, 1870, ii. 879 f.). The worst form was the setting up of altar against altar. For Augustine's general attitude towards schism see P. Batiffol, in *The Constructive Quarterly*, v. [1917] 30–55.

[1] Cyprian is praised by Augustine because (in spite of the unjust claims of Stephen, bishop of Rome) he did not break the unity of the Church by separation. He is regarded as a typical instance of the 'unschismatic temper' (Augustine, *de Bapt.* v. 25–36; cf. Jerome, *adv. Lucifer.* 25).

[2] Cf. *ad Ephes.* 4, *Smyrn.* 8, *Trall.* 3. 'Ignatius is the incarnation, as it were, of three closely connected ideas: the glory of martyrdom, the omnipotence of episcopacy, and the hatred of heresy and schism' (P. Schaff, *Hist. of the Church; Ante-Nicene Christianity*, new ed., Edinburgh, 1884, ii. 657).

[3] *Epp.* lxvi. 8, *de Unit.* 5; see Lacey, p. 168 ff.; Benson, p. 182; Jerome, *Epp.* cxlvi.

[4] *Adv. Hær.* III. iii. 1.

[5] III. iii. 4.

[6] *de Præscr.* 32, 36.

[7] *de Trin.* i.

[8] ii. 2 (vii. 3): 'In qua una cathedra [Romae] unitas ab omnibus servaretur . . . ut iam schismaticus et peccator esset, qui contra singularem cathedram alteram collocaret.' Cyprian has sometimes been claimed as a supporter of the 'papal' view on the strength of his use of the phrase 'Cathedra Petri' (*de Unit.* 4). But his whole argument shows that the phrase denotes, not the see of Rome, but the bishop's seat of authority in each several church. See Gore, *The Church and the Ministry*[4], London, 1900, p. 156 n., *Roman Catholic Claims*[9], p. 177 n. ff., *The Early Hist. of the Church and Ministry*, p. 250 ff.

self the title of universal bishop.[1] But, on the whole, it was steady, till at length Thomas Aquinas in the 13th cent. could say, in language which was accepted as authoritative by the whole Church in the West:

'Et ideo proprie schismatici dicuntur qui propria sponte et intentione se ab unitate Ecclesiae separant . . . Caput [Ecclesiae] est ipse Christus, cuius vicem in Ecclesia gerit summus pontifex. Et ideo schismatici dicuntur qui subesse renuunt summo pontifici.'[2]

He goes on to distinguish between heresy and schism:

'Haeresis per se opponitur fidei; schisma autem per se opponitur unitati ecclesiasticae charitatis . . . Peccatum schismatis est gravius peccato infidelitatis . . . Schisma est contra bonum multitudinis, id est, contra ecclesiasticam unitatem; infidelitas autem est contra bonum particulare unius . . . Schismatici habent aliquam potestatem quia retinent ordinem . . . Potest sacramentum tradere separatus . . . Duplex est spiritualis potestas—una quidem *sacramentalis*—alia *jurisdictionalis*' (schismatics have the former, but not the latter; cf. the whole section).

The final stage in the growth of papalism was reached in 1870, when the Vatican Council promulgated a series of decrees, one of which runs thus:

'Nos dogma esse definimus: Romanum Pontificem, cum ex cathedra loquitur—id est, cum doctrinam de fide vel moribus ab universa Ecclesia tenendam definit, ea infallibilitate pollere qua Divinus Redemptor Ecclesiam suam instructam esse voluit: ideoque definitiones ex sese, *non autem ex consensu Ecclesiae*, irreformabiles esse.'[3]

No doubt such claims were, in themselves, not new. The bull *Unam Sanctam* of Boniface VIII. at the beginning of the 14th cent. had claimed for the pope absolute authority, but this was repudiated in the next century by the Council of Constance, which demanded that the pope should obey its decisions in matters of faith. The Vatican decree makes the pope independent of Councils.[4]

3. Revolts from Rome.—Absolutism, in Church as in State, tends to produce restlessness and eventual revolt. And it is roughly true that the majority of the 'schisms' from the 11th cent. onwards have come about as the result, direct or indirect, of the absolutism which finds its chief expression, in matters ecclesiastical, in the Church of Rome. The first great revolt was the separation of the Eastern Church from that of the West. Up to the 11th cent. the external unity of the Church had been, on the whole, maintained. The various schisms—Montanism, Novatianism, Donatism—had not seriously impaired that unity. But in 1052 the long-standing differences, partly racial, partly ecclesiastical, between Rome and Constantinople were brought to a head by the formal excommunication of the Eastern Church by Pope Leo IX. The position taken up, and held ever since, by the autocephalous Churches of the East is that the Western Church, by introducing innovations regarding the foundations of Church government, separated herself from the Mother Churches of the East, which are the true heirs of the old undivided Church.[5] It has been argued that this separation was not a pure schism, since a point of doctrine was involved. But the addition of the *Filioque* clause to the Nicene Creed was not, in itself, important doctrinally. In the words of Laud it was 'but a question in manner of speech, and therefore not fundamental.'[6] The protest of the East was chiefly against its insertion in an ecumenical creed on purely Western authority—that of Pope Nicholas I. Thus the separation of East and West was, fundamentally, a protest against papalism.[1] In the West external unity was maintained, not infrequently by force, till the 16th cent., when a considerable part of Europe broke away from the papal obedience. In England the Reformation was conservative in character. Episcopacy was retained. The ancient creeds of the Church were kept as the authorized expression of the faith. The public services were founded on the primitive offices. But elsewhere, save in Scandinavia, Episcopacy was rejected. In Germany the reforming movement took the form of Lutheranism (*q.v.*); in Scotland and, to a limited extent, in France Calvinism (*q.v.*) became the accepted form of Protestantism. So far as England is concerned, the last stage in the separation from Rome was reached when, in 1570, Pope Pius V. published his bull of excommunication, *Regnans in Excelsis*. By the bull the Anglican 'schism,' hitherto regarded as provisional, was made definite.[2]

4. Post-Reformation schisms.—The reign of Queen Elizabeth saw the rise of Puritanism (*q.v.*) and Presbyterianism (*q.v.*) *within* the Church of England. In the latter part of this reign the Puritan party became influential, and it grew still further in strength during the next reigns, though there was, as yet, no considerable secession *from* the Church. Congregationalism (*q.v.*), from small beginnings in Elizabeth's reign, became prominent during the Commonwealth. It would have nothing to do with the parochial system. The visible Church was, in its view, made up of faithful men and women, and of such only,[3] freely gathered together into congregations, each congregation being autonomous. Thus, in one of its main features, it resembled Donatism. In 1633 the first congregation of Baptists[4] was formed by a secession from the Congregationalists. Both these bodies were democratic and therefore farther removed than the Anglican Church from Roman Catholic autocracy. The final separation between that Church and Puritanism was brought about by the 'fatal' Act of Uniformity of 1662. From this Act Dissent took its rise. The next great secession was that of Methodism (*q.v.*), under the leadership of John Wesley. He himself declared that he lived and died a member of the Anglican Church, but his action in ordaining bishops and presbyters made separation inevitable. 'Ordination,' in Lord Mansfield's words, 'is separation.' Since that time numerous separated bodies have come into existence in Britain, America, and the British colonies. This 'fissiparous tendency' has been ascribed to the 'centrifugal force of Protestantism.' Probably, however, since it is found chiefly among Anglo-Saxons, it is, in essence, racial—the result of a strong individualism, and perhaps also of a certain self-regarding temper and an impatient zeal against evil in the Church. Nor must it be forgotten that the Anglican Church has in the past displayed something of the arrogant spirit which brings about schisms. She has too often shown a want of sympathy with new ideas

[1] *Epp.* viii. 30 ('ad Eulogium'); cf. F. Homes Dudden, *Gregory the Great*, London, 1905, ii. 224 ff.

[2] *Summa*, II. ii. 39.

[3] Sess. iv. cap. iv.; see art. INFALLIBILITY.

[4] See Gore, *Roman Catholic Claims*[9], p. 122. Those members of the Roman obedience who refused to accept this decree formed the 'Old Catholic' body (see art. OLD CATHOLICISM).

[5] See art. EASTERN CHURCH.

[6] *A Relation of the Conference between William Laud, Archbishop of Canterbury, and Mr. Fisher the Jesuit*, London, 1639, § 9; Laud, *Works*, Oxford, 1849, ii. 27.

[1] The 'schism' of Antioch in the 4th cent. did not result in a permanent separation from the main body of the Church, and the 'Great Western Schism' (1377-1417) was not, strictly speaking, a schism at all, since it did not involve any denial of papal authority, but was a dispute as to which of the rival popes had the right to wield that authority.

[2] Roman Catholic theologians sometimes distinguish between active and passive schism, the former being a deliberate separation from the Church on the part of the schismatic, the latter the lot of those whom the Church rejects by excommunication. Thus the Anglican Church can say: 'Schisma patimur, non fecimus.'

[3] 'The kingdom of God is not to be begun by whole Parishes, but rather by the worthiest were they never so few' (Robert Browne, *A True and Short Declaration*, Middelburg [1583]; see art. BROWNISM).

[4] See art. ANABAPTISTS.

and new movements. In striving after uniformity she has, not infrequently, sacrificed unity.

5. The ethics of schism.—Two opposite views have been held in regard to schism on its ethical side. (1) There is the view, first formulated by Irenæus in the passage quoted at the beginning of the article, that schism is so great an evil that nothing can justify it, and that no reforms brought about by schismatics can make up for the harm caused by the schism.[1] (2) The opposite view is that churches, like commercial undertakings, are all the better for competition, and that schisms are desirable in that they promote a healthy rivalry—that in short 'a plurality of independent Christian communities in the same country is the ideal state of things.'[2] The latter view has been largely abandoned during the last few years by Nonconformists as well as by Churchmen. The words of Richard Baxter, 'He that seeth not the necessity of unity knoweth not the nature of the Church,'[3] represent, on the whole, the attitude of the great majority of thoughtful people at the present time. 'We have at least ceased to be proud of our divisions,' says a leading Nonconformist. 'A great longing possesses many of us to break down the barriers which separate us one from another.'[4] And indeed it is difficult, if not impossible, to maintain this view if the teaching of the Bible is accepted. Just as the prophets of the older Dispensation deplored the division between Israel and Judah (Is $11^{12f.}$, Ezk 37^{16}, Jer 3^{18}, Hos 1^{11}), so our Lord and the NT writers constantly put forward unity in the Church as the ideal (Jn $10^{16.17}$, esp. vv.$^{20-23}$, Eph 4, Ro $16^{17f.}$, Gal 3^{28}). Moreover, the metaphors used to describe the Church—family, vine, body, temple, etc.—all emphasize the thought of oneness in Christ. There are, further, the practical evils of division—overlapping, waste of power, and rivalry, often degenerating into mutual hostility. In regard to the former view, it may be admitted that schism is an evil, since it is contrary to charity and that unity which is Christ's ideal for the Church, and is in many cases an act of disobedience to lawful authority. But the question remains, At whose door does the sin lie in any particular case of schism? The selfish and arrogant temper which is both the cause of schism in others and itself schismatic may be found in the body from which separation is made as well as in that which separates. In the case of the 'Anglican schism' the contention of the great Anglican divines of the 17th cent.—Hooker, Jewel, Jeremy Taylor, and the rest—is that the Church of England was compelled by the arrogant demands of Rome to break away from her obedience, and that, if that Church has separated from Rome, she has never 'swerved either from the word of God, or from the Apostles of Christ, or from the primitive Church.'[5] It may be thought that the English reformers displayed too much impatience and were over-hasty in some of their proceedings. In no ecclesiastical quarrel is one party wholly in the right. But, when all deductions are made, it remains true that 'we were justified [in our separation from Rome] because the only terms on which we could retain communion with Rome were sinful terms.'[1] The Dissenters took up much the same position in regard to the Church of England. They contended that it was impossible for them to remain in communion with her, since they honestly and *ex animo* believed that they would be committing sin if they did so.[2] The extremists among them went so far as to declare that the Church of England had ceased to be a Christian Church. In like manner the separation of the Free Church of Scotland from the Established Church in the 19th cent. was regarded by the secessionists as the assertion of a great spiritual principle which made it impossible for them any longer to remain members of the Establishment.

If, then, schism is sometimes justified, it is yet clearly contrary to the ideal of our Lord and His apostles. The principle of schism has rarely been defended. At the present time the evils of separation are becoming felt more perhaps than at any previous era in the history of the Christian Church, and suggestions are being made in various quarters with the view of healing the divisions of Christendom. These are, as yet, for the most part tentative, although in Australia the question of the reunion of the Australian Church in communion with the Church of England and the Presbyterian Church seems to have advanced beyond the tentative stage.[3] But, before any large plans for reunion can be carried into effect, it would seem necessary that the various separated bodies should make it quite clear what they regard as essential and what they are prepared to sacrifice. Rome, officially at least, demands submission to the authority of the pope as the only condition of reunion. The Anglican Church, following the lead of the American Episcopal Church,[4] has, in the 'Lambeth Quadrilateral' of 1888, laid down 'as a basis for reunion' the following principles: (1) the acceptance of the Holy Scriptures as the rule of faith; (2) the acceptance of the Apostles' and Nicene Creeds as the sufficient statement of faith; (3) the recognition of the two sacraments, Baptism and Holy Communion; and (4) the recognition of the historic episcopate.[5] In March 1917 the 'Federation of Evangelical Free Churches of England,' wishing 'to seek closer federation with one another for the better witness to, and service of, the Gospel,' adopted the reports of four Committees which were drawn up with the object of promoting 'unity and communion . . . with other branches of the Church of Christ.' By action such as this the ground is being cleared and the hope of ultimate reunion and the healing of schisms brought nearer to realization. But it will take time and demand the exercise of much faith and patience before the consummation comes about. We must

[1] See Gore, *Roman Catholic Claims*⁹, p. 128; L. Duchesne, *Autonomies ecclésiastiques; Eglises séparées*², Paris, 1904.

[2] See *The Life and Letters of Fenton John Anthony Hort*, London, 1896, ii. 428; he is referring to the position taken up by W. F. Moulton.

[3] R. Baxter, *The Cure of Church Divisions*, London, 1670, p. 66; cf. Preface, § 3, and the whole treatise.

[4] R. A. Aytoun, in *The Free Catholic*, Birmingham, April 1917, p. 56; cf. R. Baxter, *The True and Only Way of Concord*, London, 1680; R. J. Campbell, *A Spiritual Pilgrimage*, do. 1917, p. 298 ff.; P. T. Forsyth, *Lectures on the Church and the Sacraments*, do. 1917 ('We look forward to an Œcumenical Christianity').

[5] Jewel, *Works* (Parker Society), Cambridge, 1848, iii. 59 ff. For other references see A. J. Mason, *The Church of England and Episcopacy*, Cambridge, 1914, ch. i.: 'There is no Catholic principle which can justify us in supposing that either the . . . Eastern Church or the Anglican Church has been guilty of the sin of schism, in that sense in which schism is the act of self-withdrawal from the Church catholic' (Gore, *Roman Catholic Claims*⁹, p. 137).

[1] Mason, p. 542.

[2] W. B. Selbie, in *Mansfield College Essays*, London, 1909, p. 29 ff. and the authorities there quoted. 'In the case of the protestant dissenters the whole argument turned upon the point whether the terms of communion with the church of England were or were not sinful. Church writers were ready to admit that if they were *thought* to be sinful, those who thought so were bound *in foro conscientiae* to secede' (Mason, p. 542).

[3] H. Lowther Clarke (archbishop of Melbourne), in *The Constructive Quarterly*, v. 19 ff.

[4] See Lacey, p. 216 ff. The document of the American bishops, drawn up in 1886, differs somewhat in form, though not in essentials, from that emanating from the Lambeth Conference.

[5] 'Episcopacy has been the instrument of the Spirit . . . [but] it is conceivable that it may be changed out of recognition or that another instrument may be found. You may hold with unhesitating faith that the Church of Christ is one, and that its unity will, in good time, be made manifest, but it may be unwise to pin your faith exclusively to episcopacy' (Lacey, p. 48).

not make the old mistake of identifying unity and uniformity. In the early Church there was practical unity combined with a great variety of local use and custom. And at the present time certain 'Uniat' Churches of the Roman obedience have their own rites. 'In una Fide nihil officit consuetudo diversa.' And, finally, we must recognize that 'the necessary prelude to reunion is not a common formula but a whole-hearted acceptance of a common principle of thought and conduct.'[1] The unity of the Church must be put on a religious rather than a theological basis. We must recognize that all Christians are brothers in Christ, and this recognition will enable us to promote *τὴν ἑνότητα τοῦ πνεύματος ἐν τῷ συνδέσμῳ τῆς εἰρήνης* (Eph 4^3).

LITERATURE.—In addition to the literature mentioned in the art. the following may be consulted: J. Bramhall, *Works*, Oxford, 1842, i. 84 ff.; H. Thorndike, *Works*, do. 1844, i., and others in the Library of Anglo-Catholic Theology (Oxford, 1842–63); W. Saywell, *Reformation of the Church of England Justified*, Cambridge, 1688; J. de Launoi, *Epistolæ Omnes*, do. 1689 (preface); T. A. Lacey, *The Unity of the Church*, London, 1898; T. M. Lindsay, *The Church and the Ministry in the Early Centuries*, do. 1902; R. Sohm, *Kirchenrecht*, Leipzig, 1892, i.; Newman Smyth, *Passing Protestantism and Coming Catholicism*, London, 1908; E. Maguire, *Is Schism Lawful?*, Dublin, 1915; W. Palmer, *A Treatise on the Church of Christ*², London, 1842; J. J. von Döllinger, *Lectures on the Reunion of the Churches*, tr. H. N. Oxenham, do. 1872; A. Chandler, *The English Church and Reunion*, do. 1916; *Our Place in Christendom* (various writers), do. 1916; the art. 'Schism' in *PRE*³, Schaff-Herzog, *CE*, *Catholic Dictionary*⁹ (London, 1907), *Protestant Dictionary* (London, 1904); *Pan-Anglican Congress Reports*, vii. (London, 1908) 50 ff.

H. W. FULFORD.

SCHLEIERMACHER.

SCHLEIERMACHER. — Friedrich Daniel Ernst Schleiermacher was born in Breslau in 1768 and died in Berlin in 1834. He is among the most important and influential of German theologians and has been called, not without reason, the father of modern theology. The boldness of his new departures, the wide range of his thought, and his experimental method mark him out as a pioneer.

1. Life and character.—Like many great men, Schleiermacher owed more to his mother than to his father. His mother, *née* Stubenrauch, was a woman of keen intellect and deep piety; she guided her son's earlier education, and throughout her life the two were knit together by bonds of the closest affection. His father, Gottlieb, was chaplain to a Prussian regiment in Silesia. His duties took him frequently away from the home and so left the family largely to the mother's care. He was a Reformed theologian of the old school and of a stern and unbending orthodoxy. As might be expected, plain living and high thinking were the rule in his household. The young Schleiermacher began his school-days at five years of age. In 1783 he was sent along with his brother and sister to a Moravian school at Niesky in Upper Lusatia and two years later to the Moravian College at Barby. In his many journeys the father had come into close contact with the Moravians and coveted for his children the pious atmosphere and healthy moral discipline of their educational system. To the son also this was at first equally congenial, but later the bonds began to chafe his restless spirit. He confesses to a constitutional scepticism, or itch for inquiry, which caused him no little mental disquiet and ultimately led to a temporary breach both with his teachers and with his father. He declined to bow to their authority and insisted on his own intellectual and spiritual independence, but always in the most filial and reverent spirit. At the same time he was deeply influenced by the Moravian teaching and tone, and to this he owed the strain of deep piety which is so marked in all his writings. In 1787, with the full consent of his father, Schleiermacher left Barby and entered the University of Halle. At that time Halle was a centre of rationalism under the influence of Semler and Wolf. Schleiermacher attended their lectures and those of Eberhard, from whom he learned that love of Plato for which he afterwards became conspicuous. He also studied NT criticism, but neglected the OT, to his lasting disadvantage. But his main interest was in the work of Kant, Jacobi, and Spinoza. Even as a student he began a reconstruction of Kant's system on lines suggested by his study of Plato, while from 'the holy and blessed Spinoza' he derived the foundation ideas of his ethical system. This eclectic course of study left him, at the end of his university career, with little more than the hope of 'attaining, by earnest research and patient examination of all the witnesses, to a reasonable degree of certainty, and to a knowledge of the boundaries of human science and learning.'[1]

In 1790 Schleiermacher obtained his licentiate and became tutor in the house of Count Dohna at Schlobitten in W. Prussia. For such a position his independent spirit was not altogether suited, but there is no doubt that he gained considerably in ease of manner and *savoir faire* from the home life of the Dohna family. In 1794 he was ordained and became for a time assistant to his uncle, the aged pastor of Landsberg-on-the-Warthe. Two years later he moved to Berlin to become chaplain to the Charité Hospital. This early sojourn in Berlin was the most formative period in his career. His ecclesiastical duties were largely formal, and he spent most of his time in philosophical and theological study and in intercourse with a wide and charming circle of friends. This drew him out of himself and completed the process of refinement begun at Schlobitten. It was the time when the Romantic movement was at its height, and Schleiermacher's sensitive and imaginative spirit was deeply influenced by it. His intimacy with F. Schlegel and his rather dangerous platonic friendship with Eleonore Grunow, the wife of a Berlin pastor, stirred his emotional nature to its depths and enriched his human sympathies. The firstfruit of this period of fermentation was the epoch-making work, *Reden über die Religion*, issued in 1799, in which, as against its 'cultured despisers,' he vindicated the place of religion in man's nature and laid the foundations of a theology based upon experience. The following year appeared the *Monologen*, in which he outlined his ethical system and asserted the freedom of the human spirit in its relations both with society and with the universe. Both books show the influence of his deeper studies in Spinoza and Fichte.

In 1802 Schleiermacher left Berlin in order to become pastor in the little town of Stolpe in Pomerania. The change was altogether to the advantage of his moral and spiritual development. It released him from the too fascinating literary and æsthetic influences of Berlin and gave him time to think and to cultivate his soul. While at Stolpe, he completed the translation of Plato which he had begun along with Schlegel—a task which confirmed him in the belief that he was dealing with the greatest of the philosophers. There, too, he published the first of his strictly philosophical works, *Grundlinien einer Kritik der bisherigen Sittenlehre*—a Herculean labour which produced but little effect owing to its obscurity of style and its purely negative and critical spirit. He passes in review the systems of Plato and Spinoza, Kant and Fichte, and decides very strongly in favour of the two former; but even these he considers deficient in that they give no complete account of the laws and ends of human life as a whole. What Schleiermacher desiderated and

[1] F. Weston (bishop of Zanzibar), *The Fulness of Christ*, London, 1916, p. 5.

[1] Letter to his Father, Dec. 1789.

sought himself to supply was a moral system which would regard the universe as a realm of ends. During this period also he paid more attention to preaching, which he regarded as the best means of bringing his personal influence to bear on the general sense of mankind in the mass. He sought by it to bring home to men the power of religion, especially in its ethical and practical aspects.

In 1804 Schleiermacher returned to his old university, Halle, as preacher and professor of theology. In that home of rationalism his reputation as a *Romantiker* and a pietist caused him to be regarded at first with some suspicion. But he soon won his way to a considerable reputation as lecturer and preacher. The fine dialogue, *Weihnachtsfeier*, which he published in 1806, served to illustrate his growing appreciation of the fundamentals of Christianity and also the confusion which still marked his theology. It is a strongly imaginative work and shows traces of a vein of real poetry. At Halle he also busied himself with patriotic political utterances, drawn from him by the need of the times, and with schemes for Church reform—a subject in which he remained deeply interested all through his life. In 1806 the University of Halle was temporarily suspended owing to Napoleon's invasion, and Schleiermacher retired to the island of Rügen. After the battle of Jena he returned to Berlin and was soon afterwards appointed pastor of the Trinity Church. The following year he married the widow of his friend Willich, with whom he lived very happily, in spite of the disparity in years (he was old enough to be her father). In 1810 he took a leading part in founding the university of Berlin and was at once called to fill the chair of theology. He was also elected secretary to the Academy of Sciences. He lectured on almost every branch of theology as well as on philosophy and philosophical introduction. He also preached regularly on Sundays, and his preaching speedily won for him a foremost place in the national life. The force and fire of his sermons, their sound common sense, and their bearing on the needs and duties of the nation at a time of danger and humiliation won for them a wide hearing and a generous appreciation. At the same time Schleiermacher was deeply concerned with the reorganization of the Prussian Church and became a lifelong advocate of union between the Lutheran and Reformed Churches. He became a great personage in the life of Berlin both social and official. The firstfruits of his new position appeared in the small volume entitled *Kurze Darstellung des theologischen Studiums* (1811). In this he surveyed the whole field of theological inquiry in quite a new way and laid down the lines for all future systematizing of the subject. It was a most important and fruitful new departure. Ten years later he issued his monumental theological work, *Der christliche Glaube nach den Grundsätzen der evangelischen Kirche*. This was an attempt to reform and restate Protestant theology on lines suggested by the *Reden*, making religious experience, or the sense of dependence on God mediated through Jesus Christ, the norm of dogmatic theology rather than the Creeds, the Fathers, or the unaided human reason. It met with much criticism from both evangelicals and rationalists; but Schleiermacher defended his positions with vigour and masterly skill, and there is no doubt that the fundamental ideas of his work have entered into the warp and woof of modern theological thought. He may have no disciples in the strict sense of the term, but every theologian is his debtor. The *Christliche Glaube* went through two or three editions in its author's lifetime, each of which was greatly altered. It should be read in connexion with his defence of it published in letters to his friend Lücke in *Studien und Kritiken* for 1829. In the same year Schleiermacher lost his only son —a blow from which he never recovered. He was now an old man; but he persevered in his manifold labours and controversies and retained his full mental vigour to the end. He died in 1834 after a few days' illness, full of years and of honours.

In appearance Schleiermacher was short of stature and slightly hump-backed. His face was grave and strongly marked, but very mobile and full of fire and expression, while his movements were quick and nervous. He had a ready and satirical wit, but it was never malicious. He kept his friendships well and was of a most affectionate nature, and he bore no grudge against his opponents. He prided himself on a certain philosophic calm and on a complete control of his emotions. At the same time he felt strongly and was often moved by conviction into lines of conduct that were by no means to his advantage. He gives the impression of a strong, fervid soul, a deeply Christian spirit, and an intellect of the widest range and sweep. Germany has never failed to do him honour, and in recent years there has been a remarkable revival of interest in his works, which are now more widely studied than perhaps ever before.

2. Work.—(*a*) *Philosophy.*—Schleiermacher has been called the prince of *Vermittlers*, but this is more true of him as a philosopher than as a theologian. In theology he was a pioneer, and in striking out his own line he was not concerned merely to mediate between extremes. In philosophy, on the other hand, he sought quite frankly to give equal weight to the idealistic and realistic elements in the Kantian position and to allow for the *a priori* as well as for the empirical factor in knowledge. Quite in consonance with this position, he made no attempt at a systematic philosophy, but was content rather to sow seeds for future thinkers and to approach philosophy from the side of his religious and theological interest. His aim was to unify the world of being and the world of thought, the real and the ideal, in God.

The materials for his philosophy are to be found in his *Dialektik*, in the criticism of previous ethical systems, and in his *Aesthetik*. The first and last named, published from his pupils' notes, are materials and nothing more. His epistemology distinguishes between the form and material of knowledge, the former being given in the 'intellectual function' and the latter through sensuous perception. The forms of knowledge, which correspond with forms of being, are concepts and judgments, and knowledge is developed by induction and deduction. Knowledge is of phenomena; and Schleiermacher definitely repudiates the Hegelian theory as to the originative power of pure thought independently of the phenomenal world.

God is the great unifying principle in the universe. In Him real and ideal are one; and He is to be conceived neither as separated from, nor as identical with, the world. But, just as absolute knowledge, the complete identity of thought and being, is an ideal which can never be wholly realized by our finite minds, so we are incapable of knowing God as He really is. He is the great First Cause, mirrored in the universe and in human souls.

> 'The usual conception of God as one single being outside of the world and behind the world is not the beginning and the end of religion. It is only one manner of expressing God, seldom entirely pure and always inadequate. . . . Yet the true nature of religion is neither this idea nor any other, but immediate consciousness of the Deity as He is found in ourselves and in the world.'[1]

Though Schleiermacher urges that philosophy is not subordinate to religion, it should be remem-

[1] *Reden*, tr. Oman, *On Religion*, p. 101.

bered that his chief interest is in the latter, and that he always confessed himself a dilettante in philosophy. The unconscious aim of all his speculation is to vindicate the need and worth of religion and the innate power of the religious consciousness. Far more important than any of his strictly philosophical works is the practical application of his philosophy found in the *Reden*. There he seeks the justification of religion, not in any dogmatic ideas, but in the religious consciousness of man.

'If man is not one with the Eternal in the unity of intuition and feeling which is immediate, he remains, in the unity of consciousness which is derived, for ever apart.'[1]

Religion is the necessary and indispensable third to science and art, because it accompanies, if it does not produce, both knowledge and action. Whatever advances true art and science is a means of religious culture. The whole world is the mirror of the individual spirit, and the being of God is involved in the very idea of our personality. The soul, through meditation and self-contemplation, enters into union with the Eternal. This union is an act not of will or of intellect, but of feeling, and it is in this feeling, or consciousness, that religion consists. If we come to analyze it, we find it to be a feeling of absolute dependence on the Divine; and in the true exercise of this feeling piety is found. The communion of all those who practise this piety is the true Church, and the various religions of the world represent the different forms assumed by this fundamental religious consciousness. The Christian religion represents not only the striving of all finite creatures towards the unity of the whole, but also the action of God in response to this striving. It is essentially a religion of redemption and reconciliation with holiness as its goal. Of this Jesus Christ is the one Mediator to men. At this point the argument of the *Reden* merges into that of the *Christliche Glaube* and is carried on in strictly theological terms. Before leaving the *Reden*, however, we should note that they belong to Schleiermacher's Romantic period, and that he modified his position considerably as time went on. They should always be read in the light of the notes and corrections which he afterwards published.

Next to theology, Schleiermacher's chief interest was in ethics. As we have already seen, his earlier efforts were confined to the criticism of previous attempts at a moral philosophy. He fails to find in any of them a complete and systematic treatment and relation of moral states and actions. He therefore sets himself to supply these deficiencies and to give a coherent and exhaustive view of the entire world of human action. The subject-matter of ethics is the action of reason upon nature; and the good at which ethics aims is found in an agreement between the two. The subject assumes certain forms such as the doctrine of goods, the doctrine of virtue, and the doctrine of duty, according to the point of view from which ethical problems are approached. The force from which all moral action proceeds is virtue, and its function is to further the highest good of man found in the agreement between reason and nature. There are four great provinces of ethical action—organization, property, thought, and feeling; to them correspond four forms of ethical relation—legal right, sociability, faith, and revelation; and to these again correspond four ethical organisms—State, society, school, and Church, the common basis of all of which is found in the family. The duties which emerge in the system thus elaborated are those of love and law, vocation and conscience. Stated thus briefly, Schleiermacher's exposition

[1] *Reden*, tr. Oman, *On Religion*, p. 40.

seems somewhat mechanical in form, but there is plenty of warmth and actuality in the way in which he works it out. Generally speaking, it presents a lofty and really valuable discussion of ethical aims and relations, and it is animated throughout by motives of the purest idealism. It cannot, however, escape the charge of vagueness, owing to the use of terms like 'nature' and 'reason' without any very definite interpretation being attached to them. They are too generally used as abstract symbols and as though they had a fixed and recognized value. At the same time it cannot but be acknowledged that Schleiermacher here makes a fruitful and permanent contribution to the development of ethical philosophy.

(*b*) *Theology*.—It is in the realm of dogmatic, or of theology proper, that Schleiermacher's chief work was done. As we have already seen, he may be regarded as the first modern systematic theologian, and in this respect he follows the great example set by Origen among the ancients. In his *Darstellung* he sets out the whole vast field of study in an ordered and comprehensive fashion which formed the model for many who have followed in his steps. His great work *Der christliche Glaube* (1821, 2nd ed. 1831) is an impressive monument, not only to his method, but to his grasp of the whole field of theology. It marks a new departure by repudiating from the outset the traditional view of Christian theology which made it consist of a number of fixed doctrines that must be accepted on faith. Schleiermacher would not allow such an interpretation. To him Christianity was not a body of doctrine in the first instance, but a condition of the heart—a mode of consciousness making itself known in devout feeling and notably in the feeling of dependence on God. The experience thus engendered, which is that not merely of any chance individual but of the Protestant Christian Church as a whole, gives to Schleiermacher a positive and stable foundation for his exposition of the Christian faith. No doubt he is here open to serious criticism as the father of a method and system too purely subjective and individual. Such criticism, however, is partly disarmed by his exposition; and, in any case, his attitude may be excused as a natural reaction from the intense dogmatism of his predecessors.

His doctrine of God owes much to Spinoza, especially when he expounds the relation of God to the world, of the *natura naturans* to the *natura naturata*, in terms of an immanence which makes all things subsist through one. In a note to the *Glaubenslehre* he defends his peculiar type of theistic pantheism as follows:

'If we keep pantheism to the customary formula, One and All, even then God and the world remain distinct, at least in point of function; and therefore a pantheist of this kind, when he regards himself as part of the world, feels himself with this All dependent on that which is the One.'[1]

In this way he reaches a conception of God as the 'somewhat' on which we depend, the correlative unity to the multiplicity of the universe. He ascribes to Him causality and omnipotence, but cannot conceive Him out of relation to His world. To do so would be mere mythology. It is from the divine causality, which to a large extent is to be identified with the totality of natural causes, that Schleiermacher derives both the actions and the attributes of God. The distinctions in them are due to our consciousness, and not to any distinctions in the Divine. This implies an ultimate conception of God very like Spinoza's Substance and apparently quite incompatible with anything of the nature of personality. At the same time Schleiermacher concedes to devout feeling (*Föm-*

[1] Quoted by Pfleiderer in his *Development of Theology*, Eng. tr., p. 110 f.

migkeit) what he cannot grant on any other terms, and in the *Glaubenslehre* he never explicitly denies what he had stated in the *Reden* as to the necessity of a personal conception of the Divine Being to devout feeling or to the enjoyment of communion with God. This apparent inconsistency is excused by his desire to interpret the Christian system as a whole; but it does not evade the criticism that he tended to reduce Christianity to the dimensions of his philosophical theory.

Schleiermacher's Christology is closely related to his doctrine of grace and redemption. One of its great merits is that he discusses the Person of Christ not as an abstract psychological problem, but always in its bearing on the Christian consciousness and on the work of redemption. He finds a link between his theology and his doctrine of Christ in the fact that Jesus is related to men in such a way that 'their conscious blessed relation to God is ascribed solely to Him as the author of it.'[1] Jesus Christ is distinguished from all other men by His essential sinlessness and absolute perfection and by the completeness of His God-consciousness. He is therefore the one perfect revelation of God, and His life is a miraculous phenomenon in a world of sin, only to be explained as a new creative act of God. At the same time His nature must not be regarded as differing in kind from ours, though He attains to a full spiritual vigour such as we cannot show. In Him human nature reaches its perfection; and His function is to impart to us that perfect God-consciousness which is normative in His own life. In his treatment of the historical personality of Jesus and His relations with both God and man, Schleiermacher shows a warmth and glow which bear witness to the fact that he is speaking out of a very real and deep experience. Imperfect as his Christology may seem according to some standards, it has the great merit of resting on the appeal which Christ makes to the soul of man and on the effect which He has produced on the consciousness of believers throughout the ages.

It is in the intensified consciousness of God which comes through Christ to men, translated into the consciousness of the Church, that Schleiermacher finds the Holy Spirit. The Holy Spirit, he says, 'is the union of the Divine Being with human nature in the form of the common spirit of the community, as animating the collective life of believers.'[2] In other words, that saving principle which showed itself in the life of the individual Jesus Christ becomes in the community the Holy Spirit of God and works for the redemption of men.

The need for redemption arises from the sin of mankind, which Schleiermacher regards as the opposition between flesh and spirit, or between the lower and the higher self-consciousness or God-consciousness. The sin of Adam was but the first emergence of a tendency inherent in our human nature and existing alongside our native God-consciousness. Escape from sin can only be by strengthening the God-consciousness and so gradually overcoming the hindrances which are due to the sense-consciousness. Jesus Christ is the supreme Redeemer because He possessed the God-consciousness in a unique degree and so is able to impart it to others. The total impression of His personality has the effect of delivering men from the contradiction between the higher and the lower in their consciousness, and so reconciling them to the highest. Salvation is thus an inward process, the source and ground of which is Jesus Christ.

Schleiermacher lays considerable stress on the function of the Church, or Christian community, in originating and maintaining the Christian life.

[1] *Glaubenslehre*, p. 91.

[2] *Ib.* p. 121.

The Church is the sphere within which opposition between the spirit and the flesh is overcome, and by providing the means of grace such as prayer, worship, etc., the Church furthers the Kingdom of God on earth. The position of the Church with regard to the future life and the final consummation of all things Schleiermacher only tolerates as 'tentative efforts of an insufficiently authorised faculty of surmise in conjunction with the reasons for and the considerations against them.'[1]

Such, then, are the dry bones of a theological system which is worked out with immense amplitude of detail, intense conviction, and rare breadth of view. Schleiermacher has had few immediate followers, but his work has provided a quarry in which every theologian since his time has been able to dig and find treasure. He was certainly in advance of his day and, like all pioneers, was slow in coming to his own. But his eager, reverent, and scientific spirit could not be denied, and his influence was never greater, especially in Germany, than it is to-day.

LITERATURE.—I. *GERMAN.*—Schleiermacher, *Theol. Works*, 11 vols., Berlin, 1836–50, *Sermons*, new ed., 5 vols., do. 1871–75, *Philosophical and Miscellaneous*, 9 vols., do. 1835–64, *Werke*, selected and ed. O. Braun and J. Bauer, 4 vols., Leipzig, 1910; C. A. Auberlen, *Schleiermacher, ein Charakterbild*, Basel, 1859; H. Bleek, *Die Grundlagen der Christologie Schleiermachers*, Freiburg i. B., 1898; C. J. Braniss, *Über Schleiermachers Glaubenslehre*, Berlin, 1824; W. Bender, *Schleiermachers philosophische Gotteslehre*, Worms, 1868; T. Camerer, *Spinoza und Schleiermacher*, Stuttgart, 1903; C. Clemen, *Schleiermachers Glaubenslehre*, Giessen, 1905; W. Dilthey, *Leben Schleiermachers*, Berlin, 1870; L. Jonas and W. Dilthey, *Aus Schleiermachers Leben, in Briefen*, 4 vols., do. 1860–63; M. Fischer, *Schleiermacher*, do. 1899; G. Fricke, *Über Schleiermacher*, Leipzig, 1869; A. Frohne, *Der Begriff der Eigentümlichkeit oder Individualität bei Schleiermacher*, Halle, 1884; E. Fuchs, *Schleiermachers Religionsbegriff und religiöse Stellung*, Giessen, 1901; O. Geyer, *Schleiermachers Psychologie*, Leipzig, 1895; J. Gottschick, *Über Schleiermachers Verhältniss zu Kant*, Tübingen, 1875; E. Huber, *Die Entwicklung des Religionsbegriffs bei Schleiermacher*, Leipzig, 1901; A. Kalthoff, *Schleiermachers Vermächtniss an unsere Zeit*, Brunswick, 1896; F. Kattenbusch, *Von Schleiermacher zu Ritschl*, Giessen, 1903; O. Kirn, *Schleiermacher und die Romantik*, Basel, 1895, 'Schleiermacher,' in *PRE*³; H. Mulert, *Schleiermachers Weihnachtsfeier*, Halle, 1906; A. Ritschl, *Schleiermachers Reden über die Religion und ihrer Nachwirkungen auf die evangelische Kirche Deutschlands*, Bonn, 1874; K. Rosenkranz, *Kritik der Schleiermacherischen Glaubenslehre*, Königsberg, 1836; J. Schaller, *Vorlesungen über Schleiermacher*, Halle, 1844; D. Schenkel, *Friedrich Schleiermacher: ein Lebens- und Charakterbild*, Elberfeld, 1868; F. M. Schiele, *Schleiermachers Monologen*, Leipzig, 1902; E. Spranger, *Schleiermacher, Fichte, Steffens*, do. 1910; E. Schürer, *Schleiermachers Religionsbegriff*, do. 1868; G. Stephan, *Die Lehre Schleiermachers von der Erlösung*, Tübingen, 1901; H. Süskind, *Der Einfluss Schellings auf die Entwicklung von Schleiermachers System*, do. 1909; K. Thiele, *Schleiermachers Theologie und ihre Bedeutung für die Gegenwart*, do. 1903; G. Thimme, *Die religionsphilosophischen Prämissen der Schleiermacherischen Glaubenslehre*, Hanover, 1901; E. Troeltsch and others, *Schleiermacher, der Philosoph des Glaubens*, Berlin, 1910; G. Wehrung, *Die philosophisch-theologische Methode Schleiermachers*, Göttingen, 1911; G. Weissenborn, *Darstellung und Kritik der Schleiermacherischen Dogmatik*, Leipzig, 1849.

II. *ENGLISH.*—Schleiermacher, *A Critical Essay on the Gospel of Luke*, tr. C. Thirlwall, London, 1825; *Brief Outline of the Study of Theology*, tr. W. Farrer, Edinburgh, 1850; *Christmas Eve*, tr. W. Hastie, do. 1890; *On Religion: Speeches to its Cultured Despisers*, tr. J. Oman, London, 1893; *Introductions to the Dialogues of Plato*, tr. W. Dobson, Cambridge, 1836, *Selected Sermons*, tr. Mary F. Wilson, do. 1890; *The Life of Schleiermacher as unfolded in his Autobiography and Letters*, tr. F. Rowan, 2 vols., London, 1860; R. Munro, *Schleiermacher: Personal and Speculative*, Paisley, 1903; W. B. Selbie, *Schleiermacher: a Critical and Historical Study*, London, 1913; G. Cross, *The Theology of Schleiermacher*, Chicago, 1911.

W. B. SELBIE.

SCHOLASTICISM.—'Scholasticism' is the term usually employed to denote the typical products of Christian thought in the West under the cultural and other historic conditions which characterized the Middle Ages. The mediæval period may be understood to extend from the 8th to the 15th century. During this period a group of definite tendencies in the history of philosophical and theological reflexion can be traced; they attain to their full strength and development

[1] *Glaubenslehre*, p. 159.

during the 12th and 13th centuries and thence decline in energy and effectiveness.

In a wider reference the term 'scholasticism' has been used to include mediæval Jewish and mediæval Arabian thought. Reference to these movements, except in their influence on Christian thought, falls outside the scope of this article. Both the Jewish and the Arabian philosophy of the period are entirely under the influence of Aristotle and Neo-Platonism. No distinctive national characteristics appear in them. They are, moreover, largely moulded by the fact that their founders and exponents were not priests but students of medicine and physical science. Two names are of outstanding importance—Avicenna (980–1037) and Averroes (1126–98), these names being originally grotesque Western corruptions of the Arabic names. The position of Avicenna (*q.v.*) is not far removed from that of pure Aristotelianism. Averroes (*q.v.*) is more independent and stands out as the most powerful and influential among the Arabian thinkers.[1]

In addition to its accurate historical sense, the adjective 'scholastic' has acquired a special meaning as descriptive of a kind of reflexion or discussion characterized by excessive formality or rigidity of method, or excessive intellectual subtlety, or punctiliously systematic development of minute details devoid of real significance. These defects, however, are not peculiar to historic scholasticism; and they are specially typical of it only in its decadence. Here we find unlimited analysis leading to endless distinctions corresponding to no real differences in the nature of things; elaborate discussion of questions having no relation to reality; and a terminology which went far beyond what was required for defining genuinely philosophical ideas or discriminating really scientific distinctions.[2] Hallam observes: 'The Aristotelian philosophy, even in the hands of the Master, was like a barren tree that conceals its want of fruit by profusion of leaves. But the scholastic ontology was much worse. What could be more trifling than disquisitions about the nature of angels, their modes of operation, their means of conversing?'[3] As a historic judgment, this is a partial and biased statement. The questions discussed in historic scholasticism were not all merely trivial or merely verbal.[4]

Scholastic reflexion involved certain general assumptions: (*a*) that absolute objective truth can be attained by the human mind (in the great age of scholasticism, *e.g.* in Aquinas, we may express the position as a claim to re-think the thoughts of the divine mind); (*b*) that the first principles or premisses of truth are revealed in Scripture and developed as Catholic doctrine by the Fathers of the Church, or, where philosophy extends beyond theology, may be ascertained by reflexion on the teaching of Aristotle; (*c*) that every principle must be worked out to its full logical issues. In estimating scholasticism, we must avoid two fundamental errors. The schoolmen did not limit themselves to discussion of merely immediate inferences from the dogmas of the Church; even in theology their work reveals remarkable variety and (within certain limits) freedom of thought. Nor is it true that in their distinctively philosophical speculations they were guided only by the doctrine of Aristotle. In philosophy and in theology alike they assimilated a stream of Neo-Platonist influence through the Fathers (especially Augustine), through the work of John Scotus Erigena and his Latin translation of pseudo-Dionysius (see below), and through the Arabians.

We must remember that, although an immense amount of ancient learning and ancient intellectual discipline had been lost, the Church never wholly lost the tradition of ancient education. What survived of ancient thought came to the Middle Ages through the Church. The Fathers, from the 2nd cent. onwards, were educated men, some of them trained in the best schools of their time. And the mediæval ecclesiastics inherited at least from the greater Latin Fathers educational and intellectual ideas akin to those of the ancient world.[1]

Hence, when Charlemagne, after consolidating his empire in the West, conceived the design of founding schools which should be centres of learning and mental cultivation, he naturally turned to the monasteries and with the help of such men as Alcuin established schools in connexion with most of the abbeys in his kingdom.[2] The name 'scholastic,' *doctor scolasticus*, given at first to teachers of the cloister schools, was afterwards given generally to teachers of systematic theology and philosophy following the tradition of the schools. At first the 'philosophy' consisted only of the elements of grammar, logic, and rhetoric, the *trivium* of the 'seven liberal arts,' of which the *quadrivium* consisted of geometry, arithmetic, astronomy, and music.

It has been said that the main objects of philosophy and theology are identical, though the method of treatment is different.[3] This may be admitted; but historically scholastic theology and scholastic philosophy must be distinguished. The former claims to be founded on the doctrine received by the Church from Scripture and the Fathers and taught as authoritative. Its detailed historical treatment belongs to the history of Christian doctrine and forms part of any standard work on that subject.[4] Scholastic philosophy, on the other hand, has its own first principles, claiming to be intuitive truths of reason. It embraces many questions wholly independent of theology, although its methods and conclusions were employed in the explanation of various dogmas. The distinction does not involve complete separation.

The scholastic age falls naturally into two periods owing to the fact that all the most important logical, metaphysical, and scientific writings of Aristotle came into the hands of Western thinkers for the first time during the latter part of the 12th century. It is convenient also to subdivide the periods as follows: (i.) the 8th, 9th, and 10th centuries, where we find (except in the case of Erigena) only the undeveloped germs of later problems and controversies; (ii.) the 11th and most of the 12th cent., where the conclusions of metaphysical logic are more and more consciously and deliberately applied to the elucidation of theological dogma; (iii.) the 13th cent., the great age of scholasticism, after the assimilation of the new Aristotelian materials, where we find strenuous endeavours to construct a comprehensive system based on an alliance of philosophy and theology; (iv.) the 14th and 15th centuries, where the alliance breaks down under the influence of Duns Scotus (who belongs historically to the previous period) and Ockham. The mutual independence of philosophy and theology involved the doctrine of the twofold nature of truth and led to the decline of scholasticism, which resolved itself ultimately into a formal perfecting of system with loss of vitality of thought.

The literature available up to the middle of the 12th cent. to stimulate and assist philosophical speculation was scanty. The facts have been well established since the work of Jourdain.[5] Of Aristotle the earlier schoolmen possessed only the two simpler parts of the *Organon*—*i.e.* the *Categoriæ* and *de Inter-*

[1] For the literature of the subject consult the standard histories named below. The following may be mentioned here: A. Schmolders, *Essai sur les écoles philosophiques chez les Arabes*, Paris, 1842; E. Renan, *Averroès et l'Averroïsme*[4], do. 1882; M. Joel, *Beiträge zur Gesch. der Philosophie*, Breslau, 1876: I. Husik, *Hist. of Jewish Mediæval Philosophy*, London and New York, 1916.

[2] Cf. Erasmus, *Stultitiæ Laus*, Basel, 1676, p. 141 ff.

[3] *View of the State of Europe during the Middle Ages*[9], London, 1846, ii. 488.

[4] Cf. J. Rickaby's brief but instructive sketch, *Scholasticism* (Philosophies Ancient and Modern), London, 1908.

[1] Cf. J. Vernon Bartlet and A. J. Carlyle, *Christianity in History*, London, 1917, p. 352 ff.

[2] On the work of Alcuin see C. J. B. Gaskoin, *Alcuin*, London, 1904; A. F. West, *Alcuin and the Rise of the Christian Schools*, do. 1892; J. Bass Mullinger, *The Schools of Charles the Great*, do. 1877; and *DNB*[3], *s.v.* 'Alcuin.'

[3] A. S. Pringle-Pattison, in *EBr*[11] xxiv. 346 ff., art. 'Scholasticism.'

[4] An extensive collection of brief extracts from the scholastic writers, classified under the various heads of doctrinal theology, is given in K. R. Hagenbach, *A Hist. of Christian Doctrines*, Eng. tr.[5], Edinburgh, 1880–81, ii. 106 ff.

[5] *Recherches critiques sur l'âge et l'origine des traductions latines d'Aristote*[2], Paris, 1843.

pretatione, together with Porphyry's *Isagoge*, or 'Introduction,' to the former (all these in Latin translations by Boethius); a summary of Aristotle's *Categories*, *Categoriæ Decem*, wrongly attributed to Augustine; two commentaries by Boethius on the *Isagoge*; and his own short treatises on the elements of formal logic. Boethius was the principal source for the text-books which maintained the logical tradition of the cloister schools, such as those of Cassiodorus and Isidore of Seville. Regarding Plato, their information was derived from the *Timæus*, or part of it, in the Latin translation of Chalcidius and his commentary, from Apuleius (*de Dogmate Platonis*), and from the writings of Augustine. Hence what little they knew of Plato came from sources moulded by Neo-Platonic influence.

Isidore of Seville († 636) is also of importance as the author of three books of 'Sentences' (*Sententiæ*) or doctrinal passages from the Fathers, systematically arranged. This and a few similar compilations circulated in the schools as material for whatever doctrinal reflexion was possible. The more elaborate work, Πηγὴ γνώσεως, by John Damascene (*fl.c.* 700), representing the Eastern Church, is the classical example of a systematic logical presentation of patristic teaching; but this was not in the hands of the earlier schoolmen. Such books suggested the plan or scheme which was carried out later in the *Liber Sententiarum* of Petrus Lombardus. It is not our purpose to refer to the history of theological doctrine except where it directly involves the conclusions of philosophical reflexion.

I. *FIRST PERIOD.*—Among the theological discussions of the first period we find in the eucharistic and predestinarian controversies of the 9th cent. the beginnings of an opposition that was destined to develop with great significance—that of faith (or authority) and reason. From this point of view we touch briefly on the subjects named, before passing to the logical and philosophical issues which were being opened up.

1. Eucharistic controversy.—In 831 Paschasius Radbertus, abbot of Corbie, published what was the first formal exposition and defence of the strict doctrine of transubstantiation; *i.e.*, that the substance of the bread and wine becomes converted into the substance of the body and blood of Christ, the same body in which He lived, suffered, rose, and ascended. This stupendous miracle takes place under the outwardly visible form ('sub figura') of bread and wine. There is nothing contrary to nature in this, because the essence of nature consists in the entire obedience of all things to the divine will ('ut a quo est semper ejus obtemperet jussis'). This uncompromising and absolute supernaturalism was contested by Ratramnus, a monk of the same abbey. While fully acknowledging an objective supernatural process in the eucharist, Ratramnus endeavoured to rationalize the doctrine as far as possible. The body and blood of Christ are present 'in mysterio'; *i.e.*, the Scriptural expressions are figurative and are to be spiritually understood. The elements after consecration produce an effect on the souls of believers which they cannot produce by their natural qualities, but this effect presupposes spiritual susceptibility on the part of the recipients; and, when the believer has attained 'ad visionem Christi,' he will no longer need such external means of perceiving what the divine love has achieved for him.

2. Predestinarian controversy.—The predestinarian dispute of the 9th cent. gives a more vivid picture of the conflict between reason and authority. In this case the Church employed the resources of human reason to counteract the unauthorized conclusions of the predestinarian Gottschalk. John Scotus Erigena, layman and independent thinker, was employed as the chosen advocate of the dogma decreed by authority.

'The force of reason evidently began to be acknowledged and felt as an antagonist which the Church had fostered within its own system, and against which the Church had need to fortify itself with the weapons of the same temper. The expedient was found to be of dangerous effect; since the philosophy of Erigena served to scatter the seeds of still more dangerous perplexity to the creed of the Church.'[1]

3. Nominalism and realism.—As with the problem of authority and reason, so with that of nominalism and realism and other logical and philosophical issues which occupied the attention of the later schoolmen. These problems were present in germ in the scholastic writings of the 9th and 10th centuries; but their implications were unknown, and their connexion with the fundamental principles of religion and ethics was not even suspected.

The problem at issue in the opposition of nominalism and realism was that of the objective significance of universals. The universal (general, generic or specific, typical) consists of those fundamental qualities, activities, uniformities of the object which it shares with others. When these are abstracted and generalized by our thought, the class-concept is formed. This consciousness of the universal is an act of thought; it is the consciousness that certain qualities realized in the individual thing are also realized in a whole group. Nominalism is the general theory that the universal has no existence outside our thought.

(*a*) Extreme nominalism may be expressed in the words of a modern writer: 'the only generality possessing separate existence is the name';[1] not even in the thought of the knower is there anything general; the universal is merely a *flatus vocis*. (*b*) Moderate nominalism, or conceptualism (*q.v.*), holds that universals exist, but only in thought; the universal is a *conceptus mentis significans plura singularia*. Both kinds of nominalism are included in the dictum, 'Species non sunt nisi termini apud animam existentes.'[2] Realism holds, on the contrary, that the universal has a being of its own, which is objectively given. (*c*) Extreme realism holds that the common nature of a group of beings—*e.g.*, man—exists *ante res*, distinct from and independently of the particular things of experience which exemplify that common nature. (*d*) Moderate realism means that the universal is an objective principle *in rebus*, common to the many different individuals and constituting them into a class. The schoolmen identified their problem with that which appeared to be at issue between Plato and Aristotle. The interest of the Greek thinkers, however, was different. They were concerned to show that the real is universal and to explain as far as possible how the universal became individualized in space and time. The schoolmen, on the contrary, started from the subjective side.

Cousin[3] and others have rightly pointed to a passage in Boethius' Latin translation of the *Isagoge* of Porphyry as suggesting the question to the scholastic thinkers. The essential sentences are these: 'de generibus et speciebus illud quidem . . . sive in solis nudis intellectibus posita sint. . . . et utrum separata a sensibilibus an in sensibilibus posita et circa haec consistentia, dicere recusabo.' Nominalism and the two forms of realism are here indicated.

These theories were not apprehended in their full significance in what we have called the first period; as Cousin observes, the two systems were, as yet, merely two different ways of interpreting a phrase of Porphyry. Moreover, the influence of Boethius was indecisive. He refuses to argue to a definite conclusion, although his incidental statements tend sometimes towards moderate realism, sometimes towards moderate nominalism. It is clear, however, from the earliest remains of scholastic thought that there existed in the schools a nominalistic and a realistic tradition. A collection of incidental comments on Porphyry, *e.g.*, has come down to us from early in the 9th century. It has been attributed, probably incorrectly, to Rabanus Maurus († 856), under whose influence the school at Fulda had become an intellectual centre of some importance. Its authorship may be assigned to one of his pupils.[4] Its statements show a distinct tendency to moderate nominalism (*e.g.*, the genus is defined as *substantialis similitudo ex diversis speciebus in cogitatione collecta*), and the important principle is asserted, 'Res non predicatur.' A similar general observation may be made in reference to Heiricus (Eric) of Auxerre, originally a student at Fulda. On the other hand, at the close of the 9th cent. we find realism definitely taught at Auxerre by Remigius. What is individual and what is specific exists only by participation in the universal, which is the substantial unity of the individuals included under it (*e.g.*, 'Homo est multorum hominum substantialis unitas').

4. Erigena.—The system of John Scotus Erigena 'stands by itself in the 9th century like the pro-

[1] R. D. Hampden, *The Scholastic Philosophy in its Relation to Christian Theology*[3] (*BL*), Hereford, 1848, p. 36 ff.

[1] A. Bain, *Mental and Moral Science*[3], London, 1884, p. 179.
[2] See Prantl, *Gesch. der Logik im Abendlande*, iv. 16.
[3] *Ouvrages inédits d'Abélard*, Introd. p. 56.
[4] For references see F. Ueberweg, *Hist. of Philosophy*, Eng. tr.[4], London, 1874–75, i. 368 f.

duct of another age.'[1] Possessed of a high degree of intellectual originality, he endeavoured, in the spirit of Origen, to lay a philosophical foundation for theology; but his speculative genius led him into methods and conclusions hostile to the general tendency of ecclesiastical doctrine. His fundamental principle is the identity of faith and reason, so that philosophy and theology are manifestations of the same spirit. But theological doctrines are symbolic expressions of the truth; and the traditional doctrines, when taken up into his system, are treated very freely.

Erigena's speculative conceptions were profoundly influenced by his study of an anonymous writer who, under the name of 'Dionysius the Areopagite' (Ac 17[34]), had issued in the second half of the 5th cent. a short series of works which afterwards had a considerable influence on mediæval thought.[2] The writer combines Christian conceptions with the emanation system of Plotinus, without giving up the tri-unity of God. God, as Absolute Being, is beyond all conceivable human predicates: this is the principle of 'negative theology,' which Dionysius distinguishes from 'positive theology,' where a symbolic knowledge of God and a gradual approximation to His image are admitted to be possible. Both the negative and the positive theology are valid and do not conflict when each has its proper place.

Erigena's chief speculative work is entitled *de Divisione Naturæ*. His system is based on the idea of the absolute immanence of God; the divine is exclusively real, and the world of experience in space and time is but a 'theophany,' an appearance of God. By *natura* he means the sum of all that is, regarded not as a mere aggregate, but as a unity. It embraces four types of being: (1) that which creates and is not created—God as source of all being; (2) that which is created and which creates—the world of 'ideas' or ideal rational principles, active in and from God, after which finite things are fashioned; (3) that which is created but does not create—the world of finite individual things; (4) that which neither is created nor creates—God as goal and end of all being. The whole realm of created being has no independent reality; it exists, but it exists in God. Creation and revelation are one. The four stages form a process from God to God, which through our finiteness we think of as in time; but in itself it is eternal and beyond time altogether.

Like 'Dionysius,' Erigena combines a negative and a positive theology. Real being—in other words, absolute perfection—belongs to God alone; all else has only partial or imperfect being. No predicate applicable to finite being is applicable to God; He is above and beyond all qualities that we experience in finite being. Hence ultimately we can say what God is not rather than what He is. On the other hand, the whole realm of created nature is in its measure a 'theophany,' whereby we may attain to a knowledge of God, perceiving His being through the being of created things, His wisdom through their order and harmony, His life through their activity and movement. This is a basis for an interpretation of the doctrine of the Trinity. God in His essential being is Father, God as realized Wisdom is Son, God as universal life and activity is Spirit. Erigena finds a reflexion of this Trinity in man; but further analysis of the conception is beyond the scope of this article.

The logical structure into which these principles are wrought is that of an infinite hierarchy of forms or types of existence, from the material objects of sense to the absolute being of Deity; and this graded scale of beings, in which each lower form proceeds from the forms above it, is completely parallel to the graded scale of logical conceptions in their successive orders of universality. Hence 'intelligitur quod ars illa, quae dividit genera in species et species in genera resolvit, quae διαλεκτική dicitur, non ab humanis machinationibus sit facta, sed in natura rerum ab Auctore omnium artium, quae vere artes sunt, condita, et a sapientibus inventa.'[3] Erigena is therefore a realist; universals are *in rebus* as the ground of their existence and *ante res* as ideal constituents of the second division of 'nature' (see above).

From the ethical point of view, this is equivalent to a hierarchy of degrees of value or perfection; and increase in perfection means increase in being. Evil as such has no real being at all; it is mere appearance. Nevertheless Erigena cannot interpret the doctrine of sin without admitting its reality. The will of the individual represents to itself something as real and good when it is neither. This is sin; but, if the representation is false, the will that represents it is real. Deliverance from sin is the discovery made by the sinner of the illusoriness of what he aims at. To become one with God through becoming like Him is the chief end of man, which humanity as a whole can attain by purification, enlightenment, and completion, with the help of the Logos.[4]

II. *SECOND PERIOD*.—The second of the four periods into which the history of scholasticism may be divided for our present purpose is marked by the appearance of men who were prepared to apply the distinctions of human logic to the elucidation of theological dogmas, and who thereby created scholastic philosophy in its distinctive forms. The speculations and discussions thus opened up may be grouped under the heads: (1) faith (or authority) and reason, (2) nominalism and realism, (3) dualism (of soul and body). Three leading thinkers of the period are the subjects of separate articles.[1]

1. Faith and reason.—Among the few names representing any original mental activity in the barbarism of the 10th cent. that of Gerbert († 1003 as Pope Sylvester II.) is prominent, not however in connexion with specially logical or philosophical questions. He had become acquainted with the work of the Arabians in Spain and Italy and had acquired an amount of knowledge such as to expose him to the suspicion of intercourse with the powers of darkness. He has the merit of urging the importance of the study of physical science and mathematics.[2] His pupil Fulbert founded the school of Chartres, which for two centuries was a centre of humanistic culture. Among its famous students was Berengarius of Tours († 1088), who was animated by a genuine impulse towards freedom of thought. This appeared in his general attitude towards cultural education and particularly in the fact that he adopted, developed, and defended the interpretation of the eucharist previously put forward by Ratramnus, which had also been defended by Erigena in his work *de Eucharistia*. Any detailed account of the prolonged controversy thus aroused belongs to the history of the doctrine of the sacraments;[3] but what is important to note is that Berengarius defended his position on philosophical grounds, and these grounds are found to involve the essential principle of nominalism. He denied the possibility of transmutation of the 'substance' while the former 'accidents,' or physically perceptible qualities, remained; and his argument was simply a specific application of nominalism. He does not appear to have investigated the question apart from this particular application of it. But it was at once perceived that the question was no mere technicality of logic, but was of momentous significance. The perception of its importance was intensified when Roscellinus, after defending nominalism as a general principle (see below), applied it to the interpretation of the doctrine of the Trinity, with results disastrous to the traditionally orthodox conception. He found in metaphysical individualism an immediate inference from nominalism. Defining 'person' as *substantia rationalis*, he concluded that, if the usage of language permitted, we ought to speak of three Gods, since the three Persons could be united only in name or abstract idea.

The controversy aroused by Berengarius ended in the complete triumph of the transubstantiation doctrine by an act of ecclesiastical authority. But the position of Roscellinus and its theological implications required to be met with the armour of reason. This led to a philosophical assertion of extreme realism by Anselm and William of Champeaux (see below), which held its ground until the more moderate doctrine of Abelard became the accepted principle of the schools. And from the time of Anselm the relation of faith and reason became a fundamental problem.

Anselm's solution is best expressed in his own words:

'Desidero intelligere veritatem Tuam, quam credit et amat cor meum. Neque enim quaero intelligere ut credam, sed credo ut intelligam. Nam et hoc credo, quia nisi credidero non

[1] Pringle-Pattison, in *EBr*[11] xxiv. 347.

[2] Cf. O. Siebert, *Die Metaphysik und Ethik des Pseudo-Dionysius Areopagita*, Jena, 1894.

[3] *De Divisione Naturæ*, iv. 4.

[4] On Erigena see R. Adamson and J. M. Mitchell, art. 'Erigena,' in *EBr*[11]; R. L. Poole, art. 'Scotus,' in *DNB*[2]; and the standard histories named below.

[1] See artt. ANSELM, ABELARD, BERNARD.

[2] Cf. K. Werner, *Gerbert von Aurillac, die Kirche und Wissenschaft seiner Zeit*[2], Vienna, 1881.

[3] See art. EUCHARIST (to end of Middle Ages).

intelligam.'[1] 'Quanto opulentius nutrimur in sacra Scriptura, . . . tanto subtilius provehimur ad ea quae per intellectum satiant. . . . Nam qui non crediderit, non experietur; et qui expertus non fuerit, non intelliget.'[2]

In this connexion he contrasts *cognitio audientis* and *scientia experientis*. Faith is regarded as before all else a condition of the emotions and the will; but it is a positive duty, for those who are capable of it, to seek a comprehensive understanding of the content of faith:

'Negligentia mihi videtur, si, postquam confirmati sumus in fide, non studemus quod credimus intelligere.'[3]

How Anselm was prepared to apply these principles is seen especially in his development of the arguments for the being of God, in *Monologium* and *Proslogium*, and his investigation of the doctrine of the Atonement in *Cur Deus Homo*. The principle is *fides praecedens intellectum*. This resembles some quite modern theories; but it should be noted that *fides*, to Anselm, means not only the religious truths to be derived from Scripture, and not only the personal religious experience of the believer; it means also the dogma as defined and authorized by the Church.

The position of Abelard is fundamentally different. Reason is not (as with Anselm) restricted to the explanatory treatment of what is in any case established as faith. The difference may be expressed by saying that reason is constitutive and even decisive of religious truth. The rule of truth is found in thought. Hence Abelard had a very high opinion of the religious and moral value of Greek philosophy. He regarded the Greek thinkers as the creators of a genuine religious tradition which was improved and widened by the Christian revelation. This view was not based on any real historical knowledge of ancient thought and its possible affiliations any more than the opposite view of the Fathers (that the Greek thinkers borrowed from the books of Moses). Abelard knew little of these thinkers; his estimate of their importance is an application of his general doctrine of reason and revelation. 'Nolo sic esse philosophus,' he says, 'ut recalcitrarem Paulo, non sic esse Aristoteles, ut secludar a Christo; non enim aliud nomen est sub coelo, in quo oporteat me salvum fieri'; but, unless faith comes to a rational consciousness of its own true nature and grounds, it lacks stability and full efficacy. The motto 'Intelligo ut credam' comes to mean, for Abelard, 'I seek to understand in order that I may believe more, and believe more fully and worthily.' His work *Sic et Non*, in which conflicting passages from the Fathers were arranged in opposition to one another, was compiled not to suggest scepticism but to promote rational inquiry; 'dubitando ad inquisitionem venimus, inquirendo ad veritatem.'[4] Yet, contrary to his own intention, the formal and theoretic precedence of knowledge to faith tended to mere intellectualism in theology and actually produced it.

At the opposite extreme to Abelard stands Bernard of Clairvaux. He contended for the existence in the human mind of an immediate inner apprehension of religious truth, with a distinctive certainty of its own. Many of his statements suggest a position akin to that of Anselm—*e.g.*, *de Consideratione*, v. 3, where it is said that faith holds the truth in a latent and implicit form; knowledge holds it in an open and explicit form, having both the truth and the distinct comprehension of it; faith is a spontaneous and assured intimation of truth that is not yet opened up before the mind in clear analysis and outline. The contrast emphasized appears to be between an implicit and an explicit form of the same truth. It would, however, be an error to assimilate the position of Bernard to that of Anselm. The former is a mystic; standing on the basis of a mystical view of religious belief, he represents a reaction against the influence of the 'dialecticians,' and especially those among them who had been influenced by Roscellinus and Abelard. The same attitude to contemporary logic was maintained through the 12th cent. at the monastery of St. Victor, near Paris, and especially by the three 'Victorines,' Hugo, Richard, and Walter; whereas the keynote of constructive scholasticism was sounded by Anselm in his solution of the problem of the relation of faith and knowledge.

2. Nominalism and realism.—The general meaning of these opposed theories has been concisely stated above. Roscellinus appears to have been the first to formulate nominalism as a general theory of the nature of universals. For knowledge of his doctrine we have to rely on the statements of his opponents, Anselm and Abelard. He is charged with making the universal a mere word, *flatus vocis*.[5] Taken strictly, this is a denial of any real connexion between similar things; their similarities become merely unessential accidents, and real knowledge is impossible. It is one thing to deny the hypostatization of an 'accident' like colour or wisdom, and another thing to deny the foundation in reality of all genera and species.

'The human race is not a word, or, if it is, we are driven to assert that there is really nothing common and identical in all men—that the brotherhood and equality of the human family are mere abstractions, and that, since individuality is the sole reality, the sole reality is difference, that is to say, hostility and war, with no right but might, no duty but interest, no remedy but despotism.'[1]

It is probable that some statements of Roscellinus suggested these consequences, but it is not probable that he intended them. These statements, and the heterodox theological conclusions alluded to above, discredited nominalism.

Anselm made no attempt to think out the difficulties of realism. He found in it what appeared to be the sole means of rationalizing dogma, and he adopted it accordingly. Universals, to him, are *in rebus* as objectively real and active principles and *ante res* as ideal principles in the divine mind. William of Champeaux († 1121) may be regarded as the founder of realism as an independent doctrine. He held it in its most extreme form, in which its pantheistic tendencies were plainly apparent. The individual has no independent being, but is only an 'accident' of the real being which is the universal. From this position he was driven by the criticism of Abelard. His final position is not clear. Opposite views of its meaning are taken by Cousin and Rémusat, on the one hand, and Prantl and Hauréau, on the other.[2]

It scarcely needs to be said that 'mediating views' found frequent acceptance, sometimes among men who had little insight into the real problem at issue. John of Salisbury[3] († 1180) gives an analysis of nine different views of the nature of universals.[4] The most interesting of the mediating theories is that of Gilbert of Poitiers († 1154), whose carefully thought out doctrine does not appear to differ in any essential point from that of Abelard.

Abelard perceived that general ideas or concepts are involved in all thought and are the instruments of all knowledge. This is so because they have an objective basis in the similarities of individual things; and the mind attains to conceptual knowledge by comparing individual things with one another. The universal, therefore, is more than a mere name. It is a predicate (*sermo*) and for that very reason cannot itself be a 'thing.' Moreover, it is a natural predicate, 'quod de pluribus natum est praedicari.'[5] The fundamental similarities of things are not accidental, but are due to the fact that the Creator formed them according to pre-existing types or ideals which in fact constitute the divine plan of the world. This type of moderate realism found sufficient acceptance to put the controversy into the background until the time of Ockham. Its place was taken by the problem of 'matter and form.'

Realism appeared to be satisfactory so long as interest was concentrated on those aspects of things which make them wholes or unities *inter se*—the universe as a whole, the State as a whole, the Church as a whole. The subsequent revival of nominalism indicates the rise of a new consciousness of individuality, which can be traced in the doctrines of Duns Scotus (who was not a nominalist) and of Ockham (see below).

3. Dualism.—The schoolmen inherited from Augustine the conception of body and soul as two

[1] *Proslogium*, 1. [2] *De Incarnatione Verbi*, 2.
[3] *Cur Deus Homo*, i. 2. [4] Cf. Bartlet and Carlyle, p. 439 f.
[5] Cf. Prantl, ii. 78.

[1] Cousin, Introd. p. 106, quoted by Pringle-Pattison, in *EBr*[9] xxi. 421.
[2] See also J. H. Löwe, *Der Kampf zwischen Realismus und Nominalismus im Mittelalter*, Prague, 1876; and Bäumker, *AGPh* x. [1896] 257.
[3] *Metalogicus*, ii. 17 ff.
[4] For details reference must be made to the larger histories.
[5] Cf. Prantl, ii. 181.

substances, entirely different and even opposed in character, so that no knowledge of the soul could be gained from its relations to the body; and in his work they saw how fruitfully the inner life of mental, moral, and spiritual fact could be studied as an experience. The reaction against 'dialectic' also helped to create a psychological interest, especially among the mystics. These men, in their religious aspirations and their struggles after the enjoyment of divine grace, became vividly conscious of an inner experience of a wider range; and they endeavoured to describe it. In doing so they employed a medley of Neo-Platonic and Augustinian terms and ideas; but incidentally, and amid much that was extravagant, they arrived at genuinely psychological results. John of Salisbury, man of affairs and cultured ecclesiastic rather than mystic, went farther and worked out the outlines of a systematic psychology based on a notion of development akin to that of the modern 'associationist' school.[1]

III. *THIRD PERIOD.*—The logical and speculative impulses lying behind all these discussions were exhausted by the middle of the 12th cent. through lack of material. Historical and scientific knowledge scarcely existed; and the logical impulse and the kindred interest in systematic methodology had to feed on themselves, or, at the most, had to turn back on the dogmas of the Church and analyze them into details of ever-increasing complexity, or, again, had to devote themselves to the systematic collection and arrangement of patristic authorities in the many works of which the *Liber Sententiarum* of Peter Lombard († 1164) and the *de Articulis Catholicæ Fidei* of Alan de Lille or de Insulis († 1203), are conspicuous examples—the former, *instar omnium*, destined to become the authoritative text-book for the teaching of the Fathers.

At the same time an epoch-making change was maturing. During the first half of the 12th cent. the remaining logical treatises of Aristotle—the *Analytics* (both parts), *Topics*, and *Sophistical Refutations*—gradually and silently found their way into the schools. This by itself would not have brought about a great change; but in the course of the century the chief works of the Arabian thinkers were introduced into France from Jewish sources.[2] This came about as a consequence of the struggle with Muhammadanism, in the nearer East, and of the Crusades. And this knowledge of Arabian and Jewish thought carried with it a knowledge of the contents of almost all the Aristotelian treatises, including the *Metaphysics*, *Ethics*, *de Anima*, and the works on *Physics* and *Natural History*. At the beginning of the 13th cent. new and better translations from the Arabic were made, followed by translations direct from the Greek. These enabled the schoolmen 'to distinguish the genuine Aristotle from the questionable accompaniments with which he had made his first appearance in Western Europe.'[3] Arabian Aristotelianism was conceived in a Neo-Platonic sense; and in its most distinctive forms it implied the entire immanence of the Deity in an eternal matter and excluded the possibility of personal immortality and of creation as an individual act 'from nothing.'

[1] The history of mediæval psychology is beyond the scope of this article; but reference may here be made to Siebeck's valuable contributions to this study in his series of articles on the beginnings of modern psychology in the scholastic age, in the *Zeitschrift für Philosophie und philosophische Kritik*, dealing with the period from Augustine to Duns Scotus: xciii. [1888] 161 ff., xciv. [1888] 161 ff., xcv. [1889] 245 ff.; and in his series of notes on scholastic psychology in *AGPh* i. [1887] 375 ff., 518 ff., ii. [1888] 22 ff., 180 ff., 414 ff., 517 ff., iii. [1889] 177 ff. Further references are given below, under Duns Scotus and Ockham.

[2] See references given above for mediæval Arabian and Jewish thought.

[3] Pringle-Pattison, in *EBr*[11] xxiv. 353[a].

The first effects of this immense acquisition of new material are seen in a stream of confused and erratic speculation, the leading tendencies of which are revealed in the materialistic pantheism of Amalric of Bena († 1207) and David Dinant († 1215?), which was strenuously combated (along with Averroism, from which it was derived) by Albertus Magnus and Thomas Aquinas. The doctrine of Amalric, we must add, was not identical with that of David;[1] and the doctrines of both must be distinguished from the tenets of the Amalricians, a widely extended sect animated by an antinomian fanaticism which exposed its adherents to fierce persecution after the Lateran Council of 1215.

The result of all this was that, along with Averroism, the study of all the Aristotelian writings except the purely logical treatises was proscribed by the Church. It is the merit of the so-called mendicant orders, Dominican and Franciscan, that they used all their power and influence to capture Aristotle for the Church. This result was achieved after a long struggle, which may be said to have ended in 1253 in the establishment, under papal authority, of two professorial chairs of the Aristotelian philosophy in the University of Paris.[2] Thus Aristotle, after being suspected and condemned, was placed on the same level with Augustine and came to be regarded as the forerunner of Christ in matters of nature, as John the Baptist had been in matters of grace. From the point of view of orthodox theology, therefore, it became necessary to combine adherence to Aristotelianism with fundamental criticism of Averroism and with justification of the doctrines of a transcendent creative God and of the immortality of the soul. This was a main part of the endeavour of Albert and Thomas.

None the less the stream of opposition to Aristotelianism was maintained during the 13th cent. by a succession of thinkers who, while making full use of the tools of analysis provided by the Aristotelian logic, advocated an Augustinian or Christianized Platonism as the true philosophical setting for the dogmas of the Church, as against the philosophical principles derived from the *Metaphysics* of Aristotle. Among these must first be mentioned Alexander of Hales († 1245), Franciscan, who appears to be the first schoolman to face the problem of organizing Christian thought in full view of the wealth of Arabian and Aristotelian material now available. This he did, with genuine power, in his *Summa Universæ Theologiæ*. His pupil and successor, John of Rochelle, illustrates a growing psychological interest in his *de Anima*, written in view of Aristotle's treatise and the Arabian and Greek commentaries on it. He was succeeded in Paris by John of Fidanza, or 'Bonaventura' († 1274), Franciscan, contemporary and friendly critic of Aquinas, who organized and defended the principles implied in mysticism, especially the doctrines of the Victorines (see above), and whose distinctive position and influence belong to the history of that subject. William of Auvergne († 1249) and Henry of Ghent († 1293) must also be named as significant exceptions to the main tendency represented by the two great thinkers to whom we have now to refer.

It is generally admitted that the highest level of scholastic thought is found in the work of the two great Dominicans, Albertus Magnus (1193–1280) and his pupil Thomas Aquinas (1227–74). The greater part, in quantity, of Albert's work consists of paraphrases and commentaries on Aristotle, in which all the writings of 'the Philosopher,' as he was now called, are systematically dealt with. So far as theology and philosophy are concerned, the systems of Albert and Thomas need not be separated. Thomas[3] entered into his master's labours with an intellect finer, if not more powerful, than that of Albert;[4] and he was able to take a more comprehensive view of the whole field.

[1] Cf. *EBr*[11] xix. 123 ff., art. 'Mysticism'; and C. Jourdain, *Mémoire sur les sources philosophiques des hérésies d'Amaury de Chartres et de David de Dinan*, Paris, 1870.

[2] H. Rashdall, *Universities of Europe in the Middle Ages*, 3 vols., London, 1895, esp. i. 345 ff.

[3] See art. AQUINAS and references there given.

[4] See J. Sighart, *Albertus Magnus, sein Leben und seine Wissenschaft*, Regensburg, 1857; and J. Bach, *Das Albertus Magnus Verhältniss*, Vienna, 1881.

It is noteworthy that the interests of Albertus Magnus embraced physical science. Here he advocated genuine empirical research, which he was able to engage in himself not without success, as his treatise *de Vegetalibus* shows. This interest in *a posteriori* inquiry was exceptional among the schoolmen as a whole. They would have admitted that these inquiries had a rightful place and a utility of their own. But, just as to-day there are mathematicians, with no taste for physical research, who revel in those developments of pure mathematics which have no connexion with such research, so the typical schoolmen preferred abstract argument to concrete investigation. This points to a fundamental weakness of scholasticism; and it sometimes led the schoolmen to attempt to determine, by abstract *a priori* argument, matters which should have been determined by observation or historical probability.[1]

The ablest and most original critic of the Thomist system was the Franciscan Johannes Duns Scotus (1270?–1308), of British origin, who taught at Oxford, Paris, and Cologne. The Franciscan edition of his works, published at Lyons in 1639, occupies 12 volumes, but contains much that is not genuine. His *Opus Oxoniense* consists of his own commentary on the *Liber Sententiarum*; the *Opus Parisiense* is a similar commentary, worked over by other hands. The miscellaneous *Questiones quodlibetales* have also been worked over.

Duns Scotus is not the subject of a separate article, and special reference will be made to his doctrines under the heads named below.[2]

The main problems of this third period of scholasticism may be viewed under the following heads: (1) faith (or authority) and reason; (2) realism and nominalism; (3) intellect and will; (4) matter and form, or the problem of individuality.

1. Faith and reason.—Albertus Magnus laboured earnestly to show that reason and revelation are neither identical nor mutually opposed, but harmonious, in the sense that certain doctrines, while not contrary to reason, are yet beyond reason. The human mind can completely know only those things the principles of which it carries within itself; hence there are some truths inaccessible to unaided human reason. Aquinas develops this fundamental conclusion and defines more precisely the doctrines which are beyond reason. He finds them to be the Trinity, the creation of the world out of nothing, the Incarnation, and the immediate inferences which follow from these.

'Et in his, quae de Deo confitemur, duplex veritatis modus. Quaedam namque vera sunt de Deo, quae omnem facultatem humanae rationis excedunt, ut Deum esse trinum et unum. Quaedam vera sint, ad quae etiam ratio naturalis pertingere potest: sicut est Deum esse, Deum esse unum, et alia hujusmodi, quae etiam philosophi demonstrative de Deo probaverunt, ducti naturalis lumine rationis.'[3]

Further,[4] he says that it is possible for natural reason to refute arguments against these supra-rational truths and even to produce considerations determining the mind towards their acceptance, since natural reason cannot be contrary to the truths of faith. Our unaided reason can discover and establish by argument a great body of truth, including natural religion and ethics; but the truths distinctive of faith are revealed to, not discovered by, the human mind. The principle underlying the supernaturalism of St. Thomas may be expressed thus: God is the chief end of man, but He is a transcendent end (*finis superexcedens*):

Man, the finite being, 'ordinatur ad Deum, sicut ad quendam finem, qui comprehensionem rationis excedit; finem oportet esse praecognitum hominibus, qui suas intentiones et actiones debent ordinare in finem.'[1]

This principle shows that he never intended to assert an absolute separation, much less an opposition, between the two kinds of truth.

In the hands of Duns Scotus the distinction widens and deepens; the range of philosophical and religious truth that can be demonstrated by the unaided reason is significantly restricted. This consequence flows from his theory of the primacy of will. For him theology is essentially practical; it points to salvation from sin by an appeal to the will. The part played by the intellect is reduced; and he finds that in addition to the Trinity, the creation at the beginning of time, and the Incarnation, the following articles of faith cannot be rationalized: the knowledge of God as omnipotent; the knowledge of God not only as infinite but as the chief end of man (*i.e.* as divine in the sense required by religion); and the knowledge of the incorruptibility and immortality of the soul. In all this there is implied the assertion of a breach between reason and faith, which had effects more far-reaching than Duns Scotus intended. Reason could claim unlimited scope and freedom so long as the finality of 'faith' was formally granted. Any doctrine, however sacred, might be intellectually analyzed and discussed; *e.g.*, atheism might be shown at length to be 'reasonable,' provided that the opposite affirmation of 'faith' was acknowledged. Hence some historians regard the position taken by Duns Scotus as the beginning of the decline of scholasticism.

2. Realism and nominalism.—The age of Albert, Aquinas, and Duns Scotus presents a substantial unanimity upon this question in the moderate realism which had been implied in the position of Abelard and was defended independently by the Arabians. Avicenna taught that the universal arises through comparison in thought; 'intellectus in formis agit universalitatem,' but there is a *genus naturale* as the basis of the *genus logicum*, and the *genus naturale* was *ante res* in the thought of God. Similarly Averroes: the universals are *in rebus*, but are posited as universals first by the intellect:

'Intellectus officium est abstrahere formam a materia individuata.'[2]

The position of Albert is not different:

'Universalis dicitur ratio non ideo quia tantum fit in nobis sive in mente nostra; sed ideo quia est res . . . quae in collatione accipitur, quae est in multis et de multis, quam collationem facit ratio.'[3]

So, again, Aquinas:

The universal is 'commune multis,' but it is not something 'praeter multa, nisi sola ratione.' It is 'aptum natum de pluribus praedicari.' 'Intellectus agens causat universale abstrahendo a materia.' In this sense, 'cognito singularium est prior quoad nos quam cognitio universalium.' Before creation universals existed in the eternal intellect of God.[4]

In Duns Scotus we find the same doctrine, but with a stronger emphasis on realism:

'Universale est ab intellectu, universali autem aliquid extra correspondet, a quo movetur intellectus ad causandum talem *intentionem* [*i.e.* the universal as an act of thought]. Effective est ab intellectu, sed materialiter sive occasionaliter sive originaliter est a proprietate in re; figmentum vero minime est.'[5]

3. Intellect and will.—In this regard the opposition between Aquinas and Duns Scotus is precise. The former teaches that intellect and will are never separated either in God or in man, but in man their union is imperfect. Intellect is superior to will because it involves knowledge, contemplation, rational intuition, and is *per se* related to reality;

---

[1] For a grotesque example of this, taken from the writings of Albert himself, see Rashdall, *Universities of Europe in the Middle Ages*, i. 464 f.

[2] The following authorities may be referred to: R. Seeberg, *Die Theologie des Johannes Duns Scotus*, Leipzig, 1900; H. Siebeck, 'Die Willenslehre bei Duns Scotus und seinen Nachfolgern,' in *Zeitschr. für Philos. und phil. Kritik*, cxii. [1898] 179 ff.; E. Pluzanski, *Essai sur la philosophie de Duns Scot*, Paris, 1887; A. Ritschl, 'Johannes Duns Scotus,' in *JDTh* x. [1865] 298 ff.; K. Werner, *Johannes Duns Scotus*, Vienna, 1881 ('Die Scholastik des späteren Mittelalters,' i.), also *Die Psychologie und Erkenntnisslehre des Johannes Duns Scotus*, do. 1877, and *Die Sprachlogik des Johannes Duns Scotus*, do. 1877.

[3] *Contra Gentiles*, i. 3.

[4] *Ib.* i. 9.

[1] Cf. *Summa*, I. qu. i. art. 1.

[2] Albertus Magnus, *de Prædicabilibus*, ii. 3; Prantl, ii. 348 ff.

[3] Albertus, *Summa*, I. xlii. 2.

[4] Aquinas, *Summa*, I. xvi. 7, lxxxv. 3; *c. Gentiles*, I. xxvi. 4, etc.

[5] Cf. Prantl, iii. 207 f.

will is determined by the perception of good, and this perception is an intellectual act, so that will is dependent on intellect. Moral freedom means that, by an intellectual act of analysis and comparison, various possible lines of action are revealed and one of them is perceived to be the best; the will then decides for the latter. In God the union of reason and will is perfect. The divine will is the total expression in action of the divine wisdom and in this sense is determined wholly by the divine nature, which is absolute goodness;[1] an alternative choice would be less good and therefore comparatively evil. This conception is applied to explain the origin of the moral law, which is a divine command. God commands it because it is good; but the goodness which is commanded is not foreign to the divine nature; it is an expression of the wisdom which is God. The chief end of man is conceived by Thomas, as by Aristotle, in intellectualistic terms. It is a rational intuition rising to a vision of God, from which love of God follows. The poetic expression of this ideal is given once for all in the *Paradiso* of Dante.

According to Duns Scotus, this dependence of will on intellect destroys freedom of choice and responsibility. He was led to this conclusion because he conceived the growth of ideas in the mind, after the manner of empirical psychology, as a natural process, so that the dependence of will on such a process involved determinism. If the will is free at all, its action must be wholly unrestricted. The intellect presents to the will the possibilities of its choice; but the will is absolutely autonomous; it is 'motor in toto regno animae, imperans intellectui.' And, as with the human will, so with the divine. Just as little can Duns Scotus admit a determination of the will of God even by His wisdom. The divine will is determined by nothing beyond itself; it acts *ex mera libertate*, free from every kind of necessity. And this will of God is the *summa lex*. Hence there is no necessity for the existence of the universe under its present constitution, forms, and relations.

Nevertheless two statements are made, in reference to this theory of Duns Scotus, which require important qualification: (*a*) it is sometimes said that he places the intellect at the mercy of arbitrary will, and (*b*) it is almost always said that, according to his teaching, a thing is good only because God has willed and commanded it, which is understood to mean that God might have made good evil and evil good.

(*a*) He does not teach that God 'could' make a square round or make contradictories identical; this is expressly denied.[2] But (*b*) God could have given to real beings other essences or natures than those which they actually have; and then, the natures of things being different, the laws of the universe would be other than they are.[3] It follows that, under the supposition stated, the laws of morality would be changed. Assuming that the content of duty depends on the constitution of human nature, it follows that, if human beings were constituted differently in certain fundamental ways, then the content of morality would be fundamentally altered. There is, however, no evidence that Duns Scotus intended to teach that morality could be determined differently by the will of God, human nature being constituted as it is.

This anti-moral conclusion was, however, actually derived from the statements of Duns Scotus. It was argued that nothing is, in itself or *per se*, either righteous or sinful, but only because God has commanded or forbidden it; and that the divine commands are made known to men only by the Church.[4] What Duns Scotus did was to affirm an entire subordination of the speculative to the practical order, in a way that reminds us of Kant. But his position is different from that of Kant. He offers us a critique not of speculative reason as such, but of certain special uses of speculative reason. He has therefore been called a 'dogmatist Kant.'

[1] Cf. *Summa*, I. xix. 3, 10.
[2] Cf. commentary on *Liber Sententiarum*, I. dist. 43, qu. 1.
[3] *Ib.* III. dist. 37, qu. 1.
[4] Cf. W. Windelband, *Hist. of Philosophy*, Eng. tr.[2], London and New York, 1907, p. 332 f.

4. The principle of individuality.—This question involves the distinction of matter and form which the schoolmen derived from Aristotle.[1] In Aristotle it is a distinction of two aspects of experience. In the hands of the schoolmen it becomes a division of the world into the spheres of two different real principles. In effect it becomes a distinction of two worlds. All beings in nature are composed of matter and form. 'Matter' is indeterminate and merely potential; it may be this or that. 'Forms' are equivalent to the constitutive laws of things; they are in all individuals of the kind or class and are essentially general. Averroes had laid down the principle that there is no form without matter and had based on it a system of pantheistic idealism indistinguishable from materialism.

Any subsistent being having a nature of its own, incommunicable to any other, is an individual. Such a being of rational grade is a person. Hence the metaphysical problem: Can we explain or conceive the means by which a being acquires individuality involving a nature that no other being can possess? The conclusions of Aquinas may be summarized as follows. Pure forms, real and active, exist only in the immaterial world. God is pure form and is unique and absolute genus and individual *per se*. The angels are relatively pure forms, each of whom is at once species and individual. Mankind belongs to both worlds and consists of matter and form in individual union. Hence men are members under a genus. How does their individuality arise? Individuality depends on matter *signata quantitate*, *i.e.* determined in reference to time and space. The matter of a man's body has been determined as to quantity by ante-natal hereditary and other influences. Matter, so determined, requires form to produce the individuality of *this* man, *this* embodied soul. The difficulty here soon became apparent. It is hard to avoid the conclusion that individuality depends on matter in a sense which puts immortality out of the question. But Aquinas and Albertus Magnus strenuously defend the incorruptibility and immortality of the soul against the materialistic implication of Averroism.

Duns Scotus appears to have seen more clearly than Aquinas that the problem of individuality is of central importance in any philosophy. It may be argued that from the nature of the case the problem is insoluble, since we cannot 'dig up the roots of our own being.' But the real nature and tendency of a philosophy depend on its grasp of the nature of this problem. In reference to the Thomist solution, Scotus affirms that all finite or created beings consist of form and matter: but there is an incorporeal matter. Formless *materia primo-prima*, *i.e.* matter as God created it, does not exist in isolation. It is *subjectum omnis receptionis*, the *radix et seminarium* of the world; rational souls are its 'flower' and pure intelligences (angels) its 'fruit.' *Materia secundo-prima* is the substrate of becoming and change. Scotus appears to have conceived of a series of forms determining the universal and primal matter. The result is a conception of nature as consisting of beings ever striving towards more complete and perfect individuality. Its unity consists in the order of its parts and the harmony of all bodies. The highest type of embodied existence is the human organism, because it is the organ of the rational soul.

[1] Cf. J. Royce, 'Latin and Scholastic Terminology,' in *DPhP*[2] i. 628 ff.

In criticizing the solution advocated by Aquinas, Scotus introduces a third principle, neither matter nor form, which he calls *hæcceitas*, and which is spoken of as if it produced or created the concrete individuality of the self-existent thing (*e.g.*, the soul of the man *qua* individual). The conception is thus stated by an interpreter of Scotus:

'Haecceitas est singularis . . . nihil aliud est nisi quidam modus intrinsecus qui immediate contrahit et primo quidditatem ad esse . . . et nominatur differentia individualis.'[1]

At first sight such statements appear to be open to two criticisms. (*a*) This is merely an illusory 'explanation' which consists in naming over again the fact to be explained: 'Socrates is an individual because he has individuality'; (*b*) more fundamentally, it is a case of the mischievous fallacy of treating the concrete existence involved in individuality as a logical quality like the differentia of a genus which makes it a species. On examination it appears that neither of these criticisms is relevant to the writer's real intention.

'The individual form (*hæcceitas*) is for Duns Scotus an original fact; no further question as to its ground is permissible. He designates individuality (both in the sense of individual substance and in that of individual occurrence) as the contingent (*contingens*); *i.e.* as that which cannot be deduced from a universal ground, but can only be verified as actual fact. For him . . . the individual is the form of all reality by means of which alone universal matter exists.'[2]

We find therefore two divergent tendencies in Scotus. His conception of *hæcceitas* implies that the real is the individual, while his theory of matter as always *informed* implies that the real is the universal.

In many respects Duns Scotus is the most important Christian thinker of the Middle Ages. Different aspects of his work have been dealt with as indicated in the references given above; but no monograph yet exists adequate to his significance as a critic of contemporaries and predecessors and as an original thinker. Nevertheless it has been said with much truth that 'in Scotus, great Schoolman as he was, Scholasticism overreached itself, and entered upon a subtlety which was the beginning of its decline.'[3] In every problem which he takes up Scotus tends to multiply divisions and distinctions to the utmost possible extent, until the essential factors of the question seem, as it were, to be reduced to impalpable particles and the real issues are lost sight of. Hence it is often far from easy to trace the fundamental and essential portions of his argument.

The opposition of principle between Aquinas and Scotus, even in questions of pure philosophy, went deep enough to perpetuate itself in two antagonistic schools. And, when it is remembered that matters of acute theological controversy, arising out of the doctrines of Incarnation and Atonement, were also involved, and that the respective doctors were impressive representatives of two different religious orders, it is easy to account for the feuds of 'Scotists' and 'Thomists' during the generation following the death of Scotus.[4]

There is, however, one fundamental question in which Aquinas and Scotus are in agreement, and in which they represent the position of the schoolmen as a whole. We may describe them both as strong realists, if we use this term, not in special reference to the question of universals, but as it is used in recent philosophy; in other words, they assume as an axiom that there is an immediate apprehension of the world as beyond and independent of the knowing mind. The distinction of understanding (or intellect) and sense, as two different modes of knowing, is always insisted on; but in each case the mind is directly related to the objectively independent world.[5] It might seem that this position was not tenable by Aquinas and Scotus, who speak as if they held a doctrine of what in recent times has been called 'representative perception.' Aquinas in particular speaks as if the interaction of the mind and the external object produced in the mind a copy of the object which is universalized by the intellect and becomes a permanent mental possession.[1] We find, however, that Aquinas is prepared to reconcile this view with the immediate objectivity of conception and of perception.

'In the process of understanding, the intellectual impression received in the potential intellect is that *whereby* (*quo*) we understand; just as the impression of colour received through the eye is not that *which* (*quod*) is seen, but that *whereby* (*quo*) we see. On the other hand, that *which* (*quod*) is understood is the nature of things existing outside the mind, as also it is things existing outside the mind that are the objects of visual perception.'[2]

In brief: our sensations and our ideas are not the objects of our knowledge but the instruments or means by which we know; or rather they are themselves the knowledge.

IV. *FOURTH PERIOD.*—Scholasticism in the proper sense of the term culminates in Thomism. Granting the inviolability of the system of ecclesiastical dogma, reason could do no more; and from this point of view the position taken by Duns Scotus already marks the beginning of the end. The decline of scholasticism is further marked by what is usually described as a 'revival of nominalism.' This expression is admissible only if we remember that it is not the nominalism of Roscellinus (whether understood as 'extreme' or as 'moderate'), but a nominalism newly thought out by a man whose ability, originality, and acumen are not inferior to those of any of the thinkers whom we have already named—William of Ockham.

William of Ockham was of British origin and was born towards the end of the 13th century. He became a member of the Franciscan order and was a pupil of Duns Scotus in Paris. He shared in the revolt of the Franciscans against Pope John XXII., which came to a head in 1322; and afterwards he supported Louis of Bavaria in the latter's famous contest with the same pope. During his life-time he was best known for the position which he took up against the Vatican: but his work as philosopher and theologian was influential enough to earn him the titles of *Doctor invincibilis* and *venerabilis Inceptor*. He became head of the order in 1342 and died about 1349.

During the years 1330–43 he issued a series of elaborate works circumscribing and limiting the authority of the pope. The issue with the Franciscan order concerned the duty of evangelical poverty. John XXII. had issued formal declarations condemning this practice; and the Franciscans maintained against him the ideal of strict imitation of Jesus in His poverty and obedience. The issue with Louis of Bavaria involved the whole question of the pope's authority as against that of the emperor. These works were theological as much as political; they served the purpose of the emperor and his supporters, because Ockham, in effect, cut at the root of the spiritual as well as the temporal supremacy of the pope. The temporal supremacy is openly and deliberately attacked. Independent civil power is declared to be as much an ordinance of God as spiritual power; and the authority of the State is affirmed in a manner which partially anticipated Hobbes.[3]

A brief comparison with the position of Aquinas may here be made. According to Aquinas, morality and social life are based on that *lex naturalis* which is an expression of the divine wisdom, and which the unaided reason of man can apprehend and realize in conduct. The State is the ordered, organized social life for which human nature is intended, and its proper end is to realize natural virtue. Natural virtue is only the preparation for man's higher destiny which grace offers him in the community of the Church; so that the State is subordinate to the Church as the *preambula gratiæ*. It is noteworthy, as Windelband[4] points out, that in Dante this relation of subordination has become one of co-ordination. But in Ockham the two powers are separated, as are reason and faith (see below). In the world of sense the civil State is supreme.

[1] Cf. Prantl, iii. 219, 280, 290.
[2] Windelband, p. 341 f.
[3] Rickaby, p. 27.
[4] For detailed information respecting these reference must be made to the standard histories named below.
[5] In reference to Aquinas and Scotus this statement requires little or no qualification; but it scarcely need be pointed out that for a nominalist the objectivity of conceptual knowledge becomes the more questionable the more thoroughly his nominalism is carried out.

[1] Cf. *c. Gentiles*, in Rickaby's annotated tr., *Of God and His Creatures*, London, 1905, pp. 38, 122.
[2] *C. Gentiles*, ii. 75; Rickaby, *Scholasticism*, p. 45.
[3] Cf. S. Riezler, *Die literararischen Widersacher der Päpste zur Zeit Ludwigs des Baiers*, Leipzig, 1874; T. M. Lindsay, 'Occam and his Connection with the Reformation,' in *British Quarterly Review*, lxxv. [1872].
[4] P. 327.

Ockham's philosophical and theological works consist mainly of commentaries on the *Liber Sententiarum* and on the logical treatises of Aristotle. It is a mistake to underestimate the importance of these as compared with his political writings.[1]

1. Ockham and Duns Scotus.—The nominalism of Ockham is best viewed in contrast with the logical realism of Duns Scotus. If we isolate this element, with its implied intellectualism and universalism, in the thought of Scotus and examine its tendencies *per se*, we obtain a doctrine which in some respects is an anticipation of Hegelianism, pointing as it does to the identity of the conceived with the real and of logical with causal dependence. Against these conclusions and all that they imply Ockham maintains a continuous polemic. Negatively, his position involves a protest against the 'hypostatization of abstractions' (to borrow a modern phrase)—in other words, against the tendency to treat an idea derived by abstraction from perceptual experience as if it could have a substantial existence *per se* or even could correspond to (or be a copy of) anything having such existence.[2] He finds this fallacy in all forms of logical realism.

Hence he argues that the class-concept or universal cannot be what realism affirmed it to be. He resolved it into contingent acts of sense-perception related directly to external objects. Such an act leaves behind it a trace or disposition (*habitus*), resembling itself, in the mind; and, when several such acts, or their traces, occur together, the common elements are assimilated. But these common elements are merely *consimilia*. The intellect is nothing but a derivative continuation of this primary sense-elaboration of given material: 'intellectus operationem suam incipit a sensibus, neque enim non sentiens intelligit.'[3] Its procedure is always the same; abstracting from the variable particulars of perceptual experience, it retains the common or permanent elements, and the only existence which the concepts have consists in these ever-recurring mental acts of abstraction, which by the help of language can be combined into propositions and syllogisms. Universals are therefore artificial products of our mental activity, although indispensable to mental discourse. A universal has no existence or meaning but what it derives from the particular concrete thing or group of things whose place it takes ('pro quibus supponit'). As mental act it is *una res singularis* or *intentio singularis*; and therefore 'non est universale nisi per significationem quia est signum plurium.'[4] Universals are 'ficta quibus in esse reali correspondent (vel correspondere possunt) consimilia.' A common name is therefore like an algebraical symbol; it is a purely denotative term whose meaning is accepted on the basis of normal experience.

Notwithstanding all this, Ockham firmly adheres to realism in the modern sense.[5] He expressly repudiates anything resembling the later doctrine of 'representative perception' (that we know things by the intervention of mental copies). He appears to assume, as an ultimate position, that the mental act (whether *perceptio rei* or *intellectio rei*) and the objective fact are necessarily related to each other, and that truth consists in the completeness of this relation. The question which he appears to leave unanswered concerns the real basis of the *consimilia* whose objectivity he admits.

'Take the simplest possible instance. One stone falls to the earth when allowed to drop; another does the same. Is there any real connexion? If there is none, then it was a chance coincidence. If a million stones fell to the ground under the given conditions, it would be a chance coincidence, and would afford no *reason* whatever for supposing that the next stone would do the same. The events would be independent in their real nature. And Science would be impossible. If, on the other hand, they are not independent, if there is a real connexion, then it is a real universal. It proves on examination to be a Law of Nature.'[1]

2. The authority of reason.—The doctrine of the twofold nature of truth appears in its ultimate form in Ockham's writings and was indeed an inevitable consequence of his view of the nature of reason. If reason consists only in the analysis and combination of facts of sense-perception, then no article of faith (whether of natural or of revealed religion) can be rationally demonstrated. Ockham endeavours to show this in his *Centiloquium Theologicum* and in *de Sacramento Altaris*. In the case of some dogmas his conclusion is that they are not only indemonstrable but irrational. The idea of God, though not irrational, is one whose truth cannot be demonstrated. It is a composite idea whose parts have been abstracted from various aspects of normal experience.[2] The mind can form the idea of God only by the artifice of abstraction. We can therefore have no knowledge of the Supreme Being in Himself; we can acquire only a purely relative notion, whose truth-value remains an open question. There is no reason to believe that such arguments imply an 'ironical scepticism' concealed 'under the mask of a most rigid orthodoxy.'[3] Ockham holds that the soul has a faculty of its own for apprehending supersensuous truth. This is the significance of his metaphorical distinction between man as *viator mortalis*, limited to the world of sense, and man as *beatus*, endowed with the privilege of faith. There is no doubt that the distinction of truth *secundum rationem* and truth *secundum fidem* was used by others as a means of attacking faith while appearing to acknowledge its authority, and that Ockham's influence actually contributed to the spread of theological scepticism; but mysticism rather than scepticism is the characteristic effect of his teaching; and it is significant that an adherence to nominalism on Ockham's lines, a rejection of metaphysics, and a mystical doctrine of the basis of religious belief are combined in Pierre D'Ailly (Petrus de Alliaco, 1350–1425) and in Johannes Gerson (1363–1429).

Of Ockham we may say that, while his manner of expression and method of exposition are thoroughly scholastic, his thinking reveals a new mental energy and a wholly modern spirit. His appeal is constantly to experience. His central doctrine, that the individual is the real, implies that investigation is directed to the concrete actual fact. No free development of this tendency was possible except partially in the field of psychology, because the scholastic method and assumptions still ruled; but none the less Ockham may be described as one of the pioneers of scientific opposition to scholasticism.

3. The new learning.—As early as the 13th cent. the Franciscan Roger Bacon, at Oxford and Paris, had criticized the tendency of scholasticism and endeavoured to improve contemporary methods of studying theology. He appealed to sound common

1 A view of Ockham's system as a whole can be obtained from a compilation issued in 1422 by Gabriel Biel († 1495, usually described as 'the last of the scholastics') under the title *Epitome et Collectorium ex Occamo super libros quatuor Sententiarum* (Tübingen, 1495). No good monograph on Ockham has yet appeared; and some of his writings have never been printed. We may name Werner, *Die Scholastik des späteren Mittelalters*, Vienna, 1881–87, iii.; Siebeck, 'Die Erkenntnisstheorie Occam's,' in *Archiv für Gesch. der Phil.* x. [1897] 317 ff.; Ritschl, 'Die nominalistische Gotteslehre,' in *JDTh* xiii. [1868] pt. 1; and (especially for references to existing sources of information) Poole, art. 'Ockham,' in *DNB* xli. 357 ff.

2 The expression usually attributed to Ockham, 'Entia non sunt multiplicanda praeter necessitatem,' is not to be found in his published writings, but is an accurate formulation of his intention.

3 Biel, I. dist. cxi. qu. 6.

4 Prantl, iii. 337.

5 Cf. above, III. *ad fin.* ('epistemological realism').

1 S. H. Mellone, 'Real Kinds and General Laws,' in *Mind*, new ser., xx. [1911] 248 ff.

2 Cf. Biel, I. dist. iii. qu. 2 ff.

3 Hagenbach, ii. 133.

sense, experience (outward and inward), and knowledge of nature and of humanity. In the second half of the 15th cent. the times were ripe for Roger Bacon's influence to come to its own. The restoration of classical studies tended to set the human mind free from absorption in one-sided theological and philosophical speculation and limited the excessive dominion of Aristotle over human thought. Scholasticism implies a Church unified and supreme, and a centralized learning employing exclusively one ancient language; but the spread of Greek literature, especially after the capture of Constantinople in 1453, exerted a profoundly transforming influence on the study of theological and philosophical subjects and promoted a reaction against the mediæval interpretation of Greek metaphysics, against the method of deduction from conceptions taken as authoritative assumptions, and against the rigidity of monastic Latin. Interest in the investigation and interpretation of nature found ever-widening scope for its effective development. Philosophy, finding a place for itself by the side of theology, claimed to be an independent secular science whose special task was the knowledge of nature; and natural science began to exert a decisive influence on the development of philosophic thought. The invention of printing (about 1440) and the discovery of America (1490) are only two out of many historic events converging to effect what was at bottom a revolution in the history of nations which necessitated a new development of religious and philosophic thought.

It is scarcely accurate to speak of a 'revival' of scholasticism in the 17th century. In 1563 the Council of Trent declared Thomism to be authoritative in reference to the essentials of philosophic truth. This, however, excluded the Church from the new movements of the time and reduced philosophy to a condition of stagnation in the seminaries. Half a century later a few writers of outstanding ability lent distinction to the movement in the Spanish peninsula, where the Thomist tradition had maintained itself most strongly: such were Gabriel Vasquez of Alcala († 1604) and Francis Suarez of Granada († 1617); but nothing that could be described as a 'revival' took place.

A certain turning-point in the history of scholasticism is marked by the publication of the papal encyclical *Æterni Patris* in 1880. In this Leo XIII. urged the intelligent study of Thomism on clergy and laity as wholesome alike for religion, philosophy, and civil life. Movements in this direction have been initiated and have not been fruitless. The *Revue Néoscolastique*, published (until 1914) at Louvain under the editorial supervision of M. de Wulf, throws interesting sidelights on what may be expected of a reformed scholasticism in the hands of Roman Catholic scholars of competence. The same observation may be made in reference to the *Revue Thomiste*, carried on by the Dominican Fathers since 1894 and published at Paris.

LITERATURE.—Within the limits of this article it has been possible to give only a concise summary of the most essential facts and to indicate sources from which reliable guidance for further study may be obtained. Numerous references have already been given for particular thinkers or particular aspects of scholasticism. The following notes relate to works where the subject as a whole is dealt with historically.

Among the most recent authorities must be mentioned: **F. J. Picavet**, *Esquisse d'une hist. générale et comparée des philosophies médiévales*[2], Paris, 1906; **C. Bäumker**, *Die europäische Philosophie des Mittelalters* (in series 'Allg. Gesch. der Phil.'), Leipzig, 1909 (cf. also Bäumker, *Beiträge zur Gesch. der Phil. des Mittelalters*, Münster, 1891 ff.); **M. de Wulf**, *Hist. de la philosophie médiévale*[2], Louvain, 1905, *Les Philosophes du Moyen Age: Textes et Études*, do. 1901 ff.; **F. Ueberweg** and **M. Heinze**, *Grundriss der Gesch. der Philosophie*[10], 4 vols., Berlin, 1906–09, esp. vol. ii. (the existing Eng. tr. is from Ueberweg[3]). Among older standard authorities must be mentioned: **B. Hauréau**, *Hist. de la philosophie scolastique*, 3 vols., Paris, 1872–80; **A. Stöckl**, *Gesch. der Philosophie des Mittelalters*, 4 vols., Mainz, 1861–67 (more briefly in *Lehrbuch der Gesch. der Phil.*[2], do. 1875); **V. Cousin**, *Ouvrages inédits d'Abelard* (General Introduction), Paris, 1836. The accounts given by **J. E. Erdmann** and **W. Windelband** in their Histories of Philosophy are good; and the older work of **A. H. Ritter** is not yet obsolete. Indispensable to the special student are **A. L. M. Jourdain**, *Recherches critiques sur l'âge et l'origine des traductions latines d'Aristote*[2], Paris, 1843; and **K. von Prantl**, *Gesch. der Logik im Abendlande*, 4 vols., Leipzig, 1855–70.

S. H. MELLONE.

SCHOPENHAUER.—I. Life and works.—Arthur Schopenhauer (1788–1860) was born at Danzig on 22nd Feb. 1788. He was the son of Heinrich Schopenhauer, an intelligent and successful merchant, who with the help of a brother created a business which held a position of preeminence among the chief mercantile firms in the famous Hanse town. The grandfather, Andreas, was a large farmer, who began to add merchandise to his agricultural work. The family was of Dutch origin, and, curiously enough, this was also true of the maternal side of the house. The name of Arthur Schopenhauer's mother was Johanna Henriette Trosiener. She was an attractive young woman, not only gifted intellectually by nature, but educated (largely through the instrumentality of a Scottish minister) in a much more thorough manner than was customary at the time. She became an authoress of some renown in later years.

Young Arthur had an ideal training for a child both at home in a villa near Danzig and in a farmhouse which his father had acquired in the territory enclosed between the Baltic Sea and the arms of the Vistula. But this happy life was soon interrupted. The first partition of Poland in 1772 had given Danzig an autonomy, which was, however, an autonomy only in name, since Frederick the Great exerted himself by various exactions to make mercantile life difficult and irksome. After his death in 1786 things did not improve, and finally, after the second partition of Poland in 1793, Danzig ceased to exist as a free city, and the Schopenhauer couple, with their five-year-old boy, hastily departed and took up residence in Hamburg. Thus Arthur Schopenhauer passed the most impressionable part of his life, from 1793 to 1807—from his fifth to his twentieth year—in another great commercial city. This time was broken between the years 1797 and 1799, when he was taken by his father to Paris and Havre and was left at the latter town in the household of a commercial correspondent of the firm. The elder Schopenhauer was 'advanced' in his views and deeply impressed by the literary life of France, and more especially by the fame of Voltaire and his contemporaries. On his return the boy attended a school conducted on commercial lines, but, despite his father's strongly expressed desire, his inclinations were towards authorship and in no way towards commerce. On the promise of a long tour to France and England, however, he allowed himself to be coerced into an engagement to devote himself after all to commercial pursuits. Whilst in England he was boarded with a clergyman at Wimbledon and brought away with him a very unfavourable impression of an English boarding-school.

After leaving England, the Schopenhauer family went through France and Switzerland to Vienna and thence to Berlin. Arthur and his mother then proceeded to Danzig, where Arthur tried to learn the elements of business training. Subsequently he rejoined his father in Hamburg, and, on the conclusion of his seventeenth year, entered the office of a merchant there. He himself states that never was there a worse mercantile clerk, for his mind was continually fixed on other subjects, and more especially on the subject of phrenology, then engaging much attention in Hamburg owing to the lectures of Gall the phrenologist. In April 1805 the dead body of the elder Schopenhauer was found in the canal; whether this had resulted from an accidental fall from a granary or not was never known. At any rate Schopenhauer had suffered serious money losses, resulting probably from the speculation that was then being carried on in the city, and the family was left in a less prosperous condition than it might have been. The widow, with her only daughter, aged ten, was glad now to be able to live a new and freer life wherein she might realize some of her social and literary aspirations. She and her child went in 1806 to Weimar, where she entered on a life of interest and happiness in the intellectual circle of men and women who had gathered round Goethe. On the social side this intellectual movement developed in great measure into the romanticism which characterized German society in later years.[1]

But Arthur Schopenhauer was left at Hamburg apparently in the depths of depression—the depression that followed him all through life in one form or another. His mother, who always regarded her son from a curiously detached and impersonal point of view, consulted her friend Fernow and on his advice gave her consent to his leaving his ledger and giving himself to classical study. At nineteen the young man entered the gymnasium and studied there with boys considerably his juniors. As this experiment was not successful, he went to Weimar, where he devoted himself to that Greek and Latin learning which (more especially the Greek) meant so much to him in later life.

Schopenhauer had already developed qualities of self-assertiveness and fault-finding which made him difficult to live with, and his mother had none of the maternal devotion that overlooks such faults or tries to remedy them. Hence the relationship between mother and son was strained in the extreme. The mother was satisfied with the position which she had attained and anxious to enjoy to the full her newly-found freedom; the son was critical, introspective, and gauche, never content with what was before his hands and always looking for something that was not to be found. In addition there was a mental side to his woes which his mother might have recognized, had she been less engrossed in her personal interests and happiness. It may have been inherited from a father who, with all his ability, was subject to outbursts of passion; his uncles, too, were mentally abnormal.

At the age of twenty-one Schopenhauer received his patrimony, which gave him the means of living in simplicity without dependence on professional gain. He enrolled as a student of medicine at Göttingen, but before long turned to philosophy, devoting himself specially to the study of Plato and Kant. He soon migrated to the young university of Berlin, where he worked under Schleiermacher, Wolf, and Fichte (though there perhaps was never a more critical student) and also did some clinical work in the hospital. In 1813 he was little moved by the call to arms, and, when Berlin was endangered (after Lützen), he fled for refuge to Dresden and subsequently to Weimar and then to Rudolstadt, where he composed his first published work, the philosophical treatise *Ueber die vierfache Wurzel des Satzes vom zureichenden Grunde* ('On the Fourfold Root of the Principle of Sufficient Reason,' Rudolstadt, 1813), as an essay to qualify for his doctorate of philosophy at Berlin. Later, and in an altered form, it was made a part of his system of philosophy. In this treatise we have much that forms the basis of Schopenhauer's philosophy. We certainly find here what was characteristic of his teaching—the substitution of his doctrine of sufficient reason for Kant's system of the categories as constitutive of experience. In this book, too, we have the first statement of that conception of the world as will, the first step towards the notion of intelligence as a secondary result developed by will.

[1] See *ERE* iv. 359 f.

The great aim of the philosopher, though only twenty-five years of age, was to escape from the turmoil of war. In 1813 he left his inn at Rudolstadt and returned to his mother's house at Weimar, but the experiment was so disastrous that in May 1814 he left that house for good. The mother died twenty-four years later, never having seen her son again. Her qualities were fundamentally different from her son's. She was spoiled in early youth and, released from the trammels of a married life in which love had played little part, she found pleasure in surroundings which gave her opportunities for displaying her undoubted talents and social gifts. The son resented her male friendships and was morose and rude to those whom he met in her house. Schopenhauer's views of women are well known. He looked upon them as incapable of undertaking any responsibility—as creatures to be kept in subjection and regarded as unmoral rather than immoral. His own experiences certainly were far from happy. He never married, and it was perhaps as well that he did not. His nature was sensual; he was perpetually brooding over sexual matters and wrote of them in great detail.

Schopenhauer came into relation with Goethe at Weimar over a subject of interest to both—the theory of colour. He wrote an essay on the subject, which he sent to Goethe and which was published at Leipzig in 1816 under the title *Ueber das Sehen und die Farben* ('On Vision and Colours'). This treatise was in some degree in harmony with Goethe's conception of the nature of colour.

From 1814 to 1818 Schopenhauer was at Dresden, where he lived in a constant state of contemplation and self-immersion. His own notes describe the nature of that life—a life which he regarded as one continual struggle between diverging principles all endeavouring to assert themselves whilst only one could ultimately prevail. Hence came that constant consciousness of defeat to be overcome only by giving up the struggle as useless that associates Schopenhauer's name more almost than any other with the doctrine of pessimism.[1] He longed for relief such as the ascetic succeeds in reaching, although it meant mere withdrawal into negativity. He soon became convinced that his system was the great system of metaphysics and ethics combined for which the ages had been waiting. He had reached beyond the science of the day, which was no science but the 'philosophy of the barber's man,' to what towered above the sensible—the supersensible. Hence his attitude of certainty regarding his creed, an attitude which the common man called arrogance. His philosophy became fixed and certain in his mind, and he believed that he had only to wait for its recognition by the world. He had, however, to wait some time. *Die Welt als Wille und Vorstellung* ('The World as Will and Idea'), Schopenhauer's greatest and most important work, fell to all appearances dead in an unappreciative world. Most of the first edition, which appeared at Leipzig in 1819, was sold as waste paper. Another edition was, however, printed with considerable emendation in 1844. Nothing discouraged the author, so completely certain was he that he had found the truth in its entirety.

In 1818 Schopenhauer made a journey to Italy which greatly influenced his later life, though his

[1] See art. PESSIMISM AND OPTIMISM, § 5.

diary is full of somewhat morbid introspection and melancholy observation. Next year, while still in Italy, he heard that the parental business-house at Danzig had failed, and that his mother and sister had accepted a composition. Characteristically he would have none of this and held out for full payment to himself with such vigour and determination that in the end—three years later—he obtained it even with interest. He was indignant with the women, who were not willing to join him in the fray, and ceased for years even to correspond with them. Though riches came to him, his nature was not an enviable one as regards his wealth, for he was ever suspicious and distrustful.

Schopenhauer had a desire to be connected with a university, and in 1820 he tried to teach as *privat-docent* in Berlin, but without success. He became involved in disputes with Hegel and other fellow-teachers, and even threw a fellow-lodger downstairs, and had to pay her a substantial annuity till her death. Another visit to Italy was paid in the winter of 1822–23; then he returned to Munich and after some further travel settled in Berlin again in 1825. He made overtures for translating Kant's works into English, but with no practical result. In 1831 he went to Frankfort-on-the-Main to escape from an outbreak of cholera in Berlin and finally settled there.

He lived for many years a curiously ordered life, writing, reading, and taking exercise. He was devoted to animals and sensitive to their ill-treatment; he loved his dog, which the children named 'Young Schopenhauer' and which was his constant companion in his daily walks. His only diversion was music or the play, more especially the former. In 1836 he published at Frankfort a small book entitled *Ueber den Willen in der Natur* ('On the Will in Nature'), which was intended to be a corroboration of his theory of truth from the scientific point of view. It endeavoured to demonstrate the nature of will as the *prius* of the organism.

In 1838 a Norwegian society offered a prize for the proof of the existence of free will derived from the evidence of consciousness, and the prize was to his great satisfaction awarded to Schopenhauer. Unfortunately for his *amour propre*, he was not so successful in his competition for a Danish prize. He suspected a plot against him on the part of those who were inspired by the special objects of his hatred and jealousy—Fichte, Schelling, and Hegel, the so-called transcendentalists. His jealousy for his own reputation and desire for recognition amounted to a disease.

He published at Frankfort in 1841 two essays under the title *Die beiden Grundprobleme der Ethik* ('The Two Fundamental Problems of Ethics'). In them he formulates his scheme of morality, morality signifying the inevitable consequences which are realized when man reaches self-consciousness. Man has to become aware that life is self-delusion, and morality becomes inward self-abnegation and renunciation of the world as it has hitherto been known to us.

It was Schopenhauer's great work *The World as Will and Idea* that made him famous. It was through this, the result of a life's reflexion, that its author hoped for recognition for himself and defeat for his 'transcendental' opponents. Hegel was dead, and he hoped Hegelianism would die likewise. At first the success of his work was not very apparent, and the revolutionary years that followed soon after its completion tended to depress him. With the republican system of government he had no sympathy, and he dreaded losing his own possessions. Gradually, however, he found disciples here and there. One article which appeared in the *Westminster Review*,[1] and which introduced Schopenhauer to English readers as an opponent of the German transcendentalism expounded by Coleridge, specially delighted him. Gwinner, his literary executor and biographer, was a faithful follower and disciple.

The World as Will and Idea passed into three editions before its author's death. Some admired the work because of its views on art and music, others because of its exposition of sexual love, others looked upon the book as providing a new sort of faith for those who had rejected the old. The work that probably first succeeded in bringing popularity to its writer was, however, *Parerga und Paralipomena* (not very respectfully translated as 'Chips and Scraps'), which was published at Berlin in 1851. The book was made up of a number of essays on various topics, full of wit and sarcasm, and there was something in it to suit every taste. The date of the third edition of *The World as Will and Idea* was 1859, and a second edition of *Will in Nature* appeared in 1854 and of *The Two Fundamental Problems of Ethics* in 1860, so that before his death Schopenhauer at least had the satisfaction of finding his work appreciated. His portrait was painted in 1855 by a French artist named Lunteschutz and in the following year by Goebel. The latter is the portrait best known in its reproductions. The author's mother and sister died before success came, and he led a lonely life in spite of having many admirers. He lived comfortably and worked hard, although in a well regulated way, until his death, which took place on 21st Oct. 1860 from heart failure.

2. Teaching. — One can best make Schopenhauer's point of view intelligible by comparing it with that of Bergson, to which it has considerable analogy. Bergson holds that the ultimate reality is a creative *élan* which, operating in time (which is for Bergson real and ultimate but is in the nature of duration and not formal or spatialized time), gives rise to intelligence. Schopenhauer held that the ultimate reality or thing-in-itself was will, which developed itself into intelligence. Both consider that we have a direct intuitive apprehension of the existence of the *nisus* which is thus revealed to us not indirectly through knowledge, but directly. But Schopenhauer, agreeing with Kant, held that time, like space, was only a form of knowledge, while Bergson, agreeing with the denial of the reality of space, treats time not only as real but as of the very essence of the creative evolution of the *nisus*. The world arises for Schopenhauer when there has been evolved a nervous system sufficiently organized to be the instrument of knowledge. The will thus governs ruthlessly. If a man wishes to reach a state of rest, he can acquire it only by an absolute renunciation of the will to live. He may, if he struggles hard enough, attain to a condition of *nirvāṇa*—a state of non-being where the will has vanished and knowledge only is left. We see in this doctrine the influence of the Indian religions, and of Buddhism in particular, upon Schopenhauer's mind.

Schopenhauer teaches that we do not in the phenomenal world come into contact with the ultimately real. The intellect constructs that world according to a 'principle of sufficient reason.' It is by direct intuition that we apprehend that which is not phenomenal, and here we arrive at that *nisus*, or will, which is quite apart from the intellect and is something not in time nor determined by motives—the activity that underlies the whole universe. The will expresses itself in every phenomenon in nature, even in inorganic nature.

[1] April 1853, pp. 388–407, 'Iconoclasm in German Philosophy,' by John Oxenford.

But the body is distinguished from the rest of nature by the circumstance that by direct intuition we are aware of will as realized in it. Thus we have a conception of the universe as, on the one hand, a phenomenal construction by the intellect, and, on the other, as will—both conscious will and will revealed in the world in different stages and forms. In music and the arts universals somewhat analogous to the ideas of Plato more especially disclose themselves as stages in the self-realization of will.

Science, Schopenhauer affirms, can be learned by any one, but from art we get only what our nature brings to it. Science only teaches us how and why a thing has become what it is, how it is strictly limited in its sphere; art reveals the truth in a way that science cannot attempt to do; it teaches us, indeed, by its revelation of the truth, the unreality of the world and its manifestations. Schopenhauer was of course very largely affected by the romanticism of the day. The scholar, he tells us, is but the man who has painfully acquired certain knowledge; the genius has vision and sees the world in all its aspects and is also able to observe himself. Schopenhauer, however, follows out his theme to a point which may seem to us exaggerated, but which may be explained by the romantic reaction against the morality of culture and convention which had before this held the field. The old conventional morality he regards as selfishness of a refined sort. The will is really at the basis of all human nature, and the intellect is but a subordinate element in it. Art gives us the truest revelation of will and its stages as the meaning of life—a revelation which cannot be arrived at by any mere reasoning. The world is but an object in relation to a subject. It is from direct intuition of self that some glimpse into the nature of reality may be had, and this shows us that it is will that is the reality behind the illusionary things of sense.

Schopenhauer being naturally disposed to melancholy, his teaching turned into the pessimism that is associated with his name. The will struggles for self-assertion in existence, and this ends in a world-wide struggle in which no satisfaction for the individual is to be found. The will is inherently blind, and there is no release from the world of torture but by discovering the error of striving after the happiness of the individual and realizing our identity with other beings by finally renouncing the will and abstracting from individual desires. This is the only means of escape from the misery of the world, and artistic contemplation such as we experience in music helps it.

Schopenhauer has been regarded as an artist or a poet as much as a philosopher. Indeed, he himself has said that his philosophy is 'philosophy as art.' This explains his way of looking at philosophy as representing the vivid impression of a genius and his attitude of detachment as the teacher of a doctrine which could not be wholly carried out in practical life. We can understand how, after the period of disillusionment which followed the outbursts of 1848, men might take refuge in views such as Schopenhauer's, and we can also understand why his teaching did not take yet firmer hold as a system, even while it influenced very deeply contemporary thought and criticism. Schopenhauer has never founded a school; but as a critic he has an important place in the history of thought. He really represents one line of possible development of the Kantian system, while Fichte and Hegel (*qq.v.*) represent another and a very different one.

LITERATURE.—**Arthur Schopenhauer**, *Sämmtliche Werke*, ed. J. Frauenstädt, 6 vols., Leipzig, 1873–74, ed. E. Grisebach[2], 6 vols., do. 1892, *The World as Will and Idea*, tr. R. B. Haldane and J. Kemp, 3 vols., London, 1883–86, [3]1896; **Helen Zimmern**, *Arthur Schopenhauer: his Life and his Philosophy*, do. 1876; *The Wisdom of Schopenhauer*, selected and tr. Walter Jekyll, do. 1911; **W. Wallace**, *Life of Arthur Schopenhauer*, do. 1890, art. 'Schopenhauer,' in *EBr*[9]; **J. E. Erdmann**, *Versuch einer wissenschaftlichen Darstellung der Gesch. der neuern Philosophie*, Riga, 1834–53, iii. 381–471; **A. Foucher de Careil**, *Hegel et Schopenhauer*, Paris, 1862; **J. Frauenstädt**, *Briefe über die schopenhauer'sche Philosophie*, Leipzig, 1854, *Neue Briefe über die schopenhauer'sche Philosophie*, do. 1876; **R. Haym**, *Arthur Schopenhauer*, Berlin, 1864; **Friedrich Nietzsche**, *Unzeitgemässe Betrachtungen*[2], vol. ii. pt. 3, 'Schopenhauer als Erzieher,' Leipzig, 1893; *Baltaser Gracian's Hand-Orakel und Kunst der Weltklugheit aus dessen Werken gezogen von Don V. J. de Lastanosa und aus dem spanischen Original übersetzt von A. Schopenhauer nachgelassenes Manuscript*, ed. J. Frauenstädt, Leipzig, 1862; *Briefwechsel zwischen Arthur Schopenhauer und Johann August Becker*, ed. J. K. Becker, do. 1883; **Frauenstädt**, *Schopenhauer-Lexikon: ein philosophisches Wörterbuch, nach Arthur Schopenhauer's sämmtlichen Schriften*, 2 vols., do. 1871; *Two Essays by Arthur Schopenhauer: I. On the Fourfold Root of the Principle of Sufficient Reason. II. On the Will in Nature*, Eng. tr., London, 1889; **Emil Reich**, *Schopenhauer als Philosoph der Tragödie*, Vienna, 1888; **James Sully**, *Pessimism: a History and a Criticism*, London, 1877; **Richard Wagner**, *Beethoven; with a Supplement from the Philosophical Works of Arthur Schopenhauer*, tr. E. Dannreuther, do. 1880; **David Asher**, *Arthur Schopenhauer: Neues von ihm und über ihn* (Letters, etc.), Berlin, 1871; **Wilhelm Gwinner**, *Arthur Schopenhauer aus persönlichem Umgange dargestellt*, Leipzig, 1862, *Schopenhauer's Leben*[3], do. 1910, *Schopenhauer und seine Freunde*, do. 1863, *Denkrede auf Arthur Schopenhauer*, do. 1888; **Frauenstädt**, *Arthur Schopenhauer; von ihm; über ihn: ein Wort der Vertheidigung von E. O. Lindner und Memorabilien, Briefe und Nachlasstücke*, Berlin, 1863, *Aus Arthur Schopenhauer's handschriftlichen Nachlass*, Leipzig, 1864, *Arthur Schopenhauer; Lichtstrahlen aus seinen Werken: mit einer Biographie und Characteristik Schopenhauer's*[7], do. 1891; **T. B. Saunders**, *Schopenhauer: a Lecture*, London, 1901; *The Art of Controversy and other Posthumous Papers*, sel. and tr. T. B. Saunders, do. 1896; *On Human Nature: Essays on Ethics and Politics*[2], sel. and tr. Saunders, do. 1902; *Religion, a Dialogue; and other Essays*[2], sel. and tr. Saunders, do. 1890; *The Wisdom of Life*[8] (being pt. i. of *Aphorismen zur Lebensweisheit*), tr. with preface by Saunders, do. 1902; *Counsels and Maxims* (being pt. ii. of *Aphorismen zur Lebensweisheit*), tr. Saunders, do. 1890; *The Art of Literature: a Series of Essays* (from the *Parerga*), sel. and tr. with preface by Saunders, do. 1891; *Studies in Pessimism; a Series of Essays*[4], sel. and tr. Saunders, do. 1893; *Essays of Schopenhauer*, tr. Mrs. R. Dircks, do. 1892; **W. Caldwell**, *Schopenhauer's System in its Philosophical Significance*, Edinburgh, 1896; *Pensées, maximes et fragments: traduit, annoté et précédé d'une vie de Schopenhauer* (by J. Bourdeau), Paris, 1880; *Selected Essays of Arthur Schopenhauer: with a biographical Introd. and Sketch of his Philosophy* (by E. B. Bax), London, 1891.

E. S. HALDANE.

SCHWENCKFELDIANS.—See SECTS (Christian).

SCIENCE.—I. Definition and characteristics.—Science is a system of knowledge defined partly by its subject-matter of more or less objective facts, but mainly by the methods by which its data are reached and by the extent to which its conclusions can be experimentally tested. Science is gained by observation (including, according to some, introspection) and by experiment, but also by reflecting (with every available technical aid) on the data thus supplied. Typically scientific knowledge is of such a kind that it can be verified by competent inquirers who repeat the observations and experiments and make them the subject of independent reflexion. In this respect, as in some others, science is a 'social phenomenon,' as it has been phrased. The verification requires, primarily, normally constituted minds; it also demands a certain competence—the fruit of discipline; it also desiderates some degree of freedom from prejudice and from the limitations imposed by the current errors of the age. Many sagacious astronomers were satisfied with the Ptolemaic system, and many sincere naturalists believed that they had evidence of the validity of the Linnæan conception of the fixity of species. Science moves asymptotically towards adequate accuracy.

Science is also essentially communicable knowledge; indeed the possibility of it depends on man's capacity for consulting with his neighbours. Yet it cannot be supposed that the range of communicability is to be limited either by the man in the street or by the man in the cloister. The average man does not find the science of Newton's *Principia* very communicable, because he does not know the technical language and cannot follow the argument. On the other hand, the accurate and astoundingly practical knowledge which a clever cattle-breeder has of the eugenic merits of an animal is often not communicable. It proves itself to be sound, like an artist's intuition, but the diagnoses involved have not been made the subject of scientific analysis, and they do not enter into the fabric of communicable science. Furthermore, knowledge does not become scientific until it is detachable from merely personal conviction, until it can be de-personalized. Those possessed by a burning enthusiasm for a conclusion, as unquestionable to them as the noonday sun, are often disappointed by the cold douche of scientific scepticism which demands personal de-polarization. The fact is, finally, that, if a conclusion is to form part of science, it must be stripped of every trace of an emotional halo. The emotional context may be essential to a sane synoptic view; it is irrelevant in science.

2. Aim of science.—The beginning of science involves a process of selection from the data of the personal thought-stream. Attention is concentrated on vivid sense-impressions whose external references are localizable in space and definable in time. The routine of these sense-impressions is observed and registered, and externalized (in most cases) as natural objects and occurrences. Whatever be the precise psychology of the beginning of scientific knowledge,[1] its pursuit depends on processes of selection and abstraction, detachment and definition. In this way there is built up a perceptual framework and then a conceptual system—the counterpart of the outer world, which empirical science at any rate must treat as real. The moment at which any part of this working 'thought-model' becomes definitely scientific is when it admits of formulation and is seen as part of a larger whole, when, as Aristotle said, from a great number of experiences one general conception is formed which will embrace all similar cases. The note of science is struck when uniformities of co-existence or succession are detected and formulated, when there is 'a unification of diverse phenomena through their reduction to a common law.' Science is essentially descriptive formulation. Its aim is to describe the impersonal facts of experience in verifiable terms as precisely and completely as possible, as simply as possible, and as consistently as possible. In its universe of discourse it keeps to experiential terms or verifiable symbolical derivatives of these. It answers the question 'How?' rather than the question 'Why?'. J. H. Poynting puts it thus:

> In science 'we explain an event not when we know "why" it happened, but when we show "how" it is like something else happening elsewhere or otherwise—when, in fact, we can include it as a case described by some law already set forth.'[2]

As Karl Pearson has said:

> 'The law of gravitation is a brief description of *how* every particle of matter in the universe is altering its motion with reference to every other particle. It does not tell us *why* particles thus move; it does not tell us *why* the earth describes a certain curve round the sun. It simply resumes, in a few brief words, the relationships observed between a vast range of phenomena. It economises thought by stating in conceptual shorthand that routine of our perceptions which forms for us the universe of gravitating matter.'[3]

The true nature of scientific explanation is well suggested by Kirchhoff's famous statement of the aim of mechanics: 'to describe completely and in the simplest manner the motions that occur in nature.' It must be recognized, however, that the end of science is not reached in the formulation of things as they are; it has also to describe how they have come to be. Its formulations have a historical or genetic, as well as an immediate, reference. They deal with the course of events. See art. NATURAL LAW.

[1] See art. EPISTEMOLOGY.
[2] *Report of the British Association, 1899*, p. 617.
[3] *Grammar of Science*[2], p. 99.

What has just been said in regard to the past holds also of the future. The more complete a science is, the greater the power of prediction. Thus Helmholtz has written:

> 'We call our ideas of the external world *true*, when they give us sufficient information about the consequences of our actions throughout the external world, and bring us to proper conclusions regarding its expected changes';[1]

and Hertz said that it was the task of science to deduce the future from the past, the quality of scientific symbols being such that their intellectually necessary consequences correspond to occurrences.[2]

A scientific hypothesis *works* when it serves to sum up the observed facts in terms consistent with the rest of the scientific framework, and when deductions from it are verified in subsequent experience. If the contradictory of a deduced proposition should be verifiable, the hypothesis would have to be discarded or modified.

The primary aim of science is to see things clearly, consistently, and connectedly, to formulate, to discover laws. It reveals coherence and continuity. Its motives are curiosity, a dislike of obscurities, a desire for unity. But science as an intellectual system and endeavour has grown out of practical lore, and the desire of mastering circumstances remains as one of its mainsprings. On the other hand, while the pursuit of science will last as long as human curiosity, it is admitted by most that the crown of science is its contribution to the enrichment and betterment of human life. It is of interest to quote from a great investigator, H. A. Rowland, the following sentence:

> 'The aims of the physicist, however, are in part purely intellectual: he strives to understand the Universe on account of the intellectual pleasure derived from the pursuit, but he is upheld in it by the knowledge that the study of nature's secrets is the ordained method by which the greatest good and happiness shall finally come to the human race.'[3]

Trotter's excellent definition of a science sums up the matter: 'a body of knowledge derived from experience of its material and co-ordinated so that it shall be useful in forecasting and, if possible, directing the future behaviour of that material.'[4]

3. The scientific mood.—The scientific study of a subject implies a certain intellectual attitude or mood, which need not, however, be regarded as the only way of approaching a subject. Thus the æsthetic or artistic approach and the purely practical approach are not less legitimate than that of the scientific investigator. The characteristic features of the expert scientific investigator, or of any one desirous of having a scientific knowledge of a subject, may be described as a passion for facts (which implies a high standard of accuracy and a detachment from personal wishes); a cautious thoroughness in coming to a conclusion (which implies persistent scepticism and self-elimination in judgment); a quality of clearness (which implies a dislike of obscurities, ambiguities, and loose ends—what Faraday called 'doubtful knowledge'); and a less readily definable sense of the inter-relations of things, which discerns tentatively at least that apparently isolated phenomena are integral parts of a system. When Sir Michael Foster, in his Presidential Address to the British Association in 1899, said that the qualities which distinguish the scientific worker

[1] Quoted by H. Höffding, *Modern Philosophers*, Eng. tr., London, 1915, p. 125.
[2] *Ib.*
[3] *Amer. Journ. Sci.* viii. [1899] 411.
[4] *Instincts of the Herd*, London, 1916, p. 11.

are truthfulness, alertness, and courage, he was perhaps stating the case too generally, but he was making the point that the scientific mood does not necessarily imply expert knowledge of any particular science. It is often exhibited in a high degree by business men. Science is verifiable knowledge, systematized and generalized. As Benchara Branford puts it:

'Science is born anew in that wonderful world within each man when with deliberate will he succeeds in thinking about the principles of his work in the great world without in a clear, logical, and systematic way, and courageously puts his conclusions to the test of experiment; and the so-called sciences are the written records of such thinking, only more extensive, clear, systematic, and consistent, and more true to reality because they have been tested by countless experiments and experiences in the race.'[1]

Perhaps, however, Huxley went too far in this direction when he spoke of science as 'organized common-sense,' for common-sense is often very easy-going as regards both its facts and its inferences. A corrective suggestion of the difficulty of being scientific is given in Karl Pearson's statement:

'The scientific man has above all things to strive at self-elimination in his judgment, to provide an argument which is as true for each individual mind as for his own. The classification of facts, the recognition of their sequence and relative significance, is the function of science, and the habit of forming a judgment upon these facts, unbiassed by personal feeling, is characteristic of what may be termed the scientific frame of mind.'[2]

4. The methods of science.—The first step in the scientific study of a problem is to get at the facts, to collect data. The virtues here are precision and exhaustiveness of observation, patience to go on collecting, impartiality to whatever is forthcoming, watchfulness against the deceptions of the senses, and humility to learn from previous mistakes made by ourselves and others. Common faults are hastiness, vagueness, acceptance of second-hand evidence, mixing up the immediate data of experience with inferences, and, worst of all, picking and choosing the facts that suit a preconceived theory.

A second step is accurate registration of the data. Science begins with measurement. Lord Kelvin said that 'nearly all the grandest discoveries of science have been but the rewards of accurate measurement and patient, long-continued labour in the minute sifting of numerical results.' Here come in instrumental aids to our senses, impersonal methods of registration such as photography, confirmatory observations by others, and various devices for securing accuracy. There is a quality of character involved, and it is very interesting that Clerk Maxwell should have referred in one and the same sentence to 'those aspirations after accuracy in measurement, and justice in action, which we reckon among our noblest attributes as men.' There is an ethical factor in the development of what has been called 'the scientific conscience.'

A third step is bringing the data into the most useful form. They may be so numerous that some statistical or graphic device is required for dealing with them. A very simple illustration is plotting out a curve which shows at a glance the general outcome of a multitude of measurements. It may also be that the data are not fully useful until they have been further analyzed or reduced to simpler terms, to a common denominator with other sets of facts with which they have to be compared. There is a familiar opportunity for fallacy here, for in reducing facts to simpler terms something may be lost sight of, as when we reduce a physiological fact to a series of chemical and physical facts. But, while the reduction of phenomena to their common denominator cannot be accomplished by violence, it must always be attempted within the limits of the reasonable. Scientific description must be as *simple* as possible.

'To get away from appearances, to read the physical fact behind the sensuous effect, is one chief aim of science.'[1]

So far the methods have been observational and descriptive—representing what Lord Kelvin used to call the 'Natural History' stage of study. But the essential step is generalization and formulation, which brings the study to the stage of 'Natural Philosophy.' A whole series of occurrences is seen to have a uniformity, which is called their law. A formula is found that fits them all, or, more frequently, a new set of facts is shown to be in conformity with a previously established law. A set of occurrences is unified by the discovery of the causal relations that make them one; a puzzling phenomenon is shown to be a disguised form of a well-known case; a body of facts is fitted into its place in the growing system of ordered natural knowledge. In the discovery of a formula that fits, the investigator is often helped by a flash of insight; but often he has to try one key after another until he finds one that works the lock.

'Bounded and conditioned by co-operant Reason,' Tyndall[2] said, 'imagination becomes the mightiest instrument of the physical discoverer. Newton's passage from a falling apple to a falling moon was, at the outset, a leap of the imagination.'

In other cases one hypothesis after another, one trial after another, may have to be made before a solution is found. And, whether the formulation is reached imaginatively or laboriously, whether it comes as a brilliant deduction from some previously established law or as a patient induction from many particulars or from an intricate interlacing of induction and deduction, it has to be tested and re-tested, criticized and verified, before it is allowed to rise to the rank of a theory. For a discussion of the logic of science we may refer to an essay by T. Case. Taking Newton's *Principia* as a supreme illustration, he shows that the method is neither the deductive Aristotelian nor the inductive Baconian, but both; it is the interaction of induction and deduction in a mixed method.

'The full title, *Philosophiæ Naturalis Principia Mathematica*, implies a combination of induction and deduction. It is also a combination of analysis and synthesis: it proceeds from facts to causes as well as from causes to facts.'[3]

Views of science are apt to swing from an extreme of objectivism to an extreme of subjectivism. On the one hand, it is sometimes forgotten that man forges the tools or refines the concepts which he uses in discovering and formulating the order of nature, that a great deal of the experimenting is experimenting with ideas and symbols in his own head, and that he labours under the difficulty of being immersed in the system which he describes, of being a product of the evolution which he analyzes. We can no more escape from anthropomorphism than we can from our shadow. Especially in the less exact sciences, such as biology, the danger is great that provisional concepts—*e.g.*, 'the struggle for existence'—often borrowed from human affairs, may lead to fallacy. It must be admitted that, while there are few who now think of the laws of nature as governing the universe, as our forefathers phrased it, there are many who think of science as more objective and 'pure' than it actually is.

But the other extreme is that of those who over-emphasize the subjectivity of science. Impressed with the fact that man builds up his science by the sweat of his brow, inventing and trying concept after concept till he attains to an intellectual grasp of the facts, they exaggerate this into the doctrine that 'scientific truth is the creation of

[1] *Janus and Vesta*, p. 185. [2] *Grammar of Science*[2], p. 6.

[1] Arthur J. Balfour, *Theism and Humanism*, London, 1915, p. 79.
[2] *Fragments of Science*, p. 131.
[3] In *Lectures on the Method of Science*, p. 15.

the human mind and not of outer nature.'[1] But this misses what is characteristic of man's scientific formulation of the order of nature, that it must be verifiable by all normally constituted minds, that it must form a reliable basis for prediction, if not also for control. The order of nature is no human invention, though the formulations of it are often premature and inadequate. The concepts and symbols which man uses are not the happy thoughts of genius, but the outcome of other concepts which have survived a long process of trial and error, of testing and verifying. Between the two extremes of objectivism and subjectivism a reasonable position is tenable.

5. Scope of science.—Much confusion and unprofitable discussion might be avoided if the word 'science' were more frequently used with a qualifying adjective—chemical and physical science, exact science, mathematical science, natural science, biological science, mental and moral science, social science, abstract science, and so on. For investigators differ so widely in their outlook on the world that there can be no agreement as to the boundary lines of science. To many workers in chemical and physical science it seems doubtful whether biology and psychology are sciences at all, and to talk of political science seems to some the height of absurdity. What is just in this austere position is the recognition that in the domain of things, as treated by chemistry and physics, measurements can be made with extraordinary precision, analyses can be made with approximate completeness, formulations can be made with practical exhaustiveness, and, given a knowledge of the conditions, predictions can be made with remarkable success. So it is with the exact sciences—gravitational astronomy being the finest instance. When we pass to living creatures and their behaviour, to human societies and their inter-relations, we find that accurate measurement and precise registration are more difficult, analysis is very imperfect, formulation is only provisional, and prediction is in most cases hazardous. Moreover, test-experiments similar to those which are so valuable in the chemical and physical sciences are often difficult or impossible in biology, psychology, and sociology. The areas of greatest certainty in biology, *e.g.*, are in most cases those where chemical and physical methods are applied to the description of chemical and physical processes occurring in connexion with organisms. The discovery of methods, concepts, and formulæ for dealing with matter and energy is, as Bergson insists, far from having its counterpart in the realm of organisms or in the kingdom of man. The view taken in this article is the common-sense one, that science includes all knowledge, communicable and verifiable, which is reached by methodical observation and experiment and admits of concise, consistent, and connected formulation. In regard to one order of facts the application of scientific methods has gone far, in regard to another order of facts it has just begun, but the incipient science has no reason to be ashamed beside her full-grown sister. An exact science is like a solar system, a young science is like a nebula, but we see no reason why the student of dreams may not be as 'scientific' as the student of rocks, provided that he does not allow assertion to outstrip evidence and understands what he knows. The temptations not to be scientific increase, however, in proportion to the availability of precise methods, and it is interesting to notice that one of the kinds of scientific 'discovery' is finding a method that can be used in the investigation of a previously more or less refractory set of facts. Even the most advanced science is, in Spencer's phrase, 'partially unified knowledge'; the most living science is that in which the process of unification is most continuous.

Of importance is the distinction, on which emphasis has been laid by Clerk Maxwell[1] and others,[2] between dynamical and statistical knowledge in physics. It corresponds to the distinction between physiological and biometric knowledge in biology, to the distinction between the study of individuals and the study of averages in social affairs. The two are complementary, but in many cases our knowledge of natural occurrence is almost entirely statistical.

Another saving clause of importance relates to scientific symbols. The modern physicist visualizes all that his analysis can be applied to in terms of groupings and displacements of ultimate particles—the atomistic view of nature; and he is able with a good scientific conscience to assure us that there are such things as atoms.[3] The modern physicist can speak of the actuality of the atom, just as the geologist can speak of the actuality of the mountains. But this is a modern achievement, for until a few years ago the atom was only a symbol, a probably real working hypothesis. And, while the reality of the atom has been experimentally verified, there remain many useful working symbols that have not reached this stage. Thus the 'determinants' in Weismann's theory of heredity and the 'ceptors' in some theories of immunity are working symbols. Yet these symbols never live long if they are fanciful or arbitrary; they are retained only if experiment shows that they correspond in some measure to reality by forming a trustworthy basis for prediction and control. The history of science shows in an eloquent way how provisional symbols gradually attain to the dignity of realities.

6. Classification of the sciences.—It is useful to have in the mind some well-defined map of knowledge, which may suggest inter-relations, counteract partial views, and help towards the fulfilment of Plato's demand that the true lover of science shall be interested in the whole of his subject. But the particular form of the classification—whether after Comte or Spencer, Bain or Pearson, or Geddes—is probably of less importance than its personal quality. For the classification which we have in our mind must express part of our philosophy. Its boundary-lines will, for instance, express our conclusions as to the autonomy or dependence of biology and of psychology, our decisions on the difficult problems of vitalism and materialism, our views as to the distinctiveness of sociology or its subordination to biology, and so on.

Another general idea of importance is that a science is defined not by its subject-matter, as is often erroneously contended, but by the methods, fundamental concepts, and formulæ used in working with the material. Two or three sciences often deal with the same material; thus the chemist, the physicist, and the biologist may work with different ends in view, and in correlation if they are wise, at one and the same material, such as contracting muscle. A chemist, for purposes of his own, may devote his life to the study of the aromatic substances in flowers, and yet never ask a single botanical or biological question. It is a confusion of thought to map out territories as preserves of particular sciences, though every one recognizes broadly that there are three great orders of fact, viz. the domain of things, the realm

[1] J. B. Baillie, in *HJ* xv. [1917] 359.

[1] A paper in *The Life of James Clerk Maxwell*, by L. Campbell and W. Garnet, London, 1882, ch. xiv. p. 434.

[2] J. T. Merz, *History of European Thought in the Nineteenth Century*, ii. 599.

[3] See J. J. Thomson, *The Atomic Theory* (Romanes Lecture), Oxford, 1914.

of organisms, and the kingdom of man—the cosmosphere, the biosphere, and the sociosphere, as some have said.

It is useful to separate off, first of all, the abstract, formal, or methodological sciences, which deal with necessary relations between abstract concepts or between propositions, 'irrespective of the special nature of the concrete objects for which the ideas stand or to which the propositions refer.' They are deductive rather than inductive, ideal, not experiential, they are not directly based on the data of observation or experimentation. They deal with methods of inference, they supply intellectual instruments of investigation, they afford criteria for testing the consistency and completeness of scientific descriptions. They comprise especially mathematics (including statistics and graphics) and logic; and it appears to many that a place should be found here for a department of metaphysics, a criticism of categories, or a study of explanations as such.

The other sciences are concrete, descriptive, experiential, sciences of phenomena in contrast to sciences of formal relations. It is useful to recognize five fundamental and general sciences—chemistry, physics, biology, psychology, and sociology. Chemistry is mainly the science of the different kinds of matter, their transformations, affinities, and interactions; it is *par excellence* the science of molecules, atoms, and corpuscles. Physics is in the main the science of the transformations of energy. Biology is the science of the structure and activity, development and evolution, of organisms, including man as organism. Psychology is the science of the subjective aspect of behaviour, of man and animals. Sociology is the science of the structure and life, growth and evolution, of societary forms or of communities. There is something to be said for recognizing only three fundamental or general concrete sciences—chemistry and physics in one, biology and psychology in one, and sociology the third; but the fivefold scheme is the more convenient in the present state of science.

(*a*) Dependent on the five general sciences are the special or derivative sciences; thus botany, zoology, and protistology are special sciences within the rubric of the general science of biology. A great part of astronomy and most of meteorology must be ranked under physics, a great part of mineralogy under chemistry. These special sciences are to be distinguished from sub-sciences like morphology, physiology, and embryology, which are subdivisions of biology, or of botany and zoology when these are separated off. (*b*) Many of the derivative sciences deserve a compartment for themselves, being synoptic or combined sciences, using the methods and concepts of several sciences for their own particular purposes. Thus geology is a synoptic science, the focusing of several sciences on the study of the earth. Geography in the same way is a circle intersecting four or five other circles for a particular purpose. Anthropology is another good example of a combined or synoptic science. When it is practically convenient to segregate off a particular field of inquiry, a science may arise which has no radical characteristics of method. Thus the sublime science of astronomy is but a focusing of mechanics, thermodynamics, optics, and chemistry on the particular phenomena of suns, planets, and the like. (*c*) Lastly, it seems useful to keep the term 'applied science' for any department of a special science or for a combination of parts of several special sciences, directly oriented towards practical issues—*e.g.*, those of the arts and crafts. Thus agricultural science and medical science, the science of engineering, and the science of education are in great part applied sciences and are neither more nor less scientific on that account. As Huxley always insisted, 'applied science' is nothing but the application of 'pure science' to detailed practical problems.

7. Correlation of the sciences.—A counteractive to the impression of heterogeneity which a study of the classification of the sciences gives us is found in a recognition of their unity or, better, their correlation. They are parts of one endeavour to understand the order of nature and human life within it. They work into one another's hands, they react on one another, they are different modes of one rational inquiry. Several of them may deal with one and the same subject and yet not exhaust it. But it is begging many questions to insist that there is only one science of nature, which describes things and changes of things in terms of ideal motions, expressible in mathematical formulæ. This is false simplicity; it does not really work.

In seeking to understand and thus in some measure to control a difficult system, such as a living organism, the methods of several different sciences may be used in correlation. From the biological side the organism may be studied in its morphological, physiological, and embryological aspects; a deeper appreciation may be gained by studying its behaviour and the mental aspect of that. Many physical and chemical processes that contribute to the resultant which we call living may also be analyzed apart, and thus bio-physical and bio-chemical aspects receive their share of attention. Moreover, the creature has to be studied in its inter-relations with its appropriate environment, both animate and inanimate. It has also to be studied in its time relations; it is an heir of the ages, a historic being. The results of the various inquiries have to be pooled, or rather integrated. For the total scientific view must not be one that dissolves the organism; it must be one that makes its unity stand out conspicuously. The sciences are most scientific when they are most correlated, for they mutually correct one another, and our appreciation of the depth of reality is enhanced. New life came to astronomy and again to physiology when each established its correlation with chemistry; and biologists look with equal interest to such modern correlations as bio-physics on the one hand and psycho-biology on the other. One of the promising methods of scientific discovery is to effect new contacts or correlations.

If vital phenomena can be adequately described in chemical and physical (*i.e.* ideally mechanical) terms, a unification of biology and physico-chemistry has been effected. But the unification is not established by demonstrating that chemical and physical processes in an animal are in line with those in a thermodynamic engine. The applicability of chemical and physical methods to the study of vital processes is admitted by all; the utility of chemical and physical formulæ in the description of what goes on in living creatures is admitted by all; but the question is whether the chemical and physical concepts are adequate for anything like complete description of the behaviour of the animal, and whether we can deduce the behaviour of the animal from laws which apply equally to the animal and to the thermodynamic engine, to the flower and to the star.

We quote Arthur O. Lovejoy's statement of this point:

'Scientific unification, then, takes place in so far as diverse classes of phenomena come to be recognised as deducible from a single, relatively simple generalisation concerning the correlation of certain variables—provided that in each particular case the actual natures or values of the variables be known. And unification fails of attainment in so far as two or more kinds of phenomena appear (in the light of existing knowledge) as un-deducible from any single, already verified law, even were the actual values of the variables referred to by any such law precisely ascertained for the phenomena in question. When two or more comparatively specific laws are, in this latter sense, incapable of being deduced from any common, more general law—in other words, are not, thus far, unified—we may speak of those laws as being discontinuous with one another.'[1]

And, as the same author points out, another mode of discontinuity will emerge in this connexion if it should be shown that the motion of matter in a living cell does not correspond in its uniformities with the motion of inorganic matter. We have seen that what the animal does may be in conformity with the laws of thermodynamics and yet not be deducible from them; but there will be further discontinuity if it be shown that the motion of particles in the organism sometimes neither follows from nor conforms to the motion of particles in an inorganic system like, say, a whirlpool.

Treating of the work of science, A. E. Dolbear writes:

'By explanation is meant the presentation of the mechanical antecedents for a phenomenon in so complete a way that no supplementary or unknown factors are necessary.'[2]

Now, what many biologists are impressed with, *e.g.*, in regard to the higher reaches of animal behaviour, is the present *necessity* of invoking other than mechanical factors, such as memory and a power of learning.

Thus it may be said that the ideal of one science of nature—the ideal of Descartes, of Hobbes, of Leibniz—has given place to an ideal of correlation rather than of unity. There has, indeed, been much profitable breaking down of artificial partitions, many a useful discovery of a common denominator bringing apparently disconnected facts into comparable relationship, but the possibility of making physiology a branch of physics, psychology a branch of physiology, and so on, has not been realized. Moreover, the measure of abstractness which marks each science makes it impossible that a unified scientific view of the world can be attained by merely pooling the results of each kind of exploration. The chemical, the physical, the biological, and the psychological formulations of an organism, *e.g.*, cannot be left as accretions to an aggregate of knowledge; they must be correlated; and this is what some would call 'the philosophy of the organism.'

8. Limitations of science.—Science is knowledge gained by certain methods; to apply these methods usually demands a partial or abstract consideration of the subject-matter; 'Divide et impera' is the scientific rule. This is a self-imposed limitation of science—that its descriptions and formulæ refer to abstracted aspects of things. We can no more in actuality separate a living organism from its environment than we can remove a whirlpool from the river, yet for scientific purposes the abstraction has to be made; and up to a certain point—*e.g.*, in analytical anatomy—it is made profitably. The same is true in more exact spheres: the concept of mass is essential in dynamics; we treat of the mass of a body as if we had the body under the influence of gravitation only. But in actual observations and experiments we can never really secure the entire absence of electrical, magnetic, and other forces. To put it in another way, science works with 'ideal systems,' and this is one of its limitations. Thus in a general way it may be said that science aims at practically convenient representations of certain aspects of facts, deliberately abstracted from other aspects.

The terms of scientific formulation are in diverse degrees far from being self-explanatory. In biology it is necessary to speak of 'organism,' 'protoplasm,' 'heredity,' and so on, but these terms obviously require further analysis or definition—which the biologist is indeed trying to work out. In more exact sciences there are secret-hiding terms like 'gravitation' and 'chemical affinity.' It is true that the terms of scientific description are continually undergoing a process of simplification, but how limited is our comprehension of the fundamental terms like 'matter,' 'energy,' 'inertia,' 'life,' 'consciousness'! Thus a good deal of what is called scientific 'explanation' consists in reducing unusual unintelligibility to order rather than to understanding.

Another limitation concerns origins. The scientific treatment of an order of facts begins, not at the beginning—that is impossible—but from something 'given,' which is not explained. The biologist begins with the first organisms, or with the first visible organisms, or with the first visible organisms upon the earth. But what was their origin? The chemist begins with the chemical elements, but what is meant by being an element and what was the origin of the fourscore of them? Matter has seemed to many easy-going minds a firm basis to start from, but what is matter, and what has been its history? Must there not have been a differentiation of various forms of matter, and may there not have been a pre-material state of things? This necessary limitation of science has been well stated by Arthur Shipley:

'No body of scientific doctrine succeeds in describing in terms of laws of succession more than some limited set of stages of a natural process: the whole process—if, indeed, it can be regarded as a whole—must for ever be beyond the reach of scientific grasp. The earliest stages to which Science has succeeded in tracing back any part of a sequence of phenomena itself constitutes a new problem for Science and that without end. There is always an earlier stage and to an earliest we can never attain. The questions of origins concern the theologian, the metaphysician, perhaps the poet.'[1]

Another limitation has to do with causal sequences. In ordinary scientific discourse, as Bergson points out, three different meanings of the term 'cause' are common. A cause may act by impelling (one billiard ball striking another), or by releasing (a spark exploding the gunpowder), or by unwinding (the relaxing of the spring turning the cylinder of a gramophone and having the melody as effect).

Now 'only in the first case, really, does cause *explain* effect; in the others the effect is more or less given in advance, and the antecedent invoked is—in different degrees, of course—its occasion rather than its cause.'[2]

The only cases where a scientific account is complete are cases of mechanics, where the resultant is just a new form of the components, where we can say with a clear intellectual conscience, 'Causa aequat effectum.' In the great majority of cases all that science can say is, 'If this, then that'; and it is a very useful thing to be able to say. One particular totality of condition changes into another, but, when the chains of sequence are intricate, it is no longer plain that the resultant must be as it is and not otherwise. Science shows that a certain collocation of antecedents and no other will result in a certain collocation of consequents and no other; but it is only in the case of mechanical sequences that we fully know how it is that the consequents emerge from the often very different antecedents.

We have seen, then, that limitations are involved in the inevitable abstractness of science, in the residual or radical mysteriousness of its fundamental concepts, in what has to be taken as 'given,' and in the difficulty of giving complete causal explanations except in the case of purely mechanical sequences. But there are limitations of other kinds. Thus a reasonable humility of mind may be fostered by remembering how limited is our range of exact data. An admission of this may be cited

[1] 'The Unity of Science,' *Univ. Missouri Bulletin*, i. [1912] 17.
[2] *The Machinery of the Universe*[2], London, 1911, p. 12.

[1] Schuster and Shipley, *Britain's Heritage of Science*, p. 276.
[2] *Creative Evolution*, Eng. tr., p. 77 f.

from an address delivered about the end of the 19th cent. by a distinguished physicist, Henry A. Rowland:

'It is a curious fact that, having minds tending to the infinite, with imaginations unlimited by time and space, the limits of our exact knowledge are very small indeed. In time we are limited by a few hundred or possibly thousand years; indeed the limit in our science is far less than the smaller of these periods. In space we have exact knowledge limited to portions of our earth's surface and a mile or so below the surface, together with what little we can learn from looking through powerful telescopes into the space beyond. In temperature our knowledge extends from near the absolute zero to that of the sun, but exact knowledge is far more limited. In pressures we go from the Crookes vacuum still containing myriads of flying atoms to pressures limited by the strength of steel, but still very minute compared with the pressures at the centre of the earth and sun, where the hardest steel would flow like the most limpid water. In velocities we are limited to a few miles per second. In forces to possibly 100 tons to the square inch. In mechanical rotations to a few hundred times a second.'

Finally, there is a sense in which science, if not asymptotic, is bound to remain approximate. A scientific law formulates an observed routine in the order of nature, and, if it has been established with due care, there is no going back on it unless the properties of the materials observed should change. It may be, however, that the law was only an approximate 'fit' and left residual phenomena, a recognition of which subsequently led to a re-statement of the law. So Kepler improves on Copernicus and Newton on Kepler. Even when the formulation fitted well and may have come to be regarded as of universal application, the extension or the intensification of research may show that it does not apply beyond certain limits. Thus the law of gravitation, which must be very near to perfect accuracy when applied to planetary distances, may not hold either for very minute molecular distances or for immense stellar distances. Even generalizations which work well and must bear a close correspondence to reality, since they afford a basis for effective prophecy, may require some modification, in their setting at least, in the light of some new fact or idea of great magnitude. Thus Frederick Soddy writes:

'It sounds incredible, but nevertheless it is true, that science up to the close of the nineteenth century had no suspicion even of the existence of the original sources of natural energy. . . . The vista which has been opened up by these new discoveries [of the radioactive properties of some substances] admittedly is without parallel in the whole history of science.'[2]

And Max Planck writes of the principle of the relativity of time:

'With the revolution which it brings about in our conception of the physical universe no other is comparable, in range and profundity, except that due to the introduction of the Copernican astronomy.'[3]

Finally, it may be useful to remember that, according to current and probably well-warranted scientific belief, there was once a time when what happened upon the earth might have been formulated in its immediacy with apparent exhaustiveness in terms of the dynamics of particles. But ages passed and living creatures emerged; new formulæ, as it seems to us, became necessary. Ages passed and intelligent creatures commanded their course; again a new aspect of reality required a new science. Ages passed and man emerged—with self-consciousness, language, reasoning capacity, and a social heritage. Science must always be asymptotic, for its subject-matter is evolving.

9. Science and feeling.—There is a natural antithesis between the scientific and the emotional mood; when either is in the saddle, it must keep the other at a spear's length. Science is essentially unemotional and impersonal, and its analytic, atomizing or anatomizing, methods are apt to be, in their matter-of-fact-ness, destructive of artistic unities and poetical interpretations. But, when science makes minor mysteries disappear, greater mysteries stand confessed. Science never destroys wonder, but only shifts it, higher and deeper. For one object of delight whose emotional value science has inevitably lessened—as Newton spoiled the rainbow for Keats—science gives back double. To the grand primary impressions of the world-powers, of the immensities, of the pervading order, and of the universal flux, with which the man of feeling has been nurtured from of old, modern science has added thrilling impressions of manifoldness, intricacy, inter-relatedness, and evolution. Science has supplied art and poetry with far more raw materials than have yet been utilized. Science is ever widening and clarifying the emotional window. There are great vistas to which science alone can lead, and they make for elevation of mind. In this and in other ways science may be epigrammatically called 'one of the humanities.'[1]

10. Science and philosophy.—A scientific system is the formulation or description of methodically observed sequences and inter-relations within groups of occurrences that admit of being measured or precisely registered. A philosophical system is the outcome of interpretative reflexion on the whole data of our experience. Science is characteristically impersonal, or, in any case, it must admit of being readily de-personalized by competent minds; but a man's philosophy must always have a personal note. To the influence of Kant, of the correlated 'philosophies of nature,' and of Hegel may be traced the fact that science and philosophy drew apart in the 19th cent., and more markedly in Germany than in France or England. Moreover, the rise of biology was giving a new completeness to science, and a fresh vigour possessed scientific inquiry as a whole. It naturally followed that scientific investigators began to resent the way in which philosophy called the tune that it wished science to play. More technically, science became less receptive to regulative concepts insinuated by philosophy into the scientific workshop. A diagrammatic example was the philosophical declaration that there could not be more than seven planets. For a time, indeed, it was in the interests of progress that science should be on the defensive against philosophy; but now there is more need for it to be afraid of thinking that it can dispense with its partner. It is well and good to ride the marches; 'I ask not proud Philosophy to tell me what thou art'; I shall scrutinize for myself. But there is a tendency on the part of science to forget its limitations, to be unaware of its assumptions, and to be easy-going in the criticism of its own categories. The truth is that science and philosophy are complementary. From the analytic descriptions which science gives we cannot but go on to the more synthetic endeavour of forming some coherent picture of the whole scheme of things and thoughts. Beyond the attainment of knowledge there is the unending search after truth.

A modern philosophy worthy of the name must take account of all the far-reaching results of scientific inquiry, of all the general conclusions of science in regard to the nature and genesis of the inorganic, the organic, and the human. A modern philosophy is inadequate which has not been influenced by the principle of the conservation of energy, by the doctrine of organic evolution, by the outstanding facts of heredity, and so on. On the other hand, philosophy justly reserves the right of critically scrutinizing the scientific conclusions which it uses in building up its interpretative system. Thus the principle of the conservation of energy, formulated in reference to the transfor-

1 'The Highest Aim of the Physicist,' in *Amer. Journ. Sci.* viii. [1899] 408.
2 *Harper's Magazine*, December 1909, p. 53.
3 *Acht Vorlesungen über theoretische Physik*, Leipzig, 1910, p. 119; quoted by Lovejoy, p. 7.

1 See Baillie, in *HJ* xv. 353.

mations of physical energies, must not be allowed to foreclose discussion of the question whether mind and body (if these be recognized as admissible scientific or philosophical terms) can interact in a way that really counts. And the answer given to that question, or to some similar question more satisfactorily phrased, affects the general philosophical or metaphysical theory that one has of the world as a whole. Science may help philosophy by bringing into prominence the results that seem to be of the most radical significance, and also by inquiring whether the facts of the case, from the scientific outlook, are congruent with the interpretations which philosophy puts upon them. On the other hand, philosophy may help science by criticizing its categories and its logic. For philosophical discipline develops a critical faculty which is different from that cultivated by ordinary scientific methods though we lessen none of the emphasis with which we have indicated that the acquirement of the 'scientific conscience,' most practicable in the discipline of the natural sciences, is of fundamental value in the solution of human problems. Especially in the spheres where it remains less exact science requires the rigorous application of a higher logic, a methodology, a critique of explanations, which some have called metaphysics. Many of the greatest discoverers of new knowledge seem to have had singularly little philosophical sense.

A. E. Taylor gives a luminous statement of the relation between science and philosophy:

'The work of the Philosophy of Nature and of Mind only begins where that of the experimental sciences leaves off. Its data are not particular facts, as directly amassed by experiment and observation, but the hypotheses used by experimental science for the co-ordination and description of those facts. And it examines these hypotheses, not with the object of modifying their structure so as to include new facts, or to include the old facts in a simpler form, but purely for the purpose of estimating their value as an account of ultimately real existence. Whether the hypotheses are adequate as implements for the calculation of natural processes is a question which Philosophy, when it understands its place, leaves entirely to the special sciences; whether they can claim to be more than useful formulæ for calculation, *i.e.* whether they give us knowledge of ultimate Reality, is a problem which can only be dealt with by the science which systematically analyses the meaning of reality, *i.e.* by Metaphysics. We may perhaps follow the usage of some recent writers in marking this difference of object by a difference in terminology and say that the goal of experimental science is the description of facts, the goal of Metaphysics their interpretation. The difference of aim is, however, not ultimate. Description of facts, when once we cease to be content with such description as will subserve the purpose of calculation and call for the description of the fact as it really is, of itself becomes metaphysical interpretation.'[1]

One of the deep facts of experience, persistently impressive to the thoughtful, is that science is possible at all—and on so grand a scale; that nature is so amenable to scientific formulation. This raises questions for philosophical consideration, but it must also be looked at through scientific spectacles. Experiential science does not attempt to explain consciousness, but it is not quite accurate to say that science simply accepts in a naive sort of way the wonderful fact of its own existence. To be asked 'How is this marvellous fabric of science to be explained in terms of evolutionary formulæ?' is like being asked to account for some very complex and relatively perfect structure like the human eye. All such questions must be treated historically: science and the eye must be regarded as the results of long processes of evolution, vastly older than man. Science has its roots in prehuman capacities of 'learning,' of intelligently profiting by experience. It has grown from very elementary inferences relating to man's everyday practical problems. The acquisition of the early lore and the expansion of it had assuredly survival value; and inborn curiosity has been from first to last a stimulus to inquiry. Registration of gains in language and records, in instruments and permanent products, made cumulative advance secure. We are only hinting at an ætiology of science. But, when we go back to the possibility of it all, the metaphysical problem remains: the strands of naturally-determined sequence having woven themselves into an intelligible pattern, which human reason slowly and laboriously discovers, is it conceivable that they might have tied themselves into a knot baffling all disentanglement? In any case it is possible to suppose that our planet might have remained permanently beclouded like Jupiter, and then, as Poincaré points out, we should never have seen the stars and might never have advanced far in deciphering the order of nature. Various attempts, such as Lachelier's (1871), have been made to explain this 'correspondence' between the intrinsic order of nature and man's capacity for deciphering it, but it seems doubtful if we get beyond some device which dissolves rather than solves the problem. It looks like a frontier-problem for man's intellect. We may find ultra-scientific reasons for believing that nature is the embodiment of a divine thought and purpose, one evolutionary expression of which is man's increasing recognition of the order of nature. The Logos, or Mind, or Reason, thus postulated at the beginning, reappears in the form of science later on.

[1] *Elements of Metaphysics*[2], p. 192.

11. Science and religion.—Science is empirical in method and aim: it seeks to discover the laws of concrete being and becoming and to formulate these in the simplest possible terms. These terms are the immediate data of experience or verifiably derived therefrom. The scientific 'universe of discourse' does not include transcendental concepts; its aim does not include attempting to give ultimate explanations.

Religion, on the other hand, implies a recognition—practical, emotional, and intellectual—of a higher order of reality than is reached in sense-experience. It means the recognition of an unseen universe, which throws light on the riddles of the observed world. In the scientific light of common day are seen the hosts of the Assyrians encompassing the city; the opened religious eye sees the mountains crowded with the chariots of God. Unless religion is altogether illusory, the metaphor of this illustration expresses a cleavage. The religious language is not scientific language, but with different concepts and necessarily more metaphorical; its aim is not the scientific aim, for it seeks after interpretation, not description. In short, science and religion are incommensurables. As a diagrammatic illustration of misunderstanding, we may refer to the title of a book, *God or Natural Selection*—so obviously a false antithesis. But to call scientific formulation 'incommensurable' with religious interpretation is not to concede to the old-fashioned impossible solution of having idea-tight compartments in our intellectual voyages. Just as a novel scientific generalization is not incorporated into our scientific system unless it is consistent with previously established conclusions or unless the latter are susceptible of re-adjustment so as to admit the new idea harmoniously, so at a greater height, where philosophical discipline is invaluable, a religious idea, such as that of a Divine Creator, must be congruent with the rest of our world-picture. Here, both learned and laity have to face the moral obligation of clear thinking—which to be valid must be in conditions of organismal freedom.

Men are led to religion along many pathways—from the perplexing contradictions of the moral life, from an appreciation of the facts of history, and from what is experienced by the three main types of mankind: at the limits of practical endeavour, of emotional expression, or of intellectual inquiry. When we think of the last-named pathways to religion — from baulked struggle, over-strained emotion, and baffled search after clear understanding—it is not difficult to see why the rapid development of science should have worked, for a time of transition at least, against religion. For science has given man an astonishingly increased mastery over nature; science with its numerous analytic triumphs has tended to diminish, in the shallow-minded, the sense of wonder, and science has dispelled much of the darkness which used to oppress man's mind. Moreover, the scientific mood has been widely diffused; it has a growing fascination of its own; it easily comes to preoccupy the mind and thus tends to crowd out the æsthetic, the poetic, the religious moods. The practically important conviction is that religious interpretation and scientific analysis are equally natural and necessary expressions of the developing human spirit.

12. Science and life.—In what has been said of the aim of science the primary purpose of understanding and the accessory purpose of controlling have been recognized. As Bacon said of Salomon's House in the *New Atlantis*:

'The end of our foundation is the knowledge of causes and the secret motions of things; and the enlarging of the bounds of human empire, to the effecting of all things possible.'

It is unwise to separate the two aims too strictly, for all the sciences, including mathematics, sprang from concrete experience of practical problems, and many theoretical advances have contributed largely to the relief of man's estate. As Branford has well said:

'Science ultimately sprang, and is continually springing, from the desires and efforts of men to increase their skill in their occupations by understanding the eternal principles that underlie all dealings of man with Nature and of man with his fellow-men. . . . And if science ultimately has sprung from, and is continually springing anew from, occupations, science has repaid the debt both by rendering those who follow her teaching more skilled in their occupations and by actually giving rise by her discoveries to absolutely new types of occupations. One of the great conditions of human progress is this unceasing reciprocal relationship between occupation and science, each constantly producing and being produced by the other.'[1]

The practical utility of the sciences is so great that there is danger in exaggerating utilitarian criteria. It is profitable to remember the distinction drawn by Bacon long ago between those results of science which are light-giving (*lucifera*) and those which are of direct practical utility (*fructifera*), regarding which he said so admirably:

'Just as the vision of light itself is something more excellent and beautiful than its manifold use, so without doubt the contemplation of things as they are, without superstition or imposture, without error or confusion, is in itself a nobler thing than a whole harvest of inventions.'[2]

A second point is the historical fact that the kind of investigation whose results Bacon called *lucifera* is the surest, and sometimes even the shortest, road to that other kind of result which he called *fructifera*. The most 'theoretical' researches have often had practical results of extraordinary magnitude. The quiet thinkers in the scientific cloisters are, like the poets, the makers and shakers of the world. This is admirably discussed in R. A. Gregory's *Discovery*, where it is shown, *e.g.*, that wireless telegraphy, the telephone, aeroplanes, radium, antiseptics, antitoxins, spectrum analysis, and X-rays were all discovered in the course of purely scientific and very theoretical investigation.

The old discouragement expressed in the saying that increase of knowledge is increase of sorrow has been replaced by the hope of science as contributory to human welfare. This is pithily expressed in Herbert Spencer's well-known sentence: 'Science is for Life, not Life for Science.' While we may not be able to say of any specialized line of scientific inquiry that it is not of value to human life, there are undoubtedly some that are more promising and urgent than others. The pursuit of knowledge sometimes stands in need of being socialized, *i.e.* of being oriented in relation to the needs of the State. As Bacon said in a famous passage in *The Advancement of Learning*:[1]

'This is that which will indeed dignify and exalt knowledge if contemplation and action may be more nearly and straitly conjoined and united together than they have been.' And the passage preceding this ends by declaring that what is sought in knowledge should be 'a rich storehouse for the glory of the Creator and the relief of man's estate.'

The duty of science to provide knowledge 'for the relief of man's estate' has its counterpart in the duty of the State to utilize the resources of science. That this duty is only half realized is certain.

'Whether we think of the more effective and less wasteful exploitation of the Earth, or of the gathering in of the harvest of the sea, or of making occupations more wholesome, or of beautifying human surroundings, or of exterminating infectious diseases, or of improving the physique of the race—we are filled with amazement at the abundance of expert knowledge of priceless value which is *not* being utilised.'[2]

Just as many ills that the flesh is heir to are met no longer with fatalism and folded hands, but by confident therapeutics and preventive medicine, so over a wide range there is a promiseful application of all kinds of science for the amelioration of the conditions of human life. Man is only beginning to enter into his kingdom; much suffering, depression, and poverty is remediable; the potency of the influences of improved nurture, in the widest sense, has not as yet been adequately appreciated. The idea of a scientific control of human life is gripping men's minds with fresh force, and, instead of meeting suffering and disharmony by apologetic justifications of the ways of God to men or by submitting to them as means of discipline, a nobler piety is insisting on their reduction and, it may be, eventual disappearance. It is man's part to build up, as he is doing, a scientific systematization of knowledge which will increasingly form the basis of a control of life. The implications of this ideal have been well set forth by L. T. Hobhouse in his *Mind in Evolution*[2] (London, 1915), *Development and Purpose* (do. 1913), *Morals in Evolution* (do. 1906). He speaks of the mundane goal of the evolutionary movement as being the mastery by the human mind of the conditions, internal as well as external, of its life and growth.[3]

Thus, without any depreciation of the other factors that make towards a good life, one may emphasize the ethical value of science. For science judiciously applied removes gratuitous hindrances to the good life and opens portals. Science well taught and well learned means an introduction to the ever-expanding interest and wonder of the world. In many cases, as William Archer[4] has said, 'vice is a refuge from boredom, from that sense of emptiness and tedium that overtakes the idle brain, or the brain benumbed by soulless, uninteresting labour. But boredom, in this wonderful world, can only result from ignorance, or from—what is much the same thing—irrelevant, inert, burdensome knowledge.' On broader grounds still, he goes on to argue that in the building up of character a part is normally played by apprehension of the world as it is and as it has come to be.

1 *Journ. of Education*, June 1904; see *Janus and Vesta*, p. 186.
2 *Novum Organum*, cxxix.

1 Bk. i. 2 Thomson, *Introd. to Science*, p. 249.
3 *Morals in Evolution*, ii. 280.
4 *Knowledge and Character*, Moral Education League, London, 1916, p. 5.

LITERATURE.—A. Aliotta, *The Idealistic Reaction against Science*, Eng. tr., London, 1914; J. M. Baldwin, *Darwin and the Humanities*[2], do. 1910; H. Bergson, *Creative Evolution*, Eng. tr., do. 1911; E. Boutroux, *Science and Religion in Contemporary Philosophy*, Eng. tr., do. 1909; B. Branford, *Janus and Vesta*, do. 1916; L. Busse, *Geist und Körper, Seele und Leib*, Leipzig, 1903; T. Case, 'Scientific Method as a Mental Operation,' in *Lectures on the Method of Science*, ed. T. B. Strong, Oxford, 1906; W. K. Clifford, *The Commonsense of the Exact Sciences*[4], London, 1904, *Lectures and Essays*, 2 vols., do. 1879; F. Enriques, *Problems of Science*, Eng. tr., Chicago and London, 1914; R. Flint, *Philosophy as Scientia Scientiarum, and a History of the Classification of the Sciences*, Edinburgh, 1904; Michael Foster, President's Address, *Report of the 69th Meeting of the Brit. Association, 1899*, London, 1900, p. 2 ff.; R. A. Gregory, *Discovery: or, The Spirit and Service of Science*, London, 1916; J. S. Haldane, *Mechanism, Life, and Personality*, do. 1913; L. J. Henderson, *The Order of Nature*, Cambridge, U.S.A., and London, 1917; A. Hill, *Introduction to Science*, London, 1899; L. T. Hobhouse, *Development and Purpose: an Essay towards a Philosophy of Evolution*, do. 1913; T. H. Huxley, *Collected Essays*, 9 vols., do. 1893–94, *e.g.*, 'Method and Results,' 'Science and Education'; W. Stanley Jevons, *The Principles of Science: a Treatise on Logic and Scientific Method*[3], do. 1879; James Johnstone, *The Philosophy of Biology*, Cambridge, 1914; J. Lachelier, *Du Fondement de l'induction*, Paris, 1871; E. Ray Lankester, *The Kingdom of Man*, London, 1907, *The Advancement of Science*, do. 1890; A. O. Lovejoy, 'The Unity of Science,' *Univ. Missouri Bulletin*, i. [1912] 1–34; E. Mach, *The Science of Mechanics*[2], Eng. tr., Chicago, 1902, *Contributions to Analysis of the Sensations*, Eng. tr., do. 1897; J. T. Merz, *A Hist. of European Thought in the Nineteenth Century*, 4 vols., Edinburgh, 1896–1914, *Religion and Science; a Philosophical Essay*, do. 1916; St. George Mivart, *The Groundwork of Science, a Study of Epistemology*, London, 1898; C. Lloyd Morgan, *The Interpretation of Nature*, Bristol, 1905, *Instinct and Experience*, London, 1912; P. Natorp, *Die logischen Grundlagen der exakten Wissenschaften*, Leipzig, 1910; W. Ostwald, *Vorlesungen über Naturphilosophie*[3], do. 1906; R. Otto, *Naturalism and Religion*, Eng. tr., London, 1907; Karl Pearson, *The Grammar of Science*[3], do. 1911; E. Picard, 'La Science moderne et son état actuel,' in *De la Méthode dans les sciences*, Paris, 1909; H. Poincaré, *Foundations of Science* (containing his *Science and Hypothesis, The Value of Science, Science and Method*), Eng. tr., New York, 1913; J. J. Poynting, Presidential Address to Mathematical and Physical Science Section, *Report of the Brit. Association, 1899*, London, 1900, p. 615 ff.; A. S. Pringle-Pattison, *The Idea of God in the Light of Recent Philosophy* (Gifford Lectures), Oxford, 1917; Bertrand Russell, *Mysticism and Logic*, London, 1918; G. Sandeman, *Problems of Biology*, do. 1896; A. Schuster and A. E. Shipley, *Britain's Heritage of Science*, do. 1917; W. T. Sedgwick and H. W. Tyler, *A Short History of Science*, New York, 1917; C. von Sigwart, *Logic*[2], Eng. tr., 2 vols., London, 1895; J. Y. Simpson, *The Spiritual Interpretation of Nature*, do. 1912; Herbert Spencer, *First Principles*[6], London, 1900; J. B. Stallo, *The Concepts and Theories of Modern Physics*, do. 1882; Carl Snyder, *New Conceptions in Science*[2], New York and London, 1903; *Lectures on the Method of Science*, ed. T. B. Strong, Oxford, 1906; A. E. Taylor, *Elements of Metaphysics*, London, 1903, [2]1909 (with valuable discussion of science); D'Arcy W. Thompson, 'Magnalia Naturæ,' Presidential Address to Zoology Section, *Report of the Brit. Association, 1911*, London, 1912, p. 395 ff., *On Growth and Form*, Cambridge, 1917; J. Arthur Thomson, *Introduction to Science*, London, 1912, *The Bible of Nature*, Edinburgh, 1908; John Tyndall, *Fragments of Science*, London, 1871 (including essay 'On the scientific Use of the Imagination'); J. von Uexküll, *Bausteine zu einer biologischen Weltanschauung*, Munich, 1913; James Ward, *Naturalism and Agnosticism*, 2 vols., London, 1899, *The Realm of Ends*, Cambridge, 1911; A. D. White, *A Hist. of the Warfare of Science with Theology*[15], London, 1905.

J. ARTHUR THOMSON.

SCOTISM.—See SCHOLASTICISM.

SCOTTISH PHILOSOPHY.—The specific doctrines of the Scottish school of philosophy come to us from the second half of the 18th cent. and are immediately associated with Aberdeen. Before that date, indeed, there were Scots philosophers who made their mark in various lands and in diverse circumstances of life; but this fact does not bring them within the range of the school that we are now considering. The term 'Scottish philosophy' is properly restricted to a certain type of Scottish thinking and must not be so extended as to include any and every philosopher (Hume, *e.g.*, or Hutcheson, or Thomas Brown) who happened to be by birth or by residence a Scotsman. It is the name for the philosophy of 'common sense,' characterized by its devotion to psychology, its adherence to the inductive method in philosophical research, and its determination to find in human nature itself the guarantee for truth. It owed its great impulse, in the 18th cent., to Thomas Reid, in Aberdeen, and was supported and expounded by several of his colleagues in the Aberdeen Philosophical Society—mainly by George Campbell, James Beattie, and Alexander Gerard. It was called forth by opposition to the principles and reasoning of David Hume; and, while having as its chief aim the due appreciation of the moral and religious tendencies of man, it paid full regard to the theoretical or speculative side of human nature. It was opposed to Hume, but, at cardinal points, to Locke and to Berkeley also, and to what Reid called 'the ideal system,' in all its forms. It was a spiritualistic philosophy, cautious and measured, designed to meet scepticism and to remove doubt by an appeal to what it conceived to be most fundamental in man's constitution.

Its appeal was to 'first principles,' intuitively apprehended. Experience was by no means ignored, but it was not looked upon as sufficient in itself for everything. While explaining much in human life, it needed itself to be explained: it could not account for principles that it itself presupposed, and whose authority was drawn from another source. That is what is meant by 'common sense.' The name has often been criticized, as though the use of it as a leading term ruled the Scottish philosophy out of court as a philosophy. It covered (so the critic has averred) a mere otiose acceptance of the unsifted opinions and beliefs of the plain man. But that is an entire misconception and could hardly have been entertained if due attention had been paid to the history of philosophy. Aristotle had employed the term 'common sense' as the designation of the synthetic power of the human mind in the unifying of experiences that come to us through the separate senses (sight, hearing, touch, etc.), in memory, and in 'the common sensibles' (rest, motion, etc.); and he had maintained the intellect (νοῦς) to be the *fons et origo* of first principles, regarding it as a native psychical activity, without which knowledge could not be, and through which alone experience becomes intelligible. So the Scottish philosophers held with regard to their doctrine of 'common sense.' The term indicates the native power and activity of the mind, which is necessary if experience is to be possible. In like manner, the Stoics, in their theory of knowledge, had laid stress on 'common consent' (*consensus gentium*) as the test of primary conceptions. They did not by this mean that the plain man, *qua* plain man, is to be the arbiter of truth; but, holding, as they did, that men everywhere share in reason and that reason is ultimately stored in the primal source of all things and is drawn by man therefrom, they maintained that there must be truths in which men in general share, and which, consequently, by the very fact that they are '*common* notions' (κοιναὶ ἔννοιαι), have an authority higher than experience alone could give—an authority that is all their own. It was sympathy with these thinkers (Peripatetic and Stoic) or with thinking on these lines that led the Scottish school to look for support to 'common consent' and to adopt the name of 'common sense' as designative of their philosophy.

I. *IN THE 18TH CENTURY.*—**1. Thomas Reid.**—The first and, in certain respects, the greatest of the Scottish philosophers was Thomas Reid.

He was the second son of the minister of Strachan, Kincardineshire, and was born there on 26th April 1710. On his mother's side, he was a member of the notable Deeside family of Gregory (akin to Rob Roy), of whom no fewer than fourteen became professors in Great Britain. He was educated at the parish school of Strachan in earlier days and, later, at the Grammar School of Aberdeen. He entered Marischal College and University in 1722 and graduated M.A. in 1726. Thereafter he studied Divinity, with a view to entering the ministry of the

Church of Scotland, and was licensed as a preacher of the gospel by the Presbytery of Kincardine O'Neil in 1731. From 1733 to 1736 he occupied the position of librarian of Marischal College. In 1737 he was presented by the Senatus of King's College and University to the parish of New Machar, adjoining Aberdeen, where he remained as minister till 1751. During his ministry he carried on and developed his philosophical and intellectual studies. He was expert in mathematics: his first publication was his 'Essay on Quantity,' contributed to *The Philosophical Transactions of the Royal Society of London* in 1748. But he exercised his thoughts also with the philosophies of Locke, Berkeley, and Hume, and laid the foundation of those literary writings which were ere long to bring him into fame. In 1751 the Senatus of King's College elected him regent or professor in succession to Alexander Rait. For thirteen years he continued at his post in Aberdeen, teaching Moral Philosophy and Logic but also Natural Philosophy and Mathematics (for a 'regent' in those days carried his pupil through the whole of the curriculum). In 1764, with an established philosophical reputation, he was appointed professor of Moral Philosophy in Glasgow University in succession to Adam Smith, who had resigned the chair; and he continued in this position till his death, although he retired from active duty in 1787. The order of publication of his writings was: *An Inquiry into the Human Mind, on the Principles of Common Sense* (Edinburgh, 1764), *Essays on the Intellectual Powers of Man* (do. 1785), and *Essays on the Active Powers of Man* (do. 1788). With the last of these works his literary career closed, although he did not yet cease to prosecute his studies with vigour. In 1796 he went to Edinburgh on a visit to his attached relative Dr. Gregory, returning to Glasgow in his usual health and spirits. In the end of September of that year, however, he was seized with illness, and, after several strokes of paralysis, he died on 7th October, in the eighty-seventh year of his age.

It was during his professorship in Aberdeen that, in co-operation with a few other congenial souls, he founded the Aberdeen Philosophical Society ('The Wise Club,' as the vulgar dubbed it), in which the Scottish philosophy took definite form, and which, therefore, demands here our explicit recognition. The society lasted somewhere over fifteen years, holding its first meeting in the Red Lion Inn, Old Aberdeen, on 12th January 1758, and finally disappearing in (or soon after) 1773, the last of the extant minutes of the society being dated 9th March 1773. Spread over these years, the total number of members was only fifteen (excluding the single honorary member in the person of James Trail, bishop of Down and Connor, elected in 1768). The object of the society, as at first constituted, is declared in rule 17 (in Reid's own handwriting and probably formulated by him):

'The Subject of the Discourses and Questions, shall be Philosophical, all Grammatical, Historical, and Philolological [*sic*] Discussions being conceived to be forreign to the Design of the Society. And Philosophical Matters are understood to comprehend, Every Principle of Science which may be deduced by Just and Lawfull Induction from the Phænomena either of the human Mind or of the Material World; All Observations and Experiments that may furnish Materials for such Induction; The Examination of False Schemes of Philosophy and false Methods of Philosophizing; The Subserviency of Philosophy to Arts, the Principles they borrow from it and the Means of carrying them to their Perfection.'

Philosophy, then, was the end, but it included the principles of science; and, as a matter of fact, most of the members of the society were intimately conversant with science in one or other of its branches (some of them being recognized scientific authorities), and all were imbued with the scientific spirit. The contributions of members to the *Proceedings* of the society were either 'discourses,' fully written out and read, or 'questions,' proposed for discussion, the former to be inserted by the writer himself in a book, and an abstract of the latter to be similarly inserted by the member who proposed the question and opened the discussion—any failure to do so in either case to be visited with a money fine, and the fine to be repeated, meeting after meeting, till the requirement was fulfilled. The minutes of the society are still extant and also portions of the MS books in which discourses and discussions were inserted (they are preserved in the Aberdeen University Library); and from them we can quite well see the wide range of the topics that came up for consideration. If philosophy, psychology, ethics, and natural theology supplied subjects for discussion, so also did political economy, jurisprudence, natural history, education, medicine, physics, chemistry, and even agriculture; and through all we can trace the gradual shaping of the writings that the world was later to know as Reid's *Inquiry*, Campbell's *Philosophy of Rhetoric*, Beattie's *Essay on the Nature and Immutability of Truth*, Gerard's *Essay on Taste* and his *Essay on Genius*, and John Gregory's *Comparative View of the State and Faculties of Man with those of the Animal World.*

The key to Reid's philosophy is to be found in the phrase, 'the principles of common sense.' Common sense is a function of reason, and its office is 'to judge of things self-evident,' which Reid identified with 'judging of first principles'; and it is conceived as 'purely the gift of Heaven,' not requiring practice and rules for the efficient use of it. First principles are of two kinds (so the *Inquiry* lays down), according as they refer to contingent or to necessary truths. The characteristic of the second class of truths is that they are necessary and immutable, and their contrary is impossible; and of the first that they are mutable, 'depending upon some effect of will and power, which had a beginning and may have an end.' Contingent truths have a wide scope and include mental states given to us in consciousness, and the existence of objects of consciousness, the trustworthiness of memory, personal identity, the existence and nature of external reality as testified by the senses, the freedom of the will, the ability of our 'natural faculties' to distinguish truth from error, the possession of life and rationality by our fellow-men as manifested outwardly in their countenances, voices, and gestures, the propriety of paying a certain amount of deference to human testimony and to authority in opinion, and the instinctive belief in the uniformity of nature. On the other hand, the first principles of necessary truth have reference to the axioms of grammar, of logic, of mathematics, of 'taste' (æsthetics), and of morals, and to the great metaphysical principles that Hume had called in question, viz. the existence of mind and of body as the subject of conscious thoughts and of material qualities respectively, the law of causality, and the legitimacy of inferring design and intelligence in the cause from marks of them in the effect.

First principles are to be considered as laid in the structure or constitution of the human mind. They are, therefore, inscrutable and inexplicable, beyond the power of critical analysis, and to be accepted by us as given without comment or question.

Hume was the writer against whom this doctrine of first principles was specially directed; but not Hume alone, for the 'ideal system' of Berkeley also seemed to have scepticism embedded in it, and Berkeley and Hume drew their inspiration from Locke. What had happened, previous to Reid, in the development of British philosophy was this: Locke had laid it down that knowledge is 'the perception of the connexion of and agreement, or disagreement and repregnancy of, any of our ideas.'[1] On this basis Berkeley had shown that, if ideas are all that we can attain to in knowledge, 'matter' (as the metaphysician understood it) must be dispensed with, although he still retained 'spirit,' as being essentially active—an agent. Accepting Berkeley's doctrine of matter, Hume proceeded, on what he conceived to be the logical outcome of Lockean principles, to discard spirit also, maintaining that change, fleetingness, succession, holds as much in the realm of mind as in the realm of matter, and that, if matter be merely phenomenal, so also is mind. In neither case is there

[1] *Essay*, bk. iv. ch. i. sect. 1.

real permanence or true causation; there is only a flow or succession of ideas, held together as a continuity by custom or association.

'What we call a *mind* is nothing but a heap or collection of different perceptions [Hume's name for states of consciousness] united together by certain relations, and suppos'd, tho' falsely, to be endow'd with a perfect simplicity and identity.'[1]

Substance of the soul there is none; and 'the question concerning the substance of the soul' is 'absolutely unintelligible.'[2]

Such was the logical outcome of philosophy, working on Locke's principles, as interpreted by David Hume. What, then, required specially to be done (so it appeared to Reid) was to prove that the Lockean conception of knowledge, accepted both by Berkeley and by Hume, was erroneous; that in knowledge we have more than 'ideas' and are indubitably in contact with reality. Accordingly, Reid set himself strenuously to the analysis of external perception and to a sustained criticism of what he called, in his own terminology, 'the ideal system'—a system that he found not only in Locke, Berkeley, and Hume, but also in Descartes, Malebranche, and many others. His first point was insistence on the distinction between bare sensation and perception proper in the perceptual process. He laid it down with emphasis that sensation is purely subjective—a mere feeling that can have no existence except in a sentient conscious mind; but perception is objective and knowledge-giving, taking us out of ourselves and indicating an object whose existence is independent of its being perceived. When, *e.g.*, I smell a rose, my sensation of smell is subjective, dependent on my sentient organism; but my consciousness of the smell as emanating from the rose gives objectivity—has reference to something that is an existent not-me. The beginning in sense-perception, therefore, is not made with bare sensation, to which objectivity is somehow tacked on afterwards—not, to use his own term, with simple apprehension—but with judgment, with 'a natural and original judgment.' I judge that the sensation is effected by an existent something outside and independent of myself. Sensations thus become 'signs' of the qualities of external objects, or 'suggest' the objects. The suggestive power is of two kinds, according to the two kinds of qualities of matter. In the case of the secondary qualities (taste, smell, sound, etc.), the suggestion is simply of *a* cause of the sensation, without any revelation being made of the exact nature of the *quality* of the object that causes it (my sensation of the scent of a rose does not *resemble* the quality in the rose that produces the scent). On the other hand, in the case of the primary qualities (hardness, solidity, extension, etc.), the sensation actually indicates, though it does not resemble, the quality of the object (its hardness or softness, roughness or smoothness, etc.) and thereby gives us true insight into objective reality.

This distinction of the two kinds of qualities in objects Reid put to great use, although he did not claim to have originated it (it is to be found in Locke and in Descartes and goes back at any rate to Democritus). It lies at the root of his contention of our unshakable conviction in external existence as obtained through sense-perception and supplies his answer to the idealism of Locke, Berkeley, Hume, and the other upholders of 'the ideal system,' which seemed to shut us out from external reality altogether, restricting us to 'ideas' in our own minds, outside of which we cannot get.

But, while in perceptive experience we get the existence and nature of external reality, we get also (so Reid taught) the existence and nature of the percipient's self or ego. The subject and the object in perception, though related, are not identical. The percipient subject is sentient and conscious, has all the qualities that we recognize in a real agent (is active and has 'power'), and is in many ways contrasted with the object. This fact, that the subject is in essence activity, energy, active power, introduces to us Reid's conception of causality and cause and brings out the nature of his opposition to Hume in regard to these. Causality, according to Hume, is mere uniform sequence guaranteed by custom, consequent on repetition, and involving an instinctive tendency to believe in uniformity of succession—which, however, has no rational basis and is not infallible, although it is for practical purposes indispensable. In causation there is 'conjunction,' indeed, but not 'connexion'—so Hume had phrased it. That view appeared to Reid to be wholly mistaken. It reposed simply on the physicist's conception of causation as found by observation of nature and natural events—a conception that does not refer to efficient causation at all, but only to general laws.

'In natural philosophy . . . we seek only the general laws, according to which nature works, and these we call the causes of what is done according to them. But such laws cannot be the efficient cause of anything. They are only the rule according to which the efficient cause operates.'[1]

However adequate this conception may be for the man of science, it is not sufficient for the philosopher. The origin of our idea of cause (so Reid held) is not mere sequence, however uniform, but personal volition—the individual's own consciousness of what takes place when he exerts himself in an act of will; and, although sequence is involved in it, there is involved also the exercise of power—an ultimate experience, which cannot be further explained. The principle of causality, therefore, becomes more than the generalized expression of observed facts: it is a first principle of necessary truth, expressive of the causal *nexus* and assuming the form that 'whatever begins to exist *must* have a cause which produced it.' If this be so, then, it appeared to Reid, the doctrine of Hume is irrelevant: it ignores the point to be explained, and is, consequently, ineffective.

Attaching to the principle of causality, in the view of Reid, is that of design as involving a designer. It is a first principle of necessary truth 'that design and intelligence in the cause may be inferred, with certainty, from marks or signs of it in the effect.' On this ground is the existence of God assured to us. From the world as a vast complex effect, manifesting intelligence, goodness, and purpose, we may legitimately infer 'an eternal intelligent First Cause'—an all-wise, all-good, all-powerful Creator. Here efficient and final causation are inseparably bound up together.

The same philosophical spirit that characterized Reid in his intellectual speculations characterized him also in his moral philosophy. To him it appeared that, unless there were some immutable foundation on which men could rely in ethics, some principles of human character and conduct that were indisputable, that were natural to men and must be taken for granted as being self-evident, we could put no certain trust in morals. These common-sense principles of morals include the freedom of the will, as the foundation of responsibility and moral approbation and disapprobation, and the deliverances of conscience as an innate faculty in man, determining duty, right and wrong, and the like, purely on the ground of intuition, and the rejection of interest or utility as the ultimate explanation of morality.[2]

[1] *Treatise of Human Nature*, bk. i. pt. iv. sect. 2.
[2] *Ib.* bk. i. pt. iv. sect. 5.

[1] Reid's *Works*, ed. Hamilton[2], Edinburgh, 1849, p. 57.
[2] *Ib.*[2], pp. 586–590.

'The testimony of our moral faculty, like that of the external senses, is the testimony of nature, and we have the same reason to rely upon it.'[1]

For the positive doctrines of ethics Reid is very largely indebted to Butler, whose doctrines of conscience, anger, and resentment, etc., as laid down in the *Sermons*, he reproduces. The characteristic of *The Active Powers* does not lie in its doctrinal originality, but in its telling criticism of opposing views, its analysis of ethical phenomena, and its keenness of psychological insight.

These are the central points in Reid's philosophy. Where its weakness lies is obvious. In the first place, its enumeration of first principles is open to criticism. It is neither logical in the arrangement nor exhaustive: it is not sifted or determined by any rational ground, so that thinkers in general might be induced to accept it, but it savours not a little of Reid's own likes and leanings. In the next place, its appeal to consciousness as the ultimate testifier is to the *mature* consciousness—the consciousness of the adult—neglectful of the fact that the mature consciousness has at the back of it a long experience, which counts for much. It, further, ignores the fact that the individual consciousness is also social, and that the influence of heredity is of high importance. Lastly, it lends itself very readily to the loose and superficial thinker, who has simply to appeal to 'the inner light' in man for support to any prejudice or opinion that he himself may hold firmly.

Nevertheless Reid's teaching has its distinct place and value in the history of philosophy. It was the opportune insistence on the fact that more than sensation is necessary for the explanation of knowledge—that there is needed also the native activity of the mind (just as Kant, somewhat later, declared), and that the mind grasps reality and is not restricted to 'ideas.' To Reid an object implied a subject; thinking involved a thinker, and sentience a sentient. His philosophy is strong also in its psychology and its analysis of psychical processes and states, and in its recognition of the necessity of rising from psychology to metaphysics, and not, contrariwise, of sacrificing psychology to metaphysics. It is Baconian in its method—inductive and experiential—and is very suspicious of theories that are not adequately supported by facts. Hence it is robust and, in large measure, effective in its criticism. Reid's judgment is eminently sober and balanced: he hardly ever allows feeling to carry him away. He is a sound thinker, as distinguished from a deep and from an intellectually adroit thinker. His mental movements are, not infrequently, cumbrous and his literary style tedious; but he is patient and persistent and adheres closely to the point. He is also singularly fortunate in discovering the weak links in his opponent's arguments. He is fair and straightforward (sometimes even blunt) in his criticism; he is aided by humour on occasion, but he is rarely captious. He respected, while he criticized, his adversary; and Hume himself acknowledged that he was a gentlemanly antagonist. His end in arguing was truth, not victory; and that means a great deal.

2. George Campbell.—Next to Reid in intellectual ability, in balance of judgment, and in keen psychological insight is George Campbell.

Like Reid, Campbell was a son of the manse, his father, Colin Campbell, being one of the ministers of Aberdeen. He was born in Aberdeen, on Christmas Day, 1719, and was educated at the Grammar School of Aberdeen and at Marischal College, which he entered in 1734, taking his M.A. degree in 1738. After graduating, he was articled to a writer to the signet in Edinburgh, but later decided to abandon Law for Theology, and, in the last year of his term as law apprentice, attended Divinity classes in the University of Edinburgh. Returning to Aberdeen, he enrolled himself, in accordance with the usual custom, as a student under both professors of Divinity—King's and Marischal. While a student of Divinity in Aberdeen, he founded a Theological Club, among the members of which were Alexander Gerard and James Trail (the future bishop of Down and Connor). He was licensed as a preacher of the gospel on 11th June 1746, and was ordained minister of Banchory-Ternan, Kincardineshire, on 2nd June 1748. While a country minister, he conceived a plan of translating the Gospels and wrote part of his *Philosophy of Rhetoric*. In 1757 he was appointed to one of the city charges in Aberdeen. The Theological Club was by this time extinct; but he entered with zest into the foundation of the Philosophical Society, of which he was an original member. In 1759 he was appointed principal of Marischal College and in 1771, on the transference of Alexander Gerard to King's College, was elected professor of Divinity, and held the office in conjunction with the principalship, but resigned his parochial charge. The Divinity chair was, however, connected with the college kirk of Greyfriars, so that his ministerial duties did not entirely cease. In 1795, 'owing to age and growing infirmities,' he resigned his Divinity professorship and soon after, on receiving a pension from Government, the principalship of the university. But he did not long enjoy his retirement. On 31st March 1796 (the year in which Reid died), he fell suddenly ill and, two days after, 'was seized with a shock of palsy,' and expired on 6th April, in his seventy-seventh year.

Campbell was distinguished as (*a*) a preacher, (*b*) a theologian, and (*c*) a philosopher.

(*a*) His preaching was characterized by solid thought, carefully elaborated and effectively presented, and enforced by sustained reasoning of a keenly argumentative kind. One of his sermons to which special interest attaches is that delivered before the Synod of Aberdeen on 9th Oct. 1760. The subject was miracles, and the discourse consisted of a reply to Hume and formed the groundwork of Campbell's *Dissertation on Miracles*. Another historical sermon was preached in 1776 on the day of the national fast held on account of the American War. It dealt powerfully with the duty of allegiance and strongly denounced the conduct of the colonies. Three years later (*i.e.* in 1779) he again intervened in a public crisis, and his attitude was greatly to his honour. The question of the repeal of the Roman Catholic penal laws was being debated, and people were much agitated over it. Campbell issued *An Address to the People of Scotland* (which formed no. 4 in the 'Tracts for the People' series), eagerly urging the claims of toleration. The result was that he provoked the hatred of an Aberdeen mob, which rushed excitedly to his house and smashed his windows.

(*b*) Campbell's fame as a theologian rests partly on his *Lectures on Ecclesiastical History* (published posthumously, 2 vols., Aberdeen, 1815), but mainly on his work on *The Four Gospels* (2 vols., London, 1789), being an original translation of the Gospels, together with learned preliminary dissertations and critical and explanatory notes. The very idea of a new translation of Scripture showed liberal and progressive thought, anticipatory of later critical requirements, though the execution hardly answered the conception. The dissertations are unique for the time and strikingly scholarly, raising Campbell at a bound to the first rank of Biblical critics. Their merit was at once recognized; they were accepted as authoritative not only in Scotland, but in England also, and continued to be the standard exposition of the subject for many years at Oxford.

(*c*) Campbell's philosophy was that of the Scottish school. As a member of the Aberdeen Philosophical Society, he was present at the first meeting on 12th Jan. 1758, and he continued a member down to the date when the minutes stop (9th March 1773). He read many papers and initiated many discussions, most of them having a bearing on the philosophical and literary positions ultimately embodied in his published works. The Scottish strain in his thinking comes out most clearly in his *Philosophy of Rhetoric* (2 vols., London, 1776). The plan of the treatise, in the words of the preface, is:

[1] *Works*², p. 590.

'On the one hand, to exhibit, he [the author] does not say, a correct map, but a tolerable sketch of the human mind; and, aided by the lights which the poet and the orator so amply furnish, to disclose its secret movements, tracing its principal channels of perception and action, as near as possible, to their source: and, on the other hand, from the science of human nature, to ascertain, with greater precision, the radical principles of that art, whose object it is, by the use of language, to operate on the soul of the hearer, in the way of informing, convincing, pleasing, moving, or persuading.'

This kind of psychological inquiry was precisely to the liking of the Scottish philosopher; and, as the handling proceeds, many opportunities occur for the application of the principles distinctive of the school. Bk. i., which deals with the nature and foundations of eloquence, affords an excellent example. The two sources of Eloquence recognized are intuition and deduction. Under the head 'Of Intuitive Evidence' the mathematical axioms, consciousness, and common sense are handled; and it is here that we find, though on a less extensive scale, an enumeration and exposition of primary truths or first principles precisely after the manner of Reid.

But the Scottish standpoint is apparent in Campbell elsewhere than in the *Rhetoric*. The *Dissertation on Miracles* (Edinburgh, 1762) is as much philosophical as theological. The foundation argument is an appeal to common sense, or 'the primary principles of the understanding.' Hume had argued against the reasonableness of belief in miracles on the ground that such belief must rest on the evidence of testimony, but no amount of testimony is sufficient to prove a miracle, inasmuch as the evidence of testimony is based on experience, and experience 'firm and unalterable' has established the laws of nature, whereas a miracle claims to be a violation or suspension of these laws. To most people, perhaps, it would seem sufficient to reply to this that Hume's argument contains both a *petitio principii* and an *ignoratio elenchi*. To assert that the experience which has established the laws of nature is 'unalterable' is simply to beg the question; whereas to define a miracle as a violation or a transgression or even a suspension of nature is to mistake the character of a miracle, and, consequently, any argument based on that definition is beside the point. But this was not exactly how Campbell faced the problem. The stress in his reply was laid on this—that, so far is it from being true that our belief in testimony rests solely on experience, the reverse is the case: our belief in testimony (we see it in the unstinted credulity of children) is antecedent to experience and often needs experience to correct it or to tone it down.

'To say, therefore, that our diffidence in testimony is the result of experience is more philosophical, because more consonant to truth, than to say that our faith in testimony has this foundation. Accordingly, youth, which is inexperienced, is credulous; age, on the contrary, is distrustful.'[1]

When the objection is raised that such primitive credulity is inexplicable, he admits the fact, but maintains in substance that we must begin with something, must have some original grounds of belief, and this primitive credulity is one of the original grounds of belief, as the law of causation and the uniformity of nature are two others. This is precisely a reply forged in the Scottish school of philosophy and shows Campbell to be a true associate of Reid.

3. James Beattie.—Great though the reputations of Reid and Campbell were, they did not equal that of Beattie. This was not in strict accordance with merit, but was partly due to favouring fortune or the chapter of accidents.

James Beattie, the son of a small farmer at Laurencekirk, Kincardineshire, was born there on 25th Oct. 1735. His early education was acquired at the parish school of Laurencekirk, aided by instruction in classics from the parish minister. In 1749, at the age of fourteen, he enrolled himself as a student at Marischal College, Aberdeen, having gained the first bursary at the annual competition, and, after four years' study, graduated M.A. in the spring of 1753. The same year he became schoolmaster of Fordoun, adjoining Laurencekirk, in which post he remained five years, prosecuting studies in Divinity at the same time with a view to the ministry (which he did not ultimately enter). It was while schoolmaster of Fordoun that he began to reveal himself as a poet. In 1758 he left Fordoun for Aberdeen, having been appointed by the magistrates of the city one of the masters of the Grammar School. This position he held for two years only; for in 1760 he became a professor in Marischal College. The chair to which he was presented was that of Natural Philosophy; but, by a happy accident, before the session began, the chair of Moral Philosophy fell vacant by the transference of Alexander Gerard to the chair of Divinity. To Gerard's vacant chair Beattie accordingly was appointed, where he found the work that was proper and congenial to him. In 1761 he was duly elected a member of the Philosophical Society, to which he contributed essays and questions for discussion; and he continued a member till the society ceased.

In 1770 appeared the *Essay on the Nature and Immutability of Truth*—a work which, contrary to his expectations, brought him immediate fame. It sold rapidly, reaching a third edition within two years, and was translated into French, German, Dutch, and Italian. It was praised by English statesmen and English men of letters—such as Lord Chatham, Burke, Samuel Johnson, Garrick, and Sir Joshua Reynolds — and won for Beattie the friendship of these distinguished men and others. It was eulogized by Church dignitaries, including the two archbishops and Dr. Porteous of Chester, afterwards bishop of London, and brought forth offers of ecclesiastical preferment on the condition of his taking Holy Orders. Above all, it attracted the attention of George III. and led to Beattie's having several interviews with the king and to his obtaining a royal pension of £200 a year. Honours were now showered upon him. Oxford conferred upon him the degree of D.C.L. and made his work a text-book; Sir Joshua Reynolds painted his portrait as part of the famous allegorical picture of the Angel of Truth pushing down Voltaire and two other sceptics (now the prized possession of the University of Aberdeen); and he was lionized and welcomed everywhere as the philosophical champion of the faith. That last phrase gives the main reason of the extraordinary popularity of the *Essay on Truth*. The treatise was an exposition of the principles of Common Sense as a safeguard against sophistry and scepticism, accompanied with an unsparing and slashing criticism of Hume's philosophy —a philosophy that had seemed to religiously-minded people to undermine by invincible logic the groundwork of morality and religion alike.

The year 1771 saw the publication of the first book of *The Minstrel*, the second being issued three years later. This poem at once raised Beattie to a high place as a poet in the public estimation and had, like the *Essay*, a rapid circulation.

Other books of Beattie were: *Dissertations, Moral and Critical* (London, 1783), *Evidences of the Christian Religion* (Edinburgh, 1786), and *Elements of Moral Science* (2 vols., do. 1790–93)—all popular and commanding a wide circle of readers.

Beattie as a man of society makes a pleasing picture to the imagination; for, while moving in the highest social circles in the land and lauded by the leaders in thought and in letters, he never allowed himself to be carried away. He remained to the end unassuming and humble, being fully cognizant of his own limitations. His domestic life was clouded during many of his later years by the sad and long-continued illness of his wife, who suffered from mental derangement. Meanwhile, his own health gave way, and he had to carry on a struggle (and manfully he did it) against many physical infirmities. The situation was aggravated by the loss of his two sons—both of them very promising youths and dear to his heart. The elder, James Hay, had the religious seriousness and the philosophical tastes and aptitudes of his father and not a little of his father's humane and amiable disposition. So precocious was he that, at the age of nineteen, he was appointed his father's assistant and colleague in the chair of Moral Philosophy. But three years later, on 19th Nov. 1790, he died of lung complaint, at the age of twenty-two. The younger son, Montagu, was cut off even more prematurely, dying of a fever, after a brief illness, on 14th March 1796, aged eighteen. All this told severely on Beattie; his nerves became shattered, vertigo settled on him as his constant companion, and his memory began to give way. Paralysis overtook him; and, after repeated strokes, occurring at intervals over several years, he died in Aberdeen, on 18th Aug. 1803.

Of Beattie as a poet little need be said. *The Minstrel*, in both the parts of it (the intended third was never written), was praised by high authorities at the time and is appreciated by competent judges still. It has won this note of immortality: it appears, in selected passages, in the popular books of quotations at the present day. The same is true of his *Hermit*.

As a philosopher, Beattie has not attained the immortality that his contemporaries predicted. Yet his writings do not deserve the contemptuous neglect that has overtaken them. The principles of his *Essay on Truth* are those of Reid, although not so judiciously handled. They are expressed, however, in a harmonious Addisonian style, which

[1] *Dissertation*, p. 12.

drew forth the approbation of the greatest literary men of the day. The ultimate appeal with Beattie is to common sense; but the effect is spoiled by two defects: (1) his tendency to identify the philosophical principle with the plain man's unsophisticated 'intuition' (that is Beattie's favourite term) and his setting it forth as a kind of inner light or inward feeling, competent of itself to guide a man in any circumstances of life; and (2) the occasional exaggeration and vehemence of his language, especially when he has Hume in view, thereby giving ground for Hume's complaint that Beattie 'had not used him like a gentleman.'

Vehement language in philosophy is apt to arouse in one a suspicion of a lack, in the person who employs it, of that philosophic calmness and 'indifferency to truth' which are indispensable to clear thinking and to a due understanding and appreciation of an opponent's standpoint. On the other hand, the weakness of the conception of an inner light is manifest. The sceptic may reasonably enough feel that *his* doubt cannot be dispelled by another man's intuition; nor is a criterion like Beattie's of very much use if, on the occasion of a difference of opinion or belief arising between two men, each can appeal to the criterion as declaring in *his* favour. Nor is the application to the doubter of the general proposition that 'what everybody sees is indisputable' of very much avail, if the doubter can honestly say, 'But *I* do not see.' That, surely, cannot rightly be said to be seen by everybody which even one man fails to see.

The weakness of the appeal was early felt in Beattie's own day. In Aberdeenshire John Skinner of Linshart, author of *Tullochgorum*, turned the doctrine of the inward infallible light into sprightly Latin verse, set to the tune of 'Tullochgorum,' and treated it with pawky humour, the sting of which was removed by the laudatory epithet applied to Beattie in the catching refrain of 'Doctissime Doctorum.' On the other hand, Joseph Priestley seized the opportunity to turn the Scottish philosophy into ridicule, joining Beattie not only with Reid but also with James Oswald (who in his *Appeal to Common Sense in behalf of Religion* [2 vols., Edinburgh, 1766–72] had made such an unscientific and unphilosophical application of common sense to religion as to render him a ready butt to sarcasm and flippant wit).

'When we see,' said Priestley, criticizing Beattie, 'how miserably bewildered the bulk of mankind are, one would think that this principle of truth is like the god Baal, who when he was most wanted, and ought to have made a point of being present, to assist his worshippers, was asleep, or on a journey, or engaged some other way.'[1]

Beattie's claims as a philosopher are usually tested by his *Essay on Truth* alone. But his other philosophical works ought to be taken into account also. In particular, the *Dissertations* and the three essays in literary criticism (on poetry, laughter, and classical learning) appended to the quarto edition of the *Essay on Truth* (Edinburgh, 1776) show keenness of psychological insight and sobriety of judgment that are far from common. They also show Beattie's style at its best and put it beyond question that there is real critical power in that school of literary criticism in Scotland (headed by Lord Kames) to which Beattie belonged, and which was sufficiently important to arouse the jealousy of Voltaire and to draw forth his scorn.

4. Alexander Gerard.—Of the Aberdeen philosophers of the 18th cent. Gerard alone remains to be noted.

Alexander Gerard, son of Gilbert Gerard, minister of Chapel of Garioch, Aberdeenshire, was born in 1728 and died in 1795. He graduated M.A. at Marischal College in 1744. In 1752 he was appointed regent or professor of Moral Philosophy in that university, having acted for the two previous years as substitute for the then professor, David Fordyce. In 1760 he was transferred to the chair of Divinity, which he occupied till 1771, when he was appointed professor of Divinity in King's College. He was not, like Reid and Campbell, an original member of the Aberdeen Philosophical Society, but he joined it at its fifth meeting—on 8th March 1758. At Marischal College he showed himself a keen advocate of university reform, and it was mainly owing to him that Marischal College gave up the 'regenting' system in 1755 and substituted that of the professoriate. His views on academic teaching may be seen in his *Plan of Education in the Marischal College and University of Aberdeen, with the Reasons of it* (Aberdeen, 1755)—a work that was translated into German in 1770. While professor of Divinity in Marischal College, he was elected Moderator of the General Assembly of the Church of Scotland (1764); and, while professor of Divinity in King's College, he held the office of one of His Majesty's chaplains in ordinary for Scotland.

Gerard attained distinction both as a theologian and as a philosopher. His two theological works are: *Dissertations on Subjects relating to the Genius and the Evidences of Christianity* (Edinburgh, 1766) and *The Pastoral Care* (London, 1799). The former consists of two lengthy dissertations, the first dealing with the suggestive manner in which Christ and His apostles proposed the evidences of their mission, and the second with Christianity as confirmed by the opposition of infidels. The topics are ably treated, and the presentation is effective from the writer's point of view. If the book has only a historical interest now, it is simply because the modern spirit is rather impatient of such formal disquisitions as are here to be found and is more likely to be impressed by the living power of the gospel as manifested in the daily lives of believers. The lectures on pastoral theology were published, after the author's death, by his son Gilbert (who succeeded his father in the chair of Divinity in King's College) in 1799. They are full of wise counsel and sane judgment and have still an interest for all who are curious to know what was expected of a Scottish pastor in the days of parochial catechizing and at the moment when 'fellowship meetings' had made their appearance in the land and were as yet looked upon with suspicion by the older generation of divines.

But, besides being a trusted theologian, Gerard had a considerable reputation as a philosopher. This arose from his *Essay on Taste* (London, 1759) and his *Essay on Genius* (do. 1774). These two writings are marked by the analytic power of the Scottish philosophers and show the same calm, well-balanced judgment as was characteristic of Thomas Reid. Gerard, indeed, lacked Reid's faculty of sustained thinking, and one can hardly conceive him as the originator of a system; but he could handle a theme adroitly and with penetration and in a style that is pleasant to read. Special interest attaches to the *Essay on Taste* because it enunciates views that met with much acceptance in Scotland and in France, resolving beauty, 'at least in part,' into association. In like manner, the *Essay on Genius* enjoyed much popularity. In it he traces the origin of genius to the associating power of the imagination, and devotes space to a consideration of the laws of association following Aristotle—thereby giving occasion to Sir William Hamilton's complimentary remark on Gerard, that 'of the later British philosophers, indeed, there is hardly to be found another, who has studied the works of Aristotle more attentively and to better effect.'[1] But the most notable fact about this essay is that it specially attracted the attention of Immanuel Kant and affected his doctrine of genius as laid down in the *Kritik of Judgment*.[2]

[1] *Examination of Dr. Reid's Inquiry*, etc., p. 128.

[1] Reid's *Works*², p. 900, note 10.

[2] See Otto Schlapp, *Kants Lehre vom Genie und die Entstehung der 'Kritik der Urteilskraft,'* Göttingen, 1901, pp. 9, 244, 417, 441, etc.

II. *IN THE 19TH CENTURY.*—Two thinkers in the University of Edinburgh have great distinction in connexion with the Scottish philosophy in the 19th cent.—Dugald Stewart and Sir William Hamilton. Previous to either, in the second half of the 18th cent., was **Adam Ferguson** (1723–1816), who accepted Reid's 'common sense' teaching and reproduced it without appreciable modification. His reputation was mainly that of a moral philosopher, inculcating Stoical ethics, mellowed by the emphatic assertion of the importance of the benevolent affections and the reiterated insistence on the need of taking full cognizance of the essentially social nature of man.[1] His eloquence and his broadened sympathy attracted many hearers to his lectures, and elicited general admiration. He had also a reputation on account of his work on the *Hist. of the Progress and Termination of the Roman Republic* (3 vols., London, 1783). His books were widely read. Yet his fame has long since gone, and his works repose peacefully on the shelves. There remains only the laudatory epitaph on his tombstone (read by every passer-by) in the cathedral graveyard of St. Andrews, written by Sir Walter Scott, which, however grandiloquent and extravagant it may appear to us to be, does quite well represent the general opinion of Ferguson's contemporaries.

1. Dugald Stewart.—

Dugald Stewart was the son of Matthew Stewart, professor of Mathematics in Edinburgh University, and was born in Edinburgh on 22nd Nov. 1753. His school and university education was received in his native town. As a student in Arts, he proved himself expert in mathematics and in philosophy. By the professors of philosophy he was instructed in Reid's principles; and he had his views expanded and confirmed later by attendance on Reid's lectures in Glasgow. In 1772 and for the three succeeding years he taught the class of Mathematics in Edinburgh as substitute for his father, whose health was beginning to fail; and in 1775 he was definitely associated with him as professor of Mathematics. In 1778, in addition to his mathematical duties, he conducted the Moral Philosophy class, in lectures of his own, during Ferguson's absence in America. In 1785, on Ferguson's resignation, he was appointed professor of Moral Philosophy. The active duties of the chair (which extended to Political Economy, as well as to Ethics) he discharged for 24 years (1785–1809); at the end of that time, without actually resigning the professorship, he had a colleague appointed in the person of Thomas Brown. Relieved thus of the active work of the chair, he retired to Kinnell House, Linlithgowshire, which was placed at his service by the Duke of Hamilton, and devoted himself to developing and finally formulating his philosophical views. On Brown's death in 1820 he retired altogether from the professorship, and John Wilson ('Christopher North') was—mainly on political grounds—elected his successor, in opposition to Hamilton. In 1822 he was attacked by paralysis, which, however, did not impair his intellectual powers; but a second stroke in 1828 ended his life. He died in Edinburgh on 11th June 1828.

His chief literary works are: *Elements of the Philosophy of the Human Mind*, i. (London, 1792), ii. (do. 1814), iii. (do. 1827), *Outlines of Moral Philosophy*, a students' text-book (Edinburgh, 1793), *Philosophical Essays* (do. 1810), *Dissertation on the Progress of Metaphysical Philosophy*, written for the 'Supplement' of the *EBr* (pt. i. in 1815, and pt. ii. in 1821), *The Philosophy of the Active and Moral Powers* (Edinburgh, 1828). The great edition of his *Collected Works* is that by Sir William Hamilton (11 vols., do. 1854–60, including the supplementary vol. of *Translations*).

Dugald Stewart was a strict adherent of the Scottish philosophy, but with characteristics of his own both in metaphysics and in ethics. First of all, like the rest of the school, he based his thinking on psychology, pursued on the inductive method. The psychology was Reid's, for the most part; but it is marked by a fuller and more sympathetic appreciation of association than Reid had shown. He carefully explains association and felicitously and copiously exemplifies its influence on all the parts of our mental being—our speculative conclusions, our judgments in matters of taste, our active powers and moral judgments. Although thus advanced in his regard for association, he stopped short of carrying the principle fully into the ethical sphere. This was specially noted and criticized by Sir James Mackintosh,[1] who set himself to prove that Stewart's refusal to acknowledge the power of association in the formation of conscience was a needless timidity; for conscience would be equally authoritative and equally entitled to be regarded as natural to man, whether it be conceived as derivative, and explained from the side of the associationist, or as original, and explained from the side of Butlerian intuitionism. The great point is that, if it be derivative or acquired, it is universally and necessarily acquired.

While accepting the general principles of the Scottish philosophy, Stewart entered a protest against its terminology. He did not approve of Reid's terms 'common sense' and 'instinct,' nor was he wholly enamoured of Beattie's 'intuition.' He saw how easily these words might encourage the belief that the Scottish philosophy was nothing more than an appeal to vulgar opinion and might create the impression of superficiality and lack of scientific precision. And so for the accredited phraseology he substituted the expression, 'the Fundamental Laws of Human Belief; or the Primary Elements of Human Reason.' This, doubtless, is to some extent an improvement, for it brings out the fact explicitly that psychology is the groundwork of the Scottish mode of thinking, and it emphasizes the rational aspect of the procedure. But the term 'laws' is not particularly happy in expressing what are held to be necessary *truths*—the indispensable *conditions* of belief; and there is a certain incongruity in designating them both 'laws' and 'elements.' But, further, Stewart objected to Reid's describing primary beliefs as 'first principles.' They are more like 'axioms' than 'principles,' he held; for the term 'principle' conveys the idea of some fact or some supposition from which a series of consequences may be deduced, whereas from fundamental laws of belief 'no inferences can be deduced for the further enlargement of our knowledge.' As regards primary beliefs themselves, however, it is to be remarked that Stewart is far more cautious than Reid in restricting the number of them.

Reid's doctrine of natural realism, in connexion with perception, was reproduced by Stewart almost to the letter and therefore does not call for special consideration. But it is different with Stewart's treatment of the epistemological question of the nature of the mathematical axioms and of mathematical or demonstrative reasoning. It was customary to regard the axioms, intuitively apprehended, as the foundation of mathematics; but Stewart, who was himself a mathematician, saw the importance of laying the stress on the definitions. These, he maintained, not the axioms, are the principles of mathematical science, but the axioms are not to be ignored; although they are not the foundation of mathematical demonstration, they are presupposed or implied in all mathematical reasoning, and, if their truth were challenged, further progress would be impossible.

'From what principle are the various properties of the circle derived, but from the definition of a circle? From what principle the properties of the parabola or ellipse, but from the definition of these curves? A similar observation may be extended to all the other theorems which the mathematician demonstrates; and it is this observation (which, obvious as it may seem, does not appear to have occurred, in all its force, either to Locke, to Reid, or to Campbell) that furnishes, if I mistake not, the true explanation of the peculiarity already remarked in mathematical evidence.'[2]

Consequently, he strongly opposes the view of mathematical evidence 'that it all resolves ultimately into the perception of identity [A=A]; and that it is this circumstance which constitutes

[1] See his *Principles of Moral and Political Science*, 2 vols., Edinburgh, 1792.

[1] In his *Dissertation on the Progress of Ethical Philosophy*, Edinburgh, 1836, pp. 324–334, 353–400.

[2] *Elements of the Philosophy of the Human Mind*, pt. ii. ch. i. p. 302.

the peculiar and characteristical cogency of mathematical demonstration.' The peculiar cogency in the case, he holds, depends on definitions and hypotheses. By adding hypotheses to definitions he meant to bring out the circumstance that the propositions to be established in mathematics are not, like those in the other sciences, expressive of facts or concerned with actual existence, but deal simply with 'the logical filiation of consequences' which follow from given suppositions or assumptions.

When we turn to Stewart as a moral philosopher, we find him eagerly engaged in arguing the two questions of the moral faculty (his own name for conscience, and preferable, in his view, to Hutcheson's term 'moral sense') and the moral standard. His doctrine is pronouncedly intuitionist. He maintains that we have an immediate apprehension of moral qualities—right, wrong, duty, obligation, etc.—and that this apprehension is ultimate and is in itself the guarantee of moral value, altogether apart from consideration of consequences. Nevertheless, he sets forth the moral faculty, not as a simple but as a complex thing, consisting of three elements: (*a*) the perception of an act as right or wrong, (*b*) an ensuing emotion of pleasure or of pain, and (*c*) a perception of the merit or the demerit of the agent; and he has a considerable appreciation of the power of association in relation to our moral judgments; nor can he refrain from joining the utilitarian on occasion and appealing to consequences. As the intention of the agent is the chief factor in estimating the moral character of an action, the question of the freedom of the will inevitably crops up, and a long section is devoted to the handling of it. Not deeply, but very interestingly, he marshals the arguments *pro* and *con* and clinches his reasoning by a detailed examination of the antithetic position of the necessitarian. This became the model for the treatment of the subject in Scotland for a full generation. But Stewart set the example also in psychological analysis of ethical notions. Accepting from Reid (who simply followed Aristotle) the twofold division of our mental powers into intellectual and active, Stewart was more successful than Reid had been in finding a place in his philosophical scheme for the sentiments and emotions. Under the heading 'Our Desires,' he treats of the commanding instinctive propensities of knowledge, society, esteem, power, and emulation; and the no less important impulses of love of kindred, friendship, patriotism, pity to the distressed, resentment, and anger come under 'Our Affections.' This is by no means an exhaustive enumeration of the emotive forces of our being, nor does the handling show the keen insight of (say) Spinoza in pt. iii. of his *Ethica*; but it is a distinct advance on what had previously obtained in Great Britain.

A very marked characteristic of Stewart's prelections as a moral philosopher was the large place that he assigned in his teaching to the treatment of natural theology—dealing with the being and attributes of God, the soul and its future existence. This was, no doubt, due partly to his conviction of the intimate relation between ethics and religion (though he did not base the former on the latter), but partly also and chiefly to the circumstances and requirements of the time. When Stewart began his professorial work, it was the eve of the French Revolution; and all the while that he actively discharged the duties of the Moral Philosophy chair, scepticism and atheism, connected with that great political upheaval, were rampant. He felt it to be his duty, therefore, in teaching inquiring youth, to try to mould and strengthen their characters by high spiritual principles, while instructing and developing their minds. And so successful was he in his effort, and so great was his fame, that he attracted to his class-room not only students from the various parts of Scotland and England, but also students from the United States of America, and from France, Switzerland, the north of Germany, and other regions of Europe.

Stewart occupies a very distinct place in the school of Scottish philosophy. He was neither a deep nor an original thinker, but he was an elegant and eloquent expositor, who did great service to the study of philosophy by attracting general attention to it, by stimulating the youth to think, and by creating in them a love of high ideals—truth, virtue, and liberty. His own personality counted for much. He was a man of deep convictions and elevated views, and a master of style (in spoken address and in writing), fluent and harmonious. Enthusiastic himself, he could arouse enthusiasm in others. His scholarship was great: indeed, previous to Hamilton, he was the most learned of the Scottish philosophers. His facility in apt quotations, selected with unerring literary instinct and drawn from a wide range of reading, is quite exceptional. And yet 'his learning,' as Veitch correctly puts it, 'was more of an accomplishment than an inspiring originating element in his philosophy.' He was fortunate in being able to gauge and to minister to the intellectual and moral needs of the age. The fact that he made a lasting impression on such men as Lord Cockburn, Lord Brougham, and James Mill is testimony enough to his ability and worth; and the imposing monument erected to him on the Calton Hill of Edinburgh testifies to the high esteem in which he was held by the community.

2. William Hamilton.—The greatest name in the Scottish school of philosophy in the 19th cent. was that of Sir William Hamilton. Endowed with a powerful intellect and a strong will, Hamilton added to his natural capacities unrivalled erudition. He had all the qualifications of a successful writer of a history of philosophy. His position as a psychologist and as a metaphysician is outstanding. While retaining the fundamental principles of Reid's philosophy, he engrafted on them some of the distinctive tenets of Kant, with which he was among the first in Great Britain to be intimately acquainted. Although not more reliable in judgment than Reid, or keener in analytic faculty, he went deeper into the consideration of speculative problems; and he had the advantage of a singularly extensive knowledge of Greek and of Scholastic philosophy and of German thought. The result was that, while adhering to the Scottish school, he promulgated doctrines of his own which Reid would not have acknowledged. To psychology and metaphysics Hamilton added logic—in which Reid showed no special originality, as may be seen from his 'Brief Account of Aristotle's Logic.'[1] Here also he was an original expositor and innovator; and, although his logical system, in its specific positions (such as the quantification of the predicate), has not been generally accepted, it aroused an interest in the subject that has had lasting effects. To his other merits has to be added that of a lucid style—inflated, indeed, and overloaded with terms of classical formation, Johnsonian to a fault, yet attractive to the student beyond anything that the accredited philosophical text-books of the time could claim. His power of incisive, even vehement, criticism has also an attraction in its way; but his personal animosities—his intolerance, let us say—sometimes narrowed his view and misled him in the interpretation of opponents, and his vast scholarship was prone to make him accept authority for argument.

[1] *Works*^{2}, pp. 681–714.

A son of Dr. William Hamilton, professor of Anatomy in Glasgow University, Hamilton was born in Glasgow on 8th March 1788. His early education was received in his native city, including his Arts curriculum at the university and attendance on several of the medical classes (Chemistry and Anatomy), supplemented later by a brief attendance on medical classes in Edinburgh, with a view to Medicine as a profession. In 1807 he proceeded, as Snell Exhibitioner of Glasgow, to Balliol College, Oxford. Here he developed his learning, according to a plan of study devised by himself. The result was an unusually intimate knowledge of Aristotle and his commentators and of the history of philosophy. Both the number and the nature of the books on which he offered himself for examination with a view to his degree surprised the examiners; 'and after a trial of many hours, besides the honours of the University, he received the thanks and the public acknowledgment of the examiners, that he had never been surpassed either in the minute or the comprehensive knowledge of the systems on which he had been examined.'[1] He graduated 'In literis humanioribus,' in class I. This was in 1810. Abandoning the idea of entering the medical profession, he devoted himself to the study of Law, and, in 1813, became an advocate of the Scottish bar, with his residence henceforth in Edinburgh. Now, as always, learning was supreme with him, and, with the Advocates' Library at his command, he had ample opportunities of pursuing it. On this account he never aimed at, nor did he acquire, an extensive practice as an advocate. In 1816 he established his claim to the title and style of Baronet of Preston and Fingalton. In 1820 he became a candidate for the chair of Moral Philosophy in Edinburgh University on the death of Thomas Brown, but, being a Whig, was unsuccessful against John Wilson, a Tory. Next year, however, he was appointed to the chair of Civil History. It was not till 1836 that he was elected professor of Logic and Metaphysics—a dignity that he retained for the next twenty years.

Hamilton was late in life in appearing as a philosophical author: indeed, he was forty-one years of age when his first great production, the article on 'The Philosophy of the Unconditioned; in reference to Cousin's Infinito-Absolute,' saw the light, in the October number of the *Edinburgh Review*, 1829. To that review and to *Blackwood's Magazine* he made contributions on a variety of topics; and he also ventilated his opinions frequently in separate pamphlets or brochures. Education and the ecclesiastical movements of the time (ending in 'the Disruption'), as well as philosophy, greatly interested him, and he strongly advocated university reform. While busily engaged in formulating and elaborating his maturer thought in that storehouse of learning, the 'Notes' or 'Dissertations' in his edition of Reid's *Works*, he was stricken by paralysis, and the edition had to be brought out, in 1846, with the 'Notes' unfinished. Fortunately, his infirmity, while limiting his physical power, left him in full possession of his mental faculties; and he was able to go on with his university work till the end came on 6th May 1856.

His leading writings are his annotated edition of *The Works of Thomas Reid* (Edinburgh, 1846, [2]1849), *Discussions on Philosophy and Literature, Education and University Reform* (London, 1852, [2]1853), *The Collected Works of Dugald Stewart* (11 vols., Edinburgh, begun to be published in 1854 and completed by Veitch in 1860), *Lectures on Metaphysics and Logic* (4 vols., Edinburgh and London, 1859-60, published posthumously and edited by Mansel and Veitch).

Hamilton's great contributions to the Scottish philosophy were his searching and extensive handling of consciousness in note A ('On the Philosophy of Common Sense') in Reid's *Works*[2] (pp. 742-803) and his recasting and elaborate exposition of Reid's doctrine of natural realism in connexion with the perception of an external material world, in several of the other notes and elsewhere. To the philosophy of common sense were now given a precision and a fullness of statement that it did not possess before; and Reid was presented in a fresh and telling setting, although, in the process of amendment, he was sometimes transformed almost past recognition, and not infrequently the corrections suggested are doubtful improvements.

The final appeal made by Reid in his philosophy was to consciousness. So, too, by Hamilton. But what is consciousness? What are the tests of it? How is it conditioned and limited? What is its veracity—the intrinsic worth or value of it? In answering these questions Hamilton went back in part to Descartes, in part to the Greek philosophers, especially Aristotle and the Stoics; but he laid under contribution the whole of his vast reading, and he brought to bear on the subject his own acute and independent thinking.

To him consciousness is a sort of knowledge. But knowledge is of two kinds—immediate and mediate. Immediate knowledge is concerned with what is here and now present to the mind of the individual percipient. Its testimony is infallible and cannot be disputed; it must simply be accepted. Mediate knowledge is derivative—a consequence of, or deduction from, what is ultimate. It is knowledge at the second remove.

[1] Villers, in Veitch's *Memoir of Sir William Hamilton*, p. 60.

The tests of the data of consciousness, the criteria of the principles of common sense, the notes or characters by which we are able to distinguish our original from our derivative convictions, are laid down as four in number: (1) incomprehensibility—*i.e.*, there is nothing more fundamental than themselves, nothing higher to which they may be referred or by which they may be explained; (2) simplicity—the opposite of what is compound and therefore derivative; (3) necessity and absolute universality—securing unwavering conviction and excluding doubt; (4) comparative evidence and certainty—inasmuch as they are fundamental, and all else is known and believed through them. Valid as these tests are in themselves (although there are difficulties in the consistent application of them), they are obviously not mutually exclusive, but overlap: the first and the third include the other two.

Hamilton set himself with great energy to purify and strengthen Reid's doctrine of external perception—the central problem in his theory of knowledge. The vacillation and looseness of Reid's utterances here (especially in the *Inquiry*), more particularly the vagueness attaching to his double application of the term 'sensation' and his disconcerting statement that sensations are the *signs* of external objects, seemed to throw doubt on Reid's genuine adherence to natural realism—the doctrine of the immediate apprehension of external reality in sense-perception. The question would ever and anon suggest itself, Was Reid not, after all, a representationist, like his opponents, although the *tertium quid* between object and percipient was not with him an 'idea' but a 'sensation'? This ambiguity Hamilton proceeded to clear away. He reaffirmed Reid's distinction between sensation (subjective) and perception proper (objective) in the perceptive process and enunciated the law of the inverse ratio—the more fully we are engrossed with the one, at any moment, the less alive are we to the other, and *vice versa*; but he also explicitly formulated and repeatedly asserted the mutual implication of subject and object, Ego and non-Ego, in sense-perception: each is given, and each immediately, in the individual act of perceiving, and, while given in mutual relation, they are given also as distinct and contrasted—they are one in knowledge, but opposed in existence.

This, on the face of it, put natural realism in a direct and unambiguous way. But, unfortunately, in working out the subject in detail Hamilton enunciated qualifications and modifications that went far towards nullifying his original position. An excellent example of this is the case of visual perception of distant objects.

Here he alleged that 'As *not here present*, an immediate knowledge of an object *distant in space* is likewise [*i.e.* as well as an immediate knowledge of the *future*] impossible. For, as beyond the sphere of our organs and faculties, it cannot be known by them in itself; it can only therefore, if known at all, be known through something different from itself, that is mediately, in a reproductive or constructive act of imagination.'[1] Again, 'To this head we may refer Reid's *inaccuracy in regard to the precise object in perception*. This object is not, as he seems frequently to assert, any distant reality; for we are percipient of nothing but what is in proximate contact, in immediate relation, with our organs of sense. Distant realities we reach, not by perception, but by a subsequent process of inference founded thereon: and so far, as he somewhere says, from all men who look upon the sun perceiving the same object, in reality, every individual, in this instance, perceives a different object, nay, a different object in each several eye.'[2] This, clearly, was a sad departure from strict natural realism, and

[1] Reid's *Works*[2], p. 810[b]. [2] *Ib.* p. 814[a].

the critics seized upon it. None more effectively, or more facetiously, exposed it than Samuel Bailey[1] (1791–1870), who vividly pictures Hamilton lecturing to his class, consisting (say) of 100 students, whose eyes are directed towards the master. On Hamilton's doctrine, each student sees a different professor from what is seen by each of the others (indeed, two professors, for each student has two eyes), and, on the principle of the veracity of consciousness (to which Hamilton made constant appeal), he has a right to trust his own perception, so that there are 100 Sir William Hamiltons (not to insist on 200, 'a different object in each several eye') in the professorial garb. On the other hand, according to the doctrine that a distant object is not really perceived at all, but only inferred, no Sir William Hamilton is seen by the students, and the learned professor may literally be described as 'disappearing in the crowd.' These and other Hamiltonian inconsistencies Bailey discards and, in substituting his own view of strict natural realism, declares that our perception of external objects 'is a simple and primary act of consciousness not susceptible of any analysis or explanation,' and that it is 'vain trying to express the fact more simply or fully than by saying that he [the percipient] perceives the object.'[2] 'That there are external objects perceived,' he maintains further, 'is a primary fact, which admits neither of being proved nor of being disproved';[3] and he holds that this view of external perception is the only one that, on the lines of natural realism, secures absolute consistency.

But Hamilton essayed, further still, to strengthen and support the Reidian realism. He took up Reid's distinction of primary and secondary qualities of matter and worked it out with unparalleled minuteness in note D of his Reid's *Works*[2] (pp. 825–875, 'Distinction of the Primary and Secondary Qualities of Body'), carefully estimating the evidential value of each. He analyzed the qualities into primary, secundo-primary, and secondary, and laid great stress on the second. His distinctive point lies in the strong and explicit way in which he takes account of the human body as an animated organism, the seat of sensation, and the necessary instrument and condition of external perception—a factor in the perceptive act equally indispensable with the mental factor. Perception (he lays down) is the apprehension, in and through the organism, of resistance and extension. In thus laying our knowledge of resistance and extension (the leading qualities of externality or real being) in the organism, Hamilton anticipated the epistemology of the present day. But, further, one may observe that, while it is so that sensation would be unintelligible if the body were eliminated (man being not merely mind, but mind *plus* body), it is of importance to remember that the body occupies a very peculiar position: it is in one aspect subjective and in another objective. To this fact the psychology of to-day, which is above all things genetic, has become alive. The body as sensitive organism, with the organic sensations, is of the utmost significance in the genesis of the conception of the individual 'self.' The body is to the individual primarily the self, from which the completed notion of self takes its start, and which must still be taken account of even after we have reached the higher and developed idea.

Not yet was Hamilton's work in the interests of natural realism complete: it had a negative as well as a positive side. He did not regard it as enough to establish a position; he conceived it necessary also to beat down all opponents. Hence he carried on a vigorous polemic against representationists of all types—especially against what he called the 'cosmothetic idealism' of Thomas Brown. His criticism is always keen, but not always valid; indeed, not seldom it rests on an obvious lack of ability to realize and appreciate the opponent's point of view. Yet it served the purpose of bringing out Hamilton's own doctrine and of setting in a clearer light certain difficulties and dangers that beset the speculative thinker when engaged with theory of knowledge.

Truth, then, according to Hamilton, rests on the testimony of consciousness; from this source emanate such metaphysical principles as those of causality and substance. This is the teaching of common sense. But what gives to consciousness its authority? Simply the fact that it is a necessary and fundamental part of the native structure of the human mind. To impugn the veracity of its primary cognitions or to suppose them false would be 'to suppose that we are created capable of intelligence, in order to be made the victims of delusion; that God is a deceiver, and the root of our nature a lie.'[1] The only valid way of rebutting or disowning the data of consciousness would be to show, if possible, that the primary deliverances are contradictory of each other—either that they are incoherent among themselves or that there is an irremediable conflict in their consequences.

Hamilton was not satisfied with simply buttressing the philosophy of Reid; he put forth doctrines of his own. The centre of his independent speculation was the relativity of knowledge. 'To think,' as he put it, 'is to condition'; and so knowledge of the unconditioned is for us impossible. 'The last and highest consecration of all true religion is an altar—Ἀγνώστῳ Θεῷ—"*To the unknown and unknowable God.*"'[3] Yet, by the necessities of the case, we are driven to the belief in an unconditioned reality, lying beyond the conditioned. But, if the absolute and the infinite are incognizable by us, if they cannot be construed to thought, what are they? The one is simply the negation of the relative and the other the negation of the finite. Of each we have 'a negative notion' and nothing more. For anything further we are thrown upon faith — faith, however, not as irrational and unjustifiable credulity, but in the philosophical sense of the term as a rational trust, the spontaneous adherence of our nature to the conviction that behind all that is relative is the absolute, and that what appears is simply the manifestation, under conditions of finite experience, of what is.

The law of the conditioned is expressed thus: 'The Conditioned is the mean between two extremes,—two inconditionates, exclusive of each other, *neither of which can be conceived as possible*, but of which, on the principles of contradiction and excluded middle, *one must be admitted as necessary*.'[2] It testifies, therefore, to the inevitable weakness or limitation of the human faculties, but it does not charge them with being deceitful. On the other hand, the value that is claimed for it is not that it solves all intellectual puzzles, but that it enforces the fact that we must not take the capacity of thought as the measure of existence or maintain the realm of knowledge to be coextensive with that of faith. Which of the contradictory alternatives in any case is to be accepted by us (*e.g.*, whether liberty or necessity in the problem of the will) it cannot say; that must be determined on other grounds—such as the testimony of consciousness. Instances of contradictory alternatives both of which are inconceivable by us are to be found in connexion with space and time. It is impossible to conceive space as absolutely limited, as a complete totality. However far we may in thought push out the boundary of space, and however much we may try to regard space as completed there, we find ourselves constrained to represent to ourselves a space beyond. In like manner, we cannot conceive space as infinitely immense, as boundless. So with time. An absolute beginning of time and an endless duration (an infinite past) are alike inconceivable. But perhaps the application of the conditioned to the principle of causality is, in some respects, the

1 *Letters on the Philosophy of the Human Mind*, 2nd ser., pp. 54–56.
2 *Ib.* p. 57. 3 *Ib.*, 1st ser., p. 141.

1 Reid's *Works*[2], p. 743b. 2 *Discussions*[2], p. 15 n.
3 *Ib.* p. 15.

most interesting, as it shows strikingly Hamilton's departure from the position of the Scottish school on this important point. Reid and his disciples had regarded causality as a necessary principle—a primary positive affirmation of the mind, whose rejection in thought is impossible. But Hamilton refuses to accept this view and maintains that the judgment of causality, though *a priori*, is not original and positive, but derivative and negative—negative as a mental impotence, determined by the law of relativity. It is thus simply a corollary of the law of the conditioned, as applied to a thing thought under the form or mental category of 'existence relative in time.'

'We cannot know, we cannot think a thing, except under the attribute of *Existence*; we cannot know or think a thing to exist, except as *in Time*; and we cannot know or think a thing to exist in Time, and think it *absolutely to commence or terminate*. Now this at once imposes on us the judgment of causality. Unable positively to think an absolute commencement, our impotence to this drives us backwards on the notion of Cause; unable positively to think an absolute termination, our impotence to this drives us forwards on the notion of *Effect*.'[1]

This has not seemed conclusive even to Hamiltonians themselves; and it does not appear to be an undoubted improvement on Reid.

The difficulty with the doctrine of the conditioned in general is that it is impossible to see (1) how it can be legitimately fitted into the philosophy of the Scottish school, which Hamilton so vigorously upheld, and (2) how it can be made consistent with itself or agreeable to fact. A merely negative notion is psychologically impossible. To conceive a thing as existing at all is to that extent to conceive it positively; the conception may be vague, but it is positive. On the other hand, the distinction between knowledge and faith in order to bring back from the side of practical need what is incompetent to intelligence (a heritage from Kant, who inherited it from the Schoolmen) is vicious. Our nature is *one*, else there can be no such thing as truth.

Yet the doctrine of the conditioned, although vehemently attacked by J. S. Mill and others, had no small influence on subsequent British philosophy. It told in two quite different directions. On the one hand, it stimulated Dean Mansel, who accepted it in its entirety and made it the basis of his famous Bampton Lectures on *The Limits of Religious Thought* (London, 1858). On the other hand, it was taken up by Herbert Spencer (who, however, discarded the doctrine of 'the negative notion') and issued in his presentation of the ultimate reality as the unknown and the unknowable, worked out in his *First Principles* (London, 1862). This agnosticism, inherent in Hamilton's teaching, would certainly have staggered Reid.

The Hamiltonian philosophy, excepting the agnostic side of it, was a real power in Scotland during the second half of the 19th century. It lay at the root of the professorial prelections of Hamilton's two former assistants—Thomas Spencer Baynes (1823–87) in St. Andrews, and John Veitch (1829–94) in Glasgow—and of his favourite post-graduate student, A. Campbell Fraser (1819–1915) in Edinburgh. Of these three Veitch came forward as the avowed defender of Hamilton against the criticism of J. S. Mill;[2] and Fraser carried forward the principles of Reid to this striking theistic conclusion:

'True philosophy is . . . the moral and religious venture which accepts and applies the principles of common sense, in the assurance that, in genuine submission to their inspired authority, we cannot finally be put to intellectual or moral confusion. Faith in God is latent even in the perceptions of external sense, in which Reid found the first example of the operation of this inspiration. Alike in the outer world of the senses, and in free or responsible agency in man, filial faith, ethical or theistic, may be justified by reasoning, although it cannot be reached by logic as a direct conclusion from premises. It is our primary postulate, and not an object of logical proof; therefore credible in reason while it is not demonstrable.'[1]

This thesis is worked out in detail in Fraser's Gifford Lectures on the *Philosophy of Theism* (2 series, Edinburgh, 1895–96, reproduced, in an amended form, in 1 vol. in 1899).

3. But, altogether apart from Hamilton and his modification of Reid, Reid's philosophy during the 19th cent. was powerful abroad. Through Royer-Collard, Jouffroy, and Victor Cousin, it became supreme in France. In Germany it was highly thought of by Fichte; and Schopenhauer said of the *Inquiry*:

'Thomas Reid's book is very scholarly and well worth reading, ten times more so than anything that, taken in all, has been written since Kant.'[2]

In America it was kept alive by James McCosh, Noah Porter, and others.

III. *In the 20th century*.—At the present time the Scottish philosophy, after an eclipse in Great Britain, has come into view again. Not that Reid would now shape the lectures of any professor of philosophy in any of the universities, as he did formerly; but there is a marked tendency in many quarters to refer to him and quote him with respect and to claim his support as something worth having. A fillip to a fresh interest in him was given, in the end of last century, by A. Seth [Pringle-Pattison], in his Balfour Lectures on the *Scottish Philosophy* (^{2} 1890). This was followed by Henry Laurie's *Scottish Philosophy in its National Development* (1902), and by T. M. Forsyth's *English Philosophy* (1910); and, quite recently (1915), we have had a book of very judicious *Selections from the Scottish Philosophy of Common Sense*, by G. A. Johnston. It is, further, significant that the 'new realism,' however far from Reid it may be at many points, delights in attaching itself to him on occasion; and it would not be difficult to affiliate Bergson's doctrine of intuition to Reid's teaching. Certainly, modern movements in philosophy are suggestive in this connexion.

LITERATURE.—The works of the various writers of the Scottish school of philosophy have been duly enumerated in the text and need not be restated here. The following books (mostly additional to those mentioned in the text) may be noted.

I. *Biographical*.—A. C. Fraser, *Thomas Reid* (in 'Famous Scots' series), Edinburgh and London, 1898; William Forbes, *Account of the Life and Writings of James Beattie, LL.D.*^{2}, 3 vols., Edinburgh, 1807; Margaret Forbes, *Beattie and his Friends*, London, 1904; John Small, *Biographical Sketch of Adam Ferguson*, Edinburgh, 1864; John Veitch, *Memoir of Sir William Hamilton, Bart.*, Edinburgh and London, 1869.

II. *Expository*.—James McCosh, *The Scottish Philosophy*, London and New York, 1875; John Veitch, *Hamilton* (in Blackwood's 'Philosophical Classics'), Edinburgh and London, 1882; Andrew Seth [Pringle-Pattison], *Scottish Philosophy*^{2}, do. 1890; Henry Laurie, *Scottish Philosophy in its National Development*, Glasgow, 1902; T. M. Forsyth, *English Philosophy: a Study of its Method and General Development*, London, 1910; James Seth, *English Philosophers and Schools of Philosophy*, London and New York, 1912.

III. *Critical*.—Joseph Priestley, *An Examination of Dr. Reid's Inquiry, Dr. Beattie's Essay, and Dr. Oswald's Appeal*, London, 1774; Henry Calderwood, *The Philosophy of the Infinite*, Edinburgh, 1854; Samuel Bailey, *Letters on the Philosophy of the Human Mind*, 2nd ser., London, 1858; J. H. Stirling, *Sir William Hamilton: being the Philosophy of Perception: an Analysis*, do. 1865; J. S. Mill, *An Examination of Sir William Hamilton's Philosophy*^{2}, do. 1865; John Grote, *Exploratio Philosophica*, pt. i., Cambridge, 1865; David Masson, *Recent British Philosophy*^{2}, London, 1867.

WILLIAM L. DAVIDSON.

SCRIBES.—'Scribes,' as the title of a distinctive order in Judaism, denotes the character and vocation of a class which flourished between the return from the Exile in the middle of the 5th cent. B.C. and the collapse of the Jewish State under the Romans six centuries later.

---

[1] *Discussions*^{2}, p. 618 f.

[2] See his *Memoir of Sir William Hamilton*, and also his *Hamilton*, in Blackwood's 'Philosophical Classics.'

[1] *Thomas Reid*, p. 158.

[2] *Die Welt als Wille und Vorstellung*, Leipzig, vol. ii. ch. ii., Eng. tr., London, 1883–86.

I. Origin and development.—In the sense of secretaries, who kept minutes, wrote letters, and even superintended the royal archives, there had been 'scribes,' or *ṣōpherîm*, under the Hebrew monarchy, as under the Persian. These functionaries might be little more than clerks like the Roman *scribæ quæstorii* or letter-writers; when attached to the army, as they still were in the Maccabæan age (1 Mac 5^{42}), they probably corresponded to subordinate officials like provost-marshals or quartermasters, who might be in charge of accounts and army-lists of men and booty. But at court the *ṣōpher* often held a more responsible position, as a secretary of State. Since his main business consisted in managing the royal correspondence, he was called 'the scribe,' the man who could write. What he wrote, as a rule, was letters for other people. They dictated; he transcribed. It was only after the fall of the monarchy that circumstances arose which led to the development of 'scribes,' in a new and technical sense, as a religious order in Judaism. These circumstances were the consolidation of the Jews as a community of the Law,[1] and the consequent need of expert students who should interpret the Tôrāh and apply its authentic decisions to the changing, varied conditions of the people.[2] It is unnecessary for our present purpose to tell over again the familiar story of this religious transformation. The point is that the *ṣōpherîm* of the post-Exilic age were not court officials, but men of the Book, charged with the task not only of copying its contents but of enforcing its administration as a code, of elucidating its bearing upon questions of practical conduct, and of instructing the bulk of the nation on their duties to its regulations. They had to be competent in a variety of ways, but the fundamental requirement for scribes was that they must be proficient in the oracles of the Law.[3]

Since γραμματεύς in Egypt covered practically all officials who had to deal with documents, from secretaries to registrars and clerks, as well as military officers, the LXX translators were free to employ this Greek term as a rule for the Hebrew *ṣōpher* in both of the senses already noted. The Vulgate *scriba* led to the English rendering 'scribe,' which in modern times has a connotation narrower than its original scope, and certainly narrower than the range of the Jewish *ṣōpher's* activities. The editing and transmission of the sacred text was only one of his functions. The *ṣōpherîm* were *literati*, not mere copyists in the mediæval monastic sense of 'scribes.' They were bookmen, authors. Even their editing involved knowledge, scholarship, and commenting. Furthermore, the supreme importance of the Tôrāh for national life led them to be educationalists and jurists. But these functions varied according to the exigencies of the day; now one element, now another, was prominent in the vocation of these exponents of the Tôrāh.

The 'scribe' as a professional penman, who took down what was dictated, was of course a familiar figure (Ps 45^{1}); later he became the *libellarius* of Judaism, who copied scrolls, phylacteries, etc. On the other hand, the scribes who tampered with the text of Deuteronomy (Jer 8^{8}) and a private secretary like Baruch (Jer 36^{26}) were more than copyists or clerks of this kind. Both lines of activity continued in the post-Exilic vocation of the scribes, but their functions became still more ramified and specialized as Judaism was driven back upon itself. The conventional idea of the Jewish scribes is twofold: that they were dull drudges, and that they were the deadly antagonists of Jesus. The former is a misapprehension; and to understand the latter it is necessary to survey their rise and scope within post-Exilic and particularly post-Maccabæan Judaism.

The origin and the development of the scribes during the post-Exilic period are still uncertain at several points; it is difficult, from the extant data, to determine the changes which passed over them as a class or even the tendencies which gradually shaped them into a class. But the general outline is fairly clear. Previous to the Maccabæan movement they seem to have been associated mainly with the priests. During the Exile the interest in national literature as an organ of continuity and unity stirred the scribes. The Tôrāh was compiled and edited by sacerdotal authorities, especially under the influence of Ezekiel, the outstanding priest and prophet of Judaism in Babylonia. Ezra himself was of priestly descent, and Levites (cf. 2 Ch 34^{13}) supported him in his endeavour to stamp the Law upon the conscience of the community. Indeed, the very formation of the Priestly Code expressed the conviction that 'in the future the delivering act of God would have to be preceded by a thorough sanctification of His people';[1] and, as this holiness involved the scrupulous and minute pressure of the Law upon life, the interests of the scribes from Ezra onwards and of the priests coincided, although the former acquired a broader and more popular position in the nation, since the cultus was no longer the be-all and end-all of religion. M. Jastrow[2] has shown that in a passage like Lv 13–14, as elsewhere in the Priestly Code, the addition of glosses, comments, and illustrations, which characterize the Mishnāh and the Gemārā, can be already traced. At this period the scribe and the priest had much in common, and this affinity continued. Thus Simon the Just (beginning of 3rd cent. B.C.), who flourished among the last of the primitive scribes entitled 'men of the Great Synagogue,'[3] was high-priest. For the most part, during this period, and even down to the time of Sirach, a scribe might be a priest, and a priest might be a scribe. Their interests were largely the same, but the scribal interest in the Law-book was naturally wider than that of the priests. The scribes were not yet the rigid canonists that they afterwards became. During the Greek period, in fact, they were often indistinguishable from the 'wise men.' The sketch of the ideal scribe in Sir 38^{24}–39^{11} suggests at any rate that his functions were not invariably associated with the scholastic study of the OT text or confined to Biblical interpretation. The scribal aim, according to Ezr 7^{10}, was threefold: 'to seek (search, study) the Law of the Lord, and to do it, and to teach in Israel rules and duties.' But Sirach ignores Ezra, perhaps 'because the only public services assigned to Ezra by the record were such as it would have equally depressed Ben Sira to speak of, and grieved his disciples to hear.'[4] Sirach correlates the Law with wisdom; his scribe has humanist interests as well as personal piety; he travels abroad, associates with courts and kings, and draws the materials of his knowledge and instruction from wider sources than the Tôrāh and its sacred tradition; he is a man of culture, with education and experience of the world. This portrait may be a protest against some contemporary tendency in scribism; it is possible to take it as an implicit criticism of elements which seemed to Sirach unduly narrow. But it is safe to infer that hitherto the line of demarcation between scribe and wise man was not sharply drawn, and perhaps that even the exclusive study of the Law had not yet amounted to anything like a characteristic feature of the scribes. It is obvious that the ordinary scribe was not absorbed in the regulations of the cultus; the obligations of the Tôrāh were much wider than the sacrificial ritual. Yet neither was he confined to the general study of the Law as an exclusive code of conduct and devotion. The scribal movement as yet had affinities to the wisdom-movement; if we cannot identify the 'wise men' or sages of Judaism at this period with the contemporary scribes, we are still less able to think of them as two independent

[1] *ERE* vii. 455, 587. [2] Cf. *ib.* vii. 855 f.
[3] *Ib.* ii. 97, 565 f.

[1] Cf. T. K. Cheyne, *Jewish Religious Life after the Exile*, New York and London, 1898, p. 80 f.
[2] *JQR* iv. [1914] 357 f. [3] *Pirqē Ābhôth*, i. 2.
[4] Cheyne, p. 210.

companies of teachers. Both made themselves responsible for teaching true 'wisdom' to the people, and both enjoyed a measure of religious intuition; it was not yet a case of tradition *versus* humanism or fresh inspiration.[1] There were scribes who had cosmopolitan interests, and scribism was still unidentified with Biblicism.

Sirach's enthusiasm for the vocation of scribe prompts him to sketch an attractive outline. He claims that the vocation of scribe requires culture and leisure such as are impossible to tradesmen and artisans and peasants; these people, he admits, are useful in their place—no city can get on without them—but (38^{33}–39^{11})

'None seeks them for advice on public affairs,[2]
and they hold no rank in the assembly;
they do not sit on the judicial bench,
and have no knowledge of law and justice;
they do not expound the requirements of wisdom,
nor grasp the proverbs of the wise.
What they understand is their handiwork,
and their thoughts are for the practice of their craft.
Not so he who sets himself to the fear of God
and ponders the Law of the most High,
who explores the wisdom of all the ancients
and is absorbed in the prophets of old,
who treasures the teaching of famous men
and reflects on what is deep,
who probes for the secret meaning of proverbs
and is familiar with enigmatic parables,
who serves great men
and appears before princes,
who travels in foreign lands,
testing what is good and what is evil among men,
who is careful to pray to the Lord that made him
and entreats mercy from the most High,
who opens his mouth in prayer
and makes supplication for his sins.
If it seems good to God most High,
he shall be made wise with the spirit of understanding.[3]
He pours out a double measure of wise sayings,
and gives thanks to the Lord in prayer.
He understands parables of the wise,
and meditates on their mysteries.
He sets forth the requirements of wisdom,
and glories in the law of the Lord's covenant.
Many praise his intelligence,
and his name shall never be blotted out;
his memory shall not pass away,
and his name shall live from generation to generation.
The congregation proclaims his wisdom,
and the assembly publishes his praise.
If he lives on, he shall be reckoned happier than a thousand,
and when he dies, his name and fame are ample.

The Maccabæan reaction against Hellenism was a turning-point in the evolution of the scribes.[4] Their vocation was at once contracted and intensified. The aristocratic priesthood lost the confidence of the people owing to their laxity, and the scribes now found themselves in opposition[5] to the sacerdotal authorities, obliged to uphold and enforce the Law at all costs. One outcome of this development was the popularization of the Law, which was no longer a predominantly sacerdotal interest. Another was the recruiting of the scribes from the ranks of the people; they became more and more a lay order[6] —no longer men of leisure who looked down upon manual labour, but for the most part students of the Law who supported themselves by a trade, declining to accept remuneration for their labours. This is a decisive change; it marks the rise of the scribes as we know them in the NT and the Mishnāh, where their power and sayings are now chronicled, and the legend of their unbroken succession is urged. To quote only one proof of their significance: we find that the thirteenth Benediction of the *Shemoneh 'Esreh*, which in its present form preserves an interesting memento of the Jewish community at the Maccabæan period,[1] definitely includes the scribes:

'Towards the righteous [*ṣaddikîm*] and the pious [*ḥasîdîm*], towards the elders of thy people the house of Israel, towards the remnant of their scribes [*sōpherîm*] . . . may thy tender mercies be stirred, O Lord our God.'[2] This is an incidental but remarkable proof of the tenacious memory which Judaism cherished of their Maccabæan rôle.

Then and thereafter the scribes contributed materially to the preservation of genuine religion under the Law. They deserved the grateful homage of posterity. The new conditions narrowed their horizon;[3] the older humanistic outlook passed away, and, when the Law, as the embodiment of all that man required to know and read, preoccupied their minds, the freer spirit of the former scribes waned; but this was the price paid for the intensity with which they enforced the claims of the Law, and the scribes probably did not regret it, in view of their fresh prestige and power within the nation. Cosmopolitan culture was now suspect. Any centrifugal tendency was resisted. Nothing mattered, if they could prevent the religious tone of Judaism from being secularized and preserve its unity from disintegration. Down to the revolt of Bar-Cochba, Greek was not eschewed entirely, it is true. But the stress of their study lay elsewhere.

2. Functions.—According to the *Bābā Bāthrā*, 14*b*, 'the men of the Great Synagogue wrote Ezekiel, the Twelve (prophets), Daniel and Esther. Ezra wrote his own book and the genealogies of the Book of Chronicles as far as (the mention of) himself.' Whatever basis (if any) underlies the rabbinic tradition that the great convocation of Neh 8–10 was an institution called 'the Great Synagogue,' which superintended the codification and administration of the Law for a generation and more, the early 'scribes' did undertake authorship. Sirach, himself a scribe, argues[4] that 'those who read [the Scriptures] must not only become skilled themselves but must also, as lovers of learning, be able to serve outsiders by speaking *and writing*.' 'The scribe,' as the man who describes and records things in heaven as well as on earth, was the title of Enoch in the book of Enoch; and the author of 4 Esdras (14^{50}) applied it to Esdras. The scribes, in fact, edited and composed; it is to them that we owe books like Chronicles, Jubilees, the Aramaic Aḥikar, and even some of the early Apocalypses—not merely compilations and extracts, but expositions and original works of a semi-Biblical kind. But, as time went on, when the canon was practically closed, and the exigencies of the situation made the Law more and more the business and bosom of the national life, the scribes ceased to produce literature; originality of this kind was not merely irrelevant, it was inconsistent; and their prominent services to practical religion were rendered eventually in what a modern would term (*a*) the-

[1] Cf. J. Wellhausen, *Israelitische und jüdische Geschichte*[6], Berlin, 1907, p. 195 f.

[2] It is this practical knowledge of the world, combined with the sway of a teacher over youth, that probably leads Josephus to call them *σοφισταί*—not at all, of course, in a derogatory sense. He attributes the popular rising against Herod and his golden eagles to the influence of two Jerusalem scribes. In one account (*BJ* I. xxxiii. 2) they are called *σοφισταὶ κατὰ τὴν πόλιν, μάλιστα δοκοῦντες ἀκριβοῦν τὰ πάτρια, καὶ διὰ τοῦτ᾽ ἐν παντὶ τῷ ἔθνει μεγίστης ἠξιωμένοι δόξης . . . τούτοις οὐκ ὀλίγοι προσῄεσαν τῶν νέων ἐξηγοῦμενοις τοὺς νόμους.* The other account (*Ant.* XVII. vi. 2) describes them as *ἐξηγηταὶ τῶν πατρίων νόμων, ἄνδρες καὶ δήμῳ προσφιλεῖς διὰ παιδείαν τοῦ νεωτέρου.* But in Sirach's day the scribes had not yet taken so active a part in stirring up public opinion, and indeed their normal function was always that of pedagogues rather than demagogues.

[3] Scribes who breathed this atmosphere would look back to a prophet like Ezekiel as their prototype; they would carry on the divine inspiration for teaching men religion, which had been degraded by prophets who had become fanatics, demagogues, and visionaries.

[4] Cf. *ERE* ix. 553 f. [5] Cf. *ib.* 553[b].

[6] By the time that the Chronicler wrote they must have been formed into gilds or families (cf. 1 Ch 2^{55}).

[1] Eleazar, one of the great Maccabæan martyrs (2 Mac 7^{12}), was a distinguished scribe, and the *Test. XII Patr.* (Levi 8^{17}) predicts Maccabæan 'priests and judges and scribes.'

[2] Cf. I. Abrahams, *Annotated Edition of the Authorised Daily Prayer Book*, London, 1914, p. lxv.

[3] A partial historical parallel is the Protestant scholasticism which followed the rediscovery of the Bible after the Reformation; it was not altogether devoid of mysticism, and it helped to preserve religion during a transition period, but it could not furnish a permanent basis for the development of a living faith.

[4] Prol. 3 f.

ology, (*b*) education, and (*c*) jurisprudence, all three revolving round the study of the Law as Tôrāh or authoritative instruction.

(*a*) *Theology.*—The scribes edited, fixed, and transmitted the Hebrew text in an authoritative form, emending[1] it when necessary. In view of the Samaritan schism, this became specially important. They also elaborated and codified a system of common or traditional law, interpreting the written Tôrāh, explaining or explaining away its discrepancies, and clearing up its ambiguities; the technical term for this was '"to make a fence to the Thorah": to surround it with a margin of casuistry; to evolve the principles which underlay its words; to develop and apply its decrees, accommodating them to the varied requirements of the time.'[2] This function arose from the valuation of the Law. Wittingly or unwittingly, a man might infringe the Law in a dozen ways, as he ate, as he acted on the Sabbath, and so forth; consequently precautions had to be taken, and additional restrictions set up, to prevent such transgressions. It was an elaborate and delicate business, but the scribes were equal to it, as their record proves. They 'fenced' the Tôrāh. This amplification of the Law was at first conveyed orally (παράδοσις), for there could only be one *written* Law, but, as the oral law professed to do no more than draw out what was implicit in the Pentateuch, it was supposed to possess Mosaic authority in its punctilious regulations for faith and conduct. The nation was living under very different conditions from those in which the original Law had been drawn up; old regulations had to be modified or even abrogated, and fresh religious sanctions and prohibitions were necessary, in order to preserve the faith from being contaminated. Now it was the scribe's business to adjust these to the written Law somehow, by reading them into the text or by altering the text, in order to invest them with an authority equal to that of the text. He had also to put the meaning of the Hebrew code into the current Aramaic dialect. The work required ingenuity and mental as well as moral aptitude. Thus Ezra (Ezr 7[6]) is called 'a ready scribe in the law of Moses,' *i.e.* apt in interpretation, skilful, quick-witted, and shrewd. Scribes often differed in their views,[3] and the echoes of controversy as well as of diplomatic evasions linger in the Mishnāh, where we can also overhear them often in their fanciful and artificial manipulation of texts, for the sake of edification. The better spirit of their work is described sympathetically by Lauterbach in the *Year-book of Central Conference of American Rabbis*, xxiii. [1913] 249–287, 'The Ethics of the Halakah.' Their aims are justifiable historically. Fundamentally the motive of their work was sincere and legitimate. The conception of revelation as embodied in a sacrosanct code left no other alternative open to the religious leaders of Judaism than to claim Mosaic authority for practical inferences and deductions drawn from what this complicated code said or did not say, about minute and central things alike. These regulations were laid down for the sake of a genuine nationalistic piety. But the method involved serious dangers and abuses. It made religion unduly complex and scholastic; it at once encouraged and tampered with scruples; it tended to subordinate the fundamental moral obligations to ritual niceties; and occasionally among its indirect effects were externalism and rigidity.[4] To be Biblical is not necessarily the same thing as to be spiritual. The attitude of the scribes in the Gospels is the first, though not the only, illustration of this truth upon a large scale.

(*b*) *Education.*—The equally responsible task of diffusing religious knowledge among the people devolved naturally on those who were responsible for determining the standards of piety; and the scribes, as νομοδιδάσκαλοι or πατρίων ἐξηγηταὶ νόμων (Josephus), or ἱερογραμματεῖς or καθηγήται, gave themselves faithfully to this task. They imparted their teaching by means of addresses delivered not only in the synagogues[1] but in private houses (their own and other people's) and in the open air, as well as at the Temple. They were not confined to their headquarters at Jerusalem. Among those who came to examine the mission of Jesus, *e.g.*, were 'Pharisees and teachers of the law who had come from every village of Galilee and Judæa and Jerusalem' (Lk 5[17]). R. Johanan, according to Jerus. *Shabbāth*, 16, spent several years in Galilee as a teacher, though he was distressed to find the Galilæans sadly indifferent to his legalism. The activities of the scribes were wide-spread, within and beyond Palestine, and the weekly reading of the Law in the synagogues furnished them with an opportunity for reaching the common people with religious instruction in the shape of *halākhôth*. If Lauterbach[2] is right in his hypothesis, these *halākhôth* remained strictly expositions of or comments on the Law, down to the period of Simon the Just, after which abstract *halākhôth*, or independent traditional laws, were more and more taught in Mishnāh form (lacking Scripture proof). The object of the latter was to justify practices and customs which had sprung up in the nation, and which could not be furnished with any precedent either in the Law or in tradition. These later 'scribes' first found official authority in the Sanhedrin under Antigonus of Socho. But the change in the form of the *halākhôth* left the educational aim unaltered. The individual under the Law constantly required the scribe to explain his duties and interpret the bearings of the code in any given case. Ezra's supporters (Neh 8[8]) 'read in the book in the law of God distinctly, and gave the sense, so that the people understood what was read,' *i.e.*, they supplied a running commentary to elucidate the text. This expository function was maintained and developed by the later scribes; they busied themselves with *halākhāh* rather than with *haggādāh*; 'what the scribes say' carried weight in popular esteem, not because they posed as authorities or claimed inspiration, but because they taught what they had received as the orthodox and original meaning of the Law, which had to be evolved from it by means of their tradition. Such was their regular and distinctive rôle. The congregational worship of the synagogues did something to familiarize Jews with the Law, but the masses required an ampler education in the principles and practice of their religion, and generations of expert scribes must have thrown themselves into this mission of popular instruction. Whether or not they took any direct part in the education of children,[3] they trained men to their own profession; their disciples or scholars, endowed with a retentive memory and an implicit deference to tradition, carried on their work and were proud to do them honour. The influence which they possessed ultimately among the people

1 By the 3rd cent. A.D. these corrections of the ancient text were called *tiķķune ṣōpherîm* (cf. *JE* viii. 366 f.).

2 C. Taylor, *Sayings of the Jewish Fathers*[2], Cambridge, 1897, p. 111.

3 Cf. J. Z. Lauterbach, in *JQR* vi. [1915] 304 f.

4 The *halākhāh*, of course, was constantly changing—once scruples start, they go on. But the innovations only added to the network of the Law, and (theoretically at any rate) the individual 'dragged at each remove a lengthening chain.' The παράδοσις πατρῷα or πρεσβύτερων, long before it was put into writing (cf. H. L. Strack, *Einleitung in den Talmud*[4], Leipzig, 1908, p. 10 f.), claimed authority as emanating from Moses and regulated the practical life and worship of the devout.

1 Cf. art. SYNAGOGUE.

2 *JQR* vi. 23 f.

3 Cf. *ERE* v. 195.

and the deference which they received may be illustrated from two sentences of their severest critic. 'The scribes and Pharisees sit on the seat of Moses; so do whatever they tell you, obey them' (Mt 23[2f.]). This was spoken by Jesus to the people. It is not ironical. Jesus recognized the validity of the Law as a divine instruction for the people, and even the need of obeying the scribes in so far as their precepts and principles were true to the spirit of the Law; what He objects to is the failure of the scribes to practise what they preached, *i.e.* to live up to their ideal (see Ezr 7[10], quoted above). Again, in a different tone He charges them with using their powerful influence and authority to prevent people from becoming adherents of His cause: 'Woe to you jurists! you have taken away the key that unlocks the door of knowledge; you have not entered yourselves, and you have stopped those who were entering' (Lk 11[52]). The difference between their methods and those of Jesus was plain to any audience. When the people were impressed by the difference between Jesus and the scribes in teaching—'He taught them like an authority, not like the[1] scribes' (Mk 1[22], Mt 7[29])—the meaning is that Jesus showed an originality and an independence which were foreign to the scribes. He had a direct intuition of God, which made His message convincing.

'His teaching is fresher and more instinct with genius than that of the Rabbis, of whose teachings we have records in the Talmud and Midrash.'[2]

They taught with authority, but appealed strictly to precedent and tradition. One of the virtues of Joḥanan ben Zakkai, *e.g.*, according to the eulogy in *Sukkāh*, 28*a*, is that 'he never uttered a word which he had not heard from the lips of his teacher.' But Jesus did not speak in inverted commas. Thus, *e.g.*, none of His parables is even exegetical, whereas most of the scribes' parables start from an OT text. Jesus elsewhere denounced them for their self-righteousness, their hypocrisy, their ostentation, and their unscrupulousness. 'Beware of the scribes! they like to walk about in long robes, to get saluted in the market-places, to secure the front seats in the synagogues and the best places at banquets; they prey upon the property of widows and offer long unreal prayers' (Mk 12[38-40]). If the charge of avarice refers to legacies which rich widows were induced to contribute to the support of rabbinical study, the scribes were guilty of the same conduct as disgraced the Roman clergy in Jerome's day. The other charges can be illustrated from the pages of Josephus and of the Talmud. Paul's only allusion to them (1 Co 1[20]) is in an OT quotation; it echoes the saying of Jesus in Mt 11[25]. But not all were degenerate. There were those among the scribal teachers who were not unwilling to keep an open mind or unable to appreciate the prophetic spirit of Jesus Himself (cf. Lk 10[25f.], Mk 12[28f.]); the scribes seem even to have furnished the primitive Church with some recruits (cf. Mt 13[52] 23[34]),[3] one of whom at least is known by name (Tit 3[13]: Ζηνᾶν τὸν νομικόν).

(*c*) *Jurisprudence.*—As the Law ruled the Jewish community, it was naturally the scribes (νομικοί) who took a leading place in pronouncing judgment upon what was permissible or unorthodox and in helping to enforce penalties upon those who broke the Law and tradition. They would exercise a strong indirect influence by their expert interpretations. They would not only discuss and decide cases of casuistry, but also investigate error and even upon occasion sentence an offender. Their ranks, as well as those of the priests, supplied members to the supreme court of the Sanhedrin (*q.v.*) at Jerusalem, which would formally ratify their interpretations as binding on the community. As responsible for the government and orthodoxy of the nation, they extended their jurisdiction to the provinces; thus, *e.g.*, we find that Jesus, whom they suspected of blasphemy and of lax intercourse with disreputable creatures like tax-gatherers, is threatened by their interference even in Galilee, and subsequently is condemned by them in the capital. This administrative authority fell to the scribes after their allies, the Pharisees, had become the governing party in the land. There must have been Sadducæan scribes, for both Sadducees and Pharisees appealed to the interpretation of the Law, but the development of the oral tradition and the popularity of the Pharisaic view of the Law gave special scope to the activity of the scribes, and we are not surprised to find 'the scribes and the Pharisees' so closely and constantly associated in antagonism to a prophet like Jesus. After the fall of Jerusalem this judicial power waned.

'After the last desperate struggle of the Jews for liberty under Hadrian, A.D. 132–135, the Scribes, no longer able to find a practical outlet for their influence in the guidance of the State, devoted themselves to systematizing and writing down the traditional Law in the stage which it had then reached. This systematization took shape in the collection which is called the Mishna.'[1]

When the Jewish State collapsed, the scribes passed finally into the rabbis.[2] But under Herod the Great and his immediate successors their judicial authority was in full play. Juristic influence attached to the scribes from an early period in their history,[3] and the paramount position of the Pharisees increased it. To what extent it survived the catastrophe of A.D. 70 seems uncertain, although the juridical activities of the scribes must have been restricted then[4] and less vital than their work at Jamnia and elsewhere on behalf of the Tôrāh. It is remarkable that the only mention[5] of them in the Fourth Gospel (Jn 7[53]–8[11])—or, at any rate, in an early Christian fragment which has become attached to the Fourth Gospel—is in connexion with their responsibility for public morals. 'The scribes and Pharisees brought a woman who had been caught in the act of committing adultery.' They asked Jesus for His opinion on the offender, not because they felt uncertain themselves,[6] but in the hope of drawing from Him a verdict which might convict Him of unorthodoxy. They intervened against the disciples (Ac 4[5]) and against Stephen (Ac 6[12]) in virtue of their judicial authority, and with this mention they pass out of the NT; like the first allusion to them in the NT (Mt 2[4]), it is sufficient to emphasize the fact that they were not literary recluses and to correct the impression, suggested by their English title, that they were no more than religious men of letters.

LITERATURE.—The phases and functions of scribism are discussed in all treatises on the history and religion of Judaism, particularly in connexion with the Pharisees (*q.v.*). Some of the older special literature is chronicled by Schürer (*GJV*[4] ii. 372 f.). Among recent contributions the following are noteworthy: **W. D. Morrison**, *The Jews under Roman Rule*, Lon-

[1] Matthew reads 'their' (αὐτῶν); he recognizes Christian γραμματεῖς.

[2] C. G. Montefiore, *The Synoptic Gospels*, London, 1909, ii. 555.

[3] The difficult saying in Mt 13[52] may perhaps be intelligible in the light of Is 22[15], where γραμματεύς (A) renders the Hebrew term for 'house-steward'; taken thus, it would tally with the following allusion to stores, the 'scribe' being not a man of the pen but a steward. The 'kingdom' probably denotes the moral and religious experience of Christian disciples, and the 'the old and new things' may refer to the order of grace in nature, as exemplified in the preceding parables.

[1] *OTJC*[2], p. 50. [2] Cf. *ERE* vii. 593.

[3] See Sirach's testimony above, § I.

[4] Cf. H. P. Chajes, in *REJ* xlix. [1899] 39 f.

[5] On the 'scribism' attacked and exposed in the Fourth Gospel see E. A. Abbott, *The Founding of the New Kingdom*, Cambridge, 1917, p. 286 f.

[6] Cf. *ERE* i. 130[b].

don, 1890, p. 273 ff.; A. Réville, *Jésus de Nazareth*, Paris, 1897, i. 89 f.; W. R. Smith, *OTJC*, lect. iii.; O. Holtzmann, *Die jüdische Schriftgelehrsamkeit zur Zeit Jesu*, Giessen, 1901; D. Eaton, in *HDB* iv. 420 f.; J. D. Prince, in *EBi* iv. 4321–4329; M. Seligsohn, in *JE* xi. 123 f.; J. W. Lightley, *Les Scribes: Etude sur leur origine chez les Israélites*, Paris and Cahors, 1905; H. L. Strack, in *RE*³ xvi. 775–779; W. Bousset, *Die Religion des Judentums*², Berlin, 1906, p. 186 f.; J. Mitchell, in *DCG* ii. 582–584; G. A. Smith, *Jerusalem*, London, 1908, ii. 364 f., 386 f.; B. Stade and A. Bertholet, *Biblische Theologie des AT*, Tübingen, 1911, ii. 335 ff.; A. Marmorstein, *Die Schriftgelehrten*, Skotschau, 1912; H. Lesêtre, in Vigouroux's *DB* v. [1912] 1536–1542; G. H. Box, 'Scribes and Sadducees in the New Testament,' in *Exp*, 8th ser., xv. [1918] 401 f., xvi. [1918] 55 f.

JAMES MOFFATT.

SCRIPTURE.—See BIBLE, INFALLIBILITY, INSPIRATION, REVELATION.

SCYTHIANS.—**1. Name.**—Scythian (Σκύθης, derivation unknown) has meant variously (1) a nomad tribe inhabiting the steppes north of the Black Sea from about the 7th to the 1st cent. B.C.; (2) this tribe with the various peoples in and round the steppe that it had subjugated; (3) any barbarian, especially a nomad, from the north-east quadrant of the world;[1] (4) later geographers—*e.g.*, Ptolemy—unwilling to drop the name, found a place for it in N. Asia, but common usage still connected it with the Black Sea; and (5) the Byzantines called new invaders like the Goths and Russians by the classical name of Scythians. In this article it will be used in (1), the narrowest sense. For the nomads of N. Asia the Persian inscriptions and Greek authors using Persian sources employ the term 'Saka,' which is possibly the same word as 'Scyth.'[2]

2. Geography.—Herodotus gives two mutually irreconcilable descriptions of Scythia.[3] The general meaning is that Scythia extended from the Danube to the Don and inland to the edge of the forest, a line running E.N.E. from the Bukovina to about Samara. In the western half were Tyritæ on the Dnestr, and south to north, from Olbia at the mouth of the Bug to the government of Kiev, stretched tribes called Callipidæ, Alazones, Scythæ Georgi, Scythæ Aroteres, all probably representing an older partly agricultural population and subject to the Royal or nomad Scyths. These ranged over the eastern half between the Dnepr, the Sea of Azov, and the Don, and over the northern part of the Crimea, the southern part of which was held by the non-Scythian Tauri. Round the borders of Scythia so defined dwelt Getæ south of the Danube, Agathyrsi in Transylvania, Neuri in Volhynia and the government of Kiev, Androphagi north of Chernigov, Melanchlæni north of Tambov, Budini with a trading settlement, Gelonus, on the middle Volga above Samara, Sauromatæ east of the Don, and Mæotæ east of the Sea of Azov.

3. History.—The tradition of a very early Scythian empire in Asia,[4] if it has any foundation, probably goes back to Hittite rule. The real historian of the Scyths is Herodotus. He gives three legends as to their origin: the first two, variations of the same tale, represent them as autochthonous and seem really to belong to a settled tribe, not to nomads; in the third story the Massagetæ on the Oxus and Jaxartes, perhaps, as says Aristeas, quoted by Herodotus, themselves impelled by Issedones and Arimaspi farther east, drove the Scyths out of Asia across the Araxes (Volga?) into Europe against the Cimmerians in S. Russia. These were cut in two, part driven west to join the Thracians, part forced through the Caucasus. The Scyths pursued these and, missing their way, found themselves in Media, which they ruled for 28 years. Then the Medes (*q.v.*) expelled them by the rising ever after commemorated at the feast called Sacæa,[1] and they returned to their own S. Russia. This story finds confirmation in Assyrian records. Asarhaddon's inscriptions (680 B.C.) tell of Gimirrai, north of Urartu (Ararat), attacked from the north by Aš-gu-za-ai (or Iš-ku-za-ai) and thus forced to invade the vassal state of Man and incur the enmity of Assyria. The latter made friends with the Ašguzaai and used them not only to drive the Gimirrai west, but in the next generation against the Medes and apparently against Egypt, so that parties of them plundered Ascalon[2] and held Bethshan, hence called Scythopolis.[3] Gimirrai is clearly the Gomer of Gn $10^{2f.}$ and the Cimmerii of Herodotus; Ašguzaai = Ashkenaz (אשכנז, miswritten for אשכוז) and Scyth. The incursion into Palestine is referred to in Jeremiah (4^{3}–6^{20}; cf. Ezk 38–39^{16}). It is, however, possible that some of these invaders were not true Scyths penetrating the Caucasus, but Sacæ from the east of the Caspian.[4]

So the Scyths returned from Media to S. Russia and re-established their lordship over the slaves whom they had left behind. We know nothing of their history for over a century but the tale of Anacharsis (*c.* 530 B.C.), who was so attracted by the life of the Greeks now established in colonies along the Euxine coasts that he actually journeyed to Greece, but on his return was slain by his kinsfolk for being untrue to their ancestral customs. According to Herodotus, Darius, king of Persia, about 512 B.C. marched through Macedonia and Thrace, crossed the Danube, leaving the Ionians with orders to guard his bridge for 60 days, and invaded Scythia. Enticed by the Scyths as far as the river Oarus (Volga?), he began eight forts, but, leaving them unfinished, turned west again and was led round the edges of the country, through the lands of the border nations who had refused to help against the invader. Meanwhile the Scyths had tried to get the Ionians to desert and destroy the bridge, but they kept it in being even beyond the date promised. Finally Darius, unable to come up with the Scyths and running short of provisions, abandoned his wounded and baggage and returned hastily to the bridge. Ctesias and Strabo make much less of the expedition, which was probably a more or less unsuccessful demonstration meant to protect the new Persian conquests and magnified to exhibit the poor spirit of the Ionians and the advantages of nomad warfare. In revenge the Scyths made a raid that reached the Thracian Chersonese, drove out Miltiades, and even proposed to Cleomenes of Sparta a joint invasion of Asia. During the 5th cent. Scythian archers were employed as police in Athens. They are often represented on painted vases, but it is hard to distinguish their equipment from that of Persians, Amazons, and the like.

Shortly before the time of Herodotus Scyles, the Scythian king, undeterred by the fate of Anacharsis, had married a Greek wife and adopted Greek ways. He came to a like end, and his successor, Octamasades, is the last of the line whom we can name. We have hardly any glimpses of Scythia during the 4th and 3rd centuries B.C.; in the latter part of the 4th the Sauromatæ were still east of the Don or just crossing; in 179 B.C.

[1] Of our two first-hand authorities, Hippocrates, *de Aëre, Aquis et Locis*, 24–30, keeps to (1), save that he includes as Scyths with a difference their eastern neighbours, the Sauromatæ; Herodotus, i. 103–106, 215 f., iv. 1–144, vii. 64, varies between (1) and (2); both expressly reject (3), the ordinary Greek use found in the other authors, who make but passing allusions to Scyths or wrote after their disappearance.

[2] Cf. Herod. vii. 64.

[3] iv. 16–20 and 99–101.

[4] Tr. Pomp. *ap.* Justin, i. 1, ii. 2 ff.; Diod. Sic. i. 55, ii. 43.

[1] Strabo, XI. viii. 4.

[2] Herod. i. 105.

[3] Josephus, *Ant.* XII. viii. 5.

[4] See H. Winckler, *Altorientalische Forschungen*, Leipzig, 1893–1906, i. 484 ff., 'Kimmerier, Ašguzäer, Skythen'; H. R. Hall, *The Ancient Hist. of the Near East*, London, 1913, pp. 495, 511.

Gatalus ὁ Σαρμάτης (the first occurrence of this form usual in later Greek writers and universal in Latin), now clearly in Europe, joined a league of Pontic states.[1] Long before this the Scyths' centre of gravity seems to have shifted westwards; their king, Atheas, defeated the Triballi on the lower Danube, but was himself defeated by Philip of Macedon (339 B.C.).[2] In an inscription *c.* 200 B.C.[3] we find the Scyths asking the men of Olbia for protection against the attacks of Galatæ and Sciri, invaders from Central Europe. In its last definite appearance the name Scyth is applied to the people of King Scilurus. Coins suggest that the kings of a Scythian remnant about the Danube mouth regained a certain amount of power and that the last of them, Scilurus, became suzerain over Olbia and extended his dominion as far as the Crimea. Inscriptions show that he had a kind of capital at Kermenchik, near Simferopol, entered into close relations with the Tauri, and threatened the city of Chersonesus. The latter called in the help of Mithridates and thereby defeated Palacus, son of Scilurus.[4] The Scythian element in the kingdom of Scilurus scarcely amounted to more than a name; and, when Strabo, rejecting the tradition of Herodotus, makes a fresh survey of the north coast of the Euxine, he finds no real Scythians there and speaks only of various Sarmatian tribes.

4. Physical characteristics, customs, etc.—Hippocrates,[5] discussing the effect of climate upon human physique, describes the peculiarities of the Scythians, whom he finds as little like other men as are the Egyptians. The special points are a close mutual resemblance, a reddish (πυρρός) complexion, a fatness, slackness, and excess of humours, a look as of eunuchs, and in certain cases a sexual indifference that amounts to actual impotence. This disease was well known; Herodotus[6] says that it was incurred through the sack of the temple of Derceto at Ascalon, but Hippocrates declares it to be a disease just like any other disease, and due to excessive riding. Men thus afflicted took their place absolutely among the women and were called 'Enarees.' He adds that all this applies only to the most noble and rich among the Scyths. The women, he says, always sit in waggons, whereas among the Sauromatæ they ride astride and take their share even in war.

Herodotus[7] gives a full account of Scythian customs; almost always he has in view the nomad Scyths, but some details seem to contradict their general scheme of life and are more probably true of the agricultural Scythians near Olbia, whence Herodotus seems to have obtained his information. The life of the nomad Scyths was conditioned by the necessity of tending their beasts; chief of these was the horse, used for riding (alone of the ancients the Scyths used geldings) and also to supply meat and mare's milk, kumys, cheese, butter, and butter-milk (τυρός and βουτυρός are perhaps Scythian loan-words), while the oxen drew the great waggons in which the women lived. They also ate sheep and game, but eschewed the pig. They used some vegetable food—grain, onions, garlic, and wild bulbs; when they could get it, they drank wine, and, unlike the Greeks, they drank it neat. For cooking they used great cauldrons; or they cooked an animal in its own skin, burning the bones at the same time. Of their dress he tells us only that they wore belts and trousers and pointed caps (*cyrbasia*). Their great weapon was the bow, with arrows and quiver, used from horseback; accordingly it was not a simple self-bow but a rather short bow with a complicated curve compared to that of the north coast of the Euxine. They also used darts, short swords (*acinaces*) or daggers (ἐγχειρίδιον), and axes (*sagaris*). For defence they had shields and scale-armour.

Their political organization consisted of an over-king, under-kings, nobles, freemen, and slaves. The women of the Scyths themselves rode in the waggons and had apparently much less freedom than those of the other nomad peoples (Sarmatæ, Massagetæ, and the like), and among them we hear of Queens Tomyris, Zarinaia, Amage, and Tirgatao. The kings were polygamous and married foreign women. On his father's death the son took over his wives, excepting of course his own mother. Their warlike tactics are proverbial—retiring before an invader, wasting the country, cutting off his supplies, harassing his rear, enticing him by feigned flight, and gradually exhausting him, while the nomads carry their supplies with them and are perfectly mobile. When they attack other countries, they leave no forces to guard their own, being quite independent of their base and so able to concentrate all their strength upon one point. But, when Thucydides[1] says that, as the most numerous people of the world, they could, united, vanquish any other nation, he exaggerates both their number and their power.

5. Religion.[2]—The Scythians reverenced chiefly Tabiti (=Hestia); next to her Papæus (=Zeus) with his wife Apia (=Ge); after them Goetosyros (=Apollo), Argimpasa (=Aphrodite Urania), and Ares. Thamimasadas (=Poseidon) was peculiar to the Royal Scyths. They raised no statues, altars, or temples to their gods, except to Ares. Their general way of sacrificing was as follows: the beast, usually a horse, took his stand with his fore-feet tied together; the sacrificer pulled the end of the rope from behind and brought him down; then he called upon the god and strangled the victim. Ares was worshipped in the form of a sword set on a platform of brushwood three furlongs square, heaped up in each district; besides horses and sheep they sacrificed to him one out of every hundred prisoners, pouring his blood upon the sword. The Ares cult suggests the more settled tribes of W. Scythia, where masses of brushwood would be obtainable; the native name is not given, and this points to a different source. The Scythian pantheon tells us very little; we do not know what aspect of the multiform Greek deities answered to the Scythian, nor can we establish the true form of the names of the latter.

6. Witchcraft.—Witchcraft[3] played a great part in Scythian life. The wizards divined with bundles of sticks, and the Enarees by plaiting bast. If the king fell sick, it was because some one had sworn by the royal hearth and had broken his oath, thus bringing down upon the king the deity's vengeance. Accordingly the wizards were called in to name the perjurer, and he escaped with his life only if he could adduce two sets of wizards to declare him innocent. If wizards were judged to have brought a false accusation, they were burnt on a pyre set on a cart.

The ceremony for taking oaths and swearing blood-brotherhood is widely spread: the parties mix their blood with wine in great cups, put therein a sword, arrows, an axe, and a dart, and, after praying long over it, drink it together.

7. Funeral customs.—In the case of the kings funeral customs[4] are very magnificent and cruel; the burials take place in the land of the Gerrhi, near the great bend of the Dnepr, and to this region the king is brought, wherever he may have died. The body is embalmed and put on a waggon. Its attendants disfigure themselves and all whom they meet, as they bring it from tribe to tribe to the appointed place, where it is laid in a great square pit under a roof of wicker-work. They strangle and lay in the vacant space one of the dead man's

[1] Polybius, xxv. ii. [xxvi. vi.] 12.
[2] Justin, ix. 2; Strabo, VII. iii. 18; he may have been king of the Getæ, who are constantly mentioned in this region; but some Scythians held the Dobrudzha, or it would not have gained the name of Little Scythia.
[3] *CIG* ii. 2058; V. V. Latyschev, *Inscr. Oræ Septent. Ponti Euxini*, Petrograd, 1885, i. 16.
[4] Strabo, VII. iii. 17, 18, iv. 3, 7, and a Chersonesan inscription (Latyschev), i. 185, *c.* 106 B.C.
[5] *Loc. cit.* [6] i. 105. [7] iv. 50–75.

[1] ii. 96. [2] Herod. iv. 59–62.
[3] *Ib.* 67–69. [4] *Ib.* 71–73.

concubines, his cup-bearer, cook, groom, and messenger, also horses, set by him his cups of gold (they make no use of silver or bronze) and firstlings of all his possessions and over all they raise a great mound. After a year they slay 50 of his favourite servants, free Scyths all, and 50 horses, stuff them and set them in a circle round the mound. An ordinary Scyth when dead is carried about on a waggon to visit his friends, who feast the dead man and his attendants, until, after 40 days, he is laid in his grave.

One or two other customs may be worth mention: that by which a Scyth who has slain an enemy in war drinks his blood and scalps him, the scalp being a voucher in the distribution of booty, and the making into cups of the skulls of private adversaries vanquished in combat before the king show an extreme of barbarism; in iv. 73–75 Herodotus seems to describe three separate customs under one—a ceremonial purification from the taint of a corpse, the usual vapour-bath still popular in Russia, and a custom of intoxication with the vapour of hemp; he adds that the women whitened their skin with a paste of pounded cypress, cedar, and frankincense, which suggests considerable luxury and wide commercial connexions.

This picture of Scythian life is supplemented, and on the whole confirmed, by the results of excavations made in S. Russia during the past hundred years. Though no tomb can be said exactly to correspond to the ritual described by Herodotus, nearly every point can be paralleled from some burial or other. From Podolia and the south part of the Kiev and Poltava governments, south to the Euxine and the neighbourhood of the Greek cities of the Crimea and east across the Dnepr and Don to the valley of the Kuban along the north slope of the Caucasus, we find groups of barrows of every size up to 70 ft. high and 400 ft. across. The best are mostly about the bend of the Dnepr, just where we should seek the land of Gerrhus. The oldest contain skeletons coloured red and a few pots, but the rich contents of the greater number show them to be tombs of nomad people in touch with Assyrian, Iranian, and Greek civilization and dating from about the 7th cent. B.C. to the period of the great migrations. Most of them have been plundered, either just after their construction or by successive generations of tomb-robbers, but a few have kept their treasures, at any rate in part, to reward scientific investigation. We may take as an example the latest great find, made by N. I. Veselovski in 1912–13.[1]

The tumulus Solokha is 15 miles south of Nicopol in the middle of the Gerrhus group. In the centre had been the tomb of a woman arrayed in all her finery (now stolen) and supplied with drinking-vessels, a cauldron, and a gridiron, and near by two horses with gold trappings. In the south-east part of the mound, approached by a deep shaft and a covered way, was a larger chamber, containing the body of a king or chief, by him his sword-bearer, and another servant near the entrance. A little to the west was a second pit with the skeletons of five horses and a groom by them. Clearly the queen had died first, and the king had later been put into the same barrow. Other examples show that, if the king had died, his wife would have immediately followed him into the grave. The king's grave-goods were wonderfully rich: he wore a great lion-ended torque and five gold bracelets; some 300 gold plaques with repoussé designs, flowers, beasts, and human figures were sewn on to his pall; above his head lay a bone-handled knife, a rusted sword, a coat of mail, a pair of greaves, a wooden cup to which gold plates had been nailed; by his shoulder lay a bronze Greek helmet; by his right arm two iron lances and a copper mace; by his leg a leather *gorytus* (combination quiver and bow-case); by his right hip two iron swords, one of them with a gold haft and a peculiar sheath. Not far from his right shoulder was a wonderful golden comb of the finest Greek work, adorned with figures of three warriors; near by stood seven silver cups with men or animals in relief. In niches in the wall of the chamber, among other things, were ten Greek wine-jars, three great cauldrons with beef and mutton bones, and another amphora, a colander, and a silver-mounted drinking-horn; a special hiding-place held a *gorytus* of repoussé silver, bearing a wonderful representation of Scythians in combat and containing 180 arrow-heads, and a great golden saucer with a central boss, animals in repoussé all round, and an obliterated Greek inscription. The whole may be dated *c.* 300 B.C.

The general inventory of the other great tombs is much the same and is dictated by the same ideas as the funeral rites described by Herodotus, illustrating them in such details as the presence of wooden tabernacles over the body, the remains of the funeral car and the funeral feast, etc. Discrepancies are the presence of silver and bronze and the rarity of any kind of axe. As to their style, the objects found are (1) a few Assyrian and perhaps Iranian, (2) archaic Ionian, (3) native Scythic, (4) 'finest' and Hellenistic Greek. Some of the last are of extreme beauty, and they are important as being easily dated and as presenting detailed representations of Scythians. Women's gear and things of general use are mostly of this class; weapons (except the *goryti*) and horse-trappings are usually of the other three. The native craftsman, though utterly failing to imitate the finest Greek work, succeeded better with the Ionian style, but imported into it a grotesque element recalling Upper Asia and Siberia, sometimes even China; he was very fond of animals, especially reindeer, and beasts and birds of prey, so foreshadowing the beast style of the great migration period. The most interesting types (both known also in Siberia) are the cauldron and the short sword with a heart-shaped guard; its sheath has a side projection and a separate tip necessary for a special way of suspending it from the belt; just such are shown upon bas-reliefs at Persepolis.

8. Ethnic origin.—The Scythians and Sarmatians used to be regarded as the ancestors of the Slavs; these are rather to be found among their north-west neighbours, the Neuri, the northern tribes adjoining being probably Finns. Niebuhr, and after him Neumann, struck by the many detailed resemblances in custom, took the Scyths to be Mongols or Turko-Tatars. Müllenhoff declared them, on the basis of the few names and words preserved, to be Iranians. No doubt Iranians formed the great bulk of the steppe population before the great migrations; this is proved by the foreign names in Greek inscriptions from Olbia and Tanais, most of which can be explained from the Iranian language of the Ossetes, a people now confined to the central Caucasus, but undoubtedly a remnant of the Sarmatians.[1] But it looks as if in the true Scyth dominant caste there was an element similar to the Huns, early Turks, and the like; this type is suggested by Hippocrates (εὐνουχοειδέσταττοι),[2] by 5th cent. Greek terra-cottas of Sacæ from Memphis, showing that the Mongoloid type was already not confined to the extreme north-east of Asia, and by certain representations of natives found in Solokha. These all have beards, but this feature is quickly introduced by any crossing with Iranian blood. If the rulers were non-Aryan, it would explain why many words—*e.g.*, the god names—do not lend themselves to Iranian interpretation, though indeed no suggestions are very convincing. Similar customs too are mostly the product of similar physical conditions. Still the balance of the evidence inclines to the view that, while the steppe-population—*e.g.*, the Cimmerians and agricultural Scythians—was predominantly Iranian, the actual name Scyth belongs to a horde akin to the Turko-Tatars, which made great inroads in the 7th cent., was decadent by the 5th, and gave way in the 3rd to the Sarmatians with Iranian views of religion, of kingship,[3] and of the freer position of women natural among nomads.

[1] See *Illustrated London News*, 3rd January, 14th February, 1914; and S. Polovtseff, in *RA*, 1914, i. 164.

[1] See art. OSSETIC RELIGION.

[2] *Loc. cit.* (30).

[3] M. I. Rostovtsev, *Iranism and Ionism*, London, 1913. The author is projecting a general account of things Scythian in English.

The substitution of the Sarmatians was a change of name rather than of population or general mode of life, and the 'Scythic' tombs belong at least as much to Sarmatians as to Scyths.

LITERATURE.—K. Neumann, *Die Hellenen im Skythenlande*, Berlin, 1855; K. Müllenhoff, *Deutsche Altertumskunde*, do. 1898–1900, iii. 101 ff.; O. Peisker, *The Cambridge Medieval History*, i. [1911] 323–359; Imperial Archæological Commission, Petrograd, *Antiquités de la Scythie d'Hérodote*, 1866–73, *Compte rendu*, 1859–88 (French), 1889– (Russian), *Bulletin* (Russian), 1901– ; N. P. Kondakoff, J. Tolstoi, and S. Reinach, *Antiquités de la Russie méridionale*, 3 pts., Paris, 1891–92; E. H. Minns, *Scythians and Greeks*, Cambridge, 1913.

E. H. MINNS.

SEA, SEA-GODS.—See WATER, WATER-GODS.

SE'ADIAH.—Se'adiah b. Joseph, the most prominent *gāôn* of the Jewish academy at Sura, inaugurated a new epoch in all branches of Jewish learning. He was born in Dilāẓ, Upper Egypt, in 892 and died at Sura in 942. Originally his name probably was Sa'īd (سعيد=Fortunatus), a form which he uses acrostically in some of his earlier writings. Later he adopted the Hebrew form סַעְדְיָה, or, fuller, סעדיהו (=Se'adiah; the commonly accepted pronunciation, Saadya, is therefore incorrect). He is often surnamed al-Fayyūmī, *i.e.* 'of Fayyūm' (the Egyptian province near which Dilāẓ is situated), for which, owing to a mistaken identification by Se'adiah of Fayyūm with the Biblical Pitom,[1] Hebrew sources, especially those of Ḳaraite origin, usually substitute ha-Pitomi. Earlier mediæval Hebrew authors, particularly Abraham Ibn Ezra, mostly refer to Se'adiah simply as 'the *gāôn*,' without thinking it necessary to mention the name.

1. Life.—Of Se'adiah's origin and family relations very little is known. In some recently discovered documents whose authors were inimical to Se'adiah the claim is made that he was of non-Jewish origin, while he himself traces his pedigree to Shelah[2] and to the Mishnic teacher Ḥanina b. Dosa.[3] None of these assertions has any historical basis. The truth appears to be that Se'adiah was of humble Jewish parentage, his father, a pious and learned man, deriving his livelihood from some trade. A son of Se'adiah, Dosa by name, made a great reputation for himself as a scholar and is often referred to also as *gāôn*.

The circumstances of Se'adiah's youth and earlier education, both Jewish and secular, are likewise a matter of conjecture, as indeed is all our knowledge of the inner history of the Jews in Egypt during that period. It is quite certain, however, that the Ḳaraites (*q.v.*) had settled in various parts of Egypt at a very early time, and that, in their eagerness to make converts to their cause among the Rabbanites, they displayed a considerable literary activity in the various branches of Jewish studies, especially Hebrew grammar, Bible exegesis, calendar, and theology, which in turn served as an incentive to the intellectual elements among the adherents of traditional Judaism to devote themselves to the same courses of study, so as to be able to defend tradition with the same scientific weapons as their adversaries used. Se'adiah, who, as his subsequent career shows, was of a fearless and somewhat contentious character, took up the fight against Ḳaraism while still a very young man, which brought upon him the wrath and persecution of the fanatic devotees of the new creed. It was no doubt the persecution of the Ḳaraites that forced Se'adiah to leave his native country in the year 915 and to emigrate to the East. Here we lose trace of him for a while, but from certain letters of his, written about seven years later, we learn that he had lived in Palestine, probably in the city of Tiberias, renowned as the seat of the Masorites. There he came in contact with numerous scholars, among them the famous Masorite Moses ben Asher, and a certain 'Abū Kathīr Yaḥya ibn Zakariyya, who, according to the report of the Arabian polyhistor 'Alī al-Mas'ūdī († 957), became Se'adiah's teacher. This 'Abū Kathīr, with whom al-Mas'ūdī had a disputation on several religious-philosophic questions,[1] probably introduced Se'adiah into the field of philosophy, in which he was later to become the first and foremost exponent of mediæval Jewry. Se'adiah's association in the East with the Jewish philosopher David ibn Merwān al-Muḳammaṣ must likewise have influenced him in that direction.

In the years 921–923 we find Se'adiah embroiled in the fierce struggle that had broken out at that time between the Palestinian *nasī*, Ben Meir, and the heads of the Babylonian academies, Ben Meir trying to wrest from the latter the supremacy which they held over all Jewry, especially their old prerogative of fixing the calendar, and to restore it to the Palestinian authorities. Being a man of great influence, Ben Meir had almost succeeded in bringing over the communities to his side, and it was only through the energetic intervention of Se'adiah, who sent out circular letters and wrote a special work in defence of the Babylonian cause, that Ben Meir and his following met with a crushing defeat. In reward for this, Se'adiah was joined as an *'allūf* (chief judge, third in rank below the *gāôn*) to the staff of the Sura academy, in which position he remained until 928. In that year the gaonate had become vacant through death, and the then exilarch, David b. Zakkai, appointed Se'adiah to the office. It was not very long, however, before a bitter quarrel broke out between the new *gāôn* and the exilarch on account of an illegal procedure by the latter in a certain lawsuit which was calculated to bring him great profit, and which Se'adiah, as an upright man, would not countenance. The exilarch, as was customary in those times, excommunicated the *gāôn* and appointed another man as his successor (*c.* 930). Se'adiah, by the power vested in him, retaliated in kind and declared David b. Zakkai to be no longer exilarch. Babylonian Jewry was immediately split into two opposing factions, the one siding with the exilarch, the other with the *gāôn*. For two years Se'adiah maintained himself in the office in spite of all opposition, but finally the exilarchal party, headed by the very wealthy and learned Aaron Sargāda (שכנארה), who offered a heavy bribe to the *khalīfah* for Se'adiah's deposition, succeeded in having him definitely removed from the gaonate (beginning of 933). Se'adiah then retired into private life, devoting himself entirely to his scientific work (933–937). In the meantime the strife which divided Babylonian Jewry continued unabated and often degenerated into open fights and even street riots. Some of the prominent men of the Baghdād community, finding the situation unbearable, urged a certain Bishr b. Aaron, father-in-law of Sargāda and a man of great influence, to try to bring about a reconciliation between the exilarch and Se'adiah, and Bishr succeeded in effecting this. Se'adiah was reinstated in his office (937), but held it for only five years. The excitement and suffering that he had undergone during the seven years of war with the exilarch had undermined his health and in 942 he died, as is reported, of melancholy, at the age of fifty, two years after the death of David b. Zakkai.

Se'adiah was undoubtedly one of the greatest men that mediæval Jewry ever produced. His universal mind embraced all branches of human knowledge cultivated by Jews and Arabs of his

[1] Ex 1[11]. [2] 1 Ch 4[21]. [3] *Ābhôth*, iii. 9 f.

[1] Goldziher, *REJ* xlvii. [1903] 41.

time. With him begins a new epoch in the history and development of Jewish learning and literature. He was the first scientific writer in the fields of Hebrew grammar and philology, Biblical exegesis, and synagogal liturgy, the first systematic expounder of Talmudic lore, and above all the pioneer and path-finder in the field of Jewish religious philosophy. His forceful personality left an indelible impress upon his age, and his literary achievements exercised a lasting influence on subsequent generations throughout the Middle Ages, even down to our own time.

2. Works.—It is impossible here to give an adequate appreciation of Se'adiah's very extensive life-work. Besides, most of his writings have come to us in fragmentary form or are known only from quotations in the works of later authors. The following is a general description of his more important works. Those of minor importance or not sufficiently known are referred to summarily.

(*a*) *Hebrew philology.*—(1) *'Agrōn*, a Hebrew dictionary in two parts with the special view of facilitating versification, preceded by a rhetorical introduction in pure Biblical Hebrew, in which the author briefly summarizes the history of the Hebrew language, deplores its neglect by the Jews of his day, and urges them to devote themselves again to its study and cultivation. Se'adiah wrote this work, his first production so far as is known, in his twentieth year (913), while yet in Egypt. Several years later he issued the work in an enlarged edition, containing also portions treating of the various themes of poetry, under the changed title, *Kitāb al-shi'r al-'ibrānī* ('Book on Hebrew Poetry'), and added an Arabic introduction which is of great historical value. Apart from a few very short fragments of the book, only the two introductions, nearly complete, have been preserved and were published by A. Harkavy, in *Studien und Mittheilungen*, Berlin, 1891, v. 40–57. For numerous bibliographical and other details see H. Malter, *Life and Works of Saadia Gaon*, Philadelphia, 1919, *s.v.* 'Agron.'

(2) *Kutub al-Lughah* ('Books on Language'), a grammatical work in twelve parts, the oldest work known on Hebrew grammar, of which, however, only fragments are extant; see W. Bacher, *Die Anfänge der hebräischen Grammatik*, Leipzig, 1895, pp. 38–62; Malter, Bibliography, i. 2.

(3) *Tafsīr al-sab'ina lafẓah al-farīdah* ('Explanation of the Seventy Isolated Words'). In this little work, which was published several times, the author explains on the basis of later Hebrew (Mishnāh) the Hebrew and Aramaic words which occur in the Bible only once or very rarely. The list actually contains the explanation of 91 words; hence the word *sab'ina* must be a scribal error, or represents the original number, which was later increased by the author or others; see Malter, Bibliography, i. 3.

(*b*) *Bible translation and exegesis.*—Se'adiah's translation of the Bible into Arabic, accompanied by extensive Arabic commentaries—the first in the Arabic language—ushered in a new epoch in the history of Judaism and to some extent of civilization in general. For, just as the Septuagint had been instrumental in bringing about that blending of Jewish and Greek thought know as Hellenism, so did Se'adiah's translation and interpretation of the Scriptures prepare the way for the inauguration of the famous Spanish-Arabic period in the history of the Jews during which they had again become the mediators between the Orient and the Occident and themselves made original contributions to all branches of mediæval science. Se'adiah's translation became the standard Arabic Bible for all Arabic-speaking Jews as well as for the Christian scholarly world down to our time.

The translation of the Pentateuch is contained in the Polyglot Bibles of Constantinople (1546), Paris (1645), and London (1657). In the Paris edition the Arabic text was translated into Latin by Gabriel Sionita, and the Hebrew characters of the *editio princeps* were transliterated into Arabic, which was the cause of innumerable mistakes in the text. A later edition (Jerusalem, 1894–1901), under the title תאג, Hebrew כתר תורה (see *JQR* xiv. [1902] 584, n. 1), is based on other MSS, in the possession of Yemenite Jews. A critical edition with Se'adiah's Arabic introduction appeared in Paris (1893) as the first volume of the *Œuvres complètes de R. Saadia ben Iosef Al-Fayyoûmi*, edited by J. Derenbourg. Genesis and Exodus in a somewhat different recension were published by P. de Lagarde from a Leyden MS in his *Materialien zur Geschichte und Kritik des Pentateuchs*, Leipzig, 1867.

Of the long commentary on the Pentateuch numerous fragments have been discovered among the Genizah MSS within the last twenty-five years and were sporadically published, partly with English translations, by various scholars. For a detailed description see Malter, Bibliography, *s.v.* 'Bible.'

Of Se'adiah's translations of and commentaries on other Biblical books the following have been preserved:

Isaiah, first poorly edited by H. E. G. Paulus, Jena, 1790–91 (see S. Munk, *Notice sur Rabbi Saadia Gaon*, Paris, 1838, p. 29 ff.). Joseph and Hartwig Derenbourg edited the translation and the extant portions of the commentary as vol. iii. of *Œuvres complètes*, Paris, 1896 (containing also a French translation of the Arabic text).

Psalms.—Extracts with a German translation were published by G. H. A. von Ewald in his *Beiträge zur Geschichte der ältesten Auslegung*, i. 9–74, 154–160. Psalms 1–20 were published by S. H. Margulies (Breslau, 1884); 21–41 by S. Lehmann (Berlin, 1901); 42–49, 84, 87, 88 by T. Hofmann (*Die korachitischen Psalmen*, Stuttgart, 1891); 50–72 by S. Baron (Berlin, 1900); 73–89 by S. Galliner (Berlin, 1903); 107–124 by J. Z. Lauterbach (Berlin, 1903); 125–150 by B. Schreier (Berlin, 1904). Thus only Pss 90–106 are still awaiting publication, which was announced by E. Weil. All these editions, except that of Hofmann, bear the title *Saadia Al-fajjûmi's arabische Psalmenübersetzung*, and all contain also Se'adiah's commentary on the respective Psalms. A double introduction to this work by Se'adiah was published by S. Eppenstein in *Festschrift zu Ehren des Dr. A. Harkavy*, Petrograd, 1908, pp. 135–160 (cf. *MWJ* viii. [1881] 1–19, 61–91).

Proverbs, translation and commentary, forming the sixth volume of *Œuvres complètes*, edited and translated into French by J. Derenbourg and M. Lambert, Paris, 1894 (cf. Jonas Bondi, *Das Spruchbuch nach Saadia*, Halle, 1888; B. Heller, *REJ* xxxvii. [1898] 72–85, 226–251).

Job, translation and commentary, was first edited by J. Cohn (Altona, 1889) and then again with additional material and copious notes by W. Bacher in vol. v. of *Œuvres complètes* (Paris, 1899), which contains also a French translation by J. and H. Derenbourg.

Daniel.—The translation was edited by H. Spiegel (*Saadia al-Fajjûmi's arabische Danielversion*, Berlin, 1906). The commentary exists in MS. Extracts from it were published by S. A. Poznański, *MGWJ* xlvi. [1902] 415 f.; cf. the Hebrew periodical *Ha-Gōren*, ii. [1909] 92–103.

There appeared also translations, partly with commentaries, of *Canticles*, *Ruth*, and *Esther* (cf. A. Merx, *Die Saadjanische Übersetzung des Hohen Liedes*, Heidelberg, 1882; M. Peritz, *Zwei alte arabische Übersetzungen des Buches Rûth*, Berlin, 1900; Poznański, *MGWJ* xlvi. 364–372), but they do not represent the original text of Se'adiah. They are later editions of the *gāôn's* works by anonymous authors who often modified and amplified the original wording; for further details see Malter, *s.v.* 'Five Scrolls.'

(*c*) *Liturgy.*—In his desire to strengthen traditional Judaism and to further the religious life of the Jews in the Diaspora, Se'adiah set himself the task of collecting all the ancient standard prayers and hymns as well as the liturgical productions of famous synagogal poets (Yannai, Eleazar, Ḳalīr, and others) and arranging them systematically in a so-called *Siddûr* or *Sēder* ('Order of Prayers') for the whole year.

In this work, which was first discovered by Steinschneider (1851) in a Bodleian MS and is as yet unpublished, Se'adiah embodied several liturgical compositions of his own. Some of these, among them a lengthy didactic poem on the 613 precepts of the Tōrâh (תר״יג מצות), the so-called *'azhārōth* ('exhortations') on the same subject, and two highly poetical Hebrew prayers (*baḳḳāshōth*), were published in J. Rosenberg's *Ḳōbēẓ*, Berlin, 1856; cf. also *Œuvres complètes*, ix. [Paris, 1897] 57–69; J. Bondi, *Der Siddūr des R. Saadia Gaon*, Frankfort a. M., 1904. A considerable number of liturgical compositions by Se'adiah were incorporated in the various rituals still in use in the synagogues. Some, more recently discovered, appeared in periodicals and other publications. For a detailed enumeration and description see Malter, *s.v.* 'Liturgy.' Here is to be mentioned only Se'adiah's 'Poem on the Number of Letters' in the Bible, which was repeatedly published and commented upon, by Buxtorf the Elder in his *Tiberias*, Basel, 1620, p. 183 ff., and C. D. Ginsburg, in *The Masoreth ha-Masoreth of Elias Levita*, London, 1867, pp. 271–278, and especially by J. Derenbourg in *Manuel du Lecteur*, Paris, 1871, pp. 139, 235 ff.

(*d*) *Halākhā.*—Se'adiah's work in this specifically Jewish field of learning was of the greatest importance, setting an example to future generations in the scientific and systematic treatment of the vast Talmudic material. Unfortunately most of his writings in this line have been lost, only three having been preserved, as it appears, in a complete form, while the others exist only in small fragments or are known from extracts and quotations in the works of later authors. So far as can be seen from the existing material, Se'adiah's Halākhic writings were divided into three classes: (1) methodology, (2) interpretation, and (3) codification of the Talmud.

(1) Of the works belonging to the first class we possess only the Hebrew translation of the originally Arabic *Interpretation of the Thirteen Hermeneutic Rules* (פרוש י״ג מדות), published first by S. Schechter in the periodical בית תלמוד, iv. [Vienna, 1885] 235–244 and re-edited by J. Müller in *Œuvres complètes*, ix. 74–83. Another methodological work, *Introduction to the Talmud*, no longer exists; cf. L. Ginzberg, *Geonica*, i. 163.

(2) None of the works of the second class (commentaries on the Mishnāh and various tractates of the Talmud) has been preserved, with the exception of a very short *Commentary on the Tractate Berākôth*, containing merely lexical notes. It was edited from a Genizah MS by S. A. Wertheimer, Jerusalem, 1908; cf. Ginzberg, p. 164.

(3) About a dozen treatises representing the third group of Se'adiah's Talmudic writings are known by name, but only the *Treatise on Inheritance* (כתאב אלמוארית) has come down to us, edited by J. Müller (*Œuvres complètes*, ix. 1–53). The treatise is preceded by a philosophic introduction. Of some of the other treatises fragments have come to light—e.g., *On Testimonies and Contracts, On Usury* (H. Hirschfeld, *JQR* xvi. [1904] 294, xviii. [1906] 119 f.), etc. Mention must also be made of Se'adiah's *Responsa* (decisions in legal and religious questions), about 50 of which were published by J. Müller, pp. 87–142; cf. Malter, *s.v.* 'Halakah' D.

(*e*) *Calendar and chronology.*—The question of calendar was the subject of perpetual controversy between Ḳaraites and Rabbanites, and Se'adiah as the chief exponent of the latter has repeatedly treated of the matter in his polemical writings (see below) as well as in monographs, of which, however, only fragments have been preserved.[1]

A treatise on chronology under the title *Kitāb al-Ta'rīḫ* was published by A. Neubauer in *Mediæval Jewish Chronicles*, Oxford, 1887–95, ii. 89–110; cf. W. Bacher, *REJ* xxxii. [1896] 140 ff., xlix. [1904] 298 ff.; A. Marx, *REJ* lviii. [1909] 299 f. Two other treatises are known only by the titles; cf. Malter, *s.v.* 'Chronology.'

(*f*) *Philosophy.*—Se'adiah dealt with special problems of philosophy in nearly all his extant works, particularly in his commentaries on various books of the Bible. Here we are concerned, however, only with two of his works which represent his religious philosophic system as a whole.

(1) *Tafsīr Kitāb al-mabādī* ('Commentary on the Book of Creation'), so far as known the first scientific attempt to unravel the mysteries of this obscure Hebrew treatise, called *Sēfer Yeṣīrah*, which the popular belief ascribed to the patriarch Abraham. In a lengthy introduction Se'adiah gives a historical account of the various theories of Greek thinkers as to the origin of the universe. The theory of the *Sēfer Yeṣīrah* he identifies with that of Pythagoras, from which it differs only in so far as, in addition to the ten numerals of the latter, it postulates also the 22 letters of the Hebrew alphabet as the origin and essence of creation. Se'adiah devotes much space to the elucidation of this fantastic theory, which he endeavours to harmonize with the teachings of Judaism. He does not, however, subscribe to the views of the *Sēfer Yeṣīrah*, accepting instead that of the *Tôrāh*, which teaches a *creatio ex nihilo*. Very interesting is Se'adiah's interpretation of the fourth chapter of the book, according to which the first thing that God created was a certain pneumatic substance, which differed from the visible air that surrounds us by its greater tenuity and by its sublimity. This pneumatic substance, or ether, which he probably adopted from the Stoics, pervades all existence, even the interior of the most solid bodies. It is through the medium of this sublimated air that God is omnipresent. Figuratively speaking, this air is 'the throne of God's Majesty,' the agency of the divine spirit that animates and sustains all creation. Scripture designates it by the term *kābôd*='glory,' as it is said (Is 6³): 'The whole earth is full of his glory.' By means of it the word of God is communicated to the prophets. The Rabbis of the Talmud coined for it the term *shekīnāh* (שכינה).

The Arabic text of the commentary was edited with a French translation by M. Lambert, *Commentaire sur le Séfer Yesira*, Paris, 1891. A Hebrew translation by an author of the 12th cent. exists in MS only. Portions of another translation are embodied in the *Commentary on the Sefer Yeṣirah* by Judah b. Barzillai of Barcelona (1135), ed. S. Halberstam, Berlin, 1885; cf. Malter, *s.v.*

(2) *Kitāb al-'Amānāt wal-'I'tiḳādāt*, in the Hebrew translation of Judah Ibn Tibbon (1186), *Sēfer ha-Emūnôth we-ha-Dēôth* ('Book of Philosophic Doctrines and Religious Beliefs'), Se'adiah's most important philosophic work, written in Baghdād during the time of his seclusion (about 933). The Arabic text was published for the first time by S. Landauer (Leyden, 1880), while the Hebrew translation is accessible in seven editions (*ed. pr.* Constantinople, 1562), some of them with commentaries. J. Fürst translated the Hebrew text, with the exception of the last chapter, into German (Leipzig, 1845). Parts of the Arabic text were translated into German by P. Bloch (*Vom Glauben und Wissen*, Munich, 1879, containing the introduction and the first chapter) and W. Engelkemper (*Die religionsphilosophische Lehre Saadja Gaons*, etc., Münster, 1903, third chapter). An older Hebrew translation, usually called 'The Paraphrase,' with a very peculiar terminology, is as yet unpublished. This translation was the basis of Berechiah ha-Naḳdān (*c.* end of 12th cent.), who epitomized the whole work in two separate volumes, which were edited with an English translation by H. Gollancz under the title *The Ethical Treatises of Berachya*, London, 1902.

One of the main features of this great work of Se'adiah is its fundamental theory that philosophy and religion not only do not contradict each other, but actually support and supplement each other in the propagation of truth. For reason and religion sprang from the same divine source, and neither therefore can teach anything that is incompatible with the teachings of the other. With this theory as a basis, Se'adiah sets out to examine the various philosophic doctrines which seem to be at variance with the teachings of the Mosaic religion and endeavours to prove that the supposed antagonism is due either to fallacious reasoning or to a misinterpretation of the religious documents. In a long introduction he discusses the sources from which all human knowledge is derived and then divides his book into ten sections, in which the following problems are dealt with:

(1) The creation of the world. Four proofs are adduced for the *creatio ex nihilo*, while twelve contrary theories by various Greek and Muhammadan thinkers are refuted with much detail.

(2) Having demonstrated the necessity of presupposing the existence of God as a Creator, Se'adiah proceeds to a discussion of God's unity and uniqueness, as well as the other divine attributes. In this connexion he refutes the Christian dogma of the Trinity as a misinterpretation of the three attributes of life, power, and knowledge.

(3) The purpose of creation was to make all created beings happy. As a means to the attainment of happiness, the divine commandments of the Holy Scriptures were revealed to man. The necessity and reliability of prophecy are defended against the contrary views of a Hindu sect (Brāhmans), likewise the authority of the Biblical law against the contentions of Christian and Muhammadan theologians that it was abrogated.

(4) The question of free will is here minutely discussed. Man is a free agent, hence responsible for all his actions. Se'adiah tries to reconcile this view with the omnipotence and omniscience of God. Numerous passages of the Bible are interpreted in the light of this theory.

(5) Men are now divided into ten classes according to their religious and moral bearing in life. Special effort is made to vindicate the idea of God's justice, seeing that the righteous often suffer, while the wicked prosper (theodicy).

(6) This section contains Se'adiah's system of psychology. Six theories of Greek philosophers regarding the essence of the human soul are discussed. Against these, the author presents his own theory, that the soul is a separate entity created by God at the moment when the body, its habitat, is about to enter this world. He thus denies the pre-existence of the soul. He further investigates the mutual relation of soul and body, defends the idea of the immortality of the former, discusses the phenomenon of death and the state of the soul after death, and finally refutes the theory of transmigration of the soul.

(7) In this section Se'adiah tries to prove the possibility of the resurrection of the dead from the point of view of nature, reason, and the Bible. The closing portion contains the answers to ten questions that have a special bearing on the doctrine of resurrection.[1]

(8) Here the author takes up the Jewish doctrine of Israel's ultimate redemption by the promised Messiah, proving it from Bible and Talmud. He argues against those who claimed that the Messianic prophecies were fulfilled during the time of the Second Temple and also against the Christian doctrine of the Messiah.

(9) On reward and punishment in the future world. Se'adiah proves from reason, Bible, and Talmud that all inequalities will be adjusted in the world to come and then devotes much space to the discussion of thirteen eschatological questions.

(10) The tenth section represents Se'adiah's system of ethics. He describes thirteen different theories regarding the course which one should choose for oneself in life and shows that any of these theories, if applied dogmatically and one-sidedly, is bound to prove harmful. Man should live in accordance with his natural inclinations, but keep them under strict control and surveillance, carrying out all functions of life in the proper time and place and refraining therefrom when reason so demands.

(*g*) *Polemic works.*—(1) *Kitāb al-Radd 'alā 'Anān*, 'Refutation of 'Anān,' the founder of Ḳaraism (760), written in 915. The book is known only from quotations; see Poznański, *JQR* x. [1898] 240 ff.

(2) *Kitāb al-Tamyīz*, 'Book of Distinction,' probably Se'adiah's most important and most voluminous polemical work, written in 926 and directed against schismatic teachings of the Ḳaraites. Several fragments were published by S. Schechter, *Saadyana*, Cambridge, 1903, pp. 30–34; and H. Hirschfeld, *JQR* xvi. 98 ff.; cf. also Poznański, *JQR* x. 246–251, 262–274.

[1] See Malter, *JQR*, new ser., iii. [1912–13] 500–509; cf. art. CALENDAR (Jewish).

[1] The seventh section exists in two entirely different recensions, the one of which is contained in the edition of Landauer (see above), while the other, on which is based also Ibn Tibbon's Hebrew translation, was edited from another MS by W. Bacher, in the *Festschrift zum achtzigsten Geburtstage M. Steinschneider's*, Leipzig, 1896, pp. 98–112.

(3) *Kitāb al-Radd 'alā Ibn Sâḳawaihi*, 'Refutation of Ibn Sâḳawaihi,' of which several fragments have come to light; see *JQR* xiii. [1901] 655–667, xvi. 100, 112; Poznański, *The Karaite Literary Opponents of Saadiah Gaon*, London, 1908, pp. 4–8.

(4) *Kitāb al-Radd 'alā al-Mūtaḥāmil*, 'Refutation of an Overbearing Aggressor,' perhaps the same Ibn Sâḳawaihi. A fragment was published by Hirschfeld, *JQR* xviii. 113–119; cf. Poznański, *JQR* x. 254 f.

(5) *Kitāb al-Radd 'alā Ḥayawaihi* (*vulgo Ḥiwi*) *al-Balḫī*, 'Refutation of Ḥiwi of Balkh.' A considerable portion of the book, written in Hebrew rhyme, was recently published by I. Davidson under the title *Saadia's Polemic against Ḥiwi Al-Balkhi*, New York, 1915, to which edition the reader is here referred for further details.

(6) *Sēfer ha-Gālui*, an apologetic work written in Biblical Hebrew and directed against David b. Zakkai and his party. About three years later Se'adiah added an Arabic translation of and commentary on the Hebrew text and wrote an Arabic introduction in which he sketched the contents of the work. The introduction, in which verses from the original book of Sirach are quoted, and of which only a few lines are missing at the beginning, was published by Harkavy in *Studien und Mittheilungen*, v. 150–181. Part of the same introduction was published from another MS with an English translation by H. Malter, *JQR*, new ser., iii. [1912–13] 487–499. Several fragments of the work itself, both Hebrew and Arabic, appeared in various periodicals; see, for the bibliography, Malter, *Life and Works of Saadia*, *s.v.*

LITERATURE.—Besides works mentioned in the body of the article, the following may be referred to:

i. *BIOGRAPHIES IN GENERAL.*—W. Bacher, *JE* x. 579–586; S. Bernfeld, *R. Sa'adyah Gaon* (Hebrew), Cracow, 1898; W. Engelkemper, *De Saadiæ Gaonis vita*, etc., Münster, 1897; S. Eppenstein, *Beiträge zur Gesch. und Literatur im geonäischen Zeitalter*, Berlin, 1913, pp. 65–148; M. Friedländer, 'Life and Works of Saadia,' *JQR* v. [1893] 177–199; A. Geiger, *Wissenschaftl. Zeitschr. für jüd. Theologie*, v. [1844] 267 ff.; M. Joël, 'Saadias,' in his *Beiträge zur Gesch. der Philosophie*, Breslau, 1876, Anhang, pp. 34–44; D. Kohn, *Toledot R. Sa'adyah Gaon* (Hebrew), Cracow, 1891; S. J. L. Rapoport, 'Toledot R. Sa'adyah Gaon,' in *Bikkūrē ha-'Ittim*, ix. [1828] 20–37; M. Steinschneider, *Cat. Lib. Heb. in Bibliotheca Bodleiana*, Berlin, 1852–60, cols. 2156–2224, *Die arab. Literatur der Juden*, Frankfort, 1902, pp. 47–69; T. Tal, in *Lezingen gehouden in de Vereeniging voor Joodsche Letterkunde en Geschiedenis*, The Hague, 1887, pp. 1–66; S. A. Taubeles, *Saadia Gaon*, Halle, 1888; I. H. Weiss, *Dor Dor we-Doreshaw*, iv. [Vienna, 1887] chs. 14–16.

ii. *LINGUISTICS AND EXEGESIS.*—W. Bacher, *Abraham Ibn Esra's Einleitung zu seinem Pentateuchcommentar*, Vienna, 1876, *Leben und Werke des Abulwalîd*, Leipzig, 1885, p. 93 ff., *Die Bibelexegese der jüdischen Religionsphilosophen des Mittelalters vor Maimuni*, Strassburg, 1892, pp. 1–44, and in Winter and Wünsche, *Die jüdische Litteratur*, Berlin, 1897, ii. 138 ff., 243 ff.; L. Bodenheimer, 'Das Paraphrastische der arabischen Übersetzung des Saadia,' in *Monatsschrift*, iv. [1854] 23–33; L. Dukes, in Ewald and Dukes, *Beiträge zur Gesch. der ältesten Auslegung und Spracherklärung des AT*, Stuttgart, 1844, ii. 5–115; A. Schmiedl, 'Randbemerkungen zu Saadia's Pentateuchübersetzung,' in *MGWJ* xlv. [1901] 124 ff. (cf. p. 565 f.), xlvi. [1902] 84 ff.; M. Wolf, 'Zur Charakteristik der Bibelexegese Saadia Alfajûmi's,' in *ZATW* iv. [1884] 225, v. [1885] 15.

iii. *LITURGY.*—H. Brody, *JQR*, new ser., iii. [1912–13] 83–99 (cf. p. 119 f.); L. Dukes, *Zur Kenntniss der neuhebräischen religiösen Poesie*, Frankfort, 1842, p. 53 f.; I. Elbogen, *Studien zur Gesch. des jüdischen Gottesdienstes*, Berlin, 1907, pp. 83, 122 ff., *Der jüdische Gottesdienst*, etc., Leipzig, 1913, pp. 294, 321–325, 361, 364; A. Kohut, *Die Hoschanot des Gaon R. Saadia*, Breslau, 1893; L. Landshuth, *'Ammūdē ha-'Abōdāh*, Berlin, 1857–62, i. 286–299; S. D. Luzzatto, *Litteraturblatt des Orients*, Leipzig, 1851, p. 387 f.; A. Neubauer, in *Ben Chananja*, vi. [1863] 552 ff., in *Semitic Studies in Memory of A. Kohut*, Berlin, 1897, pp. 388–395; N. Steinschneider, *Der Siddur des Saadia Gaon*, do. 1856, *Cat. Bodl.*, cols. 2203–2217; L. Zunz, *Literaturgesch. der synagogalen Poesie*, Berlin, 1865, pp. 93–98.

iv. *HALĀKHĀ.*—Z. Frankel, *Entwurf einer Gesch. der Literatur der nachtalmudischen Responsen*, Breslau, 1865, p. 81 ff.; L. Ginzberg, *Geonica*, New York, 1909, i. 162–167; J. Müller, introd. to vol. ix. of the *Œuvres complètes de R. Saadia*, Paris, 1897.

v. *CALENDAR AND POLEMICS.*—J. H. Bornstein, מחלקת רב סעדיה גאון ובן מאיר, Warsaw, 1904; A. Epstein, *REJ* xlii. [1901] 179–210, xliv. [1902] 220–236; cf. also *JQR* viii. [1896] 684–691, xii. [1900] 502–554, 703–705; *ExpT* xi. [1899–1900] 454–458, 521 f., 563; *JQR*, new ser., iii. [1912–13] 500–509, v. [1914–15] 543–557.

vi. *PHILOSOPHY.*—S. Bernfeld, דעת אלהים, Warsaw, 1897, pp. 113–134; M. Eisler, *Vorlesungen über die jüdischen Philosophen des Mittelalters*, Vienna, 1870–83, ii. 1–43; J. Guttmann, *Die Religionsphilosophie des Saadia*, Göttingen, 1882; S. Horovitz, *Die Psychologie bei den jüdischen Religionsphilosophen des Mittelalters*, i. 'Von Saadia bis Maimuni,' Breslau, 1898; I. Husik, *A Hist. of Mediæval Jewish Philosophy*, New York and London, 1916, pp. 23–47; D. Kaufmann, *Gesch. der Attributenlehre*, Gotha, 1877, pp. 1–90; H. Malter, חרעות במהות חנפש, etc., in the Hebrew monthly הַשִּׁלֹחַ, xxvi. [Odessa, 1912] 128–137; P. J. Müller, *De Godsleer der Middleeuwsche Joden*, Groningen, 1898, pp. 59-89; S. Munk, *Mélanges de philosophie juive et arabe*, Paris, 1857–59, ii. 477 ff.; D. Neumark, *Gesch. der jüdischen Philosophie des Mittelalters*, Berlin, 1907–13, i. 429–469, 536–551; D. Rau, 'Die Ethik R. Saadjas,' in *MGWJ* lv. [1911] 385–399, 513–530, 713–728, lvi. [1912] 65–79, 181–198 (incomplete); M. Schreiner, *Der Kalâm in der jüdischen Literatur*, Berlin, 1895, pp. 5–22; A. Schmiedl, *Studien über jüdische insonders jüdisch-arabische Religionsphilosophie*, Vienna, 1869, pp. 100–103, 134–138, 172–175, 223–225, 252 f.

HENRY MALTER.

SEAL AMULETS.—See SCARABS.

SECESSION.—See PRESBYTERIANISM.

SECOND ADVENT.—See PAROUSIA.

SECOND ADVENTISM.—This article will sketch the history of speculation about the return of Christ. Belief in His return has long been a widely accepted Christian tenet, but there have been many different opinions as to the time and manner of His appearing. These varying views fall into two main classes. One type of thinking regards the Second Advent primarily as a spiritual experience already realized through the descent of the Holy Spirit upon the disciples after the resurrection of Jesus—a 'return' repeated in the experience of successive generations of Christians. This interpretation is frequently supplemented by belief in a visible coming of Christ at an indefinite historical moment in the far distant future, after the gospel by its transforming power has gradually brought the world to a state of millennial perfection. The second type of opinion insists that the promised return of Christ has not yet taken place, but may be momentarily expected. In the meantime the world constantly deteriorates. Only by Christ's literal coming can the millennium be established and righteousness made to prevail upon the earth. The latter opinion is commonly designated pre-millenarianism and the former post-millenarianism. Since for pre-millenarians Christ's return is as yet in no sense realized, but is an imminent event greatly to be desired, they have usually been much more diligent than post-millenarians in their efforts to determine the date and manner of the Second Advent. It is mainly with pre-millennial teachings that we are here concerned.

1. Jewish antecedents.—Contemporary Judaism furnished a point of departure for early Christian belief in the return of Christ. Even the older prophets had announced the coming of a day when Jahweh would catastrophically intervene in the affairs of the world, much as the Christians of NT times depicted the imminent advent of their Lord Jesus Christ. But this type of imagery was developed most fully in the apocalyptic literature of later Judaism, whence it passed over into Christianity. Dn 7[13f.] seems to have been a particularly influential passage: 'I saw in the night visions, and, behold, there came with the clouds of heaven one like unto a son of man. . . . And there was given him dominion, and glory, and a kingdom, that all the peoples, nations, and languages should serve him.' Other apocalyptic writers revelled in descriptions of divine intervention when either God Himself or His heavenly Messiah would visibly appear descending from heaven to earth to inaugurate a new régime. This event was to be foreshadowed by a series of terrifying phenomena. Fearful wars would drench the world in blood, the heavens and the earth would be shaken, and the light would fail from sun, moon, and stars. Resurrection of the dead, the execution of judgment, and the inauguration of a new world were to occur in connexion with the advent of God or of His Messiah. Certain apocalyptists inserted an interregnum of bliss—sometimes 400 years, sometimes a millennium—

between the end of the present world and the final establishment of the new heaven and the new earth. Occasionally attempts were made to fix the date of the end, earlier estimates being revised from time to time in the light of subsequent events. Other seers were less confident of their ability to forecast exactly the hour of coming disaster, since this knowledge was not permitted to mortals, but in the signs of their own times they found ample evidence of the imminence of the event.[1]

2. Jesus on His return.—Jesus was baptized by John after hearing him announce the imminence of the judgment (Mt 3^{7-10}, Lk 3^{7-9}). Apparently the Baptist shared in the apocalyptic thinking of contemporary Judaism and awaited expectantly the impending catastrophe that was to end the old order and establish the new. But whether Jesus was so heartily in sympathy with this view that He predicted His own early return from heaven in apocalyptic fashion is still a debated question. One school of interpreters stoutly maintains that the Gospels correctly represent Jesus as teaching that He would return while men of His own generation were still alive (Mk 9^{1}).[2] Other interpreters are of the opinion that Jesus did not announce His early return in apocalyptic fashion, but that the prominence of this idea in the Gospels is due to the work of the disciples, who consoled themselves with this faith after Jesus' death.[3] While Jesus did not predict His own coming, He may on this interpretation have entertained current Jewish apocalyptic hopes and have expected an early intervention of God to inaugurate a new heavenly régime upon earth. A third view, more in accordance with popular opinion, is that Jesus, in speaking of His early return, used the apocalyptic phraseology of His time, but attached to it a deeper and more spiritual meaning. He was to return in spiritual power, and the new kingdom on earth was to be established by a gradual process of growth begun during His own career and continued by successive generations of His disciples working under the direction of His spirit.

3. NT teaching.—Belief in the Second Coming was popular among the Christians whose opinions are preserved in the NT. An expectation of Christ's early return in glory is frequently expressed in the Epistles of Paul. The Thessalonians are admonished to prepare for the approaching end of the age, waiting for the Son of God from heaven (1 Th 1^{10} 2^{19} 3^{13} 4^{15-18}). The present age is to end in a terrible outbreak of lawlessness to be followed by the coming of the Lord (2 Th 2^{1-12}). The Corinthians are advised to delay their litigations, awaiting the judgment presently to be inaugurated by Jesus when He returns. Since the time is short, it is unwise for them to become involved in family relationships such as marriage and the care of children. Within their own lifetime Christ will appear, the dead will be raised, judgment will be enacted, and the new age will be established (1 Co $1^{7f.}$ 4^{5} 5^{5} 7^{29-35} 15^{24-28} 16^{22}). This glorious day is at hand, and wise Christians will hold themselves in readiness for the imminent advent of the Lord (Ro 13^{12} 14^{10}, Ph $1^{6.\ 10}$ 4^{5}, 1 Th $5^{1-11.\ 23}$).

The Synoptic Gospels and Acts show a similar interest in the Second Advent, which is expected to occur during the lifetime of personal disciples of Jesus (Mk 9^{1} 14^{62}, Mt 16^{28} 26^{64}, Lk 9^{27} 22^{69}). Jesus is thought to have had in mind His own return when He spoke about the destruction of the Temple (Mk 13^{5-37}, Mt 24^{4-36}, Lk 21^{8-36}). The agonies experienced in the Jewish revolt of A.D. 66–70, which resulted in the destruction of the Temple, were interpreted as signs of the approaching end. Very soon after this disaster the Son of Man would appear with His angelic host to establish His kingdom upon earth. In the meantime certain preliminaries had to be completed, such as preaching the gospel to all the peoples living around the Mediterranean (Mk 13^{10}), and the exact date of the end could not be known by mortals, but in Mark's opinion it was so near that the men of that generation ought to be living in constant readiness for its coming (13^{30-37}). Similarly, Acts opens with the announcement that the disciples shall see Jesus return in like manner as they beheld Him going into heaven (1^{11}). Peter interprets the Pentecostal endowment of the Christians as a fulfilment of OT prophecies of the last times (2^{17-21}), and on still another occasion he admonishes his hearers to repent in preparation for the advent of Christ (3^{19-21}).

In Revelation the Second Coming is vividly portrayed. 'Behold he cometh with the clouds; and every eye shall see him' is the persecuted Christian's consoling hope (1^{7}). The things seen by John will 'shortly come to pass' and Christ will 'come quickly' ($22^{6f.\ 12.\ 20}$). The trials through which Christians are passing in John's own day are regarded as signs presaging the final period of distress to precede Christ's advent. He will come riding upon a white charger and accoutred with heavenly armour. The armies of heaven are to accompany Him, but the sharp sword that proceedeth out of His mouth will itself be sufficiently deadly to strike down all His enemies. The nations of the earth will fall in the terrific carnage to take place at Christ's coming (19^{11-21}). At this point John introduces a Jewish idea not explicitly mentioned in any other NT book. After His triumph Christ sets up an interregnum upon earth, dwelling with the martyred saints for 1000 years before the final judgment is staged and the New Jerusalem established. The actual date of the expected advent is vaguely indicated by John in his apparent reference to the imperial succession between his own day and the end of the present age (17^{10-14}). After the death of the present emperor his immediate successor will rule for 'a little while' before the final imperial 'beast' appears who holds dominion until overthrown by Christ. If, as seems probable, John was writing in the nineties under Domitian, he doubtless expected the Second Advent to occur not later than the second decade of the 2nd century.

Other parts of the NT also entertain the hope of Christ's coming. Readers of James are admonished to await patiently the advent of the Lord which 'is at hand,' and the judge 'standeth before the doors' (5^{7-9}). The author of Hebrews expects Christ to appear a second time to them that wait for Him to complete their salvation, and even as he writes the day seems to be 'drawing nigh' (9^{28} 10^{25}). In 1 Peter Christians are encouraged to suffer persecution, confident in the belief that the end of the present world is near. Suddenly Christ will appear, coming upon the clouds to destroy sinners and receive the faithful in His new kingdom (1^{3-7} $4^{7.\ 12f.\ 17f.}$ 5^{4}). Against sceptics who are losing faith in the Second Advent 2 Peter urges that delay is no sufficient ground for doubt, since with the Lord a thousand years are but as a single day (3^{1-13}).

[1] For a more extended statement of Jewish opinion on this subject see R. H. Charles, *A Critical Hist. of the Doctrine of a Future Life*², London and New York, 1913, chs. v.–viii.; S. J. Case, *The Millennial Hope*, pp. 80–98; P. Volz, *Jüdische Eschatologie von Daniel bis Akiba*, Tübingen, 1903; Schürer, *GJV*⁴, Leipzig, 1902–11, ii. 579–651.

[2] *E.g.*, W. Sanday, *The Life of Christ in Recent Research*, Oxford, 1907; E. F. Scott, *The Kingdom and the Messiah*, Edinburgh and New York, 1911; A. Loisy, *Jésus et la tradition évangélique*, Paris, 1910; A. Schweitzer, *Gesch. der Leben-Jesu-Forschung*, Tübingen, 1913.

[3] So, notably, W. Wrede, *Das Messiasgeheimnis in den Evangelien*, Göttingen, 1901.

The Gospel of John treats the Second Coming in a unique way. The idea rarely occurs. There is one reference to an hour when all that are in the tombs shall hear the voice of Jesus and come forth to judgment ($5^{28f.}$); but this is not the dominant teaching of the book. Elsewhere the return of Jesus is thoroughly spiritualized. He will 'come again' to receive His own at death, but not to introduce an apocalyptic kingdom upon earth ($14^{2f.}$). The kingdom He establishes is one of 'truth' (18^{37}), which is already inaugurated through His work upon earth. Those who hear His words and believe thereby acquire eternal life immediately, and those who reject incur, by that very act, a present and final judgment ($5^{24f.}$). Jesus indeed returns to earth after His death, but His return is a spiritual act affecting the personal religious living of successive generations of disciples and is not to mark a cataclysmic reversal of the present order of existence.

4. Early patristic opinion. — Throughout the 2nd and 3rd centuries many Christians continued to cherish the hope of an early visible return of their Lord. They not only reproduced the first disciples' vivid expectation of His early advent, but they frequently dwelt upon the idea of His millennial rule as depicted in Revelation. The *Didache* warns its readers to watch lest they be taken unawares by the Lord's sudden coming, which is to occur in truly apocalyptic fashion.[1] Hegesippus reported that Jesus' brother, James, just before the latter's execution, declared that Jesus was about to come upon the clouds of heaven, and the grandchildren of Jude also defined the Messianic kingdom in similar apocalyptic imagery.[2] Both Ignatius and Polycarp believed themselves to be living in the last times when Christ would suddenly appear to execute judgment upon the Christians' persecutors and to reward the faithful.[3] The so-called *Epistle of Barnabas* represents the last day as at hand, when the present world along with the evil one shall be destroyed by the returning Lord. Almost 6000 years are thought to have elapsed since creation, these years corresponding to the six days of creation week. The seventh day of 1000 years is about to begin with the Second Advent.[4] Papias also looked for a return of the Lord, when the earth would be made fabulously fruitful.[5] Hermas describes a beast seen in his vision and marked by four colours, black representing the present evil world, red signifying impending destruction by blood and fire, gold typifying faithful Christians tried by the testing fire, and white denoting the new coming age. The end is thought to be near. Even Jesus had lived in the last times, and in Hermas' day the tower representing the Church was so near to completion that the labour upon it had to be suspended for a brief period awaiting the return of Christ to inspect the structure. But this delay is not to be long.[6]

Among the early apologists, Justin is a confirmed believer in the Second Advent. He finds two advents of Christ predicted by the prophets—the one already past when He came as a dishonoured and suffering man, the second when He shall come from heaven with glory, accompanied by His angelic host.[7] This consummation is being delayed temporarily to allow more sinners to repent, and Justin thinks that the dispensation of grace may endure even long enough to include some who are not yet born.[1] But persecution of Christians will continue until Christ comes to destroy His enemies and dwell with the saints 1000 years in Jerusalem.[2] Irenæus agrees with Barnabas in placing the end of the world and the return of Christ 6000 years after creation. The date of the advent is not fixed more definitely, but the hostility of Rome is to continue until Christ comes to abolish all evil and establish His millennial reign.[3] The Montanists[4] were also enthusiastic believers in the early return of Christ, and their excesses did much to arouse opposition to the doctrine. Tertullian predicts a decline of the Roman power to be followed by the rise of the Antichrist, who will make war upon the Church until Christ suddenly appears, coming in glory upon the clouds to establish the saints in power upon earth. Already men are living in the 'last times.'[5] Hippolytus fixes the date of the Second Advent at 500 years after the birth of Christ, which is said to have taken place 550 years after creation.[6] Commodian looks for an early return of the Lord. The impending seventh persecution of the Christians is expected to introduce the tribulation of the last days. Then two Antichrists are to appear in succession, ruling for a short time before Christ's advent.[7] Lactantius dwells at length upon the events to precede the return of Christ which will occur 6000 years after the creation. He believes that at most the present world cannot endure beyond another 200 years, and the end is to be expected daily.[8] Other expectant pre-millennialists are Victorinus of Pettau,[9] Methodius of Olympus in Lycia,[10] and the Egyptian bishop Nepos.[11]

5. Early opponents of millennialism.—The idea of an early return of Christ to establish His millennial reign upon earth gradually grew unpopular as the Christian movement gained in power. While Christians remained few in numbers, and during periods of severe persecution, the only possible triumph for the new religion seemed to lie in the hope of the Second Advent. But, as Christianity became more influential, gradually rising to a position of supremacy in its world, the need for a catastrophic intervention of God disappeared. The Second Advent as a tenet of faith was not necessarily abandoned, but stress was placed upon the power of the Church to effect a gradual transformation of the present world, and the visible return of Christ was pushed far into the future.

The first opposition to Second Adventism seems to have come from the Gnostics, who were averse to the idea of any reunion of souls with restored physical bodies even in a millennial kingdom.[12] The excessive enthusiasm of the Montanists also provoked opposition to millenarianism, even causing the book of Revelation to fall into disfavour in certain circles. This is probably the reason for its rejection by the Alogi and apparently also by the Roman presbyter Caius, who calls it the work of the heretic Cerinthus.[13] But Origen was the first Christian writer to attempt a thoroughgoing refutation of vivid and literalistic Second Advent hopes.[14] He did not reject the Biblical writings commonly cited in support of these hopes, but he offered an allegorical type of interpretation by which all Scripture could be made to yield a spiritual meaning, teaching that the present world was to endure indefinitely, being

[1] Ch. 16.
[2] Eusebius, *HE* II. xxiii. 13, III. xx. 6.
[3] Ignatius, *Eph.* xi. 1, xvi. 1 f., *Mag.* v. 1; Polycarp, *Phil.* ii. 1 f., v. 2, xi. 2; *Martyr. Poly.* ii. 3, xi. 2.
[4] iv. 1–3, vi. 11 ff., vii. 9 ff., xv. 1–9, xxi. 3.
[5] Irenæus, *Hær.* v. xxxiii. 3 f.
[6] *Vis.* I. iii. 4, II. ii. 7 f., III. viii. 9, ix. 5, IV. i.–iii., *Sim.* iv. 1–8, ix. 5, 12, 3.
[7] *Apol.* i. 52, *Dial.* 110.

[1] *Apol.* i. 28.
[2] *Dial.* 39, 81; see also *Apol.* i. 45, 51 f., 60, ii. 7 f., *Dial.* 30 f., 80, 113, 121, 138 f.
[3] *Hær.* v. 25–36.
[4] See art. MONTANISM.
[5] *Apol.* 23, *de Spectac.* 30, *adv. Marc.* iii. 24, *de Resurr.* 24 f.
[6] *Frag. Dan.* ii. 4 ff.
[7] *Instr.* 43–45.
[8] *Div. Inst.* vii. 14–26.
[9] *Com. on Rev.*
[10] *Conviv.* ix. 5.
[11] Eus. *HE* vii. 24.
[12] See art. GNOSTICISM, § 4 f.
[13] Eus. *HE* iii. 28.
[14] E.g., *de Prin.* II. i. 3, xi. 2, III. vi. 9; see also *ERE* i. 317b.

gradually transformed by the power of the Christian gospel into a new ideal order of existence. The anti-millennial polemic was taken up by Dionysius of Alexandria. He did not completely reject the book of Revelation, but he did affirm that it was unintelligible to him and that it was not the work of John the Apostle.[1] Until the time of Athanasius the book of Revelation remained in disfavour with the churches of Syria and Palestine, while Origen's method of dealing with the Second Coming prevailed in the East.

Second Adventism was given a new turn by the Donatist Ticonius in his commentary on Revelation. He maintained that the return of the Lord would not occur until the true Church—meaning the Donatist Church[2]—had established itself in the world, successfully resisting both paganism and the false Church Catholicism. The book of Revelation was allegorically interpreted as a detailed forecast of this conflict. Although Ticonius, who wrote about the year 380, expected Christ to reappear soon, he made the intervening history of Christianity, gradually attaining perfection in its conflict with the world, the process by which Christ's kingdom was to be established upon earth. This notion was transformed and restated by Augustine.[3] He dismisses the view that Christ is yet to come to inaugurate a millennial reign upon earth. The Kingdom has already been established by Christ's first advent, when He bound Satan (Mk 3^{27}), and His coming 'continually occurs in His church, that is, in His members, in which He comes little by little and piece by piece, since the whole Church is His body.' When the Church has reached the climax of its growth, the present world will be transmuted by a fiery bath transforming corruptibility into incorruptibility and revealing the New Jerusalem which is from heaven 'because the grace with which God formed it is of heaven.' The work of Augustine (*q.v.*) virtually eliminated all realistic Second Adventism from the main stream of Roman Catholic thinking, and his views have also been widely current in Protestant circles.

6. Revival of interest in adventism. — When taken literally, Augustine's identification of the Church with the ideal earthly kingdom of Christ implied that the millennium would close about A.D. 1000, and that the final coming of Christ in judgment might then be expected. The approach of this date awakened a revival of interest in Second Advent hopes, and for several years thereafter more or less vivid expectations were frequently entertained; *e.g.*, the efforts of the Crusaders to gain control of the Holy Land owed not a little to the feeling that the imminent end of the world made it necessary for Christians to be in possession of that sacred territory when the Lord returned.

At the close of the 12th cent. a noteworthy reinterpretation of adventism is given by Joachim of Floris, who looked for the return of Christ to inaugurate His millennial reign upon earth in the year 1260.[4] This date was determined by reckoning the 1260 days of Rev 12^6 as the equivalent number of years that the true Church would remain concealed before the end. Stirring events of Joachim's own day, such as the aggressions of the Saracens, the Crusades, and the rise of the monastic orders, all became signs of the times fulfilling the predictions of the book of Revelation. Joachim's writings were regarded by his admirers as a new Scripture, and so incurred the hostility of the papacy; but his views gained wide currency among the Franciscans, who found the hostile papacy also prefigured among the signs of the last times in Revelation. The various Protestant movements took up this notion with avidity. Also the disturbed conditions preceding the Reformation tended to increase the conviction that the Second Advent was approaching. Militz of Kromeriz, a forerunner of John Hus, looked for the end between the years 1365 and 1367. In the next century the Hussite wars strongly stimulated advent hopes among the Bohemians, resulting in the rise of the Taborite movement and the formation of the sect known as the Bohemian Brethren.[1] The Thirty Years' War gave fresh stimulus to these hopes and called forth from the famous Comenius the prediction of an early return of Christ. Wyclif (*q.v.*) also regarded the papacy as the power of Antichrist, and other signs of the times were taken to imply the nearness of Christ's advent. The reformers in Germany and Switzerland often spoke of the Antichrist papacy, but they did not as a rule draw the logical conclusion that the literal Second Advent was imminent. Millenarianism was branded as a Judaistic heresy by both the Augsburg and the Helvetic Confessions.[2]

In the British Isles adventism was advocated more freely, the book of Revelation furnishing a basis for new speculation on the date of the Lord's return. John Napier[3] predicted the coming of the end between the years 1688 and 1700. In the next generation Joseph Mede[4] concluded from the data in Revelation that the present course of history would close about the year 1660. Isaac Newton[5] refrained from specifying an exact date, but he looked for an early consummation of the present age. William Whiston[6] less cautiously fixed first upon the year 1715, then upon 1734, and later upon 1866, as the date for the inauguration of the millennium. The same type of interpretation was advocated in France by Pierre Jurieu,[7] who sought to comfort the persecuted Huguenots by predicting the downfall of the Antichrist Roman Church in the year 1689. In Germany the Lutheran prejudice against adventist speculation was overcome by the Pietists. C. Vitringa,[8] who drew largely upon the English interpreter Mede, was specially influential in reviving German interest in this subject. But J. A. Bengel[9] did most to confirm that interest. From the figures and images of Revelation he concluded that a preliminary millennium would be inaugurated in 1836, when Satan would be bound for 1000 years. Then would follow the millennial kingdom proper, closing with the end of the world and the final judgment. Bengel exerted a powerful influence not only in his native land but also in England, where his commentary was translated at the special request of John Wesley. Thus advent speculations attained increasing popularity in various Protestant circles and have persisted down to modern times. The general method of the interpreter is to discover in Revelation a forecast of the entire history of Christianity up to his own day, noting especially those predictions that are believed to point to events of his age which convince him of the nearness of Christ's return to inaugurate the millennium.

7. Millenarian sects. — During the last two centuries advent teaching has occasionally furnished an incentive for the formation of separate sects.

[1] Eus. *HE* vii. 24 f.
[2] See art. DONATISTS.
[3] *De Civ. Dei*, xx.
[4] See art. JOACHIMITES.

[1] See art. HUSSITES.
[2] See art. CONFESSIONS, vol. iii. pp. 845 ff., 859 ff.
[3] *A Plaine Discovery of the whole Reualation of Saint John*, Edinburgh, 1593.
[4] *Clavis Apocalyptica una cum commentario in Apoc.*, Cambridge, 1627.
[5] *Observations upon the Prophecies of Daniel and the Apocalypse of St. John*, 2 pts., London, 1733.
[6] *An Essay on the Revelation of St. John*, Cambridge, 1706.
[7] *L'Accomplissement des prophéties, ou la délivrance prochaine de l'église*, 2 vols., Rotterdam, 1686.
[8] *Ἀνάκρισις apocalypsios Joannis apostoli*, Franeker, 1705.
[9] *Erklärte Offenbarung Johannis*, Stuttgart, 1740, Eng. tr. by John Robertson, London, 1757.

Even as early as the time of Cromwell the Fifth Monarchy movement appeared as a religio-political party devoted to 'King Jesus' and ready to fight in order to prepare the world for His coming. In Germany at Elberfeld the Ronsdorf sect, founded in 1726, included a group of people who held themselves in readiness for the revelation of the new kingdom from heaven in the year 1730. The Shaker communities which trace their origin to Ann Lee, who emigrated from England to America in 1774, consisted of communistic groups who lived in the expectation of the near end of the world and the early return of Christ.[1] In the next century under the leadership of Christoph Hoffmann,[2] a new sect known as the Friends of the Temple, or People of God, emerged in Germany. Believing that Christ was about to return, they proposed to rebuild the Jerusalem temple in preparation for His coming. The beginning of the 19th cent. witnessed the rise of strong millennial sects in Great Britain. A movement was begun by Edward Irving, a popular Scottish Presbyterian preacher in London, which came to be known as the Catholic Apostolic Church (or the Irvingites). In 1823 Irving published a book[3] which attracted considerable attention and led to the holding of a series of yearly conferences at the home of Henry Drummond, a wealthy London banker living in Albury. From these beginnings grew the idea of forming a new spiritual Church ready to receive Christ at His coming—an event which Irving had predicted for the year 1864.[4] A kindred movement arising in Ireland and England between the years 1827 and 1831 received the name of Plymouth Brethren (or Derbyites). Its aim was to restore the simplicity and purity of primitive Christianity in preparation for Christ's imminent return. An elaborate scheme of events to take place in connexion with the end of the world was derived from the imagery of Daniel and Revelation.[5]

The year 1830 marks the beginning in America of the Church of Jesus Christ of the Latter-Day Saints (or Mormons). The founder, Joseph Smith, is alleged to have received a new revelation from God instructing him to found a new community that would constitute a present city of Zion ready for Christ when He returns to set up His millennial reign. In the meantime the spiritual gifts of apostolic times were to be revived, and the original conditions of life in the early Church were to be restored. This movement began at Fayette in the State of New York, but the sect finally settled down to await the advent of Christ at Salt Lake City in the State of Utah.[6] A group of adventist sects resulted from the work of William Miller of Low Hampton, New York. He began public preaching in 1831, boldly proclaiming that Christ would presently appear in visible form to establish His millennial reign. This event was first predicted for the year 1843, but was later postponed to 22nd Oct. 1844. The failure of this prediction led to dissensions, and a branch known as the 'Seventh-Day Adventists' was formed in 1845, while the original body took the name 'Evangelical Adventists.' A separatist body of Seventh-Day Adventists was organized in 1866, bearing the name 'Church of God.' The cause of separation was unwillingness on their part to regard one of their revered teachers, Mrs. Ellen Gould White, as an inspired prophetess. Another branch of adventists, formed in 1861, is known as 'Advent Christians.' Two kindred bodies are the 'Life and Advent Union,' organized in 1862, and the 'Age-to-Come Adventists,' organized in 1888. Of similarly recent origin is the Russellite movement, resulting from a propaganda of the late 'Pastor' C. T. Russell, who in 1886 began a series of volumes on the general subject of 'the millennial dawn.' He maintained that the return of Christ and the inauguration of the millennium had taken place invisibly in the year 1874, and the end of the world was to occur in 1914. His disciples interpret the outbreak of the world war in 1914 as the fulfilment of their founder's prediction.

1 See art. Communistic Societies of America, § 2.

2 *Gesch. des Volkes Gottes*, Stuttgart, 1855, and *Mein Weg nach Jerusalem*, 2 vols., do. 1881–84.

3 *Babylon and Infidelity foredoomed of God*, 2 vols., London, 1826.

4 See art. Irving and the Catholic Apostolic Church.

5 See art. Brethren (Plymouth).

6 See art. Saints, Latter-Day.

8. Modern non-sectarian adventism.—During the last half century some of the most vigorous forms of adventist propaganda in Great Britain and America have been conducted, not by separate sects, but by leaders within the different Protestant communions. These teachers revel in the study of prophecy, particularly in the interpretation of Daniel and Revelation. When studied with the adventist insight, these books and other Scriptures are found to yield specific predictions of all the outstanding events in history. Fulfilments of Scripture in recent times are emphasized and used as justification for predicting the early return of Christ and other happenings incident to a catastrophic end of the world. In the year 1878 this type of interpretation received a strong stimulus in England from the publication of the widely used book of H. Grattan Guinness,[1] who, on the basis of an extensive reckoning of data, predicted that the end of the present world will occur not later than the year 1923. Contemporarily with the work of Guinness similar teachings were being advocated with vigour in America. In New York in 1878 a group of adventists representing membership in ten different Protestant bodies met for a 'prophetic conference.' An active literary propaganda on behalf of belief in the early advent of Christ was also begun, typical works of that time being J. A. Seiss, *The Last Times* (Philadelphia, 1878), and W. E. Blackstone, *Jesus is Coming* (New York, 1878, ^{3}1908). Advocates of these opinions took fresh courage with the outbreak of the world war in 1914. The horrors of the war, readily suggesting the predictions of apocalyptic prophecy regarding the agonies of the last times, revived an expectation of the end of the world. In the autumn of 1917 a group of English clergymen issued a manifesto declaring that in their opinion the signs of the times gave clear indications that the visible return of the Lord was at hand. In Canada and the United States the same view found wide acceptance and was made the subject of numerous 'prophetic' conferences, tracts, and books.

See artt. Antichrist, Eschatology, Parousia.

Literature.—H. Corrodi, *Kritische Gesch. des Chiliasmus*^{2}, 4 vols., Zürich, 1794; L. Gry, *Le Millénarisme dans ses origines et son développement*, Paris, 1904; A. Chiapelli, *Le idee millenarie dei cristiani*, Naples, 1888; H. C. Sheldon, *Studies in Recent Adventism*, New York, 1915; S. J. Case, *The Millennial Hope*, Chicago, 1918; L. Atzberger, *Gesch. der christlichen Eschatologie innerhalb der vornicänischen Zeit*, Freiburg, 1896; E. Wadstein, *Die eschatologische Ideengruppe Antichrist, Weltsabbat, Weltende und Weltgericht*, Leipzig, 1896; W. Bousset, *The Antichrist Legend*, Eng. tr., London, 1896; H. Preuss, *Die Vorstellung vom Antichrist im späteren Mittelalter, bei Luther und in der konfessionellen Polemik*, Leipzig, 1906; F. W. Evans, *Compendium of the Origin, History . . . of the United Society of Believers in Christ's Second Appearing* [Shakers], New York, 1853; E. Miller, *History and Doctrines of Irvingism*, 2 vols., London, 1878; W. B. Neatby, *A History of the Plymouth Brethren*, do. 1902; W. A. Linn, *The Story of the Mormons*, New York, 1902; I. C. Welcome, *Hist. of the Second Advent Message and Mission, Doctrine and People*, Yarmouth, Maine, 1874; J. N. Loughborough, *Rise and Progress of the Seventh-Day Adventists*, Battle Creek, Michigan, 1892; E. Kalb, *Kirchen und Sekten der Gegenwart*^{2}, Stuttgart, 1907; J. F. Silver, *The Lord's Return seen in History and in Scripture as Premillennial and Imminent*, New York, 1914.

S. J. Case.

1 *The Approaching End of the Age*, London, 1878, ^{10}1886.

SECRET SOCIETIES.

SECRET SOCIETIES (Introductory).—In whatever ways religious brotherhoods have been evolved in primitive societies, their main purpose, as at higher levels, has been to attain a closer link, on the part of those composing them, with the divinities, for the ultimate benefit of society. While the social units of the family, the clan, the tribe, have a protective value for those individuals within them and are usually consolidated with the help of religious and magical rites, additional protection and closer communion with divinity is sometimes sought by closer groupings of men, although the form of these groupings may have been determined by other causes (see below). Such fraternities are common among savage tribes. Their purpose is to ensure closer connexion with gods or spirits and greater power in dealing with them. Ritual performances at stated times are gone through. Some moral and religious teaching is connected with the initiatory rites. Such fraternities are frequently engaged in promoting law and order, all the more so because of the mystery which surrounds their actions. Admission is usually gained after severe and protracted initiations and by large payments. The element of mystery which surrounds the doings of these fraternities, their assemblies, and the actions of their members, is an essential feature of their existence in certain areas. It has added to the respect in which they are held and has led to the heightening of the mystery as a means of adding to the prestige and influence of the societies. With the aid of masks, dresses, and sacred objects which no uninitiated person may see with impunity, the members of the society show that they are in intimate relationship with gods or spirits or that these are actually among their ranks. Ultimately, where law and order are concerned, they rule by terror, with the natural result that their powers are abused. These fraternities are found mainly among the N. American Indians, with whom their religious functions are most in evidence, and among the Melanesians and W. African tribes, with whom the aspects of maintaining law and order are more apparent. They are also found in some parts of Polynesia.

Most students of these religious associations now believe that there is some connexion between them and the totemic clan system, especially in N. America. Where totemism is declining, or where the ritual of a totem clan is diffused among other clans, or where amalgamation of totemic clans has taken place, a new grouping may occur—the religious fraternity with ritual borrowed from that of the earlier clans. The connexion is genetic as well as psychological. F. Boas says:

> 'The close similarity between the clan legends and those of the acquisition of spirits presiding over secret societies, as well as the intimate relation between these and the social organization of the tribes, allow us to apply the same argument to the consideration of the growth of the secret societies, and lead us on to the conclusion that the same psychical factor that moulded the clans into their present shape has moulded the secret societies.'[1]

As the clan system loses its rigidity, the esoteric fraternity is made possible. At all events, as J. G. Frazer says, we can hardly doubt that the totem clan and the fraternity are akin.

> 'They have their root in the same mode of thought. That thought is the possibility of establishing a sympathetic relationship with an animal, a spirit, or other mighty being . . . from whom [a man] receives . . . a gift of magical power.'[1]

But these fraternities have some connexion also with the wider tribal organization, especially, according to Webster, where the government of the tribe by headmen is passing over to a more autocratic form of government by chiefs. Here the societies, as in Africa and Melanesia, provide social restraints and enforce law. The point of connexion here as well as with the totemic clan is the elaborate ritual of initiation at puberty to tribal or totemic mysteries, which occurs also as a main aspect of these fraternities. All were once initiated, and all are sometimes still initiated into the lower grades of the association. But sometimes membership in all the grades is limited, as it certainly is in the upper grades which possess the inner mysteries and 'control the organization in their own interests.'[2] The grades now correspond to the system of age-classifications with their respective initiations, as found where no such fraternities yet exist. The real difference between totem-clan and fraternity is that the latter ignores the rigid limits of the former. The totem system is hereditary—a man is born into his totem clan and the members are kinsmen. The fraternity may be partly hereditary, but far more usually entrance to it is not dependent on birth, the members are not necessarily kinsmen, but voluntary associates. Admission depends on purchase, on a man's status or prowess, or on the connexion between a candidate and the spirit-guardian of the group, usually through a vision.

In totemism and tribal organization we find much that is common to the secret associations and *vice versa*—*e.g.*, age-classifications, on the one hand, and grades, on the other; the secret lodge; the *sacra* (dresses, masks, ritual objects, the bull-roarer which frightens off non-members of totem-kin or religious association); elaborate initiation rites; and the possession of supernatural power by the members, generally used for the public good.[3]

In parts of Melanesia where totemism flourishes the fraternity is unknown; where it does not exist, the latter is found.[4] Similarly the fraternities of the Pueblo Indians spring directly from the union of totemic clans into the tribe, the clans still existing as fraternities and preserving their ancient ritual, but adding new members from without the clan. 'The snake dance is simply a form of clan totemism having special modifications, due to environment, to fit the needs of the Hopi.'[5]

LITERATURE.—This is mentioned in the notes. See also A. van Gennep, *Les Rites de passage*, Paris, 1909, p. 109 ff.; L. Frobenius, *Die Masken und Geheimbünde Afrikas*, Halle, 1898.

J. A. MACCULLOCH.

SECRET SOCIETIES (African).—I. *INTRODUCTORY*.—**1. Definition.**—In its strictest sense the term 'secret society' is applied in Africa to the body of persons concerned in the admission, by means of initiation ceremonies, of youths (or maidens) to full tribal or adult rights. The words are also applied to purely religious confraternities (which often serve social ends), to bodies with mixed religious and social functions, and to purely social organizations. Any survey of the facts must reckon not only with this looseness of termi-

[1] 'The Social Organization and the Secret Societies of the Kwakiutl Indians,' *Report of U.S. Nat. Mus. for 1895*, Washington, 1897, p. 662.

[1] *GB*[3], pt. vii., *Balder the Beautiful*, London, 1913, ii. 273.
[2] H. Webster, *Primitive Secret Societies*, New York, 1908, pp. 75, 83, 93.
[3] Cf. Frazer, *Totemism and Exogamy*, London, 1910, iii. 547; Webster, 'Totem Clans and Secret Associations in Australia and Melanesia,' *JRAI* xli. [1911] 483.
[4] Webster, *JRAI* xli. 499, 505.
[5] J. W. Fewkes, *19 RBEW* (1900), p. 1009.

nology, but also with the circumstance that a society which is secret in one area may be found in another with precisely the same functions, rites, and general environment, save that the element of secrecy is lacking.

It will be seen in the course of the survey that the features which bring the societies to a common denomination are not any community of function, but the identity, from a formal point of view, of the rites of the associations which practise initiation or make it a condition of entry into the society, and the identity of the character of the relations which these societies, in respect of one or more points, maintain, as a rule, between themselves and the profane world. The secrecy which they uphold as a means of separating themselves from the non-initiated may refer to almost any point in the complex. Primarily, no doubt, it is to the non-public nature of the rites of initiation that the term refers, or to the veil which is drawn over the nature of the proceedings of fully-initiated members; but it may imply no more than the knowledge of a password or other sign of the duly admitted associate of a confraternity, or the limitation of membership to one or other sex, or even the use of a mask or masks by one or more members, when they appear in public.

It must be borne in mind that for a society with social or political aims secrecy is well-nigh indispensable. Such a society, especially where, as is normally the case, the power, by the operation of a system of age grades, of seniority by purchase, or in some other way, is concentrated in the hands of the few, is in reality a long step in the direction of aristocratic government; the secrecy in which its deliberations are wrapped not only enhances its power by confining the knowledge of its projects to a limited circle, but also casts a glamour round it, which tends to make it more formidable by obscuring the real limits of its power; add to this the fact that supernatural allies are claimed by or ascribed to such a society, and there is no further need to look for explanations of their common element of secrecy.

The same considerations apply to the more purely religious associations; and to them must be added the fact that the right to prepare a charm, to use a spell, to call upon a deity, or to officiate as a priest is a form of wealth, jealously guarded and purchasable at a price. Diviners, doctors, and priests, even more than the ordinary man, have an interest in keeping their secrets inviolate; and it is not surprising to find that their attitude is that of possessors of a trade secret, to be divulged only to those who themselves become members of the gild. In the Ibo area we find, in fact, that the blacksmith and the doctor, like the ordinary man, form their own societies and admit candidates under like conditions; indeed the process of equalization has gone so far that the *ozo* ('blacksmith') title is simply the highest in the hierarchy and does not imply any expert knowledge of the blacksmith's craft.

There is, however, another reason for the secrecy with which many societies surround themselves; and it is perhaps the original reason. All rites of initiation, all membership of any society whatsoever, imply a certain amount of separation from the outside world, a certain affiliation to a new world; this aspect is specially prominent where it is a question of admitting a youth to full tribal rights, a rite expressed from the native standpoint in the guise of a belief in his death and resurrection in the initiation bush. Rites of sacralization imply separation from the profane world; the separated person becomes tabu, for he is a danger to those who do not share his sanctity and is himself endangered by contact with the outside world, until he is restored to it by rites of desacralization.

This ground for secrecy may also play a part where to our eyes purely political considerations are concerned. The paramount chiefs of Sierra Leone undergo a period of separation, just as do youths in their progress to manhood, before they assume the reins of power; this is, however, an intrusion, from the European point of view, of the religious sphere into the realm of politics.

2. Sources. — It is generally recognized that anthropological data collected by the casual voyager are far from reliable even in matters which, so to speak, lie on the surface. It is not surprising, therefore, that much of our material on secret societies fails to attain anything like a reasonable standard of accuracy; for not only is the traveller as a rule debarred from actually seeing what he undertakes to report, but the information which he gathers, usually through an interpreter, from the native population is of necessity derived from non-members where a rule of secrecy is imposed upon a society; and it only needs a little experience in such matters to discover that the wildest reports as to the powers of members are current in the mass of the population. Where the observer has confined himself to a record of the simple occurrences that passed under his own eyes, he may indeed attain a higher standard of accuracy; but his account is inevitably one-sided. It is clear that we have only inadequate accounts of Mumbo Jumbo (Mama Dhiombo); inquiry must show that he acts as a representative of a society, of which he may be the most conspicuous, but is not necessarily the most important, member: his duties are not confined to those appearances which have struck the observer; for he exercises functions inside the society; he may be the operator at the festivals of circumcision or excision.[1] In any case he is only a portion of the institution; our descriptions fall as far short of the truth as would the observations of a traveller who described the functions of the man in possession without mentioning that his authority is delegated, that he is the humble embodiment of the judicial power of the State.

A conspicuous example of the errors into which some authors have fallen is afforded by Golbéry's account of Poro;[2] he says that it is found among five Fula-Susu peoples between the Sierra Leone River and Cape Mount. His location is accurate; but the tribes are neither Fula nor Susu; nothing seems to have been recorded of any society among the Fula, who probably have not in the area mentioned by Golbéry even the isolated villages found in the Timne country. The Susu are separated by the Timne, Limba, and Koranko from the area mentioned; of these three tribes the only one which has Poro is the Timne; but the Timne areas in which the society is found are not those in contact with the Susu; and it is certain that the Timne themselves have borrowed Poro; finally, the Susu society is the well known Simo, now decadent.

II. *DISTRIBUTION.*—In the survey of societies which follows nearly all those for which we have full reliable evidence are noticed; but they are scarcely a tithe of those mentioned by the authorities or known on good evidence to exist. Secret societies appear to abound in French Niger territory and Upper Senegal, but we have so far only a summarized statement of their nature. They are equally numerous in Senegambia and French Guinea; a score of them can be mentioned by name as existing in Sierra Leone—not of course all so important as Poro and Bundu; and we have good accounts of one or two societies of the Kru. From Liberia to the Slave Coast there is a great gap either in our knowledge or in the chain of secret societies, which are represented by only a few religious associations like those which practise the cults of Abirewa and Yewe. Much remains to

[1] Cf. below, II. 3.

[2] S. M. X. de Golbéry, *Fragmens d'un voyage en Afrique*, Paris, 1802, i. 114–122.

be learnt of the Yoruba societies, and most of those of the Edo peoples are mere names. The populous Ibo area, again, is comparatively bare of societies, if we except the dancing and gymnastic maskers and the 'titles'—a kind of age grade in which a rise in rank is attained by payment, often on a considerable scale. From Calabar through Kamerun to the Congo we find societies in swarms: they are found south of the Congo also, but to what extent is not clear. In the interior the Baya and other tribes have initiation schools, and secret societies are reported from the west of Tanganyika. Initiation schools exist among the Yao, Baronga, Basuto, and many other S. African tribes. The Ruanda have an apparently isolated secret society of a religious type; age grades are fully developed among the Masai, the Wanyika, and other tribes of the east, and among the Kru in the west; they are also found among the Ibo, the Edo, and many tribes of the Guinea Coast, but play a smaller part in the life of the people; the grades of secret societies, in so far as these embrace the majority of the population, may be in effect age grades, though arrived at in a different way.

For an adequate survey of the secret societies we must consider them not only from the point of view of outward form and function, but also in their origin, both topographical and psychological. For such a study the materials are at present too scanty; we can only sketch the distribution of some of the main types.

1. Poro.—The Poro society is found in three tribes—Bulom, Mendi, and Timne; but it seems clear that it is indigenous only in the first, or possibly the first two, for it is not known over a considerable part of the Timne area. The Bulom people speak a language of the same type as the Timne—with classes of nouns and prefixes—but there is no doubt that they preceded the Timne in their occupation of the area; the Mendi are at present, linguistically, an offshoot of the Mandingo group, somewhat aberrant in type; but it is more than possible that the main stock of the Mendi was originally allied to the Bulom and drifted away from them in language owing to foreign influence. Another member of the Bulom family, Kisi, has already made some progress in the same direction. It may be regarded as fairly probable that the Poro society has not come to this area from without, but is a native institution; the mention of *Purrus campus* by Ptolemy[1] suggests a great antiquity for it.

(*a*) *Bulom.*—There is little reliable information as to Bulom Poro; but it appears to differ considerably from Mendi Poro.

The *yafe* is said to eat the candidates, whose heads he first breaks; when they are about to come out, the *yafe's* belly is beaten, *i.e.*, a heap of clothes is made and tied tightly, and dragged round the town by the members, who beat it with sticks: some of them call on the *yafe*, who remains in the bush, to hand over the children whom he has taken. The boys are then carried into the town, and the adult members return to the bush; here they uproot trees or break off branches, to represent the efforts of the *yafe* to escape. The boys are kept for three nights in a special house and then put in the *bari*, or meeting-house; they may now walk out accompanied by an initiated member, but must wear long caps to protect their heads, which are said to be very soft, and they must carry on conversation through their guide, for they are yet ignorant of the ordinary language. Finally they receive new names, and Taso (one of the dignitaries of the society and the speaker of the *yafe*) releases them from the restrictions and enables them to come into everyday life again.[2]

(*b*) *Mendi.*—An account of Mendi Poro (or Poi) is given by Alldridge.[3]

Candidates are brought or come to the 'bush' (*kamera*) and are introduced, through a mat door, by a messenger (*wujak*), who puts questions as to their ability to perform impossible feats, and after three attempts they are drawn inside; the bush is divided into compartments, and the same ceremony is gone through a second time. Here the candidate says which section of Poro he elects to join; there are three of these, divided in two cases into subsections; one is for chiefs and has the actual power, one for dignitaries, and one for the mass of the people. When the time comes for the candidates to reappear, the 'devil' marches round the town collecting gifts and then returns to the bush, where dead silence is kept for a time; it is said that the 'devil' has fainted. While he is in the town, all non-members must shut themselves in their houses; the 'devil' makes doleful sounds on a reed covered with spider's web, and these are explained by saying that the 'devil' is about to give birth to the candidates, for he becomes pregnant when they go into the bush. The twisted fern ropes worn by the boys are fastened in the top branches of trees when they come out, and it is said that the 'devil' has gone that way to the sky. When the boys come out, they are allowed to seize live stock, etc., for one day only.

One of the Poro dignitaries is known as Taso; he wears a hat decorated with the skulls and thigh-bones of his predecessors and surmounted by an inverted cone of feathers. When Taso dies, he must be buried in the bush; as no woman may see his dead body, the women withdraw from the town till the funeral is over. Certain women, however, who have fallen sick through penetrating the mysteries of Poro, are initiated into the society, and henceforth enjoy certain privileges.

Poro is said to be put upon fruits and other objects when medicine or some symbol of the society is put on or near them to forbid their use.

(*c*) *Timne.*—There are three kinds of initiation ceremonies in the Timne Poro society, corresponding to the occasions when candidates are introduced.

(1) The first form is used when the *banika* (a screen of grass on the right of the road leading from the village, with the *fari*, a similar screen opposite to it) is to be rebuilt. Quite young children are eligible, and the rites last only one day, or, at most, two or three. The messenger, Raka, seizes the candidate, who is known as *ansuku akbañ*: another name is *egbipe Araka* ('captive of Raka'), but this is a forbidden term. Boys initiated in this way receive no Poro marks; it is probable that they have previously been circumcised; but, if not, it would be necessary to perform the operation as a part of the ceremonies. Raka usually comes in the day-time to carry off the boy, who remains behind the *banika* till about six in the evening. When the rebuilding is finished, water is brought, the boys are washed, and loin-cloths and kerchiefs are put on them; after they have been perfumed, they are taken back to the town and sit in the *bari* for two or three nights, holding *kasimori* (short canes with cloth on each end) in their hands. Rice is brought, and the new members are shown by the initiates (*ansimori*) how to eat, for they pretend to put the *kasimori* into the rice and to be quite helpless, at any rate in some areas.

(2) The second form is also an abbreviated rite; the candidates must be at least five or six years old; it is used when some important person is performing ceremonies and is known as *bankalo*, from the name of the house to which the candidates are taken by already initiated men and boys, who push them three times and at the fourth attempt make them enter, right foot first. When they are taken to the Poro bush, the candidates lie face downwards and are marked: cold ashes are used to outline the herring-bone pattern which is cut between the shoulders with a hook; this is called *angkal* and should meet on the breast-bone; near the waist, at the foot of the line down the spine, is a small triangle. A new name is then given to the candidate, who is called *sokokant* (Poro member in the bush) or by the women *sogbaninga*. Each night they return from the Poro bush to the *bankalo* till the marks are healed, which should take about a week. When they are to be taken out, the door of the house is opened at 6 a.m. and each candidate holds by the waist the one in front of him; the leader is called Banabum; all but him stoop forward as they proceed to the *banika*. Here they stand facing the older members and are washed and dressed as in the former rite. Instruction in Poro law has already been given. They return to the *bari*, holding *kasimori*, and sleep there two or three nights, after which they are released.

(3) The main Poro bush is known as *amporo dif* ('Poro kills'); the candidates are seized by Raka or the *krifi* ('devil'), and the first boy taken is called *atəlpi amporo*; a guardian (*kumra*) is appointed to look after each lot of boys; only wholly uninitiated persons are taken, not those who have undergone either of the previous rites; no woman or uninitiated person may see them, and they live in the *kamambwi* (house in the Poro bush) behind the *banika*. Poro at this stage is called *amfǫk*, 'wrapped' (*i.e.* not public). They are told by Pa Kashi (=Taso) that the *krifi* has eaten them and that nothing may be told to the women; in this form of initiation the candidate is not pushed in through the door by the *ansimori* (initiates). After some months in the bush they make hats of the inner bark of a tree (*Thalia geniculata*, Linn. or *Palisota thyrsiflora*, Benth.) put in the ashes and plaited; taking boys out of Poro

[1] iv. 1. 10.

[2] See also *Freetown Royal Gazette*, v. [1825] 225, vi. [1826] 188; *Proc. Roy. Irish Acad.*, 3rd ser., xv. 36 f.

[3] *The Sherbro and its Hinterland*, London, 1901, pp. 124–138.

is called *atai asəndir* ('drying of the hats'). Poro now ceases to be *amfok*, and the candidates wear black (in some localities white) cloth. They come out holding each other by the waist like the *ambankalo* and are taken out in the same way; they are now *ansimori*.

Women who have got mixed up with Poro are also initiated and receive marks; only married women appear to be eligible. They are called *mambori* ('tortoise-shell') and receive new names like men.

The Poro bush is usually on the road to the west of a village, but may also lie between the two parts into which many villages, especially in Muhammadan areas, are divided. The dignitaries of the society differ from chiefdom to chiefdom.

In one place, in addition to the chief, who is the head, the following personages figure in the rites: Sumano, Kagbinti, Faramancha, Kashi, Yamba, Raka Banabum; there may be more than one of the lower grades. Sumano is elected by all the members and initiated into his functions at the *borom-asar* (hut for the worship of ancestors, with stones representing the dead); he appears to be the principal judge when a case comes before the Poro society. Kashi is said to be chosen by his predecessor and initiated at the *borom-asar*, and he offers sacrifices to consecrate his cap, which is adorned with the skulls and thigh-bones of offenders against Poro law. He is a doctor, and is said to help women in difficult labour; he is subject to certain tabus; he is said to have a kind of magical fire that will fly through the air and kill people, provided he knows where his intended victim is; he must not lie down till this *tumpaň* returns, or he may be killed by it himself. Raka's body is spotted with white clay, and he carries a fibre shield and a sword.

The central figure of the society, the *krifi*, has no distinctive dress; he speaks through a horn of corkwood with spider's web over the hole; he is said to enter a box only large enough for a child. They say that the *krifi* eats candidates or gives birth to them, and, when Soko (Poro) men run, they say the *krifi's* belly shakes. He is said to have a son, Bunu, who is always crying out.

Poro members appear (i.) in order to dance or plunder the property of an offender, (ii.) to bury a member, and (iii.) to seize candidates; they accompany the *krifi*. The members have also a certain amount of control over the chief. In the Timne country the Poro society (and the corresponding Ragbenle society in non-Poro areas) is the upholder of the chief's power. Singularly few tabus are incumbent on the members, beyond the prohibition to communicate Poro secrets; they may not abuse a member as *limpi* ('uncircumcised'), nor throw water over one, nor tell one that he has not been initiated. The only other tabu is on the use of the old name of a man. Of the important legislative and judicial functions of Poro little is known beyond the information, not necessarily very reliable, given by Golbéry and other old writers. Poro appears also to play a certain rôle as a mutual assistance society, and a member can call upon his fellow-members for aid in difficult work, precisely as in other parts a man can call upon those of his own age grade.

Although there is some reason to believe that the Human Leopard society stands in some relation to Poro, where both exist in the same area, it is certain that Poro is found beyond the limits of the Leopard society, and equally certain that the Human Leopard society exists to-day in areas, like the Bulom shore, where Poro is unknown. The Timne tradition clearly points to their having obtained Poro from the Bulom, who occupy the coast south of Freetown, but have now dwindled on the coast to the north till few if any communities exist that have held themselves distinct from the invading Timne. The non-existence of Poro in this area at the present day suggests that it is to the Mendi that we should look for the origin of the society. Some light may perhaps be thrown on the matter when examples of the secret Poro language are available for study.

How far the whole male population was in former days enrolled in the society it is difficult to judge. At the present day the spread of Muhammadanism and Christianity exercises a restraining influence; but even in non-Muhammadan areas in former days, as the rules regarding secrecy imply, there must have been men who were not members of the society.

2. Cannibal societies.—Although the Human Leopard society is commonly regarded as a thing apart, it is merely one of many magico-religious societies; its rites have developed in a special direction. It has been said that this society is not more than fifty years old, and this may well be true of it in its present form; but the *borfima* was originally a Mendi war-medicine formed of the viscera of dead enemies, to which a cult was addressed. At the present day the *borfima* is composed in part of the remains of human victims, in part of other objects; blood from a candidate is rubbed on the *borfima*; he takes an oath by it to preserve secrecy; fat from the *borfima* is also rubbed on his skin together with the mashed leaf of a tree called *nikili*; the mark of the society is cut upon the upper thigh or the buttocks. Victims are sometimes provided by members, sometimes seized by a man dressed in a leopard-skin; the corpse is shared out, portions being sent to absent members, but not farther than can be reached before daybreak; a man who has a *borfima* must eat of the victim; others can do so if they wish; as a rule a man who has no *borfima* does not touch the blood of the victim. The head of the victim is the perquisite of the chief; generally speaking, chiefs join the society in order to obtain *borfima*, which is believed to bring favour with the government and riches; the victim's head gives them authority over their people.

A cannibal society of another type is seen in the Nga of the Aduma (Ogowe River), which exists for the purpose of eating the bodies of dead members, if our information is to be relied on.[1]

3. Tenda.—In French Guinea the Tenda have secret religious societies which form the sole means of government; there appears to be no doubt that their object is to render worship to certain divinities and to obtain their protection; from one point of view the term 'secret society' is a misnomer; for the whole tribe and even slaves who have been reared in the country are initiated, practically without exception. There is, however, an element of secrecy within the society, for there are three grades, apart from the dignitaries, and the lower grades are said to be completely ignorant of the rites of the higher grades; there are, moreover, one or more secret languages. It is uncertain how far women are initiated; but, when members are on the march, they utter a distinctive cry to warn the women of their coming; it may therefore be inferred that they are at most incompletely initiated.

The three degrees are distinguished by their dress or ornaments; admission to the lowest grade coincides with the rite of circumcision, about the age of nine or ten, so that the society appears to partake of the character of a puberty group as well as of a religious association. But the rite of initiation is largely a family matter in the case of males. Admission to the second degree follows about the age of fifteen; the candidates are absent in the bush for several weeks and on their return they are separated from their families, with whom they have hitherto resided, and take up their quarters near the chief. The rite is begun by a sacrifice and consists in the tatuing upon the cheek of the tribal mark; after this any man of the village of the candidate may beat him with a stick; each village which uses the *opeda* (initiation ground) then marshals its candidates, and on their way home they are again liable to be beaten; they are lodged in a hut some 200 yards from the village, and the previously initiated members of their grade await them there. When, a fortnight later, the new initiate returns to the village, he is privileged for the first six days to insult and beat any woman whom he meets. The admission to this grade constitutes the real initiation into the ranks of the adult males, for the youths are told in advance that it involves death and subsequent resurrection; promotion to the next grade takes place when the new initiates reach the hut mentioned above: there is therefore only one group of the second grade in existence at any one time, viz. those who were initiated at the last gathering in the *opeda*; they are promoted as soon as the next group

[1] See also below, 15, Ngil.

of the first grade is advanced to the second grade, which does not happen every year. The head of the society in each village is known as *nemba*, but he never appears in public in this capacity; his agents are the *lukuta*; the *akore* are another class of functionary and, like the *lukuta*, are to be found in each village, from two to eight in number according to its size. The *lukuta*, who may not be seen by women save at certain seasons, appear in public in a bark dress which completely covers them; their function is to carry out the decisions of the *nemba*, to supervise the sacrifices offered by the women before the farming season, to secure the observance of customary law in criminal matters, etc. The *akore*, on the other hand, wear no disguise, but must observe silence when they proceed on a mission; they are concerned with quarrels between husband and wife, but an important part of their functions is to accompany girls after the ceremony of initiation, which consists in the excision of the clitoris, performed by a man.

It must also be remarked that, though the chief of a village is not necessarily one of the dignitaries, he plays an important rôle; it is probable that he nominates the dignitaries, and he can certainly issue orders to them. Moreover, among the Bassari, one of the constituent tribes of the Tenda nation, communal houses are provided for the *faleg* (second grade), the *dyarar* (third grade), and the *dyarar asonkaf* (older unmarried men of this grade). The girls of the village are free to enter these houses and pass the night there, but whether only after initiation at the age of seventeen is not made clear. War and even simple quarrels are forbidden when the initiation rites are proceeding, in the months of June and July.[1]

4. Belli-Paaro.—For the Vai, Gola, and adjacent tribes we have not only the good modern account of Büttikofer,[2] but also narratives by Barbot[3] and Dapper,[4] which go back about 250 years and show us how little change has come over the institution in the intervening centuries. Belli-Paaro is the Vai name for the boys' initiation school, to which the Sande of the girls corresponds; and, though we learn from Dapper of judicial proceedings and ordeals with which are associated the *Belli-mo* (*i.e.* 'Belli man [or priest]') and others, it seems clear that the institution is primarily an initiation school; that this is so may be inferred from the fact that Belli-Paaro and Sande are treated as co-ordinate and complementary.

Boys may enter the bush of their own free will; otherwise they are carried off by the *sova* or *soba*, who is perhaps known to the women under the name *njana* and appears to be regarded as an ancestral spirit. Circumcision is usually performed in the first year of life (by a woman), but a boy not yet circumcised must undergo the rite on entering the Belli. He is informed that he is killed by the spirit when he enters the bush, but returns to life again and receives a new name and the tribal marks. There is a considerable amount of real education, not only in dance and song, with, perhaps, acrobatics, but also in the use of weapons, in the endurance of hunger, thirst, and pain, together with a knowledge of the tribal religion and customary law. Residence in the bush may last from some months to several years, and the release takes place at the end of the rainy season, in October to November, when there is abundance of food for the celebrations. When they come out, the boys wear bark caps, which come down over their eyes; they pretend to be ignorant of the life to which they return. The *sova* appears in a leaf dress and wooden mask and performs all sorts of dances.

No one who has not been through the bush enjoys civil rights, according to Dapper, who also says that the school is held only once in twenty or twenty-five years; he adds that the candidates are killed and roasted in the bush and incorporated in the company of spirits. If a man is accused of theft, murder, or other crime, the *Belli-mo* administers the poison ordeal to him.[5]

5. Kru.—Although the Kru tribes lying to the east of the Vai and Gola have given up circumcision and have no schools of initiation, their territory is not without interest from the point of view of secret societies. In the first place, they have a well-marked system of age grades, under which two classes, the patriarchs and the Sedibo, are the legislature and executive of the nation, with classes of youths and boys below them; admission to all except the lowest class is gained by payment, but the fees are small, and practically every male joins the Sedibo as soon as he marries. Side by side with these classes are secret societies for magico-religious and judicial purposes, such as the hunting out of witches, the detection of thieves, etc. The Kwi-Iru ('children of departed spirits') admit males of all ages except the very young; a 'father' presides over the society, who is not visible or known except to members and who wears a mask during the day. The society comes out at night to find witches, who strip naked and visit houses or dance upon the graves of their victims. Persons found wandering abroad are seized by the Kwi-Iru and put on the top of a house in readiness for the sass-wood ordeal next morning; it is of interest to note that this is one of the functions of the *Belli-mo* among the Vai. The Kwi-Iru society is employed by the Sedibo in its official capacity.

A second society is known as the Deyabo; Deya men are said to be possessed.

A novitiate of three months is necessary, during which continence must be practised; a grass loincloth is the only article of clothing, and the candidate eats and sleeps apart. As a test a fowl's head is cut off and its blood put upon the candidate's eyes; the head is then thrown into the bush, and the candidate must find it, under the penalty of having his symptoms of possession—apparent death, gnashing of teeth, etc.—declared to be unreal or simulated. After passing this test he changes his dress and occupies himself with the manufacture of charms, the discovery of thieves, etc. The societies are in fact associations of diviners such as are common in other parts of Africa.[1]

6. French territories. — We have little or no detailed information as to the secret societies in the French territories of the Niger and Upper Senegal; but M. Delafosse[2] has published an excellent summary, which makes it clear that they are numerous in this area. Delafosse classifies them under three heads: (1) social and non-secret, (2) social and religious at once, and (3) purely religious.

(1) The first class celebrates its ceremonies in public, though its meetings for discussion are private, but the societies embraced in it correspond so exactly to the secret societies proper of other areas that it is necessary to include this kind of society in our survey. Each society is under a genius; it is composed of two or more age grades; it is confined to one sex and concerns itself with circumcision or excision rites. Thus there is one grade for the uncircumcised, who dance dressed in leaves or grass and use the bull-roarer, known as the 'dog' of Ntomo (the name of the society); above them comes the grade of the circumcised, much more important; the adult males form another grade, and it is incumbent upon them to assist each other in all cases; there is a very powerful grade composed of men in middle life; and finally the grade of old men. The women, on the other hand, have only two grades.

(2) In the case of religious societies grades are unknown, all members being on the same level. There are special burial rites for members, who have their own passwords; women are admitted, but only rarely. The rites are semi-secret and confined to initiates; but some ceremonies are public. To this class belongs the Mandingo society known as Kore, which exists for sexual purposes; among the Senufo is a society which prepares its members by a seven years' initiation for authority in the tribe.

(3) The last class is composed of societies devoted

[1] *Rev. d'ethnog. et de soc.* iv. [1913] 31 ff.
[2] *Reisebilder aus Liberia*, Leyden, 1890, ii. 302–308.
[3] A. and J. Churchill, *Collection of Voyages and Travels*, London, 1744–46, v. (containing Barbot, *Description of the Coasts of North and South Guinea*), 126 f.
[4] *Description de l'Afrique*, Amsterdam, 1686, pp. 268–270.
[5] Frobenius, *Die Masken und Geheimbünde Afrikas*, pp. 116–120.

[1] H. H. Johnston, *Liberia*, London, 1906, ii. 1068, 1072; J. L. Wilson, *Western Africa*, do. 1856, p. 129.
[2] *Haut-Sénégal-Niger*, 1st ser., Paris, 1912, iii. 119.

to certain cults or to the practice of certain magico-religious rites. Some are confined to one sex, some initiate both sexes indiscriminately; some are absolutely secret, some secret for women only, while non-initiated men may follow their doings. As examples of these societies may be mentioned the Mandingo Tyi-wara, which practises the non-secret cult of the genius of agriculture, and the Koma society, formed to resist enchanters (*suba*). Masks are worn by the representatives of the genius and his satellites; special instruments of music are in use, and the meetings are held at night in the sacred bush.

In the absence of detailed information it is useless to attempt to discover the centre or centres of origin of these different types or to speculate as to the ethnical conditions that have given rise to them.

7. Yewe.—If initiation societies exist on the Gold and Ivory Coasts, little or nothing has been recorded of them, and the almost complete absence of masks from these areas supports the view that there is a real gap in the distribution of societies. In Jaman masks are used in connexion with the cult of Sakrobudi,[1] and girls are dedicated to certain 'fetishes' at Krobo.[2] In Dahomey, however, an important religious secret society took its rise, which has since spread over parts of Togoland. This is the cult of Yewe, which appears to be a mixture of the worship of Xebieso, Voduda, and Agbui. The area is remarkable for the number of different languages spoken in it, often by quite small communities, and it is probable that the secret languages, of which more than one are used by the priests according to their original divinity, are in reality survivals of otherwise extinct local forms of speech preserved for a special purpose. Both sexes are admitted to the society, which has three grades: Husunuo for males, Yewesiwo and Vodusio for females, and Hundeo or Hunovio for both sexes.

The initiation ceremony consists in drinking water; certain emblems are also exhibited, such as a piece of iron wrapped in a cloth, which represents Yewe, a double axe, the emblem of So, a ram's horn, a holed stone, a long stone, and a bent iron. These are dipped in holy water, and the candidate is touched with them; the drinking of the water is sometimes explained as the taking of the god into the body of the candidate. A female candidate is shaved, washed, and rubbed with oil; she then receives a new cloth and a new name in place of her old one; during her sojourn of six months in the bush she learns the use of poisons and the secret Yewe language, known as Agbuigbe, which is said to be spoken as an ordinary language in Avleketi, near Dahomey. When the time comes for the candidate's release, a feast is made, and presents are offered to the priest.

It is incumbent upon members to assist each other in every way and to inform against all who speak ill of Yewe and his followers. Among the reasons which lead people to enter the service of Yewe is the freedom from restraint and even from ordinary law enjoyed by the members, who thus escape, *e.g.*, the penalty for non-payment of debt, which consisted in being buried alive or, at best, in death. If it is desired to compel an influential man to join the community, a small pot is buried in one of his fields; when this is dug up later, he has no choice but to become a priest. From motives of policy the chiefs endeavour to stand well with the Yewe society, even if they are not members. If a non-member insults a female member, the latter becomes *alaga* (a wild woman); she lives in the bush all day, returning to the Yewe house at night; if she is not 'brought home' soon, she is said to change into a leopard, and her enemy is soon compelled to make terms. In like manner the aid of Yewe may be invoked in legal cases by throwing over the defendant's head a ring made of oil-palm and other leaves; this compels the Yewe priest to take the matter up, and as a result the loser is compelled to pay three times the amount of the original demand, which is extorted from him, if necessary, by torture.

There is no doubt that the Yewe cult is alien to a large part of the area in which it prevails, and the complex is probably of comparatively recent origin; but there is good reason to believe that some at least of the elements which go to form it are of considerable antiquity.[1] This rise of a new cult is by no means an isolated phenomenon; for in recent years there have been similar manifestations on the Gold Coast, where the Abirewa 'fetish' gained great influence for a time; in like manner in Nigeria the cult of Isinegba has come down from the north. There can be no doubt that, generally speaking, this spread of a religion is a common occurrence in Africa; but, whereas one cult attains great influence and social importance, another, like the cult of Esu in the Yoruba-Edo area, has little beyond a kind of magical significance and brings no further profit to its votaries than the sense of protection against the evils of this life which the putting up of the image of Esu outside the house brings.

From the point of view of the present article, stress must be laid upon the fact that, before a man can take up the worship of a deity, a rite of some sort must as a rule be observed, which may range from a full-blown ceremony of initiation, parallel in every respect to that of an initiation society proper, to a simple transfer of a piece of earth in a pot to symbolize the transference to a new owner of the right to call upon the divinity represented by the piece of earthenware. The explanation of the secrecy of the rites lies on the surface: the social importance of the cult is increased and the authority of its officers enhanced by shutting the door upon the outside world.

It is perhaps not without significance that on the Gold Coast and in adjacent areas, where secret societies of the ordinary type appear to be wanting, these mushroom religions seem to attain their greatest development.[2]

8. Ogboni, Oro, Egũgũ.—In the Yoruba area we find a political secret society supported by a secondary organization with police duties; the latter has a parallel in the Zangbeto society of Porto Novo and more or less close analogues in parts of the Ibo area and the Congo. The government of the country is in the hands of the Ogboni, or elders; they are the heads of important families, but are accepted for membership only if reliable and capable men; the rank is said to descend from the oldest brother to the youngest, provided the latter is old enough and otherwise qualified. The Eda image is the amulet of the society, and a human sacrifice is offered on it at the initiation of a candidate, who is sometimes called upon to drink the blood of the victim. She is their goddess and is equated with Odudua of Benin city. The Oro society, composed of males only, carries out the decisions of the Ogboni, more especially among the Egba; members indicate their coming by swinging the bull-roarer, and, as soon as they hear this, all women must shut themselves up in their houses under pain of death, though they may see the instrument by day and even carry it. Criminals are usually disposed of in such a way that nothing more is seen of them than their clothes, high up in the branches of forest trees, where they were torn off as Oro hurried their wearers through the air;

[1] R. A. Freeman, *Travels and Life in Ashanti and Jaman*, London, 1898, p. 148.

[2] D. Kemp, *Nine Years at the Gold Coast*, London, 1898, p. 165.

[1] H. C. Monrad, *Bijdrag til en Skildring af Guinea-Kysten*, Copenhagen, 1822, describes the proceedings of a woman who feels herself insulted by her husband or some other person, and they bear a close resemblance to those of the *alaga*.

[2] *Zeitschr. für afrikan. und ocean. Sprachen*, iii. [1897] 157–185; Frobenius, *loc. cit.*

in this case Oro is said to have devoured the bodies. When the body is found on the ground in the bush, no one is allowed to bury it. The central figure of the Oro society wears a white mask and a long gown hung with shells; his voice is heard from morning till night on the days on which he appears.

Egũgũ is another secret society of the Yoruba and, according to some, is associated with the Zangbeto of Porto Novo.[1] Egũgũ appears at an annual festival, a kind of All Souls' Day, and also at burial ceremonies, and is the police power of the Yoruba;[2] in the territory of neighbouring tribes the mask also appears as a kind of diversion, without any significance, for the purpose of obtaining money for its wandering owners. The mere appearance of a mask does not justify us in speaking of a secret society; in the Ibo territory the *mauṅ* come out at burial ceremonies, but there is nothing worthy of the name of a secret society associated with them, though all knowledge of the fact that the masker is only a man is kept in the strictest manner from the women of the tribe; when, a few years ago, the ritual prohibitions of a portion of the Ibo nation were abolished by sacrifices in the presence of the Ezenri, the one point which it appeared important to the men to retain was the concealment of the real nature of the *mauṅ*, though among the prohibitions thus summarily abolished was that of marriage with one's sister and similar fundamental ordinances.

9. Ovia.—According to R. F. Burton,[3] Oro was in existence at Benin; but this seems to be a misinterpretation of what the author saw. Okiason or Akpoka was the name given to men who used to wander at night during a certain season of the year, carrying an axe or, according to another account, a hammer, with which they used to kill people to procure certain portions of the bodies with which the king made 'medicine.' There is, however, no evidence of the use of a mask by members of this body. It is perhaps more probable that what Burton saw was the Ovia celebrations, which Fawckner[4] saw at Gwatõ and described as the 'dance of the great devils,' adding that no one ventured out at night when they were about for fear of being killed or maltreated. As the Ovia society at the present day dances in public only in the day-time and performs nocturnal rites in the Ovia enclosure alone, with the exception of one night, it seems probable that the author was misled, if he did not confuse the Ovia members with the Okiason.

According to tradition, Ovia was a woman, the wife of a certain king of Yoruba land, who was hated by her mates; by a trick they caused her to fall into disfavour with her husband, who turned her away, whereupon she began to weep and melted into water. She ordered that no woman should know the secret of her cult or enter the Ovia camp; hence she is worshipped by men only, and women hold aloof from the rites, except on two occasions: when the ceremonies are about to begin, at the beginning of the dry season, women come to the camp of Ovia to rub the house; and on one night during the subsequent rites they enter the camp and sing while the men dance; they also understand, unofficially, the secret language which is spoken by the men whenever they are wearing their dresses. Although the mask of the chief figure of the society is known as the 'mother' mask, he is always addressed as 'my father,' and the women in their songs speak of him as *ogie* ('prince'); there is therefore some doubt as to the facts, and it would be rash to lay any stress for purposes of interpretation on either the male or the female character of the principal figure.

There are four grades in the society: a boy joins at the age of seven or eight and remains one year in Oyo, the first grade, paying in kind to the value of perhaps ten shillings; a sacrifice is offered, and the boy marks his face with chalk; he is henceforth an Owiovia ('son of Ovia'); he remains seven years in the second grade, Igbe, admission to which costs only sixpence; the other two grades, equally easily attained, are Ixino and Urewa. The head man of the village is usually but not necessarily the head of the society; the second man wears the Ovia hat and, on certain occasions, a net mask and other ritual apparel. He, like the third man in the society, is selected for his knowledge of the rites.

The camp of Ovia consists of an enclosure, a house, and a small screened portion of the bush, where the elders meet to discuss during the ceremonies. In the Ovia house are kept the musical sticks (*akpasiko*), bull-roarers (*emilovia*), and, when the rites are in progress, the dresses, consisting of long clothes with a net mask, and enormous hats decorated with red parrots' feathers. Both in the nocturnal dances and in the procession of the masked Ovia round the village, which women are allowed to see, prayers are offered for the welfare of the community, and a ceremony is performed, for male children only, to prevent them from suffering from convulsions; when the child is handed back to the mother, she pours water on his head; otherwise she may not touch him. In the other daylight dances the Ovia mask does not appear, but the other members dance in their hats and masks every morning and evening in their own village.

The Ovia society clearly differs in a marked degree from any of those which have hitherto come under notice; it wears masks but is not a bugbear for the women; it has neither legislative nor police functions; although Ovia receives a cult of a kind at ordinary times, a shrine being kept outside the house of such people as worship him (or her), the object of the annual celebration does not appear to be the recognition of a divinity, for the annual rites in honour of Ake, *e.g.*, largely made up of sacrifices, may be regarded as the normal type of this description of rite. There is some evidence for the view that the object is to avert evil and bring good, for all the supplications emphasize this aspect; but it seems improbable that any such customs could have grown up round such a nucleus. On the whole it appears more probable that the ceremonies are connected with the growth of crops, though next to no evidence can be produced in favour of this view; at most we can quote a passage in one of the songs to the effect that 'our prince shall grow like a young palm-tree.' In accordance with this interpretation is the saying that Ovia 'dies' when the ceremonies are at an end.

10. Other Edo societies.—Innumerable masks are found in various parts of the territory of the Edo-speaking peoples, some isolated, some associated with organized groups, some appearing in connexion with initiation ceremonies, some at certain seasons of the year, some on the occasion of funeral rites, some apparently quite sporadically; but few, if any, are of much significance, and little information has been or, probably, can be obtained about them; the masks are the property of individuals, who readily dispose of them for a few shillings apiece. Their local character is shown by the fact that at Otua, where, as elsewhere in this area, age grades are of some importance in the life of the community, only one quarter of the ten or twelve of which the town is composed has a certain set of highly decorative and somewhat costly masks, for use when, every three years, a new 'company' comes in. They dance at any time they please for the next three months, and women and children are not permitted to approach the *elimi* house; but beyond this there is no special element of secrecy.

At Fugar maskers, one male, the other female, appear at the initiation of girls, which consists merely in a festival to celebrate their putting on clothes for the first time; cowries are given to the maskers. The wearer of another mask is permitted to kill any goats that he sees, and this feature recalls the licence permitted to the newly-circumcised in many parts of W. Africa; it seems not improbable that such celebrations are only a faded reproduction of customs practised at an earlier date. The maskers are called *alimi* ('dead people').

11. Ibo societies.—When we pass eastwards to the Ibo area, masks are equally common; some are associated with burial rites and do not appear to

1 *Annales de la propagation de la Foi*, v. [1831] 194.

2 Frobenius, *loc. cit.*, and *Und Afrika Sprach*, Berlin, 1912, i. 55; Baudin, in *Les Missions catholiques*, xvi. [1884] 257.

3 *Abeokuta and the Camaroons Mountains*, London, 1863, i. 195.

4 *Narr. of Capt. James Fawckner's Travels on the Coast of Benin, W. Africa*, London, 1837.

belong to any organized society; others are worn by dancers, who have no functions, however, resembling those of the members of secret societies of other areas; all maskers appear to be known indiscriminately as *mauṅ* ('dead people'); many, if not all, of them appear during the day, and the only element of secrecy is the concealment of the knowledge of their identity from the women. So much of the Ibo life has been borrowed from Benin that we may conjecture that these masked figures do not represent anything that ever played a more important part in tribal life. It is possible, however, that the societies to which they may have belonged have been overshadowed by the rise of the custom of taking 'titles.' These correspond roughly to generation grades or age grades, for originally a man took his first title after the death of his father; by a series of changes, however, of which the tradition is preserved, a man rises from grade to grade by payment, the only limitation being that he must have attained maturity; but even in this case the rule is not universal; for, apart from the fact that a father may purchase a a title for his son, some of the titles, or at any rate their material benefits, are inheritable. In practice the system of titles provides the most profitable and indeed the only method of investing money, if we except the purchase of wives; in a rich community like Awka the highest grade may cost hundreds of pounds, and, as all subsequent members contribute the like amount, naturally in kind, not money, and their instalments are shared among the existing members, the result is the creation of a system of annuities.

From another point of view, these titles correspond to trade gilds; for the highest grade is that of *ozo* ('blacksmith'); it may be mentioned that a large proportion of the population of Awka is composed of blacksmiths, and it is possible that the customs, which have there attained perhaps their greatest development, also came from there originally, or were at the very least deeply influenced in their evolution by the fact that the blacksmiths of Awka, like the doctors (another grade) of the neighbouring town of Nibo, wandered far and wide over the face of the country in the practice of their trade, the doctors indeed without let or hindrance even in time of war. The Awka ceremonies have clearly influenced those of the towns immediately to the west of the Niger; but from the fact that the Udo bush figures largely in the Awka ceremonies and that an Udo (bush) was also of some importance in the rites of Benin connected with the worship of beads, it might be argued that Benin was the centre of origin; but much stress cannot be laid upon the point, for there is no evidence that the blacksmiths of Awka were in the habit of visiting Benin. The native explanation of the meaning of the first grade is that it indicates the freeborn status of the holder, and this is perhaps the most likely origin for this group of customs.

12. Egbo.—Although the Egbo society of Calabar is one of the most famous secret societies, we are singularly ill-informed as to the initiation ceremonies; there are, according to some authorities, ten or eleven grades, which are attained by purchase; but of the rites which actually admit the purchaser to the mysteries of the grade nothing seems to have been recorded. In some respects the society resembles the hierarchy of the Ibo titles; but there is an important difference; for the Egbo society is represented by a masked figure and thus stands nearer such societies as Poro. One tradition says that Egbo originated in a market situated between Calabar and Kamerun, where the traders decided to form it as a means of upholding order; but, quite apart from the fact that the African market is by nature orderly, this can hardly explain the existence of the masked figure, a non-human personage, nor yet the circumstance, reported by one author,[1] that Egbo comes out only at full moon, apart from circumstances of civil disorder. Each grade is said to have its own 'spirit' and its own day; on the day of the highest grade all houses have to be shut, and any one who wishes to go out must purchase the right.

The most striking and probably the most important side of the Egbo society was its judicial procedure;[2] a non-member had to purchase the protection of a member before his claim could be brought before the society; or he might even give himself to an important chief as a slave as a means of ensuring success. The intervention of the society could be secured by touching a member on the breast or by striking the big Egbo drum. In any case, the power of the society once invoked, a meeting had to be called and the case heard. When judgment was given, a representative of the society proceeded at once to the house of the loser; and not until the penalty had been exacted might any one of the inmates of the house leave it, even though they were wholly innocent of the matter in respect of which the charge was brought.

Like Poro, the Egbo society protected by its symbol the property of any one who put it in their charge; and here we see a side of the institution which recalls the tabu.[3]

13. Ndembo and Nkimba.—In the Lower Congo area the main societies, sometimes under other names, are Ndembo and Nkimba. There does not seem to be any ground for regarding the former as a puberty society; for both sexes join, and some persons pass through it several times. According to J. H. Weeks,[4] the object of joining is to escape from disease or malformation.

The candidate feigns death in some public place and is carried to the bush, where his body is said to decay till only one bone is left, which is kept by the doctor, who is supposed to raise him again from the dead. He receives a new name, is taught to eat, to feign complete ignorance, and to use a secret language, the vocabulary of which, however, is very limited.

There is more doubt as to the position of Nkimba, but good authorities assert that it has nothing to do with circumcision. Unlike Ndembo, mutual assistance is one of the objects of the society. It also aims at inuring youths to hardship; some societies (for there are many of the name, all restricted to males) check the power of the chiefs; in some cases the licence permitted to the members is the attraction, for they are allowed to assault travellers and rob them, in accordance with the principle that the candidates are separated from this world and therefore not amenable to ordinary law.

The candidate is drugged, dressed in a palm-leaf apron, whitened with clay, and taught a secret language, far more extensive than that of Ndembo; he also learns botany and spells, and hunts witches.

Like the Ndembo, the society is under a *ngaṅa* ('doctor'); there is therefore some ground for regarding it as different in character from an initiation school, especially as it is not necessary for all members of the tribe to pass through it; on the other hand, it is not necessary to suppose, with Weeks, that its objects were originally identical with those of Ndembo, unless the derivation of the name from *lemba*, 'to deliver,' should be well founded. It is, however, of some importance that Nkita, which is a local name for Nkimba, also means a power that inflicts disease and malformations.

[1] J. Thormählen, in *Mittheil. Geograph. Gesellsch.*, Hamburg, 1884, p. 332.

[2] Frobenius, p. 87.

[3] P. Amaury Talbot, *In the Shadow of the Bush*, London, 1912, p. 37 ff.; H. M. Waddell, *Twenty-nine Years in the W. Indies and Central Africa*, do. 1863, p. 247 ff.

[4] *Among the Primitive Bakongo*, London, 1912, p. 159.

Nearly the whole of our information regarding the Congo and Kamerun area is tainted with suspicion owing to the contradictions of the various authorities and still more to the new facts brought to light about the Fang societies by H. Trilles.[1] From his study it appears that there is a sharp line of demarcation between societies of priests and societies of sorcerers or witches. Both are secret, in a sense, but the meetings of the former, though closed to the profane, are held openly, and their place of meeting is known; sorcerers, on the other hand, who have a different kind of initiation, meet in private, for to be known as a sorcerer involves the poison ordeal and probably death. Totems, or animal protectors, are associated with both kinds of society; but the priest has an animal species forbidden to him *qua* priest, while the sorcerer has an individual animal familiar; the life of the priest is in no way bound up with his animal species, that of the sorcerer is linked to that of his familiar. There are human victims, whose blood is mixed with that of one of the 'totems' at the initiation of the priest, but only this ritual cannibalism is practised by the society; the sorcerers practise food cannibalism, and the rites may have in view magical purposes as well. Perhaps the most important difference is that the society of priests has a species of animal tutelar sacred to it, as it were, a totem, while the sorcerers are guarded by a spirit, possibly of a dead human being, as the name *engungure* is the same for both. Each society has an inferior grade of initiates, who assist in all the rites, but are not priests or sorcerers; the initiation of youths is distinct from the initiation rites already mentioned and precedes them.

It is clear at the outset that some of the distinctions drawn by Trilles cannot be applied to other areas—*e.g.*, the use of a protecting spirit by sorcerers only—but it is uncertain over what extent of territory his criteria will apply; it is probable that the features which he describes are not confined to the Fang, for it is common for elements of culture to spread laterally, without distinction of tribe, over a wide area. Until more exact data are to hand, it is impossible to deal at length with the societies of the region from the Cross River to the Congo.

It remains to be seen how far the distinctions drawn by Trilles are valid; for, although he distinctly states[2] that Ngil is a sorcerers' society, he also appears to imply[3] that it is a priests' society; and he formulates the same opinion without ambiguity in another work.[4] It seems clear that Ngil comes into the village openly, to detect thieves and murderers and punish unfaithful wives; not only so, but an initiate of Evodu, which is recruited in the three societies, Ngil, Ngan, and Akhun—themselves made up of devotees of Bieri, the national god, whose cult is confined to the warriors—acts, at least sometimes, as operator in the circumcision rites;[5] and Ngil must therefore, as the author says, be a grade of priests. On the other hand, it is affirmed with equal decision that the rites of initiation into Ngil include obscene practices, which are cited as a mark of sorcery. Further inquiry is needed before the distinction drawn by Trilles can be regarded as established.

14. Gabun.—North of the Congo, in the Ogowe region, are found secret societies too numerous to describe in detail. It has already been mentioned that masks appear at burial rites in parts of W. Africa; among the Balimba, Malanda is specially associated with funeral rites and the dead.

Fourteen days after the death of a member of a family a house is built on the edge of the bush by men only; a male figure is carved; the corpse disinterred, the brains are mixed with chalk and the body is tied to the side wall, while the image is at the closed end of the house. Women are warned not to look at Malanda, and the elders announce his coming in the morning. Twenty boys sit down on a long log; when they are exhausted, they are blindfolded and taken to the bush house; here a bundle known as *yaka*, consisting of brains and chalk, is opened and the new mixture added; this is then used as an ointment and smeared on the breasts of the candidates, vertically for those who are not 'witches,' horizontally for 'witches.' A six-foot pit is dug with a tunnel leading under the wall, into which the corpse is put; the skeleton is exhumed later, divided vertically, and the two portions are laid apart parallel to each other; the boys, formed into two companies, step over the remains, and an oath of secrecy is administered to them.[6]

15. Ngil.—The account of the initiation ceremonies is not free from obscurities, but it is clear that the same rites are undergone both by associates of the society, whose course of training is short, but includes two stages, and by the candidate for the position of Ngil, selected some six years younger than the age at which associates join, and trained to the work by constant association with the actual Ngil, whom he accompanies when a summons calls him from the bush.

After candidates of both classes have undergone various trials, they are secluded in the bush and are tortured by ants, flogging, etc. Those who pass these tests undergo a second period of seclusion, during which they provide a victim, sometimes a younger brother, but more often a mother, sister, or daughter (it is not explained how a candidate at the age of eighteen can do so); a euphorbia is cut down and the stump hollowed; into this is allowed to drop the blood of the victim, sacrificed by the novice himself and mingled with the sap; the members drink of the mixture, and then the victim is cooked and eaten. During this rite the novice is partially intoxicated with the sap of a tree called *ava* and a sort of fungus; but it is somewhat singular that there is no mention of any belief in death and resurrection.

It has already been mentioned that Evodu (possibly the origin of Voodoo, but cf. Dahomé *vodun*, 'fetish') is a higher grade; the highest of all is called Kouṅ; it is said to have only three members—rulers of the waters, of the winds, fire, and fecundation, and of the earth and men respectively. In the view of Trilles[1] the higher grades are clearly priestly in their character; and the Kouṅ grade comes near, if it is not actually identical with, the divine king of J. G. Frazer; it is therefore a curious and interesting problem to ascertain whether the Ngil society is really one of priests or of sorcerers, or whether it combines features of both.[2]

16. South-east Congo.—Masked figures play an important part in the south-east Congo, but it is not clear how far we can speak of a real secret society; from the reports of the earlier authors the mask appears to be the property of certain families; among other functions the Mukish is a rain-maker, prepares counter-magic, expels evil spirits, and exercises judicial functions; it might therefore be supposed that it is a case of a witch-doctor with special powers; it must, however, be remembered that the *ngaṅa* presides over the Ndembo and Nkimba; and, as it is expressly stated that Mukish directs a circumcision school, there is no reason for questioning the justice of the epithet 'secret society' in connexion with this masker.

17. Imandwa.—The Ruanda of E. Africa have an important society, the Imandwa, primarily religious in its nature, as it depends on the worship of *imandwa* (men, birds, etc.) and *angombe* (a grove, also a mortal hero); the aim of members, however, is to obtain success in life and other social objects, and all are sworn to secrecy. A sponsor is necessary, who becomes the representative of the *angombe*; other members invited to be present become the *imandwa* of the *angombe*; the profane are kept at a distance while the ceremonies are proceeding.

The candidate is thrown into the air, and a threat is made to cut him up; he receives a new name and enters into a blood-bond with his sponsor. The rites completed, the new initiate is transferred back to the world of men, and a feast is celebrated. Some time after another series of rites is held, which the missionary to whom we owe our knowledge of the society terms 'confirmation.'[3]

18. Labi.—The duplication of initiation ceremonies mentioned above, though unusual, is not without parallel, for the Baya and other tribes of the hinterland of Kamerun proceed in the same way.

A boy joins the Labi at the age of eight or ten; they have their own villages and their own farms; their secret language, made up in part of contributions from the dialects of other tribes, is intertribal in character; and candidates carry a basket shield covering the body from the head to the knee. After six months' instruction they are taken to the river and dropped through traps made of leaves; when they are half-asphyxiated, they are fished out again and wounded with a spear so guarded with a bark sheath that the point penetrates less than half an inch. The eyes, nose, and ears of the Labi are then washed to indicate that their senses have undergone a change. At a later stage the Labi return to the bush, covered by their shields, and receive a physical and moral education; when they again come out, they are free to marry.[4]

1 *Le Totémisme chez les Fâṅ*, p. 436.
2 Pp. 453, 463.
3 P. 441.
4 *Quinze Années chez les Fâṅ*, Lille, 1912, p. 210, though on p. 200 Ngil figures as a society of sorcerers.
5 *Ib.* p. 212.
6 R. H. Nassau, *Fetichism in W. Africa*, London, 1904, p. 250 ff.; cf. pp. 128, 247, 320; Frobenius, *loc. cit.*

1 *Quinze Années*, p. 214.
2 *Ib.* p. 174 ff.
3 *Anthropos*, vii. [1912] 273, 529, 840, viii. [1913] 110, 754.
4 *La Géog.* xvii. [1908] 453-457; E. A. Lenfant, *La Découverte des grandes sources du centre de l'Afrique*, Paris, 1908, p. 198.

19. Area south of the Congo. — Ordeals like those recorded for the Baya are a frequent feature of initiation ceremonies outside Africa. More elaborate kinds have been found among the Bushongo by Torday; candidates have to pass through a tunnel in which are a human leopard, a blacksmith with a furnace and hot iron, and other tests of courage. More commonly, especially in S. Africa, the ordeals consist in frequent beatings (explained as intended to harden the boys) and fasts.

Among the Basuto the candidates are associated together as a company with a young chief; they are brought back from the fields, where they hide, by armed warriors, and huts are built in the bush for them; after circumcision they are exercised in the use of arms; tribal rules are inculcated, and they undergo long fasts; the initiation over, the huts are burned, and the initiates leave them without looking round, for they are leaving their old life behind and are now at liberty to visit their families, especially their mother's brother, who gives them a spear and a heifer. Until they marry, they live in the men's house near the chief's hut and are assigned to works of public utility. In some at least of the tribes the solidarity of the company thus initiated is very marked; they may not eat food alone if some of their fellows are near, and they may not give evidence against a companion; the young chief chooses his councillors from them. An uninitiated man is reckoned as a child and may neither inherit property nor marry a wife.[1]

20. Masai, etc.—When we come to tribes like the Masai, the rites are less complicated, but the system has hardened into a hierarchy of age grades—so much so that a youth cannot be circumcised unless his father has joined the appropriate class, that of the old men. It is possible, however, to vary the age of circumcision on other grounds, such as poverty. There appears to be a good deal of uncertainty as to the number of age grades; either they vary from place to place or, what is perhaps more likely, each company, composed of the initiates for a period of five years (the interval between two series of rites), may also bear names, as in Nigeria, and these names have been confused with the more fundamental age grades. Apart from a few days of seclusion there is little or nothing in the age grades of the Masai which would justify the epithet 'secret.'

The Wanyika, on the other hand, have a well-developed political organization, on the basis of age grades, which seems to deserve the name better; some of the grades are in reality castes, for the *babasi* (wizards) form the highest rank; the next below them, the *fisi*, perform judicial functions and swear criminals on the hyena, from which they take their name, and protect the crops with the emblem of the hyena.[2]

21. Women's societies.—Apart from societies open to both sexes there are associations open to women only, some (probably the great majority) of the nature of initiation schools, others social or magical in their functions. For obvious reasons less information is available about women's societies: women do not inform the male inquirer of their doings, and female anthropologists in W. Africa have been few.

In Sierra Leone the female initiation society is known as Bundu; there is reason to suppose that it was originally a Mendi institution; from them it passed to the Timne; they in their turn are handing it on at the present day to the Limba, among whom the practice is confined to certain areas, together with the clitoridectomy which is the central feature of the rites of Bundu. Initiation schools for women are also found among the Vai and Gola, on the Lower Congo, among the Basuto and other S. African tribes, the Wayao of British Central Africa, and in all probability over a wide area of French Guinea and Senegambia; but reliable information is to hand for the Tenda people only. Both among the Wayao and among the Masai the stages of female initiation are regulated to some extent by the age of the candidate, though the age grade is less important for women than for men. The women's society not unnaturally exercises a certain amount of control over men, especially married men; males are of course forbidden to approach the bush and culprits have to buy themselves free on pain of falling victims to disease.

Among the Mpongwe an influential society exists, in some respects like the political organizations of the men. It is known as Njembe and appears to be feared by the men; it claims to discover thieves, but its main object is said to be to protect women against hard usage on the part of the male portion of the community.

There are also a certain number of magical and religious societies membership of which is confined to women; among the Timne the Raruba society sprinkles the farms with 'medicine' in order to procure good rice; the Attonga society of the Bulom is concerned with the cult of ancestors. Societies have also been recorded among the Ibibio.

Among the Mendi a society exists to which both men and women are admitted; but two distinct sides appear to be confined each to one sex; the male Humoi society has a 'devil' on which oaths are taken; the female Humoi society punishes offences against the marriage regulations known as *simongama*, as well as breaches of its own rules; in such cases the male offenders enter the house of the women's society.

III. *THEORIES OF ORIGIN.* — Secret societies have been discussed in three monographs. The first author to deal with them was Leo Frobenius, whose main thesis was the manistic nature of the secret society; he based this contention largely upon the feigned death and resurrection of the novice and also upon the rôle played by masked figures, interpreted as visitants from the spirit world, if not actually ancestral ghosts. He was followed by H. Schurtz, who referred age grades and secret societies to the operation of a 'gregarious instinct,'[1] assuming as axiomatic the essential identity of phenomena such as the men's house, age grades, initiation schools, and religious confraternities; he failed to observe that the identity of the rites is conditioned by the identity of their aim—to transfer a human being from one condition of life to another — and not by the functional homogeneity of the societies; a gregarious instinct no more explains the existence of secret societies than it explains the existence of armies; in each case we have to look for the ulterior motive which suggests to man the desirability of combining with his fellows. Hutton Webster starts with the idea that secret societies are everywhere lineal descendants of primitive initiation ceremonies, and he regards as degenerate many forms which may equally well be rudiments awaiting the opportunity for further development.

A different course is taken by van Gennep, who puts aside the questions of origin and function and shows that the rites on which stress has been laid owe their identity to the primitive conception of initiation, which persists in the great religions in the notion of rebirth, and not to the character of the society to which they admit the novice.

It is clear, from the survey of societies in the preceding pages, on which side the truth lies. There can be little doubt that the contention of Frobenius is in part justified, though it may be

[1] D. Kidd, *The Essential Kafir*, London, 1904, p. 206; H. A. Junod, *The Life of a South African Tribe*, do. 1912, i. 71–99.

[2] A. C. Hollis, *The Masai*, Oxford, 1905, p. 294 f.; *Brit. E. Africa Report*, 1897, p. 10; M. Merker, *Die Masai*, Berlin, 1904, p. 60 ff.

[1] This instinct, however, is well marked among the Chinese of the present day, who appear to form societies merely for the sake of forming them.

questioned whether it is true of the majority of societies that they are founded on a primitive type, in which an ancestral spirit figured as the genius or the presiding deity of the society, or in which, it may be, the unity of the society expressed itself in the belief that its spiritual power was concentrated in a human being possessed by, or reincarnating, such a spirit. If it is true that the spirit which protects a society is often, as among the Vai, expressly affirmed to be ancestral, there does not, on the other hand, appear to be good ground for treating the fiction of death and resurrection as a proof of the manistic element in secret societies; for the same feature is found among tribes which, unlike the natives of Africa, lay no stress on the cult of the dead and do not appear to connect their initiation ceremonies in any way with their dead ancestors. In any case, if this feature is manistic in Africa, it should be possible to produce evidence of explicit native beliefs on the subject, instead of inferences from rites and other controversial evidence.

If, with Webster, we assume the clan initiation ceremonies to have been the prototype of secret societies, it does not follow that we must admit the lineal descent of all societies from such rituals; for nothing seems clearer than that in primitive society one institution is formed on the model of another, already known.

To take a concrete case, Ibo women have societies, with few functions, the very names of the dignitaries of which are derived from the corresponding dignities (quite distinct from the 'titles' mentioned above, II. 11), which in some parts are under the *obi*, the rulers and judicial authorities of a town. Not only so, but the names of the men's titles themselves are clearly derived from the neighbouring Edo, a memorial of the time when the effective authority of the king of Benin extended as far as the Niger.

Not less important is the fact that in some regions secret societies exist side by side with initiation schools, though the latter are in this case commonly found in the less pretentious guise of a circumcision bush, the ritual of which is limited to the actual operation, a period of rest for the healing of the wound, and a few rites when the new initiates rejoin the society as men (or women). The question is of course complicated by the fact, just pointed out, that institutions travel from tribe to tribe; in fact a big river is often a more important frontier for customs than the boundary between tribe and tribe, even when they belong to entirely different linguistic stocks. But the actual diversity of form and function in societies with secret rites is too great to make it a tenable hypothesis, apart from good evidence, that they have all been derived from a single type, though it is of course true that earlier types of cult societies must necessarily have influenced the development and form of later types. It is also necessary to recognize that the form no less than the functions of a society may undergo radical change, as we see in the case of the Human Leopard society, originally a warriors' league, which may possibly have had its rise in rites intended to protect the slayer against the evil influences of the slain.

We may perhaps sum up the position by saying that to trace all secret societies to a single origin is probably as mistaken as to trace all forms of religion to a single source or to seek to unlock all the mythologies by a single key. It seems clear that age grades, burial clubs, initiation schools, religious confraternities, occupation groups, and magical societies have all contributed to the mass of diverse elements grouped under secret societies; it cannot be definitely laid down that any one of these took an earlier type as a model; as we find all in their rudimentary stages in various parts of Africa, we must, unless we suppose that these rudiments are derived from the fully developed societies of other tribes, suppose that they are the seed from which, in other areas, secret societies have been evolved, and that all are equally primitive, though not necessarily equally old. As a conspicuous case of a society which cannot be reduced to a late form of the primitive initiation society may be cited the maskers that appear at burial ceremonies or are concerned, like Malanda, with a cult of the dead. Not only is there nothing in the proceedings of this society or of the simpler forms to suggest that they are derived elements, which figure in funeral rites as intruders from another sphere, but we find simpler forms still, in which the mask itself is missing and the genesis of the custom becomes plain.

In parts of the Kukuruku country in Nigeria, after a man's death a masked figure appears in the town to perform certain rites; in the case of a hunter he carries a gun; a skull of some animal is put on the ground at a little distance, and the masker imitates the actions of the hunter in tracking it; as he retires a dog is sacrificed and he steps over the corpse, perhaps to signify that the dead man, whose representative he is, has now to leave the society of his fellow-men; the explanation given by the natives is that it is killed to make the ground smooth for the dead man, alluding probably to the journey of the soul. Although but a single masker figures in the scene, there is already the germ of a society; for, before he appears, a swarm of boys dash across the open space in which the scene is enacted, carrying green branches, but for what purpose does not appear.

In this scene we have the germ of a dramatic representation, perhaps, or the nucleus of a society specially concerned with funeral rites, such as we meet in the Yoruba and Congo areas; but even this simple ceremony is not the most elementary form; for the representative of the dead man wears a red costume and a net mask; he is differentiated from his fellows. Farther to the south, again, among the Edo proper also, the dead man has his representative, but only on the last day of the burial rites.

One of the family puts coral beads on his neck, and many cloths around his loins, with a white cloth on the top; while the rest of the family are dancing, this *nodiraia* sits down; he may not sleep till day breaks, under pain of dying himself; at daybreak a ceremonial gate is made by the young men; the 'father' is summoned and takes his seat on a chair from which they raise him; all proceed along the road, and the young men pass round his head sticks which they afterwards throw into the bush.

Here we find the same elements as in the Kukuruku area; the dead man has his representative; at the end of the ceremonies the figurehead is conducted from the house, passing through the gate to typify his separation from the living, and is then divested of his manistic character by the ordinary rite of purification, which consists in passing sand, an egg, a chicken, or some other object, round the head, and throwing it away.

In the Ibo country and probably elsewhere, when the time arrives for 'second burial,' the dead man is summoned to the house, and a chalk line is sometimes drawn from the *ajoifia*;[1] the customs just mentioned are the obvious counterpart of those of the Ibo; the dead man, who is conceived of as hovering near as long as the rites are in progress, must be sent to his own place—a familiar rite in Indonesia—and one way of doing so is to send him on his way symbolically by means of a human representative.

Intermediate between the rites just described is a ceremony from another part of W. Africa, where we see perhaps the germ of the mask.

The Ishogo of French Congo have a secret society, Bwiti, which is found among the Bavili and many other peoples as well, and corresponds to the Bieri of the Fang, who include in it a cult of ancestors, represented by a skull, and of the totem, represented by some portion of its body; it is in a sense a national cult of the Fang, all warriors being initiated into it.[2] Among the Ishogo a dance is held during the funeral ceremonies; at night all torches are suddenly extinguished; dead silence falls upon the dancers, and one of them calls the dead man by name; an answer comes from the edge of the bush, where an initiate of the society has

[1] *JRAI* lxvii. [1917] 209 f.
[2] Trilles, *Totémisme*, pp. 4, 212, 530.

concealed himself. At other times the corpse is paraded round the village—a custom found among the Ibo and other tribes, though not in the same form; an initiate of the society raises the dead man on his shoulders and covers himself from head to foot with plaited palm-leaves, so that only the face of the corpse remains visible; women look on and applaud, but how far they penetrate the secret is left uncertain.

Here, then, we have in its clearest form the beginnings of disguise, and it is no long step from using the dead man to represent himself to taking a mask to wear as his representative; the mere fact that precisely in this part of Africa the corpse is left unburied several days suggests that, with the coming of a speedier burial, the rites would take some other form which must necessarily imply the representation of the dead man by some other means. It seems clear that the secret society associated with the cult of the dead, or with burial rites, can be traced back to its very beginnings.

But, even in the relatively few cases where the spirit of the secret society is specifically declared to be ancestral in its character, we cannot assume that it was acquired in the same way as the masked figure of the burial society was, on the hypothesis just suggested, developed. Where the spirit is not ancestral, it is far simpler to suppose that it was acquired on the analogy of the personal protective deity; it is not without interest that the *atet tot* of the Timne of Sierra Leone, although it is reckoned among the *wanka* (protective charms) by the native, is really a woman's *krifi* (spirit or genius), and that she acquires the right to it precisely as though a secret society were in question; although it appears to be primarily a kind of fertilizing spirit, it also keeps thieves at a distance and in this way recalls the tabu side of a secret society's activities.

There can be very little doubt that some, at least, of the judicial and police societies have originated in societies which are concerned with burial ceremonies and the cult of the dead. There need be no hesitation in accepting such an origin for Oro and Egũgũ, the Yoruba societies; for not only are both specially associated with burial ceremonies, but other societies of less importance, like Eluku, are obviously of similar origin, and other burial rites, such as *iyaku* and *ipeku*, are clearly of the same order without having developed a fully-fledged secret society; the object of all these ceremonies is to dismiss the dead man to his own place—and in this they seem to correspond to the Edo and Ibo custom of 'second burial'—and celebrate the funeral ceremonies; it is uncertain how far participation in the rites is limited, in the simpler forms, to relatives or others nearly related to the deceased; but there is evidence to show that they are specially connected with occupation groups (hunters, farmers, etc.)—a conclusion to which the Kukuruku facts also point; and from this stage to the secret society proper the path is not a long one. The name Oro is given apparently to the spirit of the deceased, which is deemed to inhabit the house till the rites are performed, as well as to the human participants in the rites; Oro is worshipped annually by each household at home, and there is also a presiding Oro of the town; the parallel with the ancestor-cult of the Ibo is therefore fairly close. In some of the rites a figure dressed in white appears when people assemble and call upon the dead man; this is the case among the Owu section of the Egba in the rite known as *igba irana*. No such usage has been recorded among the Oro rites; but the Oro shout, *mã mũ*, is heard in the house of the dead man, and the essential identity of the rites may be inferred.

The existence of two or more societies conjointly among the Yoruba is explained by the fact that they were originally localized societies or cults, Egũgũ at Oyo, Oro among the Egba, and Eluku (Agemo) at Ijebu; as communication became easier, these customs spread to a greater or less degree, and their judicial side assumed a greater importance until finally their funerary significance became altogether obscured. How far the same process will enable us to account for the existence of other judicial societies, like Poro and Egbo, it is difficult to say; only the record of the intermediate stages in the Yoruba customs enables us to lay down the course of development undergone by Oro and Egũgũ; the continued existence of these intermediate steps is conditioned among the Yoruba by the relatively large size of the tribe—at the present day perhaps 2,000,000, including aberrant dialects—compared with that of other tribes which have developed analogous institutions.

It must be admitted that the tutelary genius theory of the spirit of the secret society is not completely satisfying as an explanation, for the simple reason that the initiation school must, unless appearances are deceptive, be the most primitive type of African secret society; if this is so, it is a mere assumption that the tutelary genius of individuals was known at the time when the initiation school came into being. It should be observed, however, that, where a spirit is associated with initiation, viz. in the Sudanese area in the main, we also find the tutelary genius in a well developed form; where, on the other hand, as in Bantu regions, the tutelary genius appears to be unknown, the spirit of the initiation school is also absent; we cannot be sure that the tutelar of the initiation society is not an afterthought or derived from other ideas. When we look at the societies of the Fang, we see another starting-point—not remote in itself from the tutelary spirit, perhaps even the germ of the idea in other areas—for the tutelar of the secret society; here each society of *ngaña* has a 'totem' (*be mvame*), just as each individual *ngaña* has his *mvame*—in each case a species of animals, plants, etc.; we need not here inquire how far it is accurate to apply the term 'totem' to this conception; it is sufficient that the society has assumed a protector on the analogy of already existing tribal groups; for we must suppose that clans preceded societies of priests. Even if the example has not been widely followed, the analogy holds good; for it proves that some secret societies have deliberately assimilated themselves to other groups by securing a protector.[1]

At present too little is known of migration in Africa generally, especially in West Africa, and too little in the way of analysis of culture has yet been accomplished for it to be possible to say how far we can refer the origin of secret societies, in whole or in part, to the clash of cultures; but it is certainly worthy of note that Kamerun, the territory in which the Bantu languages meet the Sudanese, is one of the main foci of these associations. Similarly in the Senegambian and Western Coast area, a second area of high development, we have the point of contact between the Sudanese prefix languages, which correspond in structure to Bantu, and the non-inflecting group, of which the Mandingo tribes are the main representatives. But even a brief discussion of the question is not possible within the limits of this article.

IV. *Classification.*—From the formal point of view, secret societies naturally fall into three classes according to whether they are confined to males or to females or are open to both sexes; generally speaking, the religious or magical society tends to be open in this respect; initiation schools are naturally the reverse; but no rule can be laid

[1] The relations between totemism, secret societies, and the belief in tutelars are a matter for further inquiry. Interaction may well have occurred at more than one point.

down, for even societies like Poro, which are commonly regarded as a means of keeping the women in subjection, admit them under certain circumstances. The position of societies with regard to the admission of one or both sexes may turn out to be a valuable means of discriminating between such bodies according to their origins.

Less important in a way, but from the practical point of view equally if not more weighty, is the question whether the members of a society are all equal or are ranged in grades, attained by purchase or by seniority; for where graduation according to rank or seniority obtains we come near the beginnings of an oligarchy.

From the point of view of origin, again, it is of much importance to know whether the society is supposed to be under the guardianship of a spirit, human or non-human, or has as its leader and director a doctor or magician, recognized as a human being by initiated and uninitiated alike.

From one point of view, to classify societies according to the rites which serve to admit the novice to membership is to have regard to the function, and not the form, of the society, notably in the case of initiation schools, in which these rites alone form the *raison d'être* of the society; but, from another point of view, classification according to the ritual ordinances of the society is a merely formal procedure. It is of importance, *e.g.*, to know how far circumcision or other mutilations are necessary antecedents to or steps in the admission to full membership; for there is at least a probability that such societies, whatever their function, were at the outset bodies concerned with the admission of youths to the privileges of manhood. It must not, however, be forgotten that such matters are in the hands of the elders of the tribe; and in at least one case the rite of circumcision has been separated from the initiatory ceremonies for reasons of policy; we cannot therefore argue that no society which does not practise the rite, or a substitute for it, can be regarded as equivalent to or derived from an initiation school. Conversely, especially where circumcision is performed as a rule about the age of physiological puberty, it may well have happened that a society which embraced the manhood of the tribe for any reason would come to arrogate to itself the right of circumcising the youths and thus take on the aspect of an initiation school.

From the point of view of function, the classification is comparatively simple, though in practice the lines are by no means clearly drawn, as can be seen by reference to more than one example quoted above. The form of all societies except the age grades is religious, inasmuch as there appears to be, except possibly in a few initiation schools, a spirit leader of the society; and, even where the overt reference to religious ideas is absent, as in simple circumcision rites, there is always in the foreground the ever-recurring idea of holiness, which demands the separation of the candidates from the outside world. If, therefore, we undertake to classify the societies according to their functions, it must be understood that these religious elements are deliberately put in the background, and that only the actual aims, which are not necessarily the same as the avowed aims, of the association taken into account.

Broadly speaking, the societies fall into two main groups—religious and social; but it must be observed that the ultimate object of nearly all is worldly prosperity or political power; for, whatever be the facts as regards primitive races in other parts of the world, the Negro is religious, not from any obvious need or overwhelming desire to satisfy a spiritual side of his nature, but in order to secure himself from bodily ills, to add to his wealth in wives, children, and material property, to fortify himself against his enemies, human or non-human, and to secure the favour of those in authority over him, in the present day more particularly of the white man. But these ultimate objects are attained through a series of intermediate devices such as the acquisition of a tutelary deity, either personal or collective (in the sense of the genius of a society), the obtaining of 'strong medicine,' the acquisition of secret knowledge, and the like. Classifying the societies according to these immediate aims, we may divide them broadly into these two classes; but, as has already been pointed out, there are many with a mixed character. To the purely religious societies belong the Yewe-worshippers and the adherents of the Imandwa cult; the cult of Bieri among the Fang differs from these in being national, but confined to the warriors. We may perhaps add a third type, the burial societies, with aims probably allied to the worship of ancestors, though their object is somewhat obscure. Side by side with the religious societies, and operating with the same class of forces, are the magico-religious societies with, in some cases, agricultural objects; of a different type are the Human Leopard society and its congeners; other societies, especially in the French Niger territory and in the Congo, practise protective rites against the arts of diviners, witches, and other workers of evil; others, again, have in view the averting or cure of diseases or malformations or the driving away of evil spirits by making it appear to them that the area is already occupied by a spirit, viz. the masker.

The initiation societies may perhaps be placed midway between the purely religious and the purely social groups, the more so as the element of religion is a varying one in them and sometimes, according to our authorities, completely absent. Their primary purpose is no doubt to change the child into a man or woman.

To the social type of society belong the age grades of the Kru, Masai, Galla, and others, and the corresponding type of society, admittance to which is by purchase, such as the 'titles' of the Ibo; intermingled with these are some societies which may almost be classed as castes, in so far as they are limited, at least in theory, to certain occupations, such as blacksmiths. It will be remembered that blacksmiths occupy in many areas a peculiar position, like musicians in the Western Sudan; they are occasionally a pariah class, but more often, as among the Ibo, have succeeded in making their society the head of the hierarchy formed by the 'titles.' In more than one case the blacksmith is the operator in the initiation rites; this is probably the case in the society, among others, commonly known as Mumbo Jumbo, which is more properly termed Mama Dhiombo; here there can be little doubt, from the report of a recent author, that the blacksmith is the initiator of girls and performs the operation of clitoridectomy.[1] To these occupation groups belong also the diviners' society of the Kru, classified, from another point of view, among magico-religious societies, perhaps the *ngaña* of the Congo, and even from one aspect the witches or wizards. It has already been pointed out that the rites of initiation of doctors, priests, and diviners follow closely the type of secret society ceremonies; so, too, do the rites of coronation of kings and chiefs and those of admission to Muhammadan confraternities and similar institutions.

There is a large and important class of legislative, judicial, and, in general terms, political societies, of which Poro and Egbo may be mentioned as the best known. These in some aspects come very

[1] C. Monteil, *Les Khassonké*, Paris, 1915, p. 237.

near the age grades of such tribes as the Wanyika. An interesting variant of this type is seen in the Ogboni society of the Yoruba, with its subsidiary, Oro, which is the executive force. With the relation between Ogboni and Oro may be contrasted the relation subsisting between the Poro society and the paramount chiefs of Sierra Leone, who in non-Poro areas have in like manner the Ragbenle society at their back, though it is far less powerful, partly because it is far more restricted in numbers. The chief is often the head of Poro, but it is not precisely his executive staff; for, while the society supports the chief and, as a body, carries out decisions approved by him, it also claims the right to restrain him under certain circumstances, though it does not go so far as to depose an unworthy chief. The relations between Ragbenle and Poro are somewhat obscure; for there is some antagonism between them, quite apart from the fact that a chief is as a matter of customary law associated with either one or the other; it is a recognized rule that a Poro chief cannot rule in a chiefdom where the Ragbenle society holds the reins; on the other hand, there is a method by which he can divest himself of his Poro quality and thus fit himself for his duties. Possibly this antagonism arises from the fact that Poro, as has been pointed out above, is an alien society, whereas Ragbenle is probably a native institution. This does not explain how it comes about that Poro and Ragbenle are mutually exclusive; if Ragbenle existed when Poro was imported, it is not apparent why it should have altogether vanished from the territory where the chiefs are connected with Poro. In some cases these police forces seem to exist independently, as among the people of Porto Novo, where the night guard is the Zangbeto society. In the Ibo country west of the Niger the Onotu, 'dignitaries,' are the executive for many purposes; they are sometimes reinforced by a police force known as Anikamwadu; but the element of secrecy is here very slight.

In all the cases so far passed in review it may be assumed that the society is, so to speak, in full vigour; we can discern rudimentary forms, but there is nothing to lead us to suppose that there is any decadence at work. When, however, we find the Yoruba Egũgũ appearing, in the Ibo country or at Freetown, among the descendants of the freed slaves brought to Sierra Leone, whose original home was the Slave Coast, we are at once confronted with a new feature; the awe-inspiring figure of the secret society has become the diversion of the populace, though even now the enjoyment has in it something of the feeling, so evident in some of the diversions of our own children, that there is an element of danger.

In the same class perhaps, though the decay has not proceeded so far, are many or most of the dancing societies of the Ibo, which turn out on a day of festival to make a show and perform feats of gymnastics, such as climbing a palm-tree, dressed up as monkeys, and descending head first with the most ridiculously lifelike imitation of the real animal. In E. Africa the masker's rôle is slightly different, for he has become the court fool; and the same tendency is to be seen in parts of the Congo territory.

Finally, outside all the groups already indicated, we find the secret societies of boys and girls among the Yoruba and Edo, formed, without serious purpose, in imitation of the societies of their elders, but carried on less in sport than in a spirit of deadly earnest, though without conscious aim.

V. *ELEMENTS OF THE COMPLEX.*—It is apparent that there can be no large common element in societies so variously constituted and with such diverse ends as those surveyed here; but there are certain features which demand notice, if only because some authors have drawn conclusions from them which the facts do not warrant.

(*a*) *The men's house.*—Stress has been laid upon the existence of the men's house by Webster, who argues that its presence indicates that in the past secret initiation ceremonies have been practised. Now, in the first place, the men's house is in many cases not in the bush or remote from the village, but in the very centre of the village; it is the meeting-place of the men, who have far more leisure than the women for sitting down and talking; it is sometimes the guard-house; in any case it does not resemble the temporary structures, destroyed after the rites are over, which serve for the initiation of youths. Not only so, but in the Ibo country, where the men's house does not, strictly speaking, exist, each compound has its men's house (*obu* or *ogwa*), though women are not forbidden to enter. Moreover, in this area the function of the men's house proper is fulfilled by seats of rough logs in an open space at the meeting-point of important roads; here men, and sometimes women, sit in the cool of the evening, smoking and discussing things in general; it cannot seriously be maintained that this village meeting-place is necessarily a decadent feature, derived from the initiation bush, which, be it noted, exists side by side with the meeting-place. Webster regards the men's house as designed, among other things, to enforce the separation of the young men and maidens, despite the fact that it is in some cases, notably among the Masai, the spot where the unmarried of both sexes practise free love; so far from initiation necessarily meaning that the youths are cut off from sexual indulgence, it very often means that then for the first time they are free to choose temporary mates; but, above all, Webster's argument disregards the fact that initiation rites are coincident, not with physiological, but with social, puberty; in fact in some tribes sexual intercourse is permitted both before and after the rites, but not during them.

The existence of a bachelors' house indicates that the inmates have entered upon another stage of life; there is no longer room for them, perhaps, in the paternal dwelling, or, if there is, their freedom of action is hampered. That this is so is clear from the fact that among the Ibo, where the bachelors' house is unknown, the bachelor's house is an ordinary feature. Here the youth lives at his ease, and entertains his female friends, to whom his father's house is forbidden as a resort for sexual purposes; if his mother chance to die before he marries a wife, she is buried in or near her son's house. It is certain that it cannot be interpreted in the same way as the common dwelling.

It is possible that the men's house has in some places developed into the temple; but the house dedicated to a god answers a natural need; it is found in areas where the men's house exists quite apart from it; it is situated in the village, not without; and there is no reason for deriving it from any more remote origin than the need of housing a deity, of having a place where he may be sought with offerings and prayers.

(*b*) *Seclusion in forests.*—Other authors have laid stress upon the fact that the masked figure emerges from the bush, and that the forest conceals the *arcana* of the secret society. But to emphasize this point is to ignore the conditions; there may be some slight evidence of tree-worship in Africa, but the placing of the initiation school of youths among trees is not one of the proofs. For, in the first place, over large parts of W. Africa there is no open country; all is either bush or town; if, therefore, it is necessary to escape the gaze of the profane, it can be done only by seeking quarters in the bush. The use of a leaf dress is equally meaningless in this connexion; for the tribes which do not use skins had of necessity to use vegetable products for clothing; to this day bark-cloth is woven, and for some magical operations banana-leaves are assumed as a garment; but this does not mean that the tree from which the bark is taken is sacred, still less that the banana is the object of a cult. Still farther from the truth, if possible, is the argument that the bull-roarer is evidence of tree-worship.

The real meaning of initiation rites, and consequently, among others, of the rites of secret societies, has been admirably set forth by van Gennep (*Les Rites de passage*) as first a transition of the novice from the world of the profane to the sacred world; then, after a period of instruction and ceremonies destined to mark the revolution that is coming over the nature of the candidate, a rite of separation from the world in which he has been living; then another one of redintegration into the world of the profane. Here, then, we have the explanation of the pretended death and resurrection, of the secret language, of the new name, of the ignorance feigned by the novice when he is restored to his relatives, and, finally, of the mutilations which will form a permanent memorial and proof of the change that has been undergone.

It must not, however, be supposed that these rites present themselves to the Negro under this aspect; to take only one example, circumcision, which is by no means universally practised, is not viewed by the native as anything but the removal of a useless or even hurtful appendage; but such transformations of belief are a commonplace in the history of primitive creeds.

A full analysis of the ceremonies would take us too far; but it may be pointed out that among the rites of separation is the carrying off of the novice, unresisting and even willing, to seclusion in the bush; this is sometimes preceded, sometimes followed, by a pretended death, which in some areas may possibly be produced by drugs. Widely spread too is the custom of wearing white paint, all clothing being discarded; this is worn in some areas as a mourning colour also; it is doubtful if we should interpret it as a means of assimilating the novice to the spirit world.

(*c*) *Tabus.*—During the period of residence in the bush a number of food tabus are enforced; the Ndembo, *e.g.*, may eat neither fish nor flesh; water may be used to rinse the mouth, but not otherwise. It may be noted in passing that some of the rites of redintegration consist in the public breaking of these tabus; the Ndembo member swallows an egg as part of the ceremony of the return to the village. He also touches a girl's hand; for one of the things most strictly forbidden to the novice is to touch a woman or to see a woman's face; the women therefore avoid the novice or hide their faces; this is a general rule which applies to other than initiation schools.

In connexion with the banning of women by the majority of societies, a curious fact may be mentioned (as it is rare to hear anything of the origin of the societies, parallels may be numerous, though it would be unwise to assume that this is the case). Both the Ovia society of the Edo and the Egbo society of Calabar are said to have been founded by women; in fact Egbo is said to have been a women's society at first; and to this day an old woman of the ruling family helps to bring the Egbo spirit back, when it flees from a town at the death of an important member. It is not necessary to take these stories at their face value; they may be no more than ætiological myths to explain why women are now excluded, and they may be deformed in the telling; but native traditions of origin have hitherto been unduly neglected. There is a vague story that women brought Poro to the Timne country; but here we are on somewhat different ground, for there is no question of the origin of the society, and women are admitted to it under certain circumstances at the present day.

There are certain cases—in the Yewe society, *e.g.*—where the novice must not only observe food tabus, but must drink water as part of his initiation; for by so doing he receives the god into his body.

(*d*) *Education.*—In some cases symbolic rites are performed to indicate that the eyes of the novice are now open; but a more general feature is the instruction in tribal lore and customs, in the duties of tribesmen, or of members of the society, and, generally speaking, the education of the candidate in native morality, as well as in the arts of dance and song. In this connexion the ordeals, of which examples have been given above, are of much importance.

(*e*) *Dress, lustral rites, etc.*—During the period of residence in the bush it is often permitted to the novices to come out, wearing a special dress; and during these excursions, sometimes after the final departure from the bush, they are at liberty to seize domestic animals at will.[1] It has been suggested that this is indicative of the fact that the novices are outside the law, because outside the community; but the custom is practised on other occasions, such as an interregnum in the course of marriage rites, after a theft in the market, and so on; and, though these customs are not all African, the whole group of rites needs to be surveyed before any final theory can be put forward.

There is less uncertainty as to the meaning of the ignorance feigned by the novices when they leave the bush; it is of a piece with their use of a secret language; they have been separated from this world and have come into it again; and, like infants, they have everything to learn. In fact, in an Akikuyu rite the novice undergoes a ceremony of rebirth and lives on milk, though, oddly enough, the rite takes place before circumcision; but in this tribe changes have been made in the rites by the old men.

Another series of rites—washing, donning of new clothing, burning of the bush huts—is partly to separate the novice from his life in the other world, partly to fit him to re-enter the everyday life of the tribe.

(*f*) *Secret language.*—Specimens of the languages have been recorded in Nigeria, on the Congo, and elsewhere. Broadly speaking, we may say that we find languages of three types: (1) old languages retained for cult purposes only, (2) languages made up in part of words from other dialects, in part of other elements, (3) languages in which the ordinary language is changed by the addition of a prefix or suffix, by a change of class in the noun, by a change of vowel, or a change of consonant. In this connexion it should be remembered that a kind of back slang is found at more than one point in Africa, notably among the Swahili and the Ibo.

(*g*) *The masker.* — Despite a vastly increased knowledge of Africa, there are many points of detail on which we are not much better informed than when Frobenius published his monograph in 1898. We can say that masked figures are associated with many societies in French territories since opened up, but in most cases we have few or no details. On the whole, however, it may safely be said that from Senegambia to the Ivory Coast, and from the Slave Coast through Kamerun to the Congo and beyond, with extensions of unknown depth in the hinterland of the Ivory Coast, masked figures are found which, at least in some cases, represent the tutelary spirit of the society with which they are associated. How far this applies to the masked figures of the Tenda, which are not the central figures of the society, but merely the executive power—and this is probably not a solitary instance—it is difficult to say; but it is certain that

[1] *E.g.*, see C. Lasnet, *Une Mission au Sénégal*, Paris, 1900, pp. 50, 65, 77, 89, 101, 127, 145.

in a large number of cases (Poro, Oro, many of the Kamerun societies, etc.) a supposed spirit occupies the chief place.

In a small number of tribes, notably the Vai and Gola societies, the spirits of their ancestors are associated with the societies and initiation rites, though how far they are identified with the masked figure is not quite clear. In parts of Kamerun, on the Congo, and perhaps over the greater part of S. Africa there does not seem to be any masked figure, and we may perhaps infer that there is no tutelar; the boys are in charge of a *ngaña*; the power is said, in the case of the women's society of the Ogowe, Nyembe, to reside in the society as a body. We can hardly argue that the masked figure has disappeared owing to external or internal causes. There are therefore two, if not three, types of society from this point of view.

It is of some importance to note that, so far as the distribution of personal tutelary deities is known, it coincides, to a large extent, with the area in which societies have their tutelary geniuses; of course the absence of a society tutelar where no society exists does not disprove a causal relation in other areas. It is clear that such a conception may have been developed in a society which had originally no central figure at all, or one which associated the ancestors with their initiation schools, or had other ideas, such as are perhaps indicated by the earth figures of animals used by some of the Central African tribes; in this connexion it may be noted that similar practices are found among the Fang, whose societies seem now to be of a well-developed religious type.

There is of course no necessary connexion between the wearing of a mask and the idea of a tutelar, though in many parts of the world the wearing of masks is associated with the impersonation of deities, demons, or the spirits of the dead. But, so far as Africa is concerned, some masks are definitely connected with the dead (Ibo, etc.), while others, equally unconnected, so far as can be seen, with a secret society, have no apparent animistic significance; this is the case with many of those worn in connexion with circumcision. It is a notable fact that in some areas (and those the most remote from European influence, such as the bend of the Niger) women do not fear masks; they may know who is inside and see the masker dress and undress. How this state of things has arisen it is difficult to see. Among the Ibo, where the mask is associated with the dead—it is known as *mauñ*, 'dead person'—women at ordinary times do not dread it, though they may not know who is inside; at certain times of the year, however, maskers pursue them and they flee in terror. Among the Senufo and Mande public masks are worn at circumcision and for harvest work; society masks, not to be seen by women, are worn at burial, during the actual rites of circumcision, at harvest festivals, during the building of furnaces, etc.; we are at present ignorant of the origin of this state of things; but it seems to denote either that the masks are of different origin—some derived from outside, some of genuine native origin—or that, if both are home products, they are not at the same period of development.

Frobenius has argued that Oceanic masks have created or influenced those of Africa; this means a considerable antiquity for the Oceanic masks; but, if the view put forward by Rivers to account for the secret societies of Oceania is correct, we could hardly admit them to be of an age to warrant this hypothesis even if Oceanic influences were otherwise proved; there may of course have been Oceanic masks before the rise of the present societies, but, in view of the wide distribution of masks—Australia alone is almost completely lacking in them, though the ceremonial garb of the Central tribes comes near masking—it seems unnecessary to derive African masks from elsewhere until it has been made clear that their technique makes their external origin probable.

Prima facie it seems likely that one aim of the initiation society would be to bring the new 'man' into relation with the ancestors of the tribe. To discuss the relation of initiation ceremonies to the belief in reincarnation is beyond the limits of this article.[1]

It has been pointed out above that we have every reason to regard the masker who figures in burial rites as an original type; but it is equally true that a masker is associated with the simplest circumcision rites, where there is no question of a society; it is true that in certain cases circumcision is associated with the cult of ancestors; the novices who rub themselves with white clay mix with it the ashes of their ancestor's bones in the Gabun area; but, generally speaking, we have no reason to regard the association of the rite with the ancestral cult as very close. It might therefore appear that we have here a second origin for the use of the mask; the argument would be difficult to meet if there were any reason to suppose that circumcision was an original possession of the Negro race; but among both Sudanese and Bantu tribes there are many which either do not know the rite at all or regard it with dislike if they do know it (Tamberma, Moba, Bassari, Gurunsi, Baganda, etc.). It is by no means clear how the rite spread; but it is at least permissible to suppose either that the use of the mask came with the rite or that it was developed after the rite was borrowed from elsewhere. In this connexion the public character of some circumcision masks, noted above, is very significant. In neither case are we compelled to regard the use of the mask at circumcision as a primitive African custom independent of the cult of the dead. At the same time, it must be recognized that the circumcision mask has probably served as a starting-point for the masker of the initiation schools, who has in certain instances been associated, possibly as an afterthought, with the cult of ancestors. There is no reason to suppose that the mask is in Africa frequently associated with the cult of divinities; nor, except in the Congo, is there any suggestion that the masker represents a non-human spirit; it is hardly possible to see the starting-point of the use of the mask in a belief confined to a small area.

In so far as initiation societies are independent of circumcision (it should not be forgotten that the substitutes for circumcision—the knocking out of the teeth and the like—are not associated with a mask), and in so far as the mask has played a part in the formation of initiation schools, we have, it may be, a mask of indeterminate origin; in all other cases the probability is that the mask is ultimately referable to a cult of ancestors or at least of the dead. The figure who wears the mask appears to be the protector of the society, assumed on the model of the totem, or of the individual tutelar, except in the case of simple religious societies, where the masker may represent the god of the society.[2]

VI. *INFLUENCE OF THE SOCIETIES.*—We know too little of the rise of the great empires of Africa to say how far the bond of unity created by intertribal societies helped in welding together the various parts. The support given to Timne chiefs by the Poro and Ragbenle societies suggests that their influence may at times have been

[1] See artt. INITIATION, TRANSMIGRATION.
[2] Cf. also art. MASK.

important. Less open to question is their stimulus to the growth of an organized police, which we find at more than one point; but it is in the general government of the tribe that their most important function lay in many areas; thus there is no doubt that Egbo was the equivalent of a judicial body with far more influence than the ordinary chief; and the same may be said of Poro. Even a religious association like the Yewe society exercises great social influence. In the case of age grades the government of a tribe is naturally vested in the highest ranks.

Not without importance too is the rôle played by the societies in setting up a feeling of solidarity apart from ties of tribe or kinship; mutual aid among members of the societies is a normal feature; and, if this aid sometimes aimed at defeating justice, the final result was probably not much worse than in areas where societies were unknown and the votes of the judges were bought by the highest bidder. It is a normal feature of Negro life that certain people, *e.g.*, the father-in-law, can call upon their sons-in-law and others for aid in farm work and other recurring or occasional tasks; where age grades exist, a man can in many cases call upon the men of his own grade or company for similar assistance; and no one who has seen the helplessness of the individual in some tribes before the ravages of wild animals among his crops will underrate the importance of mutual aid. Even where the secret society has not directly brought about this state of things, it may well have served as a model for other societies; it is certainly not without significance that both among the Yoruba and on the Congo, two of the chief areas of secret societies, co-operative societies for wife-purchase and other ends have been described by various authors.

How far the virtues of the unsophisticated native are due to the training received in the initiation schools is perhaps an open question, though many authorities lay stress upon the excellence of the teaching. At the same time it should not be forgotten that tribes without any such means of influencing the minds of the young show an equally high state of morality; by this is to be understood not necessarily sexual morality, which varies enormously from one part of a tribe to another, but the general respect for the native code of morals, such as honesty, truthfulness, and like virtues, which in contact with European influence disappear only too quickly.

LITERATURE.—The foregoing is based in part on unpublished material. The older literature will be found quoted at length in a monograph by **L. Frobenius**, *Die Masken und Geheimbünde Afrikas* (=*Abh. der Kaiserl. Leop.-Carol. deutschen Akademie der Naturforscher*, lxxiv.), Halle, 1898, pp. 1–278; on this is based to a large extent **H. Schurtz**, *Altersklassen und Männerbünde*, Berlin, 1902. Further references will be found in **H. Webster**, *Primitive Secret Societies*, New York, 1908; **A. van Gennep**, *Les Rites de passage*, Paris, 1909, pp. 93–164. Additional references are given in the footnotes. On the general question consult *GB*[3], and **A. Lang**, *Myth, Ritual, and Religion*, London, 1887.

On French Guinea: *Anthropologie*, xvii. [1906] 428; *Annales de la propagation de la Foi*, lv. [1883] 254.

On other French territories: **L. Desplagnes**, *Le Plateau central nigérien*, Paris, 1907; **M. Delafosse**, *Haut-Sénégal-Niger*, Paris, 1912; **L. G. Binger**, *Du Niger au golfe de Guinée*, Paris, 1892.

On Sierra Leone: **N. W. Thomas**, *Anthropological Report on Sierra Leone*, London, 1915; *Ars Quatuor Coronatorum*, xii. [1899] 66–97; **J. A. Cole**, *Revelation of Secret Orders*, Drayton, Ohio, 1886; *Proc. Roy. Irish Acad.*, 3rd ser., xv. [1908] 36.

On Nigeria: **N. W. Thomas**, *Anthropological Report on the Edo-speaking Peoples of Nigeria*, 2 pts., London, 1910, *Anthropological Report on the Ibo-speaking Peoples of Nigeria*, do. 6 pts., 1913–14; *Edinburgh Review*, ccxx. [1914] 103; **R. E. Dennett**, *At the Back of the Black Man's Mind*, London, 1906, pp. 199, 209, *Nigerian Studies*, do., 1912; *Nigerian Chronicle*, Lagos, 1910 ff.; **A. B. Ellis**, *Yoruba-speaking Peoples of the Slave Coast of West Africa*, London, 1894.

On Kamerun: *Rens. Colonials*, 1913, p. 394; *Deutsches Kolonialblatt*, x. [1899] 852, xi. [1900] 800.

On Gabun, etc.: **H. Trilles**, *Le Totémisme chez les Fâñ*, Münster, 1912, p. 426 ff.; *Les Missions catholiques*, xxvii. [1895] 198; **G. Tessmann**, *Die Pangwe*, Berlin, 1913, ii. 45 ff.; *Austr. Assoc. Adv. Sci.* vi. [1895] 589.

On Congo Free State: **L. Bittremieux**, *Die geheime Sekte der Bakhimba*, Louvain, 1911; *Revue des questions scientifiques*, 3rd ser., xii. [1907] 451–522; **E. Torday** and **T. A. Joyce**, *Les Bushongo*, Brussels, 1912, pp. 82–85, 87; **E. Pechuël-Loesche**, *Volkskunde von Loango*, Stuttgart, 1907, pp. 96, 248, 452; **Dennett**, *At the Back of the Black Man's Mind*, p. 132.

On Angola: **L. Magyar**, *Reisen in Süd-Afrika in den Jahren 1849–1857*, Buda-Pesth, 1859, p. 267.

On S. Africa: **H. A. Junod**, *Les Ba-ronga*, Neufchâtel, 1897, p. 428; **A. Merensky**, *Beiträge zur Kenntniss Süd-Afrikas*, Berlin, 1875, pp. 135, 139; **G. Fritsch**, *Die Eingeborenen Süd-Afrikas*, Breslau, 1873.

On E. Africa: **D. Macdonald**, *Africana*, London, 1882, i. 127; **K. Weule**, *Wiss. Ergebnisse*, Berlin, 1908.

On secret languages: *Globus*, lxvi. [1894] 117–119; Thomas, *Specimens of Languages from S. Nigeria*, London, 1914; *Anthropos*, viii. [1913] 779.

On N. Africa (Muhammadan confraternities): **O. Depont** and **X. Coppolani**, *Les Confréries religieuses musulmanes*, Algiers, 1897; *RHLR* xlv. [1902] 11.

N. W. THOMAS.

SECRET SOCIETIES (American).—In the social economy of the tribes of America, as among primitive peoples elsewhere, secret societies are important agencies. Such societies are invariably the vehicles of esoteric rites, and normally of an exoteric display, in the form either of public ceremonials or of badges or other symbols by means of which their members are identified. In their simplest and earliest forms such rites are those which mark the progress of the individual from status to status in his own clan. Above them in generality of relation are rituals symbolizing the creation or cementing of ideal kinships between the members of different clans or tribes. In a third category are to be placed the still more general 'religions' which rest, one might say, upon a conversion rather than an initiation and in which the social relationship is nearly obliterated; they are mysteries universalized to such a degree that they may be regarded as veritable revelations or dispensations. None of these three stages has clear-cut boundaries: the clan rite melts into the tribal, the tribal into the intertribal, and the intertribal rite into the religion; indeed, the self-same rite may at an early period of its history be a clan rite and in its last development a general religion.

1. Social background. — In American Indian tribes are found various types of societies, broadly divisible into social societies, or institutional divisions of the tribe, and 'esoteric fraternities,' or secret societies. Organizations of both types are vehicles of religious mysteries, though it is naturally in the secret society that the sense of cult becomes eminent.

In a manner the tribe itself may be regarded as a secret society having several degrees or 'lodges,' through which the tribesman passes in natural course. The most significant passage is from childhood to maturity, at the period of puberty. Puberty rites, especially fasting and vigil, are almost universal among the American tribes, but formal initiation into tribal mysteries is not so common as in other parts of the world or, we may presume, as it once was in America. The annual rites of the California Maidu, in which the fast of the youth was accompanied by instruction in tribal lore and myth by the old men and was followed by a dance of the neophytes, is one of the few clear-cut instances of tribal initiation. The *huskanaw* of the Virginia Indians, described by early writers, was probably a similar rite; one of its curious features was the administration of an intoxicating drink—a veritable water of Lethe—which was supposed to take from the youth all memory of his former life. The Yuchi Indians, confederates of the Creeks, had a puberty initiation accompanied by rites strongly suggestive of the Creek *Busk*, or festival of the new fire, at which all old scores were supposed to be settled and tribal activities begun anew. Garcilasso de la Vega[1] describes an interesting Inca rite of initiation for young nobles.

Age classes for both men and women are found in many tribes, each class forming a separate society with its own characteristic functions and dances and with its own appropriate initiation. Closely associated and in part identical with these were the military societies, whose membership was determined in part by age, in part by war record. Among the Plains peoples of N. America from four to twelve such societies occur in single tribes. One of the most famous was the Dog Men society of the Cheyenne, whose members came to be known as 'Dog Soldiers,' renowned for courage and endurance. Again, there are societies of a purely convivial nature, often with membership of both sexes, whose main purpose is entertainment or the preservation of some custom. Societies made up of tried warriors and of men approved in counsel have a political turn, dominating the affairs of the tribe and often establishing, by their habit, an ideal of decorum. Thus the Raritesharu of the Pawnees regards itself as the earthly counterpart of the star council forming the constellation Corona Borealis.

The members of this society are chiefs, and they 'are permitted by the star chiefs to paint their faces with the blue lines [symbolizing the heavens] and to wear the downy feather [symbolizing the breath of life] on the head. The members of this society do not dance and sing; they talk quietly and try to be like the stars.'[2]

Societies of the type sketched are the natural outgrowths of tribal life, though frequently they are borrowings from neighbouring tribes. They commonly possess rites—dances and songs—peculiar to themselves. Entrance to membership is not automatic, but is more or less a matter of qualification and selection and is accompanied, as a rule, by ceremony. Thus, while their general nature is that of tribal degrees, they approach in character the secret societies in stricter sense.

As distinguished from the social societies, the secret societies (or 'fraternities,' as they are often called, although membership is often of both sexes) are such as have in charge some religious mystery. To be sure, in a life where nearly every activity is accompanied by religious observances this is not a clear criterion; and, in fact, the secret societies tend to assume a social importance, *i.e.* to become priesthoods. Thus, the Bow priesthood of the Zuñi is not only a society charged with its own esoteric ritual, but it has in charge the military affairs of the pueblo. The various fraternities which execute the rain-dances may similarly be regarded as priesthoods endowed with special appeals to the gods of rain and vegetation. Perhaps most such societies are the custodians of presumably therapeutic powers, ministering to the health or luck, not only of their own membership, but also of their tribes-fellows. Nevertheless, there is a fair distinction of these societies from those of a more social cast; their secret ceremonies tend to take the form of a teaching and transmission of a mystery, their public ceremonies the form of a dramatic display, and they demand of their initiates a special qualification, often in the nature of a supernatural sign or an exceptional experience.

The origin of secret societies is various. Where tribes are formed by the agglomeration of small groups or clans, the separate clans retain, in the tribal organization, the distinctive rites which they brought to it, forming the priesthood or sect of these rites; and, even after the clan system has broken down, ritualistic precedence is likely to be confined to descendants of the original bringers of the rites. The relation of the societies to the clan system appears most distinctly, perhaps, among the Iroquois, in some tribes of whom each clan had its own society. In general, the societies flourish as the clan organization decays, forming, as it were, a kind of mystery creed in substitution for the older gentile religion—though, even in a community where the societies are so important as in Zuñi, in certain cases membership to office still depends on clanship. The whole development is curiously reminiscent of the ancient mysteries of Eleusis, which, long after they had become open to the whole Attic State, and indeed to strangers, were still in the hands of the hierophantic Eumolpidæ and Kerykes.

But, while there is this residual relationship of the secret society to the clan, as an institution the societies seem rather to represent a new social order breaking through the rigid *encadrement* which clanship produces. The societies not only bring together members of the same tribe who are of different clans, but pass from tribe to tribe and even from linguistic stock to linguistic stock, vastly broadening the members' sense of relationship and introducing a spiritual kinship and a religious solidarity far beyond the reach of secular organization. As reflecting this function, the conditions of eligibility cease to be physical or political and become spiritual or supernatural. Sometimes a revelation to a group of people is the cause of the formation of a society. A curious illustration is that of the Struck-by-lightning fraternity of Zuñi, which originated in 1891 when five men, one a Navaho, and two women were rendered senseless by lightning striking the house in which they were—their common experience leading to their formation into a theurgical society. Among the Omaha all persons who have seen a buffalo in a dream become members of the Buffalo society, endowed with therapeutic powers. Membership in the various animal societies of the N.W. Coast Indians is commonly determined by some supernatural encounter with the beast-being that gives its name to the society. Again, a man may join a society as a consequence of being restored to health by its medicine—as is the case with the Zuñi skatophagic Galaxy fraternity. An individual is not necessarily restricted to membership in a single society, and in some cases, at least, the membership includes nominal Christians.

Thus the secret society holds a middle place in the Indian's religious economy between the more primitive group-rites reflecting clan and tribal organization and those broader intertribal dispensations, or 'religions,' for which the societies seem to prepare the way by their emphasis upon spiritual kinship rather than blood-relationship or political subordination.

2. Ritual form and content.—The formal rites of the societies are of a magical, therapeutic, and devotional character, with a turn for entertainment which assumes the form of dramatic portrayal. Purgation, continence, and fasting are the common preparations for initiation into and participation in these rites. Ceremonial lodges are erected or maintained for the secret rites; the public rites take place in the open. In the pueblos the several societies have their separate *kivas*, or underground chambers, while the public dances take place in the plazas. Masking and mummery are found from the east to the west, their highest developments occurring among the totemic tribes of the north-west of North America and in the pueblos of the south-west; among the ancient civilized peoples of Mexico and Peru; and among the tribes of north-western Brazil, although many other South American tribes, even including the Fuegians, have mask ceremonies. Symbolic paint-

[1] *Royal Commentaries*, Hakluyt Society, 1869, vi. xxiv.-xxviii.
[2] *22 RBEW*, pt. 2, p. 235.

ing of face and body, costuming, and the elaboration of ceremonial emblems are universal. A survey of the rites and usages brings before one constant suggestions of the Dionysiac development of the Greek theatre. The Kwakiutl of British Columbia divide the year into a sacred and a profane period; during the former personal names and indeed the whole social organization of the tribe are changed; the members of the societies—the 'seals,' or *mystæ*—form a group by themselves; initiates are supposed to be spirit-seized and in a kind of Bacchic frenzy tear the bodies of animals with nails and teeth or, in the case of the 'cannibals,' bite into the flesh of human beings (formerly slaves were slain and eaten). Again, in the pueblos of the United States the ceremonials centre in persons who personate and may, indeed, be said to embody gods and ancients, whose legendary acts they depict; and it is interesting to observe that satirical mockery and clownish acts, often obscene, are introduced into the festivals.[1]

The content of mysteries varies indefinitely. In the pueblos the most important ceremonies are dramatic prayers for rain and corn, accompanied by portrayals of the struggle of man with primal monsters. Feats of legerdemain, especially arrow-swallowing and sword-swallowing, are features of many performances, representing that acquisition of theurgic power which is one of the chief aims of society membership. Not all members are equally endowed, and two ranks are maintained in many societies, the higher being composed of the doctors. Knowledge of herbs and of such true medicinal art as primitive peoples possess is commonly imparted, a frequent name for the organizations, among the whites, being 'medicine societies.' Of these the most carefully studied, and perhaps the most elaborate in organization, is the Grand Medicine society, or Midē'wiwin, of the Ojibwa, a society both ancient and wide-spread in the Algonquian tribes. It is a secret society of four degrees, or 'lodges,' each higher degree taken by the initiate imparting to him added therapeutic and magical powers; these powers consist in a practical knowledge of herbs, in powers of communion with the supernatural—powers that might be described as clairvoyant, clairaudient, mediumistic, prophetic; and it is rather curious to find much of the paraphernalia and repertoire of the spiritualistic sect in use by the Midé shamans—all these powers centring in the idea of help and healing from a more than human source.

The mythologic background of the Midé mysteries may be characterized as the portrayal of the path from earth to heaven, as it was established in creation and as it is perpetuated in the ordinations of the creative powers. Knowledge of this 'Way' is the source of spiritual accomplishment. A similar idea underlies the important mystery of the Plains tribes, which is best known from Alice C. Fletcher's Pawnee version.[2] This extraordinary ritual—perhaps the most elaborate evolved by any American Indians — is not the possession of a secret society, in any formal sense, but has been passed from tribe to tribe by participation and preserved by priestly tradition. It presents surprising parallels to the Eleusinian mysteries—or to what is known of the latter.

The essentials of the rite are a mystic representation of the union of Father Heaven and Mother Earth and the resultant birth of a Spirit of Life, primarily a Corn-spirit. This event is in part a kind of theogonic myth, but in a nearer sense it is regarded as a forthfiguring of animal procreation and human parenthood—*i.e.*, it is a dramatic prayer for food and children; and thus it becomes a symbol of the perpetuity of life, tribal and individual.

The rite is undertaken only in the open season, spring, summer, or autumn, when life is astir. It falls, like the Eleusinian mysteries, into three parts: first, a period of purification and of the preparation of the *sacra*; second, a journey, in which the party of the 'Father,' bearing the *hako* (the sacred articles) and singing the 'songs of the Way,' are led by the Corn-spirit to the abode of the 'Son'; and third, the final ceremonies, consisting in part of a public festival, in part of a secret mystery—a dramatic portrayal of the birth of a sacred child. It is interesting to note that the *sacra* include winged wands—emblems of the evangels, mediating between Earth and Heaven—and an ear of corn, the symbol of the spirit of fruitfulness and life.

As in Greece the season of the mysteries was a season of truce, so the *Hako* was a ceremony of peace. War parties turned aside when they saw the bearers of the winged wands, and the bringing of the ceremony from tribe to tribe was a kind of pact of peace, symbolized by the 'Father' of the one tribe adopting as his 'Son' that man of the other to whom the rite was borne; chiefs commonly personated these rôles.

The further step, found in the classical mysteries, of symbolizing a life to come does not appear in this ceremony. It is not, however, without parallel in American mysteries. Zuñi boys are initiated into the Kotikili society, membership in which is necessary in order that a man may enter the dance-house of the gods after death. The initiation ceremony appears to symbolize a re-birth; girls are rarely initiated. The Omaha Shell society centres in a mystic revelation of the gift of life—first, of successful hunting, food, in this world; second, assurance of happy entrance into a life to come.

3. Religious sects.—The demarcation between such intertribal mysteries as the *Hako* ceremony and the somewhat more open sects or dispensations usually called 'religions' is a wavering one. Thus the 'Drum religion' of the Ojibwa appears to have originated in the peace-pact ceremony between this people and the Sioux. It has developed, however, into something more; it has become a religion not only of peace, but of righteous living.

Wiskino, owner of one of the sacred drums which are the symbols of this religion, said: 'I will keep this drum in my house. There will always be tobacco beside it and the drum pipe will always be filled. When I smoke at home I will use the pipe that belongs to the drum. My friends will come to my house to visit the drum. Sometimes my wife and I will have a little feast of our own beside the drum, and we will ask the drum to strengthen us in our faith and resolution to live justly and to wrong no one. When my wife and I do this alone there will be no songs. Only special men may sing the songs of the drum, and my part is that of speaker.'[1]

But, in the majority of cases, aboriginal 'religions' are the outcome of prophetic revelations and, in so far as they are reformatory, may even be hostile to the older rites. When Handsome Lake, the Seneca prophet, undertook to reform his tribe's religion, the societies were ordered to dissolve and the old mysteries to be discarded. Gradually, however, they re-asserted themselves, and the older religion came to be regarded as a sort of Old Dispensation in contrast to the New Religion. Kanakuk, the Kickapoo prophet, whose revelation was to lead to a land of peace and plenty in this world and show the 'Way' to happiness in the next, enjoined a similar break with old traditions; and in a degree this is true of the 'religions' of all the famous Indian prophets—Tenskwatawa ('the open door'), Smohalla, Wovoka—men whose primary intention appears to have been a doctrine of Messianic salvation, but whose followers, under the press of white encroachment, have been led to regard it as the credo of a pan-tribal revolt in this world as well as of spiritual freedom in the next. Cf. artt. COMMUNION WITH DEITY (American), PROPHECY (American).

LITERATURE.—The most comprehensive survey of the general subject of secret societies is H. Webster, *Primitive Secret*

[1] Cf. art. DRAMA (American).
[2] 'The Hako,' *22 RBEW*, pt. 2.

[1] *Bull. 53 BE* (1913), p. 143; cf. art. MUSIC (American).

Societies, New York, 1908. H. Schurtz, *Altersklassen und Männerbünde*, Berlin, 1902, and A. van Gennep, *Les Rites de passage*, Paris, 1909, give admirable analyses of special phases of the subject. For N. America see esp. J. G. Frazer, *Totemism and Exogamy*, London, 1910, iii. 457–498, 'Secret Societies among the Indians of the United States,' and pp. 499–550, 'Secret Societies among the Indians of North-West America'; *Bull. 30 BE*, artt. 'Military Societies,' 'Secret Societies'; *The Mythology of All Races*, x. *North American*, Boston, 1916 (H. B. Alexander); and, for detailed reports, esp. *RBEW* vii. (1891), 'The Midē'wiwin' (W. J. Hoffman); xi. (1894), 'A Study of Siouan Cults' (J. O. Dorsey); xiv. (1896), 'The Ghost-dance Religion' (J. Mooney); xv. (1897), 'Siouan Sociology' (J. O. Dorsey), 'Tusayan Katcinas' (J. W. Fewkes); xxi. (1903), 'Hopi Katcinas' (J. W. Fewkes); xxii. (1904), 'The Hako' (A. C. Fletcher); xxiii. (1904), 'The Zuñi Indians' (M. C. Stevenson); xxvii. (1911), 'The Omaha Tribe' (A. C. Fletcher and F. La Flesche). The writings of F. Boas are the first authority for the customs of the Indians of the North-West Coast, esp. 'The Social Organization and the Secret Societies of the Kwakiutl Indians,' *Rep. U.S. National Museum for 1895*, Washington, 1897; while a summary of the subject for this interesting section is given by E. Sapir, 'The Social Organization of the West Coast Tribes,' *Trans. of the Royal Soc. of Canada*, ix. [1915]. The writings of F. Cushing, J. W. Fewkes, and M. C. Stevenson describe the societies of the Pueblo Indians; and for the societies of the Plains tribes Clark Wissler, 'Societies of the Plains Indians,' *Anthrop. Papers of the Amer. Mus. of Nat. History*, xi. [1916], is the most comprehensive study. For a survey of the *Hako*, comparatively considered, see H. B. Alexander, *The Mystery of Life*, Chicago, 1913. Important articles are *American Anthropologist*, new ser., xi. [1909], 'Secret Societies of the Seneca' (A. C. Parker), and xii. [1910], 'The Great Mysteries of the Cheyenne' (G. B. Grinnell). For Central and S. America the materials are scattered in many sources, old and recent. A select bibliography, classified by regions, will be found in *The Mythology of All Races*, xi. *American (Latin)*, Boston, 1919 (H. B. Alexander). A number of artt. describing mask and similar ceremonies will be found in the *Comptes rendus* of the Congresses of Americanists, Paris and elsewhere, 1878 ff. Among recent descriptive works of special pertinence may be named, Th. Koch-Grünberg, *Zwei Jahren unter den Indianern. Reisen in Nordwest-Brasilien, 1903–1905*, 2 vols., Stuttgart, 1909; Karl von den Steinen, *Unter den Naturvölkern Zentral-Brasiliens*, Berlin, 1897; and Thomas Whiffen, *The Northwest Amazons*, New York, 1916.

H. B. ALEXANDER.

SECRET SOCIETIES (Melanesian and Polynesian). — **1. Melanesian.** — Secret fraternities abound in Melanesia. Initiation is an arduous process, and women are rigorously excluded. The members of these fraternities do not appear to have a secret cult, but they are regarded as being in close association with ancestral ghosts. These are represented by the members, clad in special dresses and masks, terrifying to the uninitiated. Like the African societies, these fraternities are powerful in maintaining law and order; and, apart from the power of the chiefs, they form the tribal government, holding courts, exacting fines—the delinquent being visited by the masked persons—and imposing tabus on certain places and on fruit-trees.[1] Possession of a sacred enclosure (*tareu*) was general among these societies, with a lodge-room where the dresses were prepared, where the members met, and whence the spirit-personators emerged. No woman, uninitiated man, or boy might approach the *tareu*.

Among these fraternities the Duk-Duk of New Britain, the Solomon Islands, and the Bismarck Archipelago is well known.

Its chiefs decide when the ceremonies are to begin and the number of boys to be initiated. These are then collected on the beach, where preliminary ceremonies take place, including striking the youths so that they sometimes faint or even die. Then they are taken to the *tareu* with their entrance fee, and there admission to the society takes place. To each candidate is appointed a Duk-Duk guardian, and they learn about the masks and dresses, dances, and secrets. All this continues for some weeks, and then Duk-Duk is supposed to be sick and near death, and the dresses are burnt.

Where crimes against native law have been committed, Duk-Duk exacts fines, though this frequently degenerates into gross extortion. But the people fear Duk-Duk so much that they submit. For the same reason the tabu of Duk-Duk on fruit-trees, which may be had for a fee, is widely respected.[1]

Another society is the Ingiet, or Iniat, of the Bismarck Archipelago, with many local branches, each presided over by a *tena kikiuwana*, or magician, whose help is available in time of sickness. He possesses knowledge of the spirits and power of controlling them, also the secrets of the dances and of magic ritual; and by his magic he can cause death.

The members of the society meet in a place called *marawot*, in which the dances take place, but which the uninitiated may not visit on pain of death by the spirits. A special part of it is visited by the *tena* alone and contains the images of the fraternity, the abode of dangerous spirits. Certain foods are tabu to members. The nature of this fraternity is little known, though witchcraft seems to be its main purpose. Initiation takes place in the bush, where the youths are fed with certain foods which are tabu to them ever after. These are pork, shark, turtle, and dog, and may represent earlier totems.[2]

In the eastern islands of Torres Straits the Bomai-Malu organization has two divisions—'shark men,' who are the principal men of the order, and another class of singers and drum-beaters. At the ceremonial ritual songs and dances take place, and there is an exhibition of masks to the newly-initiated, who are also taught religious and social duties. The society punishes sacrilege or breaches of discipline.[3]

2. Polynesia.—In Polynesia something analogous to these fraternities was that of the Areoi of the Society and neighbouring islands. The origin of the Areoi was the subject of myths and was connected with the gods.

The brothers of Oro, Orotetefu and Urutetefu, were made by him the first Areoi. One of them had transformed himself into a pig and a bunch of feathers as gifts to Oro, afterwards assuming his original form, though the gifts remained. A pig and a bunch of feathers were therefore important offerings in the Areoi festivals. At first there were ten Areoi, nominated by the two brothers, and chosen from different islands, with power to admit others to the order. The principal Areoi in later times bore the same names as they. The tutelar deities of the fraternity were Oro and his brothers.

There were seven classes of ascending rank in the society, indicated by different tatus, and numerous servants attended each class. Wives of the Areoi were also members, but infanticide had to be practised by all members according to the orders of Oro's brothers, who lived in celibacy.

Admission to the order was supposed to be directed by divine inspiration during a long novitiate. Then the candidate, in an excited state, appeared at one of the public Areoi exhibitions and, having been approved, was given a long period of probation. He received a new name and had to murder his children. During his stay in the lower grades he learned the sacred songs, dances, and dramatic exhibitions. Admission to the various grades was costly, and the higher grades were most expensive of all. Admission took place in the *marais*, or men's houses, a sacred pig being put in the hands of the postulant and offered to the gods. Then the tatu marks were put on him, and feasting, dances, and pantomimic displays followed.

The mysteries of Oro were celebrated by the fraternity, the hymns describing the life of the gods, but the highest secrets and cult were known to members of the upper grades alone. The members were believed to be allied to the gods, yet they indulged freely in lusts. They were supported by chiefs and people, and for them was reserved the fabled sensuous Elysium of the future, Rohutunoanoa, on a mountain in Raiatea. Special ceremonies marked the death and funeral of a member. After elaborate sacrifices the members set out for other islands to perform their plays, or *upaupa*—dramatic recitals of the divine myths, with dances and hymns, often of an obscene character. Special houses were erected, and the members were sumptuously entertained by the chiefs at the expense of the people.[4]

[1] G. Brown, *Melanesians and Polynesians*, London, 1910, p. 270 ff.

[1] Brown, p. 60 ff.; R. Parkinson, *Dreissig Jahre in der Südsee*, Stuttgart, 1907, p. 567 ff.

[2] Brown, pp. 72 ff., 273; Graf von Pfeil, *JAI* xxvii. [1897] 181 ff.

[3] *Reports of the Cambridge Anthropol. Expedition to Torres Straits*, Cambridge, 1908, vi. 169 ff.

[4] W. Ellis, *Polynesian Researches*², London, 1832–36, i. 229 ff. R. P. Lesson, *Voyage autour du monde sur La Coquille*, Paris 1838–39, i. 421.

Parallel institutions were known in the Marianne and Caroline islands.

LITERATURE.—Besides the works mentioned in the notes, see H. Webster, *Primitive Secret Societies*, London, 1908, and 'Totem Clans and Secret Associations in Australia and Melanesia,' *JRAI* xli. [1911] 482 ff.

J. A. MACCULLOCH.

SECTS.

SECTS (Buddhist). — In none of the older books—the four *Nikāyas, e.g.*, or the *Sutta Nipāta* —is there any mention of sects. Divisions or dissensions in the order are referred to as follows. He who stirs up such dissensions is guilty of a 'black act' (*kammaṃ kaṇhaṃ*).[1] When diversities of opinion exist, it is not a suitable time for effort or energy in self-training.[2] Four reasons—not complimentary—are given for members of the order approving of such divisions.[3] In one passage 'ten points' (*dasa vatthūni*) are given as constituting such a division in the order (*sanghabhedo*). These are: the setting forth as truth what is not truth, and *vice versa*; as a rule of the order what is not such a rule, and *vice versa*; as the word or the practice or the precept of the Master what he had not said or practised or enjoined, and *vice versa*.[4] The same ten points are elsewhere stated to result in harm to the laity.[5] Here it is said that by means of these ten points members of the order drag others after them, draw them asunder, hold separate sessions of the chapter at which the formal business of the order is conducted, and recite the *Pātimokkha* (the 227 rules of the order) at such separate sessions. This is a step towards the foundation of a sect. It is not merely a difference of opinion; it is also an innovation in the conduct of business. But there is no question so far of a sect in the European sense—*i.e.* of a body of believers in one or more doctrines not held by the majority, a body with its own endowments, its own churches or chapels, and its own clergy ordained by itself. In the *Vinaya* we get a little farther, but it is still no question of a sect. Devadatta (*q.v.*), to whose schism the 17th *khandaka* is devoted, did not originate a sect of Buddhists; he founded a separate order of his own, whose members ceased to be followers of the Buddha. At the end of the chapter, or *khandaka*, devoted to this subject we are told of the Buddha being questioned by Upāli as to what amounts to a division in the Saṅgha (the order). The reply is the repetition of the above-mentioned ten points, but with eight other points added—points in which *bhikkhus* put offences against a rule of the order under a wrong category, calling a minor offence a serious one, and so on. Thus we get eighteen occasions for dissension in the order, leading up to the holding of separate meetings of the chapter of the order.

Unfortunately we have no historical instance of this having actually happened. There is, however, a case put in illustration of the working of one of the later rules. It occurs in the 10th *khandaka*,[6] the whole of which is concerned with this matter of dissension in the order. There may be some historical foundation for this case, but it is more probably, like so many others, purely hypothetical. It is as follows:

[1] *Aṅguttara*, ii. 234, iii. 146, 436, 439.
[2] *Ib.* iii. 66, 105.
[3] *Ib.* ii. 229.
[4] *Ib.* i. 119.
[5] *Ib.* v. 73 f.
[6] *Vinaya*, i. 337–342 (tr. *SBE* xvii. 285–291); cf. *Majjhima*, iii. 152 ff.

A *bhikkhu* (no name is given) thought he had broken one of the rules (which of the rules is not specified). His companions in the settlement thought he had not. Then they changed their minds: he thought he had not broken the rule, they thought he had, and, when he refused to adopt their view, they held a formal meeting of the order and called upon him to retire—in fact, expelled him. The *bhikkhu* then issued an appeal to other members of the order dwelling in the vicinity, and they took his side. All this being told to the Buddha, he is reported to have said to the expelling party that they should not look only at the particular point in dispute; if the supposed offender be a learned and religious man, they should also consider the possibility of his being so far right that, in consequence of their action, a dissension might arise in the order. He also went to the partisans of the supposed offender and told them, in like manner, that they should consider, not only the particular question, but the possibility of their action leading to dissension. Now the party of the supposed offender held their chapter meetings within the boundary; the other party, to avoid meeting them, held their meetings outside the boundary. The story ends[1] with the restoration, at his own request, and at a full chapter held within the boundary, of the expelled *bhikkhu*.

It should be remembered that the order was scattered throughout the countryside, which was divided, for the purpose of carrying out its business, into districts, each about equal in size to two or three English country parishes. Meetings were held as a rule once a fortnight, and every member of the order dwelling within the boundary of the district had either to attend or send to the chapter the reason for his non-attendance. The meeting was quite democratic. All were equal. Each member present had one vote. The senior member present presided and put the resolutions to the meeting; but he had no authority and no casting vote. He was simply *primus inter pares*. If, then, as in the case just put, a meeting of some only of the resident members in a district was held outside the boundary, all the proceedings of such a chapter became invalid. It will be seen, therefore, how very important the fair fixing of such boundaries (*sīmāyo*) was to the preservation of the freedom and self-government of the order.

Another fact should also be remembered. No one of the 227 rules of the order refers to any question of dogma or belief or metaphysics. No member of the order had any power over any other (except by way of personal influence) in respect of the opinions which the other held. There was no vow of obedience. Of all religious orders mentioned in the history of religions the Buddhist was the one in which there was the greatest freedom, the greatest variety, of thought. One consequence of this, we find, was that, as the centuries passed by, an increasing number of new ideas, not found in the earliest period, became more prevalent among the members of the order. The rules of the order concern such matters of conduct as were involved in the equal division of the limited personal property, held socialistically by the order, among its several members. They are mostly sumptuary regulations or points of etiquette.[2] Beliefs or opinions are left free. And this spirit of freedom seems, as far as we can judge, to have survived all through the centuries of Buddhism in India and China.

[1] *Vinaya*, i. 345 f.
[2] See art. PĀTIMOKKHA.

About 100 years after the Buddha's death there was a formidable dissension in the order, which led to the well-known Council of Vesāli. This dissension was raised by a party of the *bhikkhus* resident there who put forward their ten points (*dasa vatthūni*). It is quite possible that they chose the number ten, and made use of the technical term 'ten points,' in deference to the tradition of the older, and quite different, ten points explained above. Their points were ten relaxations in the sumptuary rules of the order. The manner in which the contest was carried on by both sides, and was finally settled, is related in full in the last chapter (a supplementary chapter) in the *khandakas*.[1] In this, the oldest, account of the matter there is no mention of the starting of any sect. Each individual on both sides was at the beginning of the controversy, and remained at the end of it, a member of the Buddhist order.

The next work to be considered is the *Kathā Vatthu*, edited for the Pāli Text Society, and translated under the title of *Points of Controversy*. The book, probably of gradual growth, was put into its present shape by Tissa in the middle of the 3rd cent. B.C.; and it discusses about 200 questions on which different opinions were then held by different members of the order. About a score of these are questions as to the personality of a Buddha; another score are on the characteristics of the *arahant*, the fully converted man, who has reached, in this world, the end of the Ariyan 'path.' Three questions are on the nature of the gods, and four on the nature of the Saṅgha. The rest are disputes on points of cosmology, psychology, or ethics. The whole gives a valuable picture of the great diversity of opinion in the order, sometimes on questions which now seem unimportant, but for the most part on matters of the greatest interest for Buddhists who wished to understand, in detail, the scheme of life unfolded in the more ancient books. No one will dispute the evidence of this collection of 'points of controversy' as to the abounding life of the new movement and the wide liberty of thought involved in its teaching. But opinions may differ as to the advantages and disadvantages of the complete absence of any authoritative power in the order. We can find in the 'points of controversy' the germs of almost all the astoundingly divergent and even contradictory beliefs which grew in power and influence through the succeeding centuries, and which, though always put forward under the name of Buddhism, resulted in the fall of Buddhism in India, and in its transformation in Tibet, and still more in Japan, into rival sects. The only authority recognized by both sides in each of these 'points of controversy' is the actual wording of the more ancient documents of the Pāli canon; and in many cases the controversy turns on diverse interpretations of ambiguous terms in that wording. Of course all the supposed disputants in the book are members of the one Buddhist Saṅgha. There is no mention of sects, or even of differing schools of thought.

Unfortunately, after the date of the *Points of Controversy* there is a gap of many centuries before we get any further evidence. The few books still extant which date nearest to the canon are four or five centuries later; and they—*e.g.*, the *Divyāvadāna*, the *Netti*, and the *Milinda*—do not consider the matter worthy of their attention. Then suddenly, in the 4th and 5th centuries of our era —*i.e.* about 1000 years after the founding of Buddhism—we find the famous list of eighteen 'sects' supposed to have arisen and to have flourished before the canon was closed. These are at first simply lists of names.[1] The list is first found in Ceylon; but similar lists of a later date—three of them from Tibetan, five from Chinese, sources—have also been traced.[2] Each list contains eighteen names. But the names differ; and the total amounts to nearly thirty. All the lists agree that the Theravādino, 'those who hold the opinions of the Elders,' was the original body out of which the others gradually arose. The order in which they are said to have thus arisen is set out in tabular form in the introduction to the *Points of Controversy*.[3] A few details of the opinions maintained by some of these schools, or tendencies of thought, are given either along with the lists or in the commentary on the *Points of Controversy*. These are curt and scrappy, often obscure, and not seldom contradictory. But one general conclusion we may already safely draw. Precisely as in the earliest days of Christianity the most far-reaching disputes were on the details of Christology, so among the Buddhists the most weighty ones were on the personality of a Buddha; and the greatest innovations came, in India, from the pagan region in the extreme north-west.

Apart from these questions of doctrine there is a remarkable silence about other differences. There is not a hint of any difference in church government, in dress, in ritual, in public or private religious observances, in finance, in the custody of buildings or property, in the ordination or the powers of the clergy, or in the gradation of authority among them. This silence is suggestive.

Now in the oldest regulations of the order a whole *khandaka* deals with the duties of the brethren towards other brethren who propose, on their travels, to stay at any settlement occupied by the order.[4] It is entirely concerned with questions of courteous treatment on both sides—that of the residents and that of the 'incoming' or 'outgoing' *bhikkhus*. Every member of the order is to be equally welcomed. No inquiry is to be made as to opinion. The relation is to be one of host and guest. The story told by the Chinese pilgrims to India shows that in the 4th cent. of our era, and again in the 7th cent., these customs were still adhered to.[5] At the time when the pilgrims were in India monasteries had taken the place of the older settlements. Brethren belonging to different 'sects' (according to the lists of eighteen above referred to) were found dwelling in the same monastery.

If we take all this evidence together, it is possible to draw only one conclusion. There were no 'sects' in India, in any proper use of that term. There were different tendencies of opinion, named after some teacher (just as we talk of 'Puseyites'), or after some locality (as we used to talk of 'the Clapham sect'), or after the kind of view dominant (just as we use 'Broad' or 'Low' Church). All the followers of such views designated by the terms or names occurring in any of the lists were members of the same order and had no separate organization of any kind.

The number eighteen is fictitious and may very probably be derived from the eighteen moral causes of division set out above. As the so-called sects were tendencies of opinion, the number of them was constantly changing, and at no time or place which we can fix were more than three or four of them of any great importance. Two or three could, and did, exist at the same time, not only in the same monastery, but in the same mind.

[1] Tr. in *Vinaya Texts*, iii. (*SBE* xx.) 386–414; see also art. COUNCILS (Buddhist).

[1] *Dīpavaṃsa*, v. 39 ff.; *Mahāvaṃsa*, ch. v.
[2] See Geiger's tr. of the *Mahāvaṃsa*, p. 277.
[3] Pp. xxvii, xxxvi–xxxvii.
[4] Eighth *khandaka*, tr. in *Vinaya Texts*, iii. 272–298.
[5] All the passages relating to this matter have been tabulated and summarized by the present writer in an art. in *JRAS*, 1891.

The expression of these ideas was at first in Pāli. Very little of this has survived. But later there are Sanskrit books, mostly as yet not edited, containing detailed statements of the most trustworthy kind of the views of the Sarvāstivādins (*q.v.*), and perhaps of some others.

The condition of things is very much the same in all Buddhist countries at the present day, and even in China. In Ceylon,[1] *e.g.*, there are said to be three 'sects'—the Siamese, the Burmese, and the Rāmañña. They all belong to the same order (Saṅgha). The Siamese — so called because its members were originally ordained by Siamese *bhikkhus* — admit only high-caste laymen to the order and habitually wear their upper robe over the left shoulder only, differing in both these points from the early Buddhists. The members of the other two confraternities reject both these innovations, and the Rāmañña *bhikkhus*, who are very few in number, claim to be particularly strict in the observance of all the ancient rules. But the religious and philosophical opinions of all three are practically the same. We have no information as to the financial arrangements. Probably each *bhikkhu* recognized by any of these three confraternities would be legally entitled to his share in any land or other property held by the order as a whole. They may, and do, take part together in public religious services, such as the preaching of *Baṇa* (the Word). They hold separate meetings of the chapter for the admission of new *bhikkhus*. The laity look upon them all with equal respect, considering them as members of the one Saṅgha. There is said to be, in quite recent years, a tendency in the Siyama Samāgama (the Siamese confraternity) to break up into, or give rise to, other small confraternities. In Burma[2] there have been continual differences of opinion (*e.g.*, on the question of boundary, *sīmā*). Certain *bhikkhus* have also claimed a superior orthodoxy on the ground that they had been trained either in Ceylon or by others who had been admitted there. But nothing is known of the establishment of any sect apart from the order; and the old differences have now been settled. Of Siam and Annam we know very little; the conditions there seem to have resembled those in Burma.

In all these countries discussion has tended to recur to the ancient faith. In China[3] the deification of the symbols of the old ideas, begun already in India, has been carried on until Chinese Buddhism, to a careless observer, seems to have relapsed altogether into polytheism. But that is true only of the multitude. The more thoughtful members of the order, even in China, have been able always, in different degrees, to see behind the deified symbols. There are practically only two schools of thought—the mystics and the Amidists (the believers in Amitābha). Every member of the order belongs more or less to both schools; and at the present day the whole order, being thus both mystic and theistic, has arrived at more or less of unity, even of opinion. But the history of the differences and innovations all through the centuries shows as yet (the present writer cannot say what further research may not discover) no evidence at all of any 'sects' in our sense of the word. The order has been, and still remains, one.[4]

In Japan[5] the case is different. There is a Japanese work, apparently of the 19th cent. of our era, giving an account of twelve separate sects—separate either in dress, in beliefs, in church government, or in finance. We have this little

[1] See art. CEYLON BUDDHISM.
[2] See art. BURMA AND SIAM (Buddhism in).
[3] See art. CHINA (Buddhism in).
[4] On this question see the admirable summary of R. F. Johnston, *Buddhist China*, London, 1913, ch. v.
[5] See art. JAPAN, II. 2.

work in two European translations, one into English by Bunyiu Nanjio,[1] and one into French by R. Fujishima.[2] Its author or authors are lamentably deficient in even the most elementary knowledge of historical criticism; and they do not make clear whether, or how far, all these sects are really existing now. But it gives the names and dates of the teachers who introduced each of the sects from China and the names of the books (mostly Chinese translations of late works in Buddhist Sanskrit) on which they respectively rely. The oldest of these works is the *Abhidharma-koṣa-vyākhyā*, of about the 12th cent. of Indian Buddhism, and the latest is the *Sukhāvati-vyūha*, of unknown date. It is curious to note that these authorities breathe the same spirit. There are differences on minor points, but not such differences as are adequate in themselves to explain to a European the breaking up into different sects. Lafcadio Hearn unfortunately refuses to say anything about it.[3] Possibly the formation of a new sect was the expression of personal devotion to a new teacher. Or possibly the real cause of division was not so much religious or philosophic differences as difference in systems of church government. But the fact remains that in Japan there are sects. The Saṅgha has been broken up. See also artt. HINAYĀNA, TIBET, SARVĀSTIVĀDINS.

LITERATURE.—*Aṅguttara*, 6 vols., ed. R. Morris and E. Hardy, *PTS*, Oxford, 1885–1910; *Vinaya Piṭakaṃ*, 5 vols., ed. H. Oldenberg, London, 1879–83; *Majjhima-Nikāya*, ed. V. Trenckner and R. Chalmers, *PTS*, 3 vols., Oxford, 1888–99; *Vinaya Texts*, tr. Rhys Davids and H. Oldenberg, do. 1881–85 (*SBE* xiii., xvii., xx.); *Kathā Vatthu*, *PTS*, do. 1894–97; *Points of Controversy* (tr. of last), *PTS*, London, 1915; *Dīpavaṃsa*, ed. H. Oldenberg, do. 1879; *Mahāvaṃsa*, ed. and tr. W. Geiger, *PTS*, do. 1908–12.

T. W. RHYS DAVIDS.

SECTS (Chinese).—I. *INTRODUCTORY.*—There are eight religions in China: (1) Confucianism, the most ancient, grew out of the religion of the mythical past in the days of Yao and Shun (2356 B.C.); (2) Taoism, the philosophic, mystic, and magical, arose about the 6th cent. B.C.; its founder, Lao-tse, was contemporary with Confucius; (3) Buddhism was introduced by the Chinese emperor who invited missionaries from India in A.D. 61; (4) Muhammadanism: Muhammad's maternal uncle came to China as religious ambassador in 628; in 757, after helping to put down a serious rebellion, 4000 Uigur Muslims settled in China; this was five years after al-Mansur had founded Baghdād, the city of the Khalīfahs, which was destroyed by the Mongols in 1258; (5) Nestorian Christianity: Alopen, with a group of Syrian missionaries, arrived at Sian-fu in 635; they were encouraged by the Government and spread widely; (6) Manichæism came from Babylon about this time; (7) Lāmaism appeared in China in the Mongol dynasty (1280–1368); (8) Wahhābī Muslims arrived in 1787.

These were the main streams of religion, but each had many sects.

II. *HISTORY AND ENUMERATION.*—**1. General.**—By a secret sect one generally understands an esoteric religion known only to the initiated. In almost every country, and in connexion with most religions, there have been secret sects, with their mysteries, initiatory rites, and so forth. In China also they have existed for many centuries. Sometimes they have implied a protest or revolt against established authority which demanded uniformity of opinion and practice in religion and politics. The secret sects are chiefly religious, and the secret societies chiefly political; but the two are intimately

[1] *Short Hist. of the Twelve Japanese Buddhist Sects*, Tokyo, 1887.
[2] *Le Bouddhisme japonais*, Paris, 1889.
[3] *Japan: an Attempt at Interpretation*, New York, 1904, p. 230.

connected with one another in China. Most of the chief secret sects have at one time or another been involved in politics, and taken a large part in many revolutions, or have been supposed to do so by the Government. Many were almost purely religious, the members living ascetic lives, abstaining from meat, and trying to acquire merit. Some originated in the early ages, and nearly all have grown out of the old Taoism, Buddhism, and ideal Confucianism, as is seen by their names. The Mahāyāna, Maitreya, White Lotus, Perfect Intelligence, are manifestly more Buddhistic; the Eight Diagrams is more Taoistic and Confucian.

We find a very large number of sect names, but the number of parent sects is small. Each larger community had many offshoots, which frequently took other names; and the same sect seems to have been known by different names at different times. When scattered by persecution, they took new names to mislead their persecutors.

The Buddhist element, with some admixture of early Christianity, seems to have predominated; and that is natural when we consider that Buddhism, both primitive and higher, preached a doctrine of salvation for all, in this life and the life to come, and thus satisfied the yearnings of the people. It taught that love to all that lives and breathes and the performance of good works were the means of obtaining this salvation, which was for any one who chose. So there arose lay communities whose members helped one another on the road to salvation. There were communities for abstaining from animal food, so as to avoid taking life, for rescuing animals from death, for the worship of particular saints, etc.; but the aim of all was the same, viz. the attainment of salvation. In the early days salvation was sought in the conventual life, but the State destroyed thousands of the monasteries and forced the inmates out into the world. The search for truth and immortality, however, was not easily suppressed; those whom the State tried to suppress formed the sects and because of persecution were obliged to hold their meetings in secret. Apparently dispersed and destroyed, they sprang up under another name. Their rites consisted chiefly in reciting formulas and Buddhist *Sūtras* and in burning incense, their practices in vegetarianism and the performance of good works. If the State had left them alone, they would have been harmless, but persecution more than once forced them into rebellion.

There have also been in China societies, like the famous Heaven and Earth Society (Tien-ti Hui) and the Kwo Lao Hui, which are confessedly of a political nature with revolutionary objects, though there is much that is Buddhistic in their origin and symbolism. They are of the class of religious societies which the State persecutes for heresy, which therefore closely fraternize for mutual help, and which are denounced by the State as hotbeds of rebellion and mutiny.

It will be well here to give a list of the principal secret sects known in China, bearing in mind that about many of them very little is known, as the Government has burnt their books again and again, and that probably they include some which are only branches of a larger community. De Groot[1] mentions the names of 68. The chief ones were: (1) Mahāyāna, (2) Maitreya, (3) Pai-lien, or White Lotus, (4) Pai-yun, or White Cloud, (5) Hung Yang (one of the Lo Hwai sects), or Red Ocean, (6) Pai Yang, or White Ocean, (7) Sien-tien, or Pre-Celestial, (8) Wu-wei, or Non-acting (natural), (9) Fen-hiang, or Incense-Burners, (10) Kin Tan Kiao, or Pill of Immortality, (11) Mi Mi Kiao, or Very Secret, (12) Pah-kwa, or Eight Diagrams, (13) Lung-hwa.

[1] *Sectarianism and Religious Persecution in China*, index.

Of secret societies we may mention: (1) Tien-ti Hui, Triad or Heaven and Earth Society, (2) Taipings, (3) Kwo Lao Hui, (4) Reform Society.

A large part of our knowledge of the sects is gleaned from Government persecution decrees. These reveal some interesting phenomena of Chinese religious life; they tell us with what undaunted zeal the sects sent out their branches in different directions, how indestructible they were, how powerful an organization bound together the numerous fraternities, how strong must have been the influence of the religion which effected all this, and how the sects, arming in self-defence, often made the Sons of Heaven tremble upon their throne.

2. The principal sects.—(*a*) *Mahāyāna.*—Just as Christianity arose out of Judaism and in its early days was referred to as a Jewish sect, so the Mahāyāna sect arose out of primitive Buddhism. The doctrines of primitive Buddhism, as taught by the first disciples of Śākyamuni, were afterwards known as the Hīnayāna (*q.v.*), the Smaller or Southern Vehicle, because largely followed in Ceylon and Burma in the south of Asia. The new school of Buddhism was called Mahāyāna (*q.v.*), the Greater or Northern Vehicle, because followed mainly in the north of Asia, China, Tibet, and Japan. Its chief sacred book, *Ki Shin Lun* ('Awakening of Faith'), was written by Aśvaghoṣa (called in Chinese Ma-ming Pusa) about the end of the 1st cent. of the Christian era. This is about the same size as the Gospel of Mark and is of immense importance. From it we find what striking contrasts there were between the old and the new Buddhism.

(1) The old Buddhism was atheistic; the new was theistic; (2) the old Buddhism taught salvation by man's own efforts; the new trusted also in the help of God; (3) the old Buddhism believed that men should retire from this evil world and seek their own salvation; the new believed that the highest virtue consisted in living in the world and seeking to save others; (4) the old Buddhism believed in the necessity of possible countless transmigrations before final deliverance; the new taught that men passed into paradise immediately after death, without transmigration.[1]

(*b*) *Maitreya.*—This must have originated from the study of a remarkable prophecy of Śākyamuni Buddha, which strongly reminds one of the Jewish prophecies of the coming Messiah. In the 'Diamond Sutra' (*King Kang King*), ch. vi., he speaks to this effect:

'Five hundred years after my death, there will rise another Teacher of religion (Maitreya) who will produce faith by the fulfilment of this prophecy. You should know that He will plant the root of His teaching, not in one, two, three, four or five Buddhas, nor in ten thousand Buddhas, but plant it at the root of all the Buddhas; when that One comes, according to this prophecy, then have faith in Him at once, and you will obtain incalculable blessings.'[2]

(*c*) *White Lotus* (*Pai-lien*).—This is the most notorious of all the sects. It seems to have been identical with the White Ocean and Incense-Smelling sects and to be closely connected with others, such as Perfect Intelligence and Mahāyāna. De Groot says:

'Possibly it is the greatest religious corporation in China, embracing all the others, or at least the chief ones.' It has flourished over a very wide area, if not over the whole realm. 'It has for centuries had a leading part in China's history, both as the chief object of persecution and as the mightiest rebel power.'

It existed in China as early as the 4th century. The goal of its members, like that of most of the sects, was salvation in the western paradise. The patron saint was Maitreya, the coming Buddha, the Messiah, for whom all longed, and who was to bring deliverance from oppression and persecution and restore the Church of Buddha to its ideal glory. For several ages we hear little of it, but in the 11th cent. the sect was patronized by the

[1] See Richard, *The New Testament of Higher Buddhism*, p. 48.
[2] *Ib.* p. 131.

then reigning emperor. It is mentioned in the 15th cent. as making common cause with rebels, and its members were severely persecuted. It had gradually grown to be a great power and could lead out armies. Because of the violence of the persecution it rose and helped to bring about the downfall of the Yuen (Mongol) dynasty. It sent thousands of its members against the Mings during the great insurrection and largely sapped that dynasty and led to its downfall. It was said to have no fewer than 2,000,000 adherents in Shantung, Shansi, Honan, Shensi, Szechuen, and Chihli.

(*d*) *Lo Hwai*.—These include the *Sien-tien* ('Pre-Celestial') and *Wu-wei* sects, which are either identical or closely connected.

The members of the Sien-tien sect claim that it dates back to before the very earliest days of Chinese history, and that its founder was the primeval power which ruled the universe, Wu-kih, without beginning or end.

The papers of the sect relate how Wu-kih in far remote antiquity himself came down to earth to save men and spirits from the ocean of suffering. At different times he sent Buddhas and prophets to bring salvation to men. Later he spoke to the Buddhas of the suffering people and said, 'There are countless millions to be saved . . . I do not know who will descend to the earth and lead my children of both sexes to their home.' Then the patriarch Lo, moved with compassion, said, 'I will descend into the world and live there to bring salvation to your children and lead them back to their home.' The ancient father, joyful and cheered, handed to the patriarch Lo his instructions. He accepted them and descended to the earth, there cleared the waste, and made the doctrine shine clear and bright.

This was in the 16th century A.D. Wu-kih's earthly name was Lo Hwai; his clerical name Wunkung ('striver after the eternal'). He was born in Shantung, studied religion under wise Buddhist teachers, and settled in the cave of the White Cloud Mountain near Nanking, where he accepted the Buddhist commandments and received ordination. He went to Peking and published a book which showed that salvation was for every one, lay or clerical. He held meetings in Peking, but was arrested; he gave proofs of supernatural power. The MSS give a most interesting account of a discussion which he had with a foreign priest from Tibet; it shows us that the prophet's religion does not attempt to bring salvation to its adherents by making them indulge in active worship of saints and deities with offerings of food and incense, with drums and lights. They have no images, no temples, no prayers; they seek perfection and bliss exclusively in 'words of truth uttered by heaven and earth,' *i.e.* by the study of *Sūtras* explaining the natural order which bears sway within the all-embracing and yet empty universe, the only temple which this sect acknowledges. To be admitted to the 'realm of Wu-wei' and abide there is the ideal aim of the members. Identification with the world's course is the chief principle of the Sien-tien sect. We read in the MSS that heaven and earth, mountains and rivers, are its gods, winds and clouds its incense, thunderclaps its drums, sun and moon its sacrificial lamps, flowers and fruits its meat-offerings, seas and lakes its drink-offerings, and the universe its temple.

The practices of the sect are not quite in accord with its principles. It builds no temples or altars, nor does it make any carved or painted images of its gods or saints. Each member worships in his own house before a burning oil-lamp the god of his choice, presenting burning incense-sticks and offering sacrifices of fruit and vegetables, in spite of Lo Hwai's teaching that these are superfluous. Each member is required to occupy himself with his own perfection without forcing perfection upon others; so active propagandism is rare. Any one who professes the principles of the sect is simply admitted as a member; nothing is required of him but a solemn promise to keep the Five Commandments of Buddha; no other ritual or form of initiation has to be gone through. The various groups which constitute the sect are simply guided by the more learned and older members; there are no religious ranks or titles; the members call each other brothers and sisters. It is essentially a domestic religion. The members, mostly well-to-do people, meet where they please, men with men and women with women. There are larger meetings, where the adherents recite Buddhist *Sūtras*, formulas, and numerous names of Buddha, to promote self-perfection and salvation; but they do not beat hollow drums or metal balls. There is also pious conversation, particularly about the Five Commandments. The chief of these is, 'Thou shalt not kill anything that has life'; therefore vegetarianism is an absolute principle of this sect. The members also buy caged birds, fish, and other animals, and set them at liberty, whilst reciting part of a *Sūtra*, and loudly proclaiming the deed to the gods and spirits of sky, water, and earth, that they may enter it to their credit in the book of rewards and punishments.

The members of the Sien-tien sect show marked sympathy for Christian doctrine; many of them are acquainted with the gospel; to some Wu-kih is the same as Jahweh; some identify Jesus with Lo Hwai, their latest Messiah, sent down to the world from the Most High for the salvation of men, who worked miracles there, suffered at the hands of the authorities, died, and ascended to heaven. They generally show themselves eager to be informed about the Christian faith.

Edkins[1] says that in some places the sect has temples, but they are destitute of images and contain only the common Chinese tablets to heaven, earth, the emperor, parents, and teachers. He also says that they exhibit more depth and reality in their convictions than is common in other sects in China.

(*e*) *Eight Diagrams*.—This sect flourished principally in the north of China—in Honan, Chihli, and Shantung—and we hear of it chiefly in connexion with great rebellions, especially those of 1786 and 1813. It is one of the great sects which included or were closely connected with several others—*e.g.*, Red and White Yang. One protocol says that the Eight Diagrams is 'also called the Lung-hwa Society.' It is subdivided into eight great sections, distinguished by the names of the diagrams. Each section had its own ruling chief, one of whom was the general head of the sect. A Government decree says of it that the Great Light is worshipped every morning, and that the members recite formulas and *Sūtras* in order to escape dangers by sword and arms, fire and water.

In 1786 there was a great heresy hunt in Honan and Chihli, where this sect flourished. This was followed by a rebellion which, prisoners confessed, was caused by exasperation at the terrible persecutions. Many thousands of members were tortured and killed, and others were banished as slaves to Central Asia. But even in exile the brotherhood continued to flourish. Again in 1813 the Diagram sects in despair rose in open rebellion and stormed the palace in Peking; they were butchered in myriads. Their leader was held in high honour by them. He taught his followers a formula which he considered of the utmost importance—'Unbegotten Father and Mother in the home of the Immaterial Void.' He urged them to repeat it morning and evening; it would ward off all danger from arms, fire, and water, and ensure the success of every undertaking.

(*f*) *Lung-hwa*.—The following account, taken from De Groot, is given in great detail, not because

[1] 'The Wu-wei Sect,' in *Trans. RAS*, China Branch, vi. [1858] Oct.

the Lung-hwa is more important than other sects, but because we have access to a manual which fully sets forth its constitution, aims, and practices. Our intimate knowledge of other sects is scanty, and this is probably fairly typical. This sect, though one in aims and principles with the Sien-tien, is very different in many respects. Its institutions are entirely moulded upon Buddhistic monasticism; it possesses everything appertaining to a complete religious system—founder, prophets, pantheon, commandments, moral philosophy, initiation and consecration ceremonies, religious ritual, writings, a theology, a paradise, and a hell—everything borrowed partly from Mahāyānistic Buddhism, partly from old Chinese philosophy and cosmogony.

(1) *Organization.*—The Lung-hwa sect is thoroughly ritualistic. The founder is supposed to be the patriarch Lo Hwai, although it existed long before he lived on earth. The aim is that of the other sects, viz. salvation. It possesses a much larger number of adherents than the Sien-tien sect, and they are drawn chiefly from the middle and lower classes. They worship a number of gods and goddesses and make carved and painted likenesses of them. At the head are Wu-kih and two others, generally represented as three old men, each holding in his hand the Eight Diagrams arranged in a circle. The meetings are most often held in the chief apartment of an ordinary dwelling-house, called the vegetarian hall. The Amoy branch of the sect, to whose MSS we have access, acknowledged a head living near Foochow, whose title is Khong-khong ('empty'). He has received Buddhist ordination and lives in celibacy with other pious men, who devote themselves to salvation work and perform ceremonies for the redemption of dead members and their relatives. Those next in rank are heads of communities; then come those who travel about and edify the members. These three ranks are celibate, but dress like the laity. Then follow other ranks down to the ninth degree, to which all novices belong. Most members quickly rise to the eighth or seventh degree. All ranks but the highest can be attained by both men and women, in accordance with the great Mahāyāna principle that the way of salvation is open to all. They look upon one another as brothers and sisters. Each parish has a leader who has charge of the altar bearing the images. The hall is kept very clean, in striking contrast to the dirt of the people's homes; for they say that the holy doctrine of purity may be housed and practised only in clean surroundings. In strict obedience to the Mahāyāna command to propagate the doctrines and principles of salvation, they are zealous in enlisting new members. Many are widows who give themselves, heart and soul, to devotion and piety.

(2) *Initiation.*—The admission of candidates is considered very important, as it opens the door to salvation in paradise. In Amoy the ceremony is called 'taking refuge.' Each candidate must be introduced by a well-known member—the 'introductory master'—to warrant his good faith, in order to guard against the danger of exposing the sect to treason by admitting untrustworthy people. Their books fully describe the most interesting initiation-ritual, of which only a short account can be given here.

As a rule several candidates are admitted at once. They first place an offering of fruit and vegetables before the altar, and the leader offers incense and candles and humbly invites the saints to enter their images and so attend the ceremony. Then comes a short sermon on the excellence of Buddha, followed by an examination of the candidates. The leader exhorts them to cast themselves into the arms of the Three Refuges—'Buddha, Dharma, and Sangha; believe in them and admit them into your hearts. Ye may not seek or find them outside yourselves.' The candidates have now entered religion, and the way of salvation lies open before them, but they cannot make the slightest progress in it except by faithful obedience to the principal commands which are now to be solemnly accepted. These Five Commands are (1) against taking life (this is most important because of the belief in transmigration, according to which any living creature may contain the soul of one who in a former life was a man); (2) against stealing; (3) against unchastity; (4) against lying; (5) against the use of spirituous liquors and of certain plants. The candidates are then taught the special *Sūtra*, consisting of 28 characters, called the 'Dharma Jewel,' and they call down a curse upon themselves if they lose this jewel. When they have taken the vow, the introductory master addresses them, exhorting them never to sin against the Three Refuges or the Five Commandments, never to allow themselves to lose anything of the Dharma Jewel; 'Then, O disciples, the vow ye have taken will become for you a lake of lotuses red and white, across which you will travel to the West, to go out and go home into the company of the Buddhas. To those who refine their conduct nothing but Heaven belongs, Hell is not their share a second time. May your six roots (perception of eyes, nose, mouth, ears, body, and mind) remain pure and clean, and the five parts of your bodies (sinews, bones, skin, flesh, and hair) enjoy quietness and health, your homes be pure and happy, the inmates enjoy rest and peace. May all your undertakings be crowned with success, may happiness and blessedness come down upon you in profusion.' A general *Sūtra* reading brings the initiation to a close. The wishes just pronounced are written down in the form of a prayer; the paper is lighted at one of the candles and placed on the ashes of the incense-burner. This prayer reaches its destination, the gold lotus throne of Wu-kih.

There are also rituals for initiation into the higher grades, in which the candidates take further vows.

(3) *Meetings.*—The meetings do not generally take place at fixed dates, and, if persecution threatens, none may be held for months together or the members may meet only at night. There are thirteen worship days in honour of special saints, among them being the patriarch Lo, the god of heaven, Kwanyin, the sun, Sākyamuni, the lord of hell, the moon, and Amita Buddha. On these days, in the early morning, cups of tea are placed on the altar to refresh the saints. When enough people are present, the service begins. Rice, vegetables, fruit, and tea are placed on the table in front of the altar, with fragrant incense. The members arrange themselves in long rows, men on one side and women on the other. With closed eyes and the palms of their hands pressed together before their breasts, they recite formulas and extracts from the *Sūtras*, one of them tapping on a hollow wooden bowl at every syllable and on a metal bell at the first word of every strophe. Then, two by two, first the men and then the women, they come forward and salute Buddha and the saints, touching the floor nine times with their foreheads. After this the dishes are removed, and they sit down to eat this vegetable meal.

(4) *Ceremonies for the dead.*—At some of their services there are ceremonies to convey departed souls to the Paradise of the West. A small barge composed of bamboo and paper is made; after *Sūtra* readings and invocations the ship is burned. 'Thus, through fire and flame, the Bark of Wisdom plies across the Sea of Transmigration to the promised Paradise where the Highest Intelligence prevails.' At some meetings members recite the *Sūtra* of 'Repentance of the Thousand Names of Buddha,' the object being to obtain pardon of sins by exciting internally, at the invocation of each name, a feeling of deep repentance.

(5) *Private worship.*—Members also recite *Sūtras* in their own homes. Most of them have only learned by heart the sound of the characters and do not know their meaning; but this does not matter; there is mighty salvation-working power in them, and perhaps there are myriads of unseen spirits listening to the recital and obtaining salvation thereby. The Mahāyāna code commands that they shall be recited in all times of sickness or when the realm is in danger; in times of rebellion; on the birthdays of parents, brothers, and religious teachers; during conflagrations and inundations, when storms harass ships, or giants and devils bring distress; also when one is struck by disasters or punishment; during epidemics, etc. Many women in their homes recite them before the image of Kwanyin, having first washed their faces and hands and put on clean clothes. Sometimes they place a cup of dry tea on the altar, and, when the recital is over, pour hot water on the tea and drink it as highly beneficial to health; or they put it away as medicine for future use. Sometimes a short invocation to Buddha or the saints is used and has the same power. It is quite usual to vow to recite, say, 1000 *Sūtra* fragments if a prayer is granted. The sectaries use rosaries to count the number of recitals. For those who cannot read or learn there is an easy way of obtaining salvation: they repeat hundreds and thousands of times the name of a saint, especially that of Amita Buddha. There are ceremonies for saving the dead by prevailing on Kwanyin to convey them to the western paradise—most interesting, but too long to be given here.

These accounts of the practices and beliefs of some of the sects are enough to give an idea of what sectarianism in China is and to point out the religious spirit which has created it and kept it alive in spite of cruel persecution. The sects have often been ranked by foreigners among the various secret societies and seditious clubs which were at work at the overthrow of the reigning dynasty; but this is largely untrue and unfair. In the MSS of the sects quoted above there is not one word about resistance and revolt, but much about being faithful to the powers that be.

Edkins,[1] writing of the books of the sects in Shantung, said that there was much therein in favour of loyalty and no word against the Government. He said that they were of a mixed Buddhistic, Taoistic, and Confucian character, containing admonitions to goodness, to loyalty, to devotion and submission to parents, to chastity, together with exhortations to abstain from the killing of living beings, from sins of the tongue and pen, from spirituous drinks and opium. The smaller religious sects all have one goal in common; they spring, partly at least, out of the common desire to know the Infinite and the Eternal. Not only do men who rank as philosophers feel after God, but

[1] *Chinese Recorder and Missionary Journal* for 1888.

many of the weary combatants in the battle of life, familiar with poverty and hardship, also feel inexpressible longings to know what and who God is. Such must have founded and developed the various so-called secret sects of China and by their manifest faith in what they teach have drawn into communities multitudes of followers. It is among these sects that the movement of religious thought is most active.

3. The principal secret societies.—(*a*) *The Triad Society, or Tien-ti Hui* (*Heaven and Earth Society*).—This was always confessedly of a political nature with revolutionary objects; but it has also a Buddhistic religious character and has to be reckoned among the religious societies which the State persecuted for heresy. It was first heard of in 1789. William Stanton[1] gives a full account of this society. He says that its membership consisted of about equal numbers of Cantonese, Fukienese, and Hakkas. Its flag bore the legend 'Rebel against the Manchus, restore the Mings.' By 1832 its influence was felt from Formosa to Hunan, from Kiangsi to Kwangsi. In 1850 its members helped the Taiping movement. The Taiping rebellion was not a Triad rebellion, but the Taiping leaders availed themselves of the help of the society. For more than a hundred years this society has been a source of constant anxiety to officials.

(*b*) *The Taiping rebels.*—Religious persecution was the main cause of this rebellion. The first signs appeared in Hunan in 1836; by 1850 the insurgents numbered 8000 in Kwangtung alone. It is sometimes said to have been a Christian movement. The leader, Hung Siu-tsuen, had imbibed some Christian ideas from a pamphlet written by a Christian, a convert of Dr. Milne of Malacca; and the writings of Hung Siu-tsuen are certainly tinged with Christian ideas and contain confused allusions to Biblical characters, mixed up with heathen and Confucian philosophy. But it was really a rebellion against the persecuting dynasty—'the effort of a desperate people to throw off a yoke of bloody intolerance and tyranny.'[2] If it had been successful, there would probably have been religious freedom; but it was washed out in seas of blood and such devastation as converted large parts of the country into a desert.

(*c*) *The Kwo Lao Hui.*—This society arose about 1891 and was inimical to the foreign reigning dynasty. Hunan, Hupeh, and Szechuen were hotbeds of the movement. Very many of the Government soldiers joined it, with the result that the Government feared to try its strength with it lest the soldiers should go over to the other side.

(*d*) *The Reform Society.*—Another society, small but of great importance, was the Reform Society, which arose in 1894–95. A few earnest and brilliant young men read Mackenzie's *History of the Nineteenth Century*, and other books on Western civilization and progress, translated by the Christian Literature Society, and were filled with a desire to introduce reforms into China. Leading statesmen and scholars in Peking and the provinces studied these books eagerly, as did also the young emperor Kwang-su. A Reform Society, consisting of more than a score of the leading Hanlins, was formed in Peking, as well as branches in Shanghai and Wuchang. The leading spirits were Tan Tsu-tsung, Kang Yu-wei, and Liang Ki-chiao. Tan, the son of the governor of Hupeh, was an earnest Christian. Kang Yu-wei, called 'the Modern Sage of China,' had thousands of student followers; he wrote a series of brilliant reform edicts, which the emperor issued. Liang was a distinguished journalist, who spread widely over China the ideas of reform. The reactionary party in Peking was greatly alarmed at the rapid spread of these ideas and persuaded the empress dowager to seize the reins of government. The emperor was made a prisoner, the office of the reformers was sealed up, and six of the leaders were executed, among whom was Tan Tsu-tsung. Kang Yu-wei and Liang Ki-chiao narrowly escaped with their lives.

[1] *The Triad Society.* [2] De Groot, p. 555.

III. *PERSECUTION OF SECTS.*—Many writers about China have said that Confucianism is most tolerant to other religions; but a very little investigation shows how mistaken they were, and that, on the contrary, it persecuted on principle. For fifteen centuries the State insisted on the necessity of stamping out heresies. Sound doctrine was regarded as harmony with *Tao*, or the course of the universe. This *Tao* has no co-equal; hence there is no room for any second set of rules; if by chance another set should arise, it is necessarily 'not correct' and must be suppressed. The Confucian classics might be called the only Bible for religion, politics, and ethics during almost twenty centuries—the treasury of dogma, outside of which no truth ever was, is, or will be.

1. From the time of Mencius. — The sage Mencius, who lived 200 years after Confucius, laid upon all future ages the duty of persecuting heresy, and he himself violently attacked heretics. He declared that heresy was everything which departed from the teachings of the Sages, and particularly of three of them, viz. Yu the Great, Cheu-kung, the principal author of the *Yih King*, and Confucius, and that their teaching must be rigorously upheld for all time. According to Chinese logic and the immutable Confucian doctrines, the Government is *bound* to doom to death all religions, customs, and ethics which are not mentioned in the classics and, so far from being tolerant, is bound to be absolutely intolerant, not only of religious sects, but also of the great systems of Taoism and Buddhism.

This was the teaching, but was it carried out? A cursory glance at the Government edicts and the reports of officials for 2000 years reveals a tale of almost incredible horror—of persecutions in which men, women, and children, innocent and guilty, were barbarously destroyed, the total mounting up to millions. Buddhism, as an imported religion, suffered more than Taoism. It was at times in favour, and even patronized by the emperor; at other times it was violently persecuted, its temples and gods were destroyed, and priests and nuns scattered.

2. From the 5th to the 17th century.—The persecutions during these centuries were specially fierce during the Tang and Ming dynasties and were mostly directed against the Buddhists. Some were at the instigation of individuals—of Fu-yeh in 624; of Yao-tsung, under the emperor Ching-tsung, 705–710; of Han-yu in 819; and of a Taoist doctor, Chao Kwei-chin, in 844.

(*a*) *Tang dynasty.*—It was impossible for the Government to root out Buddhism and Taoism, so its policy was to repress and weaken, to make it difficult for people to enter the monastic life or to build temples. About 845 the emperor decreed that more than 4600 monasteries and convents should be demolished, and that the 260,000 monks and nuns should return to secular life; their best lands were to be confiscated and the slaves divided among the families that paid ground-tax twice a year. The result was to scatter the devout priests and nuns who were zealous for their religion and to encourage the formation of secret associations throughout the country. It was further ordered that whoever surreptitiously shaved, as priests and nuns did, should be sent back to secular life, that the religious teacher should be severely beaten, and both teacher and pupil sent to exile with hard labour for three years. All exhibitions of exorcism and witchcraft and the use of holy candles and holy water were forbidden, and those practising such things were condemned to exile on the distant frontiers.

(*b*) *Ming dynasty.*—It was during this dynasty, in 1511, that the famous 'Law against Heresies' was promulgated.

'It was specially enacted to keep the laity free from pollution by heretical doctrines and practices, and to destroy everything religious and ethical which was contrary to the Confucian standard.'[1]

This law declared that the leaders of sects should be punished by strangulation; the less prominent were to be beaten with long sticks—a very severe punishment, which most often resulted in death. Others were to be banished to the frontiers and to wear cangues for life, which of course meant beggary, as the wearing of a cangue prevented any kind of work; others were to be sent as slaves to Muslim *begs* in Central Asia, for the rulers knew how Muslims hated Buddhists and Christians; others were to be banished to malarious regions in S. China. The Government raged blindly against religious communities in general without any discrimination between degrees of heresy. The prefects were ordered to ransack villages and hamlets for heretical sects and prosecute them under fear of severe penalties if they were lax. Also rewards were offered to heresy hunters. Some sects were specially mentioned, as White Lotus, Red Yang, etc. The 'Law against Heresies' has always been considered to be in force against Christians. This terrible law was taken over unaltered into the penal and civil code of the Manchu dynasty.

In 1394 members of the White Lotus sect were threatened with death. In 1458 the emperor Yung-tsung decreed that any who had taken the tonsure without Government sanction were to be sent into 'everlasting banishment to the garrisons,' and 690 Tibetans were sent away. Monasteries were again demolished and images destroyed; it was even ordered that the bones and teeth of Buddha, with other holy relics, should be burned outside the walls. Later it was decreed that no young men should enter the clerical state, and that the Buddhist monasteries should be allowed to crumble to ruins, all permission to repair them being withheld.

In the middle of the 16th cent. the White Lotus sect came into full activity, and orders were given rigorously to attack it. It was branded and outlawed for ever as a political body of the utmost danger to the Government; from that day it was delivered unconditionally to the persecution of a merciless mandarinate. The patience of the sects was thoroughly exhausted; for centuries the Government had trodden down, harassed, and persecuted their members; so at last they broke out into open rebellion.

De Groot has fully proved that the Ming dynasty, in oppressing and persecuting the non-Confucian religions, conducted itself quite systematically and with rigid determination.

3. From 1664 to 1912.—There was very fierce persecution under the Manchu dynasty, and especially under two of the very ablest and most illustrious emperors, Kang-hi and Kien-lung. Kang-hi published a great encyclopædia and a famous dictionary. Kien-lung, the conqueror of Burma, Nepāl, Tibet, and Kashgaria, rivalled his grandfather in this respect and published histories and other works. But they were both fiendish persecutors of every form of heresy, and the cause of the first great outbreak of the White Lotus sect. De Groot says that Kang-hi was the cause of the death of nearly a million people.

[1] De Groot, p. 135.

It is impossible to mention here the numerous edicts and waves of persecution which swept over the land, but it is a tale of incredible cruelty and horror; none were too obscure to escape. The Government records themselves reveal a picture of awful persecution, of tremendous rebellions called forth by these cruelties—rebellions smothered in blood. The people saw their revered religious leaders and elders, their parents and children, brothers and sisters, dragged into dungeons, beaten, tortured, strangled, beheaded, cut to pieces alive, banished; harmless religionists had prices set on their heads and were hunted down as dangerous beasts. Simple membership of a sect was punished with deportation and slavery. These persecutions were often inspired by fear, for the Government almost identified heresy with sedition and rebellion.

Many sects are mentioned by name in the persecution edicts: Eight Diagrams, White Lotus, Mahāyāna, Muhammadans, Wahhābīs, Lo Hwai, Christians. Christians were persecuted as members of a heretical sect, thus coming under the 'Law against Heresies,' which was not specially directed against them; but later special edicts were promulgated against them as followers of a foreign religion, and therefore rebels.

From 1794 to 1802 there was a great heresy crusade, especially in the five provinces of Szechuen, Hupeh, Honan, Shensi, and Kansu. The people were slaughtered by hundreds of thousands, and the country was 'pacified,' as we read in *An Account of the Pacification of the Religious Rebels.*[1] In the next reign it was the same, and the cruelties and horrors provoked the great Muhammadan rebellion, in quelling which millions perished and large portions of the country were devastated. The next emperor, Tao Kwang, followed the same course; we hear of persecutions of the Tribute Rice Society, Red Yang, White Lotus, etc. White Lotus at times seems to be almost a general term for secret sects. These new persecutions in their turn gave rise to the Taiping rebellion; and so the tale goes on. We have the Government records up to 1875, and they still reveal fresh edicts against the sects. From 1861 to her death the great empress dowager, during the greater part of the time, was responsible for the action of the Government, and the usual edicts continued to be issued to the end.

From 1842 onwards European Powers interfered to protect the Christians, and forced the Chinese Government to sign treaties of toleration, giving Christians the right to live unmolested in the exercise of their religion. So from that date the 'Law against Heresies' did not apply to them. But, in spite of treaties, much persecution went on and was winked at, and often encouraged, by officials. In 1900 there was the outburst against foreigners and Christians, instigated by the empress dowager, and known as the Boxer Rising.

LITERATURE.—T. T. Meadows, *The Chinese and their Rebellions*, London, 1856; J. J. M. de Groot, *Sectarianism and Religious Persecution in China*, 2 vols., Amsterdam, 1903–04 (of this the present writer has made extensive use); Timothy Richard, *Kin Tan Kiao* (*China Mission Handbook*), Shanghai, 1896; Li Hung Chang, *Foreign Relations in the Eighties*, Tientsin, *c.* 1880; Anon., *Death Blow to Corrupt Doctrines*, Hunan, 1870; Chow Han, *Infamous Calumnies against Christianity*, tr. T. Richard, *Shanghai Mercury*, reprint, Shanghai; T. Richard, *The Relation of the Chinese Government to Christian Missionaries*, do. 1890; *Blue Books of the Chinese Government* (*King Shih Wen*), tr. Arnold Foster, do. 1891; John Archibald, *The Sung Pu Massacres*, Hankow, 1892; *Chinese Riots*, ed. T. Richard, *North China Daily News*, reprint, Shanghai, 1891; William Stanton, *The Triad Society*, Hong Kong, 1900; T. Richard, *The New Testament of Higher Buddhism*,

[1] Wei Yuen, 1842; this occurs in ch. vii. of the *Shing wu ki*, 'Description of Military Operations.'

Edinburgh, 1910; P. Y. Saeki, *The Nestorian Monument in China*, London, 1916; W. J. Clennell, *The Historical Development of Religion in China*, do. 1917.

TIMOTHY RICHARD.

SECTS (Christian).—A sect, strictly speaking, is a group of people following some leader, whether his influence be permanent and world-wide (*e.g.*, Calvin) or local and temporary (*e.g.*, Antoinette Bourignon). The group may maintain its footing within an organized communion, like the Clapham Sect; it may, actively or passively, take up separate existence, like the Jansenists. The subject has been clouded by heresiologists in all ages, who heaped together nicknames in two or three languages, sometimes coining new titles, so that an obscure group known only for a score of years may be labelled in several ways—after their founder, after another leader, by the name which they themselves chose, and by two or three epithets flung at them by their enemies. Epiphanius, Philastrius, Theodoret, Prædestinatus, have had many imitators such as Ephraim Pagitt; and even modern compilers are more content to give alphabetical lists of hundreds of sects in the United Kingdom and the United States than to offer any clue to their relations, their importance, or their doctrines. The present article will deal chiefly with such minor parties as claim notice and are not described elsewhere in this Encyclopædia, either separately or in art. HERESY (Christian). It will, however, be necessary in telling of the twigs to observe their ramification and to mention afresh some of the larger branches from which they are the offshoots.

I. *EARLY*.—Information for the first 300 years was long due chiefly to four Greeks—Clement at Alexandria, Hippolytus at Rome, Irenæus at Lyons, and Eusebius at Cæsarea—though Tertullian at Carthage adds something for the West. But Syriac, Armenian, and Arabic scholars are enabling us in a few cases to go behind these hostile reporters and to learn at first hand. In this nascent period Christian thought was much influenced by previous religions and philosophies, and three groups show clear traces of Judaism, Zoroastrianism, and Buddhism; to these Ebionite, Manichæan, and Gnostic classes we may add the Monarchian.

The primacy of Jerusalem was lost by the catastrophe of A.D. 70, and no leader arose with the influence of James. Therefore the Christians of Jewish origin were soon out-numbered, and, since many of them clung to an observance of their Law, they came to be regarded askance. Even the fact that they had an ancient Aramaic gospel, *Secundum Hebræos*, when it became known by Jerome translating it, intensified the disposition to regard them as schismatics or heretics, who added to the sacred four an unnecessary fifth. Nor was much gratitude shown, except by Origen, to Theodotion, who revised the LXX, or to Symmachus, who made a new Greek version of the OT. Eusebius indeed took umbrage[1] at a commentary by Symmachus, regarding it as an attack upon Matthew, with a bias against the Virgin Birth; but probably it was a commentary on the Aramaic gospel.

Jewish thought ran in other channels than did Greek, and the difference was well marked in the domain of wedded life, which Jews insisted on, but Greeks and Copts disparaged. The **Jewish Christians**[2] admitted with most Jews that sacrifice was necessarily obsolete, but they circumcised, and prayed towards Jerusalem. Apparently they did not appreciate the writings of Paul, with his polemic against the Law. The points that did interest them emerge in the *Periodoi Petrou*, source of the *Clementine Homilies* and *Recognitions*, and in the *Anabathmoi Jacobou*. The test-question was what they thought of Jesus; the Greeks discerned two groups: the Nazarenes, who agreed with them, and the Ebionites, who were content to acknowledge Jesus as the Messiah and to say nothing as to pre-existence or deity.

Much less is known as to how these Jewish Christians appeared to the old Jews: the references in the *Mishnāh* and the two *Gemaras* have been sifted by R. T. Herford.[1] Among the Minim must be included the Jewish Christians, expressly said in A.D. 550 to be purely Palestinian, not Babylonian. The cleft between them and the old Jews was so deep that Rabbi Tarphon would not enter their houses or read their books, laying it down that a copy of the Law written by them should be burned, as they were worse than idolaters. About A.D. 200 they met in their own synagogues, clad in white, barefoot, with phylacteries, and read the Law. About 350 they had discarded the Law, and declared that only the Ten Words had been given at Sinai. To Jesus they attributed such utterances as 'I am God,' 'I am the son of man,' 'I will go up to heaven.' Many discussions are reported as to the duality of the Godhead, with comments on OT passages; the influence of the Epistle to the Hebrews can readily be recognized. Orthodox Jews were advised, 'If the son of the harlot say to thee, There are two gods, reply, I am He of the Red Sea, I am He of Sinai.' For a remarkable body largely recruited from Jewish Christians see art. ELKESAITES. Another body just outside the Christian border was the Dosithean, followers of a Messiah to the Samaritans, nearly contemporary with Christ. They continued to emphasize the Law, especially on points relating to the Sabbath; they were known in Persia, and in Egypt as late as A.D. 588.

In the Euphrates valley arose several blends of religion. The **Mandæan** (*q.v.*)[2] still survives near Basra, as army chaplains reported with surprise in 1917. **Manichæism** (*q.v.*) had a powerful influence in the Roman Empire. An old soldier, Acuas, from the Persian wars taught it in Palestine about A.D. 273,[3] and its aftermath appeared in sporadic mediæval sects.

At the beginning of the Christian era fusion of belief was taking place very generally in Egypt, Syria, and Asia Minor. It was to be expected that some thinkers would take up a few Christian elements, and many schools developed,[4] though there were Gnostics who had no Christian tinge, such as the Borbori, or dirt-eaters.

Alexandria had three famous **Gnostic** teachers. The indigenous system of Pleroma (*q.v.*), emanations of pairs, redemption by re-absorption, was tinged with Christianity by Basilides and Valentinus (*qq.v.*). Carpocrates also deserves notice, for Irenæus tells us that his followers coined and appropriated the term 'Gnostic.' He was indebted to Plato rather than to Egypt, and distinctly taught one supreme God, whence emanated the makers of the world. Into this came souls which had previously dwelt among Ideas, having had fellowship with God; pure souls, such as Homer, Pythagoras, Plato, Aristotle, Jesus, Paul, strove to recall those Ideas and resist the influence of the world, even by magical arts; among the influences that would enchain them was to be ranked the Law of Jahweh. Transmigration of souls enabled all to rejoin the supreme God, who might welcome a few elect souls direct. Such teaching was developed by his son, Epiphanes, and others, on the topic, What were the influences to be resisted;

[1] *HE* vi. 17.

[2] See art. EBIONISM.

[1] *Christianity in Talmud and Midrash*, London, 1903.

[2] The art. MANDÆANS discusses also the terms Hemerobaptist, Christians of St. John, Sābians. For other Sābians see art. HARRANIANS.

[3] Epiph. *Hær.* lxvi. 7.

[4] See *ERE* vi. 215.

if all human actions are indifferent, the true Gnostic ought to experiment with all, so as to find out what really helped him. In some quarters this doctrine served as a pretext for immorality, which was then charged by Christians against all Carpocratians, and by outsiders against all Christians. One party of these antinomians, rejecting the theory of a demiurge, was named **Antitactæ** by Clement.[1]

Marcus was perhaps an Alexandrian, but he taught in Asia Minor, and is known chiefly through Irenæus, who had to do with the **Marcosians** in the Rhone valley. He introduced many Pythagorean speculations with numbers. On the authority of women who repented and returned to the Church, Irenæus charged them with conjuring tricks in worship and with immorality; though they denied this. Hippolytus with independent knowledge in Rome deliberately reiterated the charge. They lingered into the 4th century. Men and women were chosen by lot to prophesy or to baptize; their rite for this was to pour oil and water on the head, in the name of the unknown Father of all, truth the Mother of all, and Him who came down upon Jesus.

Antioch was the centre of Saturninus, who was heir of Simon Magus through Menander.[2] He was frankly dualist, conceiving Jahweh as the chief of the seven creators made by the good God, and Christ as sent by Him to depose the seven. Bad men, made by the rival god, were redeemable by Christ on condition of stern abstinence from all sensuous pleasures. It obviously followed that Christ was not of flesh and blood at all, but appeared only in the likeness of man.

This line of thought was developed by Tatian, and, because he used water at the Lord's Supper, his followers were labelled **Hydroparastatæ** or **Aquarii**, and, by distortion, Saccophori, Accaophori; while a sect of **Encratites** (*q.v.*) affiliated to him. His services to Aramaic Christianity in preparing the *Diatessaron* facilitated his views spreading down the Euphrates and paved the way for the great development of Christianity in Persia termed by the Greeks **Nestorianism** (*q.v.*). This great communion, with its mission-work in mid Asia, China, and down the Persian Gulf to the coasts of India and Ceylon, deserves to be more deeply studied in its own documents.[3] In this period only one exponent claims attention, Bardaisan of Edessa. He is known to us chiefly at second hand through Greeks, and it is agreed that we cannot reconstruct his theology from them, even with the added light from Ephrem; but his disciple Philip summarized his views in *The Book of the Laws of the Countries*, available now in Syriac. Bardaisan was of high rank, perhaps once a priest in the great temple of Atargatis at Mabug (Hierapolis). A Jewish colony produced a Syriac version of the Hebrew Scriptures, different from the Aramaic targums; the earliest converts to Christianity were doubtless won from this circle, and Bardaisan joined them. He seems to have won over some followers of Cucojo, who had built upon foundations laid by Valentinus.[4] His influence with the royal house of the Abgars greatly improved the standing of Christians in the kingdom. On its subjugation by the Romans, and a persecution by Caracalla, he went as a missionary to Armenia and wrote a history of that land which became the basis of Greek accounts. He also took advantage of an embassy from India to publish some knowledge of Indian religions, and thus prepared the way for the later missions. Accessory to this main work of propagation was his devotion to Christian song. Pliny vouches that there had been hymns before, but it was Bardaisan who deliberately wrote and collected 150 Christian hymns to match the 150 Psalms of Jewish worship.[1] Only Greek ignorance has attributed to Arius the honour discerned by Hahn as due to the Syrian, the *primus hymnologus*. Later ages kept up the tradition, so that the Syrian communion is the richest in this department of worship. Of Bardaisan's own writings none survives, unless the splendid 'Hymn of the Soul' in the *Acts of Thomas* is due to him; this is not distinctly Christian, though open to a Christian interpretation. His son, Harmonius, followed up his work, and the Christianity of Edessa was of this school till Ephrem of Nisibis settled there about 363 and set himself to transform it parallel with Nicene orthodoxy, writing new hymns to the Bardaisanian tunes.

In the 4th cent. the Gnostic theory of archons, or rulers, over the various heavens was blended with Ebionite teaching so as to identify the seventh archon with Jahweh and to make the devil his son. The leader was Peter of Judæa, a hermit near Jerusalem, who was excommunicated by Epiphanius.[2] His teaching and several books were taken by Eutactus to Armenia, where they had some vogue; but no more is heard of these **Archontici**.

Another Syrian had transferred his energies to Rome about 140, preceding Tatian. The teachings of Cerdo are reported by Irenæus and by Hippolytus. In his day there was no canon of Christian literature, and he perhaps began one by an edition of Paul's letters (evidently collected by some one with a purely Ægean outlook) accompanied by the historical introduction furnished by Luke. The Jewish Scriptures were nothing to him, for the God of the Jews was not the God proclaimed by Christ. He seems to have stereotyped the dogma, already denied in the Johannine Epistles, that Christ had no flesh, only an astral or docetic body. Cerdo seems to have gathered no party, but those who sympathized with him in the unorganized state at Rome found a leader in Marcion;[3] possibly some **Marcionite** teachings have been ante-dated and attributed to Cerdo.

In opposition to all the dualist schemes of Gnostics and Manichæans, some Greeks emphasized the unity of the Godhead, and the name **Monarchian** has been generalized to cover all such schools. The problem to be solved was the relation of Christ to God; two solutions were offered—a dynamic and a modal.

The former was first taught in Rome by Theodotus of Byzantium, a close student of Euclid, Aristotle, and Galen, who eschewed allegory and interpreted Scripture on straightforward lines. His view was that Jesus was an ordinary man till the Spirit entered Him at baptism. This idea was elaborated by a namesake, a banker, who, to meet He 2^{16}, suggested that Melchizedek was the heavenly mediator for angels; this permitted the name **Melchizedekites** to be attached to his followers. He attempted a separate organization in Rome and was fortunate enough to obtain as bishop a confessor, Natalius; but the latter repented and was reconciled to Zephyrinus. The same views were taught in Rome by Artemon, but nothing more is heard of the movement after 250.

A vague account of some **Alogi** is given by Epiphanius two centuries later; he describes them as disbelieving the Logos doctrine as taught in Jn 1; he links them with the former Theodotus,

[1] *Strom.* iii. 526 ff.

[2] From a misreading of this man's name seems to have been coined the title of an imaginary sect, the Adrianistæ.

[3] See also P. Y. Saeki, *The Nestorian Monument in China*, London, 1916.

[4] Ephrem, *Against Heretics*, ch. xxii. p. 485.

[1] See art. HYMNS (Syriac Christian).

[2] See *Hær.* xl.

[3] See art. MARCIONISM.

but gives no details of place or of positive tenets. It does not appear that any one has quoted in this connexion the saying by Paul of Samosata: 'The Word is greater than Christ, for Christ became great through wisdom.'[1] As to the earlier state of Jesus, the Antiochene bishop declared:

'Mary did not bring forth the Word, for Mary was not before the ages, but she brought forth a man on a level with ourselves. It is the man who was anointed, not the Word. . . . By his unflinching, unblenched will and resolution, he made himself like unto God; and having kept himself free from sin, he was made one with Him.'[2]

The same line of thought is found a few years later in an argument professedly addressed to Mani by Archelaus, a Syrian bishop, which has come by tortuous channels not likely to modify the thought on this head:

'Doubtless Jesus was less than John among those born of women, though in the kingdom of heaven he was greater. . . . Tell me on whom the Holy Spirit came as a dove, who is it that was baptized by John. If he was perfect, if he was Son, if he was Power, the Spirit could not have entered even as kingdom cannot enter kingdom. . . . It was the Christ of God that descended on him who was Mary's son.'[3]

Archelaus infers that the Christ may descend on any man who lives a life like Jesus; he agrees with the doctrine of Mani on this point, though he denies that Mani is such a man:

'The Spirit dwells in a man, and descends and stays . . . and this often happens, even as you were professing lately that you yourself are the paraclete of God.'[4]

From such a clear utterance we may look back and discern the same doctrine held in the days of Justin.[5] Tarphon (Trypho) mentions the theory, held not by himself but by others, that Jesus can be shown to have been born as a man from men, and be proved to have been raised to the dignity of Messiahship by election. There is even an isolated passage in Hermas,[6] which may indeed be inconsistent with other passages in the same book, that is quite clear to the same effect:

When Jesus had laboured with the Spirit and had co-operated with it in everything, behaving boldly and bravely, then God chose Him as a partner with the Holy Spirit and took the Son as adviser, 'for all flesh, which is found undefiled and unspotted, wherein the Holy Spirit dwelt, shall receive a reward.'[7]

A different theory had been worked out in Asia Minor by Praxeas and Noetus. Holding the thorough deity of Christ and the absolute unity of God, they completely identified the two. They charged Hippolytus and Tertullian with being Ditheists and were in return labelled **Patripassians** or **Theopaschites.** By personal visits Praxeas won a few followers in Rome and many in Carthage. Epigonus, a disciple of Noetus, won in Rome Cleomenes and Sabellius of Libya, who spread the theory in Africa.[8] Beryllus of Bostra seems to have held kindred views, which Origen convinced him were untenable. And the same Father opposed some views held in Arabia, that the soul dies with the body and will share in its resurrection.[9]

All sects thus mentioned, except the last, crystallized on some point connected with the person of Christ. But the actual lowering of Christian life and the growth of a bureaucracy brought forth a conservative revivalist, Montanus of Ardaba in Mysia.[10] He emphasized some original features that were being dropped—*e.g.*, that the end of the age might be speedily expected (whereas Gnosticism was concerned rather with beginnings), that faith was more important than knowledge, that a high standard of morals must be maintained by rigid discipline, that the Spirit still spoke through many believers. On the other hand, he laid stress on martyrdom, virginity, widowhood; and he invented a distinction between venial sins after baptism, which could be forgiven by the Church, and mortal sins, which could not. It is singular that most of the old features which **Montanism** (*q.v.*) sought to preserve were therefore opposed and driven out, while nearly all the innovations of its founder were afterwards adopted by his opponents. Two of his helpers were Maximilla and Priscilla, whose names were used to denote sections of his followers that were said to have women not merely as preachers but also as priests and bishops. Because some at Ancyra seen by Jerome used cheese with bread at the Lord's Supper (or probably at a love-feast), they were called **Artotyritæ.** Others who practised meditation, and, like the Hindus, found special attitudes to promote this, were mocked at as **Papalorhynchitæ** or **Tascodrugitæ**; the latter word has been deformed into Ascodrugitæ, Ascodrupitæ, Ascodruti, Abrodici, Ascitæ; the former gave rise to variants, Passalorhynchitæ, Dactylorhynchitæ.

A fresh impulse was given to the demand for purity of life when the churches had leisure to recuperate after the Decian persecution. Many had apostatized, and the question became urgent on what terms they might be re-admitted to fellowship. A lenient policy was adopted in Rome, where the question was fought out. The leader of the stern party, Novatian, was chosen rival bishop, and soon the whole Christian community ranked itself on these lines. N. Africa and Asia Minor were strongholds of the puritan **Novatianists** (*q.v.*), and this geographical alignment suggests that they absorbed most Montanists. They regarded the others as apostate, incapable of regenerating any one by baptism; and therefore they baptized any candidate for admission, disregarding any previous ceremony performed by an 'apostate.' The same issue arose after the Diocletian persecution, and matters came to a head in N. Africa, where rival bishops were elected at Carthage. The stern party, or **Donatists** (*q.v.*), probably absorbed the local Novatians; they held their own, though the State patronized the others. Not till the Vandal invasions of the 5th cent. did both parties cease to be important. Various hard names flung at the Donatists were Montenses, Campitæ, Rupitæ, and Cotopitæ, Cothopithæ, Cutzupitæ, or Gotispitæ.

II. *ALONGSIDE ESTABLISHED CHURCHES.*—When Constantine recognized that the Christians were the most virile party in his empire, and decided to found a new capital near the provinces where they were strongest, he initiated a State policy of uniformity which created new sects by the score. The Greek world speculated, the Roman emperor strove to crush independence of thought, till the Arab gave both something else to think about. The rivalry of Alexandria, Antioch, and Constantinople expressed itself in theological formulas; each city fathered a great division of the Christian world, which has its representatives still. Very few doctrinal questions arose elsewhere, and even the Pelagian controversy came to its height among the Greeks. All other divisions turned on the personality of Christ.

As Illingworth says, neither the universality nor the unity of human personality was adequately understood in pre-Christian ages.[1] Greek thought was first forced to the problem by the absolutely unique case of Jesus Christ, and had no general theory as to the personality of an ordinary man. Origen was the first great thinker, and Alexandria

[1] F. C. Conybeare, *The Key of Truth*, Oxford, 1898, p. xcv.
[2] *Ib.*
[3] *Ib.* pp. xcviii, xcvii, citing *Acts of Archelaus*, ch. 49 f.
[4] *Ib.* p. xcix.
[5] *Dial.* xlviii.
[6] *Simil.* v. 6.
[7] For the later development of this Christology in Armenia see art. PAULICIANS; John of Damascus refers to its adherents as Doxarii or Aposchistæ. For Spain see art. ADOPTIANISM.
[8] See art. MONARCHIANISM.
[9] Eus. *HE* vi. 37.
[10] See *ERE* viii. 828.

[1] *Personality, Human and Divine* (*BL*), London, 1894, p. 8.

continued to lead in speculation until the views of Arius threatened to wreck Constantine's hope of a united empire. The development for the next two generations has been described in art. ARIANISM; three leaders deserve mention afresh. Aëtius of Antioch, bred in the strictest school of Aristotle, urged that Christ must be radically unlike God, and gathered a party of **Anomœans, or Exucontians.** His most illustrious follower was Eunomius of Cyzicus, whom he won at Alexandria about 350; and this man organized their sympathizers, consecrating new bishops; with his death in 395 the sect died out.[1] Theophronius of Cappadocia taught within their bounds that there were limits to God's knowledge, which was absolute only as regards current events;[2] his followers were named **Agnoëtæ.**

From the theories propounded by and against Apollinaris and his followers[3] were coined the titles **Dimœritæ, Anthropolatræ, Sarcolatræ, Vitaliani, Synusiastæ, Polemiani, Valentiniani.** The extreme anti-Arians at Alexandria separated under Coluthus in 319, but were induced to reunite in 324 by Hosius.

The latter leader with his friend Potamius, in Spain, still confronted with great missionary tasks, put out a manifesto urging that speculation should cease, and that all non-Scriptural terms should be disused; this led to the Synods of Ariminum and Seleucia in 359, when Acacius of Cæsarea led most of the Greeks to allow that the Son was like the Father, and thus provided for the Semi-Arians the new name of **Homœans.** But his influence waned within ten years.

An extraordinary interlude towards the end of the 4th cent. was connected with the name of Origen. Epiphanius of Salamis devoted some attention to him in his treatise on heresies and visited Palestine to destroy his influence. With Jerome at Bethlehem he succeeded, but Rufinus at Olivet had been a pupil of Didymus, who filled Origen's chair; and John, the patriarch of Jerusalem, regarded Epiphanius as intruding in his province. One result was that Rufinus returned to Italy and translated many of Origen's books into Latin, editing them freely. The controversy was complicated by Dioscorus and other Nitrian monks supporting the Origenists, while the Scetan monks went so far in their opposition that Theophilus, the patriarch of Alexandria, led soldiers to attack some monasteries and nearly lost his life. The one point that emerged was that Origen had denied that God had a human form, so that the Scetan-Jerome party could be called **Anthropomorphites.** As Chrysostom sided with John, the contest rapidly became personal, and Theophilus proved recreant to the traditions of Alexandria. As soon as Chrysostom was ruined by Epiphanius, the whole dispute died.

Older theories were revived, Photinus of Sirmium teaching afresh the Unitarian views of Paul of Samosata, and Marcellus of Ancyra reviving the doctrines of Sabellius. In 381 the Council of Constantinople pronounced against them, and also condemned a new theory of Macedonius,[4] late bishop of the city, who had begun to develop a doctrine of the Holy Spirit, whom he held to be a creature, ranking with the angels. It is the first sign of interest in the question which much later was to serve as a pretext for the rupture of East and West. Some of his followers were said by Philastrius to be unsocial at meals, and were therefore named **Adelophagi** by Praedestinatus.

As Christ was thus studied and dissected, till the reality of His human career was obscured by theories as to His nature, religious feeling turned

[1] See *ERE* v. 575. [2] Socrates, *HE* v. 24.
[3] See art. APOLLINARISM [4] See art. MACEDONIANISM.

to His mother. Some Thracian women who had migrated to Arabia revived in her honour the custom of offering cakes to the Queen of Heaven (*q.v.*) and were termed **Collyridians** (from κολλυρίς). Though their worship was condemned (as of women only?), the impulse to Mariolatry was strong. Helvidius of Rome maintained that after the birth of Jesus Mary bore children to Joseph; he and all who opposed the rising tide were blamed by Epiphanius[1] as **Antidicomarianites.** This led to the great controversies of the Nestorians and the Eutychians.[2] That section of the E. Syrian Church which has submitted to Rome, under the Syro-Chaldaic patriarch of Babylon, is now known as the **Chaldæan.**

The political problem of the emperors was to hold together Egypt, Syria, Asia Minor, with the earlier conquests of Rome. About the year 500 these were submerged by northern invaders, Theodoric ruling from Ravenna; the Goths were won by Arian missionaries, and it was a question whether the cities still in their midst, with Athanasian churches, would succumb or would leaven their conquerors. The conversion of the Franks was a great step towards solidifying the West, and the emperors saw that it was advisable to conciliate Rome. They secured this by doctrinal concessions only at the expense of grave disaffection throughout the East. In Egypt there was indeed a State Church upheld by force, a manifest token being that the patriarch of Alexandria was also governor of the province; but nearly the whole population scoffed at it as Melkite. The people were heartily Monophysite and were so disgusted with the time-serving of their patriarch Mongus that some abjured his authority and became known as **Acephali.**

Apart from these extremists, the Copts continued to subdivide on various questions as to the body of Jesus. That this did not function naturally, but only by constant exercise of the will to lay aside divine attributes, was a view put forward at Alexandria by Julian of Halicarnassus and supported by the Syrian Philoxenus of Mabug. When the Coptic patriarch died, Julian put forward Gaianus as a candidate and secured him the post. Their followers were thereupon nicknamed **Aphthartodocetæ** or **Incorrupticolæ**; but the tenet as stated by Stephen Niobes was that, because Christ united the two natures, humanity obtained the privilege of being uncreate. This raised the question whether the human nature of Jesus had been created or was uncreate, and the opponents called one another **Actistetæ, Ctistolatræ.** The party which held that Christ's body was ordinary was headed by Severus, who, though for six years patriarch of Antioch, had experience of Rome and of Constantinople, and was Alexandrian by education and residence. In the contest for the Coptic patriarchate of Alexandria, when Theodosius failed to hold the post, their party was styled **Phthartolatræ, Corrupticolæ.** On their line of thought came next the question whether Christ's mind was ordinary, or whether He was potentially omniscient and simply declined to know certain things. The Kenotists,[3] who took the second alternative, were known as **Agnoëtæ,** or were called after their leader, Themistius Calonymus the deacon. When these bodies, including the **Esaiani,** numbered about a dozen, they were dismissed in despair by cataloguers as **Diacrinomenoi, Hesitantes.**

Another cause of fission in Egypt late in the 6th cent. was still the relation of the three persons of the Trinity. Damian, the Coptic patriarch, taught that, while the three unitedly were God, each separately was not; his adherents were known

[1] *Hær.* lxxviii. [2] See art. MONOPHYSITISM.
[3] See art. KENOSIS.

sometimes by his name, sometimes as **Angelitæ**, from Angelium their chief church, or they were laughed at as **Tetraditæ, Condobauditæ.** Their chief opponent was John Philoponus, lay philosopher, who so emphasized the distinction of the three natures that the unity escaped notice, and his enemies readily styled him a Tritheist. He became involved also in a dispute on the resurrection with Conon of Tarsus, who held that the bodily form would not be resumed, only the material. On this line of thought the **Christolytæ** held that the body and soul of Christ fared as most do, and that only the divine nature ascended to heaven.

From a very different standpoint, another party earned the name of **Tetraditæ**; some Palestinian followers of Origen about 542, who followed up his doctrine of pre-existence and attributed divinity to the soul of Christ before the Incarnation, preferred the name **Protoctistæ.** In reaction the **Isochristi** taught that ultimately all would become like Christ; because in the course of the controversy two different monasteries became ranged against one another, they are also known as **Neolaurites.** The Abyssinian Church has steadily followed the Copts and has contributed nothing of more than local acceptance.

Theodosius, the Coptic patriarch, in 543 consecrated at Constantinople the Syrian Jacob as bishop of Nisibis. For thirty-five years he organized and ordained throughout Syria, so that the Monophysites of that land are often called **Jacobites.**[1] Not much original thought is recorded of this section; the works of Barsanuphius, an anchorite of Gaza, may be worth consulting; they are ascetic and doctrinal; those of Timotheus Ælurus of Alexandria were translated into Syriac and thence into Armenian; large numbers of sermons, hymns, and letters by Severus of Antioch are extant, and others by Jacob of Sarug. Philoxenus of Mabug about 508 revised the *Peshitta* in a most literal fashion, and a century later Thomas of Harkel edited the revision at Alexandria, adding the critical marks of Origen.

In 540 an Armenian council was held, which pronounced for Monophysitism and incorporated in the *Sanctus* the test phrase 'who wast crucified for us.' Under Heraclius this was abandoned, but from 728 communion with the Jacobites was restored. There are also remarkable relics of the Adoptian view, for the anniversary of Christ's birth is not observed, except for some mention on the great feast of the Baptism, 6th Jan.; the Julianite view of an incorruptible body was combined with this, as assumed in baptism. The Paulicians (*q.v.*) always objected to their rivals' worship of the Cross (Armenian, *Chazus*); therefore the term **Chatzitzarii, Chazinzarians (Staurolatræ)** seems to denote no small sect, but the Established Church of Armenia as viewed by the Paulicians.

Justinian sought to reconcile the Monophysites and so cement together the empire that his generals had re-conquered, and he called the fifth ecumenical council at Constantinople in 553 to ratify a compromise—his condemnation of Theodore of Mopsuestia, Theodoret, and Ibas in the 'Three Chapters.'[2] The whole West disagreed, however, and the assent of Rome was won only by retaining its bishop in exile, and on his death by nominating Pelagius, a pliant successor. He was excommunicated by nearly all the West, the lead being taken by Paulinus of Aquileia, but after his speedy death the scandal began to heal. The great influence of Rome gradually secured the acceptance of the council, so that the dissentients were presently termed schismatics. The Lombards encouraged the bishops of Aquileia to revive their former title of 'patriarch'; not until 698 was the division healed, when the whole cause was unintelligible. Two rival lines of bishops, however, bore the mere title of patriarch till 1751.

Timotheus of Constantinople, in his *Reception of Heretics*, about the end of the 6th cent., describes some Melchizedekites of Phrygia, who observed the Sabbath day; as they touched no one, they were popularly called **Athingani.** This reads as if they observed the Jewish rules of cleanliness, but the information is too scanty to trace their origin and tenets.

In the last days of Greek power the emperor Heraclius asked whether the will of Christ was single or double. The Monothelete controversy[1] occupied the attention of the theologians for half a century; all the while Islām was driving the Greek troops out of Egypt and Syria, with the hearty good will of the natives, so that the State Church there fell irretrievably. The community which held longest to the single will dwelt on Lebanon, and is known as **Maronite.** It speedily fell out of touch with Greek thought, reverting to the Syriac language, in which the liturgy is still chanted; but under Muslim rule the people speak Arabic. In the 12th cent. the Maronites adopted Dithelism as the price of Crusading help, but they were not thoroughly organized under Roman influence till 1743. Until recent troubles there were nearly 250,000 on Lebanon, with 70,000 more in Syria, Cyprus, and Egypt; about 2000 monks of St. Anthony and 1100 secular priests are under their patriarch. A curious result of all these divisions is to be seen in the title 'patriarch of Antioch,' borne to-day by six rivals: besides the Græco-Arab or Melkite and the Syrian Catholic, a Latin is to be found at Aleppo, a Greek at Damascus, and a Syriac at Diarbekr.

The views of Pelagius as to the effect of sin on mankind[2] were canvassed in the West behind his back; he himself set them forth at Bethlehem and Lydda, and was supported by Julian of Eclanum and Theodore of Mopsuestia. His follower Celestine, ordained at Ephesus, was at last condemned there in 431. But the Greeks declined to follow Augustine, and presently were classed as Semi-Pelagians. One of the classical works on heresy, written in the West, in its catalogue of wrong opinions, leads up to predestination, which is then stated, and opposed from the Semi-Pelagian standpoint. And the famous test of Catholic doctrine, that it has always been believed by everybody everywhere, was formulated to indicate that Augustinianism was a heresy. From Marseilles (Massilia), the headquarters of these Western leaders, they were often called **Massilians, Massalians,** or **Messalians**; the controversy was closed in 529 at Orange in that district. Before then the opinions of Augustine against free will had been exaggerated by monks at Hadrumetum to the pitch of antinomianism; after them was coined the title **Adrumetians.**

Lucifer of Cagliari in Sardinia stemmed the tide of laxity, somewhat on the lines of the Donatists, opposing the restoration to office of those who had given scandal; but his objection was on the score of Arian doctrine more than of apostasy. The protests of his followers were last heard in 384.

In S. Gaul and Spain, where the West Goths spread, we hear much from the 5th to the 7th cent. of certain **Bonosians,** organized with bishops. Apparently they followed Bonosus of Sardica, who flourished from 392 to 430. At first he simply taught that Joseph and Mary had children, but he was finally classed with Marcellus and Photinus. As his views were accepted in Spain, we infer that he held the old Adoptianism.

[1] See art. MONOPHYSITISM. [2] See *ERE* iv. 191 f.

[1] See art. MONOTHELETISM.
[2] See art. PELAGIANISM AND SEMI-PELAGIANISM.

Spain produced one leader in **Priscillian**[1] about 375. His opinions are certainly distorted by his opponents, who flung at him such epithets as Gnostic and Manichæan. Pamphlets of his discovered in 1885 show that he was a mystic, precursor of Santa Teresa. What really annoyed his neighbours was his asceticism, especially his strong views on the relation of the sexes, which he thought should be purely spiritual, whence the names **Abstinentes, Spiritales**; his world was not yet ripe for lay celibacy, and he was condemned at Saragossa, and finally beheaded at Trèves (385), the first victim of a new law against heretics. From Augustine we hear of a few Africans who lived as he advised, in foster-families, receiving adopted children; he called them **Abelonii, Abeliani, Abeloitæ.** If there be any truth in the tales told to Epiphanius about the **Adamiani**, reported to worship naked in the hot baths, and to maintain their virginity, they also may have reduced Priscillian's views to practice. A very different position was taken up by Jovinian of Milan, who opposed celibacy, fasts, the exaltation of martyrdom, the classification of sins; condemned at Rome and Milan, he was banished by the emperor. A pamphlet that he issued was controverted by Jerome,[2] whose abuse is our chief source of information. In the same way we hear of another Spaniard, Vigilantius, who wrote against prayers to the saints and other heathen practices, against celibacy of the clergy and monasticism; Jerome's wit coined for his followers the names **Dormitantes, Nyctages.** Vigilantius continued working at Barcelona unhindered.

Less fortunate had been **Aërius** of Pontus half a century earlier, known to us only through Epiphanius.[3] Not only had he opposed fasting and prayers for the dead, but he asserted that bishops and presbyters were one order, one honour, one dignity. He was excommunicated, and his followers were driven into practical communism till their extinction. Audæus of Syria was another contemporary reformer and missionary to the Goths of Scythia; but to quartodeciman and very ascetic practices he joined the theory that, as man was made in the image of God, therefore God must have a material shape; his **Anthropomorphite** followers are heard of till about 500. Of the **Apostolici**, or **Apotactici**, in Asia Minor we know only from Epiphanius that they were celibate communists, using the *Acts of Andrew* and *Acts of Thomas*; from the nickname Saccophori it would appear that they were mendicants. In the Theodosian law against heretics they were grouped with Encratites.

Mesopotamia, Syria, and Armenia saw during the 4th and 5th centuries a mystic movement of the Massilians, who sacrificed even self-support to constant prayer, as the means whereby the Holy Spirit entered and perfected, giving full knowledge of divine things and of the future. They were known also to the Greeks as **Euchites** (*q.v.*), **Euphemites, Choreutes**, or, after some leaders, as **Adelphians, Lampetians, Marcianites, Eustathians.** Akin to them seem to be the **Hypsistarians**, or **Cœlicolæ**, in Asia Minor, though they attracted attention by their worship of light, their rules as to food and the Sabbath, their opposition to images. The **Agonyclitæ** of the 7th and 8th centuries, who would not kneel at prayer, but preferred to stand, and often to dance, were forerunners of the dervishes, as also of many revivalist bodies in the 18th, 19th, and 20th centuries, known derisively as Jumpers.

Quarrels between the patriarch of Constantinople and the pope of Rome as to jurisdiction over the Jugo-Slavs led to the formulation of charges on each side, when the name **Azymites** was used by the Eastern to blame the Roman use of unleavened bread at the Mass, and the Western retorted with **Fermentarii.** Trivial as the allegations were, the rupture of 1054 was complete and final. Fresh causes of difference have been added, notably one in the 14th century. The monks of Athos had adopted the Hindu methods of contemplation, which were attacked by Barlaam when sent to inspect them; the **Hesychasts** held that they could attain the vision of that uncreated light which was revealed on the mount of transfiguration, while Barlaam declared that this infringed on the accepted doctrine of God. After debates before the emperors (1341–51) the Eastern Church adopted the Hesychast view.

Since the establishment of the Holy Roman Empire it might appear that sects in W. Europe were few. But this view is superficial, as will appear by a comparison with the modern Roman Catholic Church. This is often regarded as homogeneous, but is in fact highly complex; its different branches are often as remote from one another as most Protestant bodies. In the same Canadian city will be found churches frequented by Irish and churches frequented by French, with decided antipathy, although the language and ritual used are the same in both. An English town will be worked partly by secular priests, partly by a regular order; their relations are as fraternal as those of Methodists with Presbyterians. The various monks, canons, and friars are traditionally rivals, not only of the seculars, but of one another, and they have been supplemented by numerous modern foundations. In England alone there are 19 chief superiors of the principal religious orders and congregations, while a single archdiocese has 31 different congregations of women, even overlapping in the same towns.

Thus in the Middle Ages we have to consider three sorts of movement—(1) those always independent of Rome, (2) innovations adopted and moulded by Rome, (3) reforms discountenanced by Rome. (1) Of the first class there were dualists inheriting Eastern doctrines, like the **Bogomils** and **Cathari**, and pantheists like the **Brethren of the Free Spirit** (*qq.v.*). With the last should be classed the followers of **Amalric**, though he lived and died in the Roman communion. Lecturing in Paris, first on philosophy and then on theology, he developed the principles of John the Scot. Three propositions attributed to him were condemned by the university, and then, on appeal, by the pope, so that he formally recanted them: God is everything; a Christian must believe that he is a member of Christ; to those constituted in love no sin is reckoned. He died about 1207, and his followers seem to have advanced rapidly. They taught that the Son inaugurated a second era, in which the Mosaic Law was abolished (and this became the pretext for antinomianism); that the third age, that of the Spirit, was just beginning with God incarnate in them; that hell was a consciousness of sin, and that the believer was freed from this by his regeneration, which was the promised resurrection. But these versions of their mystic pantheism come only from the records of the Inquisition, which began to work among them in 1209. The Lateran Council condemned them six years later, and in 1225 Pope Honorius and the Council of Sens condemned afresh the great work of John the Scot.[1] The Amalrician philosophy filtered into several of the Béguine sisterhoods.

[1] See art. PRISCILLIANISM.

[2] *In Jovinianum.*

[3] *Hær.* lxxv.

[1] For the whole movement consult A. Jundt, *Hist. du panthéisme populaire au moyen âge et au xvi*e *siècle*, Paris, 1875; and B. Hauréau, *Hist. de la philosophie scolastique*, 2 vols., do. 1872–80.

(2) For the great leaders whose programmes were accepted, and whose followers were organized with the sanction of Rome, see art. RELIGIOUS ORDERS (Christian).

(3) In the third class fall several millenarians[1]—**Wyclifites, Hussites, Brethren of the Common Life, Waldenses,** all described in separate articles. There remain to be noticed various evangelical groups following leaders who cared little about remaining in outward communion; they were chiefly of the 12th century.

Tanchelm preached in the Netherlands till 1124, Eudo de Stella in Brittany till 1148; but three disciples of Abelard (*q.v.*) produced more famous results. Peter of Bruys, a priest, taught for twenty years in S. France; the authorities who neglected to suppress him were thus adjured:

'In your parts the people are re-baptized, the churches profaned, the altars overthrown, crosses burned; on the very day of our Lord's passion meat is publicly eaten, priests are scourged, monks imprisoned and compelled by terrors and tortures to marry.'[2]

When Peter was lynched, his work was continued by a Cluniac monk, Henry of Lausanne, at first with some episcopal sanction, as the scandalous lives of many clergy needed checking by public opinion; but Bernard of Clairvaux (*q.v.*) suspected his work, and after about fourteen years had him imprisoned in 1148. Arnold of Brescia did similar work in N. Italy, France, Switzerland, and in 1145 obtained a commanding position at Rome; ten years later he was sacrificed to the pope by the emperor. The **Arnoldists** maintained themselves, chiefly in Lombardy, for some two centuries; they contemptuously rejected the clergy as of bad life and therefore unable to administer useful sacraments; they equally rejected the theory of the efficacy of any sacraments. Their stress on the laying on of hands is an obvious corollary from their attempt to revert to primitive models as depicted in the Acts of the Apostles.

About 1183, when the French troops were trying to suppress the Brabançon brigands, they were followed up by volunteer bands linked into a brotherhood on the basis of a revelation; they wore a leaden image of the Madonna of Puy, and their distinctive mark was a white cowl, whence they were named **Capuciati.** The name was speedily transferred by Thomas of Walsingham to the English followers of Peter of Pattishall, an iconoclast who advised that it was needless to bare the head before the host.

With the 13th cent. the virility of the papal system waned. When emperor and pope quarrelled, the Italian physician **Marsilius,** eminent at the university of Paris, produced a work, *Defensor Pacis*, which put plainly for scholars, politicians, and theologians the truths hitherto maintained chiefly by the Waldenses. A democrat and Bible student, he would take away all clerical power and wealth, subjecting even bishops and pope to the civil power; as a historian he showed the growth of papal power and denied any Petrine prerogative. Ludwig of Bavaria naturally protected with the sword one who protected him with the pen; he was crowned emperor in Rome in the name of the Romans; he deposed Pope John XXII.; he installed a new pope, Nicholas V. But his adoption of the principles of Marsilius was premature, and in a way was but an episode in the Guelph-Ghibelline strife. The book was a different matter; not only did it circulate among scholars, but it was rendered into French, Italian, and English. Not only was it known to Wyclif, the Parisian promoters of the general councils, and Luther, but even to the commonalty it showed that great scholars could demand a reformation in head and members, to sweep away usurpation, in the name of the apostles.

1 See artt. ENTHUSIASTS (Religious), § 3, and SECOND ADVENTISM.

2 A. H. Newman, *Manual of Church History*, Philadelphia, 1900, i. 560.

III. *MODERN.*—With the Reformation of the 16th cent. the ostensible unity of Western Christendom disappeared. The Roman communion was soon strengthened by new orders, notably the Jesuits (*q.v.*); and it has discountenanced other new movements, such as the Jansenist and Modernist.[1] But, whereas during the Middle Ages force could usually be invoked[2] to crush teachers of whom the Curia disapproved, in modern times that has been possible only in certain localities, especially under the banners of Spain and Austria. Each century has seen great new leaders, all of whom are separately treated in the present work, as also are some minor teachers; but of the first age only three seem to need mention here.

Nicolaus von Amsdorf (1483–1565) exaggerated Luther's insistence on faith, saying that good works, when done on purpose to win salvation, were absolutely harmful; he was disowned by most of his communion. Younger in years but more antique in thought, Heinrich Niclaes (1502–80?), an Amsterdam merchant, seems to have been introduced by David Joris to mediæval mystics. Taking up headquarters at Emden (1540–60), he taught that he was an incarnation of God in Christ to found the **Familia Caritatis,** whose members themselves partook of divinity and could become perfect. It was elaborately organized on the hierarchical pattern, but adherents were allowed to conform outwardly to any Church. Thus Plantin of Antwerp became a convert, and printed most of his books. These were all rendered into English, for Niclaes and Vitel of Delft did much work in Essex and London, especially after 1570. Fifty years later Edmond Jessop published a popular account based on good authority, in his *Discovery of the Errors of the English Anabaptists*, which shows development of the Familist movement. Even in 1652 the books of 'H.N.' were reprinted, but very few new adherents were won. The Friends have always found much that was congenial in the Familists, and the most sympathetic studies are by Robert Barclay[3] and C. Fell Smith.[4] John Cameron (1577–1625) taught in ten cities, and his system was popularized by his pupils, especially Moyse Amyraut.[5]

On the whole, minor sects could maintain themselves in Europe only under special conditions; Poland and Holland gave a certain amount of toleration, and England later. New countries naturally afforded refuges, and thus were predisposed for the appearance of new sects. To guard against this, the Inquisition was peculiarly active in the New World.

It might be expected that new lands under Protestant control would be sectarian museums, but this is hardly the case; in Victoria only 8054 people returned themselves in 1911 as outside the well-known Churches. Canada has become the home of refugees from all N. Europe, and displays many immigrant sects; but it seems to have originated none. The United States is so large, so old, so active, and so well investigated, that the whole modern period can best be studied with this continent in view.[6] The facts dovetail with every

1 See artt. JANSENISM and MODERNISM.

2 See art. INQUISITION.

3 *The Inner Life of the Religious Societies of the Commonwealth*, London, 1876, p. 25 ff. with bibliography.

4 *DNB* xl. 427.

5 *ERE* i. 404.

6 The regular censuses of 1900 and 1910 contain much valuable information. On the latter a popular book has been published by H. K. Carroll, *The Religious Forces of the United States*, New York, 1912; but, while it professes to be 'revised and brought down to 1910,' it is difficult in many places to tell whether the figures are not even of 1890. Moreover, the accuracy of the figures has often been doubted, and grave

permanent European movement of the last two centuries. That America chiefly reproduces, and only slightly modifies, the conditions of the Old World will be evident by enumerating the 22 denominations which have more than 50,000 communicants each. They are named here in order of their size: Roman Catholic, Baptist, Methodist, Lutheran, Presbyterian, Disciples of Christ, Protestant Episcopal, Congregationalist, Reformed, United Brethren, German Evangelical, Latter-Day Saints, Evangelical bodies, Eastern Orthodox, Friends, Christian Connection, German Baptist Brethren, Adventist bodies, Church of Christ (Scientist), Unitarians, Universalists, Mennonites.

The 'other Protestant bodies' in 1906 had not 250,000 members; their church property was small and heavily in debt; their permanence is uncertain, for, though 42 new sects appeared in twenty years, by immigration, division, or organization, yet 15 disappeared, and 30 more decreased so rapidly that many are probably extinct already. They have four times as many ministers as most Protestant sects, and have multiplied remarkably since 1890, especially in Pennsylvania, Ohio, Massachusetts, and Illinois. A fifth of them are in a thousand isolated groups with no distinctive principles, and they are classified in the census report as 'Independent Churches.' They indicate the presence of new life, but the results are too amorphous to be described. Even among the others, from the 78 'Christian Israelites' up to the tens of thousands of Winebrennerian members in the 'Church of God,' many appear negligible in practice, for on their own official showing they do no work at home or abroad.

Since the adoption of the constitution in 1789 perfect religious freedom has been assured throughout the United States. This arose not only from the highly miscellaneous character of the population, but from the fact that two States had been deliberately founded in order to secure homes for those who respected the rights of conscience. The French of Canada, Acadie, Louisiana, the Spanish of Mexico and California, the Dutch of New Amsterdam, the Swedes of New Jersey, and the second wave of English in Virginia, indeed belonged to their respective Established Churches, but these have not been the determining factors. The Pilgrim Fathers (*q.v.*) of Plymouth and the Puritans[1] of New England have had their story often told. Even more important for our theme are Rhode Island and the Providence Plantations, with charters, first from the Commonwealth, then from Charles II., assuring a welcome to all; the Jews found guaranteed to them here not merely an asylum, but equal opportunities. This tiny province was so hemmed in by intolerant Puritans that it offered no scope to develop its principles, and the wider application was made by William Penn, whose work is too little appreciated in England. In 1677 he was joint-proprietor of West New Jersey, and, desiring population, he joined George Fox and Robert Barclay in a journey to the lower Rhine, Hanover, Brandenburg. Becoming proprietor of Pennsylvania in 1681, he decided to make it a greater Rhode Island. Numerous German pamphlets were written, and the response was beyond expectation; before long there were more than 50,000 German sectarians in the province, with hardly one Reformed or Lutheran minister.

> 'Still throughout his peaceful country
> Traces linger of all lands
> Which here sent their early settlers
> In strange headgear and quaint costumes.'[1]

After long obscuration their story has at last been told.[2]

Caspar Schwenkfeld (1490–1561) was a Silesian noble, a lay reformer influential with the Duke of Liegnitz.[3] Influenced at first by Hus and Tauler, he approved the early doings of Luther; but, when the latter threw in his lot with the princes, he feared that the promotion of purity of life was being subordinated to the construction of a new ecclesiastical machine. He therefore published his *Ermanung dess missbrauchs etlicher fürnempster Artikel des Evangelii*—a treatise on the abuse of the Gospel for the security of the flesh; and in 1525 at a discussion with Luther and Bugenhagen he charged the former with receding from his own doctrine in the preface to the Magnificat, 'No one can understand God or God's word, unless he has it directly from the Holy Spirit, and no one has it unless he experiences and is conscious of it.' Fully agreeing with this, Schwenkfeld laid such stress on inner experience that he quite disused, and advised the disuse of, baptism and the Lord's Supper, as not being any means or vehicle of grace; thus he took no part in the Zwinglian or Anabaptist controversies.

> 'God must Himself, apart from all external means, through Christ touch the soul, speak in it, work in it, if we are to experience salvation.'[4]

He was reluctant to accede to any confessions, objecting to the many new formulas, and also challenging the old Greek definitions as to the person of Christ with some arguments in 1539 'that Christ according to His humanity is to-day no creature, but absolutely our God and Lord.' This doctrine of the deification of the flesh of Christ was central with him, and his followers took from it their own title, **Confessors of the Glory of Christ**. Theologians also disagreed with his doctrine of 'a double word of God, namely, an inward, eternal and spiritual word, and an outward and perishable word of the scriptures or letter.' He further challenged the external mechanical view of justification by faith, as though men had bought an indulgence from Christ and thereupon continued in sin; he taught that the elect are not esteemed justified before God entirely through imputation, but are actually made just; that the Lord is our righteousness not as outwardly believed in, but as enjoyed in faith by His inward working and life.

As the Duke of Liegnitz found that he was falling out of line with other reforming princes, Schwenkfeld left in 1529, and after five years at Strassburg went to Swabia. His followers were recruited largely from Anabaptist and Boehmenite circles, and included many of the upper ranks. He did not attempt to organize them or to ordain ministers, warning that no outward unity or uniformity in doctrine, ceremonies, rules, or sacraments could make a Christian church.

errors have been discovered during 1918. The official Bureau of the Census, in the department of Commerce and Labor, conducted special inquiries into religious conditions in 1906 and in 1916. Few of the last returns, so far as they relate to the minor bodies, are available for this article, which draws largely from the Report on *Religious Bodies, 1906*, pt. i. 'Summary and General Tables,' pt. ii. 'Separate Denominations, History, Description, and Statistics'; *Bulletin* 103, 'Religious Bodies, Introduction, Summary, Diagrams,' Washington, 1910. So far as the returns of 1916 have been published, they show no general change in the situation.

1 See art. PURITANISM.

1 William King Baker, *William Penn and Gulielma*, London, 1917, p. 231.

2 See J. F. Sachse, *The German Pietists of Provincial Pennsylvania*, Philadelphia, 1895, *The German Sectarians of Pennsylvania*, 2 vols., Philadelphia, 1899–1900; with these may be read W. J. Hinke, *Life and Letters of the Rev. John Philip Boehm*, Philadelphia, 1916.

3 *Collected Works*, 1564, 1566, 1570; studies in G. Arnoldt. *Kirchen- und Ketzerhistorie*, 4 vols., Frankfort, 1700–15; W. H. Erbkam, *Gesch. der prot. Sekten in der Reformationszeit*, Gotha, 1848; O. Kadelbach, *Ausführliche Gesch. Kaspar von Schwenkfelds*, Lauban, 1861; C. Gerbert, *Gesch. der Strassburger Sectenbewegung*, Strassburg, 1889; R. H. Grützmacher, in *PRE*[3].

4 *Schriften*, i. 768.

'When we come together, we pray with one another . . . we teach and also converse with one another, and ask questions concerning Christ, and afterwards in writing respecting the divine Trinity, the kingdom of God. . . . We busy ourselves also with the right understanding and exposition of holy scripture according to the mind of the Spirit. . . . The true knowledge of Christ must be expected not only out of the scriptures, but much more from the gifts of grace revealed by the Father; yet so that this revelation should always be in unison with and unite with the witness of the scriptures.'[1]

Persecution from all parties not only limited their numbers to about 5000, but also exterminated them outside Swabia and Silesia. The Jesuits from 1719 attacked them there and greatly depressed them till Frederick conquered the duchy and restored their property. Meanwhile many fled; some took refuge with Count Zinzendorf in Saxony and helped to rejuvenate the Unitas Fratrum (1722–35). Some 200 from Görlitz, just across the border from Herrnhut, went by Hanover and England to Philadelphia, settling about ten miles north. Barclay thinks that Fox was indebted to Schwenkfeld for some of his leading ideas, which were taught (1624–30) by Hans de Rijs and other Waterlander Mennonites near Amsterdam, and may have reached England by way of the General Baptists; but he offers no evidence on the last point. They were so unconscious of any external connexion that in the colony of the English Friends they maintained their German speech and worship, and indeed still belong to the 'Pennsylvania Dutch.' In 1895 they founded a board of missions to propagate their faith in the United States and elsewhere; lately the fields have been India, China, and Japan. In 1910 they numbered 306 communicants.

Jean de la Badie[2] (1610–74) was another noble trained by the Jesuits, successively a Catholic canon, Huguenot professor at Montauban, pastor at Orange, Geneva, London, Middelburg. By 1668 he was suspended, and he began a separatist church, which migrated to Amsterdam. His most prominent adherent was Anna Maria van Schürmann of Utrecht, whose *Eukleria*[3] contains the best exposition of his views. These included the usual separatist tenets, with a belief in the gift of prophecy and communism; no distinction was drawn between the days of the week, all being spent in the loftiest way possible. A remarkable departure from Calvinism was that, as marriage is between the regenerate alone, their children are free from original sin. About 60,000 people were supposed to sympathize with these views, but, when Gilbert Voet, rector of Utrecht university, drove the leaders into exile, only a few score went with them from 'the garden of souls planted at Amsterdam' to be watered at Herford, and, after transplantation to Bremen, to fruit at Altona. Cornelis van Sommelsdyk, whose sisters were in the community, offered his castle of Thetinga in W. Friesland, but, before the gift took effect, la Badie died at Altona in 1674. Anna van Schürmann then led the wanderers, between 300 and 400, to the castle, where they settled down to a happy community life, of which in 1677 William Penn gives a glimpse in his *Travels*.[4] Anna died next year, and in 1679 a colony of **Labadists** was taken to America by Pieter Sluyter. More converts were made there, one of whom presented Bohemia Manor at the head of Chesapeake Bay. Sluyter's rigid rule of the community was distasteful, and his traffic in slaves and other chattels brought the movement into disrepute, so that the settlement broke up in 1722. Its more spiritual side has been depicted by Whittier in *Andrew Rykman's Prayer*.[1] Sommelsdyk had become governor of Guiana, and in 1680 he invited a second colony, which faded away soon after his death in 1688. The communist life at Thetinga ended soon after these emigrations; the last Sommelsdyk died in 1725; and with the death of the last 'speaker' seven years later the movement practically ended. Yet a few Frisian Labadists still journey annually to the ruined castle; in the crypt of Wieuwert church, hard by, the bodies of five or six of the community are exhibited, and at Franeker town hall many portraits, pictures, and books of Anna van Schürmann are preserved.

The community had been offered a home on the island of Nordstrand by **Antoinette Bourignon**, whose influence had been in the Netherlands and in Holstein; she also was buried at Franeker in 1680.[2] Her system was distinctly personal; she was the 'bride of the Spirit,' the 'woman clothed with the sun,' the 'channel of revelation.' Yet she was original only on one point: the human nature of Christ was dual, and one part was liable to sinful corruption; similarly every man has a dual nature, one part being distinctly good; as the will is entirely free, any one may throw the balance on the right side and obtain perfection here. Her teachings were digested by her disciple Pierre Poiret, and published in 7 vols. at Amsterdam in 1687, *L'Œconomie divine, ou système universel.* An English version of her *Traité admirable de la solide vertu*, published in London in 1699, indicates influence in Britain; George Garden, who had been professor at King's College, Aberdeen, and minister of St. Nicholas Church in that city, was deposed from the ministry in 1701 for maintaining Bourignonist doctrines; in 1711 the General Assembly of the Church of Scotland framed for all probationers an abjuration of these tenets. Thereafter the movement won no more adherents.[3]

Penn's journey in 1677 introduced him to Spener, who for seven years had borrowed from the Rynsburgers (*q.v.*) the idea of colleges of piety, which spread from Frankfort through Saxony. The new zeal for Bible study made the **Pietists** widely known and rather unpopular. The Frankfort Land Company therefore bought from Penn a block of land north of Philadelphia between the Schuylkill and the Delaware, as a Pietist settlement. F. D. Pastorius led out the first emigrants in 1683; the name of Crefeld was transplanted by some Mennonites to their new settlement; others were Krisheim, Sommerhausen, Germantown. By 1688 Pastorius saw that these Pilgrim Fathers to Pennsylvania had made their footing sure; his Latin ode to their descendants has been englished by Whittier:[4]

'Think how your fathers left their native land,—
Dear German-land! O sacred hearths and homes!—
And, where the wild beast roams,
In patience planned
New forest-homes beyond the mighty sea,
There undisturbed and free
To live as brothers of one family.'

Among the curious bodies that migrated from Germany was one group which declined this family life. John Kelpius, a graduate of Altdorf, had drunk deep of the Rosicrucian cup; after intercourse in London with the Philadelphians[5] he headed a band of 40 men—pilgrims, students, peasants—to Germantown. It is remarkable that

[1] Barclay, p. 245.
[2] Best recent accounts by B. B. James, *The Labadist Colony of Maryland*, Baltimore, 1899; Una Birch, *Anna van Schurmann, Artist, Scholar, Saint*, London, 1909; W. J. Kühler, *De Beteekenis van de Dissenters in de Kerkgeschiedeniss van Nederland*, Leyden, 1913; J. Dirks and B. J. Veenhoven, *De Oudheidkamer op het Stadhuis te Franeker*[2], Franeker, 1902.
[3] The first part of this work was published at Altona in 1673, the second at Amsterdam in 1685.
[4] *An Account of William Penn's Travails in Holland and Germany, anno 1677*, London, 1694, p. 163.

[1] See also J. F. Sachse, *The German Sectarians of Pennsylvania*, vol. i. ch. vi.
[2] See M. E. S., *Etude sur Antoinette Bourignon*, Paris, 1876.
[3] See *ERE* x. 537.
[4] See *The Pennsylvania Pilgrim*, 1872, with a historical preface in prose.
[5] See *ERE* ix. 836 f.

in 1694 they found no meeting-house in all the province, except those of the Friends. On the Ridge they soon erected a log-house 40 ft. square, truly oriented; it included a hall for worship, a school-room, 40 cells, with an observatory on the roof. Here the band entitled themselves **The Contented of the God-loving Soul.** Kelpius himself, however, desired a more solitary life, and Whittier[1] has well sketched how

> '. . . painful Kelpius from his hermit den
> By Wissahickon, maddest of good men,
> Dreamed o'er the Chiliast dreams of Petersen.
>
> Deep in the woods, where the small river slid
> Snake-like in shade, the Helmstadt Mystic hid,
> Weird as a wizard over arts forbid,
>
> Reading the books of Daniel and of John,
> And Behmen's Morning-Redness, through the Stone
> Of Wisdom, vouchsafed to his eyes alone.'

Some of the 40 forsook the brotherhood before the death of Kelpius in 1708; a few lingered on till the death of Matthaei in 1748. The philosophy of Kelpius was best represented to English readers in the works of Robert Fludd[2] (1574–1637), who built on the foundations of Paracelsus. He taught that there are three realities, God, the world, man; that man and the world correspond in all respects and act mutually, so that natural law rules absolutely in the spiritual sphere; that man and the world proceed from and will return to God. The subject was complicated, being advertised and at the same time discredited by a hoax in 1615, when J. V. Andreæ published at Cassel anonymously *Fama Fraternitatis*, a history of an imaginary secret society said to be 200 years old. It does not appear that the speculations of Fludd were ever reduced to practice except by the followers of Kelpius.

George Keith, an Aberdonian Friend, himself tinctured with these mystic views through Helmont, found spiritual religion at a low ebb in Pennsylvania and at length drew off several followers. On his return to carry out a similar reform in London, where he failed and presently conformed to the Established Church, the leadership fell to H. B. Koester, a learned Westphalian, and he organized the body by the first baptismal service held in the province. But at the end of 1699 he returned to Germany, and the **Keithians** melted into the English Baptists in Pennsylvania, some ordinary, some Seventh-day.

While most of the German princes suppressed new sects, there was one illustrious exception, Casimir of Wittgenstein-Berleburg, about 40 miles east of Cologne. Hither flocked the converts of the untiring evangelist E. C. Hochmann of Lauenburg (1670–1715), and of the mystic chemist J. C. Dippel (1673–1734). Under the leadership of J. F. Haug several scholars made in 1726–42 a revision of the German Bible, in eight folio volumes with abundant notes and illustrations. Despite its heavy cost, this Berleburg Bible became very popular with the nonconformists, both in Germany and in Pennsylvania, though it was greatly undersold by the Canstein Bibles from Halle.

Another outgrowth of the Collegiant and Pietist movements became manifest in 1708. At Schwarzenau in Westphalia five men and three women had met at the mill of Alexander Mack, and had come to the conclusion that they must found a new Church by baptism. One was chosen by lot to baptize Mack, who in turn baptized the others; the procedure was closely akin to Smyth's foundation of the General Baptists at Amsterdam in 1609, except in the detail that the Germans adopted immersion. Many other collegia found their way

[1] In *The Pennsylvania Pilgrim*.

[2] See J. B. Craven, *Robert Fludd the English Rosicrucian*, Kirkwall, 1902; see also art. ROSICRUCIANS.

to the same point, and little companies of German Baptists arose, in no way connected with the Mennonites or with the German Anabaptists. As the State disapproved of all dissent, twenty families went out to Germantown in 1719, and four years later, on Christmas Day, Peter Becker organized the first **German Baptist Brotherhood** in the province, partly from the immigrants, partly from new converts. Six years later Mack himself arrived, and within a few years all the communities from Germany came over, some of them numbered by hundreds. Thus they were enabled to maintain their own customs, love-feasts, feet-washing, the kiss of charity, and a generally austere life, aloof from all politics. The English population has always regarded these **Dunkers, Dunkards,** or **Tunkers** with good-humour as harmless and amusing. The annual minutes from 1742 show that they were pioneers in education, and published Sunday-school books when Raikes was a child; since 1870 this activity has been strongly developed. Their ministers are in three classes, the highest being termed 'bishops'; a few in the cities are paid, but in the country service is gratuitous. Since 1876 they have undertaken missionary work, now maintained in Scandinavia, France, Switzerland, India, China. The progressive policy, however, led to strain, and in 1882 a few of the 'Old Order' left on the one hand, more of the 'Progressives' on the other, the main body being now styled 'Conservatives.' Since 1908 these have adopted the official title, **Church of the Brethren;** they number 61,101 communicants, there being 8089 Progressives and 4411 of the Old Order.

In 1725 some Welsh Seventh-day Baptists came to settle near one of the German Baptist churches, and this resulted three years later in a remarkable movement headed by Johann Conrad Beissel, once a journeyman-baker in the Palatinate. He believed in the power of the press, and began with a German book on the Sabbath,[1] then encouraged both Benjamin Franklin and Christoph Saur to begin printing. He made a new settlement on the Cocalico, and imbibed ideas both from the Labadists and from the Rosicrucians. Uniform cells were built, monastic garb was adopted, evangelistic pilgrimages were undertaken. A large community building was erected at Ephrata, providing cells for the brethren on the ground-floor, then a hall for devotions, and cells above for the order of 'spiritual virgins.' This was soon outgrown, and many new buildings arose, making the **Ephrata community** famous for its architecture, its industries, and its piety. The organization was rather complicated, for a brotherhood of 40 was instituted, while there was also a secular congregation distinct from the two regular orders. Mysticism became ever more rife; *e.g.*, the stateliest of the edifices had doors only 60″ × 20″, because 'narrow is the way that leadeth unto life,' and iron was not used because, according to the Rosicrucian philosophy, it symbolized darkness and night.

Zinzendorf tried in 1741 to amalgamate the many German sects in America, but found that the tenacity which they had developed under persecution resisted his efforts. There was a struggle between the industrial and the pietist elements in Beissel's community, leading to the victory of the latter and the disuse of many mills. Both, however, co-operated in producing the German Bible, the first in a European tongue to be printed in the New World; Saur obtained his type from Frankfort, but his paper bears the watermark of the community, and to them he sent back the sheets to be bound. Soon the Ephrata press published hymn-books and many other works on religion and

[1] *Mystyrion Anomias*, Philadelphia, 1728, tr. into English by Michael Wohlfarth, 1729.

theology, up to the massive folio of the Mennonite martyrology. Books of mystic theology were also published, setting forth the Platonic view that man was originally male and female, and that the unity would be regained in the body of Christ.

Conrad Beissel had a brother Johann Peter, who lived at Gimbsheim in the Palatinate, a few miles north of Worms, west of the Rhine. This district was a hotbed of sectarianism in the early 18th cent., and correspondence between the brothers brought about a great pietistic revival and organization. The accession of a new Count Palatine in 1743 led to persecution, and by 1751 most of the community emigrated to Pennsylvania; some joined the Ephrata group, and others founded a new colony on the Bermudian in York county, where it gradually lost its peculiarities.

By 1786 Ephrata had abandoned its communist principles, and the two regular orders were dying out, never having numbered more than 300. In 1814 the secular congregation was organized and incorporated as the **German Seventh-day Baptists**; but apparently even by adding four regulars they numbered only 50. The centre of gravity shifted to Schneeberg, now Snow Hill, where there is a valuable library. A third church exists at Salemville; the total membership of the antique community is 194.

It is curious that, whereas the province was founded to secure religious freedom, the State in 1794 passed a Sunday law under which this harmless people was persecuted at intervals for half a century. Whittier forgot that they were Seventh-day Baptists when he put into the lips of Sister Maria Christina of Ephrata what he mistakenly styled the *Hymn of the Dunkers*, in which he also transferred to dawn what was really a midnight service; but the spirit is right.

> 'Lo! rising from baptismal flame,
> Transfigured, glorious, yet the same,
> Within the heavenly city's bound
> Our Kloster Kedar shall be found.
> He cometh soon! at dawn or noon
> Or set of sun, He cometh soon.
> Our prayers shall meet Him on His way:
> Wake, sisters, wake! arise and pray.'

George Whitefield and Wesley's missionaries ministered chiefly in their own tongue, but an atmosphere of revival was produced in which Swiss and German settlers were rejuvenated, so that new bodies were born which still survive: five claim brief notice.

Some Swiss immigrants of 1750 were affected by a revival twenty years later, and the converts were immersed in the Susquehanna, whence they became known as **River Brethren**. In many respects they suggest a Mennonite origin. They are chiefly in Pennsylvania, Ohio, and Kansas, and number 3427; they maintain missions in Rhodesia.

Another Swiss Mennonite, Martin Böhm, cooperated with P. W. Otterbein, a Prussian Reformed minister, in another revival deeply influenced by Methodist evangelism. This led to a conference in 1789, and the formation in Maryland eleven years later of the **United Brethren in Christ**. The body now has become mainly English-speaking, and numbers about 225,000 members in 23 northern States, in two groups, one conservative, one modern. They subscribe nearly $100,000 for missions in Japan, China, the Philippines, Porto Rico, and Sierra Leone.

A Lutheran revivalist, Jacob Albright, under similar influences paralleled their work in his own communion, winning converts who organized in 1807; after his death they took the title, **Evangelical Association of North America**. They too have become mainly English and Methodist; they number 133,313 in all the northern States; at a cost of $28,323 they maintain missions in Japan, China, and Germany.

The **German Evangelical Protestant Church** originated about the same time and is still growing; two-thirds of its 36,156 members are in Ohio and Pennsylvania, Cincinnati being the centre. A mission in India is sustained by $27,183.

John Winebrenner was a Reformed pastor at Harrisburg in 1820, but had to retire owing to his evangelistic proclivities. In 1830 he and five friends founded the **Church of God**, with Baptist doctrines and Methodist polity. There are 22,511 members, chiefly in Pennsylvania, Ohio, Indiana, subscribing $2036 for a mission in India.

The outbreak of the French Revolution led to a recrudescence of religious thinking and the formation of a few sects with some permanence: three lay movements deserve attention. In the north of Sweden the population was so sparse that one parish covered 6500 square miles: the lack of priests caused the rise of 'readers,' and these gradually developed a decided hostility to a paid ministry, and a great complacency. It is not clear that they survive in their native home. In Norway the peasant Nielsen Hauge (1771–1824) proved a very Bunyan, and the strength of his movement may be judged by the emigration to the northern States in America, where **Hauge's Synod** of Norwegian Lutherans was organized in 1846; to-day there are 14,730 communicants. On the other hand, Baroness Krüdener (1766–1824), who attracted much attention in religious circles throughout Central Europe, was driven by the civil authorities from Paris and Switzerland to Riga, Petrograd, and the Crimea; but she never visited the New World. Her influence was that of the evangelist and healer; her only attempt at constructive work, an eirenicon between Protestants and Catholics in Switzerland, failed completely. Her followers soon died out. No new sect made good its footing on the Continent, though some continued to linger on till the increasing uniformity of the 19th cent. made existence almost impossible.

Another series of emigrations began with the wave of revolution in 1848. C. F. Spittler of the Basel mission sent a celibate colony of mechanics to Jerusalem. From their *Brüderhaus* they hoped to evangelize the world, but the missionary fervour seems to have been deflected to archæology and patriotism. A small remnant of the Hussites (*q.v.*), who had survived in Moravia and had not been influenced by Zinzendorf, migrated to Texas in 1848; there they are known as the **Evangelical Union** of Bohemian and Moravian Brethren; they still use their native tongue for worship. Some German-Swiss went to America in 1850, and are known as the **Apostolic Christian Church**, numbering about 4500. Germany saw a **New Apostolic Church** founded in 1862, which migrated entire to America a generation later; it numbers about 2000. The adoption of general military service in Europe caused two Mennonite colonies to quit Russia for S. Dakota about 1874. The **Brüderhof** had originated in Tirol early in the 16th cent., and, when expelled from Moravia, had remained encysted for over three centuries, with German speech and communist customs. The **Brüdergemeinde** were of more recent origin in Russia, and are of the Baptist genus.

In 1885 two bodies of Swedish dissenters found it wise to leave home; the **Evangelical Free Mission** and the **Evangelical Mission Covenant** are now chiefly along the northern border of the United States. Fifteen years later the **Church of the Lutheran Brethren** and a body of Finns followed the example, and by 1903 there had also departed some Slovak Lutherans.

The perpetuation of sects on American soil is

assisted by the perpetuation of European languages for worship, a factor hardly realized by English readers. To mention only the chief tongues, there are 4,500,000 Church members who never worship in English, but only in German, Polish, French, Italian, Norse, Swedish, Spanish, Bohemian, Slovak, Lithuanian, or Dutch; while 3,000,000 more use these tongues jointly with English. Americans in 1918 for other reasons began a vigorous campaign for the use of English solely; if this succeeds, some of the smaller bodies are likely to merge with others to which they are really akin.

While sects originally European can often be studied best on American soil, there are also others which arose west of the Atlantic. Henry Alline, of a Rhode Island family which moved to Nova Scotia, did great evangelistic work between 1775 and his death in 1784. He is said to have held the view that the Creation was after the Fall, in which all souls had personally shared; but this was never adopted by any number, and his **Allinite** converts formed the raw material for the ordinary Baptist churches that soon grew to great strength in the province. Of more permanent sects which claim fewer than eight per thousand of the population there are a number of small bodies to be found chiefly in Indiana, Oregon, Kansas, Ohio, Maine, Massachusetts, Iowa, Pennsylvania, Nebraska, Washington, New Hampshire, California, Oklahoma, Vermont, and Illinois. Altogether they aggregate 35 per 1000, and seven of them may be noticed.

The great revival caused reactions against New England orthodoxy. A Methodist in Virginia, a Baptist doctor in Vermont, and Presbyterians in Kentucky and Ohio independently discarded all theologies and concentrated on the Bible. By 1806 they were aware of one another, and their adherents entered into friendly relations, adopting as their name only the Biblical term 'Christians,' which others either pronounce with the first *i* long, or expand into **Christian Connection.** Ohio and Indiana contain half their 90,718 members; N. Carolina and Virginia are the stronghold of a southern group which separated on the question of slavery in 1854. One of the original leaders passed over to the Disciples of Christ;[1] and, after long confusion of the two bodies by outsiders, actual union took place in 1917. The polity being congregational, with conferences chiefly advisory, no great difficulty presented itself.

In 1831 William Miller of Low Hampton, New York, began lecturing on the second advent of Christ, which he expected in 1843. His influence extended from Lake George over New England, but after the non-fulfilment of his second prediction a conference at Albany in 1845 revealed differences which led in time to the formation of seven sub-divisions of **Second Adventists,** of which only two are at all numerous.[2] The mortality of the soul is held by 25,816 'Advent Christians'; 29,000 observe the seventh day of the week as Sabbath and have other Jewish proclivities as to diet and prophecy; they are very aggressive, spending about $400,000 a year on missions all over the world. The 'Adonai Shomo,' an Adventist community formed in Massachusetts in 1876, expired in the first six years of the present century.

About 1880 Mrs. Beekman, an Illinois lady, announced herself as the spiritual mother of Christ in the Second Coming, and identified Him with G. J. Schweinfurth. This man accepted the honour, and for about twenty years found three or four hundred people to form the **Church Triumphant.** This too was dead by 1906. This evanescent movement recalls the handful of Dumfriesshire people who from 1784 till the death of Elspeth Buchan in 1791 believed that she was 'the woman clothed with the sun.'[1]

[1] See *ERE* iv. 713.

[2] See art. SECOND ADVENTISM.

The American civil war revealed the existence of many conscientious objectors to fighting. A Methodist minister, J. V. B. Flack, preached to these, and in 1864 a convention was organized almost on this one issue, for all questions of faith and polity were set aside in view of the diverse origins of the adherents. As the war was forgotten, members dropped off, and the **Independent Churches of Christ** in Christian Union are important only in Ohio, Missouri, Indiana, and Iowa, with some 18,000 members in 1906; next census may show them flourishing again.

In 1867 several Baptists and Methodists in Arkansas and Illinois withdrew and united; twenty years later they adopted a confession and rules; they number about 913, and call themselves the **Social Brethren Church.** Other secessions from the Methodists are the **Heavenly Recruit Church** of 1885; the **Apostolic Holiness Union** of 1897, near Cincinnati, with mission work; the **Missionary Church Association** of 1898, near Berne in Indiana; the **Christian Congregation** of 1899, near Kokomo in Indiana; the **Apostolic Faith Movement** of 1900, near Los Angeles; the **Church of Daniel's Band,** near Michigan and in Canada; these together seem to number about 5000 members, if they still exist.

In 1873 the Protestant Episcopal Church lost two bishops, who founded the Reformed Episcopal Church (*q.v.*) on an ultra-evangelical basis. A seminary was planted at Philadelphia, and mission work was undertaken to the southern negroes and in India. Work was extended in 1877 to England, and, as there was another small body of similar origin from the Established Church in 1844, known as the Free Church of England, the two united in 1918. The resultant **Free Reformed Episcopal Church** of England uses a revised version of the Book of Common Prayer, and is dividing the country into dioceses. One of its bishops has long ministered in a small iron building, and there appears no great probability of any extensive growth.

The **Reformed Catholics** arose in New York during 1879, but show little vitality. They may be compared with the Old Catholics of Europe,[2] who received accessions from 1898 onwards in the German provinces of the Austrian Empire. This **Los von Rom** movement seems, however, to have been anti-Slav, and reinforced Protestants quite as much, the tendency being to pave the way for these provinces to join the German Empire; this having been practically attained by other means, it is doubtful if the movement will continue. In America the Reformed Catholics, after absorbing the Old Catholics, number only 2100 communicants. Parallel movements have taken place in the province of Quebec and in the Philippines.

Another remarkable reaction of America on England is the **Old Baptist Union.** In Rhode Island **General Baptists** arose during the interregnum, and by 1729 were strong enough to form a yearly meeting. In the same year a similar step was taken by others in Virginia and N. Carolina, planted by 'Messengers' from England. Not all of these adopted Calvinism, and the remnant are known as **Original Freewill Baptists,** numbering now nearly 40,000. The northern group decided in 1880 to replant their principles in England, disregarding both the parent body,

[1] J. Train, *The Buchanites from First to Last*, Edinburgh, 1846.

[2] See *ERE* ix. 483 ff.

which had dwindled to a handful of Unitarian churches, and the New Connexion of Evangelicals. They retained as their banner the Confession of 1660, but in organization revived the term 'bishop' for their presiding officers. After a generation they claim about 35 churches in England, 15 in America, and 7 missionaries abroad; but the English churches seem kaleidoscopic, and the census returns of 1910 show no trace of any in America, though in 1906 there were 649 **General Six-Principle Baptists.**

We now return to denominations in Britain and begin with the **Religious Societies.**[1] Under Charles II. several young Churchmen of London and Westminster, scandalized at rampant evils, betook themselves to their ministers for advice. Getting none useful, they joined in a weekly meeting for worship and the study of the Bible, and presently adopted rules. On the practical side they relieved the poor, freed prisoners, helped students and orphans; by 1678 it was needful to have two stewards for these purposes. Against popery they established special services at St. Clement Danes, conducted by eminent city divines, and by the close of the reign of James II. there were 39 of these societies in or near the two cities. To avert gossip and suspicion of their being Jesuits in disguise, they explained their aims and methods to the bishop and obtained his goodwill. With the accession of William and Mary they widened greatly, opening up relations with Francke of Halle and helping to found societies in other parts of the United Kingdom. Specially notable were those at Dublin (soon numbering 300 persons), at Cambridge, and at Oxford: they published their prayers that these ancient and famous nurseries of piety and learning might by the conduct of those students designed for holy orders render themselves renowned in the world. These societies were of laymen, like that founded by Francis of Assisi or the Collegiants; with the patronage of Queen Mary they increased to more than 100 in England and Ireland. They established more than 100 free schools in London, and subscribed to the colonial work of the Society for the Propagation of the Gospel. A remarkable off-shoot was the **Societies for Reformation of Manners,** which supplemented the positive work of the original, by helping to enforce the laws against Sunday traffic, music-houses, and brothels; dissenters were admitted as members of these newer bodies. The Religious Societies, like the Pietists, had to defend themselves from the charge of being a society within a society, of refining upon a reformed Church; they replied that they bound themselves to attend the common prayer and to communicate monthly, and that all new rules were to be approved by three clergy; they were also advised to choose a clergyman as director of each society, who should often attend the weekly meetings. They flourished for more than thirty years after the accession of Queen Anne, publishing their own hymn-books, until from one of their number, the **Holy Club** of Oxford, arose leaders who developed them even more, and made 'the wine ferment too strongly for the skins' of the parent Church.

Thirteen Oxonians, known in derision also as Methodists, founded four distinct bodies, led by **Benjamin Ingham**, the **Countess of Huntingdon,**[2] **George Whitefield**, and **John Wesley.**[3] It is curious that the pioneer steps in these movements, taken by Benjamin Ingham of Ossett (1712–72), should be the least known. He had Anglican orders, and was one of the party which in 1736 went out to work in Georgia; on the way he met some Moravian missionaries, who transformed his ideals. Returning to England, he was one of those who in May, 1738, founded a new religious society in Fetter Lane, where the Moravian influence was strong. After a visit to Herrnhut he returned to Yorkshire, and, finding no access to pulpits of the Established Church, preached in any available place or in the open air. By 1740 he had been formally excluded from public service in the diocese; and by that year he had founded 50 societies, linking them to the Moravians. The second phase of his career opened with his marriage in 1741 to Lady Margaret Hastings, sister of the Earl of Huntingdon; this led to the conversion of the countess, and the spread of religion among the aristocracy. Seven years later he issued at Leeds a hymn-book for the use of the societies, but in 1753 he severed his connexion with the Moravians. After a year or two, while his local work was in harmony with Wesley, he took the momentous step of definitely organizing a new connexion—the **Inghamites.** His plan was largely modelled on the Moravian, and over the 80 new societies which he had gathered he was appointed general overseer. In this capacity he ordained to the ministry two of his helpers, William Batty and James Allen—a precedent followed only in 1783 within the circle round the countess, and only in 1784 by Wesley. For the new body the *Kendal Hymn-Book* was edited by Allen in 1757, and this date perhaps represents the culmination of the work. Hearing how Sandeman was developing the work of Glas[1] in Scotland, Ingham sent Batty and Allen to examine it. They heartily appreciated it, and in their attempt to leaven the Connexion were most successful. He published at Leeds in 1763 a *Discourse on the Faith and Hope of the Gospel* to arrest the change, but this failed to provide any clear programme that justified separate existence. The organization broke up, the societies became Sandemanian, Methodist, or Baptist, and it does not appear that any second general overseer was appointed. To-day the original church may still be found at Salterforth, near Barnoldswick; also six more congregations within three miles of Colne, where in 1908 a new building was erected; the old graveyard at Wheatley Lane in Pendle Forest has many relics. The only other English congregation is at Kendal; but emigrants from Colne have built a church at Farringdon, two miles from Brantford, Ontario. The whole body probably numbers about 2000.[2]

Another minor leader in the Methodist revival was William Cudworth (1717–63). After a year in charge of Whitefield's school at the Tabernacle he worked independently, and by 1747 superintended five London congregations, known collectively as the **Hearers and Followers of the Apostles.** He was invited to Norwich in 1751, and made this city his headquarters, building the Pentagon chapel on Margaret Street, while his helper James Wheatley built a tabernacle, opened by Whitefield. Cudworth had begun printing extracts from Luther, Puritans, Baptists, then published his own views, and many collections of hymns, including some by his adherents. His sixty pamphlets record disputes with Crookshanks, Wesley, Anne Dutton, Moravians, Whitefield, Relly, Sandeman, Law; also his sympathy with Hervey and John Erskine of Edinburgh. His travels embraced not only East Anglia, but the shires of Leicester, Derby, and Stafford. His ablest lieutenant was Robert Robinson, who, however, was repelled by the renewed immorality of Wheatley, and in 1759 left for Cambridge Baptist church. When therefore

[1] Josiah Woodward, *An Account of the Rise and Progress of the Religious Societies*[4], London, 1712.
[2] See art. HUNTINGDON'S (COUNTESS OF) CONNEXION.
[3] See artt. METHODISM, WESLEY.

[1] See art. GLASITES (SANDEMANIANS).
[2] See *NQ*, Jan. 1918.

Cudworth died, on tour in 1763, his connexion slowly disintegrated. The church near Covent Garden is last known in 1778, the Norwich Tabernacle passed to the Countess of Huntingdon, the Pentagon heard very different doctrine before 1840 and soon afterwards was replaced by All Saints church. Yet his views on assurance and saving faith were reprinted for the Free Church of Scotland at the Disruption, and A. A. Bonar edited his chief work in 1851. A sketch with bibliography appears in the *Transactions* of the Congregational Historical Society for 1918, vii. 363.

The **Welsh Calvinistic Methodists** regard themselves as belonging to the Presbyterian family, but their peculiar isolation deserves some notice.[1] About 1735 Howell Harris, a layman of Trevecca, Daniel Rowlands, curate of Llangeitho, Howell Davies, an itinerant clergyman, and William Williams of Pantycelyn, a deacon who was refused priest's orders, led a great revival, which was at once labelled 'Methodist,' and thus turned their attention to George Whitefield. He was asked to preside at an 'association' in Glamorgan, and this meeting of 1742 crystallized the movement. Methods and names were arranged so as to hold aloof from the old dissent and not to clash with the Established Church system. Despite bitter opposition by mobs and magistrates the work extended, and spread into N. Wales. By 1751 there was a severe check owing to a split between Harris and Rowlands; the former had had no theological training, and expressed himself so unconventionally on the divinity of Christ that the trained clergy would not work with him. He then settled at Trevecca, built a huge community-house, and preached daily, till he accepted a commission in the Brecon militia and was sent on service to different parts of England. Evangelizing there, he came into contact with the Countess of Huntingdon, for whom he prepared an ancient building at Trevecca, which she used as a college for the training of ministers. In 1768 this was inaugurated, and for a few years the little town was a centre of great influence. But, as the Wesleys and Fletcher preached Arminian doctrine, the Methodist movement fell finally into two divisions in 1771. The Calvinists in England either remained within the Established Church or were drawn into the Countess of Huntingdon's Connexion; in America they mostly formed separate churches which on the whole became Baptist. In Wales all the converts who did not join the Baptists or the Congregationalists held together and formed by degrees the Welsh Calvinistic Methodists, who affectionately style themselves 'Yr Corff,' '*The* Body.'

A great binding force has been an *Annotated Family Bible.* The Society for the Promotion of Christian Knowledge had issued in the 18th cent. only five editions of the Bible, totalling at most 70,000 copies. Peter Williams revived the old Genevan plan, and prepared a Bible with a commentary, printed and published at Carmarthen. It proved abundantly useful; it prompted Thomas Scott, John Fawcett, John Brown of Haddington, and others to do the same for readers of English; in its 38 editions it is still a great bond for the Calvinistic Methodists, though the editor himself was expelled for heresy in 1791. By that year Thomas Charles of Bala was the leader; known to Englishmen by his appeal which resulted in the British and Foreign Bible Society, he rendered constant service in Wales by promoting education, both by itinerant daily teachers and by residents on Sunday. He lived to see an important step in 1811, when Ingham's precedent was again followed, and preachers were ordained by the authority of representatives of the churches, Charles himself presiding. This led to most of the ordained clergy's ceasing to work with the body and to the withdrawal of several rich and influential families. A confession of faith was approved and published in 1823, and rules of government which had been growing for a generation were codified. A theological institute was opened at Bala, and the community-house at Trevecca was converted into a second college—not to be confounded with the Countess's college once in an older building there. The two colleges are now conducted at Bangor and Aberystwyth, in connexion with the University of Wales.

In 1840 foreign mission work was begun, and the Khasia hills, on the confines of Bengal and Burma, were chosen. A very large proportion of the population has been won to Christianity; the Connexion contributes about £16,000 yearly for this work. A little evangelism is also carried on in Brittany, whose kindred language attracts other Welsh bodies also.

With 1864 the two associations of N. and S. Wales united to establish a General Assembly. This has since entered into sisterly relations with the Presbyterian Church of England, and its churches east of Offa's Dyke often bear the legend 'English Presbyterian' in addition to the Welsh title. In America a single church was formed in 1826, and a General Assembly took shape in 1869; there are nearly 13,000 adherents.

The French Revolution brought together and stirred into activity a number of wealthy evangelicals, chiefly within the Church of England, many of whom lived at Clapham, London, whence arose the name of the **Clapham Sect**. John Thornton had done much to circulate Bibles and to buy advowsons; his son Henry became first treasurer of the Bible Society and of what became the Church Missionary Society. Zachary Macaulay by managing a Jamaican estate became sensitive to the evils of slavery. The Clapham Sect promoted the colony of Sierra Leone, of which Macaulay was governor from 1792 to 1799; he was also secretary to the company till 1808. William Wilberforce took up the cause, and in 1801 founded the *Christian Observer*, which advocated the abolition of the slave trade, and of which Macaulay was first editor. Hannah More in 1792 wrote a pamphlet on *Village Politics* which had great circulation and influence, and led in 1799 to the foundation of the Religious Tract Society. Her original interest was in village education, and she founded schools in Somerset from 1789 onwards. Charles Grant, an East India merchant, wrote in 1792 a pamphlet on the toleration of missions and education in India; in 1813 he secured in the new charter of the East India Company a grant for such education; he also promoted the building of churches in India and of Sunday-schools in Scotland. Wilberforce also furthered education, and founded a society for the better observance of Sunday. His brother-in-law, James Stephen, published in 1824 the first volume of his memorable work, *Slavery in the British West India Colonies Delineated.* The last leaders of the emancipation movement died in 1833, when slavery in the empire was on the verge of extinction; their other interests were safe in the hands of societies which have not taken shape as independent churches. The way was thus cleared for the Oxford Movement (*q.v.*).

During 1917 three groups of churches in Great Britain united under the title **Churches of Christ**, which had previously been borne by the English group. The oldest had previously been known as **Scotch Baptists**—a title peculiarly misleading, as most of its churches were in Carnarvon and Lan-

[1] W. Williams, *Welsh Calvinistic Methodism*², London, 1884.

cashire, one being in Yorkshire. The movement was due to Archibald McLean between 1765 and 1812, but only the one church in Edinburgh with which he was associated still upholds in Scotland the necessity of more pastors than one, which was the chief distinguishing feature of the group; and this one church is not concerned with the southern alliance, but is in harmony with all other Baptists in Scotland. For a few decades this view was propagated by many Scottish immigrants to England, and their churches were dotted along the west coast, in Birmingham, and in London. While several Welshmen preferred to stereotype their organization on that of Ephesus at one of Paul's visits, and thus disrupted a promising movement associated with Christmas Evans in N. Wales, yet the Scotch Baptist group had shrunk greatly. The third group, the **Disciples of Christ** (*q.v.*), sprang from American influences, and the vigorous efforts of these for reunion have succeeded in amalgamating the others.[1]

The chief ecclesiastical developments north of the Tweed[2] are described in the art. PRESBYTERIANISM. One movement, however, was away from that fold. From the United Secession Church in 1841 was suspended James Morison of Kilmarnock, whose views as to the universality of the Atonement, the nature of faith, and the work of the Spirit in salvation were not sufficiently Calvinistic. Three other ministers being also deposed, the four met in 1843 and formed the **Evangelical Union of Scotland**, for mutual aid and for training successors. They were soon joined by nine students from the Congregational Academy, and then by eight churches from the Congregational Union of Scotland. By 1889 there were nearly 100 churches, and seven years later these, with eight exceptions, joined the Congregational Union.

Among the Dutch there was no new religious movement till the 19th century. The churches then seemed to be settling into conventional respectability or moderatism, so that Mennonite, Lutheran, Calvinistic, and Arminian ministers began to interchange. The poet Willem Bilderdyk and the minister Hendrik van Cock headed a conservative reaction which resulted by 1834 in a separation. Leave was obtained with difficulty to form a new Christelyke Gereformeerde Kerk, marked by intense study of the Bible, strict adhesion to the standards of Dort, and a certain mystical strain. A similar movement in 1880 coalesced twelve years later. Meanwhile many of the Boers in Cape Colony had joined this **Dutch Reformed Church**, which there became better known as 'Dopper.' In the mother-country there is a seminary at Kampen, and the adherents are about 4 per cent of the population, ranking next to the former State Church and the Roman Catholics.

It seems as if the centrifugal forces have now been largely spent, and it is obvious that strong forces are at work for integration. The barriers between the Calvinistic and the Arminian Baptists have been taken down both in England and in America; the divisions of Methodism hardly spread outside England, and are quickly being healed there; so too with Presbyterianism. International bodies have arisen to promote fraternal intercourse of the great churches of the same faith and order, and in every part of the British Empire conferences are being held to see how far the movement towards unity may go speedily. Under these circumstances it would appear that any small sect which holds aloof is likely to become of mere local or antiquarian interest.

LITERATURE.—See the sources quoted throughout.

W. T. WHITLEY.

[1] The native movements are being investigated by T. Witton Davies of University College, Bangor, who expects to publish a short monograph through the Baptist Historical Society.

[2] See W. Grinton Berry, *Scotland's Struggles for Religious Liberty*, London, 1904.

SECTS (Hindu).—**1. Introduction.**—The study of the Hindu sects presents difficulties of many kinds: the imperfect enumeration of these religious orders, the secrecy with which many of their rites of initiation and their ritual and devotion are conducted, the fact that the doctrines of some sects merge in or overlap those of others. But, if we are to arrive at any real knowledge of Hinduism as a religious system, it must be studied in its multitudinous sects. For a consideration of Hindu sectarianism see *ERE* vi. 700 ff., ix. 257, 619; and see separate artt. AGHORĪ, BAIRĀGĪ, GORAKHNĀTH, GORAKHPANTHĪ, GOSĀĪN, KABĪR, KABĪRPANTHĪS, KAṚĀ-LIṄGĪS, LINGĀYATS, NĪMĀVATS.

The difficulty of obtaining statistics of the religious orders is great.

'It may be asked why, when the term [Hinduism] covers such a multitude of beliefs and diversity of races, an attempt has not been made to disentangle them by a return of sect. . . . In the first place, there is a bewildering maze of sects which overlap each other in a most extraordinary way. There are the two main divisions of Saiva and Vaishnava; and it has been said that all Hindus belong to one or other of these, but this does not seem to be correct. There is, for example, the Sākta sect, which owes its origin to the Tantrik developments that infected both Buddhism and Hinduism, chiefly in North-East India, about the seventh century of our era. This cult is based on the worship of the active producing principle of nature as manifested in one or other of the goddess wives of Siva; it is a religion of bloody sacrifices and magic texts. This ritual is laid down in the mediæval scriptures known as Tantras, in one of which it is expressly stated that the Vedas have become obsolete. It would be incorrect to treat the followers of this cult as Saivas. The same remark applies to the Smārta [*q.v.*], Ganpatya and Saura [*q.v.*] sects, as well as to the numerous minor sects such as the Pānchpiriya [*q.v.*] and Kartābhaja, which it would be equally wrong to allocate to either of the above main heads. Secondly, there is the practical impossibility of obtaining a complete return of sect. Of the great mass of Hindus, only a relatively small minority belong definitely to special sects, and still fewer have any idea that their peculiar cult differentiates them in any way from ordinary Hindus.'[1]

Sectarianism, in fact, so far as the mass of the rural population is concerned, depends largely on the local Brāhmans who perform the rites of public and domestic worship. With this is coupled the easy toleration which the Hindu feels towards those whose beliefs and usages differ from his own.

'There is no doubt a certain amount of hostility felt by the leaders and the inner circle of devotees against the adherents of their rival sects. It is due to this that devout Vaishnavas of the Vallabhachari sect are careful that they do not pronounce the Gujarati word *shivavun*, "to sew," lest they may indirectly utter the name of Shiva and show him reverence. The head of the Shaiva sect, the Shankaracharya of Dwarka, similarly shows hostility to the Swaminarayan and other Vaishnav leaders, and the brawls between them sometimes result in legal notices, apologies, and even criminal proceedings. But beyond these lies the great mass of the people who, while showing special reverence to the god of their sect, their *ishta deva*, worship also all the gods of the Hindu pantheon. A Shiva Brahman, for instance, visits Shiva's temples and also visits Vishnu *mandirs* and Mata temples. A Vaishnav makes obeisance to the Rama and Krishna idols of his sect, and also visits Mahadeo and Mata temples, and similarly *Devi-upasaks* [worshippers of the goddess Devi] have no objection to reverence Mahadeo or Krishna. The Gujarat Hindu is very religious and very tolerant. He worships not only his own and other people's gods, but also shows reverence to Musalman Pirs [saints] and Christian *padris*. He abstains from insulting the religious feelings of others, and avoids anything that may bring on him the wrath of any deity.'[2]

Hence in this article no attempt can be made to give an exhaustive account of the doctrines and practices of Hindu sectarians; all that can be done is to classify the sects into a series of groups, based on the worship of the sectarian gods. These groups are: Śaivas, worshippers of Śiva-Mahādeo; Sāktas, worshippers of various forms of the mother-goddess; Vaiṣṇavas, worshippers of Viṣṇu in his various incarnations (*avatāra*), especially those of Kṛṣṇa or Rāma; and some reference is made to those who worship a *guru*, or religious teacher.

[1] *Census of India, 1911*, vol. i. pt. i. p. 114 f.

[2] *Ib.* xvi. *Baroda*, pt. i. p. 74 f.

2. The Śaiva sects.—The cult of Śiva, being in its nature colder and less ecstatical than those of his consorts or Viṣṇu, presents fewer sectarial developments.

Of these the more important groups—Aghorī, Gosāīn, Lingāyat, Sannyāsī—are described in separate articles. The Daṇḍīs, who take their name from the wand (*daṇḍ*) which they carry, and the Vaiṣṇava Tridaṇḍīs 'are the only legitimate representatives of the fourth *āśrama*, or mendicant life, into which the Hindu, according to the instructions of his inspired legislators, is to enter, after passing through the previous stages of student, householder, and hermit.'[1] The term Paramahaṁsa, 'the great swan' (which can separate water from milk, truth from falsehood), is a general title of notable ascetics of every sect, but it is specially applied to the higher grades of Sannyāsīs, and more particularly Daṇḍī Sannyāsīs. Members of these orders can attain this grade only after twelve years' probation; they devote themselves to the search for the supreme Brahma, without regard to pleasure or pain, heat or cold, satiety or want. In proof of having reached this ideal of perfection, they wander about in all weathers, and do not speak even to indicate any natural want; some even go about naked, affect to live without food, or eat only when fed by others; some refuse food unless they are fed by a virgin (*kumārikā*) with her own hand; when they die, their corpses are buried or set afloat in a river.[2] For the Jogī, or Yogī, see artt. YOGA, YOGIN; H. A. Rose, *Glossary of the Tribes and Castes of the Punjab and N.W. Frontier Province*, ii. 388 ff.

In a lower grade are those who practise various kinds of disgusting mortifications.

'As a part of their *tapascharyā* or austerities, some Sādhūs undergo many inconveniences, pains, and sometimes terrible tortures. Some called Panchatapas or Panchadhūnī sit under the open sky girt about with five small fires.[3] Sometimes only four fires are lighted, the sun overhead being regarded as the fifth one. Some sit and sleep on a bed of spikes, called *kanaka-sayyā*; some, called Tharashrī, stand leaning on some kind of rest for days or weeks together. Sādhūs known as Ūrdhha-mukhī hang downwards from the bough of a tree for half an hour or more. Those known as Ūrdhvabāhu keep one or both their arms erect over head till they are reduced to a shrunken and rigid condition. Some practise *ashṭadanḍvata*, that is, applying the eight parts of the body—the forehead, breast, hands, knees, and insteps—to the ground, and thus measuring the ground, go on a long pilgrimage by slow and laborious marches. Some called Jaladayā sit a whole night immersed in water. Some called Phalāhāri live upon fruits, others called Dūdhāhārī subsist on milk alone, while those known as Alonā never eat salt with their food. As aids to meditation, a number of *āsan* or postures, *e.g. padmāsan* or lotus posture, have been devised. Some Sādhūs perform pro-purificatory rites known as *netī karma*, drawing a thread through the mouth and one of the nostrils with the object of cleaning the nasal fossæ; *dhotī karma*, swallowing a long strip of cloth, and after it has reached the stomach drawing it out again with the object of cleaning out the stomach; *brahma dāṅtan*, cleaning the throat with a long and thin green stick used as a brush; *brajotē karma* and *ganesh kriyā*, for flushing the colon without instrumental aid.'[4]

3. The Śākta sects.—In the simplest acceptation of the term, Śāktism 'is the worship of force (Skr. *śakti*) personified as a goddess and subordinately in all women.'[5]

The best known Śākta sects are the Dakshiṇāchārī, 'right-handed,' or more respectable group; the Vāmāchārī, 'left-handed'; and the Kaulā, 'belonging to a family, ancestral,' the extreme Śāktas.[6]

'When the worship of any goddess is performed in a public manner, and agreeably to the *Vaidik* or *Paurāṇik* ritual, it does not comprehend the impure practices which are attributed to a different division of the adorers of Śakti, and which are particularly prescribed to the followers of that system. In this form it is termed the *Dakshiṇa* or right-hand form of worship. The only observance that can be supposed to form an exception to the general character of this mode is the *Bali*, an offering of blood, in which rite a number of helpless animals, usually kids, are annually decapitated.'[1]

The Vāmī or Vāmāchārī adopt a ritual of an unusual kind, and contrary to what they dare publicly avow. The practices of what are known as the Cholīmārg or Kānchulipanth, the 'boddice' sect, represent a form of debauchery which cannot be described.[2] The same is the case with the Kaul of Bengal.[3]

4. The Vaiṣṇava sects.—The cult of Viṣṇu, particularly in his manifestations as Rāma or Kṛṣṇa, has produced a number of sects, of which only a few examples can be given.

The Vaiṣṇavas are usually divided into four groups or sects (*sampradāya*), of which the most ancient and respectable is that of the Śrīsampradāyī or Rāmānujī, founded by Rāmānuja (*q.v.*), or Rāmānujāchārya, born in 1017 at Parambattur, near Madras. The distinctive mark of his teaching was his assertion of a triad of principles (*padārtha-trityam*): (1) the supreme spirit, Parabrahman or Īśvara; (2) the separate spirits (*chit*) of men; (3) non-spirit (*achit*). Viṣṇu is the supreme being; individual beings are separate spirits; the visible world (*dṛiśyam*) is non-spirit; all these have an eternal existence and are inseparable. Yet *chit* and *achit* are different from Īśvara, and dependent on Īśvara.[4]

'This Sampradāya is divided into two sects, the Tenkalai and Vadakalai ['southerners' and 'northerners']. They differ on two points of doctrine which, however, are considered of much less importance than what seems to outsiders a very trivial matter, viz., a slight variation in the mode of making the sectarial mark on the forehead. The followers of the Tenkalai extend its middle line a little way down the nose itself, while the Vadakalai terminate it exactly at the bridge. The doctrinal points of difference are as follows: the Tenkalai maintain that the female energy of the Godhead, though divine, is still a finite creature that serves only as a mediator or minister (*parushakāra*) to introduce the soul into the presence of Deity; while the Vadakalai regard it as infinite and uncreated, as in itself a means (*upāya*) by which salvation can be secured. . . . The Vadakalai insist on the concomitancy of the human will in the work of salvation, and represent the soul that lays hold of God as a young monkey which grasps its mother in order to be conveyed to a place of safety. The Tenkalai, on the contrary, maintain the irresistibility of divine grace and the utter helplessness of the soul, till it is seized and carried off like a kitten by its mother before the danger that threatened it. From these two curious but apt illustrations the one doctrine is called *markaṭa-kiśora-nyāya*, the other *marjāla-kiśora-nyāya*; that is to say, "the young monkey theory," the "kitten theory."'[5]

Next come the Rāmānandī or Rāmāwat (*q.v.*), disciples of Rāmānanda, who is said to have been born in the 13th cent. A.D. They worship Viṣṇu in the form of Rāma, singly or conjointly with his wife, Sītā. His twelve disciples were drawn from all classes of Hindus, and among them Kabīr, Rāī Dās, and Tulasī Dās (*qq.v.*) are best known.

The sect known as Brahma Sampradāyī, Madhva (*q.v.*), or Madhvāchārī, owes its origin to Madhvāchārya, a S. Indian Brāhman, born in 1199. This sect is therefore popular in that part of India. Like other Vaiṣṇavas, Madhva identified Viṣṇu with the supreme spirit, as the pre-existent cause of the universe. But his special doctrine was duality (*dvaita*), as opposed to the non-duality of the opposing sect founded by the great Vedāntist, Sankarāchārya[6] (*q.v.*).

The Vallabhāchārya (*q.v.*) or Gokulastha Gosāīn sect was founded by Vallabhāchārya, who is said to have been born in the Champāranya forest, near Benares, in 1479. Its cultus is devoted to the

1 H. H. Wilson, *Select Works*, i. 192; cf. Jogendra Nath (Bhattacharya), *Hindu Castes and Sects*, p. 376.

2 *Census of India, 1911*, xiv. *Punjab*, pt. i. p. 113; *ib.* xvi. *Baroda*, pt. i. p. 88 f.

3 Manu, *Laws*, vi. 23.

4 *Census of India, 1911*, xvi. *Baroda*, pt. i. p. 86; M. Monier-Williams, *Brāhmanism and Hindūism*⁴, London, 1891, p. 88; W. Ward, *A View of the History, Literature, and Mythology of the Hindoos*², ii. 367 ff.

5 Monier-Williams, p. 180; H. H. Wilson, i. 240 ff.; Jogendra Nath, p. 409.

6 Jogendra Nath, p. 409 ff.

1 Wilson, i. 250 f.

2 *Census of India, 1911*, xvi. *Baroda*, pt. i. p. 176; *ib.* xiv. *Punjab*, pt. i. p. 110.

3 Jogendra Nath, p. 411 ff.

4 Monier-Williams, p. 119 f.

5 F. S. Growse, *Mathura*³, p. 193 f.; cf. *ERE* ix. 185.

6 Monier-Williams, p. 103; Wilson, i. 139 ff.

worship of Kṛṣṇa in the form of Bāla Gopāla, the child who played with the Gopis, or cow-herd maids of Mathura.

'Unlike other Hindu sects, in which the religious teachers are ordinarily unmarried, all the Gośāins among the Vallabhāchāryas are invariably family men and engage freely in secular pursuits. They are the Epicureans of the East, and are not ashamed to avow their belief that the ideal life consists rather in social enjoyment than in solitude and mortification. . . . The scandalous practices of the Gośāins and the unnatural subserviency of the people in ministering to their gratification received a crushing *exposé* in a *cause célèbre* for libel tried before the Supreme Court of Bombay in 1861.'[1]

5. Sects of modern origin.—The vigorous growth of sects in modern times may be illustrated by a few examples out of many.

The Kumbhipatiā sect, founded by Mukund Dās in Orissa, first attracted attention about 1874. Their name is derived from the practice of wearing the bark (*pāt*) of the yellow cotton-tree (*kumbhi*). Their founder was inspired with the idea that, if the image of Jagannāth were destroyed, it would convince the Hindus of the futility of their religion. As a result of this teaching, a band of his followers made an ineffectual attack upon the temple. There seem to be traces of Buddhism in this cult, with a substratum of phallism, and a strong antagonism to Hinduism and to Brāhmans.[2]

Guru-worship appears among the Rāmdē Pīr sect. The members worship a horse named after their founder, along with his foot-impressions (*pādukā*), before which incense is burnt, and a lamp fed with butter is kept burning.[3] Other sects display a curious combination of Christian with Hindu or Musalmān doctrines and practices. In the Panjāb the Chetrāmī sect, founded by Chetrām († 1894), recognizes a Christian Trinity consisting of Jesus, the Holy Spirit, and God, while a second consists of Allāh, Parameśvar, and Khudā, Creator, Preserver, and Destroyer, based on the Hindu conception of Brahmā, Viṣṇu, and Śiva. They often carry a long rod surmounted by a cross, and practise a form of baptism. The sect is said to be persecuted by both Hindus and Muhammadans.[4] Still more remarkable is the Nikalsaini or Narangkariā sect, which sprang up in the Panjāb after the defeat of the Sikh army at the battle of Gujarāt in 1849. In order to secure the patronage of the celebrated General John Nicholson, who fell at the siege of Delhi in 1857, they attached themselves to him and took his name, though he is said to have flogged some of the members for their audacity. It is doubtful whether there was actually a cult of Nicholson, and the sect does not appear in recent returns.[5]

6. Sectarial marks.—Each sect uses as its outward symbol a mark (*tilak*) usually made on the forehead.

In the Central Provinces that of the Śaivas, which is believed to be of phallic origin, consists of two or more horizontal lines with or without a dot below or above the lines or on the middle line, and with or without an oval or half oval, a triangle, a cone, or any other pointed or arched figure having its apex upwards. The figure of a crescent moon or that of a trident (*triśūla*) also marks some Śaivas. These marks are made by hand or by metallic stamps with ashes collected from the sacrificial fire, or from burnt cow-dung, sandalwood paste, or turmeric steeped in a solution of lime-juice and saltpetre. The ashes used are said to represent the disintegrating force associated with Śiva. Vaiṣṇavas usually make two perpendicular lines on their foreheads with or without a dot or circle between them. They also mark on their bodies the emblems of Viṣṇu: the discus (*chakrā*), the conch (*sankhā*), the mace (*gadā*), and the lotus (*padmā*). They have other signs which are coloured red, yellow, or black, and are made with sandalwood paste or charcoal taken from a fire in which incense has been burned before an image. Clay brought from sacred places is also used in the same way, especially by the lower castes, as sandal is considered to be too holy for them. Separate marks also indicate the subdivisions of the Vaiṣṇava sects. Thus, among the Rāmānujas, the Vadakalai, or 'northerners,' make a simple white line between the eyes, curved like the letter U, to represent the sole of the right foot of Viṣṇu, and a central red mark emblematical of Lakśmī, while the Tenkalai, or 'southerners,' have a more complicated device symbolical of both feet of the god, which are supposed to rest on the lotus. The complete Tenkalai symbol has the appearance of a trident, the two outer prongs painted with white earth standing for Viṣṇu's two feet, the middle painted red for his consort Lakśmī, and the white line over the nose representing the lotus. The sect marks of Madhvās and Vallabhās are the same as those of the Vadakalai, but the Madhvās, instead of a red line in the centre, have a black one made with charcoal taken from incense burned before an image of Viṣṇu. Vaiṣṇavas also brand their breasts, arms, and other parts of their bodies with stamps representing the two chief emblems of Viṣṇu, the lotus and the conch shell. These instruments are made of copper, brass, or silver, and are heated to a temperature sufficient to singe the skin and leave a deep black mark on it. These brandings are done chiefly at holy places like Dwārkā, Brindaban (*qq.v.*), and Udki. The Śāktas have no distinctive marks, using those of the Śaivas.[1] There are local variations in other parts of the country.[2]

7. The character of the ascetic orders.—Many members of these orders are men of high character, learned students of Indian theological literature, and, as *gurus*, or religious preceptors, exercise a healthy influence over their disciples. But the character of some sects is indifferent.

'Looked at with the light of common sense and unbiased judgment, the net result of their so-called reformations is that they let loose on society an army of able-bodied beggars, with the most preposterous claims on the charity and the reverence of the laity. Moral teaching of any kind seldom forms a part of the programmes of our prophets. They teach their followers to sing some songs which either tend to corrupt their morality, or to make them indifferent to work for the production of wealth. The most important part of the discipline enforced by our "incarnations" on their lay followers consists in requiring them to paint or brand their bodies in some particular manner, and to show every possible honour to their spiritual guides and to the begging mendicants. The monks and nuns of every sect are only so many licensed beggars.'[3]

LITERATURE.—The best general accounts of Hindu sects are those of H. H. Wilson, *Select Works*, i. London, 1861, and Jogendra Nath (Bhattacharya), *Hindu Castes and Sects*, Calcutta, 1896. Much information will be found in older works, such as W. Ward, *A View of the History, Literature, and Mythology of the Hindoos*[2], 2 vols., Serampore, 1815–18, and J. A. Dubois, *Hindu Manners, Customs, and Ceremonies*[3], Oxford, 1906. Among modern works the following deserve mention: H. A. Rose, *A Glossary of the Tribes and Castes of the Punjab and N.W. Frontier Province*, vols. ii. and iii., Lahore, 1911–14; R. V. Russell, *The Tribes and Castes of the Central Provinces of India*, 4 vols., London, 1916; E. Thurston, *Castes and Tribes of S. India*, 7 vols., Madras, 1909; W. Crooke, *The Tribes and Castes of the N.W. Provinces and Oudh*, 4 vols., Calcutta, 1896; H. H. Risley, *The Tribes and Castes of Bengal*, 2 vols., do. 1891; *BG*, esp. ix. pt. i. [1901]; F. S. Growse, *Mathura*[3], Allahabad, 1883; J. C. Oman, *The Mystics, Ascetics, and Saints of India*, London, 1903. The following reports of the Census of India are valuable: Punjab: *Census of India, 1891*, xix.; *Census of India, 1901*, xviii.; *Census of India, 1911*, xiv. 2 pts.; Bengal: *Census of India, 1901*, vi.; *Census of India, 1911*, v. 3 pts.; Baroda: *Census of India, 1901*, xviii.; *Census of India, 1911*, xvi. 2 pts.; Central Provinces: *Census of India, 1911*, x. 3 pts.

W. CROOKE.

1 Growse, p. 284; Karsandas Mulji, *Hist. of the Sect of the Maharajas or Vallabhacharyas*, London, 1865.
2 *Census of India, 1911*, v. *Bengal*, pt. i. p. 211 ff.
3 *Ib.* xvi. *Baroda*, pt. i. p. 82.
4 Rose, ii. 137.
5 *PNQ* ii. [1885] 181; *NINQ* v. [1895] 146.

1 *Census of India, 1911*, x. *Central Provinces*, pt. i. p. 79 f.
2 See *ib.* v. *Bengal*, pt. i. p. 252 ff., with illustrations of the marks; *BG* ix. pt. i. [1901] p. 534 ff.
3 Jogendra Nath, p. 359.

SECTS (Jewish).—Since the reorganization of Judaism after the destruction of the Temple by the Romans there has been little or no sectarianism, in so far as the monotheistic principle of Judaism is concerned. There have been groups which bear some of the marks of sects, but they deserve to be described rather as parties, which indeed have often been divided as regards very important concerns of the religious life. There is, however, no general term in Rabbinic Hebrew for 'sect' corresponding to the *αἵρεσις* of Josephus.[1] Josephus treats the groups in Judæa less as political parties than as philosophical schools. In the new Hebrew the word *kath* (כַּת) denotes 'class,' 'band,' and only rarely 'sect' in the earlier literature. Similarly with *'aguddâh* (אֲגֻדָּה), which denotes 'party' on the disruptive side, just as *ḥaburah* (חֲבוּרָה) denotes it on the side of 'union.' In modern Hebrew the Biblical word *miphlagah* (מִפְלַגָּה) is often employed both in the wider sense of 'party' and in the more specific sense of 'sect.'

In ancient Palestine there co-existed a number of local cults, and North and South (Israel and Judah) were divided religiously as well as politically. Within each division there were groups of devotees, such as Nazirites (*q.v.*), prophetic gilds, Rechabites ([*q.v.*] whose existence as late as the 12th cent. is recorded by Benjamin of Tudela), and even castes such as the Nethinim (*q.v.*). The resettlement after the Babylonian exile gave importance to the Samaritans (*q.v.*), afterwards divided into groups, among them the Dositheans. There may also have been proselytes of incomplete degree, though here the difference was of the nature of variety in status and obligation rather than sectarian.

With the later part of the Greek period the most famous parties, often described as sects, appear. The Ḥasidim played a conspicuous part on behalf of the Maccabæan rising,[2] while the Hellenists to a certain extent went into opposition. Not that this opposition lacked complexity. For Freudenthal has shown that there were 'orthodox' among the Hellenists, while Philo as a Hellenist denounced some of the antinomianism of his class. According to some authorities, the 'fearers of God' mentioned in various late passages of the OT were Greeks who adopted monotheism. Others consider the title a synonym for 'proselytes.' The Pharisees and the Sadducees (*qq.v.*) (of whom the Boethusians were a subdivision) then came into vigorous life. Whether there was a Zadokite sect (similar to the Samaritan or Sadducæan Dositheans) at the early period is still a matter of controversy. Side by side with these were the Essenes (*q.v.*), who have their counterpart in Philo's Therapeutæ (*q.v.*) and similar Egyptian groups, including the Abelites. The Pharisees, it is generally held, should hardly be considered a sect, as they gradually absorbed a preponderant majority of the Jews. During the Roman War there came into temporary being parties such as the Zealots (*q.v.*) and Sicarii, which, however, were mainly political groups.

With the birth of Christianity (which was regarded by the Romans as a sect of Judaism) we are met by the Judæo-Christian sect, known as Mînîm.[3] This term also applies to Gnostics (*q.v.*), some of whom were pre-Christian. They are described under various titles—Naasseni, Elkesaites (*q.v.*), Cainites, Ophites (*q.v.*), and so forth. The Judæo-Christians also assumed various designations such as Nazarenes, Ebionites (*qq.v.*). It is very doubtful whether we should regard the Epicureans[4] as a heretical sect.

[1] See art. HERESY (Jewish). [2] See art. HASIDÆANS, HASIDISM.
[3] See also art. HERESY (Jewish).
[4] See art. APOSTASY (Jewish and Christian).

With the 7th cent. arises the great Ḳaraite (*q.v.*) schism, which has some affinity with Sadduceeism. In Persia a sect of 'Isavites (an offshoot of these were the Yudghanites) was a forerunner of Ḳaraism. Within the Ḳaraite body there were also many subdivisions. In contrast to the Ḳaraites the great bulk of traditional Jews are known as Rabbanites. There were also wide differences within the Rabbanites, especially from the 12th cent. onwards, as regards the pursuit of metaphysics; the Maimonists and anti-Maimonists were respectively the friends and foes of this study, which was so prominently advanced by Maimonides (*q.v.*). Then the development of the Ḳabbala (*q.v.*) led to the growth of various groups of mystics, the Ḥasidim of the 18th cent. being the most important. Earlier the great Messianic movement of Shabbathai Ṣebi[1] had separative consequences, so that, even apart from the Frankists, one might almost speak of the Shabbathaian sect (who are not to be confused with the Sabbatarians). The Shabbathaian movement has left permanent traces, for there are descendants of the adherents to Shabbathai in the Donmeh of Salonica. Similarly, the Chuetas of Majorca have left their modern offspring. These were the result of the work of the Inquisition, which led to various groups of Crypto-Jews, more particularly the Maranos, who conformed externally to the Church but remained secretly Jews, often with debased theology, waiting for a favourable opportunity to throw off the mask. There had earlier been a similar phenomenon of Crypto-Muhammadans. There have been groups, similar to the pre-Islāmite Jewish communities in Arabia, which are ethnic rather than sectarian (as, *e.g.*, the Chazars, the Krimchaki of the Crimea, the Daggatuns of the Caucasus, the Falashas of Abyssinia,[2] and the Cochin Jews[3]). These are sometimes described in religious terms. Thus in China the Jews were the Tiao Kiu Kiaou ('the sect which extracts the sinews' [Gn 32^{33}]), and the Bene-Israel (*q.v.*) of Bombay were called the Shanvār Teli ('Saturday oil-pressers') in allusion at once to their occupation and to their ritual.

Within the Synagogue there grew up varieties of rite (*minhag*) as between Palestine and Babylonia, and these perpetuated themselves between the Westerns (Ashkenazim) and Easterns (Sephardim). These differences do not constitute sectarianism, and they co-exist (with many others) in the same communities. Similarly it is inappropriate to describe the post-Mendelssohnian *haskalah*, or the modern liberal movements, as sectarian.[4]

LITERATURE.—W. Bacher, 'Qirqisani, the Qaraite, and his Work on Jewish Sects,' *JQR* vii. [1894] 687–710; S. Schechter, *Documents of Jewish Sectaries*, 2 vols., Cambridge, 1910; artt. in *JE* on the various sects named; H. Graetz, *Hist. of the Jews*, Eng. tr., 5 vols., London, 1891–92 (see Index, American ed., 6 vols., Philadelphia, 1891–98, *s.v.* 'Sects'); the historical works of M. Jost, though superseded by that of Graetz, are still of value. It is important to note the title of his work: *Gesch. des Judenthums und seiner Sekten*, 3 vols., Leipzig, 1857–59. Some interesting sketches of modern Jewish communities may be read in E. N. Adler, *Jews in Many Lands*, London, 1905.

I. ABRAHAMS.

SECTS (Russian).—I. *RASKÓL.*—1. **The term and its signification.**—The term Raskól ('separation,' 'schism,' 'dissent') is applied in Russia to those ecclesiastical groups and organized communities which took their rise in the 17th cent. in consequence of the liturgical reforms introduced into the Church of Moscow by the patriarch Níkon (1652–58), and which in part still maintain their separation from the Russian Orthodox State Church. These bodies are more correctly de-

[1] See art. MESSIAHS (Pseudo-), vol. viii. p. 585 f.
[2] See art. AGAOS.
[3] See art. JEWS IN COCHIN (Malabar).
[4] Cf. art. LIBERAL JUDAISM.

scribed as 'the Raskól of the Old Ritual'; they call themselves Old Ritualists or Old Believers (*Staroobrjádtsi, Starovêri*), claiming to be the true heirs of the Old Muscovite Church as it was before Níkon introduced his reforms. Since that Church, however, was the Orthodox Church (*Pravoslávnaja Zerkovj*), Old Ritualism really asserts—as against a State Church which has departed from the true faith—that it alone is the Orthodox Church, that in fact it is *the* Church, the true Catholic and Apostolic Communion, in relation to which all other ecclesiastical bodies are heretical.

The rise of this powerful dissenting movement was due, as indicated above, to a liturgical reform. In the Eastern Church, however, and especially in the Russian Orthodox Church, the distinctive quality of religion consists in ritual,[1] and no line of demarcation is drawn between ceremony and doctrine. Hence any attempt to alter the outward form of worship was to admit that the Church had erred, and could therefore no longer claim to be the infallible vehicle of divine salvation. Church and dissent were here at one. Previous changes had claimed to be simply a restoration of the original forms; and Níkon's reform purported to be no more; it was merely more thorough-going and more extensive. Níkon himself shared the prevailing conviction that the true character of the Church found its sole warrant in the 'orthodox' ritual. To ascribe to him a more liberal attitude towards the cultus is to show a complete misunderstanding of the matter at issue. To us the warring parties may seem to be fighting about trifling liturgical points; to themselves the very nature and standing of the Church were involved. It was this fact that made the conflict so bitter and ruthless; and thus it was no original divergence of opinion, but rather the long-continued strife, that at length generated unmistakable differences in the character of the two parties—differences in their religious spirit, their temperament, and their mental tendencies.

2. Inadequate explanations.—The usual theory has been that the schism was due to the blind dependence upon tradition, the ignorance, and the fanaticism which, as was almost natural in a predominantly ritualistic communion of that age, characterized the Muscovite Church. Níkon's reforms seemed akin to the work of the Illumination, and were therefore suspect from the outset, so that resistance was certain. Such is the explanation given by most Russian writers on the subject, and it might indeed be called the 'official' theory, *i.e.* the theory hitherto current among the authorities of both Church and State. It is nevertheless quite inept. For one thing, it fails to explain how the reforming party could have diverged so far from the principles of their Church as to propose the changes in question, and how, again, the resistance to the changes developed into a movement without parallel in Russia. The cardinal defect of the theory, however, is its failure to recognize the undoubtedly religious forces which lay at the root of the Raskól.[2] Finally, the hypothesis of mere ignorance and fanaticism is confuted by the facts of history. In Russia historical investigation of the Raskól has all along been cramped and fettered by the obstructive attitude of the authorities, and the State Church was quite content with a view which saw in the movement a merely mischievous revolt against the Church and the justifiable changes introduced by its former patriarch.

[1] See art. RUSSIAN CHURCH.

[2] It is in view of this religious factor that, in opposition, *e.g.*, to F. Kattenbusch (*Lehrbuch der vergleichenden Confessionskunde*, Freiburg, 1892, i. 235), we regard the Raskól as well worth the attention of Western learning.

Russian scholars themselves felt that the theory was inadequate, and sought other explanations; but, while they produced many interesting and ingenious hypotheses, they consistently undervalued the historical material and its investigation, and their work was stimulative rather than fruitful in positive results. Thus, for instance, Old Ritualism was capriciously brought into connexion with previous heretical movements in the Russian Church;[1] or its political aspect was accentuated;[2] or the social factor in its rise was unduly emphasized;[3] or, finally, attempts were made, under the powerful advance of Russian nationalism from 1870 onwards, to represent it as a product of the distinctively Russian spirit, *i.e.* of independent and genuinely native beliefs in the religious sphere.[4]

3. The Russian Church prior to the Raskól.—In order to gain a proper understanding of the rise of Old Ritualism, we must glance at the history of the Russian Church before the 17th century.

(*a*) *Alliance with national sentiment.*—Russia was evangelized from Byzantium, and for centuries the Russian Church was entirely under the Byzantine influence—organized by immigrant Greeks, governed by the Greek metropolitans of Kiev, and subject to the ecumenical patriarch, who nominated these metropolitans. As was inevitable, the influence and predominance of the Greeks declined and at last passed away. Their position in the Church was irreconcilable in particular with the rise of a strong native State, which made Moscow its capital. The Church itself succeeded in making a close alliance with the national movement, and its complete emancipation from the authority of Byzantium was only a matter of time. Nor could the princes of Moscow in common prudence leave the choice of the metropolitans in the hands of the patriarch of Constantinople, who frequently acted with an eye to his own advantage. Moreover, the political and ecclesiastical conditions of the Byzantine empire were not such as to evoke the respect of the Russians. Thus the Church of Moscow was in the way of becoming autocephalous—a natural process, but in this case complicated by the attempts then being made to unite the Greek Church with the Roman.

(*b*) *Growth of anti-Greek feeling.*—Among the members of the Reunion Council held at Florence in 1439 was Isidore, a Greek who had shortly before been elected metropolitan of Moscow. He was in favour of the union between Constantinople and Rome, and on his return to Moscow tried to carry it into effect there. Among the Russians, however, whom the Greeks had taught to regard the Roman Church as impiously heretical, the bare mention of union raised a perfect storm of indignation. Then Prince Vassilij of Moscow, himself apprehensive of the Florentine Union, appointed—only indeed after long hesitation—the first autocephalous metropolitan of Russia (Jonas, bishop of Riazan, 1448). Although the Florentine Union was, as regards Byzantium, barren of all practical result, it generated among the Muscovites the too-welcome conviction that the Greeks had become the betrayers of orthodoxy and had sold themselves to the Latins. This belief firmly held its ground in Moscow until the 17th century. The capture of Constantinople by the Turks and the fall of the Byzantine empire were regarded as confirming it: God's righteous judgments had fallen upon a faithless people. The belief served as a formula which at once explained the divergence, mainly liturgical, of the Greek Church from the Muscovite, and harmonized with the spirit of self-reliance now found in Moscow. All these circumstances conspired to develop an excessive ecclesiastical and national pride among the Muscovites, prompting them to look down upon the Greeks with scorn, and to regard themselves as the only orthodox and God-pleasing people on earth, and, steeped in self-complacency and crude superstition, they sank deeper than ever in mere stagnation and torpidity.

(*c*) *The idea of 'the third Rome.'*—Belief in the Greek apostasy and the fall of the Byzantine empire served to create still another idea, the importance of which in Russian life can hardly be exaggerated—the idea of Moscow as 'the third Rome.' Muscovy was now the only orthodox country in the world. The prince of Moscow was thus the legitimate successor of the Byzantine emperor. By God's unchangeable decree the Roman emperor was still the defender of the orthodox imperial Church. But by reason of Rome's unfaithfulness the headship

[1] P. Meljnikov, in W. Keljssijev, *Record of the Accounts of the Raskól brought to the Notice of the Government* [Russ.], 1860.

[2] A. Zhuravljóv, *Complete and guaranteed Information regarding the ancient Strigolniki and the modern Raskólniki* [Russ.], Petrograd, 1794.

[3] A. Shtchapov, *State and Raskól* [Russ.], 1862 (never completed because of the author's banishment to Siberia); W. Andrejev, *The Raskól and its Significance in the History of the Russian People* [Russ.], Petrograd, 1870.

[4] Cf., *e.g.*, J. Júsov, *The Russian Dissenters, the Orthodox, and the Spiritual Christians*, Petrograd, 1882; A. Prugavin, *Raskól and Sectarianism in the Life of the Russian People*, Moscow, 1905, *Old Ritualism in the latter Half of the 19th Century*, do. 1904 [all Russ.].

of God's kingdom upon earth had passed over to 'the second Rome,' Byzantium, and, in turn, to the princes of Moscow. Thus these princes (and later the tsars) laid claim to the hegemony of the world. Nor was this merely the overweening belief of politicians and ecclesiastics; it came to be a conviction of the whole people. It was largely fostered by an apocalyptic conception then prevalent in Russia, viz. that Moscow was not merely the third but the *final* Rome. Should Moscow fall away, as Rome and Byzantium had done, then the dread end of all things would be at hand; Moscow was the κατέχον of 1 Th 2[6], and its constancy and faithfulness protected the world against the irruption of the divine judgment. It was under the dominance of the idea of Moscow as the third Rome that Ivan IV. (the Terrible) adopted in 1547 the title of tsar; and on the same ground was established the patriarchate of Moscow, since the orthodox emperor must by divine decree have at his side the imperial patriarch. It remains merely to emphasize the fact that this idea, besides enormously intensifying the national self-esteem, added powerfully also to the Church's sense of its importance. It also greatly strengthened the impression that only by rigid adherence to perfect orthodoxy—*i.e.*, in especial, absolute ritualistic purity—could the empire maintain its sovereign claims. Heresy of every kind, even the slightest liturgical departure from 'the faith of the fathers,' was not only a blow at the Church, but also a menace to the supremacy of Moscow as the third Rome.

(*d*) *The demand for social improvement.*—The accession of the second Romanov, the youthful Alexis (1645–76), saw the emergence of forces which gravitated towards a remodelling of the whole State, and the removal of the rigid barriers which hitherto had shut Moscow off from all non-Russian civilization. The appalling despotism of Ivan IV. († 1584), the extinction of the Ruric dynasty, and the anarchy during the interregnum (1610–13) created a sense of dissatisfaction with existent forms of life and a feeling of insecurity. Projects for ameliorating the life of the people by culture and education had now the support of the court.

(*e*) *The rise of a pro-Greek attitude and the opposition to it.*—But what concerns us in this connexion is the fact that the tsar and his *entourage* completely changed their attitude towards the Greeks, the orthodoxy of whom they now once more admitted. Our knowledge of how this was brought about is naturally rather meagre; we simply find ourselves before the accomplished fact. From about 1648 a more conciliatory attitude towards the Greeks becomes clearly noticeable at court, and was in part due to certain Greek hierarchs then present in Moscow, notably Paësios, patriarch of Jerusalem. He and others believed that in supporting the philo-Greek influences at the court of Moscow they were working in the interests of their own country, and, in particular, furthering the project of using the Russians to deliver Constantinople from the Turks and to restore the Greek empire. Paësios frankly announced this plan in his first interview with the tsar. He expressed the wish that God might assign to the tsar 'the highly exalted throne of the great emperor Constantine, your ancestor,' and that the tsar might, 'like a new Moses,' liberate the faithful from the Turkish yoke. The tsar and his counsellors could not but be impressed; they resolved upon an alliance with Greece and Greek culture, and coupled with this the idea of the third Rome in the sense that the liberated and restored Byzantium should have the Muscovite tsar himself as its head. These designs were not without a certain grandeur. They might be made a powerful instrument in breaking down the popular prejudice against the Greeks. It was forgotten, however, that, to the popular mind, the acknowledgment of Greek orthodoxy could not but seem an abandonment of the idea of the third Rome, or even a lapse of Moscow into the heresy so fatal to the Greeks. 'The third Rome,' hitherto a religious conception, had now become a political one.

(*f*) *Efforts to win the clergy for the pro-Greek attitude.*—If the cause was to succeed, it had to win the support of the Church. This was far from easy; for in the clergy was concentrated all the racial and religious conceit of the Muscovites. Thus a group of priests who had gathered round the tsar's confessor, the philo-Greek Vonifátjev, and who were earnestly bent upon social and religious betterment, were altogether unaware of the philo-Greek aims of the court, and, as was subsequently seen, were simply steeped in the traditional prejudice against the Greeks. It was from this group that the later leaders of the Raskól were drawn—its proto-popes (chief priests, proto-presbyters) Ivan Nerónov, Avvakúm, and others—and to it belonged also the archimandrite (abbot) of the new Monastery of the Saviour in Moscow, Níkon, who (born in 1605, of peasant parentage, at Veljemánovo in what is now the government of Níshni Nóvgorod) had risen by his undoubted ability and his vast energy to a position in which he had the tsar's intimate friendship and confidence. Níkon, however, was won over by the pro-Greek party—a fateful event, for the tsar believed that he was precisely the man to carry out the plans of reform. Having been appointed in 1649 metropolitan of Nóvgorod, the leading diocese of Russia, he was in a manner designated as the successor of the incompetent patriarch Josiph, and the vigour and ability of his administration added to his *prestige* alike at court and throughout the Church.

The tsar, however, could not yet prosecute his ends publicly, and meanwhile sought to prepare the way. His principal agent in the process is said to have been a Muscovite monk named Arséni Suchánov, a man of outstanding culture and of great influence in the Church. In the summer of 1649 this monk was sent to the East, accompanied by Paësios (who was returning to Jerusalem), to form a final opinion regarding the Greek Church and to lay this before the tsar. On his return he handed to the tsar a written account of his discussion with the Greek divines at Térgovite in Moldavia—*Prênije s Grekami* ('Controversy with the Greeks'). His verdict was altogether adverse, confirming the views generally prevalent in Moscow. Now, in thus employing Suchánov, did the tsar and his intimates really desire to obtain an impartial judgment regarding the Greeks before launching their pro-Greek policy? If so, it is strange that Suchánov's verdict had no effect. What was the actual object of that mission? The only adequate answer is that the philo-Greek party hoped for a reversal of Suchánov's views under the influence of the shrewd and capable Paësios. In that case they would be able to claim that a recognized authority of the Muscovite Church had now discerned the baselessness of the prejudice against the Greeks. Doubtless the tsar and his advisers were bitterly disappointed, and, if Suchánov did not fall into disfavour, it was owing to a circumstance of interest to us at this point. In his *Discussion* he had set forth the theory of the third Rome quite unambiguously, affirming that the authority of the empire had been definitely transferred to Moscow, and that the patriarch of Moscow was now the chief bishop of the Church. The pro-Greek party, while not conceding Suchánov's reason for supporting that theory, viz. the apostasy of the Greeks, were not disposed to disown so forceful a champion of the supremacy of Moscow.

4. The real origin of the Raskól.—Now the deeper cause of the Old Ritualistic movement was this change of attitude on the part of the leading political and ecclesiastical authorities towards the Greeks and the Greek Church, and their endeavour to apply their pro-Greek views in the work of reforming the Church of Moscow. The reform roused the fanatical opposition of the conservative classes, who, believing that they were defending the orthodoxy of the Church as well as the stability of the throne, and desiring to save their metropolis from the fate of Rome and Constantinople and avert the terrors of the Last Judgment, resisted with such vehemence that a conflict of unparalleled passion and virulence was the result.

5. How the reform was carried out.—(*a*) *Níkon's methods.*—On the death of Josiph (15th April, 1652) Níkon was appointed patriarch, and was consecrated on 25th July; his promotion was approved even by those among the Old Ritualists who became his bitterest enemies. The pro-Greek party at the court had thus gained their end; the elected head of the Church of Moscow was ready to carry out their plans. Níkon set himself to the work with a will. He acted with unexampled brutality, trampling upon all opposition, and ignoring the religious feelings of the people.

His ruthless methods cannot be explained wholly by his character, though he was certainly a man of harsh and rigid disposition, without patience, without the capacity of truly estimating his opponents. The deeper explanation of his actions is twofold: (1) in spite of his devotion to the cultus, he was not a man of truly religious temperament; (2) the reform was for him only a means of attaining certain ends of a politico-ecclesiastical character, his real object being to strengthen the authority of the patriarchate, even against the monarchy itself.

Thus, when Níkon entered upon office, he exacted with the sanction of the tsar an oath of inviolable obedience from the boyars and the synods. The tsar would doubtless regard this as merely a preparatory step to the work of reform, but Níkon had something more in view. The great aim of his administration was to liberate the hierarchy of Moscow, which had hitherto been a passive instrument of the monarch, and to get the reins of power into its hands. In the patriarch, as set forth by Níkon, is concentrated a power not less than divine; in him lies the source of all political and monarchical authority. Níkon exploits the theory of the third Rome by regarding the patriarch of Moscow as having been proclaimed the supreme hierarch of Christendom; and, if the tsar should become the recognized head of the world empire, what would be the position of the patriarch, the occupant of the sacred office from which were derived the jurisdiction, power, and authority of tsar and State alike?

(*b*) *His guiding principle.*—Níkon was no sooner installed in office than he began his revision and correction of the liturgical books. His guiding principle was to substitute the Greek liturgical practice of the day wherever it differed from the Muscovite. In Moscow scholars had long been engaged with the variant and often inaccurate texts, but all attempts to construct a correct and uniform edition had been thwarted by the general lack of education and also by the prevailing belief that there was one original sacred text, which required only to be restored. This belief was associated with another, viz. that in the ritual there could be but one single 'true' form, which was likewise the original; this had been given by God, and any departure from it impaired its sacred and sanctifying power, and might even obstruct the divine activity conjoined with it. 'It is the duty of all of us, as orthodox Christians'—so writes a leader of the Raskól, the relatively enlightened deacon, Feódor—'to die for a single A' (in the liturgical texts). As regards the question of different versions and various readings—natural in a liturgy so extensive and of so long a growth—the Muscovites scorned the very thought of a historical account of the liturgy: there could be but one form. By what means, then, was a uniform text to be secured? By going back to the sacred original, said the Muscovites, quite unaware that no such original existed. Such views, of course, excluded the very possibility of emendation; all that could be done was to eject the more glaring blunders.

Even so the cry of heresy was always ready to break out. Thus, at the beginning of the 16th cent., the Greek monk Maximos, a learned and noble-minded man, who had sought to rectify the formularies, was condemned by two synods (1525, 1531), and spent 26 years in a Moscow prison. In 1551 'the Hundred Chapter Synod' (held at Stogláv) ordered the priests to have the texts copied only from 'good' models, thus showing its own incapacity to deal with the prevailing confusion. The establishment of the first printing press in Moscow (1563) merely increased the disorder. Under the first of the Romanovs, Michail, the printing of the liturgical texts went assiduously forward, but only multiplied the variant editions. When Dionissi, abbot of the Trinity Monastery near Moscow and a cultured Greek scholar, constructed an emended text on the basis of the Greek form, he and his two assistants were convicted of heresy by a synod (Moscow, 1618), and imprisoned. The texts brought out under the patriarchs Philarét (1619–33), Joasaph I. (1634–40), and Josiph (1642–52) were by no means uniform, and did nothing to relieve the situation.

Níkon's emendation, on the other hand, had a prospect of success, since it followed a definite principle. But to the Muscovites the principle itself could not but be obnoxious. In face of this difficulty Níkon committed the blunder of giving an influential position in the work of revision to a Greek monk named Arsénios.

This Arsénios was proficient in the Slavic tongues, but otherwise an arrogant adventurer. He had been a pupil of the Propaganda in Rome, but had been reconciled; had subsequently gone over to Islâm and been reconciled again; and then, on coming to Moscow to seek his fortune, had been thrown into prison. The work of revision was thus discredited from the outset.

(*c*) *His first proceedings.* — Shortly after the beginning of the Easter fast of 1653 Níkon began the work of changing the ritual by issuing a decree substituting the Greek mode for the Muscovite in two rites, viz. the practice of bowing during a certain prayer (that, so called, of Ephraem Syrus) and the sign of the cross. In Moscow the sign of the cross was performed by two fingers of the right hand (representing the twofold nature of Christ), while in the Greek Church three fingers were used (representing the Trinity). In Moscow, moreover, the sign of the cross was in many cases the only act by which the uncared-for masses could manifest their religion and take part in worship; it was regarded as sacrosanct and inviolable; in its genuine form, as was said by a later writer among the Old Ritualists, was contained 'the whole secret of the faith.' Nor need we wonder at this, when we learn that the synod of 1551 had decreed as follows: 'If any one does not bestow his blessing with two fingers, as Christ did (!), or does not make the sign of the cross [in the same way], let him be accursed.' Thus Níkon's innovation seemed to expose believers to the Church's anathema; the Church was being betrayed by her own patriarch!

(*d*) *Clerical opposition.*—Hostility broke out at once, and was so vehement as to compel Níkon temporarily to desist; and it was not till 1656, when he was at the height of his power, that he sought to enforce the change in the sign of the cross. The rising opposition, however, revealed the malcontents. It had its source in the Vonifátjev group referred to above. Vonifátjev himself, it is true, shared the pro-Greek sentiments of the patriarch, and remained silent; but his friends raised a protest. Níkon did not hesitate to rid himself of these adversaries by degradation and the ban. Nerónov was excommunicated, Avvakúm was sent to Siberia; the group was broken up; Níkon had triumphed. But his ruthless policy was ill-advised, for these revered men, thus dispersed throughout the country, carried the opposition to the most remote places, and everywhere evoked fresh loyalty to the old rites. They now belonged to a class which in Russia has never failed to exercise a great influence—the class of 'sufferers,' those who bear injustice in silence.

In face of the growing resistance Níkon found it advisable to convene synods to give countenance to his measures. The first of these was held at Moscow in March or April 1654, the tsar being present, and this was followed by a series ending with the Great Synod of 1666–67. At the synod of 1654 the patriarch was supreme and despotic. In his inaugural address he summoned the assembly to make the 'divine law' operative in the Church of Moscow, to restore that Church to its pristine glory, to cancel all the 'innovations' that now disfigured it, the 'innovations' specified being all of a liturgical character and of little or no significance. The main point, however, was the reforming principle, for which Níkon obtained the sanction of the synod. This was that the 'Greek and Old Slavonic' books were to form the standard. In point of fact, however, it was only the Greek texts then in use in the Greek Church that Níkon had in his mind. The synod was a mere blind. The presence of the tsar, and his supporting vote, made opposition difficult. Pável, the revered bishop of Kolomna, who ventured very cautiously to express an opinion at variance with Níkon's, was dismissed from office, and finally banished. Here again Níkon showed his imprudence, for he furnished the adherents of the old institutions with a martyr.

(*e*) *Popular opposition.*—Opposition was not confined to the clergy. The course of events shortly after the synod of 1654 shows that a vague antagonism was stirring the masses, and that the soil was being prepared for the astonishingly rapid upgrowth of the Raskól.

In the late summer and autumn of 1654 Moscow was stricken with plague. The tsar had taken the field against the Poles, and the court, including the patriarch (who was also vicegerent), had left the city. Now Níkon, immediately after his accession to office, had started a campaign against the so-called 'Frankish' pictures of the saints, *i.e.* such as were not Byzantine, but painted from Western models. These his agents searched out, and destroyed or disfigured. On 25th August an excited mob appeared in the Kremlin carrying icons that had been disfigured by Níkon's orders; their fury was directed against him as the arch-iconoclast, and against the printing establishment where heresies were under his direction foisted into the liturgical texts. It was on his account that God had sent the plague! This disturbance was quelled, but the trouble remained. The patriarch, however, simply seized the occasion to treat the opposition more harshly than ever, and, when the tsar and he returned to Moscow (Feb. 1655), he resolved to proceed more energetically upon his chosen path.

(*f*) *Níkon's further proceedings.*—His co-adjutor and adviser for some years after this was the patriarch Makarios of Antioch, a wily and time-serving Arab, who had come to Moscow that year for the purpose of raising funds. He devoted himself entirely to Níkon's will, covering the patriarch's reforming measures with his own authority. He played cleverly, and for his own pocket effectively, the part of a zealot for orthodoxy. On Orthodoxy Sunday, 1655, he began his work by pronouncing, in conjunction with Níkon, the solemn curse of the Church upon the Frankish icons, and upon all who made them or tolerated them in their houses. On the same day Níkon fiercely inveighed against the traditional Muscovite sign of the cross; it was not 'orthodox,' the 'true' form of the sign being found among the Greeks; and this was in turn solemnly confirmed by Makarios.

Níkon then sought to sustain his proceedings by convening another synod (Moscow, March 1655). This assembly, apprehensive of his vengeance, agreed to all his proposals, though not without mutterings. Besides a number of trifling liturgical changes, the synod was asked to endorse three measures of rather more importance:

(1) The creed generally used in Moscow was to be purged of its non-'orthodox' additions, *i.e.* it was to be superseded by the Greek form;[1] (2) the non-'orthodox' sign of the cross in practice in Moscow was to give place to the 'true' form, *i.e.* that used in the Greek Church; (3) the hitherto operative rule of the Muscovite Church according to which members of another communion, already baptized by sprinkling, could join the Russian Orthodox Church only by rebaptism was to be abrogated, and thus, as against the view prevailing in Moscow and explicitly confirmed by the patriarch Philarét, viz. that only a baptism by triple immersion was 'Christian,' baptism by sprinkling was not to be recognized.

These decisions of the synod could only strengthen the impression that the Church of Moscow had broken with her past and her traditions, and yielded herself wholly to the Greeks. Had not the head of the Church openly declared in the synod: 'I am a Russian, and the son of a Russian, but in faith and conviction I am a Greek'?

Immediately after the synod of 1654 Níkon had applied to the ecumenical patriarch Paësios for advice, but he did not wait for a reply, although he speaks of the answer as having been laid before the synod of 1655, and as containing a distinct approval of his proceedings. In point of fact, Paësios warned Níkon against precipitation, and enunciated a principle not understood in Moscow, viz. that ritual differences need not involve divergence in belief, and that variations in the liturgy did not as such imply heresy. Níkon simply ignored this, and at once published the resolutions of the synod of 1655, as well as the revised form of the liturgy. The printing was hurriedly done and corrections had to be made, so that the various issues differed from one another, and the existing confusion was made worse.

While Makarios of Antioch remained in Moscow, he was Níkon's preceptor in the details of the Greek liturgical practice, and the forms of the latter were forthwith forced upon the Church of Moscow. As regards the sign of the cross, however, Níkon felt that the resolutions of a synod were not enough. Hence at the festival of St. Melatios (12th Feb. 1656), in the presence of a large congregation, including the tsar and the court, he denounced the two-finger form as indicative of the Armenian heresy.

The sting of this statement lay in the fact that the Armenians were regarded in Moscow as heretics of a peculiarly obnoxious type. The *Kirillova Kniga* ('Book of Cyril'), a work highly esteemed, denied that they were Christians at all; they did not observe the Lord's Supper; intercourse with them polluted the Orthodox. Should a Christian pass an Armenian church while service is going on, he must stop his ears to the diabolic strains; if an Armenian enters an Orthodox church during the liturgy, the service must at once be broken off; and so forth.

On Orthodoxy Sunday, 1656, Níkon once more had the curse applied by Makarios to the hitherto prevailing form, subsequently confirming it in a document signed by the Antiochene and other three Eastern prelates. Finally, he secured the ratification of all his liturgical changes at a synod of Russian bishops in Moscow (23rd April–2nd June 1656), which in particular condemned the Muscovite form as a 'Nestorian heresy.' All his modifications were then inserted in the new edition of the liturgical texts (1656–58), all the forms obtaining hitherto being suppressed.

Other changes regarded as peculiarly repugnant were: (1) the substitution of Ἰησοῦς for Issús; (2) the alteration of the form of the Cross; (3) the use of five hosts (prosphoræ) instead of seven in the Mass. Most of the changes are so slight that nothing but intense hatred of the reform generally could have magnified them into questions of faith. But, as Níkon's principle itself was mere apostasy, even the change of a letter was a mark of wickedness.

(*g*) *Níkon's fall, and the enforcement of the reform by the tsar.*—Thus in a short time Níkon had effected his reform, and above all had prepared for further advance by recognizing the Greek Church as the sole Orthodox norm. We hear little regarding the success of the process. The higher clergy, and doubtless many of the lower, acquiesced. The external nature of the reform, however, was such as to prevent its winning the masses. Resolutions, decrees, and new editions were of no avail there. What the people saw was simply that one ritual had been superseded by another; the new one was called 'true'; the old 'heretical.' Religious inertia together with custom would, it was believed, bring about the acceptance of the reforms. And, even if a smouldering excitement and dissatisfaction existed among the people, legal measures would keep them in check. Moreover, an event took place which strengthened the popular hope that the reform was a mere passing phase of things: Níkon, already at variance with the tsar, demitted office in July 1658, and left Moscow for a convent. The Church remained without a head till 1667. For over eight years an ever more embittered struggle was carried on between the tsar and Níkon as to the relations between the power of State and Church—till, in fact, Níkon was finally condemned (12th Dec. 1666) by the great synod of Moscow presided over by Paësios of Alexandria and Makarios. During that prolonged conflict the adherents of the old system still hoped that the change would be reversed. The tsar was meanwhile *de facto* head of the Church; was it not incumbent upon him to overthrow the work of the most dangerous enemy of his own purposes and the Muscovite State? It was a vain hope; the tsar might disagree with the methods of the reform, but the reform itself was his own policy. The whole situation becomes obscure: the reforms were not repealed, nor were they enforced; the tsar appeared to make friendly overtures to the opposition, the enemies of Níkon; he recalled Avvakúm from Siberia, and treated him with ostentatious kindness. It was only in the closing years of the struggle that the tsar, now determined to crush Níkon by means of the Greek hierarchs, once more resorted to stern measures. In 1664 the leaders of the opposition, including Avvakúm, were imprisoned, some of them suffering bodily disfigurement. At length Alexis summoned an assembly

[1] Apart from some insignificant features, the main point here was that, whereas the Muscovite form of the Nicæno-Constantinopolitan creed contained the words, 'And in the Lord the Holy Ghost, the true and the life-giving,' the text of the Greek Church omitted the adjective 'true.'

of Russian ecclesiastics (Moscow, 1666), which solemnly reconfirmed Níkon's reform. He called upon it to recognize (1) the orthodoxy of the Greek patriarchs, (2) the orthodoxy of the Greek liturgical books, and (3) the decisions of the all-important synod of 1654. The synod also cited the opponents of the reform, and condemned those who would not submit, Avvakúm among them. Finally, in 1667, Níkon's reform and the foregoing resolutions were ratified by a synod presided over by the patriarchs of Alexandria and Antioch, and, towards its close, by the recently elected patriarch of Moscow, Joasaph; here too the Church's curse was pronounced against the adherents of the old ritual.

6. The religious character of the opposition.—That the reaction against the reform was not more theological in character, but became a popular movement, and one vehemently hostile to the State Church, is explained by the peculiarly ritualistic bent of Orthodox Russian piety. Here the liturgy is not so much the expression and vehicle of divine wisdom—an aspect which is more prominent in the Greek Orthodox type of religion, and which to some extent mitigates the detrimental results of mere ceremonialism; in the Muscovite communion the liturgy, even in its minutest details, is a divine operation, a divinely revealed medium of intercourse with the sanctifying power of God.[1] Thus the Muscovites felt that Níkon's subversion of holy tradition in some sense maimed the activity of God, even as it debarred the faithful from access to Him. Again and again was heard the bitter outcry that Níkon had brought perdition upon all the Russian saints who had been 'saved' by the older rites. Accordingly, we cannot but admit that the resistance to the reform sprang from forces genuinely religious in character. The adherents of the old tradition believed that they were defending the Church as the infallible agent of salvation, and fighting for that assurance of their salvation which the Church guaranteed. Their conception of salvation, their ideas of religion in general, were, no doubt, stunted and defective; but a Church has ever the sects which befit it; they are bone of its bone and flesh of its flesh. The perversion of the religious spirit among the Russian people comes out but too clearly in the Raskól, but the guilt of that perversion lies with the Church itself.

Again, it is these genuinely religious forces in the Raskól that enable us to understand the intrepid loyalty with which its partisans, in spite of the most inhuman treatment, clung to their faith. Similarly, we come to understand how the writings of the earlier Old Ritualists, notwithstanding their occasional absurdities and their blind fanaticism, show more of the spirit of true religion than is found among the reformers. As things were, that fidelity to the old was a more distinct indication of a living religion than was the facile acceptance of the new.

7. Avvakúm as champion of the opposition.—In spite of all these things, the reform might still have proved successful; the masses might have become habituated to the changes. To the personality of Avvakúm alone, the present writer believes, was due the fact that Old Ritualism did not collapse, but increased in power. A man of extraordinary energy and resolution, he was indefatigable in the defence of the 'old faith.' His life was a series of afflictions heroically borne—banishment, hunger, ill-usage, the suffering and death of his followers—till at last he died a martyr at the stake in 1681. But what made him the most outstanding figure in the Raskól was the conviction that he was not merely a servant of God, but also a prophet—one who in visions and ecstasies received the counsel of God—or rather a divinely commissioned messenger possessing absolute authority over his adherents.[1] This conviction enabled him to invest Old Ritualism with a vitality that defied persecution. Ultimately the process of events brought about so wide a severance between the mother Church and the Raskól that all attempts at reunion have proved futile.

8. Old Ritualism as a sect, and its disruption into denominations.—The resolution of the synod of 1667 greatly widened the cleavage between Church and Raskól by its enactment of excommunication and coercive measures against the latter. In the eyes of the Old Ritualists, the Church had now renounced God, and had become 'the woman drunken with the blood of the saints.' At first the State was regarded as less culpable; it had been seduced by the Church. But the latter attitude was soon abandoned in face of persecution. A decree of the regent Sófja in 1685 ordered the 'stiff-necked' sectarians, after three warnings, to be burnt, and those who did not denounce them to be knouted; those who recanted were set free if they found a sponsor. The cruel penalties inflicted by the patriarch Jakím (1674–90) fomented the fanaticism of the Old Ritualists to madness, and hundreds and even thousands, believing that the end of the world was imminent, sought death by burning or starvation. Some fled to the forests and desert places; others betook themselves to Poland, Sweden, Austria, Prussia, or even Turkey. Those who remained sought to form themselves into an organized community. But, as none of the Russian bishops had joined the Raskól, a hierarchic order was impossible; and without that, again, a Church was impossible. Without an episcopate and a priesthood how could an excommunicated multitude become a Church? The priests of the 'old ordination' began to die out, and could not be replaced without bishops. The early leaders of the Raskól had tried to grapple with the difficulty, but without success. Avvakúm was disposed to recognize priests who had been ordained subsequently to the reform, but had renounced their errors, while Feódor, his companion in suffering (and eventually his fellow-martyr), absolutely rejected the ordination of the State Church—certainly the more consistent view. The question led at length to the division of the Old Ritualists into two large and mutually hostile groups, the Bezpopóvtsi ('priestless') and the Popóvtsi ('priestly').

(*a*) *Bezpopóvtsi.* — The Old Ritualists who gathered together in the district of Pomórje, in the government of Olónez—a region hitherto sparsely populated and almost churchless—solved the problem of the priesthood by reducing the number of the sacraments to two, baptism and confession, which could be dispensed by laymen, the Mass, etc., being simply omitted in their priestless service. Their example was largely followed by the Raskól throughout the empire. It was theoretically vindicated as a provisional policy (*c.* 1700) in a work still highly esteemed by the sect, viz. *Pomórskije Otwěti* ('Answers from Pomórje'), which divided the sacraments into (1) those indispensable for salvation — baptism, confession, and communion, and (2) the useful—unction with the myron, the 'oil of prayer,' marriage, and ordina-

[1] Once, when an attempt was made to make some paltry liturgical change in the Solovietski monastery (which refused to accept Níkon's reform until 1676, after a siege of eight years), the monks cried out in their despair, 'Woe! they are taking away our Christ.'

[1] This conviction may be illustrated by a vision in which heaven and earth and all created things appeared as having been enclosed in his body by God. In an account of this sent to the tsar (1669) he says: 'Seest thou, Autocrat, thou . . . dost govern the Russian land, but to me the Son of God . . . has subjected heaven and earth?'

tion; and communion might be replaced by the desire for it ('spiritual communion'). This again was brought into logical connexion with the doctrine that the kingdom of Antichrist was at hand. The priesthood, originally a gift of God's grace, had been destroyed by Antichrist, as was to be expected in the tribulation of the last days. Here, be it noted, Antichrist was not a person, but the age that began with Níkon's reform; Church and State were the organs thereof. This attitude of the Bezpopóvtsi to the ruling powers was aggravated by the reforms of Peter I. Believers fled from an unclean world; and those who left the Church for the Raskól were baptized as heathen. As might be expected, dissensions arose, and fresh disruptions. These were due mainly to two questions: marriage and the relation to the State. As there were no priests, believers had to accept celibacy as a binding law; as a matter of fact, it was adopted as a principle, and communities were organized on the monastic model. In practice, however, some sought to retain marriage, while theoretical celibates sometimes gave themselves to the worst immoralities. Then the demand of the State for a recognition of its authority (especially by prayer for the tsar), the impracticability of complete isolation, and the compromises resulting from business relations, tax-paying, military service, etc., created new difficulties.

The more important sub-sects of the Bezpopóvtsi are as follows:

(1) *The Pomórtsi* (from Pomórje; see above), organized towards the end of the 17th century. Among their characteristics were the monastic pattern of their communities, rejection of marriage and of prayer for the tsar, as also the readiness of their members to die by burning themselves. The body became wealthy; it provided teachers for other Old Ritualistic groups, and in fact came to be a kind of centre for the entire priestless section. In process of time it became less rigid: prayer for the tsar—under compulsion, it is true—was countenanced by some, marriages originally contracted in the State Church, as well as irregular unions, were tolerated, and a community which arose in Moscow at the end of the 18th cent. actually permitted regular marriage. These are the Brátchniki ('having marriage'), or novo-('new')Pomórtsi.

(2) *The Feodossêjevtsi*, so named from their founder Feodóssi Wasséljev, originally one of the Pomórtsi († 1771), who instituted independent communities in W. Russia. Originally allied with the Pomórtsi, they broke away in a controversy regarding the form of the inscription upon the cross. The questions of prayer for the tsar and marriage widened the gulf, the Feodossêjevtsi maintaining the original strictness of the Pomórtsi themselves. In 1752 a synod declared the absolute necessity of celibacy. This denomination found its most powerful support in the establishment in 1771 of the Preobrazhénsk Institution in Moscow, its leader here being the uneducated but shrewd Iljá Kovylin, under whose almost unlimited authority it rapidly increased in wealth and influence, while it adhered to a most rigid rule of celibacy (married people were admitted to baptism only after divorce). The serious spread of immorality led Kovylin, by his insistence on the merits of penitence, virtually to exonerate it. After his death a kind of tolerance was granted to loose unions, but the persons concerned remained formally outside the community, and were absolved only on their deathbed. This question of marriage is still a fruitful source of dissension and disruption in the group.

(3) *The Philípovtsi*, founded in the first half of the 18th cent. by a certain Philip, who had been expelled on personal grounds from the Pomórtsi. Its distinctive tenets are somewhat obscure; but it rejects marriage and prayer for the tsar. When in 1743 a military expedition was sent to the settlement, Philip and his adherents burned themselves, with the result, however, that the sect increased. It is characterized by fanatical and divisive tendencies.

(4) *The Stránniki* ('wanderers') or *Bêguni* ('runners'), founded not later than the latter half of the 18th cent. by a certain Jevfími, are the extremists of the Raskól, rejecting all compromise with Antichrist. The members must pay no taxes, must not deny their nonconformity or let their names appear in the Government list of the Raskólniki, must receive no official papers, must (in one group) possess no money, and have no intercourse with members of the State. Jevfími, for his salvation's sake, adopted rebaptism, and baptized his followers, thereby devoting them to a life of wandering and homelessness. While the other Bezpopóvtsi find Antichrist in a period of history, the Stránniki see it embodied in the succession of tsars from Peter I. State and Church are in its power; the Church is Satan's prophet. Disputes arose after the founder's death in 1792, ending with the triumph of a more tolerant party, and leading to the recognition of two classes of members, viz. (i.) those who keep the whole law and are under obligation to wander without rest, and (ii.) those 'who have discerned Christian doctrine' without practising it. The latter have homes and property, must be hospitable to 'wanderers,' and are not baptized till shortly before death, when, by being removed to some place associated with wanderers, they formally adopt the more extreme law. The Stránniki likewise have split up into sub-sects.

(5) *The Nêtovtsi* ('deniers'), or *Spássovo soglássije* ('community of the Redeemer'), probably arose about 1700. They deny that the laity can take the priest's place in all cases. They have no worship, no sacraments; the Church, they believe, has forfeited God's grace. Still, they permit baptism and marriage in the State Church, though they do not regard this performance of the two sacraments as orthodox, and seek to make good all defects by the prayer, 'May God let his grace be effective!'

The fanaticism and ignorance of the Bezpopóvtsi have given rise to numerous less important denominations, many of them doomed to a brief existence.

(*b*) *Popóvtsi.*—This section of the Raskól differs from the Bezpopóvtsi in regarding a priesthood as essential to the existence of a Church, and from this all other differences result. When the priests ordained prior to the reform died out, others who joined the sect were admitted on renouncing their errors. This necessarily led to modifications of the doctrine of Antichrist, who was here believed to be an actual personage of the final age. Moreover, as such priests could be recognized only in virtue of their baptism (in the State Church), rebaptism was not universally required in the case of ordinary members who passed from the State Church to the sect. The Popóvtsi are accordingly less rigid in their renunciation of the State, though they hate it no less intensely.

The priests who deserted the State Church for the Raskól did so secretly and as runaways, and hence the Popóvtsi are also called Bêglopopóvtsi, *i.e.* the Popóvtsi who are served by fugitive priests. Many of these priests made the change not from conviction but from motives of material gain, and there was among them a large disreputable element. Such men could have no good influence upon their flocks, and, though retained as instruments, were often despised and merely tolerated—a circumstance which led to an even more formal conception of religious worship and to the transference of directive control to the laity.

Flourishing centres of the sect, with churches and monasteries, were established in the following localities: (1) the island of Werka, government of Mogiljóv (broken up in 1733; rebuilt, then finally destroyed under Catherine II.); (2) Starodúbje, gov. Chernigov; (3) the Don district; (4) the river Irgíz, gov. Sarátov; (5) the Rogóz Institution in Moscow (the present headquarters of the Popóvtsi). The position of the sect, nevertheless, remained insecure, depending as it did on the attitude of the Government, which was sometimes tolerant (as under Catherine II. and Alexander I.), sometimes repressive (as under Nicholas I. and Alexander III.). Moreover, doubts arose as to whether a Church could exist without bishops, and the unworthy element in the priesthood created scandals. These things, together with the difficulty of obtaining accessions to the priesthood during persecution, suggested the idea of an independent hierarchy, and in the 18th cent. many unsuccessful attempts were made to secure a bishop from the Eastern Church.

The situation became critical from *c.* 1825. By an enactment the sect was permitted to retain priests who had joined it prior to 1826, but later accessions were heavily penalized, and, though clandestine additions could not be altogether prevented, utter collapse seemed imminent. The arrogance, greed, and ill-behaviour of the dwindling group of priests added gravely to the difficulties. Then in 1838 a synod assembled at Moscow resolved to take energetic steps towards instituting an Old Ritualist hierarchy; and, after long delays, this design was eventually realized in 1844, largely through the instrumentality of the devoted Pjotr Velikodvórski (Pável). Ambrosios, metropolitan of Bosnia, a Greek by birth, then living poverty-stricken in Constantinople, resolved to join the sect. In apprehension of Russian espionage, he left Constantinople secretly, and under Austrian protection became the first Old Ritualist bishop in the monastery of Bêlokríniza in the Bukovina. The Russian Government took fright, and their machinations led in 1848 to his being banished to Zill, where he died in 1863. Meanwhile, however, he had ordained several bishops for the Russian hierarchy, while his successor Kirill did the same for Old Ritualists in Turkey and Rumania, and in 1849 sent to Russia its first Old Ritualist bishop, Sofróni of Simbirsk, who secretly ordained others. The new hierarchy, however, was not too well received in Russia; some of the imported priests as well as of the laity saw in it a menace to their respective positions; its legitimacy was loudly questioned, while certain of the bishops themselves gave offence by their avarice and ambition.

What lay at the root of all the trouble, however, was the fact that many of the Popóvtsi had come to be influenced by ideas prevalent among the Bezpopóvtsi, and with a view to settling all perplexities a council of bishops sent out in 1862 a 'circular letter,' which had been composed by Ilarion Kabánov ('Xenos'). This pastoral, rejecting the doctrine that the State Church is ruled by Antichrist, expressly acknowledges the competency of its priests, and asserts that it serves the same God as the Raskól (denied by certain of the Bezpopóvtsi on the ground that 'Ιησοῦς had been substituted for 'Issús'); the real sin of the Church was its having excommunicated the Old Ritualists in 1667, and its 'new doctrines.' In thus recognizing the Church, the Popóvtsi were of course seeking to vindicate the legitimacy of their new hierarchy. The result, however, was further dissension, and eventually a division into Okrúzhniki ('adherents of the circular') and Neokrúzhniki (its opponents). The latter have now sunk into insignificance. The Okrúzhniki, on the other hand, have an organized hierarchy throughout Russia; its head is the archbishop of Moscow, and it has bishops in most of the great cities. The metropolitan of Bêlokríniza has only an honorary primacy, and it has been proposed to make the archbishop of Moscow a metropolitan. The Church of the Popóvtsi has thus become a counterpart of the State Church, and claims to be the genuine National Church. It has a vigorous communal life, which it directs by means of schools and a press, and its leading circles are in part open to progressive thought.

A small group of the Popóvtsi has never recognized the new hierarchy; it retains the name of Bêglopopóvtsi (see above). Another insignificant section, the Jedinovêrtsi ('of one faith'), made an alliance with the State Church in 1800, and had the 'old rites' conceded to them. Being scattered over the country, and having no hierarchy of their own—as, indeed, by their acceptance of the canonical regulations they cannot have, since one diocese cannot have two bishops — they have no real standing. Some sense of alienation between the members of the 'sect' and the Church is but natural in view of their divergent history.

Thus the Russian State Church has found its position challenged by a multitude of sects, some of them strong and well-organized. It certainly conducted a 'mission' to them, but on spiritual lines it has always shown an amazing incapacity. Down to 1905, when freedom of conscience was conceded to all, its great instrument was State coercion; and even since it has striven by legislation or local pressure to limit that freedom as far as possible. How the abolition of the State Church, and the ruin and misery of the whole country, brought about by the revolution of 1917 will react upon the whole religious situation it is impossible to predict.

LITERATURE.—The following are some of the more important Russian works dealing with the Raskól: **Platón** (P. G. Levshin), *Short Hist. of the Russian Church*, 1805, ii.; **D. Opótski**, *The Causes of the Rise of Raskól in the Russian Church*, St. Petersburg, 1861; **S. Solovjóv**, *Hist. of Russia*, Moscow, 1870; **Philarêt** (Gumilevskij), *Hist. of the Russian Church*[6], St. Petersburg, 1895; **A. Shchápov**, *The Russian Schism of Old Ritualism*, 1859; **Makári** (Bulgákov), *Hist. of the Russian Raskól*[3], St. Petersburg, 1889, *Hist. of the Russian Church*, do. 1910, xii.; **N. Ssubbôtin**, in his periodical *Brátskoje Slóvo* ('The Fraternal Word') and *Materials for the History of Raskól*, 9 vols. (a work of the utmost value in the scientific study of Raskól); **N. Ivanovski**, *Manual of the Hist. of, and the Polemic against, the Old Ritual Raskól*, 2 vols., Kazañ, 1905; **E. Golubinski**, *Our Controversy with the Old Ritualists*, Moscow, 1905 ff.

Non-Russian writers, as A. Leroy-Beaulieu, P. Strahl, L. Boissard, and F. Kattenbusch, merely reproduce the views prevalent among Russian historiographers, and independent and scientifically developed conclusions are not to be looked for in their works.

Works (in Russian) which, while sometimes differing in details, deal with Old Ritualism on strictly scientific lines, and in particular recognize the philo-Greek movement as a powerful factor in the rise of the Raskól, are: **N. Kaptenev**, *The Nature of the Relations between Russia and the Orthodox Orient in the 16th and 17th Centuries*[2], Moscow, 1914, *The Patriarch Níkon and his Opponents in the Emendation of Church Rites*[2], do. 1913, *The Patriarch Níkon and Czar Alexis Michailovich*, 2 vols., Sergiev Posad, 1909–12; **E. Golubinski**, *op. cit.*; **P. Miljukóv**, *Sketches from the Hist. of Russian Civilization*, ii.[5], St. Petersburg, 1916; **W. Kluchévski**, *A Course of Russian History*, iii.[3], Moscow, 1916.

A. BARON VON STROMBERG.

II. *OTHER SECTS.*—The sects which diverge from the Orthodox Church of Russia not merely in ritual but also in doctrine are gradually becoming more and more distinct from Raskól in its various denominations. They may be classified thus: (*a*) native sects: (i.) secret, including (1) the Khlysti, or Men of God, and (2) the Skoptsi; (ii.) public, including (3) the Doukhobors, and (4) the Molokani; (*b*) sects based upon foreign influences, the most important being (5) the Judaizers and (6) the Stundists.

1. Khlysti.—See art. MEN OF GOD, vol. viii. pp. 544–546.

2. Skoptsi.—The earliest known Skoptsi (*skopets*, 'eunuch'), 34 in number, were discovered in 1772 in villages around Orjól, in the districts of Belev and Aléxin belonging to the government of Tula, and in the district of Kosjólsk in the government of Kalúga; other 27 persons, though known to be castrated, evaded legal detection. All of them were Khlysti, led by the female teacher Akulína Ivánovna. The claim of having originated the practice of castration was made by André Ivanov Blochín, a runaway peasant thirty years of age and a professional beggar, who belonged to Brásovo in the district of Sevsk (Orjól). Having joined the Khlysti in 1769, he had mutilated himself because he found it difficult to fulfil the leading rule of that sect, viz. absolute sexual abstinence; and along with an assistant whom he had castrated—the untraced Kondráti Triphonov, or Nikiphorov, of Stolbishche, a village near Brásovo—he had in the course of four years won over the 60 others referred to above. The Khlystic female teacher already named and the Moscow 'Christ' whom she followed had not opposed this new propaganda, and in point of fact their own helpers had submitted to the rite. Blochín was knouted in Bogdanovka, where he was then resident, and sent to Nerchinsk in Siberia; his dupes, with the exception of two, were released.

In 1775, however, another Skoptsi community was discovered in a district far removed from the localities of the earlier movement, viz. in the village of Sosnovka (government of Tambov). A peasant named Kondráti, who styled himself 'the hermit of Kiev,' and his henchman Alexándr

Shilov were singled out as its founders, and were banished; the two had already been at work in the districts of Tula and Aléxin in the government of Tula, and, as regards Aléxin, in the very place where castrati had been discovered in the prosecution in 1772, viz. Luginin's linen factory in Aleshnja. Most Russian scholars identify this Kondráti with that earliest assistant of Blochín who had evaded capture in the former prosecution, but it seems more likely that he was none other than Blochín himself, since he was known among his later adherents in Petrograd by his real name, André Ivanov, and his self-confidence is difficult to explain on the theory of his being any one's disciple. Moreover, we see from the *Sorrows*[1] of Kondráti Selivanov (as he called himself in Petrograd), who is to this day regarded by the Skoptsi as their sole founder and their first leader, that the author had fled from the grasp of the law and at length reached the government of Tula. Here, however, he was still harassed; for the Khlysti, doubtless remembering what they had suffered in 1772 in consequence of his propaganda, wished to deliver him to the authorities. Nevertheless, he succeeded in winning fresh adherents from among them in the village of Aleshnja, where their local leader, Akulína Ivánovna—no doubt identical with the Akulína mentioned above—and her assistant, the 'prophetess' Anna Románovna, acknowledged him as 'Christ,' probably because he had suffered the knout (in Khlystic usage = crucifixion) and banishment, though he himself, as being the first to revive the forgotten teaching of Jesus regarding self-mutilation (Mt 19^{11f.} 18^{8f.}), accepted the dignity in a sense that excluded the other 'Christs' of the Khlysti, and then in turn recognized Akulina Ivánovna as the Mother of God, and Shilov as John the Baptist. Having been sent a second time to Siberia, on the way he brought himself, by further amputation, to the state of complete mutilation (the 'tsaric seal,' in contrast to the 'little seal,' *i.e.* simple castration), and then, in imitation of Pugachov, he assumed the designation of Tsar Peter III. Hardly anything is known of the twenty-two years he spent in Irkutsk. He returned, in a most adventurous fashion, to Russia in 1797. It appears that certain rich Skoptsi merchants in Petrograd availed themselves of Paul I.'s whimsical desire to interview those who claimed to be his father—there were fifteen such pseudo-Peters—and were permitted to bring Selivanov before him, but the impression which the fanatic made upon the tsar was such that the latter sent him to a madhouse. He was not discharged till the accession of Alexander I. From 1802 he lived with one or other of his followers in the rich commercial circles of Petrograd, and at length one of these, Solodóvnikov by name, built a kind of palace for him, where his adherents—alike those of the capital itself (now to be numbered by hundreds in consequence of a vigorously renewed propaganda) and those who came there as pilgrims from all parts of Russia—revered and worshipped him as 'Christ Peter III.'; for, while, during Selivanov's exile, the sect had expanded but slowly and only in the central provinces—with ramifications in Petrograd, Riga, and Odessa—the systematic propaganda now directed by him soon extended it over all Russia. In Petrograd it gained a certain footing also among the aristocracy. Madam de Tatárinova, while rejecting castration, introduced the Skoptsi form of worship into her 'Brotherhood in Christ.'[2] But, when castration was found to be making headway among officials and military men, Selivanov was thrown into the notorious cloister-prison of Susdal, and this town became the centre of the sect until his death in 1832. Since then the Skoptsi have contrived to keep secret the locality of their headquarters.

From the time of Selivanov's labours in Petrograd the sect has had numerous adherents not only among the peasantry, but also among the merchants and money-changers of the cities. Many of these are wealthy, and, as they have no children, their wealth passes by will from one to another, and tends to accumulate in the hands of individuals who use it in support of the work of promulgation and the policy of secrecy. Their attitude towards castration has varied between rigour and laxity. At the present day not only catechumens, but also many members in full standing, especially women, still remain unmutilated, availing themselves of the dispensation by which the operation may be again and again deferred. To-day, in fact, it is only a decided minority of the 100,000 Skoptsi that have submitted to the rite. Persecution has driven many of them to Rumania, where they have centres at Galatz and Jassy, and where, as foreigners, they are tolerated. Here, in 1872, arose a new 'Christ,' Lísin by name, who founded a party known as the New Skoptsi. In the course of a missionary journey into Russia Lísin, together with numerous helpers and followers, was arrested and banished to Siberia, and the movement collapsed. The Skoptsi have found recruits not only among the Orthodox Russians, but also among the Lutheran Finns of Ingria, and many Skoptsi of both classes are now resident in villages of their own in the government of Yakutsk, where they were forcibly settled. Selivanov himself, to judge from his appearance and character, was not of pure Russian descent, but of Russo-Finnish blood. Such half-breeds, as well as the pure Finns, find a peculiar attraction in the sect; the Finns are in fact temperamentally disposed to religious fanaticism.

Selivanov's claim of symbolic identity with Tsar Peter III. was accepted by the Skoptsi as literal fact, for they believed that Peter had been conspired against by Catherine II. because of his impotence, and had thus undergone Messianic sufferings. In order to lend this an air of plausibility they fabricated an absurd story in which certain other personages of the imperial family and the court were made to play a part. Akulína Ivánovna was identified with the tsaritsa Elizabeth, who was the virgin mother of Peter III. Napoleon was the son of Catherine II. and the Devil, was living in Turkey, and would return as Antichrist. When the number of the 144,000 virgins (Rev 14^{1-4}, but interpreted as 'castrated ones') is complete, Christ Selivanov will come from Siberia, will ring the Tsar bell in Moscow, gather around him all the Skoptsi, quell the Antichrist advancing from Turkey, and establish a Skoptsi kingdom upon the earth; only after these things will come the end. Apart from their ideas regarding Christs and the last things, the teaching of the Skoptsi differs from that of the Khlysti only in substituting mutilation (for which support was found also in Is 56^{3-5}, Wis 3^{14}, Col 3^{5}) for sexual abstinence. The idea that Adam and Eve were created sexless, and that the halves of the forbidden fruit were grafted upon them—as testicles, or as breasts—after the Fall (whence the necessity of restoring the disfigured image of God by the knife), is not received by the whole sect. Their original practice of operating with a red-hot knife was grounded on Mt 3^{11}, but the use of the cold knife was introduced while Selivanov was still living—a consequence, as the Skoptsi say, of his capitulation to human weakness. The mutilation of women likewise was subsequently

1 Ed., together with his 'Epistle,' by the present writer as *Die geheime heilige Schrift der Skopzen*, Leipzig, 1904.
2 See art. MYSTICISM (Christian, Russian), § 4.

performed in a less severe manner, and this was recommended, though not prescribed, by Selivanov. The assertion that the Skoptsi mutilate their proselytes against their will or after they have made them insensible is a calumny. The organization of the sect is much more rigid than that of the Khlysti. Its members constitute a centralized and strictly exclusive association, with well-developed methods of concealment, self-preservation, and expansion, and capable of acting throughout the whole Russian empire with astonishing unity and consistency. While their form of worship is externally almost identical with that of the Khlysti, the practice of ecstasy, borrowed from the latter, is now on the wane.

3. Doukhobors.—See art. DOUKHOBORS, vol. iv. p. 865 ff.

4. Molokani ('milk[moloko]-drinkers').—The origin of the Molokani has not as yet been made out. The hypothesis that they were an offshoot from the Doukhobors, and separated from them by surrendering the residue of Khlystic ecstasy which these still retained and attaching supreme importance to anti-ritualism in contrast to the ritual (including the seven sacraments) of the State Church, is very probable, and seems to find some corroboration in the fact that, as the Molokani themselves represent, Semjon Uklé-in, whom they regard as their founder, married (*c.* 1750) the daughter of Pobiróchin, the leader of the Doukhobors. But the use of the name 'Molokani' is of earlier date, having been applied by the Russian people as early as the 17th cent. to all sectaries who drank milk and ate non-fasting foods during Lent. Moreover, the Molokani *Confession of Faith* printed at Geneva in 1865 says that the sect designated as such is of earlier date than Uklé-in. As far back as the 17th cent. it had been brought by a physician to Moscow from England. A certain Matvé Semjónov was the first Russian who spread abroad the 'worship of God in spirit and in truth,' and for this he was broken on the wheel. His teaching, however, was carried to the government of Tambov by some of his pupils, and, although they were at once and finally got rid of, their teaching held its ground there. Now, if this account is correct, what Uklé-in did was simply to give a fresh impetus to an existing denomination. Himself originally a Doukhobor, he made a stand, in the village of Goréloje, against the claim of Pobiróchin, the leader of the Doukhobors, to be the Son of God, and against their contempt for Holy Scripture. Fleeing before Pobiróchin's 'angels of death,' he reached Rübnoje, a village in the same government, and won many adherents there. Having chosen from among them 70 'apostles,' he led them in solemn procession into Tambov, there to make war against the 'idols' (icons, the saints' pictures of the Orthodox Church). He was arrested, but regained his liberty by an ostensible reconciliation with the Church. Thereafter he directed his propaganda from the village of Raskásovo as a centre, and extended it to the provinces of Voronesh and Saratov. During his lifetime he gained some 5000 followers, and after his death a succession of zealous disciples diffused his teachings throughout Central and S.E. Russia. In 1805 a portion of the Molokani were settled in the Molotchna, in Taurida; and there they founded the prosperous villages of Novovasiljevka, Astrakhanka, and Novospassk, in which by 1833 their number had reached 3000.

Molokanism was originally a simple Bible Christianity marked by anti-ritualistic opposition to the State Church. It gave full recognition to the Church's leading doctrines of the Trinity, the Incarnation, and the God-manhood of Christ. Uklé-in accepted also the virgin-birth of Jesus, though he believed that the body of Jesus was not of the common human type, but was a spiritual one, like that of the archangel Raphael when he accompanied Tobias; on this point, however, the *Confession* of 1805 is entirely orthodox. That *Confession* also recognizes the moral perfection of Adam and the doctrine of original sin, as does also the *Foundations of the Molokany Doctrine*, published fifty years later. As regards the appropriation of redemption, the sect is far removed from Protestantism. It adhered rather to a naive legality, which it based equally on the OT and the NT. While it gave a symbolic interpretation to many of the OT commandments, it accepted others —*e.g.*, the prohibition of the use of pork—quite literally. Recently, however, the Molokani have been affected by the unitarianism of W. Europe, largely through the efforts of the able A. S. Próchanov († 1912), a physician who, educated at Dorpat, exercised a powerful influence upon them by his journal *Duchóvny Christianín*, founded in 1906. The unitarian leaven makes itself felt in the *Confession of the Spiritual Christians commonly called Molokani*, which was drawn up at the general congress of the Molokani held at Astrakhanka in 1905, was recognized as binding upon all 'spiritual Christians' (the only name that they apply to themselves), and so printed and published. The doctrine and worship of the sect are set forth by it as follows:

'God is the Good. Evil has no independent existence, but is merely the negation of God. God is not a trinity, but a unity, and the apparently trinitarian formula of Mt 28[19] simply sets forth the one God in His threefold relation to the world and man. The innocence of the first man consisted in his ignorance of evil and good alike, in which he resembled the animals, whereas the innocence of Christ was a conscious and voluntary righteousness. Thus the Fall, although it resulted in man's loss of communion with God, was in reality a step forward, and man, having become like God in the knowledge of good and evil, has now to win that communion by his own efforts (Mt 11[12]). But, while God has left man free to do either good or evil, it is the latter that is mainly preferred by him (Eph 2[1f.]); he feels that God is alien to him and that His law is coercive and hard to obey. He violates it constantly, and thus regards God as his incensed Lord, who is to be propitiated by sacrifice. In the fullness of time, however, Christ came, and revealed to us our nearness to God; called God Father and spoke of us as His children (Jn 20[17], Ro 8[14]); changed the covenant of fear into the covenant of love (Ro 8[15], He 2[14f.]), so that goodness comes to have a meaning for us, and the law of compulsion becomes the law of liberty (Gal 5[1]). He thus showed us the way to blessedness, and sealed His word with His death on the Cross. The Church which He founded is the community of those who believe in God; and in virtue of that belief all members of the Church are equal, so that the hierarchy of the Græco-Russian Church has no standing in it. The presbyters or bishops ("overseers") appointed by the "spiritual Christians" are not priests, but merely the servants of the ordinary members, and receive no remuneration for their voluntary labours. Christ instituted no visible sacraments, not even Baptism or the Lord's Supper, and the NT passages upon which these two sacraments are said to be founded are to be interpreted spiritually, *i.e.* as referring to the initial and continued apprehension of God's word; the Church's practice of fasting must also be wholly discarded.

We do not use the sign of the cross, for we regard it as quite uncalled for. All that it does is to tire the hands, whereas Christ has bidden us endure the spiritual cross, *i.e.* the sufferings appointed to us.

The Sabbath was given for relaxation and divine worship; but good works may be done on the Sabbath, as appears from the example of Christ in contrast to the Pharisaic hallowing of the Day (Mt 12[4-13]). It is specially necessary, however, to refrain on that day from evil deeds, unchastity, and drunkenness (Eph 5[18f.]). As, in conformity with the witness of Holy Writ, the first day after the Saturday is kept sacred in place of the Sabbath by Christians of all creeds in commemoration of Christ's resurrection, we likewise do this.

We recognize only the tradition given in the Holy Scriptures —not the traditions and writings of the Fathers of the Græco-Russian Church (Ro 1[22]), or the multitude of ceremonies in which its worship consists, for man should worship God in spirit and in truth (Jn 4[24]). In our assemblies the worship of God begins with the Lord's Prayer, spoken by the presbyter. Then follows the reading of Scripture, the presbyter reading the verse, the congregation then singing it, and this is continued for several hours. Thereafter begins common prayer, which the presbyter recites while the congregation kneels (Lk 22[41], Ac 20[36]), and the service closes with the singing of psalms. Our worship of God takes place in our own houses; for we do not think that a building can give sanctity to an assembly; it is rather the assembly that sanctifies any place where it is held. The Ten Commandments must still be obeyed, for Christ did not abrogate them (Mt $5^{17f.}$). Hence God alone is to be worshipped. Nowhere does Scripture authorize the worship of any besides Him—not even of the Apostles of Christ, though they wrought miracles, or of the angels (Ac $10^{25f.}$, Rev $22^{8f.}$); and if not the former while they were still alive, all the less now when they are dead; while if not the latter, then all the less the so-called saints. In conformity with the 2nd Commandment, we have no images or icons. When the Græco-Russian Church puts forward the plea that it does not worship the images themselves, but the holy men portrayed by them, the defence is quite invalid, for in that case the images would all be regarded as of equal worth, or, at most, those which show the best painting and the most accurate representation would be the more highly prized, while, in point of fact, it is the badly painted, old, and grimy ones that are preferred. The worship of saints' images, said not to have been made by hand of man but to have come into existence miraculously, is commanded on pain of anathema. We simply do not believe that there are such things at all, for God is Spirit and not man, and would not therefore concern Himself with the making of idols, and the less so because He even forbids men to do it. The worship of images is prohibited by Holy Writ in its entirety (Ac 17^{29}, 1 Co 10^{7}, Ps 115^{4-8} 134 $[135]^{15-18}$, Wis 13^{9-19} 14^{8-17}, Ep. of Jer 3–12, Rev 9^{20}). The worship of human corpses conflicts with Gn 3^{19}. Even if the body in which Christ the Saviour passed His earthly life had by chance been preserved, we would not worship it, for we revere Christ for His divine spirit and understanding, and not for His perishable body, even were it turned to stone.

The 2nd [3rd] Commandment forbids oaths of all kinds, and the 5th [6th] includes the prohibition of war and capital punishment. Marriage was instituted by God Himself (Gn 2^{18-22} 1^{28} $2^{23f.}$, Mt 19^{3-9}), and God is likewise the source of the ordinances relating to those with whom sexual intercourse is not to take place (Lv $18^{6-18.\ 22f.\ 29f.}$, Sir 9^{3-9} 23^{22-27}, 1 Co 6^{15-20}). Our mode of contracting marriages we take from To 7^{10}. After the parents have given their blessing, Ps 113 [114] is sung, and a prayer recited. The bridal pair then express their mutual consent, promise to be faithful to each other, and not to separate (1 Co $7^{10f.}$). Thereafter To $8^{5f.}$ and Eph 5^{22-33} are read. The ceremony closes with an exhortation to the married pair, and then Ps 132 [133] is sung by all present. Although Christ Himself remained unmarried, He did not regard many as being capable of this, and therefore never urged it upon His disciples. Monasticism has against it both Scripture (Mt 19^{12}, 1 Co $7^{1f.}$) and the example of Christ. If monks and nuns seclude themselves in convents in order to engage in the worship of images, God punishes them by abandoning them to unchaste conduct (Ro $1^{24.\ 26f.}$).

We believe in the resurrection of the dead and in a life to come (according to Mk $12^{26f.}$, 2 Co 5^{1}, Ps 55^{17-19}, Mt 24^{30}, Jn $5^{28f.}$, Rev 20^{12-15}, Ac 24^{15}), and accordingly we pray that their sins may be forgiven them (2 Mac $12^{44f.}$). When a member of our community dies, we pray and sing Ps 23 [24] and 145 [146], and, at the funeral, Ps 83 [84], in conformity with Ac 8^{2}, Sir $38^{16f.\ 23}$.'

At the present day the Molokani are very numerous not only in Taurida, but in the Caucasus region and in E. Siberia (to which their ancestors were banished), and they are to be found in many other parts of Russia. It is computed that they number in all over half a million. As a result of dissensions regarding what are mainly minor distinctions, they have split up into a considerable number of denominations.

5. Judaizers.—The founder of this group is generally supposed to have been a member of the Molokani named Sundúkov, a peasant from the village of Dubóvka in Saratov, and a pupil of Uklé-in. As early as the 15th cent., however, we can trace a 'heresy of the Judaizers' in Nóvgorod and Pskov (Pleskau), which spread from these cities eastwards to Moscow. This was founded by two learned Jews, Sharija, an astrologist and Kabbalist, and Moishe Chapusha, a Talmudic scholar. Its doctrinal basis was a fusion of Jewish and Christian elements, the former being by far the more predominant. It drew adherents even from the highest circles of Russian society; thus Sosima, the metropolitan of Moscow, and also the *fiancée* of Grand Duke John III. gave it their support. In 1490 and 1554 it was condemned by ecclesiastical councils in Nóvgorod and Moscow respectively. Gennadi, archbishop of Nóvgorod, and Josiph, abbot of the Volokolámsk monastery, made such onslaughts upon it that at length it disappeared from view, although it possibly survived in a state of concealment. At a later day ecclesiastical writers still occasionally refer to Judaizing groups, and it is possible that as a result of Jewish propaganda the sect may have repeatedly experienced a revival. In 1738 two Jews, by name Boruch and Faivist, diffused Jewish doctrines among the Orthodox, and, among other activities, built a Jewish school in Smolénsk for the use of the humbler classes among the Russians. The Judaizing sect of the present day, however, has no traceable connexion with these earlier movements, but took its rise independently from the soil of Molokanism, which regards the OT as a valid standard equally with the NT. Sundúkov, in fact, took the step of ranking the former above the latter, and this was certainly due in part to Jewish influence. He won numerous adherents among the Molokani. The authorities made their first discovery of Judaizing Molokani (called by the rest Subbótniki, 'Sabbatarians') in 1797 in Alexandrovka, a town in the north of the Caucasus region, where even by that time they were more numerous than the Orthodox. In 1814 proceedings were taken against them in Jélez, in the province of Orgól, and incidentally certain Jews belonging to Saratov were implicated as proselytizers. All the accused were found to be circumcised. They had connexions with fellow-believers in the province of Voronesh. One of their missionaries who had been arrested stated that they then numbered about 400 in the province of Saratov; in 1818 some 500 were identified in Voronesh, but by 1823 they had increased in that government to over 3700. In one particular village in Transcaucasia there lived at that time more than 7000 Subbótniki, while in the government of Archangel, *i.e.* the remote opposite quarter of the country, the entire Orthodox population of certain large villages had gone over to them. At the present day they possibly number 100,000. Many live in Siberia, as in the outskirts of Irkutsk and Minusinsk. As regards European Russia, they are particularly numerous in the middle and lower Volga districts, in the Crimea, in the region of the Don, and in the entire Caucasus area. Since the proclamation of religious liberty in 1905 their missionary activity has greatly expanded, and their agents are now penetrating the south-western region—as far as the government of Kiev—where previously they were not to be found. While a number of them eventually conformed in all respects to Judaism, learnt Hebrew, used the Hebrew Bible, and had their religious services conducted in that language by highly remunerated rabbis, yet the real Subbótniki—also called Karaims or Karaimites—remained Russians in all things, using their native language in all religious functions, and adhering only to some of the Jewish practices, as, *e.g.*, the laws regarding food, though indeed they are all circumcised. Their partial observance of Jewish customs is connected with the fact that, while accepting the Bible, they reject the Talmud. They do not look for a Messiah, and those who have gone wholly over to Judaism regard them as lost, declining all connexion with them either in eating or in marriage.

6. Stundists.—Stundism is an evangelical movement among the Russian peasantry of the south-west, and, according to Russian ecclesiastical writers, it is due to the propaganda of German evangelical, chiefly Lutheran, pastors who labour in the German settlements of that district. These Lutheran ministers in particular, however, in view of the legal restrictions under which the Lutheran Church was tolerated in Russia until the proclamation of religious freedom, refrained on principle from proselytizing work among the Russians, and long usage has made it easy for them latterly to maintain their practice in this respect. The only exception was found in the case of the Reformed pastor Bohnekämper, who in the Odessa district of Kherson (from 1824 onwards) conducted his pietistic devotional 'hours' (*Stunden*) in the Würtemberg manner, not only for German settlers but also for Russian peasants. It was not till the time of his son and successor, Karl Bohnekämper, however, that any religious movement of the kind arose among the Russians themselves (1862); and that the rise of Stundism was due to him is admitted by the well-known religious and theological writer Hermann Dalton,[1] who at that time was superintendent of the Reformed Church in Russia. The movement, however, under the direction of zealous Russian leaders like Ivan Rjaboshapka, Gerásim Balaban, and the brothers Zibulski, presently freed itself from all connexion with the Reformed Church, became purely Russian in character, and, spreading at first from the government of Kherson to that of Kiev, soon extended over the south-western and central regions of the country. According to the annual reports presented to the tsar from 1873 to 1885 by M. Pobêdonostsev, chief procurator of the Holy Synod, Stundist communities, notwithstanding the most rigorous measures taken against the movement by the powers of Church and State, were then to be found everywhere in the areas indicated. It was during these years too that Stundism became more consolidated by union with the Russian Baptist body, which likewise owed its rise to W. European influence, and since then it has also been designated Stundo-Baptism. The relatively few who held aloof from this union were those who sought to maintain the original link of connexion, not indeed with evangelical pastors, but with the pietistic *Stundenhalter* ('those who *hold hours* of devotion') among the Swabian colonists, and these are now the 'Stundists' strictly so called in contradistinction to the Stundo-Baptists. The latter body, again, maintains its Russian character by keeping itself distinct from the Baptist group which originated in the work of Johann Gerhard Onken and his auxiliaries (Käbner, Lehmann, Willer, Ondra, Priezkau, Fischer, Schulz, Köniz, and Liebig) among the German colonists in Russia. The most outstanding agents of the Baptist movement among the Russian Stundists were André Miller and Vasili Ivanov, presbyter in Baku. The movement, as embodied in Stundo-Baptism, has also infected the south-east of Russia. More especially in the Caucasus region and in Siberia it carries on a strenuous and successful propaganda among the numerous Molokani residing there (to whom it has the right to preach), and also among the Orthodox, its chief missionaries being W. Pavlov and D. Masajev, a wealthy man of some celebrity. While generally at one with W. European Baptists in doctrine and worship, it devotes itself largely, in its conflict with the State Church, to fighting against the worship of images. The hotheadedness of some of its adherents has prompted them now and again to lay violent hands upon the saints' images of the Church, with the result that the sect has frequently suffered severe persecution, to which, it is true, it was exposed also in the days of Pobêdonostsev. The Stundists are now a vast multitude; they are to be met with even in the north of Russia. Reliable statistics as to their numbers are not to be had, and it is a debatable point whether they are to be reckoned by the million or only by the hundred thousand, though the latter would probably be the more correct.

[1] *Evangelische Strömungen in der russischen Kirche der Gegenwart*, Heilbronn, 1881.

LITERATURE.—(i.) Of works dealing with the Skoptsi, in addition to those cited in vol. viii. p. 546, the most important are: **E. Pelikan**, *Forensic-Medical Investigations of Skoptsism and Historical Notices regarding it* [Russ.], St. Petersburg, 1872, Germ. tr. by N. Ivanov, Giessen, 1876; **K. Grass**, *Die russischen Sekten*, vol. ii. 2 pts., *Die weissen Tauben oder Skopzen nebst geistlichen Skopzen, Neuskopzen*, etc., Leipzig, 1909–14; **N. G. Wysozki**, *The First Skoptsi Trial: Materials relating to the Earliest History of the Skoptsi Sect* [Russ.], Moscow, 1915.

(ii.) Works dealing with the Stundists: **A. Roshdéstvenski**, *South Russian Stundism* [Russ.], St. Petersburg, 1889; **H. Dalton**, *Der Stundismus in Russland*, Gütersloh, 1896; **S. Stepnják-Kravtshinski**, *Der Stundist Pavel Rudenko*, Geneva, 1900, ²St. Petersburg, 1907 (=first part of *Collected Works*).

(iii.) The other sects have not been dealt with in monographs of a comprehensive kind, but short accounts of them will be found in the following general works: **Vladimir Anderson**, *Orthodoxism and Sectarianism* [Russ.] (*An Historical Sketch of Russian Religious Dissent*), St. Petersburg, 1908; **T. Butkévitch**, *Survey of the Russian Sects and their Denominations* [Russ.], Kharkov, 1910, ²1915; *The Russian Sectarians, their Doctrine, Worship, and Modes of Propaganda: Fraternal Work by Members of the Fourth Pan-Russian Missionary Congress* [Russ.], ed. M. Kalnev, Odessa, 1911.

K. GRASS.

SECTS (Samaritan).—Some of the tendencies that gave rise to sectarian movements within Judaism were also at work among the Samaritans (*q.v.*). This was natural, since the general development in many respects ran along parallel lines. The things that Jews and Samaritans had in common, such as the worship of Jahweh as the only God, the recognition of the Law with what it embodied of the prophetic spirit, and the consequent observation of the Sabbath, the other festivals, circumcision, and the dietary rules, were more important than those in which they differed. In spite of strong antipathy and more or less careful avoidance of commerce, analogous methods of interpretation, exchange to some extent of ideas and customs, and exposure to the same external influences were inevitable. Hegesippus, who flourished in the time of Eleutherus (A.D. 175–189) and appears to have been a Christian Jew, looked upon 'the sons of Israel' as a whole and counted the Samaritans as one of their seven sects. When he enumerated among these, in addition to the Pharisees, the Sadducees, the Samaritans, and the Galilæans (probably the Jewish Nazaræans of Epiphanius), also Essenes and Baptist communions like the Masbothæans and the Hemerobaptistæ,[1] he may have thought of the latter chiefly as Jews, but probably had no intention of denying that they had likewise representatives in Samaritan circles. Just as Jewish sects arose from such causes as the adoption, in one form or another, of the Persian doctrine of the resurrection of the dead, speculation concerning the desirable changes in the calendar or the mode of observing the festivals, doubts in regard to the permissibility of offering sacrifices in a sanctuary that had been desecrated and had an illegitimate or otherwise unworthy high-priesthood, opposition to animal sacrifices and to the use of animal food, abstinence from a second marriage or marriage with a divorced wife, preference for the celibate life, and the introduction of baptism as an initiatory rite for proselytes and frequently repeated ceremonies of purification, so similar tendencies seem to have occasioned schisms among the Samaritans. Nor is it at all improbable that they were at an early time affected by the currents of thought which later crystallized in the great Gnostic systems, though at first this incipient Gnosticism is likely to have appeared in a relatively crude form.

According to Epiphanius, there were four Samaritan sects, viz. Essenes, Sebuæans, Gorothenes, and Dositheans. Of the **Essenes** he gives, in this connexion, no description, evidently regarding their tenets as substantially identical with those of Jewish Essenes (*q.v.*). It is not impossible

[1] Eusebius, *HE* iv. 22.

that they were the earliest of these sects. Their name seems to designate them as 'quietists' (חַשָּׁאִי). The etymologies of Herodianus (*οἰκιστής*) and Suidas (*πολίτης*) have no value; the generally assumed connexion with the Hasidæans (*q.v.*) is improbable; a Rechabite descent (Epiphanius, Nilus, Hilgenfeld) cannot be proved; and there is no basis for Lincke's theory that they were originally a tribe settled in Samaria.[1] But there is no reason to doubt that there were Essenes in Samaria as well as in Judæa. The desecration of the temple on Mt. Gerizim by Antiochus IV. in 168 B.C., and its destruction by John Hyrcanus *c.* 120 B.C.,[2] must have deeply affected the Samaritans; and it is not unlikely that some of them were opposed to a rebuilding of the temple, and, seeing in its destruction a judgment upon the worldly character and policy of the pontificate, were led to reject the sacrificial cult, and adopted the doctrines of the Jewish Essenes. As neighbours of the Sebuæans they seem to have followed them in the matter of the calendar.

The **Sebuæans** may well have been actuated by such a motive as Epiphanius assigns for their departure from the orthodox custom as regards the festivals, though he is no doubt wrong as to its date. Their origin is to be sought, not in the Persian, but in the Seleucid period. Even if a party of Galilæan Jews was rescued by Simon in the time of Judas Maccabæus[3]—and this has been questioned by Wellhausen[4]—it is by no means certain that the whole Jewish population was removed, and many Jews no doubt settled both in Galilee and in Samaria during the reigns of John Hyrcanus and Alexander Jannæus. Conflicts would naturally arise when these went to Jerusalem at the same time as the Samaritans went to Mt. Gerizim. To eliminate this cause of friction the Sebuæans placed the Passover in the autumn. In doing so they may not only have desired to show their loyalty to the Seleucid rulers to whom Samaria belonged, and who began the year on the 1st of Tishri (Apellæus), but also have acted in harmony with their interpretation of Nu $28^{18ff.}$, which obviated a distinction between a civil and an ecclesiastical year. If this is the origin of the sect, Lagarde's[5] explanation of the name as derived from *šebu'ay*, one who counts the year as beginning with the 1st of Tishri, when God's oath (*šebu'a*) to Abraham (Gn 22^{16}) was celebrated on Mt. Gerizim, is to be preferred both to the older derivation from *šabuoth*, 'weeks,' and to that from *sabu'in*, 'Baptists,' adopted by Brandt, Bousset, and Holl; and the schism is perhaps more likely to have taken place early in the 1st cent. B.C. than after Pompey's conquest of Palestine. The result of this change in the calendar was that the Passover came to be celebrated in the autumn and the Feast of Tabernacles in the spring (Nisan, Xanthicus). Only some of the Essenes followed them in this innovation. It is not known whether they practised baptism; Abu'l Fatḥ[6] testifies that they opposed the innovations of Baba Rabba and preserved the ancient traditions of the Samaritans.

The **Gorothenes** are said to have adhered to the orthodox calendar. Their differences from the main body of Samaritans are not indicated. Possibly the name gives a hint. It may be derived from גֵּירוּת (Syriac *giurutha*), 'a body of foreigners,' 'proselytes.' The objection that proselytes do not form a sect is scarcely valid. If they were received into the religious community by baptism, they may have been regarded, and even have considered themselves, in spite of their conversion, as a separate body, not quite on a par with 'the sons of Israel' according to the flesh. The Gorothenes may have been looked upon as a Samaritan branch of the Masbuthæans, so named from *masbu'tha*, *masbu'itha*, 'baptism.' As to the age of proselyte baptism, the prevailing view at present is that it antedates the Christian era; the researches of Brandt have especially tended to confirm this opinion.

Concerning the **Dositheans**, the fourth sect mentioned by Epiphanius, we possess a certain amount of information from native Samaritan as well as Christian, Jewish, and Muslim sources. Unfortunately, Abu'l Fatḥ, a Samaritan who wrote his *Chronicle* in Arabic in 1355, while familiar with the later customs and ideas of the sect, could only report, without critical sifting, the current traditions concerning their earlier history. The accounts of Dositheus and his followers by Hippolytus (whose lost work was known to Photius and apparently used by pseudo-Tertullian), Origen, Jerome, Philaster, Epiphanius, and Eulogius are often confused and contradictory; the references in *Pirqē de R. Eliezer* and *Tanḥuma* yield little that is dependable for the earlier period, as Büchler especially[1] has shown; and those in Mas'ūdī and Shahrastānī, repeated by Abu'l Fida and Makrizi, are important chiefly for the later period. Various attempts have been made, on the basis of this material, to reconstruct the earlier history. It has been supposed that there were two or three different sects, each founded by a Dositheus. Krauss[2] mentions ten men bearing this name. This scholar identifies the founder of the sect, which continued to exist into Muslim times, with Theodosius, one of the two Samaritans who, according to Josephus,[3] disputed with Andronicus before Ptolemy VII. Philometor (181–145 B.C.) and were put to death by this king for failing to prove that the true temple was on Mt. Gerizim. There is no evidence to prove either the identity of the two or the historical character of the legend. Another Dositheus is supposed by Krauss to be a disciple of Simon Magus and founder of a Christian sect referred to by Origen. Montgomery[4] rejects the identification with Theodosius, but thinks that the first founder of a Dosithean sect may have opposed the Jews in Egypt at some time before the Christian era, while another Dositheus founded a different sect in the beginning of this era, the latter being distinguished by its belief in a resurrection, its practice of the ritual bath, and its inclination to asceticism and mysticism. But most of the ancient testimony connects Dositheus with Simon Magus (*q.v.*) either as his teacher or as his disciple. When the *Clementine Recognitions*, Philaster, pseudo-Tertullian, and Jerome derive the Sadducees (*q.v.*) from the Dositheans, it is to be remembered that they imagined absence of a belief in the Resurrection to be an innovation, and, as they knew some Dositheans in their own time to reject this doctrine, they charged them with having started this heresy. They evidently thought that Dositheus had appeared some time before the public ministry of Jesus and had been a predecessor of Simon Magus. This is indeed likely to have been the fact. As the importance of Simon Magus waxed, that of Dositheus waned, and the latter was relegated to a secondary place as disciple of the former. Dositheus may have been a *goët*, regarded by a Samaritan party as the *taheb*, or Joshua returned to life, to lead a new conquest and fulfil the promises given to Abraham; and Krauss[5] may possibly be right in connecting him with the insurrection quelled by Pontius Pilate in A.D. 35.[6] There does not seem to be any real need

1 *Samarien und seine Propheten*, p. 114 f.
2 Jos. *Ant.* XIII. ix. 1.
3 Mac $5^{21ff.}$
4 *Israelitische und jüdische Geschichte*[7], Berlin, 1914, p. 247 f.
5 *Mitteilungen*, iv. 134 ff.
6 *Annales Samaritani*, p. 131.

1 *REJ* xliii. 50 ff.
2 *Ib.* xlii. 32.
3 *Ant.* XIII. iii. 4.
4 *The Samaritans*, p. 262 ff.
5 *REJ* xlii. 36.
6 Jos. *Ant.* XVIII. iv. 1.

of assuming a second Dositheus. In view of the strong evidence to the contrary from different periods, it cannot be successfully maintained that all Dositheans believed in the Resurrection. The Dositheans known to Epiphanius 'confessed a resurrection,'[1] and there are other indications of this belief in the history of the sect. At the time when the Samaritans generally accepted this doctrine (4th cent. A.D.), it is natural that it should also have been adopted by some of the Dositheans, and that they should have ascribed it to the original founder. But this seems to have been a temporary development within the sect. From Eulogius to Shahrastānī there is no trace of it. Even the omission of the formula, 'Blessed be God forever,' may, as Montgomery intimates,[2] be due to a desire the more emphatically to deny a life beyond. Neither a transient belief in some circles in the resurrection of the dead, nor the later legends clustering about the founder, nor the older peculiarities mentioned by Epiphanius, such as abstinence from animal food, sexual continence, and mysticism, can justify the assumption of a second Dositheus and a separate sect. Rigoristic interpretation of the Law, ritual washings, asceticism, and a penchant for mystical literature found their way into many of these sects; and the descriptions of the Dustan, or Dositheans, by Abu'l Fatḥ and the Arabic writers show the perseverance of such characteristerics in the main body of the followers of Dositheus. Abu'l Fatḥ mentions a number of minor sects apparently sprung from the Dositheans. They were distinguished by such names as Abunai, Katitai, Sadukai, Foskutai, sons of Yosudak, followers of Aulian, and disciples of Sakta ben Tabim; the Katitai declared the Law to have been abolished, the Saktai did not visit Mt. Gerizim, and the followers of Aulian were communists.

Was there a Simonian sect among the Samaritans? The existence of a religious body known as **Simonians** is not in doubt. It is clear that Justin,[3] Irenæus,[4] and Hippolytus[5] believed Simon Magus to be the founder, and inferred from Ac 8^{9-25} that he and the multitudes who acclaimed him 'the great power of God' were Samaritans. The historical character of Simon Magus has been questioned in modern times, and the origin of the sect ascribed by some scholars to a Christian Gnostic of the 2nd century.[6] There is not sufficient evidence, however, to maintain either of these positions. In Samaritan tradition, manifestly influenced by Christian sources, Simon is remembered only as a wonder-worker and an opponent of Christianity. If Simon was actually baptized into the name of Jesus, this would inevitably tend to break up the Simonians as a Samaritan sect; and, if as a Christian his thought continued to move in the direction of later Gnostic speculation, this would naturally affect his fellow-converts among the Samaritans, and would, after all, best account for the characteristics of the Simonian sect described by Justin, Irenæus, Origen, and Hippolytus.

LITERATURE.—**Justin**, ed. J. C. T. de Otto, 3 vols., Jena, 1876–81; **Hippolytus**, *Philosophumena*, ed. P. Cruice, Paris, 1860; **Origen**, ed. P. Koetschau, 5 vols., Leipzig, 1899–1913; **Eusebius**, ii. ed. E. Schwartz, do. 1903; *Clementis Homiliæ*, ed. P. de Lagarde, Göttingen, 1865; *S. Clementis Romani Recognitiones*, ed. E. G. Gersdorf, Leipzig, 1838; *Clementis Romani Recognitiones Syriace*, ed. Lagarde, do. 1861; **Epiphanius**, ed. Karl Holl, do. 1915; other patristic writers in Migne, *PG*; **E. Vilmar**, *Abulfáthi Annales Samaritani*, Gotha, 1865; **Silvestre de Sacy**, *Chrestomathie arabe*², 3 vols., Paris, 1827; **S. Krauss**, 'Dosithée, et les Dosithéens,' in *REJ* xlii. [1901] 27 ff.; **A. Büchler**, 'Les Dosithéens dans le Midrasch,' *ib.* p. 220 ff.; **T. G. J. Juynboll**, *Commentarii in historiam gentis Samaritanæ*, Leyden, 1846, *Chronicon Samaritanum*, do. 1848; **J. Grimm**, *Die Samariter und ihre Stellung in der Weltgeschichte*, Munich, 1854; **J. W. Nutt**, *Fragments of a Samaritan Targum*, London, 1874; **M. Appel**, *Quæstiones de rebus Samaritanorum sub imperio Romano peractis*, Breslau, 1874; **G. Salmon** and **J. M. Fuller**, art. 'Dositheus,' in *DCB*; **R. A. Lipsius**, *Die apokryphen Apostelgeschichten und Apostel-legenden*, 2 vols., Brunswick, 1883–84; **A. Hilgenfeld**, *Die Ketzergeschichte des Urchristentums*, Leipzig, 1884; **Paul de Lagarde**, *Mitteilungen*, Göttingen, 1884–91, iv. 134 ff.; **J. Kreyenbühl**, *Das Evangelium der Wahrheit*, 2 vols., Berlin, 1900-05; **K. F. A. Lincke**, *Samarien und seine Propheten*, Tübingen, 1903; **P. W. Schmiedel**, 'Simon Magus,' in *EBi*; **W. Bousset**, *Hauptprobleme der Gnosis*, Göttingen, 1907; **J. A. Montgomery**, *The Samaritans the earliest Jewish Sect*, Philadelphia, 1907; **W. Brandt**, 'Die jüdischen Baptismen,' *ZATW* xviii. [Giessen, 1910].

N. SCHMIDT.

[1] *Hær.* i. 13.
[2] P. 262.
[3] *Apol.* i. 26, 56, ii. 15.
[4] I. xxiii. 4.
[5] vi. 15.
[6] See art. SIMON MAGUS.

SECTS (Zoroastrian).—The emergence of distinct and properly called sects in the Zarathushtrian fold cannot, apparently, be definitely traced before Sasanian times (226–652 A.D.).

It must not, however, be inferred from this fact that complete uniformity of creed and religious practice obtained in Mazdæism before that period, or at any time from the days of Zarathushtra to the end of the Parthian domination. Throughout the Avesta passages occur revealing conditions of strong religious conflict in thought and usage. It is true that the chief opponents of the orthodox Mazdayasnians, especially in the *Gāthās*, were the adherents of the old naturalistic religion, led by the *kavis* and *karapans*—the priests of the nature pantheon. Still it would scarcely be safe to assume that the gulf that separates the rival parties is, in all instances, as wide as that which divided nature-worship from the Mazdæism of Zarathushtra or his immediate followers. Two considerations should be given their due weight in the interpretation of allusions to religious antagonists in the Avesta. In the first place, the degree of vehemence with which religious opponents are assailed and denounced is not always a true measure of the essential difference of the rival creeds; for the bitterest denunciations of the Zarathushtrians of the Avesta can be paralleled in the mutual anathemas of the various sects of almost every religion. And it is significant that the connotation which tradition[1] assigns to the names *kavis* and *karapans*, viz. 'blind' and 'deaf' respectively, exactly corresponds to the epithets with which Mihr Narsih,[2] the minister of Yazdagird II., stigmatizes those who did not hold the belief of the Mazdayasnians; and yet that dignitary immediately proceeds to set forth as part of the Mazdayasnian creed a doctrine which, as we shall see below, those in the direct doctrinal succession of the Gāthic Zoroastrians must have entirely repudiated.

Secondly, a religious community which recognized equally, as the basis of its creed and practice, the polytheistic *Yashts* and the monotheistic *Gāthās* could scarcely expect to achieve anything approaching unity of faith or religious usage. Hence there must have existed, even from late Achæmenian times, between the two extremes of Gāthic Mazdayasnians on the one hand and those converts who remained but little removed from nature-worship on the other, a large number of communities holding as many varieties, professedly, of the same creed. Nevertheless our only definite evidence of this is the presence of these divergent oracles in the same canon.

The establishment of Zarathushtrian Mazdæism as the state religion by the Sasanians (*q.v.*) no doubt gave a new impulse to the process of systematization and closer definition of religious dogma, and hence the cleavage between the

[1] See W. Geiger, *Civilization of the Eastern Iranians*, tr. Dārāb D. P. Sanjānā, London, 1885–86, ii. 49 f.
[2] See Elisæus, *The History of Vartan*, tr. C. F. Neumann, London, 1830, p. 11 ff.

different teachings would be more distinctly revealed. The Pahlavi literature, strange as it may seem, contains no explicit allusions to the sects, known from other sources to exist in the Zoroastrian Church of Sasanian and early Muslim days, though the influence of the doctrines of the sectaries is discernible in some of them. With one exception—the small tract called *'Ulamā-i-Islām*,[1] whose author was almost certainly a member of the sect of which he writes—we are dependent for our knowledge of the sects of Zoroastrianism upon non-Zoroastrian works, of which the most extensive is that of the Muslim historian Shahrastānī[2] († A.D. 1153).

In addition to the two great heretical sects, the Manichæans and the followers of Mazdak, which really represented distinct religious systems, and are therefore treated in this work under their respective titles, Shahrastānī describes the tenets of two main sects which deviated from the position of the Zarathushtrians as represented in the Avesta.

1. Zarvanists.—By far the more important of the two were the Zarvanists. They derived their appellation from Zrvan or Zarvan (mod. Pers. زروان), Time, whose place in their conception of theogony is generally regarded as the distinctive doctrine of the sect. In the Avesta,[3] it will be remembered, 'the Good Spirit' is said to have created 'in endless time' (*zrvan akarana*), indicating, probably, that he was gifted with 'boundless time,' or eternity, as an attribute. In other passages[4] Zrvan[5] is praised as a *yazata*, or lesser divinity. According to the Zarvanist theory, he is neither an attribute nor a deity, but a primal source of deity, a *fons deitatis*. Moreover, not only did Ormazd owe his existence ultimately to Zrvan, but Ahriman also was derived from the same source. Thus it was sought to resolve the dualism which the orthodox faith seemed to have failed to achieve.[6] As to the details of the Zarvanist theogony there seemed to have been no unanimity. According to the *'Ulamā-i-Islām*, the origin of Ormazd from Zrvan was not direct, but mediated by the union of fire and water, which were first created, although creation was, according to this sect, a function not of Zrvan, but of Ormazd, as in the orthodox faith.

Shahrastānī and the Armenian writers[7] make no mention of any intermediary, but describe in a somewhat naive manner the conception and birth of Ormazd and Ahriman from Zrvan. According to the Armenian account, Zrvan had offered sacrifices for 1000 years in the hope of begetting a son who would bring creation into being. Shahrastānī extends the period during which Zrvan had whispered that desire to himself to 9999 years. At the end of the period all agree that misgiving assailed Zrvan and from that doubt Ahriman was conceived, although Ormazd was simultaneously generated in the womb through Zrvan's knowledge. When Zrvan realized this, he vowed to give the sovereignty to the first-born; whereupon Ahriman, although at the time the farther from the birth, perforated the womb and became the first-born. When he stood before his father to claim the sovereignty, Zrvan despised him on account of his ugliness and depravity and endeavoured to repudiate him, but owing to his vow he was constrained to grant him the lordship of the world, though in a somewhat limited form, for 9000 years.

The Zarvanists were by no means agreed among themselves as to the origin of Ahriman or as to his function in the scheme of things. Some held, according to Shahrastānī, that there was some evil principle in God eternally. Others maintained, according to the *'Ulamā-i-Islām*, that Ahriman was a fallen angel, thus agreeing with the Biblical conception. We may legitimately suspect Christian influence here. It is equally clear that the Zarvanists differed as widely among themselves as to the motive of Zrvan in the creation of Ahriman. Some held that his function was to prove to Ormazd the absolute power of Zrvan; others maintained that the two spirits were necessary for the production of variety in creation: while others again despaired of discovering the *raison d'être* of Ahriman, and regarded his existence almost as a mishap. In addition to their distinctive doctrine of theogony the Zarvanists had developed a system of cosmology which also differed in important respects from that of the Avesta.[1] The *'Ulamā-i-Islām* relates that, in the great conflict between the powers of light and the forces of darkness, seven demons were taken captive and chained to the heavens, but Ormazd changed their names and assigned to each of them a special sphere in the sky. The names prove to be the same as those given to the *apakhtars*, or planets, in the *Bundahishn*. These the Zarvanists evidently regarded as inimical to man, whereas they held the constellations to be friendly and helpful to him.[2] F. Spiegel[3] contends strongly that it was in their cosmology rather than in their theogony that the Zarvanist tenets differed from the accepted teaching of the Zoroastrian Church of Sasanian times. We may admit that Zarvanist cosmology may have been their major contribution to Zoroastrian thought, and that evident traces of Babylonian astrology can be detected in their teaching; but we can scarcely go so far as Spiegel[4] does in saying that their peculiar views on the nature of God were a matter of indifference in the Zoroastrian Church of the Sasanian period.[5] Nor do the special mention which the Zarvanist creed receives in the edict of Mihr Narsih and the fact that in his refutation of heresies Eznik confines himself to the Zarvanist doctrine warrant the conclusion that they were co-extensive with the whole or even the major part of the Church of those days. The latter fact may only prove that their theological doctrine was regarded by Eznik as by far the most pernicious.

Finally, there is much to connect the Zarvanist teaching with the strong fatalistic element that runs through some of the Pahlavi books.[6] Eznik explains the term 'Zrvan' as signifying 'fortune' (*bakht*). Theodore of Mopsuestia[7] similarly interprets the name (Ζαρουάμ ὅν ἀρχηγὸν πάντων εἰσάγει ὅν καὶ τύχην καλεῖ). The modern Persian term, روزگار, especially in the *Shāhnāmah*, signifies both 'time' and 'fortune'; and the frequent employment of *sipihr*, 'heavens,' and *charkh* in the same

1 *Fragmens relatifs à la religion de Zoroastre: extraits des manuscrits persiens*, ed. J. Mohl, Paris, 1819, pp. 1–5, Germ. tr. J. Vullers, Bonn, 1831, pp. 43–67.
2 *Kitābu'l-Milal wān-Niḥal*, Arab. text by W. Cureton, 1846, Germ. tr. T. Haarbrücker, Brunswick, 1850.
3 *Vend.* xix. 33.
4 *Ib.* xix. 44, 55; *Ny.* i. 8, etc.
5 As to the antiquity of Zarvanism, N. Söderblom (*La Vie future, d'après le Mazdéism*, Paris, 1901, p. 248, note 2) reminds us that Berosus relates that Zrvan was a king, from which it is concluded (see M. Bréal, *Mélanges de mythologie et de linguistique*, Paris, 1877, p. 214) that Zarvanism goes back to the 4th cent. A.D.
6 Paulus Persa tells us that in his day (6th cent. A.D.) many opinions were held as to the nature of God: 'There are some who believe in only one God; others maintain that he is not the only God. Some teach that he possesses contrary attributes,' etc. (*Logica*, *ap.* J. P. N. Land, *Anecdota Syriaca*, Leyden, 1862–75, vol. iv., Lat. tr. p. 2).
7 Eznik (5th cent.), tr. in John Wilson, *The Parsi Religion*, Bombay, 1843, p. 542 f.; also Elisæus, *op. cit.*

1 See art. COSMOGONY AND COSMOLOGY (Iranian).
2 Cf. *Maīnōg-ī-Khraṭ*, viii. 17 (ed. E. W. West, *SBE* xxiv. [1885] 34).
3 *Eran. Alterthumskunde*, Leipzig, 1871–78, ii. 184.
4 *Loc. cit.*
5 See also J. H. Moulton, *The Treasure of the Magi*, Oxford, 1917, p. 189.
6 See art. FATE (Iranian).
7 *Ap.* Photius, *Bibl.* 81.

book, as metaphors for 'fate' and 'chance,' evidences perhaps the fatalistic tendency of Zarvanist astral lore. It may therefore be unnecessary to assume the existence of a separate sect of fatalists.[1]

2. Gayomarthians.—The other sect, clearly of far less importance, was the Gayomarthians. For their tenets we are almost entirely beholden to Shahrastānī's account. They believed in the existence of two principles or beings, Yazdān (God, *i.e.* Ormazd) and Ahriman. Yazdān is eternal, Ahriman derived and created. The origin of the latter is accounted for in much the same way as in some of the views attributed to the Zarvanists. A thought that crossed the mind of Yazdān, as to the kind of being his rival (if such existed) would be, was not in harmony with the nature of light, and thus darkness (which was called Ahriman) resulted from that thought. The essential opposition in the nature of the two beings inevitably led to a bitter conflict between them, just as is related in the Avesta. The new element here, however, is that an angel appears as mediator, and peace is made between the warring spirits on condition that the lower world, or earth, should belong to Ahriman for 7000 years, but that at the end of the period he should surrender it to light; yet those who were in the world before peace was made were to be assigned to the evil one.

Then there appeared the man Gayomarth and the ox; but both were killed, and in the man's place there sprang up a plant, *rībās*, and from the root of the plant sprang a man, *mīsha*, and a woman, *mīshāna*. They were the parents of the human race. In the place of the ox there came the domestic and other animals. Man as yet was only spirit, but now he was allowed the option of being carried away to the realms of Ahriman, on the one hand, or, on the other, of being clothed in bodily form and entering upon the conflict with Ahriman, with an assurance of the support of light and of final victory over the forces of darkness and entrance into the state of resurrection.

3. Saisāniya.—From the Zarathushtrians, *i.e.* apparently the orthodox section of adherents of Mazdæism, there originated at the time of Abu Muslim Sāhib-u'd-Dawlah († A.D. 755) a small sect which Shahrastānī calls Saisāniya or Bihāfridiya. Their founder was a certain Khawwāf from the neighbourhood of Nishapur. His secession seems to have been due mainly to his objection to next-of-kin marriage (*khvētōk-das*) and the drinking of wine, in which it is natural to suspect traces of Muslim influence. Shahrastānī also says that he was strongly opposed to fire-worship, which brought upon him the wrath of the *mobed*, at whose bidding probably Abu Muslim ordered him to be put to death. His followers are credited also with aversion to killing and eating the flesh of any animal until it was old. They acquired for their own possession the houses of strangers, and were lavish in their expenditure. After the death of their founder we have no record of the doings of this sect, but Shahrastānī relates that they believed him to have ascended on a yellow horse to heaven, whence he would return to take vengeance upon his enemies.

A Persian work entitled *Dabistān-i-Mazāhib*, written by Muhsin-i-Fāni in the 17th cent., claims to supply us with an account of some thirteen or fourteen Parsi sects. For two reasons, at least, no discussion of those sects is included in this article: in the first place, the historical value of the *Dabistān*, and especially of the *Dasātir* (whence the materials of the *Dabistān* in that part of it are drawn), has been seriously impugned by some of the highest authorities;[1] in the second place, inasmuch as we have no other account or mention of those sects by which to compare and check notices so overlaid with purely legendary lore as we find Muhsin-i-Fāni's account of the Parsi sects to be,[2] we do not possess the necessary data to pronounce a considered opinion upon them.

The reader may consult that work in the original Persian, of which many lithographed texts exist, or in the English translation of D. Shea and A. Troyer, *The Dabistān or School of Manners*, 3 vols., Paris, 1843.

LITERATURE.—In addition to the works already referred to, see L. C. Casartelli, *La Philosophie religieuse du Mazdéisme sous les Sassanides*, Louvain, 1884, Eng. tr., Bombay, 1889; *Avesta: Livre sacré du Zoroastrisme*², tr. C. de Harlez, Paris, 1881, Introd. pp. lxxxiv–lxxxviii.

E. EDWARDS.

1 See, however, M. N. Dhalla, *Zoroastrian Theology*, New York, 1914, pp. 205–208.

SECULARISM.

1. Antecedents.—Secularism may be described as a movement, intentionally ethical, negatively religious, with political and philosophical antecedents. Founded with the express intention of providing a certain theory of life and conduct, it follows that in its positive aspect it is ethical. Since it undertook to do this without reference to a deity or a future life, and thus proposed to fulfil a function of religion, apart from religious associations, it may be regarded as negatively religious. Its origin, however, was primarily due to certain political conditions and philosophical influences.

Politically, secularism sprang from the turmoil which preceded, and still more from that which followed, the passing of the Reform Bill in 1832. Its matrix was provided in the somewhat incoherent socialism of Robert Owen and his followers and in the ill-fated Chartist movement. It came to birth shortly after the collapse of the revolutionary hopes which had been inspired in the extreme Chartists by the Continental revolutions of 1848. It was, therefore, in some measure, a recognition of the necessity of attempting to further social and political progress by the quieter methods of organization and education.

It is impossible to ignore the fact that serious social wrongs produced the reaction of which secularism was one of the fruits. The selfishness of the wealthy and influential classes, the unreasoning opposition to political and religious freedom, the stolid dogmatism of theology, were all powerful irritants; and it is not to be thought strange that, among the working-classes, consciousness of such a state of things begot not only extreme political theories, but the tendency to anti-religious reaction. Secularism was essentially a protest-movement. It possessed the vehement character of all such movements and the driving-force of the passions which they arouse. At the same time, it inherited the inevitable defects—the tendency to destructive rather than constructive action, the warping influence of heated feeling, the limited outlook, and the negationism—which inhere in all movements that are primarily reaction against established facts. Although it is true that secularism was an attempt to provide a positive policy, its positive nature was based upon a specific limitation of range and outlook, rendered possible only by reason of prejudice against the religious implications of life and conduct, which secularism refused to take into consideration. It proved impossible, therefore, as the history of secularism shows, for the movement to disentangle itself from the political and social passions out of which it arose.

The philosophical roots of secularism run back

1 E. G. Browne, *A Literary Hist. of Persia*, London, 1902–06, i. 53–56; also A. W. von Schlegel, *Réflexions sur l'étude des langues des Asiatiques*⁴, Bonn and Paris, 1832, p. 51 f.

2 This remark is not necessarily applicable to other than the accounts of Parsi sects.

to the 'associationist' school of James Mill (*q.v.*) and Jeremy Bentham, with an anti-theistic strain inherited from Thomas Paine and Richard Carlile. Secularism also reveals the influence of positivism (*q.v.*), of which it was in part the English re-echo. Although avoiding the positivist religion and refusing to constitute humanity as a deity, it espoused a theory of knowledge essentially positivistic. This influence was, however, imported into secularism chiefly at second hand, through G. H. Lewes and J. S. Mill (*q.v.*) in particular. The principles of secularism were submitted to the latter and received his approval. It was, accordingly, the British utilitarians who were philosophically the sponsors of secularism.

Whilst the main impulses of the movement were derived from the social and political conditions which roused its founders to rebel against the accepted doctrines of life and thought prevalent in their day, its collateral influences were philosophical. This was necessarily so, since its avowed separation from religion made it incumbent upon secularism to establish its claim to furnish a theory of life and conduct by an appeal to philosophy, and especially ethics. Positivism supplied a conception of knowledge affording a basis upon which it was held that religious considerations could be ruled out, and utilitarianism (*q.v.*) lent itself to a non-religious explanation of the motives and ends of conduct. In these theories, therefore, the requisite ground for secularism was given.

2. The founders.—Secularism owes its name, and in large measure its existence, to the life and labours of George Jacob Holyoake.

Holyoake was born in Birmingham in 1817. His parents were hard-working artisans, and his upbringing was religious. The atmosphere of the town of his birth and the circumstances of his own childhood aroused in him strong social and political convictions, which were fanned into flame by the passing of the Reform Bill in 1832, at which time Holyoake was an impressionable lad of fifteen. He became estranged from the Churches because of their lack of social sympathy, and made his first ventures into political life as an Owenite 'social missionary.' Subsequently he was associated with Chartism (*q.v.*), and after the failure of that movement his later years revealed him as an advanced Radical. About the year 1841 he definitely abandoned belief in God, and his antipathy to Christianity was deepened by a somewhat unjust term of imprisonment imposed upon him at Cheltenham for 'blasphemy.' At the same time Holyoake never appears to have felt himself in sympathy with the dogmatic atheism of his day. His atheism was rather agnosticism (*q.v.*), and in one of the many periodicals with which he was from time to time associated, *The Reasoner*, he wrote: 'We are not infidels if that term implies rejection of Christian truth, since all we reject is Christian error.' During his life he was frequently in association with Christians who shared his social and political sympathies, and his attitude towards the 'Christian socialism' of Maurice (*q.v.*) and Kingsley reveals his union of aim so far as socialism was concerned, equally with his dislike of the doctrinal significance which he felt was conveyed by the term 'Christian.' For many years Holyoake was honourably connected with the welfare of the co-operative movement.[1] In middle life he settled in London as a bookseller, and among his many interests the struggle of Italy for freedom found a characteristic place. He counted in the circle of his friends both Garibaldi and Mazzini, and busied himself with promoting the unlucky 'English Legion' that sailed to their assistance. In later life he settled at Brighton, where he died in 1906, agitator and enthusiast to the end, welcoming almost with his last breath the Liberal victory at the General Election early in that year.

During his long life Holyoake was associated more or less sympathetically with the men whose anti-Christian propaganda was the storm-centre of the 19th cent.; and yet at the same time he maintained, especially in his later life, cordial relations with eminent supporters of Christianity, including W. E. Gladstone, who regarded him as an honest and single-minded opponent. None of the associates of Charles Bradlaugh was so generally esteemed among their opponents as Holyoake, and a number of attacks made upon him by members of his own party are significant testimony to the fairness and independence of Holyoake's judgment.

[1] See art. Co-operation.

Among Holyoake's companions in establishing secularism may be named Charles Southwell, Thomas Cooper (afterwards converted to Christianity), Thomas Paterson, and William Chilton. The movement originated in 1849, and was expressly regarded by Holyoake as an alternative to atheism.[1] In 1850 Holyoake met Bradlaugh, and in the subsequent year coined the term 'secularism,' after some hesitation as to the merits of 'netheism' and 'limitationism' as alternatives, 'as best indicating that province of duty which belongs to this life.' Secularism was intended to differentiate Holyoake's anti-theistic position from Bradlaugh's atheistic pronouncements, and, although Bradlaugh, Charles Watts, G. W. Foote, and other atheists were identified with the secular movement, Holyoake always endeavoured to make it possible that the social, political, and ethical aims of secularism should not necessitate subscription to atheistic belief, in the hope that liberal-minded theists might, without prejudice to their theism, join in promoting these ends—an attitude to which he persisted in clinging, despite the small success which it achieved.

3. Principles.—The essential principle of secularism is to seek for human improvement by material means alone. It holds that such means are the more important, because the more proximate; and that, independently and in themselves, they are adequate to secure the desired end.

Secularism arose and developed at a period when the relations of science and religion were beginning to be regarded as those of sharp opposition. In harmony with that notion, it proclaimed the independence of secular truth. Secular knowledge is founded upon the experience of this life and can be maintained and tested by reason at work in experience. It conceived that, just as mathematics, physics, and chemistry were 'secular' sciences, so it would be possible on the same lines to establish a secular theory of the conduct and welfare of life, and to add the instruction of the conscience to instruction in the sciences, in a similar manner and on similar conditions.

The relations of secularism to religion were accordingly defined as mutually exclusive rather than hostile. Theology professes to interpret the unknown world. Secularism is wholly unconcerned with that world and its interpretation. It deals with the known world interpreted by experience and neither offers nor forbids any opinion regarding another life. Neither theism nor atheism enters into the secularist scheme, because neither is provable by experience. In so far as Christianity is moral, secularism has common ground with it, but it offers a basis for morality wholly independent of all Christian belief and one that will appeal to those who, for various reasons, are dissatisfied with theology. It submits that complete morality is attainable by, and can be based upon, secular considerations alone, just as all the uses for which the house was designed can be fulfilled without reference to the architect who may have designed it. It does not assert that there is no light elsewhere, but that such light adds nothing to the pursuit of human ends. Unless dogma actively interferes with human happiness, secularism is content to leave it to flourish or perish as it may.

Historically, secularism has been intermingled with atheism throughout its course, but Holyoake always insisted that the two were distinct. On secularist principles, he was willing to associate with Bradlaugh and equally ready to associate with any theist who would unite with him in seeking the mutual improvement of the race by secular means. He regarded both theism and

[1] See art. Atheism, § 6.

atheism as what would now be called 'overbelief.' In contrast with Holyoake, Bradlaugh considered that secularism was bound to contest theistic belief and that material progress was impossible so long as 'superstition' so powerfully manifested itself.

Secularism held that its principles could be established and sustained by the intellect as principles of reason and intelligence equally applicable to all humanity. It contended that morality was based upon reason and that error lay in knowledge rather than intention. Holyoake thought it possible to establish material conditions which would eradicate poverty and depravity. With the utilitarians he held it as self-evident that morality was the conduct which establishes the common welfare, and he thought that science could teach the laws of happiness equally with the laws of health. To that end we must be guided by reason, believing not what we desire, which gives the condition neither of certainty nor of uniformity, but that which reason can vindicate. To fulfil this function, reason must be left unfettered. Ethical and religious research must be as free as scientific research. There must be no penalties, legal or spiritual, for any investigation, criticism, or publicity. In this aspect of a reasonable theory of life secularism fulfils a function which it regards religion as imperfectly serving. It 'takes truth for authority, not authority for truth' and 'substitutes the piety of usefulness for the usefulness of piety.' What is best for man will be determined by reason tested by experience and will surely be approved by 'the Author of humanity.' The new piety exhibits itself in self-help and 'vexes not the ears of the All-wise with capricious supplications.'[1] Recognizing that we are wholly ruled by general laws, man's duty is to study them and live by them.

4. Progress and prospects.—The influence of secularism was most apparent during the middle of the 19th cent., when the movement flourished to a not inconsiderable extent among its allies in the anti-Christian reaction of the period. Latterly it has decayed rapidly and has almost disappeared from independent existence, being merged in such organized rationalism (*q.v.*) as now represents the more recent phases of the secular spirit. It is significant that the best days of secularism coincided with the definitely anti-religious propaganda of those of its sympathizers who, like Bradlaugh, joined with secularism what Holyoake refused to regard as essential to it, namely atheism. The atheistic controversy ended, the old animosities centred in it have softened, a less extreme view of the opposition of science and religion has prevailed, and with these things much of the *motif* of secularism has passed away. It is not likely to revive as an organized movement. The question is rather whether its spirit and principles are destined to continue in being. Secularism proposed a limitation of human knowledge and interest to the material sphere — an attitude which, whilst possible, and indeed often actual, in practice, is impossible to justify or establish from the theoretical standpoint, as secularism essayed to do.

In practice there are millions whose interests and concerns are confined to the material aspects of life. This attitude is practicable because they have no conscious theory of life and conduct. No such theory is needed. It is its absence that makes practical secularism possible. The weakness of secularism lies in the fact that it offers needless and insufficient reasons to mankind for doing what they can and will do without requiring reasons. It is much the same as if one should propose to afford a philosophical basis for the natural realism of 'the plain man,' which regards the evidence of the senses as indisputable testimony to the existence of an external reality which is what it appears to be. In practice no such basis is needed. In theory it cannot be given; for the first steps in philosophy reveal the insufficiency of 'the plain man's' assumptions. So it is with secularism. Many are secular in practice, but any theory of life or conduct is bound to discuss the questions which secularism attempts to ignore. Though Holyoake claimed that secularism was a theory of life and conduct, in reality it is the renunciation of one, like agnosticism, with which it is closely allied. As such it is needless, and it fails because it has no place to fill. In practice one can limit one's interests without a theory of limitation, and negate without a theory of negation. When, however, we propose to ask why we should limit our knowledge, we are obliged to take up an attitude of reception or rejection, not merely one of ignoring, in face of the claims of religion to afford a knowledge of other than material concerns. In this matter Bradlaugh acted more consistently than Holyoake, and his action is confirmed by the fact that secularism was most vigorous when linked with anti-religious views. The attempt to ignore rather than deny religion is impractical, because religion embraces both secular and spiritual concerns. Religion denies the secular conception of life, and that conception cannot establish itself without defeating the claim of religion to control life. It is an impossible proposition to maintain that there may be a God, but that He does not concern material existence. Whoever believes in God believes in Him *ex hypothesi* as the greatest of all realities. Whilst it is true that in practice a believer in God may be sufficiently inconsistent to neglect the implication of his belief upon conduct, it is impossible to construct a satisfactory theory to justify this course. It is for this reason that a secularism which does not include a definitely anti-religious theory is bound to fail.

From the philosophical side, the weakness of secularism, as Holyoake presented it, consists in an inability to appreciate the distinction between fact and value—a failure which is perhaps attributable to the dogmatic certainty which characterized the claims set forth in the name of science in the middle of the 19th century. Whilst 'facts,' *i.e.* abstractions from experience considered by themselves, as science regards them, may be treated as matters of intellectual knowledge alone, the worth and permanence of values are posited only by an act of faith. In attempting to construct an ethical system of facts, analogous to mathematics or chemistry, to deal with knowledge and not with faith, secularism reveals its ignorance of a fundamental distinction. It proposed to decide between competing values by a standard of fact, and spoke of truth and reason without any clear understanding of the relation of these terms to value, as if they gave self-evident proof of the existence of values and obvious means of distinguishing between competing values. Whilst utilitarianism — the philosophical theory which gave most impetus to secularism—prevailed, it was possible to uphold, to some extent at least, the secularist ethic, but the collapse of utilitarianism involved the failure of the movement based, on the philosophical side at least, upon its premisses.

For these reasons it does not seem apparent that secularism is destined to survive as a theory of life and conduct, and it must be regarded as a movement arising out of, and passing with, the conditions of its time. Whilst its ethical aims were honourable, it lacked an adequate basis upon

[1] Holyoake, art. 'Secularism,' in Chambers's *Encyclopædia*.

which to establish itself as a permanent feature of human thought.

LITERATURE.—G. J. Holyoake, *Principles of Secularism*, London, 1859, *The Trial of Theism*, do. 1858, *The Limits of Atheism*, do. 1861, *The Origin and Nature of Secularism*, do. 1896. See also *The Secular Review*, vol. i., do. 1876–77, *The Present Day*, 3 vols., do. 1883–86, both ed. by Holyoake, whose autobiography is contained in *Sixty Years of an Agitator's Life*, 2 vols., do. 1892, and in *Bygones worth Remembering*, 2 vols., do. 1905; J. McCabe, *Life and Letters of George Jacob Holyoake*, 2 vols., do. 1908; C. W. F. Goss, *Descriptive Bibliography of the Writings of G. J. Holyoake*, do. 1908; R. Flint, *Anti-Theistic Theories* (Baird Lecture for 1887), Edinburgh, 1879, pp. 211–249.

ERIC S. WATERHOUSE.

SEEKERS.—The Seekers, in the narrowest use of the term, formed a small sect of the Independents during the period of the English Commonwealth. In a broader and more accurate sense of the word, the name 'Seeker' covers a movement or tendency, both Continental and English, extending from the time of the Reformation in Germany to the middle of the 17th cent., the definite sect of the Seekers in England being the historical culmination of this movement.

The definite Seeker tendency, with its characteristic group of ideas, first comes to light in the writings of Sebastian Franck (1499–1542), a humanistic reformer of Schwabia. Franck[1] describes groups of Christians among the Anabaptists who desire to allow baptism and other ceremonies to remain in abeyance until God gives further commands, and those persons, he says, suspending for the time external ceremonies, *wait* and *seek* for fuller light. Dirck Coornhert, a Dutch theologian and reformer, born in Amsterdam in 1522, strongly developed the Seeker tendency, and through his influence the Seeker attitude took an important place in the thought of an interesting section of Dutch dissenters. Coornhert considered the existing Church, with its divisions, external organization, and outward ceremonies, as only an interim Church, and he held that the faithful shall quietly wait for the true apostolic, authoritative Church to be divinely commissioned, endowed, and inaugurated. The Seeker attitude, emphasized in the writings of Coornhert, was taken up by the societies of Dutch Collegiants, or Rynsburgers (*q.v.*), in the 17th cent. and made a central feature of this interesting movement. Daniel Van Breen, Adam Boreel, and Galenus Abrahams of the Amsterdam Collegium, or Society, were the leaders of this Seeker movement in Holland, though the most developed expression of it is found in a tract entitled *Lucerna super candelabro* (Amsterdam, 1662), probably written by Peter Balling, a Collegiant of Rynsburg, and translated into English by the Quaker, Benjamin Furley, under the title, *The Light on the Candlestick* (London, 1665). This tract and 'the Nineteen Articles' (1658) with their 'Further Exposition' (1659), issued by the Amsterdam Collegiants, give the fullest available account of Continental Seeker views. The visible Church, with its doctrines, or 'notions,' as they named them, its external organization, its outward ceremonies, is here thought of as devoid of real authority and spiritual power, as lost in the wilderness and in an apostate condition, while the true believer is one who waits and seeks for the Church of apostolic power which in the fullness of time God will establish with freshly-commissioned prophets whose authority will be verified by miraculous gifts. The same ideas reappear, in a more developed stage and in more cohesive form, in the groups of English Seekers during the Commonwealth.

The word 'Seekers,' as the name of a sect, with its definite religious connotation, first appears in England in *Truth's Champion* (London, 1617),

[1] *Chronica*, Strassburg, 1531.

probably written by John Morton, where 'Seekers' are described as a people opposed to everything external, who do not need to 'hear preaching nor read the Scriptures.' Even before this date, however, Bartholomew Legate, an English cloth-dealer, whose trade took him to Holland, had taught definite Seeker ideas. Henoch Clapham[1] makes Legate say that God is soon to give a new revelation through 'myraculous apostles' and a 'myraculous ministry' and that until this commission appears there is 'no true Church,' 'no true baptism,' 'no visible Christian.' Until God acts, man can only wait and seek. Legate plainly held the group of ideas which formed part of the Continental movement traced above. He was burned at Smithfield in 1612 as a heretic, suspected of holding Arian views.

Ephraim Pagitt gives an adequate account of the Seeker position:

> 'Many have wrangled so long about the Church that at last they have quite lost it, and go under the name of *Expecters* or *Seekers*, and do deny that there is any Church, or true minister, or any ordinances.'[2]

Edwards's *Gangræna* (London, 1646), Richard Baxter's accounts in *Reliquiæ Baxterianæ* (do. 1696), John Jackson's *A Sober Word to a Serious People* (do. 1651), and John Saltmarsh's *Sparkles of Glory* (do. 1648) give further and somewhat fuller description of the Seeker movement of the time. The following passage is sympathetic and on the whole a fair description of the main features of the movement:

> 'Firstly, they seek the mind of God in the Scriptures. Secondly, they judge that prayer and alms are to be attended to, and for this purpose they come together into some place on the First-days as their hearts are drawn forth and opportunity offers. Then they seek, firstly, that they may be instruments in the hand of the Lord to stir up the grace of God in one another, by mutual conference and communication of experience: and secondly, to wait for a further revelation. Thirdly, to hold out their testimony against the false, and for the pure ordinance of ministry and worship. They behave themselves as persons who have neither the power nor the gift to go before one another by way of eminency or authority, but as sheep unfolded, and as soldiers unrallied, waiting for a time of gathering. They acknowledge no other visible teacher but the Word and works of God, on whom they wait, for the grace which is to be brought at the revelation of Jesus Christ.'[3]

It is, however, through the writings and documents of the early Quakers that it has been possible to discover the extent of the movement in England and at the same time to find the real characteristics of the sect of Seekers.

The First Publishers of Truth, printed in 1907, which contains a historical account of the rise and spread of Quakerism, contains the fullest available accounts of the Seekers. They appear in these documents to be a sincere, earnest, spiritually-minded people, who have turned away from outward things and are endeavouring to discover the will of God and His divine leading by waiting in silence for the light to break forth. They are described as 'a seeking and religiously inclined people.' They appear to have had large meetings in the West Riding of Yorkshire, in Westmorland, and also in Bristol. Their meetings seem to have been held with long periods of silence and with opportunity for free, spontaneous, and unprepared messages, though there were evidently leaders in the local groups who often, probably usually, preached to them and interpreted to them the spiritual nature of Christianity as they conceived it. The Seeker groups described in the early Quaker documents went over almost entirely to the new movement inaugurated by George Fox, and the leaders of the Seeker societies became after 1652 the foremost preachers in the early Society of Friends (*q.v.*). From having been 'seekers' they now believed that they had become what

[1] *Error on the Right Hand*, London, 1608.
[2] *Heresiographie*, London, 1645, p. 128.
[3] Jackson, p. 3.

Cromwell once called 'happy finders.' After 1652 there is no indication of the continuation of a separate sect of Seekers, and the characteristic ideas which formed the body of their propaganda henceforth disappear from religious tractarian literature in England, though they continued somewhat longer to find expression in Holland.

LITERATURE.—J. C. van Slee, *De Rijnsburger Collegianten*, Haarlem, 1895; Hermann Weingarten, *Die Revolutionskirchen Englands*, Leipzig, 1868; D. Masson, *Life of Milton*, 6 vols., London, 1859–80; *The First Publishers of Truth*, ed. for the Friends' Historical Society by Norman Penney, do. 1907; *The Swaledale Papers*, in Devonshire House Library, given in extract in an art. by W. C. Braithwaite in *Journ. of the Friends' Historical Society*, v. [1908] 3 ff.; George Fox, *Journal*, ed. N. Penney, 2 vols., Cambridge, 1911, *The Great Mystery of the Great Whore*, London, 1659 (see esp. 'Epistle to the Reader,' written in 1658 by Edward Burrough); Rufus M. Jones, *Studies in Mystical Religion*, do. 1909, *Spiritual Reformers in the Sixteenth and Seventeenth Centuries*, do. 1914; William Charles Braithwaite, *Beginnings of Quakerism*, do. 1912.

RUFUS M. JONES.

SELF.—See PERSONALITY, EGO.

SELF (Buddhist).—In Buddhism the use and content of the term 'self,' both as separate word and as prefix, coincide largely with its use and content in Western religions and ethics. But the former system has some interesting features of divergent development to show—linguistic, psychological, ethical, and metaphysical.

Linguistically, *e.g.*, there is in Pāli the useful compound *atta-bhāva*, 'self-state' or 'self-hood,' meaning personality, individual life, the bodily and mental organism.

'I cannot remember, since I have had experience through this *attabhāva*, all its characteristics and habits; how then should I remember my various former existences?' [1]

'. . . each of the five organs of sense derived from the four great elements, included in the *attabhāva*.' [2]

It was consonant also with the old *Sutta* diction to use *atta* alone in this sense,[3] but the compound term superseded it.

It was used, wrote Buddhaghoṣa, 'both for the body and for all the corporeal and mental factors, foolish folk including these in the notion they hold that "This is myself" (or "my soul").' [4]

Again, there is the Pāli idiom of the dual self, a form of speech which corresponds to no psychologically conceived parallel, but in which one *atta* functions (instead of a personal pronoun) as the subject, the other as the object:

'These are the penalties of wrong-doing: self upbraids self.' [5]

'Any virtuous layman established in the fourfold peace can, if he will, confess self to self as being assured of happy rebirth.' [6]

'To whom is the self not dear? To evildoers, for . . . though they may say "Dear to us is the self," yet that which a foe would do to his foe, that do they by self to self.' [7]

'By self incite the self, examine self
By self; self-guarded thus, watchful of mind
And happy shalt thou live. For self of self
Is warder, unto self hath self recourse.
Therefore train well thyself.' [8]

Here we have a mode of psychical activity, known to psychological analysis, which bifurcates the unitary concept of the self, setting a self which is the accretion and outcome of experience—the 'character'—over against the self of the present moment, and so on.

Thus used, the former 'self' at times takes the place of our term 'conscience.'

'Doth self reproach thee not as to morals?' [9]
'There is not anywhere a place throughout the world
Where evil deeds may secretly be done.
The self doth know thee, Man, whether in truth
Thou didst it, or if it be false. O friend,
Thy better self [1] thou hold'st in mean repute,
Who within self hid'st evil from thyself.' [2]

'"Self-known" applies to one who reflects:—"Thus far am I in faith, morals, learning, self-surrender, insight, ready speech."' [3]

There are two adjectival forms of *atta*, neither of which has the meaning of our 'selfish.' The one, *attaniya*, is simply the adjective of relation, the other, *ajjhattika* (*adhi-att-ika*), is the same. But they are used in different connexions. The former is used with reference to soul, or ontological self. The latter is a purely psychological term, and is opposed to whatever is 'external' to one's self, corporeal and mental. Thus *ajjhattika* phenomena are the activities of the five senses and of the ideating factor or mind. External phenomena are objects of sense and images—mental constructions objectified. The former phenomena are 'self-referable, one's own, referable to the person, bodily and mental.'[4] And, because the corporeal factor is included, our modern term 'subjective' does not always form a fit rendering.

It is clear from the foregoing linguistic considerations that, whatever restrictions the religious philosophy of Buddhism imposed upon the metaphysical implications of the term and concept of 'self,' the use of it as a convenient label for the totality of any living individual was by that philosophy both approved and exploited. As such a label, it belonged to the stock of terms and ideas called *sammŭti*, or 'of conventional usage.' The Buddhist scholar used it as such. Philosophically speaking, it did not mean for him an ultimate unitary principle, continuing self-identical amid a stream of transient manifestations. Contrariwise, it was merely a name-and-concept binding together and labelling a transient aggregate of factors. For him the ultimate principles, material and psychical, were not in the bond or label, but among those factors. But even they were evanescent, ever-changing.[5] And as to the name-labels he judged that

'These are merely names, expressions, turns of speech, designations in common use in the world. Of these he who has won truth makes use indeed, but is not led astray by them.' [6]

The ethical implications of *atta* have been already dealt with in art. EGOISM (Buddhist).

LITERATURE.—C. A. F. Rhys Davids, *Buddhist Psychology*, London, 1914, pp. 26 f., 140 f., *Manual of Buddhist Psychological Ethics*, do. 1900, pp. xciv, 207, n. 1. The Pāli texts are published by the Pāli Text Society.

C. A. F. RHYS DAVIDS.

SELF-ASSERTION AND SELF-SUBJECTION. — **I. Primary instincts.** — Self-assertion (or self-display) together with its opposite, self-subjection (or self-abasement), has been classed by many modern psychologists with the primary instincts of human nature—the instincts which, either directly or indirectly, are the prime movers of all human activity. The term 'instinct' has, unfortunately, not yet acquired a fixed meaning.[7] For the purposes of this article the definition of McDougall may be considered useful.

He defines it as 'an inherited or innate psycho-physical disposition which determines its possessor (1) to perceive, and to pay attention to, objects of a certain class, (2) to experience an emotional excitement of a particular quality upon perceiving such an object, and (3) to act in regard to it in a particular manner, or, at least, to experience an impulse to such action.' [8]

Of the three parts of the psycho-physical disposition it is the second that is most stable and unchanging.

1 *Majjhima Nikāya*, ii. 32. 2 *Dhammasangaṇi*, § 597 f.
3 *E.g.*, *Poṭṭhapāda-Sutta, Dialogues of the Buddha*, i. 259; cf. n. 3; *Saṃyutta Nikāya*, i. 89, and citations below.
4 *Atthasālinī*, p. 308. 5 *Aṅguttara Nikāya*, i. 57.
6 *Ib.* iii. 211. 7 *Saṃyutta Nikāya*, i. 72.
8 *Dhammapada*, 379 f.
9 *Saṃyutta Nikāya*, iii. 120, etc.; *Aṅguttara Nikāya*, iii. 255, etc.

1 *Kalyānaṃ*; comparative not in the Pāli.
2 *Aṅguttara Nikāya*, i. 149. 3 *Ib.* iv. 114.
4 *Dhammasangaṇi*, §§ 1207, 1044; cf. *Majjhima Nikāya*, i. 421 f., where physical elements of the anatomy are called *ajjhattika*.
5 See art. REALITY (Buddhist).
6 *Dīgha Nikāya*, i. 202 (tr. *Dialogues of the Buddha* [*SBB*, London, 1899], i. 263); in this connexion the art. SOUL (Buddhist) should be consulted.
7 Cf. art. INSTINCT.
8 *An Introd. to Social Psychology*7, London, 1913, p. 29.

'The emotional excitement, with the accompanying nervous activities of the central part of the disposition, is the only part of the total instinctive process that retains its specific character and remains common to all individuals and all situations in which the instinct is excited.'[1]

Not only has the emotional excitement of each instinct a specific character, but it always expresses itself by the same symptoms. McDougall describes the emotion characteristic of self-assertion by the term 'elation,' its opposite by the term 'self-subjection.' Ribot[2] uses the terms 'positive self-feeling' and 'negative self-feeling' to describe them. Positive self-feeling gives an impulse to the display of size, strength, and other traits of the self, whereas negative self-feeling leads to shrinking, self-effacement, submission, self-abasement. Drever[3] questions McDougall's statement that the affective part of these instincts is always an emotion. There is no evidence, he contends, that the complex experience denoted by that term is always present when the instinct is active. The positive self-feeling invariably present is more accurately described by the term 'interest' (a feeling of worth-while-ness) than by the term 'emotion.' The emotion of elation, according to him, is experienced only when self-assertion or self-display (which is the term Drever prefers) has met with its suitable response in the submissive attitude of those before whom self-display is made.

Drever[4] employs the following five tests in determining from a psychological point of view whether any particular instinct is to be considered primary, and the two instincts under consideration meet all five:

'(1) Irreducibility by introspective analysis to simpler components.
(2) Arousal of impulse and emotion, with its specific and unmistakable expressive signs, by specific objects or specific kinds of objects, prior to individual experience of these objects.
(3) Manifestation in the early months of child life.
(4) Wide diffusion in the animal world.
(5) Occurrence in exaggerated form under pathological conditions.'[5]

McDougall relies on the fourth and fifth. His discussion, however, implies the use of the first, while we find illustrations of the five in the examples that he gives of the operation of the instincts. His treatment of self-assertion and self-subjection is the most full and satisfactory that we possess. Ribot's treatment—which preceded McDougall's—is briefer and less thorough. Drever has improved on McDougall's analysis in some particulars. A good account of the significance of self-assertion and self-subjection in the social and ethical development of the child is given by Baldwin.[6]

These instincts are essentially social in nature. Their excitement depends on the presence of others. In the case of man the *idea* of others, without their actual presence, may cause elation or subjection with their corresponding manifestations. One may 'show off' before an imaginary gallery of spectators, or even before one's self in a mirror, as if he were another person. But the display is always to, and the shrinking from, some one's notice—usually some one of the same kind. A barnyard cockerel struts before other fowls, a hen among her chicks; a small dog crawls submissively towards, or away from, a big dog; but he will also slink away with his tail between his legs from a man who has shown disapproval of him. Generally, however, the instinct of subjection is excited by the presence of one of the same kind who is perceived to be in some respect superior, whereas the instinct of self-display is excited by another of the same kind who is perceived to be inferior. In the case of animals the superiority or inferiority is chiefly in size or strength, but other striking characteristics, such as the tail of the peacock, may be organs for the self-display of their owners, and may produce subjection in others. The self-display of animals occurs mainly, though not exclusively, during the mating season. Darwin,[1] in his interesting description of this instinct, regards it as a manifestation of the courtship instinct. The two should not, however, be identified.

Self-assertion and self-subjection come into operation at an early age in children. A child will crow and otherwise display its powers and become elated at the admiring applause of the family group, whereas the absence of applause or inattention will reduce it to silence and cause it to shrink out of sight.

Pathological cases show the operation of both the instincts in an exaggerated form. In certain mental diseases—*e.g.*, general paralysis of the insane—'exaggeration of this emotion and of its impulse of display is the leading symptom.' In other mental diseases the patient exhibits exaggerated symptoms of self-abasement. He 'shrinks from the observation of his fellows, thinks himself a most wretched, useless, sinful creature,' etc.[2]

2. Emotional complexes. — Instincts may be excited singly or in combination. In human beings they are seldom excited singly. When two or more are excited together, their emotions may fuse so as to form a complex emotion in which the various constituents modify one another. In the new emotion the various constituents may be detected; yet the whole is not a quasi-mechanical sum of the constituents, but a new emotion having a special emotional tone. Among the examples given by McDougall is admiration (*q.v.*). This he analyzes into the two primary emotions of wonder and negative self-feeling. Wonder he considers to be the emotion which is the affective part of the instinct of curiosity[3]—the instinct whose impulse is to cause us to approach a relatively novel object and to contemplate it. But we approach an admired object slowly and with hesitation, *i.e.* submissively. For admiration is elicited when the novel is in some respect superior. It is therefore most frequently excited by a person perceived to be superior to ourselves, whom we do not fully understand. McDougall maintains that in our admiration for books and works of art there is always present the thought of the maker. Admiration of natural objects implies the personalization of natural powers or the postulate of their Creator. The presence in admiration of the submissive attitude with the attendant negative self-feeling is an indication of this. Admiration qualified by fear is awe (*q.v.*). When the power which excites awe is beneficent towards us and excites gratitude (*q.v.*), we experience reverence (*q.v.*)—the religious emotion *par excellence*.[4] McDougall's account of reverence is scarcely satisfactory. Wonder, negative self-feeling, and fear are clearly elements in it; but gratitude is not essential. What is essential is respect. Respect depends on the recognition of some personal excellence other than size or power. Benevolence is such an excellence, so is righteousness; and a manifestation by a being of either towards even another may suffice to qualify our

[1] McDougall, p. 34.
[2] *The Psychology of the Emotions*, Eng. tr., London, 1897, pt. ii. ch. v.
[3] *The Instinct in Man*, Cambridge, 1917, pp. 156 ff., 192.
[4] *Ib.* ch. viii. [5] *Ib.* p. 173.
[6] *Social and Ethical Interpretations in Mental Development*[4], New York and London, 1907, pp. 13 ff., 204 ff.

[1] *The Descent of Man*, 2 vols., London, 1871, ch. xiii.
[2] McDougall, pp. 64–66.
[3] Drever (p. 200) seems right when he says that the word 'curiosity' describes not only the impulse but the emotion attending it better than the word 'wonder.' Wonder is itself complex. In its simplest and most elementary form he thinks it is 'baffled curiosity.' The relatively novel rouses the instinct of curiosity. If the 'enquiring impulse' is not satisfied, 'wonder is developed,' curiosity, however, remaining an element in it.
[4] McDougall, pp. 128–135.

awe into reverence. We can respect another only if he is seen to respect himself. Indeed McDougall suggests that our 'respect for another is a sympathetic reflexion of his self-respect.'[1] Hence positive self-feeling qualified by a sense of personal worth enters into reverence. So it is an emotion possible only to a person conscious in some degree of his moral dignity or worth. Reverence for God the Father is attainable only by the man who is conscious of the value of 'sonship.'

McDougall suggests that 'the fundamental distinction between religious and magical practices is not, as is sometimes said, that religion conceives the powers it envisages as personal powers, while magic conceives them as impersonal; but rather that the religious attitude is always that of submission, the magical attitude that of self-assertion; and that the forces which both magical and religious practices are concerned to influence may be conceived in either case as personal or impersonal powers. Hence the savage, who at one time bows down before his fetish in supplication, and at another seeks to compel its assistance by threats or spells, adopts toward the one object alternately the religious and the magical attitude. The same fundamental difference of attitude and emotion distinguishes religion from science, into which magic becomes transformed as civilization progresses.'[2]

This theory cannot be justified. We have seen that in one of the highest forms of religious emotion—reverence—positive self-feeling in the form of respect is present. Durkheim[3] maintains that there is an element of respect in the fear of the primitive for his gods. And he shows that the religious rites of the Australian totemists have as one of their functions the strengthening of the divine principle in the totem and the ensuring of the reproduction of the totemic species. Their worshippers are as necessary to the gods as the gods are to the worshippers.[4] And in the higher religions (*e.g.*, Christianity) the worship and service of men are believed to be needed by their God. Hence the attitude cannot be one of pure submission. McDougall is probably right in saying that the magical attitude is self-assertive. Does not that distinguish it from both the religious and the scientific attitudes? For surely intellectual humility is a characteristic of the scientific mind. There is a confident assertion of power in the propounding and following out of hypotheses, but there is also a readiness to submit to facts, and a subjection of self to truth, even when truth demands the surrender of cherished beliefs and hopes. In the application also of scientific knowledge to practical affairs the scientific man can impose his will on nature only by obeying nature's laws. Positive and negative self-feeling are constituents of scientific and religious emotion.

3. The self-sentiment.—The emotions not only fuse to form new emotional complexes; they also compete with and inhibit one another. In comparatively undeveloped minds, such as those of animals and very young children, positive and negative self-feeling would simply preclude one another's appearance, or, if both appeared, one would expel the other from the mind. In bashful behaviour, which appears in a child's third year, neither succeeds in expelling its opposite. Both continue to be excited by different aspects of a situation—that constituted by a self in relation to other selves—but because of their opposite characteristics, and the opposite types of behaviour to which they lead, they do not fuse. The impulses to self-display and self-effacement struggle to check each other's manifestations. Such a struggle seems to imply the organization of the two dispositions into a system. The bond of union is the idea of the self, and a rudimentary form of the consciousness of self is therefore a condition of the union and consequent struggle. To such a system of dispositions organized about the idea of an object modern psychologists, following Shand, have given the name 'sentiment.'[1]

'When any one of the emotions is strongly or repeatedly excited by a particular object, there is formed the rudiment of a sentiment.'[2]

For example, the admiring applause of a child's nurse gradually develops the '"Am I not a wonder?" consciousness,' and the child will acquire the habit of displaying its powers and expect applause each time it does so. One that is always petted, admired, and allowed to have its own way may acquire the self-assertive habit to an excessive degree, will become what is called a 'spoilt' child. It will come to think of itself as a being superior to others, to whom all must always defer and submit. About its idea of self—an idea essentially social in character, for it is the idea of the self in relation to others—its emotions will become organized with positive self-feeling central and dominating. In the self-sentiment so formed it will tend to include all the emotions that are of service to its ends, and to exclude all those which are useless or antagonistic; *e.g.*, it will feel fear when the satisfaction of positive self-feeling is threatened, anger when it is obstructed, elation when it is satisfied, and sorrow when it is frustrated.[3] Signs of fear, admiration, gratitude, and deference in others it will welcome, but it will tend to restrain the impulses to exhibit them itself, and to feel the corresponding emotions. A fully-formed sentiment of this type is the cause of pride (*q.v.*) in its extreme and most objectionable form. But it never happens that the self-sentiment excludes negative self-feeling entirely. That would be possible only if a child were born devoid of the instinct, or never perceived persons in any way superior to itself. Where, however, this instinct is weak or its exercise much inhibited, a whole series of emotions into which negative self-feeling enters is only faintly felt—*e.g.*, admiration, reverence, respect, gratitude, humility. There would be comparative indifference to praise and blame—concern for either implies a recognition of the superiority of those who bestow it—and consequently little knowledge of other men, inasmuch as the motive for closely observing their attitudes and the expression of their opinions would be largely lacking. Further, there would be great ignorance of self, for we learn to know ourselves by comparing ourselves with others, by observing their attitudes towards us, and accepting their opinions about us. Moreover, weakness in negative self-feeling indicates incapacity to appreciate ideals (truth, beauty, goodness) and to devote the life to any great cause; for these ends imply the vivid realization of a form of personal life superior to one's own, which realization involves the consciousness of present inferiority and submissiveness.

In the case of the ordinary man negative self-feeling becomes incorporated with positive self-feeling, in varying degree, in the self-sentiment, because in the social environment the growing boy inevitably meets some who are superior to himself. Authority especially, represented by parents, teachers, etc., imposes its will on the boy; and above all the authority of society as a whole which 'with a collective voice and irresistible power distributes rewards and punishments, praise and blame, and formulates its approval and disapproval

[1] McDougall, p. 161. [2] P. 306.

[3] *The Elementary Forms of the Religious Life*, Eng. tr., London, 1915, pp. 206 ff., 346 ff.

[4] Cf. J. G. Frazer, *The Magic Art and the Evolution of Kings*, London, 1913, i. 31.

[1] Some distinguish between simple and complex sentiments. 'A "simple" sentiment consists of a single emotional tendency associated with an idea or idea complex' (Drever, p. 215 f.). The term 'emotion' is reserved for an experience on the perceptual level, 'sentiment' for an experience on the ideational level (cf. *ib.* ch. ix.; see also art. SENTIMENT).

[2] McDougall, p. 163.

[3] Cf. A. F. Shand, *The Foundations of Character*, London, 1914, bk. i. ch. iv. f.

in universally accepted maxims.'[1] Owing to the incorporation of these two emotions in the self-sentiment,

'all persons fall for the child into one or other of two classes; in the one class are those who impress him as beings of superior power, who evoke his negative self-feeling, and towards whom he is submissive and receptive; in the other class are those whose presence evokes his positive self-feeling and towards whom he is self-assertive and masterful, just because they fail to impress him as beings superior to himself. As his powers develop and his knowledge increases, persons who at first belonged to the former class are transferred to the latter; he learns, or thinks he learns, the limits of their powers; he no longer shrinks from a contest with them, and, every time he gains the advantage in any such contest, their power of evoking his negative self-feeling diminishes, until it fails completely. When that stage is reached his attitude towards them is reversed, it becomes self-assertive; for their presence evokes his positive self-feeling. In this way a child of good capacities, in whom the instinct of self-assertion is strong, works his way up the social ladder.'[2]

This account of the progress of a boy to manhood must be qualified by the fact that the self-sentiment is not the only one that moves him. Of special importance are the various love sentiments —love of parents, children, friends, home, country, church, God. At the basis of all the love sentiments is the primary emotion of tender feeling with its impulse to protect — an emotion and impulse which may lead to concern and care for others irrespective of their relation to the self-sentiment. This impulse may legitimately be called altruistic, and often leads to self-sacrifice.[3]

4. Extension and moralization of self-sentiment.—The moral character of the self-sentiment will depend largely on the idea of self about which it is organized together with the thoroughness of the organization depending on this idea. The idea of the self in all but its most rudimentary forms is essentially a social product, developed by interaction with other persons and involving constant reference to them; it is, in fact, a conception not merely of one's self but of one's self in relation to other selves. The relationship may be conceived to range from complete exclusion, through opposition, sympathy, co-operation in various degrees, to inclusion partial or complete.[4] The self conceived as an exclusive monad is not a defensible conception; but it has been maintained on theoretical grounds, though rarely assumed as a working conception in the actual affairs of life. Usually, as we saw above, a certain measure of antagonism and conflict of interests is felt to exist between self and others. The self, however, may identify itself with others—*e.g.*, a mother with her children; a boy with his family, school, or college; a man with his church, his country, and even with humanity. The group with which the self is identified becomes included, more or less firmly, in his self-regarding sentiment. The success or failure of the group may rouse his positive or negative self-feeling. He is concerned for its success or failure as he is for his own. He judges it to be his own, and feels and acts accordingly, when that group comes into relations of antagonism to, or co-operation with, other groups. Hence his emotions and actions, although in form self-regarding, are in effect other-regarding with respect to the group included in his self-regard. Thus, on the one hand, his conduct becomes moralized and socially valuable, through the extension of his self-regarding sentiment to include the interests of ever-increasing numbers of his fellow-men; the moralization may proceed, on the other hand, in what may be considered a more internal direction—*i.e.*, he may identify himself with the abstract sentiments which are suggested to him, or which he has thought out for himself (*e.g.*, the sentiments of truth, goodness, beauty), and incorporate them in the self-sentiment. They become his own ideals and represent the self that he wills to be—to realize them is to realize himself, to express them is to express himself. So he submits himself to them, strives to express, propagate, and defend them, is elated when their power triumphs over the impulses of himself and others, and is cast down when they are defeated.

Care for others and devotion to ideals may, and do, spring from other motives—the sentiment of love in its various forms, active sympathy which impels a man to seek to bring the feelings and actions of his fellows into harmony with his own, and his own into harmony with theirs—and these are essential moral and social motives. But these receive great reinforcement when their objects are included in the idea of self, and concern for them is incorporated in the self-sentiment. Conversely, the latter is raised to a higher level and becomes more comprehensive and adequate as a guide of conduct by the inclusion of the love sentiments within it. It is possible for a man to take pride in the thought of himself as a lover, and seek consequently to develop the love sentiments in his character. Some ethical writers have adopted this method of reconciling the claim of egoism and altruism. They maintain that the individual should seek his own good, but should conceive his good to include the good of others. Another method is to unite the self-regarding and other-regarding sentiments in a more general sentiment, the sentiment of the perfection of life—not one's own merely, but all life. One's chief concern may still be with one's own life, not because one thinks it more valuable, but because self-perfection is more within the individual's power, and by concentrating chiefly on that he will do most to promote the universal life. His efforts would have the advantage of reinforcement by the strongest human sentiment—the sentiment of self.

5. Sentiment for self-control.—Any one of the many sentiments which are formed in an adult consciousness may become sufficiently powerful to dominate large portions of a man's life — *e.g.*, avarice, ambition, love of a person, of home, church, art, science—and to inhibit all impulses which are inconsistent with, or irrelevant to, its end. But the sentiment which seems capable of meeting most of the situations in life, and of rendering an individual practically independent of passing solicitations, is the self-sentiment, when that incorporates a high ideal of life including a sentiment for self-control. Self-control is itself a particular development of the self-sentiment, and in virtue of it a man takes pride in realizing his ideal of self in all circumstances. It is the sentiment of self, according to McDougall,[1] which is roused into activity when we are said to determine by an effort of will to act along the line of greatest resistance.

'The conations, the desires and aversions, arising within this self-regarding sentiment are the motive forces which, adding themselves to the weaker ideal motive in the course of moral effort, enable it to win the mastery over some stronger, coarser desire of our primitive animal nature and to banish from consciousness the idea of the end of this desire.'[2]

It is not correct to say that only this sentiment enables us to act along the line of greatest resistance;[3] but we may say that, when, by the incorporation of the ideal of perfection of life including self-control, this master sentiment has been formed and become dominant, perhaps after many conflicts,

'it becomes capable of determining every conflict so certainly and easily that conflicts can hardly arise; it supplies a determining motive for every possible situation, namely, the desire that I, the self, shall do the right.'[4]

The subsequent struggles are no longer moral

[1] McDougall, p. 196. [2] *Ib.* p. 194.
[3] Cf. *ib.* ch. x.; Shand, bk. i. ch. iv. [4] Cf. art. EGO.

[1] Pp. 230, 246 f. [2] P. 248.
[3] Cf. art. SELF-SATISFACTION. [4] McDougall, p. 262.

conflicts, but intellectual efforts to determine what is right and most worth doing.

LITERATURE.—In addition to the literature given in the footnotes cf. A. F. Shand, 'Character and the Emotions,' in *Mind*, new ser., v. [1896] 203 ff., 'M. Ribot's Theory of the Passions,' *ib.* xvi. [1907] 477 ff.

DAVID PHILLIPS.

SELF-CONSCIOUSNESS.—This word is used in two senses, one of which has been sufficiently treated in art. CONSCIOUSNESS, and alluded to in art. COMMON SENSE. The question whether all consciousness may or may not be reduced to self-consciousness or how far by common sense, philosophically understood, the 'various impressions received' are 'reduced to the unity of a common consciousness' does not concern us here. Social and psychological observation shows that some persons are much more drawn than others to observe the workings of their own minds. The tendency and habit of introspection (*q.v.*) produces a type of mind and character capable (if literary abilities are superadded) of writing first-rate autobiography.[1] It is also valuable in helping the growth of medical and psychological knowledge, since patients who can observe their own symptoms, and artists or thinkers who can distinguish and remember their own impressions, are able to collect much valuable material for the scientific investigator. In common parlance, however, the word stands for something more pronounced than a tendency to introspection. The self-conscious person of the strongly marked type is one whose interest in the world and in society is inseparable from his personal status and individual inclinations and dispositions. Commonly this exaggerated self-consciousness accompanies a very exaggerated opinion of one's own character and abilities. But the reverse may sometimes happen, as personal responsibility for misfortunes may loom as large in the consciousness as personal credit when the event is good. In these cases it may rise to the height of mania.[2] In general, self-consciousness implies an intense sensitiveness to the opinion of friends and of society, and a constant fear of appearing in a ridiculous or undignified position, which causes diffidence in social intercourse and sometimes abnormal shyness. It becomes immoral only when the self (with its peculiar personal desires and aversions) is the one object the satisfaction of which is sought throughout life.[3] The tendency to excessive self-consciousness should be counteracted in young people by stimulating active interest in scientific and social pursuits, by extending and quickening the sympathies, and by imposing such disciplinary force as may lead the individual to regard himself as a not-all-important member of human society.

LITERATURE.—See the works cited in footnotes; also literature under CONSCIOUSNESS, COMMON SENSE.

ALICE GARDNER.

SELF-CONTROL.—See ETHICAL DISCIPLINE.

SELF-CULTURE, SELF-DISCIPLINE.—The principle that there is a right self-love, though not ignored by Greek ethics, was first brought into prominence by Christianity.[4] Self-love is a duty implied, first, in the revelation of the archetype of manhood in the incarnate Christ; secondly, in the 'royal law,' 'Thou shalt love thy neighbour as thyself' (Ja 2^8). True or reasonable self-love is in fact a part of the love of God, and coincides with it. We are to love ourselves as God loves us; having regard both to what He would have us be and to what we are on the way to become.

[1] See G. Misch, *Gesch. der Autobiographie*, i., Leipzig, 1907.

[2] See S. Baring-Gould, *The Tragedy of the Cæsars*, 2 vols., London, 1892, *passim*.

[3] G. Meredith, *The Egoist*.

[4] See *e.g.*, Plato, *Legg.* 731 E; Arist. *Eth. Nic.* IX. viii. 7.

'Tales nos amat Deus, quales futuri sumus Ipsius dono, non quales sumus nostro merito.'[1]

And this self-love involves a proper reverence and care for the personality—body, mind, and spirit. Self-culture, self-development, is a moral duty which has gained in significance in proportion as the idea of personality (*q.v.*) has been emphasized by modern philosophy.

1. Self-discipline.—Negatively, self-love takes the form of due self-discipline, including all that the Greek comprehended in the word *σωφροσύνη*—soberness, temperance, and chastity; the temper of sobriety in judgment and in the estimation of self (Ro 12^3, 2 Co 10^5); the habit of restraint in the indulgence of desire and in the enjoyment of pleasure.[2] In any case the aim of self-discipline is the cultivation of moral and spiritual power through the process of strengthening, renewing, and educating the will. In Christian language, the end of discipline is freedom, the unhindered dominion of the spirit in the personality.

The good man, says J. Smith, 'principally looks upon himself as being what he is rather by his soul than by his body; he values himself by his soul, that being which hath the greatest affinity with God, and so does not seek himself in the fading vanities of this life, nor in those poor and low delights of his senses, as wicked men do; but as the philosopher doth well express it, *ὅση δύναμις φεύγειν ἀπὸ τοῦ σώματος βούλεται, καὶ ἀπὸ τῶν σωματικῶν παθῶν εἰς ἑαυτὸν συννεύειν*.'[3]

Thus the discipline of self begins with conversion and repentance—*i.e.* with an effort of will in the direction of self-purification; with the process which St. Paul describes as 'putting off the old man' (Eph 4^{22})—the counterpart in the moral life of the individual of that which has already been mystically accomplished in Christ (Ro 6^6, Col 3^{10}). We may observe that here emerges the distinctively Christian idea of a new self, which is to be 'put on' as a garment. The process of casting away the old nature is in fact crowned by the 'putting on of Christ' (Ro 13^{14}, Eph 4^{24}, etc.). In connexion with this subject the threefold ordinance of asceticism needs consideration. Prayer, fasting, and almsgiving are duties expressly commended by Christ Himself as efficacious aids to holiness. For the process of *κάθαρσις* is followed by *γυμνασία* or *ἄσκησις* (Ac 24^{16})—the systematic effort implied in such passages as 1 Co 9^{27}, 1 Ti 4^7, He 5^{14} 12^1; and fasting, almsgiving, and prayer stand in a natural relationship to the three great spheres of Christian duty—towards *self*, towards *our fellow-man*, and towards *God*. These duties must be understood in no narrow or merely technical sense. Aquinas well says:

'Omnia quae aliquis facit ad refrenandum seipsum in suis concupiscentiis, reducuntur ad jejunium; quaecunque vero fiunt propter delectationem proximi, reducuntur ad eleemosynam; quaecunque vero propter cultum Dei fiunt, reducuntur ad orationem.'[4]

Further, the very words *γυμνασία* and *ἄσκησις* remind us that the discipline of self is a continuous and prolonged process; the state of grace is one of unceasing warfare, demanding the qualities of the soldier and of the athlete—power to 'endure hardness,' readiness to meet emergencies, vigilance, sobriety, courage. Hence the frequency of military imagery in the NT and in early Church writers.[5] The need of self-discipline is involved in the very fact that the Christian is beset by sleepless spiritual foes (Eph $6^{11ff.}$, 1 P 5^8, 1 Jn 5^{19}), and that the new personality can only through exercise and discipline attain to its full development and acquire true spiritual liberty.

Self-discipline, then, implies the training of the

[1] Conc. Araus. ii. can. 12.

[2] See artt. TEMPERANCE, SOBRIETY, MODERATION.

[3] *Select Discourses*, Cambridge, 1660, p. 387.

[4] *Summa*, I. ii. qu. cviii. 3 ad 4; see artt. PRAYER, FASTING, CHARITY.

[5] See Ro 13^{12}, 2 Co 10^5, 1 Th 5^8, Eph $6^{11ff.}$, 2 Ti $2^{3ff.}$; and A. Harnack, *Expansion of Christianity in the First Three Centuries*, Eng. tr., London, 1904, ii. 19 ff.

will, the right education of which is a matter affecting much more than the welfare of the individual. For in all social advance 'human will is the great factor, and . . . economic law and moral law are essentially one';[1] and a man is contributing to the solution of public problems by personal self-discipline. In this task religion supplies man's will with motives and helps, bringing within his reach the incalculable 'powers of the world to come' (He 6[5]): impelling him to make great ventures of faith and heroic endeavours to live as God would have him live. For the most part it is by the fulfilment of plain, obvious, and even trivial duties that the will is braced and strengthened; and, as regards the control of appetite, weakness of will is often the result of the persistent neglect of minor obligations.

Christian self-discipline—*e.g.*, of temper, manners, behaviour under stress of difficulty or trial—'is a work of the Holy Spirit, and is in virtue of prayer, and tends to establish the soul in God. Any small act of self-repression done in the grace of prayer will have some result of communion with God, and will leave a capacity for a closer union with God than before. The occasions for our daily self-discipline are mostly unimportant and un-observed. But the littleness of the opportunity is no measure of the grace developed.'[2]

As we have seen, asceticism means that process of education or discipline by which the will is enabled to acquire or regain its rightful supremacy. Asceticism properly understood has no quarrel with pleasure as such.

'Its war has never been against pleasure, but against disturbing passion, and artificial wants, and weak dependence upon external and accidental things; its aim has been, not to suffer, but to be free from the entanglements of self, to serve the calls of human pity or Divine love, and conform to the counsels of a Christ-like perfection.'[3]

2. Self-culture.—Positively regarded, the spirit of self-love implies the duty of self-culture, the 'ordered use' of every gift and endowment which man has received. Self-culture includes the proper care of the body, the training of the intellect and imagination, the education of taste and of the faculty of judgment, and the training of character. Its general aim is to make both mind and body suitable instruments for the service of God and of mankind. A man is morally bound to make his personality all that it is capable of becoming. This is a debt owed to God, who has His ideal for us, and to society, which has a right to claim our service.

(1) *The care of the body* includes all that will tend to its preservation and development as a facile instrument of the spirit—self-control or temperance, and the maintenance of the due relation between work and recreation. As regards bodily strength and vigour, Dorner wisely observes that what we should aim at is not 'to make ourselves capable of great momentary achievements but rather to cultivate *endurance* within the limits of our individual strength.'[4] He points out that bodily endurance 'is the great support of ὑπομονή,' a virtue which holds a very high place in the NT conception of the Christian character, and is most conspicuous in the human example of our Lord Himself.

(2) *The culture of the intellect and imagination*, the education of judgment and taste, come next under consideration. The general aim of self-culture has been well described as 'openness of mind to the idea of humanity and its highest interests.'[5] The process of culture consists in such a development of our spiritual nature as may correct all one-sidedness or inordinate bias due to special training or to some peculiarity of temperament. This seems to be implied in such a passage as 1 Co 9[22], 'I am made all things to all men.' The truly cultured man[1] possesses the faculty of judgment, the capacity which is the great aim of all liberal education. The power of forming a sound judgment implies not merely a wide knowledge of many subjects, but a true estimate of one's own mental limitations, and a due sense of the diversity of method employed in different departments of knowledge.

The culture of the imagination is a prominent feature in the Platonic ideal of education.[2] Plato teaches with great emphasis that art has an ethical aspect and that the æsthetic faculty needs a deliberate and serious discipline from childhood onwards. He even insists that, in the ideal State, poets and artists ought to be restrained from hindering the cause of true culture by feeding the imagination of the citizens with unworthy or immoral representations.

They are to be required, he says, 'to express the image of the good (τὴν τοῦ ἀγαθοῦ εἰκόνα) in their works, and prevented from exhibiting the forms of vice, intemperance, meanness, or indecency' under penalty of expulsion from the community.

The Christian spirit, on the one hand, claims as its own the apostolic utterance, 'all things are yours' (1 Co 3[22]); on the other, it regards the gifts of nature and civilization — art, literature, the drama, etc.—as a heritage to be used under a serious sense of responsibility. 'All things' are the heritage of God's children, but they are to be used or enjoyed under the guidance of the Spirit and as ministering to spiritual ends. They are to be contemplated and judged in union with the mind of Christ (1 Co 2[12f.]).

In modern times a sense of the importance of the proper culture of imagination has been developed by the wide diffusion of culture and by deeper insight into the theory of education. We appreciate better, perhaps, than formerly the power of imagination to kindle passion and to influence conduct by feeding upon worthy or unworthy ideals. St. Paul seems in Ph 4[8] to recognize the duty of cultivating imagination aright.

(3) The most important part of true self-culture is concerned with *the training of character.* When St. James (3[2]) speaks of the 'perfect man' he implies that every character has an ideal completeness, the attainment of which depends upon the measure of a man's self-control. Self-discipline thus lies at the root of every advance in true culture. The central element in personality is will, and character grows by acts of moral decision, by the constantly renewed 'dedication of the will to goodness,' by persevering adhesion to truth and right. Thus character tends towards stability and fixity in proportion as it comes under the restraining and inspiring domination of a single aim and motive. Obedience is in the eyes of Christ at once the organ of religious knowledge and the condition of moral progress. He appeals, generally speaking, not so much to emotion or to intellect as to will. He calls upon a man to act and to follow Him. The perfect man is in fact he whose body, soul, and spirit act in obedience to a single principle—the love of God (Ro 5[5])—and the goal of all self-culture is singleness of heart and purpose, the bringing of every impulse, inclination, and thought into subjection to the obedience of Christ (2 Co 10[5]).

Self-development, self-realization, self-culture —these are generally regarded as typical ideals of the Hellenic spirit. Hellenism is sometimes contrasted with 'Hebraism' to the disadvantage of the latter. 'Hebraism stands to us for moral

[1] H. George, *Progress and Poverty* (*Complete Works*, New York, 1904, i. 508).
[2] G. Congreve, *Parable of the Ten Virgins*, London, 1904, p. 99.
[3] J. Martineau, *Types of Ethical Theory*[2], Oxford, 1886, ii. 381.
[4] *System of Christian Ethics*, § 60.
[5] Dorner, p. 481.

[1] Aristotle's ὁ περὶ πᾶν πεπαιδευμένος (*Eth. Nic.* I. iii. 5).
[2] *Rep.* 401 B f.

discipline; Hellenism for the culture of the human, the sensitive love of the beautiful and the joy of living.'[1] The antithesis, however, is at best superficial. The real reconciliation with Hebraism of all that is admirable in Hellenism is to be found in the NT. There we learn that the realization of self is a gradual process—a progressive self-surrender:

'progressive self-identity with that spirit of the Incarnate which, being the very Spirit of God in, and as, human character, is found to be the consummation of the perfectness of the self of every man.'[2]

The Christian is 'heir of both ideals.' He loses the world and forsakes it, only to receive it back transfigured and ennobled (Mk $10^{29f.}$, Lk $18^{29f.}$).

LITERATURE.—J. Butler, *Sermons upon Human Nature*; W. R. Inge, *Personal Idealism and Mysticism*, London, 1907, lect. iv.; R. C. Moberly, *Atonement and Personality*, do. 1901, ch. ix.; Hugh Black, *Culture and Restraint*, do. 1901; Newman Smyth, *Christian Ethics*², Edinburgh, 1893, pt. ii. ch. ii.; F. G. Peabody, *Jesus Christ and the Christian Character*, New York and London, 1905, ch. vi.; I. A. Dorner, *System of Christian Ethics*, Eng. tr., Edinburgh, 1887, §§ 56–65; G. H. S. Walpole, *Personality and Power*, London, 1906; H. Rashdall, *The Theory of Good and Evil*, Oxford, 1907, ii. 171 f.

R. L. OTTLEY.

SELF-DENIAL.—See SELF-SACRIFICE.

SELF-DISCIPLINE.—See SELF-CULTURE.

SELF-EXAMINATION.—See INTROSPECTION.

SELF-EXPRESSION.—**1. Description and definition.**—Morality and religion at their best and fullest are actuated by no particular 'motive'; they seek for the most part no conscious end or reward. They are the natural behaviour of a healthy personality. Kindliness, good-will, and service desire no 'wages'; they ask only 'the wages of going on, and not to die.'[3] Worship, reverence, and religious contemplation in a nature that has found itself issue forth spontaneously like the flow of springs of water and songs of birds.

There is an autodynamic quality in life as a whole that seems to be the direct source of its urge, its passion for novel conquests, its sense of freedom, and its joy in self-realization. The power of self-expression is not a force or agency impelling life from behind, nor an external stimulus accounting for its present behaviour, nor an end existing outside it leading it on. It is a descriptive aspect of life itself. The entire organism is, in the words of Lloyd Morgan, 'a going concern.'[4]

By 'self-expression' one does not mean 'spontaneity,' or 'self-activity,' or 'self-determination,' in so far as these terms indicate that conduct is independent of causal connexions. Every mental act or state has its inner or outer excitations, its immediate and remote causes, and observes the laws of association. When, however, all these conditioning factors of a certain phenomenon are summed up, they do not fully and completely account for the output. There is, in addition, a moving, self-creating something that is of the very stuff of which life is made. The environmental factors, immediate and remote, of an act are not its sole causes; they are the necessary and ever present conditioning factors of its amount and quality.

2. Philosophical setting.—The fact of self-expression is in harmony with Aristotle's energy concept of the nature of reality.[5] Pure spontaneity, however, rarely if ever happens.

'There is not any motion independent of things themselves, for change invariably takes place in accordance with the laws of substance.'[6]

[1] Black, *Culture and Restraint*, p. 17.
[2] Moberly, *Atonement and Personality*, p. 246.
[3] Tennyson, *Wages*.
[4] *The Interpretation of Nature*², London, 1906, p. 132.
[5] *Metaphysics*, bk. vii. ch. 11. [6] *Ib.* bk. x. ch. 9.

The notion that reality as a whole is in the last analysis an urgent something with spontaneity has been steadily gaining ground since Kant. It doubtless received an impetus as the result of the *Critique of Practical Reason* and the *Metaphysic of Morality*, in which a good will is proclaimed as first in the world in primacy and in worth. Hegel's 'creative reason' is absolute self-activity moved by 'an inner necessity to set forth in itself what it inherently is.'[1] Schopenhauer, differing, as he thought, *in toto* from Hegel as to the nature of the stuff of which the world is made, is at one with him in finding it centre in a moving, self-creative principle—'the will . . . a blind incessant impulse . . . the thing-in-itself, the inner content, the essence of the world.'[2]

3. The energy concept of nature and life.—The inevitable outcome of the evolutionary science of the last half-century and more has been to lay the foundations wide and deep for appreciation of the significance of spontaneous self-expression as a characteristic of mentality. Nature as a whole has a dynamical aspect that is fundamental. The synthesis of the physical and biological sciences shows the evolutionary process to be energy or manifestation of its modes of expression.

'The evolution of life may be rewritten,' says Henry Fairfield Osborn, 'in terms of invisible energy, as it has long been written in terms of visible form. All visible tissues, organs and structures are seen to be the more or less elaborate agents of the different modes of energy.'[3]

There are no longer two basal categories of being—matter and energy—as in Spencer's synthetic philosophy; matter, along with all other static existences, has gone by the board.

'The reality of matter, as formerly conceived, is now abandoned, and the invisible becomes the everyday reality of the scientific laboratory.'[4]

Essentially all physicists and chemists accept the electron theory of matter. Its supposed attribute of self-existent stuff has been dissolved in the universal flow of energies. At bottom energy alone remains. D'Arcy W. Thompson has set forth this profound scientific change of front in these words:

'Morphology then is not only a study of material things and of the forms of material things but has its dynamical aspect, under which we deal with the interpretation, in terms of force, of the operation of Energy . . . Matter as such produces nothing, changes nothing, does nothing . . . The spermatozoon, the nucleus, the chromosomes or the germ-plasm can never act as matter alone, but only as seats of energy and as centres of force. And this is but an adaptation of the old saying of the philosopher: in the beginning was a divine and creative essence rather than matter.'[5]

It is the conviction of modern students like Osborn and Thompson that the energy concept applies equally to the physical universe and to mentality. A description of the entire continuity in the evolution of the various types of energy is the task of J. M. Macfarlane in a recent significant work, *The Causes and Course of Organic Evolution*.[6] The energies range through the connected series—the thermic, electric, biotic, cognitic, cogitic, and spiritic. In such a scheme self-expression is the spontaneous manifestation of these energies in human personality. This conception runs centrally through the voluntarism of Paulsen, the creative evolutionism of Bergson, and the vitalism of Driesch. After passing in review various modern scientific tendencies in their bearing upon the ontological problem, Paulsen exclaims:

'Spontaneous activity everywhere! Your inert rigid matter, movable only by impact, is a phantom that owes its existence,

[1] *The Phenomenology of Mind*, tr. J. B. Baillie, London, 1910, ii. 814.
[2] *The World as Will and Idea*, tr. R. B. Haldane and J. Kemp, Boston, 1887, i. 354.
[3] *The Origin and Evolution of Life*, New York, 1917, p. 17.
[4] G. W. Stewart, 'A Contrib. of Modern Physics to Rel. Thought,' *HR* (American ed.) lxviii. [Oct. 1914] 278.
[5] *On Growth and Form*, Cambridge, 1917, p. 14 f.
[6] New York, 1918.

not to observation, but to conceptual speculation. . . . The human mind is but the highest development on our earth of the mental processes which universally animate and move nature.'[1]

4. Biological evidences of self-expression.—The behaviour of all organisms, plant and animal, indicates that each of them is a centre of energies that want only to meet an appropriate situation to be released. They are touched off by fitting excitations somewhat after the way in which a finely adjusted gun is discharged by the pressure on the trigger. The growth of seeds, the development of plants, the explosion of instinct tendencies, the flow of vegetative functions during sleep and waking, the universal restlessness of organisms, their demand for new and better adaptations, the creative intelligence in science and industry, the willed activities of a highly conscious and self-conscious personality, are all—like the auto-dynamism of radio-active substances on the one hand and the spontaneity of moral, æsthetic, and religious valuation on the other—manifestations of self-expression.

Careful experimental and observational studies of lower organisms prove to many students of genetic psychology that spontaneity is a basal characteristic of life. No one has pursued the study of protozoa and metazoa with greater thoroughness than H. S. Jennings. He claims that behaviour arises as much from internal as from external factors.

'Activity occurs in organisms without present specific external stimulation. The normal condition of Paramecium is an active one, with its cilia in rapid motion; it is only under special conditions that it can be brought partly to rest. Vorticella, as Hodge and Aikins showed, is at all times active, never resting. . . . Even if external movements are suspended at times, internal activities continue. The *organism is activity*, and its activities may be spontaneous, so far as present external stimuli are concerned.'[2]

It has become progressively possible to describe the behaviour of the entire organism, including its highest mental operations, in terms of the complication, through development, of physical and chemical reactions.[3]

The theory maintained by 'behaviourists' and 'tropists' is not at variance with the point of view herein set forth, if one keeps in mind two facts: (1) 'matter,' the subject of discourse of physics and chemistry, is dynamical, perhaps even auto-dynamical; (2) the inner factors of worth and value in mentality should help to interpret the lower orders of reality, even of the inorganic world, as truly as the mechanical aspects of behaviour help to describe the higher functions.

By keeping in mind that internal and external factors never exist apart from one another, it is possible to escape the excesses of both vitalism and mechanism.

'The spontaneous activity, of course, depends finally on external conditions, in the same sense that the existence of the organism depends on external conditions. The movements are undoubtedly the expression of energy derived from metabolism.'[4]

5. Physiological evidences of self-expression.—Muscles and cells of the body seem to be centres of energy. The electrical stimulation of a nerve of a live animal will 'cause' an output of contraction fifteen to twenty-five thousand times the work-value of the stimulus. The embryo heart of a developing chick begins to beat, touched off presumably by the normal salt solution with which it is bathed, before the nerves reach it from the central nervous system.

6. Self-expression and play.—The impulse to play is the best criterion of health. It is, at its best, almost pure spontaneity. Most theories of play miss this point, which is the heart of the problem. Play may indeed be an act of imitation; it does often anticipate adult activities and prepare for them;[1] it harks back not infrequently to old anthropological types of behaviour;[2] it furnishes relaxation, rest, and recuperation of the easily fatigued higher mental powers that are overwrought by the demands of civilization.[3] More central than all these is the energy concept of play. Every normal organism has a high potential of energy. It is activity. Play is self-realization. Through a spontaneity of activity life is coming into its own and fulfilling its destiny.

It is somewhat beside the mark to call play the toppling over of excess of energy from unused faculties that are well nourished, as Herbert Spencer has done—the 'tendency to superfluous and useless exercise of faculties that have been quiescent.'[4] For it is the very nature of play, just as of work, to find its supreme satisfaction in the use of its powers to the point of complete exhaustion.

7. Self-expression and art.—With the substitution of the energy concept of play for the superfluous activity theory, the claim of Spencer and many other students, that art is the evolved play of cultivated minds, seems well founded.

'I do but sing because I must,
And pipe but as the linnets sing.'[5]

The prevailing social-utility interpretations of primitive art falsify the soul of it.

'"He makes good songs," say the Hopis. "Everybody likes Tawakwaptiwa." The poet's answer to the question, "How do you make your songs?" was like the answer made by many a Hopi singer: "When I am herding my sheep or away in the fields, and I see something that I like, I sing about it."'[6]

The great modern artist, like the primitive, usually feels himself and his art to be the organ of some inner necessity which is his truest being and at the same time more than himself. Richard Wagner's compositions are always of that sort.

'The sound and sturdy man, who stands before us clad in the panoply of actual body, describes not what he wills and whom he loves, but wills and loves, and imparts to us by his artistic organs the joy of his own willing and loving.'[7]

One further picture of the mind of the true artist will suffice:

'I have once, perhaps not inaptly, called the composer "God's stenographer." With feverish haste he attempts (for what can man do more than attempt the expression of the sublime?) to jot down the harmony of the spheres. He is compelled to articulate in the manner that seems to him their only true expression the Truths that transport him to ecstasy. There is but One more divine than this Reproducer. Him we call Creator!

If it be true that the composer is God's stenographer, we may consider the instrumental artist as His interpreter. It is for him as a medium to express the music of the spheres, the endless story of Nature, of Love and Life. Every time he climbs to the platform he is there to fulfil his mission to tell you the story again, and it is through his universal love and the all-compelling sympathy of his Art that the people are attracted to him and he is made to live in the hearts of men and women!'[8]

The most extensive and consistent presentation of the expressionist theory of art is that by Colin McAlpin:

'Art, at root, is the expression of man's feelings. The world of art is but the world of expression. And expression is at once the deepest and divinest necessity of our being. . . . All high and noble expression, whether in art or actuality, is but the escapement of an inner spiritual solicitude.'[9]

---

1 F. Paulsen, *Introd. to Philosophy*, tr. F. Thilly, New York, 1898, p. 101.
2 *Behavior of the Lower Organisms*, New York, 1915, pp. 283–294.
3 Consult, *e.g.*, J. B. Watson, *Behavior*, New York, 1914; and on 'tropisms' see J. Loeb, *The Mechanistic Conception of Life*, Chicago, 1912.
4 Jennings, p. 284.

1 K. Groos, *The Play of Animals*, Eng. tr., New York and London, 1898.
2 C. Stanley Hall, *Adolescence*, new ed., London, 1911, i. 202 ff.
3 G. T. W. Patrick, *The Psychology of Relaxation*, Boston and London, 1916, pp. 29–95.
4 *The Principles of Psychology*3, London, 1890, ii. 630, § 534.
5 Tennyson, *In Memoriam*, xxi.
6 N. Curtis, *The Indians' Book*, New York, 1907, p. 481 f.
7 *The Art of the Future* (C. D. Warner's *Lib. of the World's Best Literature*, New York, 1897–99, vol. xxvi. p. 15513).
8 Arthur Hartmann, in *The Musical Observer*, April, 1917.
9 *Hermaia: a Study in Comparative Esthetics*, London, 1915, pp. 1–3.

8. Self-expression and work.—In work as truly as in play there is satisfaction through 'escapement of an inner solicitude.' Work and play draw from the same fountain. They have more of likeness than of difference. Real play is exacting and exhausting, like work. That kind of work which counts for most is happy, contented, and buoyant because it is either life-giving in itself or moves towards a purposeful end that lightens the toil. It is done in the play attitude. Here lies the crux of a true interpretation of self-expression. Spontaneity is both serious and cheerful. As sometimes described, it is too thin and weak to function profoundly in the serious business of life with its tough struggles, defeats, and dearly-bought victories. The superficial romanticism, *e.g.*, of Rousseau and Novalis feels like an aroma, an efflorescence, or a gay holiday deliverance from the slavery of a work-a-day world. It openly rebels against the plodding programme of common life and the slavery of duty, conscience, and obligation, and lands in a 'romantic primitivism' with its 'delightful sense of having got rid of all boundaries and limitations whatsoever.'[1]

On the contrary, the energy concept of self-expression regards play, work, art, and religion as having a far more rugged constitution. Spontaneity in these human interests involves the stress and strain, the sweat and drudgery, the pain and tragedy of the world as truly as its moments of joyous self-realization. They are only part of the creative energy of the world.

'So far as the creative power of energy is concerned we are on sure ground: in physics energy controls matter and form; in physiology function controls the organ; in animal mechanics motion controls and, in a sense, creates the form of muscles and bones. In every instance, some kind of energy or work precedes some kind of form, rendering it probable that energy also precedes and controls the evolution of life.'[2]

In like vein Bergson:

'Reality is a perpetual growth, a creation pursued without end. Our will already performs this miracle. Every human work in which there is invention, every voluntary act in which there is freedom, every movement of an organism that manifests spontaneity, brings something new into the world.'[3]

9. Struggle and conflict in morality and religion.—The game of living out the personal, social, and ideal values is not an easy one because, in one aspect, it is bound up in nature's drama that has throughout the element of movement through opposition and resistance accompanied not infrequently by cataclysm. There is, furthermore, the disturbing fact that mentality is always prognosticating lines of possible improvement, anticipating more desirable situations that are at variance with old systems of habits and conventions. Hence the conflict. Duty usually presents herself initially as a stern lawgiver, a 'rod to check the erring and reprove.' Religion not infrequently has its birth through cries and groanings of the spirit. These hard experiences are but morality and religion in the making. When they discover themselves, they issue into naturalness, grace, and beauty.

'The life of the saints has always been a mystery to the non-religious. The joy, equanimity, and triumph which they have shown in the face of apparent suffering, discouragement, obstacles, and grief is one of the wonders of the human spirit. It makes work play; it makes torture pleasure; and it makes faith the beginning of life. One side of religion is humiliation, confession, and petition; another is praise, thanksgiving, and adoration. . . . Where grace aboundeth, there aboundeth joy. This is one of the beauties of the biography of the stricken and long-suffering who have found an abiding comfort in religion.'[4]

10. Morality and religion as spontaneous self-expression.—Self-expression is a dominant and central human instinct. It is more than an instinct, the impelling, creating something—call it energy, personality, world-will, God-life, or what you will—that is the real within the phenomenal. Morality and religion are forms of self-expression—morality when it plays through social values chiefly, and religion when it centres in ideal values predominantly. They are among the higher, more refined, rationalized, idealized, spiritualized forms of self-expression.

'Only in some such view is it easy to understand the meaning of much that passes under the name of religion. From this standpoint one can take a sympathetic attitude toward dancing, shouting, boisterous music, ecstasy, and the like which accompany lower forms of religion; and in higher forms, the prominent place of music and other arts of reverie and contemplation, of ritual, of missionary activity, and of worship—the pure uprush of the spirit in the contemplation of high things, which is perhaps the centre and heart of religion. One may regard religion as consisting essentially in the spontaneous act of the soul in response to its most intimate sense of absolute worth.'[1]

LITERATURE.—See the works cited in the footnotes.

EDWIN D. STARBUCK.

[1] I. Babbitt, *The New Laokoon*, Boston and London, 1910, p. 82 f.
[2] Osborn, p. 10 f.
[3] *Creative Evolution*, Eng. tr., London, 1912, p. 252.
[4] C. E. Seashore, 'The Play Impulse and Attitude in Religion,' *AJTh* xiv. [1910] 505-520.

[1] E. D. Starbuck, 'The Play Instinct and Religion,' *HR* (American ed.) lviii. [Oct. 1909] 278.

SELFISHNESS.—See SELF-LOVE.

SELF-LOVE.—The term 'self-love' is peculiarly associated with 18th cent. ethical speculation; indeed its employment by the English moralists of that period forms a distinguishing feature of their writings. In all such cases the term was understood to have reference (though by Butler other references were also included) to the question as to the disinterestedness or otherwise of the benevolent affections.

The prominence of this question was originally due to the influence—carried over from the previous century—of Thomas Hobbes (*q.v.*), who had made self-love the ultimate object of all human action, had rejected the notion of disinterested virtue, and had represented the affections as only so many forms of self-love. The ascendancy of the selfish philosophy, however, gave rise, early in the 18th cent., to a reaction against it. The latter movement was of the nature not so much of a direct attack on the then dominant tendency as of an attempt to show that the principles of Hobbes and Mandeville required to be considered in relation to certain other principles, and to be reinterpreted accordingly. Shaftesbury, Hutcheson, and Butler (*q.v.*), the protagonists of the new school, were so far in agreement. But the last-named thinker differed from the two others in respect to the point of view from which he regarded the diversity of elements in human nature, and it is to this peculiarity that the more technical character of Butler's doctrine of self-love is mainly to be attributed. Though in his exposition benevolence, self-love, and conscience are regarded as primary constituents of human nature, yet the moral quality of each of these is made to depend (and this especially applies to self-love) on what it is in relation to the rest and to the whole of which it forms part, rather than on what it is in itself. Thus, with regard to benevolence, Butler's attention does not centre exclusively, as did that of the intuitive school of moralists, in the self-evidencing superiority of the claims of benevolence over those of self-love; whilst, on the other hand, with regard to self-love he is even more express in insisting that it demands recognition, on the ground that it serves a necessary and salutary purpose in the economy of human nature. Butler indeed is concerned not so much with self-love as with its relationships. The sporadic character of his references to the subject may perhaps thus be explained.[2] The definition given of self-love in

[2] 'It is perhaps to be wished that he could have found occasion to gather into one *conspectus* all the important and leading propositions on the subject [self-love] scattered about his Works' (W. E. Gladstone, *Studies subsidiary to the Works of Bishop Butler*, Oxford, 1896, p. 62).

Sermon xi.,[1] however, contains a sufficiently positive statement as to its nature:

'Every man hath a general desire of his own happiness. . . . [This] proceeds from, or is, self-love; and seems inseparable from all sensible creatures, who can reflect upon themselves and their own interest or happiness.'

Note that it is not here said that self-love itself produces happiness. Happiness, in Butler's view, is procurable only by the attainment of 'those objects which are by nature suited to our several particular appetites, passions, and affections.' All that self-love can do is to serve as an indirect agent; its office is, in Butler's expressive phrase, to 'put us upon' obtaining our own happiness. Thus, in the case of hunger, the particular desire is for food; self-love is but the general concern for our own welfare which prompts us to gratify the particular desire.

The argument is that 'all particular appetites and passions are towards *external things themselves*, distinct from the *pleasure arising from them*.'[2]

This is a matter of great importance not only for the right understanding of Butler's view, but also as bearing upon subsequent ethical theories, these being divisible into two classes according as they do, or (as with Butler) do not, represent that the motive of all our actions is the appeasing of pain and the gaining of pleasure.[3]

Note further the presupposition involved in the last words of the definition, viz. those relating to the reflective character of self-love. This is the feature referred to when Butler speaks of the 'cool principle of self-love.' In so speaking he means something more than that, in the interests of self-love, we should reflect before we act. His intention rather is to explain the function served by reflexion in bringing to light the total interests of our being, and to emphasize the fact that it is only with these that self-love is concerned. For, in one sense, our own self-love is at the bottom of everything we do, *i.e.* in the sense that 'every particular affection' is a man's own, and 'the pleasure arising from its gratification' is his own pleasure, so that 'no creature whatever can possibly act but merely from self-love.'[4]

As distinguished from this, 'cool,' or (as it is elsewhere and perhaps better called) 'reasonable,' self-love expresses the judgment of our whole being, after taking into account 'the relations and respects which the parts have to each other.'

The two leading points with regard to the positive nature of self-love having thus been determined, viz. that it is the desire for happiness and that this desire leads to reflexion, with the result that we are enabled to act in conformity with our own self-interest in the most comprehensive sense, we are next invited to consider the relation in which self-love stands to benevolence.

'There is a natural principle of benevolence in man,' says Butler, 'which is in some degree to society what self-love is to the individual.'[5]

He, of course, admits that self-love may assert itself at the expense of benevolence, but this is so, he urges, only in the same sense in which self-love may assert itself at the expense of any other particular appetite, passion, or desire.

'The idea of self-love . . . can no otherwise exclude goodwill or love of others, than merely by not including it, no otherwise, than it excludes love of arts or reputation, or of any thing else.'[6]

This, no doubt, is carrying the distinction between self-love and the particular affections to its furthest lengths. But, when Butler's argument is disencumbered of his peculiar psychology, there need be no difficulty in accepting his general conclusion, as, *e.g.*, in the following passage:

'That any affection tends to the happiness of another, does not hinder its tending to one's own happiness too. That others enjoy the benefit of the air and the light of the sun, does not hinder but that these are . . . one's own private advantage.'[1]

Moreover, there is truth in this assertion of his:

Though 'there is indeed frequently an inconsistence or interfering between self-love or private interest, and the several particular appetites, passions, affections, or the pursuits they lead to,' yet 'this competition or interfering is merely accidental; and happens much oftener between pride, revenge, sensual gratifications, and private interest, than between private interest and benevolence.'[2]

And, again, he is fully justified in impugning the theory of Hobbes that benevolent affection and its pleasures are merely a form of the love of power, and in maintaining that 'the love of power manifests its consequences quite as much in cruelty as in benevolence.'[3] In respect to Hobbes, however, it is of more importance to note that Butler mitigates the supposed mutual opposition of self-love and benevolence by holding, with Aristotle, that man is naturally a social animal:

'That mankind is a community, that we all stand in a relation to each other . . . is the sum of morals.'[4]

And these two principles of self-love and benevolence are, we are told, so far connected that 'we can scarce promote the one without the other' and 'self-love is one chief security of our right behaviour towards society.'[5]

There remains to be considered the more positive association of self-love with morality which, from Butler's point of view, means its relation to conscience. Conscience, like self-love, is called a principle of reflexion, but, in the case of conscience, the principle is that 'by which men distinguish between, approve and disapprove their own actions.'[6] They both lead us the same way, though the fact that they do so awaits its perfect manifestation in the final distribution of things. This, though it may be disputed, cannot be regarded as a forced or arbitrary conclusion, since throughout his whole demonstration Butler exhibits the parts of human nature as having been designed by God for the furtherance of a common purpose and in the interests of the moral order. The coincidence of duty and interest is 'implied in the notion of a good and perfect administration of things.'[7] No doubt, passion or interest may rebel against the authority of conscience, but this is a mere usurpation, 'a violation of the constitution of man.' Again, we may submit only to such restraints as tend to our own interests and convenience. It is right that we should do so, says Butler, for our own happiness is the measure or end of virtue. Only, it is not vice but virtue that promotes happiness, and self-love does, in its true sense, accompany virtue.[8] However, apart from these statements regarding the harmony of virtue and self-interest, the higher character of self-love sufficiently appears from the mere consideration of the purpose for which, according to Butler, it exists.

'Surely there is nothing ignoble in conceiving,' says Gladstone (paraphrasing his master), 'of the Christian world as a garden divided into plots, each of which represents an individual soul, and is committed by the supreme Gardener, to the special care of that same soul. Self-love, then, in the only commendable sense, is our view, taken with the eye well purged from disturbance and obstruction, of what God has committed to every one of us as our principal work in life.'[9]

[1] 'Upon the Love of our Neighbour,' *ad init.*

[2] *Loc. cit.*

[3] Cf. on Butler, with reference to this question, A. Bain, *Mental and Moral Science*[3], London, 1884, p. 575; and, on the other side, T. H. Green, *Prolegomena to Ethics*[3], Oxford, 1890, p. 240, and likewise the whole of ch. iv. of bk. iii. in the latter volume; also H. Sidgwick, *Methods of Ethics*[6], London, 1901, ch. iv.

[4] *Loc. cit.*

[5] Serm. i., 'Upon Human Nature.'

[6] Serm. xi.

[1] Serm. xi.

[2] *Ib.*

[3] Cf. Bain, *Mental and Moral Science*[3], p. 574.

[4] Serm. ix., 'Upon Forgiveness of Injuries.'

[5] Cf. W. Lucas Collins, *Butler* (Philosophical Classics for English Readers), new ed., Edinburgh and London, 1901, p. 54 ff.

[6] Serm. i.

[7] Serm. iii., 'Upon Human Nature.'

[8] Cf. Collins, p. 53.

[9] *Studies*, p. 102. At the same time, on p. 63 of this work too much is claimed for self-love under its religious aspects.

Self-love gradually ceased after Butler's time to retain the technical significance which he first had imparted to it. Hume[1] has an interesting discussion on the subject, whilst Price[2] confirms the teaching of Butler. And there are frequent references to self-love (which, however, is not always called by this name) in other writings of the period previous to the rise of the utilitarian school of ethics dating from Jeremy Bentham. But the subtlety of Butler's conception is peculiar to himself. An altogether grosser, though no doubt a more easily comprehensible, view as regards the claims of self acquired wide vogue not long after Butler's death, owing to the influence of Paley. Butler's psychological method, typically illustrated by his treatment of self-love, passed out of favour. More recently the study of the mind in the light of anthropological and physiological researches has changed the point of view from which ethical questions had been previously regarded. Not only so, but, even if we confine ourselves to the field of ethics pure and simple, we shall find that utilitarians and transcendentalists are agreed in ascribing to such speculations as those of Butler on human nature a purely historical value.

This, however, being admitted, or partly admitted (for there are at all events many side-issues on which these speculations throw light), the subject of this article, both on its own account and on account of its treatment by the English school of moralists (especially during the period which is of chief significance in connexion with it), will be found to present numberless attractions alike to the student of ethics and to the student of history, all the more so inasmuch as the interest taken in it during the 18th cent. is embodied in the literature of the period not less than in its philosophy, and was not more a favourite topic of discussion in England than it was abroad.

See also artt. SELF-CULTURE, SELF-DISCIPLINE, SELF-REALIZATION, SELF-SACRIFICE.

LITERATURE.—Anthony Ashley Cooper (third Earl of Shaftesbury), *Characteristics of Men, Manners, Opinions, Times*, 3 vols., London, 1711, and frequently reprinted; Francis Hutcheson, *A System of Moral Philosophy*, 2 vols., Glasgow and London, 1755, esp. bk. i. chs. 1 and 3; J. Butler, *Sermons and Remains*, ed. E. Steere, London, 1862, *Works*, 2 vols., ed. J. H. Bernard, do. 1900; T. Fowler, *Shaftesbury and Hutcheson*, do. 1882; Leslie Stephen, *Hist. of English Thought in the 18th Century*[2], 2 vols., do. 1881, ch. ix.; T. H. Green, *Works*, ed. R. L. Nettleship, 2 vols., do. 1885–88, vol. i. pp. 325–331; Matthew Arnold, *Last Essays on Church and Religion*, do. 1877, pp. 111–114; artt. 'Butler, Joseph' and 'Ethics' in *EBr*[11]; art. 'Butler, Joseph' in *DNB*; artt. 'Butler' and 'Hobbes' in *ERE*, in addition to the works already cited in the course of this article.

C. A. WHITTUCK.

SELF-PRESERVATION.—The term 'self-preservation' is used in ethics to denote (1) a particular duty and (2) the highest principle of conduct. In the first sense the term explains itself, referring to the duty, recognized to some extent by most systems, of preserving one's own life so far as is consistent with the demands of the highest good. The self to be preserved is here usually interpreted as the physical self or life, and the duty is taken to include the use of all means necessary for its maintenance—the care of health and the avoidance of unnecessary risk, as well as the more serious and unusual measures necessary for self-defence against violence. Even the more extreme forms of religious ethics, in which resistance is forbidden, usually recognize the care of the body as a duty. In some of the Oriental types of mystical pantheism or nihilism, however, which place the goal of life in the loss of selfhood and the freedom from the illusion of individuality, even this moderate care for the self ceases to have merit. The self, as ordinarily conceived, is to be neglected or suppressed in order that the one Being may be all in all. The evil selfhood to be overcome is essentially the individual will with its desires, rather than the mere physical body, but the latter, as the bearer of these desires, is also to be at least kept down to the lowest level consistent with bare life. So also in Western pessimism, with its conception of the world as a mistake, there can be no recognition of a positive duty of self-preservation. The negation of the will to live involves only a temporary and conditional tolerance of physical life.

When used as the supreme principle in ethics, the term 'self-preservation' has generally had certain specific implications not commonly present in its usage as a particular duty. In the first place, systems which make morality consist in self-preservation are essentially individualistic, whatever may be their final conception of the self. They conceive of morality as a product of selves, which develop it as a means to their own preservation. Social action may be shown to be necessarily involved in final and adequate action for the self, but it is involved as means and not as end. In Spinoza's system this is not unambiguously the case, but in the typical systems of the class it is fundamental. In the second place, such systems imply a struggle between individuals in which the conditions of self-preservation become the recognized laws of morality. The supreme good for each individual is thus his survival in the struggle for existence, and his supreme duty is the acquirement of power for this end. The ideal is in some sense the strong man, and right is made equivalent to might. In the third place, these theories emphasize the genetic or historical aspects of the problem. They are theories of how morality with its restraints came to be, and they are, accordingly, symptomatic of changes taking place in moral living, expressions of attempts to transvalue old values and find new meanings for life. In this sense they are revolutionary systems—ethics of revolt.

It is these implications that distinguish the concept of self-preservation from the similar terms 'self-development' and 'self-realization,' in both of which idealistic meanings are involved. In self-development the self is regarded as having a positive content which is unfolded on occasion of the stimuli furnished by experience, whereas in the self-preservation theories its content is determined by the environment. Self-determination is the implication of self-development. Similarly, the theory of self-realization (*q.v.*), as held by T. H. Green and his school, implies a conception of the self as rational and universal, and sees in morality the progressive unfolding of a single rational life. It is thus the direct antithesis of the individualism and naturalism of the self-preservation theory.

The representatives of this type of ethical theory are found in modern philosophy, not in ancient thought. It is true that some of the sophistic theories seem to express this revolutionary and individualistic tendency, but in general their emphasis seems to have been on self-interest rather than on self-preservation, on advantages to be gained rather than on a life to be conserved. They tend, therefore, to be hedonistic rather than biological or metaphysical. The individualism of the Hellenistic period took the form, not of revolt, but of abstention and withdrawal from active life. The Epicurean, while an individualist, had no taste for the active life, the good, as conceived by him, being the result, not of struggle, but rather of compromise.

It is not till the late mediæval, or early modern, period that we find typical theories of self-preserva-

[1] *An Enquiry concerning the Principles of Morals*, London, 1751, appendix ii.

[2] *A Review of the Principal Questions and Difficulties in Morals*, London, 1758, ch. iii.

tion. They arose as the expression of the growing gap between the Church and secular civilization, with the consequent necessity of finding a natural sanction for moral and political law. Even within the limits of late Scholasticism we find nominalistic political theorists taking the fallen state of mankind as conceived by the Church as the basis for a doctrine of sovereignty in which the State figures as the power necessary to control and further the interests of naturally unsocial individuals. The confusion of the religious wars emphasized still more the radically unsocial character of human nature, so that it is not surprising to find a complete doctrine of self-preservation put forward by Thomas Hobbes in his *Leviathan*, in the midst of the English civil wars.

According to **Hobbes**, individuals are reaction-machines, conveying the motion furnished by the stimulus inwards to the brain and heart, whence it is returned to the muscles, and issues in action either towards or away from the stimulus. The tendency towards the object is desire or appetite; the tendency away from it is aversion. The former, which is accompanied by a sense of pleasure, is 'a corroboration of vital motion and help thereto,' and its object we call good; the latter is accompanied by a sense of displeasure, and its object we call evil. Good and evil thus get their whole natural significance from their relation to the life of the individual, and have no meaning in themselves. The fundamental and necessary impulse of every individual is directed towards those objects and activities that minister to the preservation and enlargement of life, so that we may 'put for a general inclination of all mankind a perpetual and restless desire of power after power that ceaseth only in death.' As a consequence, the natural condition of mankind is one of struggle, in which the only consideration is survival. The evils of such a war of all against all are so great and apparent that reason dictates conditions of peace, and men agree to renounce their natural rights of free offensive, in order that there may be a common power able to preserve order and make possible the values of peace. If the fundamental natural right is that of self-defence, its complement is the fundamental law of nature, 'to seek peace and follow it.'[1] All obligations go back to the primary fact that his own life is each man's nearest concern, and whatever is to be demanded of him must be demanded in the name of his own preservation. That social co-operation is the best means to accomplish this end is eternally true, but, until there is an organized State to compel peace, social morality can be only an ideal for the individual, and his actual practice must rely upon force and fraud as the means necessary for survival in war-time. Yet, while law-observance is, under almost all conditions, best for the individual, and hence has the strongest sanction, Hobbes recognizes that obedience is not an absolute obligation. There can be no gain to the individual in losing his life, and hence no reason why he should not resist the State when it threatens his life. Under these conditions we revert to the state of nature again, and use force and fraud to escape the extreme penalty of the law. The State has a right to crush us, but we have an equal right to resist, since social morality has only a conditional and conventional obligation. This reservation of the individual's right of self-defence (which is, of course, subversive of Hobbes' whole theory of State absolutism) illustrates well the essential characteristics of the self-preservation theory—its individualism, its naturalism, and its revolutionary character. Hobbes conceives of the end as the conservation of the individual life, for the sacrifice of which nothing can compensate. All that a man hath will he give, and should give, for his life. And, similarly, this life is identified with the physical life and its actual desires. An ideal or universal self can have no meaning in Hobbes' sensationalistic psychology. Selves are sharply distinct, and their relations are those of barter. So, too, the revolutionary or anarchic character of the doctrine is involved in its atomic individualism and its recognition of no ideal basis for the unity of society.

[1] *Leviathan*, ch. xiv.

These implications of the doctrine are brought out more clearly by comparison with a system whose principle seems identical with that of Hobbes, is, indeed, historically related to it, but whose development is different—so different that some would refuse to place it in the same class with his. This is the system of **Spinoza**. Like Hobbes, Spinoza assumes that the essence of each thing is its tendency to be, to persist in its being, its *conatus sese conservandi*. Whatever is done must in some way be the outcome of this inevitable tendency of each thing to be itself. It is inconceivable that anything could do anything else than be itself. Hence the virtue of the individual can consist only in the most complete self-expression.

'As Reason requires nothing contrary to Nature, it requires that each love himself, seek his own advantage, what is really for his own advantage, and desire all that which really raises man to greater perfection, and, to speak generally, it requires that each endeavour to maintain his own being as far as possible. . . . The foundation of happiness consists in this, that the man is able to preserve his own being.'[1]

Virtue does not consist, therefore, in self-abnegation or in mere negative control of passions, but in self-expansion and the attainment of positive good. The good man is the strong man. Repentance, humility, as signs of weakness, have only a slight value, and pity, so far as it is a mere feeling, is to be discouraged. This self-assertion, however, is not anti-social, since man is most useful to man. Moreover, man can be useful to man only in so far as he is himself a positive force and has something of his own to give. To be anything for another, one must be oneself. The good, therefore, Spinoza, with Hobbes, conceives, not as absolute, but as relative to the nature whose good it is. We do not desire things because they are good, but they are good because we desire them. No object of desire is in itself bad, but it may become bad when considered in relation to the whole system of desires with the satisfaction of which it may interfere. For man, as conscious, is able to form a concept of himself as a whole and hence of his total or ultimate good, which then becomes the object of his reflective pursuit. It is in his conception of the nature of the self and of its power that Spinoza differs from Hobbes and makes his classification difficult. For the self is essentially a rational self and, in so far as truly conceived, is one with the infinite nature of God. The more clearly it thinks, therefore, the more it is itself and the more adequately it expresses the nature of God. The more adequately, in turn, it conceives itself, the less is it in subjection to the power of the passions. The man who takes a thinking view of things knows himself and all things as modes of God and therefore absolutely determined both in nature and in existence by the divine nature. Knowing this absolute necessity of things, he ceases to be moved by things as individual, and fixes his contemplation on the order of nature as a whole. In this life of thought he is more truly active and himself, and therefore finds in it his highest joy. This joyful contemplation of the necessary order of things is the intellectual love of God and man's highest good. He is then free from the bondage of passion and

[1] *Ethica*, pt. iv., prop. 18, schol.

self-controlled. And, in so far as he is freed from his passions, he ceases to contend with others with whom he is united, in so far as they too have come to the recognition of their place in the necessary order of the world.

With Hobbes the tendency towards self-preservation and the power necessary to ensure it lead to the establishment of an external control through fear of which men restrain, but do not extirpate, their inordinate desires. With Spinoza the same tendency leads to the development of a rational view of the self and the world, which itself suffices to control the passions and make possible a common life. In the doctrine of Hobbes morality is a mere tool of which the individual makes use for his private ends, and which, under certain conditions, he may reject. In Spinoza virtue is itself blessedness. The knowledge which is power is not, as with Bacon, a power to do, but a power to be—the insight which is alone able to make man master of his passions.

The influence of Hobbes and Spinoza upon their age is to be found chiefly in the antagonisms which they aroused, and it is not till we come to the middle of the 19th cent. that we have again instances of the doctrine of self-preservation. And here it is not as expressions of political conditions that we find them, but as applications of the principles of biology to ethics. This is strictly true of the motives of **Herbert Spencer**, but in the case of Nietzsche the biological analogy is of secondary, rather than primary, importance.

The biological theory of evolution[1] has affected ethics in two ways: (1) by its contribution to the study of the development of morality, through which it has supplemented the older associationalist account of the genesis of conscience; and (2) by its suggestion of a new standard of morals, through which it has attempted to render the older utilitarian doctrine more exact. Spencer's *Data of Ethics* is concerned with both these problems, but the treatment of the latter is the more distinctive. His quarrel with the utilitarians, as he explains in a letter to J. S. Mill, is based upon the unscientific character of pleasure as a standard of conduct.

'The business of Moral Science [is] to deduce, from the laws of life and the conditions of existence, what kinds of action necessarily tend to produce happiness, and what kinds to produce unhappiness.'[2]

Morality is only the latest phase of life in general; its laws, therefore, are only developments of the general laws of life. These laws of life are the conditions of self-preservation as they have been developed in the struggle of individuals and groups for existence. All life is striving to persist and to grow, and the moral life is only the final and self-conscious stage of the resulting development. A moral life is one that conduces to greater life, measured, not in mere length, but in breadth, or complexity, of activities as well. As biology, psychology, and sociology grow more exact, we shall have a more scientifically worked out system of morals in place of our empirical or rule-of-thumb system. Life and more life is thus the end suggested by the evolutionary theory. No distinction of quality can be recognized without destroying the value of the exact quantitative method. The breadth of life, which is recognized as one of the dimensions, means, not width of rationally interesting activities, development of a broadly human point of view, but only variety and complexity of biological activities so far as these promote survival. If conflict were to arise between these two dimensions of length and breadth so that the individual should have to choose between them, it would seem that the fundamental principle of self-preservation would demand the sacrifice of breadth to length. Spencer's assumption that no such conflict can arise is perhaps due to his pre-occupation with the absolute ethics of ideal conditions. Certainly breadth of life cannot have equal value with length as a factor in determining quantity of life as the criterion of the moral, nor can any meaning be given to the idea of their multiplication into a single product. In the absence of any fixed unit, the very conception of quantity of life remains even more indefinite than the pre-scientific idea of the greatest happiness, which it was devised to supplant.

But, while Spencer emphasizes the fact that human conduct is what it is because the struggle for existence has so shaped it, and while therefore the end of self-preservation would seem to be the test of good and bad conduct, he yet insists that life is not in itself a value, but that it is pleasure alone that justifies it. Remove the pleasurable feeling from even the longest life and it would have no more value than a handful of dust. The universal object of desire is pleasure. There seem therefore to be two ends of human action: from the biological point of view, life is a ceaseless struggle to preserve and increase itself; from the psychological point of view, it is a search for pleasure. That the individual is not torn in two by this dual tendency is due to the fact that the two aims actually coincide—that, in the long run and under ideal conditions, pleasure-producing actions are also life-preserving. It must be so, Spencer urges, because the creature who took delight in conduct not conducive to life would be eliminated. This, of course, is no proof that pleasure is the universal object of desire, but only that, granting it to be such, the coincidence of its conditions with those of self-preservation can be explained. The implication is that the real determinants of conduct are mechanical, and that our conscious aims and interests are wholly fixed by the conditions of survival. It is physical life that unfolds itself in personal and social conduct, and it is to its laws that our conscious aims are to be adjusted. Its laws, moreover, are not so much expressions of its own nature as forms impressed upon it by the environment. Although the term 'self-preservation' seems to imply self-assertion and individual initiative, actually, as conceived by Spencer and the evolutionists, it has no such meaning. The self, whether we think of it as moulded by the direct action of the environment or as picked out by natural selection (and Spencer uses both theories), has no character of its own, makes no contribution to the result, but is wholly the product of the impersonal world-forces outside it. The forms of moral conduct are selected *for* man, not *by* him. It is the universe that is asserting itself, not individuals, and a universe in which there seem to be no real selves, but only 'others.'

The doctrine of **Friedrich Nietzsche** can be called one of self-preservation only in so far as he makes use of the biological conceptions of struggle and survival to support his thesis. As in the case of Hobbes, self-preservation is almost too negative a term to apply to that will-to-power which Nietzsche makes the essence of each individual being. The intellect and its creations have no independent value, but are only instruments in the service of this instinctive life. There is no purpose discoverable in the world at large; we are here, and our only intent is to fight our way to ever greater power. Unlike Hobbes, he can see no value in peace and ordered morality. All restraint, as a lowering of life, is bad. Nor is Nietzsche a hedonist in his individualism: it is not pleasure that gives value to life, rather almost is it pain. It is the glory and excitement of combat, the

[1] See art. EVOLUTION (Biological).

[2] *Principles of Ethics*, pt. i. ch. vi. § 21.

struggle itself, the sense of strength, that make it worth while. To eliminate this struggle, to make life comfortable and safe, is to take from it all that gives it its terrible charm. Hence our social morality and our religions of sympathy and renunciation are to be condemned as encouragements to the weak and inferior. This slave-morality of the herd is to be replaced by the master-morality of the higher man, and its supreme command is, 'Be hard.' Nietzsche's doctrine is thus one of pure individualism; the self to be preserved is the natural self of impulse, and its goal is the attainment of power in the abstract—not power for the realization of any final end, but power as power, empty of any end which might give meaning to its possession. It is the dream of the adolescent, impatient of restraint but unconscious of his ends. His ideal, therefore, in spite of its not making use of the name itself, is perhaps, in its individualism, its naturalism, and its anarchism, the most typical of the theories of self-preservation.

In Nietzsche, too, can be clearly seen both the strength and the weakness of these systems. They are strong in so far as they lay emphasis upon the actual self-preservative instincts and tendencies necessary for existence. Any order of life, whatever its ideal, must be rooted in the actual motive forces of human nature, must appeal to some real interest of the individual, or else remain a meaningless and remote idea, powerless to affect life. It is this that those thinkers feel and provide for—a real interest in the given ideal—under the obvious assumption that there can be no nearer and dearer interest to a man than his own self.

But they are weak in so far as they fail to recognize the reality of any other self than that which finds expression in the natural instincts of man—in so far as they refuse to admit a self whose interests are not individual, but reflectively social. Apart from the recognition of the reality of a direct interest in an over-individual good, Nietzsche rightly sees that there can be no such thing as moral obligation; hence his characterization of his doctrine as immoralism. Individualism made absolute renounces its claim as morality, and is indeed unable consistently to plead its cause. Self-centred and antagonistic selves can have no common good and therefore no basis for co-operative action or rational obligation. There may be an over-lordship based upon might, but no reasonable organization expressing the natural interests of all in a common life, and consequently no ground for a moral appeal for the recognition of any law not actualized by force.

The assumption upon which all these theories rest, however, that the individual is essentially and wholly a self-seeking creature, is not tenable in the light of our present psychology. The contention of Butler, as well as of the moral sense writers, that the other-regarding impulses are as fundamental as the self-regarding, has been borne out by all recent analysis. The fact that our desires are *our* desires by no means implies that we ourselves are their objects. The contrary rather is true, that our tendencies are naturally directed upon objects other than the self, and that conscious self-seeking is a secondary and reflective product. There is no reason against, but, on the contrary, all the evidence for, the fact that the social good is as immediate and natural an object as the private good, and, with this granted, the theories of self-preservation lose their plausibility.

LITERATURE.—Hobbes, *Leviathan*, London, 1651, *Human Nature*, do. 1650; Spinoza, *Ethica*, Amsterdam, 1670, *Tractatus Politicus*, do. 1670; Spencer, *The Principles of Ethics*, 2 vols., London, 1892–93; Nietzsche, *Beyond Good and Evil*[2], Eng. tr. (vol. v. of *Complete Works*, ed. O. Levy), Edinburgh, 1909, *The Genealogy of Morals*, Eng. tr. (*Complete Works*, xiii.), do. 1910, *Thus Spake Zarathustra*, Eng. tr. (*Complete Works*, iv.), do. 1909; H. Sidgwick, *Outlines of the Hist. of Ethics*[5], London, 1902, ch. iv., *The Methods of Ethics*[7], do. 1907, bk. i. ch. vii.; R. A. Duff, *Spinoza's Political and Ethical Philosophy*, Glasgow, 1903; Warner Fite, *Introd. Study of Ethics*, New York, 1903, ch. iv.; W. R. Sorley, *On the Ethics of Naturalism*, Edinburgh and London, 1885, pt. ii.; J. Watson, *Hedonistic Theories*, Glasgow, 1895, ch. ix.–xi.; J. Dewey and J. H. Tufts, *Ethics*, New York and London, 1908, ch. xviii. § 2; Havelock Ellis, *Affirmations*, New York, 1915; H. L. Stewart, *Nietzsche and the Ideals of Modern Germany*, London, 1915; H. H. Joachim, *A Study of the Ethics of Spinoza*, Oxford, 1901, pt. iii.; G. Croom Robertson, *Hobbes* (vol. x. of Blackwood's 'Philosophical Classics'), Edinburgh and London, 1886; Leslie Stephen, *Hobbes*, London and New York, 1904, ch. iii. f.; F. Tönnies, *Hobbes Leben und Lehre*, Stuttgart, 1896; J. N. Figgis, *Studies of Political Thought from Gerson to Grotius*, Cambridge, 1907, ch. vi. f.

NORMAN WILDE.

SELF-REALIZATION.—1. 'Self-realization' is a term so vague and indefinite in connotation that some writers on ethics (*e.g.*, Sidgwick) consider that it would be well to expunge it from the vocabulary of ethical science. This indefiniteness is largely due to the ambiguity of the word 'self,' and also partly caused by the vagueness of 'realization.' The self can indeed be defined with varying degrees of narrowness or of comprehensiveness—a fact which is often expressed, in loose and inaccurate phraseology, by the assertion that each individual has many selves, such as the bodily, the animal, the rational, the social, self. 'Realization,' again, is a word which, in this connexion, may be taken to include or to exclude what is usually called 'self-suppression' or 'self-sacrifice.' Thus, before any precise meaning can be attached to the compound term 'self-realization,' it is necessary first to define precisely what is meant by 'self' and 'realization' respectively.

If (i.) the self be understood predominantly as sentient, and the individual's highest good be accordingly taken to be pleasure, self-realization will consist in so living as to secure for oneself the maximum of pleasurable feeling. This was the doctrine of the Cyrenaics (*q.v.*), and the more degenerate members of that school tended to identify self-realization with what would more correctly be called self-indulgence. The better Cyrenaics, however, did not restrict pleasure to the pleasures of sense, but rather had higher forms of pleasure—*e.g.*, that of friendship—in mind. Similarly the Epicureans (*q.v.*) repudiated sensualism or slavery to the lower desires and passions, while adopting a hedonism akin to that of the Cyrenaics.

If (ii.) man's rational nature be regarded as the truest expression of the self, and the highest individual good be accordingly sought in the control of the lower or animal 'self' by right reason, then self-realization will consist in the attainment of rationality or reasonableness and will involve suppression of many impulses and desires: the whole self, or the self in all its spheres of conative activity, will thus not be 'realized.' Anti-hedonistic ethic, proceeding on these lines, culminates in emphasis of self-sacrifice or self-discipline, even self-mutilation—in emphasis on the fact that we can only enter into the higher life halt or blind. Self-realization, according to this doctrine, is realization of the rational self at the expense of the sentient self. In ancient Greece the Cynics (*q.v.*) maintained such a view as this. They held that virtue is the chief good, and that virtue makes the human being independent of the vicissitudes of worldly fortune. The Cynics went on to teach that self-realization consists in living in the natural state, or according to nature. The Stoics (*q.v.*) also advocated realization of the rational self as the highest end, and, like the Cynics, inculcated freedom from the good or ill fortune which life may bring; but they saw the means to this end in repression of the elements of feeling, desire, and emotion. This was their chief difference from the Cynics; they differed from the Epicureans, to whom they were most directly opposed, in emphasizing the supremacy of reason over feeling. Virtue, for the Stoic, consisted in the assertion of the rational side of man, and largely in extirpation of the passions, till 'apathy' was attained. A similar ethic was taught, within the modern period, by Kant (*q.v.*), and indeed by many rationalists and intuitionists.

As against both of these one-sided theories, each of which does full justice to but one side of our complex nature, the eudæmonism (*q.v.*) of Aristotle may be instanced. This philosopher held that happiness is the chief good, and regarded happiness as the outcome of life according to virtue. In eudæmonism it is rather (iii.) the whole self that is to be realized, and writers of the eudæmonistic school emphasize, more than do most ancient hedonists, the place of pleasures of the mind, while at the same time they assign more value than did the Stoics to the external goods of life and the æsthetic (as distinguished from the strictly ethical) adornments of conduct and character. Thus eudæmonism sees in self-realization, at any rate far more completely than do hedonism and rationalism, the complete development of all sides of the self, and discountenances the extirpation of any.

From what has been said it will appear that self-realization, in one form or another, is adopted as the chief good by all forms of egoism, as distinguished from altruism and systems which emphasize (iv.) the social self. In the broadest sense, self-realization will denote development of personality to the utmost, 'personality' being here used to refer to fully actualized human nature, as contrasted with the individual life of the child, the savage, or the non-rational animal. All of these inevitably seek self-realization of a kind—at least they aim at self-preservation, and at self-betterment in some sense. But the broader self-realization, or complete attainment of personality, will consist partly in synthesis or co-ordination of the conative elements of experience, and partly in the development of all the capacities of the soul. The former of these processes involves progressive control of impulse, desire, and passion, with a view to securing a full and untrammelled life for the whole self, inclusive of the higher faculties of reason, will, and moral sense. It is the means of securing that the momentary self, or, more correctly, the passing impulse or desire of the moment, indulgence or pursuit of which would mar the happiness and well-being and thwart the abiding purpose of the whole self or personality, be not allowed to have free play. For passing impulses and present passions often conflict with the attainment of enduring happiness; and desires frequently conflict with one another. If the agent in his completeness, *i.e.* as rational, volitional, and moral, as well as sentient and appetitive, be the controller of every kind of factor of his moral experience, he can effect realization of his higher or better self such as otherwise may be unattainable. The latter of the processes included in the attainment of self-perfection will involve the full use of all the individual's 'talents' or endowments, whether they be few or many, great or small, in that these may be instrumental to the completest moralization and perfecting of the self.

2. The various possible senses of 'self-realization' having now been enumerated and defined, we may turn to the further question whether any of them be adequate as a description of the highest good, and notice briefly some of the chief criticisms which the conception has received.

In the first place, it must be admitted that self-realization is very seldom actually before the mind of a moral agent when he is about to perform a moral act. Moral acts are almost always done without any consciousness on the part of the agent, at the moment, of self-realization; that is not set up by him as the final cause of his action. He chooses the course of conduct which he pursues as good, rather than as good for him. So, unless we commit 'the psychologist's fallacy,' or confound the 'psychic' and the 'psychological' standpoints (*i.e.* the standpoint of the agent at the time of his action with the standpoint of the external observer or of universal, scientific, knowledge), we must deny that self-realization is an end or a final cause that we ever set before us or by which we are ever motived, save in exceptional cases. And, if it be retorted that self-realization does not profess to be the end or the good which is consciously in view for the moral agent himself, but is nevertheless, objectively speaking, a realization of the agent's self, whether the individual know it or not, we then encounter the difficulty that all our moral acts, whether good or bad, must be regarded as stages in the assertion or realization of the self. There are objects of quite different ethical value in which a self may find its satisfaction or realization; or, as it is commonly expressed, there are different selves, or aspects of the self, to be satisfied; there is always, in moral action, a choice between the realization of one or another element in the whole self, unless self-realization be a mere empty form without content. This point has already been touched upon in the foregoing description of the various partial meanings of the self, and it has been remarked before that self-realization in actuality always involves self-negation.

In so far as self-realization is identified with self-satisfaction (*q.v.*), it may be urged that there is satisfaction of a kind for some individuals in that which is not good; and the more settled principles of individual lives, with which the momentary act may be contrasted and be found in conflict—the permanent 'self'—are not always or necessarily the best. Permanency of satisfaction, if we regard the self which is to be realized as the permanent self, is but one mark among others of the good act, moreover, when the permanent self is the better man. And, if we contemplate the whole self, rather than the self as the permanent (in contrast with the momentary), we are reminded that the whole self is never realized; as such, it cannot be, for our earliest moral teaching is directed chiefly towards the securing of our self-suppression, and 'the manifold temptations which death alone can cure' arise from conflict within the whole self which never can be wholly eliminated, in the case of most of us, while life lasts. We cannot enter into life 'whole'; the only question is, What kind of 'a whole' are we to be?

3. We pass now to a difficulty which has not been foreshadowed in our initial account of what self-realization may be understood to mean—a difficulty which arises when we turn from egoistic theories to altruistic, or even to all ethical systems which see the highest good in the *common* good. Self-realization is obviously incapable of being identified with the highest good by the altruist, for whom conduct is good in so far as it subserves the realization of other selves than one's own. And, without going to the extreme of literal altruism, we may, and nowadays generally do, demand that social activity have at least some place in the ethical ideal. If altruism fails to take note of the ethical element involved in personal culture, purely egoistic theories, which regard self-realization alone as exhaustive of the ethical ideal, fail to take note of the 'social self' in man, and of the place which devotion to the common welfare occupies in a complete and adequate account of the moral life. There is much that is to be desired because it is good, though not because it is good for the particular agent bent exclusively on the realization of himself. The chief good must be desired by some self and for some self; but not necessarily by some self for itself. Thus self-realization alone, unless the term be used so broadly and vaguely as to include the extinction of self—as in the case of the patriot who dies for his country—cannot be the whole of the ethical end. Not realization, whether assertion or development, of the self is the essential rule of conduct, but rather the use of the self and all its powers and talents for the furtherance of the common, as well as of the individual agent's, welfare. Contribution and service thus take the pre-eminence over self-development and self-culture in the ethical ideal; and realization of the self can enter into the end only in so far as self-realization is compatible with, and conducive to, the common good. To seek one's own life merely is to lose it. Attainment of the end doubtless involves self-development and self-realization; but such development presupposes an end which is not the self.

Indeed the rational self is by no means rational, nor the whole self whole, if it be conceived as an independent unit; or, rather, an isolated rational individual is inconceivable. The realization of the individual self, as we know it, demands life in society; for without social intercourse there is no rationality, so thoroughly are we 'members one of another.' Our true self, regarded either as the rational self or as the whole self, can fully develop itself only by being also the social self, or by striving for social ends, which involves much sacrifice of the individual self. 'Looking at the matter, therefore, from this point of view, it might be better to describe the ultimate end as the realization of a rational universe, rather than as self-realization.'[1]

Christianity of course accentuates the idea that we are 'members one of another'; also the truth that self-sacrifice enters largely into the effort to attain to the highest end. It thus sees in that end something more than the realization of the individual self. And this something-more arises from man's relation to God as well as from his relation to his fellow-men. At the same time Christianity, through its doctrine of eternal life and its hope of immortality, is able to present an ideal of self-realization which escapes the inadequacy characteristic of such ideas of it as have as yet been discussed, in that it is one which embraces them and transcends their mutual conflictingness. For the Christian faith, in the doctrines just mentioned, recognizes yet another 'self' than those with which we have hitherto been concerned, viz. the eternal self or the self of the life to come, which may be realized only through devotion to the common good, and even through devotion unto death. Only, perhaps, when hope of an after life is thus presupposed can we reach a sense of 'self-realization' which is wholly compatible with the end as represented in non-egoistic systems of ethics; otherwise, from the point of view of such systems, self-realization will be but a means to an end.

But even in the light of a future life and of relation to a personal God we cannot now conceive fully how the distinct ideals of self-realization and of the social good can be reconciled and combined in one. Further consideration of how these ideals arise and are conditioned will enable us to appreciate the importance of this problem which seems to be ignored by the general assumption that there is but one absolute moral ideal or end presupposed in objective moral valuation.

Three levels of valuation are to be distinguished, each having its peculiar cognitional conditions and presupposing a different kind of abstraction from the effective-conational attitude called 'valuing.' At the sub-personal level we apprehend worths determined by individual feeling which we refer to the bodily self, and not to the self as person. Here the end is happiness, and our ethic is hedonism. At the personal level we apprehend worths determined by feelings, the presupposition of which is the ideally constructed self, and attainment of the ideal which now emerges involves sacrifice of the ideals of sub-personal valuation: pleasure must be subordinated to virtuous disposition. Personal dispositions have intrinsic value, and such objects may acquire absolute worth. These are internal to the self, and recognition of them is conditioned by abstraction from all instrumentality of the virtuous disposition to attainment of the common good. Their pursuit beyond certain limits is superfluous from the common or over-individual standpoint, though obligatory from that of the individual who is an end to himself. Finally, the self may participate in the valuations of his fellows, and play the rôle of the over-individual self or the impartial observer. He then contemplates exclusively the social good, and his intrinsic personal values have now to be sacrificed to the over-individual values of society. Of course the personal and the social ideals will at many points coincide; but they will not necessarily do so in all situations. And here the problem arises, Is there any absolute criterion or standard of preference for the one ideal over the other when, in concrete situations, they may conflict or be incompatibilities for the individual will? Such an *a priori* ground of preference seems to be beyond the range of our knowledge, and it becomes a question whether ethics is entitled to speak of one only absolute moral ideal, rather than of a plurality of them which cannot be unified. A philosophy of values may require a single supreme value; but from such a theoretical absolute there is no possibility of transition to an empirical unity of conscious ends and felt values. Perhaps the only direction in which we may look for a solution of this difficulty is in identification of the individual will with the metempirical will of God. Ultimate ends and their coalescence, it would seem, must be made intelligible otherwise than by logical subordination of the one to the other, and neither self-realization nor sacrifice to the social end can be the final word of ethics.

LITERATURE.—The text-books on ethics—*e.g.*, J. S. Mackenzie, *A Manual of Ethics*[4], London, 1900; A. E. Taylor, in *IJE* vi. [1895–96] 356 ff.; W. M. Urban, *Valuation: its Nature and Laws*, London, 1909.

F. R. TENNANT.

SELF-RESPECT.—I. Ethical import.—Self-respect is regard for one's existence, one's worth and dignity as a human person. As such it is a phenomenon both of civilization and of primitive society, although in its highest and most distinctly operative form it is a feature chiefly of the ethical life of the supposedly free and independent individual of modern times. It is here a high concern for one's personal honour and personal honesty, and for the due satisfaction of the powers and capacities of intelligent and active personality as a conscious possession. It is connected with the instincts and propensities of the 'self-feeling' (*Selbstgefühl*, *amour-propre*), with the various 'emotions of self' that are recognized and treated of by nearly all psychologists.

[1] Mackenzie, *Manual of Ethics*[4], p. 295.

'Whatever name we may give them,' says Ribot,[1] 'these emotional forms are reducible to one primary fact of which they are the embodiment in consciousness—viz., the feeling (well-founded or not) of personal strength or weakness, with the tendency to action or arrest of action which is its motor manifestation.'

They may also be connected with the instinct of conservation, the will to live. They are finally connected, however, with the feeling and the idea of individuality and personality. It is in the latter idea (or reality) that the self-preservative instinct 'attains to the full consciousness of itself, and becomes incarnated in the idea of the ego.'[2]

The primary self-feeling of the human individual[3] is no doubt an undifferentiated feeling. It may be connected with the feeling of the body (its increasing size, strength, power, etc.) or with the value of its activities to the tribal or family group in question. But in its higher and later developments this self-feeling is no doubt connected with the sense (or reality) of personality (*q.v.*), with one's conscious existence as a person among conscious persons. Where this sense is lacking, as it may be in some men of science or in moral weaklings, as well as in a Caliban, a Buddhist, or a mystic, there will be no such thing possible as self-respect, or even the sense of self-agency. The reality, however, at nearly all stages of civilization, of that manifestation of personality which we call self-respect is attested by evidence from all races.[4] We all, whatever our views about the universe, desire to be recognized and respected by our fellow-men, and we all dislike being ignored, or injured, or slighted by them. In ordinary life a man or woman without a self-respecting efficiency and sense of agency, without the reliability of the autonomous morality due to self-respect, is not looked upon as a responsible, or desirable, associate or servant.

And 'according to current ideas men owe to themselves a variety of duties similar in kind to those which they owe to their fellow-creatures. They are not only forbidden to take their own lives, but are also in some measure considered to be under an obligation to support their existence, to take care of their bodies, to preserve a certain amount of personal freedom, not to waste their property, to exhibit self-respect, and, in general, to promote their own happiness.'[5]

2. Development of the self-feeling.—The inevitable and the actual associations of the phenomena of self-respect with the various psychical tendencies underlying such terms as 'self-determination,' 'self-realization,' 'self-esteem,' etc., all tend to emphasize its connexion with that general growth in self-control, in rational self-love, in character, in the sense of personality, which forms such a large part of the study of genetic psychology or genetic sociology. Self-respect is undoubtedly a kind of development of the self-feeling that, at its lower levels, passes down into simple physical selfishness (natural egoism) and that has progressed from the second stage of self-interest and self-love to the third stage of a broad ethical force, or influence, that 'impels the individual to the pursuit of larger and more appropriate ends of activity.' At this last level it becomes a high, inward guarantee of objectively moral conduct. The very fact, however, that it has even here certain grave dangers and possible excesses and defects shows that it must indeed be studied in connexion with that entire development of the sense of individuality and separate personality which is our human birthright and which means the possibility of erring as well as of achieving and attaining. Self-esteem—Gall claimed a certain 'bump' for it in the brain—is probably the nearest expressive equivalent for self-respect; for the latter is clearly above some aspects of self-activity—above self-satisfaction or self-admiration, *e.g.*, and above even self-control and self-realization. And it is also a more ethical phenomenon than self-sufficiency, or that mere inward initiative and autonomy of which a confused thinker like Nietzsche would have us make so much. For there are very clearly many definite ethical norms and criteria of that true self-respect or that true self-esteem in which we all so thoroughly believe for ourselves and others. And, again, although a development of the sense of duty under which we are all brought up, self-respect is a still more reliable guarantee of really good conduct than the mere sense of binding duty. The latter will keep a man doubtless within the limits of what is definitely owed to others who have claims upon him—superiors, dependents, the law, God, and so on. But it is only an inward self-respect that will guarantee the higher conduct that may have to rise above what is definitely prescribed or demanded.

3. A phase of moral evolution.—We may see an important confirmation of the theory of the actual and the necessary connexion of self-respect with the different physical and intellectual forms of selfishness and self-interest in Henry Bradley's finding[1] that self-respect originally meant (1) 'a private, personal, or selfish end,' then (2) 'self-love, self-conceit,'[2] and finally (3) that ethical regard for one's person and position which is implied, *e.g.*, in John Hill Burton's phrase about the 'Scot Abroad'—'the well-becoming pride and self-respecting gravity.' And, with a further use of the same distinction—emphasized by moralists—between (1) the 'external,' (2) the 'internal,' and (3) the 'teleological' aspects of the moral standard, we may point out again that, even where morality is apparently sunk in external law or custom, we can still see there the self-respect that all human beings have either as physical existences or as members of some social group—the self-respect, *e.g.*, of some 'savage' female beauty, or the pride of an Aryan conqueror, a Brāhman, a Pharisee, a well-born Greek, a Spaniard, an Englishman. But, properly speaking, we are pointing out that self-respect belongs to, and remains on, that second great stage of moral evolution which we call 'internal' morality, the stage where morality has passed from 'instinct' and 'custom' to 'insight' and 'reflexion,' to inward or voluntary self-determination. Morality is never, properly speaking, morality at all as long as it is based upon mere natural instinct (self-defence, *e.g.*, protective anger, personal effort) or on mere custom (the law of the tribe or that of one's social set). Nor do we have morality on the basis of mere desire or emotion, mere feeling. Nor is morality mere duty or prescribed morality.

It is established and invested with a dignity and a controlling power only when 'it ceases to be wholly dependent on the fitful play of emotion, or on any externally imposed standard of duty; and possesses as well that higher appeal which lies in an inward sense of self-respect.' This inward sense 'disclaims the mean, the base, the cruel, not alone because injurious to others, and attended by the condemnation of others, but because of the scorn of self that would follow.' 'The morality that is based upon the resolution to be true to our own better selves has a greatness, a spaciousness, a completeness, that no other morality can approach. For no other moral sanction can so keenly probe into the shadiest corner of our minds, and ferret out the lurking meannesses of motive. Supreme then over most secret lives, it has power to stifle wrong that no other check could influence.'[3]

4. Defects and excesses.—But just at the very point of its true and proper function it is essential to refer to the defects and excesses and limitations of self-respect, and to connect them all with the fact of the undoubted superiority of the third stage

[1] *Psychology of the Emotions*, p. 239. [2] *Ib.* p. 240.
[3] Animals are credited by psychologists with pride, jealousy, a sense of esteem or lack of esteem, and so on, but not with a sense of selfhood or personality.
[4] See Westermarck, *MI* ii. 137–139, 141. [5] *Ib.* ii. 265.

[1] In *OED*, *s.v.* 'Self-respect.'
[2] For rational self-love see Aristotle and Butler.
[3] A. Sutherland, *Origin and Growth of the Moral Instinct*, i. 63, 69.

of morality, the 'teleological,' the morality of enlightened love, the morality of the spiritual impulse after perfection. Owing to the fact of the purely natural and purely conventional basis of much self-respect, there may well be, and there often actually is, in ordinary daily life what may rightly be called (1) an entirely non-moral self-respect—the self-respect for the body, *e.g.*, or the pride in one's inherited social position. Both these things are obviously a self-respect into which the sense of duty or choice or volition has hardly as yet entered. There may also be (2) a quasi-moral self-respect—the false pride, *e.g.*, of a man who will not acknowledge a mistake, of the man who cannot bring himself to share a reduced meal with a time-honoured friend, or of the man who works hard to pay contracted debts out of a dread mainly of the personal disgrace of the bankruptcy court. And there may be the endless forms of (3) pseudo-self-respect to be associated in one form or another with egoism and with imperfect moral training—the desire, *e.g.*, to make a correct 'appearance' and to insist upon forms of etiquette and politeness rather than on reality, or the mere inward adoption of some purely conventional, outwardly prevalent, fashionable, mode of thinking and acting. These three forms are all different from the true self-respect that holds up before the self only that which it holds up—in courage, wisdom, justice, and kindness—before others. From the study of the lives of men who have professed an unswerving allegiance to diverse sets of supposedly fixed first principles; from the study of the lives of men who, like Jean Jacques Rousseau, have professed to see through all conventional and established 'principles'; from the study of the effects upon the minds and souls of the adherents of systems like Stoicism, Pharisaism, Puritanism, Brāhmanism, casuistry, transcendentalism, idealism, rigorism; from the study of the effect upon men of different forms of pride, we become aware, in fact, that the ideal of self-respect constantly requires enlargement, revision, and modification from (1) fresh knowledge of new conditions, (2) increased sympathy with beings different from oneself, (3) the imperative character of some actual duties to actual people. These last often cannot be set aside in the interest of any superman morality whatsoever.

Self-respect, in short, must progress with time and with the gradual unfolding of the possibilities and necessities of human nature. The intellectual and ethical approval of mankind can be expected only for true self-respect, viz. that which takes invariably what is to-day called the 'social' conception of the 'self' (as simply one being in a society of selves) and grasps the fact of the experimental or tentative character of even the best of our morality—the law was made for man, and not man for the law. Our self-respecting ideals are often poor things when compared with the dictates of divine goodness, of a real inward goodness of heart. An absolute belief in self-respect as the final standard takes, too, an unduly optimistic view of human nature, in ignoring its necessary and actual imperfections and the limitations of its knowledge. Like the egoist in general, the man who is all for self-respect will probably do right as long as this coincides with his own notions of the fitness of things—in general or in detail. But there is no guarantee of his doing so when this is no longer the case, or when it can no longer be the case. Both the morality of simple duty and the morality of sympathetic love are here probably superior. The morality of a so-called high or lofty self-respect has often collapsed into the meanest, basest, and cruellest of actions. And, again, in view of the diversity of actions to which an imagined self-respect may lead men, we must remember that society would fall to pieces if each person were to become a law to himself or herself.

Self-respect, in other words, although a perfectly well marked and necessary phenomenon in the evolution of morality from the stage of instinct and custom to that of conscience and insight (character and freedom), can become, if regarded as a supreme determining principle, a fetish, an idol, a stumbling-block, a rock of offence. It must pass into an operative and a sympathetic sense, an emotion, for the life of duty and achievement that we undertake for one another, as members of a 'kingdom of persons,' a 'realm of ends'; when things come to a pass, self-respect is other-respect, respect for others who are also persons, who have also self-respect, and who are worthy of it.

5. Sociological aspects.—As for some of the promised sociological aspects of a true self-respect, it follows from what has been said and implied about the true self being the social self that every self-respecting man must pursue certain impersonal, or supra-personal, common ends. Self-respect is obviously a social force of great importance, for it makes a man respect his work, his calling, his associates, his family, his 'shop,' his school, his town, his neighbourhood, his country, humanity. It involves a kind of loyalty or love to all these great personalizing and civilizing agencies. It is a cohesive force, and the person who possesses it is a valuable person, sociologically speaking—a good citizen, a good neighbour. He can be counted upon for his share of the common task, of the 'white man's burden.' And, again, in the matter of social reform, it has been discovered very definitely to-day that all the philanthropy that stops short of inculcating in the so-called down-trodden, in the poor, in the vicious, in the inefficient, in the discontented generally, a self-respect that may become a lever to efficiency and service is really wasted, and that the social problem is really the problem of adjusting our social machinery and our educational arrangements so that the unfolding of the powers and capacities of personality (a vital part of the idea of self-respect) may become a possibility for all those who are born into any society.

LITERATURE.—See the elaborate works of E. Westermarck (*MI*, 2 vols., London, 1908) and L. T. Hobhouse (*Morals in Evolution*, 2 vols., do. 1906) on the evolution of morality.

The various histories of Greek philosophy (Zeller, Gomperz, Burnet, Cornford, and Grant's ed. of the *Ethics* of Aristotle) may be consulted for the story of moral philosophy from Socrates (the importance of self-knowledge) to Aristotle, Stoicism, and Christianity. Plato's theory of virtue as the sense of an inward harmony of the soul, and his idea that it is better to suffer wrong than to do wrong, is all an elaborate theory of self-respect for one's soul and its functions. To Aristotle the ethical life as the conscious realization of function is practically a lofty kind of self-respect, rising to its height in his famous conception of the 'high-souled man.' The self-respect of the 'wise man' of the Stoics, the idea that the wise man is as necessary to God as God is to him, the idea of solitary self-contemplation (seen at its height in Marcus Aurelius), is in many respects the highest form of self-respect that the world has ever seen.

By way of contrast to Greek ethics, which is all a kind of idealization of the natural reason-endowed man, and to the ethics of naturalism generally, consult the many works on Christian ethics, for to Christianity, as to Buddhism, not self-respect, but self-surrender and self-abnegation are the beginning of the morality of the spirit. See F. Paulsen, *System of Ethics*, Eng. tr., London, 1899, for a comparison of the Greek, Christian, and 'scientific' elements in the modern moral consciousness; Butler, *Fifteen Sermons upon Human Nature*, do. 1726, for the legitimate place in the moral life for rational self-love; and Adam Smith, *Theory of the Moral Sentiments*, do. 1759, for the 'sympathy' theory of conscience.

Kant's ethical system is practically founded on a rational self-respect. See J. G. Fichte, *Popular Works*[4], tr. W. Smith, 2 vols., London, 1889, for an attempt to found German national culture, and the 'vocation of man' generally, upon the consciousness of the inward dignity of our power of self-determination. A. Schopenhauer (*The World as Will and Idea*, tr. R. B. Haldane and J. Kemp, 3 vols., London, 1883–86; various volumes of Essays, tr. T. Bailey Saunders, do. 1890–1902; W.

Caldwell, *Schopenhauer's System in its Philosophical Significance*, Edinburgh and New York, 1896) despised the absence of self-respect and legitimate pride even in the ordinary man, although his moral principle is sympathy. See **F. Nietzsche** (*Beyond Good and Evil*, Eng. tr., Edinburgh, 1907, and *The Genealogy of Morals*, Eng. tr., do. 1910) for the self-respect of the superman (cf., however, **H. Lichtenberger**, *La Philosophie de Nietzsche*, Paris, 1898, and **W. M. Salter**, *Nietzsche, The Thinker—A Study*, New York, 1917, on the spiritual, or even Christian, interpretation that may be put upon Nietzsche's and other similar attempts to transcend ordinary morality). **Goethe's** life may profitably be studied for the limits and the limitations of the inevitable egoism of an attempt to found the conduct of life on the idea of a kind of cultural self-respect, a natural and untrammelled self-development. See also **A. E. Giles**, *Moral Pathology*, London, 1895; **A. Sutherland**, *The Origin and Growth of the Moral Instinct*, 2 vols., do. 1898 (the latter work has an excellent chapter on the different phases of self-respect); **A. E. Taylor**, *The Problem of Conduct*, London, 1901 (a penetrating examination of the theoretical and practical flaws in the Anglo-German 'idealistic' or 'self-realization' theory of morals); the artt. 'Self-activity,' 'Self-consciousness,' 'Self-exhibition,' 'Self-love,' 'Personality,' etc., in *DPhP*, and in works on psychology; **W. McDougall**, *An Introd. to Social Psychology*[7], London, 1913; **T. Ribot**, *Psychology of the Emotions*, do. 1907; **A. Bain**, *Mental and Moral Science*[3], do. 1884. See the terms *αἰδώς*, *αὐτάρκεια*, *μεγαλοψυχία* in **Liddell and Scott**; also the 'Three Reverences' in **Goethe**.

The whole subject is a comparatively new one, for in ancient times and in the Middle Ages there was no such separation of the self from society as has existed (with questionable consequences) since the Reformation and the French Revolution.

W. Caldwell.

SELF-RIGHTEOUSNESS.—'Self-righteousness' is a term which figures little in philosophy, though the philosophical discussion of righteousness always raises the question, and requires by implication an examination of the self and the other-than-self as possible sources and bases of righteousness. The resources of one's own human nature are the nearest and most obvious refuge for the seeker after moral rightness and power. On the other hand, a mystical humanist or a passionate believer in human brotherhood may feel that the rightness of an individual, if it could exist and maintain itself in a self-centred form, would sin against ideal human unity or human sympathy; and thus, sinning against these things, it would already have marred itself, and would no longer be perfect rightness. Still more with the man to whom 'to live is Christ' (Ph 1[21]), or who in some other way is saturated with the realization of a personal God, the thought of a self-centred righteousness is difficult to entertain, even with an effort and for a passing moment. It belongs to a world which the long habit of dependence and communion has made strange to him. His highest conception of right is the doing of what is right by God, the doing, for the sake of God, of what is right in the sight of God.

A man would lose much by complete independence of his fellows, if such a thing were possible. (He would, of course, begin life as an adult. If he started as a child, his independence would be ruined at the start.) How would a man's character stand if he had never trusted another for help and never felt one thrill of gratitude for help received? If he had to the full the power to serve others without needing them, he would be only half human. And here again we have a contradiction in terms; for then he would not have the sympathetic insight which is necessary for the highest service and the truest justice. If it may be so put, there is nothing a man needs more than his needs. H. Weinel made a far-reaching remark when he said that St. Paul 'had the art of beautiful acceptance.' It expresses much of his charm and the whole of his religion. For it is in religion above all that a man's needs are the last thing he can afford to lose. With God there can be no possibility of a man serving and not needing. A completely self-centred righteousness is therefore, in dealing with Him, inconceivable from the outset.

It is often said that, since character can have reality only in interaction with other characters, and this is relative, self-contained righteousness is impossible. So it is; but, if the distinction may be made, a self-*centred* righteousness would still remain conceivable—interacting in the form of help bestowed on others, but not received from them, and owing to other characters, not its source, but merely an opportunity for outflow. 'I give tithes of all that I possess' (Lk 18[12]) is not self-contained, since the speaker gives; but it is self-centred, since he speaks as if he receives nothing. What he 'possesses' is treated as an absolute starting-point (though in reality it was first accumulated from outside). On this assumption there is a centrifugal but not a centripetal movement. It was therefore necessary to show (1) that this flow in one direction only, though conceivable at the first blush, would not be the flow of a complete righteousness towards other men, since essential qualities like gratitude and some forms of loyalty and faith—to say nothing of humility and readiness for contrition—would be lacking; and further, to show (2) that in relation to God self-centred righteousness is out of the question entirely, except as a poor and pitiful fragment, and vitiated at that—in any case, something quite inadequate for acceptance before God and 'justification.' And, in practice, such a righteousness, lacking help human and divine, is likely to be a far greater failure than mere logic requires. If finally (3) we go behind such righteousness as the man really has, it turns out that, just as it is inadequate, so it was never original. We can trace the influences for good which formed its source. In regard to goodness, as in regard to goods, he has nothing which he has not received (1 Co 4[7]).

If we look at the term 'self-righteous' in ordinary use, it is found to be employed with several different shades of meaning: (1) in condemnation of those who, in their own judgment, by reason of their superior character and deeds, are 'not as other men are' (Lk 18[11]); it is implied by the critic that this self-approval is due to exaggerated self-esteem; (2) in (unjust) condemnation of those who maintain their own moral convictions when they differ from those around them; they may be personally humble, and even humble in an unusual degree; (3) in a distinctly religious reference, of those, such as the Pharisees, whose claims are concerned not so much with character in itself, or with moral principles purely as moral, as with their supposed standing in relation to God. Not only are they in enjoyment of superior knowledge of Him or favour with Him, but they have in some sense earned it. They are His servants, but they cannot help knowing that they are profitable servants (Lk 17[10]). Usually they speak, and stand, and look as if they had never done a wrong; but, curiously enough, a similar state of complacency is sometimes attained by a man who, after an outstanding and degraded career as a sinner, has experienced an outstanding and distinguished conversion. He must have been singularly worth saving from the one career and for the other.

As regards all three, the ultimate question is that of God. (1) The man who really is better than his neighbour by the grace of God robs God if he obscures the fact. His self-righteousness is to assert the fact as of his own doing. His righteousness is to 'let his light shine before men,' and, when the question of credit arises, to insist that they give it all to the 'Father who is in heaven' (Mt 5[16]). (2) It is righteousness, and not self-righteousness, to stand with quiet, lofty inflexibility by a truth which we did not make, but which has 'come' to us, most of all when it 'cometh down from the Father of lights' (Ja 1[17]), and when our attitude is that we *cannot* be 'disobedient unto the heavenly vision' (Ac 26[19]). (3) The Pauline (and Christian) attitude is that native goodness, saintly heredity, preservation from falling, are all of grace, free and undeserved; that rescue after falling is also all of grace; and that there can never be a spark of self-righteousness in any man while he is giving grace its due. But its due is his absolute all. 'When ye shall have done all, say, We are unprofitable servants' (Lk 17[10]).

The peculiarity of the Pauline position is its strong emphasis, founded deep in Paul's experience, on the utter impossibility in practice of real and full self-centred righteousness. Not only so, but the righteousness which is partly self-centred and (as in Paul's case) most earnestly religious is also doomed to tragic failure and disappointment. 'In me [that is, in my human nature] dwelleth no good thing' (Ro 7[18]). Hence no amalgam of the God-given and the self-achieved will stand the tests of life or the final light of God. It must be grace, all grace, and nothing but grace.

It is a hard doctrine for men to grasp. Self-righteousness reveals its terrific strength in the form of the universal instinct of self-defence. Except when the admission of 'sin' is a mere convention, it is very rarely admitted while it can possibly be denied or while the question can possibly be shelved. In practice the everyday question is always: 'How can I justify myself?' If grace is ever to be triumphant, this attitude must be systematically undermined, not only in theology, but in philosophy and in life. And teachers of ethics might give serious attention to the question whether self-defence, take it for all in all—prejudiced and unscrupulous self-defence, as it nearly always is—should not rank as one of the deadly sins. Certainly it is the deadly enemy of repentance and of the Pauline Christianity of grace alone.

LITERATURE.—See artt. RIGHTEOUSNESS, EXPIATION AND ATONEMENT (Christian), FORGIVENESS (NT and Christian), GRACE, PHARISEES, and the literature there mentioned.

C. H. WATKINS.

SELF-SACRIFICE.—The subject of self-sacrifice is one which has many aspects and many developments. It is originally an instinct of human nature, the evolution of which can be traced from earliest data. Its power and manifold forms are demonstrated on every page of human history. It arrests our attention at the outset of our ethical inquiry. Its relation to the contrary instinct of self-preservation (*q.v.*) covers a large area in the field of ethical controversy. Its rational stimulation, direction, and control are of serious moral importance, while its relation to religion also shows us that it is of the profoundest significance and loftiest interpretation. In fact, there is hardly any limit to our search for indications of the working of the principle or to the application of its claims 'in heaven above or earth beneath.'

1. Primary facts.—To say that self-sacrifice is an instinct of the human race does not do full justice to the elementary facts. In the animal world also, side by side with instincts that are fierce and cruel, are those of parental, conjugal, or generic fidelities which make self-sacrifice necessary. Nay more; it is a law of nature itself: 'Except a grain of wheat fall into the earth and die, it abideth by itself alone: but if it die, it beareth much fruit' (Jn 12[24]). Indeed, the daisy and the guelder-rose have been used as illustrations of the statement that floral beauty depends upon the principle, since the ray florets become neutral.[1] It is with the human aspect of self-sacrifice, however, that we are here concerned. Self-sacrifice lies at the foundation of our social institutions; for there is no relation into which a man can enter with his fellows which does not proclaim 'None of us liveth to himself, and none dieth to himself' (Ro 14[7]). Not only so; in the limited range of a man's deeds, which seem at first sight to concern himself alone, life presents alternatives which require self-sacrifice in the choice of the higher, since that must be called self-sacrifice which surrenders the pleasure of the moment for nobler ends. In the most thorough or absolute sense of the word it may fairly be argued that there is no such thing as self-sacrifice or that, if there is, it is neither to be desired nor to be approved. There is always some interest or advantage larger or higher than that which short-sighted selfishness would choose, and with this the Ego, or self, identifies its own. Consequently the controversy originating with Hobbes and the Cambridge Platonists is transformed at last to the question, What is the legitimate meaning of self-realization? And we have to deal with the egoism of Nietzsche, as opposed to the social idealism of modern interpretations of Christianity. But it is clear that the essential contrast between selfishness and self-sacrifice remains. The question is, Why should a man forgo that which he naturally would prefer, and why should he voluntarily endure that which he naturally would avoid? And the actual facts of life show how differently men respond. Thus the alternative of following the higher or lower self is present from first to last. From prudential self-control we quickly pass to all the forms of altruistic conduct. Combined with these, or apart from these, there is the conscious aspiration after intellectual or spiritual excellence, for which a man will surrender the ease or pleasure, or even the safety, of the present moment. Even the miser or the ambitious man may be regarded as making a sacrifice of immediate self-pleasing; but in thinking of self-sacrifice we eliminate those cases which have no evidence of altruistic intention. There are innumerable occasions when no prudence is sufficient motive or explanation of conduct that is commendable. When there is obviously no coincidence with the natural desires of the man who does a heroic deed, we cannot deny the distinct character of his conduct.

2. Excessive forms.—We must not pass by the fact that psychologically the instinct has sometimes asserted itself irrationally, and that asceticism (*q.v.*) for its own sake has been judged to have merit. Eastern religions like Buddhism and Hinduism, as the result of theories of good and evil, have set out to achieve such self-renunciation that asceticism becomes a virtue apart from any social consequences. According to these theories, matter is the cause of evil and must be subdued in bodily life, so that spiritual exaltation is measured by neglect of the body and indifference to pain, or by such renunciation as leads to passive endurance. Through the influence of Alexandrian philosophy such ideas found their way into Jewish ethics in the customs of the Essenes (*q.v.*), and through these they found a place in early Christian thought. In monasticism (*q.v.*), with its fasting and celibacy, they have exercised a lasting influence.

But the sentient self is not necessarily evil, and severities such as those of St. John of the Cross and Suso are not reasonable. 'Negative mysticism' of this type is ethically pernicious.[1] Martyrdom may be sought with morbid desire, and even in ordinary life there may be an assumption that so-called unselfishness is in all cases saintly. It is this that gives to Nietzsche the opportunity to sneer at Christianity as slave-morality—so

[1] See Greville Macdonald, *The Religious Sense in its Scientific Aspect*, London, 1903, pp. 106–125.

[1] See W. James, *The Varieties of Religious Experience*, London, 1902, p. 306; Illingworth, *Christian Character*, p. 184 ff.

necessary is it to remember that the social relation gives value to morality. Against either egoism or altruism alone the same criticism may be urged; for both alike tend to the futile isolation of the individual, by disregard of social relations. It follows, not that morality has no reference to ideals, or that the individual has not direct relation to such ideals, but that social value is the direct and necessary criterion of conduct, and that it must be the object of rational judgment.

3. Rational forms.—We have only to begin with the individual as a centre and pass to wider and wider circles of social life to discover how expansive may be the claims for self-sacrifice and the emotions that attend its manifestations.

(*a*) Within the limits of a man's own life, besides the self-control and self-denial whereby each one is normally fit for the ordinary duties of life, there are more special demands that may be made. It may be very difficult to decide in particular cases; but, so far as a man's self-development may be of service to his fellows, either by increased capacity or as an exceptional example, any renunciation he may make of part of life's possibility is worthy, whether as athlete, artist, or saint.

(*b*) In the family the mutual rights and obligations of parents to each other, of children to their parents, and of parents to children, of brothers and sisters, etc., may require, or give the occasion for, trivial and passing or constant and complete devotion. Without such recognition of mutual dependence, service, and sacrifice, these ordinary social ties soon become intolerable and destructive. Certain expectations are generally recognized; but the extent of such claims of one life upon another for its comfort or success, for relief of suffering, or even for its continued existence, is a problem ultimately decided in each case by the individual concerned with making the sacrifice. Such problems often require the sanest and most delicate moral judgment. They afford opportunities of stupidity or of nobility, but certainly of patience and of heroism, which have always been recognized as of supreme moral worth.

(*c*) Near akin to the relations of the family are those of friendship—the voluntary loyalties to which we commit ourselves in comradeship and in the accidental partnership of risks on land and sea. These again have certain obvious and acknowledged obligations; but the finest examples may be on the fringe of uncertainty.

(*d*) Next we may put the positive self-sacrifice required by our work or calling. To be fit for our tasks, in health as far as possible, in capacity as far as may be legitimately sought or expected, will mean for each one such self-direction in the employment of his time and energy that he will have to make sacrifice not only of his lower self, but also of his own tastes and pleasures, and even of those family and social engagements which otherwise might be not only harmless but praiseworthy. Duty involves self-sacrifice. It is part of the discipline of our social life; yet here again there are in different men different standards and different estimates of what is requisite in the discharge of duty. In some cases there is such a grudging submission to what is required that there is no ethical value of self-sacrifice at all. In others there is an exaggerated interpretation of what duty means, so that the most heroic fidelity has been modestly explained as only doing what was duty. Certain callings make greater demands than others—*e.g.*, those of doctor, nurse, sailor, or soldier. Further, the vicarious suffering involved in the risks of life hardly finds a place in an analysis of self-sacrifice; yet in the choice of a calling in which such risks are run, or which distinctly sets out to lessen them, there is at least potential self-sacrifice. It does not follow that all engaged in such callings—*e.g.*, the life-boat and fire-brigade services—are actuated by such motives; but it must be recognized as a possibility.

(*e*) Besides the occupations of life there are also actual citizenship and concern for the welfare of the State, in which a man may be so disinterested as not only to forgo ease and prosperity, but, sacrificing all the rewards of ambition, to endure cruelty, shame, and obloquy, either from the external foes of his country or from those within the State itself who do not understand or do not share his purposes. This may lead to pain and hardship, and even to death itself. Paulsen[1] endeavours to show that Regulus might have acted as he did for his own sake; but it does not amount to more than showing that the sacrifice was made by reason of self-identification with all that promoted the highest honour of Rome. The same analysis or explanation might be made in all such cases.

A. B. Bruce[2] elaborates the thought of progress by sacrifice, as an outstanding law of social life.

'Sacrifice is the cost of progress; it is the instrument of redemption; not otherwise is real advance attainable.' Renan is quoted: 'There are always voluntary victims ready to serve the ends of the Universe.'[3]

'The social mass stagnates, clings tenaciously to old ways however barbarous or bad, obstinately resists movement; whence comes suffering in some form to the man who urges it to move. He suffers because he belongs to a social organism, or closely knit brotherhood, in which the pulse of a common life beats. He cannot escape from the vital influence of the corporate body. It will either assert its power over his soul, controlling his thoughts and affections, or, if his spirit be free, it will act vindictively in the sphere of his outward lot. He must either be a comrade in full sympathy with his people sharing their prejudices, errors and vices, or he must be a victim, suffering for their ignorance and sin. . . . All this is portrayed in Isaiah liii. It is He who is brought as a lamb to the slaughter who divides the spoil with the strong. But when one has grown to many, the power of resistance, if not the noblest conceivable, is the one which most readily suggests itself to brave, fearless and conscientious men. He, who came not to send peace but a sword, knew the sacrifice involved in such struggles. It is better to die fighting for liberty than to live the life of a slave.'[4]

(*f*) Philanthropy provides a distinct group of cases; it may be apart from patriotism or civic sentiment. Sympathy with any sort of sufferers has caused men and women to endure hardship and make sacrifice of all that is desirable or dear to the human heart. Children, slaves, prisoners, lepers, the poor, the sick, the dying, have evoked such devotion. When philanthropy has been associated with moral and religious enthusiasm, it has produced reformers, missionaries, and martyrs whose stories are the pride of the Christian Church.

Thus from earliest intimations of a great law of our being which may be instinctively and blindly obeyed we see there has been evolved a more and more conscious and deliberately rational acceptance of the necessity for self-sacrifice. The intellectual insight and foresight may vary immeasurably and be out of all proportion to the volitional and emotional elements in the acts of obedience.

'To preach to a man not to devote himself is like preaching to a bird not to make a nest, and not to nourish its young.'[5]

This may be true of many natural forms of self-sacrifice, and of the man who has accepted the position with passionate response to the demand; but it does not follow that we are to withhold our appreciation of such conduct, or that we are capable of passing judgment on the merit of any particular case. It certainly is a fact that a greater self may be developed with loftier aims than personal pleasure, and that there may be a rational acceptance and interpretation of the necessity for

[1] *System of Ethics*, Eng. tr., London, 1899, p. 247.
[2] *The Providential Order of the World*, London, 1897, ch. xii.
[3] Cf. Carlyle's Essay on Burns.
[4] See Bruce, p. 359; cf. on war F. D. Maurice, *Social Morality*, London, 1869, lect. xi.; P. T. Forsyth, *The Christian Ethic of War*, do. 1906.
[5] Renan, *Dialogues et fragments philosophiques*, Paris, 1876, p. 32.

the self-sacrifice involved which greatly enhances its moral value.

It is this growth of the 'conjunct self,' or social self, this over-self, or cosmic self, which tends to a reconciliation between egoism and altruism.[1]

'There is some *affirmation* in every act of sacrifice and no man can make a fine sacrifice until he has a true value of himself.'[2]

Asceticism is the mystic search for self-realization gone astray in introspection and become self-destructive, parasitic. Its search is justified, but its aim must be positive, not negative, comprehensive, not exclusive, cosmic, not ascetic.

4. Significance.—The great facts of self-sacrifice cannot be gainsaid or explained away. No cynical interpretation of human nature can reduce them to forms of natural egoism. Altruism is established. Egoistic hedonism long ago surrendered to larger views of utilitarian and evolutionary ethics of the social organism. From H. Spencer, L. Stephen, and S. Alexander to H. Rashdall, G. E. Moore, and modern socialists the well-being of the community is emphasized. Individualism from Goethe to Schopenhauer and Nietzsche has always implicit reference to an external order which after all holds the individual in tyrannous necessity, while idealism from Kant to Eucken has its kingdom of ends or its constructive endeavour. We may not agree with the pragmatist that truth and goodness are identical, or that the value of goodness is an experiment; but its humanistic note is unmistakable, and the self-activity, whether of Bergson or of Eucken, whether creative or spiritual, whether pluralistic or monistic, is far too great to be self-centred or to exclude what we mean by self-sacrifice. This is not the place to do more than indicate the bearing of the subject on general philosophical and ethical inquiry; but its significance cannot be overlooked. We do not commit the interest of morality to merely emotional instincts, any more than we leave the definition of its goal to the pure rationalist. It is when the intellectual concept of duty has supervened upon the mere emotional impulse of primitive man that morality begins. It is the rational estimate of social content that is the task of moral consciousness. Whereas certain generalizations are established, and some have crystallized into laws, it is in the individual consciousness that the questions of casuistry arise. Morality is not simply subjective. Its objective reference or goodness is the basis of its value.

'To arrive at a perfectly truthful moral judgement as to the rightness or wrongness of particular acts, we should form a conception of human life as a whole, and then ask what mode of action in any given circumstance will promote that true good.'[3]

The difficulty is, How far is every man bound to make sacrifice for the good of others? That is a matter of moral vocation. And vocation is determined partly by a man's external circumstances and the needs of human society, partly by his moral and intellectual capacity.

5. Christian emphasis. — The objectivity of moral values must ultimately lead us to metaphysical problems which are beyond the scope of the present article; but those interests which conflict with our own immediate pleasure arm themselves, so to speak, with the sanctions of religion; and it is an indisputable fact that the Christian religion is pre-eminent in its treatment of this aspect of conduct. It is not in providing rewards and penalties whereby selfishness may be restrained and self-sacrifice encouraged that the ethical value of Christianity is discovered. It is in its treatment of the moral conflict as a whole that we understand its message.[4]

By the supreme demand for faith and love, and the truths which justify that demand, Christianity seeks to overcome the natural antagonism between selfishness and self-sacrifice. Its apparently complete and exacting thoroughness of demand is intelligible only in view of the willing espousal of the interests, or 'universe,' of the Kingdom of God. The renunciation of worldly goods is required if earthly possession prove an impediment to a man's rising to the plane of character to which Christ sought to lift men (Lk $14^{15ff.}$). Any loss, even of eye or hand, is preferable to any faltering in choice between the call of the Kingdom of God and earthly or merely material pleasure or gain. Natural relations are second to those which have spiritual value (Mt 12^{48}). Worthiness for discipleship is tested by this superiority of attachment (Mt 8^{22} 10^{37}). All is focused in fidelity to Christ, which, while it may mean conflict (10^{35}), yet has abundant recompense (19^{29}). Such self-denial was to be to the uttermost, 'even to the scaffold' (10^{38}), while on four distinct occasions is recorded the utterance, 'He that loveth his life shall lose it; but whoso shall lose his life for my sake the same shall find it' (10^{39}, Lk 9^{24} 17^{33}, Jn 12^{25}). Christ's own death was a free act of love and surrender in the fulfilment of a divine purpose. It was not an irresistible destiny (Jn $10^{10.18}$, Mt 26^{53}); yet there was oneness with the Father's will in His eternal purpose. Personal love which Christ inspires is the great lever or dynamic of self-sacrifice among His followers (2 Co 5^{14}, 1 Jn 3^{16}, Ph $2^{4ff.}$, etc.). In Christ's sacrifice of the Cross are the pledge and promise of the victory of divine love and wisdom in the affairs of men and the assurance that in all self-sacrifice and suffering purposes of divine wisdom are supreme.

LITERATURE.—It is difficult to attempt a survey of the literature on this subject. On the elementary forms of temperance or self-control precepts abound among all sorts of moralists.

Plato's teaching on σωφροσύνη and the sacrifice of the individual to the State may be sought in his works, and in books that deal directly with his teaching. Of his works see esp. *Protagoras*, *Gorgias*, *Philebus*, and the *Republic*. See also Aristotle's teaching on self-restraint (ἐγκράτεια) in *Nicomachean Ethics*, iii., vii., x.–xii., and also on friendship. The relation of pleasure to moral rightness runs through the whole history of ethics. The Roman Stoics rise to a high level in their teaching of self-control and endurance.

The *Imitatio Christi* of Thomas à Kempis is a typical and familiar example of the more distinctly religious aspect of self-denial from the Christian point of view; but ascetic ideas of fasting, chastity, dress, etc., are to be found in the practical advice of Christian writers in apostolic and mediæval times. Benevolence as a specific Christian virtue is continually emphasized. As indicating the controversy originating in Hobbes, reference may be made to his and his opponents' works (see art. ETHICS) and to the subsequent writers on egoism and altruism down to the present time, esp. H. Spencer, *Data of Ethics*, new ed., London, 1906; L. Stephen, *The Science of Ethics*, do. 1882; S. Alexander, *Moral Order and Progress*, do. 1889; H. Sidgwick, *The Methods of Ethics*6, do. 1901; H. Rashdall, *The Theory of Good and Evil*, 2 vols., Oxford, 1907; G. E. Moore, *Principia Ethica*, Cambridge, 1903; B. Kidd, *The Science of Power*, London, 1918; E. Westermarck, *MI*, ch. xxxiv., 'The Altruistic Sentiment.'

For writers on Christian ethics see art. ETHICS AND MORALITY (Christian). The following may be added: J. Seeley, *Ecce Homo*, new ed., London, 1905: J. Stalker, *The Ethic of Jesus*, do. 1909; R. L. Ottley, *Christian Ideas and Ideals*, do. 1909; J. R. Illingworth, *Christian Character*, do. 1904; C. F. D'Arcy, *Christian Ethics and Modern Thought*, do. 1912; W. S. Bruce, *Formation of Christian Character*, Edinburgh, 1902; F. G. Peabody, *The Approach to the Social Question*, New York, 1909; H. C. King, *Ethics of Jesus*, do. 1910; A. E. Balch, *An Introd. to the Study of Christian Ethics*, London, 1905; W. N. Clarke, *The Ideal of Jesus*, Edinburgh, 1911; A. B. D. Alexander, *Christianity and Ethics*, London, 1914; R. M. Jones, *Social Law in the Spiritual World*, New York and London, 1904; H. S. Nash, *Genesis of Social Conscience*, New York, 1902; also J. B. Baillie, 'Self-sacrifice,' *HJ* xii. [1914] 260 ff.; H. Walker, 'Triumph and Tragedy,' *ib.* xiv. [1915] 135 ff.; C. L. Maynard, 'Love and the Law,' *ib.* xv. [1917] 479.

A. E. BALCH.

SELF-SATISFACTION.—In every volition man seeks self-satisfaction; so many have contended. Thus T. H. Green says:

'If it is a genuine definition that we want of what is common to all acts of willing, we must say that such an act is one in

[1] See art. ALTRUISM.

[2] R. M. Jones, *Social Law in the Spiritual World*, p. 103; cf. M. Maeterlinck, *Wisdom and Destiny*, London, 1908, § 63 ff.

[3] H. Rashdall, *Ethics*, London, 1913, p. 71.

[4] See *HDB*, *s.v.* 'Self-surrender.'

which a self-conscious individual directs himself to the realization of some idea, as to an object in which for the time he seeks self-satisfaction.'[1]

A voluntary act 'is the putting forth of the man or self in desire,' and desire is distinguished from a 'mere solicitation,' such as the hunger impulse, which a man may have in common with animals, by this, that in desire the man identifies himself with the impulse.[2] The object which a man desires and aims at is, therefore, 'an idea of personal good,'[3] 'a better state of himself,' 'a certain idea of himself—of himself doing or himself enjoying,'[4] 'a good of himself *as himself*.'[5] In all conduct to which moral predicates are applicable, whether it be virtuous or vicious, a man is 'an object to himself.'[6] So every form of self-satisfaction appears good to the man who seeks it. True good is true or abiding self-satisfaction, *i.e.* 'the satisfaction of the fully realized or perfected self.'[7] J. H. Muirhead likewise maintains that the object of desire and volition is 'a form of self-satisfaction':[8]

'It is only as involved in one's own that one can desire one's neighbour's good: it is only as his good enters as an element into *my* conception of *my* good that I can make it an object of desire and volition.'[9]

In form this is an egoistic view of human nature,[10] and may be classed with psychological hedonism.[11] For, according to the latter also, a man always seeks his own satisfaction in the form of pleasure or avoidance of pain. Green and those who agree with him, however, maintain that the true good of the individual is a common good and non-competitive. Hence true satisfaction can be attained only by such a life as increases the true satisfaction of other members of the community.

The 'egoistic' psychology in its various forms has been called into question. Most writers on psychology and ethics seem to accept the general contention that volition involves the satisfaction of desire;[12] that desire implies the idea of an object to the realization of which we have an impulse; and that desire arises when there is an interval between the consciousness of the impulse and its realization, or a delay to its satisfaction. But the following are highly disputable propositions: (1) the idea of self is present to consciousness whenever we have a desire; (2) the self identifies itself with every desire; (3) every desire is for the satisfaction of the self.

Green lays great stress on the unity of the self; he often writes as if the self were a single principle always more or less completely present in the consciousness of a man; that all his desires and volitions are consciously related to it; and that consequently the idea of self is a constituent element in each of them. But the unity of the self should be conceived rather as an ideal—an ideal which becomes actual only through the progressive organization of its constituent instinctive tendencies, emotions, and ideas. The latter conception is to be found in Green, and it is the conception most characteristic of his system, especially when he discusses the moral ideal.[13] But the disputable propositions mentioned seem to depend on the former abstract conception of its unity.

Now the self-regarding sentiment—an organization of emotional dispositions with their impulses about the idea of self[1]—is rarely, if ever, so comprehensive and thorough as to embrace all the desires of the mind. Until this comprehensive sentiment is formed, however, it cannot be said that the idea of self is present whenever a man desires anything; nor can it be said therefore that he identifies himself with the object of desire; still less is it true that every desire is for the satisfaction of the self, and that the good sought is the good of the self. The adult mind is capable of forming a multitude of sentiments[2] into which the idea of self does not enter, and any particular desire may find a place in, or be taken up by, one or more of these. Sometimes a desire owes its origin not to any single impulse, but to the organized dispositions forming a sentiment. And, unless the precise relations of a desire to these dispositions is discovered, its constituent elements cannot be known. Consider, *e.g.*, the following series: a simple desire for food, a desire for food for myself, a desire for food for my child, a desire for food for a stranger. These are evidently different desires on account both of the ideas that determine them and of the impulses to the realization of the ideas. The idea of self enters as a determining factor into the second and third; it need not enter into the first and fourth. The impulse that necessarily enters into the first is the hunger impulse, and this is usually the only one if the impulse is satisfied without delay. Into the second there may enter, in addition to the hunger impulse, some of the other conations organized in the sentiment which is excited by the idea of the self—*e.g.*, the impulses to enjoy the pleasure of eating, to preserve life, to render myself efficient. The hunger impulse does not enter into the third, nor does any one of the conations just mentioned. Other impulses related to my idea of myself are brought into play, such as the impulse springing from my sense of responsibility as a father, my self-respect, my concern for the approbation of others, etc. Into the fourth, the desire to procure food for a stranger, not one of the impulses mentioned above need enter. The motive force may spring from affection for children with its impulse to protect and succour. It may even spring from hatred of a man whom I consider responsible for the child's destitution, or from the thought that my enemy will be annoyed by such behaviour on my part. The emotions, with their attendant impulses, which are organized in the self-regarding sentiment are not excited in these cases. Of course it may be said that all these emotions spring from my own being; they are elements in what is called my total self; but to say that is very different from saying that the idea of my self-satisfaction is the object of desire sought in volition. It is indeed possible for hatred of enemies and affection for children to be included in the self-regarding sentiment. A man can take pride in the thought of himself as one who hates enemies and has affection for children. When this happens, the self-regarding sentiment may be stimulated by the sight of any hungry child. Whether this wider sentiment is actually stimulated in any particular case will depend on certain conditions.

(1) The first of these is the existence of a sufficient motive. If, *e.g.*, the need of the child can be satisfied with comparative ease, there will exist no motive for putting the wider sentiment into operation. But, if food is difficult to obtain, and if it is

[1] *Prolegomena to Ethics*, Oxford, 1883, § 154.
[2] *Ib.* § 146 f. [3] *Ib.* § 115. [4] *Ib.* § 95.
[5] *Ib.* § 112. [6] *Ib.* § 115.
[7] *Ib.* §§ 171, 234. There are expressions in Green's works suggesting a conception different from this, and inconsistent with it. For a detailed examination of Green see H. Sidgwick, *Lectures on the Ethics of T. H. Green, Mr. Herbert Spencer and J. Martineau*, London, 1905.
[8] *The Elements of Ethics*[3], London, 1910, § 18.
[9] *Ib.* § 67. [10] Cf. art. EGOISM.
[11] See artt. HEDONISM and ETHICS, § 6.
[12] Cf. B. Bosanquet, *Psychology of the Moral Self*, pp. 78–80, for a different view of some deliberate volitions.
[13] See *Prolegomena to Ethics*, bk. iii.

[1] See art. SELF-ASSERTION AND SELF-SUBJECTION.
[2] For an account of this specialized use of the term 'sentiment,' meaning an organized system of emotional dispositions about the idea of some object, see art. SENTIMENT; A. F. Shand, in *Mind*, new ser., v. [1896] 203 ff., xvi. [1907] 477 ff., and *The Foundations of Character*, *passim*; W. McDougall, *An Introd. to Social Psychology*[7], London, 1913, ch. v. f.

necessary to face discomfort or danger to obtain it, affection or hatred may be an insufficient motive. There will then be need for reinforcement of the will by the thought of a man's reputation, his honour, his self-respect. (2) Another condition is opportunity for deliberation. This implies sufficient time and concentration of attention to realize the situation fully and to call up the forces organized in the self-regarding sentiment. 'Falling into temptation' is not infrequently due to insufficient deliberation. (3) The third condition is the thoroughness of organization of the self-regarding system. If the system is loosely constructed its strength will be small, and what strength it has will not be effectively mobilized to reinforce its constituent desires at need.

Perhaps it is possible for the idea of self to be so comprehensive, and so completely articulated, as to include every good that the individual considers he ought to seek, and the self-regarding sentiment consequently to be so systematically and thoroughly organized as to determine all his fully deliberated volitions. Still opportunity would be lacking, and motive would be wanting, to call it into operation to determine every volition. Hence it is incorrect to define volition 'as the supporting or the re-enforcing of a desire or conation by the co-operation of an impulse excited within the system of the self-regarding sentiment.'[1] This definition would apply only to fully deliberate action—*e.g.*, 'action along the line of greatest resistance.'

It may be contended nevertheless that, although a man does not always aim at self-satisfaction, he ought to do so; he would be acting on a sound ethical principle in doing so. For, it may be urged, the true good for any individual is the abiding satisfaction of the perfect self, a good which is not only his own, but the good of others also. To realize this good, he ought constantly to aim at organizing all his impulses in relation to such an ideal of self as will bring his life to complete unity. Moreover, the sentiment organized about this ideal is an emotional system powerful enough to give a man mastery over all the vagrant solicitations of desire, and the only one that is powerful enough.

Now it must be admitted that an ethical principle of this type has obvious merits. A man inevitably seeks his own satisfaction in some measure. Could he be led to seek this in a way that increases the satisfaction of others, there would be great gain. Especially desirable is the idea of enlisting the strongest force in human nature—the self-regarding sentiment—in the service of every virtue. But, in the first place, is what appears good to men in every stage of their life a good common to all, and non-competitive? In a world of men developing ideally this might be the case. But is it true of the world as we know it? And, if it is not, is a man likely to live the best life by aiming always at satisfying himself? In particular, is this ideal likely to be a good principle of guidance for a man in process of forming his character? Is it possible for him to include in his idea of what will satisfy himself all the ends at which he should aim, and in the right proportion or degree? He will often be called upon to act with others and for others. Have we good ground for thinking that what will satisfy them will agree with his conception of what will satisfy him? If it does not, may not the judgment of many of his associates be superior to his own during his immature years?

Again, how is a man to obtain right conceptions of the virtues, of the ends, and of the ideals which he and others should seek, except by submitting to the instructions, the suggestions, the approbation and disapprobation of others—except, in other words, by striving to satisfy them and by bringing his own satisfaction into line with that of others? A more adequate general rule of conduct is Kant's maxim:

> 'So act as to treat humanity, whether in thine own person or in that of any other, in every case as an end withal, never as means only.'[1]

And it should follow that their satisfactions should be treated as ends in themselves. Indeed, it is because their satisfactions are recognized by him as ends in themselves, and therefore independently good, that concern for them can be included by a man in his self-regarding sentiment.

LITERATURE.—In addition to the literature already cited, reference may be made to B. Bosanquet, *Psychology of the Moral Self*, London, 1897, lectures vii.–ix.; F. H. Bradley, *Ethical Studies*, do. 1876, essays ii., vii.; H. Rashdall, *The Theory of Good and Evil*, Oxford, 1907, vol. i. bk. i. ch. ii.; A. F. Shand, *The Foundations of Character*, London, 1914, *passim*; see also artt. CONSENT, SELF-REALIZATION.

DAVID PHILLIPS.

SEMI-ARIANISM.—Semi-Arians is the name given to a party in the Arian controversy who, in spite of their name, were less Arian than Athanasian, and eventually by their mediating policy reconciled those who, at heart orthodox, were divided by mutual suspicion due in part to misunderstanding of their respective terminology. In the Arian dispute the Creed of Nicæa failed to reconcile the 'conservatives' of the East to the theologians of Alexandria and Rome, because the use of the word ὁμοούσιος, besides being unscriptural, appeared to countenance the Sabellian heresy that the Trinity was an 'economic' manifestation of three aspects of the Godhead. This was the real cause of the downfall of the Nicene party, which culminated in the expulsion of Athanasius from Alexandria in 356. But the triumph over Athanasius did not give the bishops who had opposed his teaching the position to which they had aspired. On the contrary, they found themselves supplanted by the genuine Arians, who had used them to condemn Athanasius in the interest of extreme subordinationism. It became evident that the creed to which the Church would be called upon to submit would pronounce the Son not merely inferior to the Father, but essentially unlike Him (ἀνόμοιος). The supporters of this view, Eunomius and Ætius, were called Anomœans, and those more cautious in expressing their views Homœans because they declared the Son like (ὅμοιος) the Father. The word οὐσία, which with its compound ὁμοούσιος had appeared in the Nicene Creed, was proscribed, and its use in defining the Godhead forbidden. These decisions, emanating in 357 from Sirmium, where the emperor Constantius was at this time, provoked the bishops of Asia Minor, under the guidance of Basil of Ancyra, to assemble under his presidency in 358 at Ancyra, where the synod in its letter condemned ὁμοούσιος or ταὐτοούσιος ('of identical essence') as Sabellian, but declared the Son to be of like essence with the Father (ὁμοίας οὐσίας). Hence is derived the word ὁμοιούσιος as opposed to ὁμοούσιος of Nicæa;[2] and those who adopted it are popularly known as the Semi-Arians.

The leaders of this party were George of Laodicæa, Eustathius of Sebaste, Eusebius of Emesa, and Basil of Ancyra; and to them the wiser of the Nicene supporters extended a friendly hand because they perceived that the *homoiousian* doctrine often expressed what they themselves really meant. The labours of Hilary of Poictiers in Asia Minor during his exile, and the publication of the *de Synodis* by Athanasius, did much towards bringing about a mutual understanding. In addition to this, the Arianizing policy of Con-

[1] McDougall[7], p. 249.

[1] *The Metaphysic of Morals*, § ii., tr. T. K. Abbott, *Kant's Theory of Ethics*[6], London, 1909.

[2] See art. ARIANISM, § 3 ff.

stantius during the last two years of his reign alarmed the Semi-Arians and drove them to make common cause with the orthodox. It was clearly recognized that the surrender of the Nicene formula by the Westerns at Ariminum and by the Easterns at Seleucia had made Homœan if not Anomœan Arianism possible as the creed of the Empire and had thereby put those who upheld the complete divinity of the Son, though questioning the Athanasian mode of expression, at a disadvantage; and after the Synod of Constantinople, in 360, the Homoiousians found themselves a persecuted party. Constantius died in Nov. 361, and the Homœan settlement was upset by the return of the banished bishops at the accession of Julian.

For the next twenty years the Arian question was being settled in favour of the Nicene Council, mainly by the efforts of a new generation whose leaders were the three Cappadocian fathers, Basil of Cæsarea and the two Gregorys (of Nyssa and Nazianzus). The point of issue among modern scholars is the manner in which the difficulty of explaining the relation of the Son to the Father was ultimately solved. Harnack maintains:

'It was not the *Homoousios* which finally triumphed, but on the contrary the *Homoiousian* doctrine, which fixed on the terms of agreement with the *Homoousios*. The doctrine which Hosius, Athanasius, Eustathius, and Marcellus had championed at Nicæa was overthrown.'[1]

In other words, the so-called Semi-Arians really triumphed over the fathers of Nicæa at Constantinople in 381 by allowing the word ὁμοούσιος to stand explained as the equivalent of ὁμοιούσιος. This view has been strongly opposed by J. F. Bethune-Baker in his *Meaning of 'Homoousios,'* a reply to the theory advocated by Harnack in his *History of Dogma*. The argument which Harnack adduces in support of his theory is as follows:

The first step towards union was the publication of Athanasius' *de Synodis*, written in 359. Here he shows his true greatness; for, whilst he concedes nothing, he shows himself concerned not for formulæ but for principles. He recognizes that whoever grants that the Son is in nature of *like* quality with the Father and springs from the substance of the Father is not far from the ὁμοούσιος, but he is too keen-sighted not to point out that ὁμοιούσιος either involves an absurdity or is dogmatically incorrect. In 362 Athanasius held the small but very important Council of Alexandria, at which it was decided that all who accepted the ὁμοούσιος should be admitted to the Church, whatever their past errors might have been. In addition it was declared in the *Tomus ad Antiochenos* that, provided the ὁμοούσιος was acknowledged, the question as to whether there were three ὑποστάσεις in the Trinity or only one might be left open. This, according to Harnack, was probably the largest concession that Athanasius ever made. It marked a complete change; for, whereas the old orthodoxy had started from the substantial unity of the Godhead in which was a mysterious plurality, it was now permissible to make the threefold nature of the Godhead the starting-point and from its unity to arrive at the conclusion that the God is one. This distinction is expressed by the terms ὁμοούσιος and ὁμοιούσιος respectively; and thus, by permitting both views to be held by those who professed to be Homoousians, the Homoiousians, whose opinions were really expressed, obtained a footing in the Church.

The decision at Alexandria satisfied the followers of the scientific theology of the day who admired Origen, notably Basil of Cæsarea and his friends. In his letter to Apollinarius Basil declares that he prefers the words 'unchangeably alike in essence' (κατ' οὐσίαν) to ὁμοούσιος; but Apollinarius convinced him that ὁμοούσιος is more correct. Basil, however, does not use the word in the Athanasian sense, nor is he particularly desirous to employ it. But the great contribution of the Cappadocians was that the Trinity consists of persons (ὑποστάσεις) who partake of an οὐσία which they hold in common.[2] The unity of the Godhead, as the Cappadocians conceived it, was not the same as the unity which Athanasius had in his mind; for, while Athanasius, like Augustine, thought of a personal God living a threefold life, the Cappadocians certainly thought of three quite distinct persons sharing a common οὐσία as men do. They preserved the unity by insisting on the monarchy of God the Father. Thus through them the influence of Origen was exerted on the side of a 'scientific' orthodoxy, which triumphed over the arid and formal Aristotelianism of Eunomius; but it was a triumph of Neo-Platonism rather than of the Athanasian system.

The Meletian schism[1] at Antioch was due to the compromising attitude of the Synod of Alexandria; for Meletius represented the Homoiousians and was for this reason distrusted by the Alexandrians and Westerns, always suspicious of the τρεῖς ὑποστάσεις of the Cappadocians. The Arianizing policy of the emperor Valens (364–378) brought the supporters of the old and new orthodoxy of the East together, and, after delegates had been sent to Liberius at Rome, a union was effected at Tyana in 367. In 370 Basil became bishop of Cæsarea in Cappadocia and the leader of the Christians of Asia, and succeeded in blending the orthodoxy of Athanasius with the science of Origen, commending both by his support of the ascetic life. The basis of all his work, to quote Harnack, was 'to unite the orthodoxy of the East and the West on the basis of the *Homoiousian* interpretation of the *Homoousion*.' The death of Valens and the accession of Theodosius as emperor of the East (19th Jan. 379) was marked by the triumph of orthodoxy; nevertheless at the Council of Constantinople (381) Meletius of Antioch, though distrusted by Rome and Alexandria, acted as president and was highly honoured by the emperor. At this council the Nicene Creed gained an unqualified victory so far as terms were concerned; but, again to quote Harnack:

'The community of substance in the sense of equality or likeness of substance, not in that of unity of substance, was from this time the orthodox doctrine of the East.'[2]

The Council, as is well known, accepted the baptismal creed of Jerusalem. It assuredly did not put it forward as a new creed; and till the Council of Chalcedon there is no mention of it as a synodal creed, though it appears in the *Ancoratus* of Epiphanius, published 374. It was the work of Cyril, bishop of Jerusalem, whose experiences it appears to reflect. Eventually it superseded the creed of the Council of Nicæa, and became the liturgical creed of the Church. The point on which particular stress is laid is that the explanation of μονογενῆ—τοῦτ' ἐστὶν ἐκ τῆς οὐσίας τοῦ πατρός—is omitted, though ὁμοούσιος is retained. It is argued that the words ἐκ τῆς οὐσίας were far more offensive to the half-friends of the ὁμοούσιος than the word itself, as encouraging a Sabellian theory of the Sonship of Christ; that the omission of the obnoxious phrase, together with the anathemas appended to the Nicene Creed, expressed the real belief of Christian neo-orthodoxy; and that 'the Christological formula in the Creed of Jerusalem . . . is thus almost homoiousian even although it retains the ὁμοούσιος.[3]

Such, then, is Harnack's opinion, to controvert which Bethune-Baker published in 1901 a contribution to the Cambridge *Texts and Studies* on *The Meaning of 'Homoousios' in the 'Constantinopolitan' Creed*. In dealing with the opinions of Basil of Ancyra, Bethune-Baker labours to show that this bishop was at heart in agreement with Athanasius, and that his formula ὅμοιον κατὰ πάντα was in reality equivalent to ὁμοούσιος in the Athanasian sense, nor have the Cappadocians any reason to be ashamed if this Basil is the father of their theology. Turning to Meletius, who was chosen to preside over the Council of Constantinople but died before its conclusion, Bethune-Baker shows that as early as the Council of Antioch in 363 he accepted the word οὐσία in the Athanasian sense, and, before the council in 381, he and his party were in full agreement, so far as doctrine was concerned, with Damasus of Rome and Ambrose. After this comes a careful discussion of the correspondence between Basil of Cæsarea and Apollinarius, which Basil explains was between two laymen, before he was a bishop or Apollinarius a declared heretic (*c.* 358–362).

[1] *Hist. of Dogma*, Eng. tr., iv. 82.
[2] See art. CAPPADOCIAN THEOLOGY.

[1] See art. MELETIANISM. [2] iv. 97. [3] See *ib.* p. 99.

Basil appeals for guidance. His exact words, as rendered by Bethune-Baker, are these:

'Now to express this conception [of the *οὐσία* of the Son] it seems to me that the term *ἀπαραλλάκτως ὅμοιος* ("like without any variation") is better suited than the term *ὁμοούσιος*.'[1]

Here, however, the stress is not on the 'likeness,' but on the unchangeability. 'In this,' says Bethune-Baker, 'he is but following in the steps of Athanasius,' who maintained that *ὁμοιούσιος + ἐκ τῆς οὐσίας = ὁμοούσιος*. Basil was careful never to confuse *φύσις* with *οὐσία*, and he expressly repudiates the notion that 'likeness' can describe the relation between the three *ὑποστάσεις* and one *οὐσία* of the Godhead. As regards the omission of *ἐξ οὐσίας τοῦ πατρός* from the Creed, Bethune-Baker points out that it is really identical with *ἐκ θεοῦ*, and that, when the danger of Arianism had passed, the phrase could be dropped without injuring the faith. He sees consequently no evidence that the creed of the Church changed between the Council of Nicæa and that of Constantinople, or that Athanasius represented the old, and the three Cappadocians the new, orthodoxy. To decide between opinions so divergent as the above is no easy task, as they represent two view-points so different. Bethune-Baker, however, does not seem to do sufficient justice to the fact that the Cappadocians represent a progress on the crude Athanasianism which the bishops of the East found difficult to accept till explained philosophically. The history of Semi-Arianism shows that the Arian controversy was one of the few which were decided by reason rather than authority. If the Creed of Nicæa prevailed, it was not because it was backed by the authority of the first general council, but because—granted the premisses accepted on both sides—it gave the best logical explanation of the point at issue. But, even when the correctness of the Nicene formula is admitted, it is evident that at its first appearance it gave rise to great and not unwarranted difficulties. Certainly it was in some cases impossible for some ardent Nicenes, notably Marcellus and Photinus, to free themselves from the charge of Sabellianism. It was not till the Creed of Nicæa was proved, after repeated experiments and failures, to be the only possible explanation of the relation of the Son to the Father that it was finally accepted; and the clearing up of obscure and contradictory doctrines connected with the Creed was due in no small degree to the Semi-Arian party.

LITERATURE.—Epiphanius, *Hær.* lxxiii.; Athanasius, *de Synodis, Tomus ad Antiochenos*; correspondence between Basil and Apollinarius in J. Dräseke, *Apollinarios von Laodicea: sein Leben und seine Schriften*, Leipzig, 1892 (*TU* vii. 3), p. 100 ff.; letters of Athanasius and Basil; Gregory of Nyssa (*PG* xlv.); Gregory of Nazianzus, *The Five Theological Orations*, ed. A. J. Mason, Cambridge, 1889; the Church historians: Socrates, Sozomen, Theodoret, Rufinus; H. M. Gwatkin, *Studies of Arianism*², Cambridge, 1900; T. Zahn, *Marcellus von Ancyra*, Gotha, 1867; A. Harnack, *Hist. of Dogma*, Eng. tr., London, 1894–99, iv.; J. F. Bethune-Baker, *The Meaning of 'Homoousios' in the 'Constantinopolitan' Creed* (*TS* vii. no. 1), Cambridge, 1901; A. Robertson, *Prolegomena to St. Athanasius: Select Works and Letters*, in 'Nicene and post-Nicene Fathers,' Oxford, 1892; F. Loofs, *Leitfaden zum Dogmengeschichte*, Halle, 1906; G. Krüger, *Lucifer, Bischof von Calaris*, Leipzig, 1886.

F. J. FOAKES JACKSON.

SEMINOLES.—The Seminoles (Creek for 'wanderers,' 'runaways'), now numbering about 600, and living in the Everglades, a swamp, or, rather, shallow sea studded with islets, in the southern portion of the State of Florida, belong to the American Indian stock of Muskhogeans (*q.v.*). Originally inhabiting what is now the State of Georgia, they broke away from the Creeks in 1750, and migrated to their present home, having been pressed farther and farther south by the whites.

1. Religious beliefs.—The Seminole believes in a Supreme Being; he also believes in God's Son (obviously the result of Christian teaching centuries ago), that the Son of God came on earth 'long time ago to live with the Indians and to make them good Indians and to prepare them for the "big sleep" when E-shock-e-tom-e-see (God) calls them hence'; he believes that the Supreme Being lives above the clouds, and that, when the Great Spirit calls him hence, his spirit will make its last journey to the happy hunting-grounds of his fathers, winging its way over the seven-coloured rainbow of the heavens, which is the 'highway of the Great Spirit.' The Seminole believes in a future existence, In-li-ke-ta (heaven or home), to which the Indians go after death. Here they may 'hunt, hunt, hunt, plenty deer, plenty turkey, plenty bear find and cool water ojus (plenty) all the time. Bad Indians, after big sleep, hunt, hunt, hunt deer, turkey, bear—no find 'em, hot water drink all the time.' The Seminole regards the Supreme Being as the 'giver and taker of life.' His religion is sacred to him and is based on the Indian's unwritten code, 'not to lie, not to steal, not to kill, and to think with God.'

Missionaries have attempted to work among the Everglade Seminoles; they receive most respectful attention, for their reverence to God will not permit the Seminoles to laugh at these messengers; their language contains no oath nor any word to express disrespect to the Great Spirit. Their idea of the Bible, however, is vague, because it is regarded as the work of the white man. 'Injun no make book—me think good Injun find happy hunting-ground all right.' No converts have been made by the white missionaries, and the Seminole clings tenaciously to his own religion.

2. Festivals.—The festivals of the Seminoles are all of religious interest, the principal one being the Green Corn (maize) Dance, which occurs annually in June at the time of the full moon. All men who have violated their laws may be reinstated at this time by undergoing certain ordeals. The transgressors appear before the council a short time before the dance, and, if they are forgiven, they are allowed to join in the feasting and dancing. The 'black drink,' which is an emetic made from herbs, is taken by all the tribe on the first day of the dance. This cleanses them and enables them to celebrate the feast to the fullest extent; its purpose may be to remove from the body all substances that may interfere with the full working of the rite which is to be celebrated.

A picturesque feature of this festival is the dancing and playing round the festal pole, which serves as a goal. The players take sides, both men and women participating in the game. The object of the game is to strike the pole with the ball, which is knocked with a racket of bent hickory having a netted pocket made of deer thongs. The ball is tossed and caught in the netted pocket, and then hurled at the pole. The opposing side endeavour to prevent the ball from touching the pole. When the ball strikes the ground beyond the line of play, the scamper for it causes great excitement, the victor having the next play. A score-keeper stands by the pole, keeping a record of the play. As the twilight falls, the players end the game. Then the feast begins, the men, women, and children each having a position designated for them—a peculiar arrangement which is employed at no other time. The joyous ball game is followed by the dance on the night of full moon, when the men and women dance from dark until sunrise. When this dance is over, the circle about the pole is perfectly symmetrical and a well-defined pathway is made by the running and dancing. It probably has some symbolical meaning—*e.g.*, to help the sun to revolve, to assist the growth of the crops.

Another festival of importance is the Hunting Dance, which occurs in cycles—once every four years. The festival is for sorrowing, rejoicing, and purifying. Old fires are allowed to go out; not a spark must remain. New fire is produced artificially; this is the sacred fire and must be made with the ancestral flint-rock. The new fire is presented from one band to another as a token

[1] P. 41.

of friendship. Then they assemble round the fires, singing and dancing.

On the nights of this festival men, women, and children gather at the council lodge. Camp fires burn round the dancing square, in the centre of which is the sacred fire, and at each corner a pole, where the dancers assemble. The leader starts a weird melody, as the Owl Song, and from the shadows of the oaks emerge the dusky forms of the Seminoles in the most fantastic dress. Yards and yards of brightly-coloured ribbons float from the head, neck, and shoulders of the women and children. The men likewise are in brilliant coats and enormous turbans, and wear leggings gracefully adorned with thongs of deerskin, with moccasins fresh and new. Nor are the children neglected; with swirling ribbons and bright red dresses that reach to their slim ankles, they come bubbling with joy and laughter, ready to be assigned their places in the dance circle. The dancers lock hands, and mark time as they take up the chant.

All members of the festival must work. They must leave the camp at daybreak and hunt or work till noon. The men hunt large game; the boys go for hares and squirrels; while the women pick potatoes or hunt hogs, and the very small children 'hunt' water and bring in wood.

3. Mythology.—The Seminole tradition of God's Son coming to live with the Indians is that the Son of God (E-shock-e-tom-e-see-e-po-chee) stopped at the most southern point of Florida, where He was met by three medicine-men, who carried Him on their shoulders, while He sowed the seeds of the *koonti* root, which the Seminole regards as God's gift to His red children. The *koonti* is found only in this southern section of Florida, and grows luxuriantly; it resembles the sago-palm, and from its roots a starch-like substance is prepared which makes delicious little cakes. According to the legend, the Indians were in a starving condition; the ground was parched, no corn grew, and the game had all left. While the Indians waited for the *koonti* to grow, God rained down bread, 'heap plenty,' which the Seminoles gathered and ate. In describing this bread, which came down each morning, the chieftain said: 'Littly bread; white man's biscuit all the same, good, every Indian eat plenty.'

The Seminole's conception of the creation is as follows:

'Long time ago, E-shock-e-tom-e-see (God) took seeds and scattered them all around in a rich valley bordering a river. By-and-by, God saw fingers coming up out of the ground and many people, "heap too many," came up from out of the sand. Some went to the river and washed, washed, washed "too much"; it made them weak and pale; this was the *es-ta-had-kee* (white race). Others went to the river and washed *not* too much; they returned full of courage, "strong heap"; this was the *es-ta-chat-tee* (red race). The remainder, "no wash, lazy too much"; *es-ta-lus-tee* (black man).'[1]

4. Marriage and burial customs.—The Seminoles, like other American Indian tribes, are classified by *gentes.* The lineage is traced through the mother. The child belongs to the *gens* which the mother represents, and, should a squaw and her husband separate for any cause, the children belong unconditionally to the wife. A young brave dare not marry a girl from his own *gens*; he must select one from another clan. The young Seminole is shy and bashful in his courtship, and, having resolved to marry, he conceals his first overtures with all the cunning of his race. His intention is secretly conveyed to the girl's parents, and, should there be no objection, the young woman is at liberty to accept or reject—no Seminole girl is forced into marriage. The lover with permission to woo shows some token of affection. The sending and receiving of a present constitutes betrothal, and the bride-to-be shows her appreciation by making a shirt or tunic and presenting it in return. Marriage with the Seminoles is an affair of the heart and not of the purse. The day is fixed by the parents of the girl; the groom goes to the bride's home at the setting of the sun, and, taking her by the hand, he agrees to maintain her and to live at her camp. When the young couple build their own wigwam, they must build it at the camp of the wife's mother, and not among the husband's relatives. Marriage laws are held sacred, but divorce is permitted where some incompatibility of temper is found. Either party may marry again, but the marriage must meet with the approval of the council.

Separation by death has its laws: a squaw losing her husband must abstain from matrimony for one year, during which she must remove her heavy strands of beads and must live with dishevelled hair; her long black tresses, worn over her face and shoulders, cause her to present a pitiable, forsaken appearance. On the death of his squaw a husband may not hunt for four days, and for four moons must appear in mourning, *i.e.* without his many neck-cloths and his turban.

When a member of the band dies, the body is carried by two men to the place of interment at sunrise the following day. The corpse is placed on a base of logs with the face to the rising sun, and a pen of logs is built over it. The rifle and accoutrements are placed by the side of the dead man, and a bottle of *sofka* (the Seminoles' tribal dish) is buried with him, that he may eat on his last journey. Into the keeping of the Great Spirit, who lives above the clouds, the mourners commend the bivouac of the dead, making a sacred fire at each end of the grave. They then return to the camp, the women loudly wailing and tearing their hair.

5. Tribal organization. — The government among the Seminoles is largely in the hands of the medicine-men, who are important personages among all bands. According to their legends, Christ was sent to live with the Indians 'to make them good Indians,' but, when the Son of God was killed by the wicked Spaniards, as their traditions tell them, it became the duty of the medicine-men to teach the Indians and to impart the Great Spirit's wishes to His red children. The medicine-men act as advisers, priests, and doctors. The Spartan spirit is supreme; each camp has its council, and no event having any connexion with the good conduct and life of the members is allowed to go without the advice and verdict of the council. In the case of the Everglade Seminoles so strict has been the obedience of the tribe that the amount of crime has been infinitesimal, involving only minor punishments. Their laws, though unwritten, are well understood, undeviatingly enforced, and unmurmuringly obeyed.

The Seminole squaw is entitled to first claim as an American suffragist. She is a good counsellor in the camp life, and has a voice in the tribal laws; she has absolute control over the children, and is supreme in the management of the home. The money which she makes is hers to do with as she likes. If a squaw wishes to divorce her husband and can prove that she has just cause to do so, she can not only divorce him but name his punishment.

6. Character, dress, and food.—The Seminoles are gentle, kindly, and hospitable. They live a life of utmost purity, for the death penalty would follow any breach of virtue. The women are as chaste and modest as perhaps are the women of no other race to-day. Not a drop of the white man's blood courses through the veins of an Everglade Seminole.

In personal appearance the Seminole is far above the average. Many of the men are more than six feet in height, but so symmetrically proportioned that one loses sight of their height. Their features are good, their hands and feet remarkably small, their voices soft and low.

The Seminole dress consists of a tunic, highly decorated with narrow bands of red, close-fitting leggings, and moccasins. The turban, picturesque and oriental in its effect, is the insignia of the race and is worn almost constantly. It is made from enormous handkerchiefs or small woollen shawls, wrapped round and round the head and held in position by a band, often of beaten silver, encircling the whole. Another char-

[1] See M. Moore-Willson, *The Seminoles of Florida*, ed. New York, 1919, p. 163.

acteristic of the dress is the numerous handkerchiefs worn knotted loosely about the neck—the more handkerchiefs worn, the greater pride does the Seminole feel in his costume. The women, on the other hand, wear no head-dress or moccasins. Beads of many colours—and many pounds in weight—are the Seminole woman's badge of distinction, and she never appears without them. When the little papoose is one year old, she is given her first string with its 'first-year bead.' This bead is always larger than the rest and of different colour. A string of beads is allowed for each year until she marries, and at her marriage her mother gives her many new strands. A string of beads is always a reward for any prowess, and a mother is allowed two strings for each child born. In full dress many of the squaws wear from twenty to thirty pounds of glass beads, the colours of which blend in perfect harmony. When the squaw reaches middle life, she begins to take off her beads, one string at a time, until only one string is left. She is now an old squaw, too old to work, and the single strand is made up of the life beads and is buried with her.

Sofka is the tribal dish of the Seminoles: it is a stew containing the nutriment of many foods. The *sofka* spoon or ladle, made of wood, is a valued household article, and the authority of the women is seen again here, for a spoon cannot be sold or taken from camp without their consent. The different households have differently shaped and carved spoons, each band having its own particular style, or Seminole 'coat of arms.'

LITERATURE.—Clay MacCauley, 'The Seminole Indians of Florida,' in *5RBEW* [1887], pp. 469–531, art. 'Seminole' in *HAI*; Minnie Moore-Willson, *The Seminoles of Florida*, New York, 1910, [6]1916.

M. MOORE-WILLSON.

SEMI-PELAGIANISM.—See PELAGIANISM AND SEMI-PELAGIANISM.

SEMITES.

—'Semites' is a term applied to a group of nations, partly living and partly dead, who live or have lived in Western Asia and Eastern Africa. The name is based on the fact that several of these nations or parts of them are said in Gn 10 to be descended from the patriarch Shem. While the name was suggested by Genesis, the classification of modern scholars does not coincide with that of Genesis, but is based on linguistic and racial characteristics. Thus in Genesis Elam is classed as a son of Shem, but the Elamite language shows that the Elamites belonged to a different race. Canaan is in Genesis classed with the sons of Ham, but linguistically and racially the Canaanites are now known to be Semites. Through a confusion of the Egyptian *keš* (Nubia) and the Babylonian *kaš* (the Kassite country) the author of Genesis was led to class the Babylonians as Hamitic, but we now know that the Babylonians were at least half Semitic. The peoples counted as Semitic are the Akkadians,[1] Assyrians,[2] Amorites, Canaanites (*q.v.*), Aramæans,[3] Phœnicians (*q.v.*), Carthaginians, Hebrews,[4] Ammonites, Moabites, Edomites, Nabatæans, Arabs, Sabæans (*qq.v.*), or South Arabs, and Abyssinians.[5] Whether the Egyptians should be counted as Semitic is a moot question.

The languages of these peoples, excepting the Egyptians, are very closely related—as closely as French, Italian, Spanish, and Portuguese are to one another. Notwithstanding considerable racial mixture in some of the nations speaking those languages, as in Babylonia and Abyssinia, there is a good degree of similarity in their physical and mental characteristics. This similarity is, however, difficult to define. The attempt of Renan[6] to define them has been criticized by Nöldeke,[7] because it attributed to the whole Semitic race characteristics of Hebrews and Arabs. In Assyria and N. Africa[8] some of these supposed characteristics, such as inaptitude for political and military affairs, have not manifested themselves. The Semitic nations possessed skulls of similar shape, and all exhibited intensity of faith.

[1] See art. SUMERO-AKKADIANS.
[2] See art. BABYLONIANS AND ASSYRIANS.
[3] See art. SYRIANS. [4] See art. ISRAEL.
[5] See art. ABYSSINIA.
[6] E. Renan, *Hist. générale des langues sémitiques*, pp. 7–17.
[7] *EBr*[11], *s.v.* 'Semitic Languages.'
[8] Islām has carried the Arabic language over N. Africa, where it is now spoken by many peoples who are non-Semitic.

I. Relation to the Hamites.—The problem of the origin of the Semites, as well as the question whether the Egyptians were Semites, is closely bound up with the relation of the Semites to the Hamites.[1] According to the Africanist Meinhof,[2] 47 Hamitic languages, comprising 71 dialects, are spoken in Africa to-day. Through the labours of Reinisch, Stumme, Motylinski, and others the structure of several of these languages is known to the scholarly world. The tribes speaking them are scattered over N. Africa and penetrate the central Sahara to its southern side, and over E. Africa along the Red Sea through Abyssinia and Somaliland. One school of philologists count ancient Egyptian and its daughter, Coptic, as belonging to this group[3]—a view shared by certain anthropologists.[4] Friedrich Müller divides them into (1) the Egyptian group (Egyptian and Coptic), (2) the Libyan group (Tamesheq), and (3) the Ethiopic group (Bedza, Galla, Somali, Saho, Chamir, etc.). Sergi classifies them as follows:

I. *Eastern branch.*	II. *Northern branch.*
1. Ancient and modern Egyptians (Copts, Fellahin), excluding the Arabs.	1. Berbers of Mediterranean, Atlantic, and Sahara.
2. Nubians, Bejas.	2. Tebus or Tubus.
3. Abyssinians.	3. Fulahs or Fulbés.
4. Gallas, Danákal (Dankali), Somalis.	4. Guanches of the Canaries.
5. Masai.	
6. Wahuma or Watusi.	

It should be noted that the Abyssinian language (Ethiopic) is not properly included in this group, since it and its daughters (Amharic, Tigre, Tigrena, and Harari) are clearly Semitic tongues. Fulbé was classed by Müller as a Nubian language, but Meinhof claims that it is partly Hamitic, forming a bridge between the Nubian and Hamitic groups.[5] W. Max Müller holds[6] that Sergi's Northern group should be classed as Libyan languages rather than Hamitic, while Erman and his school[7] claim that Egyptian (with its descendant Coptic) must be counted a Semitic language that has suffered great deterioration from contact with African dialects. That there is kinship with Semitic is, no doubt, true, but it is a question whether it is confined to Egyptian, and whether it cannot be more satisfactorily explained on the basis of a common Hamito-Semitic ancestry than by the theory of a pre-historic Semitic invasion of Egypt. The kinship of the Semitic and Hamitic peoples is revealed by the following phenomena of language:

(1) The pronouns, which in the languages of the world are the most *sui generis* of all the parts of speech, are in these two groups so nearly akin as to be practically identical. This identity is common to the Semitic tongues, to the Libyan and Berber dialects, to the dialects of Somaliland, and to early and late Egyptian and Coptic. The Egyptian pronoun is no more pronouncedly Semitic than that of the other Hamitic tongues. Indeed, the pronoun in early Egyptian texts is not so similar to the Semitic as is that found in the later texts, whereas, on the theory of Erman, the exact reverse should be the case.[8]

(2) The Semitic languages possess but two tenses, one formed by affixing pronominal particles to a verb stem, to express completed action, and one formed by prefixing pronominal particles, to express incomplete action. In Arabic five forms of this second or imperfect tense are known, in Ethiopic and Assyrian two, while in Hebrew and Aramaic sporadic instances of a second form survive. In Assyrian (and Akkadian) the so-

[1] The term 'Hamite,' like 'Semite,' was suggested by Gn 10, but in modern parlance is applied to a group of peoples whose languages are related. The group is only partially identical with the Hamitic nations of Genesis.
[2] *An Introd. to the Study of African Languages*, map opposite p. 159.
[3] *E.g.*, F. Müller, *Grundriss der Sprachwissenschaft*, Vienna, 1876–84, iii. 226 ff.
[4] G. Sergi, *The Mediterranean Race*, p. 41.
[5] P. 47.
[6] *EBr*[11], *s.v.* 'Hamitic Races and Languages.'
[7] Cf. A. Erman, in *ZDMG* xlvi. [1892] 93–129, and *Ägyptische Grammatik*[3], Berlin, 1911, p. 1; also A. Ember, *ZÄ* xlix. [1911] 87 ff., l. [1912] 86 ff., li. [1913] 110 ff.; J. H. Breasted, *Hist. of Egypt*[2], New York, 1909, pp. 7, 25, 26.
[8] Cf. F. Müller, pp. 253 ff., 353 ff.; or the comparison made by the present writer in *JAOS* xxxv. [1915] 215 ff.

called perfect form—that which originally expressed completed action—has been relegated to the expression of states of being, and completed action is expressed by one of the imperfect forms. In other words, in Assyrian and Akkadian the so-called perfect may be seen in process of elimination.[1]

In the Hamitic languages, for nearly all of which we possess no ancient literature, there is considerable variety. Somali, Afar (Dankali), Saho, and Kabyle have preserved both the perfect made by afformatives and the imperfect made by preformatives.[2] The Galla has preserved only the perfect form, modifying it to express different shades of meaning.[3] Bedauyé, Shilḥish, and R'edamès have eliminated the perfect, as the Akkadian and Assyrian were doing, and express the various shades of thought by modifications of the imperfect.[4]

Egyptian, like Galla, has entirely lost the imperfect. All its verb formations are made on the analogy of the Semitic perfect, by affixes to the verb stem. There is a considerable number of these, and one of them, the so-called pseudo-participle, is a survival of the real Semitic perfect.[5] In the Pyramid Texts it is used as a transitive verb like the ordinary Semitic perfect; in the texts of the Middle Kingdom it has become an intransitive or passive, like the perfect form in Akkadian and Assyrian; in the later language it is often replaced by other constructions.[6] These constructions consist primarily of a verbal noun to which the suffix form of the pronoun is appended: thus *śedemi*, 'I will hear'; *śedemk*, 'thou wilt hear.' The participial form of the verbal stem imparts to the combination a future meaning. Other meanings are obtained by variations of this norm. *Śedemenef* has an aoristic significance; *śedemwf* a passive meaning; *śedemynf* is also a passive; *śedemḥarf* expresses resultant action; *šedemk'f* expresses wishes.[7] These forms, made on the analogy of the Semitic perfect, have entirely displaced the imperfect, and, in the later language, the perfect. The so-called pseudo-participle (perfect) is practically unknown in Coptic. Erman and Ember explain this phenomenon in Egyptian on the supposition that there was a pre-historic invasion of Egypt by Semites from Asia, who for a time imposed their language on the Egyptians, and in course of time this Semitic tongue was largely submerged by African tendencies of speech furnished by the pre-Semitic elements in the population. The argument from the comparison of general grammatical forms is reinforced by comparisons of the Egyptian and Semitic vocabularies, by which it is proved that the roots of many Egyptian words are identical with the roots of many Semitic words. As the roots by which these same meanings are expressed in the other Hamitic tongues are quite different, the argument from vocabulary appears at first sight to have considerable force.

In reality the argument from vocabulary is fallacious. For the other Hamitic dialects we have no literature for the early time. It is all modern—millenniums later than the Egyptian. In all living languages words become obsolete, giving way to others. There is no evidence that Semitic roots did not appear in the other Hamitic dialects 4000 or 5000 years ago; or that they would appear in Egyptian, if Egyptian had remained a non-literary language, and we knew it only as a spoken dialect to-day. The argument from vocabulary must, therefore, be discarded.

If, now, the verbs of the two groups of languages are viewed broadly, it appears that it is not necessary to posit a Semitic invasion of Egypt in order to explain the existence there of the pseudo-participle. Another explanation seems more natural. Had there been such an invasion, it is difficult to explain why it should not have imparted to Egyptian the Semitic imperfect as well as the Semitic perfect. There is no early Semitic dialect from which the imperfect is lacking, and Semites entering Egypt must have carried this with them. On the other hand, the presence of the perfect form in other Hamitic dialects, and the analogy of the Galla language, which has lost the imperfect formation, show that the phenomena of Egyptian are paralleled in Hamitic, though not in Semitic. The phenomena find a more satisfactory explanation on the supposition that the Semites and Hamites are descended from a common stock, and that the Egyptians are a branch of the Hamitic stock.

This view of the matter receives confirmation from a consideration of the larger aspects of the verbal stems in Semitic and Hamitic. There are indications in Coptic that certain Egyptian stems formed an intensive by doubling the middle radical, as do the Semitic languages.[8] This formation has survived in the Berber dialect of R'edamès,[9] where it is employed to express habitual action, and in Bilīn[10] and Chamir,[11] at the other extreme of the Hamitic territory, where it expresses intensity as in Semitic. These dialects of Somaliland also, like Hebrew, form *pilpels*. Again, Egyptian forms a *niphal*,[1] like Hebrew, Arabic, and Assyrian, by prefixing the letter *n*. A similar form is found at the two extremes of the Hamitic peoples in Saho[2] and Shilḥish.[3] In Tamesheq,[4] the dialect of R'edamès,[5] Bedauyé,[6] and Saho,[7] the *n* is changed to *m* (in most languages the two sometimes interchange). The formation is also present in Bilīn,[8] where the *n* is changed to its kindred liquid *r*. Egyptian also forms causatives in *s*, like the Semitic,[9] but this is paralleled in Bedauyé,[10] Bilīn,[11] Chamir,[12] Saho,[13] Tamesheq,[14] R'edamès,[15] and Shilḥish.[16] It seems to the present writer, therefore, that we are justified in regarding the Egyptians as a Hamitic people. It seems also clear, however, that the Semites and Hamites were, at some remote epoch, one stock.

2. The Semitic cradle-land.—At least five different theories as to the cradle-land of the Semites have been put forward.

(1) Babylonia has been regarded as the earliest home of the Semites by von Kremer,[17] Guidi,[18] and Hommel.[19] Von Kremer noted that the word for 'camel' is common to all the Semitic dialects, whereas they have no common name for the date-palm or the ostrich. He concluded that in remote antiquity the Semites migrated from the great central table-land of Asia near the sources of the Oxus and the Jaxartes, and first settled in Babylonia, whence they were by migration scattered to the other Semitic lands of history. Similar linguistic arguments led Guidi and Hommel to fix the first centre of Semitic life in Babylonia, though Hommel afterwards shifted it to Upper Mesopotamia. Driver[20] was at one time inclined to accept this view. Linguistic considerations, especially those based on vocabulary alone, form, however, too insecure a basis of induction for the solution of so large a problem.

(2) The most widely accepted theory at the present day is that Arabia was the cradle-land of the Semites. This theory was defended in 1861 by Sprenger,[21] and was afterwards advocated by Sayce,[22] Schrader,[23] de Goeje,[24] and Wright.[25] It is based on the observed facts that mountaineers do not become nomads, and that people do not migrate from a fertile country like Babylonia to a sterile land like Arabia. From time immemorial wave after wave of Arabs has poured forth from Arabia to the more fertile contiguous lands, and there is no evidence that the course of migration was in a large way ever in the other direction. Moreover, the Arabic language has preserved a far larger proportion of the peculiarities of primitive Semitic speech than the other Semitic tongues.

(3) A third theory, which may be regarded as a modification of the second, is that the original home of the Semites is to be sought in Africa, and that Arabia was the earliest Asiatic home and

1 Cf. H. Zimmern, *Vergleichende Grammatik der semitischen Sprachen*, Berlin, 1898, p. 82 ff.; or C. Brockelmann, *Grundriss der vergleichenden Grammatik der semitischen Sprachen*, Berlin, 1907–12, i. 504 ff.

2 Cf. L. Reinisch, *Die 'Afar-Sprache*, 3 vols., Vienna, 1886–87, *Die Sprache der Irob-Saho in Abessinien*, do. 1878; H. Stumme, *Handbuch des Schilḥischen von Tazerwalt*, Leipzig, 1899, p. 55.

3 Müller, p. 291 f.

4 Reinisch, *Die Beḏauye-Sprache in Nordost-Afrika*, 4 vols., Vienna, 1893–94; Stumme, *op. cit.*; and A. de Calassanti-Motylinski, *Le Dialecte berbère de Rédamès*, Paris, 1904.

5 Erman, *Ägyp. Grammatik*³, § 280.

6 K. Sethe, *Das ägyptische Verbum*, Leipzig, 1899, ii. 1.

7 *Ib.* §§ 278–324.

8 Sethe, p. 344.

9 Calassanti-Motylinski, p. 33.

10 Reinisch, *Die Bilīn-Sprache in Nordost-Afrika*, Vienna, 1882, p. 21.

11 Reinisch, *Die Chamirsprache in Abessinien*, Vienna, 1884, p. 46.

1 Erman, § 271; Sethe, § 357.

2 Reinisch, *Sprache der Irob-Saho*, p. 7.

3 Stumme, p. 70.

4 F. Müller, p. 273.

5 Calassanti-Motylinski, p. 33.

6 Reinisch, *Beḏauye-Sprache*, p. 130.

7 Reinisch, *Sprache der Irob-Saho*, p. 7.

8 Reinisch, *Bilīn-Sprache*, p. 27.

9 Erman, § 270; Sethe, § 350.

10 Reinisch, *Beḏauye-Sprache*, p. 126.

11 Reinisch, *Bilīn-Sprache*, p. 22.

12 Reinisch, *Chamirsprache*, p. 46.

13 Reinisch, *Sprache der Irob-Saho*, p. 6.

14 F. Müller, p. 270.

15 Calassanti-Motylinski, p. 33.

16 Stumme, p. 69.

17 Cf. his 'Semitische Culturentlehnungen aus dem Pflanzen- und Thierreiche,' in *Das Ausland*, iv. [1875] nos. 1 and 2.

18 Cf. his 'Della sede primitiva dei popoli Semitici,' in the *Proceedings of the Reale Accademia dei Lincei* for 1879.

19 *Die Namen der Säugthiere bei den südsemitischen Völkern*, Leipzig, 1879, p. 406, and *Die semitischen Völker und Sprachen*, do. 1881–83, i. 63.

20 *Treatise on the Use of the Tenses in Hebrew*, Oxford, 1881, p. 250 n.

21 *Leben und Lehre des Mohammad*, Berlin, 1861–69, i. 241 ff., and *Die alte Geographie Arabiens*, Bern, 1875, p. 293.

22 *Assyrian Grammar*, Oxford, 1872, p. 13.

23 *ZDMG* xxvii. [1873] 397–420.

24 *Het Vaderland der semitische Volken*, Leyden, 1882.

25 *Lectures on the Comparative Grammar of the Semitic Languages*, Cambridge, 1890, p. 8.

distributing centre of this race. This theory has been advocated by Palgrave,[1] Gerland,[2] Bertin,[3] Nöldeke,[4] Brinton,[5] Morris Jastrow,[6] Keane,[7] Ripley,[8] and Barton.[9] It is based in part on the linguistic evidence of relationship between the Hamitic and Semitic languages already discussed, in part on similarity of physical characteristics (such as the form of the jaw and the slenderness of the calf of the leg), and upon data secured by an ethnographic study of the peoples of the Mediterranean basin. In the opinion of the present writer, this is the most probable theory, and accounts best for all the facts.

(4) Another theory, which is an extension of the second hypothesis and reverses the third, is that Arabia was the original home of the Semites and that the Egyptians were formed by Semites who migrated to Africa and mingled with an earlier Negroid population of the Nile valley. This view has been advocated by Wiedemann,[10] de Morgan,[11] Erman,[12] Breasted,[13] and Ember.[14] It is based, as already explained, on the fact that old Egyptian has a form of the verb which corresponds to the Semitic perfect, and that the vocabularies of Egyptian and its daughter, Coptic, are much more nearly related to Semitic vocabularies than are those of other Hamitic languages. As already pointed out, these linguistic facts are more satisfactorily accounted for in another way.

(5) A. T. Clay is the protagonist of the view that the cradle-land of the Semites was Amurru (also read in cuneiform, *Uru*), a region which lay between Syria and Mesopotamia.[15] His arguments are based mainly on his interpretation of proper names. He contends that the names of antediluvian patriarchs in Babylonia — Kalumum, Zagugib, Armû, Etana, Piliqam (=Peleg), Lugalbanda, Dumuzi, Bilqa-mesh (Gilgamesh), and Enkidu—are Semitic names. He also claims that it can be shown that Humbaba (Humba) is not an Elamite god, but a despot whose palace was in the cedars of Lebanon.[16] Clay also contends that the prominent Babylonian gods are of West Semitic origin, viz. Adad, Amurru (Uru), Anu, Antu, Ashur, Dagan, In-Urta, Ishtar, Mash, Shamash, Urru, Zababa, etc. He further holds that, apart from the eruption of Muhammadans from Arabia in the 7th cent. A.D.—the impetus of which was to plunder the world—there have been no examples of spilling-over from Arabia into the fertile lands.[17]

With reference to this theory three observations seem to be necessary. (*a*) The positive evidence for it is of the most unsubstantial philological character. It is based on possible phonetic changes in proper names. The wider and more fundamental linguistic phenomena, which point to kinship between the Hamites and Semites, and which must be taken into account in any adequate theory, are ignored. (*b*) The contention that the Islâmic eruption from Arabia is the only historical one is scarcely true to the facts. That was the most spectacular, but, as is well known to those who have lived on the border of the desert, the migration from Arabia to the more fertile lands has been silently going on from time immemorial, and is in progress still. (*c*) Even if the theory were true, it does not prove that Arabia was not the cradle-land of the Semitic race; it would only localize that cradle-land in that part of N. Arabia that may have at one time been called Amurru, or the land of the Amorites.

3. Relation to Indo-Europeans.—It was formerly assumed (and the view is still widely held) that all human beings were descended from a single pair. Where this view prevails, it is naturally supposed that at some time, not too remotely anterior to the dawn of history, the Semites and the Indo-Europeans formed one people. It is unnecessary to say that there are many problems connected with the origin of both the Indo-Europeans and the Hamito-Semitic stock that are still unsolved; but, in spite of this, the advance in knowledge that is made from decade to decade tends to show that there is no demonstrable relationship between the two divisions of the human race. A comparison of their languages points to this negative conclusion. It seems probable that tri-literal roots (*i.e.* roots consisting of three consonants, vowels being disregarded) were the basis originally of all Hamito-Semitic words. To the Indo-European mind this peculiar method of conceiving a vocal root appears most peculiar and foreign. There is no uniform tri-literality to Indo-European roots, and no such disregard of vowels. Indo-European roots sometimes consist of a single letter, and that a vowel.

Again, the whole interest in the actions of persons and the method of expressing that interest are different. To the Indo-European mind the time of an action is important; hence in the languages belonging to this group the tense-system is well developed. It is in these languages possible to make it clear whether an act is still going on, began in past time and is just reaching completion, was completed in past time, was completed in the past before some other event in the past, is still to happen, or will be completed in the future before something else happens. In some of the languages a seventh tense, expressive of momentary or timeless action, also exists. In contrast to this, the Hamito-Semitic languages had but two tenses, and primarily neither of these expressed time. One indicated that an action was complete, the other that it was incomplete. To make a narrative vivid a speaker might use of a past action the form of the verb denoting incompleteness; or to make a future deed seem certain he might employ the verbal form denoting completed action. The interest of the Hamito-Semitic mind in the time of an action was of the slightest. While the Hamito-Semite cared little for the time of an action, he was intensely interested in other phases of human activity. Whether a deed was done simply or under such strong emotion that the act was intensive, whether one did it of his own free will or some one else caused him to do it, whether he did it for himself or on himself, whether he was caused to do it for or on himself—these were the things that to the Hamito-Semitic mind seemed important. In the verbs of the languages of these races there are forms for the expression of all such shades of meaning. The Arabic, in which the most elaborate system for the expression of such shades of thought has survived, has no fewer than fifteen forms or 'stems' of the verb for this purpose. Six of them are of comparatively infrequent occurrence, it is true, but the existence of any such form is indicative of a different interest, a different psychological make-up, and a radically different method of conceiving and expressing thought from that which underlies the Indo-European verb-system. If we suppose that the two groups of races formed one people after the development of human speech (or, at least, after the development of any of the existing families of languages), it is

1 *EBr*[9], *s.v.* 'Arabia.'
2 *Iconographic Encyclopedia*, i., *s.v.* 'Ethnography.'
3 *JAI* xi. [1882] 431 ff.
4 *EBr*[11], *s.v.* 'Semitic Languages.'
5 *The Cradle of the Semites*, and *Races and Peoples*, p. 132.
6 See his art. in Brinton, *Cradle of the Semites*.
7 *Ethnology*, p. 392, *Man, Past and Present*, Cambridge, 1899, p. 490.
8 *The Races of Europe*, p. 376.
9 *A Sketch of Semitic Origins, Social and Religious*, ch. i.
10 In J. de Morgan, *Recherches sur les origines de l'Egypte*, Paris, 1897, i. 219, 223, 228.
11 *Ib.* p. 196.
12 *SBAW* xix. [1900] 350 ff., and *Ägyptische Grammatik*[3], p. 1 f.
13 *Hist. of Egypt*[2], pp. 7, 25, 26.
14 *ZA* xlix. 87 ff., l. 86 ff., li. 110 ff.
15 See, *e.g.*, his *Amurru, the Home of the Northern Semites*, *Miscellaneous Inscriptions from the Yale Babylonian Collection*, New Haven, 1915, and *The Empire of the Amorites*, New Haven, 1919.
16 *Empire of the Amorites*, p. 87 f.
17 *Ib.* ch. ii.

hardly conceivable that they should have differed so radically in the conception and expression of thought, or should have transformed the daughter-tongues of a once common speech into languages that differ so widely in the most fundamental elements of speech. The conclusion seems forced upon us that, if there is any kinship between the Indo-European group and the Hamito-Semitic group, the ancestors of the two must have separated far back in the history of *homo alalus*, before the beginnings of language. We can trace the Hamito-Semitic stock to the great Mediterranean race. The origin of the Aryans is far less clear. It is probable that, wherever the human species originated, whether, as Haeckel and others think, in a continent that once occupied the area of the Indian ocean, or, as Quatrefages thought, on the roof of the world north of the Himalayas, or, as Gerland and Brinton held, in the Mediterranean basin, or, as Giddings holds, in 'a tropical or sub-tropical zone which reached half-way around the earth from Java north-westerly to England,' it had spread over most of the globe before human speech was developed. In that case the Aryan speech and the Hamito-Semitic speech are entirely independent developments in different centres. Probably there were other independent centres of development also. The older custom of classing all non-Indo-European and non-Hamito-Semitic languages together and calling them 'Turanian' was based largely upon our ignorance of such languages.

4. Classification. — Classifications of Semitic nations are based by scholars upon peculiarities of their languages when compared with one another. The languages fall into five groups, as follows:

1. The Mesopotamian group.
    - (1) Akkadian (spoken in Babylonia).
    - (2) Assyrian.
2. The Aramaic group.
    - A. East Aramaic.
        - (1) Babylonian Aramaic (Babylonian Talmud).
        - (2) Mandæan.
        - (3) Syriac.
        - (4) Modern dialects spoken in Kurdistan and Urumia.
    - B. West Aramaic.
        - (1) Dialect of Samal and Ya'di.
        - (2) Inscription of ZKR.
        - (3) Jewish Aramaic (Biblical).
        - (4) Palmyrene (inscriptions).
        - (5) Nabatæan (inscriptions).
        - (6) Jewish Palestinian (Targums of Onkelos and Jonathan, Jerusalem Talmud, Targumim and Midrashim).
        - (7) Christian-Palestinian Aramaic.
        - (8) Samaritan.
        - (9) Dialect of Ma'lula in the Lebanon.
3. Canaanitish group.
    - (1) Phœnician.
    - (2) Hebrew:
        - (*a*) Biblical.
        - (*b*) Mishnaic.
    - (3) Moabitish.
4. The Arabic group.
    - A. North Arabic.
        - (1) North Arabic inscriptions.
        - (2) Classical Arabic.
        - (3) Modern dialects (innumerable).
    - B. South Arabic.
        - (1) Minæan and Sabæan (inscriptions).
        - (2) Mehri.
        - (3) Soqotri.
5. Abyssinian.
    - (1) Abyssinian inscriptions.
    - (2) Ethiopic (*Ge'ez*).
    - (3) Modern dialects:
        - (*a*) Tigre, Tigrina.
        - (*b*) Amharic.
        - (*c*) Hariri, Guraghe.

A comparison of these groups of tongues seems to most scholars to show that groups 1, 2, and 3 are more closely related to one another than they are to groups 4 and 5, and that there is a closer kinship between groups 4 and 5 than there is between either of these groups and 1, 2, and 3.

Most Semitic scholars, therefore, divide them into Northern Semites and Southern Semites. The Northern Semites, according to this classification, fall into three groups:

Eastern.	*Central or Aramæan.*	*Western or Canaanite.*
Babylonians	Syrians	Amorites
Assyrians	Damascenes	Canaanites
	Nabatæans	Phœnicians
	etc.	Carthaginians
		Hebrews
		Ammonites
		Moabites
		Edomites.

The Southern Semites are the Arabs, South Arabians, and Abyssinians. This classification rests on a sound linguistic basis. The South Semitic languages have some peculiarities, such as broken or internal plurals, that are entirely wanting in North Semitic. The grouping of the Northern Semites also rests on the fact that the languages of each group, while differing in many respects from those of the other groups, form among themselves only dialects of the same language.

Another classification has been adopted by some scholars—*e.g.*, Hommel[1] and Clay[2]—who divide the Semitic nations into East Semites and West Semites, the former embracing the Babylonians and Assyrians, and the latter including all the others. This division rests upon the fact that the Babylonians are supposed to have separated from the rest of the Semitic stock long anterior to any other division among the Semites, so that their language, having a longer time in which to develop peculiarities, differed (according to hypothesis) more widely from the primitive Semitic norm than any other Semitic language. This classification is not so satisfactory as the other. While it is true that the languages of the East Semites have some peculiarities that are *sui generis*, they are on the whole more nearly related to those of the Aramæan and Canaanitish Semites than to those of Arabia and Abyssinia.

5. Characteristics.—It is not easy to sum up the characteristics of an individual; it is well-nigh impossible accurately to sum up those of a race. Sayce, *e.g.*, declared the Semitic characteristics to be intensity of faith, ferocity, exclusiveness, and imagination. It is doubtful, however, whether Semites have ever been more ferocious than other peoples who were at the same stage of civilization as the Semites when they committed the atrocities that impress the modern man. Ferocity is characteristic of all ancient nations and of all barbarous nations. As to the other characteristics mentioned, the Aryans of India—to cite but one example—have probably surpassed the Semites in intensity of faith, in imagination, and in exclusiveness.

We shall tread on safer ground if we note certain features of Semitic social organization, religion, and art, and seek from these to discover characteristics.

(1) *Social organization.*—(*a*) The earliest social organization of the Semites was of a matriarchal type. Marriage was polyandrous, and the relations between the sexes were, from a modern point of view, ill regulated.[3] This organization was in a sense forced upon them by the sterile environment of their cradle-land, Arabia, where the struggle for existence was most intense, driving them into a barbarous sort of civilization in advance of other savages, but making a high civilization impossible. Mentally developed by this struggle earlier than all other peoples except their Hamitic kinsmen, they were prevented by their surroundings for centuries from attaining the highest civilization. Their desert and oasis environment impressed

[1] F. Hommel, *Die semitischen Völker und Sprachen*, i., 'Die sprachgeschichtliche Stellung des Babylonisch-Assyrischen,' in *Études archéologiques, linguistiques et historiques dédiées à C. Leemans*, Leyden, 1885, pp. 127–129, and *Aufsätze und Abhandlungen*, Munich, 1892, pp. 92–128.

[2] Clay nowhere makes a clear statement on the subject, but in *Amurru* and *The Empire of the Amorites* (*passim*) speaks of the 'West Semites' as though he took the classification for granted.

[3] Barton, ch. ii.

their minds with the great contrast between the fertile oasis and the sterile desert. Nothing seemed to them so divine as the power to give life, either vegetable or animal. They deified that power. A matriarchal society led them to regard the chief deity of fertility as a goddess. She gave the date-palm; she gave children; she gave the increase of the camels, goats, and sheep. Every act that in this rudely organized society tended to create life was sacred to her. The name of this goddess as Ishtar, Ashtar, Ashtart, Attar, Ashtoreth, or Athtar is the one divine name that is universal among Semites. No other deity commanded the devotion of all Semites as she did. She was on the side of life; the desert was death. Her worship continued in all Semitic lands far down into historical times, though in S. Arabia and Abyssinia she was transformed into a god. The less well regulated and barbarous sexual customs and orgies of the earliest times were protected by the reverence and devotion felt for her, and so were continued as sacred services in all Semitic countries well into the historical period. In Israel they were eradicated only by the ethical teaching of the prophets, reinforced by the providential disasters that befell the nation at the hand of Assyria and Babylon.

The worship of mother-goddesses and the matriarchal organization were not peculiar to the Semites; the former has been found in all parts of the world; the latter was coupled with it among the Hittites, Cretans, Celts, and others. The peculiarly sterile cradle-land of the Semites gave to the Semitic mind a stronger bent in this direction than is found among most other peoples. At its worst this manifested itself in such sexual orgies as the prophets denounced, though these could be paralleled, if not exceeded, by those of the Saivites of India. At its best this tendency is seen in that delight in offspring and devotion to family that is characteristic of the Jews to this day. It is this which also makes every Arab jubilant at the birth of a son. Among all peoples the perpetuation of race has become at some stage of development a chief care. Among Semites this care has been, for the reasons mentioned, more all-pervasive and persistent.

(*b*) While the Semites made considerable advance in the earlier forms of social organization, they contributed little, if anything, to the larger forms of political organization that build up successful and stable empires. Their long struggle for existence as small units in the desert led them to work out several forms of clan organization and developed in them a strong clan spirit. These organizations allowed the individual a good degree of freedom. The *shaikh*, or leader, was only *primus inter pares*. He had only such authority as the public opinion of his clan was willing to enforce. When more favourable circumstances permitted the construction of empire, Semites proved themselves capable warriors and despots, able to establish temporary dominion over an extensive territory. Examples of this are to be found in the empire of Sargon of Agade, that of the first dynasty of Babylon, that of Assyria, that of the Neo-Babylonians, and the various dominions of the Muhammadan khalīfahs. In a lesser degree the empire of King David of Israel also illustrates it. These empires were built up by cruel and bloody conquest (though not more cruel than other conquests equally ancient) and were absolute monarchies. It has been well said that the 'Semitic form of government was a despotism tempered by assassination.'[1] There are inherent weaknesses in such a political order. Everything depends upon the energy and character of the despot. Weakness in him causes immediate decay of the State. For this reason every Semitic state has led a chequered career, and the Semites have contributed little to the political philosophy of the world. In making this statement it is not forgotten that in modern European countries Jews here and there have proved themselves able and far-seeing statesmen, and have made contributions to sound political philosophy. They have done this, however, under the stimulus of a non-Semitic environment, and it is hardly proper to credit their achievements to their Semitic ancestry.

The failure of Semites to make a large contribution to the advanced political development of the world may be attributed in part to the early period in human development during which Semitic states flourished. There is, however, little in their history to lead one to suppose that, had they held the hegemony of the world at a later and more advanced period, the case would have been different. The aptitude for such leadership, except under outside stimulus, was apparently not theirs. The Code of Ḥammurabi, however, and some of the laws of the Jewish Pentateuch exhibit an aptitude for working out certain primary problems of social justice. The Pentateuch at least has had extensive influence upon Western civilization. If, then, they have lacked ability to develop a broad political philosophy, they have made a valuable contribution to the realization of social justice.

(2) *Art*.—In the field of art the productions of the Semitic peoples are on the whole not of the highest rank. While there are one or two exceptions to be noted below, broadly speaking, wherever we find the work of pure Semites, unstimulated by contact with other races, it is crude; it lacks artistic beauty. This is true of Semitic architecture, of Semitic modelling, and of the arts generally. It is true that pottery, bronze work, and the silver vase found at Telloh (Lagash) in S. Babylonia[1] are as excellent as any work of the kind known to us from a time equally ancient, but these were produced, if not by pure Sumerians, by Semites with a large admixture of Sumerian blood. The same remark applies to the busts, stelæ, and beautifully carved seal cylinders of the kings of Agade. Similarly, the art of the Muhammadan Arabs is in many respects very fine.[2] The mosque of 'Umar at Jerusalem is wonderfully beautiful, and the Alhambra of Spain—to mention but one example of Muhammadan art in that land—is one of the artistic wonders of the world. Such creations were not, however, the work of unaided Semitic genius, but were due in large measure to the genius of Persians and others, whom Islām had absorbed. When Phœnician civilization was at its height, Phœnician art attained a degree of barbaric finish, but it was seldom beautiful and probably never original. The Phœnicians were the carriers of the Levant for a time, and their artistic impulses were derived from Egypt or Mesopotamia. The OT echoes with the praises of the beauty of the temple of Solomon, and undoubtedly it was, like the temple of Melkart at Tyre described by Herodotus, a building of barbaric splendour. Could it be restored, however, the modern architect would not find it beautiful. Its reputation is due largely to the fact that it was the grandest building that the Hebrews, whose buildings lacked all artistic beauty, had ever seen. Whatever beauty the buildings with which Herod the Great adorned Palestine may have possessed (and their remains prove that they were beautiful), it must be remembered that Herod drew his inspiration from Hellenic models and probably employed Hellenic architects.

[1] C. H. Toy, in his lectures at Harvard University.

[1] See art. ART (Assyro-Babylonian).
[2] See art. ART (Muhammadan).

The one real exception to the inartistic character of Semitic work is found in the figures of animals from the palaces of the Sargonid kings of Assyria (722–626 B.C.), especially those from the palace of Ashurbanipal (668–626 B.C.). Here animals in action are not only carved more successfully than elsewhere in the ancient world up to that time, but they commend themselves for their beauty and success when judged by modern standards. The action of horses, wild asses, lions, etc., the pose of their bodies, and the delineation of their straining muscles leave little to be desired. The great artistic ability of many Jews in modern times, in music, painting, etc., is not a real exception to the general artistic inaptitude of the Semites, for such artistic production is due to the stimulus of their modern, non-Semitic environment. In general, then, it must be said that, though Semites all through their history have proved apt pupils whenever stimulated by the artistic achievements of other peoples, when left to themselves they are characterized by artistic inaptitude.

(3) *Literature.* — In literature Semitic talent shines more brightly than in art, though aptitude is not manifested for all varieties of literature. Semitic literatures were produced only by the Babylonians and Assyrians, the Hebrews, and the Arabs.[1] While the Babylonians developed a large mythological literature and constructed at least two epic poems, they produced nothing that takes rank among the literary masterpieces of the world. These poems are remarkable for their antiquity, but are the literary productions of men who were still in the childhood of the race. How much of them is due to Semitic and how much to Sumerian genius it is often difficult to tell. There is a certain art in Assyrian chronicle-writing, but there are also great faults which exclude these productions from the realm of literature. Neither the Babylonians nor any other Semitic people produced dramatic poetry. Neither the book of Job nor the Song of Songs in the OT constitutes an exception to this statement. These Hebrew compositions, which have often been claimed as examples of Semitic drama, really belong to other classes of literature. The Semite was too serious and matter-of-fact in his make-up to enjoy acting. The real contribution of the Semites to the universal literature of the world was made in quite another realm —the religious. The literature of the Hebrews that has survived is contained in the OT. This, along with the NT, is the most widely circulated book in the world. It is not of equal literary merit in all its parts. Some of its books, such as Leviticus and Chronicles, contain little in themselves to attract the general reader. The Psalter, the book of Job, and parts of the prophetic books are, however, among the literary treasures of the race. They constitute the gems of Hebrew poetry. The great Hebrew poets possessed the art of simple, direct expression. In terse phrases they set forth emotional experiences with a power almost unequalled. Their figures, drawn from the homely things of common life, are of universal appeal. No other book of religious devotion has been employed by so many people of widely different races, circumstances, and civilizations to voice the confessions, praises, and aspirations of worship as the Hebrew Psalter. To have given this to the world is in itself a great achievement. It is not, as is popularly supposed, the work of one great poet; in it the work of unknown and unnumbered poets is enshrined. Different in character as the work of these bards often is, different as are their points of view, in the Psalter their work is blended into a whole of wonderful richness and beauty, forming a book that is at once the model and the despair of all subsequent writers of devotional poetry.

Of Arabic literature taken as a whole it must be said that much of it was composed by Muhammadans of Persian stock. There is, however, one book, the *Qur'ān* (*q.v.*), the greatest contribution to the world's literature in the Arabic tongue, that is purely Semitic in origin. Its author, Muhammad, was an Arab of the Arabs. Such outside stimulus as he had came from Jews and the OT—purely Semitic sources. While, as judged by the standards of literary form, the *Qur'ān* leaves much to be desired, it possesses in the original a certain rhythm and assonance that is not unpleasing and that is regarded by the Arabs as remarkable. This is, of course, untranslatable, and the subject-matter and arrangement (or rather lack of it) are such that in translation the *Qur'ān* seems confused and often incoherent. Nevertheless the book is treasured by about one-sixth of the inhabitants of the world as their supreme book, so that, whatever a non-Muhammadan may think of it, he must confess that its author possessed in a marvellous degree the genius to interpret life to men of a certain stage of culture.

As creators of religious literature which appeals to all sorts and conditions of men, the Semites are without peers among the nations of the world.

(4) *Religion.* — Behind religious literature lies religion, of which literature is the expression. As Semites have given the world its best religious literature, it is not surprising that they have given it its best religion. Of the four monotheistic religions of the world — Judaism, Zoroastrianism, Muhammadanism, and Christianity—three are of Jewish origin. Zoroastrianism, the fourth, is the least satisfactory and successful. Renan held that the Semites possessed a racial tendency to monotheism, but it has long been recognized that this claim is unfounded. Among primitive Semitic tribes a kind of henotheism is found, but this by no means denies the existence of other spirits and gods, or leads to a disinclination upon occasion to worship them. When tribe conquered tribe in that clash of interests through which larger states are built, polytheism as gross and uninspiring as any in the world flourished among Semites. That they have become the religious teachers of the world is due to the character, inspiration, and genius of a few individuals. But, just as it is the immortal glory of the Greeks to have produced Æschylus, Sophocles, Euripides, Phidias, Socrates, Plato, and Aristotle, so it is the glory of the Semites to have produced Amos, Hosea, Isaiah, Jeremiah, Ezekiel, Muhammad, Jesus, and Paul. Such men do not spring from a religiously barren soil or flourish in a wholly hostile environment. If it be objected that Jesus was not altogether of the earth, it should be remembered that nevertheless He was 'of the seed of David according to the flesh,' and His mission would have been fruitless had not the ethical monotheism of the Hebrew prophets prepared the way for Him. Even though the Semites possessed no general tendency to monotheism, they produced individuals who had the vision to perceive this truth and the ability to lead a goodly number of their fellows to accept it. This monotheism as taught by Jesus and Paul, and later in a less exalted form by Muhammad, has created two of the religions of the world that make a universal appeal. Men of almost every race are found in the ranks of Christianity and Muhammadanism. No other monotheism has been able to do this. Buddhism, the other religion that aims at universality, is unstable in its conception of God. Primitive Buddhism worshipped no deity. Some later Buddhists practically worship many gods; some revere a philosophical Absolute.

[1] See artt. LITERATURE (Babylonian) and (Jewish).

To sum up in a definition the religious possibilities and tendencies of the Semites is impossible. We can only say that in one Semitic people (and in another in a far lesser degree) they possessed the power of transmuting the dark mire of primitive Semitic nature-worship, often gross in its forms, into the pure white lily of the world's best religion.

LITERATURE.—E. Renan, *Hist. générale des langues sémitiques*³, Paris, 1863; A. H. Keane, *Ethnology*, Cambridge, 1896; D. G. Brinton, *Races and Peoples*, New York, 1890, *The Cradle of the Semites*, Philadelphia, 1890; T. Nöldeke, art. 'Semitic Languages,' in *EBr*¹¹; A. A. Gerland, art. 'Ethnography,' in *Iconographic Encyclopedia*, i.; W. R. Smith, *The Religion of the Semites*², London, 1894; W. Z. Ripley, *The Races of Europe*, New York, 1900; G. Sergi, *The Mediterranean Race*, London, 1901; G. A. Barton, *A Sketch of Semitic Origins, Social and Religious*, New York, 1902, 'Tammuz and Osiris,' in *JAOS* xxxv. [1915] 215 ff.; A. Erman, 'Die Flexion des ägyptischen Verbums,' in *SBAW* xix. [1900] 317–353; A. T. Clay, *Amurru, the Home of the Northern Semites*, Philadelphia, 1909, *The Empire of the Amorites*, New Haven, 1919; C. Meinhof, *An Introd. to the Study of African Languages*, London, 1915.

GEORGE A. BARTON.

SENĀPANTHĪS.—The Senāpanthīs were an Indian Vaiṣṇava sect, an offshoot of the Rāmāwats, having been founded by a barber named Sena or Senānanda (usually shortened familiarly to Senā), one of the twelve apostles of Rāmānanda.[1] Their tenets did not differ from those of other Vaiṣṇavas, and their existence as a separate sect is due to the fact that Senā himself and his descendants exercised considerable influence as family *gurus*, or religious preceptors, of the then rājā of Bāndhogaṛh, or Rīwā, in Baghelkhaṇḍ, and his successors. According to tradition, the rājā was Bīr Singh, who reigned A.D. 1500–40. But Senā's teacher, Rāmānanda, flourished in the 14th cent.,[1] and the alleged dates of master and pupil are therefore incompatible. Either Rāmānanda lived later than is supposed—which is unlikely—or else it was not Bīr Singh, but some predecessor, to whom Senā acted as *guru*.

The story of the rājā's acceptance of Senā as his *guru* belongs to the group of Vaiṣṇava legends, of which there are many examples, in which the deity is represented as impersonating a devotee in order to save him from some censure or other calamity.

Senā, a devout Vaiṣṇava, was originally the rājā's barber. One day, intent on his duty of showing hospitality to wandering holy men,[2] he neglected to attend his master at the usual time for the performance of the necessary tonsorial functions. Rāma himself accordingly took his form, appeared before the rājā, and did Senā's work, without the rājā being aware of the change of identity. Subsequently, when Senā, knowing nothing of what had occurred, arrived and began to apologize for being behind time, the rājā discerned the true state of affairs, and, falling at Senā's feet, elected him as his spiritual guide.

The sect is believed to be now extinct.

LITERATURE.—Nābhā Dāsa, *Bhaktamāla* (63), with Priyā Dāsa's commentary; the best ed. is that of Sitārāmaśaraṇa Bhagavān Prasāda, Benares, 1905, p. 765 ff. A summary of the statements in the *Bhaktamāla* is given by H. H. Wilson, *Sketch of the Religious Sects of the Hindus*, ed. R. Rost, London, 1861, p. 118 f.

GEORGE A. GRIERSON.

SENECA.—

1. Life and character.—L. Annæus Seneca (4 B.C.–A.D. 65), the second of the three sons of the rhetorician Annæus Seneca, was born at Corduba in Spain. He received a considerable inheritance from his father, and by the favour of Nero amassed enormous riches, the disposition of which was the cause of much heart-searching.[3] Among his teachers he mentions particularly Sotion,[4] the pupil of Sextius, from whom he learnt to follow the recommendation of Pythagoras by becoming a vegetarian.[5] Subsequently, after practising the habit for a year, he abandoned it at his father's request.[6] The chief impulse to Stoicism came from Attalus, of whom he speaks with profound respect.[7] In due course Seneca became an advocate and passed through the initial stages of official life with success.[1] In the year 41 he incurred the enmity of Messalina, and was banished to Corsica, where he lived in exile for eight years. In 49 Agrippina procured his recall and employed him at court as tutor to the young Nero.[2] His subsequent career as imperial minister, the decline of his influence after the death of Burrus, his withdrawal from court, his implication in the conspiracy of Piso, and his forced suicide, belong to Roman history and do not require a more particular description.[3] He devoted the last few years of his life entirely to literary labours, whereby he essayed to promote the practical lessons of Stoicism.[4]

His character is variously estimated. While we cannot feel for Seneca the whole-hearted respect which he might have earned by a more unswerving courage, it should be remembered that the age in which he lived and the position which he occupied made it impossible for a Stoic to remain in public life without abating somewhat the rigidity of his principles. In order to retain his influence over Nero he may have thought it necessary to acquiesce in certain of his proceedings which it was impossible to restrain.[5] In this spirit, that it is useless to strive after the unattainable, Seneca declares that Zeno's recommendation of political activity does not apply when the State is so depraved as to be past healing. The wise man's motive is the service of his fellow-man, and in favourable conditions public life offers a wider opportunity than is open to the private citizen. If that avenue is closed, he will endeavour to be useful to his neighbours, or at least to improve himself.[6] Even his most bitter enemies admitted that Seneca's administration was honest and his advice inspired by a desire for good.[7] Tacitus, in describing his death, leaves us in no doubt of his admiration,[8] and his own writings sufficiently demonstrate the sincerity of his ardour in the pursuit of virtue.

2. Relation to Stoicism.—Seneca's influence in the history of human thought is due to his position as the earliest exponent of Roman Stoicism.[9] Although Cornutus and Heraclitus are represented by writings which are still extant, their subject-matter was of comparatively trivial value, whereas Seneca's works gave a fresh impetus to the spread of philosophy among the educated classes by laying stress upon its supreme importance as a practical guide for conduct, so that he became the forerunner of the movement which was subsequently developed by Musonius, Epictetus, and Marcus Aurelius. The framework of the Stoic system was taken over bodily, and it is beyond question that, though claiming a nominal independence,[10] he did not originate any fresh development on the strength of his own authority.[11] The theoretical side of Stoicism was to be cultivated at most as a legitimate object of curiosity, and for the purpose of stimulating its students to struggle onwards in the pursuit of virtue; the establishment of exact scientific knowledge was a matter of secondary interest.

Adopting this attitude, he was at liberty to express his profound contempt for the subtleties of logic on which Chrysippus had toiled so laboriously. He devoted one of his letters[12] to the discussion of the Stoic paradox that wisdom (*sapientia*, φρόνησις) is a good, but the possession of wisdom (*sapere*, φρονεῖν) is not. Holding that nothing but the corporeal exists, the Stoics nevertheless made an exception in favour of the incorporeal notion (λεκτόν, including φρονεῖν) which is intermediate between the corporeal utterance on the one hand and the corporeal mind on the other. This position was defended by a process of artificial reasoning which Seneca expounded but refused to follow. He brushed aside the distinction between *sapere* and *sapientia* as repugnant to common sense, and apologized for having spent so much time in discussing it. 'Let us pass by these ingenious triflings and hasten to pursue what will be of some profit to us.'[13]

3. Physics and metaphysics.—A much greater value is attributed to physics, which, though it

1 See art. RĀMĀNANDĪS, RĀMĀWATS.
2 See *ERE* x. 570ᵇ, note 2.
3 J. E. B. Mayor on Juvenal, x. 16, in *Thirteen Satires*, 2 vols., London, 1888–93.
4 *Ep.* xlix. 2.
5 *Ib.* cviii. 19.
6 *Ib.* 22.
7 *Ib.* 13.

1 *Dial.* XII. v. 4.
2 Tac. *Ann.* xii. 8.
3 *Ib.* xiv. 52 ff.
4 *Ep.* viii. 1–3.
5 Tac. *Ann.* xiii. 2.
6 *Dial.* VIII. iii. 3.
7 Dio, lxi. 4.
8 *Ann.* xv. 62 ff.
9 See art. STOICS.
10 *Dial.* VII. iii. 2. Seneca claimed to be an eclectic and was ready to accept even from Epicurus what he himself approved. See *Ep.* xii. 11, with Summers's note.
11 R. D. Hicks, *Stoic and Epicurean*, London, 1910, p. 14.
12 *Ep.* cxvii.
13 *Ib.* cxvii. 30.

does not directly assist the formation of character, nevertheless elevates the mind by bringing it into contact with the majesty of divine truth, whereas logic shrivels and contracts the mind without sharpening it.[1] In a similar spirit he propounded a discussion on the nature of causality, defending the Stoic conception of its unity against the plurality of Aristotle.[2] He met the objection that such controversies do not assist us to extirpate emotion, which is the final aim of moral action, by saying that, so long as they are not employed pedantically, they elevate the mind by freeing it from its earthly burdens. 'Would you forbid me to claim a share in heaven? Must I live with my head bowed to the earth?'[3]

Among the works of Seneca which have been preserved are the *Naturales Quæstiones* in seven books, which deals chiefly with the phenomena of meteorology. This work is not the product of independent research. It is derived largely from Posidonius,[4] and the perfunctory method of treatment suggests that the actual results were regarded as comparatively unimportant. Seneca professed that his interest in physical science arose from its value in strengthening moral convictions and purifying the soul.[5] He was always ready to pass from the merely material explanation of natural objects to the evidence which they afforded in support of Stoic pantheism. The similarity of the microcosm to the macrocosm and, in particular, the correspondence of God's relation to the world with that of the soul to man[6] were themes on which Seneca never wearied of expatiating.[7] The philosophic expression of these ideas treats God as a material air-current (πνεῦμα, *spiritus*), which permeates every part of the universe[8] and is the ultimate source of every variety of life and movement.[9] Hence the importance attached to the theory of tension as the peculiar characteristic of the action of spirit, giving at once unity to our bodies and growth and vigour to trees and crops.[10] Thus, we need not raise our hands to invoke an absent deity. No good man is apart from God: 'nay, he is close at hand, he is with you, he is within you.'[11] The divine origin of our souls explains the Stoic belief in immortality. After its release from the body the soul is gradually purged of the taints received in its mortal career,[12] and rises to the purer region of the celestial æther, where it enjoys daily converse with other blessed spirits.[13] Finally, at the period of the world-conflagration (ἐκπύρωσις), when everything is resolved into the fiery essence, the immortal souls, sharing in the general effacement, are absorbed in the divine unity.[14] Concerning the fate of those souls which have become debased through wickedness we have no certain information. Seneca, as we might expect, will have nothing to do with the mythical horrors of Tartarus;[15] on the other hand, he recognizes the moral value attaching to a belief in a system of future rewards and punishments.[16] He was entirely in accord with the rest of the school in refusing to condemn the observances of the State religion, but he was keenly alive to its abuses.[17] It is the inward spirit, rather than the outward ceremony, that counts. The futility of prayers to the gods as ordinarily rendered is expressed by Seneca as vigorously as by Juvenal;[1] but the value of prayer as an act of resignation to the will of heaven and of self-examination before retiring to rest is abundantly acknowledged.[2] The sum of our religious duty is to seek out the divine will, to mould ourselves in the likeness of the gods, and to submit unhesitatingly to their decrees.[3] No act of ours can deflect the unchangeable progress of destiny in fulfilment of God's purpose. Therefore, according to the lesson conveyed in Cleanthes' verses,[4] which Seneca rendered into Latin,[5] true piety consists in a willing surrender of what the stubborn must yield perforce.[6] This attitude of mind is expressed by Seneca in terms of epigram: 'I do not obey God but agree with Him';[7] 'True liberty is obedience to God.'[8] In his conception of the divine nature Seneca did not deviate from the lines prescibed by the early Stoics, as when he declared that our constitution is a unity identical with God, whose partners and members we are,[9] or that Nature, Fate, and Fortune are merely different names for God, corresponding to the various manifestations of His power.[10] His attitude differed from that of the early Stoic masters in so far as he laid a greater stress on the ethical bearing of theology, on the care of God for man, and on the duty which man owes to God. Thus, by dwelling insistently on the opposition between body and spirit, by describing the body as a prison-house from which the spirit is eager to escape, or as an adversary with whom a perpetual struggle must be maintained,[11] he speaks in a style which reminds us forcibly of Plato.[12] He even goes so far as to abandon the Stoic doctrine of the soul's unity by reverting to Plato's triplicate division, with the same splitting of the irrational element into the passionate and the sensual.[13] It should be remembered, however, that Seneca was here reproducing the teaching of Posidonius, who restricted his adherence to Platonism by assigning to the soul a separation not of parts but of faculties.[14]

4. Ethical teaching.—We may now pass to the ethical side of Seneca's teaching, to which he attached the highest importance on the ground that conduct rather than theoretical conviction is the proper aim of philosophy.[15] In this branch Seneca repeats, without any sign of faltering, all the most characteristic of the Stoic doctrines. Virtue is realized in a course of life directed with uniform consistency, which is impossible without a scientific knowledge of nature.[16] The perfect control of the inner man is shown by harmoniousness of action.[17] Yet the act itself is unimportant except as a token of the purpose which inspires it; no action can possibly be virtuous unless it proceeds from a healthy and upright will.[18] The modified degree of value (ἀξία) assigned to health, riches, family, reputation, and the like, which, though essentially indifferent and even on occasion harmful, are deserving of general preference (προηγμένα, *producta*), is recognized by Seneca; if he loosely called them 'goods,' he was for the moment using popular language, and was well aware that they have no claim to be so described.[19] But this qualified approbation of

1 *Ep.* cxvii. 19. 2 *Ib.* lxv. 2 ff.
3 *Ib.* 20.
4 A. Schmekel, *Die Philosophie der mittleren Stoa*, Berlin, 1892, p. 14, n. 5.
5 *Nat. Quæst.* iii. præf. 17 f.
6 *Ep.* lxv. 24. 7 Schmekel, p. 401 ff.
8 Frag. 16.
9 *Dial.* VII. viii. 4, *Nat. Quæst.* III. xv. 1.
10 *Nat. Quæst.* II. vi. 6. 11 *Ep.* xli. 1, lxxiii. 16.
12 *Dial.* VI. xxiv. 5. 13 *Ib.* xxv. 1.
14 *Ib.* xxvi. 6; E. V. Arnold, *Roman Stoicism*, Cambridge, 1911, p. 268.
15 *Dial.* VI. xix. 4. 16 *Ep.* cxvii. 6.
17 *Nat. Quæst.* II. xxxv. 1, *de Benef.* I. vi. 3.

1 Arnold, p. 235; see art. PRAYER (Roman).
2 *Dial.* v. xxxvi. 1–3. 3 *Ep.* xcv. 47–50.
4 H. von Arnim, *Stoicorum Veterum Fragmenta*, Leipzig, 1903–05, i. 527.
5 *Ep.* cvii. 11. 6 *Dial.* I. v. 4–6.
7 *Ep.* xcvi. 2. 8 *Dial.* VII. xv. 7.
9 *Ep.* xcii. 30. 10 *De Benef.* IV. viii. 3.
11 *Ep.* lxv. 16, 21 f., *Dial.* VI. xxiv. 5.
12 *Phæd.* 66 B ff., 79 C, *Rep.* 611 C.
13 *Ep.* xcii. 8.
14 Schmekel, p. 257; E. Zeller, *Hist. of Eclecticism in Greek Philosophy*, tr. S. F. Alleyne, London, 1883, p. 65 f.
15 *Ep.* xx. 2. 16 *Ib.* xxxi. 8.
17 *Ib.* lxxiv. 30. 18 *Ib.* xcv. 57.
19 *Ib.* lxxiv. 17.

externals does not derogate from the absolute sufficiency of virtue for happiness, on which Seneca unhesitatingly insists.[1] The earlier Stoics had exalted the figure of the wise man as an ideal portrait for imitation. Admitting that the instances of his actual appearance in life were very few,[2] they pointed to the traditional accounts of Heracles and Odysseus, and to the examples set by Socrates and Diogenes. Seneca proudly adds that nowhere could so complete a pattern be found as in the life and death of Cato the younger.[3] He even went so far as to approve the paradox that there is a sense in which the wise man is superior to God: the latter owes His freedom from fear to the bounty of nature, the former to himself.[4]

Notwithstanding the vehemence with which Seneca advocated these lofty principles, his paramount interest was to extract from them the stimulus which they might afford to the self-improvement of his readers. His writings are not to be regarded as philosophical treatises whose chief aim was to instruct. They rather resemble the utterances of a popular preacher—moral essays circulated to assist a propaganda in favour of Stoicism. They belong to that branch of philosophy—held by some to be a useless excrescence—which was known as advisory (παραινετική), being intended to mark out the course of conduct prescribed for the various contingencies encountered in actual life.[5] At the same time Seneca devotes a long letter[6] to the support of his contention that these particular recommendations are insufficient unless they are accompanied by a statement of the broad principles of philosophy upon which their validity depends. To such considerations must be traced his constant refusal to put too severe a strain upon human weakness. The emphatic manner in which he enlarges on the advantages of wealth to the wise man, and admits that the younger Cato made no attempt to conform to the standard of frugality set by his elder namesake,[7] exhibits a temper far removed from the Cynical proclivities of Zeno.[8] Cato himself, in spite of his claim to the possession of the highest wisdom, is blamed for the useless sacrifice of his life to his principles.[9] In their relations with the court or with other persons in authority, Seneca recommends to his readers a degree of complaisance not far removed from servility.[10] He recognizes that all emotion is sinful, and should be extirpated rather than moderated;[11] and he consequently accepts the view that in the infliction of punishment pity must give way to reason. He who spares the evil injures the good.[12] But Cicero's mockery of the rigidity and inhumanity of Stoicism[13] has no relevance to one who could write: 'Wherever there is a man, there is room for benevolence,'[14] or: 'Make yourself beloved by all while you live and regretted after your death.'[15] Another illustration may be taken from the discussion of the question when suicide is expedient (εὔλογος ἐξαγωγή). Here, as is well known, the Stoics had framed rules to meet particular cases, based upon the moral indifference of life and death.[16] Seneca's writings show that in his time, even if suicide could occasionally be justified, there was more frequently a danger that Cato's example would encourage a morbid craving for death; and his manly protest in favour of a healthy endurance of hardship[17] cannot fail to earn approval.

[1] *Ep.* lxxiv. 26, lxxxv. 57. [2] *Ib.* xlii. 1.
[3] *Dial.* II. ii. 1. [4] *Ep.* liii. 11.
[5] *Ib.* xciv. 1. [6] *Ib.* xcv.
[7] *Dial.* VII. xx. 3, 4.
[8] Frag. 168 f. (von Arnim, i. 239, 268).
[9] *Ep.* xiv. 13. [10] *Dial.* IV. xxxiii. 1, *Ep.* xiv. 7.
[11] *Ep.* cxvi. 1. [12] Frag. 114.
[13] *Pro Mur.* 60 ff. [14] *Dial.* VII. xxiv. 3.
[15] *Ib.* V. xliii. 1. [16] Von Arnim, iii. 768.
[17] *Ep.* xxiv. 25.

It is unnecessary to trace the signs of Seneca's moderation and humanity which pervade his discussions of the varied duties of daily life (καθήκοντα); the examples already given are sufficiently typical. But a single remark on the method of teaching morals is worth recording. The teacher is advised to exaggerate the severity of his precepts from consideration of the fact that human weakness is certain to fall short of the standard proposed.[1] Thus the occasional practice of asceticism was recommended as a countercheck to the growth of luxury,[2] in the same way as Apollodorus described the adoption of the Cynic life as a short cut to virtue.[3]

The practical outlook of Seneca's philosophy is nowhere more clearly shown than in the care with which he analyzes the conditions of progress towards virtue. Starting from the dogma which contrasted the wise man as the sole possessor of virtue with the multitude of fools,[4] and being forced to admit that the appearance of a wise man was as rare as the birth of the phœnix,[5] the Stoics were bound to admit the value of an approximation towards the ideal, if any practical advantage was to issue from their system. This was not a development in the later history of the school, but was clearly recognized by its earliest masters, Zeno and Cleanthes.[6] In Seneca it is hardly too much to say that it has become the central point of his teaching. The true end of philosophy is not to convince of ignorance by force of reason, but to heal sickness and weakness by patient discipline. We do not aim at virtue as a distant goal; rather, the effort itself is inseparable from the attainment.[7] The task of philosophy is, by means of continual admonition as well as by general precept,[8] to prevent the inborn capacity for good from becoming choked and blinded by adverse influences. Virtue is not the gift of nature, but the product of art.[9] It is not to be won by passive acceptance of the truth, but conviction must be strengthened by obedience to its particular behests. By the ingathering of the fruit of self-knowledge the mind of the postulant must be transformed in its outlook upon virtue.[10] Seneca more than once distinguishes the various grades of progress without fixing any strict lines of demarcation. In one passage[11] he speaks of those who are entirely untrained as subject to continual storms of passion resembling the Epicurean chaos. They are contrasted with those who have made progress in the right direction and are described as sometimes rising aloft in their heavenward journey and again sinking to the earth. There is a third class, comprising those who have reached the confines of wisdom: they are in harbour—to change the metaphor—but not yet on dry land. In another place[12] the three classes of apprenticeship are differently described. The highest grade are those who have mastered their passions, but are as yet inexperienced in the practice of virtue. They have ceased to fear a relapse into evil, but are not yet confident in their security. The second class have conquered the greatest evils, but are not yet secure against relapse. The third class consists of those who have only partly overcome their temptations. They may be free from avarice, lust, and inordinate desire, but they are still subject, wholly or partly, to the domination of anger, ambition, and fear.

Seneca's ethical treatises may be described as follows. (1) Twelve books of *Dialogues*, addressed

[1] Arnold, p. 364. [2] *Ep.* xviii. 5 ff.
[3] Diog. Laert. vii. 121.
[4] Zeno, frag. 148 (von Arnim, i. 216).
[5] *Ep.* xlii. 1. [6] Hicks, p. 89.
[7] *Ep.* lxxxix. 8. [8] *Ib.* xciv. 31 f., xcv. 36.
[9] *Ib.* xc. 44. [10] *Ib.* vi. 1, xciv. 48.
[11] *Ib.* lxxii. 9 f. [12] *Ib.* lxxv. 8 ff.

to various friends and relatives, treating of such subjects as providence, anger, and happiness, and comprising three on consolation. The name 'dialogue' is a misnomer, for the only trace of a debate is the occasional appearance of *inquis, inquit*, etc., which are found also in the other works. (2) The three books on *Clemency* dedicated to Nero, and the seven books entitled *de Beneficiis*. (3) A collection of 124 moral *Letters* addressed to Lucilius. These brief moral essays belong to the period subsequent to Seneca's retirement from court (A.D. 62) and contain the ripest fruit of his experience and wisdom.

LITERATURE.—The works of E. V. Arnold, R. D. Hicks, and A. Schmekel have been mentioned above. For Stoicism in general see E. Zeller, *Stoics, Epicureans, and Sceptics*, tr. O. J. Reichel, London, 1880. For the Roman period C. Martha, *Les Moralistes sous l'empire romain*[7], Paris, 1900, and S. Dill, *Roman Society from Nero to Marcus Aurelius*, London, 1904, may also be consulted. The best editions of Seneca's ethical treatises are: *Epistolæ*, ed. O. Hense, Leipzig, 1898, *Dialogi*, ed. E. Hermes, do. 1905, *de Beneficiis et de Clementia*, ed. C. Hosius, do. 1900. The *Naturales Quæstiones* have been edited by A. Gercke, do. 1907.

A. C. PEARSON.

SENECA INDIANS.—See IROQUOIS.

SENSATIONALISM. — Sensationalism is a theory of knowledge which regards the mind as a passive receptacle, deriving its entire content from the senses, or from some foreign agency through the senses; also called 'sensualism' (Germ. *Sensualismus* regularly), though the latter term is oftener used to denote the kindred theory of ethics, and still oftener a particular moral disposition. As a theory of the origin and growth of knowledge, sensationalism in modern philosophy is combined with associationism,[1] which gives an account of the processes by which the materials given in sensation are built up into knowledge. As a theory of the validity of knowledge, it merges into empiricism (*q.v.*), which, though it may admit other elements in knowledge, allows only those ideas to be true or valid which are certified by sense-experience. As a doctrine concerning reality, it becomes phenomenalism, the view that nothing can be known except that which appears to the senses, which involves the denial of all knowledge 'in the strict sense of knowing,' either agnosticism (*q.v.*) or scepticism. In its less critical form, however, it may be allied with dualism (*q.v.*), the view being that a real external world communicates a knowledge of itself through the senses to an otherwise empty mind; or with materialism (*q.v.*), where the mental processes are identified with the physical.

1. Primitive thought.—Before the rise of philosophical reflexion man knew no other way by which knowledge could enter the mind than by the senses. Even knowledge of spiritual beings and of mysterious things not normally in contact with the senses, but derived in some extraordinary way, as in dreams and visions, was regarded as communicated through the senses.

'As with souls, so with other spirits, man's most distinct and direct intercourse is had where they become actually present to his senses in dreams and visions. The belief that such phantoms are real and personal spirits, suggested and maintained as it is by the direct evidence of the senses of sight, touch, and hearing, is naturally an opinion usual in savage philosophy, and indeed elsewhere, long and obstinately resisting the attacks of the later scientific doctrine.'[2]

The sensationalist view of revelation could be abundantly illustrated from the earlier history of all religions. Biblical revelation is generally represented as communicated through the senses. Isaiah received his prophetic message, first at least, as a vision of the 'Lord sitting upon a throne, high and lifted up, and his train filled the temple' (Is 6[1]); and St. Paul treasured memories of 'visions and

[1] See art. ASSOCIATION.
[2] E. B. Tylor, *PC*[3], London, 1891, ii. 189.

revelations of the Lord' (2 Co 12[1]). 'The word of the Lord' conveyed to the ear was a still more familiar form of revelation. It is, however, open to question how far these expressions had come to be used metaphorically. But in ordinary, unphilosophical thinking it is still assumed that all knowledge comes into the mind under some form of sensation. And, in this respect at least, modern spiritism (*q.v.*) is a reversion to primitive and popular thought.[1]

2. Indian philosophy.—On the whole the Indian systems of philosophy are monistic and mystical, but some reactions to sensationalism have also issued from them.

The Buddhist doctrine of the soul is thoroughly atomic and phenomenal, and all its knowledge is derived through the senses, though consciousness as something distinct from the senses seems also to play a part.

'Sensations, perceptions, and all those processes which make up the inner life, crowd upon one another in motley variety; in the centre of this changing plurality stands consciousness (viññâṇa), which, if the body be compared to a state, may be spoken of as the ruler of this state. But consciousness is not essentially different from perceptions and sensations, the comings and goings of which it at the same time superintends and regulates: it is also a Sankhâra, and like all other Sankhâras it is changeable and without substance.'[2]

The Lokāyata (*q.v.*), the doctrine of the Chārvākas or Nāstikas, combined a thorough-going sensationalism with materialism.

'Their views were revived in more recent times by a sect who named themselves Çunyavadins, or nihilists, their one comprehensive doctrine being, all is emptiness.'[3]

3. Early Greek philosophy.—Speculative philosophy in the West applied itself at first to questions of being rather than of knowing, to inquiry into the material cause of the world as object. But the mind could not long reflect upon this problem without stumbling upon the question of its own powers to discover the truth as to external reality. When Heraclitus said that reality was a process of ceaseless becoming, and Parmenides that it was bare identity or pure being, philosophy was on the threshold of the problem of knowledge, for the world as it appeared to the senses was in each case contrasted with the philosopher's conception of its truth and reality, which must therefore have arisen from some other source than the senses, and it involved a presumption that the witness of the senses was unreliable or at least insufficient. In this way the earlier Greek philosophers arrived at a distinction between thought and perception which should, and in the main did, lead away from sensationalism. All thought or knowledge of truth was participation in the common world-reason, the λόγος of Heraclitus or νοῦς of Anaxagoras. The Pythagoreans, by their identification of knowledge with numbers, were the first to make a clear distinction between 'thought' and 'perception.' Yet in effect the distinction did not amount to much, because all mental processes, whether of thought or of perception, could as yet be defined only in physical terms. The common world-reason was thought of as fire or atoms or a kind of fluid in motion, and it could enter the mind of each individual only through the senses, though there must be a response of like to like in the mind. Perception was a purely physical process, the movement of effluxes (ἀπορροαί) from external objects (through the air) to the senses, through which they entered the mind. Although the pre-Socratic Greek writers were undoubtedly feeling

[1] See, *e.g.*, Oliver Lodge, *Raymond, or Life after Death*, London, 1916.
[2] H. Oldenberg, *Buddha*, Eng. tr., London, 1882, p. 253 (cf. p. 231 ff.); cf. G. F. Moore, *Hist. of Religions*, Edinburgh, 1914, i. 292 f.
[3] Moore, p. 323 f.; cf. M. Monier-Williams, *Hinduism*, London [1897], p. 224 ff.; G. S. Brett, *A Hist. of Psychology Ancient and Patristic*, do. 1912, p. 202 f.; cf. art. MATERIALISM (Indian).

after a theory of knowledge which did justice to the original contribution of the mind itself, the disability which their materialistic categories imposed upon them rendered it impossible for them to define any real difference between thought and perception, and compelled them therefore to derive the whole content of the mind from outside through the senses. 'These metaphysical rationalists maintained all of them in their psychology a crass sensationalism.'[1]

4. Protagoras and Aristippus.—The first sensationalist philosophy consciously advanced as such was apparently that of Protagoras (*c.* 480–411 B.C.). It was but a short and obvious step from the position of his predecessors to eliminate altogether the distinction between thought and perception, and to reduce the whole mental process to perception, which, again, was only a kind of mutual motion between the object and the mind. But, if perception is the whole of knowledge, and if it is only a motion between the mind and its object, a *tertium quid* which is different from both, there can be therefore no knowledge either of the perceiving subject or of the perceived object. Knowledge then means only the perceptions of the moment in any individual mind, and it may be called indifferently true or false, for it can have no reference to any universal standard. Man, the individual at any moment, is the measure of all things. Such at least is the interpretation of this famous saying of Protagoras given by Plato. The identification of knowledge with sense-perception is seen to lead to the relativity of all knowledge and to scepticism as to the possibility of any valid universal knowledge.[2] But the perception included not only the cognitive elements in the mind, but also its feelings and desires; and the individual and momentary states of the mind become the criteria of ethical and social values. Aristippus the Cyrenaic seems to have been the first to develop the ethical implications of sensationalism and to teach that the pleasure of the moment is the sole criterion of moral action and the only good. Afterwards it became a commonplace of this school that sensations and feelings are one class of mental facts, and that they constitute alike the motives and criteria of action and the content and criteria of thought.[3]

5. Sensationalism and materialism. — While Socrates and Plato were endeavouring to disentangle knowledge from the relativity of perception, and to set up a realm of ideas eternally true and valid, the atomists, Leucippus and Democritus (*c.* 460–360 B.C.), turned in the opposite direction, and sought for truth and reality in the atomic elements of sense-perception. Little is known of the former, but Democritus (*q.v.*) taught that objects and minds alike were composed of atoms, and all their relations, including perception and thought, were the mechanical motions of atoms. The only difference was that the mind was composed of a finer, smoother kind of atoms than the body, which were called the fire-atoms. And, although Democritus distinguished between thought and perception, and between the genuine or clear (γνησίη) knowledge of the primary qualities and the obscure (σκοτίη) knowledge of the secondary qualities (and also apparently opposed the relativist doctrine of Protagoras, holding that 'in the apprehension of the ultimate properties of the atoms we have objective knowledge'),[4] yet he had no means of making these distinctions effective on the basis of his doctrine of atoms. In fact he fell back upon the old doctrine of effluxes (ἀπορροαί) for his explanation of both perception and knowledge. Objects sent forth images or copies (εἴδωλα, δείκηλα) of themselves, which were thus impressed upon the fire-atoms of the soul. The only difference between sensation and thought lay in the form of the atoms and their rate of motion. The coarser atoms, moving more violently, produced sensation, while the thought-atoms are finer and their motion is more gentle. This may not be literally sensationalism, but in principle it is, for the mind itself is only a vague kind of sensorium which receives impressions directly from the external world.[1]

Antisthenes, the founder of the Cynic school, though he did not share the materialistic tenets of Democritus, seems to have held a theory of knowledge, not unlike his, which may be designated 'atomic realism.'

He is said to have conceived 'existence as made up of isolated individual elements, corresponding to which were isolated indivisible acts of apprehension. Psychologically these acts of apprehension were of the nature of perception.'[2]

The Epicureans (*q.v.*) were, however, the true heirs of Democritus. They adopted the doctrine of effluxes along with his theory of atoms. The soul is only a body made of finer and more mobile atoms, and as such it is capable of receiving impressions from other bodies. Its sensations are the effects produced upon it by the effluxes or images that emanate from other bodies and impress themselves upon it quite literally. All differences in sensations and in their qualities are due to differences in the form and motions of the external atoms in other bodies. It has been suggested that Epicurus seems to admit, in an obscure way, some original motion or self-determination of the mind. He also recognizes some objects, such as gods and apparitions, as being of too fine a texture for the senses to perceive them, and as being able to impress themselves directly upon the mind. But these points and their significance are rather obscure in Epicurus, and his teaching seems to come as near as possible to pure sensationalism. Morality as well as knowledge rests upon sensation, for feeling is a kind of sensation, and conduct should be determined so as to secure the most pleasurable or undisturbed state of feeling (ἀταραξία).[3]

6. Stoics and sceptics.—Although Plato and Aristotle had strongly criticized the whole sensationalist theory, and had developed an alternative view of knowledge as being the product of the self-activity of the mind or reason, yet materialistic metaphysics, with the accompanying theory of knowledge through sense-images, persisted down to the later periods of Greek philosophy, more through the influence of the Stoics than of the Epicureans.

The Stoics (*q.v.*) generally, though with some exceptions, held that the soul as well as the body was material. While their theory of knowledge is more complex and indefinite than those already noticed, involving not only reason and sense-perception, but many intermediate stages, yet they allowed no absolute distinction between sense-perception and reason, and made all knowledge to rest on sense-perception. The human mind is originally a *tabula rasa*. Its first ideas are derived from the impressions or stamp (τύπωσις) made by the external world upon the soul through the senses. Out of these sense-impressions the mind builds up its intuitions or preconceptions, and its notions, which constitute its store of ideas. Yet some kind of activity is also attributed to the mind itself, and some of its presentations (φαντασίαι), or ideas, are the product of that activity, and not derived from the senses. It is

1 W. Windelband, *Hist. of Philosophy*, Eng. tr., London, 1893, p. 65.

2 For a discussion of Plato's interpretation of Protagoras see John Watson, *An Outline of Philosophy*², Glasgow, 1898, p. 303 ff.; cf. R. Adamson, *The Development of Greek Philosophy*, Edinburgh and London, 1908, p. 71. See also art. PROTAGORAS.

3 Brett, p. 63 f.

4 Adamson, p. 66.

1 Windelband, p. 114 f.

2 Adamson, pp. 79-83.

3 Lucretius, *de Rerum Natura*, iv. 725 ff.; Brett, p. 182 ff.

characteristic of the Stoic philosophy that it wavers between materialism and spiritualism, and its theory of knowledge reveals the same inconsistency. Zeno and Cleanthes seem to have regarded the mind as purely passive until sensations made their impressions upon it, as seal upon wax. But Chrysippus taught that 'the result of sensation was not an impression but a modification of the mind.'[1] And the mind exercises further activity in retaining the sensations, and, by a kind of association, working them up into preconceptions (προλήψεις), which constitute a body of common or innate ideas that become the common heritage of men, the universal λόγος at the basis of all human knowledge, and the criterion of truth. But the Stoics had another test of the truth of an idea, which was also an original contribution of the mind, in the doctrine of conviction—the view that certain ideas (φαντασίαι καταληπτικαί) carried with them the evidence of their own truth. All these original activities of the mind of course carried the Stoic philosophy far beyond the sensationalism with which it began its explanation of knowledge.

Some of the sceptics (*q.v.*), such as Arcesilaus and Carneades, while generally opposed to Stoicism, and rejecting in particular its doctrines of conviction and of innate ideas, yet developed, from the initial Stoic sensationalism, their own doctrine of suspense of judgment and of the uncertainty of any truth. All knowledge was derived from the senses, and, since the senses were relative to changing conditions, they were unreliable, and all knowledge derived from them was likewise unreliable.[2] While the sceptics from Pyrrho downwards questioned the trustworthiness and validity of both conception and perception, their general line of attack was the relativity of the senses, and the consequent uncertainty of all ideas as being derived from them. The ten τρόποι, or points of view, for the criticism of knowledge enumerated by Sextus Empiricus, which Diogenes Laertius referred to Pyrrho, but which may have been collected and perfected only by Ænesidemus, nearly all turn upon the uncertainty of the senses.[3]

7. Asclepiades and Galen.—The later medical schools of the Greeks, in so far as they dealt at all with the problem of knowledge (and most of them attached themselves to some school of philosophy), naturally recognized the full significance of the senses; and some of the best known writers derived knowledge primarily or entirely from the senses. Asclepiades adopted the Epicurean philosophy and identified the soul with 'the activities of the senses taken collectively.'[4] Galen, though an eclectic in philosophy generally, leaned towards the Stoics in his epistemology and adopted their doctrine of spirit and of reason (νοῦς) as regulative principle; like them also he practically identified reason with sensation, derived its material content from sensation, and placed the initiative to knowledge in sensation; but again he also recognized some element of attention as being original in mind and a condition of knowledge.[5]

8. Ecclesiastical writers.—The natural dualism of common sense, fortified by the Platonic philosophy, persisted down to modern times, and with it therefore the obvious tendency to derive all knowledge of the external world through the senses. On the other hand, the Platonic-Stoic doctrine of the λόγος, which had been developed more especially in the schools of Alexandria, and amalgamated with Biblical doctrines of revelation, provided for a knowledge of spiritual things and of ultimate reality in supersensible ways, whether by the participation of the human mind in the universal λόγος, by inspiration of the Holy Spirit, or by immediate vision of God, so that we find but few traces of theoretical sensationalism in the writings of the Church Fathers.

[1] Brett, p. 168.
[2] E. Zeller, *The Stoics, Epicureans, and Sceptics*, Eng. tr., London, 1870, ch. xxiii.
[3] A. Schwegler, *Hist. of Philosophy*[2], Eng. tr., Edinburgh, 1868, p. 135 f.
[4] Brett, p. 285.
[5] *Ib.* p. 287 ff.

Tertullian, however, was influenced by the Stoic philosophy; he adopted the doctrine of the corporeity of the soul and with it a partially sensationalist theory of knowledge, but he combined with it a supernatural doctrine of revelation. He maintains a distinction between the intellect and the senses, but only to the extent of the difference of their objects, corporeal things being the objects of sense and incorporeal ones the objects of the intellect. Both are alike faculties of the mind, and the intellect can obtain its knowledge of the incorporeal only through the sensations of the corporeal.[1] No very precise theory can be derived from Tertullian's writings, and his sensationalism was even less thorough-going than that of the Stoics. For he held the soul to be rational in its natural condition. God had endowed it with common intelligence, and, when it was true to itself, it ever bore witness to the fundamental truths of religion.[2] Moreover, the Christian revelation contains truths supernaturally conveyed to the mind, which are contrary to all sense and reason, and which are to be believed because they are impossible.[3]

The same mingling of opposite tendencies appears, but rather more obscurely, in Arnobius. He affirms, in opposition to Plato's doctrine of reminiscence, that man acquires all his knowledge from outside, and that, if left to himself, he would ever remain as ignorant as a block of stone. Yet he also emphasizes the supernatural character of Christian truth.[4] His disciple Lactantius, while revealing traces of Stoic influences, has divested himself entirely of its sensationalism.

The position of the Christian Fathers may then be stated summarily as follows: they all rejected Epicureanism and pure sensationalism; most of them adopted the Platonic philosophy with its idealist theory of knowledge in the form of the λόγος doctrine, but a group of early Latin writers followed the Stoic teaching and in some cases adopted their modified sensationalism, though they coupled with it an emphatic supernaturalism—Tertullian's Montanism is an outstanding illustration—and so they anticipated the theory of Hobbes and others who would make sensationalism the basis of a rigid theological orthodoxy. The soul could receive ideas of God and the truth of religion only through authoritative revelation. Yet it was the Platonic philosophy that predominated in the thought of the early Church and formed the basis of the prevailing orthodoxy, which was scarcely challenged until the rise of modern philosophy. But the principle of authoritative orthodoxy is essentially the same as that of sensationalism. It requires that the mind should passively receive its content from outside. The Platonic doctrine of immanent reason was submerged by a naive, popular, unarticulated sensationalism, which, rather than any philosophical theory, asserted itself in Catholic orthodoxy.

The sacramental doctrines of the Church, which are also sensationalist in principle, implying that all grace, power, and virtue enter into the soul from outside through the senses, may reveal the more direct influence of Tertullian, for they are largely the product of the West, whose thought he mainly influenced.

[1] *De Anima*, xviii.
[2] *De Test. Animæ*, 2, *Apol.* 7.
[3] *De Carne Christi*, 5.
[4] *Adv. Gent.* ii. 17 ff., 74 ff.

'Tertullian makes grace reach the soul through the body and the corporeal media . . . Tertullian's sacramental theory follows the lines of his theory of knowledge, which like Locke's emphasises the creative action of matter upon mind.'[1]

Subsequent developments of the doctrine and practice of the sacraments only tended to increase the dependence of the soul upon external agencies.

Ecclesiastical ethics also became predominantly hedonistic, though the pleasures and pains which should regulate conduct were largely relegated to another world.

9. Nominalism and sensationalism.—The mediæval Church therefore presents this paradox, that its doctrines are derived from a spiritual revelation and the life that it inculcates should issue from the communion of the soul with God, while its method of teaching and practice involves that the soul should be the passive receptacle of truths and virtues communicated to it from outside by physical agencies through the senses. Mysticism (*q.v.*) was a practical protest against this view, and the prevalent philosophy, traditional and contemporary, was its antithesis. The only significant and, in the present connexion, relevant development in mediæval thought was the controversy about the reality of universals. The realist view generally accepted preserved the Platonic tradition and maintained that *genera*, or universals, were substantially real. The mind therefore by its general concepts directly apprehended ultimate reality. Roscellinus in the 11th cent. criticized this view, and held that individual things alone are real. It is doubtful whether he went so far as to maintain that universals were mere sounds (*flatus vocis*), as Anselm declares that some of his contemporaries did. But this theory is an epistemological atomism which, naturally if not necessarily, leads to sensationalism. If the individual reals are exclusively found in the world of sense, then they can be known only through the senses. And thorough-going nominalism,[2] if such there ever was, would necessarily identify all conceptions with sense-perceptions, for names are only heard or seen. Both Anselm and Abelard state that 'there were men who allowed their thinking to go on entirely in corporeal images,' 'but who these men were, and how they carried out their theory, we do not learn.'[3] Nominalism was revived in the 14th cent. by William of Ockham in the form called terminism. And he overlaid the sensationalism which is the obvious result of his terminism with intellectual scepticism. Real things are still held to be singular. Universals exist only in the mind (subjectively); they are related to real things only as signs or symbols representing them, and these symbols alone are the objects of knowledge. There are indeed two orders of such signs—direct signs of individual things (*intentio prima*), *i.e.* sensations, and the indirect or general sign (*intentio secunda*), *i.e.* the universal concept, built up by the mind from the direct signs. Knowledge consists of these universal concepts, which are the creation of the intellect rather than the contribution of the senses, but it is therefore not knowledge of the real world. The objective world lies outside the mind and is in contact with the senses, but the senses cannot convey it to the mind. Knowledge, being therefore a very uncertain representation of reality, was easily forced to make way for dogmatic orthodoxy.[4]

It is uncertain whether there were in mediæval times recrudescences of pure sensationalism. It has been alleged that the Cathari and the Albigenses reproduced the materialistic atomism of Epicurus and Lucretius.[1] But enough has been written to show that for the mediæval mind sensationalism was on the whole an alien theory. Scholasticism (*q.v.*), in so far as it was philosophical, was, on the contrary, inspired by confidence in the reasoning powers of the intellect to demonstrate all the fundamental positions of theology.[2]

10. Transition to modern philosophy. — The chief conditions of the new beginnings of philosophic inquiry in the 16th and 17th centuries, from which modern philosophy as such issued, were, on the one hand, a realization of the barrenness of the dogmatic and scholastic methods as instruments of knowledge, and, on the other, a determined search for a more fruitful method. The problem of knowledge has therefore been always central in modern philosophy, and the progress of philosophy has consisted mainly in the increasing realization of the import of this central problem. Modern philosophy is humanistic; man has realized that the world is primarily his own experience, and his search has been for the meaning or value of that experience. At first that meaning seemed to appear in certain ideas in the mind, and more particularly in certain general ideas.[3] But, as there were ideas in the mind which clearly were not true, the problem was to discover a criterion by which true or valid ideas could be distinguished from false. Some sought such a criterion in the ideas themselves, in their clearness or consistency or in some other self-evidencing quality. Others sought it in the origin of the ideas or in their causal relation to a reality beyond them or in their correspondence with that reality, thus reverting to the old division between thought and reality. Sensationalism was one of the answers given to the latter form of inquiry. All ideas were derived from sensations; they were copies of impressions made upon the mind by the external world. Or, if there were still a doubt about external reality, the ideas were just the sensations and their copies, and no criterion of truth could be found; the inquiry must end in scepticism. This theory was the most characteristic contribution of British thought to philosophy from the 17th to the 19th century. It also determined the nature of the most important movements of French philosophy during the same period.

11. Humanism.—As a tendency in thought and literature humanism (*q.v.*) preceded and conditioned the rise of modern philosophy. It is not therefore strange to find some anticipations of the sensationalist theory in the transition stage. The return to nature through human experience necessarily brought the sensations into prominence as media of knowledge. The new interest in the study of nature and in the development of physical science led to a new appreciation of such knowledge as seemed to enter the mind by way of the senses. At first this new kind of knowledge was regarded as an addition to the dogma of the Church, subordinate to it, and, in all cases of apparent contradiction, to be corrected by it.

Two representative Roman Catholic writers who held such views were Telesius (1508–88) and Campanella (1568–1639). Both were interested in the development of natural science and held that such knowledge could be derived only from the senses. Campanella taught that God spoke to us by two codes—the living book of nature and the written book of Scripture. We appropriate the contents of the latter by faith and of the former

1 J. V. Bartlet and A. J. Carlyle, *Christianity in History*, London, 1918, p. 165 f.

2 See art. REALISM AND NOMINALISM.

3 Windelband, p. 297.

4 R. Seeberg, art. 'Ockam,' in *PRE*[3] xiv. 260 ff.; M. de Wulf, *Hist. of Mediæval Philosophy*, Eng. tr., London, 1909, pp. 158–198, 420–425.

1 De Wulf, p. 219.

2 H. O. Taylor, *The Mediæval Mind*[2], London, 1914, ii. 450 ff., 463 ff.

3 See art. IDEA.

by observation through the senses. Pierre Gassendi (1592–1655), another Roman Catholic, revived the Epicurean philosophy generally and with it the sensationalist view of knowledge. Erdmann states that 'the later sensationalists in England and France have borrowed much from him.'[1] Yet he was no thorough-going sensationalist, for as a priest he acknowledged the authority of the Church in religious matters, and even in his philosophy he seems to regard both the imagination and the intellect as independent contributors to knowledge.[2] But the Roman Catholic writers of this period had not as yet defined the line of demarcation between theology and science, between dogmatism and empiricism, between knowledge acquired by faith or belief and that derived through the senses. Nor is it easy to estimate the significance of their submission to the Church or to faith side by side with their pursuit of philosophical empiricism, how far the former is purely formal, and how far the latter is regarded as the whole of knowledge, 'in the strict sense of knowing.'

12. Bacon.—Francis Bacon ([*q.v.*] 1561–1626) occupies his unique position as a pioneer of modern thought because he consciously set himself to define the sphere of scientific knowledge and insisted upon the empirical and inductive method of inquiry as the only source of scientific knowledge. He did not, however, analyze the psychological processes involved in such inquiry, and still less the epistemological problem; but, from his comparison of his method to the activities of the bee, which both gathers and constructs, rather than to those of the spider or the ant, it may be inferred that he was neither an *a priori* rationalist nor a sensationalist, but an empiricist in the present sense of the term. Moreover, he leaves the whole field of religious knowledge as such to authority and revelation. Yet his teaching is not irrelevant to the present subject, for his exaltation of empirical knowledge tended to enhance the importance of the senses as organs of knowledge and prepared the way for subsequent developments along sensationalist lines.

13. Hobbes.—Thomas Hobbes ([*q.v.*] 1588–1679) emancipated himself completely from all scholastic and theological admixture with his philosophy. He was the first modern writer to propound a thoroughly sensationalist theory of knowledge, and he based it upon an atomic, mechanical, and materialist view of the mind.

> 'The thoughts of man . . . are every one a *representation* or *appearance*, of some quality, or other accident of a body without us, which is commonly called an object. . . . The original of them all, is that which we call SENSE, for there is no conception in a man's mind, which hath not at first, totally, or by parts, been forgotten upon the organs of sense. The rest are derived from that original.'[3]

Sensations are produced by the impressions made by external bodies or objects upon the organ proper to each sense, and this impression, which is itself a motion, sets up a motion in the body which permeates inwards to the brain and heart, and produces there a reaction which, because it is directed outwards, seems to be some matter without, and this seeming or fancy is that which men call 'sense.' It is, however, not the object, nor any image of the object, but the effect of the interaction of the object and the organ; it is an idea, phantasm, or fancy, and therefore quite subjective. Hobbes rejected the old Greek and scholastic view of the image or species or form as proceeding from the object through the sense-organ to the mind. The whole content of the mind is derived from these effects of the impact of the objects upon the sense-organs.

> They re-appear first in imagination, which is 'nothing but decaying sense,' or sense weakened by the absence of the object, and, 'when we would express the decay, and signify that the sense is fading, old, and past, it is called memory.' When these imaginations or thoughts follow one another, either casually, 'unguided, without design, and inconstant,' or 'as being regulated by some desire and design,' they are called mental discourse. But it is only imaginations that have been associated together in sense that can become associated in thought. 'We have no transition from one imagination to another, whereof we never had the like before in our senses.'[1]

This is the general principle which was later developed into the doctrine of the association of ideas, but Hobbes did not analyze further the principle of association. Up to this point he regards the mental processes of man and beast as being alike. But man by the invention of speech has the means of summing up many experiences and sequences in a few signs, which therefore render it possible to combine them voluntarily in a variety of ways other than this natural order; and this is reasoning and science.

> 'For REASON, in this sense, is nothing but *reckoning*, that is adding and subtracting, of the consequences of general names agreed upon for the *marking* and *signifying* of our thoughts. . . . Reason is not, as sense and memory, born with us; nor gotten by experience only, as prudence is; but attained by industry; first in apt imposing of names; and secondly by getting a good and orderly method in proceeding from the elements, which are names, to assertions made by connexion of one of them to another; and so to syllogisms, which are the connexions of one assertion to another, till we come to a knowledge of all the consequences of names appertaining to the subject in hand; and that is it, men call SCIENCE.'[2]

Thus Hobbes derives the whole of man's faculties and knowledge from the senses and 'study and industry.' But why ideas should be associated and assertions connected by any rule he does not explain, nor does he seem to have been aware that they needed to be accounted for. It was by overlooking this problem that he was able to make his theory so complete. Concerning any knowledge of the super-sensual Hobbes was frankly agnostic.

> 'Therefore there is no idea, or conception of anything we call *infinite* . . . the name of God is used not to make us conceive him, for he is incomprehensible . . . a man can have no thought, representing any thing, not subject to sense.'[3]

So the field of religion was free for the temporal ruler to impose upon all citizens his authoritative dogmas.

Several minor writers in the 17th cent. resemble Hobbes in their tendency to subordinate reason to sensation, to adopt the formula, 'Nihil est in intellectu quod non prius in sensu fuerit,' to cast doubt upon both sensation and reason, and so to exalt religious faith and authority—*e.g.*, François de la Mothe le Vayer (1588–1672), Pierre Daniel Huet (1630–1721), Pierre Bayle (1647–1706). It does not follow that these were influenced by Hobbes, nor did they work out the theory with the thoroughness and fullness of Hobbes.

14. The doctrine of ideas.—But the main current of modern philosophy, from Descartes (1596–1650) to Spinoza (1632–77), was rationalist and dogmatic. The most important elements in knowledge and in the mind were regarded as original, innate, and independent of sense-experience. The philosophy of Hobbes seemed to be isolated and barren. Yet in one respect the Cartesian philosophy shared with it the function of preparing the way for British empiricism and its French offshoots. It supplied that 'system of ideas' which became the starting-point for Locke and his followers. Cartesians and empiricists held in common that the unit of the content of consciousness was the 'idea' or 'image,' regarded as individual, atomic, a *tertium quid* between subject and object, representing the latter to the former. For both schools the problem of know-

[1] J. E. Erdmann, *Hist. of Philosophy*, Eng. tr., London, 1891, i. 605.
[2] G. S. Brett, *The Philosophy of Gassendi*, London, 1908, pp. 125–141.
[3] *Leviathan*, pt. i. ch. 1 (*English Works*, ed. W. Molesworth, London, 1839–45, iii. 1).

[1] *Leviathan*, pt. i. ch. 2. [2] *Ib.* pt. i. ch. 5.
[3] *Ib.* pt. i. ch. 3.

ledge was to discover the origin, validity, and relations of these ideas as they made up the content of the mind.

15. Locke.—John Locke ([*q.v.*] 1632–1704), though himself neither a sensationalist nor intending to be one, was the true originator of modern sensationalism. For Hobbes had no successors, and, notwithstanding similarities in their theories, Locke regarded himself as the antagonist rather than the follower of Hobbes. But he recognized his affinities with Descartes and some indebtedness to him, and the sensationalism that developed from his teaching stands rooted in the idealism of Descartes rather than in the materialism of Hobbes.

Besides the dualistic assumption common to Descartes and Locke, and their common recognition that the problem of knowledge is the starting-point of philosophy, 'we are certainly justified in seeing the influence of Descartes in the presupposition which Locke accepts as axiomatic, needing neither discussion nor defence, that apart from the unique presence of the mind to itself, and the cognisance of self which results therefrom, the only immediate objects of the understanding are "ideas"; while these ideas are apprehended by the mind to which they are present as signs or representations of a world of things beyond it.'[1]

It was when Locke inquired into the nature of the mind and the validity and origin of its ideas that he diverged from Descartes and laid the foundation of empiricism and sensationalism. For Descartes's abstract conception of the mind as a thinking substance he substitutes conscious experience, and whereas Descartes regarded most, and in a sense all, ideas as innate, Locke made them all dependent on sense-perception. His problem was to discover what knowledge was certain as distinct from opinion or error; as he puts it, 'to inquire into the original, certainty, and extent of human knowledge, together with the grounds and degrees of belief, opinion, and assent.'[2]

He first examines and rejects the whole doctrine of innate ideas and principles, as it had survived from scholasticism, in Descartes, the Cambridge Platonists, Lord Herbert of Cherbury, and contemporary philosophical schools.[3] This doctrine assumed certain general ideas as being originally present in the mind and therefore true, and providing the foundation from which all knowledge can be deduced. Such ideas, if they exist, must then be universally given, and Locke's first line of attack was to show that these ideas are not universal, and therefore neither innate nor certain. Having thus disposed of the prevalent criteria of certainty, he seeks a new criterion and discovers it in the origin of all ideas from sensation. He supposes the mind to be a *tabula rasa*, 'a white sheet of paper, void of all characters'; it then passively receives all the materials of knowledge from experience, either as ideas of sensation or as ideas of reflexion, which is 'the perception of the operations of our own mind within us, as it is employed about the ideas it has got,'[4] and which might be called an internal sense. He adds:

'The understanding seems to me not to have the least glimmering of any ideas which it doth not receive from one of these two. External objects furnish the mind with ideas of sensible qualities, which are all those different perceptions they produce in us; and the mind furnishes the understanding with ideas of its own operations.'[5]

'Nihil est in intellectu quod non prius in sensu fuerit.' So far Locke's system seems to be purely sensationalist. But, as T. H. Green has elaborately demonstrated, Locke could not build up his system of knowledge merely out of these abstract ideas of sensation and reflexion in an otherwise empty and passive mind.[6] Yet it does not seem that this was Locke's intention. Besides ideas, he recognizes many original capacities and permanent activities of the mind.

'The first capacity of human intellect is, that the mind is fitted to receive the impressions made on it.'[1]

'Notice' or attention is affirmed as a condition of sensation and reflexion, and in the formation of complex and general ideas such processes as 'compounding,' comparison, and abstraction are required and affirmed. Locke's assumption of the knowledge of two substances, of an intuitive knowledge of the self, of demonstrable knowledge of God, and of the abstract principles of mathematics and morals implies much that he did not profess to derive from the senses. His importance in the history of sensationalism therefore comes out clearly in the use which his successors made of his new way of ideas.[2]

16. Partial developments from Locke.—Two Irish bishops were among the first to attempt to reduce Locke's doctrine of ideas to consistency, but in opposite directions.

(1) Peter Browne, bishop of Cork († 1735),[3] adopted Locke's doctrine of the *tabula rasa* and the principle 'Nihil est in intellectu,' etc., but saw that the original powers and intuitive knowledge which Locke attributed to the mind were not consistent with these. He therefore reduced all psychical functions to sensation; the impressions made upon the senses were the only original elements of knowledge, and everything else was built up out of these. Supersensible knowledge we can obtain only by analogy, by transferring sensible relations to the supersensible. Browne has been regarded as a link between Locke and both the British associationists[4] and the French sensationalists.[5]

(2) George Berkeley (*q.v.*), bishop of Cloyne (1685–1753), set himself to reduce Locke's system to self-consistency and at the same time to turn it into a polemic against materialism. He broke down the traditional epistemological dualism, and argued that, since ideas were the objects of knowledge, there was no reason for supposing any such objective external substance as the Cartesians and Locke had assumed from scholasticism to be the cause of sensations. He would thus remove the occasion for making the mind dependent upon matter and for drawing materialistic inferences from Locke's system as some were doing. There is nothing but mind and its ideas.

Human knowledge consists of 'either ideas actually imprinted on the senses; or else ideas perceived by attending to the passions and operations of the mind; or lastly, ideas formed by help of memory and imagination, either compounding, dividing, or barely representing those originally perceived in the aforesaid ways.'[6]

These correspond to Locke's ideas of sensation and of reflexion, simple and complex. But these ideas are themselves the objects of knowledge. We can have no knowledge or evidence of any substance behind them which causes them.

'Some truths there are so near and obvious to the mind that a man need only open his eyes to see them. Such I take this important one to be, viz. that all the choir of heaven and furniture of the earth, in a word all those bodies which compose the mighty frame of the world, have not any subsistence without a mind—that their *being* is *to be perceived or known*.'[7]

But, besides all that endless variety of ideas or objects of knowledge, there is likewise something

[1] James Gibson, *Locke's Theory of Knowledge*, Cambridge, 1917, p. 222.
[2] *An Essay concerning Human Understanding*, London, 1690, bk. I. ch. i. § 2.
[3] Gibson, p. 41. [4] *Essay*, II. i. 4. [5] *Ib.* II. i. 5.
[6] *Treatise of Human Nature*, ed. T. H. Green and T. H. Grose, London, 1878, General Introd. i. 1–130.

[1] *Essay*, II. i. 24.
[2] A. Seth [Pringle-Pattison], *Scottish Philosophy*[2], Edinburgh, 1890, pp. 15–32.
[3] *The Procedure, Extent, and Limits of the Human Understanding*, London, 1728.
[4] Windelband, pp. 440, 454.
[5] R. Falckenberg, *Hist. of Modern Philosophy*, Eng. tr., London, 1895, p. 246; Erdmann, *Hist. of Philosophy*, ii. 137 ff.
[6] *Principles of Human Knowledge*, § 1, in A. Campbell Fraser, *Selections from Berkeley*[6], Oxford, 1910, p. 32 ff.; *Works*, ed. Fraser, new ed., Oxford, 1901, i. 257.
[7] *Principles*, § 6.

which knows or perceives them[1]—*i.e.* the mind or spirit—and there is no other substance. Berkeley's whole world therefore consists of perceiving minds and their ideas. It was he who brought out explicitly the fact that sensationalism is essentially subjective, that mere sensations and their copies could give no knowledge of any reality beyond themselves. But he did not think it possible to interpret experience by means of sensations or ideas alone, for he assumed the spiritual substance or mind which perceives, and especially the divine spirit who causes our ideas and gives them objective order and reality.[2] Of these, however, we can have no ideas, but only notions; and here Berkeley introduces terms and principles that contradict and transcend the doctrine of abstract, passive ideas.

17. Spread of sensationalism.—At this point it will be simpler to abandon the chronological order and to trace separately the main lines of the development of sensationalist theory, in France and Britain. Very few traces of the theory are found elsewhere.

Windelband mentions some followers of Spinoza, 'both physicians and natural scientists, such as the influential *Boerhaave* of Leyden,' in Holland, who developed tendencies to materialist sensationalism on the basis of the master's parallelism of attributes. In Germany 'as early as 1697, a physician named Pancratius Wolff taught in his *Cogitationes Medico-legales* that thoughts are mechanical activities of the human body, especially of the brain, and in the year 1713 appeared the anonymous *Correspondence concerning the Nature of the Soul* (*Briefwechsel vom Wesen der Seele*), in which, screened by pious refutations, the doctrines of Bacon, Descartes, and Hobbes are carried out to an anthropological materialism.'[3] But the general trend of German philosophy has been remote from sensationalism.

In Italy the traditions of humanism were strengthened by the introduction of Locke's ideas through the teaching of Antonio Genovesi (1712–69) and the translations of Francesco Soave (1743–1816). 'The translations of the writings of Bonnet, D'Alembert, Rousseau (?), Helvetius, Holbach, de Tracy, and above all, the philosophical works of Condillac gave a powerful impulse to the doctrine, and the philosophy of the senses became predominant in the universities and colleges of the Peninsula.'[4] Condillac resided in Italy from 1758 to 1768, and his teaching was propagated in a modified form by his disciples Melchiorre Gioja (1767–1829) and Gian Domenico Romagnosi (1761–1835).[5]

In America Locke's philosophy, though not unknown, found no outstanding advocate. The important contributions of American thought to philosophy are deeply influenced by British empiricism, but they belong to its post-sensationalist stage.

18. French materialistic philosophy.—In France the theory assumed its crudest form and developed into naive materialism. Starting from Locke, it took the opposite turn to Berkeley's idealism, eliminated the subject, and at last identified consciousness with the material object.

(1) Montesquieu (1689–1755) and Voltaire ([*q.v.*] 1694–1778) brought with them from England in 1729 the ideas of Locke and his circle, and applied them, the former mainly to politics, and the latter to general religious and moral doctrines.

(2) Condillac (1715–80) and Charles Bonnet (1720–93) developed the doctrine of ideas into sensationalism. Both taught that sensations are the whole content of the life of the mind. Both employed the illustration of the statue, which, through being endowed successively with one after another of the five senses, became a conscious being, and thus showed how all our ideas could be derived from outside through the senses. Both urged that Locke's ideas needed to be supplemented by principles of association in order to construct them into a mind. Both held the mind to be inactive and devoid of ideas in itself, and until it is affected by sensations. But Bonnet's analysis of the mental processes was more thorough, and his account of them is at once more adequate and less coherent. He recognizes original and ultimate elements of mind and body which are incompatible with his sensationalist theory of knowledge. He affirmed the self-conscious unity of the Ego, which distinguishes it from matter, and held that the soul, though it derives all its ideas from sensation, has for its essence the capacity of thinking (*cogitabilité*) which responds on the occasion of sensation.

'On the other hand, he emphasizes more strongly than Condillac the dependence of psychical phenomena on physiological conditions, and endeavours to show definite brain vibrations as the basis not only of habit, memory, and the association of ideas, but also of the higher mental operations.'[1]

Neither of these writers, however, discovered these doctrines to be inconsistent with their religious beliefs.

(3) A more sceptical turn was given them by the Encyclopædists (*q.v.*) Diderot (1713–84) and D'Alembert (1717–83), who popularized Locke's theories in France and modified them in a materialistic direction. Diderot at last reduced all psychology to physiology of the nerves. Helvetius (1715–71) inferred from Condillac's theory (*a*) that self-love is the only motive of human action, and (*b*) that man is morally a creature of his environment. All men are the same in self-love and sensibility, and differences between men are entirely due to the impressions made upon them through the senses. Hence the importance of such education and legislation as will make the desired impressions.

(4) J. O. de la Mettrie (1709–51) was the first to transform the sensationalist theory into an unqualified dogmatic materialism. He identified mind with brain and reduced all psychical activities into mechanical functions of the brain proceeding inward from the senses.[2] Similar ideas, reducing thought and volition to sensation, sensation to motion, and all existence to matter, were propounded as a polemic against all religion by Baron d'Holbach (1723–89).[3] Essentially the same views are found in the writings of A. L. C. Destutt de Tracy (1754–1826) and Pierre J. G. Cabanis (1757–1808), with the difference that the latter regarded mental processes as chemical rather than mechanical processes. The universal prevalence of these views in the cultured circles of France in the 18th cent. cannot be better illustrated than by the following summary statement of Cabanis:

'Nous ne sommes pas sans doute réduits encore à prouver que la sensibilité physique est la source de toutes les idées et de toutes les habitudes qui constituent l'existence morale de l'homme: Locke, Bonnet, Condillac, Helvetius, ont porté cette vérité jusqu'au dernier degré de la démonstration. Parmi les personnes instruites, et qui font quelque usage de leur raison, il n'en est maintenant aucune qui puisse élever le moindre doute à cet égard. D'un autre côté, les physiologistes ont prouvé que tous les mouvemens vitaux sont le produit des impressions reçues par les partis sensibles: et ces deux résultats fondamentaux rapprochés dans un examen réfléchi, ne forment qu'une seule et même vérité.'[4]

(5) Mention should also be made here of Maine de Biran (1766–1824), who started from the standpoint of Condillac, but developed a theory of immediate consciousness of the Ego as a more fundamental element in knowledge than sensations, and was thus led from sensationalism to mysticism.

19. Positivism. — The French sensationalist-materialist tradition passed down through the 'ideologist' F. J. V. Broussais (1772–1838) and the phrenologist F. J. Gall (1758–1828) to Auguste Comte (1798–1857), the founder of the positive philosophy.[5] Gall's main thesis was the complete dependence of all mental processes on brain conditions; hence his attempt to localize psychical processes and characteristics in particular parts of the

1 *Principles*, §§ 2, 7.
2 *Ib.* § 26 f.; cf. *Selections*[6], p. xxxiii.
3 Windelband, p. 454; F. A. Lange, *Gesch. des Materialismus*, Leipzig, 1887, pp. 260–270.
4 Vincenzo Botta, in F. Ueberweg, *Hist. of Philosophy*, Eng. tr., London, 1874, ii. 481.
5 *Ib.* p. 483 ff.

1 Falckenberg, p. 249.
2 *L'Homme machine*, Leyden, 1748.
3 *Système de la nature*, London, 1770.
4 *Rapports du physique et du moral de l'homme*[3], Paris, 1815, i. 72.
5 See art. POSITIVISM.

brain. Yet he rejected materialism, and did not inquire into the nature of mind or body, but confined himself to phenomena. Nor was he a complete sensationalist. He held that connate tendencies, both intellectual and affective, belonged to the organic structure of man. Yet the basis of those tendencies was physical, and all ideas and feelings were causally dependent upon physical processes, though not identical with them.[1] Comte followed Gall in making psychology a branch of biology, and to some extent he accepted phrenology as the science of mind. But he enunciated no clear view of the process or criterion of knowledge. He rejected the method of psychological observation of internal consciousness as being impossible. Beyond the biological study of physiological conditions of thinking, we can know the human mind only by observing other people. But he is emphatic that all knowledge is in its nature phenomenal and relative. The positive philosophy is the complete system of the sequences and co-existences of phenomena. Knowledge therefore must be co-extensive with sense-experience, though it is not necessarily identical with sense-experience. But in his sociological doctrine Comte derives all mental characteristics from the physical environment, which again presupposes the sensationalist theory. On the other hand, his polemic against empiricism as a collection of isolated facts, his demand for method and unity in knowledge, for philosophy as distinct from science, and especially his conception of humanity as a universal whole, stand in contradiction to the epistemological atomism implied in his phenomenalism.[2]

20. Final scepticism.—David Hume ([*q.v.*] 1711–76) took his stand on the central position of Locke, on the doctrine of ideas, and proceeded carefully to eliminate all *a priori* assumptions. The epistemological dualism of Descartes and Locke is worked out to its logical issue in the scepticism of Hume. Berkeley had shown the futility of assuming an external substance of which nothing could be known. Hume applied the same logic to the spiritual substance or self (assumed by Berkeley) and to all its qualities, and he therefore reduced the human mind to 'perceptions'—a term which corresponds to 'ideas' in Locke and Berkeley. Of these there are two kinds:

'Those perceptions, which enter with most force and violence, we may name *impressions*; and under this name I comprehend all our sensations, passions and emotions, as they make their first appearance in the soul. By *ideas* I mean the faint images of these in thinking and reasoning.'[3]

Both impressions and ideas may be either simple or complex.

'All ideas are deriv'd from impressions, and are nothing but copies and representations of them.'[4]

Hume is careful to point out that by the term 'impression' he does not mean to express the manner in which the lively perceptions are produced.[5] The only difference between impressions and ideas consists in the greater force or liveliness of the former.

'That our senses offer not their impressions as images of something *distinct*, or independent, and *external* is evident; because they convey to us nothing but a single perception, and never give us the least intimation of anything beyond.'[6]

The mind knows nothing but the perceptions themselves. Yet Hume sometimes unguardedly assumes some cause of our impressions of 'sensation,' but insists that its nature is unknown.

[1] G. H. Lewes, *The Hist. of Philosophy*[3], London, 1867, ii. 394–435.
[2] E. Caird, *The Social Philosophy and Religion of Comte*[2], Glasgow, 1893, ch. ii.; *The 'Positive Philosophy' of Auguste Comte*[3], freely translated and condensed (from the *Cours de philosophie positive*), by Harriet Martineau, 3 vols., London, 1896; J. S. Mill, *Auguste Comte and Positivism*[5], London, 1907.
[3] *A Treatise of Human Nature*, ed. Green and Grose, i. 311.
[4] *Ib.* p. 327. [5] *Ib.* p. 312, note. [6] *Ib.* p. 479.

'Sensations arise in the soul originally, from unknown causes.'[1] Again, the mind itself is nothing but perceptions.

'When I enter most intimately into what I call myself, I always stumble on some perception or other, of heat or cold, light or shade, love or hatred, pain or pleasure. I never can catch *myself* at any time without a perception, and never can observe anything but the perception.'[2]

All general ideas, such as substance, self, and causation, are therefore nothing but the customary association of ideas. Hume thus modified the sensationalist theory in two important respects. (*a*) In the endeavour to render it consistent, to eliminate all *a priori* assumptions, he made its inherent scepticism explicit and complete. There can be no knowledge of any ultimate reality.[3] And (*b*) in the search for some principle of order and unity among ideas he enunciated the famous doctrine of the association of ideas. General ideas, such as substance and causation, cannot be derived from impression; they are due to an illusion of the imagination, which arises in turn from the customary connexion of ideas in the mind—*i.e.*, ideas that have often occurred together tend to recur in the same relation and order.

'The qualities from which this association arises, and by which the mind is after this manner convey'd from one idea to another, are three, *viz.* Resemblance, Contiguity in time or place, and Cause and Effect.'[4]

But here again sensationalism breaks down, for these principles cannot be derived from the atomic perceptions which alone were supposed to be the original data of consciousness.

They are a kind of attraction whose 'effects are everywhere conspicuous; but as to its causes, they are mostly unknown, and must be resolved into *original* qualities of human nature, which I pretend not to explain.'[5]

The same argument applies to the philosophical relations which Hume attributes to intuition.[6] It has been suggested that his purpose was not so much to maintain the sensationalist theory as to afford 'a *reductio ad impossibile* of accepted philosophical principles'—*i.e.* of the Cartesian and Lockian system of ideas. At least, he did not regard it as a possible working philosophy of life. He takes it for granted and as practically necessary that, whatever influence his sceptical argument may have on his reader's mind, 'an hour hence he will be persuaded there is both an external and internal world.'[7]

21. The associationists.[8]—So far were Hume's successors, however, from recognizing any contradiction between his analytic and his synthetic principles that they developed and applied the doctrine of the association of ideas in detail to demonstrate and perpetuate the sensationalist theory of the origin and nature of ideas.

(1) David Hartley (1705–57) related the law of association to corresponding nerve processes. He substituted it for Locke's ideas of reflexion as the constructive function of the mind. Though affirming a correspondence between the 'vibrations' of the nervous system and the sensations, ideas, and motions of the mind, he would not dogmatize on the relation between mind and body, nor reduce the one to the other.

'It is sufficient for me that there is a certain connection of one kind or another between the sensations of the soul, and the motions excited in the medullary substance of the brain.'[9]

Yet in making the external impression upon the sense-organs the primary cause of sensation, and therefore of all ideas, he gave his system a materialist bias.[10]

[1] *A Treatise of Human Nature*, i. 317; cf. Seth, p. 46.
[2] *Ib.* p. 534. [3] *Ib.* p. 505.
[4] *Ib.* p. 319. [5] *Ib.* p. 321.
[6] *Ib.* p. 373. [7] *Ib.* p. 505; cf. Seth, pp. 66–70.
[8] Cf. art. ASSOCIATION.
[9] Quoted by Lewes[3], ii. 350.
[10] *Observations on Man, his Frame, his Duty, and his Expectations*, 2 vols., London, 1749; cf. Lewes[3], ii. 348 ff.

(2) Joseph Priestley (1733–1804) and Erasmus Darwin (1731–1802) advocated Hartley's theory of association, but pushed the general doctrine of ideas in a materialistic direction. Priestley identified psychical with physical processes and sought to reduce psychology to nerve physiology.[1]

(3) Thomas Brown (1778–1820) identifies consciousness with 'a variety of sensations and thoughts and passions, as momentary states of the mind, but all of them existing individually, and successively to each other.'[2] These atomic elements are built up into knowledge by means of 'suggestion' or association of ideas. Knowledge of both mind and matter is relative.[3] Yet, inconsistently, Brown under the influence of Reid recognizes certain 'instinctive' or 'intuitive principles' from which he derives such conceptions as identity and uniformity.

'These principles of intuitive belief . . . are as it were an internal, never-ceasing voice from the Creator and Preserver of our being.'[4]

Here the doctrine of ideas and Reid's principles of 'common sense' stand side by side without any such attempt as Kant had made to merge them into a living unity.

(4) James Mill[5] (1773–1836) produced 'the most systematic attempt that has been made to explain all mental phenomena by the association of ideas.'[6] He reveals no doubt or scruple, such as Hume and Brown had, that by sensations, ideas, and association he has given a complete account of consciousness, without leaving a remainder. He might be called the only complete sensationalist. Consciousness consists of sensations, ideas, and trains of ideas.

Sensations are those feelings 'derived immediately from our bodies, whether by impression made on the surface of them, or unseen causes operating on them within'; ideas are 'the feelings which, after the above mentioned feelings have ceased, are capable of existing as copies or representatives of them.'[7]

The entire content of consciousness, all principles of knowledge and morality, are built up of those two kinds of feelings, by means of the one principle, 'the grand comprehensive law,' of the association of ideas by contiguity. If anything resists such analysis, it is due to no defect in the principles, but to our ignorance—'the term instinct, in all cases, being a name for nothing but our own ignorance.'[8]

(5) John Stuart Mill (1806–73) applied these principles of his father's psychology to the problem of knowledge in a more thorough fashion in his *System of Logic*,[9] and to ethics in his *Utilitarianism*.[10] 'His work contains the most thorough-going exposition of empiricism as a theory of knowledge which has ever been written.'[11] The two positive principles of his exposition are sensations and association, but he found it necessary to admit certain 'inexplicable' principles, which could not be derived from those two. All knowledge of the external world as a 'permanent possibility of sensation' is derived from sensations, association, and expectation; and the last element is 'both psychologically and logically a consequence of memory,' but whence is memory? In explaining the mind's knowledge of itself he makes memory fundamental and original, and both it and the self which it constitutes (and therefore also the expectation derived from it) are admitted to be original principles that cannot be derived from sensations.

'That there is something real in this tie, real as the sensations themselves, and not a mere product of the laws of thought without any fact corresponding to it, I hold to be indubitable. . . . But this original element, which has no community of nature with any of the things answering to our names, and to which we cannot give any name but its own peculiar one without implying some false or ungrounded theory, is the Ego, or Self.'[1]

Thus, while the sensationalist or (as Mill calls it) the psychological theory is put forward as the only possible explanation of the phenomena of knowledge, of both subject and object, it is admitted that it does not explain the most fundamental conditions of all knowledge, the self and its unity, and the unity and reality which the self bestows upon objective experience. Mill had moved from the traditional atomism of his school to the affirmation of the original synthetic unity of self-consciousness as the basic fact in experience and knowledge.

22. Evolutionary psychology.—The theory of evolution led to new emphasis being laid on the organic unity of the mind. On the other hand, some empiricists thought that it gained time for sensationalism. Factors in experience which it was now admitted could not be analyzed into sensations and their copies in one individual consciousness might be so analyzed if sufficient time was allowed for their development, and the new theory provided indefinite time.

(1) Herbert Spencer ([*q.v.*] 1820–1903), while adopting the main principles of sensationalism and associationism, under a somewhat changed terminology, for the explanation of the phenomena of the mind, definitely affirms a new position as to its metaphysics. The mind as observable consists of feelings or sensations and their relations or ideas, 'each with their varying degrees of relativity, revivability and associability.'[2] He emphasized the organic unity and continuity of all mental phenomena, from the lowest to the highest, both in the individual and in the race. But he recognizes much in mind that cannot be derived from experience. (*a*) Instincts, intuitions, general forms of knowledge, and principles of morality cannot be derived from the experience of the individual, but they are the product of the long experience of the race. They are *a priori* for the individual, but *a posteriori* for the race.

E.g., 'the belief in an external world is the outcome of reflex intellectual actions established . . . during that moulding of the organism to the environment which has been going on through countless millions of years.'[3]

(*b*) The criterion of truth, which he calls 'the inconceivability of the opposite,' is laid down as an abstract principle without any attempt to derive it from experience. Indeed, by its nature, it stands as a judge above all the deliverances of experience.[4] (*c*) The mind itself, as the substance of which consciousness is a modification, is unknown and unknowable; yet it has to be assumed as the reality of which feelings and ideas are but symbols.[5]

The last two factors Spencer does not profess to derive from experience. He rather exaggerates the distinction and separation that are now made between psychology and the metaphysical problems of epistemology and ontology.

In respect of the first point 'Spencer is open to his own objection to empiricism when he assumes that the race at any stage of its development could be subject to external influences in the absence of any existing organisation to receive these influences and determine their results.'[6]

Spencer and others of his school, while denying all knowledge of ultimate reality and affirming a dis-

[1] In *Hartley's Theory of the Human Mind on the Principles of the Association of Ideas*, London, 1775, and other works.
[2] *Lectures on the Philosophy of the Human Mind*[19], Edinburgh, 1858, lect. xi. p. 67.
[3] *Ib.* lects. vi. and ix. pp. 34, 55.
[4] *Ib.* p. 79.
[5] In *Analysis of the Phenomena of the Human Mind*, 2 vols., London, 1829, new ed. with notes by J. S. Mill, do. 1869.
[6] H. Höffding, *A Hist. of Modern Philosophy*, Eng. tr., London, 1900, ii. 371.
[7] *Analysis*, new ed., i. 223.
[8] *Ib.* i. 376.
[9] London, 1843, [9]1875.
[10] London, 1863, [12]1891.
[11] Höffding, ii. 404.

[1] *An Examination of Sir William Hamilton's Philosophy*[3], London, 1867, p. 256; cf. chs. xi., xii.
[2] *The Principles of Psychology*[5], 2 vols., London, 1890, §§ 65–128, 475*c*, 480 ff.
[3] *Ib.* § 475*j*.
[4] *Ib.* §§ 413–433.
[5] *Ib.* §§ 58–63.
[6] Höffding, ii. 476.

tinction between mental and material phenomena, show a marked tendency, notwithstanding, to assimilate psychical phenomena to physical processes. Spencer calls the primitive unit of consciousness a 'nervous shock,' and at least supposes the possibility of regarding it as a molecular motion.[1]

(2) T. H. Huxley (1825–95) reveals this tendency most clearly. He accepts in the main Hume's account of the mind.[2] The ideas, however, are 'symbols in consciousness of the changes which take place automatically in the organs.' While agreeing with Spencer that we can know nothing of the substance of mind or body, he prefers the materialistic terminology, 'for it connects thought with the other phenomena of the universe.'[3]

(3) Alexander Bain ([*q.v.*] 1818–1903) carried forward the empiricist tradition of the Mills, but he consciously and deliberately repudiates the old theory that sensations alone, even with the aid of association and evolution, can account for knowledge, whether of the individual or of the race. He for the first time drew a clear distinction between the psychological and the epistemological aspects of the problem. Since his time the psychological study of consciousness has been pursued as a pure science without raising the questions of the ultimate origin and validity of ideas or of the ultimate nature of mind. These have been left to metaphysics. He thus defines the empirical theory of the origin of ideas:

> 'All ideas may be accounted for by our ordinary intellectual powers, co-operating with the senses; not confining ourselves, of course, to the individual lifetime. In fact, the empiricist, in adopting the *nihil est in intellectu* etc., would take along with it, as an essential of the dictum, the amendment of Leibniz—*nisi intellectus ipse*. Nay, more; he would also postulate as being equally co-present, all the emotional and volitional workings of the mind; and, having done so, he would endeavour to dispense with every other pretended source of our ideas.'[4]

What he contends for is that ideas are valid only when certified by sense-experience.

> 'The empiricist may not quarrel with intuitive or innate ideas; his quarrel is with innate certainties[5] . . . the *apriorist* and the empiricist part company, not so much on the fact of intuitive suggestions, as on their value as truths. Intuition, if it means anything, implies that its suggestions are true of themselves, are their own evidence, without the verification of experience, and may therefore be made to override experience[6] . . . the empiricist's test of Validity, and the only test that he can acknowledge . . . is consistency, or, *the absence of contradiction, throughout a sufficiently wide range of conscious experience.*'[7]

Sensationalism, as a theory either of the origin of ideas or of the content of the mind, is no longer maintained. And the empiricism that posits sense-experience as a criterion of truth does not rely on the senses alone, nor does it regard sensations and ideas as abstract and individual elements of thought. Present-day theories of consciousness in one essential respect all stand at the opposite pole from sensationalism, in that they regard consciousness, not as an aggregate of atomic feelings or ideas, but as an organic unity; and this living *intellectus ipse* with all its powers, conscious and subconscious, is the starting-point of all current theories of knowledge.

23. Wider implications of sensationalism.—(1) In relation to religion the theory may involve the denial of all religious values, when it assumes a materialistic form, or it may lead to the denial of religious knowledge 'in the strict sense of knowing,' which has been its most usual effect.[8] (2) For its ethical significance see art. HEDONISM.

[1] *Psychology*3, §§ 270–272, 475.
[2] T. H. Huxley, *Hume*, London, 1879, pt. ii. ch. ii f.
[3] J. Ward, *Naturalism and Agnosticism*2, London, 1903, i. 19, 179; for a trenchant criticism of the whole sensationalist philosophy in its later developments see vol. ii. pt. iii.
[4] *Dissertations on Leading Philosophical Topics*, London, 1903, p. 135 f.
[5] *Ib.* p. 134. [6] *Ib.* p. 140. [7] *Ib.* p. 142.
[8] See artt. MATERIALISM, AGNOSTICISM.

(3) In social philosophy and politics the theory has been adapted to different and even opposite purposes. Naturally and logically it leads to individualism (*q.v.*) and in an extreme form to anarchism (*q.v.*). Hobbes, however, combined an anarchist view of society in its natural state with the doctrine of the social contract to bolster up State absolutism. With Comte the paradoxical combination of sensationalism with an organic and absolutist conception of society was an accident of history, because he had inherited his mental philosophy from Condillac and his social ideals from the Roman Catholic Church. More recent tendencies to combine naturalism (*q.v.*) with socialism (*q.v.*) or with absolutism (*q.v.*) are equally illogical. Condillac's philosophy found its appropriate expression in the French Revolution. Locke's doctrines were the *apologia* of the English Revolution. The Mills were the prophets of 19th cent. radicalism.

> 'The doctrines of individual freedom and human equality . . . [were] interpreted and formulated in terms of abstract individualism, by men who had been bred on the philosophy of pure sensationalism which dominated the eighteenth century. . . . Reducing experience to isolated impressions and ideas, this philosophy treats society as an aggregate of mutually exclusive units, each pursuing as sole end his own individual pleasure.' 'Through the influence of Hegel and of Comte, and partly through the reaction of biological conceptions upon philosophy and general thinking, the nineteenth century has seen the definitive abandonment of the individualistic or atomistic view' of the relation of the individual to society.[1]

LITERATURE.—Besides the histories of philosophy and other works named in the course of the article: R. Adamson, *The Development of Modern Philosophy*, 2 vols., Edinburgh, 1903; G. M. Stratton, *Theophrastus and the Greek Physiological Psychology before Aristotle*, London, 1917; H. Siebeck, *Gesch. der Psychologie*, 2 vols., Gotha, 1880–84; D. C. Macintosh, *The Problem of Knowledge*, London, 1916; L. J. Walker, *Theories of Knowledge*, do. 1910, T. M. Forsyth, *English Philosophy*, do. 1910; G. Villa, *Contemporary Psychology*, Eng. tr., do. 1903; J. S. Mackenzie, *Elements of Constructive Philosophy*, do. 1917; A. Bain, *The Senses and the Intellect*4, do. 1894, *The Emotions and the Will*3, do. 1880; Thomas Reid, *Works*3, with Notes and Supplementary Dissertations by Sir William Hamilton, Edinburgh, 1852; P. Janet and G. Séailles, *Hist. de la philosophie*, Paris, 1887, Eng. tr., 2 vols., London, 1902.

T. REES.

SENSE.—'Sense' is the name for the receptivity of living organisms to external physical impressions, resulting in what are called sensations. The organism of which it is composed is called the 'sensorium,' and is located in the periphery of the body in the case of most of the senses, though there are internal organs of sense which represent similar functions and reactions. In all cases it represents the organism which reacts against external stimuli of some kind. The brain-centres are the points to which impressions or physiological actions are communicated before sense responds, and may be a constitutive part of sense in the exercise of function, though they are not the usually accepted part of sense physiologically understood. As a function of the organism, however, sense denotes a process of mental action distinguished from the acts of inner consciousness or the reflective function of the mind. With the organism which connects the inner with the outer world, it implies the actions by which knowledge of this outer world is obtained.

Physiologically sense, or the sensorium, is divided into six separate organs: the organs of vision, of hearing, of touch, of taste, of smell, and of temperature. Until recently it was supposed that the senses were limited to five, but the thermal sense has been added to the other five as having a distinct neural organism of its own, and it has been suspected that even the feelings of pleasure and pain have their own separate sensorium. Six senses, however, have been fully established. Each of these has its own peculiar

[1] A. Seth Pringle-Pattison, *The Philosophical Radicals and other Essays*, London, 1907, pp. 63 f., 42.

stimulus or cause for its action. Undulations of light affect vision; undulations of the air and material objects affect hearing; contact of objects affects touch, and the same affects taste; and smell seems variously affected by corpuscular emanations and other modes of stimulation; while the thermal sense is affected by the supposed undulations of ether that constitute heat. The structure of each sense is adapted to its specific stimulus and responds accordingly. Hence the various ways in which the external world appears to the same subject of consciousness.

Sense is the source of our knowledge of an external world. It may not be the sole function involved in that knowledge, but it is the primary function in the occurrence of it, and we can only suppose either that all knowledge of the external world would be excluded without sense or that it would be different from what it is if any other source were substituted for sense. But, whatever the facts, as things are at present constituted, sense is the intermediate agency in affecting our knowledge of reality, though it is accompanied by other mental functions of an interpreting kind. Sense is thus the portal through which knowledge comes, even though it does not determine the whole of its nature. In the Lockian system sense was the only original source of knowledge; in the Kantian system this source was supplemented by the active and constructive functions of the understanding, which, though they added nothing to the matter of knowledge, determined the form which it would take. In both, sense-experiences represented the limitation of all knowledge; *i.e.*, the material of all knowledge came through sense, but the processes for systematizing it were in the intellectual functions.

LITERATURE.—J. G. Mackendrick and W. Snodgrass, *Physiology of the Senses*, London, 1893; Michael Foster, *Text-book of Physiology*[5], 4 pts., London, 1888–91, pt. i.[6], 1893, pt. ii.[6], 1895, pt. iii.[7], 1897.

JAMES H. HYSLOP.

SENSIBILITY. — Sensibility has two important meanings. The first denotes the capacity for receiving sensory impressions, and the second denotes the emotional function of the mind. It is indicated in the division of mental functions into intellect, sensibility or emotion, and will. The former meaning of the term is exhausted in the definition, but the latter refers to one of the most important of the mental functions.

Considered as the second division of mental functions, the sensibilities are of two general kinds: those which accompany or follow the exercise of function and those which precede and influence action. The first type we may call reflexive emotion or feeling, and may subdivide into pleasures and pains. The second type may be called impulsive emotion or passion, and may be subdivided into desires and repulsions. Pleasures, normally considered, are reflex concomitants of healthy function; pains, of unhealthy function. This characterization, however, is only general, and describes those feelings which the normal person has to keep in mind when adjusting his life to its best tendencies. Desires are impulses or longings towards the possession or attainment of objects, and repulsions are antipathies towards them. They are the immediate motives to action or restraint. The main service of the reflexive emotions is their part as indices, in their normal action, of our adjustment to environment, and hence they serve as guides to the actions which are directly associated with welfare. The impulsive emotions serve as incentives to the realization or prevention of consequences in this environment, and so are initiatives of volition, as pleasures and pains are the consequences of it.

LITERATURE.—J. M. Baldwin, *Handbook of Psychology*, ii., 'Feeling and Will,' New York, 1891; G. F. Stout, *Analytical Psychology*, 2 vols., London, 1896–97, ch. xii.; W. Hamilton, *Lectures on Metaphysics*[2], 2 vols., Edinburgh, 1860.

JAMES H. HYSLOP.

SENSUALISM.—See ETHICS AND MORALITY.

SENTIMENT.—As used in everyday speech, this word (from *sentire*, 'to feel') refers to the emotional sources of our more complex ethical and social judgments. It covers a wide range of spiritual meanings which exercise a powerful influence in the individual and collective life of mankind; for in a real sense it may be said that 'sentiment' controls judgment in many questions of manners and morals, making us alive to the bane or blessing of life's contacts and loyalties. The more precise definition of the word carries us into the field of the psychological and ethical sciences, especially in their sociological relations, where the description and explanation of the phenomena involved are more fully set forth. The main facts are as follows.

(*a*) The psychological genesis of sentiment is involved in the mystery that surrounds the beginnings of our more developed forms of feeling and emotion—*e.g.*, love, hate, admiration, etc. On the one hand, it is to be differentiated from sensation and perception, but partakes of their nature, like other psychical reactions, for mental life develops in the unity of the Ego. Sensation, in its origin, is a form of feeling, but, as it develops, is almost wholly confined to the activity of the physiological mechanism of sensibility. Perception, in its elementary manifestations at least, depends partly on the senses and partly on the understanding. Sentiment, however, in all its forms, involves an element of judgment, inchoate indeed in its simpler forms but nevertheless real, into which values, deeply tinged by the more complex emotions and even by passion, enter, these values centring about objects, either real or ideal, that appeal to us on the ground of their abstract truth, beauty, or goodness. Consequently our sentiments will always be found to possess a predominant tone of pleasure or pain. This is true, of course, of all psychical reactions called judgments. But the pleasure-pain feature of sentiment differs from other phases of mental activity in this: it is induced, in the self-development of the individual, by association with objects about which we have come to feel strongly, or about which we have formed judgments, or which have proved acceptable and agreeable to all persons of culture. This will become clearer as we proceed with our analysis. Meanwhile, it is obvious from this general statement that the nature of sentiment, from the purely descriptive point of view, is extremely complex, and its genesis obscure.

(*b*) Following the clues afforded by sympathetic and careful insight, A. F. Shand[1] called attention to a fact which long eluded the notice of psychologists, namely, that our sentiments are really highly organized systems of emotions, arising in us in connexion with the various classes of objects that excite them; that as systems, and not merely vague emotional reactions, they possess an exceedingly complex structural or psycho-physical disposition, in which function and structure are continuous. On this point W. McDougall observes:

> 'The structural basis of the sentiment is a system of nerve-paths by means of which the disposition of the idea of the object of the sentiment is functionally connected with several emotional dispositions. The idea, taken in the usual sense of the word as something that is stored in the mind, may therefore be said to be the essential nucleus of the sentiment, without which it cannot exist, and through the medium of which several

[1] See 'Character and the Emotions,' *Mind*, new ser., v. 203–226.

emotional dispositions are connected to form a functional disposition.'[1]

In other words, the object which occasions the sentiment is, subjectively, organically connected with our emotional life and with the processes of ideation. Continuing, McDougall says:

'The oftener the object of the sentiment becomes the object of any one of the emotions comprised in the system of the sentiment, the more readily will it evoke that emotion again, because, in accordance with the law of habit, the connexions of the psycho-physical dispositions become more intimate the more frequently they are brought into operation.'[2]

Illustrations abound in the ethical and religious life. Thus the sentiments aroused and appealed to in ritual, religion, and art are so strong because they depend in so large a measure upon truth, beauty, and goodness, and the repetitive forms of memory which, structurally, are only applications of the laws of habit. On that ground alone they are among the most powerful reinforcements of the moral life—'allies,' as William James calls them, of the soul.[3] Of this truth the persistence of religious systems is sufficient proof. In the same way the collective principle in social law, with its strong imitative tendency, may also be viewed as the medium for the development of the sentiments and their inbred emotional dispositions, and at their least valuation serve the practical purpose of providing the emotions with a bridge between mechanical routine and the higher creative ideals or sentiments of the mind.

(*c*) This very complexity of sentiment, however, precludes a naturalistic interpretation of a function which so obviously depends on our judgments of value. While somatic reactions, or systematically organized 'dispositions,' form the more or less fixed structural basis of sentiment, it would not be in accordance with the facts of common experience to say that they adequately explain its essential nature. As spiritual forms of feeling, the sentiments clearly contain certain highly abstract ideal elements, freed at times from immediate dependence on the bodily organism and its reflex actions. For not only have our sentiments, as already stated, a predominant tinge of pleasure and pain; not only does this feeling-tone depend on emotional dispositions organized about objects (or ideas), towards which we have learned to react in a habitual manner; they also involve vision of a creative sort. Thus the patriot may be said to love his country; this love is a sentiment entering into all his thoughts; pain and pleasure, love, pride, admiration, etc., are evoked by the object, entering into the warm psychoses which arise in him as he thinks of it. But, in addition to these reactions, he has a vision of still higher values. He thinks of his country, not merely as the concrete collective medium of his own self-preservation, but, under the influence of sentiment, as right and true, nay, as perfect and good. This may sometimes be an exaggerated estimate, to be modified by more mature reflexion, but sentimentally that is his deliberate judgment—the vision inspired by a passion of love which is creative of ideals. Sentiment, in this higher sense, is an ideal feeling closely akin to the artist's feeling for beauty, to the feeling of moral approbation, and to other more or less abstract or mystical emotions of religion.

No complete list of the sentiments can be made without reference to these fundamental creative ideals, or judgments of value, such as the intellectual sentiment, the æsthetical sentiment, the ethico-religious sentiment, and their combinations. In mentioning them in this connexion it must be borne in mind that they are also active in the general conditions and adjustments that underlie the normal development of mental life; that temperament, culture, and environment also qualify the expression of the sentiments as of other mental elements and products. The point is that there are also ideal elements in all our sentiments which do not necessarily involve the activity of self-reference—*i.e.* do not refer to specific organized objects, but arise in us through intuition or vision, direct or indirect, of ideals, and exercise a profound influence in their evolution. Of course, the particular form of self-reference which sentiment proper reveals is found only when an emotion has acquired strength or value by reason of the object or idea with which it is associated; but, in this total complex, ideals of truth, beauty, perfection, and goodness are ever creatively at work.

(*d*) A final word may be said on the relation of sentiments to character. If character be the product of the total effort of self-realization (*q.v.*), it is undoubtedly true that the sentiments, organized into a harmony or system under ideals, constitute a large part of what is properly called character. The sentiments alone do not, of course, constitute the whole of character; that would be sentimentalism. Will, feeling, intellect — in a word, self-control—must enter in and often modify and direct sentiment, or at any rate supplement it with ideals. If, as W. Hartsen says truly, 'a man without feeling would certainly have no intellect as well,'[1] it is equally true that a man without sentiment would have no character. Yet character is not wholly a matter of sentiment. That would be equivalent to reducing character to our organized dispositions and emotions; but character depends on conation and will, on the complete fashioning of the personality in the light of some ideal of conduct higher than routine, which has become strongly entrenched and has acquired a habitual predominance in the personal life. A sentiment, it is true, may become so strong as practically to control the will, but this would not result in a well-rounded personality; it might conceivably lead to a narrow, selfish, or mean type—the tyrant or dictator, *e.g.*—which could hardly be called moral. For the higher results of character the sentiments must be brought into the service of a concrete ideal and organized under the control of the will. This ideal must also attain to such a predominance by sheer force of love that conflicting inhibitions or interfering unorganized desires will be overcome. Character thus grows in strength and beauty, and approximates to perfection and goodness. A sentiment, therefore, may well be a controlling motive of behaviour, but character depends, ultimately, on the habit of self-control and loyalty. We cannot therefore be too careful in selecting the sentiments, or the single sentiment, which is to attain the dignity of a fixed habit through the choice of the will. The reinforcement of religion will be found necessary to the realization of the ideal self, because it is in God we live and move and have our being. If to this we add the sentiment of love, proclaimed the rule of conduct by Jesus, we have the aim and motive of all true character clearly indicated, in which sentiment and character become one.

LITERATURE. — G. T. Ladd, *Psychology, Descriptive and Explanatory*, New York and London, 1894, ch. xxii.; W. McDougall, *Introd. to Social Psychology*[4], London, 1911, chs. v., vi., and ix., p. 258 ff.; J. E. Harrison, *Ancient Art and Ritual*, do. 1913, ch. vii.; A. F. Shand, 'Character and the Emotions,' *Mind*, new ser., v. [1896] 203 ff.; G. F. Stout, *A Manual of Psychology*[3], London, 1913, bk. iv. ch. ix.; A. E. Davies, *The Moral Life* (Publications of the *Psychol. Rev.*, i.), Baltimore, 1909, ch. vi.; W. Wundt, *Ethics*, Eng. tr., London, 1897–1901, vol. ii. pt. i. ch. i.; James Sully, *Outlines of Psychology*, New York, 1898, p. 384 ff.; C. Lloyd Morgan, *The Springs of Conduct*, do. 1885, pt. iii. ch. ii.

H. DAVIES.

[1] *Introd. to Social Psychology*[4], p. 126 f. [2] *Ib.*
[3] Cf. J. E. Harrison, *Ancient Art and Ritual*, ch. vii.

[1] *Grundzüge der Psychologie*, Berlin, 1874, p. 19 f.

SEPARATIST SOCIETY.—See COMMUNISTIC SOCIETIES OF AMERICA.

SERAPHIM.—See DEMONS AND SPIRITS (Hebrew).

SERINGAPATAM (Skr. Śrīrangapattana, 'city of the holy pleasure-place').—Seringapatam is a city in Mysore District, Mysore; lat. 12° 25′ N.; long. 76° 42′ E.; situated on an island in the river Kāverī. In the earliest times Gautama Ṛṣi is said to have had a hermitage here, and he worshipped the god Ranganātha, 'lord of pleasure,' whose temple is the principal building in the fort. The earliest temple is said to have been erected by Tirumalaiya, under the Gangā dynasty, A.D. 894. About A.D. 117 the whole site was granted by one of the Chola kings to Ramānujāchārya, the celebrated Vaiṣṇava apostle, and in 1454 the Ranganātha temple was enlarged, the materials of 101 Jain temples being used for the purpose. The place is remarkable for the two famous sieges in 1792 and 1799, the British forces being under the command of Lord Cornwallis and General Harris; in the latter attack the Sultān Tīpū was slain. His remains and those of his father Haidar 'Alī rest in a mausoleum (*gumbaz*) in the garden known as the Lāl Bāgh, where prayers are still offered.

LITERATURE.—B. L. Rice, *Mysore*, rev. ed., London, 1897, ii. 294 ff.; F. Buchanan, *A Journey from Madras through the Countries of Mysore, Canara, and Malabar*, do. 1807, i. 60 ff.; M. Wilks, *Historical Sketches of the South of India*, Madras, 1869, ii. 241 ff., 358 ff.; G. B. Malleson, *Seringapatam; Past and Present*, do. 1876; *IGI* xxii. 179 f. W. CROOKE.

SERPENT-WORSHIP.

Introductory (J. A. MACCULLOCH), p. 399.
Indian (W. CROOKE), p. 411.
Teutonic and Balto-Slavic (E. WELSFORD), p. 419.

SERPENT-WORSHIP (Introductory and primitive).—The cult of the serpent exists in many forms, whether of a single serpent or of a species, of a serpent embodying a spirit or god, of a real or imaginary serpent represented in an image, of a serpent as associated with a divinity (a chief god or one of many), or of a purely mythical reptile. All these may be traced back to the cult of actual serpents, which, however, easily become a fitting vehicle for a spirit or god. The origin of the cult is to be sought in the effect which all animals more or less had upon the mind of early man—a feeling that they were stronger, wiser, subtler than he; in a word, uncanny. This was especially true of the serpent because of its swift yet graceful and mysterious gliding motion without feet or wings, unlike that of any other animal,[1] its power of disappearing suddenly, the brilliance and power of fascination of its eye, its beauty and strength, the sudden fatal consequences of its bite or of its enveloping folds, the practice of casting its skin, which suggested its longevity or even immortality. All these contributed to arouse feelings of wonder, respect, fear, to produce worship, and also to make the serpent a fit subject of innumerable myths. In the various forms of the cult there is often found a sense of the animal's beneficence, probably because myth easily attributed to it wisdom, secret knowledge, magical power, healing properties, and inspiration. As an animal dwelling in holes in the earth, its chthonic character was suggested—it was the cause of fertility (also because it was thought to give or withhold water), and became the embodiment of a fertility daimon or earth-spirit; hence also a guardian of hidden treasure or metals.[2] In so far as the serpent is a revealer of the arts of civilization, this is probably because, where it was worshipped, it was often grafted on to a mythic culture-hero or eponymous founder. Totemism sometimes lent its aid as a factor in developing respect for serpents, if not actual cult. Ancestor-worship also assisted, in so far as certain snakes haunting houses or graves were associated with the dead. Myth connected the serpent with the waters, either because some species lived in or near them or in marshy ground, or because the sinuous course and appearance of a serpent resembled those of a river, or with the lightning, because of its swift, darting motion and fatal effects. Some serpents are harmful, others are harmless; and perhaps this is one main reason why both in cult and in myth some are objects of fear and their evil traits and appearance are exaggerated or associated with demoniac beings, while others are beneficent and helpful.[1]

Man's fancy and man's dreams about such an animal as the serpent must also be taken into account in considering the origins of the cult.

This is illustrated by an account from Papua, where a native recently dreamt that a large snake living on a volcano accused him of killing snakes and alligators and offered, if he promised never to do so again, to give him a herb to cure all diseases. The native went about announcing this, but some natives still disbelieved and shot an alligator, which remonstrated with them. Snakes and alligators now go unharmed.[2]

Here the common fancy of the solidarity of animals leading them to avenge the death of a single animal and the consequent respect paid to them are seen. This and other fancies are embodied in a dream, and might easily be the origin of a cult, as they actually are of a prohibition.

Classical writers had various theories as to the origin of the cult, from that of Diodorus that the snake was worshipped because he figured in banners or was figured on banners because he was a god, to the shrewder remarks of Philo Byblius quoted by Eusebius (see § 1 (*t*)).

Practically every aspect of serpent-worship, myth, and legend, and of human attitude to the serpent, is shared by other reptiles—*e.g.*, the crocodile, to some extent the lizard, and here and there large eels.[3]

While some form of awe or reverence for the serpent is wide-spread, the actual worship varies in intensity in different regions. Fergusson supposed the cult to have originated among the Turanian peoples of the lower Euphrates and to have spread thence to every part of the old world where a Turanian people settled, while no Semitic or Aryan people adopted it as a form of faith, its presence among these being 'like the tares of a previous crop springing up among the stems of a badly-cultivated field of wheat.'[4] Fergusson's

[1] Cf. Pr 30[19].

[2] Perhaps also because the lightning (=serpent) was supposed to produce gold.

[1] See, however, C. Hose and W. McDougall, *The Pagan Tribes of Borneo*, London, 1912, ii. 68 ff.

[2] G. Murray, *ARW* xv. [1912] 628.

[3] See *ERE* i. 430[b], 509, 514[a], ii. 352, iii. 563, vii. 239[a], viii. 357[b], ix. 279, 341[a], 346[a], 511[a], 528[a]; J. F. McLennan, *Studies in Ancient History*, 2nd ser., London, 1896, pp. 272, 274, 409; Hose-McDougall, *loc. cit.*; R. B. Dixon, *Oceanic Mythology* (=*Mythology of all Races*, vol. ix.), Boston, 1916, pp. 55, 120; E. Shortland, *Traditions and Superstitions of the New Zealanders*[2], London, 1856, pp. 57, 73; W. W. Skeat, *Malay Magic*, do. 1900, p. 282 ff.; H. Callaway, *The Religious System of the Amazulu*, do. 1884, p. 217; H. Ling Roth, *JAI* xxii. [1893] 27; W. W. Gill, *Myths and Songs from the S. Pacific*, London, 1876, p. 77.

[4] J. Fergusson, *Tree and Serpent Worship*, p. 3.

theory is hardly borne out even by the facts known to him, still less by newer knowledge now available. More recently Elliot Smith suggests a theory of migration by which, along with megalith-building, terrace culture, and many other things, serpent-worship originated in Egypt about 800 B.C., was spread thence by the Phœnicians to India, the Far East, and the Pacific islands, and eventually reached America.[1] Investigation along the line of this new theory may have fruitful results.

1. Worship of the serpent. — The distinction should be noted between the worship of the animal itself and its worship as the embodiment of a god or spirit. Sometimes also a god appears as a serpent, or the animal is the symbol or attendant of a god who is probably the anthropomorphic form of an earlier serpent, such as is often the guardian of a sacred place or temple.

(*a*) *Australian.* — In Australia the serpent is often a totem and occurs in myth, but is not worshipped, except perhaps by the Warramunga tribe of N. Central Australia.

The Wollunqua is a huge mythical totem-snake, father of all snakes, and lives in a water-hole, whence it may emerge to destroy men. The men of this totem do not call it by its real name, lest they should lose their power over it, and they perform ceremonies like those used by others for increasing their totems. By these rites the Wollunqua is pleased and will not come forth to destroy. A large keel-shaped mound, resembling it, is made. The men walk round it, stroke it, and then hack it to pieces. At a visit paid to the water-hole the men, with bowed heads, solemnly begged the Wollunqua to do them no harm. Here something approaching worship, with prayer and ritual, is indicated.[2]

Some New South Wales tribes believe in the existence of two snakes, 40 miles long, found on the way to the other world or in it. They are killed and eaten by the dead, but are immediately reproduced. The blacks fear them.[3]

But among the Australians generally and other low races—Veddas, Andamanese, and Fuegians—to judge by the reports of the best observers, there does not appear to be any cult of the serpent.[4] Bushman paintings show huge snakes and other animals, sometimes with humps, on which baboons, men, and mythical creatures are painted, but we do not hear of a cult.[5]

(*b*) *Palæolithic.* — How far serpent-worship existed in pre-historic times is uncertain. Serpents are found among the animals figured by artists of the Palæolithic period. Two figured on *bâtons de commandement* may possibly be eels.[6] But in other instances even the species is recognizable. One of these occurs on an armlet, perhaps as a charm;[7] another is surrounded by an ornamental border.[8]

It is hardly likely that these animals were represented, as in S. Reinach's theory of Palæolithic art, in order to attract them, but the representations might have been for some such magical rite as that of the Arunta. The serpent with the ornamental border might suggest that the reptile was the object of a cult. N. Pinsero,[9] while disbelieving that Palæolithic man had a religion, found religious sentiments in anthropoid apes, which, he held, worship serpents and bury them with a supply of insects in their graves as a provision for a future life! In Mesolithic times the serpent had become a symbol, as on the painted pebbles of Mas d'Azil.

(*c*) *African.*—All over Africa the serpent is worshipped either in itself or as the embodiment of a god.

The cult of the snake at Whydah, Dahomey, may be taken as typical of W. Africa. The heavenly serpent Dañh-sio or Dañh-gbi, the rainbow, confers wealth on men, and is represented by a coiled or horned snake of clay in a calabash. It is also represented by the python. The monster python, grandfather of all snakes, dwelt in a temple or 'snake-house,' containing many snakes, and to it kings and people made pilgrimages with many costly gifts. The python-god is immortal, almighty, omniscient; valuable sacrifices and prayers are offered to it and oracles are received from it; and, with the exception of the priests, only the king can see it, and he but once. It is invoked for good weather, fertility of the crops, and increase of cattle. The whole species was reverenced, and a man who killed such a snake was put to death. The god had a thousand snake-wives or priestesses, and all girls of about twelve whom the older priestesses could capture at the time of millet-sprouting were kept in seclusion and taught the sacred rites, and figures of serpents were traced on their bodies. The serpent was said to have marked them. Later they were put into a hut, where the serpent was supposed to visit and marry them. Girls and women attacked by hysteria were supposed to have been touched by the serpent and thus inspired or possessed. The people had also smaller serpents, not so powerful as Dañh-sio, but adored by them.[1]

A similar cult exists among the Brass River people, where the tribal- and war-god Ogediga was a python, and pythons were so sacred as to be allowed to commit all kinds of depredations, while by an article of the treaty of 1856 white men were forbidden to kill them. The python is the tribal- and war-god and has a numerous priesthood, and is supposed to contain one of the many spirits.[2] The local god Djwij'ahnu among the Tshi appears as a serpent attended by other snakes, and human sacrifices were formerly offered to him. If he did not appear, special sacrifices were made to propitiate him.[3] The cult also exists among the Mpongwes, Bakali, Ashanti, and Niger tribes. In Fernando Po the chief god is represented by a cobra, which can inflict disease or death, give riches, etc. A skin of one is hung up annually in the market-place, and children are made to touch it, perhaps to put them under its care.[4]

Among the Baganda the god Selwanga was represented by a python with priests and mediums. It was kept in a temple, fed with milk by a woman, and then a medium, possessed by the god, gave oracles interpreted by a priest. Sacrifices were made to it, and sterile women obtained children through its power. The wife of the chief god Mukasa was a pythoness, sister of Selwanga. The Bageshu had a similar cult of a serpent Mwanga in a temple on a hill, visited by childless women.[5] Many other African tribes have a serpent cult.[6] In Madagascar serpents are looked upon with superstitious fear and are supposed to be emissaries of the god Ramahalavy.[7]

The Voodoo serpent-cult in Haiti and elsewhere reproduces these W. African cults, one of the names of Dañh-sio being Vodunhwe. The will of the god is communicated through a priest and priestess, and the cult takes place at night when the serpent is shown in a cage; offerings are made to it; the worshippers implore its aid; and the priestess, standing in the cage, becomes inspired and gives oracles. Dances and an orgy follow, and sometimes a child is sacrificed—'the goat without horns.'[8] The Bush Negroes of Dutch Guiana reverence a good divinity in the snake Papagado, which must not be hurt in any way, and the snake generally occupies a prominent position in their thoughts.[9]

(*d*) *Polynesian.* — In New Zealand and other Polynesian islands the snake is seldom met with,

---

1 G. Elliot Smith, *The Migrations of Early Culture*, Manchester, 1916, *The Influence of Ancient Egyptian Civilization in the East and in America*, London, 1916.

2 Spencer-Gillen[b], pp. 226 ff., 495

3 E. Palmer, *JAI* xiii. [1884] 291.

4 No reference to it occurs in such works as the following: A. W. Howitt, *The Native Tribes of S.E. Australia*, London, 1904; C. G. and B. Z. Seligmann, *The Veddas*, Cambridge, 1911; E. H. Man's exhaustive art. on the Andaman Islanders in *JAI* xii. [1883] 69 ff., 117 ff., 327 ff.; P. Hyades and J. Deniker in *Anthropologie et ethnologie* (=*Mission scientifique du Cap Horn*, vol. vii.), Paris, 1891.

5 G. W. Stow, *The Native Races of S. Africa*, London, 1905, pp. 32, 202; R. N. Hall, 'Bushman Paintings in the Ma-Dobo Range,' *Geographical Journal*, xxxix. [1912] 594. The snakes have giraffe heads, and similar snakes are also incised on rocks. The paintings are said to be sacred.

6 T. Wilson, 'Prehistoric Art,' in *Annual Report of the Smithsonian Institution for 1896*, Washington, 1898, pp. 388, 400.

7 Cf. below, § 4 (*a*).

8 E. Piette, *L'Anthropologie*, vi. [1895] 408, xv. [1904] 149, 174.

9 *La psicologia dell' uomo preistorico*, Palermo, 1895, quoted in *L'Anthropologie*, viii. [1897] 334.

1 A. B. Ellis, *The Ewe-speaking Peoples of the Slave Coast*, London, 1890, pp. 60, 148 f.; J. A. Skertchly, *Dahomey as it is*, do. 1874, p. 54 f.; C. de Brosses, *Du Culte des dieux fétiches*, Paris, 1760, p. 25 f.; W. Bosman, *A Description of the Coast of Guinea*, Eng. tr., in J. Pinkerton, *General Collection of Voyages and Travels*, London, 1808–14, xvi. 493 ff.; R. F. Burton, *A Mission to Gelele, king of Dahome*, do. 1864, i. 59 f., ii. 92; J. C. M. Boudin, *Etudes anthropologiques*, pt. ii. p. 57 ff.

2 Burton, i. 61; M. H. Kingsley, *West African Studies*, London, 1899, p. 483; letter of Bishop Crowther, cited in McLennan, p. 524; A. G. Leonard, *The Lower Niger*, London, 1906, p. 329.

3 Ellis, *The Tshi-speaking Peoples of the Gold Coast*, London, 1887, p. 41.

4 T. J. Hutchinson, *Impressions of W. Africa*, London, 1858, p. 196 f.

5 J. Roscoe, *The Baganda*, London, 1911, pp. 318, 322, 335, *JRAI* xxxix. [1909] 188.

6 See *ERE* i. 57[a], 166[a] (Agaos), ii. 511[b] (Berbers), vi. 491[b] (Galla).

7 C. S. Wake, *Serpent Worship*, p. 88.

8 Boudin, p. 78 ff.; S. B. St. John, *Hayti, the Black Republic*, London, 1884, p. 185 ff.

9 L. C. van Panhuys, *Actes du ive Congrès internat. d'hist. des religions*, Leyden, 1913, p. 55.

but in Tonga the water-snake is the embodiment of a god and is reverenced.[1]

(*e*) *Melanesian.*—There are traces of snake-worship in Melanesia.

Among the Koita of British New Guinea harmful mythical beings called *tabu* are seen as snakes, corresponding to the beings called *paipai* which cause sickness among the Roro-speaking tribes. Snakes are also used by sorcerers.[2] In Fiji the supreme god Ndengei had a serpent as his shrine, and was thought to exist as a vast serpent in a cave, fed by an attendant. Hogs and human victims were formerly offered to him, and he gave oracles through a priest and sent rain. Ratu-mai-Mbulu also lived as a serpent in a cave, where food was offered to him yearly.[3] A *nitu*, or spirit, in the form of a mythic snake Bunosi, to some extent a creator though born of a human mother, is holy and is worshipped with sacrifice in Lavelai in the Solomon Islands.[4]

In San Cristoval *figona* (spirits) have serpent incarnations, and one of them, Agunua, is supreme and creator. Other snake *figona* are female. Firstfruits are offered to a snake called Kagauraha, a representative of Agunua, while there are other rites and prayers for relief from sickness, from bad seasons, for growth, etc. Kagauraha and her brood live in a special house, from which women are excluded. A pig or human sacrifice is offered, and the serpent gives oracles. In other places certain *figona* incarnate in serpents are worshipped, but are said to be local representations of Agunua, who is 'all of them.'[5]

(*f*) *Dayak.*—Among the Dayaks the serpent embodies an *antu*, or spirit, and is occasionally worshipped. When a spirit enters into a snake, the animal becomes a deity and spirit-helper of an individual, but there is no tribal cult.[6] The Kenyahs of Borneo regard Bali Sungei as embodied in a serpent in a river, causing it to swirl and capsize boats. Hence he is feared.[7]

(*g*) *Ainu.*—Among the Ainus the cult is directed to a mythical snake-king, father of all snakes. Snakes cause the evils of child-birth, and their spirits may possess one who has slain them. Madness is caused by a snake entering the body, and women bitten by snakes become subject to hysteria, and sometimes act as witch-doctors.[8]

(*h*) *American Indian.*—The American Indians believe in a huge serpent, sometimes worshipped,[9] but among the northern tribes mainly the subject of myths.

He is horned or feathered,[10] the horn being the thunder-bolt, and he is generally malevolent, though not always so. Sometimes he is a personification of the lightning, more often of the waters, ruling them and their powers, and in Chippewa myth he is connected with the flood. More beneficent beings are in conflict with him, and sometimes slay him—the Great Hare (Algonquins),[11] the Thunderer who hates all noxious beings (Iroquois),[12] Manibozho (Chippewas).[13] Sometimes he is placated to avoid his malignancy, as with the Musquakies, with whom the great Rain-Serpent is the cause of drought and ancestor of all snakes, and to whose fish-totem clan he is propitious.[14] But in the drier regions he is the Rain-Serpent who sends the needed rain to fertilize the maize, and he is one of the gods.

With the Zuñi dramatic ritual symbolizes the coming of Kóloowisi, the Plumed Serpent, of whom an image is carried in procession. Water and grain are made to drop from it, and the water, symbolizing rain, is drunk by candidates for initiation; the grain is planted separately from the rest of the seed.[15] Among the Hopi the serpent is called Palülükon, and the fertilizing of the maize by him is dramatically represented.[16]

Corresponding to the Rain-Serpent is the snake Sisiutl of the Kwakiutl (N.W. Pacific coast)—a serpent with a horned head at each end of its body, and a human horned head in the middle. To touch, see, or eat it is certain death, but it brings power to those who enjoy supernatural help. It is frequently represented in carving and painting.[1]

Most of the tribes pay some form of cult and give offerings to the rattle-snake, the species almost exclusively honoured and universally represented in early and later art.[2] Where it is not actually worshipped, it is respected and not killed.

The Delawares, Lenin Lenapé, and others call it 'Grandfather,' and among the Algonquians it was the king of snakes, who gave prosperous breezes and was the symbol of life in their picture-writing.[3]

The most curious aspect of snake-worship is that of the Hopi and kindred tribes. Perhaps originally a form of totem-ancestor-worship, the cult is now a dramatic prayer for rain and growth, but the worship is paid to mythic ancestors, the snake-youth and snake-maid, Tcuamana, who are personated in the rite.

Rattle-snakes, the elder brothers of the snake-clan, are collected and ceremonially washed after prayer. Symbols representing clouds, rain, and lightning, and corn and other seeds are set out in the *kiva*, where a secret ceremonial is performed with hundreds of snakes. In the public ceremony the priests of the snake fraternity carry the snakes in their mouths, and these are sprinkled with sacred meal as a prayer-offering. The snakes are then sent off to the cardinal points, in order that they may carry the prayers for rain to the powers below. The members of the clan claim immunity from snake-bite, because the snake is their totem. This snake-dance has no connexion with the cult of the Plumed Serpent already referred to.[4] The Natchez also venerated the rattle-snake as a form of the Great Spirit and placed its image in the temple of the sun.[5]

Among the animal mounds of Wisconsin one represents a serpent, 1000 ft. in length. It is conspicuously situated, and, like all the other mounds, was fitted for the performance of ceremonies before a large multitude.[6]

(*i*) *Mexican.*—In Mexico, before and after the Aztec immigration, the snake was an important religious symbol.

Living rattle-snakes were kept in the temples and fed with the flesh of human sacrificial victims.[7] Several of the higher gods were partially of serpent origin or had been associated with older serpent-gods. Huitzilopochtli, an anthropomorphic humming-bird deity, was born of Coatlicue, whose name signifies 'serpent,' and snakes were associated with his image and ritual.[8] In times of danger his image was covered with a snake-skin, and the priest carried a wooden snake as his symbol on his festival. The walls of his temple had snakes carved in relief, and its circuit was called *coatepantli*, 'the circuit of snakes.'[9] Perhaps the snake-aspect of this god was derived from the serpent-cult of the Otomis, whose highest god, Mixcoatl, was a serpent-divinity.[10] In one of his aspects Quetzalcoatl seems to be identical with the Plumed Serpent of the Hopi, and a snake-god of Yucatan, Cuculcan, may have been merged into him. His name means 'feathered serpent'; his image had a snake beside it; and the entrance to his temple represented the gory jaws of a huge serpent. When he left Mexico for the fabled land of Tlapallan, he journeyed in a boat of serpent skins.[11] At the feast of the god Tlaloc little hills of paper and wooden snakes were placed on his altar, and his image held a golden serpent.[12] The goddess Cihuacohuatl, or 'serpent woman,' was said to have borne twins at the beginning of the fourth world-age, from whom the earth was peopled. Hence twins were called 'snakes.' She was also called Tonantzin, 'our mother,' and was represented with a great male serpent beside her.[13]

---

1 W. Mariner, *An Account of the Natives of the Tonga Islands*, London, 1817, ii. 139; J. Williams, *Narr. of Missionary Enterprises in the South Sea Islands*, do. 1838, p. 547.

2 C. G. Seligmann, *The Melanesians of British New Guinea*, Cambridge, 1910, pp. 183, 302.

3 B. Thomson, *The Fijians*, London, 1908, p. 114; T. Williams, *Fiji and the Fijians*, do. 1858, p. 217 f.; cf. *ERE* vi. 14b. For the cult in Banks Islands and the New Hebrides see *ERE* viii. 533b and cf. ix. 337b; in New Guinea, ix. 346a; in New Caledonia, ix. 338.

4 G. C. Wheeler, *ARW* xv. [1912] 348 ff.

5 C. E. Fox and F. H. Drew, *JRAI* xlv. [1915] 135 ff.; cf. *ERE* viii. 533.

6 H. Ling Roth, *The Natives of Sarawak and British N. Borneo*, London, 1896, i. 188; Hose-McDougall, ii. 90 f., 114.

7 Hose-McDougall, ii. 15; for Annam see *ERE* i. 541b.

8 J. Batchelor, *The Ainu and their Folklore*, London, 1901, pp. 301, 356 ff.; *ERE* i. 251.

9 See *ERE* i. 324b.

10 For horned snakes and their rationale see *ERE* iii. 503b, 568b, vi. 793a.

11 H. B. Alexander, *N. American Mythology* (=*Mythology of all Races*, vol. x.), Boston, 1916, p. 44.

12 J. G. Müller, *Gesch. der amerikan. Urreligionen*, Basel, 1855, p. 47.

13 E. G. Squier, *American Review*, new ser., ii. [1848] 392 ff.; Müller, p. 131.

14 M. A. Owen, *Folk-lore of the Musquakie Indians*, London, 1904, pp. 36, 110 f. For the Rain-Serpent revered by the Kickapoos see *ERE* i. 324b.

15 M. C. Stevenson, *23 RBEW* [1904], p. 94 ff.

16 See *ERE* vi. 785b, 786a, and, for such divine serpents among the Huichols, vi. 829a.

1 F. Boas, 'Social Organization and Secret Societies of the Kwakiutl Indians' (*Report of U.S. National Museum*), Washington, 1895, p. 371.

2 D. G. Brinton, *The Myths of the New World*3, Philadelphia, 1896, p. 130; W. H. Holmes, *2 RBEW* [1883], p. 289.

3 Brinton, p. 142.

4 J. G. Bourke, *The Snake Dance of the Moquis of Arizona*, London, 1884; J. W. Fewkes, *JAFL* xvi. [1901] 82 f., *15 RBEW* [1897], p. 304, *19 RBEW*, pt. 2 [1900], pp. 624, 965 ff., 1005 ff.; M. C. Stevenson, *11 RBEW* [1894], for the dance among the Sia. Cf. *ERE* vi. 785 f.

5 Müller, p. 62.

6 G. F. Wright, *The Origin and Antiquity of Man*, London, 1913, p. 148 ff.

7 Bernal Diaz, quoted by Southey, notes to *Madoc* in *Poetical Works*, London, 1860, v. 432; F. Lopez de Gómara in S. Purchas, *Purchas His Pilgrimes*, Glasgow, 1905–07, xv. 536.

8 Joseph Acosta, in Purchas, xv. 312 f.

9 *Ib.* p. 319 f.; *NR* iii. 321.

10 Müller, p. 485.

11 W. Prescott, *Hist. of Mexico*, London, 1909, i. 383; Müller, pp. 486, 577 ff.; *NR* iii. 281, 449; Lopez de Gómara, in Purchas, xv. 547.

12 Müller, p. 502.

13 *Ib.* pp. 484, 514; Brinton, p. 143; *NR* iii. 352.

(*j*) *Mayan.*—The Mayan god Votan was probably in one aspect a variety of the Plumed Serpent, and his image represented him as a bird above and a serpent below. This culture-god was said to have built 'the city of the serpents' and to have written a book proving that he was one of the Chanés, or serpents.[1] In Mayan MSS and carvings the rattle-snake alone is represented as a symbol and is called the 'serpent-king.'[2]

(*k*) *Central American.*—Among the peoples of Central America living snakes were worshipped.

Human victims are said to have been offered to a living serpent-god by the Zacatecas.[3] Near Uxmal is a spring where, according to Indian belief, an old woman sits and exchanges water for little children, whom she gives to a serpent to eat. She is perhaps the anthropomorphic form of a serpent-god to whom children were offered.[4] All over this region, in Honduras and Nicaragua, the remains of temples show colossal feathered serpents, sometimes with a human head in the jaws, as at Uxmal, sculptured on the walls and cornices, and sometimes running the whole length of the building. Quetzalcoatl or Cuculcan is also depicted holding feathered serpents or with these coiled round his body. Such serpents are also seen painted on rocks in Nicaragua.[5]

(*l*) *Peruvian.*—In Peru the pre-Inca race venerated serpents and painted them on temples and houses, and offered human hearts and blood to them. They were also represented on the temples of the Inca kingdom, where reverence for snakes was wide-spread, and the spotted wood-snake was kept in the temple of Pachacamac.[6] The god of riches, Urcaguai, was regarded as a snake, in which form he was said to have appeared, and his snake-image in the form of a horned and hairy rattle-snake was revered in a building called the 'snake-house.'[7]

(*m*) *S. American Indian.*—The native Indians of S. America have always shown certain reverence for serpents.

Among the Caribs, who believed that the spirits of the dead transmigrated into snakes, images of snakes existed. Rakumon, one of the men drawn from the thigh of the first man and god Loguo, became a snake with a human head and twined himself round trees, the fruit of which he ate and gave to others. Afterwards he became a star. Star and snake are connected in Carib myth—the star shows by its position the time of the year's fruitfulness, the snake symbolizes the renewing of vegetation through the fertilizing rain.[8] The serpent is also a common symbol in the ruins of the old temples of the more civilized tribes—*e.g.*, the Muyscas, among whom the priests in processions wore masks of snakes and crocodiles.[9] The Chibchas believed in a large snake which issued from a lake, and they made offerings of gold and emeralds to it. A snake-cult was also observed by neighbouring tribes, and the Canari believed themselves descended from a snake dwelling in a lake, to whom offerings of gold were made.[10] The great boa was worshipped by tribes in Brazil, and one tribe living near the borders of Peru kept one in a pyramidal temple, fed it with human flesh, and prayed to it.[11] Of the snake called the manima a 16th cent. traveller in Brazil says that the natives to whom it showed itself regarded themselves as blessed and believed that they would live long.[12] The tribes of the Issa-Japura district believe that the anaconda is evil and the embodiment of the water-spirit, the *yaca-mama*, mother of the streams, who bars their passage. Hence they go in fear of the reptile, which occupies in Amazonian folk-belief the place of the sea-serpent elsewhere.[13] Many myths and tales about serpents exist among the various tribes.[14]

(*n*) *Chinese.*—In China serpents, like other animals, occasionally have temples dedicated to them, this cult being apparently connected with the belief in metamorphosis;[15] but on the whole they are feared.

Their forms are frequently the embodiments of evil spectres, which cause misfortune, illness, and death, or are instruments of punishment. Snakes cause illness by sending their souls into the bodies of men, and sick people are alleged to vomit vipers. The serpent is also a common wer-animal;[1] in early times snakes with human or partly human form—a human face, a wolf's body, birds' wings, and moving like a snake—were known. Transformation of men into snakes and of snakes into men is a very old belief. In many stories, however, in spite of the generally evil aspect of the serpent, apparitions of snakes have proved to be propitious.[2] The dragon as the giver of rain is worshipped in time of drought, and also in spring and autumn by certain mandarins by command of the emperor. He has a temple in Peking, and is regarded as a great benefactor and the venerated symbol of good. In the ritual, when rain is prayed for, a large image called the 'Dragon King' is carried in procession, and incense is offered to it. Boats in the shape of a dragon also play an important part in the Dragon Boat festival and in the procession of the Five Rulers. The symbol of the dragon is a common religious and artistic *motif*: the five-clawed dragon was the emblem of the imperial power, the protecting deity of the emperor, whose body was called the dragon's body, his throne the dragon's throne, etc. The true dragon is never all visible at once, but only his head or tail, the rest of his body being enshrouded in clouds.[3]

(*o*) *Japanese.*—The Japanese frequently worship the serpent as a mysterious being, often the embodiment of a spirit or god.

It has an important place in mythic history as progenitress of the Mikado's ancestry. Myth hardly distinguishes between snake and anthropomorphic god, the forms being interchangeable. Some divinities still assume serpent form—*e.g.*, the goddess Bentem, to whom certain snakes are sacred and are her servants and confidants—and where certain snakes live famous temples have been built.[4]

(*p*) *Cretan.* — There are traces of a former serpent-divinity in Crete.

Images of a goddess, with snakes twined round the body and head-dress, have been found. Sometimes votaries holding snakes dance before her. She is probably an earth-goddess, lady of the wild creatures, and an anthropomorphic transformation of an older serpent-divinity. It is unlikely that the figures represent snake-charmers, as has been supposed.[5] On the Mycenæan cylinders of Cyprus the goddess of Paphos is associated with a pillar entwined by a serpent, and Pausanias describes an image of Artemis holding serpents.[6]

(*q*) *Egyptian.*—Among worshipful animals the serpent predominated in Egypt, either because of its supposed good qualities or through fear of some species; and the cult of the cobra and asp occurs in the earliest times.

The figure of the serpent appears as a personal or house-protecting amulet all through Egyptian history. The cobra or *uræus* was a symbol of fire or the solar disk; hence this serpent decked the forehead or crown of the solar god and of kings, his representatives, was carried by priests and priestesses of Ra, or itself occurred crowned on standards. It was identified with the flaming eye of the god; hence 'eye' and 'asp' became synonymous, and two eyes or serpents were called 'daughters of the sun-god.'[7] The sun-god is also figured as a serpent or a double asp, and, like the solar orb, the *uræus* was sometimes represented with wings. Serpents guarded the groves and gates of Amenti, breathing fire against the wicked, as well as the pylons of the heaven of Osiris. A serpent was the embodiment of certain goddesses—*e.g.*, Rannut, goddess of fertility and the harvest, perhaps because snakes found in corn-fields were regarded as local spirits in snake form and were fed; Mertseker, goddess of the necropolis at Thebes; Buto and Nekheb, guardians of Upper and Lower Egypt. It was associated with Isis and Nephthys, because these goddesses were later identified with Uazet, the *uræus*-goddess, who was gradually absorbed into all the goddesses. Hence all goddesses were adorned with or represented by the *uræus*, or as a serpent a goddess is associated with a god.[8] Qeb, god of the earth, was master of snakes and had a serpent's head.[9] Live serpents were kept as guardians or sacred animals in shrines and temples behind a sacred veil or in a small cell. These serpents were mummified

[1] Müller, p. 487 f.; *NR* v. 159.
[2] Brinton, p. 130.
[3] Müller, p. 483 f.
[4] J. L. Stephens, *Incidents of Travel in Central America*, London, 1841, p. 425.
[5] E. G. Squier, *Nicaragua*, New York, 1852, i. 317 f., ii. 36; Stephens, *Incidents of Travel in Yucatan*, London, 1856, i. 302, ii. 304 ff., 312; T. Gann, *19 RBEW*, pt. 2 [1900], p. 663 ff. See also *JRAI* xlii. [1912] 17 ff. For other Central American serpent-gods see *ERE* iii. 308a.
[6] Acosta, in Purchas, xv. 307, 388; Garcilasso de La Vega, *Royal Commentaries of the Yncas*, ed. C. R. Markham, London, 1869–71, *passim*.
[7] Müller, p. 366; Brinton, p. 142.
[8] Müller, pp. 210, 221.
[9] J. B. von Spix and C. F. P. von Martius, *Reise in Brasilien*, Munich, 1823–31, iii. 258, 1272; Müller, p. 436.
[10] T. A. Joyce, *South American Archæology*, London, 1912, pp. 28, 66, 156.
[11] Müller, p. 258; Garcilasso de La Vega, in Purchas, xvii. 388.
[12] Purchas, xvi. 497.
[13] T. W. Whiffen, *The North-West Amazons*, London, 1915, p. 231.
[14] E. Nordenskiöld, *Indianerleben: el Gran Chaco*, Leipzig, 1912, pp. 110, 288; cf. *ERE* ii. 836a, 837b.
[15] J. J. M. de Groot, *The Religion of the Chinese*, New York, 1910, p. 124.

[1] See art. LYCANTHROPY, § 1.
[2] De Groot, *The Religious System of China*, Leyden, 1892–1910, iv. 215 f., v. 626 ff.
[3] J. Doolittle, *Social Life of the Chinese*, London, 1866, i. 281, 292, ii. 55 f., 117, 264 f.
[4] W. E. Griffis, *The Religions of Japan*, London, 1895, p. 31 f.; *Kojiki*, tr. B. H. Chamberlain, Yokohama, 1883, *passim*; *ERE* ix. 238b.
[5] *BSA* x. [1904] 223; *PEFSt* [1916] 207; C. H. and H. B. Hawes, *Crete the Forerunner of Greece*², London, 1911, pp. 102, 123, 139; S. Reinach, in *L'Anthropologie*, xv. [1904] 274; cf. *ERE* i. 142.
[6] Paus. VIII. xxxvii. 4.
[7] W. Max Müller, *Egyptian Mythology* (=*Mythology of all Races*, vol. xii.), Boston, 1918, p. 29.
[8] E. A. Wallis Budge, *The Gods of the Egyptians*, London, 1904, i. 92, 100, 441 f.
[9] Max Müller, p. 42.

or, like those sacred to Amon, buried in the temple.[1] Offerings of fruit, cakes of flour and honey, flowers, and incense were made to serpent-divinities. *Uræi* figured as temple-guardians, often in the form of a cornice or frieze. In heaven was supposed to exist the serpent Sati or Bata, the serpent 'of millions of years,' into which the soul of the dead identified with Osiris could transform or identify itself.[2] Divine beings have sometimes a serpent's head. The serpent was much represented in later times as its cult increased, sometimes in pairs, and then often with the heads of Sarapis and Isis. Stars were regarded as snakes or these were their symbols.[3] Generally the serpent was regarded as an ἀγαθὸς δαίμων connected with life and healing. So even now 'it is believed that each quarter in Cairo has its peculiar guardian-genius or Agathodæmon, which has the form of a serpent.'[4] In early times dwarf figures like Bes tear up and devour serpents—symbols of hostile powers; and the heavenly gods are said in one myth to have left the earth because of the serpents who drove them away—primeval reptiles of the abyss or a serpent of the earth-god or a serpent created by Isis.[5] There is also a confused reference here to a serpent of great size embodying darkness and evil, enemy of Ra and the gods and destroyer of souls. This is Apap, referred to from early times, and probably a reminiscence of the python.[6] Apap dwelt in the ocean over which travelled the divine boat of Ra, which he sought to upset, or in that part of Hades through which the god travels daily. Ra daily attacks and slays him, and the destruction is described with grim realism.[7] The dead fought Apap and other demoniac serpents with Ra's aid, and protected by amulets and formulæ of repulsion.[8] In other forms of the myth gods (often with serpents' heads) attack and bind Apap under the earth or sea. Apap tended to be identified with Set, attacked by Horus. These myths may be connected with the Babylonian myth of Bel and Tiamat. Apap was also devourer of the souls of the wicked, and was head of all powers hostile to the sun. Serpents of demon aspect met the soul on its way to the other world, but against those the *Book of the Dead* provided a way of escape. Horus, as protector against venomous snakes, was called 'stopper of snakes' and is represented holding snakes in his hand. Hence amulets of the god in this aspect were worn as protectives.[9]

(*r*) *Babylonian*.—In Babylonia there is little trace of worship of the serpent.

Herodotus[10] speaks of a live serpent worshipped there, but this may be a reminiscence of the conquest of Tiamat by Bel-Merodach.[11] Ea had the serpent as symbol and was called 'god of the river of the great snake'—*i.e.* the deep or the Euphrates. The names of the river in early inscriptions show the connexion of the serpent with Ea and also with Innina, his daughter, whose name is interchangeable with that of the snake, the anthropomorphic transformation of which she probably was.[12] Serpents abounded in marshes at the mouth of the river. Serakh, god of corn, was a snake-god. Sala, consort of Rimmon, had a name meaning 'goddess of reptiles.' Certain goddesses associated with the under world are depicted with serpents in their hands.[13] Among what appear to be emblems of gods on boundary-stones recording sales of land a snake is a prominent figure—possibly symbolizing Ea.[14]

On the whole the serpent tended to assume or already generally had an evil aspect in Babylonia.

This is seen especially in the myth of Tiamat, of Sumerian origin, and in 'the evil serpent' or 'serpent of darkness,' often identified with her, or 'the great serpent with seven heads.' Tiamat represented the primeval, anarchic waters, as a monster dragon or raging serpent, which Merodach conquered and slew or, in another version, subdued and bound.[15] Among her forces were 'the dragon, the great serpent, the devouring reptiles.' Traces of this myth are found in the OT as a survival or borrowing. The serpent is associated with the deep, is called by various names—Leviathan, Behemoth, Rahab, as well as dragon or serpent—and is represented as conquered by Jahweh,[16] or as bound by Him or set in the sea and again to be conquered.[17] This being is apparently identified with historic nations (Babylon, Egypt, Assyria), and is sometimes duplicated,[1] and it has many heads. Other references to 'the dragon that is in the sea' may imply Tiamat's consort, Kingu.[2] Monstrous forms of reptiles and serpents are mentioned by Berosus as existing in early times in Babylon. Horned serpents occur in Chaldæan monuments, and winged dragons on the lintel of a doorway of the palace of Sennacherib. The demoniac or evil aspect of the serpent is seen also in the myths of Labbu and of Etana, and in the serpent which steals the plant of life from Gilgameš, while demons were often given a serpent form.[3] The seal with an erect serpent between two seated figures on either side of a sacred tree still lacks interpretation, though some have supposed it to represent a Babylonian version of the Fall story.[4] Serpents were believed to guard holy places and were set up on entrances of temples and palaces.

(*s*) *Canaanite and Hebrew*.—In Canaan serpents of brass or terra-cotta and actual serpents' heads have been found. These suggest a cult, and perhaps a pit in which was a serpent of brass may have been a serpent shrine.[5]

Ashtart, like the Cretan goddess, is represented with serpents in her hands. These brass serpents recall the Hebrew brazen serpent, which has been variously explained as a pre-Israelite image of a serpent embodying the spirit of a well,[6] adopted by the Hebrews; as an early Hebrew image connected with healing worshipped down to the days of Hezekiah, who destroyed it; as a totem of the family of David,[7] or the symbol of a serpent tribe; or as originally a representation of Tiamat, later misunderstood and associated with healing.[8] Was it the image of an actual serpent or of a spirit (*jinn*) embodied in a serpent? Probably the latter, as the fiery serpents of the ætiological myth explaining its origin[9] suggest demoniac beings in serpent form, such as are still believed in by the Arabs. The cult of every form of creeping thing and abominable beast portrayed on the walls of the Temple may have been a recrudescence of an earlier Hebrew cult or a borrowing from exterior sources.[10] Serpents or dragons, as in Arab belief, were doubtless also connected with wells, giving or withholding the waters, and in Syria springs are named after serpents, or as in Palmyra a female serpent-demon dwells in a spring and can hinder its flow.[11]

The fiery flying serpents of Nu 21^{8} and Dt 8^{15} are still known to Eastern superstition, and are mentioned by Herodotus[12] as inhabiting the desert. A serpent of this kind is threatened against Philistia, and is mentioned as a creature of the land of trouble and anguish.[13]

The talking serpent of Gn 3 represents a primitive stage of thought, while the story supplies an ætiological myth answering the questions, Why are serpents and men at enmity?, and Why does the serpent crawl instead of walk? It is doubtful whether the serpent was intended in the original story to be evil. More likely he was a divine being, with superior knowledge and a kindly desire to help man to knowledge denied him by other divinities. A later recension made his act have evil consequences, and therefore he himself had evil intentions. The story doubtless arose with a people to whom the serpent was sacred, and who were impressed with its wisdom.

Frazer connects the story of the Fall with myths of the origin of death (the 'perverted message' group) and of the cast skin (the serpent casting its skin renews its youth and never dies, and hence was considered immortal).[14] He assumes that in the earlier form of the story there were two trees, one of life and one of death. God wished man to eat the former and so become immortal, but man, misled by the serpent, ate the fruit of the other tree and so forfeited immortality. The serpent ate of the tree of life and so lived for ever.[15]

The connexion of the serpent with the devil is nowhere hinted at in OT, but appears first in Wis 2^{24}, and was a Rabbinic conception,[16] with profound influence on Christian and Gnostic thought. The idea of a chaotic force, personified—*e.g.*, as a dragon (Tiamat)—hostile to creative divinities, was more or less combined with this. Hence such a conception as Rev 12, esp. v.[9]. Here is also the idea of a dragon hostile to a heavenly goddess and her son (Leto, Apollo, Pytho; Isis, Horus, Typhon or Set; Marduk, Tiamat—here the goddess is lacking). These various ideas recur in Christian and Gnostic literature, and language is exhausted to express the evil character of the devil-serpent or dragon. Partly because of the myth of the

1 Ælian, *de Nat. An.* x. 31, xi. 17; Herod. ii. 74.

2 H. Brugsch, *Religion und Mythologie der alten Ägypter*, Berlin, 1885–88, p. 180; W. R. Cooper, *Trans. of Victoria Institute*, p. 340; Budge, ii. 377.

3 A. Dieterich, *Eine Mithrasliturgie*, Leipzig, 1903, p. 71; Plut. *de Is. et Osir.* 74.

4 E. W. Lane, *An Account of the Manners and Customs of the Modern Egyptians*, London, 1836, i. 289.

5 Max Müller, pp. 62, 64, 76 f., 79 f.

6 G. Maspero, *The Dawn of Civilization*, Eng. tr., London, 1894, p. 34.

7 *Litany of the Sun*, ch. 2; *Hymn to Ra*; *Books of the Overthrowing of 'Apop*; cf. *ERE* viii. 266ª.

8 *Book of the Dead*, ch. 32, 39.

9 See, further, *ERE* v. 245.

10 v. 23.

11 Cf. H. Gunkel, *Schöpfung und Chaos*, Göttingen, 1895, p. 320 f.

12 A. H. Sayce, *The Religion of the Babylonians* (*HL*), London, 1887, pp. 134, 139, 284; cf. *ERE* viii. 636ª for Ea as 'the great serpent of heaven.'

13 Perrot-Chipiez, ii. *Chaldée et Assyrie*, pp. 367, 804; Diod. Sic. II. ix. 5.

14 H. C. Rawlinson, *WAI*, London, 1870, iii. pl. xlv.

15 See *ERE* iv. 128ᵇ, 598.

16 Ps 74^{14}, Is $51^{9f.}$.

17 Ez $32^{2f.}$ $29^{3f.}$; cf. Job 38.

1 Is 27^{1}.

2 These mythical references are still found in Rev 12^{3} (possibly influenced also by the Greek myth of Pytho and Leto) $13^{2.4.11}$ 16^{13} 20^{2}.

3 *ERE* ii. 315 f., vi. 644ª; M. Jastrow, *The Religion of Babylonia and Assyria*, Boston, 1898, p. 262 f.

4 See *ERE* v. 714ᵇ; Perrot-Chipiez, p. 97.

5 H. Vincent, *Canaan d'après l'exploration récente*, Paris, 1907, pp. 117, 174 f.; *ERE* i. 792ᵇ; *PEFSt* [1903], pp. 42, 222, [1906], p. 119.

6 Cf. the serpent stone at a well (1 K 1^{9}).

7 W. R. Smith, *JPh* ix. [1880] 99.

8 *EBi.* col. 3388.

9 Nu $21^{8f.}$.

10 Ezk 8^{10}; cf. Wis 11^{15}.

11 W. R. Smith², p. 168 f.

12 ii. 75.

13 Is 14^{2} 30^{6}; cf. 2 Esd 15^{29}; for the connexion with the seraphim see *ERE* iv. 595ᵇ.

14 See § 6 (*f*).

15 J. G. Frazer, *Folk-Lore in the Old Testament*, London, 1918, i. 45 ff.

16 A. F. Gfrörer, *Gesch. des Urchristenthums*, Stuttgart, 1838, vol. i. pt. i., 'Das Jahrhundert des Heils,' p. 388.

dragon cast into the abyss, partly because of the existing conception of death as a devouring monster, Hades is often described or depicted as a dragon.

(*t*) *Phœnician and Arabian.*—For the Phœnicians we have the evidence of Eusebius, quoting Philo of Byblus:

Taautos (the Egyptian Thoth), and after him the Phœnicians and Egyptians, divinized dragons and serpents, because they of all reptiles have the strongest respiration and a certain fiery nature. Their swiftness and variety of movements, in spite of possessing no feet, their longevity, their power of renewing their youth, all contributed to the respect in which they were held. The Phœnicians called the serpent Agathodaimon, and it was adopted into the mysteries and temples. Sacrifices were offered to serpents, and they were regarded as great divinities and mediators.[1] This evidence is supported by the fact that Tyrian coins show the serpent in connexion with trees, pillars, and altars,[2] while Asklepios, the Greek serpent-god of healing, was identified with Eshmun, a Phœnician god with similar functions.[3]

In Arab belief the *jinn* are embodied in snakes, especially those haunting houses and thickets, appearing and disappearing suddenly.[4] The prophet says in the book *Mishkâta 'l-Maṣabêḥ* that such snakes are *jinn*, some infidels, some believers. They must be asked to leave; if they refuse, they are infidels and may be killed.

(*u*) *Greek.*—In Greece serpents were regarded as guardians of graves, sanctuaries, and dwellings, and were kept there or represented in symbol.

Snakes were sacred because heroes or the dead generally might appear as serpents; certain gods had once been snakes or might become visible as such; and snakes were associated with them in myth, ritual, and art. The snake as a chthonian animal—'a son of the earth'[5]—was associated with fertility, and had been early reverenced as house-spirit, *οἰκουρὸς ὄφις*, or earth daimon, or *ἀγαθὸς δαίμων*, promoting fertility, and hence worshipped or at least fed.[6] Eponymous founders regarded as heroes were thought of as snakes or as having twy-nature, like Cecrops,[7] Kychreus of Salamis,[8] and Erechtheus of Athens.[9]

The presence of snakes in sanctuaries and in the rites of certain divinities suggests that these had once been worshipped as snakes.

Snakes were kept in shrines sacred to Asklepios (whose name may be connected with *ἀσκάλαβος, ἀσκάλαφος*='snake')[10] and were fed by virgin priestesses. They gave omens of health and plenty.[11] In these shrines the snake (=the god) suggested a cure to the sufferer in dreams or gave fruitfulness to women, and the child was believed to be begotten by the god. Asklepios appears as a snake in myths and art as well as in the sorcery of Alexander of Abonoteichos,[12] and in stories of the founding of temples. The snake is also his symbol, twined about his staff, or side by side with him. Asklepios had once been a divine snake, giving fertility and health before he became anthropomorphous. He was brought from his sanctuary at Epidauros to Sicyon in the form of a snake, and an embassy went from Rome to Epidauros and brought back a serpent which caused a plague to cease and received divine honours.[13]

In some of his aspects Zeus had snake form, as certain bas-reliefs show—Zeus Ktesios, the fertility-giver, Zeus Meilichios, and Zeus Sosipolis, who as a child was placed by Eileithyia before the army of Elis when the Arcadians invaded it, and vanished into the ground as a snake. A sanctuary was afterwards built on the spot.[14] Snakes fed by a naked virgin priestess lived in Apollo's shrine at Epirus and were said to be descended from the Pytho, and to be play-things for the god. If they took the honey-cakes with which they were fed, the year would be fruitful; if not, the reverse.[15] Demeter had the snake Kychreus as her attendant at Eleusis, probably an old local snake-god, and as goddess of the Phigalians in Arcadia she had snakes twined in her hair, and her chariot was drawn by winged snakes. The Erinyes, as chthonic beings, are called *δράκαιναι*, and had the form of snakes, or snakes were coiled in their hair.[16] In so far as they originated from ghosts, their snake form is obvious.

Zeus as a serpent violated Persephone, who then gave birth to Dionysus (Sabazios),[1] a god with occasional snake form,[2] in whose rites women put snakes in their hair or round their bodies, or rent them asunder.[3] The god was doubtless embodied in the snakes, for 'the symbol of the Dionysiac orgies is a consecrated serpent.'[4] In Roman myth the parallel was the violation of the Bona Dea by her father Faunus, and a consecrated serpent was placed beside her image in her ritual.[5] Sabazios, the god of Asia Minor kindred to Dionysos (or some personal name of whom was read in Greek as 'Dionysos'), was represented as a snake along with Cybele.

Some divine beings were represented as partly snake in form—besides those already mentioned, Typhon, Boreas, Hecate (also with serpents in her hair), and the giants.[6]

Snakes kept in shrines were fed with honey or honey-cakes, as the ghosts were also propitiated with the same food.[7]

(*v*) *Roman.*—Among the Romans a serpent-cult is mainly connected with the animals as embodying the genius, and snakes were kept in large numbers in temples and houses.[8] The Greek cult of the serpent Asklepios probably influenced the Romans, as the embassy to Epidauros just mentioned suggests. A more native aspect of the cult is seen in the serpent-cave at Lanuvium, whither virgins were taken yearly to prove their chastity. If the serpent accepted the offerings brought by them, their chastity was proved and also a fertile season ensured, as at Epirus.[9]

A survival of an older cult or totem-clan rite is probably to be seen in the yearly procession of men with coils of live serpents before the image, hung with serpents, of St. Domenico of Foligno at Cocullo, near the territory of the ancient Marsi snake-clan. The people claim immunity from snake-bite as well as power over serpents, as did the Marsi.[10]

(*w*) *Celtic.*—Among the Celts details of a serpent-cult are lacking.

A horned serpent is figured with twelve Roman gods on a Gallo-Roman altar, and the serpent frequently occurs along with images of Celtic gods who hold serpents in their hands or present a torque to two ram-headed serpents.[11] These gods are probably all forms of an underworld god; hence the chthonic character of the animal as his symbol or vehicle may be suggested. The ram-headed serpent accompanies a goddess of fertility on a monument at Epinal.[12] What myth was told of such twy-natured serpents is unknown, but the ram has been supposed to be connected with a cult of the dead or with the god of the under world.[13] Serpents were entwined round oaks in the Druidic grove described by Lucan. The serpent also occurs on a group of Scottish monuments regarded as of the Christian period, either alone or with the doubly bent rod.[14] These symbols are probably derived from the pagan period, but their meaning is unknown.

W. Stukeley, in his works on Avebury and Stonehenge, advocated the theory that the megaliths there were connected with serpent-worship, but archæologists see no reason for dissociating these from similar remains known to be burial-sites. A similar theory has been connected with a so-called 'serpent-mound' near Oban.

Dragons and serpents are mentioned frequently in Celtic myth and story in association with lochs or sacred trees, and in many saintly legends they are overcome by the saints. A white serpent is king of the snakes in Celtic lore.[15]

(*x*) *Ophite.*—Reference may here be made to the cult or symbolism of the snake among the groups of Gnostics collectively known as Ophites.

With some of these the serpent was a symbol of evil. This was the case with some groups described by Irenæus, with

---

[1] Philo, *ap.* Eus. *Præp. Evang.* i. 10.
[2] T. Maurice, *Indian Antiquities compared with Persia, Egypt, Greece*, London, 1796–1806, vi. 273.
[3] W. W. F. von Baudissin, *ZDMG* lix. [1905] 459 f.; see also art. PHŒNICIANS.
[4] W. R. Smith², pp. 120, 129, 133; E. W. Lane, *Arabian Society in the Middle Ages*, London, 1883, pp. 28, 35; cf. *ERE* i. 669ᵇ.
[5] Herod. i. 78.
[6] Cf. J. E. Harrison, *Themis*, Cambridge, 1912, p. 283; cf. *ERE* vi. 404ᵇ.
[7] Aristoph. *Wasps*, 438; see *ERE* iii. 270.
[8] Paus. I. xxxvi. 1.
[9] See Herod. viii. 41; *Vita Apollon.* vii. 24; *Orph. Hymn.* xxxii. 11.
[10] O. Gruppe, *Die griech. Mythologie und Religionsgeschichte*, Munich, 1897–1906, ii. 1444.
[11] Ælian, *de Nat. An.* xi. 2.
[12] See *ERE* i. 306ᵃ.
[13] Paus. II. xi. 8, III. xxiii. 7; Ovid, *Metam.* xv. 5; Livy, x. 47.
[14] Paus. VI. xx. 3, 5.
[15] Ælian, *de Nat. An.* xi. 2.
[16] Eur. *Iphig. in Taur.* 286; Æsch. *Eum.* 126, *Choeph.* 1044 ff.

[1] Clem. Alex. *Protr.* 2; Arnobius, v. 21; Diod. Sic. iv. 4, v. 75.
[2] Eur. *Bacch.* 1017.
[3] *Ib.* 101, 687; Athen. v. 28; Clem. Alex. *Protr.* ii. 12; Galen, *de Antid.* i. 6, xiv. 45.
[4] Clem. Alex. *Protr.* ii. 12.
[5] Macrob. I. xii. 24; Plut. *Cæsar*, 9.
[6] Hyginus, *Fab.* 166; Lucian, *Philops.* 22; Paus. v. xix. 1, VIII. xxix. 3.
[7] Herod. viii. 41; Paus. IX. xxxix. 11; Aristoph. *Clouds*, 506; Lucian, *Dial. Mort.* iii. 2; Philostr. *Vita Apollon.* viii. 19.
[8] Pliny, *HN* xxix. 72.
[9] Ælian, *de Nat. An.* ix. 16; Propert. *Eleg.* iv. 8.
[10] M. C. Harrison, *FL* xviii. [1907] 187; Pliny, *HN* vii. 2.
[11] *RA* xxx. [1897] 313, xix. [1882] 322.
[12] J. L. Courcelle-Seneuil, *Les Dieux gaulois, d'après les monuments figurés*, Paris, 1910, p. 80.
[13] See J. A. MacCulloch, *Religion of the Ancient Celts*, Edinburgh, 1911, p. 166.
[14] J. Romilly Allen, *The Early Christian Monuments of Scotland*, with introd. by J. Anderson, Edinburgh, 1903, pt. i. p. xxxiii, and plates.
[15] For the serpent's egg in Celtic lore see *ERE* iii. 297ᵃ, 413ᵇ.

whom the son of Ialdabaoth was Nous ὀφιόμορφος, from whom were derived spirit, soul, and mundane things, and the cause of all wickedness. Hence, as the enemy of mankind, he was not honoured by these groups of Ophites.[1] In the system of Justin, Naas, or the serpent, is the principle of evil, commits adultery with Eve, and afflicts the spirit of Elohim in man.[2] The Severians also regarded the serpent as evil and the vine as the product of intercourse between it and earth—perhaps the reflexion of a pagan myth.[3]

Others regarded the serpent as good, thus reverting unconsciously to the belief adumbrated in the Semitic Fall myth of the wise serpent, because his action produced good results in disobedience to the Demiurge, or he represented an intelligent principle—*e.g.*, in the case of the sect which identified Sophia and the serpent.[4] To the Peratæ the Son and the serpent were identical, and the Naassenes worshipped Naas as the moist principle which is good and in which all things subsist.[5] An actual cult of a serpent was probably limited to a few extremists—*e.g.*, some described by Epiphanius; the others regarded the serpent merely as a symbol of higher powers.

Epiphanius says of this group: 'They keep a living serpent in a chest, and at the time of the mysteries entice him out by placing bread before him. The door being opened, he comes forth and having ascended the table he twines himself round the bread. This they call a perfect *sacrifice*. They not only break and distribute this among the votaries, but whoever desires may kiss the serpent. This they call the Eucharist, and they conclude by singing a hymn through him to the Supreme Father.'[6]

On Ophite gems the serpent is frequently represented in various aspects; *e.g.*, the Egyptian god Chnubis, identified with Iao Sabaoth, is depicted as a serpent with a human head.

In the apocryphal *Acts of Philip* the apostle is said to have preached in Ophioryma (Hierapolis), 'where they set up images of serpents and worshipped them,' and his persecutors are 'children of the serpent,' or Echidna, who is identified with the devil. Finally Philip and John expel the serpent—a distorted reading of fact, for the serpent-cult must have continued in Hierapolis long after apostolic days.[7] This serpent-cult was probably connected with that of Cybele. On coins of Hierapolis snake-emblems appear, or Cybele presents a cup to a snake, and in the *Acts* serpents are called 'sons of the goddess'—*i.e.* her sacred animals or representatives. Wine was offered to a viper in the temple.[8] Possibly the Gnostic reverence for the serpent was influenced by the pagan cult of a goddess associated or identified with a snake.

2. The serpent as embodiment of the dead.—Certain snakes haunt houses and burial-places, and partly for this reason they are thought to embody ghosts of the dead, returned to their old abodes or lingering round the grave.

(*a*) *Lower races.*—This is a common Bantu belief, and with the Zulus the *amatongo* are the dead in snake form, the reptiles having come out of their bodies. If a man sees a snake on his son's grave, he says, 'This is my son,' and snakes in houses are identified with the dead by marks or scars once borne by these. They cause a happy feeling to the living, who sacrifice to them and feed them with milk.[9] Among the Thonga woods where ancestral chiefs are buried are tabu, and the dead frequently appear as snakes. Sacrifice is made to them from time to time.[10] Among the Eastern Bantu spirits sometimes take this form for mischief. Such a snake is killed, because this slays the ghost or prevents its further embodiment, but an apology is made to it.[11] The Suk regard the appearance of a snake in a house as denoting that the ghost is hungry, and that, if it is not fed, all in the house will die. But such a snake may be killed outside the hut.[12] The El Kiboron, a Masai tribe, think that the bones of married men become a snake and return to the hut, where they are fed with milk.[13] Ghost-snakes are fed with honey and milk by the Akikuyu, and, if one is accidentally killed, the elders are summoned, a sheep is killed, and all must partake of it, the culprit wearing part of the skin lest his wife and children die.[14] The Nandi kill snakes in houses, but, when one is found on a woman's bed, it is the spirit of an ancestor and an omen that her next child will be safely born. It is fed with milk.[15] Among the Bahima the bodies of dead princes and princesses are thought to produce snakes, which are cared for in temples by the priests.[1] The Kafirs venerate the python, because it embodies the spirit of a dead chief; to slay a python was punishable by death.[2] Medicine-men and the rich among the Masai become snakes when the body decays, reappear in their huts, and are fed with milk.[3]

The belief occurs sporadically in N. America, the Moquis holding that men of the Rattle-snake clan become rattle-snakes at death, and the Apaches that snakes are connected with the elders or dead men of the tribe.[4] The snake is sometimes identified with the soul, as when seen coming out of a dead person's mouth. Several S. American tribes also have this belief. Women who look upon the Jurupari mysteries of Brazilian tribes become serpents or crocodiles at death, instead of going to paradise.[5]

Among the Tami of New Guinea spirits may be called up as snakes which give oracles through a seer, and among the Papuans of Geelvink Bay, who make images of the dead in which the spirit resides and communicates with the living, those of dead women are represented holding a serpent with both hands.[6] In Kiriwina (E. New Guinea) a chief may appear as a snake in a hut and is honoured but also asked to go, as his appearance is a bad omen.[7] In central Melanesia the dead may appear as snakes—*e.g.*, in a sacred place—and are held sacred, and in the Pelew Islands such snakes are never killed. According to New Britain belief, the dead are men by day and snakes by night.[8]

In Indonesia soul-substance, as distinct from soul, may animate snakes which come out of holes from the under world.[9] The Dayaks believe that spirits (*untu*) appear as snakes, and, if they enter a house, it is to carry off the living. But they are fed, and anything found in their mouths is kept as a charm.[10] With the Ibans of Borneo, who believe in a man's *ngarong*, or secret spirit-helper, usually an ancestor, the *ngarong* may be a snake, and all of the same species are reverenced by the individual who is helped.[11]

(*b*) *Japanese, Chinese, and Arabian.*—Ancestral snakes are also believed in by the Chams and Assamese,[12] and in older Japan and China there are legends of snakes appearing from graves or in coffins, as if the belief also existed there.[13] This is also an occasional Arab belief, for in Upper Egypt at Shaikh Haredi, the tomb of a saint of that name, in cases of sickness a virgin was sent to it and a serpent came forth, hung about her neck, and was carried to the sick man's bedside. Another account says that several women visit the place once a year, and the serpent twines round the neck of the loveliest.[14] In ancient Egypt it was the privilege of the dead to assume any form by means of 'words of power,' and among them were those of serpent or crocodile.[15]

(*c*) *Greek and Roman.*—Among the Greeks the snake was the symbol of the grave and of the spirit contained in it, especially spirits of worshipful heroes, often represented in art and tradition as snakes or accompanied by snakes, their doubles. The idea was doubtless derived from the fact that snakes haunted tombs. In legends snakes were seen close to the dead or crawling from their beds, or the dead turned into snakes (Cadmus and Harmonia).[16] There was also a theory that the marrow of the dead became a snake.[17] A woman or goddess (Hygeia, daughter of Asklepios) feeding a snake with milk is a common Greek artistic *motif*, recalling the savage custom of thus feeding spirit-snakes and perhaps arising from a similar custom in Greece. Analogous to this among the Romans was the symbolizing of the *genius* or *juno*—the guardian-spirit or other self—as a snake, and the keeping of tame snakes in large numbers in temples and houses.[18] The snake is already figured on Etruscan monuments, and it was painted on the walls of Roman houses, sometimes approaching

1 Iren. *adv. Hær.* I. xxviii. 3 (ed. Harvey).
2 Hippolytus, *Refut. omn. Hær.* v. 20 f.
3 Epiph. *adv. Hær.* 45.
4 Iren. I. xxviii. 8.
5 Hipp. v. 11 f.; v. 4.
6 Epiph. i. 37; cf. art. OPHITISM.
7 *Acta Apostolorum Apocrypha*, ed. R. A. Lipsius and M. Bonnet, Leipzig, 1891–1903, ii. pt. 2; W. M. Ramsay, *The Cities and Bishoprics of Phrygia*, Oxford, 1895–97, i. 87.
8 *Acta Ap. Apoc.* II. ii. 51.
9 Callaway, *Religious System of the Amazulu*, pp. 8, 12, 196 ff., etc.; E. Casalis, *Les Bassoutos*, Paris, 1859, p. 246; D. Leslie, *Among the Zulus and Amatongas*², Edinburgh, 1875, pp. 47, 120.
10 H. A. Junod, *The Life of a S. African Tribe*, Neuchâtel, 1912–13, ii. 351 ff.
11 D. Macdonald, *Africana*, London, 1882, i. 62; J. Macdonald, *JAI* xxii. 114.
12 M. W. H. Beech, *The Suk*, Oxford, 1911, p. 20.
13 M. Merker, *Die Masai*, Berlin, 1904, p. 202; cf. also *ERE* viii. 482ᵃ.
14 C. W. Hobley, *JRAI* xli. [1911] 408.
15 A. C. Hollis, *The Nandi*, Oxford, 1909, p. 90.

1 J. Roscoe, *JRAI* xxxvii. [1907] 101 f.
2 Stow, p. 148.
3 Hollis, p. 307. For the Nyanja belief, resembling the Egyptian (see below), see *ERE* ix. 420ᵇ.
4 J. G. Bourke, *FL* ii. [1884] 435 f.
5 *ERE* i. 383ᵇ, ii. 836ᵃ.
6 G. Bamler, in R. Neuhauss, *Deutsch Neu-Guinea*, Berlin, 1911, iii. 516; J. G. Frazer, *The Belief in Immortality*, London, 1913, p. 308.
7 G. Brown, *Melanesians and Polynesians*, London, 1910, p. 238 f.
8 R. H. Codrington, *The Melanesians*, Oxford, 1891, p. 178 f.; P. Rascher, *AA* xxix. [1904] 209 f.
9 *ERE* vii. 238ᵇ.
10 E. Dunn, *Anthropos*, i. [1906] 182.
11 Hose-McDougall, ii. 90; E. H. Gomes, *Seventeen Years among the Sea Dyaks of Borneo*, London, 1911, p. 143.
12 E. Aymonier, *RHR* xxiv. [1891] 267; *ERE* i. 538ᵃ, iii. 348ᵇ.
13 *Nihongi*, tr. W. G. Aston, London, 1896, i. 210; De Groot, *Rel. System of China*, iv. 218.
14 F. L. Norden, *Travels in Egypt and Nubia*, Eng. tr., 2 vols., London, 1757, ii. 28 f.; R. Pococke, *A Description of the East*, in Pinkerton's *Voyages*, xv. 269.
15 E. A. W. Budge, *Egyptian Magic*, London, 1899, p. 230.
16 Plut. *Cleomenes*, 39; Porph. *Vita Plot.* 103, ed. Didot; Ovid, *Metam.* iv. 563 f.
17 Plut. *loc. cit.*; Ovid, *Metam.* xv. 389; Pliny, *HN* x. 84 [64]; cf. *ERE* vi. 653ᵃ.
18 W. W. Fowler, *The Roman Festivals of the Period of the Republic*, London, 1899, p. 104; Pliny, *HN* xxix. 72; Servius, *ad Æn.* v. 95.

an altar. Doubtless all this was connected with an older belief in the ghost embodied in a snake. Æneas, seeing the snake coming out of his father's tomb and tasting his offering, was perplexed as to whether it was the *genius loci* or an attendant on his father.[1] In some cases life was supposed to be dependent on the safety of the house-snake; *e.g.*, when the tame serpent of Tiberius was devoured by ants, he drew the augury from it that he must guard against attack from the multitude.[2]

(*d*) *Russian*.—In Russia the presence of snakes in a cottage is a good omen. They are fed with milk, and to kill them is a sin. This is apparently a relic of the time when a belief in ancestral snakes existed among the Slavs, Lithuanians, and Wends.[3]

3. Serpents in the mysteries.—The ritual use of a serpent in Asiatic and Greek mysteries is connected with the aspect of certain divinities as snakes.

In the initiation to the rites of the Phrygian Sabazios, whose symbol and embodiment was a snake, a golden snake was let down into the bosom of the candidate and taken away again from the lower parts. Clement of Alexandria calls this 'the serpent gliding over the breast'—this serpent crawling over the breasts of the initiated being the deity.[4] This rite was also adopted in the Dionysiac mysteries.[5] In these a snake was carried in a *cista*, the snake being the god himself. The *cista*, with the snake emerging from vine leaves, is represented on coins of the cities of Asia Minor of the Roman period, and Clement speaks of the *cista* in which was a snake, the symbol of Dionysos Bassareus, having previously spoken of the box in which the Kabeiroi exhibited the φαλλός of Dionysos to the Tyrrhenians to worship.[6] In the Arretophoria, performed for the fertility of women and fields, 'sacred things which may not be named were carried about, made of cereal paste, *i.e.* images of snakes and of the forms of men,' viz. φαλλοί.[7] Snake and φαλλός are here parallel as symbols of a deity, under both of which Dionysos was represented.[8] In the Eleusinia, according to Clement of Alexandria, some object was taken by the initiate from a *cista*, put into a basket, and from the basket again put into the chest.[9] This object has been conjectured to be a φαλλός, for a representation of the mystic basket shows a φαλλός among fruit, and Dieterich thinks that what was done with the snake—drawing it through the bosom—was also done with the φαλλός.[10]

The rite was one expressive of sexual and mystic union with the god, as Zeus or Sabazios as a serpent had entered εἰς κόρης κόλπον. The god was hailed as ὑποκόλπιε, according to an Orphic hymn. 'In relation to the god both men and women were as female.' In such a rite snake and φαλλός were one and the same, and women imitated the divine action. Such rites may have given rise to the stories of sons born of human mothers by divinities in the form of a serpent.[11]

The *cista* of the mysteries of Isis may also have contained a snake.[12]

Besides the above, certain facts point to the connexion between serpent and φαλλός.[13] In Algonquian myth, at creation, the φαλλός of Geechee Manito-ah being in his way, he wrung it off and threw it into the bush, where it became Wau-kau-thee, the Rain-Serpent.[14] Elsewhere in America the φαλλός 'was correlated or identical with the serpent.'[15] If the boundary-stones in Babylon were phallic, the presence of the serpent wreathed round them is significant. The figure of Nergal as a monster on a Babylonian plaque shows the φαλλός as a serpent, and 'the serpent of conception' is spoken of in certain texts.[16] In India the serpent—*e.g.*, in the Saiva cult—is associated with sexual powers, and in the temple of Viśveśara at Benares the *liṅgam* is sometimes represented with a serpent coiled round it.[17] C. Schoebel, following certain Talmudists, Agrippa of Cologne, and others, identifies the tree of knowledge, serpent, and φαλλός in the narrative of Gn 3.[18] The connexion of snake and φαλλός is perhaps one reason, added to the snake being regarded as an earth-spirit, why it is so commonly associated with fertility, as so often noted above.[1]

4. The serpent in magical rites.—It is not surprising that such a mysterious animal as the serpent should be used in magical rites, and in some languages the word for 'serpent' has derivatives or cognates referring to magic or intercourse with demons, while the serpent is often a symbol of culture-gods and gods of wisdom, and is connected with healing.

(*a*) The common idea that the representation of a noxious being will drive off that being or other noxious creatures is perhaps one explanation of the brazen serpent story in Nu 21[6ff.].

In Egypt a serpent-head amulet guarded its wearer from snake-bite in this world and the next. The *uræus* on the crown was supposed to throw itself on the king's enemies, and to have compelling power over the gods when the *uræus* crown was placed by Nut on the head of the deceased.[2] In Athens snake-amulets are placed on the newly-born to protect them against snake-demons.[3] Perhaps the golden serpents which Clement of Alexandria condemns as a female decoration were really worn as amulets.[4] Gregory of Tours tells of a bronze serpent found in a Paris sewer on the removal of which snakes infested the city.[5] Among savages, too, amulets resembling snakes, or a snake tatued on the body, protect against snake-bite.[6] In Romagna serpents, head downward and interlaced, are painted on walls to keep away the evil eye.[7]

(*b*) The skin of the snake forms a part of the American Indian 'medicine-bag,' and medicine-men among the Nandi receive power from snakes carried in their bag.[8] A wand in the form of a snake was used by Egyptian magicians, and also in the death ritual to heal the wound made by the adze in opening the eyes and lips of the deceased. Buried with him, such a wand gave him power over the dead.[9] The skin of a serpent is also mentioned as a magico-medical remedy by Marcellus in the 4th cent., and it has still such properties in modern Tuscany.[10]

(*c*) Eating a serpent's flesh, or anointing with its fat, or applying part of its body to the wound, was a remedy against snake-bite among Greeks, Romans, Arabs, Jews, American Indians, Abipones, Thonga, and other races, and is also found in folk-medicine in many lands still—an example of the principle that like cures like.[11]

Hence fennel cured snake-bite because snakes ate it.[12] Again, part of the war medicine of the American Indians was a fragment of a serpent, to give skill in war. Its blood was given to women in child-bed, because, the snake being immortal, the blood had vital influences.[13] Here, too, the virtue of the 'serpent's egg' and of the so-called adder's stone may be noticed.[14]

(*d*) The serpent is associated with healing rites over a wide area, for no very obvious reason, but perhaps because of its supposed wisdom.

This is seen in the case of the Greek Asklepios and other divinities and in the Semitic association of serpents with healing springs. In Madagascar a god of healing was patron of serpents, and his priest carried a serpent in the procession of the god.[15]

As the snake sloughed its skin, this became a folk-explanation of its connexion with Asklepios. The sloughing symbolized the healing art.[16]

(*e*) Omens are often drawn from the sight of serpents, and it is often considered unlucky to see one, as among the Kenyahs and Thonga and many other peoples.[17]

1 Verg. *Æn.* v. 84; cf. F. B. Jevons, *Plutarch's Romane Questions*, London, 1892, p. xlvii f.; *ERE* ii. 24[b].

2 Suet. *Tiberius*, 72.

3 See art. SERPENT-WORSHIP (Teutonic and Balto-Slavic).

4 Arnobius, *adv. Gentes*, v. 21; Clem. Alex. *Protr.* ii. 16; Firmicus Maternus, *de Err. prof. Rel.* 11; cf. Justin Martyr, *Apol.* i. 27.

5 See art. MYSTERIES (Greek, Phrygian, etc.), § 1 (*c*).

6 L. Anson, *Numismata Græca*, London, 1911, pt. i. p. 936; Clem. Alex. *Protr.* ii. 19; cf. Plutarch, *Alex.* 2.

7 Schol. on Lucian, *Dial. Mer.* ii. 1; cf. J. E. Harrison, *Prolegomena to the Study of Greek Religion*, London, 1903, p. 122.

8 Gruppe, p. 1423.

9 Clem. Alex. *Protr.* ii. 21.

10 Dieterich, *Eine Mithrasliturgie*, p. 125 f.

11 Cf. Dieterich, p. 123 f., *de Hymnis Orphicis*, Marburg, 1891, p. 38; Gruppe, pp. 866, 1423; Ramsay, i. 94, 293; see also below, § 6.

12 Cf. Ovid, *Amor.* ii. 13; Juvenal, vi. 537; see also art. MYSTERIES (Egyptian).

13 Cf. E. Gerhard, *Griech. Mythologie*, Berlin, 1854–55; *ERE* v. 829.

14 Owen, p. 36.

15 Brinton, p. 177, *Nagualism*, Philadelphia, 1894, p. 49 f.

16 See § 1 (*r*); Perrot-Chipiez, p. 363 f.; *ERE* ii. 644, note ‖.

17 Crooke, *PR*[2] ii. 124; M. Monier-Williams, *Brāhmanism and Hindūism*[4], London, 1891, p. 439; J. H. Rivett-Carnac, *JASB* lii. [1879] 13.

18 *Le Mythe de la femme et du serpent*, Paris, 1876.

1 See art. PHALLISM.

2 See art. CROWN, vol. iv. p. 341; H. M. Tirard, *The Book of the Dead*, London, 1910, p. 28.

3 Gruppe, p. 902.

4 Clem. Alex. *Pæd.* ii. 13.

5 Greg. of Tours, *Hist. ecclés. des Francs*, French tr., Paris, 1874, viii. 33.

6 See *ERE* iii. 395[b], i. 538; cf. Brinton, p. 133.

7 Leland, p. 168. In Annam serpents are painted on the body to prevent snake-bite (*ERE* i. 538[b]).

8 Hollis, p. 51.

9 Tirard, p. 26.

10 Leland, p. 283.

11 Pliny, *HN* xxix. 71; Gruppe, p. 1274; *ERE* viii. 253[a] (Arabs); *JE* xi. 203 (Jews); M. Dobrizhoffer, *An Account of the Abipones*, Eng. tr., London, 1822, ii. 290 f.; Junod, ii. 317, 419.

12 Pliny, *HN* xix. 23.

13 Brinton, pp. 133, 140.

14 See *ERE* iii. 297[a], 113[b]. For love-philtres made from serpents' flesh see *ERE* i. 542[a].

15 J. Sibree, *The Great African Island*, London, 1880, p. 268.

16 J. G. Frazer, *Pausanias's Description of Greece*, London, 1898, iii. 66; see also art. DISEASE AND MEDICINE.

17 Hose-McDougall, ii. 73, 79; Junod, ii. 489; *ERE* i. 526[b], 541[b].

(*f*) Power over snakes is sometimes ascribed to sorcerers, or the snake is used by them as a 'sending'—a creature sent forth to produce disease, to wound, or to kill.[1]

Serpents were thus sent as agents of his anger by the Malagasy deity already mentioned.[2] In Calabar a tribe levied toll on all who passed. Refusal to pay resulted in a snake being sent after them, which tied their legs, and the people then came and robbed them. Medicine-leaves also protect houses in Calabar, and fetishes among the Baganda; and, if any robber approaches, snakes rush out at him.[3] Bushmen sorcerers are said to be able to whistle up snakes, which coil round their neck in the presence of spectators.[4] The Chiriguano believe that they would never die unless, *inter alia*, bitten by a snake—really a sorcerer in that form.[5]

(*g*) Charms and magic formulæ are often used as remedies for snake-bite or as protection against snakes.[6]

(*h*) As certain snakes are susceptible to musical, rhythmical sounds or movements, these are used by snake-charmers to exhibit their power over them.

This has occurred in Africa and in many Eastern lands from ancient down to modern times; among the American Indians charming was used by magicians to prove their intercourse with unseen powers and the power given them by these so that they handled snakes with impunity.[7] Possibly snake-charmers produce some cataleptic or hypnotic state in the animals.[8] The supposed immunity of the charmer should be compared with that seen in the case of the Hopi, the devotees in the Dionysiac mysteries, the Psylli and Ophiogenes, and the *kebeet* among the Abipones.[9]

5. Demoniac and mythical serpents and dragons.—Although the serpent is frequently worshipped, its harmful character and the repulsion which it arouses, its frequent large size and strength, and the mystery of its movements have often caused a sinister character to be given it, and made it an embodiment of demoniac powers. Because of the brightness of its eye and its power of fascination over animals the serpent was commonly supposed to have the evil eye. The larger species, possibly also the dim memory of extinct species or species no longer found in any region, affected man's imagination, and both fear and fancy gave rise to a belief in mythical serpents or dragons of vast size and powers, and often the cause of various natural phenomena. They have frequently many heads; they have wings and feet; and they breathe fire and smoke. Demoniac and mythical serpents are often the object of belief where a cult of serpents exists, showing that very different emotions are aroused by serpents of various kinds.

Some examples of demoniac and mythical serpents have already been referred to. The Sea Dayaks of Sarawak tell of a huge snake which came down from heaven and fed on the rice. A man slew it and ate its flesh; the result was the deluge.[10] Another myth tells how the python was once the most poisonous of snakes, and killed a man who took fish from its fish-pond. Thinking afterwards that he had come to life, it vomited its poison into the sea, where a snake, Ular Berang, swallowed some of the poison, and the sea-snakes took the rest. The Ular Berang is rarely seen, but is very dangerous.[11] Certain snakes, like other animals, possess *badi*—*i.e.* a bad spirit or mischief of a dangerous kind—while the *badi* of some large trees is a more individual spirit which may appear as a snake.[12] Both in Burma and in Borneo dangerous snakes are held to be embodiments of evil spirits.[13] Among the Negrito tribes of Borneo eclipses are caused by a python trying to swallow sun and moon or to embrace the latter.[14] According to the Ibans, the Flood was the result of men's wounding a huge python. Soon after the rain caused a flood which drowned every one except a woman.[1] The American Indian myth of the great horned serpent[2]—the embodiment of lightning or of the waters, and slain by a god or hero—is perhaps a variant of the myth of chaos, represented by a monster, and overcome by a god. In Musquakie myth a huge snake with hard, white scales, deer's horns, and spitting fire, rose from a lake, but was vanquished by the hero, Hot Hand.[3] In the arid south-west region, where the cañons are quickly flooded, men are said to have lived underground at one time, but to have been driven to earth's surface by a huge snake which caused a deluge.[4] In other American Indian myths (Ojibwa, etc.) serpents who have slain the hero's brother cause a deluge when the hero avenges them.[5] On the other hand, in British New Guinea, Raudalo, king of snakes, put an end to the deluge by pursuing the waters to their accustomed bed.[6] A Toba Battak myth tells how a great serpent lay on the primeval ocean and engulfed the earth at its creation by turning it over. But the Heavenly Maid caused eight suns to dry up the waters and then pinned the serpent to a rock.[7] The Thonga believe in the vast snake, Buwumati, dwelling in lakes invisibly and heard crying when rain falls. If any one should chance to see it, he dies.[8] The Mexican sun-god Tonatiuh cut in pieces the coloured wood-snake, as Manco Capac in Peru and Bochica in Bogota slew the serpents of the waters.[9] The Ayni believe that evil spirits are incarnated in serpents, as do also the Ibibios of S. Nigeria.[10]

The monstrous demoniac serpents of Babylon and Egypt have already been described.[11] But Egyptian myth knew also of a beneficent serpent, its body overlain with gold, and 30 cubits in length, living on an island, where it apparently was the guardian of the dead, just as serpents guarded the under world and are figured on tombs as guardians. A human-headed *uræus* of large size is sculptured on an Ethiopian temple.[12] In Greece Typhon, son of Tartaros and Gaia, was demon of the whirlwind and possessed 100 serpent-heads. He attacked Zeus, who felled him with a thunderbolt and set Ætna upon him. His consort was Echidna, half-woman, half-serpent, whose progeny were the Sphinx, Chimæra, Hydra, and the Dragon of the Hesperides.[13] Hydra, with nine heads, dwelt in the swamps of Lerna, laying waste all the land till Heracles slew it. Heracles also slew the dragon or snake of the Hesperides, which is represented as twined round a tree from below which issues a well; therefore it is guardian of the waters.[14] Jason, Perseus, and Cadmus were also slayers of dragons in Greek myth. Python, a dragon born of Gaia, sought to kill Leto because he learned that her son would be fatal to him. Zeus interfered, but Leto's son Apollo slew the Pytho at Delphi, where he buried the body and instituted the Pythian games.

Behind this lies the myth of the cult of a prophetic snake at Delphi, embodiment of a goddess. The combat with Apollo has been explained as the seizing of the oracle by a tribe of Apollo-worshippers, who changed the shrine to his. The shrine in N. Greece where serpents, the god's play-things, were fed by virgin-priestesses may also have been an ancient shrine of a snake-goddess.[15]

Ancient Persia, in its dualistic scheme, regarded some animals—*e.g.*, the serpent—as of the evil creation, while certain others were created to destroy them. It also embodied the evil power in a mythic dragon created by Angra Mainyu to destroy the faithful—the dragon Azi Dahāka, three-headed and immensely strong, sometimes also identified with Babylon (Bawri) or the Arabians.[16] He was conquered by Atar, son of Ahura Mazda, a personification of fire,[17] or, in another myth, by Thraētaona, who bound him on Mt. Demavend. At the end of time he will escape and destroy a third of mankind, cattle, and sheep, as well as water, fire, and vegetation, but will be slain by Keresāspa.[18]

---

1 Seligmann, *Melanesians*, p. 282; Junod, ii. 467 (Thonga); *ERE* i. 251^{a} (Ainus); de Groot, *Rel. System of China*, v. 851 (China); cf. art. LYCANTHROPY, vol. viii. p. 218^{a}.

2 Sibree, p. 268.

3 From information supplied by the Rev. J. K. MacGregor; Roscoe, *The Baganda*, p. 15.

4 T. Hahn, *Tsuni-‖Goam*, London, 1881, p. 80.

5 G. E. Church, *Aborigines of S. America*, London, 1913, p. 237.

6 Tirard, p. 99; Seligmann, *The Veddas*, p. 197 f.

7 Brinton, p. 131; Müller, p. 277 (Brazil); *ERE* i. 792^{b}.

8 Cf. *ERE* i. 434^{b}.

9 Dobrizhoffer, ii. 67.

10 I. H. N. Evans, *JRAI* xliii. [1913] 469 f.; E. Dunn, *Anthropos*, i. 17.

11 N. Annandale and H. C. Robinson, *Fasciculi Malayenses*, London, 1903–06, pt. i. p. 88.

12 *Ib.* pp. 100, 104.

13 *ERE* iii. 25^{a}, vii. 250^{b}.

14 W. W. Skeat and C. O. Blagden, *Pagan Races of the Malay Peninsula*, London, 1906, ii. 203, 224. A dragon-like monster is supposed to swallow candidates for initiation in New Guinea (see *ERE* viii. 826^{a}, reff.).

1 Hose-McDougall, ii. 144; cf. H. Ling Roth, *Natives of Sarawak*, i. 301.

2 See § 1 (*h*).

3 Owen, p. 4; cf. *ERE* vi. 885^{a} for a Huron mythical serpent.

4 Alexander, *N. American Mythology*, pp. 161, 299 ff.; cf. *ERE* iv. 547^{b}.

5 *Ib.* pp. 274, 301; Frazer, *Folk-Lore in the Old Testament*, i. 302.

6 A. Ker, *Papuan Fairy Tales*, London, 1910, p. 30; cf. W. W. Gill, *Journ. of the Polynesian Soc.*, xxi. [1912] 61 (Cook Island version); G. Turner, *Samoa a Hundred Years Ago*, London, 1884, p. 288.

7 J. Warneck, *Religion der Batak*, Leipzig, 1909, p. 28; cf. *ERE* vii. 796^{a} for the dragon of the Laos. The Bunun of Formosa have also a myth connecting a huge serpent with a deluge (Frazer, *Folk-Lore in the Old Testament*, i. 232).

8 Junod, ii. 318.

9 Müller, p. 566.

10 *L'Anthropologie*, iv. [1893] 431; P. A. Talbot, *Geog. Journal*, xliv. [1914] 296.

11 For a Hittite mythical serpent see *ERE* vi. 725^{b}.

12 W. M. F. Petrie, *Egyptian Tales*, London, 1895, ii. 818; G. Maspero, *Contes populaires de l'Egypte ancienne*, Paris, 1882, p. 133 f.

13 Hyginus, *Fab.* ch. 151, 152.

14 J. E. Harrison, *Themis*, p. 431.

15 *Ib.* pp. 428, 433, 436; L. R. Farnell, *CGS* iii. 9 f., iv. 181; W. S. Fox, *Greek and Roman Mythology* (=*Mythology of all Races*, vol. i.), Boston, 1916, p. 178; *ERE* ix. 493^{b}.

16 *SBE* iv.[2] [1895] 258 f., xxiii. [1883] 60.

17 *Yasht*, xix. 47 f.

18 *SBE* v. [1880] 119; *Dīnkarṭ*, ix. 13. 5; cf. ix. 15. 1 ff.; *Bundahiś*, xxix.; cf. Rev $8^{7f.}$ 9^{15} $20^{2.7f.}$; see also *Yasna*, ix. 11; *Yasht*, xix. 40 f.

In Firdausi's *Shāh Nāmah* Azi Dahāka is an Arab king with a dragon-like face and two snakes on his shoulders, the product of the kisses of Iblis. These were fed with human flesh. The poem follows closely the Armenian Zoroastrian version of the myth, in which Hruden (Thraētaona) is the conqueror of Azi.[1]

Dragons exist frequently also in Hindu, Teutonic, Slavic, and Celtic myth and folk-tale, in Mandæan and Manichæan mythology—in both cases derived from Babylonian or Persian belief—and also in Gnosticism.[2]

In the *Pistis Sophia* the disk of the sun is described as a great dragon with his tail in his mouth—an Egyptian conception;[3] and dragons form the rudder of the ship of the moon. The outer darkness, where souls incapable of redemption are cast, is a great dragon encircling the earth, with its tail in its mouth, and containing twelve chambers of punishment. So in a Gnostic system described by Epiphanius[4] the archon of the lowest heaven is a dragon encircling the earth and swallowing souls which have not knowledge. Both in Gnostic and in Catholic prayers for deliverance of the soul on its upward way there is mentioned the opposing dragon or serpent. The dragon as Hades in *Pistis Sophia* is probably a reminiscence of the Egyptian Apap. In the *Apocalypse of Baruch* there is a huge dragon in the third heaven and also in Hades. Its belly forms Hades, and the dragon devours the wicked.[5]

The Gnostic idea of the dragon or serpent as an evil world-principle, identical with the devil, encircling the earth and holding it in his power,[6] may be referred to in the *Hymn of the Pearl*, ascribed to Bardesanes. The pearl is in the sea, hard by the serpent.[7] The sea is the mythic chaotic deep, which, encircling the world, is sometimes compared in Babylonian mythology to a snake—'the river of the snake.'[8] This idea is also found in Egypt, where the myth of Apap bound in the deep is also figured as that of the ocean itself representing Apap bound, girdling the earth and keeping it together, yet ever trying to burst his bands and destroy it.[9] A Ptolemaic writer, Horapollo, says that the Egyptians represented the universe as a serpent devouring its tail—a subject depicted also in Gnostic gems.[10] In Rabbinic belief Leviathan was coiled round the earth, and the sea appeared to Alexander, when carried into the air by griffins, as a snake encircling the earth.[11] So, too, the *mið-garðr's-ormr* of the Edda, the serpent encircling the earth, is probably the ocean.[12] The Sia believe in cosmic serpents, one for each quarter and one for each earth and heaven.[13] The serpent was one of the symbols of the elements in Mithraism.[14]

6. Myths about serpents.—(*a*) *Earthquakes.*—The previous idea of the serpent coiled round the earth is perhaps connected with a series of myths in which earthquakes are caused by serpents or dragons which support the earth or swell underground, and whose movements shake the earth.[15]

In Polynesian myths the sea-serpent, by standing erect, raised the sky from the earth—the two having previously cleaved together.[16]

(*b*) *The serpent and the waters.*—In many myths a dragon or huge serpent lays waste the land, until the king offers his daughter in marriage to the knight who will slay it. Or a maiden must be given to it at intervals; at last it is the turn of the king's daughter, and then the monster is slain by a hero or saint or divinity. In some of these tales the serpent lives in a lake and keeps back the water-supply. In others a water-spirit does this, or the spirit is embodied in a serpent. Such tales are found in ancient Babylon and Greece, in all European countries, as well as among Negroes, Mongolians, Japanese, Ainus, Kabyles, Eskimo, and American Indians.[17] They have a basis in fact—in the terror inspired by huge serpents, perhaps propitiated by human sacrifice. Instances of such sacrifices occur sporadically, and divine serpents fed with human flesh have already been referred to. The association of huge serpents with water is in accordance with wide-spread belief.

Bushman belief connected a monstrous horned snake with the waters, and in Hottentot myth fountains contain a snake, and they dry up if it is killed.[1] Arab belief associated the *jinn* in serpent form with medicinal waters, and in Neh 2[13] a 'dragon's well' is mentioned, probably a sacred pool with serpent guardian.[2] In the Greek myth of Cadmus the dragon guarded the well of Dirce, and the Styx was also believed to be guarded by dragons. In Annam the spirit of the waters appears as a serpent, which also takes human form.[3] Celtic myth knows of dragons and serpents in lochs,[4] just as in Guiana and Zuñi tales a serpent lives in a pool sacred to him.[5]

Other myths speak of a serpent-race, like the Indian Nāgas, dwelling under water, and capable of assuming human form.[6] The *dracs* of French folk-lore and water-dwelling snakes in Montenegrin belief are hostile to men, like those of Cambodian and Laotian belief.[7]

(*c*) *The serpent and creation.*—Sometimes the serpent figures as the origin of the world (cf. the Tiamat myth) or as creator.

In the Netherland Islands the serpent which pushed up heaven from earth was cut in pieces, which became the islands, and its blood the stars. In Bushman myth snakes were struck by Cagn and became men. A Saliva myth tells how the Caribs sprang from the flesh of serpents. Among the S. Massim a huge snake cut to pieces is said to have been changed into the reefs.[8] In the Solomon Islands Kahausibware, a spirit in snake form, made men and animals, but was chopped to pieces by a woman, when good things became bad and death entered. The Sioux myth of the first men tells how their feet grew in the ground like trees till a great snake set them free as men.[9]

(*d*) *Origin.*—The origin of snakes themselves is sometimes mythically related.

They were made from fragments of the god Angoi, slain by another god (S.E. Borneo); from the breast of the child of a sky-maiden and a mortal, cut in two (Ifugas of the Philippines, Mandaya); or from a bark-cloth twisted and filled with thorns (E. Africa).[10]

(*e*) *Rainbows and eclipses.*—The rainbow is regarded as a great snake among the Semang (who think that the places where it touches earth are unhealthy to live in), the Shoshone, the Australian aborigines, the Dahomans, the ancient Persians, and many other races.[11] Eclipses are often regarded as caused by the efforts of a serpent or dragon to swallow the sun or moon.[12]

(*f*) *The serpent and immortality.*—The serpent was believed to have no fear of old age,[13] or to be immortal, because it casts its skin,[14] apparently renewing its life. According to many 'origin of death' stories, man was meant to be immortal by the same process, but the serpent received the boon because the messenger sent to man told the serpent this secret, or snakes heard the message and men did not, or because the creator was angry with them.[15] Hence the cast skin of a serpent is a powerful 'medicine.' Among the Lenguas of Para-

1 Cf. *ERE* i. 800[a], iv. 620[b].
2 Cf. § 1 (*x*).
3 Cooper, p. 375.
4 *Adv. Hær.* 26. 40.
5 See, further, art. Mouth, vol. viii. p. 869[a].
6 Cf. *Acts of Thomas*, in *Apoc. Gospels, Acts, and Revelations*, Edinburgh, 1873, p. 407; Origen, *c. Celsum*, vi. 25, 35.
7 A. A. Bevan, 'The Hymn of the Soul,' in *TS*, vol. v. no. 3, Cambridge, 1897.
8 Sayce, p. 116.
9 Max Müller, pp. 104, 106.
10 Cooper, p. 335.
11 *EBi*, col. 1132; J. Grimm, *Teutonic Mythology*, Eng. tr., London, 1882–88, ii. 794.
12 Grimm, *loc. cit.*
13 Stevenson, *11 RBEW*, p. 69.
14 *ERE* viii. 758[b]; see 355[a], 359[b], 360[a], for a Malay cosmic snake.
15 *Ib.* i. 491[b], v. 128[b], vi. 14[b]; *ZE* xvii. [1885] 32 (Bogobos); J. E. Erskine, *Journ. of a Cruise among the Islands of the W. Pacific*, London, 1853, p. 47 (Fiji).
16 Turner, *Samoa*, pp. 284, 288, 292.
17 *ERE* vi. 645[b] (Bab.), 855 (Japan); Ovid, *Metam.* iv. 662 f. (Perseus and Andromeda); the numerous variants are cited in MacCulloch, *CF*, p. 381 ff.

1 Stow, p. 131; Hahn, pp. 53, 77.
2 W. R. Smith[2], p. 168; cf. Jos. *BJ* v. iii. 2.
3 E. S. Hartland, *LP* i. 121 f.; cf. *ERE* vii. 796[a] (Laotians).
4 MacCulloch, *Religion of the Ancient Celts*, p. 188.
5 See § 7 (*a*), (*b*).
6 W. R. S. Ralston, *Russian Folk-tales*, London, 1873, p. 116 (Slavic); P. Rascher, *AA* xxix. 234 (New Britain); Keysser, in Neuhauss, *Deutsch Neu-Guinea*, iii. 202.
7 Gervase of Tilbury, *Otia Imperialia*, in G. W. Leibnitz, *Scriptores Rerum Brunsvicarum*, Hanover, 1710, i. 987; M. E. Durham, *JRAI* xxxix. 97.
8 A. Lang, *Myth, Ritual and Religion*[2], London, 1899, i. 170 (Bushman); J. Gumilla, *Hist. naturelle, civile et géographique de l'Orénoque*, Avignon, 1758, i. 152 (Saliva); Seligmann, *Melanesians*, p. 382.
9 *ERE* viii. 536[a] (Solomon Islands); see also § 1 (*e*); G. Catlin, *The N. Amer. Indians*, new ed., London, 1876, i. 280.
10 Dixon, p. 176 f.; Macdonald, *Africana*, i. 294.
11 Skeat-Blagden, ii. 203, 224; Howitt, p. 431; Alexander, *N. Amer. Mythology*, p. 139; Crooke, *PR*[2], ii. 144; Purchas, xv. 304 (Peru).
12 See *ERE* i. 492, viii. 360, also art. Prodigies and Portents; for the snake as the bridge to paradise see *ERE* ix. 457[b].
13 Plutarch, *de Is. et Osir.* § 74.
14 See § 1 (*t*).
15 The tales are found in New Britain, Bismarck Archipelago, Annam, Borneo, among the Arawaks and the Tamanachiers of the Orinoco; see Frazer, *The Belief in Immortality*, p. 69 f., *Folk-Lore in the Old Testament*, i. 66 ff.; I. H. N. Evans, *JRAI* xliii. 426; Dixon, p. 117 f.

guay all animals, except fish and serpents, are thought to share immortality with men.[1]

In a wide-spread myth a hero restores a friend by using a plant which he has seen a serpent use to bring back another serpent to life, as in the Greek story of Polyidus and Glaucus.[2]

(*g*) *The serpent and the language of birds.*—A common belief existed that eating the flesh or heart of certain snakes, especially of a fabulous white snake, gave the eater wisdom or a knowledge of beast language. As the serpent was regarded often as an embodiment of supernatural wisdom, to eat its flesh caused transference of that to the eater. The serpent was supposed to know beast and bird language, as Democritus thought, because it was generated from the mixed blood of birds.

This belief forms the theme of innumerable folk-tales and existed in ancient times. The gift could also be conferred by a grateful serpent licking the ear of a man, as in the Greek myth of Melampus, or in other ways.[3] In many quarters the snake is believed to give inspiration through its spirit, or to cause possession,[4] and in all parts of the world—Central America, Mexico, among the Haidas and Tlingits, in New Ireland, New Zealand, and the Solomon Islands—representations of a man holding a snake, a lizard, or a frog with its tongue to his tongue are found.[5] The idea is probably that of receiving inspiration from the animal.

(*h*) *The serpent and the magic stone.*—There is a wide-spread belief in the king of serpents who wears a jewelled crown — a magical possession which men try to win.[6]

On such a huge serpent wearing a golden crown the earth was founded, according to a Borneo myth.[7] That the serpent has in its head a jewel or magic stone much coveted by adventurous men, who try to obtain it, is the subject of many tales in India, Malaysia, and Indonesia, and among the American Indians.[8] In Sinhalese myth the stone is dropped by the serpent to give it light; in a similar Nigerian myth, to attract its prey, when the seeker is able to obtain it by craft.[9] Among the Roro-speaking tribes of British New Guinea a sorcerer obtains a black stone from a snake after ritual preparation and by worrying it till it drops the stone, when he runs off with it, pursued by the snake. The stone kills any one touched by it. This bears some resemblance to the Gaulish method of obtaining the 'serpent's egg.'[10] Other tales speak of a magic ring in a serpent's mouth which, once obtained, grants every wish.[11] The Dayaks keep anything found in the mouth of an ancestral snake as a charm.[12]

Somewhat analogous is the Andamanese belief that a small snake produces streams of oxide of iron and white clay by emitting a fluid when disturbed.[13]

(*i*) *The serpent and treasure.*—Another common belief is that dragons lie upon gold, or guard treasure, or have magic possessions—a common Teutonic and Scandinavian belief, shared by the Arabians (the winged serpents guarding incense-trees), and by the Greeks (the dragon-guardian of the golden apples of the Hesperides), Romans, Chanés of S. America, and the tribes of E. Africa.[14]

Because of this mythical connexion with treasure, as well as because deities or heroes with some serpent-attribute—Quetzalcoatl, Kneph, Ea, Indra, Cadmus—were pioneers of civilization and taught men mining and agriculture, A. W. Buckland thought that serpents may have played some part in aiding man to discover metals, and hence were worshipped.[1]

(*j*) In a number of stories having a very different provenance, but showing a certain parallelism, a small worm or snake taken into a house grows to monstrous form and is with difficulty got rid of.[2] Or the snake enters the body of a person, causing great discomfort.[3]

7. Woman and the serpent.—In folk-tale and myth, and occasionally in ritual, woman is brought into relation with the serpent, which is often her lover or husband. This is but one aspect of the world-wide myths in which an animal marries a woman, though frequently the animal is a god in disguise or a being now human, now animal, often as a result of enchantment. But in many instances, especially among savages, the snake is a snake *sans phrase*, because of the method of thought by which no clear distinction is drawn between human and animal forms,[4] possibly also because of the connexion of snake and φαλλός.

(*a*) Of the first series the European examples are mainly variants of the Beauty and the Beast cycle, and the serpent is a youth bewitched to serpent form till a maiden releases him from the enchantment by kissing him or burning his snake-skin.[5]

Greek mythology contains similar stories, though here the serpent is usually a god in disguise.[6] A similar myth was told of Faunus in Roman mythology, possibly because serpents were kept in the temple of the Bona Dea.[7] Both Greek and Roman legend related that gods as serpents were fathers of well-known personages by human mothers.

Olympias, wife of Philip, was approached by the god Ammon as a serpent, and gave birth to Alexander the Great. A serpent was found lying by her as she slept, and, as Olympias was given to the cult of Dionysos, in which serpents figured, the germ of the legend may be found in this.[8] The mother of Aristomenes had united with a god in serpent-form, as also the mother of Aratus. In her case the serpent was Asklepios, and a figurine of her sitting on a serpent existed in the temple of Asklepios at Sicyon.[9] Augustus was the son of a serpentiform deity, and his mother could never get rid of the spots left by the serpent on her body.[10] A similar legend was told of the mother of Scipio the elder.[11] Possibly all such stories arose from the use of serpents in the cult of Dionysos, or from the fact that barren women visited the temple of Asklepios.[12]

According to Athenagoras, Kore, daughter of Rhea, had a monstrous aspect and horns. Then he tells how Zeus did violence to Rhea, who changed herself to a δράκαινα to escape him, when he now became a dragon. In that form also he violated Kore.[13] Reinach sees here two parallel traditions, and thinks that Zeus and Kore had both serpent form and that Zagreus was hatched from an egg as a horned serpent.[14] Parallels from savage folk-tales exist.

In a New Guinea tale a youth is enabled to take serpent form and obtains a girl, afterwards resuming human shape. Or a serpent can take human form and marry human brides.[15] In a Zuñi tale Kóloowisi, the serpent-god, catches a girl, but takes human shape, renouncing his serpent-skin.[16] In Polynesian legend such tales are told of a huge eel which can take human

1 W. B. Grubb, *An Unknown People in an Unknown Land*, London, 1911, p. 125.
2 Hyginus, *Fab.* 136; Pliny, *HN* xxv. 5; Grimm, *Kinder- und Hausmärchen*[9], Berlin, 1870, no. 16; for numerous variants see *CF*, p. 82; J. Bolte and G. Polivka, *Anmerkungen zu den Kinder- und Hausmärchen der Brüder Grimm*, Leipzig, 1913, i. 126 ff.; Frazer, *Pausanias*, iii. 66.
3 Philostr. *Vita Apoll.* i. 20, iii. 9; Pliny, *HN* x. 70; Apollodorus, i. 9. 11; for folk-tale variants see Bolte-Polivka, i. 131 ff.; Frazer, *AR* i. [1863] 166 ff.
4 See § 1; Roscoe, *The Baganda*, p. 318 ff.
5 W. H. Dall, 'On Masks, Labrets, and Certain Aboriginal Customs,' *3 RBEW* [1884], pp. 103, 111 ff.; A. W. Buckland, *JAI* xxi. [1892] 29.
6 Grimm, *Teut. Myth.* ii. 686 f., 1219 f., *Household Tales*, tr. M. Hunt, London, 1884, ii. 77; F. S. Krauss, *Sagen und Märchen der Südslaven*, Leipzig, 1883–84, nos. 62, 107; *ERE* i. 526[b].
7 Dixon, p. 159 f.
8 Crooke, *PR*[2], ii. 143; Dixon, p. 328; Skeat, *Malay Magic*, p. 303; De Laborde, *Relation des Caraïbes*, Paris, 1674, p. 7; *ERE* i. 526[b], iii. 395[a], 503[b].
9 W. L. Hildburgh, *JRAI* xxxviii. [1908] 200; Leonard, *The Lower Niger*, p. 192; cf. Grimm, iv. 1492.
10 Seligmann, *Melanesians*, p. 282; cf. art. CHARMS AND AMULETS (Celtic), vol. iii. p. 412.
11 Dixon, p. 163.
12 E. Dunn, *Anthropos*, i. 182.
13 E. H. Man, *JAI* xii. 155.
14 Grimm, *Teut. Myth.* ii. 689 f., iii. 978 f.; Herod. iii. 107; Phædrus, iv. 19; Nordenskiöld, p. 288; Macdonald, *Africana*, i. 360.

1 A. W. Buckland, *Anthropological Studies*, London, 1891, p. 104 f.
2 W. Mapes, *de Nugis Curialium*, ed. T. Wright, London, 1850, dist. ii. cap. 6; F. Liebrecht, *Zur Volkskunde*, Heilbronn, 1879, p. 66; W. Henderson, *Notes on the Folk-Lore of the N. Counties of England*, London, 1879, p. 287; F. H. Cushing, *Zuñi Folk-tales*, New York, 1901, p. 93; G. Turner, *Samoa*, p. 243; Codrington, p. 403.
3 Seligmann, *Melanesians*, p. 382 (New Guinea); Junod, ii. 229 (Thonga).
4 See art. METAMORPHOSIS, § 3.
5 W. Webster, *Basque Legends*[2], London, 1879, p. 167; A. de Gubernatis, *Novellini popolari*, Milan, 1883, no. 14; Ralston, *The Songs of the Russian People*, London, 1872, p. 174, *Russian Folk-tales*, p. 116; J. H. Knowles, *Folk-tales of Kashmir*, London, 1888, p. 491.
6 Arnobius, *adv. Gentes*, v. 22; Diod. Sic. iv. 4, v. 75.
7 Macrob. i. 12. 24; cf. Plut. *Cæs.* 9.
8 Plut. *Alex.* 3; Lucian, *Dial. Mort.* 13; cf. *ERE* vii. 193[a].
9 *Paus.* II. x. 3, IV. xiv. 7.
10 Suet. *August.* 94; Dio Cass. xlv. i. 2.
11 Livy, xxvi. 19; Aul. Gell. vii. 1.
12 See § 1 (*t*).
13 Athen. *Leg. pro Christianis*, ch. 20; Clem. Alex. *Protr.* ii.; cf. C. A. Lobeck, *Aglaophamus*, Königsberg, 1829, p. 547 ff.
14 S. Reinach, *Cultes, mythes et religions*, Paris, 1905–12, ii. 60.
15 H. H. Romilly, *From my Verandah in New Guinea*, London, 1889, p. 78; Seligmann, *Melanesians*, p. 397.
16 Cushing, p. 93.

form.[1] Similar tales of snakes that can take human shape and marry girls are told among the Kafirs, Formosans, and Negroes of Jamaica.[2] A Rabbinic idea was that, through intercourse of the serpent with Eve, her descendants were corrupted, the serpent having then almost the form of a man.[3]

(*b*) In the second group the serpent has no human form, and the tales, mainly of savage provenance, are extremely realistic and disgusting.

Examples occur among the tribes of New Guinea, the Admiralty Islanders, Eskimo, American Indians, and Guaranos.[4] Echoes of such stories are found in early Christian literature—*e.g.*, the *Acts of Thomas*, where a dragon or snake loved a girl. In the *Visio Pauli* faithless virgins must endure the embraces of serpents in hell.[5]

(*c*) These tales may be connected with actual custom and belief.

The python god Dañh-gbi of the Ewe has many priestesses, and is supposed to marry young novices secretly. According to one writer, the girl is placed in a pit with serpents and told that one will take human form—really one of the priests.[6] The Onyckolum compel a woman to marry, saying that, if she does not, she will marry the great snake Aké.[7] Among the Akikuyu, at the worship of the snake-god, who requires wives, women and girls go to the huts built for him, where, however, the priests visit them. The children are fathered on the god.[8] Girls at initiation among the Basutos are taken to a stream where they are told a great serpent will visit them.[9] The Hottentots believe in a serpent with human organs which visits women in sleep, and a somewhat similar belief is found among the Macusi.[10] A 16th cent. treatise on Brazil says that barren women among the Indians were struck on the hips with a snake, with which soothsaying was also observed, as a means of their having children.[11] Some Australian tribes believe in a serpent which attacks women.[12] In many other instances the serpent seems to be associated with the fruitfulness of women [13]—*e.g.*, in Greece women slept in the temple of Asklepios and thought themselves visited by the serpent-god in their dreams, and their offspring was believed to be the result of this visit. Again, virgin or married priestesses are often associated, though not exclusively, with serpent shrines or ritual, in some instances probably because the serpent representing an earth-goddess was best served by women. The shrines of the pre-Apollonic Pytho and of Gaia, later consecrated to Apollo in N. Greece, the shrine at Lanuvium, that at Shaikh Haredi in Egypt, the temple of the python in Uganda, as well as the ritual of the Thesmophoria, and the wives of the serpent in Dahomey, are cases in point. The ritual with serpents in the Dionysiac mysteries and 'the snake gliding over the breast,' with the meaning already referred to, doubtless give rise to some of the Greek myths. It is also certain that women had serpents as pets among the Greeks and Romans, and that lascivious practices were followed with them. Perhaps these snakes as well as those at Dahomey were trained to these practices.[14]

(*d*) Conversely a man is sometimes the lover of a snake-mistress.

The Koranas believe that the first man and a snake lived together.[15] In Hudson's Island the sea-serpent as woman and earth as man united, and their progeny was the race of men.[16] The Snake clan of the Pueblo Indians is believed to be descended from a snake (alternatively snake and woman) and a man who gained access to the *kiva* of the Snake people. When they assumed snake form, he seized the fiercest, which changed to a beautiful girl, the Snake Maid—a personification of underworld life which fertilizes the maize. The snakes to which she gave birth changed to men and women, ancestors of the Snake clan.[1] In Japan stories of men's wives that are also serpents or dragons at times exist in the early mythology and in popular belief.[2] So in the Greek story the mistress and bride of Menippus is a lamia or serpent, and disappears when discovered by Apollonius.[3] In some folk-tales and ballads a girl is enchanted so that she appears as a reptile until a youth kisses her, when she is retransformed, and in the parallel tales where the hero is thus bewitched.[4] Hindu folk-lore has examples of beings (*e.g.*, the *nagas*) who are women by night and serpents by day.[5] In other instances we have a composite being, half-woman, half-serpent in the lower part of the body. Herodotus cites a myth regarding the origin of the Scythians, progeny of Heracles and Echidna, who was a serpent from the waist down.[6] Such composite beings are known also in India, but the typical example is found in the well-known tale of Mélusine, who, married to Raymond, asked that she should spend one day each week in seclusion. One day he spied upon her and saw her in a bath, half-woman, half-serpent, and, when he called her 'odious serpent,' she left him for ever. In one version she had been cursed by her mother, a fay, to assume this form every Saturday.[7] The story belongs to the 'supernatural bride' cycle, but Mélusine has parallels in Greek nymphs who are serpents from the waist downwards, in Egyptian art, and in the sirens—half-woman, half-fish—the form also of the Semitic Derceto or Atargatis, of Triton, and of Oannes.[8]

The converse form, in which divine beings have snake-faces, is of frequent occurrence in Egypt, as well as *vice versa*. They are also referred to in the so-called Mithras liturgy; and in some mediæval representations of the Fall the serpent has a human head and arms, or even two such heads, to address Adam and Eve at once.[9] Among the Araucanos the servants of Pillan, the chief god, are snakes with men's heads.[10]

(*e*) The fondness of snakes for milk has perhaps given rise to a belief in their sucking the breasts of women, but in certain cases the practice may have been an erotic perversion.

The Hottentots believe that serpents come by night for women to suckle them, and bite them if they refuse.[11] The Mayas believe in an imaginary snake Ekoneil which glides into houses of nursing mothers, covers their nostrils with its tail, and sucks their breasts.[12] In Welsh tradition the wings of mythical flying snakes arose because they had drunk women's milk spilt on the ground and had eaten sacramental bread.[13] The story of Caradoc, which forms part of the French Perceval cycle, relates how a serpent fastened on his arm and sucked away his life. He was saved by a young maiden presenting her breast to the serpent, which took the nipple in its mouth. Cador then cut off its head, but with that also the nipple, which was magically replaced by one of gold.[14] A close parallel exists in a Gaelic folk-tale, and less close in a Scots ballad,[15] but it is probable that the source is Celtic, as the name of the wife of the Welsh Karadawe is Tegau Eurfron, Tegau 'with the golden breast.' The Egyptian goddess Neit is represented with a crocodile at either breast, and in French mediæval architecture serpents are represented sucking the breasts of women. Women are seen by visitors to hell suckling serpents as a punishment for refusing nourishment to their children.[16] Some frescoes in Byzantine churches show a parallel to this.[17] Lucian says that in Macedonia women pressed serpents in their hands and gave them the breast.[18]

(*f*) In some instances menstruation is ascribed to the bite of a reptile or other animal.

1 Gill, p. 77.
2 G. N. Theal, *Kafir Folk-lore*, London, n.d., p. 29, cf. p. 47; *FLJ* v. [1887] 152 f. (Formosa); W. Jekyll, *Jamaican Song and Story*, do. 1907, p. 102; cf. *ERE* i. 321.
3 *JE*, *s.v.* 'Fall.'
4 Romilly, pp. 107, 120; J. Meier, *Anthropos*, ii. [1907] 654; H. Rink, *Tales and Traditions of the Eskimo*, Edinburgh and London, 1875, p. 186 ff.; C. G. Leland, *Algonquin Legends of New England*, Boston, 1885, pp. 266, 274 ff.; E. Petitot, *Traditions indiennes du Canada nord-ouest*, Paris, 1886, pp. 16, 407; *ERE* i. 321b; W. H. Brett, *Legends and Myths of the Aboriginal Tribes of British Guiana*, London, 1880, p. 64. Cf. also H. L. Joly, *Legend in Japanese Art*, London, 1908, p. 140; Ælian, *de Nat. An.* xii. 39; cf. vi. 17; Ralston, *Songs*, p. 173 f.
5 C. S. Boswell, *An Irish Precursor of Dante*, London, 1908, p. 231, suggests an origin of these ideas in travel tales of Indian serpents, preserved by Greek naturalists.
6 W. W. Reade, *Savage Africa*, London, 1863, p. 540; see § I.
7 *JAI* xxix. [1899] 22.
8 Cf. J. G. Frazer, *GB*3, pt. iv., *Adonis, Attis, Osiris*, London, 1914, i. 67 f.
9 Casalis, p. 283.
10 Hahn, p. 81; H. H. Ploss and M. Bartels, *Das Weib*8, Leipzig, 1905, ii. 334.
11 Purchas, xvi. 457.
12 A. Featherman, *Social Hist. of the Races of Mankind*, London, 1881–91, ii. 75.
13 See above, § I.
14 Boudin, p. 68 ff.; C. A. Böttiger, *Sabina*, Leipzig, 1806, ii. 188 f.
15 Hahn, p. 62.
16 Turner, *Samoa*, p. 288.

1 Bourke, *Snake-Dance of the Moquis*, p. 177; Fewkes, *16 RBEW* (1897), p. 304.
2 Joly, p. 377; *Kojiki*, ed. Chamberlain, p. 127.
3 Philostratus, *Vita Apollon.* bk. 4; cf. Burton, *Anatomy of Melancholy*, pt. iii. sec. 2, mem. 1, subs. 1; and Keats, *Lamia*.
4 See E. S. Hartland, *The Science of Fairy Tales*, London, 1891, p. 240 f.; MacCulloch, *CF*, p. 257; W. Scott, *Minstrelsy of the Scottish Border*, London, 1839, p. 345 f.
5 Crooke, *PR*2, ii. 137; J. F. Campbell, *My Circular Notes*, London, 1876–79, ii. 186.
6 Herod. iv. 8.
7 T. Keightley, *The Fairy Mythology*, reprint, London, 1900, p. 480 f.; S. Baring-Gould, *Curious Myths of the Middle Ages*, do. 1884, p. 471 ff.
8 J. E. Harrison, *Themis*, p. 281; *A Guide to the Egyptian Collections in the British Museum*, London, 1909, p. 273; *ERE* ix. 843a. Cf. the third world-power in the Gnostic system of Justin (half-female, half-serpent), and Error (half-woman, half-serpent) in Spenser's *Færie Queene*, I. i. 14.
9 Dieterich, *Eine Mithrasliturgie*, pp. 12 f., 71; A. N. Didron, *Christian Iconography*, Eng. tr., London, 1886, ii. 140.
10 R. E. Latcham, *JRAI* xxxix. 347.
11 Hahn, p. 81.
12 *FLJ* i. [1883] 256.
13 E. Owen, *Welsh Folk-Lore*, Oswestry, 1896, p. 349.
14 Gaston Paris, 'Caradoc et le Serpent' in *Romania*, xxviii. [1899] 214 ff.
15 J. F. Campbell, *Popular Tales of the W. Highlands*, Edinburgh, 1890, i., Introd. p. lxxxix; F. J. Child, *English and Scottish Popular Ballads*, Boston, 1882–98, pt. i., p. 176 f., no. 301.
16 In the *Apocalypse of Peter*, *Apoc. of Esdras*, and *Apoc. of Mary*.
17 L. Heuzey, *Annuaire de l'Assoc. pour l'encouragement des études grecques*, Paris, 1871, p. 118.
18 Ploss-Bartels8, i. 484 ff.

This is shown by images from New Guinea in which a crocodile or snake enters or emerges from the female organ.[1] Among the Chiriguanos, at a girl's first menstruation, women try to drive off with sticks 'the snake which has wounded her.'[2] Among the Macusi girls at this time are not allowed to go into the woods lest they be amorously attacked by serpents. Basuto girls at this period dance round the image of a snake.[3] Certain families at Kumano in Japan send their female children to the mountains to serve the god Susa-no-wo. When they show signs of puberty, a dragon is said to come and glare at them.[4] In Portugal menstruation is traced to a serpent, or women are thought liable to the bite of a lizard at this period.[5] Cognate with these beliefs is the superstition current in Germany in the 18th cent. that the hair of a menstruous woman, if buried, becomes a snake, and the gypsy custom whereby unfruitful women become fruitful by spitting on and sprinkling with menstrual blood the place where they have seen a snake.[6] It is also believed among the Orinoco tribes that serpents try to have connexion with menstruous women; hence they are forbidden to go into the forest. Such a woman who died of jaundice was believed to have thus exposed herself to the attack of a snake.[7] Among the Matacos a cure for snake-bite is to drop menstrual blood into the wound.[8]

Reinach suggests that the hostility between the serpent's seed and the seed of the woman, *i.e.* the daughters of Eve (Gn 3[15]), originally referred to some such myth of the origin of menstruation.[9] The rationale of such myths is probably to be found in the connexion between snake and φαλλός, the latter drawing blood at devirgination; menstrual blood was supposed to be produced by a similar wounding by a snake.

8. Children and serpents.—The test of the legitimacy of children by the Psylli[10] is paralleled by Greek myth.

When Alcmene bore Heracles and Iphicles, respectively sons of Zeus and Amphitryon, the latter placed two serpents in the bed to see which was his son. Iphicles fled—a proof that he was son of a mortal.[11] In another version Hera sent the serpents to destroy the infant Heracles, who strangled them.[12]

In many tales which suggest a source for these myths serpents appear friendly to children, and visit or play with them.

Pausanias tells how a prince at Amphiclea, suspecting a plot against his child, put him in a vessel. A wolf tried to reach him, but a serpent coiled round the vessel and kept watch. The father killed it; but, learning the truth, he made a funeral-pyre for it.[13] Vopiscus[14] tells of a snake attached to a boy and regarded as his familiar, and Spartianus[15] has a similar tale. Pliny tells a story of an asp in Egypt regularly fed. The son of the house died through the bite of one of its young ones, whereupon the asp killed it.[16] O. W. Holmes[17] cites some 17th cent. instances of the alleged friendliness of snakes for children. In Calabar a woman found a snake in her child's cradle, which the priests declared to be Ölaga, a local god.[18] House-snakes in Germany were supposed to watch infants in the cradle and sip milk out of their bowl.[19] Numerous parallels to Grimm's *Märchen* with this incident of the snake and child exist and are doubtless connected with the fact that house-haunting snakes are regarded as spirits of ancestors.[20]

9. Serpent origin of men.—Tribes, clans, and rulers were sometimes supposed to be descended from serpents, as in the instances of the Hopi Snake clan and the Scythians, already cited.

The Psylli were an African clan known to classical writers; in their bodies was a virus deadly to serpents, its smell rendering them senseless. To test the legitimacy of their children, they exposed them to serpents, and, if these did not avoid them, the children were illegitimate, *i.e.* not of the clan. Serpent-descent is indicated here.[21] In Senegambia there is a Python clan, and each child is supposed to be visited by the python within eight days after birth.[1] In the case of the El Kiboron clan of the Masai, who do not kill snakes, and the married men of whom are supposed to become snakes after death, it is believed that snakes never bite members of the clan—another indication of serpent descent.[2] A clan in Phrygia was called Ophiogenes, because they were descended from the eponymous goddess Alia and a serpent—probably the god Sabazios in that form.[3] At Parium another clan bore the same name, probably for a similar reason, and the males of the clan could heal a person bitten by a snake by touching him. The saliva of some of them had the same effect.[4] Whether the name Ophiusa, formerly applied to Rhodes and Cyprus, and the stories that Tenos, Crete, and Seriphus once swarmed with serpents, denote that serpent clans dwelt there is uncertain. The Caribs were descended from a water-spirit, with both human and serpent form, and a girl, whose child was ancestor of the Carib race.[5] The Hudson Bay islanders believe that men are descended from earth (the male) and a serpent.[6] If the name Eve (Ḥavvah) is equivalent to 'serpent,' the belief in serpent descent may have been held by the Hebrews or some branch of them.[7]

Probably such legends are connected with totemism, since, where this exists, the snake is often a totem, and the immunity from snake-bite attributed to some of the clans referred to may be explained from the belief that the snake species would not hurt its fellow-clansmen, who also would protect it. The healing of snake-bite by such people,[8] as well as their power of handling snakes with impunity (as among the Hopi), is curious. But some of the myths may be related to a cult of a serpent as chief god, from whom men believe themselves descended.

The Peruvians were progeny of the divine sun-serpent and his consort, and a similar myth existed among the Mexicans.[9] Kings and rulers also had a serpent origin in some instances—from a serpent-god or an ancestor conceived as a serpent. In Abyssinia the royal line began with the serpent Arwe; the semi-human serpent Cecrops was first king of Athens and ancestor of the Cecropidæ; and the Mikados of Japan were also believed to have serpent descent.[10]

These myths should be compared with those of serpent and woman unions,[11] with others in which a serpent has human children,[12] and with a third group telling how serpents and other reptiles were once men, afterwards transformed to reptile shape.[13] In others, again, women give birth to snakes, and in the Welsh laws of Hoel (A.D. 928) a woman declaring a man to be father of her child says, 'May I be delivered of a snake, if it be not true.'[14]

LITERATURE.—Articles in *ARW*, *passim*; W. W. von Baudissin, *Studien zur semitischen Religionsgeschichte*, Leipzig, 1876–78, i. 255 ff.; J. C. M. Boudin, *Études anthropologiques*, 'Culte du serpent,' pt. ii., Paris, 1864; P. Cassel, *Drachenkämpfe*, Berlin, 1868; W. R. Cooper, 'Observations on the Serpent Myths of Ancient Egypt,' in *Journal of the Transactions of the Victoria Institute*, London, vol. vi. (1872); J. B. Deane, *The Worship of the Serpent traced throughout the World*², do. 1833; J. Fergusson, *Tree and Serpent Worship*, do. 1868; A. de Gubernatis, *Zoological Mythology*, 2 vols., do. 1872; T. Hopfner, *Der Tierkult der alten Ägypter*, Vienna, 1914; E. Küster, *Die Schlange in der griech. Kunst und Religion*, Giessen, 1913; C. F. Oldham, *The Sun and the Serpent*, London, 1905, *Ophiolatreia*, do. 1889; F. L. W. Schwartz, *Die altgriech. Schlangengottheiten*, Berlin, 1858; E. B. Tylor, *PC*⁴, 2 vols., London, 1903; C. S. Wake, *Serpent Worship and other Essays*, do. 1888; A. Wiedemann, *Der Tierkult der alten Ägypter*, Leipzig, 1912. See also artt. ANIMALS, vol. i. p. 525 f., FALL (Ethnic), vol. v. p. 714 f.

J. A. MACCULLOCH.

SERPENT-WORSHIP (Indian).—**1. Importance and variety of the cult.**—The cult of the serpent in India is of special importance; in no

[1] Ploss-Bartels⁸, i. 484 ff.

[2] *Lettres édifiantes et curieuses*, new ed., Paris, 1780–83, viii. 333.

[3] H. H. Ellis, *Studies in the Psychology of Sex*, London and Philadelphia, 1897–1910, ii. 237.

[4] W. G. Aston, *Shinto*, London, 1905, p. 206.

[5] Ploss-Bartels⁸, ii. 484; H. H. Ellis, ii. 237.

[6] H. H. Ellis, ii. 237; H. von Wlislocki, *Volksglaube und religiöser Brauch der Zigeuner*, Münster, 1891, pp. 66, 133.

[7] F. S. Gilig, *Saggio di Storia Americano*, Rome, 1780–84, ii. 132 f.

[8] Nordenskiöld, p. 107.

[9] *Cultes, mythes et religions*, ii. 398.

[10] See below, § 9.

[11] W. S. Fox, *Greek and Roman Mythology*, p. 79.

[12] Hyginus, *Fab.* 30.

[13] Paus. x. xxxiii. 5.

[14] *Aurelianus*, c. 4.

[15] *Severus*, c. 1.

[16] Pliny, *HN* x. 96 [74].

[17] *Elsie Venner*, Cambridge, Mass., 1861, ch. xvi.

[18] Communicated by Rev. J. K. MacGregor.

[19] Grimm, *Teut. Myth.* ii. 686; cf. Olaus Magnus, *Hist. de gentibus septentrionalibus* (1555), bk. xxi. cap. 48.

[20] Grimm, *Household Tales*, ii. 76. For the variants see Bolte-Polivka, ii. 459.

[21] Varro, in Priscian. x. 32; Pliny, *HN* vii. 14.

[1] *REth* iii. [1885] 397.

[2] Merker, p. 202.

[3] Ælian, *de Nat. An.* xiii. 39; Ramsay, ii. 593.

[4] Strabo, XIII. i. 14.

[5] Brett, p. 64.

[6] Turner, *Samoa*, p. 288.

[7] Nöldeke, *ZDMG* xlii. [1888] 487; J. Wellhausen, *Reste arab. Heidenthums*², Berlin, 1897, p. 154; H. Gressmann, *ARW* x. [1907] 359 f.

[8] See art. NUBA, vol. ix. p. 402ᵇ.

[9] McLennan, p. 527; see also above, § 1.

[10] Fergusson, p. 33; Diod. Sic. i. 28; Griffis, p. 31.

[11] See above, § 7.

[12] Seligmann, *Melanesians*, p. 408 (S. Massim).

[13] Leland, p. 110; cf. *ERE* i. 320ᵇ; Skeat, pp. 54, 285; Lang, i. 170, ii. 36.

[14] Wheeler, *ARW* xv. 348 (Solomon Islands); De Groot, *Rel. System of China*, iv. 217; Seligmann, *Melanesians*, p. 397 (S. Massim); A. W. Haddan and W. Stubbs, *Councils and Eccl. Documents relating to Great Britain and Ireland*, Oxford, 1869–78, i. 253.

other part of the world is it more widely distributed or developed in more varied and interesting forms. This results from the wide distribution of the reptile.

India is the only country in the world inhabited by all the known families of living snakes. The chief characteristic of the reptile fauna of the Indian region is the great variety of the generic types and the number of their species, the latter amounting to no fewer than 450, which is nearly one-third of the total number of species known in the world, referable to about 100 genera, of which the majority do not range beyond the limits of India.[1]

2. Origin of serpent-worship.—The abundant distribution of these reptiles and the serious loss of life caused by them sufficiently explain the fear with which they are regarded and the respect and worship paid to them. The animal is dreaded and revered on account of the mysterious dangers associated with it, its stealthy habits, the cold fixity of its gaze, its sinuous motion, the protrusion of its forked tongue, and the suddenness and deadliness of its attacks. It haunts houses, old ruins, fields, and pools. It is particularly dreaded by women, whose habits of walking barefoot in fields in the early dawn and groping in the dark corners of their huts render them specially exposed to its malice. Its long life and its habit of changing its skin suggest ideas of immortality and resurrection, or of purification, one festival being held at the time when its skin is sloughed.[2]

Attempts have been made to prove that serpent-worship was introduced into India by Scythian and other invaders from Central Asia. J. Tod,[3] relying on authorities now obsolete, traced its origin to a so-called Tāk or Takshak tribe of Central Asia. But an examination of the latest authority on the Scythians[4] shows that, while a serpent barrow and the use of the snake as an ornament or symbol are found among this people, there is no indication of a general cult of the reptile. On the whole, the wide distribution and loss of life caused by the snake in India warrant the conclusion that the cult is probably local.

3. Distribution of serpent-worship.—During the census of 1891 some attempt was made to collect statistics of the numbers of the followers of the various serpent-cults, but without much success, because these merge in other types of animism prevailing among the lower classes.

In the United Provinces of Agra and Oudh 35,366 persons were recorded as worshippers of the *nāga*, and 122,991 as worshippers of the snake-hero, Gūgā Pīr, with other groups less numerically important; in the Panjāb 35,344 persons were said to worship Gūgā.[5] The results from other Provinces equally failed to indicate the wider distribution of the worship.

Some of the more important types of cult, according to their local distribution, are the following.

(*a*) *North-West Frontier.*—

In Abisāra, the modern Hazāra country, Strabo speaks of two enormous snakes, probably kept in a temple as objects of worship.[6] A Kāfir legend tells of the destruction by Imra of an enormous snake in the Bashgul valley, whose tracks are to this day indicated by some light quartz veins, which show distinctly against the darker ground of the rocks; a tarn was formed by the blood flowing from the snake's severed head.[7] In Baluchistān the mountain known as Koh-i-Mārān, 'peak of snakes,' and the petrified dragons of Bisūt and Bāmiān indicate an ancient cult.[8]

(*b*) *Kaśmīr.*—In Kaśmīr and the neighbouring hills there is evidence of wide-spread worship.

The early legends are full of tales of snake-gods, especially in connexion with water-springs.[1] The Chinese pilgrim Hiuen Tsiang (or Yuan Chwang) states that, as Kaśmīr is protected by a dragon, it has always assumed superiority among neighbouring people.[2] Abul Faḍhl, the historiographer of Akbar, records that 'in seven hundred places there are graven images of snakes which they worship and regarding which wonderful legends are told.'[3] Legends still abound of dragons, particularly in connexion with springs.[4] It was at one time supposed that all Kaśmīr temples were originally surrounded by artificial lakes as abodes for the Nāga water-deities, but this theory is now abandoned.[5]

(*c*) *The Panjāb.*—In the Panjāb, both in the plains and in the hill country, snake-worship has prevailed from ancient times.

Ælian[6] tells how Alexander the Great found in many places snakes kept in caves and worshipped; the people implored the king to spare them, and he consented to do so; one of enormous size is described.[7] The city of Taxila (Skr. *Takshaśila*, 'hewn stone,' or more probably 'rock of Takshaka,' the great Nāga king, or 'rock of the Takkas,' a snake-worshipping tribe) was apparently the site of a snake-cult which has been localized at a fountain near Ḥasan Abdāl.[8] The tradition of snake-worship still exists among the Gaur Ṭagā tribe of N. India, which claims descent from the Takkas.[9] Another centre of the snake-cult is Safīdon in the Jīnd State, the name of which is supposed to mark the snake holocaust by Janamejaya (Skr. *sarpa-damana*, 'snake-subduing').[10] Serpents, again, are connected with the widely spread legends of Rājā Rasālū and Niwal Dāī.[11] The famous iron pillar at Delhi, erected about A.D. 415, is said to have sunk into the earth so as to rest on the head of the serpent Śeṣa, which supports the world; the king Prithivī Rājā, to make its position certain as a pledge of the permanence of his dynasty, ordered it to be taken up, when blood and flesh of the snake's head were found adhering to it—an omen which foretold his ultimate defeat.[12] In the Panjāb plains snake-worship is widely spread.[13] In the Chambā State it is associated with the cult of Devī, the mother-goddess; she is not connected with springs like the *nāgas*, or serpent deities, but it is common to find a Nāga and a Devī temple side by side and common attributes are assigned to both. There is in Maṇḍī, another hill State, a close connexion between the cult of Śiva and that of the *nāgas*, the latter being his, or Kālī's, favourite servants. In Kulū the rainbow is called Buḍhī Nāgan or Nāgin, 'the old female snake,' which points to the *nāga* being regarded as a rain- or water-god, as is usually the case in the Simla hills; but in Chambā he is described as a whitish-coloured snake that frequents house-walls, is said to drink milk; and, being regarded as a good omen, he receives worship (*pūjā*) and incense is offered to him.[14] In the Panjāb hills the cult of the cobra, and in one place that of harmless snakes, is prevalent. The Nāga temples, according to C. F. Oldham, are not dedicated to the serpent, but to the Nāga Rājās, the ancient rulers of the race.[15] The Gaddis, Ghirths, and the people of Churāh worship the snake; the people of Kanaur pray thus to Nāges Deotā: 'O thou, who livest within the wall, who livest in holes, who canst go into a vessel, who canst swiftly run, who livest in the water, on the precipice, upon trees, in the waste land, among the meadows, who hast power like the thunderbolt, who livest within the hollow trees, among the rocks, within the caves, be victorious!'[16]

(*d*) *United Provinces.*—In the United Provinces of Agra and Oudh among the chief centres of the cult may be named Mathurā, Ahichhatra, and Benares.

Mathurā was a scene of *nāga*-worship, as is indicated by the local statuary and the legends of Kṛṣṇa as a slayer of dragons.[17]

[1] G. Watt, *Dict. of the Econ. Products of India*, London and Calcutta, 1889–93, vi. i. 429; *IGI* i. [1907] 269 ff.; J. Fayrer, *The Thanatophidia of India*, London, 1874.

[2] J. Fergusson, *Tree and Serpent Worship*², p. 259; *PR*² ii. 123 ff.

[3] *Annals and Antiquities of Rājasthān*, popular ed., London, 1914, p. 86.

[4] E. H. Minns, *Scythians and Greeks*, Cambridge, 1913, pp. 328 f., 410, 427 f. and other passages noted in the Index.

[5] *Census of India, 1891*, xvi. *N.W. Provinces and Oudh*, Allahabad, 1894, pt. i. 211 f., xix. *Punjab*, Calcutta, 1892, pt. i. 104 f.

[6] xv. 28; J. W. McCrindle, *Ancient India as described in Class. Literature*, London, 1901, p. 34 f.

[7] G. S. Robertson, *The Kāfirs of the Hindu-Kush*, London, 1896, p. 388.

[8] A. W. Hughes, *Balochistan*, London, 1877, p. 5; C. Masson, *Journeys in Balochistan, Afghanistan, the Panjab*, do. 1842–43, ii. 357, 395.

[1] Kalhaṇa, *Rājataraṅgiṇi*, tr. M. A. Stein, London, 1900, i. 6, 37 f., ii. 462.

[2] S. Beal, *Si-yu-ki*, London, 1884, i. 148; T. Watters, *On Yuan Chwang's Travels in India*, London, 1904–05, i. 261.

[3] *Āīn-i-Akbarī*, tr. H. S. Jarrett, Calcutta, 1891, ii. 354.

[4] W. R. Lawrence, *The Valley of Kashmīr*, London, 1895, pp. 170, 289, 294 f., 299 n.; cf. § 7 (*a*).

[5] Lawrence, p. 170; V. A. Smith, *A Hist. of Fine Art in India and Ceylon*, Oxford, 1911, p. 46.

[6] περὶ ζώων ἰδιότητος, III. xxi.

[7] McCrindle, p. 145.

[8] McCrindle, *The Invasion of India*², London, 1896, p. 343; Beal, i. 137; Watters, i. 241 f.

[9] H. M. Elliot, *Supplement to the Glossary of Indian Terms*, Roorkee, 1860, p. 420 ff.

[10] R. C. Temple, *Legends of the Panjāb*, Bombay, 1884, i. 414 ff.

[11] *Ib.* i. Introd. xvii; *FLJ* iii. [1885] 61.

[12] W. H. Sleeman, *Rambles and Recollections of an Indian Official*, Oxford, 1915, p. 499; H. C. Fanshawe, *Delhi, Past and Present*, London, 1902, p. 264 f.

[13] D. C. J. Ibbetson, *Punjab Ethnography*, Calcutta, 1883, p. 114 f.

[14] H. A. Rose, *A Glossary of the Tribes and Castes of the Punjab and North-West Frontier Province*, i. [Lahore, 1911] pp. 331, 400, 419.

[15] *The Sun and the Serpent*, p. 84 ff., with numerous photographs of snake-shrines.

[16] H. A. Rose, *Glossary*, ii. 269, 294, 214, 454; *NINQ* ii. [1884–85] 91; *Census of India, 1901*, xvii. *Punjab*, pt. i. pp. 119 f., 129; *do. 1911*, xiv. pt. i. p. 120.

[17] Smith, p. 138 f.; F. S. Growse, *Mathurā*, Allahabad, 1883, p. 57 f.

At Jait, in the Mathurā District, there is an image of a five-headed *nāga*, whose tail was said to extend seven miles underground, until the belief was dispelled by excavation.[1] Ahichhatra, 'umbrella of the dragon Ahi,' the great ruined city in Rohilkhand, like many other places of which the names are connected with the *nāgas*—Nāgpur, Nāgaur, Nāgod, etc.—has a legend of an Ahir whose claim to kingship was attested by a snake shading him with its expanded hood.[2] In Benares Śiva-Mahādeva is worshipped as Nāgeśvar, 'Lord of *nāgas*,' with a serpent twined round his image; the Nāg Kuān, or 'serpent-well,' lies in one of the oldest parts of the city and is surrounded by snake symbols.[3] In Dehra Dūn the local folk-lore is full of tales of the *nāgas*.[4] The Agarwālā caste of traders perform the worship of Āstika or Āstīka Muni, a sage descended from the snake, and call themselves *nāga-upasāka*, 'snake-worshippers.'[5] Similar worship is performed by many other castes and tribes.[6] In Oudh Nigohan, in the Lucknow District, is a centre of the cult.[7] There are numerous traces of *nāga*-worship in the Himālayan districts of the United Provinces, but now chiefly connected with the special cults of Viṣṇu and Śiva.[8]

(*e*) *Bengal.*—

In Bengal the goddess Manasā (Skr. *manas*, 'mind'), or Bishahrī (Skr. *viṣahari*, 'remover of venom'), holds the foremost place. If her worship is neglected, some one in the family is sure to die of snake-bite; she is worshipped by placing an earthen pot marked with vermilion under a tree; clay images or snakes are arranged round it, and a trident is driven into the ground; sometimes the plant named after her is taken as her emblem; sometimes she dwells in a *pīpal*-tree (*Ficus religiosa*); in places where snakes abound a special shrine or a separate room is dedicated to the goddess; her sister, Jagat Gaurī, has also power over cobras and other snakes, and Ananta Deb is king of the snakes in Orissa.[9]

(*f*) *Central Provinces and Central India.*—In the Central Provinces and Central India the snake-cult is widely spread.

At Sāgar worship is offered to Nāg Deo, the serpent-god, sometimes at a shrine, sometimes at the snake's hole, by adoring him and making an image of him with butter and cow-dung on the house wall; people of the Nāth tribe carry about snakes during the Nāgpañchamī[10] festival and receive fees for allowing them to be worshipped.[11] The Kawars greatly dread a mythical snake with a red crest on its head, the mere sight of which is believed to cause death; it lives in deep pools in the forest known as Śeṣakuṇḍa, and, when it moves, it sets fire to the grass along its track; if a man crosses its path, he becomes black in colour and suffers excruciating pains, which end in death, unless he is relieved by the *baiga*, or medicine-man; in one village where the reptile recently appeared the owner never dared to visit his field without first offering a chicken.[12] The cobra is specially worshipped by the *barais*, or betel-growers, who associate the tendrils of the plant with Vāsuki, queen of serpents; and the cobra is the tutelary god of the nomadic Kaikāris.[13] In Central India almost every village has a platform built over a snake's hole, to the occupant of which is offered a wicker cover which protects the snake; a brilliant coloured picture represents the snake when it is absent; some persons tie a thread of fourteen knots round the wrist and arm and go to worship at the abode of the snake, making an image of the reptile in sacred grass, which they worship; Bhils and Bhilālas worship the python and never injure it; there are legends of families said to be immune from snake-bite and able to cure it.[14] In the month of June, the first month of the rains, snakes frequently appear; in this month the Goṇḍs try to kill a cobra, and will then cut off the head and tail, and offer them to Nāg Deo, inside the house, while they cook and eat the body, supposing the eating of the snake's body will protect them from the effects of eating any poisonous substance throughout the year.[1] In Berār the cult prevails more among the people of the plains than among those of the hills, metal or clay images of snakes are worshipped, sometimes on an ant-hill, and, should a cobra be seen, it is regarded as a good omen; twigs of sacred trees are fixed round the ant-hill, a yellow thread is wound round them, and within the circle offerings of grain and milk are laid; the simplest form of worship is pouring milk on an ant-hill.[2]

(*g*) *Assam.*—In Assam the most remarkable form of serpent-worship is that of U Thlen, a gigantic snake which demands to be appeased by the sacrifice of human victims, and for whose sake, even in recent times, murders have been committed.

It lived once in a cave near Cherrapunjī, and was tamed by a man who used to place lumps of meat in its mouth. Finally this hero, having heated a piece of iron red-hot, induced the reptile to devour it, and so killed it. He cut up the body, and sent pieces of it throughout the country, with orders that the people were to eat them. Wherever this edict was obeyed, the land became free of the *thlens*. But one small piece remained which no one could be induced to eat, and from this sprang a multitude of *thlens*, which still infest the neighbourhood.

When a *thlen* takes up its abode in a family, there is no means of getting rid of it, though it occasionally departs of its own accord, and often follows property when it is given away or sold. The *thlen* attaches itself to property, and brings wealth to its owner, but on condition that it is supplied with human blood. The murderer cuts off the tips of the hair and the finger-nails of the victim with silver scissors, and extracts in a bamboo tube a little blood from the nostrils, which is offered to the *thlen*. This offering must be constantly repeated. In order to drive it from a house, all the money, ornaments, and other goods must be thrown away, and no one dares to appropriate such things lest the *thlen* should follow them. Persons who are supposed to keep *thlens* are regarded with awe, and no one will even mention their names lest ill luck should follow. The superstition is probably of very ancient date, and it is supposed to be connected with the primeval snake-cults of Eastern and Further India.[3]

Among the Meitheis the ancestor of one clan, Pākhangba, manifests himself as a snake. 'When it appears it is coaxed on to a cushion by the priestess in attendance, who then performs certain ceremonies to please it.' Among the same tribe the *nōngshā*, or stone-dragons, symbolize the luck of the State.[4]

Among the Lusheis a man acquires the right to heaven by slaying certain animals; when a snake coils round the antlers of a *sāmbhar* stag, the man sitting on the coils is conveyed to heaven.[5] The Rabhās worship a serpent-god which once dwelt in a cave and was propitiated by the annual sacrifice of a boy and a girl.[6]

(*h*) *South India.*—In no part of India is the cult more general than in S. India.

Here we find the *kāvu*, or snake-grove, which resembles the *nāgavana* of N. India.[7] 'A clump of wild jungle trees luxuriantly festooned with graceful creepers is usually to be found in the S.W. corner of the gardens of all respectable Malayālī Hindus. The spot is left free to Nature to deal with as she likes. Every tree and bush, every branch and twig is sacred. This is the *vishattum kāvu* (poison shrine) or *nāgakotta* (snake shrine). Usually there is a granite stone (*chitra kuṭakallu*) carved after the fashion of a cobra's head set up and consecrated in this waste spot. Leprosy, itch, barrenness in women, deaths of children, the frequent appearance of snakes in the garden, and other diseases and calamities brought about by poison, are all set down to the anger of the serpents. If there be a snake shrine in the garden, sacrifices and ceremonies are resorted to. If there be none, then the place is diligently dug up, and search is made for a snake stone, and if one is found it is concluded that the calamities have occurred because of there having been a snake shrine at the spot, and because the shrine had been neglected. A shrine is then at once formed, and costly sacrifices and ceremonies serve to allay the serpents' anger.'[8]

1 Growse, p. 74 f.

2 Cf. § 7 (*e*); A. Führer, *Monumental Antiquities and Inscriptions in the N.W. Provinces and Oudh*, Allahabad, 1891, p. 28. For other examples see E. S. Hartland, *Ritual and Belief*, London, 1914, p. 323.

3 M. A. Sherring, *The Sacred City of the Hindus*, London, 1868, pp. 75, 87 ff.

4 *IGI* xi. [1908] 212.

5 W. Crooke, *Tribes and Castes of the N.W. Provinces and Oudh*, Calcutta, 1896, i. 18 f.; *NINQ* ii. 157, 202.

6 Crooke, *TC* i. 109, 122, 131, iv. 352.

7 *NINQ* iii. [1893–94] 179, iv. [1894–95] 130.

8 E. T. Atkinson, *The Himalayan District of the N.W. Provinces of India*, ii. [Allahabad, 1884] p. 835 f.

9 *Census of India, 1901*, vi. *Bengal*, pt. i. p. 195 f.; W. J. Wilkins, *Modern Hinduism*, London, 1887, p. 225 f.; *NINQ* i. [1891–92] 166; H. H. Risley, *Tribes and Castes in Bengal*, Calcutta, 1891, i. 41, 84; W. Ward, *View of the Hist., Lit. and Religion of the Hindoos*[2], Serampore, 1815, ii. 140 f.; J. Wise, *Notes on the Races, Castes, and Trades of Eastern Bengal*, London, 1883, pp. 138, 219, 260.

10 See below, § 13 (*f*).

11 *Saugor Gazetteer*, Allahabad, 1907, i. 43.

12 *Eth. Surv. Central Provinces*, vii. [Allahabad, 1911] 44; R. V. Russell, *Tribes and Castes of Central Provinces*, London, 1916, iii. 399.

13 *Eth. Surv. Central Provinces*, i. 8, iv. 27; Russell, ii. 195 f., iii. 299.

14 Russell, iii. 25, 483 f.

1 Russell, iii. 101.

2 *Report on the Census, 1881, Berar*, p. 48.

3 P. R. T. Gurdon, *The Khasis*[2], London, 1914, pp. 98 ff., 175 ff.; *Census of India, 1901*, iv. *Assam*, pt. i. 49; *FL* xx. [1909] 419; *PNQ* i. [1883–84] 63.

4 T. C. Hodson, *The Meitheis*, London, 1908, p. 100 ff.

5 *Census of India, 1911*, iii. *Assam*, pt. i. p. 140 f.

6 *Ib.* i. 145.

7 Somadeva, *Kathā-saritsāgara*, ed. C. H. Tawney, Calcutta, 1880, i. 312.

8 W. Logan, *Manual of Malabar*, Madras, 1887, i. 183. For references to snake shrines and stones in S. India see E. Thurston, *Castes and Tribes of S. India*, Madras, 1909, ii. 206, v. 173, vii. 385 (with a photograph); J. Dubois, *Hindu Manners, Customs, and Ceremonies*[3], Eng. tr., Oxford, 1906, p. 641 f.; T. K. Gopal Panikkar, *Malabar and its Folk*[2], Madras, 1904, p. 145 ff.; L. K. Anantha Krishna Iyer, *The Cochin Tribes and Castes*, do. 1910–12, ii. 81 ff. (with illustrations); P. Percival, *The Land of the Veda*, London, 1854, p. 207 ff. (with illustrations); *FL* viii. [1897] 284 f.; V. Nagam Aiya, *Travancore State Manual*, Trivandrum, 1906, i. 169, ii. 59; *Census of India, 1901*, xxvi. *Travancore*, do. 1903, pt. i. 99; C. Achyuta

Serpent-worship in S. India is of early date, if the Aioi of Ptolemy[1] take their name from Skr. *ahi*, 'a snake.'[2] An inscription at Banavāsī, in Kanara, records the erection of a cobra stone in the middle of the 1st century A.D.[3]

In Tanjore the worship of the cobra is common at the present day. People of the higher castes consider it a sin to kill a cobra, this offence being followed by childlessness, while children may be obtained by its worship. The Vellālas make an old woman cry aloud in the backyard that a sacrifice will be offered to the cobra next day, with a prayer that the offering may be accepted. Generally in the evening cooked jaggery, rice, and an egg, with a burnt offering of butter, are laid out for its acceptance.[4] In Bellary the worship was formerly more common than at present; snake stones may be seen in every village, but few of them seem to receive much attention. Vows, however, are made before them to procure children, and, if a child is afterwards begotten, it is given an appropriate name—Nāgappa, Nāgammā, etc.[5]

(*i*) *The Deccan and W. India.*—In the Deccan and W. India the cult assumes various forms.

One of the favourite guardian-deities in the Deccan is Nāgobā, 'father snake.'[6] In Gujarāt, to make amends for chance injury to a snake resulting in barrenness or loss of children, childless women worship an image of the serpent on the bright fifth of every Hindu month; this is done for one or three years, and at the final service a cobra is drawn on the ground with rice, and a silver snake is laid on the drawing; the woman and her husband bathe, dress in white clothes, and worship; after this the wife buries an iron image of a cobra at a place where four roads meet.[7] At Thān in Kāṭhiāwār the twin snake-brethren are worshipped.[8] Khāmbda in Kāṭhiāwār owes its fame to the shrine of the Khambdio Nāg, or snake; it is supposed to guard the village, which therefore needs no gates; snakes are frequently seen near the gateway and are never molested.[9] Bhuj, the chief town of Cutch, is said to take its name from the 52-yard snake which the people used to worship and feed every day with rice and milk.[10]

(*j*) *The forest tribes.*—As will have been seen from instances already given, the worship is common among the forest tribes.

The Goṇḍs in Chhatisgaṛh worship images of snakes every three years by setting out a vessel of milk for the cobra.[11] Members of this tribe are said to have always appeared naked before the shrine of their god Sek Nāg or Śeṣa Nāga.[12] The cult is common among the tribes of the Vindhyan ranges.[13] Some Bhīls, however, in W. India are reported to kill snakes when they have the chance, and the Khalpās of Gujarāt are reported not to reverence them.[14]

4. The Nāgas.—The chief serpent-worshipping race in ancient India is known as the Nāgas, who appear both in history and in folk-lore, and to whom much vague speculation has been devoted.

(*a*) *The Nāgas in history.*—One of the latest authorities, C. F. Oldham, distinguishes between the Nāga demi-gods in heaven and the Nāga people on earth, the former being assumed to be the deified ancestors of the latter. He concludes that the Asuras and the Sarpas, 'serpents,' of the *Rigveda*, the Asuras and Nāgas of the *Mahābhārata* and Manu, and the Asuras, or demons, of Brāhmanical tradition all represent hostile tribes, who opposed the Aryan invaders, and that the Asuras were Dravidians.[1] Others regard the race of Nāgas as of trans-Himālayan origin, who adopted the snake as their national emblem, and hence gave their name to the cobra.[2]

'The great historical fact in connection with the Nāgas . . . is the fierce persecution which they suffered at the hands of the Brahmans; the destruction of serpents at the burning of the forest of Khandava, the terrible sacrifice of serpents which forms the opening scenes in the Mahābhārata, and the supernatural exploits of the youthful Krishna against the serpents sent to destroy him, are all expressions of Brahmanical hatred towards the Nāgas. Ultimately this antagonism merged into that deadly conflict between the Brahman and the Buddhist, which after a lengthened period of religious warfare terminated in the triumph of the Brahman. From these data it would appear that the Nāgas were originally a race distinct from the Aryans and wholly without the pale of Brahmanism; that those who became Buddhist were either crushed or driven out of India during the age of Brahmanical revival, and that the remainder have become converts to Brahmanism and appear to be regarded as an inferior order of Kshatriyas.'[3]

Much of this is little more than speculation, and all that can be stated with confidence is that the Nāgas appear to have been a foreign, perhaps non-Aryan, people, found chiefly in N. India, but occupying other parts of the country.[4] They were powerful in Central and S. India.[5] Castes like the Maravans, Agamundaiyans, and Kallans in Madras are possibly descended from them.[6]

(*b*) *The Nāgas of folk-lore.*—In Buddhist tradition, folk-lore, and art we have frequent references to the Nāgas, personages half-human, half-divine. In the legends chiefs and kings are mentioned who displayed special reverence for Buddha; his alms-bowl was their gift; their kings approach and consult the Master.[7] The folk-tale collections of Somadeva, *Kathā-sarit-sāgara*, and the *Jātaka*[8] abound in tales of the Mélusine and other types in which Nāgas figure.

The king of the Nāgas dwells amidst dance and song in a happy land; 'filled with troops of Nāga maidens, gladdened constantly with their sports day and night, abounding with garlands and covered with flowers, it shines like the lightning in the sky. Filled with food and drink, with dance and song and instruments of music, with maidens richly attired, it shines with dresses and ornaments.'[9] Their palaces are under water, or beneath the roots of a great tree, or under the Vindhyan hills.[10] Their king wears a magic ring and he spits fire;[11] he is offered honey, fried grain, and frogs, but dares not eat them;[12] the erection of ancient buildings is attributed to them, apparently because they were regarded as foreign artificers.[13]

5. The historical development of serpent-worship.—Serpent-worship in a fully developed form does not appear in the *Rigveda*, but it is found as an element of religion in the *Yajurveda*.[14]

'But there can be no doubt that a belief in serpents had its origin in the Veda, though the serpents meant there were at first the serpents of the dark night or the black clouds, the enemies of the solar deities, such as the Aśvins, and not yet the poisonous snakes of the earth. The later development of these serpents and the idea of pacifying them by sacrificial offerings is likewise, as has been well shown by Dr. Winternitz, thoroughly Aryan, nor is there any necessity for adopting that laziest of all

Menon, *Cochin State Manual*, Ernakulam, 1911, p. 190; B. L. Rice, *Mysore, a Gazetteer compiled for Government*, Westminster, 1897, i. 454 ff., *Mysore and Coorg from the Inscriptions*, London, 1909, p. 202 f.; for the Komatī cult of *nāgas* see H. V. Nanjundayya, *Ethnographical Survey, Mysore*, monograph no. vi. p. 29.

1 i. 9.

2 J. W. McCrindle, *Anc. India as described by Ptolemy*, Calcutta, 1885, p. 54.

3 *BG* xv. ii. [1883] 261; for early snake images and inscriptions in Mysore see B. L. Rice, *Mysore and Coorg from the Inscriptions*, pp. 15, 115, 202 (with illustrations).

4 *Tanjore Gazetteer*, Madras, 1906, i. 70.

5 *Bellary Gazetteer*, Madras, 1904, i. 64.

6 *BG* xiv. [1882] 397, XVIII. iii. [1885] 386.

7 *Ib.* IX. i. [1901] 379 f.; cf. below, § 7 (*b*).

8 J. Burgess, *Report on Ant. of Kāṭhiāwād and Kachh*, Bombay, 1876, p. 87 ff.

9 *BG* viii. [1884] 510; for other snake-shrines see *ib.* pp. 558, 663.

10 *Ib.* v. [1880] 216 n., 218; Marianne Postans, *Cutch*, London, 1839, p. 100 ff., describes the rite.

11 *JASB* LVIII. [1890] iii. 281.

12 J. F. Hewitt, *Ruling Races of Prehistoric Times*, London, 1894–95, i. 87 f.; for Goṇḍ serpent-worship in the Central Provinces see *Central Provinces Gazetteer*, Nagpur, 1870, Introd. lxvi; *NINQ* i. 93.

13 *NINQ* i. 146.

14 *BG* IX. i. 305, 346.

1 Pp. 31, 45, 55.

2 E. T. Atkinson, *Himalayan Gazetteer*, Allahabad, 1884, p. 373 f.

3 J. T. Wheeler, *Hist. of India*, London, 1867–81, i. 147, 411, ii. 630.

4 *BG* IX. i. 450 n., 458 n., where they are identified with immigrants from Central Asia.

5 *Central Provinces Gazetteer*, introd. lxviii; V. Kanakasabhai, *The Tamils Eighteen Hundred Years Ago*, Madras, 1904, p. 39 ff.; Rice, *Mysore Gazetteer*, i. 274, 454.

6 *Trichinopoly Gazetteer*, Madras, 1907, i. 120. For further accounts and speculations regarding the Nāgas see A. Cunningham, *The Stūpa of Bharhut*, London, 1879, p. 23 ff.; F. C. Maisey, *Sanchi and its Remains*, do. 1892, p. 60 ff.; B. H. Baden-Powell, *The Indian Village Community*, do. 1896, pp. 95 ff., 169 n.; Oldham, p. 53 ff.

7 A. Grünwedel, *Buddhist Art in India*, London, 1901, p. 43 ff.; T. W. Rhys Davids, *Buddhist India*, do. 1903, p. 220 ff.

8 Cambridge, 1895–1913.

9 *Jātaka*, vi. 150.

10 *Ib.* iv. 281; Somadeva, ii. 149.

11 C. H. Bompas, *Folklore of the Santal Parganas*, London, 1909, pp. 90, 130; *Jātaka*, i. 206.

12 *Jātaka*, vi. 95.

13 *Upper Burma Gazetteer*, Rangoon, 1900, I. i. 279; Grünwedel, p. 208.

14 A. A. Macdonell, *A Hist. of Sanskrit Lit.*, London, 1900, p. 182.

expedients, that of ascribing all that seems barbarous in Indian religion to the influences of the aboriginal inhabitants of the country of whom we know next to nothing.'[1]

E. W. Hopkins remarks that in Vedic times 'serpent worship is not only known, but prevalent.'[2] We meet with references to Ahibudhnya, the serpent of the deep, and to Ahi, another designation of the demon Vṛtra; in the later *Saṃhitās* the serpents (*sarpaḥ*) are a class of divine beings.[3] The post-Vedic Rāhu, the eclipse demon, is, in modern belief, a serpent.[4] The *Atharvaveda* contains numerous charms against serpents and a rite of propitiation on the full-moon day of Mārgaśīrsha; they are recognized as gods, and called euphemistically 'biting ropes.'[5] In later tradition many legends are connected with them, like that of Nahusha, turned into a serpent because he insulted the Ṛṣi Agastya.[6] A series of tales describes the enmity between Garuḍa, the chief of the feathered race, and the Nāgas.[7] Garuḍa has been compared with the Sīmurgh of Persian and the Rukh, or Roc, of Arab tradition, the latter of which attacks snakes,[8] and with the Hebrew Cherub.[9] It has also been suggested that the bird was the totem of tribes hostile to the Nāgas.[10] In the *Brāhmaṇas* serpents, as developed objects of cult, occupy a prominent place, and in the *Mahābhārata*, amidst a mass of folk-tradition, the divine snakes are grouped with other celestial powers.[11]

6. Serpents in the later orthodox cults.—The serpent is closely associated with Brāhmaṇical Hinduism, Buddhism, and Jainism.

(*a*) *Brāhmanical Hinduism.*—

The association of the snake with Śiva's symbol, the *liṅga*, is very intimate.[12] A brazen serpent surrounds the great *liṅga* at the Rājput shrine of Eklinga.[13] As symbols of Śiva's energy, they appear in the remarkable Naṭarāja image.[14] In the Himālaya Bhairava, one of the Śaiva group of deities, is represented by a coloured stick in the form of a hooded snake, and Śiva himself, as Rikheśvar, lord of the Nāgas, is surrounded by serpents and crowned with a chaplet of hooded snakes. If, in ploughing, the share injures or kills a snake, a short ritual is prescribed to appease the lord of the snakes. Gaṇeṣa, the Mātṛis or Mother-goddesses, and Kṣetrapāl, the field guardian deity, are first worshipped on the spot; then the figure of Śiva in his form as Mṛityuñjaya, 'he that overcomes death,' is drawn on cloth, and with it that of the snake-god; both are worshipped, the snake spell (*sarpamantra*) is recited, and a fire-sacrifice (*homa*) is made.[15] The Lingāyats (*q.v.*), as Śaivas, naturally worship snakes.[16] Other deities are also associated with the serpent. At Ter, probably the ancient Tagara, the hooded snake accompanies an association of Śiva, Viṣṇu, Brahmā, and Sūrya, the sun-god, and Śakti Devi, impersonation of the female energy at Chitrārī in the Chamba State, bears a bell and snake in her right hand.[17] At Jaipur, in Orissa, Kālī is represented with her hair brushed back under a snake fillet and surmounted by a distended head of a cobra,[18] while in S. India Bhadrakālī's image, with two wings, is covered with serpents.[19] Probably in commemoration of his feats as a dragon-slayer, a living snake guards Kṛṣṇa's shrine, and at Pandharpur his consort, Rādhā, holds snakes in her hands.[1] Viṣṇu resting on Ananta or Śeṣa, the world-serpent, is a common subject in religious art. He sleeps upon the serpent whose heads support the world, during the intervals of creation.[2] In his form Nārāyaṇa, at Bālājī in Nepāl, his image has a snake-hood projecting over the water.[3]

(*b*) *Buddhism.* — The records of the Chinese Buddhist pilgrims supply numerous examples of the serpent-cult in Buddhism, particularly as guardians of trees and springs.

Two dragon-kings washed the infant Buddha; the dragon grants a site for monasteries in his lake; the Nāga Rājā, Muchilinda, protects Buddha with his folds.[4] On the Bodh Gaya rails the *nāga* spreads his hood, and at Bharhut a king with a five-headed snake-hood kneels before an altar behind which is a tree.[5] At the Sarpa (or serpent) cave, excavated about the time of Aśoka, a three-headed serpent of a very archaic type appears.[6] In W. India the Śaiva Buddhist converts preserved their original snake-worship.[7] In the records of the Chinese pilgrims we find Buddhist *śramanas* worshipping the *nāga* and conducting rites at *nāga* shrines.[8] A favourite gift at modern Buddhist pagodas in Burma is a representation in gold of the Lord Buddha, with a hooded snake raising itself over him.[9]

(*c*) *Jainism.*—

In Jainism the symbol of the Tīrthakara Pārśvanātha is a serpent (*sarpa*).[10] The colossal statue of Gomatesvara at Śrāvana Belgola (*q.v.*) is surrounded with white ant-hills from which snakes emerge.[11] The Nāgamalai, or snake-hill, is said to be the remains of a great serpent formed by the magic art of the Jains, and prevented by the power of Śiva from devouring the Śaiva city of Madura, and at the Rāmatīrtha stands a Jain image covered by a cobra with expanded hood.[12]

(*d*) *Sikhism.*—Sikhism also has associations with the snake.

Guru Har Gobind, as a child, destroyed a cobra sent by an enemy to attack him, and he killed a monstrous python which in its previous birth had been a proud *mahant*, or prior, who embezzled the property of his disciples; Guru Har Rai acted in the same way to a python which in a previous existence had been a *paṇḍit* who used falsely to vaunt the power of the Vedas.[13]

7. The serpent in its various manifestations.—The snake-cult assumes many forms.

(*a*) *Controlling water.*—The belief that serpents live in, guard, and control water—lakes, springs, and rivers—is a belief common to many races.[14]

In the records of the Chinese pilgrims a *nāga* rides on the winds, passes through space, and glides over the waters; another brings fertilizing rain; on a mountain pass 'there are poison dragons, who when evil-purposed spit poison, winds, rain, snow, drifting sand, and gravel-stones'; other wicked dragons are restrained from sending rain-storms; people resort with their shamans to the tank of the Nāga Rājā Elāpātra, and by cracking their fingers and praying they obtain rain or fine weather.[15] Many lakes and tanks in N. India are sacred to serpents.[16] All the wells in Kaśmīr, especially hot springs, are associated with snake-worship.[17] The Nāga Mahāpadma is the tutelary guardian of the largest Kaśmīr lake, the Vulur.[18] The sinuous motion of the snake suggests its connexion with rivers, as in Burma, where three snakes, one of which is cut into three pieces, produce three rivers and four canals, and in Sikkim, where the course of the river Tīsta is straight because the king of serpents led it into the plains.[19]

---

1 F. Max Müller, *Contrib. to the Science of Mythology*, London, 1897, ii. 598 f.
2 *The Religions of India*, ed. Boston and London, 1902, p. 154, quoting *Rigveda*, xi. 9, viii. 6, 7, where it is combined with tree-worship (see below, § 12).
3 A. A. Macdonell, *Vedic Mythology*, Strassburg, 1897, pp. 72, 148, 152; J. Muir, *Original Sanskrit Texts*, London, 1868–70, i. 95 f.
4 Macdonell, *Ved. Myth.*, p. 160; E. Thurston, *Ethnog. Notes in S. India*, Madras, 1906, p. 289; cf. W. W. Skeat and C. O. Blagden, *Pagan Races of the Malay Peninsula*, London, 1906, ii. 235.
5 *SBE* xlii. [1897] 151 ff., 425, 487, 552 ff., 605, 640, 43, 119, 126, 162, 147.
6 Muir, i. 67 ff.
7 Somadeva, i. 182 f., ii. 312; *Jātaka*, vi. 93, 102.
8 R. F. Burton, *Book of the Thousand Nights and a Night*, ed. London, 1893, iv. 357 f.
9 *HDB* v. 644; art. HINDUISM, § 5 (*b*).
10 Oldham, p. 81 f.
11 Hopkins, pp. 251, 376.
12 J. R. Rivett-Carnac, 'The Snake Symbol in India, especially in Connection with the Worship of Śiva,' *JASB*, 1879, i. 17 ff.
13 Tod, popular ed., i. 427.
14 V. A. Smith, *Hist. of Fine Art*, p. 251.
15 Atkinson, ii. 777, 851, 913.
16 Thurston, *Castes and Tribes*, iv. 257.
17 *Arch. Surv. Rep.* 1902–03, pp. 201, 241.
18 W. W. Hunter, *Orissa*, London, 1872, i. 269.
19 Thurston, *Castes and Tribes*, ii. 406.

1 G. Oppert, *On the Orig. Inhabitants of Bharatavarsa or India*, London, 1893, p. 138; *BG* xx. [1884] 463.
2 H. H. Wilson, *Vishnu Purana*, London, 1840, p. 205; V. A. Smith, *Hist. of Fine Art*, p. 162 f.
3 P. Brown, *Picturesque Nepal*, London, 1912, p. 181.
4 Beal, i. Introd. I., i. 149, ii. 128; Watters, ii. 128 f.
5 J. Fergusson, *Hist. of Indian and Eastern Architecture*, London, 1910, i. 105 n., 107 n., i. 33.
6 J. Fergusson and J. Burgess, *Cave Temples of India*, London, 1880, p. 69.
7 *BG* xi. [1883] 336 n.
8 Beal, Introd. xli.
9 Shway Yoe [J. G. Scott], *The Burman: his Life and Notions*, London, 1882, i. 189.
10 J. G. Bühler, *On the Indian Sect of the Jainas*, Eng. tr., London, 1903, p. 71; Oldham, p. 177.
11 V. A. Smith, p. 268 f.; E. Thurston, *Omens and Superstitions of S. India*, London, 1912, p. 135.
12 *Madura Gazetteer*, Madras, 1906, i. 7; *Vizagapatam Gazetteer*, 1907, i. 335.
13 M. A. Macauliffe, *The Sikh Religion*, Oxford, 1909, iii. 39, iv. 188, 282.
14 J. A. MacCulloch, *CF*, p. 258 n.; J. G. Frazer, *Pausanias*, London, 1898, v. 44 f.
15 Beal, i. 25, 64, Introd. xxix, xli, i. 122, 137.
16 *PR*² i. 43 f.; Somadeva, ii. 225, 415.
17 Lawrence, p. 22; F. Drew, *The Jummoo and Kashmir Territories*, London, 1875, p. 130.
18 Kalhaṇa, i. 174, ii. 424.
19 *Upper Burma Gazetteer*, I. ii. 504; L. A. Waddell, *Among the Himalayas*, London, 1899, p. 111.

(*b*) *The chthonic snake.*—The snake living in crevices of the earth is often identified with deceased ancestors and is regarded as chthonic.[1]

Marmots in the Himālaya are credited with the power of producing storms because they live in the bowels of the earth with the *nāgas* that cause thunderstorms.[2]

In the *Brāhmaṇas* 'they chant the verses (seen) by the Queen of the Serpents (*sarpa-rājnī*), because the earth is the Queen of the Serpents, for she is the Queen of all that moves (*sarpat*).'[3]

Thus the snake becomes associated with fertility and eroticism.[4] Therefore the cult is largely in the hands of women.

Among the Komatis of Mysore women worship snake images set up in performance of vows, and believed to be specially efficacious in curing sores and giving children.[5]

Hence snake-worship is often performed at marriages, as among the Bedars of the Deccan by married women, by Brāhmans in Kanara, by Lambādīs in Madras.[6] The cult of earth fertility-goddesses, like Ellammā or her impersonation, the Mātangī, is accompanied by snake symbols.[7] This is specially the case with the house-snake, which is regarded as the family-genius.[8]

(*c*) *Snakes representing ancestors.*—The conception of the snake as a fertilizer is, again, connected with the belief that the spirit of an ancestor, which takes shape as a snake, is re-embodied in one of the successors.[9]

In the Central Provinces Sonjharā women will not mention the name of the snake aloud, just as they refrain from naming their male relatives.[10] When Mandalay was founded, the king of Burma ordered that a pregnant woman should be slain in order that her spirit might become the guardian *nat* of the city; offerings of fruit and food were made to her spirit, which was supposed to have taken the shape of a snake.[11] In the Central Provinces it is said that a man had three wives, who were cremated with his body. 'While they were burning, a large serpent came up, and, ascending the pile, was burnt with them. Soon after another came up and did the same. They were seen by the whole multitude, who were satisfied that they had been the wives [of the deceased] in a former birth, and would become so again after this sacrifice.'[12]

When Chitor was stormed by the Muhammadans (A.D. 1313), the Rājputs, with their wives and children, perished by fire in an underground chamber. 'Superstition has placed as its guardian a huge serpent, whose venomous breath extinguishes the light which might guide intruders to the place of sacrifice.'[13]

(*d*) *Snakes guardians of treasure.*—The chthonic snake is naturally guardian of treasure buried in the earth. This incident often appears in folklore.[14] J. Forbes tells a ghastly tale of a snake which actually occupied a cavern in which treasure was supposed to lie.[15]

(*e*) *Snakes identifying and protecting kings or heroes.*—The basis of this belief, according to one suggestion, is that, as representing the ancient rulers, they naturally protect their successors.

The Nāgasiās of the Central Provinces derive their name from the *nāg*, or cobra, and assert that a cobra spread its hood to protect the tribal hero from the sun.[16] The claim to the throne of Sanga, the hero of Mewār and Kehar of Jaisalmer, was recognized in the same way.[17] The same tale is told of the great chief Holkar,[18] and of the infant Buddha, whose image at Sārnāth represents him sheltered by the coils and hood of a three-headed snake.[1] The world-snake, Śeṣa, protected the infant Kṛṣṇa from a rain-storm.[2]

(*f*) *The snake as a healer.*—Throughout India the *nāga* is invoked to heal disease of all kinds, particularly loathsome sores. Hence parts of its body are valued as remedies.

Among the Taungthas 'there is but one medicine current, the dried gall bladder and the dung of the boa-constrictor, which is supposed to be, and is used as, a remedy for everything.'[3]

In the Garo hills the skin of a certain snake, when applied to the part affected, cures pain.[4]

(*g*) *The snake-jewel.*—The snake has in its head a jewel possessing magical powers.[5]

'It is sometimes metamorphosed into a beautiful youth; it equals the treasure of seven kings; it can be secured only by cowdung or horsedung being thrown over it; and if it is acquired the serpent dies. . . . Its presence acts as an amulet. . . . It protects the owner from drowning . . . allowing him to pass over rivers dry-shod.'[6]

Snakes make precious stones, like those in Malabar, which are formed by divine serpents blowing on gold in the depths of the earth.[7]

8. Places immune from snakes.—Like Sardinia, Ireland, and other places, certain localities in India are immune from snakes.[8]

It is believed that no poisonous snakes exist in those parts of the Kaśmīr valley from which the peak of Harāmak is visible.[9] On the Ratnagiri and Talaimalai hills venomous snakes are said to be innocuous.[10] The family saint of the Kaliār Rājputs in the Panjāb is Kāla Sayyid; any one sleeping near his shrine must lie on the ground lest he be bitten by a snake; but, if a snake bites a man on a Kaliār's land, he will suffer no harm.[11]

9. Snakes and totemism.—The worship of the serpent seems to have originated independently of totemism.[12] Descent from the snake, the use of its name as a sept title, the tabu which prevents its slaughter, and the respect paid to it when dead all appear in India.

(*a*) *Descent from the snake.*—

The Muāsīs and Nāgvansīs of the Central Provinces claim descent from a male and female snake, and the Hajjām barbers of Bombay from the world-serpent, Śeṣa.[13] Some Nāgar Brāhmans in Nimar are said to be the offspring of Brāhmans and Nāga women; some Brāhmans for this reason refuse to eat with them, and in Baroda they call their women Nāg-kanyā, 'snake-maidens.'[14] In Burma there are people who say that they are descended from the egg of a *nāga*.[15] The Gandhmālīs believe their ultimate ancestor to have been a cobra; hence they specially observe the Nāgpañchamī festival[16] and eat no cooked food on that day.[17] A group of Vellālas in Madras say that they spring from a Nāga-kanyā;[18] and the ruling family of Chota Nāgpur claim their origin from the serpent Pundarīka Nāg.

(*b*) *Septs and sub-castes named after the snake.*—Nāg is a common title of caste-sections in Bengal, Madras, and other parts of India.[19]

(*c*) *Tabu against killing snakes.*—This is partly general and partly confined to groups which claim descent from the serpent.

According to Manu, killing a snake degrades the offender into a mixed caste, and a Brāhman must give a spade of black iron.[20] In Madras a cobra is popularly believed to be a Brāhman;

1 *CGS*, Oxford, 1896, i. 290, v. 37; *JHS* xix. [1899] 205.
2 Waddell, p. 219.
3 *Aitareya Brāhmaṇa*, ed. M. Haug, Bombay, 1863, ii. 358 f.
4 A. E. Crawley, *The Mystic Rose*, London, 1902, p. 192 ff.
5 *Eth. Surv. Mysore*, vi. [Bangalore, 1906] 29; Thurston, *Omens*, pp. 124, 133, 128.
6 *BG* xxiii. [1884] 96, xv. i. [1883] 171; Thurston, *Omens*, p. 136.
7 Thurston, *Castes and Tribes*, iv. 306, 300.
8 E. S. Hartland, *Primitive Paternity*, London, 1909–10, i. 169, 172; J. C. Lawson, *Modern Greek Folklore*, Cambridge, 1910, p. 259 f.
9 *PR*[2] i. 179; Hartland, i. 169, 176; Frazer, *GB*[3], pt. v., *Spirits of the Corn and of the Wild*, London, 1912, ii. 288, 294 f., *Totemism and Exogamy*, do. 1910, ii. 634.
10 Russell, iv. 510.
11 *Upper Burma Gazetteer*, I. ii. 35.
12 W. H. Sleeman, *Rambles and Recollections*, p. 29.
13 Tod, popular ed., i. 215.
14 *Jātaka*, i. 179, ii. 214; F. A. Steel and R. C. Temple, *Wide-awake Stories*, Bombay and London, 1884, p. 295; Bompas, p. 158; T. K. Gopal Panikkar, p. 59; *BG* I. i. [1896] 461.
15 *Oriental Memoirs*[2], London, 1834, ii. 18 ff.
16 Russell, iv. 258.
17 Tod, popular ed., i. 236, ii. 203.
18 J. Malcolm, *A Memoir of Central India*, London, 1823, i. 144.

1 *Arch. Surv.* 1904–05, p. 85.
2 *Vishnu Purana*, ed. Wilson, p. 503.
3 T. H. Lewin, *The Hill Tracts of Chittagong*, Calcutta, 1869, pp. 78, 98.
4 *Asiatic Researches*, iii. [London, 1799] 41.
5 MacCulloch, *CF*, p. 41; J. Grimm, *Teutonic Mythology*, Eng. tr., London, 1882–88, iii. 1220, iv. 1686.
6 *PR*[2] ii. 143 f.
7 Gopal Panikkar, p. 59.
8 Frazer, *Pausanias*, v. 325 f.
9 Lawrence, p. 155.
10 *Trichinopoly Gazetteer*, 1907, i. 5, 285.
11 Rose, *Glossary*, ii. 441.
12 Frazer, *Totemism and Exogamy*, ii. 500 ff., iv. 35 f.
13 *Chhatīsgarh Gazetteer*, 1909, pp. 117, 309; *Census of India, 1911*, vii. *Bombay*, pt. i. 261.
14 *Nimar Gazetteer*, 1908, i. 66; *Census of India, 1911*, xvi. *Baroda*, pt. i. 308.
15 *Upper Burma Gazetteer*, II. ii. 135; H. H. Risley, *The People of India*, Calcutta, 1908, p. 101.
16 See below, § 13 (*f*).
17 Russell, iii. 19.
18 Thurston, *Castes and Tribes*, vii. 382; Sarat Chandra Roy, *The Mundas and their Country*, Calcutta, 1912, p. 136 ff.; for similar legends of descent from a snake-god see *GB*[3], pt. iv. *Adonis, Attis, Osiris*, London, 1914, i. 80 ff., pt. iii. *The Dying God*, do. 1911, p. 132 f.
19 Risley, *TC* ii. 120; Thurston, *Castes and Tribes*, v. 134 f.
20 *Laws*, xi. 69, 134.

it is a deadly sin to kill it, and the offence necessitates an extreme form of penance.[1] The Badagas of the Nīlgirī hills will not kill a snake nor pass near a dead one.[2] In W. India, in spite of its destructive nature, a cobra is never killed; when one appears in a house, the people bow to it and pray it not to harm the inmates; at the most, if it is caught, it is put in an earthen jar, and this is laid in a lonely spot; the Vāṇis of Ahmadnagar, if they wish to get rid of a cobra, have it caught with round wooden scissors and set at large in a neighbouring field.[3] One penalty for killing a snake is leprosy, and this disease attacks any one who destroys its eggs by disturbing the ground in which it dwells, or by setting on fire jungle or grass in which it lives and breeds.[4]

Among the Khatrīs of the Panjāb a snake was once born to one of the Abrolā sept, and another fed the ancestor of the Chhotrās; both septs worship and will not kill the reptile.[5] In the Central Provinces the Hatwās are descended from a snake, belong to the Nāg *gotra*, will not kill a cobra, will save it from death at the hands of others, and sometimes pay snake-charmers to release those which they have captured; an oath by the snake is their most solemn form of affirmation.[6] The same tabu prevails among the Nāgesh sept of the Kaltuyās in Bengal and the Nāgbel sept of the Nāhals in the Central Provinces.[7]

(*d*) *Respect paid to dead snakes.*—In the Central Provinces, if a Parjā of the snake sept kills one accidentally, he places a piece of new yarn on his head, praying for forgiveness, and deposits the body on an ant-hill where snakes are supposed to dwell.[8] In Travancore, if a dead cobra was found, it was burned with the same ceremonies as a man of high caste.[9] In W. India a special rite (*nāgabali*) is performed by those who desire children, by those who suffer from bodily disease, who have killed a snake, or whose nearest relative has died from snake-bite.[10]

10. Persons dying from snake-bite.—The person dying of snake-bite is considered tabu, because his body has been occupied by the snake-god. Hence the corpses of such persons are usually disposed of in a way different from that observed by the group.

Among the Sāgars of Bombay those who die of snake-bite are cremated on the village common, probably in the hope that the spirit may depart at once, and, if this is not done, it is said that they will fail to receive absolution.[11] The Jātapu Kandhs generally burn their dead, but those dying of snake-bite are buried.[12] In parts of the Central Provinces, if a person has died by hanging, drowning, or snake-bite, his body is burnt without any rites, but, in order that his soul may be saved, a fire-sacrifice (*hom*) is performed after the cremation.[13] In N. India a person dying in this way is believed to be re-born as a snake in the next life. In order to avoid this, an image of a snake is made of silver, gold, wood, or clay, offerings are made to it, a Brāhman is fed, and a prayer is made to Vāsuki Rājā to release the soul.[14]

11. Magical cures for snake-bite.—In Baroda an expert is summoned who applies charmed cowdung ashes to the bite, and, with a charm, ties knot after knot on a thread; if the patient is restless, he dashes some handfuls of water on his eyes, and tries to force the snake to leave his body; after this treatment the snake explains why it bit the man; if the injury which prompted the snake to bite was trivial, it agrees to leave the patient; if severe, it refuses to leave, and death follows; members of a Nāgar Brāhman family are expert in this treatment.[15] In the *Atharvaveda* there are numerous charms for the exorcism of snakes from houses or against snake-bite; a central feature of such charms is the invocation of the white horse of Pedu (Paidwa), a slayer of serpents.[16] A favourite means of cure is by the 'snake-stone,' which is supposed to suck the poison from the bite.[17]

1 Thurston, *Omens*, p. 124; Dubois, p. 114 ff.; cf. *GB*³, pt. ii. *Taboo and the Perils of the Soul*, London, 1911, p. 221 ff.
2 J. W. Breeks, *An Account of the Primitive Tribes and Monuments of the Nīlagiris*, London, 1873, p. 104.
3 *Census of India, 1911*, xvi. *Baroda*, pt. i. 67; *BG* xvii. [1884] 40.
4 Thurston, *Omens*, p. 124.
5 Rose, *Glossary*, ii. 516, 519.
6 Russell, i. 367.
7 *Census of India, 1901*, vi. *Bengal*, pt. i. 415; Russell, iv. 260.
8 Russell, iv. 373.
9 Frazer, *Totemism and Exogamy*, i. 21, quoting J. Canter Visscher, *Letters from Malabar*, p. 162; Thurston, *Ethnog. Notes*, p. 288.
10 J. M. Campbell, *Notes on the Spirit Basis of Belief and Custom*, Bombay, 1885, p. 366 ff.
11 *Eth. Surv.* no. 113 [Bombay, 1908], p. 4.
12 *Census of India, 1901*, xv. *Madras*, pt. i. p. 157.
13 *Jubbulpore Gazetteer*, Nagpur, 1909, i. 137.
14 *NINQ* iv. [1894–95] 130.
15 *Census of India, 1911*, xvi. *Baroda*, pt. i. 67 f.
16 *SBE* xlii. 425 f., 27 f., 461, 487, 552 ff., 605 f.; for other remedies of the same kind see Thurston, *Omens*, p. 95; *PR*² i. 239; *FL* xxi. [1910] 85.
17 H. Yule and A. C. Burnell, *Hobson-Jobson*², London, 1903, p. 847 ff.

Certain clans, families, and individuals claim the power of curing snake-bite or are closely identified with the snake.[1]

Such are the Kir of the Central Provinces,[2] the Snake-tribe in the Panjāb,[3] and the Bodlās in the same province.[4] Ghāsīdās, the founder of the Satnāmī (*q.v.*) sect, is said to have been gifted in the same way.[5] Among the Todas certain men have a reputation for curing snake-bite; the limb bitten is bound in three places with a cord of woman's hair; with a piece of a certain tree the healer strikes the limb, repeating an incantation.[6]

Various charms are used to repel the attacks of snakes. These are often made in the shape of the reptile.

Such is the *nāgapatam*, the most primitive form of ornament worn by Nāyar women in S. India, which represents a hooded snake.[7] Men and women in Vizagapatam are very fond of wearing earrings of brass or gold wire twisted to symbolize a snake, with one end flattened out and pointed to represent the head.[8] The head ornament of a Marāthā Brāhman woman bears in the centre an image of a cobra erect, representing Śeṣa Nāga, the serpent-king.[9] Ladākhī women wear, as their national head-dress, a snake-shaped plaited strip of red cloth.[10] In Bengal a *karabi* root (*Nerium odorum*), pulled whilst the breath is held, on the night when the snake-goddess, Manasā, is worshipped, protects the wearer from snake-bite, but its efficacy lasts only one year.[11] A rosary made of the vertebræ of snakes is used in Tibet for necromancy and divination.[12]

Many sacred places are in repute for the cure of snake-bite.

In the Central Provinces a visit to the shrine of Bhīlat Bābā, a local saint, cures possession by devils and snake-bite.[13] That of Mahā Siddhā, 'the great saint,' has the same reputation in Berār.[14]

With the same object *ex votos* in the form of snakes are often dedicated.

Brāhmans in Madras offer images of snakes to appease the wrath of Rāhu during an eclipse, and in Tamil temples models of snakes, especially those coiled *in coitu*, are offered to propitiate serpents.[15] Coiled snakes are constantly represented on Indian temples.[16]

12. Tree- and serpent-worship.—The connexion between tree-worship and serpent-worship has probably been overstated by J. Fergusson;[17] but some instances are forthcoming.

In Buddhist times 'the tree-deities were called Nāgas, and were able at will, like the Nāgas, to assume the human form; and in one story the spirit of a banyan tree who reduced the merchants to ashes is called a Nāga-rājā, the soldiers he sends forth from his tree are Nāgas, and the tree itself is "the dwelling-place of the Nāga."[18] This may explain why it is that the tree-gods are not specially mentioned in the Mahā Samaya list of deities who are there said by the poet to have come to pay reverence to the Buddha.'[19] On the Bharhut *stūpa* are various reliefs of *nāgas* engaged in worshipping sacred trees or possibly the Buddha immanent in them.[20] A similar subject from S. India is described by Tod.[21]

In Mysore 'the stones bearing the sculptured figures of serpents near every village are always erected under certain trees, which are most frequently built round with a raised platform, on which the stones are set up, facing the rising sun. One is invariably a sacred fig, which represents a female, and another a margosa, which represents a male; and these two are

1 Cf. Frazer, *Totemism and Exogamy*, i. 133.
2 Russell, iii. 483 f.
3 *PNQ* ii. 91; cf. *GB*³, pt. v., *Spirits of the Corn and of the Wild*, ii. 316 f.
4 Rose, *Glossary*, ii. 115.
5 *Raipur Gazetteer*, 1909, i. 80.
6 W. H. R. Rivers, *The Todas*, London, 1906, p. 267.
7 Thurston, *Castes and Tribes*, v. 366; *Census of India, 1901*, xxvi. *Travancore*, pt. i., p. 325; L. K. Anantha Krishna Iyer, *The Cochin Tribes and Castes*, ii. 101.
8 *Vizagapatam Gazetteer*, i. 69.
9 *Eth. Surv. Central Provinces*, viii. [1911] 95; *BG* XVIII. i. [1885] 54.
10 *Census of India, 1911*, xx. *Kashmir*, pt. i. p. 61 n.
11 *Mem. ASB* i. [1905] 233.
12 L. A. Waddell, *The Buddhism of Tibet*, London, 1895, p. 209.
13 *Hoshangabad Gazetteer*, 1908, i. 291.
14 *Berar Gazetteer*, Bombay, 1870, p. 192; *PR*² i. 220 ff.
15 Thurston, *Omens*, pp. 43, 160, *Ethnog. Notes*, p. 353 f.
16 *Asiatic Researches*, vi. [1801] 389 (with illustrations); *PNQ* ii. 73. For similar offerings of images of snakes and phalli see J. E. Harrison, *Themis*, Cambridge, 1912, p. 266; Somadeva, i. 8; for *ex voto* offerings, in Himālayan snake-shrines, Oldham, p. 101 f.
17 *Tree and Serpent Worship*².
18 *Jātaka*, iv. 221 ff.
19 Rhys Davids, p. 232, with illustration of Buddha preaching to *nāgas* in a sacred tree.
20 Cunningham, p. 26 f., plates xxviii., xxix.
21 Popular ed., i. 462.

married with the same ceremonies as human beings. The bilpatre [*vilva-bilva-pattra*] (*Ægle marmelos*), sacred to Śiva, is often planted with them.'[1]

In Bellary it is said that the five Pāṇḍava brethren concealed their arms on a *sami*-tree (*Prosopis spicigera*), and that their weapons turned into snakes and remained untouched till they returned.[2]

13. Worship and propitiation of snakes.—The worship and propitiation of snakes are so closely connected with orthodox and unorthodox cults that it is often difficult to disentangle them.

(*a*) *Worship of the living snake.*—

A snake temple at Calicut contains several live cobras, which are fed by priests and worshippers; they are carefully protected, and allow themselves to be handled and made into necklaces by those who feed them; they are venerated as representing the spirits of ancestors.[3] The worship of living snakes is also found in Mysore and at Vaisarpadi near Madras, where crowds of votaries assemble, generally on Sundays, in the hope of seeing the snakes preserved in the temple-grounds.[4] In the island of Nainativoe, Ceylon, consecrated snakes used to be tenderly reared by the Pandāram priests, and fed daily at the expense of their votaries.[5] At Bhāṇḍak, in the Central Provinces, a cobra appears in the snake-temple on all public occasions, and similar cases are reported from Rājamundrī, Sambalpur, and Manipur.[6]

(*b*) *Snake temples.*—Temples in which snake-worship is performed are numerous.

At the most ancient temple in Bilāspur and in Chhattīsgarh the only image is that of the cobra.[7] At Nāgarcoil, in Travancore, is a temple of the snake-god containing many stone images of snakes; snake-bite is not fatal within a mile of the temple; at Mannarsala the sacred enclosure contains several living cobras.[8] At Nimbargi, in Bījapur, a woman saw her cow dropping its milk on a serpent's hole; she was ordered in a dream to build a temple over it, and to close its doors for nine months; but in her impatience she opened it prematurely, and found that a half-finished image of Sītārām and a *liṅga* had sprung from the ground—a legend obviously invented to explain the form of the image.[9] Among the Jādejā Rājputs of Kachh the chief procession is that of the Rāv to the snake temple in Bhuj fort.[10] A curious illustration of the fusion of Islām with animism is found in the snake mosque near Manarghāṭ, at the foot of the Nīlgirī hills, where an annual festival is held and alms are collected for the mosque.[11]

(*c*) *Snake-worship at ant-hills.*—Snake-worship is often conducted at ant-hills supposed to be the home of snakes.[12]

The Dhangars of the Central Provinces say that the first sheep and goats came out of an ant-hill, and, to stop the damage which they caused to crops, Śiva created the first Dhangar; hence they revere ant-hills, never remove them from their fields, and at the Divālī, or feast of lights, worship them with offerings of rice, flowers, and part of the ear of a goat.[13] Some tribes in Madras worship snakes by pouring milk on ant-hills.[14] The worship of the ant-hill at marriages and the custom of bringing the lucky earth from them are possibly connected with the fertility cult of snakes or of ants, because they multiply in great numbers.[15]

(*d*) *Propitiation of snakes.*—

In N. India the Agarwālā branch of traders, who have a legend of snake-descent, have an annual rite for propitiation of snakes at which various ceremonies are performed, and sesamum charmed with a spell is sprinkled in the house to preserve the inmates from snake-bite.[16] In Central India, to propitiate the snake-god Nāgdeo, milk is placed by Bhīls near the hole of a cobra.[17] A solemn annual service to propitiate the Nāga rain-deities is held in Tibet.[18] In an important cycle of folk-tales a monster or dragon is appeased by the periodical sacrifice of a victim, often a girl, who is finally rescued by a hero.[1] Frazer regards the tales as reflecting a real custom of sacrificing girls or women to be the wives of water-spirits, who are often conceived as great serpents or dragons.[2]

In the worship of serpents it is important to note that the offerings made to *nāgas* are not such substances as are usually eaten by snakes, but things suitable for the food of men.[3] In S. India among the rites performed by the twice-born classes are *nāga-pratishṭha*, the worship of the cobra in the form of a carved stone image, and *nāgabali*, or the performance of the obsequies of a dead cobra with all the formalities observed in ordinary funeral-rites.[4]

(*e*) *Worship of snake-heroes.*—Many deified snake-heroes are found in India.

Such are Gūgā or Guggā Pīr in the Panjāb and Rājawa and Soral in Hoshangābād.[5] In the Central Provinces the Bharias worship Karuā, 'the black one,' the cobra who, they say, was born in the tribe; he hid in the house-oven because he happened by accident to see one of his brothers' wives without her veil, was burnt to death, and is now deified by the tribe.[6] Another worthy of the same class is Bhīlat, a deified cowherd, whose disciples are believed to be able to cure snake-bite with the long sticks which they carry.[7]

(*f*) *Snake-festivals.*—The chief snake-festival is that known as the Nāgpañchamī, 'dragon's fifth,' in N. India and Nāgara-panchamī in S. India, because it is held on the 5th day of the light half of the month Srāvana, or Sāvan. Its occurrence in the rainy season is possibly connected with the power of the snake to give rain.

In S. India, on the eve of the festival, worship is rendered with offerings of flowers and incense at snake-holes, and milk is poured into them; the stone images of snakes under sacred trees are visited with reverence; on the day of the feast these images are washed, milk, curds, etc., are poured on them, flowers are presented, and other offerings made.[8] In the Central Provinces, during the month of Srāvaṇa, a man must be sent on a certain day to eat cakes at the shrine of the snake-god and return; if this is neglected, the family will be attacked by cobras.[9] In other parts of the Province Brāhmans on the day of the feast must not cut vegetables with a knife, but only with a scythe, and may not eat bread baked on a griddle; the priest comes to the house in the morning, and, if he tells the owner to do something ridiculous, he is bound to do it; on that day every guest who eats in the house must be branded on the hind-quarters with a burning stick, the host doing this stealthily; schoolmasters take their boys to a stream, where they wash their slates, worship them, come home, and eat sweetmeats.[10] Wrestling contests are held on this day, and it is suggested that this is done because the movements of the wrestlers resemble the writhing of a snake.[11] In the Deccan, on the first day of the feast, images of snakes are painted on the walls of the house, worship is offered to them, and an old woman recites a legend explaining the origin of the rite.[12] In the Himālayan districts of the United Provinces Śiva is worshipped under the title of Rikheṣwar, as lord of the *nāgas*, in which form he is represented as surrounded by serpents and crowned with a chaplet of hooded snakes; the people paint figures of serpents and birds on the walls of their houses, and seven days before the festival steep a mixture of wheat, grain, and pulse in water; on the morning of the Nāgpañchamī they take a wisp of grass and, tying it up in the form of a snake, dip it in the water in which the grain has been steeped, and place it with money and sweetmeats before the pictures of the serpents.[13]

At the temple of Jagannāth (*q.v.*) at Puri 'the supremacy of Vishnu is declared in the festival of the slaughter of the deadly cobra-da-capello, Kālī-damana, the familiar of Śiva and his queen.'[14] Viṣṇu, in the form of Ananta, 'the infinite,' the snake-god Seṣa, is worshipped at the feast of the Anant Chaudas, on the full moon of Bhādon, which, like other snake-festivals, falls in the rainy season.[15] A remarkable rite in N. India is that of the *guṛuī*, when girls go to a tank or stream and float dolls, which are beaten by the boys with long switches, possibly a purgation, fertility, or rain cult.[16] A similar rite is known as

---

1 Rice, *Mysore Gazetteer*, i. 455.
2 *Bellary Gazetteer*, i. 64.
3 M. A. Handley, *Roughing it in S. India*, London, 1911, p. 70 f.
4 Rice, i. 455; Thurston, *Ethnog. Notes*, p. 283.
5 J. E. Tennent, *Ceylon*², London, 1859, i. 373.
6 *IGI* viii. 59; *Census Rep. Berar, 1881*, p. 48.
7 *Central Provinces Gazetteer*, 1870, Introd. lxv. 86.
8 Thurston, *Omens*, p. 92; Aiya, *Travancore State Manual*, iii. 589.
9 *BG* xxiii. 667 f. 10 *Ib.* ix. i. 136.
11 Thurston, *Castes and Tribes*, vii. 105 f.
12 For rites at conical mounds compare the Greek *omphalos* and other sacred mounds (Harrison, *Themis*, pp. 384, 396 ff.; Frazer, *Pausanias*, v. 314 ff.), and the bell-shaped mound in marriage and other rites among the pagan Malays (Skeat-Blagden, i. 189, ii. 57, 67, 72 ff., 83).
13 Russell, ii. 480.
14 Thurston, *Castes and Tribes*, i. 196, ii. 256 f., vi. 236, 356.
15 *Eth. Surv. Mysore*, ix. 6, xxii. 8, xiii. 8; L. K. Anantha Krishna Iyer, ii. 376.
16 *NINQ* ii. 202. 17 *Eth. Surv.*, 1909, p. 30.
18 Waddell, *Buddhism of Tibet*, p. 508; for a similar rite among the Pullavans of S. India see Anantha Krishna Iyer, i. 153 f.

1 E. S. Hartland, *LP* i. chs. i.–iii.; Frazer, *Pausanias*, v. 143 ff., who gives Indian parallels.
2 Frazer, *Lectures on the Early Hist. of the Kingship*, London, 1905, p. 184; *GB*³, pt. i., *The Magic Art*, do. 1911, ii. 155 ff. For human sacrifice in snake-cults see above, § 3 (*g*).
3 Oldham, p. 29 f.
4 Above, § 9 (*d*); *Census of India, 1911*, xxi. *Mysore*, pt. i. p. 89.
5 *PR*² i. 211 ff., ii. 140; for a full account of the cult of Gūgā see Rose, i. 143 ff.
6 *Eth. Surv.* iii. [1907] 33; Russell, ii. 247.
7 *Nimar Gazetteer*, 1908, i. 59.
8 *Eth. Surv. Mysore, s.v.* 'Besthas,' p. 11; Thurston, *Omens*, p. 124.
9 *Damoh Gazetteer*, 1906, i. 38.
10 *Chhindwāra Gazetteer*, 1907, i. 55 f.
11 *Nāgpur Gazetteer*, 1908, i. 94.
12 Balaji Sitaram Kothare, *Hindu Holidays*, Bombay, 1904, p. 24 ff.
13 Atkinson, ii. 851. 14 Hunter, i. 131.
15 *Mem. ASB* i. 174 f. 16 *NINQ* i. [1891–92] 73.

godhan in Bihār.[1] In other parts of N. India people go about begging during the rainy season for two and a half days, during which time they do not sleep under a roof or eat salt; the object is said to be to avert the danger of snake-bite.

14. The snake in Hindu religious art.—Representations of the snake and its worship appear throughout Hindu religious art.

Figures of the Nāga Rājā, often in connexion with those of Buddha, appear in many cave-temples.[2] The figures of the *nāgas* at Ajanta (*q.v.*) are specially interesting.[3] A favourite subject is Viṣṇu as Nārāyaṇa resting on the world-snake, Śeṣa.[4]

15. The snake in folk-lore.—The snake naturally plays a leading part in the folk-lore of India. Here only a few instances can be given.[5]

The snake knows the powers of life-giving plants, and the language of birds and animals can be acquired by eating some part of the flesh of a serpent.[6] According to Philostratos of Lemnos, their hearts and livers were eaten in India, and knowledge of the language and thoughts of animals was thus attained.[7] According to the Santāls, the power of understanding the speech of animals is given by Manasā, king of serpents.[8] In another Santāl tale a snake teaches a woman an incantation which, if used when dust is thrown into the air, will cause the person against whom it is aimed to be burned to ashes.[9] Omens are naturally taken from snakes. In Madras a person should postpone his journey if he sees a cobra or a rat-snake; and in Kumaun, when a snake crosses a man's path, he must tear a rag from his clothing and place it on the trail of the reptile; if he fails to do so, he falls sick or suffers some other evil.[10] In Madras any one who dreams of a snake is considered to be proof against its bite; if a man dreams of a cobra, his wife or some other near female relative has conceived.[11] If a man has marks of a snake on his right foot, or a woman on her left, they are incarnations of some deity.[12] In the Panjāb some snakes which drink buffaloes' milk are so swift as to be able to bite a galloping horse; two-headed snakes are common; there is a snake which poisons the breath of a sleeper, strikes him with its tail, and is able to remove from the bedside sticks which might be used against it.[13] The Sanskrit names for the snake, *dṛig-visha*, *dṛishti-visha*, 'having poison in the eyes,' imply that it can poison by a mere glance.[14] The hamadryad is supposed to pursue its victim over hill, dale, and water.[15] Among the Todas a person whom a snake has bitten must not cross a stream; if it is absolutely necessary that he should cross, he must be carried over it.[16] The same people explain eclipses by the fact that a snake once hunted a hare, which took refuge in the moon; the moon promised to protect it. 'The snake still goes sometimes to catch the hare in the moon, and when he goes the moon becomes dark and some people fire guns and send up rockets and the Todas shout.'[17]

The Kadu Gollas of Mysore believe that, if a woman in her courses enters the house, they will be bitten by snakes or stung by scorpions.[18] In N. India a snake is said to become blind on seeing a pregnant woman.[19] In the Konkan the bite of the rat-snake is poisonous on Sunday, but harmless on other days; if it is in a field with a buffalo, whichever sees the other first will survive, while the one first seen will die; when buffaloes bathe, this snake sucks their milk under water.[20] One snake in Ratnagiri can kill people by merely casting its shadow on them from a tree or the roof of a house.[21]

LITERATURE.—To the knowledge of the writer no comprehensive monograph on serpent-worship in India has been published. Some aspects of the subject have been investigated by J. Fergusson, *Tree and Serpent Worship, or Illustrations of Mythology and Art in India*², London, 1873; C. F. Oldham, *The Sun and the Serpent*, do. 1905; W. Crooke, *PR*², do. 1896, ii. 121 ff.; A. de Gubernatis, *Zoological Mythology*, do. 1872, ii. 388 ff. For other references see *EBr*¹¹ xxiv. 676 ff. Some of the abundant and scattered literature on the subject has been quoted in the article.

W. CROOKE.

1 G. A. Grierson, *Bihār Peasant Life*, Calcutta, 1885, p. 400.
2 Fergusson-Burgess, *Cave Temples of India*, pp. 156 f., 306, 317, 325, 331, 343, 421; Grünwedel, pp. 29, 94, 106 ff., 133.
3 Grünwedel, p. 43 ff.
4 *Arch. Surv. Rep.* 1905–06, p. 114; J. Fergusson, *Hist. of Ind. and Eastern Arch.*, i. 341; Smith, *Hist. of Fine Art*, p. 162 f. For other sculptures see A. Cunningham, *The Stūpa of Bharhut*, and *The Bhilsa Topes*, London, 1854; F. C. Maisey, *Sanchi and its Remains*.
5 See *PR*² ii. 141 f.
6 *GB*³, pt. iv. *Adonis, Attis, Osiris*, i. 186, pt. v. *Spirits of the Corn and of the Wild*, ii. 146; J. A. MacCulloch, *Rel. of the Anc. Celts*, Edinburgh, 1911, p. 149 n.
7 McCrindle, *Anc. India in Class. Literature*, p. 194.
8 A. Campbell, *Santāl Folk-tales*, Pokhuria, 1891, p. 22.
9 Bompas, p. 153.
10 Thurston, *Omens*, p. 25; *NINQ* ii. 136; for other omens from snakes see J. E. Padfield, *The Hindu at Home*, Madras, 1896, p. 288 ff.
11 Above, § 7 (*b*); Thurston, *Omens*, p. 20.
12 *NINQ* v. [1892–93] 17.
13 Malik Muhammad Din, *Rep. Bahawalpur State*, Lahore, 1908, p. 8 f.
14 Cf. *FL* xvi. [1905] 150.
15 H. Yule, *Narr. of the Mission to the Court of Ava*, London, 1858, p. 100 n.; Thurston, *Castes and Tribes*, vii. 136.
16 Rivers, p. 267.
17 *Ib.* p. 593.
18 *Eth. Surv.* xiv. [Bangalore, 1908] 14.
19 *NINQ* v. [1895–96] 70.
20 *BG* XVIII. i. 75.
21 *Ib.* x. [1880] 50.

SERPENT-WORSHIP (Teutonic and Balto-Slavic).

— I. *TEUTONIC.* — **1. Lombard snake-worship.** —In the 7th cent. St. Barbatus melted down the golden image of a viper, which the Lombards worshipped in secret. Unfortunately we know nothing further of this cult.[1]

2. Wisdom and healing powers.—The Teutons, like most other peoples, believed in the wisdom of the serpent and in his powers of giving health and strength.

Hother, the adversary of Balder, came to his enemy's camp, and heard that 'three maidens had gone out carrying the secret feast of Balder. . . . Now they had three snakes, of whose venom they were wont to mix a strengthening compound for the food of Balder, and even now a flood of slaver was dripping on the food from the open mouths of the serpents.' The eldest maiden refused to give the food to Hother, 'declaring that Balder would be cheated, if they increased the bodily powers of his enemy.'[2]

Saxo also tells us how Roller saw his mother preparing a meal for himself and his step-brother Eric. 'He looked up at three snakes hanging from above . . . from whose mouths flowed a slaver which dribbled drops of moisture on the meal. Now two of these were pitchy of hue, while the third seemed to have whitish scales . . . Roller thought that the affair looked like magic. . . . For he did not know that the snakes were naturally harmless, or how much strength was being brewed for that meal.' Eric chooses the broth made from the dark snake, 'judging the feast not by the colours but by the inward strengthening effected,' and so he attains 'to the highest pitch of human wisdom,' knowledge of animal language, and success in war.[3]

Somewhat similar results come from the eating of the heart of the snake or dragon, Fâfnir, by Sigurd the Volsung.[4] We find a parallel for this superstition of the potency of the snake's slaver in the Lithuanian custom of putting their sacred house-snake on the table and letting him touch their food.[5]

3. The snake and the soul.—The cult of the house-snake probably prevailed at one time among the Teutons.

'Plenty of old tales are still told of *home snakes* and *unkes*. On meadows and pastures, and even in houses, snakes come to children when alone, sip milk with them out of their bowl . . . they watch infants in the cradle, and to bigger children they shew treasures: *to kill them is unlucky*. . . . If the parents surprise the snake with the child, and kill it, the child begins to fall away, and dies before long.'[6]

'In some districts they say every house has two snakes, a male and a female, but they never shew themselves till the master or mistress of the house dies, and then they undergo the same fate.'[7]

The cult of the house-snake is a wide-spread religious practice, and seems to be a form of ancestor-worship, arising from the notion that snakes embody the souls of the dead. In some Teutonic legends and superstitions the snakes appear to embody the souls of those who are still alive—a survival perhaps of the primitive belief in the 'external soul.'

Paul the Deacon tells the story of King Gunther, whose 'soul crept out of his mouth in the shape of a snake . . . passed a little brook and entered a mountain, afterwards returning again to the mouth of the king. . . . The king in the meantime had dreamt that he crossed a bridge over a river, and arrived in a mountain full of gold. The treasure . . . was afterwards actually lifted.'[8]

Several Northern stories appear to contain reminiscences of the custom of rearing house-snakes.

Thora, daughter of Herodd, king of Sweden, at the command of her father, 'endured to rear a race of adders with her maiden hands,' which grew until they became a public nuisance and were killed by her wooer, Ragnar Lodbrog.[9] According to the version of the story in the *Saga of King Ragnar Lodbrok*,[10] the

1 Grimm, *Teutonic Mythology*, tr. Stallybrass, ii. 684.
2 Saxo, tr. Elton, p. 93.
3 *Ib.* p. 158 f.
4 *Volsunga Saga*, in *Die prosaische Edda*, ed. Wilken, p. 182.
5 See below, § II.
6 Grimm, ii. 686.
7 *Ib.* p. 687.
8 See Saussaye, *Religion of the Teutons*, p. 297.
9 Saxo, p. 364 f.
10 *Fornaldar Sögur Nordrlanda*, Kaupmannahöfn, 1829, i. 237 f

princess kept a snake in a box, with gold under him. The snake grew until he encircled the whole room, and the gold grew with his growth

Both snakes and dragons (which often play a very similar part in popular belief) are frequently supposed to bring wealth or guard gold.

Fâfnir was originally human, but guarded his treasure by lying on top of it, in the form of a great snake or dragon.[1] The dragon in *Beowulf* kept watch over treasure in a burial-mound.

It is probable that originally the dead man was thought to appear in the form of a snake or dragon guarding the treasures that were buried with him in his grave.

Saxo tells of another snake-rearing princess:

'Siward, the king of the Goths, is said to have had . . . a daughter Alfhild, who showed almost from her cradle such faithfulness to modesty, that she continually kept her face muffled in her robe. . . . Her father banished her into very close keeping, and gave her a viper and a snake to rear, wishing to defend her chastity by the protection of these reptiles.'[2]

Saxo has probably misunderstood the king's motive. Sacred snakes are often tended by virgin priestesses, who are supposed to be their wives, the fundamental belief being that women 'can conceive by the dead in the form of serpents.'[3] A legend recorded by Grimm[4] is noteworthy in this connexion:

'Once, when a woman lay asleep, a snake crept into her open mouth, and when she gave birth to a child, the snake lay coiled tightly round its neck, and could only be got away by a milk-bath; but it never left the baby's side, it lay in bed with it, and ate out of its bowl, without doing it any harm.'

4. The snake in the other world.—Saxo gives a detailed account of Thorkill's visits to the other world:

After crossing the bridge which divided the world of men from the world of monsters, he came to the dwelling of Geirrod where 'the flooring was covered with snakes.' Afterwards Thorkill and his companions went to visit Utgarda-Loki. They came at last to a cave of giants, situated in a land of eternal night. 'The entrance was hideous, the door-posts were decayed . . . the floor swarming with snakes.' Then in another cavern 'he beheld a number of iron seats among a swarm of gliding serpents. Next there met his eye a sluggish mass of water gently flowing over a sandy bottom. . . . Again . . . a foul and gloomy room was disclosed to the visitors, wherein they saw Utgarda-Loki, laden hand and foot with enormous chains. . . . They could scarcely make their way out, and were bespattered by the snakes which darted at them on every side.'[5]

We may compare this with the description of the place of punishment in the Prose Edda:

'In Corpse Strand there is a great and evil hall, and the doors face the north; it is all wrought of snake-backs, but the snake-heads look into the house, and breathe out poison, so that the poison-streams run along the halls, and oath-breakers and murderers wade those rivers as it is here said:

'"I know a hall standing
Far from the sun
In Corpse Strand,
The doors face north
Poison drops fall
In from the windows."'[6]

'There Niðhöggr devours
The corpses of the departed.'[7]

Niðhöggr lives with a great number of snakes in the spring Hvergelmir under the great World-Tree, the Ash Yggdrasil.

'The Ash Yggdrasil,
Suffers hardships
More than men know . . .
Niðhöggr crawls underneath.'[8]

'More snakes lie
Beneath the Ash Yggdrasil
Than unwise fools can think of . . .
I think they will always
Be spoiling the boughs of that tree.'[9]

The conception of the universal tree was perhaps suggested by tree-sanctuaries such as the Upsala sanctuary and the great Romove sanctuary of the Baltic peoples.[1] The above-quoted lines point to the conclusion that at one time it was customary to keep snakes in these sanctuaries; we know that a sacred serpent was kept at Romove.[2] Snakes evidently appear in the other world because they embody the souls of the dead. Two of the snakes who gnaw Yggdrasil's Ash are called Ofnir and Svâfnir—names which are also given to Odin, the god of death.[3]

5. The world-snake.—Just as the sacred tree seems to have given rise to the idea of a universal world-tree, so probably the sacred snake gave rise to the idea of Miðgarðsormr, the great world-snake, which lies in the sea, coiled round the whole earth.

Miðgarðsormr, Hell, and the wolf Fenrir are children of Loki and adversaries of the gods. At the end of the world Miðgarðsormr will come up on to the land, breathing out poison. Thor, the thunder-god, will do battle with him and be killed by his poisonous breath.[4]

6. Conclusion. — We know something of the beliefs about snakes prevalent among the Teutonic peoples, but practically nothing about the ritual of the snake-cult. The Teutons seem to have regarded the snake as possessed of special gifts of knowledge and healing power; but on the whole its malignant aspect seems to be predominant. The snake is clearly regarded as an embodiment of the soul, and so comes to be connected with death, the land of the dead, and the powers of destruction.

II. *LETTISH, LITHUANIAN, AND OLD PRUSSIAN.* —**1. The house-snake.**—The cult of the house-snake was one of the 'almost incredible things' which Jerome of Prague related to the Council of Basel (1431–37) when describing his experiences as a missionary among the Lithuanians. Each *paterfamilias* had his own serpent in a corner of the house, to which he gave food and did sacrifice.[5]

In the middle of the next century Joannes Meletius (Menecius) gives similar evidence:

'Moreover the Lithuanians and Samogitæ keep snakes warm under the stove, or in a corner of the steam-room where the table stands. These snakes they worship as they would a divine being; and at a regular season of the year the sacrificers summon them forth to share the meal. They come out and climb up over a clean cloth and sit on the table. When they have there tasted the several dishes, they go down again and hide themselves in their holes. When the snakes have gone away the men gladly eat up the dishes of which they have had a first taste, and expect that for that year all things will turn out happily for them. If, however, the snakes have not come in answer to the prayers of the sacrificer, or have refused to taste the dishes placed on the table, then they believe that in that year they will suffer some great calamity.'[6]

About thirty years later Alexander Guagnini describes the worship of house-snakes, which was still kept up by many of the country people in Samogitia.

They reverenced a particular kind of snake 'with four tiny feet, like lizards, and black and fat in body, called in their native tongue *givojitos*.' Guagnini tells the story of a pagan, living in a village near Vilna, who, having been persuaded by a Christian to kill his sacred snake, was horribly deformed, because, as he said, he 'laid wicked hands on the serpent, his domestic god.'[7]

The Letts also were in the habit of rearing and worshipping house-snakes, which were so tame that they could not harm man or beast belonging to the house; even the children would play with them and have them in their beds.[8] It was the duty of the Lettish goddess Brehkina to cry out to all who entered: 'You must leave the milk-

1 *Volsunga Saga*, ed. Wilken, p. 175.
2 P. 274.
3 J. G. Frazer, *GB*³, pt. iv., *Adonis, Attis, Osiris*², London, 1914, i. 90; cf. *ib.* pt. v., *Spirits of the Corn and of the Wild*, do. 1912, ii. 17 f., pt. i., *The Magic Art*, do. 1911, ii. 149 f.; C. F. Oldham, *The Sun and the Serpent*, do. 1905, p. 154.
4 ii. 686.
5 Pp. 344–356.
6 *Völuspd*, 38.
7 *Gylf.* lii. 88.
8 *Grimnismdl*, 35, quoted in *Gylf.* ed. Wilken, p. 23.
9 *Ib.* 34, quoted in *Gylf.* p. 23.

1 Cf. art. NATURE (Teutonic); H. M. Chadwick, in *JAI* xxx. [1900] 30.
2 See below, § II.
3 *Grimnismál*, 54, in *Die Lieder der älteren Edda*, ed. Hildebrand and Gering, p. 93.
4 *Gylf.* xxxiv. 37 f., li. 82.
5 *Scriptores Rerum Prussicarum*, 5 vols., Leipzig, 1861–74, iv. 239.
6 *FL* xii. [1910] 298.
7 *Respublica sive status regni Poloniæ Lituaniæ Prussiæ Livoniæ*, Leyden, 1627, p. 276.
8 *Scriptores Rerum Livonicarum*, Riga and Leipzig, 1848, ii. 441.

mothers [*i.e.* house-snakes, toads] unharmed in the house.'[1]

Matthæus Prætorius quotes from Bretkius a detailed description of the consecration of the house-snake.

'A *weidulut* or *maldininks* is called, who brings with him one or more snakes. Thereupon the table is laid, and a *kauszele* [*i.e.* bowl] full of drink, and a can of beer set out.' The *weidulut* prays and the snake creeps up on to the table. 'Soon he makes a circle round the snake, which thereupon lies as if dead, until the *weidulut* has finished his prayers, which are many. Then the snake is sprinkled with beer out of the consecrated *kauszele* and after that it moves again, and, on the command of the *weidulut*, touches some of the food and gets down from the table by means of a towel. The *weidulut* notices the place that the snake will occupy and hallows it by prayer. Thereupon the snake establishes itself in its place. The host, however, with the *weidulut* and the inmates of his house, is joyful and concludes this consecration with much drinking and all manner of amusements.'[2]

Erasmus Stella and Guagnini call the sacred serpents of the Baltic peoples *penates*. It is almost certain that here, as elsewhere, the cult of the house-snake was a form of ancestor-worship. The Lithuanians named their house-snakes *givojitos*, *givoitos* (cf. above), 'the living ones' (cf. Lith. *gyvatë*, 'snake,' derived from Lith. *gyvas*, 'living'). It is therefore highly probable that they shared the almost universal idea that the snake, owing to his power of sloughing his skin, is immortal and a fit embodiment for the spirit of the dead, the ever-living ancestor.[3] The association of the *paterfamilias* with a special snake, and the Lettish term *peena maates* (cf. below), point to the same conclusion.

The snake as household god or ancestral spirit would naturally further the interests of his own family at the expense of others. The Letts, we are told by Fabricius, reared huge serpents which would steal milk-pails from neighbouring herds and bring them back to their own people.[4] From the same authority we learn that these people knew how to injure their enemies' crops by magic arts, but he does not state that they used snakes for the purpose. Prætorius, however, gives an interesting piece of evidence for such practices among the Lithuanians in the 17th century:

A certain man who had been a servant in Insterburg, near Lithuanian Georgenburg, told how various villages in the neighbourhood still kept (though in great secrecy) a *moninink*s. At certain times in the year, usually spring or autumn, this *moninink*s called the people together and collected various snakes through magic prayers, and charmed them by certain magic characters. The table was then laid, food and drink set out, a special place prepared for the snakes, and milk set out for them. The snakes were brought up on to the table, and at the command of the *moninink*s touched all the food, after which the feast took place and was concluded with much drinking. After the meal each person present told the *moninink*s the name of his enemy, and how he wished him to be injured. 'If some one wished his enemy's grain to be injured in the field, the *weideler* took a snake in his two hands, charmed it anew, prayed again some magic prayers, and let it dart away to the door or window, with these words: *Szmiksst per Esze, i.e.*, Go through the fields . . . thereupon the specified corn, and other grain in the field was injured through hail. . . . If the *weideler* said: *Szmiksst per arnida*, then the supply of bread was injured.'[5]

This seems to be a survival of beliefs and practices connected with the house-snake.

2. The sanctuary-snake.—The serpent cult was not confined to the house. In Samland, it seems, large numbers of snakes were reared in an oak-wood in honour of the gods.[6] Prætorius[7] explains that *zaltones* were snake-charmers, who had charge of the snakes consecrated to Padrympus. This information, however, can scarcely be drawn from personal observation, as Prætorius tells us elsewhere that in his day Padrympus was no longer invoked by name.[1] Padrympus, or Potrimpus, was one of the deities to whom the famous Romove sanctuary was consecrated. In his honour a snake was kept in a large jar, crowned with sheaves of corn, and fed with milk by virgin priestesses.[2] Grunau's account of Old Prussian beliefs has perhaps been regarded with undue scepticism. In this case his statement is supported by the evidence of comparative religion. In diverse parts of the world snakes are tended by virgins, who apparently are considered as their wives.[3] The custom of giving milk to serpents is even more universal, most likely because milk is the food of children. The fundamental idea seems to have been that the dead could be born again into their own families. We find traces of this belief among the Scandinavians and elsewhere.

'Behind the Greek notion that women may conceive by a serpent-god seems to lie the belief that they can conceive by the dead in the form of serpents.'[4]

Hence the snake's influence over human fertility. The term *peena maates*, 'mothers of milk,' suggests that some such conception prevailed among the Letts. The word *maates*, 'mothers,' is due to the Lettish preference for female deities.

It is easy to understand why the snake was the peculiar treasure of Potrimpus.

Among the Ewe-speaking peoples of the Slave Coast 'a close connexion is apparently supposed to exist between the fertility of the soil and the marriage of these women to the serpent. For the time when new brides are sought for the reptile god is the season when the millet is beginning to sprout.'[5]

Snakes are commonly credited with power over the weather and the crops; Potrimpus is an agricultural deity — one of the many agricultural deities whose cult was ultimately merged into that of Zemynele (Lettish, *semmes maat*, 'mother of earth'), the great earth-goddess. It is worth noting that the name Potrimpus may be connected with Old Prussian *trumpa=fluvius*, and that David tells us that 'flowing waters were appropriated to him.'[6] Water-spirits are often thought to have the appearance of snakes, and, like Potrimpus, they 'have an especial taste for human blood.'[7] Possibly Potrimpus was originally a water-snake deity. This, however, is mere conjecture.

It is not improbable that at one time the serpent was a common feature of Northern sanctuaries, but here again we have no conclusive evidence.[8]

3. The god of healing.—Michalo, a Lithuanian writer of the 16th cent., believed that his nation was of Italian origin on account of the striking similarity of Lithuanian and ancient Roman rites, 'especially on account of the cult of Æsculapius, who is worshipped in the form of a serpent—the same form in which formerly he migrated from Epidaurus to Rome.'[9] This serpent-god can be none other than the Ausschauts who in the 16th cent. was still worshipped by the Sudavians in Samland, and who is equated with Æsculapius in the *Constit. Synod. Evangel.* of 1530. His name occurs in various forms:

'Ausceutum deum incolumitatis et aegritudinis.'[10] Auschleuts (also Auschkauts) 'der Gott aller Gebrechen, Krankheiten und Gesundheit.'[11] 'Auszweitis, nach Bretkius Auszweikus, ein Gott der Kranken und Gesunden, von sweikas gesund, sweikata Gesundheit.'[12] This derivation is probably correct.

[1] *Mag. der lettisch-literärischen Gesellschaft*, VI. xiv. 144.
[2] *Deliciæ Prussicæ*, ed. W. Pierson, Berlin, 1871, p. 35.
[3] See J. G. Frazer, *GB*³, pt. vi., *The Scapegoat*, London, 1913, p. 302 ff., pt. iii., *The Dying God*, do. 1911, p. 86, *The Belief in Immortality*, do. 1913, i. 60, 69 ff., 74 f., 83.
[4] *Script. Rer. Livon.*, ii. 441.
[5] Cf. *Delic. Pruss.*, p. 36.
[6] Lucas David, *Preussische Chronik*, ed. E. Hennig, Königsberg, 1812, i. 62.
[7] P. 46.

[1] P. 18.
[2] Simon Grunau, *Preussische Chronik*, ed. M. Perlbach, Leipzig, 1876–77, i. 28.
[3] Cf. *GB*³, pt. v., *Spirits of the Corn and of the Wild*, London, 1912, ii. 17 f., pt. i., *The Magic Art*, do. 1911, ii. 149 f.; Oldham, *The Sun and the Serpent*, p. 154.
[4] *GB*³, pt. iv., *Adonis, Attis, Osiris*², London, 1907, i. 76 f.
[5] *Ib.* i. 59.
[6] i. 87.
[7] See *GB*³, pt. i. *The Magic Art*, ii. 150, 155 f.
[8] Cf. above, § 1.
[9] *Respublica Poloniæ Lituaniæ Prussiæ Livoniæ*, p. 265.
[10] Meletius, *Epist. ad Sabinum* (*FL* xii. 296).
[11] David, i. 91.
[12] Prætorius, p. 27.

David gives us a further piece of information about Ausschauts. He describes in detail the usual harvest festival at which four special gods were invoked.

If, however, the harvest was unsuccessful, the priest prayed 'to their excellent and most mighty god Auschkaut, that he would intercede for them with the above-named four gods: Pergubrius, Perkunus, Schaystix and Palwittis.' Every one must then contribute some barley, for the brewing of the beer, and atonement must be made for every breach of village law. The women then brought bread (made from the first crop of wheat) for them to eat at their consecrated feast. The festival lasted until all the beer had been consumed.[1]

There is a parallel to this in the customs of the Ewe-speaking people.

'They invoke the snake in excessively wet, dry, or barren seasons; on all occasions relating to their government and the preservation of their cattle; or rather, in one word, in all necessities and difficulties in which they do not apply to their new batch of gods.'[2]

4. The mythical serpent. — The worship of actual, living snakes may develop into the belief in an imaginary, idealized serpent, and so give rise to snake- or dragon-myths. Some such process may be traced in the customs and superstitions of the Letts, recorded by Fabricius and Paul Einhorn.

'Some of them rear dragons, in their houses, which steal crops, which they bring back to their own people; others nourish huge serpents, etc.'[3]

Paul Einhorn seems to have been much puzzled as to the true nature of the Lettish house-dragon, of whose appearance and habits he gives a detailed description:

'This nation has also had just such an evil and horrible god of wealth [*i.e.* as Pluto], whom they call Puke . . . but the Germans . . . call him the dragon.' This dragon was still kept by many people even in Einhorn's day. He would steal riches and crops and bring them to the people who entertained him. 'He is fiery-red in appearance and flies quietly through the air like a burning fire.' 'He is red when he is hungry; when he is well-fed with the corn he has stolen, he is quite blue and horrible to see. If any householder wishes to keep him and gain wealth through his services, he must prepare a special chamber for him . . . which must be kept perfectly clean . . . nobody must enter there, except the master of the house, and those whom he will have within . . . not every one must know what sort of a chamber it is.' He must always have the first share of all beer and bread and other food, otherwise he will consider himself insulted and burn down the house. He is often to be seen in the evening, but those who keep him do so in great secrecy, and either cannot or will not say much about him.[4]

The Lettish *puke* may be compared with the Lithuanian *aitwars*. Opinions seem to have differed as to the appearance of this being.

'The Aitwars, or Incubus, is described by the Nadravian peasant as having human shape, but with incredibly large hands and feet.'[5]

The Nadravians draw a distinction between the *aitwars*, the *barzdukkas*, and the *kaukuczus*, who bring wealth and crops to people.

'The Barsdukkai live beneath, the Aitwars above, the earth. These Barsdukkai look like men, but the Aitwars *has the appearance of a dragon or great snake, with fiery head.*'[6]

The *aitwars*, like the *puke*, sometimes does good and sometimes ill to those with whom he lives. He is in the habit of stealing. He flies through the air. He must have the first taste of all food. Occasionally he burns down the house in which he lives.[7] It is dangerous to have an *aitwars* in the house during a thunder-storm, because Perkunus, the thunder-god, is likely to strike him for being too familiar with men, and, since it is owing to men that he is punished, he will revenge himself by burning down their home.[8]

5. Conclusion.—We have some detailed descriptions of the ritual, but little direct information as to the ideas which lay behind the serpent-cult of the Letts, Lithuanians, and Old Prussians. To a certain extent we can supply this gap in our knowledge by comparison with the beliefs and rites of other peoples, there being no important feature of Baltic serpent-worship for which we cannot find parallels elsewhere. The Lithuanians, Letts, and Old Prussians seem to have credited the snake with healing powers and with influence over the weather, crops, and human fertility. The souls of the dead were probably thought to be incarnate in snakes. The serpent, in its malignant aspect, seems to have played little part in Baltic religion, unless, perhaps, we may trace it in the superstitions connected with the *aitwars* and the *puke*.

1 David, i. 92.
2 W. Bosman, 'Description of the Coast of Guinea,' tr. from Dutch in J. Pinkerton, *General Collection of Voyages and Travels*, London, 1808-14, xvi. 494.
3 Cf. above; Fabricius, in *Script. Rer. Livon.* ii. 441.
4 'Ein christlicher Unterricht,' *Script. Rer. Livon.* ii. 624.
5 Prætorius, p. 13.
6 *Ib.* p. 29.
7 *Ib.* p. 30.
8 *Ib.* p. 21.

III. *SLAVIC.*—The Slavic snake-cult was probably very similar to that which prevailed among the Baltic peoples.[1]

According to Afanasief, Russian peasants 'consider it a happy omen if a snake takes up its quarters in a cottage, and they gladly set out milk for it. To kill such a snake would be a very great sin.'[2]

Popular superstition preserved the belief that the snake brings wealth and has the gift of healing. In Slavic fairy-tales the power of the snake depends on its possession of 'living waters.'[3]

Certain features of the old cult of the house-snake survive in the superstitions connected with the *domovoy*, a house-spirit not unlike the Lithuanian *aitwars* and the Lettish *puke*.[4] The *domovoy* lives behind the stove, but may be found wherever fires are lighted. He hides behind the stove in the daytime, but comes out at night and eats the food that has been left out for him. He is in the habit of robbing neighbouring peasants for the sake of his own people; occasionally he even harms those of his own household, sometimes going so far as to burn down the house. His close connexion with the domestic hearth, and the fact that he appears at times in the likeness of the master of the house, show that he is really an ancestral spirit. He is usually thought of as in human shape, but

'in White Russia the Domovoy is called *Tsmok*, a snake, . . . This House Snake brings all sorts of good to the master who treats it well and gives it omelettes, . . . if this be not done the snake will burn down the house.'[5]

Dlugosz, in his *History of Poland* (15th cent.), mentions a certain 'deus vitae quem vocabant Zywie.'[6] Brückner[7] suggests that this Zywie, and also perhaps 'Siwa dea Polaborum' mentioned by Helmold, may be really the house-snake. Both names may be derived from *zivb* (cf. Lith. *gywas*, 'living'; cf. Lith. *gywâte*, 'snake').

The snake, as the 'living one,' was often supposed to embody a dead man's soul, and so came to be connected with death, and to assume a malignant character. It is this aspect of the snake that appears in Slavic fairy-stories.

'In that kingdom in which Ivan lived there was no day, but always night: that was a snake's doing.'[8] 'The Serpent [Zmyei] is described in the stories as "winged," "fiery," "many-headed" . . . he is spoken of as guarding treasures of bright metals and gleaming gems, and as carrying off and imprisoning fair maidens.' He is the great antagonist of the hero. 'In some of the stories he bears a surname which points to his connexion with the Deity of the Hearth, being called Zapechny, or Zatrubnik, or Popyalof—from *pech* [the stove], or *truba* [the stove-pipe or chimney], or *pepel* [ashes].'[9]

The snake seems to be similar to, or even identical with, other evil beings who figure in the stories, especially 'Koshchei the Immortal' and the flying witch, or Baba Yaga.

1 See above, § II.
2 W. R. S. Ralston, *The Songs of the Russian People*[2], p. 175.
3 *Ib.* p. 174 f.
4 See above, § II., and art. DEMONS AND SPIRITS (Slavic).
5 Ralston, p. 125.
6 *Historiæ Polonicæ*, Leipzig, 1711-12, i., *Opera*, ed. Cracow, 1873, x. 47 f.
7 *Archiv für slav. Philologie*, xiv. [1892] 179.
8 Ralston, p. 176.
9 *Ib.* p. 174.

'In the Ukraine the flying witch is usually called a snake; in a Slovak tale the sons of a Baba Yaga are described as "baneful snakes." One of the tastes which characterize the snake of fable is sometimes attributed to the Baba Yaga also. She is supposed "to love to suck the white breasts of beautiful women." Like the Snake, also, she keeps guard over and knows the use of the founts of "Living Water"—that water which cures wounds and restores the dead to life. . . . But, as a general rule, the Baba Yaga is described as a being utterly malevolent and always hungering after human flesh. According to some traditions, she even feeds on the souls of the dead. The White Russians, for instance, affirm that "Death gives the dead to the Baba Yaga, with whom she often goes prowling about."'[1]

LITERATURE.—I. *Die prosaische Edda*[2], ed. Ernst Wilken, Paderborn, 1912; *Die Lieder der älteren Edda*[3], ed. K. Hildebrand and H. Gering, do. 1912; Saxo Grammaticus, *Hist. Danica*, i.-ix., tr. O. Elton and F. Y. Powell, London, 1894; J. Grimm, *Teutonic Mythology*, tr. J. S. Stallybrass, 4 vols., London, 1882-88; P. D. Chantepie de la Saussaye, *The Religion of the Teutons*, tr. B. J. Vos, Boston, 1902; J. G. Frazer, *GB*[3], Index, *s.vv.* 'Serpent,' 'Snake.'

II. J. G. Frazer, *GB*[3], Index, *s.vv.* 'Serpent,' 'Snake'; C. F. Oldham, *The Sun and the Serpent*, London, 1905; *EBr*[11], *s.v.* 'Serpent-Worship'; *Mag. herausgegeben von der lettisch-literärischen Gesellschaft*, VI. xiv. [1868]; see artt. OLD PRUSSIANS and NATURE (Lettish, Lithuanian, and Old Prussian) for further literature.

III. W. R. S. Ralston, *Songs of the Russian People*[2], London, 1872; A. Brückner, 'Mythologische Studien,' iii. in *Archiv für slav. Philologie*, xiv. [1892].

ENID WELSFORD.

SETTLEMENTS.—I. Origin and development.

— Settlements (university, college, public school, or generically social) represent an attempt made by the Christian spirit in the latter part of the 19th cent. to obviate one of the gravest moral and social dangers attendant on the growth of great cities. In the days of small towns all classes—the feudal chief or lord of the manor, the leading citizens, the tradesmen, the working people—were housed not very far apart. In the cluster of villages which afterwards expanded into the metropolis there was a similar juxtaposition of the various social grades. This meant always the possibility, and often the reality, of neighbourly relations. Rich and poor, high and low, were personally known to each other and could be mutually helpful. But the expansion of the town and the absorption of the adjoining villages almost entirely swept away the old neighbourliness. The well-to-do chose for their residence the most desirable regions, where the soil, the elevation, the salubrity of the atmosphere, made for the general amenity of life. The less desirable areas were left to the inflowing tide of the wage-earning poor. Thus arose that menace to civic stability and negation of Christian neighbourliness known as the residential separation of the classes. Revolutionary Paris had shown what fearful evils might result. It was to bridge over the social chasm thus formed that the settlement came into being. It was the direct outcome of the Christian spirit.

The first modern settlement practically began when the Rev. Samuel Barnett and his well-to-do bride decided to accept the living of St. Jude's, Whitechapel, which the then Bishop of London described as the worst parish in his diocese, inhabited mainly by a criminal population, and one which had, he feared, been much corrupted by doles. Animated by as profound a spirit of Christian self-sacrifice as any Francis or Damien, the pair who were married on 28th January 1873 entered on their work in Whitechapel on March 6 of the same year. Two years later they paid their first visit together to Oxford, when they talked over to the men 'the mighty problems of poverty and the people.' Mrs. Barnett writes: 'We used to ask each undergraduate as he developed interest to come and stay in Whitechapel and see for himself: and they came, some to spend a few weeks, some for the Long Vacation, while others took lodgings in East London.' Among these men was Arnold Toynbee (1852-83), who stayed with the Barnetts rather oftener than the other men, and once for a few weeks took rooms in Commercial Road; but his health was too fragile to bear the pain and strain of residence, and the experiment soon ended.

[1] Ralston, p. 162 f.

It was in the rooms of Mr. Cosmo Lang (afterwards Archbishop of York) that the undergraduates in Oxford 'first gathered to support the founding of a settlement to enable men to live with the poor.' After eleven years of service at St. Jude's in Whitechapel, the settlement premises having been built, Canon Barnett consented to become its Warden. On the anniversary of Arnold Toynbee's death, 10th March 1884, when Balliol Chapel was filled with men to do honour to his memory, and after Barnett had spoken on Arnold's example, the idea came to Mrs. Barnett and to Mr. Bolton King, 'Let us call the settlement Toynbee Hall.' So the first settlement began in the spirit of Arnold Toynbee. And of him Benjamin Jowett wrote:

> 'The "imitation of Christ" was to him the essence of Christianity; the life of Christ needed no other witness. His labours among the poor were constantly sustained by the conviction that some better thing was reserved both for them and for us: he saw them as they were in the presence of God; he thought of them as the heirs of immortality.'[1]

Thus, prompted by the ethical and religious motive, the first university settlement at Toynbee Hall was founded in 1884. The aim of this, as of every true settlement, was to heal the breach between the classes, to bring at least representatives of all classes into helpful contact, to create a better mutual understanding, to promote by personal friendship and social study a truer civic synthesis. In other words, the settlement is designed to bring those who have many social advantages, such as education, influence, leisure, or wealth, into touch with those who have few social advantages or none, to become acquainted with the real needs of the people, to supply where lacking the elements of social leadership, and to smooth down the rough edges of social antagonism.

This general idea is capable of vast variation. There are in the British Isles nearly 50 settlements; in the United States, it is reckoned, more than 400. Kindred institutions have sprung up in Paris, Berlin, and other cities on the Continent. Almost every settlement has developed differently. The two chief causes of difference are the difference of the neighbourhood and the difference of the staff. Some settlements are pre-eminently academic; they have become a permanent resident society for university extension. Others have been intensely ecclesiastical in motive. Others, again, have been what may be termed broadly religious, shading off into merely ethical or cultural centres. A number of settlements, particularly in America, have been chiefly training schools for social workers. American settlements are often on a larger scale than British. With characteristic munificence money is poured out on large buildings and in many salaries. Perhaps the most important work of the American settlements has been the development of a common spirit and of a civic unity amid the crowd of different nationalities and languages among which they were planted.

Women's settlements, both in England and in America, have done excellent work, chiefly among women and children, in tending invalid children, in providing children's country holidays, maintaining maternity societies, co-operating with employment exchanges and care committees, training and shepherding domestic servants, health visiting, relief committee work, and training of social workers. Where the women's settlement works in conjunction with the men's settlement, the effect

[1] Arnold Toynbee, *Lectures on the Industrial Revolution*[3], London, 1887, prefatory memoir, p. xvii.

upon the neighbourhood is greater. Greatest of all is that produced by settlements in which the residents are men and women, and sex is regarded as no barrier to co-operation.

2. Religious motive.—The religious motive is undoubtedly dominant in the chief workers. Graham Taylor, president in 1918 of the National Federation of American Settlements, reports:

'If the Settlement undertook either to encroach upon the prerogatives of the Churches or to show preference for any one cult or creed by maintaining religious services itself, it would forfeit its own prerogative of being common ground for all, and might be promptly and disastrously ostracized. We seem to be shut up to one of two courses: either to take the whole crowd along with us together as far as they will go, stopping short of religious divisive points; or to take far fewer as much further as we would like to, and run the risk of having no following at all as the racial transformation becomes more rapid and radical. We increasingly feel and express the broadly religious spirit, which seems to actuate Protestant, Roman Catholic, Jew and Ethical Culturist alike. But it would be impossible to agree upon any creed or ritual which would be a common denominator among us.'

A worker in the oldest settlement in Great Britain says that the dominant note in the founders was religious, in the majority of the first residents ethical.

'Religion is easy in a strictly denominational Settlement, hard in an undenominational or inter-denominational, unless the Head, like Samuel Barnett or Jane Addams, has sufficient spiritual force to give unity and expression to the various impulses and goodwill of the residents. Without such a Head, religion and even ethics evaporate.'[1]

3. Schemes of residence. — The scheme of residence is varied. The common idea of a post-graduate sojourn in the slums, to enable university men and women to learn, in a few months, how vast masses of their fellow-countrymen live, was soon found to be insufficient. Permanent residents were needed to secure permanent effects, and to introduce to the general life of the neighbourhood those residents who stayed for a shorter period. Much is to be said for the ideal expressed in the homely phrase that resident households should be scattered over the neighbourhood to be helped 'like currants in a cake.' The difficulty is to get households in sufficient number and of sufficient courage to settle in the derelict district. Experience proves that such families are few. The combination of permanent settlers with a succession of sojourners has been found to be the most useful. The influence of residents is saved from becoming occasional, haphazard, or sporadic by the continuous presence of the permanent staff, who, again, are saved from sinking into the merely parochial rut by the continual advent of fresh life, with different horizons and new points of view.

4. Methods.—There is no limit to the methods employed by the settlements in their endeavour to integrate the local society. The general principle is that, wherever the settlement comes upon an unsatisfied need, it aims, so far as its resources in friends and funds permit, to meet that need. Almost every form of educational appliance has been used, from university extension to the humblest kindergarten. Some settlements have been almost exclusively educational, partaking more of the nature of a polytechnic than the usual social colony.

All kinds of social clubs for men, for women, for youths, for girls, for boys, for children; boy scouts, girl guides; lectures and discussions on all social topics; reading circles; study circles; organizations for promoting thrift, co-operative purchase, co-operative travel; adult schools, brotherhoods; concerts, art exhibitions; classes for instruction in almost every subject; 'people's drawing-rooms'; in seasons of distress, distribution of relief; medical missions, hospitals, old age homes, holiday homes, lodging houses are among the variegated forms of service undertaken by settlements. Residents very often take some part in local government, as town councillors, poor law guardians, school managers, members of care committees and distress committees.

[1] Letter to Mrs. Barnett from private secretary of Canon Barnett.

5. Results.—(*a*) *Social and civic.*—A generation of settlement service permits one to speak of its results. Settlements have created, in almost every district where they have been at work, a better social atmosphere. They have brought higher ideals into active touch with most sides of local life. They have done much to purify and humanize most of the forms of local administration. In American cities, where civic corruption had flourished, the work of the settlements has been in this direction vigorous and effective. Hull House, which is one of the greatest settlements in the United States, has, under the intrepid leadership of Jane Addams, rendered exceptional service in checking local abuses, and in preparing the way for the civic regeneration of the Lake City. Settlements have been especially useful as social laboratories wherein experiments have been carried out that have afterwards been taken over by the municipalities.

The cripples of London, *e.g.*, had been entirely overlooked by the metropolitan education authority. But the Passmore Edwards Settlement, under the direction of Mrs. Humphry Ward, the Bermondsey Settlement, and the Browning Settlement took up the care of cripples in their neighbourhoods, gave them the only training that they had received, and together brought such pressure upon the London School Board that in its last days it began the work of providing for the instruction of cripples. The work was continued under the London County Council on lines that had been initiated by the settlements. Similarly, the vacation schools were introduced into London under the Passmore Edwards Settlement by Mrs. Humphry Ward. In the most central district of London they were developed by the Browning Settlement, with the aid of the municipal tramway, into a method of transporting the children of the slums day by day, for the whole day, to the school-houses, parks, and commons of the more salubrious suburbs. From this experiment the settlement has developed a further suggestion (and won for it before the war influential support) that, except for infants, there should be no schools provided in the central districts, but that boys and girls should be carried out every day by the municipal tramways to schools provided for them in the more healthy outskirts, where their playground would be the common or the heath. The holiday schools have first been recognized, and to some extent imitated, by the education authority, besides being widely copied in other cities of Great Britain. The feeding of necessitous children, carried out on scientific lines by some of the London settlements, supplied a valuable precedent and experiment to the London County Council before it finally decided to adopt the Act of Parliament. Settlements have been frequently visited and studied by municipal authorities, when devising schemes for the welfare of their school-children and of the poor in general. The more active settlements are continually engaged in making different kinds of experiments. The fittest that survive the crucial ordeal of practice are then commended for adoption by local authorities.

As settlements came into being to remedy the evil consequences of the residential separation of the classes, it is specially worthy of note that the measures that promise the ultimate extinction of slums have received their chief currency under settlement auspices.

It was from a settlement that the idea was launched that improved locomotion offered the first step to meeting the housing difficulties of our great cities, and from the same centre this idea was pressed, in a series of conferences, upon the municipal bodies of the metropolitan area as well as upon the general public. As a consequence, the fatal idea of increasing the central congestion by erecting residential barracks in the heart of great towns, where the site would be much more profitably employed for industrial and commercial purposes, was abandoned; and electrical and other improved forms of transit have not merely relieved the congestion of the central districts, but have brought all parts of the urban area into closer and easier touch with one another, have made possible a wise reconstruction at the centre, and have offered opportunity for judicious town-planning in the new suburban areas into which the population is flowing. A garden suburb, with dwellings let at rents ranging from the lowest to the highest figure, so that members of all classes can reside near each other, is a fitting culmination of the career of Mrs. Barnett, one of the initiators of the settlement movement. If only the population now being dispersed by swifter and cheaper means of transit round the circumference of our great cities were housed under these conditions, then the chief menace to the life of great cities would be removed.

(*b*) *Political.*—In the political life of the nation settlements have left their enduring mark. Many statesmen have owed much of their new outlook on life to the months or years they spent as residents in a settlement; and with this new social sense they have infected their comrades in Parliament and Cabinet. First-hand acquaintance with the needs of the people has also impelled settlements to seek and press for practicable measures that will meet these needs, and as a consequence settlements have done much to supply what has been termed the 'raw material of legislation.' As distinguished from the academic socialism of certain middle-class societies and from the revolutionary visions promulgated under the red flag, the demands of settlements for legislation bear the impress in almost every point of an actual social environment and of the reaction of that environment on minds continually handling concrete facts.

In Great Britain, before there were many representatives of organized labour in the House of Commons, the needs of the unemployed were voiced chiefly by settlements, and it was in response to a settlement's appeal that Queen Alexandra initiated the Queen's Fund for the Unemployed (1905), which first provided work for the workless on a national scale. From a settlement resident in a poor law union, noted as the classic instance of aged poverty, sprang the national movement which resulted in the enactment of old age pensions. This achievement was the more remarkable in that it followed the practical abandonment of the reform by both the historic parties in the State, as one that involved insuperable difficulties, financial and other. By stripping it of its partisan associations, and by an appeal characteristic of settlements to all good citizens, notably to organized labour and to organized religion, a measure was carried through with the practically unanimous support of the entire nation. It was also the experience of a settlement in its own homes for the aged which proved that it cost much less to provide the aged with a pension and with homes of their own than it did to sustain them in the workhouse with its attendant disfranchisement and degradation. The bill to establish national old age homes in place of the workhouse bore the mark of the settlement which initiated it, in that it was backed by representatives of the five parties then existing in the House of Commons. Unexpectedly and unintentionally national old age homes were made legally possible by the Housing Act (no. 2, 1914), passed without opposition shortly after the European war began.

(c) *Influence on Church and Labour.*—On ecclesiastical life the influence of settlements has been pronounced. A large number of ministers of religion have, as residents, acquired an intimate knowledge of the conditions under which the poor live, with inevitable reaction upon their teaching and the attitude of the Church. There has been in consequence a greater emphasis laid on the social teachings of Christianity. The present Bishop of London (Dr. Ingram) bears the ineffaceable marks of the experience which he acquired as head of Oxford House in Bethnal Green. What is known as the Institutional Church (*q.v.*) in its distinctive methods owes much to the settlement. It has been humorously described as a settlement that does not require from its workers residence on the spot. Central missions in great cities have adopted many forms of social service first introduced by the settlement. The new religious synthesis implicit in settlement life has not yet found widely recognized expression in theology.

Graham Taylor does not think that settlements have affected the religious, much less the theological, development of the United States. But the whole social movement in which they have their part does influence the thinking, the teaching, and the methods of the Church, especially through its nurture and evangelism, both of which, however, are very predominantly individualistic.

The settlement may be regarded as the outcome of that drift in English religious life roughly known as the Broad Church movement. The spirit of Frederick Denison Maurice (*q.v.*), operating through Charles Kingsley and his fellow-workers, took effective shape in Samuel Barnett and the settlement. But the spirit of social cohesion, which is the essence of the settlement, could not be restricted to any one ecclesiastical compartment. It has found expression in groups that are High Church, Roman Catholic, Quaker, and Congregational.

Constrained by its working-class environment, the settlement has been brought into ever closer and closer touch with the leaders of Labour and with their religious inspirations. But the leaders of the working-classes in Great Britain have for the most part sprung from that great religious awakening of the people which swept through all the Churches and may be broadly described as the Methodist movement. The lay preachers whom it inspired became the spokesmen and artificers of the new industrial democracy. Under the pressure of the social needs, which they most keenly felt and most ardently strove to meet, the individualistic tendencies of Methodism were corrected, and their religious demands assumed a social tinge entirely akin to the spirit that actuated the settlements. So at one of the London settlements were held for a number of years (1910–15) a series of 'Labour Weeks,' in which the first seven days in May were devoted to a series of appeals for personal religion by Labour members of Parliament. The speakers comprised nearly all the most important and influential Labour legislators. Visitors from over-seas spoke of the meetings as 'a revival of the old primitive Christian enthusiasm,' and remarked upon the distinctive stress laid by all speakers on personal devotion to Jesus Christ and on the ideal of the Kingdom of God on earth. The proceedings were published in English, Danish, Finnish, Spanish, and German, and have been circulated round the world. They were welcomed with a chorus of approval by the archbishops and other leaders of Churches in England, Scotland, and the Continent. Invitations were arriving, asking the settlement to organize similar 'Labour Weeks' in Norway, Finland, and in different parts of Germany, and in some cases preparations were in train, when the war broke out. It was felt that here was something more than either Methodist or Broad Church movement had advanced. Here was veritably vocal and manifest the *Labour movement in religion.* The series before the war culminated in an 'International Labour Week' (1915). Among the speakers then were M. Vandervelde (the elective head of Continental socialism), Jean Longuet (the grandson of Karl Marx and a French socialist deputy), Einar Li (a delegate from the social democratic parties of Norway and Sweden), and Hans Wirz (the editor of the official organ of the Swiss social democracy). They joined with their English colleagues in extolling the religion of Jesus Christ, in varying notes, from that of reverent agnosticism to the full assurance of evangelic faith. After the war the movement was resumed at Browning Hall in September 1919, when an International Conference on Labour and Religion endeavoured to elicit and make explicit the religion implicit in the Labour movement.

6. Effect of the war.—The seismic changes consequent upon the war will inevitably produce great transformations in the social landscape, and correspondingly affect the future of settlements. The claims of the war having intercepted the supply of residents, both men and women, settlements have been reduced to carrying on their work with the minimum of assistance; and they are necessarily affected by the general uncertainty as to what will happen in the future. The trend of legislation and administration suggests the happy prospect of the eleemosynary work of settlements being abrogated or undertaken entirely by the State. In Great Britain, if the reforms promised by the Government are carried out in respect of education and housing and the elimination of the liquor traffic, a large part of the previous work of settlements will be ultimately no longer necessary.

In the transitional period of reconstruction the social experience and local knowledge of the settlements ought to make them of priceless value to the nation. The social situation which will follow the time of transition is too uncertain to be sketched in any probable forecast. Even if the dreams of Labour were fulfilled, or if our great cities were so designed and rebuilt as to make each of them a magnified garden suburb, wherein all classes dwell together in nearness and neighbourliness—which most people will consider a very remote possibility—there would still remain important functions for the settlement to discharge. It would still be needed as a social and equal meeting-ground of all classes, of all economic grades, of differing degrees of culture, of varying schools of opinion, of all the religious bodies. Mrs. Barnett considers that the war has made the work of settlements more than ever valuable as centres of union of classes. The social unity which has been precipitated by the war needs to be made permanent by the settlements. The warden of an East End settlement[1] feels that amidst all social changes the settlement should remain as a sort of civic bishopric, a centre of local synthesis, a spiritual counterpart to the administrative unity which centres in the town hall or county council chamber, wherein all the local endeavours to supplement and spiritualize the action of the State, as well as all forms of independent religious and educational activity, might find a congenial home, an exchange of ideas, and a common centre for local initiative and propaganda. The head of a Chicago settlement[2] judges that the initiative, interpretation, and common denominator furnished by such little groups of well-qualified personalities as are found in settlement residence promise to be indefinitely necessary. Another leader in the movement in Great Britain[3] suggests that, however radically political action may readjust the interior relations of society, the settlement will for generations yet have a great part to play in bringing the inspiring influences of art and the teaching of history into the life of the people. Certain it is that those who have had the greatest experience of settlements are most ready to admit that the defects in our social system which the settlement is intended to remedy are likely to persist for generations yet to come, and that consequently it will be long before it can be said that the occupation of the settlement is gone. Whatever be its place in history, the settlement has supplied another chapter in the annals of high purpose and resolute self-sacrifice and what has been termed 'social chivalry.'

LITERATURE.—Samuel A. Barnett, *Settlements of University Men in Great Towns*, London, 1884; S. A. Barnett and Mrs. Barnett, *Practicable Socialism*², do. 1894, *Towards Social Reform*, do. 1909; Henrietta Barnett, *Canon Barnett, His Life, Work and Friends*, do. 1918; F. C. Montagu, *Arnold Toynbee: a Study*, Baltimore, 1889; Arnold Toynbee, *Lectures on the Industrial Revolution of the 18th Century in England*³, London, 1890; Jane Addams, *Philanthropy and Social Progress*, New York, 1893, *The Spirit of Youth and the City Streets*, do. 1909, *Twenty Years at Hull House*, do. 1910; Graham Taylor, *Religion in Social Action*, New York, 1913; J. M. Knapp, *Universities and the Social Problem* (preface by Sir John Gorst), London, 1895; Alfred (Viscount) Milner, *Arnold Toynbee: a Reminiscence*, do. 1895; Will Reason, *University and Social Settlements*, do. 1898; G. Montgomery, *Bibliography of College, Social, University and Church Settlements*, Boston, 1900; Charles Booth, *Improved Means of Locomotion as a First Step towards the Cure of the Housing Difficulties of London*, London, 1901; *Browning Hall Conference: Report of Sub-Committee on Housing and Locomotion in London*, do. 1907; F. H. Stead, *How Old Age Pensions began to be*, do. 1909, *The Labour Movement in Religion*, do. 1914, *No More War: a Settlement Novel*, do. 1917; records of Labour Week at Browning Hall by the foremost Labour leaders: *Labour and Religion*, do. 1910; *Christ and Labour*, do. 1911; *The Gospel of Labour*, do. 1912; *To the Workers of the World*, do. 1913; *The Soul of Labour*, do. 1914; addresses by M. Vandervelde, Jean Longuet, Einar Li, Hans Wirz, and others, in *Together at Last, The International Reconciliation of Labour and Religion*, do. 1915; *The Religion of the Labour Movement*, do. 1919; anon., *Twenty-One Years at Mansfield House*, do. 1911; Browning Settlement, *Eighteen Years in the Central City Swarm, 1895–1912*, do. 1913; record of Science Week at Browning Hall: *Science and Religion*, by seven men of science (Sir Oliver Lodge and others), do. 1914.

F. HERBERT STEAD.

[1] Douglas Eyre of Oxford House, Bethnal Green.
[2] Graham Taylor.
[3] Mrs. Barnett.

SEVEN DEADLY SINS.—Greek philosophy tended to regard evil as a necessary defect of human nature rather than as moral wrong. Christian thought, on the other hand, though not uninfluenced by Greek speculation, followed the guidance of Hebrew Scripture and inclined more to the view of sin as a principle of rebellion on the part of free agents against the divine will. Christian teachers, brought face to face with actual cases of delinquency, naturally became more concerned with the relations of sin to the Church's creed calling for disciplinary rather than speculative treatment. At an early period in ecclesiastical history an attempt was made to fix and classify those faults of conduct which were subversive of the law of the Church and perilous to the salvation of its members. These, though their number was not at first defined, came to be called 'the deadly sins.' They occupy an important place in the order and discipline of the Roman Catholic Church and, along with the cardinal virtues, constitute its moral standards and tests. As several of these vices are separately treated in this work,[1] this article will be confined to a consideration of (1) the nature, (2) the history, (3) the unity, and (4) the general influence of the classification on literature and life.

1. Definition and nature.—Mortal, or 'deadly,' sins were so named in contradistinction to 'venial,' or pardonable. They are such as wilfully violate the divine law, destroy the friendship of God, and cause the death of the soul. In this they differ from venial sins, which, though tending to injure the higher life, do not of themselves involve eternal death. Mortal sins cut off the perpetrator entirely from his true end; venial sins only impede him in its attainment. According to Stoic teaching, all sins are equally heinous, and without distinction in regard to nature and consequences. The early Church, however, in accord with Scripture, contended that, in respect both of character and of effects, some sins are graver than others. Augustine affirms that he who commits a mortal sin transgresses (1) in regard to a grave matter, (2) with clear knowledge of the evil, (3) with deliberate desire ('deliberata complacentia').[2] The distinction between mortal and venial sins was based on 1 Jn $5^{16f.}$. Though the apostle clearly recognizes a difference in the character of sins, it is questionable if the passage can justify the inferences which the later usage of the Church has deduced from it. But this passage does not stand alone. In the letter of the apostolic council to the Gentile

[1] See artt. ACCIDIE, ANGER, COVETOUSNESS, ENVY, PRIDE.
[2] *De Gen. c. Man.*, ii. 14. 21, viii. 19. 20, *Enarr. in Ps.* 129^5; Kachnik, *Ethica Catholica Generalis*, p. 368; *Catech. Aust.*, qu. 762.

churches (Ac 15) four things are forbidden: believers are to abstain from things offered to idols, from fornication, from things strangled, and from blood (murder). These constantly reappear as an outline of a scheme of sins so grave as to exclude the sinner from communion. In other portions of the NT are lists of condemned actions—Mt 15[19], Mk 7[21f.], Ro 1[29-31], Gal 5[19ff.], 1 Co 5, 2 Co 13, Rev 21[8]. In these it is difficult to find a principle of selection. The vices mentioned by Paul in Romans may be regarded as falling under the heads of selfishness, malice, pride, indifference to others. In other Pauline passages works of the flesh are emphasized—impurity, impiety, hatred, excess—while in Revelation falsehood, idolatry, unfaithfulness, impurity, and cowardice are mentioned. In general, it may be said that the sins of the NT are the ordinary vices likely to be prevalent in a semi-pagan society. The NT doctrine of sin (*q.v.*) is clearly ethical rather than ecclesiastical.

2. Origin and history.—As the Church grew in variety and complexity of character, it became necessary to define more clearly the difference between various sins. By some of the early Fathers (Clement and Hermas) the question was raised whether there were not some kinds of sin which, if committed after baptism, could never be forgiven.

(*a*) *Treatment of early Fathers.*—Hermas is the earliest writer who offers any sort of classification. In one passage[1] he gives a list of twelve virtues with their corresponding vices. The parallel is, however, not exact. The significance of his classification is (1) that it indicates within the Church a growing sense of the ethical as distinguished from the ecclesiastical import of sin; and (2) that it names some vices which suggest the germs of the classification of deadly sins as afterwards defined—*e.g.*, ἀπείθεια, ἀπάτη, and λύπη. To Tertullian, a severer moralist than Hermas, we owe the earliest recognition of the distinction between mortal and venial sins. Cyprian, an ecclesiastic rather than a moralist, adds little to the systematic treatment of sin, and is naturally more interested in the bearing of the Church's discipline upon offences. Not till we come to Augustine, the greatest authority upon the problem of evil, do we find the nature and variety of sin treated with fullness. But even he affords no fixed classification. The meaning and origin of evil, rather than its legal or judicial aspect, chiefly concern him. Moral guilt, he tells us, depends entirely on the will and takes its shape from the character of the individual offender. You cannot formulate a definite law for all forms of evil. Sins generally are of three kinds, he says—those which arise from infirmity, those flowing from ignorance, and those depending upon innate viciousness. In one passage he recognizes three principal types—*voluptas carnis*, *superbia*, and *curiositas*.[2] In another passage he traces all sin to *cupiditas* and *timor*,[3] while in a third he divides vices into three general classes—sins of thought, of word, and of deed, ascribing all alike to *concupiscentia*.[4] The germs of the list, as it was ultimately fixed, are undoubtedly latent in the writings of Augustine, but neither in his nor in those of Basil or Chrysostom, who have much to say of the evils of their age, is there any direct reference to the sevenfold hierarchy of sins.

(*b*) *Influence of monasticism.*—The earliest mention of the classification comes from the monks of the Egyptian desert. In the intense struggle with the flesh of which the cloister was the arena the catalogue of principal vices which afterwards held an established place in mediæval ethics was first framed. Although the *peccata capitalia* were eight or more (sometimes regarded as eight 'states' or 'motions' of the soul), the fascination for mystical interpretations characteristic of mediæval thinking, and especially the sanctity attached to the number seven by Oriental peoples, led to its adoption as the perfect circle both of virtues and of vices. In a passage in Origen's *Hom. in Jeremiam* the seven nations of Palestine whom Israel overcame are spoken of as types of the sins of the soul. Cassian[1] refers to this as the view entertained by Serapion, a hermit of Egypt. According to Serapion, there are really eight *principia vitia*, but he explains that the seven nations of Canaan typify the seven deadly sins. On being asked why, if there are only seven nations, there are eight sins, he replies: besides the nations of Canaan there is Egypt itself, which 'stands in the elementary condition of the soul under the influence of sin'—the basis of all evil, the conquest of which gives entrance into the true monastic life. The seven others constitute the elements of the after ascetic conflict. The list as mentioned by Cassian is essentially a list of vices besetting the monastic life. The ascetic character of the deadly sins long prevailed in the East. In the West, however, largely under the influence of Gregory the Great, the deadly sins lost their monastic limitation. Their scope was widened, and they were regarded as tests of life generally. Alcuin, a follower of Gregory, maintained that laymen not less than monks ought to strive after a life of virtue, and that to all men those sins were perils.

3. Unity and relation of sins.—From Gregory's time onwards, while there are differences in the number and names, the list of the *principia vitia* is practically fixed. Gregory himself generally speaks of seven, separating *superbia* from the others as the root or 'leader' among the powers of darkness. The catalogue is commonly notified by the catchword, *saligia*, composed of the initial letters of the following: *superbia* ('pride'), *avaritia* ('covetousness'), *luxuria* ('lust'), *invidia* ('envy'), *gula* ('gluttony'), *ira* ('anger'), *acedia* ('sloth'). Gregory is not content with describing the seven 'rulers' or 'spirits of wickedness,' as Nilus of Sinæ calls them; he sets forth their unity and connexion. They are to be regarded as successive stages in a downward course of evil. Pride comes naturally first, since it is really the source of all the others. Selfishness or egoism is the root of all sin. Pride leads to vainglory, vainglory to envy, envy to anger, anger to melancholy, and that again to avarice. Gluttony and lust follow as natural consequences. Thomas Aquinas discourses with great fullness and acuteness upon the seven deadly sins,[2] which he places over against the seven cardinal virtues. After his time most scholastic writers treat of them, though the list does not always occur in the same order, and sometimes different interpretations are given to different sins. *Superbia* is variously explained. By some it is regarded as vainglory; for others it stands for selfishness generally. So also *tristitia* has sometimes been substituted for *acedia*, in regard to the interpretation of which there has been considerable difference of opinion.

It is hard to say on what principle the classification has been made. The list is somewhat arbitrary and can hardly be regarded as exhaustive. It is strange that 'lying' does not occur. *Timor*, 'fear,' is mentioned by Aquinas as a defect of the virtue of courage, implying a lack of fidelity. It is obviously a grave fault, and heads the list of evils in Rev 21[8] which exclude from God and His salvation; yet it has no place in the catalogue of mortal sins. So, too, it is difficult to understand

[1] *Sim.* ix. 15. [2] *Enarr. in Ps. 8*, § 13.
[3] *Enarr. in Ps. 79*, § 13.
[4] *C. duas epist. Pelag.*, i. 13. 27.

[1] *Collationes*, v. [2] *Summa*, II. ii.

why luxury and gluttony are classed as co-ordinate vices with envy, sloth, and avarice. There is a sense in which all sins are spiritual and psychical; but some are more purely mental, while others are more immediately carnal or fleshly. These are indiscriminately mixed in the classification. At first sight it may not be obvious why *acedia*, 'sloth'—the thankless distaste of life, the general feeling of apathy and irritation arising from a low bodily tone—should be regarded as a sin, and especially as a fault so grave as finally to separate the person affected by it from God. But, as we come to examine this state, we see that, even more than an outbreak of passion or coarse excess, it may be the outcome of deep-seated selfishness and the cause of alienation from, and rebellion against, God, which proves that sin in its most selfish form has been gradually though unconsciously eating into the heart.

It has been said that the classification reveals its monastic origin, but, though the separate sins are such as could be dealt with in a definite legal way, they do not represent outward acts alone. They really stand for moral conditions of the soul by no means exclusively connected with the monastic life. They cannot be regarded as laying special emphasis upon ascetic practices. All of them have a social aspect and may be considered as the perils and tests of every one, whether he be a monk or a layman living his life among the ordinary conditions of the world. The classification can hardly be said to bear witness in any excessive degree to a special age or particular order of ecclesiastical life. It includes the obvious and common sins which belong to all men and to all times and traces them back to pride of self, the source from which all other forms of sinfulness really flow—that self-assertion which is the point at which the human will breaks away from allegiance to God.

4. Influence on literature and life.—It is not wonderful that 'the seven deadly sins' have deeply impressed the consciousness of Christendom and left their mark upon literature and art. Our own poets—Chaucer, Shakespeare, Dunbar, Burns, and others—allude more than once to the familiar catalogue, and every reader of Dante knows that the 'mortal vices' enter largely into the texture and framework of the *Divina Commedia*.[1] Though the use of the list disappeared in England after the Reformation, Protestant divines of every Church and ethical writers of Britain and the Continent have acknowledged the spiritual importance of a classification of sin reached after centuries of discussion by some of the acutest intellects of the race.

LITERATURE.—Works of Augustine, Origen, Cassian (*Collationes*), Gregory (*Moralia* on Job), Aquinas (*Summa*, II. ii.); modern writers: O. Zöckler, *Das Lehrstück von den sieben Hauptsünden*, Munich, 1893; T. B. Strong, *Christian Ethics*, London and New York, 1896; H. L. Martensen, *Christian Ethics*, Eng. tr., 3 vols., London, 1881–85; W. Gass, *Gesch. der christl. Ethik*, 2 vols., Berlin, 1881–87; J. Kachnik, *Ethica Catholica Generalis*, Olmütz, 1910; T. von Häring, *The Ethics of the Christian Life*[2], Eng. tr., London, 1909; J. Stalker, *The Seven Deadly Sins*, do. 1901; H. Sidgwick, *Outlines of the Hist. of Ethics*[5], do. 1902.

A. B. D. ALEXANDER.

SEVEN SLEEPERS.—1. Content of the legend.

—The legend of the Seven Sleepers is one of the most wide-spread and pleasing of hagiographical legends. The elements of the story common to the earliest texts are briefly as follows:

The emperor Decius comes to Ephesus and there revives the worship of idols, commanding that all, and especially the Christians, should offer sacrifices to them; some Christians abjure the faith, others remain steadfast and suffer tortures. Seven youths (or, according to some texts, eight),[2] who live in the imperial palace and whose names are variously given,[1] are accused of being secretly Christians, and, when brought before Decius, refuse to sacrifice to the idols. In the hope that they may waver in their resolution, Decius grants them a respite and then leaves Ephesus. The youths leave the city and hide in a cave in the neighbouring Mount Anchilus.[2] One of them, Diomedes (or Iamblichus), disguised in rags, goes down into the city, to inquire about what was happening in it and to buy food. Decius, returning after a short time to Ephesus, orders the youths to be conducted to his presence. Diomedes informs his companions of the order; sadly they take food, and then they all fall by divine Providence into a deep, long sleep. When Decius cannot find the youths in Ephesus, he summons their parents, who try to excuse themselves for the flight of their sons, and tell that they are hidden in a cave on Mount Anchilus. Decius orders the entrance of the cave to be blocked with large stones, so that the youths may be buried alive. Two Christians, Theodore and Rufinus,[3] write the story of the young martyrs on metal plates, which they place under the stones closing the cave. After 307 years,[4] in the reign of the emperor Theodosius II., a heresy breaks out, led by a bishop Theodore,[5] denying the resurrection of the dead, and the emperor is greatly perturbed. Then God suggests to Adolius, the proprietor of the field where the cave is, to build a sheepfold for his flocks; for this purpose the workmen use the stones which close the entrance of the cave and thus the cave is reopened. God awakens the youths, who think that they have slept only one night, and exhort each other in turn to suffer martyrdom at the hands of Decius, if need be. Diomedes goes down to Ephesus as usual, and is so surprised to see the cross over the gates of the city that he asks a passer-by if it is really Ephesus. He is anxious to return to his companions with the news, but first he buys food, paying for it with the money he had about him, which was of the time of Decius. The vendor and the market-people, seeing the ancient money, think that the youth has found a hidden treasure and wish to share it with him; they drag him with threats through the city; many people assemble, and the youth looks in vain among them for some one of his acquaintance. The bishop and the governor question Diomedes, who narrates the whole story, and invites them to come to the cave and see his companions. They climb the hill and find the two tablets of lead, which confirm the youth's story; they then enter the cave and find his companions alive and shining in appearance. Theodosius is informed of what has happened and comes to Ephesus to the cave. One of the youths, Maximilian (or Achillides or others), tells him that, in order to demonstrate the truth of the resurrection, God had caused them to fall asleep and then resuscitated them before the Judgment Day: after this the youths fall asleep in death. A basilica was erected on the spot.

The legend in this form is clearly Christian, but it is strange, as Heller observes, that in many points, and especially in regard to the resurrection, the references are rather to the OT than to the NT.

2. Diffusion.—The legend occurs in numerous Oriental and Western texts, showing the close intellectual relations between the East and the West, but it is not always easy to arrange the texts in definite groups, and to determine exactly their interdependence.[6]

(*a*) *Oriental.*—(1) *Christian.*—The Christian Oriental literatures in which the legend occurs are: Syriac, Coptic, Arabic, Ethiopian, and Armenian. The most ancient texts are the Syriac, which are divided into two groups: (i.) *Acta* and prose accounts, (ii.) poetical elaborations. The second group is represented by a homily by James of Serūgh, which has reached us in two somewhat varying forms. Of the *Acta* four distinct texts are known; the earliest seems to be one, half of which is contained in a codex of the British Museum, belonging to the latter part of the 6th century. Since James of Serūgh died in 520 (there is no reason to doubt the authenticity of the homily), and it is natural to suppose that the *Acta* were earlier than the poetic elaboration, we may believe that the Syriac prose account arose at the end of the 5th or, at latest, at the beginning of the 6th century.

Only a single fragment of the legend is known in Coptic so far; it represents about a quarter of the complete text. There are various indications that the Coptic text is closely related to the Syriac *Acta*, though not directly, but through the medium of a Greek text.[7]

[1] *Purg.* xviii. 132, *Infer.* vii. 123, etc.
[2] Cf. M. Huber, *Die Wanderlegende von den Siebenschläfern*, p. 91 ff.

[1] Huber, pp. 91, 492.
[2] For variant names see Huber, p. 97.
[3] *Ib.* p. 99.
[4] For variants (353 years, etc.) see Huber, p. 100 f.
[5] *Ib.* p. 101.
[6] *Ib.* pp. 104 ff., 509, 527 f.
[7] *Ib.* p. 549.

Two MSS are known in Arabic Christian literature, showing two distinct texts;[1] but the Ethiopian translator (see below) had at his disposal a third and better text. The Ethiopian translation,[2] two codices of which may be traced back to the 15th cent., must have been made at the beginning of the 15th or perhaps at the end of the 14th cent., and it forms one of that rich series of hagiographical texts whose translation from the Arabic was inaugurated by the metropolitan Salāmā.[3] The general fact of the Ethiopian literature in its second period, viz. that hagiographical texts of no local saints were translated from the Arabic, and, in particular, the change of letters in the proper names—changes which are easily explained by supposing the Arabic script—leave no doubt that the Ethiopian text is derived directly from an Arabic text.

There are two Armenian texts, the shorter one certainly not later than the first half of the 13th cent., the other, much longer and more important, appearing in the *Sufferings* (*Labours*) *and Martyrdom of the Saints*, attributed to Gregory Vgayasēr, the second Armenian patriarch of this name[4]—a work belonging to the second half of the 11th cent. and probably dependent on Syriac and Greek sources.[5] Gregory's legend of the Seven Sleepers is probably to be traced to a Greek text.

The present writer does not know whether the Georgian literature, closely connected with the Armenian, possesses a text of the legend.

Besides these full accounts there is more or less brief mention of the legend in many later historical and hagiographical works of the same literatures.[6]

(2) *Muhammadan.*—In the Arabic Muhammadan literature the legend appears in two quite distinct forms: (i.) in the Qur'ān[7] and (ii.) in the later literature. (i.) The Qur'ān account is short and disjointed, omitting important points and adding details which are wanting in the other text. Its source is undoubtedly oral tradition; it goes back probably to Christian monks, and from them directly or indirectly the story reached Muhammad, who attached great importance to it because of its value for the belief in the resurrection—a belief often inculcated in the Qur'ān. A certain resemblance to the homily of James of Serūgh, which must have been very well known and often repeated among the Syrian monks, confirms this supposition. The passage in the Qur'ān has given rise to much research among the Arabs, and many exegetical, historical, and geographical texts attempt to settle a point about which great uncertainty prevailed, viz. the whereabouts of the cave. (ii.) The later legend agrees generally with the ancient Christian texts, viz. the Syriac *Acta*, except for the inevitable contaminations occasioned by the Qur'ān account. Considering the peaceful relations which existed between learned Muhammadans and Christian Syrians (who possessed the *dhimmah*, 'protection'), it is natural that the former should have received the account from the latter.

The long Muhammadan text starts for the most part from Muhammad b. Ishāq († 768).[8] In other texts—*e.g.*, the *al-Kisā'ī*—the legend is mixed and confused with others.[9] There are noteworthy Haggadic elements, especially in the Arabic texts.[10] The legend is mentioned more or less briefly in many Muhammadan (Arabian, Persian, etc.) literary works, but they generally merely copy or abridge the above-mentioned sources.

(*b*) *Byzantine and Western.*—In the Byzantine literature the legend is merely mentioned by Theophanes (758–816), but it is narrated at length, in a form corresponding to the Syriac, in a MS of the 9th century. There are three distinct texts published critically by Huber.[1] The story occurs in Photius[2] and afterwards in the *Menaea* and other texts.[3]

In the Latin West there is a very short account in the *de Situ Terræ Sanctæ* (520–530) of the deacon Theodosius,[4] while Gregory of Tours († 593 or 594) narrates at length the *Passio* of the Seven Sleepers and says: 'Quam Syro quodam interpretante in Latinum transtulimus,' giving thus his authorities.[5] But the long Latin legend is already found in MSS which go back to the 9th cent. and have been frequently copied—which shows the great popularity of the legend in the West; it is also narrated more or less shortly in many subsequent writings.[6] Huber[7] concludes, contrary to all probability, that the legend was written originally in Latin, though he does not exclude the possibility of its being a translation from the Greek—which is far more probable. Thanks to the Latin text, the legend found its way into the mediæval literature of the West, first in the homily and *Passio* of Aelfric (bet. 1020 and 1025).[8]

Texts are found in Anglo-Saxon, mediæval and modern English, mediæval and modern High German, ancient Norse, Swedish, French, Italian, Spanish; there is also a mediæval Irish translation from the *Passio* of Gregory of Tours. These texts are partly prose and partly verse, and some (Spanish and Italian) are in dramatic form. There is also a dramatic elaboration in Latin *senarii* by an author of the 17th century.[9]

3. Cult.—The Seven Sleepers have taken a place in Christian worship as much in the East as in the West, giving rise to short liturgical texts, hymns, and commemorations in the martyrologies,[10] but the day of their commemoration varies greatly.[11] According to the legend, a church was erected above the cave by the emperor Theodosius; a church dedicated to the Seven Sleepers was built at Rome, on the Appian Way, and several in Germany.[12] Marseilles[13] and other cities boasted of possessing their relics.[14] There are miniatures representing them in the *Menologion* of the emperor Basil II. in the Vatican library, but the celebrated Vettori gem, now lost, does not seem to have represented them.[15]

Muhammadans also venerate the Seven Sleepers,[16] and their names occur, more or less disfigured, on amulets.

4. Parallel myths and legends.—A characteristic motive of the legend—the long sleep[17]—is of wide occurrence in ancient myths and legends, such as the myth of Endymion, of the Nine Sleepers of Sardinia recorded by Aristotle,[18] and especially the story of Epimenides.[19] But a greater resemblance to the story of the Seven Sleepers appears in the Talmudic legend of Onias (Ḥoni) Ha-Me'aggel,[20] who sleeps for 70 years and is convinced of the

1 Huber, p. 17.
2 *Ib.* pp. 36, 542.
3 See E. Littmann, in *Gesch. der christl. Litt. des Orients*², Leipzig, 1909, p. 205.
4 Huber, pp. 37, 544.
5 See F. N. Fink, in *Gesch. der christl. Litt. des Orients*², p. 113; R. Graffin and F. Nau, *Patr. Orient.* v. [Paris, 1910] 350.
6 Huber, pp. 6 ff., 17 ff., 36 f.
7 xviii. 8–26.
8 Cf. Huber, pp. 18–32, 537.
9 *Ib.* p. 251 ff.
10 B. Heller, *REJ* xlix. [1904] 190–203; Huber, p. 458.

1 *Beitrag zur Siebenschläferlegende*, ii. There is nothing to justify the doubt that Zacharias of Mitylene has narrated the legend in Greek and that this ancient text has been lost (Huber, pp. 10, 37). As for John of Ephesus (native of Āmid or Diarbekr), he wrote his story in Syriac, not in Greek.
2 *Bibl.* cod. 253.
3 Huber, p. 38 ff.
4 *Ib.* p. 84.
5 Cf. *ib.* pp. 59, 499 ff.
6 *Ib.* p. 72.
7 *Ib.* p. 568.
8 *Ib.* p. 155.
9 *Ib.* pp. 155–214.
10 *Ib.* pp. 1, 7, 36 f., 85, 90, 136.
11 *Ib.* p. 136.
12 *Ib.* p. 142 ff.
13 *Ib.* p. 154.
14 *Ib.* pp. 145, 153.
15 *Ib.* p. 139.
16 *Ib.* p. 308.
17 *Ib.* p. 376 f.
18 *Phys. ausc.* iv. 11.
19 For other analogous legends see Huber, pp. 128–136, 395 ff., 435, 443.
20 *Ib.* pp. 403, 418.

truth of Ps 126[1], and in the story of Abimelech,[1] whom God caused to sleep for 66 years, to spare him the sight of the destruction of the Temple under Nebuchadrezzar. The legends of men translated alive to the other world also show some connexion.

5. Criticism of the legend.—The historicity of the story of the Seven Sleepers was first questioned by Baronius († 1607) and then by Tillemont and others, against whom Assemani tried to defend it. Recently many have come to the conclusion that the legend is simply derived or developed from ancient Indo-Germanic myths.

It was generally maintained that the earliest text was Greek and of Greek provenance, but in 1886 Nöldeke produced evidence that the Greek was a translation of an original Syriac text; and this was confirmed by the observations of Ryssel and Heller.[2] As arguments against the Greek origin of the legend we may notice (1) that the earliest texts of any length are Syriac, going back perhaps to the end of the 5th cent.; (2) that it seems impossible that in an important region at the very heart of the Eastern Empire there would be narrated with imaginary circumstances (such as heresy), and with the gravest anachronisms, facts which had happened not more than a half century before and which would be remembered by many of the men of the time. Besides, the legend had a definite aim—to inspire belief in the resurrection of the body, an aim which would in such circumstances be totally missed; further, the topographical data are not accurate for Ephesus. The same applies in the main to other localizations, such as Arabissos[3] and Palestine.[4] On the other hand, the anachronisms and the historical and topographical mistakes are not surprising in Syrians who lived in the distant confines of the empire or beyond it, and it is noteworthy that the first historian to narrate the legend, John of Ephesus, was a native of Amid. Moreover, from the witness of Aphraates[5] it can be proved that the oriental Syrians, from the first half of the 4th cent., believed that the dead did not enter into reward or punishment until after the resurrection and the judgment; that, while in death the 'heavenly spirit' received at baptism returned to God, the 'animal spirit' remained buried with the body in a sleep, tranquil for the just and troubled for the sinner. For men accustomed to this order of ideas the re-awakening of the Seven Sleepers had an evidential value which it could not have for others. And we may suppose that the 'heresy' was some local dissension among the oriental Syrians. Further, although the legend is clearly Christian, it is not improbable that parallel legends of long sleep, etc., and especially the Jewish stories of Ḥoni and Abimelech, both inspired the author of the legend and procured for it the belief of the people; the influence which Judaism had in Mesopotamia (Adiabene) from the beginnings of the Syriac literature agrees with this.

LITERATURE.—The two special works dealing with the legend of the Seven Sleepers—John Koch, *Die Siebenschläferlegende, ihr Ursprung und ihre Verbreitung: eine mythologisch-literaturgeschichtliche Studie*, Leipzig, 1883; and I. Guidi, 'Testi orientali inediti sopra i Sette Dormienti di Efeso,' *Memorie della R. Accademia dei Lincei*, Classe di Scienze morali stor. e filolog., 3rd ser., vol. xii., Rome, 1885—are carefully considered and epitomized in Michael Huber, *Die Wanderlegende von den Siebenschläfern*, Leipzig, 1910 (valuable for its rich material of every kind, sometimes not closely connected with the legend; but the hypotheses and conclusions of the author cannot be accepted without great reservations. On p. 214 is a complete bibliography, from C. Baronius and S. Le Nain de Tillemont, down to the various articles of T. Nöldeke, V. Ryssel, B. Heller, M. J. de Goeje, J. Clermont-Ganneau, etc.; to this bibliography the reader may be referred).

I. GUIDI.

[1] Huber, pp. 407, 422.

[2] *Ib.* pp. 457, 460, 469. The same conclusion can be drawn from passages where, corresponding to a regular expression in the Syriac, there is an unusual expression in the Greek; *e.g.* (P. Bedjan, *Acta Martyrum et Sanctorum*, Paris, 1890–96, i. 306) ܡܛܠ ܕܟܠ ܡܠܟܘܬܐ ܐܠܗ̈ܝ ܦܠܚܝܢ ܐܢܬܘܢ ܗܘ ܡܢܟܪܝܢ ܐܢܬܘܢ ܡܢ ܪܒܘܬܐ ܕܦܠܚܘܬܐ ܕܡܠܟܘܬܝ ; (Huber, *Beitrag*, ii. 31) ἐπειδὴ ἐξεκόψατε ἑαυτοὺς ἀπὸ τῶν μεγίστων θεῶν ξένοι ἔστε ἀπὸ τῆς μεγαλοσύνης τῆς βασιλείας μου; (Bedj. 314) . . . ܢܚܢܩܐ ܒܪܚܡܗ̇ ; (Hub. 40) πιεζομένοις ἐν τῇ μήτρᾳ; (Bedj. 317) ܚܕ ܠܚܕ ; (Hub. 44) εἰς τῷ ἑνί; (Bedj. 219) ܠܗܠ ܘܠܗܠ ; (Hub. 46) ὧδε καὶ ὧδε, etc.

[3] M. J. de Goeje, *K. Akad. v. Wetensch.*, Afdeeling Letterk., IV. iv. [Amsterdam, 1901] 13–33; Huber, p. 233.

[4] J. Clermont-Ganneau, *Comptes-Rendus de l'Acad. des Inscr. et Belles Lettres*, 4th ser. xxvi. [1899] p. 564–574; Huber, p. 235.

[5] Graffin, *Patr. Syr.*, Paris, 1894–1907, i. 396, 402, 294.

SEVEN VIRTUES (or GIFTS OF THE SPIRIT).

—The mediæval Church not only formulated the 'seven deadly sins' as the sources from which all other sins might be derived, but also enunciated the seven chief virtues as the main types of all possible excellences.

1. The cardinal virtues in Greek philosophy.—The 'classification of the virtues' dates from Greek times. The Greeks named four virtues only—wisdom, courage, temperance, justice—as fundamental. Plato, in whose *Republic*[1] they first definitely appear, implies that they were already traditional in his day. Though not invented by Plato, it was his rare insight that singled out these qualities, already current in popular thought, as constituting the central core of morality. Plato attempts to show that these virtues are primary or 'cardinal' (*cardo*, 'hinge') because they correspond to the natural constitution of the soul, and therefore form the four sides of a symmetrical character. Virtue, according to Plato, is the health or harmony of the soul. As the soul is composed of three powers—intellect, feeling, will—so corresponding to these are the virtues of wisdom, temperance, and courage. These three qualities, however, have reference more particularly to the individual life. But, as man is also part of an organism, justice is conceived as the social virtue — the virtue which regulates the others. Aristotle[2] opposed the theory of Plato that virtue is innate; it is acquired by habit, and is not the same for every man, but is determined by the circumstances of the individual. Aristotle therefore considerably enlarged the list of the principal virtues, and specially includes in their number 'magnanimity,' or generosity. He drew a sharper distinction than Plato between the intellectual virtues and those dependent upon the emotions. The Stoic school followed Plato, conceiving the cardinal virtues as constitutive of 'the life according to nature.' Since Plato's day his theory has been generally accepted by moralists, though from time to time other virtues have been added, and a place has frequently been found for 'benevolence.' Among ethical writers benevolence was first prominently mentioned by Thomas Aquinas in the 13th cent., there taking the form of love and being placed, as we shall afterwards see, with the other two of the Pauline triad, faith and hope, above Plato's list. It was early felt, especially by those influenced by monotheistic thought, that, while the will is strong for courage and temperance, and the insight of the intellect just and wise, true morality is not less a matter of the heart and feelings. However keen the mind and strong the will, there is no security that they can compass moral action unless emotion be their

[1] Tr. B. Jowett, *The Dialogues of Plato*, Oxford, 1871, iii. 306 ff.; see also v. 200 ff. (*Laws*), i. 142 (*Protagoras*).

[2] *Nicom. Ethics*, bk. ii. 1, beginning.

ally; and indeed, where the mind and will alone rule and the heart is denied expression, the moral character lacks completeness; as Paul says, 'Love is the fulfilment of the law.' Like the other cardinal virtues, 'benevolence' has been variously interpreted, being identified by early monotheism with charity, and only later receiving a larger significance. It has been maintained, however, by some that the Platonic list is adequate and compact, covering the whole field of morality. There is no need for the special mention of benevolence or charity, since a proper conception of justice involves all forms of generosity. It is true, we must 'be just before we are generous.' But there is no such thing as bare justice. He who is just naturally recognizes the claims of others; and benevolence, charity, and even kindness and mercy are the implicates of true justice.

2. Virtues of NT.—The NT does not elaborate a system of ethics. Christ and His apostles deal with moral questions as circumstances dictate. While several passages set forth a catalogue of virtues (Mt 5^{1-16}, Ph 4^8, Gal $5^{22f.}$, 1 Co 13, Col $3^{12f.}$, 2 P 1^{5-7}), these summaries are not systematic or formal, though they are characterized by a remarkable similarity in spirit and tone. They usually emphasize what have been called the 'amiable graces,' and derive all excellence of character from the spirit of love. Conspicuous among the moral ideas constantly recurring in the apostolic writings are the three virtues of faith, hope, and charity (1 Co 13, 1 Th $1^{2f.}$, Col $1^{3.5}$, Ro 5, 1 P, He 10^{22})—which suggests that these were regarded as moral conditions of the Christian life. They connect man with God and form the mainspring of the type of character which Christ sought to create. These graces are not set in opposition to the classical virtues. Paul at least, who had some acquaintance with Stoic philosophy, was not likely to be ignorant of the place that the latter held in Greek and Roman morals. There is no repudiation of them in the NT. All are mentioned, at least separately if not in conjunction, and indeed strongly commended.

3. Recognition by the Church of the cardinal virtues.—When Greek philosophy began to exercise its influence in early Christianity, it is not surprising that the cardinal virtues, so long regarded as the basal elements of character, should gradually find a place in Christian ethics. But the early Fathers, being persuaded that these virtues had reference to man's mundane life alone, added to them the Pauline graces as expressive of man's relation to the spiritual world. The four first were consequently called 'natural,' the three last 'supernatural' or 'theological' virtues. The adoption of the cardinal virtues did not come about immediately. The problem before the Church was a complex one. Though Christianity might be willing to acknowledge what was good in the moral teaching of the ancient world, it could not ignore the associations which clung to many of the ideas and practices of pagan times. If, then, the Church was to assimilate any of the existing data of morals, it was bound to impose upon them its own interpretation and to bring them into harmony with its own system of belief. Only gradually, therefore, did there come about a spirit of mediation between the old morality and the new. The earliest sub-apostolic writers were disposed to emphasize the contrast and to repudiate everything that savoured of pagan ethics. Among the first to draw attention to the importance of the cardinal virtues was Origen, who, though mentioning them as indispensable to the moral character, made no attempt to give them a distinctively Christian significance. With Ambrose, whose *de Officiis*—practically a reproduction of Cicero's book bearing the same name—is the first real treatise on Christian ethics, a change of attitude becomes apparent. An effort is now made to connect the Platonic virtues with Christian ideas. 'Wisdom,' he maintains, is primarily theological as having God for its object. 'Fortitude,' or courage, is essentially firmness in withstanding the seductions of the world. But, strongly influenced by OT notions, Ambrose does not relinquish the narrower martial view of the term. 'Temperance' retains the Stoic meaning of 'observance of due measure' in all conduct, while also the Stoic idea of justice, as the union of all human interests, is enlarged to embrace the notion of Christian benevolence.

4. Transformation under Christianity.—There are undoubtedly indications in this earliest treatise on Christian ethics of the transforming influence of Christian thought, but it is in the writings of Augustine, Ambrose's greatest pupil, that the decisive step is taken of Christianizing the virtues. The old names frequently recur, but they are now employed in a new sense and are directed to a new object—viz. the vision of and devotion to God. Faith, hope, and love are now introduced and regarded by Augustine as the formative factors of Christian virtue, while the four earlier virtues are but the different aspects in which the love of God manifests itself.

> Thus he defines fortitude as 'love cheerfully enduring all things for the sake of God; temperance, love keeping itself entire and inviolate for God; justice, love serving God only and therefore controlling all else that is subject to man; prudence, or wisdom, love discriminating between those things which assist and those things which retard its approach to God.'[1]

Under the influence of Ambrose and Augustine the cardinal virtues henceforth form a generally accepted scheme for the Christian treatment of systematic ethics. The triad of Christian graces is frequently simply placed at their side. Sometimes the 'seven gifts of the Spirit' enumerated by Is 11^2 are added, while over against them are arrayed under the head of the 'seven deadly sins' (*q.v.*) the forces of wickedness. It is possible to trace the effects of Augustine's teaching upon the writings of Gregory the Great, who by his frequent use of allegory prepared the way for scholasticism. But it is when we come to the schoolmen themselves, and particularly to Thomas Aquinas, that we discover the full effect of Augustinian thought. The scholastics go back to the old sources of moral speculation. Aristotle is *par excellence* their 'master.' In Aquinas Aristotle reappears; but it is Aristotle read in the light of Augustine. The Aristotelian division of the soul and the doctrine of the 'mean' are preserved, but the cardinal virtues are now referred to the supernatural end of man and are derived from the divine gifts of love.

Thus, in the development of Christian truth, the cardinal virtues have come to hold an acknowledged place. But they have undergone a marked transformation. The Christian cannot afford to neglect them. They stand as essential qualities. But, baptized into the spirit of Christ, they are endowed with a new meaning and worth. The religion of Jesus has so profoundly modified the moral ideas of the past that they have become new creations. The old moral currency was still kept in circulation, but it was gradually minted anew.[2] Courage is not disparaged, but it is shown to be not less real when evinced, not on the battlefield, but in the conflict of the soul. Temperance is still the control of the physical passions, but it is widened out to embrace the right placing of the affections. Wisdom is no longer the selfish cal-

[1] *De Mor. Eccl.* 25.

[2] Strong, *Christian Ethics*, p. 139 ff.

culation of worldly prudence, but the true interpretation of the things of God. Justice involves, as before, the suppression of self in conflict with the rights of others; but the source of it lies in giving to God the love which is His due and in finding in the objects of His regard the subjects of our thought and care.

5. Unification. — Can the virtues be unified? May it not be shown that the various aspects of the 'good' are but different manifestations of one principle? Augustine was the first to recognize the great Christian truth that it is man's relation to God that gives cohesion and unity to the moral life; and he was but true to the spirit of the NT when he re-affirmed the Pauline triad—faith, hope, and charity — as the primary and co-ordinating elements of Christian character. According to him and later moralists, these qualities were not simply added to the classical virtues, but so fused and incorporated with them as to create the spiritual disposition which penetrates the entire personality and qualifies its every thought and act. So essential are these graces to the Christian life that, as we have seen, they were called 'the theological virtues'; because, as Aquinas says, 'they have God for their object, they bring us into true relations to God, and they are imparted to us by God alone.'[1] They are but different manifestations of one virtue, three facets of one gem, the supreme passion of the soul and lord of its emotions; and, like justice in the Platonic theory, the intimate spirit of order alike in the individual and in society, harmoniously binding together all the other virtues. Faith, hope, and love are one, and are at once the root and the fruit of all moral excellences. They constitute the attitude and spirit of the man whom Christ has redeemed. But, if they are to be called 'virtues,' it must be in a different sense from what the ancients understood by virtue. They are not elements of the natural man, but spiritual states which come into being with a changed moral character. They connect man with God and constitute him a member of a new spiritual order. Hence these graces must not be considered as outward adornments merely. They are radical and inherent in the Christian. They claim the whole man. They re-create and transfigure all his powers of mind and heart and will. They do not supersede or render superfluous the natural virtues. They transmute and complete them, giving them coherence and purpose by directing them to a divine object.

LITERATURE.—In addition to the works given in the Literature of art. SEVEN DEADLY SINS, see general works on Christian ethics: F. Schleiermacher ([2]Berlin, 1834), R. Rothe, ([2]5 vols., Wittenberg, 1869–71), I. A. Dorner (Berlin, 1885), K. R. Köstlin (do. 1887), Newman Smyth ([3]Edinburgh and New York, 1894), S. G. Mezes (*Ethics, Descriptive and Explanatory*, New York, 1901), J. C. Murray (*A Handbook of Christian Ethics*, Edinburgh, 1908), A. B. D. Alexander (*The Ethics of St. Paul*, Glasgow, 1910, *Christianity and Ethics*, London, 1914); also relevant portions of histories of philosophy: E. Zeller (*Philosophie der Griechen*[4], 4 vols., Leipzig, 1876–1909), J. E. Erdmann (Eng. tr., 3 vols., London, 1900), A. Schwegler (Eng. tr.[10], Edinburgh, 1888), A. B. D. Alexander (*A Short Hist. of Philosophy*[2], Glasgow, 1908); F. C. Baur, *Church History*[3], Eng. tr., 2 vols., London, 1878–79; J. A. W. Neander, *General Hist. of the Christian Relig. and Church*, Eng. tr., 10 vols., do. 1850–58; J. Stalker, *The Seven Cardinal Virtues*, do. 1902; R. L. Ottley, *Christian Ideas and Ideals: An Outline of Christian Ethical Theory*, do. 1909; J. R. Illingworth, *Christian Character*, do. 1904; T. H. Green, *Prolegomena to Ethics*[5], Oxford, 1906.

A. B. D. ALEXANDER.

SEX. — **1. Phenomena of sex.** — The general phenomena of sex as exhibited by the higher animals are familiar to all. The individuals of a species are divisible into two groups, males and females. Biologically the essential property of the male is that he comes to carry a certain type of minute cell known as the spermatozoon. So also is the female the bearer of a peculiar form of cell known as the ovum. Death is the lot of these cells except of such as chance to fuse one with another. Through the fusion of two gametes, a sperm with an ovum, the combined product, the zygote, receives an impetus to growth, and a new individual results. The bearing of one or other of the two types of gamete is the fundamental distinction between the two sexes, and in some of the lower animals—*e.g.*, sea-urchins—no other is to be found. But in the higher animals the sexes are further differentiated in a number of ways. Appropriate ducts and glands, differing in the sexes, facilitate the transference of the sperm from the male to the female, while in the latter sex further elaborate mechanisms are often found, serving to nourish the embryo before and after the time of birth. Besides such sexual differences as are directly subservient to the needs of the developing zygote, and are generally termed 'primary' sexual characters, there are many others of a less essential nature. The gayer plumage and the song of cock-birds, the mane of the lion, the horns of the stag, and the beard of man are well-known examples of a host of features in which the male sex differs from the female. Characters of this sort, not directly concerned in the formation and nutrition of the embryo, are termed 'secondary' sexual characters. They offer special problems of their own, especially in man, where mental characters as well as physical are doubtless to be included in this category. Owing to their social and ethical importance, a more detailed account of them is given below.

2. The reproductive process.—The process by which a new individual results from the fusion between two gametes—spermatozoon and ovum—is frequently termed 'sexual reproduction,' but from a comparative standpoint the term is not strictly accurate. Reproduction in most of the lower and smaller forms of animals is brought about by division. In the most minute forms, such as the protozoa, the whole animal divides into two portions of equal or nearly equal size, each of which becomes a fresh individual. In more complex yet still lowly animals, such as polyps and certain worms, the division is unequal, resulting in the production of one or more smaller portions or buds which eventually grow up into the adult form. In forms of life which are yet more complicated, in which the various organs are more highly differentiated, the place of the bud is taken by a single cell, the egg. Reproduction consists in the formation of numbers of eggs, which in some species develop straight away into fresh individuals of the species. In some cases only one sex is known, and reproduction may be regarded as the formation of numerous internal buds which sever their connexion with the parent while still in the unicellular stage. In higher animals the eggs are incapable of further development under normal conditions unless they fuse with another cell, the spermatozoon, though, as will appear later, even the eggs of such highly organized creatures as the frog can be artificially stimulated to develop without the intervention of the male. Reproduction has been accomplished with the formation of the eggs and sperms; the fusion with the sperm, by which the eggs are stimulated to develop, is a distinct phenomenon. It is comparable to the curious and complicated process known among the protozoa as conjugation, of which the biological significance is still a puzzle. The discovery of this phenomenon, coupled with the pronounced speculative tendencies prevalent among zoologists at the close of last century, led to the production of much literature on the question of the

[1] *Summa*, II. ii. qu. 62, art. 1.

origin of sex. With the fashion then in vogue of arranging comparable phenomena in a series from what was judged the most primitive to that considered the most highly specialized, it was inevitable that attempts should be made to construct a scale with the simplest protozoon at one end and man at the other. Moreover, it was argued how each step in the scale should theoretically confer an advantage on the species which took it, thus bringing the whole process into line with natural selection operating upon the required variations of which the existence was assumed. But, while biologists remained so ignorant of the nature of variation, these essays failed to carry conviction among the more critically minded; and with the renewal of interest in the experimental study of variation and heredity, they have for the present been relegated to the background. The feeling prevalent among biologists to-day is that, if attention is concentrated upon the experimental analysis of the nature of sex, the question of its origin, in so far as there can be certainty in this matter, will gradually solve itself.

3. Parthenogenesis.—Parthenogenesis (*q.v.*), the development of an egg without fertilization by a sperm, is a phenomenon which invites attention in connexion with sex. Various experiments show that even in the vertebrate the egg alone may contain all the constituents necessary for a fresh individual, provided that the appropriate stimuli are forthcoming. Eggs which are naturally parthenogenetic usually differ from normal eggs in extruding one polar body instead of two, and it was suggested by Weismann that the retention of the second polar body was a form of auto-fertilization. In view of the facts of artificial parthenogenesis, this thesis can hardly be maintained, since development occurred after the extrusion of both polar bodies. Moreover, in the honey-bee the eggs which produce the drones are undoubtedly parthenogenetic, and at the same time form two polar bodies.

4. Importance of the ovum.—The study of parthenogenesis suggests the question whether the gametes found in the two sexes are of equal value in so far as the next generation is concerned. The matured ovum can be induced to develop without the sperm. Can the sperm be induced to develop into a fresh individual without fusing with an ovum? So far no medium has been found in which the sperm will develop except the cell protoplasm of the egg. Boveri's experiments[1] showed that a fragment of egg protoplasm is all that is required in certain species. But, until the sperm can be shown to develop in some other medium, it is possible to maintain the view advocated by some writers that the ovum is the all-important gamete, the sperm an accessary which is not always essential. There are certain characters which, on this view, are carried independently by either egg or sperm, and such characters generally exhibit some form of Mendelian heredity. But the essential characters which determine the capacity for existence reside in the cell protoplasm of the ovum, and there alone. The factors which determine the colour of the eyes or hair, the shape of the nose, or perhaps the grade of mental ability, are to be found in either ovum or sperm. But the factors which decide the existence of lungs or a backbone reside only in the cell protoplasm of the egg. In short, as one writer has expressed it, we are vertebrates because our mothers were vertebrates.

5. Mendelian nature of sex.—With the outburst of experimental work that followed the rediscovery of Mendel's paper on heredity,[2] attention was early turned to analyzing the nature of sex by the new methods. Indeed Mendel himself had suggested in his letters to Nägeli that the inheritance of sex might follow the same lines as that of other characters. The heterozygous dominant mated with the recessive gives equal numbers of heterozygous dominants and recessives. In such matings these are the only two forms of individual produced in so far as a given character is concerned. If therefore one sex could be regarded as a heterozygous dominant and the other as a recessive, the rough equality of numbers in which the two sexes are usually produced, as well as the normal absence of transitional forms, would receive a simple explanation. For since, from the nature of the case, the mating must always be of the same type, viz. heterozygote × recessive, only males and females of the same constitution can be formed. The question then arose which sex was to be regarded as the heterozygous dominant and which as the recessive. The matter was decided by a study of the inheritance of certain characters which have been termed 'sex-linked' or 'sex-limited.' As an example of this type of heredity, we may take the following case from poultry:

In certain breeds of fowl the plumage is completely black; in other breeds, such as the Plymouth Rock, the plumage is 'barred.' Across each individual feather run alternating transverse bands of black and white, the sum total of which give the bird its characteristic barred appearance. 'Barring' (*B*) behaves as a simple dominant to black (*b*). Barred cock × black hen produce barred offspring of both sexes; and, when these are mated together, the F_2 generation consists of barred and black in the ratio 3 : 1,[1] thus establishing the recessive nature of black. But the remarkable fact of the case is that all the blacks are females. The explanation now generally adopted is that the female is heterozygous for a sex factor (*F*) which the male does not possess. When a female which is heterozygous for the barring factor, and therefore in constitution *FfBb*, comes to form gametes, the cell division is of such a nature that the factors *F* and *B* will not enter into the same gamete. The gametes which are formed in such a bird are therefore of the two kinds *Fb* and *fB* only. The heterozygous male (*ffBb*) forms gametes of the two kinds *fB* and *fb*. It is clear, therefore, that every F_2 bird which is homozygous for *b* (=*bb*) must at the same time be heterozygous for *F*, *i.e.* must be a female. This view of the case is confirmed by the result of mating barred hens with black cocks. In every case, no matter how 'pure-bred' the barred hen was, this mating has given barred cocks and black hens only. The barred hen, however bred, is always heterozygous for the barring factor (*B*), and, since she transmits this factor only to her sons, never to her daughters, it must be supposed that her gametes are of two sorts from the point of view of sex, viz. those which give rise to males and those which give rise to females. There is at present no evidence from experimental breeding for regarding the spermatozoa as other than of the same type from the point of view of sex—in other words, the male may be considered as homozygous. Breeding experiments have shown that the same holds good also for pigeons and for certain moths.

6. Experiments with Drosophila.—There is, however, another group of cases where the breeding evidence points to the converse condition holding good—the male is the heterozygous and the female the homozygous sex.

The little pomace-fly (*Drosophila ampelophila*) normally has red eyes. Some years ago a white-eyed variety appeared, at first only in the male sex. Breeding experiments showed that white was recessive to red. From the cross red-eyed female × white-eyed male all the offspring were red-eyed. When these F_1 flies were mated, the F_2 generation was found to consist of reds and whites in the ratio 3 : 1, but all the whites were males. Subsequently white-eyed females were produced, and these, when mated to any red-eyed male, gave only red-eyed females and white-eyed males. The case is the converse of that of the barred poultry. The male must be regarded as the heterozygous and the female as the homozygous sex for some factor, transmitted along Mendelian lines, upon which the manifestation of sex depends. Many other characters in *Drosophila* have recently been shown to follow the same type of inheritance as that of the white eye.

This type of transmission is of special interest owing to the fact that it is found in man also. The heredity of certain human defects, notably hæmophilia and colour-blindness, appears to be precisely parallel to the series of sex-linked *Drosophila* cases, and, so far as the evidence goes, we are forced to conclude that in man also the male is the heterozygous and the female the homozygous sex.

[1] Cf. below, § 9. [2] Cf. art. HEREDITY, § 7.

[1] Cf. art. HEREDITY, § 7.

These two groups of cases, the bird-moth group and the man-fly group, at present stand sharply apart. It is, however, difficult not to believe that future work will reveal them as forming part of some more general scheme. Indeed, attempts have already been made to effect this synthesis by the assumption of selective fertilization. On this view, the difference between the sexes would depend upon more than one factor, the male and the female being heterozygous respectively for different factors. This involves the assumption of two classes of sperms and two classes of eggs, such that the sperm of class *A* would fertilize the ova of class *A* to give females, and the sperm of class *B* would unite with the ova of class *B* to give males. In the absence of direct evidence, however, any attempt at explanation based on selective fertilization cannot be regarded as having more than a suggestive value. Nevertheless, the idea that the manifestation of sex depends upon definite factors distributed among the gametes along the well-known Mendelian lines of segregation is an idea that is already firmly based upon a secure foundation of fact.

7. The X chromosome.—During the past few years a notable advance in our knowledge of the phenomena of sex has been made by American workers, among whom should be mentioned more especially E. B. Wilson and T. H. Morgan. It was discovered that in many insects the number of chromosomes in the individual cells is different in the two sexes. Where this was the case, the number and arrangement in the female were symmetrical, so that all the ova formed were alike in these respects. In the male, however, the number was less, and asymmetry occurred, so that two classes of sperm were formed. The sperms with the lower number of chromosomes united with the ova to form the number characteristic of males, while the sperms with the higher number, on fusing with ova, gave the number characteristic of females. The deduction was made that the males were heterozygous for sex, forming two classes of sperm which were male-determining and female-determining respectively. This conclusion has been strengthened by recent work on *Drosophila*, where microscopical examination of the germ cells has accompanied experimental breeding. In this fly there is a certain type of chromosome, the so-called X chromosome which, like all the other chromosomes, is duplicated in the cells of the female, but represented by a single number only in the cells of the male. Every gamete formed in the female therefore contains an X chromosome, whereas one half of the sperms contain it and the other half are without it, its place being taken by a chromosome of a different type. This accords with the breeding work on the pomace-fly, which, as already stated, indicates that the female of this species is homozygous and the male heterozygous for sex. The two kinds of gametes produced by the same individual male and differing in their sex-determining properties, which are postulated to explain the results of breeding experiments, have been shown actually to exist as the result of independent histological work, and we are led to suppose that the factor upon which the manifestation of sex depends can be definitely identified as attached to a particular element in the gamete—the X chromosome. It may be mentioned that Morgan and others are inclined to take a quantitative view of sexual difference and to suppose that the formation of a female results when the zygote receives two X chromosomes (normally one from each gamete), and a male when the X chromosome enters from one side only. Whether this hypothesis will hold good generally must be left for future work to decide.

8. Sex-determination.—The problem of sex-determination—a problem which for centuries has excited deep interest—may be regarded as in large measure solved by the results of recent work. We now know that the sex manifested by any given individual depends upon the nature of the two gametes through whose conjugation the individual was formed. This is decided at the moment of fertilization, and there is no reason for supposing that any subsequent event can influence the fundamental sexual nature of the zygote produced, though, as will appear later, extrinsic influences may lead to modification of secondary sexual characters. The various attempts before the present century to solve the problem were largely based on the assumption that external influences (exerted either upon the parent or upon the developing offspring at an early stage) could determine the sex to which the latter was to belong. This assumption was not unnatural at a time when the most critical technique available was unable to distinguish any sexual difference in the early embryos of mammals and other animals. The newly-formed creature was regarded as indifferent with respect to sex, differentiating into male or female only at a somewhat later stage. In attacking the problem, the method adopted was generally statistical. A possible cause affecting the determination of sex was suggested, and statistics of births were collected when the suggested cause was in operation, to be contrasted with similar statistics brought together when the cause was operating either slightly or not at all. Since the greater part of available statistics refer to man, it was for this species that most of the work was done. Many authors have seen in nutrition the determining cause of sex; and it was held that a richer and more abundant nutrition of the embryo tended to lead to the production of females, while underfeeding the mother, in the case of mammals, tended to increase the output of males. Many statistics have been collected on this point, but, while some of them appear to offer support to the contention, others are directly opposed to it. Nor does the experimental evidence that exists for smaller vertebrates, such as rats, mice, and frogs, indicate that nutrition appreciably affects the sex ratio. That it should do so is not inconceivable, even though sex is determined at fertilization, for it is possible that different conditions, particularly unfavourable ones, may be better resisted in the earlier embryonic stages of one sex than of the other. On this view, a change in the external conditions would not have affected the determination of sex, but would have brought about an alteration in the sex ratio through an increased mortality among the early embryos of one sex as compared with those of the other.

9. The theory of auto-regulation.—Among the theories of sex-determination based upon statistical data mention may be made of Düsing's theory of auto-regulation. The assumption is made that the newly-formed gametes of either sex tend to produce individuals of the same sex as that from which they are sprung, whereas older gametes tend to produce the opposite sex. Thus the more freshly produced sperm has a greater tendency to give rise to male individuals than older sperm which has been for some time in the ducts. A stallion whose services are much utilized should produce more male offspring than one which is more rarely put to the mare. The fewer the males in a species, the oftener they serve the females, and in consequence the younger are the sperms they emit; and, as the younger sperms give rise to more males, the tendency is for a dearth of this sex in any generation to be compensated for by an increase in the next. The net result is an auto-regulation of the sex ratio, which is maintained at the level that is most advantageous to the species.

The leading idea in Düsing's theory, that the determination of sex depends upon the relative maturity of the gamete, was borrowed from Thury, though by him it was applied to the female sex only. According to this author, ova freshly liberated from the ovary have a stronger tendency to produce females than ova which have become staler; the latter more often give rise to males. When first enunciated, the few statistics available strongly supported the idea, and 'Thury's law' had an immediate vogue; but, as fresh and unconformable data came to hand, it fell into disrepute. More recently, however, the idea has been revived in connexion with certain experimental work. Richard Hertwig and his pupils have shown that it is possible to raise the proportion of males in frogs by delaying fertilization of the ova. As they became staler, the ratio of males increased, and in some cases the offspring were all of this sex. It is possible that in stale ova the chromatin, in which the sex-determining factors presumably reside, becomes impaired, while the cell protoplasm as a whole retains its vitality. If this were so, the sex would be determined by the entering sperm alone; and, if we suppose the male sex in the frog to be the recessive one, the resulting offspring would be male. Such a view receives some support from the work of Boveri on the fertilization of sea-urchins. By shaking the eggs it is possible to fragment them so that some pieces are produced which contain no chromatin. Boveri found that such pieces were penetrated by the sperm with the production of normal though undersized larvæ. The chromatin of the male alone is sufficient for the production of a new individual, though the sperm cannot develop except in unison with the cell protoplasm of the egg. There appears to be good evidence in some cases for an alteration in the sex ratio when the ova are stale, but whether the explanation suggested will be found to hold good can be decided only by fresh observations.

10. Secondary sexual distinctions.—Throughout the animal kingdom the primary distinction between the sexes—the bearing of either ova or spermatozoa—is nearly always accompanied by other differences of a more or less deeply seated nature. In some of the lower animals the sexes are so unlike as to have been regarded as belonging to entirely different groups. Among the vertebrates, with which we are chiefly concerned, the secondary sexual distinctions are often striking enough. They vary greatly from species to species, being very marked in some and practically non-existent in others. In pheasants and in many breeds of poultry the cock is totally different in appearance from his hens, while in pigeons it is often exceedingly difficult, if not impossible, to distinguish the sexes by means of external features. But, remarkable as these sexual differences often are, they were for long taken as a matter of course, and excited little attention until an explanation of the forms of life in terms of evolution through natural selection was formulated by Charles Darwin. Then it began to be felt that some of these secondary sexual characters offered a difficulty. The mane of a lion or the antlers of a stag might conceivably be brought about by natural selection acting within the species. Both may be serviceable in combat, and the better endowed male is enabled to drive off his rivals and satisfy his sexual instinct, leaving progeny which tend to inherit and transmit their father's advantages. But of what conceivable use was the gorgeous plumage of the male bird of paradise or of the cock pheasant in a stern struggle for existence? Would not the possessor of such adornments rather be placed at a disadvantage? The theory of natural selection demands that, if a thing exists, it must exist in virtue of its utility either to the individual or to the species. It was in terms of the species rather than of the individual that Darwin put forward his subsidiary theory of sexual selection. Beauty appeals to the æsthetic taste of the female. Beauty in the male excites her and renders her more apt for mating. Though the more gorgeous male may, through his striking beauty, be at a disadvantage in the struggle for existence, yet this is more than counterbalanced by the exciting effect which his superior attractions exert upon the female. She is the more readily induced to mate and to leave progeny, whereby the species gains, even though the more conspicuous male runs greater individual risks. Moreover, if the æsthetic ideal of the female is high, variation in the direction of more pronounced beauty of plumage or song will always meet with its reward, and the cumulative effect of sexual selection will constantly heighten sexual distinctions. The reality of sexual selection turns upon the exercise of choice by the females, and, though Darwin assiduously collected all the facts that he could, it cannot be said that the theory is firmly based. In some cases, such as that of the black-cock (*Tetrao tetrix*), observations on the courtship habits favour the idea that the female exercises a definite choice. On the other hand, there are many observations which tell against the theory. In some species of birds, such as peafowl and turkeys, the male is conspicuous from the female in plumage as well as in the persistence with which he parades his plumes in the breeding season; yet it is a matter of common observation that the hens show no apparent interest in the performance. Again, many of the characteristic so-called courtship actions of the male, as well as the exercise of his song, frequently commence after mating has already taken place. Among lepidoptera, where most marked sexual dimorphism is often found, there is some experimental evidence against its being in any way concerned with a choice exercised by the female. Males deprived of the wing scales, or painted with a colour to obscure their characteristic pattern, have been found to be just as acceptable to the female as normal ones.

Since the publication of Darwin's book more attention has been paid to the behaviour of animals in relation to the breeding period. Particularly has this been the case with birds, where courtship actions are usually more marked and observation is less difficult. Fresh facts suggested that these actions doubtless serve as an aphrodisiac, by means of which the male advertizes his readiness to mate and attempts to stimulate the female to a like condition. A more brilliant coloration in the male may serve to enhance the display, but it is not a necessary condition. The male of the little sober-coloured warblers, where the sexes are alike, goes through postures similar to those found in species such as the sun bittern (*Eupyga helias*), where the beautifully marked cock is quite distinct from the hen. On the other hand, it seems certain that in many cases the elaborate display does not serve as a direct incentive to pairing. An excellent example of this is afforded by the great crested grebe, recently studied with much care by J. S. Huxley and others. Many curious and definite posturings take place continually in this species during the breeding season. As both sexes take part in them, the term 'mutual display' has been applied to these performances. They are quite distinct from the posturings which lead up to the act of coition, and Huxley has suggested that, if we are to attribute to them a purpose, we may suppose that they serve to keep the two individuals of the pair together during the mating season. Whether this speculation be adopted or not, it is clear that these peculiarities of behaviour are dependent upon the enhanced activity of the sexual glands and probably upon the hormones[1] secreted in greater abundance during the breeding period of the year. They are of interest in showing that alterations in the metabolism of these glands may act as a stimulant to performances which, though not directly connected with reproduction, are normally in abeyance. They open up a suggestive line of inquiry on the influence of the hormones produced by the sex glands in stimulating phases of mental activity usually regarded as outside the sphere of sexual influence.

11. Wallace's view of sexual diversity.—Wallace, who put forward the theory of natural selection at the same time as Darwin, definitely rejected the theory of sexual selection. He took up a totally different standpoint with regard to sexual diversity, and considered that it is due rather to the female having diverged from the male than *vice versa*, as Darwin held. On his view, the female is less brilliantly coloured than the male owing to greater need of protection. The hen pheasant on the nest is less conspicuous in her own dress than if she were decked out in the plumes of the cock. The more sober her costume, the less likely she is to attract the attention of enemies. Her coloration is protective, and, having a utility value, it can be supposed to have been brought about through the action of natural selection. On Wallace's view, natural selection represses in the female the brilliant colours and patterns which survive only in the male. He leads us to infer that in earlier times the female was as splendid as the male, but he cannot offer, in terms of natural selection, any satisfactory explanation why these magnificent and conspicuous colours should ever have arisen in the first place. It is true he suggests that they are correlated with greater vigour, and that this has a selective value which more than counterbalances the dangers due to increased conspicuousness; but this can hardly be regarded as more than a conjecture.

12. Goodale's experiments.—When we turn from theories regarding the origin of secondary sexual characters to the nature of the characters themselves, we are met with a considerable body of facts which have been accumulated for the most part during the present century. In studying these characters the first point to be decided is the extent to which their manifestation depends upon the sexual glands themselves. An obvious method of attacking this question is to remove the glands and note the effect produced on the secondary sexual characters. Experimental castration has been performed in a number of animals, for the most part domestic ones, and on the whole more frequently in the male sex than in the female. The results are not always free from ambiguity, due to the difficulty of removing the gland completely; for even a small piece of testis or ovary will often proliferate and invalidate the experiment. Perhaps the most interesting and instructive operations are those which have been performed on domestic poultry and on ducks by Goodale in America. This observer took the precaution of using pure breeds, in which the secondary sexual differences are very marked. The testes and the ovary were in certain cases successfully and completely removed, the latter being an operation of considerable difficulty. The breeds used were the Brown Leghorn in poultry, a race very similar both in the males and in the females to the wild *Gallus bankiva*, while in ducks recourse was had to the Rouen, a variety very like the wild mallard in both sexes. In both of these species castration of the male was practically without effect upon its plumage. The Rouen drake, however, did not assume the 'eclipse plumage' which is normally exhibited for a short time at the close of the breeding season. In the Brown Leghorn the comb failed to reach the size characteristic of uncastrated cocks, and there was a tendency to develop the brooding instinct—a fact well known where caponization is practised. In neither species, however, was there any evidence for the acquisition of female plumage as the result of the operation. The removal of the ovary from the hen offered a sharp contrast to these results. The Rouen duck assumed more or less completely the characteristic plumage of the drake, even to the small curly sex feathers of the tail. And not only did she acquire the male breeding plumage, but, in one case at any rate, she moulted annually into the male eclipse plumage, as does the normal male. The Brown Leghorn hen also assumed the totally distinct and far more gorgeous feathering of the cock with its flowing hackles and tail sickles, but the comb remained small, and the general build of the body remained that of the hen. The result of this work is to show that removal of the sex gland in the female leads to the assumption of the male plumage, whereas the normal male plumage is retained when the testes are taken out. The significance of this will be referred to below.

13. Effects of castration.—Striking results have also been obtained in other animals. The stag, with its great antlers, obviously invites experimental treatment, and castration work has proved that the development of these structures is dependent upon the presence of the genital gland. The precise result obtained depends upon the age at which the operation is performed. Castration of the young fawn before the formation of the frontal tubercles completely prevents the growth of the horns. If development of the antlers has already begun, the operation hinders further growth. They remain covered by the velvet and are never shed. Castration of the adult stag results in the precocious shedding of the antlers. They may be replaced by small imperfect ones, and these are never shed again.

In Herdwick sheep, a breed with horned rams and hornless ewes, castration of the young ram prevents the further growth of horns. On the other hand, castration of the ewe does not lead to the formation of horns, from which it must be inferred that this case is not strictly comparable with those of the duck and the fowl.

In man castration is an operation rarer to-day than in times gone by, though it is still practised in China and among certain sects in Russia. The principal effect is to arrest sexual development, and its consequences depend upon the stage at which it is performed. Generally speaking, apart from its effect in stunting the sexual organs themselves, it results in a deposition of fat over certain parts of the body; the skeleton is modified without, however, becoming feminized; the larynx does not develop normally, and the voice fails to break if the operation takes place early enough. The hair is also affected. It fails to develop in the axillary and pubic regions, while on the head it is abundant and falls out less readily than in normal men. With the possible exception of this last point, it cannot be said that eunuchs show a tendency to develop female characters as the result of castration.

The influence of the sex gland upon the development of secondary sexual characters among mammals and birds is confirmed by what is known for certain lower vertebrates. The dorsal

[1] Cf. below, § 14.

fin of the male newt and the thickened skin pad on the thumb of the male frog are characters which are also affected by castration. It would appear, therefore, that among the vertebrates the dependence of these characters upon the sex gland is a general feature, and the recognition of this has recently led to a physiological explanation.

14. Hormone production.—One of the most interesting and striking advances in modern physiology is that connected with what are termed 'internal secretions.' Certain glandular structures occur in the human body which, though evidently forming a secretion, are unprovided with a duct to carry it away. The function of these bodies, among which the most conspicuous is the thyroid gland of the neck, long remained a puzzle. They were known to be affected in the case of certain diseases. Cretinism, *e.g.*, was found to be associated with an abnormal condition of the thyroid gland, while an unhealthy state of the adrenals was closely connected with Addison's disease. The function of these glands was eventually elucidated by the experimental method. It was found that removal of the thyroid quickly led to death. Death, however, could be averted either by transplanting another thyroid into the patient—whether in the original or in some other position did not matter—or else by injecting an extract of the gland. The experimental results made it clear that these ductless glands elaborate various substances essential to the life of the organism. These substances leave the glands by means of the blood stream instead of through proper ducts, whence the application of the term 'internal secretion.' The active principle in the secretion is spoken of as a 'hormone,' referring to the changes which their output awakens in the organism. Later experiments have shown that hormones are produced not only by the ductless glands but also by glands possessing a more obvious function. The pancreas, *e.g.*, in addition to elaborating a digestive secretion which flows into the intestine, produces a hormone of which the cessation leads to symptoms of acute diabetes in the patient.

15. Hormones and sexual structures.—Not the least important of the hormones are those set free from the genital gland, and it is to them that we must look for the link which connects the secondary sexual characters with the sex gland itself. The ovary and testis are not merely the organs in which the germ cells mature. They also contribute substances which exercise a profound effect upon the general metabolism of the individual. In the testis the hormone is probably elaborated by the so-called interstitial cells, the packing material in which the sperm tubules lie embedded. This, however, cannot be ascertained through direct experiment, because it is at present impossible to remove these cells without removing the whole testis. In the ovary, however, the inquiry as to the seat of hormone production has been pushed a stage farther. When an ovum matures in a mammal, there is formed round it from the follicle cells of the ovary a comparatively large vesicle known as the 'Graafian follicle.' After the rupture which accompanies the liberation of the ovum this vesicle, which is on the surface of the ovary, becomes transformed into a body known from its colour as the *corpus luteum.* The subsequent fate of this body depends upon what happens to the liberated ovum. If this is not fertilized, the *corpus luteum* is rapidly absorbed. If, however, fertilization occurs, the *corpus luteum* increases in size and persists during pregnancy. Recent researches have shown that this body is to be regarded as a temporary gland producing an internal secretion of which the action is twofold, viz. to bring about changes in the wall of the uterus which allow of the formation of a placenta, and to stimulate the mammary gland to increased activity.

It is clear that the genital glands give rise to hormones which produce a marked effect upon the sexual structures in the female that are directly concerned with the development and nutrition of the fœtus. How far their influence stretches to secondary sexual characters is not easy to determine in mammals, where these differences are not so marked as they frequently are in birds. Ovariotomy in the human female might be expected to yield interesting data, but, as the operation is of comparatively recent origin, and is resorted to only in abnormal cases after the adult state is attained, not much is yet to be learned from it. Though satisfactory instances of complete removal of the ovary are rarely available for study, there are many cases on record where the gland has atrophied through either old age or disease. The human female under such conditions may exhibit male characteristics in the gruffness of the voice and in the development of hair on the face. So also the hind may develop horns, and the mare may acquire the development of the canines which is a normal feature of the stallion. It is interesting that among such birds as fowls and pheasants the assumption of male plumage to a greater or less degree is known to accompany degeneration of the ovary through disease or old age.

16. Transplantation experiments.—Besides the method of castration, the method of transplantation has also been used in connexion with these studies. Castrated male rats can be distinguished from normal males. If, however, the testis of another individual be grafted into the body of a castrated animal at an early age, it is stated that such animals exhibit the characters and instincts of a normal male. Steinach, to whom we owe these observations, made some further experiments which are of the highest interest and importance. Into the young male rat he transplanted, after castration, the ovaries and oviducts of the female. It is stated that the graft succeeded, and that the animal became literally feminized. The quality of the hair and the adiposity were feminine; the mammary glands were such as are found in the young female; even the instincts were more or less inverted so that the impression of a female was produced on other rats.

One other transplantation experiment deserves mention here as illustrating a different method of attacking the problem. In the experiments just outlined the gland of one sex was grafted into the body of the other and the effects on the sexual characters were noted. In the following experiment the reverse procedure was adopted, and a structure showing a secondary sexual character was grafted on to an individual of the opposite sex. In the male newt the dorsal fin enlarges during the breeding season and becomes markedly serrated. When the dorsal fin of the female, which normally undergoes no alteration at this period, is grafted on to a male, it can produce the characteristic serrated edge, doubtless under the influence of the testis.

17. Castration of insects.—While the intimate connexion between the sexual glands and secondary sexual characters is beyond doubt in vertebrates, this connexion is by no means so certain in another of the great groups of the animal kingdom—the insecta. Several investigators have studied by the method of castration the common gipsy-moth (*Lymantria dispar*). The subject is a favourable one, for the sexual dimorphism is marked, the male being far smaller and darker than the female, and having also the peculiar feathered antennæ characteristic of many male moths. The sex glands are already differentiated in the caterpillar. Removal of them at this stage produces no apparent effect on the metamorphosed insect. For, though it is not possible to distinguish the sexes in the larval stage, the insects derived from castrated caterpillars were all either normal males or normal females in appearance. Further, transplantation of the sex glands in the larvæ failed to produce any effects on the adult insects. By this method were obtained females normal in every way—in the complicated sexual ducts as well as in the secondary sexual characters—but with a testis in place of an ovary. Similarly others of the operated insects turned out to be normal males, except that they contained ovaries instead of testes. Since the castration and transplantation was done in the larvæ before any sexual characters had appeared, it seems natural to conclude that they are independent of any hormone produced by the sex glands. In support of this view are the results of some experiments with crickets (*Gryllus campestris*). Removal of the sex glands, at a stage before the adult condition was reached, had no effect upon any of the structural features peculiar to either sex. More noteworthy was the absence of any change in the sexual instincts and behaviour. Both sexes after castration attracted the opposite sex and mated, and the female took the same care of her empty egg-capsules as the normal female does of her full ones. On the other hand, there is some evidence that the secondary sexual characters may be affected by castration in bees. Certain species of *Andrœna* are at times attacked by the little parasitic insect *Stylops*. The parasite does not prevent them from leading their normal active life, but affects the sex gland and renders them sterile. As the result of this 'parasitic castration,' as it has been called, definite changes are produced in the female bee, such as the reduction of the pollen-brushes, but the most noteworthy change is in the clypeus above the upper lip. This, which is normally black in the female, may assume the yellow colour characteristic of the male. Since the parasite does not attack the bee until after the metamorphosis, this change is brought about after the adult state has been reached.

18. Sex transformation in crabs.—Parasitic castration is not uncommon among certain crabs, in which it is brought about by another crustacean belonging to the group Rhizocephala. The results, which were discovered by A. Giard and studied later in more detail by Geoffrey Smith, are of remarkable interest, and are at present unparalleled in any other group of the animal kingdom. The effect of the parasite on the female is a reduction of the sexual modifications characteristic of this sex. The abdomen becomes narrower, and the biramous abdominal appendages, with the long hairs to which the eggs are stuck, become much smaller. But the animal is obviously a female and shows no approximation to the male. In the male, however, parasitic castration produces a very different effect, for it brings about a strong tendency towards the development of female characters. The large male claws diminish to the size of the female ones; the peculiar intromittent organ—a modified appendage—is much reduced; the biramous hairy abdominal appendages, normally absent in the male, are more or less strongly developed. Most remarkable of all is the fact that such males, on getting rid of the parasite and once more developing a sex gland, may form an ovary in place of a testis. Briefly, the effect of the parasite is to change a male into a female.

Castration experiments, so far as they have gone, serve to bring out certain points in connexion with the nature of sexual characters. In the first place, there are good grounds for supposing that different groups of the animal kingdom are not all on the same footing. In vertebrates both the primary sexual characters, such as the genital ducts, and the secondary sexual characters are intimately connected with the functioning of the sexual gland. This is also true of the crustacea, with this difference, that, whereas in the vertebrates the female may take on the secondary sexual characters of the male, among the crustacea it is the male which can assume the sexual characters of the female. Among insects, on the other hand, it appears that both the primary and the secondary sexual characters are developed independently of the sex glands.

19. The stage of differentiation.—Since experimental work of the kind outlined above is directed primarily towards an analysis of the constitution of the two sexes, we may inquire how far these may be supposed to have been brought into line with one another—how far sexual characters are due to a fundamental difference in hereditary constitution, and how far they are due to different hormones acting specifically upon a similar constitution. It is well known that among vertebrates each sex possesses in a rudimentary condition the primary sexual characters which are well developed in the other. Embryology has shown that the genital organs are laid down upon a common plan. It is not until a certain stage is reached that the female elements predominate in an individual which is to become a female, and the male elements in one which is to become a male. In the earlier stages the embryo is hermaphrodite in so far as the sexual characters are concerned. It is tempting to suppose that the one essential difference in the earliest stages is that of the sex gland itself, that this is decided at fertilization, and that, as it develops and produces its internal secretions, it stimulates one portion of the originally hermaphrodite set of sex characters and inhibits the development of the other. Though there are difficulties at present in putting this view to the experimental test, nature herself has performed a most interesting experiment which bears upon the point. Animals that normally produce a single offspring at a birth not infrequently produce two. Where these are not twins proper—*i.e.* enclosed in the same chorion, of the same sex, and presumably derived from a single ovum—they are most frequently one of either sex. Cattle, however, rarely produce a male and a female at a birth. Where one of the two is a normal male, the other is commonly what is called a 'free martin,' an animal which in its sexual characters is predominantly male, but is always sterile. Since described by John Hunter more than a century ago, the free martin remained a puzzle to the biologist, and its nature has only just been unravelled through the observations of F. R. Lillie. It now seems certain that it is really a female which develops abnormally owing to a connexion established at an early stage between its blood-vessels and those of the male embryo that lies beside it in the uterus. It is suggested that the testis of the male develops more rapidly than the ovary of his sister, so that its internal secretions reach the latter through the vascular connexion just referred to, inhibit the development of the ovary and its secretions, and stimulate the growth of the male portion of the originally hermaphrodite sexual apparatus. But, though the secretions affect all the sexual characters, they cannot change the fundamental nature of the sexual gland. The ovary is inhibited in its growth; but it remains an ovary and not a testis. It would clearly be of great interest to determine whether the influence of ovarial hormones acting at an early stage would lead to the development of the female portion of the genital ducts in a male embryo. At present there is here a serious gap in our knowledge.

20. Inhibitory factors.—If we regard the embryo as potentially a hermaphrodite with regard to the primary sexual characters, of which the ultimate form is determined by the activity of the sex gland itself, we are naturally led to inquire whether we can regard the secondary sexual characters in the same light. Does the young chicken of either sex, *e.g.*, contain the same complete set of factors for such characters, and is the different result in the two sexes due to the stimulation of different parts of the set by the ovary and testis respectively? Though this may be true in respect of some of the secondary sexual characters, such as the size of the comb and wattles, which are definitely altered in the male as the result of castration, there is probably a simpler explanation for the plumage. The facts given are in accordance with the view that both sexes contain the same set of characters for plumage, but that the female in addition contains a factor which inhibits the development of the male type. If the action of this inhibitor is dependent upon an ovarian hormone, we can understand why the castrated female should develop male plumage.[1] Plumage in the fowl offers a further point of interest in that the female feathering is found in the males of certain breeds, notably Sebright Bantams, Henny Game, and Campines. In heredity henny plumage in the cock behaves as a simple dominant to normal cock plumage. In terms of the 'presence and absence' theory,[2] the henny cock must be supposed to contain an additional factor which acts as an inhibitor just as it does in the hen. This view is supported by castration experiments, for removal of the testes from a henny cock causes him to develop normal cock plumage. The inhibitor of cock plumage, when present, must be supposed capable of being activated by a hormone which is found in both of the sex glands. Normally the factor for inhibition, *i.e.* the factor upon which the secondary sexual difference depends, is linked with a factor for femaleness, so that the characteristic male plumage is repressed only in this sex. If this inhibitor did not exist, it is probable that the fowl, like the pigeon, would not exhibit sexual differences in the plumage.

The great interest of this poultry case is to demonstrate that a secondary sexual character may depend upon one or more distinct hereditary factors, transmissible at times independently of sex, inoperative unless stimulated by a hormone from the sexual gland, but activated through the gland of either sex indifferently. Such sexual characters are on a different footing in the organism from those which develop from a common hermaphrodite basis through the differential activation by one or other of the sex glands. In the latter the difference is brought about by a different sex gland acting through its hormones on similarly constituted individuals; in the former the difference depends upon an unlikeness in constitution which can be expressed in terms of hereditary factors.

21. Transference of sexual characters.—To what extent the interpretation of the case of the fowl's plumage will be found applicable to cases of secondary characters in other vertebrates it is not yet possible to say, for in no other instance has the analysis of such a character been pushed so far. Nevertheless, there is some evidence of the transference of sexual characters from one sex to the other that is so distinctive a feature of the poultry case. It has already been mentioned that certain male characters may appear in the female as the result of degenerative changes in the ovary through old age or disease.[1] Cases are also on record where male characters make their appearance in females presumably normal as regards the state of the ovary. The hens of poultry and pheasants are sometimes spurred; excessive development of hair on the face may occur in women; antlers are occasionally found on the hind, a condition normal in the reindeer. Among sheep the horns, which in certain breeds are a sexual character of the ram, are in others common to the ewe. Conversely, the cock is sometimes spurless; the stag may fail to develop antlers; there are breeds of sheep in which the ram is hornless like the ewe; the smooth face of the woman is not infrequent in the man, and at times he may show the mammary development of the opposite sex. Many striking cases occur among birds, where habits generally characteristic of one sex may be found in the other. Thus the male ostrich shows the brooding instinct as well as the female, and this is occasionally found in the uncastrated cock among domestic poultry. More remarkable still is the case of the Phalarope, in which the more gaily coloured female does the courting, while the male attends to the duties of incubation. Such instances of transference could be largely added to, but those given serve to illustrate the point that at any rate a substantial proportion of so-called secondary sexual characters depend upon specific hereditary factors which may at times be transmitted independently of the factor for sex.

22. Gynandromorphism. — The phenomena of gynandromorphism and of hermaphroditism among animals in which the sexes are usually separate afford some further material for the analysis of sexual characters. Gynandromorphs are most common among insects. An individual may be completely male on one side and completely female on the other, which often results in a striking appearance where the sexes are markedly different. Both sex glands may coexist in the same body in a normal state, nor does this condition appear to affect the sexual characters. This lack of influence is in accordance with the evidence already given in connexion with castration experiments.

Complete lateral gynandromorphism probably depends upon some abnormality either in fertilization or in an early cleavage stage. One suggestion put forward is that fertilization is delayed till after the first cleavage, and that only one of the first two cells is fertilized. The female part of the gynandromorph is then regarded as derived from the fertilized half, and the male part as developing parthenogenetically from the unfertilized half. Another suggestion is that the egg is penetrated by two sperms, one of which unites in the normal way with the egg-nucleus, while the other develops independently. Besides lateral gynandromorphism, insects may exhibit a form of gynandromorphism in which the secondary sexual characters of the two sexes are jumbled up together. In the gipsy-moth, *e.g.*, insects occur with the wings presenting a mosaic of the darker male and the lighter female patterns. In such individuals the sexual glands and ducts are normal, and fertility is unimpaired. These mosaic forms are normally produced as the result of the mating between the European form (*Lymantria dispar*) and the Japanese one (*Lymantria japonica*), and the proportions in which they appear can be brought into line with Mendelian principles. Goldschmidt, who made numerous breeding experiments with these species, offers an interesting interpretation of his results. While the factors for the secondary sexual characters are hereditarily independent of the sex factors themselves, those derived from *Lymantria japonica* are

[1] Cf. § 12. [2] Cf. art. HEREDITY, § 8.

[1] Cf. § 15.

more potent than those from *Lymantria dispar*. When the secondary sexual factors of *Lymantria japonica* come to be associated with the sex factors of *Lymantria dispar*, or *vice versa*, the normal equilibrium between the two sets of factors is disturbed and gynandromorphous individuals result.

Lateral gynandromorphism is extremely rare in vertebrates, and never so complete as among insects. In view of the influence exerted on sexual characters by the sex glands, this is not surprising. For, since the hormones circulate freely in the general blood stream, a difference in the sexual characters of the two sides of the body would be very remarkable. It is not improbable that, when we know more of the functions of the sympathetic nervous system, the few cases on record will eventually receive a somewhat different explanation. Partial gynandromorphism is, however, not rare among vertebrates. One of the commonest forms which it takes is the association of the external genitalia of the female with the male gland and ducts. In such cases the testis generally fails to descend with the scrotum, nor does it contain ripe spermatozoa. The gynandromorphism may be less marked, taking the form known as hypospadias. The male is then generally fertile, and there is evidence that the condition is hereditary. It may be that some abnormality of the sex gland, such as the failure to develop this or that particular hormone, lies at the bottom of the various forms of gynandromorphism. Again, it may be that the sex gland itself is normal, and that some hereditary factor has been dropped out from the complex which is concerned with the sexual characters. Which view is to be taken must depend largely upon the results of future experimental work.

23. **Mentality and sex.**—For social and for ethical reasons the experimental analysis of sex is of fundamental importance. Recent research has demonstrated that there is reason for supposing that mental qualities are inherited on the same lines as physical ones. Owing to the newness of the methods involved and to the difficulties in procuring satisfactory data, little progress has yet been possible, but there is good evidence already in existence for regarding some forms of feeble-mindedness and musical sense as recessive to the normal condition. There is no doubt that, as time goes on, the analysis of mental qualities will be placed upon a more satisfactory basis, though, as this analysis must be based upon human material, the time will necessarily be long. Mentality, as every one knows, differs profoundly in the two sexes. A vast amount has been written on this subject; endless speculations have been devoted to it; but little of value has been evolved. To-day we begin to recognize that what is required is experimental analysis—analysis of mental traits on the one hand, and analysis of the sexual mechanism on the other. Consider, *e.g.*, the case of intellectual achievement by the two sexes, upon which so much has been written. Achievement of the first rank stands almost without exception to the credit of the male sex. In the things of the intellect the male is the creative sex. The fact is beyond dispute; but, when we seek to explain why it is so, we obtain very little satisfaction from those who have discussed it. Before we can begin to understand it, we must have some analysis of the nature of intellectual activity—whether it depends upon definite hereditary factors, like so many other qualities, and, if so, in what way these factors are transmitted. Are they sex-linked, as is known to be the case for colour-blindness, and is the woman of outstanding intellectual attainment rare for the same reason that a colour-blind woman is rare? Or are they dependent upon the activity of the sex gland, either directly or indirectly through the influence of some inhibitor which itself is activated by the gland? Again, are they acted upon differently by the ovarial and by the testicular hormones? Until we can answer such questions as these, further discussion is idle.

LITERATURE.—Works dealing with the nature of sex in its biological aspect are very numerous. Ample bibliographies are given in several of the volumes of the appended brief list, which, either from authority or modernity, will be found of especial value to those who wish to inquire further on this subject: C. Darwin, *The Descent of Man*, 2 vols., London, 1871; L. Doncaster, *The Determination of Sex*, Cambridge, 1914; P. Geddes and J. A. Thomson, *The Evolution of Sex*[2], London, 1901; T. H. Morgan, *Heredity and Sex*[2], New York, 1914. To these may be added the following list of books or papers more especially mentioned in this article: E. Bataillon, *Arch. de Zool. Exper.* xlvi. [1910] 101–135; K. Düsing, *Jenaische Zeitschrift*, xvii. [1884] 593–940; R. Goldschmidt, *Zeitschr. für induktive Abstammungs- und Vererbungslehre*, viii. [1912] 1–62, xi. [1914] 280–316; H. D. Goodale, Publ. no. 243, Carnegie Inst. of Washington, 1916; O. Hertwig, *Arch. für mikroskop. Anat.*, lxxxii. [1913] pt. ii. pp. 1–63; J. S. Huxley, *The Auk*, xxxiii. [1916] 142–161, 256–270; F. R. Lillie, *Journ. Exp. Zool.*, xxiii. [1917] 371–452; J. Loeb, *Artificial Parthenogenesis and Fertilization*, Chicago, 1913: G. W. Smith, 'Studies in the Experimental Analysis of Sex,' pts. i.–xi., *Quart. Journ. Micr. Science*, 1910–1914; A. R. Wallace, *Darwinism*, London, 1889.

R. C. PUNNETT.

SHADOW.—See SOUL.

SHAFI'ITES.—See LAW (Muhammadan).

SHAHĪDS.—As applied to Sikhs the term *shahīd* means 'martyr,' just as it does in the case of Muhammadans, and it appears to have been in use as early as the time of Guru Govind Singh.[1] The Shahīds are first found as an organized company in 1734 as one of the five which constituted the Ṭarū Dal, or young army of the Sikhs. Its leaders were Dīp Singh, Natha Singh, Gurbaksh, and others.[2] But among the Sikhs the name Shahīd is generally confined to the disciples and followers of Dīp Singh and Sadā Singh. Dīp Singh was a Khāra Jāṭ of Pohupind in Lahore and became one of the Khālsa's earliest adherents. He fought under Guru Govind Singh and Banda. At Damdama he acquired learning, and Sadā Singh became his disciple. At this time the imperial governor of Lahore had set a price upon the Sikhs' heads, but Dīwān Kaura Mal Khatri warned them of an impending attack. Dīp Singh dismissed all his followers who had earthly ties, and only 60 men remained with him. With these he encountered the imperial troops till all the Sikhs had fallen, Dīp Singh continuing to fight even after his head had been struck off. Thereby he earned the title of Shahīd, and the imperial governor, alarmed by a dream, sought his pardon and bestowed Pohupind in *jāgīr* upon his sister Mālan. The place where she burned the bodies of the fallen at Amritsar is still known as the Shahīd Būnga. Other accounts connect the story with Sudhā or Sadā Singh, and make Karm Singh and Dharm Singh, Sindhū Jāṭs, his disciples.[3] According to Khazān Singh, this Shahīd was killed fighting with the governor of Jullundur.[4] Khazān Singh also says that Shahīd Dīp Singh took possession of the Siālkot tract in 1759, and made it over to his disciples Diāl Singh and Natha Singh, who eventually assigned it for the maintenance of the shrine of the Ber of Bābā Nānak at that town. Sudhā Singh, who succeeded Dīp Singh as head of the *misl*, was killed in 1762, and Karm Singh was then elected its head. In 1763 he occupied Shāhzādpur and other tracts in

[1] M. A. Macauliffe, 'The Rise of Amritsar and the Alterations of the Sikh Religion,' in *Calcutta Review*, 1881, p. 74, or *Selections from the Calcutta Review*, 2nd ser., Calcutta, 1896, p. 100.

[2] Khazān Singh, *Philosophic Hist. of the Sikh Religion*, Lahore, 1914, i. 237.

[3] D. G. Barkley, in *PNQ* ii. [1884] 1110; cf. Lepel Griffin, *The Rajas of the Panjab*[2], Lahore, 1873, p. 46 f., and W. Wynyard, *Ambāla Settlement Report*, Lahore, 1859, § 83.

[4] i. 281.

Ambāla, and in 1778 the *nawāb* of Rānia assigned him twelve villages for the maintenance of his shrine, on condition that the Sikhs should abstain from raiding his territory. On Karm Singh's death in 1794 he was succeeded by his son Gulāb Singh, and the territories of the *misl* in the neighbourhood of Shāhzādpur became hereditary in his family.

For Muhammadan *shahīds* see art. SAINTS AND MARTYRS (Muhammadan in India).

LITERATURE.—See the sources quoted in the footnotes.

H. A. ROSE.

SHAIKH.—See PIR.

SHAKERS.—See COMMUNISTIC SOCIETIES OF AMERICA.

SHAMANISM.[1]

SHAMANISM.[1] — Shamanism is the name given to the native religion of the Ural-Altaic peoples from Bering Straits to the borders of Scandinavia. Weakened through the progress of Buddhism, Islām, and Christianity, it still exists even among tribes professing these faiths. On the whole, it is in a more or less moribund condition; and, although its nature was everywhere much the same, its development varied in different tribes. Analogous phenomena are found among the Eskimo, and also among many American Indian tribes, whose medicine-men are often called shamans by investigators. How far it exists elsewhere, either as a system of religion or with its various aspects more or less reproduced, is discussed below.

The word 'shaman' appears to be derived from the native Tungus name for the priest or medicine-man, *samân*, used also with other names among the Buriats and Yakuts. *Samân* has been thought to be an adaptation of the Pāli *samana* (Skr. *śramaṇa*), a Buddhist monk or mendicant, through the Chinese *sha mên*, but evidence is lacking. Still less likely is the derivation from Persian *shemen*, an idol or temple. Other native names are: Yakut, *oyun*, fem. *udayan*; Buriat, *bö*, fem. *odeyon*, *utyyan*; Altaian, *kam*; Ostyak, *senin*, fem. *senim*; Samoyed, *tadibei*; Lapp, *noid*.

1. What is shamanism?—The primitive religion of these tribes is polytheism or polydæmonism, with strong roots in nature-worship, and generally with a supreme god over all. While the shaman exercises certain priestly functions, his main powers are connected with healing and divination. These he exercises by virtue of his intimate relations with the supernatural world. Certain spirits aid him, possess him, are at his command. He has direct intercourse with spirits, and actual (bodily or spiritual) access to the spirit-world. With the aid of these he obtains knowledge superior to that of ordinary men, and can overcome or drive out hostile spirits or powers. All his magical acts are done by virtue of his power over or influence with spirits. And generally, during the exercise of his powers, the altered mental state of the shaman is in evidence. Through auto-hypnotism, caused by different methods, a state of trance or alternate personality is produced. The initiation of the shaman has also distinctive features. Though his functions and methods are more or less paralleled in many other regions, there are differences. The medicine-man of other tribes may use other methods, on the one hand as far as magic is concerned, on the other as far as an empirical medical science is concerned—sweat-baths, herbal remedies, crude surgery, and the like. And, while the shaman has priestly functions, the priests of other faiths have characteristics and functions in which they differ from him. On the whole, the Ural-Altaic shaman, as priest but much more as magic-wielder, is distinguished by his active relation to the spirit-world and by his regular consecration to his office. He is a mediator between gods and spirits on the one hand and men on the other. He knows the secrets of gods and spirits, often malevolent, and the well-being of all depends on his power to cajole or overcome them by various actions, rites, and sacrifices. By these he can enlist the services of spirits. Among the Yakuts a shaman has an *emekhet*, or guardian-spirit, a divinity or the spirit of a dead shaman, who aids and advises him. In other cases he may have many spirits in his control, and the more of these he has the more powerful he is.

2. The shaman.—In some tribes (Samoyeds, Ostyaks) the office is hereditary; in others a predisposition to it suffices. The youth shows signs of it in childhood, which are thought to prove that he has been chosen by the spirits[1] (Tunguses, Yakuts, Altai tribes). Among the Buriats, while any one may become a shaman or be chosen by the gods, the office is usually hereditary. Both systems are also found among the Lapps. Yet, whether hereditary or selected, the youth generally shows a predisposition to the office. He is nervous, moody, irritable, dreamy, given to hallucinations and trances, or he is epileptic. The Tungus youth declares that a dead shaman has chosen him in a dream as his successor, but he also shows himself crazy, timorous, and stupefied. Similarly among the Yakuts he gabbles like a maniac, takes to the woods, jumps into fire or water, injures himself with weapons. Among the Ostyaks the shaman chooses one of his sons according to his fitness, but the youth then spends his time in practices which irritate the nervous system and excite the imagination. The Buriat hereditary shaman shows special signs as a child: he is subject to fits and trances, has visions, and is fond of solitude, and it is then thought that his soul is with the spirits, being trained by them. On the whole, the shaman is abnormal, neurotic, and epileptic; his functions are based on his abnormal qualities and aggravate these in turn. But in any case a period is devoted to training and austerities. The youth may live for a time in the woods in a half-crazy state, practising austerities or shamanist exercises.[2] In addition he is usually taught for a longer or shorter period by an old shaman regarding the different kinds of spirits and the manner of summoning them.[3] Thus the whole preliminary period is given up to methods which augment the abnormal state and still more separate the postulant from other men. These methods, including aggravation of the nervous system, trances or fits, austerities, communion with spirits, visits to the spirit-world in trance, acquisition of knowledge from the spirits, are reproduced in the rites of the shaman, once he is consecrated to his office.[4]

Then follows the consecration to his office.

'The shaman assumes an exceptional position, takes vows upon himself, becomes the property of spirits who, though subject to his summons, have yet full power over him.'[5]

Among the Yakuts an old shaman takes him to a hill or an open field, clothes him in shaman's dress and gives him the tambourine and drum-stick, and, setting him between nine chaste youths and nine chaste maidens, makes him promise that he will be faithful to the spirit who will fulfil his prayer. He tells him where the spirits dwell, what diseases they cause, and how they may be appeased. Then, having killed a sacrificial animal, he sprinkles the candidate's dress with the blood. The spectators finally feast on the flesh.[6]

Among the Buriats the ceremony is much more elaborate, and has already been fully described.[7]

3. Functions of the shaman.—The shaman may be regarded as one whose priestly, prophetic, and magico-medical functions have not been differenti-

[1] For particular forms of shamanism see artt. BURIATS, OSTYAKS, SAMOYED, TUNGUS, YAKUTS.

[1] See *ERE* x. 281.
[2] *ERE* x. 124a.
[3] Cf. *ERE* iv. 777b.
[4] A. van Gennep, *Les Rites de passage*, Paris, 1909, p. 153.
[5] V. M. Mikhailovskii, 'Shamanism in Siberia and European Russia,' tr. O. Wardrop, *JAI* xxiv. [1895] 90.
[6] Mikhailovskii, p. 86.
[7] See art. BURIATS, § 30.

ated. As to his priestly functions, while he acts occasionally as sacrificer and takes part in public and family sacrifices, his presence as priest and sacrificer is of secondary importance to his other functions. He performs sacrifices from time to time, and at these carries on dialogues with the gods, but there are many sacrifices at which his presence is not essential, and which are offered, *e.g.*, by the elder of a tribe or head of a household. As far as the shaman is concerned, his connexion with sacrifice is mainly the fact that he knows what sacrifices will be pleasing to the gods on any particular occasion and the right means of appeasing them, since they are most particular about the form of sacrifice and prayer. Sacrifice is an important part of the shamanistic rites of healing and divination, but the shaman merely directs the nature and method of the offering from his knowledge of the gods and spirits. In healing, after the magical ceremonies, aided by the presence of spirits, it is indispensable to appease the gods who have relieved the patient, and the shaman decides what offerings are to be made to them.

The priestly functions of the shaman, and their connexion with magic, may be seen from his actions at the great sacrifice to the god Bai-Yulgan among the Altai.

On the first evening a *yurta* is prepared in a place selected by him, and a young birch-tree, with the lower branches lopped, is set up in it. A cattle pen is made outside, and a horse is chosen, which is held by a man called 'the holder of the head.' The shaman waves a birch twig over it, thus driving its soul to the gods, accompanied by the holder's soul. Then he assembles the spirits in his tambourine, sits on the image of a goose, and is supposed to be pursuing the soul of the horse upon it. Having captured the soul, he blesses it, and with the aid of assistants slays the horse. The bones and skin form the offering; the flesh is eaten by the shaman and the company. Next evening, having fed the spirits in the tambourine, he cleanses the souls of all present by certain rites, and prepares the head of the household to understand the prophecies which he is about to utter. In a state of ecstasy he describes how he is mounting the heavens on the soul of the victim or on the goose. He describes what he sees in the heavens, prophesies and utters secrets learned there, and, finally, having reached the ninth or even the tenth or twelfth heaven, he invokes Bai-Yulgan, learns whether he accepts the sacrifice, and obtains information regarding the coming weather, the harvest, etc., as well as the sacrifices which will then be required. He now falls exhausted. Frequently a third day is devoted to feasting and libations to the gods. The number of heavens scaled by the shaman depends upon his powers.[1]

In this rite the prophetic powers of the shaman are seen, and these, as well as his healing powers, distinguish him from a regular priest. While divination may be practised by means of a shoulder-blade, a stick covered with runes, or the flight of arrows, the method of foretelling the future, supplying information regarding the winning of success or averting of misfortune, or explaining the perplexities of inquirers is the *séance*, or what is locally known as *kamlanie.*

In this the shaman, his assistants, and the spectators are collected in a darkened hut. The dress necessary to the occasion is donned. The shaman beats his tambourine, summoning the spirits, and collects them in it. He sings, dances, cries out, converses with the spirits, and by these means proves his inspired state. He rushes round till he falls fainting and produces delirium. While he is in this state, the spirits reveal their will to him or give him the desired information.[2] He foretells the future and declares the will of the gods. When he awakens, he remembers nothing of what has passed. During the performance voices and noises of various kinds are heard, and these are believed to be produced by the spirits. Or, again, the shaman will allege that he is rising through the heavens, pushing aside the stars, and he describes his experiences. Rhythmic songs, prayers, and adorations are used by the shaman in the *kamlanie.*

The healing powers of the shaman, while they are partially medical, are mainly connected with the belief that diseases are caused by spirits which have lodged themselves in the sufferer. Hence the purpose of the ceremonies is to placate them or drive them out.

The shaman may take over the spirit causing the disease into himself, and indicate the necessary sacrifice, into which he now conveys it; or he may decide that the patient's soul has left his body or been carried off to Erlik's realm. Wherever it is, during the course of the performance he pursues it, even to its prison with Erlik, who may release it for certain sacrifices or may demand another soul in its stead. This soul is ensnared by the shaman and taken to Erlik, and its owner now dies. Such a performance is lengthy and expensive. Or, again, after much smoking, tambourine-playing, noise-producing, and singing (by which the shaman brings down his guardian-spirit), he dances and sings, and, having discovered the cause of the illness, is assured of the help of powerful spirits. Still dancing and beating the tambourine, he approaches the patient, expels the possessing spirit or sucks it out, and drives it away. Finally, sacrifice is offered to propitiate the gods who have relieved the sufferer. Among the Samoyeds, if it is thought that the supreme deity Num has sent the illness, the shaman refuses to oppose the divine will, but in other cases he will persuade a *tadebtsi* (spirit) to go and implore Num to lend his aid.[1]

At all such *séances* the spectators are much impressed by the whirling, dancing, singing, screaming, tambourine-playing, and ecstatic behaviour of the shaman, and believe that spirits are present. Equally they believe in all that he is asserting—his flight through the air or into the heavens and his visits to distant regions. They are terror-struck, and their nerves are much affected. Frequently the shaman proves his power by conjuring tricks, or by being bound and then released by the spirits whom he has summoned, or by thrusting knives into his body. But this 'does not exclude the possibility of a profound conviction on the part of the shamans that they are chosen by the spirits, have intercourse with them, and possess a mysterious power over the forces of nature.'[2]

In the south of Siberia mystery-plays in which the shamans are the actors are common. Among the Altaians the shaman's supposed journey to Erlik's realm is acted in the most dramatic fashion. This dramatization is also found among the Buriats, the shaman acting the part of the deity and other personages.[3] At the *séances* the dialogues carried on by the shaman with the spirits—their voices being produced by himself—are also of a highly dramatic character. Here we approach what is fully developed among many American Indian tribes—the dramatization of the life of the gods by members of a mystery-cult who represent the various divinities.

4. The shaman's dress and accessaries.—At his ceremonies the shaman wears a special dress—a coat hung with iron, rattles, rings, and representations of mythical animals, or with twisted handkerchiefs representing snakes, a mask, a breastplate, a hat, and embroidered stockings. All these have a definite meaning and purpose, and often a mystic character. Among the accessaries are a tambourine and a drum-stick. The tambourine has a cross-bar hung with rattles and is decorated with figures of a symbolic kind, intimately connected with shamanistic beliefs and mysteries. The spirits give this tambourine to the shaman, and spirits are called up by it and collected in it, while on it he is carried through the air. Horse-staves of wood or iron, specially prepared and decorated, are also used in the rites, and on them the shaman flies to heaven.[4]

5. Organization.—Shamans do not appear to be organized into an ecclesiastical caste or hierarchy, but they have varying grades and are held in differing degrees of respect according to their powers and their relation to the gods and spirits. Among the Buriats there is a distinction between hereditary shamans and those who have become shamans for some accidental reason. Among the Buriats also there are 'white shamans,' *i.e.* those who serve the good *tengris* of the west, and 'black shamans,' *i.e.* those who serve the evil *tengris* of the east. The former are honoured as those who can help men through their influence with beneficent powers; the latter are feared, because

1 V. V. Radlov, *Aus Sibirien*, ii. 20 ff.
2 Cf. *ERE* x. 124b, 125a.

1 M. A. Castrén, *Reiseerinnerungen*, Petrograd and Leipzig, 1853, p. 194 ff., quoted by Mikhailovskii, p. 143; cf. art. OSTYAKS, vol. ix. p. 580b.
2 Mikhailovskii, p. 138. 3 Cf. art. BURIATS, § 27.
4 For details of all these see artt. BURIATS, vol. iii. p. 16b, OSTYAKS, vol. ix. p. 580b, DRUM, vol. v. pp. 90b, 94a; Mikhailovskii, p. 78 ff.

through the evil spirits they may work ill to men —*e.g.*, steal their souls—and they are sometimes murdered for their evil deeds. Their lore is of a much more secret character than that of the white shamans, and there is a standing feud between them. Female shamans are also found among the Tunguses, Ostyaks, Buriats, and Yakuts, though with the last they are regarded as inferior to the male shamans, yet are preferred for the cure of mental disease. Among the Kamchadals the place of the shaman was usually taken by specially gifted old women.[1] The importance of the shaman is sufficiently upheld by the nature of his training and experience, his consecration, and the ceremonies performed before awed spectators. Usually implicit faith is put in him, except among the Chukchis, where his functions are limited to healing and conjuring.[2] The ideas concerning a shaman's death also reveal the manner in which he is regarded. Possessed by spirits, shamans do not die by the will of the gods, but by their demons being sent to kill each other. The elaborate nature of the funeral continues these ideas. Their burial-places in groves are inviolate and sacred, and dead shamans are the objects of a cult with sacrifices, while the dead shaman protects his people against the spirits of hostile shamans.

Although shamanism is described as moribund, it still exercises considerable power both in Buddhist Tibet and among nominally Christian tribes.

6. The shaman among the Eskimo.—The position and function of the so-called shaman among the Eskimo are analogous to those just described. The shades of the dead and supernatural beings called *tunghät* are controlled or owned by certain men, and even women, among the Eskimo of Bering Strait. The more of them each shaman, or *tun-gha-lĭk*, can subject to his will, the more powerful does he become. Usually a man becomes aware of spirit-power by remarkable circumstances in his life. He then goes to an old *tun-gha-lĭk*, in order to secure control of powers sufficient to enable him to announce himself as a *tun-gha-lĭk*, or he practises his art in private. In some districts he causes the death of a new-born child, steals its body, dries and preserves it, thus gaining control of its shade as a very powerful helper. Through his power over the spirits he drives off evil influences, or joins with other shamans in doing so if these influences are too strong. Both shades of the dead and shades of animals come at his call, and he claims to journey to the land of the dead and reports what he has seen there, the shades and spirits being visible to him. Like the Asiatic shaman, he knows what rites and sacrifices will be acceptable to the shades and spirits; hence his instructions are usually followed in the observance of festivals and ceremonies. He can change the weather, and cure the sick by means of incantations and performances. He is feared, and his advice is usually obeyed; but, if he uses his powers for bad ends or fails in what he sets out to do, the results may be fatal for him. Amulets and fetishes possess virtues which are secured to them by his means.[3]

Similarly among the Central Eskimo the *angakok* (plur. *angakut*) is protected by the spirits, especially by the spirit of the bear, which is acquired by a mysterious ceremony. These spirit-helpers, the indwellers of things, or *inue*, are known as *tôrnak* (plur. *tornait*). The chief office of an *angakok* is to discover the cause of sickness, misfortune, or death.

Within a darkened hut he sits down, his body shakes, and inhuman sounds are heard. He invokes the *tornait* with singing and shouting, and then announces what the atonement must be. Questions are also asked of the *tornait* regarding the cause of sickness. Ventriloquism appears to be used in such *séances*. Or the *tôrnak* is heard approaching, the hut shakes, and the *angakok* is supposed to fly with the spirit to distant regions. Or, again, the *angakok's* body is tied up, while he invokes the *tornait*. His body remains motionless, while his soul flies off, and on its return the thongs are found untied. In the Sedna feast, as in shamanistic rites, the *angakok* allows, or pretends to allow, his body to be pierced with harpoons. Sedna and other spirits come while the *angakok* is busy praying. He falls into a trance, and on awakening promises the help of the good spirits against the *tupilak*. The hardest task is to drive away Sedna, and this can be done only by the most powerful *angakut*. The *angakok* performs jugglery, and in the songs and incantations uses a sacred language. Most of the *angakut* believe in their powers, and in the *séances* go into ecstasy and trance.[1]

Among the Greenland Eskimo the *angakut* are said to obtain power by applying to an exalted spirit, who makes the *inue*, or invisible rulers, become their *tornait*, or helping and guardian-spirits. The *angakut* give counsel on all supernatural affairs, as well as in matters of daily life, and procure good weather or success in hunting by invoking a *tôrnak* and conciliating the *arnarkuagsak*. They cure the sick by extraordinary actions, give oracles, and use conjuring. The spirit *séance*, with use of the magic drum, and the bodily or spirit flight of the *angakok* are also found here. The *angakut* are the authorized teachers and judges in all questions of religious belief.[2]

7. The American Indian shaman.—Among the American Indians the most complete parallel to Asiatic shamanism is found among the tribes of the north-west, the priestly character being also here combined with it. The shaman performs religious functions and is also healer through being possessed by a supernatural being. He bears the name of this spirit and imitates its appearance. At a *séance*, by throwing himself into an ecstatic condition, he learns from the spirit the cause of sickness (which is then got rid of by blowing upon the patient or by other methods) or things and events hidden and future. The shaman has also the power of recovering the soul; he proves his powers by a variety of conjuring tricks. Yet, even where shamanism was strongest (Tlingit, Haida, Kwakiutl, Tsimshian), the chief was apt to act as priest—*e.g.*, in secret society performances.[3] On the whole, the shaman of the north-west tribes is still less of a priest than he is in Asia.[4]

The greatest development of shamanism is found among the Tlingit, with whom the shaman's spirit-helpers are many, as compared with the single helper of the Haida shaman. He has several masks, each representing one principal spirit, together with lesser spirits for each feature. He is specially aided by the spirit of the crest-animals of the family to whom these emblems belong. In the treatment of the sick the shaman draws out the material object which caused the sickness, not a spirit tormenting the patient. This method, including sucking out the disease, is also followed among the Haida, Tsimshian, Songish, and other tribes,[5] but the *séance* as used by the Asiatic shaman is lacking. Where the disease is judged to be caused by the absence of the soul, after singing, use of the rattle, dancing, etc., the shamans go to the place where the soul is supposed to be, or one of them sends his *tl'k·'ā'yin*, or guardian-spirit, after it (Songish), or dispatches his

1 Mikhailovskii, p. 68. 2 *Ib.* p. 131.

3 E. W. Nelson, 'The Eskimo about Bering Strait,' *18 RBEW* [1899], pt. i. pp. 388, 427 ff.

1 F. Boas, 'The Central Eskimo,' *6 RBEW* [1888], pp. 592 ff., 604.

2 H. J. Rink, *Tales and Traditions of the Eskimo*, Eng. tr., Edinburgh, 1875, pp. 39, 59 ff.; F. Nansen, *Eskimo Life*, Eng. tr., London, 1893, p. 283.

3 J. R. Swanton, *HAI* ii. 523.

4 A. H. Keane, *Man, Past and Present*, Cambridge, 1899, p. 376.

5 F. Boas, 'First General Report on the Indians of British Columbia,' in *Report of 59th Meeting of British Association*, London, 1890, pp. 848–855.

own soul to catch it (Chiliwack).[1] The soul is then restored to the patient. The Tlingit shaman can put spirits into material objects and send these out to do mischief. He locates supplies of food, aids in war, and fights hostile shamans by means of the spirits. The succession is from uncle to nephew, the nephew receiving his uncle's spirit in a trance after the burial. Offerings are made at the graves of shamans, and their houses in the forest are avoided lest the intruder should be made sick. The shaman's power is more dreaded among the Tlingit than among the Haida.[2]

With the Chinooks gods are invoked by the shaman for the cure of the sick, and the search for the soul by the souls of shamans is also practised. Here also, not an invading spirit, but a material object, causes sickness and is removed.[3]

Among the Dénés shamanism of this type is prevalent, with the curious addition (found also among the Eskimo to some extent) of the patient's confession of sins to the shaman.[4] With the Cherokees the type of shamanistic methods of healing resembles those already detailed, but there is appeal to the spirits to aid the shaman rather than compulsion or control over the spiritual world.[5]

Among many tribes the shaman's functions were divided among different kinds of shamans. With the Maidu (among whom all the children of a shaman must become shamans, else the spirits would kill them) there are a class of curative shamans and another class known as dreamers, who hold communion with spirits and ghosts. During the winter the latter have *séances* in darkened houses, when they hold converse with spirits. One who has not a shaman for his father goes to the mountains and there performs certain ceremonies, as do also shamans who wish to obtain more powerful spirits.[6] Or, again, as with the Ojibwa, there is the *midē'wiwin*, or society of the shamans, in which the candidate for admission is supposed to die and come to life again full of spirit-power. The members use incantations and exorcisms and administer remedies. There are, again, the *jĕssakīds*, prophets or jugglers, who speak with the *manidōs* in a hut at a *séance*. The hut shakes violently, and the voices of the spirits are heard from it. There are also *wâbĕnōs* (who prepare charms) and herbalists, but only the *midé* are combined in a society. A similar division is found among the Menomini—the *mitäwit* (society of shamans), the *tshiśaqka* (jugglers), and the *wâbĕnō*. The magical feats of the *midé* and *mitä'v* are done by the help of their *manidōs*, the power possessed by the shaman's 'medicine,' which typifies his tutelary spirit. The *jĕssakīds* at the *séance* obtain information from the spirits—*e.g.*, regarding sickness, the person causing it, its cure, etc. They also remove the substance causing sickness by sucking, after singing incantations and using the rattle.[7] Divisions of a similar kind are found among the Chippewas and Delawares.

With the Chippewas the method of healing included a fast on the part of the shaman and the erection of a medicine-lodge for him, into which the patient was brought. The shaman chanted to his tambourine, causing a spirit to descend. The spirit entered the patient and removed his sin, already confessed to the shaman, and also inserted his soul which had escaped. Sucking out the material cause of disease was also used.[1]

These mystery-societies are found among all but the lowest tribes, and the aim of their ceremonies is physical and spiritual well-being. The rites are frequently shamanistic in character.[2]

Among the tribes of the eastern plains the shaman is merged in the priest. There are societies which work at healing and use definite remedies, yet invoke supernatural powers. There is also a limited number of men who conduct the national rituals.[3] In more advanced tribes the shaman gives way to the priest, or is merely a medicine-man or wizard—*e.g.*, in the Navaho, Hupa, Apache, Choctaw, Hopi, and other Pueblo tribes, and the Natchez. Here the priest's authority is not based on individual action. He works for the tribe, or is associated with a society. But here, too, these priest-healers perform long ceremonies and medicine-dances for healing or life-giving, as in the mystery-societies of other tribes.[4]

In general, except among the tribes of the north-west (where possession of or by spirits as the fundamental fact in healing and wonder-working marks the true shaman) and in the case of mystery-societies where shamanistic methods are in vogue, the medicine-man is more in evidence than the true shaman. While not always unaided by spirits, he uses more empiric methods than those found among the Asiatic tribes—*e.g.*, the sweat-bath, bleeding, bathing, sucking, noises, and gestures. Even the north-western shaman has little to do with directing sacrifices, and the general belief that illness is caused by sorcery rather than by a spirit possessing the patient divides both the theory and the method of cure from those used in Asia.

A somewhat closer parallel to the Asiatic shaman is found among some S. American tribes. With the natives of Guiana the office of *piai* or *paje* is usually hereditary; but, if there is no son, the *piai* chooses a boy, preferably an epileptic, and subjects him to a course of fasting, vigils in the forest, drinking tobacco liquor, and lessons in ventriloquism. He is now able to work himself into a mad frenzy, to converse with *kenaimas*, after invoking them by chants, and to overcome them. By drinking tobacco-juice he falls into a trance, in which he believes that he is received into the company of the spirits and consecrated by them to his office. He also learns the tribal traditions and the properties of plants. His insignia consist of a rattle, various crystals, a kind of doll, and other things, which are tabu, and would lose their power if profaned. All evil is produced by *kenaimas*, human or superhuman, and by his power over them the *piai* gains great influence. He can call up and question the spirit of any Indian or dispatch his own spirit to question an absent tribesman or to speak with spirits. In cases of illness, where blowing off the evil spirit is not sufficient, other methods are resorted to. A healing *séance* is held in a dark hut, where fearful noises are produced for hours. Winged creatures seem to approach the house, enter by the roof, and fly off again. These are the *kenaimas* coming and going, and each one must give an account of itself and promise not to trouble the patient. At a later time the *piai* produces, *e.g.*, a caterpillar, which represents the possessing *kenaima*. In curing, the *piai*, by singing to them, calls up spirits to aid him. They are his friends, who inform him whence the disease

[1] Boas, 'Second General Report on the Indians of British Columbia,' in *Report of 60th Meeting of British Association*, London, 1901, p. 579 ff.

[2] J. R. Swanton, 'Social Conditions, Beliefs, and Linguistic Relationship of the Tlingit Indians,' *26 RBEW* [1908], p. 463 f.; see also art. HAIDA, § II.

[3] Cf. art. CHINOOKS, §§ 1, 5, 6.

[4] E. Petitot, *Traditions indiennes du Canada nord-ouest*, Paris, 1886, p. 278; see also artt. DÉNÉS, CARRIER INDIANS.

[5] See art. CHEROKEES, §§ 6, 7.

[6] *HAI* ii. 523.

[7] W. J. Hoffman, 'The Menomini Indians,' *14 RBEW* [1896], pt. i. p. 66 f., *7 RBEW* [1891], p. 149 ff.; R. M. Dorman, *The Origin of Primitive Superstitions*, p. 363; cf. art. OJIBWA.

[1] Petitot, p. 434.

[2] H. B. Alexander, *North American Mythology* (=*The Mythology of all Races*, vol. x.), Boston, 1916, p. 270 f.

[3] *HAI* ii. 523; see artt. ALGONQUINS, vol. i. p. 323b, and HURON, vol. vi. p. 885b.

[4] Cf. art. DISEASE AND MEDICINE (American), § 4; see also G. B. Grinnell, *Pawnee Hero Stories and Folk Tales*, London, 1893, p. 350 f., for a similar distinction between priests and shamans.

comes, whether from another spirit or a wizard. If from a bad spirit, he gets one of the helpful spirits to remove it. The *piai* is also employed to drive off *kenaimas* from a village. He fixes the appropriate times for attacking enemies, and can transform himself to animal shape or make himself invisible. The natives firmly believe in the powers of the *piai*, he believes more or less in them himself, and he exerts his influence in autocratic ways and shares with the headman the authority in a village. He is respected and feared, as arbiter of life and death, and when dead his spirit is propitiated.[1]

In other tribes the methods used are less clearly those of a shaman and more those of the medicine-man.[2] But in some tribes a regular priesthood exists, the members of which also practise medicine and cure, and have spirits in their service.[3]

8. The shaman in Malaysia. — Among the different peoples of the Malay Archipelago and Malay Peninsula shamanistic methods are common, and both sexes act as shamans. Priests, *i.e.* officiants in purely religious services, are sometimes a separate class, but they sometimes also act as shamans.[4] The office of shaman is often hereditary; it may also fall to men to whom spirits have revealed themselves or whom spirits have chosen, and who have been trained by another shaman. Some are self-created and do not possess a familiar spirit. To prove their calling, the shamans fast or use other means, by which they pass into trance, ecstasy, or an abnormal mental state, acting as if possessed.

The process of initiation in the case of a Dayak *manang* includes the committing to memory of the traditional lore and incantations; his treatment as a sick man by other *manangs* (he thus learns how to feel a disease in the body and to apply charms); the alleged taking out of his brains by the *manangs*, in order to wash them and give him a clear mind to penetrate the mysteries of evil spirits.[5]

The methods of curing sickness, which is caused by spirit-possession or by an object in which a spirit resides, are various: sometimes the spirit is extracted from the patient in the usual fashion of the medicine-man and propitiated by prayer and sacrifice; sometimes the shaman falls into a trance or ecstasy, and then ejects the spirit with the help of his familiar spirit; or sometimes the familiar spirit indicates the method of treatment to the shaman. When the sickness is caused by the wandering of the soul, the shaman recaptures it by a variety of means—*e.g.*, by sending his soul, when in trance or a dreamy state, after it to Hades or wherever it may be. He describes its wanderings while it is absent, and on reviving shows the soul (or a small object), which he pretends to replace in the patient.[6] Spirits are also driven off by chanting or by the familiar spirit of the shaman. Oracular messages are also obtained through conversation and communion with spirits or gods. To some extent the Malaysian shaman, male or female, acts, like the Asiatic shaman, as mediator between men and the supernatural world.[7]

The native names of the shaman are numerous—*e.g.*, Malay, *pawang*; Dayak, *belian*, *basir*; Iban, *manang*; Battak, *sibaso*; Kayan, *dayong*. Most of these use the 'sending'[8] to kill or harm others, and can change themselves into tigers.

1 W. E. Roth, 'An Inquiry into the Animism and Folk-lore of the Guiana Indians,' *30 RBEW* [1915], p. 328 ff.; E. F. im Thurn, *Among the Indians of Guiana*, London, 1883, pp. 211, 224, 328 ff.; cf. art. PAMPEANS, vol. ix. p. 598a.

2 See art. PATAGONIANS, vol. ix. p. 669b.

3 See artt. CHILE, vol. iii p. 548a, BRAZIL, vol. ii. p. 836a.

4 H. Ling Roth, *The Natives of Sarawak and British N. Borneo*, London, 1896, i. 282; cf. *ERE* viii. 347a, 364b.

5 Ling Roth, i. 280 f.

6 C. Hose and W. McDougall, *The Pagan Tribes of Borneo*, London, 1912, ii. 29 f.

7 See Ling Roth, i. 259 ff.; Spencer St. John, *Life in the Forests of the Far East*, London, 1862, i. 199 ff.; artt. MALAY ARCHIPELAGO, § 2, MALAY PENINSULA, § 14.

8 See art. LYCANTHROPY, § 5.

9. Shamanistic methods elsewhere.—One of the main aspects of shamanism, viz. possession (*q.v.*) by spirits or divinities for a particular purpose, is of wide occurrence. Among the Ainus the wizard or medicine-man, when called in to explain the cause of illness, works himself into a frenzy, falls into a trance, and tells why the disease has come and who sent it. He makes charms to be worn by the patient in order to drive away the possessing demon. In a state of trance he also prophesies as the mouthpiece of the gods.[1] Zulu diviners in their performances sometimes use the trance and are the mediums through which the spirits speak in a whistling voice, explaining the cause of illness or whatever is inquired about. The spirits go to secure the buried poisons causing the illness and fight with the spirits of the place where they are buried.[2] In other parts of Africa the phenomena of possession, often in connexion with rites of an elaborate and prolonged kind, are reproduced by priests, priestesses, medicine-men, or magicians, or, as among the Baganda, by mediums associated with the priests or particular gods, for healing the sick or giving oracles.[3] The Maori *tohunga*, or priest, was similarly possessed or inspired; and in Polynesia generally, where the priests were called 'god-boxes' because possessed by the gods, they used the method of frenzy, which proved their possession, in order to discover the cause of illness or in announcing the will of the gods.[4] In Fiji and other parts of Melanesia similar methods were in use, often in connexion with a *séance*.[5] The Vedda *kapurale* has the necessary power to call the *yaku*, or spirits, to accept the offerings. He invokes them, dances round the offerings, and then, in a semi-trance condition, he becomes possessed by them. They speak through him, announcing their acceptance of the offerings, and promise success in hunting. Others present may also become possessed by them.[6] In the religion of many Dravidian tribes, with their cult of spirits and demons, these possess the frenzied magician for the time being and utter their communications through him.[7] Such are only a few examples drawn from a wide field; the phenomena are met with in many of the higher religions also.[8] Sometimes, too, persons not specially marked out as priests or medicine-men become possessed or simulate the phenomena, and hold converse with spirits.

10. Conclusion.—The phenomena of possession are to a large extent based on the theory that sickness and diseases, especially those of a nervous and epileptic character, result from a spirit having entered the patient and speaking through him. He was regarded therefore as inspired, and in some cases such persons themselves become shamans—to use the word in a wide sense. It was easy then for others either to simulate the

1 J. Batchelor, *The Ainu and their Folk-Lore*, London, 1901, p. 308, *The Ainu of Japan*, do. 1892, p. 197.

2 H. Callaway, *The Religious System of the Amazulu*, London, 1884, pp. 259 ff., 280, 348 f.; A. Lang, *The Making of Religion*, do. 1898, p. 75.

3 R. H. Nassau, *Fetichism in W. Africa*, London, 1904, p. 72 f.; D. Macdonald, *Africana*, do. 1882, i. 61; J. Roscoe, *The Baganda*, do. 1911, p. 278; see also artt. BANTU AND S. AFRICA, § 6, NEGROES AND W. AFRICA, § 4.

4 *Old New Zealand*, by a Pakeha Maori (F. E. Maning), London, 1863, p. 137 f.; W. Ellis, *Polynesian Researches*², do. 1832–36, i. 372 f.; W. W. Gill, *Myths and Songs from the S. Pacific*, do. 1876, p. 35; G. Brown, *Melanesians and Polynesians*, do. 1910, pp. 224, 246; cf. artt. POLYNESIA, § 15, POSSESSION (Introductory and Primitive), § 7.

5 T. Williams, *Fiji and the Fijians*, London, 1858, i. 224; R. H. Codrington, *The Melanesians*, Oxford, 1891, p. 219 f.

6 C. G. and B. Z. Seligmann, *The Veddas*, Cambridge, 1911, pp. 209 f., 230, 'The Vedda Cult of the Dead,' *Transactions of the Third International Congress for the Hist. of Religions*, Oxford, 1908, i. 62 f.

7 T. H. Lewin, *Wild Races of S.E. India*, London, 1870, pp. 215, 242, 285, 301; cf. artt. DRAVIDIANS (N. India), § 3, BENGAL, § 24.

8 See artt. POSSESSION, and PRIEST, PRIESTHOOD.

phenomena of possession or, by a special training for the purpose, to reproduce them and to believe themselves (and to be believed by others) possessed by spirits and their mediums of communication. Such persons are probably often mentally unstable and subject to hysteria.[1] The main aspects of the Asiatic shaman's procedure as well as the idea of possession by spirits are found to be of well-nigh universal occurrence in connexion with healing, discovering the will of spirits or gods, or prophesying. One may occur without the others, or, again, all are found as parts of the practice of a wonder-worker. This suggests, therefore, that the shamanism of the Ural-Altaic tribes is but a specialized and highly elaborated form of a universal practice—a form associated with a full and varied religion, polytheism and polydæmonism, of which it is an essential and central part, and connected with sacrifices and the use of liturgical prayer, chant, and hymn formulæ. It probably formed the religion of the early Mongol-Tatar peoples, and others akin to them—*e.g.*, in China and Tibet, where much of it is still reproduced—and it is still very largely connected with the religion of the Malaysian tribes. Whether among the Eskimo and certain American Indian tribes it is a native growth, or has been the result of influences from Asiatic peoples, or has been brought thence in early times, is uncertain.

Keane says that the American Indian medicine-man is 'a sort of Asiatic shaman in embryo, arriving in the late Stone Age, and afterwards diverging in various directions from his Siberian prototype.'[2]

While retaining the word 'shamanism' as descriptive of the religion of the Ural-Altaic tribes, we must none the less admit that the practices of the shaman are found in greater or less completeness over a wide area. At the same time the methods of the medicine-man and the magician, as distinct from the shaman, are also found everywhere, and frequently enter into shamanistic practice. While the shaman's methods are connected with the cult of spirits, and are therefore semi-religious and not fundamentally magical, but rather mysticism of a primitive kind, seeking intimate communion with the spirit-world, those of the medicine-man are partly magical, partly empiric with the use of naturalistic modes of healing, and are not necessarily connected with spirit-help, though they may be used against hostile spirits. No doubt the differing methods are often interchangeable, and, as often, the various functions of shaman, medicine-man, and magician are shared by different classes of men in one tribe. Priests, too, sometimes combine these various functions in themselves, apart from their purely religious work. On the whole, it is better to use the word 'shaman' to denote one whose procedure is based on the fact that he is *en rapport* with spirits or has them at his command, and to consider the medicine-man as one who acts generally by methods in which the aid of spirits is not essential. The Asiatic shaman is a highly specialized user of shamanistic methods.

LITERATURE.—Besides the works mentioned, see John Abercrombie, *The Pre- and Proto-Historic Finns*, London, 1898; R. B. Dixon, *JAFL* xxi. [1908] 1 f.; R. M. Dorman, *The Origin of Primitive Superstitions*, Philadelphia, 1881, ch. i.; J. R. Swanton, *HAI*, Washington, 1907–10, art. 'Shamans and Priests,' ii. 522 ff.; W. J. Hoffman, 'The Midē'wiwin or "Grand Medicine Society" of the Ojibwa,' *7 RBEW* [1891], p. 143 ff.; L. M. Langlès, 'Recueil des usages des Mantchoux (ou Rituel),' in *Notices et extraits des MSS de la Bibliothèque Nationale*, Paris, 1787–1912, VII. i. 291 f.; E. Lehmann, *Mysticism in Heathendom and Christendom*, Eng. tr., London, 1910; V. M. Mikhailovskii, 'Shamanism in Siberia and European Russia,' tr. O. Wardrop, *JAI* xxiv. [1895] 62 ff., 126 ff.; V. V. Radlov (W. Radloff), *Aus Sibirien*, Leipzig, 1884; G. G. Roskoff, *Das Religionswesen der rohesten Naturvölker*, do. 1880; W. Schott, 'Über den Doppelsinn des Wortes Schamane und über den tunguschen Schamanencultus am Hofe des Mandju-Kaiser,' *ABAW*, 1842; E. B. Tylor, *PC*⁴, London, 1903. See also artt. BURIATS and literature cited there, DEMONS AND SPIRITS, DISEASE AND MEDICINE, FINNS (Ancient), LAPPS, OSTYAKS, POSSESSION, and PRIEST, PRIESTHOOD.

J. A. MACCULLOCH.

[1] See artt. MALAY ARCHIPELAGO, § 2, POSSESSION (Introductory and Primitive), § 1.

[2] *Man, Past and Present*, p. 378 f.

SHAME.—Shame is an emotion of self-abasement experienced by one who is conscious of acting contrary to, or below, the standards which he approves and by which he knows others judge him. This sense of self-abasement is stronger than in the related states with which it is often confused—modesty, bashfulness, shyness, and coyness. These are marked rather by hesitation, caution, and inhibition. They arise through consciousness of being under the gaze of others whose attitude is that of curiosity or superiority or searching criticism. But shame involves a sense of unworthiness and demerit. Like these kindred states, it may arise in connexion with matters of sex, but it is also found in a great variety of situations not concerned with sex. The sense of shame consists in the consciousness of failure and exposure before other persons in connexion with a point of honour or of strong self-esteem.

Darwin discussed blushing as an expression of this emotion. Other accompanying signs are the drooping of the body, lowering of the head, and averting the gaze. The subject tends to hide, to escape notice, and, in extreme cases, to inflict injury upon himself as a kind of self-imposed retributive punishment. Modern psychologists have shown that all emotions involve more or less of a conflict of opposing impulses. McDougall has treated shame in terms of the conflict between positive and negative self-feeling. He says:

'Shame, in the full sense of the word, is only possible when the self-regarding sentiment has become well developed about the idea of the self, its attributes and powers. Then any exhibition of the self to others as deficient in these powers and attributes, which constitute the self in so far as it is the object of the self-regarding sentiment, provokes shame. The self may appear defective or inferior to others in all other respects and no shame, though perhaps bashfulness, will be induced.'[1]

W. James noted this fact and pointed out[2] that the man who has great proficiency as a pugilist or as an oarsman may be shamed to death if there is one rival in all the world who can excel him. On the other hand, a puny little fellow who has no athletic prowess or ambition is not depressed by the fact that every one can surpass him. In the fraction of self-esteem represented by success over pretensions shame results when success is inadequate to the pretensions.

Interesting manifestations of the outward behaviour expressive of shame in man may be seen in the lower animals. An observer noticed that on more than one occasion when he was approaching his home after an extended absence his dog would rush towards him, barking threateningly as he would at a stranger. When he came nearer, the dog would suddenly lower his head to the ground, rub his nose with his paw, and, after a moment, bound forward with all his usual signs of friendliness. Children reflect their environment and training in the acts and circumstances in which they show shame. Apparently there are no innate endowments determining the feeling. In well-regulated homes children shrink from being discovered with muddy clothes, dirty faces, holes in their stockings, and the like. A child is ashamed to be seen with a nursing-bottle after having learned to eat. A boy of fourteen was willing to stay at home from school and assist his mother, but was painfully humiliated when his school-mates found him in the house washing dishes. Sensitiveness to awkwardness, to social blunders, and to one's appearance in the eyes of others, particularly of the opposite sex, is greatly intensified in adolescence, and hence

[1] *An Introd. to Social Psychology*⁷, p. 147 f.

[2] *Psychology*, New York, 1890, i. 310.

the sense of shame is often greatly deepened. It is doubtless on account of the dawning consciousness of sex in this period that capacity for shame in these matters is so much increased as compared with the earlier years.

The Freudian psychology has thrown new light upon the conflict of such impulses as those involved in shame. In this view, normal persons are subject to the play of many antagonistic tendencies. In their waking life the upper stratum of consciousness, representing the higher self, acts as a censor to exclude from the stream of thought ideas of a baser sort. But in dreams the suppressed tendencies may be released and 'arouse the upper personality to feelings of horror and remorse.'[1] At times this actually happens in waking life; a person's lower tendencies get expressed, the evil deed is committed, and the better self suffers keen remorse and shame.

Social psychology emphasizes the fact that one's social group furnishes the determining influences in forming an individual's standards of taste and conduct. The infringement of the conventions, or *mores*, is likely to be accompanied by shame. The divergencies among races in reference to the situations in which they experience this emotion are astonishing and give weight to the impression that education and environment are the chief factors.

'Though the Bakairi of Central Brazil have no feeling of shame about nakedness, they are ashamed to eat in public: they retired to eat, and hung their heads in shamefaced confusion when they saw him [the white man] innocently eat in public.'[2]

Sumner gives many illustrations from various sources.

LITERATURE.—C. R. Darwin, *The Expression of the Emotions*, London, 1872; T. A. Ribot, *Psychology of the Emotions*, Eng. tr., do. 1897; W. McDougall, *An Introd. to Social Psychology*[7], do. 1913; E. B. Holt, *The Freudian Wish and its Place in Ethics*, New York, 1915: W. G. Sumner, *Folkways*, Boston, 1906; Vladimir Solovyof, *The Justification of the Good*, London, 1919.

E. S. AMES.

SHAMMAI.—Shammai was a famous Jewish teacher of the 1st cent. B.C., the most distinguished contemporary of Hillel (*q.v.*), to whose views on Halākhāh as well as on many a point of general Jewish theology he was almost invariably in diametrical opposition. The two men are usually coupled together in the Talmud, and the antithesis between them was reproduced, often with actual violence, for a considerable period after their lives, in the two opposing schools which they founded and which figure prominently in Rabbinical literature as Beth Hillel and Beth Shammai. The influence exerted by these schools on the subsequent evolution of Jewish legalism is paramount.

According to the Mishnāh,[3] Shammai held the office of vice-president (*ab beth din*), whilst Hillel was president (*nasi*) of the Synhedrion—Shammai having succeeded a certain Menaḥem, who, according to Josephus,[4] was a great sage endowed with prophetic power, and in his childhood had foretold that Herod would one day rule over the Jews. The Talmud, however, makes no mention of this point. Graphic emphasis is given in the Rabbinic records to the marked contrast between the hasty, excitable, and uncompromising temper of Shammai as compared with the imperturbably sweet and patient nature of Hillel. In T.B. *Shabbāth*, 31*a*, three analogous illustrative anecdotes are given of this:

(*a*) A heathen comes to Shammai and Hillel in turn with the request that he be admitted as a convert to Judaism, whilst believing only in the 'written' and not in the 'oral' Law. Shammai reproachfully shows him the door, whereas Hillel by his kindly treatment wins him over to Judaism and a belief in both 'Laws.' (*b*) A heathen wishes to be taught the whole 'Law' (and thus become a proselyte to Judaism) whilst 'standing on one foot,' *i.e.* in a very brief space of time. Whereas Shammai, before whom he first appears, gives him a sound trouncing with a builder's measuring-rod that he happens to be holding in his hand at the moment, Hillel receives him into the Jewish faith with the advice, 'That which is hurtful to thee do not unto thy neighbour. This is the whole Tôrāh. All the rest is commentary. Go and learn.' (*c*) A heathen is desirous of becoming converted to Judaism, with the object of ultimately becoming eligible for the office of high-priest. Shammai rejects him outright, whereas Hillel admits him, whilst at the same time tactfully convincing him of the futility of his ambition to become high-priest. It was Shammai's bad temper, says the Talmud in summing up, that 'put this man out of the universe' (*i.e.* made him forfeit the bliss reaped by a convert to Judaism), whereas it was Hillel's meekness that brought him near to dwell beneath the wings of the Shekhinah.

In all probability the truest interpretation of these contrasts is to say that they point to the rigid, uncompromising attitude of Shammai towards the things of religion exclusively, and that they have no reference to his personal temper or character. That the latter was by no means so bitter and misanthropic as is popularly imagined is proved by the motto ascribed to him in *Ābhôth*, i. 15, 'Receive all men with a cheerful countenance.' A statement in T.B. *Bābhā Bathrā*, 134*b*, shows that Shammai could, on occasion, show real meekness even towards subordinates such as his disciples. Shammai was the redoubtable upholder of inherited custom, a relentless follower of the old beaten tracks, to depart from which was to call forth his measureless rage.

Further striking instances of Shammai's exceptionally stringent veneration for the letter of the Law are the following:

Mishnāh *Sukkāh*, ii. 8, relates that, when once his daughter-in-law gave birth to a son on the Feast of Tabernacles, Shammai pierced a hole through the roof of the chamber in which she lay, thus converting the room into a ritual *sukkāh* ('booth') so as to enable the new-born infant to fulfil the religious precept of Lv 23[42], 'Ye shall dwell in booths seven days; all that are home-born in Israel shall dwell in booths.' This was opposed to the dominant Rabbinic view, which maintained that the obligation did not become incumbent upon a child until he had reached at least some rudimentary stage of reasoning power.

To similar effect is the story in T.B. *Yômā*, 77*b*, which relates that Shammai on a certain Day of Atonement refused to handle food even in one of his hands in order to feed his young son (who was exempt from the ordeal of fasting by reason of his tender age), because such handling of food would entail the preliminary ritual washing of the hand in question. The sages, however, out of a feeling of sheer humanity, 'decreed' that it was his duty to perform the ritual washing of both his hands in order to feed the child and avoid risking its life through so long an abstention from food.[1]

That, nevertheless, such instances of uncompromising obedience to traditional formulæ can consist with a fine and lofty idealism in religious outlook is proved by a Baraita in T.B. *Beṣa*, 16*a*, as follows:

'They said concerning Shammai the Elder that throughout all his days whatever he ate was in honour of the Sabbath. Should he alight upon a fine beast, he would say "Let this be for the Sabbath." Should he afterwards find a finer one, he would leave it and partake only of the first.'

The observance of the Sabbath was to Shammai the welcome opportunity of the soul's joyous union with God. Hence the smallest act performed during the week was felt to have some bearing upon the Sabbath's sanctified joy.

The Mishnāh *Eduyôth*, i. 1–4, mentions three Halākhic questions disputed between Hillel and Shammai. These refer to (1) *niddah* (laws concerning female impurity), (2) *ḥallah* (laws concerning the priest's share of the dough, as alluded to in Nu 15[17-21]), and (3) *mĭkveh* (laws relating to the ritual bath). The views taken by Shammai on some of the points in connexion with these show that he was, at times, capable of adopting the more lenient standpoint in Halākhāh.[2]

There is an interesting allusion in *Sifrē*, Deut.

[1] E. B. Holt, *The Freudian Wish and its Place in Ethics*, p. 15.
[2] H. H. Ellis, 'The Evolution of Modesty,' in *Psychological Review*, vi. [1899] 137.
[3] *Hagigāh*, ii. 2.
[4] *Ant.* xv. x. 5.

[1] Cf. *Tôseftā*, ed. M. S. Zuckermandel, Magdeburg, 1877; *Yômā, ad loc.*
[2] Cf. Mishn. *Hagigāh*, ii. 2; T.B. *Shabbāth*, 15*a*; T.B *Niddah*, i. 1.

§ 203,[1] to three Halākhic laws which Shammai deduced exegetically from the words of Scripture, one of which is that a ship going on a long voyage should not start later than three days previous to the Sabbath.[2] This he deduced from Dt 20^{20}.

Many of Shammai's teachings and maxims are probably incorporated in those handed down in the name of the school which he founded—the Beth Shammai. The Halākhic decisions of this school reflect all the stringency of their founder. In all the 316 controversies between it and its rival, the Beth Hillel, as alluded to spasmodically throughout the domains of the Rabbinic literature, the Shammaites took the lenient view in only 55 cases. The Mishnāh generally prepares the reader for these 'leniencies' of the Shammaites by an introductory remark such as 'The following are of the lenient views of Beth Shammai and the stringent views of Beth Hillel.'[3] Judæa was, at the period of the existence of these schools, the storm centre of much political faction; and the Shammaites, as was perhaps natural, carried their religious austerities into the arena of the current politics. They particularly hated the Roman domination and the Roman system of taxation. They were merciless in their opposition to all intercourse with Romans or with Jews who showed countenance to Roman laws and practices. In order to carry these views into effect, they sternly forbade Jews to buy any article of food or drink from their non-Jewish neighbours. Such bitter hostility did these and other Shammaite stringencies arouse in the minds of the conciliatory Hillelites that, as the Talmud relates in many parallel passages,[4] 'the day on which the Shammaite enactments gained the ascendancy over the Hillelites was as unfortunate for Israel as the day on which the golden calf was worshipped.'

The Talmud nowhere affixes a date to the beginning or ending of these disputes; but internal evidence shows that they were carried on for some time after the destruction of the Temple by Titus. The 'war of the schools' resulted in victory for the Hillelites over the Shammaites.[5] The Halākhāh was fixed in accordance with the Hillelite view, and ratified by all subsequent Rabbinic codifiers.

LITERATURE.—I. M. Jost, *Gesch. des Judenthums und seiner Sekten*, Leipzig, 1857–59, i. 261–270; H. Graetz, *Gesch. der Juden*[3], Berlin, 1878, iii. 213 f., 275–278, notes 23, 26, Eng. tr., London, 1891–92, ii. 101, 131–133; I. H. Weiss, *Dor Dor we-Dorshaw*, Vienna, 1871–91, i. 163 f., 170–174, 177–187; W. Bacher, *Die Agada der Tannaiten*, Strassburg, 1890–1903, i. 11 f., 14–25; A. Geiger, *Judaism and its History*, tr. Charles Newburgh, New York, n.d., pp. 116–118; A. Schwarz, *Die Controversen der Schammaiten und Hilleliten*, Karlsruhe, 1893; A. Hyman, *Toldoth Tannaim Ve 'Ammoraim*, London, 1910, iii. 1118–1120.

J. ABELSON.

SHANS.—See BURMA.

SHAPE-SHIFTING.—See METAMORPHOSIS, LYCANTHROPY.

ASH-SHA'RĀNĪ or Sha'rāwī, Abū-l-mawāhib 'Abd al-Wahhāb b. Aḥmad b. 'Alī al-Anṣārī ash-Shāfi'ī ash-Shādhilī, rarely al-Aḥmadi ash-Shinnāwi al-Ash'ari (MS Leipzig-Vollers, no. 353), was born in the month of Ramaḍān, A.H. 898 (899) near Qalqashanda, in the delta of the Nile, and spent his youth in Sāqiyet Abū Sha'ra, in the same neighbourhood. He traced his genealogy back to the rulers of Tilimsēn (Tlemcen) in the times of the saint Abū Maaldyan (Médine), about A.H. 600, and even to the Khalifa 'Alī. An ancestor is said to have migrated from Tilimsēn into Upper Egypt, where ash-Sha'rānī was born near Behnesa, according to another account. At the age of twelve he went to Cairo, where he studied seventeen years in the mosque of al-Ghamri; from there he betook himself to the *madrasa* of the mosque Umm Ḥawand. Egypt had passed in 923 (1517) into the hands of the Ottomans, and the writings of ash-Sha'rānī often speak of the condition of the country, which became worse and worse under the new rule. It was his life in the mosque Umm Ḥawand that made him famous. He won friends, and made enemies who were jealous of his reputation. About this time, in the year 931, began also his literary activity. The report that he was a weaver in private life is due to a misunderstanding on the part of Von Kremer. His whole life was consecrated to devotional exercises and to teaching. He repeatedly made the pilgrimage to Mecca, first in the year 947, then again in 953 and 963. He mentions only one journey undertaken by him in Upper Egypt. His reputation grew extraordinarily when a Coptic patron founded for him (with unjustly gotten money!) a school and a house for the poor, where ash-Sha'rānī worked to the close of his life (cf. *Description de l'Egypte*, 'Plan du Caire,' fig. 8; Baedeker's plan, D 2). His popularity became boundless; great officials consulted him on important matters; the pious multitudes filled his school and environment; even the theologians (*'ulamā*) who were hostile to him were forced to change in great part their attitude. In the year 960, as he felt his death draw near—he believed like other pious people that he would die at the age of sixty-three like the Prophet—he began to write his autobiography (see below). But he lived ten years longer, and died in Jumādā I. 973. His funeral was as magnificent as only a popularly venerated saint could receive. He was buried in the basin (*fasqīya*) of his mosque-school, which later was named after him and still exists. He was four times married—successively, it would seem, not simultaneously. Of his sons, Ḥasan seems to have died early, but 'Abd ar-Raḥmān survived him, and died A.H. 1011.

The extraordinary significance of ash-Sha'rānī lies in the fact that he was practically and theoretically a mystic of the first order, and at the same time a prominent and original writer in the field of theology and jurisprudence. His writings number over seventy. Among these he names twenty-four that were entirely original (*ibtikār*), their central idea having previously been treated by no one. The fields of his literary activity were, first, mysticism, *i.e.* Ṣūfism (*at-taṣawwuf*), then law, dogmatics, the Qur'ān, tradition, poetry, and even grammar and popular medicine. The most characteristic feature of his nature, both from a theoretical and from a practical standpoint, is mysticism. His teachers and patterns in the practice of Ṣūfism were Afḍaladdīn, Ibrāhīm āl-Matbūlī, 'Alī al-Ḥauwāṣ al-Burullusī, and 'Alī al-Marṣafī—especially al-Ḥauwāṣ. Like him, ash-Sha'rānī claimed the gift of miraculously hearing *all* things, and thus of knowing also the secrets of his fellow-men, of foreseeing things to come, and of warning like a prophet. In his youth ash-Sha'rānī gave himself to an austere asceticism, hunger, watching, scourging, miserable food and clothing. Like the Christian Stylites, he used often to climb the mast (*ṣārī*) of the mosque al-Ghamrī and remain swinging there, to escape sleep. He distinguishes three degrees in the Ṣūfī life: the beginner (*murīd*), the *shaikh*, and the saint (*walī*). But the highest rank of the *walī* is still far from the lowest rank of the prophet. Within the domain of the Ṣūfīs he distinguishes a narrower (esoteric) and a broader (exoteric) circle,

[1] Ed. M. B. J. Friedmann, Vienna, 1864, p. 111*b*.
[2] Cf. Tôs. *'Erûbhîn*, iii. 7; T.B. *Shabbāth*, 19*a*.
[3] See Mishn. *Eduyôth*, iv. 1.
[4] Cf. Mishn. *Shabbāth*, i. 4; T.B. *Shabbāth*, 17*a*; T.J. *Shabbāth*, i. 3*c*; Tôs. *Shabbāth*, i. 16 f.
[5] T.B. *Berakhôth*, 36*b*; T.B. *Beṣah*, 11*b*; T.B. *Yebhamôth*, 9*a*.

and a stricter and a looser practice. The great multitude of them, that is without understanding, is called by him *al-qaum*, 'the people'; the non-Ṣūfī multitude is called, with a synonymous expression, *al-ḥalq*. We must not communicate to the *qaum* all truths and mysteries; that would be to throw pearls before swine. Also in ethical and ritual things we must allow them a certain latitude (*taḥfīf*), because they cannot bear everything. The austere manner of life (*tashdīd*) is only for the strong. The Ṣūfīs must lead a solitary, despised, and modest life; the Prophet (as he was in the Meccan period of his life) must be their comforting pattern. They must as a rule have no intercourse with the great ones of the world; only few have the gift of safely doing so. Envy and jealousy reign among the *ḥalq*, and disputing (*jidāl*) among their men of learning; peace, harmony, forgiveness, humility, patience, on the contrary, rule among the *qaum*; they know nothing about learned disputes, because they have full certainty. The Ṣūfī mode of life is necessary for the attainment of holiness; but the highest gifts, ecstasy (*jadhb*) and revelation (*kashf, fatḥ*), cannot be attained through actions, but only through divine grace.

A main point which separates Ṣūfīs from orthodox Muslim men of learning (*'ulamā*) is their conception of revelation. While the *'ulamā* regard revelation as closed with the Qur'ān and content themselves with explaining the tradition founded by the Prophet and built up by the great masters (*mujtahidīn*), the Ṣūfīs believe in the possibility of a continuous God-given revelation (*ilhām, kashf*). Thus an ever-flowing mystical knowledge and verity (*ḥaqīqa*) stand here over against the law (*sharī'a*), which rests on tradition and is closed. The *'ulamā* confine themselves to speculation and rational thinking (*naẓar, fikr*); the Ṣūfīs by their path attain full contemplation (*shuhūd*) of the truth. The *walī* assumes the rôle of the *mujtahid* of the more ancient times. The *'ulamā* reject all this as sorcery (*siḥr*), madness (*junūn*), and heresy (*zandaqa*). The Ṣūfī hermeneutics also are determined by this conception of revelation. The sense of a passage of the Qur'ān may be not only external (*ẓāhir*), but also internal (*bāṭin*). The inner sense may take as many as seventy forms. It is intelligible, then, how the belief in miracles among Ṣūfīs assumes fantastic forms even in a man of such high standing as ash-Sha'rānī. When he was a child he was saved from drowning by a crocodile, which took him on its back. Another time he scared a crocodile away by jumping into the water. Like the Prophet (*Qur.* lxxii.), ash-Sha'rānī received from God the privilege of having the *jinn* (cf. art. DEMONS AND SPIRITS [Muslim]) as hearers at his lectures. Many of his works were occasioned, in apocalyptic fashion, by visions; among others, *Kashf al-ḥijāb war-rān* was suggested by a *jinnī* in the shape of a dog, who delivered a letter to him. On the authority of 'Abd al-Ghaffār al-Qūṣī, he tells as a perfectly credible story that a man who had spoken disrespectfully of the Khalīfas Abū Bakr and 'Omar was transformed by God into a swine. In A.H. 923, he had a trance (*jadhb*) in Cairo, in which he received the gift of hearing and distinguishing all voices (like his teacher al-Ḥauwāṣ); he also perceived how the animals and the stones and the fishes of the Mediterranean praised God (cf. St. Francis of Assisi). The gift of having a share in such wonders (*karāmāt*) rests on Ṣūfī theory and practice; the *'ulamā*, therefore, cannot attain thereto. On the question of the freedom of the will and its relation to the omnipotence of God, he contends against the Mu'tazilites; God 'creates' the actions of men; only the 'appropriation' (*al-iktisāb*) is left to them.

He regards al-Junaid (d. A.H. 297) as the greatest representative of the earlier mysticism, because he knew how to reconcile the law (*sharī'a*) with his views. Ash-Sha'rānī himself belonged to the brotherhood (*ṭarīqa*) of ash-Shādhilī (d. 656), which is still widely spread in Egypt and in the Maghrib. He quotes very frequently from the works of the principal Ṣūfī writers (al-Qushairī, al-Yāfi'ī, Ibn al-Jauzī, etc.). The epithets cited above from a Leipzig MS hint at his pattern, Aḥmad al-Badawī, the great saint of Ṭanṭa, at his teacher Muḥammad ash-Shinnawī, and at al-'Ash'arī (*q.v.*), the great theologian of old Islām. He names such men, for example, as Ibn Taimīya and Faḥr ad-Dīn ar-Rāzī as antagonists of mysticism.

How numerous his writings are has already been pointed out. A good many data have come down to us concerning their order in time, but these do not all agree. It would seem that many writings existed in different editions. His earliest work is apparently a methodology for lettered Ṣūfīs (*Al-anwār al-qadsīya*), composed in 931. His activity closed with a collection of biographies of all famous Ṣūfīs, and with his own autobiography (*Laṭā'if al-minan*). Several MSS have been preserved of most of his works, and even autographs of some of them are still extant.

As would naturally be expected, most of his works are devoted to mysticism. But almost all which deal with other topics, like law or dogmatics, serve the interests of mysticism in so far as ash-Sha'rānī endeavours to harmonize his mystical ideas with the other ruling views. His attitude is partly an apologetic and defensive one, meeting the objections brought by the *'ulamā* against the Sūfīs, and partly one of reconciliation, showing that the doctrines of the Sūfīs, far from contradicting 'the law,' are rather its completion and development. Through these efforts ash-Sha'rānī evolves such ideas as are far above the average level of Islāmic theology, and secure for him an abiding place in the history of religion. He touches the principle of Protestantism, when in his 'Hodegetics' (*Ad-durar al-manthūra*) he exhorts his readers to study the earlier, shorter original texts dealing with the sciences rather than commentaries and later works of a diffuse verbosity. Several of his writings are marked by a far-reaching doctrinal and practical tolerance. Instead of treating Christians and Jews with the usual scorn and haughtiness, he praises their modesty and presents them as good examples to the Muslims. Although he himself was a member of the Shāfi'ite 'school' (*madhhab*), yet two of his most significant writings, *Al-mīzān* and *Kashf al-ghumma*, seek to harmonize the four great *Madhāhib*, and to demonstrate that all four are justified and stand on a common basis. Similarly his main dogmatic work (*Al-yawāqit wal-jawāhir*) seeks to reconcile the conceptions of the Sūfīs (*ahl al-kashf*) and of the dogmatists (*ahl al-fikr*). He would contend only against philosophers and heretics, who shake the foundations of the law (*sharī'a*). Several of his other works (*Lawāqiḥ al-anwār*; *Sawāṭi' al-anwār*; *Al-qaul al-mubīn*; *Al-kibrīt al-aḥmar*) deal with the great mystic Ibn al-'Arabī (d. 638). Two others (*Al-jawāhir wad-durar* and *Durar al-ghauwāṣ*) deal with the sayings of his master al-Ḥauwāṣ; two similarly of his teacher al-Matbūlī; in the *Tanbīh al-mughtarrīn* the morals and manners of the good old times are held before his lax contemporaries as a mirror; his *Mashāriq al-anwār* exhorts to a greater moral strictness. The above-mentioned biographical work, *Lawāqiḥ* (*lawā'iḥ*) *al-anwār*, generally known under the simpler name of *Aṭ-ṭabaqāt* (*al-kubrā*), had also a pedagogical aim, in that he portrays in it 426 (in the last edition 442) of the pious of the past, from Abū Bakr and the

Companions of the Prophet down to his own times. He composed also a mystical *Dīwān*, which has not yet been sufficiently investigated. It is owing to his tolerance and fear of God that he often warns against *takfīr*, *i.e.* charging a fellow-man with being an unbeliever (*kāfir*). He gives evidence of true courage when in his *Baḥr al-maurūd* he dares to attack the cupidity, the ostentation, the office-seeking and moral indifference of the *'ulamā*. In the same work he rises above the prevailing ideas of Islām by declaring monogamy to be better than polygamy, and in his autobiography he demands of men chastity before marriage. His conception of brotherly love among believers does not differ at all from that of primitive Christianity; and he reaches the highest summit of theological thought when he looks for a progressive perfection of Islām at the hands of theologians who have a real calling to this task.

The influence of ash-Sha'rānī over his contemporaries and upon the ages after him has been extraordinarily great. And yet his doctrinal and ethical requirements were too ideal to inspire faith in their practical realization, and his mystical views were altogether too subjective to encourage any one to maintain and develop them. It is not quite correct to speak of a 'sect' of Sha'ranians, as some do; but the number of those who have fed on the riches of his ideas is immense. He was still living when his writings had spread as far as the regions of Takrūr (central Sūdān, Wadai, Dārfūr), and at present they are studied in the Maghrib with a perhaps greater devotion than in Egypt. The best evidence for his Maghribite extraction is his fervour for theological questions, and the close affinity of the bent of his mind with that of the people of the West. He was a reforming spirit such as Islām has seldom seen.

His biography was written soon after his death by al-Munāwī (d. A.H. 1031). MSS of it are preserved at London in the British Museum, and at Berlin. Another account is preserved in the *Shadharāt adh-dhahab* (MS at Cairo, iv. 808–811). Many of his works have been printed at Cairo, among them the 'Balance' (*Al-mīzān*), the 'Dogmatics' (*Al-yawāqīt wal-jawāhir*), his biographical work (*Aṭ-ṭabaqāt*), several times his autobiography (*Laṭā'if al-minan*).

LITERATURE.—G. Fluegel, 'Scha'rānī nach d. Yawāqīt wal-jawāhir,' *ZDMG* xx. [1866] 1–48, xxi. [1867] 271–274; Perron, 'Balance de la loi musulmane ou esprit de la législation islamique et divergences de ses quatre rites jurisprudentiels par le Cheikh El-Charani,' *Revue Africaine*, xiv. [1870] 209–252, 331–348. J. D. Luciani published from the papers of Perron a fragmentary and freely rearranged translation of the 'Balance' (*Mīzān*), Algiers, 1898; A. von Kremer, 'Notice sur Sha'rany,' *JA*, 1868, vi. 11, 253–271; F. Wüstenfeld, *Die Geschichtsschreiber der Araber und ihre Werke*, Göttingen, 1882, no. 530; K. Vollers, 'Ša'rāwi und Ša'rāni,' *ZDMG* xliv. [1890] 390 ff.; 'Alī Mubārak, *Al-ḫiṭaṭ al-jadīda*, Cairo, A.H. 1305, v. 34, xiv. 109–113; C. Brockelmann, *Gesch. der arab. Litteratur*, Weimar and Berlin, 1898–1902, ii. 335 ff.; D. B. Macdonald, *Development of Muslim Theology, Jurisprudence, and Constitutional Theory*, London, 1903, pp. 279–283.

K. VOLLERS.

SHAVING.—See TONSURE, HAIR AND NAILS, HEAD.

SHEBA.—See SABÆANS.

SHEEP.—See ANIMALS.

SHEKINAH.—'The majestic presence or manifestation of God which has descended "to dwell" among men' is known as the Shekinah.[1] The word as well as the conception originated after the close of the Hebrew canon,[2] and is characteristic of Jewish theology. The term is first used in the Targum, where it forms a frequent periphrasis for God, considered as dwelling among the children of Israel. Jewish philosophy regards the Shekinah as a suitable expression for a divine intermediary between God and the world.[1] In the Talmud the Shekinah is regularly the source of inspiration. The Rabbis affirm that the Shekinah first presided in the Tabernacle prepared in the wilderness by Moses, into which it descended on the day of its consecration, in the figure of a cloud.[2] It passed then into the sanctuary of Solomon's Temple on the day of its dedication by this king in Israel, where it continued till the destruction of the Temple and Jerusalem by the Chaldæans,[3] and was not afterwards seen there any more.

There are innumerable references to the Shekinah in the Talmud. According to the Rabbis, 'the Shekinah is omnipresent.'[4] This contention is inferred from the phrase, 'Behold the angel that spake with me went forth and another angel went forth to meet me.' Since it is not said 'after him,' but 'to meet me,' it shows that the Shekinah is omnipresent, and, therefore, sends his messengers from wherever they happen to be. Again, tradition teaches that Rabbi Josi said:

> 'The Shekinah has never descended below, nor have Moses and Elijah ever ascended on high; for it is said (Ps 115^{16}): "The heavens, even the heavens, are the Lord's: but the earth hath he given to the children of men."'[5]

The context explains that the Shekinah in the Temple stopped short ten handbreadths of the earth, and Moses and Elijah a similar distance from the heavens.

There are several conflicting theories regarding the Shekinah among the Israelites. According to several Rabbinical theories, the Shekinah rested continuously upon Israel throughout her wanderings.[6] In the first place the Rabbis tell us:

> 'In three[7] places did the Shekinah rest upon Israel: in Shiloh, Nob or Gideon, and the everlasting house (the Temple), and all these three were in the portion of Benjamin; for it is said (Dt 33^{12}): "The Lord shall cover him (Benjamin) all the day long."'

And again we read:

> 'In the days of Ezra, the Shekinah did not rest (visibly) in the Temple; for it is written (Gn 9^{27}): "God shall enlarge Japheth, and he shall dwell in the tents[8] of Shem." Although God enlarged Japheth (*i.e.* counted his descendants, the Persians, worthy of building the Temple), yet the Shekinah rests only in the tents (built by the descendants) of Shem.'

And thirdly:

> 'Rabbi Simon ben Yoḥi said: "Come and see how beloved Israel is by the Holy One, blessed be He. Wherever they are banished, there the Shekinah[9] is with them"; as it is said (1 S 2^{27}): "Did I (God) plainly appear unto the house of thy father when they were in Egypt?" etc. When they were banished to Babylon, the Shekinah was with them; as it is said (Is 43^{14}): "For your sake I have sent to Babylon." And when they will be redeemed the Shekinah will be with them, as it is said (Dt 30^{3}): "Then the Lord thy God will return with thy captivity"; it is not said: He will cause to return, but He will return.'

Rav Ḥisda says:

> 'The Shekinah used to rest with each individual Israelite

1 *JE* xi. 258; see also Schechter, *Some Aspects of Rabbinic Theology*, p. 38.

2 See *HDB* iv. 487.

1 Maimonides, *More Nebuchim*, i. 28; also P. Volz, *Der Geist Gottes*, Tübingen, 1910.

2 *Berēshith Rabbāh*, iii. 9; so also Num. *Rabbāh*, xiii. 6; *Shabbāth*, 87*b*; *Sanhedrin*, 103*b*; Gen. *Rabbāh*, lxxx. 12.

3 Targ. to Hag 1^{8}; Jerus. *Ta'ănîth*, 65*a*.

4 *Bābhā Bathrā*, 25*a*; *Berākhôth*, 10*a*; so also *Meḥilta* on בא (ed. Friedmann, Vienna, 1870); *Berēshîth Rabbāh*, lxviii.; Deut. *Rabbāh*, ii. 10; Lam. *Rabbāh*, i.; *Yalquṭ* on Is 6; *Qiddūshîn*, 31*a*.

5 *Sukkāh*, 5*a*; cf. also variant in *Yalquṭ* of Zechariah, p. 77 (ed. E. G. King).

6 Midrash on Ps 89; *Yalquṭ*, § 833; *Sôṭāh*, 5*a*; *Rōsh Hashshānāh*, 3*a*; *Megillāh*, 29*a*; cf. also *Yalquṭ* on Ca 6^{2}; *Ta'ănîth* (Jerus. Talmud), ch. ii.

7 *Zebahîm*, 118*b*.

8 *Yômā*, 9*b*.

9 *Meg.* 29*a*; Num. *Rabbāh*, vii. 10. It might be well here to compare the somewhat fanciful and imaginative interpretation found in Lam. *Rabbāh* (Introd. xv.), and to note a Rabbinic inconsistency as shown in a passage in Lam. *Rabbāh* (Introd. xxix.), where a different interpretation is given: 'Before Israel was redeemed from Egypt they dwelt by themselves and the Shekinah dwelt by itself. When they were redeemed, the Shekinah and Israel became one. *But when Israel went into captivity the Shekinah again separated from them.*'

before Israel sinned, for it is written (Dt 23^{14}): "For the Lord thy God walks in the midst of thy camp." But after they had sinned, the Shekinah departed from them [1] (individually), as it is said (Dt 23^{14}): "That He see not the nakedness of anything in thee, and turn away from thee."'

Rabbi Ḥanina, however, held a different view.

He insisted 'that the Shekinah rested among the Israelites in the midst [2] of their uncleanliness,' for our sages tell us that, when a certain Sadducee remarked to him, 'Now surely the Temple is no more and you cannot cleanse yourself from your uncleanliness, you are defiled, and therefore, God no longer dwells with you; for it is written (La 1^{9}): "Her filthiness is (abideth) in her skirts,"' he replied: 'Come and see what is written concerning them (the Israelites) (Lv 16^{16}): "Who (God) remaineth among them in the midst of their uncleanness"'; *i.e.*, even when they are unclean the Shekinah rests among them.

Again, other Rabbis contend that the Holy Spirit disappeared from Israel only after the death of the last prophets, Haggai, Zechariah, and Malachi; the Holy Spirit departed from [3] Israel, but they were still availing themselves of the daughter (echo) of a voice for the reception of divine communications.

The wrong administration of justice causes the departure [4] of the Shekinah from Israel, for it is said (Ps 12^{5}): 'On account of the oppression of the poor and the sighing of the needy, now will I arise (*i.e.* depart), saith the Lord.'

'Whoever prays behind his Rabbi and whoever salutes or returns the salute of his Rabbi,[5] and whoever contends against the school of his Rabbi, or broaches anything which he had not heard from his Rabbi, he causes the Shekinah to depart from Israel.'

'The righteous in the [6] presence of the Shekinah are compared to a rushlight in the presence of a torch.' But, 'compared with Shekinah, man is the same that an ape is [7] compared with man.' '"And I praised mirth" (Ec 8^{15}) teaches that the Shekinah does not rest with people when in a melancholy mood, in illness,[8] hilarity, levity, when gossiping, or when indulging in idle talk, but with those who rejoice in the performance of a work which is alike meritorious and joyous.' Again, it is said that 'the Shekinah rests only upon one who is wise, physically strong, materially rich, and of high [9] stature.'

'Whoever passes from the synagogue to the debating-room, and from the debating-room to the synagogue, is worthy to [10] receive, and does receive, the presence of the Shekinah; for it is said (Ps 84^{7}): "They go from strength to strength; he shall be seen unto God in Zion."' Whoever 'engages in the study of the Law [11] by night has the Shekinah before him; for it is said (La 2^{19}): "Arise, cry out in the night . . . pour out thy heart like water before the Lord."'

Rabbi Pinḥas ben Yair said:

'The study of the Law leads to circumspection, circumspection leads to diligence, diligence leads to freedom from guilt, freedom from guilt leads to asceticism (or Esseneism), asceticism leads to purity, purity leads to sanctity of life, sanctity of life leads to meekness, meekness leads to the fear of sin, fear of sin leads to holiness, holiness leads to the acquisition of the Holy Spirit,[12] the Holy Spirit leads to the resurrection from the dead; but the greatest of all is sanctity of life.'

Yet Rabbi bar Rav Ada said [13] in the name of Rav Yisḥak:

'Whence is it proved that God is present in the synagogue? From the text (Ps 82^{1}): "God stands in the congregation of the mighty."'

This text further proves that the Shekinah rests with ten people who join in prayer,[14] for the ten spies are called a congregation (Nu 14^{27}). And whence is it proved that the Shekinah rests with a judicial tribunal consisting of three? From the text (Ps 82^{1}): 'He judgeth among the Gods.' And whence is it proved that the Shekinah rests with two [15] who are engaged in studying the Law? From the text (Mal 3^{16}): 'Then those that fear the Lord will converse one with the other, and the Lord will listen.' And whence is it proved that the Shekinah [1] rests even with one who is engaged in the study of the Law? From the text (Ex 20^{24}): 'In every place wherein I shall make mention of my name I will come unto thee (singular) and bless thee.' Yet our Rabbis taught [2] that a priest who does not speak by the Holy Spirit, and upon whom the Shekinah does not rest, should not be consulted oracularly. Abaii said:

'In every generation there are never less than thirty-six righteous men, who receive the presence of the [3] Shekinah; for it is said (Is 30^{18}): "Blessed are all those who wait upon Him."' [4]

Rabbi Ḥama bar Ḥanina said:

'When God causes His Shekinah to rest upon anyone, He chooses for that purpose [5] only distinguished families in Israel; for it is said (Jer 31^{1}): "At that time, saith the Lord, I will be a God to all the families of Israel." It is not said: "to all Israel," but, "to all the families of Israel."'

'Puah' (Ex 1^{15}) is another name [6] for Sarah. She was so called because she spake intuitively by the Holy Spirit (from 'to observe,' or 'to perceive'); as it is said (Gn 21^{12}): 'In all that Sarah saith unto thee, hearken unto her voice.' Whoever pronounces the blessing over the [7] new moon at the appointed time receives, as it were, the presence of the Shekinah. Whosoever gives his daughter to a disciple of the wise is as if he clings to the [8] Shekinah.

'Whoever is present at a banquet to which a disciple [9] of the wise is invited, enjoys, as it were, the effulgence of the Shekinah.'

That the Shekinah [10] supports the sick is proved from the text (Ps 41^{3}): 'God will support him upon the bed of illness.' Any one coming to visit a sick person should not sit either on the couch or on the footstool or on a chair,[11] but should sit wrapped up (a sign of reverence) on the ground, because the Shekinah rests above the couch of a sick person; as it is said (Ps 41^{3}): 'God will support him upon the bed of illness.' The hospitable reception [12] of strangers is preferable to that of the Shekinah.

Rabbi Yitshak says:

'Whoever commits [13] sin in secret, presses, as it were, against the feet of the Shekinah: for it is said (Is 66^{1}): "The earth is my footstool."'

He that strikes the cheek [14] of an Israelite strikes, as it were, the cheek of the Shekinah; for it is said (Pr 20^{25}): 'He that strikes a man, strikes the Holy One.' [15] He that gives way to anger makes no account [16] even of the presence of the Shekinah; for it is said (Ps 10^{4}): 'The wicked, when his anger arises, cares for nothing; not even God is in all his thoughts.'

'Four sets of men receive not [17] the presence of the Shekinah: the set of scoffers, the set of mendacious, the set of hypocrites, and the set of slanderers.' 'And Hannah answered and said: No, my lord' (1 S 1^{15}). Illa said: 'Some think that [18] Rabbi Yosi bar Ḥanina said it: that Hannah spake in the following sense: "Thou art neither lord, nor does the Holy Spirit rest upon thee, because thou dost suspect me in this matter, and hast formed such an uncharitable opinion of me. . . . Neither the Shekinah, nor the Holy Spirit is with thee."'

---

1 *Sôṭāh*, 3*b*; cf. *Sifre*, 120*b*; *Abhôth de R.N.* i. 58*a*; *Yalquṭ* on Ezk 36; Ex. *Rabbāh*, xv. 5, xxiv. 3; *Sifre* on Dt 32^{5}; cf. also *Yalquṭ* on La 3^{3}.

2 *Yômā*, 57*a*; cf. *Sanh.* 107*a*, however, which disputes the above contention; cf. also *Targ.* to Jer 33^{5}.

3 *Yômā*, 9*b*.

4 *Shabbāth*, 139*a*; Midrash *Teḥillim*, 12^{2} (ed. Buber, Wilna, 1891); *Sifra*, 91*a* (ed. Weiss, Vienna, 1862).

5 *Berākhôth*, 27*a*; so also 17*b* and 5*b*.

6 *Pesāḥîm*, 8*a*; cf. 117*a*.

7 *Bābhā Bathrā*, 58*a*.

8 *Shab.* 30*b*; cf. also *Sanh.* 102*b* and 103*a*.

9 *Shab.* 92*a* and 92*b*; cf. also Lev. *Rabbāh*, vii.; *Tanna d'be Eliahu*, p. 104 (ed. Friedmann, Vienna, 1900).

10 *Mô'ēd Kāton*, 29*a*.

11 *Tamid*, 32*b*.

12 *'Abōdah Zārāh*, 20*b*.

13 Cf. *Yalquṭ* on Ps 87^{3}; *Ber.* 7*a*.

14 *Ber.* 6*a*; *Ab.* 3, 9.

15 *Ab.* iii. 3; *Yalquṭ* on Ps 82.

1 *Suk.* 28*a*; cf. also *Ab. Zar.* 3*b*; *Yalquṭ* on Is 31^{6}; Num. *Rabbāh*, xix. 4; *Yalquṭ* on La 3.

2 *Yômā*, 78*b*.

3 *Sanh.* 97*b*; so also *Suk.* 45*b*.

4 The numerical value of 'HIM' is thirty-six.

5 *Qiddûshîn*, 70*a*.

6 *Sôṭāh*, 2*b*.

7 *Sanh.* 42*a*.

8 *Qîd.* 31*a*.

9 *Ber.* 64*a*.

10 *Shab.* 12*b*.

11 *Nedarîm*, 40*a*.

12 *Shab.* 127*a*.

13 *Qîd.* 31*a*; *Ber.* 43*b*; *Hagîgāh*, 16*a*.

14 *Sanh.* 58*b*.

15 Neither the Hebrew nor the Greek translation gives a satisfactory rendering of this verse. The present writer has therefore translated it somewhat differently from the ordinary rendering of the AV, translating מוּקָשׁ as a derivative of the Talmudic נָקַשׁ 'to smite,' 'to strike,' and taking ילע in a figurative sense as well in order to bring out the meaning of the Rabbis.

16 *Ned.* 22*b*.

17 *Sanh.* 103*a*.

18 *Ber.* 31*b*.

'And Esther stood in the inner court[1] of the king's house' (Est 5^{1}). Rabbi Laive said: 'When she reached the chamber of the images, the Shekinah departed from her; she then exclaimed (Ps 22^{1}): "My God, my God, why hast thou forsaken me? Dost thou perhaps judge inadvertent and compulsory transgression in the same way as thou dost[2] presumptuous sins? Or is it because I called him (Ahasuerus) dog?" as it is said (Ps 22^{20}): "Deliver my soul from the sword, and my darling from the dog." She then (by way of making amends) called him lion, as it is said (Ps 22^{21}): "Save me from the lion's mouth."'

'For a period of six months[3] David was afflicted with leprosy; for it is said (Ps 51^{7}): "Purge me with hyssop, and I shall be clean; wash me, and I shall be whiter than snow." At that time the Shekinah departed from him; for it is said (51^{12}): "Restore unto me the joy of thy salvation." And the Sanhedrin kept aloof from him; for it is said (119^{79}): "Let those that fear thee turn unto me." That the affliction lasted six months is proved from 1 K 2^{11}, where it is said: "And the days that David reigned over Israel were forty years: seven years reigned he in Hebron, and thirty and three years reigned he in Jerusalem"; whereas in 2 S 5^{5} it is said: "In Hebron he reigned over Judah seven years and six months." The reason why these six months are omitted in Kings is, because during the period he was afflicted with leprosy.'

The Talmud proves that the Shekinah did not exist during the second Temple in the following way:

Why is it that the word ואכבר, 'And I will be glorified' (Hag 1^{8}), is without the letter ה, whilst another reading has it? It intimates the absence of five things from the second Temple, which existed in the first,[4] viz. (1) the Ark, the Mercy Seat, and the Cherubim; (2) the fire from heaven upon the altar; (3) the visible presence; (4) the Holy Spirit; (5) the Urim and Thummim.

LITERATURE.—*JE* xi. 258; *HDB* iv. 487–489; J. Abelson, *The Immanence of God in Rabbinical Literature*, London, 1912, chs. iv.–xii.; G. Dalman, *Die Worte Jesu*, Leipzig, 1898; F. Weber, *Jüdische Theologie*², do. 1897; S. Schechter, *Some Aspects of Rabbinic Theology*, London, 1909, ch. xiv.; lexicons of Buxtorf, Levy, Kohut, and Jastrow.

JULIUS J. PRICE.

SHEOL.—See ABYSS, ESCHATOLOGY, STATE OF THE DEAD.

SHEWBREAD.—

1. **Terms.**—In the older sources, 1 S 21^{6} (Heb. 7), 1 K 7^{48}, we find לֶחֶם הַפָּנִים, 'bread of the face (or presence [*i.e.* of God]),' EV 'shewbread,' RVm 'presence-bread.' This term is also used in the Priestly Code (P), Ex 25^{30} (לֶחֶם פָּנִים) 35^{13} 39^{36}, and in 2 Ch 4^{19}. In Nu 4^{7} it is abbreviated into *happānīm*. In 1 Ch 9^{32} 23^{29}, Neh 10^{33} (Heb. 34), we have לֶחֶם הַמַּעֲרֶכֶת, EV 'shewbread,' AVm 'Heb. bread of ordering'; in 2 Ch 13^{11} *ma'ărekheth leḥem*; in 1 Ch 28^{16}, 2 Ch 2^{4} 29^{18}, we have *ma'ărekheth*, and in Ex 40^{23} *leḥem*. *Ma'ărekheth* is from ערך, 'to set in order,' and is used in the concrete sense of 'row' or 'pile.' As the Babylonian monuments show sacred tables with piles of bread, it is probable that *ma'ărakheth* means 'pile.' In Lv 24^{6} the shewbread consists of two *ma'ărakhōth*, EV 'rows,' RVm 'piles.' Hence, *leḥem hamma'ărekheth*, etc., mean 'pile-bread' or 'row-bread.' In 1 S 21^{5} (Heb. 6) the shewbread is called לֶחֶם קֹדֶשׁ, EV 'holy bread,' as distinguished from לֶחֶם חֹל, 'ordinary,' EV 'common bread.' In 2 Ch 2^{4} (Heb. 3) we have תָּמִיד מַעֲרֶכֶת, '*ma'ărekheth*, continually present,' and in Nu 4^{7} *leḥem hattāmīdh*, EV 'the continual bread,' as being always on the table.

In NT the shewbread is ἄρτοι τῆς προθέσεως, Mt 12^{4}, Mk 2^{26}, Lk 6^{4}; and in He 9^{2} ἡ πρόθεσις τῶν ἄρτων, 'bread of the setting out,' 'the setting out of bread,' EV 'shewbread,' in He 9^{2} RVm, 'Gr. the setting forth of the loaves.' These are LXX renderings of *leḥem hamma'ărekheth*, etc., and also of *leḥem pānīm*, though the latter is also rendered by the LXX literally ἄρτοι τοῦ προσώπου and ἄρτοι ἐνώπιοι, 'loaves of the face.' Other LXX renderings are οἱ ἄρτοι οἱ προκείμενοι, Ex 39^{18}, 'the loaves set forth,' and οἱ ἄρτοι τῆς προφορᾶς, 'bread of the offering,' in 3 K 7^{34} (Heb. and Eng. 1 K 7^{48}). Vulg. follows LXX with *panes propositionis*, 'the loaves of setting forth,' etc.; Luther has *Schaubrot*, hence probably 'shewbread' in Tindale's NT (1526), He 9^{2}, and in other English versions. This rendering may be due to the idea that the loaves were set forth to be shown to God.

With two exceptions the shewbread is said to be placed upon a 'table'; but in 1 K $6^{20.\ 22}$, Ezk 41^{22}, we read of an altar which is clearly the table of the shewbread and not the altar of incense, which does not appear till the latest strata of the Priestly Code. In Mal $1^{7.\ 12}$ 'the table of Jahweh' may be the table of the shewbread, but is more probably the altar of burnt-offering, or may include both.

[1] *Meg.* 15*b*. [2] *Sanh.* 107*a*.
[3] *Yōmā*, 22*b*; Jerus. *Ta'ăn.* 65*a*; the hyssop is presented for the purification of lepers.
[4] The numerical value of the letter ה is five.

2. **Nature.**—The shewbread consisted of two rows or piles, each containing six loaves or cakes of bread made after a special recipe (Lv 24^{5-9} P). The post-Biblical Jewish authorities, Josephus, Philo, Mishnāh, and Talmud,[1] state that the shewbread was unleavened, and in view of Lv 2^{11} P, which prescribes that a *minḥāh*, or bloodless offering, shall always be unleavened, it seems likely that this was the case with the shewbread, at any rate after the Exile, though possibly not in primitive times. In one passage in the Priestly Code, according to our present text, the shewbread is spoken of as אִשֶּׁה. This term is explained by J. G. Wetzstein[2] as for *'insheh*, from *'enosh*, 'man,' and this view is accepted by König;[3] but it is rejected by the *Oxford Hebrew Lexicon* and most scholars. *'Ishsheh* is usually explained as EV 'offering made by fire,' which would imply that the shewbread was burnt; it could hardly be called a 'fire-offering' because it had been baked. But there is no suggestion elsewhere that it was burnt, and the idea is inconsistent with the statements everywhere else that it was eaten. In the immediate context, Lv 24^{7}, the incense placed with the shewbread is called *'ishsheh*; probably some confusion between the shewbread and the incense led to a slight corruption of the text, the original having merely stated that the incense was *'ishsheh*.

The shewbread was placed upon a table or altar and was renewed weekly (Ex 26^{35} 40^{22}, 1 S 21^{6} (Heb. 7), 1 K 6^{20-22}). Probably the original text of 1 K 6^{20-22} stated that the table was cedar (Ezk 41^{22}, 'altar of wood'), and this may very well have been the case in the pre-Exilic sanctuaries, 1 K 7^{48} being late and the Chronicler, as usual, antedating the conditions of his own times.[4] In the description of the table in Ex 25^{23-30} it is made of *shittim* (acacia) wood and overlaid with gold. Probably this was the case with the table in the post-Exilic temple; it is not likely that the statements of 1 K 7^{48} and Jos. *Ant.* VIII. iii. 7, to the effect that there was a table of solid gold, are literally true. According to Ex 25^{29}, there were various utensils on the table, and, according to Lv 24^{7}, incense on, or by the side of, the loaves. In Lv 24^{6}, 2 Ch 13^{11}, the epithet *ṭahor* is applied to the table; as this term is frequently applied in P to the gold used for the tabernacle, it is probably applied to the table as being overlaid with 'pure' gold.

3. **History.**—The antiquity of the shewbread is shown by the mention of it in 1 S 21^{6} (Heb. 7), where it appears in the sanctuary at Nob in the time of Saul. In this passage it seems that the shewbread was placed hot upon the table, and that the stale bread, after it had been removed from the table, might be eaten by any one in a state of ceremonial cleanness, and not merely, as in later times, by the priests. This passage belongs to one of the older sources of S, compiled some time before 750.

We next meet with the shewbread in the Temple of Solomon (1 K 6^{20-22} 7^{48}; the former of these passages belongs to an early source, before 700, and establishes the presence of the shewbread in Solomon's Temple). From analogy we may conclude that it was also a feature of the sanctuary at Shiloh and other early Israelite shrines. Ezk 41^{22} includes the table in the specifications for the restoration of the Temple; no doubt the temple built by Zerubbabel had such a table; there is

[1] Dillmann, *Exodus und Leviticus*³, p. 653 ff.
[2] In an excursus to F. Delitzsch, *Bibl. Commentar über die Psalmen*⁴, Leipzig, 1883, p. 889, Eng. tr., London, 1889, iii. 435 ff.
[3] *Hebräisches und aramäisches Wörterbuch zum AT*, Leipzig, 1910.
[4] Cf. C. F. Burney, *Notes on the Heb. Text of the Book of Kings*, Oxford, 1903, p. 73 f.

positive evidence for its presence in the post-Exilic temple somewhat later. It is mentioned in Neh $10^{33\ (\text{Heb. } 34)}$; 1 Mac 1^{22} mentions it among the spoils carried off by Antiochus Epiphanes; 1 Mac 4^{49} tells us that Judas Maccabæus replaced the table when he cleansed and refurnished the Temple. The statement of 2 Ch 4^{8} (cf. 1 Ch 28^{16}, 2 Ch 4^{19}, 'tables') that Solomon made ten tables is an example of the Chronicler's passion for exaggerating numbers. A writer whom Josephus quotes under the name of Hecatæus of Abdera,[1] apparently belonging to the 3rd cent. B.C., speaks of a golden altar in the Temple, doubtless the table of the shewbread. The pseudepigraphal *Letter of Aristeas*,[2] variously dated from about 200 B.C. to after A.D. 33,[3] gives an elaborate account of a table of gold and precious stones said to have been presented to the Temple by Ptolemy Philadelphus (285–247 B.C.). The incident and the table are both imaginary, but they may add something to the evidence for a table of gold in the Second Temple. The table is mentioned in Philo[4] and Josephus.[5] There are also details and discussions concerning the table and the shewbread in the Talmud and other post-Biblical Jewish literature. No doubt the table and the rite continued till the final destruction of the Temple by Titus; the table is shown on the Arch of Titus, as part of the spoils taken by him from the Temple. There is no mention of shewbread in connexion with the temple at Heliopolis or that at Elephantine, but, as the available evidence is scanty, it is possible that the rite may have been observed in either or both of these sanctuaries.

4. Significance.—There is no official or even express statement as to the significance of the rite. The terms are got from the arrangement of the loaves (*maʿărekheth*) or the position of the table (*pānīm*). There is no ground for the view sometimes held that the loaves were called 'presence-bread' because they symbolized the presence of God with His people. P speaks of them as *qōdesh qodāshīm*, 'holy of holies,' *i.e.* as belonging to the group of most sacred things, probably partly because of proximity to the inner shrine, the Most Holy Place, partly because of the ancient and unique character of the rite, as far as the Temple worship was concerned.

In the absence of any express statement we can only attempt to deduce the significance of the shewbread from analogy and other *a priori* considerations. The setting out of food on a table in a temple before the shrine or image of a deity is found in many religions.[6] Jer 44^{19} etc. speaks of the cakes (*kawwanim*) baked by Jewish women for the Queen of Heaven (*q.v.*); and Is 65^{11} of those who set in order (*ʿarakh*) a table for a deity Gad, RV 'Fortune.' There were at Rome *lectisternia*, or festivals at which banquets were spread for the gods—a practice perhaps introduced from Greece. Babylonian ritual included the setting forth of loaves—twelve or a multiple thereof—before the deity; these were to be sweet, *i.e.* unleavened, and made of a special kind of meal.[7] No doubt the rite in Israel was a survival from the time when the deity was thought of as actually consuming the food offered to him. Even Lv $21^{8.17}$ H speaks of the sacrifices as *leḥem 'Elōhīm*, 'the bread of God,' doubtless metaphorically. It has been suggested that hot bread (1 S $21^{6\ [\text{Heb. } 7]}$), fresh from the oven, was used so that the deity might enjoy the fragrance. But would there be any agreeable fragrance at the end of a week? The idea that Jahweh consumed the food would be obsolete long before our documents were composed. In historical times the shewbread was an ancient established fact, accepted as a matter of course, part of the divinely prescribed worship, and therefore binding and efficacious, apart from any explanation or justification. For most that would be sufficient, but thoughtful men would find the rite significant in the different ways in which it appealed to them. To Philo[1] it seems to symbolize the earth, as the lamp-stand does heaven; *i.e.*, the presence of the loaves symbolizes the dominion of Jahweh over earth and heaven. Josephus says that the twelve loaves denoted the year with its twelve months.[2] Cyril of Jerusalem treats the shewbread as a type of the Eucharist.[3]

LITERATURE.—A. Dillmann, *Die Bücher Exodus und Leviticus*³, Leipzig, 1897, pp. 653 ff.; S. R. Driver, *The Book of Exodus*, Cambridge, 1911, pp. 203 f., 272 ff.; A. H. McNeile, *The Book of Exodus*, London, 1908, pp. xc, 164 ff.; A. R. S. Kennedy, *HDB*, *s.v.* 'Shewbread'; I. Benzinger, *Hebräische Archäologie*, Freiburg i. B., 1894, pp. 387, 397, 401, 425, 432, 443; W. Nowack, *Lehrbuch der hebräischen Archäologie*, do. 1894, ii. 207, 241.

W. H. BENNETT.

1 *C. Apion.* i. 22.
2 §§ 52–72.
3 H. T. Andrews, in R. H. Charles, *Apoc. and Pseud. of the OT*, Oxford, 1913, ii. 100 ff.
4 *Vit. Mos.* iii. 10, etc.
5 *Ant.* III. vi. 6, etc.
6 W. R. Smith, *Religion of the Semites*², London, 1894, p. 225 f.
7 Cf. the *soleth*, EV 'fine flour,' of Lv 24^{5} (*KAT*³, pp. 600, 629; A. Jeremias, *OT in the Light of the Anc. East*, Eng. tr., London, 1911, ii. 114, 135).

SHĪʿAHS.—1. The name.—The term 'Shīʿah' is a collective term meaning 'party' or 'following,' which has been applied to the partisans of the family of ʿAlī, the cousin and son-in-law of the Prophet Muḥammad, since the early days of Islām, when they first constituted themselves a sect. The full name would be Shīʿah 'Ahlu-'l-Bait, 'followers of the Prophet's kindred.' Much more frequently used in the beginning was the term 'ʿAliite'—a term which is primarily of political implication as referring to the claims of ʿAlī's family to the khalīfate. 'Shīʿahs' to-day has a directly religious reference. It describes the smaller of the two great divisions of Muhammadanism, which adheres to the twelve (or seven) *imāms* of the family of ʿAlī. For the Shīʿahs these *imāms* are infallible religious leaders. The Shīʿahs are found at the present time in large numbers only in Persia and in India.

2. Origin.—Despite the claims of the Shīʿahs and the traditions offered in proof of them, there is no reliable trace of any utterance by the Prophet which points to ʿAlī or his descendants as his successors in the leadership of Islām. The Shīʿahs assert that Muḥammad definitely nominated ʿAlī and his descendants at the Pool of Al-Ghadīr and that on different occasions he indicated his preference for ʿAlī. Veiled references in the Qurʾān, when interpreted allegorically (*tawīl*), are made to place ʿAlī next to the Prophet in excellence and far above all other men. The Prophet is the sun and ʿAlī is the moon. The course of events in the days of the Prophets and afterwards so strongly contradicts these arguments that they may be set aside, and the development of the ʿAlid claims may be studied in the light of historical facts.

Muḥammad refused to name his successor, and the two first khalīfahs, Abū Bakr and ʿUmar, were elected by the Muslim community (*Ijmāʿ*), the latter on the nomination of his predecessor; the third choice was indecisive, and the khalīfate was offered to ʿAlī on condition that he pledged loyalty to the traditional interests of Islām. In his answer he was uncertain, and the choice passed to ʿUthman. Meanwhile, ʿAlī's wife, the Prophet's daughter Fāṭimah, had presented a claim to Abū Bakr for some crown lands as her inheritance from her father's estate. The claim had been refused

1 *Vit. Mos.* iii. 10.
2 *Ant.* III. vii. 7; similarly Zimmern, Jeremias, etc., connect them with the twelve signs of the zodiac (see reff. above).
3 A. Plummer, *HDB* iii. 145.

by the khalīfah Abū Bakr, and the family of 'Alī felt aggrieved at the treatment shown them. When 'Uthman was elected, the umpire of the election, Abd-ar-Rahmān, warned 'Alī against using his nearer kinship to the Prophet as a basis for special consideration. This probably marks the emergence of a claim in favour of the 'Ahlu-'l-Bait. The weakness and failure of 'Uthman's reign ranged the stronger forces of Islām against him, and among them 'Alī and his friends. 'Uthman's governor in Syria, Mu'āwiyah, was of Umayyad descent like the khalīfah himself. In the natural course of things he very probably would have seized the power from 'Alī on 'Uthman's death in any case. But, when 'Alī and his party lent their countenance to the conspiracy which robbed 'Uthman of his life, Mu'āwiyah gave himself out as the avenger of 'Uthman's blood. Even then, when the way was once more open for him to be elected khalīfah, 'Alī was not willing to stake anything on his legitimist rights. He would have evaded election had it been possible. The rebels and his friends almost compelled him to accept. Up to this point, therefore, events make it clear that no belief in a divine right of the 'Ahlu-'l-Bait to succeed the Prophet existed, and consequently there could be no Shī'ah or party which held that belief. It is also clear that the causes at work after 'Uthman's death were tending to produce a violent schism in Islām. On the one hand there was a powerful usurper, Mu'āwiyah, with the irresistible appeal of blood-revenge and the vindication of the khalīfate—the holiest authority which Islām possessed. On the other were arrayed the partisans of democratic rights, who were prepared to resist Mu'āwiyah's usurpation, and standing with them the duly elected khalīfah 'Alī, whose supporters were now forging arguments looking towards the establishment of the divine right of 'Alī and his family to rule over the Muslim community. The two sides came into armed conflict. Mu'āwiyah cursed 'Alī in the Friday service at Damascus, and 'Alī denounced Mu'āwiyah at Kūfa. The decisive clash came at the battle of Ṣiffīn (36 A.H. ; A.D. 657), and at that time the bungling management of a golden opportunity by 'Alī's representative, Abu Mūsā, left 'Alī without the support of the democratic rights party and legally deposed in the eyes of his own friends. The former withdrew from the army and gave themselves to anarchist excesses which were a constant hindrance to 'Alī's cause. The withdrawal of these Khārijites,[1] as they called themselves because of their protests against both khalīfahs, left 'Alī's supporters a homogeneous party, a Shī'ah. The party was sufficiently formed to hold together from this time forwards. The assassination of 'Alī (40 A.H.) greatly diminished its political hopes, but the total reaction of the events gave added strength to the spirit and numbers of the group.

3. The Shī'ah imāms.—With the death of 'Alī the khalīfate ceased to be an attainable end for the Shī'ahs. For a few brief months al-Ḥasan, the elder of the two sons of 'Alī and Fāṭimah, maintained a shadowy rule in Kūfa and then resigned (41 A.H.) and betook himself to Medīna. In 61 A.H. the younger son, al-Ḥusain, yielded to the flimsy assurances of the Kūfans and left Mecca on the fatal adventure which, they said, was to set him upon the throne in Kūfa. The overwhelming of his little host by the troops of the Umayyad khalīfah, Yazīd ibn Mu'āwiyah, at Kerbelā extinguished the 'Alid hope of political dominion. The Shī'ahs made the best of necessity and gave themselves now to an ambition for religious leadership. The representatives of the house of 'Alī became the indispensable religious heads of Islām, the *imāms* of the believers. The history of the centuries that followed the death of Ḥusain is a history of intrigue actuated by religion. The 'Alids, when they acted on their own motive, were not often successful, but their claim to religious leadership gathered about them a following and made them useful instruments in the hands of men opposed to the existing form of government. In Persia they lent themselves at an early date to the nationalist movement, which in time displaced the Arab domination by purely Persian rule. In this way Shī'ism ultimately became the national religion of Persia.

(1) Al-Mukhtār in 64 A.H. is the first adventurer to employ the Shī'ahs for his own purposes. He gave himself out as the avenger of the martyred 'people of the House' and professed allegiance to a son of 'Alī, Muḥammad ibn al-Hanafīyah, whose mother was one of the wives taken by 'Alī after the death of Fāṭimah. Al-Mukhtār declared Ibn al-Hanafīyah to be the Mahdī (*q.v.*), the founder of a new order of justice and peace. The direct heir to the imāmate, 'Alī ibn Ḥusain, Zainu 'l-'Ābidīn, was but a child, and it seems to have been agreed that Ibn al-Hanafīyah should be recognized for the time being. In 68 A.H. the Shī'ahs were admitted to standing at the *hajj* in Mecca and Ibn al-Hanafīyah was acknowledged as their *imām*. Thus within a few years of al-Ḥusain's death the Shī'ahs were an acknowledged sect of Islām along with other sects or parties. Al-Muhktār's effort was shattered by his defeat at Kūfa in 67 A.H. He had championed the cause of the Persian Muslims (Mawālī) and had been supported by the Shī'ahs. His defeat bound the interests of the two groups much more closely together than they had been.

(2) The second important instance of a use of the Shī'ahs to serve the ends of designing politicians is found in the campaign of Abu Muslim, the chief agent in bringing about the overthrow of the Umayyad dynasty and the accession to power of the 'Abbāsids. Abu Muslim, the general of the revolting army in Khorāsān, while ostensibly conducting a revolution on behalf of the 'Alids, was really the agent of the family of 'Abbās. By kindling the hopes of the 'Alids he gained the support of the Persian Muslims and fought a campaign which brought Arab control in Persia to an end; but, instead of winning the ascendancy for the house of 'Alī, he secured the throne for Abu 'l-Abbās and settled the khalīfate in the keeping of the 'Abbāsids for 500 years.

(3) A third illustration of the ease with which the religious preoccupation of the Shī'ah leaders placed them at the mercy of political schemers is afforded by the case of the eighth *imām*, 'Alī ibn Mūsā ar-Riḍā, who was a favourite of the khalīfah al-Mamūn, was named his successor, and was married to his daughter. Al-Mamūn admired his piety and valued his counsel, but these qualities were quite second in importance to the opportunity afforded of extending his influence and strengthening the support of the reigning dynasty. The motive of policy which led him to exchange the colour of his royal standard from its traditional black to the 'Alid green was the motive which led him to show favour to the leading representative of the 'Alid family. This was made clear when public dissatisfaction became acute, and he took an early opportunity to get rid of the *imām*—the Shī'ahs say by giving him with his own hand a bunch of poisoned grapes.

(4) The most startling instance of this use of the religious aims of the Shī'ahs is perhaps that supplied by 'Abdallah ibn Maimūn, the founder of the Ismā'īlian sect of the Shī'ahs (260 A.H. ; A.D. 873–874). This man of far-reaching political vision laid plans to found a world-empire by destroying the power of the spiritual authority existing in Islām and, on the basis of a more rigorous and unified religious authority, securing that unquestioning obedience which would be the factor of might in the new state. As a starting-point for carrying this plan into effect, he made use of a small unaggressive sect of the Shī'ahs who insisted on recognizing as the seventh Shī'ah *imām* either Ismā'īl ibn Ja'far aṣ-Ṣādiq or Ismā'īl's son, Muḥammad. With the seventh *imām*, whichever it might be, the succession was thought to end, and because of that fact the seventh *imām* was said not to have died and thus brought the imāmate to extinction but to have withdrawn into concealment and to exercise his indisputable authority as a 'Hidden *Imām*' through chosen representatives in each generation. The Hidden *Imām* was also the Mahdī who at the end of the age would regenerate the world. 'Abdallah ibn Maimūn claimed for himself and his successors the position of a chosen legate of the Mahdī. He thereby put forward the highest claim to exercise spiritual authority. The discipline which he formulated for the novitiate of the new order was thoroughly adapted to secure the obedience that he wished to obtain. The Ismā'īlians, as they had previously existed, were absorbed in the re-organized sect and became a mere pedestal to serve the vaulting ambition of the Maimunīyah group and its leader.

Within the history of the Ismā'īlian sect the political purpose of revolutionary leaders has been prompt to avail itself of Persian mysticism in some of its Shī'ah modifications. The sect of the Hashīshīn, or Assassins (*q.v.*), in the 12th and 13th

[1] See art. KHAWĀRIJ.

centuries A.D., the Carmatians (*q.v.*), who were contemporary with the first century of Ismāʽīlian history, and the Fāṭimids of N. Africa, who established their new capital, al-Mahdīyah, in A.D. 909, are all instances of the point in question, viz. that religious Shīʽism lent itself to the ambitious ends of political leaders all too readily. The succession of the Shīʽah *imāms* is shown as follows:

(1) ʽAlī (35 A.H.–40 A.H.), (2) al-Ḥasan, (3) al-Ḥusain, (4) ʽAlī, Zainu ʼl-ʽĀbidīn, (4) Muḥammad ibn al-Hanafīyah, (5) Muḥammad al-Bāqir, (5) Abu Hāshim, (6) Jaʽfar aṣ-Ṣādiq, (7) Mūsā ibn Jaʽfar, (7) Ismāʽīl ibn Jaʽfar or Muḥammad ibn Ismāʽīl, (8) ʽAlī ibn Mūsā ar-Riḍā, (9) Muḥammad al-Jawād, (10) ʽAlī al-Hadī, (11) Al-Ḥasan al-ʽAskarī, (12) Muḥammad al-Mahdī (disappeared in A.D. 878).

These, except ʽAlī and his sons and Riḍā, were not men of note in public affairs, but, as being in the line of succession to the imāmate, they all are reputed to have possessed in pre-eminent degree the character and gifts of saints.

The Hanafīyah imāmate comprises only five *imāms*. The last of the five is reported on ʽAbbāsid authority to have transferred his claim to the imāmate to Muḥammad ibn ʽAlī the ʽAbbāsid. His father, Ibn al-Hanafīyah, is regarded by his followers as the Hidden *Imām*.

The Ismāʽīlī imāmate includes only seven *imāms*, the seventh becoming 'the Hidden One.'

The regular Shīʽahs, who form a very large majority of the whole number, are designated as the Ithnā-ʽasharīya ('Twelvers'), to distinguish them from the Ismāʽīlians, who, as they hold to only seven *imāms*, are called Ṣabʽiya ('Seveners'). The 'Twelvers' are generally called the Imāmīyah.

The law of succession in the imāmate has been fairly consistent. The *imām* inherits the grace of his office from ʽAlī as the legitimate successor of the Prophet and is, as well, the heir of the Prophet through his daughter Fāṭimah. He is of the descendants of Ḥusain, the younger son of ʽAlī and Fāṭimah. He is regularly the eldest son of his father. It was the departure from this rule that caused the Ismāʽīlian schism. The imāmate of Ibn al-Hanafīyah claims to be legitimate, though it has no connexion with Fāṭimah. It deems the connexion with ʽAlī sufficient. The Zaidīyah sect of Shīʽahs seem to have a better argument in claiming that the imāmate need not be restricted to the line of Ḥusain and need not observe the law of primogeniture. Their own founder, Zaid, a grandson of Ḥusain, was not a first-born son.

4. Later history of the Shīʽahs.—The early ʽAbbāsid khalīfahs were disposed to be friendly towards the Shīʽahs. Their attitude towards foreigners and foreign learning was sympathetic and their view and outlook liberal towards those who differed from them. By profession they were Sunnites, but in practice their attitude was much more generous than that of the orthodox leaders of their day. In the khalīfate of al-Manṣūr, the second of the ʽAbbāsid rulers, the Muʽtazilite school of thought took its rise. It was the Persian response to the cultures of the East and West as these began to make their influence felt in Persian Muslim circles. It cultivated the spirit of criticism and encouraged the testing of traditional views by an appeal to reason. The Muʽtazilah flourished especially in the reigns of al-Mamūn, al-Muʽtasim, and al-Wāthiḳ (198–232 A.H.; A.D. 813–847). In the bitter rivalry between the Sunnites on the one hand and the Muʽtazilah and Shīʽahs on the other it was assumed that the two last shared the same opinions, and Sunnī orthodoxy opposed the one in proportion as it opposed the other. Both schools were essentially Persian and both refused to be bound by the Tradition and Consensus as held by the Sunnīs. They both favoured speculation and the dialectic method of proof. Unfortunately, the apologetic industry of the orthodox party showed a zeal in creating an effective literature and in organizing a propaganda, while their opponents trusted in the intrinsic reasonableness of their views. In the conservative reaction which set in under al-Mutawakkil (232 A.H.) both Muʽtazilites and Shīʽahs suffered severely; and they seemed to be put at a still greater disadvantage when the great tradition collections of the Sunnīs were put in circulation. Al-Bukharī issued his *Saḥīḥ* before 256 A.H. (A.D. 870) and Muslim his collection with the same title a few years afterwards. These works constituted the foundation of all later works of law and seemed to afford a body of proof which could not be controverted. The Muʽtazilah and Shīʽahs alike suffered when Abuʼl Ḥasan al-Ashʽarī (*q.v.*), who had been trained under Muʽtazilite teachers, turned their own weapons against the Muʽtazilah (*c.* 300 A.H.) and framed his system of doctrine along traditional (*i.e.* Sunnite) lines. His formulation of orthodoxy became the standard throughout Sunnite Islām and has maintained its position down to the present time. Such Muʽtazilism as remained at the close of the 4th Muslim century has been absorbed by the Shīʽahs, and scholars are disposed to find in modern Shīʽism a fair representative of the old speculative and dialectical spirit of the Muʽtazilah.

The Shīʽahs enjoyed a period of prosperity when the Buwaihids came to assume the real power under the khalīfate of al-Mutīʽ (334 A.H.; A.D. 946). These princes were of Shīʽah faith, and Shīʽism was protected and encouraged by them while they retained their power in Baghdād (until 447 A.H.; A.D. 1055). During the Buwaihid régime there appeared an interesting propagandist organization which seems to have aimed at a more rational and systematic presentation of Islām as it was understood by the Muʽtazilite-Shīʽah scholars. This society was known as the 'Brethren of Purity' (Ikhwān aṣ-Ṣafā). Their views were set forth in a series of treatises numbering about 50 or 51 in all. These treatises were widely known, if we may judge from the number of copies which still survive.

The Shīʽah faith had suffered from lack of political prestige in Persia until the entrance of the Buwaihid princes upon the scene, and after their time Shīʽism again suffered eclipse as the Seljuks, who were Sunnites, assumed control. The brilliant triumph of the Safawid Shāh Ismāʽīl (A.D. 1499–1502) established a new order of things and made the Shīʽah religion what it has continued to be since that date—the national religion of Persia. The one ruler who seriously threatened the secure hold of Shīʽism on the country was Nādir Shāh (A.D. 1736), whose aims were purely secular. With an eye to the control of a vast empire, he proposed to abolish the distinction between Sunnites and Shīʽahs, have both regarded as equally orthodox, and Shīʽism placed upon the same footing as the great schools of Sunnite Islām, as a fifth school alongside the four already accepted as orthodox. The proposal met with vigorous opposition and was given up, though Nādir Shāh's treatment of the Shīʽah hierarchy in Persia to the end of his reign showed that he was very little concerned with the prosperity of the Shīʽah or any other form of religion.

The accession of the Safawids brought to the throne a line of Ṣūfī[1] saints—a fact which suggests a strong reason for the persistence and spread of Shīʽism. The Ṣūfī mysticism has had a specially close relation to Persia and the Shīʽah form of Islām, and the sects of the Shīʽah have taken much of their distinctive character from Ṣūfism.[2]

[1] See art. ṢŪFĪS.

[2] Cf. the emphasis laid on *gnosis* in the Ismāʽīlian sect and the complete submission to authority which the Shīʽah sects make prominent in their requirements.

An even more important factor in the growth of Shi'ism is found in the features of the system which provide for powerful emotional revivals of religion. The Shi'ahs have always lived in the emotional atmosphere of martyrdom. The memory of the martyred founders of the sect, of the sufferings of the *imāms*, and of the confession witnessed by the great saints is much cultivated, and the annual feasts of commemoration are marked by demonstrations of feeling observed nowhere else in Islām. The greatest of all these memorial feasts is the *Muḥarram*, which is specially devoted to the martyrs of Kerbelā, pre-eminent among them the *imām* Ḥusain. The feast in honour of 'Alī at Nejef and that observed at Meshed for the *imām* Riḍā are impressive by reason of the outward show of ceremonial and even more because of the display of intense feeling. Another factor calculated to excite interest and enthusiasm to a marked degree is the Mahdist expectation which has been constantly present in Shī'ah circles. It is not confined to the Shī'ahs, but has been specially active among them. The fanaticism of the Ismā'īlian movement was stimulated by Mahdist hopes which centred in the seventh *imām*. The Carmaṭian excesses were connected by the Carmaṭians themselves, in some part at least, with the service of the Mahdī. The Fāṭimid empire in the Maghrib was founded by Sa'īd ibn Aḥmad, who claimed to be the Mahdī, and Mahdist fanaticism promoted its extension. Other instances might be adduced. Generally speaking, the alleged withdrawal of the *imām* and his continued existence as al-Ghāib ('the Hidden *Imām*') have contributed to make the hope of the Mahdī an abiding incentive to religious interest.

The most important outgrowths of the Shī'ah party are: (1) the Zaidīyah sect; (2) the Ismā'īlians; (3) their offspring, the Carmaṭians; (4) the Fāṭimids; (5) the Druses (derived from the Faṭimids); (6) the Hashīshīn, or Assassins (a development within the Ismā'īlian sect); (7) in quite modern times the Shaikhī sect and its derivatives, the Bābīs and Bahāīs.

(1) *Zaidīyah*.—The Zaidīyah (*q.v.*) professed to follow Zaid, the grandson of al-Ḥusain, as their *imām*. They established a principality in Tabaristān and ruled there as *imāms* from A.D. 864 to 928. They were then driven out by the Sunnite Samanids. Another division of the Zaidites organized a Shī'ah state in Yemen with its centre at Ṣa'da and later at Ṣan'ā. The date of the foundation was 280 A.H. (A.D. 892), and the independent Zaidī state still exists. The Zaidites demand that the *imām* shall be a descendant of Fāṭimah as well as of 'Alī, but otherwise they are the most liberal of the Shī'ahs and in many ways are indistinguishable from the Sunnites, though they do not desire to be known as Sunnīs. Unlike other Shī'ahs, they admit the validity of the election of the first two khalīfahs, Abū Bakr and 'Umar. They provide also for the possibility of there being two *imāms* in a given age, in order to meet the needs of regions far removed from one another. The liberal attitude of the Zaidīyah is a survival of early Mu'tazilite teaching.

(2) *Ismā'īlians*.—Reference has been made in passing to the Ismā'īlian sect, or 'the Seveners.' The movement was started by 'Abdallah ibn Maimūn, al-Qaddaḥ ('the Oculist'), who died in 261 A.H. (A.D. 874). He gave himself out as the representative or 'helper' of the Hidden *Imām*, Muḥammad ibn Ismā'īl. He professed to be inspired and to have the power to perform miracles. His professed mission was to prepare a people for the Hidden *Imām*, who was to return to visible manifestation shortly and, as the Mahdī, remove wickedness and bring righteousness on earth. To realize his mission, he sent out missionaries (*du'ā*, sing. *dā'ī*), who were to disguise their purpose, take up an ordinary calling, and cultivate acquaintance with as many as they could reach. With a view to winning confidence, they were instructed to profess sympathy with the beliefs of those whom they approached. They were then to raise questions and suggest difficulties. When the new-found acquaintance showed anxiety for further light, the missionary was to hint at the possibility that a source might be found which would give the desired explanations and lead on to fuller knowledge. Gradually the inquirer was brought to ask that he might be led to the coveted teacher and was induced to pledge secrecy and unreserved acceptance of the teacher's authority. The conversion to the Ismā'īlī attitude was readily realized when an inquirer had advanced thus far, and ere long the head of the sect had added to his subjects another who was bound to him in full submission until death. The discipline of the novice came to have a fixed and elaborate order of stages, of which only those leading to the self-surrender of the candidate to the Ismā'īlī head are known. These comprise the first four and leave the remaining three or more to be guessed. The latter are thought to have led to the complete renunciation of all positive belief and worship and to a sole devotion to the *imām* and his earthly representative.

(3) *Carmaṭians*.—'Abdallah ibn Maimūn made his headquarters finally at Salamiya in Syria, and to that point the numerous *du'ā* made their reports. One of these men secured the conversion of Ḥamdan Ḳarmaṭ, who started the sect known as the Carmaṭians (*q.v.*) in Irāq before 277 A.H. They were Ismā'īlians with immediate obedience to their own chiefs but a more comprehensive submission to the *imām* Mahdī. Their ravages continued to terrorize Islām for a century, when they were finally crushed. Their attack on Mecca and seizure of the Black Stone is one of the acts in history which are regarded with horror by all Muslims. Nor is the sacrilege regarded as having been made right by the return of the Black Stone (A.D. 949) some twenty years after it had been taken away. The spoilers claimed to be acting in obedience to the Mahdī in both the removal and the restoration of the stone. The power of Mahdism to secure obedience to authority is thus illustrated.

(4) *Fāṭimids*.—Among the missionaries sent out from Salamīya was Abu 'Abdallah, who was to prepare the rude tribes of the Maghrib for the reign of the Mahdī and the acceptance of his 'helper.' This man, Abu 'Abdallah, in 289 A.H. sent word that the Berber tribes were ready to take up arms in the cause of the Mahdī. The head of the Ismā'īlīyah at Salamīya, Sa'īd ibn Aḥmad, a grandson of 'Abdallah ibn Maimūn, led an expedition to N. Africa, and after a period of conflict succeeded in establishing himself as the Mahdī, giving himself out as the lineal descendant and heir of Muḥammad ibn Ismā'īl, the Hidden *Imām*. As such, he took the name Ubaidallah. The new capital which he founded was called the city of the Mahdī, al-Mahdīya. These are the steps which culminated in the foundation of the Fāṭimid dynasty. It was the most ambitious and enduring of the Shī'ah dynasties, as the foundation is dated from the foundation of al-Mahdīya (297 A.H.; A.D. 909), and the empire continued until Saladin, a Sunnī Kurd, entered Cairo as a conqueror (567 A.H.; A.D. 1171). The Fāṭimids had been ruling in Cairo since 450 A.H. (A.D. 1058). They held the throne for 270 years altogether; the Safawid dynasty in Persia is the only other great Shī'ah line of rulers. It lasted for 234 years (A.D. 1502–1736).

The Ismā'īlite views of the Fāṭimid rulers did not take root and spread in the Maghrib and Egypt. The Kabyles and *fellahīn* assimilated the clear-cut appeal to traditional authority which the Sunnite system offered more readily than they did the Ismā'īlite theosophy. To-day Egypt follows the school of ash-Shafi'ī, while the Maghrib is Malikite in its views.

(5) *Druses and Nusairīyah*.—A noteworthy development within Shī'ism under the Fāṭimids is represented by the Druse sect. The khalīfah al-Ḥākim (386–411 A.H.; A.D. 996–1021) was a strange and probably unbalanced individual who alternately favoured and persecuted Shī'ahs, Jews, and Christians, and finally, under the influence of Ḥamza and Darazī, two Ismā'īlī emissaries, gave himself out to be God incarnate, who had appeared in the flesh in order to establish an entirely new order of things in the world. He sought to impose his view upon the people of Egypt, but the attempt provoked violent revolt. Al-Ḥākim disappeared mysteriously in A.D. 1021, and his lieutenants were driven out of Egypt. Darazī picked up a following in the Lebanon region of Syria and a sect of Ḥākim-worshippers, borrowing its views and practices from Muslim, Christian, and pagan sources, was formed. This sect assumed the name of its organizer, Darazī—a name which the West has slightly modified into Druzes or Druses. They are not generally counted as Muslims; they are distinguished from Shī'ahs and Ismā'īlians, and are sometimes reckoned as a Christian sect.

The Nusairīyah, who have long been found in the Lebanons between Tripoli and Antioch, are of Shī'ah origin, but the heathenism of their environment has been rank and persistent and has over-grown the Islāmic elements to such an extent that the sect is frequently regarded as a development of paganism rather than of Islām. They are worshippers of the natural forces for whom 'Alī is the moon-god and the 'commander of the heavenly host' (stars). The family of 'Alī constitute the supreme objects of worship. Muḥammad is only a 'veil,' though with 'Alī and Selmān he forms the Nusairī trinity. The sect accepts the Qur'ān, but adopts an extravagant allegorical interpretation (*tawīl*).

(6) *Assassins and Metāwile*.—Much more important from the historical standpoint is the order of the Hashīshīn, or Assassins (*q.v.*), which arose within the Ismā'īlian sect in the 11th Christian cent. and continued to spread terror throughout Persia and Syria until they were destroyed by the Tatars under Hulagu Khan in A.D. 1256. The Assassins held the opinions of the Ismā'īlīyah and seem to have been organized to assist any who might be favourably disposed towards their sect and to do away with such as were opposed to them or their friends. The Grand Master, or Shaikh of the Mountains (*Shaikh al-Jebāl*), exercised complete authority over all the ranks under him and was served with blind fidelity, in particular by the *fedāis*, or rank-and-file, who executed the Master's commands without being informed as to their motive or aim and often with fearful consequences to themselves as well as to their victims. The crushing of these militant Ismā'īlians left the sect an ineffective body and robbed it of its savage spirit. There are still followers of the Ismā'īlī faith in Syria, Persia, and India, all recognizing the noble head of the order, the Aga Khan, who claims descent through the Assassin leaders from Fāṭimah, the Prophet's daughter. The seat of the Aga Khan was formerly in Persia, but is now located

in Bombay. Some of the Indian Ismā'ilians, the Khojas, are not, strictly speaking, 'Seveners.' They have been described as followers of the 'twelve' *imāms*.

The Metāwile, who form a considerable body in the Lebanon region at the present day, are the descendants of an old Shī'ah colony, possibly of Persian origin. They display the exclusiveness of the Shī'ahs, marry among themselves, receive instruction and religious ministrations from the Sayyids (professed members of the family of 'Alī) who have been trained in Irāq, and exhibit physical and social characteristics which distinguish them from their orthodox neighbours. These 'friends of 'Alī,' as their name describes them, live in small communities, and their places of worship and ceremonial are of a modest character.

(7) *Shaikhīs.*—The Shaikhī sect took its rise in Persia in the early years of the last century. They are Ithna-'ashariyah ('Twelvers') by profession, but hold an exaggerated belief in the divinity of the *imāms*, especially of the *imām* Mahdī. The sect is of interest because from it sprang Mirza Muḥammad 'Alī, the founder of the Bābī sect—an eclectic religious enterprise which renounced connexion with conventional Islām and struck out a path for itself. From Bābiism has sprung in its turn Bāhāism, which aims at being a universal religion. Bābiism was founded in 1844–45, and Bāhāism in 1892. These sects are not recognized or tolerated by the Shī'ahs.[1]

5. Shī'ah doctrines.—The cardinal tenet of Shī'ahs is that of the imāmate, and the chief duty is the acknowledgment of the true *imām*. Shī'ism centres religious authority in an inspired person, whereas the Sunnīs find their authority in the Qur'ān as interpreted by the Sunnah and the Consensus, or *Ijmā'*. The *imāms* of the Sunnīs are the four orthodox founders of schools, Abu Ḥanīfa, Malik ibn Anas, ash-Shafī'ī, and Aḥmad ibn Ḥanbal. They are infallible interpreters of the Qur'ān and Sunnah and represent the Consensus of Islām. This Sunnite teaching the Shī'ahs criticize as advocating dependence upon the fallible opinion of men for whom no claim of inspiration is made, who lived several generations after the Prophet, and whose several presentations of the agreed opinion of the Muslim community are vitiated by serious discrepancies. The Shī'ahs claim that the presence of the inspired *imām* is the only sure guarantee of right guidance. Nor is the fact that the last *imām* has withdrawn and is now the 'Hidden One' a bar to the effective exercise of his authority. He is still in the world and in contact with his chosen agents, who have the right to pronounce *ex cathedra* an opinion on any matter affecting the *shār'*, or canon law. They are the media whose voice correctly interprets the view and will of the *imām*. In theory the Shī'ah doctrine of authority should be more satisfactory than that of the Sunnites. It unifies authority and makes it consistent. Neither the *khalīfah* of the Sunnīs nor the Shāh of Persia has religious authority except as an executor of ecclesiastical decisions and a purely civil administrator.

The contest between the Shī'ahs and the Sunnīs turns largely on their different modes of choosing their religious authority. The Shī'ahs assert that the imāmate is settled on the basis of divine right inhering in the family of the Prophet, and that 'Alī, as the cousin of Muḥammad and the husband of his daughter Fāṭimah, was the first *imām* by divine right. After him his sons al-Ḥasan and al-Ḥusain inherited the right in order, and after them the *imāms* descended from them in order down to the 'Hidden One,' who left no visible successor. There are variant theories of the imāmate according as the line of al-Ḥasan is admitted as eligible, or the Hashimite family in the more comprehensive sense, or Ismā'īl ibn Ja'far, or as the use of the mode of popular election when necessary is allowed; but in all these cases the Shī'ahs hold to the special *a priori* right of the individual chosen. It is because of the right that he is chosen. The Sunnite explanation is that the *khalīfah* of the Prophet is 'the commander of the community of believers,' but not an infallible source of religious direction, and that he is chosen

[1] See art. BĀB, BĀBĪS.

by the suffrages of the Muslim community (*Ijmā'*) and finds his right to office in that fact.

Along with this legitimist claim, the Shī'ah *imāms* are declared to have a right by virtue of the nomination of 'Alī and his house by the Prophet at Kum Ghadīr. With this goes the further claim that the celestial light substance which was lodged in Muḥammad was likewise received into the souls of the *imāms* in succession. This was the substantive basis of their dignity, prophetic insight, and infallibility in matters of religion. They were sinless, and, because of the 'light' within them, some deemed them incorruptible and immortal. Their character and divine mission in a world like ours brought upon them persecution, wickedly inflicted, but borne for the sake of others, and availing to atone for the sins of penitent believers.

The extreme sect of the Shī'ahs exaggerated the enduement of the *imāms* and claimed that some or all of them were of divine nature or incarnate manifestations of God. In this belief they offered to them divine honours. Among the Ismā'īlians the Ghulā, or Ghālia ('Exaggerators'), group were more common than elsewhere. We have seen how easily such views develop in connexion with Mahdist movements. Commonly the leaders of such movements make claims for themselves that imply a superhuman origin and nature. The 'Alī Ilahīya sect, which still has followers in Persia and India, takes its name from its belief in the deity of 'Alī.

The imāmate among the Shī'ahs is officially represented in Persia by the *mujtahids*. When Sir John Malcolm wrote his *History of Persia* (1815), there were in that country very few of these final authorities on canon law. This was probably due to the action of Nādir Shāh in the 18th cent. in confiscating for state purposes the ecclesiastical funds and lands, thus diminishing greatly the income available for the maintenance of the Shī'ah hierarchy. At the present time the former sources of income have been restored to a large extent, and the number of *mujtahids* has been greatly augmented. In some of the large cities there are as many as four or five. Their interpretation of the canon law, or *shar'*, is accepted, and the *mujtahids* are careful to respect the decisions of the members of their own order, so that conflict of interpretation on points of importance is not common. The *qaḍīs* and *shaikhs ul-Islām*, who are responsible for the administration of the customary law, or '*urf*, accept the word of the court of *sharī'a*, and the Shāh, who imposes or confirms the sentence in important cases, acts as the canonists have recommended, unless the vague distinction between the functions of the canon law and the customary law gives him an excuse for exercising his personal authority. The exceptions are numerous, and all the weight of public sentiment in favour of the *shar'* and its venerated interpreters, the *mujtahids*, has been needed to check in some measure the despotic exercise of the prerogative of the Shāh. The constitution of 1905, as placing restriction upon the autocratic power of the throne and the alleged exclusive rights of the hierarchy in Persia, has been resisted by both and at the present time has little regulative force in the politics of the country. The *mujtahids* are chosen by the people and appointed by the Shāh. They are therefore men of outstanding reputation and held in esteem by the laity. It is required that they shall have had a long and thorough training in the schools of the law, including a period of many years at the best known of the Shī'ah schools at Kerbelā. Exhaustive knowledge of 'seventy sciences' and study extending through 'eighteen years' is the way in which popular report phrases the prerequisites of the *mujtahid's* office. These higher clergy are expected to maintain a reputation for sanctity, humility, and reverent gravity. They speak little and affect meditation habitually. Those well able to judge regard them as probably sincere, but professionally or conventionally pious. Apart from their activity as jurisconsults and judges, they have an important place in state functions and the greater religious ceremonies; they are also available for private ceremonies and legal transactions where the parties are of some social significance.

The inferior religious functionaries are the *mullās* (*q.v.*). They include a large number of men of excellent legal training and of sincere character, but as a class the *mullās* are not held in high respect, and a great many impostors are found. They have no fixed stipend and must depend on what they can collect in fees for their services, on gifts, and on charity. They execute deeds of sale, contracts, documents connected with marriage, and wills. They also perform the marriage ceremony, conduct funerals, and perform other minor religious rites. They are consulted by those needing advice and officiate at public prayers. In small places and among the nomad tribes in Persia they try cases and adjudicate disputes, their decision being subject to revision by the nearest higher authority such as the *qaḍī* or *shaikh ul-Islām*.

The Sayyids among the Shīʿahs are the nobility who trace their descent from ʿAlī and Fāṭimah. They draw stipends from the state in Persia, and in other places are regarded as entitled to support by the gifts of the faithful.

In their legal usage there is little difference between the Shīʿahs and the Sunnīs on the whole. The most pronounced variation is found in the permission of *muʿta* marriage. This has its justification for the Shīʿahs in *Qurʾān* iv. 28: 'It shall be no crime to make agreements over and above the law' (of marriage)—a verse which the Sunnīs contend was later abrogated by the Prophet. The Shīʿahs deny this. The prohibition of *muʿta* marriage attributed to the khalīfah ʿUmar is not recognized as having any authority with them, as they deny the validity of ʿUmar's claim to his office. This form of marriage permits a man to enter into a legal contract with a woman that they should live as man and wife for any period of time upon which they may agree. The sum of money is paid over, and all obligations on either side cease when the term of the contract has expired. The lawful offspring of such marriages are reckoned to the father. Divorce is not permitted. The women who lend themselves to this kind of union are of humble social standing and in many cases of indifferent reputation. The custom seriously affects the happiness and purity of the marriage relation and tends to degrade the character of those who participate in it. At the same time, as having full legal status with the Shīʿahs, it is not viewed as discreditable by the lower clergy, who themselves practise this mode of marriage.

The sanction of equivocation in the religious life is carried out systematically by the Shīʿahs. Muḥammad had approved *taqīyah* under special and extreme circumstances. The Shīʿahs regard the practice of it as a positive obligation. The term implies that, where one is likely to suffer or the safety of religion requires it, the believer should suitably protect himself or his faith by accommodating his profession of religion to the views of those with whom he has to deal. This practice of *taqīyah* or *kitmān* ('concealment') is the result of the early persecution of the Shīʿahs in Persia and has been confirmed ever since by their ill-treatment when present in Mecca and Medīna for the ceremonies of the *ḥājj*. The advocacy and practice of such a principle as this have a decidedly damaging effect upon the Shīʿah character.

The mutual hatred of the Sunnīs and Shīʿahs is of long standing. It is tending to diminish on the Shīʿah side with the growing contact of the Persians with foreigners and is now not so noticeable in large cities and in parts where Christian churches are conducting missions as it is in more remote parts. One fruitful cause of friction has been the Sunnīs' use of the Sunnah against the Shīʿahs. It has been claimed that the Sunnī traditionists have falsified some traditions and forged others, in order to prove their own position and discredit their opponents; but as a matter of fact the Sunnah which the Shīʿahs profess to follow is commonly adjudged unreliable. The standard collections of traditions were prepared to oppose the great Sunnī collections and were compiled at a late date. The evidences of manipulation are unmistakable.

The ablutions before prayer (*wuḍū*) are somewhat different from the Sunnī practice. The feet are not washed, but wiped, while the hands and arms are washed in an upward direction, towards the elbow, and not downward towards the finger ends. There is a slight change in the formulas of prayer and the order in which they occur.

The laws of marriage, inheritance, and slavery are not in all details the same as the Sunnī laws.

The *ḥājj* may be performed by proxy among the Shīʿahs, and much more practical importance is attached to the *ziyārah* ('visitation') to the tombs of pre-eminent Shīʿah saints than to the Meccan pilgrimage.[1]

LITERATURE.—F. J. Bliss, *The Religions of Modern Syria and Palestine*, Edinburgh, 1912; E. G. Browne, *A Literary Hist. of Persia*, 2 vols., London, 1902–06; T. J. de Boer, *Hist. of Philosophy in Islam*, Eng. tr., do. 1903; M. J. de Goeje, *Mémoire sur les Carmathes du Bahraïn et les Fatimides*², Paris, 1886; R. Dozy, *Het Islamisme*, Leyden, 1863, French tr., *Essai sur l'hist. de l'islamisme*, Paris, 1879; *EBr*⁸, *EBr*⁹, *s.v.* 'Mohammedanism,' *EBr*¹¹, *s.vv.* 'Mahommedan Religion,' 'Shiʿites,' 'Caliphate'; I. Goldziher, *Mohammed and Islam*, New Haven, 1917; T. P. Hughes, *DI*, London, 1895; D. B. Macdonald, *Development of Muslim Theology, Jurisprudence, and Constitutional Theory*, do. 1903; J. Malcolm, *Hist. of Persia*, 2 vols., do. 1815; D. S. Margoliouth, *The Early Development of Mohammedanism*, do. 1914; W. Muir, *The Caliphate: its Rise, Decline, and Fall*, new and rev. ed., do. 1915; A. Müller, *Der Islam im Morgen- und Abendland*, 2 vols., Berlin, 1885–87; R. A. Nicholson, *A Literary Hist. of the Arabs*, London, 1907; T. Nöldeke, *Sketches from Eastern History*, Eng. tr., do. 1892; E. Sell, *The Faith of Islam*², do. 1896; P. M. Sykes, *The Glory of the Shia World*, do. 1910; C. Snouck-Hurgronje, *Mohammedanism*, do. 1916; N. von Tornauw, *Das moslemisches Recht*, Leipzig, 1855; G. van Vloten, *Recherches sur la domination arabe, le Chiitisme, etc.*, Amsterdam, 1894; A. von Kremer, *Gesch. der herrschenden Ideen des Islams*, Leipzig, 1868; E. M. Wherry, *A Comprehensive Commentary on the Qurán*, 4 vols., London, 1896.

WALTER M. PATTON.

SHILLUK.—I. Geographical and general.—The Shilluk country forms a narrow fringe on the west bank of the Nile from Kaka (between 10° and 11° N.) in the north to Lake No in the south. From Kodok to Taufikia the Shilluk also occupy the east bank, and their villages extend about 35 miles up the Sobat river, principally on the north bank. Their territory is almost entirely a grass country; hence cattle are their wealth and principal care, and, although a considerable quantity of dura is grown, not enough is harvested to provide fully for the really dense population, and scarcity is by no means unusual. A census taken in 1903 gave a population of nearly 40,000 possessing over 12,000 head of cattle and nearly 64,000 sheep and goats. No doubt the number of cattle returned was unduly low, but, making all allowances, the Shilluk are poorer in cattle than the Dinka.

The Acholi, or Gang, and the Lango of Uganda speak dialects of Shilluk, but it is not clear whether the Shilluk migrated northward from the neighbourhood of Lake Victoria or their 'cradle-land' lay between the lake and their present territory, emigration taking place in both direc-

[1] See also art. LAW (Muhammadan).

tions. The latter hypothesis is perhaps the more probable.

The Shilluk are tall long-headed Negroids, usually with coarse features and broad noses, but it is not uncommon to meet men, especially members of chiefs' families, with shapely features, including relatively thin lips, noses that are anything but coarse, and well-modelled foreheads. While it would be premature to assert that the Shilluk aristocracy represents a conquering, predominantly Hamitic stock, there is little doubt that, as far as the Nilotic tribes are concerned, the maximum of Hamitic blood is to be found among the Shilluk—a matter worth remembering when comparing their social organization and religious ideas with those of kindred tribes such as the Dinka. The Shilluk are probably the best-organized people in the Anglo-Egyptian Sūdan; they alone of the black tribes offered a constant and determined opposition to the Mahdī and his followers; their king is absolute head of a state, whose territory is divided into districts, each administered by a chief directly responsible to the sovereign and acting as his proxy.

On account of the important part played by the king in the Shilluk religion, it is necessary to give some account of the royal family and its relation to the general organization of the people. The aristocracy of the Shilluk nation consists of the king (*ret*), his children (*niăret*), his grandchildren (*ni'ăret*), and his great-grandchildren (*kwaniăret*). Royal descent is not recognized beyond four generations. Nyakang was the first of the Shilluk kings, and all subsequent rulers are his descendants, the present king being his twenty-fifth successor in the twelve generations that, according to the royal genealogy, have existed since his time. The Shilluk have always paid their king high honour, so that even now he keeps up considerable state and has much authority. He usually rides a donkey, and never moves without a body-guard of from twelve to twenty men, more or less well armed, and all ready to obey his commands implicitly. In the old days his word was law, and his decisions are still obeyed in all matters coming before him; *e.g.*, the fines of cattle that he imposes are paid with reasonable speed.

Polygamy is prevalent, and a large number of the *tukl* in Fashoda—the royal burgh—are the residences of the king's wives, who are very numerous. His sons, too, take many wives, but the royal daughters must remain unmarried, the alleged reason being that it is unfitting that the daughter of a king should marry a commoner, while she could not marry a *niăret*, since this would be incest. When one of the king's wives is pregnant, she remains at Fashoda until the fourth or fifth month; she is then sent to a village, not necessarily her own, where she remains under the charge of the village chief until the child is weaned, when she probably returns to Fashoda. She usually takes a certain number of servants and cattle with her to the village in which she will be confined, and these are generally left there after her departure, becoming the property of the child, who is invariably brought up in the village where it is born, in which it should also be buried. This rule applies equally to all royal children of either sex, in whatever part of the Shilluk territory they may happen to die.

2. The Shilluk high god.—The Shilluk recognize a high god whom they call Juok. He is formless and invisible, and, like the air, is everywhere at once; he is far above Nyakang (in whom the Shilluk religion centres[1]) and men alike; nevertheless, it is only through Nyakang that men can approach him, performing the sacrifices to Nyakang which cause him to move Juok to send rain. Although the name Juok occurs in many greetings—*e.g.*, *Yimiti Juok!*, 'May Juok guard you!'—and although a sick man may cry *Er ra Juok?*, 'Why, O Juok?', it seems doubtful whether he is ever worshipped directly; and, although some Shilluk may vaguely associate the dead with him, this feeling does not appear to imply any dogma concerning a place of the dead or their condition. It should be noted that Westermann[1] gives a prayer to Juok, but the ritual accompanying it is the same as that practised in the case of possession by one of the early divine kings of the Shilluk, while the words of the prayer seem to reflect a common enough confusion between Nyakang, his son Dag, and Juok.

[1] Cf. below, 3.

3. The cult of Nyakang.—J. K. Giffen[2] gives the following account of the origin of Nyakang:

> In the beginning Juok created a great white cow, Deung Adok, who came up out of the Nile. She gave birth to a man child, whose grandchild, Ukwa, married two sisters, of whom one, Nikaiya or Nyakai, whose lower parts were those of a crocodile, gave birth to Nyakang, who inherited his mother's saurian attributes.

In spite of the animal element attributed to Nyakang in this legend (apparently collected on the Sobat), the writer feels confident that the majority of Shilluk think of Nyakang as a divine or semi-divine being, entirely human in form and physical qualities, though, unlike his recent successors, he did not die, but disappeared. Moreover, in spite of the fact that the objects kept in his shrine are fit for the use only of a creature with a human body, the writer is convinced that to many of his worshippers, including some at least of his priests, Nyakang, though the founder of their nation, is now essentially a spiritual being.

It is convenient to begin a description of the cult of Nyakang by considering certain shrines which exist in many Shilluk villages, but which are not shrines of Nyakang. These consist of groups of two or more huts of the same circular form and much the same size as those of which the village is composed, but they are more neatly thatched, and their miniature spires terminate in an ostrich egg from which there projects the blade of a spear; moreover, the fence surrounding them is kept in specially good repair. These huts, with the enclosed area, are sacred; for, with the exception of the old people concerned in keeping them clean, no one enters the enclosure, or even approaches it, without due cause. Each enclosure constitutes a shrine, sacred to a dead king, one of the huts being built over his grave, while the others are used by those who attend to the upkeep of the shrine. Nyakang and his son Dag, who did not die but disappeared, have many shrines called 'graves'; Nyakang has no fewer than ten, the most celebrated being at Akurwa and Fenikang. The former consists of two huts, the latter of five. The shrines of Nyakang do not differ in appearance from the grave-shrines of the later Shilluk kings, and they are all spoken of as *kengo Nyakang*, 'the grave of Nyakang,' although it is well known that no one is buried in them.[3] The *kengo Nyakang* are looked after by certain men and old women, the real or reputed descendants of the companions of Nyakang. All are responsible for keeping the shrines clean, but in addition the men act as priests, killing the sacrifices and disposing of the bones, which they cast into the river. The contents of the *kengo* vary, but they always

[1] *The Shilluk People*, p. 171.

[2] *Anglo-Egyptian Sudan*, London, 1906, p. 197.

[3] The word *kengo* is applied only to the graves of kings and their children, the graves of commoners being spoken of as *roro*; a similar verbal distinction is made with regard to the death of kings, who are said not to 'die' but, like their ancestor Nyakang, to 'go away.'

include certain sacred spears called *alodo*, representing those used by Nyakang and his companions. At Akurwa the shrine contains the effigy and stool of Nyakang.[1]

The shrine at Fenikang, as already mentioned, consists of five huts; one of these is in a special sense the house of Nyakang, which, in his spirit form, he is thought to inhabit. It is distinguished by a number of very rough paintings on its outer wall, some of which could be recognized as representing animals, but the writer could not learn that the paintings had any special significance. Before the door of this hut are a number of elephant tusks, the broad ends of which are thrust into the ground; within it there are skins on the floor as if for Nyakang to rest upon. Some of the sacred 'spears of Nyakang' appear to be kept in the hut, and there is an extremely sacred stool in this shrine, which seems to be kept there, though it may perhaps be preserved with some of the sacred spears and a number of elephant tusks in one of the other huts of the shrine. The other huts are used by the guardians of the shrine and for storing the dura brought as offerings when the crop is cut.

The graves of the kings and the *kengo Nyakang* are alike the site of the performance of certain ceremonies which show the intimate relation, amounting sometimes to confusion, which exists between Nyakang and subsequent kings. Thus it is usual for the harvest ceremony to be performed at the royal grave-shrines as well as at the shrines of Nyakang, though it is recognized that this is not absolutely necessary. Again, each king soon after his installation sends, or should send, presents to the grave-shrines of his predecessors, treating these in the same way as he treats the shrines of Nyakang, though the presents need not be so lavish. Finally, sick folk send animals to be sacrificed as offerings at the shrines of their kings, just as they do at the shrines of Nyakang.

The writer may now anticipate the conclusions to which the remainder of this article will lead, and point out that the actual working religion of the Shilluk is a cult of Nyakang depending upon the acceptance of the following beliefs: (i.) the immanence in each king (*ret*) of the spirit of Nyakang, simply spoken of as Nyakang; (ii.) the conviction that the king must not be allowed to become ill or senile, lest with his diminishing vigour the cattle should sicken and fail to bear their increase, the crops should rot in the fields, and man, stricken with disease, should die in ever increasing numbers.

It follows that the *ret* of the Shilluk must be numbered among those rulers whom J. G. Frazer has called 'divine kings,' and, though, as in many instances in other countries, every precaution is taken against accidental death—*e.g.*, they may not take part in battle—the Shilluk kings are (or were) killed, in order to avoid those disasters which their senescence was thought to bring upon the State.

4. The killing of the king and the transmission of the divine spirit.—Although there is not the least doubt that the kings of the Shilluk were killed ceremonially when they began to show signs of old age or ill health, it is extremely difficult to ascertain exactly what was done, and there is no doubt that a good deal of Shilluk folklore is enshrined in the accounts commonly given of the killing of the *ret*. According to these, any *niăret* has the right to attempt to kill the king, and, if successful, to reign in his stead. The killing could take place only at night, for during the day the king would be surrounded by his friends and his body-guard, and no would-be successor would have the slightest chance of harming him. At night the king's position was very different. Alone in his enclosure with his favourite wives, and with no men to protect him, except a few herdsmen whose huts would be at a little distance, he was represented as passing the night in constant watchfulness, prowling fully armed, peering into the shadows, or standing silent and watchful in some dark corner. Then, when at last his rival appeared, the fight would take place in grim silence, broken only by the clash of spear and shield, for it was said to be a point of honour for the *ret* not to call the herdsmen to his assistance.

[1] Cf. below, 4.

Many commoners will give some such account as the above, and, though nothing of the sort occurred during the recent period before the Mahdia, it is probable that these tales reproduce with tolerable fidelity a state of affairs which once existed among the Shilluk, or among their ancestors before they occupied their present territory. One survival of the conditions outlined does, indeed, seem to remain. It is commonly believed that the king keeps awake at night and sleeps only by day, and the sleepy condition of the king on the few occasions on which the writer saw him seemed to confirm this report.

In recent times the leading part in the killing of the *ret* has been assigned to the members of certain families called *ororo*, said to be the descendants of the brothers of Oshalo, the third king of the Shilluk. It is generally believed among well-informed Shilluk that their fourth king, Duwad, was the first to be killed ceremonially, but, according to one account, Tugo, the seventh king, was the first to suffer. Absolutely reliable information concerning the actual killing of the *ret* during recent times is not forthcoming. It is said that the *ororo* and some of the chiefs announce his fate to him, after which he is taken to a hut specially built for the occasion, and strangled. The reasons determining the *ororo* to act are said to be the ill health of the *ret* or his incapacity to satisfy his wives, which is regarded as an undoubted sign of senescence. Concerning this there are two popularly received accounts. One states that his wives would themselves strangle the *ret*, but this is incorrect; the other is to the effect that the wives notify their husbands' shortcomings to some of the chiefs, who tell them to inform the *ret* of his approaching death. It is widely believed that this is done by spreading a piece of cloth over his face and over his knees as he lies sleeping during the afternoon. If we ignore these discrepancies and recent practice, there is little doubt that the old custom was to take the *ret* and a nubile maiden (or perhaps two) to a specially built hut, the opening of which was then walled up so that the inmates, left without water or food, died of starvation and suffocation. This practice was said to have been given up some five generations ago on account of the sufferings of the *ret*, who was so distressed by the stench arising from his companion's body that he shouted to the people outside the hut commanding them on no account to leave his successor to die slowly in such a manner.

For a long time no public announcement of the king's death is made, but the news spreads gradually. As already stated, no information was obtainable as to who actually killed the king, or by whom and under what circumstances he was brought to his birthplace where he would be buried and his grave-shrine erected. It must, however, be remembered that Fashoda has not always been the home of the king, for, although it is uncertain how the change was brought about, there is no doubt that formerly each Shilluk king reigned and was buried in the village in which he was born and in which his afterbirth was buried. Some months after the king's death, when decomposition was judged to have proceeded so far that little but the bones would be found, the hut was broken open by the *ororo*, a grave was dug, and the bones of the king and of his companion were placed in it, after being wrapped in the skin of one of the oxen sacrificed. A hut was built over the grave, and one or two others were put up within the enclosure for the attendants on the new shrine which had thus arisen. Westermann[1] states that this ceremony was the public notification that the king had disappeared, and he describes the sacrifice by drowning of a man and woman, who were placed in a canoe with many spears, cattle, bells, beads, and pottery vessels. The canoe with its load was towed into the middle of the river and sunk.

During the interregnum which occurs after the death of a *ret* the most important chiefs decide all comparatively small matters, great affairs standing over until the appointment of a new king. The election appears to be in the hands of not more than eight or ten men, none of whom are *ororo*; the evidence is not clear whether their choice is thought to be inspired, but certain portents might occur if the wrong man were chosen. The king-elect and a number of big chiefs wait for the return of two or three chiefs, who go to Akurwa near the northern limit of the Shilluk country to bid the Akurwa people bring the sacred four-legged stool from the shrine of Nyakang in their village, and also his effigy called 'Nyakang,' which is kept wrapped in a piece of *dammur*, *i.e.* the common cotton-cloth of the Sūdan. The effigy and the sacred stool are carried southward towards Fashoda; each night the effigy is placed upon the sacred stool, but by day the objects are borne upon men's shoulders, and as they march the men sing songs that Nyakang has commanded them to sing.[2] The party bearing the sacred objects may seize anything they like on the way, but it seems that their wants are so freely provided for in the villages which they pass that they scarcely exercise their prerogative.

There is a shallow, generally dry, *khor* near Kwom, which is the scene of a sham fight between the Akurwa men bringing the effigy and the folk waiting with the newly-elected *ret*, in which the former are victorious. No reason could be given for this 'old custom,' as it was called, but immediately after it the king-elect is escorted to Fashoda. Certain of the Akurwa men now enter the shrine of Nyakang with the stool, and, after a short time, come out and place it on the ground outside the entrance to the shrine enclosure; they now place the effigy of Nyakang on the stool, the king-elect holding one leg of the stool while an important chief holds another. Near him stand two of his paternal aunts and two of his sisters, while he is surrounded by a crowd of *niăret*, *ni'ăret*, *kwaniăret*, and *ororo*. The Akurwa men carry the effigy into the shrine, and the *ororo* lift up the king-elect and place him upon the stool, on which he remains seated for some time, perhaps till sunset, when the Akurwa men take the sacred stool into the shrine and the *ororo* escort the new king to three new huts specially built for him. The king stays in one of these, or perhaps within the enclosure, for three days; on the fourth night the *ororo* take the king quietly, almost stealthily, to the royal residence. The three newly-built huts which were occupied by the king are broken up (perhaps by the *ororo*) and their fragments thrown into the river.

5. Reverence for trees.—Special regard is paid to trees that grow near the shrines of dead kings. This is not remarkable, for the Shilluk country is in the main bare, with few shade-trees, so that any tree growing in or on the outskirts of a village is preserved and the ground becomes to some extent a meeting- and squatting-place. But the Shilluk attitude to trees growing near the grave-shrines of their kings appears to be something more than an appreciation of the grateful shade, though there is no regular cult. When a tree has grown, or is believed to have grown, near a shrine shortly after its erection, *i.e.* within a few months or years of the burial of a 'divine king,' it is thought that the tree has sprung from one of the logs used in making the grave, and in such cases the connexion between the tree and the dead king is one that would easily suggest itself.

In the case of an old tree at Kodok which grew near the grave of Nyadwai, the ninth king, a 'big' sacrifice was made when it fell down, and its trunk and all its fragments were carefully thrown into the river. This is not done to produce rain or to influence the crops, but it was said that, if any one burned the wood of this tree, even accidentally, he would sicken. In this connexion reference may be made to the fact that the bones of certain sacrifices are carefully gathered and disposed of in the same way. There was (1911) no hut over the grave of Nyadwai, probably because it is situated some little distance from the present native village and is surrounded by Government offices and houses, but it had a fence round it, and a young tree that had appeared at some distance from the stump of the old tree was regarded with respect. The old tree did not really spring from the grave of Nyadwai, since it was admitted that during his lifetime it stood near his house, and that he would often sit under it; nevertheless, there is a general feeling that it is associated with his grave, and this feeling is so strong that many Shilluk at one time or another spoke of Nyadwai being buried under the tree, though his grave must be nearly a hundred yards away. It should be remembered that the due growth of the crops, *i.e.* of the most important part of the vegetable world, depends on the well-being of the 'divine' king, so that there is nothing surprising in a strong, almost religious, feeling for any tree growing near a shrine.

6. The appearance of the Shilluk kings in animal form.—Nyakang, Dag, and Nyadwai all appear as a white bird called *okak*, or rarely as a giraffe; if the animal comes straight towards the village in which the shrine stands, exhibiting no sign of fear, it is concluded that it is a spirit animal, and the attendants at the tomb sacrifice a sheep or perhaps even a bullock. Father Banholzer[1] adds 'long-bodied grasshoppers' and 'a kind of snake called *red*' as forms in which Nyakang appears. The writer is indebted to Dr. Lambie of the American Mission for pointing out that unusual behaviour on the part of almost any land animal will lead the Shilluk to look upon the creature as a temporary incarnation of Nyakang.

Thus, 'if a little bird flies into the midst of a crowd of people and is not frightened, or attracts some one's notice in a special manner, they say "Nyakang."'[1]

Occasionally Nyakang appears as a bull. A very old Shilluk of the royal family said that, when he was a youth, fifty or more years ago, Nyakang appeared as a white bull; the king ordered sacrifices to be made in addition to those already offered by the local chief. Dr. Lambie adds that unusual behaviour on the part of a water animal will be put down to the animal containing the spirit of Nikaiya (Nyakai).

Reference may here be made to the Shilluk attitude towards the crocodile. This animal is generally spared, as some of the worst man-eaters are believed to be men whom other crocodiles have taken, and very dark coloured crocodiles are supposed to be either man-crocodiles or their descendants. Further, there is a firm belief in the crocodilian attributes of the ancestors of Nyakang already recorded.[2] Nikaiya lives in the river, and is definitely associated with the crocodile, and, though in old days she would assume human form, and at times come to the village by night in all friendliness, she might seize a man or woman and bear him or her off to her home in the river, and there change her victim into a crocodile to be a

[1] P. 136.

[2] Nyakang appears in a dream to one of the guardians of the shrine at Akurwa and prescribes the songs to be sung; further investigation will probably show that songs play an important part in the tribal lore of the Shilluk, and that there is a sort of epic commemorating the great deeds of the royal family.

[1] In a personal communication to the present writer.

[2] Above, § 3.

spouse to one of her crocodile relatives. Nyakai brings luck to those whom she visits by night to ask for fire; if a barren woman bears a child after such a visit, it will be called Nyakai, and the father will take a sheep and kill it and throw it into the river. Nyakai is known by her short, stout figure and great muscular development, and by the fact that she 'eats' (mouths) her words. That the river is the true home of Nyakai, even in her most spiritual form, is shown by the sacrifice made to her on another occasion. Just as a sacrifice would be made at the shrine of Nyakang, or at the grave-shrine of any king, if Nyakang or one of the Shilluk kings had appeared in a dream, or if one of the kings had 'possessed' a man, causing him to become ill, so, when Nyakai takes up her abode in a man or woman, the sacrifice is made by throwing a live sheep with its legs tied together into the river.

The Shilluk do not eat the flesh of the lion, leopard, hyena, a species of monitor lizard (*varanus*), and a fish called *shuro*. The last prohibition is directly attributed to Nyakang, who told his people to bring him all the fish that they caught in the river. Although they brought him many fish, they kept back one, and Nyakang, who knew this, as in a dream men know things happening at a distance, told his people that this fish should always be unlawful food to them.

7. Oaths.—Oaths are sworn by Nyakang or on one of the holy spears from a shrine of Nyakang. Westermann[1] notes that the latter form is used only in judicial procedure. A sheep is killed and both parties are smeared with its blood, after which they swear by the spear, perjury being followed by death. In swearing by Nyakang his name is often coupled with that of one of the villages in which he has a shrine; *e.g.*, a man may swear by 'Nyakang of Akurwa.' The early kings may also be invoked by name, especially Dag.

8. General remarks.—Juok, the high god of the Shilluk, must not be confused with the *jok* (ancestral spirits) of the Dinka (*q.v.*), whose worship is so important a part of the Dinka religion. It is at first sight somewhat surprising that, although in the case of important men the funeral customs are by no means short or lacking in ceremony, there is no considerable cult of the dead among the Shilluk. The explanation is no doubt to be sought in the development of the cult of Nyakang and the divine kings in whom his spirit is immanent. Thus, while the Dinka commonly attribute sickness to the action of an ancestral spirit, the Shilluk regard the entrance into the body of the spirit of one of their kings as the commonest cause of sickness. Probably only the early kings are thought to produce illness in this manner, and the few cases with which the writer became familiar were held to be possessed by Dag, the son and successor of Nyakang.

One of these cases, a woman who recovered after two sheep had been sacrificed to Dag, wore bead anklets, and amidst the beads there were threaded small pieces of the ear lobes of the sheep. These anklets were considered protective against future possession by Dag. A chief who had been badly used and imprisoned by the king was treated in exactly the same way. On his release his friends brought him beads, sheep were killed, and he now wears the beads and pieces of the ears of the sheep in exactly the same manner as the woman.

The men and women called *ajuago*, though they too have immanent in them the spirits of the early Shilluk kings, seem to form a class apart. They have the power of healing the sick and do a brisk trade in charms, of which almost every Shilluk seems to wear a considerable number. When a man first becomes *ajuago*, he is taken ill, perhaps waking up trembling and agitated from a dream (in which he may afterwards say the spirit came to him). He consults an *ajuago*, who may tell him, 'No, you are not ill; you have the spirit of Dag within you.' A long and complicated ceremony is then performed in order that the spirit may not affect him so severely, for without this ceremony the spirit would be so strong in his body that he would not dare to approach his women. It was impossible to discover with certainty the exact nature of the change effected by the ceremony, but the informant, one Akon Achol, who had in him the spirit of Dag, seemed to think that, after the ceremony, the spirit which had previously attacked his body in the rudest fashion became attached rather to his spirit or soul.

[1] P. xliii.

One ancestral spirit may be immanent in many *ajuago* at the same time, often passing at the death of an *ajuago*, or shortly afterwards, into one of his children, who thus becomes an *ajuago* like his or her father. It was said that *ajuago* of the female sex should not marry if they were unmarried at the time that the spirit came to them; they would be allowed to take lovers, but, like the king's daughters, they should not bear children. But it seemed that women very seldom became *ajuago* in their youth, and it is certain that married women who are *ajuago* do not leave their husbands, and continue to bear children. The following information on this matter was volunteered by a usually reliable informant: the husbands of women who are *ajuago* have access to their wives only during the dark half of the month, for 'Nyakang and Dag only come during that half of the month when the moon is bright.' Unfortunately the writer was unable to follow up his information or even to verify it.

LITERATURE. — P. W. Hofmayr, 'Religion der Schilluk,' *Anthropos*, vi. [1911] 120 ff.; C. G. Seligmann, *The Cult of Nyakang and the Divine Kings of the Shilluk* (*Fourth Report of the Wellcome Research Laboratories*, vol. B.), Khartum, 1911; D. Westermann, *The Shilluk People, their Language and Folk-lore*, Philadelphia and Berlin, 1912.

Since this article was written, an officer of the Sudan Civil Service who witnessed the installation of the Shilluk king Fafite wad Yor on Jan. 17, 1918, has published an account of what he saw (P. Munro, 'Installation of the King of the Shilluks,' *Sudan Notes and Records*, Khartum, 1918, vol. i. no. 3). The author gives further details, the chief discrepancies noted being that an effigy of Dag is brought from Akurwa with that of his father Nyakang, and that the mock battle with dura stalks takes place after the installation.

C. G. SELIGMAN.

SHIṆS.—See art. DARDS. Here it may be noted that, since the art. DARDS was written, it has been ascertained that the correct spelling of this name is 'Shiṇ,' not 'Shīn.' Similarly, their language is Shiṇá, with the stress-accent on the last syllable, not Shīnā. G. A. GRIERSON.

SHINTO.—1. Early history and general features.—Shinto, *i.e.* 'the way of the gods,' is the old native religion of Japan before the introduction of Buddhism and Confucianism. Its affinities, as the analogy of race and language would lead us to expect, are with the religions of Northern Asia rather than with the ancient Chinese cult. Shinto agrees with the former in making the sun the chief object of worship, though this is in itself by no means conclusive, as sun-worship is common to most nations in the barbaric stage of development. It is more significant that it has nothing to correspond with the two chief deities of ancient China, the personal Supreme Deity called *Shangti* and the more impersonal *Tien* or Heaven. In Japan, Heaven is not a god, but the region where the gods reside. There are more definite indications of a connexion between Shinto and the old religion of Korea. Some Shinto gods are of Korean origin, and others have Korean associations.

Writing was practically unknown in Japan before the 5th cent., and the myths and rituals of Shinto were transmitted by oral tradition only, chiefly by the Nakatomi and Imbe, hereditary priestly corporations attached to the Mikado's court. We also hear of *katarihe*, or reciters, who recited 'ancient words' at the *Ohonihe*, or coronation ceremony, and doubtless on other occasions. In A.D. 712, a quasi-historical work called the *Kojiki* was compiled by Imperial order. It contains much mythical matter. The *Nihongi*, a similar compilation, completed in 720, is our other chief authority for the myths of Japan (see the Literature at the end of this article). The prayers and rituals of Shinto were not committed to writing until the beginning of the 10th century. The *Yengishiki*, compiled at this time, describes the chief ceremonies, and gives the text of a number of prayers called *norito*. The picture of Shinto presented by these and other less important works is tolerably complete, and has the great advantage for us of having been drawn by the Japanese themselves.

When we compare Shinto with the great religions of the world, it must be deemed perhaps the most rudimentary cult of which we have an adequate written record. It has not advanced beyond a crude polytheism; its personifications are vague and feeble; there is little grasp of the conception of spirit; it has scarcely anything in the shape of a moral code; it practically does not recognize a future state, and generally gives little evidence of deep thought or earnest devotion. It is, nevertheless, not the religion of a primitive people. Long before Shinto had assumed the shape in which we know it, the Japanese had possessed a settled government and a fair degree of civilization. They were already an agricultural nation, a circumstance which has profoundly affected their religion. The degree of their material civilization is indicated by the mention in the old records of bridges, iron, copper, mirrors, bellows for smelting metal, weaving, silk culture, and brewing. Their degree of mental culture may be gathered from the fact that Chinese learning had reached Japan early in the 5th century, if not sooner, and Buddhism towards the middle of the 6th century. The Shinto of this early period is a State religion. We hear but little of the popular beliefs and practices.

It is impossible with Herbert Spencer to refer all classes of deity to one origin, namely, the worship of humanity, as ghosts or ancestors. As Pfleiderer, d'Alviella, and other Continental scholars have clearly pointed out, there are two currents of deity-making thought. One is the personification of natural objects and phenomena, the other the deification of men. Shinto, which has been described as exclusively a cult of ancestors and deceased sovereigns, has in reality little of this element. It is in the main a worship of nature. The man-deities are of more recent origin and of minor importance. These two classes of deities may each be subdivided into deities of individuals, of classes, and of qualities, all of which are exemplified in Shinto. The sun-goddess is a deified individual object; the gods of trees and herbs represent classes; the god of growth (*Musubi*) is a personification of an abstract quality. *Temmangu* is a deified statesman; *Koyane* is the deified type of the Nakatomi priestly corporation; *Ta-jikara no wo* ('the male of hand-strength') is a human quality personified and raised to divine rank.

The Japanese word for God is *Kami*. It means 'above,' 'superior,' and may therefore be compared to the Latin *superi* or *cœlicoli*, the Greek *οὐρανίωνες*. It suggests the theory that celestial objects were the first deities. Motoöri, the great modern Shinto theologian, says:

'The term *Kami* is applied in the first place to the various deities of Heaven and Earth who are mentioned in the ancient records, as well as to their spirits (*mi-tama*) which reside in the shrines where they are worshipped. Moreover, not only human beings, but birds, beasts, plants and trees, seas and mountains, and all other things whatsoever which deserve to be dreaded and revered for the extraordinary and pre-eminent powers which they possess, are called *Kami*. They need not be eminent for surpassing nobleness, goodness, or serviceableness alone. Malignant and uncanny beings are also called *Kami*, if only they are the objects of general dread. Among *Kami* who are human beings I need hardly mention Mikados. . . . Amongst others there are thunder (in Japanese *Naru kami* or the Sounding God); the dragon, the echo (called in Japanese *Kodama*, or the Tree-Spirit), and the fox, who are *Kami* by reason of their uncanny and fearful natures. The term *Kami* is applied in the *Nihongi* and *Manyōshiu*, a collection of ancient poetry, to the tiger and wolf. Izanagi gave to the fruit of the peach, and to the jewels round his neck, names which implied that they were *Kami*. . . . There are many cases of seas and mountains being called *Kami*. It is not their spirits which are meant. The word was applied directly to the seas or mountains themselves, as being very awful things.'

There may be recognized in Shinto, as elsewhere, three successive stages of the conception of divinity in nature. First, the god, a natural object as the sun, is regarded as sentient, and direct worship is paid to it. This is probably what Comte meant when he described the first stage of religion as fetishism. But the word 'fetish' has been used of so many things, notably of the material object representing a deity, that its use is undesirable when precision is aimed at. Secondly, the god is thought of as an anthropomorphic being; and, thirdly, it is conceived, not as the natural object itself or its presiding deity, but as a spiritual emanation (*mitama*) from him, which resides in his temple on earth and otherwise exercises an influence there. There is much confusion in all mythologies between these different stages. The first and second are confused in the Shinto sun-myth. When we are told that the sun-goddess by retiring to the rock-cave of Heaven caused darkness all over the world, it is evidently the sun itself that is intended. Yet in the same story she does many things which have no meaning, if not said of a purely anthropomorphic being.

The passage just quoted from Motoöri illustrates another kind of confusion, namely between the god and his *mitama*. The doctrine of the *mitama* (the *Shekinah* of the Jews) is plainly of secondary origin. It is due to the attempts of thoughtful men to reconcile such facts as the presence of the sun-goddess at the same time in the sky and in her temple at Ise. It is a step towards the conception of the omnipresence of Deity. But it is not prominent in Shinto. On the whole, the ancient Japanese gods (like Homer's) are very material beings, modelled, not on ghosts or spirits, but on living men. There is a myth in which the god *Oho-na-mochi* has an interview with his own *mitama* or spiritual double, resulting in the latter being settled in the shrine of Miwa. But the people disregard this distinction and speak of the god worshipped here simply as Oho-na-mochi. A god may have two *mitama*, one in his beneficent, the other in his sinister, aspect, or many, according to the number of shrines at which he is worshipped. The special place of residence of the *mitama* is the *shintai*, or god-body, which is a sword, a stone, a mirror, or other material object deposited in the shrine, usually in a box which is rarely or never opened. Some ignorant worshippers confound the *shintai* with the *mitama*, just as in France the peasant speaks of the host as 'le bon Dieu.'

Shinto has practically no idols, not because the ancient Japanese were specially enlightened, but because they had no art before sculpture and painting were introduced from China, and because they realized very feebly the personal character of Divinity. The deities are very numerous, as is always the case in nature-worship. For, although a monotheistic nature-worship, as, for example, of the sun, is conceivable, yet in practice the same feeling leads inevitably to the cult of other natural phenomena as well. The number of Shinto deities is constantly fluctuating. Some are forgotten, and are re-established under new names. Or wholly new gods may be added to the pantheon. A deity is frequently cut into two by a fissiparous process; or, on the other hand, two distinct deities may come to be regarded as identical. Their character is very ill-defined. A well, a tree, or a mountain may have worship paid to it without having an individual name or any indication of sex or number. Japanese grammar greatly neglects these two distinctions. The wind-god is sometimes a single male deity and sometimes a married pair; the sea-god of Sumiyoshi is either one or three. The rain-storm god, *Susa no wo*, has in modern times been made into a sort of trinity. *Musubi*, the god of growth, was split up into several deities.

The general character of the Shinto deities is beneficent. But even a good deity may send plague or disaster if offended by neglect or disrespect. There is no evil deity, though Susa no wo, the rain-storm, shows some tendency to represent the evil principle generally. Their functions also are very much confused. Generally speaking, the nature-god in course of time acquires the functions of a providence that watches over human affairs. The sun-goddess is not only looked up to with gratitude for warmth and light, but is supposed to grant bodily health and success in business to her devotees. She also gives protection from foreign invasion, and many other blessings which have no conceivable relation to her nature-functions. *Inari*, the grain-god, is in one place the patron-god of swordsmiths. At another, he has a reputation for recovering stolen property. Very often a god is worshipped simply as the deity of a particular shrine, nothing more being known of him. Few people are aware that the very popular *Suitengu* of Tokio is in reality three several deities of widely different origin and character. Shrines may have their deity changed, as was the case with the well-known *Kompira* of Shikoku, without detriment to their popularity.

2. Ancestor-worship.[1]—The worship of ancestors in Japan is an importation from China, and has no place in the older Shinto. There are, however, in the *Nihongi* cases of the worship (whether divine or otherwise is not clear) of deceased Mikados by their successors, and at a later date they were certainly regarded as *Kami*. Even living Mikados claimed a titular divinity, though without miraculous powers. We may probably trace these practices to Chinese influence. When a modern Japanese says that Shinto is ancestor-worship, he is no doubt thinking of the *ujigami* cult, which unquestionably formed an important part of it. In ancient times the local chieftainship and the offices of the central government were hereditary in certain families. The result was that the official designation came to be equivalent to a family name. These families or clans had each its special deity, called *ujigami*, or 'surname-deity,' for whose worship the members were from time to time convened. The *ujigami* might be and often was a nature-god. But even when he was a man-deity he was in most cases not a deified individual, but only a type. *Koyane* and *Futodama*, for example, are simply personifications of the families or clans whose ancestors they were feigned to be. They correspond to such conceptions as John Bull and Tommy Atkins. This is not true ancestor-worship.

3. State of the dead.—A land of Yomi or darkness is frequently mentioned in the ancient myths. Several of the gods are said to have gone there at death. In the old times Yomi was probably only a sufficiently transparent metaphor for the grave. There is little to show that the ancient Japanese believed in a future state of existence. A story in the *Nihongi* implies that the question was an open one, but that some people believed that the dead could execute vengeance on those who were their enemies during life. It is true that in pre-historic times it was the custom to sacrifice wives and attendants at the tombs of deceased Mikados. To some this will appear a conclusive proof of a belief in their continued existence in another state. But if we reflect on the motives of our own funeral observances, we may see reason to doubt this. Was the sacrifice of a wife to a Mikado intended for his personal satisfaction any more than the primroses laid before Lord Beaconsfield's statue are meant for the gratification of his sight and smell? The rituals make no mention of a future state. There are no prayers that after this life we may enjoy eternal felicity.

[1] See art. ANCESTOR-WORSHIP (Japanese).

4. Animals in Shinto.—Animals may receive worship for their own sakes as terrible or uncanny beings. It is for this reason that the tiger, the serpent, and the wolf are called *Kami*. But they have no temples and no regular organized cult. They may also be honoured for their association with some deity as his servant. The deer, the monkey, the pigeon, the tortoise, etc., are held sacred to various deities. The gods in myth often assume the form of animals, as the cormorant, the *wani* (dragon or sea-monster), the deer, the snake, etc. There is no definite evidence that totemism was known.

5. Supreme Being.—Shinto has no Supreme Deity. There has been, however, a tendency to exalt some of the gods to a supreme position. The sun-goddess is described as the most exalted of all the gods. Especially in modern times she has received an increasing degree of honour as a general providence, her special solar quality being left in the background. There was once an attempt to raise *Kuni-toko-tachi* to the position of Supreme Deity, simply because he is the first god in point of time of the *Nihongi*. Infinite knowledge and power are not recognized as attributes of Shinto deities.

6. Myths.[1]—The chief religious ideas embodied in the myths of Japan are, firstly, the conception of various parts and aspects of the material universe as sentient beings, or presided over by sentient beings; and, secondly, the doctrine that reverence and obedience are due to the wise sovereign, whose rule confers on his people blessings comparable to the sun's warmth and light. This, we take it, is the real meaning of the story which traces the descent of the Mikados from the sun-goddess. The *Nihongi* begins with a philosophical essay of later date, which bears manifest traces of Chinese inspiration. It describes the evolution of Heaven and Earth from a chaotic egg-shaped mass which contained germs. The purer part became thinly diffused and formed Heaven, while the grosser element sank down and became Earth. Thereafter divine beings were produced between them.

There is great confusion in the various versions of the myths in regard to the earlier deities. The *Nihongi* calls the first god *Kuni-toko-tachi* ('land-eternal-stand'), and says that he was produced by the transformation of something in form like a reed-shoot, which was brought forth between Heaven and Earth. The other mythical records give different names to the first deity. *Kuni-toko-tachi* was succeeded by a number of other deities of whom little is known. Most of them, from their names, seem to be nature-gods.

It is not until the seventh generation that Japanese myth really begins with the creator pair, *Izanagi* and *Izanami*. At the behest of the other gods, these two stood on the 'floating bridge of Heaven' (the rainbow), and, thrusting down the 'jewel-spear of Heaven' (a phallus, according to some), groped with it in the chaos below. The brine from the spear-point coagulated and formed an island, upon which the divine pair descended and built a house with one central pillar. Then, the male deity turning by the left and the female deity turning by the right, they went round this central pillar until they met at the other side.

[1] Cf. art. COSMOGONY AND COSMOLOGY (Japanese).

The female deity thereupon spoke first and exclaimed, 'How delightful! a lovely youth!' The male deity was displeased at the woman for having spoken first, so they went round the pillar a second time; and, having met anew, the male deity spoke first and said, 'How delightful! a lovely maiden!' Thereupon they became united as husband and wife. Another account says that, in consequence of the ill-luck produced by the female deity having been the first to speak, the child which was born to them was a leech, which they placed in a reed-boat and sent adrift. The author of this story probably had in mind an ancient marriage rite. The house built by them is the hut specially erected by the ancient Japanese for the consummation of a marriage. Izanagi and Izanami then proceeded to procreate the various islands of Japan, the deity of trees, the deity of herbs and grasses, the sun-goddess, the moon-god, the god *Susa no wo* (by one account), the earth-goddess, the water-goddess, the wind-gods, the food-goddess, the fire-god, and others. In giving birth to the last-named deity, Izanami was injured so that she died. Izanagi, in his rage and grief, drew his sword and cut the newborn fire-god into pieces, a number of other deities being generated by his doing so.

On her death, Izanami went to the land of Yomi or Hades. She was followed thither by her husband. But he was too late to bring her back, as she had already eaten of the cooking-furnaces of Yomi. She forbade him to look at her, but he disregarded her prayer. Breaking off the end-tooth of the comb which he had in his hair, he made of it a torch, and looked in where his wife was lying. Her body was already putrid and swarmed with maggots, and the 'Eight Thunders' had been generated in various parts of it. Izanami was enraged at her husband for exposing her nakedness, and sent the 'Eight Thunders' and the 'Ugly Females' of Yomi to attack him. Izanagi took to flight and used various expedients to delay his pursuers. He first flung down his head-dress. It became changed to grapes, which the 'Ugly Females' stopped to gather and eat. Then he threw down his comb. It turned into bamboo-shoots, which the 'Ugly Females' pulled up and ate before continuing their pursuit. Izanami herself overtook him at the 'Even Pass of Yomi,' where the formula of divorce was pronounced by Izanagi, and their final parting took place. On returning from Yomi, Izanagi's first care was to bathe in the sea, in order to purify himself from the pollutions which he had contracted by his visit to the Land of the Dead. A number of deities were generated by this process. The sun-goddess was born from the washing of his left eye, and the moon-god from that of his right, while *Susa no wo* (the rain-storm) was generated from the washing of his nose. To the sun-goddess Izanagi gave charge of the 'Plain of High-Heaven,' and to the moon-god was allotted the realm of Night. Susa no wo was at first appointed to rule the sea; but he preferred to rejoin his deceased mother Izanami, and was therefore made the Lord of Ne-no-kuni, *i.e.* the Root or Nether Country, another name for the Land of Yomi. Susa no wo, before proceeding to take up his charge as Ruler of the Nether Region, ascended to Heaven to take leave of his elder sister the sun-goddess. By reason of the fierceness of his divine nature, there was a commotion in the sea, and the hills and mountains groaned aloud as he passed upwards. The sun-goddess, in alarm, arrayed herself in manly garb, and confronted her brother armed with sword and bow and arrows. The pair stood face to face on opposite sides of the River of Heaven. Susa no wo then assured his sister of the purity of his intentions, and proposed to her that they should each produce children by biting off and crunching parts of the jewels and swords which they wore and blowing away the fragments. Eight children born in this way were worshipped in after-times as the Hachōji or eight princely children. From one of them was descended Hoho no Ninigi, who came down from Heaven to rule the world (*i.e.* Japan), and became the ancestor of Jimmu Tennō, the first Mikado.

Susa no wo's subsequent proceedings were very rude and unseemly. He broke down the divisions between the rice-fields belonging to his sister, sowed them over again, let loose in them the piebald colt of Heaven, and committed nuisances in the hall where she was celebrating the solemn festival of firstfruits. The climax to his misdeeds was to flay a piebald colt of Heaven and to fling it into the sacred weaving-hall where the sun-goddess was engaged in weaving the garments of the deities. She was so deeply indignant at this last insult that she entered the Rock-cave of Heaven and left the world to darkness. The retirement of the sun-goddess to the Rock-cave of Heaven produced great consternation among the heavenly deities. They met on the dry bed of the River of Heaven (the Milky Way) and took counsel how they should entice her from her seclusion. By the advice of *Omoi-kane no Mikoto* ('the thought-combiner' or 'counsellor-deity'), the long-singing birds of the Eternal Land (cocks) were made to utter their prolonged cry before the door of the cave. *Koyane no Mikoto*, ancestor of the Nakatomi, and *Futo-dama no Mikoto*, ancestor of the Imbe, dug up by the roots a five-hundred-branched true Sakaki tree of Heaven, and hung on its higher branches strings of jewels, on its middle branches a mirror, and on its lower branches pieces of cloth. Then they recited their liturgy in her honour. Moreover, *Ame no Uzume* ('the dread female of Heaven') arrayed herself in a fantastic manner and, standing on a tub which resounded when she stamped upon it, performed a (not very decent) mimic dance and gave forth an inspired utterance. The sun-goddess wondered how Ame no Uzume and the other gods could be so jolly while the world was wrapped in complete darkness, and peeped out from the half-opened door of the cave. She was at once seized by *Ta-jikara no wo* ('male of hand-strength') and prevented by main force from re-entering, to the great joy of all the deities.

Susa no wo was then tried by a council of gods, who mulcted him in a fine of a thousand tables of purification-offerings. They also pulled out the nails of his fingers and toes, and banished him to the land of Yomi. Finally, *Ame no Koyane*, the ancestor of the Nakatomi, recited his *Ōharai* or great purification liturgy. After his banishment Susa no wo went to the province of Idzumo. Here, like another Perseus, he slew the eight-headed serpent of Koshi (having first made him drunk) and delivered his intended victim, a young maiden who subsequently became his wife. Eventually he entered the Nether Land.

Susa no wo had 181 children. One of these was *Oho-na-mochi* ('great-name-possessor'), also called *Oho-kuni-nushi* ('great-country-master'). He dwelt in Idzumo, and with the aid of his *mitama* reduced to order this part of Japan. Associated with him was the dwarf-deity *Sukuna-bikona*, who came floating over the sea in a tiny boat, clothed in bird-skins. To these two is attributed the origin of the art of medicine and of charms against the powers of evil. The dynasty of Susa no wo was not recognized by the Gods of Heaven, who sent down several other deities to subdue and govern the world, *i.e.* Japan. Ultimately Oho-na-mochi and his son *Koto-shiro-nushi* ('thing-know-master,' or 'governor') agreed to yield the government to *Hoho no Ninigi,* a grandchild of the sun-goddess, who accordingly descended to earth on a mountain in the western island of Kiushiu. He was attended by the ancestors of the five *be,* or hereditary government corporations, viz. the Nakatomi, the Imbe, the Sarume, the mirror-makers' *be,* and the jewellers' *be,* to which some accounts add several others.

Hoho no Ninigi took to wife the daughter of a deity whom he found there. When the time came for her delivery, she shut herself up in a doorless shed, which, on the birth of her three children, she set fire to, with the object of clearing herself from certain suspicions which her husband had entertained of her fidelity. 'If,' said she, 'the children are really the offspring of the Heavenly Grandchild, the fire cannot harm them.' The children and their mother came forth unhurt, and were thereupon recognized by Hoho no Ninigi as his true offspring and wife. One of these children, named *Hohodemi,* was a hunter. He exchanged his bow and arrows for the fish-hook of his elder brother, but lost the latter in the sea. This led to his visiting the palace of the sea-god *Toyotama-hiko,* and marrying his daughter. A child of this union was the father of Jimmu Tennō, the first human sovereign of Japan. With him history is supposed to begin. But in reality the annals of Japan for nearly a thousand years longer are deeply permeated by legend.

7. The pantheon.—(i.) *NATURE-GODS.*—(*a*) *The sun-goddess* is the most eminent of the Shinto deities. She is called the Ruler of Heaven, wears royal insignia, and is surrounded by a court of ministers and functionaries. Yet she is hardly what we should call a Supreme Deity. All important celestial matters are determined not by her fiat, but by a council of the gods. The sea and the land of Yomi are beyond her jurisdiction. Her Japanese name is *Ama-terasu no Oho-kami* ('the Heaven-shining Great Deity'). She is also called *Ama-terasu hirume* ('Heaven-shining-sun-female'), or, more briefly, *Hirume.* Another name is *Ama-terasu mi oya* ('Heaven-shining-august-parent'). In modern times Tenshō-daijin, the Chinese equivalent of Ama-terasu no Oho-kami, is more common. Under this name her solar quality is practically forgotten, and she is simply a great deity whose seat is at Ise. The *shintai* or material token of the sun-goddess is a mirror, called the *yata-kagami* ('eight-hand-mirror') or *hi-gata no kagami* ('sun-form-mirror'). It is kept in a box in the great shrine of Ise, and is treated with the greatest reverence, being even spoken of as 'the great God of Ise.'

The *yata-garasu,* or 'eight-hand-crow,' is a bird sacred to the sun. It is identified with the Chinese *yang-wu,* a three-legged crow of a red colour which inhabits the sun. Ama-terasu is only one of many solar deities mentioned in the old records. *Waka-hirume* ('young-sun-female,' probably the morning sun) and *Hiruko* ('sun-youth') may be given as examples. *Hiruko* may also mean 'leech-child.' Hence the legend according to which the first child of Izanagi and Izanami was a leech.

Susa no wo, a name which has been interpreted variously as the 'male of Susa' (a place where he was worshipped), and as the 'impetuous male,' has been the subject of much speculation. Dr. Buckley of Chicago has shown that he is a personification of the rain-storm. This explains the violent character given to him in myth, and his quarrel with the sun-goddess. Hirata identifies him with the moon-god; and it is true that myth often associates the darkness of the storm with the gloom of night—represented by its presiding deity, the moon. This view may be correct; but if so, it had been forgotten in the time of the *Kojiki* and *Nihongi,* which distinguish clearly between the moon-god and Susa no wo. Susa no wo appears in a beneficent aspect as the rescuer of a Japanese Andromeda from a great serpent, and as the provider of fruit and other useful trees for mankind.

Tsukiyomi, the moon-god, is not one of the greater gods of Japan. The name means 'moon-darkness,' or perhaps 'moon-reckoner.' There is a myth in which he is represented as the murderer of the food-goddess, and therefore alienated from his sister, the sun-goddess. His *shintai* is a mirror. Star-worship is hardly known in Shinto.

(*b*) *Earth-worship.*—There are several cases in which the earth is worshipped directly, without attributing to it sex or distinct personality, or the addition of name or myth. The *Ji-matsuri* ('earth-festival') is a ceremony by which it is sought to propitiate a plot of ground selected for building or for bringing under cultivation. A secondary phase of earth-worship is where the deity is a god who rules, or who has made the country. Oho-na-mochi, the great god of Idzumo, is the chief deity of this class. His name means 'great-name-possessor,' a merely honorific title. He is also called *Oho-kuni-nushi* ('great-land-master'), or *Oho-kuni-dama* ('great-land-spirit'). His temple ranks next in importance after the shrines of Ise, and is supposed to be visited by all the other gods annually in the tenth month. His *shintai* is a necklace of jewels.

(*c*) *Mountain-gods.*—Most mountains have their deity, but few have more than a local importance. The deity of Fujiyama, *Sengensama,* and that of Mount Aso in the province of Higo are the best known.

(*d*) *Sea-gods.*—A triplet of sea-gods was produced by Izanagi when he washed in the sea after his return from Yomi. They are named *Soko-tsu wata-dzu-mi* ('bottom-sea-body'), *Naka-tsu wata-dzu-mi* ('middle-sea-body'), and *Uha-tsu wata-dzu-mi* ('upper-sea-body'). They are frequently spoken of and depicted as if they were only one deity. Their chief shrine is at Sumiyoshi, near Osaka. They are prayed to for prosperous voyages.

(*e*) *River-gods* have no individual names. They are called generically *Midzuchi* or 'water-father.' As in other countries, they are usually conceived of as having the form of snakes or dragons. Two rain-gods are mentioned in the *Nihongi.* They have also dragon-form. But any god may be prayed to for rain. All wells are more or less deified. Offerings are made at the present day to the house-well on the morning of New Year's day. The wells from which water is drawn for the great ceremonies of Shinto are worshipped. The element of water is also deified on account of its use in sacrifice.

(*f*) A *wind-god* is mentioned in the *Nihongi* as having been produced from Izanagi's breath, but the *norito* or rituals recognize two wind-gods, male and female. They were much prayed to for good harvests.

(*g*) The *fire-god, Kagutsuchi* ('radiant father') or *Ho-musubi* ('fire-growth'), is worshipped at Atago, a hill near Kioto, and other places. He is supposed to protect against conflagrations. *Futsu nushi* is probably another fire-deity. He it was who was sent down from Heaven to prepare Japan for the advent of Hoho no Ninigi, the grandchild of the sun-goddess. His chief shrine is at Kadori in Eastern Japan. Associated with him in myth and worship is a god called *Take-mika-tsuchi,* whose shrine is at Kashima, also on the east coast. Take-mika-tsuchi ('brave-dread-father') is a personification of thunder. But in modern times both these gods are universally recognized as *war-*

deities. Futsu nushi's material token or *shintai* is a sword. There is a separate worship of *thunder* under the name of *Naru-kami*, or the 'sounding-god.' The domestic *cooking-furnace* is worshipped as a god all over Japan. Sometimes it is a single deity, sometimes a married pair. There is no *shintai.* The furnace *is* the deity.

(*h*) Next after the sun-goddess, the *goddess of food* is the most important deity of Shinto. To her the outer shrine of Ise is dedicated. She is called *Uke-mochi* ('food-possessor'), or *Uka no mitama* ('spirit of food'), with numerous aliases. The *sake-god* is sometimes identified with the food-goddess (*sake* is brewed from rice), and at others is a distinct deity. Notwithstanding the difference of sex, *Inari* or the rice-god may be regarded as a variant of *Uke-mochi.* Every village and many private houses have small shrines in honour of him. He grants his worshippers agricultural prosperity; but, as is so often the case with nature-deities, his functions have been extended so as to cover many things which have nothing to do with grain, such as the restoration of stolen property, wealth, domestic harmony, etc. The *shintai* varies. Very often it is a round stone, which has the advantages of being cheap and durable. The fox is associated with him as his messenger or servant, and the vulgar regard the figures of this animal which are set up before his shrine as the deity himself.

(*i*) *Tree-gods.*—Individual trees of great age and size are universally worshipped. A *Kami-gi* ('god-tree') is frequently planted before shrines, not, however, as a god, but as an offering. The older records mention a god of trees named *Kukunochi* ('trees-father'), and a deity of herbs and grasses called *Kaya no hime* ('lady of reeds'). These gods were prayed to before cutting wood or reeds for building or thatching.

(*j*) The *house* is deified, sometimes as one, sometimes as two, deities. A special sanctity attaches to the central pillar—corresponding to our 'king-post.' There is also a god of the *privy* and of the *gate.* The latter had some importance in the palace. One of the *norito* is addressed to him or them—the number is uncertain.

Izanagi and Izanami, who occupy so conspicuous a place in myth, are in ritual comparatively unimportant deities. The present writer regards them as personifications of the Chinese *yin* and *yang*, or positive and negative principles of nature. They are therefore of later date than the gods whose parents they are feigned to be. *Musubi*, the god of growth, represents the conception of a god immanent in the Universe, and not, like Izanagi and Izanami, external to it. Musubi became split up into two deities, *Kami-musubi* ('divine growth') and *Taka-musubi* ('high growth'), supposed by some to be a married pair. Subsequently a still further subdivision took place. Their worship at one time flourished, but is now almost extinct.

(ii.) *MAN-GODS.*—*Take minagata*, the very popular deity of Suwa in the province of Shinano, is one of the few ancient gods who, with some probability, may be assigned to the class of deified individual men. He was a son of Oho-na-mochi, who refused allegiance to the sun-goddess's grandchild, and fled to Shinano, where he was afterwards worshipped. The present high priests are regarded as his descendants and incarnations. There is no shrine, but only a rock-cave—perhaps a dolmen. The war-god *Hachiman* is also stated to be a human being deified, viz. the Mikado Ôjin, a very legendary personage. The authority is an oracle delivered hundreds of years after his death. This god is unknown to the Shinto of the *Kojiki* and the *Nihongi.* Other legendary heroes who were deified in subsequent times are: *Jimmu*, the first Mikado; *Jingo*, the empress who is supposed to have conquered Korea; her counsellor, *Takechi no Sukune*; and *Yamato-dake*, the hero-prince who subdued eastern Japan. The best known indubitable example of a deified human being is *Temmangu*, who presides over learning and caligraphy, and is the special god of schoolboys and pedagogues. He was a statesman, born A.D. 845. Owing to slanderous accusations by a rival, he was exiled to Kiushiu, where he died. Great calamities followed. To propitiate his angry ghost, a cult was instituted in his honour, which continues to this day. It may be suspected that the worship of Confucius in China had much to do with that of Temmangu in Japan.

The man-gods of the older Shinto are not deified individuals, but types. The sun-goddess is represented as attended by the gods of the five *be* or hereditary government corporations. These included Koyane, the so-called ancestor, but really a type, of the Nakatomi priestly gild; Futo-dama ('great offering'), the ancestor of the Imbe who prepared the sacrificial offerings; and Toyotama ('rich-jewel'), the ancestor of the jewel-makers. *Sukuna-bikona*, a dwarf deity who is associated with Oho-na-mochi in worship and myth, is probably also a deified type—a sort of Æsculapius or father of medicine.

The *phallic deities* are the chief representatives of the class of deified human qualities. Originally a symbol of the procreative power, the phallus came to represent lusty animal vigour generally, the foe to death and disease. Hence its use as a magical appliance to repel pestilence. It is mainly in this prophylactic capacity that it figures in Shinto, where it is deified under the name of *Kunado no kami* ('god of the come-not place'), and has a special ritual. Kunado no kami had no shrines, but in the shape of a natural phalloid boulder or carved wooden pillar was worshipped by the roadside, especially at cross-ways. Hence he came to be regarded as the god of roads and the guide and protector of travellers. The honours still paid to the *Dōsojin* ('road-ancestor-deity') are a survival of this cult, which, in spite of official discouragement, is not quite extinct in eastern Japan. The kteis is represented by the peach, the bean, and the rice-grain, which are used magically to keep off diseases or—what is the same thing—demons. The peach flung by Izanagi to drive back the 'Thunders' which pursued him from Yomi was deified for its services.

8. Priesthood.—Herbert Spencer's saying (*Sociology*) that 'in early stages of social evolution the secular and the sacred are but little distinguished' is well illustrated by Shinto. The *Jingikwan*, or 'department of religion,' whose officers discharged the chief religious functions of State Shinto, was simply a Government bureau like any other, though it took precedence of the rest, and its proceedings were as much matters of State as the collection of taxes or the administration of justice. The very word *matsurigoto* ('government') is only another form of *matsuri* ('a religious festival'). Hirata says that 'the worship of the gods is the source of Government, nay, it *is* Government.'

The chief priest of Shinto is the Mikado himself. In some of the most important ceremonies he takes the leading part. But from the most ancient times his religious functions have been delegated. In the Jimmu Tennō legend we are told of a *michi no omi*, or 'Minister of the Way,' who acted as 'ruler of a festival' in honour of the god Taka-mi-musubi. The chief vicars of the Mikado were the family, or rather hereditary corporation, called the Nakatomi, of which the Fujiwara, so famous in later times for the number of poets, statesmen, and empresses which it furnished, was a branch. The Nakatomi held the chief offices of the Jingikwan, and exercised a control over the local priesthood, if we may call them so. The *Imbe* were another hereditary corporation. Their chief business was to prepare the offerings for the State ceremonies. The name *Imi-be*, or 'religious purity department,' has reference to the care with which they avoided all ritual impurity in doing so. The *urabe*, or diviners, correspond to the Roman college of augurs. Their business was to divine, by means of the marks on a scorched tortoise-shell or deer's shoulder-blade, all matters which might be referred to them by the higher religious officials. The priests of local shrines were called *Kannushi*, that is, *Kami-nushi* or 'God-master.' Their duty was to recite the usual prayers, and to attend to the repairs of the shrine. The *Kannushi* are not a caste, though some of the most important posts are usually held by Nakatomi. They are not celibates, and wear their distinctive dress only when engaged in worship. Even this is not a sacerdotal costume, but only an old official garb of the Mikado's court.

There were several kinds of priestesses. The highest in rank was the *saiwō*, a princess of the Imperial blood, who was consecrated at the beginning of every reign to the service of the sun-goddess at Ise. A similar appointment was made to the shrine of Kamo near Kioto, where the Mikado's *ujigami* ('surname-god') was worshipped. Both these offices have long been extinct. At all the principal shrines young girls called *Kamu no Ko* ('God-child') or *miko* are consecrated to the service of the gods. They dance the *kagura*, cook the food for offerings, and occasionally become the medium of inspired communications. The greater shrines had also *Kami-be* attached to them. These were peasants who tilled the glebe-lands. Recent statistics give the number of Shinto priests as 14,766. Their duties are light and their emoluments scanty. Many of them have other sources of income.

9. Worship.—In Shinto, as in other religions, the forms of divine worship are, with scarcely an exception, adaptations of the forms of respect to living men. The most common of these is obeisance. The Shinto worshipper bows twice before and after he makes his offering. Kneeling is also known. Clapping hands, primarily a sign of joy, became first a general form of respect to sovereigns and others. More recently it has been confined to divine worship. The number of hand-clappings is minutely prescribed in the rituals. Offerings 'in token of respect,' as one of the rituals has it, by way of bargain for future blessings, or as a ransom for ceremonial shortcomings, consisted of food or drink, as rice, salt, *sake*, flesh, fish, fruit, vegetables, etc.; offerings of clothing, whether in the shape of woven fabrics, of yarn, or of garments, of hemp, and mulberry-bark fibre or silk, held a very important place. They were represented in later times by the *ohonusa* or 'great offerings,' which consisted of two wands placed side by side with hempen fibre depending from the one and strips of paper from the other. The latter are made of mulberry-bark fibre, and represent the cloth which was formerly made of that material. The well-known *gohei*, which consist of one wand with paper strips attached to it, are a simplification of the *ohonusa*. The assertion so often made, that the white colour of the paper is symbolical of purity, has no foundation. The *gohei* are in modern times the objects of much superstition. The god on ceremonial occasions is supposed to descend into the *gohei*; they are flourished in order to avert evil influences, and even placed in the domestic shrine and worshipped. *Gohei-katsugi* ('*gohei*-bearer') is the Japanese phrase for a superstitious man. Swords, jewels, and mirrors are offerings of a more permanent character. The *shintai*, which in so many cases consist of these objects, were doubtless originally simply offerings. *Human sacrifice* formed no part of the Shinto State religion as described in the ancient records. But there is evidence that such offerings were not unknown, especially to the river-gods. In the *Yengishiki* lists of offerings we also find mention of agricultural implements, slaves, horses, and carriages, or rather palanquins.

10. Shrines.—The Shinto shrine is by no means a costly edifice. Many of the smaller ones are quite portable. In 771 a 'greater shrine' had only 18 feet frontage. The more important shrines have usually a number of smaller edifices attached to them, such as a gallery of votive pictures, a small oratory where the envoy of the Mikado performs his devotions, a stage for the *kagura* or sacred pantomimes, and *massha* or shrines for dependent or associated deities. The *Yengishiki* enumerates 3132 official shrines. At the present day there are nearly 200,000 Shinto shrines in Japan, of which but a small proportion have priests or revenues. The well-known *tori-i* or honorary gateway seen before them is no doubt an imitation of the Chinese *pailoo* and the Indian *turan*. It is not mentioned in the *Kojiki* or the *Nihongi*.

11. Prayer.[1]—Of private individual prayer there is little mention in the old records. But a considerable collection of the religious formulæ called *norito*, read at festivals and other occasions by officials on behalf of the Mikado, have come down to us from a great but unknown antiquity. They are addressed sometimes to individual deities, sometimes to special categories of deities, and sometimes to the gods generally. They comprise petitions for rain, for good harvests, for preservation from earthquake and conflagration, for children, for health and long life to the sovereign, and peace and prosperity to the empire. Moral and spiritual blessings, or happiness in a future state, are undreamt of. There are also announcements of the appointment of a priestess, or of the beginning of a new reign. At the present day the Shinto gods are prayed to when a new piece of ground is reclaimed, on building a house or sowing a rice-field. There are prayers for prosperity in trade and for domestic happiness, making under Buddhist influence vows to give up drink, gambling or profligacy, thanking for escape from shipwreck or other danger.

12. Rank of deities. — In the 7th century a system of official ranks was introduced into Japan from China, and applied to gods as well as men. A curious result was that many gods stood lower in the hierarchy than the higher grades of officials. There is a case of a volcano-god being propitiated with the equivalent of a D.S.O. In the 11th and 12th cents. there were wholesale promotions of deities. A few of the greater deities, as the sun-goddess and food-goddess, did not share in these honours.

13. Kagura is a pantomimic dance commemorating some incident of the mythical narrative. Important shrines have stages and corps of girl dancers for this purpose.

14. Pilgrimages[2] are common to Ise, where are the shrines of the sun-goddess and food-goddess, Idzumo (Oho-na-mochi and Susa no wo), and to various mountains, as Fujiyama, Nantai, Kompira, etc.

[1] See art. PRAYER (Japanese).
[2] See art. PILGRIMAGE (Japanese).

15. Purity and morals.[1]—It cannot be doubted that the ancient Japanese had some ideas of morality. There is evidence that theft, lying, and adultery were condemned by them. But there is scarcely anything in Shinto by way of a moral code. There is no direct moral teaching in its sacred books. A schedule of offences against the gods, to absolve which the ceremony of 'Great Purification' was performed twice a year, enumerates: incest (within narrow limits of relationship), bestiality, wounding, witchcraft, and certain interferences with agricultural operations. The other offences mentioned are of a purely ceremonial character. Shinto therefore would appear to be an exception to the rule stated by Pfleiderer (*Philosophy of Religion*), that 'the beginnings of all social customs and legal ordinances are directly derived from religion.' The ceremonial purity of Shinto greatly resembles that of the Mosaic dispensation. Actual personal dirt was considered disrespectful to the deities, and hence bathing and putting on fresh garments are constantly prescribed among the preliminaries of worship. The consummation of a marriage produced defilement, and a separate hut was built for this purpose so that the dwelling might not be rendered unclean. Shinto has no marriage ceremony. There is a modern custom of sousing with buckets of water on New Year's day men who have been married during the previous year. Virgins were selected as priestesses. There is a case of a princess's appointment as such being cancelled for unchastity. Menstruation and childbirth caused uncleanness. The death of a relative, pronouncing or executing a capital sentence, touching a dead body, eating food prepared in a house of mourning, disease, wounds, leprosy, or sores involved various degrees of ritual impurity. These ideas were inconsistent with religious rites at funerals. The Shinto burial service, much heard of during the Russo-Japanese war, is a modern innovation, dating after the Restoration of 1868. Eating flesh was in ancient times not regarded as causing uncleanness, but later, under Buddhist influence, it became so. Impure food communicated its uncleanness to the fire with which it had been cooked. To avoid chances of such impurity, fire was made afresh with a fire-drill for use in the more important sacrifices. Certain calamities, such as snake-bite and the stroke of lightning, were regarded as indicating the displeasure of the gods, and therefore as unfitting the victim for their service. At one time when a man's house was destroyed by fire he became temporarily unclean. There was a special avoidance (*imi*) of impure things for a specified term in preparation for the festivals.

Lustration, the most natural and universal means of restoring purity, is well known in Japan. The use of salt is another. Spitting (there was a god of spittle) is a symbolical expulsion of impurity. Breathing on an object, such as a garment or a human figure, which is then cast into the sea, has the same result. The idea of ransom is also implied in the last ceremony.

16. Ceremonies.[2]—These are combinations of the elements of worship described above. The greatest Shinto ceremony is the *Ohonihe* or *Daijowe*, which corresponds to our coronation. It is the solemn religious sanction of the Mikado's sovereignty. The kernel of this rite was the offering by the Mikado in person to the gods, represented by a cushion, of rice and *sake*, which were then partaken of by himself and subsequently by the court. The rice came from two provinces selected by divination. Everything in the Ohonihe ceremony was in duplicate, so that, if one part was vitiated by some accidental impurity, the other might escape. *Urabe* or diviners from the capital superintended the ingathering of the rice, which was done with great ceremony by a staff of local officials. It was then brought to the capital, where special buildings had been erected for its reception and for the accommodation of the very numerous officials concerned. Here, too, everything was done in duplicate. The ceremony included frequent purifications, prayers to the eight gods, which included amongst others the harvest-gods, the god of growth, and the food-goddess, and the recital of 'ancient words' and *norito* of blessing.

The *Nihi-name* or 'new tasting,' when the rice of the new season was first partaken of, was the same as the Ohonihe, except that it was performed annually and with much less pomp. Something of the same kind was performed by the local officials and also by the people. Conscientious persons would not eat the new rice until after this celebration. The *Ahimbe* and *Kanname* were different forms of the same ceremony. The festival of *Hirano* is believed to have been in honour of Image no Kami ('the goddess of new food') and of the gods of the kitchen boiler and cooking-pan. In later times the sun-goddess, the hero Yamato-dake, and the Mikados Chiuai and Nintoku were recognized as the deities of Hirano.

The *Toshigohi* ('praying for harvest') was a very important festival. It was in honour practically of all the gods, and was celebrated in the chapel of the Imperial palace by a Nakatomi as representing the Mikado.

The *Tsukinami* is described as a 'thanksgiving service for the protecting care of the gods.' The name means 'monthly,' but it was really performed only twice a year. It resembles the Toshigohi.

The *Kiü* ('praying for rain') was addressed to the gods of 85 shrines, and included the usual offerings of cloth-stuffs. To a few a black horse was offered in addition, no doubt symbolical of the black clouds which usher in rain.

Other ceremonies were for 'the offering of clothing' to the sun-goddess at Ise, on the occasion of the rebuilding of the Ise shrines; for 'blessing the great palace'; in honour of the sacred mirror preserved in the palace; and for 'calming the august spirit,' in other words, for long life to the Mikado.

The *Ohoharahi* or 'Great Purification' ceremony, by which the nation was solemnly absolved twice a year from its ceremonial sins, was one of the most important and ancient of the Shinto rites. It is mentioned in the *Nihongi* under the date A.D. 200, which, although legendary, implies a great antiquity. The *Ohoharahi* consisted in the recital by a Nakatomi on behalf of the Mikado of a *norito*, which recounts the divine origin of the dynasty and the authority given to the sovereign to absolve his people from all offences to be committed by them. These offences are enumerated and their absolution is declared:

> 'As the many-piled clouds of Heaven are scattered by the breath of the Wind-Gods: as the morning breezes and the evening breezes dissipate the dense morning vapours and the dense evening vapours: as a huge ship, moored in a great harbour, casting off its stern-moorings, casting off its bow-moorings, drives forth into the great sea-plain: as yonder thick brushwood is smitten and cleared away by the sharp sickle forged in the fire,—so shall all offences be utterly annulled.'

The reading of this formula was accompanied by the offering of ransom-objects, which after the ceremony were taken away and thrown into a river, where certain gods took delivery of them and dispatched them to the sea. Thence they were ultimately transferred to the land of Yomi. In the case of the purification of the offences of individuals, the culprit was obliged to supply the needful offerings, which thus became the equivalent of a fine.

[1] Cf. artt. PURIFICATION (Japanese), ETHICS AND MORALITY (Japanese).
[2] Cf. art. MAGIC (Japanese).

The *Michiahe* ceremony was in honour of the phallic Sahe no Kami (preventive or prophylactic deities). The *norito* of this rite called upon them to prevent evil spirits (diseases personified) from entering the capital from the Nether country, *i.e.* the land of Yomi. Offerings of cloth-stuffs and food are made to them for this purpose.

The *Mikado no Matsuri*, or festival of the august gate, was addressed to the guardian deities of the palace gates, adjuring them to prevent the entrance of noxious things.

The *Hoshidzume* ('fire-quieting') ceremony was performed on the last day of the sixth and twelfth months. The *Urabe* kindled a fire by means of a fire-drill, and read a *norito* in which the fire-god was reminded of the divine authority of the Mikado, and of the means provided for his coercion and control by his mother Izanami. This intimidation is followed by bribery: 'To the end that thou mayest control thy transports against the Palace of the Sovran grandchild, I offer thee bright cloth,' etc.

The above by no means exhausts the list of Shinto ceremonies. In modern times there are many local celebrations much resembling in character the carnivals of Southern Europe. Fun and jollity are more prominent here than religion.

17. **Magic.**[1]—There are two kinds of magic in Japan, the religious and the non-religious. The latter is probably the first in order of time. It is closely associated with medicine. Sometimes a magical procedure, non-religious in itself, acquires a religious character by being represented as taught or practised by a god. The novelist Bakin, writing early in the 19th century, applies the term *majinai* ('magic') indiscriminately to exposing books in the sun to keep away bookworms, to curing a toothache by turning over a pebble on the road, and to swallowing the ashes of an old almanac as an antidote to poisonous fish. 'If,' he says, 'the master of a house before going to bed goes round calling out, "Beware of fire," the spirit of the words will fill the house, and it will be preserved against fire and robbery.' The principle of 'sympathetic magic,' described in Frazer's *Golden Bough*, is illustrated by the case of a round stone (supposed to be the *shintai* of a rainfall-god) which causes rain to fall when water is poured on it. Whistling to raise the wind is another example. If a married woman is childless, the old women of the neighbourhood assemble and go through the form of delivering her of a child, represented by a doll. Relief from local ailments is obtained by rubbing the corresponding part of a god's image. The well-known witchcraft of ill-treating a figure of the intended victim with the intention of making him suffer accordingly is common in Japan, and may be practised either with or without the assistance of a deity. There are no pacts with demons or coercion of spirits in the older Shinto literature.

The magical power of the symbol, as if it possessed some of the actual powers of the thing it represents, is also exemplified. Roof-tiles are impressed with a pattern of bubbles—suggestive of water—as a preventative against fire. The talismans used for various purposes may have been originally symbols, though we cannot now trace their origin. The sea-god gave Hohodemi a tide-flowing and a tide-ebbing jewel, by which he could make the tide flow and ebb at pleasure. The waving of a magic scarf had the effect of keeping off snakes and centipedes. The modern witch twangs a small bow in her magical summoning of spirits. The *shime-nawa*, a cord made of rice-straw which has been pulled up by the roots, is well known as a preventative of evil spirits. It is suspended before shrines, round sacred trees, and at the New Year in front of every dwelling-house. Some superstitious people wear one on their persons. The magic use of set forms of speech independent of their meaning is illustrated by the recital of the numerals from one to ten as a safeguard against disease. A Japanese in a thunderstorm calls out, *Kuhabara*! ('Mulberry grove!'). Here, however, the idea is to suggest to the thunder-god that the place is a mulberry grove—which is never struck by lightning. Some magic is condemned by Shinto, not for its want of efficacy, but for the evil purposes to which it was put.

[1] Cf. art. MAGIC (Japanese).

Divination[1] is magic which has the special purpose of revealing the unknown. It may be either religious, or, like our palmistry, non-religious. The modern Japanese writer Hirata defines it as 'respectfully inquiring the heart of the gods.' The 'Greater Divination,' practised in the olden times, consisted in drawing conclusions according to certain rules from the lines which appear in a deer's shoulder-blade when scorched by fire—a practice known to the Chinese, Kalmuks, the ancient Greeks and Germans, and even in Scotland, where it is called 'reading the speal.' In later times a tortoise-shell was substituted for the deer's shoulder-blade. The religious element of this divination consisted in a prayer to Koyane, the diviner's god, to grant a true result of the procedure. *Tsuji-ura* ('cross-roads divination') was performed by going out to the highway, planting a stick to represent Kunado, the phallic deity of roads, and then interpreting the casual utterances of the passers-by as an answer. The *mikayu-ura* ('august-gruel-divination') consisted in plunging reeds into a gruel made of rice and red beans, and divining from the way in which the rice grains entered the reeds the crops which it would be best to sow. *Caldron-divination* predicts good or ill fortune from the sound made by a boiling caldron. *Omens* are frequently mentioned in the old histories. Earthquakes, floods, and storms were supposed to portend war. White animals and three-legged birds were lucky. The *ordeal* of boiling water is frequently mentioned. *Dreams* reveal the future; but, like Pharaoh's, they usually require interpretation.

18. **Inspiration.**—We have no record of the circumstances under which such grains of divine truth as Shinto contains became known to the Japanese. Most Shinto oracles, however well intended, bear the plain stamp of imposture. Inspiration is called in Japanese *kangakari* ('God-attach'). This term implies that the god takes possession of the prophet, or oftener prophetess, and uses him or her as a mouth-piece. The oracles were very often used for political purposes. The empress Jingō was inspired by a god to advise her husband to invade Korea. By another ancient oracle, the sun-goddess directed that a shrine should be erected to her in Ise. In A.D. 672 warning was given by certain gods of the approach of a hostile army. The deities concerned were rewarded by an increase of rank. In A.D. 1031 certain abuses in the management of the Ise shrines were condemned by a virgin priestess when in an inspired condition. The Buddhist priests who converted Shinto to their own purposes made large use of oracles. The circumstances as noted leave no doubt that by *kangakari* or inspiration the hypnotic trance is meant. It is still practised in Japan. The *miko*, or young virgins attached to the shrines, give inspired utterances; and there are strolling mediums of indifferent character who will fall into a hypnotic state, real or assumed, and for a trifle communicate

[1] Cf. art. DIVINATION (Japanese).

messages to their clients from any gods or spirits of deceased men that may be desired.

19. Later history.—Shinto and Buddhism at first held aloof from one another, or showed a mutual antagonism. But in the 8th cent. the Mikado Shomu, when about to found the Buddhist temple of Tōdaji at Nara, sent a Buddhist priest named Gyōgi to the shrine of the sun-goddess at Ise with a present of a Buddhist relic. Gyōgi brought back an oracle, which was interpreted to mean that the sun-goddess identified herself with the Buddha Vairochana—described as the personification of essential *bodhi* and absolute purity. This was the first case in Japan (the same principle had already been applied in China to Lao-tse and Confucius) of the recognition of the *Kami* as Buddhist *avatars* or incarnations. Systematized, it formed the basis of the teaching of a new sect called *Ryōbu* Shintō. Its chief founder was the famous Kōbō Daishi (died A.D. 835), a Buddhist saint to whom is ascribed the invention of the Hiragana Syllabary, and writings and paintings innumerable. The Ryōbu had great vogue down to the end of the 18th century. It is really much more Buddhist than Shinto. The only Shinto deity it gives importance to is Kuni-toko-tachi, a very colourless personage, to whom the *Nihongi* gives the first position in point of time. The *Yui-itsu* Shinto was a branch of the Ryōbu. It was established about the end of the 15th cent. Other sects were the *Deguchi* and *Suwiga* Shinto, both of which arose in the 17th century. The former introduces into Shinto the principles of the *I-king*, a Chinese book of divination, while the latter is penetrated with principles derived from the Chinese Sung dynasty philosophy.

The encroachments of Buddhism were not confined to doctrine. Buddhist priests took charge of all the Shinto shrines except a few of the most important, such as those of Ise and Idzumo. Many elements of Buddhist ceremony were combined with the native rites. The architecture and ornaments of the shrines were given a Buddhist character. For many centuries most of the Mikados, the high priests of Shinto, assumed the Buddhist tonsure. In the 17th cent. there was a great revival of Chinese learning in Japan, much to the neglect of Buddhism, by the educated classes. It reached a climax towards the end of the 18th cent., when a reaction set in, which Mabuchi, Motoöri, and Hirata took advantage of to recall the attention of the nation to the old pure Shinto of the *Kojiki* and the *Nihongi*. They succeeded to some extent, especially in discrediting the Ryōbu and other Buddhist forms of Shinto. But this was in reality a reactionary movement. The older faith was wholly inadequate to meet the spiritual wants of a nation long familiar with the religious thought of India and China—both far richer in spiritual and ethical purport than Shinto. Their propaganda, however, did much to reanimate the old belief in the Mikado's divine descent and authority, and undoubtedly contributed to bring about his restoration in 1868 to his position as a *de facto* sovereign.

In the last century two popular forms of Shinto—so-called—sprang up. One of these is called the *Remmonkyō* ('lotus-gate-doctrine'), because, like the lotus growing in the mud, it remains pure in a wicked world. The other is the *Tenrikyō* ('teaching of the Heavenly Reason'). It has high moral aims. Both these sects have made rapid progress, and claim great numbers of adherents. They are not really Shinto, but owe whatever vitality they possess to elements borrowed from India and China. At the present day, Shinto as a religion is practically extinct. It cannot compete with Buddhism, which has of recent years awakened to new life. And now there is a new and still more formidable rival in the field—Christianity—which has already about 130,000 followers, and is spreading every day. Shinto is kept alive mainly by the popular festivals and pilgrimages, of which religion forms but a small part. To Shinto also belongs the religious element in the cult of the Mikado, and the sensibility to the divine in Nature, which is characteristic of the Japanese nation.

LITERATURE.—The student may safely disregard everything written on Shinto in European languages before Sir E. Satow's articles in *TASJ*, 1874 to 1881. The older authorities, especially Kaempfer, are grossly inaccurate and misleading. *GENERAL*: W. E. Griffis, *The Religions of Japan*, London, 1895; W. G. Aston, *Shinto*, do. 1905; F. Brinkley, *Japan and China: their History, Arts, and Lit.*, London, 1903–04, v.; M. Revon, *Le Shinntoïsme*, Paris, 1905. *MYTHS*: *Kojiki*, tr. B. H. Chamberlain in *TASJ* vol. x. Supplement, 1883–1906; *Nihongi*, tr. W. G. Aston, 2 vols., London, 1896 (*Trans. Jap. Soc. of London*, Suppl. i.); Karl Florenz, 'Japanische Mythologie' in *Mittheilungen der deutschen Gesellschaft für Natur- und Völkerkunde Ostasiens*, Tokyo, 1901. *CEREMONIAL*: 'Ancient Japanese Rituals,' by Satow in *TASJ* vols. vii. and ix., continued by Florenz, vol. xxvii. pt. i. *INSPIRATION*: P. Lowell, *Occult Japan*, Boston, U.S.A., 1895. *LATER HISTORY*: 'Revival of Pure Shinto,' by Satow in *TASJ* vol. iii. Appendix; papers on the Remmonkyô and Tenrikyô sects in *TASJ* vols. xxiii. and xxix. 1. B. H. Chamberlain and W. B. Mason, *Japan*[8], London, 1907 ('Murray's Hand-books for Travellers'), contains a valuable account of religious belief and practice. See also N. Hozumi in *Japan by the Japanese*, ed. A. Stead, London, 1904, p. 282 ff.; G. A. Cobbold, *Religion in Japan*, London. 1894; and F. von Wenckstern, *Bibliography of the Japanese Empire*, Leiden and Tokyo, 1895–1907, pp. 52–59.

W. G. ASTON.

SHIPS AND BOATS.

SHIPS AND BOATS.—The art of navigation often has a religious or magical aspect. The building and launching of vessels may be accompanied by definite rites at various stages of their progress, and ships and boats are often used in ceremonies connected with social events, especially in connexion with death. Boats also come occasionally into rites of divination and medicine. In some places certain ships or boats are sacred or parts of a vessel may have special sanctity. Religious and magical motives often influence the decoration of vessels and may be the cause of features of their construction.

1. Rites of building and launching.—These take place in many parts of the world, varying from such relatively simple ceremonies as accompany the launching of a large vessel among ourselves to prolonged rites accompanying every important stage in the building and preparation of a vessel for use.

In the island of Ambrim in the New Hebrides, ceremonies take place at the felling of the tree from which the canoe is to be made, at the beginning of the hollowing of its trunk, when the outrigger is affixed, and on other occasions. Ceremonial feasts are held every five days during the process of construction, and, when the canoe is ready, it is taken in stages spread over several days to the clearing in the forest where all the important religious rites of the people are held. Both here and on other occasions the maker of the canoe calls upon the ghosts of canoe-makers of former times, asking them to take the canoe under their protection, and certain of the pigs killed during the rites are believed to serve as food for these ghosts.

When the canoe is launched, rites are performed, in one of which a procession marches five times round the canoe, and the contents of coco-nuts are poured over various parts of it. The canoe is taken on ceremonial visits to neighbouring villages, where pigs are killed and ceremonies take place. When the canoe returns after being launched, fruits are thrown at its occupants. This seems to be the degenerate remnant of ceremonial combats which in the neighbouring Banks Islands form an important feature of ceremonial voyages of the canoe round the island where it is made.[1]

In New Caledonia ceremonies take place during the building of a large canoe and also when it is launched, and those who take part in the rites have to be continent.[2] During the construction of a canoe in Eddystone Island, in the Solomons, various rites are performed to give speed and durability. In one of these leaves are hung over the canoe and creepers tied to it, and insects are placed in the caulking, both leaves and insects being used in groups of four. Prayers are uttered similar to those of other religious rites of the island, in which

[1] W. H. R. Rivers, *Hist. of Melanesian Society*, Cambridge, 1914, i. 171.

[2] R. P. Lambert, *Les Missions catholiques*, xii. [1880] 215.

the appeal is probably to the ghosts of former canoe-makers.[1] In several of the Solomon Islands slaves are killed or the heads of enemies are taken in connexion with the building or launching of a new canoe. In Fiji human victims were killed and eaten when a canoe was launched.[2]

In some parts of the Papuan Gulf of New Guinea a beheaded corpse is held over the bow of a new canoe so that it is covered with blood, while elsewhere man-killing raids take place when a new canoe is made, and in some cases the blood of the victim is used to 'paint' the canoe. In the Namara district they kill a pig and a cassowary before killing the human victim. In the north of Papua no human victim is killed, but the canoe is painted red before it is launched. A formula is sung continuously as a canoe is being made and a feast is held on its completion. Conchs are blown at the launching, after which the owner is paddled about sitting on the platform of the canoe. When the Binandele fell a tree from which to make a new canoe for a raid, they address it in the name of a dead man, saying that they are cutting it down to be able to visit his slayers.[3]

In Polynesia the whole process of making a canoe had a ceremonial character. Songs were chanted as it was adzed, and in Tahiti any slip, such as an inaccurate stroke or the use of an implement on the wrong side, would not merely be enough to stop the work temporarily, but might lead to the permanent abandonment of a canoe when almost finished. A fault, even a hesitation, on the part of the canoe-maker in the utterance of his formulas would have the same result.[4] Feasts to gain the favour of the *atua* were held before cutting down the tree from which the canoe was to be made, and at the beginning and at every important stage in its construction. A special canoe was made as an offering to the *atua* and a human victim sacrificed.[5] In the Austral Islands the god Poere, who filled the springs with water, was invoked with offerings of fish when a canoe was launched,[6] and the Maoris performed rites at the launching of a canoe by means of which it was placed under the protection of the gods.[7] In the Hawaiian Islands the choice of a suitable tree was determined by the dream of a priest (*kahuna*) while sleeping before the shrine. Before the tree was cut down, pigs, coco-nuts, fish, and kava were offered to the gods with prayer, and the whole process of building was accompanied by rites.[8]

Among the Kayans of Borneo the operation of boat-building is preceded by the taking of omens, and is liable to be stopped if these are inauspicious.[9]

Similar rites have been recorded from various parts of Africa. Thus among the Baganda an oracle is consulted before the tree to be used in the making of a canoe is felled, and rites take place during this process, one feature of which is the necessity for continence on the part of the makers. The owner together with the builders eats the meat of the sacrificed animal on the shore near the canoe. When it is launched, a hut is built as a shrine for the spirit of the canoe. Goats or fowls are killed so that their blood may run along the keel, and this blood mixed with beer is placed by the side of the hut which serves as a shrine for the canoe-spirit. The first journey of the canoe is to the shrine of a god.[10] Among the Banyoro a man or an ox is eaten before the tree, while the body of a human victim is left by the tree-roots. When the canoe is ready to be launched, a sheep or fowl is killed so that the blood runs into the vessel.[11] Among the Baronga of S. Africa sacrifices must be made to the ghosts of ancestors buried in the forest before a tree therefrom is cut down to serve as material for a canoe.[12]

Both in Oceania and in Africa the rites of building and launching are definitely connected with spiritual beings. In Melanesia these are certainly the spirits or ghosts of dead ancestors, who form the basis of the religious cult of this part of the world. Both in the New Hebrides and in the Solomons there is evidence that the ghosts are those of former canoe-builders, probably starting with that of the original introducer of the art. In Africa the spirit to which offerings are made during the processes of building and launching is clearly connected with the tree from which the vessel is made. The spirit of a large canoe is thought to be the spirit of the tree, which clings to the timber, and especially the keel.[1] Among the Baronga, another Bantu people, the necessity of offerings is connected with the dead who have been buried in the forest from which the tree used for the canoe is taken. This suggests that the tree- and canoe-spirits of other Bantu peoples may have been derived from the spirit or ghost of the dead.

[1] A. M. Hocart, MSS.
[2] W. T. Pritchard, *Polynesian Reminiscences*, London, 1866, p. 372.
[3] A. C. Haddon, in a personal communication.
[4] J. A. Moerenhout, *Voyages aux îles du Grand Océan*, Paris, 1837, i. 501.
[5] W. Wilson, *A Missionary Voyage to the S. Pacific, 1796–98, in the 'Duff,'* London, 1799, p. 377 ff.
[6] W. Ellis, *Polynesian Researches*², London, 1833, iii. 364.
[7] Elsdon Best, *Trans. and Proc. New Zealand Institute*, xlviii. [1915] 452.
[8] David Malo, *Hawaiian Antiquities*, Honolulu, 1903, p. 168 ff.
[9] C. Hose and W. McDougall, *The Pagan Tribes of Borneo*, London, 1912, i. 202.
[10] J. Roscoe, *The Baganda*, London, 1911, p. 386.
[11] Roscoe, *The Northern Bantu*, Cambridge, 1915, p. 79 f.
[12] H. A. Junod, *The Life of a South African Tribe*, Neuchâtel, 1912–13, ii. 20.

A similar connexion between a canoe and the spirit of the tree from which it is made occurs in Polynesia. In the Hervey Islands the songs chanted while a canoe is being made are said to have been addressed originally to the tree-spirit;[2] and the necessity for the propitiation of the tree-spirit in Samoa is seen in the case of a tree which had been cut down as suitable for the keel of a canoe not being used through fear of the *aitu* of the grove in which the tree was growing.[3] It may be that this was the original belief of the canoe-makers of Melanesia, and that it has since been replaced by the propitiation of ancestors which is characteristic of the religion of that region.

The ship or boat is often the object of religious or magical ritual after it has been built and launched, but it is usually difficult to tell how far such rites pertain to the vessel itself and how far they form part of the ritual of warfare, fishing, or other purpose for which the vessel is to be used. In Eddystone Island rites are performed during the making of a canoe which are designed to promote success in the fishing for bonito, which is one of the favourite pursuits of the islanders; and in many places the nature of rites in which a boat is concerned shows that they are designed to promote the success of fishing or warfare rather than the safety of the vessel. Among the Baganda, however, fish are definitely offered to the canoe; they are killed in the vessel with the words 'This fish we offer to you,' and, if the fishing fails after the omission of this offering, a propitiatory ceremony is held in which fish are offered with a confession of wrong-doing.[4]

2. Death-rites.—In the rites so far considered the vessel itself is the main purpose. Ships and boats also frequently enter into rites the purpose of which is wholly different. Thus the use of boats is very frequent and prominent in death-rites.[5]

In Melanesia the bodies of the dead are often placed in canoes at some stage of the funeral-rites or the dead are interred in their canoes. In the New Hebrides a canoe is loaded with objects which may be of use to the dead and is then sent adrift during the course of the death ceremonies; and a similar proceeding takes place as part of the highly complex and prolonged ceremonial in which initiates gradually rise in rank as members of a fraternity connected with a cult of the dead.

In New Britain the corpse of an important man is laid in a boat which, with its contents, is sunk far out at sea. The dead were also sent out to sea in canoes in several islands of Polynesia, such as Samoa and Niué. In other cases the corpse, while undergoing desiccation, was left in a canoe or placed on the platform of a double canoe. In other islands of Polynesia a body was interred in a canoe or in a hollowed log of wood representing a canoe.[6] In the Lau region of the Fijian archipelago the bodies of chiefs were placed in great canoes and dragged to almost inaccessible caves.[7]

The Malanau, a Klemantan people of Borneo, put the property of a dead man and sometimes the corpse also in a canoe and send it out to sea.[8]

The use of a canoe is frequent in the death-rites of America, especially in the southern continent, the bodies of the dead being frequently interred in canoes.[9]

In Asia there are only a few traces of the use of boats in death-rites. In the Nicobar Islands the dead are sometimes

[1] J. Roscoe, in a personal communication.
[2] W. W. Gill, *The Southern Pacific and New Guinea*, Sydney, 1892, p. 22.
[3] J. Fraser, *Journ. and Proc. Royal Society of New South Wales*, xxiv. [1890] 203.
[4] Roscoe, *JAI* xxxii. [1902] 56.
[5] See art. DEATH AND DISPOSAL OF THE DEAD (Introductory and Primitive), vol. iv. p. 430.
[6] See Rivers, *Hist. of Melanesian Society*, ii. 269.
[7] T. R. St. Johnston, *The Lau Islands*, London, 1918, p. 23.
[8] *TES* ii. [1863] 32.
[9] G. Friederici, *Die Schiffahrt der Indianer*, Stuttgart, 1907, p. 110.

buried in the hull of a canoe.[1] Pieces of reed in the walls of Indian tombs are said to serve as boats;[2] and the Ainus of Japan say that an object which looks like a spear, placed over a grave, is really a boat-oar.[3] A double canoe was used in the death-rite of a king of Kandy, but only as the means of taking a horse or an elephant on a river in order that its rider should deposit the ashes of the king in the stream.[4]

In Africa the use of boats in funeral-rites is less frequent than in Oceania or America. The Egyptians from the Vth to the XIIth dynasty included models of ships among the furniture of a tomb. The Bakongo use an old canoe as material for a coffin;[5] and a priest of the Ibo in the Asaba district on the Niger is buried in a canoe or a model of a canoe is put into his coffin, the practice being accompanied by a prohibition against the use of a canoe by a priest while he is alive.[6]

The use of ships in funeral rites was very prominent in ancient Scandinavia. The vikings used a ship as a funeral pyre. They put the body of a dead leader in his ship and sent it out burning to sea. The ship was also used for interment. Funeral-mounds have been found to contain large sea-going vessels on which the bodies of the dead had been placed, together with numerous animals and other objects for the use of the dead. One such vessel found at Oseberg contained the bodies of two women, one probably of high rank and the other her attendant. Around the Baltic old stone burial-places occur in the form of boats. Models of boats, sometimes in gold and often in large numbers, are found in the ancient interments in this region.[7]

3. Boat-processions.—Ships or boats sometimes took an important place in ceremonies.

In Greece, at the general Panathenaic festival, held every fourth year, a ship on wheels was taken in procession with a robe fastened to its mast to be presented to Athene. At Smyrna, during the feast of Dionysus in the spring, a sacred ship steered by a priest of the god was carried aloft round the market-place.[8]

There is no direct evidence of similar processions in ancient Egypt, but a ship was prominent in the rites of Isis, and representations of boat-shrines on sledges in ancient tombs and a golden model of a boat on wheels from the XVIIth dynasty point to the occurrence of processions similar to those of Greece.[9] Such processions still take place in modern Egypt. Three take place every year in Luxor, the chief of which is in honour of Abu'l Heggag, a *shaikh* who is said to have journeyed from Keneh to Cairo in a stone boat about 700 years ago. A procession in which a boat is used occurs in a Sinhalese ceremony performed by the Muhammadan Moormen of Ceylon.[10] Ship-drawing cavalcades occurred in Europe in the Middle Ages and were forbidden by a proclamation at Ulm as late as 1530.[11] Relics of such processions survived in Suabia until the middle of last century.[12] Boats burned in China to carry away evil influences are previously carried through the streets in procession.[13]

4. Boat-races.—In several parts of the world boat-races seem to have or to have had a religious significance.

In Siam regattas are held from the results of which prognostics are drawn,[14] and in China races of dragon-boats are believed to produce rain.[15] In Hermione in Attica boat-races were held in honour of Dionysus of the Black Goatskin, and races were held at Sunium. Races rowed in sacred boats round the promontory of Piræus formed part of the training of the Athenian youth.[16] Boat-racing took place also at the Isthmian and Panathenaic festivals.[17]

5. Divination by means of boats.—In several islands of the Solomons the swaying of a canoe forms a means by which the people determine whether their ancestors favour an enterprise that they are about to undertake, the movement doubtless depending on automatic movements of the occupant of the canoe similar to that of table-turning. In one part of Eddystone Island the movements are believed to be produced by a crocodile, and in others by a shark or by a mythical octopus-like creature.

6. Boats and medicine. — In some parts of Indonesia rites are performed to cure disease, especially epidemic disease, in which small vessels, often elaborately constructed, are sent out to sea and are believed thus to carry away the disease.

In Sarawak such a boat is made of sago-pith, and an image in human form is placed therein. A 'sorcerer' is then called upon to discover the abode of the evil spirit who is causing the disease and the place propitious for sending the boat adrift. The sorcerer takes the image from the boat and instructs it what to say to the spirit. After spitting betel juice on the image, he replaces it in the boat, which is allowed to float away.[1] A similar practice occurs in Eddystone Island, where a leaf resembling a canoe, in which ashes, some thatch, and shells are placed, is sent out to sea to carry away an epidemic disease.

Thanksgiving offerings may also be floated out to sea.[2] In China the boats which are burned on the sea-shore in order to take away evil influences[3] have the form of dragons.

It is noteworthy that the custom of banishing disease by sending it to sea in a boat occurs in Indonesia and Melanesia. In both those regions the dead or their property are sent out to sea in boats. The relation between the two practices raised by their common distribution is reinforced by the custom of Sarawak in which an image placed in the disease-boat is instructed to speak to the spirit. It suggests that the spirit or ghost to whom the occurrence of epidemic disease is ascribed is that of a dead ancestor or hero who lives across the water, to whom a message is sent by means similar to those by which he himself is believed to have travelled after death.

7. Sacred ships and boats.—In several of the rites which have been described special sacred vessels are used.

In Melanesia only certain canoes are tabu to women, thus showing some degree of sacred character, and canoes are often also tabu to women in Polynesia. In the Duke of York Island in the Bismarck Archipelago sacred canoes called *pidik* were formerly made with much ceremony, and leaders of the *Dukduk* or ghost-cult of that region were carried in it to all the surrounding villages.[4] Sacred canoes form a definite feature of Polynesian religion. In Tahiti certain canoes, apparently made by the chiefs, were specially dedicated to the *atua*. They were called *marae*, the word otherwise used for 'temple'; a human victim was sacrificed when they were launched, and they were not allowed to touch any soil but that of the *marae* to which they were carried from the sea. They had a platform, also called *marae*, on which were laid the bodies of those slain in warfare.[5]

In ancient Greece a sacred vessel went every year from Athens to Delos. During its absence Athens was in a state of purification and no criminal could be killed; this occasion was the means of delaying the death of Socrates. When the vessel started on its voyage, its bows were crowned with flowers by the priests of Apollo.

The doge of Venice had a sacred galley, the *Bucentaur*, from which was performed at the feast of the Ascension the ceremony of marriage with the sea, into which a ring was thrown.

In two widely separated parts of the earth, Scandinavia and China, vessels were used, more or less sacred in character, which took the form of dragons, and similar vessels are represented in the sculpture of ancient India.[6] It is a question whether the *dreki*, or dragon-ship, of the vikings had a special build or differed from other vessels only in having a dragon-head at the bow and a 'tail-fin' at the stern. Vessels of this kind were especially associated with the chiefs, and it was in them that dead chiefs were buried or cremated. The Veneti of Brittany appear to have had similar vessels.[7] The dragon-boats of the Chinese also had a sacred character and were apparently believed to be associated with rain-making.

1 W. Campbell, *My Indian Journal*, Edinburgh, 1864, p. 442.
2 See *ERE* iv. 475b, 479a.
3 J. Batchelor, *The Ainu of Japan*, London, 1892, p. 209.
4 J. Davy, *Account of the Interior of Ceylon*, London, 1821, p. 162.
5 J. H. Weeks, *Among Congo Cannibals*, London, 1913, p. 317.
6 N. W. Thomas, *JRAI* xlvii. [1917] 183.
7 G. H. Boehmer, *RSI* for 1891, p. 557 ff.
8 Pausanias, I. xxix. 1.
9 *ERE* iii. 226, v. 243b, 856.
10 C. G. Seligmann, in *Essays and Studies presented to W. Ridgeway*, Cambridge, 1913, p. 452 ff.
11 O. Schade, *Die Sage von der heiligen Ursula*, Hanover, 1854, p. 81.
12 E. Meier, *Deutsche Sagen, Sitten und Gebräuche aus Schwaben*, Stuttgart, 1852, p. 374.
13 M. W. de Visser, 'The Dragon in China and Japan,' *Verhandelingen der koninklijke Akademie van Wetenschappen te Amsterdam*, Afdeeling Letterkunde, xiii. 2 [1913] 70.
14 *ERE* v. 887b.
15 De Visser, p. 85.
16 Pausanias, II. xxxv. 1.
17 P. Gardner, *JHS* ii. [1881] 90, 315; J. E. Harrison, *ib.* vi. [1885] 26.

1 W. M. Croker, *Sarawak Gazette*, nos. 120 and 121, quoted by H. Ling Roth, *The Natives of Sarawak and British North Borneo*, London, 1896, ii. 284.
2 Hose-McDougall, ii. 134.
3 See above, § 3.
4 G. Brown, *Melanesians and Polynesians*, London, 1910, p. 92.
5 Moerenhout, i. 526.
6 F. C. Maisey, *Sanchi and its Remains*, London, 1892, p. 58.
7 E. Magnússon, *Notes of Shipbuilding and Nautical Terms of Old in the North*, London, 1906, p. 42.

Tradition in several places tells of stone boats.

The *shaikh* in whose honour boat-processions still take place in Egypt[1] is reported to have travelled in a stone boat, of which relics are still shown. Stone boats are prominent in the stories of Irish and British saints.[2] Petrified boats occur in the legends of Indonesia;[3] and one of the legendary heroes of Ruviana, in the Solomon Islands, is said to have turned his war-canoe into stone.

8. Sacred parts of vessels.—In several places the hinder end of a vessel has a sacred character.

In the Maori canoe the stern-thwart might be occupied by the priests, and this part was also believed to be occupied by the spirit under whose protection the vessel had been placed. In the Marquesas the image of a god was placed in the hinder part of the canoe.[4] In the boat-burials of the vikings the dead were placed in houses erected behind the mast, and the Roman war-galley had a portion of the stern set apart as a temple.

In other cases sacred objects of various kinds are placed in the bows, suggesting a more or less sacred character of this part of the vessel.

In the island of Dobu in the D'Entrecasteaux group (S.E. New Guinea) the bow of a canoe is dedicated to war and the stern to peace. If a canoe of any size were brought to a place bow first, it would mean war.[5]

Among the Baganda sanctity appears to attach to the keel. The spirit of the tree from which the canoe is made is believed to cling especially to the keel, and the blood of the goat killed at the launching is allowed to run along this part of the vessel.[6]

The decoration of ships and boats often has, or has had, a religious significance.

Sometimes, as in Samoa, the figure-head in the form of an animal may indicate the village or district to which the canoe belongs, but more often (and perhaps also in Polynesia) the human being or animal represented is believed to protect or guide the vessel. The natives of the north-west coast of N. America adorned the bow and stern of their canoes with elaborate totemic patterns in painting or carving.[7]

The presence of an eye upon the bows, which in ancient Egypt portrayed the eye of Osiris, seems elsewhere in the Mediterranean, India, China, and N. America to have become a mere decoration, but it is possible that it still possesses a religious significance. Objects placed in the bows, such as the head of an albatross, sharks' tails, horse-shoes, etc., may in some cases be only trophies, but more frequently they are amulets designed to ensure a fair wind or other benefit.

The intense conservatism of sailors, which has done much to perpetuate special types of vessels and details of their structure, is probably connected with the belief in the religious or magical significance of the objects that they have preserved. On the other hand, the strength of the religious sentiments connected with boats has in some cases led to the disappearance of all means of navigation. There is little doubt that the complete absence of sea-going vessels, even in certain islands where they would seem to be indispensable, is due to the sacred character of the art of boat-building. When those who knew the appropriate formulas and rites have died, the people have forgone the highly useful art of navigation rather than make vessels destined to misfortune owing to the absence of the due religious rites.[8]

LITERATURE.—See the authorities quoted in the footnotes.

W. H. R. RIVERS.

SHOES AND SANDALS. — Most savage peoples wear no covering on the feet, except where the climate is excessively cold—*e.g.*, among the Eskimo, Samoyed, and Gilyaks (but not the Fuegians). How soon the custom of covering the feet arose in pre-historic times is uncertain, as the perishable nature of the material used would not tend to its preservation. Increasing civilization led to the use of some form of sandals, but even among the early Greeks these were not always worn, and among cultured Hindus a foot-covering, especially of leather, is disliked. Clement of Alexandria wrote that bare feet are in keeping for a man, except when on military service, and he quotes the Greek proverb, ὑποδεδέσθαι τῷ δεδέσθαι.[1] We have to consider here the use of sandals and shoes in religious ritual.

1. Ritual putting off of shoes.—On two occasions in the OT a command is given, 'Put off thy shoes from off thy feet, for the place whereon thou standest is holy ground'—first to Moses, second to Joshua, on both occasions in presence of a theophany, making the surrounding place holy or tabu.[2] The priests also probably officiated in the Temple with bare feet.[3] Parallels from other religions may be cited before suggesting the rationale of the custom.

No one was permitted to enter the temple of Britomartis in Crete unless barefooted, and a similar prohibition forbade the carrying of shoes into the holy place of Alectro at Ialysos in Rhodes, and into the temple of the Tegean mother.[4] Several other instances from Greek ritual might be cited, and the custom was a general one.[5] Worshippers at Rome went barefoot in honour of Cybele, and also in the cult of Isis, as pictures at Herculaneum show.[6] While nothing is said of the priests in Roman sacrificial ritual, the suppliant offering a sacrifice to obtain a favour required to have his feet bare and hair dishevelled.[7] Ovid cites an instance of a place where formerly stood a sacred grove, still approached with naked feet—an instance of the tenacity of custom.[8] In Egypt the priests, when officiating in the temples, frequently removed their sandals.[9] A similar custom holds in India, where, *e.g.*, at the temple of Dākor in Gujarāt a visitor must remove his shoes before ascending its steps.[10] The practice is also found with the Muslims, who remove their shoes at the door of a mosque, carrying them in the left hand, sole to sole.[11] Similarly, on entering a house, Muslims leave their shoes on the *durḳā'ah*, or lower part of the floor, before stepping on the *leewān*, or upper part, and they also remove them before stepping on a carpet or mat.[12] In some instances the sacredness of the threshold demands that it be not touched with the foot when crossing it; hence among other rites that of taking off the shoes is sometimes found.[13]

The sandals or shoes which have been in contact with common ground must not be brought into contact with sacred ground, first, lest any dirt or the contagion of the outer secular world should be brought in, and probably, as a secondary reason, to avoid carrying away the sacredness of the holy place upon them. The latter would, of course, prevent their being used afterwards in ordinary life. For the former reason the feet are washed also where shoes are not ordinarily worn as well as where they are, before entering a sacred place.[14] These customs are parallel to the precautions taken among savages to remove the outward contagion from a stranger before admitting him to the village or house.[15] But the question of archaic

[1] See above, § 3.
[2] C. Plummer, *Vitæ Sanctorum Hiberniæ*, Oxford, 1910, i. Introd. p. clv and p. 227.
[3] W. J. Perry, *The Megalithic Culture of Indonesia*, Manchester, 1918, pp. 45, 48, 124.
[4] Elsdon Best, *loc. cit.*
[5] W. E. Bromilow, *Rep. Austral. Ass.*, vol. xii. p. 470.
[6] J. Roscoe, in a personal communication.
[7] A. P. Niblack, *RSI* for 1887–88, p. 295; G. Vancouver, *A Voyage of Discovery*, London, 1798, ii. 303.
[8] W. H. R. Rivers, 'The Disappearance of Useful Arts,' *Festskrift til E. Westermarck*, Helsingfors, 1912, p. 109.

[1] Clem. *Pæd.* ii. 12.
[2] Ex 3^5, Jos 5^{15}; cf. Ex 19^{12}, Ec 5^1.
[3] See art. FEET-WASHING, § 1.
[4] W. Dittenberger, *Sylloge Inscr. Græcarum*^{2}, Leipzig, 1898–1901, no. 357; Solinus, *Collectanea rerum memorabilium*, ed. T. Mommsen, Berlin, 1874, xi. 8; Ovid, *Fasti*, i. 629.
[5] See O. Gruppe, *Griech. Mythologie und Religionsgeschichte*, Munich, 1897–1906, p. 912; C. A. Lobeck *Aglaophamus*, Königsberg, 1829, i. 249; J. G. Frazer, *GB*^{3}, pt. viii., *Spirits of the Corn and of the Wild*, London, 1912, ii. 45.
[6] Prudentius, *Peristeph*, 154; W. Smith, *Dict. of Greek and Roman Antiquities*^{3}, London, 1890–91, *s.v.* 'Calceus.'
[7] A. Réville, *Prolegomena of the Hist. of Religions*, tr. A. S. Squire, London, 1884, p. 126.
[8] Ovid, *Fasti*, vi. 395 ff.
[9] J. G. Wilkinson, *Manners and Customs of the Ancient Egyptians*, ed. S. Birch, London, 1878, ii. 336.
[10] M. Monier-Williams, *Brāhmanism and Hindūism*^{4}, London, 1891, p. 144.
[11] E. W. Lane, *Arabian Society in the Middle Ages*, ed. S. Lane-Poole, London, 1883, p. 146, *An Account of the Manners and Customs of the Modern Egyptians*^{3}, do. 1846, i. 118.
[12] Lane, *Modern Egyptians*^{3}, i. 55.
[13] See art. DOOR, § 1 (*c*).
[14] See art. FEET-WASHING, § 1. The Talmud directs that no person should approach the Temple with dirt on the feet (*Yᵉbamōth, 6b*).
[15] See Frazer, *GB*^{3}, pt. ii., *Taboo and the Perils of the Soul*, London, 1911, p. 102 ff.; A. van Gennep, *Les Rites de passage*, Paris, 1909, p. 35 ff.

usage also must be considered. Before any foot-covering was worn or in the period of transition (*e.g.*, in Homeric Greece) all religious rites must have been performed barefoot, after washing the feet. Hence it may have been thought wiser to continue the practice after sandals were in common use, and the cause just considered would also affect the practice. In the same way stone knives continued to be used ritually long after metal was used in ordinary life.

In some magical rites sandals had to be laid aside and the feet washed.

Ovid relates that they were removed by the man who threw beans as a ransom for himself and his friends from the ghosts at the Lemuria.[1] Horace describes how Canidia practised her rites of sorcery with bare feet and dishevelled hair, and Pliny says that *selago* was gathered in Gaul by one who went with newly-washed unshod feet, and who wore a white robe.[2]

This putting off of shoes, in conjunction with wearing the hair unbound and also a loose robe, points to the fear of hindering the magical action through any knot or constriction. In the same way all garments had to be loose in Greek sacrificial ritual.[3]

Another reason for putting off the shoes or sandals was that this was a sign of grief or mourning, and hence the right attitude in those who approached the gods and their sacred places in humility. The custom is found in religious ritual where grief or humility was to be shown.

The women in the procession through the town mourning with Demeter went unshod, and so did the Locrian virgins (who served as slaves) in approaching the βωμός of Athene.[4] In drought a procession and ritual called *nudipedalia* was intended to propitiate the gods by this token of humiliation and sorrow.[5] Many other instances of this are known.[6] In actual mourning rites going barefoot was used by both Greeks and Romans; *e.g.*, Suetonius describes how the young nobles who removed the ashes of Augustus from the pyre were barefoot.[7] Bion describes Aphrodite wailing for Adonis as ἀσάνδαλος, and Autonoe was unshod at the death of Actaion.[8] It was also a token of distraction, as when the Roman vestals fled from Rome with the sacred utensils.[9] Among the Hebrews to go bare-footed was also a sign of mourning.[10]

2. Ritual wearing of special shoes.—Dress could be washed before visiting a sacred place, but this was impossible for sandals or shoes, unless these were merely of linen, as in a rite described by Herodian.[11] Hence they were removed, as we have just seen, or special shoes were worn in the sanctuary or sacred place. These as well as a special dress might be there provided for the worshipper, unless he was rich enough to supply them for himself.[12] This is found in savage as well as in ancient custom.

At the annual ceremony of the new fire among the Creek Indians the priest wore a pair of new buckskin moccasins instead of going barefoot. These were made by himself, and were stitched with the sinews of the animal from whose hide the material was procured. They were kept carefully in the sacred enclosure and used only at the festival.[13] In Mexico the woman representing the goddess Iyacatecutli wore white sandals, and sandals fastened with buttons and cords were worn by the victims sacrificed to Huixtocihuatl, and so also in other instances.[14] In old Chinese ritual a great officer, on leaving his state and crossing the boundary, had to prepare a place for an altar and there wore shoes of untanned leather and special garments.[15] Persons consulting the oracle of Trophonius, after being washed and anointed, put on a linen shirt and shoes of the country—ὑποδησάμενος ἐπιχωρίας κρεπῖδας.[1] In the procession at the Andanian mysteries the sacred women had to wear no other shoes than those made of felt or of the skins of the sacrificial victims.[2] Similarly at a late Syrian rite in which boys were initiated they wore slippers made from the hide of a sacrificed animal.[3] As a customary foot-gear the wife of the *flamen Dialis* wore shoes made of the skin of a sacrificial victim or of one killed, never of one dying a natural death.[4] Herodotus says that the Egyptian priests were not allowed to wear any other shoes than those made from papyrus—ὑποδήματα βύβλινα. In other cases they were made of leaves of palm.[5]

The last examples have perhaps some connexion with rites in which at a sacrifice the worshipper stood or knelt on the victim's skin.[6] In the Greek, Roman, and Egyptian instances the reason for wearing special shoes or sandals, not of leather, was connected with the idea that anything made of the hide of animals dying a natural death—*i.e.* not slain or sacrificed—would defile a sacred place. This is expressly stated by Ovid and Varro,[7] and it also would be a reason for going unshod where the feet were not covered with some other material. The skin of sacrificed animals might be used, as some instances have shown.

In ancient India, where probably, as in modern India, it may have been the usual custom to go barefoot because of the supposed impurity of leather,[8] the king who had performed the *rājasūya* rite must never stand on the earth with bare feet.

'From the throne-seat he slips into the shoes and on shoes (he stands), whatever his vehicle may be, whether a chariot or anything else. For verily he who performs the Râgasûya is high above everything here, and everything here is beneath him;—therefore this is for him a religious observance: as long as he lives he does not stand on earth (with bare feet).'[9]

Here the real reason probably was connected with sacredness as a result of the rite, which must not be contaminated by direct contact with the ground. Another rite in connexion with a king's consecration ordained him to wear shoes of boar's skin at the investing.

The reason assigned is that the gods once produced a boar from a pot of *ghī*. Hence 'cows readily take to a boar,' because 'it is their own essence (life-sap, blood)' to which they are taking. Thus the king 'firmly establishes himself in the essence of the cattle: therefore he puts on shoes of boar-skin.'[10]

The Parsi sacred books ordain that 'walking with one boot as far as four steps is a *Tanâpûhar* sin,' or forbid this lest grievous harm should happen to the soul. The true reading here appears to be 'without boots,' or 'with only a single covering on the feet'—*i.e.* inner boots of thin leather over which an outer pair were worn out-of-doors. Modern Parsis understand it as walking without boots.[11] In another passage the reason is clearly stated—one is not to walk without boots because, if one treads on dead matter while wearing them, he is not polluted.[12] Touching the ground—*i.e.* unconsecrated ground—with bare feet is most offensive to the Parsi and a sinful act:

'It is not desirable for those of the good religion . . . to put a bare foot upon the ground, because it is a sin, and injury occurs to Spendârmad, the archangel.'[13]

3. Removing one shoe.—In some instances in Greek ritual we find that one shoe was removed.

Ovid describes Medea, before her invocation of the powers which will help her to obtain herbs for the renewal of youth, as having her feet—probably one foot—bare, hair and garments

1 Ovid, *Fasti*, v. 432.
2 Hor. *Sat.* I. viii. 23; Pliny, *HN* xxiv. 11 (62).
3 J. Potter, *Antiquities of Greece*[12], London, 1832, i. 266; cf. art. KNOTS.
4 Callimachus, *Hymn.*, vi. 124; Plutarch, *de Sera Numinis Vindicta*, 12.
5 Tertullian, *Apol.* 40.
6 See Gruppe, p. 912, for other reff.; C. Weinhold, 'Zur Gesch. der heidn. Ritus,' in *Abh. der königl. Preuss. Akad. der Wissenschaften*, Berlin, 1896, p. 17.
7 Suet. *Aug.* 100; cf. *ERE* iv. 506*a*.
8 Bion, i. 20; cf. Nonnus, *Dionysiaca*, v. 374.
9 Flor., i. 13. 10 Is 20[2f.], Ezk 24[17. 23], 2 S 15[30].
11 Herodian, v. v. 10; W. R. Smith[2], p. 453.
12 J. G. Frazer, *Pausanias's Description of Greece*, London, 1894, v. 202.
13 J. Adair, *The Hist. of the American Indians*, London, 1775, p. 82.
14 *NR* ii. 326, 395 f.
15 *Lî Kî*, II i. 10; *SBE* xxvii. [1885] 104.

1 Paus. IX. xxxix. 8.
2 *Ib.* IV. i. 5 f.; Dittenberger, no. 388.
3 W. R. Smith[2], p. 438.
4 Servius on Vergil, *Æn.* iv. 518; Festus, p. 191, ed. C. O. Müller, Leipzig, 1839.
5 Herod. ii. 37; cf. Apul. *Metam.* 2.
6 Lucian, *de Dea Syria*, 59; W. R. Smith[2], p. 438; for other examples see Lobeck, i. 244.
7 Ovid, *Fasti*, i. 629; Varro, *de Ling. Lat.*, vii. 84.
8 Monier-Williams, p. 396.
9 *Śatapatha Brāhmaṇa*, v. v. 3 (*SBE* xli. [1894] 128).
10 *Ib.* v. iv. 3.
11 *Shāyast-lā-Shāyast*, iv. 12 (*SBE* v. [1880] 288); *Dīnā-ī Maīnōg-ī Khraṭ*, ii. 37 (*SBE* xxiv. [1885] 11); cf. *Dīnkarṭ*, ix. 1 (*SBE* xxxvii. [1892] 182).
12 *Shāyast-lā-Shāyast*, x. 12 (*SBE* v. 320).
13 *Sad-dar*, xliv. 1 (*SBE* xxiv. 307).

floating loosely.[1] Vergil's account of Dido assisting at the rites ordained by the sorceress before her death is in the same terms —'unum exuta pedem vinclis, in veste recincta.'[2]

The purpose here seems to be, as in parallel instances, to permit the free action of magical influences by loosening all knots (*q.v.*) and bonds which might be conceived to restrain it, though why one foot only should be unshod is not clear. Greek ritual of purification sometimes prescribed that the right foot should be bare and resting on the skin of the sacrificial victim, probably in order that there might be free communication between the suppliant and the sacrifice.[3] A similar custom of having one foot bare existed among the warriors of the Aetolians and the Anagnini.[4]

The latter, as described by Vergil, fought entirely naked, but the right foot was shod in the raw hide of a bull.[5] Thucydides also tells how 200 men of Platæa, having only one foot shod, surprised the Spartans and broke their line.[6] Similarly Perseus, in attacking the Gorgon, wore only one shoe.[7]

Possibly the account given by Herodotus of the occasional appearance of Perseus among the Chemmitæ within his temple near Neapolis, when a sandal worn by him, two cubits in length, was sometimes found there, may have some connexion with this custom. After its discovery all Egypt flourished.[8]

Frazer considers this warrior custom to be a form of consecration or devotion observed by men in great danger, and cites also an instance of the pagan Arabs cursing with one foot bare.[9]

The story of Jason relates that, when he was crossing a swollen stream, one of his sandals stuck in the mire. He proceeded on his way to the house of the usurper Pelias, who recognized that he was the man with one foot shod by whom it was announced that he should die. This is probably a legend arising out of the ritual act in question.

The story of Rhodope, whose shoe, taken by an eagle, was dropped by it in the bosom of Psammetichos, who sought its owner through all Egypt,[10] is a version of the myth of Aphrodite and Hermes, and an early variant of the well-known folk-tale of Cinderella or Aschenputtel, of which there are innumerable examples.[11]

Hermes fell in love with Aphrodite, but to his grief she proved obdurate. Zeus, in pity for Hermes, sent an eagle which took her shoe while she was bathing and brought it to Hermes. Aphrodite sought it, and eventually Hermes won her.[12]

Gruppe connects this story, as well as those of Jason and Perseus, with such rites as have been referred to, and in particular with some mystery-legend and a mystery-ritual in which the sandal is a badge, as it is the token of recognition in the folk-tales. The rite or rites may also explain the numerous representations of Aphrodite or Hermes binding or loosing their sandals, or of Aphrodite chastising Eros with a sandal. Hermes himself might be considered as μονοκρηπίς like Jason,[13] and possibly in the story the eagle is the god himself, since Zeus transformed him to that shape, according to one version of the myth of Leda. The rite may also account for such place-names as Sandalion and the like.[14] As a token of recognition sandals, armour, and weapons were placed under a stone by Aigeus where Aithra might show them to her son by him, Theseus, when he was of age.

Sandals were often consecrated both to Aphrodite and to Hermes.[15] In art and myth the sandals of Hermes are winged and 'carry him over sea and the boundless earth, with the blasts of the wind.'[16] Perseus and Pan also had winged sandals.

1 Ovid, *Met.* vii. 182.
2 Verg. *Æn.* iv. 518.
3 J. G. Frazer, *GB*³, pt. ii., *Taboo*, p. 311.
4 Macrobius, *Satur.* v. xviii. 13 f.
5 *Æn.* vii. 689.
6 Thuc. iii. 22.
7 Artemid. *Oneir.* iv. 63.
8 Herod. ii. 91.
9 *GB*³, pt. ii., *Taboo*, p. 312; I. Goldziher, *ZDMG* xlvi. [1892] 5. Is there any connexion between this custom and that of cursing while standing on one foot? (see *ERE* iii. 300b, 413a).
10 Strabo, xvii. 1; Ælian, *Var. Hist.*, xiii. 32.
11 J. and W. Grimm, *Kinder- und Hausmärchen*⁹, Berlin, 1870, no. 21; J. Bolte and G. Polivka, *Anmerkungen zu den Kinder- und Hausmärchen der Brüder Grimm*, Leipzig, 1913, i. 165 ff.; R. Köhler, *Kleinere Schriften*, Weimar, 1898–1900, i. 274; and M. R. Cox, *Cinderella*, London, 1892, give the variants of the story.
12 Hyginus, *Astronomica*, ii. 16.
13 Artemid. *loc. cit.*
14 Gruppe, p. 1332.
15 *Ib.*
16 Homer, *Il.* xxiv. 341 f.

The shoes of swiftness, 'seven-leagued boots' of many folk-tales, transporting the wearer swiftly from one place to another, resemble Hermes' winged sandals. They are magic properties of the gods appropriated by men, or imaginative exaggerations of the primitive sandal protecting the foot of the swift runner. In a Norse tale they are made by Hermodr from the skin of the soles of her feet.[1]

4. Magical rites with shoes.—The supposed dislike of spirits to leather,[2] as well as the magical virtues attributed to the shoe itself, accounts for its use in various magical rites.

It is placed heel upwards on the top of a house in India by the poor to ensure protection; and hailstones are beaten with a shoe by a wizard during a hail-storm to cause it to cease.[3] Again, the origin of throwing a shoe at a wedding for luck may be traced to some idea of scaring off demons who might cause barrenness, or of enhancing fertility.[4] According to a German superstition,[5] shoes placed wrong-wise at the head of the bed prevent the *alp*, or nightmare, from pressing one during the night. The shoes, or one shoe, are often untied at a wedding, with the idea that the unbinding of the knot will counteract evil influences.[6] Other superstitions are of a very varied kind. If the wife puts on her husband's slippers on the wedding-day, she will have easy labour, in Teutonic belief.[7] In Sicily shoes made out of wolf-skin for a child render it lucky and courageous.[8] An ancient Greek method of bringing back a faithless lover was to get a witch to fumigate his sandals with sulphur and to use incantations over them.[9]

The sandal of Perseus was a relic in Egypt and, when found, ensured the prosperity of the land.[10] So the dervishes at Old Cairo preserve a huge shoe as that of their founder.[11] Sandals and shoes of Christian saints have also been reverenced as relics.

5. Symbolism of the shoe.—Among the Hebrews putting off the shoe was a confirmation and symbol of a renunciation or transference of rights. It was removed from a man by the widow of his brother when he refused to take her as wife, as an act of contempt, and his family was known as 'the house of the unsandalled one.'[12] On refusing to redeem land the shoe was removed by the man himself, and apparently the seller of land gave his shoe to the buyer as a symbol of the rights given up by him.[13] In Arab usage a man divorcing his wife said, 'She was my slipper and I cast her off.'[14] If the phrase, 'Over Edom will I cast my shoe,'[15] signifies a symbol of taking possession of the land, this would also be a Hebrew custom, resembling one reported from Abyssinia, and parallel to putting the foot on the neck of a captive, or placing the figure of a captive on the lining of a sandal, as in ancient Egypt, signifying that he was trodden under foot.[16] But the meaning of the phrase, by analogy with 'Moab is my wash-pot,'[17] may rather be that of throwing a shoe to a slave to carry or clean.

6. Shoes of the dead.—As the dead were frequently supposed to take a long and rough journey to the other world, they were often provided with shoes. This is already found in later pre-historic times, and it continued as a general custom in various parts of Europe.[18] It also occurs

1 J. Grimm, *Teutonic Mythology*, tr. J. S. Stallybrass, London, 1882–88, ii. 871, iv. 1569; MacCulloch, *CF*, p. 221, note 3; J. Arnason, *Icelandic Legends*, tr. G. E. J. Powell and E. Magnússon, London, 1864–66, p. 397.
2 See artt. Changeling, vol. iii. p. 359b, Incense, vol. vii. p. 202a; Crooke, *PR*² ii. 34.
3 Crooke, *PR*² i. 80, ii. 34.
4 Cf. E. S. Hartland, *LP* i. 171.
5 Grimm, *Teut. Myth.* iv. 1795.
6 T. Pennant, *A Tour in Scotland*, in J. Pinkerton, *A General Collection of Voyages and Travels*, London, 1808–14, iii. 91; C. Rogers, *Social Life in Scotland*, Edinburgh, 1884–86, iii. 232.
7 Grimm, *Teut. Myth.* iii. 1175.
8 Gruppe, p. 805, note 2.
9 Lucian, *Dial. Meret.* 4. For other superstitions see Grimm, *Teut. Myth.* iv. 1805, 1809; R. Hunt, *Popular Romances of the West of England*³, London, 1881, p. 409; Crooke, *PR*² ii. 34. For divination with a shoe see J. G. Frazer, *GB*³, pt. vii., *Balder the Beautiful*, London, 1913, i. 236. For German betrothal-customs with the shoe see Grimm, *Deutsche Rechtsaltertümer*³, Göttingen, 1881, i. 214.
10 Herod. ii. 91.
11 G. Rawlinson, *Hist. of Herodotus*³, London, 1875, i. 147.
12 Dt 25⁹ᶠ.
13 Ru 4⁷ᶠ.; for Arab usage see reff. in *EBi* iv. 5196.
14 W. R. Smith, *Kinship and Marriage in Early Arabia*, Cambridge, 1885, p. 269.
15 Ps 60⁸.
16 Wilkinson, ii. 337.
17 Ps 60⁸.
18 See *ERE* ii. 19a, iv. 417b.

sometimes among savage tribes, among whom generally no shoes are worn.

Some of the tribes of lower California put shoes on the feet of the dead, so that they may be ready for their long journey.[1] In Scandinavian and Teutonic regions such shoes were known as *hek-skô* (Old Norse) or *Todtenschuh*—the latter name surviving as a general one for the funeral-rites long after the custom itself had ceased.[2] In some cases, as in Yorkshire, it was thought that one who gave a pair of new shoes to a poor man during life would meet an old man after death who would present him with the same shoes at the edge of Whinnymuir, the region full of thorns and furze—'ower flinty steeans, thruff monny a thorny brake,' which otherwise the spirit would have to traverse 'wi' shoonless feet.' This belief is illustrated by the 'Lyke-Wake Dirge,' various versions of which are sung in the north of England.[3] Elsewhere—*e.g.*, in Brittany—Death personified is supposed to grease the boots of the man whom he comes to fetch, like a good servant, so that he may travel along Death's high-road.[4] Lucian's story of the ghost of the dead wife who appeared to her husband and complained that one of her slippers had not been burned on the funeral pyre is interesting in this connexion.[5]

7. Concealing the shod or unshod foot.—In China and among the Chuvashes (Turks of the Volga) it is considered indecent to show a foot unshod or without stockings. This idea is connected, in China, with the enforced smallness of the feet, which has probably an association with sexual attraction.[6] Clement of Alexandria recommends the women of his time to wear shoes, as it is not fitting for their feet to be shown naked.[7] In Spain, whence it passed into Italy, it was considered immodest for ladies to show their feet even when shod, and several 16th and 17th cent. writers refer to this—*e.g.*, Brantôme, who maintains that a beautiful foot 'portoit une telle lasciveté en soy,' and Madame d'Aulnoy.[8]

LITERATURE.—There is no special work dealing with this subject. See also art. DRESS.

J. A. MACCULLOCH.

SHRINES.—See SAINTS AND MARTYRS.

SHROVE-TIDE, SHROVE TUESDAY.—

I. *SHROVE-TIDE.*—The name Shrove-tide is given to the week before the First Sunday in Lent. Shrove Tuesday is the day before Ash Wednesday, and it gathered up in itself in the later Middle Ages the customs and the practices which formerly characterized the whole week. Shrove-tide was the season of confession, absolution, and reconciliation before the solemnities of Lent and Passion-tide and Easter, a time of purification and of joy.

The name is derived from Anglo-Saxon *scrifan*, 'to shrive.' There is a passage in the *Capitula incerti authoris* printed by Spelman from a Corpus Christi College, Cambridge, MS which illustrates both the practice of Shrove-tide and the origin of the name. The *Capitula* follow upon the Canons of Ælfric, and may belong to the same period, *i.e.* the 10th century. The Anglo-Saxon text is only a paraphrase of the Latin. The Latin text reads:

'Haebdomeda prima ante initium Quadragesimae, confessiones Sacerdotibus dandae sunt, poenitentia accipienda, discordantes reconciliandi, et omnia jurgia sedanda, et dimittere debent debita invicem de cordibus suis, ut liberius dicant, *Dimitte nobis debita nostra, sicut et nos dimittimus debitoribus nostris*: et sic ingredientes in beatae Quadragesimae tempus, mundis et purificatis mentibus ad sanctum Pascha procedant.'

The Anglo-Saxon paraphrase begins thus:

'On thaere nyhstan wucan ær halgan nyht scealge hwa to his scrifte gan, and his dædum ge andettan and his scrift him sceal swa scrifan swa he thonne on his dædum gehyreth.'[1]

The Latin *capitulum* states clearly that confessions are to be made in the week before the *initium Quadragesimæ*. There is a liturgical difference between the *caput jejunii*, the title of Ash Wednesday, and the *initium Quadragesimæ*, the title of the First Sunday in Lent. The original fast of 36 days began on the Monday after the First Sunday in Lent. After the time of Gregory the Great Ash Wednesday became the first of the four supplementary fast-days with the title *caput jejunii*.

F. Cabrol explains the difference:

'Tommasi explique du reste cette apparente contradiction en disant que le carême antique avec ses trente-six jours de jeûne commençait en réalité le lundi de la première semaine; le premier dimanche était, en ce cas, le commencement du carême, d'où la secrète de ce dimanche: *sacrificium quadragesimalis initii solemniter immolamus.*'[2]

The First Sunday in Lent in the *Gelasian Sacramentary* is called 'Dominica in Quadragesima [V æ] Inchoantis initium.' This is preceded by the Shrove-tide prayers: 'Orationes et preces a Quinquagesima usque ad Quadragesimam.' Wednesday has the title, 'In Jejunio. Prima Statione. Feria iv.,' and the prayer, 'Inchoata jejunia, quaesumus, Domine.' There is no reference to Thursday. Friday has the title 'Feria vi. in Quinquagesima,' and the prayer, 'Da, quaesumus, Domine, fidelibus tuis jejuniis paschalibus convenienter aptari.' Saturday has the title 'Feria vii. in Quinquagesima,' with the prayer, 'Observationis hujus annua celebritate laetantes, quaesumus, Domine, ut paschalibus actionibus inhaerentes, plenis ejus effectibus gaudeamus.'[3]

These prayers and titles illustrate the liturgical difficulty involved in the throwing back of the Lenten fast to Ash Wednesday and the breaking up of the week of Quinquagesima. The Shrove-tide customs are a witness to the earlier use, and the *gaudeamus* of the Saturday prayer preserves the note of joy even in the shadow of Lent.

The double tradition of the beginning of Lent is witnessed in the terms 'Carnisprivium Vetus' and 'Carnisprivium Novum,' which are found in documents illustrating the history of Dauphiné at the close of the 13th century.[4]

The terms 'Shrove-tide' and 'Shrove Tuesday' are still in common use. The following note in a curious Cambridge record, *Bedell* (*Matthew*) *Stokys' Book*, written about 1557, gives the name of Shrove Sunday to the First Sunday in Lent. It 'describes the Cambridge Ceremonies in Lent' and illustrates the older tradition when the Shrove-tide customs were not confined to Shrove Tuesday.

'Ashwenssdaye:—First, the Bedels erlye in the mornynge, every one in their severall Coursis, shall toll or cause to be tolled in every Colledge, Howse, Hall or Hostell, where eny determiners be, the bell to gather the Companye together, and so shall brynge them to St. Maries Churche before viii. of the Clocke etc. etc. . . . Item, All the determiners dothe sytte in the New Chappel within the Schooles from i. of the Clocke untyll five, upon the Mondaye, Twesdaye, Wensdaye, and Thursdaye in the weeke before Shrove Sondaye . . . and from three to 4 all they have a Potation of Figgs, Reasons, and Almons, Bonnes and Beer, at the charge of the said determiners.'[5]

The Monday before Ash Wednesday was called Collop Monday or Shrove Monday.[6] And in a Latin and English Vocabulary printed from a

1 *NR* i. 569.
2 Grimm, *Teut. Myth.* ii. 835 f., iv. 1550.
3 Sir W. Scott, *Minstrelsy of the Scottish Border*, London, 1839, p. 299 f.; *County Folk-Lore*, ii., *Examples of Printed Folk-Lore concerning the North Riding of Yorkshire, York and the Ainsty*, collected and ed. Mrs. Gutch, do. 1901, p. 224 ff.
4 Grimm, *Teut. Myth.* ii. 844.
5 *Philops.* 27.
6 H. Ploss and M. Bartels, *Das Weib*⁸, Leipzig, 1905, i. 173 ff.; O. Stoll, *Das Geschlechtsleben in der Völkerpsychologie*, do. 1908, pp. 44 f., 621 f.; S. Reinach, 'Pieds pudiques,' *Cultes, mythes, et religions*, Paris, 1905–12, iv. 105 ff. See art. AUSTERITIES, vol. ii. p. 234.
7 Clem. *Pæd.* ii. 12.
8 P. de B. de Brantôme, *Vies des dames galantes*, ed. H. Vigneau, Paris, n.d., 3me discours; Comtesse d'Aulnoy, *Relation du Voyage d'Espagne*, The Hague, 1715, p. 125 f.; Reinach, *loc. cit.*

1 H. Spelman, *Concilia*, London, 1639–64, i. 610 f.
2 *DACL*, *s.v.* 'Caput jejunii.'
3 *The Gelasian Sacramentary*, ed. H. A. Wilson, Oxford, 1894, pp. 15–17.
4 Du Cange, *Glossarium*, Paris, 1733, *s.v.*
5 C. Wordsworth, *The Ancient Kalendar of the University of Oxford*, p. 29 f.
6 J. Brand, *Popular Antiquities*, ed. H. Ellis and J. O. Halliwell, i. 62.

Trinity College, Cambridge, MS of the 15th cent. there is the word 'Shrofday':

'Carniprivium . . . shrofday, quia a tunc privamur carnibus.'[1]

The name 'Carniprivium' is given to Quinquagesima Sunday.[2]

The Shrove-tide rhymes recorded by Brand from the neighbourhood of Salisbury show that 'shroving' was as popular a custom in the early part of the year as 'souling' was, and is still, in the Midlands in November.

'Shrove Tide is nigh at hand,
And I am come a shroving;
Pray, Dame, something,
An Apple or a Dumpling,
Or a piece of Truckle Cheese
Of your own making,
Or a piece of Pancake.'[2]

The observation of Shrove-tide has affinities with the Continental carnival.

II. *SHROVE-TIDE REVELS.*—Shrove-tide was a season of revelry and sport in court, college, and country-side.

1. Court.—Fungoso, a court aspirant in Ben Jonson's *Every Man out of his Humour*, refers to those revels in a letter to his father.

'I desire you likewise to be advertised, that this Shrove-tide, contrary to custom, we are always to have revels; which is indeed dancing, and makes an excellent shew in truth.'[3]

In the same play Carlo Buffone, speaking of Macilente, says:

'Ay, this is he; a good tough gentleman: he looks like a shield of brawn at Shrove-tide, out of date, and ready to take his leave.'[4]

This is evidence for the year 1599. There were costly revellings at Hatfield in 1556:

'In Shrovetide, 1556, sir Thomas Pope made for the lady Elizabeth, all at his own costs, a great and rich masking in the great hall at Hatfield, where the pageants were marvellously furnished.'[5]

For 28th Feb. 1587–88 we have the following information:

Francis Bacon 'assisted in getting up the masque which was presented to the Queen by the gentlemen of Gray's Inn.'[6]

These revels were well rooted in the observance of the court. In 1512 there is a notice in the *Percy Household Book*:

'The Clergy and Officers of Lord Percy's Chapel performed a play before his Lordship upon Shrowftewesday at night.'[7]

The ruder sports were also encouraged in still earlier times by the court and the nobles. Among the royal household accounts of Henry VII. there is this entry under date 2nd March, 1492:

'Item to Master Bray for rewards to them that brought Cokkes at Shrovetide, at Westmr. xx^{s}.'[8]

And in a MS Life of Thomas Lord Berkeley (1352–1417), among his recreations, we are told:

'Hee also would to the threshing of the Cocke, pucke with Hens blindfolde and such like.'[9]

2. College and school.—In a British Museum MS entitled *Status Scholæ Etonensis* (1560) it appears that Shrove Tuesday was kept as a holiday. The cook brought in the pancake (*laganum*) and fastened it to a crow. The meaning is obscure.

'Die Martis Carnis-privii luditur ad horam octavam in totum diem: venit Coquus, affigit laganum Cornici, juxta illud pullis Corvorum invocantibus eum, ad ostium Scholae.'[10]

There was also a Shrove Monday custom at Eton, called Bacchus. The upper form boys wrote poems 'either in praise or dispraise' of Bacchus. The

[1] Thomas Wright, *Anglo-Saxon and Old English Vocabularies*, ed. R. P. Wülcker, London, 1883, pt. i. col. 571.
[2] Brand, *loc. cit.*
[3] *Plays of Ben Jonson*, 'Every Man's Library,' vol. 489, p. 106.
[4] *Ib.* p. 119.
[5] J. Nichols, *Progresses and Public Processions of Queen Elizabeth*, London, 1788–1805, ii. 19, quoted by Lucy Aikin, *Memoirs of the Court of Queen Elizabeth*[4], do. 1819.
[6] J. Spedding, *Account of the Life and Times of Bacon*, London, 1878, i. 32 f.
[7] Brand, i. 65.
[8] *Ib.* i. 79.
[9] *Ib.*
[10] *Ib.* i. 83.

poems were fastened to the inner doors of the College.[1] The revels at Merton College, Oxford, are described by Anthony Wood under date 1647–48:

'Shrove-Tuesday, Feb. 15, the fire being made in the common hall before 5 of the clock at night, the fellowes would go to supper before six, and making anend sooner than at other times, they left the hall to the liberties of the undergraduate, but with an admonition from one of the fellowes (who was then principal of the undergraduates and postmasters) that all things should be carried in good order. While they were at supper in the hall, the cook (Will. Noble) was making the lesser of the brass pots ful of cawdle at the freshmen's charge, which after the hall was free from the fellowes was brought up and set before the fire in the said hall. Afterward every freshman, according to seniority, was to pluck off his gowne and band and if possible to make himself look like a scoundrell. This done, they were conducted each after the other to the high table, and there made to stand on a forme placed thereon: from thence they were to speak their speech with an audible voice to the company: which if well done, the person that spake it was to have a cup of cawdle, and no salted drinke: if indifferently some cawdle and some salted drinke; but if dull nothing was given him but salted drinke or salt put in college bere, with tucks to boot. Afterwards when they were to be admitted into the fraternity, the senior cook was to administer to them an oath over an old shoe, part of which runs thus: "Item te jurabis quod penniless bench non visitabis."'

A note adds: 'This was the way and customs that had been used in the college, time out of mind, to initiate the freshmen: but between that time and the restoration of K. Ch. 2 it was disused, and now such a thing is absolutely forgotten.'[2]

W. Huddesford[3] refers to similar customs prevailing in the university about 1772. Thomas Hearne, in his *Reliquiæ*,[4] mentions customs of this kind at Brasenose and Balliol.[5]

The grammar schools were not behind the colleges in their observance of Shrove-tide. The sports were rougher, and were similar to those of the country-side. Stowe, on the authority of W. Fitzstephen, refers to the ancient practice of cock-fighting and playing at the ball or bastion.[6] Sir John Sinclair in his *Statistical Account* produces a witness for Scotland, the minister of the parish of Kirkmichael, Perthshire:

'Foot-Ball is a common amusement with the School-boys, who also preserve the custom of Cock-fighting on Shrove-Tuesday.'[7]

In Lancashire and Cumberland the 'Cock-penny' formed a part of the stipend of grammar school masters. At Lancaster Grammar School and at Burnley, Clitheroe, Whitehaven, and Millom this gratuity was paid by the scholars at Shrove-tide. The Yorkshire rhymes may refer to this custom:

'A nick and a nock,
A hen and a cock,
And a penny for my master.'

In Scotland the schoolmaster claimed the 'fugees,' or runaway cocks.[8]

Joseph Addison, in the year 1684 or 1685, took part in another Shrove-tide custom at Lichfield Grammar School. This was known as 'barring-out' the master. It was a custom practised at Christmas and Shrove-tide, and links the Bacchanalian customs of Shrove-tide with the Saturnalian licence of Christmas.[9]

3. Country-side.—(1) *The Holly-boy and Ivy-girl.*—This custom is one of the most important links in the chain of evidence for the origin of the Shrove-tide revels. It survived in Kent at the close of the 18th century. It is described in *The Gentleman's Magazine* for 1779:

'Being on a visit on Tuesday last [Shrove Tuesday] in a little obscure village in this county, I found an odd kind of sport

[1] Brand, i. 62.
[2] *Life and Times of Anthony à Wood, described by Himself*, Oxford, 1891–1900, i. (Oxford Hist. Soc. Publications, xix.) 138.
[3] *Lives of those Eminent Antiquaries, Leyland, Hearne and Anthony à Wood*, ed. T. Warton and W. Huddesford, 2 vols., Oxford, 1772.
[4] *Reliquiæ Hernianæ*, ed. P. Bliss, 2 vols., Oxford, 1857.
[5] *Life and Times of Wood*, i. 140, n. 8.
[6] J. Stowe, *Survey of London*, ed. J. Strype, London, 1720, i. 247.
[7] *Statistical Account of Scotland*, Edinburgh, 1791–95, xv. 521.
[8] Brand, i. 70, 72.
[9] *Ib.* pp. 70 f., 441–450.

going forward: the Girls, from eighteen to five or six years old, were assembled in a crowd, and burning an uncouth effigy, which they called an *Holly-Boy*, and which it seems they had stolen from the Boys, who, in another part of the village, were assembled together, and burning what they called an *Ivy-Girl*, which they had stolen from the Girls: all this ceremony was accompanied with loud huzzas, noise, and acclamations. What it all means I cannot tell, although I inquired of several of the oldest people in the place, who could only answer that it had always been a sport at this season of the year.'[1]

There is a reference to a similar custom in Barnaby Googe's translation of Naogeorgus's *Popish Kingdome* (1570):

'Some others make a man all stuft with straw or ragges within,
Apparayled in dublet faire, and hosen passing trim.
. . . .
They hurle him up into the ayre, nor suffring him to fall,
And this they doe at diuers tymes the citie over all.'[2]

(2) *Cock-fighting.*—This was one of the most widely prevalent sports on Shrove Tuesday. The Cumberland practice is described by W. Hutchinson:

'The party whose Cocks won the most battles was victorious in the Cock-pit; and the prize, a small silver bell, suspended to the button of the victor's hat, and worn for three successive Sundays. After the Cock-fight was ended, the Foot-Ball was thrown down in the Church-yard.'[3]

The monasteries did not favour these sports. Cock-fighting is forbidden in the *Customary of St. Augustine's, Canterbury*:

'Nec interesse luctis, pugnis, vel duellis hominum, animalium vel avium.'[4]

(3) *Throwing at cocks.*—The question is asked in *The British Apollo*: 'How old and from whence is the custom of throwing at Cocks on Shrove Tuesday?'[5] An epigram by Sir Charles Sedley, 'On a Cock at Rochester,' in *The Gentleman's Journal* of Jan. 1692–93 suggests a sacrificial origin, veiled under later lore:

'May'st thou be punish'd for St. Peter's crime,
And on Shrove Tuesday perish in thy prime.'[6]

The custom was retained at Heston in Middlesex on Shrove Tuesday in 1791:

'The owner of the cock trains his bird for some time before Shrove Tuesday, and throws a stick at him himself, in order to prepare him for the fatal day, by accustoming him to watch the threatened danger, and by springing aside avoid the fatal blow. He holds the poor victim on the spot marked out by a cord fixed to his leg, and at the distance of nine or ten yards, so as to be out of the way of the stick himself. Another spot is marked, at the distance of twenty-two yards, for the person who throws to stand upon. He has three *shys*, or throws, for twopence, and wins the cock if he can knock him down and run up and catch him before the bird recovers his legs.'[7]

The word 'cock-shy' is a survival of this brutal sport. In the parish accounts of Pinner in 1622 is the entry: 'Received for Cocks at Shrove-tide, 12s. 0d.' The money collected was applied in aid of the poor rate.[8]

(4) *Thrashing the hen.*—In Robert Baron's *Cyprian Academy*[9] this practice is referred to as a Shrove-tide sport:

'By the Maskins I would give the best Cow in my yard to find out this Raskall. And I would thrash him as I did the Henne last Shrove Tuesday.'

Thomas Tusser, in his *Five Hundreth Pointes of Good Husbandrie* (1573), says:

'At Shroftide to shroving, go thresh the fat Hen,
If blindfold can kill her, then give it thy men.'

Tusser Redivivus has a note explaining these lines:

'The Hen is hung at a fellow's back, who has also some horse-bells about him; the rest of the fellows are blinded, and have boughs in their hands, with which they chase this fellow and his Hen about some large court or small enclosure. The fellow with his Hen and bells shifting as well as he can, they follow the sound, and sometimes hit him and his Hen.'[1]

(5) *Stone-throwing.*—This was a custom in the Scilly Isles. When the cock-shying was ended, boys threw stones against the house-doors. Heath, the authority on whom this rests, says that it was practised also in Cornwall and in Spain.[2] This may be compared with the custom of 'Lent crocking' in Dorset and Wilts.[3]

(6) *Pancakes.*—This remains in most parts of England the only relic of the old Shrove-tide customs. In *Poor Robin's Almanack* (1731) it gave its name to the day:

'St. Taffy is no sooner gone
But *Pancake day* is coming on.'[4]

At Baldock, in Hertfordshire, it was called Dough-nut day.[5] *The Gentleman's Magazine* for 1790 refers to the 'pancake bell.'[6] In a tract of 1690 it is said that at York 'all the apprentices, journeymen, and other servants . . . had the liberty to go into the Cathedral, and ring the Pancake-bell.' This bell had originally been rung to call the people to church for the confession of sin.[7] In Scotland, according to Frederick M. Eden, crowdie used to take the place of pancakes.[8] Brand and Ellis give several versions of the pancake rhymes.

(7) *Carting.*—In 1555 'an ill woman who kept the Greyhound in Westminster was carted about the city.' In 1556 'were carted two men and three women.' This seems to have been a recognized punishment for persons of ill-fame. In a comedy, *Tottenham Court*, written by Thomas Nabbes in 1638, we find:

'If I doe, I have lesse mercy than Prentices at Shrove-tide.'[9]

(8) *Football.*—The Derby football play is described in *The Penny Magazine* for 6th April, 1839. A similar Shrove-tide custom was practised in Perthshire:

'Every year on Shrove Tuesday the bachelors and married men drew themselves up at the Cross of Scone, on opposite sides. A ball was then thrown up, and they played from two o'clock till sunset' . . . One goal was the so-called 'dool' on the moor, the other was the river. The game in early times covered the whole town.[10]

(9) *Rope-pulling.*—In 1846 this was an old Shrove-tide custom at Ludlow. The tug-of-war was between the Corve Street Ward and the Broad Street Ward, and lasted from four o'clock till sunset.[11]

III. *FOLK-LORE ANALOGIES.*—The Christmas customs are acknowledged to be survivals in part of the old Saturnalia. The 'servants' holiday' in N. Staffordshire has points of contact with the liberty and licence allowed by masters to their slaves in the midwinter revels. Dekker, in his *Seven Deadly Sins of London* (1606), refers to the same licence at Shrove-tide.

'They presently (like Prentices upon Shrove Tuesday) take the lawe into their owne handes and do what they list.'[12]

In the records of Norwich mention is made of the Shrove-tide revels as the closing of the revels of Christmas:

'John Gladman . . . on Tuesday in the last ende of Crestemesse [1440] vizt. *Fastyngonge Tuesday*, made a disport with hys neyghbours, havyng his hors trappyd with tynnsoyle and other nyse disgisy things, corroned as Kyng of Crestemesse, in tokyn that seson should end with the twelve monethes of the yere.'[13]

This name 'Fastyngonge Tuesday' recalls the Scotch 'Fasten's Eve' and the German *Fastnacht.*

1 Brand, p. 68.
2 *Ib.* p. 66 f.
3 *Hist. of the County of Cumberland*, Carlisle, 1794–98, ii. 323; Brand, i. 71.
4 E. Maunde Thompson, *Customary of the Benedictine Monasteries of St. Augustine, Canterbury, and St. Peter, Westminster*, London, 1902–04, i. (Henry Bradshaw Society, vol. xxiii.) 154.
5 London, 1708, vol. i. no. 1.
6 Brand, i. 73 f.
7 *Ib.* p. 77.
8 *Ib.* p. 80.
9 London, 1648, p. 53; Brand, i. 80.

1 D. Hilman, *Tusser Redivivus: a Calendar of the Twelve Months*², London, 1744, p. 80; Brand, i. 80.
2 Brand, i. 81.
3 R. Chambers, *Book of Days*, i. 239.
4 Brand, i. 81.
5 *Ib.* p. 83.
6 P. 953.
7 Brand, i. 85.
8 *The State of the Poor*, London, 1797, i. 498.
9 Brand, i. 89 f.
10 *Statistical Account of Scotland*, xviii. 88; Brand, i. 91.
11 Brand, i. 92.
12 *Ib.* p. 88.
13 F. Blomefield, *Topographical Hist. of Norfolk*, ed C Parkin, London, 1739–75, ii. 111; cf. Brand, i. 68.

The German form dates only from the 18th cent., and is a corruption by assimilation of *Fasenacht*, *vasenaht*, *vaschane*, preserved in the form *Fasching* in Bavaria and Austria. It is derived from *fasen*, *faseln*='Possen treiben zu Grunde,' *i.e.* an end of all trifling and farcing.[1]

In Germany the Monday in Shrove-tide is called *Rosenmontag* and *Hirsmontag*, the latter name derived from the revellers masquerading as deer.[2] The Sunday before is called the *Grosser Fastelabend* or *Rinnetag* or *Funkensonntag*. The writer adds:

'Die dort üblichen Lustbarkeiten, Maskeraden, Tänze, Schmausereien und dergl. wurden bald . . . ausgedehnt, schliesslich durch Verbindung mit den üblichen Frühlings-, Neujahrs- und Dezemberfasten noch weiter zurück auf die Zeit von 7 Januar ab oder (z. B. in Venedig) seit dem 26 Dezember, doch so, dass sich das Hauptleben in den letzten Wochen oder Tagen vor dem Aschermittwoch abspielt.'[3]

The Holly-boy and Ivy-girl of Kent are the most important links with the German *Fastnachtsmann*, or *Prinz Karneval*—itself a memory of the Saturnalian king who, after a reign of 30 days, was burnt as a sacrifice to Kronos (Saturn):

'Es wirken aber hier wie anderswo noch ältere Sitten nach; die Fastnachtsbräuche erinnern nicht selten an die an den römischen Saturnalien, den altitalischen noch lange in christlicher Zeit bestehenden Luperkalien und den germanischen Frühlingsfesten üblichen Lustbarkeiten. Wenn z. B. hier und da der Fastnachtsmann oder "Prinz Karneval"—eine Strohpuppe—öffentlich verbrannt, geköpft, oder gesteinigt und am Aschermittwoch begraben wird, . . . so sieht man darin teils die Nachwirkung eines älteren gemein-germanischen Balder-Kultus, teils das Fortleben des Saturnalienkönigs, der 30 Tage lang als Spottkönig herrschte und dann dem Kronos als Opfer dargebracht wurde.'[4]

Zscharnack adds:

'No wonder that the Church protested as much against these revels as against those of the New Year.'

It is to be noted that in Italy Liber, the Latin Dionysus, has a female deity Libera as his associate. The Kentish Holly-boy was accompanied by the Ivy-girl. The Liberalia were held in Rome on 17th March;

'Old women, crowned with ivy, sold cheap cakes (*liba*) of meal, honey, and oil, and burnt them on little pans for the purchasers.'[5]

The English evidence from the Ivy-girl and the pancakes adds support to the suggestion of Zscharnack as to the affinity of the Shrove-tide revels with the earlier cults.

The association of cock-shying with some national event, the feud between the English and the Danes,[6] or the long wars between the English and the French,[7] will not stand the test of the wider study of folk-lore. N. W. Thomas, in his study of the folk-lore of animals, says:

'The cock is one of the most important sacrificial victims. . . . The cock figures in spring ceremonies in Europe. . . . The cock is sometimes used in the expulsion of evils. Modern Jews sacrifice a white cock on the eve of the Day of Atonement. We may probably interpret in the same sense the numerous European customs in which a cock or hen is hunted or beaten.'[8]

Thus the throwing at the cock, the thrashing at the hen, and the punishment of persons of ill-fame seem to be different aspects of the spring rites of purification. The cock was also associated with the Celtic god Sacellus and with the Gaulish Mercury. It was tabu to the ancient Britons. There may thus be a link with the ancient rites of Gaul and Britain.

The presence of conflation of primitive cults in the Shrove-tide revels—the traces of different strands of ritual tradition—does not weaken the argument for affinity. Every custom is important to build up the evidence. It will then be found that folk-lore has the last word in our old English sports and revels.

[1] *RGG*, *s.v.* 'Fastnacht.'

[2] Cf. the Abbot's-Bromley horn-dance in Staffordshire and a similar horn-dance at Mohaçs on the Danube. They may be traceable to the cult of the Celtic god Cernunnos, of whom there are vestiges from the Danube to Brittany. The legend of Herne the hunter in Windsor Park may perhaps be akin to the same ancient cult.

[3] *RGG*, *s.v.* 'Fastnacht,' vol. ii. col. 839.

[4] *Ib.*

[5] A. O. Seyffert, *Dict. of Class. Ant.*, ed. H. Nettleship and J. E. Sandys, Oxford, 1891, art. 'Dionysos.'

[6] Brand, i. 73.

[7] *Ib.* p. 78.

[8] *ERE* i. 515[b].

LITERATURE.—J. Brand, *Observations on Popular Antiquities*, new ed. by H. Ellis, with additions by J. O. Halliwell, 3 vols., London, 1849; W. Hone, *The Every-day Book*, 2 vols., do. 1830; R. Chambers, *The Book of Days*, 2 vols., do. 1863–64; *DACL*, Paris, 1908–11, art. 'Caput jejunii'; Christopher Wordsworth, *The Ancient Kalendar of the University of Oxford* (Oxford Hist. Soc. Publications, xlv.), Oxford, 1904; *RGG*, Tübingen, 1909–13, *s.v.* 'Fastnacht,' vol. ii. col. 838.

THOMAS BARNS.

SIAM.—The kingdom of Siam (Mu'ăng Thăi, Săyám Pra : thet[1]) occupies the centre and includes the greater part of the Indo-Chinese peninsula. It extends from 20° to 6° N. lat., and covers an area of 600,000 sq. kilometres, although it has hardly 7,500,000 inhabitants. It is bounded on the north by the Shan States (under English rule) and the kingdom of Laos (under French rule); on the east by the Mekong river, which is the frontier between it and French Cambodia; on the south by the Gulf of Siam; and on the west by British Malaysia and Burma. Mountainous on its northern and western confines, it is simply the valley of the beautiful Menam river, which waters and fertilizes it.

Politically and historically it is divided into three parts:

(1) Siamese Laos, including the upper valley of the Menam and the right bank of the middle Mekong with the entire basin of its tributary, the Sĕ-Mun, is a mountainous district through which flow rivers unsuitable for navigation owing to rapids, and which is very rich in timber and dye-wood, and sparsely peopled by about 2,000,000 inhabitants, almost all Laotians and closely related ethnographically and linguistically to the Siamese.

(2) The Siamo-Malay peninsula (and islands) between British Burma and Malaysia, which has only 1,106,640 inhabitants, of whom some are Siamese, the majority Malay, and the rest the débris of aboriginal and semi-civilized populations (Semangs, etc.), is a mountainous country, cut up by rugged cliffs, poor in vegetation, but very rich in deposits of tin, argentiferous galena, wolfram, coal, and gold; its chief exports are swallows' nests, the feathers of rare birds, tortoise-shell, fish, elephants, and oxen.

(3) Siam proper, extending from 13° to 18° N. lat., is formed by the middle and lower valley of the Menam. It is in this vast plain, composed of limestone hills, furrowed by navigable rivers, and indented with ports and creeks, that the pure Siamese element is concentrated. Its population totals about 4,000,000. It is the open door for the kingdom of the Thais to the free seas of China and India, affording it communication with the Far East on the one side and Europe on the other. There also is found the capital of Siam, Bangkok, between the two branches of the Menam at its mouth in the Gulf of Siam, and 40 kilometres from the sea. In 1909 Bangkok had 628,675 inhabitants, of whom 200,000 were Chinese, Annamese, and Cham, and 1600 European. The Venice of the Far East, as it has been rather pretentiously called, is built on piles in numerous canals and arms of rivers from 200 to 300 metres broad and 10 to 12 deep, and is dotted with thousands of barges, steam-boats, junks, and sailing-boats—not to mention the cargo-boats and merchant vessels anchored in its port. The general appearance of its bamboo huts forms a contrast with the brilliance of its gilded pagodas and multi-coloured pyramids, but it is gradually being transformed into a modern town: it is entirely lit by electricity and already has 120 kilometres of coach-roads,

[1] In this art. Pallegoix's system of transcription for the native names has been followed (except that his *j* has always been rendered *y*); if it is not the best, it is at least the best known.

some of which are very beautiful, and 40 kilometres of electric tramways.

1. Origin.—The Siamese are a branch of the ethnic family of the Thais, 'free men,' whose other branches are the Shans, the Laotians, the Lus, the Pou-Thais, and other Thai races in the north of Tongking. They all seem to have come down from the high plateaux of Tibet and Yunnan into the Indo-Chinese plain and towards the sea, following the valley of the rivers Menam, Mekong, and Song-Khoi. Gradually, but irresistibly, they drove the aboriginal races before them and forced towards the coast the other Indo-Chinese races—Annamese, Chams, Cambodians (Khmers), Peguans (Mons), and Burmese. The Siamese branch passed from the upper valley of the Mekong to the middle valley, which it disputed for centuries with the Laotians and the Khmers, then to the entire basin of the Menam, where it became permanently settled—not without mixing with numerous Chinese, Malay, Khmer, Mon, and Burmese elements.

2. History.—The early history of Siam is not very well known. According to the annals and chronicles of Siam, it may be divided into two periods. The first, rather legendary, extends from the beginning to the founding of Ayuthia (*c.* 1350). A collection of fables and traditional legends dating back to the 5th cent. B.C. give as the ancestors of the present kings some of the Buddha's first disciples. In this period the names of dynasties and capitals are very variable, facts being constantly mingled with supernatural interventions. Even at this early period the Siamese princes who were vassals of the kingdom of Cambodia were trying to escape from its power, and at one time they were at war, at another in union, with China; their contests with the Laotians were even more lively.

With the foundation of Ayuthia, although the date given by the Siamese annals (A.D. 1350) is now disputed, we come upon more real history. In 1514 Ayuthia was reduced to ashes by a fire which lasted three days. In 1532 conquered Cambodia became tributary, and its capital Lovêk was occupied; but a new and much more dangerous enemy, Pegu, appeared against Siam. In 1543 the king of Pegu laid waste the whole of Siam, besieging Ayuthia in vain. In 1555 he seized the whole of Siam and Ayuthia after nine months of siege, devastating it to such an extent that only 1000 inhabitants remained. But in 1558 the Siamese throne was occupied by a talented young Phra: Nărèt prince, who freed his country from the Peguan yoke, restored Ayuthia, conquered the whole of Laos and Cambodia, and in his turn took possession of Hangsavada, the capital of Pegu. He died in 1593.

His successors became embroiled in intrigues and bloody strifes. In 1656 one of them, Phra: Narai, tried to restore the kingdom with the help of a European prime minister, a clever Greek adventurer Constance Phaulkon (or Falcon). At his instigation Phra: Narai opened his ports to Spanish, Portuguese, English, Dutch, and French merchants, and sent two embassies to Louis XIV. to ask for a commercial treaty and an alliance based on mutual help which would enable him to modernize his subjects by force if not with their consent. A plot of Siamese mandarins, who were anxious about their privileges and jealous of the rights accorded to strangers, ended in the death of the king and the massacre of Constance Falcon.

Intrigue and civil war began once more. The king of Ava, taking advantage of the opportunity thus afforded, came with his Burmans, laid waste the whole of Siam, and took Ayuthia, which was burned down, while its vanquished ruler died of hunger and despair in the surrounding woods. A clever usurper, Phaya Tak, rallied the Siamese at Chantabun, delivered Siam, and took his stand in the present capital Bangkok (or Thanaburi). He recaptured Laos and a part of the peninsula of Malacca, and overcame the Burmans on several occasions, but the mandarins became suspicious of his influence and had him assassinated. The ancient dynasty regained power; the king of Vieng Chang (Laos) was beaten and put into an iron cage at Bangkok; the Cochin-Chinese were conquered.

In 1851, when King Mongkuṭ, who had been long confined in a monastery to save his life from the jealousy of a usurper, ascended the throne, he set himself to restore Siam by bold modernization. He learned the European languages, surrounded himself with European counsellors, and, after purifying and reforming his clergy, removed the most notorious abuses of his mandarins; he also tried to enrich his country by increasing its production of rice and by concluding friendly and commercial treaties with the great European Powers. This one-time monk was the real creator of modern Siam. His son, Chulālongkorṇ (1868–1910), educated like a European and having travelled extensively in Europe, continued his work. With the help of his younger brother, Prince Damrong, he multiplied schools, benevolent institutions, works of public utility, and modern processes of agriculture and industry. His son Vajirāvudh, who succeeded him in 1910, and has been brought up with equally broad views, is continuing the work of his father and his grandfather in close friendship with the two European Powers established in Indo-China, viz. Britain and France.

3. Physical features.—In spite of frequent admixtures with neighbouring peoples, the Siamese race preserves a distinct type. The Siamese is of medium height, and has a supple body, vigorous and well-proportioned. Both sexes are olive-coloured, with narrow upper-foreheads, broad faces with thick lips, and black well-lacquered teeth. Their hands are well-shaped but rather large, and they have long red-coloured nails. Their hair is glossy black, but coarse and not very thick; the men have their heads shaved, except a big tuft on the top, and they always shave their beards. The women also shave their heads except a big tuft which they wear on the top, not so high as that of the men, and which they comb, pomade, and perfume carefully. This method of wearing the hair is still seen, but the Siamese of both sexes now tend to copy the Cambodians and wear their hair cut short. Among the upper classes, in imitation of the Europeans, the men wear their hair quite short, or even have their heads shaved, while the women let their hair grow long and twist it up behind. The children of both sexes still have shaved heads, except for a pretty lock of hair on the top which their parents adorn with small garlands of flowers and large gold or silver pins. This lock of hair is shaved with great ceremony at puberty.

4. Dress.—Except in the case of very small children, the Siamese do not allow nakedness. Both men and women wear a *languti*, or lower garment, arranged in the form of wide breeches, the material of which (cotton, silk, etc.) varies according to means; the breast is covered with a vest with sleeves, or among the women by a scarf worn crosswise over the shoulders. All go barefooted as a rule, except princes and mandarins, who wear embroidered slippers. The custom of wearing European shoes is gradually spreading. People in good circumstances shade themselves from the sun with a parasol; ordinary people content themselves with huge hats of palm-leaves. Both men and women have a passion for jewels.

5. Character.—The Siamese character has been variously judged. Pallegoix, who perhaps knew them best because of his long residence in Siam, credits them with a spirit of charity, humanity, and gentleness, not only towards men, but towards animals, and a happy, timid, thoughtless, irresolute, and rather childish disposition; they have a horror of shouting and quarrelling, and are fond of amusement; they are great beggars, but also willingly give to those who ask from them. They have great respect for authority and old age and deep reverence for their kings. As regards the accusations made against them that they are fonder of borrowing than of repaying, that they are humble with the powerful and harsh towards the weak, that they sometimes prove too clever in business, and that they are dishonest and glory in their dishonesty, as is exemplified by the Siamese proverb, 'Trade is the business of the Dutch, arts and industry that of the Chinese, war that of France, and cleverness that of the Siamese,' it is only fair to remark that similar accusations have been made, and not always justly, against many European races; lastly, the worst faults of the Siamese seem to be those of the despotic government under which they are bowed down rather than those of the race itself.

6. Dwelling-places.—As a rule the Siamese live in bamboo huts built on piles and covered with a roof of interlaced palm-leaves; they are poor and simple, but often very clean. They are raised about a metre from the ground, with access by a bamboo ladder. The hut itself is divided by bamboo partitions into two or three compartments; and under it are kept the supplies of rice, household utensils, and domestic animals. Merchants prefer to build their huts on a bamboo raft so that they can be removed at pleasure; many of the canal- and river-dwellers have house-boats. The rich build their houses in the Chinese style of wood or brick with pillars of iron-wood and floor and framework of teak; they require two or three houses in order to afford separate accommodation to their family, slaves, and cooks.

Before building a house, the Siamese must first consult the diviner to find out in what direction he must build. He must avoid a place with piles sunk in the earth—the debris of a former building; he must not use pillars of teak, and among the pillars of iron-wood he must avoid those with exudations of resinous oil. The rungs of the ladder, the doors, windows, rooms, partitions must all be of odd number. Every house that violates these rules is unlucky and should be demolished.

The furniture consists of thin mats and cushions for lying on, benches, some boxes, earthenware articles, baskets, hampers, and knives. The rich, however, especially since the modernization of Siam, have carved beds, mattresses of floss silk, arm-chairs, tables, furniture inlaid with mother-of-pearl, tapestries, curtains, and carpets, costly weapons, as well as vases of valuable workmanship or material, cups of all shapes and materials, sometimes beautiful plate, a great many clocks, musical-boxes, pianos, gramophones, and other inventions of modern genius.

7. Food.—The Siamese are as a rule very temperate, like all the natives of the Far East: they live on rice, fresh or dried fish, and fruits; they season their dishes with a sauce or curry made with red allspice. They eat very little meat, but all kinds—poultry, water-birds, stags, buffalo- or ox-flesh dried in the sun, tortoises, frogs, crocodiles, bats, serpent-boas, rats, etc.—and drink pure water or tea, and sometimes arak or rice-brandy.

8. Arts and trades.—The Siamese are good cultivators and good sailors in smooth water, but disinclined to coasting either from headland to headland or close to the shore; they also fish and hunt. Intelligent, skilful, and manageable, they would make excellent workmen if their sense of initiative had not been killed by the custom of the court and the mandarins of monopolizing them at a ridiculous price as soon as they possess any manual skill. Some do artistic wood-carving and metal-working; others make barges and canoes; the women weave materials for clothing. During the reigns of the last three kings efforts have been made to develop national industry.

9. Tobacco and opium.—The Siamese smoke tobacco, and, in spite of the stern edicts of King Chulālongkorṇ, many are still addicted to opium. This the authorities combat very strongly, although they do not always set an example of abstinence.

10. Religion: Buddhism.—The Siamese are one of the most religious races of the religious East. Their religion, like that of Cambodia, is Southern, or orthodox, Buddhism, with Pāli as its sacred language, and called Sinhalese Buddhism. Under this very deep-rooted Buddhism there still remain traces of Brāhmanism and innumerable animistic survivals. Buddhism seems to have been introduced into Cambodia and thence into Siam in A.D. 422 (965 of the Buddhist era). For many years the whole Buddhist theology of Siam was based on the *Trai Phûm*, 'The Three Places,' which is not an original Pāli work, but a compilation in Siamese of works and commentaries on the Buddhist Pāli canon, composed at the request of King Phaya Tâk (1767–80). The *Trai Phûm* is divided into three parts: (1) the first treats of the universe in general and the earth in particular; (2) the second of the heavens and their inhabitants; (3) the third of the hells and their various punishments. Since the theological reform carried out in the 19th cent. under the auspices of King Mongkuṭ the *Trai Phûm* has had very little orthodox value.[1]

The fervour of the Siamese is shown by the multiplicity and richness of their pagodas, the number of their monks, and the esteem in which they are held. The pagodas, especially those of Bangkok, are most impressive with their forests of bell-turrets, above which towers a central pyramid 60 to 80 metres high, their trunks of white elephants at the corners, their coverings of polished tiles, their gilding, and their coloured porcelains. But connoisseurs find in them a too evident intrusion of Chinese statuary and decorative art. They are high colonnaded buildings, with recurved roofs, the walls, painted in fresco on the inside, sheltering great statues of the Buddha as well as *stūpas* of various dimensions. As a rule the pagodas are veritable monastic towns built in the middle of beautiful gardens dotted with ponds; their principal ornament is one or more temples dedicated to the Buddha. The monastic enclosure also contains a funeral-pile for burning the dead, rooms for preaching and for the temporary accommodation of pilgrims and strangers, out-houses, and hundreds of little wooden and brick houses where the *bonzes* of the pagoda live.

The monks, usually called by the earliest European travellers *talapoins* (*tala: păt*, the fan which they always carry) or *bonzes*, and by the Siamese *phra:*, 'great,' *chăo thăi*, 'lords,' *phĭkhu* (Pāli *bhikkhu*), *phĭsu* (Skr. *bhikṣu*), 'mendicants,' are more than 100,000 in number, attached to about 20,000 monasteries throughout the whole of Siam. The rule to which they conform is, as in Cambodia, the 27 articles of the *Patimôk* (Pāli *Patimokkha*) and the commentaries of the *Phra: Vinăi* (Skr. *Vinaya*). At their head is the *śăngkhărăt* (Skr. (*saṅgharāja*), nominated by the king, who is the 'protector and preserver of Buddhism' in the kingdom. The *saṅgharāja* has jurisdiction over all the monks in Siam, but interferes as little as possible in their affairs; it is he who decides, in agreement with the king, in all religious controversies and litigations; and he presides at the assembly of the chiefs of pagodas when the king convokes it to discuss theological reforms. Under the *saṅgharāja*, but independent of him, are the abbots (*somdet chao*) of the royal monasteries, also nominated by the king. Each abbot governs his monastery assisted by a vicar (*chao khŭn pălat*) and a chief secretary (*chao khŭn sămu*). Under them are the *bonzes* who have been ordained, and under them, again, the *nen* or *sama: nén* (Pāli *samaṇera*), novices under twenty years of age, who wear the yellow robe, but are not yet obliged to observe more than the eight Buddhist commandments.[1]

The pagoda in Siam is not only the sanctuary of prayer; it is also the centre of culture. This culture is essentially Indian, as, until the arrival of the first Portuguese navigators, Siam was completely within India's sphere of influence; it received its first civilization from the Brāhmans of India, and then from merchants from Malabar and Coromandel, and, along with Cambodia and Laos, it remained permeated with this Indian civilization until the east coast of Indo-China accepted Chinese civilization. There are still extant noteworthy archæological witnesses of this primitive Hinduization of Siam in the monuments of its former capitals, Savankhalôk, Sukhôkai, and Lopburī. The former and present religion of Siam (Brāhmanism and Buddhism), its sacred language (Pāli), its civil institutions, its writing, its arts, and its literature come from India. In the 13th cent. the Thai alphabet, the prototype of the present alphabet, was invented by the help of Brāhman *gurus* on the model of the Indian writing already in use in the country. All this civilization has been preserved and diffused up to the present day by the monks, who are as a rule the educators of the people, as the Christian monks were in Europe in the Middle Ages. The *văt* (monastery) is still the only school in isolated villages, although in the large towns modern schools have been established, with special teachers to initiate the Siamese into Western culture. In spite of the welcome given to this culture, every boy, from the humblest subject to the king, still continues to go to the pagoda at the age of puberty to receive a Buddhist initiation, with religious and domestic ceremonies which recall the first Christian communion. The Buddhist monastery, on the whole, has always maintained in Siam, even during the most troubled times, the inclination for spiritual life and culture. It is naturally more concerned with the boys than with the girls, although in 1767 there were convents of *bhikkhunī* ('nuns') flourishing in Ayuthia, in which a great many women and girls received an elementary education; at the present day wealthy families, especially those of court officials, give a very good education to their daughters, some of whom are fairly elegant Siamese writers.

11. Reforms of Buddhism.—The establishment of Christian missions in Siam introduced Western culture, which was received, especially at court, with genuine enthusiasm, particularly the astronomy and mathematics taught by the Jesuits. So also the preaching of Christianity, as well as that of Islām, always received complete tolerance, except when it was believed to be a cloak for dangerous political designs. The embassy of Louis XIV. was so well received that for a moment that monarch thought that the whole of Siam would be converted to Christianity; young Siamese were sent to the Louis le Grand College, and one of them there sustained a thesis in Latin at the Sorbonne. In 1767 the destruction of Ayuthia and the dynasty reigning there aroused a violent reaction; Siam became a hater of foreigners. But with the establishment of the present dynasty in 1787, with Bangkok as its capital, the former Siamese civilization revived, and the kingdom was opened to the influence of Western civilization. The great author of this double evolution—at one and the same time traditional and modernist—was King Mongkuṭ. But this former *bhikkhu* remained at the same time a proud nationalist and a fervent Buddhist, who longed for a revival of Buddhism

[1] For the facts concerning Siamese Buddhism cf. the artt. CEYLON BUDDHISM and CAMBODIA.

[1] See art. MONASTICISM (Buddhist).

in Siam. He reformed the monastic discipline in an orthodox sense, grounding himself on the original sources; and he organized the teaching of Pāli in the monasteries with examinations in sacred hermeneutics and theology. He attempted more—the modernization of Buddhism—in concert with his minister the Phra: Klan Chao Phaya Thipakon. In 1869 the latter published a work entitled *Kichanukit*, 'Book explaining Things clearly,' in which he posits four truths (pain, the origin of pain, destruction of this origin, and the way leading to this destruction), which are in germ all the teaching of the Buddha. He denies the authenticity of the *Jātakas* and the five stories of the *suttas* forming the *Suttapiṭaka*. For him there emanate from the Buddha only the Four Noble Truths (enumerated above) and the *Paramattha, i.e.* the substance of the *Abhidhammapiṭaka*, or superior doctrine.

This doctrine as well as a royal plan of reform based thereon caused uneasiness among the traditionalists of Siamese monasticism, but, though not in reality very workable, at least it had the excellent effect of forcing the Siamese theologians to learn Pāli scientifically, to get closer to the texts of the Buddhist canon, and to renew their theology.

King Chulālongkorn continued the work of his father by printing and editing at his own expense the whole of the Pāli *Tipiṭaka*,[1] copies of which were lavishly distributed among the scholars and scientific establishments of Europe and America. Under the direction of his brother, Prince Damrong, the Vajirañana National Library regularly publishes Pāli texts, works on Buddhism, and researches on the historical and religious past of Siam after the best European methods.

Thus Siam is taking possession of its glorious past at the very time when it is turning towards a brilliant future in conjunction with the great European nations, enlightened by their civilization, but anxious to keep politically independent of them.

12. Brāhmanism.—Although Brāhmanism has not played such an important part in the history of Siam as in that of Cambodia, it has had great influence. An inscription engraved on an ancient statue of Śiva tells of a curious attempt to restore this ancient religion in Siam: in 1510 the king of Kămpheng-Phĕt, Dharmāśoka, in spite of his ultra-Buddhist name, substituted the worship of Śiva for that of Buddha in his states. Probably this religious transformation in a vassal principality of Ayuthia was specially designed to make final a declaration of independence of the rebel vassal prince. But it is not to this factitious action that the important remains of Brāhmanism on Siamese soil are due, whose living witnesses are the *phrams*, or Brāhmans of the king of Siam, similar to the *bakus* of the king of Cambodia. They are said to be descended from the persecuted Brāhmans of India who fled first to Pegu and then to Siam during the course of the 5th and 6th centuries of our era. They are believed to preserve their primitive type; and there are only about 80 of them living near their special temple, the Vat Bôt Phram, or 'pagoda of the sanctuary of the Brāhmans'—a collection of three miserable brick buildings in an enclosure. The main ornament of this temple consists of colossal statues of the Hindu *trimūrti*; their chief is called in Siamese Phra: Mâhâràxàkhruvitthi (Skr. Mahārājaguruviddhi). They marry, and wear their long hair tied behind; they worship the Brāhmanic deities, and once a year they ceremonially parade through the town with them amid the ignorant respect of the people. Their rôle in the royal palace is exactly the same as in Cambodia, but not so influential. They compose in Sanskrit the official names of the princes, mandarins, towns, temples, palaces, and elephants. In the great ceremonies of the palace, clad in white robes, with long conical caps on their heads, and carrying their Brāhmanic statues in their hands, they occupy as honourable a position as the *bonzes*; they also preside at coronations; and they consecrate the water which is drunk every year as a sign of fidelity by the great mandarins and high officials. Certain of them, called *hôn, hôra* (Skr. *horā*; cf. Gr. ὥρα), are the astrologers and diviners of the king, charged with astronomical and astrological computations, announcing rains or drought, and lucky or unlucky hours and days. Besides the *phrams* we must also mention the *àcàr* (Skr. *āchārya*), the lay teachers of the pagodas.

1 39 vols., Bangkok, 1893.

13. Popular religion.—Although the Siamese are excellent Buddhists, they preserve a mass of survivals of ancient animism. To whatever class of society they belong, all believe in good and bad spirits (*phí*); and the spirits in whom the people are most interested are those which do not seem to have any connexion with Buddhist mythology. The malignant or formidable *phís* are much more numerous and more venerated than the good spirits. Among the latter the best known are the *phí nang măi*, female tree-spirits who dwell in certain beautiful forest-trees. It is said that those good fairies often fill the alms-bowls of monks on pilgrimage when they lay them at the foot of the trees which the spirits inhabit.

Evil spirits are divided into three classes: (1) the 'autogenous' *phí*, those which are not derived from any human being, although some human beings, especially sorcerers, may succeed in keeping them in their power; (2) the *phís* which are the spirits of the dead (spectres, ghosts, demons, etc.); (3) the *phís* belonging to other worlds, which cannot be seen on earth, but which for many people exist as really as if they were seen and heard.

The most common and the most dangerous of all are the second class—the *phí lok*, or spirits of the dead. Having escaped from the body at death, they inhabit abandoned houses and ruins, always on the outlook for living beings to harm or frighten. They can make themselves visible or tangible. They nearly always take up their position at the foot of a person's bed, trying to pull him from it, seizing him by the big toes, etc. One of them, whom many people claim to have seen, is the *phí pret*, from 10 to 16 metres in height, who is the spirit of a malefactor. Having a mouth as small as the eye of a needle, he is constantly in a state of inanition, and looks like a skeleton. He appears at night and, instead of speaking, gives a low whistle. The *phí tai hông* are the spirits of persons who died a sudden or violent death or of still-born children. They are often confused with the *phí tai ha*, who are rather the ghosts of people who have died from cholera or a sudden illness. They are all horrible and malignant, and yet the people do not always avoid the places where they are said to be, because the possession of a *phí phrăi* (the 'essence' of a *phí tai hông*) is a formidable power. To get this a sorcerer goes by night to the place haunted by the *phí tai hông*, conjures him up by incantations, and immediately puts a lighted torch under his chin, so that the heat may cause the grease to flow from his chin into a vessel. This grease, mixed with perfumed oils, forms a magic pomade, by means of which the sorcerer can make people go mad or become amorous, ruin them, or bring dangerous illness upon them. According to the Siamese, a man possessed with a *phí phrăi* suddenly becomes mad, shouts, gesticulates, and tries to break everything round about him; ordinary means being powerless to calm him, they send for the sorcerer to exorcize him; the sorcerer takes a nail and applies the point of it to the big toe of the victim, who begins to shout, although the point has only pressed against the skin; the sorcerer presses with the nail a little more to make the place untenable by the *phí phrăi*; then he drives his nail into a piece of wood, so that the *phí phrăi* feels itself pierced through or is forced to enter the nail; the patient begins to howl, then after a quarter of an hour he quietens down, and is normal and cured. The *phí kŭman* (Skr. *kumara*) is the spirit of a fœtus or of a child dying at birth; the greatest precautions must be taken to bury this abortion to prevent the spirit from returning to haunt the body of the mother and cause her death. The little corpse is folded in two, enclosed in a large pot for cooking rice, covered with paper and leaves on which have been written charms (*mantras*) in Pāli, and buried in the wood; or it may, after being enclosed in the vessel, be given to a sorcerer, who, armed with a sword, carries it to the bank of a river, loads it with imprecations, and then, after breaking it in two with a stroke of the sword, abandons it to the current. The *phí kra : sú* selects as its home the body of certain women (sorceresses), which it leaves at night to look for food, eating the very stones. According to some, it is inoffensive; according to others, it is very dangerous, devouring embryos in the womb. Some claim that these *phís* are the spirits of women who have died in the jungle and come back to haunt the place. The *phí ka : háng*, which appears in the form of a man with the wings and tail of a bird, is also an evil spirit. So also is the *phí pong khang*, a kind of vampire like a black monkey, which dwells in the jungle and sucks the blood from the big toes of sleeping people. The *phí kaong koi* does the same; so that any one who wishes to sleep in the jungle is recommended to keep hold of his feet. These spirits may be forced to obey certain clever sorcerers, who send them to torment their enemies. The *phí pã*, special invisible demons of the jungle, cause fever or dysentery in those who rest there during the night. The *phí khămôt*, a kind of will o' the wisp, in the form of a red star seen in desert places at night, causes mirages and makes people fall into a hole which they take for a house; it also loves to deceive boatmen with its false light and wreck them. The *phí ăm*, the nightmare ghost, sits on the chests of sleepers, especially travellers in the *salas*,[1] and makes them utter inarticulate cries. There are also several wandering spirits, *chăo phí*, *thepharăk* (Skr. *devarakṣa*), for whom the people erect small brick and wooden buildings, called *śan chăo*, 'house of the master.' People living near a *śan chăo*, both men and women, are often possessed by the *phís* who have chosen to dwell in them, and they deliver oracles, cure illnesses, etc.

The *kŭn* (Skr. *guṇa*) is a sort of possession compelling its victim to throw away outside a piece of meat or skin, which forces itself into the body of some person, and harms him if he is not freed from it by means of incantations. Both the bewitched person (*tuk kŭn*) and the bewitcher, moreover, may find themselves in a very bad state if they do not paralyze the malignant effect by periodical and regular incantations.

A certain spirit, the *thàn vèt suvăn*, is regarded as the chief of all; he resembles a *yăk* (Skr. *yakṣa*), or fierce giant, inhabits the sky, is armed with a heavy iron club, and is believed to send smallpox to children.

Among the 'autogenous' *phís* we may mention the *phí ru'en*, the guardian angel or spirit of the house. There is one for each house, and it is sometimes heard whispering to itself; it may be seen in the shape of a man; a small building is dedicated to it in every house.

The water-spirits (*phí năm*) are also very much respected. Small rafts are frequently seen, bearing figurines representing a family with a man, woman, children, offerings of betel, rice, and flowers, dotted with little tapers, floating on the surface of the rivers; this is a tribute of the faithful to the water-spirits. During serious epidemics it is to the spirits of the cross-roads that offerings are dedicated. Of course in Siam, as in Cambodia, a whole series of spirits of a purely Buddhist character are worshipped—the *pisat* (Skr. *pisacha*), the *pret* (Skr. *preta*), the *yăk* (Skr. *yakṣa*), the *raxei* (Skr. *rakṣasa*), the *khrŭt* (Skr. *garuḍa*), and the *nàk* (Skr. *naga*). It is evident also that, with some differences in names, the system of superstitious beliefs is identical in the two countries.

14. Amulets.—Rich and poor wear amulets: these are sometimes *phà pra : chiet*, or bands of cloth which they roll round the head and neck, sometimes necklaces made of seven amber or gold beads, sometimes *ka : krŭt*, or small gold or silver plates engraved with diagrams or sacred formulas and worn on consecrated cords (this is in fact the only clothing of very young children), sometimes circles of thin artistically woven bamboo thongs. All these objects are intended to ward off illnesses and all kinds of witchcraft; and there are also *kayă sith* (Skr. *kāya + siddhi* ?), amulets of invisibility, and *ka : phan*, talismans of invulnerability. The women also wear across their shoulders necklaces soaked in lustral water by the *bonzes*; among the poorer classes strings of consecrated cotton thread are substituted.

15. Sorcerers. — Sorcerers (*módu*), sorceresses (*thao*), and diviners (*mothai*) are consulted in all the important actions of life. They are believed to be able to command certain spirits, to send them into the bodies of human beings, or to chase them away. The spirit by their enchantments hides itself in a buffalo-skin reduced to the size of a pea, which the enemy is made to swallow; soon, under the effect of the spirit's power, the body of the bewitched man expands, swells, and bursts, unless another sorcerer counteracts the witchcraft.

The sorcerers practise spells by means of tiny clay figurines (*pha : yon*) representing the person whom they wish to harm; they stick a pin or a nail through the heart or the head and then bury them. A person can thus either free the victim from an illness or give him an illness from which he will die in a very short time. These sorcerers are also skilled in making love-philtres (*săne, ya phĕt*). It is held that they often make alliance with thieves, facilitating burglaries by causing the whole family to sleep soundly by means of a spell. Most of the formulas used by the sorcerers are in distorted Pāli and are often incomprehensible even to the person who utters them.

16. Medicine.—Siamese medicine originated in India, and tradition says that it was introduced by Khomarabhacca, who lived in the time of Buddha. He wrote medical treatises which were regarded as sacred and to-day are translated into Siamese in the pagodas under the name of *Rôkha: nĭthan* (Skr. *Roghānidāna*). Being essentially Indian, this science is philosophical and theoretical. The human body is supposed to be composed of four elements (wind, water, fire, earth), and health depends upon the equilibrium or non-equilibrium of these elements in the body. Nowhere in these books do we find systematic descriptions of diseases; there is no real knowledge of anatomy, physiology, or surgery, which is in the hands of timid bone-setters, with dressings of coconut-oil and cotton. Midwifery is not quite so rudimentary; but the barbarous and unhygienic custom of keeping a fire burning near the lying-in woman persists in Siam, as in Burma, Cambodia, Annam, and the whole of Indo-China. Except in the case of women of high rank, with whom everything is done in the European fashion, every pregnant Siamese woman is laid on a small bed near a fire in a dark room with no outlet for the smoke; she remains there thirty days for the first child, twenty-five for the second, ten for the third, and five for the others. The women are keenest to maintain this cruel custom, thinking that it improves the beautiful pale yellow colour of their skin.

Knowing their superstitious disposition, we are not surprised that the Siamese attribute the non-equilibrium of the four elements and hence their illnesses to spirits, and consult the sorcerer rather than the doctor; besides, the sorcerer is often the ordinary doctor. They also believe that illnesses are the consequences of deeds, either in this life or in a previous one, and that the best of remedies is to do good works (*thăm bŭn*, Skr. *puṇya*). In all serious illnesses two tapers are offered to the god of medicine.

The Siamese also practise Chinese medicine. The Chinese system consists in taking the pulse and using bundles of medicinal plants; the Siamese system makes drugs of powders and pills of flowers, roots, and medicinal woods dissolved in lukewarm water. The most extraordinary substances, like those to be found in ancient pharmacopœias, abound in Siamese medicine.

In a word, Siamese medicaments, whether of mineral, vegetable, or animal origin, aim at adding to or taking away from the constitutive elements what they lack or what they have in excess. In a single prescription, therefore, the Siamese doctor may use more than a hundred substances all mixed together.

The doctors (*mó*) are divided into *mó luang*, or royal physicians, and *mó ràtsădon* (Skr. *rāja + dāna* ?), or people's physicians. The royal doctors (physicians and surgeons), with a chief at their head, are divided into squads, who in turn remain in the palace and follow the king and court. They all receive a salary from the king, and their office passes to their children. Their knowledge must

[1] Shelters at the entrances to villages for the use of strangers and travellers.

have been very much enriched by the European scientific information which the Wang Lang Medical College (*văng lăng* = 'palace') provided at Bangkok for students. The doctors of the people, who are numerous and specialized, and often take up their art without the slightest medical preparation, include the *mó nŭet*, or masseurs, and the *mó phí*, or exorcists.

17. Superstitious beliefs.—(*a*) *General.*—The superstitions of the Siamese are as numerous as those of the Cambodians (which they resemble in the most curious way).

One of their chief preoccupations is to make themselves invulnerable: they claim that a ball of solidified mercury—probably an amalgam of lead or tin—carried on the person protects against all weapon-wounds; princes and nobles always carry this in their girdles; eaglewood beads are also considered a good preservative.

Rice has a lucky character and plays an important part in all domestic and official ceremonies. It is the symbol of fecundity in the marriage rites, and of happiness in others. The Siamese bestow on the rice-goddess, a second Ceres, worship based on the belief that she presides at the sprouting of this cereal in the fields; the children are taught to reverence her before meals, and in many families they even murmur a prayer in her honour before eating.

Agriculture has always been an object of great reverence, and gives rise to the rite (as in China) of ceremonially tracing a furrow at the beginning of the agricultural year (*rèk na*). Formerly it was the king himself who performed this rite; to-day it is the minister of agriculture. It takes place at the beginning of May—the period fixed for the cultivation of rice throughout the whole kingdom. Harvest takes place without ceremony, but it is closed by a sacrifice in which as an offering to the deities very well-filled ears of rice are burned. With the rice-ceremonies we may connect the burlesque festival of the *ókya khăo*, 'king of the rice,' which also takes place in May–June. While the real king remains within his palace, a mock king usurps his prerogatives for three days amid joy and feasting. The subjects of the new king scatter themselves over the port and the town, laying violent hands on the Chinese junks and ships that happen to be there, entering houses and bazaars, and taking possession of all that they find unless the owners make haste to buy everything back from them. But—most interesting of all—this rice-king goes into a field in the middle of the town and traces a furrow with a gilded plough. Above this field there has been erected a high swing; the minister of agriculture, who accompanies the ephemeral sovereign, takes his stand on the swing, amid the silence of the crowd, and balances himself in it in order to invoke celestial blessings on the field and all the crops of the year.[1] The rice-king mounts it in his turn and balances on it amid the laughter, shouting, and tom-tom beating of the people. The 'king' also leans against a tree-trunk, standing on his left foot and holding his right foot up as high as his left knee. Then a cow is brought, before which are spread rice, potatoes, beans, etc.; the food towards which it first turns will be scarcest and most expensive during the year.

Certain trees are worshipped on account of their antiquity or the Buddhist memories which they recall—*e.g.*, the *phó*-(=Skr. *bodhi*)tree (*Ficus religiosa*)—or because they are regarded as the dwelling-place of a powerful *phi*.

To the Buddhist beliefs must be attributed the pity that all the Siamese have for animals and the horror that they feel at their slaughter even by the laity; the rich buy barges full of fish at certain times in order to throw them back into the water, or cages full of captive birds which they set at liberty in the precincts of a pagoda. From a similar motive every eighth and fifteenth day of the month hunting and fishing are strictly forbidden, and on those days nobody would dream of selling, buying, or eating flesh.

(*b*) *White elephants.*—The best known of the Siamese superstitions connected with animals is the veneration of white elephants (*xang phu'ek*). It still seems entirely Buddhist, recalling the white elephant in which the Buddha became incarnate. Monkeys and 'white' sparrows (*i.e.* albinos) are also treated with respect, but not to such a degree as the white elephant, the possession of which is a promise of happiness for the king and the whole kingdom. During the 16th and 17th centuries the kings of Siam, Cambodia, Pegu, and Laos waged unending wars with each other for the possession of white elephants.

When a white elephant is discovered in the kingdom, the person who captures it is exempted by the king from royal corvées until the third generation, and receives a number of gold pieces; then a deputation from the court along with musicians goes with ceremony to fetch the majestic luck-bringer to Bangkok, on a raft garlanded with flowers, where it is fed with cakes and sugar-canes and receives from all sides so much respect that European travellers thought at one time that the Siamese worshipped the white elephant. Its arrival in the capital is the sign for great festivities. The Brāhmans bathe it with lustral water and choose the pompous Sanskrit name by which it will henceforth be called, for, on entering the royal stable it also receives the title of 'great mandarin.' Its covers are of velvet; it eats and drinks from a gold or silver basin fruits and choice herbs; its teeth are hooped with gold, and it often wears a precious diadem; a whole suite of slaves and followers bustle round it, and, when it takes a bath, it is shaded under a sumptuous red and gold parasol. Its slightest ailments are tended by the royal physicians; its death puts the whole court and kingdom into mourning. Servants suspected of having been careless with it are mercilessly put to death. The figure of the white elephant adorns the Siamese flag at the present day.

The tiger, which is very much dreaded by the Siamese because of its power and its ferocity, is always addressed with respectful fear, but is put to death whenever possible. An enormous fresh-water lizard (*Monitor elegans*) is believed to bring misfortune to any one who meets or touches it.

(*c*) *Portraits.*—The Siamese are afraid to see a painting or a photograph of themselves; they think that it may be made use of in black magic. It is most probably this superstition, which is almost universal in the Far East, that is responsible for the non-existence of coins bearing the representation of the sovereign in Brāhmanic India, thus depriving us of valuable historical evidence. King Mongkuṭ has done much to modify this prejudice against portraits: he has been photographed on several occasions with the dignitaries of his court, and he has had coins struck with a representation of himself. It is only fair to mention that in 1686 the Siamese who were sent as ambassadors to the court of Louis XIV. were not afraid to allow their portraits to be painted, for the picture of the whole embassy is still to be seen at Versailles; but these men—their voyage itself proves it—were exceptional.

(*d*) *Treaties.*—When a treaty is signed between the king of Siam and another party, the latter must immediately take charge of the copy of the treaty signed by the king without letting it remain in any intermediary dwelling-place for fear of bringing misfortune to the place.

18. Human sacrifices.—In Siam, as in Cambodia and Burma, tradition claims that the foundation of a new town always required a human sacrifice: when the walls were almost completed,—just when the gate was being put into position—it is said, the voluntary or involuntary sacrifice of one or even of three victims had to be obtained. As voluntary victims were usually not to be found, a great mandarin accompanied by guards used to post himself near the gate repeating his future name in a loud voice; if a passer-by, thinking that he was being summoned, turned his head in their direction, he was regarded as designed by fate, and he was seized and taken away. After a short retreat and a sumptuous banquet the victim or victims thus obtained were solemnly taken to the gate and buried alive under a foundation beam.

19. Festivals.—See art. FESTIVALS AND FASTS (Siamese).

20. Organization of family life.—(1) *Relations of the sexes.*—Marriage in Siam takes place early, usually at 15 years of age for girls and 17 for boys. The law allows polygamy, and the rich take full advantage of it; following the king's example, they have regular *harīms*; but the poor are almost always monogamous. Moreover, only one of the numerous wives of a Siamese holds the rank of legitimate spouse, the one who was first wedded according to the solemn betrothal (*khan māk*), and brought a dowry instead of being bought. Even if others are afterwards wedded with similar ceremonies—which is very rare—they are, as com-

[1] This swing-rite seems to signify, as in India, the alternation of the seasons.

pared with the first wife (*miâ luâng*, 'chief wife'), only 'little wives.' As a rule it is the chief wife who chooses the wives of the second rank; the husband always asks her advice and her approval on this point, and she treats them as young sisters or as docile servants; even the favourite takes care not to go against the traditional dignity of her who is the only 'mistress of the house.' Further, only the chief wife and her children can inherit from the husband. It is therefore the position of the woman rather than that of the man that determines the legal status of the children.

(2) *Betrothal.*—Marriages are often arranged by the parents, but often also the young man makes his choice and then speaks to his parents. If his choice is approved, his parents request two trustworthy friends to sound the girl's parents. Though they are well received, it does not follow that they at once obtain a decisive answer; it is proper for the parents of the girl to ask leave to consult her, to reflect, not to appear in too great haste; it is only at the third of the requests, repeated at regular intervals, that they decide to agree. Then the conditions are discussed: the future husband must give a sum of money which his future parents-in-law will either keep for themselves, if they are poor, or give to the girl as a dowry to help her when she begins housekeeping. He must also present to his fiancée jewels according to his wealth, and sometimes also a house or a barge. When all this is settled, the betrothal (*khan māk*)—always very solemn—takes place; the young man, accompanied by his friends, all dressed in their finest clothes, enters a barge, decorated with flags, to convey to his fiancée's house appropriate gifts, such as betel, areca, and rice-cakes; on his arrival he greets all his future family, the dowry is counted, and the wedding-day fixed.

(3) *Marriage.*—This is a purely domestic ceremony; the State never interferes with it, and religion only occasionally by prayers and aspersions of lustral water on the young couple by the *bonzes* if they have been invited. The marriage is primarily a kind of 'wedding-party,' at which the parents and friends assemble at the house of the girl's parents to eat, drink, and be merry for one or two days according to the wealth of the couple. During a certain time, from one to three months, the young couple as a rule live near the girl's parents in a cottage which the man had to build for the purpose before the marriage. As the Siamese law gives parents absolute control over their children, and a greedy father might often take advantage of this to sell his daughter, under the pretext of marriage, to a man whom she hated, there is a custom to counterbalance this; when a pair of lovers cannot obtain their parents' consent, they elope, and go and live together some distance away; their union being thus affirmed, they return, preceded by two trustworthy friends to intercede in their favour, and ask their parents' forgiveness. The young man then presents his parents-in-law with the usual gifts and the marriage is concluded. If the parents persist in refusing, the young people repair to the judges, who generally arrange things in their favour. Marriage is forbidden between near relatives except in the case of kings, who are allowed to wed their half-sisters to maintain the purity of the royal line.

Although in Siam the wife never goes out with her husband, she is quite free to go and come indoors and out, is seen at the theatre, carries on business if need be, and is almost always consulted by her husband in all important undertakings. Legally the husband has the right to sell a wife whom he has bought; he cannot sell the chief wife, who brought him a dowry, except when the woman, having consented to the contracting of the debt, has thus become surety for it; but both cases are very uncommon.

(4) *Divorce.*—Divorce (*yă*) exists, but is seldom practised. It cannot take place until after an attempt at reconciliation before the seniors. The guilty husband must sign a written agreement to alter his conduct; if he does not improve, divorce is granted. In cases of adultery (much rarer than in Laos) the man may send his wife away after giving her a letter of divorce (*nang-sŭ'yă*) with his seal upon it. Divorce almost always takes place by mutual consent; the woman takes back her dowry; the common property and the children are divided—unless the children are grown up and show a preference for father or mother. When there are no children, the man returns to his parents.

(5) *Birth.*—The birth of a child is accompanied by various superstitious rites. Whenever it is born, it is washed, its arm is bound with bands of consecrated cotton, its horoscope is taken, and the name given is always an ugly one so as not to arouse the jealousy of the evil spirits; in the event of illness the name is changed in order to baffle the *phi* who is angry; the child is always breast-fed; every month its head is shaved; its body is washed daily, and is left naked except for one or two gold or silver necklaces, with small metal plates bearing mysterious characters and serving as amulets; girls also wear another gold or silver, or sometimes copper, plate, shaped like a heart and hung on a chain or string round the waist. At the age of four or five years a little tuft of hair is allowed to grow, which in the case of both sexes is shaved at the age of puberty in a great ceremony which is both religious and domestic.

(6) *Shaving of the fore-lock.*—After the diviner has fixed the most favourable day and hour for the ceremony of shaving the fore-lock (*kôn chuk*), the parents send cakes and flowers to all relatives and friends to invite them to the festival. A gunshot or petard-reports open the ceremony. The *bonzes* come and recite prayers on the head of the child, who is decked with all the jewels procurable; he is sprinkled with lustral water, then one of his near relatives shaves his fore-lock, while hired musicians play their most lively tunes. All the guests congratulate the newly-tonsured boy on his entrance into the world of young men, and place money for him in a plate; this is put aside to buy jewels for the boy's fiancée, unless the parents are very poor, when they use it themselves. Then, for a day or more, they eat, drink, smoke, play, and attend cock-fights or theatrical shows in honour of the new young man or woman.

At the tonsure of a royal prince (Pāli *cūlā-kantana maṅgala*, 'festival of the shaving of the fore-lock') all Bangkok goes on holiday. On the appointed day the prince, dressed in a red *languti* covered with jewels, and surrounded by armed soldiers and a long procession of children of his own age of all nationalities, wearing their national costume and each carrying a lotus-flower in his hand, goes in a gilded palanquin to the king's apartments. He prostrates himself before his father, who raises him up, and leads him by the hand to prostrate himself before the ashes of his ancestors in the temple of the palace. For three days in succession the same ceremonies are repeated; on the fourth day, in front of the ancestral tombs, the Brāhmans sprinkle him with lustral water, and divide his fore-lock into three locks (in allusion to the Hindu *trimūrti*); the king cuts the locks, and almost immediately the Brāhmans shave the boy's head. At the last stroke of the razor two Brāhmans sound the conch. Then the prince, accompanied by the king, goes in procession to a gilded pavilion on the top of an artificial mountain of pyramid shape, which symbolizes Mount Kailāsa, the famous peak of the Himālayas whither the god Śiva repaired at the shaving of the fore-lock of his son, Gaṇeśa. In this pavilion, in the presence of the royal family and all the high court officials, the prince purifies himself in a bath which seems to represent the Ganges; then he is sprinkled by the king and the highest persons in the assembly on the head, shoulders, and the whole body with five ewers of lustral water (in allusion to the five great rivers that issue from the Himālayas). The musicians at the foot of the mountain play a triumphal march; a Brāhman wipes the prince's face, and a crown of pure white cotton is placed on his head. Everybody descends, and the religious ceremony is over. The secular festivals now begin, and last for several days. The whole ceremony of shaving the top-knot is a Brāhmanical survival in a population for centuries Buddhist, which Buddhism not only has tolerated, but has made an effort to preserve. On the day after the shaving of the top-knot the young people usually enter the pagoda as novices, tradition requiring that all, even the kings, should have worn the yellow robe for a time. Although King Mongkuṭ spent years in the monastery, his son, King Chulālongkorṇ, imbued with Western ideas, would not stay more than three days, and would not have his eyebrows and his head completely shaved—which scandalized the most pious of his subjects.

Girls, after the shaving of their top-knot, return until marriage to the shelter of their parents' homes.

(7) *Parents and children.*—The relations between parents and children in Siam are as a rule marked on the one side by affectionate care and on the other by profound respect and deference. Infanticide is almost unknown, and the idea of parricide never enters their minds. Of course the law gives parents complete power over their offspring; although a man cannot sell his chief wife as a slave to pay his debts, unless she was aware of the contracting of these debts and had agreed to it, he can at any time sell his daughter as a slave temporarily or permanently to settle any kind of debt; this happens most frequently in the case of gambling debts.

(8) *Disposal of the dead.*—The most general method of disposal of the dead in Siam is cremation. When a Siamese is so ill that he cannot swallow rice, he is regarded as dying, and monks are summoned to his bedside to sprinkle him with lustral water, and to prepare him for death by the reading of sacred texts on the vanity of human things. His friends shout in his ears, '*Arahang! arahang!*', 'The saint! the just!' (Pāli *arahaṃ*, 'the saint,' 'he who has obtained lasting happiness'), in order to procure for him a better future lot. At his last breath his family and friends weep and mourn aloud for half an hour; then the corpse is bathed, and a *tical* (piece of money) is put into the mouth; the body is wrapped in a piece of white cloth and put into a coffin, covered with gilt paper and bits of glass, and dotted with little tapers. After two days it is taken down into the street by an opening at the side of the house—not by the door—and they carry it round the house running; the dead man has now become a dreaded spirit; it is their aim to make him forget the road from his house in order that he may not return to torment the living. Then the coffin is placed on a catafalque, and to the sound of plaintive flutes it is conveyed, amidst the relatives and friends in pure white mourning dress and with shaved heads, by barge or by land, to the funeral pile of the pagoda where it is to be burned. There, after renewed prayers, the person whose duty it is to burn the corpse washes its face with coconut-water and then places it on the pile, where it is consumed, while all present mourn. The few bones that are left after cremation are put into an urn, which is placed in the house, near the little altar of the household gods. The funeral ends with a banquet and entertainments of all kinds, including even theatrical performances. Among the rich these festivals may last for three days; many poor people ruin themselves in order to do things well on such occasions.

The funeral of a prince or a king requires no less than ten or twelve months' preparation; it costs enormous sums and gives occasion for rejoicings which the people long remember. The corpse is slowly dried by injections of mercury and placed in a golden urn; a huge pavilion of teak-wood is erected, on which the urn is to be placed and which symbolizes Mount Meru; its pillars, framework, and roof are covered with gold and silver leaves and inlaid with glass-work. Under the roof of the central pavilion there are other pavilions or kiosks for the king, princes, monks, high officials, and eminent strangers invited to the ceremony. The king's one is very large and contains reception-rooms and special apartments—even a bathroom. Under a special verandah are the valuable gifts which the king presents to the monks or to the other persons invited—sometimes including European agricultural machinery of the most up-to-date kind.

The cremation begins in the interior of the palace by a solemn procession of the relics of the Buddha and the ashes of the royal ancestors, to which strangers are not admitted. The relics of the Buddha are then enthroned on an altar situated above and in front of the remains that are awaiting cremation; the ashes of the royal ancestors are placed in the royal pavilion. Then the monks recite the whole day sacred texts in Pāli, holding the silver cord by means of which they communicate with the urn containing the mortal remains. The people outside share in the festival, receiving gratuitous refreshment and entertainment.

On the following day the monks again recite Pāli texts, while holding the silver cord; outside the people are being entertained to scenes from the *Rāmāyaṇa*, Chinese shadow-plays (*nang*), marionettes (*hûn*), and Peguan dances; but they also attend sermons preached by the monks, before scrambling for the lemons containing pieces of silver which the king throws to the crowd—one of the great attractions of the ceremony.

Next day, to the sound of guns and plaintive music, the mortal remains leave the pagoda, followed by a procession of great magnificence. They are carried three times round the pyramid and laid on the gilded throne or altar in the central pavilion; four groups of monks recite texts from the *Abhidharma*; outside the entertainments continue for four nights and four days.

At the end of the fifth day the gilded altars are removed from the throne of the central pavilion, or *phra:man*, and the provisional altars which are to be burned are substituted; on these are laid the bodies in sandalwood caskets amid sweet-scented flowers. The king sets fire to the pile for his near relatives by means of a fire kept perpetually burning in the pagoda. Then all the great personages throw sweet-scented wood and gilt-paper ornaments into the pile. Outside the games continue.

Next day the ashes are collected and in procession are thrown into the river from the top of a pagoda. The bones which have not been entirely consumed are placed inside a golden urn and returned to the pyramid on the altar which was set up for the purpose.

On the following day the relics of the Buddha, the remains of the royal ancestors, and the debris of the new cremation are again taken in procession along the road to the palace and the pagodas—their fixed dwelling-place.

For the last twenty years or so, after funerals, when they appear traditionally in white, with shaved heads, the princes have adopted the custom of wearing black mourning-clothes, like Europeans.

There is another method of disposing of the dead which is sometimes required by the most fervent Buddhists, viz. the partial offering of their bodies to vultures. If it is arms or legs that are to be offered, the part is, in the case of a prince, cut up into small pieces, put on a golden plate, and presented thus in the Vat Sakêt of Bangkok to the swarms of vultures which fly incessantly round this sacred charnel-house.

21. Political and civil organization.—(1) *King.*—Siam is governed by an absolute king, supreme judge and legislator, 'owner of the earth and its inhabitants,' whose despotism is moderated only by the mildness of Buddhist beliefs, secular traditions, and popular revolts. This king is called the *phra:*, 'the august,' 'the divine,' 'the sacred'; his subjects, whatever their rank, approach him on their knees and elbows and speak without daring to raise their eyes. The crown is hereditary; nevertheless within the space of 450 years, thanks to popular revolutions and court intrigues, Siam has been governed by four different dynasties. The order of succession is badly regulated; in theory the crown comes to the eldest son of the queen or the first wife; in reality the king appoints his heir; if he fails to do so, the great mandarins and ministers choose a king from the royal family.

(2) *Second king; royal family.*—Next to the king comes the second king, corresponding to the *uparāja* or the *obbarać* of Cambodia; he is a brother of the king, and has insignia, several attributes of royalty, special revenues, a house, and a court of his own. In time of war he used to be made generalissimo; this led certain European travellers to call him the 'war-king.' His authority is very slight, and even the officials of his palace are nominated by the real king. In reality the second king is the first and most respected of the twelve *krom*, or princes of high blood, brothers of the king, who surround the sovereign. Beneath them are ranged 200 or 300 other members of the royal family, with high titles, low revenue, and no authority whatever. At the fifth generation the descendants of royal race return to the common mass of subjects.

(3) *Mandarins.*—Nobility is not hereditary in Siam, so that the king can choose his mandarins or ministers. In former days their rank was indicated by the shape of their betel-box, the shape and material of the gold or silver crowns encircling their ceremonial *mokot* (Skr. *mukuṭa*), a sort of astrologer's peaked cap of white cloth, the arrangement of their *balon* (a highly ornamented shore-boat), the adornment of their swords, and the number of slaves who followed them; and they formed six classes. At the present day they are headed by the two *somdet chao phra : ya*—three words meaning 'lord,' 'king,' 'prince'—or great ministers, the one generalissimo (the *chakkra*), and the other admiralissimo (the *kra : lahôm*). Under them come five secondary ministers, *chao ph(r)a : ya*, who govern the palace, and look after the sacred and royal storehouses (*phra : khlăng*), agriculture (*phŏllăthèp*, Skr. *bāladeva*), law-suits, and the Peguans and other Asiatics not belonging to Siam. These ministers, assisted by more than 20 *pha : ya* or *phya*, are placed at the head of the important services of the capital. The governors of provinces are lower still, with the generic title of *chao mu'ăng*, 'lords of the country,' and with great powers. They are both prefects and high judges, treasurers and controllers of taxes. They are nominated and dismissed at will by the king. All those officials are obliged to drink the water of allegiance twice a year. Great oppressors of the people, they are restrained only by the fear of royal punishment.

(4) *Justice.*—As in Cambodia, justice is slow and costly, although, according to the code, all cases ought to be settled in three days. At the foot of the scale justice is administered by the village-chiefs (*kăm năn*), then by the governor of the province, to whom one may appeal from them. From him one may then go to Bangkok to the *lakhonban* (Skr. *nagarapāla*), presided over by the minister of justice. A special tribunal deals with European cases.

(5) *Codes of laws.*—Since the time of King Phra : Nărèt the Siamese codes have been collected into four volumes. This compilation, which is strikingly similar to the Cambodian one, is divided into three parts: (*a*) *Phra : tămra*, a list of officials, their prerogatives and duties; (*b*) *Phra : thămnun*, a collection of ancient Siamese institutions; and (*c*) *Phra : ràxă kămnot*, 'Book of Royal Ordinances,' the laws promulgated or revised under Phra : Nărèt. Divided into *lakkhăna*, or sections, they treat of theft, slaves, marriage, contracts and debts, trials and disputes, and inheritances. In all these laws, which are wise and well suited to the customs of the country, there are few specially Hindu traits.

A methodical modernized revision, in the light of European and Neo-Japanese codes, has been made of the *corpus* of Siamese laws under the excellent supervision of King Chulālongkorn; he himself has written the preface. The work is in course of publication, and European translations of it are beginning to be produced.

(6) *Ordeals.*—Trial by ordeal is still adopted in some cases—*e.g.*, trial by clay.

In order to discover a thief, a sorcerer asks two *ticals* (about two francs) from the person who has been robbed. He lights a candle and places one of the coins at either side; then he mutters a magical formula, and, taking a bar of clay, raises it several times above his head, reciting formulas. He then measures it with his little finger and breaks it into pieces a little over three centimetres long; he gives one piece to each of the suspected persons and orders them to chew it and then spit. The one who cannot do so is declared guilty.

There are also ordeals by water, boiling oil, melted tin, fire, etc.

(7) *Penalties.*—There is a great variety of penalties, including, besides imprisonment,—for life or for a time—public exhibitions, ignominious parades, corporal punishment (flagellation, mutilation, etc.), and death by beheading or by drowning. Old authorities tell that a popular punishment was 'frying' the culprits in a huge copper filled with coconut-oil. The death penalty cannot be pronounced except after royal approval. Crimes of *lèse-majesté* and *lèse-religion* call forth the direst punishments.

(8) *Slavery and statute labour.*—In former times the slave was a slave by birth; now he becomes a slave by voluntary contract, by sale (of a daughter by her parents), or because of insolvency, conviction, or legal confiscation. Since 1890 children born in slavery become exempt from law on their twenty-first birthday. All free healthy men subjected to the 'royal service' are liable to statute labour. On his accession every sovereign orders all adult males to be tatued on the wrist with a special sign. At the age of seventeen they are registered. They owe three months per annum of statute labour for the execution and repair of public works, but this must never occupy more than one month per quarter, so as not to hinder their agricultural operations. They may redeem themselves by means of a payment of 50 francs per annum; they have much to put up with from the bad faith and the greed of the royal officials. The hereditary serfs are undoubtedly the descendants of ancient criminals; the crown reserves them for its service. They have one month of work, during which they are fed, one month's rest, and so on. Often they can buy back their service for a certain sum. Their person is inviolable, and therefore their insolence is often great; they can run into debt and become the slaves of their creditors. The Asiatic 'slaves'—Peguans, Annamese, Cambodians, Chams, Laotians, and descendants of former prisoners of war—owe three months of military service in the year, and never leave the kingdom. Others are simply paid in money or in kind. The Chinese, duly inscribed in a special list and undergoing certain civil formalities, are subject to only one tax, the payment of which is certified by a wax seal applied to a string round their wrists.

LITERATURE.—H. Alabaster, *The Wheel of the Law: Buddhism illustrated from Siamese Sources*, London, 1871; A. Bastian, *Die Völker der östlichen Asien: Studien und Reisen*, vol. iii., 'Reisen in Siam im Jahre 1863,' Jena, 1867; C. Beyer, 'About Siamese Medicine,' *Journ. Siam Society*, iv. pt. i. [Bangkok, 1907], p. 1; J. Bowring, *The Kingdom and People of Siam*, 2 vols., London, 1857; R. Chalmers, 'The King of Siam's Edition of the Pāli Tipiṭaka,' *JRAS*, Jan. 1898, pp. 1–10 (cf. C. R. Lanman, *PAOS*, April, 1895, pp. ccxliv-ccciv); L. Finot, *Recherches sur la littérature laotienne*, Hanoï, 1917 (from *Bull. de l'Ecole française d'Extrême-Orient*, xvii. no. 5); E. Fournereau, *Le Siam ancien*, 2 vols., Paris, 1895–1908; O. Frankfurter, *The Kingdom of Siam*, New York, 1904 (published on the occasion of the St. Louis Exhibition); G. E. Gerini, *Siam . . . A descriptive Catalogue of the Siamese Section at the International Exhibition . . . in Turin, 1911*, Eng. rev. ed., Hertford, 1912, and various artt. in the *Bangkok Times*; N. Gervaise, *Hist. naturelle et politique du royaume de Siam*, Paris, 1688; E. Hamy, 'Note sur une statue ancienne du dieu Çiva provenant des ruines de Kămpheng Phĕt' (and bearing an inscription translated by Father Schmidt), in *REth* vii. [1888] 363–372; A. J. Irwin, 'Some Siamese Ghost-lore and Demonology,' in *Journ. Siam Society*, iv. pt. ii. [1907] p. 19 ff.; S. de la Loubère, *Du Royaume de Siam*, 2 vols., Paris, 1691, Eng. tr., *A New Historical Relation of the Kingdom of Siam*, 2 vols., London, 1693; E. Lorgeou, 'Les Suphasit [=moral proverbs] Siamois,' in *Bull. de l'Athénée oriental*, nos. 1–3 [1881]; J. B. Pallegoix, *Description du royaume Thai ou Siam*, 2 vols., Paris, 1854, and *Grammatica linguæ thai*, Bangkok, 1850; A. Pavie, *Contes siamois et laotiens*, Paris, 1918; I. Taylor, 'Some Account of the Trai Phum,' in *Journ. of Ind. Archipelago*, v. [1854] 538–542.

ANTOINE CABATON.

SIBERIA, SIBIRIAKS, SIBERIANS.—I. *SIBERIA.*—**1. Origin of the name.**—The name Siberia is usually considered to be derived from one of two sources: either from the Russian term for 'north,' Sievier, Sivir, Sibir, or from Sybir-Isker, the name of the chief town of the Tatar dominion which the Russians found in Siberia at the time of her conquest. But as a matter of fact the first hypothesis seems superficial, since the early Russians knew Siberia under the name not of North but of Yugra. By this term must be understood the land which in the 9th and 10th centuries stretched from the river Vychegda in the west to the Upper Irtish in the east. In the 15th cent. the geographical boundaries of Yugra changed; it was confined to the eastern side of the Ural, between the rivers Sygva, Konda, and Lower Ob (*i.e.* the lands north of 58° N. lat.). It is only after the 15th cent. that the Russian chronicles begin to abandon the name Yugra for that of 'Siberian lands.' Meanwhile the name Sybir as capital of the Tatar khanate appears on old maps of 1367 (unknown origin) and 1459 (Fra. Mauro); and under the last Tatar khan, Kuchum, in the 16th cent., the name was also used for the whole khanate. When, in 1583, Isker or Sybir was taken by the Cossacks of Yermak, the Russians adopted the name Sybir for the whole of the conquered territory, including Yugra. A new derivation of the word Siberia has been suggested by E. Blochet. He considers that the people known in the ancient Chinese annals as the Jwen-Jwen were the same as the people called Ib-Ib, Ibim, Ibil, Ibir, and that the last word is identical with Sybir.[1]

2. Geographical position.—By the name Siberia is understood the country between the Arctic shore and the Central Asiatic mountains and steppes from north to south, and the Ural Mountains and the Pacific Ocean from west to east. Under the administrative division of the Russian Government up to 1917 it denoted a much smaller territory, viz. the governments of Tobolsk, Tomsk, Yeniseisk, Irkutsk, Yakutsk, and Trans-Baikal. All the lands east of these were called the 'Far East Country.' From a geographical and ethical point of view, however, this division is artificial, and we shall here take Siberia to include the Far East country, *i.e.* as being composed of the governments of Tobolsk, Tomsk, Yeniseisk, Irkutsk, Yakutsk, Trans-Baikal, Amur, the sea-coast, and the island of Sakhalin. The Caspian-Aral steppe country, with Turkestan and Transcaspia, forms under this division Russian Central Asia.

3. History.—The material relating to the earliest history of man in Siberia and the adjacent countries is only beginning to be unearthed. Whether palæolithic man existed there is still unproved, though the Russian archæologist Savyenkoff declares the stone implements found by him along the Middle Yenisei to be of palæolithic types.[2]

The earliest epoch that is fairly well defined is that of neolithic kitchen-middens and pictographic writings on the cliffs, which are probably of the same date. These are met with chiefly in S.W. Siberia, between the rivers Ishim, Tobol, Yenisei, Abakan, and Kemchik.

The bronze age remains discovered in the Minusinsk country in S.W. Siberia and the Altai come next in antiquity. Besides bronze implements, the graves of this period contain implements of copper and gold and burial masks of gypsum.

While the neolithic remnants can be associated with the people whom one can call the Palæo-Siberians, who are even now living to a large extent in a neolithic state of culture, it is very doubtful whether they had anything to do with the highly developed culture of the bronze age. It is more probable that Central Asiatic influences are responsible for it, either 'Aryan' or 'Turanian' or both.

Following on the bronze age we find remnants of the iron age spread over a much wider area: in fact all S. and W. Siberia is rich in iron implements and weapons, and also in memorial stones with Turkic-Uigur inscriptions. These can be ascribed without hesitation to the Neo-Siberians of Turkic (Turanian) affinities.[3] One of these Turkic tribes, the Yakut, are even now in the stage of iron culture, owing to their isolation since they migrated to the north-east.[4] It is difficult to ascertain what was the distribution of the Palæo-Siberians at the time of the Minusinsk bronze culture, but it is fairly certain that it was the iron age people who were responsible for the forced migration of the Palæo-Siberians to the north-east; some of the tribes to whom the introduction of iron has been ascribed still survive in S. Siberia and Central Asia. These are the Kirghiz, called by the ancient Chinese 'Khakas.'

Politically, S. Siberia was from time immemorial directly or indirectly subject to China, till in the 7th cent. A.D. the Turkic khans became strong enough to free themselves from Chinese supremacy and to deprive the Palæo-Siberians in the north of their freedom. In the north-west Siberia had been in the power of the Yugra and the Samoyed and then under the domination of Turks, and in the south and east under Turks, Chinese, and Mongols when the Russians appeared there as conquerors in the 16th century. Moreover, the peaceful migration of the Finnic and Great Russian tribes to W. Siberia, as far as the Ob, had been in progress since the 10th and 11th centuries. This natural colonization was stopped for the time being when in the 13th cent. Russia was over-run by the Turkic Tatars; but soon after the fall of the Golden Horde the Russian attitude changed again from defensive to offensive. In the 15th cent. the Yugra lands were subdued by Moscow, and in the 16th cent. W. Siberia as far as the Ob. Between 1613 and 1648 the Russians moved from the Ob to the Pacific. This conquest was not effected by the sweeping advance of an imperial army like that of Alexander the Great or Jenghiz Khan, but was the result of successful raids by small bands of Cossacks, which were the more effective since the aboriginal tribes, with the exception of the Turkic khanate of Siberia and the Kirghiz and Kaizak states, had no strong State organization and unity. Thus all opposition came from the Neo-Siberians of the steppe country and W. Siberia. The Samoyed, Tungus, Yakut, Buriat, and Palæo-Siberians could offer hardly any resistance to the invasion. It was not the efforts of the Cossacks and the regular army, however, that won Siberia for Russia, but the unceasing and steady stream of emigrants from the Volga to the Ob and the Yenisei. This voluntary migration never reached as far as the Pacific, and that is why the Russian domination of the Pacific was due to strategical and political methods rather than to colonization.

Though the first Russian reached Amur in the 17th cent. (Okhotsk was founded in 1647), it was not till the time of the governor Muravieff-Amurski, in the middle of the 19th cent., that the Far East was conquered from both a strategic and a diplomatic point of view. Forcible colonization followed, but even after railways were constructed the Sibiriak and Russian workmen could not nearly hold their own in numbers against the overwhelming preponderance of yellow labourers.

4. Exploration.—The information about Siberia found in Chinese historians is still very little known and needs much interpretation; these historians are concerned chiefly with E. Siberia. Again, mediæval travellers like Marco Polo knew of Siberia only by hearsay. The first modern traveller who explored Siberia was Herberstein in the 16th cent. and then Messerschmidt (1719–27), who included in his party the Swede von Strahlenberg. The MSS of Messerschmidt have never been printed or fully used. Next come Dutch, English, and Danish travellers, whose explorations were confined to the sea-route between Asia and Europe, and Asia and America. In fact, from the time of the Novgorod Republic the northern sea-route from the West to Siberia was a matter of constant experiment. This route was established in the 16th cent. by the Muscovites, the Dutch, and the English. For a short period all colonization followed this route, and an international trade-station was established along the river Taz, east of the Bay of Ob, early in the 17th century.

The first study of the customs and religion of the aborigines we owe to Gmelin, Steller, Pallas, and Georgi, all of whom visited Siberia in the 18th century. But it is the travellers of the 19th cent., especially Middendorff, Radloff, Adrianoff, Schrenk, Czekanowski, Klements, Bogoras, Jochelson, Sternberg, and others, who have collected information which enables us to understand the present religious systems of Siberia.

5. Classification of inhabitants.—From the historical survey of Siberia it follows that we can find there representatives of all the peoples who at various times dominated the whole or part of this vast country, viz. the Palæo-Siberians, the Neo-Siberians, the Chinese, the Russians, and the Japanese.

(*a*) By the name *Palæo-Siberians* we mean the most ancient stock of Siberian aborigines who were pushed to the north and north-east by the

[1] 'Les Noms des Turcs dans l'Avesta,' *JRAS*, 1915, pp. 305–308.

[2] I. T. Savyenkoff, *The Palæolithic Epoch in the Neighbourhood of Krasnoyarsk* (in Russian), Krasnoyarsk, 1892.

[3] M. A. Czaplicka, *The Turks of Central Asia*, Oxford, 1918, pp. 97–108.

[4] See art. YAKUT.

Neo-Siberians advancing from Central Asia, especially the Finnic and Turkic peoples.[1] The Palæo-Siberians are also known as Northern and North-Eastern Palæo-Asiats.[2] Neither of these terms is intended to indicate absolute community of race or linguistic identity between the various peoples who formed the original population of the country. We find among them both the hairy Ainu and the beardless Chukchi; and we include here also the Eskimo, who in physical type, language, and culture form a wedge between the Palæo-Siberians living in Asia and their kinsmen in America who are known as the north-western Amerinds. Hence this grouping of remnants of different races is merely justified historically and geographically, though to a large extent culturally as well.

This group contains the following tribes:

(1) The Eskimo, on the Asiatic shore of Bering Strait, (numbering 1415 in 1911); also the whole of Arctic America from Alaska to Greenland. Their total number is 25,000.

(2) The Aleut, in the Aleutian Islands and Komandor Islands (1232).

(3) The Gilyak, near the mouth of the Amur and in the northern part of the island of Sakhalin (4298).

(4) The Ainu, in the island of Yezo and the southern part of Sakhalin (1457).

(5) The Kamchadal (Itelmen), southern part of Kamchatka (2182).

(6) The Chukchi, on the Chukchi Peninsula, between the Anadyr river and the Arctic Ocean (12,968).

(7) The Koryak, south of the Chukchi, between the Anadyr river and the central part of Kamchatka (7943).

(8) The Chuvantzy, on the Upper and Middle Anadyr (569).

(9) The Yukagir, between the Lower Yana and the Lower Kolyma rivers (about 723).

(10) The Ostyak of the Yenisei, the most westerly of all, on the Lower Yenisei, between the Lower and the Middle or Stony Tunguska (1021).[3]

To this day 92 per cent of the Palæo-Siberians know no language but their own, and only 40 per cent of them are nominal Christians. They are said to be dying out only in cases where they have given up their native industries and taken up the life of a Russian colonist.

(*b*) The term *Neo-Siberians* will cover the peoples who, from a linguistic standpoint, made up Castrén's[4] 'Ural-Altaic people'; but the people speaking Ural-Altaic languages are not limited to Siberia. By Neo-Siberian, therefore, we mean those of the Ural-Altaic peoples who originally came from Central Asia or E. Europe, but have been in Siberia for at least the last 1000 years, and are now sufficiently differentiated from the kindred peoples of the region of their origin to deserve a generic name. The Neo-Siberians include:

(1) The Finnic tribes of Siberia, viz. the Vogul between the Ural Mountains, Berezoff, and Tobolsk, and the Ugrian Ostyak between the mouth of the Ob, the Yenisei, and Tomsk.

(2) The Samoyedic tribes, living along the Arctic shore between Cheskaya Bay in European Russia and the Khatonga river in Siberia, extending southward to the Abakan steppes.

(3) The Turkic tribes, inhabiting S.W. Siberia, and represented by one of their nations, the Yakut, in E. Siberia.

(4) The Mongolic tribes, including the Western Mongols or the Kalmuk, the Eastern Mongols or the Khalka, and the Northern Mongols or the Buriat of Baikal.

(5) The Tungusic tribes, scattered all over E. Siberia as far west as the river Taz and as far south as the southern frontiers of Manchuria.[5]

The native population, both Palæo- and Neo-Siberian, formed in 1911 only a small percentage of the total number of inhabitants—in Siberia proper 10·9 per cent, and in the Far East country 20·6 per cent (in the Aral-Caspian steppe country 60 per cent). This means that the number of Palæo-Siberians in 1911 was 32,000; of Neo-Siberians, 949,000 in Siberia and the Far East (and 2,200,000 in the steppe country); while the European or semi-European colonists number some 8,000,000 in Siberia and in the Far East (and 1,500,000 in the steppe country). Thus, while in the steppe country the native element predominates, in Siberia it forms a quite unimportant percentage from an economic point of view. The strength of the Russian colonists lies in their birth-rate. Statistics of 1910 show that for each 100 Russian colonist women 11 children were born, while in the Turkic tribe of Yakut, which is supposed to be the most prolific of the native tribes, the number of children for the same number of women was only 9 and among the Kirghiz only 6.

(*c*) The name *Sibiriak* is used for those Siberian colonists who have lived in the country for at least one or two generations, and have won the name of 'old settlers,' 'Starojily' (*stary*, 'old,' *jil*, 'lived'). The new emigrants are called 'Novosiely' (*novy*, 'new,' *sielo*, 'village'). Several E. European nations have a share in the composition of the Sibiriak nation. The largest infusion is of Great Russian blood, and then Little Russian or Ukrainian, but it also includes Finns, Poles, White Russians, various Caucasian natives, and many Neo-Siberian peoples, especially those of Turkish blood.

Generally speaking, the ethnical classification corresponds to the distribution of the chief religious creeds. The Palæo-Siberians are in the main shamanists, and have only begun to be converted to the Russian Orthodox Church on the borders of their territory.

The Neo-Siberians are Muhammadans in W. Siberia, Lamaists in E. Siberia, shamanists in inaccessible parts of the country, and Russian Orthodox only where they are fused with the Sibiriaks. The farther south we go into Central Asia, the more general becomes the Muhammadan religion. The Sibiriaks are followers of various Christian Churches. Christianity in Siberia is represented chiefly by the Russian Orthodox Church (about 8,000,000 members in 1911); then by various Russian schismatic sects numbering at least 350,000; the third place is occupied by the Roman Catholic Church (about 90,000 in 1911).

These statistics, however, must be taken with some reserve. They are based on the general census of 1897 and on the additional census of the local statistical committees. Since the political purpose of this work was to show the success of the Russian Orthodox Church and to depreciate all other Christian Churches as well as the schismatics from Orthodoxy, it may be taken as certain that the number of the schismatics is about ten times greater than it appears. Moreover, to belong officially to the Russian Orthodox Church in Siberia in many cases means merely to combine the superstitious beliefs of shamanism with some of the ritual of the Russian Orthodox Church.

II. *THE SIBIRIAKS.*—While emigration from Russia to Siberia since the construction of the Trans-Siberian railway has followed a definite plan, and was, in a way, compulsory, the same cannot be said of the early emigration. Thus, inquiring into the origin of 776 districts of the Yeniseisk government, we find that 674 of them were started by free emigrants and only 102 arose as the result of the old Russian Government order —*i.e.* were composed of political and criminal exiles and those Russian peasants who were brought by the Government Immigration Committee. The first category is called 'Po-volye' ('of free will'); the second category consists of those who came 'Po-nyevolye' ('not of free will').

[1] M. A. Czaplicka, *Aboriginal Siberia*, Oxford, 1914, p. 15 f.

[2] L. von Schrenck, *The Natives of the Amur Country* (in Russian), St. Petersburg, 1883, pp. 255–257; see also Germ. tr., *Die Völker des Amur-Landes*, St. Petersburg, 1891.

[3] Cf. artt. AINUS, ALEUTS, ESKIMOS, GILYAKS, OSTYAKS.

[4] M. A. Castrén, *Reiseberichte und Briefe aus den Jahren 1845–49*, St. Petersburg, 1856.

[5] See artt. BURIATS, FINNS (Ancient), FINNO-UGRIANS, IMAGES AND IDOLS (Lapps and Samoyeds), KOREA, MONGOLS, OSTYAKS, PASTORAL PEOPLES, SAMOYED, TUNGUS, TURKS, and YAKUT.

1. **Colonization.**—The earliest colonists are to be found in W. Siberia. We can trace a remarkable regularity in the free and undirected colonization of the pre-railway period. The inhabitants of the steppes of S. Russia moved to the steppe regions of Siberia, while the people from the forest region settled in the *taiga* (dense forest). The government of Tomsk has received immigrants chiefly from the governments of Kursk, Voronej, Tamboff, Chernigoff, and Poltava. The government of Tobolsk has been peopled chiefly by the natives of the governments of Vitebsk, Mogileff, Chernigoff, Orel, and Poltava. Again, the steppe country is almost entirely populated by the immigrants from the southern or steppe provinces of European Russia, the governments of Poltava, Tavris, Ekaterinoslav, and Kherson. Thus it may be seen that Siberia, especially W. Siberia, has been peopled by the Great Russians no less than by the Little Russians or Ukrainians. The Far East contains but few old settlers, with the exception of the Siberian Cossacks; the Russian element there consists chiefly of peasants brought straight from Russia in the middle of the 19th cent., called, in contradistinction to the Starojily and Novosiely, by the name of 'Starosiely.'

Of all the inhabitants of Siberia the least susceptible to assimilation are perhaps the Cossack communities. Their origin is different from that of the European Cossacks, who were once in the 15th and 16th centuries national units. The Siberian Cossacks were formed as voluntary regiments composed of the most adventurous elements of the Russian State, and were used for the purpose of conquering Asiatic lands, safeguarding the frontiers, or keeping watch over the people exiled to Siberia. They are more devoted to the Orthodox Church, except those who belong to the Muhammadan creed, than the Sibiriaks.

The Siberian Cossacks met the European Cossacks when the latter were sent as political exiles after each of their national risings, and through this contact the Siberian Cossacks adopted some of the national traditions and the schismatic spirit of the European Cossacks. Up till 1917 the social position of the Siberian Cossacks was better than that of either the colonists or the natives, since they were richly endowed with land and lived under their special Cossack organizations, and hence formed a community within a community. They are made up of eight units: (1) the Yenisei unit, with its centre at Irkutsk (numbering 30,000 members of both sexes); (2) the Ussuri unit, with its centre at Vladivostok (34,000); (3) the Semirechie unit, with its centre at Viernyi (45,000); (4) the Amur unit, with its centre at Blagovyeshchensk (50,000); (5) the Siberian unit, with its centre at Omsk (180,000); (6) the Trans-Baikal unit, with its centre at Chita (270,000); (7) the Orenburg unit, with its centre at Orenburg (530,000); and (8) the Ural (Yaik) unit, with its centre at Uralsk (900,000). The half-breeds of Russian-Buriat blood form a special group called 'Karymy.' Among the ethnological curiosities of the Siberian colonial world are the people who live in 17 villages of the Bukhtarminsk district in the Altai. In the middle of the 17th cent. all people of Russian origin who were wanderers and had no identity books were banished there. They formed a colony of their own, called themselves 'Bezimyennye,' *i.e.* 'nameless,' intermarried with the Altai Turks, adopted their culture and beliefs, and became practically independent of the Russian Government. Towards the end of the 18th and the beginning of the 19th cent. they were compelled to become Russian subjects again, but under the same conditions as the local aborigines—*i.e.*, their own 'steppe Duma' was their direct administrative body. In this way they enjoyed more freedom than the other Sibiriaks.

We do not find many Russian old settlers in the steppe country or in Turkestan. The Russian element is represented there by Russian officials, who seldom became amalgamated with the local population, and by the Cossacks. One class of the old Russian administration, the Orthodox clergy, included a fairly large number of Sibiriaks.

Within the Sibiriak group the class distinctions of European Russia are unknown, since the institution of serfdom never penetrated beyond the Urals. According to their occupation, the Sibiriaks are divided into town people, country people, and Cossacks. The Cossacks number some 2,000,000 (in all Asiatic Russia). The Sibiriaks have some mental qualities in which they differ from the Great and Little Russians even more than they do from a physical point of view. These are a sense of equality, a national tolerance, energy and enterprise, and the power of becoming wealthy. They lack the great religious feeling and mystical attitude to Church and State so often found in European Russia. The Sibiriak attitude of tolerance has played a large part in the racial history of the nation. Peoples who seldom, if ever, intermarried on the other side of the Urals—*e.g.*, the Poles, Letts, and Great Russians—mix freely with one another in Siberia. Many Neo-Siberians, especially the Yakut, the Buriat, and the Tatars, merge willingly with the Sibiriaks. Even some of the Palæo-Siberians, especially the Chukchi and the Kamchadal, have begun to take part in this great fusion.

On the other hand, if it is difficult to find in European Russia a representative of a fairly pure Great Russian type, it is easy to find this in the colonies of 'Old Believers'[1] in the Southern Altai and Trans-Baikal, since their religious beliefs have evolved a custom of endogamy and have protected them from any foreign admixture. On the other hand, among the Orthodox colonists in some cases the administrative orders of the Russian Government have made forced inter-racial marriages—*e.g.*, the ukase of 11th Feb. 1825, which ordered the local officials to buy children of the female sex from the aborigines for wives for the colonists in view of the preponderance of the male over the female population among the Russian colonists.[1]

[1] See art. RUSSIAN CHURCH, vol. x. p. 871[b].

2. **Religious life.**—There is scarcely any evidence of the religious life of the early settlers in Siberia. Many of them must have been Christians already, but they do not seem to have been imbued with the missionary spirit, nor have they left material relics in the way of churches and eikons. The official propagation of Orthodoxy supported by the military and material help of the Russian Government began in the 16th and was at the height of its development in the 17th century. In 1620 the archbishopric of Siberia and Tobolsk was founded at Tobolsk.

The Raskol,[2] or schism from the Russian Orthodox Church, has had unusual success in Siberia from its very beginning (17th century). The first serious supporter of Raskol, Bishop Avvakum, was exiled in the second part of the 17th cent. to Siberia, where he was so earnest in propagating his ideas and opposing the official translation of the Bible (under supervision of the patriarch Nikon) that he was exiled still farther away into Dauria. To convert the heathen, and still more to effect the conversion of the schismatics, the Russian Government built as many as 32 monasteries in Siberia alone, 17 of which still exist; and in 1727 a bishopric of Irkutsk was founded. As regards the aborigines, their conversion has often been effected by such material means as freedom from *yassak* (tribute) or provision of flour and clothing. At the same time there are records of some true missionaries of real Christian spirit who acquired native languages (Tatar, Kalmuk, Yakut, and Buriat) for the purpose of spreading the gospel, and who incidentally have also added to ethnological literature. The number of Siberian saints and holy eikons does not correspond to the enormous numbers of monasteries and churches. In the 19th cent. there were added some 34 religious houses to the 11 administrative divisions of the Siberian Church, of which 21 were nunneries.

Among the few local saints of whom Siberia can boast is St. Innocent, the first bishop of Irkutsk, who was an active missionary among the Buriat and Tungus; 26th Nov. is celebrated as his day. His tomb was opened 70 years after his death, and the body was said to have been found unchanged. At present his remains (*moshchi*) are kept in the Voznesensky monastery in Irkutsk. This monastery is usually compared by the Sibiriaks to the Kieff-Pecherskaya Lavra at Kieff in European Russia.

Another patron saint of Siberia is Simeon of Verkhoturye. The son of a boyar at the court of Tsar Boris Godunoff, young Simeon migrated across the Urals and settled in the village of Merkushino near Verkhoturye. He was a wandering tailor by profession, spreading the gospel among the people for whom he worked. It was chiefly for the holiness of his character that he was beloved during his life and proclaimed a saint after his death. He died in 1642, and in 1704 his corpse, apparently still uncorrupted, was carried to Nikolayeff monastery in Verkhoturye. Many miracles are said to have been performed at his tomb.

The third patron saint of the Sibiriaks is the only one with whom a story of martyrdom is associated. He is Basil of Mangazeya, once an important trading station on the river Taz, west of the Yenisei. He was a merchant's assistant, and his master, wrongly suspecting him of theft, tortured him to death and flung his body on to the

[1] In the Far East there are even now about 650 women to every 1000 men.

[2] See art. SECTS (Russian).

tundra. Then a religious youth, who had not met Basil in life, living along the Yenisei, was ordered in a vision by the Holy Spirit to bring Basil's body to the monastery of Turukhansk. Awakening from his sleep, the youth arose, went alone across the cold country, and brought back the body. It was found that Basil had been martyrizing himself by wearing an iron-bond ring round his waist. His body is an object of worship to all N. Siberians.

Thus a bishop, a pilgrim of noble birth, a merchant's assistant, and a later saint, the old man Daniel of Achinsk (1845), a holy hermit sometimes identified with Tsar Alexander I., complete the number of local patron saints for the Orthodox Sibiriaks.

Besides the tombs of the saints, there are in Siberia places recognized as holy on account of the eikons they possess. The eikon of Abalak, some 25 versts from Tobolsk, has an especial attraction for pilgrims, not only from Siberia but also from European Russia. It represents Mary the Virgin with child, and has a drawing of St. Nicholas in the right corner, and one of Mary of Egypt in the left. It originally came from S. Russia, but its early history is rather vague. All the other eikons which are regarded with peculiar reverence are copies of this eikon—*e.g.*, those in Kurgan, Tomsk, and Omsk.

The sect known as the Old Believers is spread in groups all over Siberia, but is most numerous in the Verkheudinsk district of the Trans-Baikal territory (where they are called 'Semyeynye,' from *syemya*, a 'family,' because they were exiled in whole families in the reign of Catherine II.), in the Barnaul, Biisk, and Zmeinogorsk districts of the Tomsk government, in the southern districts of the Tobolsk government, and in the Blagovyeshchensk district of the Amur territory. The Old Believers of the Altai region of the Tomsk government are called 'Polaki,' which is the Russian name for Poles, since they, not unlike the Poles, live in communities apart. The Old Believers form for the most part the most stable and best organized element, and, together with the political exiles, though but a small percentage of the 8,000,000 Sibiriaks, exercise a great moral influence and have contributed some of the best qualities of the Sibiriak nation.

III. *THE PALÆO-SIBERIANS.*—Some of the Palæo-Siberians are dealt with under separate headings;[1] here we shall confine ourselves to those who, before the publication of the results of recent ethnological research, were practically unknown in scientific literature—*e.g.*, the Chukchi, the Kamchadal, the Koryak, the Yukagir, and the Aleut.

The first four tribes have more in common racially and culturally than the other Palæo-Siberians, and are also more akin to the American Indians on the other side of the Bering Straits, called the North-Western Amerinds. The North-Western Amerinds are commonly divided into: (1) Northern tribes: the Tlingit, Haida (*qq.v.*), and Tsimshian; (2) Central tribes: the Kwakiutl and Bellacoola;[2] and (3) the Southern tribes: the Coast Salish,[2] Nootka,[3] and Chinook (*q.v.*). The Eskimo form culturally a wedge between the Palæo-Siberians and their American cousins. A short examination of the points of similarity between them will not only prove their cultural affinity, but also throw some light on their religious beliefs and practices. Whether further investigations will decide that the original home of these two groups was N. America or N. Asia, and will accordingly call them all Palæo-Americans or Palæo-Siberians, does not alter the fact that their affinity is closer than can be ascribed to the influence of mere environment. The Palæo-Siberians, *e.g.*, are more like the people on the other side of the Bering Straits than they are like those Neo-Siberians (Tungus and Yakut) who live under the same climatic and geographical conditions.

1. Cultural affinity with N.W. Amerinds.—Culturally there is a resemblance between the boats and dwellings of the peoples on both sides of the Bering Sea. Their large skin boats are of the same structure and material, though the Koryak boats, with 'their flaring sides and semi-circular stern and bow,' and the Kamchadal wooden dug-outs are of different types. The dwellings of the Palæo-Siberians are of two main types. The first is the 'jawbone house,' the skeleton of which is composed of the ribs and jawbone of a whale or of driftwood and trees, where such material is available. These are covered with sods and earth, forming a house half underground. It is divided into three compartments inside, and has a square entrance through the roof and through two underground corridors, one for summer and one for winter. It was universal round the Bering Sea, but is now found only among the Koryak, Kamchadal, some Chukchi, and some of the Amerinds on the borders of the forest. But remnants of these underground houses can be found among all N.W. Amerinds, and mention of them is made in their myths. At present the Tlingit, Tsimshian, and Haida have quadrangular log huts. The second kind of house is typical of the Chukchi, and is called their 'genuine house.' It is a double skin tent, round outside and square inside. The Eskimo snow house is not found among other tribes, though the Koryak 'jawbone house,' when covered with snow for winter, may appear to be similar outwardly. Of all the peoples of these two groups the Koryak possess the richest mythology, just as they excel in the art of engraving human and animal figures in motion. In mythology the most characteristic feature of both groups is the Raven myth cycle, which appears in Eskimo mythology only in imported incidents.

The Raven or Big Raven was sent to the earth by the Supreme Being, who is identified with the sun or thunder. Big Raven married a young girl, called Miti, who was abandoned by her father, the Twilight, and their children were the ancestors of the Koryak. Big Raven is supplicated and propitiated only in the supreme crises of life for protection from malicious spirits.[1] In Chukchi mythology the Raven is called 'one self-created' His wife becomes a woman and gives birth to four sons. Then Raven decides to create the earth, and does so by throwing his excrement down below him. Afterwards he teaches the people on the earth how to live and multiply.[2] Almost all the Koryak and many Tlingit myths deal with the life, travels, and adventures of Big Raven and his family.

Another point of resemblance between the peoples of the N. Pacific culture is their tradition relating to the remote era when there was no difference between men and animals. There are, however, some Asiatic elements among the Palæo-Siberians unknown to the N.W. Amerinds—*e.g.*, religious dualism and the sacrifice of reindeer and dogs to the chief deities. Again we find evidence of the great influence of the American Indian culture in general on the N.W. Amerinds in their totemic poles, ceremonial masks, and in the variety and richness of their facial painting, all of which are peculiar to totemistic people and hence do not exist among the Palæo-Siberians.

If we take into consideration the fact that the Palæo-Siberians make reindeer breeding their chief occupation and are merely incidentally hunters and fishermen, and the fact that the art of reindeer-

[1] See artt. AINUS, ALEUTS, ESKIMOS, GILYAKS, and OSTYAKS.
[2] See art. SALISH.
[3] See art. VANCOUVER ISLAND INDIANS.

[1] W. Jochelson, 'The Koryak, Religion and Myths,' in *Memoirs of the American Museum of Natural History: The Jesup North Pacific Expedition*, vol. vi. pt. 1, Leyden and New York, 1908.
[2] W. Bogoras, 'The Chukchee,' *Jesup N. Pacific Exped.*, vol. vii. pt. ii. [1910] p. 155 ff.

breeding is unknown (and seems impossible) on the American continent, we shall here find the essential economic explanation of the difference between the religious ceremonies of these two groups. In any case the N.W. Amerinds must have separated from the Palæo-Siberians before the appearance of the Eskimo along the Bering Straits. At what time and whence the migration of the Eskimo to the Pacific shore took place is difficult to determine, but traces of a long influence of Arctic geographical environment on their culture point to the conclusion that they must have been settled there for many centuries.

The question whether the Palæo-Siberian languages (with the exception of the Ostyak of the Yenisei) are nearer the N.W. American than the Ural-Altaic tongues has not been sufficiently studied because we cannot find any similarity even between the Indian languages which were formerly believed to exist. The Indian languages used to be called polysynthetic and incorporating, in contradistinction to the Ural-Altaic group; but it is now known that there is great grammatical variety among them. All the same, incorporation and polysynthetism, as well as the division of substantives into animate and inanimate, are features especially strongly marked in N.W. American as in Palæo-Siberian languages.

As to their physical type, F. Boas[1] thinks that the colour of the skin and of the hair, and the shape of the head and of the face, are remarkably alike in these two groups, and he even suggests that the physical type of these Indians is nearer to that of their Asiatic brethren than to that of the Californian or Mississippi Indians. The materials of the Jesup North Pacific Expedition that have as yet been worked out have shown that the Chukchi, who are the nearest neighbours of the N.W. Amerinds, resemble them more than do the other Palæo-Siberians. So, *e.g.*, the Ainu and the Yukagir are short-statured, the Kamchadal and Koryak under medium stature, while the Chukchi and the N.W. Amerinds are above medium stature. The Ainu, Yukagir, Koryak, and Kamchadal have medium-sized heads, the Eskimo are long-headed, while the Chukchi and the N.W. Amerinds are comparatively broad-headed. The colour of the skin of the N.W. Amerinds is much lighter than that of the other Indians and more like that of the Palæo-Siberians, and their noses, though prominent, do not resemble the typical eagle-like nose of the American Indian and are again more of the N. Pacific type.

The chief difference between the Neo- and Palæo-Siberians, besides the stature and the head-form (the Neo-Siberians are taller and more broad-headed), is that the Mongolian flat bridge to the nose and the Mongolian fold in the inner corner of the eyelid occur more often among the Neo- than among the Palæo-Siberians. Then the Neo-Siberians have the Mongolic straight black hair and sparse beards and moustaches which are not allowed to grow, while the Palæo-Siberians have often wavy hair and beards which they always encourage to grow.

2. The Chukchi country and people.—Of all the people of N.E. Asia, the Chukchi form both in physical type and in culture the essence of what is called Palæo-Siberian. We shall therefore consider them primarily and deal with the other Palæo-Siberians only so far as they differ from the Chukchi.

The name Chukchi is derived from Chuchu, 'rich in reindeer,' but this name is used of both the Reindeer Chukchi and the Reindeer Koryak, while Lyiyilylyt, 'those of genuine language,' is the name used by Chukchi alone, whether Reindeer or Maritime.[2] According to the Chukchi traditions, they were formerly a coast people, who, however, always had domesticated reindeer. But the facts that they keep so many dogs without making practical use of them as most of the Arctic people do, that the snake appears so often in their folk-tales (there are no snakes in their present abode), and that the climatic names of the months do not correspond to the changes of climate in their present locality seem to point to their original home being farther south. The Chukchi are, generally speaking, not a coast people; out of a total of 12,000 only some 1100 live on the Pacific and some 2000 on the Arctic shore. Hence three-fourths of them are reindeer-breeders and only one-fourth live by maritime industries.

1 'Physical Types of the Indians of Canada,' *Annual Archæological Reports*, Toronto, 1905, p. 84.

2 Bogoras, p. 11.

The Chukchi live in the far north-east of Siberia from the river Indigirka to Bering Straits in the east and to the Anadyr and even as far as Kamchatka in the south. But east of the river Omolon they are found only sporadically on the coast of the Bering Sea, and the Asiatic Eskimo (1600) occupy part of the shore, while south of the Anadyr the land is really Koryak. Farther within Chukchi territory to the south-west of Chaun Bay lives the tribe of Chuvantzy (probably the same as the half-mythical Chaachet), who are intermediary between the Chukchi and the Yukagir. Another people who are probably mixed with the Koryak more than with the Chukchi are the Lamut of the Tungus group. The Tungus group divides on the Middle Kolyma the Yukagir from the other Palæo-Siberian peoples.

It is perhaps owing to the splendid physical health and great fertility of the Chukchi[1] and their great reindeer wealth, partly also to the persistence of their language, which they have imposed not only on the Koryak of Kamchatka and the Asiatic Eskimo, but even on the Russians on the Anadyr, that the Chukchi occupy the predominant position among the natives of N.E. Siberia.

The so-called 'Chukchi Territory,' which has never been forcibly subdued by the Russians and hence enjoys a fictitious legal autonomy, lies west of the rivers Chaun and Anadyr to the river Omolon, and was probably the whole extent of the Chukchi land in the 17th century. If we believe Wrangell,[2] the Asiatic Eskimo formerly occupied a much larger space on the Arctic shore, but were driven away by the Chukchi. After the advent of the Chukchi it is probable that they migrated towards the Pacific Coast and also north-eastwards. Possibly it is to the latter event that those traditions are due which are common to all the peoples of N. Siberia, about the tribes which migrated north. Some native tribes believe that an unknown people live in Wrangell Land and the other islands; others that they are extinct as the half-mythical Shelagi from whose name is derived Cape Shelagsky on the Arctic coast. The Shelagi are said to have been Chukchi, while other extinct tribes of N.E. Siberia (Omoki, Khodyntsy, Anauli, Kongenyty) were clans of the Yukagir tribe.[3] Bogoras[4] gives a list of village names from the Arctic and Pacific Coast Chukchi, which indeed are Eskimo in sound and in a sense support the theory that the Eskimo were formerly more widely extended, spreading east as well as west. The Chukchi land stretches to the tundra and northern fringe of the forest country; its climate is dry and cold, the average winter temperature being 31° F. (Nijne-Kolymsk), and the average summer 52° F. On the Pacific the climate is less dry, the average in winter being 8° F. and in summer 54° F.

We can take the Chukchi as physically the most free from foreign admixture among the Palæo-Siberians, and in this connexion it is interesting to consider the anthropometric results obtained by the Jesup North Pacific Expedition.[5] The average height of the men is 162·2 mm., and their cephalic index averages 82. Their cheek bones are much less prominent than those of the Tungus or Yakut, and the low Mongolian nose bridge and Mongolian eyelids occur only very rarely. Their hair—and in this respect the Koryak can be put in the same class with them—is wavy and sometimes even curly. Beards are more frequent than among the Tungus and Yakut, and, contrary to the customs of the latter, are allowed to grow freely. The colour of their hair is less dark as the Pacific is approached, while their complexion is bronze-red, and their ideal is to be as 'red as blood.'

3. Material culture.—The elements of four cultures can be observed in the Palæo-Siberian tribes: the Asiatic, the N. Pacific, the Eskimo, and the American Indian.

The domesticated reindeer is a purely Asiatic element, common to Neo- and Palæo-Siberians. Among the Palæo-Siberian reindeer-breeders one sometimes finds a light portable tent, similar to the tent of Neo-Siberians. The underground houses are a N. Pacific element. The skin boats and harpoons are of Eskimo origin, while the

1 In 1897, 10 per cent of the families had no fewer than five children living (Bogoras p. 35).

2 *Journey to the North Coast of Siberia and to the Arctic Sea, 1820–24* (in Russian), St. Petersburg, 1841.

3 W. Jochelson, 'The Yukaghir and the Yukaghirised Tungus,' *Jesup N. Pacific Exped.*, vol. ix. pt. i. [1910] p. 18.

4 P. 22.

5 *Ib.* p. 33.

dug-outs, the basket- and rug-making, and the occasional ceremonial masks are of American origin.

With the exception of the Ainu all the Palæo-Siberians are reindeer-breeders. In most of their legends—*e.g.*, those of the Chukchi—they always appear as owners of reindeer. Now many of the Gilyak, Chukchi, and Koryak have reindeer no longer and rely on hunting and maritime industries for their livelihood. Together with the reindeer we find the dog used for draught purposes and to provide clothing.

4. Social organization.—The social structure among the Palæo-Siberians is of a less regular character than among the N.W. Amerinds. We do not find here the strictly exogamous, totemistic clans of the Tlingit, Haida, and Tsimshian, but rather organizations resembling those among some Salish and Athapascan tribes in N.W. America. On the whole, the family is the most regular unit. Only the Gilyak have now a distinct clan organization, though the Yukagir and Chukchi might have had such an organization in the past. The Chukchi live in local groups based on community of economic interests, reindeer-breeding, hunting, fishing. The reindeer-breeders are naturally more nomadic than the maritime people. Thus there is no word for 'family' among the Chukchi, and the people living together are called 'those in the house.' There is, moreover, the term *varat*, meaning 'those who are together,' which relates to those who take part in blood-revenge, but, as this unit changes its members very often in practice, it is the relatives in the paternal line, and, failing them, those on the maternal side, or 'group-marriage' companions, that are held to the duty of taking revenge for blood. The Koryak family is organized on the principle of seniority, the father being the head of the family. On the whole, all Palæo-Siberians, with the exception of the Ainu, are patriarchal. Even what looks like a matrilocal arrangement, when the bridegroom goes to live for a time or permanently in his father-in-law's house, is seen by closer study to be merely the way of procuring a wife by 'serving' for her.

The Gilyak clan is called *khal*, 'foot-sack' (used in travelling), and is a group of people united by marriage ties, common cult, responsibility for blood-revenge, or its compensation, and common tabus. The clan is divided into three exogamous sub-clans. Clansmen prefer to live together, and the relationship within the clan is classificatory. They carry on together bear-hunting, trapping of sables, and fishing.

5. Marriage.—On the whole, marriage among the Palæo-Siberians tends to be endogamic. The Gilyak marriage regulations are the most complicated. Within the clan they are endogamic, while the sub-clans are exogamic. Cross-cousin marriage seems to have been the original custom, and the third clan originated probably when one of the two sub-clans could not produce the necessary number of females.

The people who are in the relation of *angey* (wife) and *pu* (husband) have the right of sexual intercourse, if the individual husband is away.[1] This 'group-marriage' arrangement is questioned by some investigators, who think that it amounts to this, that, if a woman betrays her husband with her 'potential' husband, it is considered less blameworthy than if she had done so with a stranger.[2]

Another kind of 'group-marriage' is to be found among the Chukchi. It is in the nature of a supplementary union. Several men married individually join a group, and each man belonging to such a group may exercise the right of a husband when visiting the camp if a husband is away. No two brothers can belong to the group, but the people joining the group, if not relatives before, become so and call themselves 'companions in wives.' Some marriage rites are performed on this occasion, though shorter than in the case of individual marriage. These supplementary unions are seldom arranged between people living in the same camp. The custom of levirate is common among most Palæo-Siberians.

In some respects marriage customs among all the Palæo-Siberians are similar. Thus they all tend to endogamy, with the exception of the Gilyak at present and possibly the Yukagir in the past. The *kalym*, or bride-price, which occurs occasionally, was introduced by the Neo-Siberians, since it is by serving for her that the wife is obtained among most Palæo-Siberians. In connexion with this custom the bridegroom goes to live permanently or temporarily in his father-in-law's house, and his position in the family and the name by which he is called are secure only after the first child is born. Among the Koryak, Kamchadal, and Kuril the ceremony which gives the husband full rights to his wife is the act of 'seizing' her. It is different from marriage by capture and consists in a fight of the bridegroom with the bride and several other women, in the process of which the bridegroom must tear the clothes of the bride, who is carefully wrapped up for the occasion, and touch her sexual organs with his hand. This symbolic ceremony has been compared[1] to the somewhat similar ceremony of the Lillooet and Thompson Indians in N.W. America. According to recent investigators[2] of this region, the most essential marriage ceremony in these tribes is for the bridegroom to touch the bride's naked breast or heel, for, since the usual sitting position is squatting on the heels, touching these practically corresponds to touching her sexual organs. This symbolic action, together with the preliminary attack on the man by the women, may possibly be placed in the same class as the tortures during the initiation of the youth. In all these cases the men are entering on a new phase of life, and have to pass through a period of probationary sufferings, which in the case of couvade are merely symbolic.

6. Religion.—The Palæo-Siberians are typical shamanists. By shamanism (*q.v.*) is meant a religion based on animistic and pre-animistic conceptions in which the person of the shaman, or medicine-man, plays an important rôle. The shamanism of the Palæo-Siberians differs from that of the Neo-Siberians in its (*a*) religious conceptions, (*b*) ceremonies, (*c*) shamanistic accessaries, (*d*) ideas of gods and spirits.

(*a*) *Religious conceptions.*—The pre-animistic beliefs, *i.e.* beliefs in a somewhat chaotic unpersonified supernatural power, are more often met with among the Palæo-Siberians, especially among the Chukchi and Koryak, than among the Neo-Siberians, with perhaps the exception of the Samoyed, who are the most primitive of the Neo-Siberians.[3] Thus the Palæo-Siberians are, as it were, at a more primitive evolutionary stage of their beliefs, and their objects of worship are

[1] L. Sternberg, *The Gilyak* (in Russian), St. Petersburg, 1905, pp. 32–35.

[2] A. N. Maksimoff, *Group-Marriage* (in Russian), Moscow, 1908, p. 41.

[1] A. N. Maksimoff, 'Concerning a Certain Marriage Ceremony,' *Etnograficheskoe Obozrénie*, no. 79 (in Russian), reprint, Moscow, n.d.

[2] J. Teit, 'The Thompson Indians of British Columbia,' *Jesup N. Pacific Exped.*, vol. i. pt. iv. [1900] p. 323 ff., 'The Lillooet Indians,' *ib.* vol. ii. pt. v. [1906] p. 268; F. Boas, 'The Indian Tribes of the Lower Fraser River,' *Report of the British Association*, 1894, p. 458.

[3] See art. SAMOYED.

slightly different, corresponding to the difference of geographical environment. The worship of the sun and sky is not as developed as among the Neo-Siberians, and the animals which play a part in their religious belief are pictured fantastically, not realistically.[1] It is curious and hard to explain why the reindeer, which plays such a unique rôle in the life of the Palæo-Siberians, is neither worshipped nor venerated, and does not in any way enter into the religious life of the people except as a sacrificial animal. In the case of the horse, which occupies a similar position among the inhabitants of Central Asia, it is quite the reverse.

Animism among the Palæo-Siberians is in the highest state of development.

'Even the shadows on the wall constitute definite tribes and have their own country where they live in huts and subsist by hunting. The rainbow and sun-rays have "masters" who live above on the highest part of the rainbow and at the place where the sun's rays emanate, and descend to earth along these paths of light.'[2]

Even such things as the voice of an animal, the sound of the drum, or human speech, have an existence independent of the object which produces them.[3] Anything which formed part of a body—*e.g.*, a lock of hair which has been cut off or even the human or animal excrement—has a soul of its own, or, as the Chukchi say, it is 'having a voice.' These objects 'having a voice' do not entirely lose their qualities as material objects.

'A stone endowed with a "voice" would simply roll down and crush a man against whom it had a grudge.'[4]

It is not quite clear, however, whether objects belonging to one man, as household utensils, have an independent life like natural objects or whether they are spirit-guardians of the family to which they belong. For it is stated by Jochelson that among the Koryak these household objects may warn the people of the house of danger and attack their enemies.[5]

(*b*) *Ceremonies.*—In their religious ceremonies the Palæo-Siberians differ from the Neo-Siberians in that their prayers are simpler and less regularly offered. Reindeer and dogs are usually slaughtered for sacrifice, and occasionally a substitute for reindeer is made of willow-leaves or even of snow. In this respect and in the method of slaughtering the sacrificial animal the Palæo- and Neo-Siberians do not differ very much. The bear ceremony which is such a feature of N. Asia seems to have originated among the Palæo-Siberians, since nowhere is its ritual so rich and complicated as among the Ainu and Koryak. The bear ceremony has a dual nature: the bear is the sacrificial animal and at the same time receives the sacrifice.

Before the bear is slaughtered, women perform a ceremonial dance round his cage, and ceremonial food is given to him. Then the woman who acts as the bear's foster-mother performs a little drama of sorrow at his departure. Again, after the animal is slaughtered for the sacrifice to the spirit of the wood, a series of sacrifices to the victim are made.[6]

Bear-sacrifice and the sacrifice to the fire or new fire are common to all the Palæo-Siberians, whether living on the coast or farther inland. Another ceremony common to them all is the wolf-sacrifice, though the latter is more often found among the Reindeer people. But the wolf-sacrifice has not the dual character of the bear-sacrifice, since no sacrifice is made to the wolf.

After the wolf has been killed, food is presented to him and a ceremonial dance is performed to the beat of the drum. Its meaning is expressed by the prayer addressed to the High Being on such occasions by the Koryak: 'Be good; do not make the wolf bad.'[1] Further, the festival does not end, as the bear-festival or the whale-festival performed among the Palæo-Siberians, with equipment for the homeward journey and the invitation to repeat its visit the following year. The wolf, which does not serve as food and is a danger to the reindeer herd, needless to say, is not encouraged to return, but, the spirit of the dead wolf being particularly malignant, must be carefully propitiated at the ceremony.

The wolf-festival therefore must be looked upon, not as a fertilization ceremony, but as a preventive measure. Together with the wolf, a reindeer is killed, and the bodies of both are placed on a high platform. This symbolizes that the High Being is propitiated that he may not allow the wolf to attack the reindeer.

In comparing the ceremonies of the Palæo- and Neo-Siberians, we must first note the lack of maritime ceremonies among the latter. Of these ceremonies the most important are the whale-festival, celebrations connected with the launching of the boats in the summer, and putting them away for the winter—all known to the Koryak, Chukchi, Eskimo, Kamchadal, and Aleut. Then each maritime tribe has its own conception of the spirit of the god-owner of the sea or of the sea-animals. The Chukchi have even two conceptions of such a god. One is the powerful old woman who lives at the bottom of the sea, called 'the mother of the walrus'; her mouth was adorned with two walrus-like tusks, one of which got broken; and she was so angry that she limited the number of sea-animals. Sad to say, when her other tusk breaks, all sea-animals will perish.[2] This goddess bears a faint resemblance to the goddess Sedna of the Eskimo, but, as the picture of the latter goddess is fuller, it is probable that the Chukchi borrowed her from the Eskimo. The chief 'being of the sea' of the Chukchi, Keretkun, is an old man with a family. A similar idea is attached to the Kachak of the Asiatic Eskimo, who possibly borrowed the god and the ceremonies connected with him from the Chukchi. The Keretkun ceremonies are more detailed and elaborate. The ceremonies last at least three days, and an image of Keretkun is made which is burnt at the end of the ceremonies. Feasts, shamanizing, exchange of presents, and finally an orgiastic dance between the members belonging to the 'additional' marriage group, complete the proceedings. The 'group marriage' arrangements are usually made at this ceremony.[3]

The annual ceremonies of the Reindeer Palæo-Siberians are not unknown to Neo-Siberian reindeer-breeders. The economic rôle of the spring and autumn boat ceremonies of the maritime peoples corresponds to the fawn ceremony in the spring and the ceremonies attending the return of the herd from the summer pastures in autumn. But, though there exists a faint conception of a god-owner of the reindeer, he does not occupy the position of Keretkun, nor are there any special ceremonies connected with him. The fertility of the reindeer herd apparently depends more on keeping certain tabus during the spring and autumn festivals as well as permanent tabus connected with reindeer-breeding than upon sacrifices to the god or spirit of the reindeer.

The annual ceremony of sacrifice to the fire is performed to gain two objects: (*a*) to obtain the new fire or the continued welfare of all those who gather round it, and (*b*) to consecrate a new fetish representing the hearth, which fetish is considered the protector of the hearth and herd, and is anointed with the sacrificial blood and fat.

Though the Palæo-Siberians obtain fire by the use of a flint and steel, the sacrificial fire is obtained by the drilling method, which may point to the fact that that was the original way of ob-

1 M. A. Czaplicka, 'The Influence of Environment upon the Religious Ideas and Practices of the Aborigines of Northern Asia,' *FL* xxv. [1914] 34 ff.
2 Bogoras, p. 281.
3 Jochelson, *Jesup N. Pacific Exped.*, vol. vi. pt. i. p. 117.
4 Bogoras, p. 280.
5 Jochelson, *Jesup N. Pacific Exped.*, vol. vi. pt. i. p. 117.
6 B. Pilsudski, 'Bear Festival among the Ainu,' *Sphinx*, May, 1908.

1 Jochelson, p. 89 f. 2 Bogoras, p. 315 f.
3 Czaplicka, *Aboriginal Siberia*, p. 292 ff.

taining fire among them. The fire-board, on which the drill is turned by means of the bow, is usually made of dry wood and shaped in human form. This fire-board acquires magical power after the new fire is obtained on it, but, to make this magic power work to protect the hearth which it symbolizes, it is necessary that bloody sacrifices of animal victims be offered to it and that an incantation be pronounced over it. The implements used in this ceremony are considered sacred, and even the dust obtained by the drilling is carefully gathered up, 'for it is considered a sin to scatter it.'[1]

(*c*) *Shamanistic accessaries.*—The Palæo-Siberians differ from the Neo-Siberians more in the accessaries used at the religious ceremonies by the shamans than in their religious conceptions or in their actual ceremonies. This again is to a great extent due to the influence of geographical environment, since in the accessaries of the Neo-Siberian shaman the influence of the Central Asiatic environment can still be traced. The ceremonial dress of the shaman—*e.g.*, the ceremonial drum—and the representations of the gods and spirits are very often adorned with or made of metal among the Yakut or Tungus, but not among the Palæo-Siberians, unless of course the latter have borrowed it from the former, as the Yukagir have borrowed it from the Yakut. On the other hand, the form of the drum shows an independence of environment and expresses the tribal individuality. The Chukchi and Eskimo drum is round and its diameter is only from 40 to 50 centimetres. It is very light and has no rattles, which are such an important part of the Neo-Siberian drum. The typical Neo-Siberian drum is of course oval in shape and much greater in diameter, and has protuberances on the outer circle of the rim, which, according to the Yakut, represent the horns of the shaman's spirit. Needless to say, the shamanistic garments of the Palæo-Siberians are, on the whole, much simpler than those of the Neo-Siberians.

(*d*) *Ideas of gods and spirits.*—The highest gods of the Palæo-Siberians are less anthropomorphic than those of the Neo-Siberians. They all have animal characteristics, for the line of demarcation between the human and animal worlds is very obscure. Thus, *e.g.*, the Raven (called, in Chukchi, Kurkil, in Koryak, Kutqi, in Kamchadal, Kutq) takes the form of an animal more frequently than that of a man. He is certainly worshipped as a god by the Koryak, and was worshipped by the Kamchadal till their religion decayed under the influence of the Russian Orthodox Church. But there is also a name in Koryak for the Supreme God, identified with the universe, with the dawn, and with strength. He seems to be above Big Raven and to have sent Big Raven to earth to arrange human affairs. It is Big Raven, therefore, who is considered creator and plays the chief part in religious ceremonies. Among the Chukchi and N.W. Amerinds the Raven has not such a high position and is of more importance in myths than in religious ceremonies.

Religious dualism, so well marked among the Neo-Siberians, is here less defined. There are spirits, as the *kelet* of the Chukchi or *kelau* of the Koryak, who are mostly malicious, and bring disease, death, and all sorts of misfortune. The half-mythical giants dwelling on distant shores and endangering the existence of the Chukchi are also called *kelet*, but the shamanistic spirits are apparently *kelet* too, and these obviously cannot be definitely malicious, at least towards the person on whose behalf they are used by the shaman. So *kelet* may after all mean only 'spirits'; and there is another class of spirits, *vairgit*, which are often benevolent, but *aqam-vairgit* means 'bad spirits,' the same as *kelet*, which seems to point to the fact that *vairgit* also is the name of a class of spirits without a well-defined character. All the celestial bodies are *vairgit*, but, while the sun is a benevolent *vairgin* (singular of *vairgit*) imagined as a man in a radiant garment, the moon is a malicious *vairgin* and could be called a *kele* (sing. of *kelet*), assuming that this class of beings is more malicious than the *vairgit*. Of all the celestial bodies the Polar Star is held in the highest esteem. Her house is in the zenith, higher than the other stars, and she is called 'Motionless star' or the 'Sole-stuck star.' *Kelet* and *kelau* are fond of the human liver, which accounts for that part of the Chukchi funeral rites which demands the opening of the abdomen of the corpse and the search, especially in the liver, to discover which *kele* has killed the man. At the same time the Chukchi believe that the chief soul (*uvirit*, 'belonging to the body') resides in the liver, though other parts of the body have their own souls. A disease in any part of the body is supposed to be caused by lack of a soul in that particular part. The Koryak have no conception corresponding to that of the Chukchi *vairgit*. The soul of a dead man goes to a world above or below the earth, but the soul of a man who was strangled or had otherwise a violent death resides, according to the Chukchi, in the *aurora borealis*. A shaman can easily wander from our world to a world above or beyond ours or anywhere else, for there are many other worlds. All the celestial bodies are inhabited by people. In the time of Big Raven, *i.e.* when he was sent from the sky to create the world and man, and afterwards when he lived among the peoples and taught them industries, every one had the power to pass from one world to another.

[1] Jochelson, *Jesup N. Pacific Exped.*, vol. vi. pt. i. p. 33.

LITERATURE.—In addition to the works referred to in the footnotes the following may be consulted: *Asiatic Russia*, ed. by the Immigration Committee of the Department of Agriculture (in Russian), St. Petersburg, 1914; N. Agapitoff and M. N. Khangaloff, 'Materials for the Study of Shamanism in Siberia' (in Russian), *Memoirs of the East Siberian Section of the Imperial Russian Geographical Society*, Irkutsk, 1883; J. E. Fischer, *Sibirische Geschichte von der Entdeckung Sibiriens bis auf die Eroberung dieses Landes durch die russischen Waffen*, St. Petersburg, 1768; O. Finsch, *Reise nach West-Sibirien im Jahre 1876*, Berlin, 1879; J. S. Georgi, *Bemerkungen einer Reise im russischen Reich in den Jahren 1773 und 1774*, St. Petersburg, 1775; S. P. Krasheninnikoff, *Description of the Country of Kamchatka*[3] (in Russian), do. 1818; F. Nansen, *Through Siberia*, London, 1914; P. S. Pallas, *Reise durch verschiedene Provinzen des russischen Reichs*, 3 vols., St. Petersburg, 1771–76 (*Travels through Siberia and Tartary*, London, 1788, vol. ii. of *The Habitable World Described*, ed. J. Trusler, do. 1788–89); P. J. Strahlenberg, *Der nördliche und östliche Teil von Europa und Asien*, Stockholm, 1730.

M. A. CZAPLICKA.

SIBYLLINE ORACLES.—1. The Sibyl.

—The *Sibylline Oracles* form one of the curiosities of ancient literature. The belief that certain women are possessed with an occult power, however derived, that enables them to predict the future is indeed common to many races of men. But the Sibyl was no ordinary witch, or prophetess, or 'damsel possessed with the spirit of divination'; rather she seems to have gathered into her person all the mystery and reverential awe which attach to a communication from an unknown and intan gible world. Not that she was ever regarded or worshipped as a goddess. In her essence she was always an old woman compelled by some hard fate to be the organ of communication between some god and man. She was venerated, but she was never envied; and the children's game of question and answer, 'Sibyl, what would'st thou?' 'I would I might die,' sums up the strange mixture of awe and pity with which she was regarded. But it was not so much the Sibyl herself as her message that aroused the curious interest of the ancient world. She might appear in person, as she did to Tarquin, but her great importance to men lay rather in the collections of her writings, which were looked upon as providing in some inscrutable way superhuman answers to all kinds of questions, when approached with due reverence and ceremony.

There are Sibyls connected with many different towns and localities. The earliest is undoubtedly that of Erythræ[1] in Asia Minor; she is connected by tradition with Apollo, and her prophecies dealt with Helen and the Trojan war. It may be, indeed, that the Sibylline tradition originated in a kind of rivalry with the cycle of Homeric poems. The most famous Sibyl next to the Erythræan is that of Cumæ in Campania.[2] She it was who in the well-known story appeared to Tarquin, and of whom Vergil wrote in *Eclogue* iv. and *Æneid*, vi. The Sibyl third in importance was associated with Delphi.

2. Classical Sibylline verses. — It is probable that Sibylline verses, when once they had obtained a vogue, multiplied rapidly, and in course of time collections were made. Their general character seems to have been more or less stereotyped. As befitted an old woman who had seen a good deal of the seamy side of life, the tone of the Sibyl was generally pessimistic, and prophecies of disasters in different places formed her stock-in-trade. This is plainly brought out by the testimony of Heraclitus, as cited by Plutarch,[3] who specifies among the 'many mirthless things' prophesied by the Sibyl 'many revolutions and transportations of Greek cities, many appearances of barbarian armies, and deaths of leading men.' Another special device was the division of the history of the world into generations, usually ten in number, sometimes corresponding with the metals, or assigned to various gods.[4]

As far as can be ascertained, all Sibylline verses were written in Greek, and there were undoubtedly early collections in Greece. The Erythræan Sibyl had various imitators, among the most famous of whom was a certain Musæus of Athens, whose writings were collected, at Pisistratus's command, into one book by Onomacritus. Aristophanes has several allusions to the Sibyl scattered through his writings, and Plato speaks of her with distinct respect. But it was at Rome that the influence of Sibylline writings as a political force was most pronounced. Their history begins with the visit of the old woman to Tarquin, and his purchase of three of the nine books which she brought. These were buried in the ground for safe custody, probably in the temple of Capitoline Jove. They were consulted first of all at rare intervals, but later every three or four years. In 82 B.C. the Capitol was destroyed by fire, and the Sibylline books perished entirely. Seven years later three men were sent out on a special mission to Erythræ to bring back any Sibylline verses that they could find. A thousand lines or so were discovered, and others were brought from other places, and out of the materials thus collected the *xv viri sacris faciundis* were deputed to make a selection.[5] This selection was in later years subjected to a searching criticism by Augustus, who rejected all but a small residuum. This was carefully guarded, but the best days of the *Sibylline Oracles* were over, and they became more and more neglected; and, although they enjoyed a temporary revival of popularity under Aurelian and later under Julian, they never really regained their hold over the credulity of man. They were finally burned by Stilicho in the principate of Honorius.

3. Jewish adaptations.—If the history of the *Sibylline Oracles* had been confined to Greece and Rome, it would still have been a very curious and interesting phenomenon in the ancient world. But their main interest to the modern student lies in the fact that their form and, to a considerable, though uncertain, extent, their substance were copied by Jewish, and later by Christian, writers mainly for the purpose of propaganda. It says a good deal for the influence of the ancient Sibyl that such a device should have been put in practice, and it says still more for the credulity of the ancient world that it should so largely have served its purpose. The Jew who first hit upon the expedient of borrowing the authority of the Sibyl for the propagation of his national faith lived in Egypt, and probably in Alexandria, in the first half of the 2nd century B.C. He was therefore a contemporary of the author of the book of Daniel, and of that of the original section of the book of Enoch. His work is seen in the main portion of bk. iii., beginning at line 97. His method of procedure is worthy of note for its strange mixture of OT history and ancient legend, the latter probably borrowed from ancient Sibylline writings. So the destruction of the Tower of Babel is followed by the reign of Cronos, Titan, and Iapetus, and the birth of Zeus. Then, after passing summarily over the rise of different world-powers, he comes to his main theme in Jewish history. This is all put in the future tense as representing a prophecy of the Sibyl. In the rest of the book there is a strange mixture of ancient oracles, more or less contemporary history, eschatological details, and especially extravagant praise of the Jewish nation, and a description of the happiness of the members of it.

How far these Jewish Sibylline writings had a direct value as a proselytizing force we have no means of knowing. But at a time when Greek culture and the study of Greek literature were more and more coming into vogue, when superstition was rife, and when there was a good deal of scepticism abroad as to the value of the gods of Rome, it is not hard to imagine that the indirect influence of these Sibylline verses on cultivated minds may have been considerable. The Romans seem to have been always impressed with the Jewish religion ever since their first contact with it, and there may well have been many who would be disposed to view with sympathy the suggestion that in the ancient and venerable Sibyl might be found a point of union between the austere and moral religion of the Jews and the literature of ancient Greece, which was being increasingly studied and adapted. At the same time we must remember that till 82 B.C. the official collection of Sibylline verses was being preserved with the utmost secrecy at Rome. It is probable, therefore, that the Jewish portions were studied in Eastern lands, and more especially at Alexandria.

4. Christian Sibyllines.—But the chief argument for the success of the Jewish Sibylline verses as a means for proselytizing lies in their imitation by Christian writers. As the Christian writers of the 1st and 2nd centuries, following St. Paul's line of argument, boldly took over as the heritage of the Christian Church the special privileges given of old to the Jews, so the Jewish Sibyl was impressed into the service of the Christian faith. In the books that have come down to us we have therefore three elements: (*a*) fragments of oracles of unknown antiquity, possibly stretching back into a remote past; (*b*) Jewish oracles of the last two centuries B.C. and the first two centuries A.D., dealing partly with contemporary history put in

[1] Pausanias, x. xii. The Sibyl's head appears on ancient Erythræan coins.

[2] Justin, *Cohort. ad Graecos*, 37, gives a description of the Sibyl's grotto at Cumæ.

[3] *De Pyth. Or.* vii. (561).

[4] Servius, on Vergil, *Ecl.* iv. 4.

[5] Tac. *Ann.* vi. 12.

the form of prophecy, partly with Jewish teaching and propaganda, and partly with the eschatological conjectures that played so conspicuous a part in the thought of that transitional age; (*c*) Christian writings, sometimes a few lines sandwiched in between Jewish or pagan writings, sometimes extending to long continuous sections, as in bk. ii. and especially in bk. viii. These Christian writings deal largely with the life and work of Christ, but in them also eschatology plays a leading part. Bk. vii. is evidently tinged with Gnostic thought.

It cannot be said that the Christian Sibyllines have made any marked contribution of their own to the general literature. And yet the early Fathers laid very great stress on the witness of the Sibyl to Christ. For the most part they regarded her as undoubtedly inspired, but they drew a distinction between her and the prophets of the OT. The latter were, to some degree at any rate, conscious interpreters of the message of God, though exactly how far their human thought and language had moulded their message was not always clear. But the Sibyl was but a mouthpiece—by her own confession an unwilling mouthpiece—of the oracle of God;[1] and consequently her testimony was all the more striking as being anything but spontaneous. It will readily be seen than an argument like this, in so far as it appealed to the critical instinct of the time, would have a real apologetic value. To our minds it may well appear strange that verses which seem obviously so late should be regarded as possessing the reverence of hoary antiquity. But we must remember the Sibylline tradition stretching back into centuries far away, the air of mystery which had always surrounded it, and above all the credulity of the average man in the matter of literary records.

The first mention of a Sibyl in a Christian writer appears to be in Hermas.[2] The writer sees an old woman splendidly arrayed, holding in her hands a book from which she reads. He takes her to be the Sibyl, but is told that she is the Church. The passage is interesting as showing the idea of the Sibyl's personality. According to Justin,[3] Clement of Rome referred to the Sibyl's prophecy that the world should be judged by fire. Justin himself has several allusions to her,[4] and does not doubt that she spoke under divine inspiration. Theophilus is the first to preserve fragments i.–iii. Athenagoras has at least one quotation from the fragments. Clement of Alexandria cites freely from most of the books, but it is noticeable that he never mentions the specially Christian bk. viii. He could hardly have omitted to do so had it been extant at the time, or had he not had suspicions of its genuineness. Soon after his time the Christians fell under the suspicion of coining oracles in their own favour. Celsus[5] roundly accused them of interpolating and faking many passages in the ancient and genuine Sibylline writings, and Lucian makes merry over the idea of Christian oracles, and produces some very clever parodies. Here is one on the gematria of the *Sibyllines*:

Εὐξείνου πόντοιο παρ' ἠϊόσ' ἄγχι Σινώπης
ἔσταί τις κατὰ Τύρσιν ὑπ' Αὐσονίοισι προφήτης
ἐκ πρώτης δεικνὺς μόναδος, τρισσῶν δεκάδων τε,
πένθ' ἑτέρας μόναδας καὶ εἰκόσαδα τρισάριθμον
ἀνδρὸς ἀλεξητῆρος ὁμωνυμίην τετράκυκλον.

The name is Ἀλέξανδρος (Α=1, λ=30, ε=5, ξ=60).[6]

The force of these onslaughts upon the Christian teaching of the Sibyls will be felt when it is remembered that some Christian writers went so far as to make St. Paul himself appeal to the testimony of the Sibyl.

[1] Cf. *Sib.* iii. 3–7, etc. [2] *Vis.* ii. § 4.
[3] *Quæst. et resp. ad Orthodoxos*, 74.
[4] *Apol.* i. 20, 59. [5] Orig. *c. Cels.* vii. § 56.
[6] For such puzzles in the *Sibyllines*, cf. i. 140–146, 326–331.

ἐπεὶ ὅτι καθάπερ Ἰουδαίους σώζεσθαι ἐβούλετο ὁ θεὸς, τοὺς προφήτας διδοὺς, οὕτω καὶ Ἑλλήνων τοὺς δοκιμωτάτους, οἰκείους αὐτῶν τῇ διαλέκτῳ προφήτας ἀναστήσας, ὡς οἷοί τε ἦσαν δέχεσθαι τὴν παρὰ θεοῦ εὐεργεσίαν. τῶν χυδαίων ἀνθρώπων διέκρινε, δηλώσει πρὸς τῷ Πετροῦ κηρύγματι ὁ ἀπόστολος λέγων Παῦλος· Λάβετε καὶ τὰς Ἑλληνικὰς βίβλους, ἐπίγνωτε Σίβυλλαν, ὡς δηλοῖ ἕνα θεὸν καὶ τὰ μέλλοντα ἔσεσθαι.[1]

After this there are few allusions to the Sibyl in the Greek Fathers. But among Latin writers there are frequent quotations. Lactantius is a mine of Sibylline verses. Constantine's speech to the elders at Nicæa, as recorded by Eusebius, abounds in allusions. Augustine discussed seriously the Sibyl's claim, and, finding nothing in her whole poem that advocated the worship of false gods, he decided that she must be included in the number of those who belong to the City of God.[2]

5. MSS.—The great majority of MSS of the *Sibylline Oracles* date from the 15th cent.; only two appear to belong to the 14th, and none are earlier. The first printed ed. is that of Xystus Betuleius (Basel, 1545), containing bks. i.–viii. 485. The first ed. to contain the whole of bk. viii. is that of Johannes Opsopœus (Paris, 1599). The last four books were discovered by Angelo Mai and published in 1817, in his *Scriptorum veterum nova collectio*. The fragments, six in number, are preserved in Theophilus, *ad Autolycum*, and in Lactantius.

Of the many edd. of the *Oracles* special mention should be made of the monumental work of C. Alexandre (*Oracula sibyllina*, 2 vols., Paris, 1841–56) and of the most recent ed., that of J. Geffcken (Leipzig, 1902). Geffcken built upon the unpublished work of Mendelssohn, and both in this ed. and in various magazine articles he has rendered valuable service to the problem of the text.

6. Contents.—A brief summary of the different books is subjoined. Of the fragments only the first and third are of any considerable length. They are quoted by Theophilus as occurring 'at the beginning of [the Sibyl's] prophecy,' and therefore it is possible that they formed an introduction to bk. iii. They are certainly of early date, and their theme is the majesty of God, especially as seen in the works of creation, the folly of idolatry, and the wisdom of worshipping God.

First and second books.—Bks. i. and ii. are best treated as a unity, the division between them being found in no early MS. The general scheme is to give a summary of the world's history from the earliest times to the end. This purpose is not fully carried out. Bk. i. indeed recounts six generations, up to and including the Flood, but then a new generation (of Titans) arises, and the intervening history is omitted till the coming of Christ. Bk. ii. begins with a short introduction, and then describes the coming of the tenth generation, which is to witness the breaking down of the dominion of Rome. There is to ensue a period of deep peace, and afterwards Christ is to appear, heralded by a star, and is to distribute rewards to those who have proved themselves worthy. At this point 92 lines are inserted, mostly from pseudo-Phocylides, which have no obvious connexion with what precedes or follows. Four transitional lines intervene, and then commences a new section which is occupied principally with eschatological details. Many of these details are closely parallel to the descriptions in the Apocalypse of Peter.

The most probable view of these books is that in their original scheme they form a Jewish work dealing with the ten generations of man, but that this scheme was for some reason abandoned half-way through, and the interest of the writer passed to eschatology. The book, being thus left as a kind of medley, was further confused by the insertion of various Christian elements. In its present form it is therefore late, and is to be ascribed probably to the 2nd cent. A.D. The section from pseudo-Phocylides (ii. 56–148) is obviously an insertion, and has possibly displaced iii. 1–92.

Third book.—Bk. iii. is the most important, and in some ways the most perplexing, of the Sibylline writings. It is obviously composed of several different elements, but great uncertainty exists as to the exact character of them. The following division of the book is suggested:

1–62. An introduction written by a Jew living probably in Palestine about 80 B.C.
63–92. A Jewish or Christian eschatological section from the end of the 1st cent. A.D.; a very much later addition to the book.
93–96. A Jewish or Christian fragment.
97–161. A passage overworked from the Babylonian Sibyl.
162–294. A Jewish passage dating from 140 B.C. or a little earlier.
295–488. A collection of prophecies on the whole Jewish and anti-Roman. The bulk deals with the years 170–140 B.C., and seems to have been composed about the latter date, though some sections may be much

[1] Clem. Alex. *Strom.* vi. 5. [2] *De Civ. Dei*, xviii. 23.

earlier. Lines 464–488 are considerably later and may be dated about 80 B.C.

489–829. Another Jewish collection incorporating several ancient oracles, but dating on the whole from 140 B.C., or very near that time. The eschatological element is strongly marked towards the end, and the hortatory tone is more noticeable. The ending bears signs of interpolation.

Lines 1–96 can hardly be homogeneous in themselves. One section (46–62) appears to belong to the same date as the section 464–470, *i.e.* about 80 B.C. But lines 62–92 are obviously late and cannot be placed earlier than the 1st cent. A.D. Indeed their eschatology is to be compared with ii. 165 ff. The first part (8–45) comes nearest in thought to frag. i., while 92–95 seem to be, like v. 256–259, a Christian interpolation.

The middle section (295–488) is mainly historical in its allusion and has very little direct teaching. The history has to do partly with Antiochus Epiphanes and the struggles of his successors, but partly with the events of the next century. Lines 350–355 seem to refer to the Mithradatic war, and 464–470 bring us in all probability to the stirring times of Sulla. But more ancient writings are incorporated—*e.g.*, 401–418, 419–432—and oracles on various lands are interspersed. The view of Rome is interesting. She is regarded with bitter hatred, and the writer looks forward with savage joy to her discomfiture at the hands of Asia. This goes far beyond the unfavourable view of Rome expressed in the first of the three divisions (175 ff.).

There is no sign of any special interest in Egypt, though the struggles between the brothers Ptolemy, Philometor and Euergetes, seem to be alluded to in line 316. The writer seems to belong to Asia, and perhaps to Phrygia.

With regard to the question of date, lines 97–294 and 489–829 represent, with possible interpolations, the oldest portions of the book and reflect very much the same date, though lines 97–294 are probably a little earlier. The standpoint of this section is that of an Egyptian Jew of about 140 B.C., who sees in the recent troubles of his nation a parallel to the Babylonian captivity, and in their reviving fortunes under Simon Maccabæus a type of their former deliverance under Cyrus. Imbued with the same kind of spirit as that which prompted Aristobulus some twenty years before to maintain that all the flower of Greek philosophy and poetry was in some way dependent on the Jewish Scriptures, he begins with an ancient Sibylline writing (97–154), which he introduces by a few lines dealing with the Flood and the Tower of Babel, and then goes on with an account of the fortunes of the Jews and the prosperity that is in store for them. Certain other nations are mentioned, but only one at any length. The Romans have already made their mark in Eastern history and have inspired terror of their arms. The moral obliquities ascribed to them in line 184 ff. may be out of place here, or they may be grossly exaggerated. But we cannot say certainly that they were entirely unfounded.

In line 489 *ad fin.* the country most in the writer's mind is not Rome, but Greece. In true Sibylline style he leads up to his main theme by allusions to various other lands, but Greece forms evidently his main theme. A great disaster has lately overtaken it. A barbarian land has laid it waste, and its long history seems to have closed in irretrievable catastrophe. This can hardly refer to anything but the expedition of L. Mummius in 146 B.C., which was crowned by the capture and destruction of Corinth. Other allusions make for the same date (*c.* 140 B.C.); these will be found in 607–615, 732–740, and in the general idea of the renewed prosperity of the Jewish race. The writer is a patriotic Jew, well-versed in OT prophecy. His interests are largely eschatological. He believes intensely in the coming of Messiah, he foresees further troubles and a fresh determined onslaught on the Holy City by the evil powers of the world; but beyond that he looks forward to a reign of peace and happiness, in which the nation shall dwell contentedly around its restored Temple, and the peoples of the world shall bring their gifts and offer their sacrifice of praise. The whole spirit of this writing seems to reflect the exuberant hope of the days of Simon Maccabæus.

Fourth book.—Bk. iv. deals with the same kinds of subjects as bk. iii., but in much shorter compass. The history of man is divided into twelve generations, and catastrophes on various cities and countries are foretold. Among these catastrophes earthquakes play a noticeable part, and it is probable that the severe earthquake which ruined Laodicea in A.D. 60 is comparatively fresh in the writer's mind.[1] The destruction of the Temple is presupposed (116 ff.), and the curious belief in the return of Nero points to a date not long after A.D. 70. We may with considerable confidence assign the book to about A.D. 80. The author appears to be chiefly interested in Asia Minor. His religious position is marked by (*a*) rejection of temples or shrines, (*b*) rejection of sacrifices, (*c*) belief in the imminence of a final judgment, to be followed by a reign of the just upon earth, (*d*) insistence on ceremonial washings. Formerly the author was widely believed to have been a Christian, but the prevailing opinion now sees in him a Jew, possibly an Essene.

Fifth book.—Bk. v. falls into two unequal divisions: (*a*) 1–51, (*b*) 52–531. In section (*a*) the writer goes through a list of the Roman emperors, whom he identifies by their initials, as far as Hadrian. Section (*b*) is for the most part taken up with the regular Sibylline prophecy of woes on various lands and cities, but there are certain sections which seem to stand out as striking a different note. Such are 228–246, an address to Ὕβρις, 260–285, a panegyric on Judæa, and 256–259, a Christian interpolation.

The characteristic of section (*b*) is bitter hatred against Rome and a strong vein of patriotism for Judæa. Mingled with the hatred for Rome there is also a marked bitterness against Egypt, where there had apparently been a recent persecution of Jews. Lines 411–413 refer to the belief, attested elsewhere, that Titus, on his way home after the capture of Jerusalem, would die the moment he set foot on Italian soil.

The expectation of the return of Nero appears in both sections, but in 33 f. Nero is still the historical personage, while in 137–154 and 361–385 he is invested with superhuman traits.

Section (*a*) appears to date from the middle years of the principate of Hadrian, when Rome could be regarded with favour by a patriotic Jew. Section (*b*) is the work of a Jew living in Egypt, and writing shortly after the suppression of the rebellion of Bar Cochba in A.D. 132.

Sixth book.—Bk. vi. is a short hymn describing the ministry and death of Christ. Its date is probably towards the end of the 2nd century A.D. The following may be reckoned as peculiar features: (*a*) the appearance of fire at the Baptism of Christ (line 6); (*b*) the dove at the Baptism specified as white (7); (*c*) the reference to Adam and Eve having seen Christ (18); (*d*) the taking of the Cross into heaven (27). The anti-Jewish feeling is noticeable. Judæa is called the 'land of Sodom' (21).

Seventh book.—Bk. vii. has come down in a fragmentary condition. It falls into three divisions, 1–50, 51–95, 96–162, each beginning with detached oracles of woe and passing on to some definite religious teaching. The author is deeply tinged with Gnosticism. He believes in three towers in heaven, which are the dwelling-place of the three 'Mothers of God'—Hope, Piety, and Worship (71–73). He enjoins quaint ceremonies, prayers, and incantations (76–91). He is familiar with the Gnostic ogdoad (140). His eschatology is marked by sternness. Fire is to play an important part at the end of the world, and the torments of the ungodly are apparently to be eternal. The date may be tentatively placed in the first half of the 3rd cent. A.D.

Eighth book.—Bk. viii. is the most definitely Christian of all. It falls into two main divisions at line 216. The first is marked by a bitter hatred against Rome, whose miserable end is expected at a definite day, *i.e.* A.D. 195. This date is arrived at by counting the numerical value of the letters of ΡΩΜΗ=948, and reckoning from the foundation of the city. The theme of the fall of Rome leads on to eschatology, in which special features are the return of Nero Redivivus and the dominion of a woman apparently regarded as the incarnation of evil. A 'holy son' is to slay the wicked woman by launching upon her the waters of the great deep, and is to save mankind in a second ark. In the resurrection that is to follow there is to be a perfect life of communism and happiness. The author is probably a Christian, though there is little distinctively Christian in his outlook.

The second division is frankly and avowedly Christian, and contains the famous acrostic on ΙΗΣΟΥΣ ΧΡΕΙΣΤΟΣ ΘΕΟΥ ΥΙΟΣ ΣΩΤΗΡ ΣΤΑΥΡΟΣ, the five first letters of which form another acrostic, ΙΧΘΥΣ: hence the common symbol of the fish for Christ as noticed by Tertullian and Augustine.[1] This acrostic is the basis of the whole division, and it is expanded by various details of the life and especially of the death of Christ, and rounded off by an eschatological section. Between 358 and 455 there is inserted an independent section dealing with the nature of God and the worship due to Him. There are no certain marks of date in this division of the book, but it may be placed somewhere in the 3rd cent. A.D.

The last four books.—The last four bks., xi.–xiv., are mainly historical, and of less interest. Bk. xi. begins with the Flood, dated in the fifth[2] generation, and proceeds at once to the story of the Tower of Babel in the tenth generation. Then comes a rapid survey of successive empires beginning with Egypt and the Exodus. The second half of the book deals principally with Rome, especially in its connexion with Egypt.

The writer is evidently an Egyptian patriot, who traces his country's history down to the loss of her independence. He is probably an Alexandrian Jew, and perhaps a proselyte. His chief model is bk. iii., especially in its historical portions. The latest mark of date is the reference in line 160 to the extension of the Roman empire to the Tigris and Euphrates, which occurred in the principate of Hadrian.

Bk. xii. follows a simple scheme. Beginning with eleven lines taken bodily from the commencement of bk. v., it proceeds to give a short history of the Roman emperors from Augustine to Elagabalus, each emperor being indicated by the numerical value of his initial. The history is usually straightforward, though there are occasional inaccuracies—*e.g.*, in the statement that Caligula was put to death in an outburst of feeling occasioned by the execution of a Vestal Virgin, and that Vespasian was murdered. There are a few Christian passages; *e.g.*, 30–36 speak of the Incarnation, and 196 ff. refer to the story of the Thundering Legion. But the religious side is not emphasized. The writer is little more than a versifier of history. His date is probably in the reign of Alexander Severus (A.D. 222–235).

Bk. xiii. continues the history from the reign of Alexander Severus to about the reign of Tacitus (A.D. 275). After a

[1] Cf. Tac. *Ann.* xiv. 27.

[1] The acrostic is quoted in Eusebius, *Const. Or. ad Sanct. Coet.* xviii., and a Latin tr. is found in Augustine, *de Civ. Dei*, xviii. 23.

[2] Reading πέμπτην (so Rzach) for πενίην in line 7.

stereotyped introduction the book begins so abruptly that it is evidently mutilated. The history is narrated so allusively that the identification of the references is frequently attended with great difficulty. There is much more of the Sibylline woes on various places than in the preceding book. The religious teaching is again very slight. The writer seems to be a Jew rather than a Christian, and possibly he is an Alexandrian. He writes under the spell of the consternation caused by the capture of Valerian by Sapor, the Persian king, and the troubles and upheavals of the second half of the 3rd cent. are faithfully reflected in his lines. But throughout all the enumeration of troubles there runs a vein of hope and confidence. The writer by no means despairs of the Roman empire (contrast 46–49 with viii. 148–150).

The style is somewhat conventional, but not without a certain vigour. There are allusions to earlier books, and the vocabulary is 'Sibylline,' but we find no such patchwork of borrowed fragments as in the preceding book.

Bk. xiv. evidently sets out to be a continuation of bk. xiii., and therefore it starts with the death of Odenatus (lines 12–17) and the reign of Aureolus (18–20). But after this no scheme of history has been propounded that can be adapted to the allusions to the names of emperors. It is possible to pick out one or two here and there that seem to fit, but in the general chaos of the book it appears to be an unprofitable task to do so. Either the writer lived about the 6th or 7th cent. A.D. and had a very inaccurate knowledge of history or, if he is writing about A.D. 300, he is giving rein to a very vivid imagination. In either case his work can hardly be pronounced worthy of serious study.

LITERATURE.—i. *Edd. of text.*—**Xystus Betuleius**, *Sibyllinorum Oraculorum Libri octo*, Basel, 1545; **Johannes Opsopœus**, Σιβυλλιακοὶ Χρησμοί, Paris, 1599; **Servatius Gallæus**, Σιβυλλιακοὶ Χρησμοί, Amsterdam, 1689; **Angelo Mai**, Σιβύλλης Λόγος ιδ', Milan, 1817, *id.* Libri xi.–xiv. (*Scriptorum veterum nova collectio*, iii. 202 ff.), Rome, 1828; **C. Alexandre**, *Oracula Sibyllina*, 2 vols. in 3 pts., Paris, 1841–56, *id.*, abridged ed., do. 1869; **J. H. Friedlieb**, Χρησμοί Σιβυλλιακοί, Leipzig, 1852; **Aloisius Rzach**, Χρησμοί Σιβυλλιακοί, Vienna, 1891; **J. Geffcken**, *Die Oracula Sibyllina bearbeitet im Auftrage der Kirchenväterkommission*, Leipzig, 1902.

ii. *Artt. in dictionaries.*—**F. Schwally**, in Pauly-Wissowa; **E. Reuss**, in *PRE*[2] xiv. [1884] 179 ff.; **S. Krauss**, in *JE* xi. 319; **J. H. A. Hart**, in *EBr*[11] xxv. 19; **P. J. Healy**, in *CE* xiii. 770; **W. Bousset**, in *PRE*[3] xviii. [1906] 265 ff., and Schaff-Herzog, x 396 ff.; **J. R. Harris**, in *HDB* v. 66; **J. Moffatt**, in *DAC* ii. 477.

iii. *Works dealing with the text and explanation of the Oracles.*—**B. Thorlacius**, *Libri Sibyllistarum veteris ecclesiæ crisi, quatenus monumenta Christiana sunt, subjecti*, Copenhagen, 1815; **F. Bleek**, 'Ueber die Entstehung und Zusammenhang der uns in acht Büchern erhaltenen Sammlung sibyllin. Orakel,' *Theol. Zeitschr.* i. [1819] 120 ff., ii. [1820] 172 ff.; **A. F. Gfrörer**, *Philo und die Alexandrin. Theosophie*, Stuttgart, 1831, ii. 121 ff.; **J. H. Friedlieb**, *De Codicibus Sibyllinorum manuscriptis in usum criticum nondum adhibitis commentatio*, Breslau, 1847; **R. Volkmann**, *De oraculis Sibyllinis dissertatio*, Leipzig, 1853, *Lectiones Sibyllinæ*, Pyritz, 1861; **H. Ewald**, *Abhandlung über Entstehung, Inhalt, und Werth der sibyllin. Bücher*, Göttingen, 1858; **A. Hilgenfeld**, *Die jüdische Apokalyptik in ihrer geschichtl. Entwickelung*, Jena, 1857, p. 51 ff., 'Die jüdische Sibyllen-Weissagung,' in *ZWT* iii. [1860] 313 ff., 'Die jüdischen Sibyllen und der Essenismus,' in *ZWT* xiv. [1871] 30 ff.; **R. H. Klausen**, *Æneas und die Penaten*, 2 vols., Hamburg, 1839–40; **G. Volkmar**, *Commentar zur Offenbarung Johannis*, Zürich, 1862; **E. Reuss**, 'Die christl. Sibyllen,' *Strassburger Revue der Theologie*, May, 1869; **J. Larocque**, 'Sur la Date du troisième livre des Oracles sibyllins,' *RA*, new ser. xx. [1869] 261 ff.; **H. Dechent**, *Ueber das erste, zweite und elfte Buch der sibyllin. Weissagungen*, Frankfort, 1873, 'Charakter und Geschichte der altchristl. Sibyllenschriften,' *ZKG* ii. [1878] 481 ff.; **W. Hildebrandt**, 'Das römische Antichristenthum zur Zeit der Offenbarung Johannis und des vten sibyllin. Buches,' *ZWT* xvii. [1874] 57 ff.; **F. Delitzsch**, 'Versuchte Lösung eines sibyllin. Rätsels,' *Zeitschr. für luth. Theol.* xxxviii. [1877] 216 ff.; **T. Zahn**, 'Apokalyptische Studien,' *ZKWL* vii. [1886] 32 ff., 77 ff.; **B. Badt**, *Ursprung, Inhalt, und Text des ivten Buches der sibyllin. Orakel*, Breslau, 1878; **O. Zöckler**, *Die Apokryphen des AT*, Munich, 1901, p. 477 ff.; **E. Maass**, *De Sibyllarum indicibus*, Berlin, 1879; **A. C. Bang**, *Voluspá und die sibyllin. Orakel*, tr. from Danish, Vienna, 1880; **J. Rendel Harris**, *The Teaching of the Apostles and the Sibylline Books*, Cambridge, 1885; **M. S. Terry**, *The Sibylline Oracles*, tr. from Greek into English blank verse, New York, 1890; **L. Mendelssohn**, 'Zu den Oracula Sibyllina,' *Philologus*, xlix. [1890] 240 ff.; **S. A. Hirsch**, 'The Jewish Sibylline Oracles,' *JQR* ii. [1890] 406 ff.; **H. Diels**, *Sibyllin. Blätter*, Berlin, 1890; **K. Buresch**, 'Die pseudosibyllin. Orakel und ihre letzte Bearbeitung,' *Jahrb. für class. Philol.* xviii. [1891] 529 ff., 'Zu den pseudosibyllin. Orakeln,' *Jahrb. für class. Philol.* xix. [1892] 273 ff., 'Krit. Brief über die falschen Sibyllen,' *Philologus*, li. [1892] 82 ff., 422 ff., 'Pseudosibyllinisches,' *Rhein. Museum für Philologie*, xlvii. [1892] 329 ff.; **W. J. Deane**, *Pseudepigrapha*, Edinburgh, 1891; **Rzach**, in *Wiener Studien*, iv. [1882] 121 ff., xii. [1890] 190 ff., xiv. [1892] 18 ff., 145 ff., xv. [1893] 77 ff., xvii. [1895] 310, *Krit. Studien zu den sibyllin. Orakeln*, Vienna, 1890; **E. Fehr**, *Studia in Oracula Sibyllina*, Upsala, 1893; **E. Schürer**, *GJV*[3] iii. 421 ff., *HJP* iii. 271 ff.; **M. Friedländer**, *REJ* xxix. [1894] 183 ff., *Gesch. der jüd. Apologetik*, Zürich, 1903, p. 31 ff.; **F. Blass**, 'Die Sibyllin. Orakel,' in E. Kautzsch, *Apocryphen und Pseudepigraphen des AT*, Tübingen, 1900, ii. 177 ff.; **J. Geffcken**, *Komposition und Entstehungszeit des Oracula Sibyllina*, Leipzig, 1902; **H. C. O. Lanchester**, 'The Sibylline Oracles,' in R. H. Charles, *The Apocrypha and Pseudepigrapha of the OT*, Oxford, 1913, ii. 368 ff.

iv. *Works dealing with quotations from the Sibyllines in the early Fathers.*—**C. L. Struve**, *Fragmenta librorum Sibyllinorum quæ apud Lactantium reperiuntur*, Königsberg, 1817; **F. Vervorst**, *De carminibus Sibyllinis apud sanctos Patres disceptatio*, Paris, 1844; **G. Besançon**, *De l'Emploi que les pères de l'église ont fait des oracles sibyllins*, Montauban, 1851; **Alexandre**, *Excursus ad Sibyllina*, Paris, 1856, p. 254 ff.

v. *Translations.*—(*a*) *English.*—**J. Floyer**, *The Sibylline Oracles, translated from the best Greek Copies*, London, 1731; **Terry**, *The Sibylline Oracles*, New York, 1890.

(*b*) *French.*—**S. Champier** and **J. Robertet**, *Oracles de la Sibylle*, Paris, 1702–03; **A. Bouché-Leclercq**, in *RHR* vii. [1883] 236 ff., viii. [1884] 619 ff., ix. [1885] 220 ff.

(*c*) *German.*—**J. C. Nahrung**, *Neun Bücher sibyllin. Propheceiungen, aus der griechischen in die deutsche Sprache übersetzt*, Halle, 1819; **J. H. Friedlieb**, *Die sibyllin. Weissagungen vollständig gesammelt*, Leipzig, 1852.

(*d*) *Italian.*—**V. Antolini**, *Oracoli Sibillini, tradotti dal Greco in versi Italiani*, Viterbo, 1775.

(*e*) *Latin.*—**S. Castalio**, *Sibyllina Oracula de Græco in Latinum conversa et in eadem annotationes*, Basel, 1546; **A. Mai**, *Sibyllæ Libri xiv. Græca et Latina*, Milan, 1817.

(*f*) *Spanish.*—**Baltasar Poreno**, *Oráculos de las doze Sibilas. Profetisas de Christo nuestro Señor entre los Gentiles*, Cuença, 1621.

H. C. O. LANCHESTER.

SICKNESS.—See DISEASE AND MEDICINE.

SIDGWICK (HENRY).

—I. **Life.** — Henry Sidgwick was born in 1838 at Skipton in Yorkshire, where his father, the Rev. William Sidgwick, was headmaster of the Grammar School. He came of Yorkshire stock, and there is a tradition that in the last generation one might hear this family referred to in the neighbourhood of Skipton as 'the good and great Sidgwicks.' William Sidgwick's wife was Miss Mary Crofts, also of Yorkshire descent, and it is told of her that she was a beauty and a wit. Her third son, Henry, the subject of this article, was three years old when his father died. Henry's sister, Mary, became the wife of her cousin, E. W. Benson, afterwards archbishop of Canterbury, and his youngest brother Arthur, a brilliant classical scholar, was Reader in Greek in the University of Oxford. Henry Sidgwick's life is most admirably set before us by his brother and his wife, Arthur Sidgwick and Eleanor Mildred Sidgwick, in *Henry Sidgwick: a Memoir by A. S. and E. M. S.*

In Sept. 1852 Henry Sidgwick went to Rugby, and from there, in Oct. 1855, to Trinity College, Cambridge. He won the Bell and Craven Scholarships—the latter the 'blue ribbon' among Classical scholarships at Cambridge—and in Jan. 1859, having taken both the Classical and Mathematical Triposes, he came out 33rd Wrangler and Senior Classic, and also won the first Chancellor's Medal. In October of the same year he was elected a Fellow of Trinity. Henry Sidgwick felt at that time no difficulty in making the declaration required from all Fellows of Colleges on admission, that he was a member of the Church of England, and he was appointed an assistant tutor in Classics, being then a little over 21 years of age. Thus began that life of academic teaching which he carried on for over forty years.

In an autobiographical fragment dictated in his last illness, which is included in the *Memoir*, Sidgwick, referring to his membership of 'The Apostles,' says:

'In the Michaelmas term of my second year an event occurred which had more effect on my intellectual life than any one thing that happened to me afterwards: I became a member of a discussion society—old and possessing historical traditions—which went by the name of "The Apostles" . . . [The spirit of this Society] 'gradually absorbed and dominated me. I can only describe it as the spirit of the pursuit of truth with absolute devotion and unreserve by a group of intimate friends, who were perfectly frank with each other. . . . Absolute candour was the only duty that the tradition of the society enforced.'[1] 'It came to seem to me that no part of my life at Cambridge

[1] P. 34.

was so real to me as the Saturday evenings on which the apostolic debates were held; and the tie of attachment to the society is much the strongest corporate bond which I have known in life. I think, then, that my admission into this society and the enthusiastic way in which I came to idealise it really determined or revealed that the deepest bent of my nature was towards the life of thought—thought exercised on the central problems of human life. But many years elapsed before the consciousness of this led me to embrace the study of philosophy as my life's work.'[1] In the same fragment he describes the 'central and fundamental aim' of his life as 'the solution, or contribution to the solution, of the deepest problems of human life. The peculiarity of my career has been that I have sought light on these problems, and that not casually but systematically and laboriously, from very various sources and by very diverse methods.'[2]

In 1869 Sidgwick had come to feel that he could no longer honestly declare himself to be a member of the Church of England. His secession from the Church was perhaps a foregone conclusion, but his future life seemed only the more deeply devoted to an unwavering passionate allegiance to truth. He resigned his Fellowship. His reasons for doing so were recognized and respected, and he retained the post of college lecturer. It was considered that this action of Sidgwick's was one of the influences which led to the removal of religious tests in the University in 1871.

In 1885 he was re-admitted a Fellow of his college, having been elected to the Knightbridge Professorship of Moral Philosophy two years previously. In 1876 Sidgwick had married Miss Eleanor Mildred Balfour, sister of Mr. A. J. Balfour.

To attempt to give here anything like an adequate list of Sidgwick's occupations and activities would be out of place, but three main directions of sustained and fruitful activity—in addition to his philosophic or moral sciences work—must be mentioned, each of which would in itself have made a good life's record. These are (1) his work for the education of women, chiefly in connexion with Newnham College—work crowned with most signal success; to him women's education in Cambridge owes an immeasurable debt; (2) his work in University matters generally; he was, as has been said, one who led the leaders, and he took his full share of ordinary business. It may be noted how excellent his work in this connexion was—how accurate, able, and thorough. He was one who 'sought peace and ensued it,' but he always stood up for the right and strove valiantly for it, and in this

'His strength was as the strength of ten
Because his heart was pure.'

(3) His interest in psychical research must also be referred to. There is perhaps no part of Sidgwick's work which shows in a more marked measure the initiative and courage which were so characteristic of him. His was a brave and candid spirit—in bondage to no fears, no weaknesses, no hypocrisies. Psychical research was, as Sidgwick indicates, to some extent connected with that search after enlightenment, that study of the central problems of human life, to which he had deliberately chosen to consecrate his chief effort. To this choice he remained true, with an unswerving devotion, an inexhaustible patience.

We must regard as an important part of this study and devotion the labour which he bestowed upon the affairs of the Moral Sciences Tripos and all connected with it. Philosophy was his main interest; and among philosophical subjects it was ethics that had the first place in his thought, and in ethics that his most successful and influential work was accomplished.

In May 1900, in the full vigour of mental power, with so much accomplished, yet so much still to do, with life so full of interest, happiness, and promise, Sidgwick received his death-warrant from his physician—with grief and pain indeed, but with an indomitable sweetness and unselfishness and 'a most moving courage.'

'For nearly a fortnight he told no one but his wife. It was easier to carry on life in a normal manner when no one knew. But he began to set his affairs in order.'[1]

He wrote for the Oxford Philosophical Society a promised paper on T. H. Green, which, said one of those who heard it read on 19th May, was 'the most lucid, sincere, and impressive piece of philosophic criticism it had ever been my privilege to hear.'[2] And so, fulfilling his ordinary engagements, doing what he could to prepare against the contingency of an unfavourable result of the operation which he decided to undergo, comforting his friends, he bore the suffering and weakness of the last stage of life with 'unbroken patience and the simplest unselfish fortitude.'[3] He died on 28th Aug. 1900 at Terling Place, Essex, and was buried in the village churchyard at Terling.

2. Writings and philosophy.—We may begin our account of Sidgwick's main ethical doctrines and conclusions with a summary in his own words of the scope of the subject:

'The subject of Ethics, most comprehensively understood, includes (1) an investigation of the constituents and conditions of the Good or Wellbeing of men considered individually, which chiefly takes the form of an examination into the general and particular species of (*a*) Virtue or (*b*) Pleasure, and the chief means of realising these ends; (2) an investigation of the principles and most important details of Duty or the Moral Law (so far as this is distinguished from Virtue); (3) some inquiry into the nature and origin of the Faculty by which duty is recognised and, more generally, into the part taken by Intellect in human action, and its relation to various kinds of Desire and Aversion; (4) some examination of the question of human Free Will. It is connected with Theology, in so far as a Universal Good is recognised, inclusive of Human Good, or analogous to it; and again, so far as morality is regarded as a Code of Divine appointment. It is connected with Politics, so far as the wellbeing of any individual man is bound up with the wellbeing of his society; and again with Jurisprudence—if this is separated from Politics—so far as morality is identified with Natural Law. Finally, almost every branch of ethical discussion belongs at least in part to Psychology.'[4]

In his great work, *The Methods of Ethics* (1874), Sidgwick has given us a full and lucid discussion of these topics, and has gathered up the results of previous ethical thought; and both in that book and in the *History of Ethics* we have a dispassionate, penetrating account of the work of earlier moralists, from the pre-Socratics down to Herbert Spencer, T. H. Green, and German post-Kantians. This critical history, brief as it is, is unique and invaluable. But it is to *The Methods of Ethics* that we must go if we are to learn, as fully as we can, the doctrine of this great English moralist.

Of the three questions, (1) What ought I to do?, (2) How do I know what I ought to do?, (3) Why should I do what I see to be right?, it is as an answer to the second that Sidgwick has laid out his scheme of treatment in *The Methods of Ethics*; hence the title of the book.

'My object,' he says, 'in the present work is to expound as clearly and as fully as my limits will allow the different methods of Ethics that I find implicit in our common moral reasoning; to point to their mutual relations; and where they seem to conflict, to define the issue as much as possible.'[5]

In his view, until the logical question, the question of method, is answered, it is not possible to offer a reasoned answer to the primary question, What ought I to do?

'In deciding what they ought to do,' he says, 'men naturally proceed on different principles, and by different methods. There are two *prima facie* rational Ends, Excellence or Perfection and Happiness. . . . It is also commonly thought that certain Rules are prescribed without reference to ulterior consequences. The Methods corresponding to these different principles reduce themselves in the main to three, Egoism, Intuitionism, Utilitarianism. These methods we are to examine separately, abstracting them from ordinary thought, where we find them in

[1] P. 35. [2] P. 33 f.

[1] *Memoir*, p. 584. [2] *Ib.* p. 586, n. 1.
[3] *Ib.* p. 598.
[4] See *Outlines of the Hist. of Ethics*[5], p. 10 f.
[5] *The Methods of Ethics*[7], p. 14.

confused combination, and developing them as precisely and consistently as possible.'[1] The end of egoism is the happiness of the agent; the end of utilitarianism is the general happiness. The method which proceeds on the assumption that 'certain rules are prescribed without reference to ulterior consequences' is called intuitionism—more precisely, dogmatic intuitionism.

It is this common-sense ethics—the dogmatic intuitionism of popular morality—that Sidgwick examines in bk. iii., in ch. xi. of which he sums up his results, and concludes that the maxims of common sense do not possess the characteristics required in scientific axioms; for they are sometimes tautologous, sometimes vague, sometimes inconsistent with one another—to every rule, or almost every rule, exceptions are allowed.

'The maxims of Wisdom and Self-control are only self-evident in so far as they are tautological: nor can we state any clear, absolute, universally-admitted axioms for determining the duties of the Affections: and as for the group of principles that were extracted from the common notion of Justice, we cannot define each singly in a satisfactory manner, still less reconcile them: and even the Duty of Good Faith, when we consider the numerous qualifications of it more or less doubtfully admitted by Common Sense, seems more like a subordinate rule than an independent First Principle . . . similarly with other virtues . . . The common moral maxims are adequate for practical guidance, but do not admit of being elevated into scientific axioms.'[2]

The search for rules which can be accepted as scientific axioms, for 'some deeper explanation *why* . . . conduct commonly judged to be right is so,' for 'some rational synthesis' of commonly accepted precepts, leads the inquirer from dogmatic intuitionism to that phase of intuitionism called philosophical—

a method which, 'while accepting the morality of common sense as in the main sound, still attempts to find for it a philosophic basis which it does not itself offer; to get one or more principles more absolutely and undeniably true and evident, from which the current rules might be deduced, either just as they are commonly received or with slight modifications and rectifications.'[3]

Such principles Sidgwick finds in Kant's Categorical Imperative: 'Act as if the maxim of thy action were to become by thy will a universal law of nature,' and in Samuel Clarke's rule of equity and rule of love or benevolence. Kant's Imperative gives the *form* of a law or general rule: 'What is right for me is right for anyone else in similar circumstances.' The Rule of Equity is:

'Whatever I judge reasonable or unreasonable for another to do for me; that by the same judgment I declare reasonable or unreasonable that I *in the like case* should do for him.'[4]

This maxim is simply a precise statement of the 'Golden Rule' of the gospel: 'Do unto others as ye would that they should do unto you.' The Rule of Universal Love or Benevolence declares:

'Every rational creature ought in its sphere and station, according to its respective powers and faculties, to do all the Good it can to all its fellow-creatures: to which end universal Love and Benevolence is . . . plainly the most direct, certain, and effectual means.'[5]

'Love your neighbour as yourself' perhaps sums up the Rules of both Equity and Benevolence. The Maxim of Prudence, or rational self-love, is that 'one ought to aim at one's own good on the whole.' These maxims are among those 'absolute practical principles, the truth of which, when they are explicitly stated, is manifest.'[6]

'Hereafter *as such* is to be regarded neither less nor more than *Now*'[7] is a self-evident maxim of impartiality educible from the Maxim of Prudence. It is self-evident too that 'whatever action any of us judges to be right for himself, he implicitly judges to be right for all similar persons in similar circumstances.'[8] As regards the Rule of Equity, Sidgwick says of it:

'Common Sense has amply recognised the practical importance of the maxim: and its truth, so far as it goes, appears to me self-evident.'[1] 'And it is evident to me that as a rational being I am bound to aim at good generally,—so far as it is attainable by my efforts.'[2]

It is found (*a*) that of the commonly received maxims of duty most, when closely examined, 'contain an implicit subordination to the more general principles of Prudence and Benevolence: and (*b*) that no principles except these, and the formal principle of Justice or Equity, can be admitted as at once intuitively clear and certain; while, again, these principles themselves, so far as they are self-evident, may be stated as precepts to seek (1) one's own good on the whole, . . . and (2) others' good no less than one's own, repressing any undue preference for one individual over another. Thus we are brought round again to the old question with which ethical speculation in Europe began, "What is the Ultimate Good for man?"—though not in the egoistic form in which the old question was raised. When, however, we examine the controversies to which this question originally led, we see that the investigation which has brought us round to it has tended definitely to exclude one of the answers which early moral reflection was disposed to give to it. For to say that "General Good" consists solely in general Virtue,—if we mean by Virtue conformity to such prescriptions and prohibitions as make up the main part of the morality of Common Sense—would obviously involve us in a logical circle: since . . . the exact determination of these prescriptions and prohibitions must depend on the definition of this General Good. . . . For example, Common Sense may seem to regard Liberality, Frugality, Courage, Placability, as intrinsically desirable: but when we consider their relation respectively to Profusion, Meanness, Foolhardiness, Weakness, we find that Common Sense draws the line in each case not by immediate intuition, but by reference either to some definite maxim of duty, or to the general notion of "Good" or Wellbeing. . . . Other qualities commonly admired, such as Energy, Zeal, Self-control, Thoughtfulness, are obviously regarded as virtues only when they are directed to good ends.'[3] Again, 'Wisdom is insight into Good and the means to Good: Benevolence is exhibited in the purposive actions called "doing Good": Justice (when regarded as essentially and always a Virtue) lies in distributing Good (or evil) impartially according to right rules. If then we are asked what is this Good which it is excellent to know, to bestow on others, to distribute impartially, it would be obviously absurd to reply that it is just this knowledge, these beneficent purposes, this impartial distribution.'[4]

What, then, is the Good, that which is ultimately and intrinsically good—good in itself?

This—the question debated in the ethical controversy of ancient Greece—assumed that any 'rational individual would make the pursuit of his own good his supreme aim: the controverted question was whether this Good was rightly conceived as Pleasure or Virtue, or any *tertium quid*.'[5] . . . 'Which of the objects that men think good is truly Good or the Highest Good?'[6]

As we have just seen, the commonly accepted rules of virtuous conduct involved a reference to good otherwise determined. There remain, therefore, pleasure and the *tertium quid* (if any).

Now, pleasure is 'Feeling which is *in itself* desirable, and which is apprehended as desirable by the sentient individual at the time of feeling it,' and happiness is pleasure and the absence of pain. At the end of ch. ix. of bk. i. in which the meaning of good is closely discussed, Sidgwick reaches this conclusion:

In the view of common sense 'beauty, knowledge and other ideal goods, as well as all external material things, are only reasonably to be sought by men in so far as they conduce either (1) to Happiness or (2) to the Perfection or Excellence of human existence.'[7]

Other objects of pursuit do not seem to be in themselves intrinsically and ultimately good. Fame, *e.g.*, which is so eagerly pursued, is not 'an object which it is reasonable for men to seek for its own sake. It only commends itself to reflective minds either (1) as a source of Happiness to the person who gains it, or (2) a sign of his Excellence, moral or intellectual, or (3) because it attests the achievement by him of some important benefit to society, and at the same time stimulates him and others to further achievement in the future . . . a man is commonly thought to benefit others either by making them happier or by making them wiser and more virtuous.'[8] Similar considerations are recognised in the case of other commonly accepted sources of happiness—*e.g.*, health, wealth, social position.

As to human perfection or excellence, it is not 'in accordance with Common Sense to regard Subjective Rightness of Will, or other elements of perfection as constituting Ultimate Good.' Subjective rightness of will—a man's will to do what he thinks is right—is compatible with the most

1 *The Methods of Ethics*[7], p. xxiii.
2 *Ib.* p. xxxii. 3 *Ib.* p. 102.
4 *Boyle Lectures* (1705), London, 1719, p. 67.
5 *Ib.* p. 72.
6 *The Methods of Ethics*[7], p. 379.
7 *Ib.* p. 381. 8 *Ib.* p. 379.

1 *The Methods of Ethics*[7], p. 380. 2 *Ib.* p. 382.
3 *Ib.* p. 391 f. 4 *Ib.* p. 393. 5 *Ib.* p. 92.
6 *Ib.* p. 106. 7 *Ib.* p. 114. 8 *Ib.* p. 9.

mistaken views as to what *is* right. A fanatic may be a most dangerous and mischievous person.

'And what has been said of Virtue seems . . . still more manifestly true of the other talents, gifts, and graces which make up the common notion of human excellence or Perfection. . . . Reflection shows that they are only valuable on account of the good or desirable conscious life in which they are . . . actualised, or which will be somehow promoted by their exercise.'[1]

'What is ultimately good or desirable must be desirable Consciousness,' *i.e.* either (1) happiness or (2) relations of the conscious subject to something objective, something that is 'not merely consciousness'—*e.g.*, the relation of the mind to truth (in cognition), to beauty (in contemplation of beauty), to freedom or virtue (in volitions to realize virtue or freedom). To Sidgwick it seems clear that such objective relations of conscious subjects are not in themselves ultimately and intrinsically desirable.

In bk. iii. ch. xiv. he appeals first to the intuitive judgment of the reader, 'after due consideration of the question when fairly placed before it: and secondly to a comprehensive comparison of the ordinary judgments of mankind. As regards the first argument, to me at least it seems clear after reflection that these objective relations of the conscious subject, when distinguished from the consciousness accompanying and resulting from them, are not ultimately and intrinsically desirable; any more than material or other objects are, when considered apart from any relation to conscious existence. Admitting that we have actual experience of such preferences as have just been described, of which the ultimate object is something that is not merely consciousness: it still seems to me that when (to use Butler's phrase) we "sit down in a cool hour," we can only justify to ourselves the importance that we attach to any of these objects by considering its conduciveness, in one way or another, to the happiness of sentient beings.

The second argument, which refers to the common sense of mankind, obviously cannot be made completely cogent; since, as above stated, several cultivated persons do habitually judge that knowledge, art, etc.—not to speak of Virtue—are ends independently of the pleasure derived from them. But we may urge not only that all these elements of "ideal good" are productive of pleasure in various ways; but also that they seem to obtain the commendation of Common Sense, roughly speaking, in proportion to the degree of this productiveness. This seems obviously true of Beauty; and will hardly be denied in respect of any kind of social ideal: it is paradoxical to maintain that any degree of Freedom, or any form of social order, would still be commonly regarded as desirable even if we were certain that it had no tendency to promote the general happiness. The case of Knowledge is rather more complex; but certainly Common Sense is most impressed with the value of knowledge, when its "fruitfulness" has been demonstrated. It is, however, aware that experience has frequently shown how knowledge, long fruitless, may become unexpectedly fruitful, and how light may be shed on one part of the field of knowledge from another apparently remote: and even if any particular branch of scientific pursuit could be shown to be devoid of even this indirect utility, it would still deserve some respect on utilitarian grounds; both as furnishing to the inquirer the refined and innocent pleasures of curiosity, and because the intellectual disposition which it exhibits and sustains is likely on the whole to produce fruitful knowledge. Still in cases approximating to this last, Common Sense is somewhat disposed to complain of the misdirection of valuable effort; so that the meed of honour commonly paid to Science seems to be graduated, though perhaps unconsciously, by a tolerably exact utilitarian scale. Certainly the moment the legitimacy of any branch of scientific inquiry is seriously disputed, as in the . . . case of vivisection, the controversy on both sides is generally conducted on an avowedly utilitarian basis.'[2]

Though it has to be allowed that common sense is disinclined to admit happiness (=sum of pleasures) to be the ultimate Good, yet this can be explained by considering (1) that the term 'pleasure' is very commonly used in a bad sense and with a restricted scope; (2) that many pleasures depend on our experiencing desires for other things than pleasures; (3) that, when happiness is taken as the ultimate Good, it is often supposed that what is meant is that each individual should pursue only *his own* happiness; (4) 'from the universal point of view no less than from that of the individual, it seems true that Happiness is likely to be better attained if the extent to which we set ourselves consciously to aim at it be carefully restricted.'[3]

As the result of this appeal to common sense,

[1] *The Methods of Ethics*[7], p. 395.

[2] *Ib.* pp. 400-402.

[3] *Ib.* p. 405.

Sidgwick concludes that we are justified in considering that common sense is disposed to accept happiness as the ultimate Good.

It may seem almost superfluous to insist on men's ineradicable belief in the value of happiness. Our desire that virtue should be rewarded—rewarded with happiness, that is—that there should be a heaven for the good, answers some of the deepest demands of our nature. We are convinced that the 'wages of virtue' ought not to be 'dust.' What we wish to those we love is 'long life and *happiness*,' 'many *happy* returns,' and so on. Long life without happiness is not desirable, and an hour, a day, a week, of torturing pain, or even of simple discomfort or mere indifference, is in itself entirely undesirable.

Sidgwick's argument has eliminated every alternative except happiness; and he points out that the acceptance of cognition of objective truth, contemplation of objective beauty, and so on, as ultimate Good, instead of happiness, would leave us without any 'criterion for determining the comparative value of different elements of "Good".' He concludes that 'the Intuitional Method rigorously applied yields as its final result the doctrine of pure Universalistic Hedonism.' Thus the utilitarianism of Bentham and Mill is provided with that intuitional basis which it had previously lacked, and the effort of thought which has so fully explained and systematized the maxims of common sense has also accomplished a further great constructive achievement, and has succeeded in unifying intuitionism and Benthamite utilitarianism. The 'consilience' is very impressive.

The problem that occupied the ethical schools of Greece is thus solved: it is seen that virtue consists in the promotion of happiness (pleasure and absence of pain); as far as human conduct is concerned, the practice of virtue is the best means to the general happiness, and 'that most excellent of all practical principles, the active principle of benevolence,' as Butler calls it, the principle which aims at the happiness of others, is the root and support of common-sense morality. And not only so, but—since this fundamental principle is in essence no other than the Golden Rule of the Gospels—we have here the coalescence of intuitional hedonism with Christian ethics. This unification, though recognized by Sidgwick, was not emphasized by him; but it furnishes a striking confirmation of the view which he reached as the result of systematic and profound reflexion on ethical thought.[1]

This is perhaps the most convenient place for some further consideration of that doctrine of the dualism of practical reason to which reference has already been made. This dualism is regarded by Sidgwick as the final ethical difficulty—'the profoundest problem of Ethics.'[2] He accepts as intuitively certain the maxims of reasonable self-love and of rational benevolence, but he does not find in his moral consciousness 'any intuition, claiming to be clear and certain, that the performance of duty will be adequately rewarded and its violation punished,' though he feels a 'desire, apparently inseparable from the moral sentiments, that this result may be realised.'[3] He has not been able to reach the desideratum of the practical reason—a reconciliation of the individual with the universal reason. There seems to be no clear and certain intuition that the action most conducive

[1] A most interesting autobiographical account of the steps by which Sidgwick arrived at his 'Utilitarianism on an Intuitional basis' is to be found in the preface to the sixth and subsequent edd. of *The Methods of Ethics*, and in *Mind*, new ser., x. [1901] 287 ff.

[2] *The Methods of Ethics*[7], p. 386, note 4.

[3] *Ib.* p. 507.

to the agent's good *is* always coincident with that most conducive to the good of others, no convincing and indisputable metaphysical or theological proof. Again, it is not found that such invariable coincidence is supported by an appeal to experience, that 'inseparable connection between Utilitarian Duty and the greatest happiness of the individual who conforms to it' can 'be satisfactorily demonstrated on empirical grounds.'[1] His conclusion is:

The discussion of the 'profoundly difficult and controverted question' with which we are here concerned 'belongs rather to a treatise on General Philosophy than to a work on the Methods of Ethics: as it could not be satisfactorily answered without a general examination of the criteria of true and false beliefs. Those who hold that the edifice of physical science is really constructed of conclusions logically inferred from self-evident premises, may reasonably demand that any practical judgments claiming philosophic certainty should be based on an equally firm foundation. If on the other hand we find that in our supposed knowledge of the world of nature propositions are commonly taken to be universally true, which yet seem to rest on no other grounds than that we have a strong disposition to accept them, and that they are indispensable to the systematic coherence of our beliefs,—it will be more difficult to reject a similarly supported assumption in ethics, without opening the door to universal scepticism.'[2]

We may observe that it is practical dualism which alone among ethical doctrines clearly sees, honestly recognizes, and fairly faces the claims (for the individual agent) of both self and others, and it gives a clue to the mixture of good and evil that is in men, and does not leave us with a hopeless puzzle—self-love and benevolence are recognized as both natural and both rational.

There is another consideration, which is not insisted on by Sidgwick, but which appears to be of great interest and importance in its bearing on the dualism of practical reason. It is this. Whoever accepts the end of rational benevolence—*i.e.* the happiness of others—can accept it only on the ground that each individual's happiness is *to him* ultimately and intrinsically valuable, valuable in itself, and, since a man cannot directly experience any happiness but his own, this belief in the value for others of their own happiness must be based on his recognition of the value for himself of his own happiness. The reasonableness of benevolence implies the reasonableness of self-love. If we start from rational benevolence, we are irresistibly led back to self-love as our starting-point, and in the precept 'Love your neighbour as yourself' we find the same implication that love of our self is logically prior to, and sets the standard for, love of our neighbour.

On the other hand, as Sidgwick points out, the egoist who 'puts forward, implicitly or explicitly, the proposition that his happiness or pleasure is Good, not only *for him* but from the point of view of the Universe . . . may be brought to accept Universal happiness or pleasure as that which is absolutely and without qualification Good or Desirable.'[3]

This reciprocal implication of the 'two chief or superior principles' of conduct is striking, and is another instance of the 'consiliences' which are so impressive in Sidgwick's ethical construction.

Sidgwick's account of the relation between ethics and politics is highly interesting and important. The two are in his view so closely connected that they are in fact parts of one whole—*i.e.* the science of conduct, of what ought to be done.

'Ethics aims at determining what ought to be done by individuals, while Politics aims at determining what the government of a state or political society ought to do and how it ought to be constituted.'[4]

The relation between ethics and politics is in the utilitarian view particularly close, and must in any case be such that some common measure can be applied in both departments; otherwise hopeless confusion will result. It is imperative that any satisfactory theory of ethics should have a corresponding theory of politics, and that any theory of politics should be considered in relation to ethics. Further, the two must be harmonious; for, unless they have a common principle and the same conception of ultimate human good, they cannot pretend to divide between them, and to regulate without inconsistency, the whole region of human conduct.

[1] *The Methods of Ethics*[7], p. 503. [2] *Ib.* p. 508 f.
[3] *Ib.* pp. 420, 421. [4] *Ib.* p. 15.

In *The Elements of Politics* Sidgwick has given us an indispensable supplement to the ethical work published seventeen years previously, accepting the same fundamental principle—the principle of rational benevolence, the supreme aim of which is the promotion of the general happiness. The aim is all-embracing—'the happiness or well-being of humanity at large.' In the preface to the *Politics* Sidgwick explains that what he has tried to provide is 'a book which would expound . . . the chief general considerations that enter into the rational discussion of political questions in modern states.'

'The Theory of Politics as here expounded is concerned with human societies regarded as possessing Government. Its primary aim is to determine what the constitution and action of Government *ought* to be: accordingly its method is not primarily historical, but deductive, based on psychological propositions not universally and absolutely true, but approximately true of civilised men. It has two main divisions: one concerned with the Functions of Government, internal and external, and the other mainly with its structure.'

The part played by the dualism of the practical reason is different in politics from what it is in ethics.

According to this dualism, 'Reasonable Self-love and Conscience are the chief or superior principles in the nature of man, because an action may be suitable to this nature, though all other principles be violated, but becomes unsuitable if either of those is.'[1]

In the case of the individual agent it seems to be theoretically possible that the good of the agent may conflict with the good of the whole, and experience seems to confirm this view. Common sense admits the possibility and the actuality of self-sacrifice. A man may give his life for others; many a man has done this and more.

The statesman as such is not subject to this division in the counsels of practical reason. He exists for the good of the governed in the political community to which he belongs. The promotion of the good of his community (with of course a due regard to the good of the larger whole of which it is a part) in his *raison d'être.*[2] But for him too the dualism is, from a different point of view, momentous. Though as statesman he is not liable to be faced with the conflict (which emerges primarily as a conflict of motives) between interest and duty, between the happiness of self and the happiness of others, yet, since the community which he administers consists of individuals who are one and all liable to this conflict, it is his business to reconcile the conflict to the utmost of his power, to make it for the interest of individuals to do that which, if they would do it, would be for the good of the whole—to furnish at any moment motives sufficiently strong to induce individuals at that moment to do what is for the general good. In proportion as the attainment of happiness for self and the attainment of it for others are—so far as the power of government extends—made coincident in any community, in proportion as they are promoted by the same course of action, in that proportion is the community well organized and well governed, to that extent do the members of the community enjoy what Kant calls the 'Supreme Good'; they are both virtuous and happy. The great problem for rulers, as for teachers, is to promote this coincidence of well-doing and well-being. Herein lies much hope for the future—the reduction for the individual agent of the conflict between self-love and rational benevolence does

[1] We have seen why Sidgwick would here substitute rational benevolence for conscience.

[2] See essays on 'Public Morality' and 'Morality of Strife' referred to below, p. 505a.

seem to be to a very considerable extent in the power of rulers and educators.

Sidgwick's posthumously published *Development of European Polity*, which is 'an evolutionary study of the development of polity, within the historical period in Europe, beginning with the earliest known Græco-Roman and Teutonic polity and carried down to the modern state of Europe and its colonies as the last result of political evolution,' has an interesting relation, complementary and illustrative, to *The Elements of Politics*; and in this connexion mention may also be made of three admirable essays on 'Public Morality,' 'The Morality of Strife,' and 'Luxury,' in the volume entitled *Practical Ethics: a Collection of Addresses and Essays.*

These exemplify the 'practical' effort of the author 'to bring into a more clear and consistent form the broad and general agreement as to the particulars of morality which we find among moral persons, making explicit the general conceptions of the good and evil in human life, of the normal relation of a man to his fellows, which this agreement implies.'[1]

Besides the books already mentioned, four volumes on philosophical subjects were published after Sidgwick's death, namely, *Philosophy, its Scope and Relations* (1902), *Lectures on the Ethics of T. H. Green, Mr. Herbert Spencer and J. Martineau* (1902), *Lectures on the Philosophy of Kant and other Philosophical Lectures and Essays* (1905), and a volume of *Miscellaneous Essays and Addresses* (1904), selected from already published work.

The lectures on Green, Spencer, and Martineau are to some extent supplementary to *The Methods of Ethics*, as the early editions of that work were published before Green's *Prolegomena to Ethics* (1883), Spencer's *Principles of Ethics* (1879–93), and Martineau's *Types of Ethical Theory* (1885).

The Kant volume contains lectures on 'The Metaphysics of Kant,' 'The Metaphysics of T. H. Green,' 'The Philosophy of Mr. Herbert Spencer,' and five reprinted essays. The *Lectures on Philosophy, its Scope and Relations*, were intended as an introduction to the study of philosophy, an 'attempt to define the Scope of Philosophy and its relation to other studies' and that relation between theoretical and practical philosophy which Sidgwick regarded as the profoundest of philosophical problems.

This volume exemplifies the stress on comprehensiveness and articulation of view which pervaded Sidgwick's teaching as well as his writings, and is of such exceptional importance in the moral sciences.[2] Although his writings on metaphysical topics are of great value and interest, he never published any book on the subject; he had not formulated any metaphysical system. In addition to the books referred to above, Sidgwick published (between 1860 and 1900) a large number of articles, reviews, and pamphlets, a list of over 130 of which is given at the end of the *Memoir*. One of these was the article on 'Ethics' in the *EBr*[9], which was expanded later into the *Outlines of the History of Ethics*; and among them we find a remarkable series of ethical reviews and articles which are models of philosophical criticism and literary form. The range of topics of the other articles is very wide, taking in history, classics, literature, psychology, logic, biography, economics, psychical research, education, theology, law, and sociology. It may be permitted to make special mention of three—(1) 'A Dialogue on Time and Common Sense' (reprinted in the Kant volume from *Mind*, new ser., iii. [1894] 441 ff.), which is a gem both as philosophy and as literature; it is very characteristic—full of wit and wisdom, graceful and subtle—and gives a very suggestive idea of what Sidgwick's talk was like; (2) 'The Ethics of Religious Conformity,' and (3) 'Clerical Veracity' (both in the volume of *Practical Ethics*)—which are for a different reason of particular interest, since they deal with a difficulty which is poignant and many-voiced in the Anglican Church.

3. Appreciation.—We find in Sidgwick's work a rare combination of learning and originality, of imaginativeness together with good judgment, sense of perspective, and comprehensiveness of view, of unsparing pains and intense and vivid interest. It would not be too much to say that he took great joy in his work. We find, too, a generous capacity of intellectual sympathy and appreciation and an extraordinary freedom and boldness. Thought was to Henry Sidgwick his native element—a medium in which he moved at ease. Hence his swiftness and sureness of mind, his analytical and critical power, his insight and constructive force. He never misses the point, never fails or falters. In *The Methods of Ethics*, *e.g.*, there are no slack places, no confusions slurred over, no difficulties shirked—the whole is as coherent as a living organism. Analysis and comparison only serve to bring into greater relief the articulation of the parts and the living thought which animates them. No summary, not even the author's own admirable analytical summaries of contents, no quotations even, can convey an adequate idea of the excellence and interest of the work, which is perhaps the best extant treatise on ethics, a classic for all time. The book is difficult, but it repays the closest study, and that it receives full meed of recognition as indispensable for students of philosophy is evidenced by the fact that since its publication in 1874 a steady demand for it has continued, and an eighth edition was published in 1914.

What one feels in reading not only *The Methods of Ethics* but also Sidgwick's other writings (we may indicate in particular here *The Elements of Politics, The Principles of Political Economy*, and *Outlines of the History of Ethics*) is that confusion and muddle have been cleared away, dark places illuminated, logic and coherence introduced. *The Methods of Ethics* gives the clue to all Sidgwick's work; in it method—logical procedure—is fundamental.

To a close student Sidgwick's ethical writings reveal, as perhaps no other records of him do, the spirit and mind of their author. They are his most considered intellectual output—his great and lasting monument. They breathe throughout absolute sincerity, a steady belief in goodness and enthusiasm for it, an unrelaxing pursuit of truth, with a grasp, insight, and fullness of knowledge in which the student learns to place a confidence that is never betrayed. His writings are educative in the same sense as his oral teaching and his work as an examiner were. They compel inquiry, and stir honest effort in the learner from first to last. A full and interesting account of Sidgwick's lecturing is given in ch. v. of the *Memoir*. We may extract a few sentences from a speech there quoted of F. W. Maitland, one of Sidgwick's most distinguished pupils:

'I feel safe in saying that within the field [of teaching] that was most properly his own Sidgwick's work has borne excellent fruit. . . . I believe that he was a supremely great teacher. . . . I believe that no more truthful man than Sidgwick ever lived. I am speaking of a rare intellectual virtue. However small the class might be, Sidgwick always gave us his very best . . . as the terms went by, we came to think of lecture-time as the best time that we had in Cambridge; and some of us, looking back now, can say that it was in a very true sense the best time that we ever had in our lives. . . . The matter of the lectures, the theories and the arguments, might be forgotten; but the method remained, the spirit remained, as an ideal—an unattainable ideal, perhaps, but a model of perfect work.'[1]

Sidgwick's letters, as given to us in the *Memoir*, help, in a delightful fashion, to fill out our picture of him—they reveal his thoughts and moods of the moment, the growth of his opinions, his changes of view; they show how constant and loyal and affectionate he was, how friendly with his friends, how full of fun and of interest in current life and thought, especially university matters, politics, and of course books, how vivid and active, how unselfish and generous in small things and in great. They bring home to us in unexpected ways how large-minded he was and how large-hearted; and they are so sympathetic and so responsive that they often seem to tell us as much about his correspondent as they do about himself. His was a soul touched with divine fire, and men felt in him a purity of heart which no evil could invade. Truth and right were to him the 'pearl of great price,' and he had the crowning happiness of a wife like-minded with himself.

LITERATURE.—The following is a list of Sidgwick's published books: *The Methods of Ethics*, London, 1874, [2]1877, [3]1884, [4]1890, [5]1893, [6]1901, [7]1907, [8]1914; Supplements to *The Methods*

[1] P. 8.

[2] It may be pointed out that the 'moral sciences' at Cambridge included moral philosophy, *i.e.* ethics and politics, metaphysics, psychology, logic, and—previous to 1905—political economy.

[1] P. 305 f.

of Ethics, to 1st ed., 1877, to 2nd ed., 1884; *The Principles of Political Economy*, do. 1883, ^{2}1887, ^{3}1901; *The Scope and Method of Economic Science* (presidential address delivered to the Economic Science and Statistics Section of the British Association at Aberdeen, and republished in *Miscellaneous Essays and Addresses*), do. 1885; *Outlines of the Hist. of Ethics for English Readers*, do. 1886, ^{2}1888, ^{3}1892, ^{4}1896, ^{5}1902, reprinted 1906, 1910, 1916; *The Elements of Politics*, do. 1891, ^{2}1897, ^{3}1908; *Practical Ethics: a Collection of Addresses and Essays*, do. 1898; *Philosophy, its Scope and Relations: an Introductory Course of Lectures*, ed. James Ward, do. 1902; *Lectures on the Ethics of T. H. Green, Mr. Herbert Spencer and J. Martineau*, ed. E. E. C. Jones, do. 1902; *The Development of European Polity*, ed. Eleanor Mildred Sidgwick, do. 1903, ^{2}1913; *Miscellaneous Essays and Addresses*, ed. Eleanor Mildred Sidgwick and Arthur Sidgwick, do. 1904; *Lectures on the Philosophy of Kant and other Philosophical Lectures and Essays*, ed. James Ward, do. 1905. (The last five books were published posthumously.) A list of articles, reviews, pamphlets, etc., is given in the *Memoir*, pp. 617–622.

The biography written by his brother and his wife, *Henry Sidgwick: a Memoir by A. S. and E. M. S.*, London, 1906, gives a detailed account of Sidgwick's life, consisting largely of extracts from his own letters. It does not include any description or evaluation of Sidgwick's ethical and other philosophical writings. At the end of the *Memoir* (p. 623) is a list of the biographical notices of Sidgwick which had appeared previous to 1906.

Objections to Sidgwick's utilitarianism (sometimes referred to by him as utilitarianism on an intuitional basis) have been summarized and replied to by E. E. C. Jones in art. 'Rational Hedonism,' in *IJE* v. [1894–95] 79 ff., and 'Discussion on Same,' *ib.* pp. 218 ff., 376 ff., and art. 'Professor Sidgwick's Ethics,' in *Proc. of the Aristotelian Society*, new ser., iv. [1903–04] 32 ff.

E. E. CONSTANCE JONES.

SIDHE.—See FAIRY, CELTS.

SIEVE.—1. Sieves used in rain-making ceremonies.—Sieves, and especially winnowing-fans,[1] are frequently employed by primitive peoples for magico-religious purposes, such as rain-making.

Among the Ainus, *e.g.*, when rain is urgently needed, the people are gathered together and the master of the ceremonies appoints certain men to head small companies to execute particular functions. It is the duty of one of these parties to take sieves and scatter water about with them,[2] just as Buddhist monks, during the ceremonies to promote the fertility of the earth, 'pour water into little holes in the floor of the pagoda as a symbol of the rain which they hope Buddha will send down on the rice-fields.'[3] In comparatively recent times (1868) Russian peasants in the Tarashchansk districts are known to have dug up the corpse of a Raskolnik (Dissenter), and to have beaten it, exclaiming, 'Give us rain!', while others poured water on it through a sieve in imitation of a shower of rain.[4] In times of drought in S. India the Kâpu women 'tie a frog alive to a new winnowing fan made of bamboo. On this fan they spread a few margosa leaves, and go singing from door to door, "Lady frog must have her bath. Oh! rain-god, give a little water for her at least." This means that the drought has reached such a stage that there is not even a drop of water for the frogs. When the Kâpu woman sings this song, the woman of the house brings a little water in a vessel, pours it over the frog which is left on the fan outside the house, and gives some alms. The woman of the house is satisfied that such an action will soon bring down rain in torrents.'[5]

2. Sieves used as cradles.—It was a regular custom among the Greeks and many other people to employ a winnowing-fan as a cradle for infants.[6]

In Java the midwife places the newly-born child in a bamboo basket like the sieve used for separating the rice from the chaff. As she does this, she knocks with the palms of both hands on the basket in order that the child may not be timid. Then she exhorts the child, saying, 'Cry not, for Njaï-among and Kaki-among [two spirits] are watching over you.' Next she addresses the two spirits, saying, 'Bring not your grandchild to the road, lest he be trampled by a horse; bring him not to the bank of the river, lest he fall into the river.' The object of the ceremony is said to be that these two spirits should always guard the infant.[7]

Similarly in Laos, when a child has been born in a house, it is laid upon a rice-sieve and placed by the grandmother or other near female relative at the head of the staircase or ladder leading to the house. There the woman calls in a loud voice to the spirits to come and take the child away or for ever to let it alone, stamping on the ground violently to make it cry. The precaution, however, is taken of tying strings round its wrists

[1] See art. FAN.

[2] J. Batchelor, *The Ainu and their Folk-lore*, London, 1901, p. 333.

[3] GB^3, pt. i., *The Magic Art*, London, 1911, i. 251.

[4] *Ib.* p. 285.

[5] E. Thurston, *Castes and Tribes of Southern India*, Madras, 1909, iii. 245.

[6] The *mystica vannus Iachhi* is fully treated in art. FAN, § 2.

[7] GB^3, pt. v., *Spirits of the Corn and of the Wild*, London, 1912, i. 6.

on the first night after birth, lest the spirits should take the invitation too literally. If the infant should fail to respond to the treatment, it is regarded as an evil omen. If, on the other hand, it behaves naturally and lifts up its voice, all will be well. 'On the day after its birth the child is regarded as being the property no longer of the spirits, who could have taken it if they had wanted it, but of the parents, who forthwith sell it to some relation for a nominal sum—an eighth or a quarter of a rupee perhaps. This, again, is a further guarantee against molestation by the spirits, who apparently are regarded as honest folk that would not stoop to take what has been bought and paid for.'[1]

The same notion of rescuing a new-born infant from the power of evil spirits is seen in the Panjâb custom of putting a new baby into an old winnowing-basket (*chhaj*) with the sweepings of the house and dragging it out into the yard. After this has been done, the child will bear the name of 'Winnowing-basket' (Chhajju) or 'Dragged' (Ghasitâ). The object of this procedure is probably to deceive the spirits by rendering the child unrecognizable. The same may perhaps be the intention of a ceremony employed among the Gaolis of the Deccan. As soon as a child is born, it is bathed and then laid on a sieve for a few minutes. On the fifth day the sieve, with a line and *pan*-leaves on it, is taken outside the house and, after the worship of Chetti has been performed, is thrown away.[2]

In Upper Egypt a newly-born child is merely dried, not washed, and immediately laid upon a corn-sieve; beside its head the knife with which the umbilical cord has been cut is laid, and corn is scattered round about. This is intended to drive away the *kasina*, the child's evil brother or sister from the spirit-world. On the morning of the seventh day the child is again placed on a sieve, tapers are fixed on metal plates and on the point of a sword, and the child is carried in procession through the whole house, while the midwife scatters wheat, barley, peas, and salt for the wicked spirits. The child is then shaken on the sieve, in order that it may lose fear for the rest of its life.[3]

Children born in an unlucky month (Faosa) among the Tanala people of Madagascar are either buried alive in the forest or placed in a winnowing-fan along with certain herbs and washed in water medicated with some of the same herbs. The ceremony is thought to avert the threatened ill-luck. Similarly the Chinese of Foo-Chow set a lad suffering from smallpox in a large winnowing-fan, placing a piece of red cloth on his head and on the cloth some parched beans. The beans (whose name in the local dialect is identical with the name for smallpox) are allowed to roll off to represent the passing away of all traces of the disease from the boy's body.[4]

3. Sieves used in marriage-rites.[5]—Among the Naoda, a caste of ferrymen in the Central Provinces of India, a winnowing-fan together with certain other articles is passed by the mother in front of the bridegroom to keep off evil spirits and scatter them to the winds like chaff. The Rajjhars in the same district exorcize the bridal pair by touching the head, breast, and knees of the bridegroom with a winnowing-fan, a pestle, and a churning-stick.[6]

4. Divination by sieves.—There was an early form of divination known as coscinomancy (κόσκινον, 'sieve'; μαντεία, 'divination'), or, as it is described in *Hudibras*, 'the oracle of sieve and shears, that turns as certain as the spheres.' A sieve was suspended, held by a thread or by the points of a pair of shears stuck into its rim; the movement, turning, or fall of the sieve at the naming of the person suspected of a crime, coupled with the repetition of an incantation or other magic formula, decided the guilt or innocence of the person.

In the Highlands of Scotland, on Hallowe'en, the young people until recently assembled in one of their houses for the express purpose of ascertaining future events by divination. In the Lowlands also similar customs prevailed at this season. In order to cause the apparition of a future husband or wife, it was necessary to visit a barn alone and secretly, taking care to open both doors or, better still, take them off their hinges, to guard against complications that might arise on the arrival of the stranger. Having done this, the diviner takes a sieve (*wecht* or *waicht*) and goes through the action of winnowing corn. After this has been done three times, the 'future husband or wife will pass through the barn, entering at the windy door and passing out at the other.'[7]

5. Conclusion.—From the foregoing examples it would seem that the sieve or winnowing-fan

[1] Carl Bock, *Temples and Elephants*, London, 1884, p. 258 ff.

[2] GB^3, pt. v., *Spirits of the Corn and of the Wild*, i. 7.

[3] C. B. Klunzinger, *Upper Egypt: People and Products*, Eng. tr., London, 1878, p. 185 ff.

[4] GB^3, pt. v., *Spirits of the Corn and of the Wild*, i. 9.

[5] For the use of the *liknon* see art. FAN.

[6] R. V. Russell, *The Tribes and Castes of the Central Provinces of India*, London, 1916, iv. 284, 407.

[7] GB^3, pt. vii., *Balder the Beautiful*, London, 1913, i. 236.

figures in magico-religious cults primarily as a symbol of fecundity. Sieves in the Stone Age appear to have been simply jars pierced with holes, and therefore they may have been used for carrying water. In this way their connexion with rain-making ceremonies is readily explained, since the dripping of the water from the vessel would be calculated to suggest to the primitive mind the falling of rain. Thus the instrument would soon come to be regarded as a means of controlling the weather.[1] But the custom of carrying water in a sieve was apparently also anciently connected with virginity and a fertility cult,[2] and, consequently, at a very early period the implement may have been used to promote fertility and growth. This view is supported by the connexion between the sieve and the winnowing-fan—an article intimately associated with corn, the symbol of growth and fertility.[3] Moreover, when a winnowing-fan is used as a cradle, it is not infrequently surrounded by corn or fruit to emphasize the desire to communicate to the infant the power of fecundity and growth. The sowing of seed was unquestionably regarded by the ancient Greeks and other primitive people as analogous to the begetting of children, just as in Germany barley and flax seed are sown over stunted children to make them grow.[4] It seems, therefore, that infants were cradled in sieves and winnowing-fans originally to promote fertility, and that the notions of rescuing them from evil influences and of purification are only later interpretations (suggested by the separating function of the fan) that have arisen to explain the custom. In the Bacchic ritual the earlier conception is clearly indicated on the monuments by the appearance of the implement filled with fruitage together with the male organ of generation.[5] Here the winnowing-fan, from which Dionysus derived his surname, is unmistakably represented as the emblem of creative energy. In the Athenian marriage ceremonies the fact that the boy who carried the *liknon* was obliged to have both parents alive suggests that the basket was a fertility charm to induce the birth of children and natural wealth. The symbolism of the *liknites*, of fruit, and the child point to the same conclusion. It is not without significance that the implement has been used in recent times in Scotland as a means of producing an apparition of a future husband or wife.

LITERATURE.—The literature has been given in the footnotes.

E. O. JAMES.

[1] Cf. art. RAIN.

[2] J. E. Harrison, *Prolegomena to the Study of Greek Religion*, Cambridge, 1903, p. 621 f.

[3] *Ib.*

[4] W. Mannhardt, 'Kind und Korn,' *Mythologische Forschungen*, Strassburg, 1884, pp. 351–374.

[5] See art. FAN, vol. v. p. 755b, fig. 3; Harrison, *Prolegomena*, p. 518 ff., *JHS* xxiii. [1903] 296; L. R. Farnell, *CGS*, Oxford, 1896–1909, v. 243.

SIKHS.

I. History.—One of the most striking of the creeds in India, which, arising on its own soil, protested against her dominant Brāhmanism, is the Sikh religion. Socially and politically as well as in religion Sikhism opposed the influence of the Brāhman and the system which he taught and represented. Its founder, Nānak (*q.v.*), the first *guru*, was born in A.D. 1469, fourteen years before Luther; the traditions of his earlier life picture him as leading the life of one meditatively careless of the things of this world until he received a definite call to a divine mission as the expounder of a new doctrine. Teaching that Hindu and Muhammadan differed in no essentials of faith, he set out on a series of pilgrimages to the four points of the compass and made a fifth and last allegorical visit to the saints (*siddhs*) of Gorakhnāth (*q.v.*). These pilgrimages may have extended far beyond the confines of modern India, and indeed it is claimed that he visited not only Ceylon and Kashmīr, but also Russia, Turkestan, and Mecca. His preaching was intensely monotheistic and largely directed against the pretensions of priestcraft. He reproached his Hindu compatriots who lived upon alms wrung from the people, and he taught the dignity of labour. He composed religious hymns, being thus the first contributor to the *Granṭh* (*q.v.*), but his teaching had no political aims.

Before his death in 1538 Nānak had installed as his successor Angad, like himself a Khatrī by caste, and his disciple, but not of his kin by blood. Angad invented the Gurmukhi alphabet[1] and enlarged the *Granṭh*, but he remained a humble religious teacher, earning a livelihood by twisting coarse twine into rope. He died in 1552 or 1553.

Angad installed as *guru* Amar Dās, who began to organize the new sect and develop its teaching. He divided the country into 22 sees (*manja*, lit. a couch or large bed), and maintained a public refectory at which all ate without distinction of caste. He also reformed the Brāhmanical rites at marriage and death, forbade pilgrimages and similar extravagances, pronounced against *sati*, and separated the Sikh recluses, or Udāsīs (*q.v.*), from the laity. Having added largely to the hymns of the *Granṭh*, he bestowed the apostolic succession on his son-in-law, Rāmdās.

Guru Rāmdās succeeded in 1574, and is said to have entered into closer relations with the emperor Akbar than his predecessor. The biographers of that tolerant ruler do not indeed allude to the *gurus* or their teaching, but his broad-minded policy doubtless encouraged the new sect to develop its religious activities, while it gave it no provocation to enter the political arena. Rāmdās founded Rāmdāspur, later known as Amritsar, the sacred capital of the Sikhs, and in 1581 he was succeeded by his youngest son, Arjan Dev. With his accession Sikhism entered on a new phase. He laid aside the garb of a *faqīr*, dressed in costly attire, and organized a system of tithing his followers. His energy succeeded in sending disciples to trade and spread the faith as far afield as Turkestan, and it gained many adherents in Kābul and Kandahār as well as in India generally. Nevertheless Arjan Dev was able to maintain amicable relations with Muhammadans like the famous saint Mīān Mīr, and his chief opponents were a Hindu, finance minister to the Mughal governor of Lahore, and his eldest brother, Prithi Chand,[2] who never forgave him his own supersession in the *guru*ship. Unfortunately he entered into an obscure conspiracy with Khusro, son of the emperor Jahāngīr, and expiated his assistance to the rebel with his life.

In 1606 Rāmdās's only son, Hargobind, succeeded him. He rejected for good the tokens of a *faqīr* and wore two swords, one denoting *faqīrī*, or spiritual, the other *amīrī*, or secular, authority. He built the first Sikh stronghold, and many whom want and misgovernment had driven from their homes flocked to his standard. But, if he was the first of the *gurus* to take up arms against the Mughals, he met with scant success as a leader, for Jahāngīr is said to have kept him a prisoner at Gwalior for twelve years until that emperor's death in 1628. Even then he obtained his liberty only by sacrificing his treasures.[3]

Hargobind died in 1645 and was succeeded by

[1] This alphabet is derived from the Śarada, through the Tākrī alphabet of the Panjāb hills and the Landa of the Panjāb (G. A. Grierson, *JRAS*, 1916, p. 677).

[2] The founder of the Mīna sect.

[3] The Sikh accounts represent Mīān Mīr as having reconciled him to Jahāngīr, and this is the version of the *Dabistān* (tr. A. Troyer, Paris, 1843, ii. 274), which adds that he continued in the imperial service under Shāh Jahān.

his grandson, Har Rai, his son, Gurditta, having entered the Udāsī order and thus being disqualified to succeed to a secular office. He too entered into relations with a rebellious scion of the Mughal dynasty, Dārā Shikoh, and on his defeat he sent his son, Rām Rai, to Delhi to negotiate a pardon. The lad was still a hostage in the hands of Aurangzīb when his father died, and either on that account or because he had in fear of ill-usage misquoted a verse of the *Granṭh* he was disqualified by his father, who designated his second son, Har Kishn, as his successor. This son too was summoned to Delhi, where he died after vaguely appointing as his successor one 'at Bakāla,' a village on the Biās river.

No fewer than 22 Khatrīs of the Sodhī sept claimed the *guru*ship, but it was awarded to Tegh Bahādur, the only Sodhī who divined that a devout follower had not fulfilled a vow made in distress. He was duly installed, but, saying that he was unworthy to wear his father's sword, he proclaimed his ambition to be styled Degh Bahādur, or 'lord of the vessel,' the *degh* which symbolizes the world. His accession led to many dissensions. Rām Rai had founded a sect of his own, which still endures in the Dehra Dūn. Dhir Mal, probably an older brother of Guru Har Rai, who had refused to acknowledge his accession, had possession of the *Granṭh* and supported Rām Rai's pretensions to the *guru*ship. This opposition from his own kin compelled Tegh Bahādur to seek a refuge in the Jaswān Dūn beyond the Siwālik hills, and there in 1665 he founded Anandpur. Nevertheless he was able to make progresses through the Mālwa of the southern Panjāb, the Kurukshetra, eastern and lower India, while his influence extended even to Ceylon. But the intolerance of Aurangzīb led to his seizure and execution at Delhi in 1675.[1]

We now come to the 10th and last *guru*, Govind Singh, founder of the militant Sikh theocracy. Born at Patna in 1666, and installed at Anandpur in 1676, he made momentous changes in Sikh ritual and polity. His policy was to raise the Sikhs to one and the same high caste, the Khālsa. To this end he chose five faithful followers, whom he initiated with the *khanda pahul*, 'whetting by the two-edged dagger.' These five in turn initiated the *guru* himself, and he thus placed initiators and candidate on the same level.

In this rite the candidate bathes and dons clean clothes. He is seated in an assembly generally convened for the purpose, and a Sikh who is regular in his observance of Sikh rules of conduct stirs with a dagger some sugar in water in an iron basin, while chanting verses from the *Granṭh*. This solution is called *amrit* (whence the rite is sometimes called *amrit chhuknā*, 'to be filled with nectar') and is sprinkled on the candidate's hair and body. He is also given some of it to drink and is made to repeat certain vows which constitute the *rahat*, or Sikh rules of conduct. The *amrit* is believed to confer immortality and to make the initiate a son of Govind Singh and a Singh ('lion') or true Kṣatriya. He also becomes a son of Mātā Sāhib Devi, the childless wife of that *guru* who was promised the motherhood of the whole Khālsa. The *pahul*, erroneously derived by J. D. Cunningham[2] from the Greek πύλη, 'gate,' is generally regarded as a baptismal rite, but the bathing is merely to obtain ceremonial purity. The use of the dagger is doubtless intended to communicate soldierly qualities to the initiate. The Baloch have at birth a very similar practice. The *amrit* confers immunity in battle. The *charn pahul* (see below) conveys the sanctity of the *guru* to his disciple.

[1] Recent research has shown that the network of Sikh organization had been spread by Tegh Bahādur's predecessors as far east as Patna and even Dacca, which became a *huzūr sangat*, or provincial *sangat*, at first under the pontifical throne at Anandpur and later under the *takht*, or archiepiscopal throne, at Patna. When Tegh Bahādur visited Dacca in 1666, he found prosperous *sangats* at Sylhet, Chittagong, Sandīp, Lashkar, and elsewhere, and by the time of Guru Govind Singh Dacca had earned the title of 'the home of Sikhism.' The *takhts* were four, viz. Anandpur, Amritsar, Patna, and Nander (in the Nizām's Dominions, Deccan [Gurbakhsh Singh, *Sikh Relics from Eastern Bengal*, Dacca, 1915, p. 225 f., 1916, p. 376 ff.]).

[2] *Hist. of the Sikhs*, p. 74 n.

The *guru* assumed the suffix of Singh instead of his Hindu affix, Rai, at initiation, and all initiates take that suffix. His five initiators were a Khatrī and four men of castes generally regarded as Śūdras who had offered their heads in his service. Various versions of this choice of the *panj piāras*, 'the five beloved ones,' of the *guru* are current. That of the *Panth Prakāsh* relates that the *guru* called for Sikhs willing to offer their heads for his sword, the goddess, and five came forward. The *guru* took them one by one into his tent, and, emerging with his sword dripping with the blood of a goat, tested their devotion by pretending that he had killed each in turn.[1] But the Sikhs who seek to retain the cult of Devi and to reconcile it with the *gurus*' monotheism say that one of the five was actually sacrificed to the goddess at Naina Devi, and this is the version current in the Simla hills, where Sikhism never found a footing.[2] In requital the Devi promised him the success of his sect. Guru Govind Singh was a man of considerable learning. A Gurmukhi, Sanskrit, and Persian scholar, he deputed five Sikhs to learn Sanskrit at Benares, and had many important Sanskrit and Persian works translated into the *bhāsha*, or vulgar tongue. In accord with his democratic policy, he abolished the system of collecting tithes through *masands* (collectors), which Guru Arjan had organized, and the system was maintained only by some dissident Sikh sects. He was, moreover, a military leader of parts. His refusal to pay tribute in any form to the *rājā* of Bilāspur, from which state Tegh Bahādur had purchased the site of Anandpur, led to his first battle. He defeated the *rājā* in 1682, but his victory cost him the hostility of many of the hill states in the mountainous country which forms the north-east corner of the Panjāb. Among them he found some allies, but his teaching made no headway among the ancient Hindu polities of those states, and his only effective ally was the *rājā* of Sirmūr, a state lying west of the upper Jamna, who allowed him to found Paonta in the Kiārda Dūn of that state in 1684. Had Sikhism succeeded in winning over the hill people, its history might have been different, but the influence of their Rājpūt overlords and Brāhmanical priests was too firmly planted to allow a democratic theocracy to make converts among them. Guru Govind Singh sought support in other directions. He enlisted 500 Muslim Pathāns, but they failed him at a crisis, as did the Udāsīs whom he had fostered. His military position was weak. It lay in the *dūns*, or valleys, of the outer Himālayas; behind him were the hill *rājās*, jealous of one another, but still more jealous of a plainsman preaching a new creed. On his widely extended front he was opposed to the decadent but still organized and powerful authority of the Mughals. He was not without supporters among the Muhammadans of the plains, notably the *pīr* of Sādhaura and other spiritual notables. But the Mughals, by a well-conceived campaign in conjunction with the hill *rājās*, drove the *guru* out of Anandpur, and in the flight of the Sikhs his children were captured. They were buried alive at Sirhind, and their martyrdom made that thriving city for ever accursed in the eyes of the Sikhs. The *guru* himself escaped to the south of the Sutlej and, on Aurangzīb's death, threw in his lot with Bahādur Shāh, whom he helped to defeat Prince 'Azim. This ensured him tolerance, if not favour, but in 1708 he was treacherously stabbed by a Pathān who had been reared in his family, and he died soon afterwards.

[1] Gokal Chand Narang, *Transformation of Sikhism*, Lahore, 1912, p. 79.

[2] *Simla Hill States Gazetteer*, Lahore, 1904, 'Bilāspur,' p. 13 f.

Before his death a new and devastating force had arisen in 'Banda, the Bairāgī.' Born at Rājauri, the capital of an ancient principality in the Jammū hills, Lachhman, as he was first named, became a Bairāgī and then a Yogi with the style of Madho Dās, and in the latter character he acquired skill in the occult sciences. Meeting Guru Govind Singh on the Godāvārī in S. India, he became his slave (*banda*), but not his disciple, with the title of Banda Bahādur, 'the lord slave.' On him the *guru* bestowed his own sword, bidding him observe strict continence and truthfulness and avoid schism, the use of a cushion in the Sikh temple, and the title of *guru*, but enjoining on him brotherly love and peace with the Singhs. These behests Banda did not obey. He married, and started a sect of his own, the Bandāī Singhs; he substituted for the *khanda pahul* the *charn pahul*, in which the initiate drinks water used in washing his *guru's* feet; and for the war-cry of the true Singh, '*Fatih wāhe-guru jī kī*,'[1] he enjoined the cry, '*Fatih daras* (or *darshan*) *fatih dharma*,' 'Victory to religion and the faith!' He donned royal dress and lorded it over the Sikhs, instead of regarding himself as merely an equal and a brother. He also ceased to enforce the Singh rule against cutting the hair, and exhorted the Sikhs to abstain from flesh, though Govind Singh had encouraged its use for military reasons. But this does not complete the tale of Banda's backslidings. The Sikh *gurus* had been installed by a special rite, in which five pice and a coco-nut were placed before the *guru*-designate, while his predecessor and appointer circumambulated him four times. By this rite the spiritual light of Guru Nānak had been transmitted to his successors, and on the forehead of each in turn the *tilak* (coronation mark) was made by a member of a family of cultivators in which the office was hereditary.[2] Guru Govind Singh had installed the sacred *Granth* itself as his sole successor, but Banda claimed to be the eleventh *guru*. This and his other heresies in the end alienated the true Singhs, and, though in his earlier years as a soldier-saint Banda had won notable successes against the Mughal government, even taking Sirhind and sacking it with merciless slaughter of the Muslims, his career ended in defeat and failure. At its zenith in 1714 he had convened a royal *darbār* at Amritsar and assumed kingly robes with an aigrette in his turban, and the country from Lahore to the banks of the Jamna had passed into the possession of the Singhs. Banda had also succeeded in extorting some kind of allegiance from the hill *rājās*, and indeed he found in the hills a refuge in time of stress and a retreat for religious meditation, to which he seems to have abandoned himself at critical moments when he might have followed up a success or organized territory already won. But his character lacked consistency. While, on the one hand, he chastised the heretic Rām Rāīas, on the other, he dealt mercilessly with Muhammadan towns whose inhabitants had befriended Guru Govind Singh. The true Singhs, the Tat Khālsa, the elect of the elect, separated themselves from Banda, who left them Amritsar and retired to Gurdāspur, nearer the hills, where his strength lay. Thence he carried on a predatory warfare until the Tat Khālsa reluctantly appeared in arms with the Muhammadans against him. This ensured his downfall, and in 1716 he was probably captured and put to death at Delhi. Tradition says that he was executed with every circumstance of cruelty, but it also avers that by a mental process he triumphed over his physical sufferings, resuscitated himself, and retired to the banks of the Chenab in his native state of Jammū. There his tomb is still held by his descendants, and his followers are still to be found in the Panjāb under the name of the Banda-panthis.

[1] The form usually given is '*Wāh Gurū jī kā Khālsa, Wāh Gurū jī kī fatih*' (Narang, p. 120; but cf. Khazān Singh, *Philosophic Hist. of the Sikh Religion*, p. 219).

[2] Its founder, Bhāī Budhā, was so named by Guru Nānak when he expressed fear of an early death. Owing to the *guru's* prophecy or gift of long life, he survived to install the first five successors of Guru Nānak. The 'light' of the *gurus* is sometimes called *barqat*, a term borrowed from Islām.

Banda's death left the Singhs without a secular leader, and, though most of the Bandāīs rejoined the true Khālsa, they had no definite policy. Their forays provoked reprisals, and a price was offered for every Sikh head. Farrukhsiār attempted to conciliate them and assigned tracts of territory to some at any rate of their leaders. One of them, Kapūr Singh, accepted (contemptuously, some say) the Muhammadan title *nawāb*, and he with many of the other leaders formed what was known as 'the veteran army' (*budhā ḍal*), while the younger (*tarū ḍal*) organized itself into five companies, the Shahīds (*q.v.*), Amritsarias, Dallewālīās, Rāmdāsīās, and another. The *budhā ḍal* clung to Amritsar, and many of both *ḍals* settled down to cultivation, but the younger generation found itself pressed for subsistence, and sought an outlet in Rājpūtāna. The Muslim governors seized the occasion to harass the veterans, and in revenge the two *ḍals* recombined and ravaged the whole of the northern Panjāb. Upon the distracted province fell Nādir Shāh's invasion of 1738–39. The Sikhs did not respond to the Mughal governor's request for aid to oppose him, but they harassed him on his retreat and refused to surrender their booty. This led to fresh persecution, and Ahmad Shāh's inroads found the province still more rent by internecine strife than those of his predecessor. Finally the Mughal governor, Adīna Beg, sought Sikh aid and with it recovered a fraction of the province, but, distrusting his allies, he called in the Marāthās, who overran it, driving the Durrānis across the Indus, in 1757. On Adīna Beg's death, in the following year, the Sikhs killed his principal minister and made themselves independent in the central and north-eastern Panjāb.

By this time their old division into two armies had disappeared, and of the five companies only one, the Shahīds, remained, twelve new *misls* (confederacies) having taken the place of the five companies. Of these twelve, however, four are more correctly to be described as *dehras* (militant orders), like the Shahīds, who formed the oldest and at one time the most important *dehra*. No attempt had been made to revive the *guru*ship, but Nawāb Kapūr Singh, who was childless, bequeathed his honours and the leadership of the Khālsa to Jassa Singh, Ahlūwālīā, saying that he was destined to be a *bādshāh*, 'king,' a title subsequently accorded him by his own followers. Yet, although he had been treated by Mātā Sundri, a widow of Guru Govind Singh, as her own son, he did not aspire to any authority over the Khālsa and was content to be elected head of the Ahlūwālīā *misl*, although he struck coin in the old Mughal mint at Lahore with the inscription in Persian: 'Struck in the world by grace of the Everlasting: Jassa, the Kalāl,[1] seized Ahmad's country.' Initiation by him was highly prized, and Rājā Amr Singh of Patiāla was one of his initiates. Ālā Singh of Patiāla consented to take the province of Sirhind on lease from Ahmad Shāh in 1767, with the title of Rājā-i-rājagān Mahindar Bahādur, the Muhammadan chiefs of Māler Kotla and Raikot fearing the Sikhs too much to undertake its charge. This paved the way for the

[1] Kalāl = Ahlūwālīā; see below.

organization of the Sikh territories south of the Sutlej into Sikh kingships, the principal being the Phūlkīān states (Patiāla, Nābha, and Jīnd), Farīdkot, Kalsia, and the now extinct chiefship of the Bhāīs of Kaithal. But Muhammadan states like Māler Kotla, Raikot, and many religious institutions whose incumbents had befriended the Sikhs from time to time, were tolerated and protected.

Meanwhile to the north of the Sutlej the introduction of a monarchical system (for which Kapūr Singh and Jassa Singh had paved the way) and the authority of the *Granṭh* materialized, as it were, in a *gurumaṭṭa*, or cabinet. This institution is by some ascribed to Guru Govind Singh, who had declared that wherever five orthodox Singhs were assembled the *guru* must be deemed present. But probably the first *gurumaṭṭa* as a council of state was held at Amritsar in 1762. It was convened by the *granṭhis*, or exponents of the *Granṭh*, or, according to others, by the Akālīs (*q.v.*). Its precise functions were ill-defined, but it certainly exercised some judicial powers. In 1765 a national council held at Amritsar proclaimed the Khālsa the supreme religion and minted coins with the Persian legend: *Degh wa Tegh wa Fatih nusrat bedrang—Yāft az Nānak Guru Govind Singh*, 'Guru Govind Singh received from Nānak the *degh*, the sword and unfailing victory.' Thus the Sikhs marked their rule as a theocracy, democratic in principle and owning no allegiance to an earthly king. The failure of Ahmad Shāh's last invasion in 1767 left them masters of the Panjāb from the Jamna to the Indus.

With these events the religious development of Sikhism may be said to have closed. The next phase in its political history is the transformation of the *misls* into hereditary chiefships or clans. The ruling family of the Kapūrthala state is descended from Jassa Singh, 'Bādshāh'; that of Kalsia from the elected chief of the Karori-Singhi, or Panjgaṛhia, *misl*; and those of the Phūlkīān states and other fiefs from Phūl, the founder of the *dehra* of that name. The Rāmgaṛhia *misl* founded by another Jassa Singh, who was a carpenter by caste, gives its name to the Sikh carpenter caste generally, just as all Sikh Nebs or Kalāls aspire to be called Ahlūwālīās. The founders of the Nishānānwāli *misl* were the standard-bearers of the Khālsa, but its chiefship soon became hereditary and Ranjīt Singh extinguished it in 1808. The Dallewālīā *misl* was founded by a Khatrī surnamed Rāthor on account of his valour, and from his village it took its name, but a Jāṭ was elected its chief, his descendants divided its territories, and their disunion enabled Ranjīt Singh to annex nearly all its possessions.

The secularization of the possessions of the Khālsa and the inveterate tendency of the leaders of *misls* to treat their territories as private estates paved the way for the rise of Mahārāja Ranjīt Singh, chief by inheritance of the Sukarchakīā *misl*. Its territories, which were considerable, lay in the north of the province, but of his fellow-chiefs several were more powerful, and it was only by the exercise of great natural abilities, astuteness, and good fortune that he was able to weld the Sikh states north of the Sutlej into a kingdom. He extended its power to the Afghān frontier beyond Peshāwār, conquered Kashmīr, and effectively reduced the hill states to submission. He also extended his power over the south-west Panjāb, but south of the Sutlej a British protectorate of the cis-Sutlej states barred his ambitions. Autocratic though his power was in reality, he continued to mint coins bearing the Khālsa legend, and, while he appointed Muhammadan *qāzīs* and *muftīs*, he upheld Sikhism as the State religion.

2. Theology and ritual.—The distinctive tenet of Sikhism is monotheism, and, though the existence of the countless gods and goddesses of the Hindu pantheon is not denied, their worship is not inculcated and may be said to be implicitly condemned. The *Granṭh* repeatedly condemns idolatry. Nevertheless the masses worship the *Granṭh* itself in almost the same way as Hindus worship images. It is, however, difficult in India to draw the line between worship and reverence. Sikh theology is somewhat nebulous. Guru Nānak's idea of God is pantheistic rather than theistic, but he displayed an utter disregard of form and formal theology. He respected every religion so far as its real essence was concerned, but despised mechanical worship in any aspect. Guru Govind Singh made Sikhism more formal. He forbade smoking and cutting of the hair at any period of life. As a uniform he prescribed the wearing of the five *k's*, viz. the *kes* (long hair), the *kachh* (short drawers ending above the knee), the *kara* (iron bangle), the *kripān* (sword),[1] and the *kangha* (comb).

The Sikh retains the Hindu reverence for the cow, but is generally a meat-eater and disregards most of the Hindu ceremonial in the preparation of food. A merciful regard for animal suffering, however, makes him eschew all flesh not killed by a single stroke of the sword or jerk of the neck.[2] Female infanticide was sternly prohibited by the *gurus*, and Sikh women are permitted to acquire education, especially in the semi-sacred Gurmukhi script. At weddings the Hindu ritual is discarded, no Brāhman need be employed, and Vedic texts are dispensed with. The worship of Ganesh and the planets is not allowed, and in recent years an agitation for an independent marriage ritual led to the passing of the Anand[3] Marriage Act (Act 1 of 1909). In this rite the *Ādī Granṭh* is circumambulated in lieu of fire, and texts from it are recited to sanctify the union as emblematical of that between the soul and the Supreme. Metempsychosis is a cardinal tenet in Sikhism, and each successive *guru* was Nānak; indeed Guru Hargovind so signed himself. Where Sikhism has failed as a social force is in the abolition of the caste system. Nānak did not attempt its condemnation. He observed its rules and was content to preach that God cared not for a man's caste but for his deeds. Guru Govind Singh abolished it in theory, but in practice Sikhism fully recognizes caste distinctions, though at initiation, and in theory after it, all Singhs may be equal.

3. Sects and orders.—Sikhism is rent by schisms so that it is difficult to enumerate all its sects and movements. Two great groups may be distinguished: the Nānakpanthis,[4] or Sikhs of Nānak, are merely Hindus who follow Nānak's teaching; the Sikhs of Guru Govind Singh are the Singhs, the Khālsa or Tat (wā) Khālsa.[5] With the Nānakpanthis may be roughly equated the Sahijdhāri,[6] 'easy-going' Sikhs; and with the Khālsa the Kesdhāri Sikhs, *i.e.* those who wear the long hair (*kes*). These two groups are tending to separate, though a Kesdhāri will still take a Sahijdhāri girl to wife. The Rām Raīās[7] have not much following in the Panjāb. The Hindālis,[8] once influential,

[1] Some authorities give the *khanda* (steel knife), but this is an error, due to the use of the *khanda* in the *pahul* rite.

[2] *Jhaṭka*, a sudden shake, a jerk; cf. *jhaṭ*, a moment, snatch, or sudden attack.

[3] *Anand* means 'joy,' and is the equivalent of the Urdu *shādi*. Used at first by the lower classes in widow re-marriage and similar non-ritual unions, the tendency is now to bring it into vogue among the higher classes.

[4] H. A. Rose, *Glossary of Panjab Tribes and Castes*, Lahore, 1914, iii. 152 f. They are to be distinguished from the Nānakputras and the Nānakshāhis (*ib.* p. 155).

[5] *Ib.* p. 460.
[6] *Ib.* iii. 343.
[7] *Ib.* p. 307.
[8] *Ib.* ii. 325.

lost ground by throwing in their lot with Ahmad Shāh Abdāli, and they are now called Narinjani, or 'worshippers of the Bright One (God).' The Nirankārīs,[1] a modern sect, revived Nānak's teaching, though they respect the later *gurus* also. The Gangūshāhis,[2] who refused initiation from Guru Govind Singh, the Mīnās,[3] or 'deceitful' followers of Prithi Chand, and the Dhirmalias,[4] founded by Dhir Mal, elder brother of Guru Har Rāi, are all schismatical sects. The Sanwal-Shāhis[5] are followers of a disciple of Guru Nānak, and are found chiefly in the south-west Panjāb; the Sewapanthis[6] are confined to the Sindh Sāgar Doāb. The Kūkas[7] are an extremist sect whose tenets are kept secret, but they disclaim female infanticide. Orders rather than sects are the Dīwāna Sādhs,[8] or 'ecstatic saints,' the Nirmalās and Udāsīs (*qq.v.*). The term 'Rāmdāsi'[9] has various meanings, but it is usually applied to a weaver or tanner who has been converted to Sikhism. Mazhabi[10] is similarly applied to a converted sweeper.

4. Present conditions.—The Sikhs have now a central association, called the Chief Khālsa Dīwān, with its headquarters at Amritsar and local societies (Singh Sabhas) all over the Panjāb and at some places beyond it. They have also at Amritsar the Khālsa College, and at Tarn Tāran and Gujrānwāla two theological seminaries receive grants from the Dīwān. They possess 33 girls' schools, a newspaper (the *Khālsa Advocate*), orphanages, a tract society, and a Khālsa Young Men's Association, besides a Sikh Bank. Attempts are also made to help the depressed classes.[11]

LITERATURE.—See the works referred to in the text and especially Khazān Singh, *Philosophic Hist. of the Sikh Religion*, 2 vols., Lahore, 1914; M. A. Macauliffe, *The Sikh Religion*, 6 vols., Oxford, 1909; J. D. Cunningham, *A Hist. of the Sikhs*, London, 1849, reprinted, Oxford, 1918; Sewarām Singh Thapar, *Sri Gurū Nānak Dev*, Rawalpindi, 1904; Rup Singh, *Sikhism, A Universal Religion*, Amritsar, 1911, *Bhai Mahnga or the Search after Truth*, do. 1911. The Gurmukhi literature is now very voluminous.

H. A. ROSE.

SIKKIM.—Sikkim is a small country lying between Nepāl and Bhutān and between Tibet and India, and consists of the larger part of the mountain valley of the Tīsta river. It is a land of steep and lofty ridges and peaks and of deeply cut valleys. The area is only 2818 sq. miles, and, while its lowest elevation, at the junction of the Tīsta and the Rangīt, is about 700 ft., its highest, the top of Kinchinjunga, is 28,146 ft. This range of elevation implies an immense variety of vegetable life and also of insect and bird life. Other animal life is rather restricted in both individuals and species, most probably by the influence of the hordes of leeches which infest the jungles and roads in the rainy season. The rainfall is abundant, and the forests are thick, but from 2000 to 5000 ft. these have been to a great extent cleared to make way for cultivation. Apart from agriculture there are no industries, though an attempt is now being made to develop the mineral resources (mostly copper) of the country.

The population at the 1911 census numbered 87,920. It also is varied, but consists principally of immigrants from Nepāl. There are 20 Nepālese castes (many of which are really tribes) represented. Besides these there are Tibetan and Bhutānese tribes, and Lepchās, the so-called aborigines of Sikkim. Nepālis, Tibetans, and Bhutānese are described elsewhere.[12] It need only be said here that the Nepālis profess Hinduism of the type found in Nepāl. They are recent immigrants and have not had time to develop any peculiar features or to build any but insignificant shrines. The Bhutānese, migrant herdsmen, are very few. The Tibetans came into the country in the 17th cent. and usurped the government. They have now much Lepchā blood in them, which, however, has not sufficed to improve them. They brought Lāmaism (*q.v.*) with them, with Lāmaistic literature, and introduced the elements of civilization. It has been said that it was a tribe of robbers that entered Sikkim as the first colonists, and it is easy to believe this. They are a dishonest race in speech and act, given to bullying and violence, but thorough cowards, filthy in their persons, habits, and conversation, and generally tainted with venereal disease. Both polygamy and polyandry are common among them. Needless to add, they are priest-ridden to a degree, and their priests are, with some exceptions, exemplars to the flock in all their vices. There are over 40 monasteries and nunneries.

The origin of the Lepchās (in their own speech Rong, 'valley men') is not known with certainty. They are thought to have come from somewhere on the borders of Tibet and Burma. According to their own traditions, they came to Sikkim from the east in company with the Jimdars (who went on to Nepāl and who share this tradition) and the Mech (who settled in the plains at the foot of the hills). The Lepchās settled in Sikkim, which they called Ne-lyang (='cave country'), and lived a primitive life in its deep forests, keeping no cattle and cultivating very little, but living mainly on forest produce. They claim yet to be able to live wherever the monkey lives. The Lepchā is gentle, inoffensive, and timid, fond of solitude, with no peculiar arts or industries; indeed he is not at all fond of work. His speech is Mongolian and monosyllabic, though during years of Tibetan dominance many Tibetan words have been introduced. His faith and his folklore are, like his speech, certainly Mongolian, and now more or less Tibetan. Lāmaistic Buddhism of the unreformed Nying-ma-pa is generally attributed to him, but it is its animistic, not its Buddhistic, elements that appeal to him. There is still extant a tradition of a former religion in which the Lepchās believed in a good spirit, but preferred, for prudential reasons, to worship bad ones. One may also hear sometimes of Lepchā scriptures, written by a king of Rokangkorung, in which the king appears as a kind of Lepchā prophet. But, as the Lepchā alphabet is the Tibetan one slightly modified by an early Tibetan king of Sikkim, this tradition is of doubtful value.

It is very difficult to say how much of the folklore is originally Lepchā and how much is Tibetan. Many of the stories of jackals and tigers are common to the two peoples. It is interesting to note that there was a tribe of very foolish Lepchās like our wise men of Gotham. But the inquirer is sure to be informed that these 'great fools' are extinct. One of their achievements was to build a tower meant to reach the sky. When it was very high, the builders on the top called down for more stones and those below thought they were being told to cut away the foundations. They did so, and the tower fell and killed half the tribe. The site and ruins are still shown. There is also a flood tradition, in which a Lepchā family is saved by the mountain Tendong ('the uplifted horn') elevating its summit, on which they were perched, above the rising waters. As the flood passed away, the uplifted horn again contracted.

LITERATURE.—J. W. Edgar, *Report on a Visit to Sikkim and the Tibetan Frontier*, Calcutta, 1874; C. Macaulay, *Report on a Mission to Sikhim and the Tibetan Frontier*, do. 1885; *The Gazetteer of Sikkim*, do. 1894; J. D. Hooker, *Himalayan Journals*, 2 vols., London, 1854; L. A. Waddell, *The Buddhism*

[1] H. A. Rose, *op. cit.* iii. 171.
[2] *Ib.* ii. 178.
[3] *Ib.* iii. 104.
[4] *Ib.* ii. 238.
[5] *Ib.* iii. 380.
[6] *Ib.* p. 397.
[7] *Ib.* ii. 500.
[8] *Ib.* p. 243.
[9] *Ib.* iii. 306 f.
[10] *Ib.* p. 75.
[11] J. N. Farquhar, *Modern Religious Movements in India*, New York, 1915, p. 340 f.
[12] See artt. NEPĀL, TIBET, BHUTĀN.

of Tibet, or Lamaism, do. 1895, *Among the Himalayas*, do. 1899; J. Claude White, *Sikhim and Bhutan*, do. 1909; L. S. S. O'Malley, *Bengal, Bihar and Orissa, Sikkim*, Cambridge, 1917; P. Brown, *Tours in Sikkim*, Calcutta, 1917.

W. G. MACKEAN.

SILENCE.—Silence, as an aid to worship or as a method of preparing the soul for spiritual experiences, has been practised among larger or smaller groups in almost all periods of religious history and in almost all parts of the world. It was given an important place in the Pythagorean societies and probably also in the Orphic circles in Greece. Pythagoras is said to have made silence the form of initiation into his religious order, requiring the initiate to remain silent and listen for an entire year—some say even three years. Socrates, at least the Socrates of Plato, refers frequently to the importance of silence, and he appears to have practised silence as a form of inward culture. One striking account of Socrates in an intense long-continued silent meditation is given in the *Symposium*.[1] Plutarch, too, pronounces silence the best way to wisdom and far superior to speech.

The OT contains many references to the value of silence as a preparation for spiritual vision or revelation. Many of the prophets and leaders of Israel were prepared for their mission by the discipline of silence, and the voice in the stillness was felt to be a clearer revelation of God than earthquake, fire, or storm. The most emphatic passages on the value of silence, however, are to be found in the Psalms and in the later period of Hebrew literature, *i.e.* after the Exile:

'Be still, and know that I am God' (Ps 46[10]); 'Praise is silent for thee, O God' (65[1]); 'Keep thou silence at the presence of the Lord God' (Zeph 1[7]); 'The Lord is in his holy temple: let all the earth keep silence before him' (Hab 2[20]); 'Keep thy foot when thou goest to the house of God; for to draw nigh to hear is better than to give the sacrifice of fools [*i.e.* talk] . . . Be not rash with thy mouth, and let not thine heart be hasty to utter any thing before God' (Ec 5[1f.]).

The later uncanonical books show an increasing appreciation of silence. One passage from the book of Wisdom (18[14f.]) must suffice:

'When all things were in quiet silence and night was in her swift course, Thine Almighty Word, O Lord, leaped down from heaven.'

The practice of silence is implicit rather than positively explicit in the NT. Christ prayed frequently apart alone, and sought the opportunity for quiet communion. He also enjoined upon His followers the practice of retreat from noise and disturbance to the silent closet for solitary prayer. There seem to have been periods of silence in the meetings of the primitive Christian Church, though this is implied rather than overtly stated or emphasized in the accounts. The worshippers of Mithra, as was true of the initiates in all the mystery religions, exalted silence. The preparatory instructions to these initiates contained these directions:

'Lay thy right finger on thy mouth, and say Silence! Silence! Silence! Symbol of the living, imperishable God.'

Egyptian mystical worshippers called God 'the Lord of the silent' and addressed Him thus:

'Thou sweet Well for him that thirsteth in the desert; it is closed to him who speaks, but it is open to him who is silent. When he who is silent comes, lo, he finds the well.'[2]

Many of the Christian Fathers encouraged the practice of silence and appreciated its value as a way of cultivating the spiritual life. Ignatius of Antioch, Clement of Alexandria, Gregory of Nazianzus, and Gregory of Nyssa especially dwell upon its use. Gregory of Nazianzus says:

'To speak of God is an exercise of great value, but there is one that is worth much more, namely to purify one's soul before God in silence.'[3]

[1] 220 B.

[2] Quoted from J. H. Breasted, *Development of Religion and Thought in Ancient Egypt*, New York and London, 1912, p. 356.

[3] *Orat.* xxvi.

Augustine refers in many places to the need for retirement, solitude, and silence, if the soul is to find God. The most impressive passage on the effect of silence is the famous one in the *Confessions* describing 'the sweet communion' which he and his mother, Monica, had at Ostia just before her death:

'When in one's body the storm of the flesh is silenced, when the voices of land and sea are hushed, and the canopy of heaven is silent; when the soul is mute within itself; when the dreams and fancies of the imagination are silent; when every tongue, and every sense, and all that is perishable, is silent; and when the Creator speaks, not through any of these, but speaks Himself directly, and we thus hear His voice, not from any man's lips, and not from the lips of angels, not in thunder and darkness, and not in unintelligible parable, but hear Him whom we adore in these things, Himself alone apart from them all, even as we have risen above them, and, in rapturous flights of thoughts, have reached the eternal wisdom which is highly exalted above them all; if then this condition could be a lasting one, and all other thoughts and imaginings of a different nature could be banished for ever, and the beholder were thus carried away, consumed, swallowed up in joy, and the soul's yearning satisfied, would not then this be the moment to which these words apply, "Enter thou into the joy of thy Lord"?'[1]

Mystics in all ages, whether Christian, Neo-Platonic, Persian, Indian, Arabic, or mediæval Jewish, have made large use of silence and have considered it a way to find God. A well-known passage from Hierotheus—a pseudonym for a Syrian mystic of the 5th cent.—furnishes a good example of the Neo-Platonic attitude:

'To me it seems right to speak without words, and understand without knowledge, that which is above words and knowledge; this I apprehend to be nothing but the mysterious silence and mystical quiet which destroys consciousness and dissolves forms. Seek, therefore, silently and mystically, that perfect and primitive union with the Arch-Good.'[2]

Thomas à Kempis in the *Imitation* expresses in striking words what all Christian mystics say in one form or another:

'In silence and in stillness the religious soul grows and learns the mysteries of Holy Writ. There she finds rivers of tears wherein she may wash and cleanse herself night after night that she may be more familiar with her Creator, . . . Whoso, therefore, withdraweth himself from his acquaintances and friends, God will draw near unto him with His holy angels. . . . Shut thy door behind thee, and call unto thee Jesus thy Beloved. Stay with Him in thy cell: for thou shalt not find so great peace elsewhere.'[3]

The Roman Catholic mystics of the Counter-Reformation and the Quietists of the 17th cent. show an increased appreciation of silence, and they made the practice of the presence of God in silence the very centre of their religion.

In the monastery silence was a large element of the religious life. St. Benedict made very strict rules regarding the practice of silence for the monks of his order, and all other monastic orders laid strong emphasis upon it and set apart periods of 'great silence.' The Cistercians were especially strict in their observance of silence, while the Reformed Cistercians, or Trappists, carried their demands for silence to excessive lengths of strictness, some of them taking perpetual vows of silence. The Carthusian monks, in their periods of purity and strictness, lived as contemplatives and spoke little.

The members of the Society of Friends (*q.v.*) have given a greater place to silence than any other Protestant sect. They took from the 'Seekers' (*q.v.*) of the English Commonwealth period the custom of sitting silent in meetings for worship, and they considered silence essential to worship and a preparation for all public service. George Fox, their founder, practised silence and solitary meditation during his long period of search for light on his own path, and, when he went out to gather others to the truth which he had found, he insisted that those who gathered about him should first learn to sit still and listen.

[1] Bk. ix. ch. 10.

[2] Quoted from W. R. Inge, *Christian Mysticism*, London, 1899, p. 103.

[3] Bk. i. ch. 20.

On one occasion he sat in silence for 'some hours,' in order 'to famish' the people 'from words.' At last he 'was moved of the Lord to speak,' and the people were 'reached by the Lord's power, and word of life.'[1]

Robert Barclay, the most distinguished of the early defenders and interpreters of Quakerism, wrote from his own experience a striking account of the power of this Quaker silence. He says:

'Sometimes, when there is not a word in the meeting but all are silently waiting, if one come in that is rude and wicked, and in whom the power of darkness prevaileth much, perhaps with an intention to mock or do mischief, if the whole meeting be gathered into the life, and it be raised in a good measure, it will strike terror into such an one, and he will feel himself unable to resist; but by the secret strength and virtue thereof, the power of darkness in him will be chained down: and if the day of his visitation be not expired, it will reach to the measure of grace in him, and raise it up to the redeeming of his soul. . . . For not a few had come to be convinced of the truth after this manner, of which I myself am a true witness, who not by strength of arguments, or by a particular disquisition of each doctrine, and convincement of my understanding thereby, came to receive and bear witness of the truth, but by being secretly reached by this life. For when I came into the silent assemblies of God's people, I felt a secret power among them, which touched my heart, and as I gave way unto it, I found the evil weakening in me, and the good raised up: and so I became thus knit and united unto them, hungering more and more after the increase of this power and life, whereby I might feel myself perfectly redeemed.'[2]

After the writings of the Continental Quietists, Molinos, Madame Guyon, and Fénelon, became the favourite books in Quaker circles, and as a result of this influence the whole Society became permeated with quietistic ideals, especially in the period from 1760 to 1830, Friends came to regard this silence as the essential mark of spiritual life and as the one way to communion with God. The favourite texts of the Bible for Friends of this period were those on silence and stillness, and silence seemed almost to possess magic power. Many meetings were held year after year without any interruption of the silence, and the only public vocal utterances in many Quaker communities were heard when visiting ministers came from a distance on itinerant service. This Quaker quietism largely yielded place before the evangelical wave which swept over the Society of Friends in the first half of the 19th cent., the great exponent of this movement being Joseph John Gurney of Norwich (1788–1847).

In recent times silence as a method of communion has been given a new and growing place in the Church of England. This modern practice of silence had its beginnings in New Zealand, was transmitted to London, was taken up in many churches in England, and later became a feature in some of the Episcopalian churches of America.

Carlyle, in rhapsodical manner, has expressed an appreciation of silence which has many parallels in literature but which may be taken as a striking literary estimate of the moral and spiritual value of silence:

'Silence and secrecy! Altars might still be raised to them (were this an altar-building time) for universal worship. Silence is the element in which great things fashion themselves together; that at length they may emerge, full-formed and majestic, into the daylight of Life, which they are henceforth to rule . . . do thou thyself but hold thy tongue for one day: on the morrow, how much clearer are thy purposes and duties; what wreck and rubbish have those mute workmen within thee swept away, when intrusive noises were shut out! Speech is too often not, as the Frenchman defined it, the art of concealing Thought; but of quite stifling and suspending Thought, so that there is none to conceal. . . . Speech is of Time, Silence is of Eternity. Bees will not work except in darkness; Thought will not work except in Silence.' . . . 'Silence, the great Empire of Silence: higher than the stars; deeper than the Kingdoms of Death! . . . The great silent men! . . . A country which has none or few of these is in a bad way. Like a forest that has no roots; which had all turned into leaves and boughs;—which must soon wither and be no forest.'[1]

LITERATURE.—Joan M. Fry, *The Communion of Life*, London, 1910; Cyril Hepher, *The Fellowship of Silence*, do. 1915, *The Fruits of Silence*, do. 1915; L. Violet Hodgkin, *The Surrender of Silence*, do. 1915; Charles Courtenay, *The Empire of Silence*, do. 1916; L. Violet Hodgkin, *Silent Worship*, do. 1919.

RUFUS M. JONES.

SILENOI.—In the recently discovered *Ichneutæ* of Sophocles Silenos is the leader of the Satyr-Trackers. Though the art-form, origin, and exact connotation of the Satyr are still open to question, the nature and art-form of the Silenoi have, thanks to recent investigations, been clearly defined. In fig. below, from the François vase,[2] are represented and, happily, inscribed three Silenoi. They form part of the cortège of Dionysos, who brings back to Olympus Hephaistos, mounted on a mule; they are characteristically employed: one carries a wine-skin, another plays the double-flute, and the third harries a nymph. These inscribed Silenoi have characteristic equine ears, up-springing tail, and hooves. This leaves no doubt that, whatever be the art-form of the cognate Satyrs[3] (*q.v.*), the Silenoi are in the 6th cent. B.C. horse-daimons. In horse-breeding countries the horse is a familiar 'daimon of fertility'—witness the October-horse of the Romans and our own hobby-horse. On the original of fig. above the Silenoi are markedly ithyphallic.

Happily the explanation of Silenoi horse-daimons is now confirmed by philology. O. Lagercrantz[4] has solved the long riddle. Σιληνός with its by-form σιλανός is derived from the Indo-Germanic **kēl*. The word σιληνός is Thraco-Phrygian, a 'satem' language, so the sigmation of the velar-guttural is all in order. The Greek cognate κήλων naturally preserved the guttural, and clinches the argument. According to Hesychius, κήλων = ὀχεύτης, the horse as stallion; according to Archilochos,[5] the he-ass

ἡ δέ οἱ σάθη
ὡσεί τ' ὄνου Πριηνέος
κήλωνος ἐπλήμμυρεν ὀτρυγηφάγου.

[1] *Journal*, ed. Norman Penney, Cambridge, 1911, i. 28.
[2] *Apology*, London, 1678, prop. xi. sect. 7.

[1] *Sartor Resartus*, bk. iii. ch. 3, *On Heroes*, Lect. iv.
[2] In the Museo Greco-Etrusco, Florence; see *Wiener Vorlegeblätter*, 1883, Taf. 3; and A. Furtwängler and K. Reichhold, *Griech. Vasenmalerei*, Munich, 1904–09, i. 58, Taf. 11 and 12. Fig. above is reproduced from J. E. Harrison, *Prolegomena*, fig. 116, p. 376.
[3] This difficult question is fully discussed by E. Kühnert, in Roscher. The best résumé and resolution of the problem is in A. B. Cook, *Zeus*, Cambridge, 1914, i. 695–705.
[4] 'Zur Herkunft des Wortes Silen,' in *Sertum Philolog. Carolo Ferdinando Johansson oblatum*, Göteborg, 1910, pp. 117–121; for other suggested derivations see P. Kretschmer, *Glotta*, ii. [1910] 398.
[5] Bergk, *Poetæ Lyrici Græci*, Leipzig, 1878–82, frag. 97.

In Thraco-Phrygian κήλων attained the semi-divinity of a capital letter, Silenos in Greek never.

That originally the Silenoi were ass-daimons as well as horse-daimons is abundantly clear from the myths of the two arch-Silenoi, Marsyas and Midas. S. Reinach[1] has shown that the flaying of the flute-playing Silenos, Marsyas, was in its origin not the savage punishment of a rival, but the sacrifice of a sacred ass. The skin was preserved for its magical properties, and shown at Celænæ in the time of Aelian.[2] He further suggests, though the etymology is not quite certain, that the name Marsyas is connected with μάρσυπος, from which comes our 'marsupial.' Marsyas became human in Græco-Roman art,[3] and carried his own hide in the form of a wine-skin—a figure exactly parallel to the first Silenos in fig. above. The skin of Marsyas may well be the origin of the famous 'peau d'âne' of French literature.[4]

Even more unimpeachable is the evidence of King Midas, who judged the case of the Silen Marsyas and who caught 'Silen' in his rose-gardens. Midas, says Philostratos[5] in telling his story, 'had something of the race of satyrs about him, witness his ears.' By the time of Philostratos the word 'satyr' is loosely used to cover any half-animal daimon. The asses' ears mark Midas for us as a Silen, in ass- not horse-form. We think of the ass as the patient burden-bearer, and it surprises us that he should figure as fertility-daimon side by side with the splendid horse, but to the ancient Greek (as to the modern) it was the mule that was beast of burden; the ass was primarily sire of the useful mule and ever prone, as Simonides of Amorgos[6] says, πρὸς ἔργον ἀφροδίσιον. It may well be, as Reinach[7] suggests, that the ass-daimon was the primary basis of the Silen, and that the horse-form was due to a later blend with the popular horse-Centaur. The connexion of ass and Silen was remembered down to Alexandrian times. In the great Dionysiac procession of Ptolemy II. Silens and Satyrs alike are mounted on asses, not horses.[8]

Midas in popular legend is a Phrygian, but Herodotus[9] knew that his real home was in Europe, not Asia. The Macedonians claimed that Silenos was caught by Midas in his wondrous rose-gardens overshadowed by Mt. Bermios. The magic roses as fodder for the ass live on in Apuleius.[10] The spring in which Midas mixed the wine to snare Silenos is placed by Athenæus[11] (on the authority of Bion) on the borderland between the Mædi and the Paonians. Its name was Ἴννα, and the name is instructive; ἴννος is Greek for a mule, the sire being a stallion, the dam a she-ass.[12] Silenoi are constantly associated with springs and rivers; the old interpretation[13] was that they simply *were* springs; but the ass- and horse-form points to a wider fertility connotation.

Midas, the ass-eared Silen, is a Phrygian, and, like all other Phrygians, before he passed from Europe into Asia, he was a Brigian[14] of Indo-European stock, but, like Dionysos, Thracian, not Greek. It is now clear why the word 'Silenos' is from the Thraco-Phrygian 'satem' form of an Indo-Germanic root. The sanctity and sacrifice of the ass—so strange to the Greeks—were familiar to the Thraco-Phrygians. A portion of the Thraco-Phrygian stock dwelt about the great snow peak of Bora[1]—the modern Nidje, 2000 ft. high, the highest point between Haliakma and the Axios; hence its name, which means simply 'mountain,' the guttural form surviving in Russian *gora*, 'mountain.' Here was the home of the Silenoi; witness the coins of Macedonia. It was to these Hyperboreans that Apollo, and Perseus before him, fared and saw them 'sacrificing splendid hecatombs of asses.' In these feasts, Pindar[2] tells us, Apollo took special joy and—most instructive for our purpose—'the god laughed aloud to see the romping licence of the monstrous beasts.'[3] The Silen is dissolute even in old age; and yet as flute-playing Phrygian, countryman of the Thracian Orpheus, he is redeemed always by the spirit of music and mysterious prophetic wisdom. It was not for his snub-nose only that Socrates was dubbed Silen.

LITERATURE.—In the Lexicons of Roscher and Daremberg-Saglio Silenos must be sought under 'Satyroi'—a serious defect in method tending to confuse the known with the uncertain. O. Gruppe, *Griechische Mythologie*, Munich, 1897–1906, discusses Silenos under 'Pan, Satyroi, Silenos.' The same defect must be noted in the present writer's discussion of the horse-shaped Silenoi in *Prolegomena to the Study of Greek Religion*, Cambridge, 1903, pp. 380, 389. In the articles of the Lexicons will be found full references to the older literature, in which the Silenoi are explained as either *Quell-* or *Berg-daimonen*. The references for the new view are given more conveniently in the text. Indispensable to the study of the ass- and horse-forms, though not dealing directly with the Silenoi, is A. B. Cook, 'Animal Worship in the Mycenæan Age,' *JHS* xiv. [1894] 81–169. He there figures (fig. 1) the ass-demons of Mycenæ which are the nameless ritual ancestors of the Silenoi.

J. E. HARRISON.

SILENT TRADE.—See GIFTS (Primitive and Savage).

SILVER.—See METALS AND MINERALS.

SIMON MAGUS.—Simon Magus, the subject of an episode in the first evangelization of Samaria recorded in Ac 8[9-24], appears in ecclesiastical tradition under three aspects: (1) as a false Messiah, who practised magical arts and subsequently attempted, by the aid and with the sanction of Christianity, to set up a rival universal religion; (2) as the founder of a Gnostic sect; (3) as a travesty of the apostle Paul. Our information about him is derived from three distinct types of early Christian literature—the heresiologists of the 2nd to the 5th cent. A.D., the Clementine literature, and the apocryphal *Acts of SS. Peter and Paul*. The first two features of the tradition are present in a greater or less degree in each of those sources; the last occurs with certainty only in the *Clementine Homilies* and *Recognitions* and possibly in the apocryphal *Acts*.

I. The narrative of Ac 8[9-24].—In Acts Simon is described as a man who had bewitched the people of Samaria by his sorcery, 'giving out that himself was some great one: to whom they all gave heed, from the least to the greatest, saying, This man is the great power of God.' At the preaching of Philip, Simon believed and was baptized; but later, when Peter and John came down to Samaria to confer the gift of the Holy Ghost upon Philip's converts by the laying on of hands, he offered the apostles money, saying, 'Give me also this power, that on whomsoever I lay hands, he may receive the Holy Ghost.' Peter cursed him for his presumption and bade him repent; the

1 'Marsyas' in *Cultes, mythes, et religions*, Paris, 1905–12, iv. 42.
2 *Var. Hist.* xiii. 21.
3 See coin of L. Marcius Censorinus representing a statue of Marsyas in the Forum (Roscher, *s.v.* 'Marsyas,' p. 2444, fig. i.).
4 Reinach, p. 44.
5 *Vit. Apoll.* vi. 27. 2.
6 7 [8]. 49.
7 P. 37.
8 Athen. v. 31, p. 200.
9 viii. 138.
10 *Metam.* iii. 85; and in Lucian, *Lucius*, 54.
11 ii. 23, p. 45 C.
12 Schrader, *Reallexikon der indogerman. Altertumskunde*, Strassburg, 1901, p. 534, *s.v.* 'Maulthier.'
13 L. Preller and C. Robert, *Griech. Myth.*[4], Berlin, 1894, i. 729 ff., followed even by Lagercrantz, p. 117, though his own new derivation shows the inadequacy of the old view. O. Jessen, in his art. 'Marsyas' in Roscher, still holds that Marsyas is merely a *Quell-dämon*.
14 Herod. vii. 73.

1 O. Schroeder, 'Hyperboreer,' *ARW* viii. [1905] 83.
2 *Pyth.* x. 31 ff.
3 γελᾷ θ' ὁρῶν ὕβριν ὀρθίαν κνωδάλων.

incident concluded with Simon's request for the apostles' prayers on his behalf.

The authenticity and integrity of the narrative in Acts are suspect on several grounds. (1) The text shows traces of interpolation. In v.[11] *προσεῖχον* and *ἐξεστακέναι* look like an echo of *ἐξιστῶν* in v.[9] and *προσεῖχον* in v.[10a], and the verse simply repeats the sense of the foregoing narrative. (2) The commotion caused by Simon in Samaria, resulting in the adhesion of the whole city and the declaration that he was the great power of God, must be an exaggeration, since it is quite out of proportion to the importance of the representative of a common type of impostor. (3) There is no close to the story: nothing is said as to what became of Simon after his repudiation by the apostles. (4) It has been urged that the theory implicit in vv.[14-18], that the power of conferring the Holy Ghost belonged exclusively to the apostles, is an unhistorical transference of the ideas of a later age into the conditions of the primitive Church.

According to the theory that the text has been interpolated, Simon was at first represented merely as desirous of acquiring Philip's miraculous powers. His acclamation by the people as the great power of God, his confronting with Peter, and the suggestion that his purpose was to purchase equality with the apostles are relegated to a later version of the story, whose motive has thus been fundamentally recast.

2. Simon in ecclesiastical tradition.—(*a*) *Justin.*—In the 2nd cent. A.D. a cycle of legends concerning Simon's doings in Rome grew up as a sequel to the story of Acts. Justin Martyr[1] is our earliest authority, and his evidence should carry considerable weight, since he was a native of Nablus (Shechem) in Samaria,[2] though allowance must be made for misrepresentation natural to a champion of orthodoxy and an apologist of the Church. Justin describes Simon as a native of Gitta in Samaria, who was acknowledged almost universally by his fellow-countrymen as the transcendent God 'above all principality, power, and dominion,'[3] but does not definitely connect him with the impostor of Acts. He was the master of the heretic Menander of Capparatæa,[4] who taught in Antioch that his followers should never die, and was accompanied in his travels by a woman named Helena, who had formerly been a prostitute and whom he declared to be 'the first intelligence' proceeding from himself. For Simon claimed to be and was accounted a god both in Samaria and elsewhere. He had won the favour of Cæsar (presumably Claudius),[5] and a statue was erected to him as god on an island in the Tiber by command of the Senate,[6] bearing the inscription 'Simoni Deo Sancto.'

Justin has confused Simon with the old Sabine deity Semo Sancus, who presided over compacts.[7] His mistake can be checked with absolute certainty, thanks to an accident of Roman archæology. In the year 1574 the base of a statue was discovered on an island in the Tiber, with the following dedication inscribed on it:[8]

'Semoni | Sanco | Deo. Fidio | Sacrum | Sex. Pompeius. S.P.F. | Col. Mussianus | Quinquennalis | Decur. | Bidentalis | Donum. Dedit ‖.'

(*b*) *Tertullian and Origen.*—The ecclesiastical writers of the next two generations add little but detail to Justin's account. His story of the statue which the Romans dedicated to Simon became part of tradition and is repeated by Irenæus and almost all later authorities. Tertullian[9] identifies Simon the heretic with the Simon who had been cursed and expelled by the apostle Peter, attributes his magic art to the service of angels, as Justin had ascribed it to the help of demons, and says that he

1 *Apol.* i. 25, 26, *Dial. cum Tryph.* cxx. 16.

2 *Dial. cum Tryph.* cxx. 16: οὐδὲ γὰρ ἀπὸ τοῦ γένους τοῦ ἐμοῦ λέγω δὲ τῶν Σαμαρέων, κ.τ.λ.

3 *Ib.*: ὅι θεὸν ὑπεράνω πάσης ἀρχῆς καὶ ἐξουσίας καὶ δυνάμεως εἶναι λέγουσι.

4 *Apol.* i. 26.

5 Cf. *Dial. cum Tryph.* cxx. 16, Καίσαρι προσομιλῶν, with *Apol.* i. 26, ἐπὶ Κλαυδίου καίσαρος.

6 *Apol.* i. 56: τὴν ἱερὰν σύγκλητον.

7 See Ovid, *Fasti*, vi. 213.

8 The inscription is given in Baronius, *Annales*, Lucca, 1738–46, ad annum 44, i. 306. Tillemont doubts this solution (*Mémoires*, Paris, 1693-1712, ii. 482).

9 *De Idol.* 9, *de Fuga*, 12, *de Anima*, 34, *Apol.* 13.

ransomed Helen of Tyre to console himself for the loss of the powers which he had desired to purchase of the apostles. Origen,[1] like Justin, places Simon in a series of pretenders to divine honours, who had appeared since the ascension of Christ, and puts him in the line of the Samaritan Messiahs—Theudas, Dositheus, and Cleobius.

3. The tradition of Simon's conflict with St. Peter in Rome.—Hippolytus is the first ecclesiastical writer to connect the tradition of Simon's sojourn in Rome with the tradition of St. Peter's presence there. Justin alludes to the disillusionment of the Roman people,[2] but Hippolytus gives the earliest extant version of the legend of Simon's conflict with Peter, his final defeat, and death.[3] His narrative, however, disagrees completely with the legend of Simon's flight and fall from heaven in the presence of the emperor Nero, which was accepted later. Hippolytus makes no reference to the conflicts of Simon and Peter in Syria, and only in passing mentions the opposition of the Apostle in Rome. Simon taught sitting under a plane-tree and, in order to convince his hearers and to escape exposure, promised that, if he was buried alive, he would rise again the third day. A trench was dug and Simon was buried, but the test failed. This version of the legend of Simon's death is perhaps parodied in the apocryphal *Acts of SS. Peter and Paul*[4] by the story of Simon's undertaking before Nero to rise again after he had been beheaded and of his successful imposture by substituting a ram for himself.

The earliest connexion of the death of Simon with the incident of his attempted flight extant in ecclesiastical tradition is found in Arnobius (fl. *c.* 310).[5] Peter invoked the name of Christ, and Simon was precipitated from his fiery chariot. This account varies from later tradition in that Simon does not die outright as a consequence of his fall, but is conveyed to Brunda (=Brundisium) and there, overcome by his sufferings and by shame at his failure, casts himself down a precipice. The pre-Catholic *Actus Petri cum Simone*[6] agrees with Arnobius in prolonging Simon's life after his fall, but attributes his death to the assistance of the physicians of Terracina. This writing must belong to the earlier part of the 3rd cent. A.D., since Commodian[7] (fl. 250) alludes to the dog which, being made to speak by Peter's command, betrayed Simon's presence in the house of Marcellus and prophesied his overthrow. The *Syriac Didascalia*,[8] which was later expanded into the *Apostolic Constitutions* and is dated about the end of the 3rd cent., *i.e.* slightly earlier than Arnobius, describes Simon's attempted flight, but seems to imply that he survived his fall, from which he suffered a broken ankle, since it relates that, while many turned away from him, others clave to him. The same document and also Eusebius[9] refer to a previous contest between Peter and Simon Magus in Palestine, but there is no reason to suppose that either had any other source of information than the narrative of Acts. Eusebius's account of Simon's overthrow is ambiguous. Philaster[10] (*c.* 380) is the earliest writer who definitely alludes to previous conflicts in Palestine other than that recorded by St. Luke: he mentions the flight of Simon from Jerusalem to Rome and his challenge to Peter before Nero, ascribes his fall to the intervention of an angel at the prayer of Peter, and makes his death immediate. Philaster apparently did not derive this information from his chief source, the lost syntagma of Hippolytus (*c.* 200). Cyril of Jerusalem[11] is the earliest of the Fathers to attribute the fall of Simon to the joint prayers of the apostles Peter and Paul, as it is recorded in *Passio Petri et Pauli*.[12] The author of the work *de Excidio urbis Hierosolymitanæ*[13] draws upon the apocryphal *Acts* for a number of incidents in his account of Simon. The *Apostolic Constitutions*[14] weaves together all the strands which were finally combined in the legend of Simon Magus.

4. Difficulties in identifying Simon the Gnostic with the Simon of Acts.—From Irenæus onwards the Fathers of the Church are unanimous in ascribing to Simon Magus the origin and author-

1 *C. Celsum*, i. 57, vi. 11.

2 *Apol.* i. 56. 3 *Phil.* vi. 20.

4 *Passio SS. AA. Petri et Pauli*, ed. R. A. Lipsius and M. Bonnet, Leipzig, 1891-1903, chs. 32, 57.

5 *Adv. Nationes*, ii. 12.

6 Lat. version, ch. 32; Gr. version, ch. 3.

7 *Carmen Apologeticum*, i. 613; cf. *Actus Petri cum Simone*, chs. 9, 11, 12.

8 vi. 8, 9 (p. 100 f., ed. P. A. de Lagarde, tr. A. C. Headlam, *HDB* iv. 521, *s.v.* 'Simon Magus').

9 *HE* ii. 13 f. 10 *Hær.* 29.

11 *Catech.* vi. 14. 12 52-55.

13 iii. 2, ascribed to Hegesippus, but probably by Ambrose.

14 vi. 7-9.

ship of heresy.[1] But, in addition to his character as the progenitor of heresy in general, the authorship of a particular Gnostic system is also attributed to Simon. There are serious difficulties in accepting the tradition that the Simon of Acts was the founder of the sect called by his name and professing these doctrines.

Simon's attempt to purchase the power of the apostles occurred in the reign of Claudius; but Hegesippus[2] asserts that Gnosticism arose in the times of Trajan, after the sacred choir of the apostles had ceased. The heretic Menander is universally represented as the disciple of Simon, and Justin Martyr[3] in the reign of Antoninus Pius (A.D. 152) mentions that some of Menander's followers were still alive. One of the sayings attributed to their founder by the Simonians, which has every appearance of being genuine, is inconsistent with the hypothesis that he is the Simon of Acts. The Gnostic Simon[4] claimed to have appeared as the Son in Judæa, where he simulated death, to have descended in Samaria as the Father, and to have visited the Gentiles as the Holy Spirit. He seems to have held the doctrine of metempsychosis; but his claim of identity with Jesus rules out the possibility of his reappearance as an incarnation of the Father in the reign of Claudius. Moreover, writings were current in this sect under the name of Simon in which two passages from St. Paul's epistles are quoted (1 Co 11^{32}, Eph $6^{14ff.}$), and allusion is made to the parable of the lost sheep.[5] If the identification of the Simon of Acts with the founder of the Simonian sect is maintained, his system would be distinguished from all other Gnostic sects in this respect, that it arose before St. Paul had re-interpreted Christianity to the Gentiles; yet the speculations attributed to Simon are in their main outlines closely akin to the Gnostic systems of the 2nd cent. A.D., except that Simon himself is substituted for Christ in the part of the Redeemer. Simon is the subject of the Gnostic speculations current in the Simonian sect and cannot be regarded as the author of them, at least in their developed form. Nevertheless, after Justin the Fathers agree in identifying the leader of the Gnostic sect with the Simon of Acts and in making Samaria the scene of his first activities.

5. Sources from which our knowledge of Simon's doctrine is derived.—Two independent traditions profess to preserve the teaching of Simon, the one betraying the influence of Alexandrian allegory (Hippolytus), the other of Syrian and Babylonian religion (Irenæus, Epiphanius, Theodoret). The former survives only in the fragments of a book ascribed to Simon and entitled *The Great Announcement*, which are preserved by the author of the *Philosophumena*.[6] The contents of this work, which is written in the form of an allegorical commentary on the Pentateuch, consist chiefly of cosmological speculations. The latter tradition is derived ultimately from a lost treatise of Justin against all heresies,[7] which is the common source underlying the account of Simon's doctrines given by Irenæus, Epiphanius, Theodoret, and pseudo-Tertullian. Epiphanius seems to have had access to the original document whence Justin drew his information, since by an awkward transition he twice introduces Simon as speaking in the first person. Hippolytus was also acquainted with this treatise of Justin and supplemented his use of *The Great Announcement* by quotations from it. *Phil.* vi. 19 f. repeats the story of Helen's deliverance as given by Irenæus, sometimes with verbal coincidences. The central theme of this tradition is a myth of redemption.

6. Cosmogony of 'The Great Announcement.'—*The Great Announcement* professes to solve the riddle of the universe by a theory of emanations.

The principle of all things is fire,[1] a boundless power so compounded of two natures, the one hidden and the other manifest, 'that the hidden are concealed in the manifest portions of the fire, and the manifest derive their being from the hidden.' The cosmos, or ordered universe, originated as the self-realization of the unbegotten fire and is arranged in a series of three successive worlds, in which the lower is a reflexion of the one above. An intermediate world mirrors the primal world and is itself the paradigm of the lower world of sense. It is difficult to decide whether Simon conceives of the three worlds as co-existing together or simply as stages in a process of evolution. For the infinite and self-existent Power is the source of all finite and manifold existence, since it includes all things potentially within itself from eternity. 'This,' says Simon,[2] 'is one power, divided above and below, generating itself, making itself grow, seeking itself, finding itself, being mother of itself, father of itself, sister of itself, spouse of itself, daughter of itself, son of itself, μητροπάτωρ, the root of the entire circle of existence.' The originating principle of the universe is styled 'the Standing One,' ὁ ἑστὼς, στάς, στησόμενος.[3]

The highest world was unfolded from the Unbegotten Fire by means of three pairs of roots called respectively Mind (Νοῦς) and Thought (Ἐπίνοια), Voice (Φωνή) and Name (Ὄνομα), Reason (Λογισμός) and Desire (Ἐνθύμησις).[4] In each of the six roots the infinite Power resides simultaneously and in its entirety, potentially but not actually: the roots are regarded as aspects of the Supreme, having no independent existence of their own, while their addition together is necessary to complete the fullness of his being.[5] Together with their source these six roots, which are named 'Powers' (δυνάμεις), constitute a hebdomad. The intermediate world is also composed of a hebdomad, the head of which answers to the boundless Power of the primal world and is similarly styled 'the Standing One.' He, like his prototype, is both male and female and generates a similar chain of three pairs, or syzygies, of emanations, which are named Æons. The roots of this second world—Heaven and Earth, Sun and Moon, Air and Water[6]—correspond to the hierarchy of abstract principles in the primal world and form the archetypes or ideal patterns of the phenomena of the sensible world. The lower world came into being from chaotic matter quickened by the breath of the seventh Power of the intermediate world, who is identified with the Spirit wafted over the face of the waters, 'an image from an incorruptible form which alone reduces all things to order.'[7] The angels and authorities were charged with its government.

By obscure and confused imagery *The Great Announcement* attempts to explain the procession of the two upper worlds from their sources.[8] In the bisexual nature of Power Silence, the female element, which alone possesses the power of conceiving and producing new beings, was originally concealed within the male element, as the thought is concealed within the mind, and was called 'Silence invisible, incomprehensible,' because she has no independent existence until her emission as Thought, just as the thought conceived by the mind becomes comprehensible only by utterance. Each of the roots, like the principles from which they proceed, has a double aspect and is both male and female, since each is the offspring of, and therefore the cause of conception to, that which is above it, and each controls and is a source of being to the Power or Æon below.[9]

Simon's system has been called an 'anthropological pantheism.'[10] In attempting to explain the presence of a multiplicity of being within the indivisible and all-embracing unity of the supreme principle of the universe, he has recourse to the analogy of the processes of human consciousness. In this respect the Gnostic doctrine of emanations anticipates the later theology of the Church, which sought to illustrate the distinctions within the Trinity from the traces of the divine image in man's constitution.

7. Doctrine of redemption in 'The Great Announcement.'—The anthropology of *The Great Announcement* is developed in a paraphrase of the Bible narratives of the Creation and the Fall.

[1] Iren. *adv. Hær.* I. xxiii. 2 (Massuet)=I. xvi. 2 (Harvey): 'Simon autem Samaritanus ex quo universae haereses substiterunt'; cf. Hipp. *Phil.* vi. 20; Eus. *HE* ii. 13; Cyril Hier. *Catech.* vi. 14; Epiph. *Hær.* 21; Augustine, *Liber de Hær.* 1; Theodoret, *Fab. Hær.* i. 1; pseudo-Tertullian, *adv. Omnes Hær.* 1.

[2] Eus. *HE* iv. 7.

[3] *Apol.* i. 26.

[4] Iren. *Hær.* I. xvi. (xxiii.) 1; Hipp. *Phil.* vi. 19; Theodoret, *Fab. Hær.* i. 1: καὶ Ἰουδαίοις μὲν ὡς υἱὸν φανῆναι, πρὸς δὲ Σαμαρείτας ὡς πατέρα κατεληλυθέναι, ἐν δὲ τοῖς ἄλλοις ἔθνεσιν ὡς πνεῦμα ἅγιον ἐπιφοιτῆσαι. Cyril of Jerusalem (*Catech.* vi. 14) says that Simon claimed to have appeared as the Father on Mt. Sinai, as Christ Jesus in seeming but not in the flesh among the Jews, and afterwards as the Paraclete whom Christ promised to send. He has misquoted his authority, confused possibly by some reminiscence of Sabellianism or Montanism.

[5] Epiph. *Hær.* xxi. 3; Hipp. *Phil.* vi. 14.

[6] Hipp. *Phil.* vi. 7–20.

[7] Justin, *Apol.* i. 26. 8: σύνταγμα κατὰ πασῶν τῶν γεγενημένων αἱρέσεων.

[1] Hipp. *Phil.* vi. 9 (p. 247, Cruice).

[2] *Ib.* vi. 17 (p. 259, Cruice).

[3] The same designation occurs for Simon's supreme God in Clem. Alex. *Strom.* ii. 11, p. 456: τὸν Σίμωνα τῷ ἑστῶτι, ὃν σέβουσιν, ἐξομοιοῦσθαι τρόπον βούλονται.

[4] Hipp. *Phil.* vi. 13 (p. 251, Cruice). Both Irenæus and Epiphanius call the second partner in the first pair of roots Ἔννοια, Hippolytus Ἐπίνοια (=Afterthought).

[5] *Ib.* vi. 17 (p. 258, Cruice).

[6] *Ib.* vi. 14.

[7] *Ib.* vi. 15.

[8] *Ib.* vi. 18 (p. 261 f., Cruice).

[9] *Ib.* vi. 18.

[10] Kreyenbühl, *Das Evangelium der Wahrheit*, i. 240.

The seventh Power of the intermediate world, the Father of all, moulded man by taking dust from the earth and fashioned him after His own image and likeness. The image of the Father is the organizing principle in man, since by it alone he attains actuality, just as the Spirit wafted over the face of the waters, *i.e.* Ἐπίνοια, with which it is identified, is the organizing principle of the world of sense.[1] Hence man was originally compounded of two elements—a spiritual and an earthly—and was both male and female, reproducing the nature of the Father, in whose likeness he was made. The primal man, as the image of God and the microcosm, remains in the intermediate world; he is the ideal copy of the men of earth, whose present condition explains their need of redemption. For they are in a fallen state and no longer reflect the perfection of their archetype, since the sexes have been separated. Redemption was apparently represented as the reunion of the sexes, *i.e.* the renewal of man in his original likeness to the Father. Unfortunately the doctrine of redemption survives only in an isolated and very obscure fragment of *The Great Announcement.*[2] Man's nature is the theatre of a conflict arising from the combination within him of two mutually hostile elements, the divine spark both animating and at the same time striving against the previously existing matter from which he was fashioned. Lest it should free itself by returning upwards to its source, whither it continually tends, the soul was divided, and the two parts were imprisoned in male and female bodies. The soul, thus maimed and entangled and subject to changeable generation, is powerless to raise itself into the upper world, until after passing into many bodies it discovers and is conjoined with its affinity. Redemption consists in the deliverance of man from slavery to finite things and his restoration to his original home, and is effected by the gradual reunion of the sexes; the completion of the process would coincide with the regeneration of all things.

8. Affinities of 'The Great Announcement' with Greek philosophy and pagan religion.—The system of *The Great Announcement* is an attempt to reconcile two incompatible things. The popular theology and science of Hellenism provide the matter, but the form of its presentation is determined by reverence for the inspired traditions of its author's nation. In order to commend alien doctrines to his countrymen, he had to discover them in their Scriptures, and allegory supplied the means of penetrating beneath the surface to the deeper meaning which they enshrined. But this device has scarcely modified the substance of the thought, though the violent expedients of interpretation required, while heightening the sense of mystery, have rendered its presentation unnecessarily obscure. As Hippolytus points out,[3] in affirming that fire is the principle of the universe 'Simon' is following Heraclitus, and his teaching about the manifest and hidden properties of which it is composed is simply an echo of Plato's speculations concerning the intelligible and the sensible and Aristotle's distinction between δύναμις and ἐνέργεια. The theory of redemption by the reunion of the sexes is borrowed from the *Symposium*[4] and assimilated by taking Plato's irony seriously. In adopting the method of allegory to reconcile the Jewish Scriptures with Greek science Simon had a forerunner in Philo, and therefore coincidences of thought as well as of expression are not surprising in the two writers. Philo also designates God 'the Standing One'[5] and interprets the story of Adam's creation by reference to the myth of a primal man[6] who is a hermaphrodite. But the use of allegory also opened the door for the immediate influence of Græco-Oriental religion and mythology. For the pretensions of *The Great Announcement* to scientific culture are merely superficial. The history of Greek philosophy had completed a circle. Having arisen as an interpretation of mythology, it had once more become the handmaid of a religion which discovered in primeval tradition a revealed wisdom anticipating all the conclusions of science. The ultimate source of the speculations of *The Great Announcement* is to be found in the cosmogonies of the Greek and Oriental religions modified by astrology. In Orphic speculation the bisexed Phanes begot Heaven and Earth of Night, who as the child and companion of Zeus corresponds to Ἐπίνοια. Zoroastrianism differentiated a hierarchy of personal attributes within the Supreme and depending from Him like links in a chain. And the Egyptian priests, by combining native speculations with Plato's theory of ideas, interpreted the myth of Isis and Osiris as a parable of creation, the child Horus representing the perceptible world which is the image and reflexion of the κόσμος νοητός.[1] The prevalence of Chaldæan astrology, which named the planets after the most important gods of the nations and, by thus identifying the stars with persons, reinforced its teaching as to the influence of the stars on the destiny of the world, made it possible to ascribe personality to cosmological potencies as the rulers of this world (ἀρχαί), each of which presided over particular periods of time (αἰῶνες), while the pessimism which it fostered drove men to depreciate the world of sense as a derivative reflexion of the world of abiding realities under the tyranny of apostate angels.

1 Hipp. *Phil.* vi. 14.
2 *Ib.* vi. 17 (p. 259 f., Cruice).
3 *Ib.* vi. 9 (p. 247, Cruice).
4 Plato, *Symp.* 17 f.
5 *De Nominum Mutatione*, I. 586 (Mangey).
6 *Legg. Allegor.* I. 49 (Mangey).

9. The myth of Helen.—The myth of Helen's redemption, which forms the common tradition of the heresiologists, appeals to the authority of the Greek legend of Helen of Troy, in the shape in which the sceptical mock reverence of Stesichorus[2] developed it. Justin once refers to his lost account of the Simonian doctrine, when he relates that Simon was worshipped as 'the god above all principality, power, and dominion.' Irenæus, Theodoret, and Epiphanius[3] agree in identifying Simon with the supreme God and Helen with Ἔννοια, the first conception of His mind and His agent in creation. Through her He created the angels and archangels, who in turn created the world of men and were charged with its government. Her fall, and consequently the origin of evil in the world, was due to the rebellion of these spirits. For, as she was proceeding forth, they seized her and detained her on earth by imprisoning her in a human body and subjecting her to a series of transmigrations. The motive of the angels is variously given in our different authorities. Irenæus attributes their act to jealousy, because they were unwilling to be looked upon as the progeny of any other being, Epiphanius to concupiscence. In the course of time Ἔννοια passed into the body of Helen of Troy; according to his interpreters, Simon wished to signify by this that Ἔννοια 'was the object of universal pursuit and the eternal cause of strife, wasting the life of her foes until they recant.'[4] Helen was identified with the lost sheep of the parable; for at each new incarnation her ignominy increased until she passed into the body of a prostitute at Tyre.[5] Meanwhile the angels misgoverned the world in their rivalry for pre-eminence. And therefore the supreme God descended, deceiving the successive ranks of the world-ruling angels who barred His passage by 'transfiguring himself in the form of the dwellers of each heaven,' until at last He appeared in the similitude of a man among men and was deemed to have suffered death in Judæa. Simon rescued Helen from her shame and was thus reunited to his affinity, who throughout the ages was awaiting the advent of her consort and redeemer.[6]

10. The conception of salvation.—The myth of Helen is only vaguely connected with the salvation which Simon brought his adherents. Hippolytus declares that Simon, having purified Helen, brought salvation to men by his own discernment (διὰ τῆς ἰδίας ἐπιγνώσεως).[7] Epiphanius records that Simon interpreted the story of the wooden horse as a symbol of the self-destruction wrought by the ἄγνοια of the Gentiles.[8] Salvation therefore consists in γνῶσις. It is possible that the descent of

1 Plutarch, *de Is. et Osir.* 53–56.
2 Hipp. *Phil.* vi. 19 (p. 265, Cruice).
3 Iren. *Hær.* I. xvi. (xxiii.); Theodoret, *Fab. Hær.* i. 1; Epiph. *Hær.* xxi.
4 Cf. Hipp. *Phil.* vi. 19; Renan, *Les Apôtres*, Paris, 1866, ch. xv.
5 Eus. *HE* ii. 13; Hipp. *Phil.* vi. 19; Iren. *Hær.* I. xvi. (xxiii.) 2.
6 Philaster, *Hær.* 29: 'expectabat artem virtutem aliam, id est Magi ipsius Simonis præsentiam.'
7 *Phil.* vi. 19 (p. 263 f., Cruice).
8 *Hær.* xxi. 3: ἔθνη . . . ἕλκουσιν ἑαυτοῖς τὴν ἀπώλειαν.

the Supreme through the ranks of the angels was regarded as initiating a process of redemption; for it was necessary that the redeemer should assume every form of creation that harmony might be restored to the world. In the end Simon promised to bring the world to naught along with the angels. But the dissolution of the world is anticipated by Simon's followers and salvation is partially realized as an already present boon. Origen says that Simon took away from his followers the fear of death, but has probably confused him with his disciple, Menander, who promised his followers that they should never die.[1] The promise of an indefectible salvation sanctioned an antinomian ethic.[2] Simon taught that the precepts of the law and the prophets were inspired by the angels in the desire to reduce men to slavery, but those who believed on him and Helen, since they were delivered from the sinister tyranny of the law, were free to act as they would. For men are saved by his grace and not by good works. The antinomianism of the Simonians issued in libertine conduct and a compromise with heathenism,[3] possibly also in licentious rites.[4] Their docetic theory of the Saviour's passion presupposed that matter was irredeemably corrupt. The soul of the redeemed could contract no pollution from the deeds of the body, and therefore purity of life was a matter of indifference. 'All earth is earth and it makes no difference where any one sows, provided he does sow.'[5]

11. Pagan sources of the myth of Helen.—Epiphanius, when he ascribes the imprisonment of Helen to the concupiscence of the angels, probably has in mind the story of the seduction of the daughters of men by the Watchers, to which the book of Enoch[6] attributes the origin of sin and the fall of mankind. The fundamental ideas of Gnosticism were probably derived from Jewish apocalyptic; but it appealed to the sympathies of the pagan world by the tolerant eclecticism which allowed it to adopt and combine elements from the most diverse religions. The original of Simon's Helen is the moon-goddess of Syria and Babylonia. In the *Clementine Recognitions* Helena is always translated 'Luna.'[7] The theory that Simon was accustomed to borrow from paganism is corroborated by the assertion of the Fathers that he and Helena were worshipped by their sect with the attributes of Zeus and Athene and received the cult-title κύριος and κύρια.[8] Baur suggests that Simon transferred to himself and his consort the cult of the Phœnician sun-god and moon-goddess, Melkart and Astarte; it only required a slight alteration to confuse his own personal name, which was formed from the same root, with that of the former (שֶׁמֶשׁ). But, apart from this theory, there existed a wide-spread cult of the moon-goddess (σελήνη) in Syria and Egypt under the name of Helene; she was identified with Aphrodite, Atargatis, and the Egyptian Isis, who was often represented with horns to betoken her relation to the moon.[9] One feature of the myth of Helen can be traced to the very ancient connexion of the religion of Osiris with Syria (especially with Byblus).[10] According to legend, Isis spent ten years in a brothel at Tyre during the course of her wanderings in search of the scattered limbs of her husband.[11] The imprisonment of Helen is thus only a variant of the many myths relating the degradation of the Queen of Heaven, which all originally symbolized the waning of the moon. The orbit of the moon was, according to the astronomy of the time, the boundary between the realm of light and freedom and the realm of fate. Helen therefore, as the moon-goddess, was suited to be the source of all the distress of the sublunar world.

12. Relation of the myth of Helen to 'The Great Announcement.'—There is no reason to doubt the trustworthiness of Hippolytus or to discredit the authenticity of his quotations from *The Great Announcement.* Writings[12] purporting to be the composition of Simon were certainly current in the sect called after him. And the two traditions of his teaching, though divergent, show unmistakable points of contact. At the head of both systems stand the same pair of beings, the Supreme God with His companion Ἔννοια or Ἐπίνοια, who acts as His agent in the creation of the lower world; and the theosophical speculations of *The Great Announcement* provide a cosmic setting in which the drama of Helen's redemption can be enacted. The greatest divergence appears in the conceptions of salvation respectively characteristic of the two traditions. Whereas *The Great Announcement* regards redemption, consisting in the reunion of the sexes, as the goal to which all things tend and as a universal process whose completion will result in the salvation of all men, in Justin's account the deliverance of Helen is indeed brought about by reunion with her affinity, but this is not co-ordinated to the redemption of the believer as either symbolizing its method or guaranteeing its fulfilment. For salvation is acquired for Simon's adherents simply by faith in himself and his companion. Nevertheless the fundamental idea is the same in both conceptions. The visible world is in a state of distress and tension owing to the mixture of two incompatible elements, and harmony can be restored only by retrieving the spiritual essence which belongs to the upper world from its captivity in the alien kingdom of matter. Just as the imprisonment of Helen, who is the animating breath of God, symbolizes the bondage of the spirit, so her deliverance typifies the redemption of the soul from thraldom to matter and fits her to act as a medium by which her children can regain freedom.

The assertion of Hippolytus[1] that Simon concocted the myth of Helen to conceal his shame from his adherents can be dismissed as a calumny, since, if his disciples followed the example of their master's licence, as the same author states, such a device would be gratuitous. Perhaps the speculations of *The Great Announcement* may be taken as the esoteric doctrines of the sect, the myth of Helen as the popular teaching intended to attract adherents. The allusion to a Greek legend and the adoption of a heathen cult were calculated to appeal to the Hellenized and semi-pagan inhabitants of Samaria; the obviously symbolical form in which this teaching was cast would awaken curiosity by suggesting the possession of deeper mysteries to be imparted later. Eusebius[2] distinguishes the cult of Simon and Helen from τὰ ἀπορρητότερα, the more secret mysteries of the Simonian sect; Epiphanius[3] has distorted the charge that the sectaries were initiated into delirious doctrines by imputing to them the practice of licentious rites.

13. Date and place of composition.—We possess no exact criterion for determining which of these two forms of teaching is prior to the other in date. Since both refer to the NT, both, in the form in which they reached the knowledge of the ecclesiastical writers, must have been composed long subsequent to Simon's historical activities in Samaria. And therefore, since the hypothesis that the leader of the Gnostic sect is a distinct person from the Simon of Acts is entirely unsupported by any proof, both *The Great Announcement* and the myth of Helen must be regarded as products of the Simonian sect fathered on its reputed founder. The starting-point of these speculations was probably the universally attested tradition that Simon claimed divine honours and associated with himself a woman named Helen, whence his followers were sometimes known as the Helenians.[4] Much of the substance of the myth of Helen possibly goes back to the Samaritan

[1] *C. Celsum*, vi. 11. [2] Iren. *Hær.* I. xvi. (xxiii.) 2.
[3] Origen, *c. Celsum*, vi. 11. [4] Epiph. *Hær.* xxi. 4.
[5] Hipp. *loc. cit.* [6] *Ethiopic Enoch*, chs. vi.–ix.
[7] *Rec.* ii. 5–15; cf. *Hom.* ii. 23. John the Baptist's 29 male disciples, with Helena, who counts as half a day, symbolize the 29½ days of the lunar month.
[8] Hipp. *Phil.* vi. 20; Epiph. *Hær.* xxi. 3; Iren. *Hær.* I. xvi. (xxiii.) 3; cf. *Hom.* ii. 23.
[9] Plutarch, *de Malignitate Herodoti*, 12; Pausanias, III. xix. 10; Strabo, xvii. 1; cf. Bousset, *Hauptprobleme der Gnosis*, p. 78 ff.
[10] Cf. Cyril Alex. *Comment. in Isaiam*, xviii. 1 ff.
[11] Epiph. *Ancoratus*, 104.
[12] Epiph. *Hær.* xxi. 3, mentions writings current under the name of Simon; cf. *Clem. Rec.* ii. 38: 'tuis scripturis propriis'; Jerome, *in Mat.* 24[5]: 'Haec quoque inter caetera in suis voluminibus scripta dimittens: Ego sum sermo Dei, ego sum speciosus, ego paracletus, ego omnipotens, ego omnia Dei'; *Apost. Const.* vi. 8: οἴδαμεν ὅτι οἱ περὶ Σιμώνα καὶ Κλεόβιον ἰδώδη συντάξαντες βίβλια 'επ' ὀνόματι Χριστοῦ καὶ τῶν μαθητῶν αὐτοῦ περιφέρουσιν εἰς ἀπατήν; *Præfatio Arabica ad Concilium Nicænum*: 'Sibi autem perfidi isti Simonitae Evangelium effinxerunt quod in quatuor tomos secantes, librum quatuor angulorum et cardinum mundi appellarunt.'

[1] *Phil.* vi. 19. [2] *HE* ii. 13. [3] *Hær.* xxi. 4.
[4] Celsus, *ap.* Origen, *c. Celsum*, v. 62.

Simon himself. For the two references to the NT, by which Helen is compared to the lost sheep and St. Paul's description of the Christian armour (Eph $6^{14ff.}$) is adduced to justify her identification with Athene,[1] may very well be portions of the propaganda of his later followers embodied in the traditional exposition of his teaching. *The Great Announcement*, on the other hand, must have been composed later than the 1st cent. A.D., since its quotations[2] from the NT (1 Co 11^{32}, Mt 3^{10}) are an integral part of the text. There is no difficulty in accepting Samaria as the place of its composition, in spite of its use of Alexandrian allegory, since the Samaritans readily adopted the methods by which the Jews of the Dispersion attempted to reconcile their religion with Greek culture.[3] Just as they imitated the pragmatism of such apologetic historians as Eupolemus and Artapanus[4] in harmonizing the traditions of their race with Greek mythology,[5] so some unknown Samaritan perhaps borrowed from Philo the science of allegory to transform the Pentateuch into a vehicle of Hellenistic theosophy.

14. Relation of the Simonian system to other forms of Gnosticism.—Harnack regards Simon as the founder of 'a new religion, and that a world-religion, upon the principle of embodying all the important articles of the older ones.'[6] Lipsius dismisses the system attributed to Simon as 'an obvious adaptation of the earlier popular Christian Gnosticism, as it was propagated in Syria about the time of Trajan.'[7] The Simonian in its main outlines resembles other Gnostic systems, but is an early and original version of the common type.

Apart from his character as the author of heresy in general, Simon is regarded by the Fathers as in particular a heretic from Judaism. Hegesippus places him at the head of a list of Jewish heresiarchs.[8] Tertullian[9] contrasts him with Marcion and Valentinus and classes him with Hebion, as a typical representative of Jewish and Samaritan heresy. His hostility to Judaism is manifested chiefly by his disparagement of the prophets and his rejection of the moral law. Epiphanius[10] attributes to Simon's followers the doctrine that the God of the Jews was one of the angels of the lower world who created man; but this doctrine, if it ever found a place in the teaching of the sect, is not one of the original tenets of Simonian Gnosticism, and must have been introduced later, probably owing to the influence of Marcion. For Simon's sense of the antagonism between the law and grace did not issue in the antithesis of a just God, the creator of the lower world, and a good God, the creator of the world of light. And just as he is less logical than Marcion, so his hostility to Judaism is less radical than that of the Ophites. The strained interpretation of Scripture characteristic of Simon's system is not peculiar to him, and his use of a pagan legend is parallel to the Gnostic Justin's allegorical interpretation of the myth of Heracles by which Herodotus prefaces his account of the Scythians.[11] But he accepts the Pentateuch as containing a true revelation, and does not read it backwards like the Ophites, who worshipped the serpent as a benefactor for persuading men to taste of knowledge and reverenced the sinners of the OT as saints.

Nevertheless the Simonian system is most closely akin to Ophitism and to Valentinianism, in which the leading characteristics of primitive Gnosticism tend to recover their central position. It must be assigned to a comparatively early date in the history of Gnosticism, since its dualism is by no means absolute. The origin of evil is subsequent to creation; the lower world was willed by the supreme God, and His immediate companion was charged with the task of bringing life to quicken it. And, just as the creation of the lower world is not attributed to the malice of a subordinate demiurge, low in the scale of divine being, or to an act of rebellion in heaven, so the conception of a mediator in redemption is absent: the Most High Himself descends to seek and redeem His companion. In respect of the doctrine of a primal man, Simon's system is closely similar to that of the Ophites. For in that system primal man, who in Simon's system is the image of the Supreme, is identified with the supreme God Himself, and His immediate companion, second man, is His thought[1] (ἔννοια). Simon, however, unlike the Ophites, practises a rigid economy in the number of persons whom he brings upon the stage; this simplicity indicates an early date by contrast with the many differentiations of God among whom the successive parts in the drama of redemption were distributed by the later Gnostics. The actors are reduced to the two essential persons—the fallen deity and the saviour, Helen and Simon; and therefore primal man plays no part in the fall or in redemption, as in the system of Valentinus. But Helen (Ἔννοια) is a variant of the fallen female principle whom Valentinus named Sophia or Achamoth. The Fathers were quick to notice points of similarity: pseudo-Tertullian identifies Helen with Sapientia;[2] Simon himself is reported to have called her Προύνικος and Holy Spirit.[3] The earthly degradation of Helena emphasizes the thought that the exile of the fallen goddess here below, as the thrall of her own creation, itself calls for a redeemer. In the system of Secundus,[4] a disciple of Valentinus, Sophia is distinguished from her abortive offspring Achamoth, and remains throughout in the upper world, where she is redeemed by becoming the saviour's bride. This transference of scene from the earthly to the celestial world is the product of reflexion and marks the Valentinian as a later version of the myth of a fallen goddess.

The points of contact with the earlier forms of Gnosticism are more frequent in the case of the myth of Helen than in that of the system of *The Great Announcement*. The device, *e.g.*, by which Helen's redeemer escaped the notice of the world-ruling angels resembles the descent of Jesus, as it was sung by the early Naassene sect of the Ophites;[5] the theory of emanations in *The Great Announcement* resembles Valentinus's developed doctrine of syzygies. The doctrine of transmigration does not play so conspicuous a part in most Gnostic systems as in *The Great Announcement*, where it is represented as a process by which the seeds of divine light are sifted and purified from their imprisonment in evil matter; perhaps the theory was originally employed to justify the one feature which is absolutely peculiar to this system. For the identification of the supreme God and His consort with historical persons distinguishes the doctrine of the Simonians as unique in the many forms of Gnosticism.

[1] Iren. *Hær.* I. xvi. (xxiii.) 2; Epiph. *Hær.* xxi. 3.
[2] Hipp. *Phil.* vi. 14, 16.
[3] According to *Hom.* ii. 22, Simon Magus was educated at Alexandria.
[4] Cf. fragments preserved by Eusebius, *Præp. Evang.* ix. 18, 27.
[5] Cf. the fragments of a Samaritan historian preserved by Alexander Polyhistor, in J. Freudenthal, *Alexander Polyhistor* (*Hellenist. Studien*, i. ii.), Breslau, 1875, p. 82.
[6] *EBr*^{9} xxii. 80^{b}.
[7] *Die apokryphen Apostelgeschichten und Apostellegenden*, ii. 36.
[8] *Ap.* Eus. *HE* iv. 22.
[9] *De Præscr.* 10.
[10] *Hær.* xxiv. 1, attributed to Basilides borrowing from Simon.
[11] Hipp. *Phil.* v. 25; cf. v. 7 for a similar use of Homer by the Ophites.

[1] Iren. *Hær.* I. xxix.
[2] Ps.-Ter. *Hær.* i. 1.
[3] Epiph. *Hær.* xxi. 2.
[4] Iren. *Hær.* I. xi. 2.
[5] Hipp. *Phil.* v. 10.

15. Simon Magus in the character of a Gnostic in the 'Clementines.'—The chief catchwords of Simonian Gnosticism were known to the author of the original work which underlies the *Clementine Homilies* and *Recognitions*. Both versions of this early Christian romance give accounts of Simon's history,[1] which agree so closely that they must have been derived from a common source.

Simon, a native of Gitta in Samaria, was educated in Alexandria, where he learned the wisdom of the Greeks and became an adept in magic. He later became a disciple of Dositheus, the successor of John the Baptist, and supplanted him in the leadership of the sect. He announced himself to be the highest Power, exalted above the creator of the world, and called himself 'the Standing One,'[2] signifying that he would be established for ever and would never see corruption. He associated with himself Helena, who is called Luna in the *Recognitions*, and had been the only female disciple of John the Baptist. According to his account, she had come down from the highest heavens and was Wisdom, the mother of all things; the Greeks and barbarians who fought at Troy were contending for an image of the truth, being ignorant that she was the consort of the one and only God, with whom she dwelt in heaven.

The *Clementines* are acquainted with the distinctive catchwords of Simonian Gnosticism in each of its forms; but, since this acquaintance is only superficial, no attempt is made to avoid confusion with other similar systems. Helen is confused with the Sophia of Valentinus, and her identity with Helen of Troy is explained by the theory that the object of contention between the Greeks and barbarians was a phantom of the celestial Wisdom, not by the theory of transmigration. The claim that Simon himself was the supreme God is confused with the distinction between the supreme God and the subordinate creator, which is characteristic of later forms of Gnosticism, but is not original in the Simonian. Subsequently in the romance Simon expounds the doctrine of an unknown and perfect God and contrasts Him with the creator, whose imperfection and weakness are manifest.[3] St. Peter is the champion of the Monarchian theory in the form in which it was developed early in the 3rd cent., and especially at Rome in the controversy of the Church with Gnosticism. Moreover, doctrines similar to those taught by his historical disciple, Menander, are placed in the mouth of the Simon of the *Clementines*. Menander promised his followers that they should never die. Similarly Simon is represented as denying a future resurrection, since the knowledge of its heavenly origin makes the soul at once superior to its bodily prison.[4] Simon is attacked in the *Clementines*, not as the leader of a particular Gnostic sect, but as the author and typical representative of Gnostic heresy in general.

16. The attack on St. Paul under the mask of Simon Magus.—In addition to this hostility to Simon Magus as the representative of Gnosticism, which is the fundamental characteristic of the disputes between St. Peter and Simon described in the *Clementines*, there are undoubted traces of a veiled attack on St. Paul, most frequently in the disguise of Simon, but in one instance under cover of the designation 'the enemy' (ὁ ἐχθρὸς ἄνθρωπος). St. Paul is attacked (1) for having stirred up persecution against the infant Church; (2) on account of his claim to equal authority with the apostles in virtue of the personal call heard in the vision on his way to Damascus; (3) for his opposition to the original apostles and their emissaries, in particular for the rebuke which he administered to St. Peter at Antioch.

(1) In the *Recognitions*[5] Paul the persecutor is referred to as 'the enemy'; and, since the section in which this designation is used in the *Recognitions* also occurs in the table of heads given in the last chapter of the third book, it must also have stood in the lost *Circuits of Peter*, which underlies both the *Homilies* and the *Recognitions*. St. Peter describes how an enemy raised a tumult in the temple and thus interrupted the preaching of James, when the conversion and baptism of the people at Jerusalem was imminent; after throwing James headlong from the top of the steps, this man was dispatched with a mission from Caiaphas to Damascus. The designation does not occur in the *Homilies*, but in the epistle[1] prefixed to the book St. Peter, its putative author, attributes the rejection of his own preaching to the lawless and babbling teaching of the enemy. This is an allusion to St. Paul, not in the character of a persecutor of the Church in his unconverted days, but as the apostle of the Gentiles.

(2) In other portions of these works, when the disguise of Simon is adopted, the hostility to St. Paul is much more covert. In one passage of the *Homilies*,[2] in which this hostility is generally more violent than in the *Recognitions*, St. Peter refutes Simon's contention that revelation in visions is more certain than that given in personal intercourse. There is an obvious allusion to St. Paul's vision on the road to Damascus and to the claims to an equal apostolate which he based upon it. After suggesting that the real purpose of his vision of Jesus was to confound him as the adversary of the faith, St. Peter proceeds: 'But if he made you an apostle after a brief discipleship in a single vision lasting but an hour, prove it by preaching His message, by interpreting His doctrines, by loving His apostles, by not contending against me, His companion.' But St. Paul supported his authority not merely by the single vision on the road to Damascus; he also claimed to have visions[3] subsequent to his conversion. This claim is perhaps disparaged in the *Recognitions* by words put into the mouth of St. Peter,[4] when disputing with Simon concerning the power of imagination to rise above the apprehension of things perceived by the senses: 'But if you think that there is easy access for your mind above the heavens, and that you are able to conceive the things that are there and to apprehend that immeasurable light . . .' The miracles which St. Paul wrought are perhaps discredited by ascribing Simon's ascendancy over his followers to his skill in magic.[5]

(3) (*a*) During the earlier part of his mission to the Gentiles at least St. Paul was involved in bitter controversy with opponents who claimed to be emissaries of the apostles, and sometimes even with the original apostles. His opponents accused him, on the one hand, of undue laxity in dispensing his converts from fulfilling the obligations of the Jewish law and in allowing them to compromise with heathenism by eating meats offered to idols, and, on the other hand, of a desire to establish his own authority and to make capital out of an insincere profession of Christianity by preaching himself rather than Christ,[6] which issued sometimes in undue severity in the exercise of the power to which he pretended.[7] Some of their taunts are quoted in St. Paul's apologias. He was accused of pleasing men and not God,[8] and was referred to as an 'enemy' (ἐχθρός)[9] and a 'deceiver' (πλάνος).[10] Similarly, according to the *Clementines*, it is Simon's whole mission to commend himself under shelter of his professed allegiance to the truth which the apostles teach; St. Paul's supposed laxity in the matter of meats offered to idols is parodied in an episode at Tyre, where Simon is reported to have entertained the people to a feast on sacrificial flesh;[11] Simon is also called the 'enemy' and the 'deceiver,' who misleads his converts into receiving him as a friend and a preacher of the truth.[12]

(*b*) St. Paul perhaps sometimes provoked his opponents by the strong terms of condemnation with which he retaliated. 'I would,' he says, 'they were even cut off which trouble you';[13] and he pronounces a curse on any one, though an angel from heaven, who should preach any other gospel than that which he had preached.[14] In the *Homilies* and *Recognitions* the charges levelled by St. Paul at his opponents are retorted on Simon Magus. Just as he called them 'false apostles . . . transforming themselves into the apostles of Christ,'[15] so St. Peter denounces Simon as a false apostle, who opposes the true (ψευδαπόστολος).[16] In the *Recognitions* there is an echo of the phrase which St. Paul used to expose the seductions of these false teachers: 'for Satan himself is transformed into an angel of light.'[17] Simon, since he is the Devil's minister, is described as 'the Evil One transforming himself into a splendour of light.'[18] On one occasion St. Paul denounced one of the original apostles himself. The passage in the *Homilies*[19] in which St. Peter confutes Simon's theory of the greater certainty of a revelation obtained in visions is a counterpart to St. Paul's withstanding St. Peter at Antioch.[20] St. Peter says that Simon had pitted himself against a solid rock, the foundation of the Church, and was slandering the preaching which he had heard from Christ, and then, referring to a phrase used by St. Paul to the Galatians,[21] he proceeds, 'or

---

1 *Hom.* ii. 22–26, *Rec.* ii. 5–15.
2 ὁ Ἑστώς (*Hom.* ii. 22, *Rec.* ii. 7, 72).
3 *Rec.* ii. 38–70, esp. 53 ff.; cf. *Hom.* ii. 2, xvi. and xviii.
4 *Rec.* ii. 13, 57, *Hom.* ii. 22.
5 *Rec.* i. 70–73 ('homo inimicus').

---

1 *Ep. Petri*, 2.
2 xvii. 19.
3 2 Co 12^{2-4}.
4 *Rec.* ii. 65.
5 *Ib.* ii. 9, x. 66.
6 2 Co 5^{11} 4^{5} 1^{12}.
7 2 Co 1^{24} 2^{1} 10^{8} 13^{10}.
8 Gal 1^{10}.
9 Gal 4^{16}.
10 2 Co 6^{8}.
11 *Hom.* vii. 3.
12 *Ib.* ii. 18: καὶ ὁ ἐχθρός ὡς φίλος ἀποδέδεκται. . . . καὶ πλάνος ὢν ὡς αληθεύων ἀκούεται; cf. *Hom.* xviii. 10 for Simon's pleasing of men: ἐπειδὴ ἀρεσκόντως τοῖς παροῦσιν ὄχλοις οὕτως ἔφης.
13 Gal 5^{12}.
14 Gal 1^{8}.
15 2 Co 11^{13}.
16 Cf. *Hom.* xvi. 21, *Rec.* iv. 24: 'pseudoprophetas et pseudoapostolos.'
17 2 Co 11^{14}.
18 *Rec.* ii. 18.
19 xvii. 19.
20 Gal 2^{11-21}.
21 Gal 2^{11}: κατεγνωσμένος.

if you call me "condemned," you accuse God who revealed the Christ to me.'

St. Paul in the person of Simon is attacked not for repudiating the law, but for his opposition to the original apostles, which he justifies by a claim to equality with them. It is true that St. Peter, in the epistle prefatory to the *Homilies*, describes his doctrine as lawless; but his real sin is the assumption of the right to expound the law in opposition to the twelve apostles whose peculiar prerogative it is, as the custodians of the teaching of 'the True Prophet' and His personal disciples.[1] It is the mission of St. Peter to resist the false apostle, Simon Magus, as Moses resisted the magicians in Egypt,[2] and to warn his hearers not to listen to any preacher who has not received a testimonial from James, the Lord's brother. The offence of this false gospel is recognized as inevitable; for the True Prophet in His last charge to His apostles had foretold that a preacher of error must necessarily precede the true gospel in order that by his overthrow the truth might be the more clearly established.[3] Simon Magus, like St. Paul, is a chosen vessel, but of the Evil One.[4] He is the deceiver who is chosen by the Devil to go as St. Peter's forerunner to the Gentiles with a counterfeit gospel.[5] Simon Peter, according to the *Clementines*, is the real apostle to the Gentiles, who brings them the salvation to which they have been called by following in the footsteps of Simon-Paul and correcting the errors which he teaches.[6] The contest between St. Peter and his adversary in both forms of the romance ends in the complete defeat of the latter, when Faustinianus, the father of Clement, in the form of Simon publicly recants his errors at Antioch in language reminiscent of St. Paul's style.[7] The sham Simon confesses that he was brought to make this avowal because an angel of God had scourged him by night; this is an allusion to the affliction which St. Paul attributed to an angel of Satan sent to buffet him.

In the episode of the *Recognitions* which describes the persecution of the Church by St. Paul in his unconverted days the future apostle, under the designation of 'the enemy,' is clearly distinguished from Simon, since he himself denounces the apostles as disciples of the magician.[8] Moreover, the theory that Simon plays a providential part in the dissemination of the true gospel as the false forerunner of the apostles is only a particular application of the Helxaistic doctrine, generally characteristic of the *Homilies*, that good and evil necessarily go in pairs.[9] But there can be no doubt that St. Paul is attacked under the mask of Simon Magus; for, whereas elsewhere in these books Simon does not believe in Jesus at all, in these passages he is represented as falsely claiming to have received a commission from Christ in opposition to the claims of the original apostles.

17. Modern critical theories based on the equation Simon = Paul.—Starting from the evidence which the *Clementines* afford of a veiled attack on St. Paul in the person of Simon Magus, inspired by Jewish-Christian or Ebionite hatred of the Apostle of the Gentiles, Baur put forward the theory that the figure of the arch-heretic and false apostle Simon Magus was simply invented by his opponents as a caricature of St. Paul, and that the traditions of a conflict between St. Peter and Simon Magus had their origin in the contest between St. Peter and St. Paul. Baur was followed by the critics of the Tübingen school—Volkmar, Hilgenfeld, Lipsius, Zeller, and others. And more recently his thesis has been defended by Kreyenbühl, Krenkel, Preuschen, and Schmiedel. The theory consists of two main contentions: (1) the story of Simon Magus in Acts is a modification of a Jewish-Christian tradition, whose original anti-Pauline tendency has been forgotten; and (2) the ecclesiastical traditions of St. Peter's travels and labours among the Gentiles, and especially of his martyrdom at Rome, are unhistorical and had their origin in the journeys and labours of St. Paul.

1 *Rec.* ii. 55, iv. 35. 2 *Rec.* iii. 56, iv. 35.
3 *Hom.* xi. 35, ii. 17 f.: πρῶτον ψευδὲς δεῖ ἐλθεῖν εὐαγγελίον ὑπὸ πλάνου τινός. St. Peter is ὁ μετ' ἐκεῖνον ἐληλυθώς, καὶ ἐπελθὼν ὡς σκότῳ φῶς, ὡς ἀγνοίᾳ γνῶσις, ὡς νόσῳ ἴασις.
4 *Rec.* iii. 49: 'Et ideo magis deflendus est Simon, quod vas electionis factus est maligno'; cf. Ac 9^{15}, σκεῦος ἐκλογῆς.
5 *Hom.* xi. 35, ii. 17 f., *Rec.* iv. 34.
6 *Rec.* iii. 65, 68. 7 *Rec.* x. 61, 66 = *Hom.* xx. 13, 19.
8 Cf. *Rec.* i. 70.
9 *Hom.* ii. 15, 33, xix., xx. *passim*; cf. *Rec.* iii. 59–61, viii. 53.

(1) The story of St. Peter's resistance to Simon Magus at Samaria was originally intended as a counterpart to St. Paul's condemnation of St. Peter at Antioch,[1] representing the victory of the Prince of the Apostles and the complete discomfiture of his opponent. The rapid conversion of Simon is intended to question the genuineness of St. Paul's sudden change from a persecutor to a disciple. The personal pretensions of Simon Magus are distortions of the claims of St. Paul. Simon Magus proclaiming himself to be some great one, and acclaimed by the Samaritans as 'the great power of God,' is St. Paul claiming that he lives by the power of God, or that the power of Christ rests upon him, or that his gospel is the power of God.[2] St. Paul's pretensions to equality with the apostles are caricatured in the request of Simon to receive the power of conferring the Holy Spirit by the laying on of hands. For Simon offering money for this power is really St. Paul attempting to purchase the apostleship by the contributions of the Gentile churches to the poor saints in Jerusalem.[3] St. Peter's rebuke to Simon is understood only when it is seen to be a reflexion on the conduct of St. Paul. 'Thou hast neither part nor lot in this matter' is a refusal to acknowledge his right to the κλῆρος τῆς ἀποστολῆς.[4] 'I perceive that thou art in the gall of bitterness' is an allusion to his bitterness in controversy. This theory presupposes that tendency in an opposite direction is also present in the Acts; that St. Luke in fact wrote the work as a pamphlet in defence of St. Paul, suppressing some facts and modifying others, with the object of representing the relation of the original apostles to his master as always harmonious. He has inadvertently preserved legends of an anti-Pauline tendency owing to the fact that their original purpose has been forgotten.

(2) Lipsius maintained that the tradition of St. Peter's mission to the Gentiles and martyrdom at Rome was an Ebionite fabrication, whose motive was a desire to detract from the glory of St. Paul's labours by misrepresenting him as the false forerunner of the preacher of the true gospel, which corresponded to the standards of Jewish-Christian orthodoxy. St. Paul is already subordinated to St. Peter in Acts, since the latter is there represented as initiating the mission to the Gentiles. The legend of St. Peter's visit to Rome was later adopted in a Catholic sense, when it was realized how easily it might be used to subserve the interests and ambition of the Roman Church. Its intention was thereby fundamentally transformed. Whereas originally the purpose of St. Peter's presence in Rome was represented to be the final discomfiture of the false apostle, *i.e.* Simon-Paul, in the Catholic version of the legend St. Paul is introduced as co-operating with him in the foundation of the Roman Church and as his second in the contest with Simon.

18. Arguments used in support of the Tübingen theory. — Three arguments have been chiefly urged in support of Baur's thesis that the legend of Simon Magus originated in a distortion of St. Paul: (1) there is evidence of a bitter polemic against St. Paul in his lifetime, emanating from Jewish-Christian circles; (2) the *Clementine Homilies* and *Recognitions* embody traditions of a time much earlier than the date of their compilation; (3) all the versions of the apocryphal *Acts of St. Peter* betray a similar hostility to St. Paul under the mask of Simon Magus, and go back to the same cycle of legends as the *Clementines*, since the legend of St. Peter's travels in Palestine and the legend of his visit to Rome presuppose each other.

(1) That St. Paul was engaged during his lifetime in bitter controversies with opponents who disparaged his claims to be an apostle and appealed against him to the authority of the original apostles is sufficiently attested by the evidence of his own epistles. The internal evidence of his own writings is corroborated by external evidence. Epiphanius[5] mentions certain fictitious discourses current among the Ebionites, in which St. Paul was accused of being the son of a Greek father and mother and which ascribe to him an exaggerated hostility to the law, due, as they assert, to his disappointment in failing to obtain the hand of the priest's daughter in marriage, after he had become a proselyte. Evidences of an attack on St. Paul, sometimes veiled and sometimes open, have been discovered in the Apocalypse, in the Gospels, and in certain incidents recorded in Acts. It is ultimately against him that the condemnation of the Nicolaitans is directed in the Revelation of St. John;[6] his laxity had led men to violate the commands of the Apostolic Council at Jerusalem, to eat things sacrificed to idols, and to commit fornication; his phrase, 'the depths of God,' is parodied in the condemnation of those of Thyatira 'who know not the depths of Satan.'[7] St. Paul is the enemy in the parable, who oversowed the wheat with tares.[8] St. Luke in the Acts has attempted to wrest to St. Paul's honour certain episodes invented to discredit him, but their original

1 Gal $2^{11ff.}$. 2 2 Co 12^{9} 13^{4}, Ro 1^{16}, 1 Co 1^{18}.
3 Ac 11^{29} 24^{17}, 1 Co 16^{1}, 2 Co 8^{4}, Ro 15^{25}, Gal 2^{10}.
4 Cf. Ac 1^{25}. 5 *Hær.* xxx. 16.
6 Rev $2^{6.15}$. 7 Rev 2^{24}; cf. 1 Co 2^{10}.
8 Mt 13^{25}.

intention can be detected; *e.g.*, the incident of his deification at Derbe[1] originally parodied his claims to speak with the authority of Christ; his champion goes out of his way to explain the reasons of St. Paul's light imprisonment under Felix,[2] which was probably urged against him to his reproach. The story of St. Paul's contest with the sorcerer Elymas or Bar-jesus in Cyprus[3] is introduced to counterbalance the story of St. Peter's conflict with the magician Simon, and 'thus anticipates the later apocryphal legends in which St. Paul in alliance with St. Peter combats a caricature of himself.'[4]

(2) It is contended that the *Clementine Homilies* and *Recognitions* preserve the earliest form of the legend of St. Peter's conflict with St. Paul in the disguise of Simon Magus, and therefore embody a Jewish-Christian myth of the 1st cent. all but contemporary with the first generation of Christians The *Homilies* and the *Recognitions* relate the story of the wanderings of Clement of Rome in Egypt and Palestine in search of the lost members of his family, during which he accompanies St. Peter and witnesses his conflict with Simon Magus at Cæsarea and Laodicea. Neither gives the romance in its original form, but both are recensions of a common written source, the *Circuits of Peter*, known to Origen[5] (*c.* 240), which itself had an archetype in the *Preachings of Peter* (*c.* 200). Whether any of these versions was made at Rome has not been decided; there is a general tendency among recent critics to accept the opinion that they were all composed in Syria. The *Circuits of Peter*, fragments of which have been preserved by Epiphanius,[6] presents no very definite sectarian features, and the view has been maintained (*e.g.*, by C. Bigg) that the *Homilies* represent a recast of an orthodox work by an Ebionite editor. But it is probable that the Ebionite features, including the hatred of St. Paul, were present in the *Preachings of Peter*, the earliest known ancestor of the whole literature. Lipsius proposed to bridge the gulf of over 100 years which separates this work from the 1st cent. A.D. by conjecturing the existence of an earlier Ebionite *Acts of Peter*, and supported his hypothesis by the contention that the account of Simon Magus given in the *Apostolic Constitutions* is a summary of the contents of this book. But the discovery of the *Syriac Didascalia* disproved his hypothesis; for this work (the earlier form of the *Apostolic Constitutions*), the composition of which was contemporary with that of the *Preachings of Peter*, contains no reference to a visit of Simon Magus to Cæsarea. Lipsius's attempt to reconstruct an original 1st cent. romance relating the contest between St. Peter and Simon has since been abandoned, and the champions of the Tübingen theory now have recourse to the hypothesis of an oral tradition. The *Homilies* are undoubtedly composite and embody elements of the tradition not contained in the *Circuits*—*e.g.*, the dispute with Apion concerning idolatry; the hypothesis of an oral source, it is maintained, would explain the confusion of characteristics in the person of the Simon of the *Homilies* and *Recognitions*.

(3) The legend of St. Peter's contest with Simon at Rome and his subsequent martyrdom is given in a series of apocryphal *Acts*. The earliest of these, the *Actus Petri cum Simone*, is a heretical composition; the πράξεις Πέτρου καὶ Παύλου, preserved in two recensions, is an orthodox recast of the legend.[7] St. Paul appears in both forms of the legend: in the earlier he departs from Rome for the evangelization of Spain, before St. Peter's arrival; in the latter he acts as St. Peter's second in the dispute with Simon and is martyred with him.

(*a*) These books preserve traces of a polemic against St. Paul under the mask of Simon similar to that carried on in the *Clementines*. In the *Actus Petri cum Simone* St. Peter denounces Simon as a cheat and an impostor,[8] using the very same term (*planus*) with which Simon was stigmatized in the *Clementines*, and St. Paul by his opponents. Moreover, this term of reproach is used of St. Paul himself and coupled with that of *magus* by apostate Christians,[9] who had been misled by Simon. Simon is also called 'the enemy.'[10] Traces of hostility to St. Paul are more numerous in the Catholic *Acta*, which perhaps represents an orthodox recension of a document of distinctly anti-Pauline tendency, since Paul is associated with St. Peter to combat his own caricature. St. Paul in the disguise of Simon is attacked for his inconsistent attitude to the question of circumcision.[11] Simon warns the emperor Nero against the apostles, because they are circumcised. The apostles answer that Simon himself is circumcised and suggest that his object is to deceive souls by his strict conformity to the Jewish law. The favour which Simon enjoys with Nero is perhaps a reflexion on the mild treatment which St. Paul was supposed to have secured during his captivity at Rome by his recommending obedience to the power of the emperor. The pretended beheading of Simon and his trick of substituting a ram for himself[1] are possibly malicious perversions of the legend of St. Paul's martyrdom. The story of Simon's attempted flight perhaps originated in St. Paul's claim to have been caught up into the third heaven in a vision. For in the *Actus Petri cum Simone*[2] the object of Simon's flight is not to regain his ascendancy over the people by a proof of his magical powers, but to manifest his divinity by ascending to God, whose power he is.

(*b*) The conflicts between Simon and St. Peter are located in the Clementine literature entirely in Palestine and Syria; in the apocryphal *Acts* in Rome. But the Roman contest is not a mere echo of the Syrian. For the books of apocryphal *Acts* presuppose earlier conflicts in Palestine; the *Clementines* foreshadow a final conflict in Rome. The *Clementines* regard St. Peter's commission to follow and refute Simon as the divinely appointed method of bringing salvation to the Gentiles. St. Peter continually contemplates Rome as the goal of his travels,[3] and his adversary prophesies that Rome will be the scene of his crowning glory, when he will be adored as a god.[4] The apocryphal *Acts*, and especially the *Actus Petri cum Simone*, mention a previous victory of St. Peter over Simon in Judæa and give details of one incident[5] which place it beyond doubt that these allusions do not refer exclusively to the contest recorded in Acts.[6] Lipsius found in this agreement of the *Clementines* with the apocryphal *Acts* an argument in support of his hypothesis of 1st cent. Ebionite *Acts of St. Peter*; but, now that this hypothesis has been abandoned, the original oneness of the tradition underlying these two classes of literature is still urged in support of the theory that the veiled attack on St. Paul under the mask of Simon Magus in the *Clementines* derives from a 1st cent. legend orally handed down, since the anti-Pauline interest seems to be the basis on which they agree.

19. The theory that Simon-Paul = Simon of Cyprus.—The attempt to answer the objection, Why was the name Simon adopted to conceal St. Paul?, has given rise to an ingenious theory. Originally it was supposed that the name was given him to contrast him with St. Peter as the false Simon with the true. But later the suggestion was made that it was given him at the time of his imprisonment under Felix. Josephus[7] mentions a courtier of Felix, a Jew of Cyprus, named Simon, whom he used as a go-between in his intrigue with Drusilla, the wife of Azizus, king of Emesa, since he pretended to be a magician. It is just possible, though very improbable, that this person may have been the same as Simon of Gitta, Josephus having confused his native place with Kition, *i.e.* Cyprus. But that St. Paul was ever accused of using the disguise of this man's name for the purpose of doing such a favour for Felix is out of the question. Those who maintain the theory disagree as to who were responsible for the calumny, Kreyenbühl attributing it to the Jews who accused St. Paul before Felix, Krenkel to his Jewish-Christian opponents.

20. Criticism of the Tübingen theory.—Pushed to its logical conclusion, this theory amounts to a denial that the Samaritan sorcerer ever existed; he originated as a caricature of the apostle Paul, and his later characteristics either arose out of the *rôle* which the Apostle of the Gentiles was represented by Jewish-Christian hatred to have played in the early history of the Church or were added when his connexion with St. Paul had been forgotten and the tradition had been adopted by the Catholic Church. Simon Magus became the father of heresy, because St. Paul was attacked in his person as the typical false apostle, whose mission is to oppose the true; since Gnosticism was the most serious danger to the Catholic system in the 2nd and 3rd centuries A.D., it was inevitable that the arch-heretic should be represented as a teacher of Gnostic error.

Preuschen[8] has discovered the origin of the conception of Antichrist as a false teacher—as opposed

1 Ac 14^{11-13}. 2 Ac 24^{22-26}.

3 Ac 13^{6}.

4 Krenkel, *Josephus und Lucas*, p. 186.

5 *In Matth.* iii. 894 (Delarue), 'Petrus apud Clementem.'

6 *Hær.* xxx.

7 *Acta Apostolorum Apocrypha*, i., ed. R. A. Lipsius and M. Bonnet, Leipzig, 1891–1903.

8 Ch. 12: 'planum et deceptorem.'

9 *Ib.* ch. 4: 'Et magis Simone se exaltante in quibus faciebat . . . Paulum magum vocantes, alii planum, et tam magnae multitudinis constabilitae in fide omnes dissoluti sunt.'

10 *Actus Petri cum Simone*, ch. 5: 'inimicus'; *Passio SS. AA. Petri et Pauli*, ch. 43: πρόδηλος ἐχθρός ('hostem et inimicum domini').

11 *Passio SS. AA. Petri et Pauli*, ch. 42 ff.

1 *Passio SS. AA. Petri et Pauli*, chs. 31 f., 56.

2 *Actus Petri cum Simone*, ch. 31.

3 *Hom.* i. 16, *Rec.* i. 13, 74, iii. 64 f., 69; *Epistle of Peter*, 1 (St. Peter chosen as the fittest to evangelize the West).

4 *Rec.* ii. 9, iii. 63.

5 *Actus Petri cum Simone*, chs. 5, 9, 17.

6 *Ib.* ch. 17 (the imposture practised on Eubola). The allusion to conflicts in Judæa, Palestine, and Cæsarea in *Passio SS. AA. Petri et Pauli*, ch. 28, is of course a reference to the *Clementine Recognitions*.

7 *Ant.* xx. ii. 3. 8 In *ZNTW* ii. [1901] 169 ff.

to the earlier conception of him as a persecuting monarch—in the figure of Simon-Paul, and appeals to the evidence of the Christian apocalypses. Simon Magus is detected in the Antichrist of the Christian *Apocalypse of Elias*, in the second beast of the Revelation of St. John,[1] who deceived the people of the earth by his signs and caused men to worship an image of himself, and also in a false teacher prophesied in the *Sibylline Oracles*.[2] The latter foretell the advent of a beast (Βελίαρ) from the Sebastenes, who would mislead three classes of men—the elect, the lawless Hebrews, and the Gentiles. If the mention of the Sebastenes (*i.e.* the people of Augustus) alludes to Samaria (Sebaste), the passage must be an interpolation, since it is inserted in a context which probably refers to the triumvirs and Cleopatra, *i.e.* to a time before Octavian had assumed the name Augustus, though it is possible that allusion is made to the events of A.D. 70. But it is improbable that, even if Simon is a caricature of St. Paul, he was so important a figure at this early date as to be identified with Antichrist. The passage more probably alludes to the worship of the emperor. Most of the defenders of Baur's thesis, while still maintaining that St. Paul is attacked in the disguise of the sorcerer, have been convinced that Simon was a historical personage, whether they identify him with the Samaritan impostor whose doings are recorded in the earlier uninterpolated version of the story in Acts or with the hypothetical 2nd cent. leader of a Gnostic sect.

Nevertheless it is still contended that the Pauline features in the composite figure of the Simon of the *Clementines* are older than the Gnostic, and are in fact the cause of the vitality of his legend. By the time that the earliest Clementine romance was written St. Paul's peculiar contribution to the development of Christianity had been forgotten, and the uniqueness of the part that he had played in the mission to the Gentiles was obscured by the growing reverence of the Catholic Church for St. Peter. And yet it is just this claim of St. Paul to be the Apostle of the Gentiles that is traversed and distorted in the controversy of St. Peter with Simon Magus. The *Clementines* repeat the reproaches which were made against St. Paul in his lifetime. Schmiedel[3] thinks it 'a psychological impossibility' that any one should venture to attack the memory of a now revered apostle in the 3rd cent. A.D. But this is exactly what the author of the *Recognitions*, at least, has done; the allusion to St. Paul's persecution of the Church is too obvious for the writer to have repeated it without realizing that he was bitterly attacking the memory of the Apostle of the Gentiles under the name of 'the enemy.' Moreover, the currency among the Ebionites of writings which attacked St. Paul without any disguise is well attested for a period much later than the date of the composition of the *Clementines*.[4] It is more probable to suppose that the terms with which St. Paul is reproached—'the deceiver' and 'the enemy'—were handed down in the Ebionite sect through long generations of conscious hatred, against the adversary of their sectarian narrowness, than that they survived because they were embedded in a tradition whose original intention was no longer understood. The intensity of the hatred manifested against St. Paul in the *Clementines* is due to the fact that it was still felt; their inability to make any progress or to forget any prejudice was the distinguishing characteristic of the Ebionites. The intense hatred manifested against Simon Magus as the representative of Gnosticism is self-explained.

1 Rev $13^{11\text{-}16}$.
2 ἐκ δὲ Σεβαστήνων ἥξει βελίαρ μετόπισθεν (*Orac. Sibyll.* iii. 63).
3 *EBi* iv. 4549.
4 Epiph. *Hær.* xxx. 16.

The figure of the champion of Gnostic error was chosen as a disguise for St. Paul, probably because certain tenets characteristic of this heresy—*e.g.*, the antinomianism—were supported by an appeal to his epistles and arose from an exaggeration of his doctrines. An Ebionite of the 2nd or 3rd cent. could justify the long cherished hatred of his sect and discredit its object by pointing to the results of his teaching. Moreover, whenever the figure of Simon Magus was adopted as a disguise of St. Paul, he was most probably regarded as a distinct historical person, since the sting of caricaturing an adversary under the name of another consists in the historical infamy associated with that name.

The *a priori* improbability of the theory is corroborated by a closer examination of the evidence on which it rests. In the dispute at Laodicea described in the *Homilies*, where the attack on St. Paul is most violent, Simon is the mouthpiece of the doctrines of Marcion. An innuendo against St. Paul would not be out of place, since Marcion's antithesis of the law and grace was simply an exaggeration of Paulinism. In the apocryphal *Acts of Peter* Simon, so far from representing a rebellion against Jewish-Christian exclusiveness, is a champion of Judaism in its controversy with the Church. This work probably belonged to the Leucian collection, and, if so, there is positive evidence that it could not possibly have been written under Ebionite influence; according to Photius,[1] the Leucian *Acts of Peter* taught that the God of the Jews was evil and that Simon was his minister. Moreover, the contention that St. Paul was introduced into the later recensions of the Acts with the object of distinguishing him from Simon is untenable, since the tradition of his association with St. Peter at Rome, mentioned by Dionysius of Corinth,[2] is older than the tradition of St. Peter's encounter with Simon at Rome, of which Hippolytus gives the earliest extant account. Justin Martyr's authority for the visit of Simon to Rome is weakened both by his mistaken conjecture about the statue and by the confusion which makes him date it in the reign of Claudius. Probably the story of this visit is entirely legendary, and the later traditions about it arose by the transference from Syria to Rome of the scene of St. Peter's victory in the conflict with Simon. For both the *Clementines* and the earliest extant version of the *Acts of Peter* reproduce Justin's story of the statue,[3] just as they are both acquainted with some of the catchwords of the Gnostic system ascribed to him.

21. The real Simon Magus.—In each of the three types of early Christian literature from which our information about Simon Magus is derived he is represented to have claimed divine honours and to have set up a rival religion to Christianity after his encounter with the apostles, by attempting to transfer to himself the worship which men paid to Jesus.

The founder of the Gnostic sect of the Simonians himself claimed to be the supreme God, and this claim distinguishes the system attributed to him from all other forms of Gnosticism. Justin's mistake about the statue was probably suggested by his knowledge of this claim. Simon and his consort were worshipped by their followers with the attributes of Zeus and Athene. The *Clementines* represent the object of his journey to Rome to have been that he might there be adored as a god. The story of Simon's flight was perhaps invented

1 *Bibliotheca*, cxiv.
2 *Ap.* Eus. *HE* II. xxv. 8; ταῦτα καὶ ὑμεῖς διὰ τῆς τοσαύτης νουθεσίας τήν ἀπὸ Πέτρου καὶ Παύλου φυτείαν γενηθεῖσαν Ῥωμαίων τε καὶ Κορινθίων συνεκεράσατε, κ.τ.λ.
3 *Rec.* ii. 9, iii. 63; *Actus Petri cum Simone*, ch. 11 (Marcellus erects a statue 'Simoni Juveni Deo'), ch. 4 (the acclamation of his followers, 'Tu es in Italia deus').

with the purpose of ridiculing his pretended apotheosis. In the *Actus Petri cum Simone* Simon undertakes to fly to God, after he had been exposed by St. Peter, and leaves the earth with this invocation to the Father:

'Me, the Standing One, thy son, they wished to overthrow; but having refused to agree with them, I have come to thy self.'[1]

The self-immolation of Peregrinus Proteus[2] on his pyre at the Olympic games had familiarized the Christians of the 2nd cent. with the pagan craze for deification. The details of the episode were probably suggested by an anecdote of Suetonius:[3] at games held in the presence of Nero an acrobat personated Icarus and, when he fell, besprinkled the emperor with his blood.

Origen[4] tells us that the Simonians never confess Jesus as the Son of God, but say that Simon is the power of God. It is difficult to understand why Simon was ever regarded as a Christian heretic. For, though he claimed that Jesus was an incarnation of himself, he is more frequently represented as rivalling the religion of Christ's followers and travestying His passion. Simon's promise to rise again the third day, after he had been buried or beheaded, which is related with variations in detail both by Hippolytus and in the apocryphal *Acts*, is a parody of the resurrection of Jesus Christ, and is the early version of the story of Simon's death which was later superseded by the legend of his attempted flight. His aspect as a false Christ is older than his aspect as a false apostle.

Considering the independence of the three classes of documents to which we owe our information about Simon, there is a strong presumption that the points in which they agree contain the original kernel of truth. And these points of agreement tend to vindicate the authenticity of St. Luke's account of his doings. The author of Acts probably obtained his information about this incident in the early history of the evangelization of Samaria from Philip the Deacon, to whom its inception was due, while staying in his house when accompanying Paul to Jerusalem.[5] Simon Magus was a Samaritan Messiah similar to Dositheus and Cleobius, with whom he appears to have had some connexion; he assumed some of the cognate traits of the pagan θεῖος ἄνθρωπος. Celsus[6] had seen such enthusiasts in Samaria and heard them proclaim their gospel:

'I am God, or the Son of God, or the Divine Spirit. The dissolution of the world is at hand, and I come. . . . I desire to save and ye shall behold me again coming in the power of heaven. Blessed is he, whoso pays me reverence now, but on the rest I will cast everlasting fire.'

Later, when he came into contact with Christianity, Simon conceived the idea of using the new movement for his own ends. The gospel of the Samaritan saviour already contained in germ the peculiar doctrines of Gnostic salvation, and it was natural that his later followers approximated more and more to the common type of Christian Gnosticism, with which it had always had close affinity; but this approximation never entirely obscured the original relation of the sect to its founder or the central place which he occupied as the object of worship. Simon probably owed his reputation as the father of heresy to the fact that he is the only heretic mentioned in the NT and that he opposed the apostles, to whom, according to the theory of the 2nd cent., was committed the custody of the catholic and apostolic faith.

22. Subsequent history of the Simonian sect.—According to the Fathers, Simon was succeeded in the headship of the sect by his disciple Menander.

[1] *Actus Petri cum Simone*, ch. 31.
[2] Lucian, *de Morte Peregrini*; cf. Tertullian, *ad Martyras*, 4: 'Peregrinus qui non olim se rogo immisit.'
[3] Suetonius, *Nero*, 12; cf. Dio Chrysostom, *Orat.* xxi. 9.
[4] *C. Celsum*, v. 62.
[5] Ac 21[8ff.].
[6] *Ap.* Origen, *c. Celsum*, vii. 9.

The Simonians were also known as the Helenians[1] and the Ἐντυχηταί.[2] They were ill famed for their practice of magical arts.[3] The author of the tract *de Rebaptismate* says that they made fire to appear on the water when they administered baptism.[4] The history of the sect is a record of dwindling numbers. Justin Martyr mentions a school of Simonians existing in Rome in the time of Antoninus Pius. Theodoret[5] asserts that they spread chiefly in Syria, Phrygia, and Rome. Origen[6] says that in his time (*c.* A.D. 230) Simon had no followers anywhere outside Samaria, and not more than 30, if that, in his native land. But his evidence must be discounted, since Eusebius[7] speaks of them as still numerous in the reign of Constantine, though compelled to conceal themselves or to dissemble their faith. Epiphanius[8] says that Gitta had by his time sunk from a populous town into a village, and that there were still some Simonians in existence.

23. The survival of the legend of Simon Magus.—The encounter of Simon Magus with the apostles in Samaria was quoted by the canons of the Church as the stock instance of the sin of attempting to purchase or confer spiritual gifts or preferment in return for money, and 'simony' (*q.v.*) became a technical term of ecclesiastical law. Simon's reputation as the author of heresy lived on long after the last remnant of his sect had vanished. In a Byzantine Psalter of the 9th cent. A.D. the overthrow of Simon Magus by St. Peter is depicted as the Biblical prototype of the triumph of orthodoxy won over the errors of the iconoclasts at the 7th Ecumenical Council of Nicæa.[9] The story of Simon Magus survived in the popular mythology of the Middle Ages and contributed some elements to the legend of Faust. Faust, like Simon, enjoyed the companionship of Helen of Troy, and the incident of the *homunculus* which he made by chemistry originated in the legend that Simon had fashioned a boy from air and, having slain him, used his soul for the purposes of magic.[10]

LITERATURE.—(1) On Simon generally the articles in the dictionaries: R. A. Lipsius, in Schenkel's *Bibel-Lexicon*, v. 301 ff.; W. Möller, in *PRE*[2] xiv. [1885] 246 ff.; H. Waitz, in *PRE*[3] xviii. 351 ff.; G. Salmon, in *DCB* iv. 681 ff.; A. C. Headlam, in *HDB* iv. 520 ff.; P. W. Schmiedel, in *EBi* iv. 4536 ff.; A. Harnack, in *EBr*[9] xxii. 78 ff.; St. George Stock, in *EBr*[11] xxv. 126 ff.; J. E. Roberts, in *DAC* ii. 493 ff.

(2) On the Gnostic system attributed to Simon: A. Hilgenfeld, *Die Ketzergeschichte des Urchristenthums*, Leipzig, 1884; F. Legge, *Forerunners and Rivals of Christianity*, London, 1916, vol. i. ch. vi.; W. Bousset, *Hauptprobleme der Gnosis*, Göttingen, 1907.

(3) On the Tübingen theory: (*a*) F. C. Baur, 'Die Christuspartie in Korinth,' in *Tübinger Zeitschrift für Theologie*, 1831, pt. iv. p. 116 ff.; A. Simson, *Zeitschrift für die historische Theologie*, xi. [1841] 15 ff.; G. Volkmar, in *Tübinger Theologische Jahrbücher*, xv. [1856] 279 ff.; R. A. Lipsius, *Die Quellen der römischen Petrus-Sage*, Kiel, 1872, *Die apokryphen Apostelgeschichten und Apostellegenden*, Brunswick, 1887, ii. 28 ff.

(*b*) Later developments: E. Preuschen, *ZNTW* ii. [1901] 169 ff.; J. Kreyenbühl, *Das Evangelium der Wahrheit*, Berlin, 1900–05, i. 174–284; M. Krenkel, *Josephus und Lucas*, Leipzig, 1894, pp. 178 ff.

(4) On the *Clementines*; G. Uhlhorn, *Die Homilien und Recognitionen des Clemens Romanus*, Göttingen, 1854; A. Hilgenfeld, *Die clementinischen Recognitionen und Homilien*, Jena, 1848; F. J. A. Hort, *Notes Introd. to the Study of the Clementine Recognitions*, London, 1901; C. Bigg, 'The Clementine Homilies,' in *Studia Biblica*, ii. [1890] 157 ff.; A. C. Headlam, in *JThSt* iii. [1901] 41 ff.; G. Salmon, in *DCB*, *s.v.* 'Clementine Literature,' i. 567 ff.

[1] Celsus, *ap.* Origen, *c. Celsum*, v. 62.
[2] Clem. Alex. *Strom.* vii. 17.
[3] Iren. *Hær.* I. xvi. (xxviii.) 3.
[4] Pseudo-Cyprian, *de Rebaptismate*, 16.
[5] Theodoret, *Fab. Hær.* i. 1 f.
[6] Origen, *c. Celsum*, vi. 11, i. 57; in vi. 11 Origen says that Simon had no followers anywhere in the world, and Dositheus only 30.
[7] Eus. *HE* ii. 13.
[8] Epiph. *Hær.* xxi.
[9] The Barberini Psalter in the Vatican; cf. J. B. Bury, *A Hist. of the Eastern Roman Empire*, A.D. 802–867, London, 1912, p. 432.
[10] *Hom.* ii. 26, *Rec.* ii. 15.

(5) On Simon and the Faust legend; T. Zahn, *Cyprian von Antiochien und die deutsche Faustsage*, Erlangen, 1882, esp. pp. 110–116.
G. N. L. HALL.

SIMONY.—**1. Definitions.**—'Simony' is a word of somewhat varied meanings. The most general definition of it perhaps is 'buying or selling spiritual gifts or offices'; and it is named from Simon Magus (*q.v.*), who, when he 'saw that through the laying on of the apostles' hands the Holy Ghost was given'—some outward manifestation seems to have accompanied the gift, over and above the laying on of hands—offered them money that they might give him the same power (Ac 8[18ff.]). The evil here mentioned has proved to be of wide ramifications in the Christian Church, and it may safely be said that no age and no country has been quite free from it; when it is suppressed in its more obvious forms, it takes a veiled form and becomes the more difficult to overcome.

In its primary sense simony is the buying or selling of sacraments or sacramental ordinances—*e.g.*, the exacting or paying of money for baptism or the Eucharist, or especially for the conferring or receiving of holy orders, including the episcopate. But the term was soon extended so as to include more indirect forms of the same evil, such as the buying or selling of ecclesiastical offices, and the exacting or giving of undue promises in order to obtain ordination or preferment, even if no money passes, and the improper procuring of presentations to benefices. At a somewhat later date distinctions were made between *munus a manu*, when money or something of value is given or received, *munus ab obsequio*, when promises are exacted or given for the performance of the duties of a benefice in some way which the particular Church has not prescribed, and *munus a lingua*, when preferment is given or procured, not because of the merits of the person presented, but because of the influence of an outside party.

2. Early period.—The earliest known instance of simony after NT times is that of Paul of Samosata in N. Syria, bishop of Antioch A.D. 260–270, and a celebrated Monarchian heretic.[1] Simony certainly appears to be included in the charges made against him by the bishops in their letter quoted by Eusebius.[2] Paul enriched himself at the expense of the Church, but no doubt this was chiefly owing to his holding the office of *ducenarius* under Zenobia, queen of Palmyra, and to his selling justice in that capacity. There was, however, not much temptation to simony as long as the Church was poor, and suffering under persecution. In the 4th cent. the evil began to show itself in widely separated parts of the Christian world. At the Council of Elvira or Illiberis in S. Spain (*c.* A.D. 305) fees for baptism were forbidden; the gift received gratuitously by the priest (*sacerdos*) was not to be made a gain of.[3] The practice of exacting baptismal fees was also blamed in the East. Gregory of Nazianzus in Cappadocia[4] (A.D. 381) refers to candidates for baptism being kept back thereby; he says that baptismal offerings are not necessary, for the real offering is oneself. The *Apostolic Constitutions*, a Syrian work written *c.* A.D. 375, speaking of Simon Magus and of his trying 'to obtain the invaluable (ἀτίμητον) grace by purchase,' bids its readers avoid oblations to God's altar which do not come from a good conscience;[5] and this is found, expressed less explicitly in the *Older Didascalia* (3rd cent.) from which the later writer borrows.[6] The *Apostolic Canons* (*c.* A.D. 400, from the same school as, or perhaps compiled by the author of, the *Constitutions*) forbid giving or receiving the episcopate, presbyterate, or diaconate for money, and mention Simon Magus.[1] The Council of Sardica (the modern Sofia in Bulgaria; *c.* A.D. 347) denounces bribery in the election of a bishop,[2] and forbids the translation of bishops from one see to another, as this (it says) is always done from avarice, for 'no bishop has been found to go from a better to an inferior see';[3] translations were evidently common in practice. But the genuineness of these canons is disputed.

An extension of simony already appears in the 4th century. At the Council of Antioch *in encæniis* (A.D. 341) a bishop is forbidden, even on his deathbed, to appoint his successor;[4] and in the *Apostolic Canons*[5] a bishop is forbidden to give the episcopate to his brother, son, or other kinsman, or to ordain those whom he himself desires (so explicitly the Latin, and less plainly some texts of the Greek), for the gift of God may not be sold by him or made a matter of inheritance.

From the 5th cent. onwards we have numerous indications of the prevalence of simony. At the ecumenical Council of Chalcedon (A.D. 451) not only is ordination for money to any order (including those under the diaconate) strenuously forbidden, for it is turning the grace which cannot be bought (τὴν ἄπρατον χάριν) into merchandise, but equally are those who give or accept bribes for appointments to Church stewardships and other ecclesiastical posts condemned, as well as the middlemen who negotiate these transactions.[6] The *Novellæ* of the emperor Justinian I., issued A.D. 534 to 565, prescribe an oath against simony to be taken at the consecration of a bishop by the elect and by the electors.[7] A large number of councils deal with the subject.[8] A Roman synod under Pope Symmachus, held A.D. 499 soon after his election, forbade canvassing and promises of votes before papal elections in the life-time of the reigning pope[9]—an early instance of what became a notorious evil in the Middle Ages. The 2nd Council of Orleans (A.D. 533 or 536) forbids ordination for money.[10] The 3rd Council of Braga (in Portugal, A.D. 572) forbids bribes for ordination, and the exaction of fees for baptism, chrism (confirmation), and the consecration of a church.[11] At the Council of Rheims (*c.* A.D. 625) a bishop is forbidden to take anything from another Church for his own advantage or for that of his Church.[12] At the 4th Council of Toledo in Spain (A.D. 633) bishops are forbidden to appropriate Church property;[13] and the 8th (A.D. 653) strongly condemns simony.[14] At the 11th (A.D. 675) the demanding, or even accepting, of fees for baptism, chrism, and ordination is forbidden.[15]

Nor was the East less emphatic. The 'Trullan' Council of Constantinople (A.D. 691 or 692) forbids ordination for money or the demanding of compulsory fees for the Eucharist.[16] The 2nd Council of Nicæa (A.D. 787) was strong against simony,[17] whether in the case of a bishop demanding money or the like from other bishops or clergy or monks or in the case of any one obtaining a position in the Church by payment.

1 See art. SAMOSATENISM.
2 *HE* vii. 30.
3 Can. 48.
4 *Orat.* xl. 25, 'de Bapt.'
5 iv. 7.
6 F. X. Funk, *Didascalia et Constitutiones Apostolorum*, Paderborn, 1905, i. 226 f.

1 Can. 29 [30]; these canons are probably based on earlier regulations.
2 Can. 2.
3 Can. 1.
4 Can. 23.
5 Can. 76 [75].
6 Can. 2.
7 cxxiii. 1, cxxxvii. 2.
8 Most of the following references may be seen in C. J. Hefele's *Hist. of the Councils of the Church*, Eng. tr., 5 vols., Edinburgh, 1872–96, and all in J. D. Mansi's *Sacrorum Conciliorum . . . Collectio*, 31 vols., Florence and Venice, 1759–98.
9 Hefele, iv. 51.
10 Can. 3, 4.
11 Can. 3, 4, 5, 7.
12 Can. 21.
13 Can. 33.
14 Can. 3.
15 Can. 8, 9.
16 Can. 22, 23.
17 Can. 4, 5.

But perhaps the writer in the early period who deals most with the subject is Pope Gregory the Great (A.D. 590–604). In his epistles he constantly speaks of it, especially with reference to ordination. He declares that in parts of Gaul and Germany no one was ordained without a fee,[1] and so also in Achaia[2] and Epirus.[3] He exhorts Brunichild, queen of the Franks, to prevent ordination for money, and 'selling the Holy Spirit.'[4] Gregory declares in his letter to Isaac, patriarch of Jerusalem,[5] that he has heard that in the Churches of the East no one is ordained without bribes. In ii. 23 he urges an Illyrican bishop not to allow any ordinations for money or entreaties (here we have the *munus a lingua*), but only for merit. In ii. 48 he says that the Donatists bribed a Catholic bishop in Numidia to allow one of their own bishops to be appointed in the place where he lived; and in iii. 48, writing to the same correspondent (Bishop Columbus), he strongly deprecates the ordination of boys, and all venality in ordination or 'influence or entreaty.' In iv. 27, writing to Januarius, bishop of Cagliari (Calaris) in Sardinia, he forbids the receiving of any fee for ordinations, marriages of clerics, or the veiling of virgins (nuns), unless it is voluntarily offered. A Roman synod under Pope Gregory (A.D. 595) forbade any compulsory payment for the pallium—the vestment sent by the papal see to archbishops, at least from the 6th cent. onwards.[6]

Accusations of simony against individuals in this period must be received with some caution. It was very easy to charge a theological opponent with this crime. A few instances may be mentioned. For that of Paul of Samosata see above. Ambrose accuses the Arian bishop, Auxentius, of simony.[7] At Chalcedon Ibas, bishop of Edessa, was accused (falsely) of taking money for ordinations, as well as of spending the money of the Church on himself.[8] Maximus, bishop of Salona in Illyricum (Dalmatia), was accused to Gregory the Great of having been consecrated bishop by simony,[9] but was afterwards declared innocent. In many such cases it is obvious that a charge of simony was a convenient weapon when the real accusation was one of heresy or schism.

Most of the prohibitions of the Councils in this period on the subject of simony were embodied in the *Corpus juris canonici*.

3. Mediæval period in the West.—The form of simony which chiefly gave trouble in the Middle Ages was the buying and selling of ecclesiastical preferment. But two councils in the 12th cent. deal with compulsory fees: that of Tours (1163) forbids the exaction of payment for the admission of monks, or for appointments to monastic or clerical posts, or for burials, chrism, and unction with holy oil;[10] the 3rd Lateran Council (1179), for enthroning bishops, installing abbots, instituting presbyters to benefices, burials, benediction or marriages, or for the other sacraments.[11] Thomas Aquinas[12] (1226–74) treats of simony at some length. He defines it as buying or selling anything spiritual or annexed to what is spiritual (*spirituali annexum*), since spiritual grace, being freely given, cannot be equated to any earthly price.[13] It is therefore simony to give or accept anything for the sacraments as a price, though not as a stipend for priest's sustenance.[14] It is clear from the objections which Aquinas answers that it was the common practice to exact money for the

1 *Ep.* v. 53, 55, 57. 2 *Ib.* v. 58.
3 *Ib.* vi. 8.
4 *Ib.* ix. 11; see also, for ordinations in Gaul, ix. 106, 109, 110, xi. 55, 59, 61.
5 *Ib.* xi. 46. 6 Hefele, iv. 427.
7 *C. Auxent.* 21. 8 Hefele, iii. 362.
9 Gregory, *Ep.* vi. 3, etc. 10 Can. 6.
11 Cap. 7. 12 *Summa Theol.* II. ii. qu. c.
13 *Ib.* art. 1. 14 *Ib.* art. 2.

sacraments—for baptisms and masses, for absolutions under the name of penance, for ordinations, marriages, and so forth. And a widely spread practice such as this perhaps prevented the 'angelic doctor' from showing with his usual perspicacity the real distinction in these cases between simony and an innocent offering. A priest might demand fees for baptism on the plea that it was the only way by which he could get his living, but the demand would be simoniacal; if the fee is exacted as a condition of giving the sacrament, it comes under the head of simony, though a free-will offering is permissible and laudable. Aquinas goes on[1] to observe justly that accepting and giving anything for the support of those ministering spiritual things is not simony unless there is any intention of buying or selling. Here comes in the same distinction as that made above. In art. 4 Aquinas explains what he means by buying or selling things which are 'annexed to what is spiritual,' and gives as an example that a bishop who demanded as a condition of collating a person to a benefice that part of the income thereof should be paid to himself would be guilty of simony. He then goes on[2] to deal with *munus ab obsequio* and *munus a lingua*, terms which had been in use long before his day; both these, he says, are simoniacal just as if money were received and paid.[3] Finally Aquinas deals[4] with the proper penalty for simony, for which see below, § 6. It is noteworthy in view of the history of the times that the question is raised whether the pope can commit simony. Aquinas answers[5] that the pope can incur the guilt of simony like any other man, for the higher the place filled, the greater the sin. The things of the Church are his only as dispenser, not as possessor.

That in England simony was considered a grave offence during this period is seen from the *Salisbury Cathedral Statutes* of 1392,[6] which, though only mentioning these cases incidentally, refer them expressly to the cognizance of the bishop himself. It was one of the regulations at Salisbury that the clergy were not to receive the oblations of the laity on Easter-day even after Mass, because it indicated avarice;[7] this was to prevent simoniacal exactions (see below). The extent of simony in mediæval England is seen by the denunciations of Chaucer (*c.* 1340–1400) in his *Canterbury Tales*. The 'Persones Tale' (*de Avaritia*) says:

> It 'is the gretteste sinne that may be, after the sinne of Lucifer and of Antecrist' . . . 'be it by catel, be it by procuringe, or by fleshly preyere of his freendes,' *i.e.* by *munus a lingua*, of which Chaucer says that, if the nominee is worthy, it is not simony.

There were, indeed, many exceptions. Not all the clergy were guilty in this respect. Of the 'poore persone of a toun' Chaucer says:

> 'Ful looth were him to cursen for his tythes,
> But rather wolde he yeven, out of doute,
> Unto his poure parisshens aboute
> Of his offring, and eek of his substaunce.
> He coude in litel thing han suffisaunce.'[8]

The evil of simony had been prevalent all over the West under Popes Boniface IX. (1389–1404) and John XXIII. (1410–17), and the Council of Constance on 21st March 1418 decreed the vacation of offices obtained thereby; but the decree was half-hearted, and had little effect.[9] Offices in the curia were openly sold under Innocent VIII. (1484–92);[10] and the elections to the papacy of Alexander VI. (1492), and of Julius II. (1503) were openly

1 Art. 3. 2 Art. 5. 3 See above, § 1.
4 Art. 6. 5 Art. 1.
6 Ed. C. Wordsworth and D. Macleane, London, 1915, p. 304.
7 W. H. Frere, *The Use of Sarum*, Cambridge, 1898–1901, i. 162.
8 *Prologue*, i. 485 ff.
9 M. Creighton, *Hist. of the Papacy*, London, 1882–94, i. 402, 418.
10 *Ib.* iii. 154.

promoted by bribes.[1] A stronger effort to abolish the evil was made by the Council of Trent in the 16th century. Bishops were forbidden[2] to receive money for ordinations or for letters dimissory, or the like, though their notaries might charge certain fees; and so[3] with regard to benefices and other ecclesiastical posts, and the making of conditions (the *munus ab obsequio*; see above, § 1). The council in sess. xxii. ('Decr. de observandis et evitandis in celebratione missae') forbids the importunate exaction of alms for masses as being simoniacal.

The extension of the meaning of 'simony' is illustrated by some chapters of the *Scotichronicon* of the Scottish historian John of Fordun, written c. A.D. 1385.[4] Thus an abbot who gained his office by undue persuasion, and another who procured the succession to his office for his nephew,[5] are judged to have been guilty of simony, even though no money passed. And this name is even given to the offence of a layman of Richard Cœur de Lion's court who received gifts from Saladin. It is also applied to the case of a monastery of women which would admit only nuns who brought a certain dowry to the community.

In mediæval Scotland offerings by parishioners came to be regarded as dues, and were exacted in spite of explicit regulations to the contrary, that 'neither sacraments nor sacramentals' (*e.g.*, sprinkling of the people with holy water or benediction by the priest at Mass) 'were to be sold.'[6] It was the custom (though explicitly forbidden by law) for the priest to retain the host in his hand on Easter-day till the communicant paid his dues.[7] Offerings for masses, baptisms, burials, confession (called in England 'shrift-silver'), and the churching of women were common, and were exacted as of right, the priest refusing otherwise to officiate or to absolve.[8] A relic of a quasi-compulsory offering by women when churched is still found in the last rubric of that office in the Book of Common Prayer; the woman 'must offer accustomed offerings' (in 1549 'her chrism [chrisom, the white garment of the baptized child], and other accustomed offerings'). The exaction of 'kirk richts and Pasche offrands' and the withholding of the sacraments till they were paid was denounced at the last provincial synod of the unreformed Church in Scotland, held in 1558.[9] In 1483 a Scottish Act of Parliament was passed to prevent money being taken out of Scotland to pay for promotion and for pleas in Rome; for no ecclesiastic could expect preferment without paying the cardinals and officials in Rome. A striking instance is the appointment of a bishop of Brechin in 1488, the deeds relating to which are printed in the appendix to the *Registrum Episcopatus Brechinensis*.[10]

4. The East.—As the Church in the West became richer, the form which simony took had reference chiefly to the presentation to benefices. But in the East, especially in the Far East, it seems that the ecclesiastical authorities have had to deal with the evil chiefly in connexion with the exaction of what are called in England 'surplice-fees'—the exaction, not as a matter of free-will offering, but of right, of money for baptisms and other offices. In many cases the Eastern clergy have had to live principally on those fees. And, it is to be feared, the exaction of money for ordination (under whatever name the fees are charged) has been very common. Yet the decisions of the *Apostolic Canons* (which were believed to have apostolic authority) and of Chalcedon[1] are held to be still binding.

In Egypt simony was first introduced as a regular system by the Coptic patriarch Michael (Chail) III. (A.D. 881–884), who exacted large sums from bishops-elect to meet the demands of the Musalmān government, and this system continued for several hundred years.[2] In India, among the Christians of Malabar, one of the efforts of the Synod of Diamper under the Portuguese (1599) was directed towards the extirpation of simony.[3]

With regard to the other minor Eastern Churches, it may suffice to quote the canons of two of them. The West Syrian (Monophysite or Jacobite) canons given by H. Denzinger[4] say that a bishop may not receive a gift for ordination or for giving judgment; for in this and similar communities the civil authorities allow the bishop to be somewhat of a judge in ecclesiastical or quasi-ecclesiastical matters, such as marriage and divorce. Further, priests and deacons are forbidden to receive a gift from those to whom they distribute the sacraments;[5] and those who confer or receive the priesthood by payment of a gift are to be submitted to the penance of adulterers and fornicators.[6] The East Syrian (Nestorian) *Sunhadhus*, or Book of Canon Law, deals with ordinations to the episcopate, presbyterate, or diaconate, effected by bribes,[7] and with improper appointments to the episcopate of persons who have been under penitential discipline;[8] and forbids the exaction of fees for baptism, 'because baptism is spiritual circumcision,' though it allows the giving of voluntary offerings.[9] In spite of canons, however, bribery for ordination has always been the bane of the Far Eastern Churches. A particularly bad case occurred in the 6th cent., when one Abraham was consecrated through simony bishop of Beith Lāphaṭ in the south of Persia, with the result that he and his three consecrators were excommunicated by two succeeding patriarchs.[10]

5. Modern Anglican regulations.—After the Reformation simony comes into view in England almost entirely with regard to preferment, but the statute 31 Elizab. cap. 6 imposed fines on those who conferred or received holy orders simoniacally, as well as voiding presentations to benefices so made. In the English canons of 1604 an oath is directed to be taken by those who are about to be admitted to office, that they have not obtained it by simoniacal payment, contract, or promise.[11] This applies to ordinations as well as to admissions to benefices and other ecclesiastical offices. The same oath is prescribed in the present canons of the Church of Ireland.[12] Under modern conditions this regulation serves indirectly to protect the clergy from undue pressure by patrons of livings to make promises not required by the Church for the performance of their duty (the *munus ab obsequio*). This is seen very clearly in the canons of the Episcopal Church in Scotland. A provision of long standing enacts that no promise

1 *Hist. of the Papacy*, iii. 159 f., iv. 60; for many other instances see B. Platina's *Lives of the Popes*, ed. W. Benham, 3 vols., London, 1888.
2 *Canones et decreta*, sess. xxi. 'de Reform.' § 1.
3 Sess. xxiv. 'de Reform.' §§ 14, 18.
4 viii. 35–38; ed. W. Goodall, Edinburgh, 1759, i. 486 ff.
5 See above, § 2.
6 J. Robertson, *Concilia Scotiæ: Statuta Ecclesiæ Scoticanæ*, Edinburgh, 1866 (Bannatyne Club), ii. 52; J. Dowden, *The Medieval Church in Scotland*, Glasgow, 1910, p. 179.
7 *Registrum Episcopatus Aberdonensis*, Edinburgh, 1845 (Spalding Club), ii. 33.
8 Dowden, p. 180.
9 *Ib.* p. 183; this chapter has many other interesting instances of the simoniacal exaction of fees.
10 Edinburgh, 1856 (Bannatyne Club); Dowden, p. 328.

1 Above, § 2.
2 M. Fowler, *Christian Egypt*, London, 1901, pp. 76, 98.
3 G. B. Howard, *The Christians of St. Thomas and their Liturgies*, Oxford, 1864, p. 39.
4 *Ritus Orientalium*, Wurzburg, 1863–64, i. 488, can. 124.
5 *Ib.* i. 493, can. 29.
6 *Ib.* i. 495, can. 32 f.
7 viii. 6.
8 viii. 5.
9 vi. 6, can. 7.
10 W. A. Wigram, *An Introd. to the Hist. of the Assyrian Church*, London, 1910, p. 193 f.
11 Can. 40.
12 Can. 25.

other than the ordinary canonical subscriptions is to be required or given in the case of an episcopal election as a condition of the election, or of the confirmation of the election by the comprovincial bishops.[1] Another, dating from 1911, forbids (with certain reservations) any bishop, priest, or deacon about to be admitted to an office or order to make any promise, or to lay himself under any obligation inconsistent with his retaining his lawful liberty of judgment in performing his duties.[2]

But there is a danger of simony, direct or indirect, to which any system of ecclesiastical patronage is liable unless stringent precautions are taken. The sale of advowsons and of next presentations has given much trouble in the Church of England. The prohibition of the sales *in toto*, if the system of patronage is maintained—and there are at least equally great dangers in popular election of the clergy by the parishioners—would lead to the patronage in many cases being held by persons who had no interest in the parish. On the other hand, if patronage is bought and sold indiscriminately, simony must be the result. One way in which this has in the past been the case is by exacting a resignation bond from the presentee to a benefice—*i.e.* a promise to resign after a definite period. General resignation bonds have long been forbidden, but a statute of the early part of the 19th cent. (9 Geo. IV. cap. 94) allowed such a bond to be given if it were in favour of some person named in the bond. The great reform in this matter was effected in England in 1898, when the English Benefices Act, among other provisions, required sales of advowsons to be registered, forbade sales of next presentations, or sales by auction of any right of patronage except as part of an estate, and invalidated agreements to exercise a right of patronage in favour of a particular person. The new declaration against simony was of a very stringent character.[3] For this reform the Church of England is chiefly indebted to the persistence of Archbishop E. W. Benson, who, however, did not live to see the Act passed.[4]

6. Penalties for simony.—In the earlier authorities the penalty prescribed, in the case of all parties concerned, was excommunication for laity and monks (who at first were almost always laymen, and therefore judged under that category), and, in addition, deposition and deprivation for the clergy. But, as time went on, the penalty of excommunication seems by degrees to have been relaxed. Aquinas in his *Summa*[1] says that the proper penalty for simony is for a man to be deprived of that which he has got thereby, as is laid down in canon 2 of Chalcedon.[2] And the Nestorian *Sunhadhus*[3] decrees deposition,[4] and only in some cases excommunication.[5] In England the Elizabethan statute[6] imposes fines and voidance of the benefice.

But the Council of Chalcedon,[7] saying that a layman or monk who has been guilty of simoniacal transactions is to be anathematized, and that the cleric is to be deposed, says also that the bishop who receives the money endangers his own office (βαθμός). Excommunication is also prescribed in the Sardican canons;[8] in the *Apostolic Canons*,[9] expressly for both giver and receiver 'as Simon Magus [was excommunicated] by Peter';[10] also at the 3rd Council of Braga.[11] Subsequent practice, however, varied. The 2nd Council of Orleans orders deposition of a priest ordained simoniacally, without mentioning the punishment of the ordainer;[12] the Council of Rheims orders deposition of a bishop appropriating the property of other Churches, saying that he is to be deposed 'as he cannot be excommunicated.'[13] The 8th Council of Toledo[14] adds imprisonment in a monastery to excommunication ('anathema'); the 11th[15] in some cases adds a flogging. The 'Trullan' Council mentions only deposition,[16] and so the 2nd Council of Nicæa[17] in some cases, though in others[18] excommunication is added. The Council of Tours[19] only says that simoniacs will have their portion with Simon [Magus]; so the third Lateran, substituting Gehazi for Simon.

LITERATURE.—This has been given in the course of the article.

A. J. MACLEAN.

1 Can. iii. 17. 2 Can. xii. 2.

3 A. C. Benson, *Life of Edward White Benson*, London, 1900, ii. 103 n.

4 For an account of the opposition in Parliament to the proposals, and of the whole movement for reform, see *ib.* ii. 92 ff.

1 Above, § 3. 2 Above, § 2. 3 Above, § 4.
4 viii. 6. 5 vii. 5. 6 Above, § 5.
7 Can. 2. 8 Can. 1, 2. 9 Can. 29 [30].
10 So Can. 76 [75].
11 Can. 3: 'anathema sit danti et accipienti.'
12 Can. 4. 13 Can. 21; see above, § 2.
14 Can. 3; above, § 2.
15 Can. 8. So, perhaps, Gregory the Great, *Ep.* iv. 27.
16 Can. 22, 23; above, § 2.
17 Can. 4. 18 Can. 5. 19 Above, § 3.

SIN.

SIN (American).—There is, of course, no such thing as an aboriginal critique, or science, of conduct in America. Accordingly, among the American Indian peoples there is no conscious demarcation of classes of offence with respect to responsibility and object, such as is represented by the civilized man's conception of crime as offence against law, vice as offence against society, and sin as offence against the divine in nature or in human nature. Sin, vice, crime, pollution, and even misfortune, are, for the American Indian, all embraced in the category of evil; the range of the things which he recognizes as evil (and also as good) is, in the broad, equivalent to the range of things evil (and good) recognized by other races of men; but he did not, aboriginally, make a reflective separation of these things into classes. For this reason, it is impracticable to treat the native Americans' conceptions of sin except as related to their general notions of morality, of which subject this is a special continuation.

1. Pollution.—It is a commonplace of the study of primitive thinking that the notions of spiritual and material, of psychical and physical, are not clear-cut, and that the distinction is, therefore, no more significant than it was to those Ephesians whom Heraclitus satirized for their purifications by blood. It is, indeed, perfectly natural to the animistic or pantheistic frame of mind to conceive physical nature as susceptible of giving or of receiving spiritual taint, and hence to imagine that the spiritual taint may be removed by physical purifications. This notion of uncleanness and its medicine, as pertaining both to men and to things, is as universal as is religious ceremonial. Nor can it be dismissed as mere superstition while we repeat—and with reason—that cleanliness is next to godliness.

The American Indian does not differ from the rest of the human race in respect of this confusion of spiritual and physical. Notions of pollution and purification are a part of his habit of mind and the explanation of much of his ritual. Birth and death, the functions of sex, preparation for war, for great hunts, for sowings and reapings, and above all for the great clan and tribal festivals, are everywhere attended with purificatory ceremonies—among which are abstinences, fastings, sacrifices, catharsis and emesis, and dedicatory rites such as painting of the body and face with symbols, bathings, aspergings, anointings, and sacramental feasts. The Indian stands before his lodge at the dawn in order that the young and growing sun may strike him with the rays of its vigorous youth, and make him strong; he strokes his child with green vegetation that its life may be green and flourishing.

'The old Indians,' writes a missionary to the Sioux, 'continuously bathed their feet in dew and snow, and their bodies in snow and rain and "sacred living water." The purpose of this was more to "keep the perceptions keen" than to keep the body clean.'[1]

The rite of baptism as practised by some of the Plains tribes, by the Aztec, and by the Maya was governed by a similar motive.

Thus, in the *Hako*, the officiating elder 'makes certain wet lines on the face of the child.' These signify that the sustaining of life through the power of water comes from Tira'wa atius, *i.e.* from Father Heaven.[2] Bishop Landa says of the Yucatec that they named their baptismal rite *caputzihil*, meaning to be 'born anew'; and he adds that 'they have such a respect for it that those who have sins on their conscience or who feel themselves inclined to commit a sin, confess to the priest in order to be in a state to receive baptism. . . . They believe that they receive therefrom a disposition inclined to good conduct, that it guarantees them from all temptations of the devil, with respect to temporal things, and by means of this rite and a good life they hope to secure salvation (*gloria*).'[3] Another most interesting rite described by Landa[4] was the feast of 1 Zac (February), in which expiation for the shedding of blood in the chase was made: 'for they regarded as abominable all shedding of blood apart from sacrifices.'

Pollution of places and things is, of course, recognized along with pollution of persons. The destruction of old utensils and the preparation of new for new undertakings or for the new year is connected with such a conception, of which perhaps the clearest symbol is the sweeping of sacred or festival precincts—a feature of the Creek *Busk*, and of numerous festivals of the Pueblo, Aztec, Maya, Inca, and other tribes with elaborate rituals. One of the most affecting anecdotes of the Mexican Conquest is related by Bernal Diaz.

A few days after Cortes' entry into Tenochtitlan a group of the Spaniards were conducted by Montezuma to the summit of the great *teocalli* overlooking the market-place. There the Mexican monarch first proudly indicated the wealth and populousness of the rich valley over which he ruled, and then brought the strangers into the presence of his gods. Cortes seized the occasion to demand permission to erect there a Christian cross. 'You will see,' he said in effect, 'how these symbols of the devil which you have placed here will wither before the symbol of the true faith.' Montezuma indignantly refused, upbraiding the Spaniards for their impiety; and when they departed he remained behind to perform expiation and cleanse the temple of the sin wherewith it was tainted.[5]

2. Vice and crime.—Even among peoples with a scientific ethics the conception of vice (as a social offence punishable by public opprobrium) and of crime (as physically punishable, by law) is not wholly distinguished from the conception of sin (as offence against God or nature). Vices and crimes, though they may be punishable evils, are not regarded as sins when there is no guilty motive; and sin, at the other extreme, exists where there is temptation to guilt, entertained without resistance, even though it may eventuate in no vicious or criminal action. Nevertheless, in the great mid-realm of conduct most offences are regarded as having the twofold character of social offence punishable by society and sinful offence to be answered by the mercy of God or by the conscience. The practical problem of the distribution of responsibility is so complex that it forms to-day one of the greatest and least-settled fields of ethical controversy.

Such being the case among the more advanced, it is certainly not to be expected that primitive peoples should make any clear distinction between the two types of offence—least of all, in view of the fact that primitive societies, almost without exception, are theocratic in their sanctions: a people whose customs are regarded as established and sustained by tutelar or patron gods, or by ancestral heroes become divine, must inevitably regard offences against society as offences against divinity, and all social offences, therefore, as sins. This is the prevalent American Indian notion. Murder is punished for the appeasement of the *manes* of the murdered rather than for injury to the tribe. Impurity, and especially sexual perversion, was regarded in many localities as an abominable impiety, to be atoned only by bloodshed (though it may be suspected that the charge of this offence was sometimes brought, as by the Aztec against the Huastec and by the Inca against the Yunca, mainly as an excuse for bloody conquest). Disobedience to tribal custom has all the taint of blasphemy, and Indian legends abound with incidents of supernatural retributions for tabus defied.

Perhaps as clear a notion as may be gained of the range of Indian moral ideas is suggested by native terms for types of persons.

Thus the Omaha tribe have words to designate: (*a*) on the side of good: an unselfish person, a self-controlled person, a straightforward or truthful person, a willing, a sympathetic, a courteous, a hospitable person; (*b*) on the side of the bad: a liar, a thief, a quarreller, a glutton, a meddler, a libertine, a boaster, a talebearer, a beggar, and, again, an impudent, an obstinate, a stingy, a discourteous person. 'Religion and ethics, closely interwoven, pervaded the life of the tribe, and in judging the evidences of constructive thought on these topics one should not consider them apart from the natural and social environment of the people.'[1] Of the kindred Sioux Beede says that the old Indians made much of humility (*igluhukuniciye*) and charity (*wacantkiye*), and in another connexion he gives the interesting information that the soul of 'a willful suicide cannot dwell in any living object; a suicide, who does his deed willfully, is painless and hopeless, sole, alone and exclusive, an "aristocrat" in all but the ability to make others serve him.'[2]

Both the virtues and the offences give an enlightening glimpse into the Indian's conception of the spiritual sociality of the world. Moral standards and moral enlightenment varied, and still vary, greatly from tribe to tribe; but it is probably true that everywhere the maintenance of custom rested upon the entirely theological grounds given to Knud Rasmussen by the old Eskimo:

'We observe our old customs, in order to hold the world up, for the powers must not be offended. We observe our customs, in order to hold each other up; we are afraid of the great Evil. . . . Men are so helpless in the face of illness. The people here do penance, because the dead are strong in their vital sap, and boundless in their might.'[3]

1 A. McG. Beede, *Toward the Sun*, Bismarck, 1916, p. 63.
2 *22 RBEW* [1904], pt. 2, p. 217.
3 *Relacion de las cosas de Yucatan*, Paris, 1864, ch. xxvi.
4 Ch. xl.
5 Bernal Diaz del Castillo, *Hist. Verdadera de la Conquista de la Nueva España*, Madrid, 1632, ch. xcii.

1 A. C. Fletcher and F. La Flesche, 'The Omaha Tribe,' in *27 RBEW* [1911], p. 603 f.; cf. also F. Boas, 'Tsimshian Mythology,' in *31 RBEW* [1916], pp. 443-453, one of the fullest analyses of the moral and religious ideas of an American Indian tribe, as shown in its myths.
2 Pp. 79, 141.
3 K. Rasmussen, *The People of the Polar North*, London, 1908, p. 124.

3. Sin, confession, and penitence.—The conception of sin in the more precise sense, as offence against divine powers, calling for repentance and inner regeneration, is by no means absent from the Indian consciousness. In a number of localities, and especially in the more civilized native states, confession and penance under priestly supervision were important rites in pre-Columban times. Nor can we suppose that the institution of these rites in Christian forms by the first missionaries would have received the hearty and conscientious favour which the mission relations attest, had there not been in the aboriginal disposition some natural intuition of their significance. As a matter of fact, impiety, blasphemy, and a willingness to do evil were thoroughly reprobated; while, on the converse side, the Indian sought by every means to find favour and enlightenment from the higher powers by which he deemed himself to be surrounded and sustained. Probably no human race has laid such general stress upon the significance of visions, won in fast and solitude, as a form of inspiration; in many tribes it was the common practice for a man or woman in trouble to seek help and consolation by this means, while it was no less general for each individual, on approaching maturity, to conduct a similar quest of his life's helper, making a kind of consecration of his strength to the tutelar power.

There are stories, not a few, of pagan Indians, visited by remorse for some crime, and expiating it even by self-inflicted death; stories, too, of entire change of character as a result of vision or of some similarly intimate experience. But for the more doctrinated conception of sin and responsibility it is necessary to turn to the ritualized religions of the semi-civilized nations—at least, for pre-Columban practices. Thus, Las Casas, describing the religion of the Guatemalans, whom he knew intimately, presents their compunctions and penitences as worthy examples of piety to the Spaniards themselves,[1] while the similar practices of the Yucatec and Mexican peoples are described by Landa, Sahagun, and other writers. Of the Yucatec Landa says:

'The Yucatec knew naturally evil when they committed it, and they believed that it was in punishment for sin and evil that death came to them, as also illness and suffering. They had the custom of confession, and when they were in the mind for it, it was made in the following manner. When, in consequence of illness or something else, they were in danger of dying, they confessed their sins; but if they forgot to think thereof, their nearest relatives or friends reminded them of it. Thus they told publicly their sins to the priest, if he were present; if not, to their fathers and mothers, wives to their husbands, and husbands to their wives. The faults of which they most commonly accused themselves were theft, murder, weaknesses of the flesh, and false testimony. But it often happened, when they came to recover, that there arose quarrels between husband and wife, because of their infidelities, and with those who had caused them. Men confessed their delinquencies (*flaquezas*), except those which they had committed with their slaves, for they said that it was permitted to use those who belonged to them as they willed. They did not confess sins in intention, although they regarded such as evil; and in their counsels and preachings they preached their avoidance.'[2]

Sahagun gives many prayers which are penitential or confessional in tone, and describes the numberless penitences imposed by the priests. Formal confession, it appears, was made primarily to the god Tezcatlipoca, 'Smoking Mirror,' the invisible and impalpable deity who penetrates all things and sees even into the recesses of the heart.

'Thou, Lord, who art father and mother of the gods and oldest of divinities, know that hither comes thy vassal, thy slave; weeping, he approaches with great sadness; he comes plunged in grief, recognizing that he has fallen into error, that he has fallen into vile sins and grave derelictions meriting death; he comes deeply pained and oppressed with all this. Our merciful master, who art the sustainer and defender of all, receive in penitence and hearken to the anguishes of thy slave and vassal.'

After this prayer the priest exhorts the penitent to tell all, omitting nothing for shame or weakness; and, when the confession is made, he assigns the penance according to the gravity of the sin. Sahagun says that the confessors kept secret what was confessed to them, stating that it was not to them but to their god that the sin was confessed: 'they had not confessed to man, but simply to God.' Nevertheless, it appears that confession and penance relieved the culprit from civil penalties (again an instance of the confusion of crime and sin); and, when Spanish priests replaced the native with the Christian confession, the Indians expected the certificate of confession, which they asked of the fathers, to satisfy any legal complaint against their conduct. As in Yucatan, confession was not frequent, but only with approaching age or fear of calamity; but they at least 'believed themselves obliged to confess once in their life, and this, *in lumine naturali*, without having any previous notion of the faith.'[1]

The narratives of the French Jesuits and other Roman Catholic missionaries to the wilder tribes uniformly describe the enthusiasm with which the confessional was welcomed by the Indians, and their willingness to undergo penance for their faults. This, of course (though there is some evidence for a pagan practice of confession even among very primitive Indian tribes),[2] does not argue any previous acquaintance with the rite, but it does indicate a ready comprehension of its meaning—for which there is some analogy in such pagan customs as that described in the 'Relations' of the mission to the Hurons:

'They address themselves to the Sky, paying it homage; and they call upon the Sun to be witness of their courage, their misery, or of their innocence. But, above all, in the treaties of peace and alliance with foreign nations they invoke, as witnesses of their sincerity, the Sun and the Sky, which see into the depths of their hearts and will wreak vengeance on the treachery of those who betray their trust and do not keep their word. So true is what Tertullian said of the most infidel nations, that nature in the midst of perils makes them speak with a Christian voice,—*exclamant vocem naturaliter Christianam*,—and have recourse to a God whom they invoke almost without knowing him,—*Ignoto Deo*.'[3]

The 'Relation of 1653-54' contains a number of affecting narratives of Indian conversions, and in the midst an account of the reception of the confessional rite, not without its amusing features. Says the good father:

'When winter expires in giving birth to spring, all our hunters betake themselves, with all their goods, to the banks of the great river, at the cove or harbor which we call Tadoussac; and here, a public confession is held, without gehenna [rack], without torture, and without any coercion. There is said to be a country where the cold is so great as to freeze all words uttered there; and, when spring approaches, upon these words thawing out, there is heard, almost in a moment, all that was said during the winter. Whatever may be the foundation of this story, it is true that all the evil that has been committed during the winter in these great woods is told to the father publicly in the month of April. The first-comers recite aloud the confessions of those who follow, and this from a zeal which they feel for Christian justice.'[4]

Incidents of zeal for confession and baptism are related by many missionaries, and often in connexions that leave no manner of doubt that the candidates conceived the religious significance of the rite correctly, judged by the standards of the Church; *i.e.*, the purification sought is clearly conceived by the Indian as an inner and spiritual change, not as a mere release from external taint and public obloquy. In the older native rites there are many elements that represent a conception of regenerated life. In most cases, it is

[1] *Apologética Historia de las Indias*, ed. Serrano y Sanz Madrid, 1909, ch. clxxx. p. 473.
[2] Ch. xxvii.

[1] B. de Sahagun, *Hist. general de las cosas de Nueva España*, Mexico, 1829–30, bk. i. ch. xii.
[2] See 9 *RBEW* [1892], p. 465, note 8.
[3] *Jesuit Relations*, xxxiii. ['Lower Canada, Algonkins, Hurons, 1648-49'] 225.
[4] *Ib.* xli. ['Lower Canada, Iroquois, 1654-56'] 189 ff.

true, the native prophet or preacher promises material as well as spiritual advantages; but the latter are nearly always present. The Indians have learned lessons of religion from both Roman Catholic and Protestant missionaries, and their native prophets have adopted elements from both forms of Christianity, but obviously because of a distinctly native foundation upon which to build.

'Long time I knew nothing—just like an animal,' said one convert to such a semi-Christian native creed. 'I was a drunkard, was a thief, and a robber. When I joined this religion, I was told to be good. . . . I prayed and was sick—my soul was sick. I prayed to God and he pays me for that. . . . A good Christian man in the dark sees a light toward God. God makes a fog—a good Christian man goes straight through it to the end, like good medicine. I believe this religion. It helps poor people.'[1]

The form of the idea underlying this expression is Christian, but its substance is the universal one of a human conscience, first oppressed by the sense of sin, then redeemed by an intimate and buoyant consciousness of grace received.

4. The origin of sin.—Theology is, of course, no primitive science. Nevertheless, the problems with which the theologian must deal are too elemental in human life not to have appealed to the minds of men in all grades of reflective advancement. Among them no problem is more universally felt than is that of the origin of evil: how comes it that men are tried with suffering, and above all oppressed by their own inescapable shames? This is the problem of the tales of Pandora and Eve, of Job and of Œdipus, as well as of the Epistles of St. Paul; and it is the problem at the heart of many of the most ancient myths of the aboriginal peoples of the New World.

Not infrequently in American myth an age of innocence preceded the present condition of men. Thus the Cheyenne tale of the 'Great Medicine'[2] tells of a paradisal age when men were naked and innocent, amid fields of plenty, followed by a period in which flood, war, and famine ensued upon the gift of understanding. In the usual N. American stories death and evil come into the world as the result of sortilege, but there are many examples in which moral motives enter—as in the Eskimo tale in which man is given choice between eternal life in eternal darkness or mortality blessed by the light of day, and chooses the latter. Probably the most beautiful of all these tales is the Wintun story of 'Sedit and the Two Brothers Hus.'[3]

Olelbis, the creator, caused the demiurgic brothers Hus to make a road to heaven, at the top placing two springs, one for internal and one for external purification. Mortals growing old could mount to these springs and there renew their youth. But Coyote—also a demiurgic power—opposes this: 'Joy at birth and grief for the dead is better,' he says, 'for these mean love.' So the road is destroyed.

Of course, in the great number of tales, it is a broken tabu that first brings the disaster of evil into the world.

But certainly, of all native American beliefs, that of most extraordinary interest in this connexion is the Aztec conception. In Mexican and Mayan myth alike the origin of the world is represented as occupying a series of cycles or ages, each, as it were, an experimental creation, and each, up to the present, destroyed cataclysmically to make place for a better effort. The present age—or 'Sun,' of the world, as the Aztec conceived it—endures by reason of the continual expiation, self-maceration, and sacrifice of human hearts, offered to gods who had made of themselves the first great sacrifice. The fullest version of this remarkable myth is in the anonymous *Historia de los Mexicanos por sus Pinturas*, though it is to be found also in the *Anales de Cuauhtitlan*, fragmentarily. The idea underlying the myth is apparently related to the notion of Anaximander that individual life (even of gods) is in some sense an arrogance and injustice to be atoned for, and a great part of the ceremonial of Mexican religion was devoted to acts of atonement. How completely the idea dominated the Mexican mind is most impressively shown by the prayers recorded by Sahagun, for the whole sixth book of the *Historia* is virtually an elaborate ritual of penitence—not so much for individual sins as for the presumptuousness of living.

See artt. COMMUNION WITH DEITY (American), ETHICS AND MORALITY (American), PRAYER (American).

LITERATURE.—In addition to the authorities cited above, see J. Mooney, 'The Ghost-Dance Religion,' in *14 RBEW* [1896], pt. 2; *Jesuit Relations and Allied Documents*, 73 vols., ed. R. G. Thwaites, Cleveland, 1896–1901; *Life, Letters and Travels of Father Pierre-Jean de Smet, S.J., 1801–1873: Missionary Labours and Adventures among the North American Indians*, 4 vols., New York, 1905. For a survey of Indian myth and full bibliographies see H. B. Alexander, in *The Mythology of All Races*, x., 'North American,' Boston, 1916, and xi., 'American (Latin),' do. 1919.

H. B. ALEXANDER.

1 *14 RBEW* [1896], pt. 2, p. 754 f.

2 *Anthropological Series, Field Columbian Museum*, ix. [1905] 34 ff.

3 Jeremiah Curtin, *Creation Myths of Primitive America*, Boston, 1898, p. 163 ff.

SIN (Babylonian).[1]

SIN (Babylonian).[1]—Free will was completely assumed by both Sumerian and Semite in Babylonia. Although the tendency to sin is attributed to man as a natural inheritance, the theologians never raise the problem of its ultimate origin in the divine order of things. The attitude of the Babylonian in this regard may be described as one of perpetual humility and concern for his frail human will, which is never sufficient to attain to the divine standards of purity. To introduce the subject in its general aspect, we cannot do better than quote from a Sumerian bilingual confessional (*eršaghunga*):

'Oh lord, my wrongdoings are many, great are my sins.[2]
Mankind is dumb knowing nothing at all.
Mankind, as many as bear names, what do they know?
Whether he has acted shamefully, whether he has acted well, he knows not at all.
. . . .
Oh my god, my wrongdoings are seven times seven, forgive my wrongdoing.'[3]

The penitential psalm from which this selection is taken is perhaps the best statement in cuneiform literature concerning the naturally sinful state of man, his abject foolishness compared with the wisdom of the gods, and his inability to avoid sin, even though his desire be set upon righteousness. Another prayer, probably employed in a magic ritual of atonement, has been recently discovered and throws more light upon the general aspect of the problem of sin:

'Who is there who forever [*is sinless?*]
Mankind as many as there be [*commit*] sin.
I thy servant have sinned and . . .
Before thee I stand and I turn . . .
Rebellious things I plot, I have set free the wicked.
I have spoken what is not good; but whatsoever is wicked thou knowest.
The food that belongs to god I have eaten.
I have trodden on the interdicted thing; evil I have done.
Upon thy vast possessions I have lifted a [covetous] face.
Unto thy precious silver my greed goes up.
I have lifted my hand and touched what should not be touched.
In my uncleanness I have entered into thy temple.
I have thus committed thy mighty abomination.
I have transgressed thy borders,[4] a thing which is obnoxious to thee.
In the wrath of my heart I have cursed thy divinity.
Wrong known and unknown I have committed.
I go about, I behold, and before me shame I obtain.
Oh my god, it is enough, may thy heart repose.
Oh Ishtar, who hast been enraged, may it be pardoned.

1 See the artt. EXPIATION AND ATONEMENT (Babylonian), vol. v. p. 637 ff., and PRAYER (Babylonian), vol. x. p. 159 ff.

2 H. C. Rawlinson, *WAI* iv. (London, 1891) 10*a*, 36.

3 *Ib.* 10*b*, 29–45. See also M. Jastrow, *Die Religion Babyloniens und Assyriens*, ii. 103.

4 *e-te-te-ḳi a-ḫat-ka.*

Oh deliver, thou who hast wrought thy heart to a mighty rage.
Thy favour which I have rehearsed be unto me for welfare.
Verily many are my wrongdoings, oh sever my bonds.
[Seven times] seven are my disgraces, but may thy heart repose.'[1]

The inborn sinful nature of man is not only due to the weakness of the will, but may be inherited.

'Oh great lord Marduk, merciful god,
Mankind as many as bear names,
Who among them learns anything by himself?
Who has not been negligent, who has not acted despicably?
. . . .
The penalty of my father, of my grandfather, of my mother, of my grandmother,
Of my family, of relations through brothers and sisters,
May it not come nigh me, but may it go elsewhere.
. . . .
O ye gods that dwell in heaven, absolve my penalty.
The great wrong which from my youth I have committed,
Oh scatter and seven times absolve.'[2]

Babylonian conceptions of sin passed through various stages of religious and ethical values during the long period covered by the Sumerian and Semitic sources. Sumerian and Babylonian doctrines concerning transgression may be divided into two great groups—(1) religious and ceremonial sin, and (2) ethical sin. The former group is naturally the more fundamental and original.

1. Religious and ceremonial sin.—A term frequently employed in religious texts for transgression is *ăg-gig*, *ág-gig*, Semitic *ikkibu* (loan-word) or *an-zillu*. The fundamental meaning of these words is 'forbidden thing,' 'sacred possession of a deity.'[3] It was apparently first employed for the food assigned to a deity or to the holy places consecrated to deities. To eat of such food or to tread upon such places without proper purification and habit constituted one of the greatest of sins.

'Have I eaten the forbidden thing[4] of my god unknowingly?
Have I trodden on the interdicted place of my goddess[5] unknowingly?'[6]

Here we touch upon the most ancient Babylonian conception of sin, an unconscious violation of the ceremonial regulations. By metonymy 'to eat interdicted food' came to mean to commit an abomination, and hence both *ikkib* and *anzillu* became synonymous with 'abomination,' 'desecration.' The terms connote always a most serious religious transgression, and in the psalm translated above the sinner connects the violation of divine law with 'thy mighty abomination I have done.'

As in Hebrew, so also in Babylonian the principal words for sin, both noun and verb, are derived from the root חטא, 'be faulty,' 'be defective,' 'fail,' 'sin.' The verb is *ḫaṭû*, and the noun *ḫiṭṭû*, *ḫiṭîtu*. The Sumerian equivalent is *šebida*, whose original meaning is unknown. In Sumerian this word invariably denotes a religious sin which entails the anger of the gods and a stain upon the soul. Hence the ritual of atonement must be employed to free man from the deadly effect of this transgression.[7] This form of sin is often contrasted with *namtag*, 'overturning,' violent transgression of civil laws and social customs. The Semitic equivalent is *annu* or *arnu*, which is best rendered by 'wrongdoing.' The discussion of this term falls under ethical sin (below, § 2). The essential difference between these two categories may be best illustrated by repeating a line from the well-known 'psalm to all gods':[8]

'Oh lord, my wrongdoings are many, great are my sins.'[1]

The spiritual and religious aspect of sin is almost invariably denoted by the words *ḫaṭû*, *ḫiṭû*, *ḫiṭîtu* in Babylonian. 'The sin which I have committed' is expressed by *šebida dib-ba-mu*, 'the stigma which I have laid upon myself' in Sumerian.[2] The ethical and religious contrast of these terms is indicated by a line of a liturgy:

ta nam-tag-ga ta nam-še-bi-da
minû annu-ma minû egî-ma,
'What was the wrongdoing? What was the sin?'[3]

Here the Semitic root עקה, 'sin' (in a religious sense), is employed. The verb *egû* has the same force in Babylonian as *ḫaṭû*, and the grammatical texts explain one by the other. The ceremonial character of sin conveyed by *egû* is illustrated by the passage, 'Who has sinned against Esagila (temple of Marduk)?' The noun *egîtu*, 'desecration,' 'ceremonial sin,' must always be interpreted in this sense.[4] In one passage *šebida* has been rendered into Semitic by a verb (*šâṭu*) which means 'be negligent,' *i.e.* neglect the rules and ceremonials of religion.

'Where has the wise not been negligent, and not committed despicable deeds?
Where has he who acted cautiously not been afflicted?'[5]

These terms are frequently employed for ethical sins, political disturbances, and law-breaking, but, when so employed, they obtain a weakened sense and become synonymous with *annu*, *arnu*, and similar words.[6]

2. Ethical and political sin.—The Sumerian noun for this type of sin, *namtagga*, means 'perversion,' 'violent disturbance of the legal order'—meanings almost invariably assigned to the Semitic translations of this word, *annu*,[7] *arnu*, *šertu*.[8] These terms may be described as denoting both wrongdoing and the punishment for wrongdoing. *Arnu* is probably a phonetic variant of *annu*, and both words appear to have been derived from a root meaning 'oppose,' whence is derived the word *anantu*, 'hostility,' 'conflict'; *šertu* has probably the meaning 'perverseness,' 'treachery,' 'dishonesty.'[9] *Arnu* and *šertu* are, therefore, the words recognized in legal procedure for violation of ethical standards and civil law; *e.g.*, a woman treacherously seeking to break a contract sues another woman concerning property; the judges convict her of *šertu*, *i.e.* treachery.[10] Another record of a lawsuit of the period of Ḫammurabi,

[1] E. Ebeling, *Keilschrifttexte aus Assur*, Leipzig, 1915, no. 45.

[2] L. W. King, *Babylonian Magic and Sorcery*, London, 1896, no. 11. See also J. Hehn, *BASS* v. [1903] 364; H. Zimmern, *Der alte Orient*, vii. pt. iii. [1905] p. 18.

[3] The Sumerian *ăg-gig* is an abstract noun derived from the root *gig*, 'exclude,' 'divide off,' 'separate.'

[4] *Ikkib ili-ia=ág-gig-ga dimmer-mu.*

[5] *Anzil ilat Iš-ta-ri-ia=amad Innini-mu ág-gig-ga.*

[6] Rawlinson, iv. 10*a*, 32–35.

[7] *Sĕbida asilal-la-e-ne=ḫiṭîti duppiri*, 'Oh remove my sin'; P. Haupt, *Akkadische und sumerische Keilschrifttexte*, Leipzig, 1882, p. 117, 7.

[8] Rawlinson, iv. 10*a*, 36.

[1] *Bêlum annū-a ma'da rabâ ḫiṭû-a*, where the Semitic version properly distinguishes the nature of *annu* and *ḫiṭṭu*, *ḫīṭu*, by the selection of its adjectives.

[2] Rawlinson, iv. 10*a*, 44, *b* 39.

[3] G. Reisner, *Sumerisch-babylonische Hymnen*, Berlin, 1896, p. 119, rev. 5.

[4] The original meaning of the verb *egû* is perhaps discovered in the obscure phrase of the fifth tablet of Creation, l. 7, *ana la epiš anni la egû manama*, 'That no one of them do wrong or go astray (?),' said of the stars. It is difficult to explain why the verbs *ḫaṭû* and *egû* ordinarily came to convey the deeper aspect of sin.

[5] *BASS* v. 640, 15–18.

[6] The terms usually employed for each type of sin cannot be brought under definitions which have no exceptions. Terms of each class are found conveying the sense of their opposite class. The rules given above are almost invariably true with respect to the Sumerian words, but the Semites employed their terms more loosely.

[7] Semitic root probably ענן, 'oppose,' after Zimmern, *Babylonische Busspsalmen*, p. 13. Derivatives of the same root are *enunu* (found as yet only in the sense of penalty for sin) and *ennîtu*, which is employed in the sense opposed to its cognate *annu*, as a synonym of *ḫīṭu*, 'religious sin.'

[8] Employed occasionally for 'religious sin' (*Šurpu*, ii. 32; Ebeling, p. 90, rev. 3 f.).

[9] Note that in *Šurpu*, iii. 12, *kittu*, 'honesty,' is contrasted with *šertu*, where a variant text has *ṣartu*, 'trickery.' The 'Chicago Syllabary' published by D. D. Luckenbill in *AJSL* xxxiii. [1917] has an entry *emedup=suḫtu* ('forgery') and *šertu*.

[10] The phrase is *šertam emēdu*, 'to lay (the decision of) treachery upon.' See M. Schorr, *Altbabylonische Rechtsurkunden*, Leipzig, 1913, p. 267, 7; see also p. 313, 33, *šertam lû immidu-niati*, 'Verily they convict us of falsehood.' The words *šertu* and *annu*, when employed with *emēdu* in legal documents, do not mean 'penalty,' as Assyriologists render them, but 'falsehood,' 'error,' 'wrongdoing.'

in which a man sues another for possession of a house, will illustrate the similar use of the word *arnu*. The judges arrange the legal proceedings, investigate the case, and convict the plaintiff of wrong or error.[1] *Arnu* is the official term employed in the great Code of Ḫammurabi and is there employed regularly in its original and legal sense, 'error,' 'wrong.' The Code also employs *arnu* in the sense of penalty for error, but not so frequently.

It is not always easy to determine the kind of sin or wrongdoing which many other terms of the Babylonian religious texts convey, such as *sillatu*, 'slander,' 'impudence,' *ḳillatu*,[2] 'contemptible conduct,' *limuttu*, 'wickedness.' The result of sin,[3] however, at least in the later period, was invariably the same. Man's protecting god abandoned him; he became the prey of disease and the prisoner of the demons. Hence elaborate rituals of atonement came into use to free mankind from the effects of religious, ceremonial, and ethical sins. These rituals have been defined and described in the art. EXPIATION AND ATONEMENT (Babylonian). In the more important rituals of atonement the penitent recites long lists of the sins which he may have committed, usually of an ethical character; *e.g.*, the second tablet of the *Šurpu* series has the following confession said for a sinner by a priest:

'Has he failed to free a prisoner and not loosed the bound?
Has he not caused him in prison to see the light?
Has he said concerning a captive, "Seize him" or concerning the bound, "Bind him"?
Is there some unknown falsehood toward god, some unknown contrariness against goddess?
Is his wrongdoing against his god, is his perversity against his goddess?
Is there hostility to the *ancestors*, hatred toward the elder brother?
Has he despised father and mother, behaved disgracefully toward the elder sister?
Has he given in littleness and *received* in largeness?
For "No" has he said "Yes"?
For "Yes" has he said "No"?'

This tablet continues the enumeration of ethical sins in such manner that it really forms a good source for an estimation of the moral standards of the Babylonians. Ceremonial sins are then recorded in detail:

'Has he strode toward a man under a curse?
Has a man under a curse strode toward his face?
Has he slept in the bed of a man under a curse?
Did he lie upon the divan of a man under a curse?'

Recitations of this kind appear to have been called 'the tablet of sins,' the tablet, according to the imprecation of one passage, being destroyed as an act which symbolized the annihilation of the demons and the expiation of sin.

'The tablet of his wrongdoing, of his sins, of his disgraceful conduct, of his curses, of his bans, be thrown into the water.'

In another ritual the penitent prays, 'Verily let be broken the tablet of my wrongdoings.'[4]

LITERATURE.—**J. Morgenstern**, *The Doctrine of Sin in the Babylonian Religion*, Berlin, 1905; **H. Zimmern**, *Babylonische Busspsalmen*, Leipzig, 1885, *Die Beschwörungstafeln Šurpu*, do. 1896, *Ritualtafeln für den Wahrsager, Beschwörer und Sänger*, do. 1900; briefly in *KAT*³, pp. 510–512; **K. L. Tallqvist**, *Die assyrische Beschwörungsserie Maqlû*, Leipzig, 1895; **R. Campbell Thompson**, *The Devils and Evil Spirits of Babylonia*, 2 vols., London, 1903–04; **W. Schrank**, *Babylonische Sühnriten*, Leipzig, 1908; **S. Langdon**, 'Babylonian Magic,' in *Scientia*, xv. [1914] 222–240; **M. Jastrow**, *Die Religion Babyloniens und Assyriens*, 2 vols., Giessen, 1905–13 (brief references to sin; see Index, p. 1097). The penitential psalms, which are the chief source for the study of this subject, are discussed in the art. PRAYER (Babylonian); **P. Dhorme**, *La Religion assyro-babylonienne*, Paris, 1910, p. 231 ff.

S. H. LANGDON.

SIN (Buddhist).

SIN (Buddhist).—The doctrine of sin, as held in Europe, is a complex idea of many strands. One or two of those strands may be more or less parallel to statements found in the earliest Buddhist texts or to ideas expressed in Indian pre-Buddhistic texts. But the doctrine as a whole, in any one of its various forms, is antagonistic to the Indian, and especially to the Buddhist, view of life.

To the Buddhist the universe is a cosmos, under the reign of law; whatever happens is a detail in an unending chain of cause and effect. The gods are as subject to this law as men. It holds good equally in the moral sphere and in the physical. Every wrong deed or word, every evil thought must work out its result, its effect; and that of its own force, quite independent of any deity. It is absolutely impossible for any conscious being to escape this result of his own act or thought, or, to phrase it in Indian fashion, of his *karma*. The application of this theory to details, and the explanations of the method in which *karma* worked, differed greatly at different times and places in India and among the different religious communities and philosophic schools that arose there.

Much has been written on the subject of *karma*. Most of it is vitiated by the erroneous assumption that there was only one theory, and that a statement in a work, say, of the 4th cent. A.D. is good evidence of beliefs held universally, say, in the 4th or 6th cent. B.C. The doctrine of *karma* is referred to as a great mystery in documents just earlier than the rise of Buddhism. It receives its first elaboration in detail in the older portions of the Pali Buddhist canon,[1] but in certain of the later portions,[2] in the 3rd cent. B.C., the point of view has changed. There is a good deal of evidence to be collected from the Sanskrit literature, both Hindu and Buddhist, dating from the 2nd to the 6th cent. A.D. No attempt has yet been made to deal with the history of the doctrine as a whole or even to collect and sift the evidence as to its form at any one particular period. E. W. Hopkins has several suggestive historical remarks on the last of the above-mentioned periods;[3] and the present writers have discussed the amount of truth that lies at the basis of the general theory.[4]

No one holding the doctrine of *karma*, in any one of its various forms, could accept the doctrine of sin. What the European calls 'sin' he would call 'folly,' a result of ignorance. And there cannot be, in his view, any forgiveness of sin; it must work out to the bitter end, and of itself, its own fruit. This is cosmic law, from which there can be no escape—not even with the help of the most powerful deity, for that deity would himself be subject to the law. Again, another implication in the European use of the word 'sin' is that of an offence against a personal deity. This a Buddhist believer in *karma* would find difficult even to understand. To him no personal deity ever made the moral law. Should a deity erroneously think he did, and then take offence against some mortal because the mortal had broken the law that he (the deity) had made, then that would be an evil deed, and would work out its effect to the shortening of the life, as deity, of the person who wrongfully took offence. Even a Buddha cannot lay down the moral law, the *Dhamma*, as something devised or created by himself. He can but interpret a law that he finds existing[5]—a law ante-dating the existence of any personal lawgiver.

The Buddhist would equate the abstraction 'sin' by every kind of collision, individual and social, with that cosmic moral law. Such collisions he would call evil, wrong, bad, demeritorious, corrupt (*pāpa*, *michchhā*, *akusala*, *apuñña*, *saṅkiliṭṭha*). And he would call them so because, as collisions or infractions, they threw back the in-

[1] *Arnam imidu-šu-ma*; Schorr, p. 262, 9; see also pp. 264, 7, 266, 21; Code of Ḫammurabi, § 172.
[2] Not to be read *ḫablatu*.
[3] Excepting, naturally, purely political errors or wrongdoings.
[4] See Zimmern, *Beiträge zur Kenntnis der babylonischen Religion*, Leipzig, 1901, pp. 23, 58 f. (corrected after Ebeling, no. 67) and p. 125, col. iii. 5.

[1] *E.g.*, *Majjhima Nikāya*, iii. 202, 207.
[2] Namely, portions of the *Khuddaka Nikāya*, especially the *Jātaka*.
[3] *The Religions of India*, London, 1896, and 'Modifications of the Karma Doctrine,' in *JRAS*, 1906, p. 581 f.
[4] T. W. Rhys Davids, *Buddhism: its Hist. and Literature* (American Lectures), New York, 1896, Index, *s.v.* 'Karma,' and *Buddhism*²², London, 1910, Index; C. A. F. Rhys Davids, *Buddhism*, ch. v.
[5] *Saṃyutta*, ii. 105; tr. C. A. F. Rhys Davids, in *Buddhism*, p. 83 f.

dividual in his long and, mainly, painful pilgrimage to higher, happier experience.

To the handicap imposed on each individual which is known among us as 'original sin' the doctrine of *karma* lends emphasis. From what has been said it is clear that no son of man can be born into the world free from the heavy mortmain of the follies and misdeeds of past lives, so far as these have not been already redeemed by unpleasant experiences. The same teaching, however, is equally insistent in the matter of the inheritance of a *plus* quantity of happy experience resulting from what we might call 'original virtue.' No lovely deed, word, or thought but brings its future reward, mundane or supramundane.

It should not, however, be concluded that sound Buddhist doctrine recognized, in the experiences of any given individual life, a mere gathering in of a predestined harvest of mixed crops, pleasant and painful, sown in previous lives.[1] That doctrine viewed every individual as a growth, or growing thing, both physically and spiritually. And all growth, while it is, on the one hand, the outcome of conditions (favourable or unfavourable to desirable growth), is, on the other hand, essentially creative. In the efforts at self-expression that we call 'creation' lay the capacity, and in the environing conditions the opportunity, of each individual to slough off the latent vices (*anusaya*) of his lower nature (called collectively the *kilesa's*), and mould for himself, *i.e.* the resultant of his present self, a lighter burden of 'original sin,' a brighter heritage of future destiny.

LITERATURE.—The foregoing remarks are gleaned from countless passages in Buddhist canonical and early commentarial literature, most of which are as yet untranslated into English. But *Aṅguttara*, i. 173 f. is discussed by Ledi Sadaw, 'Some Points in Buddhist Doctrine,' *JPTS*, 1913-14, p. 117 f., and other texts in C. A. F. Rhys Davids, *Buddhism*, London, 1912, ch. v.

T. W. and C. A. F. RHYS DAVIDS.

[1] *Aṅguttara*, i. 173 f.

SIN (Celtic).—In the Celtic sections of the artt. COMMUNION WITH DEITY (§ 3) and CRIMES AND PUNISHMENTS (§ 1) it has been shown that the Celts had clear notions on the subject of the gods' being offended by neglect, whether of an individual or of a community. Their wrath manifested itself in illness, calamity, defeat in battle, and the like; and it had to be propitiated by sacrifice, usually of human victims, for the Celts considered that, unless man's life were given for man's life, the majesty of the immortal gods could not be appeased.[2] The proof of this is found in the passages from classical observers cited in these articles.[3] How far the idea of sin against the gods had an ethical colouring we do not know, but this was probably not lacking, as the kind of crimes included among those punished by society suggests. In Gaul, too, the Druids acted as judges, and there, apart from punishment by death, excommunication from religious rites, especially sacrifice, was in common use in the case of those who would not submit to their decision. This was equivalent to outlawry, and the offender was regarded as impious and wicked.[4]

These statements receive further illustration from various mythical stories, mainly in Irish MSS. Though these have been redacted in most cases by Christian scribes, there is little doubt that, in so far as they describe the action of the gods or ideas purely pagan, they have undergone but small change through colouring by Christian conceptions. Even in such a Welsh legend as that of Nynnyaw and Peibaw transformed into oxen by God for their sins it is likely that the legend was a pagan one and that a pagan divinity was the punisher of the culprits.[1] In the euhemerized account of the relation of the Milesians to the Tuatha Dé Danann, *i.e.* of the pagan Irish Celts to their gods, the latter are said to have destroyed the corn and milk of the Milesians. To prevent this in future these made friends with Dagda, the chief of the Tuatha Dé Danann, and now their corn and milk were safe.[2] This story appears to reflect the idea that corn and milk depend upon the gods, and may be withheld or destroyed by them because of man's misdoings. The compact with Dagda suggests the fresh covenants made with Jahweh by His worshippers in the OT after they have been punished by Him for their sins. The story of the yearly destruction by fire of the fort of Tara by Aillen mac Midhna of the Tuatha Dé Danann may be based on some idea of human guilt thus punished. Aillen made every one in the fort sleep through his fairy music and then set it on fire, until he was destroyed by Fionn.[3]

The gods punished the taking of things dedicated to them, or tabu, and this may have been the subject of current stories known to classical writers. These speak of their own gods punishing the Celts for taking things devoted to them, perhaps applying to their divinities the anger of native Celtic gods.[4] Such breach of tabu was also punished with torture by the ministers of justice.[5] Trespass upon a sacred place was also obnoxious to the gods, and this is illustrated by several stories.

In one of these Eochaid, having encamped on a meadow, was told by the god Oengus, in disguise, to remove from it. He disobeyed, and Oengus sent plagues upon him, killing his cattle and horses, and threatening to slay his household if he would not go.[6] This resembles the tales of the bursting of a sacred well and its waters overwhelming an impious trespasser. Boand, wife of Nechtain, went to the fairy well which her husband and his cup-bearers alone might visit, and, when she further showed her contempt for it, the waters overwhelmed her. They now flow as the river Boyne. Similarly Sinend was destroyed for trespassing on Connla's well, the pursuing waters now forming the river Shannon.[7]

Myths of origins are here mingled with myths of punishment by the spirit or divinity of a sacred well, meted out to women to whom a sacred place was tabu. In other tales women who are the guardians or priestesses of sacred wells, and must keep them covered save when water is drawn, are similarly overwhelmed by the waters bursting forth when they fail to put the cover on, thus neglecting the ritual of the well.[8]

The breach of personal tabus, or *geasa*, is frequently described as punished by destruction or death. Heroes like Cúchulainn or Fionn broke the tabus which they had hitherto observed carefully, and this led to disastrous events culminating in death. These results are sometimes regarded as the inevitable operation of a kind of fate. The *geasa* are put upon one person by another, perhaps framed as an incantation or spell; he must obey; if not, disaster followed as it might do in the case of a curse. But the punishment, automatic though it might be, was also regarded as divine vengeance for wrong done to the gods, not always by the victim, but sometimes by his ancestors.

[2] Cæsar, *de Bell. Gall.* vi. 16.
[3] See also art. CELTS, vol. iii. p. 277 f.
[4] Cæsar, vi. 13.

[1] *Mabinogion*, i. 302, tr. J. Loth, in H. d'Arbois de Jubainville, *Cours de littérature celtique*, vols. iii. and iv., Paris, 1889.
[2] *Book of Leinster*, Dublin, 1880, 245*b*.
[3] S. H. O'Grady, *Silva Gadelica*, 2 vols., London, 1892, ii. 142 f.
[4] C. Jullian, *Recherches sur la religion gauloise*, Bordeaux, 1903, p. 96.
[5] Cæsar, vi. 13.
[6] Rennes *Dindṣenchas*, in *RCel* xv. [1894] 482; cf. xvi. [1895] 152; J. O'B. Crowe, *Journal of the Royal Historical and Archæological Association of Ireland*, 4th ser., i. [1871] 94 f.
[7] Rennes *Dindṣenchas*, in *RCel* xv. 315, 457. For further instances of punishment for the misuse of wells see P. Sébillot, *La Folk-Lore de France*, Paris, 1904–06, ii. 192; W. J. Rees, *Lives of Cambro-British Saints*, Llandovery, 1853, pp. 520, 523.
[8] Giraldus Cambrensis, *Topographia Hibernica*, ed. T. Wright, London, 1867, ii. 9; S. H. O'Grady, i. 233; J. A. MacCulloch, *The Religion of the Ancient Celts*, Edinburgh, 1911, p. 192.

The best illustration of this is found in the long, tragic Irish story of *The Destruction of Da Derga's Hostel*,[1] in which the *síd*-folk (beings of a fairy type who represent the older gods) avenge themselves upon Conaire for wrong done by his ancestor Eochaid to the god Mider. Conaire was told by Nemglan, a divinity who can take the form of a bird, of the tabus which he must observe. He became king, and at first all went well with him, and the land prospered. But the vengeance of the god began to work. Through fate or circumstances which he could not resist Conaire broke one tabu after another, until at last he was defeated in battle and himself slain. The events leading up to the final vengeance are told with great detail and realism, and Conaire is clearly shown to be the innocent victim of a divine vengeance which he could not resist.

So also the story of *Da Choca's Hostel* tells of the destruction of Cormac for breaking his *geasa*.[2] Another curious story tells how Corrchenn of Cruach slew the god Dagda's son Aedh for seduction of his wife. Dagda punished him for this by making him carry the corpse on his back until he had found a stone for the grave as long as Aedh's body.[3]

In Irish Celtic belief the fruitfulness and prosperity of the land depended largely upon the king's observing his *geasa*; this also kept misfortune from him. But this was changed into the idea that the king's goodness or the reverse affected the fertility of the country. Probably there was not much difference between the two conceptions, though some of the *geasa* detailed are of an arbitrary and, to us, unmeaning character. In any case some idea of obeying what were really divinely appointed rules seems to be implied, though perhaps the king, looked upon as a divinity, subject himself to rules, had been regarded as the source of fertility.[4]

How far the conception of retribution after death for wrongdoing was known to the pagan Celts is uncertain. Possibly cowards may have been regarded as doomed to miss the joys of the after life, since the hope of these made warriors face death without a tremor. Some characteristics of hell in Irish Christian visions of the other world and in folk-belief may be derived from pagan belief—*e.g.*, the sufferings of the wicked from cold.[5] But they may equally be of Christian origin. As the idea of transmigration after death was not unknown to the Celts, the later folk-belief that souls of the wicked appear after death as ravens, crows, black dogs, and the like may be derived from some earlier pagan myth of retribution, though here again transmigration without retribution is quite as likely as not to have been believed in.[6]

The idea of sinlessness, *i.e.* innocence from particular sin or from sin in general, occurs now and then in the mythic tales, not apparently as a reflexion of Christian ideas.

When Bran on his voyage met the god Manannan mac Lir, the latter described to him the Elysian land, on which his coracle seemed to be sailing, and its people. They were immortal and sinless, unlike Adam's descendants, and they made love without crime.[7] In another tale, cited below, the son of a sinless couple is required as a sacrifice, and he turns out to be the son of the inhabitants of such a divine land as Bran saw.

Other tales show that the gods could punish members of their own group for wrongdoing.

Aoife transformed her step-children into swans, in the pathetic story of *The Children of Ler*, and for this the god Bodb punished her by transforming her into a demon of the air.[8] In another instance the god Manannan, having fallen in love with a mortal maiden, Tuag, sent a divine Druid, Fer Figail, to bring her to him. He brought her from her home and left her slumbering on the shore while he sought a boat to carry her to Elysium. There a great sea wave sent by the god, or the god himself in that form, overwhelmed her, and Fer Figail was afterwards slain by Manannan.[1] The cause of offence is not stated, but doubtless it was that the Druid had forestalled Manannan in his love for Tuag. In another tale the goddess Becuma was banished from the gods' land because of her sin with Manannan's son. She came to earth and by spells induced Conn, king of Ireland, to succumb to her wiles and to banish his son. During the year that he remained in dalliance with her there was neither corn nor milk in Ireland—an example of the idea of a bad king causing disaster to his land (itself a divine punishment). His Druids told Conn that nothing could save the land but the sacrifice of the son of a sinless couple. This was the son of the queen of an Elysian region. She came to rescue him, bringing a cow, which was sacrificed in his stead, and she told Conn that he must renounce Becuma, else Ireland would still lose a third of its corn and milk.[2]

On the whole, the ideas which these stories reveal suggest breaches of religious ritual and custom, and of customary law, passing over, however, into more ethical conceptions, while all through bringing the gods into relation with men as punishers of their wrongdoing.

LITERATURE.—This is referred to in the footnotes. See also the chapter on 'Divine Enmity and Punishment' in J. A. MacCulloch, *Celtic Mythology* (=*The Mythology of all Races*, vol. iii.), Boston, 1918.

J. A. MACCULLOCH.

SIN (Chinese).—The knowledge of sin in China has developed in the course of her long religious history. The Chinese have always possessed 'a sense of sin and its consequences.'[3] Man is described by Chaú Chí (2nd cent. A.D.) as differentiated from the brute creation by 'the knowledge of righteousness.'[4] Mankind is thus endowed with a moral sense.[5] The emperor Tang (176 B.C.) said, 'The Great God has conferred on the common people a moral sense.'[6] But man is prone to err.[7]

1. Earliest ideas. — In the early period of Chinese history, prior to 221 B.C., sin or crime was 'the disturbance of celestial routine,' 'the celestial order forming a human guide.'

'Offences against the gods or the spirits in a vague sense were often spoken of.' 'Sin was only conceivable in the sense of an infraction of nature's general laws.'[8]

Though sin was 'a moral and spiritual delinquency,'[9] and transgressions would call down divine retribution, yet at the same time the idea of sin was vague, and the opinion has been expressed that it might be said to have no well-defined existence at all.[10]

Time and again tyrants and evil rulers have received condign punishment at the hands of those who, in accordance with the will of Heaven, overthrew their thrones and rescued the country from their misrule. Their names, sins, and crimes are set forth in the Chinese classics and histories as terrible examples of the retribution which sins or crimes against high Heaven produce.[11] The punishment for sin was a material one, meted out in this life. There was no hell or purgatory known to the early Chinese. There were some hazy ideas about a state of bliss where the good and even the bad went.

2. Terms used.—There are three principal words used for sin, *tsui*, *ok*, and *kwo*. *Ok* means evil, bad, vicious, etc.; *kwo*, to transgress, to go beyond what is right. Among the 'wealth of distinctive terms'[12] for sin, evil, transgression in Chinese the nearest to the idea of sin is *tsui*, but it also means

1 Ed. W. Stokes, *RCel* xxii. [1901] 27 ff.
2 *Ib.* xxi. [1900] 149 f.
3 Rennes *Dindsenchas*, in *RCel* xvi. [1895] 42.
4 *Leabhar na g-Ceart, or the Book of Rights*, ed. J. O'Donovan, Dublin, 1847, p. 3 ff.; see also art. CELTS, vol. iii. p. 301a.
5 Examples in A. Le Braz, *La Légende de la mort en Basse-Bretagne: Croyances, traditions et usages des Bretons armoricains*[2], Paris, 1902, ii. 91; J. Curtin, *Tales of the Fairies and Ghost World*, London, 1895, p. 146.
6 Le Braz, ii. 82, 86, 307; Rees, p. 92.
7 *The Voyage of Bran*, ed. A. Nutt and K. Meyer, London, 1895–97, i. 2 f.
8 Ed. E. O'Curry, *Atlantis*, iv. [1863] 115 ff.

1 W. Stokes, 'The Bodleian Dinnshenchas,' *FL* iii. [1892] 510 f.
2 *Eriu*, iii. [1907–08] 150 ff.
3 W. E. Soothill, *The Three Religions of China*, London [1913], p. 250.
4 J. Legge, *The Religions of China*, London, 1880, p. 97.
5 Legge, *The Chinese Classics*, Hongkong, 1861–72, vol. iii., *The Shoo King*, bk. iii. pt. iv. p. 2.
6 *The Chinese Recorder*, xxviii. [Shanghai, 1897] 483.
7 Legge, *Religions of China*, p. 102, and *The Shoo King*, bk. ii. pt. ii. p. 2.
8 E. H. Parker, *China and Religion*, London, 1905, p. 24, and *Ancient China Simplified*, do. 1908, p. 55.
9 Soothill, p. 251.
10 *Ib.* p. 247; Parker, *Ancient China*, p. 55.
11 See Legge, *The Shoo King*, bk. iii. *passim*.
12 *Chinese Recorder*, xxiv. [1893] 52.

a crime, punishment, penalty, to treat one as a criminal. Further it means a violation of order, to give occasion for blame, a wrong, fault, or iniquity, and is also applied to a violation of decorum, a breach of the laws of etiquette. It is used in a phrase nearly equivalent to 'I beg your pardon.' The ethical force of meaning of the word is thus greatly dissipated by the breadth of ideas connoted. It has been said that the task of tasks is to bring home to the native mind the sense of what sin is. Nearly all writers on the religious and ethical side of Chinese nature draw attention to this, though there are some who have found notable instances to the contrary.[1]

3. Confucian ideas.—There is not much light thrown on the subject of sin in the sayings of Confucius. He was not inclined to split hairs upon the vexed question of sin, or even to speak of sin except in connexion with the practical affairs of life. He considered that there were five capital sins besides theft and robbery, viz. malignity, perverseness, mendacity, vindictiveness, and vacillating weakness.[2] He said that of the 3000 offences against which the five punishments were directed there was not one greater than that of being unfilial.[3] This is the sin of sins. Confucianists declare that their sage was perfect and did not need to repent of any errors, and that any statement by him which might be construed to the contrary was due to his humility, but the sage had a better knowledge of himself, for he dared not rank himself with 'the man of perfect virtue.'[4] Confucius never expressed any opinion as to a future state or as to rewards and punishments for sin.[5] The Confucian doctrine of man's nature is that he is naturally formed for virtue. There is no acknowledgment of a universal proneness to evil. All Chinese scholars have not, however, subscribed to the doctrine of a sinless nature. Suen believed that the nature of man was evil.[6]

Thus Confucianism has but little room for sin in its outlook on human life. 'All fundamental views of Confucianism are optimistic, human depravity and sin are not taken into account.'[7] Sin is therefore to a great extent outside the purview of Confucianism. Virtue can be practised and evil-doing given up by all. Reformation is a sufficient panacea for sin, even for one who sins against Heaven and 'who has nowhere left for prayer,' as Confucius once said.[8] Reformation is urged by both Confucius and Mencius. The former said, 'When you have faults [or bad habits],[9] do not fear to abandon them.' The latter said that all dispatch should be used in putting an end to what one knows as wrong.[10] These and similar passages in the Classics are used as proverbs by the Chinese.[11] Confucianism considers that 'the perfecting of knowledge and the influence of some good examples is sufficient to produce a good character.'[12]

Heaven was distinctly and directly cognizant of the actions of men whether good or evil. The great Chinese philosopher Chu Hsi (12th cent. A.D.) thus wrote:

> 'Heaven knows all our good and all our crimes [sins]. It is as if Heaven noted them down and numbered them up. Your good deeds are all before God, and my evil deeds will also be before Him.'[1]

> 'Sin to the Confucianist is an offence against the majesty of Heaven, a departure from law. It is constantly spoken of as error, deflection, something to be grown out of by self-culture. . . . There is no consciousness of the deep guilt of sin, no conception' of its 'deceiving, blundering, destroying power. All men have strength, if they would only use it, to overcome the tendencies to evil. . . . Sin becomes a kind of external tarnish, that obscures the lustre of the naturally bright virtues, that can be easily brushed aside, when these virtues assume their original brilliancy.'[2]

4. Buddhist ideas.—The influence of Buddhism in China in the religious sphere has been great. In place of a hazy notion of a future state it introduced a complete system of future rewards and punishments. The description of its heavens and hells, couched in realistic terms for the common man, met a crying want in the Chinese conceptions of a future state. There was thus introduced for the first time into Chinese religious thought a definite doctrine of the future punishment of sin committed in the present life.[3] The religious terms and the new conceptions which Buddhism infused into existing terms all widened the outlook of men on sin and its consequences. The Chinese by the worship of ancestors had developed what amounted to not much more than a shadowy faith in something like ghosts. There was apparently no strong conviction about the future life, and sin had no connexion with it. A certainty took the place of vague hopes. This life was linked on to the next. A future life was the inheritance of every living being, and the happiness or misery of this future life was within the power of every one to enjoy or suffer, for rewards or punishments were conditioned by the conduct of each in the present life. The chanting of liturgies, repentance, meritorious actions, the life of an ascetic, will produce the forgiveness of sins, according to popular Chinese Buddhism.

Yet, with all that Buddhism introduced into China, the absence of a strong conviction of sin among the Chinese is doubtless due in a measure to the negative view of virtue which this religion presents. With its lack of inspiration towards goodness and its inability to strengthen man in a struggle against evil, it has had the effect of obscuring the idea of sin and has exerted a weakening effect on the moral nature. For sin, viewed from its standpoint, is more a calamity or a misfortune than a moral evil.[4] Even in the best sects of Buddhism, such as that of the Paradise of the Western Heavens, it is not deliverance from a world of sin that its followers look forward to, but deliverance from the 'bitter seas' of sorrow and suffering in this world and rescue from almost interminable births and *nirvāṇa* itself by a rapid transfer to the Land of Peace by faith in Amitabha Buddha and salvation through his name. But even in this abode of bliss sin is mentioned as being absent.

5. Taoist ideas.—In the ideal state of pristine perfection which Lao-tse (born *c.* 604 B.C.) describes, and to which mankind would revert were his philosophy carried out, good and evil were unknown. All suffering is due to a departure from this state. Chuang-tse, his eminent follower, a few centuries later also spoke of primitive innocence. In that Golden Age the people were upright and correct.[5] There was no room for sin to enter into such an Eden. But Taoism has become

1 *Reports of the World Missionary Conference*, Edinburgh and London, 1910, iv. 43.
2 Parker, *Studies in Chinese Religion*, London, 1910, p. 210.
3 *Chinese Recorder*, xxxi. [1900] 392.
4 *Ib.* xxix. [1898] 386, xliv. [1913] 289, 732; Legge, *Chinese Classics*, i., *The Confucian Analects*, bk. vii. ch. 33.
5 Parker, *Studies in Chinese Religion*, p. 211.
6 See Legge, *Chinese Classics*, ii., *Works of Mencius*, 'Prolegomena,' ch. ii. p. 82 ff.
7 E. Faber, quoted in *Chinese Recorder*, xxxiii. [1902] 166.
8 See Soothill, p. 256 f.
9 Legge, *Confucian Analects*, bk. i. ch. 8, v. 4. The same word is used for 'transgressions.'
10 *Ib.* vol. ii. bk. iii. ch. 8, v. 3.
11 See J. Dyer Ball, *Pith of the Classics*, Hongkong, 1905, pp. 2, 28.
12 E. Faber, *Hist. of China*, Shanghai, 1902, Introd. by P. Kranz, p. 7.

1 *Chinese Recorder*, xxviii. [1897], 517.
2 *Ib.* xvii. [1886] 374. 3 See *ib.* ix. [1878] 286.
4 See E. J. Eitel, *Three Lectures on Buddhism*[2], London, 1873, pp. 59, 63, 73; also *Chinese Recorder*, ix. [1878] 292; J. Edkins, *Chinese Buddhism*[2], London, 1893, p. 366; cf. art. SIN (Buddhist).
5 Soothill, pp. 48, 62, 64, 65; see Legge, *The Texts of Tâoism* [*SBE* xxxix., xl.], Oxford, 1891, pt. i. p. 325; H. A. Giles, *Chuang Tzu*, London, 1889, p. 152.

debased, superstitious, and idolatrous; among its devotees evil and sin are constantly present, and the consequences of sin have to be guarded against in this world and the next. The idea of sin is the same in Taoism as in Confucianism to a considerable extent. But, while an approving conscience is what Confucianism aimed at, the Taoist desires virtue to be rewarded by material benefits, such as long life, wealth, health, official rank, and many descendants.[1] In the fundamental doctrine that 'every creature is good in its essence' Confucianism and Taoism are at one and opposed to Buddhism. While Confucianism has simply its plane of action in the present life, Taoism 'looks beyond this world' and aims at purifying 'the heart [and the body] by special methods.'

The influence of Buddhism on Taoism has been most marked, especially in its doctrine of future rewards and punishments for sins committed in this life.

'A hell, with many apartments for multifarious tortures, has been adopted . . . as also many means, derived from the same source, for escape from the torments there. A system of merit and demerit and of retribution through spiritual agents in this life and hereafter was developed.'[2]

Through Buddhism, Taoism has borrowed the Hindu ruler of the dead, King Yama, and he presides over the nine other judges in the hell mentioned above. This development in the ideas of a future state where sin was thus dealt with took place in the 11th cent. A.D. One Taoist notion also accepted by some Confucianists and indigenous in China is of a conditional immortality. The good souls, but only they, inherit heaven, a place of happiness.

Sin, thus practically unknown in Taoism's early days, has now a definite position in its later elaborated system of beliefs. This position is shown in the popular religious tracts and books in which Taoist beliefs are the *motifs*, though, of course, tempered in some by Buddhist ideas. At the same time the latter religion is responsible for the inception and development of many of the statements figuring as Taoist. This literature has a wide circulation, and many of the tracts are very popular. One of the most widely read and best known is *Actions and Recompenses*, probably written by an unknown author in the 10th century. One passage in it is as follows:

'Transgressions, great and small, are of several hundred kinds. He who wishes for long life must first attend to strictly avoiding all these sins.'[3]

Nor is the sinner left in doubt as to what his sins are, for categories of them are given in books of this sort. They are very full, as the following will show:

'Blasphemy, simply ridiculing and breaking images of the gods, undutifulness to parents, oppression of the people, deception of the prince, lewdness of all sorts, careless scattering about of the five kinds of grain, slaughtering oxen and dogs for food, the use of false weights and measures, injuring others to benefit oneself, cheating of the good by the wicked, ill-treatment of the poor by the rich, aggravated forms of covetousness, crimes of violence, house-breaking, selling adulterated goods, cheating the simple in buying and selling, trampling lettered paper underfoot, deceiving the aged and despising the young, breaking off marriage contracts, striking and cursing grandparents,' etc.[4]

It will thus be seen that relations between the gods and mankind, dutiful regard to parents, rightful and just intercourse between mankind, business relationships, and charity, as well as offences against the laws, are all thought of in this list of sins and crimes which would subvert family order and civil life. These and similar transgressions bring their retribution according to their heinousness, for life is shortened by twelve years for great ones, and one hundred days for small ones. A regular system of accounts is adopted, and evil deeds and faults are entered to the debit of the keepers of these registers, and to their credit good actions are entered, a numerical value being assigned to each entry according to its position in the scale of virtue or evil. That the introspection, in some cases at all events, is most searching is shown by the following statement in one of these religious books:

'The most of what you do, what you say, the thoughts you think . . . are on the side of evil.'

The conflict between sin and the good in our own hearts is most strikingly stated in a philosophical work issued about the beginning of the 18th cent., and reminds one of St. Paul's reference to the subject in Ro 7[ff.]:

'When you have advanced sufficiently in knowledge of yourself, you will find it a grief. There will be, as it were, two men in your bosom. When you desire to do good, evil will come between. Again, when you wish to do wrong, a sense of shame will oppose you. Thus a battle goes on within you.'[1]

Some of the gods even are not perfect or free from sin. The gemmeous ruler of Taoism had a covetous heart, so one of his three souls had to become incarnate in 'the dusty, troublesome world.' Again, the Neptune of Taoism, the Sea Dragon, was disobedient, and his son was a drunkard, and the god of fire (originally a Buddhist god) committed theft. These stories are recounted in Taoist books published a few centuries ago.[2]

The Chinese, thanks largely to the moral teaching of Confucius, are remarkable, in comparison with many other non-Christian nations, for the purity of their religions. Yet the baser elements of human nature are to be found occasionally, so that not only are the everyday needs of life as well as riches, honours, health, prosperity, and offspring sought for from the gods, but there are a few deities worshipped by those who hope for help from them for the commission of sins and the carrying out of evil deeds. There is a small temple on the hill-side over the eastern portion of the city of Victoria, Hongkong, near some rocks which are believed, by the Chinese, to exert an evil influence on the morality of the city.[3] The goddess of this temple is the patroness of prostitution.[4] The present writer found on inquiry that the powder rubbed on the face of the image was supposed to make the worshippers who earned their living by that vice fair and attractive. There are also gods of gamblers[5] and of thieves,[6] gods of revenge[7] and of cruelty.[8] The drunkards even take as their patron saint Li Tái-pò, an anacreontic poet of former times.[9] Some men of former times who have been renowned for their evil deeds have been even deified and worshipped owing to an idea that it is well to propitiate them for fear of what they may be able to do to the living.[10] The tendency is, however, more to canonize the good.

6. Present-day popular beliefs.—The resultant of all the preceding influences is that, with his eclectic attitude towards all these elements of belief, the average Chinese has evolved a blend or amalgam of the whole as regards the religious side of his life—his ideas of sin and forgiveness of sin and all else connected with his spiritual life.

LITERATURE.—See the works cited in the footnotes.

J. DYER BALL.

1 See J. Edkins, *Religion in China*, London, 1878, p. 140.
2 Faber, in *China Review*, xiii. [Hongkong, 1884–85] 244 ff.
3 *Chinese Recorder*, xxviii. [1897] 586.
4 *Ib.* xiii. [1882] 303.

1 *Chinese Recorder*, xxix. [1898] 240.
2 See Dyer Ball, 'Scraps from Chinese Mythology,' *China Review*, xi. [1882–83] 203 ff., 282 ff., xiii. [1884–85] 75 ff., xii. [1883–84] 190 f.
3 See E. J. Eitel, *Feng Shui, or the Rudiments of Natural Science in China*, Hongkong, 1873, p. 53; also J. Doolittle, *Social Life of the Chinese*, New York, 1866, i. 292 f.
4 See H. C. Du Bose, *The Dragon, Image, and Demon*, London, 1886, p. 340, for a description of one of the goddesses of prostitution.
5 *Ib.* p. 340; also Doolittle, i. 271 f.
6 See *Chinese Recorder*, xli. [1910] 324.
7 *Ib.* 8 *Ib.* 9 *Ib.*
10 See Du Bose, p. 341 ff.

SIN (Christian).—This article in large measure presupposes what has been written in the artt. FALL and ORIGINAL SIN. It confines itself to a discussion of the Christian view or doctrine of sin as a state or power actually present in the developed moral consciousness of man. Since a modern interpretation must rest on the history of thought, our first task is to study the teaching of the NT and of great Christian minds.

I. The New Testament.—(*a*) Jewish literature of the 1st cent. B.C. and A.D. takes a sombre view of man. Constant allusion is made to the all but universal corruption, and, as man's relation to God is construed in essentially legal terms, the prevailing temper is fear of utter condemnation. Though sin may be inherited, moral freedom is intact, and man can choose whether he will or will not live righteously. The heart, not the flesh, is the seat of the inborn evil impulse (*yezer hara*); but at least the flesh makes sin intelligible, and, as Holtzmann puts it, 'there is no clear agreement whether the flesh represents a power ethically indifferent or one that somehow leads to sin.'[1] At the same time exceptional cases of sinless life are known. Each sin is an individual act, which can be weighed and numbered. Much responsibility for sin belongs to evil spirits which tempt men even to apostasy from God. But isolated offences can easily be expiated by penitence. Thus the Rabbinic mind swings between despair and pride. 'Far better were it for us,' says 4 Ezra, 'that we had not to face judgment after death' ($7^{68f.}$); on the other hand, the busy acquirer of merit thanked God that he was not like the rest of men (Lk 18^{11}). Sin is never put in relation to the love of God. Even by John the Baptist it is viewed solely as contumacy or rebellion. God is creditor, judge, king; man is debtor, culprit, subject.

(*b*) Jesus has no doctrine of sin in general; it was not abstract considerations creating an intellectual problem that He fastened on, but concrete sins. He does not speak of the Fall. But sin is a terrible fact, which is always committed against God, not merely against fellow-men (Lk 15^{18}), and the sinner is guilty. It has been said that Jesus dispersed the old morbid consciousness of sin like mist before the sun, but, if this means that He took it lightly, it is untrue. He does speak freely of good men and bad, and in the Beatitudes He implies the existence of those whom they describe. But He does not regard 'sinners' as merely one class of men among others; 'the righteous' are named so ironically. 'If ye then, being evil' (Mt 7^{11}), is one of His most arresting phrases; Peter is rebuked as 'Satan' for attempting to hold Him back from the Cross and told that he thinks like men; 'no one is good' (19^{17}), He replies to one questioner. Men must look like that to One who bids them love God with their whole heart and strength (22^{37}). The call to repent, with which Jesus' ministry opens, assumes that all have sinned, and more than once this call is repeated. All must be merciful, for all need pardon, and all will perish unless they show a change of mind. It is the man who cries 'God, be merciful to me a sinner' who is justified (Lk 18^{13}). The preaching of Jesus begins with individual acts of sin, but in addition He points to the corrupt heart which underlies them, for it is out of man's inner life that everything capable of defiling proceeds. Unless the heart is single, all is wrong. The sources of actual sin are this evil heart, stumbling-blocks put in the way by others (Mt 18^{7}), and the temptation of the devil (13^{39})—all of them influences which man can perceive and oppose. But no necessary determination to sin is even glanced at. The kinds of sin against which Jesus specially warns men[1] are unkindness, which will come up at the Last Judgment (Mt 25); the passions of anger and lust, the impure look and desire being equally wrong with the impure act (Mt 5^{28}); self-deception and unreality of thought ('Thou blind Pharisee,' 23^{26}); and moral indecision (Lk 9^{62}). Sin develops; the inner treasure of the heart becomes evil (Mt 12^{35}), and men, growing worse and worse, come to resemble a bad tree bearing fruit after its kind. God punishes sin, but far greater is the truth that men can repent and that all sins can be forgiven except that which connotes final hardening and therefore entangles men in guilt for ever (Mk $3^{28f.}$). It is when He is speaking of forgiveness that we can perceive how much sin means to Jesus. Guilt in His eyes is the heaviest of all loads, as is clear from the episode of the paralytic (Mk 2); men need pardon constantly (Mt 6^{12}); and in God's sight even disciples are laden with an overwhelming debt calling for the sheer mercy of the Father ($18^{23ff.}$).

(*c*) St. Paul, unlike Jesus, offers the data for a doctrine of sin in the sense that sin (oftenest used in the singular) is generalized from a profound interest in its nature and significance as a whole. Broadly it means what is opposed to the law of God—His will expressed in commandments—and through law man becomes fully aware of it (Ro 3^{20} 7^{7}). But law too can be generalized; it is present not merely in the Law of Moses, though its embodiment there rose most naturally in the apostle's mind, but in man's heart everywhere. All are under law; all have violated law; hence all are under sin. The sin manifested in individual acts is a power, a universal condition or tendency of human life, a principle confronting men which St. Paul virtually personifies, though it does not possess objective existence for him as 'a power in *rerum natura* but not in this or that will.' The personification is half poetic, just as in the case of death, law, or flesh. But the meaning is a terrible reality; there is a system of sin, to which all are hopelessly enslaved, their only wages death. Except for the counter-activity of the Spirit of God or Christ, human life is sinful through and through. The manifestations of this principle are variously named—transgression, unrighteousness, lawlessness, disobedience, etc.

St. Paul proves the universality of sin by several considerations: by inspection of the life of Jews and Gentiles (Ro 2 and 1); by citation of the OT (Ro 3); by deduction from the universality of death, its penalty; by regressive inference from Christ's atoning death, which implies a universal need; finally by what is to all intents and purposes a metaphysical argument about the compelling power of the flesh. This universality he does not hesitate to call a divine ordinance. The law was intended to multiply transgressions by provoking the natural antipathy of the flesh (Gal 3^{19}), and thus to lead sinners to despair of attaining righteousness otherwise than through Christ and faith.

The original element in St. Paul's teaching does not lie in what he says regarding the various types of sin, or its moral character, or its effect on man's relation to God, who reacts upon it in the doom of death. He seldom touches the connexion of sin with Satan or demonic powers, though we must not forget phrases like 2 Co 4^{4}: 'The god of this world has blinded the minds of unbelievers.' His originality in contrast to Rabbinic thought lies in his explanation of the necessity of sin. To many scholars he seems to offer two unreconciled theories. First, the necessity is due to Adam's fall—a familiar Judaistic conception made impressive by its insistence on the unity of the race

[1] *Neutest. Theologie*², i. 67.

[1] T. R. Glover, *The Jesus of History*, London, 1917, ch. vii.

for which Adam stood (Ro $5^{12ff.}$). But for St. Paul this scarcely had the importance which it came to possess for historic theology; he really glances at it by way of illustrating the solidarity of believing men with Christ. 'Sin entered the world by one man' (5^{12}) may mean that Adam created for posterity the conditions of sinning, or it may only mean that Adam's was the first sin of history. St. Paul may have conceived of him as but the first instance of the sin inherent in man's fleshly nature, which brings up the second theory. This is that the flesh is radically antagonistic to God: as has been said, it represents for St. Paul 'the virulence and constitutional character as well as the omnipresence of sin.'[1] The will of the flesh and the will of man are one thing, the tie between the two being so close that there occurs in Ro 8^3 the phrase 'flesh of sin.' It is because he is in the flesh that man does sin and can do no other. This is not a Jewish conception; according to the OT and Judaism, the flesh, so far from being the point of departure, rather by its frailty extenuates the sinner's guilt, and in any case entails no hopeless compulsion to evil. Nor is the theory traceable to the dualistic psychology of Hellenism, in which matter is opposed to mind—a view far too intellectual for the moral passion and despair of St. Paul. He does not equate sin and evil matter, or sin and sensuality, for there are spiritual sins, and he never forgets that God has created the flesh and can make it the abode of Spirit. A careful linguistic inquiry has led E. D. Burton to the following result:

'Neither the evidence of contemporary usage nor that of the New Testament itself warrants us in finding in Paul . . . the notion that the flesh is by reason of its materiality a force that makes for evil, or that a corporeal being is by reason of that fact a sinful being.'[2]

We must then believe that to St. Paul the flesh is a power productive of sin not because it *is* sin, but because sin, seated in the flesh as an alien power, utilizes it as organ and instrument. Till Christ came, the empirically sinful fleshly principle ruled; ever since, the counteractive Spirit has been victoriously on the ground. For the man who lacks the Spirit and lives on the soil of law the flesh must always be the gateway through which sin, in the shape of lust, invades experience, but this inevitable revolt against God leaves responsibility undiminished. Man's state is revealed to him by conscience, not to furnish him with an excuse, but to prove that no way to righteousness is open except God's.

(*d*) The doctrine of sin in the Johannine writings has been described as accidental or even almost wholly absent. For the writer of the Fourth Gospel, it is held, sin is a mere privation, which in itself involves no moral culpability; it is 'the natural incapacity of man to possess himself of the higher life.' It is true that we cannot identify the Johannine teaching with the Pauline. The former allows more for degrees of sin (19^{11}). Sin is indeed universal, but some men are, as it were, naturally of the truth (18^{37}) or of God (8^{47}). At the other extreme is unbelieving Judaism; in fact the sin in which the writer of the Gospel, from his historical and apologetic purpose, is chiefly interested, and upon which he generalizes, is disbelief in Christ with its inevitable judgment. It is on this ground that the Spirit convinces of sin (16^9). Those who sin purely out of blindness may come to faith if they are given sight, but the bulk of men have this condemnation resting on them that they preferred darkness to the Light now present in the world (3^{19}), and this because light, by exposing evil acts, incurs the hatred of all whose practices are corrupt. Their blindness is guilty. Such unbelievers are children of the devil, that murderer and liar from the first, in whose power the whole world lies (1 Jn 5^{19}); they have learned of their father and do his will. Not that Christians are sinless, though in principle they have broken with moral evil (3^9); on the contrary, they need pardon constantly (1^8), and are in danger of self-deceit and lovelessness; nay, such deadly sin is possible as may not bear being prayed for (5^{16}). This last almost certainly means apostasy from the faith. Obstinately disbelieving mankind make up 'the world'—a hostile system confronting God and His people which is undivine in origin and quality, though no effort is made to explain how it arose in a universe created by God. This world hates Christ because He does not belong to it (Jn $15^{18f.}$), as indeed it hates God, whom it has not known ($15^{23f.}$). Sensuality and pride are characteristic of it (1 Jn 2^{16}). This opposition of faith and worldly unbelief is primarily one of experience, but it hardens into something like a static or timeless and irreconcilable antagonism; the world cannot receive the Spirit (Jn 14^{17}), and in nature is identical with the devil. Yet, on the whole, the Fourth Gospel leaves us faced by an antinomy; on the one hand, Jesus will not pray for the world (17^9), on the other, the prospect of its being brought to faith in Christ's mission is left open (17^{21}). Such a sentence as the last, or the great prophecy that Christ will draw all men to Himself (12^{32}), could hardly have been written by one whose mind finally rested in a metaphysical or gnostic dualism.

2. History of doctrine.—Church teaching about sin is much less concerned than Scripture is with the meaning of sin in experience and under the light of Christ. Roughly, two-thirds of its interest has been given to original sin—*i.e.* the sin of Adam in its consequences for the spiritual condition and fate of mankind, this first sin having as its foil an alleged state of original righteousness on which Scripture has little to say. Yet what most troubles the Christian conscience is neither sin committed by the first human pair nor the sin with which we are born, but the actual sinfulness of our acts and persons. Abstracting so far as possible from original sin, we shall seek to indicate the main trend of thought in the Church with regard to sin as found in normal adult experience.

(*a*) Among the more important questions canvassed in the 2nd cent. were the persistence of sin in the Christian life, and the rigoristic demand that lapse into grave sin should be viewed as involving the loss of salvation—a demand eventually rejected by the great Church even in face of Tertullian's unwillingness to readmit those who had been guilty of mortal sins (fornication, idolatry, murder). East and West conceived of sin differently, though at first both held that moral evil springs out of freedom, and that freedom cannot be lost. To the Greek mind not guilt but sensuality and decay were the essential features of the misery entailed by Adam's fall. The idea of original sin was largely foreign to the East as late as the 5th century. Not even the universality of sin was a fixed point, though Origen affirmed it speculatively; Athanasius distinctly says that there were many sinless lives before and after Christ. It was universally held that baptism remits all previous sin, but the terms on which later sins were pardoned caused much difficulty.

(*b*) The greatest of all controversies over sin is that between Augustine and Pelagius. In opposition to the Manichæans, Augustine insisted on the voluntary nature of sin, which is not a natural (*i.e.* automatic) but a moral fact. An act is not sin at all if it be not voluntary. But he was the first Church teacher to declare that none the less

[1] J. Denney, in *Exp*, 6th ser., iii. [1901] 290.
[2] *AJTh* xx. [1916] 596.

it is due to a pitiful necessity. Man, cut off from God the source of all good, is impotent to do good actions. As a psychological indeterminist Augustine conceded that man may freely prefer a less evil to a greater; as a theological necessitarian he denied that without grace any right act is possible. It is sheer frivolity to talk, as Pelagius did, of pure freedom of choice as man's inalienable prerogative; the sinner's will is in the last resort the will of a slave. Not merely particular acts, but the nature, disposition, and affections of man are sinful and guilty throughout, incapable of any good. No terms can be made with Pelagius's doctrine that sin consists of individual actions only and leaves the will and nature unaffected, or that children are born sinless, or that the universality of sin (if a fact) is due to bad example or defective education, or that divine grace is requisite only in the form of instruction and the example of Christ. All this was gathered up in Augustine's religiously profound and logically rigorous doctrine of original sin together with its implications.

Sin he defines as *spontaneus defectus a bono*,[1] but (apparently in answer to the Manichæan doctrine, which made sin a substance) he describes it further as merely negative in the sense that it is a *privatio boni.* Good is being, evil is not something positive but a loss or lack of being, which needs no efficient but only a deficient cause. This privative conception of sin, never really accepted by the Church, was probably meant by Augustine to guard against the mistake of viewing sin as essential to human nature and *eo ipso* created by God. God, like one who strikes an untuned harp, is the cause of man's activity, but not of its discord with the law of righteousness. Sin at bottom is pride, while the form which the perverted will takes in every human being is concupiscence or lust. Any sin is 'mortal' in which the will turns away from God. Men are born not merely sinful but guilty, subject to God's wrath, and meriting eternal damnation. The thought of inherited guilt is no longer convincing, and must tend to evacuate guilt of its proper sense, but the religious power of Augustine's teaching as to the solidarity of mankind in sin will always make its own impression. The Church settled thereafter for centuries in a semi-Pelagianism, or, from another point of view, a semi-Augustinianism, which left the sinner with a capacity to assent to grace.

(*c*) In the following centuries also the emphasis moved by degrees from act to disposition, and mortal sin became equivalent to love of the creature instead of God. In the 9th cent., while venial sins were atoned for by a paternoster, mortal sins were changed to venial by the satisfactions of penance. Anselm made an advance of great moment by bringing out indisputably the guilt of sin, previously obscured by a tendency to construe sin as a defect and in large measure to overlook its personal relation to God; and yet even Anselm's view of guilt leans to the negative side. It is our failure to perform a duty, and the full spiritual relationship of the sinner to God is not made clear; a deficient thought of God so far concealed the full blameworthiness of sin. The older idea of sin as formally a *carentia*, or lack, persists in scholastic theology; it is what we have lost in comparison with Adam; materially it is concupiscence, though, according to Duns Scotus, this, as but the *fomes peccati*, is not itself sin.

(*d*) The Reformers strove most of all to accentuate the religious and personal character of sin as interpreted by the light of revelation. As for content, sin is want of faith, the failure to fear and love and trust God. Luther never tires of saying that mistrust of God is the gravest manifestation of our corrupt nature. He marked his opposition to the externalized doctrine of scholasticism by thus identifying sin with the 'faithless heart.' Thus the personal significance of sin was forced in upon conscience, despite the fact that in most ways the Augustinian tradition, which made original sin primary, still persisted. How inherited guilt can be reconciled with the new sense of moral responsibility is left dark; Zwingli alone protests that we cannot speak of sin (which for him embraces guilt) except when the individual will has appropriated the corrupt heritage. In the Protestant scholasticism of the 17th cent. much is said of the consequences of sin, viz. guilt (*reatus culpæ*) and punishability (*reatus pœnæ*). The penalty is death in the most comprehensive sense: (1) *mors spiritualis*, or the loss of the divine image; (2) *mors corporalis*, including sickness and outward evils as well as actual dissolution; (3) *mors æterna*, or exclusion from everlasting life with God.

The preoccupation of orthodoxy with Adam's transgression and its fruits led to undue neglect of the social power of sin. Modern thought, instead of linking our inborn evil constitution to our first parents, speaks rather of a sinful race or community in whose evil we share, and insists that in this field the idea of inheritance means that we infect those who come after as well as receive infection from our ancestors. Not only so; it is rightly held that sin spreads in other ways than by heredity, viz. through bad training, unworthy example, and tempting provocations. We must advance to the conception of the whole complex sin of humanity, in which inherited sin is only an element. The traditional idea of total depravity, while no doubt indicative of the fact that no part of our nature is unstained and that we cannot of ourselves do what is in the highest sense good, is nevertheless unscriptural and untrue to life if taken to mean that non-Christians are 'utterly indisposed, disabled, and made opposite to all good, and wholly inclined to all evil.'[1]

(*e*) Socinian and Arminian criticism of a tradition so deeply influenced by Augustine bears chiefly on original sin, but from the Socinian definition of the essence of sin as voluntary transgression of the law it is clear that sin as such is for the Socinians a narrower idea than for orthodoxy. The later supranaturalists held that sin is imputable only when free will has failed to fight and overcome the difficulties of a nature disordered by sensuous impulse. At a wider remove from orthodoxy, 18th cent. Rationalism taught that man is characterized by a certain weakness of the will to good and a certain disposition to evil, while at the same time, though in consequence of his finitude only by degrees, he is perfectible, *i.e.* can develop the feeble inborn germ of good and rise above the tyranny of desire into true liberty of spirit. The interest and importance of Kant in this field largely rest on his efforts to supply what may be called a philosophic analogue to the Church doctrine of original sin—that radical evil in man as man the timeless origin of which is symbolized by the Biblical story of the Fall. But this we must pass over. Schelling gives his own philosophic form to the antinomies of tradition, holding that, in spite of a universal necessity rooted in the dark bases of God, evil is man's choice, and every creature falls by its own guilt. To Hegel the Adamitic fall is a mythic representation of an eternally necessary process; for man, good by nature (*i.e.* ideally spirit or rationality), must, in order to realize the life of

[1] A fuller definition is this (*de duab. Anim.*): 'Peccatum est voluntas retinendi vel consequendi quod iustitia vetat, et unde liberum est abstinere.'

[1] *Westminster Confession*, vi. 4.

spirit, pass by a dialectically inevitable movement from innocence to sin and from sin to virtue. The transition from innocence to sin is due to the necessity of transcending mere nature, which, *qua* absence of will, is bad; the transition from sin to virtue is mediated by retribution and amendment. This, as McTaggart points out,[1] means that sin is not only a necessary concomitant of virtue, but a necessary element in it. Sin must lead to virtue, and there is no virtue which is not based on sin. But it will naturally be asked whether this point of view is not more æsthetic than moral, and wrong even so; whether it can be taken seriously in moments of self-scrutiny and penitence; whether, provided the actual evil of life is part of its perfection, to replace vice by virtue is not simply a blunder; and whether the conception of goodness as rooted in badness has any relevance to Jesus, His personal holiness, and His revelation of the Father against whom all sin is done.

Modern theologians have determined the concept of sin variously, yet with an all but unanimous rejection of Pelagian tenets. Schleiermacher, reporting, as he held, on the Christian consciousness, defined sin as the positive struggle of the flesh against the spirit. Man's sensuous development gets ahead of his spiritual development, and, this being God's ordinance, we can avoid making Him the author of sin only by concluding that the consciousness of guilt, which *we* trace to sin but God does not, has been given us to stimulate the desire of redemption. Schleiermacher vacillates between the view that sin is non-existent for God and that it is caused by Him; he grounds it in human nature and finds this an enhancement of its gravity, yet he is tempted to explain it as a necessary outcome of our sensuous nature. Sin, he declares, is a social fact, being 'in each the work of all, and in all the work of each.' In contrast to this conception of sin as sensuality may be placed the view, notably exemplified in Julius Müller, that it is selfishness, though in Müller's case this was supported by a curious speculation, reminiscent of Origen and Kant, according to which finite selves have not so much pre-temporally as timelessly and primordially torn themselves loose from God and made self the principle of life. This theory of sin as being in principle selfishness has had great vogue, not in conservative quarters only. Ritschl too subscribed to it, but is chiefly meritorious for his insistence on the religious character of sin. Its real nature, range, and evil are only revealed fully by the Gospel; religiously it is the lack of reverence and trust towards God, while in a moral aspect it is antagonism to His Kingdom. His contention that all forgivable sin is in God's eye sin of ignorance has been severely criticized as abolishing guilt, though Ritschl's own main charge against original sin is that such sin could not be reckoned guilty. But it has been rightly felt that, as sin is not *all* ignorance, Ritschl's formula is misleading, and gives encouragement to the notion that deliberate open-eyed transgression is too great for God to pardon. Another of his valuable ideas is that of a 'kingdom of sin,' which is not in the least a futile effort to account for sin by the universality of sin, but a clear indication of the fact that the wrongly used freedom of the individual is relative to an environment — coextensive in the last resort with human life—in which sin already prevails.

The most important English discussion of sin in recent years is that of F. R. Tennant,[2] who argues that we ought to substitute a plurality of concepts, developmental not static, for the rigid idea of sin with which theology has usually operated.

[1] *Studies in Hegelian Cosmology*, Cambridge, 1896, p. 151 ff.
[2] See his *Origin and Propagation of Sin*[2] and *Concept of Sin*.

Sin is one thing, imperfection another; and imperfection is sin only when at the same time it is volitional. 'Man is conscious before he is self-conscious, impulsively appetitive before he is volitional, and volitional before he is moral,'[1] so that natural and organic propensities provide the raw material out of which the will constructs sin. Sin and guilt are correlative and co-extensive. Penetrating and illuminative as Tennant's work is, it may be doubted whether his 'logically perfect' concept of sin will be approved by those who hold with St. Paul and Augustine, not to speak of numerous modern students of society, that men are ethically as well as physically involved in the unity of the race, and that we desert experience if we ignore either aspect of sin, the voluntary or the constitutional.

3. The doctrinal interpretation of sin.—Certain points, such as the universality of sin, have been sufficiently treated of above, but we may now consider from a theoretic point of view some larger topics which have been referred to only incidentally.

(*a*) Sin may be defined as indifference or opposition to the will of God, the refusal of faith and love. And, if the will of God be fully revealed in Jesus, it follows that the Christian estimate of sin is a new and creative one. For it declares that sin is what it is in virtue of its relation to holy love. Elsewhere sin is folly, ugliness, or sickness, not mistrust or rebellion against a love measured by the Cross. The difference is not superficial, but radical, inasmuch as it results from a new thought of God. Sin, then, is the explicit or implicit claim to live independently of God, to put something else, be it the world or self, in His place. In a moral aspect this fundamental godlessness or God-forgetfulness appears as selfishness and sensuality.

At bottom sin is a religious idea, which for that reason cannot be properly defined otherwise than by putting it expressly in relation to God. In a formal point of view the same consideration disqualifies the proposal to define it as selfishness. All selfishness is of course sin, but neither logic nor (the present writer would hold) experience justifies us in converting this proposition *simpliciter*. It is indeed very questionable whether some sins are not quite disinterested, involving no pursuit of egoistic ends at the cost of others. Thus the family affection which produces the family vendetta, or suicide committed to save the reputation of a friend, or the most odious forms of religious persecution are not obviously selfish and may actually demand true loyalty and unlimited self-sacrifice.

To define sin as sensuality is even more inaccurate. Many of the worst sins—hate, cruelty, lying, irreverence—have no close connexion with the senses; they run their course within the mind. It is of course recognized by those who prefer this definition that deliberate surrender to the force of bodily craving is not *per se* sinful; no man sins merely by taking food to satisfy hunger or by going to sleep; sensuality is the wrong gratification of bodily impulse, in contravention of higher demands. At the same time, to identify sin with sensuality, to make the two an equation, is more or less to extenuate its badness by deducing it from the natural conditions of human life. An illegitimate interpretation of the theory of evolution has probably rendered this view of sin more popular to-day than ever. Sin, it is held, is just the brute-inheritance; we move upwards by working out the beast. But every biologist who thinks clearly will grant the necessity of distinguishing two things that differ—the enlargement of faculty

[1] *Concept of Sin*, p. 155.

whereby man becomes more than an animal, and the voluntary commission of evil known to be such. But it is the first, not the second, that constitutes a rise in the scale of being. In other words, the willed commission of sin is an anti-evolutionary fact. Sin and the consequent disorder cannot be exhibited as the consistent prolongation of natural processes of development or as progressive adaptation to environment. As well might we call poverty a result of good trade, or error an example of compliance with the rules of logic. Doctrines of human development can in some real degree construct for us the probable situation—whether of race or of individual—in which sin is first committed; they can do nothing to explain its actual emergence or its religious or moral meaning once it has emerged. The argument of a few evolutionary writers, on quasi-Hegelian lines, that experience of moral evil is necessary to prepare men to appreciate good may sound imposing as a generalization, but breaks down completely when applied to definite persons and definite sins.

Men become aware of sin, first of all, as an episode, a definite evil act in which a higher will is thrust aside. As it has been put, 'it is *a* sin of which man accuses himself—a disobedience which he can isolate in his life, regarding it as a blot, a stain, an exceptional phenomenon to be dealt with by itself.'[1] But behind this is next discovered a motive or disposition which gives the act meaning and out of which the act rises; and, by His condemnation of the murderous thought and lustful desire, Jesus made an end of the conventional idea that the sinner is merely one who commits so many wrong acts. Still deeper reflexion points to a permanent character or state of personal life affording unity and basis to varied acts and dispositions or attitudes. The falsest of all heresies is Pelagianism; if life is built on atomic lines, nothing like religion or morality is thinkable. No spiritual significance can be predicated of an act if it is a bare, accidental, unrelated point, but only if it carries with it a theory of its own origin in a certain articulated character from which it springs and on which it reacts. Nor is it true to say that this is but to use a collective name for the sum of our particular sins. Character is more than its past manifestations: in scholastic phrase, *peccatum actuale* does go back and down to *peccatum habituale.* Finally it is realized that the sinful individual life is part of a wider context of vitiated social life. The sins and sinfulness of a man require for full valuation this reference to the sin of the whole race.

(*b*) Christian theology must operate with an idea of guilt which is drawn from fully conscious moral experience. The idea is not confined to individual experience, but individual experience supplies our point of departure. Guilt is personal accountability and blameworthiness attaching either to a voluntary infringement of the will of God, in so far as that will is known to us or might have been known except for previous sin, or to a condition of personal life directly or indirectly consequent on such infringements. In strictness guilt is predicable not of acts, but of persons. No act, *qua* occurrence in space and time, is in itself wrong; ultimately moral quality belongs solely to the agent and his motives. Not only so, but acts pass, while persons remain somehow identical with their own past.

In this field we must first distinguish between guilt and sin in the sense of imperfection or badness. A young child may have acquired habits of lying or dishonesty through evil training in years prior to the normal awakening of full moral consciousness; in so far it is bad or imperfect, and

[1] J. Denney, *Studies in Theology*, London, 1894, p. 80.

it would be paradoxical to describe the child as without sin, for sin is whatever contradicts God's revealed will for human life. But the child's guilt may be small.[1] There can be no sin without guilt, but in such a case by far the greater portion of guilt attaches to others. In other words, guilt does not vary directly with sinfulness, except when we contemplate the race as a whole; collective human guilt is co-extensive and co-terminous with collective human sin. When the distinction just insisted on is wholly overlooked, guilt loses meaning and gravity; though it is undeniable that the religious mind does retrospectively predicate 'unworthiness' or the quality of being unpleasing to God of acts or states which at the time, from lack of enlightenment, could not have been other than they were. A second needful distinction is that between guilt as a feeling and as a fact. The consciousness of guilt cannot be taken as an exact or trustworthy index of actual guiltiness, for many wicked men have no bad conscience to speak of, and the worst and most hardened of men, feeling his guilt the least, and hardly conscious of the reproach of God or of his personal ill-desert, might otherwise be reckoned the least guilty. Our sense of guilt ought to be proportioned to our guiltiness; we cannot assert that in fact it is so.

To be guilty, a man must have moral knowledge or appreciation of right and wrong as they concern his action; where this pre-condition is lacking, as in imbecile or infant, guilt cannot be. But the knowledge in question need not be in the present consciousness of the sinner, for we should not cease to call a man guilty whose moral perceptions had been darkened by persistent wrong-doing. Further, guilt presupposes power in the moral agent to have acted otherwise. The sin must have been avoidable. If the liar had no option but to lie, because the constitution of things forced the lie from his lips, self-reproach is out of place. In all probability the modern habit of rightly bringing action into the closest possible connexion with character tends to obscure this real avoidability of guilty sin. How, it is asked, can we be responsible for what is the necessary outcome of character? Conscience imputes guilt to me on the ground that my character, being bad, inevitably expressed itself in just this way. But this appears to be out of harmony with the utterances of the moral consciousness. What I feel in moments of penitence is not that I am bad because I could act only in this sinful fashion, but that the badness of my disposition is revealed by the fact that I could do, and did, this evil thing. My sin is not an inevitable manifestation of me, but it is an actual manifestation of those elements in me which I might have suppressed and did not. No form of determinism can consistently assign to guilt the significance it has for specifically Christian thought. Whether it be physical determinism, as in Lucretius, which makes the soul one kind of mechanical force working along with and in the midst of other forces of the same kind; or psychical determinism, as in Mill, for whom the self forms an organic mental unity, reacting according to law, like other organic unities, on the stimuli of the environment; or idealistic determinism, as it may be called, which ascribes to the self, besides this vital reaction, the logical capacity to co-ordinate and combine the motives present in consciousness—in every case the *sui generis* quality of personal action is lost sight of. Choice is confused with what is not choice at all—be it a physical event or a judgment of the understanding—whereas in fact it is the experience in which,

[1] And in principle this is the case of all; there is no young life which sinful infection has not touched long before the attainment of true moral personality.

by distribution of attention, we take up a selective attitude to the moral alternatives before us. We will to take this attitude when we sin; it is not taken for us by any interior psychical clockwork. Moral freedom is expressed in the valuation of motives, and in the last issue guilt is a word with only legal but no ethical sense unless the will produces actions without being itself produced. This is not to say that freedom is unconditioned. On the contrary, as it has been put, in all life there is involved a 'synthesis of two moments which it is wrong to take as real in themselves, the moment of necessity or acceptance of the situation and the moment of freedom or free action in the situation.'[1] Freedom, that is, is the correlative of data provided in part by our temperament and circumstances, in part by our previous moral history. We are candidates for freedom rather than completely free, but moral liberty in some real though varying measure is an essential presupposition of that culpable responsibility to God which religion names guilt. That, in spite of this real liberty, men sin so habitually is due to the accumulated power of evil impulses which they have nourished or failed to eradicate and to the incessant pressure of sin-charged social forces.

(*c*) The genesis of sin within the individual life is a problem so intricate that we must bear well in mind that no conclusion or lack of conclusion regarding the origin of sin can in the least affect our actual consciousness of its nature. Sin is on the ground, but we cannot watch it rising out of hypothetical antecedent conditions. Yet if, as we have seen, it is our own moral act, or a moral condition of our being which apart from our moral act would have no existence, the origin of sin must lie in the abuse of freedom. As it has been expressed, 'in the secret places of the human spirit takes place that strange change by which the non-moral is transformed into the immoral. We face here a mystery which we cannot explain, yet may not deny.'[2] Such abuse of freedom, however, does not occur *in vacuo*. The spontaneity of consciousness is a spontaneity of response to given factors in the world of presentation. What these factors are in this case may in part be understood if we recollect that our moral life has roots in animal nature, and is at first unformed—the process of our becoming being suffused from the very outset with a naive egoism operating in the midst of a chaotic strife between higher and lower impulses, a strife inseparable from each life's growth.[3] This confused mass of impulse, shot through by incipient movements of self-creation, is played upon by tainted social influences. These are the occasions and provocations of sin, but when we ask how they are translated into actuality the only answer is, 'By free choice.' This will seem inadequate only to minds obsessed by the idea of mechanical causation, which explains every phenomenon by some other. The will is not caused. Yet to refer moral evil to the free activity of will is less an explanation in the proper sense (all true explanation being teleological) than an implicit admission that sin is radically unintelligible—the one thing in the universe rightly to be called 'irrational,' as not merely an irreducible fact but the negation of all rationality. But, if freedom is an ultimate, we can see that the pre-condition of disobedience is also the pre-condition of obedience and of redemption. If God is love, it was necessary that sin should be possible.

[1] H. J. Paton, *Mind*, new ser., xxiii. [1914] 430; cf. W. R. Sorley, *Moral Values and the Idea of God*, Cambridge, 1919, ch. xvii.

[2] W. Adams Brown, *Christian Theology in Outline*, Edinburgh, 1907, p. 276.

[3] See especially the works of F. R. Tennant.

(*d*) Nothing in sin can be so important for the Christian mind as its relation to God. He assuredly is not the author of sin, in the sense either that it forms for Him a personal experience or that His will is equally fulfilled through human sin and human obedience. Otherwise we should need to be redeemed not by Him, but from Him. When sin, however, has once become real, like other real things it falls under the sweep of divine power and is made to serve the purpose of holy love. Thus it is permitted to expose itself in all its vileness and misery, pre-eminently at the Cross, this progressive self-revelation of evil being accompanied and more than impeded by a parallel disclosure of good. Again, sin is condemned by the divine holiness; on this subject the believing mind attains a certitude which admits of no dispute, including the insight that what religion calls the wrath of God—*i.e.* the reaction of His holiness against sin—is, in face of sin, a necessary aspect of love. This reaction takes shape in punishment; to ask whether God *must* punish sin is otiose, in view of the fact that He invariably does so. True, the old distinction of natural and positive divine penalties is unreal. Natural penalties, it was held, flow from sin by ordinary causation, habitual intemperance, *e.g.*, leading to disease; positive penalties by their striking and unusual character compel the sufferer or onlookers to ascribe them to divine agency. But all divine penalties are positive in the sense that God's will imposes them, and the fact that their incidence may be mediated by ordinary finite causes does not alter this in the least. Sin's proper punishment lies, as it were, within sin itself. It consists in the self-stultification of the evil will (for, in McTaggart's vivid phrase, sin is like drinking sea-water to quench thirst), in the persistence of evil desire, in weakness of character, in the sense of guilt, above all and decisively in estrangement from God. And, if to lose communion with God be sin's worst penalty, it is no paradox to say that no one is punished for sin as the Christian is. The social consequences of sin, like lovelessness and dispeace, are directly proportioned to the moral evil prevailing in society as a whole. But we cannot fix a proportion between sin and suffering for the individual life (Jn 9[3]). Sin always brings pain, but the pain, as the experience of Jesus proves, may strike the most innocent of all. Not only so, but to the reconciled heart external evil, instead of being annihilating judgment, may be fatherly chastisement which opens the way for a fuller revelation of divine love and thereby for the blessing of others. To the experience of death, which literature in every age proves to have been felt as the greatest of all ills, sin imparts a new penal character, which in some solemnizing measure it may retain even for the Christian, despite his recognition of it as appointed by the Father's love.

Closer to the heart of faith lie the great divine counteractives to sin, of which life and history are full. All ethical institutions which minister to community in the largest sense, such as the family, law, and the State, are here to be reckoned in; still more the emergence of great prophetic souls, deepening and refining the moral insight of the race. Above all, Jesus Christ has been here, and in the light of His person the drift of divine redeeming activity has become apprehensible by faith. His sin-conquering power is still made ours in the Holy Spirit, ever available in prayer and energizing divinely in the will of the believer, so enabling him to overcome sin and transform it into its opposite. The cardinal truth about sin is that it can be so forgiven as to be replaced by Christian goodness, and that in His Son the Father has interposed to put it away by the sacrifice of Himself.

LITERATURE.—The NT Theologies of H. J. Holtzmann (2nd ed., 2 vols., Tübingen, 1911), W. Beyschlag (Eng. tr., 2 vols., Edinburgh, 1895), P. Feine (Leipzig, 1910), H. Weinel (Tübingen, 1911), and G. B. Stevens (Edinburgh, 1899); A. Titius, *Die NT Lehre von der Seligkeit*, 4 pts., Freiburg i. B., 1895–1900; C. Clemen, *Die christl. Lehre von der Sünde*, Göttingen, 1897, i.; E. Ménégoz, *Le Péché et la rédemption d'après saint Paul*, Paris, 1882; the Histories of Dogma by A. Harnack (Eng. tr., 7 vols., London, 1894–99), F. Loofs (4 Halle, 1907), and R. Seeberg (Eng. tr., London, 1908); T. A. Lacey, *Nature, Miracle and Sin*, do. 1916; J. Müller, *The Christian Doctrine of Sin*, Eng. tr., 2 vols., Edinburgh, 1868; J. Tulloch, *The Christian Doctrine of Sin*, do. 1877; F. R. Tennant, *The Origin and Propagation of Sin*2, London, 1906, and *The Concept of Sin*, Cambridge, 1912; W. E. Orchard, *Modern Theories of Sin*, London, 1909; R. Mackintosh, *Christianity and Sin*, do. 1913; A. Ritschl, *The Christian Doctrine of Justification and Reconciliation*, Eng. tr., Edinburgh, 1900; O. Kirn, art. 'Sünde' in *PRE*3; J. Gottschick, art. 'Schuld und Freiheit,' in *ZTK* ix. [1899] 316–356; H. Rashdall, *Theory of Good and Evil*, 2 vols., Oxford, 1907.

H. R. MACKINTOSH.

SIN (Egyptian).—1. Conceptions of sin.—An idea, by no means complete, of what the Egyptians regarded as sins is afforded us by the two 'Assertions of Innocence' in ch. 125 of the *Book of the Dead*.[1] The acts and qualities therein repudiated by the deceased are murder, robbery, theft, oppression, impiety towards the gods and the dead,[2] lying, slander, dishonesty, avarice (*'wn-ib*), hasty temper, pride, loquacity, eavesdropping, adultery, and masturbation. From statements in moral treatises and other literary compositions, and in the biographical inscriptions of feudal lords and officials, we learn that to the sins enumerated in those two distinctly haphazard lists must be added injustice, partiality, disrespect for the aged and for parents, disobedience, contentiousness, rancour, ingratitude, selfishness, and drunkenness.

Some conception of the varying degree of reprobation in which the different sins were held—*i.e.* to what extent they were classed as greater or lesser offences against the gods or the community—can be gained from a study of the two artt. ETHICS AND MORALITY (Egyptian), § 13, and RIGHTEOUSNESS (Egyptian), §§ 2, 3, 4 (2), 5.

2. The origin of evil.—The Egyptians at a very early date seem to have had some conception of a Golden Age, when the sun-god ruled over the earth and when sin and evil did not yet exist.[3]

Already in the *Pyramid Texts* mention is made of 'those belonging to that first generation of the company of the righteous, that was born before anger arose, born before clamour arose, born before blasphemy arose, born before tumult arose, before the eye of Horus was wrenched out (?), before the testicles of Sēth were torn away (?).'[4]

To explain the origin of evil in the world is perhaps one of the aims of the so-called *Destruction of Mankind*.[5]

According to this tale, the sun-god Rē' (the god who was characterized by his righteousness and hatred of evil[6]) ruled at a remote age over gods and men. When he grew old, men thought blasphemously of him, so he sent down his eye in the form of the goddess Ḥathor to destroy them. After Ḥathor had for a whole day revelled in slaughter, Rē' relented and saved men from total extermination. But he henceforth refused to dwell any longer on earth, and withdrew himself to the sky.

In this legend men themselves seem to be regarded as the originators of sin, for it was as the result of their folly that the earth ceased to be under the direct rule of the perfectly righteous god.

Possibly also the above-quoted passage from the *Pyramid Texts* refers, in its original form, to this rebellion against the sun-god.[1] The reference to the quarrel between Horus and Sēth is apparently a later addition. But he who inserted it evidently held the view that all the sin and misery that prevail in the world originated, not in the acts of men, but in Sēth's murder of Osiris and his subsequent conflict with Horus.

3. The punishment of sin.—(1) *After death.*—The Egyptians had various conceptions of the punishments meted out to those who failed to obtain a favourable verdict at the posthumous trial.[2] The majority of these are sufficiently described in the art. RIGHTEOUSNESS (Egyptian), § 9 (1) (i.), (iii.), (v.). According to the *Second Tale of Khamuas*, the unrighteous dead were tortured.

'Setme saw . . . one man in whose right eye the pivot (?) of the door of the fifth hall (of Amenti) was fixed, while he prayed and uttered loud lamentation.'[3]

The man in question had been great and wealthy during his life, but after his death 'his evil deeds were found more numerous than his good deeds that he did upon earth.'[4] We read in the same tale that those who were improvident[5] during their lives suffered the pangs of hunger, while those who had led stupid, aimless existences—'the kind of men on earth whose life is before them, but God diggeth a pit at their feet to prevent them finding it'—had food, water, and bread hung over them, but as 'they were hastening to take it down . . . others dug pits at their feet to prevent their reaching it.'[6]

A point overlooked in the art. RIGHTEOUSNESS (Egyptian), § 9 (1), may here be noted. According to the above-quoted *Second Tale of Khamuas*, the actively virtuous are granted a higher award than the moderately good:

'As for him of whom it shall be found that his good deeds are more numerous than his evil deeds, he is taken among the gods of the council of the Lord of Amenti, his soul going to heaven with the noble spirits. And he of whom it shall be found that his good deeds are equal to his evil deeds, he is taken amongst the excellent spirits that serve Sokari-Osiris.'[7]

The high ethical tone of this tale (the existing version dates from the latter half of the 1st cent. A.D.)[8] is most remarkable.[9] We find no trace in it of the idea that justification after death could be attained by means of spells and ceremonial ablutions;[10] on the contrary, a man's fate in the hereafter is represented as entirely dependent upon how his life on earth had been spent. It may be pointed out at the same time that an equally high ethical standard is displayed in the description of the posthumous judgment in a composition of the feudal age, quoted in the art. RIGHTEOUSNESS (Egyptian), § 9 (1), (iii.), and also in the well-known passage occurring in one of that special group of hymns discussed below in § 6:

'Amun-Rē' who judgeth the earth with his finger . . . He assigneth him that sinneth against him to the fire, and the just to the West.'[11]

(2) *In this world.*—The Egyptian moralists warn the evil-doer that his sins will bring misfortune upon him or an untimely death.[12] The gods 'who will not ignore the deed of any person' are often represented as directly responsible for the sinner's doom.[13] A very ancient philosophical treatise informs us that the tongue of Ptaḥ 'gives life to the peaceful, death to the guilty.'[14]

1 See artt. ETHICS AND MORALITY (Egyptian), § 8; RIGHTEOUSNESS (Egyptian), § 3.
2 Cf. artt. PURIFICATION (Egyptian), v. 8 (*a*); RIGHTEOUSNESS (Egyptian), § 3 (6); ETHICS AND MORALITY (Egyptian), § 13 (10), (11), (18), (19).
3 See J. H. Breasted, *Development of Religion and Thought in Ancient Egypt*, New York and London, 1912, p. 211 ff.
4 K. Sethe, *Die altägyptischen Pyramidentexte* (hereafter cited as *Pyr.*), Leipzig, 1908–10, § 1463.
5 E. Naville, *TSBA* iv. [1876] 4 ff.; A. Erman, *A Handbook of Egyptian Religion*, Eng. tr., London, 1907, p. 29 ff.
6 See art. RIGHTEOUSNESS (Egyptian), § 6.

1 Cf. its phraseology with that of certain passages in A. H. Gardiner, *The Admonitions of an Egyptian Sage*, Leipzig, 1909, pp. 44, 78, 84, the whole aim of the sage here being to contrast the prosperous rule of the righteous sun-god with the disastrous rule of the weak Pharaoh whom he is addressing.
2 See below, § 4.
3 F. Ll. Griffith, *Stories of the High Priests of Memphis*, Oxford, 1900, p. 46.
4 *Ib.* p. 49.
5 See art. RIGHTEOUSNESS (Egyptian), § 9 (1), (iv.).
6 Griffith, pp. 45, 49 f.
7 *Ib.* p. 47 f.
8 *Ib.* p. 14.
9 *Ib.* p. 46, note on l. 6, p. 48, notes on ll. 8, 10; see also Erman, *Handbook*, p. 230 f.
10 See under § 4; see also Griffith, p. 46 f., note on l. 6.
11 *Select Papyri in the Hieratic Character from the Collections of the British Museum*, London, 1841–44, pl. lxviii. = *Pap. Anastasi*, 2, vi., ll. 5–7.
12 See art. RIGHTEOUSNESS (Egyptian), § 9 (3).
13 *Ib.*
14 A. Erman, 'Ein Denkmal memphitischer Theologie,' in *SBAW* xliii. [1911] 940.

4. The necessity for being sinless.—As has already been stated in the art. RIGHTEOUSNESS (Egyptian), §§ 5, 9, the attainment of bliss by the dead depended upon the verdict which they obtained at their posthumous trial. The judge of the dead, whether Rē' or Osiris, was characterized by his righteousness and hatred of wrong, as were also the members of the assistant judicial council. The deceased, in order to find favour in the sight of these gods and so obtain the verdict upon which his happiness depended, had also to be righteous, *i.e.* be able to show that he had led an absolutely sinless life on earth. Even an Egyptian would have regarded that as an achievement beyond the power of most men. Accordingly several ways were found of overcoming what must have appeared a very serious obstacle to salvation.[1] These were: (*a*) ceremonial ablutions, which, whether performed by or on behalf of a man during life or after death, cleansed him from his sin and made him righteous; (*b*) going on pilgrimage to Abydos or otherwise participating in the Osirian mysteries; (*c*) the recitation of magical formulæ, by means of which things alleged (*e.g.*, that the speaker was free from sin or had performed or participated in this or that ceremony), however untrue they might be, became actualities.[2]

5. The unwillingness of the Egyptian to acknowledge himself a sinner.—The nobles, officials, and private persons of the Old and Middle Kingdoms and early New Empire never seem to weary of asserting in their biographical inscriptions that, in respect of their character and conduct, they were models of perfection. To own that they were sinners or even imperfect never seems to have occurred to them. In fact they mention a fault only in order to deny that they were ever guilty of committing it.[3]

What looks like the most amazing spiritual pride may possibly be accounted for by the prevailing belief in the magical efficacy of formulæ, written or recited.[4] This belief, coupled with the idea that ceremonial purity and freedom from sin were their sole passports to posthumous happiness, naturally deterred the Egyptians from owning themselves sinners in any documents, particularly in ones so closely connected with their existence after death as were inscriptions on their tomb-chapel walls or on their funerary stelæ.[5] To allow there that they were anything but absolute perfection would be to jeopardize their chances of salvation. Indeed, if a man felt that he could not attain happiness in the hereafter unless by some means or other he convinced his divine judges that he was free from all moral and ceremonial defects, he might well have shrunk from admitting that he had any such defects even to himself.

(1) The claim of the Egyptian to moral perfection was also prompted by his desire to win the goodwill of visitors to his tomb-chapel, so that they might be ready to present him with food and drink-offerings or in lieu of these recite certain spells.[6]

(2) Those who accuse the Egyptians of unexampled spiritual pride must bear in mind that, though in accordance with custom the narrative containing these self-adulatory assertions is put into the mouth of the deceased, it was often composed under the direction of a pious son or some other surviving relative.[1]

(3) Such assertions in process of time became a convention, the stereotyped way of describing a deceased[2] or living[3] person's character, or even one's own.[4]

6. Acknowledgment of sin.—As has been pointed out, it was characteristic of the Egyptian to deny that he was guilty of sin. But certain hymns of the XIXth dynasty,[5] written on papyri or inscribed on votive stelæ, display a religious sentiment hitherto unknown in Egypt and not met with again until Christian times. The persons who wrote the hymns, or for whom the hymns were written, speak of themselves as 'humble'[6] folk, 'afflicted,'[7] 'distressed,'[8] 'in bondage,'[9] 'wearied.'[10] They confess that they are sinners deserving punishment at the hands of this or that divinity;[11] but they throw themselves on the mercy of the divinity, pleading that they are 'ignorant and foolish, not knowing good from bad,'[12] and 'disposed to commit sin.'[13]

'Punish me not for my many sins,' exclaims a suppliant of the god Amūn, 'I am a witless man. I am a man without understanding. All day I follow after my own dictates, as the ox after the fodder.'[14]

The divinities addressed are represented as chastising men for their sins.

A certain Nekhtamūn, we learn, 'lay sick unto death,' and was '[under] the might of Amūn by reason of his sin.'[15] Nefer-'abu 'was a just man upon earth,' but he 'wrought the transgression' against the Peak of the West (a Theban goddess) and she chastised him. This goddess, we are told, 'smites with the smiting of a savage lion, she pursues after him that transgresseth against her.'[16] The moon-god Thōth is said in one hymn to have punished a man for swearing falsely by him.[17] According to another, a man was smitten with blindness for a similar offence against Ptaḥ.[18]

But these divinities are always addressed as compassionate and ready to forgive.

'Be merciful to me!' cries a suppliant of Ptaḥ, 'look upon me, that thou mayest be merciful.'[19] Another suppliant appeals to Thōth as 'Merciful one, who art able to take this (punishment in the form of sickness) away.'[20] Amun-Rē', we are told, 'comes at the voice of the distressed humble one.'[21] He is as 'disposed to mercy' as is his petitioner to sin.[22] In answer to the prayer of a friend, this god heals a man whom he had smitten with sickness; for 'he passeth not a whole day wroth. His wrath is finished in a moment and nought is left.'[23] Similarly the Peak of the West is merciful to him who transgressed against her, when he turned to her in penitence.[24]

LITERATURE.—See the works cited in the text and footnotes.

AYLWARD M. BLACKMAN.

SIN (Greek).

SIN (Greek).—Sin may be defined, for our present purpose, as all conduct which by omission or by commission, in overt act or inner meaning, is offensive to the supra-human Powers.

1 See Griffith, p. 46, note on l. 6.
2 For details see artt. PURIFICATION (Egyptian), § v. 2, 8 (*b*), RIGHTEOUSNESS (Egyptian), § 10, SALVATION (Egyptian), § 2.
3 See art. RIGHTEOUSNESS (Egyptian), § 2.
4 See § 4 (*c*) above, and Griffith, *loc. cit.*
5 See Breasted, p. 167 ff., and esp. p. 169 f. It should be pointed out in this connexion that similar statements to those that follow the second 'Assertion of Innocence' in ch. 125 of the *Book of the Dead* (*i.e.* 'I have done what men command and that wherewith the gods are pleased . . . I have given bread to the hungry, water to the thirsty, clothes to the naked, a ferry-boat to the boatless. I have made offerings to the gods, and ablutions to the blessed dead') frequently occur in the tomb-inscriptions and on stelæ of the feudal age; see, *e.g.*, art. RIGHTEOUSNESS (Egyptian), §§ 2 (1), 3, 9 (6).
6 See art. RIGHTEOUSNESS (Egyptian), § 9 (6); Breasted, p. 169.

1 See Breasted, p. 167.
2 See Breasted, *Ancient Records of Egypt*, Chicago, 1906–07, ii. §§ 767–769.
3 See Gardiner, *Egyptian Hieratic Texts*, Leipzig, 1911, pt. i., p. 6.
4 *Ib.* p. 7.
5 See Erman, 'Denksteine aus der theban. Gräberstadt,' in *SBAW* xlix. [1911] 1086 ff.; B. Gunn, *Journ. of Egyp. Archæology*, iii. [1916] 81 ff.
6 *E.g.*, Erman, *Denksteine*, pp. 1088, 1091 f.
7 *Ib.* pp. 1088, 1105.
8 *Ib.* pp. 1088, 1091.
9 *Ib.* p. 1091.
10 *Ib.* p. 1108.
11 *E.g.*, 'Righteous was Ptaḥ, Lord of Truth, towards me, when he chastised me' (*ib.* p. 1102).
12 *Ib.* p. 1098.
13 *Ib.* p. 1094.
14 *Select Papyri in . . . the British Museum*, pl. lxxii. = *Pap. Anastasi*, 2, x., l. 7–xi., l. 1.
15 Erman, *Denksteine*, p. 1092 f.
16 *Ib.* p. 1098 f.
17 *Ib.* p. 1102 f.
18 *Ib.* p. 1101 f.
19 *Ib.* p. 1102.
20 *Ib.* p. 1103.
21 *Ib.* p. 1088.
22 *Ib.* p. 1094.
23 *Ib.* p. 1092 ff.
24 *Ib.* p. 1099. For a complete and accurate translation of many of these hymns, and for an admirable discussion on the question as to what influences were responsible for the unusual sentiments that the hymns display, see B. Gunn, *Journ. of Egyp. Archæology*, iii. 81 ff.; see also A. Erman, *Handbook*, pp. 78 f., 82 ff.; J. H. Breasted, *Development of Religion and Thought in Ancient Egypt*, p. 349 ff.

1. Early conceptions.—(1) *Sin and crime.*—We are accustomed to draw a distinction between sin and crime.

'All crimes,' says Hobbes,[1] 'are indeed sins, but not all sins crimes. A sin may be in the thought or secret purpose of a man, of which neither a judge, nor a witness, nor any man can take notice.'

Hobbes thus founds his distinction entirely on the difference between the overt act and the inner meaning. But it would be more in accordance with usage to define crime as an offence against the law of the State and sin as an offence against the law of God. Now in an early stage of society, when the sanction of the laws of the State is mainly their inherent validity as the ordinances of the Deity, however conceived, such a distinction could hardly emerge. But, when it does emerge, we shall find that it is by no means the case that all crimes are sins.

Thus, when Antigone buries her brother Polyneikes in defiance of the prohibition of the State, she sharply contrasts the law of man, which makes it a crime to bury her brother, and the law of God, which makes it a sin to leave him unburied. She deliberately makes her choice: she makes herself amenable to the penalty of death by committing a 'sinless crime'[2] on the ground that she owes a longer allegiance to the dead than to the living, and that the human law which she breaks is of inferior validity to the 'unwritten and unshakable laws of heaven.'[3]

And this distinction between the laws of man, which society has made for its own preservation, and the 'unwritten laws' (νόμοι ἄγραφοι) of heaven is one of much importance in the Greek doctrine of sin. The contrast is discussed in the *Memorabilia* of Xenophon, iv. 4, where we find that they differ in several ways. The 'unwritten laws' are of universal validity and their enactment must therefore be ascribed not to men but to the gods; they concern the fundamental facts of social life; they carry their own punishment with them and the penalties of their violation cannot be avoided, as the penalties established for the violation of human laws may be and are; in them that which is 'lawful' (νομικόν) is invariably also 'just' (δίκαιον). Mr. Bumble's immortal dictum applies only to man-made law.

(2) *Objective conception.*—To modern ideas the decisive criterion of sin is the consciousness of wrongdoing. An act may be foolish and mistaken, disastrous in its results to the doer and to others; but, if the doer acted with right intention and according to his best judgment, then, however we may characterize him or his act, we should certainly not employ, seriously, the terms 'sin' and 'sinner.' But from the earlier point of view the act alone is regarded. The sinner is in the position of a man who has incurred a debt. His sinfulness is not a matter of inner meaning, but an objective relation. Given the deed, the doer is a sinner, and a sinner he remains until the sin is expiated or condoned—precisely as the debtor remains a debtor until his debt is either discharged or remitted.

From this point of view it becomes even irrelevant to inquire whether the sin was incurred voluntarily or involuntarily, knowingly or unknowingly, with the best intentions or the worst.

This point of view is familiar to us in the OT. Thus, though 'Jonathan heard not when his father charged the people with the oath' (1 S 14^{27}), yet, because he did taste a little honey with 'the end of the rod that was in his hand,' he was condemned to die. So 2 S 6^{6}: 'Uzzah put forth his hand to the ark of God, and took hold of it; for the oxen stumbled. And the anger of the Lord was kindled against Uzzah; and God smote him there for his error; and there he died by the ark of God.'

We meet the same type of thought in Greek mythology. Thus Oineus sinned against Artemis by neglecting to perform sacrifice to her,[4] and the poet leaves it an open question whether his neglect was due to mere forgetfulness or was intentional:

ἢ λάθετ', ἢ οὐκ ἐνόησεν· ἀάσατο δὲ μέγα θυμῷ.

(3) *Sin and punishment.*—Closely connected with this objective conception of sin and the absence of conscious wrongdoing is the fact that the inference of sin is drawn from the punishment which sin is assumed to have evoked. As sin is inevitably punished, and punished according to early ideas directly and materially here and now, so the primitive mind easily infers that, if a man suffers signal misfortune, he must have sinned; whether knowingly or unknowingly, he must by omission or by commission have offended the Deity.

This type, again, is well known in the OT. In 1 S $14^{36ff.}$, when Saul asked counsel of God and God refused to answer him, Saul at once inferred that a sin had been committed: 'Draw nigh hither, all ye chiefs of the people: and know and see wherein this sin hath been this day.'

Precisely so in Homer, when Lycaon falls into the hands of Achilles, he says: 'Now again hath deadly fate delivered me into thy hands: surely I must be hateful to father Zeus, since he hath given me a second time to thee!'[1] So Odysseus attributes his detention to some sin that he had unwittingly committed: 'Not willingly am I detained, but I must have sinned against the deathless gods.'[2]

Just as material prosperity implies that a man is well-pleasing to the gods, so material adversity—poverty, childlessness, physical affliction—implies that he has offended them.

(4) *Collective guilt.*—Again, the guilt of the sinner is not, according to early ideas, a merely individual matter. The burden of the sinner's guilt may involve an innocent community in the wrath of heaven. Unexpiated sin cries for expiation. It may be that, only when the penalty of sin—plague or famine or both—falls upon the community, it first becomes aware of the guilt, or first has its attention called to it. Just as we read in 2 S 21^{1} 'There was a famine in the days of David three years, year after year; and David sought the face of the Lord. And the Lord said, It is for Saul, and for his bloody house, because he put to death the Gibeonites,' so in Greek literature we find repeatedly that, when some signal affliction falls upon a city, it is immediately interpreted as a judgment of an angry heaven, and it is inferred that some sin has been committed which demands expiation, and an oracle is consulted as to the nature of the unknown sin and the manner of its expiation.

The story of Oedipus may serve as an illustration. Son of Laios, king of Thebes, and Jokasta, he is exposed in infancy, is adopted and reared as son of Polybos, king of Corinth. Doubts having been cast upon his parentage, he goes to Delphi to consult the oracle. Learning that, if he returns to his home, he is doomed to slay his father and to marry his mother, he resolves not to go back to Corinth but to become a wanderer. Precisely this resolve leads him to meet his real father Laios on the road. Him he slays in ignorance, and, going on to Thebes, he marries the widowed queen, his mother, and by her has children. All this is done in ignorance. Yet the vengeance of outraged heaven visits the city with plague and barrenness of earth and beast and man. Oedipus sends to consult the oracle at Delphi and learns that the unknown murderer of Laios is in the land, and that it is the blood of Laios which occasions their affliction, and that the city must be purified either by banishing the murderer or by slaying him.[3] Thereupon Oedipus pronounces solemn sentence of outlawry upon the unknown murderer. As we shall have to recur to this point, the words in which Sophocles puts the denunciation of Oedipus, and which follow the actual formula employed in such cases, may be here quoted: 'This man, whoever he be—I forbid that any in this land whereof I hold the throne and sovereignty, either entertain or speak to him or make him a partner in prayers to the gods or in sacrifices or give him of the holy water (χέρνιψ) but all shall drive him from their homes, as he is our pollution (μίασμα)[4] . . . and I pray that he who did the deed, whether the unknown be one or hath accomplices, may evilly as he is evil (κακὸν κακῶς) wear out his hapless life. And I pray that, if with my knowledge he should share my hearth, I myself may suffer the curses which I have now invoked on these.'[5]

From the modern point of view Oedipus, inas-

[1] *A Dialogue of the Common Laws* (*English Works*, ed. W. Molesworth, London, 1839–45, vi. 37).
[2] ὅσια πανουργήσασα (Soph. *Antig.* 74).
[3] *Ib.* 450.
[4] *Iliad*, ix. 533 ff.

[1] *Il.* xxi. 82 ff.
[2] *Od.* iv. 377 f.
[3] Soph. *Oed. Tyr.* 100 ff.
[4] Cf. *ib.* 97: μίασμα χώρας.
[5] *Ib.* 236 ff.

much as he acted unwittingly, is guiltless. It was his very endeavour to avoid his awful doom that led him into it. But to the earlier conception of sin that does not at all alter the position. His acts have placed him in the position of a guilty person, and the innocent community which unwittingly harbours him shares his guilt and his punishment. The vengeance of heaven requires his expulsion (ἐλαύνειν) from the community whose gods he has offended.

It is important here to raise the question, Is the guilt which rests upon the people merely their failure to expel the guilty person, or is the community actually regarded as polluted by his presence? Obviously the answer must affect the whole conception of sin which is implied in the procedure. Now, however the matter may have been conceived in later times, there seems to be no doubt that at one period the people were regarded as actually polluted by the presence of the murderer. He is regarded as a plague-spot, a centre of contagion. He cannot take part in the worship of the gods, cannot enter the homes of the citizens without bringing contamination. If this were not already implied by such expressions as μίασμα, καθαρμός, etc., it seems to be clearly shown by such procedure as was adopted, *e.g.*, by the Athenians in the case of the murderers of Kylon.

Kylon, an Athenian noble, attempted to make himself tyrant of Athens. He seized the acropolis, where he was besieged. He and his brother made their escape. His followers were forced to capitulate. They sought sanctuary in the temple of Athene Polias, which they left only when the archons guaranteed their lives. At the instigation of Megakles they were nevertheless put to death. This brought a curse upon the city, and, in order to remove it, αὐτοὶ μὲν ἐκ τῶν τάφων ἐξέβληθησαν, τὸ δὲ γένος αὐτῶν ἔφυγεν ἀειφυγίαν. Ἐπιμενίδης δ' ὁ Κρὴς ἐπὶ τούτοις ἐκάθηρε τὴν πόλιν—*i.e.*, those of the actual murderers who were already dead were exhumed and cast beyond the borders of Attica; the family (γένος) of the Alkmaeonids was banished in perpetuity; and after that Epimenides of Crete purified the city. Thus clearly the innocent community was regarded as being itself polluted by the presence of the accursed (ἐναγεῖς).[1]

(5) *Procedure in cases of murder.*—The same sort of conception lies at the root of the Greek procedure in the case of murder and homicide. Our information is naturally fullest about that of Athens, which may be taken as typical. The legislation of Draco (*c.* 621 B.C.) appears to have amounted in general to a codifying of customary law, and his enactments appear to have possessed a quasi-religious sanction, as is already implied in the term applied to them—θεσμοί.[2] His laws relating to murder (the effect of which seems to have been to discriminate definitely between intentional and unintentional murder, and to emphasize the right of the State to exact punishment[3] instead of leaving it to the aggrieved individual) were not abrogated by the legislation of Solon (594 B.C.), who abolished his other enactments.[4] Severe as his regulations seemed to a later age—their severity Aristotle[5] considers to be their one notable feature[6]—they survived many revolutions and are the foundation of the ideal legislation in the *Laws* of Plato. It is, of course, beyond the scope of this article to examine these regulations in detail. But the significant point is that alike in Athenian law and in Plato all shedding of blood, whether voluntary or involuntary, requires, where the death penalty is not exacted, exile for a longer or shorter term, together with the performance of a ceremony of purification.

A curious procedure is that adopted in the case of a person who, being already exiled for involuntary homicide, is charged with committing another murder or with wounding with intent. Being a polluted person, he was not allowed to set foot in the land, but pleaded his case from a boat, lying off shore: ἐὰν δὲ φεύγων φυγὴν ὧν ἄρεσίς ἐστιν, αἰτίαν ἔχῃ ἀποκτεῖναι ἢ τρῶσαί τινα, τούτῳ δ' ἐν Φρεάτου δικάζουσιν, ὁ δ' ἀπολογεῖται προσορμισαμένος ἐν πλοίῳ.[1]

A similar procedure is enjoined by Plato in the case of an involuntary homicide who is driven to land by stress of weather: 'if he be wrecked and driven on the coast against his will, he shall encamp, wetting his feet in the sea, and wait for an opportunity to sail.'[2]

The procedure in the case of murder committed by a person or persons unknown is of interest as affording a comparison with Hebrew practice. The reader will remember the regulations laid down for such a case in Dt 21[1ff.]:

'If one be found slain in the land which the Lord thy God giveth thee to possess it, lying in the field, and it be not known who hath smitten him: then thy elders and thy judges shall come forth, and they shall measure unto the cities which are round about him that is slain: and it shall be, that the city which is nearest unto the slain man, even the elders of that city shall take an heifer of the herd, which hath not been wrought with, and which hath not drawn in the yoke; and the elders of that city shall bring down the heifer unto a valley with running water, which is neither plowed nor sown, and shall break the heifer's neck there in the valley: and the priests the sons of Levi shall come near . . . and all the elders of that city, who are nearest unto the slain man, shall wash their hands over the heifer whose neck was broken in the valley: and they shall answer and say, Our hands have not shed this blood, neither have our eyes seen it. Forgive, O Lord, thy people Israel, whom thou hast redeemed, and suffer not innocent blood to remain in the midst of thy people Israel. And the blood shall be forgiven them.'

It seems an adequate explanation to say that the measuring 'unto the cities which are round about' had for its object merely to determine which community was to bear the expense of the purification. All analogy indicates that the nearest city was regarded as being actually contaminated by the murder.

Now let us compare the Greek procedure in a similar case. Aristotle, describing the duties of the archon basileus, says:

'If the actual offender is unknown, the writ runs against the doer of the deed' (οἴαν δὲ μὴ εἰδῇ τὸν ποιήσαντα, τῷ δράσαντι λαγχάνει).[3]

The same sort of procedure is instituted by Plato:

'If a man is found dead, and his murderer be unknown, and after a diligent search cannot be discovered, the same proclamations shall be made as in the other cases, the death sentence shall be passed on the guilty person (τῷ δράσαντι) and proclamation shall be made in the market-place that he who has slain so and so and is guilty of murder, shall not set foot in the temples or at all in the country of the slain man, under penalty of being put to death if he appear and is known and being cast unburied beyond the borders of the country of the slain man.'[4]

The Hebrew rite is to be performed 'in a valley which is neither plowed nor sown'—*i.e.*, the guilt is to be transferred from the community to a no man's land.

Precisely so suicides are 'to be buried alone, and none shall be laid by their side; they shall be buried ingloriously in the borders of the twelve portions of the land'—as in this country they used to be buried at the crossways—'in such places as are uncultivated and nameless, and no column or inscription shall mark the place of their burial.'[5]

(6) *Guilt of animals and things.*—Guilt, again, may attach, according to early ideas, to the lower animals and even to inanimate things. To the case of the lower animals we cannot do more than allude here, as it is not very prominent in Greek records and is susceptible, perhaps, of more than one explanation. That such guilt was recognized in Greece and that animals which had caused a person's death were solemnly tried is a well-attested fact:

'And if a beast of burden or other animal cause the death of any one, except in the case of anything of that kind happening in the public games, the kinsmen of the deceased shall prosecute the slayer for murder, and the wardens of the country, such and so many as the kinsmen appoint, shall try the cause, and

---

[1] Arist. *Constitution of Athens*, 1. [2] *Ib.* 4.
[3] See art. CRIMES AND PUNISHMENTS (Greek), § 6.
[4] Arist. *Const.* 7. [5] *Pol.* II. ix. 9.
[6] Cf. Arist. *Rhet.* ii. 23; Aul. Gell. xi. 18.

[1] Arist. *Const. of Athens*, 57; cf. Suid., Harpocrat., etc.
[2] *Laws*, ix. 866.
[3] *Const. of Athens*, 57; cf. Pollux, viii. 120: τὸ ἐπὶ Πρυτανείῳ δικάζει δὲ περὶ τῶν ἀποκτεινάντων κἂν ὦσιν ἀφανεῖς.
[4] *Laws*, ix. 874. [5] *Ib.* 873.

let the beast, when condemned, be slain by them and cast beyond the borders.'[1]

And we know that elsewhere similar prosecution and punishment of animals was common in the Middle Ages.[2] But, as such punishment is capable of being explained as a mere exhibition of revenge or retaliation, it may be left out of account here.

Even more striking is the procedure against inanimate objects which had caused a man's death:

'The king and the tribe-kings also hear the cases in which the guilt rests on inanimate objects and the lower animals.'[3] 'And if any lifeless thing deprive a man of life, except in the case of a thunderbolt or other fatal dart sent from the gods—whether a man is killed by lifeless objects falling upon him, or by his falling upon them, the nearest of kin shall appoint the nearest neighbour to be a judge, and thereby acquit himself and the whole family of guilt. And he shall cast forth the guilty thing beyond the border.'[4]

The same, so to say, mechanical conception of guilt or impurity meets us repeatedly in the OT.[5] And precisely the same conception underlies the old English legal usage of *deodand*—the statutes of which were abolished only in 1846—whereby chattels such as carts and wheels which had caused the death of a man were forfeited to God, *i.e.* to the king, God's lieutenant on earth, to be distributed in works of charity for the appeasing of God's wrath.

(7) *Contamination by contact.*—Similar ideas lie at the root of many other well-attested Greek practices. The contamination incurred by contact with death or with birth is well known. Thucydides describes how the holy island of Delos was purified by the Athenians in the winter of 426 B.C. in conformity with the injunction of an oracle:

'The same winter the Athenians purified (ἐκάθηραν) Delos in accordance with a certain oracle. Pisistratus had purified it previously—not all of it, but so much of the island as was visible from the temple. But on this occasion the whole was purified in the manner following. They took up all the graves of the dead that were in Delos and made proclamation that in future no one should die in the island or give birth in it, but they must be conveyed across to Rheneia.'[6]

(8) *Unconscious communal sin.*—A further illustration of unconscious sin, which becomes known only when attention is directed to it by the affliction occasioned by it, is one of a type which is very common in Greek literature. A city is visited by a plague or famine or similar calamity. It is at once inferred that the city has somehow incurred the anger of heaven. Oracles are consulted and it is discovered that some hero belonging to the city lies dead in an alien land where his spirit cannot rest: his bones are to be brought home for burial in his own city, when all will be well.

Thus in Pindar[7] the motive which Pelias gives for the Argonautic expedition is that the soul of Phrixos cannot rest in the alien land of Colchis; he says to Jason: 'Thou canst take away the anger of the Chthonians. For Phrixos bids us go to the halls of Aietes to bring home his soul' (ψυχὰν κομίξαι). We have a historical example of this type in the case of Theseus. According to tradition, Theseus died in Skyros at the hands of Lycomedes, king of that island. When in 474–473 B.C. the island was conquered by Kimon, son of Miltiades, what were supposed to be the bones of Theseus were discovered there, and were solemnly conveyed to Athens for burial. 'The bones being conveyed home by Kimon on a ship of war, the delighted Athenians received them with splendid processions and sacrifices as if it were Theseus himself returning to the city.'[8]

(9) *The scapegoat.* — The same physical or mechanical conception of sin is implied in the wide-spread custom of the scapegoat. Just as the guilty individual, according to primitive notions, pollutes the innocent community, so the sin of the community may be put upon an individual, who then becomes excommunicate, no longer entitled to the rights and the security which belong to other members of the community. The position of the scapegoat is in most respects analogous to that of the banished murderer; only he suffers not for his own individual sin but for the sins of the community as a whole. This conception is, of course, familiar in the OT. In Lv 16 we have the ritual of atonement, in which two goats are selected and assigned by lot, one to Jahweh and one לַעֲזָאזֵל. The orthodox modern interpretation makes this mean 'to Azazel,' a devil or spirit of the waste. There does not appear to be any convincing evidence, linguistic or other, for rejecting the LXX version τῷ ἀποπομπαίῳ. Doubtless those 'outcasts' belonged to the spirits of 'the wild.' But such a dualism as the modern interpretation assumes, by which the individual Azazel could be balanced against Jahweh, seems foreign to the Pentateuch. The Greek φαρμακός is led 'beyond the borders,' and just this is the lot of the Hebrew scapegoat: הַמִּדְבָּרָה לְשַׁלַּח אֹתוֹ לַעֲזָאזֵל. If the mysterious Azazel was thus early capable of being opposed as an individual to Jahweh, it is strange that no reference is made to him in Lv 14 or 17.

In Greece, anyhow, there is no question in the case of the φαρμακός of anything of the nature of a sacrifice or offering to devils. The ritual, as we know it in the case of the Thargelia, is that two men—in later times two malefactors—are solemnly 'led forth' (ἐξάγονται), *i.e.* expelled from the community.[1]

2. Homer.—So far we have been dealing with certain early conceptions which, stereotyped and formalized in ritual and custom, continue to be, as it were, the substratum or the background of far more advanced ideas. When we turn to the literature of Greece, we find already in Homer a conception of sin which is, on the whole, remarkably advanced; and this is only another way of saying that the conception of divinity which is implied in the Homeric poem is a relatively high one. It need scarcely be emphasized that here, as elsewhere, we must distinguish between the account of the gods which is given in mythology, or their behaviour as mere *dramatis personæ*, and that conception of them which is implied in their relation to the conduct of the individual or of the community. The mythology or theogony will always preserve fossil and formal elements which reflect an earlier stage of belief. And the general history of religion shows abundantly how easily such primitive elements maintain themselves alongside of far more advanced ideas. They are not formally rejected or repealed: for many minds they do not appear to demand rejection or repeal; but in relation to the ordinary business of life they no longer correspond to the living beliefs, inasmuch as they no longer constitute the determining motives of human conduct.

(1) *Standards of duty and right.*—Duty or right action is in Homer expressed chiefly by two terms: θέμις and δίκη. These terms are not mutually exclusive, nor are they even very sharply distinguished. It is true of both words that they sometimes have no deeper significance than 'way,' 'custom,' 'use,' 'wont.'[2] But it is an easy step to the notion of 'right way,' righteousness, or duty. If we had to state broadly the difference between δίκη and θέμις, we should say with reasonable accuracy that δίκη sums up man's duty to his fellows, θέμις man's duty to the gods; or, to put it

[1] Arist. *loc. cit.*; Plato, *Laws*, ix. 873 E.

[2] E. P. Evans, *The Criminal Prosecution and Capital Punishment of Animals*, London, 1906.

[3] Arist. *loc. cit.*

[4] Plato, *Laws*, ix. 873 E; cf. Demosth. xxiii. 76; Æschin. iii. 244; Paus. I. xxviii. 10; Suid., Harpocr., etc., ἐπὶ Πρυτανείῳ; *Etymologicum Magnum*, 362. 55; I. Bekker, *Anecdota græca*, Berlin, 1814–21, 311. 15; Plutarch, *Pericles*, 36.

[5] Cf. Lv 8^{11}, Ex $29^{36f.}$ $30^{26\text{-}29}$, Lv $5^{14f.}$ $11^{33\text{-}35}$ 15^{12}; cf., in NT, Mk 7^{4}.

[6] iii. 104; cf. Callimachus, *Hymn to Zeus*, 11 ff. (the place in Arkadia where Zeus was born is holy: ἔνθεν ὁ χῶρος | ἱερός, οὐδέ τι μιν κεχρημένον Εἰλειθυίας | ἑρπετὸν οὐδὲ γυνὴ ἐπινίσσεται); for the same idea cf. Aristoph. *Lys.* 742: ὦ πότνι' Εἰλείθυι', ἐπίσχες τοῦ τόκου. So Æschylus in the *Frogs* of Aristophanes (1080 f.) is made to reproach Euripides with introducing τικτούσας ἐν τοῖς ἱεροῖς, who are put on the same level with those who are guilty of incest.

[7] *Pyth.* iv. 158 ff.

[8] Cf. Plutarch, *Thes.* 36.

[1] See art. SCAPEGOAT (Greek).

[2] Thus δίκη in *Od.* iv. 691, xi. 218, xiv. 59, xix. 43, 168, xxiv. 255; θέμις in *Il.* ix. 134, etc.

other words, *θέμις* is at most the religious aspect of *δίκη*. The individual judgments which constitute *θέμις* are called *θέμιστες*, which are regarded as being of immemorial antiquity and as, indeed, deriving their sanction ultimately from Zeus, whose ordinances they are. Thus the *Διὸς θέμιστες* of *Od.* xvi. 403 are exactly the *Διὸς ἐφετμαί* of *Il.* xviii. 569 f., and the same term is applied to the divine will as revealed in oracles.[1] In a special sense the king is the guardian of these *θέμιστες*.[2]

The *θέμιστες* are regarded as of universal validity and as regulating the conduct of all civilized men. They may be crookedly interpreted by the unjust judges,[3] but they are recognized by all men who are not beyond the pale of civilization.

Thus it is characteristic that the Kyklopes, who are otherwise outside civilization, are described as *ὑπερφίαλοι, ἀθεμίστοι*,[4] are in fact savages.[5] And precisely so 'wild War, who breaks the converse of the wise,' is described as a doer of *καρτερὰ ἔργα*—the works of Might, not of Right—and a fool or madman *ὅς οὔτινα οἶδε θέμιστα*.[6]

The transgression of these *θέμιστες* is in Homer described by the terms *ἀλιτέσθαι, ἁμαρτάνειν*.

(2) *Offences against the gods and men.*—We have now to consider what offences are regarded in Homer as sins, *i.e.* as offensive to and exciting the anger of the gods. These, we find, may be broadly classified as follows.

(*a*) Man owes certain specific duties towards the gods—certain duties which do not concern his relations to his fellow-men—the neglect of which is sin. (*α*) He must offer prayer and sacrifice. Neglect of this duty excites the anger of heaven.[7] To commence any important undertaking without due sacrifice is to court disaster.[8] (*β*) But, apart from the specific duties of prayer and sacrifice, man owes to the gods the general homage of deference and humility. Man must not seek to overstep the boundary which separates gods and men. Disregard of this boundary, encroachment on the prerogatives of heaven, is sin.

Thus Thamyris boasted that he could defeat the Muses in song and was punished by blindness.[9] So Lycurgus suffered for his insolence to Dionysos,[10] Bellerophon for his attempt to fly to heaven,[11] Ajax the Locrian because he defied Athene.[12]

(*γ*) Deliberate disobedience to the will of heaven as revealed by signs and portents is sin.[13] (*δ*) Lastly, the gods must be approached with due purity.[14]

(*b*) There are offences which are not primarily direct offences against the gods but are a violation of social duties. Briefly enumerated, these are the following: (1) the conduct of the wooers in devouring the substance of Odysseus in his absence,[15] (2) reckless or indiscriminate slaughter in war,[16] (3) use of poisoned arrows,[17] (4) adultery,[18] (5) breach of the law of host and guest,[19] (6) neglect of suppliant,[20] (7) unfilial conduct,[21] (8) insulting the dead by maltreatment[1] or by boasting over them,[2] (9) murder,[3] (10) perjury.[4]

(3) *The ethical standpoint.*—In considering the Homeric conception of sin the first feature which strikes one is the prominence of the ethical as opposed to the specifically religious standpoint. The grounds on which certain conduct is regarded as displeasing to the gods are in the main such as appeal to the general conscience of men, not any mysterious or, so to say, magical reasons which are understood only by the priest or other possessor of esoteric knowledge. Just this feature constitutes the healthy-mindedness of the Homeric religion. Nothing could less suggest the religion of a priest-ridden people. When Hector declares to Polydamas his confession of faith,

'Thou biddest me to put my trust in winged birds, which I heed not at all nor care whether to the right they fly toward the morning and the sun or whether to the left toward the misty dark. Let us put our trust in the counsel of mighty Zeus, who rules over all mortals and immortals. One bird [omen] is best—to fight for fatherland!',[5]

he is speaking in a spirit which is hardly other than the prevailing spirit in Homer.

Entirely consonant with this is the Homeric view of the nature and origin of sin. Here again the prevailing note is ethical. Sin is, indeed, a mystery, but only as evil in general is a mystery; and the genesis of sin in nations and individuals is clearly enough conceived. Put in the simplest terms, the Homeric conception of the genesis of sin is this. There is developed in man a spirit of reckless self-confidence or wantonness, *ὕβρις*, which may be the outcome of sudden or excessive prosperity or the mere rashness and impetuosity of youth and strength. This *ὕβρις* is at all points the antithesis to *αἰδώς*: *αἰδώς* is the spirit of reverence which in conduct respects the rights of others, which looks before and after and considers not what is best at the immediate moment but what is best in the end; *ὕβρις* is the spirit of irreverence, pride, wantonness, which disregards the rights of others and grasps the lust of the moment in the scorn of consequence. Hence *αἰδώς* is the spirit of *εὐνομία*, of law and order; *ὕβρις* the spirit of *ἀνομία*, anarchy. The consequence of this spirit is an obscuring of moral values, a blindness of soul, *ἄτη*, which directly leads to the commission of sin.

We need not examine in detail the use of *ὕβρις* and synonymous or associated words in Homer. It will be sufficient to say that the whole conduct of the wooers in the absence of Odysseus is denoted by this term;[6] so Agamemnon's taking away of Briseis from Achilles;[7] so the conduct of the comrades of Odysseus.[8] It is coupled with *βιή*, might or violence, in *Od.* xv. 329, xvii. 565; and this characteristic of *ὕβρις* furnishes the standing epithet *ὑπέρβιος* applied to it in *Od.* i. 368, iv. 321, xvi. 410, etc. The phrase which occurs in *Od.* xiv. 262, xvii. 431, *οἱ δ' ὕβρει εἴξαντες, ἐπισπόμενοι μένεϊ σφῷ*, well illustrates the Greek conception of *ὕβρις* as passion uncontrolled by reason or reflexion. Hence *ὕβρις* is opposed to *εὐνομία*, or the reign of law.[9] Other terms of similar connotation are *ἀτάσθαλος, ἀτασθαλίαι, ὑπεροπλίαι, ὑπερηνορέων, ὑπερηφανέων, ὑπερφίαλος*. *ἄτη* is rather moral blindness or infatuation than mere intellectual ignorance. It is a misjudging of moral values induced by *ὕβρις*. Thus in *Il.* i. 412 Agamemnon is to be made by suffering to realize his 'blindness' in dealing unfairly with Achilles. It is in fact the characteristic of *ἄτη* that it is not so much ignorance as heedlessness (*ἀφραδίη*), and, when the sinner's eyes are opened, remorse comes, as with Bellerophon.[10] So it is sometimes termed 'foolishness,' *ἀφροσύνη*—thus of the wooers.[11] Ares is called *ἄφρονα τοῦτον . . . ὅς οὔτινα οἶδε θέμιστα*.[12] That it is not mere intellectual ignorance is illustrated by *Od.* xxii. 287 ff.: *μήποτε πάμπαν | εἴκων ἀφραδίῃς μέγα εἰπεῖν, ἀλλὰ θεοῖσιν | μῦθον ἐπιτρεψάι· ἐπειὴ πολὺ φέρτεροί εἰσιν*, and xxiv. 457 ff.: *ὑμετέρους παῖδας καταπαυέμεν ἀφροσυνάων· | οἳ μέγα ἔργον ἔρεξαν ἀτασθαλίῃσι κακῇσιν*.

1 *Hom. H. Apoll.* 394.
2 Cf. *Il.* i. 238.
3 *Il.* xvi. 387.
4 *Od.* ix. 106.
5 Cf. *Od.* ix. 215, where *ἄγριον* is equivalent to *οὔτε δίκας εὖ εἰδότα, οὔτε θέμιστας*, *i.e.* recognizing no law human or divine.
6 *Il.* v. 761.
7 *Ib.* i. 65, v. 178, viii. 236 ff.: the due performance of these duties entitles a man to expect a recompense from the gods; cf. xii. 6 ff.: the Greeks built their wall without first sacrificing to the gods.
8 Cf. *Od.* iv. 351.
9 *Il.* ii. 595 ff.
10 *Ib.* vi. 129 f.
11 *Ib.* vi. 200 f.
12 *Od.* iv. 503, xi. 307; cf. v. 119, xi. 582, 576, 593, *Il.* vii. 445 ff., xvii. 98 f., xxiv. 25 ff., 607.
13 *Il.* iv. 381, iv. 408 f.; so the companions of Odysseus who devoured the oxen of Helios in defiance of an express warning, *αὐτῶν . . . σφετέρῃσιν ἀτασθαλίῃσιν ὄλοντο*.
14 *Il.* vi. 266 ff.
15 *Od.* i. 376, ii. 64, xiv. 81, xx. 394, xxii. 38, xxiii. 63, xxiv. 351.
16 *Il.* ix. 63 f., v. 757 f.
17 *Od.* i. 259 ff.
18 *Ib.* i. 46; cf. iv. 261, xxiii. 218.
19 *Il.* xiii. 623 ff., vi. 167.
20 *Il.* xxiv. 156, 569, ix. 269, 477, xiii. 213, *Od.* xiv. 283, 405, xvi. 422, xvii. 475, xxi. 27.
21 *Il.* ix. 451, xv. 204, xxi. 412, *Od.* ii. 135.

1 *Il.* xxiv. 53.
2 *Od.* xxii. 412, *Il.* xxii. 354.
3 *Il.* xxiv. 480.
4 *Il.* iii. 298, iv. 158, 235 ff., 270, vii. 351 f., xix. 259 f., 264 f., xxiii. 585–595.
5 *Il.* xii. 237 ff.
6 *Od.* iv. 627, xvii. 169, xxiii. 64, etc.
7 *Il.* i. 203, 214.
8 *Od.* xiv. 262, xvii. 431.
9 *Ib.* xvii. 487.
10 *Il.* vi. 201; cf. *Od.* iv. 261: *ἄτην δὲ μετέστενον*, and *Od.* ii. 281–284.
11 *Od.* xvi. 278; cf. xxiv. 457.
12 *Il.* v. 761.

The remark must be interpolated here that the doctrine of ὕβρις and ἄτη, as we have stated it, appears to give a one-sided view of the origin of sin as arising from excessive prosperity, sudden success, youth and strength and beauty—in a word, the goods of this life—and takes no account of the sin which springs from the ills of life. Now it must be said at once that the sins arising from prosperity are far more emphasized in Greek literature than those which arise from adversity. And the reason, we imagine, is that they struck the imagination more as being illustrated in the fortunes of great and noble houses and thus formed a more natural theme for the poet or the moralist. The sins to which ὕβρις leads have as a rule a certain splendour of audacity or magnificence of disaster which makes them memorable. Hence Aristotle, while he notes that the wealthy tend to be 'ὑβρισταί καὶ ὑπερήφανοι, being affected by the acquisition of wealth; for they feel as if they possessed all good things,' says that their crimes are not those of the malefactor, 'but crimes of wantonness or licence, as, *e.g.*, assault and adultery.'[1] He notes, too, that, while εὐτυχία, or success, tends, like wealth, to make men ὑπερηφανώτεροι καὶ ἀλογιστότεροι, it has one excellent effect in that it tends to make men religious,[2] since they attribute to the providence of heaven what is really an accident of fortune. But the effect of what we call the force of circumstances in causing sin was not ignored by the Greek moralist, and the rôle of what the Greeks call ἀνάγκη in the sphere of ethics has not had the attention paid to it which it deserves.[3]

In his *Greece and Babylon*[4] L. R. Farnell writes:

'Both [Greece and Babylon] reveal the phenomenon that marks an early stage of social morality: as the tribe of the family are one flesh, one corporate unit of life, so the members are collectively responsible, and the "sins of the fathers are visited on the children." This was the familiar law of old Hellas, and we may say of the ancient Mediterranean society; the first to make the momentous protest against it, and to proclaim the responsibility of the individual conscience, was Theognis for the Greeks and Ezekiel for the Hebrews.'

This statement is capable of misleading if it were taken to imply (1) that Theognis maintained that the children do *not* suffer for the sins of the children; on the contrary, he insists most strongly that they do; he deplores it, but he insists that it is a fact; (2) that Homer does not recognize personal responsibility. This of course is not the case. In Homer the punishment of the innocent for the guilty hardly amounts to more than that the slighted goddesses, Hera and Athene, wreak or attempt to wreak their vengeance for the judgment of Paris upon the innocent Trojans,[5] and the sin of Agamemnon in taking the daughter of Apollo's priest is visited by a plague upon the Greek army. In Homer it is always the individual sinner who is primarily responsible for his sin and only quite secondarily, if at all, his family or clan or country. There is more to be said for the vicarious doctrine, perhaps, in the case of the Hebrews. But it must be pointed out that long before the eloquent protest of Ezekiel[6] the individual sinner was primarily responsible,[7] and only in the case of the immediate sinner being unavailable does the punishment fall upon his descendants.[8] And to explain this much of family solidarity we do not need to invoke the social theories of Durkheim. The point of view is explicitly recognized by Aristotle in the much misunderstood passage in *Nicomachean Ethics*, i. 10, where he says that it would be absurd to discount the fortunes of his posterity in estimating the fortunes of the individual.[1] When Homer says of the violators of an oath,

'Even if the Olympian fulfil it not immediately, yet late he fulfils, and they pay with a heavy price, with their own heads and their wives and their children,'[2]

there is no immediate reference to the posthumous punishment of the sinner's children. And, if there were, it has to be pointed out that the leading feature of an oath was the invocation of a curse by the oath-taker upon himself and his family, and the belief in the efficacy of the curse by a blood-relation on his relatives was valid down to the latest times of which we shall here take cognizance, and it remained part of the regular formula of oath-taking.[3] Nor is there anything more surprising in this than the inclusion of innocent children in the sentence of disfranchisement on a father.[4] The special potency which belongs to the curses—and the blessings—of parents was always recognized.[5]

It is true that we have in Homer certain passages which appear to disclaim personal responsibility. In *Il.* xix. 86ff. Agamemnon says:

ἐγὼ δ' οὐκ αἴτιός εἰμι,
ἀλλὰ Ζεὺς καὶ Μοῖρα καὶ ἠεροφοῖτις Ἐρινύς,
οἵτε μοι εἰν ἀγορῇ φρεσὶν ἔμβαλον ἄγριον ἄτην,
ἤματι τῷ, ὅτ' Ἀχιλλῆος γέρας αὐτὸς ἀπηύρων.
ἀλλὰ τί κεν ῥέξαιμι; θεὸς διὰ πάντα τελευτᾷ.

And then follows the well-known personification of Ate,

πρέσβα Διὸς θυγάτηρ Ἄτη, ἣ πάντας ἀᾶται,
οὐλομένη· τῆς μέν θ' ἁπαλοὶ πόδες· οὐ γὰρ ἐπ' οὔδει
πίλναται, ἀλλ' ἄρα ἥγε κατ' ἀνδρῶν κράατα βαίνει.
βλάπτουσ' ἀνθρώπους· κατὰ δ' οὖν ἕτερόν γε πέδησεν,

which, however, adds nothing whatever to our conception of Ate, since the account of Zeus as being the victim of Ate, when Hera deceives him,[6] is a mere bit of mythology. Again, in *Il.* iii. 164, Priam chivalrously excuses Helen and blames the gods —οὔτί μοι αἰτίη ἐσσί θεοί νύ μοι αἴτιοί εἰσιν—but that does not deliver her from the bitterness of self-reproach,[7] any more than her own ascription of her infatuation to Aphrodite saves her from remorse—

ἄτην δὲ μετέστενον, ἣν Ἀφροδίτη
δῶχ', ὅτε μ' ἤγαγε κεῖσε φίλης ἀπὸ πατρίδος αἴης.[8]

Such pleas are, at most, pleas for the weakness of mortality. There is nc thought of really repudiating personal responsibility or personal guilt. If in the OT (Ex. 9^{12}) we read 'the Lord hardened the heart of Pharaoh,' we also read (v.^{34}) that 'Pharaoh . . . sinned yet more and hardened his heart,' and the guilt implied in the one formula is no greater and no less than that implied in the other. So Xanthos, the horse of Achilles, says:

ἀλλά τοι ἐγγύθεν ἦμαρ ὀλέθριον· οὐδέ τοι ἡμεῖς
αἴτιοι, ἀλλὰ θεός τε μέγας καὶ Μοῖρα κραταιή.
οὐδὲ γὰρ ἡμετέρῃ βραδυτῆτί τε νωχελίῃ τε, κτλ.,[9]

which merely means that the horses have done their best and better was not to be. If there were no question of personal responsibility, what point would there be in the protest of the river Xanthos in *Il.* xxi. 370 that he is not so guilty as the other rivers which assist the Trojans?

(4) *Punishment of sin.*—The penalties for sin, like the rewards for virtue, are normally conceived as material and are consummated here and now. Normally the good prosper, the wicked perish. The vengeance of the gods may linger, but it is sure,[10] and temporary prosperity does not shake men's confidence in the justice of heaven, though the signal punishment of the wicked is hailed as a welcome evidence of the activity of the gods.[11]

The purpose of punishment, according to Homer, is retributive and deterrent. The retributive intention is sufficiently attested by the verb which is regularly employed in reference to punishment —τίνω (ἀποτίνω), 'pay,' of the sinner; τίνυμαι of the avenger.[12] The deterrent intention is illus-

1 *Rhet.* ii. 16. 2 *Ib.* 17.
3 It will be enough here to refer to Æschylus, *Agam.* 211: ἐπεὶ δ' ἀνάγκας ἔδυ λέπαδνον, and to the admirable analysis of social and political unrest in Thucydides, iii. 82.
4 Edinburgh, 1911, p. 152. 5 *Il.* iv. 31 ff., xxiv. 25 ff.
6 $14^{12ff.}$ 18. 7 2 K 3^{27} 14^{6}, 1 K $2^{5.\ 31ff.}$.
8 2 S $21^{1ff.}$

1 See art. LIFE AND DEATH (Greek and Roman).
2 *Il.* iv. 160 ff.
3 *E.g.*, Andoc. i. 126: λαβόμενος τοῦ βωμοῦ ὤμοσεν ἦ μὴν μὴ εἶναι . . . ἢ ἐλώλη εἶναι καὶ αὐτὸν καὶ τὴν οἰκίαν; Antiphon, v. 11; Demosth. xxiii. 67: διομεῖται κατ' ἐξωλείας αὐτοῦ καὶ γένους καὶ οἰκίας, κτλ.
4 *E.g.*, the law in Demosth. *c. Meid.* 113: ἄτιμος ἔστω καὶ παῖδες καὶ τὰ ἐκείνου.
5 *E.g.*, Plato, *Laws*, xi. 931 B; cf. Lycophron, *Alex.* 125: καὶ πατρὶ (Poseidon) πέμψας (Proteus) τὰς ἐπηκόους ἀράς.
6 *Il.* xix. 95 ff. 7 *Il.* iii. 172 ff.
8 *Od.* iv. 261. 9 *Il.* xix. 409 ff.
10 *Il.* iv. 160. 11 *Od.* xxiv. 351.
12 Cf. παλίντιτα ἔργα (*Od.* i. 379, ii. 144, xvii. 51).

trated by *Il.* iii. 351 ff., where Menelaus prays to Zeus:

'O Lord Zeus, grant me to take vengeance (τίσασθαι) on him who hath first done me evil, even Alexandros, and overcome him by my hands, so that another, even among men of after time, may shudder to do evil to the host that hath shewn him kindness.'

Nägelsbach[1] compares Dt 19[19ff.]:

'Then shall ye do unto him, as he had thought to do unto his brother: so shalt thou put away the evil from the midst of thee. And those which remain shall hear, and fear, and shall henceforth commit no more any such evil in the midst of thee. And thine eye shall not pity; life shall go for life, eye for eye, tooth for tooth, hand for hand, foot for foot.'[2]

Here, as in Homer, we have the retributive and deterrent intentions combined.

(5) *Retribution in a life to come.*—But, while normally sin is punished by material affliction in this life and virtue rewarded by material benefits, it is clear that the Homeric poet was familiar also with the conception that punishment or reward awaits men on the other side of the grave. The Homeric attitude to immortality does not appear to be quite fairly represented in much modern writing. But the fact is that for Homer there is no question of immortality. The survival of the soul after death is a certainty for Homer, just as much as this present life. And, if the picture of the after life which he presents is a ghostly one, that is only because the after life cannot be imagined but in one of two ways: either (1) as a duplicate of the present life, only that pain and conflict, parting and renunciation, are done away and transience has given place to permanence, or (2) in terms of the immaterial. And, precisely as we cannot visualize an immaterial existence, our picture must be a mere suggestion of a realm of shadows.

Now, when Homer says 'hurled to the house of Hades many valiant souls (ψυχάς) of heroes and made themselves (αὐτούς) to be the prey of dogs,'[3] or when he says that the ghost of Patroklos, as it appeared to Achilles,[4] was 'altogether like himself in stature and beautiful eyes and voice,' it is actually argued, and apparently quite seriously, by some scholars that for Homer the real man, the man himself, was the living material body, of which the soul was a mere faint *Doppelgänger*. On the same principle we could easily prove precisely the same conception for even the most orthodox of Christian writers. The man we know and love is doubtless the living human presence, the immortal soul inseparate from its mortal bravery; and doubtless we cannot imagine the man himself except in the garment of mortality. Even the sincerest Christian cannot easily conceive his dead, if the dead came back, as other than disturbers and intruders on the banquet of life, as uncanny presences with whom he could not hold comfortable and familiar converse. And it is no paradox to say that the poet above all, by the very conditions of his art, is necessarily driven back upon the realm of material things, disguise it how he may, and, in exact proportion as he seeks to give to the ideal the semblance of reality and of life, he is compelled to render the ideal by the images of sense. And the society of Homer, beyond all others, is a society which seeks to avert its eyes from the unseen and mysterious dominions of the dead, and to turn them to the familiar scenes of human life and activity. But not the less the Homeric age knew that the grave is not the end—'sunt aliquid manes: letum non omnia finit'—and that, so far from the body being the man himself, it becomes, so soon as the soul leaves it, mere 'dumb dust' (κωφὴ γαῖα)[5] which must be reverently dealt with, not for what it is, but even because it was once the tenement of a beloved soul.

[1] *Die homer. Theologie*[3], p. 320.
[2] Cf. Dt 20[18ff.].
[3] *Il.* i. 3 ff.
[4] *Il.* xxiii. 66 f.
[5] *Il.* xxiv. 54.

But, of course, the relation which the after life as conceived by Homer bears to the present life was wholly different from that which Christian teaching conceives to exist. For the Christian this life is but a preparation, whether propædeutic or probational, for a better and fuller life to come; this life is transient and mortal; the reality is the eternity which lies beyond. For the Homeric Greek they are both alike realities, and they differ only in that this life is certainly transitory, that may possibly be eternal; this life certainly holds within it many things desirable, what the after life holds can only be a dim conjecture.

Within these limits the belief in the soul's survival after death could scarcely fail to have some bearing on the doctrine of sin. Where a man had refrained from all signal wickedness, he had nothing to fear from the world of the dead nor in it. Where he had distinguished himself beyond his fellows, whether for good or for evil, he might hope for a correspondingly exceptional felicity or woe beyond the grave. Our literature naturally says little of the hopes of the common man, and the 'tiresomeness of an over-peopled heaven'[1] would have been felt with more than ordinary force by the Homeric heroes. But that the terrors of the unseen world were a very real thing in the Homeric age is abundantly clear. The evidence can be neither ignored nor explained away.

Take the case of perjury. This, like other sins, may bring its punishment immediately. The violation of the truce by the Trojans is conceived as bound to lead to their defeat in battle.[2] Yet we have an unmistakable reference to the punishment of perjury after death in the under world.[3] But, we are told, the idea of posthumous punishment is non-Homeric. The examples of Tityos, Tantalos, and Sisyphos, in *Od.* xi. 576-600, occur in a late interpolation. Heroic endeavours are made to explain away the *Iliad* passages as meaning that the powers under earth punish men *in this life*, or the passages are simply excised as spurious. This is a proceeding as misleading and unscientific as it is on linguistic or other grounds unjustifiable. The truth is rather that, while in general the living have no occasion to fear any evil either from the dead or in death, yet, whenever they come into collision with the great sanctities of life—when they commit murder or sin against the fundamental ties of family—then they have to fear punishment not only in this life but also in the life to come. And in taking an oath, which is an essential and basal feature of any early system of law, the gods of the under world are directly and solemnly challenged, and it would be indeed strange if their jurisdiction were limited to this world. Surely it is not an accident that Pindar takes as the type of the happy dead those who ἔχαιρον εὐορκίαις,[4] or that Hesiod says ἀνδρὸς δ' εὐόρκου γενεὴ μετόπισθεν ἀμείνων.[5]

(6) *Atonement for sin.*—We have next to consider the mode in which atonement is made for sin in the Homeric age. The first essential feature is that the wrong conduct is intermitted, and where possible restoration or reparation is made to the aggrieved party.

Thus the daughter of Apollo's priest is restored to him.[6] Odysseus stays the anger of the gods by performing a neglected sacrifice.[7] So Agamemnon makes amends to Achilles by gifts of tripods, female slaves, etc.[8]

The next essential thing is prayer and sacrifice to the offended deity.[9] The intention of the sacrifice is purely propitiatory, and precisely the same

[1] W. James, *Human Immortality*, London, 1898, p. 83.
[2] *Il.* iv. 159.
[3] *Il.* iii. 278 f.
[4] *Ol.* ii. 72.
[5] *Works and Days*, 283.
[6] *Il.* i. 97.
[7] *Od.* iv. 581 ff.; cf. *Il.* ix. 119 f.
[8] *Il.* xix. 243 ff.
[9] *Ib.* i. 98 ff.

procedure is followed to avert impending evil.[1] Hence, too, the sacrifice may be substituted by a vow,[2] and accompanied or rather followed by hymns.[3]

The usual term for 'propitiate' is ἱλάσκεσθαι, *i.e.* to render the god ἵλεως, 'well-pleased' or 'at peace' with the worshipper. The same idea is expressed by ἀρέσαι,[4] ἀρέσσασθαι.[5] The propitiatory prayer is especially called λιτή; to pray is λίτεσθαι.[6]

(7) *Ceremonial purification.*—It is sometimes said that the ceremonial or symbolic ritual of purification, which in forms more or less repulsive we know to have been practised in later Greece and which is attested all over the world, was unknown to the Homeric age. No one, however, can maintain such a doctrine who does not approach the question with eyes wilfully shut to the obvious meaning of several Homeric passages. These are noticed in art. PURIFICATION (Greek) and need not be repeated here. But even had there been no actual reference to such practices in Homer, we should have been abundantly justified on *a priori* grounds in assuming that they existed.

The case of Theoklymenos in *Od.* xv. 223 ff. is constantly quoted as supporting the opposite opinion. This appears to be a misunderstanding of the position of a suppliant. So far as the present writer knows, the blood-guiltiness of a suppliant was inoperative outside his own country. If this were not so, how could the guilty man ever begin the process of recovering his status? The very first step in that process is usually for the suppliant to seat himself at the hearth of some person beyond the borders of his own country. If his blood-guiltiness were operative, how could he approach the holy of holies, *i.e.* the hearth of his host?[7] Usually the suppliant does not even reveal his identity before he has been a guest for some time. If his presence carried pollution beyond his own borders, could this have been tolerated? Once beyond his own land, he becomes, so far as concerns outsiders, possessed of all the rights of the suppliant; in his own land to slay him is the duty of his victim's kindred; outside his own land for an alien to slay him is a crime which brings down the vengeance of Ζεὺς ἱκετήσιος.

The well-known case of Orestes might, of course, be quoted. The festival of Pitchers (Choes), which formed part of the Anthesteria, was peculiar in that each participant drank his pitcher of wine separately. The reason given was that, when Orestes with his mother's blood upon him came to Athens during the festival, the Athenian king, not wishing to be inhospitable but unwilling to contaminate the worshippers, ordered separate pitchers of wine to be given to each.[8] But that is a quite peculiar case. It is precisely to the *Semnai Theai* at Athens that Orestes is sent by Apollo to make his peace with them.

The banishment of the suppliant, moreover, does not prevent him from offering prayer and sacrifice even to the Deity, whose sanctuaries in his own land he may no longer enter. But he must make himself an outcast, and then from beyond the pale solicit re-admission.

So we would interpret the curious instructions given to Odysseus.[9] He has offended Poseidon. He must therefore seek a land where men know not the sea nor eat food mixed with salt, who mistake the farmer's shovel (scull) for the seaman's oar (scull)—*i.e.*, he is to travel beyond the sphere of the sea-god, and there he is to make his propitiatory offering to Poseidon.

3. Hesiod.—The general framework of ideas which we have sketched in Homer is to be presumed in our study of the conception of sin in the later Greek authors. For in the history of religious ideas each new development does not cancel or repeal all that went before. Custom, with the force of an almost religious sanction,[1] is nowhere more powerful than here. The old and the new tend to persist side by side, each acting and re-acting upon the other. The present article can only aim at noting the more important points of departure and illustrating the leading tendencies.

The terminology of Hesiod is similar to that of Homer. Righteousness is δίκη,[2] and means that conduct which is in conformity with a divinely established order, which is careful of the rights of others, whether God or man. Unrighteousness is ὕβρις, ὑπερβασία, σχέτλια ἔργα, and is the conduct which ignores the rights of others and transgresses the laws of the divinely established order. The generally sober colouring of the poet's creed is redeemed from pessimism by his firm conviction that the Judge of all the earth is righteous and will not suffer unrighteousness to prevail finally.

'Now may neither I nor son of mine be righteous among men: for it is an ill thing to be righteous if the unrighteous shall have the greater right. But that I deem not that Zeus the hurler of the thunder will bring to pass.'[3]

Punishment of unrighteousness may not follow immediately after the unrighteous act, and the wicked may prosper for a time, but in the end the moral order of the world triumphs:

'It is better to pass by unrighteousness and to pursue righteousness. Righteousness in the end is better than unrighteousness, and the fool learneth it by suffering.'[4]

Dike is the daughter of Zeus, honoured and revered by the gods who keep Olympos,[5] and the observance of δίκη is the sovereign distinction whereby the race of men is divinely marked off from the lower animals, for whom the law of might (βία) is the only law.[6]

When we compare the specific sins which Hesiod enumerates with those of Homer, we are struck by the greater prominence of those which have no obvious ethical significance and are more of the nature of unreasoning tabus. On the one hand, we have the Homeric sins: perjury,[7] falsehood,[8] theft,[9] covetousness,[10] dishonouring parents,[11] unjust judgments,[12] injury to the fatherless,[13] injury to suppliant or the stranger within the gates,[14] taunting the poor with his poverty,[15] lying with brother's wife,[16] neglect of prayer and sacrifice,[17] praying with unwashed hands,[18] to which we may add idleness.[19] On the other hand, we have a whole catalogue of 'sins' which, if not severely reprobated, are at least 'unlucky,' which have no parallel in Homer—cutting the nails at a festival of the gods,[20] sitting on tombstones or other 'unmovables' (ἀκίνητα),[21] contact with water which has been used by a woman,[22] muttering at a sacrifice,[23] placing a ladle across the mixing bowl,[24] leaving the wood of a house unplaned,[25] eating from unconsecrated vessels,[26] performing certain private operations indiscreetly,[27] bringing the contagion of death into contact with birth.[28] To find in these prohibitions traces of Orphic and Pythagorean teaching, as Fick does, seems wholly mistaken. These ideas are of a type universally attested in early thought, and, if they do not appear in Homer, it is not so

1 *Il.* vi. 86 ff., 115, *Od.* xvi. 184 f.
2 *Od.* xii. 346.
3 *Il.* i. 472.
4 *Ib.* ix. 120, xix. 138.
5 *Od.* viii. 396, etc.
6 See artt. PRAYER (Greek), § 1, PROPITIATION (Greek), EXPIATION AND ATONEMENT (Greek).
7 Cf. Aristotle, *Oec.* 1344a. 11: ὥσπερ ἱκέτιν καὶ ἀφ' ἑστίας ἠγμένην.
8 Athen. x. 437 C; Callimach. *Aitia*, in *Oxyrh. Pap.* xi. 1362; Eurip. *Iph. in Taur.* 947 ff.
9 *Od.* xi. 121 ff.; cf xxiii. 265 ff.

1 Cf. 2 S 13[12]: לֹא־יֵעָשֶׂה כֵן בְּיִשְׂרָאֵל.
2 θέμις (*Works*, 137).
3 *Ib.* 270 ff.
4 *Ib.* 216 ff.; cf. 333.
5 *Ib.* 256 ff.
6 *Ib.* 276 ff.
7 *Ib.* 190, 194, 282 ff.
8 *Ib.* 322, 709.
9 *Ib.* 320, 352.
10 *Ib.* 315 f.
11 *Ib.* 185 ff., 331.
12 *Ib.* 260 ff.
13 *Ib.* 330.
14 *Ib.* 327.
15 *Ib.* 718.
16 *Ib.* 328 f.
17 *Ib.* 737.
18 *Ib.* 723 ff.
19 *Ib.* 303 ff., 309.
20 *Ib.* 742.
21 *Ib.* 750.
22 *Ib.* 753.
23 *Ib.* 758.
24 *Ib.* 744.
25 *Ib.* 746.
26 *Ib.* 748.
27 *Ib.* 727, 733.
28 *Ib.* 735.

much that they are unknown as that they are ignored.

The specific duties which Hesiod recognizes are mainly those of Homer: oath-keeping and honesty, worship of the gods by prayer and libation and sacrifice.[1] We need only notice the new dignity which he gives to work as a duty which wins the approbation of the gods,[2] who have appointed work as the lot of humanity.[3] The practice of righteousness is, moreover, given a practical or prudential intention which is less obvious in Homer:

'Work, foolish Perses, the works which the gods have appointed unto men, lest one day with children and wife thou hast to beg thy bread among the neighbours and they heed thee not.'[4]

'According to thy power do sacrifice unto the deathless gods . . . that they may have a gracious heart and mind toward thee, that thou mayst buy another's estate, not another thine.'[5]

'Take just measure from thy neighbour and give him just return, with the same measure or yet better if thou canst, that even so afterward in thy need thou mayst find him a sure help.'[6]

So the scarlet woman[7] is to be avoided for prudential reasons.

The punishment of sin is by way of temporal affliction in this life:

'Whoso ensue evil insolence and froward works, for them doth Zeus decree justice. . . . On them doth the Son of Kronos bring from heaven a grievous visitation, even famine and plague together, and the people perish. Their women bear not children: their houses decay by devising of Olympian Zeus: or anon he destroyeth a great host of them within a wall if may be, or the Son of Kronos taketh vengeance on their ships at sea.'[8]

So the righteous are rewarded by temporal prosperity:

'Their city flourisheth and the people prosper therein. And there is in their land peace, the nurse of children, and Zeus doth never decree war for them. Neither doth famine ever consort with men who deal straight judgments, nor doom, but in mirth they tend the works that are their care. For them earth beareth abundant livelihood, and on the hills the oak's top beareth acorns, the oak's midst bees: their fleecy sheep are heavy with wool: their wives bear children like unto their parents: they flourish with good things continually, neither go they on ships, but bounteous earth beareth fruit for them.'[9]

The punishment of the wicked may, of course, involve the innocent:

'Oftentimes a whole city reapeth the recompense of the evil man who sinneth and worketh the works of foolishness.'[10]

We have seen in Homer how the vengeance of Zeus may involve the sinner's wife and children.[11] So in Hesiod:

'Whoso of his will sweareth false witness and lieth, and wrongeth justice and sinneth beyond redemption, his race is dimmer in the after days; but the race of him that keepeth his oath is better in the time to come.'[12]

But this does not seem to mean much more than is already necessarily implied in the solidarity of the family, and is at any rate no such explicit doctrine of the hereditary curse as we shall find in Theognis.

As to the special agency by which retribution is effected, we have Horkos, who attends on crooked judgments (*Rechtsbeugung*)[13] and punishes perjury;[14] the Erinyes as avenging spirits;[15] Dike, who informs Zeus of the wickedness of men:

'Whenever any injureth her with crooked slighting, straightway she sitteth by Zeus the father and telleth of the unrighteous mind of men till the people pay for the folly of their kings who with ill thoughts wrest aside judgments, declaring falsely.'[16]

But we have a specially interesting development in the idea of a sort of spirits intermediate between men and gods whose function is to act as 'watchers' (φύλακες) of mortal men:

'The immortals are nigh among men and remark them that with crooked judgments oppress one another, taking no heed of the anger of the gods. Yea, thrice ten thousand immortals are there on the bounteous earth, who keep watch over mortal men: who watch over judgments and froward works: clad in mist, faring everywhere over the earth.'[1]

In Homer it is the gods themselves who 'in the likeness of strangers from another land visit in divers guises the cities of men and watch the unrighteousness (ὕβρις) and righteousness (εὐνομίη) of men.'[2]

Historically these Hesiodic φύλακες seem—but this is matter of opinion—to reappear in the φύλακες of Plato's *Republic*.[3] They seem to be rightly equated with the spirits of the golden race who, in Hesiod's account of the fall, in the form of δαίμονες,[4] exercise just this supervision over men.

The reader who turns from Homer to Hesiod is conscious of a change of atmosphere. The radiant gaiety of the Homeric world has given place to a world of most sober colouring, where the lights burn low and the shadows deepen. There is but a hint in Homer of an earlier age, a lusty springtime of the world when men were mightier than their degenerate descendants. 'As men are now'[5]—so the poet contrasts his own with the earlier age. But the contrast is merely of physical prowess. In Hesiod, on the other hand, we find a fully developed doctrine of a lost Golden Age from which men have through their folly and sin declined.[6]

4. Solon, Theognis, etc.—In the Greek poets of the period between Hesiod and the end of the 6th cent. B.C. the general conception of the nature and consequences of sin remains much as we have described it in Homer and Hesiod; κόρος, satiety, begets ὕβρις, wantonness, whence springs ἄτη, moral blindness, sin, or the consequences of sin:

τίκτει γὰρ κόρος ὕβριν, ὅταν πολὺς ὄλβος ἕπηται ἀνθρώποισιν ὅσοις μὴ νόος ἄρτιος ᾖ.[7]

Or, again, as in Homer, ὕβρις may arise from the mere thoughtlessness of youth:

ἥβη καὶ νεότης ἐπικουφίζει νόον ἀνδρός, πολλῶν δ' ἐξαίρει θυμὸν ἐς ἀμπλακίην.[8]

There is the same profound conviction of the moral order of the universe:

'O Zeus, father Zeus, thine is the dominion of heaven, and thou dost watch the works of men, lawless and lawful, and takest heed of the righteousness and unrighteousness of beasts' (σοὶ δὲ θηρίων ὕβρις τε καὶ δίκη μέλει).[9]

There is the same certainty that sin must be followed by punishment:

'Unrighteous is the mind of the rulers of the people: for them there is prepared much suffering by reason of their great insolence. For they know not to restrain satiety (lust) . . . They wax wealthy by unrighteous deeds: they spare neither holy things nor public things; they steal and rob here and there; they take no heed to the august foundations of justice, who, though she is silent, knoweth the things that are and that were afore, and in time verily she cometh to repay.'[10] 'None ever wronged stranger or suppliant and escaped the knowledge of the immortals.' Sin may prosper for a little, but 'the end is woe, and the counsel of the gods prevails.'[11]

The punishment of the guilty, we have seen in Homer and Hesiod, may involve the affliction of the sinner's connexions, his wife, his children, his city: the people pay for the sins of their rulers.[12] But now we find it explicitly stated that the sins of the fathers are visited upon the children. And this is, indeed, but the natural corollary of the conception that sin is inevitably followed by affliction. Since it appears that in this life the sinner frequently escapes punishment, while there was no lively conviction that there is any punishment after death, it was natural to conclude that the punishment must fall upon his descendants.

1 *Works*, 135, 336 ff., 465.
2 *Ib.* 299 ff.
3 *Ib.* 397.
4 *Ib.* 397 ff.
5 *Ib.* 336 ff.
6 *Ib.* 349 ff.
7 *Ib.* 373: γυνὴ πυγοστόλος.
8 *Ib.* 238 ff.
9 *Ib.* 227 ff.
10 *Ib.* 240 f.
11 *Il.* iv. 162.
12 *Works*, 283 ff.
13 *Ib.* 219.
14 *Th.* 231.
15 *Works*, 803, *Th.* 185, 472 f.
16 *Works*, 258 ff.

1 *Works*, 249 ff.
2 *Od.* xvii. 485 ff.
3 374 D, and *passim*.
4 *Works*, 122.
5 οἷοι νῦν βροτοί εἰσι (*Il.* v. 304, xii. 383, 449, xx. 287).
6 For the details of Hesiod's account of the fall the reader is referred to the art. HESIOD. Here it will be sufficient to say that in the *Works* we have two versions of the legend: (1) lines 42–105 and (2) lines 109–201.
7 Solon, frag. 4. 3; cf. Theognis, 153 f.
8 Theognis, 629 f.
9 Archilochus, frag. 84.
10 Solon, frag. 2. 7 ff.
11 Theognis, 201 f.; Solon, frag. 12. 7 ff.
12 Hesiod, *Works*, 260.

Otherwise the doctrine of the eternal and infallible justice of heaven becomes vain. God, it is inferred, takes long views. He bides His time until the cup of iniquity is full. The sword of justice may linger, but it will surely fall, if not upon the sinner himself, then upon the heads of his children or descendants.

'Not long abide for men the works of unrighteousness. Zeus beholdeth the issue of all things, and sudden as the wind that scatters the clouds in spring . . . is the vengeance of Zeus. He is not swift to anger at each thing like a mortal man, yet he who has a sinful heart escapes not his notice for ever, but is surely revealed in the end. One pays the penalty immediately, another after. And if they escape themselves and the doom of the gods overtake them not, yet surely it cometh afterward: the innocent pay for their deeds, their children or their descendants after them.'[1]

'These things [the apparent escape of the sinner from retribution] deceive the mind of men; for not at the moment of each act do the gods punish sins, but one pays the ill debt himself nor hangs woe over his dear children in the aftertime: another justice overtaketh not: ere that relentless death alights upon his eyes, bringing doom.'[2]

The doctrine seemed to be the natural issue of the doctrine of the inflexible justice of heaven. And genuine examples of the unrighteous prosperity of one generation being succeeded by signal calamity in another were common enough. Popular fancy would manufacture others, and by an easy paralogism infer a general principle. How deeply ingrained in Greek belief it was is shown by the fact that in a formal curse—*e.g.*, that pronounced by the herald at the opening of the Ecclesia and the Boule — the descendants and family of the transgressor were included:

ὅν ἐκείνοις εὔχεσθ' ἐξώλη ποιεῖν αὐτὸν, καὶ γένος, καὶ οἰκίαν.[3]

And Aristotle[4] implicitly justifies the doctrine, if regard be had only to the individual's reckoning with heaven. But, from the point of view of the innocent sufferer, it is manifestly unfair that he should pay the penalty for sins in which he had no part. The injustice of it was bound to strike every serious man.

As David cried: 'Lo, I have sinned, and I have done perversely: but these sheep, what have they done? let thine hand, I pray thee, be against me, and against my father's house,'[5] so Theognis cries: 'O Father Zeus, would that it might please the gods that he . . . who works the works of foolishness and taketh no heed of the gods might himself pay for his evil doing and that the sins of the father should not afterward be an evil for his children: that the children of an unjust father who do righteously, reverencing thine anger, who among their townsmen have loved justice from the beginning, should not pay for any transgression of their fathers. Would that this were well-pleasing to the gods: but now the doer escapes, and another afterwards bears the evil';[6] and again: 'O Zeus, I wonder at thee: thou art lord of all: . . . how can thy heart count the sinner and the unrighteous alike? . . . There is no sure sign given to men by the gods nor any certain way wherein one may walk and be well-pleasing to the gods. The sinners enjoy untroubled prosperity, while those who refrain their hearts from wickedness have poverty for their lot.'[7]

It must be emphasized that Theognis is not questioning the fact, nor is he impugning the justice of heaven, which indeed he is concerned to maintain—precisely as Jeremiah[8] makes the righteousness of God his justification for reasoning with Him:

'Righteous art thou, O Lord, when I plead with thee: yet would I reason the cause with thee: wherefore doth the way of the wicked prosper? wherefore are all they at ease that deal very treacherously?'

There in fact is the difficulty. If God is a just God, why does the sinner not pay for his sins immediately so that the anger of God should be unmistakably revealed? Why, if God is just, does the sinner sometimes escape punishment in this life altogether? If it be answered that God visits the sins of the fathers upon the children, then God is again unjust, in that He visits the guilt of the sinner upon the innocent. From this dilemma there could be no escape without a new conception of the meaning of life—that is to say, a new conception of the destiny of the soul.

That new conception of the soul, which for convenience we may call the mystic or Orphic conception, profoundly influenced the Greek doctrine of sin from the 6th cent. onwards, and the remainder of this article is chiefly concerned to illustrate the traces of that influence to be found in Greek writers of the 5th and 4th centuries before Christ.[1]

5. Pindar.—The genesis of sin is in Pindar conceived on familiar lines. Great prosperity (*ὄλβος*) is a temptation or incentive to sin. The effect is likened to that of overfeeding: satiety (*κόρος*) breeds insolence (*ὕβρις*). When *ὕβρις* finds expression in action, it leads to woe (*ἄτη*).

Thus Ixion:

εὐμενέσσι γὰρ παρὰ Κρονίδαις
γλυκὺν ἑλὼν βίοτον, μακρὸν οὐχ ὑπέμεινεν ὄλβον, μαινομέναις φρασὶν
Ἥρας ὅτ' ἐράσσατο, . . .
. . . ἀλλά νιν ὕβρις εἰς αὐάταν ὑπεράφανον
ὦρσεν.[2]

So Tantalos:

καταπέψαι
μέγαν ὄλβον οὐκ ἐδυνάσθη, κόρῳ δ' ἕλεν
ἄταν ὑπέροπλον.[3]

It may be noted that *κόρος* and *ὕβρις* come to have practically identical meanings, so that Hybris appears as mother of Koros,[4] thus reversing the Solon-Theognis version, which makes Hybris daughter of Koros.

No Greek poet lays more emphasis than Pindar does upon heredity.[5] And nowhere do we find the solidarity of the family, whether for weal or for woe, more vividly realized. The family is like a field which is fruitful or fallow in alternate generations.[6] The 'family fortune' is of great moment always.[7] Hence it is natural for Pindar to think of the destiny of a given generation as conditioned by the conduct of earlier generations—to conceive, in fact, the sin or the righteousness of the fathers being visited upon the children. But now, in several remarkable passages of Pindar, we have the nature and destiny of the soul presented in a light which alters the relative values of life and death. Unfortunately the fragmentary character of some of these passages makes their interpretation a matter of the utmost difficulty. Yet the general outlines seem sufficiently clear.

In frag. 131[8] we find a definite contrast between the destiny of the 'body (*σῶμα*) which followeth overmighty death' and the 'likeness of life' (*αἰῶνος εἴδωλον*) which 'remaineth yet alive: for it alone is from the gods. It sleepeth when the members are active, but to them that sleep in many a dream it revealeth the coming judgment for weal or woe.'

The soul, then, and the soul alone, is divine in its origin. It is a 'likeness of life,' that is to say, it is conceived as resembling the living man in such a way as to preserve its identity: it can be known among other souls as being the soul of such and such a person. It is a prisoner in the body, which hampers and impedes its activity. Its still small voice cannot be heard amid the thunder of fleshly energies; only in sleep, when these energies are hushed and stilled, it regains for a season its full efficiency. Life, this present life, is less a boon than a thorn: 'Man is well done with it soon as he's born.' Only by death can the temporary release of sleep become a permanent emancipation.

And, if one incarnation, why not many? It is an easy step to conceive the soul as undergoing a series of probationary incarnations, until it has again become worthy to be united with the divine, to return to heaven, which is its home. The

1 Solon, frag. 12. 2 Theognis, 203 ff.
3 Demosth. *Falsa Legatio*, 71.
4 *Eth. Nic.* i. 10. 1100a 29: *ἄτοπον δὲ καὶ τὸ μηδὲν μηδ' ἐπί τινα χρόνον συνικνεῖσθαι τὰ τῶν ἐκγόνων τοῖς γονεῦσιν.*
5 2 S 24[17]. 6 731 ff. 7 373 ff. 8 12[1].

1 For details the reader may be referred to the articles on MYSTERIES (Greek, etc.), NEO-PLATONISM, etc.
2 *Pyth.* ii. 25. 3 *Ol.* i. 55.
4 *Ol.* xiii. 10 (cf. Oracle in Herod. viii. 77).
5 *τὸ δὲ φυᾷ κράτιστον ἅπαν* (*Ol.* ix. 100).
6 *Nem.* vi. 8 ff., xi. 37 ff.
7 *κρίνει συγγενὴς ἔργων περὶ πάντων* (*Nem.* v. 40; cf. *Pyth.* v. 17; *Isth.* i. 40; *Nem.* iii. 40).
8 Preserved by Plutarch, *Consol. ad Apollon.* ch. 35.

number and the nature of its incarnations must depend upon its previous conduct:

'From whomsoever Persephone accepts atonement of ancient sorrow, the souls of these she sends again in the ninth year into the upper sun: from these spring glorious kings, and men excellent in strength and mightiest in wisdom: who in future time are called by men holy heroes.'[1]

How, then, can the individual best assist the emancipation of his soul? In two ways: (1) he must endeavour to abstain from unrighteousness; (2) he must be initiated in the mysteries which not merely teach him what lies beyond, but actually show him the *φέγγος ἱερόν*,[2] the holy light, the light that never was on land or sea. Then he shall know that the same heaven from which the soul came at first shall also be her final home. He sees the light and whence it flows.

'Happy is he who has seen these things ere he goes beneath the earth: he knows that the end of life is with God, even as from God was its beginning.'[3]

What now is the bearing of this doctrine of the soul upon the conception of hereditary guilt? Pindar seems to answer this question in the *2nd Olympian*.

The victor whom he celebrates is Theron of Acrapas, who as one of the Emmenidai is a descendant of the sinful house of Laios, king of Thebes. Now, even from the time that Laios was slain by his fatal son (*μόριμος υἱός*), Fate (*Μοῖρα*) has so guided the family fortune, on the whole a happy fortune,[4] that together with heaven-sent prosperity they have also endured 'woeful reverse at other times.' But 'wealth adorned with deeds of excellence . . . is a most sure light,'[5] if the possessor 'knoweth that which is to be: that the helpless souls[6] of the dead pay the penalty immediately here, while the sins done in this realm of Zeus one judges under earth, pronouncing doom by hateful constraint.' 'But equally by night as by day'—the same emphasis and order as we have noted above—'the good receive a life more free from trouble,[7] vexing not the earth with the might of their hands nor the waters of the sea, in that ghostly life. But with the honoured of the gods, even those who rejoiced in keeping their oaths, they live a tearless life, while those others endure trouble beyond beholding. But whoso have endured unto three times on either side to refrain their souls utterly from iniquity, rise by the way of Zeus unto the tower of Kronos; where round the planets of the blest the ocean breezes blow, and flowers of gold are glowing,' etc.[8]

Thus God is not unjust: if He seems so, it is 'because we see not to the end.' Sin, in the end, must be punished. The sins of the fathers affect the destiny of the children. But it is not without hope that each generation travels. And the path which each must thus hopefully travel is the same —to do justice, to love mercy, and to walk humbly with their God.

6. Æschylus.—Æschylus is much occupied with the hereditary curse, as illustrated especially in the royal house of Atreus, in which one murder is avenged by a new murder, and the new murder by yet another, and so on, seemingly without end. At times the ineluctability of fate becomes overpowering.

'Taunt answers taunt, and things are hard to read. The spoiler is spoiled, the slayer pays, and it abides, as Zeus abides upon his throne, that he who does must suffer; for so it is ordained. Who shall cast forth from the house the bread of curses? The race is glued to woe.'[9]

Indeed, if punishment is viewed in its merely retributive aspect, and if we take short views of justice, there is no seeing where the process is to stop. The last sufferer must in any case be unavenged. It is only when she is weary of the unending play of tit-for-tat[1] that Klytemnestra is fain to conclude an amnesty with the *δαίμων*, or ancestral spirit, of the Pleisthenidai, upon the basis of the *status quo*.[2]

But the retributive aspect of sin is to Æschylus merely an incident in the larger motive, which is educative. He is never tired of insisting that the end of suffering is to teach men *σωφροσύνη*, which is precisely the antithesis of *ὕβρις*.

'It is good to learn wisdom by sorrow.'[3] 'Zeus who guides men to be wise, Zeus who hath established it as valid law that by suffering men shall learn.'[4]

We have seen that Pindar conceives the soul as most active in sleep. So the Psalmist[5] says: 'My reins instruct me in the night seasons.' So Æschylus conceives that it is in the watches of the night, when the bodily energies are hushed, that the still small voice of conscience is heard, or, as he expresses it in the physiological language of his time,

'There droppeth before the heart (*καρδία*) sad memory's pain, and wisdom (*σωφρονεῖν*) cometh to men against their will.'[6]

This he describes as a *δαιμόνων χάρις βιαίως*, a favour which the gods force upon men.[7] He conceives then that the gods 'will not that any should perish,' and, so conceiving, he rejects quite definitely the old notion that mere prosperity excites the anger and the vengeance of heaven. He proclaims his 'lonely faith' (*μονόφρων*) in memorable words:

'It is the impious deed that gives birth to other deeds after it in the likeness of its kind, but the house of the righteous is blessed in its children for ever.'[8]

Prosperity is doubtless a temptation; it is no less hard a task to 'thole'[9] prosperity than to 'thole' adversity. But the good man wins through. So the ancestral curse is not a compelling cause of crime; it may aid and abet,[10] but it does not render sin unavoidable or excuse the sinner.

Æschylus is familiar with the larger faith which regarded the present life as only the gateway to a fuller life beyond. Preoccupied as he was with the problem of sin and suffering, he dwells on the unseen world mostly as a place of retribution.

'The gods are not heedless of them whose hands are steeped in blood. The dark Erinyes *in time*, when a man has prospered without righteousness, with reversal of his life's lot make him dim, and when he is among the unseen there is no avail.'[11] 'Not even in the house of Hades when he dies shall he who doeth these things escape the guilt of his sin. There too, it is said, another Zeus judges among the dead men's sins in a last judgment.'[12]

7. Conclusion.—Here we must end our study. Henceforth the Greek doctrine of sin develops in two main directions. On the one hand, sin becomes identical with ignorance, righteousness with knowledge: *οὐδεὶς ἑκὼν κακός*.[13] And this, indeed, may not unfairly be described as the characteristically philosophic doctrine. Conceiving moral rightness as essentially a matter of right knowledge, they held it to be unthinkable that a man should know the better and yet deliberately choose the worse. And, if this theory proved manifestly out of harmony with the facts, as Aristotle says,[14] that was because right knowledge was wholly or temporarily obscured by vicious appetite, and none the less the ideal to be pursued was knowledge. It did not greatly trouble the philosopher that on this view the gates of heaven were barred to the general mass of toiling mortality and that no weight was given to the great non-intellectual virtues of patience and humility and charity, all

1 Frag. 133 (Plato, *Meno*, 81 B).
2 Aristoph. *Frogs*, 445.
3 Frag. 102. O. Kern in *ARW* xix. [1919] 2–3, p. 434, is mistaken in thinking that the *ἀρχά* here refers to 'die Wiedergeburt des Mysten aus dem Mutterschosse der Unterweltsgöttin,' as if a *vita nuova* which the *mystes* has attained by contact with the objects in the holy *cista*. 'Deshalb steht *ἀρχά* ausdrücklich hinter *τελευτά*.' But the position of *ἀρχά* is due to the natural emphasis—'the end is even as the beginning' (cf. *Pyth.* x. 10: *γλυκὺ δ' ἀνθρώπων τέλος ἀρχά τε δαίμονος ὀρνύντος αὔξεται*, where the emphasis and the order are precisely the same).
4 *πατρώιον τὸν εὔφρονα πότμον* (65 f.).
5 *ἐτυμώτατον φέγγος* (101 f.).
6 *ἀπάλαμνοι φρένες* (105), *i.e.* those who have committed *ἀνήκεστα, ἀνίατα*, and are not yet redeemed.
7 *ἀπονέστερον* (110); they are not yet wholly emancipated.
8 *Ol.* ii. 58 ff. 9 *Agam.* 1537 ff.

1 *τύμμα τύμματι τῖσαι* (*Agam.* 1430).
2 *Ib.* 1534. 3 *Eumen.* 520. 4 *Agam.* 176 f.
5 167. 6 *Agam.* 178 ff. 7 *Ib.*
8 *Ib.* 737.
9 *φέρειν* is regular in the double sense.
10 *πατρόθεν δὲ συλλήπτωρ γένοιτ' ἂν ἀλάστωρ* (*Agam.* 1508).
11 *Ib.* 460 ff.
12 *Suppl.* 228 ff.; cf. 415; also *Eumen.* 267 ff., 335 ff.
13 Plato, *Timæus*, 86 D.
14 *Eth. Nic.* VII. ii. 2, 1145^b 25.

that we sum up as 'otherworldliness.' But to others it seemed as if this doctrine could lead at best only to a practical or 'political' righteousness. If the soul is indeed a wanderer from God who is her home, if her final destiny is indeed reunion with God, then knowledge such as is attainable by ordinary means seemed insufficient. The finer spirits yearned, as Plato yearned, for an ὄχημα βεβαιότερον, a λόγος θεῖος, in which to make the voyage of life, in place of the poor raft (σχεδία) of merely 'human' knowledge.[1] If the soul alone is divine, if this tenement of clay be in truth a prison, as the mysteries taught, then man must wean the soul from association with the body, must accustom her to be, so far as is now possible, 'alone with herself,' must accustom her to contemplate the things beyond, so that, when she leaves the body and arrives there, she will not gape and be dizzy,[2] but will feel at home in her surroundings.[3] If it be only in moments of exaltation and ecstasy that the embodied spirit can obtain even a glimpse of disembodied felicity, the seeker after truth cries: ὦ Μανία, ξύλλαβε.[4] The foolishness of men may be wisdom with God.

LITERATURE.—E. Rohde, *Psyche*², 2 vols., Freiburg, 1898; J. Köberle, *Sünde und Gnade*, Munich, 1905; P. D. Chantepie de la Saussaye, *Lehrbuch der Religionsgeschichte*³, Tübingen, 1905, ii.; F. R. Tennant, *The Sources of the Doctrines of the Fall and Original Sin*, Cambridge, 1903; E. Buchholz, *Die sittliche Weltanschauung des Pindaros und Aeschylos*, Leipzig, 1869; P. Decharme, *Euripide et l'esprit de son théâtre*, Paris, 1893; E. Maass, *Orpheus*, Munich, 1895; C. F. von Nägelsbach, *Die homerische Theologie*³, Nuremberg, 1884; A. Bertholet, *Biblische Theologie des alten Testaments*, Tübingen, 1911; E. D. Burton, J. M. P. Smith, and G. B. Smith, *Biblical Ideas of Atonement*, Chicago, 1919; H. Usener, *Die Sintfluthsagen*, Bonn, 1899.

A. W. MAIR.

SIN (Hebrew and Jewish).

—**1. Terms.**—We need not concern ourselves here with the numerous words denoting particular vices or with words of such wide significance as רַע, *ra'*, and its cognates (used for every variety of vice or misfortune, of moral or material evil). We confine ourselves to the ordinary, general words for 'sin.'

There is a group of terms from the root חטא—חֵטְא, חֲטָאָה, חַטָּאָה, חַטָּאת, usually translated 'sin.' The verb is also used in the purely secular sense of 'missing one's way (or aim)' (Job 5^{24}, RV, Pr 8^{36}, RVm, Job 41^{25} (Heb. 17), RV). פָּשַׁע and פֶּשַׁע are usually translated 'transgress,' 'transgression.' The verb is also used in the secular sense of 'rebel.' עָוֹן, *'āwōn*, אָוֶן, *'āwen*, and עָוֶל, *'āwel*, are all translated 'iniquity.' The usage of similar roots in cognate languages suggests that *'āwōn* and *'āwel* may have had originally the concrete sense of 'going astray.' The concrete sense of *'āwen*, 'sorrow,' 'trouble,' is still in use in the OT. רָשָׁע, רֶשַׁע, and רִשְׁעָה are usually translated 'wicked,' 'wickedness.' The original meaning of the root is doubtful; but these words and the corresponding denominative verb are regularly used in the forensic sense of 'being guilty of a crime,' 'being in the wrong in a lawsuit' (Ex 23^{1}). The use of these terms in the ethical and religious sense, 'wicked,' is an extension of the forensic usage. In LXX derivatives of *ḥṭ'* are rendered *inter alia* in various passages by ἀδικία, ἁμαρτία, ἀνομία, or the verbs, nouns, adjectives, etc., corresponding to these words. The same is true of derivatives of *p sh'* and of *r sh'*, and of the words *'āwōn*, *'āwen*, and *'āwel* themselves, except that *'āwen* and *'āwel* are not rendered by ἁμαρτία or its cognates. The derivatives of *ḥṭ'*, however, are usually rendered by ἁμαρτία and its cognates. *'Āwōn* is translated in roughly equal proportions by ἀδικία, etc., ἁμαρτία, etc., ἀνομία, etc., and seldom by anything else. *'Āwel* is usually rendered by ἀδικία and, less frequently, ἀνομία. *'Āwen*, on the other hand, is usually rendered by ἀνομία and, much less often, by ἀδικία, when understood in ethical and religious senses, otherwise by words denoting 'toil,' 'trouble,' etc. The derivatives of *p sh'* are rendered usually by either ἁμαρτία, etc., ἀδικία, etc., ἀνομία, etc., or ἀσέβεια, etc., or ἀθετέω. The derivatives of *r sh'* are most often rendered by ἀσεβής and its cognates, but also frequently by ἁμαρτωλός and cognates, occasionally by ἀδικία, etc. The Latin renderings of the Vg. are also very varied. The most common rendering for the *ḥṭ'* terms is *peccatum*; for *pesha'* and *'āwōn*, *iniquitas*, but sometimes *scelus* for *pesha'*; for *r sh'* terms, *impius*, etc. The Vg. renderings have been influenced by those of the LXX. It is noteworthy that *ḥēṭ'*, *ḥaṭṭ'āth*, *'āwōn*, and *pesha'* are, each of them, used alike for 'sin,' 'guilt,' and 'punishment,' and that *ḥaṭṭ'āth* and *pesha'* are also used for 'sin-offering.' Although the *ḥṭ'* terms are mostly used of sin against God, they occasionally denote wrong done to man; *'āwōn* and the *p sh'* terms are used of conduct, etc., either to God or to man.

A somewhat different feature is the frequent use in connexion with sin and sinners of *nābhāl*, *nebhālā*, EV 'fool,' 'folly,' LXX mostly ἄφρων, ἀφροσύνη, Vg. various; and other words of similar meaning.

Other terms for 'sin' peculiar to particular writers or periods will be noticed below.

2. General considerations suggested by the terminology.—We do not learn much from the etymology; it is often uncertain. When a word is fairly launched on its career, its meaning in actual usage is little influenced by its original etymology unless this is conspicuously obvious, and not always then. Sometimes, however, an original concrete usage persists side by side with the abstract sense derived from it, as in the cases of *'āwen*, and the roots *p sh'*, *r sh'*, and probably *ḥṭ'*. In these cases the concrete usage might continue to determine in some measure the sense of the abstract terms; *e.g.*, it would be tempting to suppose that the *ḥṭ'* words implied that sin was a futile blunder, the *p sh'* words that it was rebellion against God, and the *r sh'* words that the sinner put himself in the wrong, and to some extent this may have been the case. The fact that the LXX almost invariably renders the *ḥṭ'* words by ἁμαρτία and its cognates shows that these terms were regarded as specially denoting sin *qua* sin. Otherwise the facts in § 1 indicate that by the time the LXX was made there was no sense of any marked difference between the leading terms for sin.

It should be noticed that both the etymology and the LXX renderings indicate that sin was regarded as negative. Both *ḥṭ'* and ἁμαρτία are failure to reach an ideal standard—it is suggested that the α in ἁμαρτία, though aspirated, is privative. *R sh'* and ἀδικία are divergence from a legal standard. Both the *ḥṭ'* and the *r sh'* terms are contrasted with the צדק ('righteous') terms (Pr 10^{2} 13^{21}).[1] *P sh'* is rebellion against a lawful authority; *'āwōn* and *'āwel* are divergence from the straight course; *'āwen* is the absence of what is worthy or desirable.

Another feature is the use of the same terms for sin, guilt, punishment, and sin-offering. The usage arises out of a primitive psychology as to which it is dangerous to be dogmatic. It seems natural, however, to see in these facts an indication that sin was thought of as automatically including and working out its own fatal sequel. The terms might be extended to sin-offering as a kind of penalty. 'For the Jews sin is a power which brings ruin to sinners, because it is fundamentally identical with punishment.'[2] Sin is personified in the literature, which probably implies that it was sometimes popularly regarded as a person, a kind of evil deity. In Gn 4^{7} sin (*ḥaṭṭāth*) crouches like a wild beast lying in wait for its prey. Parallel to the familiar phrase '*ne'um YHWH*,' 'oracle of Jahweh,' we have in Ps 36^{1} '*ne'um pesha'*,' 'oracle of sin.' In Zec $5^{5ff.}$ wickedness (*rish'â*) appears as a woman.[3] In Sir 27^{10} a lion lies in wait for prey as sin (ἁμαρτία) for evil-doers.

3. Primitive ideas.—Obviously many of the Israelite ideas as to sin were held by them in common with other peoples, especially other Semitic peoples. This is most of all the case in the earlier period, before the time of Amos, *c.* 750 B.C. In this period the ideas suggested by the etymology of the terms and their concrete use would be prominent—*e.g.*, that of sin as a power automatically working out punishment. Closely connected with this is the view that suffering and misfortune, especially exceptional misfortune, are indications that the sufferer has been guilty of heinous sin. Thus in 2 S 21^{1} a grievous famine leads David to ask of what sin it is the punishment.

Further, we must bear in mind that the idea of sin in its earliest form is neither moral nor spiritual; sin is simply that of which the deity or deities disapprove. It is, indeed, often said that sin, at a primitive stage, is merely the violation of national or tribal custom.

1 *Phædo*, 85 D.
2 *Gorgias*, 527 A.
3 οὐκ ἀγνοεῖ τὰ παρόντα (*Phædo*, 108 A).
4 Aristoph. *Frogs*, 1345.

1 Cf. art. 'Righteousness' in *HDB* and *ERE*.
2 R. Smend, *Lehrbuch der AT Religionsgeschichte*, Freiburg, 1893, p. 431; cf. p. 196 and W. R. Smith, *Religion of the Semites*², p. 423.
3 Cf. Is $64^{6f.}$ (Heb. 5f.).

'In the earliest parts of the Old Testament, sin is almost invariably presented to us as nothing more than disobedience to the statutes regulating religious, social, and civil life in Israel, and a violation of the good customs in vogue among this people.'[1]

There is a large measure of truth in this view, but it is not inconsistent with what was said above. At this stage of religious development there is a very close organic connexion between deity and people; the customs and rules of national life are under religious sanction; they are the will of the deity. Men's ideas of sin depend upon their thoughts of God; for primitive peoples the deity has largely the character of an arbitrary, self-willed tyrant. There is no knowing what may please or anger Him, or what He may think fit to demand, what He may approve as piety, or what He may condemn as sin. Man may only discover that he has sinned through the punishment that crushes him.

Thus Moses is on his way to Egypt to fulfil the mission with which Jahweh has entrusted him; he is unconscious of anything that should rouse the divine anger against him. Yet Jahweh makes an onslaught on him and seeks to kill him, because he had not circumcised his son, although there is no previous command to circumcise in the document J, to which the passage belongs (Ex $4^{24ff.}$). David, when persecuted by Saul, thought it possible that, for some unknown reason, he had incurred the ill-will of Jahweh, that Jahweh had stirred up Saul against him, but might be appeased by a gift (1 S 26^{19}).[2]

Again, in the early period, the idea of sin is objective; sin consists in the performance or neglect of certain external acts.

'No occasion is taken to inquire more deeply into the nature of sin as affecting man's inner life.'[3] 'Sin is action antagonistic to God (*gottwidrige*) without any reference whatever to the question whether the actor is conscious of this quality of his action. A man does not become a sinner through the purpose of his act but through his objective doings.'[4]

The conditions of satisfactory relations with God are largely material and physical—various rites, regulations as to food and 'cleanness and uncleanness' generally, all sorts of tabus. Although most of the Levitical ordinances come to us from a later period, they probably represent very fairly the conditions of earlier times. This is implied, *inter alia*, by the prophetic denunciations of ritual. If we could compare the system of the Priestly Code with the practices in early Israel, the advantage would be with the Code. Thus the distinction with which we meet later between 'secret' sins, or 'errors' (שְׁגִיאוֹת), and 'presumptuous' sins (זֵדִים [Ps $19^{13f.}$]), or sins 'with a high hand' (Nu 15^{30})—*i.e.* between unconscious, unintentional sins and those which were conscious and deliberate—is, as we have seen in examples already referred to, ancient and primitive. The exact interpretation of ordinances as to ritual, etc., would often be known to the priests alone; moreover, the ordinances as to what was clean or unclean might easily be broken unwittingly.

In early times the principle of the solidarity of the family, tribe, or nation was strongly held; guilt attached to the kindred and fellow-tribesmen of an offender—as in the case of Achan (Jos $7^{1.\ 24f.}$) and of Saul and the Gibeonites (2 S 21). The guilt of fathers and ancestors attaches to children and descendants.

The punishment of sin may involve the death of the offender—*e.g.*, the sons of Eli (1 S 2^{34})—or some minor misfortune, as in the case of David (2 S $12^{13f.}$). Sacrifice (*q.v.*) played a large part in establishing, maintaining, and restoring right relations between God and man, but the cancelling of sin might also be effected by a suitable punishment, and partly by the spontaneous forgiveness of God.[1]

Moreover, in early times, religion was largely a matter of the tribe or nation; accordingly, as the nation incurred divine displeasure through the sin of one of its members, it could also be purged of guilt by his punishment—*e.g.*, the incident of Achan.

It is natural to see in the story of the Fall (Gn 3) an account of the origin of sin, but sin is present in the serpent before it arises in Adam and Eve; the story rather gives the first sin as the origin of suffering. The first sin is typical of the primitive idea: it is an external act, the violation of an arbitrary command. Moreover, the story of the Fall was probably borrowed from a non-Israelite source, though no very close parallel to it has yet been found. It does not seem to have had much influence on early Israelite thought, which does not assert the corruption of human nature or the alienation from God that NT and later theology attribute to the Fall.[2]

The question as to what in the way of commission or omission was reckoned sin is too large to be dealt with here; it rather belongs to OT ethics.

'This ethical ideal of the ancient Israelites is far from perfect. The patriarchs use deception toward the stranger, as if it were a lawful practice. Polygamy is not considered an evil, nor intemperance in eating and drinking a vice. Great licence in morals is tolerated. Barbarity is practised in war, and generally towards adversaries, as the case of David himself proves. Suicide does not appear culpable.'[3]

4. The period from c. 750 B.C. to c. 586 B.C., with special reference to the prophets of the 8th cent., to Deuteronomy, and to Jeremiah and (in part) Ezekiel. — The various ideas as to sin already mentioned persisted in this period; and in cases where nothing is said about them in this section it may be understood that they were held by the prophets, etc., of this period.

Probably there is little in the prophets that was absolutely new; even ideas which appear for the first time in the literature of this period may not have been new to the hearers of the prophets. The most important novelty was a change of emphasis arising out of an advance in the doctrine of God. Sin is still that which God disapproves, but the ethical nature of God is much more clearly and fully held. He is no longer concerned chiefly with material gifts and external homage—the strict observance of the etiquette of His divine court. He desires sincere loyalty and heartfelt affection from His people. He is concerned for their material, moral, and spiritual well-being, and desires that His worshippers should further His purposes by mutual goodwill and beneficence. This is summed up in Hos 6^6: 'I will have benevolence (*hesedh*) rather than sacrifice, and the knowledge of God rather than burnt offerings.' Sin has now come to mean failure as to these matters. The prophets may not actually condemn ritual, but, if they do not, they regard it as altogether subordinate. One cardinal sin is social wrong-doing, the corrupt administration of justice, the exploiting of the resources of the community in the interests of a privileged few (Am $2^{6f.}$, Hos 4^1, Is 1^{10-17}, Mic $2^{2.\ 8f.}$). Deut., indeed, has regulations as to ritual, clean and unclean things, etc., but its main interest is to provide for the needs of the poor.

Hosea's phrase, 'the knowledge of God' ($4^{1.\ 6}$ 6^6; cf. Is 5^{13}), includes what we should call fellowship and religious experience; the primitive view, as we have seen, held that sin arose from the ignorance of external ritual. Hosea and Isaiah

1 H. Schultz, *OT Theology*, Eng. tr., Edinburgh, 1892, ii. 281.
2 Cf. the episodes of the Gibeonites and of the census (2 S 21, 24).
3 Schultz, *loc. cit.*
4 Cf. Smend, p. 106f., and W. Staerk, *Sünde und Gnade*, p. 25: 'The conception of sin in older Judaism was very external and lax.'

1 Cf. again David, in 2 S $12^{13f.}$.
2 Cf. K. Marti, *Gesch. der israelit. Religion*, Strassburg, 1897, p. 198 ff.
3 C. Piepenbring, *Theology of the OT*, Eng. tr., New York, 1893, p. 36.

hold that sin arises from ignorance of the character of God and His ethical demands. Isaiah uses the old ritualistic language and speaks of that which is unclean (*ṭāmē'*) as sin, but the term is no longer merely physical, and now denotes what is morally and spiritually unsatisfactory. He also emphasizes the idea that sin is rebellion against God (1^{2-4}).[1]

As regards punishment, these prophets are concerned chiefly with the judgment on the nation, though occasionally they deal with specific individuals (Am 7^{17}, Hos 1-3, unless those chapters are entirely figurative [Is $22^{22ff.}$]). Isaiah also discriminates between classes within the nation: it is well with the righteous, but woe to the wicked (3^{10}); the nation is doomed, but a remnant will escape (10^{20}).

These prophets are for the most part so absorbed in the guilt and punishment of Israel that they mostly say nothing as to forgiveness or treat it as impossible (Jer 13^{23}). The great exception is Hosea; according to him, Jahweh pleads with His people to repent, and offers them a free forgiveness ($11^{8f.}$). There is no reference to sacrifice or any ritual conditions of forgiveness.

Ezk 18 repudiates the doctrine that children suffer for the sins of their parents.[2] Both Jeremiah and Ezekiel insist on the total and universal depravity of their fellow-countrymen in their own time, and Ezekiel extends this to Israel throughout its history (Jer 5^{1-5} 8^{6}, Ezk 16, 20).

These prophets also deal with the sins of Gentile nations. We have already mentioned the emphasis which they laid on social wrong-doing; they also denounce idolatry and other superstitions, whether connected with the worship of Jahweh or with that of foreign deities.

5. Exilic and post-Exilic Judaism.—(*a*) *Biblical, together with the Wisdom literature of the Apocrypha (in part).*—The Priestly Code and the later prophets are by no means indifferent to the ethical and spiritual aspects of sin, but we find in this literature a special interest in sins against the ritual laws (Ezk 40-48, Hag 1^{2}, Zec 6^{12} 14^{16-21}, Jl 1^{9}, Mal 1^{8} 3^{8-10}).

It is often said that the special attention given to sin-offerings in the Priestly Code is due to the deepened sense of sin in this period, but this is doubtful. In all times the idea that sacrifice atoned for sin was common; what was new in the Priestly Code was the limitation of atoning value to special sacrifices and of the efficacy of these sacrifices to sins that were not conscious or deliberate (Lv 5).

The sense of sin, of the unhappy alienation from God arising out of sin, together with the feeling of penitence, finds fuller expression in the confessions and aspirations of the Psalter, etc., than in the earlier literature—*e.g.*, Ps 51, Neh 1. On the other hand, some of the Psalms breathe a spirit of self-righteousness which seems to argue a defective sense of sin (Ps 18^{20-24}). Probably, however, in such passages the writer is thinking of Israel as the loyal servant of Jahweh, in contrast to the idolatrous heathen, and is not claiming absolute righteousness for himself.

The literature of this period shows in many ways a raising of the moral and spiritual standard. A comparison of the narratives in the Priestly Code and in Chronicles with the corresponding narratives in the earlier literature, J, E, Samuel, Kings, shows that after the Exile the Jews regarded as sinful much that was not condemned in earlier times; *e.g.*, 1 K 11^{1-8} does not seem to see anything amiss in the populousness of Solomon's harem; what was wrong was that many of the women were foreigners; but the Chronicler has suppressed this account of the harem; as far as he is concerned, one might suppose that Solomon had only one wife, Pharaoh's daughter. A high ethical standard is set in Ezk 18, Job 29, 31.

The universality of sin is asserted (Ps 14, Pr 20^{9}), though Ezk 14^{14} suggests that exceptionally righteous men, like Noah, Daniel, and Job, might be saved by their own righteousness.[1]

The OT does not develop any formal doctrine of the origin of sin, but explains sins variously according to the circumstances of individual cases. Human nature is such that man sins through the influence of different motives and causes—the pride engendered by prosperity, the distress arising from poverty (Pr 30^{9}), indolence ($26^{13ff.}$), lust (27^{20}), persuasion by men (1^{10}), etc. Sometimes, indeed, God Himself is spoken of as causing men to sin (Is 44^{18} 63^{17}, Ezk 20^{25}); but probably this is a rhetorical way of saying that God has ordained that indulgence in sin should make men more prone to sin—to put the idea in modern terms. Whether there is any real difference between the two forms of expression may be doubtful.

The literature of this period is much occupied with the relation between sin and suffering. In Dt 30, etc., Ezk 18, etc., Ps 1, etc., the doctrine is taught that a man's external circumstances correspond to his character and conduct: the righteous prospers, the sinner is unfortunate; accordingly, suffering and misfortune are indications of sin. Many of the Psalms suggest that suffering had awakened a sense of guilt in the writers—*e.g.*, $32^{4f.}$, 119^{67}. On the other hand, the book of Job, Ps 73, 37, etc., repudiate the view of close correspondence between a man's conduct and his external fortunes. Isaiah 53 represents the sufferings of the righteous as providing salvation for sinners, and as borne willingly—teaching on a much higher level than the old idea that the guilt of the sinner was shared by his kin and his fellow-countrymen, but yet in a way a development from it, involving the principle of the vicarious efficacy of suffering.

It is a natural characteristic of the Wisdom literature that it should lay stress on the moral and spiritual value of 'wisdom,' and speak of sin as 'folly.'[2]

(*b*) *Apocrypha (in part) and Apocalyptic literature.*—In spite of Job, the doctrine of inherited guilt persisted; Tobit prays that he may not be punished for the sins of his fathers.[3]

As regards the origin and causes of sin, there is as little formal theory and as great a variety of treatment as in the literature dealt with in the last section. Sin is due to the wilfulness and evil self-will of man (Sir 15^{11-20}, a passage which expressly controverts the teaching found elsewhere [2 Es 3^{20}], that it is due to God); it is an inheritance from Eve (Sir 25^{24}), from Adam (2 Es 3^{21-25})—a suggestion of the doctrine of original sin; it is due to fallen angels and demons (*En.* 9^{6} 15^{11}); the wide-spread belief in demoniac possession inevitably led to the ascription of much wrong-doing to this cause. The idea of the tendency to sin being inherited from Adam—*i.e.* of original sin (2 Es 4^{30}) as distinguished from the later Augustinian doctrine, which is really one of original guilt—regards this inborn tendency as the cause of sin, and inclines to limit the responsibility of the individual. On the other hand, the doctrine of transmigration (Wis $8^{19f.}$) maintains responsibility, even though the tendency to sin is held to be inborn.

As to its nature, sin is still regarded as rebellion against God (Wis 3^{10}), as that which is contrary to the will of God; since God had made known His

[1] Cf. Smend, p. 206; O. C. Whitehouse, *Isaiah I.-XXXIX.* (*Century Bible*), Edinburgh, 1905, p. 56.
[2] Cf. Jer $31^{29f.}$, but, on the other hand, see 15^{4}.

[1] Cf. Schultz, ii. 295 f.
[2] See Prov., Ec., Wis., Sir., etc., *passim*; cf. also above, § 1.
[3] To 3^{3-5}; cf. 13^{9}, Jth 7^{28}, Dn $9^{4ff.}$, Bar 1^{15}–3^{8}.

will to the Jews in the Pentateuchal law, sin for them consisted largely in breaking that law (Sir., Prologue, 41^{8} 49^{4}, Mac., *passim*). Wisdom, following Hosea on the one hand and Plato on the other, sees salvation in wisdom (9^{18}) and sin in ignorance and folly ($2^{21f.}$ 3^{11} 5^{4-6}). The Apocalyptic literature, again, implies that a special sinfulness attaches to men of power and wealth, kings, nobles, princes (*En.* 38^{5} 54^{2} 67^{8-13} 94^{8}).

The idea of the universality of sin is found in 2 Es 3 7^{46-56} 8^{35}:

'For in truth there is no man among them that be born, but he hath dealt wickedly.' In 3^{36}, however, there is a qualification: 'Thou shalt find that men who may be reckoned by name have kept thy precepts, but nations thou shalt not find.'

Similarly, in the Prayer of Manasses:

'Thou therefore, O Lord, that art the God of the just, hast not appointed repentance to the just, as to Abraham, and Isaac, and Jacob, which have not sinned against thee.'

Further, we find frequently in Sir. (*e.g.*, 7^{16} 8^{10}) the contrast between 'sinner' and 'righteous' which is common in Psalms and Proverbs, implying that, however universal sin may be, practically men differ so much in this respect that some may be styled righteous and others sinners. But a closer investigation shows that the distinction is often what we should call sectarian rather than moral or spiritual: the professed worshipper of Jahweh is righteous; others are sinners. Sin becomes merely the lack of external adherence to certain sectarian views and practices.

The growing belief during this period in a future life, in resurrection, and in a judgment after death gave a larger importance to the consequences of sin, extended its punishment to an indefinite period, if not to eternity, and invested it with all the terrors of supernatural torture (Jth 16^{17}, 2 *En.* 10^{6}, 4 Mac 12^{12}).

By this time sin was largely regarded as concerning the individual, but the idea of national sin, sometimes arising from wrong-doing by only a part of the people, still survives (*Ps. Sol.* 2).

According to 4 Mac 5^{20}, all transgressions of the law, whether small or great, are equally sinful; but *Jub.* $7^{21f.}$ mentions three sins as the special cause of the Flood: fornication, uncleanness, and all iniquity; there is a general tendency in this literature to lay special stress on sexual sins. This may be seen in the various lists of vices and crimes which summarize the ethical position (Wis 14^{25}, *Gr. Bar.* 8, 13, *Test. Jud.* 16–19; cf. *Test. Reub.* 3).

6. Pharisaic, Sadducaic, and Rabbinic Judaism.—It seems impossible to avoid the conclusion that Orthodox Judaism, at all times and even now, has laid undue stress on external observances; sin has largely consisted in the neglect or breaking of external laws, often concerned with matters of mere ritual. Witness the supreme importance attached to the Pentateuch and the Talmud, and the extent to which these, especially the latter, are preoccupied with the details of the ceremonial law. Naturally this tendency is exaggerated among the less advanced Jewish communities—*e.g.*, in Russia and Poland. Yet such a tendency is not necessarily incompatible with a high morality; there is an advanced ethical standard in the law and the Talmud, if only it can maintain itself side by side with zeal for ritual. Moreover, these works do not ignore the inner and spiritual side of religion. C. G. Montefiore is justified in saying:

'The Law was not a mere external law, fulfilled from fear of punishment and for hope of reward. It was the Law of the all-wise and all-righteous God, given to Israel as a sign of supremest grace. It was a token of divine affection, and in its fulfilment was the highest human joy.'[1]

This statement could be supported by quotations from Jewish writers of every period. Thus

[1] *The Synoptic Gospels*, London, 1899, ii. 503.

I. Abrahams tells us, 'Sin is uncleanness.'[1] Doubtless physical, ceremonial uncleanness was often thought of as sin; but, on the other hand, uncleanness is often a figure for spiritual corruption. There is a similar combination of the ritual and ethical in *Ābhôth*, v. 10 f., which names as the seven main transgressions neglect in the matter of tithes, of the offering of the dough-cake, and of the seventh-years fruits; corrupt administration of justice; profanation of the NAME; idolatry; incest; murder; and failure to observe the Sabbatical year. Heretical exegesis of the Pentateuch is apparently included under the corrupt administration of justice. Again, we find in *Ābhôth*, iv. 5, the pregnant saying:

'The reward of precept is precept, and the reward of transgression is transgression.'

So far we have been speaking of orthodox Judaism; such sects as the Ḥasidim and the various bodies of Reformed Jews lay less emphasis on the ritual law and more on the ethical and spiritual features of Judaism.

As regards the origin and causes of sin, later Judaism has inevitably been influenced by general speculative thought. Already in Job 9 f. it is suggested that God is responsible for injustice and wrong-doing. Later writers are often occupied with the problems which we connect with the terms 'free will' and 'divine sovereignty.'

According to Josephus, the Sadducees emphasized man's control over his actions: 'God is not concerned in our doing or not doing what is evil . . . to act what is good or evil is at men's own choice.'[2] The Essenes, on the other hand, asserted that 'fate governs all things,'[3] or that 'all things are best ascribed to God.'[4] The Pharisees occupied an intermediate position; thus, 'when they determine that all things are done by fate, they do not take away the freedom from men of acting as they think fit; since their notion is, that it hath pleased God to make a temperament (κρᾶσις, rather 'combination') whereby what He wills is done, but so that the will of man can act virtuously or viciously.'[5] Or, as *Ābhôth*, iii. 24, puts it: 'Everything is foreseen (צפן), and freewill (רְשׁוּת) is given. And the world is judged by grace; and everything is according to work.'[6]

Later Judaism, with the exception of a measure of antinomianism in some of the Jewish mystics, has always asserted responsibility and ethical obligation, but there has also been a tendency to lay some of the responsibility for human sin upon God. Sin is partly due to the *Yeṣer hara'*, יֵצֶר הָרַע, the evil nature in man; and this was implanted in him by God. The phrase is often rendered 'evil impulse' (or 'tendency'), and this is according to its usage.

'The extraordinary thing about this theory of the origin of sin is that, in the last instance, God is the cause of Sin; for, as Creator of all things, He created the *Yetser hara'* in Adam, the existence of which made the Fall possible (*Bereshith rabbah*, c. 27). . . . The Almighty is made to say: . . . "It repenteth me that I created the *Yetser hara'* in man, for had I not done this he would not have rebelled against me (*Yalkut Shim. Beresh.* 61)."'[7]

A similar view was held by Baalshem, the founder of the Ḥasidim: 'We should thus regard all things in the light of so many manifestations of the Divinity.'[8] In the Ḳabbala, too, God is the author of evil, seeing that He created both the just and the unjust, and formed man of a spirit of good and a spirit of evil.[9] Such teaching implies the universality of sin; the Talmudic statement that children of a year old are free from sin need not be taken literally.[10]

As Abrahams tells us, 'Rabbinic Judaism took over from the Old Testament a belief that disease was a consequence of sin.'[11]

Both Philo and the Rabbis follow the OT in teaching that God's desire to forgive and the divine provision for forgiveness anticipate and stimulate

[1] *Studies in Pharisaism and the Gospels*, Cambridge, 1917, p. 41.
[2] *BJ* II. viii. 14. [3] *Ant.* XIII. v. 9.
[4] *Ib.* XVIII. i. 5. [5] *Ib.* XVIII. i. 3.
[6] Cf. Ph 2^{12}.
[7] W. O. E. Oesterley and G. H. Box, *Religion and Worship of the Synagogue*[2], p. 268.
[8] S. Schechter, *Studies in Judaism*, p. 27.
[9] A. E. Waite, *The Secret Doctrine in Israel*, London, 1913, p. 81.
[10] *Yômā*, 22*b*, *ap.* Abrahams, p. 119.
[11] Abrahams, p. 108.

man's repentance.[1] The conditions of forgiveness are confession, repentance, amendment or good works. Since the final destruction of the Temple there has been no question of sacrifice, but to some extent, especially with the less enlightened, the ceremonies of the Day of Atonement have been credited with atoning value.[2] On the other hand, the prayers for forgiveness in the liturgy of the Day of Atonement illustrate the ethical and spiritual character of the Jewish doctrine of sin.

LITERATURE.—The relevant articles and sections in Dictionaries of the Bible and *JE*; the relevant sections in treatises on the theology of the OT and on Jewish theology; the art. 'Righteousness' in *ERE* and *HDB*; also F. Bennewitz, *Die Sünde im alten Israel*, Leipzig, 1907; C. Clemen, *Die christliche Lehre von der Sünde*, Göttingen, 1897; J. Herrmann, *Die Idee der Sühne im Alten Testament*, Leipzig, 1905; J. Köberle, *Sünde und Gnade im relig. Leben des Volkes Israel*, Munich, 1905; W. O. E. Oesterley, *The Jewish Doctrine of Mediation*, London, 1910; W. O. E. Oesterley and G. H. Box, *The Religion and Worship of the Synagogue*², do. 1911; S. Schechter, *Studies in Judaism*, do. 1896; W. Staerk, *Sünde und Gnade nach der Vorstellung des alten Judenthums*, Tübingen, 1905.

W. H. BENNETT.

SIN (Hindu).—**1. Vedic.**—As in the *Rigveda* is found the most developed expression in Vedic literature of the concept of righteousness, so that *Saṁhitā* contains the most elevated expression of the sense of sin and the desire to be set free from it. Varuṇa is the god to whom the sinner addresses himself, as Varuṇa is the god who is omniscient, and who of himself or by his spies knows the thoughts of men. In the hymn VII. lxxxvi. the poet with unusual earnestness asserts his anxiety to be at peace with Varuṇa, of whose anger with him he is convinced by the testimony of his friends. He assures the god that the sin which he has committed, whether his own or inherited from his father, is not deliberate; heedlessness, drunkenness, dicing, passion, and thoughtlessness are pleaded as excuses; even sleep may produce wrong-doing, and the older may be involved in the sin of the younger. The god is therefore invoked to set free the sinner from his bonds, as the calf is released from the rope which fetters it. The hymn itself does not reveal the cause of the poet's appeal, and it is most probable that the sense of sin must be considered to have been brought home to him by disease, as is admitted freely in the later hymn VII. lxxxix., but even on this assumption the hymn is not without moral value. It confesses sin, even if it seeks to explain it; it assumes the justice of the divine anger, which it seeks to remove by supplication, probably accompanied by offering, though the hymn does not expressly say so. On the other hand, it is impossible to find in it any great depth of moral feeling, and it is certainly unnecessary to see in it proof of the influence of Semitic religion on early Indian belief.[3]

Beside this comparatively elevated conception of sin as an offence against the divine majesty there appears, freely enough in the *Rigveda* and predominantly in the *Atharvaveda*, the more primitive conception of sin as a pollution which can be removed by physical means. It is not difficult to trace remains of this earlier view in the hymns to Varuṇa: from VII. lxxxix. it is plain that the sinner was afflicted by dropsy, and the watery nature of the disease can hardly have failed to suggest connexion with Varuṇa, who is even in the *Rigveda* closely connected with the waters. Nor is it unlikely that Varuṇa's power to loosen the bonds of sin is derived ultimately from the cleansing power of the waters. In another hymn the waters themselves as goddesses[4] are entreated to carry away the sin and untruth of the poet. So Agni is asked to loosen the bonds of the sinner,[1] for fire by itself is potent to destroy, by burning, evil. In place of the more complicated conception of fetters imposed by a god, the sin itself is regarded as the fetter.[2] The same conception of sin as a kind of disease is implicit in the view of inherited sin or sin which comes from contagion: sin can be obtained not merely from the father, but from the mother and other close kindred.[3] In other cases the kinship of sin to a pollution is more evident: the black bird, the harbinger of Nirṛti, the goddess of misfortune, by its excrement creates guilt on the person affected; the wailing of the women in the house of the dead creates a pollution on the kin; the lowing of the victim at the sacrifice lays on the sacrificer the burden of a sin which he must expiate.[4] Even the sins of other men may pass over to a guiltless man,[5] and in this category perhaps must be reckoned the mysterious sins caused by the gods which appear in the *Yajurveda*.[6] Sin, therefore, it is legitimate to suppose, was to the Vedic Indian primarily the actual pollution of disease present in his body, and only by a gradual process of moral development was the disease interpreted as the punishment inflicted for an act, or thought, or word, displeasing to gods who exacted obedience to moral laws.

In the methods prescribed for the removal of sin, of which the later *Saṁhitās* give full details, the material character of sin and its spiritual nature are constantly recognized in close union. The former aspect is prominent in the simple process of sin-transfer, which is one mode of removing guilt: the gods themselves set the example by transferring the guilt of the blood of the sacrifice to one man after another until it rested finally with the slayer of an embryo, the most guilty of sinners.[7] So a man seeks to transfer his own sins to others.[8] At the end of the *aśvamedha* the sins of the sacrificer are removed by an offering made on the head of a bald repulsive-looking man who stands in the water of the concluding bath; this man at the end of the whole rite is driven away into the forest, bearing with him the sins of the village out-castes.[9] Another version[10] attributes to the water of the bath, after the sacrificer has bathed in it, the power to drive away sin from those who have offended, although they themselves have taken no part in the sacrifice. Even more elaborate is the scheme of the *varuṇapraghāsas*,[11] one of the four-monthly sacrifices. The wife of the householder is enjoined to confess to the priest what lovers she has had, the declaration serving as a mode of expiation; cakes in platter form are baked, one for each member of the household, and offered in the fire, thus removing the sins of the members of the house, which are deemed to be transferred to the cakes; the ceremony is closed by a bath in which husband and wife wash each other, clearly as a species of purification, while the moral side is brought out in a prayer to Varuṇa for forgiveness for any sin committed by the sacrificer and his household, in public or in private. In the ritual of the *soma*-sacrifice there is a curious rite: the priest offers in the fire splinters of the post to which the animal victim has been tied, and with each he utters a formula asking remission

[1] Abrahams, § xix. [2] Cf. art. SACRIFICE (Jewish).
[3] As suggested by H. Oldenberg, *Die Religion des Veda*, Berlin, 1894, p. 195, n. 1.
[4] I. xxiii. 22.

[1] V. ii. 7. [2] I. xxiv. 9, VI. lxxiv. 3.
[3] *Atharvaveda*, V. xxx. 4, VI. cxvi. 3, X. iii. 8.
[4] *Ib.* VII. lxiv., XIV. ii. 59 f.; *Taittirīya Saṁhitā*, III. i. 4. 3.
[5] *Rigveda*, II. xxviii. 9, VI. li. 7.
[6] *Vājasaneyi Saṁhitā*, iii. 48, viii. 13; *Taittirīya Saṁhitā*, III. ii. 5. 7.
[7] *Maitrāyaṇī Saṁhitā*, IV. i. 9.
[8] *Rigveda*, X. xxxvi. 9.
[9] *Śāṅkhāyana Śrauta Sūtra*, XVI. xviii.; A. B. Keith, *JRAS*, 1908, p. 845 ff.
[10] *Kātyāyana Śrauta Sūtra*, XX. viii. 17 f.
[11] See A. Hillebrandt, *Rituallitteratur* (=*GIAP* iii. 2), Strassburg, 1897, p. 114 f.

of the sin which has emanated from the gods, from men, from the fathers, and from one's self.[1] But cases occur also in which an ordinary sacrifice is offered to remove sin, without recourse to magic, such as the expiation of a false oath by an offering to Agni Vaiśvānara prescribed in the *Taittirīya Saṁhitā*.[2]

This external view of sin, which clearly was the most prevalent in Vedic thought, explains the failure to rise to any distinction between neglect of ceremonial duties, natural defects, and real offences against the moral law. The only difference which is ever recognized in the texts of this period is in the relative gravity of crimes: in the *Yajurveda*[3] we find a list (varying in detail in the different *Saṁhitās*) which exhibits a scale of offenders ascending in heinousness, from the man who has allowed the sun to rise before he has performed a ritual duty, or to set before he has completed such a duty, through the man with black teeth or bad nails, the man who has married before his elder brother and the latter (ranked, however, as the more guilty), the slayer of a man, and the slayer of a Brāhman, to the slayer of an embryo. In accord with this the *Gṛhya* and *Dharmasūtras* reveal no trace of distinction between ceremonial and moral duties, though they differ for the better from the ritual of the Avesta by observing, as a rule, some degree of moderation in the penalties which they impose on sins of either kind. Naturally the tendency to invent remedies for every form of sin was developed by the priest, who found profit in these performances, and already in the Vedic period in such works as the *Sāmavidhāna Brāhmaṇa* appears a literature of *prāyaśchitta* rites intended to avert the evil consequences of error, moral, social, and ritual, by processes which in the main are those of magic, eked out with prayers and confession of fault.

It would be natural to expect to find in the *Upaniṣads*, which on the whole represent a decided reaction against the ritualism of the *Brāhmaṇas*, a careful examination of the real nature of sin and a distinction between ceremonial and morality. But the outlook of the *Upaniṣads* is almost wholly intellectual; the problem of conduct is not raised as the starting-point of discussion and inquiry, which is instead the question of the relation between the individual and the absolute, and the fundamental doctrine of the *Upaniṣads*, which merges the individual at death in the absolute, renders it difficult to find a place for considerations of moral action in the seeker of true knowledge with its resulting release from the bonds of transmigration. In contrast to knowledge, all action is of inferior worth, since it leads to rebirth. To the older view, which rewarded good deeds with heaven and punished evil with hell, there is now added the doctrine that all actions lead to their deserved fruits in the form of rebirth on earth, with or without an interval; but the moral value of this principle is greatly diminished, not merely by the fact that all action is ultimately regarded as evil, but also inasmuch as no criterion is proposed by which a man may discriminate between acts good and evil, the distinction being left to the ordinary views of men. Moreover, there does appear, though in an isolated passage,[4] the dangerous and immoral doctrine that the most evil deeds are annulled by the possession of true knowledge.

2. Post-Vedic.—In its attitude to sin Jainism is a faithful exponent of the prevailing view among the ascetics of the Brāhman community at the time when the system of Mahāvīra took definite shape. The ideal aimed at by the ascetic is to suppress all natural desire, and to Mahāvīra belongs the distinction of carrying the principle to its most complete extent. Such a doctrine, however, clearly precludes in theory the development of a sound ethical system, since it rests on the twofold basis of pure egoism and of a conception of the Ego which regards all its desires as evil and its true aim as the negation of all earthly interests. Thus Jainism has accumulated an extraordinary system of complicated restrictions, violation of any of which is a sin to be expiated; these restrictions so cover the field of human action that a layman bent on following the path of salvation must not practise agriculture or make a living by military service, a trade, crafts, teaching, singing, or music; and the avoidance of taking insect life is carried to an excess which is burdensome and irrational. But Jainism avoids the possibility inherent in the view of the *Upaniṣads* which allows knowledge to outweigh sin; its restrictions on conduct are an essential part of the system, and obedience to them is an integral element of the effort to attain enlightenment and freedom from transmigration.

In early Hinduism, as expressed in the *Mahābhārata* and the earlier *Dharmaśāstras*, such as those of Manu and Yājñavalkya, the principle is accepted that each deed brings its recompense, sometimes on earth, but more normally in a future birth; but no effort is made to set out a rationale for the distinction between meritorious and evil acts. Nor is the doctrine of *karma* without exception; there are traces of the old belief in sin-transfer: the evil king must bear responsibility for the sins of his subjects;[1] the priestly guest who meets with scant hospitality transfers to his host his evil *karma*.[2] More important is the doctrine of the effects of parental sin: it is expressly asserted that a deed may not bear fruit at once, but may defer its effect until it bears fruit in a son, grandson, or other descendant,[3] and a modification of this idea ascribes to the child a character derived from father or mother or both.[4] A wife too absorbs *karma* from her husband, and does not stand necessarily on her own merits—a doctrine expressly asserted in the *Rāmāyaṇa*[5] and implied in Manu.[6] Moreover, the epic mentions cases where the justice of the rule of retribution is assailed. Thus Kṛṣṇā asserts[7] that her misfortunes are due to the grace (*prasāda*) of the creator, who has thus recompensed an error against the gods committed by her in childhood, in a way clearly out of all proportion to the sin, while the sage Māṇḍavya[8] is so incensed by the action of Dharma, the personification of justice, in causing him to be impaled by the king as retribution for his ill-treatment of an insect in his childish days that he curses Dharma to be reborn as a Śūdra. In strict accord with this imperfectly ethical view of sin is the multitude of means by which it can be atoned for. All the sin of a king's conquest of the earth can be wiped out by sacrifices, if accompanied by large gifts to the priests such as cows and villages; and presents to a sacred bull expiate a king's breach of his oath.[9] Confession and penance avail to remove sins, even intentional crimes, but the same effect is accomplished even more simply by gifts to the priest and resort to places of pilgrimage.[10]

A further conception of the destruction of sin is

[1] W. Caland and V. Henry, *L'Agniṣṭoma*, Paris, 1905–07, ii. 388.
[2] II. ii. 6. 2.
[3] See B. Delbrück, *Die indogermanischen Verwandtschaftsnamen*, Leipzig, 1889, p. 200 ff.
[4] *Kauṣītaki Upaniṣad*, iii. 1.

[1] *Manu*, viii. 304, 308.
[2] *Ib.* iii. 100.
[3] *Mahābhārata*, XII. cxxxix. 22, I. lxxx. 2 f.
[4] *Ib.* XIII. xlviii. 42 f.
[5] II. xxvii. 4 f.
[6] v. 166, ix. 29.
[7] *Mahābhārata*, IV. xx. 7 ff.
[8] *Ib.* I. cvii. f.
[9] *Ib.* III. xxxiii. 78 f., xxxv. 34, ii. 57
[10] *Manu*, xi. 146, 228, 240 f.

developed in the *Bhagavad-Gītā* (*q.v.*), from which it passes over into the sectarian religions as a common property. The *Gītā* in effect enunciates the doctrine that the grace (*prasāda*) of the lord, coupled with the antecedent loving faith (*bhakti*) of the devotee, has power to cancel the results of actions committed in a previous birth. This doctrine attained favour through Rāmānuja (11th cent. A.D.), but he left the question of the exact relation between the devotion of the worshipper and the grace of god to become the basis of the distinction between the Tengalai sect and the Vaḍagalais. To the latter the process must begin with the act of the man who seeks liberation, while the former make grace proceed spontaneously from the god. The latter view is clearly the more common opinion of the sectarian cults generally, but, even when effort is demanded from the devotee, in no case is there an attempt to devise a moral code binding on the devotee as an essential preliminary to the exercise of grace, and the doctrine of grace in effect overthrows the whole rationale of the *karma* theory, without substituting for it any basis of a moral system.

The defect in the religious systems is not remedied by the philosophies, which in their intellectualism approach the doctrine of the *Kauṣītaki Upaniṣad*, that knowledge avails to counterbalance any and every crime. To Śaṅkara the recognition of the identity of the self with the absolute and the unreality of the whole empirical universe from the Īśvara downwards is essentially an action which cannot be explained by causal categories above which it stands, and all action alike, good or bad, is therefore in no essential relation to this knowledge. The empirical world remains, indeed, and Śaṅkara accepts it fully as real for conventional purposes, but the fact that its reality was conventional was doubtless sufficient to prevent him from seeking to examine the nature of moral judgments as actually formed by men. The other systems were equally indifferent to questions of conduct.[1]

The result of this negative attitude on the part of religion and philosophy alike can be clearly seen in the later Hinduism of the *Purāṇas* and the law digests which devote their energies to multiplying the number of sins, ceremonial, social, and moral, between which they make no distinction, but at the same time regard all these offences, of whatever degree, as capable of expiation by *prāyaśchittas*, of which doubtless the most important point was often the profit to be derived by the priest by whom the penance was enjoined and under whose direction it was carried out, or by the saving grace of a sectarian deity whose favour can be won by acts of pilgrimage or devotion of purely formal character—doctrines wholly incompatible with the development of any deep moral sense of the heinousness of wrong-doing in itself. Characteristic of this period is the glorification of all manner of sacred places, mere presence within whose limits is enough to remove all sin; there is practically no limit to the creation of *māhātmyas*, legendary accounts of the origin of the sanctity of these places and celebration of their powers, though few of them have attained such wide celebrity as the Ganges, which has sanctity above all other rivers. The mere reading of *Purāṇas* and hearing them read destroys sin—a doctrine which brings from Kabīr the indignant protest[2] that a man cannot be freed from the guilt of killing by hearing scores of *Purāṇas*. Equally efficacious, and less troublesome than pilgrimage, is the repetition of the names of the god, and *Ashṭottaraśatanāmans* and *Sahasranāmans*, claiming to be parts of *Purāṇas*, exist for all the greater and even some of the minor deities. Nor is it merely a man's own evil deeds that can thus be undone: prayer and offerings avail to rescue ancestors and descendants from the effects of their own actions. A true Vaiṣṇava, according to the doctrine of the *Brahmavaivarta-Purāṇa*,[1] who is thoroughly devoted to Kṛṣṇa, not merely acquires all knowledge and virtue, enjoys on earth superhuman powers, and goes to the world of Kṛṣṇa on death, but liberates from rebirth seven generations before and after himself. Any person who meets him on the road is cleansed by the mere fact from all the sins committed in seven previous existences, and to attain this position no course of religious exercises or devout penances is necessary; all that is requisite is the love of Hari or Kṛṣṇa and constant thought of him, subject, however, to the condition that the necessary initiatory *mantra* has been acquired from the teacher, whose profit is thus adequately secured.

LITERATURE. — See authorities under art. RIGHTEOUSNESS (Hindu), and V. Henry, *La Magie dans l'Inde antique*[2], Paris, 1909; E. W. Hopkins, artt. on 'Modifications of the Karma Doctrine,' in *JRAS*, 1906, p. 581 ff., 1907, p. 665 ff.; the views of the different schools of *bhakti* on the comparative value of works and faith are given by A. Govindāchārya, *JRAS*, 1910, p. 1103 ff.

A. BERRIEDALE KEITH.

[1] See A. B. Keith, *The Sāṅkhya System*, London, 1919, pp. 37 f., 99 f.
[2] *Sākhī*, ii. 209.

SIN (Iranian). — **I. Introductory.** — Speaking generally, it is chiefly in the matter of the respective teaching about sin (though also in some other momentous points of doctrine) that the Iranian stands in marked contrast to the Indian religious systems and approaches near to the general Christian idea. In the last we find certain well-defined elements as necessary constituents of the theory of sin. These are: (1) the idea of a Supreme Being, endowed with a will, which will requires certain acts to be performed on our part and other acts to be refrained from; (2) consequently, the idea of a moral law, which is the expression of this divine will, formulated and delivered to us as a complete system by which we, as creatures, are bound; (3) the idea of a creature having also a will, endowed with freedom of choice, *i.e.* having the power to choose between willing obedience to the moral law (or divine will) and its opposite.

Sin is nothing but a refusal, on the part of the free choice of the human will, to conform to the divine will. If one or other of these conditions is wanting, we cannot be said to have the Christian acceptation of the term 'sin.'

Here it must be noted that the moral law and the will of God are taken as identical terms. To express the idea in a familiar way, we may say that a thing is good because God wills it, and God wills it because it is good. In other words, God could not will a thing unless it were good in itself, and no thing could be good unless it were in accordance with the will of God.

It is evident that some of the Oriental systems recognize one or other of the elements of this conception of sin. But, on the other hand, we find that there are some in which the fundamental idea is a supreme law, though one that is impersonal—a blind force—yet eternal and unconscious, a kind of *fatum* or μοῖρα over-ruling the gods themselves, to which these divinities, even those in the highest rank, are subservient, and only agents. This law, influencing alike the physical and the moral order of things in the universe, evidently cannot be taken as the equivalent of the supreme and conscious will of a God who is the creator and governor of the worlds. Being unconscious, this law does not presuppose a personal will.

It will be readily understood that all such religious systems, in fact, are either entirely founded on a basis of pantheism or incline towards pantheism. It is precisely in pantheism that the

[1] See H. H. Wilson, *Works*, London, 1861–77, iii. 107 f.

'order' of things—physical and moral alike—the constant march of nature, or of the great All, to which belong and from which proceed the gods and lesser beings, perforce becomes a 'law,' a 'wheel,' an impersonal and unconscious 'way of life.'

Again, no system which fails to recognize the free choice of the human will as a necessary basis of morality can be said to possess such a conception of the idea of sin as Christians have. Such religions are nothing but systems of fatalism or systems with the tendency towards fatalism.

These remarks are true of all the Indian religions from the Vedic downwards. The striking exception is the very limited and early-forgotten system connected with the Vedic deity Varuṇa, essentially the deity of the moral law, whose *dhāman* (decree) and *vratāni* (wills or laws) are the foundations of the moral (as of the physical) law. Sin is the breaking of these laws;[1] 'we men daily do violence to thy will.'[2]

All this is singularly like the Iranian moral doctrine in both its more ancient and its more recent forms, and has been the main reason leading many scholars, from Darmesteter onwards, to equate, if not to identify, the Vedic Varuna with the Iranian Auramazda—Ahura Mazda.[3] But, whether the deities themselves be identified or not, it is clear that their ethical systems, especially as regards the doctrine of sin, are practically the same.[4]

Passing now to consider the Iranian system, we remark that the doctrine of sin in all its aspects plays a very large, we may say—at least with regard to the later epochs of its history—a preponderating, part in the Mazdayasnian or Mazdean religion and philosophy. We may consider this doctrine in three presentments: (1) in the Old Persian inscriptions of the Achæmenian kings, (2) in the sacred books of the Avesta—*Gāthās* and later Avesta, (3) in the Pahlavi exegetic and theological literatures.

2. The religion of the Achæmenian kings.—Extremely limited in extent and brief in expression as are the religious beliefs preserved in the rock-cut inscriptions of the great Darius and his successors (532–336 B.C., approximately), they yet clearly contain the notion of sin, *i.e.* of evil as a transgression of the will of the supreme deity, the creator Auramazda.

'Oh man!', says Darius, 'despise not the commands of Auramazda. Turn not away from the right path. Sin not.' The last sentence, *ma starava*,[5] contains the verb *star*, meaning 'to sin,' which occurs frequently also in the Avesta.

Of all the sins condemned by the morality of the Achæmenids the most serious is undoubtedly the lie (*drauga*). On this point the truths expressed in the inscriptions are in wonderful accordance with the notions on the subject given by Greek historians, and also with Iranian tradition itself.

E.g., Darius cries out: 'O thou who shalt be king after me, keep thou from lying! Should a man be found to be a liar, deal thou with him severely, if thou desirest to keep thy kingdom whole.'[6] All evils are attributed to lying. Darius tells us that during Cambyses' absence in Egypt 'the people became hostile and lying became widespread in the land.'[1] In another verse the same king, relating how a rebellion had taken place in many of the provinces of his vast empire, states that 'these provinces had broken into rebellion; it was lying that had made them rebellious.'[2] Therefore the king prays to Auramazda to guard his kingdom from lying, as it was one of the three chief scourges of a people: 'May A. protect this land from the hostile inroads, from bad harvests, and from lying.'[3]

Indeed the importance attached to this evil of the lie led J. H. Moulton to the belief that we may regard Drauga as a proper name and as representing the Angra Mainyu, or Evil Spirit, of the Avesta, whose absence from the royal inscriptions has been urged as one of the objections to the identification of the Achæmenian with the Zoroastrian faith.[4]

The other sins condemned by the kings are, on the one hand, rebellion of the subject against authority, on the other, despotism or cruelty on the part of the ruler.

Thus does Darius break forth with pride and say: 'A. has been my help . . for I have neither been a liar nor a tyrant.'[5]

3. The Avesta.—Whether the form of Mazdeism preserved in the Avesta was a religion exactly identical with that of the Achæmenian kings or a different one, it is certain that the worship of the god Ahura Mazda is its most essential feature, and that Zoroaster and his followers have as good a right as the Persian kings to boast of being 'Ahuramazdeans.' This Avestic religion—especially in its most ancient form, as preserved in the *Gāthās*—is essentially a religion founded on a basis of morality, in the sense which we apply to the term. In spite of the dualism which is its most notable characteristic, the Avestic system of morality differs but little from what we term the Christian conception. Evil, it is true, is conceived as produced, in the moral and physical order alike, by an independent principle, an evil creator, eternal, and independent of the good God, and termed Angra Mainyu. But the good law is that of Ahura Mazda, as revealed by him to man. The Avesta contains the whole of this code, in both its moral and its ritual aspect. Besides, there is a special and technical term continually used to describe moral good, holiness, purity, conformity to the good law (*vaṇuhi daēnā*): the term is *asha*, which, according to phonetical rules, is etymologically identical with the *ṛta* of the Vedas.[6] The opposite term *anasha* gives the adjective *anashavan*, as in the Vedic *anṛta*.

The Avesta treats the whole life of man, and the whole history of the world, as a 'spiritual combat.' Man is born endowed with free will, and at the start finds himself in the presence of two hostile armies, one of which is that of the good God, the other that of the Spirit of Evil. He must choose which of these he will serve, precisely as St. Ignatius Loyola pictures the Christian placed between the 'two camps,' or 'two standards,' of Christ and Satan. The whole life of man is a warfare, a perpetual struggle in the choice between good and evil. The Spirit of Evil may even tempt man, as he tempted the prophet Zarathushtra himself, by calling upon him to renounce the good Mazdayasnian law, and promising him a great reward, even the sovereignty of the world:[7]

'No,' the Prophet replies, 'I will not renounce the good law, not even if soul and body and life shall part.'[8]

Here we have clearly the picture of the free will

---

1 *Tava dharmā yuyōpima* (*Rigveda*, VII. lxxxix. 5).

2 *Ib.* I. xxv. 1.

3 Cf. J. Darmesteter, *Ormazd et Ahriman*, Paris, 1877; E. Hardy, *Die vedisch-brahmanische Periode der Religion des alten Indiens*, Münster, 1893; H. Oldenberg, *Die Religion des Veda*, Berlin, 1894; also R. Roth, *ZDMG* [1853] vi.

4 Cf. A. Barth, *The Religions of India*, Eng. tr., London, 1882, pp. 16–18. But W. Geiger writes: 'Ich wüsste auch nicht leicht ein Volk, das unter gleichen oder ähnlichen historischen Bedingungen zu einer solchen Höhe der ethischen Erkenntnis gelangte. In manchen Varuna-hymnen leuchten wohl auch derartige Ideen von Sündenschuld und Versöhnung des Gewissens mit der Gottheit auf; aber das sind doch nur vereinzelte Gedankenblitze, während wir es im Awesta mit einer festen und bestimmten Lehre zu thun haben, welche Gemeingut aller ist oder werden soll' (*Ostīrānische Kultur im Alterthum*, Erlangen, 1882, p. 334).

5 Formerly read *stakava*.

6 *Dar. Bh.* col. 4, § 37, 40.

---

1 *Dar. Bh.* col. 1, § 34.

2 *Ib.* col. 4, § 33, 34.

3 *Dar. Pers.* D., § 3.

4 See his *Early Zoroastrianism* (*HL*), London, 1913, and *The Treasure of the Magi*, do. 1917.

5 *Dar. Bh.* col. 4, § 63, 64.

6 The curiously exact analogy existing between *Khā ṛtasya*, 'source of justice' (cf. *Rigveda*, II. xxviii.), and *ashahe Khāō* of the Avesta (*Ys.* x. 4) has often been remarked.

7 *Vend.* xix. 23 (xix. 6 in *SBE* iv. [1895] 211).

8 *Ib.* 25, 26 (7 in *SBE* iv. 212).

making a choice between the divine law and sin. In fact, the whole of the Avesta bears witness to this doctrine.

The Vedic names for sin (*ēnas*, 23 times in the *Rigveda*, *āgas*, 18 times) in the Varuṇa cycle scarcely appear at all in the Avesta: *aenanh*,[1] *aghem* (only in derivatives, perhaps in *aghem vīmanōhim*, 'sin of unbelief').[2] But the more recent Iranian languages (see below) lead us to conjecture also the existence of a term **vināsa*. The verb *star*, 'to sin,' which occurs in the inscription of Darius quoted above, is frequent in the Avesta, whilst a substantive *stara*, 'sin,' seems to have existed.[3]

Throughout the Avesta we find specific sins enumerated with the punishment which they involve and (in the later Avesta) the temporal penances which can expiate them.

It must be noted that the moral law of the Avesta extends not only to external acts and words, but also to thoughts. This is very rarely the case in ethnical religions. It is also the reason why it is so frequently expressed in the sacred texts by the well-known formula: *humata, hukhta, huvarshta* ('good thought, good word, good deed'). Sin, on the other hand, is described by the three opposite terms: *duzhmata, duzhukhta, duzhvarshta* ('bad thought, bad word, bad deed').

Certain sins which are reckoned as of peculiar heinousness in the Avesta are said to render the one who commits them *peshōtanus*, or *peretōtanus*—a term variously explained as signifying 'whose body (*tanu*) is steeped in iniquity or has morally perished' (de Harlez), 'one who pays with his own body' (Darmesteter), or 'one whose body is forfeit, *i.e.* guilty of a sin for which there is no atonement' (Bartholomae, Moulton). The word reappears in Pahlavi in the inverted form *tanāpuhar*. What kind of sin is this, for which, be it noted, the *maximum* penalty is 200 stripes? In *Vendīdād*, xv. 1–8, we are told that there are five sins which, unconfessed and unatoned for, make one *peshōtanu*. It is a strange list indeed: teaching one of the faithful another religion; giving bones too hard or food too hot to a dog; striking, frightening, or kicking a bitch with young; having intercourse with a woman during menstruation; having intercourse with a pregnant woman. But, heinous as these sins are, they can be expiated; whilst the *anāperatha* sins are inexpiable:

'For such there is no punishment, no expiation, no purification; for these acts are inexpiable for ever, for eternity.'[4]

As such are reckoned both burning and burying dead bodies, eating of the carcass of a man or a dog, unnatural sin, self-pollution. Probably these sins, at least in the beginning, were punishable with immediate death here and eternal punishment hereafter. Otherwise it seems strange that capital punishment seems indicated for a very few sins, such as throwing a corpse into the water, carrying a corpse alone, illegally attempting to carry out a ritual purification. The guilt of other sins is reckoned in terms of the number of stripes by the *aspahē ashtra* (horse-goad) or *sraoshō-carana* ('obedience-maker') arranged in ascending scale from five for a simple *āgerepta* (act of violence) through graver assaults up to 200; breaches of contract (*mithrō druj*), up to 1000; violations of mortuary rites, up to 1000; sexual sins, 30 to 1000; ill-treatment and killing of animals, 50 to 1000; and, most astounding of all,[5] killing an otter, 10,000.[6] Whether these 'stripes' were ever inflicted or not, they had become little more than the degrees on the thermometer, indicating the comparative guilt of various sins.[1]

4. The Sasanian religion.—Instead of becoming weaker, as might have been expected, by the lapse of time, the moral system of post-Avestic Mazdeism developed further. The principal points are these:

(1) The basis of all morality is to be sought for in man's intellectual nature, and consequently in his free will. This is why children who have not yet come to the use of reason and adults bereft of reason are irresponsible. The age of reason varies from seven to eight years, inasmuch as before that time of life 'sin does not take root.'[2]

(2) All which is not according to the will of Ahura Mazda is sin.[3]

(3) Man is naturally created good, but Aharman (the Spirit of Evil) blinds him, hiding from his sight future retribution.

(4) It is owing to the fact of the soul being in the body during life that, not seeing future retribution, it commits sin; otherwise it would not commit it for any earthly consideration.[4]

(5) Aharman deceived the first human couple, *Māshya* and *Māshyōi*, and led them to commit sin by persuading them to eat the flesh of animals. So with every sinner. Thus the life of man is a spiritual conflict, an unceasing warfare.[5]

A system of moral theology and casuistic science grew up in the Sasanian schools. Here were compiled long lists of virtues including a code of duties for every state of life, as well as classified lists of sins.

For sin the generic term is *vanas*, from which is derived *vanaskar*, 'sinner,' words which have passed into the Armenian language, as *vnas*, *vnasakar*. In modern Persian and in Kurdish the word *vanas* appears, according to phonetic law, in the form *gunāh*, borrowed in the Arabic of the Qur'ān as *junāh*.[6]

The summary of the contents of the original *Nasks*, or parts of the Avesta now lost,[7] shows that some of the *Nasks* were veritable treatises of moral theology and of criminal jurisprudence, for in the Mazdean, as in other Oriental religions, no distinction is made between sin and misdemeanours of even purely civil or ceremonial nature. Hence endless chapters containing enumerations of such transgressions, their effects, and their appropriate chastisements, whether of a spiritual or of a civil nature. The enumerations of sins of all kinds are so constant and of such great length in the various Pahlavi writings that it would be tedious to repeat or even summarize them. A few examples must suffice.

One list of 30 sins is found in the *Maīnōg-ī Khrāṭ*, xxxvi., as follows:

(1) Sodomy, (2) pederasty, (3) murder of a just man, (4) the destruction of *khvētūk-das* (next-of-kin marriage), (5) unfaithfulness towards an adopted son, (6) destruction of the sacred fire, (7) destruction of the otter, (8) idolatry, (9) religious indifferentism, (10) violation of trust, (11) support of wickedness, (12) laziness, (13) heresy, (14) witchcraft, (15) apostasy, (16) demon-worship, (17) theft and abetting thieves, (18) violation of promises, (19) maliciousness, (20) oppression in order to obtain another's goods, (21) persecution of the righteous, (22) slander, (23) arrogance, (24) adultery, (25) ingratitude, (26) falsehood, (27) persecution of the helpless (or the dead?), (28) pleasure in distressing the good, (29) abetment of sin and hindering of good work, (30) regret at having done good to others.

A shorter and somewhat more intelligible list is that of *Dīnkarṭ*, III. cix. 3:

Avarice, fraud, ingratitude, discontent, disobedience, violence,

1 *Ys.* xxxi. 13. 2 *Vend.* i. 7.
3 See C. Bartholomae, *Altiran. Wörterbuch*, Strassburg, 1904, *s.v.*
4 *Vend.* iii. 39. 5 *Ib.* xiv.
6 This seems inexplicable—'de haute fantaisie,' says Darmesteter. The only explanation (surely an improbable one) we have seen suggested is that of V. Henry (*Le Parsisme*, p. 104) that perhaps the ancient Iranians tamed the otter and used it to catch fish! See also *Vend.* iv., xiii., xvi., xviii., etc.

1 See art. LAW (Iranian).
2 *Dīnkarṭ*, IV. clxx. 2; Casartelli, *Philosophie religieuse du Mazdéisme*, p. 137.
3 *Zāḍ-Sparam*, i. 13 (*SBE* v. 157).
4 *Dīnk.* IX. xvi. 3 (*SBE* xxxvii. 200).
5 Casartelli, p. 138 f. 6 *Ib.* pp. 141–150.
7 Contained in bks. VIII. and IX. of the *Dīnkarṭ*; tr. first by West in *SBE* xxxvii. and, more recently, published for the first time in the Pahlavi text with a new tr. by Dārāb Peshotan Sanjana, in vols. xv. [1916] and xvi. [1917] of the great ed. of the *Dīnkarṭ* (Bombay, London, etc., 1874–1917).

mercilessness, tyranny, heresy, spiritual blindness (*kīkīh*), spiritual deafness (*karafīh*), opposition to the law (*adātīh*), 'and other faults.'

The *Maīnōg-ī Khrāṭ*, lix., has an interesting division of predominant sins according to the four primitive 'castes' or classes of the population.

Thus the characteristic sins (1) of the *priests* are hypocrisy, negligence, idleness, attention to trifles, religious indifference; (2) of *warriors*, oppression, violence, unfaithfulness to promises, encouragement of evil, ostentation, arrogance, insolence; (3) of *agriculturists*, ignorance, envy, ill-will, malice; lastly (4) of *artisans*, unbelief, ingratitude, improper talk, moroseness, abusiveness.

Certain sins specially condemned are pride and contempt of others, adulteration of food-stuffs, unjust weights and measures, cruelty to animals, useless destruction of cattle. Intemperance and drunkenness are condemned, curiously enough, because excess in drink causes excess in eating, and the latter hinders the recitation of the *Gāthās*.[1]

Two mysterious sins or faults often mentioned in the last-quoted book and other treatises are *faraēbūt* and *aībībūt*. It is not clear what these are, though great importance is evidently attached to them. According to the *Dīnkarṭ*, the former is intellectual pride ('I know no one superior to myself'), the latter contempt of others ('This other person knows nothing, he is backward and infirm,'[2] which recalls the Pharisee of Lk 18[9-12]). Quite different explanations are given by other writers. Attempts are made at other classifications of sins; thus two classes are distinguished, one of sins which injure one's neighbour (entitled *hamēmālān*) and one of sins which injure only one's own soul (*rūbānīk*);[3] or, again, 'antecedent vices,' such as concupiscence and anger, and 'consequent vices,' such as idleness and murder—apparently what we may term internal and external sins.

5. Trend of Mazdean teaching.—Glancing over the whole mass of Mazdean teaching, Avestan and post-Avestan, concerning sin, we cannot fail to notice that, whilst that ethical system condemns practically all those forms of moral evil which we and, we may say, mankind generally hold to be deserving of reprobation, there are other acts which to us seem strangely out of place. Of course some of them are violations of religious or ritual precepts, to which the Avesta and the Mazdean priesthood attach great importance. Under this head we can easily understand why it is sinful to let the sun shine on the fire.[4] Other apparently grotesque or at least puerile condemnations of actions as sinful are those of walking with only one boot,[5] or barefooted,[6] or, still stranger, 'uno pede stando mingere'[7]—for which crimes Arṭā-ī Vīrāf, the 'Persian Dante,' saw a man suffering atrocious torment in hell,[8] as well as another tortured for eating whilst talking.[9] Of these it may be said that possibly they were originally condemned for hygienic reasons. But the most astounding condemnation as of one of 33 most heinous sins, second only to unnatural lust and murder, is that of 'breaking off a *khvētūk-das*,' *i.e.* a next-of-kin (to us incestuous) marriage.[10] This of course is only in strict accordance with the exaltation of that abominable practice, at least in post-Avestan times, to the rank of one of the most meritorious good works.[11]

(*a*) *Merit and responsibility.*—Exact ideas were held as to merit and demerit and the responsibility of the sinner. Good deeds done unconsciously or on the spur of the moment have little if any merit. The sacrifices offered in divine worship are always productive of merit (*kerfak*). Should the minister, by reason of want of attention, fail to receive any merit, the merit finds its way into a treasury of merits (*ganj*), placed in the hands of the spirits (*yazdān*), who have the power to bestow the contents on the souls of the just. The merit of good deeds, lost by sin, can be born anew in the soul after the confession, contrition, and good resolutions of the sinner. Parents are responsible for their conduct towards their children, husbands for their wives, superiors for those under them, in the event of their failing to instruct and correct them. A just man is also bound to instruct his fellow-man who is a sinner; otherwise he shares the latter's guilt and will incur great shame at the judgment;[1] similarly the husband who does not correct his wife.[2]

Proper fasting is fasting from sin, not from food[3]—a maxim in thorough agreement with Mazdean views on mortification and asceticism.

In cases of doubt as to sin the high-priest is to be consulted.[4] Elsewhere, when one is in doubt whether an act is a sin or not, the act must not be done.[5]

(*b*) *Effects of sin.* — Sin produces demons. 'Various new demons arise from the various new sins the creatures may commit,' and apparently these demons even introduce confusion into the heavenly bodies and here on earth.[6] All ruin and misery among mankind and animals come from man's sinfulness.[7] It would even appear that grievous sin could actually turn men into actual demons; a case in point was that of the wicked Afrāsyāb (the Avestan Franrasyan, the great Turanian foe of Īrān), who thus became a *dēv* and will not be saved at the end of creation.[8] Very wicked men, who have only the name of humanity and whose lives are all sinful, are called 'demi-*dēvs*.'[9]

(*c*) *Punishment in hell.*—After death the unrepentant sinner is punished in hell (Av. *daožahva*, from *duz-*, 'evil,' *ahu*, 'being,' 'life'; Pahl. *dūšahū*). Whether this hell was considered as eternal is doubtful; certainly many of the later schools contemplated its final destruction at the end of all things, and apparently the purification of those suffering in it. But in the earlier Avesta such epithets are used—especially *yavōi vīspāi*,[10] *utayūiti*—of both heaven and hell as seem to leave little doubt that the original idea was that of a real eternity of misery.[11]

In the post-Avestan literature it is the celebrated 'Inferno' of Artā-ī Vīrāf, with its minute and crude description of the gruesome sufferings of the damned in hell and its enumeration of the sins for which they are tortured, that supplies the most complete summary of late Mazdean teaching about sin and its chastisement.[12]

(*d*) *Contrition and confession.*—The means by which sin and its fatal consequences can be got rid of are contrition, purpose of amendment, and confession. True repentance (*patītīh*) is necessarily both internal and external. External duty, it is said, requires that the sin which the penitent knows that he has committed should be specifically confessed in words (*barā gūbishnō*); mental duty

[1] *Dīnk.* I. ix. [2] *Dīnk.* III. civ.
[3] *Shāyast lā-Shāyast*, viii. 1 (*SBE* v. 300).
[4] *Sad-dar*, 69 (*SBE* xxiv. 334).
[5] *Bund.* xxviii. 13 (*SBE* v. 107).
[6] *Shāy. lā-Shāy.* x. 12 (*SBE* v. 320); *Sad-dar*, 44 (*SBE* xxiv. 307).
[7] *Sad-dar*, 56 (*SBE* xxiv. 317); cf. *Vend.* xviii. 40 (*SBE* iv. 201), and Ammianus Marcellinus, xxiii. 6.
[8] *Arṭā-ī-Vīrāf Nāmak*, xxv. [9] *Ib.* xxiii.
[10] *Maīnōg-ī Khrāṭ*, xxxvi. 7 (*SBE* xxiv. 71).
[11] See art. MARRIAGE (Iranian), § 2.

[1] *Bund.* xxx. 11 (*SBE* v. 123).
[2] *Arṭā-ī-Vīrāf Nāmak*, lxviii.
[3] *Sad-dar*, 83 (*SBE* xxiv. 337). [4] *Ib.* 27 (*SBE* xxiv. 290).
[5] *Shāy. lā-Shāy.* x. 27 (*SBE* v. 328).
[6] *Bund.* xxviii. 43–45 (*SBE* v. 113 f.).
[7] *Dīnk.* VII. xvi. 2 (as quoted from Avesta *Nask* x.).
[8] *Ib.* III. cx. 13.
[9] *Maīnōg-ī Khrāṭ*, xlii. 12–16. [10] *Ys.* xlvi.
[11] See Moulton, *Early Zoroastrianism*, pp. 173–175.
[12] Cf. art. STATE OF THE DEAD (Iranian).

consists 'in his renouncing it': 'in future I will sin no more.'[1] There are two formulæ of confession, called *patēts*; one is the great *patēt*, the other the little *patēt*. Sins must be confessed in detail, according to the manner in which they have been committed, whether 'by thought, by word, or by deed' (*minishnīk, gūbishnīk, kūnishnīk*).[2]

LITERATURE.—The ideas connected with sin permeate so widely the whole Mazdean system, Avestan and post-Avestan, that it suffices to indicate all the translations of the scriptures and the commentaries upon them, and especially the *Pahlavi Texts* of E. W. West, in *SBE* v. [1880], xviii. [1882], xxiv. [1885], xxxvii. [1892], xlvii. [1897]. A useful brief summary of the chief points is V. Henry, *Le Parsisme*, Paris, 1905 (esp. ch. vi.); see also L. C. Casartelli, *La Philosophie religieuse du Mazdéisme sous les Sassanides*, Louvain, 1884, and Eng. tr. by Firoz Jamaspji, Bombay, 1889, as quoted in text, esp. chs. vi. and vii.

L. C. CASARTELLI.

SIN (Japanese). — **1. Definition.** — The old Japanese word expressing the idea of sin is *tsumi*. But *tsumi* is both less and more comprehensive than our word 'sin': on the one hand, the deeds which the most ancient Shintō enumerates as *tsumi* form only a short list, which does not cover the vast field of the actions which we regard as sins; on the other hand, the notion of *tsumi* includes three distinct categories, viz. *kegare*, 'uncleanness,' *ashiki waza*, 'ill deeds,' and *wazawai*, 'calamities.' The *ashiki waza* category corresponds in a certain degree to our idea of sin. But from the mere fact of the combination of those three things under the single word *tsumi* we see that the ancient Japanese drew no clear distinction between ritual impurities, moral faults, and certain calamities. Ritual impurity—*e.g.*, being dirty in body and clothing—was a want of respect for the gods; and calamities were regarded as signs of the displeasure of the gods for some offence, conscious or unconscious. Thus impurities and calamities became combined under the same title as actual sins, for the psychological reason that they were equally displeasing to the gods.

2. Different kinds of tsumi.—The chief sins of the oldest Shintō are enumerated in the following passage of the *Oho-harai no Kotoba* ('Words of the Great Purification'):

'As for the various sorts of offences which may be committed either inadvertently or deliberately by the heaven's increasing population, that shall come into being in the country, a number of offences are distinguished as heavenly offences: (viz.) breaking down the divisions of the rice-fields, filling up the irrigating channels, opening the flood-gates of sluices, sowing seed over again, planting wands, flaying alive and flaying backwards, evacuating excrements; these are distinguished as heavenly offences. As for earthly offences, there will be forthcoming a number of offences: (viz.) cutting the living skin, cutting the dead skin, white men, excrescences, the offence of (a son's) cohabitation with his own mother, the offence of (a father's) cohabitation with his own child, the offence of (a father's) cohabitation with his step-daughter, the offence of (a man's) cohabitation with his mother-in-law, the offence of cohabitation with animals, calamity through crawling worms, calamity through the gods on high, calamity through birds on high, killing the animals, the offence of performing witchcraft.'[3]

According to this text, the sins that might be committed by 'the heaven's increasing population' (*ame no masu hito-ra*, 'heavenly-surplus population,' a very old expression meaning the Japanese people, the origin of which appears in one of the most ancient myths of the *Kojiki*)[4] are divided into two large classes, viz. *ama tsu tsumi*, 'heavenly sins,' and *kuni tsu tsumi*, 'earthly sins.'

The seven *ama tsu tsumi* here enumerated are grouped under this generic title because they are the crimes which, in the mythology, were committed in heaven by the wicked god Susa-no-wo against the sun-goddess. This is easily seen from a simple comparison with the accounts in the *Kojiki* and the *Nihongi*, which, although differing in some minor details from each other and from the list in the Ritual of the Great Purification, are none the less essentially in agreement with this list. Breaking up the narrow embankments which separated the rice-fields and at the same time served as dams for keeping back the water, filling up the channels which conducted the water (indispensable to native cultivation), opening the ponds where it was most carefully preserved till the proper time—those were the most execrable crimes for a population of agriculturists; and that is why they put those crimes at the head of their list. No less hateful is the sowing, on a field already sown, of bad seed which will ruin the harvest.[1] The planting of wands (in the rice-fields) has already been explained.[2] As to the crime of flaying an animal alive, from the tail to the head, it is no doubt condemned not on account of its cruelty, but because of some magical reason which remains obscure, perhaps because of the evil use which might be made in sorcery of the skins thus obtained. However that may be, this crime, as well as that of evacuating excrements (*i.e.* in places not meant for the purpose) appears also in the number of wicked deeds committed by Susa-no-wo against his sister.

'He broke down the divisions of the rice-fields laid out by the Heaven-Shining-Great-August Deity, filled up the ditches, and moreover strewed excrements in the palace where she partook of the great food.' And again: 'As the Heaven-Shining-Great-August Deity sat in her awful weaving-hall seeing to the weaving of the august garments of the Deities, he broke a hole in the top of the weaving-hall, and through it let fall a heavenly piebald horse which he had flayed with a backward flaying.'[3]

The *kuni tsu tsumi*, according to the Japanese commentators, are those which have been committed since the time of Jimmu Tennō, the first legendary emperor; and it is almost certain that the difference between them and the *ama tsu tsumi* rests on a mythological basis. This explanation, if we interpret it historically, may be connected in a very real way with the diversity of races that appear successively at the origin of the Japanese people.[4] In any case we cannot agree with the simple explanation of W. G. Aston, who did away with the difficulty by attributing to the author of the Ritual a rhetorical device, viz. the breaking up of 'the long list of offences into two balanced sentences.'[5]

The list of sins in this second category comprises, first of all, 'cutting the living skin' (*iki-hada-tachi*), which includes murder and wounding; it should be noticed also that every effusion of blood meant pollution, even for the victim. The sin of 'cutting the dead skin' (*shini-hada-tachi*) is easily understood when it is remembered that, according to primitive ideas, it was particularly impure to touch a dead body, and much more so to cut it up. The next two offences concern two diseases which are repulsive and therefore displeasing to the gods: 'white men' (*shira hito*), *i.e.* doubtless men afflicted with white spots on their skin, like lepers, and also albinos; and 'excrescences' (*kokumi*, 'superfluous flesh,' 'proud flesh'), a disease which we cannot specify more definitely from the text—unless we accept the interpretation of a Japanese commentator, who combines the two crimes into one, *shira-hi toko-kumi*, 'cohabitation in broad daylight' (*shira*, 'white'; *hi*, 'day'; *toko*, 'bed'; *kumu*, 'to unite,' 'to interlace');

1 *Shāy. lā-Shāy.* viii. 8 (*SBE* v. 303).
2 Casartelli, *La Philosophie religieuse*, p. 161.
3 See Karl Florenz, 'Ancient Japanese Rituals,' in *TASJ* xxvii. pt. i. [1899]; cf. E. Satow, 'The Mythology and Religious Worship of the Ancient Japanese,' in *Westminster Review*, July 1878, p. 27 ff.; and M. Revon, *Anthologie de la littérature japonaise*[4], Paris, 1919, p. 25 ff.
4 See *Kojiki*, tr. B. H. Chamberlain[2], Tōkyō, 1906, p. 40; and cf. art. COSMOGONY AND COSMOLOGY (Japanese), vol. iv. p. 166b, and Revon, p. 41.

1 Cf. Mt 13[24ff.].
2 See art. MAGIC (Japanese), vol. viii. p. 298a.
3 *Kojiki*, p. 61 f.
4 See Revon, *Le Shinntoïsme*, Paris, 1907, p. 338 ff., esp. p. 353.
5 *Shinto, the Way of the Gods*, London, 1905, p. 300.

this view gains support when it is recalled that even the emperor could not have sexual intercourse except in the depth of night, before the first glimmer of dawn had appeared. The obscurity of the writing of those texts, in which the Chinese characters may be taken sometimes in their ideographic meaning and sometimes phonetically to represent Japanese words, prevents any elucidation of this point. There follow various kinds of incest and the sin of bestiality.[1] Then come several 'calamities,' viz. 'through crawling worms' (*hafu mushi*), *i.e.* the bite of serpents, millepeds, and other venomous creatures, all the more to be feared as the primitive hut had no floor; 'through the gods on high' (*taka-tsu-kami*), *i.e.* especially being struck by lightning; and 'through birds on high' (*taka-tsu-tori*), because, entering by the holes which every house had for the escape of the smoke from the fire, they could defile the food.[2] Next there is mentioned 'killing the animals' (*kemono tafushi*), *i.e.* not animals in general, as in Buddhism, but only the domestic animals of one's neighbour, perhaps by means of evil spells; and lastly comes witchcraft (*maji-mono seru tsumi*)[3]—a prohibition which becomes particularly clear when we think of the story in the *Kojiki* which shows that the casting of spells was known in the most ancient Japanese magic.[4]

Those are the essential sins according to the primitive Japanese conception. Obviously this list does not include all possible crimes; *e.g.*, in the case of heavenly sins, if the *Kojiki*[5] is not so complete as the Ritual, on the other hand we notice some additional sins of the same kind in the mythical accounts of the crimes of Susa-no-wo, as they are given in the *Nihongi*.[6] But the list in the Ritual is the one which authentically represents the real tradition, as is sufficiently proved by the fact that it corresponds exactly with the list of heavenly sins given in a third important book of mythology, the *Kogoshūi* (A.D. 807), a work compiled by Hironari, a Shintōist priest belonging to the old sacerdotal family of the Imibe. On the other hand, it is obvious also that Japanese morality did not condemn these few crimes only; the study of the oldest criminal law shows that its field was much wider;[7] and there is a sure proof that, besides the old religious offences, the social conscience prohibited numerous deeds not mentioned in the Ritual, viz. the fact that a single individual who at the same time had violated both the divine law and the human law was logically condemned both to a ritual expiation and to a civil punishment.[8] But, lastly, in this necessarily vague domain of morality it is the text of the Ritual explained above that gives us the most original and at the same time most correct idea of the notion of sin in pure Shintō.

3. Avoidance of sin.—*Tsumi* may be avoided by the means corresponding to the notion of *imi*, antagonistic to that of *tsumi*. This conception of *imi*, 'avoidance,' 'abstinence,' and the various religious practices connected with it, have already been explained.[9]

4. Deliverance from sin.—When once *tsumi* had been committed, deliverance from it could be obtained by the magical proceedings indicated in the Ritual of the Great Purification itself.[1] And, in fact, since the *tsumi* were regarded as infractions which must be expiated whether there was any evil intention or not (see the beginning of the text cited above), the Japanese thought that such sins must be cleansed, not by inward repentance, but by external rites, *i.e.* magical rites.

The notion of purely moral sin, as we conceive it, did not gain supremacy in Japan until Buddhism was introduced, which, along with the mystic doctrines of a superior religion, brought to the distant archipelago a new morality founded no longer on ancient magic, but on the discriminations of conscience, and thus revealed the true idea of sin, which consists not in actions but in intentions, which man avoids by virtue and atones for by repentance.

LITERATURE.—The references are given in the footnotes.

MICHEL REVON.

1 These correspond to Lv 18[7. 17. 15. 8. 23].
2 Cf. the 8th Ritual, art. MAGIC (Japanese), vol. viii. p. 297b.
3 *Ib.* p. 298a.
4 *Ib.* p. 300; and cf. Revon, 'L'Envoûtement dans le Japon primitif,' in *Bulletin de la Société d'Ethnographie de Paris*, Oct. 1913.
5 P. 61 f.; and cf. p. 286.
6 Tr. Aston, London, 1896, i. 40 ff., esp. p. 48 f.
7 See Revon, *Le Shinntoïsme*, p. 367 ff.
8 *Ib.* p. 368.
9 See art. ASCETICISM (Japanese); cf. also art. MAGIC (Japanese), vol. viii. pp. 297 (8th Ritual), 298b (14th Ritual), 299a (23rd Ritual), 299b (27th Ritual), and art. SACRIFICE (Japanese), vol. xi. p. 22a.

1 See art. MAGIC (Japanese), vol. viii. pp. 297b, 298a, (10th and 11th Rituals); cf. art. HUMAN SACRIFICE (Japanese and Korean), vol. vi. p. 857a, and, for a practical illustration of Great Purification, art. POSSESSION (Japanese), vol. x. p. 131b.

SIN (Muslim).—There are various words used in the Qur'ān to express the ideas of fault, crime, sin. The shades of meaning with which they are used seem to vary with the context. Thus, *sayyāt* means evils which may happen to a man.

'So God preserved him from the evils they had planned.'[2]

It expresses the evils which God's punishment brings.[3] It also expresses moral guilt.

'Whoso doeth evil and is encompassed with his iniquity, they shall be the companions of hell fire.'[4]

The word *dhanb* expresses all forms of unbelief and wrong actions proceeding from such unbelief. The commission of a *dhanb* constitutes one a *khāṭī*, or sinner.[5] The word *ithm* seems to imply a wrong attitude to others and so injustice.

'Avoid frequent suspicion, for some suspicions are a crime.'[6]

It denotes a wrong attitude towards God.

'He who united the gods with God hath devised a great wickedness.'[7]

The Qur'ānic idea of sin seems to be that it is pride and opposition to God. Thus Satan (Iblīs), who refused to obey the command to prostrate himself before Adam, is described as swelling with pride and becoming an unbeliever.[8]

The punishment of this rebellious pride is that those who possess it must remain in it.

'The unjustly proud ones of the earth, will I turn aside from my signs, for even if they see every sign they will not believe them.'[9]

This opposition to God may lead a man to be an atheist, a polytheist, or a simply careless irreligious person. Man does not inherit a sinful nature, but simply a weak one. Sin is not so much a disposition as a habit which men acquire because of their weakness. The willing desire of the natural heart to sin is referred to in what Joseph says of himself:

'Yet I hold not myself clear, for the heart is prone to evil, save those on whom the Lord hath mercy.'[10]

The Qur'ān marvels at the sin of man, his obstinate disobedience, and calls upon him to exercise faith and repentance, but it is deficient in its call for a broken and contrite heart.

'All through the Qur'ān, the message is that while repentance must be sincere, it is a very easy matter, while forgiveness is a question scarcely worth troubling about, so simple is its attainment. Muḥammad nowhere displays anguish of heart and contrition in the sight of a pure and holy God, and therefore does not demand that others should experience that of which he himself had no knowledge.'[11]

According to Muslim theologians, sins are of two kinds, little (*saghīra*) and great (*kabīra*). This distinction is based on the text:

'To those who avoid the great sins and scandals, but commit

2 xl. 48. 3 xxx. 35. 4 ii. 75.
5 xii. 29, 98. 6 xlix. 12. 7 iv. 51.
8 xxxviii. 74; see also vii. 73–74. 9 vii. 143.
10 xii. 53.
11 W. R. W. Gardner, *The Qur'ānic Doctrine of Sin*, p. 40.

only the lighter faults, verily the Lord will be diffuse of mercy.'[1]

Lesser sins, mere faults and imperfections such as are inherent in human nature, are all forgiven, if some good act is done.

'Observe prayer at early morning, at the close of day and at the approach of night: for the good deeds drive away the evil deeds.'[2]

Opinions vary as to the number of greater sins, but in all lists there occur: infidelity or the ascribing of partners to God, murder, theft, adultery, unnatural crimes, neglect of the Ramaḍān fast and of the Friday prayers, magic, gambling, drunkenness, perjury, usury, disobedience to parents, false witness, defrauding orphans, despair of God's mercy, continued commission of little sins, and cowardice on the field of battle before an infidel enemy. The last, however, is said not to be a sin if the enemy outnumber the Muslims by more than two to one. It is said, further, that the number of great sins has not been definitely laid down, so that men may exercise the greater caution.

If a learned man commits a little sin and thereby misleads those whom he should guide, it becomes great. If small sins are repeated inadvertently, they do not become great; but, if knowingly, they change into great sins. The greatest of all sins is the associating of another with God (*shirk*). Other sins may be pardoned, but not this. A Muslim, although he commits sins small and great, will not be left in hell for ever, provided he does not commit this sin, or declare lawful what God has forbidden.

Sins require no atonement; repentance immediately after the commission of the sin is enough.

'They who, after they have done a base deed or committed wrong against their own selves, remember God and implore forgiveness of their sins—and who will forgive sins but God only?—and persevere not in what they have willingly done amiss: as for these, pardon from their Lord shall be their recompense.'[3]

True repentance implies sorrow for sin, full purpose of amendment and restitution if wrong has been done to another. If, after repentance, a man again sins, the repentance is not lost, for sins repented of are no longer reckoned. Some deny the validity of repentance at death; others say that God accepts it even then. Infidels may be forgiven:

'Say to the infidels, if they desist [from their unbelief], what is now past shall be forgiven them; but, if they return to it, they have already before them the doom of the ancients.'[4]

With some theologians, when an infidel becomes a Muslim, the act of conversion is equal to repentance. Others say that repentance is a separate action and must be separately and definitely made. A believer who commits a mortal sin does not, in the opinion of the orthodox, become an infidel.[5]

An interesting question arises with regard to the sinlessness of prophets. The orthodox belief is that they are free from sin. The Ash'arites hold that even the power of sinning does not exist in them; the Hashāmiyyah, a sub-section of the Shī'ahs, in order to exalt the *imāms*, hold that prophets can sin: 'The prophets sin, but the Imāms are pure.'[6] The Mu'tazilites deny this, but admit that they possess some quality which keeps them from sin. All are unanimous that prophets do not commit the greater sins. As regards the lesser, some say that they may commit these before inspiration (*waḥy*) comes upon them; others that they may do so even after inspiration has come, but that such little sins in them are mere frailties and slight imperfections not really amounting to sin. To a Muslim this disposes of a difficulty in the Qur'ān

1 liii. 33. 2 xi. 116. 3 iii. 129. 4 viii. 39.
5 Ibn Khallikān, *Biographical Dictionary*, London, 1842–71, iii. 343.
6 Ash-Shahrastānī, in *Milal wa'n-Niḥal*, ed. W. Cureton, London, 1846, p. 142.

itself, for there the greater prophets are spoken of as sinning. Adam's fall is referred to thus:

'And we said, O Adam, dwell thou and thy wife in the garden, and eat ye plentifully therefrom wherever ye list, but to this tree come not nigh lest ye become of the transgressors; and Satan made them slip from it, and caused their banishment from the place in which they were.'[1]

But it is said that Adam did not really sin; he only committed a slight fault, which after all proved beneficial to mankind; for, had he remained in paradise, the world would not have been peopled, and the will of God, 'I have not created men and *jinn* except for worship,' would not have been fulfilled.[2] Further, Adam and Eve, on being convicted of sin, said:

'O our Lord, with ourselves have we dealt unjustly: if thou forgive us not and have not pity on us, we shall surely be of those who perish.'[3] Noah said: 'Unless thou forgive me and be merciful to me, I shall be one of the lost.'[4] Abraham said: 'When I am sick, He healeth me, and who will cause me to die and quicken me, and who, I hope, will forgive me my sins in the day of reckoning!'[5] Moses killed a man—an act described as a work of Satan. He repented and said: 'O my Lord, I have sinned to my own heart, forgive me.'[6]

The references to sins committed by Muhammad are numerous:

'Be thou steadfast and patient, for true is the promise of God; and seek pardon for thy sin.'[7]

Various explanations are given of this verse. Some say that it refers to remissness in the propagation of Islām; others to neglect in rendering thanks to God; but one popular explanation is that the Prophet was to seek pardon for sin merely as an act of worship and as an example of that confession of sin which was to be a portion of the worship rendered by his followers.[8] If this explanation is not enough, then it is said that the word for sin (*dhanb*) conveys the idea of a fault only, or what is technically called a little sin. The objection is that this word (*dhanb*) is used to describe the sin of ordinary people.[9] It is quite clear, in general, that the word used to describe the sin of Muhammad does not denote a mere trivial offence, but a great sin. Again, 'Ask pardon for thy sin and for believers both men and women'[10] is similarly explained. The Prophet was ordered by God to ask pardon for his sin, not because he really had committed any sin which needed pardon, but because, if he thus asked, then, in accordance with the principle that his actions form the *sunnah*, or rule of faith and practice, it would become the duty of all Muslims to confess their sins and seek pardon.[11] Another passage is:

'Verily, we have won for thee an undoubted victory, in order that God might forgive thee that which went before of thy fault and what followed after.'[12]

This reference to an earlier and to a later fault has led to many ingenious explanations, such as the fault before and after the descent of inspiration (*waḥy*); before and after the taking of Mecca; before and after the revelation of this verse. But all these still leave the fault with Muhammad; so a further explanation is given. The 'former sin' refers to the sin of Adam when Muhammad was yet in the loins of his great ancestor and the 'later sin' refers to the sin of the followers of Muhammad. Both are connected with the Prophet, as Adam was forgiven by the blessing of Muhammad and Muslims will be pardoned through his intercession. The traditions also record the fact that Muhammad prayed for the pardon of his sins. On the authority of 'Ā'isha it is said that Muhammad used often to say: 'By thy praise O God, pardon me'; 'O God,

1 ii. 33 f. 2 E. Sell, *Faith of Islām*[2], p. 245.
3 vii. 22. 4 xi. 49. 5 xxvi. 82.
6 xxviii. 15; see also Ṣaḥīḥ al-Bukhārī, Leyden, 1862, iii. 194.
7 *Qur'ān*, xl. 57.
8 See also Baiḍāwī, ed. H. O. Fleischer, Leipzig, 1848, ii. 214.
9 *Qur'ān*, ix. 103, xxviii. 78, xii. 29.
10 xlvii. 21.
11 Tafsīr-i-Ḥusaini, quoted in Sell[2], p. 246.
12 xlviii. 1 f.

I ask pardon of thee for my offence, and I ask of thee thy mercy.' On the authority of Abū Huraira it is recorded that Muhammad said: 'I ask pardon of God and repent (return) towards Him more than seventy times a day.'[1] It is said that Muhammad felt such remorse when he had committed slight faults that he called them sins when they were not really such. The reply to this is obvious. From a Muhammadan standpoint, the Qur'ān is the word of God and not of man; so it is God and not Muhammad who speaks of the Prophet's sin. Whilst, however, the Qur'ān lends no countenance to the idea that prophets cannot sin and indeed refers to their sins, there is no mention whatever of sin in connexion with Jesus Christ. He is the one sinless prophet of Islām.

The Muhammadan view of sin looks upon it as the neglect of the arbitrary decrees of an absolute Ruler rather than as an offence against an immutable moral law of right or wrong. This is the real defence for many of the actions of the Prophet. In other men they would have been sin, but they are not to be considered so in him, as God commanded him to perform them. This also accounts for the absence of any moral gradation of the great sins. Adultery is a great sin, but so is flight from a field of battle; murder is a great sin, but so is the neglect of a fast. All this shows how the Muhammadan conception of God as a despotic ruler, who lays down laws for no apparent reason but that He wills so to do, has led to a false notion about the real nature of sin. *E.g.*, associating others with God in worship is the first and greatest of the great sins, yet the angels were ordered to worship Adam. Iblīs (Satan) refused and was, in consequence, driven out of paradise.[2] The sin here did not consist in the breach of the eternal law that worship belongs to God alone, but in disobedience to a command, arbitrary in its nature and contrary to the great law of man's relation to God. Again, sin is looked upon as a weakness of human nature. The sinner is not much to blame, and God is merciful. The spirit of fatalism also deadens the conscience and makes a man accept even his failings as decreed for him. The sensual descriptions of paradise, looked upon by a few purer-minded Muslims only as allegorical, deaden the moral sense. It is difficult for the man inclined to give way to his passions to see that what is right in heaven is wrong on earth. Sin, also, is too often regarded as an external pollution which the performance of certain good actions and attention to the prescribed religious ritual can cleanse. The giving of alms is said to 'do away sins.'[3] The ceremonial ablution before the stated prayers is such a meritorious ceremony that the Prophet said: 'When the Muslim performs his ablutions, all his sins will be forgiven him.' The *hajj*, or pilgrimage to Mecca, 'cleanses the hearts of men and makes them innocent like new-born babes.'[4] There are numerous traditions[5] on the subject of sin, the result of belief in which has been to lessen the idea of its evil nature and to make the means for its removal very mechanical. Doubtless there are Muslims who have a deeper sense of sin and who believe in repentance and amendment of life, men who place little faith in all the puerile stories handed down by tradition; but the tendency of the whole system of belief and practice, of the dogmatic statements and of the alleged usage of the Prophet, is to make the Muslim attitude to sin mechanical, with outward formalism as the general rule and inward spiritual experience the rare exception.

LITERATURE.—W. R. W. Gardner, *The Qur'ānic Doctrine of Sin*, London and Madras, 1914; T. P. Hughes, *DI*, London, 1895; E. Sell, *The Faith of Islām*², do. 1907; D. B. Macdonald, *Muslim Theology*, do. 1903, Appendix 1, *The Religious Life and Attitude in Islām*, Chicago, 1909, lect. x.

EDWARD SELL.

[1] *Miskātu'l-Masābīh*, ed. Bombay, 1878; for many other similar traditions see W. St. Clair Tisdall, *The Path of Life*, London and Madras, 1912.

[2] viii. 10.

[3] ii. 273.

[4] Maulavi Rafī'ad-dīn Aḥmad, in *Nineteenth Century*, xlii. [1897] 522.

[5] *Meshkāt*, bk. i. ch. ii., quoted in *DI*, p. 595.

SIN (Roman).

SIN (Roman).—Sin, in the Christian world, implies a personal and moral relation between man and the divine power which was never realized in anything like the same degree in ancient Roman life. The sinner is to moderns not only a breaker of superhuman law, but a contemner of the majesty of a divine person. The sense of being at enmity with superhuman forces was of course conspicuous in primitive Roman religion, as in primitive religions of all ages and all lands. The condition of hostility is declared by the god against the human being for some offence which may have been given by him quite unwittingly; but the punishment which he suffers is not the less believed to be merited. Although the tragic conception of the Greek ἄτη is foreign to native Italic and Roman beliefs, yet they included the persuasion that divine vengeance often falls on a human being for some merely mechanical error apart from blameworthiness of a moral character. In the Roman *ius diuinum* of early days, as in the secular law, a casual slip in ceremonial action or utterance might entail dire consequences, comparable to those assigned to arrogant defiance or neglect of the deity. The rigidity of the religious formula was parallel to that of the legal formula, and the maxim of the Twelve Tables, 'uti lingua nuncupassit, ita ius esto,' applied in both spheres. In the field of early ancient civilization deities were realized as essentially civic, and as concerned only with the members of particular communities. It was natural therefore that offences against them should be on the same level with the offences against secular law. Each man was related to the divinities of his city rather as a citizen than as a mere person. When deities came to be conceived as non-local, the idea of offences against them grew to be larger and more refined. The old civic cults were felt by the most cultivated spirits to be crampingly formal and narrow, and men turned away from them, finding satisfaction for their needs in those more emotional and spontaneous forms of worship which spread from East to West and to a large extent supplanted immemorial civic usage. In Italy the new influences were first felt among the Greek settlements, but they had so far affected the Italic peoples that in 186 B.C. the Roman senate, as the supreme religious authority in Italy, felt constrained to suppress those 'Bacchic' brotherhoods which were regarded as constituting a 'conspiracy' against society and the State. The decrees then issued are contained in the famous extant inscription.[1]

It may be said, however, that to certain offences of special enormity the notion of sinfulness did attach in very early days among Romans, as among Greeks. An offender guilty of a crime to which the vague but awful penalty 'Sacer esto' was assigned was outlawed and might lawfully be slain, as odious to the gods, by any man's hand.[2]

The consciousness of personal defilement, as caused by the perpetration of acts forbidden by the deities, was stimulated in Italy by the Græco-Oriental worships, which became ever more popular. A feeling spread that for the welfare of the soul it was needful to seek reconciliation with heaven and deliverance from the bondage of error, by

[1] *CIL* i. 196.

[2] See art. ROMAN RELIGION.

special services and practices which would ensure divine pardon and relief from the stains contracted by the soul. The mysteries, as a special means of escape, never held the same importance in Roman culture as they acquired for the Greeks.[1] In the West the conception of sin was vivified in a high degree by the prevalence in late antiquity of the Stoic philosophy, which drew much of its spiritual effectiveness from the mystical religions of the East, transmitted through a Greek atmosphere. The ethical aspects of philosophy became dominant over the speculative teaching in the Stoic as in all the late schools of Hellas. The idea of sin was especially developed by the Stoics (*q.v.*), whose ethical doctrines took a strong hold of the later culture of Rome as of Greece. These philosophers, paying little heed to many insuperable antinomies, contrived to combine a pantheism which was technically materialistic with the conception of a personal relation to a Supreme Being, and to tinge with emotion an intellectualism which in some of its aspects remained as dry and barren as it could well be. The Stoic law of life for the individual was summed up in unswerving loyalty to a divine order of the universe, and in the composure of the will to perfect harmony with the will of God. A healthy state of the will, according to the Stoics, ensures happiness, while a recalcitrance against the divine purposes, as expressed in the ordered universe, brings misery. The Stoics brought into general use the terms for 'sin' which established themselves in the Greek world, viz. *ἁμαρτία* and *ἁμάρτημα*, and these were rendered in Latin by *peccatio* and *peccatum*, which passed into the language of Latin Christian theology. The whole duty of man was declared by the Stoics to lie in self-discipline, to the end that the will might be brought into complete accord with the will of God. A religious fervour was thus infused into the pursuit of virtue, which was a new influence in culture, and the sway of Stoic religious and moral teaching over the civilization of the Roman Empire, with its action on early Christian thought, was incalculably powerful. This was achieved in the paradoxical manner of the Stoics, in spite of their theoretic doctrine that sin has its origin in erroneous intellectual judgment. The whole field of education in imperial Roman times was permeated by a Stoic colouring, which entered deeply into early Christian literature and into all the later developments of philosophy, in which the corruption of the human soul and the need for a divine deliverance were accepted as axiomatic. This great practical achievement of Stoicism in the Roman world was accomplished in spite of some doctrines which might have been expected to work against general acceptance. Opponents of the school ridiculed their admission that the appearance in the world of the perfect man had been rarer than that of the phœnix. Again, the Stoic thesis that 'all sins are equal' (*i.e.* are of the same heinousness) was difficult to accommodate to ordinary life, and indeed it was more or less ignored in Stoic literature, as may be seen in the writings of Seneca (*q.v.*). The attractiveness of man's proper aim, in the Stoic view, was great enough to overcome the weight of the paradoxes which encumbered it. Many utterances are to be found in the later classical literature, above all in the Stoic, relating to the subject of sin, which have an almost Christian ring. The idea of 'salvation' from sin is often found in connexion with the different divinities who were customarily designated as 'saviours' (*σωτῆρες*). The notion of a 'new birth,' so eminently Christian, is encountered in connexion with the ceremony of the *taurobolium* (*q.v.*), whereby, as one inscription records, a man was 'reborn for everlasting life' ('renatus in aeternum').

[1] See artt. MYSTERIES (Greek, Phrygian, etc.), MYSTERIES (Roman).

LITERATURE.—Information on this subject is widely scattered in works bearing on ancient philosophy and religion. Specially may be mentioned E. Zeller, *Die Philosophie der Griechen*, iii., 'Nacharistotelische Philosophie [4],' Leipzig, 1903–09, and E. V. Arnold, *Roman Stoicism*, Cambridge, 1911, ch. xiv. 'Sin and Weakness.'

J. S. REID.

SIN (Teutonic).—In the old Teutonic languages, especially in the Gothic, there is no clear concept of sin as a conscious nonconformity to, or transgression of, an ideal standard of right or duty as revealed in conscience or divine law.[1] The word *syn* entered the North from western Germany. It was a derivative from *sun*, a root of several compounds with the implicated idea of a denial or an apology. Its meaning when used in cognate languages was rather uncertain. In the Salic Law[2] it was used in establishing a plea of 'Not guilty' before the court, while later it came to stand as a technical and abstract expression for the matter of the accusation itself, as we notice in *Heliand*, the Old Saxon epic of the Saviour from about 825. In the Northern languages this usage also became established by way of accommodation as Christianity was introduced. The word generally used for sin in Ulfilas' translation of the New Testament, from about 350, was *fra-vaurhts*, 'misdeed'—an idea which was readily comprehended by the Gothic peoples among which he worked as a missionary.

Thus, while it must be granted that it is difficult exactly to make out the early Teutonic idea of sin in a manner which would meet the philosophical and religious requirements of our times, and even if we allow that Teutonic literature reveals character rather than principles of conduct, this does not mean that the Teutons were callous to moral requirements. Their convictions about right and wrong were very decided, at least on certain points. With them blasphemy, *e.g.*, was a great sin, as were also perjury and adultery. There is therefore evidently a moral value placed upon man's conduct as noticed in the *Völuspa* and other Eddic songs, in the *Gylfaginning*, and in the Northern and Icelandic sagas. In the *Nibelungenlied*, the great German epic from the Middle Ages, there are few traces of strictly moral sentiments, for, while this *Lied* in its subject-matter has much in common with the *Eddas*, it brings out less of the humane character and more of the valiant and heroic.

With the earlier Teuton, as known to Tacitus, the case was different. When treating of crimes and courts he says:

> 'The nature of the crime determines the punishment. Traitors and deserters they hang on trees. Cowards and those given to debauchery they smother in filthy bogs and fens, casting a hurdle over them. In these different punishments the point and spirit of the law is, that crimes which affect the political organization may be exposed to public notoriety, while the infamous vice and the debauchee cannot too soon be removed from the light of day.'[3]

The classification which is here brought out could be arrived at only from a moral point of view. That cowards were counted infamous is evident to every student of Teutonic life and literature. Cowardice was the sin of all sins, for which there was no pardon.[4]

The eschatological views which are abundant in the later songs of the *Edda*, in the *Gylfaginning*, and in the sagas agree entirely with the grouping of sins and punishments as obtaining in this life. In Saxo's *Danish History* the place where the condemned are kept and tortured is described in the most repulsive terms, while the

[1] Moritz Heyne, *Deutsches Wörterbuch*, iii. 916.
[2] J. F. Behrend, *Lex Salica*[2].
[3] *Germ.* xii. [4] *Ib.* vi.

inmates are depicted accordingly.[1] In the *Gylfaginning* we have it set forth that the consequences of all misdeeds and crimes will follow the sinner after death, and that he will have to meet with due punishment in Nastrand, one of the dismal halls below Niflheim, where Hel rules.[2] Those who arrive at their dreadful destination are sinners of various descriptions and classes, of which nine or ten are enumerated in the *Song of the Sun*—if this poem, standing almost on the border-line between heathendom and Christianity, may be taken as a witness. From it as well as from many other records, some of undisputed heathen character, we learn that enemies of the gods, desecrators, the unmerciful, perjurers, murderers, adulterers, the covetous, the proud and the arrogant, violators of laws, and breakers of covenants are doomed to Niflhel for ever, or at least for a very long time.[3]

In the *Völuspa*[4] Nastrand and its woeful prisoners are described as follows:

'She saw a hall standing,
far from the sun,
in Nastrand;
its doors are northward turned,
venom-drops fall in
through its apertures:
entwined is that hall
with serpents' backs.
She there saw wading
the sluggish streams
bloodthirsty men
and perjurers,
and him who the ear beguiles
of another's wife.
There Nidhögg sucks
the corpses of the dead;
the wolf tears men.
Understand ye yet, or what?'

From all this it seems perfectly clear that the concept of a coming retribution in another world was fostered and entertained by the Teutons and especially by those of the north. It also goes without saying that man's moral responsibility had to be reckoned with, even though the very idea of sin was not altogether like ours. It referred less to the religious life itself—something of which we know very little in regard to the Teuton—and more to the external behaviour. The reaction upon the sinner himself from the evil deed in the first place made him an outcast from his own people and an object of punishment, while in the second the doom will follow him after death and into the dismal regions of Hel, where he will be chastised according to his deserts. Sin as a condemnation will cleave to him for ever. In the light of this, those two well-known strophes from *Hávamál*[5] may be easier of interpretation as presenting the Teutonic summing-up of the value of man's deeds and the result of his entire life:

'Cattle die, kindred die, we ourselves also die;
but the fair name never dies of him who has earned it.

Cattle die, kindred die, we ourselves also die;
but I know one thing that never dies,—
judgment on each one dead.'

LITERATURE.—**Moritz Heyne**, *Deutsches Wörterbuch*, iii., Leipzig, 1895; *Lex Salica*, ed. J. F. Behrend², Weimar, 1897; **Tacitus**, *Germanica*; **Saxo Grammaticus**, *Danish History*, books i.-ix., tr. O. Elton, London, 1894; *The Elder Edda*, tr. Benjamin Thorpe, do. 1866; **R. B. Anderson**, *The Younger Edda*, Chicago, 1880; **A. Olrik**, *Nordisches Geistesleben*, Heidelberg, 1908; **R. Hildebrand**, *Recht und Sitte auf den primitiveren wirtschaftl. Kulturstufen*², Jena, 1908; **J. A. Enander**, *Vara Förfäders Sinnelag*, Stockholm, 1894; **C. Rosenberg**, *Nordboernes Aandsliv fra Oldtiden till vore Dage*, Copenhagen, 1877-78; **V. Grönbeck**, *Hellighed og Helligdom*, Copenhagen, 1912; see also literature to artt. SACRIFICE (Teutonic) and SALVATION (Teutonic).

S. G. YOUNGERT.

SIN (Original).—See ORIGINAL SIN.

[1] Saxo Gram., Eng. tr. ed. Rasmus B. Anderson, New York, 1905, ii. 517 f.
[2] *Younger Edda*, ch. 34.
[3] *Song of the Sun*, st. 53–68; *Sig. Fafn.* ii. 4.
[4] *Völuspa*, st. 42 f.
[5] St. 76 f.

SIND, SINDH

SIND, SINDH.—The province of Sind forms the extreme north-west portion of the Bombay Presidency, consisting of the lower valley and delta of the Indus, with an area of 46,968 sq. m. and a population of 3,513,435.

1. Name.—It takes its name from Skr. *sindhu*, probably connected with the root *syand*, 'to flow,' 'the ocean,' afterwards specially applied to the river Indus.

'Sindhu in the Rigveda and the Atharvaveda often means "a stream" merely, but it has also the more exact sense of "the stream" *par excellence*, the Indus. The name is, however, rarely mentioned after the period of the Saṃhitas, always then occurring in such a way as to suggest distance.'[1]

2. History.—Sind formed an early Aryan settlement and a seat of trade with E. Africa and the Persian Gulf (*c.* 1000 B.C.), was conquered by Darius Hystaspes (521–485 B.C.), by Alexander the Great (326 B.C.), formed part of the Mauryan empire, and was occupied by the Ephthalites or White Huns in the 7th cent. A.D. It was the first part of India occupied by the Muhammadans under the leadership of Muḥammad ibn Qāsim (A.D. 712). Maḥmūd of Ghaznī occupied the valley (1024–26). After this it became the seat of a Hindu dynasty, that of the Sūmras (1053), who were overthrown by Alāu-d-dīn Khiljī about the end of the 13th century. They were followed by another Hindu dynasty, the Sammās. Finally (1592), the Mughal Akbar united the province to the empire at Delhi. Towards the end of the 17th cent. the Kalhorās rose to power in the lower Indus valley, and ruled it till the invasion of Nādir Shāh (1739). Subsequently it was held by local princes, the Tālpur Mīrs, who were defeated by Sir C. Napier at the battle of Miānī in 1843, when the whole valley, with the exception of the Khairpur State, was annexed to the British dominions.[2]

3. Ethnology.—The province is distinguished from other parts of India by the great predominance of Muhammadans, who, at the census of 1911, amounted to 75·14 per cent of the total population, Hindus being 23·83 per cent, and the balance being made up of animists, Christians, Parsis, Jews, and the so-called Hindu-Muhammadans, who follow both creeds.[3] The Sindīs may be regarded as descendants of the original Hindu population, who were converted to Islām during the reign of the Umayyad *khalīfahs*. When the province was invaded by Muḥammad ibn Qāsim, there was a large and flourishing Hindu kingdom, provided with an efficient army.[4] The foreign elements are represented by Sayyids, Afghāns, Baloch, Jāt, Meman, Khwāja, and African slaves.[5] The Hindus occupy a position analogous to that of the Musalmāns in the rest of the Presidency, being in a minority and greatly influenced by the former predominance of Musalmān ideas and culture. The Brāhmans, consisting of Pokharnās (or Pushkarnās) from Rājputānā and Sāraswats from the Panjāb, are illiterate and depraved. There are no Kṣatriyās, those claiming that position being generally Banyās who have partly conformed to Sikhism, and are really heterodox.[6] The most important Hindu caste is that of the Lohānās, of whom the 'Āmil section are clerks and writers, early immigrants from the Panjāb, as is shown by their language and its alphabet. They wear the Brāhmanical cord (*janeo*), worship the god of the Indus, Viṣṇu, or Śiva, or follow the faith of Nānak Shah (*q.v.*). The other important Banyā caste is that of the Bhātiās, who are strong in Gujarāt and Cutch.[7] There are few castes of the Śūdra group, those that exist wearing the Brāhmanical cord, applying the Hindu sectarial marks to their foreheads, and in all other respects imitating Banyās. They generally worship Śiva and his consort Devī, and employ Brāhman priests. The Sikhs include the Akālī Khālsā, or pure Sikhs, and the Lohānās. The former imitate the Panjāb devotees—never cut their hair, eat various forbidden meats, such as the domestic fowl, have the usual tabu against tobacco, anoint their hair with butter instead of

[1] A. A. Macdonell and A. B. Keith, *Vedic Index*, London, 1912, ii. 450.
[2] See Aitken, *Gazetteer*, p. 85 ff.; *IGI* xxii. 394 ff.
[3] *Census of India, 1911*, vii., *Bombay*, p. 58.
[4] Hughes, *Gazetteer*, p. 86.
[5] Burton, *Sindh*, p. 233 ff.
[6] *Ib.* p. 313.
[7] *BG* ix. pt. i. [1901] 116 ff.

oil, and eat flesh only when the animal has been killed according to the ritual (*jhaṭkā*).[1] The local Hinduism is thus of an impure type, only a few Brāhmans studying Sanskrit, while the popular faith is mixed up with Islām and Sikhism.[2]

4. The fusion of Islām with Hinduism.—We find Islām and Hinduism amalgamated here in a more remarkable way, perhaps, than in any other part of India. The Hindu will often become the disciple (*murīd*) of a Muslim, and *vice versa*; not only are the same saints respected by members of both religions, but each faith uses a different name for the same holy man. The Hindus know the river-god under the name of Jind Pīr (*zindah*, 'the living one'), while Muhammadans call him Khwājah Khiḍr; in the same way Uddhero Lāl of the Hindus becomes the Musalmān Shaikh Tahir and Lālā Jasrāj becomes Pīr Mangho. The Hindus, probably with justice, claim these worthies as their own, and the Musalmāns have only applied new names to them.

5. Worship of saints.—The distinguishing feature of Islām in Sind is the wide-spread worship of saints (*pīr*, *walī*).[3] This is largely due to the influence of Ṣūfism (*q.v.*), and is opposed to the original form of the faith. But, though they may have lost touch with orthodoxy, the Musalmāns are a religious people.

'The mass of the Sind peasantry, though they may be unacquainted with the cardinal articles of their faith, are careless or ignorant of its precepts; but, upon the whole, they strike a stranger as being more religious according to their lights than Musalmāns of almost any other part of India. They are also pre-eminent for abject devotion to Pīrs and Sayads, living or dead.'[4]

The most eminent of these saints are Lāl Shāhbāz and Pīr Mangho, or Mango.

Lāl Shāhbāz, the head of the Jalālī order, whose original name was 'Usmān-i-Merwandī, from his birthplace, was a qalandar and a rigid celibate who died at Sehwān in 1274. He was called Shāhbāz, 'the red falcon,' because, as in the legend of Abraham,[5] his colour was changed to red by his penance of sitting in an iron pot over a broiling fire for a year.[6] His tomb is much respected, and every year a girl of the Khonbatī, or weaver, caste is married to his tomb, with music, dancing, and other solemnities. She is never allowed to contract a real marriage. The rite of initiation into the order is made as humiliating as possible, in order to prepare the religious mendicant (*faqīr*) for the life which he is about to adopt. All hair on his person is removed; the tomb attendants blacken his face, hang a cord round his neck, show him a looking-glass, and ask him how he likes his appearance. He replies, 'Very much.' Then his shoulder is seared with a hot iron, his body is stripped and smeared with cowdung, and he is told to go forth into the world and beg his bread.[7]

The cult of Pīr Mango at Magar Talāo, or the Crocodile Tank, near Karāchī, is more remarkable. In the tank a number of tame crocodiles (*Crocodilus palustris*) are kept, and goat's flesh is given to them by pilgrims. Here, about the middle of the 13th cent., a Musalmān hermit caused a stream to trickle out of the rock, and Lāl Shāhbāz in like manner produced a mineral spring. Pilgrims visit the tomb of Pīr Mango, and Hindus venerate the place out of reverence for the warm water.[8]

6. Worship of the river Indus.—The cult of Khwājah Khiḍr, or Khiẓr,[9] is common in Sind, where the saint is regarded as the *numen* of the Indus. His shrine at Rohrī is said to have been built A.D. 925 by a Delhī merchant, whose daughter a wicked king tried to abduct; when she prayed to the saint, he changed the course of the river and saved her honour.[10] He is known as Jendā, or Jindā, 'the living' (*zindah*) saint. Closely connected or identical with him is Uddhero Lāl, known as Vadherā Lāl in the Panjāb, said to be prime minister (*wazīr*) of the Khwājah. A long tale is told how he saved the Hindus from persecution by a *qāẓi*, or law officer, in the time of the emperor Aurangzīb. He is also known as Shaikh Tahir, and is much respected by Musalmāns, who deny that he has any connexion with the Hindus. In another story Uddhero Lāl was an incarnation of the river Indus who rose from the water in the form of a spearman, mounted on a white horse, and was then reborn from a Banyā, or merchant woman. He overcame the Musalmāns in a religious controversy and was honoured by an annual fair.[1] This saint, in his various manifestations, is worshipped by a sect of river-worshippers (Daryāpanthī) by means of water and lights; a lamp always burns at his shrine; and at the new moon he is worshipped at the river, canal, or any piece of water, with offerings of rice, sugar candy, spices, fruits, and lighted lamps.[2] Worship of this holy man is common among the Jhabēl, a Panjāb fishing caste, and among the Lohānās of Cutch, because he is said to have saved them when they fled from Multān.[3]

7. Magical powers of saints.—Saints in Sind are regarded as workers of miracles.

They cure barrenness and diseases usually incurable by ordinary means, the remedy being to give the patient a drop of water to drink, or to pass the hand over the part affected at the shrine; they cause prayers to be granted; protect mariners and traders; appear to a person at a distance to save him from some unseen danger; calm storms, especially those that are distant; change female into male children; convert sinners and infidels to the true faith; turn men's hearts by a look, thought, or word; compel inanimate objects to act as if they possessed life and volition; benefit friends and destroy foes; exercise dominion over beasts, birds, fishes; make youths' beards grow and restore vigour to aged men; raise the dead; put the fiend to flight, and summon angels and spirits; cause trees to produce butter and honey; refine sensual to spiritual love; know men's thoughts and plans; break chains, fetters, doors, and walls; live without food, drink, or sleep; cause a single pot of water to support a caravan without sensible diminution; commute the death of a person by providing a substitute; give learning to fools.[4]

The method of venerating a saint is as follows:

The votary comes to the sepulchre (*turbat*) and makes the invocation: 'O Qalandar! O thou with a great name, well-known in both worlds! Thou listener to thy friends! Only grant me my desire, and I propose to distribute a pot (*deg*) of rice-flour, cooked with sugar and butter, to the poor in thy honour!' He visits the shrine morning and evening, and, if his need be urgent, takes up his abode at the spot, because his only chance of success lies in his perseverance, and the saint needs to be reminded of the wants of the suppliant.

LITERATURE.—*IGI* xxii. 389 ff.; E. H. Aitken, *Gazetteer of the Province of Sind*, Karāchī, 1907; A. W. Hughes, *Gazetteer of the Province of Sind*², London, 1876; R. F. Burton, *Scinde: or, the Unhappy Valley*, 2 vols., do. 1851, *Sindh, and the Races that inhabit the Valley of the Indus*, do. 1851, *Sind Revisited*, 2 vols., do. 1877; T. Postans, *Personal Observations on Sinde, the Manners and Customs of its Inhabitants and its Productive Capabilities*, do. 1843; E. B. Eastwick, *Dry Leaves from Young Egypt*³, do. 1851; D. Ross, *The Land of the Five Rivers and Sindh*, do. 1883.

W. CROOKE.

SIN-EATING

SIN-EATING.—Sin-eating was an ancient custom at funerals in Wales and the Welsh Marches. The earliest allusion to it is by John Aubrey in the reign of Charles II. He says:

'In the County of Hereford was an old Custome at funeralls to hire [have] poor people, who were to take upon them all the sinnes of the party deceased. One of them I remember lived in a cottage on Rosse-high way. (He was a long, leane, ugly, lamentable poor raskal.) The manner was that when the Corps was brought out of the house and layd on the Biere; a Loafe of bread was brought out and delivered to the Sinne-eater over the corps, as also a Mazar-bowle of maple (Gossips bowle) full of beer, wch he was to drinke up, and sixpence in money, in consideration whereof he tooke upon him (ipso facto) all the Sinnes of the Defunct, and freed him (or her) from walking after they were dead. . . . This Custome (though rarely used in our dayes) yet by some people was observed [continued] even in the strictest time of ye Presbyterian goverment: as at Dynder, volens nolens the Parson of ye Parish, the kinred [relations] of a woman deceased there had this ceremonie punctually performed according to her Will: and also the like was donne at ye City of Hereford in these times, when a woman kept many yeares before her death a Mazard-bowle for the Sinne-eater; and the like in other places in this Countie; as also in Brecon, *e.g.* at Llangors, where Mr. Gwin the minister

1 Burton, p. 317 ff.
2 *Ib.* p. 325.
3 See art. SAINTS AND MARTYRS (Muhammadan in India).
4 Aitken, p. 159.
5 *Qur'ān*, xxi. 68 f.
6 Burton, *Sind Revisited*, ii. 185 ff.
7 Burton, *Sindh*, p. 211 f.
8 Burton, *Sind Revisited*, i. 92 ff.
9 See art. KHIḌR.
10 Hughes, p. 681.

1 Burton, *Sindh*, p. 329, *Sind Revisited*, i. 294 f.
2 Aitken, p. 165 f.
3 H. A. Rose, *A Glossary of Tribes and Castes of the Punjab and N.W. Frontier Province*, Lahore, 1911, ii. 380; *BG* v. [1880] 55, ix. pt. i. [1901] 349 f.
4 Burton, *Sindh*, p. 229 f.

about 1640 could no hinder ye performing of this ancient custome. I believe this custome was heretofore used over all Wales. . . . In North-Wales, the Sinne-eaters are frequently made use of; but there, insted of a Bowle of Beere, they have a bowle of Milke.'[1]

Again, writing of offertories at funerals, he says:

'These are mentioned in the Rubrick of ye ch. of Engl. Comon-Prayer-booke: but I never sawe it used, but once at Beaumaris, in Anglesey; but it is used over all the Counties of North-Wales. But before when the corps is brought out of Doores, there is Cake & Cheese, and a new Bowle of Beere, and another of Milke with ye Anno Dni ingraved on it, & ye parties name deceased, wch one accepts of on the other side of ye Corps; & this Custome is used to this day, 1686, in North Wales.'[2]

Aubrey is also related to have given to a Mr. Bagford the following account of the ceremony as practised in Shropshire:

'Within the memory of our Fathers, in Shropshire, in those villages adjoyning to Wales, when a person dyed there was notice given to an old Sire, (for so they called him), who presently repaired to the place where the deceased lay, and stood before the door of the house, when some of the Family came out and furnished him with a Cricket, on which he sat down facing the door. Then they gave him a Groat, which he put in his pocket; a Crust of Bread, which he eat; and a full bowle of Ale, which he drank off at a draught. After this he got up from the Cricket and pronounced, with a composed gesture, *the ease and rest of the Soul departed, for which he would pawn his own Soul*.'[3]

In more recent times Matthew Moggridge of Swansea gave an account to the Cambrian Archæological Association, at their meeting at Ludlow in 1852, of the custom as lately surviving in the neighbourhood of Llandebie, about twelve or thirteen miles from Swansea.

He related that, 'when a person died, the friends sent for the Sin-eater of the district, who on his arrival placed a plate of salt on the breast of the defunct, and upon the salt a piece of bread. He then muttered an incantation over the bread, which he finally ate, thereby eating up all the sins of the deceased. This done, he received his fee of 2s. 6d., and vanished as quickly as possible from the general gaze; for as it was believed that he really appropriated to his own use and behoof the sins of all those over whom he performed the above ceremony, he was utterly detested in the neighbourhood—regarded as a mere Pariah—as one irredeemably lost.'[4]

Moggridge's account was afterwards challenged by Canon Silvan Evans and others. But, if we turn again to N. Wales, we find a ceremony there described corroborating Aubrey's account. In the *British Magazine*, vii. [1835] 399, there appeared a description said to be taken 'from a MS. book of a bishop of St. Asaph' written about a century earlier, which runs as follows:

'When the corpse is brought out of the house and laid upon the bier, and covered before it be taken up, the next of kin to the deceased—widow, mother, daughter or cousin (never done by a man)—gives cross over the corpse to one of the poorest neighbours two or three white loaves of bread and a cheese with a piece of money stuck in it, and then a new wooden cup of drink, which some will require the poor body that receives it immediately to drink a little of. When this is done, the minister (if present) saith the Lord's prayer, and then they set forward towards church.'

Pennant, writing about the year 1780, describes the same custom as practised in Carnarvonshire. He apparently uses the source used by the writer in the *British Magazine*, but adds details of his own.[5] In 1820 Robert Jones, a Calvinistic Methodist minister of N. Wales, describes it also, adding that the poor man to whom the loaf, cheese, and beer had been given over the corpse 'in return blessed and prayed fervently and earnestly with [or for] the dead man's soul.'[6] Twenty years earlier Bingley speaks of the custom, which he assigns to Carnarvonshire and some other parts of N. Wales, as having been diverted to a gift of money for procuring slips of yew, box, and other evergreens to strew over and ornament the grave during a certain period after the interment.

But still the money was 'given to the person on a plate at the door of the house where the body is standing on a bier. The gift is called *Diodlys*, for formerly, instead of it, the person used to receive from the hand of the female relative a cheese with a piece of money stuck in it, and some white bread, and afterwards a cup of drink, but this practice is now entirely discontinued; the gift however still retains its old name.'[1]

The word *diodlys* refers to the gift of the drink, as also do other Welsh words for the custom: *diawdlestr* or *diodlestr*, *diodlifft* (which Sir J. Rhys conjectured to be partly English, meaning the drink lifted over the dead), and *cwpan y meirw*, the cup of the dead.

What appear to be remains of the practice have lately been found in Herefordshire and Derbyshire.

A resident in the neighbourhood of Hay 'was invited to attend the funeral of the sister of a farmer near Crasswall [Herefordshire], and to his surprise was invited to go upstairs to the room where the body was lying. He went, with the brother and four bearers. At the bottom of the bed, at the foot of the coffin, was a little box with a white cloth covering it. On it were placed a bottle of port wine, opened, and six glasses arranged around it. The glasses were filled, and my informant was asked to drink. This he refused, saying that he never took wine. "But you must drink, sir," said the old farmer; "it is like the sacrament. It is to kill the sins of my sister." Traces of this custom are to be found at Walterstone; and near the Welsh border from Hay to Longtown port wine is drunk, exactly as described, by the bearers in the room where the body lies. Finger biscuits are provided.'[2] 'At a funeral in Derbyshire wine is first offered to the bearers who carry the corpse. This custom is strictly maintained, the guests not receiving any wine until the funeral party has returned from church.' Addy, who reports this, was told by the daughter of a farmer near Newark, formerly residing near Dronfield, 'When you drink wine at a funeral, every drop that you drink is a sin which the deceased has committed. You thereby take away the dead man's sins and bear them yourself.'[3]

In Yorkshire the custom was long preserved (and perhaps still is) of handing round wine and a special kind of sponge-cakes known as 'avril-bread' to friends attending the funeral, immediately before the procession starts from the house for the churchyard.[4] The word *avril* is derived by Skeat from *arval*, 'succession-ale,' 'heir-ale,' the name of the feast given by an heir on succeeding to property in Iceland. The shape of the biscuits differed according to locality. They were often wrapped up, that the guests might take them home, in paper printed on the outside with coffins, cross-bones, skulls, and similar emblems of mortality,[5] or (probably under the influence of the Evangelical Revival) with pious verses. The custom seems to have spread even as far afield as the island of Antigua, in the West Indies, where species of pastry called 'dyer-bread' and 'biscuit-cakes' are said to have been formerly handed round at Negro funerals, enveloped in white paper and sealed with black wax.[6] It is not known how or whence the custom was introduced. In Wales a custom is described of giving to the guests before proceeding to the churchyard spiced ale in pewter vessels somewhat larger than those used in the administration of the Lord's Supper. It was administered 'just as the Lord's Supper is administered and almost with the same reverence' to the company, all of whom took their hats off as soon as it made its appearance.[7] The custom was also observed on the Shropshire border, and in addition cakes, wrapped up in black-edged paper as in Yorkshire, were handed round.[8]

1 *Remaines of Gentilisme and Judaisme, 1686–87* (first published for the Folk-lore Society, London, 1881), p. 35 f.
2 *Ib.* p. 23.
3 J. Brand and H. Ellis, *Observations on Popular Antiquities*, London, 1813, ii. 155, quoting Bagford's letter, dated 1st Feb. 1714–15, from Leland's *Collectanea*, London, 1715, i. 76.
4 *Archæologia Cambrensis*, new ser., iii. [1852] 330.
5 *Tours in Wales*, ed. J. Rhys, Carnarvon, 1883, iii. 150.
6 *Drych yr Amseroedd*, Llanrwst [1820], p. 50.

1 N. Bingley, *A Tour round N. Wales*, London, 1800, ii. 233.
2 Mrs. E. M. Leather, *The Folk-lore of Herefordshire*, London, 1912, p. 121.
3 S. O. Addy, *Household Tales, with other Traditional Remains collected in the Counties of York, Lincoln, Derby and Nottingham*, London, 1895, p. 123 f.
4 J. C. Atkinson, *Forty Years in a Moorland Parish*, London, 1891, p. 227.
5 *Manners and Customs* (Gent. Mag. Lib.), London, 1883, p. 70.
6 *Antigua and the Antiguans* (anon.), London, 1844, ii. 188.
7 *Cymru Fu Notes and Queries*, ii. [Cardiff, 1891] 271, quoting Rhys Lewis.
8 *Ib.* p. 275.

A foreigner, describing a nobleman's obsequies which he witnessed at Shrewsbury in the early years of Charles II., states that the minister made a funeral oration in the chamber where the body lay, and 'during the Oration, there stood upon the Coffin a large Pot of Wine, out of which every one drank to the health of the deceased. This being finished, six Men took up the Corps, and carried it on their shoulders to the Church.'[1]

At Cwm Yoy, in the Black Mountain, on the way to Llanthony, the people have at a funeral what they call 'the Last Sacrament.' The coffin is brought out and placed on trestles, and beer and cake are then partaken of by the guests and persons assembled (evidently in the immediate presence of the corpse), before the funeral procession starts.[2]

The interpretation of the custom has been much discussed. Analogues are found in other countries. In the Highlands of Bavaria, when the corpse had been enswathed in a linen shroud and placed on the bier, the death-chamber was carefully washed out and cleaned. The housewife then used to prepare the corpse-cakes. Having kneaded the dough, she placed it on the dead body to rise. When it had risen, the cakes were baked for the expected guests. To the cakes so prepared the belief attached that they would contain the virtues and advantages of the dead man, and that thus his vital power was transferred to the kinsmen who consumed the corpse-cakes and so was preserved to the kin.[3] Here the identification of the food with the dead man is not merely symbolic, as in the Welsh custom; the dough in rising is believed actually to absorb his qualities, which are transmitted to those of his kin who partake of the cakes. Moreover, the consumption of the food thus identified is not confined to one official; it is extended to the kinsmen who are present, and, as might be expected in such a case, it is held to be beneficial to them; they partake for their own advantage; they run no risk on behalf of the dead.

In India, however, the official practice of taking over the sins of another is well known.

When the king of Tanjore died in 1801, his corpse was cremated as usual, together with two of his wives chosen by the Brāhmans. A portion of his bones which had not been entirely consumed was reduced to powder, mixed with some boiled rice, and eaten by twelve Brāhmans. This act 'had for its object the expiation of the sins of the deceased—sins which, according to the popular opinion, were transmitted to the bodies of the persons who ate the ashes, and were tempted by money to overcome their repugnance for such disgusting food.'[4] About the year 1884, when the funeral party of a *rani* of Chamba reached the burning ground some *ghi* and rice were placed in the hands of the corpse and consumed by a Brāhman on payment of a certain sum.[5] A British official was informed by a Brāhman at a village near Raipur 'that he had eaten food out of the hand of the Raja of Biláspúr after his death, and that in consequence he had for the space of one year been placed on the throne at Biláspúr. At the end of the year he had been given presents, including a village, and then turned out of Biláspúr territory, and forbidden apparently to return. Now he is an outcaste among his co-religionists, as he has eaten food out of a dead man's hand.'[6]

The object of eating food from the corpse's hand is not stated in these cases. In the latter the Brāhman seems to have been thought to have become possessed by the soul of the deceased, as in Bavaria the qualities of the deceased are transmitted to the kinsmen who eat the corpse-cakes.

Among the lower castes and tribes in India an offender against the ritual prescriptions of his people is expelled, but may be re-admitted on submission and the provision of a feast for his caste-fellows or fellow-tribesmen.

Among the Oraons of the Central Provinces the head of the caste *panchāyat*, or council, is called the *panua*. When an offender is reinstated, the *panua* first drinks water from his hand and takes upon himself the burden of the erring one's transgression.[1] A woman belonging to the wandering tribe of the Kaikāri, in the Central Provinces, who goes wrong with a man who is not a member of the tribe is excluded. But she may be re-admitted after being purified by a ceremony, part of which consists in being seated under a wooden shed having two doors. She enters by one of these, and the shed is then set on fire. She must remain seated until the whole shed is burning, when she may escape by the other door. A young boy of the caste then eats from her hand, and, thus purified, she is re-admitted to social intercourse.[2]

Usually the official or body re-admitting the offender eats and drinks with him. By so doing he or they take the burden of the sins of which the offender has been guilty.[3]

In Oudh, when female infanticide is practised, the infant is destroyed in the room where it was born, and there buried. The floor is then plastered over with cow-dung, and, on the thirteenth day after, the village or family priest must cook and eat his food in that room. This is considered as a *hom*, or burnt-offering, and by eating it in that place the priest is supposed to take the whole *hatia*, or sin, upon himself, and to cleanse the family from it.[4]

The ecclesiastical dominance of the Brāhmans in India has probably affected more or less all castes and tribes of the population, rendering prominent the idea of sin and practices for its removal. If we turn elsewhere, we find similar customs in reference to the dead explained as in Bavaria.

The savage tribes inhabiting the valley of the Uaupes, a tributary of the Amazon, bury their dead beneath the floor of the communal house. About a month later the survivors 'disinter the corpse, which is then much decomposed, and put it in a great pan, or oven, over the fire, till all the volatile parts are driven off with a most horrible odour, leaving only a black carbonaceous mass, which is pounded into a fine powder and mixed in several large *couchés* (vats made of hollowed trees) of a fermented drink called *caxiri*; this is drunk by the assembled company till all is finished; they believe that thus the virtues of the deceased will be transmitted to the drinkers.'[5] The like practices are reported of other S. American tribes, either at the present day or up to quite recent times. Among these the Cobeus are expressly said to observe the custom for the purpose of incorporating in their own persons all the energy of the deceased. The Caribs do so for a similar reason. Some of the Brazilian tribes hold that the soul dwells in the bones, and by means of this proceeding the departed live again in those who thus drink up the bones.[6]

So among the tribes of the Darling River, in Australia, in the course of the funeral ceremonies a piece of flesh is cut from a corpse, 'taken to the camp, and after being sun-dried is cut up into small pieces and distributed among relatives and friends of the deceased: some use the piece in making the charm called *Yountoo*; others suck it to get strength and courage, or throw it into the river to bring a flood and fish, when both are wanted.'[7] A European informant in whom A. W. Howitt had full confidence told him 'that when a boy he saw two old men secretly roasting and eating fat taken from a dead blackfellow, and they observed to him that now they would have the strength of the other man.'[8] Among the Melanesian population of the Banks Islands a morsel of a corpse would be stolen and eaten by one who desired communion with the ghost. Such an one would then become a *talamaur*; the ghost 'would join in a close friendship with' him and by its aid he could afflict any one whom he desired. 'The same name, *talamaur*, was given to one whose soul was supposed to go out and eat the soul or lingering life of a freshly-dead corpse.'[9]

In these cases the object seems to have been magical. The intention evidently was, by consuming a portion of the corpse, to appropriate some power or quality of the deceased and add it to that of the survivor. The belief in the possibility of acquiring qualities, mental as well as physical, by means of food is wide-spread in the lower culture.

1 Quoted in Brand and Ellis, ii. 153, note.
2 Verbal communication to the writer by Mr. Illtyd Gardiner, Registrar of the County Court at Abergavenny.
3 *Am Urquell*, ii. [Lunden in Holstein, 1891] 101.
4 J. A. Dubois, *Hindu Manners, Customs, and Ceremonies*3, ed. H. K. Beauchamp, Oxford, 1906, p. 366.
5 *PNQ* ii. [Allahabad, 1885] 93, quoting *The Civil and Military Gazette*, 7th March, 1884.
6 *Ib.* i. [1883] 86.

1 R. V. Russell, *The Tribes and Castes of the Central Provinces of India*, London, 1916, iv. 320.
2 *Ib.* iii. 301.
3 *Ib.* ii. 514, iii. 164, 199, 402; *Census of India, 1911*, vol. i. pt. i. p. 390.
4 *PNQ* iii. [1886] 179, quoting W. H. Sleeman, *Journey through the Kingdom of Oudh*, 2 vols., London, 1858.
5 A. R. Wallace, *Narr. of Travels on the Amazon and Rio Negro*, London, 1890, p. 346.
6 *AE* xii. [1899] 83; J. G. Müller, *Gesch. der amerikanischen Urreligionen*, Basel, 1867, pp. 209, 289; *TES*, new ser., iii. [1865] 158, 193; *Anthropos*, vii. [1912] 215; W. E. Roth, *30 RBEW* [1915], p. 158; D. G. Brinton, *American Race* [Philadelphia, 1891], p. 267.
7 F. Bonney, *JAI* xiii. [1884] 135.
8 *Ib.* xvi. [1887] 30.
9 R. H. Codrington, *The Melanesians*, Oxford, 1891, p. 222.

Among the Kiwai at the mouth of the Fly River, New Guinea, sharks, because of their ferocity, are held to be the proper kind of food for warriors in war-time; other fish are 'too soft.'[1] When a youth is initiated, among the Thonga of S.E. Africa, as a diviner, a vulture's heart is cooked with other drugs and given to him, so that he 'will be able to dream of things which are far away and go straight to them.'[2] The Omaha give a boy a turtle's heart to make his heart strong (like the shell of a turtle?); the fat about a buffalo's heart was given to children that they might have strong hearts, *i.e.* be courageous; a buffalo's liver eaten raw was said to make a man courageous, and to give him a clear voice.[3] The children of the Indians of the Paraguayan Chaco are forbidden milk, whether of the cow, goat, sheep, or mare, 'because it is supposed that the milk upon which they are nourished will influence them physically as well as in character, and the Indians have no desire that their children should in any way acquire the natures of such animals.'[4] The Caribs eat neither hog nor turtle, though both are plentiful on their islands, lest their eyes become small like those of the former, or lest they themselves become clumsy and stupid like the latter.[5] On the other hand, the Ekoi of S. Nigeria hold that the manatee's flesh confers magical properties on those who eat it.[6] The Suk of the Highlands of British E. Africa sometimes give the fat and heart of a lion to children to eat, so that they may become strong.[7] The men of various Dayak tribes eat no deer-flesh lest they thereby acquire the shy, timid character of the deer.[8] On the contrary, among the Macassarese the blood of the deer is much drunk by hunters, with or without palm-wine, apparently with the object of becoming fleet as a deer. At all events it is expressly asserted of the Torajas that their chiefs always drink in war a little blood of the foe whom they have slain, in order to become valiant and strong.[9]

But the qualities desired can also be obtained by appropriating and wearing the spoils of the dead.

The Araucanos, we are told, 'imagine that any portion of the body is endowed with the qualities of the whole. Here we have the reason of their wearing the skins or heads of wild animals: that of the puma to give them strength and valour; of the fox for cunning; of the snake to enable them to crawl unseen among their enemies; eagles' feathers to make them rapid and fearless in attack. They believe that the wearing of these articles endows the wearer with the qualities they represent.'[10] The belief is by no means confined to the Araucanos. It is probable that in the old Armenian Church the priests clothing themselves even at the altar in the hides of wolves, foxes, and other animals did so in order to invest themselves with the sanctity of the animals from which the hides were taken.[11] This seems to have been a continuation of an old heathen rite.[12]

The wearing of the spoils is, however, only one method of substitution for the more complete rite of eating the creature, whether human or non-human, in order to appropriate its qualities. Of all varieties of cannibalism (*q.v.*) the eating of dead relatives is likely to be the earliest discarded. In such a case various devices would be adopted for securing the aim of the practice.

On the island of Vate in the New Hebrides the aged were put to death by burying them alive. A hole was dug, and the victim placed within it in a sitting posture, a live pig tied to each arm. Before the grave was closed, the cords were cut, and the pigs thus liberated were killed and served up at the funeral feast. In this way they seem to be identified with the corpse.[13] Among the Todas and the Kotas of the Nilgiri Hills, at a funeral, a buffalo is killed and brought into contact with the corpse. It is afterwards eaten at the feast.[14] In Kanaur, on the Upper Sutlej, at the annual feast (*śrāddha*) in honour of the dead, a he-goat, reared in the dead man's name, is dressed in his clothes, sacrificed, and eaten by members of his kindred.[15] The Dhāngars and Basors of the United Provinces, after burying a corpse, return to the dead man's house, kill a hog, and, after separating the limbs to be cooked for the funeral feast, bury the trunk in the courtyard of the house, making an invocation to it as the representative of the deceased, and ordering him to rest there in peace and not worry his descendants.[1] In the Balkan peninsula cakes, called by the Greeks *kolyva*, made of boiled wheat and other ingredients, are eaten at funerals. These are either carried, as in Albania, in the funeral procession and eaten on the tomb or, as elsewhere, eaten at the funeral feast immediately on the return to the house. In many places they bear the image of the dead stamped upon them. It is sinful to indulge in expressions of sorrow while eating them. As each mourner takes his share, he says: 'May he (or she) be forgiven!' or 'God rest him!' In Calymnos, among the Greeks, the *kolyva* cakes are carried the day after the funeral from the house of death to the tomb, on which they are set to be distributed. The eating of *kolyva* cakes is repeated with similar ceremonies on the third, ninth, and fortieth days and again at the end of three, six, and nine months and of one, two, and three years after death, when the death rites cease.[2] In Sicily annually, on the festival of All Souls, sweetmeats impressed with images of skulls, bones, skeletons, souls in purgatory, and the like, are eaten. This is called 'eating the dead.'[3] There is a similar custom at Perugia and probably at other places in Italy.[4] Elsewhere the intention is hardly less manifest. It is customary among the Letts to serve the relatives, on the grave itself, with bread and cheese, or with beans and peas, beer and brandy.[5] In the government of Smolensk, White Russia, when the grave is filled, a white cloth is spread over it, on which a paste composed of flour, poppy, and honey is served, every one taking a spoonful.[6] In Brunswick—where the funeral meal is regarded as a pious duty to which the departed has a right, the last honour that can be paid to him—the tables are laid by ancient custom on the very spot from which the coffin has just been removed.[7] An Armenian custom, witnessed by Rendel Harris some years ago at the village of Archag, goes further, and reminds us of the Bavarian corpse-cakes. He saw there a corpse lying in the midst of the church, laid out for burial the following day. Two large flat loaves had been placed upon the body. On inquiry he learned, after some difficulty, 'that in former days the custom was to eat the bread, dividing it up amongst the friends of the deceased'—a custom which the people were apparently beginning to outgrow.[8]

The custom of sin-eating, therefore, would seem to be derived from that of eating the corpse. In all the customs just cited there is an attempt to identify the ritual food with the deceased. The same attempt is obviously made in both the British and the Bavarian customs, although the effect of consuming the food is differently interpreted. Under ecclesiastical influence, and specifically in Great Britain under influences derived from the Mosaic legislation, prominence has been given both in India and in this country to the idea of the scapegoat (*q.v.*), which is absent from the ritual elsewhere. There can be little doubt that this idea has been imported into the custom, which is probably represented much more nearly to its original form by the Bavarian rite. A funeral meal is a common incident everywhere. It is the reunion of the kin after the shock of the severance of one of its members. It does not everywhere suggest a primitive feast on the corpse itself; rather it takes the form in most cases of a feast at which the deceased is, though unseen, one of the convives—a feast given to speed the parting soul. Such may have been the feast in classic times provided at the tomb, and that at Argentière, in the department of the Hautes Alpes, France, where the table of the curé and the family is still placed in the cemetery upon the grave itself, and after the meal every one, led by the next of kin, drinks to the health of the departed.[9] But where a special kind of food or drink is provided, and where it is brought into immediate connexion with the corpse, the case is different, and we may reasonably conclude that it represents the flesh of the dead, especially where it is expressly believed

1 G. Landtman, *JRAI* xlvi. [1916] 323.
2 H. A. Junod, *The Life of a South African Tribe*, London, 1912–13, ii. 517.
3 A. C. Fletcher, *27 RBEW* [1911], p. 332.
4 W. B. Grubb, *An Unknown People in an Unknown Land*, London, 1911, p. 137.
5 W. E. Roth, *30 RBEW* [1915], p. 297.
6 P. A. Talbot, *In the Shadow of the Bush*, London, 1912, p. 2.
7 M. W. H. Beech, *The Suk, their Language and Folklore*, Oxford, 1911, p. 11.
8 A. C. Kruijt, *Het Animisme in den Indischen Archipel*, The Hague, 1906, p. 51.
9 *Ib.* p. 56.
10 R. E. Latcham, *JRAI* xxxix. [1909] 350.
11 F. C. Conybeare, *FL* xviii. [1907] 432.
12 A large collection of cases in J. G. Frazer, *GB*³, *passim*.
13 A. Featherman, *Social Hist. of the Races of Mankind*, II. i., 'Papuo- and Malayo-Melanesians,' London, 1887, p. 74.
14 E. Thurston, *Madras Gov. Mus. Bull.*, i. 179, 197, 204, iv. 11.
15 H. A. Rose, *A Glossary of the Tribes and Castes of the Punjab and N.W. Frontier Province*, Lahore, 1911, ii. 449.

1 W. Crooke, *PR*, 1896, ii. 58.
2 L. M. J. Garnett, *The Women of Turkey and their Folklore*, London, 1890–91, ii. 264; A. Strausz, *Die Bulgaren*, Leipzig, 1898, p. 451; Hartland, *LP* ii. 288.
3 *Rivista delle Trad. Pop. Italiane*, i. [1893] 239.
4 *Ib.* p. 322.
5 *ARW* xvii. [1914] 488.
6 *L'Anthropologie*, xiv. [1903], 717, citing *ZE* xxv. 650.
7 R. Andree, *Braunschweiger Volkskunde*, Brunswick, 1896, p. 227.
8 *FL* xv. [1904] 440.
9 Laisnel de la Salle, *Croyances et légendes du centre de la France*, Paris, 1875, ii. 81.

that some qualities, good or bad, of the deceased are transmitted to the eater.

Cannibalism of the kind referred to—namely, the eating of dead kinsmen—is reported from Asia, Africa, Australia, S. America, and the E. Indian Archipelago. In Europe it is reported by Strabo[1] of the ancient Irish, though he admits that his evidence is not wholly satisfactory. Nor was it always customary among peoples who practised it to await the convenience of the aged to die. They were slain and devoured. Herodotus[2] attributes this custom to the Massagetæ. Savages all over the world have been wont to put to death the aged and infirm. The traditions of the 'holy maul,' with which the son was said to knock on the head his old and useless father, point to this custom as once practised in Western Europe. There is no direct evidence to connect it with the eating of the dead. But there is a custom in Scandinavia, which was witnessed by Du Chaillu at Husum, whereby the son formally dispossesses his father and takes his place at the head of the table in spite of the father's pleas and protests. That the ceremony is performed at the table prior to partaking of a common meal is noteworthy in this connexion.[3]

LITERATURE.—In addition to the authorities cited in the footnotes reference may be made to a lengthy correspondence in *The Academy*, 9th Nov. 1895–23rd May 1896, in which the evidence on which the Welsh custom rests was fully considered; and E. S. Hartland, *The Legend of Perseus*, London, 1894–96, ii. ch. xiii. See also the art. CANNIBALISM, and the authorities there cited. E. SIDNEY HARTLAND.

SIOUANS.—While the tribal units of the Siouan family of American Indians have many ethical and religious traits in common, yet each separate tribe possesses certain highly individualized characteristics, often not at all in keeping with the views of its nearest relatives and associates. For convenience we may divide the Siouans into three great cultural groups: (1) the Plains division, including the various sub-tribes of the Dakota, Assiniboin, and Crow; (2) the village Siouans, made up of the Mandan and Hidatsa; and (3) the Southern Siouans, the principal component tribes of which are the Omaha, Ponca, Osage, Iowa, Oto, and perhaps the Winnebago.

1. Ideas of deity.—Among all these groups there are found certain fundamental concepts, which indeed are not confined to the Siouans alone. While none of them, *e.g.*, have anything corresponding to the true European thought of God, yet all hold ideas of a great supernatural power or complex of powers which controls the universe. The Dakota believe in a celestial hierarchy made up of the sun, sky, earth, and rock, each of which is called *wakan tanka*, and each has control over certain things necessary to the existence of mankind. Among the Omaha, however, the cognate term *wakonda* has a different meaning. It is used with reference to all objects or phenomena which are regarded as supernatural, and at the same time this term is also applied to the sacred and mysterious omnipresent power which animates them. This power is not infrequently personified, and is addressed in prayer as the 'power that moves,' for movement and life are to the Omaha synonymous. There can be little doubt that these ideas permeate the religious beliefs of all the Southern Siouans, and are closely related to the Algonquian *manitu* concepts.

The various agents through which the American Indian believes mysterious power to be manifested are termed *wakanda*, or, among the Dakota, *wakan*. These include a host of beings of greater or less importance, chief among whom are the Thunderbird, Whirlwind, Tree-dwelling elf, and the panther-like Water-monster. These beings are able to transfer their supernatural power to mankind, under certain conditions.

The method of approaching these deities is the same among all the Siouans. At the age of puberty the aspiring youth retires to some solitary spot, where he proceeds to fast, and in some cases, as among the Dakota, to mortify his flesh by undergoing self-torture and even mutilation accompanied by incessant prayer. This period of self-castigation is prolonged for several days, generally not ending until the supplicant has brought on a vision in which one of the *wakanda* appears to him and offers to grant him certain privileges, usually concerned with success in war and the chase. In return for this, the recipient is enjoined to observe certain tabus and always to carry about some memento of his guardian-spirit, such as the skin of the animal in whose form it appeared, or a small symbolic trinket. This object itself now becomes the seat of much, if not all, of its owner's *wakanda*, and its loss renders him helpless and no more than a common man. It also receives sacrifices and feasts and even the prayers of its owner, as being the abiding-place of his *wakanda* and the symbol of, if not the intermediary with, his dream-guardian.

It sometimes happens that an individual receives from his guardian instructions that affect the religious life of the whole tribe.

An Oto now (or very recently) living was ordered by a *wakanda* in a dream to make a shrine in which were to centre certain ceremonies that were to benefit the entire people. Accordingly, the shrine was made and the songs, prayers, and dances which this Siouan received from his mysterious source were introduced into the ceremonial and religious life, not only of his tribe, but among the Iowa and others as well. Thus have grown up societies and ceremonies of a religious nature throughout the entire Siouan stock.

2. Religious ceremonies.—Among the Siouan tribes forming the Prairie group the great religious ceremony is the Sun-dance. This function is divided into a secret and a public performance. The former takes place in a secluded *tipi*, where the priests gather for the holding of their rites, such as praying, fasting, and making ready the objects which are to form part of the paraphernalia of the participants in the public ceremony, or are to be used on the altar in the Sun-dance lodge.

On the last day of the secret observances a great ceremonial structure is erected in the centre of the camp circle; the obtaining and bringing in of the material is attended to by certain warrior societies of the tribe, the selection of the centre pole being peculiarly the task of the braves; and all is accomplished with many ritualistic observances. When completed, the structure is a huge roofless enclosure of circular form with a tall central pole. The priests now come out of their seclusion and enter the lodge, which is dedicated by elaborate rites, generally including parades by the societies of warriors. The next day the altar is set up on the west side of the lodge. Its construction differs from tribe to tribe. Among the Ponca it is a mere buffalo-skull placed with a pipe on a rectangle of clean earth from which the sod has been cut. Among the Mandan, in their cognate *okipa* ceremony, it is a large symbolic structure made in reference to mythic incidents. When the altar is completed, the priests decorate the bodies of the dancers with paint and wreaths of sage or willow-leaves about the neck, waist, head, wrists, and ankles. The performers then dance in line, gazing at the sun and incessantly blowing on eagle-bone whistles, while the dance music is sung to the tune of a drum placed near the south side of the lodge. The dancers usually fast during the entire ceremony. They also submit to painful forms of self-torture. The commonest types of this ordeal consist of slitting the skin of the breasts and inserting skewers to which thongs are attached, the thongs being made fast to the central lodge pole, and the victim then endeavouring to tear himself loose. Others drag buffalo-skulls, fastened to their backs in the manner described. The Crow, in particular, chop off joints of their fingers as offerings to the sun. These practices reached their greatest development among the Mandan, who carried the torture to great lengths. Among them individuals were often suspended from the top of the lodge by thongs and skewers. Other less physically painful sacrifices were made—*e.g.*, throwing away blankets, clothing, and other goods.

The Crow Sun-dance, unlike that of the other

[1] iv. 5. 4. [2] i. 216.
[3] P. B. Du Chaillu, *Land of the Midnight Sun*, London, 1881, i. 393.

Siouans, was not a periodical ceremony. It was held only when a mourner was especially eager to avenge the murder of a close relative by the death of a member of a hostile tribe. He was first obliged to obtain a vision of a conquered foe, which was an implied promise of his success. He was able to have this vision only through the aid of a sacred doll, which was the most important object in the entire ceremony. The owner of one of these dolls (there were several in the tribe) was hired by the person desiring to hold the dance, to take charge of the ceremonies.

Among the Southern Siouans there are many esoteric religious societies. Of these the chief was the Medicine-dance society, as it is known among the Iowa, Oto, Winnebago, and Eastern Dakota. It corresponds closely to the Midē'wiwin of the Central Algonquians. The Omaha form of this society is called Wacicka, and is based on a ritual founded on a long secret origin-myth. The object of the society is to teach its members how to secure long life on earth through the knowledge of healing herbs and medicines, and to secure their safe arrival in the hereafter through ethical and religious teachings.

The tribal religious rites of the Omaha were called *wewacpe*, a term which had reference to bringing the people into thoughtful composure. These rites partook of the general nature of prayer, and were intended to be intermediaries between the Omaha and *wakan*. An error could be adjusted only after a ceremony of contrition and retribution, as they believed that any interruption of the prescribed order of a ceremony made the culprit liable to divine punishment. All *wewacpe* rites were considered institutional and were distinct from individual rites. They were both private and public. Except for the ceremonies of the *hoⁿbe watci*, or night-dance, the performances of the esoteric societies of the tribe were not looked upon as *wewacpe*. The *wewacpe* ceremonies included those for corn or maize, those pertaining to the yearly buffalo-chase, the introduction of a child to the supernatural powers, the consecrating of male children to the thunder, and the calumet ceremony.

3. Eschatology.—Siouan beliefs as to a future existence vary greatly. The Omaha have certain theories in common with the Central Algonquians. The Dakota think that each person has four spirits: one resides in the body, and dies with it; the second always remains near the body; the third accounts for the deeds of the body, and travels south after death; the fourth always lingers with the lock of hair which the mourners cut from the head of the deceased; this lock is kept until the opportunity offers itself to the mourners to throw the bundle away in the enemies' country, when the spirit becomes a wanderer sowing death and disease among the foe. From this theory arose the custom of wearing four eagle-plumes for each enemy killed in war, one for each spirit. There are some Dakota who claim the right to wear a fifth feather for another spirit which transmigrates to the body of a child or an animal. The Dakota seem to have no theory as to what is the final abode of the four spirits, except that they travel to the south.

The Hidatsa, on the other hand, believe that, when one of their people dies, his spirit stays four nights around the camp or settlement where he breathed his last, and then goes to the lodge of his departed relatives in the village of the dead. When he has arrived, he is rewarded for his conduct on earth with the same things as are valued in this life. The 'village of the dead' is located under the earth, but, in order to reach it, the soul must cross a broad swift river on a narrow pathway. Those whose life has been evil slip off and are hurried into oblivion. In the other world the shades pursue and kill the shades of buffalo and other animals that have died.

With the Omaha the belief was held that spirits travelled over the Milky Way to the hereafter, which was a land where the environment resembles that of this world. The journey required four days and as many nights, so the mourners kept a fire burning on the grave for four nights after the interment of the deceased, that its light might cheer and guide the departing soul on its way. After a toilsome trip the spirit came to a fork in the road of the dead, where sat an old man closely wrapped in the folds of a buffalo-robe. If the deceased had been a righteous and peaceable person, the road-keeper directed him a short-cut to the hereafter. If, on the other hand, the soul was that of an evil-doer, it was sent over a rough and dreary road, where it wandered on for ever. By exception, however, the souls of the members of the two Omaha buffalo gentes were supposed to return to their eponymic ancestors.

4. Disposal of the dead and mourning customs.—While many of the Siouan tribes practised scaffold-burial, the Omaha buried their dead on hill-tops, placing the corpse in a flexed position on its side and erecting a mound over it. Some of the belongings of the deceased, such as the knife, tomahawk, or club, kettle, and the like, were placed in the tomb. In some cases a horse was strangled over the grave. Food was also placed near by. Often the male mourners met in a lodge near that of the deceased, and cut the flesh of their arms and thrust willow-twigs into the wounds. Then, with the blood dripping from their cuts, they went to the wake and sang certain funeral-songs. They then withdrew the twigs and threw them on the ground. Mourners often went on the war-path to obtain relief from grief. A man who had lost a child carried its little moccasins and placed them at the side of the body of a fallen foe, whom he had killed, in the belief that the soul of his slain enemy would guide the spirit of the dead babe to its relatives in the hereafter.

LITERATURE.—J. O. Dorsey, 'A Study of Siouan Cults,' *11 RBEW* [1894], pp. 351–544; Alice C. Fletcher and Francis La Flesche, 'The Omaha Tribe,' *27 RBEW* [1911], pp. 15–654; Alanson Skinner, 'Societies of the Iowa, Kansa and Ponca Indians,' *Anthropological Papers of the American Museum of Natural History*, vol. xi. [1915] no. ix.

ALANSON SKINNER.

SIRENS.—The symbolism of the sirens, Σειρῆνες, in literature and art is of more significance for the history of moral ideas than the etymology of the name or the pre-historic origin of the myth would be, even if we could ascertain them. We cannot. The prevailing view is that they are primarily 'the stranglers,' 'würgende Totengeister,' akin to the Keres, Erinyes, and Harpies. This, like many prevailing views of the science of mythology, is confirmed by over-stressing the evidence of Greek vases and by the assumption that the fragmentary testimony of Alexandrian and Roman writers always preserves the genuine pre-Homeric popular belief.[1] Already at their first appearance[2] the two[3] Sirens embody a conscious allegory,[4] as Cicero[5] and Horace[6] perceived. Ruskin's explicit

[1] See G. Weicker, 'Die Seirenen,' in Roscher, where all the testimonia are collected.
[2] Homer, *Od.* xii. 39, 165 ff.
[3] Dual in *Od.* xii. 167; for the three or more of later tradition, their transparent names, and varying genealogies, see A. C. Pearson on Sophocles' frag. 861; G. W. Mooney on Apollonius Rhodius, iv. 893 ff.; and Weicker, p. 602 f.
[4] See F. M. Stawell, *Homer and the Iliad*, London, 1909, p. 150, where, however, the rendering 'a spirit had put the waves to rest' is fanciful.
[5] *De Fin.* v. 18.
[6] *Ep.* I. ii. 23; cf. *Sat.* II. iii. 14.

allegorization of their song as the lure of the thirst for unsanctified knowledge and the immodesty of science,[1] for all its modern sound, is merely a development of what Homer and Cicero tell us—that they promised Odysseus, not love or pleasure, but knowledge. The notion of the fatal songstress, the lurer, the temptress, the Lorelei,[2] arises naturally in the human mind, and we cannot now recover the particular association of ideas that first clothed it for the Greek imagination in the form of the Sirens. In the earliest Greek vases that represent the scene from the *Odyssey* they are portrayed with the wings and body of a bird and a woman's head.[3]

It was a plausible hypothesis, then, that they were originally birds, symbolizing either the widespread association of the fleeting soul with the wings of a bird or the magic of the bird's song,

> 'that tells us
> What life is, so clear.
> —The secret they sang to Ulysses
> When, ages ago,
> He heard and he knew this life's secret
> I hear and I know.'[4]

Or as singers they may signify the spell of all song and eloquence, and for this reason perhaps the image of a Siren was later placed on the monuments of poets and orators—*e.g.*, Sophocles and Isocrates.[5]

Again, they are in a sense sea-nymphs inhabiting a lonely ocean isle, somewhere in the western fairyland of Odyssean adventure.[6] And the treacherous lure or the magic spell of the smiling sea was a commonplace of Greek poetry and has been familiar to the human imagination from Lucretius'

> 'Subdola cum ridet placidi pellacia ponti'

to Keats'

> 'Magic casements, opening on the foam
> Of perilous seas, in faery lands forlorn.'

Or, again, the Sirens may have blended in the Greek imagination with the wailing women who sang laments for the dead at funerals. Weicker confirms this connexion of ideas by the regret with which the souls of Homeric heroes leave 'the warm precincts of the cheerful day.'[7] It would be far more pertinent to Homer to quote Gray's *Elegy*, the last line of the *Æneid*, Matthew Arnold's *Sohrab and Rustum*, and John Masefield's *August, 1914*. However that may be, the association with death opens up infinite possibilities for speculation and sentiment. 'Before Plato could speak, the soul had wings in Homer,' says Sir Thomas Browne.[8] The primitive conception of the soul-bird is the theme of a modern monograph.[9] The analogy of the Harpies has also been used in confirmation of this association.

None of these fancies admits of proof, but their suggestions for the poetic and the moral imagination can never pass away. The name of one of the Sirens on the British Museum amphora, ἱμερόπα, recalls Alcman's 'maidens with voices that wake desire,' and Dante's 'siren of sensual pleasure' repeats in verse of more than Greek loveliness the

1 *The Eagle's Nest*, § 74.
2 'Illectos suo cantu in naufragia deducebant' (Servius, on *Æneid*, v. 864).
3 Amphora, Brit. Mus. E. 440, reproduced in Weicker's article, p. 606. This article is now the most convenient repertory of the monumental evidence. But much of it can be found also in A. Baumeister, *Denkmäler des klass. Altertums*, 3 vols., Munich, 1884–88, and in the full and learned article of C. Michel in Daremberg-Saglio.
4 R. Browning, *The Englishman in Italy*.
5 *Vita Soph.* 9, *Vita Isoc.* 13.
6 Their original home shifts with the localization of the Homeric story. The late testimonia are collected by Weicker in Roscher, p. 606. Strabo, v. 246, tells of a cult of the Siren Parthenope at Neapolis.
7 *Il.* xvi. 856, xxiii. 362.
8 *Urn Burial*, ch. iv.
9 G. Weicker, *Der Seelenvogel in der alten Literatur und Kunst*, Leipzig, 1902.

inscription ΣΙΡΗΝΕΙΜΙ on the Tyrrhenian Hydria, Louvre E 803:

> 'Io son cantava io son dolce sirena
> Che i marinari in mezzo mar dismago.'

The Sirens are not mentioned except by modern inference in Hesiod, the Homeric hymns, Pindar, or Æschylus. In the Greek lyrics they are named only in Erinna's reference to the Sirens on the tomb of her companion Baucis, and in frag. 7 of Alcman, and a new fragment of Archilochus. Sophocles speaks of them as the 'songstresses of death' and 'daughters of Phorkys.'[1] Euripides' *Helena* invokes them as 'winged maidens, daughters of earth,' to sing her sorrows.[2] And in his *Andromache*[3] 'Sirens' speeches' is rhetoric for the words of the women who lead Hermione astray.

In the fragments of Greek comedy (Epicharmus, Theopompus) it is perhaps they who tempt the famished Odysseus with descriptions of a Gargantuan feast, while he checks the eagerness of his companions by the remark that their flute-playing is rotten (σαπρά).

In Plato's *Republic*[4] the music of the spheres is produced by the concerted notes of eight Sirens, one on each circle. Plato's *Cratylus*[5] allegorizes the myth in what Ruskin[6] calls 'the divine passage in the Cratylus of Plato about the place of the dead,' which he renders exquisitely:

> 'And none of those who dwell there desire to depart thence,—no, not even the Sirens; but even they, the seducers, are there themselves beguiled, and they who lulled all men, themselves laid to rest—they, and all others—such sweet songs doth death know how to sing to them.'

Ovid[7] merely says that the Sirens were playmates of Proserpine, and that the gods granted them wings that they might continue their search for her over the sea also. In the legend of the Argonauts, as the mythographs Apollodorus[8] and Hyginus[9] tell us, Orpheus sang against the Sirens who, being defeated, cast themselves into the sea and were transformed into hidden rocks.[10] This is the origin of the long modern literary tradition, from Samuel Daniel to William Morris's *Life and Death of Jason*, in which Orpheus (or Odysseus) sings the song of virtue against the allurements of the Sirens of temptation. In the language of the LXX (Job 30^{29}, Is 34^{13} 43^{20}, Jer 50^{39}) Siren is a synonym for the wild creatures and spirits that inhabit waste places. The AV renders it by 'owls' or 'dragons.' The Christian Fathers variously allegorized these passages, and also interpreted Odysseus lashed to the mast as a symbol of the Christian clinging to the Cross of Christ to resist the allurements of the world. Bacon pronounces Orpheus' remedy of song better than Ulysses' device of stopping the ears of his crew with wax:

> 'For meditations upon things divine excell the pleasures of the sense, not in power only but also in sweetness.' Light and conscienceless literature aims 'at taking the wings away from the Muses' crowns and giving them back to the Sirens.'[11]

In Daniel's *Ulysses and the Siren* Ulysses answers the Siren in this edifying strain:

> 'Fair Nymph, if fame or honour were
> To be attain'd with ease,
> Then would I come and rest me there
> And leave such toils as these.'

Though not expressly named, the Sirens are clearly meant in the *Faerie Queene*[12] by the mermaids who

> 'fondly striv'd
> With th' Heliconian maides for maistery,'

and who invite Sir Guyon to find his 'Port of rest' in

> 'The worlds sweet In, from paine and wearisome turmoyle.'

1 Frags. 852 and 861, Jebb-Pearson.
2 *Helena*, 167.
3 Line 936.
4 617 B.
5 403 D.
6 *Time and Tide*, xxiv. § 166.
7 *Metam.* v. 552 ff.
8 i. 9.
9 *Fab.* 141.
10 See Apollonius Rhodius, iv. 893.
11 *Wisdom of the Ancients*, xxxi.
12 II. xii. 31 f.

This is a favourite motive of Renaissance epics, recurring in various forms in Ariosto, Camoëns, and Tasso. The *Sea-Fairies* of Tennyson is a lyric development of the same theme with touches taken from Catullus' *epyllium* of Peleus and Thetis. The appeal of Matthew Arnold's *New Sirens* is to scepticism and emotionalism—

' Only, what we feel, we know.'

Lowell's Sirens echo Tennyson's sea-fairies and his lotos-eaters, and their lure is

' To be at rest for evermore ! '

LITERATURE.—See the sources quoted in the footnotes.

PAUL SHOREY.

ŚIVA.—See ŚAIVISM, DRAVIDIANS (North India).

ŚIVA NĀRĀYAṆĪS.—The Śiva Nārāyaṇīs, or Sio Narānīs, are a monotheistic sect of N. India, having their centre in the Districts of Ghāzīpur and Baliā. They profess unqualified monotheism, have no formal ritual, and pay no regard to the objects of Hindu and Musalmān veneration. Their worship consists in the members gathering at a *dhām*, or monastery, where one of their *Granths*, or sacred books, is read. Adoration is then offered to the Para Brahma, or the Supreme, and offerings are made, which are devoted to the upkeep of the establishment.

They accept converts from all classes of the community—Hindus, Muslims, or Christians—and many of these adhere outwardly to the forms of their original beliefs. It is specially reported that some Indian Christians of the District of Shāhābād belong to the sect. At the present day most of the members are low-caste Hindus, but the chief *sants*, or leaders, are generally Rājpūts or Brāhmans. According to Risley,[1] the large majority of Bengali Chamārs belong to it.

The acceptance of a convert is a matter of small ceremony. No *guru*, or spiritual guide, is required. A few Śiva Nārāyaṇīs assemble to meet the postulant, sweetmeats which have previously been deposited on one of their holy books are distributed, a few passages are read from the book, and the ceremony is complete.

The sect was founded in the reign of the emperor Muḥammad Shāh (A.D. 1719–48) by one Śiva Nārāyaṇa, a Naraunī Rajpūt of the village of Chandrawār in the present Baliā District. He is said to have written sixteen Hindī works,[2] viz. *Lava Granth*, *Śānt-vilās*, *Sant ō jān Granth*, *Śānt-sundar*, *Guru-nyās*, *Śānt-āchārī*, *Śāntôpadēś*, *Śabdâvali*, *Sānt-parwāna*, *Sānt-mahimā*, *Sānt-sāgar*, *Baṛā stōtra*, *Baṛā parwāna*, *Pati parwāna*, and *Barhō Bāṇī*. The most important of these are the *Guru-nyās* and the *Śānt-vilās*. The former, compiled from the Sanskrit *Purāṇas*, gives an account of the ten incarnations of Viṣṇu, and is subdivided into fourteen chapters, of which the first six treat of the author, of faith, of the punishment of sinners, of virtue, of a future state, and of discipline. The latter is a treatise on moral sentiments. The opening lines are : ' The love of God and His knowledge are the only true understanding.'[3] In addition to these fifteen there is one more, sealing the whole, which has not yet been divulged, and which remains in the exclusive charge of the head of the sect.

The unitarianism of this sect is of the straitest kind. They acknowledge one Supreme Deity, the creator (*kartā*), whom they call the Niraṅkār Par Brahm (*i.e. nirākāraṁ paraṁ Bráhma*) and the Sant Puruṣ (*Saṭ-puruṣa*), on whose nature ' light was thrown by Śiva Nārāyaṇa.' The moral virtues of truth, temperance, and mercy are inculcated,

[1] *Tribes and Castes of Bengal*, i. 178.
[2] Wilson says twelve. In the above list the last four are not mentioned by him. He calls the *Sant ō jān Granth* the *Vajan Granth*.
[3] Risley, i. 178.

polygamy is prohibited, and sectarian marks are not used.

They claim that the emperor Muḥammad Shāh was one of Śiva Nārāyaṇa's converts and that he gave him a seal. This is still possessed by the sect, and used on *parwānas*, or precepts, issued by the heads to the faithful.

Crooke[1] and Risley[2] identify the Śiva Nārāyaṇīs with the Rai Dāsīs (*q.v.*), but this is not borne out by inquiries made by the present writer. The Rai Dāsīs are all Chamārs, but among the Śiva Nārāyaṇīs all sects are admitted. Quite possibly the Rai Dāsīs, whose tenets are not dissimilar, claim to be Śiva Nārāyaṇīs, but they by no means form the whole sect.

LITERATURE.—Except the articles of Risley and Crooke above mentioned, the only published account of this sect which has been seen by the present writer is that contained in H. H. Wilson, *Sketch of the Religious Sects of the Hindus* [vol. i. of *Select Works*, ed. R. Rost], London, 1861, p. 358 f. The present art. is based on this, but his statements are corrected and supplemented by inquiries specially made from the head of the sect at Ghāzīpur ; see *JRAS*, 1918, p. 114 ff. H. H. Risley, *The Tribes and Castes of Bengal*, Calcutta, 1891, i. 178, and W. Crooke, *The Tribes and Castes of the N.W. Provinces and Oudh*, do. 1896, ii. 185 ff., describe at length the Śiva Nārāyaṇī customs, as those of the Chamār Rai Dāsīs. The practices described differ in a few details from those given above.

G. A. GRIERSON.

SKIN.—The significance of the skin for the history of religion springs from three principal sources : (*a*) its natural pigmentation, (*b*) tatuing, etc., (*c*) sacrificial rites.

(*a*) The colour of the skin affords one of the most obvious tests of racial difference. Three recognizable pigments are found in the mucous layer between the dermis and the epidermis, viz. yellow, reddish-brown, and black.[3] But any classification of the many varieties of skin-colouration must be more or less arbitrary. A typical scheme is that of Paul Topinard,[4] who enumerates ten varieties, by dividing the white into pale, florid, olive-white, the yellow into clear, olive, and dark, the dark into coppery-red, chocolate-brown, sooty-black, and coal-black. In some countries the colour-distinction is still of great social and political importance ; this may help us to realize the religious influence of colour in earlier periods.

' The Sanskrit word for caste is *varna*, that is " colour " ; and this shows how their distinction of high and low caste arose.'[5]

As a precise morphological distinction, the colour of the skin is of secondary value.

' Used alone . . . the test of colour will lead to serious misapprehension of the real relations of various races.'[6]

(*b*) The alteration of the appearance of the skin by tatued marks and patterns is a very wide-spread custom. Lubbock[7] collects a number of examples, ranging from simple ornament to serious mutilation. He remarks that ' ornamentation of the skin is almost universal among the lower races of men.' Some would regard all these customs as springing primarily from a desire for ornamentation. Thus Westermarck says :

' We have seen how savage men and women in various ways endeavour to make themselves attractive to the opposite sex :—by ornamenting, mutilating, painting, and tattooing themselves. That these practices essentially subserve this end appears chiefly from the fact that the time selected for them is the age of puberty.'[8]

The motive to which he refers is certainly contributory, but hardly primary. It is safer to agree with Achelis, who says :[9]

[1] *Tribes and Castes of the N.W. Provinces and Oudh*, ii. 185 ff.
[2] i. 178 ff.
[3] W. L. H. Duckworth, *Morphology and Anthropology*, Cambridge, 1904, p. 348.
[4] Quoted by Duckworth, p. 353.
[5] E. B. Tylor, *Anthropology*, new ed., London, 1904, p. 69.
[6] Duckworth, p. 352.
[7] *Origin of Civilisation*[6], London, 1902, pp. 59–66. See also art. TATUING.
[8] *Hist. of Human Marriage*[3], London, 1901, p. 541.
[9] P. D. Chantepie de la Saussaye, in *Lehrbuch der Religionsgeschichte*[3], Tübingen, 1905, i. 46.

'There is no doubt that the operation has a religious significance; it is performed by the priests during the chanting of religious songs, and its origin is ascribed to the gods. . . . The custom stands in close relation to Totemism, especially since the incised figures so often represent animals: snakes, lizards, fishes, birds.'

We may also note that 'the marks or scars left on legs or arms from which blood had been drawn were probably the origin of tattooing.'[1]

(*c*) With totemism (*q.v.*) we may also connect the various sacrificial ceremonies in the ritual of which some use is made of the skin of the slain animal. A typical case is that reported by Herodotus in his account of the festival of Zeus at Thebes. He gives the current legend of an appearance of Zeus to Herakles in the disguise of a ram's fleece, with the ram's head held in front, and proceeds:

'The Thebans then do not sacrifice rams but hold them sacred for this reason; on one day however in the year, on the feast of Zeus, they cut up in the same manner and flay one single ram and cover with its skin the image of Zeus, and then they bring up to it another image of Heracles. This done, all who are in the temple beat themselves in lamentation for the ram, and then they bury it in a sacred tomb.'[2]

Here the legend has obviously sprung from the annual institution of killing the animal totem, or (if we doubt, with Frazer, the totemistic stage in this case) from the institution of killing the divine animal.[3] Frazer compares with the example given by Herodotus a custom once existing among the Indians of California of preserving the entire skin and feathers of their sacred bird, the great buzzard, when one was slain annually, to make a festal garment, also a W. African custom (Fernando Po) of hanging the skin of the sacred cobra-capella on a tree to be touched by all the children born during the previous year. It has been suggested that the OT reference to 'the horns of the altar,' in connexion with the application of the blood and the right of asylum, should be traced back to the custom of spreading the skin of the victim, with the horns still attached to it, over the altar.[4] In these and many similar practices[5] we can trace two principles of primitive thought: (1) the sacred animal is conceived as standing in the most intimate relation to the life and prosperity of the worshippers; (2) the skin is thought to contain within itself a portion of the life of the animal even after separation from the body. With such premisses, it is quite natural to reason that closer communion with the animal-god can be gained by the priest or the worshipper putting on the skin of the flayed animal as a sacred garment.[6] Robertson Smith[7] traces a survival of this in the coming of Jacob to his father in the skins of kids. Frazer[8] points out a similar use of human skin in the Mexican ritual. The chorus of the Greek tragedy were originally called 'goats' (τράγοι), and wore goat-skins to show their close relation with the goat-god,[9] whilst it was the custom even of certain Christian catechumens to stand bare-footed upon a goat-skin.[10] We may see the same circle of ideas extended to divine inspiration and divination; thus the god Faunus was supposed to reveal the future through dreams to such of his votaries as slept within his precincts upon the fleeces of sacrificed lambs.[11] A further extension of these ideas may be seen in the

[1] F. B. Jevons, *Introd. to the Hist. of Religion*[2], London, 1902, p. 172.
[2] ii. 42, tr. G. C. Macaulay.
[3] *GB*[3], pt. v., *Spirits of the Corn and of the Wild*, London, 1912, ii. 169–172, 174 f.
[4] E. Kautzsch, in *HDB* v. 620.
[5] Cf., *e.g.*, A. Lang, *Myth, Ritual, and Religion*, new ed., London, 1899, ii. 233; W. Robertson Smith, *Religion of the Semites*[3], do. 1894, pp. 435–439; Jevons, p. 338.
[6] Cf. Jevons, p. 102 f.
[7] P. 467.
[8] *GB*[3], pt. vi., *The Scapegoat*, London, 1913, pp. 288, 290, 294 f., 296 ff., 301 f.
[9] Jevons, p. 351.
[10] H. von Schubert and W. Moeller, *Lehrbuch der Kirchengeschichte*, Tübingen, 1902, i. 742.
[11] A. O. Seyffert, *Dict. of Classical Antiquities*[9], London, 1906, p. 235; cf. Gideon's fleece (Jg 6^{36-40}); see also art. FLEECE.

outstanding institutions of marriage and burial, so closely and universally linked with religion. In the Roman marriage ceremony known as *confarreatio* the skin of the slain victim was stretched over two seats, on which the bride and bridegroom had to sit;[1] Hartland[2] refers to cohabitation upon a cow-hide in connexion with a Transylvanian gipsy tribe. In ancient Palestine burial in a sheep-skin seems to have been customary.[3]

In recent years, when the king of the Shankalla tribes (Abyssinia) died, 'he was sewn up in a green hide bag in a sitting position. . . . One tribe had a custom of sewing chance strangers up in green hides and leaving them to be killed by the contraction of the skins.'[4]

The original idea of such practices is clearly to secure a closer union with the deity represented by the skin, whether for protection or for the more efficient offering of a victim. A late survival of these primitive customs among civilized peoples may be seen in the harvest custom of slaying a goat and wearing the skin to cure pains in the back;[5] this may be paralleled with the making of the skin of the totem-animal into a medicine-bag among the Mosquito Indians.[6]

Frazer suggests that the use of images may have arisen through the habit of preserving the skin of the sacred animal.

'The skin in fact was kept as a token or memorial of the god, or rather as containing in it a part of the divine life, and it had only to be stuffed or stretched upon a frame to become a regular image of him.'[7]

An example of this may be seen in the manufacture of an image in human form from the skin of some animal by the hands of the Samoyed shaman.[8] Another interesting transitional case, which seems to support Frazer's suggestion, is seen in the practice of the pearl-fishers of the Persian Gulf:

'Each boat has a sort of figure-head, called the *kubait*, generally covered with a skin of a sheep or goat which was sacrificed when the boat was first launched.'[9]

There can be little doubt that the belief in the psychical qualities of the skin, which forms the connecting link in the religious customs exemplified, has operated in many instances less easy to detect, such as the shining of the skin of the face of Moses (Ex 34^{29}), and the general attitude to skin diseases such as leprosy, in ancient times.

LITERATURE.—See the works cited in the footnotes.

H. WHEELER ROBINSON.

SKY AND SKY-GODS.—I. Universality and antiquity.—Through endless transformations and disfigurements (mythological or functional) the sky-god is found to be at the base of all the systems of the great civilized religions of the classical Mediterranean and Oriental worlds. He occupies the same place in the great systems of Asia and in the semi-civilized religions of pre-Columban America. As we find him in all the groups of so-called non-civilized religions without exception, we may safely presume that the concept of sky-god belongs to the most ancient period in the history of religious feeling, and that it is at least as ancient as primitive naturism and animistic fetishism. Whether it is even pre-animistic in its fundamental aspect is a question which must be reserved in the meantime.

The nature, rôle, and characteristics of this

[1] Servius, *ad Æn.* iv. 374; cited by W. W. Fowler, *Social Life at Rome*, London, 1909, p. 136.
[2] *LP* i. 124, note (1).
[3] S. A. Cook, *The Religion of Ancient Palestine*, London, 1908, p. 35.
[4] Reported in *The Tribune*, 25th April, 1906.
[5] *GB*[3], pt. v., *Spirits of the Corn and of the Wild*, i. 285; the instance is from Grenoble.
[6] Jevons, p. 183.
[7] *GB*[3], pt. v., *Spirits of the Corn and of the Wild*, ii. 173.
[8] A. Bastian, *Der Mensch in der Geschichte*, Leipzig, 1860, ii. 129; cf. ii. 257.
[9] S. M. Zwemer, *Arabia: the Cradle of Islam*, Edinburgh and London, 1900, p. 101.

universal sky-god may be concealed under the most diverse forms, but he is always more or less clearly recognizable to the historian of religions and always identical in essential definition. America shows him in the mythologies of the Toltecs, the Mayas, and the Incas,[1] as well as in Brazil, in the Andes, among the Caribs, in Tierra del Fuego, and at the extreme north among the Eskimo. The shamanist groups of N. Asia and the cosmogony and dualism of the Ainus show him (Pase-Kamui) similar to the sky-god (much more distinct) of the religions of China (Ti-en) and of primitive Japanese Shintō. He is related to the ancient Pulugu of the Andamans, to the Varuna of primitive India, and, towards the west, to all the pantheons of the ancient classical East. Towards the south, Australia, Polynesia, and Melanesia sometimes present deformed characteristics, as in the myths of N. America, but comparative study soon disentangles his fundamental characteristics, which are those found long ago in Chaldæa and in the Semitic and proto-Semitic world. But nowhere does his physiognomy appear more distinctly than in Africa—whether in the pantheons of ancient Egypt or in the many savage religions of the black continent. From the great Kilima of the Bantu groups to the Negritian Mahu we recognize him as always the same under a hundred different names: Ibantzu of the Congo among the Bangala, Fidi Mukulu ('the supreme being') of the sky among the Basonga, Kalaga among the Warega, Uletit among the Kuku, Kabedya Mpungu and Vilye Mukulu among the Baholos and the Balubas, etc. Dzakuta, the 'thrower of celestial stones,' of the Yorubas is only another aspect of the same sky-god; so also Waka of the Gallas is the thunder aspect of the sky-god; and Lubari is the rain aspect of the sky-god, just like Dengdit among the Dinkas, Iankupong among the Aquapins, Ropi on the Gold Coast, Oloron in Benin, Ngangmo on the Ivory Coast, and hundreds of others (Ituri in Kilimanjaro, the Bumba of the Bushongo, the great Kongola of E. Africa, the Mutabani of the Batutsi, the Kafir Inhu-Ankulu, the M'ba of the Ababua, etc.). If we ascend to the cold regions of the Finnish races, we find him again under the names of Yumala (Lapps), Yuma (Cheremiss), Yubmel (Samoyed), Tengri (Mongol), Bonga (Tunguses), and Uklo (Esthonian).

The sky-god has reigned everywhere; his kingdom still covers the whole of the uncivilized world. No historical or proto-historical motive can be assigned as the cause, and neither the migrations of races nor the diffusion of myths and folk-lore affords the slightest justification of this fact. The universality of the sky-god and the uniformity of his essential characteristics[2] are the logical consequence of the constant uniformity of the primitive systems of cosmogony. The sky-god is connected with the most ancient ideas on the composition of the world and its forces (not the universe, which is too vast for the mind of the savage, but the corner of earth which is for him the whole world). Now, everywhere we find the sky conceived in the same way—as a huge liquid mass, supported above the earth by a solid transparent substance, below which are the air, the winds, and then the terrestrial plane. Frequently this liquid mass is thought to surround the solid earth also and to form another liquid abyss below it. It is not within the scope of this article to enumerate the secondary varieties of this general structure, such as 'upper and lower abysses, vaulted skies, with superimposed compartments, divided into quarters,' etc. But, in order to understand the subject, we must emphasize the constant bond that materially united the waters of the sky either to the sea or to the fabled sources of the great rivers; so that finally all water, as well as the liquid masses which fall from the clouds, is a product of the celestial plane. The function of rain-god and water-god (sea or river) and of so many sky-gods is thus explained. The essential rôle of water in the general life of nature justifies the attributing to the sky-god of all the great natural phenomena. The power and the remarkable characteristics of the various meteorological phenomena of which the sky is the theatre are a secondary, though not less efficient, cause of the pre-eminent part assigned to it by all primitive religions.

[1] See below, § 6. [2] See below, § 5.

There is such close resemblance between the sky-god and the vital manifestations of the sky that, according to the various peoples, we find the same linguistic root meaning simultaneously the material sky, the rain, the clouds, and the sky-god (or meteorological phenomena and the sky-god), or, again, the storm, the thunder, and the sky-god (cf. Jupiter Pluvius and Ζεὺς Κεραυνός in classical mythology).

Alongside of the single sky-god we find in several systems two or more gods—*e.g.*, a god of the upper sky and a god of the lower sky (*i.e.* on the terrestrial plane); or four (or more) sky-gods in charge of quarters or geometrical divisions of celestial space; or several sky-gods, each having one of the superimposed skies as his kingdom. The study of these different systems shows that they are not primitive. Some are the product of astrological speculations or very refined astral myths; others are the result of historical circumstances having agglomerated into a single political civilization religious groups which were at one time distinct (*e.g.*, Chaldæa, Egypt, Mexico). In such cases syncretism tends to amalgamate these gods into a single being (*e.g.*, Hathor-Maut-Nut-Neith-Isis for Egypt); or theology attributes distinct characteristics and functions to each of them. Thus, among the Aztecs the sky-god Tezcatlipoca, Tlaloc, the Quetzalcoatl of Cholotlan, and the Huitzilopochtli (blue sky) of the Temochcas were originally single sky-gods, peculiar to the peoples subdued by and incorporated in the empire of the conquerors.

2. Nature and personality.—If the importance and antiquity of the concept of the sky-god are explained by the importance of the material sky, is the conception of sky-god itself explained by an exclusive application of the processes of pure and simple animism or by the usual mechanism of naturism? Neither animism nor naturism entirely explains the particular nature of the sky-god. Animism may bestow a personality on the most varied natural phenomena or on any inanimate object in nature, from hunger, plague, or a mountain-peak to a spring, a water-spout, a cyclone, or an artificially manufactured object. The sky is something more than simple matter personified.[1] Naturism in itself would only partly explain the nature of the sky-god. It has long been observed that the personal beings emanating from naturism have often a special aspect quite distinct and different from the objects or phenomena of which they are the personifications (*e.g.*, the waters, winds, sun, etc.). Personification, in its fundamental *processus*, starts from the idea that under the appearance and within or behind the material exterior there exists a being or, rather, a personal force (of course it cannot yet be conceived as immaterial), closely bound to the substance of which it is the energy and the life, unable to exist without this substance, but distinct from it and, if necessary, separable from it—at least momentarily. The sky-god is therefore radically different from the substance which forms the material sky. He lives in it; he lives by it; he is mingled with it; the physical sky is not merely his habitat—it is his very substance; but the personification of a substance is distinct and separable from the substance which it animates; it is superior to it, and yet the substance is indispensable to its existence, for without it it would return to the vortex of the impersonal forces of chaos. Does this imply that

[1] See art. PERSONIFICATION (Introductory and Primitive).

primitive man imagines a time when, as the sky was not yet in existence, the sky-god could not exist? This vital question cannot be definitely answered in the present state of ethnological information. Numerous myths of savage and semi-civilized races seem to show a sky-god existing even in primordial matter and releasing the sky by his effort. But are those myths primitive? Can primitive reasoning reach the problem of the origin of the sky? Provisionally and with great reserve, we may suggest the following solution: in the formless mass of impersonal forces there spontaneously appeared forces endowed with personal consciousness; the most efficient of these released the liquid mass from the universal chaos and formed the material sky, which has ever since been its vital substance and its special property. Such an outline, however, must be subject to constant revision, for no savage tribe has formulated the theory in explicit abstract terms; and it requires for basis the exposition of a great mass of myths, folk-lore, theogony, cosmology, and even traditional ceremonial.

3. **Rôle and functions.**—It is much easier to draw up an inventory of the functions and attributes of the sky-god. The essential characteristics are constant throughout, and this identity, both in characteristics and in evolution, is one of the points most firmly established by the comparative method in the study of religions.

The data of primitive man's actual experience and the exercise of rational (or pseudo-rational) search for its causes logically led to the series of functional attributes of the sky-god. The physical phenomena of the sky and their ascription to the personality living in the material sky were always and everywhere the starting-point, the only variations resulting from local geography and climatology.

Rain and its effects on the terrestrial surface are naturally in the first rank. As a logical result, the rôle of giving the rain, and with it the storm, thunder, lightning, and their consequences, led men to conclude that the sky-god was the author of a certain number of manifestations of life and death. Several mythologies, civilized and savage, ascribe the ownership of life (regarded as breath or as a force) to the sky-god. Sometimes they even reach the stage of regarding him as the source of every vital principle, although frequently also he shares this ownership with the earth-god. The question of death is more obscure. Primitive man does not imagine *one* death; to him there are as many kinds of death as there are material manifestations of the destruction of living things. We may say, briefly, that death as a rule is not the work of the sky-god. It is an impersonal force, superior to him, like fate; and he often seems even to oppose it. As an almost absolute rule, only death by lightning is his direct action.[1] Beyond this, the rôle of the sky-god in ordinary life approximates to the type of 'the otiose supreme being.' As a matter of fact, to his activity as first cause is ascribed all that is inexplicable, beyond the capacity of such-and-such a special spirit, all that is abnormal or specially impressive. But in practice the constant search of the human spirit for the explanation of the unknown and the infinite always tends gradually to strip the sky-god of his prerogatives or special qualities in favour of more definite and more accessible beings of secondary rank. A universal result of this is the paucity of definite worship and the almost complete absence of liturgy, sacrifices, and sacerdotal organizations connected with him, because the religious systems which have reached this stage of organization address themselves to deities already more specialized in definite functions.

Nevertheless, by the contrary phenomenon, which, however, is very logical in its consequences, the same progressive human reflexion results in attributing more and more the origin of the sensible world (or rather the organization of animate matter) to the old sky-god. By this means the conception of the creator sky-god was reached, who, once his task is finished, seems to lose interest in it and leave to other beings the duty of governing and controlling the struggling mass of living beings and the whole world of nature.

The word 'create,' of course, must here be understood in a simple and unphilosophical sense. The very idea of this restricted 'creation,' understood in the sense of modelling, making, and vivifying matter, is not a primitive speculation. It developed slowly, by the gradual addition to the original stock of the sky-god's powers of a series of new acts as reasoning and the growing search for the principle of causality established new connexions and made new deductions therefrom. The creation of the sky-god never appears as complete or absolute. He is the oldest demiurge, but he is neither anterior to nor the author of all life.

The nucleus around which has gradually accumulated the mass of facts which combine to constitute a creation seems, in the majority of cosmogonies, to be the double operation of (1) separating the luminous mass from the dark mass, light and darkness being henceforth distinct and opposed, and (2) releasing the solid elements from the liquid mass—these two operations being, in a sense, quite naturally suggested by the material appearance of the sky and the successive luminous phenomena observed by man in it, and by the universal belief in the liquid consistency of the sky resting on the transparent but solid vault of the firmament. This first series of acts of creation has a paramount influence afterwards on the appearance of the first dualistic systems.[1]

A list of the sky-gods regarded as the authors of the creation (quasi-complete or partial) of the universe would involve an enumeration of all known mythologies. To give an idea of them as briefly as possible we shall adopt the following classification.

(*a*) *Systems in which the sky-god is regarded as the sole agent in creation.*[2]—These systems may be conveniently divided into three chief groups. (1) Those in which the sky-god is asexual and has, simply on account of grammatical termination, a tendency to be conceived as a male principle. To this group belong the most elementary cosmogonies, in which living beings are supposed to be the direct product of some portion of the physical substance of the sky-god. The myths of savages all over the world, both at the present time and in the past (*e.g.*, Egypt), give us all varieties of the supposed processes: the beings are the product of the sweat of the god, of his tears, of his humours, of his vomit, etc. We have to come fairly high up to find systems that conceive the sky-god as creating by means of action, forming matter, and communicating to it by his material breath a portion of his vital substance.

(2) Those in which the sky-god is positively regarded as being of the male sex. In such cases the isolation of the god leads to the necessity of imagining that the 'creation' issues from his substance, either by drops of blood or, more frequently, by the effusion of the seminal fluid (*e.g.*, the Egyptian Tum and the Bumba of the Bushongo).

(3) Those, much more developed, in which living beings (in whole or in part) are derived by childbirth from the womb of the sky-deity—which presupposes the deity to be female. Sometimes this birth takes place directly for all (*e.g.*, the myths of the Upper White Nile); sometimes it takes place in two stages, the goddess giving birth to a

[1] Sometimes death by drowning is assimilated to death by celestial fire, chiefly in the systems in which the sea or the river is regarded as a dependent of the material sky.

[1] See artt. DUALISM, and below, § 5.

[2] It must be noted, of course, that 'to create' always means essentially to organize and vivify or fashion already existing substances. Creation *ex nihilo* is unknown to the intellect of primitive and semi-civilized man and even of civilized man at the stage of the ancient religions of the classical East.

certain number of agents, who, in their turn, couple and reproduce the chief classes of beings (*e.g.*, the Egyptian sky-goddess Hathor). This seems to be the most frequent type. We must mention that in every case the sky-goddess conceives of her own accord, without the help of a male principle (cf., *e.g.*, the most ancient Sumerian conception). Her animal or human form[1] has nothing to do with the question.

This initial position leads, in advanced religions, to the most subtle theological theories when the work of the sky-goddess has to be reconciled with the necessity of a vivifying principle anterior to her and fecundating her. The inextricable difficulties of the sacerdotal account of Theban Egypt, with Rā, the bull-god, as husband of his mother, borne by her and continually fecundating her, give a sufficient idea of these systems, whose outlines we find in more than twenty known religions.[2]

(*b*) *Systems in which the sky-god is associated with another god in the work of creation.*—Without examining the question of simultaneity or later appearance, we find a second important series of religions, in which the sky-god, in order to accomplish his work as demiurge, has associated his activity with that of another being, usually the earth-deity. We may distinguish two chief groups.

(1) The first (and the most numerous) includes cases in which the sky is a god and the earth a goddess. The world is born from their union. This is the type of the Polynesian myths of Rangi and Pépé, that of Tangaroa, and that of the Greek Gaia and Ouranos.

(2) In the second group the sky is regarded as the matrix in which beings are formed, and the earth is the fecundating principle—a sky-goddess and an earth-god (*e.g.*, Seb and Nut of the Egyptian myth, etc.).

A great number of secondary types suggest the demiurge sharing his task with several companions. He himself is sometimes relegated to the very beginning of the work in the most vague rôle (*e.g.*, in N. American cosmologies, in which the elaboration of the world seems to belong specially to certain animals, often of low species; these systems require careful study and often appear on analysis to be composite and deformed products of earlier mythologies).

We must pass over the cosmogonies in which the sky-god creates or organizes the world without producing it directly from his substance, fashioning its various substances by means of his word alone, which seizes and models the different formless energies vibrating and trembling in the universe (*e.g.*, creation by the words of the Egyptian Thōth). Those belong to a period when the sky-god no longer possesses his specially celestial characteristics and is rather a supreme god.

In order to understand the sky-god, we must notice a result of the constant confusion of the primordial celestial water with the water of the sea. In a great number of religious systems, both savage and advanced, the sky-god is confused with the sea-god, whether he takes up his abode in the sky or the sea indifferently, or whether he unites in his person sky-myths and sea-myths. This phenomenon is very marked, *e.g.*, in the Indian mythology of Varuṇa and, among savage races, in the aquatic sky-god of the Ainus (*q.v.*) and in the dogfish-god of the Benin; it is conjectured also in the Chaldæan Oannes and in the various fish-deities of the E. Mediterranean (*e.g.*, Aphrodite, mother of the world). The sea is in every case regarded as bound to the celestial mass. The latter is separated from it only above the terrestrial plane by the vault of the firmament (the 'firmament' of Genesis). The same reasoning leads uncivilized man in the interior of the continents to believe that certain large expanses of water, lakes and rivers, are derived from the celestial water (*e.g.*, the Egyptian Nile, the Congo, the Welle, the Zambesi). The sky-god, the creator of the world, often therefore dwells in the bed of their waters. In the extreme west of Africa we find the sky-god living in the lagoons on the coast, and the Ibanza of the Bangala living at one and the same time in the sky and in the depths of the river; so also Kilima in the Welle of the Monbuttu or the Ababua, etc. Such were the crocodile Sebek of ancient Egypt and the crocodile of the Shilluks or Dinkas of the present-day White Nile.

The confusion of the sky-god with the chthonian gods, which is rarer, is more difficult to explain and would require too long treatment. It is traceable in New Zealand and Polynesian myths, but its mechanism appears more clearly in Africa—*e.g.*, Kalaga of the Warega and the sky-god (at the same time the volcano-god) of the Ituri, according to the (distorted) myth of the Imandwa secret society. To put it briefly, the bond between the celestial world and the chthonian world is due to water (deep sources), fire (volcanoes), and celestial metal (iron).

4. Specific aspect and representations. — (*a*) *Natural phenomena.*—The most remarkable visible manifestations of the activity or power of the sky-god seem everywhere to have been chosen for the material expression of the god (we must say 'material expression' and not 'image'). Exceptional manifestations have naturally been in the first rank. As a matter of fact, we find lightning (all known religions), thunder (*passim*), the rainbow (*e.g.*, the Ababua), the *aurora borealis* (Eskimo), St. Elmo's fire (classical Mediterranean), the zodiacal light (eastern Egyptian delta), etc. These natural manifestations have gradually tended to become 'aspects' of the sky-god, and are the starting-point of fetishistic representations, in which the object, sometimes natural, sometimes of human manufacture, is not yet regarded as the image of the god, but as his habitat, or rather as a material covering sympathetically bound to the essential force of the 'spirit.' Such objects naturally are of infinite variety, according to the human group and the geographical position. In general, we may say that in the choice of fetishes the reasoning has been the same all the world over: the principle of material expression, *e.g.*, may be the representation of the effect to express the cause (or *vice versa*), or perhaps the part for the whole (or *vice versa*), either in time or in space. It is a curious fact that fetishistic expression has almost everywhere obeyed the same laws which separated the magic ideogram from simple pictography and thus created all over the world the first written characters based on magical value.

The most important class of natural phenomena is found in the supposed effects of the material action of the sky-god. Thus the sacred fire, the emblem of this god, is supposed to be lighted by him; detached rocks and sharp mountain-peaks are supposed to be caused by the thunder in direct relation with the force of the sky-god; and translucent stones, rock crystals, and precious stones are regarded as fragments of the celestial vault (the same principle later connected gold and silver with the solar and lunar gods). Hence also—and this throughout the whole world—the cult of the sky-god as manifest in meteorites, 'thunder-stones,' fragments of shooting-stars, 'eagle-stones,' in the meteorite fire supposed to be detached from the sky, and, by extension, in stones supposed to have fallen from the sky, standing-stones, etc. (*e.g.*, menhirs). Belief in the presence of celestial fire (and consequently of the sky-god) in flint, combined with the notions about aerolites or meteorites, gives rise later to the world-wide cult of palæolithic or neolithic tools, weapons, and instruments which are worshipped as having fallen from the sky and which become emblems of the sky-god. Two equally interesting developments are the stones on mountain-summits becoming the first altars for sacrifice to the sky-god and the worship of sacred trees regarded as celestial trees.

(*b*) *Idolatrous representations.*—(*a*) *Aniconic.*—We now pass to the representations of the sky-god by modelled or drawn imitations of his activity—*e.g.*, mimetic signs meant to reproduce the zigzags of the lightning, the contours of the sky, the triangular projection of the zodiacal light, etc. In

[1] See below, § 4.

[2] Some Polynesian mythologies avoid the problem by imagining that the single deity tears from his sides the first matter necessary for making beings.

the same connexion we find strings with curls, knots, twists, etc., and gradually there develop the thousand different forms of aniconic representations of the sky-god by magical symbolism. The fetishes formed by combinations of substances connected with celestial forces vary infinitely. Among representations of a higher character we may cite the axe, the emblem of the sky-god (*e.g.*, Minoan Crete), and the mirror, image of the sky-goddess (Japan).

(β) *Iconic.*—The representation of the sky-god tends in this way gradually to become the reproduction of characteristics regarded as those of the material spirit (if we may be allowed to use such an expression). But iconic representation began, in every place where it can be verified, by a process of pictographic expression (the term 'symbolic' is beyond the conception of primitive man) of his power or his nature, embodied in an animal figure. We cannot trace here the evolution of the zoolatrical cults. But, as far as the sky-god is concerned, we may state that his zoomorphic representation has always been the product of conventional speculation and not of a crude idea that he bore the special form of such-and-such an animal. We may suggest, with great reserve, the possibility that this god may have been invested momentarily and under certain circumstances with the aspect of the animal. But this is never his absolute and permanent material form.

It is impossible to give the animal representations of the sky-god *in extenso* here. The chief groups may be conveniently classified according to the supposed sex of the world-creator sky-god.[1] We find (i.) the great inhabitants of the celestial heights—*e.g.*, the vulture (conceived in Egypt as exclusively female and bearing without the help of a male), the female eagle (classical Mediterranean), the condor (S. America), etc.; (ii.) the females of domestic animals, and in the first place, universally adored, the celestial cow; (iii.) in the domain of sea, lake, or river (*i.e.* the aquatic region) the female shark or crocodile, the female serpent, and especially the fish. All these representations ended in hybrid forms, the best-known types of which, in the advanced religions of the classical world, are the Chaldæan Oannes, half-man and half-fish, and the Asiatic Aphrodite, Derceto, etc.

The sky-god regarded as of the male sex has given rise to identical series, also too long to enumerate. Among the most wide-spread we may mention the hawk or eagle (Egypt, classical Greece and Italy, Asia Minor, Central America, etc.), and the goat or ram (Egypt, Sudan, N. India, Dahomey, etc.). The constant association of the eagle or the ram with thunder, lightning, etc., is one of the religious phenomena most generally found in iconography.

In the composite forms the symbolic animal form remains necessary as the plastic means of expressing the rôle and power of the sky-god, but it is combined with the human aspect. The well-known series of the classical East (Egypt, Chaldæa, Assyria, Asia Minor, Greece) recur among savage and semi-civilized races all over the world. According to the usual process, all merge in two series of representations: (*a*) those in which the sky-god is gradually confused with the solar, lunar, and astral forms;[2] (*b*) the anthropomorphic pure and simple, which corresponds to an already high type of religious civilization. The sky-god, purely male or female in form, is, however, rare, precisely because one of the effects of this development of religious civilization is to relegate him to second or third rank in the divine hierarchy.[3]

5. Characteristics.—The comparative study of savage races proves that the characteristics of the sky-god (as they appear to-day among semi-civilized or as they crop up sporadically in advanced religions) are everywhere identical.

Naturally the question whether he is uncreated or self-created is beyond the scope of savage thought. It is the same with the conception of eternity. 'Indefinitely renewable duration' seems the extreme limit of the primitive mind. Even Egypt, saying of Atum Kheperā 'I am yesterday; I am to-morrow,' did not reach the theoretical definition of eternity.

Nor by definition is the sky-god anterior to any other god, spirit, or demon. The creation, partial or complete, of the material universe does not in any way imply that of the forces embodied in the names of gods, spirits, genii, demons, etc. He is neither omnipotent nor omniscient, but simply stronger or cleverer in certain special spheres. Certain gods or spirits may fight against him, and often successfully. His victory in the event of a struggle does not preclude future defeat. The most remarkable characteristic of such a sky-god is that, in all the cases that have been examined, he is manifestly weaker than a certain mysterious, impersonal, diffuse force, which among primitive races often has a name analogous to what we mean by destiny.[1]

In principle the sky-god has no moral characteristics; by definition he is indifferent. Nevertheless his constant association with the rain and the light has the universal result of giving him a beneficent aspect. At first disinterested and inaccessible or deaf to all prayer, he sometimes becomes susceptible of intervention in human affairs, and man strives to develop and define this intervention. Dualism, organizing the strife of darkness and light, of drought (or death) and fertilizing water (or life), gives him a much more definite character in more advanced religions. Nevertheless, as a general rule, the sky-god takes no interest in the material world produced by his activity and never controls the progress of this earth's various elements or the struggles of its inhabitants. Again, the development of dualism frequently results in giving him a gradually more precise activity. At this stage, however, in the progress of knowledge of the forces of the world and the principles of causality the sky-god tends to be robbed of his activity or to be divided up into new beings.

6. Evolution. — If we carefully consider the nature and character of the primitive sky-god, we find that, on the whole, he is the incarnation of the sum of primitive man's ignorance and inexperience, combined with his knowledge that the other material beings (whether they are called genii, gods, spirits, or any other name) are not powerful enough to govern the world, to have formed it, or to direct its great forces (celestial, meteorological, and hydrological phenomena, death, etc.).

The study of magic and of primitive rites leads to more definite knowledge of the forces retained by the sky-god and of the rudiments of cosmogonies explaining the mechanism of creation, and gives everywhere identical results: (*a*) the acts of the sky-god become separate personalities and gradually dismember his personality, which was originally formed of vague elements; the clearest example occurs in the series of thunder-gods taking the place of the sky-god in the rôle of 'father of beings' (*e.g.*, the Ζεὺς Κεραυνός of Hellenic myths, the Mahu of Dahomey, etc.); (*b*) the beings produced by the celestial energy—sun, moon, stars—tend to take the place and the rôle of light (conceived originally as something quite independent of them, and the direct product of the sky-god) and relegate to the background the beneficent rôle of the sky; (*c*) on the terrestrial plane the activities of various spirits and of their representations (fetishistic or iconic) take a more and more conspicuous part in the world's struggles. Their actions and the relations of cause and effect belong to the domains of water, air, earth, and under-earth rather than to the sky. But by these activities they grow in importance; their cults and magic tend to be established; organized polytheisms become possible, and they capture a portion of the vague attributes belonging as yet to the old sky-god. (Two good examples may be given: (1) among primitive races the system of

[1] See § 3 (*a*) (3), above. [2] Cf. below, § 6.
[3] Cf. below, § 6.

[1] The terms *mana* and *orenda*, largely employed by ethnological sociology, cover only a part of this conception.

the Bushongo in Africa, (2) in advanced religions the system of the Toltecs.)

The result of these three elements is that, at different rates according to the different peoples and according to the proportion in which the elements are found, there is a constant tendency to the suppression and gradual disappearance of what constituted the very distinct physiognomy of the primitive sky-god. The most striking proof of this weakening or gradual dispossession is seen in the cosmogonic and creator rôle. The progress of the religious system almost always results in substituting for creation by the sky-god the organization of the world by the sun-god, the moon-god, or one of the stellar gods. Sometimes in fact the sun-god is supreme creator. Ancient Egypt presents a very complete schema of this type of evolution. It tends to substitute Rā (the sun) for the sky-gods (such as Atum, Hor, Nut, Hathor, Anhur, Sebek, etc.); but it does not completely realize this evolution, and consigns to the more or less vague beginning the primitive activity of the sky-god. The general process in the various religious systems is from the rôle of light, the direct emanation of the sky-god, to that of the stellar groups, substituted for the initial force of this god, then to that of the separate stars, and finally to the sun, the last arrival in the series of author-gods of the world and of life.[1]

The same evolution, with the same effects, recurs when there appears, with dualism, the first representation of a moral or quasi-moral world. The sky-god, stripped of his definite beneficent activities, is superseded in the struggle against evil by the sun or by an anthropomorphic aspect of himself (usually his son—*e.g.*, the Osirian myth). The details of this evolution would require a whole volume. One of the most remarkable examples of it is the myth of Heitsi-Eibib of the Khoi-Khoin, of whom we have accounts by ethnologists as early as the year 1655. We find in him all the characteristics of the primordial sky-god rôle of rain-god, aniconic worship of rude stones, fetishism of a lithic kind, etc. Then he becomes associated with the dawn; and mythology invents a terrestrial incarnation for him. Similarly we can follow the confusion of the sky-god with the lunar cults. We find, as in the case of the Osirian myth, a later confusion with the parallel myth of Tsuni-Goab. Just as we see the dualist myth developing in Egypt under the double form Rā-Āpêpi and Horus-Set, so we see the sky-god Heitsi-Eibib struggling with Gaunab, who has become the principle of darkness and evil, while Heitsi-Eibib becomes the light which dies each day and is reborn in the east. He finally incarnates the good principles struggling against evil. This parallelism with ancient Egypt proves decisively the general direction which the evolution of the concept of the sky-god is bound to take in similar cases all over the world.

On the other hand, where circumstances have hindered this higher transformation, the rôle of the sky-god has gradually disappeared. His primordial creative activity has become as vague and fluid as the pale distant figures of Saturn, Ouranos, or Chronos in classical mythology.

In a word, after having united in himself the attributes of a supreme being, of an elementary kind, the sky-god had two chief fates—either, transformed and brought nearer to us under other names, he became the main resort of the divine activity of this world or he retained his primitive physiognomy, and his importance and his worship have been in inverse proportion to the progress of man's conceptions of the sensible world.

[1] Cf., *e.g.*, the Peruvian system and the evolution of the Chaldæan system.

LITERATURE.—There is no monograph on the subject. Observations of a general character in ancient ethnological and anthropological literature should be examined—*e.g.*, A. Bastian, *Beiträge zur vergleichenden Psychologie*, Berlin, 1868; E. B. Tylor, *PC*[4], 2 vols., London, 1903; and A. Lang, *Myth, Ritual, and Religion*, 2 vols., do. 1887. For details the reader should consult the articles in the present Encyclopædia under the names of the different nations and races.

GEORGE FOUCART.

SLANDER.—Slander has been defined as 'the utterance or dissemination of false statements or reports concerning a person, or malicious misrepresentation of his actions, in order to defame or injure him,'[1] the term being used to denote not only the act itself, but also the statement circulated, and even the consequential discredit suffered. The last meaning is, however, now commonly conveyed by the word 'scandal,' of which 'slander' is etymologically[2] only a variant form, though in modern usage 'the word [scandal] differs from the etymologically identical "slander" in not implying the falsity of the imputations made.'[3] With slander as a technical term in law we are not concerned; we shall consider only its ethical use and import.

Instances of the word are found in English books as early as A.D. 1270. In the *Lay Folks Catechism* (1375) we read of 'Sklandre for to fordo a mannes gode fame,' and in Chaucer's *House of Fame* of 'His other clarioun | That hight sklaundre in every toun.' The term has substantially the same meaning in Shakespeare, *Much Ado*, II. i 143: 'His gift is in devising impossible slanders'; the corresponding verb occurs in *The Two Gentlemen of Verona*, III. ii. 31: 'The best way is to slander Valentine | With falsehood, cowardice, and poor descent'; while of the derived adjective a forcible example is found in Milton, *Par. Lost*, xii. 536: 'Truth shall retire | Bestuck with slanderous darts.' Jeremy Taylor (1613–67), who in *The Great Exemplar* speaks of 'killing a man's reputation by calumnies or slander or open reviling,' elsewhere (*Serm.* xxii.–xxiv.) defines slander, properly so called, as 'the inventing evil things, falsely imputing crimes to our neighbour.' This he co-ordinates, as one form (*d*) of calumny, with (*a*) tale-bearing, (*b*) detraction proper, (*c*) railing or reviling, and (*e*) cursing; calumny, or slanderous and detracting speech in general, being in his view one species (ii.), co-ordinate with (i.) idle speech, and (iii.) flattery, of that 'corrupt communication' which, as reprobated by St. Paul (Eph 4[29]), forms the text of his trilogy of sermons 'On the Good and Evil Tongue.'

These quotations will suffice to indicate how slander, as understood by classical English authors, stands related to, and how far it can be distinguished in meaning from, such terms as 'calumny,' 'detraction,' and 'evil-speaking.' While no two of these terms are exactly synonymous, it is hardly possible to mark off their several denotations by any fast line. They are to a large extent interchangeable, especially 'calumny' and 'slander,' which, as distinguished from 'evil-speaking' and 'detraction,' imply falsehood in addition to more or less of either positive malevolence or reckless indifference to the injurious effect of defamatory words. Even to slander and calumny it is perhaps not essential that the allegations made should be definitely known by the speaker or writer to be false. A man is none the less a slanderer if he utters and disseminates regarding his neighbour injurious matter which he has no reason whatever, or no approximately sufficient reason, for believing to be true. If, on the other hand, it is true, he is not a slanderer, though the utterance, if superfluous and unprovoked, may still be fitly accounted 'evil-speaking,' and reprehensible as such. And it nearly always is superfluous, if it is not likely to do any positive good, or if no third party would be wronged or discredited by silence. The latter condition is, indeed, apt to be overlooked; and denunciation of indefensible conduct is often improperly censured as evil-speaking, when in reality reticence or disbelief regarding it would be grossly unfair to some wholly innocent, and perhaps actively beneficent, and deeply injured, person.

[1] *OED*, *s.v.*
[2] Skeat, *Etymol. Dict.*[4], Oxford, 1910, *s.v.*, and *OED*.
[3] *OED*, *s.v.* 'Scandal.'

Thus, on the whole, disclosure of ascertained truth is morally safer than a timid reticence, though often legally perilous. While, however, the actual truth of a statement is (on the whole and subject to important exceptions) a good reason morally for not withholding it on occasion, a mere belief on the part of the speaker that it is true is, if it be in fact untrue, a very poor defence. There is indeed a measure of malevolence, if not of dishonesty, in all readiness lightly to believe what is evil concerning one's neighbour, though there is scarcely less in perversely disbelieving palpable evidence of grievous wrong inflicted upon an inoffensive, or clearly well-intentioned, neighbour by another who is manifestly unscrupulous. In practice the false belief and the perverse disbelief are apt to go together. The same person, *i.e.*, who readily slanders a good man will often be stolidly blind to the atrocious deeds of the evil-minded. It is of the essence of slander to call good evil; and this normally finds its complement in calling evil good.

The act, or habit of thought and speech, denoted in English by 'slander' was in the languages and literatures of Græco-Roman antiquity, which were so large a factor in the constitution of European morals, represented most completely by the Greek word διαβολή. This word, in the sense of false charge or slanderous imputation, was used by the historians Herodotus and Thucydides, by the poet Euripides, by Isocrates and other orators, and somewhat scantily by the philosophers Plato,[1] Aristotle,[2] and Cleanthes the Stoic. The corresponding verb-form had a similar range. In no instance would the term seem to be technical. For purposes of ethical study the most interesting occurrences of the word are the few cited from the philosophers, and more particularly that from Cleanthes, who wrote:

> 'There is nothing, that ever was, more mischievous than slander (κακουργότερον οὐδὲν διαβολῆς ἐστί πω); secretly deceiving the man whose ear it has won, it works up odium against the guiltless.'[3]

A more trenchant epitome of the vice could hardly be given. Three centuries later Plutarch[4] writes of the fellow-countrymen of an exiled, but prosperous, statesman as 'from envy' (διὰ τὸ φθονεῖν) readily accepting the various 'slanders' (διαβολάς) circulated concerning him, thus incidentally marking what has been perhaps the most frequent, though by no means the universal, motive of calumnious allegation.

Meanwhile the term διαβολή had been employed by Greek translators of the Hebrew Scriptures and other Hellenistic writers to represent a type of speech and intention which, though not covered by any one Hebrew name, is recognized in the OT as eminently sinful, and which might be described as meditated and systematic violation of the spirit of the Ninth Commandment. The noun occurs in Nu 14^{37} (Aq.), Ps 31^{13} (Sym.), where Eng. AV gives 'slander' (PBV 'blasphemy,' RV 'defaming'), 2 Mac 14^{27}, and six times in Sir (19^{15} 26^{5} 28^{9} 38^{17} $51^{2.6}$), the verb (διαβάλλειν) in Dn 3^{8} 6^{24}. The noun, which is thus fairly frequent in the Greek OT and in the English versions is often (Sir 19^{15} 26^{5} 51^{6}), though not uniformly, rendered 'slander,' is not found in the NT. The corresponding adjective (διάβολος) is, however, used thrice in the Pastoral Epistles (1 Ti 3^{11}, 2 Ti 3^{3}, Tit 2^{3}), where RV, following the precedent of Wyclif in the last passage, rightly restores 'slanderers' for the less exact 'false accusers' of AV and most previous versions, while the same word, with the article prefixed, is of frequent occurrence and appears in the English versions as 'the devil.' It is probable that we may safely connect with this fact the exceptionally stern warning of Mt 5^{22}, and the still more tremendous language (Mk 3^{29}=Mt 12^{31}=Lk 12^{10}) touching 'blasphemy of the Holy Spirit'—an extreme form of wickedness, which, it would appear, consists in a set and wilful determination to call good evil, in despite of evidence that to any heart not utterly depraved from honesty is overwhelming. For 'blasphemy' (βλασφημία), though not identical with, is nearly akin to, 'slander.' Actually it is the more general term, signifying generically 'evil-speaking.' It becomes theological blasphemy when it has as its object God or the manifestations of His will and beneficence. And this occurs whenever works of love and mercy, due to the agency of His Holy Spirit, are perversely and malignantly attributed to the agency of the powers of evil. If, then, slander be regarded as evil-speaking envenomed by falsehood, the worst conceivable slanderer will be a personality uniting consummate ability in falsehood with unlimited readiness to speak evil of the Holy Spirit of God. While it does not fall within the scope of this article to discuss the personality of the devil, it is relevant to note that 'the devil' of the NT is before all things a 'slanderer,' an intensely malevolent perverter of truth and fabricator of untruth.

It follows that in any system of ethics claiming to be distinctively Christian no form of evil practice can be thought graver or more deadly than that of habitually traducing and slandering the guiltless and the beneficent. Nevertheless it found no place among the 'seven deadly sins' of mediæval theology, and so apparently escaped being denounced either by the scholastic doctors of Latin Christendom or even by Dante. All the more is it to the credit of English moral insight that in the last of Chaucer's *Canterbury Tales* 'the Parson' brings in 'backbiting or detraction' as a specific sin bred by the recognized 'deadly sin' of envy, and sets forth tersely and with perspicuity the several shapes that it may assume. But, notwithstanding the efforts of individual moralists, it has at no time either officially or in popular estimation ranked, as it should, with breaches of the sixth, seventh, and eighth Commandments as sin of the first magnitude. Theory apart, experience of life, justly interpreted, might warn us that, as civilization becomes more complex and more highly equipped, the slanderer's capacity for evil becomes more terrible. It may be true that modern institutions have improved the means of combating and disproving calumny. But the rapid multiplication of opportunities for censorious and derogatory comment outside the peril of the law has more than countervailed that advantage. And there has certainly in the last 200 years been no amelioration of the virulence either of envy or of other passions prompting to calumny. On the contrary, in the 18th cent. we find Butler, a singularly cautious observer, in his sermon 'Upon the Government of the Tongue,'[1] holding that a main source of much 'evil-speaking' was nothing more than 'unrestrained volubility and wantonness of speech,' which, however, 'is often of as bad effect upon the good name of others, as deep envy or malice.' And a century later Thomas Brown († 1820) taught that 'defamation' and slanderous talk arise less often from envy and malice than from 'mere flippancy' and 'the necessity of filling up with amusement of some sort a conversation that' else 'would flag.'[2] This was probably true of his own, as of Butler's, age—an age of 'conversation.' But in the present age of relentless competition and equally relentless pleasure-seeking slander has once again become, as of old, a serious

[1] *Apol.* 19 A, 20 D, E.
[2] *Rhet.* i. 1. 4, ii. 4. 30, iii. 15. 1.
[3] Frag. 586 (von Arnim).
[4] *Them.* 4.

[1] *Serm.* iv.
[2] *Lectures on the Philosophy of the Human Mind*[15], p. 567.

business, now often elaborately organized, needing therefore to be vigilantly detected and refuted, alike in public and in private life, by all lovers of truth and justice. From the individual heart the vice, or vicious propensity, whether originating in envy or, as not seldom, in contempt, or in the mere pleasure of saying pungent things, calculated to attract attention or amuse, can be extirpated only by the counteracting presence and prevalence of a love which honours one's neighbour as oneself, and, in the words of St. Paul, 'rejoiceth not in unrighteousness, but rejoiceth with the truth' (1 Co 13[6]).

LITERATURE.—In addition to authorities quoted in the art. see Ja 3[2-8]; Jeremy Taylor, *Course of Sermons*, London, 1650, nos. xxii.-xxiv.; J. Butler, *Fifteen Sermons upon Human Nature*, do. 1726, no. iv.; T. Brown, *Lectures on the Philosophy of the Human Mind*[15], Edinburgh, 1845, lect. 84, pp. 566-570; J. Martineau, *Types of Ethical Theory*[2], Oxford, 1886, vol. ii. bk. i. ch. 5, § 2, pp. 172-174.

J. M. VAIZEY HOPE.

SLAVS.—I. *DEFINITION OF THE TERM.*—The term Slav, Slavic, Slavonic, does not correspond to the term German, which denotes a group of people united by cultural and national ties, but to the term Germanic or Teutonic, which is applied to all people speaking Germanic tongues, irrespective of nationality or culture. Comparative study of the Slavic peoples and their neighbours shows that neither in physical type nor in culture and religion have the Slavs, either in modern days or in the earliest times, formed a unit or shown a greater likeness than that which is manifested by any neighbours living under the same geographical and historical conditions.

The name Slav is derived by Western writers from *sclavi*, 'slave.' This derivation, however, does not hold good in Slavic languages, and the Slavic name for Slav, *slavianin* (Russian) or *slowianin* (Polish), is more obviously derived from *slowo*—a word meaning all people who use the same words.[1] Still another derivation is suggested from *slawa*, 'glory.' The first historical mention of the Slavs does not call them Sclavi, but Vinithi, Veneti, Venethæ; the south-eastern Slavs were known as Antæ, Antes; not till the 6th cent. A.D. do we meet the name Sclavini. It is difficult to decide whether the Romans imposed the name Sclavini on the Slavs or whether the Slavic name coincided with the Roman, in sound if not in meaning. There are no proofs that the Slavs were ever subjected to the slave-trade to the extent that the Greeks or the people of Asia Minor were, and the fact that, as T. Peisker[2] explains, some Slavic tribes were ruled by the Scandinavian vikings (Slavicized into *vitez, vitiaz*) or Turkic leaders (*zupan*) does not necessarily imply that they were slaves to their kings, any more than any other subjects were slaves of their king at the beginning of European history.

II. *HISTORY.*—Historical mention of the Slavs, as of other European nations outside the Mediterranean area, is not found much before the Christian era, but the archæological evidence reaches much farther back. Still, it is very doubtful whether we have remnants of any Neolithic culture among the Slavs, or much evidence even of the Hallstatt period. We find the first historical reference to the Slavs in the *Naturalis Historia* of Pliny the Elder (1st cent. A.D.), who mentions the Venedæ or Venedi, who were undoubtedly Slavs; but it must be remembered that there are also theories connecting the Scythians with the Slavs, as well as the Neuri, Budini, and Sauromatæ of Herodotus, which, if accepted, will take the historical Slavs back to the 5th cent. B.C. But what we know about these races will not stand scrutiny by the searchlight of modern ethnological study, so we shall count the whole period before Pliny as forming part of the archæological era. In this way the history of the Slavs, or rather the history of the people speaking Slavic tongues, will be subdivided into the following periods: (1) the archæological period, to the 1st cent. A.D.; (2) the classical period, from Pliny to the 6th cent.; (3) the Byzantine period, from Procopius to the 7th cent.; (4) the period of independent Christian Slavic states, from the 7th to the 13th cent.; (5) the period of political dependency, from the Turko-Mongol invasions and the subjugation of the Eastern and Southern Slavs by the Turks to the middle of the 19th cent.; (6) the period of the realization of various Slavic-speaking peoples, from the national revivals to the present day.

For the purposes of this article we need consider only the four first periods, when the Slavs had more than mere linguistic community through their early religious beliefs and customs. In the last two periods the history of the Slavic peoples runs in separate national channels which became racially less Slavic, and politically and culturally farther apart, if we take the successive Pan-Slavist movements as springing entirely from the imperialistic propaganda of the various governments. Without going into the history of the last two periods, we shall, however, deal with the folk-lore of the Slavic people to the present day.

1. The archæological period (to the 1st cent. A.D.).—In 1837 appeared the monumental work of P. J. Šafařík on *Slavonic Antiquities*,[1] in which he gives a picture of the Slavs of the archæological period. This work marks the beginning of scientific investigation of the early history of the Slavs, as all former works on the subject were full of serious misinterpretations. It is still a subject of discussion which of the old tumuli in Central and Eastern Europe can be ascribed to the Slavs. None of the Stone Age tumuli have any peculiarly Slav characteristics, least of all the dolichocephalic skulls found in them. The so-called Slav period of these tumuli begins in the 9th century. According to Pytheas, in the beginning of the 3rd cent. B.C. Germanic tribes were already round the Baltic, so it may be assumed that the Slavic branch of the Aryan linguistic family had then already separated from the Germanic branch, and their separation from the Iranian branch of this family must have occurred even earlier, at least before the Scythian period (5th-3rd cent. B.C.). While the Slavic archæology of this period has not been sufficiently investigated to allow us to draw conclusions from it, and is bound up with the early archæology of the Aryans in general, the historical evidence of the period is only one degree better.

(*a*) *The Scythian problem.*—We find no mention of the Slavs as such in B.C. times, and can only conjecture their existence under the name of various tribes belonging to the Scythian or Sarmatian political units. Hence the early history of the Slavs is closely connected with the Scythian problem. The somewhat debatable assumption that the Scythians or Sarmatians must have left some descendants or other, and that 'there was no more obvious ancestry for the Slavs to be discerned among nations mentioned by ancient writers,'[2] is the chief ground on which the Scytho-Slavic theory is based. On the other hand, as Minns justly observes, 'this theory naturally appealed to the tendency of chroniclers to push the ancestry of their own nation back as far as possible.'[3]

Broadly speaking, the following solutions have been suggested for the Scythian problem:

(1) That all the Scyths were Turanian.—Suggested first by B. G. Niebuhr, *Kleine Schriften*, Bonn, 1828-43, i. 352 ff.; supported by K. Neumann, *Die Hellenen im Skythenlande*, Berlin, 1855; George Grote, *History of Greece*[3], London, 1851, iii. 216-243.

[1] After the great migration of the Slavs in the 7th cent., we find the name Slav in almost the same form near Novgorod (Slovyene), in N. Hungary (Slovatsu), in Pomerania (Slovinsu), and in the Balkans (Slovyenu).

[2] 'The Expansion of the Slavs' (*The Cambridge Medieval History*, Cambridge, 1911-13, vol. ii. ch. xiv.).

[1] *Slovanské Starozitnosti*, 2 vols., Prague, 1837, Germ. tr., *Slawische Alterthümer*, Leipzig, 1843-44.

[2] E. H. Minns, *Scythians and Greeks*, Cambridge, 1913, p. 98.

[3] *Ib.*; see also art. SCYTHIANS.

(2) That the Scythic nation was an artificial product evolved from the nomads of the steppes.—R. W. Macan, *Herodotus*, London, 1895, ii. 12.

(3) That all the Scyths were Iranian.—Originated by K. Zeuss, *Die Deutschen und die Nachbarstämme*, Munich, 1837; supported by A. Schiefner, 'Sprachliche Bedeuten gegen das Mongolenthum der Skythen,' *Mélanges Asiatiques*, ii. [St. Petersburg, 1856] 531 ff.; K. Müllenhoff, 'Ueber die Herkunft und Sprache der pontischen Scythen und Sarmaten,' *MBAW*, 1866, p. 549 ff., reprinted in *Deutsche Altertumskunde*, Berlin, 1870–1900, iii. 101 ff.; M. Duncker, *Hist. of Antiquity*, Eng. tr., London, 1877–82, iii. 228–246; W. Tomaschek, 'Kritik der ältesten Nachrichten über den skythischen Norden,' i. 'Ueber das arimaspische Gedicht des Aristeas,' *SWAW* (Phil. hist. Classe), cxvi. [1888] 715–780, ii. 'Die Nachrichten Herodots über den skythischen Karawanenweg nach Innerasien,' *ib.* cxvii. [1889] 1–70; A. von Gutschmid, 'Die Skythen,' in *Kleine Schriften*, Leipzig, 1889–94, iii. 421 ff. (his art. 'Scythia, Scythians' in *EBr*^{9} is an epitome of this).

(4) That the Scyths were an Aryan people who have now disappeared.—G. Rawlinson, *Hist. of Herodotus*^{2}, London, 1862, iii. 157 ff.

(5) That the Scyths were Germans.—L. Wilset, *Internat. Centralblatt für Anthropologie*, VII. [1902] vi. 353, and 'Skythen und Perser,' in *Asien: Organ der deutschen asiatischen Gesellschaft*, ii. [1902]; J. Freßl, *Die Skythen-Saken die Urväter der Germanen*, Munich, 1886.

(6) That the Scyths were Slavs.—J. G. Cuno, *Forschungen im Gebiete der alten Völkerkunde*, Berlin, 1871; J. E. Zabyelin, *Hist. of Russian Life* (Russ.), Moscow, 1871, i. 243; D. J. Samokvasov, *Hist. of Russian Law* (Russ.), Warsaw, 1884, pt. ii. pp. 1–69.

(7) That the Eastern Scyths were Mongolian and the Western Scyths Iranian and possibly ancestors of the Slavs.—V. T. Miller, 'Epigraphic Traces of Iranian Population on the North Coast of the Euxine,' *Journ. Min. Educ.*, St. Petersburg, 1886, p. 232; T. I. Mishchenko, 'Concerning the Geography and Ethnology of Herodotean Scythia,' *ib.*, 1888.

(8) That the Eastern Scyths between the Dnieper and the Don were Iranian, while the Western Scyths between the Dnieper and the Carpathians and the Lower Danube were Slavs.—P. J. Šafařík, *Slavonic Antiquities*.

Recent study of Scythian archæology and customs makes it more and more clear that the Scyths were a political unit composed of various ethnical elements. The distinction of three different kinds of Scythians had already been made by Herodotus, besides which he distinguishes various other tribes which he considered non-Scythian. Recognizing his distinctions, and assuming that the W. Scythians were Slavs, we find it impossible to class as Slavic the non-Scythian tribes of Herodotus, as, *e.g.*, the Neuri. In this case the Neuri must be considered as one of the neighbours of the Slavs, probably the Letto-Lithuanians. This, however, is not realized by Šafařík, who considers the W. Scythians and Neuri, as well as others, to be Slavs. Such inconsistencies deprive his Scytho-Slavic theory of any profound historic or ethnological value. Another argument against identifying the Slavs and W. Scythians is brought forward by T. G. Braun.[1] He says that the first historical mention of the Slavs in Pliny, Tacitus (1st cent. A.D.), and Ptolemy shows them far away from the Lower Danube. Pliny says that they live east of the Vistula,[2] Tacitus places them somewhere between the Valdai hills near Novgorod and the Vistula,[3] Ptolemy (2nd cent.) places them on the Vistula, in Sarmatia, and along the shores of the Venedic gulf (the Gulf of Danzig); but he also speaks of the Venedic mountains, probably meaning the N. Carpathians.[4] Further, if we bear in mind that the territory of the W. Scythians was the battle-ground of every tribe migrating southwards, we can see that it would not be a very good nursery for a rapidly increasing race which was to overrun half Europe by the 6th century.

But, if we are not to find ancestors of the Slavs among the Scythians, we have still to consider whether they are to be found among the non-Scythian tribes described by Herodotus, such as the Neuri and Budini.

(*b*) *The Neuri.*—Herodotus (5th cent. B.C.) tells us that the Neuri live along the rivers Hypanis (Bug) and Tyras (Dniester), north of the Scythian Aroteres;[1] and that they had been driven from their land a generation before by a plague of snakes, and had taken refuge with the Budini.[2] In the same place he tells us that once a year they became wolves for a short season. Of the land which lay beyond them he confesses his ignorance, but believes it to be desolate. Ephorus of Cyme[3] (2nd cent. B.C.), quoted by Scymnus Chius,[4] follows Herodotus, saying that they live beyond the Aroteres, and that the country beyond them is desolate. Pomponius Mela[5] (1st cent. A.D.) mentions the Neuri as living on the Tyras. He also relates the wolf-story. Claudius Ptolemy[6] (2nd cent. A.D.) speaks of the Ναύβαροι or Ναύαροι as inhabiting S. Podolia. Ammianus Marcellinus[7] (4th cent. A.D.) says that they live in the mountains north of the land of the Borysthenes (*i.e.* near Kiev).

Šafařík was the first to propose the identification of the Neuri with the Slavs.[8] He considers that their territory was just where the Wends (Slavs) originally settled. He is supported by L. Niederle,[9] Braun,[10] Tomaschek,[11] and Minns.[12]

(*c*) *The Budini.*—In iv. 21 Herodotus tells us that the Budini are living in the great country north of the Sauromatæ, east of the Tanais (Don); in iv. 108 that they are a powerful nation, with blue eyes and red hair. With them live a people called the Geloni, whom Herodotus believes to be fugitive Greeks. These people have built for themselves a town of wood called Gelonus, with temples and shrines in which they worship gods whom Herodotus believes to be Greek. Pomponius Mela[13] also mentions this wooden town of Gelonus in the land of the Budini. Rawlinson[14] gathers from the data given by Herodotus that the Budini inhabited the region round about Zadonsk and Woronetz (Saratov).

Many theories are suggested concerning the ethnology of the Budini. Rawlinson[15] holds that the Budini were either the ancestors of the Germans or else a remnant of the Cimmerians, whom he believes to be Celts. F. Lenormant[16] considers the town Gelonus to be the Asgard of Scandinavian mythology. C. Ritter[17] goes so far as to say that Budini is a religious title, and that the Budini were Buddhists. Minns[18] thinks that they were probably Finns of the branch now represented by the Votiaks and Permiaks. Of course Šafařík[19] regards the Budini and Geloni as both Slav peoples, and derives their name from *voda*, 'water' ('waterfolk'). Grote[20] supports this view. E. H. Bunbury[21] suggests that Herodotus' informant may have confused Greek and Slavic methods of worship in his account of Gelonus. Niederle[22] is also inclined to think that the Budini were a Slavic people. It is certainly more likely that the Budini were Slavic.

(*d*) *The Sauromatæ, Sarmatæ, etc.*—Herodotus[23] says that the Sauromatæ were living on the east bank of the Tanais (Don), which divided their land from that of the Scythians. They stretched northwards from Lake Mæotis (Sea of Azov) to the forest land belonging to the Budini. He relates the legend that they were descendants of Amazons conquered by the Greeks on the Thermodon, who, having been embarked for Greece, slew their

[1] *Researches in the Sphere of Gotho-Slavonic Relations* (Russian), St. Petersburg, 1899, pp. 74–77.
[2] *HN* iv. 13 (27), 97.
[3] *Germ.* 46, ed. H. Furneaux, Oxford, 1894, p. 120 f.
[4] *Geog.* iii. 5.

[1] iv. 17, 51.
[2] iv. 105.
[3] Frag. 78.
[4] Frag. 78 (*FHG* i. [Paris, 1841] 287).
[5] *De Situ Orbis*, ii. 1, ed. J. Reynolds, Eton, 1761, p. 26.
[6] *Geog.* iii. 5 (P. Bertius, *Theatrum Geographiæ Veteris*, Leyden, 1618–19, ii. 82).
[7] *Rer. Gest.* xxii. 8 (C. Nisard, *Collection des Auteurs latins*, Paris, 1878, ii. 176).
[8] *Slovanské Starozitnosti*^{2}, Prague, 1862–63, i. 224 f.
[9] *Slovanské Starozitnosti*, Prague, 1902, i. 266.
[10] P. 247.
[11] *Kritik*, II. v. 247.
[12] P. 102 f.
[13] i. 22, ed. Reynolds, p. 22.
[14] *Herodotus*^{2}, vol. iii. p. 79.
[15] *Ib.* p. 78.
[16] *Manual of the Ancient Hist. of the East*, Eng. tr., London, 1869–70, ii. 134.
[17] *Die Vorhalle Europäischer*, Berlin, 1820, p. 381.
[18] *EBr*^{11}, s.v. 'Budini.'
[19] *Slawische Alterthümer*, i. 10, 185–195.
[20] *Hist. of Greece*^{3}, iii. 325 note.
[21] *Hist. of Ancient Geography*, London, 1879, i. 193–195.
[22] i. 275.
[23] iv. 21.

captors, and drifted to Kremni on the shores of Lake Mæotis, whence they advanced up the Tanais. Hippocrates[1] (468 B.C.) places them on the shores of Lake Mæotis. The *Periplus* of Scylax, dated by K. Müller about 338 B.C., mentions in § 69[2] a tribe of 'Syrmatæ' in Europe close to the Tanais; but in § 70[3] the Sauromatæ are still in Asia on the eastern side of the river. In connexion with this we may note that Stephanus Byzantius cites this rare form 'Syrmatæ' from Eudoxus of Cnidos (4th cent. B.C.), and says that it is identical with 'Sauromatæ,' 'Surmates,' etc. The first definite mention of the Sauromatæ as in Europe is that of Polybius[4] (210 B.C.), where Γάταλος ὁ Σαρμάτης joins a great league of states in Asia Minor on the shores of the Euxine. This is the first occasion on which the term Σαρμάτης takes the place of the form Σαυρομάτης. Ephorus (2nd cent. B.C.), quoted by Scymnus Chius,[5] says that they live on the shores of Lake Mæotis. Strabo (2nd cent. B.C.)[6] has the Iazyges Sarmatæ on the Ister (Danube). His Sarmatian tribes are Iazyges-Sarmatæ, Royal Sarmatæ, and Uirgi, and the Rhoxolani, Aorsi, and Siraci beyond the Tanais. Ovid (1st cent. B.C.)[7] places the Iazyges on the Danube and the Sauromatæ in W. Sarmatia. Diodorus Siculus (1st cent. B.C.)[8] says that the Sauromatæ are still on the Don, and that they come from Media.

Before going on to the notices in writers of the Christian era, it is well to remark that it is not clear exactly when the Sauromatæ crossed the Don. In the 4th cent. B.C. the Sauromatæ were either east of the Don or just crossing. After that we get no definite information for a century and a half. Minns[9] suggests that the reason of this is that the Scyths were then fighting a losing struggle with the Sauromatæ. The Scyths, contrary to the opinion of Herodotus,[10] were good neighbours to the Pontic Greeks, but it was not safe to travel near the Euxine when the Sauromatæ were first in the ascendant. We may also notice two main divisions of Sauromatæ by the 1st cent. B.C.—the Iazyges-Sauromatæ, Royal Sauromatæ, and Uirgi on the Danube, and the other division, Sauromatæ, Rhoxolani, Aorsi, and Siraci, on the Don and the shores of the Sea of Azov and in the Caucasus.

In the 1st cent. A.D. Pomponius Mela[11] places Sarmatia between the Vistula and the Danube. Pliny the Elder[12] has the Hamaxobii (or Aorsi) and Rhoxolani on the Danube and Herecynthian Marsh, and the Iazyges in Dacia, having previously driven out the Dacians. This is confirmed by Tacitus, who tells, in *Hist.* i. 79, how the Rhoxolani, having occupied W. Sarmatia, which had been left vacant by the Iazyges, made an unsuccessful raid into Mœsia in A.D. 70.[13] In *Ann.* xii. 29 he has the Iazyges-Sarmatæ in Pannonia.[14] In *Germ.* 1 the Iazyges-Sarmatæ are between the Danube and Theiss, having driven out the Dacians,[15] and in *Germ.* 43 we find the Sarmatæ imposing tribute on the Osi in Pannonia.[16] In the 2nd cent. A.D. Ptolemy[17] has the Sarmati along the coast of Lake Mæotis, and the Iazyges Metanastæ between the Theiss and the Danube, but this is probably, as Minns points out,[18] the result of combining information of two different dates. Another 2nd cent. historian, Polyænus,[19] tells the story of Amage, queen of the Sarmatians, who reigned on the shores of the Pontus. She allied with the Chersonesians against their neighbours the Scythians. In the 4th cent. A.D. the *Hist. August. Scriptores* tells us of war waged against the Sauromatæ by Hadrian, Marcus, Maximus Regalianus, and others.[1] The 4th cent. historian Olympiodorus[2] shows that the Sarmatæ have overrun Thrace and Illyricum. Jordanes[3] (6th cent. A.D.) says that Dacia was *formerly* bounded on the east by the Rhoxolani, on the west by the Iazyges, on the south by the Sarmatæ and Bastarnæ, and on the north by the streams of the Danube. In the *de Get.* xxxvi. we find the Sarmatians on the side of the Byzantine Romans against Valentinian, emperor of Rome.[4] Procopius, however, in the 6th cent. A.D., merely mentions the Sauromatæ as a tribe of Scythians.[5]

1 *De Aer.* 17 (*Opera*, ed. H. Kuehlewein, Leipzig, 1894–1902, i. 59).
2 R. H. Klausen, *Hecatæi Frag.*, Berlin, 1831, p. 209.
3 *Ib.* p. 211.
4 *Hist.* xxvi. 6, 13, ed. L. Dindorf, Leipzig, 1866–68, iii. 436.
5 Frag. 78 (*FHG* i. 257).
6 *Geog.* VII. ii. 17, ed. A. Meineke, Leipzig, 1852–53, ii. 421.
7 *Trist.* ii. 191 ff.
8 *Bibl.* ii. 43, ed. F. Vogel and C. T. Fischer, Leipzig, 1886–1906, i. 240.
9 P. 118.
10 See iv. 76.
11 iii. 4, ed. Reynolds, p. 51.
12 *HN* iv. 12 (25), ed. C. Mayhoff, Leipzig, 1906–09, i. 337.
13 See Tac. *Hist.*, ed. W. A. Spooner, London, 1891, p. 179.
14 Ed. H. Furneaux, Oxford, 1885, p. 37.
15 Ed. Furneaux, p. 37.
16 *Ib.* p. 112.
17 *Georg.* III. vii. 5.
18 P. 121.
19 viii. 56, ed. I. Melber, Leipzig, 1887, p. 417.

Of the customs of the Sauromatæ Herodotus has a good deal to say. In iv. 110 ff. he tells us that the Sauromatian women hunted, went to war, and wore the same clothes as the men. Every woman had to kill a man in battle before she could marry. They spoke a language which Herodotus believed to be broken Scythian. These customs put together amply account for the myth of Amazonian origin.

Hippocrates[6] notes the difference between the Sauromatæ and the other 'Scythian' tribes around them. He gives the same account of the activities of the Sauromatian women as Herodotus, adding that they were not allowed to take part in religious ceremonies till they were married, and that they had no right breasts, since it was the custom of their mothers to cut these off in early childhood, to make their right shoulder and arm stronger by concentrating the strength there. When married, they gave up riding in general, but were still liable to be called up when a crisis necessitated universal tribal service. This is interesting, since these two accounts must have come from independent sources.

Ephorus[7] gives the same account of the Sauromatæ as Herodotus, from whom, most probably, he got his information.

Strabo gives a very full account of their customs. In *Geog.* ζ. 2,[8] he says that they are a mare-milking, milk-drinking, simple people, who have mixed with the Thracians and Bastarnæ beyond the Ister. In *Geog.* ζ. 17[9] he says that they are mostly nomads, though some practise agriculture, and he gives a detailed account of the Rhoxolani. They wear very little armour, and are almost naked. Their helmets and breastplates are made of ox-hide, their shields of wicker-work. They also use spears, bows, and swords. On the top of their waggons are fastened felt tents. They eat milk, cheese, and meat. They winter in the marshes round Lake Mæotis, and move up to the steppes in summer.

Diodorus Siculus[10] says that women ruled among the Sauromatæ, and he gives the usual account of their habits.

Tacitus[11] gives an account of the Rhoxolani: they use swords and poles of an extraordinary length, and wear coats of mail made of steel plates and ox-hide; they are almost impregnable to a charge, but, if knocked over, they cannot get up again. In *Germ.* 17 he says that the Sarmatæ have flowing garments like the Parthians; in *Germ.* 46 that they live in waggons, and are dirty and lazy.

Pomponius Mela says that the Sarmatians are rather like Parthians, their greater roughness being accounted for by the greater harshness of their climate; they are nomads and very fierce. He also mentions the strange habits of their women.

Nicolaus Damascenus[12] (1st cent. A.D.) tells that the Sauromatæ have a habit of eating hard for three days till they are full up.

Pausanias[13] (late 2nd cent. A.D.) gives an account of the Sarmatian breastplate, which was made of pieces of horses' hoofs. He says that the Sauromatæ, though the most isolated of the barbarians, were skilful craftsmen. They had no iron in their country and did not import any, so they used bone for the tips of their arrows and spears. They used to lasso their enemies in battle. They were nomads, and had many horses, which they used to eat and sacrifice to the local gods. In VIII. xliii. 6[14] he says that they were warlike and wicked and relates how Antonius II. punished them for wantonly breaking the peace.

Many scholars, including Šafařík and Rawlinson, have believed the Sauromatæ to be Slavs; but this theory seems weakened by the ample evidence as to the Turanian character of the Sarmatian people.

1 See ed. H. Peter, Leipzig, 1865.
2 Ch. 27 (*Hist. Græc. Minores*, ed. L. Dindorf, Leipzig, 1870–71, i. 461).
3 *De Get.* xii., ed. C. A. Closs, Stuttgart, 1861, p. 54.
4 Ed. Closs, p. 134.
5 *De Bell. Got.* iv. 5, ed. D. Comparetti, Rome, 1895–98, iii. 26.
6 *De Aer.* 17, ed. Kuehlewein, i. 59.
7 Frag. 78 (*FHG* i. 257).
8 Ed. Meineke, ii. 407.
9 *Ib.* p. 420.
10 ii. 44, ed. Vogel and Fischer, i. 241.
11 *Hist.* i. 79.
12 Ch. 16 (*Hist. Græc. Min.*, ed. Dindorf, i. 147).
13 I. xxi. 5, ed. F. Spiro, Leipzig, 1903, i. 53 ff.
14 Ed. Spiro, ii. 365.

Moreover—a fact which Šafaŕik ignores—it is impossible to regard both Scyths and Sauromatæ as Slavic, since Herodotus most definitely distinguishes the Sauromatæ from the Scyths. They have all the characteristics of the Turkic nomads of the steppes, milking mares, living on meat, milk, and cheese, wearing flowing garments, living in waggons, and using felt tents. On the other hand, that important characteristic of the Turkic people, the use of iron, is lacking.

2. The classical period (1st–6th cent. A.D.).—We have very little information about the Slavs from the classical authors. Pliny mentions them under the name of Venedi or Venedæ.[1] He only says vaguely that they, among other tribes, are reported to live east of the Vistula. He also mentions the Sirbi (Serbs), who, he says, live with the Cimmerians.[2] Tacitus[3] mentions the Venedi as living near what H. Furneaux[4] considers to be between the Valdai hills near Novgorod and the east bank of the Vistula. He hesitates whether to call them Germans or Sarmatians, but is inclined to class them with the former, because they have fixed houses, use shields, and are swift of foot—all very un-Sarmatian characteristics. He also says that they are dirty and sluggish by nature. We must remember, however, that in this case the reading of the MS is 'Veneti.' In the 2nd cent. A.D. Ptolemy[5] places the Venedæ on the Vistula, in Sarmatia, and along the shores of the Venedic gulf, which seems to have been the Gulf of Danzig. He also mentions the Veltæ on the Baltic, the Sudini and Saboci in Prussia, which tribes Minns[6] considers Slavic. Minns suggests that Ptolemy's 'Stavani,' which he places in Prussia, might be read 'Stlavani.' Ptolemy[7] also mentions the Serbi, whom he places in Asiatic Sarmatia between the Ceraunian mountains and the river Rha.

3. The Byzantine period.—The first definite use of the word Sclavini is to be found in the pseudo-Cæsarius dialogue[8] early in the 6th cent. A.D. The first account of the Slavs under the name of Sclaveni is given by Jordanes.[9] He says that the Winidæ, Sclaveni, and Antes live in Dacia, from the town of Noviodunum and Lake Mursianus to the Danaster (Dniester), and northwards to the Vistula. They dwell in woods and marshes instead of houses. The Antes are the bravest tribe, and live round the shore of the Pontus from the Danaster to the Danaper (Dnieper). Farther on he says that the Winidæ, Antes, and Sclavi formed part of the subjects of Hermanreich; they were very warlike tribes, who were then subdued, 'but now range wheresoever they will through our neglect.'[10]

The most useful of the authorities is Procopius (6th cent.). His important remarks on 5th and 6th cent. Slavic institutions are worth quoting.

'For these tribes, the Antes and Sclaveni, are not ruled by one man, but have lived from olden times under democratic rule, and for this reason they deliberate in public all that concerns their weal and ill. Both these peoples have the same laws and customs. . . . They live in miserable hovels very far apart from one another and often change their abode. They go to battle on foot and charge the enemy with small shields and javelins in their hands. Some wear neither tunic nor cloak when going to battle, but merely short breeches. They all speak the same barbarous language, and are very like one another to look at. Their mode of living is hard and uncultured like that of the Massagetæ; they are always dirty. They are not malicious or deceitful, but have something of the simplicity of the Huns. At one time the Sclaveni and Antes had only one name, for they were called the Spori in ancient days, because, I take it, they were scattered so sporadically over the land they lived in; indeed they inhabit the greater part of the banks of the Danube. That is all I have to say about these people.'[1]

1 *HN* iv. 13 (27), 97. 2 vi. 7. 3 *Germ.* 46.
4 *Germ.* p. 120 f. 5 iii. 5. 6 *EBr*[11], *s.v.* 'Slavs.'
7 v. 8. 8 *Dial.* ii. 110 (*PG* xxxviii. 986).
9 *De Get.* v. (Nisard, 429).
10 Cf. xxiii. (Nisard, 444).

Procopius also gives a good deal about the history of the Slavs.

The Slavs during the 5th and 6th centuries are constantly trying to cross the Danube, and becoming more and more successful each time: the Slavs cross the Danube, and overrun Illyricum as far as Dyrrhachium;[2] Slavs again cross the Danube and Eurus. They divide into two bands, one of which ravages Illyria and the other Thrace. The latter take the town of Toperos on the Thracian coast, and commit horrible atrocities there.[3] A number of Slavs larger than had been seen before cross the Danube and attack Naisos with the intention of invading Thessalonica. Through fear of the Germans, however, they leave Thessalonica untouched, going through the Illyrian mountains to Dalmatia.[4] As time goes on, the Romans are less able to repel them. In iii. 14[5] Justinian offers the Antes the town of Tourris and land on the Danube, if they will protect the empire from the advance of the Huns. In iii. 40,[6] however, they are in the pay of Totila, the Hun leader, and attacking the empire. Towards the end of the 6th cent. they have overrun the whole of Greece, and are in such numbers that the Romans can make no way against them.[7] In fact, in iii. 14 Procopius admits that since the death of Chilbudinus (5th cent. A.D.) nothing has been able to protect the empire from the barbarians.

Towards the end of the 6th cent. Menander tells us that the Slavs made a raid into Thrace.[8] The next year (A.D. 578) they were ravaging the whole of Greece. Tiberius, the Roman, not having sufficient forces to meet them, persuaded Baianus, leader of the Avars, to attack them in their own country, and so force them to go back and defend it. Baianus accordingly crossed the Danube and burnt the Slav villages there, whose inhabitants had fled to the caves and woods. Baianus was the more ready to attack the Slavs since he had a private grudge against them; for they had refused to pay him tribute and killed his ambassadors shortly before.

Mauricius[9] (6th cent.) has much to say on the characteristics of the Slavs. Physically they are strong, well able and accustomed to endure cold and lack of clothing and food. They have great reverence for the laws of hospitality, and are very kind to strangers and prisoners. They are armed with two javelins, wooden bows, and small poisoned arrows; some use shields. Their method of attack is by sudden raids and incursions; they rarely fight a pitched battle. They are supreme in the art of defence; when pursued by enemies or suddenly attacked, they dive under the water, and, lying on their backs at the bottom, breathe through a long reed, and so escape destruction. They live in a continuous state of defence, having several exits to their houses and burying all their superfluous goods.

Thus, in the 6th cent., we have the Slavs definitely settled in large numbers north of the Danube. There were also Slavs in the Mark of Brandenburg.[10]

There were Serbo-Croats in Dalmatia and Pannonia, invited there by the emperor Heraclius (610–640) to protect them from the Avars.[11] The Danube Slavs were making constant raids into Greece, and had practically conquered N. Illyricum.

Nicephorus Patriarchus (8th cent. A.D.) is our chief authority for the fate of the Slavs in the 7th and 8th centuries. In 626 the Avars, with large numbers of Slav auxiliaries, attacked Blachernæ in Thrace. A number of Slav women were found to be in the forces.[12] In 679 the Boyars subdued the Slavs living in Mœsia and Thrace,[13] and in 688 the Slavs who had conquered parts of

1 *De Bell. Got.* iii. 14, ed. Comparetti, ii. 292–294.
2 iii. 29, ed. Comparetti, ii. 383.
3 xxxviii., ed. Comparetti, ii. 445–450.
4 iii. 40, ed. Comparetti, ii. 457.
5 Ed. Comparetti, ii. 294. 6 *Ib.* p. 465.
7 *Hist. Arcan.* § 18, *Opera*, ed. J. Haury, Leipzig, 1905–06, vol. iii. pt. i. p. 114.
8 Ch. 24 (*Corpus Script. Hist. Byzantinæ*, ed. I. Bekker and B. G. Niebuhr, Bonn, 1829, p. 327 c).
9 *Strategicum*, xi. ch. 5, ed. J. Scheffer, Upsala, 1664, p. 272.
10 Procopius, *de Bell. Got.* ii. 15.
11 Constantinus Porphyrogenitus, *de Administ. Imperio*, ch. 31–33, ed. I. Bekker in *Corp. Script. Hist. Byz.*, Bonn, 1829–40, iii. 152.
12 *De Reb. Gest.* 13 A, in *Corp. Script. Hist. Byz.*, Bonn, 1829–55, ii. 20.
13 *Ib.* p. 24 (p. 40).

Thessalonica submitted to the power of the Romans.[1] The same author tells us that in 763 a large number of Slavs crossed the Euxine and settled at the mouth of the river Artanes.[2]

Fredegar tells us of the foundation of a Slav state in Thuringia under Samo, a Frank, in the early 7th century.[3]

The period called Byzantine, because the chief authorities for it are the Byzantines, is the most important in Slavic history; in fact, it is the only period in which we can treat the Slavs as one race, though already varying according to locality and having different names in different places. It is certain that the rapid spread of the Slavs over the Eastern Empire was facilitated by its weakness, resulting from the incursions of bearded invaders from the north under Alaric and Odovacer, and beardless hordes from the east under Attila. Whatever region it was in which the Slavs first broke away from the Aryan stock, they must have been somewhere in the forest region of the western part of E. Europe outside the route of the Asiatic steppe invaders immediately before their invasion of the Roman Empire. About the 5th cent. they had spread over the lands of the W. Scythians, Sarmatians, and Celts, and so encroached upon the territories of the Eastern Roman Empire, and later upon the Frankish Empire. In the west they crossed the Rhine and got as far as Spain; in the south-east they reached Asia Minor a century and a half later. In the north-east they were on the northern shores of the Baltic in the 1st cent., and on the Dnieper in the 6th cent. (the Antes).

Pending further archæological discoveries, there is no exact information as to the date when the Slavs began to spread westwards. This lack of information has given certain Slavic scholars the opportunity of advancing a theory that the Slavs of the Elbe region were autochthonous.[4] The views of the most prominent German scholar may be summed up by the following quotation:

'... From the beginning of the fifth, and indeed for the greater part from the end of the third century, A.D., the country westward to the Oder and southward to the Riesengebirge was abandoned by its old German inhabitants. ... It must be admitted that the Slavs found everywhere scattered remnants of the Germans, because they merely adapted the German names, *Oder*, *Elbe* (*Albi*), *Moldau* (*Walth ahva*), etc., to their own mouths (*Odra*, *Laba*, *Vltava*). For certain times and in certain districts there was a mixed population, and it is to be particularly noticed that even in the sixth century the Germans, who had long withdrawn to the South, did not admit that the East as far as the Vistula had definitely passed to the Slavs. It had not been conquered by them—only occupied by loose bands of settlers.'[5]

Since Peisker gives us a great deal of valuable historical information in this chapter on the expansion of the Slavs, it is the more important to point out where his preconceived ideas have vitiated his facts.

The axioms on which he bases his theory are: (1) that the rapid Slav conquest was due to either a Germanic or a Turanian (Avar) admixture, since the Slavs were merely the passive party; (2) that the organization of the early Slavic states was due to these two elements.

(1) His first argument is based on a quotation from Theophylactus' 'spy story': 'Three captives were brought before the Emperor Maurice having neither swords nor any other weapon, but only citharas with them. Being questioned they answered that they were Slavs from the coast of the northern ocean [Baltic Sea], whither the Khagan sent envoys with presents to ask for auxiliaries. They brought back an answer to the Khagan that he could expect no help from such a distance—they themselves had been fifteen months on the journey—and their people were absolutely peaceable. They played on the zither because they were unacquainted with weapons, their land produced no iron and therefore they lived there still and peacefully, and as the war trumpet was not understood there they played on the zither. These were obviously spies, but the fiction of their entire harmlessness could only deceive the Emperor when the story of the Khagan's embassy to the Baltic Slavs appeared natural. The whole mystification produced the widespread story of the *dove-like nature of the Slavs*.'[1]

Since Theophylactus himself considers the Slavs not so blameless as they seemed, this will hardly support his theory. Against it we have the testimony of almost all the other writers that the Slavs are good warriors, especially in defensive warfare. Nor are they lacking in savagery. Peisker ignores this evidence, however, and, when he deals with the pre-Avar conquests of the Slavs in the west, he says that the Germans for some unknown reason voluntarily abandoned their territories. Again, when he tells of the Rügen Slavs predominating over the Danes, he ascribes it[2] to the 'remarkable fusion of the viking pirates, Altaian herdsmen and Slav peasants on the island of Rügen' in 1168.

(2) As to the founding of Slavic states which took place at the end of the Byzantine period, it is true that Samo, the founder of a Slavic state bordering on Thuringia, at the beginning of the 7th cent., was a Frank, but the 'empire' was a short-lived adventure, which played no rôle in Slavic history. Peisker ascribes to it the deeper significance of a rebellion of Slavic peasants against their foreign masters, but it was equally a rebellion of the Frank chief against his own king, Dagobert. All the Slavic states which were at all permanent—as the Carinthian (7th cent.), the Croatian, Serbian, Bohemian (Lemusi), and Polish (Lakhy)—were states developed from purely local origins, and could scarcely owe much in that direction to the Avars, who, like all other Asiatic invaders, were better fighters than statesmen. The Bulgarian-Asiatic element among the Slavs who adopted this name must have been very insignificant, if the original Bulgarians changed their language and adopted Christianity so soon after settling down (9th cent. under Simeon and Samuel). Very little greater numerically was the Scandinavian element in the Kiev state, for in the third generation it amounted to the foreign dynasty, which, as is known from modern history, usually adopts the nationality of its subjects. Still Scandinavian influence in the formation of the Novgorod and Kiev states had been undoubtedly great, but its strength was due to the fact that the first Scandinavian Russ soon became Slavicized.

In the one case where Germanic influence was not sporadic, but permanent, it does not seem to have had the effect of forming a centralized state. This was the case of the most westerly Slavs, neighbours of the Germans, who lived between the Danube and Mecklenburg—such as the Sorbs of the Saale and Elbe, and the Lyutitsi and Obodritsi farther north—who never formed a state of any importance. Considering the constant disturbances coming from the steppe, we cannot but wonder how the Slavs succeeded in organizing their states, and providing at such an early period such large collections of native law based on legal proceedings rather than force.

It may be questioned whether the Avar invasion made a cleavage between the Slavs, dividing them into Northern and Southern, or whether it helped to accentuate a division already there.

4. The period of independent Christian Slavic states (7th–13th cent. A.D.).—There are two sources of evidence for the period—historical and archæological. The history of the Slavs during this period can be gleaned from local authorities of the 10th cent. or later. Among these are the Germans, Thietmar of Merseburg (10th cent.), Adam of Bremen (11th cent.), Helmold (12th cent.), and Otto of Bamberg (12th cent.), and the Danish Saxo Grammaticus (12th cent.), Fredegar, and the *Knytlinga Saga*. Others are Slavic, such as the S. Russian chronicler Nestor (12th cent.), the Bohemian Cosmas, bishop of Prague (12th cent.), the Polish-Latin *Homilies* (12th cent.), and the Polish chroniclers, Marcianus Gallus (11th–12th cent.), Vincentius Kadlubek of Cracow (13th cent.), Yanko of Czarnkov (14th cent.), and Dlugosz (15th cent.). The chroniclers, though of a later date, deal with the period which we are now considering. Besides these local sources, the Arabian travellers, al-Mas'ūdī (10th cent.) and Ibrāhīm ibn Vāsīfshāh (12th cent.), and a Spanish Jew called Ibraham ibn La'qūb (10th cent.) contribute interesting information which is much more impartial and free from bias than the Germanic and Slavic contributions.

From a historical and archæological point of view, this is the most 'Slavic' period in the history of the race, since at that time, between the advance of Attila and that of Jenghiz Khan, there were no invasions of any importance from the east or from the west—*i.e.*, there was no great infusion of Turanian blood to the Slavic stock, since the Avars were a

[1] *Ib.* p. 24 c (p. 41). [2] *Ib.* p. 44 c (p. 77).
[3] *Chron.* 48 (*PL* lxxi. 636 f.).
[4] E. Boguslawski, *Proofs of the Autochthonism of the Slavs in the Territories occupied by them in Mediæval Times* (Polish), Warsaw, 1912.
[5] Peisker, in *Cam. Med. Hist.* ii. 435.

[1] Peisker, p. 438 (Theophylactus, vi. 2). [2] *Ib.* p. 456.

military and political power, and did not amalgamate with or absorb those whom they conquered. In the west, though the Germans were by this time pushing the Slavs back before them, they were only politically supreme over the Elbe Slavs, who had never united to form a strong Slavic state, but lived in small village communities as Slavic islets in a Germanic sea.

III. *DISTRIBUTION AND CLASSIFICATION OF THE SLAVS UP TO THE PRESENT DAY.*—In dealing with the early Slavs we get more important evidence from archæological remains than from the actual notices of ancient and Old German historians. The Slavic graves in Germany and Austria have now been thoroughly studied, and a map of their distribution was made by C. Toldt.[1] They date from the 7th to the 12th cent. and are characterized chiefly by metal ornaments of the shape of the letter S (*Schlöferinge*), worn probably on the cap, which are not to be found in the graves of W. Germany, France, or Great Britain.[2] The graves not possessing this characteristic ornament have small urns without ears, ornamented with a design imitating waves. Rings are found chiefly in the graves in what is now Germany, the island of Rügen, Austria, as well as in Bohemia and Moravia, and less in Poland or White and Little Russia. Some 169 skulls have been found in the Slavic graves on the territory of what is at present E. Germany, and of these 151 are dolichocephalic and only 18 brachycephalic. As to the 'Slavic' graves of Austria, 46 out of 148 were dolichocephalic, but it is not certain how many of these can be described as Slavic. Some archæologists, among them Niederle, suppose that the Slavs formed the bulk of the population of the Danube, Styria, and Carinthia; others (chiefly Germans) think that the Slavs formed small groups among Roman, German, and Illyrian elements.

From the Elbe to the Volga in 8th cent. graves we meet with Arabian silver coins, which R. Virchow[3] considers particularly associated with the Slavic graves.[4]

The skulls from Slavic graves in the territory of the present-day Russia were also dolichocephalic, but it is difficult to say which of them can be ascribed to the E. Slavs and which to the Finns, who lived in that district before the Slavs. The population of Little Russia was dolichocephalic until the Tatar invasion. The dolichocephals of Great Russia, whether of Slavic or of Finnic origin, were affected in modern times by a fair brachycephalic 'Valdai' type from Polesia and a dark brachycephalic Little Russian type.

IV. *LANGUAGE.* — The relation of the Slavic languages to the other European tongues was clearly defined for the first time by F. Bopp,[5] but, even before, other philologists had noticed points of likeness between the Slavic tongues and Latin, Greek, German, Celtic, Letto-Lithuanian, etc. Since the publication of Bopp's work it has been generally recognized that the Slavic family of languages has developed from the original Indo-European (Aryan) common language, just as the Germanic, Celtic, Italic, Letto-Lithuanian, Albanian, Greek, Armenian, Indian, and Iranian branches did.

V. *RELIGION.*—When we speak of the religion of the Slavs, we mean their religion at the time when the term 'Slavs' meant more of a unity of language, customs, and beliefs than now—in other words, before they adopted Christianity.

1. Sources.—There are no Slavic records written in the pre-Christian era of the beliefs which the Slavs held before they became Christians, but the Slavic chronicles of the 11th–15th centuries frequently refer to the earlier religion. These chroniclers, however, were already looking at things from the point of view of either Byzantine Christians (in the case of the E. Slavs) or Roman Christians (of W. Slavs), and hence they purposely depreciated the pagan era of Slavic history. This is true of the earliest Slavic chronicler Nestor of the Russ (a proto-Russian people), and also of the Czech chronicler Cosmas of Prague, and the Pole Gallus. Even more biased are the references in the early German and Danish chroniclers—*e.g.*, Thietmar, Adam of Bremen, Saxo Grammaticus, Otto of Bamberg—and in the *Knytlinga Saga*. Further notices are found in the Eastern historians, Byzantine or Arabian, such as Procopius, Constantinus Porphyrogenitus, or Mas'ūdī, and Ibn Fadlān, but the latter often confused the E. Slavs with the Scandinavian Variags, and possibly with the Finns and Turks.

In a sense more valuable evidence may be obtained from the existing folk-lore, such as the customs connected with the change of the seasons which may be called communal, and those connected with *rites de passage* in the life of the individual. Then there is linguistic evidence, which, however, has little value unless it is connected with a survival of ritual or belief; *e.g.*, it will not do to conclude, with some folk-lorists, that, merely because *Bug*, the name of two different rivers, means in all Slavic languages 'God,' the two rivers were therefore objects of special worship. There is one more source of evidence, viz. the church records dealing with pagan practices which pass into Christian ritual, but these must be treated with no less reserve than such documents in other countries. Thus it is folk-lore with all its modes of expression — songs, sayings, epics, sculpture, drawing, dances, or games—that provides us with the most satisfactory material. This material has only begun to be utilized since the publication of Šafařík's monumental work, *Slavonic Antiquities*, in 1837, and from the very beginning the study of the past of the Slavs has been impeded by national and racial prejudices. The German scholar Peisker starts his study of the past of the Slavs with the assumption that they are nomads of Scytho-Turanian religious conceptions, while almost all Slavic scholars take for granted that, because the Slavic languages belong to the Indo-Germanic group, their religion must have been also like that of the other Indo-Germanic speaking peoples. Further, their assumption that a distinct Slavic linguistic group corresponded to a distinct Slavic race led them to expect an equal originality in the early religion of the Slavs and their present folk-lore. These ready-made assumptions prevented collectors of Slavic folk-lore from presenting it comparatively with the folk-lore of other peoples, and, on the other hand, from seeing the variety of the Slavic beliefs; *e.g.*, the god Svietovit (spelt in various ways), known exclusively to the Slavs of Rügen, was ascribed to Slavdom, and so was also Perun, who was the Scandinavian Thor, brought by them to Novgorod and Kiev.

2. Gods.—The names of the ancient Slavic gods have almost all been gleaned from Russian, Polish, or foreign authors; the Czech and S. Slav writers have contributed little to our knowledge of names famous in Slavic mythology.

All the foreign writers on the ancient Slavs

1 'Altslavengräber in Deutschland und Oesterreich,' *Korrespondenzblatt der deut. Gesellschaft für anthrop. Ethnologie und Urgeschichte*, xl. [1911].

2 M. Wawrzeniecki, *Slowianie doby przed i wczesno historycznej* (Polish), Warsaw, 1910.

3 'Über das erste Auftreten der Slaven in Deutschland,' *Korrespondenzblatt*, xxxi. [1900] 1–12.

4 The duty of Charlemagne on silver from the other side of the Elbe stopped the penetration of these coins to W. Europe.

5 *Vergleichende Grammatik*, 3 vols., Berlin, 1833–35, Eng. tr. E. B. Eastwick, London, 1845.

mention some names of deities that they came across among the Slavs whom they have known; *e.g.*, Saxo Grammaticus speaks of the gods of the Slavs of Rügen—Rugevit, Porevit, Porenuch, and Svyetovit; Helmold mentions Syetovit, Prove, Biel-Bog, and Cherno-Bog.

The authors of the 16th and 17th centuries, curiously enough, have a much larger collection of Slavic gods; thus Michaeli Frencelli (1658) describes a far greater number of gods than were known to the native and foreign travellers of the earlier period when their worship might still have been tolerated in the newly Christianized states. Frencelli describes Perun, Martsyana, Didila, Zolotaga-Baba ('golden woman'), Perenuch, Perovit, Biel-Bog, and Cherno-Bog. It is probable that the writers of the later period were influenced by the writings of the Polish historian Dlugosz, who was himself so influenced by classical mythology as to be tempted to find parallels to it in the mythology of the Slavs. Even before Dlugosz, Cosmas of Prague found a likeness between the classical and Slavic Olympus, so that in speaking of the Slavic gods he does not give them their Slavic names, but calls them Jupiter, Mars, and Bellona. Dlugosz was the first to give the Slavic equivalents, most of which do not appear in the Slavic or foreign writers before him. It is open to doubt whether any pagan cult still existed in the time of Dlugosz, 500 hundred years after the introduction of Christianity to Poland; but his deductive genius may have revealed to him from contemporary folk-lore, which must have still been very rich in his time, evidence which escaped the notice of the earlier writers. Historians of a later date merely repeat and seldom amplify his assertions.

Some Russian authors (Gizel, Popov, Glinka, etc.) believe that there were a great number of Slavic gods, and divide them into high gods, secondary gods, and spirits. Others (Nestor, Stroyev, Russov, Prigezjev, etc.) believe that there were only seven chief gods among the primitive Slavs. These were (1) Perun, the chief god, ruler of the lightning; (2) Volos (Veles), god of cattle; (3) Dajd-bog, god of wealth and success; (4) Stribog, god of wind and sometimes war; (5) Semargla (Zimtserla), goddess of cold and frost; (6) Khors (Hrs), god of sickness, sometimes of hunting and libations; (7) Mokosh (Mkosh), god of trade, often a 'gossiper.' The supporters of the seven-god system mention mostly the high gods known chiefly among E. Slavs; the supporters of Slavic polytheism mention sometimes as many as 59 (Glinka) gods and spirits, of the various Slavs, as well as names whose meaning they could not explain, and to which they could not assign any individuality—*e.g.*, Didilia, Prono, Yassa, Krado, etc.

The Russian historian N. M. Karamzin says that the old Slavs worshipped Biel-Bog ('white god') and Cherno-Bog ('black god'). This is the repetition of a statement made by Helmold that the W. Slavs made a distinction between a good and a bad god, and called the latter Cherno-Bog ('black god');[1] but we may look in vain for evidence of the cult of either of these gods in the archæological remains or in the present folk-lore. According to the great Russian folk-lorist Sakharov, who tried to introduce some system into this host of meaningless names of Slavic gods, the seven Slavic gods mentioned by Nestor ought to be called Eastern or Russ Slav gods. He attributes to the Lett or Polish Western Slavs the names of the following gods: (1) Mya, whose temple was in Gneran, (2) Gassa, (3) Lada, (4) Dzila, (5) Zyevanna, (6) Zivalo, (7) Lel, (8) Polel, (9) Pogoda, (10) Pohvist. He further considers that Svyetovit was worshipped by the Slavs of Rügen and the Wends, while the god Perkun originated with the ancient Prussians and Letts.

We may now consider the early authorities' accounts of these gods and their ritual.

The first authority to give a definite account of Slav religion is Procopius; he, of course, speaks of E. and S. Slavs. Of these people he says:

'They worship one god whom they conceive to be creator of the thunder and maker of all things; to him they sacrifice cattle and other victims. They do not recognize "Destiny," nor do they admit that she has power over men, but when death seems near them, whether it be that they are attacked by pestilence or force of arms, they vow that, if they escape, they will straightway make a sacrifice to the gods in payment for their lives. Then if they do escape, they sacrifice as they promised to do, and believe they have bought their safety by the sacrifice. However, they reverence rivers, nymphs, and other spirits, and sacrifice to them all; from these sacrifices they divine the future.'[1]

Our next authority is Thietmar, bishop of Merseburg, in the 10th cent., who speaks of the Elbe Slavs. He gives an account of the town of Riedegost, with its three gates surrounded on all sides by sacred woods and its wonderful wooden temple, the foundations of which are made of the horns of different kinds of beasts. Inside this temple are images of gods and goddesses with armour which makes them terrible to behold, and foremost among them is the chief god, Zuarasici. They have banners, which are never moved save when they lead the way to battle, and specially appointed priests to guard the gods and their treasures. When the time comes to appease or supplicate these gods, the priests sit down—the congregation stands—and, muttering spells and incantations, take lots. Then, with accompanying prayers, spears are fixed in the ground, and a sacred horse is led through them. If he steps through them, well and good; if not, trouble is imminent. The results of this augury are compared with the lots first obtained, and, if the omens agree, their fulfilment is inevitable. Thietmar goes on to say that there are as many temples in these parts as there are districts, and many single images of gods are worshipped by the people, but the city of Riedegost is the centre of the cult. Human sacrifice to appease the wrath of the gods is common.[2] Thietmar also mentions a sacred and inviolate grave at Zutibure,[3] and a sacred stick at Silivellum, in which place the people worship and sacrifice to *penates*, or domestic gods.[4] At Glomuzi was a sacred well which produced blood and ashes when war was impending.[5]

Adam of Bremen (11th cent.) gives an account of the city of Rethre (Riedegost) which is probably based on that of Thietmar. He calls the chief god 'Redigost.'[6] He also mentions the town of Iumne inhabited by Greeks, Slavs, and barbarians, where Olla Vulcani and Neptune are worshipped.[7] He tells us that in Great Estland the people worship dragons with wings, to whom they offer sacrifices of men without blemish, buying them from merchants for the purpose.[8]

Cosmas of Prague gives us information about the religion of the Czechs. He tells us that they worshipped Oreads, Dryads, and Hamadryads. Some worshipped streams, some fires, and some groves, trees, or stones. Some prayed to mountains or hills.[9] He also mentions the cult of *penates*.[10]

Helmold and Saxo Grammaticus are the chief authorities for the cult of Svantovit, who was worshipped by the people of Rügen. His temple was at Arkona on the island of Rügen. Saxo Grammaticus describes the image as having four heads and necks, two facing to the front and two behind. The beards of these heads were shaved and their hair was cut short, as was the custom of the people of Rügen. In his right hand the image held a horn of divers metals, and in the left a bow. He wore a tunic of wood reaching to the knees. Saxo describes the cult as follows. 'Once every year, after the harvest, a motley crowd from the whole island celebrated a ceremonial feast before the temple of the image and sacrificed animals as peace-offerings. The priest of the image, who was conspicuous for the length of his hair and his beard, which he wore longer than is the custom in that country, on the day before that on which

[1] *Chronica Slavorum* (*MGH*, Script., xxi.), Hanover, 1869, p. 156.

[1] *De Bell. Got.* iii. 14.
[2] Thietmar, *Chron.* vi. 17 f. (*MGH* iii. 812).
[3] vi. 26 (*MGH* iii. 816).
[4] vii. 50 (*MGH* iii. 858).
[5] i. 3 (*MGH* iii. 735).
[6] *Gesta Pontif. Hammaburg. Eccles.* ii. 18 (*MGH* vii. 312).
[7] ii. 19 (*MGH* vii. 312).
[8] iv. 17 (*MGH* vii. 374).
[9] *Chronicæ Bohemorum*, i. 4 (*MGH* ix. 34).
[10] i. 8 (*MGH* ix. 38).

he was to celebrate, carefully cleaned out with a broom the sanctuary, which he alone was allowed to enter. He was careful not to breathe in the building, and, as often as he was forced to inhale or exhale, ran to the door lest he should contaminate the presence of the god with the pollution of mortal breath. The next day, while the people watched before the doors, he took the horn from the hand of the image and looked at it carefully; if any of the liquid in it had disappeared, he judged that this portended a scanty harvest next year. With this knowledge he ordered the people to preserve their present corn for future need. If it seemed to be as full as it usually was, he predicted that the next harvest would be a good one. So then, according to the omen, he advised them to use their corn in the coming year lavishly or sparingly. Having poured the old wine at the feet of the image as a libation, he filled the empty cup with fresh wine and adored the image, pretending to be its cup-bearer. Thus doing, he prayed for an increase of wealth and victories for himself and his country in a set form of words. When he had finished he drained the cup dry at one draught with overmuch haste, and, refilling it with wine, put it again in the hand of the image.

Mead cakes were also brought forward as offerings, round in shape and almost as tall as a man. The priest put one of these between him and the people, and asked the people whether they could see him. If they said they could, he expressed the wish that they might not be able to see him next year. Then he greeted the people in the name of the image, and exhorted them to prolong their worship of the god with diligent sacrifice, promising them certain reward for their husbandry and victory by land and sea.

When these ceremonies were over, they wasted the rest of the day in luxurious banqueting, striving to turn the very sacrificial feast into conviviality and serving the victims consecrated to the god with intemperance. In this feast it was considered a religious act to get drunk, and impious to restrain oneself.'[1]

The temple of Svantovit was made of wood; it was gaily painted, and had two enclosures, the innermost having magnificent curtains instead of walls. Among the appurtenances of the god were a bridle, a saddle, and a wonderfully embossed sword. There was also a white horse, sacred to the god, which could be ridden and tended only by the priest. Since it was found covered with mire in the morning, it was concluded that Svantovit rode it during the night. Omens were taken by means of this horse in a way similar to that in which the worshippers of Zuarasici took omens with the sacred black horse; but in this case the omen was good if the horse stepped on the spear with the right foot first, and *vice versa.* Like Zuarasici, Svantovit had sacred banners which led his people to victory, the most revered of these being called *Stanitia.* Svantovit had 300 men-at-arms and horses attached to him, and always received one-third of their spoil. He was identified by the Christian monks with St. Vitus of Corvey.

Saxo Grammaticus mentions other deities in the island of Rügen closely connected with Svantovit. Such were Rugie-Vitus at Karentia (Gazz), who had seven faces and eight swords, and was so tall that Bishop Absalon could only reach his chin with his axe; Pore-Vitus, who had five heads and no weapons; and Porenutius, who had five faces, one of which was in his bosom. Rugie-Vitus was believed by the people to have the powers of Mars.[2]

Helmold also mentions Zvantevith, god of the Rugiani, and says that he is the pre-eminent deity of the N. or Elbe Slavs. In comparison with him, they consider the rest demigods. Every year a Christian is chosen by lot and sacrificed to him.[3] The king is held in very moderate estimation compared with the priest of Svantovit.[1] Merchants from abroad were not allowed to sell their goods in the market till they had offered part of them to the god.[2]

Herbord[3] (12th cent.) mentions a god Gerovitus who had his shrine at Hologost, and was worshipped by the Pomeranians; he was said to have the attributes of Mars. Ebbo[4] mentions his enormous shield which must not be touched by mortal hands, and could be moved only in case of war. He is most probably an analogue to Svantovit.

Another god who is considered to have affinities with Svantovit is Triglav of Stettin. There were four temples in Stettin, one of which was far more important than the others. It had on its inner and outer walls such wonderful embossed figures of men, birds, and animals that they seemed to live and breathe. The colours of these paintings could not be dimmed by rain or snow. The temple was full of valuables, such as drinking-cups of gold and silver, horns decorated for the purpose of drinking or made into musical instruments. One-tenth of all the booty was stored in this temple. The three other temples were less ornate, and had in them tables and chairs for meetings, for on certain days and hours the inhabitants were wont to assemble there to drink, play games, or discuss matters of importance. Near the temples were a sacred oak and a sacred fountain. The image of the god had three heads and was made of gold. Its eyes and lips were covered with a veil. This god had a sacred black horse. Divination was made in the usual way with nine lances. If the horse, when led three times across them, did not touch them, the omen was favourable.[5]

Ebbo[6] tells the story of another image of this god from Wollin, which was saved from the iconoclasm of St. Otto by the Slav priests, who gave it to a woman to hide in a lonely part of the country. He also tells us[7] that the three heads of the god denote his three kingdoms—the heavens, the earth, and the under world. Triglav was also worshipped by the Slavs of Brandenburg.[8]

Helmold also mentions the names of several other gods, such as Prove, god of the land of Aldenburg, of whom there was no image.[9] He had a secret grove surrounded by a fence, where at a certain time the people assembled with their priest and ruler for judgment.[10] This grove was so sacred that even those in peril of death could not take refuge there. Then there was Siwa (Syuna), goddess of the Polabi, and Podaga, an image which was worshipped at Pluna.[11]

Helmold says that at feasts the Slavs prayed to a divinity of evil as well as to one of good, 'professing to receive prosperity from a good god, and adversity from a bad one. Therefore in their language they call the bad god Diabol or Zcerneboch, which is Black God.'[12] He adds: 'Indeed, among the many forms of the gods to whom they attribute fields, woods, sorrows, and pleasures, they do not deny that one god rules over the others in the skies, who cares only for celestial things, the rest performing their various functions, proceeding from his blood, and enjoying distinction in proportion as they are nearer to that god of gods.'[13] He does not, however, give the name of this god.

Dlugosz[14] attempts to identify the old Slavic gods with the Greek and Roman deities. Jessis he identifies with Jove. He is the highest god, from whom is all temporal good and protection from one's enemies. Honour is paid to him above all other gods and he is worshipped with more frequent sacrifices. Liada corresponds to Mars; he is a leader and god of war. Men pray to him for triumphs over their enemies and that their hearts may be fierce; they propitiate him with a very rude sort of worship. Dzidzielia is the same as Venus, the goddess of marriage and fertility. To her men pray for sons and daughters. Nüa, or Pluto, is worshipped as god of the under world and of souls when they leave the body. He is propitiated to persuade him to admit souls to the more favourable parts of his domain. Pogoda (Zylvie, Dziewanna) is like Diana. She is worshipped as a woman and virgin by wives and

1 *Historia Danica*, bk. xiv., ed. P. E. Müller and I. M. Velschow, Copenhagen, 1839–58, i. 822 ff.
2 *Ib.*
3 *Chron. Slav.* i. 52 (*MGH* xxi. 52).

1 ii. 12 (*MGH* xxi. 96).
2 i. 6 (*MGH* xxi. 16).
3 *Vita Ottonis Episc. Bamberg.* iii. 6 (*MGH* xii. 804 f.).
4 *Ib.* iii. 8 (*MGH* xii. 865).
5 *Ib.* ii. 31 f. (*MGH* xii. 793 f.).
6 *Ib.* ii. 13 (*MGH* xii. 851 f.).
7 *Ib.* iii. 1 (*MGH* xii. 589).
8 Pulkawa, *Chronicon Bohemiæ* (*Fontes Rerum Bohemicarum*, Prague, 1893, v. 89), quoted by J. Máchal, *Slavic Mythology* (=*Mythology of all Races*, iii.), p. 353.
9 i. 52, 83 (*MGH* xxi. 52, 78).
10 i. 83 (*MGH* xxi. 75).
11 i. 52, 83 (*MGH* xxi. 52, 75).
12 i. 52 (*MGH* xxi. 52).
13 i. 83 (*MGH* xxi. 75).
14 *Hist. Polonicæ*, i. 36 f.

virgins, and as Ceres by settlers and those engaged in agriculture, who try to make corn grow by sacrifices. She is also venerated as goddess of the weather under the name Pogoda ('giver of a favourable wind'). Marzanna was, like Ceres, worshipped as the mother and goddess of corn, and held in very special reverence. Dlugosz goes on to say that those deities had shrines, images, sacred precincts, and priests allotted to them, and were offered as sacrifices cattle, sheep, baggage-animals, and even human victims taken in battle. They had religious games at regular intervals, which survived in the form of the Polish celebration at Pentecost and the 'Stado' after fully 500 years of Christian influence.

3. Spirits.—(*a*) *Spirits of the dead.*—Leo Diaconus (10th cent.) gives an interesting account of the funeral rites of the Danube Slavs of his period. He describes the scene after a battle:

'Now had night begun, and when the moon shone full, they went out over the plain and sought their dead. These they burnt beside the wall with much fuel in heaps, and with them many captives, both men and women, whom they slaughtered after the manner of their nation. Thus did they feast the infernal deities, suffocating babes unweaned and cocks in the Ister, drowning them in the waters of the river. For they say that these people take part in Greek orgies and make sacrifices and offer libations to the departed after the manner of the Hellenes, having been initiated in these mysteries by Anacharsis and Zamolxis, their own philosophers, or else by the "Comrades of Achilles."'[1]

The Arabian traveller Ibn Fadlān gives an interesting description of the obsequies of a Russian chieftain:

'When a nobleman died, for ten days his body was laid provisionally in his grave, where he was left until his shroud was prepared for him. His property was divided into three parts, one-third was given to the family, another served to defray the funeral expenses, and the remainder was spent on intoxicating drinks which were served at the funeral banquet. On the day appointed for the final obsequies, a boat was taken out of the water, and round it were placed pieces of wood shaped to the form of human beings. Then the corpse was removed from its provisional grave and, being clad with a costly garment, was seated in a boat on a richly ornamented arm-chair, around which were arranged the weapons of the deceased together with intoxicating beverages; while not only bread and fruit, but also flesh of killed animals, such as dogs, horses, cows, cocks, and hens, were put into the boat. Then one of his wives, who had voluntarily agreed to be burned together with her dead husband, was led to the boat by an old woman called the "Angel of Death," and was stabbed at the side of the corpse, whereupon the wood piled up under and around the boat was set on fire. After the boat with the dead bodies and all the other articles placed upon it had been consumed, the ashes were collected and scattered over the cairn, and a banquet, lasting for days and nights without interruption, closed the ceremony.'[2]

Similar evidence is given by Mas'ūdī.[3] Testimony is supplied by V. Kadlubek[4] that young girls tore their hair, matrons their faces, and old women their garments.

It is obvious from these few notices that ancestor-worship at a remote period was widely spread among the Slavs, who looked upon their dead ancestors as beings deeply interested in the fortunes of their children. Evidence of the persistence of this belief is to be found in the *dziadys* of White Russia and the *zadusnica* of Bulgaria in modern times. The drowned and suffocated children mentioned by Leo Diaconus are the origin of the *rusalky*, or water-spirits, of modern Russia.

(*b*) *The penates.*—Helmold[1] says that, 'besides groves and household gods (*penates*) in whom the fields and towns abounded, there were powerful gods, etc.,' alluding to the cult of *penates* among the ancient Slavs. Cosmas of Prague[2] relates the story of Czech who carried the *penates* on his shoulders to the new country, resting on the mountain of the Rzip and saying to his followers: 'Come, good comrades, and make sacrifice to your *penates*, for it is by their help that ye have been brought to this new country destined for you by Fate of old.' The Slavic name for them (*ded, dedik, deduska*, etc.), meaning 'grandfather,' shows that they had their origin in ancestor-worship. Survivals of this cult are the Russian *domovoy*, the Little Russian *didko*, the Bohemian *setek*, the Polish *skrzatek*, the Bulgarian *stopan*, and the *ludki* of the Lusatian Sorbs and Slovaks.

(*c*) *Genii of fate, the woods, water, etc.*—Of these we have few notices in the contemporary and early authorities. Procopius,[3] as we have seen, denies that they pay any reverence to 'Destiny,' but affirms that they worship rivers, nymphs, and other spirits, and even make sacrifices to them. Cosmas of Prague,[4] as we saw above, says:

'Oreads, Dryads and Hamadryads are objects of adoration and worship to this foolish and silly people'; and again: 'Some worship streams, some fires, some groves, trees, or stones. Some pray to mountains or hills.'

The modern Slavs have *genii* of fate, *rodjenice* (Croatia) and the Russian *dolya* (Serbian, *sreča*); *vily*, nymphs; *lesig*, Dryads, and the *poludnica*, who is almost an Oread. The Russian *vodyanik* is a sort of Slavic 'old man of the sea.'[5]

LITERATURE.—Modern authorities on the religion and mythology of the Slavs include the following: A. Brückner, 'Poczatki Kultury Slowianskiej,' in *Encyklopedja Polska*, vol. iv. pt. 2, Cracow, 1916; J. Dlugosz, *Historiæ Polonicæ*, 2 vols., Leipzig, 1711–12; J. Máchal, *Slavic Mythology* (=*Mythology of all Races*, iii.), Boston, U.S.A., 1918; P. J. Šafařík, *Slovanské Starozitnosti*, 2 vols., Prague, 1837, Germ. tr., *Slawische Alterthümer*, Leipzig, 1843–44; T. R. Georgevitch, 'Parthenogenesis in Serbian Popular Tradition,' *FL* xxix. [1918] 58 ff.; N. M. Karamzin, *Hist. de l'empire de Russie*, French tr., 11 vols., Paris, 1819–26; I. P. Sakarov, *The Story of the Russian People* (Russ.), 2 vols., St. Petersburg, 1841–49. See also R. J. Kerner, *Slavic Europe: A Selected Bibliography*, Harvard and Oxford, 1918; E. Kolodziejczyk, *Bibliografja Slowianoznawstwa Polskiego*, Cracow, 1911.

M. A. CZAPLICKA.

SLAVERY.

SLAVERY (Primitive).—I. *INTRODUCTORY.*—**1. Definition and scope.**—The most generally accepted definition of slavery is that it is a social system in which one person is the property of another. Westermarck takes exception to this definition:

'The owner's right over his property, even when not absolute, is at all events exclusive, that is, nobody but the owner has the right to dispose of it,' whereas 'the master's right of disposing of his slave is not necessarily exclusive; custom or law may grant the latter a certain amount of liberty, and in such case his condition differs essentially from that of a piece of property.'[6]

Now those who speak of a slave as property admit that restrictions on the exercise of the master's power are indeed common, but would say, with Nieboer:

[1] *Hist.* ix. 6 (*Corp. Script. Hist. Byz.*, Bonn, 1828, pt. xi. p. 149 f.).
[2] *Ibn Foszlan's und anderer Araber Berichte über die Russen älterer Zeit*, tr. C. M. Frähn, St. Petersburg, 1823, pp. 10–21, quoted by Máchal, p. 233 f.
[3] *Les Prairies d'or*, Paris, 1861–69, ii. 9, iii. 62 f., quoted by Máchal, p. 234.
[4] *Script. Hist. Polon.*, Danzig, 1749.

[1] i. 52 (*MGH* xxi. 52).
[2] *Chron. Bohem.* i. 2 (*MGH* ix. 33).
[3] *De Bell. Got.* iii. 14. 3.
[4] i. 4 (*MGH* ix. 34).
[5] The writer would like to acknowledge the collaboration of Miss A. B. Finch White, of Lady Margaret Hall, Oxford, in preparing this article.
[6] *MI* i. 670.

'Any restriction put upon the free exercise of his power is a mitigation of slavery, not belonging to its nature.'[1]

By 'property' this Dutch writer, who is the foremost authority on the economics of primitive slavery, means

'a power that, however leniently exercised in many cases, is in principle unlimited.'[2]

We are reminded of the following rule in Roman and Romanized modern law:

'The proprietor has had the right to do with his property whatever he is not by special rules forbidden to do.'[3]

Property in a human being, *i.e.* slavery, is equivalent to a right to all the labour of the slave.[4]

The view which regards a slave as the property of the master is not then, it seems, inconsistent with Westermarck's own position, that the essence of slavery is to be found in the compulsory nature of the slave's relation to his master; in other words:

'Slavery is essentially an industrial institution, which implies compulsory labour beyond the limits of family relations.'[5]

All would agree with the statement of this authority:

'The master has a right to avail himself of the working power of his slave, without previous agreement on the part of the latter.'[6] 'Voluntary slavery, as when a person sells himself as a slave, is only an imitation of slavery true and proper; the person who gives up his liberty confers upon another, by contract, either for a limited period or for ever, the same rights over himself as a master possesses over his slave. If slavery proper could be based upon a contract between the parties concerned, I fail to see how to distinguish between a servant and a slave.'[7]

We may combine the two kinds of definition and define a slave as a human being who is the property of another and subject to compulsory labour, beyond the limits of the family.

The expression 'primitive' is difficult to define with precision. By 'primitive peoples' we may understand certain ethnic groups which occupy a relatively little advanced position in the scale of cultural development. The groups included in the present survey will be confined to those which live in 'tribal society'—*i.e.*, that have kinship (a social relation not always synonymous with physical consanguinity) as the basis of membership in the group (clan, gens, phratry, tribe), in contrast to citizenship in political states. Admission of an outsider into the group is by 'adoption,' in contradistinction to 'naturalization.' Another criterion is the possession or lack of literary records, of history in the strict sense. Under 'primitive' will be included not only 'savages,' but also groups in a state of 'barbarism.' Our present discussion will not embrace the early stages of nations that have developed into 'civilization.' We shall consider as primitive, not only hunting tribes, but most pastoral and many agricultural societies.

2. Slavery distinguished from similar phenomena.—(*a*) *Subjection of wives.* — The status of wives among primitive peoples is often referred to as 'slavery.' Without considering here the question whether the subjection of women, particularly of wives, in primitive society is as abject as is popularly supposed,[8] it may be said that slavery as a social institution and industrial system does not exist when there are only female slaves. When women only are enslaved, the reason probably is that they are valued as women rather than as labourers; otherwise men also would be enslaved.[9]

(*b*) *Subjection of children.*—In primitive societies every family has its head, who exercises more or less authority over its members, including, of course, the young. But, no matter how complete this subjection may be, it cannot be called slavery, which, as a social institution, has a very different origin and function. Slavery is a relation beyond the limits of the family, as stated in Westermarck's definition given above.[1]

1 *Slavery as an Industrial System*, p. 3.
2 *Ib.* p. 37.
3 See also L. Dargun, 'Ursprung und Entwicklungsgeschichte des Eigenthums,' *ZVRW* v. [1884] 3.
4 Nieboer, p. 37; see also below, under 'Serfdom,' I. 2 (*e*).
5 *MI* i. 670.
6 *Ib.*
7 *Ib.* i. 671.
8 See *MI* i. ch. xxvi.
9 See Nieboer, p. 23.

(*c*) *Subjection of members of a society to its head.*—The subjects of a despotic ruler are sometimes called his slaves. To this use of the term it is to be objected that, in order to have slavery, it is necessary that the master's power should be recognized by the society.

'The whole group must approve of the custom and must enforce it; otherwise it cannot exist.'[2]

The slave lives in a society that recognizes him as a slave; slavery can exist only where there is a society of freemen. The head of a community, no matter how great his power may be, is not as such a master of slaves. Of course, a chief, like other freemen, may keep slaves of his own.

(*d*) *Subjection of tribes, provinces, or classes.*—Where a population or territory is subject to an external power, this is not slavery. The latter is the subjection of men individually and a subjection which includes the whole personality of the slave. A slave cannot live in tribal relations; he would to that extent be free. J. K. Ingram observes:

'The lowest caste may be a degraded and despised one, but its members are not in a state of slavery; they are in collective, not individual, subjection to the members of the higher classes.'[3]

This is true also of subjected tribes. Subjection of tribes as such sometimes serves as a substitute for slavery proper, making the latter superfluous.

(*e*) *Serfdom.*—Ingram says:

'The transition to serfdom took place in civic communities when the master parted with or was deprived of his property in the person of the slave, and became entitled only to his services, or to a determinate portion of them.'[4]

This is a correct statement, with this important exception, that the right, not to the services of the labourer, but to 'a determinate portion' of them, is the real differential of serfdom. For, as Nieboer points out, he who is entitled to all the services of another is his owner:

'The slave-owner may do with his slave whatever he is not by special laws forbidden to do; the master of the serf may require from his man such services or tributes only as the law allows him to require.'[5]

It may be remarked that, while it is necessary, for the purposes of discussion, to draw theoretical lines of demarcation, practically there is not a single social institution that is strictly separated from kindred institutions. The student of social phenomena still recognizes the truth in Spencer's observation:

'As the distinctions between different forms of slavery are indefinite, so must there be an indefinite distinction between slavery and serfdom, and between the several forms of serfdom. Much confusion has arisen in describing these respective institutions, and for the sufficient reason that the institutions themselves are confused.'[6]

II. *ORIGIN AND EARLY GROWTH OF SLAVERY.*

—1. Extra-tribal slavery in relation to war.—Slavery in early society may be divided into intra-tribal and extra-tribal, depending on whether or not the slave belongs to the same kinship-group as the master, *i.e.* to the 'in-group' as distinct from the 'out-group,' to use Sumner's terminology.[7] Extra-tribal slavery is first both in time and in extent. In the primitive group all members are on a footing of equality; they are 'all-one-flesh,' and practice conforms to theory. 'Custom everywhere, as a rule, forbids the enslaving of tribesmen.'[8] It is only in extraordinary cases, and after slavery of the extra-tribal form has become

1 See *MI* i. ch. xxv.; also art. CHILDREN.
2 Sumner, *Folkways*, p. 262.
3 *Hist. of Slavery and Serfdom*, London, 1895, p. 3.
4 *Ib.* p. 262.
5 P. 37.
6 *Principles of Sociology*, iii. 472.
7 P. 12.
8 *MI* i. 675.

prevalent, that a person is permitted to enslave a member of his own community.

All available evidence confirms the view, held by all students of the subject, that slavery is a sequence of war, that the earliest slaves were captives in war.[1] Now it is necessary to revise radically the traditional view that war is the constant and normal state of earliest human society. The data from pre-historic archæology (implements, art, etc.), as well as from the ethnology of latter-day 'savages,' indicate a decidedly peaceable life among primitive mankind. This is even more true if we distinguish, as it is often difficult to do, between blood-feuds and wars of communities as such. In the correlation made by Hobhouse and his collaborators it is found that the groups under the heading 'no war' were confined mainly to the lowest grade of hunting tribes.[2] As one would expect, the same groups are among those in which slavery is quite unknown.[3] When war had become a feature of the relations of human groups, the rights and immunities which prevented the enslavement of tribesmen would not operate in favour of captives from hostile bands. While there are at times mitigating circumstances, in the main it is true that 'the defeated enemy is rightless, and is treated as best suits the victor's convenience.'[4] Quarter may be refused altogether and the vanquished foes exterminated. Or, if prisoners are taken, they may be tortured, eaten, adopted, ransomed, exchanged, liberated, or enslaved. In the actual practice of existing tribes there are instances of all these modes of treatment.

Adoption, a custom which is especially common among the N. American Indians,[5] is the main exception to the rule that the life of the captive is spared in order that he may become a slave. It may be remarked here that a distinction is often made between the adult males among the enemy on the one hand and the women and children on the other. The men may be killed, while the women and children are adopted or enslaved. Adoption is probably intimately related to the beginnings of slavery. According to the theory of J. W. Powell,[6] for which there is much to be said, the latter institution is a development of the practice of adoption. The motives for keeping captives alive are not likely to have been, in the beginning, the shrewd calculations usually ascribed to primitive man, as in the following statement of Hobhouse:

'There comes a time in social development when the victor sees that a live prisoner is after all better than a dead one.'[7]

Nieboer's criticism is much to the point:

'It is not to be supposed that men, convinced of the utility of some new kind of labour, began to procure slaves in order to make them perform this labour; or that, finding some work tedious, they invented slavery to relieve themselves of this burden. Modern psychology does not account for psychical and social phenomena in such a rationalistic way.' 'Social institutions are sometimes made; but this is the exception; generally they grow.'[8]

Whatever the primary motives for enslaving vanquished enemies may have been, it is doubtless true that slavery marks 'a humanitarian improvement in the laws of war.'[9] Also, as Hobhouse observes:

'The vindictive passions must be sufficiently held in check to prevent their gratification in the moment of victory.'[10]

2. Internal conditions of the growth of slavery; occurrence in various states of culture.—No matter what may be the external relations of the group, slavery could not exist unless it conformed to the requirements of the social life of the tribe both in its purely economic and in its more distinctly moral aspects. This appears clearly from the study of the actual appearance and distribution of slavery among the uncivilized peoples of various cultural grades.

(*a*) *Among hunting tribes.*—Human societies in the hunting stage hardly ever keep slaves. Among 'lower hunters,' the representatives of the real 'primitive man,' slavery is entirely unknown.[1] Even among 'higher hunters' it is extremely rare; and its occurrence is due to certain extraordinary circumstances. Of the 83 hunting groups analyzed by Nieboer there are 65 negative and only 18 positive cases. Of the latter 15 are Indian tribes on the N.W. Pacific coast of N. America (see below). The remaining three are the Tehuelches and Abipones in S. America and the Kamchadales in Siberia.[2]

The reasons for these facts are not far to seek. As Westermarck says:

'Slaves are kept only where there is employment for them, and where the circumstances are otherwise favourable to the growth of slavery.'[3]

Now the economic state of hunting societies is decidedly unfavourable to the development of slavery.

'In the absence of industrial activity, slaves are almost useless: and, indeed, where game is scarce, are not worth their food.'[4]

In the desperate daily struggle for existence it is necessary for every man to exert his powers to the utmost, and each man, even then, can produce barely enough for himself and his family. Hence slaves, even if they were as efficient as their masters, could not produce any surplus for the use of the latter. But slave-labour is essentially inefficient in work, such as hunting, which requires great skill and application.

As Nieboer expresses it, 'a compulsory hunting system cannot exist. If a man is to exert all his faculties, there must be other motives than mere compulsion.'[5] Spencer also observes that 'the relative lack of energy, the entire lack of interest, the unintelligent performance of work, and the greater cost of supervision, make the slave an unprofitable productive agent.'[6] So too J. S. Mill: 'It remains certain that slavery is incompatible with any high state of the arts of life, and any great efficiency of labour.'[7]

This applies equally to the primitive hunting life and to modern industrialism; it is a striking instance of the correspondence between extremes.

But, even if slaves were profitable, it would be very difficult to keep them in subjection or prevent their escape. Hunting supposes a nomadic life, and the hunter who roams over vast stretches of country in pursuit of his game has not much chance to watch over the movements of his slave. And, if the slave himself were set to hunting, as he would have to be (all men being needed in that work), this difficulty would amount almost to impossibility. Moreover, a hunting slave will be much more inclined to run away than a soil-tilling slave; for the latter, during his flight, has to live upon the spontaneous products of the land, whereas the former can continue hunting, just as he has done before; his flight would not be of the nature of a flight.

Another cause for the non-existence of slavery is that primitive hunters generally live in small groups—at the most, of a few hundred persons.[8] Now such a small group would not be able to develop coercive power sufficient to keep in sub-

[1] See, among many others, Spencer, iii. 459, 470; *MI* i. 674.
[2] *Material Culture and Social Institutions*, p. 228.
[3] *Ib.* p. 30.
[4] Hobhouse, *Morals in Evolution*, i. 244.
[5] See J. N. B. Hewitt, art. 'Adoption,' in *HAI* i. 15 f.
[6] 'On Regimentation,' *15 RBEW* [1893-94], p. cxii.
[7] i. 252.
[8] P. 193 and footnote.
[9] Sumner, p. 262.
[10] i. 252.

[1] Under this head are included the Australians, Tasmanians, Andamanese, Negritos, Veddas, African Pygmies, Bushmen, Kubus, Botocudos, and Fuegians. They correspond to A. Vierkandt's *unstäte Völker* ('Die Kulturtypen der Menschheit,' *AA* xxv. [1898] 67 ff.). See Hobhouse, Wheeler, and Ginsberg, p. 30; Nieboer, p. 186 ff.
[2] P. 187 ff.
[3] i. 671.
[4] Spencer, iii. 459.
[5] P. 195.
[6] iii. 470.
[7] *Principles of Political Economy*[5], London, 1862, i. 302.
[8] See A. Sutherland, *The Origin and Growth of the Moral Instinct*, London, 1898, i. 360.

jection slaves introduced from foreign parts. A fugitive slave would very soon be beyond the reach of his master's tribe, and a relatively small number of slaves would be a danger to the power of the free tribesmen.

But there are still other, more psychical, reasons militating against the introduction of slavery among primitive hunters. Both in emotional interest and in social evaluation hunting is an agreeable and noble occupation.

Nieboer describes it as 'occupying the whole soul and leaving no room for distracting thought; offering the hunter a definite aim to which he can reach by one mighty effort of strength and skill; uncertain in its results like battle, and promising the glory of victory over a living creature. . . . It is not a work fit to be imposed upon men who are deprived of the common rights of freemen and are the property of others.'[1]

Not only the intrinsic character of the work of the hunter, but also its social worth, takes it out of the forms of labour suited to enslaved persons. Among a primitive hunting people hereditary nobility is unknown and wealth does not exist; personal qualities are the only basis of social differentiation. Besides generosity, hospitality, and wisdom in council, strength, courage, and skill form the primitive patent of nobility. The activities in which these qualities are expressed and demonstrated are hunting and (though not universally) warfare.[2] Now, to admit slaves as hunters and warriors would be to place them on a footing of equality with freemen. Public opinion could not consider as slaves those who are successful in the noble occupations of hunting and fighting; and without public opinion the masters would be unable to keep them in subjection. And a poor hunter would be of little or no use as a hunting slave.

This attitude of respect for the hunter prevents the growth of intra-tribal slavery, for no member of the tribe is so superior to any other member that he can reduce him to a state of complete subjection, unless perhaps the latter is a physical or mental weakling, in which case he would be of no value as a hunting slave. It also tends to prevent extra-tribal slavery, though here what Sumner has called 'ethnocentrism,' with the common accompaniment of contempt for people who do not belong to the 'we-group,' would act as a neutralizing force in many cases; it would be a case of contempt for the enemy and stranger against respect for the hunter and warrior. There are, however, not a few instances on record where enemies, though they are hated and feared, are not despised. Among the Indians of the central parts of N. America captives were, as a rule, either killed or adopted; in the latter case they were regarded and treated as members of the tribe.

The study of the life of the simplest grades of human society leads to the conclusion that, in the strictest sense of the word, slavery is not a primitive institution; its appearance and growth depend on social conditions which are absent in the lowest forms of human association to-day, as they undoubtedly were during by far the greater portion of the time that man has existed upon the earth.

Attention is again called to the fact, noted above, that 15 out of the 18 positive cases of slavery among tribes in the hunting stage, according to Nieboer's tabulation, are found among the Indians of the N.W. Pacific coast of N. America. Now, while these tribes are classed in the general economic and cultural grade of hunting groups, on the negative ground of their being unacquainted with cattle-breeding or agriculture,[3] they have some very important characteristics which mark them off rather sharply from hunters in the strict sense. The principal and underlying characteristic is that they get their subsistence from fishing, not from hunting land-animals. The study of these particular aborigines is of special value in that it brings out, in a notable way, several of the general causes which account for the growth of slavery. They possess many features of economic and social life the absence of which tends to prevent or retard the growth of slavery among hunting peoples. Food is abundant and easy to procure. They have fixed habitations and live in comparatively large groups. They are enabled to do so by preserving food for future consumption. Also a settled life makes the escape of slaves more difficult. Living in larger groups brings about a higher organization of freemen, and hence greater coercive power. And the preserving of goods demands additional labour, which is fit to be performed by slaves, as it does not require much skill and has to be done in or near the dwellings, so that supervision is easy. Moreover, as Nieboer remarks: 'The hope of partaking of the stored food is a tie that binds the slave to his master's house, in much the same manner as a modern labourer is bound by having a share in the insurance funds of the manufactory.'[1] Slave-trade is carried on. This facilitates the keeping of slaves. Captives taken in war usually belong to neighbouring tribes and have more opportunity to escape to their native parts than have purchased slaves, who have often been brought from a great distance. Fishing implements have been brought to a high degree of perfection; fishing has become more remunerative; and the product of a fishing slave's labours exceeds his primary wants. The more freemen devote themselves to trade and industry, the more need is there for slaves to do the ruder work of fishing, rowing, cooking, etc.

1 P. 193. J. Dewey points out that 'game and sport are still words which mean the most intense immediate play of the emotions, running their whole gamut' ('Interpretation of Savage Mind,' in *Psychological Review*, ix. [1902] 217; this art. is an admirable study of the nature and effects of the mental life of the hunting stage).

2 For a study of the *mores* of a typical hunting people see A. N. Gilbertson, 'Ethical Phases of Eskimo Culture,' *Journ. of Religious Psychology*, vi. and vii. [1913–14].

3 See Nieboer, p. 174.

(*b*) *Among pastoral tribes.*—Pastoral nomadism has been considered favourable to the growth of slavery. There is 'the mystical belief,' as Nieboer calls it, 'that the taming of animals naturally leads to the taming of men';[2] *i.e.*, it is supposed that the nomadic herdsman who has learned to domesticate animals begins also to domesticate, to enslave, men.

Thus J. Lippert holds that slavery 'first arises in the patriarchal communities of pastoral peoples'; the slaves 'were the object of an appropriation entirely similar to the appropriation of the domestic animals.'[3]

A study of the actual origin and distribution of slavery dispels speculations of this kind. Nieboer's survey shows that only one-half of the pastoral tribes of the globe keep slaves. It may be noted here that the positive cases are all found in a few definite areas, mainly N.W. and N.E. Africa, and a few tribes in the Caucasus and Arabia, while the pastoral nomads of Siberia, Central Asia, India, and S. Africa do not have slaves.[4]

The fact is that slavery is of little moment to pastoral peoples as such; among some of the slave-keeping tribes slaves are kept as a mere luxury. The chief reason for this is that, in pastoral life, subsistence depends almost entirely on capital, *i.e.*, cattle, and comparatively little on labour, and for the small amount of labour demanded free labourers are available.

'Among people who live upon the produce of their cattle, a man who owns no cattle, *i.e.*, no capital, has no means of subsistence. Accordingly, among pastoral tribes we find rich and poor men; and the poor often offer themselves as labourers to the rich.'[5]

But, on the other hand, Nieboer continues:

'There are no causes preventing them from having slaves. These tribes are, so to speak, in a state of equilibrium; a small additional cause on either side turns the balance.'[6]

The most important of such additional causes favouring the growth of slavery are the slave-trade and the neighbourhood of inferior races. It is found that the regions mentioned above as being those to which slavery among pastoral tribes is confined are exactly those where the slave-trade has for a long time been carried on on an extensive scale. The slaves are often purchased from slave-traders, and in several cases they belong to races with an inferior culture.

(*c*) *Among agricultural tribes.*—Three stages in the development of agriculture may be distin-

1 P. 205.

2 P. 292.

3 *Kulturgesch. der Menschheit*, Stuttgart, 1886–87, pp. 522, 535.

4 For list of tribes and detailed description see Nieboer, p. 261 ff.

5 Nieboer, p. 199.

6 *Ib.* p. 292.

guished in the tribal societies coming within the field of our present consideration: (1) in the first stage agriculture holds a subordinate place, subsistence being derived chiefly from other sources (hunting, fishing, gathering wild-growing plant food);[1] (2) tribes in the second stage carry on agriculture to a considerable extent, but not to the point of exclusive dependence upon it; (3) the third stage is that in which agriculture is by far the principal source of subsistence; the other, more primitive, means of livelihood hold such a subordinate place that, if they were entirely wanting, the economic state would be practically the same.[2]

A survey of the agricultural tribes of the world shows that slavery prevails extensively among them. On the other hand, there are many agricultural tribes without slaves, so that the practice of agriculture does not necessarily lead to the keeping of slaves. It is found, furthermore, that slavery is much more common among such tribes as subsist chiefly by agriculture than among the incipient agriculturists, who still depend to a considerable extent on hunting or fishing. In the first stage of agriculture a minority of tribes has slaves; the more agriculture develops, the more common slavery becomes, until in the third stage it exists in the great majority of tribes. Now it may be noted that agricultural societies of the most primitive stage bear a strong resemblance to tribes of the more specifically hunting type. Generally the business of the men is still largely hunting and warfare; the tilling of the soil is carried on mainly by the women.[3] This division of labour does not in principle differ much from that which prevails among such hunting peoples as the Australian aborigines, where the women gather fruits and dig roots. These primitive agricultural tribes are often nomadic.[4] When the products of the fields are scarcely ripe, they reap them and move on to some other place. Or they may sow something in a favourable spot as they pass, and return later to reap the fruits. The best examples of this type of agriculturists are found among some of the Indian tribes of S. America.[5]

Where agriculture is carried on without the aid of domestic animals, subsistence does not demand much capital. Where the population is scarce, as it generally is, only the most fertile and most accessible grounds are cultivated; very primitive implements are used; even the plough is used by very few tribal societies; they usually content themselves with a hoe or pointed stick.[6] And, even where agriculture is carried on in a more skilful manner, as by means of irrigation, it is not capital that is wanted, but labour. The construction of irrigation works may be a long and laborious task, but the materials cost nothing. Since subsistence is independent of capital and easy to procure, nobody offers his services to another.

'All freemen in new countries,' says Bagehot, 'must be pretty equal; every one has labour, and every one has land; capital, at least in agricultural countries (for pastoral countries are very different), is of little use; it cannot hire labour; the labourers go and work for themselves.'[1]

Hence, under such conditions, if a man wants another to work for him, he must force him to do so—in other words, he must make him a slave. This holds true of most primitive agricultural communities, *i.e.* of all those that have at their disposal more fertile land than is needed for cultivation, in order to support the actual population. But this state of things does not always exist.

In some areas every piece of arable land has been appropriated. In that case a man cannot procure his subsistence independently of a landlord. Hence 'free labourers' are available, slaves are not wanted, and slavery is not likely to exist. And, even where there are no poor persons, but every one has a share in the resources of the country, the use of slaves is not great when all land has been appropriated. When there is free land, a man can, by increasing the number of his slaves, increase his income to any extent. But, where the supply of land is limited, a landowner can employ only a limited number of labourers. As soon as there are hands enough to till his land, an increase in the number of labourers would be unprofitable. Perhaps the operation of this economic principle in primitive societies is best illustrated by conditions in Oceania, where slavery is confined to a few islands. The fact that all land had been appropriated led to a state of things inconsistent with slavery as a social and industrial system.[2]

It has been pointed out above that the need of skill and application, the intrinsic interest and excitement, and the social worth of the occupation are among the forces preventing or retarding the development of slavery among hunters. These forces are absent in agricultural life. As compared with hunting or sea-faring or even manufacture, agriculture is likely to be rather dull work, requiring patience rather than strength or skill. And there is not a single instance discovered of influence or power depending on agriculture (as distinct from ownership of land). It is an occupation that has been regarded as especially fit for women and slaves. These facts, together with the more material causes, tend to make the social life of agricultural groups favourable to the existence and growth of slavery.

3. Intra-tribal slavery.—After slavery had come to exist in its original form of extra-tribal slavery, it was extended also to some classes of cases in the in-group. The two principal causes of intra-tribal enslavement are debt and crime. In some exceptional cases a debtor who cannot pay is put to death. Much more frequently he becomes the slave of the creditor. Often, though not always, the debtor-slave or pawn has a right to become free again by paying his debt. Such is the case with the debtor-slaves (known by the Dutch name of *pandelingen*) in the Malay Archipelago. Here the creditor cannot refuse to accept the money.[3] In some cases a man will pay a debt by giving one or more of his kindred, usually children or women, into slavery to the creditor.

Slavery may be imposed as a punishment for crime, either directly or when the compensation (*wergild*) is not paid. Members of the offender's family may likewise be liable to enslavement.[4]

III. *POSITION AND TREATMENT OF SLAVES.*—While slavery may in principle involve an absolute power of the master over his slave, in practice there are undoubtedly many and marked limitations on the exercise of this power. It is found also that slaves may have certain 'rights,' determined by custom or public opinion, which the master is bound to respect. With regard to 'the power of life and death,' it may be expected that, when the slaves are war captives, the right of killing an enemy would pass into the right of killing the

[1] The tribes in this stage are the *Jägerbauern* ('hunting agriculturists') of Dargun (*ZVRW* v. 60).

[2] See Nieboer, p. 175; Hobhouse, Wheeler, and Ginsberg, p. 235.

[3] Woman's work as the primitive agriculturist is one of the most important chapters in the history of human civilization; see O. T. Mason, *Woman's Share in Primitive Culture*, New York, 1894, esp. ch. ii. 'The Food-Bringer.'

[4] This feature of primitive culture is noted by W. Cunningham (*The Growth of English Industry and Commerce*[5], Cambridge, 1915, i. 31 ff.); he remarks that 'primitive agriculture is perfectly consistent with a very migratory life' (p. 33).

[5] See Nieboer, p. 297.

[6] The *Hackbau* of E. Hahn (*Die Haustiere und ihre Beziehungen zur Wirtschaft der Menschen*, Leipzig, 1896, p. 388 ff.) as distinguished from agriculture proper or *Ackerbau*.

[1] *Physics and Politics*, London, 1872, p. 72.

[2] Nieboer, p. 315 ff.

[3] Nieboer, p. 38.

[4] See S. R. Steinmetz, *Ethnologische Studien zur ersten Entwicklung der Strafe*, 2 vols., Leyden and Leipzig, 1894.

slave; and this seems to have been true to a great extent. Yet it is to be noted that, while in descriptions of primitive peoples one repeatedly finds it stated that the master may kill his slave at pleasure, or that he is not accountable for killing him, as Westermarck says,

'This seems to mean rather that, if he does so, no complaint can be brought against him, or no vengeance taken on him, than that he has an unconditional moral right to put to death a slave whom he no longer cares to keep.'[1]

In many cases the master is expressly prohibited from killing his slave at his own discretion.[2] The slaying of another man's slave is regarded largely as an offence against the property of the master, but not exclusively so. Where the master himself is not permitted to kill his slave, the slave has the right of life, sometimes with little difference in this respect between him and a freeman.

In a surprisingly large number of instances the master does not have even an unlimited right to sell his slave. This is true especially of slaves born in the house; sometimes he may sell at will only slaves captured in war or purchased. In several instances a slave, especially if he be a domestic slave, can be sold only if he has been guilty of some crime. The cases, referred to by Westermarck,[3] where the master is entitled only to a limited portion of the services of the slave would come more strictly under the head of serfdom, though we have here border-line phenomena hard to fit into a theoretical system. Sometimes a slave is said to have the right to possess property of his own; in some of these cases he may buy his own freedom. Among several peoples it is even permissible for a discontented slave to change masters. In other instances a slave, in order to secure a new master, needs only to cause a slight injury to some one's property or commit some trifling offence, and he must then be surrendered to the 'injured' person.

'It is astonishing,' says Westermarck, 'to notice how readily, in many African countries, slaves are allowed by custom to rid themselves of tyrannical or neglectful masters.'[4]

In some places a slave becomes free by simply leaving his master, or, if he escapes from one master and selects another, it is presumed that he has been badly treated by the first one, and consequently cannot be reclaimed.[5]

On the treatment of slaves by their masters in tribal society descriptions and opinions vary widely, and there are no doubt marked actual differences among various peoples in this regard. Thus we find this judgment by two American sociologists:

'No pen will ever record the brutal history of primitive slavery through generations and even centuries of which mankind was taught to labor. The bitterest scenes of an *Uncle Tom's Cabin* would be an agreeable relief from the contemplation of the stern realities of this unwritten history.'[6]

While undoubtedly cases could be found of which such a description might be given, taken as a generalization about primitive slavery, it is a gross exaggeration. More consistent with a far greater mass of data are these words of Spencer:

'The current assumption is that of necessity a slave is a down-trodden being, subject to unlimited labour and great hardship; whereas in many cases he is well cared for, not overworked, and leniently treated. Assuming slaves everywhere to have ideas of liberty like our own, we suppose them to be intolerant of despotic control; whereas their subjection is sometimes so little onerous that they jeer at those of their race who have no masters. Assuming that their feelings are such as we should have under the same circumstances, we regard them as necessarily unhappy; whereas they are often more light-hearted than their superiors.'[7]

[1] i. 422. [2] See references, *ib.*
[3] i. 677. [4] i. 678.
[5] This phase of the subject is discussed at length in A. H. Post's works, *Grundriss der ethnologischen Jurisprudenz*, 2 vols., Oldenburg, 1894-95, and *Afrikanische Jurisprudenz*, 2 vols., do. 1887; also by S. R. Steinmetz, *Rechtsverhältnisse von eingeborenen Völkern in Afrika und Ozeanien*, Berlin, 1903.
[6] J. Q. Dealey and L. F. Ward, *Text-book of Sociology*, New York, 1905, p. 90 f.
[7] iii. 456 f.

It appears from the available evidence that the condition of slaves in primitive culture is certainly better on the whole than in civilized states, ancient or modern, especially in the negro slavery of recent centuries; of the last Westermarck says truly:

'This system of slavery . . . at least in the British colonies and the Slave States surpassed in cruelty the slavery of any pagan country, ancient or modern.'[1]

Concerning the slave among the lower races we can accept the conclusion of this authority that as a rule 'he is treated kindly, very commonly as an inferior member of the family.' Of the slavery among the fishing tribes of the N.W. coast of N. America we are told that it was of a rather mild type.

'Slaves, as a rule, were well-fed and well-treated, as was natural with valuable property' (a significant remark, of wide application). 'The condition of the bondman indeed seems generally to have been little inferior to that of his master.'[2]

After considering the evidence with regard to slavery on the Gold Coast of Africa, Westermarck declares:

'The lot of a slave is not generally one of hardship, but is on the whole far better than that of the agricultural labourer in England.'[3]

These conclusions could be confirmed by evidence from other parts of the globe.

A difference has been observed in the treatment of slaves captured in war or purchased from outside the tribe and that of slaves born within the group, especially in the house of their master. It appears that the latter are generally better treated than the former. Thus, in Central Africa, slavery is more severe in character among pastoral than among agricultural tribes, because the slaves of the former are for the most part war-captives, whereas those of the latter are slaves mostly by inheritance. Domestic slaves seem to be more favoured than slaves employed in the fields. Sumner's statement with regard to slavery in Africa would be equally true of other areas of primitive culture:

'Whenever slaves live in a family, sharing in the family life and associating freely with the male members of it in their work, religion, play, etc., the slavery is of a very light type and implies no hardship for the slave.'[4]

We may give just one typical case, outside of Africa, in N. Borneo:

'In most cases [the slaves] have been brought up as ordinary members of the family, and have no wish to leave their home. Cases of unkind treatment are very few and far between.'[5]

IV. *EFFECTS OF SLAVERY.*—The effect of slavery upon human life is well expressed by Sumner, when he says:

'Slavery, wherever it has existed, has affected all the *mores* of the society. . . . When adopted into the folkways it has dominated and given tone and color to them all.'[6]

We can speak here only of a few of its many far-reaching effects.

One result of slavery which has often been emphasized—perhaps too much so—is that, in the words of the same writer, slavery has been 'the great schoolmaster to teach men steady work'; 'slavery is a part of the discipline by which the human race has learned to carry on industrial organization.'[7] Now, while it may be true that 'man is naturally inclined to idleness,' this, as Westermarck points out, is 'not because he is averse from muscular activity as such, but because he dislikes the monotony of regular labour and the mental exertion it implies.'[8] Now, outside of hunting and fighting, and to a certain degree trading, the labour in primitive times, as in later

[1] i. 711.
[2] H. W. Henshaw, art. 'Slavery,' in *HAI* ii. 598.
[3] i. 678 f. [4] P. 269 f.
[5] Dorothy Cator, *Everyday Life among the Head-hunters*, London and New York, 1905, p. 198.
[6] P. 262. [7] *Ib.*
[8] ii. 268; cf. G. Ferrero, 'Les Formes primitives du travail,' *Revue scientifique*, ser. iv. vol. v. [1896] 331 ff.

civilizations, was monotonous and uninteresting. Men preferred to be idle if they could compel other persons to work for them, nor would any one do it unless compelled.

'The original problem,' Dealey and Ward hold, 'was how to make men work,' and they add that 'nothing short of slavery could ever have accomplished this.'[1]

In another place, however, Ward criticizes the view expressed by Spencer[2] that without slavery the stage of discipline is never reached:

'The constant spur of want is sufficient of itself to accomplish this, as is evidenced by non-slaveholding industrial societies.'[3]

It may be agreed that slavery played an important rôle in disciplining men to uninterrupted labour, but some prevalent theories as to the transmission of this capacity cannot be accepted.

Thus the sociologists just quoted set forth the view that the stronger and more adaptable persons, who could bear and survive the burdens of their enslaved existence, could 'transmit some small increment of their new-found powers of endurance to their posterity. For the capacity to labour is a typical "acquired character," that has been transmitted in minute additions from parent to offspring and generation to generation of slaves, until great numbers of men were at last born with a "natural" or constitutional power to apply themselves to monotonous tasks during their whole lives.'[4]

Now it should be observed that the contrasts so often drawn between native aptitudes of men in primitive life and in civilization are, to say the least, very questionable.[5] Even if any such difference should be established, it could not be explained in the manner set forth by Dealey and Ward. The trouble with their position is that, on their theory, capacity to labour is an acquired character, and hence, biologically considered, its transmission through inheritance is very unlikely. If there are any innate differences in regard to capacity for labour between contemporary mankind and our earliest ancestors, a more plausible kind of explanation would be found in the operation of a principle of selection, by which the more industrious type of man survived and those unfit for steady and irksome toil were, partially at least, eliminated.

The great fundamental effect of slavery on the economic activities of mankind, and through them on other social traits, is the division of labour. It is the original differentiation of human society into a governing and regulating and a governed and operating class.

Slavery 'creates a set of persons born to work that others may not work, and not to think in order that others may think.'[6]

Thus was made possible the leisure class, released from constant toil, and the historical function of this class, whatever that may have been.

'Leisure is the great need of early societies, and slaves only can give men leisure.'[7]

That the keeping of slaves furthered the augmentation and accumulation of wealth, with all the power and prestige that go with it, need hardly be said.

A further consequence of this division of labour and the social distinction based upon it is a contempt for manual labour, domestic and agricultural, and, in later stages of economic development, industrial.

To give but two typical instances: in Uganda the prevalence of slavery 'causes all manual labour to be looked upon as derogatory to the dignity of a free man,'[8] and in Dahomey 'agriculture is despised because slaves are employed in it.'[9]

1 P. 89 f.
2 In his *Study of Sociology*[9], London, 1880, p. 192.
3 *Dynamic Sociology*, New York, 1883, i. 541.
4 *Text-book of Sociology*, p. 91.
5 See on this point F. Boas, *The Mind of Primitive Man*, New York, 1911, esp. ch. iv. 'Mental Traits of Primitive Man and Civilized Man.'
6 Bagehot, p. 73.
7 *Ib.* p. 72.
8 C. T. Wilson and R. W. Felkin, *Uganda and the Egyptian Soudan*, London, 1882, i. 186, quoted in *MI* ii. 272.
9 R. F. Burton, *A Mission to Gelele, King of Dahomey*, London, 1864, ii. 248, quoted in Spencer, iii. 460.

V. *SLAVERY AND RELIGION IN PRIMITIVE CULTURE.*—Slavery, like other features of the *mores* of a people, has had the sanction of the prevailing religion. It is scarcely necessary to remind ourselves how recently slavery was not only recognized by the governments of leading nations professedly Christian, but also championed by eminent theologians as an institution of divine sanction and even prescription.

An interesting phenomenon in primitive slavery —how wide-spread has not been determined—is the securing of freedom by a slave through his devoting himself to some deity.

Among the Ewe-speaking peoples of the Slave Coast of W. Africa, *e.g.*, 'according to custom, any slave who takes refuge in a temple and dedicates himself to the service of a god, cannot be reclaimed by his owner,' but, we are told, 'as by paying a fee to the priests the owner can close the doors of all the temples in the neighbourhood to his fugitive slaves, this provision of an asylum for an ill-treated slave is more apparent than real.'[1]

A parallel to this is found in the emancipation of a serf in mediæval Europe through his taking holy orders.

A curious view of the relation between slavery and religion was put forth by A. Comte,[2] which would scarcely deserve attention or require refutation at the present time, except for the fact that it seems still to have adherents and has been repeated with approval by J. K. Ingram in his valuable work on the *History of Slavery and Serfdom.*[3]

Since, so this theory has it, the rise of polytheism was contemporary with or soon followed the formation of sedentary communities, it is concluded that that religious system was coincident in time with the system of slavery. To quote Ingram: 'There is, in fact, a natural correlation between them, as there is between fetichism and the massacre of captives, and between monotheism and liberty'; *i.e.*, 'fetichism, as a strictly local religion, tended to the extermination of prisoners, because it could not establish any spiritual tie between the victors and the vanquished sufficient to check the impulse to destruction. But each form of polytheism being of a receptive and accommodating nature, and not absolutely excluding the others, the conquerors and the conquered had sufficient community of religious ideas to admit habitual harmony, whilst there was yet a sufficient difference to maintain a certain distance between them. The submission of the vanquished implied an admission of the inferiority of his deities, and the acknowledgment sufficed to consecrate his permanent subordination.'

While there is an element of truth in these speculations, especially in the sentence last quoted, as an explanation of the cause of slavery it is wholly inadequate.

VI. *DISTRIBUTION OF SLAVERY AMONG PRIMITIVE PEOPLES BY GEOGRAPHICAL AREAS.*— Slavery is unknown in aboriginal Australia. In Oceania it is found in only a few islands and districts, being confined, in Melanesia, almost entirely to W. New Guinea, and, in Polynesia, to Tahiti and New Zealand; it probably does not exist at all in Micronesia. There is no clear evidence of slavery among the wild tribes of the Malay Peninsula, while it is of frequent occurrence in the Malay Archipelago and the Philippines. In the last-named group the most primitive and probably the aboriginal race, the Negritos, have no slaves. It is found among a considerable number of the aboriginal tribes of Indo-China and India; it is unknown among such very primitive groups as the Todas and the Veddas. In Central Asia and Siberia its existence has been proved only in the case of the natives of Kamchatka; some of the Bedawīn of Arabia and N. Africa keep slaves.

Slavery was a well-established institution in the civilized states of the American continent, in Mexico, Central America, and Peru, before the European conquest, but was very uncommon among the other aborigines. In N. America it appears to have been unknown outside of the Pacific Coast area from Bering Strait to N. California. The institution is wholly foreign to Eskimo life,

1 A. B. Ellis, *The Ewe-speaking Peoples of the Slave Coast*, London, 1890, p. 220.
2 *Cours de philosophie positive*, 6 vols., Paris, 1830–42, leçon 53.
3 P. 7.

though in Alaska it has, in a few instances, been borrowed from neighbouring Indian tribes. Its occurrence has been reported from a few scattered Central and S. American tribes.

Africa is intimately related to the institution of slavery, not only by its being the great source of supply of the slave-trade of modern European and American nations, but also by its being the continent where slavery prevails most extensively among native peoples of a primitive culture. Leaving out of consideration the civilized and semi-civilized peoples of N. Africa, Nieboer finds only two districts where there is no clear positive evidence of the practice; these are S. Africa south of the Zambesi, and the region about the Upper Nile to the south-west of Abyssinia. Particularly large aggregations of slave-keeping tribes are found on the coast of Guinea and in the district formed by Lower Guinea and the territory bordering on the Congo. It occurs equally among Sudanese and Bantu peoples. It does not exist among the Pygmies and the Bushmen, and there is no definite evidence of its occurrence among the Hottentots.[1]

LITERATURE.—The following books will give more extended discussions of the subject and references to most of the literature: H. J. Nieboer, *Slavery as an Industrial System: Ethnological Researches*, The Hague, 1900, ²1910 (references in this art. are to first ed.); E. Westermarck, *MI*, 2 vols., London, 1906–08, esp. ch. xxvii.; L. T. Hobhouse, *Morals in Evolution*, 2 vols., do. 1906, esp. pt. i. ch. vi.; L. T. Hobhouse, G. C. Wheeler, and M. Ginsberg, *The Material Culture and Social Institutions of the Simpler Peoples: An Essay in Correlation*, do. 1915; W. G. Sumner, *Folkways*, Boston, 1911, esp. ch. vi.; H. Spencer, *The Principles of Sociology*, London, i.⁴, 1893, ii.³, 1893, iii. 1896 (esp. pt. viii. ch. xv.).

ALBERT N. GILBERTSON.

SLAVERY (Christian). — **1. Introductory.** — Slavery has existed from very early times and is hardly extinct in the world to-day. Few institutions have produced greater evil, and, though in primitive and semi-barbarous communities it may have been for a time and in certain places a necessary step in human progress, in its more developed forms in the Roman empire and the New World it has been the cause of an enormous amount of suffering, most of which must be unrecorded. The causes of slavery are at first sight manifold. It may be the result of capture in war; it may be a punishment for crime or debt; or a man who is starving may sell himself or his children to buy food. But, the more we examine the subject, the more we find that the primary cause is capture in war, particularly when the war is between different races. (We shall see presently that the racial element accounts for the perpetuation of slavery or the lingering of legal and social anomalies where they would otherwise probably have disappeared.) A stronger race captures a weaker, but does not exterminate it, and the vanquished become the thralls of their victors. Only as a substitute for slaughter can slavery be said to have been a step forward in moral progress. It must be considered historically and in relation to law, economics, ethics, and theology; and the Church, in this as in other things, affected and was affected by the social and political institutions among which it grew.

2. In the Old Testament. — Slavery existed among the Hebrews, as among all the peoples of antiquity, but it appears in milder forms and was inspired by a more humane spirit than in either Greece or Rome, and there was nothing in Israel to correspond to the vast pyramids of Egypt or buildings of Assyria reared by the ceaseless labour of thralls working under the lash of their oppressors.[2] In the Semitic foreworld slaves were

[1] A distribution-map is given at the end of the second edition of Nieboer's work.

[2] For slavery in ancient Babylonia see C. H. W. Johns, *The Oldest Code of Laws in the World* (Code of Ḥammurabi, king of Babylon, 2285–2242 B.C.), Edinburgh, 1903.

probably captives in war. The Israelites from being sojourners became bondmen in Egypt and owed their deliverance to Moses. Here, as elsewhere, what is properly called slavery shades off imperceptibly into what is not. The Hebrew עֶבֶד is used of the service of servants and of slaves to their masters, of subjects serving their king, and of serving God. Its cognates in other Semitic tongues have a like variety of meanings.[1]

The OT legislation as to slavery is given in art. SLAVERY (Jewish).

3. In the New Testament.—There is no explicit condemnation of slavery in the teaching of our Lord. It would even be difficult to say how much He refers to it, as the Greek can mean 'slave,' 'bond servant,' or 'servant.' The later differentiation into free, half-free, and unfree, or free man, serf, and slave, was not definitely evolved. But it remains true that the abolitionist could point to no one text in the Gospels in defence of his position, while those who defended slavery could appeal at any rate to the letter of Scripture. Our Lord accepted the political and social conditions of His time, leaving His teaching to work out its consequences in the Christian Church and in the course of history.

In St. Paul we find more explicit references and a more developed doctrine of the relation of man to man. Thus in 1 Co 12^{13} 'were we all baptized into one body,' εἴτε δοῦλοι εἴτε ἐλεύθεροι, and in Gal 3^{28} 'there can be neither bond nor free . . . for ye all are one in Christ Jesus.'[2] But it is in the Epistle to Philemon that St. Paul's teaching is most clear. Onesimus was a runaway slave whom the apostle was sending back to his master Philemon.

The names Onesimus and Philemon are both Phrygian, and 'for some reason or other Phrygian slaves were regarded with contempt': Φρὺξ ἀνὴρ πληγεὶς ἀμείνων καὶ διακονέστερος was an old saying.[3] The name Onesimus is frequent in inscriptions.

St. Paul asks that Onesimus may be forgiven, that he may be received as he himself would have been (v.^{17}). But there is no condemnation of slavery. Nevertheless it has been rightly said that 'St. Paul does not seem quite to like the relation.'[4] Why was it that he and others were slow to condemn an institution fraught with so much evil to mankind? Three reasons may be assigned: (1) our Lord left the implications of His teaching to be worked out in time, as we saw above; (2) the immediate abolition or attempted abolition of slavery in the Roman empire would probably have led to the collapse of the fabric of society;[5] (3) the early Church was buoyed up with the hope of the immediate second coming of Christ; hence earthly things did not matter so much, and, whatever a man's condition in this world, it was generally better for him to remain in it, and be faithful to his duties towards those with whom he found himself in relation whether as a master or as a bond-servant.[6]

The more closely we examine the thought of the NT writers and understand the conditions under which they lived, the less shall we be inclined to

[1] See O. C. Whitehouse, in *HDB*, *s.v.* 'Servant, Slave, Slavery.'

[2] Cf. also Col 3^{11}.

[3] Wallon, *Hist. de l'esclavage dans l'antiquité*, ii. 61 f.; W. O. E. Oesterley, in *The Expositor's Greek Testament*, iv. [1910] 207, 'The Epistle to Philemon.'

[4] H. M. Gwatkin, *Early Church History*, London, 1909, i. 233, n. 1.

[5] Perhaps this has suggested the use of the term 'Spartacist' by the extreme socialists of the present day, as Spartacus was a leader of slave revolt.

[6] Cf. Eph 6^{5-9}, Col 3^{22}–4^{1}, 1 Ti 6^{1}, Tit $2^{9f.}$, 1 P 2^{18}. We may probably infer that St. Paul felt that there was some danger lest the new sense of spiritual dignity, and of spiritual relation between Christians of all conditions, should tend violently to destroy the old social order; he is afraid lest the conduct of Christian men should bring discredit or suspicion upon the religion of Christ.

be surprised at their attitude towards this and other social questions.

It is a mistake to say that St. Paul consciously addressed himself to the task of abolishing slavery by urging those aspects of the gospel which, in their practical application, he knew would eventually undermine it. 'It is not likely that he saw the way to its destruction at all.'[1] But this does not mean that the Apostle thought that slavery was right in itself, and a thing so anti-Christian in its nature could not permanently continue.

4. In the early Church.—There are few references to slavery in the Apostolic Fathers.

St. Ignatius says that slaves ought not to be despised, nor ought they to be puffed up: Δούλους καὶ δούλας μὴ ὑπερηφάνει· ἀλλὰ μηδὲ αὐτοὶ φυσιούσθωσαν, ἀλλ' εἰς δόξαν θεοῦ πλεῖον δουλευέτωσαν, ἵνα κρείττονος ἐλευθερίας τύχωσιν. Μὴ αἱρέτωσαν ἀπὸ τοῦ κοινοῦ ἐλευθεροῦσθαι, ἵνα μὴ δοῦλοι εὑρεθῶσιν ἐπιθυμίας.[2]

St. Barnabas does not wish slaves to be commanded with bitterness: Οὐ μὴ ἐπιτάξῃς παιδίσκῃ ἢ δούλῳ σου ἐν πικρίᾳ, τοῖς ἐπὶ τὸν αὐτὸν ἐλπίζουσι, μήποτε οὐ φοβηθήσῃ τὸν ἐπ' ἀμφοτέροις Θεόν· ὅτι ἦλθεν οὐκ ἐπὶ πρόσωπον καλέσαι, ἀλλ' ἐφ' οὓς τὸ Πνεῦμα ἡτοίμασε.[3]

The Fathers of the Church make frequent reference to slavery and generally show pity for the slave without condemning the institution. In many cases a common faith must have drawn master and slave together closer than would have been possible had one or both been heathen, for in Christ they shared a higher unity. This was intensified during persecution, when the humblest slaves amazed the Roman populace by showing a fortitude as great as that of any saint or hero.

At the persecution of Lyons and Vienne in A.D. 177 it was said of the torture of the slave girl Blandina, 'Never woman in our time suffered so much as this one.'[4] Likewise at the martyrdom of St. Perpetua in 203. 'There is something here even more significant than the lofty courage of Perpetua, which forms the front of the story. From first to last she never dreams that Revocatus and Felicitas are less than her equals and companions in Christ. Enthusiasm might have nerved the matron and the slave apart: but no mere enthusiasm could have joined their hands in death. The mischievous eccentricities of Montanism are as dust in the balance while we watch the mighty working of the power of another world in which not only the vulgar fear of death is overcome, but the deepest social division of the ancient world is utterly forgotten.'[5]

With the end of persecution Christianity was not put to so severe a test in its members, and so there was always a tendency to slip back into the standards of a world still largely heathen at heart, for the structure of ancient society lasted beyond the conversion of Constantine, though several forces were combining to shake it. It is not surprising, therefore, that the Church, and the Fathers who were her spokesmen, tended to palliate and even to compromise with, rather than to oppose, the evils of slavery, and that the thought of a spiritual society in which all earthly distinctions are of little account was not so clear to the minds of a later generation as it was to St. Paul, or to master and slave who died together in the Roman amphitheatre. It was easier to say, therefore, that the 'true slavery is the slavery of sin' than to grapple with the evils of an institution inseparable from ancient society.

As the doctrinal system of Christianity became more explicit, it may seem remarkable that its moral implications did not become more explicit too. A few quotations will show the attitudes of the Fathers, though here, as elsewhere, they vary as the spirit of each is that of a mystic, a dogmatist, an administrator, or a lawyer.

St. Irenæus says that before redemption there was no difference among men: 'Significans quoniam secundum carnem ex liberis, et ex servis Christus statueret filios Dei, similiter omnibus dans munus Spiritus vivificantis nos.'[6]

Clement of Alexandria protests against unfair treatment of slaves, quoting the proverb: Οἵα γὰρ δέσποινα τοιάδε χ' ἁ κύων,[1] and states the equality of master and slave before God. He draws out the Pauline teaching that it is the duty of slaves to obey their masters and of wives to obey their husbands, and, if those in authority are bad, the duty of submission remains the same.

Origen recalls in what terms Celsus had reproached the first Christians with the number of slaves they counted amongst them: τούτους γὰρ ἀξίους τοῦ σφετέρου Θεοῦ αὐτόθεν ὁμολογοῦντες δῆλοι εἰσιν, ὅτι μόνους τοὺς ἠλιθίους καὶ ἀγεννεῖς καὶ ἀναισθήτους καὶ ἀνδράποδα, καὶ γύναια, καὶ παιδάρια, πείθειν ἐθέλουσί τε καὶ δύνανται.[2] Christians ought to show their slaves how, while having a free spirit, they can be ennobled by religion.

Justin Martyr recalls the forgotten spirit of universal brotherhood.[3] Tertullian invokes the same spirit of world-wide charity: 'Unam omnium rempublicam agnoscimus mundum. . . . Fratres autem etiam vestri sumus, jure naturae matris unius, etsi vos parum homines, quia mali fratres.'[4]

Arnobius enforces the same truth: 'Idcirco animas misit, ut . . . expugnarent atque everterent civitates, servitutis opprimerent, et mancipárent se jugo, et ad ultimum fierent alterius altera potestatis natalium conditione mutata.'[5]

This equality of all mankind is asserted many times. St. Jerome remarks: 'Aequaliter omnes nascimur, et imperatores, et pauperes: aequaliter et morimur omnes; aequalis enim conditio est.'[6]

St. Ambrose says: 'Eadem enim natura omnium mater est hominum; et ideo fratres sumus omnes, una atqua eadem matre geniti, cognationisque eodem jure devicti.'[7]

St. Cyril of Jerusalem does not think that slavery in itself is bad: οὐχ ὅτι αἰσχύνη ἡ δουλεία, ἀλλ' ὅτι τὸ δοῦλον ὄντα, ἐλευθερίαν πλάττεσθαι, κακόν.[8]

Again, the relation of master and slave is compared by St. Cyril of Alexandria with that of the maker and the thing made: οὐ γὰρ ἄν ποτε τὴν αὐτὴν ἀξίαν τῷ δεσπότῃ φορέσῃ τὸ δοῦλον, οὐδὲ τῷ ποιήσαντι, τὸ ποιηθέν.[9]

Despite the timidity of some of the Fathers, the instinct of the Church was against slavery. It is significant that no early Christian epitaph bears the inscription 'slave.' Three Roman bishops, Evaristus, Anicetus, and Calixtus I., had been slaves. The tendency of the Fathers certainly was to urge the slave to be obedient, rather than to urge the master to set him free.

St. Augustine writes: 'Etiam sermo mihi est ad vos, servi, quicumque dominos carnales habetis, cuicumque servitii conditionem debetis. Obedite dominis vestris, diligite ex corde, non ad oculum servientes, sed ministerium ex amore facientes: quia et illos Deus constituit ut vobis dominentur, et vos ut serviatis. Bene serviate propter Deum quia de bono servitio mercedem habebitis. Si boni fueritis, meliores eritis dominis malis: quia apud Deum anima uniuscuiusque non est discernenda nobilitate, sed opere, nec genere, sed actione.'[10]

Augustine thinks that the state of slavery is the result of human sin. He discusses the question in the *de Civitate Dei*, xix. 15.

The decrees of Councils and Canons are sometimes interpreted as favourable, sometimes as unfavourable, to the slave. Did the Church hasten the powers of gradual emancipation which without her would not ultimately have borne the fruit that it did, or did she retard a change which but for her would have gone farther and achieved its end more quickly? The right view is between the two, though the truth is on the whole more favourable to the Church than otherwise. The spirit of Christianity, like leaven working within human society, always tended towards freedom: but individual Christian writers and the official decrees of Councils erred on the side of a nervous fear of disturbing established institutions. The same tendency which we see in St. Augustine in the West appears in the East in St. Gregory and St. Basil. A church of Cappadocia by common consent elected for bishop a slave of Simplicia, a rich matron, generous towards the poor, but suspected of heresy. Gregory and Basil consecrated him on the prayers of the people, but they do not boldly claim that it is right to ordain a slave without the consent of his master. That

1 M. R. Vincent, *The Epistles to the Philippians and Philemon* (*ICC*), Edinburgh, 1897, p. 166.
2 *Ad Polycarp.* iv. 3.
3 *Ep.* xix. 7.
4 Gwatkin, i. 163. The account of her martyrdom is in Eus. *HE* v. 1 (*PG* xx. 416).
5 Gwatkin, ii. 127.
6 *Contra Hær.* IV. xxi. 3 (*PG* vii. 1046); ed. W. W. Harvey, 2 vols., Cambridge, 1857, ii. 227.

1 *Pæd.* iii. 11 (*PG* viii. 649).
2 *Contra Cels.* iii. 44 (*PG* xi. 977).
3 *Apol.* ii. 1.
4 *Apol. adv. Gentes*, 38 f.
5 *Adv. Gentes*, ii. 39; for these and other references to the Fathers see Wallon, iii. 295 ff.
6 *In Ps.* lxxxi. § 4.
7 *De Noe et Arca*, 26.
8 *Cat.* vi., *de Uno Deo*, 26.
9 *Argumentorum de S. Spiritu capita* (*PG* lxxv. 1133).
10 *De Tempore*, sermo vii. 12.

a slave had to gain that consent has generally been the rule in Catholic Christianity. But in Catholic Christianity properly understood the sacraments must be great levellers, though the implications of this were not fully perceived. So St. Gregory Nazianzus extols the nobility conferred by baptism.[1]

As regards the monastic life there was less difficulty than about ordination. Free men or slaves were subjected to three years' probation.[2] If a slave fled from a monastery and sought to live elsewhere, his former master could claim him. The simple fact of sojourn in a monastery in order to enter there suspended servitude.[3]

As regards marriage, canon law annulled a marriage of slaves contracted without the knowledge of their servile conditions on the part of the priest; if this was known, the marriage remained valid. Pope Hadrian IV. (1154–59) proclaimed anew the validity of a marriage contracted without the assent of the master, but the slave must continue to serve him.

The general impression left by the study of the attitude of the Church is that it tended to make slavery milder, though not to abolish it, and, owing to its excessive care for the rights of the masters, even to perpetuate what would otherwise have passed away. But in patristic literature we meet with the exhortation to masters to treat their slaves kindly. Despite the worldly compromises with existing institutions, here as elsewhere the spirit of Christ was at work.

5. Slavery and imperial law.—It was, however, not only in the working out of the gospel precepts of the spiritual equality of all men that slavery was modified, but also because of its place in the fabric of ancient society. Slavery was the worst abuse of the Roman empire.[4] It was a heritage from ancient times vastly increased in its evil nature and its extent, and made worse by contact with the corrupt elements of Greek and Oriental life. That the slave was often better educated than his master led frequently to additional evils, for it was his interest to pander to his master's lowest vices, and he had no rights of body or soul against his owner. The existence of a large class of freedmen was a further misfortune, for their freedom was not entire—it took several generations to remove the stigma of slavery, and the freedman still retained many of the vices of the slave. After Trajan the progressive manumission of freedmen was always resisted by the enlightened emperors as a permanent conspiracy against Roman society, but, when the freedman no longer had the taint of slavery or servile vices, the danger was removed. Christian influence on imperial legislation is seen as early as Constantine, who authorized manumission in the presence of Christian people. Those who had been enfranchised in church were to enjoy the full rights of Roman citizenship. Clergy were enabled to give by their wills complete liberty to their slaves in whatever terms they pleased. Constantine elevated from the enjoyment of the Latin right to the full Roman citizenship those who had been freed in church and subsequently converted to Christianity. One of his enactments declared free a slave who should denounce a ravisher. The work of Constantine was carried on in the East by his successors at Constantinople, while in the West it was profoundly modified by the barbarians.

6. Slavery in the Eastern Roman empire.—The legislation of Justinian here, as elsewhere, was important.

'We can perceive that between the age of Gaius and the age of Justinian the feeling that man is naturally free has become stronger, and this feeling was in the spirit of Christianity. Florentius said that liberty was a natural faculty whereas servitude was a constitution contrary to nature; and this view is adopted by Justinian in his Institutes.'[1]

Justinian re-enacted the legislation of Constantine which made a master who killed or ill-treated his slave liable to punishment. Slaves who became criminals were punished more severely than were free men. He declared that slaves could not refuse enfranchisement, and forbade any Jew, pagan, or heretic to have an orthodox slave.

Basil the Macedonian (867–886) ordered the marriage of slaves to be celebrated with the benediction of the priest.

Constantinus Porphyrogenitus (945–959) fixed the price to be paid for a slave who had been brought back.

Alexius Comnenus (1081–1118) re-enacted that the blessing of the Church should be given to a slave marriage; unless this was given, he decreed that the newly-married slaves be freed. This seems to indicate that the slaves also believed themselves freed by the ceremony. But Alexius declared that in the eye of God all men are equal.

Dreadful punishments might be inflicted on the slave—mutilation of the nose and ears, or gouging out of the eyes. But slavery was less rigorous in new than in old Rome, for with the consent of his master a slave might enter the army and thereby become free.

Various terms are employed by Greek writers for slaves and slavery. Δοῦλος was, of course, the usual word; sometimes ἀνδράποδον was employed, as the equivalent of the Latin *mancipium*, or ψυχάριον, or ἀνδράκιον; *domesticus* was represented by οἰκέτης. After the 9th cent., δοῦλος is generally the equivalent of *famulus*. Constantinus Porphyrogenitus relates how the Venetians, asked by Louis I. (814–840) to recognize his suzerainty, refused, asserting ὅτι ἡμεῖς δοῦλοι θέλομεν εἶναι τοῦ τῶν Ῥωμαίων βασίλεως, δοῦλοι here being subjects. Παιδαρίσκη is used for *ancilla* (the ordinary feminine of *servus*). From the 10th cent. we find a new term, Σκλάβος. The fact that mediæval Greek, like modern English, took its word for 'slave' from the Slav peoples shows that Slavs were often captured and made use of as slaves, as they seemed to possess the toughness and docility which fitted them for servile work. (Σκλάβοι was apt to be confused with Σέρβλοι, 'Servians,' as *servi* with *Servii*.)

Slavery proper disappeared from the Eastern empire in the 13th cent.; but, as in Western Europe, serfs, not personally chattels, but tied to the land, had existed from the time of Justinian. The regular word was γεόργος, *colonus*. The emperor Nicephorus Phocas in 963 forbade religious communities to build new houses or monasteries or to acquire property with ground rents, for these estates were worked by οἰκέται, who were bought as true slaves independent of the land, but they soon came to be serfs or colons paying a fixed amount, as this was more convenient for monasteries than to work them as slaves, needing continual supervision.

The emperor Manuel Comnenus (1143–1180) prohibited all forced labour, and so seems to have abolished the colonate throughout his dominions, like Louis X. of France.

Domestic slavery disappeared by degrees because of the Christian doctrine of the spiritual equality of all men, and at length by special laws forbidding the sale of an individual freeman and punishing the homicide of a slave like that of a free man.[2] Slavery certainly had as a rule merged into serfdom from the time of Justinian, though its disappearance may not have been as complete as is sometimes supposed. It was hastened by the

[1] *Oratio*, xl., 'In Sanctum Baptisma' (*PG* xxxvi. 396 f.).
[2] *Novella*, v. 2.
[3] *Code of Justinian*, I. iii. 38.
[4] Cf. art. SLAVERY (Roman).

[1] J. B. Bury, *Hist. of the Later Roman Empire, from Arcadius to Irene*, London, 1889, i. 371. The emperor regarded himself as the protector of liberty: 'pro libertate quam et fovere et tueri Romanis legibus et praecipue nostro numini peculiare est' (quoted by Bury).
[2] For slavery in the Eastern empire see H. J. Roby, in *Cambridge Medieval History*, ii. 62–66 (a convenient summary of Justinian's legislation); E. Biot, *De l'Abolition de l'esclavage ancien en Occident*, p. 207 ff.

turmoils of the Latin empire in the East. The war against the infidel was responsible for the perpetuation of slavery. In 1344 the empress Anne agreed that the sultan Orkhan should export as slaves captives belonging to the party of Cantacuzenos.[1] It was against both the theory and the practice of the time to sell Christians as slaves to an infidel.

An interesting document quoted by Finlay records the freeing of a serf of Duke Antonio of Athens in 1437:

'Αλλὰ καὶ μᾶλλον ἔστω σοι Φράγγος ἐλεύθερος καὶ παιδία τῶν παιδίων σου ἀπὸ πάσης ὑπαροικίας τε δουλοσύνης ἀπὸ τε ἐγγαρίας κανισκίων, μουστοφοριῶν, ἐλαιοπαρουχίων καὶ ἑτέρων ἄλλων τοιαύτης ὑπαροικίας προνόμιον.

7. Slavery in the Greek Church.—A few references to the attitude of the Church in the East further illustrate slavery in E. Europe in the Middle Ages.

If a slave is made a eunuch, he is to be freed and never to be sent back into slavery[2]—a nomocanon of Photius, patriarch of Constantinople († 891).

'We do not permit slaves to be called to office without their master's knowledge, to the annoyance of the masters who possess them, for such a thing works the overthrow of households. But if a household slave ever appear worthy of obtaining a further appointment, such as our Onesimus appeared to be, and the masters agree to set him free, and send him forth from the house, so let it be.'[3]

There are various regulations about fugitive slaves in the time of Justinian.[4]

A slave shall be freed if he make known the rape of a virgin.[5] Those compelled to do something shameful shall be freed by the bishop.[6] If any one teach a slave to despise his master, let him be anathema.[7]

During the Latin empire the soil was generally cultivated by serfs, as is shown by a letter of Pope Innocent III. to the archbishop of Patros in 1209.[8]

8. Slavery and the barbarians.—The coming of barbarian tribes naturally had an effect on slavery as on other institutions, both before and after the fall of the Western empire. The small proprietor had become more and more depressed and the slave gradually emancipated, so both tended to coalesce into the serf, or *colonus*. The process was gradual and imperfect, as pure slavery did not in the West any more than in the East cease as early or as universally as has sometimes been assumed, and serfdom and slavery went on side by side for many centuries. In the disorder of the fall of the Western empire captives of war were bought and sold; so another contributory cause of slavery was added; through anarchy and privation many men were driven to sell themselves as slaves. The captives of war taken by Clovis after the defeat of the Alemanni, by Charles the Great after the defeat of the Saxons, and by Henry the Fowler and his successors after the defeat of the Slavs were sold as slaves or sometimes settled on the land as colons.

Barbarian legislation forbade Christian slaves to be sold to pagans or Jews, but otherwise tended to recognize slavery as a normal institution. In the West the marriage of slaves with the benediction of priests was refused, as it was generally interpreted to mean freedom.

The distinctive sign of slavery was short hair, and the Salic law forbade cutting the hair of individual freemen, as likewise did a capitulary of Charles the Great.

A few extracts from barbarian laws will illustrate the legislation.

The *Lex Alemannorum*, of Lothair II. (*c.* A.D. 613–622):

'XVIII. 1. Si [libera dimissa] fuerit per cartam aut in ecclesiam et post haec servo nupserit, ecclesiae ancilla permaneat.

2. Si libera Alemanna servum ecclesiae nupserit et servitium opus ancilla contradixerit, abscedat.

3. Si autem ibi filios vel filias generaverit, ipsi servi et ancillae permaneant, potestatem ad exiendum non habeant.

4. Illa autem mater eorum, quando exire voluerit, ante tres annos liberam habeat potestatem. Si autem tres annos induraverit opus ancillae et parentes eius non exadoniaverunt eam ut libera fuisset, nec ante ducem nec ante comitem nec in publico mallo transactis tres Kal. Marcias: post haec ancilla permaneat in perpetuum et quidquid ex ea nati fuerint servi et ancillae sint.'[1]

'XXXVIII. 1. Ut die dominico nemo opera servilia praesumat facere, quia hoc lex prohibuit et sacra scriptura in omnibus testatur.

2. Si quis servus in hoc vicio inventus fuerit, vapuletur fustibus.'[2]

The *Lex Alemannorum* (*c.* 817–823) decreed that, if a slave fled to a church, he was to be returned to his lord. If the slave could not be found, another or his value was to be given to his lord.[3] If a man killed the slave of any one else, he was to compound with another slave or the value of the slave.[4] Any one killing a royal or ecclesiastical slave was to compound with 45 instead of 15 *solidi*.

The *Lex Bainivariorum* of Lothair II. fixes the amount of compensation for various injuries to a slave; for killing him the amount was 20 shillings.

Dagobert I. (622–638) decreed that, if a slave was sold and, unknown to his lord, had a *peculium*, this became the property of the lord.[5]

An illustration of the amelioration of slavery into serfdom is seen in the decree that slaves of the Church shall work three days a week on the demesne and three for themselves.[6] According to the *Decreta Synodorum Bavaricarum* of uncertain date, though not later than the 11th cent., a freeman who has committed sacrilege has to get 72 men to 'do judgment' for him, while a slave has the ordeal of walking over twelve red-hot ploughshares or carrying a hot iron.[7]

In the *Leges Burgundionum* of *c.* A.D. 500 we read (II. *De homicidiis*): '3. Si servus inconscio domino hominem ingenuum occidere fortasse praesumpserit, servus tradatur ad mortem: dominus vero reddetur indempnis. 4. Si dominus huius facti conscius fuerit, ambo tradantur ad mortem. 5. Si servus ipse post factum defuerit, dominus eius pro pretio servi 30 solidos parentibus occisi cogatur exsolvere: simili de servis regis secundum qualitatem personarum circa interfectores conditione servata.'[8]

In the *Lex Frisionum* of the 8th cent. tit. I. [E. Frisia only]: '13. Si servus nobilem, seu liberum, aut litum, nesciente domino occiderit, dominus eius, cuiuscunque conditionis fuerit homo qui occisus est, iuret hoc se non iusisse, et mulctam eius pro servo, bis simplum, componet. 14. Aut si servus hoc se iussu domini sui fecisse dixerit, et dominus non negaverit, solvat eum sicut manu sua occidisset; sive nobilis, sive liber, sive litus est.'[9]

The stern side of slave legislation comes out in tit. XX. 3: 'Si servus dominum suum interfecerit, tormentis interficiatur; similiter et litus.'[10]

The general tone of this legislation can hardly be said to favour the slave, as an injured slave was viewed as a damaged piece of property rather than a wronged man. Christian influence is shown especially in the marriage laws. Thus the law of the Lombards forbade the breaking of marriages between slaves of different masters,[11] quoting Mk 10⁹. The Council of Châlons of 813 permitted the marriage of slaves, but always with the consent of their masters. Marriage, or even intercourse, between a free man or woman and a slave was sometimes punished with death. The condition of offspring of these mixed marriages varied, but was generally servile. In England it usually followed the status of the father[12] (in Cornwall one child was free, while another was a slave), while the Lombard law followed the Roman in making the child take the status of the mother.

The attitude of the Church was to encourage a

[1] G. Finlay, *Hist. of Greece*, ed. H. F. Tozer, iv. 166 ff.

[2] See G. A. Rhalles and M. Potles, *Σύνταγμα τῶν θείων καὶ ἱερῶν κανόνων*, Athens, 1852–59, i. 55.

[3] *Ib.* ii. 105 ('Canons of the Holy Apostles').

[4] *Ib.* iv. 403.

[5] *Ib.* i. 215 (Patriarch Photius).

[6] *Ib.* i. 325.

[7] *Ib.* iii. 102.

[8] *Epistolæ Innocentii Papæ III.*, ed. E. Baluze, Paris, 1682, vol. ii. bk. xiii., esp. no. 159.

[1] *MGH*, 'Leges,' iii., ed. G. H. Pertz, p. 50 f.

[2] *Ib.* p. 57.

[3] *Ib.* p. 129.

[4] *Ib.* p. 133.

[5] *Ib.* p. 322.

[6] *Ib.* p. 280.

[7] *Ib.* p. 486.

[8] *Ib.* p. 533.

[9] *Ib.* p. 657 ff.

[10] *Ib.* p. 672. With this Pertz would compare *Leg. Salicam*, XIII. 4 (ed. P. J. Merkel): 'si puer regis vel letus ingenuam feminam traxerit, de vita componat'; and 'si servus aut libertus incestum commiserit, vapuletur plagis multis' (*MGH*, 'Leges,' i. 29).

[11] See Biot, p. 269, quoting L. A. Muratori, *Antiquitates Italicæ medii ævi*, Milan, 1738–42, i. 838. Muratori thinks that marriage without consent of the lord was punished, though not declared null.

[12] See H. de Bracton, *De legibus et consuetudinibus Angliæ* (Rolls Ser. lxx.), 6 vols., London, 1878–83, ii. 1: 'De Connubiis servorum.'

master to manumit his slave, but, if the slave fled of his own accord, the rights of the master were protected. It was decreed by canon law that a slave could not be ordained without the consent of his lord. Had the Church protected the fugitive slave in all cases, a great step towards emancipation would have been made.

9. Disappearance of slavery in Western Europe.—In France the transition from slavery to serfdom took place from the 4th to the 10th cent.,[1] while serfdom went on to the Revolution. Before A.D. 1000 there are many references to slavery, but afterwards only a few.[2] It lasted longer in northern than in southern France. A charter of 1113 contains a donation pure and simple of a woman and her child to a monastery. In southern France the words *servi, ancillæ, mancipia* are not found later than the 10th cent., and even then there was no sale of individuals separate from the lands on which they worked.

In Germany a scheme of punishment was set forth by the statutes of the Council of Cologne in 1083, while the first privilege of liberty for fugitive slaves was granted by Frederick I. to Bremen in 1186. In 1220 Frederick II. pronounced against refuge in imperial towns for serfs and slaves, but in 1230 he granted it to Ratisbon and Vienna; his charter to Ratisbon leaves to the masters a period of ten years in which to reclaim fugitive slaves. But terminology is rather vague; in 1243 a donation is signed by many *servi*, but these were serfs. In the 12th and 13th centuries personal slavery tended to be extinct in western Germany. Domestic slavery was totally extinct by 1300 at the latest.

In Spain slavery was a prominent feature of mediæval society. Among the Goths slaves were employed in the army and in administrative posts. Here, as elsewhere, the Church was a slave-owner. Donations of *mancipia* were made in 812 and 891 respectively by Alphonso the Chaste and Alphonso III. to the church of Orviedo. In 966 a Count of Barcelona freed in his will all the slaves acquired by him. Wars among the lords and against the Moors led to the abolition of domestic slavery, and it seems to have disappeared from Castile in the 13th century. The marriage of slaves was independent of the will of the master.[3] Excommunication was launched against the sellers of men by tit. 24 of the national Council of Valladolid in 1322. In 1491 Moorish captives were set free, and in 1501 they were driven from Spain altogether. In 1558 an ordinance of Philip II. decreed the expulsion from Spain of Jewish slaves and those recently made Christian. Those whom Ferdinand and Isabella ejected were admitted into Portugal by John II. on the condition of emigrating after seven years under penalty of slavery. Many could not emigrate and became slaves. In 1626 all slaves were obliged to embrace Christianity, and the Moorish slaves diminished, but the slave traffic continued. Christian slaves were found in the 18th and serfdom continued to the 19th century.

The end of slavery came slowly also in Italy. The tumults of the 10th and 11th centuries prolonged personal slavery and drove small proprietors into the position of serfs. The Italian republics had Greek Saracen slaves, and the ancient annals of Venice show her as a mart of slaves bought in the East or exchanged into Eastern lands, and among these must be reckoned Christians who had been enslaved. From the 7th and 8th centuries they brought back slaves from Africa, whom they sold to other Africans or to the Moors established in Spain. This traffic went on despite the prohibition of the Church.

It is recorded in the life of Pope Zacharias (741–752): 'Contigit plures Veneticorum hanc romanam advenisse in urbem negociatores, et mercimonii nundinas propagantes multitudinem manciporum, virilis scilicet et femini generis emere visi sunt, quos et in Africani ad paganam gentem nitebantur deducere. Quo cognito idem sanctissimus pater fieri prohibuit, datoque eisdem Veneticis pretio, quod in eorum emptione se dedisse probati sunt, cunctos a jugo servitutis redemit.'

Towards 840 the emperor Lothair I. promised to prevent his subjects from making slaves in the duchy of Venice, keeping them, or selling them to the pagans. About the year 800, under the doge Urso Participato, this species of commerce was forbidden under severe penalties, but the prohibition was little respected.

Sometimes the slavery was qualified, as in one case at least the consent of the slave to be transferred from one master to another was granted.[1]

In the 14th and even in the 15th cent. Venetians bought slaves in their colonies of Istria and Dalmatia. In 1323 the explorer Marco Polo freed one of his slaves by his will. There is a contract of 1428 for the sale of a young Russian woman of thirty-three, and a law of 1446 forbade the sale of slaves to the Ragusans and Dalmatians because they sold them again to the Musalmāns. The Venetians bought and sold slaves in Asia and Africa; they were only forbidden to sell Christians to Musalmāns. The existence of slavery and especially of the practice of mutilation was one of the causes of the moral corruption of Venice, and thus probably contributed in the long run not only to the decay of the moral stamina of her people, but also to the decline of her prosperity.[2]

Not only Venice but also Pisa and Amalfi traded in slaves. The *Opuscula* of Pope Celestine V. (1294) contain various regulations; *e.g.*, the Jews can have only slaves that have been reared in the house—if they are Christians, they become free; if a priest has married a free woman, the children become slaves of the Church, which has been injured by the sin of their father. At Bologna enfranchisement was achieved in 1283; in Florence there are still traces of personal slavery in the 14th century. The statutes of Florence of 1415 permitted citizens to have slaves 'qui non sunt Catholicae fidei et Christianae.' The statutes of Lucca of 1537 declare that the master of a female slave can force one who has had intercourse with her to buy her at double the price which she cost, besides paying a fine.

In the kingdom of Naples rural slavery had been converted into the colonate which continued under Greek domination and was found there by the Normans.

So a rescript of the emperor Otto II. in 985 speaks of free men who, in default of slaves, 'ex inopia servorum,' are established as colons in the domain of the Church 'in locis ecclesiastic patrimoniis.'

In the 11th and 12th centuries many small cultivators of Naples and Bologna surrendered themselves to powerful proprietors. In Sicily slavery was disappearing in the time of Frederick of Aragon (1296–1337). His *Capitula Regis Siciliæ* order the master of a slave baptized by him to treat him as a brother and to baptize him soon after birth; if he fail to do so, the slave is to be baptized in church and declared free; female slaves must not be prostituted. Biot acutely observes:

[1] P. Allard, *Les Origines du servage en France*, p. 3.

[2] Biot, p. 336.

[3] Traces of ancient barbarity appear—not only does the father enjoy all his life the goods of his son, but he is authorized to eat him, if he finds himself in danger of dying of hunger—so it was not remarkable if a child could be sold (Biot, p. 417).

[1] B. Gamba, *Serie degli scritti impressi in Dialetto Veneziano*, Venice, 1832, p. 32, 'Instrumento di vendita d' uno schiavo scritto l' anno 1365.'

[2] See Pierre Daru, *Hist. de la République de Venise*[3], Brussels, 1840, bk. xix. § 6 f.; also, for Italian slavery in the later Middle Ages, Jacob Burckhardt, *The Civilisation of the Renaissance in Italy*[3], tr. S. G. C. Middlemore, London, 1892, p. 296 f.; Muratori, *Antiq. Ital. medii ævi.*

'Ces divers exemples nous montrent l'empreinte permanente des habitudes orientales sur le caractère italien.'[1]

It is clear, therefore, that slavery was not extinct in Europe at the close of the Middle Ages, but that commercial interests and the strife between Christian and Saracen or Turk had perpetuated it in the eastern Mediterranean. When Elizabethan adventurers and their contemporaries of other lands explored America and exploited Africa, they only transferred to fresh soil an institution which they found ready to hand. This perpetuation of a decayed ancient and mediæval abuse and its re-erection on a far vaster scale than ever before is one of the most remarkable and deplorable instances of historical continuity. Thus, when the emperor Charles V. took Tunis in 1535, thousands of men and women were killed or led away into slavery.[2] Christians and Muhammadans alike employed prisoners of war as galley-slaves. By this time negroes had already been brought from Africa to America. But slavery was destined to continue on the widest scale in English-speaking countries. In England, as in N. Europe generally, there is a gap in the institution between mediæval and modern times.

10. Slavery in Britain.[3]—The early history of slavery in Britain is obscure as everything else in primitive development, but it seems clear that slavery existed not only from Celtic but also probably from pre-Celtic times. When slaves appear, they are probably the relics of subject races. Thus it may be conjectured that the conquering Celts reduced to servitude some of the aboriginal Iberians, but it is not probable that this process was thorough-going, and more would be kept in a half-free condition or allowed to mingle with the conquering races. Early Celtic customs show us a number of slaves, but the structure of society is not really that of a slave economy, and at the English conquest of Britain slavery was rather a survival. There was hardly the clear-cut division between bond and free which marks the slavery of ancient Athens or Rome, or of the United States in modern times.

'It appears that the arrangement of society on the basis of slavery or serfdom is not so easily carried out as many suppose, and that it is, perhaps, a more complex result of historical development than even primitive democracy.'[4]

So in the undeveloped polity of pre-Conquest England slavery, though frequent, was not the economic basis of society. Slave-owning, therefore, became limited to kings and other important persons.

'With the rest of the inhabitants of Scotch and Welsh mountains and of Irish bogs, slaves might be an exceptional commodity, female slaves might even be specially sought for different purposes; but there could be no slave-holding husbandry arrangements.'[5]

We do not know enough of the details of the English conquest of Britain to be sure how the English dealt with those whom they conquered. The theory of the almost complete displacement by slaughter or driving west of the Celtic tribes is now exploded—perhaps a larger number were made slaves than is often assumed, and, if so, this would account for the longer continuance of slavery in England than on the Continent, for slaves are continually mentioned alike in Old English literature and legislation and must have been fairly numerous at the Conquest. The old English term was *þeow*, and sometimes *esne*. The story of Pope Gregory the Great and the sale of beautiful English slave-boys in the Roman Forum is too well known to need repetition,[1] but it shows that English slaves found a ready market abroad. Till after the Conquest Bristol was the chief port for the sale of slaves. But how far was Old English slavery an inheritance from early Britain and how far an importation from the Continent? Roman masters had lorded it over British slaves at Colchester and elsewhere.[2] Slavery among Teutonic tribes is described in the *Germania* of Tacitus; it is disputed whether the English tribes brought over large numbers of slaves with them to England.[3]

As the Celtic tribes were driven west, some men would doubtless be enslaved, and the survival of remnants of a former race would explain some anomalies, such as the half-free *laets* of Kent, whose exact nature is not known.[4] Many points indeed of early English slavery remain obscure. The greater number of slaves were probably in bondage to landowners.[5] Various regulations are given in the *Penitentiary* of Theodore, archbishop of Canterbury (669–690). A father compelled by necessity can hand over his son to slavery for seven years, but, if for longer, only with the consent of the son. In Alfred's laws it is decreed that slaves should not have the same holidays as free labourers, only the Wednesdays in the four ember weeks.

In a bilingual dialogue written in the 10th cent. the slave complains of his thraldom, 'Ha! ha! hard work it is, hard work it is, because I am not free' ('*hig, hig, micel gedeorf ys hyt, geleof micel gedorf hit ys, ferþam ic neom freoh*').[6]

The ravages of the Danes seem to have forced some monks to escape starvation by becoming slaves on large estates.

The manumission of slaves was common, being often done in a will—and, of course, at other times.[7]

Bishop Wilfrith, on receiving a grant of Selsey from Caedwaelha of Wessex, manumitted 250 slaves.[8] A letter of Archbishop Brihtwald to Forthere, bishop of Sherborne, begs him to order Beorwald, abbot of Glastonbury, to release a captive girl.[9]

What percentage of the population were slaves is not known, but there were probably more just before the Norman Conquest than in the other countries of W. Europe.

'If we turn to the Old English charters we shall have to recognize that up to the eleventh century, slavery and manumission from slavery are playing a most important part in social life.'[10]

Domesday Book shows 25,000 slaves in England. These were spread over the country in very unequal proportion—none in Yorkshire or Lincolnshire, 9 per cent in Kent, 24 per cent in Gloucestershire, and 18 per cent in Devon.[11]

[1] P. 441.
[2] See *The Cambridge Modern History*, vol. iii. ch. 4, 'The Height of the Ottoman Power,' by Moritz Brosch. For the attitude of Muhammadan to Christian slaves see D. S. Margoliouth, *Early Development of Mohammedanism* (*HL*, 2nd ser.), London, 1914, and for Jewish traffic in Christian slaves H. H. Milman, *Hist. of the Jews*, 3 vols., London, 1868, iii. 207–219.
[3] See P. Vinogradoff, *The Growth of the Manor*, London, 1905, *Villainage in England*, Oxford, 1892, and *English Society in the Eleventh Century*, London, 1908; F. Seebohm, *The English Village Community*, do. 1883; J. E. Lloyd, *Hist. of Wales*, 2 vols., do. 1911; B. Thorpe, *Diplomatarium Anglicum ævi Saxonici*, 3 vols., do. 1865; I. Jastrow, *Zur strafrechtlichen Stellung der Sclaven bei Deutschen und Angelsachsen* (in 'Untersuchungen zur deutschen Staats- und Rechtsgeschichte,' ed. O. Gierke), Berlin, 1878; F. W. Maitland, *Domesday Book and Beyond*, Cambridge, 1897; J. M. Kemble, *The Saxons in England*, 2 vols., London, 1849.
[4] Vinogradoff, *Growth of the Manor*, p. 27.
[5] *Ib.* p. 27.

[1] The narrative is in Bede, *HE* ii. 1.
[2] Hodgkin, *Political Hist. of England*, i. 39.
[3] Tacitus (*Germ.* 40) describes the immolation of slaves 'to ensure' secrecy in the worship of the goddess Herthus by the Continental Angli, in a 'hallowed grove' on an island, perhaps Rügen (see art. EUROPE, vol. v. p. 593). The slaughter of slaves may also have been part of the ceremony itself (see Tac. *Germ.* [cf. ed. of H. Furneaux, Oxford, 1894] *ad loc.*).
[4] See Maitland, *Domesday Book and Beyond*, p. 27.
[5] A. W. Haddan and W. Stubbs, *Councils and Ecclesiastical Documents*, iii. 202.
[6] Seebohm, *English Village Community*, p. 65. His ambition is to get an outfit of oxen from his lord and become a *gebur* instead of a *þeow*.
[7] Thorpe, *Diplomatarium*, pp. 621–651; *Crawford Collection of Early Charters and Documents, now in the Bodleian*, ed. A. S. Napier and W. H. Stevenson, Oxford, 1895, p. 132 (will of Alfwold, bishop of Crediton, † *c.* 1012).
[8] Bede, *HE* iv. 13. [9] Haddan and Stubbs, iii. 284.
[10] Vinogradoff, *English Society in the Eleventh Century*, p. 465.
[11] Vinogradoff, *Growth of the Manor*, p. 373.

But personal slavery was beginning to disappear into villeinage, and the villein was half-free; he was generally free as against all men except his lord, only attached to the land and not able to leave it. Instead of constantly watching slaves and spending care and thought in organizing their unwilling labour, the upper classes of mediæval society levied dues and services from villeins who were attached to the soil and held in order by the interests which they had in their own households.[1] Slavery properly so called became extinct in England in the 13th cent., though it still seems to have been possible from a legal standpoint. But the rural population was still 'largely unfree,' and in 1313 the bishop of Durham manumitted a scholar of the city.[2]

One feature differentiates the disappearance of slavery in England and in the Roman empire—that in England there were no *libertini*, or freedmen, though Vinogradoff thinks there may be some trace of them in the *coliberti*.

The gradual change from slavery to villeinage was accomplished by the elimination of slavery, as for a time the two institutions had existed side by side; villeinage was swept away finally at the Restoration, though it had been nearly extinct for some time before.[3]

A statute of 1547 (Edward VI.) ordered a runaway or one who lived idly for three days to be brought before two justices of the peace, marked V with a hot iron in the breast, and adjudged for two years the slave of him who bought him. The slave was to be fed, and punished if he refused to work; if he absented himself for fourteen days, he was to be marked with an S on the breast and be his master's slave for ever.

Villeins in the 13th and 14th centuries comprised a large class including not only the villeins of early times but also the degraded freeman and the half-emancipated or now nearly freed slave.[4] About 1240 there is a grant of freedom to the population of the vill of Kirby in Kendal who had previously been unfree.[5]

11. Slavery in the East Syrian Church.—Directions about slave-holding are found in the works of Ebedjesus († 1318), metropolitan of Nisibis, or Zoba.

He directs that, if any one have manumitted some of his slaves and not manumitted others, those still under the yoke shall be manumitted. If a non-manumitted slave dies, his lord shall be his heir.

This plainly shows that the slave could acquire property, presumably like the *peculium* of the Roman slaves. If the slave had sons, it would go to them, but, if not, then to his lord—not to the slave's other relatives.[6]

Mar Gregor of Melitene, known as Bar-Hebræus or Abulpharagus (primate of the Jacobites in Chaldæa, Assyria, and Mesopotamia, 1261), issued instructions on the manumission of slaves:

If a lord shall say to his slave, 'O my lord,' or to his slave woman, 'O my lady,' or 'O my sister,' or 'O my wife,' the manumission shall not be confirmed by these phrases. But, if he shall say to the slave, 'O free man,' and to the slave woman, 'O free woman,' they shall be freed. He who is sick cannot free a slave whose price exceeds a third part of his goods. If a slave belong to two lords and both say to him, 'When we die, thou art free,' he shall not be freed by the death of one, but only the half of him shall be free.[1]

The slavery here referred to may have been of a modified kind, as the slave was not devoid of property, but it is further evidence for the continuance of the institution in W. Asia in mediæval times.

12. The revival of the slave-trade in modern times.—It is remarkable that the Renaissance, which brought the minds of men back to the literature of classical antiquity, re-established in newly-discovered lands the classic institution of slavery. The first offenders were the Portuguese, but it is unlikely that the slave-trade would have developed as it did, if men had not been familiar with it in the Ottoman empire and the Mediterranean. In 1442 Gonzales brought back ten slaves and some gold dust to Prince Henry of Portugal. In 1443 Nunez Trestan sailed on an expedition to Africa and brought back fourteen slaves.

The African natives naturally resented slave-raids and resisted with all their might, but without much effect. European traders then tried to foment disputes among the natives as an excuse for making raids. In 1511 Ferdinand the Catholic gave permission to import slaves from Africa into Hispaniola. The Spaniards were led to import African slaves into America by the unsuitability of American Indian natives for labour in the mines, and also because the horrible barbarities which the Spaniards had committed nearly exterminated the American Indians in many places. The emperor Charles V. urged the importation of Africans 'because the work of one negro was more than equal to that of four Indians.' In 1517 he granted a patent to a Flemish gentleman allowing him to import each year 4000 Africans into Hispaniola, Porto Rico, Cuba, and Jamaica.

The Dominican friars in S. America protested against the cruel treatment of the slaves, but the Franciscans defended it. Pope Leo X. (1513–22) in a bull declared that 'not only the Christian religion, but nature herself, cried out against a system of slavery.'

In 1562 Sir John Hawkins sailed to Guinea, obtained 300 negroes, sold them in Hispaniola, and came back to England. Queen Elizabeth told him that, 'if any Africans should be carried away without their free consent, it would be detestable and call down the vengeance of Heaven upon the undertaking.' The French, Dutch, and Spaniards continued the trade, but there do not seem definite instances of English trading in slaves till the charter of Charles I. to the African Company in 1631, supplying negroes to the British settlements in the West Indies. In 1640 Louis XIII. issued an edict by which 'all Africans whatever who came into the French colonies, under any circumstances, were to be made slaves.' In 1655 Cromwell took Jamaica from the Spaniards and found there about 1500 whites and 1500 negroes—the natives had been exterminated. The Third African Company was established in 1622 to supply the British West Indian colonies with 3000 slaves annually, and in 1672 the Fourth African Company, but it has been estimated that at the time the Dutch trade in slaves was ten times greater than the English. Between 1679 and 1689 about 4500 slaves were imported annually to British colonies. The French supplied the Spaniards with African slaves.[2]

Francis Crow, an ejected minister who had emigrated to the West Indies, wrote from Port Royal in Jamaica (7th March

---

1 Vinogradoff, *Growth of the Manor*, pp. 332–336.

2 F. Pollock and F. W. Maitland, *Hist. of Eng. Law before Edward I.*², 2 vols., Cambridge, 1898, i. 415.

3 For villeinage see Vinogradoff in *EBr*¹¹, artt. 'Serfdom' and 'Villenage,' and *Villainage in England*; C. Petit-Dutaillis, *Studies and Notes Supplementary to Stubbs' Constitutional History*, Eng. tr., London, 1908–14, ii.; H. L. Gray, 'The Commutation of Villein Services in England before the Black Death,' in *English Hist. Review*, xxix. [1914]; E. E. Power, 'The Effects of the Black Death on Rural Organisation in England,' in *History*, iii. 10 [1918] p. 109 ff.; illustrations of servile conditions of Church lands may be found in *Cartularium Monasterii de Rameseia* [Ramsey, in Huntingdonshire], ed. W. H. Hart and P. A. Lyons (Rolls Ser., lxxix.), 3 vols., London, 1884–93.

4 Vinogradoff, *English Society in the Eleventh Century*, p. 454

5 *A Boke of Recorde or Register, Kirbie Kendell, 1575*, ed. R. S. Ferguson, Kendal, 1892 (Cumberland and Westmorland Antiq. and Archæological Society).

6 'Ebedjesu Metropolitæ Sobæ et Armeniæ,' in A. Mai, *Scriptorum veterum nova collectio e Vaticanis codd.*, Rome, 1838, vol. x. pt. i. p. 64.

1 'Ecclesiæ Antiochenæ Syrorum Nomocanon, a Gregorio Abulpharagio Bar-Hebræo,' ch. 32, 'de Manumissione Servorum,' in Mai, x. 206–210.

2 For the abolition of the slave-trade see Bandinel, *Some Account of the Trade in Slaves from Africa*.

1687): 'The greatest trade of this place lies in bringing these poor creatures from Guinea hither, to sell them to the home plantations, and to the Spanish factors that buy them at 20*l.* per head or thereabouts. They come as naked as they were born, and the buyers look in their mouths, and survey their joints as if they were horses in a market. We have few other servants here but these slaves who are bought with our money, except some from Newgate.'[1]

In 1713 the Asiento contract was signed between England and Spain. England agreed to supply Spain with 4800 slaves a year for 30 years. England was to advance 200,000 crowns and to pay a duty of 33½ crowns on each slave, and the monarchs of England and Spain were each to have a quarter of the profits. From 1713 to 1733 the number of slaves annually exported by the English from Africa was 15,000, of whom a third to a half went to Spanish colonies; from 1733 to 1753 it was 20,000. England, however, did not derive much profit from the Asiento, for in 1739 the English company was owing Spain £68,000. War intervened, but by the Peace of Aix-la-Chapelle (1748) the Asiento was to be allowed to continue four years more. By the convention of 1750 George II. gave up the privilege of continuing the treaty for £100,000.

In 1755 the negro slaves in the British West Indies numbered 240,000, while the white population was only 90,000. About 1761 feeling began to be stirred in England against the trade; the Quakers were prime movers in the agitation. In 1766 Bishop Warburton preached a sermon against the slave-trade, which 'infringed all human and all Divine law.' In 1769 Granville Sharp brought an action to decide whether a man could remain a slave in England, and it was decided in 1772 that a slave, if he set foot in England, became free. In 1787 William Clarkson, William Wilberforce, Granville Sharp, and others formed themselves into a private committee to try to abolish the slave-trade. It was soon joined by others such as William Paley and John Wesley. At this time and earlier various writers had protested against the trade, including Baxter, Pope, Sterne, and Adam Smith. In 1788 the king by an order in council directed that the Board of Trade 'should take into consideration the present state of the African slave-trade, the purchasing and obtaining slaves on the coast of Africa.' The feeling in favour of abolition gradually grew and was supported by Pitt, Fox, and Lord Grenville. In 1788 a bill was brought in for lessening the horrors of the 'Middle Passage'—the first Act of Parliament which checked the trade. It was estimated that then the annual export of slaves from Africa was 200,000, about 100,000 being sent from Africa to America and the West Indies, the remainder from the east coast of Africa to Persia and the East Indies and partly from the interior of Africa to Turkey and Egypt. In 1789 Wilberforce described the horrors of the slave-trade in the House of Commons, again emphasizing the suffering of the slaves and the loss of life in the 'Middle Passage'—about one-third of the slaves were lost *en route.* Some legislative improvements were effected in the West Indies, as public feeling had been aroused in England, but the planters resented much in the way of change.

In 1791 a Sierra Leone Company was started by Wilberforce, Granville Sharp, and Henry Thornton. The object was to form a colony of liberated slaves. Zachary Macaulay[2] went out to the colony and became governor in 1793. On his return he became secretary to the company. He was editor of the *Christian Observer*, the periodical of the 'Clapham sect,' from 1802 to 1816. This was specially devoted to the abolition of the slave-trade at home and abroad.

The motion for abolishing the trade was rejected several times by a small majority between 1795 and 1799. Opposition was strong in various quarters.

[1] *The Monthly Repository*, 1811, p. 451.
[2] See his life in *DNB*.

Thus Lord Nelson in a letter addressed to a friend in Jamaica (10th June 1805) declared himself 'a firm friend to our colonial system,' which he was prepared to defend 'against the damnable and cursed doctrine of Wilberforce and his hypocritical allies.'[1]

In March 1807 the 'Bill for the Abolition of the Slave Trade' passed both Houses of Parliament and received the royal assent. A fine of £100 was decreed for each slave dealt in.

At the Congress of Vienna of 1815 the various Powers agreed to abolish the slave-trade. But France 'was allowed to carry on a five years' traffic of insult and injury and rape and murder on the coast of Africa.'[2] The abolition took effect in 1820 and the following years, Portugal being the last in 1836. But, even after the trade was supposed to be abolished, it went on; like other evil customs, it died hard, and slavery itself was still a firmly-rooted institution.

In May 1823 Fowell Buxton in the House of Commons spoke of the 'inconsistency of British laws which permitted slavery while they prosecuted the slave-trade.' He moved that 'the state of slavery is repugnant to the principles of the British constitution and the Christian religion; and that it ought to be gradually abolished throughout the British colonies.' Canning moved in favour of the amelioration and ultimate abolition of slavery. The anti-slavery feeling was increased by the fact that the colonial legislatures had not carried out the views of Parliament for the amelioration of slaves.

Thomas (afterwards Lord) Denman said in the House of Commons that 'judicial oppression is the hardest of all evils to bear by civilized man, and in Jamaica it had reached the highest pinnacle of its power; the most horrible atrocities were consequently perpetrated with impunity in open day.' He adverted to one case in which a female slave's head was absolutely twisted off in the presence of many persons; the offender escaped conviction because the witnesses were but slaves, and their evidence could not be legally taken.[3] Two negroes were sentenced to be suspended in chains and starved to death.[4] In Barbados there was a protest of the colonial assembly against concessions to slaves.

At length in 1833 the bill for the total abolition of slavery was passed, and the slave-holders were granted 20 millions sterling compensation. On 1st Aug. 1834 slavery came to an end throughout the British empire, and 770,280 slaves became free.

An instance of a slave-holder's mentality is related by Southey. A planter 'describes the refined and elegant manner in which the operation [of branding a slave] is performed, by way of mitigating the indignation which such an usage ought to excite. He assures us that the stamp is not a branding iron but a silver instrument; and that it is heated not in the fire, but in spirits of wine.'[5]

13. In the United States.—The history of slavery in the United States of America cannot be treated here in detail.[6] The British colonies before the Declaration of Independence were all slave-holding, and it was unhappily to the mother-country that this state of things was due, for it was to her profit that slaves should be sent thither, though the colonies themselves protested.

Thus in 1760 S. Carolina prohibited further importation of slaves; the Act was rejected by the Crown, and the governors of all other colonies were warned against such legislation in future.

In the North slaves were the luxury of a wealthy few, though they were treated with great severity at times. After the slave insurrections of New York in 1712 and 1741 the culprits were broken on the wheel or burned alive. In the South, on the other hand, slave-labour was a part of the economic system. The Declaration of Independence was founded on the principle of the equality

[1] *The Monthly Repository*, 1807, p. 203.
[2] *Ib.* 1815, p. 262.
[3] Bandinel, p. 204.
[4] *Ib.* p. 208.
[5] *The Christian Reformer*, 1829, p. 285.
[6] See further art. NEGROES (United States), and *Cambridge Modern History*, vol. vii. *passim*, esp. ch. xiii., 'State Rights (1850–60),' by Woodrow Wilson.

of men. Did this apply to the slave? Two points seem clear: (1) that the founders of the new republic did not quite approve of slavery, while not seeing their way to abolish it; (2) that equality could be quite thorough-going only among whites, as the negroes were an inferior race. Soon after the Declaration it seemed as if slavery might be abolished, and again early in the 19th cent., but in each case it revived, only to gain greater power in the decade before its abolition. By then it was clear to many men that slavery could not continue indefinitely, but it was a complicated question for several reasons: (1) it was left by the constitution for each state to settle the question for itself, though the word 'slavery' was never mentioned; with the founding of new states, the question inevitably arose; (2) but it was much easier to abolish slavery in the North than in the South, as the number of slaves was so much smaller, and they were simply sold to Southern slave-holders; (3) the anti-slavery agitation became extraordinarily bitter, and the pro-slavery party was very violent. There was certainly something to be said for the slave-holders. They were not responsible for the institution, since it was an inheritance which they could not avoid. They naturally resented being viewed as blood-thirsty tyrants. If slavery was abolished, what was to be done with the blacks? If they were given the same rights as white men, Southerners naturally dreaded the result; if not, they might create equally a social, economic, and political difficulty. Slavery had become part of the fabric of Southern society, and it was very difficult to alter it.

But the abolition movement would never have gained the strength which it did nor have ultimately succeeded, had not the abuses of slavery been wide-spread and inevitably bound up with the system. No doubt many, probably most, of the Southern planters were humane men, but the slave had very little redress. He could not generally be a witness, and it was a crime to teach him to read and write. Slave insurrections occurred from time to time, though they were not frequent.

One in Virginia in 1831 was led by Nat Turner, in which 58 whites were killed. Turner was not an ill-used slave, but a religious fanatic. Greater strictness in the administration of the slave laws naturally resulted.[1]

As the cotton industry increased, slave-labour was more and more demanded. Continual difficulties arose when new states were founded—Texas (1845), Missouri (1845), Kansas and Nebraska (1854)—and a compromise was arranged. But the Fugitive Slave Act of 1850 was much more of a concession to slavery than to its opponents, for escaped slaves who imagined themselves to be in safety were ruthlessly hunted out from non-slave-holding states. In the ten years before the Civil War (1850–60) slavery, though more actively threatened, became stronger than ever, and, when war was declared, it was the avowed intention of the Confederate States to erect themselves into a slave Power. Abolitionists in the South were not allowed the right of free speech, so it is not surprising that at times their language became exaggerated. A few examples may be given of the attitude of divines on both sides.

W. E. Channing, the Unitarian anti-slavery leader, said: 'No power of conception can do justice to the evils of slavery. They are chiefly moral, they act on the mind and through the mind on the body. As far as the human soul can be destroyed, slavery is that destroyer.'[2]

Theodore Parker, also a Unitarian, wrote to Miss Frances Power Cobbe: 'You in England, I think, do not see how slavery corrupts everything. Politics, theology, literature, trade, it is the *bête noire* which threatens to devour all the flock.'[1] His position is described thus from the pro-slavery side: 'Rev. Theodore Parker supposes the case of a man who aids a slave to escape from his master and who is brought to trial for an offence against the law. He assumes he has taken the oath as a juror to try the man, and says, "If I have extinguished my manhood by my juror's oath I shall do my business and find him guilty, but if I value my manhood I shall say not guilty; then men may call me forsworn and a liar, but I think human nature will justify the verdict." We have fallen upon evil times when the teachers of our holy religion thus debase themselves and their pulpits to a level with the lowest rum-shops and their frequenters.'

Other pro-slavery utterances are remarkable, and it must not be forgotten that the ministers and members of orthodox churches in the South held slaves to the number of at least 660,000.

A Southern slave-holder wrote to Theodore Parker in 1848: 'The Bible is either inconsistent—the Almighty a changeling—or you are a horrid monster of infidelity or blasphemy in your execrable spirit of Yankee conceitedness against the South.'[2] Robert N. Anderson, a Presbyterian minister, said: 'If there be any stray goat of a minister among you tainted with the bloodhound principle of abolitionism, let him be ferreted out, silenced, excommunicated, and left to the public to deprive him in other respects.'[3] Joel Parker, of Philadelphia, was credited with saying: 'What then are the evils inseparable from slavery? There is not one that is not equally inseparable from depraved human nature in other lawful relations.'

The slave-holding South managed to get the Christian Church, on the whole, on its side.

Were the evils of American slavery as great as is popularly supposed? No doubt the exploits and execution of John Brown and the publication of *Uncle Tom's Cabin* aroused popular feeling in America and in Europe almost to fever pitch. The evils were exaggerated in that the exceptional was too often taken as normal. It was sometimes asserted that slavery was beneficial to the African as introducing him to Christianity and civilization. But in some states of the South slave-labour simply meant that the slave was worked to death, as it was most profitable to the slave-holder to use up his slaves quickly. Nothing, however, can alter the fact that American slavery meant very real abuses and was dangerous morally both to the slave-holder and to the slave, and, so long as it continued, all real progress, moral, social, and political, was impossible.

Slavery was abolished for ever in the United States in 1862, and negroes were declared completely equal with whites in 1870.

14. The final disappearance of slavery.—The abolition of the slave-trade in the British empire was followed by its abolition in other countries. Since the discovery of the New World slavery had continued in the French colonies. The *Code Noir* of Louis XIV. was more lenient to the slaves than were the codes of most British colonies. All slaves were to be baptized and instructed in the Catholic faith.[4] But many cruelties were perpetrated here as elsewhere. J. B. Labat[5] described the abuses of French colonial slavery. Spaniards seem to have been gentler and more successful in dealing with slaves than either the English or the French, and the Portuguese were often kindly in dealing with natives in Africa. But there probably was not any considerable difference between one nation and another. The *Code Noir* punished the first desertion on the part of the slave with ear-cropping and the mark of the fleur-de-lys on the left shoulder, the second with a fleur-de-lys on the right shoulder and the cutting of the leg sinew, the third with death. Slavery in French colonies was drastically reformed in 1845 and abolished in 1848. Other countries followed; the Dutch West Indies abolished it in 1863, Porto Rico in 1873, Cuba in

[1] See W. S. Drewry, *Slave Insurrections in Virginia (1830–1865)*.

[2] *Memoir of William Ellery Channing*, ed. by his nephew, 3 vols., London, 1848, vol. iii. p. 149.

[1] John Weiss, *Life and Correspondence of Theodore Parker*, 2 vols., London, 1863, i. 463.

[2] *Ib.* ii. 79.

[3] Eliza Wigham, *The Anti-Slavery Cause*, p. 55.

[4] Mary Bateson, in *Cambridge Modern History*, vol. vii. ch. iii., 'The French in America,' p. 101 f.

[5] *Nouveaux voyages aux îles de l'Amérique*, 6 vols., Paris, 1722.

1886, Brazil in 1888. It lingered longest in Portuguese colonies and in Africa — which was natural, as Africa was the source of slaves. The Republic of Liberia for free blacks was founded in 1822. Slavery was suppressed in Zanzibar in 1897, though there has been sporadic slave-raiding in the Congo Free State and probably elsewhere since then. The later 19th cent. saw practical slavery revived in the South Sea islands by Queensland adventurers till it was put down in 1884, and the Putumayo atrocities in S. America also involved practical slavery.

15. Slavery in Slavic countries. — As the very word 'slave' is of Slavic origin,[1] it is not surprising that slavery and serfdom lingered longer in Slavic lands than in W. Europe. It has been asserted by some Russians that there were no pure slaves in Russia in early times, but there were actually three classes in the rural population: (1) slaves, (2) free agricultural labourers, and (3) peasants. In the 18th cent. these were welded together into the slave class, and even then serfs were often more like slaves, as they were regularly bought and sold and advertised for sale. An extract from the *Moscow Gazette* of 1801 shows this:

> 'To be sold: Three workmen, well trained and handsome; and two girls, one eighteen and the other fifteen years of age, both of them good-looking, and well acquainted with various kinds of handiwork. In the same house there are for sale two hair-dressers—the one twenty years of age, can read, write, play on a musical instrument, and act as huntsman; the other can dress ladies' and gentlemen's hair. In the same house are sold pianos and organs.'[2]

Alexander I. (1801–25) prohibited advertisements of this sort, and Nicholas I. (1825–55) repressed them.

Again, the Turks raided Russian and Polish territory and sold their captives as slaves in the Crimea, till it was conquered by Russia in 1783. The men especially were badly treated and fed on putrid flesh; the women were employed to amuse their captors.[3] They were sold to Saracens, Persians, Indians, Arabs, Syrians, and Assyrians.

In Poland serfdom in the 14th cent. became harsher and practically developed into slavery. It lasted till the 19th century. In Serbia slavery was legal, though serfdom was more common in the Middle Ages.[4]

16. Slavery and law. — The legal aspect of slavery is clearly of great importance, and, if we are right in the definition that a slave is a human being treated as a chattel, it is obvious that the question must arise: Should he ever be regarded in the light of a human being? Primitive jurisprudence did not always see clearly the exact position of the slave. To treat a person as if he were legally a thing requires a step in legal metaphysics of which a very undeveloped mind is incapable. If a slave is only a thing, his master cannot be punished for ill-treating or killing him; if he is a thing, the slave cannot be punished either; but most codes have punished a criminous slave with severity. If a slave is once fully recognized to be a person, slavery is doomed. So the mediæval jurists regarded it as contrary to natural law and as an institution of the *jus gentium* or *jus civile*.[5] Slave codes show how far the rights of man and the facts of human nature can be perverted in the interests of selfishness.

17. Slavery and ethnology.—Where slavery has persisted, it has often been owing to the survival of a subject race, imperfectly assimilated. Where two races have been widely different and one has been subject, it has been most difficult to abolish. Thus in the United States the question still remains: How far can white and black men live happily side by side? Intermarriage of two races which are not meant to mingle, and the consequent existence of mulattoes and quadroons, only leads to further difficulties. These legacies of slavery exist to-day.

18. Slavery and economics.—This is largely outside the scope of this article, but the question arises: Is a system which puts society on a false basis likely to be economically sound? It seems clear that slavery has sometimes been the most profitable economy for the time, though the wastage of labour and of men generally brought its result in the long run; the economy of the Southern States of America before abolition was wasteful, and still more so was that of ancient Rome.

19. Slavery and morality.—In the long run slavery must have evil results alike in the master and in the slave, because it lowers the dignity of human nature, and because no man can fittingly be entrusted with absolute power; he will not always use it aright even if it is to his own interest to do so. Thus a favourite argument of slave-holders collapses.

In the narrower sense of sexual immorality slavery has been productive of untold evil. A master has power to gratify his lusts on his chattels, and it is to the interest of the slave to play up to the vices of his master. The very phrase 'The White Slave Traffic' is significant, and suggests what did and must take place under actual slavery. The corruptions of life under the Roman empire and the abuses of American slavery show that, while purity is always hard for man, slavery makes it much more difficult, and the evils which resulted from this aspect of it alone would have justified its abolition.

20. Slavery and war.—We have seen that conquest has been one of the first causes of slavery and that war has led to its recrudescence at various times. The deportations from Belgian and French towns carried out by the Germans in 1916–18 meant a species of enforced labour which may be called serfdom and seems akin to slavery.

21. Slavery and Christian theology.—Man is a spiritual being akin to his Maker. St. Paul says: 'In Christ is neither bond nor free.' Can then slavery be right? It can be shown to be contrary to the spirit of Christ's gospel, though the Church has often been too timid to deal drastically with it.[1] It was sure sooner or later to disappear, and only traces of it now survive. Though it may have been a necessary step in human progress at certain times and places, and though the wickedness of slave-holders as individuals or as a class is often exaggerated, a detailed study of its records leaves the impression that it has been definitely evil, productive of untold misery for the slave, and of deep-seated corruption alike for the slave and for his master. But even slavery may not have run its evil course in vain, if its varied fortunes and final disappearance have shown that to treat a man as if he were no man but a beast is theologically false, morally wrong, economically unsound, and politically and socially disastrous, and that there is an essential unity of aim and principle between the moral and theological precepts of the gospel and the freedom and welfare of mankind.

LITERATURE.—i. *ENCYCLOPÆDIAS*, etc.—Artt. in *HDB* ('Servant, Slave, Slavery'), *DCG*, *DAC*, *EBi*, *EBr*[11] ('Slavery' and

[1] See above, § 6.
[2] D. Mackenzie Wallace, *Russia*, new ed., 2 vols., London, 1905, ii. 114.
[3] *Ib.* i. 289 ff., quoting a Lithuanian author, Michalonis Litvani, *De Moribus Tartorum Fragmina*, Basel, 1615.
[4] H. W. V. Temperley, *Hist. of Serbia*, London, 1917, p. 87.
[5] R. W. and A. J. Carlyle, p. 38.

[1] An instance of ecclesiastical timidity is the view of Theodore of Studium, who wrote that a monk ought not to possess as a slave a man made in the image of God, and then spoils it by saying that this, like marriage, is only for seculars (quoted by Sirmondus, *Opera Varia*, Venice, 1728, v. 66). St. Thomas Aquinas compares the relation of master and slave to that of father and son (*Summa*, II. ii. qu. lvii. art. 3).

'Serfdom'); P. Larousse, *Grand Dict. universel*, Paris, 1866–90; *DACL* ('Esclavage'); *CE*; C. du F. Du Cange, *Glossarium*, ed. C. Du Fresne, Niort, 1884, 'Servus,' 'Servitium'; *Handwörterbuch der Staatswissenschaften*, Jena, 1908 ff.

ii. *General.* — P. Allard, *Les Origines du servage en France*, Paris, 1913; J. Bandinel, *Some Account of the Trade in Slaves from Africa as Connected with Europe and America*, London, 1842; E. Biot, *De l'Abolition de l'esclavage ancien en Occident*, Paris, 1840 (full, detailed, and good); J. R. Brackett, *The Negro in Maryland: a Study of the Institution of Slavery*, Baltimore, 1889; W. W. Buckland, *Elementary Principles of Roman Private Law*, Cambridge, 1912; John E. Cairnes, *The Slave Power: its Character, Career, and probable Designs*[2], London, 1863 (shows the Confederate States as a menace to civilization); R. W. and A. J. Carlyle, *A Hist. of Mediæval Political Theory in the West*, 2 vols., Edinburgh, 1903–09 (much valuable information); Thomas Clarkson, *Hist. of the Rise, Progress and Accomplishment of the Abolition of the African Slave Trade by the British Parliament*, 2 vols., London, 1808; Samuel Dill, *Roman Society in the Last Century of the Western Empire*[2], do. 1899; W. S. Drewry, *Slave Insurrections in Virginia (1830–65)*, Washington, 1900 (defends slave-owners, contains bibliography); George Finlay, *Hist. of Greece*, ed. H. F. Tozer, 7 vols., Oxford, 1877; Fustel de Coulanges, *Hist. des institutions politiques de l'ancienne France*[2], Paris, 1900–14, i.; A. W. Haddan and William Stubbs, *Councils and Ecclesiastical Documents relating to Great Britain and Ireland*, Oxford, 1869–78, i. and iii. [1871]; Thomas Hodgkin, *Political Hist. of England*, i., 'From Earliest Times to the Norman Conquest,' London, 1906; A. Luchaire, *Manuel des institutions françaises*, Paris, 1892; Charles de Secondat, Baron de Montesquieu, *L'Esprit des lois*, Genève, 1748, bk. xv.; James Montgomery, *The West Indies, and other Poems*[6], London, 1823 (a rhetorical but impassioned indictment of the slave-trade after its abolition); *The Monthly Repository*, 21 vols., and 6 vols., new ser., do. 1806–32, *passim* (shows the attitude to slavery of the English Nonconformists of the time); G. H. Pertz, in *MGH*, 'Leges,' Hanover, 1863, iii.; Lucien Peytraud, *L'Esclavage aux Antilles françaises avant 1789*, Paris, 1897; C. Pfister, in *The Cambridge Medieval History*, Cambridge, 1911–13, vol. ii. ch. v., 'Gaul under the Merovingian Franks'; G. W. E. Russell, 'A Priestess of Freedom,' in *Manchester Guardian*, 5th Aug. 1911 (sketch of Mrs. Stowe); Reinhold Schmid, *Die Gesetze der Angelsachsen*[2], Leipzig, 1858; Harriet Beecher Stowe, *Uncle Tom's Cabin*, 2 vols., Boston, 1852, and republished since in numerous edd. and trr. (a wonderful book, which, though a work of fiction, contains the best, if a somewhat highly coloured, presentation of American slavery), *The Key to Uncle Tom's Cabin*, do. 1853 (Mrs. Stowe here substantiates her statements); H. Wallon, *Hist. de l'esclavage dans l'antiquité*[2], 3 vols., Paris, 1879 (a very good monograph; emphasizes perhaps even too strongly the work of the Church in mitigating slavery); Eliza Wigham, *The Anti-Slavery Cause in America and its Martyrs*, London, 1863; James Williams, *The South Vindicated*, do. 1862 (an able but prejudiced pro-slavery work); H. Wilson, *Hist. of the Rise and Fall of the Slave Power in America*[4], 3 vols., Boston, 1872–77.

iii. *Pamphlets.*—A vast number of pamphlets, especially those by anti-slavery reformers, are a most important source of information, though they may contain overstatements. Many volumes of *Tracts on Slavery* will be found in the Cambridge University Library and doubtless elsewhere. Among the most interesting are the following: Stephen Fuller, *Two Reports from the Committees of the Honourable House of Assembly of Jamaica*, London, 1789; John Jeremie, *Four Essays on Colonial Slavery*, do. 1831; Hannah More, *The Feast of Freedom; or, the Abolition of Domestic Slavery in Ceylon*, do. 1827 (a curiosity of literature); *Representation of the State of Government . . . in the Mauritius*, by a resident, do. 1830; John Kay, *The Slave Trade in the New Hebrides*, Edinburgh, 1872.

iv. *Annual Publications.*—Statistics of the slave-holding countries in America can be found in the various volumes of the *Almanach de Gotha*, published annually (also in German as the *Hof-Kalendar*).

v. *Bibliography.* — Works on American slavery will be found in the bibliographies to *Cambridge Modern History*, Cambridge, 1902–12, vol. vii., esp. chs. 15 and 16. Much MS material must still exist in the British Colonies and also in America, and in print in the *Acts of the Privy Council* and *Calendars of State Papers, Colonial Series*.

Works noted above are either important works of reference or monographs, or are interesting from some special point of view. Other authorities are referred to in the text.

Leonard D. Agate.

SLAVERY (Greek).—**1. Introduction.**—Slavery arose in Greece, as elsewhere, from two main causes—want and war, the one operative chiefly within the community, bringing about the subjection of individuals or whole families to other individuals or families of the same community,[1] the other producing the same result mainly as between different communities. The tendency to spare life in view of ulterior advantage would vary with the stage of culture.[1] A slave is of little use to the hunter, besides being troublesome to guard; he cannot earn his keep. In this stage the victor will mostly slay his enemy out of hand, though he may retain some of his captured women as wives, *i.e.* for domestic servitude. In the pastoral stage both male and female captives, even young children, can earn their keep by tending cattle and working up their products.[2] In proportion as the sedentary agricultural stage is reached, with its hard and more continuous toil at definite seasons, the demand for 'labour' becomes more insistent. The disadvantage is that in the slack seasons the slave is 'eating his head off.' Only as the industrial stage is reached is a more continuous and economical use of such 'living machines' possible. Moreover, it is in communities strongly organized for war that forced labour or slavery attains its highest development and importance, as it is at once a main product and a main support of military organization and activities. Applying this to ancient Greece, we find that in the historic period Greece is predominantly agricultural, but with pronounced local symptoms of transition into the mercantile and industrial phase, the whole being strongly overlaid by militarism of a somewhat aimless though highly specialized type.[3] Under the conditions of ancient life, in which one must be either hammer or anvil, military organization was inevitable[4] as a standing condition of existence itself; so that slavery in some shape was apparently equally inevitable. Sparta, the state which exhibited military organization in its most intense and logical form, was therefore constituted practically as a standing army supported by what was essentially slave-labour for the most part. Even in the ideal communities sketched by the Greek thinkers, military and servile institutions together constitute the very warp and woof of the entire fabric—though this fact is kept out of sight, partly by not calling things by their true names.[5]

If the special conditions and temper of a people be such as to allow it to devolve its military obligations upon some agency (mercenaries), in order to be free for wealth-production (*e.g.*, Carthage), the result will be still the same. For, if the conditions be favourable, no limits, except such as are purely temporary in view of greater ultimate

[1] Thuc. i. 8 (speaking of primitive Greece). Cf. the experience of Attica before Solon (Aristotle, *Ath. Pol.* ii. 2; Plutarch, *Sol.* 13).

[1] Cf. art. Slavery (Primitive).

[2] Cf. Herod. iv. 2: Skythians keep blinded slaves (cf. Jg 16[21]: Samson blinded and kept at the mill; the Skythians would of course have other slaves, not blinded) to churn the milk—'for they are not tillers of the soil, but nomads.'

[3] 'It was of necessity an organization of society in which, to use the forcible words of Bagehot, "every intellectual gain was made use of—was *invested* and taken out—in war"' (B. Kidd, *Principles of Western Civilisation*, London, 1902, p. 175, quoting W. Bagehot, *Physics and Politics*, do. 1872, p. 49). Cf. Plato, *Laws*, 626 A.

[4] Ar. *Pol.* ii. 7=1267 A: ἀναγκαῖον ἄρα τὴν πολιτείαν συντετάχθαι πρὸς τὴν πολεμικὴν ἰσχύν.

[5] This is especially the case in Plato's *Republic*, which never mentions slaves as constituent elements of the construction, though Plato nowhere impugns the principle of slavery, as applied to βάρβαροι, who are πολέμιοι φύσει (*Rep.* 470 C). But the non-appearance in the *Republic* of the precise legal status and name of slavery matters little; the essential point is that of the real relationship between the elements—a dominant class set over against an inferior, and deliberately using the latter for purely self-regarding ends. No intrinsic excellence of those ends has any bearing upon the morality of such construction. Nor, again, can it be moralized, as it were by a side wind, by pretending that it involves an educative process both for the individual and for the race, or the like, which is just Aristotle's line of defence of openly recognized and confessed slavery—a defence which had not even the merit of novelty, having been invented by Perikles in the interest of the Athenian empire as a whole (see Thuc. ii. 63, and 35 f.). To say of Plato and slavery that 'in his ideal *Republic* he abolishes it silently by merely constructing a state without slaves' (G. Murray, *The Rise of the Greek Epic*[2], London, 1911, p. 37) is simply to forget both Aristotle's warning, δεῖν ἐπὶ σωτηρίᾳ γε τῆς ἀληθείας καὶ τὰ οἰκεῖα ἀναιρεῖν (*Eth. Nic.*, I. vi. 1), and what Plato himself said, ἀλλ' οὐ γὰρ πρό γε τῆς ἀληθείας τιμητέος ἀνήρ (*Rep.* 595 C). The lowest class in Plato's ideal state is practically a serf class.

advantage, are set to production—save by such factors as are themselves beyond human control.[1] Of controllable factors, one of the chief is the amount of labour available; and the problem of its supply is solved by the reduction of masses of men to serfdom, or by the importation of labourers either forced or only nominally free.

Military power, then, and the accumulation of material wealth both led, in the ancient state, directly to the satisfaction of the unceasing hunger for a fully exploitable form of labour, *i.e.* slavery.[2] This demand is everywhere strongly reinforced by the almost universal natural distaste of men for the severer forms of labour, especially for those in which the activity demanded is of a sustained, monotonous, and unexhilarating type. As a matter of fact, in whatever parade of economic logic or philosophy of social evolution the historian may indulge about it, even sometimes to the extent of defending it, the institution of slavery, for the individual slave-owner, had its *raison d'être* in his own idleness and desire for self-indulgence,[3] seeking gratification through the ruthless exploitation of the strength and capacities of others whom circumstances permitted him to control absolutely, without attendant responsibilities, except such as mere possession of a damageable property involved. As Aristotle puts it, if the shuttles could have set to work of themselves, we should have had no need of slaves.[4] It is this claim of one man to exploit another to the utmost, under a converse minimum of obligation, that constitutes the fundamental vice of the institution of slavery.

2. Slavery in Homer.—Slavery is found already established as an immemorial usage in the Homeric period, and slaves of both sexes are a staple commodity to which the victorious warrior looks for his profit, just as he will on occasion replenish his flocks and herds by foray.[5]

The Homeric slave has no rights, and is powerless against the caprice and fiat of his owner.[6] Odysseus does actually execute his erring maids without reference to any other authority. Yet, as in historic times, custom has so far ameliorated the lot of the Homeric slave as to allow him to amass property on sufferance.[7] The promise of Odysseus to give a wife and house and *κτήματα* to the loyal Eumaios and Philoitios[8] must be regarded as merely an extension of this customary tolerance, not as an indication of a practice of legal emancipation;[9] at best it would mean elevation to the status of serf. The patriarchal character of Homeric society doubtless ameliorated the servile status, but without altering its legal aspect or essential nature.[10] Though he draws these charming pictures of kindly social intercourse, Homer has also uttered one of the most truthful and famous judgments on the real significance of slavery in *Od.* xvii. 320 f.:

'Thralls (δμῶες) are no more inclined to honest service when their master's control is gone . . . for Zeus takes away half the worth (ἀρετή)[11] of a man when the day of slavery (δούλιον ἦμαρ) comes upon him.'

[1] Cf. Aristotle, *Pol.* i. 8=1256 B: ὥσπερ Σόλων φησὶ ποιήσας 'πλούτου δ' οὐδὲν τέρμα πεφασμένον ἀνδράσι κεῖται.'

[2] Cf. Herod. i. 66; Paus. IV. xiv. 4.

[3] Cf. Thuc. iii. 82 and ii. 63 f.; Xen. *Sym.* iv. 36; H. Lotze, *Microcosmus*, Eng. tr.[3], Edinburgh, 1888, ii. 373.

[4] *Pol.* i. 4=1253 B.

[5] *Il.* xviii. 28, *Od.* i. 398; cf. *Il.* xi. 677 f., *Od.* xxiii. 356 f.

[6] Cf. *Il.* ix. 449, *Od.* xix. 91 f. (Penelope threatens her maid Melantho with death).

[7] *Od.* xiv. 449 f. (Eumaios has a bought slave of his own, νόσφι δεσποίνης—whatever that may mean).

[8] *Ib.* xxi. 213 f.; cf. xiv. 62 f.

[9] Though so understood by Plut. *Quæst. gr.* 14.

[10] Cf. *Od.* vi. 84 f. (Nausikaa superintends the family washing and takes part in it with the slave ἀμφίπολοι), xvii. 256 f. (Melanthios the goat-herd sits and eats with the suitors). See also *Od.* xviii. 322 f. xv. 363 f.

[11] 'Αρετή, not to be taken here specially of moral qualities, but in the sense in which we say a man is 'no good' for a thing,

External appearance and demeanour alike were affected by servile status, in the popular conception.[1] This was also the historical Greek view, as formulated by Xen. *Mem.* IV. v. 2.[2]

3. Types of slavery in historical Greece.—In historical times Greece shows two main types of unfree status—imported slaves (δοῦλοι,[3] ἀνδράποδα, οἰκέται, often simply σώματα), and indigenous serfs (Εἵλωτες in Laconia, Πενέσται in Thessaly; other names elsewhere) — which are associated typically with Athens and Sparta respectively. Although the historical origin of Greek serfdom was identical with one of the main sources of true slavery, viz. war, the primary distinction between the two types was that, while the slave was an alien without legal rights, who could be bought and sold at will, the serf was a descendant of an earlier population settled in the land 'before the Conquest,' and was permanently and legally attached, with customary and legal rights, to what had been his ancestral soil (*ascriptus glebæ*). The two types were in general mutually exclusive, in fact though not in law. The Lacedæmonian social and political organization based upon serfdom hardly knew slavery in its ordinary sense, whereas in Attica, where there were thousands of bought slaves (ἀργυρώνητοι), serfdom was unknown — though the 7th cent. B.C. had come very near evolving and perpetuating its institution.[4] In Greece, the distinction tended to coincide with that between agriculture (carried on by serfs) and industry (carried on by slaves).

(*a*) *The Helots.*—The Helots of Laconia and Messenia (Εἵλωτες, Εἱλῶται)[5] are the best known representatives of the serf class. They were state slaves (δοῦλοι τοῦ κοινοῦ),[6] cultivators attached as perpetual hereditary appendage to the lot (κλῆρος) assigned to individual Spartiates. Hence the individual in whose interest they laboured could neither emancipate nor sell nor slay the Helots on his lot, and was bound under a curse not to exact more than the specified annual amount of produce, which was paid in kind as a first charge on the estate, the balance belonging to the serfs. The state also had a paramount claim to the service of Helots in war as light-armed troops or as rowers, or even on occasion as heavy infantry,[7] and sometimes emancipated them for good service.[8] Helots were also liable for all manner of personal service to their lords in peace and war.[9] They enjoyed, however, by customary right, if not by express convention made at the time of the conquest, their own household and family life, with a large degree of personal freedom and power of amassing wealth.[10] As they were the economic basis of the whole Spartan organization, it was imperative that they should be allowed to propagate and live in a certain measure of comfort, though doubtless there was no lack of cases of oppression.[11] The general attitude of the Spartans towards them was one of

meaning in respect of efficiency; certainly not here 'manhood,' as rendered by G. Murray, *Rise of the Greek Epic*[2], p. 37, any more than it is true to say that Homer 'speaks always of slaves with a half-puzzled tenderness' (*ib.*)—pure imagination. Cf. D. B. Monro's note *in loc.* (*Homer's Odyssey*, bks. xiii.–xxiv., Oxford, 1901)—'probably the sense [of ἀρετή] is very general'; 'Zeus takes out half the *good* of a man'; cf. *Od.* xiii. 45.

[1] Cf. *Od.* xxiv. 252: 'There shows nothing of the slave about thy face and stature.'

[2] Cf. Theogn. 535, and Aristotle's half-pathetic lament that Nature after all often blunders in her stamp (*Pol.* i. 5=1254 B).

[3] For the etymology of the word δοῦλος see M. Lambertz in *Glotta*, vi. [Göttingen, 1914] 1–18, and E. Assmann, *ib.* ix. [1917] 94 f.

[4] Cf. Ar. *Ath. Pol.* ii. 2: ἐδούλευον οἱ πένητες τοῖς πλουσίοις καὶ αὐτοὶ καὶ τὰ τέκνα καὶ αἱ γυναῖκες.

[5] The name was, by the ancients, derived from the town of Helos in lower Laconia (Strabo, p. 365), but is more probably connected with ἕλος, 'fen,' or with the root of ἑλεῖν, 'to capture.'

[6] Paus. III. xx. 6.

[7] Xen. *Hell.* VI. v. 28.

[8] Thuc. v. 34.

[9] Cf. Herod. vii. 229, ix. 10.

[10] Cf. Plut. *Kleom.* 28.

[11] Cf. Athen. 272 A.

suspicion and perpetual watchfulness.[1] They felt that they held a wolf by the ears, for the Helots, says Aristotle, were ever on the alert to take advantage of any national disaster.[2]

(*b*) *True slavery in Greece.*—As known from the Homeric and Hesiodic poems, Greece is a land of free peasant cultivators, slavery, though a familiar institution, being of comparatively little economic importance, confined chiefly to female domestic slavery, so that the Greeks themselves easily imagined a Greece which once knew no slavery.[3] Even Hesiod appears not yet to know rural slavery as a fact of any great importance in the social stratum with which he is chiefly concerned. For, in enumerating the items of capital outlay for the peasant, he mentions first the homestead, next the wife, and then the ox for the plough, and finally the 'things,' *i.e.* gear.[4] This is in accord with the historical development, for Bœotia, as well as Lokris and Phokis, was predominantly a land of free farmers even in the 5th cent. B.C., as was also the Peloponnese.

Chios had the dubious honour of inaugurating the slave-trade on a large scale.[5] It spread rapidly to the rising industrial and trading states of the Saronic gulf. As early as 600 B.C. Periander tried to check it in Corinth, probably in the interests of native labour;[6] but in vain, for the Corinthians soon earned their mock-name of χοινικομέτραι.[7] In Greece, therefore, slavery as a factor of prime importance in the national life was intimately connected with the economic revolution of the 7th and 6th centuries B.C. The transition from the agricultural to the industrial and mercantile system of national life, undermining the old static aristocratic society and the privileges of birth, and substituting a social stratification according to wealth expressed in terms of coinage (except in those states which, like Sparta, Crete, or Thessaly, applied special safeguards of the old régime), opened innumerable avenues for exploitation and stimulated a demand for cheap docile labour. The free citizen was ill adapted to meet this demand, by reason of his rapidly developing political freedom and his equality before the law with his employer.[8] He did not readily accept the subordination implied by the relationship of employer and employed.[9]

The case stood quite otherwise with the slave—an alien, and therefore without legal rights, a mere live tool (ἔμψυχον ὄργανον), in some respects indeed the more valuable just because it was alive, yet with almost as little power of protest as a lifeless instrument.[10] Hence the use of slaves became ever more prevalent, the heavier forms of labour being definitely abandoned to them (*e.g.*, the mines), and slaves becoming a lucrative and favourite form of investment; for here was found a solution of one of the great problems of ancient life, viz. how to invest savings profitably and safely. Hence prosperity and the employment of slaves went hand in hand, as mutually cause and effect.[11] The essence of the demand was not for workers who were in a legal sense slaves, that is to say, not for slavery as an institution *per se* desirable, but for cheap, docile, and fully exploitable labour; and such was to be had, in any degree

1 Xen. *Resp. Lac.* xii. 4; Thuc. iv. 80, v. 14.
2 *Pol.* ii. 9=1269 A; cf. Thuc. i. 132; Xen. *Hell.* III. iii. 6.
3 Herod. vi. 137; Timaios, *ap.* Polyb. xii. 6; cf. Athen. 264 C (true enough if referred to the sudden development of industrial slavery from the 7th cent. onwards).
4 Hes. *Works*, 405 f.
5 Athen. 265 B.
6 Nic. Dam. frag. 59.
7 Athen. 272 B—as though their chief occupation was to issue slave rations; cf. Herod. ii. 167: ἥκιστα δὲ Κορίνθιοι ὄνονται τοὺς χειροτέχνας, of whom a large porportion was servile.
8 Cf. Meyer, *Kleine Schriften*, p. 192.
9 Instructive case in Xen. *Mem.* II. viii. 5; cf. *de Vect.* iv. 22.
10 Cf. Xen. *Mem.* II. vii. 6.
11 Cf. Diod. xi. 72 (Sicily); cf. Herod. v. 31 (Naxos).

of perfection, only in the form of forced alien labour.[1] The slave class, therefore, held in the ancient industrial organization precisely the place held in modern times by free labour working under contract.

4. Sources of supply.—The sources of slave supply were chiefly war and commerce.

(1) *War.*—In dealing with a conquered town, whether Greek or foreign, Greek practice was to kill all bearing or capable of bearing arms, and to enslave the rest of the population without exception.[2] It marked, therefore, some advance when Philip in 348 B.C., instead of slaughtering the men of the Chalcidic cities, sold the population *en masse*, and when Alexander in 335 B.C., upon the capture of Thebes, sold its 30,000 inhabitants into slavery.[3]

(2) *Commerce.*—Supply of slaves through war was of the nature of a windfall. There was in addition a systematic slave-trade catering for the constant demand. The market was fed chiefly from lands on the fringe of the Hellenic world,[4] especially the hinterland of Asia Minor (Lydia, Phrygia, and Galatia), and the countries bordering the Euxine (Pontos and Paphlagonia, and above all Thrace). Syria, Egypt, Æthiopia, and even Italy,[5] were also taken in toll. The great slave marts were Samos, Chios, and Ephesus for Asia, Pagasai and Byzantion for the Balkan area; Delos and Cypros were the *entrepôts* for the human freights of the pirates and kidnappers working the eastern Mediterranean, while Corinth and Athens were the main emporia in Greece proper.[6] Probably there were regular agents in frontier towns buying whatever was offered in this line and asking no questions. War and rapine among the hill-tribes, sale of families by natives,[7] casual kidnapping, and apparently even the organized slave-raid, kept up a fairly steady stream of supply, which gradually attained enormous dimensions. It savours of irony to find that the sacred island of Delos became ultimately, perhaps as the most central, the main slave mart, so that a saying arose: 'Put in, skipper, unload—all's sold.'[8]

(3) Minor sources were: (*a*) natural increase among the slaves themselves, the status being hereditary; this was important mainly in later times; (*b*) sale of children—tolerated generally in Greece (but not in Athens, though an Athenian father might, and seemingly often did, refuse to rear a child, especially if a female,[9] and expose it); (*c*) sale into slavery, even of adults, due to the action of the law; *e.g.*, before Solon's time an insolvent Athenian could be sold into slavery by his creditor (as in Rome), or he might be retained as a bond-slave on his estate.[10]

5. Employments of slaves.—One of the most striking differences between ancient and modern slavery is the great variety of *skilled* employments for which slaves were trained in Athens, apparently with success.[11] Besides their employment, to a moderate extent, as personal attendants (ἀκόλουθοι, both in and out of doors),[12] slaves of both sexes were used for all manner of domestic service and domestic production.[13] Naturally, agriculture

1 Cf. Meyer, p. 197; Ar. *Œc.* i. 5. So Polybius, describing the advantages of Byzantion, says: 'For those commodities which are the first necessaries of existence, namely cattle and slaves, are confessedly supplied by the districts round the Pontos in greater profusion and of better quality than by any others' (iv. 38).
2 Cf. Hom. *Il.* ix. 591 ff.; Xen. *Cyrop.* vii. 5. 73.
3 Diod. xvii. 14; but contrast his savage treatment of Tyre (*ib.* 46), and of Gaza (Arr. *Anab.* ii. 27).
4 Cf. Jl 3[6] (Phœnicians sell Jews to the 'sons of the Grecians' [RV]), Ezk 27[13] ('Javan . . . traded the persons of men,' with Tyre [EV]).
5 Livy, xxxiv. 50; Plut. *Flam.* 13 (Romans taken prisoner by Hannibal held as slaves in Achaia in 194 B.C.).
6 Cf. Paus. x. xxxii. 15 (fair held at the temple of Asklepios near Tithorea in Phokis).
7 Philostr. *Vita Apoll.* VIII. vii. 12.
8 Strabo, p. 668.
9 See Newman, *Politics of Aristotle*, iii. 474.
10 Ar. *Ath. Pol.* xii. 4; cf. Dem. xxv. 57, lix. 17.
11 Cf. Xen. *Œc.* xiii. 8 f., *Mem.* II. vii. 6.
12 Cf. Theophr. *Char.* 23. It is a sign of vulgarity when Meidias 'swaggers through the Agora with three or four footmen' (Dem. *Meid.* 158).
13 Cf. Xen. *Œc.* vii. 41.

claimed many.[1] A large number were employed in all grades of public service[2]—*e.g.*, 1200 Σκύθαι as city police in Athens. At one end of the scale are slaves employed in the higher professions and skilled trades (doctors, teachers, bankers, and business-agents), at the other those doomed to the tragic horror of the Laurion silver mines. This last class it is that stands closest to Roman as well as to modern prædial slavery; the former class, on the other hand, stands very close, in external aspect at any rate,[3] to that of the free alien, or even the free citizen. Artisan slavery was, in fact, a main factor in the development of Athenian industrialism and commerce in the 6th and 5th centuries B.C.; it is here that the most important, and at the same time most obscure, problems in the economics of ancient slavery lie, viz. in the co-existence of a free and a servile artisan population, working side by side in unrestricted competition.

A peculiar and early development, best known to us from Athens, was that of a class of slaves known as οἱ χωρὶς οἰκοῦντες. These slaves 'living apart' were allowed by their master to work in quasi-independence, living upon the proceeds of their labour, under condition of paying him regularly a fixed sum (ἀποφορά).[4] Sometimes a group of such slaves worked together, under a foreman, himself a slave, mutually sharing the profits after paying the stipulated ἀποφορά.[5] These slaves, therefore, lived in practical independence, and were able to amass money, and so might ultimately be allowed to purchase their freedom. Legally, the master's rights remained unimpaired; the permission so to live was revocable, and the slave retained his earnings (so far as we can see) purely on sufferance. The system relieved the owner of responsibility, while guaranteeing him regular and high interest on his capital outlay; between him and loss of income through trade depression there stood the savings of the slave, and in the last resort the market value of the slave himself.

6. The economic problem.—Here arises a problem of particular interest, viz. that of the economic relation of slave-labour to wage-labour in Greek states, and the degree to which the latter was affected by the competition of a servile class probably greatly superior in numbers, and at least its equal in skill. Here it is necessary to avoid the exaggerations widely current in much popular exposition. Statements such as that of J. P. Mahaffy—'for each freeman with a vote there were at least three or four slaves. . . . Even very poor Athenians kept a slave or two'—belong to a pre-scientific age.[6] Equally unscientific is the sentimentalism of the 'New Hellenism,' which is bent upon 'clearing the name of Athens from one cruel reproach which has clung to it ever since the human conscience began to concern itself with these questions,' teaching that it was only late in the history of Athens, 'when the structure of her civilization became too heavy to be sustained by her own unaided efforts, that slaves and free immigrants crowded in to co-operate in the task. And these she treated in most cases, not as mere living instruments, but as "fellow-workers" with her citizens and free partners in the Empire.'[7]

We can only glance at the problem thus raised. How fundamental slavery appeared to its contemporaries, and how universally the social and economic effects which it entailed were accepted as part of the natural order of things, is shown by the fact that the most serious crisis in Athenian economic history originated in the pre-Solonian age, *i.e. before* the great development of industrial slavery in Attica.[1] It is true that 'the ultimate controlling fact in Greek politics of the 5th and 4th centuries is the evil economic condition of the lower classes, due to the competition of slave labour';[2] but analysis of social and economic facts in this regard was almost impossible, because neither in dress nor, above all, in colour were Athenian slaves marked off from the free community. Hence the standing poverty of the middle and lower class in Athens—a poverty which co-existed with a high degree of prosperity of the state as a whole[3]—is rarely, if at all, traced to its real root in slave competition.[4] From this point of view we may say that the expansion of artisan slavery, which by cheap labour took the bread out of the mouth of the free worker and threw him upon the street to subsist upon state pay,[5] with a large margin of leisure, but hardly any of wealth, closely resembled in its working the introduction of machinery into modern industry. But the bitter class war in ancient Greece[6] is waged not as between starving free artisans and their servile competitors; rather, the slave is the sign and source of the wealth which the lower classes covet, and for which the cry of γῆς ἀναδασμός and χρεῶν ἀποκοπή is raised. Hence the constant tendency of the lower classes actually to look for allies in the slave class, for the one partner desires freedom and the other wealth—both by the same means, and at the expense of one and the same foe.[7] The discussion of slavery arises, therefore, as an ethical, not as an economic, question; it originates with poets and philosophers, not with the political champion of popular rights (προστάτης τοῦ δήμου)—and this is in fact quite characteristic of the Greeks.

7. Treatment of slaves.—The readiness with which Greek slaves ran away is not to be taken as evidence of their general ill-treatment.[8] For the mere natural instinct of freedom will impel the slave to flight, often aimlessly. The Greek prædial serfs, a permanent immobile population, speaking a common language and inheriting a common tradition of national life, older and richer than that of their lords, and, above all, sharing in the essentials of contemporary Greek culture equally with them as a recognized element in the political structure, though without political rights, found life upon the whole more intolerable and more offensive to dignity than was the case with slaves proper; hence the danger of Helot insurrection was a constant and notorious factor in Lacedæmonian politics.[9]

Demosthenes[10] says that, if the barbarians who supplied the Greek slave marts could be told how civilized and humane the Greeks were[11] in their treatment of slaves, they would officially constitute the Athenians their public protectors! Apart from the singular and intolerable bathos of the orator's conclusion, it is to be remarked that his statement is an example of those naive delusions which in all ages pass current among peoples concerning themselves;[12] it is, in addition,

[1] Cf. Thuc. iii. 73; Xen. *Hell.* VI. ii. 6 (Corcyra), III. ii. 6 (Elis); see Polyb. iv. 73 ('Elis is more populous, as well as more richly furnished with slaves and other property, than the rest of the Peloponnese').

[2] To this class really belong the courtesans (ἱερόδουλοι) serving at the temples—*e.g.*, at Corinth, or at Eryx; cf. Strabo, p. 272.

[3] Xen. *Resp. Ath.* 10 f.

[4] Cf. Is. viii. 35.

[5] Cf. Æschines, i. 97.

[6] *Problems of Greek History*, London, 1892, p. 88; Mahaffy's statement is disproved by Ar. *Pol.* viii. (vi.) 8=1323 A: τοῖς γὰρ ἀπόροις ἀνάγκη χρῆσθαι καὶ γυναιξὶ καὶ παισὶν ὥσπερ ἀκολούθοις διὰ τὴν ἀδουλίαν). 'There can be little doubt that in almost all democracies a majority of the citizens were ἄποροι' (Newman, *Pol. of Ar.* iv. 568; cf., for Athens, Plut. *Per.* 11: ἐπανορθούμενος τὰς ἀπορίας τοῦ δήμου).

[7] A. E. Zimmern, *The Greek Commonwealth*[1], p. 389.

[1] Cf. Ar. *Ath. Pol.* ii. 2.

[2] G. B. Grundy, *Thucydides and the Hist. of his Age*, London, 1911, p. 106.

[3] Athens was the only state with a gold reserve (cf. Ar. *Ath. Pol.* xxiv. 1: χρημάτων ἠθροισμένων πολλῶν).

[4] But see Athen. 264 D (criticism levelled at Aristotle's friend Mnason because his thousand slaves meant that an equal number of Phocians was displaced).

[5] Cf. Ar. *Ath. Pol.* xxiv. 3, *Pol.* vii. (v.) 8=1309 A.

[6] Isocr. *Archid.* 77 f.; Polyb. iv. 17, xxxix. 8.

[7] Cf. Thuc. iii. 73; Strabo, p. 646; Diod. xiii. 48.

[8] Cf. Dio Chrys. x. 143.

[9] Thuc. iv. 80, v. 23.

[10] *Meid.* 530.

[11] Cf. *Phil.* iii. 3.

[12] Culminating, among the Greeks, in the insolent speech of Jason to Medea (Euripides, *Medea*, 536 ff.) in which he explains her indebtedness to him for bringing her within the pale of Greek civilization.

deliberate sophistry, for Demosthenes well knew that the intention of the law which he quotes, and of which he makes so much, was quite other than the advantage of the slave as such—*i.e.*, it protected him as another's property, not as being himself a person with inherent rights. Nevertheless, the comparative humanity of the Greek, and especially of the Athenian, treatment of slaves is indisputable.

The law protected the slave against ill-treatment by strangers, by allowing an owner to bring a prosecution for assault (γραφὴ ὕβρεως) [1] against the assailant. The slave is protected as a chattel of his owner. Further, having no legal personality, an Athenian slave could not put the law in operation in his own behoof.[2] Although a slave was his master's absolute property, to be disposed of by sale, gift, or bequest at his pleasure, a death penalty could be inflicted upon him, even for murder, only by a legal tribunal.[3] If a master killed his slave, he was subject to religious obligations of purification — which in practice meant little more than financial outlay.[4] Against inhuman treatment by his owner the Athenian slave could get a doubtful and temporary measure of protection by taking asylum, if he could, at the temple of Theseus, or in the precinct of the Semnai, and perhaps there obtain the good offices of the priest to induce his master to sell him to another.[5] It is clear, however, that the practical amount of legal protection was but slight, the only real restraining force being the owner's self-interest, reinforced by natural humanity, and to a certain extent by religion, which in Athens as elsewhere was very chary of interference with rights of private property.[6] The lot of the state slaves was in this respect probably more tolerable than that of the ordinary slave, as being less exposed to individual caprice; and the state employees, of various grades, naturally tended to acquire a certain independence by virtue of their official status.[7]

8. Modes of punishment.—(1) The commonest naturally was flogging.[8] This could easily become a death penalty (and is so used in Plato, *Laws*, 872 B, in cases of wilful murder of a free man by a slave). Flogging is very often the statutory penalty for slaves in the inscriptions, usually 50 strokes.[9] Sometimes flogging is combined with a fine, touching the slave's *peculium*, or with ἀπεργασία, 'working off the penalty.' [10]

(2) Short rations, and confinement of various types and degrees of painfulness.[11] Shackling was so ordinary a precaution as hardly to be classed as a punishment.

(3) Branding, applied especially to runaways.[12]

(4) Hard labour, at the mill, or, worse still, at the mines—reducing the culprit to the lowest grade of chattel-slave and practically dooming him to death.[13]

(5) Doubtless also tortures privately administered were not unexampled in the households of masters callous to public opinion.[14] But Athens seems to have known little or nothing of the hideous scenes of private torture and capricious cruelty with which Rome was familiar.

[1] Cf. Æschin. i. 15.
[2] Cf. Plato, *Gorg.* 483 B.
[3] Antiph. v. 48.
[4] Cf. Antiph. vi. 4.
[5] Cf. Plut. *de Superst.* iv. 166: ἔστι καὶ δούλοις νόμος ἐλευθερίαν ἀπογνοῦσι, πρᾶσιν αἰτεῖσθαι. Only certain temples were available for such asylum for slaves. The whole subject is very obscure (see M. H. E. Meier, G. F. Schömann, and J. H. Lipsius, *Der attische Process*, Berlin, 1883–87, ii. 625).
[6] Cf. Xen. *Mem.* II. iv. 3 f.
[7] Cf. Æschin. i. 54.
[8] Cf. Dem. xxiv. 167.
[9] *E.g.*, *CIA* ii. 841. 10; in Dittenberger², 680. 4 (Syros) it is 100 strokes.
[10] *E.g.*, at Andania (Dittenberger², 653. 75 f.).
[11] Cf. Ar. *Œc.* i. 5.
[12] Cf. Aristoph. *Birds*, 760, *Lysistr.* 331.
[13] Cf. Dio Chrys. *Or.* xiv. 233.
[14] A choice list in Aristoph. *Frogs*, 618 ff.

But there was nothing of the kid glove about the generality of Greek slave-owners.[1] Plato is dissatisfied with the older, patriarchal (*i.e.* Homeric) method, in which slaves were treated 'gently yet firmly'; he would have them kept in their place, 'not admonished as if they were freemen, which only makes them conceited.' [2]

9. Slave-torture.—Here falls to be mentioned the Attic rule, 'almost grotesque in its absurd cruelty,' [3] under which the evidence of a slave was inadmissible in a court of law unless it had been extracted on the rack by responsible officials (δημόκοινοι) [4]—themselves of course slaves.[5] Slaves who were themselves suspected of, or charged with, crime were tortured to secure a confession, but this sort of torture, frequent in all ages, even in the case of free men, needs no further remark here. Again, a master was free to torture his own slaves for his own ends, but the answers so obtained did not constitute legal evidence. The torture here in question is that applied to slaves of the parties in a suit. The views of the orators on the value of such evidence depend entirely upon the needs of the argument. Sometimes it is dismissed as worthless, but in general it is spoken of as final and unimpeachable, indeed as preferable to that given by a freeman, even under oath.[6] That citizens were exempted by Attic law from such torture [7] may indeed prove the 'superior humanity of the Athenians,' [8] but hardly in respect of their slaves.

10. Emancipation.—Aristotle, in flat contradiction of his own theoretical creed—for clearly a 'natural' slave, according to his definition, could only lose by being freed — recognized that the prospect of ultimate freedom was the slave's most powerful incentive to zeal and loyalty;[9] and the author of the Aristotelian *Economics* says: 'Slaves are willing to take trouble when freedom is the prize and the time is fixed.' [10] This principle was well established in popular usage, and various methods of emancipation were in vogue. The characteristic of these is their want of precision and the vagueness of the idea of personal freedom upon which they were based. Hence no universal legal forms were evolved, and the practical result in many cases was the highly illogical one of creating a class intermediate between those of the pure slave and the free citizen, subject to all degrees and kinds of servitudes. With all their imperfections, however, these more or less regularized, easily available, and constantly employed methods of creating free or semi-free status constitute one of the principal features of distinction between ancient and modern slavery.

(*a*) *By the state.*—The state itself sometimes conferred freedom on individuals, or even on considerable numbers, for special services, especially those rendered in defence of the country.[11]

(*b*) *By individuals.*—Emancipation by a private owner, either as an act of grace or upon payment by the slave of a sum agreed upon out of his *pecu-*

[1] As is clear from such passages as Xen. *Œc.* i. 22, *Mem.* III. xiii. 4, II. i. 17 (κολάζω πᾶσι κακοῖς, ἕως ἂν δουλεύειν ἀναγκάσω).
[2] Cf. Plato, *Rep.* 549 A, *Laws*, 778 A.
[3] J. P. Mahaffy, *Social Life in Greece*³, London, 1898, p. 241.
[4] Isocr. 361 D.
[5] Of course such torture, if ever applied, did not take place in court, but in the preliminary hearing.
[6] Is. viii. 12; cf. a remarkable passage in Antiph. vi. 25; Ar. *Rhet.* i. 15.
[7] Andoc. i. 43.
[8] J. W. Headlam, in *CR* vii. [1893] 1 ff., where he seeks to prove that 'the appeal to the Question was not a means of collecting evidence for a jury; it was an alternative method of trial; it was a kind of *ordeal*.'
[9] Ar. *Pol* iv. (vii.) 10=1330 A.
[10] 1344 B.
[11] Cf. Xen. *Hell.* I. vi. 24 (slaves on the fleet at Arginusai in 406 B.C. freed); Diod. xvii. 11 (Thebes), xx. 84 (Rhodes); cf. Dittenberger², 329. 49 (Ephesus); see A. Croiset, 'L'Affranchissement des esclaves pour faits de guerre,' in *Mélanges Henri Weil*, Paris, 1898, p. 67 f.

lium, was effected either *inter vivos* or by testament.[1] Manumission *inter vivos* naturally involved publication, as by announcement in a law-court (*ἐν δικαστηρίῳ*)[2] or other public place.[3] Proclamation by the herald in the Athenian theatre before the people became a fashionable nuisance which had to be checked by the severest penalty.[4]

(*c*) *Through a deity.* — In many places the favourite method was manumission under the form of dedication to a deity, the slave thus becoming the god's property (*ἱερόδουλος*). This was perhaps historically the oldest method. Properly and originally it was not manumission, but substitution of ownership; and originally perhaps the slave was actually transferred to the service of the temple—certainly always lighter than that of a private owner.

By far the largest and most instructive class of manumission inscriptions is that dating generally from the end of the 3rd cent. B.C. to the 2nd cent. A.D., in which the deity named appears not merely as accepting or witnessing to a dedication made to himself, but as one of the principals in a purely commercial transaction, *i.e.* as himself purchasing the slave, not to retain him as *ἱερόδουλος*, but to set him free[5]—his freedom being generally conditioned in the instrument of sale by certain obligations towards his old master. Many hundreds of such records having survived, a study of them tends to dissipate all illusion as to the real significance of slavery among the Greeks. The sale to the deity is not fictitious, for real money passes into the master's pocket[6]—perhaps the full market-price of the slave, hardly less, as agreed between slave and owner; the purchase money is of course provided by the slave himself from his *peculium* or sufferance savings. As the slave, having no legal personality, could not enter into any legal contract with his master, he must rely upon the god to act for him, *i.e.* he must entrust his priest both with the purchase money and with the carrying out of the entire transaction (*καθὼς ἐπίστευσε τῷ θεῷ τὰν ὠνάν* is the phrase used). Thus the owner could not touch the money deposited by the slave with the priest without first parting with his property in the slave to the god, under a legal contract of sale providing adequate secular safeguards against its breach. The transaction was profitable to the temple indirectly, and perhaps also directly; the owner secured his own price for his living property, and the slave got just what he was able to wring from a situation in which, in the last resort, he was absolutely powerless.

It is clear that this method of sale into freedom was simply a means of getting hold of the bulk of the slave's *peculium* and retaining his services during his best years, and of throwing him upon the world at the end of his days to fend for himself; neither humanity nor religion had much real significance in this connexion. The method is applied almost wholly in the interest of the vendor,

[1] See Aristotle's own will, in Diog. Laert. v. i. 9; cf. Dio Chrys. xiv. 440: *οἱ δέ τινες τὴν αὐτῶν τιμὴν καταβεβλήκασι τοῖς δεσπόταις*, and xxxi. 326.

[2] Dion. Hal. v. 596.

[3] Cf. Suid. *s.v.* Κράτης (*ἐπὶ βωμὸν ἀρθεὶς εἶπεν· Κράτης ἀπολύει Κράτητα*).

[4] Æschin. *Ctes.* 41.

[5] Hence the confusion of thought and phrase in the formula in use: *ὡς ἐλεύθερον ὄντα καὶ τοῦ θεοῦ*, 'free and yet the god's property.' Doubtless this method was a development of a transaction in which the god, *i.e.* his priest, with the god's own money (the temple treasure), bought in open market the slaves, male or female, required for service about the temple. Many, if not most, of the slaves donated to a temple as hierodoules must have been, or must eventually have become, too old and feeble to be of much use; but the god could no more reject such dedications, or cast them adrift, than he could refuse the cheap and flimsy offerings of the poor. Hence the Greek temples in this way served as almshouses.

[6] Cf. the almost constant formula *καὶ τὰν τιμὰν ἔχει*, or *ἀπέχει πᾶσαν*, asserting this.

who of course could have found no purchaser so complaisant as the deity with whom he deals. The vendor retained in effect what he professed to sell.[1]

11. Freedmen. — In Roman history freedmen (*ἀπελεύθεροι, ἐξελεύθεροι*) play a great part, but not in Athens or Greece generally. In Greece, freedmen were indistinguishable from ordinary domiciled aliens (*μέτοικοι*). Even as early as Kleisthenes freedmen seem to have been numerous in Athens, for he made many of them citizens.[2] Like ordinary domiciled aliens, freed slaves of Athenians must put themselves under a patron (*προστάτης*—their old master), and must observe certain obligations of service and respect towards him, details of which are unknown, and must pay to the state the alien's annual tax (*μετοίκιον*), with an additional three obols, besides performing all required military service by land or sea.[3] Standing thus to the state as a metic, and to his former owner as a client, the Athenian freedman was worse off than the Roman freedman, being in a condition intermediate between slavery and complete freedom as a citizen—an ambiguity characteristic of the Greek incapacity for clear legal conceptions, and illustrative of the extreme difficulty of naturalization in the ancient state, with its inherent conception of exclusive citizenship. If a freedman was false to his obligations, he was liable to prosecution (*δίκη ἀποστασίου*), and, if condemned, sank again into slavery, or in the other event became finally freed of obligation towards his former master—*i.e.*, he became a free metic, with freedom of choice as to his patron. A special vote of the assembly alone could elevate him to citizenship.

12. Slavery and Greek thought.—A discrimination between lower social functions (those of husbandman, artisan, trader, and the like) and higher social functions (those of administration, legislation, and war) is characteristic of Greek sentiment, though not everywhere made in practice. Of rigid coincidence of theory and practice, indeed, solitary examples were presented by Crete and Sparta, which 'sorted' the elements of the state with a thorough-going doctrinairism that appealed powerfully to the philosopher, but found itself, in Greece at large, with the exception of particular coteries, at ever greater variance with the facts of life. Nevertheless, even in such states as admitted the industrial and commercial classes to political power, popular sentiment, in its usual illogical and snobbish way, was thoroughly contemptuous of the so-called *βαναυσικαὶ τέχναι*.

To do manual work, even of such sort as did not obviously impair health and vigour, and especially to do it for pay, implied acceptance of a relation of subservience,[4] incompatible with the independence and leisure of a free man, and breeding a mean and sordid spirit. The real difference of intellectual and ethical level between some vocations and others was the solid core of truth upon which Greek philosophic thought seized, from which with merciless logic it developed a distinction between a professional ruling class and all such as engaged in the 'necessary' functions of trade and the manual arts. A separate class, or classes, must needs exist in the state for the discharge of these lower functions, and those so employed must, unless justice is to be infringed, be capable of nothing higher. The existence, in adequate numbers, of such a class is essential to

[1] This is not to say that there may not have been numerous instances in which the transaction was genuine in spirit and form.

[2] Ar. *Pol.* iii. 2=1275 B: *πολλοὺς γὰρ ἐφυλέτευσε ξένους καὶ δούλους μετοίκους* (see Newman's note *in loc.*, and vol. i. p. 231).

[3] Dem. *Phil.* i. 36.

[4] *διακονία* (Plato, *Laws*, 919 D); cf. Ar. *Pol.* i. 13=1260 A: *ὁ γὰρ βάναυσος τεχνίτης ἀφωρισμένην τινὰ ἔχει δουλείαν.*

the realization of the highest type of society, just as the household must consist of both slaves and free.[1] Unless, however, there was to be frankly accepted a dichotomy of the Hellenic race itself, such as would be fraught with the gravest menace of national disruption and chaos, there was nothing for it but to adopt the old standing division of humanity into Hellene and non-Hellene,[2] and to find therein the philosophic justification of the institution of slavery, while doing what could be done for the slave himself. The 5th cent., less troubled than the 4th with doubts, had not discovered the comfortable doctrine that slavery might be actually good for the slave, enabling him, under the mild yoke of the exponents of culture, to lead a higher sort of life than was otherwise possible for him.

The bias of Aristotle being, in general, to accept, with his own amendments, the institutions and views in which the collective experience of the Greek race had crystallized, he retains slavery in his ideal state, but retains it in an ideal form which would make it spiritually as well as practically advantageous to the highest capacities of both master and slave. The slave is an article of household property, an indispensable animate instrument,[3] of a superior sort—an instrument not of production, but of action, *i.e.* not coming solely within the sphere or purview of economics, but within that of ethics;[4] being an article of property, he belongs wholly to his master. The facts of the world show that there is a natural, and therefore just, because actually existing, principle of rule and subordination, or scheme of co-ordination in nature, both animate and inanimate.[5] There is, then, a 'natural slavery' (φύσει δοῦλον), in which the slave's bodily strength is complementary to the master's intelligence and 'virtue,' just as the union of male and female is necessary for purposes of reproduction and continuance of the species.[6] The natural slave is as far inferior to his master as the body is to the soul, or as the lower animals to man generally, so that the relation of rule and subordination which obtains between soul and body, or between men and animals, is applicable here also. The only difference, indeed, between such men and animals is that the former can listen to reason; but their best function is the obedient expenditure of their physical strength,[7] making noble life (τὸ εὖ ζῆν) possible for their master. The moral possibilities of the institution of slavery justify it—justified as it is indeed already by the mere fact of its existence as part of the teleological scheme of things. Paradoxical as it may sound, it was not every one who could be a slave in the true sense,[8] for the status properly connoted a certain spiritual as well as physical aptitude. It is less therefore upon the social or economic necessity for slavery than upon the moral benefits which through it arise for both master and slave that Aristotle insists, and he postulates for the master an intellectual and moral endowment as high as that of the slave is low. Thereby, in effect, was condemned a great deal of current slavery, in so far as it included captives, not a few even of Greek blood, taken in war, *i.e.* men in whose case mere brute force was the basis of the status. The true test of just freedom and just slavery, according to Aristotle, lay in the relative goodness and badness, *i.e.* the intellectual and moral capacities, of men. Constituted on such lines, slavery would be, for the slave, no such one-sided bargain as in actual fact it was.

Aristotle's theory, though it started from fact and claimed to return to fact, yet made shipwreck upon the rock of fact. For, in the first place, there were in Attica tens of thousands of slaves who, being in no genuine sense elements of a household, were yet in mental and moral capacity and actual output fully on a par with the free citizens who owned them and claimed the main part of the fruits of their intelligence and conscientious labour. In the second place, the ultimate basis of their status, let the theorists say what they would about laws of nature and existent right, was mere force and violence enlisted in the service of idleness and greed, and worse. Lastly, the actual moral effects of slavery, alike for slave and for slave-owner, were as a rule very conspicuously different from those desiderated by Aristotle; yet, if the institution was natural and right just because it was an objective fact, how could its fruits be logically condemned? The task of moralizing an essentially immoral institution was beyond his powers. Then as now rapacity and selfishness were apt to define right strictly from their own standpoint, and men were not slow, with grandiloquent phrase and fitful exhibition of capricious benevolence, to gloze national wrongdoing.

The noteworthy points are, not the precise amount of truth in Aristotle's attitude, but, firstly, the fact that 'the Greeks are characteristically the first human beings who felt a doubt or scruple about slavery' and that it was 'in Greece alone that men's consciences were troubled' by it, so that Aristotle found himself driven to defend the position with what forces of argument he could muster; secondly, that he makes little or no point of any supposed indispensability of slavery to the maintenance of the economic fabric of his age. And practical philosophy itself was soon to demonstrate the illusoriness of his fundamental axioms. Kleanthes was none the less a 'wise' man though he earned his living by the sweat of his brow in nightly toil as a drawer of water and kneader of bread, both reputed servile employments.[1] The Stoics demonstrated that virtue and happiness were independent of social condition,[2] thus making it clear that slaves were not essential by way of bolstering up virtue in order to save supposed higher natures from deterioration through contact with the crudities of life; thus 'slavery lost its Aristotelian *raison d'être*.'[3] Aristotle perceived clearly enough that slavery is incompatible with full human dignity, but, his thought being conditioned always by the vicious aristocratic antithesis of Hellene and βάρβαρος (though Plato could have taught him better),[4] he was unable to go on to perceive also that the concept of human dignity is either universally valid or everywhere equally worthless. He is honest enough, however, to confess that nature has left us without any practical criterion by which to distinguish the noble from the ignoble;[5] for the obvious criterion of colour, to which men in more modern times were fain to appeal, was to the Greeks unknown, or at least insignificant, and he was unwilling to fall back upon the 'verdict of history' as given by war, for that, as all Athenians knew to their sorrow, often proves far too much.

For the influence of Stoicism on slavery see art. SLAVERY (Roman).

LITERATURE.—P. Foucart, 'Mémoire sur l'affranchissement des esclaves par forme de vente à une divinité,' in *Archives des miss. scient. et litt.* iii. [1867] 375 ff.; W. Oncken, *Die Staatslehre des Aristoteles*, 2 vols., Leipzig, 1875; H. Wallon, *Histoire de l'esclavage dans l'antiquité*², 3 vols., Paris, 1879; W. A. Becker, *Charikles*, new ed., 3 vols., Berlin, 1877–78, tr. F. Metcalfe⁶, London, 1882; Julius Beloch, *Die Bevölkerung der griechisch-römischen Welt*, Leipzig, 1886; W. Richter, *Die Sklaverei im griechischen Altertume*, Breslau, 1886; W. L. Newman, *The Politics of Aristotle*, 4 vols., Oxford, 1887–1902; Fustel de Coulanges, *Nouvelles Recherches sur quelques problèmes d'histoire*, Paris, 1891; Ludwig Mitteis, *Reichsrecht und Volksrecht in den östlichen Provinzen des römischen Kaiserreichs*, Leipzig, 1891; George Foucart, *De Libertorum conditione apud Athenienses*, Paris, 1896; L. Beauchet, *Hist. du droit privé de la République athénienne*, 4 vols., do. 1897; Henri Francotte, *L'Industrie dans la Grèce ancienne*, 2 vols., Brussels, 1900; Paul Guiraud, *La Main-d'œuvre industrielle dans l'ancienne Grèce*, Paris, 1900; R. Dareste, B. Haussoullier, and T. Reinach, *Recueil des Inscriptions juridiques grecques*, 2nd ser., 2 vols., do. 1904; E. Barker, *The Political Thought of Plato and Aristotle*, London, 1906; Aristide Calderini, *La Manomissione e la Condizione dei Liberti in Grecia*, Milan, 1908; A. E. Zimmern, 'Was Greek Civilization based on Slave Labour?', in *Sociological Review*, ii. [1909] 1–19, 159–176, *The Greek Commonwealth*, Oxford, 1911; Eduard Meyer, *Kleine Schriften*, Halle, 1910; W. E. B. Du Bois, 'The Economics of Negro Emancipation,' in *Sociological Review*, iv. [1911] 303–313; Josef Kohler and Erich Ziebarth, *Das Stadtrecht von Gortyn*, Göttingen, 1912; R. v. Pöhlmann, *Gesch. der sozialen Frage und des Sozialismus in der antiken Welt*, 2 vols., Munich, 1912, *Aus Altertum und Gegenwart*², do. 1912, p. 139–198.

W. J. WOODHOUSE.

1 Ar. *Pol.* i. 3=1253 B: οἰκία δὲ τέλειος ἐκ δούλων καὶ ἐλευθέρων.

2 βάρβαρος; cf. Ar. *Pol.* i. 2=1252 B: ταὐτὸ φύσει βάρβαρον καὶ δοῦλον ὄν, and Eur. *Iph. Aul.* 1266.

3 Ar. *Pol.* i. 4=1253 B; cf. *Eth. Nic.* VIII. xi. 6.

4 *Pol.* i. 4=1254 A: ὁ δὲ βίος πρᾶξις, οὐ ποίησίς ἐστιν· διὸ καὶ ὁ δοῦλος ὑπηρέτης τῶν πρὸς τὴν πρᾶξιν. So William Morris: 'We must see industry not simply as a process of production but as a form of association,' etc., simply echoing Aristotle. See A. E. Zimmern, 'Progress in Industry,' in *Progress and History*, ed. F. S. Marvin, Oxford, 1912, p. 212 f.

5 *Pol.* i. 5=1254 A: ἐν ἅπασιν ἐμφαίνεται τὸ ἄρχον καὶ τὸ ἀρχόμενον.

6 *Ib.* i. 2=1252 A.

7 This is just the point at which Aristotle comes within hail of modern systems of 'scientific management,' such as the notorious Taylor system, the inventor of which in his defence thereof (as is pointed out by Zimmern, *loc. cit.*) unconsciously paraphrases Aristotle's defence of slavery.

8 *Pol.* i. 5=1254 B: ἔστι γὰρ φύσει δοῦλος ὁ δυνάμενος ἄλλου εἶναι.

1 Diog. Laert. 168.

2 Cf. Ar. *Eth. Nic.* I. x. 8.

3 Newman, i. 156.

4 Cf. Ar. *Pol.* iv. (vii.) 7=1327 B for Aristotle's own well-known comparison of Hellenes and Asiatics, the valuelessness of which is shown by comparing what Isocrates says on the same subject (*de Antid.* 293); cf. Plato, *Polit.* 262 D. But Plato's formal profession of faith in this matter is just as uncompromising as Aristotle's (see *Rep.* 470 C).

5 *Pol.* i. 5=1254 B.

SLAVERY (Hindu)

SLAVERY (Hindu).—Slavery is an institution fully recognized in the Sanskrit lawbooks of India. The Code of Manu (viii. 415) names seven causes of slavery, viz. capture in war, voluntary submission to slavery for a maintenance, birth from a female slave, sale, gift, inheritance from ancestor, and condemnation to slavery by way of punishment. Manu adds that wives and sons, like slaves, can have no property of their own, and that Śūdras, even when emancipated by their master, are not therefore released from servitude, because the state of dependence is innate in them. The perpetual slavery of the Śūdra class is one of the axioms of Brāhmanism, and may be traced back to the *Puruṣasūkta* hymn of the Ṛigveda (x. 90), in which it is stated that the Śūdra issued from the feet of Puruṣa, the primeval male, feet meaning service. Nārada (v. 25 ff.) gives some further details regarding slavery, and enumerates fifteen kinds of slaves: one born (of a female slave) in his master's house, one bought, one received by gift, one obtained by inheritance, one maintained during a general famine, one pledged by his rightful owner, one released from a heavy debt, one made captive in war, one won in a stake, one offering himself for a slave, an apostate from asceticism, one enslaved for a stipulated period, one becoming a slave for maintenance, one enslaved on account of his connexion with a female slave, and one self-sold. The difference between these various slaves and the class of hired servants, according to Nārada, lies in this, that the former, but not the latter, do impure work, such as removing urine and ordure, attending their naked master, handling cows, cleaning the house and the road. The first four in the above enumeration of fifteen slaves, likewise an apostate from asceticism and one self-sold, can never be released from slavery except by the favour of their owners, but the others may obtain their release by giving a compensation in money or providing a substitute. One intending to emancipate his slave has to take from the slave's shoulders a jar with water and smash it, sprinkling his head with the water, and thrice declaring him free. One superior in caste cannot be the slave of his inferior, nor is it legal slavery when a man has been sold after having been captured by robbers, or has been enslaved by force. Here it should be observed that the ancient Hindu law contains important relics of the practice of selling children for slaves which obtained amongst ancient societies. Thus it is stated by Vasiṣṭha (xv. 2) that the father and the mother have power to give, to sell, and to abandon their son, and the son bought is generally mentioned among the various substitutes for a real legitimate son. It is true that Āpastamba (ii. 13. 11) does not recognize the right to buy or sell a child, and the secondary sons generally were abolished in the more recent lawbooks, excepting the adopted son (*dattaka*; see art. ADOPTION [Hindu]). Adoption itself may be regarded as the survival of an archaic institution which owed its origin to the principle of slavery, whereby a man might be bought and sold, given and accepted, or relinquished in the same way as a cow or horse. The statements of the lawbooks on the subject of slavery are corroborated by the historical records, and V. A. Smith in his *Early History of India* observes that prædial and domestic slavery of a mild form seems to have been an institution in most parts of India from very remote times. In the time of J. A. Dubois (in India, 1792-1823), the Pariahs 'were looked upon as slaves by other castes, and treated with great harshness' (see art. PARIAH). Under British rule, slavery was not abolished at once, but gradually. Regulation x. of 1811 prohibited the importation of slaves from foreign countries into the British territories. This rule was by Regulation iii. of 1832 extended to the provinces which subsequently came into the possession of the British Government. Later on was passed Act v. of 1843 prohibiting all officers of Government from recognizing slavery. And it was finally abolished in 1860 by the Indian Penal Code, which declared the equality of all men, and provided punishment for buying or selling any person as a slave.

LITERATURE.—G. Bühler's and J. Jolly's trr. of Sanskrit lawbooks in *SBE*, Oxford, vols. ii. vii. xiv. xxv. xxxiii.; G. Sarkar, *The Hindu Law of Adoption*, Calcutta, 1891; V. A. Smith, *The Early History of India*, Oxford, 1904.

J. JOLLY.

SLAVERY (Jewish).—Slavery was one of the features of ancient and mediæval Jewish life, and there is a large crop of Jewish legislation on the subject. It is noteworthy that among the Jews treatment of the slave was never debasing or cruel. The Mosaic legislation, with its insistence upon the rights possessed by the bondman or bondwoman and its consequent limitation of the master's power over them, inculcated the duty of clemency in the master—a virtue which colours their mutual relations in all subsequent epochs. Besides this, the Jew at every turn was confronted with such injunctions as those in Dt 5^{15} 15^{15}, where the law of kindness to the slave is brought home to the Israelite by the duty to recollect how much his own ancestors had suffered during their serfdom in Egypt.

1. In OT literature.—Gn 14^{14} speaks of Abram 'arming his trained men, born in his house, three hundred and eighteen.' These 'trained men' were most probably hereditary slave property. That such slaves were, even in this early epoch, something more than the chattels of ancient Greece and Rome is evidenced by Gn 17^{23}, where 'all that were born in his [Abraham's] house, and all that were bought with his money' underwent the rite of circumcision—a clear proof that the master owed some sort of family obligation to the slave. Similarly in Ex 12^{44} the circumcised slave, by becoming a member of the family, and thus sharing its religious duties and privileges, is permitted to eat of the Passover. But the fountain-head of ancient Jewish slave legislation is Ex 21^{2-27}. A clear distinction is here drawn between the Israelitish and the non-Israelitish bondman or bondwoman, a distinction which held in all succeeding ages. An Israelite could buy a fellow-Israelite for six years only. In the seventh year he automatically received emancipation, unless he voluntarily decided to remain. Gentile slaves, however, whether male or female, could gain their freedom only if they had previously been the victims of certain specified acts of cruelty by the master. In the year of jubile[1] all Israelite slaves together with the children born to them during serfdom were, according to Lv $25^{39f.}$, to be liberated without exception; but, if the children were born of a Gentile mother, then they, like her, must remain in slavery (Ex 21^4). According to Lv $25^{50f.}$, the Hebrew slave of a non-Hebrew master had also to be freed in the year of jubile, although he should previously be redeemed, if possible, by his kindred or by his own money, the redemption price being reckoned in accordance with the number of years that had still to elapse before the arrival of the jubile. That the traffic in slaves led to numerous abuses, religious, moral, and economic, is seen from Jer 34^{8-22}, where the princes, priests, and people of Judah are divinely warned of the dire punishment which will overtake them as a result of their breach with the ordinances of the Mosaic slave legislation. There are numerous points, both of resemblance and of contrast, between the Mosaic slave laws and those of the Code of Ḥammurabi.[2]

2. In Rabbinic literature.—The status, rights, privileges, and manumission of slaves are subjects of elaborate discussion in the Talmud as well as in the subsequent mediæval code-books, such as—to mention the two principal ones—the *Mishneh Tôrāh* of Maimonides (*q.v.*) and the *Shûlḥān 'Ārûkh* of Joseph Qaro (*q.v.*). From Lv 25^{39}, 'And if thy

1 See art. FESTIVALS AND FASTS (Hebrew), § I. iv. 2.

2 See art. LAW (Babylonian), vol. vii. p. 818.

brother . . . be waxen poor, and be sold . . .,' the Talmudic authorities deduced the injunction that a Jew should sell himself into slavery only as a very last possible resort, as such an act was a stigma upon the honour of the Jewish religion, which declared through Lv 25^{55} that the Israelites were to be servants of the divine, and not of any human, master. He should not sell himself to a woman or to a convert or to a Gentile; but, should he do so, the sale is valid, and it then becomes the religious duty not only of his family but also of the Jewish community to effect his redemption. Such an act was always considered a highly meritorious one, and the social life of the mediæval Jews is studded with instances of it on the part of individuals and communities in different parts of Europe—although it should here be said that the Synagogue forbade the traffic in Jewish slaves at quite an early stage, but placed no bar on the commerce in heathen slaves. The master was religiously bound to have his non-Jewish slave circumcised. In default of this, it was the duty of the ecclesiastical authorities to have the circumcision performed. But, should such slave have been purchased from a non-Jewish master, then circumcision was optional to the slave, who, if he refused to undergo it, was not allowed to be kept longer than twelve months, after which it was incumbent upon the Jew to sell him to a non-Jewish master.[1] The object of laws like these was to make the slaves an integral part of the Jewish community. Once circumcised, they were regarded as being 'received into the fold' and bound by all the 'negative' precepts of the Tôrāh and by such 'affirmative' precepts as apply 'to stated times only.' But they were never more than a subordinate and inferior part of the community, as is proved by the limitations imposed by the Talmud and all the later codes upon their rights of intermarriage with the general Jewish population. When, however, as in the Middle Ages, the act of making Jewish converts was fraught with danger at the hands of Christian authorities (who in many places officially prohibited such conversions), the duty of circumcising slaves was entirely abrogated. According to the Talmud,[2] the master of a Jewish slave was compelled to accord him the same home comforts as he himself enjoyed.

As the *Shûlḥān 'Ārûkh* puts it, 'It is the quality of saintliness (*ḥasidûth*) and the way of wisdom for man to be merciful to his slave, not to make his yoke heavy nor to distress him, but to give him to eat and drink of all manner of foods, not to contemn him either by deed or word, not to multiply complaints and anger against him but rather to speak gently to him and lend a kindly ear to his grievances.'[3]

Self-redemption for the slave, whether Jewish or not, was always permitted, the conditions governing such an act on the part of a female differing in many material ways from those attaching to a male.

Jewish legislation, like all other systems which legalized slavery, refused to slaves all title to independent property. As the Rabbis laconically phrased it, 'Whatsoever the slave hath acquired, the master hath acquired.'[4] Whatever he may receive from others, or find by the way, belongs to the master. Should he be assailed and injured, the damages—which were a five-fold compensation for (*a*) the blow, (*b*) the pain caused, (*c*) the cost of healing, (*d*) loss of time, (*e*) the indignity—were to be paid to the master.

A subject elaborated at great length in the Talmud and the mediæval codes is the manumission of the non-Jewish slave, which became compulsory on the master's ill-treatment of him in certain specified respects. A deed of manumission had to be drawn up, and, should the master refuse to sign it, he was excommunicated. It had to be handed to the slave in the presence of two witnesses; and, should the master have expressed a merely oral intention to manumit, he could not retract, as his words were binding, and the court could compel him to write out the official deed. A curious law is the following: if the master married his slave to a freewoman, or if he put phylacteries on his head, or if he bade him read three verses in a scroll of the Law before the congregation, or if he asked him to do any of those precepts which only a freeman might perform, the slave became free and the master was compelled to give him a document of manumission.[1] To write in the future tense 'I shall manumit' was ineffectual. It must be in the past tense, 'I have manumitted.' According to Lv 25^{46}, it is the Jew's duty to retain his non-Jewish slave and transmit him as a heritage to his children. Hence it was that the Rabbis said that to manumit a 'Canaanite' (*i.e.* non-Jewish) slave was to infringe a negative precept.[2] An exception, however, was made in the case of manumission *lidbar mitzvah*, *i.e.* for the purpose of fulfilling a precept, as, *e.g.*, to complete the number of ten males required for the celebration of public worship. Should the slave express a wish to go to Palestine, the master was compelled to go with him or to sell him to some one who would consent to take him there. If a slave fled from anywhere to Palestine, he might not be brought back into serfdom; and the master was bound to manumit him. This law is based on Dt 23^{15}, 'Thou shalt not deliver unto his master the servant which is escaped from his master unto thee.' He who, living in Palestine, sells his slave to a master outside Palestine thereby enables the slave to get his freedom, as the second master is compelled to manumit him.[3] Should a Jew sell his slave to a non-Jew, the slave thereby acquires his freedom.

3. Jews and the slave trade.—The mediæval Church's objection, from the time of Constantine, against the ownership of Christian slaves by Jews did not prevent the latter from becoming, at certain epochs, the chief traders in this class of traffic. Indeed, Christians openly defied the Church by co-operating with Jews in this commerce. In the reign of Louis the Pious the Jews imported large numbers of Christian slaves into Spain and N. Africa. Likewise they acted as middlemen, supplying Christian slaves to the Muslim world and Muslim slaves to the Christian. At the zenith of the Jew's prosperity in Spain (from the 10th to the end of the 15th cent.) many of the most wealthy Spanish-Jewish families amassed large fortunes by the importation of slaves from Andalusia.[4] The circumcision of slaves often incensed the mediæval Church authorities, and bitter protests were frequently heard. As the practice was looked upon as an infringement of the law prohibiting Jews from making converts, the Rabbinical authorities made the rite of circumcision optional on the part of the bondman.

LITERATURE.—J. L. Saalschütz, *Archäologie der Hebräer*, Berlin, 1855-56, ii. 236 ff.; A. Barnes, *An Inquiry into the Scriptural Views of Slavery*², Philadelphia, 1857; M. Mielziner, *Die Verhältnisse der Sklaven bei den alten Hebräern*, Copenhagen, 1859, Eng. tr. in *British and Foreign Evangelical Review*, xi. [1862] 311 ff.; M. J. Raphall, *Bible View of Slavery*, New York, 1861; Zadoc Kahn, *L'Esclavage selon la Bible et le Talmud*, Paris, 1867; A. Grünfeld, *Die Stellung der Sklaven bei den Juden*, Jena, 1886; M. Mandl, *Das Sklavenrecht des*

1 See T.B. *Yᵉbhāmôth*, 48*b*.
2 T.B. *Qiddûshîn*, 20*a*.
3 'Yōreh De'āh,' 'Hilkōth 'Ăbādîm,' sect. 267, 17.
4 T.B. *Bābhā Mᵉṣî'ā*, 12*a*; T.B. *Qiddûshîn*, 22*b*.

1 *Shûlḥān 'Ārûkh*, 'Yōreh De'āh,' sect. 267, 70.
2 T.B. *Giṭṭin*, 45*b*.
3 *Ib*. 45*a*.
4 H. Graetz, *Hist. of the Jews*, Eng. tr., London, 1891-92, vol. iv. ch. 3.

AT, Hamburg, 1886; J. Winter, *Die Stellung der Sklaven bei den Juden*, Breslau, 1886; J. B. Lightfoot, *Saint Paul's Epistles to the Colossians and Philemon*[3], Introd. to Philemon, London, 1879; T. André, *L'Esclavage chez les anciens Hébreux*, Paris, 1892; A. Bertholet, *Die Stellung der Israeliten und der Juden zu den Fremden*, Freiburg i. Br., 1896; J. F. McCurdy, *History, Prophecy and the Monuments*, New York, 1896, ii. 168 ff.; I. Benzinger, *Hebräische Archäologie*, Freiburg i. Br., 1894, p. 123 ff.; *HDB* iv. 461 ff.; *EBi* iv. 4653 ff.; *DCG* ii. 641 f.; *JE* xi. 403 ff.; Israel Abrahams, *Jewish Life in the Middle Ages*, London, 1896, pp. 95 ff.; E. Benamozegh, *Israël et l'humanite*, Paris, 1913, pp. 589 ff.; Maimonides, *Yad Hā-hazākah*, 'Hilkōth 'Ăbādīm'; J. Qaro, *Shūlḥān 'Ārûkh*, 'Yōreh De'āh,' 'Hilkōth 'Abādīm.'

J. Abelson.

SLAVERY (Roman). — Slavery among the Romans differs from slavery in Greece in respect of the scale and the application of the institution. To these differences must be added that of greater range in time, so that the historical development of Roman slavery is both more apparent and more complex than is the case in Greece. In spite of these differences, however, the essential nature and general characteristics of the institution remain the same, so that much of what is said under the head of Greek slavery is true here also.

I. *First Period.*—We must distinguish three periods in the history of Roman slavery. The earliest, a comparatively brief phase, is that of what Mommsen calls 'the old, in some measure innocent, rural slavery,'[1] under which the farmer tilled his moderate holding in person, assisted by his sons and his slaves, and occasionally by hired hands—a system under which the slaves were comparatively few, and mainly of Italian or at least Etruscan origin. They were either war captives or born of such. There was thus 'no striking distinction, and often no distinction at all, of race, appearance, speech, or manners, no instinctive repulsion between owners and owned, which, in other regions, have supplied some of the most painful chapters in the history of human relations. Chattels at law, ritual included them not only within the pale of humankind, but to a limited extent even of the family, and the simple households of earliest Rome may have witnessed little difference in the treatment of slaves and sons.'[2]

Traces of this older humanity of relations between master and slave still linger in the household of the elder Cato in the middle of the 2nd cent. B.C., though he belongs in reality to the following period.[3] Like the housefather and landholder of old time, Cato shared the labours and coarse fare of his slaves,[4] and his wife—'if she allowed her children to be suckled by female slaves, she also allowed their children[5] in return to draw nourishment from her own breast; one of the few traits which indicate an endeavour to mitigate the institution of slavery by ties of human sympathy—the common impulses of maternity and the bond of foster-brotherhood.'[6]

II. *Second Period.* — The second stage of Roman slavery was entered upon early in the 4th cent. B.C., when the national economy of Italy began to experience a revolution, the earliest evidence of which is the enactment of the law of 367 B.C., compelling a landholder to employ along with his slaves a certain proportion[7] of free labourers. The centralized farming on a big scale which began after the Hannibalic war was probably derived from the Carthaginian slave plantation-system,[8] with which the Romans came in contact in Africa and Sicily; perhaps also, as Mommsen

1 *The Hist. of Rome*, Eng. tr., new ed., London, 1901, iii. 305.

2 C. W. L. Launspach, *State and Family in Early Rome*, London, 1908, p. 63; cf. Plutarch, *Coriolanus*, 24; see also the directions of Varro to make a place for the slaves to stroll about in and sleep (*de Re rust.* i. 13).

3 Mommsen, iii. 117 f.; see G. Ferrero, *The Greatness and Decline of Rome*, Eng. tr., London, 1907–09, i. 30.

4 Plut. *Cato Maior*, 3.

5 Probably to be understood not of the ruck of the slaves, but of the permissive family of the *villicus* (cf. Varro, *de Re rust.* i. 17. 5).

6 Mommsen, iii. 118.

7 One-third, in the law as revived by Julius Cæsar (Suetonius, *Julius Cæsar*, 42). Appian, *de Bellis civilibus*, i. 8, is the only authority referring this provision back to the Licinian law.

8 See Mommsen, iii. 307; cf. ii. 138.

suggests,[1] it was not unconnected with the recent introduction of wheat-growing. The result was the rapid expansion of slave-owning as a mode of investment—a process which simply repeated the industrial development seen in Greece two centuries earlier. The new system 'was pervaded by the utter regardlessness characteristic of the power of capital,'[2] and was 'just like that of America, based on the methodically-prosecuted hunting of man.'[3] Concomitantly, special factors were at work to divert attention from agriculture to cattle-rearing as being at once easier, more profitable, and apparently capable of unlimited development, besides being more immediately available and lending itself to the spirit of an age in which the display and spending of wealth (in some respect actually enforced by law[4]) was more congenial than the making of it by personal industry, as in the old days.[5] But, in whatever direction speculation applied itself, 'its instrument was without exception man reduced in law to a beast of burden.'[6] This expanded slave-system was applied in two main forms—to pastoral husbandry carried on by means of armed, often mounted, slave-herdsmen on great ranches,[7] and to the plantation-system proper, *i.e.* cultivation of huge estates (*latifundia*) by means of gangs of slaves,[8] working often in shackles and always under the supervision of overseers, slaves like themselves. To these types a third may be added, that of domestic industry carried on for the profit of an owner by slaves skilled in various arts or trades, or by freedmen working in part for the profit of their *quondam* master.[9]

Thus from the latter part of the 2nd cent. B.C. the slave-system of the Republic reached its acme. An enormous increase in the slave trade was the consequence of the sudden and universal demand for cheap labour—'occupiers of State land required shepherds; the contractors required labour for public works or military equipment;[10] the State required it for the public services; traders for the crews of their ships; the wealthy for domestic service or for gladiatorial shows; small proprietors and the middle class generally to relieve them of the more distasteful part of their daily work.'[11] There can be no question that the work controlled by the public companies was done mainly by slaves, and that their operations were unhampered by the organized claims of free labour; they were therefore able to choose their instruments solely with a view to efficiency. For the more technical side of the various activities in request the Roman citizen was in general never sufficiently well educated, while for the life on the great cattle-runs and sheep-walks he was if possible still less adapted. Moreover, the frequent calls to military service, 'the real industry of the Roman freeman,'[12] made it undesirable, from the employer's point of view, to use citizens even for such labour as they might be willing to undertake.[13]

The inherent viciousness of the situation was hardly felt at all at first.[14] For, while the continual wars of plunder bred and fostered a capitalistic class crying ever for labour and yet more labour, they also directed towards Italy a ceaseless and, as it seemed, inexhaustible stream of the cheapest labour in the world,[15] in the tens of thousands of slaves torn from all parts of the Mediterranean area and the north. There was perhaps hardly

1 Mommsen, ii. 77.

2 *Ib.* iii. 71.

3 *Ib.* iii. 306.

4 Dion. Hal. vii. 71.

5 Mommsen, iii. 120.

6 *Ib.* iii. 307.

7 This pastoral husbandry on slave-manned ranches or sheep-runs was rapidly extended to the provinces as they became available for exploitation; *e.g.*, Dalmatia in 155 B.C. was no sooner acquired than the Roman capitalists began the rearing of cattle there on a big scale. T. Pomponius Atticus possessed enormous cattle-runs in Epirus (Cornelius Nepos, *Atticus*, xiv. 3). It was the vast military needs of the time that made these so profitable.

8 Especially in Etruria (Plut. *Tib. Gracchus*, 8, and cf. Ferrero, iii. 302 f.).

9 Cf. the case of Crassus, who made much of his wealth by buying unskilled slaves and having them trained to various professions (Ferrero, i. 203 and 340; A. H. J. Greenidge, *Hist. of Rome*, i. 56 f.).

10 For the enormous development of the contract system in this age see Polybius, vi. 17.

11 Ferrero, i. 28.

12 Cf. Dion. Hal. ii. 28.

13 Cf. App. *de Bell. civ.* i. 7; see Ferrero, i. 28.

14 Cf. Greenidge, i. 65.

15 *Ib.* p. 82. See *ib.* p. 83 for prices; also Dio Cassius, lv. 31; Tacitus, *Annals*, xiii. 31.

any branch of trade better organized than the slave trade itself, the foster-mother of all other trades of the time.

1. Sources of supply.—'The Negroland of that period was western Asia,[1] where the Cretan and Cilician corsairs, the real professional slave-hunters and slave-dealers, robbed the coasts of Syria and the Greek islands.'[2] To such a pitch was the hunting pursued that about 100 B.C. the king of Bithynia pleaded, as a reason for his inability to supply the required military contingent, the ravages of the Roman revenue-farmers among the able-bodied population of his kingdom.[3] At the great slave-mart in Delos, where the Eastern dealers disposed of their human cargoes to Italian middlemen, as many as 10,000 head were said to have been landed and sold off in a single day.[4] Many regions must thus have been permanently depopulated and permanently depressed below the margin of cultivation.

After the overthrow of the Macedonian kingdom at the battle of Pydna Æmilius Paullus, under the senate's orders, sold into slavery, *i.e.* to the speculators or wholesale agents (*mangones*) who accompanied Roman armies for that purpose, 150,000 free inhabitants of 70 communities in Epirus which had sided with Perseus.[5] The defeat of the Cimbri and Teutones contributed a like number to the Roman slave-market.[6] Cæsar on a single occasion sold into slavery 53,000 of the Aduatuci;[7] and similarly, at the opposite extremity of the empire, Cicero, after his own petty campaign in the Taurus and the capture of the hill-fort of Pindenissus, writes to Atticus telling him how much the sale of the captives brought.[8] Titus sold 90,000 Jews into slavery in the conquest of Palestine.

2. Legal position. — In law the slave was a chattel; he was the one human being who could be owned. He is not only a chattel (*res*), but is treated constantly in the legal texts as the typical chattel. Under the republic there were no legal limitations to the master's power; *iure gentium* his rights were unrestricted. Public opinion,[9] however, and self-interest, combined with the religious sentiment connected with family life, exercised a powerful influence to the slave's advantage at a time when slaves were few and in closer relations with the master than was the case in later ages. The censors could also take note of outrageous cruelty to slaves as of other conduct unworthy of a citizen. In political and civic life the slave had no share; he could hold no public office nor sit in any public assembly; nor could he serve in the army.[10]

3. Public slaves. — A considerable number of slaves were employed in various public departments in subordinate duties. These formed a class standing somewhat apart from the rest of the slaves, and were known as *servi publici populi Romani*. They formed in fact a sort of rudimentary lowest grade of a permanent civil service, as at Athens, serving as messengers, magistrates' attendants, clerks, servants in temples,[11] assistants in the fire, water, and sewerage services, under the control of the ædiles.[12] Under the empire the employment of *servi publici* diminished, and they were superseded by freemen, except within the capital, as early as the time of Augustus.

4. Status in religion.—The exclusion of slaves from the public cults was not due to any denial of their claim to divine protection, but simply to the fact that the gods were divinities of certain special groups, *gentes*, etc., to which slaves neither did nor could belong. Hence they could not share in the *sacra* of the *gens* of their master. But slaves had a special cult of Diana, and were given special consideration at the festival of the *Saturnalia*, the most remarkable feature of which was the temporary licence granted to slaves in the household —slaves and free for the nonce exchanging rôles.[1] Within the household, slaves shared in the worship of the Lares and Penates. In the burial customs their common humanity is fully recognized, and the grave of the slave is declared as sacred as that of the freeman; he rests there with the other departed members of the family of which he was the humblest element. Hence memorials to slaves are among the commonest of funeral inscriptions. Slaves are also members (with their master's consent) of burial clubs[2] (*collegia*).

5. Marriage. — Legally slaves were incapable of marriage, but it is abundantly clear from the literary and legal texts that they habitually entered into permanent unions, which were marriage in all but their legal aspect, and were in general respected as such by their masters; and the names of legal relationships arising through legal marriage—*uxor*, *pater*, *filius*, *frater*, and the like — were freely applied in the case of slaves, even in the legal texts, but, as is expressly said, by analogy only and without legal significance. In strictness, however, any such connexion between male and female slave, or between slave and free, could only be 'cohabitation' (*contubernium*), not *matrimonium*. Hence, in the case of free persons, enslavement of either party broke the marriage tie.

6. Torture.—A slave could not be party to civil proceedings, either to sue or to be sued; this must be done through his master. Nor could a slave be accuser in a criminal case;[3] but he could 'inform,' *i.e.* make *delationes* of criminal offences, though not against his master (except, from the time of Severus, for certain specified offences; cf. the rules regarding slaves' evidence against their masters).

As a rule, the evidence of slaves was not admissible in civil cases, but there were some exceptions. Where it was admissible, it had to be taken under torture (*quæstio*), as in Greece; but recourse was not to be had to such evidence unless there was already independent evidence before the court. In criminal cases also the evidence of slaves must be elicited by torture, conducted out of court under the supervision of the *quæsitor*; it might be applied more than once.[4] But a slave could not be examined under torture to elicit evidence against his own master, or, in the case of jointly-owned slaves, against either joint-owner.[5]

7. The peculium. — Though slaves were *pro nullis* in the eye of the civil and the prætorian law,[6] they were in practice far from being nullities. Practical needs compelled recognition of a slave's individuality, and suggested those illogical com-

[1] Slaves from that region were regarded as being specially fitted for slavery owing to their great powers of endurance. Plautus commends the Syrians ('genus quod patientissimum est hominum' [*Trinummus*, 542]). Sardinians, on the other hand, were little worth (cf. Cicero, *pro Flacco*, 27 [65]; Festus, p. 322: 'Sardi venales, alius alio nequior').

[2] Mommsen, iii. 306.

[3] Diodorus, xxxvi. 3.

[4] Strabo, p. 668.

[5] Livy, xlv. 34; Strabo, p. 322.

[6] Livy, *Epit.* 68.

[7] *de Bell. Gall.* ii. 33; cf. iii. 16.

[8] *ad Att.* v. xx. 5.

[9] So even under the empire (see Sen. *de Clem.* i. 18).

[10] Death was the penalty for enrolment; cf. Livy xxii. 33 for the crucifying of 25 slaves, 'quod in campo Martio coniurassent' (see Pliny, *Epp. ad Trajanum*, 29 and 30). The state itself could of course override this rule, as was said to have been done after Cannæ.

[11] Livy, ix. 29; Tac. *Hist.* i. 43.

[12] Cf. *Lex Coloniæ Genetivæ Juliæ*, 62 (in E. G. Hardy, *Roman Laws and Charters*, Oxford, 1912).

[1] See *GB*³, pt. vi. *The Scapegoat*, London, 1913, p. 307 f.; and cf. Seneca, *Ep.* xlvii. 14: 'honores illis in domo gerere, ius dicere permiserunt et domum pusillam rem publicam esse iudicaverunt.'

[2] The *Lex collegii Lanuvini* of A.D. 133 has survived, and shows slaves as members (C. G. Bruns, *Fontes iuris romani antiqui*⁷, Tübingen, 1909, i. 388 f.; see S. Dill, *Roman Society*, p. 251 f.).

[3] Hence, to save the principle, Hadrian enacted that complaints lodged by slaves, of cruelty on their master's part, were not technically 'accusations.'

[4] Valerius Maximus, viii. 4: 'octies tortus.'

[5] Tac. *Ann.* ii. 30.

[6] But not at natural law (Ulpian, *Digest.* L. xvii. 32: 'Quod attinet ad ius civile, servi pro nullis habentur; quod ad ius naturale attinet, omnes homines aequales sunt'). Slavery is the only case in which, in the extant sources of Roman law, a conflict is declared to exist between the *ius gentium* and the *ius naturale*. It is part of the *ius gentium* because it originates in war. The Romans therefore frankly admitted that slavery was inconsistent with the highest ideals of human society. The thesis of Aristotle, on the contrary, was that slavery realized the purpose of nature as formulated in those ideals.

promises which are inherent in the Roman conception and law of slavery, and in the Greek also, though there less striking because of the paucity of documentary evidence. In Rome, as in Athens, almost any industry now carried on by free men might be and was carried on by slaves;[1] in imperial times it is hardly an exaggeration to say that Roman commerce was mainly in the hands of slaves; they carried on business (*e.g.*, banking) for their master, or were partners in firms; the whole sphere of private trading was shared by slaves in competition with free men, freedmen, and *peregrini*, before the development of the free *procurator*, or agent. It is this activity of slaves in the higher walks of mercantile and professional life—an activity which is at variance with the strict law of their status—that constitutes one of the most striking, and indeed hardly comprehensible, differences between ancient and modern slavery. For these activities demand for their exercise precisely those qualities of intelligence, industry, integrity, and mutual respect which in the conventional literary estimates of the slave are *totidem verbis* denied, and seem to moderns, partly on the basis of experience and partly through mere prejudice, incompatible with a status so degraded.

The institution which enabled the rich Roman to engage in commerce without that personal intervention which would have offended the social prejudices of his age, and at little risk, was that of the slave's *peculium*. The *peculium* was a fund which masters allowed slaves to hold and, within certain limits, to deal with as they pleased; in law it was the master's, but *de facto* it was the slave's. Originally it was simply the small savings of food and such like that a slave had a mind to make by stinting himself. Under the empire it might imply a great sum and be in any form, even including other slaves (*vicarii*) and their *peculia*, to a total value greater than that of the principal slave in whose *peculium* they were held, and whose stock-in-trade they constituted. In dealing with it commercially the slave appears as quite distinct from his master, though his capacity is purely derivative from him, ostensibly and in ordinary parlance dealing for himself, but in the eye of the law for the master's account. The *peculium* was thus a sort of property of the slave, so that upon his manumission by a living master, whether *vindicta* or informally, he took the *peculium*, unless it was expressly reserved;[2] by manumission by will it did not pass to the slave unless expressly given in the will. But alienation of the slave did not carry with it the *peculium* unless it was expressly so granted.

8. Treatment.—The mutual goodwill and even familiarity of intercourse marking the earlier domestic slavery of the Romans gradually gave place to harshness and cruelty, though the legal position of the slave remained in essentials unchanged. Life, however, does not necessarily move always on the lines of strict logic and law, and it is always open for the individual to rise above the standard of his age, so that the actual position of the slave was no doubt very often much better in fact than it was in theory.[3] In this later period also examples of happy relations between slave and master are not unknown, such as those between Cicero and his slave (later his freedman) Tiro[4]—though Cicero's general views on slavery seem to have been on all fours with those of Aristotle.[5] Such also were the relations between Atticus and his slave Alexis,[6] and between the younger Pliny and his *libertus* Zosimus.[7] But such humanity was purely personal, or at best confined to limited and cultured circles,[8] and represented neither the law nor average opinion and practice.

1 Cf. Cicero, *de Officiis*, i. 42.
2 In Greece apparently the rule was that the master manumitting or selling took the *peculium* unless he expressly waived his right (L. Mitteis, *Reichsrecht und Volksrecht*, Leipzig, 1891, p. 382).
3 Cf. G. Boissier, *La Religion romaine*3, ii. 315 f.
4 See Boissier, *Cicéron et ses amis*7, Paris, 1884, p. 113 f.; R. Y. Tyrrell and L. C. Purser, *Correspondence of Cicero*2, Dublin, 1885, i. 106 f.
5 Cf. *de Rep.* iii. 24; *de Off.* i. 42, ii. 7, and compare *ad Att.* i. xii. 4.
6 'Imaginem Tironis' (Cic. *ad Att.* xii. 10).
7 *Ep.* v. 19; and cf. viii. 16.
8 Cf. Boissier, *Cicéron*, p. 118.

For with the economic revolution and the resultant broad distinction between the *familia urbana* and the *familia rustica*[1] a greater distance had been put between master and slave.[2] The slaves working on the estate, the stronger, rougher, less cultured and less tractable element, with which the master had as a rule little personal concern or contact,[3] came to stand, in comparison with the slaves of the town house, somewhat as a penal establishment, degradation to which could be held *in terrorem* over the heads of the more favoured class.[4] The fact that the slaves on the country estate were now controlled by a *villicus*, himself a slave, was probably but an aggravation of their condition.

Cato expressly advised the sale of old, worn-out, or sick slaves for what they would fetch—the system he applied to cattle and the inanimate tools.[5] Rations of sick slaves, he suggests, should be docked—a maxim adopted on other than hygienic grounds.[6] The practical application of this advice must generally have meant the callous abandonment of ailing slaves to their fate. A slave, Cato held, should either be at work or be asleep, *i.e.* he must as far as possible be reduced to the condition of a machine.[7] Though he ate with his household slaves, his after-dinner leisure was devoted to administering to peccant slaves 'the proper number of lashes with a thong wielded by his own hand.'[8] In the same business-like spirit he allowed indeed the union or quasi-marriage (*contubernium*) of his slaves, but only at a tariff, paid out of their *peculium*—a practice which doubtless would not lack imitators.

What in Cato's régime was the outcome of a mean and unsympathetic nature was in later times the calculated product of systematic policy.[9] Although it was universally recognized that harshness and injustice failed of their end,[10] the very numbers of the slaves led to the adoption of extreme cruelty in their punishments[11] and the application of the harshest methods of control.[12] No limits were set by law, until long after republican times, and very wide limits by custom and the tone of society, to the lengths to which caprice, passion, fear,[13] or innate love of cruelty might go in punishing even the most trifling offences.

Among other things, the use of chains, no longer as a penal measure,[14] but as a normal and constant precaution, and that not only for the slaves when at work in the fields under the eye of overseers, but also when they were herded at night in the fetid *ergastulum*, and even for women, became common.[15] In Ovid's time even the house-porter was, by old custom, a chained slave.[16]

Against such treatment the slave was, until the empire brought him a measure of relief,[17] quite impotent. Flight within Italy was in general hopeless,[18] and, even if effected, could at best but

1 The distinction between the *familia urbana* and the *familia rustica* was one of occupation (and therefore of type of slave) rather than of place (*Dig.* L. xvi. 166: 'urbana familia et rustica non loco, sed genere distinguitur').
2 Cf. Wallon, *Hist. de l'esclavage*, ii. 229. For monstrous exaggeration of demeanour towards slaves by the upstart freedman see the behaviour of Pallas (Dio Cass. lxii. 14; Tac. *Ann.* xiii. 23).
3 Cf. Lucan, *Pharsalia*, i. 170: 'longa sub ignotis extendere rura colonis'; cf. Petronius, *Sat.* 37 and 48.
4 Hor. *Sat.* II. vii. 117 f.; Sen. *de Ira*, iii. 29. Condemnation to the mill (*pistrinum*) was perhaps as bad, to the quarries much worse (Plautus, *Captivi*, 998 f.). The extremity of misery was reached by the slaves condemned to labour in the mines (cf. the mines at Laurion, and see Strabo's account of the Pontic mines, p. 562).
5 Cato, *de Agric.* ii. 7: 'boves vetulos, armenta delicula, oves deliculas, lanam, pelles, plostrum vetus, ferramenta vetera, servum senem, servum morbosum, et si quid aliut supersit, vendat.'
6 *Ib.* ii. 4.
7 Plut. *Cato Maior*, 21.
8 *Ib.*; Mommsen, iii. 118.
9 Greenidge, *Hist.* i. 46.
10 Cf. Diod. Sic. xxxiv. 33.
11 Cf. Gibbon, *The Decline and Fall of the Roman Empire*4, ed. J. B. Bury, London, 1906, i. 39.
12 Cf. Tac. *Ann.* xiv. 44: 'postquam vero nationes in familiis habemus, quibus diversi ritus, externa sacra aut nulla sunt, colluviem istam non nisi metu coercueris.'
13 Cf. Greenidge, *Hist.* i. 83.
14 Their original purpose (Colum. i. 8; cf. Mommsen, iii. 70, note 1).
15 Cf. Pliny, *HN.* xviii. 4.
16 Suet. *de claris Rhetoribus*, 3; cf. Ovid, *Ars amat.* I. vi. 1: 'Janitor, indignum! dura religate catena'; but perhaps this was a mere fashionable pretence at rich houses.
17 Through the right of asylum at the emperor's statue (Tac. *Ann.* iii. 36).
18 The laws concerning *fugitivi*, and the legal interpretation of the term *fugitivus*, were very severe (see Buckland, *Roman Law of Slavery*, p. 267 f.). *Fugitivi* were pursued by hue and cry, their description being circulated and reward offered. Professional *fugitivarii* were employed to hunt them

lead eventually to the violent end of the highwayman,[1] and, if unsuccessful, to the doom of the arena or the cross, or to the more fearful forms of private execution which were among the grim secrets of the slaves' prison.[2] Mommsen has summed up the facts of this later slavery :

'The abyss of misery and woe, which opens before our eyes in this most miserable of all proletariates, may be fathomed by those who venture to gaze into such depths ; it is very possible that, compared with the sufferings of the Roman slaves, the sum of all Negro sufferings is but a drop.'[3]

9. Gladiatorial slaves. — Amid the general misery of this slave world two classes, doomed to a yet blacker depth, are to be distinguished—(1) the wretched property of the *leno* ('qui cogit invitas pati stuprum'),[4] and (2) the gladiators of all varieties, kept either by private persons or by a *lanista*[5] in his training-school (*ludus*).[6] They were bound to their master by an oath (*auctoramentum gladiatorium*) to endure burning, bonds, flogging, and death by the sword, or anything else that the master ordered.[7] Prisoners of war, slaves, and criminals (especially brigands and incendiaries) condemned to death formed the bulk of the class, which numbered in its ranks also a proportion of voluntary combatants (often freedmen).[8]

Men even of the type of Cicero[9] and the younger Pliny[10] speak approvingly of the gladiatorial combats as an education in bravery and contempt of death. 'Even a man of high moral tone like Tacitus, while he condemns Drusus for gloating over his gladiatorial shows, has only a word of scorn for the victims of the butchery.'[11] Among the Romans Seneca here also showed himself far in advance of his age, and a noble exception to its lust for cruelty.[12]

The rewards of the successful gladiator were great, exceeding even those paid in modern times to men of thews and sinews and skill of this sort—the *popularis aura*, the praises sung by famous poets,[13] and the favours of fair admirers.[14] His fighting days over, the champion gained the wooden foil (*rudis*) of honourable retirement—fortunate if he escaped the honour of dying by the hand of a lunatic emperor ;[15] more often in a last unlucky contest he heard the blood-maddened crowd roar '*Habet*' as some younger and more agile arm got home, and saw the pitiless thumbs give the signal for the fatal stroke.[1]

10. Murder of a master.—Not infrequently ill-treatment or an overpowering sense of degradation drove a slave, or even an entire household, to a desperate and bloody revenge.[2] 'As many foes as slaves' was held to be a truism,[3] even by a naturally merciful master. This led to the atrocious rule that the death of a master by the hand of one of his slaves was the signal for the summary execution of every slave in the house.[4]

Apparently this rule was so far modified that there was substituted a general liability to torture with the object of discovering the murderer, who thereupon alone would be executed. Hadrian definitely limited the torture to such slaves as had been under the same roof, or hard by, or actually in the slain man's company—those who had presumably been near enough to render help ('armis, manu, clamore et obiectu corporis').[5]

A fearful instance of the operation of the old practice was given in Nero's reign, upon the murder of the city præfect Pedanius Secundus in A.D. 61. The monstrous horror of the proposed wholesale execution of the *familia urbana* of the slain senator—400 slaves of both sexes—caused an outbreak of popular sympathy.[6] By this date a large proportion of the *plebs sordida* of Rome was tainted with servile blood. Although apparently the actual perpetrator was known to have acted alone on purely personal grounds, the senate refused to make an exception, and Nero was compelled to guard by troops the route of the condemned slaves to the place of butchery.

11. Servile revolts.—Slave conspiracies directed against the state itself, as distinguished from outbreaks against the tyranny of individual owners, were familiar to the Romans from an early date. In respect of both kinds of servile outbreak the history of Rome is in striking and instructive contrast with that of Athens.[7] Tradition carried back servile unrest even to the 6th cent. B.C.[8] and to the social and political struggles of the Roman Commons[9]—just as at the end of the republic the warring factions relied in part upon slave support. As time went on, servile insurrection became ever more possible, and ever more dangerous, through the increase in the servile and semi-servile classes.[10]

It was in Sicily, where the prædial slavery was seen in its most hateful operation, that servile revolt on a really great scale took place. The island was full of slaves herded in great gangs, branded like cattle, overworked under the lowest possible conditions of life, and in part expected or even urged to maintain themselves by violence and rapine, as was also the case on the great pastoral domains in Italy.[11] At the same time, the measure of precaution inculcated by Plato and Aristotle,[12] against bringing together men of the same race, had been quite neglected ; for the great mass of Sicilian slaves were of Syrian, or at least Asiatic, origin—a source which was reputed moreover to furnish the hardiest type of slave. The rising under Eunus, in 133 B.C., was suppressed by the consul P. Rupilius only after three years of warfare and the slaughter of over 20,000 slaves.[13] Then came the great slave war in Sicily, lasting five years, under Tryphon (Salvius) and Athenion, from 103 B.C.[14] Even more formidable was the insurrection of gladiatorial slaves[15] under Spartacus, in Italy.

12. Slaves in the civil wars.—Naturally, the slave resources of powerful houses became an instrument of political warfare also, as waged in the

down (cf. Petron. *Sat.* 97). When caught, they were branded on the forehead (*ib.* 103) or maimed or sent to the arena (cf. the story of Androcles [Aulus Gellius, v. 14]).

1 Cf. Petron. *Sat.* 111. 2 Sen. *de Ira*, iii. 3, 6.

3 iii. 308. 4 See art. PROSTITUTION (Roman).

5 Isidore of Seville (*Orig.* 10) says this is an Etruscan word meaning 'butcher' or 'executioner.' The gladiatorial spectacles were introduced from Etruria ; they were a survival of the practice of immolating slaves and prisoners at the tomb of a chieftain ; at Rome also they were for long confined to funerals. Even Atticus invested in gladiators (as did others) to let out or to sell again to the ædiles for the public games, or to such as wanted a gang of roughs as bodyguard (cf. Cic. *ad Att.* iv. 4, *ad Q. Fratrem*, ii. 4, 5).

6 Cf. Quintilian, *Decl.* ix. 21 : 'in ludo fui, qua poena nullam graviorem scelera noverunt, cuius ad comparationen ergastulum leve est.'

7 Cf. Hor. *Sat.* II. vii. 58 ; Petron. *Sat.* 117 ; Sen. *Ep.* xxxvii. 1 f., lxx. 17 f.

8 Petron. *Sat.* 45.

9 *Tusc. Disp.* ii. 17 (41) : 'oculis nulla poterat esse fortior contra dolorem et mortem disciplina' ; though Cicero in this passage adds the words : 'crudele gladiatorum spectaculum et inhumanum nonnullis videri solet, et haud scio an ita sit, ut nunc fit.'

10 *Panegyricus*, 33.

11 Dill, *Roman Society*, p. 234 ; Tac. *Ann.* i. 76 : 'vili sanguine nimis gaudens.'

12 See *Ep.* vii. 3 f., xcv. 33 : 'Homo, sacra res homini' ; *de Brevitate Vitæ*, 13 f. Among the Greeks, when the Athenians were meditating the establishment of such shows, the gentle Demonax bade them first overthrow their altar of Pity (Lucian, *Demonax*, 57) ; cf. Dio Chrys. *Orationes*, xxxi. p. 385, ed. L. Dindorf ; Plut. *Reip. ger. pr.* 29 ; Philostratus, *Vit. Apoll.* iv. 22—a remarkable passage, if true.

13 Cf. Martial, *Epigrams*, v. 25.

14 Petron. *Sat.* 126 ; Juv. *Sat.* vi. 103 f.—some of them were eager to emulate their exploits (Juv. *Sat.* vi. 246 f. ; Tac. *Ann.* xv. 32 ; Dio Cass. lxxv. 16).

15 Cf. Suet. *Caligula*, 32.

1 Juv. *Sat.* iii. 36 f.

2 Sen. *de Clem.* i. 26 ; see the fate of the *superbus et sævus dominus*, Largius Macedo, in Pliny, *Ep.* iii. 14 ; cf. Sen. *Ep.* iv. 8 ; Tac. *Ann.* xiv. 44 ; Pliny, *Ep.* iii. 14, § 5.

3 Sen. *Ep.* xlvii. 5 : 'totidem esse hostes quot servos. Non habemus illos hostes, sed facimus.'

4 Tac. *Ann.* xiv. 42 ; cf. the letter of Servius Sulpicius to Cicero in 45 B.C. (*ad Fam.* IV. xii. 3).

5 Spart. *Hadr.* xviii. 11.

6 Tac. *Ann.* xiv. 42 : 'usque ad seditionem ventum est.'

7 See art. SLAVERY (Greek), § 7. 8 Dion. Hal. v. 51.

9 Livy, iii. 15 ; Dion. Hal. x. 16.

10 Cf. Livy, xxxii. 26, xxxiii. 36, xxxix. 29—all falling within the period from 198 B.C. to 185 B.C.

11 Diod. Sic. xxxiv. 27 f., xxxviii. ; cf. G. Long, *Decline of the Roman Republic*, London, 1864–74, i. 113 f.

12 Plato, *Laws*, 777 D ; Aristotle, *Œconomica*, i. 5 ; *Pol.* iv. (vii.) 10 = 1330 A ; so also Plut. *Cato Maior*, 21.

13 Orosius, v. 9 ; details in Diod. Sic. xxxiv. 2 (5) f. ; Greenidge, *Hist.* i. 89 f. ; Mommsen, iii. 309 f. See also J. P. Mahaffy, in *Hermathena*, xvi. [1890].

14 See Diod. Sic. xxxvi. 3 f. ; Mommsen, iii. 383 f. ; Long, ii. 76 f.

15 The history of this has to be pieced together from App. *de Bell. civ.* i. 116 f. ; Plut. *Crassus*, 8 f., *Pompeius*, 21 ; Livy, *Epit.* 95 f. ; Florus, ii. 8 ; and the fragments of Sallust's *Histories* (see B. Maurenbrecher, *Sallust. Crisp. Hist. Reliquiæ*, 2 vols., Leipzig, 1891–93, *passim*) ; see also Mommsen, iv. 357 ff.

streets and environs of Rome by men like Milo and Clodius.[1] Clodius controlled the streets and the Comitia by means of his *operæ*, or 'gangs.' In 58 B.C. he legalized the so-called *Collegia Compitalicia*, or religious gilds of the lower orders, to which slaves also were admitted;[2] these received a semi-military organization.[3] In the civil wars slaves also were called into play, as by Saturninus (100 B.C.), who tried to rouse them by the offer of freedom.[4] 'The turning of slaves into soldiers is the proper work of civil war. . . . This is the final desperate act of a political party.'[5] Sulla relied largely upon the 10,000 slaves whom he had called to freedom and citizenship.[6]

The last desperate throw of Milo was his attempt to raise the pastoral slaves of S. Italy.[7] The senate itself, at the time of Catiline's conspiracy, determined to call out the gladiators of private citizens.[8] Cicero goes out of his way to boast of the protection afforded himself by the gladiators bought by Milo.[9] The assassins of Cæsar were guarded by the gladiators of Decimus Brutus.[10] In the struggle between Octavian, Antonius, and Pompeius gladiators and other slaves were freely employed, and were not seldom tricked to their destruction when they had served their purpose.[11]

III. *THIRD PERIOD.*—The second period of Roman slavery extends into imperial times for about a century. It passes insensibly into the third period, which is marked by the cessation of the military expansion of Roman power,[12] and consequently by a partial failure of the sources of slave supply. Being thus to a great extent thrown back upon the human resources already accumulated, the Roman slave-owners 'were reduced to the milder but more tedious method of propagation,'[13] and to a more careful conservation of their human property. Hence the prominence now assumed by questions of status where one or other parent was a slave. This enhanced interest in the practical problems of slavery, to which the legal genius of Rome had always given much thought, is from henceforth further complicated by the new factors calling for recognition. The result is that legislation in regard to slaves exhibits a sort of ebb and flow of humanitarianism. Although there is observable under the earlier emperors a tendency to ameliorate the servile status by legislation punishing various forms of cruelty to slaves (*e.g.*, the decree of Claudius in reference to the exposure of sick slaves), yet the legislation of Trajan was in this respect distinctly reactionary—a fact which may perhaps be connected with his renewal of external conquest. It is in Hadrian's time that the new spirit of humanitarianism and cosmopolitanism—that great social and spiritual change of so deep significance for the future of the world—in the main an outgrowth of Stoicism (*q.v.*), becomes a real factor in legislation. Hadrian is the first imperial representative of this new spirit, the operative principles of which had long before been formulated by Seneca (*q.v.*) and put in practice by that 'noblest type of a true Roman gentleman,'[14] Pliny the younger. Of Seneca it has been truly said that 'no modern has more clearly discerned the far-reaching curse of slavery.'[1]

It is significant of the seminal quality of the mind of Hellas that, although the first reasoned utterance of her philosophy on the slave question had been in defence of the 'peculiar institution,' a development of that philosophy in the fullness of time enunciated just as clearly and unmistakably the moral principles upon which the humanitarian legislation of Hadrian and the Antonines in this field was based; for these principles were no discovery of Seneca's, but had been in the air for generations before they find expression in the 'Stoic sermons'[2] addressed to Lucilius or in the earliest documents of the Christian Church. They are of course but the simple development of that assertion of the natural equality of bond and free, upon the common plane of rational humanity, which had been promulgated by the unnamed critics against whom Aristotle argues. By them slavery had been attacked, not on grounds of its inexpediency, whether social or economic, but on those of a natural justice which slavery violated or definitely impugned.[3]

1. Stoicism and slavery.—The theory of life elaborated by Stoicism was that of a spiritual city with a spiritual law, a city not made by hands, the citizenship of which was gained through spiritual insight, whether of bond or of free. Thus the classical and Aristotelian position was abandoned in two directions: the πόλις yielded place to the cosmopolis, the κοινὴ πατρὶς ἀνθρώπων ἁπάντων, and slavery, the basis of the ancient city, gave place to equality of all men in the 'dear city of God.'[4] That Roman conquest had made the Mediterranean area for the first time an actual political unity simply rendered things easier for the Stoic, by creating out of the multiplicity of city- and nation-states the single world-state, or something very like it.[5] But the same kind of opposition that is observed between Stoicism and the narrower social ideals of Aristotle is found also when Stoicism is transplanted to Italy. For the fundamental difference between Stoicism, or the religion of humanity, and early Roman thought is that the former maintained the existence of a bond of unity among mankind which transcended all the distinctions of the actual political and social organization.

2. Amelioration of slavery.—When the tramp of the legions had reached its destined limits, and the empire, in obedience to the obscure laws of its own evolution had ceased to expand, there began that slow economic process by which, through the intermediate stage of serfdom, the servile status of the producing class was changed into one of legal freedom.[6] How far the different emperors in their legislation furthering these changes, as by protecting the slave against his master, facilitating manumission, and elevating the freedman, were working with prescience under a definite conception of the economic and social tendencies of their age is a problem far too obscure to be lightly answered.[7] Here, being concerned with the bare facts, and among them with such only as are significant for culture, we must content ourselves with tracing

1 Dio Cass. xxxix. 7 f.

2 They would require their master's permission; the master would generally be glad thus to secure the support of the roughs of his quarter for his political occasions.

3 Cf. Dio Cass. xxxviii. 13.

4 Val. Max. viii. 6. 2.

5 Long, i. 461; cf. Ferrero, ii. 185.

6 App. *de Bell. civ.* i. 100.

7 Cæsar, *de Bell. civ.* iii. 21 f.; see *ib.* i. 14 for an attempt of the consul Lentulus to turn the tables on Cæsar by freeing and enrolling Cæsar's own gladiators against him. For a similar proposal, rejected by the British Government, to arm the negroes of the Southern States, and thus abolish slavery at a stroke, see W. F. P. Napier, *Life and Opinions of Gen. Sir Charles J. Napier*, London, 1857, i. 370.

8 Sall. *Catilina*, 30.

9 *De Off.* ii. 17; cf. 'manus illa Clodiana, in caede civium saepe victrix' (*pro Sestio*, 37 [79]).

10 App. *de Bell. civ.* ii. 120.

11 Cf. Tac. *Hist.* ii. 11.

12 Cf. Tac. *Ann.* i. 11.

13 Gibbon, ed. Bury[4], i. 40.

14 J. B. Lightfoot, *Colossians and Philemon*[9], London, 1890, p. 317.

1 S. Dill, *Roman Society*, p. 12, quoting Sen. *de Ira*, iii. 35: 'deinde idem de republica libertatem sublatam quereris quam domi sustulisti.' 'Seneca has never risen higher, or swept farther into the future than in his treatment of slavery. He is far in advance of many a bishop or abbot or Christian baron of the middle age' (*ib.* p. 328).

2 Cf. W. E. H. Lecky, *Hist. of European Morals*[8], London, 1888, i. 243.

3 Aristotle, *Politics*, i. 3=1253 B.

4 Marcus Aurelius, iv. 23.

5 Cf. Plut. *de Alexandri Virtute*, 6.

6 The history of the rise and development of serfdom, which falls outside the limits of this article, is given by F. de Coulanges, *Recherches sur quelques problèmes d'histoire*, Paris, 1885, and B. Heisterbergk, *Die Entstehung des Colonats*, Leipzig, 1876.

7 Cf. Ferrero, i. 365: 'The law of life was the same then as it has been in all ages. The great men of that day were just as ignorant as their fellows of the historic work of which they were at once to be the instruments and the victims'; see also what is said by J. B. Bury with reference to Justinian and his work (*Hist. of the Later Roman Empire*, London, 1889, i. 354). So, speaking of Constantine, J. B. Carter (*The Religious Life of Ancient Rome*, do. 1912, p. 116) says: 'He accomplished an extraordinary number of fateful things, yet we feel that these things did themselves through him rather than that he did them.'

the general tendency of imperial enactments and legal rules in favour of freedom.

Something was done to check subsidiary sources of slave supply by the prohibition of the exposure or sale of children or the giving of them in pledge for debt. A *lex Petronia* of the 1st cent. A.D. forbade masters to punish slaves by sending them to fight with beasts in the arena, except with the assent of a proper court. Hadrian made it illegal for a master to kill his slave, except after judgment before a magistrate;[1] Antoninus Pius held a master who killed his slave just as liable for homicide as if the slave had belonged to another. He further laid down the rule that a slave badly used might take sanctuary at a temple (*fana deorum*) or the emperor's statue[2] and thus initiate a magisterial inquiry into his case; if his complaint of excessive cruelty[3] were made good, the slave was to be sold *bonis conditionibus* to another master.[4] A series of enactments had by the time of Justinian gradually limited the master's right of punishment to reasonable castigation. Protection to the morality of slaves was strangely slow in developing. Domitian forbade the commercial castration of slaves,[5] under penalty of forfeiture of half the offender's property; Hadrian increased the stringency of the law, and allowed the slave to lodge a complaint. Justinian confirmed all this in his *Novellæ*, 142, and punished all concerned in the perpetration of the act, on whatever pretence, and declared the slave free. Protection to the chastity of female slaves was similarly long delayed, and very imperfect. Not until A.D. 428 was it made penal for *lenones* to employ their slaves in prostitution. Justinian made rape of an *ancilla aliena* a capital offence; but there is no penalty laid down for seduction of an *ancilla* by her own master.

As regards the natural relationships which arose between slaves, the marked distinction between the rules of law and the practice of everyday life has been noticed.[6] Here also law tended to recognize the validity of practice informed with natural equity. Constantine laid it down that upon division of a property the slaves were to be so distributed as to keep together parent and child, brother and sister, husband and wife, thus recognizing not only the tie of marriage but also that of blood. Justinian went farther, and not only restricted the master's freedom of action so as to benefit the slave, but gave certain rights of succession to the issue of servile or semi-servile marriages, when one or other parent was manumitted.

Here may be mentioned the mass of legislation designed in the interests of orthodoxy, from the time of Constantine onwards. Its purpose was to crush heresy and prevent proselytism to the non-Christian cults tolerated by the empire (especially was it directed against Judaism). This legislation culminates in that of Justinian consolidating earlier efforts. It provided that no Jew should acquire a Christian slave by any title whatsoever, and that, if he did acquire one and circumcised him, or indeed if he circumcised any non-Jewish slave, Christian or not, he should be capitally punished, and the slave be free. Further, no pagan, Jew, Samaritan, or unorthodox person was allowed to hold a Christian slave, but such slave was to be free, and the man was to be fined. Lastly, if any non-Christian slave or heretic joined the Christian Church, he *ipso facto* became free, without compensation to his master. This must have operated powerfully to foster the idea of the Christian faith as constituting an order within which the victims of oppression of various kinds found protection and privilege.[7]

1 Hadrian exiled for five years a Roman lady who treated her slaves with atrocious cruelty on slight occasion (*Dig.* I. vi. 2; cf. Juv. *Sat.* vi. 490 f.).

2 In later times of course the Christian Church superseded these (cf. *Codex Theodosianus*, ix. 44. 1).

3 This was held to cover not merely bodily violence or starvation rations, but also *infamis iniuria*, which would probably cover attempts to debauch an *ancilla*.

4 Cf. the Attic rule; Gaius, iii. 53: 'si intolerabilis videbatur dominorum saevitia cogantur servos suos vendere.'

5 Suet. *Domitianus*, 7.

6 Above, II. 5.

7 Cf. artt. SLAVERY (Christian) and (Jewish).

3. Influence of Christianity.—It is evident from the above that, while the legitimacy of slavery continued to be firmly held, humanitarianism made its first conspicuous advance under Hadrian and the Antonines; and that the two hundred years following the first Christian emperor were comparatively barren in this respect. The legislation of Theodosius and Justinian marked a second advance, by its abolition of the restrictions on enfranchisement and the amelioration of the condition of freedmen, and its regulations in connexion with slave marriages (through the repeal of the *Senatus-consultum Claudianum*) and the status of exposed children. But *per contra*, even under Constantine, the rights of property were still so strictly guarded that, even for crimes, slaves were forbidden to lay information against their own master—a rule to which Constantine allowed no exception, but enacted that in all such cases the slave proffering information was to be crucified unheard.[1] The emperor Gratian, under whom orthodox Christianity for the first time became dominant in the empire, improved upon this by a law 'which may rank among the most atrocious of Paganism.'[2] It provided that, if a slave accused his master of any crime, except treason, the justice of his charge was not to be examined, but the slave was to be burnt alive;[3] the same terrible punishment, under Constantine, was laid on the slave guilty of intercourse with his mistress. Even Justinian's legislation, though it is no doubt influenced by the new religion, yet has nothing to say about slavery being opposed to either the spirit or the letter of Christianity; its guiding principle is expressed in a formula that is Stoic rather than specially Christian: 'pro libertate quam et fovere et tueri Romanis legibus et praecipue nostro numini peculiare est.'

The change in sentiment and policy of which the above modifications of the law are significant, so far as they go—which is indeed not very far—was of much earlier date than the official recognition of Christianity, and even antecedent to its introduction into the empire at all.[4] Perception of this fact gives the corrective of the exaggerated estimate, or rather the false historical perspective, in which the influence of Christianity upon the slave system of the empire is sometimes presented.[5] Partly the change was the fruit of philosophy or higher thought of the time, partly it was the natural adaptation of sentiment to the existing economic facts. 'While we cannot deny that Christianity tended to discourage slavery, and to lessen the evils of slavery by humanizing the relations with masters, it is certain that the economical conditions which changed the slave system into the colonate and serf system were the chief cause. Beliefs and sentiments generally adapt themselves to facts, and facts are in turn modified by beliefs.'[6] Such humanitarian sentiments and attitude were not the exclusive property of Christianity. 'What is a Roman knight, or a *libertinus*, or a slave?', Seneca asks. 'They are mere titles, born of ambition or of wrong.'[7] '"Slaves!",' he says in one of his finest letters. 'Nay, rather they are men. "Slaves!" No, comrades. "Slaves!" No, they are lowly friends, yea our fellow-slaves. . . . Remember that he whom you call your slave sprang from the same stock, is smiled upon by the same skies, and on equal terms with yourself breathes, and lives, and dies.'[8] 'Virtue is fenced against none, but is open to all, admits all, calls to all—freeborn, freedmen, slaves, princes, exiles.'[9] In such passages as these 'Seneca preaches, with the unction of an evangelist, all the doctrines on which the humane legislation of the Antonine age was founded, all the principles of humanity and charity of every age.'[10]

1 For fragment of this law see Bruns, *Fontes*[7], i. 266.

2 Lecky, *Hist. of Rationalism in Europe*, London, 1887, ii. 238.

3 *Codex Theodos.* IX. vi. 2.

4 Cf. J. Muirhead, *Hist. Introd. to the Private Law of Rome*[2], London, 1899, p. 355: 'It may well be that that spirit [of natural right] was intensified and rendered more active with the growth of Christian belief; but not until the latter had been publicly sanctioned by Constantine, and by Theodosius declared to be the religion of the State, do we meet with incontestable records of its influence.'

5 Cf. H. Schiller, *Gesch. der römischen Kaiserzeit*, Gotha, 1883–87, i. 455; Boissier, *Cicéron*[7], p. 118; R. D. Shaw, *The Pauline Epistles*, Edinburgh, 1903, p. 313.

6 J. B. Bury, *Hist. of the Later Roman Empire*, i. 370.

7 *Ep.* xxxi. 11.

8 *Ib.* xlvii. 1, 10.

9 *De Ben.* III. xviii. 2.

10 Dill, p. 190; cf. Sen. *de Clem.* I. xviii. 3, *de Ben.* III. xxviii. 2.

Pliny the younger is like him in feeling that his slaves are of the same flesh and blood as himself,[1] and that towards them he has moral duties transcending the legal conventions of his time. His kindly letter on behalf of the repentant freedman of his friend Sabinianus[2] has often been brought into comparison with that of St. Paul addressed to Philemon on behalf of the runaway slave Onesimus.[3]

It has been pointed out[4] that the services of Christianity in this sphere were of three kinds. (1) The ceremonies and discipline of the Church ignored class distinctions; slave birth was no bar even to priesthood. This, however, is no innovation of the Christian brotherhood, for such equality of membership is found in the mystery-religions and other social-religious unions.[5] And, as in them, so in the Christian Church the obliteration of the distinction between bond and free is confessedly limited to those who come within the sacred pale; for those outside the Church, social and legal distinctions are left untouched, and therefore implicitly valid. Precisely the same attitude is forced upon the Church in modern times in dealing with similar conditions (often in deference to purely political considerations). That is to say, it has to be content to 'wait upon God,' in the sense that it must await the slow operation of what, humanly speaking, are secular causes. (2) In so far as Christianity imparted moral dignity to the servile class, by insistence upon the moral worth of just those qualities which were especially open for a slave to cultivate—obedience, fidelity, gentleness, patience, and resignation—it was but reinforcing the higher secular teaching of the time; and, like that, it found itself precisely herein most at variance with current conceptions and popular ideals of character. It would probably be correct, however, to see here the most profound and far-reaching influence of Christianity upon the social history of the empire; and not improbably much of the social hostility towards it was inspired by a perception of this fact of the inner sympathy of the new faith with the discredited and submerged sections of the population.[6] (3) The claim that the Church gave a special impetus to the movement of enfranchisement does not seem to be borne out as fully as one would wish.[7] It is at least a curious commentary thereon that the ecclesiastics 'were among the last to follow the counsels they so liberally bestowed upon the laity,'[8] and Christians continued to own slaves like their pagan neighbours. The historical fact is that slavery lasted in Europe for nearly 1000 years after Constantine—so slow is the working[9] of the moral leaven, even when, as here, economic factors conspire with religious motives in effecting the ultimate freedom of labour.

The truth is that much of what is said on this topic fails for want of historical knowledge, or through actual *suppressio veri* in the interests of prejudice. We can hardly with justice claim that the Church in its infancy and youth, advancing not by jumps but by and through human volition conditioned always by immediate facts and the forces of inherited tendency and circumstances, should have seen things more clearly than proved to be the case nearly 2000 years later when the 'three or four absolutely virtuous pages comprised in the history of nations' were written—written, moreover, largely in blood. Its action was not so much definitely official and mandatory as steadily influential for good, a *causa causans* in the heart of the individual slave-owner.[10]

4. Manumission.—Hardly anywhere better than in connexion with the manumission of slaves is the fundamental selfishness and meanness of antiquity observable. The emancipator never lost by his act, but probably in most cases stood to gain much.

Among the Romans manumission was 'less an act of liberality than an industrial speculation, the master often finding it more for his interest to share the profits of the trade or commerce of the freedman than to assert his title to the whole proceeds of the labour of his slave.'[11]

[1] Cf. Juv. *Sat.* xiv. 16; Pliny, *Ep.* v. 19.

[2] *Ep.* ix. 21.

[3] Tr. of Pliny's letter in Lightfoot, *Coloss. and Philem.*[9], p. 316.

[4] Lecky, *Hist. of European Morals*[8], ii. 66 f.

[5] Cf. Schiller, i. 455.

[6] Cf. 1 Co 1[26].

[7] When, in reference to St. Paul's Epistle to Philemon, Lightfoot says, 'The word "emancipation" seems to be trembling on his lips' (p. 321), we must hold that to be purely imaginary. The letter contains not the slightest hint that Philemon ought to set Onesimus free. The hope that he will receive him as a brother means only that the old tie should be beautified by the new relation of Christian fellowship. Certainly the phrase of v.[16]: οὐκέτι ὡς δοῦλον, ἀλλὰ ὑπὲρ δοῦλον, cannot be twisted to signify manumission. There is no evidence that the thought of an ultimate general abolition of slavery being possible or desirable had ever occurred to St. Paul (cf. A. C. McGiffert, *Hist. of Christianity in the Apostolic Age*, Edinburgh, 1897, p. 376).

[8] Lecky, *Hist. of European Morals*[8], ii. 71.

[9] 'The power of tradition in the blood is quite strong enough, often indeed is so powerful as to make progress but slow and doubtful, and to prevent the intrusion of new ideas' (P. Gardner, *Exploratio Evangelica*, London, 1899, p. 500).

[10] Cf. A. Deissmann, *Light from the Ancient East*, London, 1910, p. 290; H. Lotze, *Microcosmus*, Eng. tr., Edinburgh, 1885, ii. 469; cf. also art. SLAVERY (Christian).

[11] Mommsen, ii. 84.

Manumission was of two kinds—regular (*iusta*), and informal (*minus iusta*). Of the former class there were three varieties.[1]

(*a*) *Censu.*—This was essentially connected with the republican constitution and forms, and was probably a very ancient mode. Under the empire, with the extinction of the censorship, it is practically obsolete. In form it was simply the censor's enrolment of the slave, under a name of Roman type, on the list of citizens,[2] with his owner's assent. The slave became free and a Roman citizen. No conditions could be attached, though by means of a preliminary oath taken by the slave such could in practice be imposed.[3]

(*b*) *Vindicta.*—This mode was really a fictitious litigation or collusive action, in the form of an action brought by an *adsertor libertatis*, who claimed the slave before the presiding magistrate as a free man; the part of *adsertor libertatis*, in later times, was usually played by a *lictor*, who touched the slave with his wand (*vindicta*, or *festuca*), which gave its name to the method. As the point of the method lies in the official declaration that the slave is a free man, the freedom conferred is absolute; *i.e.*, it cannot be suspended or made conditional either expressly or tacitly, though doubtless there were ways of circumventing this difficulty so as to safeguard the claims which the master wished to retain over the services of his freedman. It was not unusual to exact from the slave to be manumitted an oath before manumission covering such services; repudiation of the oath rendered the freedman liable to penalties as a *libertus ingratus*.[4]

(*c*) *Testamento.*—This mode, by far the most important, is as old as, and therefore probably older than, the XII Tables. It differs from the preceding methods in that it is not based on fiction. It takes effect only upon the operation of a valid will, so that in general manumissions by this mode stand or fall with the will itself. Further, this manumission may be conditional or deferred (pending the event the man is a *statu liber*); the subject in the interim, until the arrival of the stated time or the occurrence of the condition, is exposed to the ordinary incidents of slavery, sale, etc., but he may not be brought into a worse condition or be deprived of his conditional right to freedom. Once effective, his liberty is irrevocable, subject to his performance of his duties as freedman.

(*d*) These were the only forms of manumission recognized as valid under the republic; but there were in use certain other less formal modes. Of such there were several varieties—*e.g.*, voluntary declaration *inter amicos*, or *per epistolam*. Such declarations were legally void, but towards the end of the republic the *prætor* intervened to protect slaves who had been declared free in this way, so that they enjoyed freedom *de facto*, though not *de iure*.[5]

(*e*) To these forms of manumission must be added one in use from the time of Constantine—the *manumissio in sacrosanctis ecclesiis*. A constitution of Constantine in A.D. 316 says that it had long been allowed for masters to free slaves *in ecclesia catholica* before the people, in the presence of the priests. By a constitution of 321 such manumission is declared to give also the *civitas Romana*. Hence it is surmised that this method was at first informal—a development of the manumission *inter amicos*. Justinian seems to have added the provision that there must also be a document signed by the master *vice testium*. This method appears to be in part a descendant of

[1] Cf. Cic. *Top.* 2: 'si neque censu, nec vindicta, nec testamento liber factus est, non est liber.' The origin of Roman manumission is unknown; it is already an established institution at the time of the XII Tables (450 B.C.). Dion. Hal. (iv. 22) credits the law about it to Servius Tullius, but little weight attaches to this.

[2] Cf. Cic. *de Orat.* i. 183.

[3] This mode could be applied only in Rome, where alone the true Roman *census* was held. Strictly the entry of the name did not confer the *civitas*; it was the fictitious renewal of the record that the man was a citizen, under his proper class; but the legal mind of the Romans detected here a nice problem.

[4] Cf. Cic. *ad Att.* VII. ii. 8; Tac. *Ann.* xiii. 26.

[5] Hence such could not dispose of their *peculium*; cf. Tac. *Ann.* xiii. 27.

the Greek mode of manumission by dedication in a temple to a deity.[1]

M. Aurelius and his brother authorized or regulated the purchase of freedom by slaves. This must have been an old practice in Rome, just as in Greece it was apparently the usual practice. The slave arranged with a third party to purchase him from his master, with money supplied by the slave, and then manumit him. The source of the purchase-money was immaterial, whether it came from the slave's *peculium* (which in law belonged actually to the vendor, his master) or from a loan advanced by a friend or even by the purchaser by arrangement with the slave. A slave so purchased was said 'suis nummis emi.'[2] The purchase was fictitious (*imaginaria*), but was winked at by the law.

IV. *FREEDMEN.*—Upon formal manumission by a valid method a slave became a freedman (*libertinus*, if spoken of with reference to class; *libertus* [=*liberatus*] in relation to his former *dominus*, who now becomes his *patronus*). In business relations with the world he was his own man,[3] but towards his old master and his family he continued to stand in a semi-servile relation,[4] under certain ties recognized by custom and law.

1. Social position.—Liberated slaves were perhaps usually set up in business or industry by their old master, who indeed in most cases liberated them to that end, and they continued to act as his confidential agents in financial undertakings, and as managers of businesses in which the *patronus* was sleeping partner. A man was thus able to profit by trade while avoiding the social stigma of direct management, and, if he was a senator, he was thus enabled to evade the Claudian law of 218 B.C., forbidding senators or their sons to engage in commerce—an enactment which drove them partly to invest their money in land, *i.e.* in slave-worked estates, partly to defeat the law in various ways through business slaves and freedmen. The Claudian law thus indirectly encouraged manumission.

Freedmen, though citizens, were in an inferior position, as they had not *connubium* with free persons, or the *ius honorum* (right of office or of sitting in the senate); nor could they as a rule serve in the legions[5] or among the equites. Their political rights were really annulled by their being restricted to enrolment in the four city tribes.[6]

2. Importance under the empire.—One of the most remarkable features of the empire was the swift rise of freedmen to wealth and power,[7] and the extraordinary importance to which individual freedmen attained, not only in the business world, but in that of imperial administration, in spite of the most violent prejudice and hatred felt towards them by aristocrats and plebeians alike. The inscriptions bear testimony to the extent to which wealth drifted into the hands of this class, just as in previous centuries it had tended to concentrate in the hands of a comparatively small section of *ingenui*, the great noble and the great contractor, and to be almost wholly withdrawn from the peasant and artisan. Since a freedman had no social standing to lose, the whole field of industry and trade, to which he had been trained as a slave,

[1] Cf. Mitteis, pp. 100, 376.

[2] Cf. Suet. *de illust. Gramm.* 13.

[3] A slave, having no legal name, had to have one made for him on manumission. He took the name (*nomen* and *prœnomen*) of his old master, adding his own slave name as cognomen; cf. Cic. *ad Att.* IV. xv. 1.

[4] A slave liberated by will was called *orcinus libertus*, and the patron's rights fell to the children of the deceased.

[5] This was the strict rule under the empire, so that a freedman, before he could be enrolled in the army, must have *ingenuitas* conferred upon him by the exercise of the imperial prerogative. But *libertini* were always freely employed in the fleet.

[6] Mommsen, i. 396 f.; details in his *Staatsrecht*, Berlin, 1874–88, iii. 436 f. Cicero in reference to this approves of the action of T. Gracchus, censor in 169 B.C., saying that otherwise 'rempublicam quam nunc vix tenemus, iam diu nullam haberemus' (*de Orat.* i. 9 [38]). Cicero, of course, exhibits all the narrow prejudices of the *municipalis eques*.

[7] Cf. Petron. *Sat.* 38: 'sed liberti scelerati, qui omnia ad se fecerunt.' In Martial's day 'freedman's wealth' has become proverbial (Mart. *Epigr.* v. xiii. 6; cf. Sen. *Ep.* xxvii. 4: 'et patrimonium habebat libertini et ingenium'); see also Juv. *Sat.* i. 102 f., xiv. 305 f.

was open to him; so that he became, from the economic point of view, the greatest enemy of the pure-blood Italian. Not only were the lower walks of trade and industry invaded by freedmen, but as capitalists and landowners on the largest scale, both in Italy and in the provinces, they became a power in the land, and were conspicuous for their liberalities to *collegia* and municipalities. It is to this class that we must turn if we wish to trace the rise of a free industrial and free mercantile element divorced from the social and political traditions of the ancient world.

'They began to be regarded as the natural free workers of the community, who surrendered a portion of their profits to their superiors to maintain the upper and middle-class Italians in a luxurious idleness.'[1]

Trimalchio, the self-made man depicted by Petronius, is in many of his traits typical of the class—of its opulence, its vulgar consciousness of success, and its utter lack of all traditions or standards, except such as were expressible in terms of money.[2]

It is under Sulla that, in the person of Chrysogonus, there first comes into view 'the artful Greek freedman . . . a sinister figure, destined to reappear again and again in the days of the Empire as an instrument of administration, and to wield enormous power.'[3] The regular use of slaves and ex-slaves as public officials began under Julius Cæsar, who installed slaves of his household as officers of the mint.[4] But the practice must go back to a still earlier date, to the time of C. Gracchus, who 'concentrated the most varied and most complicated functions of government in his own person.'[5] In these multifarious activities Gracchus must have relied upon the skill and devotion of educated slaves and freedmen, just as did the great companies of *publicani*. 'The houses of politicians like Pompey, Crassus and Cæsar were miniature government offices where numberless freedmen and slaves from the east were engaged on their master's work.'[6] It is of this class above all, both under the later republic and under the empire, that Ferrero's words hold good when he says that 'in the pages of too many modern historians the mighty host of the workers lies concealed and contemned behind the dominant personality of a few soldiers and politicians.'[7]

3. The imperial freedmen.—The system of employing in the imperial administration the household talent of the reigning emperor was a necessary concomitant of the empire itself; for theoretically the emperor was only the first citizen, and his administrative staff was simply that of his private house, with its hierarchy of slaves under departmental heads who were themselves also either slaves or freedmen.[8] He had neither ministers of state nor a trained civil service, but was in theory his own secretary of state, chancellor, and minister of foreign affairs. It was not until the reign of Claudius, however, that the 'household of Cæsar' was confounded with the commonwealth, and his freedmen placed 'on a level with himself and the laws';[9] the political importance of the emperor's personal administrative staff increased, so that his freedmen became really ministers of state, responsible solely to him, and presiding over new departments, or acting with increased power and independence abroad.[10] The three great departments of controller of accounts (*a rationibus*), presided over by Pallas,[11] secretary

[1] Ferrero, i. 340.

[2] Cf. Petron. *Sat.* 77: 'Credite mihi: assem habeas, assem valeas; habes, habeberis,' and 43: 'Ab asse crevit et paratus fuit quadrantem de stercore mordicus tollere.'

[3] Heitland, *Roman Republic*, ii. 499.

[4] Suet. *Jul. Cæs.* 76: 'peculiares servos praeposuit.'

[5] Mommsen, iii. 355.

[6] Ferrero, i. 341.

[7] i. 347.

[8] Cf. Suet. *Aug.* 67. 'It was a standing anomaly of the constitution that many offices which in a modern state would be important departments of the civil service were regarded as no more than posts in the chief citizen's household, unworthy of the dignity of any person above the rank of a freedman' (H. Furneaux, *Taciti Annalium*, ii. 38). Even under the republic 'the domestic transaction of official business was very large at Rome, for the State had given its administrators not even the skeleton of a civil service' (Greenidge, *Hist.* i. 15).

[9] Tac. *Ann.* xii. 60.

[10] *E.g.*, Felix, brother of the freedman Pallas, 'quem cohortibus et alis provinciaeque Iudaeae praeposuit, trium reginarum maritum' (Suet. *Claud.* 28; Ac 24^{24}), who 'exercised the power of a king in the spirit of a slave' (Tac. *Hist.* v. 9).

[11] Tac. *Ann.* xi. 29.

(*ab epistulis*), presided over by Narcissus,[1] and receiver of petitions (*a libellis*), presided over first by Callistus and then by Doryphorus[2]—all these being private freedmen of the emperor—originated or took their importance in this reign. The rule of these powerful and wealthy freedmen was one of the bitterest memories of the outraged aristocrats[3]—as though it had been the work of a set of mere menials rather than of men at the highest level of capacity and education. In spite of their many gross and obvious vices, the ability and immense energy of these freedmen are undeniable. The disadvantage of their use was that, for all their efficiency and fidelity to their imperial master, they were not legally state officials at all, and their actual position was a standing offence to the social prejudices of their time.

4. The augustales.—The strict exclusion of *libertini* from magistracies and priestly offices, and from a seat on the municipal senates, was a public loss, as it debarred from public life and the constant distribution of wealth entailed by office precisely the richest and most enterprising class in the municipalities. To the problem of associating this class with the social and political ideals and organization of the empire Augustus early devoted attention. To this end he opened to the ambition of freedmen a field in the municipalities of Italy and the west by means of a new institution—that of the *Augustales* and the *Seviri Augustales*.[4]

V. *ECONOMIC AND SOCIAL EFFECTS.*—Investigation of the economic effects of slavery upon the Roman community is at once one of the most important and most difficult chapters in the history of the institution. To what degree did slave labour interfere with the development of free industry? An answer to this question would involve primarily an accurate estimate of the number of slaves found in Rome at a given moment, and the proportion they bore to free adults.

We have no statistics as to the number of urban slaves, public and private; much less can we discover the total slave population of Italy or the number of freedmen. Both slaves and freedmen are spoken of vaguely as a vast multitude, so great as to awaken alarm in the mind of any one who faced the facts.[5] The statement of Athenæus[6] that 'very many' (πάμπολλοι) Romans possessed 10,000 and even 20,000 slaves is no doubt an exaggeration. The freedman, C. Cæc. Claud. Isidorus, under Augustus, lost much property in the civil wars, but left at his death 4116 slaves;[7] Pedanius Secundus had 400 slaves in his city establishment.[8] But there is no doubt that in Rome as in Athens the vast majority of the people possessed no slaves at all. A reasonable estimate puts the urban slaves at 800,000 or 900,000.[9]

'The history of the Roman Republic is largely the history of the wealthier classes.'[10] Of the poorer classes we know little, as we hear of them only in the mass, and generally only as a political instrument in the hands of the demagogues. They must have had some means of livelihood other than the cheap corn distributed by the government (which indeed was not distributed gratis until 58 B.C.). This applies still more forcibly after the number of recipients was ruthlessly cut down from 320,000 to 150,000 by Julius Cæsar,[11] to a little over 200,000 by Augustus.[12] The continued existence of the trade gilds (*collegia opificum*) in the last

1 Suet. *Claud.* 28. 2 Dio Cass. lxi. 5.
3 Cf. Pliny, *Paneg.* 88: 'civium domini, libertorum servi'; Tac. *Hist.* i. 37, ii. 95.
4 See J. S. Reid, *The Municipalities of the Roman Empire*, Cambridge, 1913, p. 511.
5 Cf. Tac. *Ann.* iii. 53: 'familiarum numerum et nationes,' iv. 27: 'urbem iam trepidam, ob multitudinem familiarum, quae gliscebat immensum, minore in dies plebe ingenua,' and xiv. 44; cf. also Sen. *de Clem.* i. 24; and Tac. *Ann.* xiii. 27, in reference to freedmen.
6 vi. p. 272. 7 Pliny, *HN* xxxiii. 135.
8 Tac. *Ann.* xiv. 43.
9 See Furneaux, i. 90; J. Beloch, 'Die Bevölkerung Italiens im Altertum,' in *Klio*, iii. [1903] 471 f.
10 Heitland, iii. 139. 11 Suet. *Jul. Cæs.* 41.
12 Dio Cass. lv. 10; *Monumentum Ancyranum*, 15.

century of the republic (though then largely misused as instruments of anarchism, *collegia sodalicia*) must, it seems, indicate that some freemen at least, in spite of the prejudice against small industry and retail trading,[1] made their living by such labour. Some indeed have gone so far as to maintain that even under the early empire a freeman could always obtain work if he wanted it[2]—in spite of the competition of slaves, and of *libertini*, who, as bound to their *patronus*, must in this connexion be reckoned with the true slaves. A large number of urban slaves worked within the great houses of the rich,[3] making them to a great extent self-supporting, but not directly competing with the small freeman, though undoubtedly restricting the field of his enterprise. Probably still larger in the aggregate was the class of slaves employed by contractors for public and private works, for public shows, and for all the activities of the various classes of *publicani*. Many of these slaves had been specially trained for their work.[4] This is the class which directly competed with free labour, for the free citizen either was not sufficiently well educated for these posts or was too independent for manual labour, apart from the fact that the stigma attaching to labour, other than agriculture, was very pronounced.[5] It was obviously as easy to hire from his master the sort of slave one wanted as to hire the services of a freeman from himself, without any certainty that he was capable of doing the work. The slave, it was certain, would do the work—his master would see to that. Hence both the skilled and the unskilled forms of labour would appear by a natural law to have been almost wholly in slave hands, except in so far as freedmen and their children, having gained special skill and habits of industry in slavery, retained a place in the industrial world. The whole tendency of the later republic and the empire was in the direction of 'permanent endowment of the unemployed.'[6] As regards the country estates, the tradition had always been that the farm should be as far as possible self-supporting;[7] but this had not implied that it should be run solely by slave labour.[8] Hired free labourers[9] were called in when extra hands were wanted, as at hay-harvest-time, or for the gathering of olives, and the vintage; Varro[10] also recommends the use of hired labourers rather than one's own slaves in unhealthy districts. Nevertheless the tendency was to make such properties more and more self-contained and self-supporting, so that even Varro's farming, which stands midway between the small farming of early times and the later plantation system, is essentially slave-farming and leaves little room for free labour. Upon the cattle-runs of S. Italy the work was apparently entirely in the hands of the half-wild herdsmen,[11] and here the economic system had sunk to a more primitive level; the same was true of Etruria also.[12] Here the exclusion of free labour

1 Cf. Cic. *de Off.* i. 42 (150); Livy, xxii. 25.
2 L. Friedländer, *Darstellungen aus der Sittengesch.*[5], Leipzig, 1881, i. 264.
3 Sall. *Cat.* 12: 'domos atque villas in urbium modum exaedificatas.'
4 Cf. the case of Crassus, from whom almost any kind of specially trained slave could be hired (Plut. *Crass.* 2).
5 Cf. Cic. *Tusc.* v. 104: 'quos singulos sicut operarios barbarosque contemnas.'
6 Heitland, iii. 451.
7 Cf. Varro, *de Re rust.* i. 22: 'quae nasci in fundo ac fieri a domesticis poterunt, eorum nequid ematur.'
8 It is curious that Vergil in his *Georgics* never mentions slaves. Perhaps the reason is that given in Sen. *Ep.* lxxxvi. 14: 'Vergilius noster, qui non quid verissime, sed quid decentissime diceretur adspexit nec agricolas docere voluit, sed legentes delectare.'
9 *Mercenarii, operarii* (Cato, *de Agric.* iv.), *conducticii* (Varro, *de Re rust.* i. 17).
10 *De Re rust.* i. 17. 11 *Ib.* ii. 10; Cic. *pro Tullio*, 14 f.
12 Plut. *Tib. Gr.* 8.

must have been absolute, for life on the cattle-run was below the culture level of the Roman populace.

Two remarkable facts stand out in this inquiry. (1) The Roman proletariat, so far as appears, never at any time complained of the competition of slave labour as depriving them of bread, though the Roman populace wanted bread badly—even Cicero, superficial as are his social and political judgments, admits that the corn-law of Gracchus was necessary.[1] (2) The Roman slave-owners, though the shrewdest men in the world, never seem to have had any doubts about the comparative advantages of slave labour. Both classes—and the same is true of Greece—persist, the one in acquiescence in, and the other in an application of, a system which is now held condemned not only in its moral basis but also in its economic results. Yet the Roman proletariat showed itself all through its history by no means unready to proceed to the most violent measures in relief of its grievances; and, on the other hand, we have no right to assume on the part of the Roman capitalists a stupid inability to gather from experience in what direction their maximum profit lay. It is undeniable that the Roman grandees found their account in the slave system as actually worked; only when the financial conditions altered, under the later empire, did slavery give place, in obedience to the law of maximum profit, to a new economic form, which indeed is very old—that of serfdom. In this connexion it must be noted that the Gracchan movement would be entirely wrongly interpreted as a protest of free labour against a slave system which deprived the freeman of the right to live by his toil. When Tiberius Gracchus cried that the beasts had their lairs, but nothing was left to Roman citizens save the air and the sunshine, that those who were styled masters of the world had no longer a clod they could call their own,[2] he was protesting, not against the slave system as such, but against a vicious system of land-distribution and of land-tenure, and his aim, like that of his brother, was not to revive the free labourer, but to re-establish the free peasant proprietor; the anonymous appeals to him were not that he should abolish the slave, but that he should restore to the poor their share of the public lands.[3] The failure of the Gracchan legislation, so far as it did fail—in proving unable to check the influx of the country population to the capital—was due to the fact that it 'offended against social ideals rather than against economic tendencies.'[4] Yet it is accepted almost as an axiom that it was the slave system, and the slave system alone, that ruined the Italian middle class of small proprietors and created the urban proletariat.

It is of course on the moral and spiritual ground, not on the economic, that slavery must ultimately be judged. That wide and deep demoralization which results for both master and slave is sufficiently obvious in the case of Rome also. On the one hand, the slave-owners, with no feeling of responsibility, except that of mere self-interest towards those who were absolutely at their mercy, fell into that despotic temper which found its logical but unexpected final expression in the insane cruelties of the successive masters of the Roman world. On the other hand, the existence in Italy of tens of thousands of men for whom all ties of race and kindred and home had been snapped at a stroke, for whom no moral standard thenceforth held good but that of their master's

[1] Cic. *de Off.* ii. 21 (72): 'frumentaria largitio . . . plebi necessaria.'

[2] Plut. *Tib. Gr.* 9. [3] *Ib.* 8.

[4] Greenidge *Hist.* i. 269.

will, for whose conduct the only sanction was corporal punishment in its most debasing forms, for the vast majority of whom life offered no faintest prospect of moral or social independence and development, meant, at its lowest valuation, a permanent and terrible menace to the whole community. The evil was accentuated by the fact that this poisoned reservoir was not fenced off by the law, nor guarded by nature's colour-signal, which only those for whom the claims of their native race and culture already stood for little dared disobey; on the contrary, from this tainted source an ever-flowing stream was directed into the free population by the way of manumission. The condition of social progress, viz. the gradual elimination of class inequality, was certainly in a degree achieved thereby, and the decay of the native population to some extent made good;[1] but it was unfortunately from the most corrupted and most pernicious class—that of the urban slaves—that the freedmen who were the active agents in transmission of the blood-taint were mainly derived.[2] The steady stream of manumissions meant that the blood of the lower and middle classes of Latin stock was, generation after generation, losing its purity and becoming contaminated into a mongrel mixture of blood derived from nearly every race in the empire—and that only after its purveyors had been for a longer or shorter time submitted to all the deleterious influences of slavery. At a comparatively early date the effect of this process was manifest.[3] To argue that such qualitative distinctions are historically and philosophically invalid, and to point to the fact that in the fullness of time the blood which Scipio reviled was destined to produce a new race,[4] is not permissible, for it was after all true that, in comparison with Thracians, Gauls, Germans, and Asiatics, the Italian peoples had been and still were the vehicles of higher culture, and that, in so far as the elements assimilated through manumission were derived from Greece, it was nevertheless from a Greece decadent and debased.[5] The criticism rightly taken, however, is directed not against the mere fact of incorporation of diverse alien material, but against the ill-regulated and fortuitous way in which the incorporation proceeded, and the absence of any selective process worthy of the name, the whole field being in fact abandoned to a capricious and haphazard operation which gave no guarantee that only those most deserving of the honour attained it—a process entirely contrary to that lengthy education through which the larger political groups within the Italian peninsula itself had been incorporated with the republic. It is surely passing strange that aliens were freely admitted to citizenship provided that they entered by the door of slavery, whereas the incorporation of individual foreigners on grounds of personal merit was the rarest thing[6] and mostly the result of jobbery. Dionysius of Halicarnassus in the time of Augustus gives remarkable expression, as the result of his own experience, to the

[1] Cf. Pliny, *Ep.* vii. 32. [2] Cf. App. *de Bell. civ.* ii. 120.

[3] See the well-known utterance of Scipio: 'cum omnis contio adclamasset, "Hostium," inquit, "armatorum totiens clamore non territus, qui possum vestro moveri, quorum noverca est Italia!"' (Vell. II. iv. 4); Val. Max. VI. ii. 3: 'Orto deinde murmure "Non efficietis," ait, "ut solutos verear, quos alligatos adduxi"'; cf. Petron. *Sat.* 122 (165 f.): 'Mercedibus emptae | ac viles operae, quorum est mea Roma noverca'; Lucan, *Phars.* vii. 404: 'nulloque frequentem | cive suo Romam, sed mundi faece repletam.'

[4] Cf. E. Meyer, *Kleine Schriften*, Halle, 1910, p. 212.

[5] Cf. Juv. *Sat.* iii. 58 f.; Cic. *pro Flacco*, 27 (65); *de Orat.* ii. 66 (265).

[6] Julius Cæsar, however, tried to encourage immigration of skilled labour (Suet. *Jul. Cæs.* 42: 'omnesque medicinam Romae professos et liberalium artium doctores, quo libentius et ipsi Urbem incolerent, et ceteri appeterent, civitate donavit'). On the other hand, he sent out a large number of *libertini* to the colony at Corinth (Strabo, p. 381).

evil effects of this indiscriminate system of manumission, with suggestions of a remedy.[1] But the collapse of the empire was not brought about by slavery,[2] but partly by the inclusion of undigested masses of barbarians[3] (who play on a larger scale within the empire the rôle previously played by slave-masses within the body politic of Italy), and partly by the vicious non-productive economic system of the empire itself.

LITERATURE.—H. Wallon, *Hist. de l'esclavage dans l'antiquité*², 3 vols., Paris, 1879; W. A. Becker, *Gallus, oder römischen Scenen aus der Zeit Augusts*, ed. H. Göll, 3 vols., Berlin, 1883; G. Boissier, *La Religion romaine*³, 2 vols., Paris, 1884; Joachim Marquardt, *Das Privatleben der Römer*², ed. A. Mau, Leipzig, 1886 [=J. Marquardt and T. Mommsen, *Handb. der röm. Altertümer*, vii.]; Samuel Dill, *Roman Society from Nero to Marcus Aurelius*, London, 1904; A. H. J. Greenidge, *Hist. of Rome during the later Republic and early Principate*, i. (all published), do. 1904; W. Warde Fowler, *Social Life at Rome in the Age of Cicero*, do. 1908; W. E. Heitland, *The Roman Republic*, 3 vols., Cambridge, 1909; W. W. Buckland, *The Roman Law of Slavery*, do. 1908; *Elementary Principles of the Roman Private Law*, do. 1912; M. Rostowzew, *Studien zur Geschichte des römischen Kolonates* (1st Beiheft of *Archiv für Papyrusforschung*, Leipzig and Berlin, 1910); Friedrich Lübker, *Reallexikon des klassischen Altertums*⁸, ed. J. Geffcken and E. Ziebarth, Leipzig, 1914 (contains many titles of recent works on various aspects of the subject).

W. J. WOODHOUSE.

SLEEP.—See DREAMS AND SLEEP.

SMĀRTAS.—**1.** The Smārtas are an important sect of Brāhmans, found mostly in the south of India, their chief seat being in the Mysore State. There are also many in the Central Provinces. They derive their name from *smṛti*, 'what was remembered,' or tradition, as distinguished from *śruti*, 'what was heard,' inspired or revealed truth, only orally and audibly transmitted. As Manu[4] explains it, *śruti* means the Veda, *smṛti* 'the institutes of the sacred law.'

The Smārtas worship the triad of Brahmā, Śiva, and Viṣṇu under the mystic syllable *Ōṃ*, and, while admitting them to be equal, exalt Śiva as their chief deity. They hold the pantheistic Vedānta doctrine of *advaita*, or non-dualism, which means that the universe is not distinct from the supreme soul. The leading tenet of the sect is the recognition of Brahma Para-Brahma as the only existing being, the sole cause and supreme ruler of the universe, and as distinct from Śiva, Viṣṇu, Brahmā, or any individual member of the pantheon; to know him is the supreme good. The attainment of complete wisdom results in *mukti*, or liberation, and re-union with the divine essence. But, as the mind of man cannot elevate itself to the contemplation of the inscrutable first cause and only soul, he may be contemplated through inferior deities and sought through the prescribed rites and exercises. This creed thus tolerates all the Hindu deities, and the worship of the following was, by Śaṅkarāchārya's express permission, taught by some of his disciples: Śiva, Viṣṇu, Kṛṣṇa, Sūrya, Śakti, Gaṇeśa, and Bhairava. The distinctive marks of a Smārta Brāhman are three parallel horizontal lines, of pounded sandalwood or of the ashes of cow-dung, on the forehead, with a round red spot in the centre. The Daṇḍīs of the north of India are an outcome of the Smārtas; they are mendicants.

The founder of the sect was Śaṅkara or Śaṅkarāchārya (*q.v.*), the celebrated Hindu reformer of the 8th cent., and apostle of the Uttara Mīmāṁsa or Vedānta. Their *guru*, or spiritual head, is the Śringeri Swāmi, designated the Jagad Guru, or priest of the world. He is a man of eminent learning and an ascetic of great sanctity, trained for his office from boyhood. His claims to reverence are admitted by all votaries of Śiva, whether of the Smārta or of any other communion. The enormous sums obtained from the piety of his disciples during his tours, on which he is often away for several years, are spent with a lavish hand in hospitality and works of charity so called. Śriṅgeri, Śriṅga-giri, or Ṛishya-Śriṅga-giri, the site of the monastery, is a most picturesque and fertile spot on the bank of the Tungā river, sheltered by the Western Ghāts, in the Koppa *tāluq* of the Kadūr District of Mysore. The *jāgīr*, or landed estate, is about 8 miles long by 6 wide.

2. Subdivisions.—The following are some of the subdivisions of the Smārtas, in certain of which are also included some members of the Mādhva (*q.v.*) sect. The Baḍaga-naḍ had their origin in the northern (*baḍaga*) districts (*nāḍ*) and speak Kannaḍa. The Deśastha are immigrants from the Mahratta country and mostly retain the use of Mahratti. The Babbūr Kamme, Kannaḍa Kamme, and Ulcha Kamme nearly all speak Kannaḍa, a few Telugu also. The Kamme country seems to have been to the east of the Kolar District. The Muliki-nāḍ or Muriki-nāḍ are from the Kaḍapa District and speak Telugu. The Hoysaṇiga, also called Vaiṣaṇiga, derive their name from the old Hoysala or Hoysaṇa kingdom and of course speak Kannaḍa. The Āruvelu, or the Six Thousand, speak both Kannaḍa and Telugu. The Āruvelu Niyogi are a branch of them who are *laukikas*, or devoted to secular callings. The Chitpāvan are Mahrattas. The Havika or Haiga are immigrants from Haiga, the ancient name of N. Kanara, and they are almost entirely confined to the west of the Shimoga District. They are now principally engaged in the cultivation of areca-nut gardens. They lay claim to original descent from the north of India. The small communities of Kandāvara, Kavarga, Koṭa and Koṭiśvara, Kuśasthala, Śiśuvarga (properly Śiṣyavarga), with the Śivalli, are all Tulu Brāhmans, immigrants from S. Kanara, the ancient Tuluva, and mostly located in the western districts. They engage in agriculture and trade and speak Tulu and Kannaḍa. The Karāḍe or Karhāḍe are Mahrattas from Karhāḍ. Some are employed in the Revenue Survey. The Konkaṇastha are also Mahrattas, from the Konkan. The Nandavaidīka are from the Telugu country and speak Telugu and Kannaḍa. The Prathamaśākhe or Madyāndina also speak Telugu and Kannaḍa. The Sahavāsi are immigrants, like the Chitpāvan, from the Mahratta country. The Sanketi are from Madura and speak a corrupt mixture of Tamil and Kannaḍa. There are two branches—the Kauśika and the Beṭṭadpur, so named from the places in which they first settled, which are in the west of the Hassan and Mysore Districts. The Sanketi reverence a prophetess named Nāchāramma or Nangiramma, who seems to have been instrumental in causing their migration from their original seats. The Haḷe Sīranāḍ speak Kannaḍa and probably derive their name from Sīra in the Tumkūr District. The Vengipuram all speak Telugu. So do the Velnāḍ, who resemble the Muriki-nāḍ. They are mostly in the south and east. The Vegi-nāḍ speak Kannaḍa.

3. Śriṅgeri.—The fortunes of Śriṅgeri, of such vital importance to the Smārtas, have had their ups and downs. It is worthy of note that the same neighbourhood was the cradle of two great states, thus proving it to be what is called 'heroic soil.' It was the birthplace of the Hoysalas, who developed into a first-rate power, arrested the Chola invasion in these parts, and finally drove the Cholas out of Mysore, thus becoming rulers of the whole country. But on the collapse of the Hoysala kingdom through Musalmān invaders from the north, in the 14th cent., an interregnum was created. Advantage was taken of this by the head of the Śriṅgeri *maṭh* to aid two princes who had been connected with the Hoysalas to found a new kingdom, which before long expanded into the great Vijayanagar empire, embracing the whole of S. India. Mādhava, surnamed Vidyāraṇya, 'forest of learning,' the abbot of Śriṅgeri, himself became the first minister, and after him the capital was first called Vidyānagara, eventually changed to Vijayanagar, 'city of victory.' It was now that the *maṭh* was endowed with lands and entered on a prosperous career. But Vijayanagar fell a prey in 1565 to a confederacy of Musalmān powers, and evil times overtook Śriṅgeri. It was reduced to ruins, and its lands were seized by any one who could get hold of them. Meanwhile the Keladi or Bednūr kings in the north-west of Mysore had been extending their power and absorbed all Kanara and Malabar, with regions beyond to the north. They, in common with all the neighbour-

1 *Ant. Rom.* iv. 24.
2 Cf. Meyer, p. 210.
3 Cf. *The Cambridge Medieval History*, Cambridge, 1911 ff., i. 544.
4 ii. 10.

ing states, had adopted the new Vīra Śaiva or Lingāyat (*q.v.*) faith, which had spread with great rapidity throughout the Kannada and S. Mahratta countries. To them, nevertheless, the *guru* appealed in person and was successful in enlisting their support. The ruined buildings were rebuilt and the lands restored. At the same time, the *guru* judiciously resolved to recognize the Lingāyats, as being votaries of Śiva, though they would have nothing to say to Brāhmans. Since that time the place has been in safety, and, after the Keladi or Bednūr kingdom was subdued, has been liberally maintained by the Rājas of Mysore.

4. Other maṭhs.—Other *maṭhs* besides Śriṅgeri were established by Śaṅkarāchārya in various parts, which are still in operation. The most notable is the Badarikāśrama at Kedarnāth in the Himālayas. This is where he died, at the early age of 32. The temple there is to this day always served by a Nambūtiri Brāhman (known as the *rāwal*) from Malabar, which was Śaṅkarāchārya's native country. Other *maṭhs* are at Dwāraka in Kathiawar, Jagannāth in Orissa, and Kumbakonam in Tanjore. There was thus one at each cardinal point of the compass.

LITERATURE.—H. H. Wilson, *Religious Sects of the Hindus*, ed. Rost, London, 1862; John Dowson, *Classical Dictionary of Hindu Mythology and Religion*, etc., do. 1879; L. Rice, *Mysore*, revised ed., i., do. 1897.

LEWIS RICE.

SMOKING.—1. Smoking to produce rain.—In primitive society, where the food-supply is governed directly by the rainfall, the attitude of man is intensely practical and calculated to produce states of emotional intensity. The emotions must find vent somehow; this they do in representative and emotional ceremonies to produce the desired result. When primitive man wants rain, he does not imitate it, but endeavours actually to make it.[1] He has learnt by observation that the gathering of clouds presages the fall of rain, and consequently, he argues, to make clouds is the equivalent of making rain. Now nothing would more readily suggest to his mind the phenomena of clouds than smoke, and it is therefore not surprising that this substance frequently figures in rain-making ceremonies.

Thus the Bechuanas burn the stomach of an ox at evening because they imagine that the black smoke will produce rain-clouds,[2] just as the Tarahumare Indians of Mexico envelop the whole country in smoke in the spring by burning the grass, in order to gather rain-clouds. Likewise the Zuñi Indians of New Mexico set fire to the grass and trees at the summer solstice in order to make a great cloud of smoke, while bull-roarers are swung and prayers offered imploring the rain-makers to water the earth.[3] Every four years in August, when the corn is a foot high, a sacred dance is performed by Zuñi maidens carrying baskets of corn, while a man of the Frog clan smokes a cigarette of native tobacco over vessels of water and stalks of green corn. The object of the rite is to ensure a supply of rain and the growth of corn.[4]

Among the Omahas of N. America, when the first thunder is heard in the spring, the Elk and Bear clans assemble in a sacred tent belonging to the Elk gens. There one of the Bear people takes a pipe from a sacred bag and hands it to one of the Elk men with tobacco from an elk bladder. Before the pipe is smoked, it is held towards the sky and the thunder-god is addressed. After the pipe has been smoked, the rain always ceases.[5]

2. Smoking to produce trance.—It not infrequently happens that various psychological experiences are produced by inhaling the smoke of certain plants—a fact that has led primitive man to regard smoking as a means of getting into communication with the spirit world. Thus in the Hindu Kush the *dainyal*, or sibyl, inhales the smoke from the smouldering sacred cedar with a cloth over her head, till she is seized with con-

[1] Cf. art. RAIN, § 8.
[2] *GB*³, pt. i., *The Magic Art*, London, 1911, i. 291.
[3] M. C. Stevenson, 'The Zuñi Indians,' *23 RBEW* [1904], pp. 20 f., 158 ff.
[4] *Ib.* pp. 41, 48, 51–57, 180 ff.
[5] J. O. Dorsey, 'Omaha Sociology,' *3 RBEW* [1884], p. 227.

vulsions and falls to the ground.[1] The smoke of the same wood is also inhaled by the prophet among the Takhas on the border of Kashmīr in order to keep off evil spirits before he utters his oracle.[2] The sacred laurel was inhaled by Apollo's prophetess before she prophesied,[3] and in Madura the woman who is to act as the medium of a spirit inhales the smoke of incense, sitting with her head over a smoking censer. Gradually she falls into a trance, and her utterances are regarded as oracular.[4] By smoking tobacco the sorcerers of Brazilian tribes raise themselves to ecstasy in their convulsive orgies and see spirits. The Bororo Indians (Brazil), *e.g.*, bless the new maize by an *aroetorrari* (medicine-man) working himself into a frenzy by dancing, singing, and incessant smoking, and in this condition biting into the husk and uttering shrieks from time to time.[5]

Among the Baganda of Central Africa a priest is set apart as the vehicle of the manifestation of the late king's spirit. The royal tomb is visited five months after the death of the king by his successor's uncle, three chiefs, and a few soldiers. One of the party enters and severs the head from the late king's body, brings it out, and puts it in a heap for insects to eat off the flesh. The skull is then washed and filled with wine and later with milk, after the former has been drunk by one of the priests. The lower jaw-bone (*lwanga*)—the special portion of the body to which the ghost of the deceased clings—is put into a separate house shaped like a bee-hive. This 'temple' containing the jaw-bone and umbilical cord (*mulongo*) of the king is divided into two compartments—an outer one, into which the ordinary people are admitted, and an inner one, where the spirit of the departed king is said to dwell. In front of the partition is a throne covered with lion- and leopard-skins, and in front of this is a rail of spears and shields and knives, keeping the entrance to the throne sacred. When the *mandwa*, or priest, who is to be possessed by the king's spirit wants to converse with the people in the king's name, he first comes to this throne and speaks to the spirit inside the inner room, telling it the business of the people. He then smokes one or two pipes, and after a few minutes he begins to rave, being possessed with the spirit, and speaks in the tones of the late king.[6]

3. Smoking to produce guardian spirits.—Young men of the Blackfeet tribe of N. America use pipes in a ceremony for acquiring a guardian spirit. They 'go up on to a hill, and cry and pray for some animal or bird to come to them. . . . They take with them a pipe and tinder and flint, and a native weed or bark for smoking (not matches or tobacco). When the pipe is filled, they point the stem to the sun and say, "Pity me, that some animal or bird may come to me!" Then they address the trees, the grass, the water, and the stones in the same manner.' The animal or bird that appears to them in their dreams becomes their guardian spirit.[7]

4. Smoking as a means of propitiation.—Smoking is employed in ceremonies to propitiate gods, animals, and stones. (*a*) *Gods.*—The Osages of N. America begin an undertaking by smoking a pipe with a prayer: 'Great Spirit, come down to smoke with me as a friend! Fire and Earth, smoke with me and help me to overthrow my foes!'[8] The Comanches of the prairies send the first puff of tobacco-smoke to the Great Spirit, and the second to the sun. The Creeks, who regard the sun as a symbol of the Great Spirit, send him the first puff of the calumet at treaties, and the Natchez chief smokes towards the east at sunrise.[9] Among the Thompson Indians of British Columbia, when the first tobacco of the season is gathered and smoked, an elderly man assembles all the inhabitants of each lodge, arranging the smokers

[1] J. Biddulph, *Tribes of the Hindoo Koosh*, Calcutta, 1880, p. 97.
[2] *GB*³, pt. i., *The Magic Art*, i. 383.
[3] Lucian, *Bis accusatus*, 1; Plutarch, *de E apud Delphos*, 2.
[4] *GB*³, pt. i., *The Magic Art*, i. 384.
[5] V. Frič and P. Radin, 'Contributions to the Study of the Bororo Indians,' *JAI* xxxvi. [1906] 392.
[6] J. Roscoe, 'Notes on the Manners and Customs of the Baganda,' *JAI* xxxi. [1901] 129 f., xxxii. [1902] 45 f.; cf. *The Baganda*, London, 1911, p. 283.
[7] E. F. Wilson, 'Report on the Blackfoot Tribes,' *Report of 57th Meeting of Brit. Assoc.*, London, 1888, p. 187.
[8] *PC*³ ii. 383.
[9] *Ib.* pp. 287 f., 343.

(male and female) in a circle while he stands in the middle. He then addresses the company, cuts up some of the tobacco, and, after mixing it with bear-berry leaves, fills a large pipe, lights it, and hands it to each of the individuals in turn, following the sun's course. Every one takes a whiff and, holding up his hands, blows the smoke between the fingers and over the breast, praying to the Tobacco Chief to be kept from sickness and death.[1]

The Hañga and Iñkĕ-sabe, or Black Shoulders clans, of the Omahas are in possession of two pipes made of red pipe-stone and decorated with porcupine quills. According to Anbahebe, the aged historian of the Omahas, the old men made seven pipes and carried them round the circle formed by the tents of the tribe. They gave the first pipe to the head of the Iñkĕ-sabe gens, and then passed on to the Hañga, to whom they handed a firebrand with which to light the pipes for the chiefs. The Bear, Blackbird, and Turtle people received no pipe because they feared them. The Eagle people, however, not being feared, were given a pipe, and the remaining five pipes were distributed among the 'good' sections of the other clans. This tradition is based on the belief that these seven pipes are symbols of peace.[2] On ceremonial occasions the two pipes kept by the Iñkĕ-sabe are brought out of the sacred bag in which they are kept with the other tribal relics, and solemnly cleaned and filled by Ictasanda men, who, while performing these functions, recite certain formulæ. They are lit by a member of the Hañga clan, and are passed round the circle of the chiefs assembled in council on tribal affairs. Both pipes are smoked by the chiefs, who blow the smoke upwards, saying, 'Here, Wakanda, is the smoke.' This is done because they say that Wakanda gave them the pipes and he rules over them.[3]

(*b*) *Animals*.—Before setting out on a bear hunt, the American Indians 'offered expiatory sacrifices to the souls of the bears slain in previous hunts. When a bear was killed, the hunter lit his pipe, and putting the mouth of it between the bear's lips, blew into the bowl, filling the beast's mouth with smoke. Then he begged the bear not to be angry at having been killed and not to thwart him afterwards in the chase.[4] The Assiniboins address prayers to the bear and offer to it sacrifices of tobacco, belts, and other valued objects. The head of the animal is often kept in camp for several days and ornamented, the pipe is offered to it, and prayer made that the natives may be able to kill all the bears they meet without harm to themselves.[5] The trader Alexander Henry has described the apologies offered by the Ojibwas to a bear which he killed near the winter camp in 1764. The animal was reminded that it was an Englishman who had done the deed and was requested not to lay the fault upon the natives. The next day the head of the bear was placed on a new stroud of blanket, pipes were lit, and tobacco-smoke was blown into the nostrils to appease her anger.[6] A similar ceremony was performed in the same district when an Englishman killed a rattlesnake. It was addressed as grandfather and smoked over, and its protection was sought for the Indians and their families.[7]

(*c*) *Stones*.—The Huron Indians of Canada offered tobacco to certain rocks, such as the one called Tsanhohi Arasta (the abode of Tsanhohi, a kind of bird of prey), which apparently stood at one time on the bank of the St. Lawrence. This stone is said to have once been a man, and it was thought that in the hollows of the huge boulder a demon dwelt. In consequence tobacco was deposited in one of the clefts of the rock by the natives as they paddled up and down the river, and the spirit was addressed thus: 'O demon, who dost inhabit this place, here is some tobacco which I offer to you. Help us, save us from shipwreck, defend us from our enemies, cause us to do good business and to return safe and sound to our village.' Likewise every spring the Mandan Indians approached a thick porous stone some 20 ft. in circumference, 'and solemnly smoked to it, alternately taking a whiff themselves and then passing the pipe to the stone.' The following morning certain marks (secretly painted on the stone during the night) were examined and deciphered.[1]

1 J. Teit, *The Thompson Indians of Brit. Columbia*, New York, 1900, p. 349.

2 *3 RBEW*, p. 221 ff.

3 *Ib.*

4 *GB*3, pt. v., *Spirits of the Corn and of the Wild*, London, 1912, ii. 224.

5 P. J. de Smet, *Western Missions and Missionaries*, New York, 1863, p. 139.

6 J. Mooney, 'Myths of the Cherokee,' *19 RBEW* [1900], pt. i. p. 446.

7 *GB*3, pt. v., *Spirits of the Corn and of the Wild*, ii. 218.

LITERATURE.—The literature has been given in the footnotes.

E. O. JAMES.

SNEEZING.—See NOSE, § 4.

SOBRIETY.—The relation of sobriety[2] to temperance and moderation (*qq.v.*) has been variously understood. Aquinas regards sobriety as a part of temperance.[3] Jeremy Taylor, on the other hand, says that sobriety 'hath within it [includes] the duties of temperance, chastity, humility, modesty, and content.'[4] The fact is that the word in its widest sense is equivalent to moderation.

> 'Nomen autem sobrietatis sumitur a mensura: dicitur enim aliquis sobrius, quasi *briam*, id est, mensuram, servans.'[5]

But, inasmuch as it is 'chiefly praiseworthy' to observe moderation in the matter of drink, since drink in a greater degree than food impedes the use of reason, sobriety may be regarded as a 'special virtue' designed to guard against 'the special impediment of reason' which is involved in excessive use of strong drink.[6]

1. As a special virtue, sobriety is a duty particularly enjoined upon the young, on women, and on the Church-ruler.[7] Speaking generally, Scripture is far from discouraging or prohibiting the use of wine. It was, indeed, forbidden to the priests at the time of their ministration and to the Nazirite during the period of his separation,[8] but generally 'wine' is regarded as the symbol of all that is most generous and joyous in human life. Its good effects, however, depend upon strictly moderate use, and St. Paul's words in Ro 14^{21} imply that there may be cases in which total abstinence is a way of showing true brotherly love; in other cases it may be a condition of personal perfection.[9]

2. In the NT use of the word *νηφάλιος* we see a gradual extension of the word 'sobriety' to other spheres. In 1 Th $5^{7f.}$ the word *νήφειν* is opposed to *μεθύσκειν*, but *νηφάλιος* in 1 Ti 3^2 is evidently understood by early commentators to imply something more than abstinence from the disabling use of strong drink. Thus Chrysostom[10] says: *νηφάλιον εἶναι δεῖ τὸν ἱερέα . . . διορατικόν, καὶ μυρίους πανταχόθεν κεκτῆσθαι τοὺς ὀφθαλμούς*. He adds that the multiplicity of cares and worldly business usually hinders the growth of this grace.[11] The wider use of *νήφειν* appears also in 1 P 1^{13} 4^7 5^8. It is used in these passages metaphorically to mean calmness of temper, watchfulness, and self-control.[12] Thus in

1 J. G. Frazer, *Folk-lore in the Old Testament*, London, 1918, ii. 69 f.

2 On the use of the word and its different Greek equivalents in the NT see *HDB*, *s.v.*

3 *Summa*, II. ii. qu. cxliii.

4 *Holy Living*, ch. ii. § 1.

5 Aquinas, *Summa* II. ii. qu. cxlix. art. 1, resp.

6 *Ib.* art. 2.

7 1 Ti $3^{3.11}$, Tit 2^6, etc.

8 Lv 10^9, Nu 6^3.

9 Aquinas, *loc. cit.* art. 3 ad 3.

10 *De Sacerd.* iii. 241.

11 *Ib.* 244.

12 Cf. 2 Ti 4^5, *νῆφε ἐν πᾶσιν*.

1 P 1^{13} the duty of 'soberness' is closely connected with that of girding up 'the loins' of the mind, checking the vague wandering of thought and speculation, etc.

Sobriety in this sense 'guards men against the "intoxication" of false prophets, against false views of ἐλευθερία, against moral and doctrinal caprices.'[1]

In the same way, St. Paul opposes to intoxication the duty of being 'filled with the Spirit.'[2] The word, however, that is more frequently used in this connexion is the verb σωφρονεῖν; the adv. σωφρόνως is also found,[3] and σωφροσύνη at least once, in this sense.[4] The grace of sobriety corresponds to the actual condition of the world, and to the fact that human life necessarily involves warfare and struggle, demanding the vigilance of a soldier and the endurance of an athlete.[5]

(1) According to the teaching of the NT, sobriety thus includes watchfulness against the great enemies of our salvation,[6] and against the danger of being overcome by the intoxicating draught of pleasure, the pressure of worldly care, the example of an evil world. This is the temper enjoined by our Lord in Mt 24$^{42-51}$, Lk 12$^{35-48}$ and 21$^{34-36}$; the wakeful heart, the girded loins, the lighted lamp are symbols of the spirit which should animate the Christian in a world full of hidden snares, deceits, and allurements.

(2) Sobriety also includes a moderate and temperate use of creatures, 'a moderate delight and satisfaction in prosperity,'[7] the temper that does not expect too much of life and is not inordinately dismayed or depressed by adversity. Bernard speaks of sobriety as the counterpart of two forms of intoxication:

'Ebrietas exterior voluptatum effusio, interior curiositatum occupatio.'[8]

Sobriety accordingly involves restraint in the matter of pleasure,[9] and the curbing of curiosity. Practically the duty of sobriety in this aspect is identical with temperance (*q.v.*).

'The sobriety of the soul consists in humility, and in being content with necessaries.'[10]

(3) A very important part of sobriety is a just self-estimate. So St. Paul insists,[11] having regard to the general needs of the community and the necessity that each individual should realize his true function and place in it.[12] Sobriety in this sense is equivalent to 'the philosophic mind' which comes with years.

'As we grow older . . . we take more and more our right place in the social organism. . . . We recognize that we are members one of another. That is a fact which involves a claim —the claim that we should love our neighbour as ourselves. We recognize that one member cannot suffer without the other members suffering with it. . . . We come to accept our limitations, internal as well as external. . . . It is only in middle age that most of us are able to say calmly of our rivals: "he must ncrease, but I must decrease."'[13]

(4) Finally, sobriety is the temper that results from a particular view of the world and of life—a view everywhere implied in Scripture, and equally removed from shallow optimism and from pessimism. There is a frame of mind which perhaps finds its typical embodiment in men like Bishop Butler.

'We should,' he says in a characteristic passage, 'propose to ourselves peace and tranquillity of mind, rather than pursue after high enjoyments. . . . The miseries of life brought home to ourselves by compassion . . . would beget in us that moderation, humility, and soberness of mind, which has been now recommended: and which peculiarly belongs to a season of recollection,[1] the only purpose of which is to bring us to a just sense of things, to recover us out of that forgetfulness of ourselves, and our true state, which it is manifest far the greatest part of men pass their whole lives in.'[2]

This temper is characteristic also of Wordsworth and the whole 'Romantic' school of poets. Christianity sanctions and encourages it, in so far as it frankly recognizes the presence and power of evil in the world, and the close relation that exists between physical and moral evil. The Christian habitually bears in mind the inevitable limitations of human nature in respect of knowledge, power, and character. The spirit described in 2 Co 6^{10} 4^{8} is this: 'sorrowful, yet alway rejoicing, perplexed, but not in despair.'[3] This is a temper which, as we have said, corresponds to the facts of life, and which is not unmindful of the divinely ordained regenerative forces which are at work in the world, counteracting the disturbing and disintegrating elements introduced by sin, sorrow, and death.[4] It is a temper which finds its characteristic view reflected in the Bible, which 'looks on the world as God's world,' and with severe truthfulness takes account of the stern and sombre aspects of human life,

'the heavy and the weary weight
Of all this unintelligible world.'[5]

Hence Bishop Wilson enjoins as 'our greatest wisdom' 'a constant seriousness of temper; an universal care and exactness of life, an indifference for the world; self-denial, sobriety, and watchfulness.'[6]

The Christian character is a union of opposites. The sobriety described above is quite compatible with fervour of spirit,[7] 'joy and peace in believing,'[8] and cheerful thankfulness 'for all things.'[9] In a world like ours all things

'Do take a sober colouring from an eye
That hath kept watch o'er man's mortality';[10]

but the reign of God is a truth which countervails the impression made on the heart by the stern and sombre facts of life. The site of St. Peter's martyrdom at Rome is marked by an obelisk bearing the inscription:

'Christus vincit; Christus regnat; Christus imperat;
Vicit Leo ex tribu Juda.'

Sobriety is the temper which has great things in view, and which, because it believes in the victory of God, learns to 'use the world as not abusing it.'

LITERATURE.—J. Butler, *The Analogy* and *Sermons*; T. Wilson, *Sacra Privata*, and *Maxims of Piety and Morality*, vol. v. of *Works* (in 'Library of Anglo-Catholic Theology'), Oxford, 1847–60; Comm. on the Pastoral Epistles.

R. L. OTTLEY.

SOCIALISM.—Socialism, with all that it implies and reveals of the desires and possibilities of human life in this world, stands in thought and history as gathering into itself tendencies, ideals, impulses, visions, and activities, theoretical and practical, which are as profoundly significant as any in our modern civilization, and the power and worth of which for the future of mankind no one would be justified in estimating on a low scale. By enthusiastic believers socialism has been described as in itself a religion; and the fact that for thousands of earnest men and women, feeling themselves crushed in the tangle and welter of human existence, something called 'socialism'—often something crude, indefinite, tinged with the violence of discontent—has been indeed substituted for religion, and made the goal of effort and the standard of

[1] C. Bigg, *The Epistles of St. Peter and St. Jude* (*ICC*), Edinburgh, 1901, p. 112.
[2] Eph 5^{18}. [3] Tit 2^{12}.
[4] Ac 26^{25}, where it is opposed to 'madness.'
[5] Cf. 1 Co 7$^{29-31}$ 9^{25}. [6] 1 P 5^{8}.
[7] G. Bull, *Serm.* xvi. (*Works*, Oxford, 1846, i. 409).
[8] *Serm.* 53 (*Opera*, ed. J. Mabillon, Paris, 1839, i. 2478).
[9] Cf. Aristotle's definition of σωφροσύνη: μεσότης ἐστὶ περὶ ἡδονάς (*Eth. Nic.* iii. 10).
[10] Wilson, *Sacra Privata* (*Works*, v. 146).
[11] Ro 12^{3}.
[12] See W. Sanday and A. C. Headlam, *The Epistle to the Romans*[5] (*ICC*), Edinburgh, 1902, p. 355.
[13] W. R. Inge, *Truth and Falsehood in Religion*, London, 1906, pp. 85, 88; see art. HUMILITY.

[1] The sermon was preached on the First Sunday in Lent.
[2] *Serm.* 6, 'Upon Compassion'; cf. *Anal.* pt. i. ch. 4.
[3] Cf. Ro 8^{28}.
[4] Cf. H. Martensen, *Christian Ethics* (*General*), Eng. tr., Edinburgh, 1885, §§ 51–58; T. H. Huxley, *Evolution and Ethics* (Romanes Lecture), London, 1893, p. 29 ff.
[5] Wordsworth, *Tintern Abbey*, 39.
[6] *Sacra Privata* (*Works*, v. 147).
[7] Ro 12^{11}. [8] Ro 15^{13}. [9] Eph 5^{19}.
[10] Wordsworth, *Intimations of Immortality*, 201.

conduct, is an indication both of the passion and the enthusiasm for humanity which lie behind all socialistic theories, even the crudest, and of the failure on the part of religion, as usually understood, to meet desperate problems and high aspirations in the life and thought of modern men and women. It would be unwise and unworthy to present socialism as an insignificant thing, whether we deal with it as a theory or complex of theories about existence, as a vision of what human society might be and perhaps ought to be, or as a comprehensive ideal to be achieved in the future. Socialism belongs to the big things of human history and endeavour.

As practically all writers on the subject have confessed, socialism is difficult to define with accuracy and brevity in such a way as to cover all that the term contains, still more all that it means for those who most sincerely and devotedly use it. Socialism has been called a religion. In modern history it stands before the observer as distinctly a 'movement,' something with its ground and origin in life rather than in thought, in the factory, the workshop, and the slum rather than in the study. But it appears equally as a theory, or more truly a complex of theories, economic and political, concerned with social existence and organization. On occasion it may advance to the rank of a philosophy. It has been described as the 'economic philosophy of the suffering classes.' Again and again, by upholders and opponents alike, it has been set in contrast with the philosophy of individualism (*q.v.*), however that may be defined. In the later years of the 19th cent. socialism became an organized political force in all Western States, with its programmes, national and international, its representatives in legislative assemblies, its parties, and its press. Socialism may, therefore, be considered in any or all of these aspects, and attempts at definition made accordingly. Further, it may be treated simply as an ideal and defined or described under the form of a Utopia. A definition that shall cover all the possibilities seems beyond attainment. The best way of approach is probably through a study of the history of socialism, as a theory and as a political force, with a steady and sympathetic eye upon the actual conditions of human existence out of which the theories developed and within which alone they could be turned to weapons of practical endeavour.

I. *HISTORICAL SURVEY OF SOCIALISTIC IDEAS.*—In this article it is impossible to treat the history of socialism with any completeness of detail. Only a survey sufficient to bring out the chief characteristics, and this mainly in the region of socialistic ideas rather than socialistic effort, will be attempted.

i. SOCIALISM A MODERN DEVELOPMENT.—It is important to recognize from the outset that socialism, as a historical fact, both in its theoretical aspects and as possessing political and practical importance, is a modern development. If socialism were so indefinite as to be only the philosophy, explicit or latent, of the suffering classes of mankind, or if we include under it any and every attempt at emancipation on the part of people in economic and social enslavement, or again any vision at any time of a better social future for humanity, any ideal 'Republic' or 'Civitas Dei' or 'Kingdom of Heaven' that imagination has bodied forth, then there has always been socialism; but it is rhetorical exaggeration to push back socialism beyond the limits of the modern period. Those limits are fairly definite. They may be taken to be, on the one hand, the French Revolution and, on the other, with less accuracy as to delimiting dates, that series of changes, in the social and economic structure of civilization, from the basis of feudalism, the land, and economically individualized production, to the basis of commercialism, capital, machinery, and collective production, which is summed up under the phrase 'the Industrial Revolution.' We need look no farther back than the last quarter of the 18th cent. for the beginnings of socialism.

ii. EARLY SOCIALISTIC THOUGHT ILLUSTRATED: ITS SOURCES.—J. T. Merz[1] points out that the historian Michelet opens his *History of the Nineteenth Century* 'by introducing three great Socialists.' It is a significant beginning, and reveals profound insight into the deeper currents of 19th cent. life and into the importance of socialism. The socialists whom Michelet names are Babeuf (1764–97), Saint-Simon (1760–1825), and Fourier (1772–1837).

These men, he says, 'emerge about the same time from the prisons of the Terror. Their ideas, to begin with, are in no wise discordant; they have the same point of departure: humanity, pity, the outlook on extreme misery. . . . Whatever opinion one may form of the three famous Utopists, we must admit that their systems, even their eccentricities, sprang from an admirable emotion, from the rising of a most generous feeling. Babeuf asks only for the division of deserted lands, abounding everywhere, in order to make them productive: *Right* is the single basis, the universal right of men to a sufficient living. Saint-Simon desires *Progress* . . . Fourier raves for *Harmony*.'[1]

Far more important than the 'systems' which these men desired or the practical demands which they made are, as Michelet suggests, the motives underlying their writings, the controlling ideas with which they worked, and the assumptions on which they rested. They aimed, in the end, at nothing less than an entire reconstruction of society, a radical alteration in the whole method and manner of human living. In so doing they established from the outset a characteristic of socialism which it has always retained, and lapse from which may truly be regarded as lapse from genuine socialism. Both as theory and as movement, socialism seeks to envisage and to establish an order of social existence totally different from that which is characteristic of modern industrial civilization. The order of social and economic life which the Industrial Revolution induced was accompanied from its inception by the demand for an altogether new order. In a sense, though not quite in the sense intended by him, the contention which, as we shall indicate, Karl Marx insisted on as so important, to the effect that the capitalistic order of life contains within itself the seeds of its own destruction, is true enough. Revolt has been with modern industrialism all along, its second self, its perpetual shadow. The mind and heart of modern life, which in the French Revolution, despite awful failures and disillusionment, received so rich an emancipation, have ever been in conflict against machinery, the peculiar force in the Industrial Revolution; and socialism represents in no small degree the persistent struggle of mind and heart against machinery. Feelings of pity, a sympathetic enthusiasm for humanity, belief in equality and brotherhood and the rights of man, distrust of 'civilization,' a strong sense of the injustice and ugliness of poverty and misery—these emotional and spiritual qualities, so potent in producing the mighty upheaval in France, lived on into the era of the factory and the machine as perpetual incentives to criticism and discontent; they are the moral springs of every consciously elaborated socialistic theory, even the most apparently materialistic, and they are the real sources of energy in every socialist movement. It is, therefore, significant that men like Saint-Simon and Fourier, who influenced socialism in the beginning, were more Utopian than scientific, more akin to the poets than to the sociologists or economists, more open to the logic of the heart than to that of the philosophy of history.

1. **Saint-Simon.**—If socialism seeks a beginning in the thought of Saint-Simon, Fourier, and their followers, we must admit that it originates from men who had a geniune passion for humanity. They sought after a complete reorganization of society which should allow human beings full opportunity to develop and display the qualities of humanity which they possessed; they believed in the natural goodness of man, in his natural ability to achieve absolute truth, and in his natural and inalienable right to full and satisfying life. The systems which they imagined as likely to give

[1] *History of European Thought in the XIXth Century*, Edinburgh, 1896–1912, iv. 472 ff.

[1] Michelet, *Hist. du XIXe siècle*, i. 1, quoted in Merz, *loc. cit.*

human nature the best chance to be itself would hardly pass muster now as in accord with received socialistic theory. Saint-Simon, *e.g.*, who directed his sense of revolt mainly against the ancient régime and viewed the approaching change to industrialism as good in itself, seems to contemplate an ordering of society in which spiritual power shall be vested in men of science, and temporal power in representatives of the property-possessing class, leaders of the new industrialism—a disastrous heresy, viewed from a later standpoint. The contrast between labour and capital, so prominent in subsequent theory, is not present to him. In the writings of his later life his interest, it is true, becomes more and more fixed on the question of the condition of the poorest classes in society. In his *New Christianity* (1825) he emphasizes this aspect of the matter repeatedly and develops the view that the main function of society is the betterment of the moral and physical existence of the poorest class: society ought to organize itself in the way best adapted for attaining this end. This was Saint-Simon's final interpretation of the Christian ethic, a true philosophy of the suffering classes, and an attempt, not noticeable in his earlier works, to place his social theories on a religious basis and present them indeed as a necessary fulfilment of Christian truth. Saint-Simon's writings contain many fruitful and brilliant ideas, and there are few of the great social problems of modern life on which he does not touch; but his schemes have historical interest only. His main contribution was to present plainly the truth that the crucial problem of the new modern world which he saw opening before him would be nothing less than the ultimate organization of society as a whole. Among his more immediate followers, in the midst of many extravagances which brought the whole complex of his ideas into disrepute, we find notions which were destined to play a great part in later socialistic thought. The definite attack on private ownership, soon to become one of the cardinal characteristics of socialism, finds emphasis, and there is development towards doctrines of extreme communism, whilst the conception that the principle of association (co-operation) must be fundamental in social organization becomes prominent; we get the first hints of the emancipation of women and of the doctrine of the political and economic equality of the sexes as necessary to worthy social life.

2. Fourier. — The underlying assumptions on which Fourier, a clearer and more systematic though less influential thinker, rested his views were much the same as Saint-Simon's. He believed in the ultimate, native goodness of human nature, and desired a social organization that should give freedom for full exercise of every individual's capacity and desire. Set free from restraints, human nature, he believed, would inevitably work towards harmony. The social system which he imagined as adequate to meet the need for freedom is interesting as representing a tendency in socialism opposed to the corresponding dominant tendency of the Saint-Simon school. Whereas Saint-Simon looked rather to centralization and what we might call bureaucratic government, by scientific experts, as the way of social salvation, Fourier envisages a tremendous development of the small, autonomous group—a kind of village commune with full local self-government—as the basis of social organization. He thought that such an arrangement would allow a greater measure of real freedom to the individual than any other method, freedom for the individual being the object of social organization.

These two tendencies, the one towards centralized government and the absolutizing of the State, the other towards group-organization and decentralization — the spreading of autonomous power over as wide an area as possible—appear again and again throughout the history of socialism and might even be taken as differentiating schools of socialist thought one from another. Saint-Simon represents one tendency, Fourier the other. Intellectually and spiritually the one thinker belongs to the camp of the bureaucrats, the other to that of the anarchists. Socialism knows both.

These early French thinkers, and we may say practically all who can be described as socialistic thinkers throughout the first half of the 19th cent., developed their ideas on the basis of a profound belief in human reason and in an underlying natural law, natural right, natural harmony of created things, due to the goodness of God or of Nature, which it was the highest business of reason to discover and to accept. In their view the ultimate principle of reality, God or Nature, had intended an orderly and harmonious creation, and as part of that creation an orderly and harmonious human society, in which man could be happy. The principles of that natural social harmony and organization existed *in rebus æternis* and only required looking for. 'Has not Nature,' exclaims Cabet, a typical socialistic thinker of the time, 'endowed us with intelligence and reason with which to organise happiness, society, and equality?' True social organization is a matter of knowledge and perception; only reveal the underlying natural principles of society to mankind, educate men's minds, and their reason will accept and act on them and all will be well.

3. Rousseau.—In all this belief in reason and natural right and order, which had and still has so much to do with the vitality of socialistic speculation, there is clearly discernible the influence of the spiritual forces that helped to bring about the French Revolution, and particularly the influence of Rousseau (*q.v.*), the father of so many of the greatest ideas in modern thought. It was very largely from Rousseau and kindred sources that the early socialistic thinkers learnt their belief in the goodness and perfectibility of human nature, their distrust of civilization and consequent demand for a new start in history, a complete change, their conviction that mankind needs and must have, and can rationally devise, a political constitution and an economic and social structure that shall give the individual full freedom of personal life, and their optimistic faith in progress and education.[1] Convinced, thus, that man was intended for happiness and was by nature a social being, and yet seeing all around them unhappiness, misery, crimes, disorders of all kinds, they could only conclude that the laws of nature had been defied or misunderstood, and that the way out of the morass was a new application of reason to the discovery of these laws and a complete reorganization of society on the basis of them. The fact that other thinkers of the period also believed in a 'natural' order for society, and thought that they had discovered that natural order in industrialism, free competition, and capitalism, does not seem to have troubled the pioneers of socialism very much. Views opposed to their own belonged, no doubt, to what Owen called 'the irrationality and insanity of the past and present state of the human race.' Although the systems of the first socialists differ considerably from one another in detail, the authors of them are agreed in the conviction that the rational order is different from the one in which they lived, and tend to reach agreement also in the belief that among the natural principles of social harmony and organization there may be found at least two which are to be regarded as axiomatic: (1) that *common property is natural* and therefore necessary to happiness,

[1] All the early socialists were great believers in propaganda and had a remarkable faith and trust in mankind's power of understanding. They thought that men had only to be shown the truth in order to act upon it.

(2) that *labour is the only title to property.* All socialistic economics may be said to be variations on these fundamental themes.

4. Robert Owen.—A very interesting and remarkable illustration of socialistic ideas, of the rationalist and Utopian kind, is to be found in the writings and the practical activities of Robert Owen (1771–1858).

Owen was a man of extraordinary capacity and great personality. His career was a varied and amazing one; in the course of it he rose to wealth and European reputation as a successful manufacturer with novel ideas of treating his workers, and sank to poverty and ill-repute as an advocate of extreme communism, a supporter of social change and militant trade unionism, and an experimentalist in communist settlements. As a 'model employer' in his famous factory at New Lanark he introduced reforms, amenities, privileges, opportunities of education, for his work-people, which showed on his part a deeply humane insight into the social problems and sadness of the new industrial era, and also laid down the lines that were later followed in many respects when legislation had to step in, perforce, to remedy some of the worst evils of competition and mechanical industry. The direction and character of his later activities may be illustrated by such facts as these: in 1825 he established, at his own expense, a communist society at New Harmony, Indiana; in 1832 he attempted, on a small scale, the establishment of 'an equitable labour exchange system, in which exchange was effected by means of labour notes, the usual means of exchange and the usual middlemen being alike superseded';[1] in 1834 he was mainly responsible for the appearance, with amazing though short-lived success, of the 'Grand National Consolidated Trades Union,' with syndicalist ideals, in 1835 for the 'Association of all Classes of all Nations,' a premonitory sign of socialistic internationalism.

Owen's socialistic thought, which chiefly concerns us, set forth mainly in his *New View of Society* (1813) and *The Book of the New Moral World* (1836), is based on the familiar belief in reason and natural right and in ultimate principles of natural social order and social harmony which reason can discover. Those principles Owen thought he had discovered, and in his writings he undertakes to explain them for the benefit of his fellows. Give, first of all, freedom to human nature, and it will develop a form of society in harmony with natural law. Systems of restriction are due to the stupidity of man refusing to follow reason; they prevent human nature doing its proper work. The present social system is a monstrous imposition which must be got rid of; enlightenment of reason and education will achieve its destruction. Owen apparently believed that there once was historically a true social order, in accordance with nature, and the new order which he desiderated was a reproduction of that first paradise. The eternal principles of natural social order were communistic. By natural right, property is common. Therefore the institution of private property must be abolished. Owen contended (and the contention has been repeated in socialist teaching time and again) that the institution of private property is the root of all divisions and separations in society, the basis of economic poverty and of the difference between rich and poor, and the source of all jealousies, rivalries, strifes, and wars; private property, he maintained, is not necessary to meet human needs, nor is competitive industry, based on private property, the best way of satisfying legitimate human wants. Co-operative labour, aided by science and machinery, would produce so much wealth that not only would all needs be supplied, but there would be abundance beyond all wants or wishes, so that 'any desire for individual accumulation or inequality of condition' would cease. This communism of the natural order Owen carried to some lengths with regard to the institutions of marriage and the family, making marriage an easily terminable contract, whilst his extreme belief in the necessity for the free play of individual preferences and feelings and his equally extreme distrust of man-made laws led him far, though with inconsistencies, in the direction of anarchism.

[1] Cf. Kirkup, *Hist. of Socialism*[4], p. 67.

Owen was not content with preaching his socialistic communism; he made valiant attempts to practise it, obsessed somewhat by the heroic, though mistaken, idea, which appears over and over again in socialist history, that the best way of destroying the present evil social order and establishing the new natural and good order is to start out at once and build 'communities' within the existing fabric of society, on the basis of the laws discovered by reason. Owen tried this method and failed, though not before he had created considerable interest and set going a stream of potent influence. A recent socialist writer has said that the promulgation of Owen's ideas on the 'community' forms a landmark and may be reckoned as the beginning of modern socialism. The claim is extreme; but without doubt the ideas which Owen expounded have played a tremendous part in socialist thought, whilst the sentiments from which his ideas drew their inspiration are characteristic, both in their good points and in their defects, of every socialistic Utopia that has been imagined, portrayed, or attempted.

Another not unimportant aspect in socialistic thought which finds remarkable illustration in the ideas of Owen may be mentioned here. He seems to have perceived with great clearness that the troubles of social existence under the new régime of machines and factories were economic rather than political; he was concerned more with the worker at his work than with the citizen in the larger life of the community. He was among the first to envisage the social situation definitely from the point of view of the economically enslaved workman. As a result, he and his followers were often thought to be lukewarm towards the agitations for political reform and the securing of the franchise, which aroused much popular enthusiasm at the time. Owen did not believe that the way to the social, and still more the economic, revolution which he desired lay through the controlling of political and parliamentary power. Political democracy appeared to him 'quite secondary to Industrial Democracy, or the co-operative ownership and control of industry answering to the economic co-operation in all industrial processes which had been brought about by machinery and factory organization, and which had removed manufacture irrevocably from the separate firesides of independent individual producers. . . . Owen and his more enthusiastic disciples were persuaded that a universal voluntary association of workers for productive purposes on his principles would render the political organization of society of comparatively trivial account.'[1]

When his isolated communities of producers failed to realize his dream, Owen hit on the idea of turning the trade unions, defensive combinations of workmen, into the voluntary communistic associations, 'National Companies,' as he called them, which should supersede both the capitalist manufacturers and the State. All that the workers had to do was to combine into such associations of producers as Owen imagined, and the capitalistic system was doomed. Just how the associations of producers were to secure the transfer of industries from the existing proprietors Owen does not seem to have made clear; he does not appear to have approved of violence, and the concept of the 'general strike' is not adopted by him, although that method was advocated by contemporaries.

In various forms this idea of voluntary co-operative associations of producers has appeared frequently in socialistic thought and effort.[2] But the notion of turning the trade unions into such associations was distinctly an inspiration on the part of Owen himself, and, as the quite recent history both

[1] Cf. Sidney and Beatrice Webb, *Hist. of Trade Unionism*, new ed., p. 139 f.

[2] We may instance the social workshops—associations of workers provided with capital by the State—conceived and attempted by Louis Blanc in France about 1848 (see his *Organisation du travail*, Paris, 1839). Ferdinand Lassalle, the founder of German socialism as a political force, advocated associations of producers working with capital supplied by the State, as a practical method of advance. We may compare also the self-governing workshops favoured by the 'Christian Socialists' in England.

of trade union theory and of socialist theory has shown, a much bigger and more fruitful idea than some of Owen's critics have allowed. The point, however, to be emphasized here is that Owen's ideas in this respect sprang from the fact that, in envisaging the social and economic problem of his time, he fixed his attention on the worker as producer, the worker at his work, more than on anything else. Freedom for the individual in his industrial life, the power of self-government and self-control there, was what Owen wanted to secure. The fact is that, like most of the Utopians of his time and since, he begins his socialism with the individual. There is another school of socialist theory which begins definitely with the concept of 'the State,' the community as a whole, 'society' as such, the 'social organism,' and so forth. The difference is very great, with regard both to the way in which the socialistic Utopia is envisaged and to the methods by which it is to be achieved.

There has been a tendency in some socialistic writers to treat almost with contempt all this earlier socialist speculation. Marx and Engels described it all alike as 'Utopian,' a term not overburdened with respect, in contrast with their own 'scientific' socialism. Others have quarrelled with it because it has no real philosophy of history, no sense of historical evolution, above all no concept of 'the State,' whilst its criticism of social conditions is rejected as sentimental. The sources of its intellectual origin in the rationalism of the 18th cent. are suspect. Its inclination towards extreme communism in economic theory and voluntaristic anarchism in political theory makes it repugnant to some types of mind. But no one can really hope to understand socialism without consideration of its early Utopian period. Ideas characteristic of all socialistic thought were then and there developed, or at least set going. But, even more significantly still, these early Utopians—and this feature is characteristic of all others like them—reflected and expressed the usually voiceless feelings and aspirations of oppressed masses, and particularly of the crushed and enslaved individual, out of which socialism most truly springs, and they never failed to waken the passion for freedom and individuality without which socialism is unrecognizable. In default of a philosophy of history and a sense of historical evolution they had faith in humanity, belief in the perfectibility of man by education, and a strong apocalyptic idealism, leading them to expect the dawn of a new era, as it were, on the morrow.

iii. EARLY SOCIALISTIC THOUGHT AND RISING DEMOCRACY. —Socialism can never be properly appreciated in any of its aspects unless it is seen in intimate connexion with the life of the working-classes of society, and its best exponents have been just those who, either through actual experience or through sympathetic imagination, have entered most fully into the feeling and passion of the working life of working people. The early pioneers of socialistic thought were the voices of new forces and new classes in society, above all of that characteristic product of the Industrial Revolution known commonly as 'the working-class,' described more technically as 'the proletariat.'

1. Emancipation of the proletariat. — Werner Sombart defines socialism as 'the intellectual embodiment of the modern Social Movement,' and the 'Social Movement' he takes to be the totality of 'all the attempts at emancipation on the part of the proletariat.'[1] That definition brings out the fact, which it is important to emphasize, that socialism is and always has been, theoretically and practically, a movement in thought and life intimately concerned and connected with certain particular social classes, roughly the wage-earning classes, economically the most insecure and menaced members in the social whole. The more modern, and so-called 'scientific,' way of regarding socialism, which would elevate it to the position of a political philosophy, or a doctrine of society, as it were, in its own metaphysical right, is really mistaken and historically incorrect. In the sources of its vitality, and in the general scope of its most characteristic ideas, socialism might not inaccurately be described as the philosophy of an oppressed social class, which was itself the product of a particular series of economic developments and a particular kind of economic organization.

[1] *Socialism and the Social Movement*, Eng. tr., Introd. p. 1.

The Industrial Revolution, which we have pointed to as one of the limits beyond which it is needless to look for socialism, created new social forces and social classes. Especially, it created, on the one side, the social class possessing capital and the power to employ labour and, on the other side, the social class possessing nothing but power to work, and dependent on the capitalistic class for opportunity to exercise that power, and so to live. There had been land-less men before: there were now capital-less men—men possessing power and skill to labour, but destitute of the economic facilities for utilizing their labour and making it productive. That was the root fact of the new situation created by the change to industrialism; it is the dominating social fact of the 19th cent. and of modern civilization. The coming of machinery, the application of science to industry, the collectivization of production by the factory system, and in the early years of the new era the amazing rapidity with which wealth was gained, affording temptation and opportunity to unscrupulous greed and selfishness, speedily intensified the new class divisions and deepened the misery of the non-possessing members of society. The story of that evolution is well known; the social history of England for certainly the first half of the 19th cent., if not more, illustrates the condition of things only too well.[1] Admittedly the new era produced 'suffering classes' and there was need and room for 'an economic philosophy of the suffering classes.' Socialism rose to answer that need. Socialistic ideas were the intellectual formulation of desires, aspirations, half-conscious longings and stirrings after freedom, fuller and better life, felt by these economically subordinate social classes. Often it is difficult to say whether a socialistic idea owed its origin to an independent thinker and was accepted by the proletariat, or whether the man who formulated the idea first discerned it germinating in the mind of the struggling proletariat itself. Socialism, at any rate, has been a live force only when there has been close interaction between its intellectual formulation in the realm of ideas and the instinctive thought and feeling of the proletariat, or, if we like the phrase better, the heart of the people.

2. The Chartist movement.—We may illustrate what we have just said, and also, perhaps, bring out some further characteristic ideas of socialism by a brief consideration of the remarkable Chartist movement which largely constituted the life of the English working-classes for a

[1] The pitiful story of these years has been told frequently, perhaps nowhere better, at any rate for the first thirty years of the century, than in the social studies of J. L. and Barbara Hammond, *The Village Labourer, 1760–1832*, London, 1911, and *The Town Labourer, 1760–1832*, do. 1917. The terrible indictment drawn by Karl Marx in *Das Kapital*, 3 vols., Hamburg, 1867–95, will always be classic. The novels of Kingsley and Dickens tell the same story, and there is a mass of other evidence.

quarter of a century, and the actual connexion of which with socialistic thought has not been as fully recognized as it ought to have been.[1]

The Chartist movement was the most complete expression of the revolutionary temper of the English working-classes, developed in them, slowly and painfully, by the bitter actual experience of what the Industrial Revolution meant in their lives. It was not the work of agitators, but the spontaneous outburst of oppressed men and women, no longer to be restrained. It was a movement of the new industrial proletariat, the first of its kind that the world had seen. Just as the Industrial Revolution itself ran its opening stages earlier and more quickly in England than elsewhere, so, quite naturally, it there earlier than elsewhere revealed within itself the power of provoking resistance and opposition inherent in its constitution; the capitalistic, competitive mode of social organization *creates* a class of people whose only hope of endurable existence consists in destroying the creature that begat them.

'The Industrial Revolution,' it has been truly said, 'obliged everybody whom it affected to think about the problems it raised, and when they addressed themselves to these problems the rich and the poor started from different standpoints: the rich from the abstractions of property, the poor from the facts of their own lives. As a result there developed two different systems of morality. For it makes a great deal of difference whether experience is passed through the sieve of hypothesis and theory, or whether hypothesis and theory are passed through the sieve of experience. The upper-class explanations ceased to be satisfying to men and women who wanted to know why they were starving in the midst of great wealth.'[2]

Instinctively and subconsciously, driven by pressure of experience, the working-classes of the new society were making, on the basis of their own needs and suppressed desires, a philosophy of social life and an economic theory which were bound to be different from those of the possessing classes. The unpropertied man *cannot* think and feel like the propertied: his psychology is different; he sees life from a totally different angle. Chartism is, historically, the first clear pronouncement of the instinctive political philosophy and economic theory of propertyless and unprivileged human beings, awakening, on the one hand, to the sense of enslavement and, on the other, to their capacity for visions and ideals. The fundamental demand of Chartism was for a total change in social and economic organization. It was a revolutionary movement, in the strict sense of being a movement not for 'reform,' leaving the basis untouched, but for radical change involving alteration of basis. It is true that Chartism is frequently presented as a movement merely for political enfranchisement, conditioned by the dissatisfaction of the working-classes with the results of the Reform Act of 1832; and undoubtedly it was a movement of demand for political democracy. The famous 'Six Points' of the Charter were all concerned with matters political, and contained no hint of economic and social demands. But the reason why Chartism, as a political programme, spread like wildfire is not contained in the political programme itself, but in the conceptions which the proletariat had now begun to cherish of the uses to which political power might be put. Political democracy was not desired for its own sake; it was desired as means to an end, and it was the thought of the end beyond the means that created enthusiasm. For twelve years at least prior to 1837, when the Charter appeared, the movement behind it had been fermenting and developing, and examination of contemporary Chartist literature seems to show conclusively that the aim of the deeper movement was nothing other than the revolutionizing of Britain in a complete socialistic sense, and further that this aim represented, not something given to or foisted upon the working-classes from outside, but their own instinctive, and now partly conscious, reaction to the conditions in which they were placed. The idea of social revolution — radical social and economic change — which gave to Chartism its emotional force was born from the heart of the proletariat. The demand for political power covered the determination to use such power, if acquired, to reconstruct society on a new basis. Democratic parliamentary reform was only a step to the larger goal. Chartism, it is true, was not an uninterrupted movement, nor systematically developed, nor were its intellectual foundations and sources the same as those of more modern socialistic-democratic thought. There was no unanimity in regard to the salient characteristics of the social revolution desired or in the envisagement of the ultimate goal. But in the course of the Chartist movement, and especially during the years of its greatest intellectual activity (1831–34), almost every permanently important socialistic idea found expression, and, more significantly, response from the working-classes, whilst the characteristic proletarian criticism of modern civilization was published in the newspapers and pamphlets of the movement.

We are not concerned here with the course of the Chartist movement itself,[1] but only with the ideas lying behind it and their relation to socialistic thought. What were the most prominent of those ideas? (1) Chartism makes evident the presence and operation of the concepts of class-consciousness, class-interest, and class-war. In the literature of the movement we find the doctrines enunciated that the working-class must stand alone and work out its own salvation, that there must be no alliance with the property-owning classes, that the interests of labour and capital are essentially irreconcilable, and that the only solvent for the misery of existence is the democratic organization of society on the exclusive basis of labour as the only title to rights, possessions, and privileges of any kind. The outburst of revolutionary trade unionism (really to be considered part and parcel of the Chartist movement) which followed the repeal of the Combination Acts in 1825, and in which Robert Owen was influential, rested on conceptions such as these. The concept of the 'general strike' as a way towards social revolution appeared, and ideas of the ownership and control of the means of production in each industry, not by the community at large, but by the workers engaged in the industry—ideas which were to have a remarkable resurrection in syndicalism—were put forward.

(2) The economic theory behind all this ferment of ideas was determined by the doctrine that labour is the real source of wealth, the only ground of possession, and that consequently the labourer has inalienable right to the whole produce of his labour. This doctrine, in various forms, had been derived by unorthodox economists like William Thompson (1783–1833) and others as an amplification of the reasoning of Ricardo, from whom the economics of unfettered capitalism and free competition also professed their origin. By thinkers drawing their inspiration from the rationalism of the 18th cent. and the theories of natural law and natural right—notably, *e.g.*, William Godwin (1756–1836)—the doctrine of the 'right of labour' had also been enunciated. But it was received by the working-classes only because it corresponded to their own instinctive reactions towards private ownership, their own sense of what was naturally right, and their own painful experience of continually toiling at the production of great wealth and receiving next to nothing of it in return. Quite clearly, if the propertyless producer of wealth achieves an economic theory at all, it will inevitably contain some proposition to the effect that the man who produces is also the man who ought to own the product, that the only title to wealth is that a man has worked for it. Equally inevitably and naturally, when it is observed that only a very small portion of the wealth produced by labour, or *ex hypothesi* so produced, is enjoyed by labour, whilst the residue goes off elsewhere into interest, rent, and profits, this departure of the product appears to be a taking away from labour of its rightful due, and almost, in fact, robbery. *That* doctrine, and economic criticism of capitalistic society, also found expression in the Chartist movement, but in the more polite form of the theory of 'surplus value,' later to be made by Karl Marx a cardinal theory of socialist economics, and to be elaborated by him with great acuteness and skill. Again, the doctrine is part of the instinctive economics of the

[1] The best treatment of the Chartist movement in its relationship to English socialism will be found in Max Beer, *Gesch. des Sozialismus in England* (far the best history of socialistic thought yet produced). Another illuminating study of Chartism is that of Mark Hovell, *The Chartist Movement*, Manchester, 1918.

[2] J. L. and B. Hammond, *The Town Labourer, 1760–1832*, p. 289.

[1] See art. CHARTISM.

proletariat. About 1835, in the *Poor Man's Guardian* and elsewhere, the declaration is to be found that, under the modern system, whilst the worker produces all the wealth, he receives only the barest minimum needed for subsistence, and sometimes not even that, whilst all wealth over and above that, the surplus, goes to the capitalist, who, with the aristocracy and priests and gentlemen, lives by the toil of the workers.

(3) The aspirations of the proletariat in the Chartist movement turned partly in the direction of desire to socialize the land of Great Britain and organize life on a basis of communistic colonies—a desire frequent enough in early Utopian socialism; partly in the direction of preparing the workers, by parliamentary reform, political organization, and education, to revolutionize and control the country in a political sense, making them ready for economic power through use and exercise of political power; and partly, again, in the direction, as we have already suggested, of the ownership and control of industry and the means to industry by the associated workers themselves—a kind of syndicalism. These aspirations received little systematic expression, but their undoubted presence illustrates characteristics of the mind of the workers in revolt on which socialism has always depended, if not for its theories, at any rate for the vigour of its practical effectiveness.

(4) Another significant feature in the movement is found in the differences of method advocated as likely to secure the desired goal. Chartism had a 'moral force party' and a 'physical force party'—names which sufficiently indicate the nature of the methods proposed. For our purpose the matter has importance as showing how thus early, in the first real movement of the modern proletariat towards social redemption, what we might almost call the two wings of socialism in all stages and in all countries make their appearance—on the one side, the tendency towards violence, insurrectionary revolution, anti-parliamentarism, distrust of politics, and ultimately a loose, communistic, group-organization of society, with suggestions of anarchism; and, on the other side, the tendency towards political reform, change by constitutional legislation and parliamentary action, evolutionary socialism, as it was called later, and ultimately a centralized, rather bureaucratic social organization.

3. Revolt against machinery.—It is not necessary to recapitulate the ideas that we have found present in Chartism. The parallelism between them and the ideas of early theoretical socialism is obvious, and it is important to notice that actual experience of misery on the part of the proletariat led, not only to the acceptance, but also to the instinctive discovery, of the same kind of ideas concerning social life and organization as had been prompted in the minds of theorists by contemplation of and sympathy with that misery. Still more significantly, just as theoretical, Utopian socialism was animated by a genuine passion for humanity and a deep sense of human beings as persons, so this proletarian, instinctive socialism, as manifested in Chartism, was everywhere fanned into a flame by a sense of outraged personality. That was the deepest motive in it; it was inspired, we may say, by hatred of the machine. For the men and women concerned in the Chartist movement machinery was the monstrous symbol of the new social and industrial and economic order in its totality.

> They felt passionately that the new power 'was inhuman, that it disregarded all their instincts and sensibilities, that it brought into their lives an inexorable force, destroying and scattering their customs, their traditions, their freedom, their ties of family and home, their dignity and character as men and women.'[1]

Proletarian socialism is a characteristic form of the revolt of mind against machinery which is the innermost thing in modern history; and the right way to see socialism is not as a system in economics or as a political philosophy, but as a movement of humanism and personalism in life, especially in the life of the working-classes.[2]

iv. 'SCIENTIFIC' SOCIALISM. — Many writers, following Marx and Engels, have spoken of the first period of socialistic thought as 'Utopian,' and of the second as 'scientific,' though the changes are often represented as much deeper than they really were. Socialistic thought, as we shall see, has never wholly lost the characteristics of its humanistic and, if we will, Utopian origins. Still, there were changes, made inevitable by various causes operating in the world of intellectual, social, and political development generally. The long-continued influence of the rationalism of the 18th cent. disappeared, about the middle of the 19th cent., before the advance of the evolutionary, scientific, and developmental point of view; historical realism displaced *a priori* speculation in regard to the problems of human life and society; political theory and philosophy were subjected to scientific method, with consequent departure from all conceptions of a 'natural order' of society and a possible displacement of the existing order by reversal at the instigation of the human will. On the continent of Europe also, at any rate, if not in Britain, the philosophy of the State, centralized and organized, as the real social entity, became prominent, whilst in Britain itself, the special home of political individualism, by the beginning of the last quarter of the century, the older view of the State in relation to the individual was dying, if not dead, and the social sense, the social conscience, the feeling of corporate and collective responsibility, were everywhere growing apace. Further, the endeavour of the working-classes to secure emancipation from industrialism became actively and prominently involved in the development of political democracy; socialism, in some form or other, became the programme of political parties, organized and forceful; and this fact also affected socialistic thinking.

Under these and similar influences, socialistic thought, as we are now to consider it, appears much more definitely than before as systematic economic theory and political philosophy. It develops a distinctively economic, rather than a purely humanistic, criticism of modern capitalistic society. Socialism is now presented not simply as a desirable social change to be striven for by those who will to strive for it, but as a necessary stage in the evolution of society, an order of social life that must supervene on the present order. On its theoretical side, in some aspects, it loses touch with the heart of the proletariat and tends to become even academic, drifting often from its original and indeed essential character as a revolutionary movement and appearing frequently as little more than an impetus towards evolutionary, gradual, and politically-engendered social reform.

1. The Communist Manifesto.—The characteristic language of this new level of socialistic thought is heard for the first time with concentrated power and the force of genuine eloquence in the famous *Communist Manifesto*, which has been called the charter of independence of modern socialism, and which is described by Werner Sombart as 'a unique document in the literature of the world.' We shall get to the heart of the most

[1] Cf. J. L. and B. Hammond, *The Town Labourer*, p. 18.

[2] We may add here two observations: (1) the Chartist movement collapsed about 1850, in failure so far as its main objects were concerned. But the ferment that it created and the ideas that were disseminated during it led to lasting results in the social life of Great Britain: we may instance the co-operative movement, and the movement for education of the people which led to the great Acts of 1870 and 1871, and, also, noticing here the special influence of Robert Owen, the legislation for the control of factories and the employment of women and children, which helped to remedy some of the worst abuses of the early years of industrialism. So far as British socialism is concerned, it is usually said to have died, at any rate as a movement, about 1848, and not to have revived again till 1880, except for the labours of the so-called 'Christian Socialists,' chief among whom were F. D. Maurice and Charles Kingsley, with their abortive efforts at 'self-governing workshops.' (2) In other countries, where capitalism has pursued a similar course, the connexion of socialistic ideas with movements of emancipation on the part of the proletariat was not unlike that illustrated by the Chartist movement, especially in the concentration of the first proletarian efforts everywhere to secure wider political power. Socialistic ideas became connected with efforts to secure political democracy, whilst industrial unrest among the workers tended to find expression in socialistic visions and efforts. That is the usual story. The years round about 1848 were years of proletarian unrest and revolt throughout Europe, and these years witnessed a vast spread of socialistic thought, thereafter soon to induce definite socialist political movements and parties, organized, national, and international.

effective and most wide-spread socialistic thought of modern times, and of working-class life even to-day, by considering the leading ideas in this *Communist Manifesto*.

After a challenging preamble, describing the fear which the spread of communism, *i.e.* socialism, is creating throughout Europe, the *Manifesto* begins by laying down the principle that all history, since the days, at any rate, of primitive tribal community of property, is the history of conflict between social classes, created by economic conditions, and distinguished from each other by the possession or non-possession of economic independence and power.

'The modern bourgeois society,' says the *Manifesto*, 'that has grown from the ruins of feudal society, has not done away with class antagonisms. It has but established new classes, new conditions of oppression, new forms of struggle in place of the old ones. Our epoch, the epoch of the bourgeoisie, possesses, however, this distinctive feature: it has simplified the class antagonisms. Society as a whole is more and more splitting up into two great hostile camps, with two great classes directly facing each other: Bourgeoisie and Proletariat.'

The development, characteristics, and achievements of capitalistic civilization, under the dominance of the social class distinguished by the possession of capital, are next described, with full regard for the amazing endeavours and results of modern industrialism.

'The bourgeoisie, during its rule of scarce one hundred years, has created more massive and more colossal productive forces than have all preceding generations together. Subjection of Nature's forces to man, machinery, application of chemistry to industry and agriculture, steam-navigation, railways, electric telegraphs, clearing of whole Continents for cultivation, canalization of rivers, whole populations conjured out of the ground —what earlier generation had even a presentiment that such productive forces slumbered in the lap of social labour?'

Under the new industrial régime economic existence, production and consumption of wealth, has become cosmopolitan, international. Home industries, national industries, are displaced everywhere by new industries which 'no longer work up indigenous raw material, but raw material drawn from the remotest zones; industries whose products are consumed, not only at home, but in every quarter of the globe.' This means, according to the *Manifesto*, the breaking down of national barriers and exclusivenesses, and the rise of 'a universal interdependence of nations'—a real internationalism of intellectual creation and a common form of civilization. But unrestricted competition rules in the realm of consumption and distribution of created wealth: there is competition on the one hand to secure markets in which the goods produced can be disposed of, and on the other hand to secure raw material to which the new vast productive forces can be applied. This means perpetual instability in economic existence. Driven by insatiable competition, the capitalistic methods of production and distribution must exploit every corner of the globe; the instruments of production are constantly being revolutionized; productive capacity overleaps itself and its opportunities, periodic crises occur, 'epidemics of over-production,' which destroy 'a great part not only of the existing products, but also of the previously created productive forces,' and threaten the whole fabric and existence of society. All this is really due to a contradiction inherent in the nature of capitalistic, competitive civilization itself —a contradiction between socialized, or collective, production, and individualistic, competitive appropriation, which tends of itself to destroy the capitalistic order of civilization, by creating conflict between the productive forces at the disposal of society and the conditions, of private ownership of capital and free competition, on which the actual existence of bourgeois, capitalistic society depends.

This inherent contradiction—and it is on this point that the *Manifesto* chiefly insists—is reflected, and indeed represented, in the struggle between the classes, bourgeoisie and proletarian, of which the one stands for the factor of individualistic ownership and appropriation, the other for the factor of socialized labour and collective production. These social classes are created by economic conditions and are differentiated from each other by economic characteristics. The bourgeois, possessing class is marked by ownership of the means of production, with consequent economic independence and control of economic power, on which follows control of political power, the institutions of government, and the organization of the State. The proletariat, on the other hand, is marked by lack of economic power and independence, concentrated in the fact of wage-labour, the basis of capitalistic exploitation, the essence of which is the compulsion placed on the wage-earning class to sell their labour-capacity, in order to subsist, at a price not only dependent on the will of the possessing class and capitalist controllers of industry, but (according to the doctrine of the *Manifesto*) tending always, by 'iron law' of the economic system itself, to approximate only to the level of the cost of subsistence needed to keep the wage-earner in being as a productive agent. Between the two classes thus characterized there is and must necessarily be mortal antagonism: their interests are opposed; their function in history is different; their destiny is not the same. As capitalistic society develops, this antagonism deepens and intensifies, capital tends to become concentrated and centralized in fewer and fewer hands, with the steady advance of large-scale organization in industry, whilst, on the other hand, the proletariat tends to be numerically constantly increased by a mass of individuals, resting at the bottom on complete unemployment and poverty, who benefit not at all by the progress of industry and the increasing facility of production, but sink deeper into misery.

'The modern worker,' says the *Manifesto*, 'instead of rising with the advance of industry, sinks deeper and deeper because of the conditions which his own class imposes upon him' (*i.e.*, because of the compulsion of the wage-system and the competition for existence among the workers). 'The worker becomes a pauper, and pauperism develops even more quickly than population or wealth.'

Such an ever-widening gulf between classes, with the steady pauperization of one class as the condition of the enrichment of the other, constitutes an inherent criticism of social organization which must in the end be disruptive. This inherent conflict 'makes it abundantly clear that the bourgeoisie [the condition of whose existence is private ownership of the means of production] is incapable of remaining the ruling class in society, and of forcing society to accept the conditions of its own existence as a general law regulating the existence of society as a whole. The bourgeoisie is incapable of bearing rule because it is unable to ensure for its slaves a bare existence, because it is forced to place them in a position where, instead of maintaining society, society must maintain them.' The only way to escape from the impasse is to resolve the fundamental contradiction in the system—viz. the contradiction between collective, socialized production and private appropriation, ownership, and control. This means either reverting to individualized production, which in view of the progress of industry is impossible, or advancing to socialization, not only of production, but also of appropriation, ownership, and control. This means, again, socialization of the means of production, abolition of private property in these respects—in a word, appropriation, ownership, and control of the socialized means of production by the socialized producing agents, *i.e.* by the proletarian class.

The rôle of the proletariat in social evolution is

to represent and work out, in unity and solidarity, the negative side of the contradiction inherent in capitalistic organization—to turn that negative into the positive of the new social order by taking over the ownership and control of the means of production, thereby emancipating itself, overthrowing class society, and compassing the real social revolution, which is not only to accord with the desire and will of the workers for freedom, but also to be a necessary fulfilment of the inherent conditions of economic development itself. The very progress of capitalistically organized industrial society creates the conditions of change and the class by which change is to be brought about; it accumulates misery, which breeds revolt, and it compels the proletariat more and more towards self-protective unity and solidarity, by which revolt can be directed to its appropriate end. The class struggle represents the developing economic situation; the main duty of the proletariat is to spread and intensify that struggle, and to hasten the inherent economic development, by cultivating class-consciousness, the sense of their destined historical function, solidarity of intention and aim, and unity.

The *Manifesto* ends with the famous appeal for unity; and, because the conditions are in essence identical wherever capitalistic industrial organization prevails, the appeal for unity is made to all workers everywhere, the call to socialism becomes international: 'The workers have nothing to lose but their chains: they have a world to gain. Workers of all lands, unite!'

2. **Influence of Karl Marx.**—This *Communist Manifesto*, drawn up in 1847 for a relatively small society of revolt in Brussels, calling itself the 'Union of the Just,' and in principle repeated in 1864 as the basis of the 'International Workingmen's Association,' the real beginning of international socialism, was the work of two men, Karl Marx (1818–83) and Friedrich Engels (1820–95), mainly the former. These two names are indelibly associated with modern socialism in all its aspects, and wherever it has found acceptance. Marxian socialism moulded and dominated the socialistic thought of the Continent almost completely, and, till a relatively few years ago, almost without question. Its influence has been less in Britain than elsewhere, though socialism in Britain was in some measure reborn from the study of Marx which occupied certain acute minds about the year 1880.[1] Marx has the greater fame, and he was a more erudite and accomplished thinker than Engels, but he owed much to Engels, and especially to the knowledge which the latter possessed of the development of industrialism in Britain. Marx, in *Das Kapital*, may be truly said to be theoretically diagnosing and formulating, in his own metaphysical and economic terms, the history of capitalistic industrial organization in Britain, and peculiarly the proletarian reaction manifested in the Chartist movement, whilst his indebtedness to English political economists, and again especially to the economists of Chartism, is well known. The leading ideas in the *Communist Manifesto* are the ideas to the elaboration of which Marx devoted his splendid intellectual faculties, and to the practical organization and spreading of which he gave his energy and his life.

(1) From amongst these ideas we may single out, firstly, the so-called *materialistic conception of history*. Marx was a student of philosophy and belonged to the extreme left wing of the Hegelian school, being influenced especially by Feuerbach. From Hegel he accepted the monistic and systematic interpretation of life and history and the (Hegelian) evolutionary theory of development, but he rejected Hegel's ideal principle of reality and substituted a naturalistic or purely materialistic principle, which he further identified with the economic factors of existence. For the Hegelian dialectic of the Absolute Idea Marx substitutes a dialectic of economic conditions and economic development: it is economic changes that determine all else, whilst the ideal elements in man's nature and life are reflexes only, or reflexions, of alterations, movements, in the play of material conditions and economic forces. History, says the *Manifesto*, is the record of the struggles of social classes; but the main point is that the existence and character of these social classes are determined by economic factors.

'The materialist conception of history,' writes Engels, expounding Marx, 'starts from the proposition that the production of the means to support human life and, next to production, the exchange of things produced, is the basis of all social structure; that in every society that has appeared in history, the manner in which wealth is distributed and society divided into classes or orders, is dependent on what is produced, and how the products are exchanged. From this point of view the final causes of all social changes and political revolutions are to be sought, not in men's brains, not in man's better insight into eternal truth and justice, but in changes in the modes of production and exchange.'[1]

Unrest of any class or group of human beings against the conditions of their existence—*e.g.*, proletarian unrest against capitalistic society—is only a reflexion of an unstable and changing condition of things, a lack of equilibrium of forces, in the economic system itself, which is pursuing the laws of its own being towards a new stage. There is, thus, determinism in the process, a certain fatality of events, which the will of man cannot finally hinder, though it may conceivably help. In any condition of social existence there is always development going on, and at some point a climax will come when the existing economic and social order will give way to another. If, at any given moment, the character of the economic forces at work in social life can be discerned and understood, if observation can lay bare the hidden dialectic of any given economic system, reveal the stage of its movement and the contradictions which it contains, then the character of the next stage, the direction of the changes implicit in the existing system, can be predicted, and, as it were, the programme and policy of human life arranged accordingly. This was the metaphysic behind the *Communist Manifesto*; it was this view of history that led Marx to the conviction that socialism could be made scientific and displayed as scientifically necessary; it was this that prompted him to search out the secret of capitalistic industrial organization, to undertake what Engels called 'the revelation of the secret of capitalistic production.' This materialistic conception of history, and the consequent conviction of some intimate connexion between socialism and science, had for socialistic thought certain ethical implications of importance which are noticed below (§ III.). For the moment we leave the theory with two observations: (*a*) it clearly serves to emphasize the undoubtedly great importance of economic, and in so far material, conditions in human history and existence, and sometimes the thoroughly deterministic power of the economic factor is overlooked; (*b*) in the applications which Marx made of his theory, especially with regard to the enhancing of the historical rôle of the proletariat, it is very difficult to decide whether he made these by virtue of scientific and impersonal loyalty to the theory or by virtue of a temperamental,

[1] *E.g.*, H. M. Hyndman, who was mainly responsible for the founding of the Social Democratic Federation in 1881, and E. B. Bax, who did much to popularize socialism. The group of brilliant and adventurous thinkers who established the Fabian Society in 1883 studied Marx, though after, rather than before, reaching socialistic ideas, and to many Marxian ideas they became strongly opposed.

[1] *Socialism, Utopian and Scientific*, Eng. tr., p. 45.

revolutionary strain in his nature which, resting on profound sympathy with human misery and hatred of oppression, made him from the outset of his career a champion of the socially subordinate and politically impotent classes.

(2) The *Manifesto* next reveals the fundamental Marxian *economic criticism of capitalistic society*. This criticism is really a restatement of the older, Utopian, humanistic criticism in terms of socialistic economics. Three intimately associated strands may be discerned in it: (*a*) the well-known doctrine of 'surplus value,' (*b*) the concept of a contradiction between collectivistic production of wealth and individualistic control and appropriation, and (*c*) the focusing of interest on the human agents in production, on the worker as a person.

(*a*) *Doctrine of surplus value.*—In the *Communist Manifesto* the main economic criticism of the wage-system, the basis of capitalistic production, is drawn, not in terms of the theory of surplus value, but in terms of the cognate doctrine of the 'iron law' of wages.[1] The general form of this doctrine, familiar enough in socialistic thought, is to this effect, that from the produce of labour only so much is distributed among the workers as is required for their maintenance, with reference to their qualities and needs not as persons but only as producers, and that the amount thus distributed is determined by the varying number of workers to be maintained, or by the number required at any given moment by the conditions of capitalistic production. By the operation of this law, it is said, the workers are permanently and necessarily excluded from participation in any increase of productivity in their own labour; under capitalism their position can never become better, but, as their number grows, must inevitably become worse, until a point of collapse is reached, when the capitalistic system must topple over through sheer inability to maintain the wage-labour on which it rests. In passing, we may remark with reference to this doctrine that, whilst it has been severely criticized by modern political economists, and whilst some of the conclusions based on it—*e.g.*, the steady pauperization of the proletariat and the approach to collapse—do not seem so far historically justifiable, it has an ethical value often overlooked. The sting of it, and its persistent appeal, as a criticism of capitalistic society, are to be found in the fact that, viewed from the side of the wage-earners, the distribution of wealth does appear to be decisively dependent, not on any principle of justice, but only on the necessity for keeping them alive—if they were not needed, they would receive nothing—and the level of wages, whatever the reasons in economic theory may be, appears to the worker practically variable only in accordance with variations in the cost of living and the demand for labour. No mere economic criticism of a doctrine like this will ever shake its force amongst people who instinctively feel that they are not receiving a fair share of the wealth which they conceive themselves to be producing. The fact is that socialistic economics, in so far as they have life in them, are not drawn from theoretical political economy, but are interpretations, in economic terms, of instinctive ethical reactions of the mind of the proletariat to the conditions of its existence.

(*b*) *Production and appropriation of wealth.*—The doctrine of the 'iron law' of wages, taken in connexion with the further doctrine that labour is the source of all value and so of all wealth that can be distributed,[2] leads to the discovery of a contradiction in the economic system between the production of wealth and its appropriation, and to the further doctrine that the surplus of wealth produced by labour, over and above the portion distributed to it for its maintenance, is held by the capitalistic class unjustifiably and to the detriment of the worker. It is this doctrine of surplus value that Marx makes central in his economic criticism of capitalistic production, and to the development and exposition of which he devotes a considerable part of his chief work, *Das Kapital.* Marx starts out definitely to analyze economic conditions on the basis of a theoretical political economy, beginning with an analysis of the concept of value. By subtle and frequently very difficult definition and argument he seeks to show that the essence of capitalistic commercialism consists in the appropriation of value, due to the expenditure of labour-power, but in excess of what is needed to replace that labour-power itself and maintain it. Into the economic intricacies of the argument we shall here make no attempt to follow him, more especially as, in effective socialistic thought, it has always been the general significance of the doctrine much more than the precise Marxian economics that has been prominent. And that general significance is clear enough, and has already been indicated.

(*c*) *The worker as person.*—More important in Marxian socialism than the doctrine of surplus value are (1) the insistence on a contradiction in capitalistic society itself, and (2), in the analysis of the significance and meaning of labour-power, the emphasizing of the worker as producer, and the concentration of interest on him and his class as dominant social facts—a concentration of interest made poignant by Marx's exposures of the iniquities of competitive industry.[1] Marx urges again and again that the disastrous peculiarity in modern industrialism is the contradiction between socialized production and individualistic appropriation. In an earlier stage of economic development, when individualized production was the rule, the worker had, in general, been himself the owner of the means to make his work effective, and consequently had exercised control over the conditions of his industry and the disposal of its product. The great change to modern industrialism meant the divorce of the worker from the means of making work effective, and consequent loss of all control over conditions of industry and disposal of the product. The workers, no longer their own masters, were driven by the exigencies of advancing conditions, on the one hand, and the fear of starvation, on the other, to accept socialized production—*i.e.* factory-labour, large-scale industry, and so forth—and dispose of their labour-power to the owners of the means of production in return for wages. Wage-labour became the rule and basis of all production, and, though nominally one of the conditions of wage-labour is that the worker shall be a free person, able to dispose of his labour-power to the highest bidder, he ceases to be free in reality—for two reasons: (1) because he no longer exercises control over the conditions of his industry and has no say in the disposal of the product of that industry, and (2) because the tendency of the competitive system itself is to exert a compulsion which makes 'free contract' impossible, whilst, inasmuch as labour-power, though treated as a commodity, is inseparable from the personal life of the worker, the loss of freedom *within* industry inevitably detracts from the free personality of the worker away from his work. This is the contradiction viewed from the side of the workers; socialized production, dependent on wage-labour, along with individualist ownership and appropriation, means the inevitable failure of society to allow and provide for the full development of free personality.

All the economic criticism of the *Communist Manifesto*, all the Hegelian theorizing and subtle economic analyzings of Marx, rest really on this fundamentally *ethical* indictment of modern industrial existence. Once more it is the sense of outraged personality, full and free development of life denied, that makes real and vital the proletarian-socialist criticism and economics. The class-consciousness of the proletariat, the unity and solidarity by which alone, according to Marx, they can put themselves in alliance with developing historical economic conditions, and accomplish, at the destined moment, the revolution which is to replace capitalist society by a new order, must rest on the realization of the fact that they are being robbed of their freedom as persons.

Marx has been subjected to severe criticism on many points, and much that he regarded as true and vital has been discarded by socialists everywhere, but no one can overestimate the value of his work. He it was who gathered up into the form of a coherent and systematic theory, with its metaphysical background (whether true or false we do not now say), its connexions with historical evolution, its scientific outlook, and its technical economics, all the hitherto mainly instinctive reactions of the proletariat mind to its new surroundings, and its hitherto mainly unsystematic and disconnected aspirations. He limited social-

[1] This doctrine originates with the physiocrats of the 18th century. Turgot, *e.g.*, writes: 'In every sort of occupation it must come to pass that the wages of the artisan are limited to that which is necessary to procure him subsistence' (quoted in Hammond, *The Town Labourer*, p. 201). Wages are determined by natural law and tend to approximate only to the bare level of subsistence. Adam Smith and Malthus give countenance to the doctrine, whilst Ricardo often seems to accept it. It can be used, and was used, as a justification of poverty, and its general acceptance is certainly one of the reasons why the possessing classes in the early days of industrialism were content to see their fellows starving and in misery. But by unorthodox economists the doctrine was used as a severe criticism of capitalistic society and as a reason for abolishing that order. Ferdinand Lassalle, following Rodbertus, made this doctrine one of the bases of his socialism.

[2] This doctrine appeared, as we have seen, in the economics of the Chartist movement. The orthodox economists, including Ricardo, are cited as authority for it. William Thompson, to whom Marx was indebted, drew practical socialistic conclusions from it in his *Principles of the Distribution of Wealth most conducive to Human Happiness*, London, 1814. The history of the doctrine is treated fully in Anton Mengers, *Das Recht auf den vollen Arbeitsertrag in geschichtl. Darstellung*, Stuttgart, 1886. The doctrine has the form of the general proposition that labour is the source of all wealth—*i.e.* other than natural resources—and the more technical form that the exchange-value of commodities, on which production for profit depends, is the result of labour expended.

[1] Cf. Marx, *Capital*, Eng. tr., 2 vols., London, 1887, pt. iii. ch. ix. f., pt. iv. ch. xv., 'Machinery and Modern Industry.'

ism, as Sombart says, 'to the movement of one particular social class, the proletariat,' and this was of the greatest importance; 'he inspired the proletariat with self-consciousness, with a trust in their own strength, and with a belief in their future'; he gave them a historical rôle and a function in the social life of to-morrow; he set before them a simple and definite goal; and he gave them, also, weapons of criticism which, though they may change their form, do not change their incisiveness and force.[1] They were to accomplish their own salvation and that of society by resolving the fundamental contradiction in modern life; socialized production must be accompanied by socialized ownership and control of the means of production; collective labour necessitates collective capital. Ownership of the means of production in industry, and control over the conditions of industry, by the workers themselves—that was the Marxian goal. That was the 'social revolution,' and the first step towards it was the development of class-consciousness and unity, and the realization of international solidarity[2] amongst the workers of the world. For fifty years Continental socialism held by Marx, in essentials, and the 'revisionist' attempt to get away from him was very soon met by the cry, 'Back to Marx!', and the discovery in him of yet more truth.[3]

v. SOCIALISTIC CONCEPT OF 'THE STATE': RECENT DEVELOPMENTS OF REVOLT. — The programmes of modern socialistic parties frequently contain, along with some statement of principles and of the goal to be reached, a series of demands for 'reforms' to be undertaken by 'the State.' The *Communist Manifesto* contained such demands, but it contained no theory of the State; socialism was there approached not from the point of view of society as a whole, but from the point of view of a class.

1. Marxian theory of the State.—Marx, despite his Hegelianism, made little use of the concept of the State in thinking out his socialism. The social revolution, for him, consists in the proletariat taking over the ownership and control of the means of production. One way of their doing this (though not for Marx the only way) is for them to acquire political power, through the development and right use of the democratic franchise and representative institutions, and to use that power for the purposes of the social revolution. What happens to the State after the revolution is not very clear. If we are to accept Engels as expressing Marx's views on the point, we must conclude that both regarded 'the State' as a product of class-society and as always in reality representing only the dominant social class, by whom its mechanism is used to subject and exploit subordinate classes. Inasmuch, then, as the proletarian social revolution abolishes all classes and class-distinctions, it of necessity 'abolishes also the State as State.' The State loses its essential function as a weapon of subjection and so ceases to exist.[4] If, behind this, anything at all is envisaged with regard to the future form of social organization, it can only be some ordering of society under 'groups,' determined by economic factors, which are autonomous and at best only loosely federated into a larger whole for certain purposes. The internationalism of Marx, and his doctrine that the proletarian has no country, would emphasize this. The political ideas involved in this view are evidently not those which emphasize the State as the main functioning organ of social life, insist on the priority of society to the individual, regard sovereignty as necessarily concentrated in a central authority, incline strongly towards the theory of centralized government and control by experts, and tend to view the 'rights' of groups and individuals, not as constituted by the effective will there present and the purposes contemplated by the groups or the individuals themselves, but as granted only or substantiated only by the sovereign power of the State as such.[1] On the Continent, where Marxian influence was strongest, however, the apparently inevitable connexion of socialism with political democracy, as evidenced in the growth of all socialistic parties everywhere, and the notion of achieving a socialist régime through acquiring and developing political power, naturally caused the idea of the State to loom large in socialistic thought; and the consequent tendency to formulate an appropriate theory of the State and society was strengthened, on the one hand, by the practical development, especially in Germany, of the absolutism of the State and, on the other hand, by the general spreading of political, and especially of sociological, views which emphasized the organic character of society and asserted, in one way or another, the priority of society over the individual.

2. British collectivism.—But it is to Britain that we have to look for the most complete development and formulation of the theory of the State in explicit connexion with socialism; and indeed the idea of collectivism, or State socialism, may be regarded as the characteristic contribution of Britain to socialistic thought, the product of a national temperament not prone to revolutionary feeling, and of a country with highly-developed political sense and long training in political traditions, and in which the working-classes, for various reasons, never have shown, save for the spasmodic outburst in Chartism and the revolutionary trade unionism of brief periods, many signs of strongly developed class-consciousness.

We cannot here discuss the intellectual and spiritual influences that have moulded British socialism and given it sources of origin very different from those elsewhere.[2] We can only

1 Cf. *Socialism and the Social Movement*, Eng. tr., p. 60 f.

2 It was Marx who gave to socialism for ever the vital concept of internationalism.

3 About the year 1900 German socialism, under the influence of E. Bernstein, showed a tendency to break with the Marxian tradition, but it was more than counterbalanced by the appearance at the same time of syndicalism in France and Italy—which professed to be, and in no small degree was, a return to pure Marxism. Cf. Georges Sorel, *L'Avenir socialiste des syndicats*, Paris, 1898, and *Réflexions sur la violence*, do. 1908.

4 Cf. Engels, pp. 75–77.

1 The profound importance of the differences in political philosophy here briefly suggested, not only for socialistic thought but also for the whole future of mankind, cannot at the present moment be overestimated. Differences of opinion as to the respective significance of society and individual, and as to the meaning of sovereignty and the functions of the State, not only divide socialistic theory into opposed parts, but actually rend the whole world.

2 Socialistic thought in Britain experienced a revival about the year 1880. Chartism failed and perished in 1850, leaving echoes only in the co-operative movement and in a tendency towards revolutionary trade unionism which was spasmodically displayed in recurrent industrial unrest and strikes between 1850 and 1880. Christian socialism maintained, to a certain extent, the Chartist criticism of competitive society, but exercised no wide influence on either Church or State. Political philosophy and economic theory in Britain were dominated by individualism and *laissez-faire*. On the other side, as influences making for a socialistic revival, must be set (1) the literary and humanistic criticism of the dominant philosophies with which the names of Carlyle and Matthew Arnold are prominently associated; (2) the work of Ruskin and his Platonizing; (3) the social theories of Comte and positivism (*q.v.*), which incidentally link British socialism with Saint-Simon, whose disciple Comte was; (4) the movement in the realm of political economy away from individualism to collectivism, to which the great authority of John Stuart Mill contributed much; Mill had not only committed himself to the view that the distribution of wealth is an artificial matter controllable by the State, but in his late writings had more than sympathized with the idea of collective ownership and control of capital; (5) the study of Marx already referred to; (6) above all, the by now manifest failure of *laissez-faire* in political life and the continued growth of State interference, coupled with the rapid development of the sense of society as an organism and the rise of a social conscience. All these influences gave British socialism its peculiar

touch briefly on its characteristic ideas; and we select, more or less arbitrarily, only a few points. Orthodox British socialism, if we may use the term, has been predominantly collectivistic, evolutionary, and parliamentary or political. Its ideal has been State socialism, the ownership and control of the means of production, land, and capital, in the interests and service of the whole community, by the community as a whole, operating through the organs of its political life, *i.e.* through a central government and officials, responsible to a representative parliament democratically elected, and, locally, through the same essential organs on a smaller scale—the State for national, the municipality for local concerns. The ideas dominating such collectivism are familiar enough.

'The essential contribution of the century to sociology,' says a leader of collectivistic thought, 'has been the supersession of the Individual by the Community as the starting-point of social investigations. Socialism is the product of this development, arising with it from the contemporary industrial evolution. On the economic side Socialism implies the collective administration of rent and interest, leaving to the individual only the wages of his labour, of hand or brain. On the political side, it involves the collective control over, and ultimate administration of, all the main instruments of wealth production. On the ethical side it expresses the real recognition of fraternity, the universal obligation of personal service, and the subordination of individual ends to the common good.'[1]

The point of view behind this is that of society as a whole rather than that of an oppressed social class. The controlling thought is of society as an organism, itself conferring individuality on its members; the law of individuality is service to the community as opposed to self-interest and self-assertion, and it is the very fact of society that provides opportunity for such service and so for the development of true individuality. Ethically society, the social organism, is the essential and necessary co-operator with the individual, and indeed the major partner and influence, in the building of a good and valuable personal life. And as the case stands ethically, so should it stand economically. Wealth, like morality, is in the end socially created; without society wealth, like morality, would be impossible; and so the wealth really created by the whole society ought to be 'owned and administered by the whole society.' The ethics and economics of collectivism both depend on the organic conception of society. As the organ of practical administration and the exercise of government, which in theory is to be self-government, collectivism envisages 'the State,' but the State as purely and completely democratic. It seeks to equate State ownership and State control with the notion of ownership and control in industry by the workers themselves, by assuming, and working towards, a fully democratic State in which the State shall be the workers, and the workers the State. Socialization of the means of production and democracy must advance together if socialism is to be realized. Although collectivistic socialists have been prone at times to regard any and every transfer of property or control of industry from private hands to the national government or the municipality as a move towards socialism, it must be said in justice to the true collectivistic theory that only when the State or lesser organ of administration concerned is truly democratic and representative of an enlightened democracy, only when and in so far as the State ceases to be oligarchical and the bulwark of a superior economic class, or an entrenched bureaucracy, can changes from private to public ownership and control be regarded as genuinely socialistic. It is, indeed, just in the slowness of the advance towards real democracy, and the failure of the organs of collective government and administration to correspond to the ideal of enlightened and educated democracy, that collectivism finds its most serious obstacles and the source of criticism most damaging to it. The upholders of collectivism have been, more often than not, primarily interested in the problems of the administration of wealth and its distribution rather than in the problems of its production, and so more concerned with the efficiency and good order of the social structure as a whole than with the individual life and personal freedom of the worker in his working existence. They have tended, therefore, almost inevitably, to lean towards uniformity in social life, to strongly centralized government, necessitating, because of the magnitude of the powers and issues involved, the continued existence of a governing class, trained in administration—in a word, a bureaucracy—and the maintenance of practically coercive authority. Like other socialistic theories, collectivism has been inspired by sympathy with oppressed social classes, but collectivism differs from other socialistic thought in the extent to which this underlying sympathy has been dominated by a highly philosophical theory of society, the social organism, and the State, which, whatever other values it may have, finds little place in the instinctive reactions of the minds of the workers to their surroundings.

The most recent developments in socialistic thought have made this fact clear. Collectivism is evidently adapted to the political mind and suitable to a purely political form of socialistic thought and activity. The approach to it as goal is evolutionary and gradual, and depends on the acquiring of political power by the workers. The reflexion of collectivism in the world of politics is parliamentary (and municipal) socialism, with its repudiation of violent and revolutionary action, its belief in constitutional methods, and its faith that the social revolution can be accomplished by stages of 'reform.' From all this, recent socialistic thought has diverged in directions which significantly mark the reappearance, of course in more highly developed shape, of earlier, original, and, as we should hold, more fundamental socialistic ideas. The divergence is best illustrated by syndicalism and guild socialism, or the theory of national guilds.

3. **Syndicalism.**—The true home of syndicalism is France. It is the product of a revolutionary national temperament, and of a country in which revolutionary hope and fervour have always lived in the working-class mind, and where socialistic thought has been prevailingly influenced by anarchist-communist ideals.[1] Syndicalism, with its persistent distrust of parliamentary socialism, revives and emphasizes the conviction that only the workers can emancipate the workers. It holds that the social revolution must be the product of the energizing will of the industrial classes,

collectivist tone and colouring. It sprang to life again as in a highly special sense a philosophy of society and the State, in opposition to individualism, with a fitting ethics and economics; and it was in proportion far less a movement originating in instinctive reactions of the working-classes. Collectivism, with all its outlook and terminology, is decidedly a product more of the study than of the factory—a theory resting much more on intellectualist bases than on the inherent aspirations and desires of a social class. And this difference is very significant.

A full, and probably final, treatment of this topic is contained in Max Beer, *Gesch. des Sozialismus*, referred to above.

[1] Sidney Webb, *Socialism in England*, London, 1890, p. 9 f.

[1] The historical origin and general significance of French syndicalism is best treated, among English writers, by G. D. H. Cole, *The World of Labour*, and *Self-Government in Industry*. Syndicalism was born and developed within the French trade union movement which made rapid and remarkable progress during the two decades before and after 1900. The inspiring personality in the movement was Fernand Pelloutier, whose *Hist. des bourses du travail*, Paris, 1902, was the chief literary influence in forming syndicalist thought. Pelloutier was a philosophic anarchist, of the school of Proudhon and Bakunin, and his whole outlook was swayed by the concepts of voluntary association of producers, group-organization with federation, and the local commune. The philosopher of syndicalism is Georges Sorel, whose chief works have been mentioned already.

operating possibly only through a 'conscious minority,' clear as to goal and method, swaying the mass. But in any case social freedom must come as result of the desire for freedom and the will to freedom, and cannot be imposed by organization from above or ensured by government. The workers must create their own society and do so by act of their own will. The end is still the fundamental socialistic end—the socializing of the means of production—but new methods are upheld. Not parliamentary but trade union activity, not political but industrial organization, not the franchise but the general strike—this is the newer socialism. The concept of the class war is rejuvenated and brought into prominence. Socialism once more is presented as the peculiar and exclusive doctrine and ideal of working-class life. The socialistic order of society must be made by the workers, through their own natural organizations, and especially through their trade unions. The divisions between social classes must be not only kept intact but deepened, intensified. Already a new society, with its own institutions, its own morality, its own point of view, is growing amongst the workers, and nothing must be done to impede that growth, but everything to aid it. Class-consciousness and the 'will-to-revolt' must be kept alive and fostered in every possible way. The goal is freedom, individual and social, and only intense desire for freedom, and the sense of freedom filched away, can lead towards that goal.

Syndicalism envisages the form of the future society as based upon group-organization, groups being determined by economic and industrial functions, workshops, factories, and industries without 'masters,' private or collective, democratically constituted, owning and controlling the means of production, and bound together by a system of local and national federation. The State as central organ of administration disappears, and power is distributed throughout a series of autonomous though interdependent industrial groups. The controlling impulse in the whole outlook is to get back closer to the individual worker in and at his work, and to move outwards to association, determined by the will of the workers and the purposes to be achieved. Syndicalist criticism of capitalistic social and industrial organization is characteristically drawn in terms of the personal life and personal freedom of the worker.

4. Guild socialism.—In Britain the parallel of syndicalism is to be found most theoretically complete in guild socialism, or the theory of national guilds, the latest of all developments in socialistic thought, and still in its early stages.

Guild socialism, says one of its leading exponents, 'sets before itself the ideal of finding that form of social organisation which will afford to the individual the fullest and freest power of self-development in an organised community. It wants men to be free, not merely in order to get good administration, but because freedom is in itself a good thing and the greatest of good things.'[1]

It believes that the State, 'in the sense of a governing authority claiming supreme power in every sphere of social organization,' is the negation of self-government. It contemplates, therefore, an organization of society on the basis of self-governing industrial groups, determined by industrial function, each democratically organized throughout, and federated into larger wholes for certain defined purposes. That form of social grouping called 'the State' will not cease to exist, but it will become one only of many groupings, divested of all intrinsic sovereignty, and with its value and significance determined simply by the purposes of man's free spirit which it can adequately and conveniently serve and by the functions of collective life which it can conveniently and adequately discharge.[1] The practical steps towards realization of this type of socialism consist mainly in the development of the existing characteristic products and organs of working-class life, viz. trade unions, the transformation of these into industrial groups (guilds), covering and including all engaged in any industry or common service, and the transference of control, with regard to all the conditions of labour, in workshop, factory, and elsewhere, from the 'employer' to such democratically organized groups of workers—a transference which, passing inevitably from socialized control of the conditions of production to socialized ownership of the means of production, would expropriate the capital-possessing class and bring about the social revolution. The only conceivable ethical justification for the existence of a capitalistic class—viz. the management and control of the conditions of production—would be gone, and the system would collapse. The main criticism of existing society by upholders of guild socialism is drawn in terms of an investigation of the moral significance of wage-labour, and a setting forth of what the inevitable condition of dependence for livelihood on the will of a possessing class means for the personality of the worker in his work, and outside—a kind of criticism which has appeared frequently throughout this article. The desire and intention behind guild socialism is to secure for the worker in his work 'the greatest chance for individual self-expression and for local initiative and experiment,' thereby increasing indefinitely his personal value, both in his working-life and outside it.

Both syndicalism[2] and guild socialism are fundamentally motivated by interest in the personal freedom and life, the true individuality, of the worker. The evil of society for both is at bottom an ethical evil, and no economic solution can be adequate unless it carries with it an ethical solution, and is indeed determined by the categories of individual freedom and personal worth as supreme for human life. Once more, in syndicalism and guild socialism the source of socialistic aspiration and theory becomes the definite sense of oppression and lack of freedom; the atmosphere of revolutionary discontent is restored; and with the emphasis again on class-consciousness and class-antagonism, in the form of the irreconcilability of the interests of labour and capital, and the conviction that the working-classes must work out their own salvation and be themselves architects of their own future, socialism resumes its character as definitely a movement of emancipation on the part of economically subordinate, and consequently ethically unfree, social classes.

II. *WHAT, THEN, IS SOCIALISM?*—We must now try to gather together the central points revealed in our endeavour to trace and illustrate historically the characteristics of socialistic thought, and this we shall do in the form of a series of propositions stated without criticism or amplification.

1. A feature of modern civilization.—Socialism is a characteristic fact, element, and feature in modern industrial civilization, and is recognizable throughout its history as an attack upon the economic, and, in so far, the ethical, bases of that civilization.

2. A revolt against capitalism.—Socialism is a movement of revolt against capitalistic, competitive, industrial and social organization, and its significant demand is for a new order of society

[1] G. D. H. Cole, in a letter to the present writer.

[1] It should be noted that in the theory of national guilds the philosophy of the State, its meaning and function, is not yet adequately agreed upon.

[2] Syndicalism, which we have treated as a characteristic product of French socialistic thought, has what may be called parallels not only in guild socialism but also in 'industrial unionism,' as promulgated, *e.g.*, by the society known as the 'Industrial Workers of the World' (the 'I.W.W.'), strong in America, Australia, and elsewhere. The common element in all these modern movements of revolt is the predominance of the ethical idea of freedom as corner-stone of doctrine, and the transference in economics of interest from consumption and distribution (the main concerns of collectivism) to production and the democratic control of conditions of production. Their envisagement of the future organization of society depends on the historical and economic national life and development in which they appear.

resting on new economic bases and emphasizing new ethical values. It is a continual criticism of the existing order, from the point of view conditioned by vision of a new order and desire for radical change. Socialism demands the complete reorganization of social and industrial existence, and is, therefore, strictly revolutionary in intention and aim, whether violent in method or not.

3. **A demand for collective ownership.**—Though varying in many details, socialistic theories are united in the conviction that the root of economic evils is to be found in the private and individualistic ownership of those things without which our human ability to labour is unproductive and uncreative, or by which that ability to labour can be utilized more effectively, made more productive, and given greater freedom in creativeness. Socialism seeks the abolition of private possession and individualistic ownership in respect of what may be called fundamentally communal goods—*e.g.*, land and capital, including under the former the material resources of nature, and under the latter all the means and instruments of production by which human labour can be more efficiently applied to those natural resources. Nothing is recognizable as socialism which does not contemplate and strive towards some radical change, not merely in the distribution of wealth, but also in the ownership of wealth and the means to wealth, and consequently some radical change also in the economic fact and the ethical concept and value of 'property' and private possession. Socialistic theories and visions of Utopia show many variations with regard (*a*) to the standards, methods, and manner of distributing created wealth among the working members of society, and (*b*) to the extent and meaning of private ownership, consumption, and enjoyment of the portion of wealth thus acquired by the individual, but all are agreed that private ownership in the definite means of production must cease, and that its place must be taken by communal or collective ownership in some shape or form.

4. **An ideal of a juster order.**—Socialism, in so far as it is a vital movement and is not turned into a merely academic philosophical theory, a political or economic dogma, and not too much entangled in parliamentarism and party politics, is a revolutionary criticism of modern society, an ideal and vision of a possible more just and equitable order of life, and an aspiration towards fuller freedom, all engendered by the division of the social structure into separate classes marked off from each other by economic differentiations. Socialism is the characteristic product of the mind, heart, and will of those social classes distinguished by the fact that they in the end own and possess nothing but ability to work, reacting towards the inevitable conditions of their existence under such a limitation. In other words, socialism, at its deepest and in its most vital elements, is the instinctive reaction of working-class thought and emotion towards an economic environment felt to be ethically evil, restrictive, and oppressive, combined with a steadily growing realization of personal worth and consequent desire for personal freedom and self-expression, to be achieved in an environment of greater economic liberty, more complete equality of opportunity, and wider, more satisfying fellowship.

5. **An ever-changing theory.** — Socialistic theories, political and economic, are formulations of these instinctive reactions. No socialistic theory in all its details is ever to be regarded as final or made into a dogma. Socialistic theory undergoes many changes and exhibits many variations, in accordance partly with general changes in the contemporary intellectual and moral outlook, but more especially in accordance with definite advances in education, culture, opportunity, and the sense of power, among the workers themselves. Socialism itself continues and will continue, finding expression in theory, in visions of Utopia, and in efforts to secure radical change, so long as the division of the social structure into economically differentiated classes remains, and so long as that division, or any similar division, is felt by any straitened and subordinate class to be a restriction on freedom and a curtailment of personality—in other words, so long as economic differentiation is felt to have an evil ethical content and significance.

6. **An ethical criticism of economic system.**—Socialism, although frequently in its theories it has expressed the truth the wrong way round, always contains the conviction that economics, economic systems, and economic theories have ethical significance, ethical meaning and value, and must be judged ultimately by ethical standards. Consequently, always, its economic criticism of society rests and depends upon an ethical criticism, implicit or explicit, and the deepest motive in all socialism is an ethical motive. It may be sympathy with the oppressed, belief in the value of humanity, faith in human nature, the desire for freedom and self-realization, the sense of personality cramped and crushed, the seeking after fellowship, or some similar motive or combination of such motives; but no economic or political theory of socialism, and no action of men under the socialistic impulse, can be rightly judged or appreciated unless it is seen continuously against the background of ethical motive. This is why the economics of socialism has, again and again, received support from quarters where the fundamental, and frequently the only, criticism of modern life has been ethical.[1] The paradoxical truth is this, that the innermost power and quality of all vital and vivid socialism is and always has been something which we can only call 'personalism,' the conviction of supreme ethical values resident in persons, and the certainty that the meaning of life is the realization of these ethical values through and by individual freedom, development, and self-expression. Not any theory of 'the State' or of the 'social organism,' nor any metaphysic of history, nor any economic theory, is the ultimate in socialism, the source of vitality and power, its root and ground in life, but always the conviction of personality, the sense of cramped and fettered existence, nay the very urge of life itself towards personality, freedom, and fellowship; and all this operating mainly, though not exclusively, through particular social classes, created during a particular period of history by arrangements in the social structure largely determined by economic factors. Socialism, as we said at the outset, is a form of the perpetual conflict of in-

[1] This significant truth can be best illustrated by the socialism of a man like William Morris, whose criticism of and revolt against modern society were fundamentally ethical, and whose socialism was born of his experience as craftsman, poet, and artist. In this article we have deliberately refrained from appealing to or noting the tremendous import of socialism of the William Morris type. It must always be remembered that behind and deeper than all political and economic socialism there is somewhere present, giving vitality to the theory, just that criticism of life, that demand for freedom and beauty, that craving for fellowship and joy in creative work, that revolt against sordidness, misery, and ugliness of a cramped existence, which Morris so gloriously and with such magnificent humanity expressed. Morris had the heart of socialism, and no critic has answered him yet. In another direction this bringing of support to economic socialism from a purely ethical criticism of society might be illustrated by the influence on socialistic thought of great individualist ethical thinkers like Tolstoi, Carlyle, and even Nietzsche, and indeed of every philosophy and movement in modern times which has insisted on the significance of life as against mechanism, and on the value of personality.

dividual mind against the tyranny of mechanical existence—a ceaseless criticism carried on by life itself against the outward forms of its manifestation, inspired by vision of new and better forms.

III. *SOCIALISM, ETHICS, AND RELIGION.*—Much energy has been wasted by socialistic writers and even more by critics of socialism in discussion concerning the relations of socialism with, and the effects of socialism upon, morality and religion, with these latter elements ill-defined or not defined at all.

1. Ethical value of socialism.—So far as socialism and ethics are concerned, the underlying purpose of this article has been to reveal the fact that, historically, socialism springs from definitely ethical motives and ethical sentiments, has an ethical value, and must be regarded as a moral force. It is the fact, also, that in all socialistic writings the dominating ethical note is that of altruism, brotherhood, love for one's neighbour, service of the community, sympathy with the oppressed. On the other hand, it is true that socialistic theorists have often seemed to favour unusual, and therefore in the eyes of many people 'immoral,' experiments, arrangements, and possibilities, with regard to certain established institutions of human life—*e.g.*, marriage and the family. It is, however, mere obscurantism to confound socialism with anything and everything that socialistic writers may have chosen to say. The issue is really simple. The motive behind the socialistic demand for a radical change in social organization is ethical. What the effect on 'morality' of such radical change as is desired would be depends on what the ultimate ethical result might be of the abolition of private property in the means of production. In so far as existing customary ethical valuations and ethical relationships depend, as they undoubtedly to a considerable extent do depend, upon the method of ownership and distribution of property and wealth, socialism with its radical change in that direction would inevitably induce many alterations and differences. Other causes—as, *e.g.*, the adoption and putting into practice of a full ethical Christianity—might produce equally noticeable changes and differences in morality. But it is obviously impossible to predict in any detail what such alterations and differences would turn out to be. Socialism is to be judged, not by any imagined consequences that might follow from its actualizing, but by the character of the need and the demand which have called socialistic theory, hope, and vision into existence. If that demand and need are really vital, if they represent and accord with the fundamental, instinctive movement of life itself, consequences must be risked. But it should always be remembered by socialists and their critics that in all probability, despite Marx and the materialistic conception of history, the ethical life of humanity, as the story of socialistic hope and theory itself actually reveals, is a deeper and more fundamental reality than the economic or political form of society, and that this ethical life is continually following its own laws of development under influence of many forces other than the strictly economic or political.

2. Variable ethical results.—Within socialistic theory itself intelligent anticipation of ethical effects and results will vary in accordance with the type of ultimate socialistic organization contemplated. The ethical results, *e.g.*, of a highly-centralized, bureaucratic, State socialism, with primary emphasis on the concepts of society, efficient order, the good of the community, the authority of the whole body, and so forth, will not be the same as the ethical results of a socialism tending towards distribution of sovereignty, decentralization, group-organization, and determination of forms of fellowship and co-operation from the effective will of the individual working outwards to wider association in conformity with purposes initiated and approved by the individual will. It is along the lines of these quite characteristic and indeed ultimate differences regarding the final form of socialistic organization that the question of the effects of socialism on morality should be discussed, allowing always, in all cases, for the extreme difficulty of prediction, and the independent movement of the ethical life in humanity itself.

3. Ethical determinism.—The tendency of much socialistic thinking and theorizing to support, often with startling inconsistencies, ethical determinism and to place exaggerated insistence on the importance of environment,[1] should be noted. Much socialism, as a result of this tendency, has, by an almost perverse devotion to abstract and now largely discredited deterministic theory, both obscured the genuinely ethical character of its origin and aim and given its opponents a ground of criticism which has served only to confuse and complicate the real issues of socialistic thought and aspiration. For this singular and, as we hold, altogether unfortunate obsession by ethical determinism there is a historical reason, which explains not only this but other curiosities of socialism as well.

4. Socialism and religion.—This reason becomes more obvious and pertinent when we consider the relations of socialism with religion. During its history socialism has been marked by very varying relations to religion and Christianity, whether as individual profession or as organized institution. The majority of professing socialists to-day would probably assert that religion is an individual and private affair outside the purview of socialistic theory; they would oppose any State organization of religion, State maintenance, or provision for religious teaching by the community, and they would contemplate religious organizations only on a purely voluntary basis, and altogether without temporal authority; it is doubtful whether many would trouble to identify their socialism with a denial of the religious hypothesis, whilst some certainly would individually accept that hypothesis. Many of the earlier Utopian socialists rested their socialism on belief in God, and strove to identify socialistic theory with Christian ethic and the gospel of Jesus. Similar efforts have been frequently made, whilst from the side of accepted religion and Christianity attempts in the same direction have been not uncommon, though, with few exceptions, what is called 'Christian socialism' has been content with criticism of conditions and advocacy of reform, or the infusing of the Christian spirit into existing institutions, stopping short of the full socialistic demand.[2]

Socialism and Christian ethic, or the gospel of Jesus, are not essentially related, either historically

[1] Robert Owen expounded and adhered to an almost naive form of materialistic determinism in ethics. Consciousness, for him, is a product merely of material organization and determined wholly by external stimulation, whilst the notion that the individual is in any way responsible for his character he regarded as vicious error. It is of course difficult to reconcile this with Owen's distrust of government, on the one hand, and his belief in education, on the other. The sources of his materialism are to be found in certain well-known aspects of 18th cent. rationalism. In later socialistic thought materialism has other origins. It is often as naive and extreme, but differently based.

[2] The socialism of Maurice and Kingsley was of the reformative type. The advanced Roman Catholic understanding of Christian ethic tends in the direction of a social organization containing socialistic elements, though officially Catholicism is mortally opposed to socialism. The only definitely Christian organization which to-day seems to advocate a full and strictly revolutionary socialism is the Church Socialist League. A desire for 'social reform' is not socialism.

or intellectually. The existence of the gospel and the Christian ethic has, no doubt, directly and indirectly, influenced and contributed to the existence of socialism, and some interpretations of Christian ethic might, and indeed would, lead to conclusions very closely similar to socialistic theory and demand; but many of the premisses and the line of argument would be different. Christianity, in its ethic, contains a social philosophy which can be and ought to be worked out independently of historical socialism. One of the mistakes of professing Christians with socialistic sympathies has been a too great readiness merely to accept a formed socialism and try by various devices to fit it into their Christian ethic or their ethic into it, whereas they should have been occupied in developing independently the social implications of their faith and gospel and in working its ethical principles out into detailed application.

5. Socialistic faith.—But modern socialism, as most widely accepted and existing as a political force and organized power, has been, especially on the Continent, almost uniformly hostile to organized Christianity, partly through theoretical antipathy to the religious hypothesis in general, but more significantly because, in practical matters, it has been thought, and not unjustifiably, by upholders of socialism that organized Christianity, in modern times at any rate, has little to its credit in the way of sympathy for the struggle of the non-possessing against the possessing classes, and much to its discredit as being a habitual supporter of the established social order and a bulwark of the existing state of things.

The theoretical antipathy of socialistic thought to the religious hypothesis in general is important. Admittedly, such antipathy has been widely prevalent in socialistic writing and thinking, especially since the time of Marx. One reason for this antipathy is obvious: socialism is primarily and indeed absolutely concerned, in all its forms, with the destiny of mankind on this earth and within the sphere of historical time. It contemplates an order of society realizable by men in earthly conditions, and to be entered upon at a date not impossibly distant by generations which will reap the fruit of present sowing. From this point of view, socialism is clearly committed to a high and indeed extreme form of ethical altruism, since any labour for socialism undertaken by an individual must be undertaken without expectation of individual reward and for the sake only of some future hour of realization in which he cannot hope to share. Thus, paradoxically and unwittingly, socialists have frequently demanded and lived by a faith (in the historical future of mankind) more difficult than most accepted religious faiths; but this exclusive interest in historical time has induced a certain blindness among socialists to some valuable aspects in the characteristic religious concepts of eternal life, the future of the soul, and man's spiritual and otherworldly destiny, whilst the feeling that interest in personal immortality and a life beyond this life may become a preoccupation leading either to disregard of this life's problems or to contentment with 'things as they are' has caused socialists again and again to turn altogether away from these necessities of religion.

6. Marxian materialism.—But there is a deeper and more subtle reason for the antipathy of much socialism to the religious hypothesis. This reason is to be found mainly in the teaching of Marx. The materialistic conception of history is obviously hostile to all theories of a spiritual origin and destiny for man and the universe, and Marx accepted the extreme materialism of the Hegelian Left with its denial of all independent spiritual values and reduction of religion to a man-made illusion. When, as was frequently the case, this Marxian materialism became confused with scientific materialism and determinism, having in reality a quite different origin, the antipathy to religion was only strengthened. But the story of this antipathy does not end there. Far more potent than the materialistic conception of history was the conviction of Marx and Engels that they had made socialism 'scientific.' In that fact lies the final secret of all the antipathy to religion and all the ethical determinism which is to be found in socialistic thought. It was and has been repeatedly assumed that between socialism and 'science' there is intimate connexion, and this assumption has been interpreted to mean that socialism must accept without question all that 'science' may say. If 'science,' therefore, declares for a materialistic hypothesis of life and the universe, socialism must follow suit; if 'science' stands for moral determinism, socialism must accept that view too, and so on all through; only very slowly has socialism begun to emancipate itself from subservience to 'science,' and to realize that between the fundamental socialistic hypothesis and demand and the utterances of 'science,' so often science overstepping its proper limits, there is no necessary connexion. The process of emancipation has been aided by the deeper understanding of its place and function which modern science has achieved for itself, and by the realization within the region of socialistic thought that in any case socialism, in one necessary aspect, is an ideal, a vision, and a hope, and so demands for its acceptance and service a measure of 'faith,' and that determinism and materialism are not the best ground on which to nourish an ideal and faith in that ideal. The most recent movements in socialistic thought show the change clearly. They, although systematic, display little respect for the earlier devotion to so-called 'scientific' argument and talk of the 'necessary truth' of socialism, and so forth, but reveal instead a new intensity of feeling, a belief in human freedom, and a dominating appeal to the power in man of creating ideals and of living and working for them in pure faith, and with an enthusiasm which, it is now recognized, a cold scientific materialism and determinism inevitably destroy.

7. Conclusion.—Socialism is one of the significant movements of modern life, naturally affected by all the varying currents of thought and feeling which go to the making of that complex modern life; and the question of the relations of religion or Christianity, and of ethics, to socialism is really part of the wider question of the relations of these things to modern existence and thought generally, and their place therein. From all such questions the fundamental issues of socialism can be, and for purposes of true appreciation should be, separated, and taken in and for themselves. Then socialism appears, as we have already defined it, as a movement, vision, hope, theory, and ideal, generated by modern conditions, motived in the deepest intent and meaning of it by ethical impulse and inspiration, and issuing in a characteristic demand for the economic reconstruction of society along well-defined lines, and in the anticipation of an earthly order of existence, based on new economic and industrial arrangements, inspired by new motives and purposes, and intended to provide a fuller and richer opportunity for the development of individual freedom, powers and qualities of personality, in a life of more intense, real, and satisfying fellowship than, thus far, the world has seen. The vital points are two: (1) understanding of the fundamental economic demand and effort involved in all socialism, viz. the abolition of private possession in the means of production, and (2) understanding of the ethical ground, need, and desire out of which that demand issues. Everything else in socialism, both in the setting forth and in the criticism of it, is subsidiary, and often merely incidental and largely irrelevant, to these two considerations.

LITERATURE.—The literature of socialism in its various phases is vast and extraordinarily dispersed. Much of the best work has taken the form of tracts and pamphlets. It has been possible only to select a very few books, more as being suggestive than as really covering the field.

i. *Historical.*—**Thomas Kirkup**, *A Hist. of Socialism*[4], London, 1909; **Karl Diehl**, *Über Sozialismus, Kommunismus und Anarchismus*[2], Jena, 1911; **Max Beer**, *Die Gesch. des Sozialismus in England*, Stuttgart, 1911, *A Hist. of British Socialism*, London, 1919; **Werner Sombart**, *Socialism and the Social Movement*, Eng. tr. from 6th German ed. by M. Epstein, do. 1909; **J. T. Stoddart**, *The New Socialism*, do. 1909 (with good bibliography); **A. V. Woodworth**, *Christian Socialism in England*, do. 1903; **Morris Hillquit**, *Hist. of Socialism in the United States*[5], New York, 1910; **Sidney and Beatrice Webb**, *Industrial Democracy*, new ed., London, 1902, *The Hist. of Trade Unionism*, new ed., do. 1920.

ii. *Theoretical.*—**F. Engels**, *Socialism, Utopian and Scientific*, tr. E. Aveling (Social Science Series), London, 1892; **Jean Jaurès**, *Etudes socialistes*, Paris, 1902; **E. Vandervelde**, *Essais socialistes*, do. 1905; **E. Bernstein**, *Die Voraussetzungen des Sozialismus und die Aufgaben der Sozialdemokratie*, Stuttgart, 1906; **J. R. MacDonald**, *Socialism and Society*, London, 1905, *The Socialist Movement*, do. 1911; **A. Schäffle**, *The Quintessence of Socialism*[9], tr. B. Bosanquet, do. 1906; **L. B. Boudin**, *The Theoretical System of Karl Marx*, New York, 1911; *Fabian Essays in Socialism*, ed. G. Bernard Shaw, London, 1889; **K. Kautsky**, *Karl Marx' ökonomische Lehren*[8], Stuttgart, 1903.

iii. *Special.*—*Syndicalisme et socialisme* (essays by various authors), ed. J. Lagardelle, Paris, 1908; **A. D. Lewis**, *Syndicalism and the General Strike*, London, 1912; **A. R. Orage**, *National Guilds*, London, 1914; **G. D. H. Cole**, *The World of Labour*, do. 1915 (good bibliography), *Self-government in Industry*, do. 1917; **G. D. H. Cole and W. Mellor**, *The Meaning of Industrial Freedom*, do. 1918.

iv. *Critical.*—**A. Schäffle**, *The Impossibility of Social Democracy*, Eng. tr. (Social Science Series), London, 1892 (pt. ii. of *Quintessence of Socialism* by the same writer); **Robert Flint**, *Socialism*[2], do. 1914 (good references to literature of socialism); **W. H. Mallock**, *A Critical Examination of Socialism*, do. 1908.

STANLEY A. MELLOR.

SOCIETAS PERFECTA.—A *societas perfecta* is a society that contains within itself all means sufficient for its support. The use of the term is derived from Aristotle, and came to mean in the Middle Ages no more than a sovereign and independent community. The term became important in the later Middle Ages, on all topics connected with the relations of Church and State. From Aristotle through St. Thomas Aquinas it filtered into Roman Catholic political theory. In the discussions that arose in consequence of the great schism at the end of the 14th cent. we find it argued that it must be possible for the Council to depose a pope, otherwise the Church would not be a perfect society, *i.e.*, if it could not get rid of an impossible ruler, or had no organ to do so. The point is that a perfect society must have within itself all sufficient means to exercise its own functions and needs no extraneous help. Therefore it must provide implicitly or explicitly for every emergency. In the period succeeding the Reformation the term became more common in regard to the relations between Church and State. We find the argument used on behalf of whichever of the two powers is at the moment depressed. Church controversialists like Bellarmine claimed all kinds of rights for the Church on the ground that it is a perfect society. When these were extended by the papalist party in such a way as practically to deny the independent existence of the State, the secular writers used the argument on their side. John Barclay,[1] *e.g.*, frequently uses this argument—the State is a perfect society no less than the Church. At that date no Roman Catholic thought of denying that the Church was a perfect society; therefore the State had within itself all powers and did not require ecclesiastical sanction or approval; therefore the deposing power claimed for the pope is iniquitous, and so forth. It was the recognition of something like this position for the State that caused the development of the doctrine of the indirect temporal power of the papacy. In theory this doctrine is very different from that of the direct power. The doctrine of the direct power of the papacy is expressed, *e.g.*, in the *Unam Sanctam* of Boniface VIII., or in the writings of Augustinus Triumphus or Bozius, who asserts that the State is a part of the Church, and that kings are servants of the papacy. The doctrine of the indirect power proclaimed by Bellarmine and Suarez allows the State an independent existence as being in some sort a perfect society, but claims an indirect power for the Church in cases in which its own interests might be concerned. The former doctrine has relation to the mediæval notion of the whole commonwealth as one society with its two departments, temporal and spiritual. The other looks forward to the modern doctrine of Church and State as two separate societies. In the 19th cent. the extreme claim of the civil power, especially in France after the Restoration, led to the development of modern ultramontanism (*q.v.*), and it was necessary to maintain the independence and inherent reality of the Church as a society. For this purpose there was the doctrine of the *societas perfecta* to hand. It was developed with great elaboration by two Jesuit writers, Tarquini and Palmieri. Later we find the official recognition of the doctrine in the encyclical of Pope Leo XIII., *Immortale Dei* (1885). Therein it is stated that the Church no less than the State is a *societas genere et jure perfecta*. The admission in regard to the State shows how different is the condition from that contemplated by Boniface VIII. The following passage from a 16th cent. papalist Simanca illustrates the way in which the doctrine was employed in controversy:

> 'Cum respublica spiritualis perfecta sit et sibi sufficiens, ut se ipsam indemnem servet, potest ea omnia facere, quae necessaria fuerint ad suum finem consequendum exercendo etiam jurisdictionem in eos qui in rebus temporalibus alioqui sibi subjecti non essent, quod quidem naturali jure cuicumque Principi facere contra aliorum rempublicam licet.'[1]

LITERATURE.—**Aristotle**, *Politics*, I. ii. 8; **Aquinas**, *Summa*, I. ii. qu. xc. art. 3, shows how the theory comes out of St. Thomas. Much use is made of doctrines of *societas perfecta* by **Suarez**, *Tractatus de Legibus ac Deo Legislatore*, Antwerp, 1613, iii.; see also **C. Tarquini**, *Juris Ecclesiastici Publici Institutiones*[3], Rome, 1875; **D. Palmieri**, *Tractatus de Romano Pontifice*[4], Prato, 1902. Discussion of the conception is found *passim* in **A. Robertson**, *Regnum Dei* [*BL*], London, 1901; and in **J. N. Figgis**, *Studies of Political Thought from Gerson to Grotius*, do. 1916, pp. 208 ff. and 264 (12).

J. N. FIGGIS.

SOCIETY ISLANDS.—See POLYNESIA.

SOCIETY OF JESUS.—See JESUITS.

SOCINIANISM.—Socinianism is the term applied to a critical and reconstructive theological movement of the post-Reformation decades, with consequent ideals of faith and morals. It was named after its master spirit, Fausto Paolo Sozzini (latinized into Socinus), a man of commanding intellect, supreme organizing ability, and unfaltering will. He led and inspired a succession of able expositors who developed and articulated his tenets. Among these the names of Völkel (his amanuensis), Schmalz, Moscorovius, and Ostorodt, who were his contemporaries, followed in later years by Johann Crell, a most prolific writer, Schlichting, Ludwig von Wolzogen, and Andrew Wiszowaty (grandson

[1] *Pietas, sive . . . pro regibus ac principibus . . . vindiciæ*, Paris, 1612.

[1] *De Papa*, printed in J. T. Rocaberti, *Bibliotheca maxima Pontificalia*, Rome, 1695–99, xiii. 277.

of Socinus), deserve a place in the record. The most important of the Socinian writings were gathered together in the *Bibliotheca Fratrum Polonorum*, edited by Wiszowaty, the first two volumes of which contain the treatises of Socinus. In the *Racovian Catechism*, issued first in Polish in 1605, the year after the death of Socinus, at Rakow in Poland, where the Socinians had a strong church and a noted college, there is to be found the most compact and clearly developed scheme of the doctrines. It is a marvel of clear, orderly, and definite statement in a time of intellectual confusion and doctrinal debate. Socinianism was an intellectual and rationalist system of Christian doctrine on a supernatural basis. It was a species of Unitarianism. The name Unitarian came into general currency through the admission on the title-page of the *Bibliotheca Fratrum Polonorum*—'quos Unitarios vocant.' It asserted the necessity and the fact of a divine revelation, maintained that the Scriptures are its authoritative record, and declared that the reason—the moral and religious nature—is the sole and final arbiter of truth. But in the beginning it was rather anti-Trinitarian than entirely sympathetic with the opinions of the Unitarian teachers of its day. Harnack, in his *History of Dogma*, ranks it, along with Tridentine Catholicism and Protestantism, as one of the three final stages of dogma. That may seem to be an exaggeration of its importance. But, when we look broadly at the historic developments of Christian doctrine, and remember how many schools of Christian thought are sympathetic with the conclusions of Socinianism, Harnack's classification is justified. The teaching of Socinus and his followers was a distinct variant from both the Roman and the Reformed doctrines, and churches of that variant remain to this day.

1. Historical setting.—The historical setting of Socinianism is of the first consequence. In every European country which was quickened by the religious and theological ferment of the Reformation a new sense of individuality, a clear realization of the discrepancy between the dogmas of the Church and the Christian experience of the times, combined with an intense moral passion, issued in a contempt for all stereotyped forms of doctrine. There was a wide-spread outbreak of independent and adventurous thought and speculation. Its expression and advocacy depended, in great measure, on the attitude of the civil rulers. Where the authorities were sympathetic, or where any measure of religious liberty prevailed, the truths which had laid hold on men's minds were publicly proclaimed, openly debated, and, when accepted, rigorously enforced upon the community. For this reason Switzerland, Transylvania, and the then large and powerful country of Poland became the haunts and sheltering homes of refugees from intolerant and persecuting lands. In Italy, under the rule of the papacy, with the merciless eye of the Inquisition watching every heretic, the expression of conviction was perilous to both life and fortune. But in Italy, as elsewhere, there were men for whom religious liberty was the breath of life. Foremost among these was the patrician family of the Sozini (as they spelled their name). They had been distinguished as jurists and canonists for several generations. They were as notable for nobility of character as for intellectual energy and dialectical skill.

Lelio Francesco Maria Sozini (1525–62), a jurist whose legal studies had led him on to researches in Hebrew and Biblical literature, broke openly with what he called 'the idolatry of Rome.' He sought the larger liberty to be found only beyond the borders of Italy. He visited all the Reformation lands and won the respect of all its leaders by his wide knowledge and sincere piety, while he gained their friendship by his personal charm. He lived at Wittenberg for a time on intimate terms with Melanchthon. He made the acquaintance at Geneva of Calvin, whom, however, he 'shocked' by the audacity of his speculations. His eager and subtle mind canvassed all the doctrinal problems of the day, reaching at last, through the confession and fate of Servetus, the central doctrine of the Trinity. Returning from his travels to Zürich, he spent three quiet years there, when his brief career was closed by his early death in 1562.

Lelio Sozini is of interest chiefly because of his influence upon his nephew, Fausto Paolo Sozzini. Lelio was the father of the doctrine, but Fausto was the moulder of the theology and the founder of the Church. To his nephew Lelio bequeathed all his property. His most precious legacy was a number of MSS and exegetical notes. His nephew acknowledged his indebtedness in generous terms. He declared that his conversations with his uncle imbued his young mind with a moral passion for the things of salvation and with a true conception of its method. He confessed that he learned from him a fair interpretation of Scripture, and he makes the express statement that Lelio's exegesis of 'Ἐν ἀρχῇ in Jn 1[1] as 'In the beginning—*of the gospel*' was the fruitful hint for a method of a new Christology.

Fausto Sozzini was born in Siena in 1539. There he spent his youth and received his education. On coming of age, he left Italy, living first at Lyons and then at Geneva, where he was enrolled as a member of the Italian congregation. In 1565 he returned to Italy, conformed to the Roman Catholic Church, and, after the custom of the time, entered the service of Isabella de Medici in Florence, who bestowed upon him both office and honour. He always referred to these twelve years as the wasted period of his life. Yet his mind had not been dormant, although he made no open sign. It is now known that the fear of losing his patrimony kept him silent. After Isabella's death he left Italy and settled in Basel to give himself entirely to the study of the Bible. There he became a centre of theological inquiry and discussion. The first outcome was seen in his treatise *de Jesu Christo Servatore*, a polemic against the evangelical teaching of the Reformers. It was written anonymously and privately circulated. A copy reached the hands of Blandrata, who was court physician in Poland, with an ambition to regulate the religious life of the people. Italians had always been welcome in Poland, where their genius in both literature and art had been admired. The religious tolerance of the rulers had made Poland a land of desire. When Blandrata sent for Socinus, he eagerly accepted the invitation, and his theological learning and deftness in practical affairs found their fitting sphere. Despite his alien birth and his hampering deafness, he so busied himself with his pen, and in debate in conferences, that he impressed himself and his convictions on the religious thought of the people. The Unitarian doctrines held the minds of the ruling classes. Socinus won them to his protest against the doctrine of the pre-existence of Jesus, and, on the other hand, overcame their objection to invoking Christ's help in prayer. The Unitarians became *invocantes—non adorantes*. The Anabaptists, with their urgent and enthusiastic zeal for individualism in religion and their imperative demand for re-baptism, had enlisted the sympathy of the masses. He purged the Anabaptists from their unreasonableness in doctrine and their excesses in morals. His writings were published pseudonymously. But, when he found himself settled in Poland, married into one of its families, and cut off from his patrimony in Italy, he acknowledged their authorship. This issued in a revolt of the masses against him, and in 1598 he was expelled from Cracow. He found shelter with friends, but the intense toil and strain of his life had prematurely aged him, and he died on 4th March 1604. It is open to question whether or not the Minor Church, as it was called, with its clear-cut and subtly argued scheme of doctrine from the hand of Socinus, might not have become supreme in Poland. But the authorities at length took up a position of keen antagonism, which issued in active persecution. Its teachers and people were scattered throughout Western Europe, finding shelter in Holland and in England, and giving birth to schools of Unitarian theology. It is only among these Unitarian communities that the modified tenets of Socinus and of his earlier followers are to be found openly avowed, but the influence of his teaching is more pervasive than is commonly realized.

2. Outline of doctrines.—The doctrines of Socinianism, because wrought out into a well-knit scheme, can be given an orderly statement. The point of view from which they should be approached is that of a theory of salvation. In this Socinus had caught the spirit of his age. That was the subject of his first treatise written in Basel. The focus of its critical attack was the orthodox doctrine of the Atonement, and to this day all churches and schools who look back to Socinus level their lance at the evangelical interpretation of the death of Christ. The most strenuous pages of the *Bibliotheca* and the most pungent sentences of the *Racovian Catechism* deal with the meaning of the sacrifice on the Cross. To stand with Socinus at his conception of the death and resurrection of Jesus as a centre enables us to sweep round the whole circle of his system.

(*a*) *The basis.*—The first feature which emerges is its basis in the Scriptures. The NT, whose authenticity, sufficiency, and perspicuity are postulated rather than argued, is the text-book. Its rational and balanced exegesis will yield proofs of its authority as a divine revelation. The witness of tradition, the declaration of creeds, and the authority of the Church are summarily set aside. All that is required is the use of 'right reason' to discover, understand, and apply the things which belong to the faith and its salvation. The OT has no authority in itself. It has a certain value for its illustrative and devotional features. But it is entirely dependent for its authentication and interpretation upon the NT Scriptures. One of the by-products of the teaching of Socinus was his method of a balanced and scholarly exegesis, and the ban which he placed on dogmatic interpretations was a service of exceeding value to Christian scholarship.

(*b*) *The doctrine of God.*—On this basis there was raised the superstructure, and its first article, in order, is concerned with the doctrine of God. Here Socinus was influenced and even controlled by his Scotist conception of the divine nature. Philosophically Socinianism was a throwback to the Scotist demand for concrete and evidenced reality, and a protest against a metaphysic which would not yield itself to almost entirely natural categories. As a consequence, the conception of God in the mind of Socinus was somewhat external, and His attributes are those which are essential to His being, rather than inherent in His character. Socinus, therefore, defined God after His nature and His will. In His nature God is 'the supreme Lord of all.' Omnipotence is not His only attribute, but it rules every other. God is an *absolutum Dominium.* There can be no question raised against God, who, however, will do no evil. Still more, as the finite cannot be a measure for the infinite, all human conceptions of the nature of God must be considered as inadequate grounds on which to base a critical or condemning judgment. It follows that God's will is an *arbitrium imperium,* a will entirely free, bound by no law that the human mind can formulate, and able to will God's pleasure, in obedience to His purposes, in ways hidden from the human mind.

'God's dominion comprises a right and supreme authority to determine whatsoever He may choose (and He cannot choose what is in its own nature evil and unjust) in respect to us and to all other things, and also in respect to those matters which no other authority can reach; such as are our thoughts though concealed in the inmost recesses of our hearts—for which He can, at pleasure, ordain laws, and appoint rewards and punishments.'[1]

Thus God is simply the great omnipotent free will, the supreme individual personality, over against whom man is also an individual personality as free in will but impotent in fact. It at once appears evident that such doctrines as predestination, original sin, the necessity of imposing a penalty or of adhering to any doctrine of forgiveness in relation to law, are swept away. God stands above all compulsion, over against man, who also is endowed with a free will to obey or to disobey. From this position it is an inevitable step to the unity of God. God is the absolute arbitrary One. 'There cannot be more beings than one who possess supreme dominion over all things.' To speak of three persons, by which Socinus always means three individuals, is to speak irrationally. Yet the Socinian doctrine was careful to utter a caveat and to suggest a limitation, with a view to giving room for its Christology. As against the personality of the Holy Spirit, there is no hesitation. The Holy Spirit is only an energy. But God may delegate His power or may share it, as He has done pre-eminently in one instance. Yet He remains single, alone, supreme, so that the Socinian argument is always unfalteringly anti-Trinitarian.

(*c*) *Doctrine of Christ.* — The Christology of Socinus is set out in regard to Christ's person or 'nature,' and His work or 'offices.' Jesus was truly a mortal man while He lived on earth, but at the same time the only-begotten Son of God, being conceived of the Holy Spirit and born of a virgin. He was separated from all other men, distinguished by the perfect holiness of His life, endued with divine wisdom and power, and was sent by the Father with supreme authority on an embassy to mankind. By His resurrection He was begotten a second time and became, like God, immortal. He was therefore glorified by God, that He might be made the chief director of our religion and salvation—in which office are comprised His supreme authority and dominion. These positions are supported by a comprehensive citation, with a confident exegesis of the relevant passages and types and symbols in the Scriptures. The strenuous and subtle argument, with its occasional violence of denial, indicates the strain clearly felt in dealing with the words of Christ and the witness of the Epistles, as these are accepted by the Church Catholic. A similar pathetic note can be heard in the protests of Martineau under the stress of the same exegetical contest. The 'offices' of Christ are three — the prophet, the high-priest, and the king. But the offices of the high-priest and the king are dismissed briefly, and the whole stress is laid upon His prophetic ministry. Jesus is our high-priest, not because of His sacrifice at Calvary, but because of His mediation and intercession after His resurrection to heaven. Jesus is the king because God has 'placed Him at His right hand and given Him all power in heaven and on earth, that He might at His own pleasure govern, protect, and eternally save those who believed in Him.' In His prophetic office Jesus has manifested and confirmed the knowledge of the hidden will of God, and His work was consummated in the new covenant, as it is found in He 8[6] and 1 Ti 2[5]. In that covenant, interpreted by Jesus, are stored the perfect pre-

[1] *Rac. Cat.*, § 3.

cepts and perfect promises of God, with the modes and grounds of our obedience to them. The precepts are both moral and ceremonial. Some of them were additions by Jesus. Others were interpretations, and a quickening of the inwardness of OT laws. The ceremonial ordinances are baptism by immersion, simply as a rite of initiation, although Socinus himself remained indifferent to the use of this sacrament, and the Lord's Supper, which is nothing more than a feast of remembrance. Through these observances the Christian believer lays hold on eternal life and receives the gift of the Holy Ghost. But Christ's prophetic office fulfilled its supreme function in His confirmation of the divine will by His perfect innocence, His miracles, and His death. With the meaning and efficacy of Christ's death Socinus wrestled in the fullness of his strength. The one thing of which he is sure is that Christ's death is not an atoning sacrifice. Christ indeed suffered for sin rather than for sinners. He was a victim of sin, a witness to its guilt, a deliverer from its power, and, therefore, He willingly 'underwent a bloody death as an expiatory sacrifice.' Because of this willing submission to the rage and fury of sin, men have a right to the remission of sins, and a new hope in God. They are drawn to Christ as their Saviour and see Him to be God's witness to His own boundless love to the human race, and are therefore led into reconciliation with Him. Every other view is rigorously analyzed. The doctrine of satisfaction, which the Reformers urged, is keenly canvassed and its difficulties are set out in an animated dialectic. The conclusion reached is that God, whose will could have chosen any mode of forgiveness which is not foreign to His nature, chose to make acceptance (*acceptatio*) of Christ's death at Calvary, but especially of its offering in heaven, the ground of forgiveness. The forgiveness of God is, therefore, not *propter Christum* and not even *per Christum*, but *gratuito*, because God was willing to accept this sacrifice. Its power consists in its revelation of the will of God and its consequent moral influence on the heart of man.

(*d*) *Doctrine of faith.*—This theory of salvation is matched by a corresponding doctrine of faith. Faith is an attitude of attention to the promises and an obedience to the precepts of God. It may be of two kinds. 'A bare assent alone of the mind whereby we acknowledge the doctrine of Jesus Christ to be true' is not attended by salvation. The faith required is that 'we trust in God through Christ, and give ourselves up wholly to obey His will.' In spite of the wide gulf between these limiting definitions and the breadth and depth of the Pauline conception, Socinus felt himself compelled to relate his conclusion to the Pauline doctrine of justification. But his reference is slight, and his logic renders his use of Paul's master word unreal, if not unmeaning. The whole system is completed by an ethical demand of high seriousness and even of austerity, although it lacks the glow and colour of an obedience which is the outflow of the adoring gratitude of the redeemed.

3. Critical estimate.—When we turn to a critical examination of the doctrines of Socinianism, we find that the contest ranges along the whole front. Socinianism has been condemned both by the judgment of history and by the witness of almost universal Christian experience. The Roman Church, with its adherence both to the method and to the content of the early creeds, and through its passionate loyalty to Augustinian doctrine, dismisses the teaching of Socinus with an unflinching denial. But it troubled the Reformed theologians of the 17th cent. and invaded all their communions, so that they grappled with it as the subtlest and strongest enemy of evangelical truth. The Christian thought of to-day no longer fears its assault, for it has discarded, once for all, the Socinian method of approaching Christian doctrine, but it maintains and must maintain its protest against its chief conclusions.

The first broad remark to make is that Socinianism was a school rather than a Church. Its congregations were associations for Christian learning rather than communions for Christian worship and service. This is confessed in the opening sentence of the *Racovian Catechism*:

> 'The Christian religion is the way of attaining eternal life which God has pointed out by Jesus Christ and it may be learned in the Holy Scriptures, especially in the New Testament.'

But the Mediæval Church and the Reformers held that the Church was a religious fellowship, a society of divine origin, founded by Christ through His atoning work for men. Within its communion and by its offices sinful men found the way to God. The Church was more important than, and prior to, the individual believer. To the Church God fulfilled more abundantly His promise of the Holy Spirit. Through its message men were called of God, and by its sacraments were sealed to His service and to communion with Him and their fellow-men. Had Socinus and his followers ever entered into this truth, they would have realized how insufficient was the basis, and how external was the structure, of their scheme of doctrine.

The view that Scripture is merely a source of information about doctrines and precepts is a shrunken conception of what both the OT and the NT have been to the Christian mind and conscience. Scripture is a means of grace, a channel through which the message of God passes to the soul of man, a meeting-ground where God and man stand, spirit in touch with spirit. Scripture has a divine power to enlighten, to quicken, to rebuke, to comfort, to give peace. The Reformation doctrine of the witness of the Spirit to the word, which is affirmed not only by Scripture itself but also by universal experience, was never upon the horizon of the Socinians, and that casts a blight upon much of the skilful exegesis of their scholars and commentators. In the same way in their doctrine of God they never rise to the height of the thought that He is the God and Father of the Lord Jesus Christ, and is so regarded, so known, and so confessed through the power of the Holy Spirit. He is not even a moral Ruler of a moral universe with laws unalterably righteous, to which He has set His seal. He is simply an 'All Highest,' for whom creation and providence and, finally, the redemption of men are simply acts of His mere pleasure, the exercise of His will. He is never a holy love, with a necessity to create and redeem, because of a self-sacrificing passion for men and a desire for their fellowship and service.

When we realize the insufficiency of the Socinian doctrine of God, we understand the reason for the limited and depreciatory doctrine of Christ's person and work. Jesus was not the Word made flesh. He was the man whose life in the flesh achieved victory over sin for Himself, whose resurrection, not by His own power but by the will and power of God, made that victory a means of salvation to men. We realize in a moment with what tremendous energy the Reformers did battle with this, as they deemed it, dishonouring conception of the incarnate and redeeming Christ. They pointed out not only that the ecstatic sentences of the NT were inconsistent with these formal statements of Socinian theology, but also that this conception was a throwback to the discredited Pelagianism of the past. They remarked upon the fact that no self-forgetting consecration and no impassioned devotion were to be found in the hymns and prayers of the still life within the Socinian churches. The truth was clear that the Socinians had no sufficient doctrine of sin. It was neither a transgression of a holy and indefeasible law nor a state of enmity to God. It was the offence of an individual man against an individual God, a private injury which God might pass by on any conditions that He might choose to impose. As a consequence the Atonement is really superfluous. All that can be said is that God has chosen to accept it in the exercise of His will as an offering through which He will be reconciled. The motive of the love of God as the source and spring of the Atonement, the fact of the divine reaction against sin, the solemn truth that a holy law cannot be broken without the breach of much else, and the necessity of a reason in righteousness for Christ's death for sinners, all lie outside the narrow path of Socinian theology. The issue of all this is that both faith and obedience, both the relationship to God and its ethical issues, are bleached of their colour. It is not accurate to say that the Socinian conception of faith is only *assensus*. That is denied, with good reason. But it is fair to say that faith never became a full-orbed and adoring *fiducia*. It never attained to a simple, unquestioning confidence in God and in His grace revealed and made potent in Christ. It never reached to that vision of His love, that venture upon His mercy, and that victory over the world which constitute the secret of the Lord. It never evoked that love which casts out fear. The final issue is seen in the fact that the ethics of the Socinian churches in all time never rise to that abandonment of joy, that quenchless zeal for Christ and His kingdom, and that glow of devotion which make up the atmosphere of believing churches and believing men. The Socinian ethics lacks the dynamic of a faith in the love of a divine Redeemer who gave Himself for men. It is unlikely that Christian theology will ever hark back to the way of the Socinian. It will never build either with his intellectual method or upon his narrow and scholastic bases. But there is a possibility that, through the application of similar methods to the self-consciousness of Christ, there may be a reaction to anti-Trinitarianism, and from that men may stand again with the Socinian to utter their denial of the deity of Jesus and all that that implies.

LITERATURE.—The reasoned apologetic of Socinianism is to be found in the *Bibliotheca Fratrum Polonorum*, Amsterdam, 1656. Vols. i. and ii. contain the letters of Socinus as well as his chief controversial works. Of these his treatise *de Auctoritate Sanctæ Scripturæ*, Rakow, 1570, which is said to be his earliest writing, and his *de Jesu Christo Servatore*, Basel, 1594, state and defend the basis of his system, and the stress-point of his thinking. In the latter it is the work, and not the person, of Christ that is expounded and argued. The simplest and clearest statement is to be found in the *Racovian Catechism* issued in Polish in 1605, published in Latin in 1609, and translated into English by John Biddle in 1652. It was afterwards revised and enlarged and reached its final form in 1680. From this ed. Thomas Rees published his Eng. tr., with a sympathetic historical introd., in 1818. A. Harnack, *Hist. of Dogma*, Eng. tr., London, 1894–99 (vols. v.–vii.), gives a full account of the historic development and theological trend of the system. Albrecht Ritschl, *Critical Hist. of the Christian Doctrine of Justification and Reconciliation*, Eng. tr., Edinburgh, 1872, deals critically with its chief features; T. M. Lindsay, *Hist. of the Reformation*, Edinburgh, 1906–07, ii., shows its historic setting and relationship to the Reformation. The standard German work is that of O. Fock, *Der Socinianismus*, Kiel, 1847. The biographies of Socinus are of especial value. The earliest (1636) by S. Przypkowski is prefixed to his works. In 1653 it was rendered into English by John Biddle (1615–62), who has been called, significantly, 'the father of English Unitarianism,' whose sufferings in an intolerant age indicate the antipathies aroused by Socinianism. A sympathetic Eng. tr. by Joshua Toulmin, with a historical introd., was published in 1777 under the title *Memoirs of the Life, Character and Writings of F. Socinus*. An illuminating study, embodying the result of recent researches, is A. Gordon, 'The Sozzini and their School,' *Theological Review*, July 1879. The various histories of Unitarianism in England and in the United States trace its connexion with Socinianism, and point out the criticism and redaction of its conclusions and the difference between their points of view.

W. M. CLOW.

SOCIOLOGY.—I. The field.—Sociology is the study of human society, which means in its most general sense the tissue of relations into which human beings enter with one another. The name suggests friendliness and co-operation, and it is true that a certain ultimate community of aim and of character underlies those relations between men which are continuously active and permanent. But these are in fact blended with dealings and feelings of a hostile or indifferent character, and, for purposes of investigation, all or any dealings of man with man, anything that conditions or proceeds from such dealings, is a social fact. 'Envy, hatred, malice, and all uncharitableness'—the unsocial or anti-social elements in one sense of the term—are unfortunately relevant to the study of social facts in the widest sense. The social relation, again, may be direct, personal and conscious, or it may be indirect and unknown or ill understood by those whom it affects. In the complexities of the world market a good harvest in the Argentine may affect the fortunes of a Norfolk farmer and possibly the employment of a labourer who would be puzzled to point out the Argentine on the map. The effect is just one element in the operation of a tissue of social relationships of which perhaps no one but the student of this particular market possesses any adequate knowledge, and it is a part of any sociological inquiry to bring to light relations of social cause and effect which without systematic investigation remain quite obscure even to those whom they most intimately affect. Thus the social relationship is potentially as wide as humanity and as various as life. In the simpler societies, it is true, physical barriers separate off different tribes and peoples so that their lives may have little or no contact with one another, but, as material civilization advances, such barriers are scaled and the range of direct and still more of indirect social interaction is progressively widened. In the study of society we may deal with anything which interests us within the whole range of this interaction, and it will be seen that by 'society' we mean something different from *a* society. Society is something universal and pervasive, a tissue, as we have called it, of relations of which it is difficult to find the beginning or the end. A society, on the other hand, is a definite collection of people united by certain special relations with one another and in some way marked off by these relations from others who do not enter into them, possessing in fact a certain unity and in general a structure and what for want of a better metaphor we are accustomed to call a certain life of its own. The formation of societies—their growth, structure, and decay, their inner history and their mutual relations—constitutes the principal part of the study of society, but not the whole. Behind societies there is always society, and the door is opened to serious fallacies if we forget the distinction. Broadly we may express the relationship by saying that it is one of the general characteristics of society that it engenders societies. Out of the tissue of social relationships emerge collections of people constituted each with a definite structure of its own distinguishing it, but by no means severing its relations with others. If society is the tissue of relationships between men, a society may be defined as a structure of which the elements are human beings living in certain enduring and defined relations to one another. Any given human being is as a rule a member of many societies—*e.g.*, family, house of business, trade union, Church, and State—and those societies may either be concentric (the smaller group being members of the larger) or intersect (*e.g.*, a world Church or an international labour organization cuts across State divisions). Running through and beyond all these societies are the social relationships that have not thrown up any organized structure. Thus the influence of science, philosophy, art, and literature is international and extremely pervasive, but, though we speak of the republic of letters or of science, this is no more than a metaphor. The mutual influence of thought and discovery among the peoples is of old standing and is very great, while such organization as it has attained in the shape, *e.g.*, of world congresses is recent and very partial. Nevertheless the tendency of social relationship to take shape in some definite organization is interesting and important here as elsewhere.

Ideally the complete subject of sociology is the entire field of these social relationships organized or unorganized. Any study is sociological which concerns itself with any branch of them, and, as human faculty is limited and the field of society vast, it is in practice necessary to divide the subject into a number of specialisms. Necessary, but a necessary evil. For one of the few generalizations that can be laid down with confidence about society is that all its different parts, however clearly distinguishable for thought, are in their actual development interwoven. The religious, the ethical, the legal, the scientific, the economic relations of life are rightly distinguished, and, if any results are to be attained, each must be studied with the minuteness and accuracy that are possible only to specialism. Yet change in any one of these relations may affect all the others, and the specialist who becomes so concentrated on his particular branch that he ignores the rest is liable to serious errors, such as, *e.g.*, disturbed for a time the development of economics. There is no fundamental difference in this respect between sociology and other sciences, particularly sciences which deal with living beings. A pathologist may specialize with success on the eye or the ear or the liver, though all these organs are part of one organism and are affected in their functions by changes in other organs. What the social specialist has to do is to cultivate his own garden without forgetting the larger field of which it forms a part and from which weeds, let us say, may spread to his own patch. Or, to drop the metaphor, he may make generalizations within his own department, but must bear in mind that these results are conditional on freedom from disturbance by influences emanating from other departments. These things are so obvious that they would hardly be worth stating if it were not for a certain pride of specialism which tends to erect the particular branch, whatever it may be, that the student has chosen into the main stem of society. Thus the economist is apt to see in the industrial and commercial relationships the true and solid foundation of society, the groundwork of its development, the root of its diseases and decay. The political philosopher is convinced that the State is society—not merely the governmental organization which serves as a shell, but the essence and spirit of society itself. The religious man will find all that is of real account in the character of the beliefs current among a people. The biologist sees racial characters everywhere, and the historian of thought is inclined to the view that intellectual development is the sole cause of profound changes in civilization. Against all these tendencies to bias sociology has to make its protest. Its fundamental thesis is that all parts of society interact, and that no pre-eminence over the remainder can be claimed *a priori* for any one element of social life. What is the extent of the influence of each is a very difficult problem to be solved inductively, and probably is destined to receive a different answer in relation to different societies and different periods.

Perhaps a single illustration may be given of the interlocking of cause and effect and the impossibility of assigning the palm of influence to a single factor. Some economists, the Marxians in particular, represent history as an economic process proceeding by an inherent dialectic determining and not determined by the rest of the social structure. But it must be apparent that the industrial structure of our own time is more and more determined by scientific discoveries; nor in the 19th cent. would the electric telegraph—one of the key processes—have arisen but for the experiments of Gauss and Weber stimulated by a theoretical interest, and derived in their turn from the purely intellectual work of Volta and many others. In our own time wireless telegraphy, a commercial innovation of the highest importance, owes its origin to the work of Hertz, which is affiliated to the purely theoretical researches of Clerk-Maxwell. So far the economic factor is dependent on the intellectual, but, if any one thinks that the intellectual factor alone determines the application of science to industry, let him ask himself why the principle of the steam engine, known to Hero of Alexandria, had to wait for the second half of the 18th cent. for its fruition. It is clear that in the 1st cent. B.C. there were men capable of devising practicable steam engines if the conditions had created a demand for them.

It would be easy but superfluous to follow the illustration farther. Let us put the point in this way. The development, say, of science is primarily self-dependent, one discovery leading on to another, but it is conditioned by many elements in the social order—*e.g.*, by religious freedom, the facility of intercommunication, and the social appreciation of intellectual work. Social prejudices, moreover, affect the fashions of scientific thought; *e.g.*, political passions have encouraged theories of race and of the struggle for existence, and national prejudices play their part. So again religion has its own evolution, but is vitally affected by science. Ethical evolution is not the same as religious, but is closely interwoven with it. Law is distinct from either, but cannot violate the ethical or the religious standard with impunity. National evolution has its own roots, but plays upon and is played upon by religious, ethical, and economic influences and even by scientific or pseudo-scientific theories of race. The existing sum of sociological knowledge includes all the scientific studies of all these departments of society. The ideal sociology which has yet to be created would be the synthesis correlating and correcting their results.

Ultimately, then, sociology is a synthesis of the social studies. In the meantime the immediate task of the sociologist is humbler and yet difficult enough. Having in mind the interconnexion of social relations, it is his business to discuss and expose the central conceptions from which a synthesis may proceed, to analyze the general character of society, examine the action of social development, and distinguish the permanent factors on which society rests and from which social changes proceed. In a wider sense sociology may be taken to cover the whole body of sociological specialisms. In a narrower sense it is itself a specialism, having as its object the discovery of the connecting links between other specialisms. In this sense the problem of sociology is the investigation of the general character of social relations and the nature and determining conditions of social development.

2. Social science and philosophy.—So much controversy has arisen as to the method of such investigation as to have in large measure blocked the path of investigation itself. The greater part of sociological treatises is apt to be taken up with questions of the logic of the science. In point of fact every science has found out its own method by experiment, and it is only by investigating social phenomena that we shall learn to distinguish between the fruitful and unfruitful methods of approaching them. Nevertheless to define the relation of sociology to other inquiries that cover or even touch the same field is to make some advance in our main problem of clearing up fundamental conceptions, and we must deal here briefly with the main issues that have been raised.

(*a*) *Questions of fact and questions of value.*—Historically the systematic investigation of social life began as a branch of general philosophy. Plato's *Republic* is a treatise on metaphysics, ethics, æsthetics, psychology, education, and political theory in one. For Aristotle ethics and politics in the narrower sense are two branches of a more widely conceived political inquiry, and are together subordinate to his conception of nature and man's place therein. To the Stoic the city of Cecrops was a microcosm within the wider cosmos which was the city of Zeus. In modern times the study of social affairs began with the criticism of political authority and was dominated by the conception bequeathed to the world by the Stoics of a law of nature, and down to our own day among the followers of Hegel the metaphysical theory of the State (*q.v.*) retains its influence. The simpler and truer view of the relations between social science and philosophy is due to the Utilitarians. For them moral philosophy was devoted to the study of the ultimate ends of human action, which they declared to be the promotion of the greatest happiness of the greatest number of those whom action can affect. Political and in general social theory were concerned with the actual relations of man in society, and this investigation would be the servant of ethics, as it would reveal what institutions made for and what were prejudicial to the general happiness. We thus get a clear distinction between three inquiries which are apt to be confused: (1) the inquiry into the nature of the good, a discussion of values; (2) the inquiry into the actual relations of human beings, a discussion of facts; (3) the inquiry into the means of utilizing our knowledge of the facts in the service of the good, the application of ideals of value to the discovered truth as to facts, the art of social improvement.

Certain fundamental questions may be raised here as to the distinction of value and fact. It may be that value (*q.v.*) is also a fact, an element in reality. We shall not pursue the discussion here, as we should be far from denying the ultimate co-ordination of all thought—a co-ordination in which the conception of what is desirable must play a part along with the knowledge of what is actual. But, in whatever sense the actual and ideal are related, they are also distinct, and of any specific inquiry we must know whether it is dealing with the one or the other. We may appropriately use the term 'philosophy' for the discussion of value, whether it be the value of methods of attaining truth or the value of modes of life and conduct, and the term 'science' for the investigation of facts and the interconnexions of fact which we seek to exhibit as laws. As social life is the medium in which all that we most value has its being, it is clear that it falls within the purview of philosophy as here described, and, if we call the study of value ethics, it follows that any social philosophy is a branch or application of ethics, as the Utilitarians justly conceived. But it is also clear that the application cannot be usefully attempted without knowledge of the facts of society, the systematic exhibition of which is the object of a social science. So far we have a justification for both the philosophic and the scientific treatment of our subject. A complete sociology would therefore embrace a social philosophy and a social science. But it would be a synthesis, not a fusion, of the two inquiries.

It is necessary to make this clear because the distinction has in fact been too often ignored. If we turn to any treatise on social philosophy, we shall find an examination of many of the elementary social institutions—government, law, property, the family, international relations, etc. These are all existing facts, institutions varying endlessly in detail and often in most essential elements from case to case. If we examine these institutions in order to discover what is in fact common to them or how they in fact differ, we are in the region of science. If we examine them to discover how far, or in which of these specific forms, they conduce to the good of man, we are in the region of philosophy. The fundamental defect of the metaphysical treatment of society, however, has been precisely that it has not distinguished these questions and that in analyzing the actual constitution of society it has seemed at the same time to determine what is and to lay down what ought to be. As against this method it must be maintained that the analysis of institutions is either an analysis of values in subordination to some explicit system of ends or an analysis of their actual form of operation in a given society. Both inquiries follow a characteristic method of general philosophy in that they examine those elementary conceptions which ordinary thought takes for granted. Both cover a good deal of the same ground. But their final goal and consequently their continuous interest is different. One thinks constantly of the good which an institution subserves, the other of the precise form which it assumes at a given time, the evolution through which it assumed that form, its interaction with other institutions, and similar questions of fact. Grave confusions arise when issues of fact are coloured by judgment of value; but, when the facts are completely and accurately stated, it is reasonable to essay their valuation, and this is the proper task of social philosophy.

Thus the whole field of society can and should be treated scientifically, and, when scientifically understood, can and should be reviewed philosophically. There is no objection to either method in itself, but only to a confusion of the two. A complete sociology, indeed, aims at a synthesis in which the two parts, though always distinct, are brought into definite relation.

The confusion of method may be illustrated by the uncritical use of terms like 'progress,' which, if it means anything, means a change to something better, a change which therefore we approve, which accords with our standard of ethical valuation. If this meaning had been kept in mind, it would have been impossible for the conception of progress as involving an unmitigated brute struggle for existence to hold its own for a day. In the scientific part of our work we had better avoid terms of distinctively ethical colouring, and with that object, in place of social 'progress' and 'retrogression,' we shall speak of 'development,' 'arrest,' and 'decay.' It may be objected that these terms still carry ethical associations, particularly if we speak, and we shall have to speak, of 'higher' and 'lower' developments. As shown farther on, there is, however, a precise and unambiguous meaning to be attached to these terms which is independent of any ethical valuation; they import differences in the internal vitality, efficiency, and extension of social organization. Whether such organization is on the whole a good or a bad thing is another question. On the method here proposed the question of the nature and conditions of social development becomes a question of social science proper, the question of the social ideal one of ethics, and the question whether actual development has been or is or may be so guided as to conform to the ideal one of the application of ethical principles to scientific results. The present article deals in some detail with the definition of social development, and only briefly indicates the ethical ideal by which the facts should be valued.

(*b*) *Law and freedom.* — Another philosophical conception which has given trouble in the scientific study of society is the conception of law. It is maintained that the object of sociology as a science is to achieve generalizations which presuppose the existence of law in the life of society, and it is questioned whether law involving necessary connexion prevails in the field of human action determined by the human will. The metaphysical question of freedom which emerges here has been generally held to be of critical importance to the status of sociology as a science. But this is an error. It is forgotten that in all sciences the 'laws' which investigation reveals are conditional. They tell us what will happen under given conditions, and enable us to predict what will actually happen at a given time and place only on the tacit supposition that our knowledge of the conditions then and there existing is adequate. Even the astronomer who predicts an eclipse for a given hour and minute speaks with the tacit reservation that the solar system remains unchanged by the irruption of a comet or other disturbing body. Whenever we apply science to practical affairs, the possibility that our enumeration of the relevant conditions is incomplete becomes a serious consideration, and the judgment of the practical man is required to round off and apply the conditional predictions of the specialist. The pathologist lays down the normal course of a disease. The family doctor, using the pathologist's results and knowing the history of the patient, forms by the union of the two a prognosis which is valuable in proportion to his discernment but is not matter of demonstrative certainty. Similarly, what sociology tells us or hopes to tell us is what will happen under given conditions. The economist, *e.g.*, shows that, if supply is reduced while demand is constant, prices will rise. This is a result reached by legitimate reasoning from certain postulates, generally verified in the workings of a modern market. But, if a food controller intervenes, or even if there is a strong appeal to patriotism or a wide dislike of 'profiteering,' a new condition is introduced and the conclusion will not hold. The motives that may stimulate the will are so various, and the complications of social life so intricate, that on any theory of the will all our sociological generalizations must be conditional in character. If people act in certain normal ways conformably to our analysis of human nature, confirmed perhaps by statistical records of actual behaviour, then on given conditions certain results will follow. Even if we assume the strictest philosophical determinism, we could not get farther than this until we knew all the possible motives to action which all possible situations might throw up. If, on the contrary, we assume an indeterminism in the old and strict sense, we are for the present no worse off. We shall still be able to say that, if the mass of men act as they ordinarily do, the results will follow. The difference would emerge only at a much later stage than sociology has reached. For, if there is a strictly indeterminate element in the will, then there is a factor which not only is not known but never can be known. In that case, while other sciences might, ideally, complete the study of their subject-matters and succeed some day in transforming their hypothetical predictions into categorical generalizations in which all relevant conditions should be known, sociology and psychology would have to leave a gap where the undetermined will operates. None the less on both sides of the gap the territory could be explored, and the generalizations obtained would be valid conditionally on a statable operation of the will.

But even this distinction admits a little too much. It overlooks the power of statistical method. If there is an element in the operation of the will which is *bona fide* indeterminate, we are in the region of 'pure chance.' Among a thousand persons confronted with a certain conflict of motives it is even odds whether any individual chooses this or that, accepts, let us say, or refuses. To deny this evenness is to take away the indifference of the will, and inclines us one way or the other. Now in such an event it is quite impossible to determine how any one of the thousand may act, but of the thousand as a whole statistical theory will tell us what the probabilities are. It will tell us that probably the number of acceptances and refusals will be approximately equal, and it will give us a precise measure of the improbability of their diverging by more than a specified amount from equality. If there are many sets of a thousand in question, a divergence in the same direction in all of them becomes increasingly improbable. The approach to certainty is asymptotic, but it is the business of inductive science to yield not only certainties but also measured probabilities, and this is possible to sociology by the use of statistics even on the assumption (which one may take as almost excluded by philosophy) of a strictly indeterminate element in volition. In fact, if the indeterminateness of the will is clearly grasped and the conception rigidly applied, it results that, while the conduct of any individual in a given case is absolutely unpredictable, the average of conduct in a large number of cases will be exactly what it would be if the indeterminate element of choice were non-existent. On the average men will act in accordance with the predominant motive. If, on the other hand, the unknown element does not act indifferently now one way and now another, it ceases to be indeterminate, and, if its effect is studied over a large number of cases, it must become measurable.

(c) *The element of individuality.* — It may be objected that the individual decision may be just the critical event — the turning-point on which great things depend. There are moments in which a single man holds issues as great as those of peace or war in his hands, and the whole future of a community will be different as he decides this way or that. The scientific view of society has sometimes been too hasty in dismissing this objection. Carried to an extreme, indeed, the objection develops with the 'great man' theory of history, the sufficient answer to which is the careful study of the careers of great men. Such study shows that in the realm of action such men have been very narrowly circumscribed by their surroundings and have attained their conspicuous position far more by clever adaptation to the movements of their time than by the power of sheer creation. On the other hand, it is false science to limit the importance of individuals on the strength of any *a priori* preference for the general and the uniform. All social cause and effect runs through the medium of individual character, and it is simply matter of empirical fact that individuals differ and that character is more strongly marked in some than in others. It is also matter of fact that the structure of all societies gives the immediate decision on various issues, sometimes issues of great magnitude, to particular persons in particular positions. In such cases the character of the individual will count. It will not count for as much as appears on the surface, for the large social causes will operate and will be sure to narrow down the choice to a fine point, but none the less at that point the attitude of the individual will be a makeweight, and it may be just the makeweight which turns the balance. There is nothing in this to conflict with the 'reign of law.' A tumbler rolls along a table, coming slowly to rest at the edge. A breath, a tremor, decides whether it stops or falls over and is smashed to atoms. Whichever happens, all is in accordance with uniform and indeed, in this example, perfectly mechanical laws, but to the tumbler the difference is catastrophic. The most rigidly mechanical view of society cannot ignore these perilous edges, and in general any one who has seen public affairs from the inside, particularly if his position is that of a critic rather than an actor, must have learnt that, while public men are much less free in the range of their choice than appears on a superficial view, yet at every stage of a movement personalities count. The vanity of one highly-placed person, the private enmities of another, the fortunes of a Cabinet intrigue, the fears of this man for his seat in Parliament, the regard of that man for his consistency, the coldness of Mr. A. to a cause which his rival Mr. B. has made his own—all these the onlooker has noted with despair as palpable influences in matters on which great public interests depend.

The European War was long attributed popularly in Britain to the Kaiser. Wilhelm II. could no more have made the war by his single decision than he could have waged it single-handed, but the gradual gravitation of his mind towards war so subtly described by M. Cambon reflected the new distribution of multitudinous psychological forces in Germany during 1913, and a decision was taken in July 1914 in which the scales wavering between very nearly equal weights moved finally to one side and at that moment the weight of the Kaiser's personality and position was amply sufficient to decide the turn.

Individuality, then, counts for something, and its effects are not altogether smoothed out by compensations into simple laws of averages because there are moments and points of turning when individuality—possibly through its weakness as much as through its strength—switches a society on the line to the left instead of on the line to the right, and great consequences ensue. This fact introduces an element of uncertainty into any science based on and resting in social generalization. But to some thinkers it is accordingly fatal to the pretensions of sociology as a science. Indeed many see in it only an illustration of a much wider truth applying not only to sociology but to all sciences that pretend to deal with life. Science, they say, deals with the universal and the measurable. It is or is destined to be mathematical in its final shape. It must have exact likenesses or graded and scaled differentiations, so that it can generalize, formulate, and predict. But life is neither uniform nor differentiated only by degrees measurable in scale. It is individual, and in each of its cases there is something unique and unseizable by the intellect—creative of essentially novel, and therefore unpredictable, developments. Even if the idiosyncrasies of individuals could be in some measure reduced to law by the fiction of averages, the life of a society to which millions of individuals contribute each in individual ways is so unique that no generalizations apply to it, and there are not those large numbers of societies which make possible the use of statistics for the calculation of average results. What we can know about a community is its history as a living organism, just as what we can know about a man is his biography. The history and the biography may be written with greater or less fullness and truth, but, the nearer they come to the real springs of life, in either case the more they will reveal these as unique, incapable of being inferred from any parallel case because there is no parallel case, incapable of revealing their own future activity because they are essentially creative in such a sense that the future need in no way resemble the past.

So far as this argument touches the claim of sociology to be a science, it may be sufficient to reply that the sphere of science is too narrowly conceived when it is identified with generalization and prediction. The function of science is to examine and describe facts impartially, accurately, and systematically. If it finds any of its facts unique, it is its business to say so. But it is only from systematic comparison that true uniqueness will emerge. If we test the action of a living organism by mechanical principles, we do or do not find a correspondence. Either the circulation of the blood corresponds to that of a liquid forced through elastic tubes, in which case the physical analogy holds and we are right in regarding the process as mechanical, or there is a measurable divergence, in which case we know what is due to the organic elements involved. It is a residual phenomenon which we identify, even if we do not explain it, only when we have contrasted the organic with the known behaviour of the inorganic. If the vitalist is right, there will always, when the physical and chemical explanation has been carried through, be such a residue, but what this residue amounts to can be known only by carrying the physical explanation as far as it will go and no farther. Similarly it is only when we have applied all the generalizations which we can legitimately make to the life of a given society that we can ascertain and measure the value of that factor, if any, which is its own peculiar individual self. Individuality, if real, will display itself as the result of scientific inquiry. We suspect its force just because we do not find uniformity. To know it, we must find out accurately what uniformity means, to what expectations it would lead us, and how far the reality differs from these anticipations. The individual is not withdrawn from our knowledge. On the contrary, knowledge begins with individuals. Generalizations are drawn from them and concern them, and the limits of generalization in turn display and delimit the field of individual differences. We come back to the caution which we advanced at the outset. Generalizations in all science are conditional, with this addendum that it is in the failure of generalizations that we discover residual phenomena.

(*d*) *Law and will.* — Scientifically, generalizations have become popularly known as laws. It is not the best of all possible metaphors, and in sociology it raises peculiar difficulties. Sociological laws are sometimes crudely confused with the law of the land. In fact, they correspond only in so far as the law of the land formulates the ways in which ordinary people do ordinarily act. Scientific laws have not the force of commands and do not impose penalties, but to seize this contrast is at once to come perilously near to a mistake of the opposite kind. If it is thought that, because sociological law is not an ordinance imposed upon the will, it is therefore something necessarily independent of the will and, if valid at all, must express something which will and must happen in the life of society, no matter what the human beings who constitute that society may think or desire, social development comes to be conceived as something proceeding fatally and even mechanically, which human beings can neither arrest, accelerate, nor modify. In opposition to that view, it must be maintained that social laws rest on and express the ways in which human beings act in their relations to one another together with the consequences of such actions. But, as human beings are capable of that reflective and deliberate action which we call the action of will, sociological laws, far from being independent of the will, must consist largely of statements of the ways in which human wills act. It follows that the mere knowledge of such laws and of the tendencies to which they lead introduces new data for consideration and possible new motives.

Malthus's law of population, *e.g.*, by showing how, under given conditions, population must increase faster than the means of subsistence, had a profound and far-reaching affect upon opinion, and finally upon action, which seriously contributed to the arrest of the increase of population. Such an effect is falsely described as a defeat of Malthus's law. It is a defeat of the tendencies which Malthus found in operation through the apprehension of the results which Malthus predicted. The law, properly stated, is a conditional generalization. If, and so long as, people act in a certain way guided by certain conditions, population will increase faster than the means of subsistence. When they take this into account, new motives come into play and the condition under which the law holds is removed.

Sociological laws therefore do not necessarily formulate processes that must occur independently of our will, but rather indicate the ways in which men act under assignable conditions and the consequences of such action. The knowledge so obtained is the necessary condition of a fuller control of the life of society by the deliberate will of human beings.

To sum up. Sociology as a science does not involve the negation of the freedom of the will, nor does it negate the individuality of societies or the uniqueness of national history. Its business in general is to give an articulate, impartial, and systematic description of the facts of social life. In these it finds features that recur and features that are unique, events attributable to widely prevalent social conditions and events attributable to the action of this or that individual; and the elements of uniformity it sums up into generalizations which hold conditionally on the character of that complex of circumstances which constitutes the individual life of a society at a given time. These generalizations express the ways in which human beings act in accordance with the promptings of human nature and the consequences of such actions; but they do not hold good if other motives come into play than those which they have taken into account. They display social life as made by man for man, not as imposed on man by a superincumbent necessity.

3. The social structure.—(*a*) *Types of society.*—We have described a society as a structure of which the units or elements are human beings living in certain more or less durable and dependable relations to one another. The definition is intended to fit a family or a State, a literary society, or the 'society' of a town or a neighbourhood. In the last case the conditions of durability and definiteness may be sometimes said to recede towards the vanishing point, and the limits which mark out one such society from another become correspondingly vague. Yet even within a society of this kind people exercise mutual hospitality in certain recognized ways and within observed limits, and the relations between them endure sometimes through a lifetime. But, when the term 'society' is used in so large a sense, very little can be said of it in general. If we want to be more precise, we must distinguish different kinds of societies, and in particular those which rest on the deeper needs of man and play the larger part in his life. Of these we may perhaps distinguish three types: (1) the effective kindred[1] growing out of the ties of parenthood and sex, forming a structure of a definite and durable kind deeply rooted in human impulses; (2) the community, which is the entire society occupying a certain territory[2] as long as it is united by certain connective relations[3] that do not extend beyond its borders; (3) what we shall call the 'association,' by which is meant not one society only or even one species of society, but rather a genus including all societies which are based on specific purposes and needs of man. Some such societies are temporary and superficial as the purposes they serve. But some are based on profound needs and must rank with those of the greatest importance to the sociologist. Of these the Churches are the most conspicuous instance. Professional and trade organizations, political parties and leagues, and finally 'institutions,' universities, colleges and schools, even great businesses and government departments, are all societies existing primarily to meet certain needs and often possessing a life and character of their own which profoundly affect the individuals who join them, and react on the other societies with which they are in contact and on the community or communities to which they belong.

(*b*) *The community.*—The centre of these three types is the community. For the family is normally, if not universally, a part of a community and intimately attached to its structure and its fortunes, while the association is by definition hardly capable of an independent life, but requires either a community or communities as its background and support. Sociology therefore is right in making the community the centre of its inquiry, though it goes wrong if it forgets that society is wider than any community and that very essential relations may transcend the communal limits.

What we have called the connective relations constituting the community consist mainly in (1) the observance of a common system of rules regulating the ordinary intercourse of life, and (2) mutual protection against both external enemies and internal breaches of the peace. Among many of the simpler peoples these two functions fall apart, the second particularly in internal relations falling rather to the kindred or quasi-kindred (*e.g.*, the totemic group). The community here consists of people who live in habitual intercourse regulated by customs which are generally observed but not necessarily enforced by organized collective action. Moreover, if there are some rules so enforced, they are often not such as ensure the protection of individuals, which is a matter for the kindred or some other constituent group. Even for purposes of external defence or aggression the community as a whole may be very slightly organized. In larger and more organized communities the enforcement of rules and the protection of its members as well as the maintenance of its own being and perhaps the extension of its borders become essential features of the community and are the first function of a distinct organ, the State (*q.v.*).

A civilized community is, in fact, always organized as a State, but the State and the community are not to be identified. By the community we understand the people in the entire fabric of their life, including their family relationships, their industry, commerce, religion, art, and relaxation. The State is the organized fabric supporting law and government. It is more than mere government—with which it is sometimes identified—while it is less than the community. It includes the executive and judicial system (with the public forces, police and military) on the one side, and the constituent authority on which government is based on the other. In a very democratic country the State may be regarded as the community as organized for those collective purposes which involve compulsion as an ultimate resort. In undemocratic countries the State is not the whole community and may be alien and unfriendly to a greater or less part of it. In many simple communities there is no government and no State. Community and State therefore are different forms of society, and on the whole the State belongs to the type of society which we have called association. It exists to meet specific needs, and it becomes confused with the community because in large and developed societies it is the organ and outer expression of its unity. Questions of the basis, origin, and development of society in general, of the community, and of the

[1] By the term 'effective kindred' the present writer means the kindred to the limit within which its tie is an actually operative force—a limit that varies remarkably among different peoples, and even in different families.

[2] Or (in the case of nomads) habitually moving in association.

[3] If a community is loosely organized, individuals or other communities like gypsies may occupy or move about in the same territory without entering into connective relations with it. Firmly organized communities, of course, bring all such relationships under control.

State should therefore be distinguished. The community is a form of society, and the State is an organ of the community. Man builds society as naturally as the bee builds the honeycomb because isolated man is an incomplete being, and societies vary in every possible way because man's nature is so various, and on all or almost all sides needs the social relation to complete its expression. As social beings the men whose lot is cast together build communities, but in the formation, maintenance, and development of these permanent structures the differences of human qualities make themselves felt. The distinction which we drew between social relations in the wider and narrower sense comes into play, and it is only so far as the tendencies making for co-operation overcome those of antagonism that the community extends, and only so far as the former gain at the expense of the latter that it can develop. Thus the conditions—psychological, historical, or environmental—that make for co-operation determine the life and character of the community, and the abstract fact that man is a social animal is only the first step in explanation. The State reflects the life of the community, in part its conscious or half-conscious need for organization, in part the actual superiority which organization confers in the struggle for existence. It is natural neither in the sense of issuing immediately from man's primitive impulses nor in that of spontaneously expressing his matured perfection. On the contrary, at all known stages it requires effort and criticism to adjust its control, whether to the lower or to the higher nature of man.

As a durable society a community is, in accordance with our definition, a structure of which the unitary elements are human beings living in defined and permanent relations with one another. It may include many subordinate societies, even the simplest communities, *e.g.*, generally including several families (at least in the narrower sense of the term). What is generally necessary to the maintenance of the community is that the several relations between individuals, families, and associations within it should be compatible with one another. However complex, they must, taken together, be self-maintaining; economically, *e.g.*, the relationship between motive and effort must so work out that the community produces enough to maintain itself. On the side of law and order its members must on the whole know what they may expect of others and what others expect of them. Even a game cannot be played without this much of mutual understanding, still less the complex business of running social life. Thus, from the simplest people upwards, every community known has its web of traditional custom, which as a whole makes up a fabric that with less or more of friction will somehow work. Thus a community is not only a structure but a self-maintaining structure—one of which the parts are always in movement and action, but on such lines that by movement and action the structure is on the whole maintained. This description is suggestive of the life of an organism, and not the less so if we consider that the structure may not only be maintained but also develop, and not only develop but also perhaps decay and even perish, so that what might seem to be an objection to our general postulate of self-maintenance falls into place as an exception which proves the rule. How far is this comparison a metaphor, and how far does it express the real essence of communal life?

The objection commonly made is that an organism is a unity possessing a life and consciousness as a whole and not in its several parts, whereas, whatever unity the community may have, the life and consciousness are manifested in its individual members. Our consciousness in its normal functioning is unitary, and we know nothing of any consciousness in our component cells. In the community, on the other hand, each component individual is a conscious being, and we know nothing of any central consciousness unless it be either (*a*) that of a ruler, who is after all one member of the community, or (*b*) the common councils and decisions of many or all members of the community acting in co-operation. Here, we may agree, is a material difference which disposes of any attempt to treat the community as a species of living organism, if that means a species of animal.

(*c*) *The organic principle.*—But there is another and more effectual way of using the term. We may define the organic in general terms and treat living beings, societies, and perhaps other things (*e.g.*, works of art) as species falling within it. An organic whole, then, is a system with a distinct character and mode of action of its own constituted by the conjoint action of parts, each in turn with a distinct character and mode of action of its own, but conditioned in the maintenance of their character and the pursuit of their activity by their mutual requirements as members of the union. The relation of whole and part requires no external agency to create or maintain it. This differentiates it from a mechanical whole in which something essential to the formation is always external. It must be said further that organic unities differ in two principal respects. (1) Some are more and some less thorough-going and intimate. In some the parts cannot exist without the whole; in others they survive its destruction, but modified or crippled in greater or less degree. Among the higher animals a cell removed from the body rapidly dies; among the lower it may survive permanently with some change of form. Viewed under this aspect, some social relations are seen to be very intimate. Indeed the sum-total of all the social relationships in which a man stands must be regarded as so deeply affecting his whole nature that, if we suppose them all cancelled, it may be doubted whether he could still be called human. Any given society, however, may embody only a fraction of these relationships, and its dissolution might not greatly affect the individual. We cannot say *a priori* how it will be in any given case but merely note that on this side the intimacy of the organic union varies in every possible degree. (2) There is, further, a variation of kind, according as the union is harmonious or constrained. Each part is so far distinct as to have its own tendencies and potentialities. It may find in the other parts the co-operative conditions necessary to fulfil these, or it may find forces which in greater or less degree distort and cramp it. Such mutual constraint—the price, so to say, of mutual development—is of common occurrence in organic unions, but necessarily involves a loss of energy and, if carried far enough, entails the risk of a break-up. The organic principle is pure or harmonious in proportion as the constraint involved diminishes.

To apply these principles to a community, it may have many constituent groups, each with a certain internal life, and these in turn are composed of individuals, each with his capacities which may or may not be fulfilled. It will suffice to consider the community in relation to the individual. What do we mean by fulfilment of capacity? Human life rests on impulses which in their higher and more definite form become purposes. Any attainment of a purpose is *pro tanto* a fulfilment of some element in our nature. But purposes may be distracted and conflicting, so that the fulfilment of one may be the frustration of others, and there is no fulfilment of the self as a whole. Hence, conversely, if there is any fulfilment of the self as a whole, it must lie in the realization of a comprehensive purpose or in a coherent system of purposes. Now, one purpose might be pursued through life to the disregard of all others. There would then be consistency of action, but no fulfilment of the mass of impulses or purposes. But, conversely, the purpose or system of purposes might be such as would give to all manner of impulses and purposes the greatest scope compatible with mutual consistency. It might indeed be a summing up of such purposes as seem in relation to one another. This would yield the most complete possible fulfilment of the self as a whole. The process of such fulfilment is the development of personality, which is thus seen to rest on the free scope of each part conditioned only by the harmony of the whole.

What is true within the single personality applies *mutatis mutandis* to the plurality of persons in a society. If we conceive a common purpose, or system, embracing all purposes of all individuals so far as they are mutually consistent, the realization of such a system would be the completest fulfilment of the life of a community. Ideally such a system would be one which should lay all elements of our nature under contribution, informing them with a spirit of unity rather than limiting them by constraint. It is clear that such a harmony could be expressed only in a religious ideal setting before humanity as a whole the meaning and value of its life. Of such an ideal all that can be said here is that the two conditions on which it rests are those which we have called harmony and freedom—fullness of scope for our many-sided nature conditioned at the lowest by the requirement of mutual consistency, or at a higher grade inspired by conscious relation to a harmonious whole.

A community will be harmonious or organic in the purest sense in proportion as it realizes these conditions—*i.e.*, as it rests upon and calls forth the personality of its members in all respects in which they are in fact capable of harmonization. Thus it will repose upon the social qualities in the narrower of the two senses given to that term. It will not admit any quality or activity incompatible with the consistent working of the whole, nor allow the restraint or stoppage of any development except on the score of such incompatibility.

Unfortunately, as we saw at the outset, the term 'social qualities' has a much wider sense; the human beings of whom society is composed do not with their whole being enter into harmonious co-operation: they are centres of independent life with interests of their own, in the pursuit of which they impinge on one another, crossing each other's paths. The various groups which they form act with a similar collective selfishness, so that we are faced by centrifugal tendencies and begin to wonder how it is that the community is kept together at all. Thinkers who start from these tendencies have, in fact, formed two main theories of the origin of social union.

(*d*) *The principle of force.*—One school rests the State upon force. Now it is true that organized society has never yet been able to dispense with force, but force itself as applied in social life is a conception requiring analysis. Where more than two or three are gathered together, force cannot be effectively exerted by a single man. It may no doubt be wielded, directed in detail, by the will of a single chief. But essentially it rests on discipline and organization, and organization involves a delicate psychological balance. Even in a disciplined army there must at bottom be a widely diffused will to obey, and, if there comes a point at which for any reason that will is shaken, the whole fabric may, as the world has seen, suddenly crumble. In a slave society there must be union among masters and overseers or privileged slaves. In an aristocratic society compromises and shifts are adopted to prevent trouble with the mass, and 'charity' plays a large part in substitution for justice, while the power of the governing class rests on an energetic development of a common will. In short, if organization involves force, it is still more true that force rests on organization, and organization on response of mind to mind, will to will. There may indeed be a large class of slaves, serfs, or subjects who have 'nothing to do with the laws except obey them,' but even here, as we get closer to the facts, we generally find that it is easier to proclaim laws than to enforce them if they are definitely out of keeping with the ingrained tendency of the mass. Repression may unfortunately play a very large part in social organization, and many of the vital social impulses may be inhibited, but there must be some seed of social co-operation, even if it is limited to a small section of the community which conceives its common good as conditioned by the subordination of the remainder. Force is not the basis of the State as such, but is the element in State organization which is the exact antithesis of the organic principle, expanding or contracting as that principle contracts or expands, but incapable of extinguishing the last germs of its life without resolving the structure into a chaos of centrifugal elements.

(*e*) *The principle of self-interest.*—Other thinkers have founded the community on self-interest, and this theory has taken two main forms. In one the organized community, the State, is based on a contract. Individual self-seeking, unable to get its way, comes to terms with others, 'so as neither to do nor suffer injustice,' and the result is an agreed system of general rules and an accepted government to enforce them. This theory, viewed in broad principle and without regard to the ingenuities of its historical exponents, covers a part of the facts. It is true that on the balance the interests of each man are in general better served by some sort of order than by anarchy, and a vague sense of this truth may even operate as a true psychological factor in securing consent to government. But as a principle the theory of contract errs by omitting the entire common interests of mankind and with it the manifold and complex relations into which human beings enter spontaneously through the development of their own impulses. Compact, express as well as implied, plays its part in public as in private life. Public transactions are affected by reciprocity, and men favour or disfavour a project of laws which does not directly touch them from a sense that the same principle might be applied in a way that would directly touch them. Indeed in this manner there is an element of self-interest in the assent nominally given to law itself. But the part played by calculating egoism is very secondary to that of the various impulses that constitute the Ego. It is true that men are more moved by something that might easily have happened to themselves than by things more remote, but this is largely because such things necessarily lie within the range of their experience and are the more readily realized in imagination. Pity is not a fear lest the like misfortune befall oneself. It is quite another kind of emotion. But it is more easily stirred by a situation in which one can readily imagine oneself or others near to one to be placed. Both for good and for evil our relations to others rest primarily not on egoistic calculation, but on direct and spontaneous impulses and emotions, and the organized life of the community represents rather the adjustment of such impulses and their reduction to order and system than a precarious balance of purely self-centred interests.

The second form of this theory played an important part at one stage in the development of economics. It was conceived that in a community in which every man was free to pursue his own interests, and enlightened enough to understand its true conditions, the play of economic forces would suffice to secure the common good. Since each knows where his own shoe pinches, it is the free purchaser in the free market who is most likely to get the shoes to fit his own feet. The workman who can sell his labour freely works to the best advantage. The employer who can secure labour freely finds the best man for the most paying job, and the most paying job is that for which at the moment there is the widest demand. Thus demand and supply, operating in a world of free, equal, and intelligent beings, adapt the efforts of each to the maximum needs felt in that world, and there is a natural harmony of interests on which the statesman should rely for the promotion of order and progress. On this theory only two comments are required here. The first is that it postulates freedom, enlightenment, and equality of opportunity, which, if obtainable, are so only by a complete system of restraint on the oppressive use of personal or class ascendancy—*i.e.*, it postulates after all organized action for the common good. The second is that this theory simulates a harmonic view of society, but is really different in principle. For in the harmonic view the interest of one is in the welfare of others. In this view the interest of each one is merely served by the others as instruments, and the correspondence assumes a kind of 'pre-established harmony' which is little short of miraculous. We must distinguish sharply between a harmony growing out of social impulses and expressed in a common purpose and a harmony resting on a mechanical coincidence of self-centred desires from which the social interest is eliminated. But, though these two forms of harmony are distinct in idea, they have something more than the name in common. It is a very important truth that even as self-centred individuals men have a certain community of interest—*e.g.*, that in the long run the trader gains by the prosperity of his customer, that high wages may mean cheap production, and so forth. These relations testify to underlying conditions of harmony in human life, whether men are aware of them or not, and the old economic theory had at least a glimpse of the truth. On the other hand, to bring these conditions to light and make them the basis of social organization a very different psychology is required.

(*f*) *The blending of distinct principles.*—Thus we find different and even opposed principles operating in the life of the community. But we must not imagine those principles either as lying side by side or as in continual conflict with one another. Men adapt themselves to their conditions, and under a system of constraint some tendencies atrophy and others develop and take a firmer hold, and one may become in time a loyal and willing slave, while another takes it as a natural right that he should be master. The actual system of society may be far from harmonious, but may be very deeply rooted in the minds of the members as they have come to be under the pressure of generations of historic development and may be strongly resistant to changes which would in fact liberate many of its suppressed potentialities and yield a fuller and more harmonious life. Such a community is highly organic in the sense that its members are deeply penetrated by its spirit, though it may be of low grade from the point of view of the harmony which it secures.

It would seem then that to define a community as an organism would be to simplify our problem too much. A community has more or less of organic character as the case may be, or sometimes more of one organic character and less of another, and is accordingly less or more subject to internal (or external) constraints. If, then, the community is not as such an organism, may we call it an organization? The term has been proposed to avoid the analogy of the animal organism, but it carries with it converse suggestions which are hardly less objectionable. All communities are no doubt more or less organized, in that they are structures in which people stand in fairly definite and durable relations in virtue of which they so act as on the whole to keep the structure in being. But the term 'organization' is apt to suggest that this structure is intelligently planned for a purpose and imposed for that purpose on an otherwise unordered people. Such organization of course plays its part within most communities at one point or another, but in the main the community grows out of the needs, and indeed the purposes, of individuals, but not out of a common purpose, while, if it achieves a common purpose, that is rather the flower of its high development than the originating cause of its being. We may speak of 'the organization of a community' in a neutral sense, leaving its base and character, whether organic or mechanical, purposive or impurposive, to be further determined. But we had better avoid defining the community as an organization. Generically a community—we fall back on our first account—is a self-maintaining structure, composed of individuals with lives and purposes of their own, but in perpetual interaction with one another. This interaction modifies the individual so far that the normal community settles down to an accepted order. How far in such order the development of individuals is subject to restraint, distorted, and suppressed, how far it is full, harmonious, and free, are questions to which the answer must differ from case to case, and in each case it tells us how far that community is in the full sense a completely developed organism.

Whatever the relative importance of the co-operative or the repressive principle in its life, the communal structure is a whole, constituted by those elements of character which its constituent individuals contribute, while it modifies those individuals to the extent to which it draws forth from them or represses the characteristics which in a different social *milieu* would have had a different history. So understood, the common life is precisely the sum-total of the individual lives as actually lived in the community.

4. The development of the community.—Structures which maintain themselves in continual process, through the interaction of their parts and by dealings with their physical or social environment, may be said to differ from one another in one or more of three principal points, and it is by such differences that we measure their development. These points are (*a*) the efficiency of their operation, (*b*) their scale or scope, (*c*) the basis or principle of their organization.

(*a*) *Efficiency.*—The term suggests an end or purpose. How far purpose can be attributed to communities as such is, as has been hinted, a doubtful question, and it cannot be discussed here. But, whether of clear purpose or otherwise, the community somehow maintains itself, and that not like a stock or stone by dull inertia, but like an organism (it does not matter for the moment whether the likeness is superficial or fundamental) by unceasing metabolism. It protects itself against enemies and against internal disorder. Its members supply themselves, largely if not principally by mutual service, with the necessaries, comforts, and luxuries of life. All this, though it may not be planned by any common will or by any single will on behalf of the community, may obviously be in fact performed with greater or with less efficiency. It is the requirement of efficiency that gives rise to the division and combination of effort, the articulation of social functions, all that we are accustomed to call organization in the narrower sense of the term. The farther differentiation proceeds, the greater is the need of some supreme regulation based on recognized principles. But without assuming a common purpose to be universal, we may say that every community in maintaining its being exhibits a degree of efficiency, high or low.

(*b*) *Scale or scope.*—Communities differ in scope. This has two principal meanings. In the first place, they differ in mere size. A living organism may consist of a single cell or of millions of cells, a community of three or four families or of a hundred million men; and it may be remarked that unity and size are not, generally speaking, easy to reconcile. Great organizations generally contain small organizations within them, and sometimes the smaller organization is the more effective unity of the two. Thus the cell is more efficiently organized than the life of some of the metazoa which are aggregations of cells acting normally as one being but capable of independent life. Many of the larger human communities have been loosely compacted, and the smaller units composing them have in history shown more vitality, more power of keeping together and maintaining themselves, than the whole to which they belonged. In the simpler societies the tribe is often a feeble and ill-organized community, as compared with the clan which is its immediate component.

But there is a less obvious sense in which communities differ in scope. They cover a larger or smaller sphere of life and activity. The total output of human energy may be relatively great or small, poor and narrow or rich and many-sided in its development. As the scientific, the religious, the imaginative interests develop, as callings are differentiated and wealth and industry grow, the scope of life extends. The metabolism that sustains the social structure is more intense, the outlook is wider, the pace faster. There always arises the question whether the old bottles will hold the new wine, or, to drop metaphor, whether the sum of the activities, at once extended and intensified, will still maintain itself as a unity or suffer disruption. The success of the community in absorbing manifold and divergent developments into the unity of its life is the measure of its scope.

(*c*) *The base or principle of organization.*—Communities differ in spontaneity. As we have seen, organization may be imposed upon elements which are indifferent to its purposes from without. The elements are then subdued, for their energies are directed by the superincumbent force into channels into which they would not naturally flow. With time their original impulse may be crushed, or it may be simply held in check to re-assert itself when the pressure is removed, while, so long as the organization remains mechanical and in proportion as it is mechanical, it is alien to the elements which are made to serve it, and herein there must be necessarily a net loss of efficiency, because by hypothesis some portion greater or less of the inherent energy of the parts is indifferent or even hostile to the purpose for which it is being used. On the other hand, the structure may spring from and express the inherent energies of the parts themselves, which spontaneously respond to one another, each eliciting from the other the output of its inherent energy for the fulfilment of its capacity. Such a structure differs from every other in that it has the root of self-maintenance and development in itself, diffused through all its parts. It is in accordance with our definition organic. As applied to society, it is easy to recognize in this description the ideal life of a community, and it is as easy to see that it is an ideal which is very imperfectly realized in any existing community, and one that is not readily reconcilable with the imperfections of human nature. It results, however, that communities are organic in proportion as their life is based upon spontaneous co-operation, and that a free co-operative commonwealth, however difficult to realize, has within it the foundations of a more complete and stable unity and of a higher efficiency than the most complete mechanical organization. It is also clear that it has within it the power of attaining a very much wider scope than the mechanical organization which is by hypothesis repressive, and which, while it may be exceedingly efficient for one purpose, must cramp human nature on other sides. Could there be co-operation in freedom, on the other hand, it would be a co-operation on all sides of life which are capable of social or harmonious expression.

But, though co-operation may be based on freedom, it would be a mistake to suppose that the most completely organic society could dispense with positive institutions, or that there could be harmony of manifold impulses without limitations and restraints. The best impulses require direction and co-operation, and even a community of saints would need a definite order in which the special functions of each person on each occasion should be indicated. The problem of freedom is not that of dispensing with all guidance and all restraint, but that of finding the lines upon which the manifold social qualities of man can develop in harmony, with the result that the restraints involved are voluntarily accepted and self-imposed. Nor is the problem of organic construction that of engendering the social impulses, which are born and not made, but that of so adjusting the framework of institutions that such impulses have free play and scope for development. This is the truth expressed by T. H. Green when he says that the direct object of legislation is to create not the common good—conceived as the free operation of a spiritual principle—but rather the conditions under which the common good may develop. Legislation cannot make men honest on principle, but commercial law may be such that honesty is the road to ruin, while it may be so reformed that the honest man becomes capable of holding his own. Industrial law may enable the harsh employer to beat down prices by sweating, and so render it impossible for any one who refuses to employ others except on a living wage to remain in the trade. When such a law is amended, it does not force anybody to be truly and spontaneously considerate in his dealings—in this sense no one can be made good by Act of Parliament—but it does enable the considerate man to play his part as an employer in industry. Thus it is no more possible to create an organic spirit than it is to make a living thing, but it is possible to open the channels along which the vitalizing fluid may run and thereby gather energy and volume. What we call free institutions are institutions which on the whole rest for their stability on this vital principle, and provide the lines upon which it can move without obstruction.

Communities, then, differ in the three essential respects of efficiency, scope, and spontaneity, nor do they tend to vary concomitantly in the three relations; *e.g.*, a community may be organically one—its common life a 'spontaneous' expression of character—but very small and very limited in the scope of its activity. Thus a little clan may stand together as one man to protect every one of its members, its unity based on spontaneous and deep-seated feeling. On the other hand, it contains only a few score of individuals, and its notions of life may be exceedingly narrow. Again, a large community may be efficiently organized upon the basis of military despotism. It is then an exceedingly formidable force in the world, and may defeat and destroy rivals who have cared more for the development of individuality and less for discipline and order. This is the victory of mechanism over the spirit which is the recurrent tragedy of human history.

Again, the life of a community may be many-sided and so rich in scope, but the greater amplitude conditioned by freedom may be purchased at the expense of organic unity. There may be an order like that of the Roman empire superimposed on heterogeneous peoples allowing great latitude for internal movements such as are illustrated in the rich religious growth of the imperial period. Such states do a service for civilization, though not quite the highest service, and their weaknesses are easy to see.

Lastly, the organic principle may be strong and penetrating, but not pure or harmonious, resting, *e.g.*, on the strong mutual development of certain qualities and a certain attitude of mind which represses other qualities of personality. Such organic character will often be found in small communities of very simple mode of life, and sometimes even, through the strange adaptability of mankind, in larger communities supporting essentially repressive systems of authority.

Thus these three features of social organization vary independently, and development may be measured by the advance in any one of them. But, considered in its fullness, it is measured by the advance in all three taken together. That is to say, the most developed community would be that which effectively achieves the most complete synthesis of the widest range of human activity, including within its membership the largest number of human beings, but in such wise as to rest most completely upon their free co-operation, thus expressing the whole of their vital energies as far as these are capable of working together in harmony. Judging by this standard, we may speak of one society as more highly developed than another, and we have in this conception a general criterion of advance in organization.

5. Complete development and the ethical ideal.—Now, the final term of development in these three respects accords with the ideal of a rationalistic system of social ethics. For, whatever the view taken in detail by the ethical rationalist, his general principle is that right conduct must form a rational system. A rational system is one applicable to all humanity in all the varied relations of its life, and its demand is for a practical consistency in character and conduct. By practical consistency, again, is meant a system of purposes which in their operation do not conflict with but support and require one another, forming a whole within which they are distinct but interdependent parts.[1] Thus such a system constitutes an organic whole, as it has been here defined, and one that embraces the whole of human life and activity. Thus for a rational ethics the good life, if actually realized in society, would form a perfectly organic unity of the widest possible scope. It follows that at bottom the ethical and the organic principle are the same thing. Thus, when we speak of 'higher' and 'lower' development in the senses here set out, the ethical implication of these terms is fully justified from the point of view of a rational ethics. But it is important to remark that the terms 'higher' and 'lower' may be used of organization without an ethical reference, implying merely the greater or less completeness, efficiency, or extent of the organization itself. From this point of view, the three characteristics here taken are the essentials. For organization, to be complete, must rest on an internal principle, and will be more or less complete in proportion as it is saturated with that principle. The principle must be efficient in governing the parts and in controlling their activities, and, completeness being thus assured, extent is measured by size and what we have called scope. Thus we arrive at the result that in fundamental principle development in social organization, considered in its fullness, coincides with ethical development as conceived by a rationalistic system. This is the fundamental proposition in the relation between sociology conceived as a science of facts and sociology as a philosophy of values. Partial developments may diverge from ethical requirements in any degree.

From this point the further treatment of the subject, which cannot be pursued here, divides into two branches. The first is philosophical and consists (*a*) in the justification of the ethical theory here laid down, and (*b*) in its expansion and application to social institutions. This is the task of social philosophy proper. The second is scientific and consists in ascertaining the condition of development, the correlation of its different branches, the causes making for its furtherance, arrest, or decay, and the principal phases of its partial achievement in the course of historic civilization.

[1] It may be objected that the requirements of a rational system would be satisfied by the subordination of all purposes to one supreme end, so that in place of a system of ends distinct but interdependent rational conduct would be of the nature of a mechanism in which every detail is a mere means to a single end. This conception can be shown to rest on an imperfect view of rationality, but in relation to ethics it is sufficient to remark that it involves a denial of all intrinsic value to personality—*i.e.* at once of conscience, of love, and of justice.

LITERATURE.—The term 'sociology' is due to Comte (see art. POSITIVISM), and the modern treatment of the subject has been greatly influenced by his work and that of Herbert Spencer. To Comte his *General View of Positivism*, Eng. tr. by J. H. Bridges, new ed., with introd. by F. Harrison, London, 1908, is the best introduction. Spencer's *Principles of Sociology*[6], London, 1900, is now mainly of historical interest, but his *Study of Sociology*[9], do. 1880, is a brilliant introduction which retains a value.

Sociological literature since Spencer's time has been exceedingly voluminous, but the subject has been pursued more successfully in its special aspects than as a whole. For this reason any adequate bibliography would be of unmanageable dimensions. Perhaps the best recent treatise, professedly sociological in aim, is R. C. McIver, *Community: a Sociological Study*, London, 1917, to which the present writer must express his obligations. Numerous text-books and introductory volumes have appeared in America, among which F. H. Giddings, *Principles of Sociology*, New York, 1898; L. F. Ward, *Outlines of Sociology*, do. 1898; J. Q. Dealey and L. F. Ward, *Text-book of Sociology*, do. 1905; F. W. Blackmar and J. L. Gillin, *Outlines of Sociology*, do. 1915; Albion W. Small, *General Sociology*, Chicago, 1905; E. A. Ross, *Foundations of Sociology*, New York, 1905; and C. A. Ellwood, *Sociology in its Psychological Aspects*, do. 1913, illustrate various methods of treatment. L. T. Hobhouse, *Social Evolution and Political Theory*, was also published in America (New York, 1911). The *American Journal of Sociology*, *Sociological Papers*, and the *Sociological Review* published by the (London) Sociological Society are the principal serial publications in English. The first volume of the *Sociological Papers* contains a valuable art. on 'The Origin and Use of the Word Sociology' by V. V. Branford. In French E. Durkheim's works, especially *Les Règles de la méthode sociologique*[6], Paris, 1912, and the volumes of *L'Année sociologique* are important, and the volumes of *La Science sociale* incorporate the principal work of the school of Le Play. In German G. Simmel, *Soziologie*, Leipzig, 1908, is a voluminous treatise, and P. Barth, *Die Philosophie der Geschichte als Soziologie*, do. 1897, a very valuable résumé. Müller Lyer, *Phasen der Kultur*, is of interest to the student of comparative sociology. The *Vierteljahrschrift für wissenschaftliche Philosophie und Soziologie* may be consulted. In England the general subject has been approached mainly from the philosophical point of view. E. J. Urwick, *A Philosophy of Social Progress*, London, 1912, and J. A. Hobson, *The Social Problem*, do. 1901, are of value to the general student. J. H. Muirhead and H. J. W. Hetherington, *Social Purpose*,

London, 1918, and **J. S. Mackenzie**, *Outlines of Social Philosophy*, do. 1918, are representative volumes (Mackenzie's *Introd. to Social Philosophy*, Glasgow, 1890, retains its value). **Westermarck**, *MI*, 2 vols., London, 1908, **L. T. Hobhouse**, *Morals in Evolution*, rev. ed., London, 1915, and **A. Sutherland**, *Origin and Growth of the Moral Instinct*, 2 vols., do. 1898, are in the main works on comparative sociology on the side of custom and ethics. **Graham Wallas**, *The Great Society*, London, 1914, is indispensable to the student of social psychology, to which the works of **Ross** (New York, 1908) and **W. McDougall** (⁹ London, 1915) under that title are suggestive contributions.

L. T. HOBHOUSE.

SOCRATES.—1. Chronology.—Socrates was put to death in the archonship of Laches (Ol. xcv. 1=400–399 B.C.). The date was given by Demetrius Phalereus in his *Register of Archons* (ἀρχόντων ἀναγραφή), which was based on official records, and is the only fact about Socrates that may be regarded as beyond the reach of controversy. The year of his birth was obtained by calculation. Plato made Socrates say that he was seventy[1] or over seventy[2] at the time of his trial, and the ancient chronologists counted back seventy archons from Laches inclusive, which brought them to the year of Apsephion (469–468 B.C.). As, however, Socrates was condemned at the beginning of the Delian festival, which appears to have fallen in March, it is safer to go back at least to 470 B.C. In any case, that year cannot be far wrong.[3] The dates show that Socrates was essentially a man of the Periclean age, and that he grew up in that wonderful time when Athens, conscious of having saved Greek liberty, became the centre of a free artistic and intellectual development that has never been surpassed. He must have seen the first performances of the *Antigone* and the *Hippolytus* and watched the building of the new Parthenon from start to finish. On the other hand, Plato and Xenophon, the writers who have most to say about him, were not born till after the high hopes of the Periclean age had been bitterly disappointed, and their youth was spent in years of disaster which ended, by the time Plato was twenty-three, in the fall of Athens and the loss of her leading place among the states of Greece. It is obvious that, if we are to understand Socrates, we must try to replace him among the surroundings of his own generation, and to do that we must carefully weigh all contemporary references to his youth and early manhood. It is only when we have done this that we shall be in possession of a test which we can apply to the evidence of men who knew him only in his old age.

Plato was born in 428–427 B.C., when Socrates was already over forty. It used to be supposed that Xenophon was older, and this is the real explanation of the general disposition to regard his evidence as particularly valuable. The early date given in older books for the birth of Xenophon is solely due, however, to an uncritical acceptance of the calculations of ancient chronologers. They fixed his ἀκμή, or *floruit*, in 401–400 B.C., the date of the *Anabasis*, and equated the *floruit*, as usual, with the fortieth year of his life. From the *Anabasis* itself, however, we learn that Xenophon must have been well under thirty in 399 B.C.[4] He insists a great deal on his youth as compared with the other generals,[5] and Proxenus was only thirty. We may confidently infer that Xenophon was younger than Plato. It is also to be remembered that he left Athens before the death of Socrates, so that he was only a lad when he knew him. His Socratic writings belong to a later date, when those of Plato, Antisthenes, and Æschines were already well known. None of the most recent writers on Socrates regard Xenophon as a first-hand authority, though they differ considerably as to his sources.

2. Early references to Socrates.—The earliest reference to Socrates now extant probably comes from a time before the birth of Plato, and certainly from a time before he was ten years old. In a book of memoirs entitled *Visits* (ἐπιδημίαι) the

1 *Crito*, 52 E.

2 *Apol.* 17 D (according to the reading of T): πλείω ἑβδομήκοντα.

3 For the chronological questions involved see F. Jacoby, *Apollodors Chronik* (*Philol. Unters.* xvi.), Berlin, 1904, p. 284 ff.

4 C. G. Cobet, *Novæ Lectiones*, Leyden, 1858, p. 534 ff.

5 iii. 1. 14, 25. For the age of Proxenus see ii. 6. 20.

tragic poet Ion of Chios said[1] that Socrates in his youth visited Samos in the company of Archelaus. If we had the context, we might be able to fix the date of this; but, even as it is, we may be fairly sure. We know[2] that Ion met the poet Sophocles (who was one of the generals) at a dinner-party at Chios during the Samian War (441 B.C.), and it is natural to suppose that his meeting with Archelaus and Socrates was about the same time. At any rate, Plato makes Socrates say in the *Crito*[3] that he had never left Athens but on military service, with the single exception of a visit to the Isthmus, and there does not seem to be any other occasion than this on which he could have been at Samos on military service during the life-time of Ion, who is referred to as already dead in the *Peace*[4] of Aristophanes, which was produced in 421 B.C.

Now this reference of Ion's is very important for what it implies. Archelaus was, in the first place, an elegiac poet, who belonged to the circle of Cimon, son of Miltiades, and the *Consolation* on the death of Cimon's wife, which survived to a later date, was attributed to him.[5] Ion of Chios belonged to the same circle, to which he was introduced when quite a lad, and certainly before the ostracism of Themistocles.[6] It may be taken for granted, then, that Archelaus was an old acquaintance of his; and so, when he mentions Socrates as being in his company, he must mean that there was a close relation of some kind between them. There is independent testimony to this, though from a later and less trustworthy source. Aristoxenus of Tarentum wrote a scandalous account of Socrates, based on the recollections of his father Spintharos, and he said that Socrates attached himself to Archelaus at the age of seventeen and followed him for many years.[7] The tittle-tattle which accompanied this may be disregarded, but it could hardly have arisen unless the relations of Socrates with Archelaus had been notorious. Now Archelaus was not only an elegiac poet, but the disciple and successor of Anaxagoras, who had introduced Ionian science into Athens immediately after the Persian Wars, but had been forced to take refuge at Lampsacus about the middle of the century.

For the date of the trial and flight of Anaxagoras see A. E. Taylor's article in the *Classical Quarterly*, xi. [1917] 81. The idea that it took place just before the Peloponnesian War is due solely to Ephorus, whose chronology is well known to be arbitrary. All the data we have point to the residence of Anaxagoras at Athens having lasted from about 480 to about 450 B.C. It is quite distinctly implied in Plato's *Phædo*[8] that Anaxagoras had left Athens before Socrates was old enough to take an interest in science, and that Socrates never had any personal relations with him. It is also clear that the earlier date is alone consistent with the statement of Plato and Isocrates that Anaxagoras was the teacher of Pericles,[9] and the fact that he was succeeded by Archelaus, who had written a poem for Cimon. Plutarch's statement about this comes from Didymus.[10]

If, then, Socrates became a disciple of Archelaus about 450 B.C., or a little earlier, it means that he was then interested in Ionian science. It would have been strange if he had not been so; for, according to all accounts, he was a man of boundless curiosity, and Ionian science flourished exceedingly at Athens in those days. We need not, however, suppose that Anaxagoras had already

1 Frag. 9 (*FHG* ii. 49). This is quoted in the *Life of Socrates* by Diogenes Laertius. The suggestion of Wilamowitz that it refers to another Socrates has now been withdrawn (*Platon*, Berlin, 1919, p. 96).

2 Frag. 1 (*FHG* ii. 46). 3 52 B. 4 836.

5 Plutarch, *Vit. Cim.* 4, where Panætius is referred to for the authorship of the poem.

6 Cf. frag. 4 (*FHG* ii. 47).

7 H. Diels, *Die Fragmente der Vorsokratiker*, Berlin, 1912, 47 A 3.

8 97 B ff.

9 Plato, *Phædrus*, 270 A; Isocrates, Περὶ ἀντιδόσεως, § 235.

10 See E. Meyer, *Forschungen zur alten Gesch.*, Halle, 1892–99, ii. 43.

developed the subtle theory of substance by which we know him best. That was more probably the work of his old age at Lampsacus, and we can see from Euripides, who was also influenced by him, that it was rather what Theophrastus calls 'the philsophy of Anaximenes'[1] that Anaxagoras had brought to Athens in his youth. According to this doctrine, the primary form of matter is 'air' (*i.e.* vapour), which becomes 'æther' and fire when rarefied, and which becomes visible in clouds when condensed, passing ultimately into water and earth. The earth was regarded as flat and as supported by the air, and the formation of the world and everything in it was explained as due to an eddy or vortex (*δίνη*) in the original 'air.'

3. **The comic poets.**—We have no further contemporary reference to Socrates till 423 B.C., when, for some reason we can only guess at present, he was burlesqued in two of the three comedies produced that year, the *Connus* of Amipsias and the *Clouds* of Aristophanes. We do not know much about the *Connus*, which takes its name from the musician Connus, the son of Metrobius, whom Socrates speaks of as his music-master in Plato's *Euthydemus*[2] and in the *Menexenus*.[3] The *Clouds* is named from its chorus, and that is composed of clouds just because of their importance as a visible form of 'air' in Ionian science. There is one very striking coincidence between the two plays. The chorus of the *Connus* consisted of 'thinkers' (*φροντισταί*), while in the *Clouds* Socrates is represented as inhabiting a 'thought-factory' (*φροντιστήριον*) with his disciples. It seems to follow that Socrates and his associates used *φροντίς* and its cognates in a way of their own, and that this amused the Athenians. Now in Attic the words *φρονεῖν*, *φροντίς*, and *φροντίζω* are employed in certain special connexions, and cannot be used in the general sense of 'think' or 'thought,' but in Ionic it was different. A glance at the Index to Diels' *Vorsokratiker* will show that *φρονεῖν* and *φρόνησις* were used by the early philosophers for *thought* as opposed to *sense* (*αἰσθάνεσθαι*, *αἴσθησις*), and we may reasonably infer that Socrates was already occupied with the distinction between sensation and intelligence at this date. From the *Clouds*[4] we learn a little more about *φροντίδες*. A 'thought' has to be born like a child, and any disturbance may cause a miscarriage. This implies that the *μαιευτική* of Socrates was already well known to the Athenians when Plato was four years old.

Plato uses the word *φροντιστής* only once, and that in a direct allusion to the comic poets.[5] Xenophon[6] makes one of his characters address Socrates as *ὁ φροντιστὴς ἐπικαλούμενος*, which is doubtless a literary reminiscence too. We may infer that Socrates had dropped the Ionic word in later life when he had given up Ionian science. In that case the *φροντίζων τι ἕστηκεν* of Plato, *Symp.* 220 C, which refers to 431 B.C., is a fine historical touch.

The *Clouds* is in no sense an attack on the 'sophists' in the sense in which that word is now commonly used. What is really attacked in the play is Ionian natural science, and Socrates is taken as the representative of that because, as every one knew, he had been the disciple of Archelaus, who was the successor of Anaxagoras. That was quite legitimate, and every one who has studied the science of those days must admit that Aristophanes was quite well informed about it, and that his caricature is based on a perfectly accurate view of its general character.

It is usual to say with Diels that the system caricatured in the *Clouds* is that of Diogenes of Apollonia.[7] He too was an adherent of 'the philosophy of Anaximenes,' and it is quite natural that there should be coincidences between him and Archelaus. The main things were common to the whole school. Specially noteworthy are the oath of Socrates by Respiration, Chaos, and Air,[1] and the references to the vortex.[2] If Socrates had been a disciple of Archelaus, these are perfectly correct allusions to the system in which he had been brought up.

There is, however, another strain in the Socrates of the *Clouds*, which has nothing to do with Archelaus or Ionian cosmology. Socrates is represented not only as a votary of science but also, and even more, as an ascetic and a teacher of strange doctrine about the soul. His disciples are pallid 'semi-corpses,' and the initiation of Strepsiades is an obvious parody of some Orphic or Corybantic ceremony. The grotesque picture of the *φροντιστήριον* is intelligible only on the supposition that Socrates was popularly regarded as the director at once of a scientific school and of a religious conventicle, and that combination inevitably suggests a Pythagorean *συνέδριον*. There can be no doubt that Pythagorean influences had reached Athens by this time. About the middle of the century the Pythagoreans had been expelled from the cities of Magna Græcia; they had tried to continue their society at Rhegion, and, when they left Rhegion, they established themselves at Thebes (Philolaus, Lysis) and Phlius (Echecrates). There were many Pythagoreans at Athens in the 4th cent. B.C., as we know from the fragments of the comic poets, who burlesqued them very much in the same way as Aristophanes had burlesqued Socrates and his associates; but our knowledge of the Periclean age is so fragmentary that it is difficult to find contemporary evidence of their presence at Athens then. It is certain, however, that Athens had concluded an alliance with Rhegion in 433 B.C., ten years before the *Clouds*, and that Rhegion was then, or had lately been, the chief seat of the Pythagorean society. It is also certain that in 428 B.C. Euripides, in his *Hippolytus*, put on the stage a study of an Orphic saint. What is still more significant is that, even before the *Clouds*, Cratinus in his *Panoptæ* had burlesqued the science of the time in the person of Hippo, who was certainly a Pythagorean. His doctrine, so far as we know it, was not indeed very orthodox, but Pythagoreanism produced many heretics, and he is called a Crotoniate, a Metapontine, and a Rhegine as well as a Samian, and that can hardly mean anything else than that he was a Pythagorean. Nor is there any real reason to doubt the genuineness of his epitaph, which is quoted by Alexander of Aphrodisias and Clement of Alexandria,[3] in which we are told that Fate had made Hippo 'equal to the gods in death.' Of course the Athenians called him an 'atheist' for that, but it is sound Pythagorean doctrine all the same. It is also credible that the quotation from him made by the learned Claudianus Mamertus of Vienne (5th cent. A.D.) is genuine; for it distinguishes soul and body in terms which strongly suggest the 5th cent. B.C.[4]

In view of this, it is noticeable that the word *ψυχή* is used very curiously in the *Clouds*. The 'thought-factory' is inhabited by 'wise souls,'[5] which would only suggest to the average Athenian the meaning 'clever ghosts.' In the *Birds*[6] Socrates is spoken of as one who practises necromancy (*ψυχαγωγεῖ*), and his disciple Chærepho plays the part of the ghost. It was clearly well known before Plato was ten years old that Socrates taught strange doctrine about the soul.

Now we are told by the scholiast on the *Clouds*[7]

[1] J. Burnet, *Early Greek Philosophy*², London, 1908, § 122.
[2] 272 C, 295 D. [3] 235 E. [4] 137.
[5] *Apol.* 18 B : *Σωκράτης, σοφὸς ἀνήρ, τὰ . . . μετέωρα φροντιστής.*
[6] *Symp.* vi. 6. [7] Burnet, § 186 f.

[1] 627 : *μὰ τὴν Ἀναπνοήν, μὰ τὸ Χάος, μὰ τὸν Ἀέρα.*
[2] 379 : not Zeus, *ἀλλ' αἰθέριος δῖνος*, 1471 : *δῖνος βασιλεύει τὸν Δί' ἐξεληλακώς.*
[3] Diels, 26 B 2.
[4] Claudian. Mamert. *de An.* 7, p. 121, 14, ed. A. Engelbrecht (*CSEL* xi.) : 'longe aliud anima, aliud corpus est, quae corpore et torpente viget et caeco videt et mortuo vivit.' See art. Soul (Greek). For the variation in nationality ascribed to the Pythagoreans see Burnet, § 185, n. 1.
[5] 94. [6] 1555 ff. [7] 96.

that the allusion to men who teach that the heavens are an oven (πνιγεύς) was taken from the *Panoptæ*, where it was expressly referred to Hippo, so it appears that Aristophanes thought it plausible to attribute Italian as well as Ionian scientific ideas to Socrates. We must always remember that these two divergent views of the world met on common ground at Athens, where they set up an intellectual ferment which was of far more importance than the excitement produced by the occasional visits of the distinguished teachers to whom the name of 'sophists' is commonly applied. They were here to-day and gone to-morrow, but the scientific schools and the religious associations were firmly established.

Of course the whole plot of the *Clouds* turns on the belief of Strepsiades that the Socratics keep on the premises two λόγοι, a weaker and a stronger, and that they can make the weaker prevail over the stronger, though its case is a dishonest one. That is a perversion of Protagoras, but it does not follow that Aristophanes attributed it to Socrates. On the contrary, much of the fun of the play depends on the fact that, when Strepsiades has been initiated, he finds himself let in for something quite different from what he had expected. The idea is that the ordinary Athenian knew there was some talk of λόγοι in the school of Socrates and took for granted that it was just what Protagoras had made familiar some years earlier. Aristophanes knew at least that it was something different, though he may not have troubled to find out exactly what it was.

It appears also from the comic poets that Socrates had somehow become impoverished about this time. They allude to his want of a new cloak and the shifts he was put to to get one. Amipsias said he 'was born to spite the shoemakers,'[1] but that only refers to his practice of going barefoot, which Aristophanes attributes to the whole school.[2] Amipsias, in the same fragment, calls him 'a stout-hearted fellow that, for all his hunger, never stooped to be a parasite.' Two years later Eupolis spoke of him[3] as 'a garrulous beggar, who has "thoughts" about everything (τἆλλα μὲν πεφρόντικεν) except where to get a meal'—another reference to the φροντιστής.

4. Antisthenes and Æschines.—So far we have made no use of any evidence later than Plato's childhood; we must now look at certain writers of Socratic dialogues who were his contemporaries. There is not much to be learnt from the remains of Antisthenes, who seems to have been considerably older than Plato and to have been attracted to Socrates mainly by the strength of his character. The most important contribution he makes to our knowledge of him is that he spoke of foreigners being attracted to Athens by the renown of Socrates (κατὰ κλέος Σωκράτους). It is important to observe that this cannot have happened at any time after the outbreak of the war. Socrates must therefore have had a Hellenic reputation before Plato was born. Antisthenes told the story about Socrates saving the life of Alcibiades, which we know from Plato's *Symposium*, and he also mentioned the fact that Socrates yielded the ἀριστεῖα to Alcibiades, but he referred the incident to the battle at Delium instead of to that at Potidæa.[4]

If we could be quite sure that Æschines of Sphettus was independent of Plato, his testimony would be of the greatest importance. Plato makes Socrates mention him as one of his followers in the *Apology*,[5] and in the *Phædo*[6] we are told that he was among the company present at his death. Whether he was older or younger than Plato we have no means of knowing. In any case it seems in the highest degree improbable that Æschines and Plato should have conspired to misrepresent what must have been notorious facts in their day, and Æschines had no philosophy of his own to commend by representing it as that of Socrates. We may therefore regard his evidence as trustworthy, so far as it goes. For our purpose the most important of his dialogues are the *Aspasia*, the *Alcibiades*, and the *Telauges*, and we fortunately know a good deal about them. In the first of these dialogues Socrates was represented as taking lessons in the art of love from Aspasia, and as recommending Callias to send his son Hipponicus to learn politics from her. Moreover, he was made to maintain that the goodness (ἀρετή) of a woman is the same as that of a man—a point which he illustrated, not only by the case of Aspasia herself, but also by that of the Persian warrior maiden Rhodogune. Plato has little or nothing to say about Aspasia, though she is represented in the *Menexenus*[1] as the instructress of Socrates in the art of rhetoric. It will, however, be observed that Æschines confirms the account given by Plato in the *Republic* of the views held by Socrates with regard to women. The *Alcibiades* is even more instructive, and, thanks to a recent discovery of Grenfell and Hunt, we now possess a considerable continuous fragment of it. In this dialogue Socrates made Alcibiades feel that he was insufficiently prepared for the ambitious projects that he entertained, and made him weep in despair 'with his head on his knees' by proving to him that he was foolish (ἀμαθής) and therefore wretched (ἄθλιος), and, still worse, ugly (αἰσχρός). What he had neglected was 'care for himself' (ἐπιμέλεια ἑαυτοῦ). Socrates himself has no ἐπιστήμη and cannot therefore impart any to others, and certain characteristic expressions, such as θείᾳ μοίρᾳ, ἐνθουσιᾶν, ἔρως occurred. The main purpose of the dialogue appears to have been to show that Alcibiades was not, properly speaking, a disciple (μαθητής) of Socrates, as had been alleged—a point made also by Plato,[2] Isocrates,[3] and Xenophon.[4] There is, of course, a striking resemblance between the dialogue and what Plato makes Alcibiades himself confess in the *Symposium*.[5] In the *Telauges* Socrates was represented in conversation with a Pythagorean of that name who seems to belong to the circle of Philolaus. He is an associate (ἑταῖρος) of Hermogenes, and Cratylus also appears to have been introduced. So far as can be made out, Socrates expostulated with Telauges for his exaggerated asceticism. Here, then, we have further confirmation of the existence of Pythagorism at Athens at this date and of the relations of Socrates with it. Æschines also confirms Plato in representing the attitude of Socrates to the extreme asceticism of the doctrine as one of comparative detachment, while Aristophanes, for his own purposes, chose to ignore the distinction between him and such persons as Telauges. Perhaps Chærepho was more thoroughgoing than his master in this respect.

5. Plato.—Up to this point we have endeavoured to picture Socrates without making use of Plato except for a few hints. We have seen that in his youth he was a follower of 'the philosophy of Anaximenes,' then represented at Athens by Archelaus, and that he was also influenced by contemporary Pythagorism. We have seen that he was believed to have belonged to the circle of Aspasia and that he did his best to influence Alcibiades. We have also seen that he had become a comparatively poor man some time shortly before 423 B.C. At that date he was known chiefly as one who taught some new doctrine about the soul and

[1] Frag. 9. [2] *Clouds*, 103. [3] Frag. 352.
[4] This is far less probable; for Socrates would be more likely to have deserved the ἀριστεῖα when he was under forty than some years later, when he was nearly fifty.
[5] 33 E. [6] 59 B.

[1] 235 E, 249 C. [2] *Apol.* 33 A. [3] *Busiris*, § 5.
[4] *Mem.* i. 2. 12 ff. [5] 215 A ff.

about the birth of thoughts (*φροντίδες*) from it. Plato was still only a child, but we can hardly doubt his statement that his uncle Charmides had already made the acquaintance of Socrates. Apart altogether from what he may have learnt by personal intercourse with Socrates himself, Plato had every opportunity of hearing about him from the older members of his own family.

We learn, then, from Plato that Sophroniscus, the father of Socrates, had been a close friend of Lysimachus, the son of the great Aristides, who belonged to the same deme of Alopece, about a mile and a half from Athens.[1] Socrates himself had a lifelong friend in his contemporary, the wealthy Crito, who belonged to the same deme.[2] The name of his mother, Phænarete, has an aristocratic sound, and so has Patrocles, the name of her son by another husband, Chæredemus.[3] This is not in the least inconsistent with the fact that she exercised the profession of a *μαῖα*.[4] Such offices were performed by women of good family, and the translation 'midwife' is quite misleading. There is no good evidence that either Socrates or his father was a statuary or a sculptor. Xenophon, at least, had never heard of such a thing, or he could hardly have avoided mentioning it when he related the advice given by Socrates to the sculptor Clito.[5] The impression left by all our best authorities is that Socrates came of a well-to-do family, that he had no definite trade or occupation, and that he associated on terms of perfect equality with all the 'best people' at Athens, and especially with the Periclean circle. His poverty belonged only to his later years; for he served as a hoplite at Potidæa (431), Delium (424), and Amphipolis (422), and must therefore have had some property of his own.

The close relations of Socrates with the family of Aristides are presupposed in the curious story of 'the bigamy of Socrates.' He is said to have been married to Myrto, the daughter or grand-daughter of Aristides, as well as to Xanthippe. This story is given on the authority of Aristotle in his *Περὶ εὐγενείας*. We know that Socrates married Xanthippe late in life; for his three sons were all young when he died, and one of them was a baby; and A. E. Taylor has shown it to be quite possible that he was then a widower, having married and lost Myrto in his youth. We must remember, however, that the age of tittle-tattle had begun by Aristotle's time, and the story in the form quoted from him by Diogenes Laertius is plainly impossible. Surely too, if Plato had known the story, and if Lysimachus had been the brother-in-law or the uncle by marriage of Socrates, he would not have made him call him simply *πατρικὸς φίλος*. The first appearance of the statement that Socrates was a statuary or stone-cutter (*λιθοξόος* or *λαξόος*) is in Timon of Phlius,[6] who belongs to the 3rd cent. B.C. and is a very unsafe authority for anything. It appears to have arisen from an almost certainly false interpretation of his references to Dædalus as the ancestor of his family.[7] The Attic hero Dædalus had nothing to do with stone-cutting or marble sculpture, but was primarily a worker in metals, and secondarily the reputed artist of wooden *ξόανα*. He was sprung from the line of Erechtheus, and the Dædalidæ were not, as sometimes asserted, a trade gild, but an Athenian *γένος*, which had given its namo to a deme not far from Alopece. The whole chapter of Xenophon referred to[8] contrasts Socrates with *οἱ τὰς τέχνας ἔχοντες καὶ ἐργασίας ἕνεκα χρώμενοι*, and the point of it is clearly that he himself was not a professional man. In the *Apology* Plato makes Socrates address himself to the *δημιουργοί* as to a hitherto unexplored class. Plato's repeated allusions to the intimacy of Socrates with Damon confirm the tradition that he was intimate with the uncle of Pericles.

Plato has very little to tell us of the early interest of Socrates in Ionian science, which is natural enough, seeing that it had ceased to be of much interest in his time, and that he knew Socrates only after he had given it up as hopeless. It is all the more remarkable that, in the autobiographical sketch which he puts into the mouth of Socrates on the last day of his life, his youthful enthusiasm for science is made quite prominent.[9] It seems unthinkable that Plato should have invented a purely fictitious account of his revered master's intellectual development, and inserted it in an account of his last hours on earth. We are told that Plato himself was not present on this occasion,[1] and we have no means of knowing whether Socrates did, as a matter of fact, say these things, but we are surely bound to believe that Plato thought they were substantially true. Such arguments do not, however, appeal to every one, and there are fortunately others of a more objective character. The whole passage has obviously been written with the greatest care. After saying how eager he had been in his youth for the kind of knowledge called natural science (*περὶ φύσεως ἱστορία*), Socrates enumerates the problems that had interested him. They were such as whether the earth is flat or round, and whether 'what we think with' is air or blood, and the like. There were also problems about the nature of the unit and what is really meant by addition and subtraction. Now it can be proved in detail that all the questions raised in this passage were eagerly discussed in the middle of the 5th cent. B.C. at Athens, and that they could hardly have excited so much interest at any other time or place. There is not an anachronism in the whole passage, and a very slight knowledge of the state of science in those days is enough to show that what is represented as puzzling Socrates is just the opposition between the Ionian theories, 'the philosophy of Anaximenes,' and the Italiote doctrines, that is to say, the Pythagorean and Eleatic systems. It was just in the Athens of Pericles and nowhere else that these came into contact. Plato does not mention Archelaus by name, though a doctrine which we know to have been his is clearly described. Socrates felt (or professed to feel) quite helpless in face of this diversity of opinion, and he came to the conclusion that he had no gifts that way. That, of course, is his 'accustomed irony.' At last he heard 'some one [Archelaus?] reading a book, as he said of Anaxagoras,' in which mind was said to be the cause of all things, but the expectations this raised in him were disappointed when he got the book for himself and found that it really assigned no causality to mind at all, but only to 'airs' and 'æthers' and the like. He determined accordingly to strike out a line of his own. All this is confirmed by the burlesque of it in the *Clouds*.[2]

In another dialogue, the *Parmenides*, Plato supplements this account of the intellectual struggles of the youthful Socrates. It is a report of a discussion between him and Parmenides of Elea, who was visiting Athens along with Zeno, and the discussion turns on the difficulties which attend the conception of sensible things as 'participating' in the forms (*εἴδη*). There is no chronological difficulty whatever,[3] and the actual occurrence of the discussion is referred to as a fact in two other passages of Plato.[4] We know that Zeno was at Athens for a considerable time, and that Pericles 'heard' him there. We also know that Pythodorus, son of Isolochus, studied under him and that other Athenians paid him large sums of money. If we remember the growing interest of Athens in the West at this date, it will not appear surprising that Parmenides, who was not only a philosopher but also a statesman and legislator in the Ionic colony of Elea, should have visited Athens along with his favourite disciple. Now it is, of course, obvious that Plato was not in a position to give an accurate report of a conversation which took

1 *Laches*, 180 E.
2 *Apol.* 33 D.
3 *Euthyd.* 297 E.
4 *Theæt.* 149 A.
5 *Mem.* iii. 10. 6.
6 Frag. 25 (Diels).
7 *Euthyphro*, 11 C, 15 B.
8 *Mem.* iii. 10.
9 *Phædo*, 96 A ff.

1 *Phædo*, 59 B.
2 For the details see the notes on *Phædo*, 96 A ff., in the present writer's edition of the dialogue (Oxford, 1911). The view that Plato is describing his own intellectual development in this passage is ludicrous. These questions were no longer of any interest even in his youth.
3 Burnet, § 84.
4 *Theæt.* 183 E, *Soph.* 217 C.

place more than twenty years before he was born, but it should also be obvious that he was not likely to represent a theory of his own as the subject of a rather damaging criticism in that conversation. It is, therefore, important to notice that the criticism of Parmenides is not specially directed against the so-called 'theory of ideas,' but rather against the view that these 'intelligible forms' can somehow be 'present' in the things of sense, or that the things of sense can 'partake of' them—a view which Plato expressly ascribes to Socrates in the autobiographical sketch of the *Phædo*,[1] though he indicates at the same time that Socrates was not clear that 'presence' or 'participation' was the right name for the relation between the sensible and the intelligible which he postulated. It is, fortunately, unnecessary to pursue this subject farther here. We are not bound to discuss whether Plato himself proceeded to 'separate' (χωρίζειν) universals from particulars or not, or whether Aristotle thought he did so or not. What is quite certain is that he never represents Socrates as 'separating' the forms from the things of sense, and that the difficulties he gets into in the *Parmenides* are due solely to his insistence on the participation of sensible things in the forms, and his refusal to take the easiest way out of these difficulties by adopting the theory of 'separation' (χωρισμός).[2]

Now in the *Phædo* it is just this coming into being and passing away (γένεσις καὶ φθορά) of particular things that interests Socrates. It never occurs to him or any of his associates from first to last to question the reality of the world of being (οὐσία); that is the postulate (ὑπόθεσις) which they all accept. The only question is the cause of becoming, and the new method by which Socrates proposed to attack it was what he called 'examination in arguments' (σκέψις ἐν λόγοις). That was, in fact, the method which had proved so successful in geometry already, and which Zeno had turned into such a deadly weapon against the Pythagorean geometry itself. What was new was its application to the consideration of other than arithmetical and geometrical problems, and in particular to the good and the beautiful. The importance of λόγοι in the work of the 'thought-factory' was well known to Aristophanes, as we have seen, though he carelessly or deliberately mixed it up with the teaching of Protagoras about making the weaker argument the stronger—a point which he still further developed when he introduced the righteous and the wicked argument in the second edition of the play. The Athenian public would certainly not distinguish the two things, and, as a matter of fact, there was something in common between them. Protagoras said that on every subject there were two λόγοι opposed to each other, and that was exactly what Zeno had shown in another sphere. The method of Socrates was to follow out the consequences (τὰ συμβαίνοντα) of these λόγοι, to 'follow wherever the argument led him,' and he transferred this method to matters of right and wrong, fair and foul. There still exists a curious document written in the Doric dialect, in which this application of the method is plainly exhibited, and which must have been composed under Socratic influence.[3]

1 100 D.

2 It is worth noting that Proclus, who was familiar with both the Academic and the Peripatetic tradition, has no hesitation in saying that Aristotle ascribed the 'theory of ideas' to Socrates. He says (*in Platonis Rempublicam*, i. 259, ed. G. Kroll, Leipzig, 1899–1901): περὶ γάρ τοι ταῦτα καὶ διέτριβεν ὁ Σωκράτης τὰ ὁριστὰ εἴδη, καὶ ὅ γε Ἀριστοτέλης φησὶν αὐτὸν ἀπὸ τῆς περὶ τοὺς ὁρισμοὺς διατριβῆς εἰς ἔννοιαν τῶν εἰδῶν ἀναδραμεῖν.

3 For the so-called διαλέξεις see Diels, 83, and A. E. Taylor's chapter on the δισσοὶ λόγοι in *Varia Socratica*, 1st ser., Oxford, 1911, p. 91 ff. The Peloponnesian War is referred to as the most recent, which dates the dialogue within fairly narrow limits. The Dorian dialect at once suggests Megara, where Euclides was developing the Eleatic doctrine under Socratic influence.

6. Early reputation of Socrates.—In the *Clouds*, as we have seen, Socrates is represented as the head of a regular school. The picture of the φροντιστήριον would be quite pointless on any other supposition, and the most natural thing is to assume that he succeeded Archelaus. His work must have been much interrupted, however, by the war. Plato makes a great point of his bravery in the field. We know that Socrates served at Potidæa, Delium, Amphipolis, and probably elsewhere, and we may take it for granted that these experiences made a deep impression on him. It is clear that he was already a celebrated man. We saw that Antisthenes spoke of foreigners being attracted to Athens 'by the renown of Socrates,' and we know who some at least of these were. There were the Eleatics Euclides and Terpsion from Megara, the Pythagorean Echecrates from Phlius, Aristippus from Cyrene, and doubtless many others (Cebes and Simmias, the disciples of Philolaus, from Thebes, and Phædo of Elis belong to a later time; for they are quite young in 399 B.C.). No one has ever disputed these facts, and they imply a great deal which is not yet generally recognized. In particular, we must remember that the attachment of the scattered Pythagoreans to Socrates must have begun in those early days before Plato was born. He had also devoted disciples among his fellow-citizens, of whom the best known to the Athenian public was the enthusiastic and eccentric Chærepho. It was he who, somewhere about this time, actually asked the oracle at Delphi whether there was any one wiser than Socrates. The oracle of course replied that there was not, and, according to Plato, Socrates at his trial attributed his mission to the Athenians to his desire to refute or confirm the truth of this oracle. He was conscious of knowing nothing except that he knew nothing, and he found at last that he was wiser than others only in this, that he knew he knew nothing, while they knew nothing either but thought they did know something. That, of course, is Socratic 'irony'; his mission was a much more serious thing, as we shall see. What is important for our present purpose is to observe that his reputation for 'wisdom' was well established before he entered on his mission at all.

To this period we must also assign the rivalry of Antiphon the sophist with Socrates, of which Xenophon has preserved some notices from an unknown literary source. He tells us[1] that Antiphon endeavoured to rob Socrates of his associates (τοὺς συνουσιαστὰς αὐτοῦ παρελέσθαι). He pointed out to him that he lived a life no slave would put up with, that he wore a cloak which was not only shabby, but the same in summer and winter, that he went barefoot and shirtless, and he argued that he was really a teacher of unhappiness. That was why he charged no fee. Here Socrates is clearly depicted as the head of a voluntary association of ascetics, much as he is in the *Clouds*. Socrates answered him as was to be expected, and he goes on to describe the way he spent his time with his associates.[2]

> 'I unroll in common with my friends the treasures of the wise men of old, which they have left behind written in papyrus volumes, and if we see anything good in them, we extract it, and think it great gain if we become friends to one another.'

This is not like anything else in Xenophon, or even in Plato, and must refer to the date of the institution which Aristophanes burlesqued as the φροντιστήριον.

It is impossible that Xenophon can be speaking here from his own personal recollections. We have no means of dating Antiphon the sophist, but the style and matter of the fragments which we possess[3] make it clear that he belongs to a time before Xenophon was born.

7. The mission of Socrates.—It is evident that

1 *Mem.* i. 6. 1 ff. 2 *Ib.* 14. 3 Diels, 80 B.

the early years of the Peloponnesian War marked a crisis in the life of Socrates, though we can determine its nature only from stray indications and inferences drawn from his later life. As we have seen, his military record was exceptional, and Plato has been careful to make Alcibiades and Laches (no mean judge) bear witness to his coolness in the face of danger and his admirable qualities as a soldier. As we have seen, Antisthenes confirms Plato's account of his saving the life of Alcibiades and declining the distinction of the *ἀριστεῖα* to which he was fairly entitled, though he transfers the incident (probably wrongly) from Potidæa to Delium. The discrepancy suggests that we are dealing with independent testimony, and it would have been difficult for Plato to put into the mouth of Laches such a handsome tribute as he does[1] to the conduct of Socrates at Delium,[2] unless his military reputation had been firmly established. That is an aspect of Socrates which should never be overlooked. We saw also from the fragments of the comic poets that Socrates had been impoverished by the war, like so many other Athenians. He cannot, however, have been reduced to real poverty before the battle of Amphipolis (422 B.C.); for he was serving as a hoplite there, which proves that he still possessed, or was deemed to possess, the property-qualification required for this service.

In the *Apology*[3] there is a much more illuminating account of the nature of the mission undertaken by Socrates than the half-serious story of the oracle already referred to. Socrates is made to say that God (not specially the god of Delphi) had assigned a certain duty to him—that of living in 'philosophy' and exhorting every one, and especially his fellow-citizens, young and old, not to care for their bodies or for money so much as for their souls, and how to make them as good as possible. To disobey that order would be to desert his post in the face of the enemy. It seems impossible to doubt that this was his real conviction. Socrates believed in his divine vocation, and the military language in which he describes it is probably due to the fact that he was on active service when the call came to him.

Now Alcibiades in the *Symposium*[4] is made to give a very circumstantial account of how Socrates at Potidæa remained in a 'rapt' for twenty-four hours, from one sunrise to the next, and we can hardly be wrong in connecting this with the mission to which he devoted himself from about this time. He was now nearly forty years old, and, though it is not to be supposed that he gave up his school at once, it is probable that the 'writings of the wise men of old' did not occupy so much of his attention as formerly. He believed himself to have received illumination from above and to be under the orders of God, and his whole life was now to be consecrated to their fulfilment. There are other indications that Socrates possessed the temperament which renders men receptive to such influence. From childhood[5] he had a 'sign' or 'voice' which seemed to be more than human. It came to him on quite trivial occasions (*πάνυ ἐπὶ σμικροῖς*) and opposed his doing something that he was about to do, but it never told him to do anything. It had to do, so far as we can see, only with the disadvantageous consequences of acts in themselves indifferent, and it is never appealed to on questions of right and wrong. Socrates naturally spoke of it as something superhuman (*δαιμόνιον*), and it must be remembered that the Pythagoreans held the doctrine of guardian spirits. On the other hand, the attitude of Socrates to it, as to

[1] *Lach.* 181 B. [2] Cf. *Symp.* 221 B.
[3] *Apol.* 28 E, 29 D ff. [4] *Symp.* 220 C ff.
[5] *Apol.* 31 C ff.

most things of the kind, is one of humorous half-belief (*εἰρωνεία*). He is made to say that the 'voice' was always right, and it is possible that he had a genuine belief in revelations of this kind. That only illustrates his temperament, however. The command which he now believed to have been laid upon him by God had nothing to do with the *δαιμόνιον*. That only warned him off undesirable actions; this issued a positive order. That might be treated lightly; this was something that he must obey even if it cost him his life, as in fact it did.

It is only from Plato that we get any intelligible account of the 'divine sign.' Xenophon[1] maintains that it gave positive directions as well as negative, and we may well believe that many followers of Socrates made much more of it than he did himself. The *Theages*, a dialogue included in the Platonic *corpus*, is evidence of that. The most important thing to notice is that he had the 'voice' from childhood, while the divine command came to him only in middle life.

We know in a general way what the mission of Socrates was. It was to convict his fellow-men of their ignorance and sinfulness (which for Socrates was the same thing), and his method was that of searching questions. Æschines and Plato agree that Alcibiades was one of those on whom he exercised his powers, and this is confirmed by the charge made later that he had 'educated' Alcibiades or that Alcibiades was his 'disciple.' Plato makes it clear that Socrates had known Alcibiades intimately when he himself was quite young and when Alcibiades was a small boy. At the time of the incident at Potidæa Alcibiades must have been twenty at least, as he was on military service, so there cannot have been more than eighteen years' difference of age between him and Socrates, and there may have been less. Charmides, Plato's uncle, was also one of the first of the lads whom Socrates sought to convert. Plato himself was not yet born.

8. The soul.—In the *Apology*[2] the burden of Socrates' preaching is that every man must 'care for his soul.'[3] The startling novelty of this requirement can be made clear only by an examination of the history of Greek ideas about the soul.[4] Here it will be enough to point out that the soul had never yet been recognized as 'the thing in us which has knowledge and ignorance, goodness or badness'; it had never been identified with the normal consciousness or character of a man. This, then, was the great discovery of Socrates, the thing which entitles him to be regarded as the true founder of the 'spiritual' view of knowledge and conduct. It is hardly necessary to insist on the importance of this for all subsequent religion and ethics.

In the *First Alcibiades*, attributed to Plato, the idea is fully developed. The first stage is 'care of oneself' (*ἐπιμέλεια ἑαυτοῦ*), and then the question arises, 'What is oneself?', the answer being that it is 'soul.' There are some reasons for believing that the *First Alcibiades* (which can hardly be Plato's) was based to a considerable extent on the *Alcibiades* of Æschines.

9. Goodness is knowledge.—The best-known Socratic doctrine, that goodness is knowledge, becomes at once intelligible in the light of this new view of the soul as the seat of both. Of course Socrates did not mean to deny the patent fact that a man may do what he knows, in the popular sense of the word, to be wrong. The question is what we mean by knowledge (*ἐπιστήμη*), and Socrates has no difficulty in showing that what commonly passes for knowledge is only belief (*δόξα*). Of course it may be a right belief (*ὀρθὴ δόξα*), and in that case it will be sufficient in

[1] *Mem.* i. 1. 2–5, iv. 3. 12–13, 8. 1. [2] *Apol.* 29 E.
[3] For *ἐπιμέλεια ψυχῆς* cf. especially *Apol.* 29 D and 30 A. It is no invention of Plato, but genuine Socratic doctrine; for it was found in Antisthenes also. Cf. also Xen. *Mem.* i. 2. 4: *ταύτην γὰρ τὴν ἕξιν . . . τὴν τῆς ψυχῆς ἐπιμέλειαν οὐκ ἐμποδίζειν ἔφη*, and the *Alcibiades* of Æschines referred to above.
[4] See art. SOUL (Greek).

ordinary circumstances to keep a man on the right road; but it cannot be trusted to do so in every case and in all circumstances, because it is not secured by a 'reasoned account of the cause' (αἰτίας λογισμῷ), as all scientific knowledge must be.[1] The man who really *knows* knows that everything worth doing is only so 'for the sake of the good,' which is the only thing it is really possible to wish for.[2] Now the only man who knows the good is the philosopher, and he is the man whose soul is in complete union with it, so that it is impossible for him to do wrong. It seems impossible to doubt that Socrates spoke in the language of passion of the love of the soul for the good and of its mystical union with it, and that the speech he is made to attribute to Diotima in the *Symposium* represents his real teaching on the subject. Such things were, of course, beyond the range of Xenophon, who had read Plato's *Symposium* without discovering what it was about, if we may judge from his own composition of the same name. We would give much for a glimpse of Plato's relations with Socrates, but he has kept himself out of the Socratic dialogues completely.

The present writer believes that we are bound to regard all the dialogues in which Socrates is the leading speaker as primarily intended to expound his teaching. This by no means excludes the possibility that Plato may have idealized his hero more or less, or that he may have given a turn of his own to a good many things. That would only be human nature, but it would not seriously affect the general impression. The principal ground for holding this view is that, at a certain period of his life, Plato began to feel that it was inappropriate to make Socrates the chief speaker in his dialogues. He is present in all of them except the *Laws*, which makes the secondary position assigned to him in the later dialogues all the more remarkable. If Plato had made Socrates the mere mouthpiece of his own speculations in the *Symposium*, it is difficult to see why he should not also have credited him with the logic of the *Sophist* and *Statesman* and the cosmology of the *Timæus*. The *Philebus*, one of Plato's latest works, is just the exception that proves the rule. Its theme is the application of Pythagorean principles to questions of morals; and, if we believe Plato, that was just the chief occupation of Socrates.

10. Trial and death of Socrates.—Though he performed all his duties as a citizen, and especially as a soldier, Socrates took no part in public life till the year 406 B.C., when the very existence of Athens was at stake. In that year he allowed himself to be nominated for the Council of Five Hundred; the lot fell upon him, and he took office. It was in the prytany of his tribe, the Antiochis, that the illegal proposal was made to condemn the generals who were accused of failing to recover the dead after Arginusæ collectively, instead of deciding each case by itself. Socrates stood alone in opposing the proposal and would not even take any responsibility for putting the question to the vote. There is no reason for supposing that he was in any way disloyal to the democracy, but he had seen it become more and more anarchical and tyrannous, and, if we may trust Plato's *Gorgias*, he now saw that Pericles himself had started it on this course. To him it was quite as repugnant that the people should act contrary to the laws as that a despot should do so, and he was bound by his deepest convictions to resist anything arbitrary. It is not therefore surprising that, when the democracy fell, Socrates did not feel obliged in any way to identify himself with its cause by leaving Athens. It may have seemed quite possible at first that the Thirty, several of whom had been among his associates, would restore the legal State. We know now that there was no chance of that, but it was not so clear then. Xenophon, who may have been in Athens at the time, has a story[3] of how Critias and Charicles called Socrates before them and told him that he must obey the law which had been ordained forbidding any one to teach 'the art of arguments' (τὴν τῶν λόγων τέχνην). Socrates replied by arguing in his customary manner with them. That was not very serious, but the affair of Leon of Salamis, twice repeated by Plato,[1] was more so. The Thirty were anxious to implicate as many people as possible in their crimes, and they sent for Socrates with four others and ordered them to bring Leon over from Salamis to be put to death. The others obeyed, but Socrates simply went home, for which he would have been put to death, if the Thirty had not been overthrown in time. That may have made him popular with the restored democracy for a little and so delayed the inevitable end, but of course Socrates remained faithful to his principles, and, when the democracy began to fall away from its original moderation, we may be sure that he did not spare his criticisms. To the men now at the head of the State he must have seemed dangerous, as a cause of disaffection among the younger men. The amnesty made it impossible for them to accuse him for his acquiescence in the rule of the Thirty, so something else had to be found to try him for. The actual accusation contained two counts: (1) irreligion (ἀσέβεια), which was explained to consist in his failure to recognize the gods recognized by the State and introducing new ones; and (2) corruption of the young. The first charge was based on the old story of his unorthodoxy contained in the *Clouds* of Aristophanes. That may seem to be going a long way back, but it must be remembered that the men who had flocked to him from all parts of Greece in the days of the φροντιστήριον were now free to visit him once more; and Plato indicates that at least Euclides of Megara, Theodorus of Cyrene, and Cebes and Simmias from Thebes actually did so. Most of these men had just recently been 'enemy aliens,' and their views were doubtless shocking to the orthodox. It was not, therefore, strange that the old scandal should be revived at this time. As to 'corrupting the youth,' that really meant encouraging them to criticize the new régime. It is not to be supposed that Anytus really wished Socrates to be put to death; he only wished him to leave Athens. Socrates, however, refused any compromise of this kind. He was not found guilty by a large majority, and it is clear that, if he had cared to propose banishment as an alternative penalty to death, as it was open to him to do, that would have been accepted. As it was, he proposed free entertainment in the Prytaneum for life, with the natural result that the majority for the sentence of death was greater than that for the verdict of guilty. Owing to the Delian festival, a month passed before he could drink the hemlock, and he spent it in conversation with his friends. Some of them were eager to get him out of prison and away from Athens, but he would not stultify himself by breaking the law. He had been legally condemned, however unjustly, and he must abide by the sentence, and so, he added, must his accusers. It is particularly noteworthy that most of the Athenians who were present at the last were men whom we know to have been associates of Socrates in earlier days. The rich young men, whom he was supposed to have corrupted, were not there. On the other hand, there was a remarkable company of foreigners—Eleatics from Megara and Pythagoreans from Thebes. It was very natural in these circumstances that Socrates should revert to the topics which had occupied him in earlier days. His mission was over, and there was no need to talk of that any more. He spoke, therefore, of the soul and its destiny, and Plato makes us feel how far he had gone beyond his former associates in his view of it. The older men say nothing at all, and Cebes and Simmias, the young Pythagoreans, though ready to be convinced, are frankly critical and inclined to

[1] *Meno*, 97 A ff. [2] *Gorg.* 466 D ff.
[3] *Mem.* i. 2. 33 ff.

[1] *Apol.* 32 D, E, *Epp.* vii. 324 E.

scepticism. When the talk was over, Xanthippe, who had been resting after sitting up with her husband the night before, was sent for to say farewell to him, and to receive his last instructions in the presence of Crito. The last scene of all is one of the great things of European literature, and must be read to be felt. Plato had ample opportunities of hearing the death of Socrates described in detail by men who were present, and it is impossible to doubt that he tried to record it as accurately as he could. The world has never quite forgotten the message that was left to it on that spring day of 399 B.C.

LITERATURE.—The Socratic problem was correctly formulated by **F. D. E. Schleiermacher**, *Ueber den Werth des Sokrates als Philosophen* (*Werke*, Berlin, 1834–64, sect. III. vol. ii. p. 287 ff.). His canon was: 'What *may* Socrates have been, besides what Xenophon tells us of him, without, however, contradicting the traits of character and principles of life which Xenophon definitely sets up as Socratic; and what *must* he have been to give Plato the occasion and the right to represent him as he does in his dialogues?' Unfortunately, this canon was overshadowed by the dictum of **G. W. F. Hegel** (*Vorlesungen über die Gesch. der Philosophie*, Berlin, 1832, ii. 69) that 'we must hold chiefly to Xenophon in regard to the content of his knowledge, and the degree in which his thought was developed.' This became untenable as soon as the date of Xenophon was settled, and the slight character of his acquaintance with Socrates was realized. **K. Joel**, *Der echte und der Xenophontische Sokrates*, 2 vols., Berlin, 1901, tried to find a test by which to judge between Plato and Xenophon in the statements of Aristotle, but this has not been generally accepted, since Aristotle did not come to Athens till a whole generation had passed away since the death of Socrates, and he could have had no firsthand knowledge about him. The literary problem was well discussed by **Ivo Bruns**, *Das literarische Porträt der Griechen*, Berlin, 1896. **A. E. Taylor** has discussed a number of points in *Varia Socratica*, 1st ser. (*St. Andrews University Publications*, no. ix.), Oxford, 1911, and a similar standpoint is adopted in the Introduction to **J. Burnet**, *Plato's Phædo*, Oxford, 1911. The most recent discussions are those of **H. Maier**, *Sokrates, sein Werk und seine geschichtliche Stellung*, Tübingen, 1914, and **A. Busse**, *Sokrates*, Berlin, 1914, which agree in rejecting the testimony of Xenophon and Aristotle in favour of Plato's. Their other results are criticized in the present writer's article on 'Ancient Philosophy' in *The Year's Work in Classical Studies, 1915*, ed. Cyril Bailey, London, 1916.

JOHN BURNET.

SODOMY.—Sodomy is sometimes defined as 'unnatural sexual relations, as between persons of the same sex, or with beasts.'[1] The word 'sodomy' meant originally the kind of wickedness practised by the inhabitants of the city of Sodom. That this was sexual intercourse between persons of the same sex is an inference based on the words of the men of Sodom to Lot (Gn 19[5]): 'Bring them [the men] out unto us that we may know them.' If 'know' (ידע) be given here a sexual meaning, as in Gn 4[1], the reference would be to unnatural intercourse. There is no actual necessity, however, for so interpreting the word 'know.' It may mean no more than 'get acquainted with,' and the wickedness which Lot is said to have anticipated that the men of Sodom contemplated may have been no more than to give the strangers a beating.

The translators of AV understood the word to cover any immoral sexual intercourse, for they rendered Dt 23[17]: 'There shall be no whore of the daughters of Israel, nor a sodomite of the sons of Israel.' The 'whore' of this passage was a *hierodoulos* (קדשה), or sacred prostitute,[2] and the sodomite was her male counterpart (קדש). The Bishops' Bible translated: 'There shal bee no whore of the daughters of Israel, neither shall there bee a whore keeper of the sonnes of Israel.' It is clear, therefore, that in Elizabethan English sodomy was not restricted to sexual intercourse with the same sex and with beasts, but was applied to intercourse between unmarried human beings also. In this article we shall assume that the term has the breadth of meaning that it had when AV was made.

1. Hebrews.—Among the Hebrews sodomy of both types existed. A law in Ex 22[19] reads: 'Whosoever lieth with a beast shall surely be put to death.' Just as a prohibition law implies that traffic in liquor has been known, and has even been customary, so the prohibition recorded in this law testifies to the existence of the thing prohibited. Similarly Lv 18[22], 'Thou shalt not lie with mankind, as with womankind: it is abomination,' is evidence that the second form of sodomy included in the *Century Dictionary's* definition at one time existed among the Hebrews. To what extent such unnatural indulgence was practised we do not know. Fortunately the veil of oblivion has fallen over the details. Sodomy of the second kind (immorality practised by men consecrated to a deity, and practised in the precincts of a temple in the service of religion) also existed in Israel down to the reform of Josiah. The term קדש, by which a sodomite is designated, means 'holy' or 'consecrated,' and indicates that he was especially devoted to a deity for that purpose. In 1 K 14[24] it is said that these sodomites 'did according to all the abominations of the nations which Jahweh drove out before the children of Israel.' This implies that men consecrated to similar service were connected with the sacred places of other western Semites. This is what we should expect, and is doubtless true. Asa, king of Judah, endeavoured to expel sodomites from the temple in Jerusalem (1 K 15[12])—a work which Josiah accomplished (2 K 23[7]). According to the most probable reading, in Job 36[14] it is said of the wicked: 'They die in their youth and perish like sodomites.' This parallelism implies that the life of sodomites was proverbially short, possibly from the fact that they contracted venereal disease. It may, however, simply refer to the destruction of sodomites by Josiah, though the first interpretation seems more probable.

The purpose of these officials is somewhat obscure. It seems probable, however, that they represented the life-giving power of the deity interpreted in a physical sense. If this were the case, barren women and perhaps also brides would resort to them.

2. Babylonia.—That behind the Babylonian civilization there lay a condition in which the type of sodomy defined by the *Century Dictionary* existed is proved by the Gilgamesh Epic, one of the heroes of which, Enkidu, is said to have eaten grass with the gazelles, with the cattle to have quaffed drink, and with the creatures of the water to have delighted his heart.[1] As the Epic goes on to tell how by intercourse with a *hierodoulos* he was enticed away from his animal companions, the narrative means, apparently, that before the coming of the woman he had satisfied his sexual appetite with the animals.

Of the existence of the equivalent of the Hebrew consecrated sodomite (קדש) there is no certain trace known to the present writer, though there is mentioned in the Code of Ḫammurabi an official who was probably a sodomite. This official is designated by a Sumerian term usually read *NER-SE-GA*, which a syllabary defines by the Semitic *manzaz pani*. The *NER-SE-GA* is first mentioned in § 187 of the Code, where it is said:

> 'One may not bring claim for the son of a *NER-SE-GA*, a temple guard (*manzaz ekallim*), or a sacred harlot (*SAL-zikru*).'

Again, in § 192 it is said:

> 'If the son of a *NER-SE-GA* or the son of a sacred harlot says to the father that brought him up or to the mother that brought him up, "Thou art not my father" or "Thou art not my mother," they shall cut out his tongue.'

The point of importance to our subject in these laws is that the children of the *NER-SE-GA* are treated exactly like the children of the sacred

[1] *Century Dictionary, s.v.*

[2] See art. HIERODOULOI (Semitic and Egyptian), § 5.

[1] Cf. P. Haupt, *Die babylon. Nimrodepos*, Leipzig, 1884, p. 9, line 39 ff.

harlot, or *hierodoulos*.[1] If the *NER-SE-GA* claimed his child, no one—not even the legal husband of the child's mother—could lay claim to the child. If the *hierodoulos* chose to bring up her child, no one—not even its real father—could deprive her of it. If, on the other hand, one adopted the son of a *NER-SE-GA* or the son of a *hierodoulos*, and the child repudiated the adopted father or mother, his tongue was to be cut out. The parallelism makes it probable that the *NER-SE-GA* was the male counterpart of the *hierodoulos* (*SAL-zikru*).

In the first of the two laws quoted the son of a *manzaz ekallim* is placed on a par with the sons of the other two. *Manzaz ekallim* has been sometimes translated 'palace guard,' but *ekallim* means 'temple' as well as 'palace,' so that the term may refer to another class of sodomites.

What is the meaning of *NER-SE-GA* and its equivalent *manzaz pani*? Muss-Arnolt defines *manzaz pani* as 'foremost place, dignitary, magnate';[2] Delitzsch as 'Frontplatz, dann als Titel: Ranghöchster, der die erste Stellung bekleidet, höchster Würdenträger.'[3] This interpretation seems to be confirmed for the later time by the phrase *manzaz pani šarri*, 'place before the king.'[4] It is, however, doubtful whether this was the original meaning either of the Sumerian expression or of its Semitic equivalent. Scholars have transliterated the Sumerian, *NER-SE-GA*; in the writer's judgment it should be read *GIR-SIG-GA*. *GA* is simply a phonetic complement. *GIR* is the sign for 'foot';[5] *SIG*, the word for 'pour out.'[6] When we remember the way in which 'feet' is employed in Hebrew as a euphemism for *pudenda*, as in Ru 3^{4-7} and Is 7^{20}, the possibility presents itself that this phrase may originally have had a meaning quite consonant with the office of a sodomite. In that case *manzaz pani* would not be a literal translation of it, but a paraphrase. It is by no means certain, however, that *manzaz pani* always means 'foremost place.' The uses of *pani* in Akkadian and Assyrian are closely parallel with the uses of *panim* in Hebrew, and in Ex $33^{14f.}$ *panim* is employed in the sense of 'presence,' or, as we should say, 'person.' The meaning is that Jahweh said to Moses: 'I will go with thee in person.' If we might apply this analogy to our phrase, *manzaz panim* would mean 'in place of the person,' and would appropriately designate a priest who impersonated a god, or who represented to the worshipper the functions supposed to be performed by a deity. If sodomites represented the life-giving functions or the fertility of a deity, as we have supposed, this would be a fitting designation of them. Herodotus tells how in the temple of Marduk in Babylon there was a couch on which the wife of the god slept at certain times, and that the oracle came only when she occupied the couch.[7] This appears to be confirmed by a text in the British Museum,[8] which speaks of the presentation of a couch for the *ziqqurat*.[9] From what we know of ancient oracles, it is hardly conceivable that at such times the god was not represented by a priest or *manzaz panim*, one who took the place of his person.

This view of the religious character of the *manzaz pani* of a god or a temple seems to be warranted by the fact that the *manzaz pani* of a king seems to have been the representative of the monarch in overseeing public work, and the *manzaz pani* of a temple was the representative of the god in looking after the affairs of the temple. Thus a pay-roll of the time of the Ur dynasty was certified to by the *GIR-SIG-GA* of the *patesi*, or ruler;[10] quantities of wool presented to the temple of Eanna at Erech were certified to by the *GIR-SIG-GA* of the temple.[11] In the year that Ibi-Sin, the last king of the dynasty of Ur, became king quantities of grain were paid as wages in behalf of the *patesi* of Girsu by a certain *GIR-SIG-GA* who acted as overseer.[12] There is no reason, however, why, just because a man was a representative of the king, there should be any irregularity in the birth of his children so that the Code would need to provide that no claim should be brought against them. It seems probable, therefore, that it is necessary to distinguish between two classes of *GIR-SIG-GA*, one of which impersonated the god in functions parallel to those of the sacred harlot, while the other impersonated or acted as the representatives of earthly rulers. It is probable that the *GIR* which occurs so often on the business documents of the dynasty of Ur as the official who *viséed* or authenticated the documents represents an abbreviation of *GIR-SIG-GA*.[13]

These etymologies represent possibilities only. While it seems probable that the *NER-SE-GA* (*GIR-SIG-GA*) was a sodomite, full proof is lacking.

3. India.—In India there seems to have been among the native races a wide-spread belief that the greatest manifestation of divine power was in the generation of life. The organs of generation consequently became to them the most revered symbols of deity. In course of time this view made its way into some forms of the religion of the Aryans. In present-day Hinduism it is most generally found among the Śaivite sects, though some of the Vaiṣṇavite sects also have adopted it. In Śaivite temples the deity is usually represented by the *liṅgam*, or phallus; the *yoni*, or vulva, is also a common religious symbol. Wherever such ideas prevail, sodomy is, or was at some time, a feature of religious services.

It is reported that in India there is a class of *faqīrs* who go entirely nude, and live apart from the people, but are held in the highest reverence. When they approach a village, the people flock about them, and the women lay aside all modesty in their intercourse with them. Especially those who desire to rid themselves of the reproach of barrenness kneel before the *faqīr*, take his private member in their hands, and kiss it.[1]

Another manifestation of sodomy is found among the Śaivite secret societies called Śaktas. To one another the members of these societies call themselves 'the perfect' and speak of outsiders as 'beasts.' Such is the ill repute of these societies at present that no respectable person will admit connexion with them. Their rites are set forth in texts called *Tantras*, in which the initiated are instructed. In one of these texts Śiva says to his wife Durgā: 'All men have my form and all women thy form; any one who recognises any distinction in caste in the mystic circle has a foolish soul.' At their secret meetings a naked woman, the wife of the chief priest, sits in the middle of the 'holy circle'—a circle composed of men and women sitting promiscuously without regard to caste or kinship. After partaking of meats, fish, parched grain, and various kinds of wines and liquors, each man is for the time Śiva and each woman Durgā. They freely copulate without regard to caste or the risk of incest. To give in detail the ceremonies of different societies would be but to repeat such indecencies.[2] The theory which underlies these societies is that man is a creature of passion, that passion is poison, but a poison that can be cured only by poison. On the principle 'Similia similibus curantur' they indulge in these orgies in order to cross the region of darkness to union with Śiva.

4. Australia.—In Australia, among a number of tribes, the conceptions out of which sodomy grew still prevail, though the customs in which they are embodied are different; *e.g.*, when a girl reaches the marriageable age (fourteen or fifteen), an initiation ceremony is performed upon her, which consists in cutting open the vagina.

Among the northern Arunta and Ilpirra the man to whom a girl has been assigned takes her, along with his father's sister's sons, and, accompanied by other men of the tribe who might have been her lawful husbands, and by a mother's mother's brother, they go out into the bush. The mother's mother's brother (who, of course, is an old man) then 'performs the operation with a stone knife, after having touched the lips of the vulva with Churinga, so as to prevent excessive bleeding.' Afterwards the old man who performed the operation, the father's sister's sons, and the other men have intercourse with the girl in the order named. The girl is then decorated and

---

[1] See art. Hierodouloi (Semitic and Egyptian), § 1.

[2] *Assyrisch-englisch-deutsches Handwörterbuch*, Berlin, 1905, p. 562a.

[3] *Assyrisches Handwörterbuch*, Leipzig, 1896, p. 457a.

[4] H. C. Rawlinson, *WAI* iv^2. [1891] 48, 4b.

[5] G. A. Barton, *The Origin and Development of Babylonian Writing*, Leipzig, 1913, no. 400^{24}.

[6] *Ib.* no. 175^{24}.

[7] i. 181 f.

[8] K. 164.

[9] Cf. *BH* ii. 635 f.

[10] Cf. *Cuneiform Texts, etc., from Babylonian Tablets in the British Museum*, London, 1899-1901, vii. 50, no. 19984.

[11] *Ib.* ix. 37, no. 21399.

[12] *Ib.* x. 48, no. 12245.

[13] This is evidently the view of Myhrmann, who in discussing the phrase *GIR-SIG-GA* (which he reads correctly) has accumulated a number of references, many of which turn out to be simply *GIR* written alone; cf. *Babylonian Expedition of the University of Pennsylvania, Series A: Cuneiform Texts*, ed. H. V. Hilprecht, iii., Philadelphia, 1910, p. 82.

[1] Quoted in *Phallism*, p. 49, from Barthélemy d'Herbelot's *Bibliothèque orientale*, Paris, 1697.

[2] Moore, *Hist. of Religions*, i. 343; Hopkins, *Religions of India*, p. 491.

taken to the camp of her allotted husband. At least once afterwards he is very likely to send her back to the same men.[1] Similar customs are found with varying details among other tribes.

In the Illiaura, after the operation is performed by the mother's mother's brother, first he, then the elder brothers of the husband, then his younger brothers have access to the girl in the order named. 'In the Kaitish tribe the operation is performed by an elder sister of the girl,' after which mother's mother's brothers, elder and younger brothers (but not in blood), mother's brothers, and those who might have been lawful husbands have access to her.[2]

In the Warramunga tribe the husband lies down with a brother on each side of him; the girl is laid across them by an elder sister; the operation is performed by a father's sister's son in the presence of all the men and women of the camp. She then goes to the camp of the man to whom she is allotted, but he has no intercourse with her for two or three days. After this she is lent for two nights to mother's mother's brother, father's sister's sons, paternal grandfather, elder and younger brothers (but not in blood), and to those who might lawfully have been her husbands. 'After this she becomes the property of the man to whom she was assigned.'[3]

The customs of the Worgaia, Bingongina, Wulmalla, Tjingilli, Umbaia, and Walpari tribes are in substantial agreement with the Warramunga customs, except that, as a general rule, the husband's father performs the operation.[4]

If the husband dies and the woman is handed over to one of his younger brothers, he lends her for a day or two to other men.[5]

In addition to the practices connected with puberty and marriage, there are in Australia other occasions on which intercourse with women other than those allotted to them is permitted to men. While certain of their ceremonies are being performed, large numbers of natives are gathered together and marital rules appear to be set aside for the time being.[6] The native name for such gatherings is *corrobboree*. In some tribes a woman is told off each day or each night to attend at the *corrobboree* ground, and all the men, except fathers, elder and younger brothers, and sons, have access to her.

Among the Arunta, when an ordinary *corrobboree* is in progress, an elder man will send his son-in-law into the bush with the elder man's wife to collect material for decoration. Ordinarily it would be unlawful for the younger man to speak to the woman or to come near her. Now he is expected to have intercourse with her, in order to cause the ceremonies to go more smoothly and to prevent the decorations from falling off. Towards night, when all is ready, the women who have spent the day at the men's camp are painted with red ochre and go to summon the other women and children for the festal night.[7]

In some tribes such sexual intercourse is much more common than in others. Among the Warramunga, *e.g.*, it is carried on night after night during the performance of sacred ceremonies. The lending of women follows certain rules which vary according to tribal conditions. Under certain circumstances women are lent only to men belonging to another division of a tribe; on other occasions only to men belonging to a man's own division of it.

An instance is recorded where, because the men of one moiety of a tribe had built a mound for another moiety, the head man of the moiety for whom the mound had been built brought his wife up near to the other group, secreted her in the bush, and escorted the head man of the other group out to have intercourse with her.[8]

On other occasions women in the Warramunga tribe are lent to men who ordinarily would not be permitted to approach them—*e.g.*, men who are sent out to bring in the bones of a dead person before the ceremony connected with the rites of burial. On this occasion the father of the dead person, or in his absence some tribal father, lends the woman. Often messengers are sent out with dead men's bones to summon other groups to the performance of some ceremony; on such occasions not only are women lent to the messengers, but a general interchange takes place. In some tribes the messengers will take women with them. When they have delivered their message, they leave them

1 Spencer-Gillen[b], p. 134. 2 *Ib.*
3 *Ib.* p. 134 f. 4 *Ib.* p. 135. 5 *Ib.* p. 136.
6 *Ib.* p. 136 f. 7 *Ib.* p. 137. 8 *Ib.* p. 138 f

a little way out in the bush, where they are visited by men of the other group, who, irrespective of class, have intercourse with them. It is, however, a prerequisite to such intercourse that they should have accepted the invitation of the messengers or should have agreed to the request that they bring. When men of one group go to exact vengeance of another group by killing a man, it is customary to offer to the messengers the use of women. If the offer is accepted, it is a sign of reconciliation; if it is rejected, it is a sign that full vengeance will be exacted.[1]

Except in the Urabunna tribe, where group-marriage prevails, the men have individual wives. Under ordinary circumstances for a man to have intercourse with a woman who does not belong to his group of lawful wives would be a very grave offence, liable to be punished by death. It is only in connexion with ceremonies and the sending out of messengers that irregular intercourse is allowed. In a few special cases the lending of women may be explained as a return for some service rendered, but in most cases it is clearly due to another motive. It is supposed to have some supernatural potency.[2]

LITERATURE.—S. R. Driver, *A Critical and Exegetical Commentary on Deuteronomy* (*ICC*), Edinburgh, 1896, p. 264 f.; E. W. Hopkins, *The Religions of India*, Boston, 1895, London, 1896, p. 491 f.; *Phallism: a Description of the Worship of Lingam-Yoni* (anonymous), London (privately printed), 1889, p. 48 f.; G. F. Moore, *Hist. of Religions*, New York, 1913, Edinburgh, 1914, i. 343 f.; Spencer-Gillen[b], ch. iv.; W. H. R. Rivers, *The Hist. of Melanesian Society*, Cambridge, 1914, i. 386 f.; E. Buckley, *Phallicism in Japan*, Chicago, 1898.

GEORGE A. BARTON.

SOLEMN LEAGUE AND COVENANT.—The Solemn League and Covenant was the formal undertaking entered into in the late autumn of 1643 by the Scottish General Assembly and Estates on the one part, and the English House of Commons and House of Lords on the other, with a view to making common cause against Charles I. in his civil and ecclesiastical policy. The agreement took the form of a religious covenant by the strong desire and insistence of the Scots,[3] who had become familiar with this more serious form of agreement in their recent ecclesiastical history. Bands had not been unknown in Scottish civil matters, the most noted being the Douglas Band and the band for the murder of Darnley in 1567. But from the era of the Reformation onwards covenants had been common and stringent. The first Covenant[4] was signed on 3rd Dec. 1557 by Argyll, Glencairn, Morton, Lorne, and Erskine of Dun. Between this date and 1643 almost twenty bands were signed or planned,[5] the most famous, perhaps, being the band of 27th April 1560 and the National Covenant of 1638. They were kindred in several respects. They were all purely Scottish in bearing and reference, and they were definite and emphatic in repudiation of Roman Catholic doctrine and practice. But the Solemn League and Covenant, while it had great similarity to those earlier bands in its strong anti-Romanism, differed in a marked way from them in its international character and in its international purpose. It was 'a Solemn League and Covenant for Reformation and defence of Religion, the Honour and Happinesse of the King, and the Peace and Safety of the three Kingdomes of Scotland, England, and Ireland.'[6]

The special form of it was not of English devis-

1 Spencer-Gillen[b], p. 139 f. 2 *Ib.* p. 140 ff.
3 Robert Baillie, *Letters and Journals, 1637–42*, Edinburgh, 1841–42, ii. 90.
4 A. R. MacEwan, *A Hist. of the Church in Scotland*, London, 1913–18, ii. 79.
5 D. Hay Fleming, *The Story of the Scottish Covenants in Outline*, Edinburgh, 1904.
6 A. Peterkin, *Records of the Kirk of Scotland from 1638 to 1650*, Edinburgh, 1838, p. 362.

ing; the substantial agreement was of English seeking. It took form comparatively late in 1643, but various steps towards it had been taken as early as the beginning of 1642. The earliest movements towards common action between the English and Scottish Puritan leaders are not known. But in the beginning of 1642, after the outbreak of rebellion in Ireland, 'the English Parliament agreed to pay both English and Scottish troops' to serve there.[1] The promise to the Scots was not kept, owing to the outbreak of the Civil War. The Scottish sympathizers with the Parliament had to find means in Scotland to defray the cost of food, clothing, and pay of the Scottish army. In Feb. 1643 voluntary contributions were asked for, and the response was general, Argyll giving £1000 sterling, and Alexander Henderson, the Covenanting leader, 1000 merks. That there were negotiations for closer relations between the English Puritans and the Scottish Covenanting party appears from emphatic protests made by Charles I. himself to the Scottish Privy Council. In these protests is to be found a strange mixture of self-deception and clear reading of the aims of the English Independents in their little sympathy with fundamental Scottish religious ideas. Thus, on 21st April 1643, the king reminds his Scottish subjects:

'Wee require our good subjects there to consider that the persons who have contrived, fomented, and doe still maintaine these bloodie distractions and this unnaturall civill warre, what pretence soever they make of the true reformed Protestant religion, are in truth Brownists, Anabaptists, and other independent sectaries, and, tho they seeme to desire a uniformitie of church governement with our Kingdom of Scotland, doe no more intend, and ar als farre from allowing the church governement by law established there, or indeed anie church governement quhatsoever, as they ar from consenting to the episcopall.'[2]

Various proposals were made to the Scottish States and General Assembly from time to time. At length, in Aug. 1643, a decisive step was taken when the English Parliament formally dispatched commissioners to Edinburgh to ask for an alliance with the Scots. The commissioners landed at Leith on 7th August. Even then the situation was singularly indefinite. 'One night all were bent to go as Redders (mediators) and friends to both, without syding altogether with Parliament.' Baillie was of the number who favoured this proposal. 'But Waristoun, his allone, did show the vanitie of that motion, and the impossibilitie of it.'[3] Alexander Henderson is usually credited with the authorship of the Solemn League and Covenant, but this assertion requires to be qualified, if not altogether put aside. The English commissioners yielded to the Scottish pressure for a religious covenant—a concession the more easily made because of the English Parliament's necessity, and because of the serious sentiments of the early Reformers both in England and in Scotland when leading statesmen saw the need not only of an alliance between the Protestants of the two countries but also of their giving this alliance a religious basis.[4] But difficulties arose after this preliminary agreement.

'When they were brought to us in this, and Mr. Henderson had given them a draught of the covenant, *we were not like to agree on the frame*; they were more nor we could assent to, for keeping a door open in England to Independencie. *At last some two or three* in private accorded *to that draught*, which all our three Committees from our States, our Assemblie and the Parliament of England did unanimously assent to.'[5]

Henderson, indeed, was spokesman for the League and Covenant in the Assembly. It 'was well prefaced with his most grave oration.'[6] But a leading spirit in the composition, if not the author of the whole document, was Archibald Johnston of Waristoun, whose *Diary* has this entry under Sunday, 22nd June 1651:

'My soule blesseth Him for making use of me in the draughte of the National Covenant, Solemn League and Solemn Acknowledgement, whereof the first scroll was from Him to me.'[1]

Hay Fleming goes so far as to suggest that the Solemn League and Covenant 'may have been entirely from Waristoun's pen.'[2] Waristoun was supremely loyal to it; and 'he looked on the Covenant as the setting Christ on his throne.'[3]

While the English commissioners were in Edinburgh, no serious changes were made in the agreement, although it was seen, as Baillie has noted, what the main drift of Vane and his associates was. On their return to England with the Scottish proposals Parliament on 28th Aug. 1643 remitted the League and Covenant to the Westminster Assembly of Divines 'to take into consideration the lawfulness of it.' Certain alterations were made.

Thus for 'according to the Word of God' was substituted the more guarded expression 'as far as in my conscience, I shall conceive it to be according to the Word of God.' There was discussion upon the undertaking 'to extirpate Popery,' 'it being a very nice business to know what Popery is, and what is meant by extirpation,' but no change was made in the clause.[4] Prelacy had an explanation added 'that is church-government by Archbishops, Bishops, their Chancellors, and Commissaries, Deans, Deans and Chapters, Archdeacons, and all other ecclesiastical Officers depending on that hierarchy.'[5]

On the main contention in the Solemn League and Covenant the contracting parties were agreed.

They condemn 'the treacherous and bloody plots, conspiracies, attempts and practices of the enemies of God . . . ever since the reformation of religion.' They discriminate the condition of the three countries. They see a remedy for the several degrees of mischief in the different countries. 'They are to endeavour to bring the Churches of God in the three Kingdoms to the nearest conjunction in religion, confession of faith, form of Church government, directory for worship and catechising.'[6]

After conjoining in milder condemnation prelacy, as above defined, with popery, the Covenanting representatives in both countries pass to a different and civil subject of treaty.

They are not only 'to endeavour mutually to preserve the rights and privileges of the Parliaments, and the liberties of the kingdomes,' but, strangely enough, considering the proximate end of the Solemn League, 'to preserve and defend the Kings Majesties person and authority, in the preservation and defence of the true religion and liberties of the Kingdomes; that the world may bear witnesse with our consciences of our loyalty, and that wee have no thoughts or intentions to diminish his Majesties just power and greatnesse.'[7]

The matter of the Covenant was so far adjusted that by 22nd Sept. it was sworn by both Houses of Parliament, and by 25th Sept. 1643 it was solemnly sworn to, in St. Margaret's, Westminster, by the Assembly of Divines and 112 members of the House of Commons. Plainly, in spite of the grave seriousness of the language and solemnity of all the procedure, there was room for conflict over the bond of union itself. The Scottish signatories did not see the irreconcilable character of particular provisions, nor the loop-holes in the portion which appeared to provide for one great international Presbyterian Church. The English representatives forgot that they were consenting to the realization of this Presbyterian ideal in spite of what they regarded as verbal safeguards. There was a certain lack of sincerity on both sides. Baillie tells us that he counselled eschewing 'a public rupture with the Independents till we were more able for them'—an advice 'which even Henderson

1 *Register of the Privy Council of Scotland*, Edinburgh, 1877–1913, vol. viii., introd. p. viii.
2 *Ib.*, vol. viii. p. 435.
3 Baillie, ii. 88 ff.
4 MacEwan, ii. 113.
5 Baillie, ii. 90.
6 *Ib.*

1 Waristoun's *Diary*, p. 72, ed. D. Hay Fleming, for Scot. Hist. Society, Edinburgh.
2 *Some Subscribed Copies of the Solemn League and Covenant*, privately printed, Edinburgh, 1918 (from the papers of the Edinburgh Bibliographical Society).
3 Bishop Burnet, *Hist. of His Own Time*, London, 1724, i. 28.
4 John Lightfoot, *Journal of the Proceedings of the Assembly of Divines* (*Works*, ed. J. R. Pitman, London, 1824, xiii. 10 f.).
5 Peterkin, p. 362.
6 *Ib.*
7 *Ib.* p. 362.

applauded.'[1] There was on the part of many of the English dislike of the Scots and antagonism to their persistence in clinging to the letter of the Covenant. 'The Independents laughed at the Solemn League and Covenant as an old almanack.'[2] Cromwell spoke 'contumeliously against the Scots intention of coming to England to establish their Church government on which Cromwell said he would draw the sword against them.'[3] The English were so clear-sighted and the Scots so idealistic, in spite of recent experience of unfulfilled promises, that the signing of the League and Covenant was followed by an undertaking to send an army into England for which the English Parliament was to pay. This led to difficulties altogether different from the theological or ecclesiastical. Early in 1644 the Scottish army crossed the Border and materially assisted the cause of the Parliament in the north of England, especially in the battle of Marston Moor on 2nd July 1644. In less than a year came the further defeat of the Royalists at Naseby, and the English Parliamentary leaders ceased to regard the Scots as necessary for the purpose of beating Charles I. and his following. Their doctrinal impatience was intensified by their growing sense of practical freedom, and their comparative political liberty led to a neglect of their pledged word in the treaty which followed upon the League and Covenant. The Puritan leaders had accepted the Covenant and the ideal of an enlarged Presbyterianism as the condition of receiving military aid, but, as the need for the latter grew less, the price to be paid seemed indifferent, not imperative. How genuine this grievance was, and how cruel, appears from complaints made to the House of Lords and from the *Records of the Commission of the General Assembly*, where the neglect of the Scottish forces was emphasized by the serious fact that the same indifference was not shown to their English fellow-soldiers. A. F. Mitchell, who, with J. Christie, edited *The Records of the Commissions of the General Assemblies* (*1646–1649*),[4] dwells upon the discouraging effects of this calculated niggardliness, and quotes from S. R. Gardiner[5] to the same purpose :

> 'Though the hard work thus devolved upon the Scots, nothing had been done to pay or to supply them. An assessment, indeed, had been made upon certain English counties for the support of their army, but not a penny had been raised, whilst Fairfax's troops received their pay fortnightly with the utmost regularity.'

The deliberate withholding of pay and supplies from the Scottish army was doubtless connected also with the Scottish attitude to Charles I. For not only was this exasperating in its marked divergence from the English Puritan antagonism ; it could not be reconciled with the treatment which the Scottish leaders meted out to Charles himself. To satisfy them he was to become a covenanted king. Yet the feeling that he was a specially Scottish sovereign, who had a right to homage and reverent national sentiment, did not fail, although Scottish 'dourness' would make no concession which might imply failure to honour the Solemn League and Covenant. A striking illustration of this somewhat illogical but very real feeling about the king, which prevailed from the negotiations about this agreement until the death of Charles and afterwards, is found at the close of a declaration of the Scottish Parliament on 21st April 1648 :

> 'And in particular this Kingdom of Scotland will now make it evident as they often declared, That their quietness, stability and happiness doth depend upon the safety of the kings Majesties Person and maintenance of his greatnesse and Royal Authority, who is Gods Vice-Gerent set over us for maintenance of Religion and ministration of justice ; Having so many bands and ties of duty and subjection to his Majestie and his government, who is our native King, from a longer series and discent of his Royall Progenitors than can be paralleld in Europe, That we resolve constantly and closely to adhere thereunto, as also to all the ends of the Covenant.'[1]

The beginning of the end of Scottish Covenanting idealism in its first stage may be said to have appeared with special significance when the English Parliament, on 19th May 1646, voted that the Scottish army was no longer needed. This led the way to that most mischievous cleavage which separated Scottish and English Puritanism. But this was augmented by the other severances which accompanied it. The Roman Catholics could not possibly have any feeling but hostility to the champions of a Covenant which bound its defenders to extirpate the whole system of popery, which looked only to the least worthy of its representatives in the 16th cent., having no regard (to speak of Scotland alone) to men like Wardlaw, Kennedy, Elphinstone, Turnbull, and Robert Reid, bishop of Orkney, and which lived in constant suspicion of something that would rival the massacre of the Eve of St. Bartholomew. Adherents of the Church of England and of Episcopacy in Scotland were considered to be little better than papists because they tended to the same doctrines and practices, and offended Covenanters by their worldliness and political subservience. The worst blow but one came when the meditated unity and approximate uniformity disappeared before Cromwell's Independent triumph, when the chosen home of Presbyterianism and the Covenant was tyrannically governed by the arch-Independent himself. Absolutely the worst calamity emerged, although it was not seen to be such, save by clear-sighted saints like James Fraser of Brea, when Charles II. was compelled to sign the Solemn League and Covenant—which his father never would do—and when the leaders of the Covenanters accepted the signature, well knowing that it was false in fact and in spirit.

The Restoration gave victory to the men and the forces most hostile to the principles which were embodied in the Solemn League and Covenant, and, as these open and determined opponents were joined by weak and sometimes worthless and worldly-minded men who had themselves been Covenanters, the ruin of the scheme of the Solemn League and Covenant was for the time assured. Baillie pathetically records the closing disaster in May 1661 :

> 'But when the House of Commons did not only vote the Bishops into the House of Lords, but the Solemn League and Covenant to be burnt with the hand of the hangman, all our hopes were turned in despaire.'[2]

This was the burning of the body of the Covenant. The spirit was not destructible. For a quarter of a century and more there were brave Scottish men and women who laid down their lives for the ideal which it embodied, and those who had marked only the errors and exaggerations of its defenders saw in the Revolution of 1688 a modified triumph of what had been contended for.

The Revolution Settlement was a modified triumph, but it was a triumph. Yet the glory of the Covenant, in the cloud of witnesses from 'the Killing Time,' long haunted the Scottish mind, and the influence of the age of the National Covenant and of the Solemn League and Covenant, consciously associated with that slightly later time of martyrdom, did much for the preparation of the

1 Baillie, ii. 117.
2 John Aiton, *The Life and Times of Alexander Henderson*, Edinburgh, 1836, p. 534.
3 Baillie, ii. 245.
4 3 vols., Edinburgh, 1892–1909 (Scot. Hist. Soc., xi., xxv., lviii.).
5 *Hist. of the Great Civil War, 1642–49*, new ed., London, 1904–05, ii. 228.

1 *Records of the Commissions of the General Assemblies* (*1648*) xi. [1892] 471.
2 iii. 470.

Disruption of 1843, which, with some admixture of frailty and fallibility, did more for Scottish religion than any other event since the Reformation.

LITERATURE.—See the sources quoted in the footnotes.

ALEXANDER LAWSON.

SOLIDARITY.—Solidarity is a bond which welds together living, especially human, beings, when they belong to the same whole or are mutually dependent upon each other. It is first of all a fact. (*a*) It is a *physiological fact*. As we advance in the scale of beings, we observe an ever more perfect co-ordination of all the parts of living organisms: primitive organisms are aggregates of relatively independent parts, while more perfect organisms are made up of parts which mutually condition each other. (*b*) It is a *social fact*. There is a bond between the child and its parents (at least between the child and its mother, since among some peoples paternity does not count), between the members of a family, a tribe, or a nation. As civilization advances, individuals, as Herbert Spencer shows, specialize and become dissimilar, but society becomes more coherent, because those specialized individuals require each other. Attempts have even been made to prove that society is an organism, similar to physical organisms, with a brain, digestive system, etc. But that is ingenious comparison rather than scientifically demonstrable truth. Not only do men of the same generation depend upon each other, but each generation depends upon those which preceded it, inherits their possessions, and profits from their labours, discoveries, struggles, and sufferings; it also suffers for their vices, mistakes, and ignorance. We owe to our ancestors the language which we speak, our customs, our religious ideas, and our artistic and scientific heritage. Besides general social solidarity, which is based on the family, nation, state, and sometimes even on larger groups, there are special solidarities—*e.g.*, that based on community of religion or profession. As a general rule, the smaller the group of men, the stronger is the bond of solidarity; but the opposite is also sometimes the case; *e.g.*, the religious bond uniting men of several nations may be stronger than the bond of national solidarity.

As is clear from what has just been said, the fact of solidarity arises both from causes which are independent of human will (this is the case especially in the natural groups) and from the voluntary action of man (*e.g.*, we create or extend a bond of solidarity by creating or extending a political or a religious organization, although the idea of establishing a new solidarity is not necessarily the predominating *motif* of these creations or extensions). In proportion as exchanges of all kinds and means of communication multiply, a bond of solidarity tends to unite the whole of humanity.

The fact of solidarity has become the starting-point of various metaphysical, theological, and moral theories.

1. Metaphysics.—One of the chief tasks of philosophy has always been to show the bond which exists between all beings, even beyond the confines of humanity. Pantheistic systems all end in a universal solidarity, since all beings are merely the manifestation of a single being, the deity. The Brāhmanic philosophy of the *Upaniṣads*, in particular, is summed up in the famous *Tat tvam asi*, 'That art thou,' which forms the foundation, adopted by Schopenhauer, of an altruistic ethic, *i.e.* in the fundamental identity of all beings.

2. Theology.—(*a*) The idea of original sin, and more particularly that of original guilt, rests on that of the solidarity of humanity with its first father. As the result of his fall, humanity has become sinful and guilty. The sin is transmitted from generation to generation as a fatal heritage. These doctrines and their history are discussed in special articles.[1] Here we shall merely observe (1) that the conception of original sin is sometimes metaphysico-physiological, as in St. Augustine, and sometimes rather juridical and moral; (2) that the way is prepared for these doctrines in the OT, where the idea of punishment inflicted on children for the faults of parents, on a people for those of its chiefs, is so prevalent that on certain occasions the prophets, especially Ezekiel, expressly attack it; this idea is also met with among a great many races; (3) that the idea of hereditary guilt is self-contradictory, but that, on the other hand, it is certain that sin is not only an individual fact, but also a collective fact, and that the sins of some are often the cause of the sins of others. The degree of guilt is to be reckoned from that of the sin, but it very often happens that habitual or present sin is imputable not so much to the one who is affected by it or who committed it as to others who, consciously or unconsciously, have determined his moral condition.

(*b*) The work of Jesus Christ has also been considered from the point of view of solidarity, not so much when it is regarded as a vicarious satisfaction (*i.e.* when emphasis is laid on the punishment of the Man-God accepted by God as the equivalent of that of all sinners) as when the idea of expiation is emphasized (*i.e.* the fact that Jesus is a member and the chief of humanity, and that, as such, He, the innocent one who had no penalty to fear, freely accepts that which sinful humanity deserved). The idea of expiation rests completely on that of the solidarity between the guilty and the innocent which makes possible the substitution of the latter for the former; and, when we say that a man is expiating his own sins, we are, in our imagination, somehow making two persons of him—a guilty man and a man who, after having admitted and regretted his sin, frees himself from it by consenting to his punishment, who freely takes upon himself the condemnation deserved by the former and blots out his mistake by sanctioning the moral law which he has violated. It is in this sense that Kant, *e.g.*, tried to rationalize the doctrine of the expiation accomplished by Jesus Christ. According to this theory, Christ became, as it were, the personification of the idea of the repentant sinner who accepts his penalty. The idea of an expiation accomplished by an innocent person for guilty ones, with whom he is connected by some kind of bond, is not specifically Christian, but Christianity has in a manner transferred it from the objective to the subjective mode, by showing that it is not the exterior fact of the suffering of an innocent one that saves the guilty, but the moral revolution that this fact produces in the heart of the latter.

3. Ethics.—The fact of solidarity has been very frequently, especially in recent times, taken as the *point d'appui* for ethical theories. Léon Bourgeois especially, in a book entitled *Solidarité*, has shown the interdependence of men in society, and the difference that exists between the distribution of the advantages which it ensures to its members and the real services rendered by one class or another to the common good. These services form between those who render them and those who receive them what in juridical language is called a quasi-contract, *i.e.* a state similar to that which results from certain contracts. The moral duty of society and its members therefore would consist, above all, in observing this quasi-contract and in paying to each the debt contracted with it. Morality, thus understood, would realize true justice and would also have the advantage of possessing a scientific character and of thus resting

[1] See artt. ORIGINAL SIN, SIN (Christian).

on a solid foundation. It may be objected to this theory that the fact alone does not create the law, and that the idea of a quasi-contract is not sufficient to produce the latter from the former. The relations between men are far too complex and unstable, their value far too much subject to discussion, to apply the idea of quasi-contract to them and to disentangle the consequences which they involve. It is impossible to triumph over all the iniquities which are included in numerous explicit contracts. Moreover, this idea of a social debt resting on a quasi-contract is much too external to become the principle of an ethic. It argues from a fact, simply as a fact, but, considered thus, it is incapable of transforming the conscience or stirring the heart. Of itself it will not prevent any one from trying to reduce his debt as much as possible, and, then, once he believes that he has paid it, allowing himself to be ruled by egoism; it at least limits as much as extends altruistic activity. Similar remarks apply to the theory of reparative justice developed by A. Fouillée in his *Science sociale contemporaine.* This philosopher insists mainly on the solidarity between the different generations of men and on the fact that this holds of the poor classes especially, because in the past they did not receive the property to which they were entitled or get the remuneration for their services which was their due. He asks, therefore, that these injustices should be redressed, but he himself recognizes the great difficulty that there is in determining the subjects of the rights which he proclaims and in determining what is due to such or such a person on account of past injustices. Thus in practice he reduces reparative justice almost to conferring the benefit of education on all, in order to put within their hands the means of rising in the social scale.

In presence of these theories we may affirm that solidarity can supply a principle of morality only if it is accompanied by a sentiment, as in the case of family or national solidarity, and to a certain extent of other solidarities also (*e.g.*, that of the members of a religious society), or if it is considered in the light of a principle of justice, it being previously understood that this principle is purely rational (*e.g.*, that of the equality of all men, from which it follows that there must be equality in their exchanges of services), or that it is a religious principle (*e.g.*, that of the love of one's neighbour for the love of God).

According to the principle which we adopt, we shall take more or less account of the fact of solidarity, and we shall consider ourselves more or less obliged to extend existing solidarities, to tighten their bonds, to obtain from them only results that are beneficial to other men, and to avoid the unfavourable consequences that might also be deduced from them in certain cases. It is only under these conditions that solidarity can pass from the state of a simple fact to that of a moral principle.

In Christian social circles the idea of solidarity is greatly insisted on as helping to persuade men to perform their duty towards the disinherited of this world. The name 'solidarities' has even been given to certain schemes which are concerned with grouping either members of a parish or all kinds of persons, rich and poor, for the purpose of mutual aid, both spiritual and material. But in these circles solidarity is regarded not as a simple social fact, but as a divine law which is specially shown forth in Jesus Christ, and that is why we are able to obtain the practical results that we do from it.

In the economic world the idea of solidarity is shown in the creation of all kinds of associations, co-operating in production, distribution, credit, etc. Some of these associations, it is true, are concerned only with the interest of the participants, and as a result they endeavour merely to create a new fact of solidarity, profitable to their members alone, not to transfer solidarity in the name of justice and love from the condition of a fact to that of a moral principle; but others endeavour to accomplish the education of their members in the sense of developing the spirit of solidarity even outside the bounds of any given association. If the principle of justice and love summons us to extend and increase the benefits of solidarity, it also summons us to suppress all its unpleasant results—*e.g.*, to wage war upon hereditary vices and diseases and get rid of all unjustified responsibilities in our laws and customs, especially in the penal law which formerly (and, in our own time, among savage races) often punished the innocent along with or for the guilty.

Solidarity is frequently contrasted with fraternity (a word which denotes merely a vague sentiment) and with charity (which implies the humiliating idea of dependence of the weak and the poor on the powerful and the rich). It is certain that the feeling of sympathy which accompanies certain facts of solidarity, and the feeling of obligation which arises from the connexion of the fact of solidarity with the principle of equal justice for all, is stronger than the general sentiment of human fraternity. As regards charity, it always retains its place alongside of solidarity, for it alone takes an interest in the unfortunates who have not the right, in certain cases at least, to invoke any solidarity, and especially the guilty ones who have disregarded it.

Perhaps, in order to avoid confusion, it would be better to keep the word 'solidarity' for the simple fact of the various bonds which unite men, and to designate the feeling which accompanies it or the principle which applies to it by the terms 'sympathy' and 'obligation,' founded on solidarity, or other equivalents.

LITERATURE.—See the sociological and moral treatises and manuals, works on Christian dogmatics, Biblical theology, and history of religions; also E. Bersier, *La Solidarité*^{2}, Paris, 1870; C. Secrétan, *La Philosophie de la liberté*^{3}, do. 1879; H. Marion, *De la Solidarité morale*, do. 1880; A. Fouillée, *La Science sociale contemporaine*, do. 1880; N. Recolin, *Solidaires*, do. 1894; R. Worms, *Organisme et société*, do. 1896; I. Izoulet, *La Cité moderne*^{2}, do. 1895; L. Bourgeois, *Solidarité*^{7}, do. 1912; C. Andler, 'Du Quasi-contrat et de M. Léon Bourgeois,' in *Revue de métaphysique et de morale*, 1897, p. 520; A. Darlu, 'Réflexions d'un philosophe sur une question du jour, la solidarité,' *ib.* p. 120, and 'Encore quelques Réflexions sur le quasi-contrat,' *ib.* 1898, p. 113. See also artt. SOCIOLOGY and ORIGINAL SIN.

E. EHRHARDT.

SOLIPSISM.—I. History of the term.

It is not known who invented the term 'solipsism' and introduced it into philosophical terminology. In 1652 an apostate Jesuit, Giulio Clemente Scotti, published under the title of *La Monarchie des Solipses* what purports to be a translation of a tract called *Monarchia Solipsorum* by one Melchior Inchofer. Crétineau-Joly[1] attributes the authorship to Scotti himself. The tract is a satire on the self-seeking policy pursued by the Jesuit order. The 'Kingdom of Self-Aloners,' *i.e.* self-seekers or egoists, is, on the model of Sir Thomas More's Utopia, described as a distant island, and an account is given of the constitution, manners, and customs of its inhabitants. The name 'solipses' is alleged to mean 'dans le langage des Magogues' the people living under the providence of many gods, the allusion being to the skill with which the Jesuits secure everywhere the favour of the powers that be. It is also punningly connected with *soleil.* Subsequently the term *solipsiste* seems to have been a current label in France for the Jesuits, with

[1] *Hist. religieuse, politique et littéraire de la Compagnie de Jésus*, 6 vols., Paris, 1844–46.

reference to their selfishness. *Solipsismus* is found for the first time in Kant's *Critique of Practical Reason* as the Latin *terminus technicus* for the German *Selbstsucht*. The passage runs:

'All the inclinations together (which can be reduced to a tolerable system, in which case their satisfaction is called happiness) constitute *self-regard (solipsismus)*. This is either the *self-love* that consists in an excessive *fondness* for oneself (*philautia*), or satisfaction with oneself (*arrogantia*). The former is called particularly *selfishness*; the latter *self-conceit*.'[1]

W. T. Krug[2] follows Kant's usage in identifying solipsism with moral egoism ('making one's own self the end of all one's actions'), but gives no references. This identification is still repeated as late as 1890 by F. Kirchner.[3] Meanwhile, some time during the 19th cent., solipsism was transferred from moral or practical egoism to theoretical (either epistemological or metaphysical) egoism, *i.e.* to the theory that I can know nothing but my own ideas and that I and my ideas are all that exists. This view was called simply 'egoism' by Wolf (who treats it, rightly, as an extreme species of idealism), Mendelssohn, Tetens, and other 18th cent. writers. The distinction between practical and theoretical egoism is clearly made by Schopenhauer.[4] Reid, Hamilton, and other English writers use the terms 'egoism,' 'pan-egoism,' 'egoistical idealism' like Wolf, as did Überweg in Germany, most of them representing metaphysical egoism as the logical consequence of Berkeley's views. Who was the first to substitute 'solipsism' for 'egoism' in this metaphysical sense cannot be determined. Campbell Fraser is said to have used the term in his lectures as early as 1874–75. It certainly became current in philosophical lecture-rooms and books in the seventies and eighties in England, Germany, and France. Its first appearance in English print is in A. Barratt's *Physical Metempiric*[5] (1883), where it is used as a familiar term. In 1892 the metaphysical sense is given exclusively in Alexis Bertrand's *Lexique de philosophie*.[6] In 1893 F. H. Bradley devotes a chapter to its refutation in *Appearance and Reality*.[7] In Italian *semetipsismo* and *psiconomismo* appear as synonyms. Nowadays it is in the theoretical sense alone that the term is used among philosophers.[8]

2. Metaphysical solipsism.—To follow in detail the development of the metaphysical theory which is now called solipsism is unnecessary. Its origins have been traced to Descartes's 'Cogito ergo sum,' to Malebranche's remark, 'Les sensations pourraient subsister sans qu'il y eut aucun objet hors de nous,'[9] to Berkeley's 'Esse est percipi.' One of the earliest and most complete formulations of it may be found in Fénelon:[10]

'Non seulement tous ces corps qu'il me semble apercevoir, mais encore tous les esprits, qui me paraissent en société avec moi . . . tous ces êtres, dis-je, peuvent avoir rien de réel et n'être qu'une pure illusion qui se passe toute entière au dedans de moi seul: peut-être suis-je moi seul toute la nature.'

Modern discussions of solipsism have been needlessly embarrassed by the paradoxical habit which many philosophers have of expressing the theory in the first person plural. 'Have we any reason to believe in the existence of anything beyond our private selves?', asks Bradley, and he goes on to use such phrases as 'our private self' (*sic*). That each of us believes in the existence of other selves, and generally of a world beyond his private self, is of course a fact. But, when the *right* to that belief is challenged, as it is by the solipsist, the scales are unfairly loaded against the challenger, if the examination of his thesis is conducted in terms which assume the truth of the belief. Solipsism appeals to the individual, and the individual must argue the pros and cons out with himself, addressing no audience until he has gained the right to believe that there is an audience to address. The thesis, then, to be examined is this: I alone exist, and all I experience and know is my own self. What, on this view, becomes of the distinction between mine and thine? Will it be possible for me to distinguish, *e.g.*, between my own body and the bodies of others? Must I claim that all things are mine? that the manifold sounds I hear are all my own voice? that I am the owner of all there is? In so far as solipsism denies the reality of others, consequences such as these might be held to follow, and a quick, if somewhat painful, refutation of it might be secured by putting the theory into practice. But the point of the questions is not to secure a cheap *reductio ad absurdum*, but to bring out, for clearness' sake, the fact that the solipsistic argument is not conducted with reference to the legal and social relations between individuals. It does not move at all in the context of 'inter-subjective intercourse.' Hence the meaning which solipsism gives to the terms 'I' and 'myself' must be quite different from the sense which these terms bear in social experience. This point is most important. There are, we may say, at least two senses of the terms 'I' and 'myself.' There is, first, the sense appropriate to the experience of living as a self among other selves, of being a member of a world of selves mutually recognizing each other. This sense, and the experience on which it rests, the solipsist in effect denies by his thesis. Hence it is not in this sense that he can use the terms in stating his thesis. What, then, is this second, solipsistic, sense of 'I'?

The answer is that 'I,' 'myself,' and all similar terms, in the solipsist's mouth, can denote only what 'this,' 'here,' 'now,' and such terms denote, viz. immediate experience in its present 'that' and 'what.' They are mere demonstratives, pointing to or expressing the feelings, perceptions, thoughts, etc., which are present in me. 'In me' here does not have the force of distinguishing my feelings from yours or another's. It is only another way of saying, 'These feelings here and now.' In short, the whole and sole point of solipsism is to declare the exclusive reality of immediate experience and to deny the possibility of transcending that experience. It is nothing but an argument for immediacy and against transcendence. To affirm that 'I alone exist' thus means that 'my,' *i.e.* 'these,' present feelings, sensations, thoughts, as bare psychical facts, are all there is. To affirm that 'I can experience or know only myself' means that these present feelings do not imply, point to, mean anything other than themselves, are not a fragment of a vaster world transcending them in existence and character. It cuts down the universe to the 'this—here—now' of immediate experience. Of modern writers no one has seen this more clearly than Bradley:

'The "this" and the "mine" are names which stand for the immediacy of feeling. . . . There is no "mine" which is not "this," nor any "this" which fails, in a sense, to be "mine."'[1]

1 *Kant's Critique of Practical Reason and other Works on the Theory of Ethics*[6], tr. T. K. Abbott, London, 1909, p. 165.

2 *Allgemeines Handwörterbuch der philosophischen Wissenschaften*[2], 5 vols., Leipzig, 1832–38.

3 *Wörterbuch der philosophischen Grundbegriffe*[2], Heidelberg, 1890: 'Der Solipsist handelt als ob er allein auf der Welt wäre.'

4 *Die Welt als Wille und Vorstellung*[3], Leipzig, 1859, i. § 19.

5 P. 25.

6 An unusual sense appears to be given to the term 'solipsism' by certain French philosophers referred to in Élie Blanc's *Dictionnaire de Philosophie*, Paris, 1906, who are said to oppose solipsism to monism 'pour désigner tout système qui admet un grand nombre d'êtres individuels, substantiellement distincts.' Leibniz's monadism would be solipsistic in this sense.

7 Ch. xxi.

8 For solipsism in the ethical sense see artt. EGOISM, SELF-LOVE.

9 *De la Recherche de la Vérité*, vol. i. ch. i. (*Œuvres*, Paris, 1871).

10 *Traité de l'existence de Dieu*, pt. ii. ch. i. (*Œuvres*, Paris, 1787–92, ii. 188).

1 Ch. xix., p. 223 of 5th ed. (1908); his chapter on 'The This and the Mine' (ch. xix.) is essential to his argument against solipsism (ch. xxi.).

To deny transcendence is to deny any reality beyond the momentary thrill of experience. It is to deny past and future except as present felt acts of remembering or anticipating. It is to deny the existence of material things, of the physical world or nature, except for this moment's colours, sounds, touches, and other sense-data. These fleeting presences are all there is of 'nature'; they are not signs or glimpses of a stable, enduring, orderly world of which they are parts. It is to deny the existence of other minds or selves, *i.e.* of centres or complexes of immediate experience other than this present one which calls itself 'I.' In short, the denial of transcendence is a denial of all inference and interpretation, nay of all judgment. For every judgment, as involving a universal, transcends the 'this' in its bare givenness or immediacy.

These sweeping denials might of themselves be regarded as sufficient to discredit solipsism. Yet many writers have been content to say that solipsism, though it carries no conviction, is theoretically irrefutable, and to justify the fact that neither in theory nor in conduct does any one proceed as if solipsism were true, by appeal to an ultimate act of faith or to a venture of the will—whether rational or irrational remaining a moot point. The pragmatist certainly has an opening here to say that the venture 'works' and is 'made true' by its success.[1] Others, like Bradley, have marshalled elaborate dialectics for refutation. Bradley certainly scores a point when he argues that the solipsist has no right to say, 'Only I and my ideas exist,' or, 'The world as I know it consists only of states of my own mind,' for immediate experience contains no such division into subject and object, into an 'I' and its ideas, into a mind and its states. These formulæ already transcend the given—the one thing which the solipsist is committed not to do, if he can avoid it. The rest of Bradley's refutation boils down to variations on the theme, 'He cannot avoid it.' He cannot, because immediate experience does not stay immediate. It transcends itself. 'I' have no choice in the matter. The right to transcendence, which the solipsist challenges, is thus ultimately justified by appeal to the fact of transcendence. But, if it comes to that, had we not better at once say with Hegel: 'The "I" is thought and the universal. When I say "I," I let fall all particularity . . .'?[2] In other words, immediate experience, the solipsist's 'I' and 'self,' is always both 'that' and 'what,' both 'this' and 'such,' both particular and universal, and it is the universal in it that ever carries it beyond itself—the life in it of the whole of which it is a part.

3. Methodological solipsism.—A few present-day philosophers advocate solipsism, not as a metaphysical thesis, but as a principle of method. Bertrand Russell, arguing that physics, if it is to be a genuinely empirical science, must begin and end with sense-data, puts forward the ideal of constructing physics on a solipsistic basis. The main point, in practice, would be the exclusion of the testimony of 'others.' The only evidence admitted would be, for each physicist, his own sense-data. A similar methodological solipsism, the point of which, however, is directed, not towards the distinction between my own experience and that of others, but towards the distinction between actual phenomena and hypothetical entities assumed as causes or grounds for phenomena ('metaphysics'), has been developed by Hans Driesch. Defining logic as 'the theory of order,' he claims that it may be 'founded solipsistically,' being concerned with the ordering of what I am immediately conscious of:

'Solipsism is the only basis of philosophy that is not dogmatic; for, let it be well understood, solipsism does not say that I "exist" as a "substance" or something else, but it only analyses the fundamental pre-phenomenon: *I have something consciously*. And this is the only fact—though not a "fact" in the usual sense—that is beyond any doubt.

Solipsism, then, is *not* dogmatic, not even in a negative manner. It does *not* say: What I consciously have is *nothing but* my phenomenon. It merely says: What I consciously have is *certainly* my phenomenon—whether it "be" anything else or not.

But now, for reasons that cannot be explained here in full, the ordering Ego tries to go beyond the limits of a pure theory of order and to establish the concept of a something that "is" *not* merely in so far as it is consciously possessed or possibly possessed in some way. Thus, for reasons of order, the theory of order gives itself up and asks for metaphysics.'[1]

The methodological solipsism of Russell and Driesch concerns, thus, only the starting-point of knowledge. Both admit the necessity for transcendence, Russell in the form of 'logical constructions,' Driesch in the form of metaphysical hypotheses.

LITERATURE.—Besides the references in the text see: J. M. Baldwin, *DPhP*, *s.v.*; R. Eisler, *Wörterbuch der philosophischen Begriffe*[3], 3 vols., Berlin, 1910; C. von Wolf, *Psychologia rationalis*, Frankfort, 1734, § 38; F. Erhardt, *Metaphysik*, Leipzig, 1894, vol. i., ch. x.; M. Keibel, *Werth und Ursprung der philosophischen Transcendenz*, Berlin, 1886; R. von Schubert-Soldern, *Grundlagen einer Erkenntnisstheorie*, Leipzig, 1884, ch. iii.; T. Reid, *Works*, ed. Sir William Hamilton, Edinburgh, 1846, Notes B and C; J. S. Mill, *An Examination of Sir William Hamilton's Philosophy*, London, 1865, ch. x. ff.; Hans Driesch, *The History and Theory of Vitalism*, do. 1914, p. 233 ff., *Ordnungslehre*, Jena, 1912, p. 2; Bertrand Russell, 'Sense-Data and Physics,' originally published in *Scientia*, vol. xvi. no. xxxvi.–4 [1914], reprinted in *Mysticism and Logic*, New York, 1918 (see esp. p. 158).

R. F. A. HOERNLÉ.

SOLOMON ISLANDS. — This large archipelago lies in the western Pacific and consists of a long chain of islands extending from 150° 40′ in a south-easterly direction to 162° 30′ E. The larger islands are mountainous, the highest point of Guadalcanar reaching to 10,000 feet. All have a volcanic basis; the island of Bougainville in the north-west has an active volcano, and the small island of Savo was also actively volcanic when the islands were visited by the Spaniards in the 16th century. This discovery was made after crossing the Pacific in the search for the source of gold and other precious objects in early times, and the islands were named after King Solomon in the idea that they may have contributed to his wealth. Many of the individual islands, such as San Cristoval, Florida, and Ysabel, still bear the names given to them by the Spanish voyagers in the 16th century. After the discovery the islands passed out of sight until last century. In 1914 the archipelago formed a British protectorate with the exception of the islands of Bougainville and Buka, which fell within the German sphere of influence. The interior of several of the larger islands is still unexplored, but the smaller islands and most of the coastal districts are now under European influence and are the seat of large plantations, chiefly for the production of copra.

1. Somatology.—In physical character the inhabitants fall into two groups sharply divided by a line passing through Manning Strait and the Russel Islands. To the north-west of this line the people are very dark, and on the whole negroid characters are more pronounced here than to the south-east, though many natives of this region combine with excessive blackness wavy hair and noses almost of European dimensions. The difference in colour and general appearance is so pronounced that natives of the two regions can be distinguished at a glance even by the most casual observer. These physical differences on the two sides of the dividing line are accompanied by definite differences in dress, especially of the women. To the east of the line the women, if they are not completely nude, wear grass petticoats, while in Ruviana, Eddystone Island, and

[1] See art. PRAGMATISM.

[2] *Philosophy of Right*, Introd., § 4, Add. (see tr. by S. W. Dyde, London, 1896).

[1] *Problem of Individuality*, London, 1914, p. 75 f.

Vella Lavella to the west they wear a remarkable garment resembling a knapsack both in appearance and in function, but covering the buttocks instead of the shoulders. These differences in physique and dress mark out the Solomons into two distinct regions which will be spoken of in this article as the Eastern and Western Solomons respectively.

Surrounding the main islands there are a number of small outliers, such as Bellona, Rennell Island, Sikaiana, and Lord Howe's Island (or Ongtong Java), in which the people are Polynesians in physical characters, but in some cases with evident indications of Melanesian mixture.

2. **Language.**—In most of the islands the languages are characteristic examples of the Melanesian family with few such aberrant forms as are frequent in the Santa Cruz Islands and the New Hebrides. In a few islands, such as Savo, Vella Lavella, and some parts of Bougainville, the languages belong to a wholly different family. They differ widely not only from those of the Melanesian stock, but also from one another. In certain respects, such as the position of the genitive, they resemble the non-Melanesian languages of New Guinea and have in consequence been assigned to the Papuan family. The people who speak these Papuan languages do not differ appreciably in physical character or general culture from their neighbours who speak languages of the Melanesian family. These exceptional languages are generally regarded as survivals of such an early linguistic diversity as is still present in New Guinea. It is supposed that these early languages have in all but a few islands been replaced by languages belonging to the general Austronesian stock and that the languages so introduced have taken on the form characteristic of the Melanesian family.

In the small outliers in which the people resemble the Polynesians in physique the language is also Polynesian in character.

3. **Social organization.**—The special form of social system in which the community is divided into two exogamous moieties with matrilineal descent occurs at each end of the group, in San Cristoval and at the northern end of Bougainville. In San Cristoval the dual organization occurs in the central part of the island. It is believed that the people of the moieties differ in physical and mental characters, and there is a definite tradition of hostility between the two. One of the moieties is held to be superior to the other; its members may not be enslaved or beaten, or subjected to other indignities, and its name is Atawa, which means 'seafarer' or 'foreigner.' These differences provide definite confirmation of the view that the dual system has arisen out of the fusion between two peoples. There is evidence that the dual system was once universal over the whole of the Eastern Solomons, but there is no sign of its presence in the Western Solomons until one comes to the northern end of Bougainville, where it occurs again in its characteristic form and closely related to the similar organizations of New Britain and New Ireland.[1]

The totemic form of social organization is more widely distributed. In San Cristoval it occurs in Santa Anna and Santa Catalina at the eastern end of the island and again at the western end, but with the striking difference that the totems of the eastern islands are mainly aquatic, while the western totems are almost exclusively birds. In each case descent within the clan is matrilineal. There are similar matrilineal clans in Ulawa, though with one or two exceptions they have no names and no totems. In Florida, Ysabel, and the western end of Guadalcanar the totemism is less definite. There are matrilineal clans each of which is connected with certain animals, often birds, but these animals are grouped with other sacred objects under the term *tindalo*, *tindadho*, or *tinda'o*, which is also the term for the ghost of a dead ancestor. In Ruviana, Eddystone Island, and Vella Lavella there is no trace of totemic organization, but this is found again in the Shortland Islands and Bougainville, where the totems are universally birds, and here again descent is matrilineal.

A third form of social organization occurs in Ruviana, Eddystone Island, and Vella Lavella, and probably in parts at least of Choiseul. Here there is no form of clan organization, but the social organization is founded on kinship or genealogical relationship.[1] In Eddystone Island a man calls all those with whom he can trace relationship his *taviti*, and it is this relationship by which marriage is regulated, a man not being allowed to marry any woman to whom he is related through either father or mother. The *taviti* of different persons form groups which overlap, and there is nothing which corresponds accurately to the descent of the dual and clan organizations.

In San Cristoval there is a remarkable form of adoption in which a boy is adopted, not as a son, but as a father, a mother's brother, or a grandfather, while a girl may be adopted as a mother or a grandmother. A child so adopted assumes the name and status of the person whose place he takes, the motive assigned for the practice being to 'keep green' the memory of a deceased person. By this process of adoption a child comes to be called father or grandfather, and it is possible that this practice accounts for certain peculiarities of the nomenclature of relationship, such as the use of a common term for the elder brother and the son's son, which elsewhere have been explained by peculiar forms of marriage.[2] These anomalous marriages, such as that with the wife of the father's father, however, occur in San Cristoval, and probably form, as in other parts of Melanesia, the starting-point of the peculiarities of relationship.

Definite hereditary chieftainship is general in the Solomons, with patrilineal succession, even where descent is matrilineal.[3] The concept of 'chief' has been much modified by European influence owing to officials expecting chiefs to take an important part in government. In their original state this seems to have been largely foreign to the ideas of the people, the main functions of chiefs being to see that ceremonies were properly carried out and that duly abundant feasts were provided on these occasions. In recent times certain chiefs, especially in Ruviana, have acquired great authority and have extended this beyond the confines of their own island or district, and it may be that these were examples of a native tendency to extend the functions of a chief to other spheres than the religious, but in most cases these functions have almost certainly been due, directly or indirectly, to external influence. In Eddystone Island chiefs and men who had taken ten heads in warfare were allowed to have a second wife.

An organization called *Matambala*, similar to the *Sukwe* and *Mangge* of the New Hebrides,[4] is known to have been present in Florida in the Eastern Solomons fifty years ago, but it appears to have been in process of degeneration and soon disappeared under European influence. There is no trace of the presence of such organizations in New Georgia, the Shortland Islands, or southern Bougainville, but they reappear as the *Rukruk*, allied to the *Dukduk* of New Britain,[5] in the northern part of Bougainville, and occur here in conjunction with the dual form of social organization. In Santa Anna the members of different totemic clans may not eat food cooked at one fire—a rule which in other parts of Melanesia holds good of the grades of the *Sukwe* and *Mangge*.

4. **Religion.**—This has an elaborate character in

[1] *ERE* ix. 336.

[1] *ERE* vii. 700. [2] *Ib.* viii. 426.
[3] *Ib.* viii. 853. [4] *Ib.* ix. 353[b].
[5] *Ib.* ix. 336[b].

rite of a simpler kind in which the tabu-sign is usually stroked with certain leaves, these movements with the accompanying formula being designed to remove from the sign the spiritual influence to which the efficacy of the tabu is due. Another kind of rite is carried out when it is desired to use the fruit of a tree protected by a tabu.

When a person falls ill, it is necessary first to discover the nature of the disease, and, if the symptoms do not make this obvious, the cause may be ascertained by the ring method of divination. Usually a number of diagnoses are made, each followed by the appropriate remedies. If it is diagnosed that a tabu of a certain kind has been broken, a man who knows the tabu carries out the appropriate treatment. This is of various kinds, the most frequent measures being to stroke or rub the body or limbs with certain leaves, usually four in number, and to spit chewed roots or tubers over the patient. The leaves used in the treatment are afterwards worn by the patient, usually suspended from a creeper round the neck. Creepers are often placed over one or other shoulder of the patient and of other people present, and similar creepers may be worn as armlets or anklets. In all cases prayers are uttered desiring that the sick man may be made well, the words used often indicating a belief in the presence of some influence within the sufferer which it is the object of the rites to expel. Usually the rites extend over four days, on the third of which nothing is done by the leech, this day being left in order to give the *tomate* or other spiritual beings an opportunity for action. Some forms of treatment should be carried out only during the waning of the moon, and in these cases the treatment is usually carried out in four successive months. When a cure has been effected, an offering is made of puddings, usually four in number. These may be burnt or put in the thatch of the house, and pieces of another pudding may be eaten by both patient and leech.

In some cases the tabu and associated treatment are connected with a shrine, but it does not appear that any ceremony connected with the tabu is performed at the shrine, though rites of other kinds may take place there.

When disease is ascribed to the agency of other spiritual beings the curative rites are much like those which follow the breaking of a tabu, the motive in most cases being the expulsion from the body of some spiritual agent by which the sufferer is possessed.

The breaking of a tabu corresponds with what we should ordinarily call theft, and there is little doubt that the institution of tabu came into being in Eddystone as a means of protecting property. There is thus in this case a definite relation between religion and morality.

6. Head-hunting.—The practice of head-hunting, which exists in Ruviana, Eddystone Island, Vella Lavella, Choiseul, and the Shortland Islands, is closely connected with the skull-cult and with the cult of ghosts. A head-hunting expedition is accompanied throughout by rites of a religious kind which begin a year or more before a proposed expedition in connexion with the new canoes which are made for the occasion. Various talismans and amulets are placed in the canoes during the expedition, and formulas are uttered and other rites performed which have definite reference to the cult of ghosts. Similar rites accompany the return of an expedition. This is followed at intervals by ceremonial dances which seem to have a definite religious character. The heads which are taken in the expedition are placed in a house constructed in a special manner, but, after they are so disposed, they are not the object of any special rites. Captives are also taken in the head-hunting expeditions. When brought to the island, these captives are adopted into families, of which they are treated as members. They may marry native women and have children. In Vella Lavella they may even become chiefs, but they are always liable to be killed to supply heads when these are needed. These *pinausu*, as they are called, are also chosen to take the leading part in certain ceremonies which are believed to be accompanied by danger, as when it is necessary in the construction of a new skull-house that the skulls shall be touched by human hands in being transferred to their new resting-place. The heads are needed at the building of a new house or a new canoe, and their use is almost certainly the survival of a former practice of human sacrifice.

7. Divination.—Divination for various purposes is practised by two chief methods. (1) In one the diviner holds an arm-ring in his hand and puts questions to the ghosts, who give an affirmative answer by movements of the arm which carry the ring round and round in a circle. This method of divination is especially frequent in religious rites, and it is by this means that those with special knowledge of disease discover what tabu has been broken or the nature of any other act by which a ghost or spirit has been offended. Before performing a rite designed either to produce or to cure an illness, the officiant will ascertain by means of the arm-ring whether the being by whose power the disease has been produced is willing to cause or cure the sickness. (2) The other method is by swaying movements of a canoe. Thus, if anything goes wrong on a head-hunting expedition, the canoe stops and its crew put questions to it, taking the swaying of the vessel to indicate an affirmative answer. It is believed that these movements are produced by a shark, crocodile, or octopus, and in Eddystone Island by a special octopus called Ngganggai. In this island these animals are *tamasa*, and there is some reason to connect this form of divination with the *tamasa vambule*, the beings by which the weather is controlled. These two kinds of divination almost certainly depend on the occurrence of movements produced without any witting intention on the part of the holder of the ring or the occupants of the canoe. They are of the same order as the automatic movements of the table-turner or the dowser.

8. Disposal of the dead.—There are many different methods of treating the bodies of the dead, over twenty varieties having been noted by C. E. Fox in San Cristoval alone. At the western end of this island, in the district of bird-totemism, the leading practice is cremation, the other chief method being to preserve the body in the house, the bones being collected when the flesh has disappeared. In other cases the body is exposed on a platform or on a rock. In San Cristoval and other islands at this end of the Solomons the body of a chief is placed in a canoe or food-bowl and buried in a square or oblong mound, called *heo*, 50 ft. or more in length. The dead body is placed in a cavity on the top of the mound, and sometimes this cavity is closed except for a shaft leading from the exterior of the mound. Sometimes there is a dolmen on the top of the mound, under which at a later stage the bones are placed. On the mound there is often a small statue of coral or stone, into which the 'soul' of the dead man is believed to go. Behind the head of these images there is an object like a pig-tail going down to the seat on which the image is represented as sitting.

Cremation and preservation of the body occur also at the eastern end of Malaita, where the body of an important man may be kept in the house enclosed either in a canoe or in a model of the sword-fish. In Florida inhumation with later disinterment of the skull is general, while in Savo this method is used only for chiefs, the bodies of the common people being thrown into the sea. In Eddystone, Ruviana, and Vella Lavella the usual method is to expose the body on a rock or small island till the skull can be removed and placed in one of the shrines already described. If a man so desires, his body can be thrown into the sea. In the Shortland Islands the bodies of ordinary people are either interred or thrown into the sea, while those of chiefs are cremated, and this is the habitual practice in the district of Buin in Bougainville. In both places the bones are collected from the ashes. In the Shortland Islands they are thrown into water, each totemic clan having its own site for the purpose, and it is believed that they are swallowed by fishes or other animals. In other cases the bones are interred, and this is the habitual practice in Buin. In Choiseul the body is either burnt or treated as in Eddystone, the practice of this island being said to have come from Choiseul.

The beliefs concerning the nature of the soul and of the existence after death vary much in different islands. The people of San Cristoval believe in two kinds of soul which in one part of the island are called *aunga* and *adaro*, the former being compared with the shadow from the sun and the latter with the reflexion from water. When a man dies the *aunga* leaves the body either at the fontanelle or by the mouth and goes to a distant place called Rodomana, of which the people have but a vague idea. The *adaro*, on the other hand, remains for some time with the body and then goes either into the jaw-bone or into a sacred stone, or, in the case of the chiefly clan, into the stone statue which is put upon the funeral mound (*heo*). In Florida the soul, called *tarunga* in life, leaves the body at death and becomes a *tindalo*, or ghost. In Eddystone Island the soul is called *ghalaghala*. It leaves the body at death, soon after which a ceremony is performed in which it is caught and put under the ridge-pole of the house. Soon after this another ceremony is performed in connexion with which the ghost is believed to go to a cave near the highest point of the island. On the eighteenth day after death the *ghalaghala* is transferred by means of another ceremony to the shrine in which the skull is kept, and still later the *ghalaghala*, now called a *tomate*, or ghost, goes to the home of the dead called Sonto, which is located in the island of Bougainville. In Vella Lavella it is believed that the ghost, here called *njiolo*, goes to the cave in Eddystone Island which furnishes a temporary resort for the *ghalaghala* of that island. In the Shortland Islands the soul, called *nunu*, is identified with both the shadow and the reflexion. When a man dies, the *nunu* becomes a *nitu*, or ghost, and goes to a place in Bougainville which is the site of a volcano. There it recovers from the effect of cremation, and with restored body returns to its own island, where it dwells in a special district. In some cases this is a place where the bones are buried after cremation. The soul in Buin is called *ura*, a word which also denotes the shadow, the reflexion, and a dream. The *ura* leaves a man when he is ill and flies in the form of a bird to the under world, where there is a tree the leaves of which represent human lives. If the soul-bird plucks the leaf representing the man whose body it has left, this man dies and the soul-bird stays in the under world. This home of the dead of Buin is the same volcano which is the temporary home of the dead of the Shortland Islands.

In all cases the life in the world of the dead differs little from that of the living. The ghosts eat, drink, dance, marry, and have children, and in some cases it is believed that they die. The nature of the life after death seems to be in no way influenced by the kind of life the man has lived, though it may be influenced by ceremonial omissions. Thus, if a man of the Shortlands had nothing burnt with him at his cremation, he would have no present to give to a being who meets him on the way to the home of the dead in Bougainville, and either he would fail to reach the place or his arrival would be delayed.

In several parts of the Solomons it is believed that pigs and inanimate objects have souls. When an object is burnt or broken at the funeral rites it is believed that the soul of the object goes with the deceased to the home of the dead.

9. Magic.—Malignant magic is less prominent than in the more southerly parts of Melanesia. In Eddystone Island, where it is called *mba*, the power of bringing disease or death by this means is ascribed to a few men and women who are also known as *mba*. They act by obtaining a portion of the food of their victim, which is then enveloped in a covering and called *penupenu*. This is kept in the clothing of the sorcerer or placed in the hot air of one of the fumaroles of the island, the motive in each case being to keep the *penupenu* warm and thus assist the occurrence of fever. When a person falls ill and it is suspected that he is suffering from the action of *mba*, the worker of the magic is discovered by divination with an arm-ring, and formerly the person indicated was slung by one arm in a tree till he confessed and revealed where the *penupenu* was to be found. Now the magic parcel is discovered by certain men who are believed to act through friendly spirits known as *tomate kuri*. These spirits know how to find the object by which the disease is being maintained in activity. It is believed that the malignant influence of the object once connected with the victim is due to the action of a spirit, which is almost certainly the ghost of a former *mba*. This variety of magic, which in many other parts of the world is supposed to depend on some virtue inherent in the magical ritual, is here ascribed to a spiritual agency, and this kind of agency is even more definitely involved in the process by which the illness so produced is cured. In the same island the injurious power of the evil eye is also ascribed to certain men and women called *njiama*, who have the power of flying from place to place and produce by means of their look a disease accompanied by bleeding from the throat which is nearly always fatal. Here again the power of the *njiama* is ascribed to the agency of a *tomate njiama*, or ghost of a dead possessor of the evil eye.

LITERATURE.—H. B. Guppy, *The Solomon Islands and their Natives*, London, 1887; A. Penny, *Ten Years in Melanesia*, do. 1887; C. M. Woodford, *A Naturalist among the Head-Hunters*, do. 1890; R. H. Codrington, *The Melanesians*, Oxford, 1891; Carl Ribbe, *Zwei Jahre unter den Kannibalen der Salomo-Inseln*, Dresden-Blasewitz, 1903; G. C. Wheeler, *ARW* xv. [1912] 24, 321, xvii. [1914] 64; R. Thurnwald, *Forschungen auf den Salomo-Inseln und dem Bismarck-Archipel*, i. and iii., Berlin, 1912; W. H. R. Rivers, *The History of Melanesian Society*, 2 vols., Cambridge, 1914; C. E. Fox and F. H. Drew, 'Beliefs and Tales of San Cristoval (Solomon Islands),' *JRAI* xlv. [1915] 131, 187; C. E. Fox, 'Social Organisation in San Cristoval (Solomon Islands),' *JRAI* xlix. [1919] 94.

The facts concerning Eddystone Island are drawn from unpublished material of the Percy Sladen Trust Expedition to the Solomon Islands by A. M. Hocart and the present writer.

W. H. R. RIVERS.

SOMA.—*Soma*, an intoxicating plant of N.W. India which was pressed (Skr. *su*, 'press,' *soma*, 'the pressing') and allowed to ferment, is supposed to be the *Asclepias acida* or *Sarcostemma viminale*, 'the expressed juice of which produces a peculiarly astringent, narcotic, and intoxicating effect.' As such it was regarded as a divine power, and, as in Mexico and Peru the *octli* and similar intoxicating plants were deified, so in India and in Persia the *soma*, identical with the Zarathushtrian *haoma*, was regarded as a god. Whether in later times the plant called *soma* was really the same as the Vedic *soma*, and whether this in turn was actually one with the *haoma* of the Avesta and the *ὅμωμι* mentioned by Plutarch,[1] is questionable. It may be that the names (indubitably identical) were retained when substitutes for the plant were used. We know that in the later period a 'substitute plant' was used in the Hindu *soma*-ritual, and the plant called *haoma* by the Zoroastrians was not the *soma* of the later cult. But originally both names and plants were the same. As early as the *Sāmaveda* it was recognized that there was a white as well as a yellow *soma*, and the latter is said in the *Rigveda*[2] to grow upon Mt. Mūjavat, where it is fostered by the storm-god. The eagle, on the other hand, is said to have brought it 'from the sky.'[3] It was mixed with water, milk, butter (*ghī*), and barley, and offered to the gods. It was at first drunk not only by the gods and the priests but also by other Aryans, and perhaps by all. Later, as the cult became more regulated, only the three upper castes were permitted to drink

1 *De Is. et Osir.* 46. 2 x. 34. 1.
3 *Rigveda*, ix. 86. 24.

soma, withal only as a religious ceremony, while *surā*, a rice-brandy, became the popular intoxicant. So important was the *soma*-cult that one whole book (bk. ix.) of the *Rigveda* is devoted to hymns in its honour. It is called the soul of the sacrifice and the delight of gods and men. It strengthens the weak, inspires the poet, prolongs life, and gives divine power to the gods. Especially is Indra (the god of strength and battle) the enjoyer of *soma*, which (or who) is regarded as his inspirer and friend. As god, Soma, like Indra, frees from danger and conquers foes, and brings wealth to the Aryan from sky and earth and air.[1]

'Soma is addressed in the highest strains of adulation and veneration; all powers belong to him; all blessings are besought of him.'[2]

Even the juice, as it filters through the sieve for purification, is addressed in terms of divine worship. Besides the ninth book of the *Rigveda* and hymns found also in other books, the *Sāma-veda* is devoted to its praise. From the descriptions it is evident that it was the yellow *soma*-plant that was used by the Vedic priests; this also is the colour of the Persian *haoma*. In the (much later) medical treatises no fewer than 24 varieties of the plant (then called) *soma* are mentioned.

Before the end of the *Rigveda* period this yellow plant (which was plucked by moonlight and bathed in water and milk, and which also had the property of 'swelling' as it was thus 'purified') became esoterically identified with the yellow, swelling, and water-cleansed moon, and in some of the latest hymns of the *Rigveda* there is no question that *soma* means the moon. From this time onward *soma* was thus used in two senses, either of the divine plant or of the moon-god, until, as in the epics, unless expressly the plant, the word *soma* means the moon. It is the moon-god as Soma who is portrayed in the *Mahābhārata* as a great warrior-god, ancestor of a race of heroes, etc. There is, however, even in this later period, the consciousness that *soma* is both plant and moon; it is no longer an esoteric doctrine, but one generally recognized; and in some mysterious way the 'moon-plant' is both moon and plant. The divine power of the Vedic Soma, who also is a war-god, made this identification easy. It has even been urged that, in the earliest period, Soma was already the moon. This is the contention of Alfred Hillebrandt, who, in the first volume of his *Vedische Mythologie*, has presented the thesis with great ingenuity. In this volume will be found the most complete analysis of the position and character of the Vedic *soma*, both as a plant (the different ways of fermentation are here described) and as the moon-god. Yet it does not seem to be proved by this treatise that Soma was at first the moon. The Iranian conception is distinctly that of a plant alone, and in most of the Vedic passages the conception is also that of a plant, albeit a divine power. The wild hyperbole of Vedic utterance permits many expressions which appear to be impossible when used of a plant, but some even of these are not applicable to the moon. Thus it is said that Soma gives the sun his light,[3] and it is not necessary to infer from this or other extravagant phrases that Soma is the moon. Soma is also said to create all things, which applies to neither plant nor moon, but is only one of innumerable lauds given to sundry gods, any one of whom at any time may be called creator, preserver, light-giver, etc., as the henotheistic poet is inspired to wilder flights of praise. Hillebrandt's main thesis, that 'everywhere in the Rig-Veda Soma means the moon,'[4] is itself an exaggeration, which he has not hesitated to carry to its logical conclusion and

[1] *Rigveda*, i. 91. 7 and ix. *passim*.
[2] W. D. Whitney, *JAOS* iii. [1853] 299 f.
[3] *Rigveda*, vi. 44. 23.
[4] Pp. 340, 450.

so predicates a lunar Haoma in the Avesta. In the *Rigveda* the prevailing thought is that the plant *soma* as an intoxicant stimulates Indra, the war-god, to slay enemies, human and divine, and, as stimulator, Soma himself may be said to be the 'foe-killer.' In one hymn Indra explains that he has drunk *soma* and is thereby nerved to do great deeds in a semi-intoxicated condition. This *soma* is the 'sharp-horned bull' (which Hillebrandt interprets as 'horned' moon), as it is said: 'Like a bull with sharp horns is thy brewed drink, O Indra,'[1] and the reason for the simile is given as 'because it bellows,' alluding to the roaring flood of juice pouring noisily into the vat. A further argument against Hillebrandt's interpretation is that the ancient name for moon (*mās*, identical with μής, μείς) is never applied to Soma. The allusion in *Rigveda*, x. 85. 3, to 'the Soma known to the priests, whereof no one eats' implies that the esoteric interpretation, to which allusion has been made, has finally in this late hymn identified plant and moon. The late *Atharvaveda* also speaks of 'the god Soma who, they say, is the moon.'[2] This is in line with the gradual mystical tendency which appears fully developed in the *Brāhmaṇas*. It is also analogous to the mystic character of the vine-worship or Dionysiac cult of Greece. Euripides says of Dionysos: 'Born a god he is poured out in libations to gods; through him men receive good.'[3] So Soma is poured out to god, being himself a god, and he gives goods and cures woes, as Dionysos in the same passage is said to be the 'cure (φάρμακον) for all woes.' 'We have drunk Soma, we have become immortal,'[4] says the Vedic worshipper, who 'knows the gods'—much like a Greek mystic.

The later moon-Soma is fabled to have married 33 (later 27) daughters of the creator-god Prajāpati (later Daksha) and to have roused the jealousy of the others by excessive devotion to one of them called Rohiṇī. The others went back to their father, who permitted Soma to take them again only on condition that he associated equally with them all. He agreed, but broke his promise, and hence was punished with a waning sickness or consumption, which causes the moon to diminish every month. This fable of the *Taittirīya Saṃhitā*[5] is popular in all later literature. The 'wives' are the signs of the lunar zodiac. As moon, Soma in the epics and *Purāṇas* is 'lord of stars and planets, of priests and plants, of sacrifices and of devotions.'[6] In this later mythology Soma is son of Atri or of Dharma, or is produced from the ocean-churning. His great exploit was the rape of Tārā, wife of Bṛhaspati, which caused the war of the gods described at length in the epics and *Purāṇas* and constantly alluded to in classical literature. According to these later legends, it was the son born of this intrigue who as Budha, *i.e.* the planet Mercury, became the ancestor of the lunar race and so, eventually, of Kṛṣṇa. The later moon-mythology gives Soma several new names or titles, the best known of which are 'crest of Śiva' (Śiva carries on his brow the crescent moon), 'hare-marked' (the Hindus see a hare in the moon), and 'lord of the lotuses.' The moon-Soma is represented as drawn in a three-wheeled chariot by ten white horses.

See also art. HAOMA.

LITERATURE. — The chief literature is contained in several notable articles of which the content is now available in the books mentioned below. It will be necessary to refer only to the masterly artt. of F. Windischmann, 'Ueber den Somacultus der Arier,' in *Abhandlungen Münch. Akademie*, iv. [1846]; and R. Roth, in *ZDMG* xxxv. [1881] 681, xxxviii. [1884] 134. The subject is treated at length by A. Hillebrandt, *Vedische*

[1] *Rigveda*, x. 86. 15.
[2] xi. 6. 7.
[3] *Bacchæ*, 272 f.
[4] *Rigveda*, viii. 48. 3.
[5] ii. 3, 5.
[6] *Viṣṇu Purāṇa*, I. xxii.

Mythologie, Breslau, 1891-1902, i., 'Soma'; and very fully (with copious extracts from preceding literature) by **J. Muir**, *Original Sanskrit Texts*, London, 1858-72, ii. 469, v. 258. For the Vedic Soma, **A. A. Macdonell**, *Vedic Mythology*, Stuttgart, 1897; and, for Soma in the epics, **E. W. Hopkins**, *Epic Mythology*, do. 1915 (both in *GIAP*), may be consulted; also **Hopkins**, *The Religions of India*, Boston, 1895, London, 1896, p. 112 f. (with preceding literature, p. 579), where, as in Muir, some of the hymns to Soma are translated and a fuller discussion may be found.

E. WASHBURN HOPKINS.

SOMALIS.—See ABYSSINIA, HAMITES AND E. AFRICA.

SOMNĀTH, PATAN SOMNĀTH.

—Somnāth (Skr. *Somanātha*, 'lord of *soma*' [*q.v.*], the famous sacred plant[1]), an ancient town in the State of Junāgarh, Kāthiāwār, Bombay (lat. 20° 53′ N., long. 70° 28′ E.), is noted as the site of the famous temple of Somnāth, the scene of the destruction of the Yādava tribe in an internecine struggle, and of the death of Kṛṣṇa, who seems to have been in this place the object of a cult independent of that of the hero of Mathurā.[2] Little is known of the famous temple before its destruction by Maḥmūd of Ghaznī (A.D. 1024–26).

According to Khondamīr in the *Habību-s-siyār*, 'Somnāt was placed in an idol-temple upon the shore of the sea. The ignorant Hindus, when smitten with fear, assemble in his temple, and on those nights more than 100,000 men come into it. From the extremities of kingdoms, they bring offerings to that temple, and 10,000 cultivated villages are set apart for the expenses of the keepers thereof. So many exquisite jewels were found there, that a tenth part thereof could not be contained entirely in the treasury of any king. Two thousand Brahmans were always occupied in prayer round about the temple. A gold chain weighing 200 *mans*, on which bells were fixed, hung from a corner of that temple, and they rang them at appointed hours, so that by the noise thereof the Brahmans might know the time for prayer. Three hundred musicians and 500 dancing slave-girls were the servants of that temple, and all the necessaries of life were provided for them from the offerings and bequests for pious usages.'[3]

'Sultān Maḥmūd, having entered into the idol-temple, beheld an excessively long and broad room, insomuch that fifty-six pillars had been made to support the roof. Somnāt was an idol cut out of stone, whose height was five yards, of which three yards were visible and two yards were concealed in the ground. Yamīnu-d-daula, having broken the idol with his own hand, ordered that they should pack up pieces of the stone, take them to Ghaznīn, and throw them in the threshold of the Jāmi' Masjid [cathedral mosque].'[4]

The common tale that the 'idol,' when broken, was found to be hollow and stuffed with diamonds and other precious stones is obviously a fable; it was really a *liṅga*, or symbol of Śiva, and such stones are never hollowed in this way.[5] The present ruined temple was built by Komārapāla in A.D. 1169, and was the second reconstruction of the temple destroyed by Maḥmūd.[6]

Another legend told that Maḥmūd carried off to Ghaznī the carved gates of the temple. At the close of the Afghān war of 1842 Lord Ellenborough, the governor-general, directed that these gates should be brought to India, and he addressed a pompous proclamation to the chiefs announcing that 'the insult of eight hundred years had been avenged.' The gates are now deposited in a room in the Zanāna court-yard of the Agra Fort. They clearly have no connexion with Somnāth, being made of Ghaznī *deodār* pinewood, bearing no resemblance to Hindu work, and being decorated with an Arabic inscription relating to the family of Subuktigīn, ruler of Ghaznī (A.D. 977–997).[7]

1 For the discussion on the identification of the plant see G. Watt, *Dict. of the Economic Products of India*, Calcutta and London, 1889-93, iii. 246 ff.; on the post-Vedic application of the name to the moon see A. A. Macdonell, *Vedic Mythology* (*GIAP* III. i.), Strassburg, 1897, p. 112 ff.

2 J. Kennedy, 'The Child Krishna, Christianity, and the Gujars,' *JRAS*, Oct. 1907, p. 951 ff.

3 H. M. Elliot, *Hist. of India as told by its own Historians*, London, 1867–77, iv. 181.

4 *Ib.* iv. 182 f.

5 M. Elphinstone, *Hist. of India*[6], London, 1874, p. 336.

6 *Progress Report of the Arch. Survey of W. India, 1898–99*, Calcutta, 1899, p. 8.

7 *Archæological Report, 1903–04*, Calcutta, 1904, p. 17; E. B. Havell, *Handbook to Agra*, London, 1904, p. 62 f.

LITERATURE.—Besides the authorities quoted above, see various accounts of the place: *IGI* xxiii. [1908] 74 f.; *BG* viii. [1884] 607 ff.; *The Āīn-i-Akbarī*, tr. H. Blochman and H. S. Jarrett, Calcutta, 1873–94, ii. 246 f.; **H. Yule**, *The Book of Marco Polo*[3], London, 1903, ii. 400 f.; **J. Tod**, *Travels in Western India*, do. 1839, p. 328 ff.

W. CROOKE.

SOOTHSAYING.—See DIVINATION, PROPHECY.

SOPHISTS.

—The sophists with whom this article deals are the paid teachers who undertook to prepare young men, by lectures or private tuition, for a public career in the city-states of Greece. Such were Protagoras and Isocrates (*qq.v.*).

1. Lives and writings.—It should always be borne in mind that the writings, save a few fragments, are lost and the sophists themselves for the most part known by the testimony of their opponents. **Prodicus** of Ceos, a countryman of the poets Simonides and Bacchylides,[1] frequently visited Athens. We read of one occasion when his speech before the Athenian senate (presumably as the envoy of Iulis, the township in Ceos to which he belonged) won great admiration, while his public lectures attracted the young and brought him large sums in fees.[2] There are allusions to the scale of payment, which ranged from half a drachma to fifty drachmas.[3] In order probably that his pupil might acquire a good prose style, Prodicus laid great stress on the accurate use of terms[4] and the careful discrimination of synonyms.[5] That his distinctions were not always logical is clear from the criticisms of Aristotle[6] and of Alexander of Aphrodisias.[7] But, besides grammar and rhetoric, he also gave instruction in ethics. One of his works, the *Horæ*, as we know from the scholiast on Aristophanes' *Clouds*, 361, contained a famous apologue, which is referred to by Plato[8] and happily preserved to us in substance by Xenophon.[9] Pleasure and virtue personified appear to the young Hercules, urging their conflicting claims on his allegiance until he decides to forgo the allurements of ease and follow the toilsome path of duty. From this it appears that Prodicus upheld the orthodox Greek morality of his day, as enforced by the poets.[10] Remarks of Prodicus on the right use of wealth are quoted in the dialogue *Eryxias*.[11] But the author of the *Axiochus* is probably mistaken when he puts into the mouth of Prodicus the well-known Epicurean maxim that 'death is nothing to us, since it does not concern the living and the dead no longer exist.'[12] From Aristophanes' *Birds*, 692, and the scholiast *ad loc.*, it may be inferred that Prodicus had somewhere sketched a cosmogony, though of its contents we are ignorant. In *Clouds*, 360, he is called a μετεωροσοφιστής, a term which there seems the counterpart of φυσιολόγος as used by Aristotle of the Ionians and other early physicists. Like them, he certainly wrote a work περὶ φύσεως,[13] of which Galen has preserved a single fragment dealing with human physiology.[14] Of his views on religion we know a little more. Philodemus the Epicurean,[15] in agreement with Cicero,[16] Sextus,[17]

1 Plato, *Protagoras*, 339 E.

2 Plato, *Hippias Major*, 282 C.

3 Plato, *Axiochus*, 366 C, *Cratylus*, 384 B; Aristotle, *Rhet.* iii. 14, 1415 *b* 15.

4 Marcellinus, *Vit. Thuc.* 36.

5 Plato, *Prot.* 337 A–C, 340 A, B, *Meno*, 75 E, *Euthyd.* 277 E, *Laches*, 197 B, D, *Charmides*, 163 A, B, D.

6 *Top.* ii. 6, 112 *b* 22.

7 *Comm. in Top.* 181. 2.

8 *Symp.* 177 B.

9 *Mem.* II. i. 21–34.

10 Cf. Hesiod, *Works and Days*, 285 ff.; Plato, *Phædo*, 68 D ff., *Rep.* ii. 363 A ff.

11 395 E, 396 E, 397 D.

12 369 B, C.

13 Galen, *de Elementis* (*Opera Omnia*, ed. C. G. Kühn, Leipzig, 1821–33, i. 487).

14 *De Virt. Physic.* ii. 9, iii. 195 (G. Helmreich).

15 *De Piet.* ch. 9. 7, p. 75 *b*.

16 *De Nat. Deorum*, i. 42 (118); cf. i. 15 (38).

17 *Adv. Math.* ix. 18, 52.

and Themistius,[1] names Prodicus as the first to base an explanation of religious rites and belief in the gods on a definite rationalistic theory. It would seem, Prodicus thought, that those natural objects which benefit us and sustain life were conceived as deities—sun and moon, rivers and springs, fields and fruits of the earth, fire and water, corn and wine. Most religious rites would then be closely connected with agriculture. This theory was more than once restated, notably by the Stoic Persæus.

Gorgias of Leontini in Sicily, a pupil of the Sicilian Empedocles, holds a very important place in the development of Greek prose style and forensic rhetoric.[2] He wrote a treatise on *Nature or the Non-Existent*, which in the manner of the Eleatic Zeno proved up to the hilt (1) that nothing exists; (2) that, if anything existed, it could not be known or conceived by man; (3) that, if anything existed and were known, it could not be divulged to another. Of this *tour de force* we have a detailed account in the treatise *De Xenophane, de Zenone, de Gorgia* (as it is wrongly entitled) in the Aristotelian Corpus[3] besides an abstract in Sextus Empiricus.[4] Despite this scepticism, Gorgias seems to have adopted and extended his master's hypothesis of perception by means of 'pores' or channels.[5] In ethics he upheld a plurality of virtues, which are differently developed under different conditions of age and sex.[6] However, unlike other sophists, Gorgias did not undertake to teach virtue,[7] but rhetoric, which he declared to be the first and most indispensable of all arts.[8] Yet his admission[9] that the art of persuasion deals with right and wrong, the just and the unjust, shows that some recognition of moral judgments, some outline, at least, of ethical theory, is required from the orator.[10] In the famous discussion with Socrates on the question whether it is better to suffer than to do wrong Gorgias stands aside: it is his pupil, the light-minded Polus of Agrigentum—'colt by name and colt by nature'—who is the opponent of Socrates. To Polus the prosperous career of the usurper Archelaus seems enviable, for have not his crimes brought him power, with its attendant wealth and fame?[11]

Thrasymachus of Chalcedon is another sophist who devoted himself to teaching rhetoric. His writings were confined, so far as we know, to speeches and an important treatise on the Art (ἡ μεγάλη τέχνη). In this direction his services were conspicuous. Critics were disposed to attribute to him rather than to Isocrates the introduction of the intermediate or mixed style, which eventually superseded both the high-flown and the bald.[12] We are told that he was rash and combative in argument, as his name suggests,[13] and this may be the reason why Plato chose him in the first book of the *Republic* to play an arrogant and offensive part in support of the definition of justice as the interest of the stronger.[14] A literary artist like Plato was not likely to miss the opening afforded by such a definition, with which we may well credit the historical Thrasymachus. But, as the dialogue proceeds, Thrasymachus becomes tamed, and at last we hear with no great surprise that Socrates

1 *Or.* 30, ed. W. Dindorf, Leipzig, 1832, p. 422.
2 See R. C. Jebb, *The Attic Orators*, London, 1876, i. p. cxxiii ff.; F. Blass, *Die attische Beredsamkeit*², Leipzig, 1887, i. 47–91.
3 979 *a* 11–998 *b* 21.
4 *Adv. Math.* vii. 65 ff.
5 *Meno*, 76 A–E; Theophrastus, *de Igne*, § 73.
6 Plato, *Meno*, 71 D ff.; Aristotle, *Politics*, i. 13, 1260 *a* 27.
7 Plato, *Meno*, 95 B, C.
8 *Philebus*, 58 A, C, *Gorgias*, 449 A, 456 B ff.
9 *Gorgias*, 454 C.
10 *Ib.* 456 C, 460 A f., 482 C.
11 *Ib.* 470 D ff.
12 Dion. Hal. *Judicium Demosthenis*, 3.
13 Aristotle, *Rhet.* ii. 23, 1400 *b* 19.
14 *Rep.* i. 338 C ff.

and Thrasymachus have never been enemies and are now very good friends.[1] In this connexion it should not be forgotten that we have a very different sentiment cited from a speech of Thrasymachus:

> 'The gods take no notice of human affairs; otherwise they would not have overlooked justice, which we see every day violated.'[2]

The spirit of this utterance is that of the book of Job. A specimen of his style is preserved by Dionysius of Halicarnassus.[3]

Hippias of Elis, like Prodicus and Gorgias, travelled about Greece, acquiring wealth and celebrity by giving lectures and taking pupils.[4] As Prodicus represented Iulis at Athens, so Hippias seems to have been the political agent of Elis at Sparta.[5] His accomplishments were varied; besides arithmetic, geometry, and astronomy, he was versed in poetry, music, mythology, philology, and history. To historians of mathematics he is known as the discoverer of a curve, called after him 'the *quadratix* of Hippias.'[6] Further, he acquired no mean skill in manual arts, if, as we are told, he appeared at Olympia with every article that he wore made by his own hands,[7] even to the signet-ring, which he had himself engraved, and the curry-comb and oil-flask of his own manufacture. He is also said to have invented a mnemonic system. That he was a learned antiquary is attested by his writings, of which the register of Olympic victors (Ὀλυμπιονικῶν ἀναγραφή) was perhaps the most important. His mode of instructing his pupils is criticized as too nearly akin to the curriculum of schoolboys.[8] As he claimed to be at home in all the learning of the age, he sought to popularize different branches of it, but the instruction so given must often have been superficial. By Xenophon[9] and by Plato (or whoever wrote the two dialogues *Hippias Major* and *Hippias Minor*) he is represented as discussing with Socrates such subjects as justice, beauty, and the peculiar Socratic thesis that injustice when voluntary is better than when involuntary. Hippias is made to appear conceited and ridiculous, but the opinions he defends—sometimes against quibbling or downright fallacy—in no way diverge from those approved by popular Greek morality.

There is little ground for supposing **Critias** the sophist to be any other than the Athenian politician who took part in the revolution of the Four Hundred and was chief of the Thirty Tyrants—that extreme oligarchical faction which, after the fall of Athens in 404 B.C., attempted to extirpate democracy by a reign of terror. It is not easy to imagine this ruthless doctrinaire giving lessons, but he certainly was a prolific writer both of verse and of prose. In the play entitled *Sisyphus*, probably by him, though some authors refer it to Euripides,[10] one of the characters sets forth speculations on the origin of the belief in the gods. The lines quoted by Sextus Empiricus[11] describe how in the beginning men lived a mere animal life without law and order; how, to prevent violence and oppression, severe penalties were enforced; but, as these could only check open crime, secret wrong-doing went unpunished until some man, shrewder than his fellows, thought to discourage

1 *Rep.* vi. 498 C.
2 Hermias, *In Platonis Phædrum Scholia*, ed. P. Couvreur, Paris, 1901, p. 239, 21.
3 *Loc. cit.*
4 Plato, *Apol.* 19 E, *Hipp. Maj.* 281 A ff., 282 D ff., 286 A.
5 *Hipp. Maj.* 281 A, B.
6 P. Tannery, *Pour l'histoire de la science hellène*, Paris, 1887, p. 247; T. L. Heath, *Euclid's Elements*, Cambridge, 1908, i. 266.
7 *Hipp. Min.* 368.
8 Plato, *Prot.* 318 D, E.
9 *Mem.* IV. iv. 5 ff.
10 Aët. I. vii. 2 (Diels, *Doxographi Græci*, Berlin, 1879, p. 298); cf. Athenæus, xi. 496 B.
11 *Adv. Math.* ix. 54.

it by proclaiming the existence of mighty and immortal beings, who see all that is hidden and hear all that is said in secret. In order to heighten the dread of them, he placed their abode in the sky, whence came the terrible thunderbolt and the beneficent rain.

These are the more eminent among the older sophists, whom we know from our chief authority, Plato. There were, however, some whom he does not mention by name, as **Xeniades** of Corinth, who, according to Sextus,[1] taught thorough-going scepticism. On the other hand, **Antiphon** the sophist, who was not the same person as Antiphon the orator,[2] was constructive, even dogmatic, and his claim to rank as a philosopher is not disputed by Philodemus the Epicurean, εἴτ' οὖν ῥητορικὸς εἴτε καὶ φιλόσοφος ἠβούλετ' εἶναι.[3] He was obviously interested in and familiar with the physical inquiries of his predecessors. He wrote a work *On Truth* in two books, the one dealing with first principles, the other with physics and anthropology. This work, if we may judge by citations of single words in Harpocration and Pollux, must have been widely read and studied. From the first book a few fragmentary utterances are cited:

'For the Word or Logos all is one. Once understand this, and you will know that for the Word nothing exists singly either of the things seen by the farthest reach of the eye or of thoughts conceived by the farthest stretch of the mind.'

'Hence it needs nothing and accepts not anything of any, but is infinite and self-sufficient.'

'The mind leads the body in the direction of health and disease, or whatever else it may be.'

Time he held to be 'a conception or measure, not a real substance.'[4] His proposal for the quadrature of the circle is criticized by Aristotle,[5] by Simplicius, *ad loc.*,[6] and by Themistius.[7] In the second book he dealt with the sun, moon, eclipses, the saltness of the sea, and other physical phenomena.

The sun he described as 'fire traversing the moist air which encircles the earth, setting when it leaves the air enkindled, rising to renew the attack when the air has again grown damp.'[8]

In spite of Anaxagoras, he adhered to the old view that the moon shone by her own light, being put out by the approach of the sun, because a stronger fire tends to put out a weaker one, and in like manner the other stars are obscured by the sun.[9] Samples of his style are furnished by Stobæus.[10] Of his ethics we can only judge by fragments of a treatise *On Concord*, which emphasize the importance of education and marriage, or point a moral against injustice and cowardice.

The anonymous sophist whom we know from Iamblichus[11] resembles Antiphon (with whom some would identify him) in his treatment of ethical and social questions. He, too, insists on the need of training to supplement natural endowment. Only by practice, begun early and long continued, can men become virtuous or successful, or acquire fair fame. The same advantages become good or evil according as they are used well or ill. Every man should practise especially two forms of self-control: (1) his honesty should be proof against bribes; (2) his courage should not shrink even from the sacrifice of life for his country. A truly good man seeks reputation, not by external distinctions, but by his own goodness. We must not think obedience to the laws cowardly or the use of might for aggression something valiant and noble. Men cannot live in isolation; they must come together in society if they are to get even a bare living; nor will this suffice if there be lawlessness, which entails worse evils than life in isolation. Hence it follows of necessity that law and right are the bonds of civil society. Imagine a superman, invulnerable in body, exempt from disease and suffering, of iron will, who might be supposed competent to use his strength for aggression and defy the laws with impunity; still, even he, if there were such an one, which is impossible, would be safe only so long as he upheld the laws; for the rest of mankind, given discipline in their superior numbers, could by force or fraud overcome him. The writer sets forth at length the contrast between the blessings of an orderly government—the confidence and security which it affords when men have leisure to attend to their private concerns and are free from alarm of civil strife or foreign war—and the opposite evils which come in the train of lawlessness. It is in such a state of anarchy and disorder that the tyrant or usurper springs up.

The fragmentary treatise entitled *Twofold Arguments* (δισσοὶ λόγοι) has been called a specimen of early eristic, but is rather a storehouse of special topics, Aristotle's εἴδη,[1] suitable for controversy, whichever side the orator or disputant may take. It cannot have been the show-piece (ἐπίδειξις) of a wandering sophist, but, as Diels says, a formal school-lecture to his pupils by one settled in a town where the dialect spoken was Doric; and it follows from i. 8 that its date is about 400 B.C.[2]

The method is to take certain pairs, good and bad, fair and foul, right and wrong, true and false, and argue in the case of each pair: first, that there is not any absolute distinction between its two members; and then, again, that there is, the conclusion in the latter case being generally reached by *reductio ad absurdum*. Thus the famous antithesis of nature and convention is presented in several distinct forms. The next theme so treated is that there is no difference in the conduct of the sane and the insane, the wise and the foolish; the next, that wisdom and virtue cannot be taught, because (*a*) one cannot impart a thing to another and keep it himself; (*b*) if they were teachable, there would be a recognized class of teachers of wisdom and virtue, as of music; (*c*) again, the sages of old would have made their sons wise, which is not the case; (*d*) many pupils of professed sophists have got no good by their instruction; (*e*) many have become eminent who never studied under sophists. Against (*a*) we can appeal to experience; schoolmasters and teachers of the lyre do both impart their special knowledge and retain it; (*b*) we answer that there is a special class of teachers, the so-called sophists; as to (*c*), there is the case of Polyclitus, who taught his own son to be a statuary; as to (*d*) and (*e*), the instances are admitted, but the inference is irrelevant. There is such a thing as natural endowment, φύσις, and, if one has enough of this, he can dispense with education. I do not say, adds the author, that virtue and wisdom can be taught, but the proofs alleged to the contrary do not satisfy me. Other arguments follow against the institution of the lot (arguments in its favour are wanting) and in support of the position that the best theorist is also the best practitioner of any art. Here negative arguments are wanting.

Of sophists eminent as dialecticians **Euthydemus** and **Dionysodorus** are familiar figures through Plato's dialogue named after the former. There were also **Bryson** of the Pontic Heraclea, a circle-squarer like Antiphon, whose pupil **Polyxenus** was asserted by Phanias to have been the author of the 'third man' argument against the theory of ideas,[3] and **Lycophron,** who held that law, so far from directly promoting civic virtue, was merely a guarantee to citizens of their mutual rights, ἐγγυητὴς ἀλλήλοις τῶν δικαίων,[4] and denied the reality of the distinction between the noble and the low-born.[5] Of rhetoricians besides **Theodorus** of Byzantium, **Evenus** of Paros, and **Licymnius** of Sicily, all three mentioned in Plato's *Phædrus*,[6] there was the Athenian **Polycrates,** whose pamphlet *The Indictment of Socrates* was written at least six years after the death of the latter, since it referred

1 *Adv. Math.* vii. 53.
2 Suidas, *s.v.*; Hermogenes, *de Ideis*, ii. 11. 7.
3 *De Poëm.* col. 187. 3 (*Voluminum Herculanensium*, Collectio altera, Naples, 1862–76, vi.).
4 Diels, *Fragmente der Vorsokratiker*3, 80 B, frags. 1. 10, 2. 9.
5 *Phys.* A. i. 185 *a* 14; cf. *Soph. El.* 11. 172 *a* 7.
6 *In Phys.* 54. 12.
7 *Phys.* 4. 2.
8 Diels, *Doxographi*, 351.
9 *Ib.* 358.
10 *Florilegium*, III. xvi. 30, lxviii. 37, xx. 66.
11 *Protrepticus*, ch. 20.

1 *Rhet.* i. 2, 1358 *a* 31.
2 *Frag. der Vorsokratiker*2, ii. pt. 1, p. 635 note.
3 *Ap.* Alex. Aphrod. in *Arist. Metaph.* i. 9, p. 84, line 16.
4 Aristotle, *Politics*, iii. 9, 1280 *b* 10.
5 Aristotle, frag. 82, 1490 *a* 10.
6 266 E ff.

to events of 393 B.C.[1] **Alcidamas** of Elæa in Æolis in his Messenian oration advanced the thesis that God and nature have left all men free, whence it would follow that slavery is unnatural and indefensible.[2]

2. Doctrine; general estimate.—In the history of popular education the sophists themselves mark an epoch. Before their time the schools taught music and gymnastics, reading and writing, but, except for the severe military training at Sparta or the peculiar discipline of Pythagorean brotherhoods in S. Italy, there was nothing beyond—no means of acquiring general culture. The recognition of the need for liberal studies and the effort, however unsystematic, to supply that need were the first-fruits of the age of aspiration and enlightenment which followed the Persian wars, when, under the leadership of Athens, literature and art blossomed anew. Among the diverse methods adopted by individual initiative the chief was the oral lecture (for which a fee was charged) on some topic of importance or interest, the theme being sometimes chosen by the audience. Under such conditions the lecturer was not only bound to be a good speaker, in order to attract hearers; he also needed much skill and practice in replying to questions and taking part in any discussion at the close. The lectures were often on language or diction or the interpretation of the poets or other matters closely connected with literature. The pupils of a Protagoras or a Prodicus were thus taught by precept and example to admire literary excellence and form a prose style of their own. In other words, they received an elementary, but indispensable, grounding in the humanities. When we reflect that the period from Gorgias to Isocrates saw the gradual fashioning and perfecting of prose, whether written or spoken, and that the names of Tisias, Thrasymachus, and Theodorus[3] mark definite stages in this process of evolution, we may fairly estimate the services of the sophists to literature as second only to their services to education. For the rest, there was a continuous change of programme, owing to the necessity of arousing interest by novelties. At different times four varieties of instruction may be distinguished. The literary and political essays of Protagoras made way for forensic rhetoric, which Gorgias brought from Sicily in 427 B.C. on his first visit to Athens, where its theory and practice became firmly established. Eristic, again, or the art of controversy, though it dates back to the Eleatic Zeno, came into prominence later than rhetoric, largely under the influence of Socrates and his disciples. Lastly in 392 B.C. arose the school of Isocrates, who, while he specially taught political rhetoric and the principles of politics, imparted to a wider circle a more comprehensive culture, not limited to any single professional routine, avoiding barren subtleties and technicalities. Some such reaction was advisable after the over-specialization which had gone on in forensic rhetoric and eristic, if the sophists were to free themselves from the charge that their whole stock-in-trade consisted of oratorical tricks and logical fallacies, with which their pupils might impose upon a jury or entrap an unwary disputant. It is not strange that great influence was exerted at the outset by teachers who awakened intellectual interests and worked upon the native Greek passion for excelling (*αἰὲν ἀριστεύειν καὶ ὑπείροχον ἔμμεναι ἄλλων*). In the 'art of words' they could offer their pupils an incomparable weapon for use in public debate or private discussion. But grammar and rhetoric were the sole studies which owed much of permanent value to the sophists. Elsewhere, as will be seen, preoccupation with the popular and the practical unfitted them for the work of original thinkers.

(*a*) *Ethics and politics.*—Quite apart from the absurdity of postulating for the sophists in common a distinctive ethical doctrine, as if the members of a whole profession ever agreed on controversial questions, or as if the rest shared the views of Lycophron on nobility or those of Alcidamas on slavery, there is little evidence that the sophists, as such, specially interested themselves in scientific ethics. For one thing, their ignorance of psychology was profound and is adduced as the cause of their errors in the theory and practice of rhetoric.[1] The opinions on morality cited as coming from them cannot always be credited to individual sophists as thinkers; they may be put forward by them as litigants or disputants. Then, again, other views have been ascribed to the sophists upon inference only; *e.g.*, their conception of the end of human action (it might be maintained) was success (*οὔ τις ἐρᾷ τὸ τυχεῖν*), but this is vague, unless we know what use is to be made of success. The undertaking to teach virtue implies, it may be said, a definite view of education, as the process by which information is imparted, just as liquid is poured into an empty jar, and not, in Plato's words, as 'the turning round of the soul's eye to the light.' It also implies the conception of virtue as something teachable, which may be thought to resolve it into a sort of knowledge. Here, again, no general conclusions are warranted, for Gorgias did not teach virtue, and Isocrates decided that it could not be taught. The apologue of Prodicus recommends the virtues or, rather, courage and temperance as means to an end, and on utilitarian grounds. Neither Prodicus nor Protagoras could define virtue itself, or any of the virtues, in a way to satisfy dialecticians like Socrates and Plato, who for that reason pronounced both to be ignorant of virtue; this was the cardinal defect of their ethical opinions. What havoc it worked can best be seen if we consider justice. How could the common good be reconciled with individual interest? The myth of Protagoras[2] rightly makes this virtue (*αἰδὼς καὶ δίκη*) to be insensibly imparted in a civilized state by the interaction of individuals living in society, growing up to obey the laws and gradually recognizing in them the voice of the State. Such views are quite in harmony with Greek tradition, which derived morality from law and law from nature or God or the divine legislator. This harmony is rudely broken by the maxim 'Man the measure,' by the divergence between the code of one state and that of its neighbours, and by the conflict of human and divine law which Sophocles had emphasized.[3] Protagoras, however, still adheres to his position[4] that the State is the ultimate authority from which the citizen derives his views of morality, holding that to be just which the law at a given time and place ordains to be just; but there is this reservation introduced, that it is no longer absolute justice, but merely relative justice, which different states from time to time lay down in shifting ordinances. Although this is a lame defence, such inquiries, whether of a Protagoras or of a Machiavelli, deal with real problems, which must be faced. If the source of law, and therefore of morality, is not divine, it follows that it is merely human; then ought men to follow the example of Hippias and refuse obedience to all but the unwritten laws of nature?[5] Polus, Thrasymachus, and Callicles—the last not a sophist, but a politician and a pupil of sophists—like the author of the *δισσοὶ λόγοι*, made great play with the antithesis of

1 Diog. Laert. ii. 38 f.
2 Aristotle, *Rhet.* i. 13, 1373 *b* 18, and schol. *ad loc.*
3 Aristotle, *Soph. El.* 34, 183 *b* 29.

1 Plato, *Phædrus*, 270 D ff.
2 *Prot.* 320 D ff.
3 *Antigone*, 450 ff.
4 *Theæt.* 167 C ff.
5 Xen. *Mem.* IV. iv. 19.

the natural and the conventional (or the legal, νόμῳ). It shocked the Greek mind to be told that institutions hallowed by old associations had merely a conventional value, and that the immutable alone was natural. If the rules of existing society are merely conventional, it may fairly be argued that obedience to them is a slave's part; the able and intelligent, the masterful and vigorous, will rise in revolt and disregard them. Therefore Polus admires the tyrant Archelaus; Critias and others plotted the overthrow of the demos at Athens; for, the constitution being part of the laws, if might makes right, a claim to rightful rule rests upon force. Or the same result can be reached in another way, by considering the effects of a revolution which has put an oligarchy or a tyrant in power. The laws will no longer be fetters imposed by the multitude on the powerful individual, nature's born ruler; they will be laid down by such a ruler for a community where he has gained the upper hand, and thus again we arrive at the definition, 'Justice is the interest of the stronger.'[1] Between these two lies the opinion formulated by Glaucon[2] of a social compact based on the recognition that all men desire to do injustice, which is good, but fear to suffer injustice, which is evil: hence the compromise of positive laws which forbid both the doing and the suffering of wrong. Lycophron, as mentioned above, also restricted the province of law to the same narrow function of guaranteeing mutual rights. When a similar problem is presented by Anonymus Iamblichi,[3] he, unlike Polus or Thrasymachus, decides that the unprincipled adventurer will be thwarted in the long run, provided the State be well-ordered and the citizens loyal. Before we condemn the sophists for corrupting youth, it will be well to remember that the doctrine that might makes right was publicly advocated by Athenian politicians and orators in the Peloponnesian War, whether the tyrant city[4] was punishing revolt at Mytilene,[5] threatening neutral Melos,[6] or justifying an aggressive policy in Sicily.[7] In short, Plato is right when in a famous passage[8] he declares that it is not individual sophists, but that arch-sophist, the public at large, that corrupts youth. For the sentiments engendered as men sit side by side in the assembly, the law-courts, or the theatre—forces against which reason is powerless—may not be, as Protagoras supposed, relatively true and right, but absolutely erroneous and dangerous. Now the discourse of Protagoras, as reported by Plato, and the fragments of Antiphon and of Anonymus Iamblichi rather suggest that these sophists in handling commonplaces presented popular morals, wherever possible, as modified by the progressive spirit of the age; *e.g.*, the deterrent purpose of legal penalties is recognized by Diodotus,[9] as well as by Protagoras,[10] and the panegyric on orderly government (εὐνομία) of Anonymus Iamblichi partly covers the same ground as the Funeral Oration of Pericles.[11] In such moral harangues it was the lecturer's or writer's interest to keep an eye on his clientèle, the parents and guardians, relatives and friends, of his scholars, and not wantonly to offend their susceptibilities.

(*b*) *Philosophy and religion.*—If sophists were not scientific moralists, far less were they logicians or metaphysicians. Preceding philosophers—Ionians, Pythagoreans, Eleatics, or pluralists—had their crude theories of physics and ontology, with which the older sophists appear to have been acquainted. At any rate, the treatises of Prodicus and Gorgias on nature (περὶ φύσεως), and the explanations of celestial and physical phenomena—motions of sun and moon, eclipses, hail, the saltness of the sea (which are cited from Antiphon's treatise περὶ ἀληθείας)—as well as the more famous incursion of Protagoras into the domain of epistemology, prove that these authors were not disinclined to pursue such studies, or, at least, as receptive rather than original thinkers, to advertise the discoveries of others. Possibly, if such a demand had been made by their pupils, they would have taught physics. This impression is strengthened by the prominent place which burlesque of physical investigations takes in the *Clouds* of Aristophanes, where the typical sophist, Socrates, swings in a basket for the better observation of things celestial (ἀεροβατῶ καὶ περιφρονῶ τὸν ἥλιον) and directs experiments to measure exactly the length of a flea's jump. From the time when this play appeared (423 B.C.), or even earlier, the study of physics declined. The Socrates of the *Phædo* says that in his youth he was acquainted with speculations, some of which we recognize as those of Alcmæon, Anaxagoras, Empedocles, Diogenes of Apollonia, but that he had long since ceased to be interested in them. Presumably contemporary sophists would have made much the same admission. If anything can be predicated of the sophists as a whole, it is that their bent was not theoretical but practical. The name they bore, when we examine its history, confirms this. Before it became specialized to designate the class of paid teachers, it had been used (by Pindar, the tragedians, and Herodotus) in a wider sense, but exclusively applied to practical men, whose wisdom had been tested by experience. To the wise bards Homer and Hesiod, to artists or experts in any department, from cooks and diviners to musicians and generals, not only to Pythagoras, Thales, and Solon, but to those shrewd men of affairs, statesmen or rulers, who were known in Greece as the Seven Sages, such as Pittacus or Periander, the name σοφιστής was thus given. There is one point, however, where the practical teacher and the original thinker were thoroughly at one, viz. their attitude to religion. From the time of Heraclitus and Xenophanes all philosophical systems had broken with the popular creeds and the legends which offended the moral standard of the time. In the ancient quarrel between philosophy and poetry, as Plato calls it, the sophists were on the side of the philosophers. Protagoras was an agnostic, unable to decide whether there are gods or no, and, if there are, what is their nature. Yet Hippias, according to Xenophon's report, believed the gods to be the authors of the unwritten laws, one of which enjoined worship of the gods.[1] The rationalistic speculations of Prodicus and Critias, noticed above, clearly assume that the popular creed has been set aside, for they deal with the further problem, how it originally arose. Nor must it be forgotten that in his burlesque Aristophanes presses the charge of atheism again and again, as when he makes Socrates, his type of the sophist, say, 'Vortex is king; Zeus has been dethroned.'[2] Similarly the aged Plato traces crimes of violence and insolence to the impiety of certain wise men (σοφοί) who maintain that religion and morality are mere convention, and that the highest right is might.[3] Other indications of the gradual change in public opinion are afforded by a comparison of Herodotus with Thucydides. Where the former is credulous, as regards divination and oracles, the latter is sceptical, for he had witnessed fruitless appeals to

[1] *Rep.* 338 E.
[2] *Ib.* 358 E ff.
[3] Diels, *Frag. der Vorsokratiker*³, 82. 6, p. 632.
[4] Thuc. ii. 63; cf. iii. 37.
[5] *Ib.* iii. 37-40.
[6] *Ib.* v. 105; cf. 85-111.
[7] *Ib.* vi. 82-87.
[8] *Rep.* 492 B.
[9] Thuc. iii. 45.
[10] Plato, 324 A.
[11] Thuc. ii. 37 ff.

[1] Xen. *Mem.* IV. iv. 19.
[2] *Clouds*, 828; cf. 264, 365, 367, 627, 1241 ff., 1509.
[3] *Laws*, x. 889 A ff.

divine justice by victims of oppression, the undeserved success of perjury and treachery, the influence of fortune in thwarting the wisest calculations.[1]

3. Charges against the sophists.—In a matter of much controversy notice must be taken of divergent views, particularly the attacks and aspersions from which Grote endeavoured to vindicate the sophists. Whatever the cause, the fortunes of the sophists declined; the second generation was not equal to the first, the pupils were less brilliant and eminent than their teachers, or, like Alcibiades, Theramenes, and Critias, attained to a bad eminence; in the 4th cent. B.C. a liberal education was sought elsewhere, in the Lyceum or the Academy; soon the very name became a term of abuse. Isocrates so applied it to the Eristics and to Plato; Lysias to Æschines (the Socratic) and to Plato; Androtion and Æschines (the orator) to Socrates, who took no fees. For one thing, the practice of charging fees touched a strong Greek prejudice, as if it meant prostitution of the mental powers.[2] This prejudice we moderns, who regard the intellectual as well as the manual labourer as worthy of his hire, can barely understand, much less share. Again, not only Aristophanes, but many worthy citizens like Anytus, a leader of the restored democracy in Athens, mistrusted what seemed to them the revolutionary tendencies of such teaching.[3] Public opinion, too, shifted, and the sophist, once hailed as a prodigy of wisdom and knowledge, an invaluable aid to the political aspirant, came to be despised as a needy adventurer, often a foreigner; if a citizen, doing little, if any, service to the State.[4] Isocrates, ensconced in his own flourishing school near the Lyceum, while claiming that what he himself taught was philosophy and culture, could afford to sneer alike at the Eristics as vendors of fallacies, who denied the possibility of falsehood or contradiction, and at those Socratics who said that courage, wisdom, and justice were identical, that none of these virtues was innate, but that there was a single science of them all.[5] With these facts before us it is impossible to agree with Grote that the name 'sophist' was brought into bad repute mainly by the persistent and acrimonious attacks of Plato and Aristotle on a deserving profession. Plato was born in 427 B.C., and in the *Clouds* (423 B.C.) the term 'sophist,' originally neutral, was well on its way to be stereotyped *in malam partem.* Very rarely has prejudice been so completely successful in changing the connotation of a word: the paid teacher became the needy adventurer, the incompetent pretender, the charlatan, or trickster, the last implication being firmly embedded in our modern words 'sophism,' 'sophistical,' 'sophistry.' In the main, however, Grote is justified in his contention[6] that the sophists were not a sect or school of conscious impostors, flattering rich youths for personal gain and corrupting general morality. Nor, on the other hand, were they, as others have imagined, systematic philosophers who based upon reasoned scepticism an anti-social ethics, sanctioning lawless aggression in politics and freeing the individual from all conventional restraints. The latter hypothesis takes something for granted at every stage, its chief error being the assumption of a school with common doctrines, an assumption no more valid for Greek sophists than for modern journalists. Nor, again, is the charge of indifference to truth justified, except in so far as it corresponds to the old count of making the weaker side the stronger (τὸν ἥττω λόγον κρείττω ποιεῖν). This, it should be remembered, is the aim of every advocate; he appears in court, not to judge his client, but to defend him. If in so doing he does violence to his conscience, if his act is immoral, it is the fault of a system, which neither he nor the sophists devised. The supposed pernicious effect of dialectic and eristic in accustoming the disputant to take either side indifferently admits of a similar answer; and, if the objection be to the use of fallacies, surely they ought not to pass unexposed and unrefuted.[1] Plato's opposition is grounded on his metaphysics. He calls sophistry at one time the sham counterpart of legislation, which is one branch of politics,[2] while in the dialogue devoted to the dissection of the sophist the latter is ultimately defined as the counterfeit of the philosopher, the pretender who, juggling with words in private, dissembles his own ignorance and entangles his hearer in self-contradiction.[3] This amounts to saying that the sophist was, like Isocrates, content with appearance and opinion (δόξα) and had not gone farther in quest of reality and science (ἐπιστήμη). There were these two educational theories, and the champion of the one was bound to condemn the other. Yet we note that six at least of Plato's provisional definitions[4] imply no discredit. If the sophist purged away false opinions, if he imparted information wholesale, retail, or pedlar-fashion, if he was a brilliant athlete in controversy, and ever on the hunt for fresh scholars to teach, he was doing the State some service; for these are traits not unworthy of the world's great educators, from Socrates to Pestalozzi.

LITERATURE.—**J. Frei**, *Quæstiones Protagoreæ*, Bonn, 1845; **F. G. Welcker**, 'Prodikos der Vorgänger des Sokrates,' in *Kleine Schriften*, Göttingen, 1844–67, ii. 393 ff.; **G. Grote**, *Hist. of Greece*, 12 vols., London, 1846–56, ch. lxvii., *Plato and the other Companions of Socrates*, 3 vols., do. 1865, *Aristotle*, 2 vols., do. 1872; **B. Jowett**, *The Dialogues of Plato*³, 5 vols., Oxford, 1892; **E. M. Cope**, 'The Sophists' and 'On the Sophistical Rhetoric,' in *Journ. of Classical and Sacred Philology*, i. [1854] 154 ff., ii. [1855] 129 ff., iii. [1857] 34 ff., 253 ff.; **N. Wecklein**, *Die Sophisten und die Sophistik*, Würzburg, 1865; **M. Schanz**, *Beiträge zur vorsokrat. Philosophie aus Plato*, bk. i., 'Die Sophisten,' Göttingen, 1867; **H. Sidgwick**, in *JPh* iv. [1872] 288 ff., v. [1873] 66 ff.; **H. Jackson**, in *EBr*⁹ xxii. 263 ff., *JPh* xiv. [1885] 173 ff.; **H. Diels**, *Die Fragmente der Vorsokratiker*², Berlin, 1906–10, ii. pt. 1, chs. 73b–83; **A. E. Taylor**, *Varia Socratica*, 1st ser., Oxford, 1911, p. 91 ff.; also the histories of Greek philosophy, as **E. Zeller**, *Philosophie der Griechen*, Leipzig, 1892, i.⁵, 1038–1164, Eng. tr., *Hist. of Greek Philosophy to the Time of Socrates*, London, 1881, ii. 394–516; **T. Gomperz**, *Greek Thinkers*, Eng. tr., do. 1901–12, i. 412–496; **J. Burnet**, *Greek Philosophy*, pt. i., 'Thales to Plato,' do. 1914, pp. 105–125; **L. Schmidt**, *Die Ethik der alten Griechen*, Berlin, 1882.

R. D. HICKS.

SOPHOCLES.

SOPHOCLES.—In studying the religious content of dramatic poetry, it is well to distinguish between (1) what is traditional or contemporary; (2) what is adapted to the dramatic situation; and (3) the poet's own contribution in thought and feeling.

1. In Sophoclean drama the gods of the national worship are still living powers, to whom contemporary piety accords an implicit belief. But special stress is laid on the universal supremacy of Zeus and the oracular truth of Apollo. Athene also holds a conspicuous place. Ares and Aphrodite are regarded chiefly as authors of destruction and misery. The Eleusinian mysteries are by this time fully recognized as belonging to the religion of the State; and Dionysus, the immediate patron of the drama, is an object of affectionate reverence. The religion of the family, coming down from patriarchal times, is prized as of the first import-

[1] R. C. Jebb, *Essays and Addresses*, Cambridge, 1907, p. 406 ff.

[2] Xen. *Mem.* I. vi. 13.

[3] Plato, *Meno*, 91 A ff.

[4] ἔργα σοφιστῶν λίαν ἀχρήστων καὶ σφόδρα βίον δεομένων (Lysias, *Or.* xxxiii. 3).

[5] Isocr. *Or.* x. 1; cf. *Or.* xiii. 1–8.

[6] *Hist. of Greece*, ch. lxvii.

[1] Cf. Plato, *Protag.* 350 C, D.

[2] *Gorgias*, 465 C.

[3] *Sophist*, 268 E.

[4] *Ib.* 218 B–237 A.

ance. Not only blood-guiltiness between kinsmen, but all breaches of domestic harmony are looked on with abhorrence, and to vindicate the honour of one's kindred is an imperious duty. It is this which gives inviolable sanctity to the laws of burial, and it is in connexion with family religion that reference is made to those unwritten laws which are of immemorial antiquity. In upholding these, Greek tragedy seems to enforce the religion of Eleusis; for, in language very similar to that of Sophocles' *Antigone* (lines 453–457), Pericles is reported to have spoken of 'those unwritten laws on which the Eumolpidæ based their instructions, laws which never may be abrogated, and of which no man can tell the origin' ([Lysias] 6. § 10; cf. Thuc. ii. 37. § 4; also Æsch. *Suppl.* 707 f.). The scene is still haunted with fears of divine jealousy or envy (Νέμεσις, Φθόνος; see art. GOD [Greek]), and God is still imagined as causing infatuation, and thus occasioning the crimes which He punishes. The sovereignty of Zeus spares none whose folly, inspired by hope and desire, misleads them (*Ant.* 604 ff.). Hence life sometimes appears a tissue of miseries from which death is the release (*Œd. Col.* 1225 ff.; cf. Herod. vii. 46). That rule is inexorable, but piety never loses its reward (*Phil.* 1444, 1445). Fate, more distinctly than in Æschylus, is identified with an inscrutable Divine Providence of which the oracles are the exponents, above all the oracle at Delphi (*Œd. Tyr.* 1329, 1330).

2. Such are the main features of traditional and contemporary religion as represented in Sophoclean drama, and to the poet's unquestioning acceptance of them he owes that high repute for piety which was awarded to him by the unanimous voice of antiquity. But the exact phase of polytheism that is reflected in each drama depends largely on *the situation*; and if the later epics on which the plays are founded had been preserved to us, it would be possible to account more fully for certain variations. Thus, while in the two *Œdipi* and in the *Electra* the Delphian Apollo is all-important, in the *Trachiniæ* the prime mover is the Dodonæan Zeus, whereas, in the *Ajax*, Athene is the chief agent, and in the *Philoctetes* the knot is solved by Heracles. And in the last-named play it is observable that the sacred place of Chrysa, the allusion to Hephæstus of the volcano, and to the Lemnian Zeus, the invocation of the earth-goddess as the great mother, and the prayer to the nymphs of stream and meadow help to complete the local colouring, while the thought of Heracles on Oeta, of the river-god Spercheius, and the Melian nymphs adds reality and verisimilitude to the person of the hero. Athene, too, while retaining her Athenian attributes (Νίκη πολιάς, l. 134), is in a special sense the guardian of Odysseus, as she is in the *Ajax*, where the Salaminian mariners by their invocation of Pan recall the islet which he made his peculiar haunt (Æsch. *Persæ*, 418). Ajax himself, on the other hand, combines with the longing for his father's hearth a deep sense of the sacredness of the rivers and other divine presences of the Troad.

In the *Œdipus Tyrannus* there is a remarkable blending of Athenian and epic with local Theban worships. Athene, *more Homerico*, is the daughter of Zeus; but it is not forgotten that she has two ancient shrines in the Cadmean city. Artemis at once presides over the Theban Agora and with her brother Phœbus roves the Lycian hills. Apollo is the Pythian prophet of Zeus, and he is also the epic far-darter. His local worship as Lyceius, the protector of the home, and as the prophet by the Ismenus, are separately mentioned. Dionysus is *par excellence* the Theban god; but Ares, to whom the Theban women in Æschylus appeal as the founder of their race, is here identified with the viewless enemy who has visited the city in the form of the plague. In the *Œdipus Coloneus*, Polynices speaks of his father's Erinys, apparently without identifying her with the dread goddesses of Colonus.

3. Behind all such associations, and shining through them, is *the religious thought of the poet*, less original and far-reaching than that of Æschylus, but in some ways more sober and mature. The 'unwritten ordinances' of the Eumolpidæ are developed in the central ode of the first *Œdipus* into the vision of an eternal law of integrity in thought and action whose violation, conscious or unconscious, leads the way to ruin. 'God sees and visits soon or late when one leaves hold of divine principles and turns to madness' (*Œd. Col.* 536 f.). Yet—it is added in a later strain of reflexion—when the error has been involuntary, though it inevitably results in suffering, the very power that punishes holds forth a better hope. The life that is crushed in this world finds acceptance in the end, is itself blessed, and becomes a source of blessing. Even destiny has a human aspect, for it is the outcome of a divine purpose, which, however incalculable, is not, as a previous generation had thought, wholly malignant. Athene, to protect her favourites and to rebuke the pride of Ajax, brings down on him a fatal blight. But her anger, had he but known it, was only for a day, and she prepares the mind of Odysseus, his rival and supposed enemy, to vindicate his honour after death. The clear and steady vision of the poet, holding firmly by the facts of experience (he lived through the Peloponnesian War), forbade him to extenuate the sadness of life, yet he saw a light beyond. The loyal heart of Antigone, the love of Deianira, the brotherhood of Teucer, the essential purity and public spirit of Œdipus, the faithful endurance of Electra, the incorruptible truth of Neoptolemus—these belong to the eternal things, however, on this 'narrow isthmus' of mortality,[1] they may be frustrated or obscured. Even the dark end of the *Trachiniæ* and the agonized reclamation of Hyllus could not hide from the Athenian audience the certainty of the glory that should follow.

The poet's sympathies are enlisted for 'the noble living and the noble dead.' Great souls by their own or others' fault may be overclouded or broken, but in the end they shall be purified and justified. Ajax is provoked into a fatal outburst, but his valour shall be held in everlasting remembrance. The innocent but rash spirit of Œdipus is unwittingly involved in a tangle of guilt from which there is no recovery in this world. But, though rejected by his kindred and nation, his end is peace, and he bestows a blessing on the after time. The same motive, the divine acceptance of inherent greatness that is rejected by men, appears once more in the *Philoctetes*.

Yet this exalted view of the divine purpose in humanity is subject to a certain limitation. The greatness admired is not that of outward position; it is essential greatness and nobility of nature. But noble qualities are still more or less associated with the accident of birth. Sophocles has not the Æschylean breadth and universality of sympathy. The inherent nobleness of Ajax, notwithstanding his offence, is vindicated by his captive bride, his illegitimate brother, and his opponent and rival, whom he suspects of being base-born. But Tecmessa was originally a princess, Teucer's mother likewise was the daughter of a king, and Odysseus was the true son of Laertes by his lawful queen. Antigone scorns Creon for his violation of eternal law, but she also despises him because he is not of the Cadmean race.

[1] Soph. frag. 146: βίου βραχὺν ἰσθμόν.

Closely akin to this limitation is the frank, untempered presentation of vindictiveness. Love and hatred in ancient life were equal powers. When Achilles drags Hector round the body of Patroclus, and kills twelve Trojan prisoners at his friend's funeral, the comment of the Greek mind would be, 'Behold, how he loved him!' So Electra's love for her father and her brother is measured by the exhortation to 'give a second stroke,' and to expose the dead Ægisthus to the dogs and birds. Ajax does not feel, as the heroic maiden in Æschylus' *Choephori* felt, that the curse he utters 'mars his perfect prayer.' Odysseus has been taught only that hatred is not to be carried beyond the grave. The peaceful end of Œdipus is not prevented, but only delayed for a moment, by the renewal of his curse against his sons.

In what remains to us of the work of Sophocles there is hardly any trace of Orphism, and the lyric poetry of the 6th cent. had comparatively little influence on his work. His materials are drawn chiefly from the epic cycle. On the subject of immortality his position is intermediate between Homer and Plato. That the Eleusinian mystic alone lives happily in Hades is strongly asserted in one fragment (753). But the feeling of Antigone is rather that of the pathetic funeral monuments in the Ceramicus. Affection looks beyond the tomb. Souls meet again in that still realm, and 'longer is the time which we shall spend with them than with the persons who surround us here' (*Ant.* 74, 75). Although the language is not consistent, the continuance, not of a mere shadow, but of the conscious self in the unseen world is on the whole anticipated. Not the body, as in Homer, but the soul is αὐτός. And while the place of departed spirits is generally spoken of as 'Hades,' in one passage, according to a later mode of thought, the dead are imagined as entering the 'vast æther' (*Ajax*, 1192; cf. the inscription over the Athenians who fell at Potidæa, B.C. 432, αἰθὴρ μὲμ ψυχὰς ὑπεδέξατο). The case of Œdipus is peculiar. He lives, like Amphiaraus, a semi-divine life, in the darkness beneath the ground. Amphiaraus, too, retains in that under world the fullness of his mind, πάμψυχος ἀνάσσει.

It remains to speak of the dramatist's conception of irreligion. Creon's impiety, like that of the generals in the *Ajax*, consists in his defiance of the burial rite. But Jocasta's case is more typical. She and Laius had disobeyed the oracle, and then sought to evade it by an unnatural deed. For a moment she tries to smother her own and her husband's anxiety by a conventional act of worship. But when her hopes are revived by false intelligence, she defies not only the prophecy but the gods who gave it, until, on the sudden revelation of the dreadful truth, she dies in despair.

Some recrudescence of pessimism, such as we find in Euripides, is reflected in some passages of the latest plays. Philoctetes, when at the lowest of his fortunes, complains that in praising divine attributes one finds evil in the gods (*Phil.* 451, 452); and the elders of Colonus descant upon the vanity of life and the infirmities of age (*Œd. Col.* 1225 f.). But these depressing sentiments are contradicted by the main tenor of both dramas.

In the last *Œdipus* there is a depth and range of religious feeling which is not equally present in the other tragedies. The magnanimity of Theseus discards the superstitious fears and scruples of the elders of the deme. Not the ritual itself, but the prayer accompanying it, is the important thing. Not the details of the ceremonial, but the pure intention of the ministrant, secures divine acceptance. Innocence of heart commends itself, in spite of involuntary pollution. And the great spirit, in passing from the upper air and light of day, is surrounded with an atmosphere of religious peace.

LITERATURE.—Gustav Dronke, *Die religiösen und sittlichen Vorstellungen des Aeschylos und Sophokles*, Leipzig, 1861; Evelyn Abbott, 'The Theology and Ethics of Sophocles,' in *Hellenica*, London, 1880; G. Gunther, *Grundzüge der tragischen Kunst*, Leipzig, 1885; L. Campbell, *Sophocles*, London, 1879 (Macmillan's 'Classical Writers' ser.), *Religion in Greek Literature*, do. 1898, *Tragic Drama in Æschylus, Sophocles, and Shakespeare*, do. 1904.

LEWIS CAMPBELL.

SORCERY.—See MAGIC, SHAMANISM, WITCHCRAFT.

SOTERIOLOGY.—In the article SALVATION (Christian) an attempt was made to trace the experience of salvation to its origins in the religion of Israel, and to depict it in the life of the disciples of Jesus and of the members of the Christian community during the apostolic age. In this article an attempt will be made to trace the idea of salvation as it manifests itself in successive periods in the history of Christian thought.

I. *THE FACT OF THE CHRISTIAN SALVATION.*—Salvation as presented in the NT consists fundamentally in a work wrought by God through Jesus Christ. In Him God gave the perfect revelation of Himself, and through Him fulfilled His saving purpose towards mankind. The saving work of God, however, is not complete as a bare fact of history. It operates as an abiding power in the experience of men, under the condition of trustful surrender to Jesus Christ, the personal Saviour and ever-living Lord. Certain features of this experience as presented in the NT are noteworthy, and determine essential elements in the Christian conception of salvation.

1. The continuity of this experience.—It stands in direct succession to the religion of Israel, not distinguishable from it in any other sense than consummation is from the earlier stages of one vital process. It begins a new development of God's saving work, whose centre and spring is always the same, viz. the exalted and living Lord; nor can its bounds be delimited, because they are conterminous with nothing less than the holy love of God. Christianity is to be identified, not by the intellectual or institutional forms with which it has been in different ages accompanied, but by the experience of salvation, which has been evoked, maintained, and furthered by trust in Christ as Redeemer and Lord. The life of the Church in salvation is continuous and forms a unity recognizable in variety. Its power of development is renewed, maintained, and defended by 'a constant spiritual return to Christ.'

2. Its differentia as a religious experience.—It is sharply distinguished from two forms of the higher life of man: (1) moralism, in which salvation is achieved by man through diligent obedience to the moral imperative; (2) mysticism, in which salvation, conceived as immediate union with God, is achieved by man through special exercises of soul which vary from the magical to the contemplative. In deep contrast with these divergent types, the Christian salvation is grounded in, and warranted by, the divine initiative and the divine sufficiency. Its origin is in the love of God, conceived as a ruling purpose aiming at a kingdom or realm in which the holy will of God shall be done. This love appears in human experience as grace, *i.e.* the action of God, in the history of the race and the individual, directed towards the salvation of man. This salvation is not the work of man, but the work of God in man, and always it evokes in man, not self-congratulation, but the sense of constraint, as of those who find themselves in a bondage which is, nevertheless, perfect freedom (2 Co 5^{14}). At the same time, this attitude towards the divine salvation is the very reverse of quietism. Its distinguishing note is the sense of power. The OT and NT alike present a picture of life thrilling with activity and crowned with victory. Out of this experience there arises a twofold interest or passion: a passion for righteousness and a passionate longing for fellowship with God. Moralism and mysticism alike come to their rights in Christianity. They take their place within the Christian salvation. They are its expression and its outcome. They are not an achievement of man; but they manifest what human life may become through the saving action of God in man.

3. Its goal: the Kingdom of God.—Salvation is never, in the Biblical literature, statically conceived. It is always described in terms of power and action. It is true that salvation consists in a transition from one state or condition to another; and descriptions abound of the misery of the one and the blessedness of the other. But both states are conceived as determined by a power governing and animating human life. The one is the condition of man in 'the world,' or the present 'age.' Here man is subject to a power of evil, which masters him, drives him, and holds him in bondage. The other is the condition of man in the Realm of God (Col 1[13]). Here man is subject to the sovereignty of holy love and penetrated by the power of the Holy Spirit. This realm of power and love is conceived as a divine reality, a supernatural order, which is not, however, abnormal. It is nature, human nature, which is in an abnormal condition, and in this abnormality physical nature shares (Ro 8[19-22]). The divine order is the truth of man and the universe, and overhangs this spatial universe, impinges upon it, and is ever ready to intervene in it, if we may use figures, which, however, wholly fail to combine ideas that are really disparate, viz. a world above time and sense, and a world conditioned by time and sense. The Realm of God, being thus conceived as a fact of a divine supersensuous order, has three aspects: it is present, progressive, and future.

(*a*) It is present to the need and the faith of men. It is to be received as an immediate gift of grace, and entered in deep humility (Mt 18[3]), through such a reversal of aim in life as amounts to a new birth (Jn 3[3. 5]) or a new creation (2 Co 5[17]).

(*b*) It is progressive as an enterprise to which God has devoted Himself and all His resources, and in which His honour is involved. To a share in this enterprise He summons all who will be saved. They are to serve it to the last limit of devotion, counting all things but loss for the glory of this achievement. Apart from a service which springs out of death to the old world and the old nature and may involve actual suffering and death at the hands of the enemies of God, there can be no salvation. Those who in one aspect are 'saved' in another are 'being saved.'

(*c*) It is future inasmuch as its victory depends on an act of divine intervention. It is impossible to omit this from any picture of salvation as an object of Christian faith and hope in the 1st cent., or in any subsequent age of the Church's history. Men cannot build the Kingdom. The Kingdom comes. Questions of time and manner are secondary and not essential to the Christian faith. The first generation of believers thought of the Kingdom as immediately to appear, and framed pictures of a literal millennium, mistaking symbolism for prediction. The point of value is that the Realm of God exists as 'the highest order of life and power in the universe.'[1] In endeavouring to represent the relation of this spiritual order to the world of time and space, it must always be conceived as imminent and described as 'at hand.' The Christian enterprise, which is, fundamentally, the vindication of the divine sovereignty in the whole domain of human life, derives from this imminence its source of urgency and its note of confidence. In preaching the gospel, in perfecting holiness in the fear of God, in waging war on behalf of righteousness, Christian men are not striving to win a salvation which is in doubt. They are building, not on the sands of human fancy, 'but on the bedrock of that Order which, however deeply it is hidden from common observation by the course of outward events, yet stands to religious faith as the most secure and final truth' (Mt 7[24f.]).[2] Salvation, therefore, lies always above and beyond and before the Christian. The paradox of a Kingdom 'come' and 'coming,' a salvation at once possessed and expected, may defy logical solution, but has never seriously perplexed those who, moving through the world of time and space, have seen and entered a region of values and powers where earthly measurements do not apply.

[1] G. F. Barbour, *A Philosophical Study of Christian Ethics*, Edinburgh and London, 1911, p. 203.
[2] *Ib.*, p. 204.

II. *THE IDEA OF SALVATION IN THE MYSTERY-RELIGIONS.*—In the Hellenic-Roman world, at the time when Christianity began its missionary career, there was proceeding what cannot be termed less than a revival of religion. The religious worship of the Olympian deities had lost whatever moral and spiritual power it ever possessed. That devotion to the city which was 'the real religion of the 5th century'[1] necessarily passed away when the independence of the city-states perished under the might of a world-empire. But religion itself never perishes. Where ancient forms of religious life have failed, the demand of the human spirit for a satisfying salvation is only the more intense and urgent.

In the 1st cent. of our era men were going behind the more formal and cultured religions to the practices and ideas of primitive times. It seems a terrible relapse into barbarism that the inheritors of the splendid Hellenic culture should seek salvation in the blood of a divine bull. Yet, in a sense, this return to a cruder and less sophisticated age was really an advance. There was a wide-spread 'failure of nerve,' as Gilbert Murray has phrased it.[2] But, when man reaches the depths of his helplessness, he is near the sources of religious strength and hope. He turns passionately to any religion, however crude its ceremonial or outrageous its mythology, which will offer confidently enough the great boon without which life is unendurable—salvation. The mystery-religions and the Gnostic sects are all of one religious type. They are avowedly religions of salvation. They are dissociated from race or nationality. They pass through the organized forms of civic or political life and reach down to the single soul. They are at once individualistic and universal. They are not so much separate religions as, at bottom, the ultimate religious need and susceptibility of man, turning away from traditional and stereotyped forms and plunging into depths of psychic experience where the human and the divine seem to be blent, or perhaps confused, in a unity too mysterious for thought or speech. While they are thus rooted in mystery, they share certain views of the nature of God and man and the world, of sin and evil, and of deliverance and blessedness which amount in fact to a fairly coherent doctrine of salvation.

(i.) God, or the divine nature, is conceived or felt to be a being or substance, far beyond apprehension or determination by human thought. He is not personal and cannot be named. Only this is certain, that, if the human spirit could attain to oneness with this ultimate divine nature, it would be emancipated from all ill and would enjoy an ineffable experience of peace and freedom and rest. (ii.) Beneath or over against God is the world, to which He stands in no living relation. It is occupied by powers which reign in the whole region inhabited by man and hold him in subjection, so that the soul is haunted by fear, and life becomes one great cry for deliverance. (iii.) Man carries within him a seed of the divine. He is at once greater and less than these sub-divine principalities and powers—greater because he is himself divine and holds, as it were, a fragment of the divine nature in himself; less, because he, *i.e.* the divine in him, is enclosed in a material fabric, which holds him at an immeasurable distance from God and is subject to all the influences which govern and tyrannize over the material world. Salvation, on its negative side, means deliverance from matter, from sense, from all that is not God. (iv.) The powerlessness of man requires a helper, redeemer, saviour. Such an one appears in all these religions, with a various ancestry, with cloudy mythologies, decorated with titles of honour, but always claiming victory over the powers that hold man in bondage. (v.) The method by which this victory is won is variously depicted in the myths. Deep through them all, however, is the thought of life won through death. The old religion of nature, glorifying the succession of winter's death and spring's resurrection, returns with fresh power to hearts weary of the artificialities of state ceremonial. Such primitive conceptions,

[1] Gilbert Murray, *Four Stages of Greek Religion*, p. 96.
[2] *Ib.* ch. iii.

too, relate themselves to profounder and more ethical ideas, of lives surrendered to shame and death and yet found again in the increased values of the welfare of the community. (vi.) Our sympathy with the mystery-religions up to this point is deep and our expectation great. It is disappointing to find that, when we ask under what conditions the individual was supposed to reach union with the divine, the reply flings us back, not merely on symbolism, but on magic, not merely on self-discipline, but on semi-physical ecstasy. The commonplace of Greek religion through this whole period is the process whereby the spark of divinity in man is reunited to its source: (*a*) ceremonial, making keen appeal to the emotional and sensuous nature; (*b*) ascetic practices, aiding the religious susceptibilities and repressing (it was hoped) the urgency of lower instincts; (*c*) ecstasy, produced by fulfilling certain physical and psychic conditions and superinducing a state of sub- or supra-consciousness in which the soul knows itself to be united to God, sunk in God, and filled with God. These are the outstanding features of the way of salvation opened to seeking souls in the mystery-religions, which were the 'forerunners and rivals of Christianity.' (vii.) When we examine the salvation itself, the result is disappointingly meagre. In phrase it is magnificent, 'deification.' In reality it disappears in vagueness. Negatively it is deliverance from mortality; positively it is union with the divine, conceived mainly as a blending of a particle of being with its abysmal source. Experimentally salvation is the mystic state, bearing the marks which William James has noted—ineffability, noetic quality, transiency, passivity. This is the real heart of the mystery-religions.[1]

Applying the ethical standard, the only valid test, we must assign to these mystery-religions a very moderate value. Their emphasis is not on morality at all, but on escape from elemental powers, a flight of the soul to the divine, which is conceived mainly through negations. In this deliverance morality is only a step, valuable not in itself, but as an introduction to a condition in which moral good does not survive, being succeeded by some psychic state which is held to be the highest blessedness of which man is capable. Morality, too, even in this secondary position, is left without dynamic. There is no inner constraint, no self-forgetful inspiration. A man is to be pure, and just, and chaste, in order that he may reach a state beyond the sphere of moral values altogether. We should not deny that the mystery-religions served religious ends in the experience of multitudes of adherents. The salvation they offered was a fragment, an element, or an instalment, of the true good. They expressed a demand and increased a desire, preparing the way for a religion which more perfectly uttered the one and responded to the other.

When we compare the ideas of salvation set forth in the mystery-religions and in Christianity respectively, we are impressed with the features common to both.

(i.) Both conceive man's highest blessedness as union with God. (ii.) Both trace man's distress to separation from God. (iii.) Both take a lofty view of one side of man's nature, as indicating affinity with the divine. (iv.) Both present the radiant figure of a Deliverer to the fainting spirit. (v.) Both trace life to its roots in death. (vi.) Both connect the deepest religious experiences with certain ritual acts. (vii.) Both place salvation in the return to God.

To infer, however, from these undoubted resemblances that Christianity was itself no other than a mystery-religion is a mistake. The hypothesis of borrowing, or even of unconscious infiltration, is not required by the facts, which, at the same time, make impossible the conception of Christianity as a bare revelation, standing naked and alone in the history of the human spirit. All religions spring from sources deep in the nature of man. Historically, however, the great religions have followed separate paths. The mystery-religions represent the highest point reached on one line of development. Christianity is the culmination of another and wholly distinct line. It is the religion of Israel, growing by continuous evolution out of the experiences of the prophets and of those, their associates and successors, who received and responded to the actings and communications of the divine love in its redeeming, saving work. The primary fact in the NT Church is the experience of salvation entered into by its members; and that experience is unique and distinctive. Its implications are essentially different from those of the mystery-religions. It is *sui generis* and cannot be explained as a composite. Christian missionaries borrowed in the 1st cent., as they do in the 20th, phrases of speech and forms of thought. How else were they to be intelligible? But they did not borrow their message; and they did not copy from foreign sources the religious experience which they sought to evoke and deepen in the lives of their converts. Between Christianity, with its distinctive view of man's case, its own special message, and its typical experience, and the mystery-religions at their highest and best there is a deep line of demarcation. On the one side, the deepest concern is ethical and personal, and the highest result is a character conformed to that of God, conceived as the impersonation of love and holiness. On the other side, the problem is primarily ontological or cosmological, and the solution is found in an experience in which the ethical and the personal are subordinated to the psychic and the ineffable. The Christian missionaries accepted the challenge presented by the mystery-religions, or rather they availed themselves of the opportunity offered in these noble and pathetic approaches towards God. Their claim was that what they had to offer took up into itself all that was best in these religions; and they invited every seeker to share in a good which satisfied a need deeper than the mystery-religions ever knew. Each point of contact noted above reveals also the breadth of separation.

(i.) *The idea of God*: to the mystery-religions a vague, remote, impersonal, unknowable, divine nature; to Christianity a living Being, with a character and purpose, personal in His actions and manifestations, known in history as loving and righteous, achieving by His own doing and suffering the redemption of man.

(ii.) *The distress of man*: to the mystery-religions mortality and subjection to hostile influences in or above the world—a separation conceived almost locally and physically; to Christianity a moral separation from the holy God, produced by man's own act involving guilt and judgment and ruin.

(iii.) *The dignity of man*: to the mystery-religions the possession in mortal frame of a veritable spark of divinity, which ever seeks reunion with its source; to Christianity a moral likeness to God, which has been defaced by sin, and yet is capable of being renewed, so that man can be restored to divine uses and fellowship.

(iv.) *The person of the Deliverer*: to the mystery-religions a mythical figure, supra-human, whose history moves in a non-human region of endeavour and achievement; to Christianity a real human being, with a genuine human experience, the reality of whose life and death constitutes the gospel, inasmuch as they are the means through which God in Him redeemed the world.

(v.) *The method of redemption*: to the mystery-religions a death which belongs to another region than that in which men suffer and die; to Christianity a death real and tragic, an actual dying, in which the utmost need of man is felt and met by One in whom divine love fulfils its redeeming function.

(vi.) *The conditions of salvation.*—In the mystery-religions there is no living relation between what the Deliverer effects for men and what men achieve for themselves. The process of salvation in reality does not need a Mediator at all. It consists in experiences which are evoked by sacraments or dramatic symbols. Such experiences are effective in proportion as they pass beyond conscious apprehension or articulate expression; and they culminate in an ecstatic state, in which the desired union with God is attained. The difference between this and the way of salvation provided in Christianity is horizon-wide. The Christian message concerns a saving action of God, which is carried out by His Son Jesus Christ. It concentrates the salvation of men in the person of Christ. The one essential condition of salvation on the part of men is that they receive, with trustful surrender, the love of God as it reaches them in Christ. This is what the Scriptures of Christianity, whether OT or NT, mean by faith. It is not a mystic state. It is radically different from ecstasy. It is not ineffable; for it is genuine only as it makes confession of its inward experience. It has 'noetic quality' only in the sense that it 'knows' by experimental acquaintance the living object of its trust. It is not 'transient,' but is the constant energy of life. It is not 'passive,' but is the inspiration of service. Everything in salvation is controlled by this exercise of faith. The ultimate object is always God. If Christ is designated as the object of saving faith, it is because God is not known at all in His saving

[1] See, further, art. MYSTERIES.

power apart from Him, and because He is inseparable from God in the believing apprehension of those who are the subjects of the divine salvation. The experience in which man, in his need, commits himself to the God who comes to him in Christ is the deepest, richest, and most fruitful of which the human spirit is capable. It embraces the whole complex of human power. It cannot, therefore, be unemotional. Precisely at this point Christianity and the mystery-religions approach most nearly and at the same time stand most widely apart. The Christian, like the devotee in the mysteries, has moments in which great tides of feeling sweep through his being, sometimes elevating him to a region of truth and reality too sacred to be disclosed to any human being. The difference lies in the source and quality of such emotional experiences. To the Christian they are privileges granted as helps to faith; but they are not, in themselves, identified with faith. They are states; faith is an action. They are products, by-products, of faith, and are not to be confused with it or prized as though they were more precious than it. The expression 'faith-mysticism' is, strictly, a self-contradiction. The act of faith is incompatible with the impersonality which is the characteristic note of the mystic state. The degree to which emotion will be the accompaniment of faith's activity will vary endlessly in individuals. The occasions too will vary. Ordinarily, however, feeling will be stirred when in symbolic action the objective saving deeds are presented to the view of believers. The so-called 'sacraments' of the Christian Church and the rites performed in the mysteries belong to different universes of religious thought and practice. Symbolism in Christianity has reference to a historic redemption and is meant to ratify the message of the divine salvation. It becomes effective in experience only on condition of faith directed to God. It has no saving power in itself. No doubt, already in NT times, there were adherents of mystery-religions who, in entering the Church, carried with them ideas of the *ex opere operato* virtue of ritual actions. But it is certain that such were not the views entertained by the leaders of the Church. W. Morgan, who is not slow to assign large influence to the mystery-religions in the developing theology of the Church, denies that the apostle Paul held any such idea of the ordinances he prized so highly. 'A memorial of Christ's sacrificial death, a means of proclaiming it—that and that alone is what the Supper signifies for Paul.'[1] The aim of the ordinances is to express and confirm faith, not to produce an ecstatic state in which self shall be absorbed in God. Paul, who was an expert in practical psychology, valued highly the raptures of religious feeling, but he was well aware of the dangers attendant upon them; and he bequeathed to the Church such a careful evaluation of the emotional element in religion as saved Christianity from being merged in the mystery-religions and from sharing their moral impotence and subsequent doom.

(vii.) *The scope and contents of salvation.*—The mystery-religions break down at this point. Escape from sense, deliverance from demons, final absorption in God are not themes which permit of enlargement. Salvation as thus conceived cannot be articulated—for the simple reason that there is nothing in it. In wide contrast, Christianity moves in a world of historical fact and ethical values. On one side, salvation is the wealth of the divine love, unfolded and conveyed in the Christ of history. On the other side, salvation is the progressive appropriation of what divine love means in life. This is all, and this is everything. There is no divine beyond that which operates in Christ. He is the Pleroma. He is not a step towards a union with God which, in its metaphysical abstraction, is supposed to be superior to the concrete spiritual realities of forgiveness, reconciliation, and moral renewal. No doubt, the people who pressed into the Church were obsessed with fear of demons and of death, and it was certainly part of the Christian salvation that they should be delivered from such torment; but this, like every other benefit, was only an issue of the new relation in which men stood to God through faith in Christ. There is no getting to an end of what may be possessed in faith; and there is no getting beyond Christ. The convert was taught that all things belonged to him, because he belonged to Christ, and Christ belonged to God. Paradoxically, Christianity, which offered a full salvation for immediate acceptance, did not proclaim itself to be the final stage of God's redemptive acting. The salvation of the mystery-religions was at once individualistic and final. Christianity, true to its Hebrew origin, was social and dynamic. Its ideal is still the Kingdom of God. Till that Kingdom shall have come, salvation is not complete. Christianity, therefore, is bound to the conception of a coming of the Redeemer to which there is no real parallel in the mystery-religions. The belief in the Parousia is an element in the essentially historical character of the Christian religion. It is a religion of the acts of God, and these acts are not closed. The greatest of them is yet to come. It will be the climax of a great redemptive movement, and in it humanity will be reconstituted and the Realm of God established in an environment suited to its divine nature.

These, then, are the elements in the Christian conception of salvation which distinguish it from that entertained in the mystery-religions—the personal, the historical, the ethical, the eschatological. To them Christianity owed its superior power and attractiveness and its final victory over its forerunners and rivals. Whether, in generations following the period of the first missionary enterprise of the Church, the mystery-religions did not win an unmarked but very real triumph, by entering into Christianity and giving it a distinct mystic quality, is another question. But that the religion whose literary record is found in the NT has its own essential qualities, placing it in a class apart from the contemporary mystery-religions and giving it religious and moral superiority over them, seems to be an ascertained historical judgment.

[1] *The Religion and Theology of Paul*, p. 224.

III. *THE IDEA OF SALVATION IN GREEK PHILOSOPHY.*—**1. Pre-Socratic.**—Reviewing the course of Greek philosophy in its three main periods, we note that pre-Socratic thinkers have scarcely faced the problem of their relation to religion. Their attitude towards the popular religion is scornful, as illustrated by the contempt poured by Xenophanes upon the polytheism of his day. This, however, means no more than that the Olympians were losing whatever divinity they had ever possessed and were passing to their doom of unreality. Philosophy itself is making direct contribution to the religious and theological inheritance upon which both Greek and Christian entered in succeeding ages. The idea of God, in Xenophanes and Parmenides, has already assumed the form which has clung to it to this day. The unity of God has become a fixed point for all subsequent reflexion—a unity conceived as the negation of all differences, an absolute principle, into which the whole intelligible world, and even the intelligence itself, is resolved and lost. Greek thought, in its first stage, has not realized the place of the self-conscious subject and has not found a spiritual unity to explain the fullness of experience and give man a position of independence and lordship in the world which hems him in.

2. Idealist constructions.—The second period of Greek philosophy is introduced by the great name of Socrates (*q.v.*). Socrates has been described as a 'philosopher by accident'; and yet he gave to philosophy and to theology at once the problem and the principle by which their course was to be determined for all time coming. He is the discoverer of reason, he gave to human subjectivity its rights. At the same time he is the fountain-head of an intellectualism which made the Greek solution of the problem of life one-sided and inadequate. Difficulties arise when we press for vindication of the positive proposition that virtue is the fruit of knowledge. It is a commonplace that knowledge in things ethical is not power; else why do we constantly approve the better and do the worse? A deeper source of difficulty is the implied relation of reason to what may be termed the raw material of the moral life—the instincts and impulses of the individual and the common practices of men acting together in society. Is there such a deep gulf between them that morality and religion will spend themselves upon a task which can never be finished, viz. the reconciliation of elements of experience which are fundamentally disparate? It can be foreseen that on such a dualism thought will ultimately break itself to pieces. Precisely this is the endeavour and the tragedy of Greek philosophy—to overcome dualism by the sheer force of dialectic and, when the task is seen to be hopeless, to appeal to supra-rational sanctions and to plunge into irrational experiences. The ethic of Socrates, illustrated by the splendour of his death, has all the nobility of a protest against unreason, all the significance of a fresh starting-point in the history of the human spirit. The individual is now the problem. His salvation becomes the vital concern, not only of religion, but of philosophy.

Plato and Aristotle (*qq.v.*) take the torch from Socrates' falling hand and bear it into regions which he never presumed to enter. The conception of an end determinable by reason bringing order into the moral life is by them extended to experience as a whole. Intelligence is treated as the ultimate source of all knowledge and all being. The ethic of Socrates is transmuted into cosmology, metaphysics, and theology. The problem of the individual, accordingly, is not explicitly central; and yet it is by reference to the individual that the grand sweep of Platonic and Aristotelian thought will ultimately be tested. Philosophy, as represented by Plato and Aristotle, reflects a form of life in which the individual personality has not yet received full recognition. Therefore the question of an adequate life for the individual remains unanswered, because it has not been asked with sufficient thoroughness. In this respect, therefore, Plato and Aristotle are not true Socratics. Their encyclopædic systems are, in a sense, a brilliant episode of thought. The true succession passed from Socrates to the era of individualism which succeeded that phase of life of which the idealism of Plato and Aristotle is the splendid record. At the same time that idealism was a necessary stage in the evolution of Greek thought; it stood as a final demonstration of the sufficiency or the insufficiency of intelligence to unify human experience and to be the dynamic of the moral and religious life of man.

In the Platonic view of knowledge and of life there are two movements—one towards concrete idealism, the other towards dualism and mysticism, the latter being proof that the former has failed to reach its goal. (*a*) Plato seeks to reach a principle of unity which will really underlie and explain the variety manifest in the universe. With respect to human life, the Platonic ideal is an organic unity, in which each individual will find his place and function and reach the perfection possible to him, through conscious identification with the dominant idea of the whole. On this side of his great effort Plato did not need to face the problem of individualism. The individual is simply found in the great whole and finds himself when he realizes where he is. There is no problem of salvation. (*b*) The other movement of Plato's thought, however, suggests quite a different view of man's place and destiny. It would appear now that the unity aimed at is not found in the differences. The ultimate reason is not wholly intelligible. The goodness of God is not adequate to its tasks, being confronted by unconquerable necessity; and this recalcitrant material makes evil an abiding quality of the scheme of things. Thus dualism and pessimism haunt an idealism which has over-emphasized the intelligence and turned it against the practical details of knowing and doing. As soon as dualism makes itself felt, the question of the individual and his salvation emerges; and its solution in one way—the way of negation and mysticism—becomes inevitable. Dualism and mysticism follow a beaten path—whether in the East or in the West, whether Indian or Greek or Christian. The rubric may vary; the essential mystery is the same, and, it cannot be too plainly stated, it is essentially different from the core of that religion whose literary expression is the Scriptures of the Old and New Testaments. The true nature of man is oneness with God. His present position is that of imprisonment within an irrational and material envelope. Immediately salvation becomes his primary concern and forms the supreme business of his life, and this salvation must always take shape as a purification (*κάθαρσις*) of the soul, its deliverance (*λύσις*) from the chains which bind it to earth and sense, culminating in that vision of the divine (*θέα τῶν ἄνω*) which is, in the very act, its reunion with the source of its true being. Phrases like these repeat themselves unendingly in the literature of mysticism. They revolve round one central idea, a universal that is abstract, without contents, union with which is denial of all the positive experiences of life. Over against this whole conception stands the Biblical idea of salvation as fellowship with the living God, realized in faith and love, manifesting itself in character and ministry, and culminating in a social order of which God is at once the head and the indwelling life.

The effort to overcome dualism fails even more conspicuously in Aristotle than in Plato. The moral life, as Aristotle portrays it, is simply a rescript of the best Greek life he knew, not ignoble by any means, but essentially narrow, and confined to a class which bases its wealth and power and leisure on the labour of those who can never share its culture and privileges. A really dominant unity ought to constitute humanity as an organism; but such an idea is repellent to the Greek spirit and is exhibited in Aristotle's social ideal. Reason uses the irrational and cannot transmute it. And, even when this ideal, such as it is, is reached, the irrational still clings to it. Virtue is not knowledge. The virtuous man has to deal with conditions which are not the creation of reason, and accordingly he can only do his best and reach, on the whole, a balance between reason and unreason. He can attain an art of living; but to reach the perfection of reason he must cease to live the normal life. It is a far cry from Athens to the Thebaid, and a farther still to Luther, doubting if he can save his soul in the world. But the abstract opposition of form and matter, of reason and sense, of the theoretical and the practical, is the philosophy which lies behind monachism and asceticism; and it is the bequest of Greek dualism, even in the hands of so concrete a thinker as Aristotle, to the Occidental world. A negative salvation achieved by flight is his message, which subsequent generations accepted only too submissively.

Plato and Aristotle reflect the life of the Greek city-state, which, already when they wrote, was showing that it could not be permanent. Its passing left the problem of the individual and his salvation in explicit and definite form. The mystery-religions met the need of the age with their own message and methods. Philosophy pursued its own path to a goal now distinctly discerned. If the great synthetic systems are gone, with the form of life they interpreted, if there is no outward organism in which the individual can find himself, there is nothing for him to do but to pass inward into his own inner life and endeavour to satisfy himself with that which he shall find therein. Here the Greek dualism suffers shipwreck. The elements which Plato and Aristotle had masterfully held together fall apart and are made the prize of opposing dogmatisms. Suppose the inner life yields us its secret and rational principle, which is also discernible as the very life of nature, then the result will be an individualism which is also a cosmopolitanism, and even a pantheism, and will be essentially religious. Suppose, however, the secret of the inner life be no more than sense and its satisfaction, the result may be delicate and beautiful, the joy of a cultured élite, or it may be gross and vile, the shame of the reckless and profligate; but it will conform to no standard of values which can approve itself objective and universal; and, whatever form it takes, it will be essentially non-religious. Between these two views of what the inner life could yield the thought of the age was divided. The latter was really a denial of the deepest demand of the human spirit. The former became the real religion of all who sought the higher life of the soul, and did afford a standing-ground and a safeguard in the midst of an alien world.

3. Stoicism.—The Stoic conception of the universe and human life is essentially religious; and the great Stoics are men with a message to the world of their day which is the outcome of a genuine and very noble religious experience. Philosophically they are monists. They surmount the dualism which even an Aristotle could not exorcize by the denial of one of its alleged constituents. The difference between form and matter is, in point of fact, unreal. It is true that the universe may be read in terms of matter; but matter is spirit and life, and the material universe is spiritual to the core. It forms a unity, in the sense that there is but one element of being—not two elements confronting one another in irreconcilable opposition. The Stoic solution of the problem of life, accordingly, is greatly simplified. The universe manifests the presence and operation of the λόγος σπερματικός, a germinative principle, which is immanent in individual existences, or rather is so one with them that they are really parts of it. The Stoic has advanced beyond Heraclitus, from whom the Logos (*q.v.*) conception is derived, in that he defines it after the type of that reason which in man is reflective and self-conscious. The universe reveals the control of a Divine Providence, the constant energy of a universal life. In God all things live and move and have their being. Man has this privilege, beyond all other beings, that he can recognize the Logos as identical with his own true self. He can make himself the willing organ of a universal principle. He can rise above the separation of his mere individuality and, ceasing from all selfish endeavour, see himself to be member of a community which includes all human beings. In this vision of himself, which he reaches by leaving behind the mere externalities and accidents of his environment and entering into the secret of his individuality, he really attains spiritual universality and lives by the impulse of the broadest philanthropy. By accepting his place in the universe he transforms fate into freedom and enjoys an independence and integrity of which no outward circumstances can deprive him. This, then, is the Stoic 'salvation.' It turns from a world which no longer provided a rational life for man, and centres the whole interest on the individual. In him it finds the presence of the same reason which is the soul of the universe. It bids him awake to the consciousness of what he is, adopt that as the will of his life, and live in entire consistency with it, *i.e.* at once with universal reason and with his own nature, for these two are one. He thus stands secure against the assaults of unreason, whether they take the form of the fury of blinded men or the stirrings of blind passion. Even those losses and afflictions which belong to an existence in time and space do not greatly move him. He is pure reason; and all things, other or less than rational, remain outside the citadel of his soul. The task of his life is simple. Positively, it is to will the universal; negatively, it is to confront the irrational with absolute refusal. The Stoic saint is an ethical absolutist; and his moral judgments admit of no qualifications. It is altogether intelligible that the Christian salvation should show affinity with Stoicism, while with Aristotle and Plato the relation is almost wholly one of contrast. The metaphysical dualism of the Greek philosophies has no true parallel in the Biblical literature; neither the problem nor the solution enters into the Christian idea of salvation. But an ethical dualism and an active victory over it, which are the central interests of Stoicism, form the very stuff of Christian experience. The incisiveness, the strenuousness, even the ethical intolerance, of a Stoic have their parallels both in Jesus and in Paul. Stoic virtue, at its sternest and most assured, might have recognized its counterpart in those 'who endured the cross and despised the shame.' A high-minded man, in the years when Stoicism and Christianity competed for the winning of souls, could have no other alternative. He must commit himself to the one or the other. Yet the defect of its Greek origin clung to Stoicism and turned its strength to weakness. After all, though it is a monism, it is born of dualism. Its unity is the unity of one element, which does not really transmute its opposite, and can do nothing with it but reject it. At its best Stoicism has the strength and weakness of asceticism. It can repress, but it cannot construct. It can command, but it cannot create. It has no inward spring of action, capable of continuous transformation of character and endless service of the ideal. It is law, not gospel. Like all honest legalists, the Stoic was bound to end in pessimism.

4. Philo and Plotinus.—The conclusion is that, since in Stoicism the guiding clue of Greek philosophy has failed us, we must seek some other. Plainly some deeper principle is wanted than reason, which can never subdue its opposite. The human spirit must seek for the ultimate unity, *i.e.* for God, not in the outer world of the universe or the inner world of the soul, but in a region that transcends both. It must cease to rely on pure thought as the instrument of its endeavour or the method of its approach. God must be held to be essentially transcendent. He cannot be immanent in it. His connexion with it cannot be immediate, but must be maintained through intermediaries. The Logos must be dethroned from its position of Lord of all and become at best the greatest of those intermediaries. Man cannot find God even by the highest form of spiritual energy hitherto practised. Philosophy itself can bring us no farther than the threshold, which can be crossed, if ever, only in ecstasy. Such an experience leaves even the purest contemplation hopelessly behind, and implies the death of the very self which irresistibly craves this final blessedness. This is the religion—it would be improperly called a philosophy—in which the Greek spirit finally sought satisfaction. It closes an epoch. In the same period Christianity is inaugurating a new experience and giving a new statement and solution of the age-long problem. These two forms of spiritual endeavour are contemporaries. Their interrelations dominate the subsequent history of thought. Greek philosophy does not stand alone at the point which it has reached. Indeed, it may be regarded as the expression of a movement which filled the Hellenic-Roman world. God was not to be found in the stereotyped religions and the systematic philosophies. He was in a beyond which must be reached, as it were, in a kind of desperation. This is the significance alike of the mystery-religions and of the closing period of Greek philosophy. The same stage, moreover, had been reached by a race whose mental qualities were widely different from those of the Greek. The religion of Israel stands apart from the theological conceptions of the Hellenic spirit. Its problem is primarily and essentially moral. It concerns the relation of man with a God who is not afar off, as a unity above all differences, but near in His righteous and merciful actions. He is not an Idea, with the impotence of impersonality, but a living Being, known in His doings. No Hebrew ever dreamed of discussing either the existence or knowableness of God—He has made Himself known; He is acting in the history of His people. What is left for man to do is to read the lesson of history and enter into the redeeming purpose of God as it grows through the centuries. There came a time, however, when it was not so easy to hold the idea of God as living, active, and close at hand. The historical revelation ceased with the destruction of Israel as a separate nationality. The voice of prophecy is still. Its place is taken by a sacred book. In it is written down the absolute truth of God. Man's business is to learn the contents of the book and hold, and do, what is therein prescribed. But God Himself is not there. He is in a heaven above. From thence He will come in a great day and vindicate Himself and establish His sovereignty. The idea of God in His bare transcendence takes growing hold of the Jewish mind. The Jew has reached the point where the Greek mind stood after the failure of Stoicism was becoming manifest. Dualism, which had been alien to his religious consciousness, has laid its malign spell on him. He, like the Greek, has somehow to bridge the chasm between the absolute and the relative, the infinite and the finite, a principle of unity and the manifold of experience. He, too, has to provide a way of salvation whereby the exiled spirit of man may regain its home in God. When he reaches this point, the Jew becomes the pupil of the Greek and takes over the Greek solution of the problem, which is common to both. The Hellenizing of an Isaiah is unthinkable. The Hellenizing of Philo Judæus was inevitable. In point of fact, dualism arrives in the natural movement of the human mind. When it is stated in its metaphysical form, there is only one solution, after philosophical reflexion has sunk exhausted under a task too heavy for it. The solution consists fundamentally in two conceptions—mediation between the transcendent God and the finite world, and ecstatic communion between man and the God who cannot be reached by exercise of rational faculty. The scheme of religious thought, accordingly, throughout three centuries has the same outline, whether we study it in a Jewish or in a Greek representative. The details, of course, vary widely, but they come under three heads; (*a*) the idea of God as transcendent; (*b*) the relation of God to the world through intermediaries; (*c*) the salvation of man through an ascent, which culminates in ecstasy.

Philo, born about 20 B.C., represents the Jewish movement, while the Greek development has its finest exponent in Plotinus (A.D. 203–269). A brief summary will illustrate the resemblance between them.

Philo.—(i.) *The idea of God*.—The transcendence of God finds in Philo[1] such strong emphasis as at once imperils His connexion with the world and His relation to man. Anthropomorphism must be scrupulously set aside. In pure and reverent thought we rise to the conception of God as One who is wholly removed from all relations, and therefore cannot be defined. We know that He is. What He is can never be apprehended in thought. He has no attributes, and such predicates as we apply to Him express only the gulf which separates Him from the sphere of things relative and finite and His removal from the grasp of our thought—ἁπλοῦς, ἄρρητος, ἀκατάληπτος, ἄτρεπτος, ἀΐδιος, ἄφθαρτος. He is the simply existent (ὁ ὤν, τὸ ὄν); He is self-sufficient (ἑαυτῷ ἱκανός) and cannot directly sustain relations with any finite being.

(ii.) *The idea of mediation*.—Between a God thus conceived and the finite world some link must be found. God is not identical with the world, nor can His pure essence be brought into immediate contact with the world. Philo finds the bridge built for him, both in Greek thought and in Jewish theology. God operated on the world in virtue of powers which are His and yet in some sense are separable from Him. For the Jew these powers are personified attributes of God. For the Greek they are the Ideas which Plato held to be the truth of things, and which later thought tended more and more to hypostatize. These intermediaries Philo concentrated in the Logos, the one mediator between the transcendent God and the finite world. The Logos is all in all for Philo. Without the Logos there could be no knowledge of God, nor any relation of God to man. The Logos is the first-born Son of God, or even the second God; and, from the other side of the contrast between God and the world, the Logos is the Heavenly Man, the Intercessor, the High Priest on behalf of man. To the Logos belong the great OT types of the divine presence and power, the manna, the living stream, the cloud, the rock in the wilderness.

The same great name, the same honorific titles, and the same typology are to be found in the NT; but the difference between Philo and the NT writers is profound. In Philo the problem is metaphysical and cosmological. The Logos links ontological opposites together. The Philonic Logos presupposes a distant Deity. In the NT the problem is moral and personal. The Logos crosses a far deeper than an ontological chasm, viz. that which yawns between two moral beings who were meant to live in harmony, one of whom has rebelled against the love which ought to have been his inward constraint and impulse. The NT Logos presupposes a God so near to man that He entered into the situation sin has made, and, as man, achieved the reconciliation. The problem is set to the divine love and to the human conscience, and it is solved not in idea, but in historic fact. The Logos of the NT is not a shadow cast by God, but the brightness of His glory, the express image of His person, not a vague speculative figure of which it is impossible to say whether it is God or other than God, personal or impersonal, but an historic personality, Jesus of Nazareth. It is with a kind of triumph not quite unmixed with scorn that the NT writers fling back on Alexandrian Judaism its august yet empty formula. The Logos? Certainly, we have heard and seen that word—not an empty name, but the living voice of a present redeeming God. 'The Logos became flesh, and tarried among us.' 'It is of what existed from the very beginning, of what we heard, of what we saw, of what we witnessed and touched with our own hands, it is of the Logos of life—it is of what we heard and saw that we bring you word, so that you may share our fellowship, and our fellowship is with the Father and with His Son Jesus Christ.' This is not philosophy at all. It is life, rising out of historic fact, fulfilling itself in experience.

(iii.) *The idea of salvation*.—On principles of dualism there is only one source of man's distress—his body, which is the tomb or prison of his soul. From the body, therefore, man must be delivered, and also from the whole activity of the soul as that is occupied with things finite; and, as action is necessarily occupied with things finite, deliverance can be accomplished only where the soul has sunk into passivity and yielded itself to the rapture of the beatific vision. The stages of this salvation are, practically, stereotyped for all these centuries. Philo named them ἄσκησις, διδαχή, φύσις, 'moral discipline,' 'contemplation,' 'ecstasy.' This is the way of salvation as conceived throughout the whole Hellenic world. There is in it no conception of an historic redemption wrought for men. Indeed, even the Logos ceases to be necessary and may be left out of account in the final step that brings emancipation. There is no call for faith, as an act of trustful commitment or as a life of personal loyalty. The contents of the Philonic salvation do not include the peace of forgiveness, the joy of reconciliation, the gladness of filial confidence.

Plotinus.—(i.) *The idea of God*.—The transcendence of God finds final expression in Plotinus.[1] What is present in Plato almost, as it were, against his will, what is the last result of Aristotle's great endeavour to present a truly organic view of the universe, what the Stoics were driven back upon, as they fought a rear-guard action against the irrationality of their environment, what Philo robed in the pieties of the OT, is for Plotinus the crown of religion and philosophy, the heart of his message to a world determined to reach God at any cost. As an idealist he climbs 'the steep ascent to heaven,' rising above every stage of existence and thought that is still mingled with the finite and the relative, seeking continually the unity which shall escape from difference. Then, when he has reached the top of the ladder, he finds it too short to reach the higher sphere, where the Absolute dwells inaccessible and unknowable. The Absolute is beyond existence, beyond good, beyond knowledge, beyond will. In the most literal sense the Absolute is ineffable. Even to ascribe unity to what is not an object for thought is an improper procedure, for to predicate is to limit. The Hebrew redeemer God says, 'I am that I am.' The Absolute of Plotinus, if He could declare anything, would say, 'I am not anything that can be expressed in any word that is intelligible to the ears of man.' The only truth that can be affirmed of such a God is that we can affirm nothing. This ultimate negation is not the humility of a worshipper, nor is it the despair of the agnostic; it is the voice of philosophy itself, declaring that unity cannot be found in differences, a philosophy which proclaims itself the ultimate, the only possible, religion. It is the voice of an epoch, finding utterance through its finest representative. This is the secret thought of the mystery-religion. All the philosophical and religious endeavours of the day have attained their utmost in thus raising an altar Ἀγνώστῳ Θεῷ; and on this the race of men has laid as an offering its aspiration and its hope.

(ii.) *The idea of mediation*.—Plotinus is not a pantheist; the finite does not live in God, though, apart from God, it would not be. It is; yet, if we are to reach God, we must leave it behind. Out of God, in some sense, it comes. Yet God cannot have any direct connexion with it, either to make it or to sustain it. The relation of a transcendent God to the world cannot be conceived except through spatial metaphors. If God is

[1] See art. ALEXANDRIAN THEOLOGY.

[1] See art. NEO-PLATONISM.

the beyond, plainly a bridge is wanted to connect Him with what is on the hither side. It is at this point that Plotinus shows himself to be no true Platonist, and to be the exponent of a new Platonism, which is fundamentally a misapprehension of Plato. It is true that Plato did not succeed in showing that the two elements with which he worked implied each other, and that to separate them was to make the solution of the problem of knowledge impossible; but he did not mean to place truth in one region, spatially separate from phenomena. 'For him, as for modern Idealism, all reality and being fall within experience, if not indeed within knowledge, and the distinction which he accepts is plainly shown by his terminology to be a distinction of aspects within the intellectual or real world.'[1] Plotinus does what Plato and Aristotle were too concrete in their thought to do: he separates truth from the world of experience and then has to build a bridge between them. For a conception of the divine immanence he substitutes a scheme of subordination, as follows: (1) the Unknowable Absolute; (2) the intelligence; (3) the world-soul; (4) the phenomenal world; (5) unknowable matter. It sounds mythological. It is mythology. It is the expedient to which a thoroughgoing dualism is necessarily reduced. When the extremes are held apart, an intermediary must be found which is not a real principle of union, but a third being externally related to each. This subordinationism pervaded the thought of the day. The attempt to make it the form of Christian thought regarding God, man, and salvation well-nigh wrecked Christianity itself.

(iii.) *The idea of salvation.*—It is difficult on principles of mysticism to understand the descent of man. But, waiving this, we can see what salvation of soul must be. It must be an ascent of man passing upward towards the fountain of truth and reality, which arises 'beyond existence.' Plotinus has nothing to add to the way of salvation which is common to all who seek to cross the chasm wrought by a dualistic view of God and the world. Its steps are stereotyped: (1) morality, conceived ascetically as purification of the soul; (2) contemplation, which thinks away all difference and apprehends the unity of the self and God; (3) ecstasy, the state, not necessarily accompanied by physical disturbances, in which the mind concentrates itself on God and reaches a condition which is indescribable, just as God Himself is ineffable. This is the beatific vision of which no report can be given, except that it is the 'life of the gods, and of godlike and blessed men, a release from all else here below, a life that takes no pleasure in earthly things, a flight of the alone to the alone.' This, then, is the highest that men can do. It is, at the same time, the exhaustion of the human spirit and the confession of its despair. The religious situation of the Western world in the first three centuries of our era presents a threefold choice: (*a*) unmitigated paganism, materialism, barbarism, in which the soul is 'lost' with an unmistakable and lamentable destruction; (*b*) the movement, of which the mystery-religions are the popular examples, and Neo-Platonism the final philosophical expression, offering a salvation for the soul, which is essentially an ecstatic experience of union with a blank and indeterminate divinity; (*c*) Christianity, the gospel of a divine love historically manifested in a human life and death, the experience of that love in the lives of men, reconciling them to God, forgiving their sins, binding them together in an organism indissoluble by force of persecution, by tyranny of space, or by the incident of death. It is true that Christianity conquered; that it still endures; and that, when the same alternatives are presented, it always wins. But it is also true that, in those very centuries in which it was winning its triumphs, it was being profoundly modified in the direction both of the mystery-religions and of Neo-Platonism. Its conception of salvation is never wholly lost. The personality of Jesus and the realism of His Cross make that an impossibility. Yet the simplicity of the gospel and the fullness of Christian experience are at once overlaid and impoverished by alien elements. Christianity becomes a mystery-religion, and theology owes more to Plotinus than to Paul.

IV. *THE IDEA OF SALVATION IN GREEK THEOLOGY.*—Recall the Greek non-Christian philosophy, which by this time was also the religion and theology of the cultured.[2] There is a wide contrast between it and the Christian religion of redemption. The NT is fully aware of this contrast. In the writings of Paul, in Hebrews, and in the Fourth Gospel we have the standpoint of men who were sufficiently acquainted with Greek thought to know that it belonged to a wholly different type of religious experience. They were perfectly willing to use its characteristic forms, if by this means they could win a hearing and present their Christ as the reality after which the best of the Greeks had earnestly sought. But they must be allowed to fill the forms with their own special message. Thus the Greek forms on Christian lips have little in common with the philosophy from which they are derived except the bare terminology. The heart of the NT is not a Logos Christology, but a soteriology that is historical and experimental to the core. The case, however, is altogether different when we pass from the NT to the scientific theology which arose in the 2nd cent., grew for three hundred years to a portentous elaboration, and created a fabric of dogma within which the Church has dwelt even to this day. The authors of it did not perceive the chasm that separated Greek philosophy from Christian experience. The form of their thinking was Greek; the matter of it was Christian. Now, when form and matter are disparate and the attempt is made to bring them together, one or other of two things will happen—either the matter will break up the form and force its way towards some higher and more adequate category or the form will subdue to itself the matter and deeply alter its value and significance. The latter alternative describes the course of Greek theology. It was meant to expound and defend the faith. It is true that it did sweep from the field all intellectual rivals; but it is not true that the faith remained victorious. The faith itself was profoundly modified; and the idea of salvation that emerges is certainly not of the NT type, while it conforms closely to prevalent Greek conceptions. The ruling ideas which we have noted in Philo and Plotinus as representative of the whole movement repeat themselves in the leading Greek theologians.

1. The idea of God.—That conception of God with which Greek philosophy terminated, viz. the Absolute, the Transcendent, the Indeterminable, governs unquestioned in the domain of Christian thought. The Fathers fall back on this abstract notion, with which to interpret the Christian faith in God, who is known in Christ, whose children believers in Christ are. It is a metaphysical envelope, in which is enclosed a religious experience. A metaphysic, essentially dualistic, is used to express and interpret a life whose glory consists in ethical oneness with the God to whom through Christ there is direct access, and of whom in Christ there is immediate knowledge. This metaphysical conception of God prevailed in Greek theology till the Council of Chalcedon closed that epoch of constructive work. It has remained to this day in spite of the reversion to the NT which marked the Reformation, in spite of that destruction of dogmatism with which Kant inaugurated the modern age; and still it confuses the issues for men who have travelled far from the conditions of Greek thought. God, as thus described, even by men who are seeking to defend Christian monotheism—Justin Martyr, Irenæus, Clement, Tertullian, Origen—is not, in the forms they use, the God and Father of our Lord and Saviour Jesus Christ, the God whose very essence is love, who by the inner constraint of His character must needs appear in human history and work out there in action and suffering the great salvation. Love and holiness, with the action and passion arising therefrom, are lacking to the Greek idea of God, and this defect makes that idea unsuited to act as the governing category of Christian soteriology.

2. The idea of mediation.—The shape which the problem of mediation will take is necessarily determined by the idea of God. With the Greek idea of God in their minds, the Greek theologians gave to the problem a distinctly cosmological character; and their solution took a predominantly metaphysical form. They have not indeed forgotten the human interest in salvation and the conviction of faith regarding the Saviour. But they have given soteriology a decidedly cosmological cast and have supposed that, if they could

[1] B. Bosanquet, *A Companion to Plato's Republic*[2], London, 1895, p. 248.

[2] See above, § II.

solve the problem of *being*, they had met the need of *salvation*.

The question, as they conceive it, is, How can God be connected with the world? In this question the whole of Greek dualism is involved, because 'God' is regarded as an entity of one kind, and the 'world' as a substance of so utterly diverse a kind that God can have no direct dealing with it, and therefore also man, as sunk in matter, can have no direct access to God. The only possible solution of such a problem is the building of a bridge between God and the world, and the question that divides the different schools, Greek and Christian, is as to the composition and structure of this bridge. Both schools indeed use one word: the bridge, or at least its central span, is the Logos. The differentia of the Christian answer is that the Logos is Christ. The main concern, therefore, of Christian theology is to contend that Christ, as Logos, is divine enough to reach the farther shore, where the Absolute dwells in the lonely splendour of His ineffable being. But by the logic of that dualism which was ineradicable in Greek philosophy it was impossible to say that the Christ Logos was *quite* God. Even supposing the distinction of λόγος ἐνδιάθετος and λόγος προφορικός were adopted, and a dwelling of the Logos in God were affirmed, yet the Logos appearing in the soul of Jesus cannot be on an equality with God. Lofty as is the rank of the Christ Logos, He is still one remove from the Absolute. There must be a subordination of Christ to God in respect of being, and therefore also of value. Precisely here, however, Greek dualism, even in Christian guise, found Christian faith sensitive, alert, and armed. The common sort of believers were perfectly certain that the Logos (whatever that might be in philosophy) was Jesus, and that Jesus, as Saviour, was as divine as God. This was a 'value-judgment' of faith, whatever theology might make of it. Yet faith had this inherent weakness, when it tried to say what God is, and what by consequence the Logos-Saviour is: it had no other idea to work with than the Greek conception of the remote and lonely Absolute. By such a presupposed dualism of God and the world, of form and matter, and by such conflicting interests of head and heart, the course of Christian thought is determined, till Nicæa, nominally at least, drove Greek philosophy from the field. The oft-told story runs in three chapters.

(1) *Subordinationism in control.*—Christ is an intermediary needed to connect God with the world. Christian faith, indeed, rejoiced to think of Jesus as the Son and Servant of God, entering the world on a redemptive mission and carrying out the Father's will of love, in life and death, thereby securing forgiveness, reconciliation, and fellowship. But, when taken up into Greek metaphysical and dualistic philosophy, this truth of religion attested in experience is turned into a doctrine of the person of Christ, which makes Him second from God in rank of being; and this is precisely the reverse of what faith meant to say. The Logos Christology is not the implicit faith of the NT, brought into clear consciousness by its own inherent logic. It is that faith stated, with the best intention, in a logic which did not belong to it. It is found in the apologists, to whom the Logos as a separate existence is numerically distinct from God, a second God, to be worshipped indeed, but not to be regarded as in the fullest sense God, subordinate to God, a kind of 'depotentiated God.' The point of these assertions is that they are not reached through a study of the inner life of Jesus and are not an attempt to enter into the secret of His self-consciousness. They are constructions based on an *a priori* conception of God which was not critically examined or experimentally evaluated. They are deductions of what the Logos must be; not a picture of the Jesus of history, who, for NT Christianity, is the Jesus of faith. Irenæus's doctrine of the person and work of Christ displays closer contact with the NT thought and life. He is clear on the fundamental Christian convictions 'that the Creator of the world and the supreme God are one and the same' and that 'Christianity is real redemption . . . effected by the appearance of Christ.'[1] But the atmosphere of the day cleaves to him. He is still operating with categories supplied to him by the last phase of Greek philosophy, with their parallels in the mystery-religions. Salvation requires participation in the being of God, and it is primarily because this being is brought within reach by the Incarnation that Christ can be Saviour. Irenæus's account of the ἀνακεφαλαίωσις is poetic and suggests truth deeper than he knew; but in him it has Neo-Platonic connotation and runs out into sacramentarianism and mysticism. The presuppositions are still ontological. Christ 'was made as we are in order that He might make us to be as He is.' It is still salvation by participation in divine essence, and to that extent it is Greek rather than Christian.

In the great Alexandrians we have the same combination of intense Christian conviction with the Greek metaphysic and the Logos Christology. Clement's description of God is as defective as anything in Philo or Plotinus. God is 'formless and nameless, though we sometimes give Him titles, which are not to be taken in their proper sense, the One, the Good, Intelligence, or Existence, or Father, or God, or Creator, or Lord'—a truly 'appalling definition.'[1] Appalling though it be, it is the climax of centuries of Greek thought, and, when it is used as starting-point, a satisfying Christian doctrine of God and of salvation becomes impossible. It is quite true that nothing was farther from Clement's mind than to attribute to Christ a reduced divinity. He desired to bring Him as close to God as possible—as close, say, as the Nous, or intelligible world, in Plotinus's trinity. Yet in the last resort Christ is not God Himself, in His own proper person, acting, suffering, saving on man's behalf. The Logos may be the immanent reason of the universe, and Clement is the typical 'Broad Churchman' rejoicing in a revelation of God to Greek as well as to Christian. But this reason has always God, in His essence unknowable, behind it. Subordinationism attends on the Greek idea of God, like its shadow. Thoroughly Greek, too, is Clement's conception of the work of Christ. Clement has not entered Christianity through the moral discipline of the OT. He is through and through intellectualist, in his views at once of need and of salvation. He 'himself had passed through no spiritual crisis; enlightenment rather than the need of forgiveness, intellectual unrest rather than an accusing conscience, drove him to the Christian faith.'[2] The source of man's distress is ignorance; hence comes the disease of sin, and man is doomed to death. The work of Christ, therefore, though Clement employs the classic language of sacrifice, is to give knowledge. This throws the actual experience of humanity into the shade, and Clement is constantly slipping towards docetism. All that is needed, from a Greek point of view, is enough humanity to convey ideas to men. Real identification with men is not needed, though, from a Christian point of view, it is the *sine qua non* of salvation.

Origen's loyalty to the full divinity of Christ is beyond question, but his scheme of thought is Greek, and it is through the Greek *a priori* conceptions that he apprehends the statements of Scripture. He is no avowed subordinationist; and yet the all but inevitable issue of his thought is subordinationism. His God is the Absolute, whom, however, after Plato, he conceives as good with inward *nisus* towards self-communication. Between this God and the world there are (i.) the Logos, produced by the will of God supra-temporally in an ineffable act of generation; (ii.) the Logos united with the pre-existent holy soul of Jesus; (iii.) these two inhabiting an incontaminate body, born of a virgin; (iv.) along with the Logos, but without any inherent necessity, the Spirit, an adjunct, borrowed from Scripture and subordinate with the Logos, though superior to all other holy beings. This is not the Christianity of the NT. It is Christianity stretched on the rack of Greek thought.

The logic of subordinationism becomes explicit in Arianism. The issue of the Greek metaphysical conception of God is now made plain. Let God be conceived as the Absolute. Let Christ be regarded as the Logos, between God and the world, and the result is inevitable—a distortion of the Christian idea of salvation and an emptying of Christian experience of its rich ethical and religious contents. Clement and Origen were great believers; but they were too much under the dominance of Greek thought to do full justice to the Christian faith in Christ or to unfold and verify the Christian experience of salvation. In Arius we have a thinker who had gone one worse than any of his predecessors. In the guise of a Christian ascetic, he is plain Greek and pagan. In him the Greek religious philosophy, in this its latest phase, is making its final stand. It understands that it must make terms with Christianity. Its terms are these: it will accept Christ as of divine rank and will apply to Him any honorific title that may be proposed, and set Him far above all men and all angelic beings, at the head of the whole creation, but it will not, either as a philosophy or as a religion, treat Him as Himself God, or a real incarnation of God, or God living and working out man's redemption. He is at His greatest a κτίσμα still; at best, a cosmological principle, but no Saviour from sin's guilt and power. This is the old heathenism, whatever its disguise. Christianity was at the crisis of its fate. To have accepted Arianism would have meant absolute defeat, the arrest of the whole movement of the human spirit Godward.[3]

(2) *Monarchianism, in vigorous defence of Christian monotheism.*—Monarchianism (*q.v.*) takes its rise as a protest against the attempt to make Christ an Æon, or intermediate being, and asserts the prevailing Christian interest in the unity and

[1] Harnack, *Hist. of Dogma*[3], Eng. tr., London, 1894-99, ii. 237.

[1] Bigg, *Christian Platonists of Alexandria*, p. 63.

[2] John Patrick, *Clement of Alexandria*, Edinburgh and London, 1914, p. 119.

[3] Cf. artt. ARIANISM, SUBORDINATION.

supremacy of God. It rightly sees that salvation is God's act only, and that to transfer the mighty work to any Saviour, divided, however faintly, from the only God, is to invalidate it and leave faith no security. But this Christian interest was defeated by the Greek idea of God. The Monarchians too are Greeks. They are working with Greek categories—the Absolute, the Monas, and the like. They set themselves a task which was really impossible—to combine the divinity of Christ with that Greek conception. A choice of paths appeared to them. They might hold the individuality of Christ and regard the divine in Him as a quality or force; or they might hold the divinity of Christ in the fullest sense, but regard it as the very presence of the absolute God. The former alternative looks at Jesus as a man inspired by God, and so, by a special line, leads round into subordinationism and makes salvation a human achievement, accomplished by moral endeavour. The latter is much more fitted, in one sense, to express Christian conviction and might seem to be no more than what adoring faith will ascribe to its divine object. In point of fact, however, when traced to its Greek original, it is an almost complete denial of the Christian verities. Here is no living God, but an expanding and contracting Monas; no Mediator between God and man, Himself man, no living Saviour and Lord. The Son has no life of His own, and, when His temporary manifestation is over, He is retracted into the Monas and lost to faith. Tertullian's vigorous protest was of value in asserting the necessity of the historic Christ for the security of the Christian salvation. But Tertullian's own Christology is still caught in the Logos scheme and assigns to Christ no more than a *portio* of the Godhead.

(3) *The victory of Nicæa.*—The intolerable consequences of Greek dualism are met by Athanasius with a flat denial. For three centuries Greek thought has assumed that God could not be brought into direct communication with anything so low as a material universe, but needed intermediaries. Christian thought had not ventured to declare that this was pure *a priori* prejudice, but gave a religious turn to Greek philosophy by declaring that Christ was such an intermediary, who, by the logic of this movement, would not be quite what God is. Athanasius is brave enough to say that the long-accepted dualism is no necessity of thought. God can create directly. There is no need of a *tertium quid*. It is true that God uses the instrumentality of His Son in the act of creation, but this is a secondary matter. The central function of the Son is not cosmological, but redemptive. His central significance in theology, as in Christian faith, is His agency in salvation. The object of the Christian worship is not the Logos of the philosophers, but the Son of God, the historic Christ, who was born, and lived, and died, and rose again. In Him God Himself entered into humanity. Therefore no phrase must be used which shall permit Him to be thought of as a creature, however near to God, or howsoever adorned with epithets. Human salvation demands that there shall be more than a bridge by which man shall pass to God; that there shall be in humanity a divine Being in becoming one with whom man shall reach oneness with God and so be saved. This, in fact, is the Christian message of salvation. 'He was not man, and then became God, but He was God and became man and that to deify us.' The Son, accordingly, is not to be thought of as an intermediary, a second God. He must be regarded as having the same substance with the Father and constituting with the Father a unity. The symbol of Nicæa makes this position explicit: 'Begotten from the Father as only begotten God from God, *i.e.* from the very being of the Father (ἐκ τῆς οὐσίας τοῦ πατρός), sharing one being with the Father (ὁμοούσιον τῷ πατρί).'

Thus the long history of Greek philosophy is brought to a close by an intuition of faith discerning the value of a fact of history. Christ is the Son of God. No cosmological scheme can content the believing heart which has found in Christ, not an introduction to God, but God Himself in the fullness of the Godhead. A cosmological bridge does not meet the need of salvation. Suppose we climb to the end of the span formed by the Logos, what guarantee have we that it will really abut on God? Rather, it is certain that, if Christ be not truly God, there will still be a chasm to cross. Well might Athanasius say, 'We are fighting for our all,' when he stood against an Arian world. Therefore historians and theologians of every shade of orthodoxy have sympathized with Athanasius and have admitted that a diphthong may mark the whole difference between Christianity and paganism.

To do this, however, and even to accept *ex animo* the Nicene Creed as a confession of faith, does not mean to be satisfied with it as a doctrine of God or of Christ or of salvation. The use of the word οὐσία has unconsciously and unintentionally reintroduced the very philosophy it was meant to exclude. God viewed as οὐσία is a static Deity, such an 'unmoved mover' as Aristotle reached through his dualism of matter and form, such an Absolute as Philo or Plotinus set in immobile and immortal blessedness beyond the manifold of experience. Such a God does not really live. He never acts. He cannot suffer. He has an οὐσία all His own. The Son shares that with the Father. Thus the affirmation of faith, that Christ is as divine as God, is construed to mean that He had a divine essence which is not man's. And, as soon as this passes into common belief, we have left NT ground and are occupying the position of the mystery-religions and of Neo-Platonism, viz. that salvation means participation in the divine Being, a participation that is effected in a supra-rational manner by vision or ecstasy. The victory which faith won at Nicæa was thus in great measure nullified by the metaphysic which remained uncorrected in the language of the creed. Faith is quite sure that Christ the Lord is as divine as the Father, whose Son and Servant He is, and as human as those whom He came to save. In that assurance there is implicit a view of divinity and humanity which thinks of them not as opposites or disparate essences, but as so related that a divine Being may have a human experience and be in the fullest sense God, being in the completest sense man, while manhood is perfected in the human experience through which God attains the ends of His holy love. This view, however, was rendered impossible by the metaphysical view of God which remained in the minds even of believing theologians, wholly uncriticized and uncorrected. The result was a theological *impasse*. The dualism which wrecked Greek philosophy has returned and has inserted itself in the doctrine of the person of Christ and in the conception of salvation bound up therewith. The Christological discussions of the 4th cent. represent the mind of man exhausting itself in alternative escapes from an impossible situation. Take the Apollinarian road and mutilate the humanity so that divinity may have room to act; take the pathway of Nestorius and place divinity side by side with its opposite and bind them together with a phrase; follow Eutyches and absorb the humanity in the divinity—in each case Greek dualism is driving faith whither it would not go, and, as soon as faith becomes aware of the coercion of logic, it revolts and, in defiance of logic, returns to its basal convictions. It cares nothing for logic; its one interest is salvation. If that be endangered, it will expel as heresy the most carefully devised Christology. This is, of course, what faith did in the symbol of Chalcedon.

'The definitions of ancient creeds . . . were an attempt to stake off the limits of that area which the Church had come to claim as reserved for faith and sacred to it; marking it off by certain assured points which she believed to be guaranteed at once by the witness of Holy Scripture and by her own consciousness of salvation in Christ.'[1]

Our estimate of Chalcedon repeats that of Nicæa. It is a victory for faith, rendered fruitless by the employment of categories useless and misleading, if employed beyond the bare purpose of negating error. They are steeped in metaphysical dualism and are unfit to bring into clear consciousness an experience in which the supposed opposites of philosophy are held together in the grasp of a living synthesis. In the article just quoted Dykes thus sums up his review of the Chalcedonian formula:

'A Being who combines in an inscrutable fashion Divine with Human properties, and of whom consequently contradictory assertions may be made, whose single Person is Divine, while His dual natures hold an undefined relation to one another: this is not a scheme to satisfy either head or heart.'[2]

In point of fact, neither the head nor the heart of the Church was satisfied with the Chalcedonian orthodoxy. When divinity and humanity are placed in juxtaposition, without any real unity

[1] J. Oswald Dykes, *ExpT* xvii. [1905–06] 7.
[2] *Ib.* p. 10.

between them, both mind and heart will place the emphasis on divinity. The primal need is for God. It is God in Christ who saves. If, therefore, God be defined in terms which make a human experience for Him impossible, the inevitable result will be that the humanity of the Saviour sinks in value and reality. Cyril had the interests of salvation at heart. But he so conceived of God that salvation was imperilled, lost its distinctively Christian character, and took a specifically Greek form. Monophysitism, expelled in name, returns in power. Christ is so one with God that He shares the divine transcendence. Hence arises a double dualism: (*a*) within the person of Christ, between His divinity and His humanity, the latter being rendered by orthodoxy more and more unreal and ineffective; (*b*) in the sphere of salvation, between the divine Christ and human beings, who find it now as hard to get to Christ as ever Neo-Platonist did to reach the absolute Deity. Christianity had appealed to Greek philosophy, and it had received its reward. The God it had found in Christ was removed to an intolerable distance; and Christ, who was one with God, shared the remoteness of the Absolute. Once more the chasm yawned; once more a bridge had to be built, or, rather, the bridge reared by the speculative genius of Plotinus was still standing. This, therefore, the human spirit was constrained to use, giving it only a new facing of Christian forms and usages, not knowing or not heeding that, in so doing, it was reverting to something that lay farther back than Neo-Platonism, in the obscurities of primeval religious feeling, and was transmuting Christianity into a revived mystery-religion.

3. **The idea of salvation.**—The Greek scheme works out as follows. (*a*) *Man and sin.*—In his innermost essence man belongs to the sphere of the divine. As in Plotinus individual souls belong to the world-soul and are one in essence with it, so in the Christian application of this thought all souls are divine in being. Their reality and their blessedness consist in their participation in the divine nature. Their separation from it would be destruction, and their salvation would be reunion with it. The whole movement is apart from ethical relationship. The goal is a good that is above moral good. The salvation, in like manner, is a process which may have morality as a stage, but reaches towards a metaphysical issue, accomplished not through rectification of moral relations, but through changes affecting essence and being. This distinction between moral values and metaphysical reality goes deep into the Greek idea of salvation and marks it off from the NT region of thought. From a pristine state of oneness with the divine nature human souls have fallen. In harmony with the Platonizing thought of his day, Origen had held the pre-existence of souls. Whether in this theory or in that of creationism, the fall of souls is wholly unintelligible. Plotinus could not give a reason for the irrational. The descent was simply part of the working of his scheme—a far-off result of the distinction of matter and form, observable in all experience. In Christian thought the Greek regard for the determining power of reason is uppermost. Greek theology remains true to the freedom of man, conceiving it as bare power of the rational nature, a power inherent, incapable of being lost. In any case the descent has been made by Adam and is made by practically every individual soul. The descent, as in Greek thought, is into the region of matter and sense and mortality. In this position freedom cannot indeed be lost, but is considerably weakened, and the soul would need assistance of some sort in its upward way, as it seeks its home in the supersensuous sphere and returns to its divine original. It is a simple and obvious situation, precisely that which Greek thought had been dealing with for centuries. Man is sunk in sense, with all its concomitant evils—mortality and subjection to demonic power. The one problem is the ascent of man. It is not the situation as the NT, with its roots in the OT, conceived it. For a mind trained in Hebraic modes of thought, for a conscience disciplined by the revelation of the divine holiness, the situation is that of man's revolt, in the pride of self-assertion, against the will of a holy, loving, and sovereign God. Greek theology is singularly lacking in its sense of the righteousness and holiness of God; and its soteriology suffers accordingly. Its captivity to Greek forms is conspicuous and disastrous.

(*b*) *Redemption.*—Plainly, what is needed by man, thus immersed in a region so foreign to his true being, is reinstatement in the sphere to which he belongs, *i.e.* the divine. The descent must be replaced by ascent, and the successful accomplishment of this process is termed 'deification.' Man must be lifted to the place to which he belongs and become what God is in His essential nature—*i.e.* immortal, free from all taint of sense. The central significance of this deification is the quality that is assigned to the divine essence. There is no rich ethical content filling the thought. Greek speculation defines God mainly by negations; and thus its conception of deification is also mainly negative. The aspiration of the soul is set on a mode of being of which nothing can be said, save that it is at the opposite pole from matter. True, this higher state is conceived as the only reality, for matter, in genuine Platonic fashion, is conceived as non-being. But, after all, mere being is scarcely a richer thought than non-being. Deification reaches being, and that is reckoned blessedness; but the contents of that blessedness are, like God Himself, beyond predication. Salvation, thus conceived as deification, can be only partial, as long as the soul has any material integument. It can never therefore be a possession. It is not, as in the NT, by a paradox, both possession and inheritance. It lies in the beyond only. Its instalments are not itself. They are only steps towards it. Only when the dead lift is complete, and the soul escapes from matter, does it reach salvation. The method of this deliverance is determined by the goal. The question for Greek thought is how to get the divine nature so near to man that man can unite himself with it and share its blessedness. There is no question of atonement and reconciliation, of a moral estrangement overcome by love, and a new moral relationship entered upon in faith. Baptized into Christianity, Greek thought proclaims the Incarnation to be the method of salvation. The divine life is in Christ—not indeed in His flesh: He has no more relation to flesh and blood than will allow the divinity, which is His only real being, to become accessible to man. The ruling thought is transformation of man's being, till he become what God is. Greek theology makes everything of the Incarnation. Yet the most damaging criticism upon it is that it does not make enough of incarnation. Deity retains its transcendence and remoteness even within the veil of flesh. It is in flesh only that man may be deified. There is no thoroughgoing human experience on the part of the Logos Christ. Even the *recapitulatio* of Irenæus, though it brings him in some aspects close to the gospel, is at bottom Greek. It means that the Incarnate One brings to actuality the divine mode of being, which is God's original plan for humanity, so that now human nature may be deified by being taken up into it. Origen shows the real drift of the tendency, for, while recognizing rather than teaching various theories of atonement, he passes beyond them to conceive of salvation as consisting in being 'interwoven with the divine essence'—a condition reached by knowledge, revealed by Christ in His capacity as teacher and hierophant. Athanasius has rejected Greek cosmology. His profoundest concern is salvation, and this requires the full deity of the Redeemer. But, at bottom, the idea of salvation and the means of deliverance are Greek. Man's distress is his mortality. Repentance alone, therefore, cannot deliver him. Life must be brought to him, that he may partake of the very nature of the Deity. Athanasius is able to give a real place in redemption to the death and resurrection of Christ, but it is not the place assigned to them in the NT. It is still the question of deliverance from mortality with which he is dealing. In the death of Christ the law of death is abrogated, and in the resurrection of Christ incorruption is guaranteed.

'By death immortality has reached to all . . . for He was made man that we might be made God, and He manifested Himself by a body that we might receive the idea of the unseen Father, and He endured the insolence of men that we might inherit immortality. For while He Himself was in no way injured, being impassible and incorruptible and very Word and God, men who were suffering, and for whose sake He endured all this, He maintained and preserved in His own impassibility.'[1]

It is devout and very Christian in its sense of debt to Christ,[2] but its metaphysic, theology, Christology, and soteriology are Greek and not NT.

The condition under which salvation viewed as deification is obtained by men is necessarily union with Christ—*i.e.* oneness in being with His divine being. There is no question here of faith committing itself to Christ and receiving in the act His unsearchable riches. There is no union of two living personalities to be mutually possessed in love, each entering into the experience of the other. It is, in the precise sense of the age-long religion of Hellas, a mystical union, a participation not in the 'benefits of Christ,' but in His very being.

(*c*) *The process of salvation.*—In a way Greek theology was more dualistic, at least after the overthrow of subordinationism, than Neo-Platonism and more at a loss to produce an effective salvation. The divine in Christ has been so completely identified with the absolute Godhead that it cannot form the link between God and man. With the practical triumph of Monophysitism, the dualism is now as much between Christ and man as it ever was in Greek thought between God and the world. The chasm is still there. The question now is, How shall the divine Christ be made accessible to man? Where and how shall man find Christ and be made one with Him? The answer comes straight from the heart of Greek religion—that primitive religion which preceded and outlasted the intellectualized Olympians of the middle period of Greek development, and which in the last stage of Greek life and thought was found mingled in a confused syncretism with all manner of Oriental cults. The very word which carried the whole meaning of Greek religion with it is employed to designate the central element in the Christian salvation. Christ is brought to man in the 'mysteries,' of which the Eucharist is the chief. No theory of His presence as yet holds the field. The crudity of popular imagination, which regards the consecrated elements as the actual flesh and blood of Christ, is below the subtlety of Greek symbolism; and transubstantiation, as an attempt to make the mystery intelligible, is still far off. No theory is needed. Suffice it that in the rite, with the aid of all well-devised circumstances, the mind of the worshipper is subdued, the emotions are stimulated, reason is silent, and the unknown Divine, too wonderful for intellectual definition, is felt to be somehow, inexplicably, there. At this point the function of the Church becomes manifest in all its soul-subduing sanctity. The Presence depends on the rite, the rite depends for its efficacy on the celebrant, and the celebrant depends for the due performance of the rite on his place in the Church. Behold the bridge between heaven and earth, the only link that can bring Christ and man together! Where is Christ? On the altar. What brought Him there? The power of the hierurge. All that Christ can do for the soul is done in the Eucharist. It is the medicine of immortality, the instrument of deification. Rapt in spirit before the altar, severed from all things of sense, in deep emotion beyond all processes of reason, almost above consciousness of self, the soul tastes salvation and almost enjoys the beatific vision, which will one day, in a moment, admit him to the immortal life and give him the object of his passionate aspiration—participation in the divine nature. This is the core of the Christian experience. Christianity stands forth confessed a mystery-religion.

It is not necessary to deny to this 'mystery' a definite religious value. Any one who has given sympathetic attention to the Russian Eucharist must have thrilled to the sense of the unseen conveyed by a ceremonial more splendid and more surcharged with inexpressible suggestion than even the Roman rite. Still it has to be noted that its ancestry is not in the NT, but in primitive Greek religion, as that was reproduced in the mystery-religions, and that its intellectual equivalent is not the teaching of Jesus or any of His apostles, but Greek philosophy, in the last stage of its development, when, as Neo-Platonism, it offered itself to every cultured intelligence as a revelation of God and a way of salvation. It is impossible also not to note the danger which haunts it—the danger that besets all mysticism—viz. the emphasis laid on the metaphysical and the reduction of the ethical to a secondary place and value. The salvation which does not find its climax in duty and virtue needs no theological acuteness to criticize it. It is condemned already.

The process of salvation, looked at from the human side, exhibits the same thoroughgoing Greek character. The question is, How shall the soul fit itself for the great moment of its deification? The answer keeps close to Neo-Platonic lines. The first step is morality. At this point Christianity presents itself as a new law; and its morality is a baptized Stoicism. The second step is knowledge. Here Christianity takes up into itself the older Greek idea of salvation by wisdom. The third step is that in which the soul goes beyond morality, and even beyond knowledge, and makes its transition from things earthly in an ecstasy. In this procedure two points of contrast with NT Christianity are to be noted. (1) There is no place for faith. The NT knows no other condition of salvation than trust in God. Whatever psychological concomitants it may have, it is a definite conscious act of the human personality in the exercise of its highest powers. A scheme which omits this trustful commitment of the sinner to the sin-bearing and sin-forgiving God is not Christian. (2) The relation of morality to salvation is inverted. Self-purification is, in Christianity, not a stage which is left behind in the final attainment; it is the issue, the consequence, and the test of the Christian salvation. A writer who has been held responsible for mysticism in Christianity declares: 'This is how we may be sure we are in Him: he

[1] *On the Incarnation*, liv. 3.
[2] So most eloquently in §§ 4, 5.

who says he remains in Him ought to live as He lived' (1 Jn $2^{5f.}$). A practical result of this inversion is seen in the two grades of Christians now recognized within the Church. The one remains in the world, to continue the race and carry on its business. The other devotes itself to the pursuit of salvation by those paths which are shut to ordinary traffic. Greek theology requires the solitary for the successful prosecution of the way of salvation devised by the Greek spirit. He alone can direct his soul, in entire withdrawal from sense, upon the divine, so as to obtain the vision of it and become one with it. And here is a strange, yet inevitable, thing. For the crowning experience the historic Christ and the actual Cross are no longer necessary. They themselves belong to time and sense and matter, and all these things are transcended. Salvation is gained in ecstatic contemplation, and that permits no object to be before it save the Absolute Deity. Unneeded, too, by the expert solitary is the Eucharist itself. Beyond all such things, linked as these are to the external, the soul passes inward and upward, till it is absorbed in God. When we have reached this point, we see that Christianity has lost all distinctiveness as a historical religion. It has ceased to have reference to persons or deeds. Even one unique Person and one atoning deed cease to have interest for it. It is manifest mysticism; and mysticism is identical in all its forms, whether Greek, Hindu, Muslim, or Christian.

V. *THE IDEA OF SALVATION IN LATIN THEOLOGY.*—The Western Church accorded to the East its special place and function as thinker and interpreter. In the controversies which marked the progress of dogma the West intervened, not as a rival specialist in speculation, but as a calm and just moderator. Chalcedon, though a settlement of Greek controversies, is a product of the Western mind, which is not versed in metaphysical subtleties, but is quite sure of the facts of faith and quite competent to say exactly what it stands for. The Greek conception of God, accordingly, passes over into the West uncriticized and unrevised. It lies behind Latin theology and its descendants and revives even after the Reformation has pointed out a more Biblical and more excellent way of thinking regarding God. That, moreover, which goes with the Greek idea of God—the conception, namely, of a salvation which consists in deification and is attained in ecstasy—remains as the highest grade of religious attainment. However elaborate the dogma, however rigid and detailed the discipline, however magnificent the cultus, the ideal of the finest religious experience remains as the mystic oneness of the soul with God, to which, ultimately, dogma and discipline and cultus are alike secondary and even indifferent. The solitary still stands above and apart from ecclesiastical Christianity and represents the highest type of the religious soul as such.

All this being presupposed and regarded as sacrosanct, Latin theology proceeds to interpret Christianity by means of its own characteristic modes of thought. These are political and social in their nature. If Greek theology was created by Greek philosophy, Latin theology was created by the Roman empire and had for its governing category the Roman imperial idea. While the idea of God, in formal Latin orthodoxy, is the Greek Absolute, taken over without revision, this empty notion is filled with contents derived from the person and authority of the Roman emperor. God is the Emperor of the universe. This is not merely a poetic image; it is a ruling principle in theology and religion, and consequences logically derived from it are binding upon mind and conscience. God is essentially will. Will takes the place of being as the deepest element in the idea of God; but it is will regarded as bare sovereignty. No doubt the Emperor of the universe will administer its affairs as the best type of Roman emperor managed his vast dominions, in the highest interests of His subjects; but the chief object of man's regard, as he contemplates God, is the tremendous operative force of His absolute will. If the universe, in one sense, is the sphere of God's imperial sway, in another the Church is His real and proper empire. As within the Roman empire, and there alone, peace and security prevailed, so only in the Church was there possibility of salvation from the evil forces that raged around it and from the unspeakable doom which awaited all beyond its pale. The heart of the empire grew chill at the thought of the barbarians, whose stroke, in those last days, had reached even the imperial city. In like manner the heart of the Christian was moved at the terror of a judgment that would surely befall him but for the sheltering walls of the city of God. His religion was a religion of fear; and salvation was deliverance from the power of Satan here and hereafter. The constitution of the Church, accordingly, becomes of first-rate religious importance. The Founder of the Church, its first great Imperator, could make no mistake. He fixed once for all its mighty ramparts. To touch them is not merely to cherish a wrong opinion, but to strike at the will of God and the very safeguards of salvation. The great security of the Church is the historic episcopate. The Scriptures, the cultus, the sacraments, all stand within the guardianship of the bishop and from him derive their salvation value and their spiritual effectiveness. The souls of men are his peculiar care. He is responsible for them to the great Head of the Church. They, for their part, have but one duty with respect to him, and that is obedience. The emperor has his double hierarchy—State officials from the loftiest to the lowliest, and the priests of the imperial worship duplicating the offices of government. So Christ has His hierarchy—bishops and presbyters, like the priests and Levites in the Jewish Temple, who are at once State officials in the ecclesiastical empire and the only celebrants in the action of Christian worship. Beneath stand the laity submissive and adoring.

Further developments follow inevitably. Salvation depends on obeying the laws of God, as they are administered by the Church. Sin means breach of these laws. Strictly speaking, sin is crime committed against the imperial majesty of heaven. Sin, therefore, like crime, must be punished, while obedience, at least if it reach large proportions, may be rewarded. Penalty and merit are brought into the relations of man to God. A man pays for his disobedience by the penalty he endures. A man's obedience is the price he pays for his security. Ominous phrases begin to be heard, 'satisfacere Deo,' 'placare Deum.' The whole system no doubt —the Church and its penitential discipline—has been brought into existence by the mercy of God. But within the system juridical and forensic principles and methods bear sway. Members of the Church live under a legal administration and have their spiritual state adjudged in terms of crime and penalty, good works and merit. In all this the NT does not come into consideration. Christianity has become the religion of the empire; but still more it has become an imperialism. We are moving throughout in a politico-legal atmosphere. The creator of the ecclesiastical soteriology is the heathen empire. In defence of the Latin theologians and churchmen it may be urged that they could scarcely help themselves.

'With the flood of new proselytes the Church acquired a constituency which could only be dealt with on legal principles: and such principles could be applied only in the way of enjoining certain observances. That alone could be practically intelligible to the mass. The assumption followed, that when these observances were passively accepted, at least without disbelief or contradiction, they would do their work, would confer and accomplish the Christian salvation. On any other view, what must become of the mass of recognized Christians? The theory which this implied settled on men's minds like a fate. Christ has furnished us with a system of church ordinances which, if reverently complied with, do mysteriously effect salvation.'[1]

This way of salvation is expounded in Tertullian and Cyprian—the one a great apologist for the faith, the other a martyr; yet the scheme itself is not Christian. Gwatkin's blunt verdict on Cyprian exhibits the relation of a Church statesman to the ideas of his day:

'Saint he is, and martyr; and the Christian Church is justly proud of him; yet his general conception of religion is much more heathen than Christian. There is no sign that he ever troubled himself to think out the ideas on which it depends. Like a practical man, he takes them from the air about him, and assumes them to be not only true but self-evident, and concerns himself only with their practical applications.'[2]

In Latin theology proper, forensic forms are confined to the application of salvation to the souls that need it. The provision of salvation is not yet brought under these forms. The ominous *satisfactio* is not applied to the work of Christ either by Tertullian or by Cyprian. This extension of the idea, however, lies close at hand; and, when Latin theology merges into mediæval, this borrowed conception will begin its career as the key to the work of Christ.

Latin theology is systematized by St. Augustine, whose magnificence none will dispute; though, if we may adopt the expression of a much-tried Scottish king, employed by him in another connexion, he has been 'a sair sanct' to the Christian Church, whether Protestant or Catholic.

In Augustine's thought we have the blending of four great influences: (i.) a deep Pauline experience, (ii.) an experimental acquaintance with the truths of Scripture, (iii.) the dominance of Neo-Platonism, (iv.) the authority of the Church. It may be predicted that a system built up under this fourfold control will be suggestive rather than satisfying and will give rise to divergent streams of thought and life. From Augustine's experience and his sympathetic reading of Paulinism there have flowed evangelical experience and evangelical theology. The appeal to experience and the grounding of salvation in the love of God may well go back to Augustine, as Augustine went back to St. Paul, and St. Paul went back to the Cross of Christ. But, when Christian experience is interpreted both through Greek dualism and through Roman imperialism, we may be certain that its characteristic features will be distorted out of knowledge.

1. The idea of God.—The idea of God takes on the qualities of its double origin: God is the Greek Absolute and the Roman Will, in either aspect, beyond the reach of man's knowledge. God is the only real. Things that exist do so only by 'participation' in the divine nature. Reality is not in time and space. History is not real development; it is simply the translation into time of the immutable will of God. The Augustinian 'predestination' is simply the Greek affirmation of the transcendence of God, brought *ab extra*, and imposed on Christian experience. The conviction of the NT believer that salvation does not depend on human initiative, but on the everlasting mercy, belongs to a totally different region of thought and cannot properly be interpreted through a Greek category.

2. The idea of sin.—Sin is explained on the old lines that go back to Plato and were ineradicable in Greek thought. Augustine was keenly aware of the guilt of sin; but his experience and the whole bent of his disposition led him to view it mainly in the aspect of disease, defilement, and moral impotency, to connect it with the body, and to lay enormous emphasis on carnality. His agony as a sinner was that he could not sever the bonds that held him, till he 'put on the Lord Jesus Christ.' Salvation was emancipation, and is interpreted chiefly as power. His problem as a man, a pastor, and a theologian is, How shall the slave of sin be set free and brought into a freedom which consists in identity with the will of God? It is because an exercised Christian knows this true liberty of the soul that Augustine defeated Pelagius; and it is because the semi-heathen knows nothing of it that Semi-Pelagianism is the working creed of a half-Christian Christendom. Yet the problem, as Augustine put it, is not stated in its real depth, and his solution is marred by intellectual puzzles.

3. The idea of the Church.—The Church confronts the soul that knows by bitter experience the helplessness of its will-power and the incapacity of its intellectual faculty. Augustine is recapitulating in his own mind the history of Greek philosophy. By the logic of Greek thought, reason is incapable of reaching God and so solving the problems of life and mind. The situation thus created demands an extra-rational authority, which shall meet the mind in its impotency, lift it into participation in the divine nature, and imbue it with divine power. This authority presented itself to Augustine and to the Latin mind in the guise of the Church, Catholic and Roman. It is the authority of God. Nothing has rights over man that is not in the hands of the Church. The gospel itself meets man with the *imprimatur* of the Church; and all redeeming and emancipating powers reach the soul through the channel of the Church's ordinances. Such a conception may be magnificent, but it is simply Roman imperialism, adapted to a use for which it is utterly unfitted and made the key to the salvation of man. It contains, too, an inconsistency with which the common man did not need to concern himself, viz. between predestination and the idea of the Church as the sphere and instrument of salvation. Augustine himself made various attempts, by distinction of the Church invisible and the Church visible and by referring all the elect to the membership of the Church, to overcome a difficulty which is really on the premisses insurmountable. Predestination and the saving power and absolute authority of the Church cannot be combined. Protestants had perfect logical right to use the one to destroy the other. In practice, however, the Church remains in the imperial position which Augustine gave it, for all who come to it with his *a priori* presuppositions.

4. The idea of salvation.—The way of salvation, as Augustine defined it, is plain and will be easy or hard in proportion to the seriousness and sincerity of the traveller. The principal points to be considered by him who would understand this matter of salvation are:

(*a*) *The idea of grace.*—This is conceived, in Greek fashion, as a divine substance or energy coming from above, descending into human nature, and working there as omnipotence in the sphere of things finite. Grace, in short, is a thing, and not a person—a thing almighty and mysterious, but still impersonal, as things are in distinction from forces personal and historic. Augustine is using a philosophical abstraction to cover the phenomena of a spiritual experience; and, in so doing, he has done all in his power to destroy it. As soon as grace is isolated in thought and regard from the historic Redeemer, the nerve of the

[1] R. Rainy, *The Ancient Catholic Church*, Edinburgh, 1902, p. 521.
[2] *Knowledge of God*, ii. 167.

Christian salvation has been cut. After that we may get an intense religious experience, bearing fruit of its own, but it will have its roots outside the NT, and its real parallel will be found in non-Christian religions.

(*b*) *The sacraments.*—These are taken over from Greek theology, as Greek theology took them from the mystery-religions. They are the vehicles by which the divine vivifying substance reaches the dead soul. Theologians will discuss afterwards with endless subtleties the relations between this substance and the Eucharistic elements. No ordinary man need occupy himself with these scholastic disputes. The mystic fact remains that he gets that substance, with its divine energy, into his lips and somehow into his soul. The whole transaction is at once physical and supra-rational and impersonal.

(*c*) *Faith.*—The nature and function of faith are defined by the relation of the soul to the Church. The Church is the object with which the soul has primarily to concern itself. The redeeming powers which will effect its salvation are administered by the Church. What the soul has to do, therefore, is to commit itself to the Church. This act of self-committal is faith. Self-commitment is, indeed, the very essence of faith, as described in the NT. But in the NT the object of faith is the personal Saviour. In Latin theology it is the Church.

(*d*) *Love.*—When faith attaches itself to the Church and devoutly employs the sacraments, grace is infused into the soul, the process being understood under the analogy of the healing art. That thing, salvation or energy, called grace is imbibed and passes into the system with healing and renewing powers. The sum and substance of these powers is love. What faith does in the NT love does in Latin theology. It is the medicament of the soul. In the strength of it the impotent man can arise, take up his bed, and walk. Nerveless before, he can now do works acceptable to God, which may properly be rewarded by the divine justice and crowned with the gift of salvation. Here is legalism to all intents and purposes. True, grace comes from without and gives power, revived from time to time in the sacraments. But the scheme itself is distinctly unevangelical and amounts to salvation by merit.

(*e*) *Mysticism.*—After all, legalism is only a stage, which suffices indeed for those who are in the world and must remain there. Their salvation is looked after by the Church. Experts, however, like Augustine and Monica, may go much farther. It is strange that the Christian salvation, as Augustine outlined it, was the introduction to an experience which is taken over from the religious philosophy which was Christianity's most powerful rival. The highest reach of religion is not attained by faith, and is even ultimately independent of the sacraments. It is taken in the final step, by which the soul abandons all earthly things, and even its own characteristic powers and exercises, and is taken out of itself in rapture. Quoting the great passage in which Augustine describes his last conversation with his mother, Edward Caird comments:

> 'How deeply Neo-Platonism must have sunk into the spirit of St. Augustine, when, in describing the highest moments of his religious experience, he adopts almost verbally the language in which Plotinus tries to depict the mystic ecstasy of the individual soul, as it enters into communion with the soul of the world!'[1]

It would appear, then, that there are just two religions, properly so called, in the world. The one is mysticism, and the other is NT Christianity. The one offers a salvation which consists in mystic communion with the Absolute—salvation by ecstasy. The other offers a salvation which consists in reconciliation to the living God and in a life of ethical harmony with Him in His character and redeeming purpose towards mankind—salvation by faith. Augustine presents the strange spectacle of a man who seeks to follow both religions and enjoy both salvations. The attempt is necessarily a failure. Evangelical faith has to be debased into legalism before the expert is free to enjoy his mystic blessedness. The common man is condemned to the one, that the religious specialist may concentrate on the other. The lamentable result is that Christianity, which was meant to reconcile men to God and to reconstitute humanity as a living organism, becomes the parent of endless dualism—the Church and the world, clergy and laity, secular clergy and the monks and solitaries. Instead of a salvation that is at once possession and inheritance, gift and task, there is presented a salvation from which the vast bulk of mankind is for ever excluded, to which those only can attain who isolate themselves from the very life which the divine purpose of mercy designed to redeem, regenerate, and restore.

[1] *Evolution of Theology in the Greek Philosophers*, ii. 288.

From the point of view alike of mysticism and of predestination, there was no real need for a historic deed of atonement as the ground of salvation; and Augustine has not concentrated his mind on the work of Christ for men as he has upon the operations of divine grace in man. The exigencies of the Pelagian controversy absorbed his energies. Yet, as a sincerely Christian mind, he adoringly recognized Christ as the Mediator, and attributed saving power to what He did. His deepest thought here is the humility of Christ, in which the love of God seeks to subdue to itself the pride of man. But his attempts at a theory are vague and wavering. He accepts the impossible idea that the Devil had rights over fallen men. These rights the Devil forfeited when he killed Christ. So those who believe in Christ are freed from the power of the Devil, for over Christ the Devil had no right. Along with this he treats the death of Christ forensically and attributes to it penal significance, but, like Tertullian, without constructing a 'satisfaction' theory. As an inheritor of Greek theology, he also retains the idea of the Word sharing our mortality, that we may be made to share in His divinity. Along these lines, however, his constructive thought does not travel. The way to a view of divine action in the redemption of man is blocked by his ruling ideas of predestination and miraculous grace; and these are due to the strain of Neo-Platonism which enters so deeply into his thought.[1]

VI. *THE IDEA OF SALVATION IN THE MEDIÆVAL CHURCH.*—The interest belonging to that great stretch of European history from Gregory I. to the close of the 15th cent. can never be exaggerated or exhausted. Nations are being born with much travail. Vast experiments in political organization and social structure are being made at enormous cost of life and suffering. The human mind is being aroused out of decadence, or awakened out of unconsciousness, and prepared for undreamed-of enterprises. The destiny of the human race is being determined amid a welter of controversy and battle, the participants in which know not the aim and guess not the issue of the conflict.

The clue, however, to these multitudinous and confused happenings is, as ever in the history of the human spirit, a religious need, together with its doctrinal expression. 'Dogmatically expressed,' says Harnack, as the story draws to its completion, 'there was a seeking for a sure doctrine of salva-

[1] Bartlet and Carlyle, *Christianity in History*, p. 423.

tion.'[1] The records of this quest cover the whole period, and the details are innumerable. The stages or aspects of it may be classed as three: (1) the function of the Church, (2) the problem of the work of Christ, and (3) the protest of mysticism.

1. The function of the Church.—This is twofold, in part political and in part specifically religious, though, in its political aspirations, it was striving to reach avowedly religious ends. (*a*) In the first place, then, the Church succeeded to the place and work of the Roman empire. The empire had been, in a very real sense, the saviour of the world. It was the barrier behind which human life could be carried on, secure from threatening destruction at the hands of barbarism and anarchy. Its splendour, its wealth, its power, its venerable age, gave the impression of superhuman dignity and seemed to be the operation in the material world of the sovereignty of God Himself. When it began to decay, men were stricken with fear. Its impending doom hung over their souls. This doom was delayed in the East for many centuries by the founding of New Rome. Because the Eastern empire stood, there was no room or need for the Church to take its place and assume its functions. The Church was confined to its hierurgical functions, and Christianity remained no more than a mystery-religion. The State, accordingly, remained supreme over the Church—a position which it maintained in Eastern Europe till the fall of the Russian autocracy set the Church at liberty; and the problem is yet unsolved as to how it will use its unaccustomed freedom. The situation in the West was very different. The empire was manifestly passing away. The later emperors did not live in Rome. Finally, even the shadow of the Western empire passed away. Nominally, the civilized world had but one head, the emperor who lived in Constantine's capital. Really, the Western world was without political unity and had no central authority. In those centuries when the empire was on its death-bed, its prestige and power began to pass to the Church. Its spirit was born again in the Church. The key to the course of European history from Gregory the Great (pope 590–604) to the dawn of the Reformation is the doctrine of the Church. In the NT the Church is a spiritual fellowship of believers with their Lord and with one another. The Church of those long and terrible centuries is a political organization framed on the model of the banished empire, controlling men by a legal system, administered by a highly centralized government. The task before it was one of appalling magnitude. On the one hand, it had to preserve whatever was of permanent value in the culture of the ancient world, while penetrating it with new ethical and religious ideas. On the other hand, it had to face the barbarian menace, to subdue those untutored races which were breaking through the crumbling walls of empire, and make them subjects of a supreme Holy Will, which might restrain their passions and renew their natures. It was, in fact, the missionary task of every age. If we can imagine India, the seat of an immemorial civilization, ringed round with savage forces threatening its destruction—an India without any British rule to hold back the enemy beyond the frontiers and to keep the peace within them—and can picture what the work of the Christian Church would be in such circumstances, we have some conception of the situation of the Church in Western Europe when the sceptre had dropped from the nerveless hands of the last Roman emperor.

Now, if the spirit of the first missionary to Europe had shaped the missionary policy of the Church at this time, it is certain that the Church would not have adopted the method of political supremacy, but would have trusted to that power of the gospel of Christ on which St. Paul relied absolutely. But St. Paul's method of evangelism had long been forgotten. Externalism had had an increasing vogue for centuries. The Church had gone to school to the empire and had learned the imperial style. No other method was thought of than to oppose force to force—the force of Roman authority to barbarian force of terror and destruction. The only possible policy was supposed to be that of gathering the world under the dominion of Rome, binding the yoke of law more securely than ever upon Rome's old subjects, and riveting it on the new races that were occupying her domain and holding all alike for ever in bondage and tutelage. There is nothing ignoble about this dream of conquest and subjugation. The dreamers of it were among the greatest of men, noble in their devotion to an end which was power, but not selfish aggrandizement. Two remarks, however, are historically justified.

(i.) This conception of the salvation of mankind differs absolutely from that set forth in the NT: in the NT salvation by faith; in the mediæval Church salvation by political domination and legal discipline; in the NT a salvation that operates from within by love and hope; in the mediæval Church a salvation that acts from without by force and terror. The one is the outcome of a long religious growth in which redemption is accomplished by a God so close at hand that He can be man and bear human burdens and gather humanity to Himself in a living fellowship, of which He is the inspiration, the energy, and the unifying principle. The other has its roots in Greek dualism and Roman imperialism and is effected by a God afar off, governing, controlling, subduing through the might of the pope, His earthly representative. We can see, by considering the course of events and the influences at work, how the one type came to be substituted for the other; but we are not warranted in concluding that the one evolves out of the other by an inherent logic, or that the mediæval Church is what Christianity was bound to become as it grew out of its NT germ.

(ii.) The dream was never quite realized, and the hour of the Church's greatest triumph preceded its final downfall. From the beginning the Church realized the need of a secular instrument in dealing with the brute forces which had to be met and coerced. Accordingly, she called into existence a secular empire, to be the counterpart, on a lower level of spiritual value, of her own imperial constitution. The empire of the universe was to be governed by a world-priest and a world-king, each holding office and exercising authority under God, the unseen Emperor. Ideally, these two authorities ought to have operated in harmony. Practically, they never did. The true genius of the Church required its absolute supremacy, the secular State, even though nominally holy and imperial, being no more than the instrument to carry out the divine sovereign Will of whose behests the Church was the depository and revealer. Such a position the empire declined to take. The Middle Ages were filled with the strife of empire and papacy. In the end victory lay with neither. The empire was destroyed by the greater skill of its papal enemies. The Church lost its imperial position in less than a century after its most violent, and even grotesque, expression—if we may credit the story of Boniface VIII. with his brandished sword and his exultant cry, 'I am Cæsar, I am Emperor.' The rising spirit of nationality would not permit absolutism, whether imperial or papal. The Church had preserved much of the past. It had formed the beginning of a new world. But it had not saved Europe, and it had destroyed itself. The failure of the Church, in its political and social endeavour, is to be traced to its radical misapprehension of the religious need of man. On presuppositions of dualism, religious and philosophical, nothing better, probably, could have been devised than the papal system. The Middle Ages are proof, on a large scale, of the inaccuracy of the diagnosis and of the failure of the remedy.

(*b*) In the second place, the Church assumed the function of mediator of salvation to the individual soul. The way of salvation, as marked out by the mediæval Church, presents the curious spectacle of contact with NT ideas together with complete inversion of them. The NT Church is the communion of saints, *i.e.* the fellowship of believers, the individual being taken by his relation to Christ out of his isolation and made a member of a living organism, in which he finds his place and work, and is disciplined, trained, and helped in knowledge and virtue. The mediæval Church is an institute of salvation, by whose machinery heathen men are made Christians, and sinners are enabled to escape eternal punishment, and even, in rare cases, to

[1] vi. 117.

attain saintship. It stands, in its divinely imparted powers and its divinely designed mechanism, apart from and above the individual and proceeds to operate upon him with a view to his salvation. The NT Church summons men to yield themselves to Christ. The mediæval Church summons men to yield themselves to its authority. It incorporates them in its organization, supplies them with divine grace, and legislates for them as they proceed to work out their salvation.

'In the mediæval Church, the individual, *qua* individual, had little or no place. His salvation was conditioned from first to last by his belonging to a corporation, in whose privileges and functions he shared, through whose sacraments his life was nourished; by whose graduated hierarchy, though but the meanest servant of the Church, he was linked to the supreme Head; whose saints shielded him by their "merits," or helped him by their intercession. Through this corporation alone was he brought into touch with his Saviour. Outside the corporation his soul was lost.'[1]

In this mediæval conception of salvation there is the practical and exquisitely skilful application of ideas which have occupied theologians from the days of Neo-Platonism, and of theories which have prevailed since Latin theology was constructed by Roman lawyers. The Church is the old Neo-Platonic 'bridge' over which the soul passes to the Absolute. The mediæval Christian knows nothing of immediate access to God. He is confronted at every turn by the Church, the mediator. All divine influences, regenerative, educative, directive, come through the medium of the Church, with whom alone the ordinary Christian has ever directly to do. Grace is not, as in the NT, a saving, operative, love of God to sinners, but a substance, as Augustine conceived it, capable of being communicated after the analogy of food or medicine, with physical and hyperphysical results of a magical kind. With such presuppositions, the process of salvation is elaborate, but quite intelligible and workable.

(i.) Grace is infused into the soul in the sacrament of baptism and the Eucharist. In the one, life is communicated, first of all, to a soul conceived of as dead. In the other, renewed communications of life are made from time to time. Properly speaking, the celebration of Mass should be accompanied by communion. But mysticism with its own logic intervenes to make non-communicating attendance a means of grace. The mystery becomes one for eye and ear, for æsthetic emotion and rapt adoring contemplation, and in this the union of soul with the divine is effected. Still the Eucharist holds its own as the peculiar medium through which the divine life is maintained in the believer; the dead soul, being now quickened with divine energy, is able to perform good works. These are meritorious in the sight of God, and by their practice the sinner is transformed into a righteous person. This progressive sanctification is crowned by justification. The way of salvation stretches before the mediæval Christian, arduous indeed and indefinitely prolonged, but plainly in view. Legal directions are abundant. A priestly director is always available. This way, accordingly, has strong attractions for pure and earnest souls who keenly desire the blessedness of union with God, are deeply aware of their ignorance and weakness, and are glad to pay the price of a humbled reason and a surrendered will. The difficulty lay in the nature of the authority to which the soul was required to bow. It was an external authority, and the method of salvation was legal and even commercial. It might well happen, therefore, to an earnest and determined spirit, as to Paul in earlier days and to Luther in the following age, that despair should settle down in darkness, unless a more excellent way were found. That way had been forgotten by the theologians of the Church. As far as mediævalism was concerned, the only alternative to legalism was mysticism—the way that plunges over a precipice into the deeps of the unknown divine.

(ii.) Grace, when it becomes exhausted through human weakness and error, has to be restored. The loss of grace is an ever recurring fact. Machinery for its recovery is a pressing need. This need was met in the sacrament of penance (*q.v.*), which, for obvious reasons, becomes of prime importance in this institute of salvation, and, in fact, is practically the salvation itself for all ordinary believers. Suppose, then, that a soul has fallen into mortal sin, and so has lost the grace infused into it at baptism or Eucharist, what must be done that the loss may be recovered? First, there must be sorrow of heart, preferably *contritio*, though *attritio* with certain conditions appended might suffice; then confession to the priest, guided by interrogatories, in which psychological skill, gained by long dealing with the secrets of human nature, aids the halting self-knowledge of the penitent; then the priestly absolution, wiping off the guilt of sin and delivering the soul from eternal damnation; next, the 'satisfaction' (*q.v.*), or the task imposed by the priest, whereby the justice of God, pursuing sin with temporal punishments in this world or the next, is 'satisfied.' By absolution, granted in view of the satisfactions which are to follow, the soul is returned to a spiritual condition which makes it fit for further infusion of grace, and the interrupted course is resumed—grace, good works, merit, justification.

A serious complication is introduced into the scheme by the granting of 'indulgences' (*q.v.*). These are the remission of the temporal punishments by authority of the pope, to whom is committed the wondrous treasury of the merits of the saints. This addition to the scheme was necessary to make it tolerable. Indulgences express the pitiful heart of the Church, refraining from legal exaction and devising means whereby God's banished ones may be restored to Him. At the same time, an indulgence, in the midst of legalism, is fraught with moral peril; and of this the practice of indulgences in the last years of the 15th cent. contains ample illustration. The mistake did not lie in the intention of the Church, but in the invincible dualism which externalized all the relations of God and man and in the end made salvation a compromise between justice and mercy.

As the centuries rolled on, the limitations of the mediæval Church became more and more evident. Profound dissatisfaction and wide-spread unrest characterized the religious life of the closing period of the Middle Ages. But deeper than discontent with the incidental features of the ecclesiastical system was the demand for a revision of the theological presuppositions on which that system rested and for a reversion to the primal redemptive forces in the might of which Christianity from its birth-hour had gone forth conquering and to conquer.

2. The doctrine of the work of Christ. — Doctrine always follows experience, reacting upon it and giving it a stereotyped form. The mediæval doctrine of salvation, accordingly, is the mediæval practice rationalized, illuminated, and fixed.

The idea of God which governs mediæval soteriology is that philosophical abstraction of being or substance, blent with the idea of political absolutism, which we have seen at work in Latin theology. The one element is Greek—the unconditioned and transcendent nature of God. The other is Roman—the will of an absolute monarch. A God of this character stands outside of His world, which is entirely dependent upon Him, while its coming into existence at all remains inexplicable. Its relation to Him, at any point of its career, is that of an empire to a distant, inscrutable, and almighty prince. In His regulation of the affairs of His dominion God is governed by no other considerations than His own absolute will. This He utters in the form of law, and the maintenance of law He delegates to designated ministers — *i.e.* the hierarchy of the Church—whom He suitably endows and equips for the unique responsibility.

Breaches of law are crimes. To meet the case of those who are guilty of breach of law but who are nevertheless the objects of the inscrutable election of the divine mercy, the penitential discipline of the Church has been divinely instituted. In the 'satisfactions' rendered by the penitent law is upheld and the conscience is awakened to a reverential sense of its demands. At the same time, this is procedure merely. It is a dealing with individuals only, and is, so to speak, empirical, and not absolute or final. Upon what does the penitential discipline rest? It must be warranted by, and be an application of, the divine dealing with the whole empire of God. That storehouse of merit, upon which the sinner ultimately depends for forgiveness and sanctification, cannot be left liable to depletion. It must be secure and inexhaustible. There must be an absolute and final vindication of the divine law and the divine honour by which God's government of the universe can be made inviolable and His preferential dealings with individuals be ratified. God, it was plain, must intervene in the history of His world so as once for all to exhibit the supremacy of His law, the unassailable dignity of His name. What

[1] Workman, *Christian Thought to the Reformation*, p. 190.

is that act which possesses such momentous import? Experimental faith had always fastened on the death of Christ. Tradition enshrined the Passion of the Redeemer in the central articles of the Creed. Once the question, therefore, was raised as to the validity of the Church's procedure in granting absolution to sinners, it could be answered only in one way: The Cross is the act which vindicates the divine law and honour and validates the Church's procedure. The awakening mind of man, however, as it seeks to make faith conscious and clear, is not content with the bare fact. It presses for a theory. What gives the Cross of Christ this amazing significance? The difference between this question and that which was the central problem of Greek theology has to be carefully noted. The Greek question is: How shall man, corrupt and dying, be united to, and made participator in, the divine nature, and so be 'deified'? The question which Latin thought made inevitable, and which now in mediæval theology was asked in the most searching form, was this: How shall man, a convicted criminal, escape the doom which follows inevitably upon transgression in the court of divine inexorable justice? Putting the matter broadly, Vernon Bartlet and Carlyle say of the Latin temper:

'Its typical product was not metaphysics but jurisprudence; and it was from this standpoint that man's relations even to God were regarded.'[1]

And these writers proceed to illustrate by quotation from Sir Henry Maine:

'Almost anybody who has knowledge enough of Roman law to appreciate the Roman penal system, the Roman theory of the obligations established by Contract or Delict, the Roman view of Debts and of the modes of incurring, extinguishing, and transmuting them, the Roman notion of the continuance of individual existence by Universal Succession, may be trusted to say whence arose the frame of mind to which the problems of Western theology proved so congenial, whence came the phraseology in which these problems were stated, and whence the description of reasoning employed in their solution.'

With special reference to the problem of salvation, the required form lies close at hand. For offences against law there must be satisfaction. The wrong-doer must make amends. This, however, in the nature of the case is impossible. Man is finite; but his offence is infinite, for it has been committed against an infinite Being. Infinite, therefore, must be the satisfaction. The need of satisfaction is met in the person and work of Christ. He is divine, and therefore His work has the required note of infinitude. He is human, and therefore His work can be viewed as rendered to God by man. His redemptive work is His death—a deed of superabounding merit; and this, since the Son has no need of it for His own purposes, is available for those whose own merits so sorely need to be supplemented. The issue of this abounding satisfaction is twofold: Godward, it makes ample amends to the divine honour—the Lord of the whole earth has made His Name to be had in reverence of all His creatures; manward, it supplies what is needed to enable the sinner, impotent in himself, to do good works, to obtain the reward of merit, and to become progressively sanctified and in the end justified. The death of Christ creates the treasury of grace and fills it with an inexhaustible supply of merit. Grace is a transferable quantity, which God employs for the benefit of His elect. By means of it He first starts them on the way to sanctification, in the sacrament of baptism; and then from time to time, in the sacrament of penance, He replenishes this store. Thus does the theory of satisfaction, as applied to the work of Christ, arise from and return to the praxis, as observed in the Church. The one interprets the other. The mediæval mind found in the satisfaction theory the very mirror of itself, a Christianity

[1] *Christianity in History*, p. 420.

intelligible to it, because it was simply the universal practice of piety, expressed in terms of thought. Precisely at this point, however, a danger threatened the theory and indeed ultimately dissolved it. Reason has undertaken to give a rationale of the work of Christ. But what are the rights of reason? It may be the handmaid of faith, or the equivalent of faith, or a power independent of faith; and, if reason be ever pitted against faith, the human spirit will be divided within itself. This is, historically, the course of scholasticism as a whole and of the satisfaction theory in particular.[1] In Anselm the satisfaction is a necessity flowing from the relation of God to the world. In Aquinas it is a method, not strictly necessary, but the most suitable for the end in view. In Duns Scotus it is grounded only in the absolute will of the Supreme Being; and the death of Christ has just the value which God chooses to put upon it. The defects of the mediæval satisfaction theory are obvious. They all flow from the non-Christian idea of God which mediæval thinkers took over from Greek thought. Mediæval thought is penetrated by dualism and is congenitally incapable of yielding an adequate interpretation of Christian experience. Its God is the Absolute and cannot act within His world. He must have a delegate. What is achieved by this Other is presented to Him, and He enjoys the satisfaction rendered to Him. He is shut out of the sacrifice He demands. Its Christ is monophysite; and incarnation is so delimited as to be made unreal. Christ is just human enough to be able to die. The sole point of interest is His death, the death of an infinite Being, from which His life falls apart, neither giving value to the death nor receiving significance from it. This whole drama of divine redemption goes on apart from humanity. It is set in operation at the Cross and is maintained in action by the Church. The Church is the proximate object of the sinner's regard. With Christ he has nothing directly to do. Faith is directed to the Church; it is assent to an outward authority conceived as the delegated authority of God; it is not a direct relation of the soul to the Saviour. The Christian life, accordingly, is treated legally. Forgiveness is not the *prius* and the motive of the believer's experience, but its difficult and precarious goal. Union to Christ is sacramental and occasional, not abiding as inward spring and energy. It belongs only to the higher substance of which man is composed and can be reached only when the dualism of matter and form has been conquered by the suppression of the one and the sole survival of the other. So closely are mediæval piety and mediæval theology bound up with a philosophy which was radically alien to the spirit of Christianity.

The satisfaction theory did not pass unquestioned even in the Middle Ages. Abelard has been much praised and also severely blamed for rejecting it and substituting for it a 'subjective' or 'moral influence' theory. He has been regarded as far in advance of his time. When all is said, however, he remains mediæval still. He has not critically revised the idea of God, which remains still involved in the dualism in which Aristotle, as well as Plato, left it. His God is still transcendent. It is true that Abelard reacts strongly against the idea of law. Over against law he sets love. But the function of love is simply the function of law with respect to the world. It is a device to secure the submission of men. The satisfaction theory keeps the world going by means of a legal discipline. For the legal discipline Abelard substitutes the exhibition of the divine love. An appeal is made to the tenderest emotions of the human

[1] See artt. SATISFACTION, SCHOLASTICISM.

heart. That appeal reaches its utmost poignancy in the Cross. There is no reason to doubt the sincerity of Abelard's personal response to the love of which he discourses so movingly. At the same time, he is still within the sphere of mediæval praxis and mediæval piety. The merit of Christ —*i.e.* the love manifest in His death—stimulates human action and makes possible merit of the same sort. Yet, of course, such merit is never sufficient and has to be supplemented by the intercessions of the Redeemer. In truth, so long as the idea of God remains where Greek thought had placed it, the theological account of redemption must remain arbitrary and unreal.

3. The protest of mysticism.—The term 'mysticism,' commonly employed to denote any religious experience which is very intense and emotional and cannot be formulated in intellectual utterance, properly implies a dualistic metaphysic—the effort to reach a unity which shall rise high above both the elements which have been set in mutual contrast.

'God, for the Mystic, is the One who is presupposed in all, God as God, as the unity above the difference of subject and object, to which everything is related and which itself is related to nothing . . . for Mysticism, the negative so decisively preponderates over the positive relation, that God and the world cannot be included in one thought.'[1]

The religion based on this philosophy gained classical expression in Plotinus and entered, essentially unchanged, into Christianity. It governed the theology of the Church. When, accordingly, we observe the phenomenon of mysticism arising in the Middle Ages, we are not to imagine that it is a protest against the piety of the mediæval Church. It is that piety in its purest form. Every mediæval Christian has before him the mystic experience of a union of substance with the divine—a union which he can never effect by any effort except the effort which is the cessation of all action; an experience which is supra-rational and supra-ethical, ineffable and incommunicable. The experience belongs to an inner region, where the soul, withdrawing from all finite things, matter, the world, the Church, and its own separate existence, finds God and is content. A mystic is out of place in any religious communion which does not ground its theology in the Neo-Platonic idea of God. Yet even that communion is not his resting-place. He will be in it and use its sacramental system. But his goal is beyond the Church and its institutions.

The mediæval Church, however, was Latin as well as Greek. If its goal is a mystical salvation, it had a legal discipline to serve as a stage on the way. The exigencies of life compelled the ordinary type of believer to remain the slave of an external system. The Church, too, was bound to keep the vast majority of its subjects in this servile condition. If every soul was a solitary, how could the Church rule the world? The Church, therefore, as the institute of salvation in the midst of a lawless world, was bound to be a legal system, holding down the individual by constraint of an external authority. But such suppression of the individual is, in essence, profoundly irreligious, for it surrenders the idea of bringing the ordinary man into immediate relation to God. The protest against externalism is mysticism, which is 'religion in its most concentrated and exclusive form . . . that attitude of the mind in which all other relations are swallowed up in the relation of the soul to God.'[2] The mediæval Church, accordingly, held within itself, side by side, legalism and mysticism —both alike the products of a non-Christian conception of God. The mediæval theologian's philosophical presuppositions rendered him helpless.

[1] Caird, *Evolution of Theology in the Greek Philosophers*, ii. 213.
[2] *Ib.* p. 210.

VII. *THE IDEA OF SALVATION IN THE THEOLOGY OF THE REFORMATION AND IN SUBSEQUENT THOUGHT.*—Scholasticism reached the height of its power in Scotism, and thence began its long decline. The history of four centuries of Christian life and thought is filled with one long endeavour to remove the static Absolute from its supremacy in philosophy and theology and to find some conception of God more adequate to the realities of religious experience. The details of this history are multitudinous. The main line, however, can be followed plainly enough; and the great epochs stand out clearly. They may be named and briefly characterized in their relation to central Christian experience as follows.

1. The return to experience.—While mediæval dualism was subjecting all human interests to the control of an absolute authority, which was held to express the sovereignty of God, these interests themselves were growing in value and were demanding a more ample recognition and satisfaction. In every department of human life and action the feature of a confident and exulting appeal to experience is most marked. Nature stands out in its endless wonder and charm, with promise of amazing rewards to all who will diligently seek them. Eager explorers give the world to humanity as the sphere of action and achievement, wherein the mind of man may grow to its maturity. Human history thrills with interest, as it records the attainments and the triumphs as well as the agonies and tragedies of real men. Nations become conscious of themselves, not as pupils of Church and Empire, but as independent personalities with careers of their own. Above all and deeper than all, the human spirit seeks to break through forms which were ostensibly means of access to God, but had proved to be barriers. Formally, the movement we know as the Reformation (*q.v.*) was an effort to purge the Church of abuses, clear away its mythology, and rectify certain points in its theology. Really, it was something other, and more, than an intellectual, or even an ethical, demand. It was a quest for reality, and the direction of this quest was towards the New Testament. In essence the Reformation was a revival of that primitive Christianity which had, indeed, never wholly faded from the Christian consciousness. Along with the piety whose roots lay in the old mystery-religions there had come down through the ages a religion whose gospel was the Gospels, whose salvation was the historic Christ, the living Lord, whose creed centred in the redemptive facts of His life, death, and resurrection, whose piety was an immediate access to Him and an endeavour to be like Him.

When absolutism, ecclesiastical and dogmatic, proved untenable, this religion became aware of itself, found human voices in which to utter its message, and stood forth out of the wreckage of the past as essential Christianity, changeless as the unchanging love of God. Such a religion reaches back to ultimate unities of history and of experience which no dualistic logic can express. The Christianity of the NT, long overlaid by dualism, is a synthesis of elements that are intelligible only when grasped in their interrelations. Its note is always unity, the unity of life. Salvation comes to the individual when he finds himself in this unity, not absorbed or lost or suppressed, but lifted out of a false separation, and so, for the first time, justified in his individuality and guaranteed in the fullness of his personality. This salvation is seen in Christ. We find God in Christ. Christ is the incarnate love of God. He is the divine forgiveness, operating in the completeness of God's moral character amid the conditions of human sin and misery. He is this because of what He actually was, and did, and suffered. Yet His existence and His power are not limited to a few years of time. He meets men always at the point where their need of God is deepest. Christianity is the historic Christ, but the historic Christ is timeless. The salvation thus presented in Christ is possessed in faith. What faith meant in Christian experience could not be understood by a theology governed by Greek and Latin presuppositions. In such a theology faith was only a preliminary step to a salvation carried on by a legal procedure and issuing finally in the beatific vision. But faith, as it deals with the personal Redeemer, is an action neither mainly intellectual, as in assent, nor emotional, as in ecstasy. It is the action in which a soul, in full self-consciousness with sober self-judgment, commits itself trustfully to the everlasting mercy, conveyed in the person and work of Christ. It is the act in which a soul passes from self-assertion to self-realization, through surrender to, and identification with, the love which, in the life and death of Jesus, authenticates itself as divine redemptive efficacy. No activity of the human spirit could be more unlike surrender to a system or ecstatic plunge into a sea of being. It has no affinities with Roman legalism or Neo-Platonic mysticism. It implies a historic revelation and a personal relation to God. It permits no machinery of mediation and has no use for either hierurgy or hierarchy. In it the soul has immediate access to the Son of God and in Him finds the Father. This experience is the direct gift of God in Christ and confers on men that priestly privilege which non-Christian religions, and the mediæval Church after them, had confined to a special and narrow caste. Without any apparatus of mysticism, the exercise of faith carries with it the blessing which is the eternal quest of the human spirit—union to God; and that not as an impossible blending of substances, but as a relationship in which the man who gives himself to God gains fullness of personal life, while he draws increasing wealth of knowledge and power from the communications of the divine Word and Spirit. Faith is generically distinct from passivity. It is an energy of the soul. It is the whole energy of the soul in the moral sphere, needing no supplement to make it a condition in man of the experience of salvation. Faith sets the soul on that moral enterprise whose goal is the accomplishment of the purpose of divine love, revealed and guaranteed in Christ. The relation of faith and works is not a problem for faith. There can be no faith which is not a dynamic issuing in service. There can be no gift of salvation which is not at the same time the summons to a redemptive task.

This salvation is accomplished as a life in the Spirit. Neither Greek mysticism nor Latin legalism had any room for the work of the Spirit. Theology added a *locus* regarding the Spirit, because of a clause in the baptismal formula and because of certain texts which it was impossible to ignore. But the application of dualism to Christianity made the NT idea of the Spirit, with its intensely Hebraic associations, utterly unintelligible. What philosophy ruled out and theology could not interpret Christian experience grasped as the simplest, divinest fact. To believe in Christ is to have the Spirit. The Spirit is not a proposition to be admitted; it is a power to be received and exulted in. In the reception of the Spirit the Christian apprehension of God reaches its deepest religious truth. God, and Christ, and the fellowship of believers are included in an experience of which the indwelling Spirit is the source and power. The Christian life is not lived outside of God, in a region where human effort is occasionally reinforced by infusion of grace. It is not drawn into the divine Being or Substance, so that a unity is reached by the suppression of man's individuality. It is lived in God as the career of a personality which has a moral function in God's universe and is called on to discharge it with entire consecration, the energy for fulfilment being supplied continually by the immanent Spirit of God. It is a life of intense and growing intimacy with God, in which self-realization becomes complete in proportion as God is discovered to be the source and sum of all moral values and powers.

The NT is full of the boldest synonyms, equivalences, and correspondences, which Greek theology could make nothing of, in which, however, Christian experience finds at once its interpretation and its nourishment. God and Christ; Christ and the Spirit; the Redeemer and the redeemed; the love which is God giving Himself to man, and faith which is man answering the approach of God; forgiveness and the new life; reconciliation and sanctification; salvation and service; salvation, present and to come—all such seeming contrasts, or even contradictions, are held together in the unity of a living experience. From the point of view of any logic known to the ancient world, Christianity was one vast paradox, an absurdity with which it was difficult to deal seriously. When, accordingly, that logic was adopted by the Church as the instrument of its self-expression, the result could not be satisfactory. The incompatibility of that logic with Christianity is registered in Chalcedon, makes Augustine the fountain-head of divergent streams, and turns the mighty structure of mediæval theology into an intolerable burden. The disappointing thing in the theology of the Reformation is that this incompatibility was not discerned, and no effort was made to substitute for the older forms others more adequate. The new life which was moving in the Church of the 16th cent. 'would have required a wholly new theology to match it, but to the production of such a theology the Protestant Church was for the time unequal.'[1]

2. The continuity of mediæval forms of thought.—Of the two strands of systematic thought which formed the traditional dogma it may be said, broadly, that in Lutheranism we have the continuation of Greek and Alexandrian theology, while Calvinism continues the line of Latin theology. In Lutheranism we have the mystical union of Christ and the believer, the *communicatio idiomatum* as a theory of Christ's person, the doctrine of the Real Presence in the Eucharist, all conceived in the vein of Greek theology. In Calvinism we have the governing principle of the divine sovereignty, conceived in the style of Roman imperialism. By means of this organizing idea a systematic theology was constructed which appealed to the interest of dogmatic completeness and was able to meet Roman dogma with a dogmatism as finished and masterful. In virtue of this conception also an ecclesiastical polity was devised which carried into the new age the old idea of the Church as an independent and imperial body, representing in spiritual things the supremacy of God, strong to resist aggression and insistent in its claim, not merely to be supported by the State, but to give to the State guidance and rule in all things pertaining to the Kingdom of God.

Lutheranism, with its individualistic and mystical tendencies, made the Church, as in the old Greek empire, subservient to the State, with portentous results in the history of Germany. Calvinism made men and nations strong to resist despotism and created nations whose passion is liberty. The retention by Calvinism, however, of the Latin idea of God made impossible any thorough revision of dogma. In the history of the

[1] Denney, *Christian Doctrine of Reconciliation*, p. 92.

attempt to make mediæval thought serve the purposes of Reformation experience there are three leading phases.

(a) *The 'satisfaction' theory.*—This is intended to solve that central problem of soteriology which Anselm was the first to face explicitly: *Cur Deus homo?* Particularly, why was the Cross necessary or, at least, divinely chosen, to meet the situation created by sin and form the warrant of human salvation in face of the judgments of a holy God and the sentence of an accusing conscience? The category of *satisfactio*, supplied by the old Latin theology and applied by mediæval theology to the work of Christ, is taken over by Calvinism without any sense of its inadequacy to represent NT truth and life. Indeed, the Calvinistic use of it is more rigidly Latin even than that common in mediæval theologians. In Anselm satisfaction is not punishment, is indeed an alternative to it. In Aquinas satisfaction is punishment of a sort. In Calvin the satisfaction made in the suffering of the Redeemer is explicitly and fully penal. The imagery is that of a court of justice—in this case divine justice—absolutely unerring and altogether inexorable in judgment. We must not allow the terror of this scheme to confuse us as to its moral quality. A Roman emperor, administering the affairs of the world in accordance with a system of law which he has ordained, is a far better God than an oriental despot whose will is caprice, or a feudal monarch punctilious as to his honour, or a pope dispensing grace for a consideration. Calvinism is making thorough work of the forensic form of thought. The real demand raised by the logical perfection of the Calvinistic scheme is for a reconsideration of the idea of God. Is the God of Jesus a magnified Roman emperor? Is this the God whom the penitent and the believing find in Christ? Is salvation purchasable by punishment or by any other device known to law? Is the Redeemer a divine Being, who is just human enough to transact business with God on a basis of strict legal satisfaction? Is justification so forensic that sanctification is only a required addendum to be carried on, out of court, by extra-legal directions and incentives? The Christian consciousness awakening to such questions will leave the scheme as such on one side, go back to the NT, live over again the experience of the first believers, and make a new discovery of Jesus, and of God in Him.

(b) *The Socinian criticism.*—Historically, the most acute and yet the most fruitless criticism of the forensic theology comes from Socinianism (*q.v.*). Socinianism is the continuation of mediæval thought in its last stage of abstractness and formalism. Its God is the Scotist impersonation of *dominium absolutum*. His will operates in a moral vacuum. Sin is no more than a private debt. Atonement is superfluous. The Socinians are simply Scotists who have no barrier of ecclesiastical authority to prohibit them from pursuing the logic of mediæval thought to its bitter end. Their system is mediæval orthodoxy turned inside out. Socinian criticism of the satisfaction theory accordingly is directed from the point of view of that absolutist view of God which was behind the Latin theology, and had not been questioned in the Reformation theology, and is a formally consistent application of it. But, since that idea is not the Christian idea of God, the Socinian criticism does not touch the heart of the Christian experience. It may be formally correct to say with Socinianism that satisfaction and remission exclude one another, that grace and merit are contradictories, but no man has experienced the divine forgiveness apart from the love that suffered on the Cross; and all the redeemed grasp in the unity of experience the *gratuito* and the *propter Christum*. It may be logically absurd to say that God made satisfaction to Himself when Christ suffered on the Cross. But the faith that receives salvation is profoundly aware that God is in that action and passion and is charging Himself with the cost of redemption. The satisfaction theory may commit the grave ethical and theological error of holding the divine attributes apart, and specially of pitting holiness and love against one another; but an experimental knowledge of God passes by all such impossible dissection and sees in Christ the whole character of God, holy in love and loving in holiness. Socinianism is individualism. Its method is that of formal logic, deducing its conclusions from assumed premisses. The strength of the satisfaction theory was its sense of the necessary relations of God and man in a moral universe. Its weakness lay in its conception of that universe as an imperial realm, governed by an absolute monarch and administered by strict judicial procedure. The Christian consciousness has accepted this conception in lieu of a better, because it has felt that here, rather than in Socinianism, moral values and redemptive forces were secured.

(c) *The Grotian compromise.*—Grotius (*q.v.*) sets out to defend the Catholic doctrine of satisfaction against the Socinian criticism. Yet he shares with Arminianism the Scotist conception of the *dominium absolutum*. God is under no obligation to inflict punishment for breach of His law. Grotius rejects the category of private right, according to which sin was a debt which it was open to God to remit at His own discretion without satisfaction. But he remains within the circle of Latin thought in regarding God under the analogy of head of the State. The State, however, is not an empire, and God is not a feudal lord; He rules with enlightened and constant regard for the welfare and happiness of His subjects. Wisdom and benevolence determine His dealings with His people. They sin, no doubt, but their sins cannot really injure God; neither His honour nor His justice requires that He shall punish sin; but, as a beneficent ruler, He cannot allow the presence of sin in His dominions. He employs penalty, accordingly, simply as the proper means towards the end in view. That end is the preservation of order and the restraint of transgression. The whole conception exactly reproduces the ideal of statesmanship, when absolutism in politics is giving way to the modern conception of a well-ordered realm, where human life and happiness are reasonably secure. It belongs to God's surpassing wisdom that He did devise an adequate scheme, by which the benefits of penalty could be secured to His realm, without the odious necessity of inflicting the extreme penalty of the law upon law-breakers. Suppose His Son, the heir to the divine dominion, Himself guiltless of any offence, were to receive in His person, not, of course, punishment, but such pains as might be a vivid and awful symbol of punishment, would not this make such a profound impression on the mind of beholders, conscious of what was appointed them by the law of the State, that they would recoil from sin and avoid those dreadful consequences of law-breaking which had received in the passion of the Redeemer so tremendous an illustration? Faith can draw nourishment from faulty metaphors and ill-drawn pictures. But surely there never was a worse doctrine of salvation than that which represents the Cross as a triumph of administrative wisdom, securing a condition of public order in which people may live leisured and pleasant lives, undisturbed by the malign activities of criminals and revolutionaries. The worst features of the Greek and the Latin conceptions of God, with the Abelardian impressionism thrown in, are reproduced in the Grotian reading of the satisfaction theory. Analogy for analogy, that of civil government is worse than that of the court-room. The latter suggests at least the inevitableness of a moral order. The former is coloured by the changeableness of political expediency. The obvious criticism upon both is that they are mere analogies, or metaphors, or illustrations, which do not and cannot express the whole Christian truth.

3. The disintegration of dogma.—The Grotian theory is the death-knell of scholasticism, whether mediæval or Protestant. It represents the exhaustion of forms of thought which had come down through the ages uncriticized and unrevised. The great upheaval of the Reformation is beginning to tell in the region of doctrinal reflexion. At first, however, the endeavour after a new theology takes destructive form. The disintegration of the dogmatic system constructed under Greek and Latin influence proceeded along various lines of thought with intensifying force, till Kant's drastic criticism re-stated the whole problem of man's relation to God and the world and demanded a new solution. Three movements within this period are of special interest and importance.

(*a*) *Pietism* is a peculiarly Continental phenomenon, which has its English parallel in Revivalism. Pietism is a revolt against three forces which had oppressed the human spirit and had hindered the deepening of Christian experience: against intellectualism, which had turned faith into the acceptance of dogmatic propositions; against institutionalism, which had subjected the individual to an external authority; against professionalism, which had made theology the province of experts and had excluded the lay mind from the privileges and responsibilities of reflective thought. It demands piety as the test of Christian standing. It asserts the need of an individual relation to God and the right of the individual to the dignity of a child of God and a freeman in the realm of spiritual realities. It stands independently related to dogma and places upon it a pragmatic valuation, according as it ministers to the wealth of the soul's inner life. In all this pietism was occupying Reformation ground. At the same time, it did not occupy precisely the same position towards dogma as did the theologians of the Reformation. They believed in systematization and were consciously constructive in their efforts. The pietists disregarded system and concentrated on those doctrines which were distinctly experiential in their import and were susceptible of psychological exposition. If they had generalized this method, they would have anticipated modern thought in a remarkable degree. As it was, their chief interest lay in the experiences of the individual soul; and their main theological work was done in connexion with the fact of conversion and the process of sanctification.

The merits and defects of pietism and its English equivalents in more recent times are patent. They awoke the conscience and appealed for faith with prophetic fervour and power. They inspired magnificent evangelistic and missionary enterprises. They set in operation humanitarian work, which endured long after the special religious conceptions that attended its beginning had been forgotten. At the same time, their conception of salvation was narrowly subjective and tended to concentrate attention on states of the soul's inner experience and to erect as standard of Christian perfection æsthetic and emotional delights rather than righteousness and truth. Such a salvation omits three-quarters of life from its purview and makes duty and virtue an annex to Christian experience rather than its product and its verification. This subjectivism has resulted, too, in a lowered conception of the Church as the sphere and instrument of the Christian salvation and in a tendency to revert towards separatism and quietism (*q.v.*). The result has been to deprive the Church of its richest and most vital elements and to condemn it to barrenness and futility. Men have been repelled alike by the narrowness of an individualistic piety and by the abstractions of dogmatic theology and institutionalized Christianity.

(*b*) *Mysticism.*—Formalism and externalism in all ages produce mysticism, and the essence of mysticism is ever the same. Accordingly, when we note the ominous development of Protestant scholasticism, we eagerly await the appearance of the mystic protest. Nor are we disappointed. Mystics confront the Protestant ascendancy and invite elect souls to draw apart from institutional Christianity and find God in the depths of their own souls. The most interesting and influential of these intense spiritual individualists were, undoubtedly, the Quakers, who found in a Scotsman, Barclay of Ury, their ablest systematic thinker. This Aberdeenshire laird dared to oppose the Calvinism which held the great majority of his fellow-countrymen in what he believed to be gross darkness. He did not mean, indeed, to deny the objective ground on which the traditional orthodoxy, Roman and Reformed alike, had based the fact of salvation. But he placed alongside of the historic fact an inward mystery, whose singular value tends to make the other unnecessary.

There is a 'two-fold redemption'; the first 'performed and accomplished by *Christ for us* in His crucified body without us,' the other 'wrought by *Christ in us*, which no less properly is called and accounted a redemption than the former.' By the first 'we are put into a capacity of salvation.' By the second 'we witness this capacity brought into act.' The historically procured 'capacity,' however, is really not needed. God has given Christ as a Light which 'enlighteneth the hearts of all for a time, in order to salvation . . . and would work out the salvation of all if not resisted.' This Light is 'a spiritual substance which may be felt in the soul and apprehended.' This Light is seen in the historic Christ, yet the history and the mystery of Christ fall apart. 'The history is profitable and comfortable with the mystery and never without it; but the mystery is and may be profitable without the explicit and outward knowledge of the history.' 'In regard Christ is in all as in a seed, yea, and that he never is nor can be separate from that pure and holy seed and light which is in all men, therefore may it be said in a larger sense, that he is in all.' Salvation, therefore, is not bound up with any historic facts; and Christ becomes other than the Jesus of history. He is the λόγος σπερματικός of old Greek thought. 'As many as resist not this light, but receive the same, it becomes in them an holy, pure and spiritual birth, bringing forth holiness, righteousness, purity, and all those other blessed truths which are acceptable to God.' 'This inward birth of Christ in man' is that by which we are 'made just' and so justified; for justification means 'making one just, and not reputing one merely such, and is all one with sanctification.'[1]

The good laird's interest in righteousness is deep and true, and his protest against the 'satisfaction' theory is intelligible. But the background of his thought is none other than Neo-Platonism. His conception of salvation would be as blank and empty as the mystic plunge into the Absolute, were it not for the accident that Barclay was a devout believer in Christ, deeply exercised in Christian experience. Quakerism has lovely fruits and has a strong fascination for all who have felt the fruitlessness of intellectualism. But in itself it has the instability and incommunicableness of the mystic rapture. The Christian salvation cannot be separated from the redemptive action of God in history. Mystics abound throughout Christendom during the 17th and 18th centuries. They provide a refuge in the midst of that dogmatism which their influence tended to destroy. They are intensely interesting personalities. But there is no advance in their thought beyond the point reached

[1] *An Apology for the True Christian Divinity*, London, 1678, prop. vii. § 3 f.

by Plotinus, and the differences between them do not obscure the identity of their central positions.[1]

(*c*) *Rationalism.* — Reflective thought has a necessary function in reference to religious experience. This function it does not exercise alone, but always in conjunction with conscience, feeling, and will.

Knowledge in the NT is 'not an abstractly intellectual view of Christianity . . . not only a deeper comprehension of the Christian revelation itself, but a deeper insight into its practical significance and obligations. . . . Some such thing—not in the sense of a speculation *a priori*, without ethical inspiration, but in the sense of an expression and interpretation of Christian faith, which shall be pervaded throughout by the spiritual virtue of that faith—seems to be set before us by the NT writers as the ideal of "knowledge."'[2]

Suppose, however, the intellectual element in this complex function of the mind were isolated from all other elements and erected into a standard of the truth and value of a living religious experience, it is plain that the result would be defective. The tendency to such false isolation and elevation of intellect lies close at hand, and theology in all ages has felt it as a temptation. When the temptation is yielded to, the result is rationalism (*q.v.*). Practically, it means 'salvation by wisdom.' Religion is cast into propositional form. The acceptance of this form is treated as the condition of salvation. Salvation is intellectualized and thereby, of course, emptied of its vital force. In post-Reformation thought prior to Kant rationalism reigned supreme. On the one side, it assumed the form of dogmatic orthodoxy and professed to be a formal and systematic presentation of saving truth. The more rigorously the logic of the understanding was applied to the fullness of religious life, the more elaborate the system became, and the less able it was to sustain its own weight. Controversies broke out, sects multiplied, weapons of mutual exclusion were employed, and salvation was disfigured by the very process that was meant to defend it. On the other side, rationalism appears as criticism of dogma. At first the movement is not directed against the content of the Christian revelation. Men like Baxter among the Nonconformists or the Cambridge Platonists among the Anglicans are in full sympathy with evangelical Christianity. But they are repelled by the Protestant scholasticism. The Cambridge men, in particular, occupied the position of the Alexandrian theologians. They are seeking to do a genuinely constructive work in theology. They have borrowed their ruling principles, however, from the Alexandrians—just as the Alexandrians borrowed from prevalent Greek modes of thought. They did not estimate correctly the nature and issues of the principles they were thus assuming, and they were brought near the result that ever haunts Greek thought, viz. the undervaluing of the historical basis of redemption and the relapse into mysticism. Their Platonism is really Neo-Platonism. Their chief value is that they created an atmosphere in which the Christian soul might grow in sweetness of spirit and tolerance of judgment. After all, however, theirs was a cloistered virtue. They were not able to interpret Christianity afresh to a generation under the control of dogmatism. The critical process took further and more aggressive shape in the movement of which English Deism (*q.v.*) is the best-known representative. This movement is as intellectualist as the orthodoxy it combated. Its aim is not to dispense with dogma, but to reduce the dogmatic system to an easier compass. Christianity is still *gnosis*; but its propositions can be cut down to a few brief statements. Salvation is still by wisdom; but the opinions offered for acceptance are such as will find the minimum of opposition from the human understanding. Such reduction of dogma has no religious value. Rather, it accentuates the essential evil of all dogma. It accentuates that 'usurpation of the understanding' which makes rationalism so strong in its attack on orthodoxy and so useless as a contribution to the higher life of the spirit. Further, a rationalism that cleaves to a few dogmas is powerless against an application of its own rigorous method, which discards all dogma and delivers the human mind once for all from all bondage to external authority. Christianity was never so near extinction as in the period which began with the Protestant dogmatic and ended with dogmatic atheism. The root of all the evil is plain. Theology has lost touch with life. It has ceased to be a real soteriology. It has betaken itself to system-building and has forgotten its true task, the interpretation of the Christian salvation as an actual experience of living men.

[1] *E.g.*, William Law and the Quakers; cf. J. H. Overton, *William Law, Nonjuror and Mystic*, London, 1881, pp. 418-420.

[2] Denney, *HDB*, art. 'Knowledge.'

4. The movement towards reconstruction.—In place of decadent scholasticism there came a great return to experience. In every department of thought there is an abandonment of scholastic methods and a recurrence to the facts of life. Physical science enters confidently into its kingdom. The historical method of study, critical in its approaches, constructive in its aim, governs procedure in philosophy and theology. Literature emerges out of pedantry and formalism and becomes vivid, human, free, and varied. Social and economic forces gain increasing practical and scientific recognition. Deeper and more influential than all these efforts after reality is the revival of religion which characterized the second half of the 18th cent., continued during most of the 19th cent., and spread through all lands occupied by daughter churches of the Reformation. As in that century when Christianity was born and in that which saw the collapse of mediævalism, so now men became deeply penetrated by a sense of the need of divine redemptive power to deliver them from the moral evils which afflicted them. All problems of life and thought were seen to run back to the ultimate problem of man's relation to God. Salvation, as in the 1st cent. and in the 16th, was an imperious demand of the human spirit. As in those two great epochs of religious history, the response to this need came in a new proclamation of the love of God, manifested in the life and suffering of the historic Redeemer. Christianity was, as it were, reborn in the consciousness of men, and something of the gladness and power of NT days re-visited the fainting Church.

Theology and philosophy in this period alike address themselves to constructive work. In such an endeavour the activities and results of the past could not be forgotten. All the greater forms of ancient thought are reproduced. Yet there are deep lines of demarcation which separate modern thought from those typical forms which, after eighteen centuries of dominance, perished under the criticism of Hume and the yet more thoroughgoing criticism of Kant. The broad distinction consists in this: that, whereas ancient thought, in its Greek and Latin forms and in its mediæval continuation, is governed by metaphysical dualism, modern thought, in all its forms, has abandoned the attempt to construct a universe out of two opposed elements. The Greek idea of an Absolute, out of relation to the finite, to be reached by a supra-rational endeavour of soul, is finally surrendered. The Absolute, however defined, must be conceived as manifesting itself in the fullness of life, to be apprehended, therefore, not by going outside of experience, but by penetrating to the heart of experience and reaching that which is at once the highest value and the supreme reality.

The problem, in one word, is reconciliation. How is man to discern and appropriate the fundamental unity through which all human interests are to be reconciled and harmonized? It is the underlying problem of economics, of social and political science, as well as of philosophy in its broadest range and of theology in its specific task. Salvation is conceived as essentially functional and organic. The effort is made to combine two aspects of salvation which had been often held apart. The one is the objective and historic: the unifying of life cannot take place in idea merely; it must be wrought out for men in a history, if it is ever to be appropriated by men as an inspiration and a power. The other is the subjective and experiential: the action in which reconciliation is achieved cannot be an isolated historic incident. Salvation is not a transaction. It is an action indeed, but such an action as is continued in the experience of men and does really organize human life into a living unity. The 19th cent. is remarkable for its interest in history. It is the period of 'lives of Christ'; so confident is it that what it needs is to be found in Him, if only He were properly understood. It is remarkable, also, for its intense concern with human welfare. The constant political upheavals which mark its course are subordinate in importance to the goal of social improvement which they are supposed, often mistakenly, to attain. No way of salvation which does not issue in the moral uplift of the individual and of society can make successful appeal to the modern mind. Atonement must be real at-onement, of man and God, and of man with man. When from the standpoint of our own day we survey the field and note the many volumes and all their plans and schemes, we perceive that, amid this bewildering variety, there is one controlling quest, viz. for a secure doctrine of salvation. This does not mean that the modern mind will ever bind upon itself the intolerable yoke of a dogmatic system. Still, as it surveys a century of varied and intense activity, as it finds all gains and values imperilled in the great disaster of a world war, as it looks forward to an era of reconstruction, it does require that the forces of redemption shall be understood, so that humanity shall be saved with a salvation which shall atone for unspeakable wrong, repair intolerable waste and injury, and comprehend all nations in mutual service and helpfulness.

Success in the effort to reach a truly organic idea of salvation has been very varied. Certain types of doctrine may be distinguished in the leading thinkers of the period. Affinities with past conceptions may be noted, with a constant reaching out after more concrete modes of thought.

(*a*) *Salvation by wisdom.*—The old Greek intellectualism has its modern representatives in Hegel and the great English thinkers who carry on the idealist tradition. Let the idea of God be conceived as that of a self-differentiating unity. Let the element of difference appear in the individual's intense consciousness of himself, with separate rights and claims. It is plain, then, what sin and salvation mean. Sin is the turning of the self against the unity which alone gives it meaning. Salvation will be the dying to this selfish self and the affirmation by the self of its oneness with the universal Self, in whose completeness all elements of difference lose their separateness and are reconciled to one another. 'Die to live' is the gospel which each individual must preach to himself. In the act in which he thus dies he enters a new life. In the life thus reached by death his sin is seen to be lifted from him. It has been already borne by the universal consciousness, of which he is by nature a partaker, to which he owes both the possibility of sin and the power of redemption. Historic Christianity sees this unity with the divine exhibited supremely in the consciousness of Christ. The ordinary man will do well to attach himself to that great discoverer of the way of salvation. But the salvation is not dependent on Jesus, and there is no need or room for trust in Him. The salvation is the discovery by the individual of his oneness with God; and it is made by sheer force of thought.

No philosophy was ever more religious. It is Neo-Platonism purged of dualism. It is Platonism interpreted, corrected, enriched. But it is not Christianity. The dualism it supposes itself to have transcended is sunk too deep in human nature to be exorcized by a formula. God is more than an idea, even than 'the Idea.' Christ is more than an illustration of a process of thought. Salvation by wisdom is for an intellectual élite. It is neither universal, final, nor effective.

(*b*) *Salvation by feeling.*—Intellectualism never fails to produce the protest of feeling. Over against the makers of systems and the keen-witted destroyers of systems stand continually the great company of the mystics. Jacobi, stirred both by the success and by the failure of Kant's critical philosophy, maintains that the mere understanding can indeed bring us only to phenomena. The realities of God and the spiritual life are inaccessible to its procedure. They are not, however, on that account out of reach. Another faculty, which sometimes he calls 'faith' and sometimes 'reason,' conducts us to the supreme realities and gives us a direct perception of them. The same mystical vein is present in Schleiermacher (*q.v.*), combined with a strong sense of the value of the historic redemption in Christ and of the organic fullness of the Christian life. Religion is neither philosophy, nor theology, nor ethic. Its source is deep beneath intellect and will. It consists in a state of soul wherein ordinary activities are suppressed and the whole being is surrendered to the overwhelming sense of the presence of the Infinite. This condition is the very essence of salvation. The Christian religion owes its supremacy to the fact that in it this sense of the Infinite and the soul's absolute dependence upon it is evoked, and maintained, in a unique degree. Christ holds the central place in this religion because He lived habitually in this consciousness of God's presence. The Church, as the fellowship of those who trace their new life to the spirit of Jesus, is the organ whereby Christ's consciousness of God is to be disseminated throughout humanity. In Ritschl's words:

> 'Redemption is the actual liberation of believers from the sin that prevails in them, by communication of the power of His consciousness of God, which the individual receives in the fellowship of those who resemble Him.'[1]

Schleiermacher's message was life from the dead to a Church dying of intellectualism. It was pietism lifted out of a narrow groove and applied to the widest problems of philosophy and religion. It communicated an impulse to theology which has never ceased to act, recalling it to its real function as interpreter of the Church's life. It was a determined effort to deliver mysticism from the twin errors which continually haunt it—the undervaluing of history and the isolation of the individual. Christ and the Church are brought within the scope of the mystic experience and are made essential to it. Yet, after all, religion, as Schleiermacher conceives it, is essentially mysticism. It implies the dualism which is the presupposition of Neo-Platonism and which recurs even in Spinozism. The Infinite does in effect absorb the finite. Salvation does mean the dissolution of the soul in the rapture of its sense of

1 *A Critical Hist. of the Christian Doctrine of Justification and Reconciliation*, Eng. tr., Edinburgh, 1872, p. 467.

the Infinite and the Eternal. The power in virtue of which man reaches the Infinite is not the intellect or the will; neither is it faith, in the NT and Reformation sense of *fiducia*. Religion is not action, nor does it urge men to activity. It is the soul feeling itself as one with God. God, in such an experience, is not viewed as personal. Schleiermacher, like all mystics, shrinks from the popular language which makes of God an individual like all other individuals, only bigger and stronger. But he carries this reverence to the characteristic mystical position that 'omnis determinatio est negatio'; and in this denial of predicates to God personality too is lost. With it there is lost also the conception of a divine end, and a divine historic action, and a redemption which is an achievement of love. In spite of the Christian doctrinal construction and the beautifully Christian spirit, we are still at the point where mysticism resolutely abides, at which salvation is an ineffable and incommunicable experience of the individual soul, not merely immediate, but unmediated by any Saviour or any saving deed. At this point mysticism and Christianity part company. It is significant that in the exhaustion which attended the close of the 19th cent., and the destruction of all institutional forms of life which has marked the second decade of the 20th cent., there has prevailed a deep and wide-spread interest in mysticism. Its historic representatives are being sympathetically studied. Its psychological elements are being analyzed. To it, as to the essence of religion, men are being recalled, and in it, it is hoped, they will unite in a community of soul which disregards divergences of ecclesiastical connexion. Sects are springing up in which—*e.g.*, 'Christian Science' (*q.v.*)—in spite of the grotesque ignorance they display, we can see that a mystic influence is at work, giving them any real value they may possess. The net result is the same as in any other era in which mysticism has arisen. Its value lies in its protest. Its weakness lies in its dualism and individualism. Its presuppositions are not those of Christianity, and its salvation is radically distinct from that with which Christianity meets the need of man—in the 1st cent., in the 16th, or the 20th.

(*c*) *Salvation by power of will.*—Stoicism, like mysticism, stands strong in a period of intellectual impoverishment and moral anarchy. It differs, at least in its primary form, by being the assertion, and not the despair, of self. Mysticism carries the denial of things finite one degree farther than Stoicism and denies the sufficiency of the finite subject. The lesson of the history of thought is that mysticism diagnoses the need of man more thoroughly than Stoicism. It is precisely within the self that the root evil lies. The self cannot be its own redeemer. Yet Stoicism has a nobility and valour of spirit lacking to mysticism. It acts as a moral tonic, when destructive criticism is rampant and religious feeling seems to have no care for the wounds inflicted by a ruthless logic. In the heart of the 18th cent. Butler proclaimed the autonomy and supremacy of conscience. Conscience is like a king issuing commands to turbulent and ill-conditioned subjects. Unfortunately, its authority is not combined with power. Any individual who chooses, however, may make conscience supreme in his own life, and, if he does, virtue will follow and be his reward. This idea of conscience is crossed in Butler with other ethical conceptions, as self-interest and the love of God. His attempt to combine them, however, would have required another psychology than was at his disposal and a different reading than he attained to of man's need and of divine redemption. As it is, he stands, a lonely figure, amid the crowd of destructive thinkers. The world of his day honoured him with a bishopric, but left his message severely alone. Not to him, but to John Wesley, on whom, it is to be feared, he looked with some degree of contempt, was the moral uplift of his generation to be due. Stoicism has no gospel, bids each man be his own Saviour, permits no objective mediation of salvation, stands erect, great, somewhat grim, and a total failure.

In Kant (*q.v.*) the destructive criticism of the 18th cent. is carried to its most drastic issues. The whole structure of dogmatism crumbles beneath his blows. He had finally demonstrated that that power of the mere understanding and that method of logical process by which the great dogmatic systems had been reared are incompetent to reach the sphere of things real. By the same rigid criticism he also demonstrated that the attack upon dogmatism is open to the same condemnation as dogmatism itself. If dogmatism is incompetent, so also is scepticism. Never was so great a destroyer. But, with him, destruction is only a preliminary step. In heart he is a builder. He belongs in intention to the period not of disintegration, but of reconstruction. He himself, however, scarcely advances beyond Stoicism; nothing is more interesting in him than his attempt to make Stoicism Christian, though, in effect, all that he does accomplish is to turn Christianity into a Stoic philosophy. Above the world of phenomena, to which alone the intellect conducts us, there is the region of ethical value, which is the sphere of reality. In the former man is an empirical object, and therefore not free. In the latter he is free, because freedom means the determination of the self by its own law; and the noumenal self gives the law to itself. Suppose, however (what is indeed the case) that man has ceased to be his real noumenal self and, by an act which on Kantian principles is really inexplicable, has allowed himself to be determined, not by the law of his real being, but by things sensuous and empirical, how shall he deliver himself? What shall he do to be saved? Kant has no answer to give except, 'Obey the moral law.' It is the law of the moral subject as noumenon. But it is his law only as an individual. It is not the revelation of God in him and in mankind. It has no regenerative force.

> 'Because he stops short of this latter conception, Kant necessarily rejects as Mysticism, or as involving the negation of moral freedom, that very idea which gives its great moral power to Christianity, viz. the idea of a real objective mediation, by which the individual is raised above himself.'[1]

It is deeply interesting to note how Kant employs Christian phraseology, 'Son of God,' 'substitute,' 'Redeemer.' But, with his presuppositions, all this is picture language only. There is no God but the good will, no gospel but the categorical imperative, no salvation save man's obedience to law, no Saviour but his own unaided power.

Kant's view of salvation suffers from his dualism, which involved a really unintelligible distinction between man noumenal and man phenomenal. It shuts man up to his subjectivity and makes impossible any real reconciliation of man to God and of man to man. Ritschl's view of Christianity is Kantian in its thoroughly ethical quality; but it seeks to get above the Kantian moralism in these two respects: it seeks to ground man's salvation in a work of God; and it exhibits salvation as fulfilment of a social task.[2] (*a*) God has before Him one purpose in His dealings with men—the creation of a Kingdom, which is the Kantian 'realm of ends,' treated not as a deliverance of the moral law, but as a fact of religious experience, and filled with the positive content of

[1] E. Caird, *The Critical Philosophy of Kant*, Glasgow, 1889, ii. 619.
[2] See art. RITSCHLIANISM.

mutual relationships and service. (*b*) This Kingdom is constituted by obedience to the divine will. It is, accordingly, a synonym for salvation. Salvation, or justification, or adoption means moral harmony with God. (*c*) This Kingdom has a history, inasmuch as God does in all ages labour for its realization. In that history Christ has a unique place. He perfectly obeyed God, was entirely faithful to His calling as Son and Servant of God, and carried His obedience to the point of death rather than forgo His oneness of will with God. On His fidelity the Kingdom depended. It is due to Christ that it exists. Salvation is a fact in human experience, which owes its permanence to Christ's loyalty to His Father. Therefore humanity is in debt to Christ and is saved only through the grace of Christ—*i.e.* through Christ's perseverance in His vocation. (*d*) The individual is saved in and through His place in the Kingdom. Salvation is membership in the community which Christ gathered about Him, and which has existed ever since, the members of which share Christ's relation to God. The Kingdom, or salvation, is prior to the individual and is a gift to him. But it is his only as he makes it his task and devotes himself to doing the will of God, which will include serving his neighbour. Unquestionably, all this is moralism of a very noble kind. Its recoil from a hard, forensic, or transactional view of the work of Christ and of man's salvation is entirely intelligible and has proved most fruitful in all subsequent soteriology. When all is said, however, it remains moralism still. It does not view sin in the aspect which it has always borne for the Christian consciousness, as a fact of such overwhelming magnitude that it involved God in the unspeakable anguish of enduring it as a load upon His heart. For Ritschl 'the sin of the world is a separable accident of the mission of Jesus.'[1] Faith, accordingly, has not the note of trustful self-commitment to the mercy of God in Christ which is struck in the NT and re-echoed in the praises of the Church in every age. It becomes 'the permanent direction of the will to the final purpose of God and Christ which the believer for his own sake maintains.' A. E. Garvie, who quotes this passage, adds, 'Individual faith is social loyalty.'[2] Thus has Ritschl separated fruit from root. Or, rather, the fruit of character grows from the root of individual moral capacity and owes to Christ and His Church no more than indirect assistance. It is an unpleasant issue of Ritschlianism that a salvation, thus conceived as moral task, seems open only to those nations which inherit Western culture. What becomes of the rest of the world does not appear; and missionary enterprise does not seem to be one of the ministries of the Kingdom.

It is significant, too, that Ritschl has omitted any place or function of the Holy Spirit in the salvation of men. Yet so deep-seated an element in the experience of the NT Church ought surely to have been embraced in a theory which turns upon the fact of the Christian community. Where, however, the work of Christ for us, and upon us, or in us, is inadequately interpreted, because of invincible subjectivism, there can be no occasion for the idea of divine power operating directly within the human spirit. Ultimately man is self-sufficient in salvation.

(*d*) *Salvation by process.*—Throughout the whole movement towards reconstruction one characteristic is most marked, the recoil from the static view of God, which had reigned unquestioned in Greek and Latin theology. Even Hegelianism did not intend to present for acceptance a motionless and impassible God, but did desire to bring the facts of life and movement into the idea of the Absolute.

Two phases of recent thought have given voice to this reaction from a static view of God. One is the magnificent activity of science in unfolding the facts of development in the universe. The other is the emphasis which is increasingly laid on social facts, forces, and ideals. The governing idea of evolution, and the prevailing social emphasis, could not fail to have profound effects on theology and to produce far-reaching influence upon older conceptions of God and of salvation. When the first shock was over, it was thought that no great harm was done. It was hoped that theology could take into itself the evolutionary view of nature and yet retain all the advantages of the old absolutist view. In like manner, theology, it was considered, could be democratized and socialized, while God could still be worshipped in His solitary supremacy. Of late, however, it has become apparent that the theological revolution cannot be accomplished so smoothly. The static Absolute is not to be so easily transmuted. If the static view goes back to Parmenides, some of the leaders of the revolution are inclined to go back to Heraclitus. Instead of a universe rigid and fixed, we are invited to behold a growing universe and to discern at its heart a growing God.[1] Instead of a God conceived as an omniscient Planner and an omnipotent Doer, we are offered a finite God, not omnipotent, but doing the best He can to overcome forces hostile to Him and gradually, very gradually, with toil and pain, winning satisfactory results. A God of this kind, we are assured, is quite intelligible and much more adorable than the distant Divinity of older thought. Human salvation, accordingly, takes on a wholly different cast from anything we have believed in hitherto. It is not a victory of divine love already won, which we appropriate and carry out into issues which God had in view when He undertook the making of the world. It is a process in which God and man are both engaged, the issue of which is by no means a certainty either for God or for man. On the whole, there is reason for hope. If we cannot be optimists, we can at least be meliorists. Things are moving; and God has grown so wise and strong, and has increased so much in moral intuition and moral power, that we are reasonably sure He will win in the end, provided He gets the help of all high-minded persons. There can be no doubt that the intellectual atmosphere is charged with ideas like these. Even before the war men like William James and Hastings Rashdall were insisting on the worthiness of the conception of a finite or limited God, who is not the Absolute. To Ward the Absolute is 'God-and-the-world.'[2] McTaggart's Absolute is a society conceived after the analogy of a College![3] H. G. Wells harks back to the analogy of a hero King, 'a young and energetic God, an Invisible Prince growing in strength and wisdom, who calls men and women to his service, and who gives salvation from self and mortality only through self-abandonment to his service.'[4] The idea of a 'young God' suggests obvious questions. Did he then come into existence, and when and how? Is his present rate of progress fixed, or, with added experience, will he be able to increase his speed?

The difficulty of attributing growth to God is intensified, if we are meant to include in it development of character.

[1] R. Mackintosh, *Albrecht Ritschl and his School*, London, 1915, p. 154.
[2] *The Ritschlian Theology*, Edinburgh, 1899, p. 321.

[1] See art. PLURALISM.
[2] *The Realm of Ends* (*Gifford Lectures*), Cambridge, 1911, p. 241.
[3] *Studies in Hegelian Cosmology*, Cambridge, 1901, p. 86.
[4] *God the Invisible King*, London, 1917, p. 114.

'It is not clear,' says Pringle-Pattison, 'whether this God is morally perfect to begin with—in which case the development and progress would consist simply in the moral enlightenment and betterment of human beings and similar races in other regions of the universe—or whether the finite God is himself conceived as growing in insight and in moral wisdom through the lessons of experience, and working out his own character as he proceeds with his beneficent work. In the latter case, one is at a loss to see why the title of God should be bestowed on an individual essentially of the human type, though, no doubt, on a larger scale and at a higher stage of development; and one is bound to conclude that such a developing demigod would give the same account of his own development as the moral and religious man among ourselves. He would describe it as a new insight into the nature of things, due to the leading of a higher God, who would be God indeed. It seems to me impossible to override the testimony of the religious consciousness on this point.'[1]

That testimony is unquestionably that God is the source of salvation, which is with Him an accomplished victory, which men presuppose in all their own moral warfare. Commenting on William James's description of his position as 'moralistic religion,' Pringle-Pattison says:

'However it may be with popular religion, the deeper experiences of religious faith and emotion—the utterances of the saints, the religious experts—appear quite irreconcilable with the pluralistic conception of a finite God, an unfinished world, and a dubious fight. In fact, it is not too much to say, with Mr. Bradley, that "to make the moral point of view absolute" is to have "broken with every considerable religion." The victory for which morality fights is for religion already, or rather eternally, won; and it is the assurance of this victory which inspires the finite subject with courage and confidence in his individual struggle. . . . As experience abundantly shows, the assurance of victory won and reconciliation achieved is the most powerful dynamic that can be supplied to morality.'[2]

The motives which prompt this hypothesis of a finite God are no doubt altogether admirable—the desire to give reality to man's moral history, and to God's sympathy with him in it, as well as the hope of clearing God's character in view of the miseries of mankind. And it may very well be that those ends cannot be served so long as we hold a static view of the Absolute. But is there no alternative to such a static Absolute except a finite growing God? It is certain that the alternative did not present itself to the saints and seers of the OT or NT. They believed profoundly in the sympathy of God with man and included suffering in the divine experience. But the background of this thought was not a demigod, fighting his way to a dubious issue. Rather it was a God of omnipotent love, realizing in time a purpose that is eternal, and doing so by Himself entering into human experience and achieving once for all the redemption of the world. Men enter on this redemption as a possession—they fulfil it in an experience of toil and suffering, in which they have the presence and sympathy of their Redeemer, and they inherit it as a completed salvation, a Kingdom that cannot be shaken.

Speculatively, the doctrine of the finite God depends on the success of Bergson's philosophy; and that stands or falls by his theory of time. It may be permitted to doubt whether that theory will hold the field against criticism. It seems as though, in his view of the future, Bergson himself has fallen a victim to the metaphor of space, and is thinking of time in the old way as a prolongation of a line into an unknown region where nothing is certain and anything may happen. Such, in any case, is the speculative implication in the theological idea of a young and energetic God, whose success is quite unpredictable. Suppose he were to fail! In that case he would himself need a Saviour, like any other beaten soul. In allowing that such a fate is thinkable we have abandoned the point of view of religion altogether and have arrived at a profound and comprehensive scepticism.

(*e*) *Salvation by historic redemption.*—We stand too near to our own period to expect co-ordinate work among the crowd of expert scholars and eager students, or to hope for such a comprehensive statement of results as shall express the Christian verities in a form adequate to the needs of men in this new age. The significant fact is that, within the generation which has not yet passed from the arena of conflict and endeavour there has been a prevailing Biblical idea of salvation, presented with careful exegetical work and with ample ethical and psychological emphasis.

Salvation is conceived broadly and deeply as personal and moral, including fellowship with God, the elevation of individual character, and the service of men in righteousness and love. This salvation, inexhaustible in redemptive and restorative power, is recognized as due to God's action in the historic Christ. The debt of humanity to Christ is regarded as unique and incomparable. By writers and preachers of every variety of theological opinion men are being summoned to Christ as the fountain-head of the influences which are to renew humanity at its centre and inaugurate, after the discipline of war, an era penitent, humble, and at the same time more wisely ordered and more hopeful. It is being perceived also, even more clearly, that God's revealing action in Christ must be accompanied by suffering. Any view of Christ which omits the element of suffering as essential to His vocation and to His abiding influence is recognized to be less than Christian. There is a growing impression that the suffering of love is the mightiest redemptive influence known to man, and that, in the winning of salvation by divine act, suffering must have the central place.

The doctrine of atonement, which modern intellectualism had neglected, is attracting earnest attention, and Christian thought is concentrating upon the Cross of Christ.

As we survey the work of Christian thinkers of the latter part of the 19th cent., to the verge of the Great War, we find that the death of Christ has been presented mainly in three aspects.

(*a*) *As a transaction.*—From this point of view, 'the atoning Christ acts on God for man.'[1] Hitherto this transaction has been described after commercial or forensic analogies. Grotius had led the way to a view of the work of Christ coloured by the idea of a modern State administered by a just and wise prince. This last type of thought harmonized with much that was burning in the hearts of Englishmen. The political revolution was proceeding. Democratic ideals were being realized. The conception of a State in which every citizen has his place and function guaranteed in law was being made the goal of practical politics. No man wrought harder in the cause of ordered liberty than R. W. Dale of Birmingham. It was natural, therefore, that his theological thinking should be controlled by the ideas which inspired his social and political action. His governing category is law, not made by man or exploited in the interest of individuals or classes, but a law of righteousness, without caprice or variableness, untouched by time or change. The Kingdom of Heaven is an eternal order. Human welfare depends on the maintenance of this order. 'In this kingdom Christ is the Moral Ruler . . . His voice is the voice of the eternal Law of Righteousness.'[2] Law, however, is threatened by the uprising of human pride and arrogance, which would upset the order and make life intolerable. Law must be vindicated, and there is no way of vindicating it save by the sequence in which suffering inevitably follows law-breaking. It belongs to the Moral Ruler in the Kingdom of Heaven to vindicate the

[1] *The Idea of God*, p. 382 f. [2] *Ib.* p. 395 f.

[1] J. K. Mozley, *The Doctrine of the Atonement*, p. 173.
[2] *The Atonement*[7], London, 1878, p. xxxii.

law which is His own voice. He has done so, not, however, in the person of the offenders, but in His own, 'not by inflicting suffering on the sinner, but by enduring suffering Himself.'[1] This is the gospel. When we lie under conviction of sin's sinfulness and are feeling the pressure of the divine judgments, we are enabled to rest on the death of Christ as 'the perfect expression and fulfilment of that submission which we know ought to be manifested by ourselves. . . . He endured the penalties of sin, and so made an actual submission to the authority and righteousness of the principle which those penalties express.'[2] The redemption of man rests on the endurance by the Moral Ruler of the actual penalty of sin. The fact of sin is so real and terrible that only a fact as tragic in its agony and as measureless in its significance as the Cross of Christ can meet it. But whether the value of that death is adequately or even fittingly expressed in terms of law and penalty, and whether Christ's relation to the Kingdom of Heaven is properly stated where He is described as its Moral Ruler, may gravely be questioned. Dale himself strove earnestly to avoid the hardness of these forms by dwelling on the unity of Christ with God and His relation to men as their representative. But surely, if these true and great thoughts are to be present in a doctrine of the Atonement, they ought to be regulative; and, if they are made so, legal categories must not be treated as determinative. Something of the old dualism remains when the love of God is confronted by His law as a power to be reckoned with. Love does not break into an order constituted by law. It is itself the basis of the order and is supreme within it.

(*b*) *As a demonstration.*—From this standpoint 'the atoning Christ acts on man for God.'[3] If the 19th cent. was marked by a great movement towards political emancipation and the reconstitution of society, it was also characterized by an intense humanitarian instinct. Love, no less than justice, was its passion. Men were becoming imbued with the spirit of pity. The hapless lot of multitudes 'damned into this world' moved noble and self-denying souls to life-long ministries of compassion. Legislation was devoted to the improvement of the position of the less favoured masses. Criminals were regarded not merely as wrong-doers, but as unfortunate in the conditions of their birth, inheritance, and social environment, or even as themselves grievously wronged by the conditions of their life. The idea of punishment was reconsidered, and prison management was revolutionized. Discipline, and not penalty, became the regulative principle for society's dealing with its outcasts; and the great end was definitely conceived as the restoration of the offender to the ranks of citizenship. Political science, the system of education, church machinery and enterprise, were controlled by moral and social ends. Internationalism was scarcely yet born; but the ideal of an organized world was growing in the minds of statesmen and political thinkers. Thoughts like these could not fail to have a profound effect on theology. They are really occupied with the redemption of men; and that is the heart of the Christian faith. The Christian salvation can be nothing, if it is not ethical and social. The great doctrine of the Atonement, admittedly the very core of Christian thought, must be thoroughly moralized and must be interpreted through that spirit of love which has awakened to such glorious efficiency in modern society. The moral theory of the Atonement, accordingly, which had never ceased as a protest against legalism and particularism, was revived in richer form than could be found in Abelard or the Socinians.

What does the world need—so the argument runs—in its sorrows, agonies, sins, but a demonstration that God loves His wayward children to the uttermost? Once a soul is convinced of this, its hardness will melt; it will turn from its sins in penitence: it will respond in love to the appealing love of God. But what can produce this conviction? The answer is: The presence of Christ in the world, in the character that was His, in the life He lived, and the death He died.[1] The sight of Christ crucified produces in the beholder repentance; and repentance is regeneration. The Atonement is 'a moral atonement, offered to repentance.'[2] This state of soul, in which the sinner's heart is broken because of sin, 'is not a condition precedent to being forgiven; it is itself forgiveness—forgiveness which separates the sinner from his past self as far as the east is from the west.'[3] It is on the basis of this state of mind being genuine that God proceeds in forgiveness.[4] The Christian life, having been thus inaugurated, is carried forward under redemptive influences, which stream from the exalted Lord. Deeply Christian as this statement is, it does not seem to have made any doctrinal advance upon Abelard.[5] The question recurs: How does the death of Christ demonstrate the love of God? Surely the force of that demonstration must lie in itself, prior to, and independent of, our response to it; and that independent value can attach to it only if in the death of Christ the love of God deals effectively and finally with the fact of sin.

(*c*) *As an experience.*—Mozley's phrase in this connexion is: 'The atoning Christ acts on God as man.'[6] Deepest of all interests in the 19th cent. was the sacred mystery of personality. A dualistic philosophy was never able to do justice to the idea of personality, either in God or in man. It translated personality by individuality, concentrated selfhood in the bare act of self-assertion, arrayed the divine Self against the human self, and viewed the relations of God and man as those of two self-centred individuals. Proceeding upon individualistic presuppositions, theology could make no more of salvation than an arrangement between two individuals—one very great and powerful, the other very small and helpless—carried through by a third, who is externally related to each of these. The Atonement is a transaction in which God inflicts suffering on Christ, and Christ endures it, the result being assigned to man, or to some men, by divine decree. Plainly this is wholly inadequate to the Christian experience of redemption through Christ and leads to such perversities of thought as that God inflicted punishment on the Son of His love, and that there was a quantitative equivalence between the sufferings of Christ and the pains which sinners would otherwise have to endure. Individualism ran its course in the French Revolution and in the commercialism which exploited the idea of individual liberty. Most of 19th cent. thought has been an effort to get away from individualism. Much of it has been vague. The study of personality has not yet reached conclusions. Two points, however, may be regarded as fixed in modern thought, turned against individualism and absolutism respectively. The one is the individual's power of sympathetic self-identification with selves other than his own, making their concerns his, with an appropriating energy to which experience presents no limits. Individuality and finitude are only margins, which fade for ever before

[1] *The Atonement*[7], p. 392. [2] *Ib.* p. 423.
[3] Mozley, *loc. cit.*

[1] R. Mackintosh, *Essays toward a New Theology*, Glasgow, 1889, p. 26.
[2] *Ib.* p. 50. [3] *Ib.* p. 50. [4] *Ib.* p. 51.
[5] Harnack, *Hist. of Dogma*, Eng. tr., vi. 79.
[6] *Loc. cit.*

the impulse of self-communicating love. This is the essence of personality. The other is the self-realization of the individual through this continuous surrender. He is not 'lost' in the process. He finds himself and reaches a fullness of being which is his own, an indefeasible possession, gained and retained in self-surrender. The self that is thus surrendered is inseparable from that to which, and for which, the surrender is made. Alone, it is a fragment whose existence is its doom. In union, it lives its own true life in power and joy. This idea of the personal life could not fail to be applied to the person and work of Christ. We need not apply to Greek or Latin theology to supply explanatory forms of thought. Love is its own interpreter. Within the experience of Jesus are to be found at once the fact and the interpretation of atonement. The key to the problem is as simple and as mysterious as sympathy—a perfect sympathy with God, and a perfect sympathy with man. This sympathy is found in Christ. This, in its manifestation and exercise, is the Christian salvation. There has been born into the heart of humanity One who gathered into His own soul the guilt of man and felt it as no sinner can, and at the same time held inviolate the holiness of God. His experience is the Atonement—a veritable sin-bearing, in which the whole character of God is at once expressed and satisfied, and through which the love of God moves triumphant over sin to its goal in the great redemption. The situation created by sin has been fully met. God in Christ has reconciled the world to Himself; and this accomplished reconciliation is offered to the acceptance of faith. The old distinction of objective and subjective, as descriptive of theories of atonement, no longer holds good. This is demonstration of love, by love's deed; but the deed is the experience of Jesus.

The often quoted language of McLeod Campbell is the classical expression of this theory of the Atonement, which, in the mind of its chief exponent, is not so much a theory as a reverent entrance into, and a devout valuation of, the experience of Him who passed through deepening pain to the supreme sacrifice of the Cross.

Christ, in this experience, uttered 'a perfect Amen in humanity to the judgment of God on the sin of man. . . . He who so responds to the divine wrath against sin, saying, "Thou art righteous, O Lord, who judgest us," is necessarily receiving the full apprehension and realisation of that wrath, as well as of that sin against which it comes forth into His soul and spirit, into the bosom of the divine humanity, and, so receiving it, He responds to it with a perfect response,—a response from the depths of that divine humanity,—and *in that perfect response He absorbs it*. . . . By that perfect response in Amen to the mind of God in relation to sin is the wrath of God rightly met, and that is accorded to divine justice which is its due, and could alone satisfy it.'[1]

With this insight into the conditions of redemption the history of the doctrine of salvation has reached its climax as far as our generation is concerned. Nothing of fundamental importance has been added to the ideas which McLeod Campbell suggested in his epoch-making book. Criticism attaches mainly to his description of the experience of Jesus as 'repentance'; but a defective phrase does not invalidate the truth of the description itself.

Commenting on this phrase, Denney, while admitting that it is an unhappy one, maintains the soundness of McLeod Campbell's central position:

'It is a description of facts in the experience of the Saviour, and of facts on which His power to reconcile us to God is essentially dependent. If He had not thus seen and felt what sin is to God, if He had not thus acknowledged God's justice in condemning it, we could never have been brought through Him to the same insight and sorrow, to the same confession and acknowledgment, apart from which the reconciliation of sinners to God is self-evidently an impossibility. For to be reconciled to God means at all events that God's mind about sin, which is revealed to us in Christ, through Christ becomes our own.'[1]

Later writers have supplemented McLeod Campbell at certain points: Moberley, by including the work of the Holy Spirit in the winning of the Christian salvation; Forsyth, by emphasizing Christ's confession of God's holiness as the element in His experience which gives it atoning value; Denney, by extending the experience of Jesus to include the act of dying, because short of this 'we do not get to that in the experience of Jesus which, as the most unfathomable proof of love, has both supreme value to God and supreme influence with men.'[2] All of them, however, are at one in their point of view. They hold all they conceive to have been valid in the older 'objective' theories, but they are seeking the ground of atonement, not in anything that happened to Jesus by mandate of an external power, but in the experience wherein He embraced the whole fact of sin and held fast the mighty and inseparable interests of the divine love and holiness. They are at one in seeking to get rid of the last remains of dualism and to exhibit the vital connexion between what was wrought for man on the Cross and what is wrought in man by the Spirit. They all vindicate the Christian salvation as being far more than the rescue of individuals, as being indeed the constitution of a redeemed humanity, in which, through the service and sacrifice of faith, individuals advance in fellowship with God and in likeness to Him. Together they express a universal human intuition that the sorrow of the world can be healed only by the infinitely greater sorrow of God.

VIII. *CONCLUSION.*—The impulse of Christian thought in every stage of its evolution has been the need of a secure doctrine of salvation. Theologians of the East and of the West, mediæval schoolmen, and men of the modern period have had no other task than to interpret the Christian experience of salvation through the eternal principles which make it valid, and so to vindicate its value and power in the redemption of humanity.

The broad lessons of this long history can scarcely be missed: a steady distrust both of intellectualism and of emotionalism; a constant return to experience and an earnest evaluation of its ethical significance; a confident appeal to Christ as the standard and test of the faith which He Himself awakens; the value to be ascribed to Scripture, because it presents a record of God's saving acts and searchingly exhibits both human need and the principles on which divine love proceeds in dealing with it; the validity of the historical method in the study of Christian doctrine for the correction of inadequacies and as an instrument of advance; and to these we may add the guidance to be got from a comparison between the Christianity of the NT and the religions which, in all places whither it has come, have met it as its rivals, and in part also its anticipations and its heralds.

In particular, it is plain that, in order to win a satisfying doctrine of salvation, thought will need to deal afresh with its great determining conception, viz. the Christian idea of God. Philosophic thought has been much concerned with the Absolute, the ultimate Unity, which may be conceived as holding together the manifold differences which appear in human experience. It has had before it, in constructing its idea of the Absolute, an ideal of logical simplicity: and so, in bold speculative adventure, it has conceived God as bare transcendence or as barren immanence—a Being so utterly above the finite that, in com-

[1] *The Nature of the Atonement*[4], London, 1873, p. 116 ff.

[1] *Christian Doctrine of Reconciliation*, p. 259 f.
[2] *Ib.* p. 270 f.

parison with it, the finite loses all meaning and value; or so completely unified with the finite that, in this identification, the Infinite loses all significance and power. In revenge upon these cold abstractions pluralism mocks at the Absolute and gives us a God who is frankly finite and growing. Christianity has suffered many things at the hands of philosophers and has been far too docile when they insisted on presenting to faith a ready-made idea of God. Its own primary concern has not been with the Absolute at all. Its own special problem is neither logical nor ontological; and it cannot afford to wait till speculative discussion has come to an end before proclaiming its remedy for the abiding distress of man. Yet it may well be that its own problem *is* the ultimate problem of the universe, and that its own salvation contains implicitly a philosophy of God's relation to the world.

Christianity begins with human experience in its concrete fullness. It does not separate elements supposed to be incompatible and then painfully put them together again. It starts with the fact of life. It asks: What is the meaning of life? What is the direction and goal of its endeavours? What is its inherent value? What hinders, and what may achieve, its consummation? If we care to call it a philosophy, it is a philosophy of value; and, in realizing ultimate values, it believes itself to have attained ultimate reality. Christianity is human experience interpreted and reproduced through the supremacy of its highest value. What is that value? Christianity has one clear and definite answer: The Cross of Christ—life won through death. The Cross is the sum of Christianity. It is the Christian salvation, as message, as experience, as doctrine.

Christianity does not seek for proofs that God is. Its vital interest is the character of God. It is confident that it can recognize God when it sees Him; and then proof of His existence will pass aside as needless. God, seen in the Cross, is recognized as love. God is, in His inmost character, One who lives in the energy of self-giving. Christianity has never entangled itself in precarious discussions as to time and its relation to eternity. But it is perfectly certain that, in the Cross, it has touched the eternal—yes, the absolute—being of God. God is love. What He does and endures in time is the outcome of the inexhaustible fountain of the divine love. Human life is the exploration of the divine being. Time is deeply significant, therefore, and history is a real movement. It is, on the one side, the progressive revelation of God and, on the other, the progressive discovery by man of the wealth of the divine character. In either aspect time is real; but in neither does it move away from God towards an unknown beyond His ken and man's. It lies within God and is comprehended by Him in its completeness in a manner untranslatable by us whose transient lives are part of its flow. But at any point, and in any experience, we touch the Eternal whose 'moving image' time is. Supremely in the Cross we reach God and know what He is in His eternal being. The epithets 'immanent' and 'transcendent' are a foreign language to Christianity. Yet, if 'immanent' means that God is always giving Himself to His world, and thereby sustaining it in whatever degree of reality belongs to its successive stages, then the God of Christianity is 'immanent,' with an intensity and seriousness which leaves Spinozism far behind. And, if 'transcendent' means, in plain words, that God knows what He is about, that He is preparing a world capable of receiving His perfect self-communication, then the God of Christianity is 'transcendent,' with a glory that belongs not to the Greek Absolute or the Roman Imperator. 'Personality,' in like manner, is a term which Christianity has not needed to express its thought of God, not because it was too concrete to apply to Him, but because it was not concrete enough. But, if by 'personality' we indicate a capacity, which men possess only in degree, of making each moment a stage towards the realization of the organic fullness of life, then the God of Christianity is personal, in a measure far above what is competent to any individual member of our race. God, understood through the Cross, is a Being capable of a human experience. His 'immanence' and 'transcendence' make Him capable of a human experience immeasurably richer and deeper than that of any individual man can possibly be. He can know what is in man as no man can know it. He can be man as no man can be. His progressive revelation is the fullness of His own inner life unfolded in and to the world. This revelation, in the very action of which God lives, makes possible, and requires for its completion, an experience of the life of man in its central depths. Incarnation is a divine necessity. Theology has never had, in connexion with this great mystery of love, the courage of its convictions. Through fear of Sabellianism it has ascribed the Incarnation to a Being who, after all is said, is not quite the same as God, and has excluded the Father, the very fountain of Godhead, from the possibility of love's supremest manifestation. Faith sees God in Jesus, 'the whole of God, who has kept nothing back which He could have given us. It is very doubtful whether the framers of the old creed ever grasped this thought. The great expounder of the old theology, Augustine, certainly did not. The failure to enter into it showed itself not merely in the doctrine of God, but also in the theories of grace.'[1] The doctrines of God, of the person of Christ, and of salvation come together at this point. The Atonement is God's experience of what sin is and of what it has wrought in His universe. This experience, which is the salvation of the world, He purchased on the Cross. In His pain, the agony of sin-bearing, the condemnation of sin is absorbed, and love flows uninterrupted to the sinner. This is God, the very God, God manifest in flesh, Himself making atonement, offering Himself a sacrifice, commending His own love, reconciling the world to Himself. Here are not two, dealing with one another across the prostrate figure of the sinner. Here is One only, the living and true God, who is love, who is wholly in Jesus.

God who thus bore the Cross did not, even in that supreme action, exhaust the possibilities of His love or cease from His immanence and retire into motionless transcendence. The same vein of thought as separated God and Christ removed the Spirit a degree farther away and made this third article in the creed an appendix rather than a climax. Yet, if we trust the NT as the classic of Christian faith, the Spirit is not separable from God. The Spirit is God in His deepest immanence and His most glorious transcendence. It is strange that to many minds the work of the Spirit is a superfluity of feeble piety, whereas in the NT writings 'the reception of the Spirit is the whole of Christianity.'[2] The blame must lie with those who sought to make the Greek Absolute do duty for the Christian idea of God. The moral universe, constituted in the love which achieved a final victory on the Cross, is sustained by the same divine energy. As God is in Christ, so God-in-Christ is in the Spirit. This is not a subtlety of the analytic Greek mind. It is the synthetic

[1] T. M. Lindsay, *A Hist. of the Reformation*, Edinburgh, 1907, i. 472.

[2] See art. 'Holy Spirit,' in *DCG*.

utterance of faith, which knows in one experience 'the grace of the Lord Jesus Christ, and the love of God, and the fellowship of the Holy Spirit.'

To the idea of God as love there corresponds in man the function of faith. The idea of the Absolute drives religion into mysticism. The idea of God-in-Christ centres religion in the act of faith. Between the mystic state and the act of faith there is this radical distinction—that the former presupposes a God transcendent, incapable of incarnation; while the latter has for its object a God immanent, who, to be Himself, must needs enter human history and, in a sinful world, must needs be a suffering Saviour and hang upon a Cross. To speak of 'Christian mysticism' is, strictly speaking, to continue that confusion of Christianity and Neo-Platonism which has diverted Christian experience from its real fountain-head and given the Christian salvation a definitely non-Christian character.

If we are to keep to the Christian standpoint, we must regard the divine love in its action towards man and faith in its action towards God as being in the deepest sense correlative. All of God's saving action is concentrated in Christ. Upon Christ, accordingly, is concentrated the whole action of man in faith. All of Christianity, as the disclosure of God's being and character, is in Christ. All of Christianity, as a human experience, is in faith. Faith is fundamentally action, and is not to be defined through intellect or through feeling. The act of faith takes place when man meets God in Christ. In that supreme moment of life's discipline the love of God is revealed in Christ as the crown of all that is highest in human aspiration and the remedy of all that is deepest in human need. Man on his part makes reply by committing himself, in the fullness of his personal being, absolutely and for ever to this redeeming and perfecting love. This action is entirely simple. The analysis which resolves it into a complex of state and feelings disguises its true nature. It cannot be dissected because it is the man in action —the man in that action which sums up the full value of life. It is also all-inclusive, and underlies and comprehends the whole experience of salvation. Mediæval dualism had to add works to faith, if it was to make up the compound which was all it could think of as salvation. Protestant theologians even have anxiously explained that the faith that saves is a faith that 'works by love.' Of course it does! Not, however, as though the faith that works by love, and therefore is saving in its quality, were one among several forms of faith. It is faith itself, in the only sense which is possible in view of the saving action of God.

It saves because it carries the man from the standpoint of an individuality which strove to maintain itself apart from God to a position in which the individual, responding to the love of God, finds his need met, his nature satisfied, and the self which he has surrendered restored to him in fullness of power and certainty of victory. Faith is therefore an act which unites the man to Christ, in a sense deeper than mysticism can ever know. A union of being or substance, so far from being the loftiest and most religious of ideas, is one of the emptiest and least significant. The vital union is that of will and character, when man shares with God His thought, purpose, and power. And this union takes place, and can take place only, in faith. God gives Himse' to man in Christ. Man gives himself to God in faith. Christ is the point of union.

The language of the NT outdoes mysticism in the daring with which it affirms the continuity of the divine saving action. Love saved the world once for all in sacrifice. Love saves the world still by the same sacrificial ministry. Faith never swerves from its acknowledgment of the finality of the Cross. But it never hesitates to declare that, in believing, the soul is united to the dying and undying Christ. The man who has given himself to Christ has been crucified with Him, and therefore he lives, with a life which is really the presence of the indwelling love. Therefore also he has this rank and function, that through him the redemption of the world is proceeding still towards its assured consummation. Love never loses its vocation. It is always redemptive, always vicarious and sacrificial. The salvation of the world is the sacrificial ministry of Jesus continued in those who in their persons 'make up the full sum of all that Christ had to suffer.'

The confidence that that divine sacrifice will be crowned by the fulfilment of God's eternal will of salvation is the religious ground of the hope of immortality and the expectation of the Parousia.

This idea of God and this function of faith are not forms of thought imposed by theology on the Christian salvation. They lie within it, as the very secret of Christianity. They came into the world in Christ. They created Christian experience in the 1st cent. and are renewing it in the 20th. The Great War, amid all its darkness and agony, illumines the eternal being of God and verifies the abiding conditions of man's salvation. The love of God, sealed in sacrifice and reproduced in sacrificial service, is the redemption of the world.

The deepening experience of the Church requires a new effort of thought to express its vital meanings. A new theology must be the issue of the growing experimental knowledge of God.

The theology of the Cross requires a reconstruction of doctrine, in which the great Christian ideas of God, Christ, the Spirit, the Atonement, Salvation, Grace, Faith, the Church, and the Last Things shall be re-stated under the governance of one principle—the love that lives in sacrifice. The reign of the Greek Absolute is over. The unity which is the perpetual problem of thought and the abiding demand of the heart is given in Christ, in whom God is present in His fullness. Through Him, also, there is open to man that union with God which is the abiding demand of the human heart, and the realization of which in the act of faith is the Christian salvation, as a present possession, an unfailing energy, and a sure and certain hope.

LITERATURE.—The student must consult the primary sources, dictionary articles, and monographs dealing with outstanding names. On the leading aspects of the theme the following will be found helpful:

(i.) *On the contact of Christianity with the religions of the Hellenic-Roman world.*—F. Legge, *Forerunners and Rivals of Christianity*, 2 vols., Cambridge, 1915; Gilbert Murray, *Four Stages of Greek Religion*, London and New York, 1912; C. H. Moore, *The Religious Thought of the Greeks from Homer to the Triumph of Christianity*, London, 1916; W. Warde Fowler, *The Religious Experience of the Roman People*, do. 1911; T. R. Glover, *The Conflict of Religions in the Early Roman Empire*[3], do. 1909; A. Harnack, *The Mission and Expansion of Christianity in the First Three Centuries*[2], Eng. tr., 2 vols., do. 1908; J. Estlin Carpenter, *Phases of Early Christianity*, New York and London, 1916; Kirsopp Lake, *The Earlier Epistles of St. Paul*, London, 1911; Percy Gardner, *The Religious Experience of Saint Paul*, do. 1911; A. Schweitzer, *Paul and his Interpreters*, do. 1912; C. Clemen, *Primitive Christianity and its Non-Jewish Sources*, Eng. tr., Edinburgh, 1912: H. A. A. Kennedy, *St. Paul and the Mystery-Religions*, London, 1913; W. Morgan, *The Religion and Theology of Paul*, Edinburgh, 1917; M. H. P. Hatch, *The Pauline Idea of Faith in its Relation to Jewish and Hellenistic Religion*, Harvard and London, 1917.

(ii.) *On the relations between Christianity and philosophy.*—E. Caird, *The Evolution of Theology in the Greek Philosophers*, 2 vols., Glasgow, 1904; J. Watson, *The Philosophical Basis of Religion*, do. 1907, *The Interpretation of Religious Experience* (*Gifford Lectures*), 2 vols., do. 1912; E. Hatch, *The Influence of Greek Ideas and Usages upon the Christian Church*[6] (*HL*), London, 1897; W. R. Inge, art. 'Neo-Platonism,' in *ERE*, vol. x. p. 307[b], *The Philosophy of Plotinus*, 2 vols., London, 1918;

C. Elsee, *Neoplatonism in Relationship to Christianity*, Cambridge, 1908; **J. Ten Broeke**, *A Constructive Basis for Theology*, London, 1914. For recent philosophy **A. S. Pringle-Pattison**, *The Idea of God in the Light of Recent Philosophy*, Oxford, 1917, and **W. R. Sorley**, *Moral Values and the Idea of God*, Cambridge, 1918, are of the highest value and importance.

(iii.) *On the history of Christian thought.*—The historical works of **Harnack, Loofs, Dorner, Fisher, Orr**; **J. F. Bethune-Baker**, *Introd. to the Early Hist. of Christian Doctrine*, London, 1903; **C. Bigg**, *The Christian Platonists of Alexandria* (*BL*), Oxford, 1886, *The Origins of Christianity*, do. 1909; **A. V. G. Allen**, *The Continuity of Christian Thought*, London, 1895; **J. Vernon Bartlet** and **A. J. Carlyle**, *Christianity in History*, do. 1917; **H. M. Gwatkin**, *The Knowledge of God and its Historical Development*, 2 vols., Edinburgh, 1908; **V. F. Storr**, *The Development of English Theology in the 19th Century*, London, 1913; **H. B. Workman**, *Christian Thought to the Reformation*, New York, 1917; **A. C. McGiffert**, *Protestant Thought before Kant*, London, 1911; **E. C. Moore**, *An Outline of the Hist. of Christian Thought since Kant*, do. 1912; **H. O. Taylor**, *The Mediæval Mind*, 2 vols., do. 1914.

(iv.) *On the doctrine of the Atonement.*—**W. Adams Brown**, art. 'Expiation and Atonement (Christian),' in *ERE*, and literature referred to; **J. K. Mozley**, *The Doctrine of the Atonement*, London, 1915 (a careful bibliography); **R. S. Franks**, *A Hist. of the Doctrine of the Work of Christ*, 2 vols., London and New York, 1918; **J. Denney**, *The Christian Doctrine of Reconciliation*, do. 1917.

T. B. KILPATRICK.

SOUL.

SOUL (Primitive).—The English word 'soul' (and its equivalent in cognate European languages), in its primary meaning, designates an entity conceived as the cause or vehicle of the bodily life and psychical activities of the individual person. The soul is assumed to exist as a spiritual substance, in rather sharp antithesis to material substances, thus giving form to the contrast of soul and body (as constituents of man) and the assumption of their separability. This is, of course, a metaphysical conception, for which, in the range of primitive culture, there is no precise equivalent. Nevertheless, there are among primitive men forms of belief (so nearly universal in occurrence that they may be said to exist by a kind of instinct of the human intelligence) closely analogous to the metaphysical conception of the soul. The contrast under regard, in the more primitive intention, is not that of material and spiritual substances (for neither of these categories is recognized), but it is very near to the reflective distinction between form and energy; the primitive man everywhere makes a quick discrimination between the perceptual aspects of things and their powers or strengths: of the former he is suspicious; the latter he fears or strives to control by magical suggestion, by persuasion, by his own occult force; everywhere his interest centres in the hidden powers of things, which are for him their prime realities, and it is no marvel to find that everywhere he figures these powers under some evanescent analogy of the senses (the blood, the breath, the shade). It is these analogic figures of the primitive imagination that bear the names usually transcribed by the word 'soul'—itself, doubtless, originally, like *anima* and other classical equivalents, a term of the same class. Nor is it surprising that beliefs so bodied forth should assume various and fantastic guise, somewhat distorting their real identity.

1. Animism.—In the animistic *fond* of human thought there is recognized in nature no aristocratic class of soul-possessing beings: everything dignified by thinghood has its own power or function—however insignificant—and therefore its own soul. Indeed, what is designated by the name of a thing, as distinguished from the perceptual image or sense-object, is in a fair sense always its soul; for the foundation of naming is the discrimination of characteristic functions or powers; so that, in the broad truth, the nouns of a language represent the congregation of those souls in nature which the people speaking it has come to recognize. This is no merely primitive trait, but is true of all practical thinking, as distinguished from speculative analysis.

There is nevertheless, even for the raw animist, a certain position of privilege for human souls. They are by no means the most powerful in nature, either for good or for bad; but they are distinctly of the most concern and the most precious to their possessors. Moreover, they are the measures of the qualities of all other souls. It is true that, in a degree, they are distorted by fantasy; but, if the essence of primitive thought be disengaged from its figures, it will invariably be found that the measures of all other spiritual activities are human psychical activities, which are in the very truest sense the substantial powers of the human soul. One might fairly say that the primitive interpretation of nature (perhaps the mature interpretation also) is best represented by a harmonic proportion in which three terms are known and one is deduced; of the known terms, the first extreme is man's mind (chiefly his conations), while the means are first his own body, as the instrument of desire, and second other bodies, or sense-objects, viewed as the instruments of those animating desires of all nature which form the inferred extreme. Indeed, it is in direct harmony with all that we know of human psychology to affirm that the immediate foundation of belief in souls is the disparity between desire and realization: the 'I' which wants what it has not is distinct from the 'I' which is engrossed in what is, and, if the latter is a physical reality, the former must be a spiritual. If the desires of the conative 'I' were never balked or obstructed, probably there would arise no conceptions of other than human souls—which, when they do arise, naturally take on the colour of what they oppose. The body itself, in its weaknesses, assumes something of this obstructive character, and thus tends to sharpen its own fission from the animating desires and idealities which define themselves as its soul, while, again, in a sort of fantastic by-play, it becomes, as it were, the host of a whole group of disharmonious spirits—animal, passional, intellective—each striving, with no small malice, for the mastery.

2. Idea of the soul.—The distinction of embodied soul and disembodied is no easy one. Even in speculative philosophies there is usually involved change of quality with the change of state—a distinction preserved, in general, by the differing connotations of the English words 'soul' and 'spirit.' There are, in fact, three groups of conceptions of the soul, differing in relation to the body. The embodied soul—variously imaged—forms the key to the first group, the disembodied soul, or spirit, to the second, while intermediate between these is the twofold group, comprising the idols, or doubles, of living bodies and the ghosts, or haunters, of dead ones. All three are common to the most primitive stages of human thinking—among living races of men, at least. For the sake of convenience, and as having a natural priority, the embodied soul, which is in some sense the body's life, may be treated first, and primarily with reference to the figures by which it is most commonly imaged.

(*a*) *The life.*—Fundamentally, the soul is the 'life' of the body. In primitive thought this is shown in custom rather than in expression, and more particularly in those customs which show an inability to conceive soul and body in disunion. South America, Africa, and Australia contain the world's most primitive populations and most utter savages. Cannibalism is found in all three continents, and in all three it is associated with the conviction that he who eats of another man's body receives into himself the life or strength of his victim. The yet more repulsive custom of devouring the bodies of dead kinsmen (also found, sporadically, in the same continents) is based upon a similar notion, namely, that the life of the kindred is thus transmitted without loss from generation to generation. Innumerable funeral customs illustrate the primitive man's inability to separate in thought the visible body from its invisible life—indeed, the whole fact of burial or other funeral honours rests upon this confusion. John Fraser's monograph[1] gives a number of striking illustrations: a son was found supporting the body of his dead father on his chest and abdomen, for the purpose, as he explained, of keeping him warm; a mother bore the mummy of her son about with her for four years; another carried the dead body of her child until it fell into decay. These are but illustrations, at the savage extreme, of that feeling that the dead body is still not inanimate which must have underlain the burial impulses of palæolithic man, as it certainly did the elaborate rites of Egyptian funerals, and in some vague sense survives in modern consciousness.

(*b*) *The life-blood.*—One of the most natural of the tropes by which the 'life' is represented is the blood (*q.v.*), the 'fountain of life.' 'But flesh with the life thereof, which is the blood thereof, shall ye not eat' (Gn 9^{4})—only, in most primitive societies, the command is the reverse, and for a sacramental reason: he who partakes of the blood, be it of man or of animal, thereby imbibes the life and the strength, and the enemy whose blood is drunk is totally conquered. It is the blood, again, that 'cries for vengeance,' and, according to the old belief, gushes from the murdered corpse at the approach of the murderer. Finally, exsanguinate shades from the world below and gods in the heavens above alike delight in the odours of blood—in good sooth a spirit, which serves to invigorate their paler being. This is the blood of sacrifice and the blood of atonement, which is, in fact, the blood of life. The most astonishing of all developments of this idea was that of the Aztec, who believed that the sun is maintained in its course and the world in its order solely by the unceasing effluvia of human blood drenching altars and shrines. Nor is there any idea more ubiquitous in literature than that of blood symbolism.

(*c*) *The heart.*—Probably closely related to the preceding trope, and equally physical, is the conception of the heart as the seat of life. Whether this is because it is the 'bleeding heart' or the throbbing heart is difficult to determine. Certainly in aboriginal American rites, where the ritual use of the heart attained its greatest extravagances, the association with the blood is very close. The burial customs of the Egyptians, with a special vessel for the heart, are only an example of a widespread custom which has survived down into civilized Europe. Of course, in later times, the added symbolism of the heart, as the seat of the higher emotions (courage, love), may be partially related to classical psychology; but the foundation of the image is certainly primitive and many-sourced. The heart is sometimes conceived as having a special soul of its own; the American Indian prophet Keokuk commanded from his followers prayers for the heart, along with others for the family, name, life, etc.

J. F. Cunningham[1] could find among the Manyema little trace of a belief in souls. 'All the Manyema would admit was: "We know there is something living in a man during his life, because we can hear it beat. If that something is the soul, we know it no longer exists in a man when he dies. That is all we know."' Walter Roth,[2] reporting on the Guiana Indians, says that among them 'originally, not only the shadow, but also the heart, the head, and the more perceptible of all the parts of the body where there is a pulsation of the arteries, as well as perhaps the blood, the spittle, the footprint, and the bone were each regarded in the light of a Spirit or Something that was part and parcel of the body, and took its departure at the material death. . . . The Warrau expression for the shadow is *amého-ko-i*, while *ak-óbi* is their word for "heart" or for the heart's Spirit which, leaving the body at death, becomes their *Hebu*, or Bush Spirit. . . . The Island Caribs . . . held strong beliefs in a connection between spirits and an individual's heart- and pulse-beats: "they talked of the latter as the Spirit of the Hand; they spoke of the Spirit-something near the heart as Gonanni or Lanichi." This one at the heart was the principal one, which after death went to the sky in company with its Icheiri, or Chemin, to live there with other Familiar Spirits, and change into a young and new body. . . . Koch-Grünberg makes the interesting suggestion that certain procedures connected with some of the death festivals point to a belief in the bones constituting the real and final resting-place of the Spirit after the dismemberment (*Zersetzung*) of the body.' But the skeleton is more intimately connected with ghost-lore than with vital souls.

(*d*) *The breath.*—'And the Lord God formed man of the dust of the ground, and breathed into his nostrils the breath of life; and man became a living soul' (Gn 2^{7}). That the conception of the life as the breath is one of the most universal is attested by the great number of terms (נֶפֶשׁ, ψυχή, πνεῦμα, *anima*, *spiritus*—to cite Hebrew and classical examples) for the soul having 'breath' or 'wind' as their primary meaning. 'To breathe' and 'to live' are virtually literary synonyms. The Roman custom of a kinsman catching the last breath of his dying kin is doubtless but a more refined form of the superstition which causes a number of groups of savages to devour sacramentally the bodies, or parts of the bodies, of dead kindred. The wind-like character of liberated souls is expressed everywhere in ghostly literature. Job 7^{7}, 'Oh remember that my life is wind,' surely has a double intention; as also Ezk 37^{9}, 'Prophesy unto the wind, prophesy, son of man, and say to the wind, Thus saith the Lord God: Come from the four winds, O breath, and breathe upon these slain, that they may live.' Primitive equivalents are not far to seek. In many American rites the aspirate, as an element in ejaculation, appears to symbolize an intensification of the 'breathing life' which it represents. 'Heru! Hotoru. He!' is a Pawnee appeal to the winds. *Hotoru* is not the ordinary word for winds, but refers to them as supernatural powers.

'They are,' say the priests, 'from the breath of Tira'wa [Father Heaven] and they give life to man . . . they bring to man the breath by which he lives.'[3]

Even the universe, in some early philosophies, is conceived as having a windy soul.

The Tepehuane, according to C. Lumholtz,[4] place the seat of the soul between the stomach and the chest, and regard its

[1] *The Aborigines of New South Wales*, Sydney, 1892, sect. viii.

[1] *Uganda and Its Peoples*, London, 1905, p. 321.
[2] *30 RBEW* [1915], p. 152 f.
[3] A. C. Fletcher, *22 RBEW* [1904], pt. 2, p. 29 f.
[4] *Unknown Mexico*, New York, 1902, i. 434.

nature as breath. This is an interesting psycho-physiological belief for a primitive tribe. A Navaho legend tells of the creation of man and woman: 'It was the wind that gave them life. It is the wind that comes out of our mouths now that gives us life. When this ceases to blow, we die. In the skin at the tips of our fingers we see the trail of the wind; it shows us where the wind blew when our ancestors were created.'[1] Another legend tells of the death of a woman; the body was buried, but 'they all wondered what had become of her breath; they went in various directions to seek for its trail, but could find it nowhere.'[2] One of the most interesting passages in this connexion is in the myth of 'Isis and Yaulilik's Daughters.' Isis is told that his first child is dead. '"I don't want to live in this world. Bring me the other boy," he says. When the younger wife brought her child, Isis took it in his arms, put the top of its head to his mouth and drew a long breath. He took the breath out of the child and it was dead. He put the second child by the first, and said: "These children are half mine, and half yours. The breath is mine, the body is yours. I have taken the breath into myself. You can have the bodies."'[3] Very curious, for its suggestion of introspection, is an image in a Pima myth which likens sorrow to 'a wind four times twisting' about its object.[4]

These American examples might be paralleled from the lore of other races.

(*e*) *Flame*.—That the living body is warm and the corpse cold is a fact which in itself is sufficient to suggest that the 'life' is of the nature of fire.

'The life in your body and the fire in your lodge are the same and of the same date,' said the Shawnee prophet to his followers; 'if you suffer your fire to be extinguished, at that moment your life will be at its end.'[5]

The brand of Meleager is a Greek analogue, as, no doubt, is the sanctity of the hearth and its fire everywhere. Swamp-fires and other phosphorescences are almost universally objects of superstitious dread, being regarded as released souls. In sacred art the flammula, nimbus, and halo all come back to the notion that spirit is luminous; while the body lives, we speak of 'the fires of life' as burning, but the freed soul is as a tongue of flame. The Zuñi say of a death that the man's 'light is cut off.'

(*f*) *The shade or phantom*.—Considered as the body's life, life-blood, breath, or vital flame, the soul is not readily thought of as enduring in separation from its physical host; but, viewed (as almost universally it is) as the body's shadow (σκιά, *umbra*) or as its phantasmic likeness (εἴδωλον, *simulacrum*), it is with difficulty that it is conceived except in some degree of separation, as the body's friendly companion (*hospes comesque corporis*) or as its bloodless and boneless shade, after death. In myth and in literature, from the classical onwards, such visualized images of the soul naturally play a large rôle, but there are multitudes of instances in superstition and in nomenclature indicating the like ideas among the most savage peoples. Tylor[6] gives Tasmanian, Algonquin, Quiché, Arawak, Abipone, Zulu, Basuto, and Old Calabar examples of identifications of 'soul' with 'shadow,' and this list might be far extended.

The Zulus, explaining, say that people have souls which are not entirely confined to the body; 'they may occupy the roof of a man's hut, and if he changes his abode his soul flits also. The people often use the word *zitunzela* (from *izitunzi*, "shadows") to express their ideas of human spirits.'[7]

Superstitions about shadows cast by the body in sunlight (noon is a particularly perilous hour, when the shadow is small) and reflexion shown in the water are common, and figure frequently in myth. Probably, also, superstitions about the eye—the evil eye of the living, the glassy eye of the dead—are intimately associated with the notion that the images caught or reflected therein are souls. It is only a developed phase of this belief

[1] Washington Matthews, *Navaho Legends*, Boston and New York, 1897, p. 69.
[2] *Ib.* p. 78.
[3] J. Curtin, *Myths of the Modocs*, Boston, 1912, p. 37.
[4] F. Russell, *26 RBEW* [1908], p. 355.
[5] J. Mooney, *14 RBEW* [1896], pt. 2, p. 678.
[6] *PC*[3] i. 430.
[7] A. H. Keane, *Africa*, London, 1904, ii. 248; cf. *JAI* xx. [1891] 120.

which leads to veneration for crystals and the practice of mantic crystal-gazing, as well as to dread of the mechanical eye of the camera, or to pictured representation of one's form and features.

'Warraus assure me that on looking at a mountain for the first time the eyes are shut to prevent the person attracting or drawing the Shadow of the Spirit toward him. When one person looks at another, the former draws or drags the latter's shadow toward him, a principle on which these Indians explain the taking of a photograph. The Island Carib corpse is laid out with two weights on the eyes, that he may not see his parents, thus making them ill. Catlin gives an amusing instance among the Conibos of the Amazon of the local medicine-man preventing him painting any more portraits by exhorting the tribesmen as follows: "These things are a great mystery, but there you are, my friends, with your eyes open all night—they never shut: this is all wrong and you are very foolish to allow it. You never will be happy afterwards if you allow these things to be always awake at night. My friends, this is only a cunning way this man has to get your skins; and the next thing they will have glass eyes, and be placed among the skins of the wild beasts and birds and snakes." (The medicine-man had been to Para or some other place where he had seen the stuffed skins in a museum.) For a pregnant woman to look at the face of a corpse will draw trouble on her unborn child. It is possible that, perhaps on principles analogous to some of the preceding, most European races have adopted the practice of closing the eyes when in the attitude of prayer.'[1] Curtin gives a Modoc myth describing the resuscitation of a dead man: 'All the bones were dead but the eyes were living'[2]—and from this life the whole was reanimated.

(*g*) *The name*.—Superstitions about names and name-souls are as wide-spread as any. It should be observed that the name is quite as physical a thing for the unlettered as is the phantasm; it is an auditory or motor-auditory image, just as the phantasm is a visual image, and it possesses a perceptual reality quite different from that of the lettered symbol of book-learned peoples; *flatus vocis* is a nominalist phrase for a word, but it is just the vocal breath (above all in the chant) which is to the primitive one of the most powerful and compelling of all agents. Says J. W. Fewkes:

'When a Tusayan priest addresses a supernatural being of his mythology he believes he must do so through the medium of some object as a prayer bearer; he breathes his wish on meal and throws this meal to the god. The prayer bearer is thought to have a spiritual double or breath body which carries his wishes.'[3]

So the name is a kind of breath-body, though not so intimately joined to the man as the breath itself. Le Jeune[4] says that the Indians sometimes change their name on recovering from a severe sickness, and the Bellacoola believe that souls receive a new name, and speak a new language, when they reach the next world. Normally, children are not truly named until they reach a certain age and are capable of discretion. V. Stefánsson[5] gives a most interesting explanation of Eskimo beliefs connected with this custom:

'As the child grows up the soul with which he was born (the *nappan*) gradually develops in strength, experience, and wisdom, so that after the age of ten or twelve years it is fairly competent to look after the child and begins to do so; at that age it therefore becomes of less vital moment to please the guardian spirit (*atka*), and accordingly it is customary to begin forbidding children and punishing them.'

The guardian-spirit which controls the child previous to this age is supposed to be some ancestral soul, and all the child's words are the utterance of this soul up to the age when its own soul assumes sway, and it is called after a name of its own. Frequently it is supposed that the name of the guardian is known, and the young child is called by this name. One of Curtin's[6] Modoc myths tells of a babe that cried continuously until addressed by its true name. These beliefs are, of course, associated with the almost universal primitive belief in rebirth, especially of very young

[1] W. E. Roth, *30 RBEW*, p. 299 f. [2] P. 34.
[3] *Rep. Smithsonian Institution*, 1895, p. 689.
[4] *Jesuit Relations and Allied Documents*, ed. R. G. Thwaites, Cleveland, 1896–1901, xvi. 'Quebec and Hurons, 1639,' p. 203.
[5] *My Life with the Eskimo*, New York and London, 1913, p. 399 f.
[6] P. 6.

children (the Aztec, *e.g.*, had a special limbo for souls of babes, who alone can be born anew). Ancestor-worship is naturally closely associated with name-souls. Probably this was what was meant by the Indian who told Le Jeune[1] that 'the body has a soul of its own which some call the soul of their Nation.' In the far Orient the Annamites at least address prayers to the clan ancestor, to the spirits of parents and grandparents to three generations, and then collectively to the soul of the family as a whole.[2] Naturally all worship of the *manes* tends to become associated with the clan name. See artt. NAMES.

3. Psychology.—The course of historic psychology has been from a psycho-physiological (such as Aristotle's) to a predominantly psychological type of theory; older speculations on the constitution of man distinguished a group of souls (nutritive, passional, intellective, and the like) associated with the several parts of the body; later theories came to assert the unity of the spiritual substance and to make of psychology, not a description of the several souls for which the body acts as a single host, but an account of the several powers or 'faculties' of the single soul. Primitive theories belong to the older type: the whole man is looked upon as composed of a group of entities, physical and psychical, which disperse with the dissolution of his body. Death is rarely regarded as the liberation of an imprisoned spirit to a more glorified existence; rather the future existence of the immortal parts is at best a kind of mutilated existence, and not even Elysium is a fair compensation for the loss of that completer manhood which is truly realized only in the flesh. The very ancient and wide-spread notion that the souls of the departed await in a kind of neutral limbo the day of their reincarnation as men is surely a reflexion of the feeling that the disembodied is somehow dismembered, while the equally common conception of the ghost as vengeful and malicious but pictures its own dissatisfaction with its unhappy state. To the primitive mind the normal man is the physical man, whose souls (for he commonly owns several) are in the nature of more or less dispensable baggage—something that he *has*, rather than *is*.

In the passage cited from Roth's account of Guiana Indian beliefs[3] it is pointed out that along with the shadow there are souls for head, heart, blood, spittle, and even footprint. Indeed, there is hardly a part of the body that is not somewhere believed to own a spiritual double, which is its life, so that the whole bodily life may be said to be possessed, as it were, in severalty. The bones, the marrow of the bones, the eyes, the hair, the belly—all are parts with which a residential soul is found associated in primitive thinking. An interesting Iroquoian conception, recorded by J. N. B. Hewitt,[4] regards the brain as the seat of the soul, and death by braining is held to render the soul stupid, implacable, and capable of committing excesses. The Maoris of New Zealand are a Polynesian instance of a primitive people seating the soul in the head. Le Jeune[5] says of the Canadian Indians: 'They distinguish several souls in one and the same body. An old man told us some time ago that some savages had as many as two or three souls; that his own had left him more than two years before, to go away with his dead relatives—that he no longer had any but the soul of his own body, which would go down into the grave with him'—nor is it difficult to imagine that, to a desolate old man whose kindred and friends were gone, his life should seem but the soul-bereft shadow of what it had been.

Belief in a plurality of souls, as associated with the one body or forming the one person, is very wide-spread, and is, indeed, a natural consequence of the variety of tropes employed to designate the spiritual entity. The heart, the flesh, the life, the name, the family, were distinguished by Keokuk. The Iroquois have separate words for the mind, soul, ghost, life, strength, brain-soul. The Haida distinguish mind, ghost, discarnate soul, and have two words for embodied soul. These are sporadic American examples. Some of the Melanesians believe that a man possesses as many as seven souls, of differing types; and belief in the possession of two or more is frequent among the primitive. An amusing instance is the Bagobo notion that man has two souls, a good and a bad, which respectively pass to paradise and hell in the hereafter; we may suspect that the moral terminus comes as a result of foreign influence. Such ideas endure into higher cultural stages. The Egyptian is notable, with its distinction of *ka* (genius), *khaibit* (shadow), *khu* (life or intelligence), *ba* (soul proper), *ran* (name), together with something like animistic personification of the mummy, heart, strength, form. But hardly less complex is the old Persian spiritual dissection of a man into body, life, form, soul, and *fravashi* (genius); or the Roman, which in addition to the *genius* of a man (fem. *juno*), distinguished the tomb-haunting *umbra*, the *manes*, descending to Orcus, and the *spiritus*, climbing to its ethereal element above, and more or less identified with the mind-soul, *anima*. Even for near moderns 'the constitution of the soul . . . is conflate of the mind, spirit and animal soul, or idolum';[1] while there is to-day a degree of separation of psychic entities implied in the meanings of 'soul,' 'spirit,' 'mind,' 'consciousness.'

The converse of the idea of the possession of multiple souls is the notion of the existence of soulless men. This is by no means an uncommon primitive notion. There are tribes, especially in Africa, apparently with no belief in souls, at any rate as in any sense separable from the body; while in numerous African and Polynesian instances women and lower-caste people are regarded as soulless. Cunningham gives a humoresque incident:

'A chief pointed at a poor peasant and said: "He have an immortal soul? I cannot believe it; but I will admit that perhaps Wakoli or Luba had a soul. Wakoli had four hundred wives!"'[2]

Obviously, in cases of reported disbelief in souls among primitive men, what is commonly meant is disbelief in a separable entity endowed with immortal life; and as to this dogma primitive men are hardly more in agreement than are civilized. On the other hand, some discrimination of body and soul, or, more exactly, of the body and its indwelling life, is as universal as is the animistic apprehension of nature. Even among peoples like the Fuegian Yahgans, among whom there is no clear evidence of a belief in the existence of gods of any sort, there is still a lively apprehension of the wandering (and more or less physical) simulacra of men.

4. Discarnate souls.—It has been remarked above that the phantasmic soul, or double, is less intimately bound to the body than are other forms. Even during the life of the body it may journey abroad, appearing to those gifted with the second sight as the co-walker (fetch, wraith, double-ganger, idolum) of the living, and visiting in dreams those for whom its master has a message or upon whom he meditates inimical action. Shamans make great use of their souls as messengers, to seek information from places remote, while prophets use them for the similar purpose of visiting the abodes of the dead or the homes of the gods. It is even advisable at times for a man setting out on a perilous task to have his soul extracted by a competent shaman and kept at home to ensure his own safe return; while sickness is caused not only by the body's becoming the host of unwelcome foreign spirits (which the shaman must extract), but often by the inconsiderate *Wanderlust* of the patient's soul, which the medicine-man's own spirit must

[1] *Jes. Rel.* xvi. 192. [2] *Anthropos*, ii. [1907] 966.
[3] *30 RBEW*, p. 152.
[4] 'The Iroquoian Concept of the Soul,' *JAFL* viii. [1895] 111.
[5] *Jes. Rel.* xvi. 191.

[1] S. Purchas, *Microcosmus*, London, 1619, ch. lviii. p. 568.
[2] P. 118.

hale home in order to ensure a cure. Sometimes, even, there are stationed on the road to the home of the dead, wardens whose business it is to turn back souls which are leaving the body before the appointed hour, while, again, a man may, by desperate effort, recover his own departing soul.

De Smet[1] gives a striking Chippewa story to this effect. A chief, left on the battle-field for slain, accompanies the war-band home, trying to make himself known to them, but all his solicitations and commands are unheeded. Arrived at the home camp, he finds his wife in mourning; he shouts in her ear, 'I am hungry! I am thirsty!' She thinks she hears a rumbling sound, but she sees no one. Frustrated in his attempts, he turns back to the battle-field, but, as he nears it, he finds a fire in his path, which moves as he moves, ever thwarting his approach. In despair he cries: 'I also am a spirit; I am seeking to return into my body; I will accomplish my design. Thou wilt purify me, but thou shalt not hinder the realization of my project. This day I will triumph over thee, Spirit of Fire!' And with a desperate effort he darts into the flame, to awake, as from a long trance, in his own weakened body.

But death itself does not result in a complete separation of soul and body—or perhaps it would be truer to say that the errant soul and the body-soul, or ghost, pursue different destinies. De Smet[2] says that many of the Indians believe in two souls, one of which is admitted to their paradise, while the other, the body-soul, hovers near the burial-place; and in another connexion he remarks that 'nothing but the hope of gain could ever induce an Indian to go alone in a burying-ground at night.'[3] Probably the original of the Bagobo belief in dual souls was of this nature—which is, in fact, the popular belief of uneducated Europeans. As among Europeans, too, it is common everywhere to find the ghost associated with the skeleton, or as wearing the pale or mutilated aspect of the dead body. Numerous tales have for their motive accounts of the commerce of the living with their dead kindred, who are skeletons by day but phantasmal ghosts by night. Not only do men meet and converse with these departed beings, but there are marriages between the dead and the living, and children are born to them, though never normal children. A Bellacoola tale of such a child describes it as a bodiless head which must never touch the ground; when it does so, it disappears into the under world. One of the most enlightening of these tales is recorded by F. Boas.[4]

A man visits the bones of the dead, which at night assume the forms of his kinsmen; their boats are full of holes and covered with moss, and they take in their nets dead leaves and twigs, which to them are fish. The man discovers that by speaking aloud—for the spirits all speak in low voices—he can reduce them to the condition of skeletons. This he does, to their annoyance, so that they send him back to the land of the living. But, disobeying their commands, he dies; and now, coming as a shade into the land of the dead, he finds that the ghosts, their canoes, and the fish that they take are like the full-bodied beings of the life that he has left.

This is an interesting effort, on the part of the aboriginals, to imagine the state of the dead, which to themselves is altogether like that of the living, and only from the standpoint of the latter is seen as a form of mutilated existence.

The notions that ghosts speak in whistling voices, that they nibble feebly at food left for them, that in stature they are manikins or doll-like, and that generally they are given to a kind of panic fear of embodied men are all found, not merely in Homer, but throughout the primitive world. Sometimes these ghosts are corpse-like in appearance; and this is especially true if the body has been mutilated. In such cases the ghost is usually vengeful, ready to wreak ill where it can. Often, however, the ghosts simply reflect the bodily condition, without any necessary malice.

[1] *Life, Letters and Travels of Father Pierre-Jean de Smet, S.J.*, 4 vols., New York, 1905, pp. 1047–1053.
[2] P. 1075.
[3] P. 941.
[4] 'Doctrine of Souls among the Chinook Indians,' *JAFL* vi. [1893] pp. 39–43.

The Pawnee have a special class of ghosts of scalped men, who avoid the abode of the happy dead and the eyes of the living for the same reason—shame of their condition. They form a sort of society of disconsolates, and address one another by terms descriptive of their estate as 'One-Hair,' 'Forehead Hair,' etc. The Zuñi, more humanly, expect to see their ancestral spirits in their natural guise.

'The old men too feeble to walk will come leaning on a cane, the mother with her son walking before her, her child led by the hand, her younger child carried on her back, the infant in her arms, and her unborn child'[1]—all not in the flesh, but in the ghost-self, just as in nature.

Sometimes the ghost, or body-soul, hovers near the burial-place in the form of a bird, an insect, or a small animal. It is interesting to find the butterfly occurring as such an embodied soul in the lore of N.W. America.[2] The same insect is common in Aztec art as a symbol of the breath, or breath-soul, shown on the lips of goddesses. From such a notion to the conception of reincarnation in animal form is but a step—a step which has been taken by primitive men the world over. Nocturnal creatures, like owls and bats, or earth-dwelling animals, such as beetles, serpents, and even worms, are forms in which souls are likely to be re-embodied. In not a few tribes these re-embodiments go progressively down in the animal scale, and may end by final departure from the earth or utter obliteration. Here, however, we are encroaching upon the field of beliefs in the future state of souls, for which the reader is referred to the artt. BLEST (ABODE OF THE), ESCHATOLOGY, INCARNATION, STATE OF THE DEAD, TRANSMIGRATION.

5. The powers of souls.—The primary function of the soul is, of course, to keep the body in life; the soul *is* the life of the body; and, although soul and body may be temporarily separated, as in sleep or trance or even with the body still wakeful and active, with no damage incurred, none the less their lasting separation is death. Further, it would appear from a considerable variety of beliefs that the soul's comfort and the fullest exercise of its powers depend upon its connexion with some sort of body. Souls haunt, in ghostly forms, even mutilated and decaying bodies; they strive, in the form of familiars or demons, to obtain an entrance into and a partial control of the bodies of the living, from which they sometimes succeed in ejecting the native owner (for the plight in which Dante pictures Friar Alberigo—soul in hell while his devil-animated body still moves in the world of men—is no marvel to the primitive imagination); while, finally, discarnate existence in the other world is commonly represented as a kind of limbo in which the spirits await rebirth as full-bodied men; or, if it be an Elysium, there is in its pallid joys always an element of dissolvent illusion. Even artificial and substitute bodies which men supply—carven blocks and the like—are attractive to the unhoused spirits, who may be lured or charmed into them, there finding a new contact with the life of men, whose idols or tutelars they become. The Indians of the N. Pacific Coast occasionally carve portraits of deceased persons, as mortuary or other memorials;[3] and they are not without legends of spirits of the deceased taking possession of these. One such legend, truly affecting, is recorded by J. R. Swanton.[4]

A young chief had lost his wife, but kept by him, dressed in her clothing, a portrait image which, out of pity for his sorrow,

[1] M. C. Stevenson, *23 RBEW* [1904], p. 236.
[2] *ZE* xxiv. [1892] 398.
[3] See C. T. Emmons, 'Portraiture among the North Pacific Coast Tribes,' *American Anthropologist*, new ser., xvi. [1914] 59–67.
[4] *Bull. 39 BE* [1909], p. 181 f.

a carver had made for him. 'One day, while he sat mourning very close to the image, he felt it move. . . . At first he thought that the movement was only his imagination, yet he examined it every day, for he thought that at some time it would come to life. . . . One day, after the chief had had it for a long, long time, he examined the body and found it just like that of a human being. Still, although it was alive, it could not move or speak. . . . The woman moved around very little and never got to talk, but her husband dreamed what she wanted to tell him. It was through his dreams that he knew she was talking to him.'

This incident is surely illuminating, both as to the motives which lead to art among primitive peoples and as to those which lead to idolatry. Here it is clearly the power of love which lures the departed soul to the man-wrought body; the complementary form, where magical compulsion is the force employed, is best illustrated by the account given by R. E. Dennett[1] of the W. African making of a 'Fetish-into-which-Nails-are-Driven':

'A palaver is held, and it is there decided whose Kulu [soul] it is that is to enter into the Muamba tree and to preside over the fetish to be made. A boy of great spirit, or else, above all, a great and daring hunter, is chosen. Then they go into the bush and call his name. The Nganga priest cuts down the tree, and blood is said to gush forth. A fowl is killed and its blood is mingled with the blood that they say comes from the tree. The named one then dies, certainly within ten days. His life has been sacrificed for what the Zinganga consider the welfare of the people. They say that the named one never fails to die. . . . People pass before these fetishes (Zinkici Mbowu), calling on them to kill them if they do, or have done, such and such a thing. Others go to them and insist upon their killing so and so, who has done or is about to do some fearful injury. And as they swear or make their demand, a nail is driven into the fetish, and the palaver is settled so far as they are concerned. The Kulu of the man whose life was sacrificed upon the cutting of the tree sees to the rest.'

Mediumistic powers are nearly akin to the soul's yearning for embodiment. Virtually all primitive men believe in such powers, though it is commonly supposed that they come by special endowment and preparation—the latter often strenuous to a degree—in many instances through death and resurrection, as is assumed. Primitive mythology abounds in tales of men acquiring supernatural strength by the thorny road of bodily destruction and restoration. By such means the soul of the medium, or shaman, is supposed to acquire the faculty of direct intercourse with the world of spirits, and usually to have as his especial agent or 'control' a genius, tutelar, or familiar spirit, whose powers reinforce his own. Indeed, it is not a little remarkable to discover virtually all the phenomena of modern spiritualism (if it be modern) among savage peoples, remote in time and place. Le Jeune's description of a Montagnais shamanistic performance, written in 1634,[2] would hold, *mutatis mutandis*, for a spiritualistic *séance* in central New York: there is the medium's cabinet, the darkened room, the singing, the winds, voices, and 'physical phenomena,' and along with these prophecies of life and death. The shaman (although Le Jeune believed him to be a great rogue) was obviously sincere. 'Enter thou thyself into the tent,' he said, 'and thou wilt see that thy body will remain below, and thy soul will mount on high.' The Seneca Indians of New York State still continue similar practices,[3] as do the Chippewa tribes in their Midḗ society.[4] The Zuñi have a curious belief that in the old times the souls of the dead used to return in the flesh to converse with the living, but their presence caused a great mortality; now they come as spirits, and only those gifted with a superior sight, their mediums, can see them.[5]

Apart from preserving the body in life, the important powers of the soul are curative and

1 *At the Back of the Black Man's Mind*, London, 1906, p. 93.
2 *Jes. Rel.* vi., 'Quebec, 1633-34,' p. 163 ff.
3 'Secret Medicine Societies of the Seneca,' *American Anthropologist*, new ser., xi. [1909] 161-185.
4 W. J. Hoffman, 'The Midḗ'wiwin,' *7 RBEW* [1891], p. 149 ff., also *14 RBEW* [1896], pt. i. p. 66 ff.
5 M. C. Stevenson, *23 RBEW*, p. 236.

clairvoyant. As clairvoyant, the soul is a kind of scout, able to penetrate times, places, and substances closed to the body.

A curious Cree tale, narrated by de Smet,[1] tells of a war party being guided on its course by a girl with blindfold eyes; 'the manitou of war was supposed to guide her.' The Chippewa have an interesting legend of having once numbered among them a flying man, a powerful magician whose 'medicine' was a feather which he could cause to enter his body, thereby enabling him to fly and spy out the enemy.[2]

Crystal-gazing is suggested in numerous rites and myths.

The N.W. Coast Indians tell of a man to whom a serpent gave a transparent stone which led him through all lands; the Spanish chronicles tell of an obsidian mirror in which Montezuma saw ominous images; the Cakchiquel employed a similar stone in testing the guilt or innocence of accused men; the Inca Yupanqui is said to have been given a crystal by the sun, in which he saw whatever he desired to discover—these are widely separated American examples.

Belief in telepathy is evidenced in many tales: 'All spoke with their hearts; hearts spoke to hearts, and lips did not move,' is a Zuñi expression.[3] Stories of 'veridical hallucinations' and prophetic visions are numerous. Of the former J. S. Polack[4] gives a number of examples—but the account of savage instances of this phenomenon would be bulky. Prophecies by shamans or mediums are still more numerous in primitive lore: there is a whole group of legendary American Indian prophecies of the coming of white men and of disaster to the native life recorded in the Spanish annals; much of this may be supposed to be apocryphal, but it is at least striking that Cortes should have been discovered by watchers posted on the coast at Montezuma's orders, on the look-out for the coming of the prophesied god, and that the first presents which the emperor of the Aztec sent to the new-comer were mainly the appropriate apparel of this god, Quetzalcoatl. Gifted souls, however, see not only into the future, but also into the past; it is thus, at least, that Mohave shamans explain their knowledge of creation; they were present at the beginning of the world, as in a dream. This belief is, of course, entirely consonant with the theory of transmigration. Naturally, in the main, clairvoyant powers are called into play to satisfy more immediate interests: to discover the fate of the absent, to recover stolen property, to find food or treasure. Dreams are regarded as great aids in all this (for the soul journeys in dreams—this is the common explanation), but, when the search is difficult, the shaman is called into service, with his more potent or active faculties.

A striking example, where the seeker was a white man consulting a Zulu doctor, is given by David Leslie:[5]

The white man's eight hunters were overdue, having been long gone on an elephant hunt, and at the solicitation of his native servants he consulted the doctor. 'The doctor made eight little fires—that being the number of my hunters; on each he cast some roots, which emitted a curious sickly odour and thick smoke: into each he cast a small stone, shouting, as he did so, the name to which the stone was dedicated; then he ate some "medicine," and fell over into what appeared to be a trance for about ten minutes, during all which time his hands kept moving. Then he seemed to wake, went to one of the fires, raked the ashes about, looked at the stone attentively, described the man faithfully, and said: "This man died of fever and your gun is lost." To the next fire as before: "This man" (correctly described) "has killed four elephants," and then he described the tusks. The next: "This man" (again describing him) "has been killed by an elephant, but your gun is coming home," and so on through the whole, the men being minutely and correctly described; their success or non-success being equally so. I was told where the survivors were, and what they were doing, and that in three months they would come out, but as they would not expect to find me waiting on

1 P. 520.
2 F. Densmore, *Bull. 45 BE* [1910], p. 98.
3 M. C. Stevenson, *23 RBEW*, p. 52.
4 *Manners and Customs of the New Zealanders*, London, 1840, i. 268 f.
5 *Among the Zulus and Amatongas*², Edinburgh, 1875, pp. 224-226.

them there so long after the time appointed, they would not pass that way. I took particular note of all this information at the time, and to my utter amazement it turned out correct in every particular. It was scarcely within the bounds of possibility that this man could have had ordinary intelligence of the hunters; they were scattered about in a country two hundred miles away.'

If this narrative is to be trusted, it certainly outdoes all that is ascribed to the tested clairvoyants of the civilized world.

The curative or psycho-therapeutic powers of souls appear in every variety of use of suggestion and hypnotism, and amid practically all peoples. These functions have their obverse use in the power to inflict disease, or even death, upon an absent or unconscious victim. All such practices are interbound with ritual and magical observances; and, indeed, they can hardly be dealt with except in connexion with such customs. See artt. DISEASE AND MEDICINE, DIVINATION, MANA, PSYCHO-THERAPEUTICS, SHAMANISM, SPIRITISM.

LITERATURE.—The literature dealing with primitive conceptions of the soul is enormous, being co-extensive with the study of primitive religion and superstition. In general, it may be said to fall into three classes: (*a*) reports on the beliefs and myths of particular tribes, from travellers, missionaries, and anthropological field-workers—abundant both in book form and in the ethnological journals (notably *JAI* [*JRAI*], *FL*, *JAFL*, *RHR*, *ZE*, and *Anthropos*); (*b*) critical and comparative studies of primitive religious ideas, of which the most important, probably in any language, are E. B. Tylor, *PC*3, 2 vols., London, 1891; A. Lang, *Myth, Ritual and Religion*3, 2 vols., do. 1899; and J. G. Frazer, *GB*3, 12 vols., do. 1911–15; with these should be named E. Durkheim, *Les Formes élémentaires de la vie religieuse*, Paris, 1912, Eng. tr., London and New York, 1915; (*c*) briefer résumés of the subject in works on comparative religion and descriptive or comparative ethnology, few being better conceived than the introductory lecture of S. Reinach, *Orpheus: Hist. général des religions*, Paris, 1909, Eng. tr., London and New York, 1909. See also the 'Literature' and bibliographical references of the artt. cited in this art.; also 'Literature' of artt. ANIMISM, GOD (Primitive and Savage), PRAYER, COMMUNION WITH DEITY. Probably the most comprehensive study since Tylor's *PC*, centring upon the idea of soul in primitive religion, is A. E. Crawley, *The Idea of the Soul*, London, 1909, containing much bibliography. The volumes of *The Mythology of All Races* (Boston, 1916 ff.) will be found of use as giving conceptions classified by racial groups.

H. B. ALEXANDER.

SOUL (Buddhist).—Few words are more ambiguous than 'soul,' as any dictionary will testify. Nor is there any one word in the religious literature of Buddhism which can be said to coincide with it in either extension or intension. The principal terms in the canonical literature which translators have rendered, sometimes or always, by 'soul' are *jīva*, *attan*, *satta*, and in the Abhidhamma section *puggala*. In the somewhat later *Questions of King Milinda*, *jīva* is preferred, and with it the rare word *vedagū* ('sentient one'). The other three terms are used, in connexion with their contexts, only when canonical passages are quoted.[1]

Jīva is literally 'living thing.' It is a term imported from the staple terms of religious schools opposed to Buddhism, and occurs only[2] in the title of one among many debatable propositions classed as erratic or heretical:

'Is the *jīva* the same as . . . (or) . . . a different thing from the bodily frame (*aññañ jīvaṃ aññaṃ sarīraṃ*)?'[3]

It may thus be fairly rendered by 'soul' in the Hebrew sense—'and man became a living soul.' But the Buddhist canonical books do not select the term *jīva* when they are uttering doctrines concerning man's spiritual nature as contrasted with his bodily and sensuous faculties. They choose one of the other three terms *attan* (nom. case, *attā*), *satta*, *puggala*. The last two mean a (living, intelligent) being, a person, and are used in ordinary discourse simply to represent any fellow-being.[1] The first is also closely connected with 'living thing' in that it means breath (Skr. *ātman*; cf. πνεῦμα, 'spirit'). In ordinary discourse it means self,[2] and in the Abhidhamma *Piṭaka*, the *Milinda*, and the *Netti* it rarely occurs in any philosophical argument. But the earlier *Sutta*-literature uses *attā* repeatedly in controversial discourse concerning a right conception of what we should call soul or spirit. At the same time, the *Suttas* show an unhesitating acceptance of the term wherever we should say 'self.'[3] These contexts lead us to infer that such discourses were uttered at a period when the speakers were making a strong protest, not against man's spiritual nature, but against a certain religious or philosophical attitude in vogue in their time, concerning that nature viewed as *attā* or *ātman*. It needs but a glance into Vedāntic literature—*e.g.*, the *Upaniṣads*, notably those reckoned to be pre-Buddhistic, and the *Bhagavad-Gītā*—to find everywhere a unique cult of *ātman* (called also *Brahman*). It was regarded as divinity universally immanent, but especially so in the human organism. Conceived materialistically as a fine substance, located in the heart, and compared as to size and shape to a variety of small objects,[4] this microcosm was held to possess, like the macrocosmic divinity, the essential qualities of permanence (quitting the impermanent body at death), immutability, bliss, and omnipotence. And to discern the essential identity of microcosm and macrocosm was to attain true insight.

E.g., 'in that subtle essence . . . all that exists has its self. It is the true. It is the self, and thou art it. . . . The infinite is bliss . . . is the self. He who loves the self . . . becomes a self-ruler; lord and master in all the worlds. The self is without decay, death, grief.'[5] 'The embodied one which is eternal . . . is not born, nor does it ever die . . . unchangeable, primeval . . . all-pervading, stable, firm.'[6]

It is on this point of soul or spirit or self, as a thing different in kind from the rest of the individual, that Buddhism joins issue with Vedāntism. To such a dualism it is in fundamental antithesis. Its philosophy of life may be said to be based on the axioms, *sabbaṃ aniccaṃ, sabbaṃ dukkhaṃ* ('all is impermanent,' 'all is [liable-to] suffering'). In no constituent of the living being was any exception to this rule of nature to be found. And, since *attā*, as currently taught, was essentially permanent, unchanging, blissful, powerful, there could be none of *attā* so conceived in the living being:

'What think ye then? Is body, is mind permanent, or impermanent?' 'Impermanent, sir.' 'Is that which is impermanent liable to suffering or not?' 'It is liable, sir.' 'But is it proper to say of that which is impermanent, liable to suffering and to change, This is of me; I am this; this is the soul (self) of me?'[7]

The individual is entirely phenomenal, governed by the laws of life. Were there in him a microcosmic emanation of the superphenomenal *ātman* or *Brahman*, he would have the power of deity to remould himself 'nearer to the heart's desire,' and thus at will to transcend those laws—

1 *The Questions of King Milinda*, tr. Rhys Davids (*SBE* xxxv.), Oxford, 1890; on pp. 41, 48, 86, 132, *jīva* is used; on pp. 86, 111, *vedagū*; on p. 45, *satta* ('being'); on p. 67, *attā*; on p. 40, *puggala*. Three centuries or so later Buddhaghoṣa has reverted to the use of *attā* (cf. *Sumangala Vilāsinī*, i. 194 f.). The need for protest mentioned below may no longer have been pressing—he wrote in Ceylon—but he was commenting on canonical arguments. He also uses *vedaka*, *kāraka* ('feeler,' 'agent'), for the soul or self-entity (*Visuddhi Magga*, xvii., xx.).

2 Rhys Davids, *Dialogues of the Buddha*, Oxford, 1899–1910, ii. 359 f., uses *jīva*, but the Buddhist origin of this *Sutta* (*Pāyāsi*) is doubtful. Cf. the term in Jainism (see art. JAINISM, 4, i. (*b*)).

3 *Dialogues*, i. 204, 254; *Saṃyutta Nikāya*, 215, 258, etc.

1 Animals are never so referred to. They would be included under the yet wider name *pāna* ('breathing thing'). But *devas* (spirits, deities), who are for Buddhists reborn mankind, would be included.

2 See art. SELF (Buddhist).

3 *E.g.*, as prefix in compounds, and in oblique cases.

4 Cf. Rhys Davids, 'Theory of Soul in the Upanishads,' *JRAS*, Jan. 1899.

5 *SBE* i. [1900] 101 f., 123 f. (*Chhāndogya-Upaniṣad*, vi. 8 f., vii. 23 ff.).

6 *SBE* viii. [21898] 45 (*Bhagavad-Gītā*, ii. 27 ff.).

7 *Majjhima Nikāya*, iii. 19 f., and elsewhere.

'If the body . . . if any of the four mental factors were the soul (self), the body . . . the mind would not be subject to disease, and we should be able to say: Let my body . . . my mind be, or not be, so and so.'[1]

Into a complex or congeries of these five varieties of functionings or faculties called *khandhas* (Skr. *skandhas*), or groups, the individual can be analyzed without residuum. In fact, according to Buddhaghoṣa,[2] it was in order to effect an exhaustive analysis for the rejection of ātmanistic dualism that the teaching at its outset adopted this fivefold classification. And, living personality being thus resolved, the teaching proceeded to repudiate any identification or coincidence of an extra-phenomenal self or soul with any one of the five. Immanence was equally rejected:

'The well-taught disciple . . . regards not the bodily qualities as *attā*, nor that they have *attā*, nor are in *attā*, nor that *attā* is in them. Neither does he hold any of these views regarding the *khandha* of feeling, nor of perception, nor of mental activities, nor of consciousness. For him each one of these *khandhas* changes, becomes other, he does not get thoughts [which bring about] a recurrence of changing *khandhas*.'[3]

The *khandhas*, bodily and mental, were thus declared to be 'empty' (*suñña*) of any unchanging essence.[4] That which was wholly impermanent and liable to suffering was also inevitably *an-attā*, 'soulless,' or, as we should prefer to say, 'without *Ātman*.'

It should not for a moment be inferred, on this account, that Buddhist teaching countenanced any belief in a total annihilation of body and mind at death. Beside the error of eternalism (*sassăta-vāda*), or indwelling immutable entity, it set the error of annihilationism (*uccheda-vāda*).[5] Beside the doctrine of *anicca* it set that of *kamma*, or the transmitted force of the act, bodily and mental.[6] The self or soul *is* the *khandha* complex, ever changing but ever determined by its (or their) antecedent character. Hence the long-drawn-out line of life is a fluctuating curve of evolving and degenerating experience, into which it is logically unthinkable to intrude an immutable factor. But annihilationism was not as prevalent an error as was eternalism. Had it been so, we may feel confident that, to the oft-repeated trio, *anicca*, *dukkha*, *an-atta*, Buddhist teaching would have added a fourth, such as *punabbhăva* ('renewed becoming'), or the like. The future state of the living is constantly referred to, but the teaching is not so much that there will be rebirth as of what kind, because of the present life, it is likely to be. And the *an-atta* doctrine is logically so much a corollary of *anicca* that, had it not been for the exaggerated eternalism of the *ātman* doctrine, we should scarcely have found *an-atta* in the rank it occupies. It would have been overshadowed by, and taken up into, *anicca-vāda* and *kamma-vāda*. We may even venture to affirm that Buddhism, in the emphasis with which it combats a tendency at once mythological and mystical in the land of its birth, has weakened itself as a doctrine for all lands and all times by not building up a more positive teaching on the spiritual nature of man.

Be this as it may, Buddhism had no quarrel with any term for the living person as a whole—*attā*, *satta*, *puggala*—so long as in these terms we see labels, binding concepts, conventions in language, holding together, for economy in thought and word, the compound that a living person at any given moment, past, present, or future, is

'"Being"! (*satta*) Why dost thou harp upon that word?
. . . . .
Mere bundle of conditioned factors, this.
No "being" can be here discerned to be.
For just as when the parts are rightly set,
The word "chariot" ariseth in our minds,
So doth our usage covenant to say
"A being" when the aggregates (*khandha*) are there.'[1]

'For these, Chitta, are merely names, expressions, turns of speech, designations in common use in the world.'[2]

In this way all these terms are frequently used in the *Suttas*. Wherever the individual was living, unless it was in the very dimly conceived spheres called the unconscious and the immaterial, he or she was still and was always a compound of *khandhas*, the body-factor varying in grossness or refinement and other qualities according to the sphere inhabited and the mental factors no less. Thus, if you were in the Brahmā heaven, you had to assume a grosser body before you could pass into and act in the lower heavens.[3] Ever the 'soul' *was* the compound, always changing, growing out from, and the inevitable result of the souls (or selves) that had been. And, so long as the earnest inquirer bore in mind this distinction between self, soul, spirit as the mutable, growing organism, revealed by philosophic truth (*paramattha-sacca*), and the name-label, *suggestive* of a fictitious immutable entity, as used in the social convention of language (conventional truth, *sammuti-sacca*),[4] he thought in conformity with the mother-tradition of his religion. The *Suttas* show no hesitation in using conventional language in connexion with man as surviving not one death only, but any number of dyings. Available words, in fact, were so utterly inadequate, during the early centuries of Buddhism (as they are still), to discourse of what is commonly called transmigration that practically no choice was left. Survival was spoken of, by Brāhman and Buddhist alike, in terms of bodily acts and states. We are at a loss to conclude which was the more remarkable—the reaching out by the mind of Gotama Buddha to ideas which it needed the philosophic growth of a later period to make more clearly articulate by new terms, or the apparent failure of his opponents to discern how very badly the current terms of transmigration, such as they used, applied to an immanent being who was eternal and immutable. In the latest book of the canon, the *Kathā-vatthu*, in the great opening discussion on the soul (*puggala-kathā*),[5] we find the materially conceived views of transmigration criticized with a mainly negative emphasis. Terms for a constructive theory seem to be still lacking.

E.g., after much discourse to show dialectically that it is impossible to find, among the ultimates of our conscious experience, a soul or person (*puggala*) apprehended as 'a real and ultimate fact,' the argument proceeds to reject any such ultimate in the mysterious but accepted procedure of rebirth:

'*Heterodox Qy.* Then is it wrong to say, "A soul (*puggala*) transmigrates from this world to another world, and from another world to this?"

Orthodox Ans. Yes',

the latter speaker having elicited the admission that there is neither an identical soul that is reborn, nor a different (*i.e.* quite other) soul, nor both, nor neither.[6]

Passing on to the *Milinda*, we find there the germ-doctrine of the founder—viz. that man, in his entirety, is never the same, yet ever the resultant of his fore-existing self,[7] stated with a growing maturity in thought and diction.

But it is not till the times of Buddhaghoṣa[8] and his successors that we find, grown out of the too negative conception of *anicca*, a positive view, made articulate by certain newly applied terms, of

[1] *Vinaya Texts*, *Mahāvagga*, I. vi. 38 ff. (*SBE* xiii. [1881] 100 f.).
[2] *Vis. Magga*, xiv., tr. in H. C. Warren, *Buddhism in Translations*, Cambridge, Mass., 1896, p. 156.
[3] *Saṃyutta*, iii. 17 f. [4] *Ib.* iv. 54.
[5] *Dialogues of the Buddha*, i. 27 f., 46 f.; *Saṃyutta Nikāya*, ii. 20 f.
[6] Cf. *e.g.*, *Saṃyutta Nikāya*, iv. 132: 'Kammaṃ,' with the three following Suttas.

[1] *Kindred Sayings* (*PTS*), London, 1917, p. 170.
[2] *Dialogues*, i. 263. [3] *Dialogues*, ii. 264.
[4] *Points of Controversy*, p. 63, n. 2; cf. artt. REALITY (Buddhist), TRUTH (Buddhist).
[5] *Ib.* p. 1 f.
[6] Tr. in *Points of Controversy*, p. 26 f.
[7] *SBE* xxv. 63 f.
[8] E.g., *Commentary on the Paṭṭhāna* (unedited).

the ever-changing being of man conceived as a causally determined series of forces and resultants, and as a growing series, in which the now passing moment is wrought up into the coming moment.

Even then, discussion on a subject so inaccessible and mysterious is still stiff and halting. Further knowledge of mediæval Pāli literature may reveal further advance in theory. But we know enough to show that Buddhist doctrine as to soul and survival has logically reconciled *anicca* and *kamma*. My 'self,' as changing constantly, undergoes at death but a relatively deeper change; my new 'body' (*rūpa-khandha*), determined by my *kamma*, becomes one fitted to that new sphere, wherever it be, in which my past thought and will have determined that my new thought, call it soul or spirit or mind, be renewed.

LITERATURE.—See references in footnotes; cf. also **C. A. F. Rhys Davids**, *Buddhism*, London, 1912, chs. iii., v., and *Buddhist Psychology*, do. 1914, chs. ii., iii.; **S. Z. Aung** and **C. A. F. Rhys Davids**, *Points of Controversy* (*PTS*), do. 1915, p. 8 f.

C. A. F. RHYS DAVIDS.

SOUL (Christian).—I. *INTRODUCTION.*—(*a*) The term 'soul' is, in this article, taken in its most comprehensive sense, as denoting the whole 'self' or personality, the essential principle of human nature, the basis of conscious, continuous, individual existence. It is clear that study of the Christian idea of the soul in this broad sense involves the psychological interpretation of all characteristic data of Christian experience. We may speak of this study as 'Christian psychology,' because there are particular groups of phenomena at different periods with which Christianity is specially concerned (notably those of the NT period), and because there are certain real or alleged aspects of human nature in which Christianity is specially interested. But the method of the study must be that of psychology in general, *i.e.* purely historical and scientific, without dogmatic presuppositions, though the ultimate problems of all psychology pass into the realm of metaphysic.

(*b*) The psychological terminology and ideas of the NT are, as we might expect, largely continuous with those of the OT and the subsequent Jewish literature. The relevant ideas of the OT may be summarized as follows:

'The idea of human nature implies a unity, not a dualism. There is no contrast between the body and the soul, such as the terms instinctively suggest to us. The shades of the dead in Sheol . . . are not called "souls" or "spirits" in the Old Testament; nor does the Old Testament contain any distinct word for "body," as it surely would have done, had this idea been sharply differentiated from that of "soul." Man's nature is a product of the two factors—the breath-soul [נֶפֶשׁ] which is his principle of life, and the complex of physical organs which this animates. Separate them, and the man ceases to be, in any real sense of personality; nothing but a "shade" remains, which is neither body nor soul. If this seems but a poor idea of human nature, we must set over against it the great redeeming feature, that there is an aspect of this nature [רוּחַ] which relates man to God, and makes man accessible to God.'[1]

The non-canonical literature of Jewish thought shows that this fundamental idea was subsequently modified in two primary ways, chiefly in relation to the new eschatological emphasis. One was the accentuation of individualism; the detachment of the individual from the corporate personality of his social group, already declared by Jeremiah and Ezekiel, was more sharply presented against the new eschatological background of moral retribution in the life after death. The other, closely related, was a clearer recognition of the ethical problems of human nature, such as those arising from the tendency to evil which is in all men as it was in Adam. On the other hand, the OT doctrine of the Spirit of God fell into practical neglect, to the great impoverishment of the doctrine of man. It is, in fact, through the recovery of this doctrine that the most characteristic advance of the NT anthropology is made (*i.e.* in the Pauline interpretation of Christian experience).

[1] H. W. Robinson, *The Religious Ideas of the Old Testament*, London, 1913, p. 83.

(*c*) It is necessary to emphasize the fact that the NT psychology is, in general, continuous with that of the OT and the Apocrypha, because some scholars (*e.g.*, Holtzmann, Lüdemann, Sokolowski) have tended to exaggerate the Hellenistic influences, especially in regard to the Pauline contrast of the inner and outer man. They interpret the contrast as a dualism, though this is essentially untrue to the Hebrew basis of Pauline thought. It is, of course, true that the reproduction of the Hebrew psychological terms through their Greek equivalents gave easier access to the Hellenistic influences of the age. But the resultant modification has been, in fact, much less than we might have expected. The Greek terms of the NT are filled with an essentially Hebrew content; the two new terms, *νοῦς* and *συνείδησις*, are really specializations from the psychological usage of 'heart' in the OT, and are not used with a Greek connotation.

II. *NEW TESTAMENT.*—**1. The psychological terms.**—The group of writings known as the NT, though emanating from a single generation, presents at least three types of psychological usage, viz. the Synoptic, approximating most closely of all to the OT; the Pauline, offering the most important and original development of the OT conceptions; and the Johannine, apparently dependent on the Pauline usage, but moving in a circle of its own. We may conveniently review the use of the chief terms in each group separately, reserving for a fourth class other noticeable occurrences in the NT. The chief terms to be considered, in order to reach the general NT idea of human personality, are four, viz. *ψυχή*, *πνεῦμα*, *καρδία*, and *σάρξ*, corresponding respectively to נֶפֶשׁ, רוּחַ, לֵב, בָּשָׂר, in the OT.

(The attached numbers signify the approximate number of cases of each usage.)

(*a*) *Synoptic.*—Ψυχή (37) denotes physical life (Mt 2^{20}), or the subject of emotional states (Mk 14^{34}), as in the OT, but in eleven cases (as Mt 10^{28}) it refers to the continuance of life after death, a usage to which there is nothing corresponding in the use of נֶפֶשׁ. Πνεῦμα (78) is used chiefly of the Holy Spirit (34, as Mk 1^{12}), and of demonic influences (32, as Mt 8^{16}), but in three instances it denotes the principle of life (Mt 27^{50}, Lk 8^{55} 23^{46}), and in seven the psychical side of life (Mt 5^{3} 26^{41}, Mk 2^{8} 8^{12} 14^{38}, Lk $1^{47.\,80}$), though on a higher level than that denoted by *ψυχή*. Καρδία (49) is used especially of personality, inner life, and character (18, as Mk 7^{21}), also of emotional (2, as Lk 24^{32}), intellectual (12, as Mk 2^{6}), volitional (9, as Mt 5^{28}) life. Σάρξ (11) is used of the physical part of human nature, with the suggestion of weakness and limitation (Mk 14^{38}; cf. Lk 24^{39}), and thus in contrast with divine power (Mt 16^{7}). Except for the use of *ψυχή* in reference to life after death, all these usages could be directly classified under the corresponding OT terms, the connotation of which they continue, though the Christian emphasis on the inner life in contrast with the outer (cf. *καρδία*) is naturally marked in NT teaching.

(*b*) *Pauline.*—Ψυχή (13) is a term very little used by Paul; of the four instances with psychical content three denote 'desire' (Eph 6^{6}, Ph 1^{27}, Col 3^{23}), and one denotes simply the emotional side of consciousness (1 Th 5^{23}). His use of the adjective *ψυχικός* (1 Co $2^{14f.}$ $15^{44\text{-}46}$) shows that for him the *ψυχή* is no more than the animating principle of the body of flesh, and the basis of its emotional experience. Πνεῦμα (146) is the most important word in his psychological vocabulary, whether as denoting supernatural influences (116, as Ro 15^{13}), or the higher nature of a Christian man under the influence of the Spirit of God (14, as 1^{9}), or a normal element in human nature (16, as 8^{16}). This distinction of *ψυχή* and *πνεῦμα* further develops the tendencies already noticeable in the later OT usage of נֶפֶשׁ and רוּחַ. Καρδία (52) denotes the inner life (15, as 1 Co 14^{25}), the seat of emotional (13, as Ro 9^{2}), intellectual (11, as 1^{21}), and volitional (13, as 2^{5}) psychoses, continuing directly the usage of לֵב in the OT, except that the two Greek terms *νοῦς* (21, as Ph 4^{7}) and *συνείδησις* (20, as Ro 2^{15}), denoting 'mind' and 'conscience' (ethical judgment), cover usages which the OT would have expressed through לֵב. Σάρξ (91) is used to imply physical or intellectual weakness, or some limitation in value (19; see 2 Co 7^{5}, Ro 6^{19}, Ph 3^{3}); in 35 instances there is some ethical reference to the connexion of 'flesh' and sin

(Ro $7^{5ff.}$), though not so as to involve a fundamental ethical dualism of 'flesh' and 'spirit.'

(*c*) *Johannine* (*Gospel and Epistles*).—Here the usage of ψυχή (13) offers no marked difference from that of the Synoptics, except that it once includes the inner life on its higher side (3 Jn 2), as נֶפֶשׁ also can (Job 16^{4}). Πνεῦμα (34) is almost confined to supernatural influences, whilst never used of demons. In one instance it is used of the principle of life (Jn 19^{30}), and in two psychically, of anger (11^{33}, RVm), and of trouble (13^{21}). Καρδία (11) follows the Synoptic usage. In the usage of σάρξ (16) the Synoptic contrast with πνεῦμα is further emphasized in the Pauline sense (1^{13} 3^{6} 6^{63} 8^{15}, 1 Jn 2^{16}), in accordance with the Johannine fondness for antithesis; the spiritual birth of the believer means the impartation of a principle of new life.

(*d*) Among other NT usages calling for notice, Petrine psychology (1 P) is interesting by its contrast with the Pauline. For Peter, ψυχή (6) denotes the whole personality, including its highest aspects (1^{22} 2^{11}); πνεῦμα (8) is used of the soul or spirit after death ($3^{18f.}$ 4^{6}); in one instance πνεῦμα denotes a meek and gentle 'disposition' (3^{4}), as imparted by the Holy Spirit, but never a normal element in human nature, as it does in Paul's usage. Καρδία (3) follows the usual Hebrew and Pauline usage, with reference to the inner life as contrasted with the outer; σάρξ (7) is used in a purely physical and non-ethical sense, unlike the Pauline characteristic connotation. The usage of terms in James follows that of the OT. In Hebrews ψυχή and πνεῦμα are named together as normal elements of human nature (4^{12}; cf. 1 Th 5^{23}), and πνεῦμα is used of 'spirits' (angels, 1^{14}, men, 12^{23}; cf. 12^{9}). The psychology of the Acts, like that of the Synoptics, shows clearly the general continuance of the OT thought and usage, apart from the use of πνεῦμα in the sense of a disembodied 'spirit' ($23^{8f.}$; cf. 7^{59}); ψυχή represents the more emotional (15^{24}), καρδία the more volitional (11^{23}; cf. 4^{32} for both) aspect of personality, whilst πνεῦμα is used like רוּחַ of the special 'energies' of personality (17^{16} 18^{25} 19^{21} 20^{22}).

From this survey it will be clear that the fundamental ideas of personality in the NT are derived from the OT; the most important advance is in the belief that essential personality, whether called ψυχή or πνεῦμα, survives bodily death. This continued personality, however, still implies a body (ct. the Greek idea of the immortality of the soul), whether the present body (its ghostly counterpart? Mt $5^{29f.}$ 10^{28}) or the 'pneumatic' body of Pauline anticipation (1 Co 15^{35-38}), more adapted to the needs of the spirit (cf. the body of the Risen Christ, which possesses new powers). The body is conceived as an integral part of the personality, whose consciousness is diffused throughout it, and differentiated into the local consciousness of its particular members (1 Co $12^{12ff.}$), as in Hebrew psychology. Thus the eye, hand, mouth, etc., have psychical and ethical qualities of their own; since the writers of the NT, like those of the OT, knew nothing of the nervous system, they could not link up sensory and motor phenomena with a central organ, as we do, or assign to the brain its true function. In regard to the psychical side of this unified life of body and soul, the survey shows that no hard and fast division was made by the NT writers; the inner life might be called ψυχή, πνεῦμα, or καρδία, though usually, and on the basis of Hebrew usage, with more or less suggestion of emotional, 'spiritual,' and volitional activity respectively. We are not warranted, therefore, in speaking of a 'trichotomy' of body, soul, and spirit, or even a 'dichotomy' of soul (spirit) and body; a soul (spirit) may be temporarily disembodied, but full personality ultimately involves the union of body and soul, here and hereafter.[1]

2. Spiritual influences.—Further light is thrown on the NT idea of the soul by relating it to its environment of general and Christian belief. First in importance ranks the belief that the soul is accessible to 'spiritual' influences of the widest range, from those implied in the crudest demonology up to the Holy Spirit as conceived in the Pauline doctrine. The cosmic environment of the soul is constituted by hosts of demonic powers, which seek to make it their battleground.[2] Christ has entered the world armed with spiritual powers (Ac 10^{38}, 1 Jn 3^{8}), to overthrow Satan and his hosts—'I, by the Spirit of God, cast out demons.' In fact, Origen ascribes the progress of Christianity up to his time to the decrease in the number of demons, owing to their defeat by Christ.[1] To an extent that we can hardly realize, the soul was conceived by the early Christian as the arena of opposing spiritual forces, so that the doctrine of the Holy Spirit claims a unique and primary place among the ideas of early Christian anthropology. We owe to Paul the fullest elaboration of this doctrine, though it is more or less common ground to the NT writers. In the Pauline anthropology the cruder demonology of the time is replaced by 'sin,' conceived as an objective and almost personalized force, enabled to enter the human personality through the relatively weaker resistance of the 'flesh.'[2] This is not conceived dualistically, as the source of evil, but as the 'base of operation' of sin (ἀφορμή [Ro $7^{8.\ 11}$; cf. vv.$^{17.\ 18}$]). The full significance of this idea is apparent only when we remember the fact indicated already, viz. that the 'flesh,' including all the members of the body, is an essential part of the personality, possessed of a quasi-consciousness of its own. Against sin, then, operating through the flesh, the Holy Spirit wages unceasing war, working from the higher side of personality, whose essential spirituality (Ro 7^{22}) it successfully reinforces (8^{2}). The whole course of the victorious campaign in the arena of the soul, whose higher nature is linked with God through faith, produces Christian experience in regeneration and sanctification. Paul has thus lifted the function of the Spirit from the popular level of tongues and miracles of healing to the ethical plane, as is seen in his recapitulation of the 'fruit of the Spirit' (Gal $5^{22f.}$). He is not concerned with the ethical and metaphysical problems of this moral development; it is enough for him that all is of God and all is of man (Ph 2^{12}); as Deissmann says:

> 'Determinists and indeterminists can [both] appeal to him; Paul himself was neither one nor the other: to him the oars meant as much as the sails.'[3]

The entrance of the soul into this higher experience is by its faith, accompanied as this is by the baptism of the Holy Spirit outwardly enacted in, or accompanied by, water-baptism. But this baptism implies a new relation to all baptized believers, who are thereby constituted the unity of the Church. In the 'corporate personality' of the Church, forcibly depicted in the Pauline parable of the human body (1 Co $12^{12ff.}$), the old social consciousness of Israel re-appears. This corporate personality, whose vital energy is the Spirit of God, forms an essential factor in the NT conception of individual personality; the soul of the baptized believer is what it is by virtue of its relation to the whole, though the complementary truth must not be forgotten, that there is direct individual access to, and fellowship with, God through Christ in one Spirit (Eph 2^{18}; cf. 1 Jn 1^{3}).

3. Summary.—We may distinguish the essential features of the NT idea of the soul from the local and temporary forms of its expression by saying that this idea assumes the unity of human nature in its material and immaterial elements, which it does not so clearly distinguish as we are inclined to do; that it emphasizes the worth of human personality, especially by the appeal to its eternal destiny; and that it finds the realization of this worth in the moral values of a society

[1] See art. ESCHATOLOGY, vol. v. p. 385 ff.

[2] For the copious evidence see Harnack, *Die Mission und Ausbreitung des Christentums*², Leipzig, 1906, Eng. tr., London, 1908, bk. i. ch. iii.; J. Weiss, 'Dämonische,' in *PRE*³ iv. 411–419.

[1] *Hom.* xv. 5, quoted by Harnack, i. 124, n. 2, Eng. tr., i. 143, n. 2.

[2] See art. SIN (Christian).

[3] *Paulus*, Tübingen, 1911, p. 126, Eng. tr., London, 1912, p. 188.

constituted through the corporate and individual surrender of personality to the Spirit of God (or Christ). The NT characteristically shows little consciousness of the problems inevitably arising within the circle of this idea of the soul, such as the method of the soul's origin, the relation of the soul's activity to God's (freedom and grace), the degree of moral development required for membership in the Church, the mediation of spiritual energies to the soul by institutions or truths respectively. The gradual emergence of these problems in the subsequent course of Christian thought has profoundly affected the history of the Church.[1]

III. *PATRISTIC AND MEDIÆVAL.*—When the Christian gospel passed out through the gate of the Jewish synagogue into the arena of the Roman Empire, an idea of the soul fundamentally Hebrew was transferred into an environment of Greek thought, with no slight consequences in the process of adaptation. Patristic thinkers were usually men trained in Greek philosophy, and they could make their apologetic and constructive work intelligible to a Greek-thinking world only through the established terms and conceptions of Greek psychology. The fundamental difference of outlook has been clearly stated by Siebeck:[2]

'For the Greeks, the soul is a product of the world, and the rational soul primarily exists to know the world as it is, and actively shape it; the soul was consequently the means to an end or ends assigned to it by the world. To the Christian, on the contrary, the world is a means for the end of salvation, which springs from the independent and characteristic nature of the soul; for him, accordingly, the soul is not a product of the world, but a creation of the transcendent God, conceived after the analogy of spirit.'

The transference brought both gain and loss—gain, in that a more scientific analysis of the Christian consciousness became possible; loss, in that some of the religious values conserved by the more primitive Hebrew and NT idea of the soul were more likely to be obscured. One general result was the development of a distinction between soul and body in marked contrast with the unity of the Hebrew idea (cf. Philo's dualism owing to similar influences), though this was usually accompanied by the retention of the Jewish doctrine of the resurrection of the body, which became an established Christian tenet.

1. Tertullian and Origen.—The influence of the Stoic and Platonic psychology on Patristic writers may be illustrated from Tertullian and Origen respectively. Tertullian (160–220), whilst naturally ascribing the soul of the first man to the divine inbreathing, follows Stoic teachers in asserting that the human soul is corporeal, and is handed on from parent to child, being begotten with the body (Traducianism). But the unity of the soul, with νοῦς as its highest function, stands over against the body, so that Tertullian is a 'dichotomist.' When the soul is seen in vision, it has the shape of the body, and even a certain tangibility. His formal definition may be quoted:

'The soul, then, we define to be sprung from the breath of God, immortal, possessing body, having form, simple in its substance, intelligent in its own nature, developing its powers in various ways, free in its determinations, subject to growth by opportunity, in its faculties mutable, rational, supreme, endued with an instinct of presentiment, evolved out of one (original).'[3]

Origen (185–254), like the Alexandrians generally, follows the Platonic idea of the soul as incorporeal and eternal; he regards it as pre-existent to the present life. From Platonic influence comes also that 'trichotomy' which Greek thought could so easily, though without warrant, read into the NT reference to 'body, soul, and spirit' (1 Th 5[23]). A third Patristic theory of the origin of the soul, which became dominant from the time of Jerome onwards, is creationism, according to which 'God is daily making souls,'[1] whilst bodies alone come by human generation.

2. Augustine.—Augustine (354–430), whilst deeply influenced by Neo-Platonism, claims a unique place in Patristic psychology by the originality and importance of his work. He is the first to realize fully and adequately that the inner life is *sui generis*, with its own intrinsic claims to introspective study; in his analysis of the mind as memory, intellect, and will he gives the primary place to the will, instead of to the intellect; his deep conception of the freedom realized through divine grace stands in sharp contrast with the superficiality of contemporary Pelagianism. His influence is supreme through the subsequent centuries until Scholasticism brings in the reign of Aristotle, and 'the Aristotelian conception of the soul as life-energy mingles with the Platonic idea of the body as the instrument of the soul.'[2]

3. Aquinas.—Aquinas (1224–75), the foremost representative of Scholasticism, combined the Augustinian anthropology with Aristotle's general idea of the soul[3] and rejected the Platonic dualism, but 'ecclesiastical dogma demanded such transformation of the Aristotelian distinctions as amounted to a religious dualism.'[4] In the elaborate system of Thomas man became a central point of contact between the two great realms of 'form' and 'matter'—the microcosm which unites them both.[5] Metaphysic thus gave support to the Christian doctrine of the soul's worth, though its formalism failed to do justice to the soul's content.

4. Eckhart.—Side by side, however, with the more rationalistic view of Scholasticism there is an approach to the realities of the soul made by mystical religion, which is of great significance for Christian thought. Thus Eckhart (1260–1327), gathering up the soul's powers into unity with God, holds that 'there is something in the soul uncreated and uncreatable,' through which the divine birth within man takes place (cf. the *synteresis* of Scholastic psychology).[6] In this return to God, involving, on the negative side, the withdrawal from sensational life, the soul's salvation consists. A natural outcome of such views would be pantheism, though Eckhart perhaps saves himself from this.[7] The insistence on the surrender of the soul to God as the source and unity (*unitas*) of its life is characteristic of mysticism (*q.v.*), and may be studied in the *Theologia Germanica*, which so profoundly influenced Luther. In fact, mediæval mysticism forms one of the principal tributaries of the Protestant Reformation, with its new emphasis on the experience of the individual soul and on the work of the Holy Spirit.

IV. *MODERN.*—**1. Lines of approach.**—From the Renaissance and Reformation onwards the characteristic feature of inquiry into the nature of the soul has been its specialization along different lines, pursued more or less independently; Christian thought tends more and more to concentrate on the religious significance of the soul.

(*a*) *Religious.*—The new emphasis on religious experience which characterized the Reformation illustrates the more subjective spirit of Protestant religion in general. The necessary objective complement of this was found in the doctrine of the Holy Spirit, as the supernatural basis of the soul's experience, though usually in intimate relation to

1 Cf. artt. PELAGIANISM, DONATISTS, PROTESTANTISM.
2 *Gesch. der Psychologie*, ii. 359.
3 *De Anima*, 22.

1 Jerome, *ad Pamm.* 22.
2 Siebeck, ii. 426.
3 See art. SOUL (Greek).
4 Klemm, *Gesch. der Psychologie*, p. 22.
5 Dessoir, *Abriss einer Gesch. der Psychologie*, p. 68.
6 Cf. art. SYNDERESIS.
7 Cf. Rufus M. Jones, *Studies in Mystical Religion*, London, 1909, p. 233.

the canon of Scripture.[1] A wider application of the doctrine of the Spirit is to be found in the Quaker doctrine of the 'Inner Light,' which Barclay defines as 'a real spiritual substance, which the soul of man is capable to feel and apprehend, from which that real, spiritual inward birth in believers arises, called the new creature, the new man in the heart.'[2] From the teaching of George Fox[3] we can see that this meant the religious evaluation of the moral consciousness—a most suggestive contribution to modern apologetic.[4] At the other end of the scale of spiritual experience we find Wesley's doctrine of the 'witness of the Spirit.'[5] Between these two experiences—the sense of morality on the one side and the glow of Christian certainty on the other—are to be found the distinctive interests of Protestantism and the tribunal of its doctrines, to whatever degree the Scriptural record of similar experience remains the formal court of appeal. A new era in the study of the soul in its religious interests was initiated when Schleiermacher (*q.v.*) recognized this. The consequent emphasis on religious experience as the basis of inquiry into the soul is one of the most significant features of present-day theology, in full agreement with the contemporary scientific interest in the psychology of religion.

(*b*) *Psychological.*—The scientific interests of 17th cent. thought, seen in the philosophy of Descartes (1596–1650), Spinoza (1632–77), and Leibniz (1646–1716), and culminating in Locke (1632–1704), involved the differentiation of physiology from psychology, and of both from the religious or metaphysical ideas of the soul. Psychology acquired the character of a distinct science, and has tended more and more in recent times to confine itself as such to the study of the actual phenomena of consciousness, whilst remitting to the theologian and the metaphysician all theories of an alleged substratum or 'soul.' No objection can be raised to this limitation, provided that it be not construed as a denial of soul or personality, in the sense of the theological or ontological postulate of the states of consciousness which the psychologist studies. In this connexion it should be noted that the assumption by Locke of a 'closed consciousness,' accessible through the physical senses alone, still tends to create a prejudice against those spiritual influences which the Christian idea of the soul essentially maintains. Against this prejudice the modern study of telepathy has exerted a useful influence, by showing the possibility of mind influencing mind, apart from the normal link of sensational knowledge. Indeed, the study of abnormal psychology (hypnosis, multiple personality, dreams and visions) may still have important contributions to render to our knowledge of personality. The modern recognition of the 'sub-consciousness' has done much to clear up certain phenomena of normal life, quite apart from the further question of a subliminal self.[6]

(*c*) *Historical.*—In our own generation a further line of approach has been opened up by the comparative study of anthropology and religion. Australian totemism, African fetishism, the psychophysiological ideas and practices of the ancient Egyptians, the demonology of Babylonia, the metaphysical ideas of the soul current in Indian religion—all these can contribute to a clearer knowledge of the Christian idea of the soul, if only by throwing into contrast its distinctive features. Before the rise of this modern study we were more or less confined to a Græcized approach to Biblical ideas, and, in particular, the psychology of the Hebrews was misunderstood. We can now see the alien origin of 'trichotomies' and other assumptions, and recognize the essential unity of man's nature in the Hebrew-Christian idea, and its contrast with Greek and other dualisms (Chinese, Zoroastrian); the emphasis of this idea on man's dependence on God, for creation, preservation, and salvation, in contrast with the scientific or philosophical interests of Greek thought; the fundamental Christian assumption of individuality, in contrast with the ultimate denial of this by Buddhism.

(*d*) *Philosophical.*—The history of philosophy in all periods shows how intimately its progress affects the theological ideas of God and man. In the modern period we may trace a growing approximation to, or recognition of, the demands of Christian faith, as seen in the rejection of materialism and naturalism, and the recognition of the reality of 'spirit.' The decline of absolute idealism, largely through its inadequate account of individuality, and the rise of personal idealism and of various forms of pluralism show that the Christian insistence on the value of the individual soul is not without its philosophic basis. The importance of the idea of 'personality' is more fully recognized in modern philosophy, and the Kantian emphasis on the essential reality of ethical experience harmonizes with the Christian claim that the moral side of personality is its highest development and supreme 'value.'[1]

2. Values and problems.—The essential features of Christian anthropology—the religious data or 'values' which any system of thought is called on to interpret—are 'its emphasis on the worth of man to God as spiritual personality, its practical recognition of an individual self, possessing moral freedom and responsibility, its condemnation of sin as that which ought not to be, its assertion of human dependence on divine aid for the realization of spiritual possibilities, its definition of personal development in terms of social relationship.'[2] The problems of the Christian idea of the soul gather chiefly around the primary postulate of the soul's reality, its relation to the body, and its relation to God.

(*a*) The term 'soul' must be taken to mean, not the unknown substratum of certain phenomena, but the spiritual entity which *is* in its distinctive activities and qualities. Such are its possession of a unique individuality, of the freedom of real initiative, of non-material content. Its development in time is part of its reality, though its ultimate nature may be conceived as timeless. Total human personality is obviously more than the self of self-consciousness at any moment, if only because of the fact of memory. Moreover, the relation of the Christian self-consciousness to other selves and to God may suggest that the soul is an entity larger than past or present experience exhibits.

(*b*) The relation of soul to body in the Christian conception of personality involves the rejection of dualism and the recognition of the body as integral to human nature, at least in the sense that the powers of the body belong to and are finally gathered up into the life of the soul. This, of course, does not mean that the soul depends on the body for its ultimate being, or dies in the physical dissolution of death, but simply that the connexion of soul and body is not artificial, temporary, and alien. The historic Christian conception of life beyond death has accordingly

1 Cf., *e.g.*, the *Westminster Confession of Faith*.
2 *Apology*, London, 1676, prop. v. and vi. § 14.
3 *E.g.*, *Journal*[8], London, 1901, ii. 185.
4 See art. FRIENDS, SOCIETY OF.
5 *ERE* iii. 329.
6 See F. W. H. Myers, *Human Personality*, 2 vols., London, 1903, *passim*.

1 See, especially, A. S. Pringle-Pattison, *The Idea of God*, Oxford, 1917, *passim*.
2 H. W. Robinson, *The Christian Doctrine of Man*[2], p. 344.

been based on the Hebrew doctrine of resurrection, rather than on the Greek doctrine of immortality. The non-Hebraic idea of pre-existence (*q.v.*) has failed to find a genuine home in Christian thought; as a speculation in regard to what lies beyond all experience, it hardly admits of proof or disproof. Christian emphasis falls on the theistic idea that soul and body alike owe their creation to God; the fact that they are in present experience so intimately interwoven suggests that they have been brought into existence together, and are complementary expressions (on different planes) of the one entity of personality. Such a view implies no surrender of the faith that the soul survives bodily death; the apparent cessation of intercourse with other embodied selves on earth would find sufficient explanation if the present relation of brain to mind be one of permissive or transmissive, not productive, function.[1] This view of the body as an integral factor, though not, in its present form, a permanent element, in the slowly-evolved self of personality, would agree with the whole evolutionary history of the world, in which human personality offers the highest values attained, and gathers up so many factors of the process. Philosophically, this implies the spiritualization of the body, as against the materialization of the soul; but both elements, body and soul, are real, and form a unity for Christian anthropology and ethics.

(*c*) The relation of the soul to God in Christian thought demands the rejection of any form of monistic absorption, as clearly as of naturalistic degradation. Notwithstanding the quasi-pantheism of some forms of Christian mysticism, and the adoption of quasi-pantheistic systems by some Christian thinkers, the normal testimony of the Christian consciousness is to a clear-cut individuality, carrying with it a real freedom, in upward as well as downward relations. On the other hand, the deeper experiences of Christian fellowship with God point to a relation of the soul to Him so intimate that the completer the surrender of the soul to its Creator and Redeemer, the fuller and richer is the soul's individual life. Whilst the process of salvation may be defined as 'God in us,' its goal is 'we in God.' The doctrine of the Holy Spirit (*q.v.*) here becomes of cardinal importance for Christian anthropology. Through 'the law of the Spirit of life in Christ Jesus' human personality realizes its larger life by voluntary surrender to God:

> 'Psychologically, it is the setting of the mind on Christ, in the revelation of His graciousness and of the infinite love of God in it, that makes it possible for the Spirit of Christ to act unto the soul's complete deliverance.'[2]

The repeated discovery is made by the Christian that the true life of the soul is hid with Christ in God—*i.e.*, that it is waiting for personal appropriation. This truth of experience shows the significance of fellowship, human and divine; in practice and in theory corporate fellowship must be held to be fundamental to the life of the soul.

The Christian idea of the soul, whilst always implying a metaphysic, is not dependent on any particular system of metaphysics, past, present, or future. All that we are entitled to say is that a metaphysic of personality adequate to explain the Christian experience must, on the one hand, do justice to the moral freedom which alone gives reality to sin and guilt, and significance to the soul's surrender to God, and, on the other hand, show the soul's kinship with God, and its constant relation to the 'Father of spirits,' so that its whole development in time becomes at once a divine as well as a human activity. To develop such a metaphysic obviously lies beyond the scope of the present article.

[1] Cf. W. James, *Human Immortality*[6], London, 1906, p. 32.
[2] G. Steven, *Psychology of the Christian Soul*, p. 264.

LITERATURE.—i. *NEW TESTAMENT.*—H. Lüdemann, *Die Anthropologie des Apostels Paulus*, Kiel, 1872; J. Gloel, *Der heilige Geist in der Heilsverkündigung des Paulus*, Halle, 1888; J. Laidlaw, *The Bible Doctrine of Man*[2], Edinburgh, 1895; T. Simon, *Die Psychologie des Apostels Paulus*, Göttingen, 1897; H. Gunkel, *Die Wirkungen des heiligen Geistes*[2], do. 1899; E. Sokolowski, *Die Begriffe von Geist und Leben bei Paulus*, do. 1903; I. F. Wood, *The Spirit of God in Biblical Literature*, London, 1904: E. H. van Leeuwen, *Bijbelsche Anthropologie*, Utrecht, 1906; E. W. Winstanley, *Spirit in the NT*, Cambridge, 1908; H. W. Robinson, 'Hebrew Psychology in Relation to Pauline Anthropology,' in *Mansfield College Essays*, London, 1909, p. 265 ff.; M. Scott Fletcher, *The Psychology of the NT*, do. 1913; H. W. Robinson, *The Christian Doctrine of Man*[2], Edinburgh, 1913; E. D. Burton, 'Spirit, Soul and Flesh,' in *AJTh* xvii. [1913] 563 ff., xviii. [1914] 59 ff., 395 ff., 571 ff., xx. [1916] 390 ff., republished, Chicago, 1918; A. S. Peake, 'The Quintessence of Paulinism,' in *Bulletin of the John Rylands Library, Manchester*, iv. 2 [1918] 285 f.

ii. *PATRISTIC AND MEDIÆVAL.*—H. Siebeck, *Gesch. der Psychologie*, 2 vols., Gotha, 1880–84 (to Aquinas; the best and fullest account); H. Weinel, *Die Wirkungen des Geistes und der Geister im nachapostolischen Zeitalter bis auf Irenäus*, Freiburg i. B., 1899; H. Delacroix, *Etudes d'hist. et de psychologie du mysticisme*, Paris, 1908; M. Dessoir, *Abriss einer Gesch. der Psychologie*, Heidelberg, 1911; O. Klemm, *Gesch. der Psychologie*, Leipzig, 1911; G. S. Brett, *A Hist. of Psychology Ancient and Patristic*, London, 1912.

iii. *MODERN AND GENERAL.*—G. A. Coe, *The Spiritual Life*, New York, 1900; F. Granger, *The Soul of a Christian*, London, 1900; W. James, *The Varieties of Religious Experience*, London and New York, 1902; L. D. Arnett, 'The Soul,' in *AJPs* xv. [1904] 121–200, 347–382; J. B. Pratt, *The Psychology of Religious Belief*, New York and London, 1907; G. B. Cutten, *The Psychological Phenomena of Christianity*, London, 1909; W. R. Inge, *Faith and its Psychology*, do. 1909; E. S. Ames, *The Psychology of Religious Experience*, do. 1910; A. Caldecott, *The Religious Sentiment illustrated from the Lives of Wesley's Helpers*, do. n.d. [*c.* 1910]; E. D. Starbuck, *The Psychology of Religion*[3], do. 1911; G. Steven, *The Psychology of the Christian Soul*, do. n.d. [1911]; H. Maldwyn Hughes, art. 'Experience (Religious),' in *ERE* v. 630–635; J. Stalker, *Christian Psychology*, London, 1914; W. Boyd Carpenter, *The Witness of Religious Experience*, do. 1916; R. Rouse and H. C. Miller, *Christian Experience and Psychological Processes*, do. 1917; P. Gardner (and others), 'The Pyschology of Religious Experience,' in *The Modern Churchman*, viii. 5–7 [Aug.-Oct. 1918].

H. WHEELER ROBINSON.

SOUL (Greek).—When we attempt to understand the development of Greek ideas about the soul (ψυχή), we are faced at once by the difficulty that there appears to be no bridge leading from the views implied in our earliest literary record, the Homeric poems, to the religious practices and beliefs of later ages. These are in many respects much more primitive, though it is also true that popular beliefs were much affected by Homer, since most Greeks were brought up on him from childhood. On the other hand, we find that the clearest thinkers among the Greeks, while they naturally rejected popular superstitions about 'souls,' were even more emphatic in their condemnation of the Homeric doctrine. In fact, the Homeric poems appear to be an intrusive and disturbing factor in the normal development of Greek belief. That is why, so long as the *Iliad* and the *Odyssey* were regarded as primitive popular poetry, it seemed impossible to account for later Greek ideas about the soul except on some hypothesis of Oriental influences. At the present day, however, it is generally agreed that the *Iliad* and *Odyssey* are not popular poetry, but court poetry, and it is perfectly certain that they are not in any way primitive. Archæological research has shown that there was a highly developed civilization in the Ægean at least 2000 years before Homer, and it has also shown that the people to whom this civilization belonged were conquered, some centuries before Homer, by invaders who probably came from the north. The civilization which Homer describes is not the old Ægean civilization even in its latest period. The Mycenæ unearthed by Schliemann is not the Mycenæ of Agamemnon, but that of his predecessors of the older race. What Homer does describe is the civilization of the new-comers, whom he usually calls Achaians, and of these only after they had already settled themselves firmly in the chief seats of the old Ægean kingdoms. It is clear, however, that these Achaians did not occupy the whole of what was afterwards called Hellas or Greece, and we may also assume that the new-comers would be numerically inferior to the older inhabitants almost everywhere, and would be gradually assimilated and absorbed. That is why, as becomes clearer every day, the later Greek civilization was in the main a revival and continuation of that which existed before the coming of the Achaians, though it was profoundly modified by Achaian influences. Hesiod was still conscious of the break. In his account of the ages of man[1] he interpolates a fifth age, that of the heroes who fought at Thebes and Troy, between the bronze age and the iron age, to which he himself belonged. That is the age with which Homer deals, and, if we remember that the heroic age is an interlude which stands by itself, it will be much easier for us to understand the development of Greek ideas about the soul. It has also to be borne in mind that Homer knows nothing of the Dorian conquest of the Peloponnese, and that, in the time of which he sings, the region later called Ionia was still in the hands of 'barbarians.'

1. Early beliefs and practices.—It is, of course, obvious that we cannot know with any certainty what the old Ægean population thought of the soul, so long as their writing remains undeciphered. We can only draw inferences from the remains of tombs, etc., that have come to light, and these may easily be misleading. Even if the inscriptions could be read, we might make mistakes. It would not be safe to infer from the inscriptions in a Christian churchyard what is really believed about the soul to-day. Still, there are certain broad statements which may be regarded as assured. The kings of Cnossus and Mycenæ were buried in elaborate state, not cremated like the Achaians of Homer; and, in early times at least, that generally points to a difference of belief about the soul. The great distinction between such beliefs depends on the answer given to the question whether the soul remains attached to the body after death or goes to a place of its own. If this question is answered in the first way, we naturally find that the body is buried in such a manner as to secure it against corruption as long as possible, and that along with it are buried weapons, implements, etc., which may be of use to the soul in its life below the ground. There will also be a mortuary cult of some kind, the main purpose of which will be to provide the soul with appropriate nourishment. All these features are met with in the Mycenæan tombs,[2] and we may fairly infer that, in those days, the 'soul' was supposed to dwell in the tomb. This is the belief we know best from Egypt, where it was carried out with rigorous logic, and where great precautions were taken to secure the preservation of the body after death. At Mycenæ the face was covered with a thin gold mask, so that we still know the features of some of the old kings; and the Egyptians also tried to make their mummies life-like. It seems to have been felt that the outward appearance of the man was the essential thing, and, so long as that was preserved, the soul could still enjoy the offerings brought to the grave. In Egypt this idea was still further developed when the image of the *ka*, or 'double,' was placed in the tomb, but we have no clear indication of that in the Ægean. The sarcophagus of Hagia Triada does, however, furnish us with a representation of the mortuary cult, which seems to prove that a belief similar to the Egyptian prevailed in Crete, and we shall see that the later Greek practices and beliefs must have been developed from some such origin.

2. Homer.—When we come to Homer, everything is changed. The 'soul' is called ψυχή and is identified with the last breath, the 'ghost' which a man 'gives up.' That is obviously separated from the body at death, so there can be no question of trying to preserve the body or its likeness, or of a mortuary cult. On the contrary, it is desirable that the body should be destroyed as soon as possible, so that the 'soul' may be quite free to depart. It seems to be feared that, so long as the body is there, the soul will be in a measure bound to it. Cremation is an obvious corollary of this view, and there can be no thought of offerings at the grave.

It was not to be expected, however, that this belief should be developed to its logical conclusions in those early days, and there are a good many survivals in Homer of something more primitive. Above all, the soul is still thought of as in some sense a 'double' of the self, and the self is frankly identified with the body. The soul, however, must somehow retain the outward appearance of the man 'himself,' since it is obviously possible to dream of the dead. This comes out best in *Il.* xxiii. 106, where we are told that the soul (ψυχή) of Patroclus stood over Achilles all night long, 'and it was marvellously like himself' (ἔικτο δὲ θέσκελον αὐτῷ). Indeed, the whole funeral of Patroclus as here described, with its human sacrifices and libations, is quite unlike anything else in Homer and reads like a survival from earlier times, with this great difference, however, that it is not to be repeated, and that no mortuary cult is to be instituted, after Patroclus 'himself' has once been burned.

It is important to observe, in the next place, that the soul (ψυχή) is not of the slightest importance during life. Homer has many descriptions of conscious processes, whether of the nature of thought, will, or desire, and he has an unusually large psychological vocabulary, as we should call it. He uses words like φρήν (φρένες), ἦτορ, κῆρ, νόος, βουλή, μένος, μῆτις with considerable precision, but these things are all parts or functions of the body. There is not a single passage where any conscious process whatever is ascribed to the soul (ψυχή) of a living man. No doubt there are places where we may translate the word by 'life,' but even then it only means life regarded as a thing to be lost.[1]

As the soul is not the seat of consciousness in life, it follows that it can have no consciousness when it has left the body, and that is the normal Homeric view. The departed soul has no midriff (φρένες) and no heart, so it is impossible for it to be conscious. It is only real enough to be capable of appearing in the dream of a living man. The souls of the dead depart to a barren, gloomy region, called 'the home of Aïdes' (*i.e.* 'the unseen one'), which is thought of as lying in the far West, and there they have only a dream-like simulacrum of life. As Apollodorus put it in his work on the gods:

> Homer 'assumes that souls resemble the images appearing in mirrors and arising in water, which are made in our likeness and imitate our movements, but have no solid substance to be grasped or touched.'

That is why the departed souls are called 'shades' (σκιαί) or 'images' (εἴδωλα).[2]

[1] *Works and Days*, 108 ff.

[2] See art. FOOD FOR THE DEAD, vol. vi. p. 66ᵃ.

[1] Cf. *Il.* xxii. 161: περὶ ψυχῆς θέον, *Od.* xxii. 245: περί τε ψῡχέων ἐμάχοντο, *Il.* xiii. 763: ψυχὰς ὀλέσαντες. A Homeric hero fights for his ψυχή, or risks it or loses it, but he does not live by it. In *Il.* ix. 401 οὐ ψυχῆς ἀντάξιον means 'no compensation for the *loss* of life.'

[2] The *locus classicus* is *Il.* xxiii. 104: Ὢ πόποι, ἦ ῥά τίς ἐστι καὶ εἰν Ἀΐδαο δόμοισι | ψυχή καὶ εἴδωλον, ἀτὰρ φρένες οὐκ ἔνι

All apparent exceptions to this normal Homeric doctrine of the soul are of the kind that prove the rule, since they are clearly attempts to adapt certain older ideas to it. The most remarkable is that of the seer Tiresias, whose departed soul is said to retain its consciousness. That, we are told,[1] however, was a gift of Persephone, who 'granted him a mind (νόον) even though he was dead.' It is, therefore, a special miracle, which only confirms the general rule. The whole story of the Nekyia in *Od.* xi. depends on the view that the souls must drink blood before they can become conscious. The blood gives them, as it were, a temporary body while it lasts, and therefore they can speak with Odysseus. Obviously, however, as Rohde says, the poet would hardly have thought of putting the matter in that way, if it had not been for the memory of the old blood-offering to the dead (αἱμακουρία). The most startling survival is the promise which Odysseus makes on the instructions of Circe[2] to offer a sacrifice to the dead when he gets back to Ithaca. According to the usual Homeric view, such a sacrifice would be altogether meaningless. We see, then, that even in Homer there are traces of an older theory of the soul than that which prevails in the poems.

The few favourites of heaven who are carried away to the Elysian field and the few great sinners who are punished in Tartarus form, on the other hand, no exception to the rule. They have been made immortal; but for Homer that means that they retain their bodies. They have become like the gods; but a god for the Greek is an 'animal' (ζῷον) and has a body. Neither the punishment of Tantalus, Tityos, or Sisyphus nor the delights of the Elysian field would be possible for disembodied souls. Immortality consists just in exemption from the separation of soul and body.

3. Hesiod.—In Hesiod we find, as might be expected, still more numerous survivals of earlier ideas. The men of the golden age became δαίμονες after death, while those of the silver age are called 'the subterranean blessed,' and we are expressly told[3] that they too 'are attended by honour' (τιμή). We are apparently to think of an earlier time, when men might become gods upon earth, and of a later time, when they might become chthonian divinities like Amphiaraus and Trophonius. All that, however, was very long ago, and no such lot is possible for souls now. The souls of the bronze age men went 'nameless to the dank house of chill Hades.'[4] Some of the souls of the next age, that of the heroes, share the same fate, while others are carried away to the 'isles of the blest,' which correspond to Homer's Elysian field.[5] So far as the present race is concerned, there seems to be no hope of any real life after death.

4. The cult of heroes.—When we come to times of which there is any real historical memory, we find everywhere a cult of 'heroes' subsisting alongside of the worship of the gods. These heroes are plainly souls which have their dwelling in the grave. It is impossible to believe that this is an innovation, or that the name 'hero' (ἥρως) has been adopted from Homer, who often uses it merely in the sense of 'free man.' It seems rather that the word has been secularized, as it were, by the Achaians, and that the cult had survived among the older population to emerge once more into the light of day when the invading Achaians had been absorbed. This view is confirmed by what we learn from Hesiod. As we saw, he knows that in distant days there were departed souls which received a cult, but he uses the word 'hero' in the Homeric sense, and therefore he cannot apply it to the 'subterranean blessed ones,' to whom it properly belongs. However that may be, the cult was always sharply distinguished from the worship of the gods. To sacrifice (θύειν) to the gods on an altar (βωμός) was to send the sweet savour (κνίσα) upwards, while to sacrifice (ἐναγίζειν) to the heroes on an ἐσχάρα was to permit the blood and libations to sink into the earth. The archæological evidence shows that the latter practice was known at pre-Homeric Mycenæ. It is quite plain that the heroes were regarded as the souls of departed men, though only a few of the departed become heroes. It is also clear that the cult of the heroes is localized at their graves, which implies that their souls dwell there. That is why the bones of heroes are transported from one place to another. The cult can take place only where they are.[1]

5. Conflicting ideas.—(1) At Athens, in historical times, we find great confusion of ideas about the soul. Attica had not been overrun by the invading northerners, and the older ideas had never been displaced by such theories as are implied in Homer. Accordingly, burial and not cremation was the orthodox Athenian method of disposing of the dead. It was prescribed and regulated in the laws of Solon, and it is the only practice strictly consistent with the due observance of the 'customary uses' (τὰ νομιζόμενα), *i.e.* the mortuary cult. On the other hand, all Athenians were brought up on Homer and necessarily had the Homeric beliefs impressed on their minds. That may be the explanation of the fact that cremation was quite common at one period (7th cent. B.C.) and was always regarded as a possible and proper method of disposing of the dead. There was, in fact, a divergence between the things an Athenian did in connexion with departed souls and the things he believed about them. The mortuary cult implied that the souls were in the grave with the body, and we know from Plato's *Phædo*[2] that ghosts were believed to have been seen in the neighbourhood of tombs. At the feast of the Anthesteria departed souls or ghosts (κῆρες) were supposed to be released from their graves and to revisit the houses in which they had dwelt. They were solemnly dismissed at the end of the festival with the words, 'Out, ghosts, the Anthesteria is over!' (θύραζε, κῆρες, οὐκέτ' Ἀνθεστήρια). All that is quite primitive; but, if an ordinary Athenian had been asked what he believed about the soul, he would doubtless have answered by talking of its departure 'to Hades's' (εἰς Ἅιδου) and of Charon and the Styx—things which imply quite a different belief. This confusion is well marked by the representation of Charon and his boat, much as he is depicted in Lucian and Virgil, on a piece of black-figured pottery which must belong to the 6th cent. B.C. This piece of pottery was evidently intended for use in the mortuary cult, and yet it is ornamented with a scene quite inconsistent with the necessary presuppositions of that cult.[3] The fact is that we should have very little knowledge of the mortuary cult at all, if it had

πάμπαν. It must be remembered that Ἀΐδης (Att. Ἅιδης, whence Hades) is a person, not a place. The name of the place is Erebos ('Gloom'). The quotation from Apollodorus, Περὶ θεῶν, given above runs thus (*ap.* Stob. *Ecl.* i. p. 420, ed. C. Wachsmuth, Berlin, 1884): ὑποτίθεται τὰς ψυχὰς τοῖς εἰδώλοις τοῖς ἐν τοῖς κατόπτροις φαινομένοις ὁμοίας καὶ τοῖς διὰ τῶν ὑδάτων συνισταμένοις, ἃ καθάπαξ ἡμῖν ἐξείκασται καὶ τὰς κινήσεις μιμεῖται, στερεμνώδη δὲ ὑπόστασιν οὐδεμίαν ἔχει εἰς ἀντίληψιν καὶ ἀφήν.

1 *Od.* x. 494.
2 *Od.* xi. 29 ff.
3 *Works and Days*, 142.
4 *Ib.* 153.
5 *Ib.* 167 ff.

1 The point of view is well brought out by the account of the bringing of the bones of Orestes from Tegea to Sparta in Herodotus (i. 67 ff.). As late as 476 B.C. the bones of Theseus were brought from Scyros to Athens (Plut. *Cim.* 8, *Thes.* 36; Paus. III. iii. 7).
2 81 C.
3 See A. Furtwängler, 'Charon, eine altattische Malerei,' *ARW* viii. [1905] 191 ff.

not been of importance in cases of inheritance, so that orators like Isæus had to mention it. The Athenian acquired such beliefs about the soul as he had from Homer, but he continued to honour his dead 'after the manner of his fathers' (κατὰ τὰ πάτρια).

(2) The Eleusinian mysteries were another source of confusion. It is not at all probable that any particular doctrine about the soul was originally implied in these; but, as Demeter and the Maid were both chthonian goddesses, it seemed natural that they should be able to secure for their votaries a more satisfactory existence in the under world than that of a Homeric 'shade.' We find that idea already in the Homeric *Hymn to Demeter*, and it was obviously capable of development. On the whole, however, it does not appear that there was any mysticism in the 'mysteries,' and the nature of the life to come which they promised was clearly modelled on Homer's Elysian field. It will be seen that, strictly speaking, this would imply that the initiated retained their bodies after death, but it is not necessary to suppose that the average Athenian troubled himself on this point.

(3) So far, we have come to nothing that can rightly be called an immortal soul. The gods alone are immortal, and that is because they have immortal bodies. It was only with the spread of the worship of Dionysus that a new idea of the soul as essentially divine, though fallen, gradually emerged. The worship of Dionysus was distinguished by its insistence on divine 'possession' (κατοκωχή, ἐνθουσιασμός) and 'ecstasy' (ἔκστασις, 'stepping out' of the body). In that there is nothing startling or beyond the range of primitive peoples. What was new was that it suggested to some Greeks an entirely new view of the soul and its relation to God. We know from the Orphic gold plates discovered at Thurii and Petelia that the soul of the departed Orphic saint (ὅσιος, καθαρός) claimed actually to be a god and to have won release (λύσις) from the 'grievous wheel' of birth by strict observance of the precepts of purity. From this point of view it followed that what we call life is really death, and that the body is the prison or tomb of the soul. Now, the followers of Orpheus were certainly numerous at Athens from the time of Pisistratus onwards, and we have always to take account of their influence. It is not clear, however, that they really went much farther than primitive spiritism in their theory of the soul. At any rate, Pindar, who was certainly influenced by the doctrine and insists that the soul alone is 'from the gods,' also calls it 'an image of life' (αἰῶνος εἴδωλον) which survives death—a thing Homer might quite well have said —and he expressly lays down that it 'sleeps when the limbs are active' (εὕδει δὲ πρασσόντων μελέων).[1] It is only in dreams that it shows its true nature during life, and it appears to be quite dissociated from the normal waking consciousness. It is not clear that an Orphic believer would naturally speak of his soul as 'I' before he died. It is rather a supernatural guest whom he entertains. The Orphic doctrine, then, is more important in this connexion for what it suggested to philosophers than for itself.

(4) Another influence, which began to make itself felt at Athens early in the 5th cent. B.C., was that of Ionian science. It must be remembered that Ionia was, comparatively speaking, a country without a past. There was no 'usage of the fathers,' as there was at Athens, to keep up the memory of older beliefs. The traditional doctrine of the soul was obviously unsatisfactory from the scientific point of view. It is true that the Ionians were led by a natural human impulse, which seems to have given rise both to science and to religion, to seek for something 'ageless and deathless' (a Homeric phrase adopted by Anaximander), but they looked for it in the world around them. Their central belief was that all the changing things of this world must be forms of one undying substance, which they called 'god'—a word which they had completely secularized. In its developed form Ionian science held that this primary substance was 'air' (*i.e.* vapour), and the soul was regarded simply as a portion of the boundless air which happened for the time being to be enclosed in a human, animal, or vegetable body. This is not, of course, to be identified with the dream-consciousness like the Orphic soul. Diogenes of Apollonia regarded the 'internal air,' which was 'a small portion of the god,' as the seat of our ordinary consciousness, and Heraclitus (who regarded the soul as fire) insisted specially on its identity with our waking life. On the other hand, it has no permanent reality of its own; it is nothing that can be called 'I' or even 'this.' It is introduced into the body by respiration, and, if it is called immortal, that merely means that it returns at death to the undying air outside us.[1]

(5) Neither the Orphic 'soul' nor the 'soul' of Ionian science was a *self* any more than the Homeric. So far as we can judge, it was Pythagoras who first regarded the soul in this way. If we are right in referring to him the doctrine of reminiscence (ἀνάμνησις) and connecting it with that of reincarnation (παλιγγενεσία), it seems to follow that he must have regarded the soul, which is the seat of knowledge, as something with a permanent individuality of its own. If so, however, his followers were not very faithful to their master's teaching. Those of them who emphasized its scientific side soon came to regard the soul as an 'attunement' (ἁρμονία) of the elements constituting the body, and of course such a theory is wholly inconsistent with its immortality, or even its individuality. The soul is simply a function of the body. Pythagoreanism, then, only added to the existing confusion of ideas.

In these circumstances, it is easy to see how it was that the Athenians of the Periclean age had no definite views about the soul at all. They continued to perform the customary rites of the mortuary cult, and they continued to use the wholly inconsistent language of Homer. Down to the very end of the century the word ψυχή is hardly found in any but its Homeric sense of life as a thing to be lost. Even in the passages where it seems to be used of the seat of feeling—what we call the 'heart'—the feelings attributed to it are always of the inarticulate kind which belong rather to the dream-consciousness than to the waking life. The idea of a real life of the soul after death is quite unknown. The orators sometimes use such phrases as 'if the departed have any consciousness of the things in this world'; but they speak very doubtfully, and it is obvious that they are thinking chiefly of the souls in the grave which were the objects of the mortuary cult. In the funeral orations delivered over those who had fallen in battle it was customary to introduce a 'consolation' for their parents, but it is never suggested to them that the souls of their sons have perhaps departed to a better life. Under the influences which have been described above, the only formula that seemed satisfactory was 'Earth to earth and air to air,' and that this was considered quite orthodox is proved by the fact that it was

[1] Frag. 131 (96), quoted by Plutarch, *Consol. ad Apoll.* p. 120 D.

[1] Cf. Theophrastus, *de Sens.* 42 (of Diogenes of Apollonia): ὅτι δὲ ὁ ἐντὸς ἀὴρ αἰσθάνεται, μικρὸν ὂν μόριον τοῦ θεοῦ, κ.τ.λ. For Heraclitus sleep was just being cut off from the surrounding fire.

employed in the epitaph on those who fell at Potidæa in 432 B.C. Plato, therefore, is historically justified when he represents the companions of Socrates as startled when they hear that their master believes the individual soul to be immortal. To them the very idea was quite unfamiliar.[1]

6. Socrates and Plato.—In the 4th cent. all this is changed. Isocrates speaks of the soul very much as we do, and it is freely identified with the normal consciousness. It is the seat of knowledge and ignorance, and it is the seat of character. It seems, then, that some one must have set forth a new view of the soul in the latter half of the 5th cent. B.C., and it is hard to think of any one who is likely to have done so except Socrates. Now it is certain from the jests of Aristophanes that Socrates was well known in 423 B.C. as a man who taught strange doctrine about the soul (*ψυχή*). His disciples are referred to in derision as *ψυχαί* in the *Clouds*,[2] and he himself is said to practise *ψυχαγωγία* in the *Birds*.[3] It is improbable that *ψυχαγωγεῖ* at this date can mean anything else than 'calls spirits' from the other world; and, unless the joke is to be regarded as intolerably frigid, we must suppose that Socrates was commonly known at this date (413 B.C.) to teach the immortality of the soul. Now, in the *Apology*, Plato makes Socrates state twice over[4] with great emphasis that the purpose of his mission was to get men 'to care for their soul' (*ἐπιμελεῖσθαι τῆς ψυχῆς*) and to make it as good as they can. It does not seem possible that he could have made Socrates say this unless the fact had been well known, and it is certain that, if Socrates did say this, he was using the word 'soul' (*ψυχή*) in a sense it had not hitherto borne. We gather that he described it as 'that in us which has knowledge and goodness' or their opposites,[5] and that he insisted that it was our true self and demanded our best care (*ἐπιμέλεια*), 'not only for the time of this life, but for all time.'[6]

Such, at any rate, is the doctrine which Plato always ascribes to Socrates and which even Xenophon has tried to express in his own way.[7] Plato himself adopted it and gave it a scientific form. For him 'soul' was above all the source of motion (*ἀρχὴ κινήσεως*). It was the only thing which could move itself and other things without being itself moved by anything else. It was, therefore, 'prior to the body' (*πρεσβύτερον τοῦ σώματος*), and the efficient cause of everything good and bad. There are, as a matter of fact, bad things as well as good, and therefore there must be more souls than one. It is not easy to distinguish in Plato's dialogues those parts of the doctrine of soul which he inherited from the Pythagoreans and Socrates and those which reveal his own convictions, but the teaching of his immediate successors and the criticisms of Aristotle prove that the point chiefly emphasized by him was that the soul is the only 'self-mover.'

It is specially to be noted that the doctrine of the 'self-mover' does not occur in the *Phædo*, and this seems to indicate that it is Platonic rather than Socratic. On the other hand, Socrates is made to expound it in the *Phædrus*[1] with perfect clearness and precision. That, however, is in a strongly Pythagorizing passage, and it may be that the Pythagoreans had to some extent anticipated Plato's theory. That seems to be suggested by what we know of the doctrines of Alcmæon, a younger contemporary of Pythagoras, who taught that the soul was immortal because it resembled immortal things, and was always in motion like the heavenly bodies.[2] Plato implies in the *Phædo*[3] that Socrates had been interested in Alcmæon's view that the brain, rather than the heart, was the seat of sensation, so he must certainly have known his theory of the soul. We may infer, however, from the silence of the *Phædo* that this aspect of it did not appeal to him as strongly as it did to Plato. It is important also to notice that in Plato the soul is always distinguished from the 'forms' (*εἴδη, ἰδέαι*). It is just the existence of souls that makes it possible for the 'forms' to enter into the world of becoming.

If these views are correct, it follows that what is called the soul from the religious and ethical point of view was clearly apprehended for the first time by Socrates, and that it became the central thing in Plato's system. To him the existence of souls was the only possible explanation of the existence of a world. The movements of the heavenly bodies implied that there was a soul of the world, which was an animate creature (*ζῷον*), and God could be understood only if He were regarded as a soul. The soul of the world, the souls of the heavenly bodies, and the souls of men, animals, and plants were all created by God; but, once created, they would never be destroyed, because that would be inconsistent with the goodness of God, who can only desire that they should become as like Himself as may be. That is, in brief, the doctrine of the soul which we owe to Greece.

7. Aristotle.—It only remains for us to say something of the reaction which followed at first on the proclamation of this doctrine. It begins at once with Aristotle, though, as usual, we can distinguish two conflicting strains in his thought. He is, in the first place, an Ionian, and he therefore rebels against the spiritual interpretation of nature. On the other hand, he had been carried away, in spite of himself, by the teaching of Plato, and the beliefs he really cares about are just those which cannot be reconciled with the rest of his system or expressed in terms of it. He begins with the body, to which the soul is related as form to matter. It is not, however, a mere function of the body, and Aristotle will have nothing to do with the doctrine that it is an 'attunement' (*ἁρμονία*). On the contrary, the body is the instrument (*ὄργανον*) of the soul; for matter is only a potency and exists only in so far as it is necessary for the realization of a form. Even so, however, soul is inseparably bound up with body, and can have no life apart from it. So far it is easy to follow, but then we are told, without any real explanation at all, that, while the most developed form of soul is mind (*νοῦς*), this mind is purely passive. There is another sense of mind in which it is 'separable from matter,' and this alone is 'immortal and everlasting.' The conflicting interpretations of this doctrine given by Alexander of Aphrodisias, Averroes, and St. Thomas do not concern us here. The fact remains that Aristotle himself gives no intelligible account of the matter, and that he puts us off with a metaphor, as he usually does when he has gone as far as his own system will take him without coming to the beliefs that he really cherished. Even the metaphor is instructive. He tells us that this

[1] For the hesitation of the Attic orators on the subject of the soul see H. Meuss, 'Die Vorstellungen vom Dasein nach dem Tode bei den attischen Rednern' (*Jahrb. für klass. Philologie*, v. [1889] 801 ff.). The usual phrase is 'if in any way the dead should acquire a consciousness of what is now happening' (*εἴ τινες τῶν τετελευτηκότων λάβοιεν τρόπῳ τινὶ τοῦ νῦν γιγνομένου πράγματος αἴσθησιν*). This explains also the doubtful way in which Plato makes Socrates refer to the subject in the *Apology*. In this, as in other matters, he outwardly respects the conventions of the Athenian law-courts. No inference can be drawn as to his real beliefs about the soul, and in the *Apology* itself these are made sufficiently clear, as we shall see. The absence of all reference to a future life in the consolatory passages of the *ἐπιτάφιοι λόγοι* was pointed out by C. Lehrs (*Populäre Aufsätze*, Leipzig, 1856, p. 331). The epitaph on those who fell at Potidæa says simply (*CIA* i. 442) *αἰθὴρ μὲν ψυχὰς ὑπεδέξατο, σώματα δὲ χθών*, with which we may compare Eur. *Suppl.* 533: *πνεῦμα μὲν πρὸς αἰθέρα, | τὸ σῶμα δ' ἐς γῆν*. For the surprise with which the companions of Socrates receive the announcement of his doctrine of soul cf. esp. *Rep.* x. 608 D: *Οὐκ ᾔσθησαι, ἦν δ' ἐγώ, ὅτι ἀθάνατος ἡμῶν ἡ ψυχὴ καὶ οὐδέποτε ἀπόλλυται;—Καὶ ὃς ἐμβλέψας μοι* ('staring at me') *καὶ θαυμάσας εἶπε· Μὰ Δί', οὐκ ἔγωγε· σὺ δὲ τοῦτ' ἔχεις λέγειν;* It is particularly to be noted that, in the *Phædo* (69 E, 70 A, 80 D), even the Pythagorean associates of Socrates are represented as quite incredulous. That is because they had adopted the view that the soul is the *ἁρμονία* of the body.

[2] 94.

[3] 1555 ff.

[4] 24 D and 30 A.

[5] Cf. e.g., *Crito*, 47 E.

[6] *Phædo*, 107 C.

[7] *Cyr.* viii. 7, 19 ff.

[1] 245 D ff.

[2] Arist. *de Anima*, 405*a* 30.

[3] 96 B.

mind comes 'from outside' (θύραθεν), which is a thoroughly Ionian way of speaking and is apparently derived from Anaxagoras. On the other hand, this doctrine lands Aristotle in a dualism which neither Anaxagoras nor Plato would have admitted. It is quite wrong to say, as Rohde does, that it is 'a mythological element derived from Plato's dogmatic system.' Even in his most mythological moods Plato never lost sight of the unity of the individual soul.

This point is frequently obscured by the stress laid on the doctrine of the 'tripartite soul,' which is used for dialectical purposes in the *Republic* and for mythological purposes elsewhere. It is almost certainly Pythagorean, and connected with the doctrine of the ἁρμονία. The three 'parts' of the soul were identified with the three intervals of the scale, the fourth, the fifth, and the octave. Even in the *Republic*, however, we are left in no doubt that the soul is really one. It is only when it is diseased that the three 'parts' seem to be independent of each other.

8. Stoic and Epicurean doctrines.—The Stoic and Epicurean doctrines are still more obviously reversions to the standpoint of early Ionian science, though they too admit inconsistent elements from other sources, such, *e.g.*, as the Stoic belief that individual souls (which were regarded as corporeal) survived till the next world-conflagration (ἐκπύρωσις). That was denied by Panætius, but reasserted by Posidonius, who adopted Platonic views wholesale. He is the source of the popular orthodoxy on the subject, as we find it represented in Cicero. For the Epicureans the atoms which composed the soul were blown away 'like smoke' at death, though Epicurus left careful directions for the observation of his mortuary cult. Such is the strength of inherited tradition.

As a matter of fact this cult was kept up more assiduously than ever, and the number of 'heroes' increased daily. The teaching of the Orphics and others had left its mark, and there were parts of Greece where almost every one seems to have been promoted to heroic honours after death. That, however, need not mean a real belief in the soul's immortality. Nor did the religious revival of the 3rd and 4th centuries A.D. really bring anything new, except the worship of strange gods. The ideas about the soul which these brought with them had long been familiar in Greece. On the other hand, there arose a strong feeling of dissatisfaction with traditional views, which the revival of Pythagorism did little to meet.

9. Neo-Platonism and its influence on Christianity.—It was only when the doctrine of Plato was again preached in its integrity by Plotinus that it once more became possible to hold a coherent doctrine of the soul. Neo-Platonism at its best owed nothing to exotic religions or popular superstition, and there is no reason to believe that Plato would have disavowed his later followers. At the end it was only the Academy among the schools of Greece that retained any vitality, and it was through the Platonists that the true Greek doctrine of the soul was passed on to Christian theology. Clement of Alexandria, Origen, and Augustine all learned in the school of Plato, and the direct influence of Aristotle was not to be felt for centuries yet. That was not what the Platonists designed. Plotinus ignored Christianity, and most of his followers were bitterly hostile to it. Nevertheless, it was on their teaching that the Catholic doctrine was based, and their teaching goes back, through Plato, to Socrates, Pythagoras, and the Orphics, who represent the genuine Greek doctrine of the soul far more than Homer or the Attic tragedians do. There are two sides of this which are essential to it. In the first place, the soul is immortal, and that is the Italiote contribution to the doctrine. In the second place, this immortal soul is just our ordinary consciousness; it is the seat of knowledge and error, of goodness and badness. That is the Ionian contribution. The two views were fused into one at Athens, the place where western and eastern influences met and reacted on one another, and this must have happened in the 5th cent. B.C.; for it was only then that the necessary conditions for such a fusion existed. The practical inference was that the soul which we know in our everyday waking life requires as much care (ἐπιμέλεια) as any Orphic votary had ever bestowed on the fallen divinity within him. Plato represents this as the burden of the mission of Socrates, and there does not seem to be any good ground for disbelieving him.

LITERATURE.—E. Rohde, *Psyche*[5, 6], 2 vols., Tübingen, 1910 (this work supersedes all the earlier literature of the subject; its only defect is that it overlooks the importance of Socrates altogether, with the result that it fails to distinguish the Pythagorean and Socratic element in Plato's writings from his own scientific teaching on the subject); A. Dieterich, *Nekyia*, Leipzig, 1893; J. Adam, in *Cambridge University Prælections delivered before the Senate*, Cambridge, 1906, p. 29 ff., *The Religious Teachers of Greece*, Edinburgh, 1908; J. Burnet, *Plato's Phædo*, Oxford, 1911, *The Socratic Doctrine of the Soul*, London, 1916, reprinted from the *Proceedings of the British Academy*, vii. [1915-16] 235 ff.

JOHN BURNET.

SOUL (Hindu). — From the very earliest moment at which we can trace the Aryan race which invaded India (perhaps in the second millennium B.C.), and became there the nucleus of the Hindu people, they already distinguished the soul from the body and believed that it survived death. The evidence is their ancestor-worship,[1] in which they laid out food for the souls of their dead ancestors to eat. The character of the food is sufficient proof that, at the time when the rite was formed, they still thought of the soul as being of the same nature as the body.

As in the case of other primitive races, their idea of survival was for long undefined; they had no conviction that the soul lasted for ever. But a change came after the rise of the heavenly gods (*devas*) among them:[2] they began to believe that the souls of their ancestors lived with or near these gods, and that was followed by the idea that some god conferred immortality on them, at least on those who had lived good lives on earth.[3] From that faith there would naturally spring the conviction that the soul was of such a nature as to be fit to live for ever.

At an unknown date, perhaps in the 7th or 8th cent. B.C., the belief in transmigration and *karma* (*qq.v.*) was formed among a small group of thinking men in N. India and gradually spread from them to the whole Hindu people.[4] The central idea of this doctrine is that of moral requital: man's soul lives many lives on earth, and reaps in a later the moral harvest which he has sown in an earlier life. As the happiness and misery of each existence are proof that the soul lived before and did good and evil actions, the theory compels the belief that the process of life and death can have had no beginning; and, as the actions of every life that is lived demand another life for their expiation, there is no escape from the conclusion that the process of repeated birth can have no end. The souls of men are thus eternal, have had no beginning, and can have no end. Each is *an indestructible eternal entity*. This is the first important idea in the Hindu concept of soul.

One element in the theory of requital is that a man who has lived a very good life may be born in his next life as a royal personage, a petty godling, or even one of the greatest gods, while, if he has lived a very evil life, he may be born in the very lowest grade of society, as a devil, an

[1] See art. ANCESTOR-WORSHIP AND CULT OF THE DEAD (Indian).
[2] See art. ARYAN RELIGION, vol. ii. p. 31.
[3] A. A. Macdonell, *Vedic Mythology*, Strassburg, 1897, p. 166.
[4] H. Oldenberg, *Die Lehre der Upanishaden und die Anfänge des Buddhismus*, Göttingen, 1915, pp. 28, 105.

animal, or even a plant. Clearly this implies that *all souls*, whether now living as gods, devils, men, or plants, *are essentially the same*, the differences between them being only elements of their temporary status, which have come on them as a result of their actions. This is the second characteristic element in the Hindu concept of soul.

The contemporaneous Hindu polytheism is clearly reflected in this notable idea. There can be no doubt that the men who formed the theory of transmigration and *karma* were polytheists. If they had been theists, the concept of the Supreme, high above all men and ordinary gods, would have exercised an influence in several directions. The process of requital would have been conceived as under his control, and the idea of the human spirit would inevitably have been formed in relation to him, while the fact is that, from the beginning, the process of *karma* was regarded as automatic, and there was no thought of a soul of a higher order, all being conceived as on a single plane.

Yet it seems to be true that at the very time when the theory of transmigration and *karma* was formed, or even earlier, another concept, which was destined to produce immeasurable results in India, was gradually taking shape[1] in a small intellectual circle in N. India—the philosophic concept of the *Brahman-Ātman*, the earliest germ of the Vedānta philosophy. At first the idea seems to have been that within, behind, and beyond the whole visible and invisible universe of man's experience and beliefs there is a spiritual existence of the most exalted order, free, intelligent, joyful. It was called the *Brahman*, the *Ātman*, or the *Brahman-Ātman*. It was sometimes said to be the source of all gods and men and the universe; at another time it was identified with the all. One of the commonest statements about it is that it alone exists: 'One there is and there is no second.'

But it was not long before the theory of rebirth and *karma* provoked a reaction.[2] While the idea of just requital was felt to be a great gain, the finer spirits soon began to regard the prospect of an endless series of births and deaths as intolerable. The question was asked, Is there no means whereby one may be released from the necessity of rebirth? In response to this desire of the spirit, a whole series of philosophic theories, each one a theory of release, sprang into being. The earliest and most significant of these theories springs from the belief in the ever free and joyful *Ātman*. Some thinker reached the conviction that his own soul was the *Ātman*—not a product of it, nor a portion of it, but the whole; and he began to teach that he who knows that his own spirit is the *Ātman* is thereby released from all bonds, and therefore from the bondage of rebirth.

This theory of the identity of the divine and the human spirit is the root of the Vedānta philosophy and first finds expression in the early *Upaniṣads*. As the source of the conception lies in the original contrast between man, bound in the toils of rebirth and *karma*, on the one hand, and God, ever free and joyful, on the other, the contrast is very clearly developed in these writings. The idea that the *Ātman* has nothing to do with *karma* and rebirth is especially prominent. Since the *Ātman* is not burdened with *karma*, it must be completely inactive—completely apart from all the temptations and toils of the sense-world. Hence, although no definite system is taught in the *Upaniṣads*, there is a broad and very general tendency to describe the *Ātman* as being not only inactive but also (1) abstract intelligence rather than an intelligent personality, (2) thought rather than will, (3) above the petty distinctions of morality. Therefore, since this was the teaching of the earliest system of release (a system which has had an immeasurable influence in India), and since it taught the identity of man's soul with this abstract impersonal intelligence, the great stream of Hindu thought has always tended to conceive the human spirit as being essentially intelligence, to regard personality, will, and emotion as belonging to the lower reaches of human nature, because they are involved in action, which leads to *karma*, and to think of morality as a set of rules belonging merely to the social life of man and therefore having little or no relation to the nature of the soul.

This tendency has produced momentous results in Indian thought and religion. The almost total neglect of the will and the extreme weakness of ethics in Hindu philosophy, and the great emphasis laid on ritualism, or on knowledge, rather than on ethical change as the way of salvation in Hinduism, are all attributable to this cause.

In spite of this broad general tendency, the teaching of the *Upaniṣads* is by no means uniform. Lines of thought running in many directions may be found, from which divergent systems sprang at later dates. One of these is the Sāṅkhya (*q.v.*) philosophy, which is a realistic dualism. There are two eternal existences, original nature (*prakṛti*) and an infinite number of individual spirits (*puruṣa*); there is no God. Each spirit is intelligence, but no more, merely a solitary, passive spectator of the operations of nature. This concept has clearly been formed from the common idea of the human soul already spoken of. But for our purpose the most interesting point is this—that in this philosophy there took shape a psychological theory which, with modifications, has been held in all forms of Indian religion. From *prakṛti*, besides the visible things of the world, there issues a series of subtle substances—*buddhi*, *ahaṁkāra*, *manas*, 'intellect,' 'egoism,' 'mind,'—and also the senses, by means of which the functions of perception, generalization, and decision are carried out. In this physical series we have the fact made plain that, according to the Hindu idea, the human spirit is not an active power which thinks and feels and wills, but is the pure light of consciousness.

At a later date another philosophy was formed known as the Vaiśeṣika (*q.v.*), which recognizes the existence of many souls and the reality of the world. In this philosophy the concept of the soul is richer and fuller than in any earlier system. Feeling and will as well as thought are recognized as its functions.[1]

The central school of the Vedānta, with which the great name of Śaṅkarāchārya (*q.v.*) is linked, is monistic, *advaita*. It interprets with strictness both the leading declarations of the *Upaniṣads*, viz. that the *Ātman* alone exists, and that the human spirit is the *Ātman*. Consequently, its doctrine of the human soul is in accordance with these standards. In Deussen's words:

> 'To it are applicable all those negative characteristics whose purpose is to secure the conception of Brahman from all ideas by which His Being might seem to be limited. Therefore the soul is, like Brahman, (1) omnipresent, or, as we should say, spaceless, (2) omniscient and omnipotent, (3) neither agent nor enjoyer (or sufferer, as the case may be).'[2]

In the theistic sects, which were formed in the early Christian centuries, the central ideas of the Vedānta philosophy—that the *Ātman* alone exists, and that the human spirit *is* the *Ātman*—are held, but they are not interpreted so strictly as in the monistic Vedānta. These systems vary amongst

[1] Oldenberg, pp. 36–104; P. Deussen, *Allgemeine Gesch. der Philosophie*, Leipzig, 1894, I. i. 159 ff.
[2] Oldenberg, pp. 124–147.

[1] J. C. Chatterji, *The Hindu Realism*, Allahabad, 1912, p. 102.
[2] *The System of the Vedānta*, Eng. tr., Chicago, 1912, p. 468.

themselves in some degree in their statement of the relation of the soul to God, four forms of theory being held, as follows: (1) *śuddhādvaita*: pure monism; this, though called pure monism, is not so strictly monistic as the *advaita*; (2) *viśiṣṭ-ādvaita*: modified monism, identity with a difference; this is the commonest point of view; (3) *bhedābheda* or *dvaitādvaita*: the relation is both monistic and dualistic; (4) *bheda*, or *dvaita*: dualism.

Yet these differences are not of much practical import, except in so far as they modify the conception of the state of the soul after release. In the monistic Vedānta, the identity of the soul with God being held in the strictest possible way, the seeming individuality of the soul in life is interpreted as an illusion, and release means the disappearance of the illusion, the complete absorption of the man in God.[1] Of the theistic sects, on the other hand, while a few teach absorption, the mass believe in the actual reality of the soul, and teach that in release the soul either enters into a mystical union with God in which individuality is not lost or spends eternity in a fellowship with God which does not in the slightest impair personality. In their account of the nature of the soul they vary between the Sāṅkhya conviction that it is a spectator, but in no sense an agent or an enjoyer, and the Vaiśeṣika theory that it wills and feels as well as acts. Yet, even if they declare the soul an agent, all the active psychological functions are still ascribed to *buddhi*, *ahaṁkāra*, and *manas*—the triple physical concomitant of the soul in Hinduism. Most of them teach that after release the soul is omnipresent and omniscient, but they differ in their account of its size, some declaring that it is atomic, others that it is infinite. The Śrī-Vaiṣṇavas, *e.g.*, the sect of Rāmānuja, teach that the soul is consciousness, but is also an agent, that it is atomic in size, and that in release it is omniscient, unrestricted in movement, and able to realize all its wishes.[2]

LITERATURE.—See the works cited in the footnotes.

J. N. FARQUHAR.

SOUL (Iranian).—Little need be added under this heading to what has been said in the art. PHILOSOPHY (Iranian), especially under § 1 (*d*) and (*e*), and the latter part of § 2, concerning the psychological analysis of the human compound—so favourite a topic in both Avestan and later literature. Of the terms *urvan*, *ahū*, *baodah*, *daēna*, *fravaši*, and in later times *khrat*, *vīr*, *hōš*, which express various spiritual faculties or constituents of man's non-material nature, the first named, *urvan* (gen. *urunō*), is generally taken as expressing most closely what we mean by our word 'soul' in the widest sense. Its form and meaning seem to have come down practically unaltered from the *Gāthās* to the Pahlavi *rūbāno* and modern Persian *ravān*. It is generally admitted that it is that element of man which remains immortal after death and bears the responsibility of reward or punishment for his actions in this life. Hence it is commonly employed in contrast to *tanū*, the body. And in a broader sense the two opposed terms are used, at least in the later literature, to indicate the spiritual and the material worlds respectively. Thus in the curious diagram of the *Dīnkarṭ* reproduced in art. DUALISM (Iranian) the whole of being (*yehevūn*) is carefully divided into two opposed parts, *rūbāno* and *tanū*. It is not only of men that *urvan* is predicated, but also, though rarely, in both Gāthic and later Avesta, of animals.[3] The soul of the primeval ox (*gēuš urvan*) was taken up into heaven after its slaughter and became the well-known tutelary genius of cattle.

After a man's death, according to the famous description of *Vendīdād*, xix., and the *Hadokht-Nask*, the soul hovers above his head for three days, but on the fourth morning sets out on its journey towards the Chinvat Bridge, which leads to the next world, and on its way meets the strange female figure, the creation and personification of the man's deeds, words, and thoughts in this life—an exquisitely beautiful damsel in the case of the virtuous soul, a horrible hag in that of the sinful soul—who ushers it either to eternal happiness or to misery and punishment.

The relationship of the *urvan* to the *fravaši* (*q.v.*), in spite of all that has been written on the subject, still remains very obscure, and probably was never very clearly defined. The etymology of *urvan* is also uncertain. It is almost certainly from $\sqrt{var}$, 'to choose,' indicating the faculty of free will.

LITERATURE.—The art. 'Urvan' in C. Bartholomae, *Altiranisches Wörterbuch*, Strassburg, 1904 (concise and full of useful information); all the ordinary translators and commentators, C. de Harlez, J. Darmesteter, etc.

L. C. CASARTELLI.

SOUL (Muslim).[1]—**I. In the Qur'ān and in popular belief.**—According to the Qur'ān,[2] Allāh, when He created the first man, breathed into him the soul (*nafs*) or the spirit of life (*rūḥ*). In Adam's soul were created the souls of all his descendants, and the act of endowing with life the embryo in the womb is thus a second creation.[3] The soul has its seat in the heart, and is accordingly often described in the Qur'ān by the phrase 'heart, hearing, and sight,' or 'hearing, sight, and heart.'[4] In particular, the heart is the abode of religious knowledge and of faith or unbelief. Should Allāh see good to leave a man in unbelief, He seals up or narrows his heart, closes his ears, and puts a veil upon his eyes;[5] on the other hand, He enlarges the heart of believers, and opens their ears to the divine revelation. As is usually the case in religious psychology, hearing is of more importance than sight, and as a rule precedes it in any mention of the two. Thus Allāh Himself hears and sees;[6] He is the hearer, the knower.[7] He expresses Himself by the eternal Word. By unanimous Muslim tradition, Muhammad received his revelation by the ear. It is by means of hearing that faith is imparted to the heart.

Besides heart, hearing, and sight, however, Allāh at the creation endowed the soul with two fundamental propensities, viz. wickedness and piety[8]—an impulse towards evil and an impulse towards good. Originally this may have implied simply that every soul has these two impulses, and that it was Muhammad's part to address his admonitions to the good impulse, the good side of the will. Gradually, however, the preaching of the Prophet comes to ignore the human will. Allāh alone has a will in the proper sense; man is a being who knows and acts, but has no volition of his own, and his whole duty is to be prudent, to give heed to God's word, and to obey it.

Moreover, as Allāh breathes the soul into the body from without, He can also separate the two, as in sleeping and dreaming or at death.[9] Of the soul's continued existence after death the Qur'ān says little to which we can attach a definite

1 Deussen, *System of the Vedânta*, p. 478.

2 A. V. Sukhtankar, *Teachings of Vedanta according to Ramanuja*, Vienna, 1908, p. 78 f.

3 E.g., *Yasna* xxxix. 2 (of cattle) and 4 (of wild animals); *Vendīdād*, xiii. 15 (of the otter), and *Yašt* xiii. 74 (of all quadrupeds, aquatic and winged animals, etc. [though here the *urunō* seem identified with the *fravašis*]).

1 For views of the soul among the Arabs of pre-Muhammadan times cf. art. ARABS (Ancient), vol. i. p. 659 ff., esp. 671 ff.

2 xv. 29. 3 xxxix. 8.

4 ii. 6, and *passim*, xvi. 80, etc., esp. xxxii. 8.

5 ii. 6, xvi. 110. 6 iv. 61.

7 ii. 121. 8 xci. 7 f.

9 vi. 60, xxxix. 43.

meaning. When the pious die, Allāh brings their souls near Himself, and keeps them there until He unites them again with their risen bodies at the day of judgment.[1]

These notices have been considerably amplified by the Tradition, and many elements have been added also by popular belief in the various Muslim lands. As it is impossible here to enter fully into details, we restrict ourselves to a few of the main features reflected in the popular theology.

As regards the pre-existence of souls, the Tradition supplies the following particulars. Between the first creation of souls in the soul of Adam and the second in the mother's womb they are kept by Allāh in His treasure-house or in a shrine attached to His throne. When their time has come, He transmits them from His heavenly realm into the human embryos. It is true that God creates a far larger number of non-human souls or spirits—those of animals, demons, angels, and devils—but it is naturally the human soul and its destiny that engage the supreme interest of man. Nor is the soul's pre-existence a subject of anything like so much concern as its future, its life after death. Here the dreams of eschatological fantasy are lavishly drawn upon. Just as here and now man is surrounded and attended by angels and spirits, so the souls of the dying are taken in charge by the angel of death, who conveys those of believers to blessedness and those of unbelievers to perdition. The soul departs from the body (on the most widely current view) by way of the mouth, while some hold that it leaves by the back of the head. Another very common belief is that the soul which at death has been carried to heaven is sent back again by God, and that it sojourns for a longer or shorter period beside the body in the grave. It is there subjected to an examination by the angels Munkir and Nakīr. If it asserts its belief in Islām—the great test is the creed, good works being of minor importance—the angels carry it aloft to heaven and set it upon a candlestick by the throne of God. The evil soul, the soul that does not know its Lord, is, on the other hand, tormented there and then, and also afterwards in hell. The souls of believers who have done evil pass into purgatory. A fairly prevalent idea is that the departed soul survives till the day of judgment in the form of a bird—the soul of the believer living in a green bird, that of the unbeliever in a black one. The souls of those who have been murdered sit beside their graves in the form of owls and cry for vengeance.

It is popularly believed that the departed soul has severed itself from the body greatly against its will; and it accordingly remains near the corpse as long as the latter is not wholly decomposed. This again affords grounds for the belief that intercourse may continue for a time between the dead and their surviving relatives. The prayers, alms, and good works of the living benefit the souls of the dead.

The synthesis of body and soul during man's earthly life is regarded as relatively loose. There is a great variety of belief as to the seat of the soul. There is no doubt, however, that the soul can leave the body during sleep. In its real nature it is known to God alone, and, as the Qur'ān says,[2] man knows but little about it. Nevertheless popular thought usually conceives of the soul as a material entity, and with this idea it conjoins speculations regarding the various classes of spirits—spirits or souls of the prophets, the angels, the *jinn*, the devils, human beings, and animals, and these in all their species and varieties. On the day of resurrection the souls of men, as belonging to their bodies, return, and enter into their renovated material frame, and thereupon Allāh assigns them for all eternity to paradise or hell, the joys or pains of which are represented, alike in the Qur'ān and in popular belief, as being of a physical rather than a spiritual character. The wicked are to burn for ever in hell without being consumed, while the good are to eat and drink for ever in paradise, and live there with beautiful youths and maidens, without weariness or satiety. The delights of paradise are accordingly those of men. As regards the blessedness that women are to expect in the beyond, the Tradition is altogether silent.

[1] lxxxi. 7. [2] xvii. 87.

2. In the theologians and the mystics.—The rudimentary notions of the Qur'ān and popular thought regarding the soul are found again in the conceptions of the theologians and mystics, there assuming, however, a number of forms varying from the grossest materialism of the masses to the extreme spiritualism of allegorical interpretation, and in part modified by the influence of Christian theology and philosophical speculation. In the theological systems too, as in ordinary thinking, the doctrine of the soul is concerned mainly with subjects like the hereafter, resurrection, hell, purgatory, and paradise. The theologians, however, are more interested than either the Qur'ān or the Tradition in the soul as a fact of experience, though they do not deal with it empirically. Their speculations regarding the nature of the soul, its properties and capacities, and its connexion with the material body are coloured throughout by views already current.

The earliest groups of Muslim theologians (*Mutakallimūn*)[1]—those of all schools, orthodox or heterodox—take a more or less material view of the soul. All that exists, from the divine spirit to the animal soul, is body or of bodily nature. With many of them this is simply the popular view, but in some thinkers—*e.g.*, Hishām—we probably must trace it to Stoic influence. Those who do not actually regard the soul as matter define it as an accident of material substance. We find this conception in the Muslim atomists,[2] according to whom the whole world consists of atoms and their accidents, and among these accidents they place souls, or the manifestations and activities of souls. Like the atoms, souls come into being and pass away again every instant. This denial of the independence and continuity of their essential nature does not impugn their immortality, but merely does away with the nexus of natural causality. It thus presents no analogy to the modern theory of actuality (Wundt, etc.). It might be more aptly compared with the Buddhistic conception, though the element of causality, which is the essential characteristic of the latter, is not recognized by the Muslim atomists. According to these thinkers, Allāh creates anew every moment the soul, or its phenomena and activities, as accidents of bodily substances (*i.e.* atoms), whether of the body as a whole, or of a number of atoms, or even of a single atom in the heart. Among those who stood apart from popular beliefs, among free-thinkers, and especially among physicians, the accidentalistic theory assumes a form in which the soul is regarded as a combination or a combining ratio of the bodily elements. On the other hand, the conception of the soul as a substance was very frequently conjoined with the doctrine of metempsychosis.

The doctrine of the soul as a purely spiritual substance constituting the essential nature of man was held by only a few of the earlier theologians—

[1] From about the 12th cent. most theologians adhere either to a mystical dualism or spiritualism, on the one hand, or, on the other, to a psychology that had developed under the influence of Aristotle.

[2] Cf. art. ATOMIC THEORY (Muhammadan), vol. ii. p. 202f.

e.g., by Naẓẓām and his school. These regarded the connexion between soul and body as being effected by the spirit of life (*rūḥ*, *πνεῦμα*): it was only by the mediation of that spirit that the soul could operate upon the body. The body is a product of the soul, or is at all events dependent upon it. The soul, in its essential nature, is simply pure knowledge and pure volition. Naẓẓām and his school usually define the soul as inward volitional action—a view which must not be identified with voluntarism in the modern sense. What they mean is, on the one hand, that the external actions of human beings are all in the stream of natural causality, and, on the other, that the soul manifests its freedom in its inner volition, and is therefore not determined directly (as most theologians held) by the supreme will of God.

The spiritualistic tendencies of the view that the soul is a substance distinct from the body are found in many of the mystics, and, somewhat tempered in form, among the theologians who were influenced by mysticism. Al-Ghazālī[1] and al-'Arabī[2] may be mentioned as two of the most prominent representatives of this view. The mystics, in the first place, have a peculiar terminology, which, while showing affinity to the usage of the Qur'ān, has been coloured even more decidedly by Hellenistic *γνῶσις* and Christian theology. Thus *nafs*, the ordinary Arabic equivalent of *ψυχή*, they bring down to the sphere of physical life, giving it the sense of 'sensuous desire' (*ἐπιθυμία*, *ὄρεξις*). Conversely, they exalt the *rūḥ* (*πνεῦμα*, *spiritus*) by making it the immaterial psychic principle. They give a meaning identical with that of *rūḥ* to the term *qalb*, 'heart.' But, when they use *rūḥ* in the sense given to it in the philosophical and medical tradition,[3] they attach an adjective—e.g., *rūḥ ḥaywānī*, 'spiritus animalis.' As regards the actual facts of the mystical psychology, again, the more salient features may be summarized as follows. The soul (*rūḥ* or *qalb*) is an immaterial substance of divine or god-like nature; it is God's image in man, light of His light. The body is a thing of inferior worth—a view found in many varieties of form. It is the soul, however, that constitutes the essential nature of man, his distinctive character. Having been created by God, through the agency either of angels or of the world-soul, it seeks the way back to God with ardent yearning. The stages of this return, leading at last to ecstasy or the *unio mystica*, are very variously enumerated.[4] The individual soul can prepare itself for union with the Supreme Essence by pious exercises, meditation, absorption in the inner life—asceticism and good works are of secondary importance, or belong to one of the lower stages. The real union, however, the ecstatic state, the illumination, the revelation of divine mysteries—all this comes in a moment, not as the reward of human merit, but as Allāh's beatific gift of grace to the soul. While the psychology of the mystics assigns a large place to the emotional factor in religion—the affective states of the soul—yet the supreme end of man's life is always represented as a form of knowledge (*γνῶσις*) won by immediate experience of the divine. This crowning intuition is reached by way of self-knowledge, for 'he who knows himself knows also his Lord.'[5]

3. In the philosophers and the physicians.—The spiritual or mystical psychology described above is found also in many Muslim philosophers, though in a different context of thought and with some difference in expression. In point of fact, mysticism had felt the influence of philosophy, while, again, both philosopher and mystic were indebted to the same sources. The philosophers most closely related to the mystics are the so-called philosophers of illumination or revelation, who derive their doctrine from Hermes, etc. In their numerous devotional or hortatory works they inculcate the soul's withdrawal from the material world and its return to God. Even the more typical Peripatetics of Islām, however, import mystical elements into their doctrine of the soul, or crown the Aristotelian psychology with mysticism. In so doing, nevertheless, they differ in two respects from the theologians and the pure mystics: they speak more of the powers or faculties of the human soul than of creation, God's grace, or resurrection, and they allow greater scope to the empirical investigation of the soul. The latter is especially true of the medical savants. Taken as a whole, the philosophico-medical psychology is a syncretism of Platonic and Aristotelian views, and here a factor of the utmost importance was the influence of Galen. The earliest document typical of this school is a little work by Qusṭā ibn Lūqā, a Syrian Christian (*c.* A.D. 835), dealing with the difference between spirit (*rūḥ*, *πνεῦμα*, *spiritus*) and soul. We are here told that the spirit spreads outwards from the heart as a subtle body and controls the functions of the organic frame. It is the breath, the spirit of life, animating the whole body, and ceasing to be when the body dies. It is likewise this spirit of life which, in a more refined form, effects the conservation, combination, and recollection of sense-perceptions in the ventricles of the brain. Thus the gathering together of sense-impressions (general sensation) and the process of representation or conception (*φαντασία*) are localized in the fore-brain; the appraisement of what is represented—reflexion and association—in the mid-brain; the faculties of memory (including recollection) and movement in the hind-brain. This spirit is quite distinct from the soul, the difference being one not of degree, but rather like that between matter and form. The soul is an incorporeal substance—the entelechy of the body conjoined with it; and, as simple substance, it is immortal. The *πνεῦμα* is its instrument, by means of which it animates the body and renders it capable of motion and perception.

These views were adopted, and even elaborated, by the Muslim philosophers of the 11th or 12th and later centuries, as well as by many theologians. Here we find in particular two characteristic developments, viz. the doctrine of the inner senses, and the doctrine of the *νοῦς* (*'aql*). As regards the former, while Galen had distinguished three inner powers of the soul as localized in the three cerebral chambers, Muslim philosophers enumerate these powers as three, four, or even five, and in the last case they find five inner senses corresponding to our five external senses. According to the dualism of the mystics and the philosophers of revelation,[1] the inner senses are to be regarded as higher spiritual faculties of the immaterial soul, while, according to the so-called Aristotelians of Islām (al-Fārābī [*q.v.*], Avicenna [*q.v.*], etc.), they stand midway between the external senses and the purely spiritual intellect (*νοῦς*, *'aql*). Schematically, the doctrine might be set forth as follows. The fore-brain is the seat of (1) general perception (*κοινὴ αἴσθησις*) and (2) the faculty of sense-presentation (Aristotle's *φαντασία*); the mid-brain that of (3) reflexion, which is not only reproductive, but capable of moulding the elements of perception and presentation into new forms by discrimination and combination (and therefore corresponding

[1] Cf. art. ETHICS AND MORALITY (Muslim), vol. v. p. 508 f.
[2] Cf. art. MUḤYĪ AL-DĪN IBN AL-'ARABĪ, vol. viii. p. 907 ff.
[3] Cf. § 3.
[4] Cf. art. ṢŪFIS.
[5] This saying is the inversion of an idea found in pseudo-Plato, *Alcibiades*, 129 ff.; it reached the Arabs through the medium of Neo-Platonism, and so passed into the general tradition.

[1] Cf. § 2.

partly to Aristotle's φαντασία and partly to Galen's διανοητικόν); in the hind-brain are localized (4) the faculty of sensuous judgment (δόξα), which deals with the particulars of perception and conception; and (5) memory, together with the faculty of recollection (*i.e.* Galen's μνημονευτικόν). Some philosophers regard (2) as recollection of the sensuous forms, and (5) as recollection of the meanings associated with these forms.

The intelligence or rational soul (νοῦς) is an immaterial principle, towering above the vegetative and animal soul, as above external and internal sense. The speculations of Muslim philosophers regarding it are almost entirely metaphysical or epistemological, and provide no fresh material for psychology. In the hands of Muslim thinkers the Peripatetic system becomes purely intellectualistic, and their doctrine of the soul virtually ignores the emotional and volitional aspects of human life. Their psychology as a whole shows little originality. Certain fresh developments, however, are found in the works of al-Haitham († 1038), who had an inkling of certain important results of modern experimental psychology (*e.g.*, laws of colour-mixture, Weber's law), and also knew something of the duration of perception and mental assimilation. His principal work deals with optics, and contains scattered observations on psychological points. He had unfortunately no successor in Muslim thought.

LITERATURE.—D. B. Macdonald, *The Religious Attitude and Life in Islam*, Chicago, 1909 (contains a good deal of psychological matter); M. Horten, *Die religiöse Gedankenwelt des Volkes im heutigen Islam*, i., Halle, 1917, ii. 1918; D. Kaufmann, *Die Sinne*, Leipzig, 1884; S. Horovitz, *Die Psychologie bei den jüdischen Religions-Philosophen des Mittelalters von Saadia bis Maimuni*, 4 pts., Breslau, 1898–1912, in *Jahresber. des jüd.-theol. Seminars*; M. Horten, *Die philosophischen Systeme der spekulativen Theologen im Islam*, Bonn, 1912; *Hermetis Trismegisti qui apud Arabes fertur de Castigatione animæ libellum*, ed. O. Bardenhewer, Bonn, 1873; M. Wolff, *Muhammedanische Eschatologie*, Leipzig, 1872 (Arabic and German); al-Ghazālī, *Ad-durra al-fākhira* (*La Perle précieuse*), ed., with French tr. by L. Gautier, Geneva, 1878 (with this should be compared al-Ghazālī's *Al-madnūn al-saghīr* and various sections of his *Ihyā 'ulūm al-dīn*); M. Asín Palacios, 'La Psicología segun Mohidín Abenarabi,' in *Actes du xive Congrès internat. des orientalistes*, Paris, 1906, iii. 79 ff.; *Kitāb maānī al-nafs: Buch vom Wesen der Seele*, ed. I. Goldziher, in *AGG* ix. [1907] 1; *Costa-Ben-Lucæ de differentia animæ et spiritus*, tr. J. Hispalensis, Innsbrück, 1878 (*Bibl. Philos. mediæ ætatis*, ed. C. S. Barach, ii.); and the Arabic original, ed. L. Cheikho, in *Traités inédits d'anciens philosophes arabes*², Beirut, 1911; S. Landauer, 'Die Psychologie des Ibn Sina,' in *ZDMG* xxix. [1875]; H. Bauer, *Die Psychologie Alhazens*, Münster, 1911 (also in C. Bäumker and G. von Hertling, *Beiträge zur Gesch. der Philos. des Mittelalters*, vol. x., pt. v.); F. Taeschner, *Die Psychologie Qazwinis*, Tübingen, 1912.

T. J. DE BOER.

SOUL (Roman).—It is difficult to form any definite or consistent idea of the way in which the early Romans thought of the soul of man either during life or after it; this is owing to the want of an early Roman literature and to the uncertainty of archæological evidence up to the present time. There are, however, certain ascertained facts of the later period of kingly government (which is also the period of the earliest religious calendar) which help us in determining the Roman idea of the condition of the soul after death, and these may possibly be taken as some evidence for the idea of the soul in the living man. The words which in the literary or Græco-Roman age were used for the soul, such as *anima*, 'breath,' cannot with certainty be considered primitive. It is quite probable that, being under the influence of an organizing priesthood and ceremonial religion, the early Romans did not trouble themselves much about their own souls or realize as vividly as many peoples have done that they possessed such a thing; the soul was of slight importance during life. There is no trace of any speculation about the soul of the living man until we come to the last century of the Republic and the introduction of Greek philosophy.

The oldest evidence for the souls of the dead is a so-called *lex regia* attributed to Servius Tullius,[1] which enacts that the son who strikes his parent must be made *sacer* to the *di parentum*, where the word *di*, as in other similar expressions, evidently means spirits, while the word *parentum* is explained in another passage of Festus[2] as meaning, according to the lawyers, three generations of ancestors, beyond which apparently the memory was not expected to go.[3] The fact that the son who strikes a parent is made over as an offering to the spirits of his immediate ancestors shows that these are conceived as (1) active, (2) conscious of morality, (3) in some degree capable of receiving sacrifice, like fully developed *dei*. But how far they reflected the nature of the soul in the living man is by no means clear. We only know that these *di parentes* were the subject of an organized festival in the month of February, which has been described in the art. ROMAN RELIGION.[4] This worship, if we may call it so, of the dead (whether burnt or buried, for both practices undoubtedly existed)[5] outside the walls in the resting-place of the family suggests a pleasant idea of the survival of the soul, which, if properly cared for, could no longer take human shape or return to trouble its human relatives. As in the case of *dei* reclaimed from wild life by settlement in farm or city, the spirits of the departed might be effectually 'laid' by yearly renewed ceremonies, and need do no harm to the survivors; and, so far as we can discover, this belief remained unaltered throughout the republican period.

But in the oldest calendar[6] we find a festival of three days (May 9, 11, 13) called *Lemuria*, of which the object seems to have been to get rid of ghosts from the house; the only information which we have about it includes no public ceremony outside the private dwelling of a family.[7] How we are to interpret this festival of the dead, or even the word *Lemur* which gave it its name, is extremely doubtful. It is safer not to attribute it to a pre-Roman race. The present writer has always inclined to the belief that, if we consider the kind of life led by the various tribes of early Italy, in which death on the battle-field or far from home must have been at least as common as death in the peace of family life, the most likely interpretation is that by *Lemures* is meant the host of the *unburied* dead whose souls were always liable to endeavour to return to the house familiar to them.[8] It was not impossible to forget and ignore entirely relatives lost in this way, who had never been subjected to the processes which ensured their peace and goodwill towards the living; and those three days gave the survivors an opportunity of getting rid of them and forgetting them for the rest of the year. Thus they were thought of as hostile. True, Ovid, in the passage where he describes the father of the family expelling them from the house,[9] calls them *manes paterni*, and *manes* no doubt meant euphemistically 'the good

1 Festus, ed. W. M. Lindsay, Leipzig, 1913, p. 260.
2 *Ib.* p. 247.
3 This probably reflects the practice of three generations living together in one house; and we may remember that this is a well-known feature of social life among certain peoples (see art. ARYAN RELIGION, vol. ii. p. 23^b).
4 Vol. x. p. 826^b.
5 See art. DEATH AND DISPOSAL OF THE DEAD (Roman).
6 See art. ROMAN RELIGION, vol. x. p. 822^a.
7 *Ib.* p. 826^b.
8 Cf. *Æneid*, ix. 214,

'Sit, qui me raptum pugna pretiove redemptum
Mandet humo, solita aut si qua id Fortuna vetabit,
Absenti ferat inferias, decoretque sepulcro,'

where the word *solita* shows how common was the fate of the unburied even in Virgil's time.
9 *Fasti*, v. 429 ff.

ones'; but the house-father may be supposed to be anxious not to irritate them. Here we may note a belief that the great host of souls (*manes*) dwelt in some doubtful sense within the earth, under the guardianship of a deity Orcus,[1] and were permitted to return to the upper world only on three days in the year, August 24, October 5, November 8. But it may be doubted whether this is really a primitive Roman belief;[2] and in any case it seems hardly possible to co-ordinate it in this form with the other beliefs which we have been considering.

From what has been said it will have been noticed that the Roman always spoke of his dead in the plural; and this is significant as showing how hard it was for him to think of the concept soul otherwise than collectively or to realize a soul in himself as an individual entity. There was, however, one exception to this, in the *genius* of the *paterfamilias*, which must be as old as the family itself. That the *genius* was in some sort a soul is not to be doubted;[3] and its peculiarity among the Latins is that it represents the mysterious power of the *paterfamilias* to continue the life of the family.

'The soul of a man is often conceived as the cause of life, but not often as the procreative power itself; and that this latter was the Latin idea is certain, both from the etymology of the word and from the fact that the marriage-bed was called *lectus genialis*.'[4]

This singularity is probably to be explained by the very early development of the idea of fatherhood, both physical and social, in close connexion with that of the continuity which the father alone could contribute to the family. Creative power was the function of the soul of the living man, if he were the head of the household; and it is possible that his wife too had a soul of the same kind, if her *Juno* is a primitive idea.[5] The connexion of snakes, both in the house and in the tomb, with the idea of *genius* need not be explained here.[6]

In what little survives of the earliest Roman literature we find no trace of thought about the soul till we come to Ennius († 169 B.C.). Ennius was a Greek of Calabria and well acquainted with Greek literature in general and with Pythagoreanism in particular; and, as in literature, so in thought, he revolutionized Rome, suggesting subjects of inquiry about which the Romans had never yet troubled themselves. One of these subjects was the nature of the soul, as Lucretius tells us:

'Ignoratur enim quae sit natura Animaï;
Nata sit, an contra nascentibus insinuetur;
Et simul intereat nobiscum morte dirempta
An tenebras Orci visat, vastasque lacunas
An pecudes alias divinitus insinuet se,
Ennius ut noster cecinit, qui primus amoeno
Detulit ex Helicone perenni fronde coronam,
Per gentes Italas hominum quae clara clueret;
Etsi praeterea tamen esse Acherusia templa
Ennius aeternis exponit versibus edens,
Quo neque permanent animae, neque corpora nostra,
Sed quaedam simulacra modis pallentia miris.'[7]

Here the first reference to Ennius seems to allude to his Pythagorean idea of re-incarnation, the second to some exposition of the Homeric idea of the shades in the nether world, which are neither souls nor bodies, but are best described in the memorable words[8] which Lucretius took from Ennius and passed on to Virgil. The inference perhaps is that Ennius had no very definite belief himself, and infected the so far unthinking Roman mind with his own agnosticism. What did he mean when he wrote the famous couplet:

'Nemo me lacrumis decoret, nec Funera fletu
Faxit. Cur? volito vivu' per ora virum.'[1]

Does he mean simply that his literary reputation will survive in the mouths of men who will repeat his verses, or, as James Henry insists,[2] that he will actually flit before men's faces like one of the Homeric shades? Without a better knowledge of Ennius than we possess, it is impossible to say. However this may be, it is certain that from this time onwards the educated class at Rome, if they troubled themselves at all on the subject, held Greek ideas of the soul, the masses retaining the primitive notions as explained above. During a century and a half of war and money-getting the Roman educated man lapsed into a condition of mind mainly indifferent but partly sceptical about the soul, as also about the gods. If he took an interest at all in such questions, it was in the Stoic idea of the soul as a part of the universal Reason, which appealed to his legal and practical instincts[3] and did not trouble him with speculations about his soul and its fortunes after death.

From this indifferentism and scepticism there came a reaction in the age of Cicero, which took the form of a revival of Pythagoreanism, *i.e.* a fresh interest in the soul and its fate. This is first seen in the *Somnium Scipionis* of Cicero, in which we find the beginning of the belief that the good and great man's soul flies upwards at death —a belief afterwards more fully expounded in the *Tusculan Disputations*, bk. i. So far there had been no sign of a view of the soul as individual: the tombs of the Scipios are monumental only, preserving the memory of the man and his deeds. But just at this time we have the first occurrence of a sepulchral inscription 'Dis Manibus'—still in the plural, but commemorating an individual person; and Cicero's apotheosis (so it must be called) of his daughter Tullia points plainly in the same direction.[4]

Yet, in spite of this reaction, the spirit of agnosticism continued, and is a marked feature of the next two or three centuries. Cicero himself was normally a doubter;[5] Cæsar was believed to be so, though he was *pontifex maximus*;[6] Catullus wrote of death as 'nox . . . perpetua . . . dormienda';[7] Lucretius in his third book glories in the Epicurean doctrine that the soul is a material thing which is put an end to at death. So too under the Empire Tacitus expresses the general feeling in *Agricola*, 46:

'Si quis piorum manibus locus: si, ut sapientibus placet, non cum corpore exstinguuntur magnae animae, placide quiescas.'

If we read through the chapter, it becomes fairly clear that what Tacitus really cared for was an immortality of good or great deeds. And a little earlier the elder Pliny had written of death[8] as the relapsing into the same nothingness in which we were before birth. In the sepulchral inscriptions of the Empire the note of doubt and melancholy is sounded again and again.[9]

'The funerary inscriptions leave the impression that, down to the final triumph of the Church, the feeling of the Romans about death was still in the main the feeling of their remote ancestors of the Samnite and Punic wars. It was a social feeling, in the prospect of a dim life dependent on the memory

1 Cf. *Orci thesaurus* in the epitaph of Nævius (E. Baehrens, *Fragmenta Poetarum Romanorum*, Leipzig, 1886, p. 296).
2 See *JRS* ii. [1912] 25 f.
3 In art. ROMAN RELIGION, vol. x. p. 845b, it is called the *numen* in the man rather than his soul; but this is simply because the Romans had no word of their own for soul in primitive times, so far as we can discover.
4 Fowler, *Religious Experience*, p. 74; some parallel conceptions may be found in art. ARYAN RELIGION, vol. ii. p. 24; A. E. Crawley, *The Mystic Rose*, London, 1902, p. 306; L. Lévy-Brühl, *Les Fonctions mentales dans les sociétés inférieures*, Paris, 1910, p. 90.
5 See art. ROMAN RELIGION, vol. x. p. 825.
6 Cf. art. SERPENT-WORSHIP (Introductory and Primitive).
7 i. 114 ff.
8 Line 123.

1 Quoted by Cicero, *Tusc. Disp.* I. xv. 34.
2 Commenting on *Æn.* xii. 234 f., in *Æneidea*, 5 vols., London, 1873–92.
3 See Fowler, *Religious Experience*, ch. xvi.
4 *Ib.* p. 385 ff.
5 *Ad Att.* xii. 18.
6 Sall. *Cat.* 51.
7 v. 6.
8 *HN* vii. 188.
9 See Fowler, *Roman Ideas of Deity*, p. 26, note 2.

of the living, a horror of loneliness and desertion, the longing for a passing prayer even from a stranger.'[1]

This horror of being forgotten by the living, though it does not give us any direct evidence of what was popularly thought about the soul, is worth consideration here, and may be illustrated in two ways. (1) It appears in the Augustan literature and especially in Horace—*e.g.*, in the last ode of bk. iii., where in 'Non omnis moriar, multaque pars mei vitabit Libitinam,' etc., he is plainly thinking of a literary immortality;[2] (2) the primary object of a multitude of *collegia* in the first three centuries of the Empire was undoubtedly to preserve the memory of their members after death.

'It is pathetic to see how universal is the craving to be remembered felt even by slaves, by men plying the most despised or unsavoury crafts.'[3]

Here the one thing we should like to know constantly eludes us—whether the soul was thought of as in any real sense surviving, whether the survivors could hope to meet their loved ones after death. The truth is that the inscriptions betray a great variety of ideas, and most of these are dim and vague, or conventionally expressed. It remained for Christianity to shape these ideas into a definite belief.

The deification of the soul of an emperor after death implies a belief in the survival of the souls of great men; but this, though we meet with it here and there in the poets, especially in Virgil, is not rooted in Roman ideas.[4] What an emperor could himself think about his soul one may see in Hadrian's well-known lines, 'Animula vagula blandula,' etc., which express rather 'regret for the sunlight left behind than any hope in entering on a dim journey into the unknown.'[5]

LITERATURE.—W. Warde Fowler, *The Religious Experience of the Roman People* (*Gifford Lectures*), London, 1911, lectures 4 and 17, *Roman Ideas of Deity*, do. 1914, ch. i.; S. Dill, *Roman Society from Nero to Marcus Aurelius*, do. 1904, bk. ii. ch. iii., bk. iv. ch. ii.; Cyril Bailey, *Some Greek and Roman Ideas of a Future Life* (Occasional Publications of the Classical Association, no. 3), Cambridge, 1915. Much information about Græco-Roman and Pythagorean ideas may be found in the introduction to Eduard Norden, *Aeneis: Buch VI.*, Leipzig, 1903, and here and there in the notes.

W. WARDE FOWLER.

SOUL (Semitic and Egyptian).—The ancient Semites recognized that man consists of two parts, an outer frame of flesh and bones and an inner impalpable part. This inner part they connected with the breath. Only gradually did they come to think of it as an entity that could exist apart from the body. In all the Semitic dialects the soul was designated by a noun derived from a root meaning 'breathe.'

Thus, in Akkadian-Assyrian, *napašu*='be wide,' 'breathe'; *napištu*='breath,' 'life,' 'soul.' In Hebrew *naphash*='take breath,' 'refresh oneself'; *nephesh*='breath,' 'soul,' 'life,' 'person.' In Arabic *nafas*='to injure by breathing upon'; *tanaffus*='to fetch a deep breath'; *nafs*='breath of life,' 'soul,' 'self.' In Aramaic *naphshā*='soul'; *ettapash*='breathe.' In Ethiopic *nephsa*='breathe'; *nephes*='soul.'

To what extent the soul was, in course of time, differentiated from the breath may be discerned by reviewing the conceptions entertained by the different Semitic peoples concerning the soul and its survival after death.

1. Babylonian and Assyrian.—In ancient Babylonia Semitic conceptions are inextricably interwoven with Sumerian. While it is probable that the Semites were first in the Tigris-Euphrates valley, the earliest literature is in Sumerian.

[1] Dill, *Roman Society from Nero to Marcus Aurelius*, p. 498; the whole of the chapter (bk. iv. ch. ii.) will be found instructive.

[2] Cf. IV. ix. 26 ff.: 'omnes illacrimabiles urgentur, ignotique longa nocte, *carent quia vate sacro*'; cf. Virg. *Æn.* ix. 446 ff., *Georg.* iii. 9, where there is a reminiscence of Ennius's epitaph.

[3] Dill, p. 258 ff.

[4] It is fully discussed in art. DEIFICATION (Greek and Roman).

[5] Dill, p. 503.

In Sumerian there are two equivalents of *napištu*—*ZI* and *ŠI*. *ZI*, the one most commonly employed, is written by an ideogram which originally pictured a reed growing by running water. This expressed life—vigorous, abundant life. The ideogram for *ŠI* was the picture of an eye. The brilliance and flash of the eye suitably expressed the vigour of one's life.

While it may be that the reasons which led to the employment of these ideograms were phonetic, it seems probable that the appropriateness of the symbols to suggest life had something to do with it. The words *ZI*, *ŠI*, and *napištu* are, in the literature, employed as the equivalents of 'life'; it is not necessary to render them 'soul.' 'Life' was distinguished from the 'body' or 'carcass' (*šalamtu*), and was apparently conceived as having after death an independent existence apart from the *šalamtu*.

In none of the Semitic languages is the root for 'life,' 'soul,' employed as the verb 'to live.' This is expressed in Hebrew by the verb *hayā*; in Arabic, *ḥayī*; in Syriac, *ḥayā*; in Ethiopic, *ḥaywa*. It is the root from which in Hebrew the word for 'animal' is derived. The Akkadian and Assyrian dialects of Mesopotamia, on the other hand, employ as the verb 'to live' the root *balāṭu*—a root which in Jewish Aramaic signifies 'stand forth,' 'project'; in Syriac, 'shut the eyes,' 'bolt the gate,' or 'breed worms'; in Arabic, 'spread or pave a house with flag-stones' (the noun *balāṭ* meaning 'ground,' 'smooth ground,' 'surface of the ground'); in Ethiopic the only occurrence of the root known to the present writer, *bāluṭ*, means 'oak.' The Mesopotamian *balāṭu*, 'to live,' seems to have closer affinities with the Arabic root *bālada*, 'remain,' 'abide,' 'dwell,' than with the Arabic *balaṭa*.

The idea involved in the Babylonian conception of living would, accordingly, seem to have been, not the possession of a soul, but the ability to stand forth as a distinct being and to occupy a habitation.

We can best ascertain the Babylonian conceptions of the soul by studying their conceptions of the life after death.[1] In common with many other peoples who buried their dead, the Babylonians believed that those who had departed this life dragged out a miserable existence in a subterranean cavern. In this cheerless abode the departed were thought to assume the forms of partially decomposed bodies; this we learn from representations of certain demons from whom Babylonians thought it necessary to guard themselves and who were, as the texts which describe them clearly show, human beings who had died. It is easy to see how early men should think of the departed as assuming the forms of skeletons or partially decomposed bodies. The fact that they did so conceive them is proof that they did not think of the soul as an entity which was altogether independent of the body. The dead, living in the earth, were thought to long for the food and drink of living beings; the dust and clay of the lower world did not satisfy them. In order to so satisfy them that they should not haunt the living and afflict them with disease, the Babylonians from the earliest times presented offerings of food and drink to the dead. The technical term for this was *SI-A-NAK*, 'pouring water on the ground.' In addition to this, an initial supply of food and drink was placed at the time of burial in the tomb with the body. Records of such offerings to the dead are found in practically all periods of Babylonian history. Their object was to keep the dead contented with their lot, so that they would not return to torment the living. When dissatisfied departed spirits did so return, they were believed to form demons and to harm the living. The spirits that came forth from the under world to trouble men were (1) those whose bodies lay unburied, (2) those who had none to present offerings for them, and (3) spirits who had, while living, never been able to satisfy their normal human desires.

The first of these classes is in the Gilgamesh epic described by Engidu, after Gilgamesh had had him called forth from the under world, thus:

[1] See art. STATE OF THE DEAD (Babylonian).

'He whose body is thrown on the plain,
    Thou hast seen, I see;
His spirit rests not in the earth;
Whose spirit has no care,
    Thou hast seen, I see;
The leavings of the dish, the remains of the food,
What is thrown into the street, he eats.'[1]

The second class is alluded to in an incantation which apostrophizes many kinds of spirits, thus:

'Or a spirit that has no care,
Or a spirit with none to make food-offerings,
Or a spirit with none to make libations.'[2]

The third class is described in the following:

'Or a demon that has no resting-place,
Or a maid that died a virgin,
Or a man that died unmarried.'[3]

'A hierodoulos who has died of pestilence,
A woman who has died in travail,
A wailing woman who has died in travail.'[4]

'He who from hunger in prison died,
He who from thirst in prison died,
The hungry man who in his hunger
Its odour smelled not,
He who the dyke of a canal
Opened and was drowned,
He who on plain or marsh-land died,
He who on the plain a storm o'erwhelmed,
The spirit-maid that has no husband,
The spirit-man who embraced no wife.'[5]

All these, whose deaths were accidental or so untimely that the natural functions of life were not fulfilled or its legitimate desires satisfied, roamed the world and were dangerous to the living.

In general, then, we may say of the Babylonian conceptions of the soul that they were vague and for the most part ill-defined. It was recognized that each man possessed an impalpable something that made him a living being, but, so long as he lived, little attention was paid to this. After death this indefinable part of man demanded food and drink. If this were not given, it might return to annoy the living. This fear of the dead led to the conception of the soul as a form of wind—whirlwind or storm-wind. Such satisfactions as the soul received were to be obtained in this life only. If they were not attained before death, the spirit would come back seeking them. It was this in part that constituted the spirits of the departed a menace to the living.

2. Hebrew.—Among the Hebrews the word for 'soul,' *nephesh*, passed through a considerable development which gave it different shades of meaning at different times.

It is employed (1) to denote the principle of life—the thing that constitutes a living being. Thus it is said (Gn 2^{7}) that Jahweh breathed into man's nostrils the breath of life and man became a 'living soul' (*nephesh hayā*), a 'living being.' As denoting a living being, *nephesh* was applied to animals as well as men, and was believed to have its residence in the blood. Thus the Hebrews were prohibited from eating the meat of sacrifices until the blood of the animal had been poured out on the ground to God, for 'the blood is the life (*nephesh*)' (Dt 12^{22-24}; cf. also Lv 17^{10-14}, Gn $9^{4f.}$). In 1 K 17^{22} 'soul' is employed to denote this principle of life, when it is said that the 'soul' of the child came into him again after Elijah had stretched himself upon him three times.

(2) 'Soul' (*nephesh*) is employed to designate the seat of the physical appetites. Thus in Dt $12^{15.\ 20.\ 21}$ it is the seat of the appetite for meat; in Dt 23^{24} for grapes; in Nu 21^{5}, Job 33^{20}, for bread; in Ps 78^{18} 107^{18}, Ec 2^{24}, for food in general; and in Mic 7^{1} for figs.

(3) The 'soul' was also regarded as the seat of all kinds of emotion—pity for the poor (Job 30^{25}), joy (Ps 86^{4}), love (Ca 1^{7}), hate (Is 1^{14}), courage (Ps 138^{3}), purpose (Gn 23^{8}).

(4) It was also the seat of moral action and of the will. Thus in Gn 49^{6} a poet sings:

'O my soul, come not thou into their council;
. . . .
For in their anger they slew a man,
And in their selfwill they houghed an ox.'

In Dt 4^{29} the 'soul' is the seat of the will to seek God; in Job 7^{15}, of the purpose to die; in Ps 24^{4}, of deceit and fraud; in Ps 25^{1}, of trust in God; in Ps $119^{129.\ 167}$, of obedience to law; in Jer 32^{41}, of the will to perform a beneficent act; in Mic 6^{7}, of sin; and in Hab 2^{4}, of pride. In some cases the 'soul' seems to be regarded as the seat of mental activity also; see Jos 23^{14}, Est 4^{13}, Ps 13^{2}.

(5) 'Soul' was also employed by the Hebrews to designate an individual man or person. Thus in Gn 14^{21} the king of Sodom said to Abraham: 'Give me the souls (persons), and take the goods thyself'; also in Lv 17^{12}: 'No soul of you shall eat blood'; Ezk 18^{4}: 'The soul that sinneth, he shall die.' From this usage it came to be employed in enumerations, as in Gn 46^{15}, where it is said that all the 'souls' of Jacob's descendants at a certain time were 33. Another result of the employment of 'soul' in the sense of 'person' was that with a pronominal suffix it came to denote 'self'; thus 'my soul,' 'thy soul,' 'his soul,' meant 'myself,' 'thyself,' 'himself.' By a curious extension of the use of 'soul' for 'person,' it came in time to denote also a person once living but now dead. This usage is found in the OT only in Leviticus, Numbers, and Haggai (see, *e.g.*, Lv 19^{28}, Nu 6^{6}, and Hag 2^{13}). Although the *nephesh* had clearly gone from the body, its long use in the sense of 'person' led to this curious application of it to a dead body.

Closely connected in usage with the term *nephesh* were the terms 'spirit' (*rūaḥ*) and 'heart' (*lebh*). Indeed some writers have held that the Hebrew conception of human nature was a trichotomy, consisting of body, soul, and spirit. This position, as the best scholars have pointed out, cannot be maintained; for, however different from 'soul' the terms 'spirit' and 'heart' may have been originally, they came in time, like the term 'soul,' to designate the whole inner, impalpable nature of man. Thus *rūaḥ* originally meant 'wind,' as in Ps 1^{4}; then it was employed to denote the 'Spirit of God,' as in Gn 1^{2}, and is extensively used in this sense throughout the OT; it was then applied to the inner life of man, and is often employed as a synonym for 'soul.' Thus the 'spirit' is the seat of various emotions—in Gn 26^{35}, of grief; in Gn 41^{8}, Ex 6^{9}, of anxiety; in Dt 2^{30}, of obduracy; in Jg 8^{3}, of hate; in Ps 32^{2}, of deceit; in Pr 18^{14}, of a lack of courage; in Jer 51^{11}, of courage; in Ezk 3^{14}, of anger; in Zec 6^{8}, of peace. Like 'soul,' 'spirit' is also regarded as the seat of moral and religious attributes or qualities: thus in Ps 34^{18} it is the seat of contrition; in Ps 51^{12}, of willingness; in Ps 51^{17}, of humility; in Is 26^{9}, of the will to find God; in Ezk 11^{19}, of teachableness; in Hag 1^{14}, of the will to work.

In late writers only *ruāḥ* ('spirit') is also employed of the seat of mentality; cf. Job 20^{3}, 1 Ch 28^{12}, Is 29^{24}, Ezk 11^{5} 20^{32}. It thus becomes clear that the uses of 'soul' and 'spirit' overlap one another. The Hebrews did not have a clear-cut psychology of the inner life of man with a well-defined terminology, but held a very simple view of the constitution of human nature and employed terms with a vagueness and an overlapping characteristic of popular unscientific thought.

The inner life of man was also by the Hebrews often designated the 'heart' (*lebh*). 'Heart' was more often employed to denote the seat of the mind or intelligence than either 'soul' or 'spirit' was; cf. Nu 16^{28} 24^{13}, Pr 6^{32} 7^{7}, etc. The heart is sometimes described as wise (1 K 3^{12}, Pr 16^{23}, Ec 8^{5}), sometimes as intelligent (Pr 14^{33} 15^{14} 18^{15}). It is also employed to designate the seat of emotions and of moral purpose: thus in Jg 16^{25} the heart is the seat of joy; in Neh 2^{2}, of sorrow; in Am 2^{16}, Ps 27^{14}, of courage; in Job 36^{13}, of godlessness; in Pr 11^{20}, of perversity; in Jer 14^{14}, of deceit; and in Pr 21^{4}, of pride. It is, therefore, like spirit, often but another name for soul.

As to the fate of the soul after death, the views of the Hebrews were akin to those of the Babylonians. The soul went with the body into the under world or Sheol, where the Hebrews before the Greek period believed that it dragged out a wretched existence (Is 14^{9-11}). It is implied that in Sheol the dead perform much the same functions as when alive. At least kings are represented as still sitting on their thrones, though worms cover them and are spread under them. The last idea is derived from the putrefaction of the body.

[1] E. Schrader, *Keilinschriftliche Bibliothek*, vi., Berlin, 1900, p. 264 f.

[2] *Cuneiform Texts from Babylonian Tablets, etc., in the British Museum*, xvi. 10; cf. R. C. Thompson, *The Devils and Evil Spirits of Babylonia*, i. 40 f.

[3] *Cuneiform Texts, loc. cit.*; Thompson, p. 38 f.

[4] P. Haupt, *Akkadische und sumerische Keilschrifttexte*, Leipzig, 1883, p. 88 f.

[5] *Cuneiform Texts*, xvi. 12; Thompson, p. 54 f.

Similarly in Ezk 32[27-32] Sheol is portrayed as a great subterranean region where the dead of all the nations are collected. They lie in helplessness and gloom, though their kings are still kings and their princes still princes. The inhabitants of Sheol were called *rephaim*, *i.e.* 'helpless (or 'powerless') ones.' After a century or more of contact with the Greeks the conception of a longer and happier life, bordering on the idea of the immortality of the soul, was entertained in some sections of the nation. The earliest approximation to this idea appears in Enoch 10[10] (before 170 B.C.), where it is said of certain wicked ones: 'They hope that they will live an eternal life, and that each one of them will live five hundred years.' The author of Enoch evidently regarded such a hope as presumptuous, for he declares in substance that this hope was vain. The author of Daniel, however, a few years later accepted the view which the author of Enoch repudiated, and definitely predicted a resurrection (Dn 12[2]). Later writers who came under Greek influence accepted it also (cf. Wis 2[23]), and it became the faith of the Pharisees, but nevertheless some of the later Psalmists adhered to the old view. One of them declares:

'The dead praise not Jahweh,
Neither any that go down into silence' (Ps 115[17]).

A similar idea is expressed in Ps 88[10]:

'Wilt thou shew wonders to the dead?
Shall the shades arise and praise thee?'

This view the Sadducees still held at the beginning of the Christian era. Jews who accepted the idea of a resurrection were not, however, able as a rule to dissociate the soul from the body; they held to the resurrection of the body.

Like the Babylonians, the early Hebrews believed that certain persons had the power of bringing the dead up from the grave. Such persons were said to be master or mistress of an *'obh*, though just what this was is unknown. It was probably a name for a departed spirit.

The classical instance of this sort of necromancy is the witch of Endor who was consulted by King Saul the night before he fell on Mount Gilboah. She brought Samuel from the earth, and when she saw him she said: 'I see a god (*elohim*) coming up out of the earth.' Saul asked her: 'What form is he of?' She answered: 'An old man cometh up; and he is covered with a robe.' Saul then perceived that it was Samuel (1 S 28[13f.]).

From this it appears that the Hebrews did not dissociate the soul from the body as much as the Babylonians did. Samuel is still in the form of an old man wearing his mantle. He is not, like Engidu, a whirlwind.

Such necromancy was practised in Israel down to the time of the Exile or later. Masters of *'ōboth* or *yidde'oni* (another term for departed spirits) practised it. They are mentioned in Is 8[19] 19[3], 2 K 21[6] 23[24], Lv 19[31] 20[6.27], Dt 18[11], and 2 Ch 33[6]. King Saul had during his reign prohibited the practice of such necromancy, and Isaiah and the author of Deuteronomy protested against it, substituting prophecy for it as a means of ascertaining the future. While the Hebrew conceptions of the soul are somewhat more clearly defined than the Babylonian, especially on the moral and religious side, they are nevertheless vague and are not for the most part clearly distinguished from the mind and other aspects of the inner life.

3. Jewish.—In post-Biblical Judaism conceptions of the soul have varied according to the environment and intellectual outlook of Jewish thinkers. They may, however, be grouped in three classes: the Hellenistic, the Rabbinic, and the philosophical.

(*a*) *Hellenistic.*—In Jewish Hellenism the conceptions of the soul were shaped by Platonic ideas. Plato's doctrine of the pre-existence of souls was accepted by the author of the *Secrets of Enoch* (23[5]) and by his contemporary, Philo Judæus. Philo accepted also Plato's tripartite division of the soul, holding that one part is rational, the second spiritual, the third the seat of desire. This tripartite division relates in Philo's usage solely to the functions of the soul. When he speaks of its composition, he regards it as dual, composed of a rational and an irrational part. The rational soul (νοῦς) was divine; the irrational, corruptible. Not all souls created by God became incarnate; the purest of them inhabited the air and were never entangled in the corruptions of the flesh. The mind or rational soul, which dwelt in the head, was, Philo believed, akin to the incorruptible 'citizens of the air.' Like them, it was incorruptible and immortal. It is the instrument by which man comes into contact with the various objects of creation and makes its way to God Himself. It sends out its streams like a fountain, and pervades the whole body. The spiritual, he believed, inhabited the chest; the soul of the desires, the abdomen. When Philo treats of immortality, it is the rational soul only that occupies his thought. The mind of man came from God and, of course, would return to God. By implication this would be true of the spiritual soul also, but apparently not of the seat of desire. We must not, however, look for logical consistency in Philo; his twofold system of classifying souls and their powers, the dualistic and the tripartite, led him to inextricable confusion.

(*b*) *Rabbinic.*—Rabbinic Judaism, as represented by the Talmud and the related literature, retained the Biblical view of the dualism of human nature, consisting of body and soul.[1] Probably on account of the influence of Platonism, the Rabbis, although they rejected Philonism, believed in the pre-existence of souls.[2] They held, however, that it was taught in Gn 2[7], and consequently believed that their view was due to Biblical teaching rather than to philosophy. At the time of conception God, so the Rabbis taught, commanded an angel to bring Him such-and-such a spirit, and the spirit or soul entered the embryo by the head.[3] The spirits which were to descend to earth to inhabit bodies were said to be kept in Araboth, the lowest of the seven heavens.[4] The spirits of the righteous dead, on the other hand, were beneath the throne of God. There was a difference of opinion as to whether the soul descended from heaven at the moment of conception or after the embryo was formed.[5] Some held that God gave the Jew a new soul every Friday and took it back again at the end of the Sabbath.[6] The Talmud seems to consider the inner nature of man as consisting of soul and spirit, but there was in the thought of the Rabbis no clear division between the two. In their opinion the power by which man distinguishes between right and wrong and his inclination to one or the other are two distinct essences which God places in the soul. They are the *yeṣer ṭōb*, or 'inclination to good,' and *yeṣer hāra'*, or 'evil propensities.'[7] Over these the soul has control, and it is thus responsible for moral action. The connexion between body and soul was held to be of the slightest. In sleep the soul was believed to ascend to its heavenly abode, where it often learned important truths. It was this belief that gave dreams their oracular significance. Nevertheless some Rabbis believed that dreams were due to psychological suggestion.[8]

(*c*) *Philosophical.*—The Jewish philosophers, who were the pupils of Arabian masters, who had in

[1] Cf. *Berākhōth*, 10*a*, 43*b*; *Shabbāth*, 113*b*, 152*b*; *Yōmā*, 30*b*; *Nedarīm*, 32*a*; *Sanhedrin*, 91*a*, 108, 110*b*.
[2] *Sifrē*, 143*b*.
[3] *Niddah*, 30*b*.
[4] *Ḥagīgāh*, 12*b*.
[5] *Sanh.* 90*a*.
[6] *Beṣah.* 16*a*.
[7] *Sifrē*, 82*b*; *Berākh.* 61*a*; *Sanh.* 91*b*.
[8] *Berākh.* 56*a*.

turn learned their philosophy from the Greeks, thought of the soul in more scientific fashion. Se'adiah (*q.v.*), who died in Babylonia in A.D. 942, denied the Platonic doctrine of the pre-existence of the soul, claiming that each soul was created at the time of the creation of its body. The substance of souls resembled that of the 'spheres,' but was of finer quality, since it has the power to think and discern, which the 'spheres' lacked. The soul needs the body as its instrument or medium of activity. By its union with the body three powers latent in the soul are set free—intelligence, passion, and desire. These are not three separate parts of the soul, each having a seat in a different part of the body, but are powers of the indivisible spirit which has its seat in the heart. Without its union with the body the soul could not attain to eternal bliss, because this reward is granted it only as a recompense for obedience to the will of God, an obedience impossible without a body.

Notwithstanding the work of Se'adiah, *Sefer Emunoth we De'oth*, 'Book of the Articles of Faith and the Doctrines of Dogma,' in the sixth chapter of which his views on the soul are set forth, the Platonic views prevailed in a debased form in most of the Jewish schools during the 10th and 11th centuries. According to a work of this period attributed to Ibn Pakuda, man has three souls—the vegetative, the animal, and the rational. The first two are derived from matter. The vegetative soul creates the body. The attribute of the vegetative soul is chastity; of the animal soul, energy; of the rational soul, wisdom. These views were accepted with variations by Ibn Gabirol and Ibn Ziddik.

Maimonides (*q.v.*), who had come under the influence of Aristotle, fashioned his conception of the soul after that Greek master. According to him, the soul is a unit possessing five faculties—the nutritive; the sensitive, by which one perceives; the imaginative, by which it has the power to form images of the things impressed on it by the senses; the appetitive, or the ability to feel either desire or aversion; and the rational, by which it acquires knowledge and discerns right and wrong. Maimonides held that the soul is indissolubly bound up with the body and at death ceases to exist. Maimonides and Levi ben Gershon (*q.v.*) held that, in addition to the soul possessed by every one, it was possible to develop, as was done by some, an acquired intellect. These views were strenuously opposed by others.

In *Zôhăr*, the most psychological of the treatises of the Ḳabbala, the Neo-Platonic theories of the soul asserted themselves.

4. Arabian.—See art. ARABS (Ancient), vol. i. p. 671 f.

5. Muhammadan.—See art. SOUL (Muslim).

6. Other Semitic races.—Our information concerning the conceptions of the soul entertained by the other Semitic nations is very fragmentary, but what there is of it goes to show that their ideas were practically identical with those of the early Hebrews and Arabs. A Phœnician inscription employs *nephesh* in the sense of 'person.'[1] The Nabatæans used the word in the same way, for there is a survival in one of their inscriptions of its employment to express the idea of self.[2] Another extension of this meaning, already traced in Arabia, was the employment of *naphsha* in the sense of 'memorial monument' or 'gravestone.' This is quite frequent.[3] It is also found among the Palmyrenes.[4] *Naphsha* had also, in the Nabatæan dialect, the meaning 'life.'[1] Of a deeper or more psychological meaning to the word among these peoples the sources reveal no trace.

The Syriac literature from the region of Edessa and the Ethiopic literature from Abyssinia are both Christian. The conceptions of the soul formally presented in these literatures are accordingly Christian. Nevertheless the usages of the languages in which the literatures are written testify that the heathen ancestors of these two sections of the Semitic race shared the views of the soul already traced in Israel and among the Arabs. In Syriac a verb formed from the root *n^ephash* meant 'to breathe,' also 'to desire.' Forms of the root were also employed in the meaning of 'natural life,' 'soul,' and 'self.'

In general the same is true of Ethiopic. *Nafsa* means 'breath,' 'blow'; *nefs*, 'soul,' 'living thing,' 'wind,' 'air'; *nafst*, 'body,' 'pudenda'; and *manfus*, 'spirit,' 'soul.' The methods of reasoning employed above enable us to deduce from these facts that the word stood for 'breath,' 'life,' 'soul,' 'person,' and 'self,' as among the other Semitic peoples.

7. Egyptian.—The Egyptian beliefs concerning the soul differed considerably from those of the Semitic peoples. It is generally held that they thought a concrete entity, invisible during life, had its residence in the human body. They called this *ba*, a word which never means 'life.' Life was denoted by quite a different word, *'ankh*. There is a verb *ba*, which means 'to cut in pieces,' and, if it had any connexion with the word for soul, the connexion is not apparent. There is also a denominative verb *ba*, 'to become a *ba*.' The *ba*, according to the usual Egyptian belief, dwelt in the body during life, but departed from it at death.[2] Some texts indicate that in parts the belief prevailed that only at death one became a *ba*. The Egyptians never developed philosophical ability; they did not form theories as to the inner composition or structure of the soul, such as were given to the world by Plato and Aristotle and were entertained by the peoples who came under the influence of these philosophers. In Egypt interest centred in the future fortunes of the soul. The conceptions on this subject at the beginning were bound up with myths which differed in different nomes. As time advanced and the establishment of the monarchy created syncretism, those myths and theories blended. They also in the lapse of time underwent development. Many of those views found expression in that medley of myths of the hereafter known as *The Book of the Dead*. Gods as well as men were thought to possess souls. The soul was the seat of strength, courage, and power in both gods and men. The favourite method of picturing the soul was in the form of a heron; in later times it was represented as a bird with a human face. Such representations on tombs enabled the survivors to place a portrait of the deceased over his grave.

In early times it was thought that, though the soul wandered abroad during the day through the under world or through the desert, on the borders of which cemeteries lay, it needed to return to the body at night or in moments of danger, as when attacked by hostile spirits. It was probably for this reason that such pains were taken to mummify and preserve the body. Departed souls were supposed to need the same kind of sustenance as in life; hence quantities of food were placed in the tomb. If a man had possessed wealth and servants in this world, he would need them in the after life. Hence, from the Vth dynasty onward, numerous servants preparing food and making all

1 *CIS* I. i. 86. 2 *Ib.* I. ii. 147.
3 *Ib.* I. ii. 115, 116, 162, 169, 192, 195, 196, 332, 333.
4 G. A. Cooke, *Text-book of North Semitic Inscriptions*, Oxford, 1903, no. 146.

1 *CIS* I. ii. 114.
2 See art. DEATH AND DISPOSAL OF THE DEAD (Egyptian).

that was useful during life are pictured on the walls of the tombs. *Ushabti* figures were later introduced for the same purpose.

The Pyramid Texts, our oldest source of information, deal with the posthumous destiny of the king. The souls of other men were thought to remain in the under world or to wander in the desert; the king was, like Osiris, transferred to the skies and placed among the gods. The reception given him there is vividly portrayed. Feasts of geese, bread, and all delicious viands are provided for him; quantities of beer are furnished for him to drink; concubines for the gratification of his desires are not lacking. Sometimes, as he was, on his arrival in the sky, but a babe to the new life, he is represented as suckled at the breast of a goddess. Later the heaven of the sky was democratized, and it was believed that all good men went thither. Old beliefs that the dead returned to the tomb or revisited his former abode survived side by side with the beliefs in the soul's celestial destiny. Sometimes a little ladder or a boat was pictured, by which the soul could climb or sail away to the stars.

In course of time it came to be believed that on its arrival in the under world the soul must undergo an examination to see whether it was fit to go to heaven. While Osiris was believed to be the great judge, he was attended by 42 assessors—one for each of Egypt's nomes. These bore such terrifying names as 'Blood-drinker,' 'Bone-breaker,' 'Shadow-swallower.' Those who successfully passed the examination and could say at the end, 'I am pure,' were transferred to the sky, where they enjoyed a material paradise such as was, in the Pyramid Texts, the lot of kings. These promises were only for the worthy. The wicked were doomed to destruction by the myriads of demons who inhabited the under world. They might be torn in pieces by the 42 terrible judges, burned in furnaces, or drowned in the abyss. These souls might themselves become demons and return to torment the living with disease and death. Against them, as against other demons, magic spells were necessary.

It has often been stated that in addition to the soul (*ba*) the Egyptians believed that a man possessed another invisible entity or double, called a *ka*. The existence of the *ka* is beyond question, but its function has until recently been misunderstood. The *ka* was a man's double. On the walls of the temple of Luxor a sculpture of the 15th cent. B.C. depicts the birth of Amenophis III. By his side is another child of the same size and appearance.[1] This was the *ka*, which accompanied him through life. The *ka* was a corporeal comrade, though an invisible one. He accompanied a man through life, as a sort of guardian genius. The *ka* preceded a man to the realm of Osiris and prepared for his reception there. When a man died, therefore, it was said, 'He goes to his *ka*.' Lest the *ka* should mistake his *protégé*, the dead was given a peculiar garment by which the *ka* might identify him. The *ka*, united with the individual whom it had protected, lived a common life with him in the hereafter. Often it was said of the dead: 'How beautiful it is in the company of the *ka*!'

LITERATURE.—**R. C. Thompson**, *The Devils and Evil Spirits of Babylonia*, London, 1903-04, i. pp. xxiv-xxxv; **S. H. Langdon**, 'Babylonian Eschatology,' in *Essays in Modern Theology and Related Subjects Gathered and Published as a Testimonial to Charles Augustus Briggs, D.D., D.Litt.*, New York, 1911, pp. 141-162; **F. Schwally**, *Das Leben nach dem Tode*, Giessen, 1892; **J. Frey**, *Tod, Seelenglaube und Seelenkult im alten Israel*, Leipzig, 1898, pp. 18-33, 188-228; **C. Grüneisen**, *Der Ahnenkultus und die Urreligion Israels*, Halle, 1900, pp. 97-100; **C. H. Toy**, *Judaism and Christianity*, Boston and London, 1890, pp. 174-176; **C. Piepenbring**, *Theology of the Old Testament*, Eng. tr., New York, 1893, pp. 160-167; **A. B. Davidson**, *The Theology of the Old Testament*, Edinburgh, 1904, pp. 199-203; **E. D. Burton**, *Spirit, Soul and Flesh*, Chicago, 1918, ch. ii.; **J. Drummond**, *Philo Judæus*, 2 vols., London, 1888, i. 318-357; **F. Weber**, *Jüdische Theologie*², Leipzig, 1897, pp. 211 ff., 225 f., 228, 341; **K. Kohler**, *Jewish Theology*, New York, 1918, pp. 213-217; **I. Broydé** and **L. Blau**, art. 'Soul,' in *JE*; **E. A. Van Dyck**, *A Compendium on the Soul*, Verona, 1906; **D. B. Macdonald**, *The Religious Attitude and Life in Islam*, Chicago, 1909, pp. 53-61; **J. H. Breasted**, *Development of Religion and Thought in Ancient Egypt*, New York and London, 1912, p. 52 ff.; **G. Steindorff**, *The Religion of the Ancient Egyptians*, do. 1905, p. 121 ff.; **A. Erman**, *Die ägyptische Religion*², Berlin, 1909, pp. 44, 47, 55, 102, 103, 276; **W. Max Müller**, *Egyptian Mythology* (=*Mythology of all Races*, vol. xii.), Boston, 1918, ch. x.; **E. A. W. Budge**, *The Book of the Dead*, 3 vols., London, 1898.

GEORGE A. BARTON.

[1] Cf. A. Erman, *Die ägyptische Religion*², p. 102.

SOUL (Teutonic).—**I. The personal soul.**—(*a*) *In life.*—The conception of a personal soul inherent in man during life and distinct from his body can be traced in popular beliefs of to-day in Germany, but the only evidence for it among the early Teutonic peoples comes from Scandinavia, and is singularly uniform in character. The mind (*hugr*) of a man is seen, on occasion, in the form of some animal usually thought to share the characteristics of the individual; thus a gallant chief will be represented by a bear, an eagle, or a bull, a bloodthirsty man by a wolf, a cunning man by a fox, a fair woman by a swan, and so on. This 'animal familiar' is called *fylgja* (fem. sing.; pl. *fylgjur*), 'something accompanying,' which we may render 'companion' or 'associate.' It can be seen (except in dreams) only by persons with second-sight, but it appears to have an objective existence.

Thus in an Icelandic story a boy stumbles over some obstacle unnoticed by him which an old man present sees to be the lad's own *fylgja*, a bear-cub (*þorsteins þáttr uxafóts*). After killing an enemy Eyjólf fell off his horse and was lamed for life; a wise man tells him that the reason of his fall was that he could not withstand the *fylgjur* of the slain man's kinsmen, whereupon Eyjólf asks: 'Do you think that their *fylgjur* are more powerful than mine and those of my friends?'[1] In another saga certain brothers are said to be awkward to contend against, as they have 'strong *fylgjur*.'

The *fylgja* has thus a protective character, and it precedes its owner on all critical occasions. Hence dreams of encounters with wild animals are taken as portending a fight with the individuals whose *fylgjur* the animals are supposed to be, and an alternative name for the *fylgjur* is 'men's minds' (*manna hugir*).

Thus a hero dreams that he is attacked by wolves, of which he kills two; the dream is interpreted next day: 'It is easy to see that these are men's minds hostile to thee,' and in the ensuing encounter he actually kills two of his opponents.[2] In *Njáls Saga* a man dreams of a great white bear entering his brother's house; he says on waking that the animal had no peer and must therefore be the *fylgja* of the peerless Gunnarr.[3]

The close connexion of this belief with that of shape-changing is obvious. When we are told that Böðvarr Bjarki fought as a bear while he sat inert in the king's hall,[4] it would seem that his *fylgja*, or animal-soul, was fighting for him; but, when the Icelandic chief Kveldúlf, of the 9th cent., is said to become a wolf at night, this appears to be rather a case of shape-changing.

So also in the case of Lára, who flew in the form of a swan above her lover in battle, chanting magic incantations so that none could wound him, until in swinging his sword he cut off the leg of the swan, and Lára dropped dead to the ground.[5]

In one essential point the conception of the external soul, or *fylgja*, follows closely that of the belief in shape-changing. The life of the *fylgja* depends on that of the individual, and dies when he dies. Though it is called his *hugr*, 'mind,' it is not the part of a man which continues a life after death. Its death is the portent of the death of its owner, and this not only when its death is seen in dreams. The freedman Thórð in *Njáls Saga*[6] sees a dead

[1] *Ljósvetninga Saga*, ch. 30.
[2] *Thorð. Saga Hræða*, ch. 6.
[3] *Njáls Saga*, ch. 23.
[4] *Hrólfs Saga Kráka*, ch. 33.
[5] *Hrómundar Saga Greipssonar*, ch. 6 f.
[6] Ch. 41.

goat, which is realized to be his *fylgja*, and he is killed the same day.

The animal-soul, or *fylgja*, which dies or disappears on the death of the body, must certainly be distinct from the *hamingja*, occasionally called *fylgjukona*, which is a kind of female tutelary genius, who on the death of one member of the family passes on to another. In an Eddic poem these are described as 'wise maidens.'[1] The practice of naming a child after a recently deceased grandparent appears to have originated in a desire to attach the family *hamingja* to his fortunes.[2] In one or two passages there is a confusion of terms, and this tutelary genius is called *fylgja*, but, as the word only means 'companion,' it is really as applicable to the *hamingja* as to the animal-soul. The *fylgja* proper, the animal-soul, is never called *hamingja*. A similar distinction between the ancestral soul and the personal soul is found in various races.

The Kafirs believe in the *idhlozi*, an individual soul unable to leave the corpse after death, and the *itongo*, a corporate soul, shared by various members of a family and making its home permanently with their descendants.[3] So among the Eskimo the individual soul of a child is distinct from the family guardian-spirit (*atka*), which is immanent in it in childhood.[4]

Ancient Teutonic literature has thus preserved to us no conception of the soul as a shade, or as a miniature, or as present in the breath or heart or blood. In modern popular superstition it is generally thought of as a butterfly, mouse, or other small creature, which issues from the mouth of a sleeper. This does not, however, resemble the Northern *fylgja*, for it survives the death of its human associate. In folk-tales it is often seen leaving its human habitation on the death of its owner.

(*b*) *After death.*—As we have seen, these *fylgjur*, or 'men's minds,' are not 'souls' in the sense of being that part of the individual which continues an existence beyond the grave. There is absolutely no mention of them in the realms of the dead, nor is there any hint that any particular part of man, such as the breath, is the seat of life both before and after death. Yet the popular belief in the Wild Huntsman and his companions, who are undoubtedly spirits of the dead, and the association of Odin (originally a god of the dead) with the wind,[5] must be connected with the idea that the spirit of man was breath or wind. Other conceptions of the realm of the dead show less consciousness of any difference between spirit and matter. It is true that the realm of Hel, the goddess of death, seems to have been somewhat shadow-like, since its guardian chides the living Hermóð for making more noise than five battalions of the dead, but, when the dead Balder gives Hermóð the ring which was burnt on his pyre, as a gift to Odin, and his dead wife sends a shift to Frigg, these articles are apparently still material enough to give satisfaction in the world of the living.[6] The practice of cremation must have originated in some definite belief about the soul's departure to another world, but Teutonic thought, like Chinese, seems to have been averse from admitting the dualism of spirit and matter, and literature gives us no hint that they can be separated. Moreover, the beliefs connected with cremation may have early crystallized into meaningless custom. When the German peasants in Voigtland put an umbrella and galoshes into the coffin of a departed friend, it is not to be supposed that they really believe these articles to be required in heaven, but merely that they have become part of the Sunday outfit in which it has always been customary to inter the body.

Constant references in ecclesiastical prohibitions show that the dead were still thought to require food and drink, and in some parts of Sweden the peasants still continue to lay such offerings in the saucer-shaped depressions on the rock slabs of ancient tombs. Neither the idea of Hel nor that of Valhöll could oust from the popular mind the older and more widely spread belief that the dead man lived on in his grave-mound. Icelandic sources show that certain families believed that they 'died into' hills, which they regarded as sacred, and a reference in *Landnáma* suggests that the young men of the family were conducted to this hill for the ceremonies associated with the attainment of manhood.[1] When continuing an existence in the neighbourhood of their burial-place, the dead seem to have been thought of as *álfar*, 'elves,' in Scandinavia, N. Germany, and the Netherlands. Sacrifice to these beings seems to have been practised in Sweden,[2] and it is once mentioned in Iceland.[3] That the continuance of the prosperity due to some fortunate king depended on the actual presence of his corpse is clear from the eagerness which different portions of his kingdom evinced for some part of the body of King Halfdán the Black,[4] and also from the story of Frode, who was embalmed after death and taken round his kingdom in a carriage.[5] In Norway the *haugbu*, or dweller in the grave-mound, is still regarded with veneration. In these cases, if the soul is thought of as separate from the body at all, it is evidently in close dependence on it. The importance of the corpse rather than the spirit is seen in the belief that dead bodies could be made by spells to utter prophecies, whereas there is no reference to calling up *spirits* to foretell the future. The refusal to distinguish between the corpse and its spirit is seen even more clearly in the beliefs about persistent ghosts—dead men who were evil in life. The ghost, if we may call it so, still possesses great physical power and can kill men; and its activities can equally well be put an end to by burning the corpse and scattering the ashes in the sea[6] or by overcoming the ghost and cutting off its head.[7]

If, as has been suggested, Jötunheim, the world of the giants, is originally a realm of the dead, and the word *jötunn* really means 'devourer,' it seems as if Teutonic thought had contemplated a world in which the dead are nothing but corpses, devoured by ogres.[8] This is a more crudely materialistic conception than most savages could boast of.

In Valhöll, which is probably a creation of the North, the *einherjar*, or warriors slain in battle and now living a new life under almost the same conditions as the old, must evidently be thought of as re-incarnated, since their dead bodies are not in Valhöll. But there is nothing spiritual about their fare of pork and ale, and their life after death is not an immortality, since they are doomed to fall again, with no further hope of renewed life, in the battle between gods and giants. We find the perpetual fighting dissociated from the belief in Valhöll in the story of Hild, who by her spells raised up the slain combatants in a great battle. At night they and their weapons turn into boulders, but every day they revive and fight, and so it shall continue till the end of the world.[9] This excessive activity on the part of the dead probably reflects the superabundant energy of the Viking age, and

1 *Vafþrúðnismál*, 48 f. 2 Cf. *Vatnsdæla Saga*, ch. 7.
3 Dudley Kidd, *Savage Childhood*, London, 1906, p. 281 ff.
4 See art. SOUL (Primitive).
5 See art. GOD (Teutonic), § 2 (*a*).
6 Snorri's Edda, *Gylfaginning*, ch. 52.

1 *Landnámabok*, ed. F. Jónsson, Copenhagen, 1900, p. 158.
2 *Heimskringla*, ed. F. Jónsson, Copenhagen, 1893–1900, ii. 171.
3 *Kormáks Saga*, ch. 22. 4 *Heimskringla*, i.
5 Saxo, *Gesta Danorum*, ed. A. Holder, Strassburg, 1886, p. 171.
6 *Laxdæla Saga*, ch. 17; *Eyrbyggia Saga*, ch. 63.
7 *Grettis Saga*, ch. 35; Saxo, ed. Holder, p. 163.
8 Cf. O. Schoning, *Dödsriger i nordisk Hedentro*, Copenhagen, 1903, and *ARW* viii. [1904] 124 f.
9 Snorri's Edda, *Skáldskaparmál*, ch. 57.

is perhaps also the foundation of the belief that persons pre-eminent in their life are reborn.

It will be seen from the above that the early Teutonic peoples were less speculative about the relations of matter and spirit than many savages. No doubt, if they had been questioned as savages are to-day, they would have produced a philosophy, but in their literature as it stands there is no recognition of any distinction between body and soul. It is, however, possible that their perception of this dualism had been clearer in the pre-literary time, and had become blurred in the Viking age owing to its intense interest in this life, to its materialism, and, above all, to its acquaintance with different forms of burial and with conflicting beliefs as to the destiny of the dead. Whereas the conception 'spirit' is not expressed in heathen Teutonic literature, the traces of animistic belief still left from a more primitive age may perhaps justify us in believing that the idea had once been more clearly formulated. Only the more enlightened classes seem wholly to have abandoned animistic beliefs, in which 'souls' are attributed not only to living beings, but also to inanimate objects.

2. Animism.—The worship of waterfalls, springs, and rocks, common all over Scandinavia, England, and N. Germany, had probably an animistic basis, as also probably had the cult of the *landvættir*, spirits of the soil. Where literature fails, archæology may serve to show that in the period immediately preceding the Viking age the distinction between matter and spirit was more clearly realized. The intentional damaging of weapons and other objects before interment with their owners, practised in the 5th and 6th centuries, suggests that souls were ascribed to the objects as well as to their owners, and that it was believed that these souls could be set free to follow their dead owner only if they too were 'killed' in some way. So the sword of the Frankish king Childeric († 481) lay broken in the grave. Perhaps the most interesting illustration of this belief is given by such S. Scandinavian bog-finds as that at Vimose in Denmark, where some 4000 objects, mostly weapons and gear, are found to have been carefully damaged before being abandoned. The same idea of setting free the spiritual counterparts of objects can be traced in certain finds in Bornholm. These contain no corpses, but consist merely of a heap of intentionally damaged objects, the personal effects of some man whose body, probably because he fell at a distance, was not available for interment.[1]

LITERATURE.—Besides the literature mentioned in the footnotes, reference should be made to the section on souls in E. Mogk's art. 'Teutonic Religion,' in H. Paul, *Grundriss der german. Philologie*², Strassburg, 1898–1913, iii. 249 ff., and to other works on Teutonic religion and folk-lore mentioned in that art.; also to Rieger, 'Über den nordischen Fylgien glauben,' *ZDA* xlii. [1898] 277 ff.; G. Storm, 'Vore Forfædres Tro pa Sjælevandring og deres Opkaldelsessystem,' *Arkiv for nordisk Filologi*, ix. [1893] 119 ff.; R. Cleasby and G. Vigfusson, *Icelandic-Eng. Dict.*, London, 1874; J. Fritzner, *Ordbog over det gamle norske Sprog*, Christiania, 1867, *s.vv.* 'Fylgia,' 'Hamingja'; J. Ihre, *Glossarium Sviogothicum*, Upsala, 1769, *s.v.* 'Fylgia.'

B. S. PHILLPOTTS.

SOUL-HOUSE.—This name is only a recent one for reference, as no original name is known. The Egyptians, like many other peoples, habitually placed food-offerings with the dead, from the time of the earliest pre-historic graves down to the present. Before the Ist dynasty it became usual to place additional food-offerings—probably at festivals—on one side of the surface mound, or *mastaba*, opposite to the slit where the soul was supposed to go in and out. The heaps of offering pottery still remain in place.[2] In other cases a mat was laid down to keep back the dust, and a pan of flour was placed on it; this was the origin of the sign *hetep* for any offering, satisfaction, or peace, a sign which appears among the earliest hieroglyphs, at the beginning of the Ist dynasty.[1] Next, a stone altar appears with a tank to hold a drink-offering (IVth dynasty), and, as sculptured offerings would never decay, the forms of cakes and other food were carved beside the tank. By the Vth dynasty the tank was looked on as a model of the living-house tank; one in the Cairo Museum has the months of high and low Nile marked on different steps. Various foreign influences came in at the collapse of IVth–VIth dynasty civilization, and it is not unlikely that African custom (see below) modified the altar of offering by providing a shelter for the soul, when it came out to feed at the tank-altar. Some time between the VIth and IXth dynasties various stages of shelters are found, modelled in pottery, about a foot across. At first it was like a Bedawi tent, a cover propped up with two sticks in front, and closed at the back and sides; in front of it is a courtyard, with a tank in the middle, and lying round this are the offerings of an ox head and haunch, round loaves, and bundles of vegetables. The tanks sometimes have holes at each corner, in which to set up poles for supporting a mat-shelter, to keep the water cool. The tent type soon passed into a colonnade with four columns, forming a verandah. Then a little box-shelter was added in the verandah, which soon developed into a back chamber. Steps were placed at the side to give access to the roof, and wind-openings to keep the interior cool. This point was reached at about the Xth dynasty.

The development continued by adding more back chambers; then small chambers on the roof, which grew into a complete second storey. The steps were continued up to reach the roof of the upper storey. Furniture was added—a chair, a couch with head-rest, an easing-stool. A servant grinding corn, and a recess for worship, are also represented. In short, we learn the exact arrangement of the peasants' houses of the XIth and XIIth dynasties. The details of construction were shown—elliptic brick-arch roofing, floors of poles and matting, mud-plastered, as at present, a flying staircase winding round curves, drip-hoodings over the windows, and crenellated walls exactly like those of the modern tombs in the same region.[2] A series of 150 examples giving every variety of development was found at Rifeh, south of Asyut. A few rather more elaborate are known elsewhere, but, as they have been imitated very skilfully by forgers, the further detail cannot be trusted.

The regular position of these soul-houses was on the surface of the ground, at the side of the grave, facing towards it, and most often at the north end. The period is from soon after the VIth dynasty, mainly about the Xth and XIth, and dying out in the XIIth dynasty. The region is at Gebeleyn, Erment, Thebes, Dendereh, and Rifeh, all south of Asyut, in the Thebaid. The most complete series of soul-houses is in the Manchester Museum.

Modern African parallels suggest that this idea came into Egypt from the south.

'Chipoka had been a person of importance . . . a ceremony was to take place for the purpose of propitiating the old chief's spirit . . . people were busied about a group of neat miniature huts, made of grass, about two feet high. The roofs of these huts, which had been finished separately, were not yet put on, and I could see that a couple of earthen jars were sunk in the

[1] Cf. K. Stjerna, *Frā filolog. föreningen i Lund: Sprakl. uppsatser*, ii. [1902] 141, 154.

[2] W. M. F. Petrie, *Tarkhan II.* (*British School of Arch. in Egypt*), London, 1914, pls. xii.–xiv.

[1] Petrie, *Deshasheh* (*Egyp. Expl. Fund, 15th Memoir*), London, 1898, p. 35.

[2] Petrie, *Gizeh and Rifeh* (*Brit. School of Arch. in Egypt*), London, 1907, pl. xiv.–xxii.E, pp. 14–20.

ground inside each. These jars were now filled with beer, and then the roof was lifted on.'[1] 'Of things which the stranger can see for himself in passing through the villages, the most noticeable are the little spirit-houses . . . where sacrifices are presented from time to time.'[2]

'Homeless *idimu* [souls] remain in the air and haunt the neighbourhood of the village. . . . It is to provide accommodation for the *idimu* that small huts are built over graves, and a clever device to keep them from wandering at night is to kindle small fires in the huts, for, if this is done, the *idimu* will remain there and warm themselves.'[3]

Lastly, what is the motive for such offerings? Three attitudes toward the dead are found in different countries:[4] (1) fear, as with the Troglodytæ, who bound the body as tightly as possible, or in the various means of breaking connexion between the house and the grave; (2) comfort of the dead, as by giving food and drink; (3) honour of the dead, as in placing on the grave a light (as in Egypt) or flowers (Europe) in the present time. There seems no trace of fear of the dead in Egypt; in all ages weapons were placed with them, or models of weapons, and also sandals (or models in a pre-historic grave) to enable the dead to travel; and in Græco-Roman times the mummy was kept in the house for twenty or thirty years and there honoured, like the present African's offering to his father's head kept in the family circle. It seems therefore only consistent to regard the soul-house as being placed by the grave to comfort the soul when it came out, and provide shelter, food, and rest for it. W. M. FLINDERS PETRIE.

SOUTHCOTTIANS.—The Southcottians are the followers of Joanna Southcott (1750–1814), a Devonian. One of her followers, herself claiming to be divinely directed to write, describes her in 1907 in these words:

'(i) She was a woman chosen by God to stand at the end of the ages in perfect obedience to Him. (ii) She was to claim the Promise made in the Fall to the Woman, that her seed (Christ) should bruise the Serpent's head and thus put an end to evil. (iii) She was in a special sense to be the bride of Christ, not the only one, but set as a type until all become brides—both men and women—and give their supreme love to Him, standing in perfect obedience as His Church.'[5]

The same authority continues that the Holy Spirit revealed to Joanna things to come, and showed her plainly of the Father; that, as the woman's hand brought the evil fruit to man, so her hand is to bring to man the good; that woman is to be saved through child-bearing; that Joanna perfectly fulfilled Rev 12 in the spiritual birth of the man child; that the Church is finally to be the man child when filled with His Spirit.

Joanna, who was of Wesleyan extraction, began prophesying in 1792, and many of her predictions were fulfilled within a few months, as was verified by a local inquiry. Publications from 1800 onwards introduced her to a wider circle, and in 1801 Thomas P. Foley, rector of Old Swinford, brought friends who conducted a systematic trial of her gifts at Exeter, and, being convinced, were hailed as the 'Seven Stars.' In Aug. 1802 she retired for a seven-day dispute with Satan, which she published. Further trials ensued in 1803 and 1804, each widening her fame. She organized her adherents, enjoining on them the observance of certain Jewish laws, notably as to the Sabbath and as to clean meats. They were presented with a signed paper, 'The Sealed of the Lord—the Elect Precious Man's Redemption—To Inherit the Tree of Life—To be made Heirs of God and Joint-Heirs with Jesus Christ. Joanna Southcott.' This was bestowed only on those who had read and accepted at least two of her major works; within five years about 14,000 persons were 'sealed.' She then challenged attention by a personal letter to every bishop, peer, and member of the House of Commons, and by letters to the *Times* and the *Morning Herald* in 1813. Next spring she announced that she was pregnant with Shiloh, and much excitement was evinced, even in medical circles, fourteen doctors being invited to examine her. But she passed away two days after Christmas.

Samuel Sibley and John Ward sought to rally her followers, the latter being believed in as late as 1892. But George Turner, himself owned by Joanna as inspired, joined with Jane Townley, her most intimate friend, in holding together the main body. Between 1840 and 1850 a controversy broke out, leading to much publication, on the question whether a spiritual child was born at the end of 1814, or whether Joanna will return, complete the year foretold, and bear a literal child. Forty years ago the London adherents were but a handful in Walworth; but a revival has taken place. With 1902 Alice Seymour, deeply impressed by the annual service on New Year's Day 1901 (Old Style), the 'lifting up of hands,' near Manchester, felt drawn to renewed study, and came to the conclusion that the prophecies 'for ten years from the fourth of the century' applied to the 20th cent., not the 19th. She therefore published two volumes in 1909 which are the foundation for sane study, and thus prompted renewed interest. The coincidences in the five years since are certainly remarkable.

Two other movements have sprung out of the original. John Wroe of Bowling, near Bradford, was accepted as successor to George Turner of Leeds in 1822, and his new revelations broke fresh ground, so that the Christian Israelites, as his followers are called, are not to be classed as Southcottians. They hold that the Ten Tribes are dispersed throughout the nations, and are to gather on the basis of the four books of Moses and the four Gospels. Perfect obedience to the Mosaic Law will procure immortality, the body not seeing death. There is no ordained ministry; propaganda is carried on especially in the open air, with a large brass band rendering plaintive music; adherents may be recognized by their long unshorn hair. They reached New York in 1844, and have excited some curiosity in Australia.

In 1875 the Chatham group of Southcottians was joined by a soldier, James White, who, after his period of service in India, returned and took the lead locally, developing further the doctrines of Joanna and of Wroe, with a communistic tinge. The name 'New and Latter House of Israel' was assumed. Though he died in 1885, his widow continued the work, and an enormous mass of brickwork at Gillingham, strong as a fort, marks the house of Jezreel. Her death three years later caused financial chaos and a cessation of work. But adherents still exist in the United States, Canada, and Australia.

LITERATURE.—The sources are pamphlets by Joanna Southcott, complete sets of which are in the British Museum, the Bodleian, and the John Rylands Library, Manchester, totalling 4500 pages. Twice as much remains of her MSS, some in a peculiar shorthand, most sealed in a large case corded up till the next crisis of world-history. Her correspondence books are also preserved. The only long studies of her which are not caricatures are: Alice Seymour, *The Express, containing the Life and Divine Writings of Joanna Southcott*, 2 vols., London, 1909; Charles Lane, *Life and Bibliography of Joanna Southcott*, Exeter, 1912. W. T. WHITLEY.

SOVEREIGNTY (Divine).—**1. Definition.**—There are three senses in which the term 'divine sovereignty' may be used, two of which need little more than mention, as they are dealt with else-

[1] A. Werner, *The Natives of British Central Africa*, London, 1906, p. 47 f.

[2] *Ib.* p. 50.

[3] E. Torday and T. A. Joyce, quoted by C. G. Seligman, 'Multiple Souls in Negro Africa,' in *Ancient Egypt*, 1915, pt. iii. p. 105.

[4] See artt. DEATH AND DISPOSAL OF THE DEAD.

[5] Alice Seymour, *The Express*, No. 1, page 27.

where; the third alone claims further treatment. (1) In polytheism (*q.v.*) we may speak of the divine sovereignty of the one god who is more or less exalted above the other gods. In Chinese religion T'ien or Shang Ti possesses an absolute pre-eminence over all gods and spirits. In Vedic religion the gods in succession are exalted by the worshippers in the type of piety which Max Müller[1] has called henotheism or kathenotheism.[2] Some of the hymns almost rise to the height of monotheism (*q.v.*). Of Varuṇa it is said:

'The mighty Varuṇa, who rules above, looks down
Upon these worlds, his kingdom, as if close at hand.'[3]

Even in Zoroastrian dualism Ahura Mazda, despite his conflict with Angra Mainyu, is assured of final triumph. It is questioned now whether Dyaush pitâ, 'Heaven-Father,' in spite of the linguistic equivalence, ever held the same place in the Vedic pantheon as Ζεὺς πατήρ in the Greek, or Jupiter in the Latin,[4] although the monarchy of these deities was very much limited by the wayward wills of the other gods. A similar position was attained among the Babylonian gods by Marduk, and the Assyrian by Ashur. The composite deity Amon-Rē was in like manner exalted in Egyptian theology, and the attempt of Amenhotep IV. to dethrone him in favour of Aten failed. This tendency to raise one god over others may be regarded as the movement from polytheism towards monotheism.

(2) In the monotheistic religions the divine sovereignty means not exaltation above other gods, but complete power over nature and man, though in the OT we can trace the process by which monolatry—the exclusive worship of Jahweh along with a recognition of other gods—passed into monotheism. In Am 1 and 2 Jahweh is Judge and Ruler of all nations even as of His people Israel. Assyria is the rod of His anger (Is 10^{5}). Cyrus is His anointed to fulfil His purpose (45^{1}). Monotheism was never as confident or challenging as in Is 40^{12-26}. The omnipotence of God is the prevailing doctrine of the OT.[5] The same doctrine is assumed in the NT, as indeed it must be in any monotheistic religion. Into any details it is not necessary here to enter.

(3) It is the third sense of the term—the exercise of the will of God absolutely, unconditioned by the will of man—that claims special attention, since this view has been challenged and defended in the history of Christian theology, as the omnipotence of God has not been, unless in dualistic systems of thought.[6] Before dealing with the doctrine of divine sovereignty in this narrower sense in Christian theology, we must note the unqualified and unreserved assertion of God's sole sovereignty in Islām.

'There is no god but God—are words simply tantamount in English to the negation of any deity save one alone; and this much they certainly mean in Arabic, but they imply much more also. Their full sense is, not only to deny absolutely and unreservedly all plurality, whether of nature or of person, in the Supreme Being, not only to establish the Unity of the Unbegetting and Unbegot, in all its simple and uncommunicable Oneness, but besides this the words, in Arabic and among Arabs, imply that this one Supreme Being is also the only Agent, the only Force, the only Act existing throughout the universe, and leave to all beings else, matter or spirit, instinct or intelligence, physical or moral, nothing but pure unconditional passiveness, alike in movement or in quiescence, in action or in capacity. The sole power, the sole motor, movement, energy, and deed is God; the rest is downright inertia and mere instrumentality, from the highest archangel down to the simplest atom of creation. Hence in this one sentence, "La Ilāh illa Allāh," is summed up a system which, for want of a better name, I may be permitted to call the Pantheism of Force, or of Act, thus exclusively assigned to God, who absorbs it all, exercises it all, and to whom alone it can be ascribed, whether for preserving or for destroying, for relative evil or for equally relative good.'[1]

This doctrine is obtruded very frequently in its most offensive form in the Qur'ān:

'God misleadeth whom He pleaseth, and guideth whom He pleaseth aright.' 'We created man upright, and then caused him to be the vilest of the vile.' 'The fate of every man have we bound about his neck.'[2]

Such statements of the doctrine without reserve or restraint might have served as warnings to Christian theologians.

2. The Pauline doctrine.—While it is in the NT that the divine sovereignty is first dealt with controversially, the unconditionalness of God's action is already asserted in the OT. God's work shall not return to Him void, but it shall accomplish that which He pleases, and it shall prosper in the thing whereto He sends it (Is 55^{11}). In contrast to other gods, He is in the heavens, and 'hath done whatsoever he pleased' (Ps 115^{3}). He does good and evil, and creates darkness and light (Is 41^{23} 45^{7} 54^{16}, Am 3^{7}). For Him 'the nations are as a drop of a bucket, and are counted as the small dust of the balance' (Is 40^{15}). None can hinder His work, and from Him none can deliver (43^{13}). The impossible to man is possible to God (Zec 8^{6}). The relation of God's action to man's activity was a subject of controversy in the Jewish schools, although it is probable that Josephus was accommodating himself to Gentile readers in the account that he gives of the difference on this question:

'The Essenes taught an absolute fate, the Sadducees utterly denied fate, and the Pharisees struck out a middle path between the two.' For 'the very expression εἱμαρμένη, which is utterly impossible to any Jewish consciousness, proves that we have at least to deal with a strongly Hellenized colouring of Jewish views.'[3]

For fate the Jew would put the will of God. Paul, in his argument in Ro 9–11, takes the middle path in asserting both divine sovereignty and human freedom; as an *argumentum ad hominem* he assumes that his opponents grant the divine sovereignty while maintaining human freedom. Had Christian theologians recognized that Paul was fighting Jewish arrogance and exclusiveness with its own weapons, that the argument is to be treated as a whole, and a dogma must not be built upon its separate statements, and that the distinctively Christian contribution is the hope of a universal mercy, they would not have given to the doctrine of divine sovereignty the place that in their systems they have assigned to it, disproportionate to the teaching of the NT as a whole, and even inconsistent with the general trend of Paul's theology.

'The argument consists of three main propositions: (1) God is absolutely free to elect or reject individuals or nations according to His own will (ix. 1–29); (2) the Jewish people, by its unbelief, has deserved its present exclusion from the blessings of the gospel (ix. 30–x. 21); (3) this exclusion is partial and temporary, as it is God's purpose ultimately to include both Jew and Gentile in His grace (xi.).'[4]

In dealing with the first proposition 'he shows how in the history of the chosen people the principle of God's unconditional election has been again and again asserted, and repels the charge of injustice by appealing to God's own words, in which He claims freedom in all His acts. While rebuking the arrogance of the creature in questioning the acts of the Creator, he blunts the edge of his argument somewhat by showing that God has used His freedom to show mercy rather than judgment. The form of the argument is not beyond criticism; Paul's exegesis cannot be accepted as strictly historical.' But, as regards the substance, we cannot escape the difficulty by say-

1 *Lectures on the Origin and Growth of Religion* (*HL*), London, 1878, p. 271.
2 See art. MONOLATRY AND HENOTHEISM.
3 Monier Williams, *Hinduism*14, London, 1901, p. 27 f.
4 Max Müller, p. 216 f.; G. F. Moore, *Hist. of Religions*, Edinburgh, 1914, i. 252, 411.
5 H. Schultz, *OT Theology*, Eng. tr., Edinburgh, 1892, ii. 150 f.; also art. GOD (Biblical and Christian), vol. vi. p. 254 f.
6 See artt. DUALISM.

1 Quoted from W. G. Palgrave by S. M. Zwemer, in *Arabia: the Cradle of Islam*, Edinburgh, London, and New York, 1900, p. 172 f.
2 Quoted in Muir, *The Coran*, ed. London, 1903, p. 52.
3 Jos. *Ant.* XIII. v. 9; Schürer, *HJP* II. ii. 14 f.
4 A. E. Garvie, *Romans* ('Century Bible'), Edinburgh, 1901, p. 206.

ing that Paul has in view only the historical fate of a nation, for he asserts unequivocally God's freedom in electing or rejecting individuals. We must insist that 'it is not the Christian conception of God which dominates the discussion'; that Paul does not carry out his principle with rigorous logic, since 'he shrinks from affirming that God fitted the vessels of wrath unto destruction, and admits that God endured them with much long-suffering,' and that 'the metaphor of the potter itself cancels the argument,' for 'the potter does not use the clay wilfully, but makes of each lump what it is fitted to become.'[1] Apart from this argument in Ro 9–11, there are passages in which Paul asserts 'a doctrine of election as regards Christian believers (Ro 8[28f.], Eph 1[4]). . . . The aim of this teaching is, however, to give the believer assurance that his relation to God does not begin in time with his faith in God's grace, but is deeply rooted, firmly fixed, in the eternal will of God. . . . Paul does not teach that God foreknows, foreordains, or elects any man unto eternal death. The responsibility for that he throws on the man himself.'[2]

We must not ascribe to Paul the deductions of a too ruthless logic, which infers that whom God does not elect He rejects, as he was concerned not with the speculative problem of the relation of divine sovereignty and human freedom, but solely with the practical assurance of God's unchanging grace.

3. Augustinianism. — Neither Paul's theology nor even his personal experience accounts wholly for Augustine's position; his previous philosophical training must be taken into our reckoning. While, as with Paul, it is man's entire dependence on God's grace that He seeks to magnify, yet he, in his controversy with Pelagianism, develops this practical assurance into a speculative doctrine which virtually denies man all freedom, and even transforms constraining grace into compelling force, fixing man's destiny solely by the eternal will of God.

'Sinful man depends,' says B. B. Warfield, 'for his recovery to good and to God, entirely on the free grace of God; this grace is therefore indispensable, prevenient, irresistible, indefectible; and, being thus the free grace of God, must have lain, in all the details of its conference and working, in the intention of God from all eternity.'[3]

'From the sinfulness and impotency of all men,' says G. P. Fisher, 'Augustine deduced the doctrine of unconditional predestination. They who believe in the Gospel with a saving faith are not merely elected to be the recipients of the heavenly reward; they are elected to be the recipients of faith (*de Prædest. Sanctorum*, 37, c. 18). Faith itself is the gift of God. All others are left in their sins—left to perish. They are not predestinated to sin, but rather to the punishment which sin deserves, from which they are not saved by electing grace. The number of the elect is fixed (*de Corrept. et Grat.* 39, c. 13). It is predetermined in the plan of God. But not all believers are of the elect. Perseverance in the new, holy life is the gift of God, and is bestowed on that portion of believers to whom God in His inscrutable wisdom chooses to grant it.'[4]

While Augustinianism triumphed over Pelagianism, yet the Church did not accept it in its entirety, for this emphasis on free grace is in inherent antagonism to the Church's doctrine and practice of 'works.'

'As over against the Pelagians,' says Warfield, 'the indispensableness of grace was quickly established; as over against the Semi-Pelagians, its prevenience was with almost equal rapidity made good. But there advance paused. If the necessity of prevenient grace was thereafter (after the second Council of Orange, 529) the established doctrine of the Church, the irresistibility of this prevenient grace was put under the ban, and there remained no place for a complete "Augustinianism" within the Church, as Gottschalk and Jansen were fully to discover.'[5]

4. The Reformers.—Augustinianism was revived at the Reformation. Luther in his controversy with Erasmus 'affirmed in almost reckless language the impotence of the human will. God's agency was asserted to be the universal cause. His will was declared to be subject to no law, but to be the foundation of right. Predestination was declared to be unconditional and to include as its objects the lost as well as the saved.' He did not attack Melanchthon, however, when he propounded

1 Garvie, *Studies of Paul and his Gospel*, London, 1911, pp. 241–243.
2 Garvie, *Romans*, p. 224.
3 Art. Augustine, vol. ii. p. 224[a].
4 *Hist. of Christian Doctrine*, Edinburgh, 1896, p. 191 f.
5 *ERE* ii. 224[a].

the doctrine of synergism (*q.v.*)—a co-operation, however subordinate, of the human will with divine grace in conversion. In truth he himself had not a consistent doctrine. On the one hand, he affirmed 'that God from eternity desires the salvation of all men,' and, on the other, the truth nearest his heart was 'that salvation is by divine grace, without merit,' which he used as a weapon against the Roman Catholic insistence on human merit.[1] The doctrine of predestination was not with Luther, as it was with Zwingli, the starting-point of his theology. It was in Calvin, however, that the doctrine of the divine sovereignty found its full expression in a logical system of theology.

'Calvin and Calvinism,' says Fisher, 'emphasize not only the freedom, the unmerited character, of grace, but equally the *sovereignty* of God in the bestowal of it. The idea is that apart from this sovereignty in the selection of the subjects of it, grace would not be grace. . . . The peculiarity of Calvin's doctrine of predestination is that it includes in it the decree of reprobation. This the Lutheran confessions exclude. . . . God has once for all determined "whom He would admit to salvation and whom He would condemn to destruction" (Calvin, *Institutes*, III. xxi. 7).'[2]

God does not merely foresee the hardening of the heart of the sinners; but Himself brings it about by the withdrawal of His Spirit and by using Satan to influence their minds and deeds. Why God does this we must not ask, as God's will is above all. Yet there is a good and sufficient reason for every divine decree.[3]

It has been disputed whether Calvin is to be regarded as a supralapsarian or a sub- or infralapsarian. The question at issue was this: Did the divine decree of election and reprobation precede (in divine thought, not in time) or follow 'the consideration of man as fallen'? While in the heat of controversy Calvin seems to commit himself to the former view, his more considered judgment inclines to the latter.

'Calvin,' says J. Orr, 'always viewed election as from a "mass" already in condemnation, while, of course, recognizing that the fall of man also was embraced in the providence of God.'[4]

5. Later doctrinal developments.—A modification of Calvinism which gave the doctrine of divine sovereignty less the appearance of arbitrariness was the doctrine of the Covenants, or the Federal Theology,[5] of which Cocceius in Holland was the leading exponent. A deduction from the doctrine of election, which Calvin himself did not make, was that the Atonement in Christ's death must be provided only for the elect. Arminianism asserted the universality of the Atonement, in God's intention, although it is not actually efficient in all. A compromise was attempted in Amyraut's 'hypothetical universalism': the Atonement is for all, and yet it is applied only to the elect; and this view found wide acceptance.[6] It is unjust to regard Arminianism as simply a revived Pelagianism, for it taught an election conditional on God's foreknowledge of faith in the individual, man's dependence on God's grace for the ability to exercise saving faith, the necessity of regeneration by the Holy Spirit for good works, the indispensableness, but not irresistibility, of grace. It is not necessary to follow in detail the subsequent controversies. The 'hypothetical universalism' of Amyraut, however, was capable of further development. If the Atonement avails for all, can it be God's purpose that its efficacy shall be limited to the elect because the operations of the Holy Spirit in producing saving faith are limited to them? The universality of the Atonement led James Morison backward to the universality of the love of God and forward to the universality of the work of the Holy Spirit: the three universalities was the battle-cry of the movement in Scotland of which he was leader. He still affirmed, however, that man was free to choose or

1 Fisher, p. 292 f. 2 *Ib.* p. 300. 3 *Ib.*
4 Art. Calvinism, vol. iii. p. 152 f.
5 See art. Covenant Theology.
6 See art. Expiation and Atonement (Christian).

to refuse this universal salvation. Starting from the conception of God as Father, as given in the revelation of Christ, and applying the conception of divine sovereignty thereto with the same logical rigour as did Calvinism, we should at last reach universalism.

6. Fatherhood and sovereignty.—Every monotheistic religion must affirm the divine sovereignty. Apart from impossibilities, metaphysical, logical, and moral, God can do whatsoever He wills. But whatsoever He wills depends and must depend on what God is. As we conceive God, so must we think of the divine sovereignty. If we think of God as Father, we must think of His sovereignty as fatherly. A doctrine of divine sovereignty that ends, as do Augustinianism and Calvinism, in the election of the few and the reprobation of the many has evidently started wrong—not from the Christian conception of God as revealed in Christ, but from a conception of sovereignty that in every country to-day which enjoys any measure of constitutional liberty would be repudiated as false. Even a sovereign to-day does not wield absolute and arbitrary power. The doctrine of election, it is argued in its favour, has its roots in the sense of man's impotence, and his dependence on God for every good; but is it in a child's trust in the father or a subject's submission to a sovereign? Must we not admit that, while the former attitude was not absent, yet it was the latter that was dominant, when the religious assurance was developed into the speculative doctrine? But does not the religious consciousness need to be allied with the moral conscience, which no less clearly and firmly affirms man's responsibility and liberty? The conception of God's Fatherhood, which implies man's moral affinity as well as his religious community with God, involves that God will so exercise His sovereignty, on which man depends, as not to deprive him of his liberty. It is no abrogation of the divine sovereignty, but only an exercise of it accordant with His Fatherhood, if He allows the activity of His will in dealing with men to be conditioned by the acts of their wills. Such a view of the divine sovereignty forbids the deduction from God's Fatherhood made by universalism; but it does leave us the hope that the Father who created man in His likeness and for fellowship, despite man's sin, has such resources in Himself, rational, righteous, and gracious, as will at last, not by the compulsion of force, but by the constraint of love, make His Fatherhood sovereign in mankind.

LITERATURE.—See the works cited in the footnotes.

ALFRED E. GARVIE.

SPACE.—The various ideas which have historically prevailed regarding the nature of space are commonly regarded as so many detached views, independent of, and mostly in conflict with, each other. In this article we propose to consider them from a different standpoint, and to regard each of those opinions or doctrines as contributing an important factor or element in the one true conception of space. In point of fact, there is scarcely a view or theory which has been put forward regarding space that does not express some important aspect of the truth.

1. History.—(*a*) *Greek philosophy.*—In early Greek philosophy the concept of space is confounded with that of matter, at any rate by the Pythagoreans. J. Burnet says:

'The Pythagoreans, or some of them, certainly identified "air" with the void. This is the beginning, but no more than the beginning, of the conception of abstract space or extension.'[1]

It still remains true that the most recent discussions as to the nature of space turn upon the relations between the two concepts, space and matter, and the objects which they denote. In modern speculations it is no longer the air, it is the ether, that is confounded with the void.

The first important conception of space which we have to notice is that of Plato. It is not necessary, for this purpose, to enter upon a discussion of the different interpretations which have been given to the Platonic philosophy in recent times. Whether we adopt the objective view of the Ideas, as the hypostatization of the universal, attributed to Plato by Aristotle, or the more subjective interpretation of Henry Jackson and R. D. Archer-Hind, based on the later dialogues, or that older view of St. Augustine, and in modern times of Cousin,[1] which combines both these interpretations, in none of these cases is the interpretation of the Platonic space essentially affected. Plato in his speculations seems to have travelled a road the reverse of that travelled by Fichte. As the latter began with an Ego which was suspiciously finite, and ended with an Absolute which had very few of the characters of Ego-hood (*Ichheit*) about it, so Plato began with an Absolute which continued itself into a world of ideas, and ended in a world-soul and a demiurge.

Space Plato speaks of in the *Timæus* as 'the receptacle, and as it were the nurse, of all becoming.'[2] 'It behoves that which is fitly to receive many times over its whole extent likenesses of all things, that is, of all eternal existences, to be itself naturally without part or lot in any of the forms. Therefore the mother and recipient of creation, which is visible and by any sense perceptible, we must call neither earth nor air nor fire nor water, nor the combinations of these nor the elements of which they are formed; but we shall not err in affirming it to be a viewless nature and formless, all receiving, in some manner most bewildering and hard to comprehend, partaking of the intelligible.'[3] 'This being so, we must agree that there is first the unchanging idea, unbegotten and imperishable, neither receiving aught into itself from without nor itself entering into aught else, invisible, nor in anywise perceptible—even that whereof the contemplation belongs to thought. Second is that which is named after it and is like to it, sensible, created, ever in motion, coming to be in a certain place and again from thence perishing, apprehensible by opinion with sensation. And the third kind is space everlasting, admitting not destruction, but affording place for all things that come into being, itself apprehensible without sensation by a sort of bastard reasoning, hardly matter of belief. It is with this in view that dreaming we say that all that exists must be in some place and filling some space, and that what is neither on earth nor in heaven anywhere is nought.'[4]

To some extent there can be no question with regard to the interpretation of this. Space is to Plato 'the other,' what in the Platonic philosophy takes the place of the *prima materia* in the Aristotelian philosophy. This interpretation has been completely established by Zeller,[5] though the opposite view, which makes primordial matter different from space, was still maintained by Gomperz.[6] But here a subtle difference of interpretation arises, which has a close connexion with recent philosophy. We may adopt a subjective view with Ritter,[7] and hold that the relation subsisting between the ideal and the sensible is 'a mere relation to the sentient,' and still, as Zeller points out,[8] the resulting view of matter can be adopted, with slight modifications apart from that theory. The Platonic theory of matter is then, in effect, as Zeller says, identical with that of Leibniz. This is the interpretation of Plato adopted by Archer-Hind, according to whom space, though the substrate and recipient of the images of the ideas, is only 'the law of our finite nature which ordains that we shall perceive all objects as extended in space,' and depends on a subjective view of the Ideas, which, following Jackson, Archer-Hind

[1] *Early Greek Philosophy*, pt. i., London, 1914, p. 51.

[1] *Du vrai, du beau, et du bien*, bk. iv., Paris, 1858.
[2] Archer-Hind, *Timæus*, London, 1888, p. 171.
[3] *Ib.* p. 179. [4] *Ib.* p. 184 f.
[5] *Plato and the Older Academy*, Eng. tr., London, 1876, ch. vii.
[6] *Greek Thinkers*, Eng. tr., London, 1901-12, iii. 366.
[7] *Hist. of Ancient Philosophy*, Eng. tr., Oxford and London, 1838-46, ii. 320.
[8] P. 311.

adopts. It is different, however, if an objective view of the nature of the Idea is taken, as was done by Maguire in his *Essay on the Platonic Idea.*[1] Maguire's theory is indeed classed by Zeller[2] along with Ritter's, and regarded as exposed to the same criticism. But, owing to the doctrine of the objectivity of the Idea, Maguire's view of the subjectivity of space approaches much more closely to the modern 'theory of objects' of Meinong and his school. Spatial *entia* are *entia rationis*, which may or may not coincide with phenomenal existence.

With regard to the remarkable phrase, 'apprehensible by a sort of bastard reasoning, hardly matter of belief,' its significance will appear hereafter. Here, however, we may say that it is closely related to Plato's conception of the world-soul. The latter is compounded of the ideal element and the element of multiplicity. It is antecedent to the world and yet in a way presupposes the element of plurality. Plato's theory of space presents in this way a close analogy to the Hegelian view, with a difference characteristic of the objectivity of ancient philosophy, as against the subjectivity of modern philosophy. In Hegel thought, by reason of the inner law of contradiction, which is its essence, expels from itself the phenomenal world, the out-of-itselfness of which is space. In Plato the 'otherness' which clings to the Idea is space. The contradiction which in Hegel is inherent in thought is in Plato adherent to the Idea. It is the infinite region of dissimilitude.

Between Plato and Aristotle there is often great similarity in statement; but the actual thought is altogether different. Space in Plato is matter, the only matter there is. Aristotle correctly represents his master here.[3] But Aristotle's doctrine is rather an identification of space with matter. It closely resembles the modern doctrine of relativity in its more moderate forms. Matter exists in space, but the space in which it exists is itself determined and produced by the matter existing in it. Space is no antecedent empty receptacle, into which the world and the things of the world are fitted. But neither is it 'soft'; it does not expand or contract any more than time. Space is 'the first unmoved limit of the containing body';[4] *i.e.*, matter exists, but exists with inherent spatial character. It is the boundary of the containing body, in its relation to the contained, that constitutes the spatial existence of the latter. When there is no containing body, space does not exist; therefore the universe is not in space. If there were no contained, there would be no boundary; therefore there must be a plenum. Aristotle's doctrine is made perfectly clear by his reply to Zeno's difficulty—that space, not being a substance, would have to be in something which is in space, and so on *ad infinitum*. To this Aristotle gives the reply that space may be in something else, as health in warm beings as a state, or warmth in body as an affection.[5]

It is in relation to the well-known paradoxes of Zeno that Aristotle's doctrine attains its full significance. These paradoxes are based on the contradictions which arise from assuming the actuality of the infinitely small. The Aristotelian doctrine implies that matter is the potentiality of space. Matter is the potentiality of actual existence. It is only through matter passing into actual existence that space exists as a reality. Matter, as infinitely great or infinitesimally small, is nothing actual. It is identical with pure potency. The infinitely little, the infinitely great, do not actually exist. This contradicts recent mathematical doctrines which treat the infinite as actual. The views of Cantor and his school have been subjected to criticism on this very point by Poincaré.[6] There is, however, an older line of argument which seems to be decisive in favour of the Aristotelian position. Actual is that which has one or other of two opposite determinations, not that which hovers in uncertainty between both. Consider the series of Grandi. If infinitely prolonged, such a series may be said to be equal to 0 *or* 1. But '*either . . . or*' cannot be actual. Actual is that which is determinate; which, in accordance with the law of Excluded Middle, possesses one or other of two conflicting characters; which is, therefore, something more than the potentiality of either. But this character cannot belong to a series which is incomplete, whose last member cannot be said to be odd or even, + or −, *i.e.* which has no last member. The same reasoning which applies to series applies also to space. As Cantor himself has pointed out, the actual infinite has been rejected not only by philosophers, but also by mathematicians, such as Gauss and Cauchy.[1] The strongest support for the actual infinite is derived from the use of convergent series in mathematics. But, if the opinion held by both Augustus de Morgan and William Rowan Hamilton be true—that the mathematical validity of the summation of such infinite series does not at all depend on convergence, as is commonly thought, but on this alternation—then it may, on the contrary, be held that the true mathematical conception is the potential infinite.[2]

1 London, 1866. 2 P. 308.
3 *Phys.* iv. 2 (209b). 4 *Ib.* iv. 2 (212a 20).
5 *Ib.* iv. 3 (210b 22).
6 *Science et méthode*, Paris, 1908, Eng. tr., London, 1914.

We therefore see in Aristotle's views an advance on those of Plato. To Plato space is a sort of logical ejection from the Idea, possessed of no independent existence. In Aristotle it has such independent existence, which it receives from that which stands over against the Idea—the *materia prima*. It receives existential reality from the latter and ceases to be a mere dialectical relativity of the Idea. At the same time, Aristotle's doctrine, by making the reality of space thus dependent upon matter, anticipates the element of truth underlying the modern theory of relativity.

The doctrine of the Stoics[3] that beyond the world there exists an unlimited void, the distinction of the Epicureans between place (τόπος) and room (χώρα), and their doctrine of the intangible nature of empty space[4] are to be regarded as important not so much in themselves as marking the next great development in the conception of space, as having an entitative though not substantial existence distinct from matter. According to Plotinus, the magnitude of things does not pre-exist in first matter. First matter has not bulk, but the 'phantasm of bulk' as aptitude for it. First matter, by its very indefiniteness, stands in an indefinite relation to magnitude. It is separately neither great nor small, but both small and great. Space is posterior to matter and bodies; therefore bodies must first be material before they can be spatial.[5] In these chapters there is much that anticipates all future speculation on the subject of space. Plotinus advances beyond Plato and Aristotle; at the same time it is the logical outcome of Aristotle's doctrine. Aristotle had carefully distinguished space as something different from matter and form. Matter as pure potentiality is prior to its expression in spatial existence. This is logically involved in his doctrine that space is in bodies—not as contained in them, but as an affection. In Iamblichus the aptitude of Plotinus is explained by the efficacy of the primal one.[6] Proclus seems to combine this with the opposed view of Porphyry, and even regards space as a body.[7] The problem of philosophy is to explain how incorporeal form must necessitate extension and matter issue in space.

(*b*) *Middle Ages.*—The Alexandrian school did not attribute to space an existence independent of matter, outside the world. The same position was maintained by St. Augustine.[8] This remains the fundamental point of view of the Aristotelianism

1 Cantor, Letter to G. Eneström, 4th Nov. 1885.
2 See R. P. Graves, *Life of Sir W. R. Hamilton*, Dublin, 1882–89, iii. 538–540, 551.
3 Diog. Laert. vii. 140. 4 *Ib.* x. 40.
5 *Enneads*, II. iv. 11 f.
6 Simplicius, *in Præd.* p. 34, ed. Basil, 1557, quoted by J. Harris, *Philosophical Arrangements*, London, 1775, p. 116; cf. E. Vacherot, *Hist. crit. de l'école d'Alexandrie*, Paris, 1846–51, ii. 61.
7 *Scholia in Aristotel.*, coll. C. A. Brandis, vol. vi. of *Opera*, Berlin, 1831–70, p. 379.
8 *De Civ. Dei*, xi. 5.

of the Middle Ages. De Wulf[1] attributes to Henry of Ghent belief in the possibility of the existence of vacuum, but only as a deduction from his theory of matter. But, within the general view of the dependence of space or extension on matter, what is most significant for the Scholastic theory of space is the controversy as to the principle of individuation. It is unnecessary here to enter into the numerous theories put forward on this subject in mediæval philosophy. It is sufficient to consider the theory of Aquinas, the different interpretations of it, and one or two of the theories opposed to it.

According to St. Thomas Aquinas, the principle of individuation is not matter in general, but *materia signata certis dimensionibus, i.e.* matter limited by dimensive quantity. There are, however, two interpretations of the phrase. According to Ægidio Colonna and others, it means matter quantitatively determined—not the mere potentiality or capacity, but the actual determination. According to Cardinal Cajetan, it means matter endowed with the proximate power of receiving such determinate quantity. The former interpretation is exposed to the objection, actually made by the realists, that such quantitative determination already implies the possession of form. The latter interpretation endows the *materia prima* with a determinate capacity or potentiality. Now the rival theory of Duns Scotus regards *hæcceitas* as the individualizing principle. This difficult conception has been explained by Rousselot[2] as a force or active type in matter. It is the reverse of St. Thomas's theory on the first interpretation; but it approximates to it on the second. To attribute to first matter a capacity or force prior to its union with form seems to require a degree of reality in matter apart from form. Notwithstanding this difficulty, Cajetan's interpretation of St. Thomas finds favour with Neo-Scholastics.[3]

The logical solution of these difficulties is to be found in the theory of aptitudinal extension put forward by Suarez,[4] that there is in first matter a natural tendency towards extension. But no more than any other Scholastic does he explain why it should be there. It does not escape the witty criticism of Geulincx on all these theories, that quantity is like the size used to stiffen the brims of hats, without which matter would become flaccid or collapse to a point.[5] Plotinus had already foreseen this criticism when he said that matter separately was 'both small and great.'

(*c*) *Cartesian and English philosophy.*—The speculations of the later Scholastics prepared the way for the doctrine of Descartes. Aquinas had held that *materia prima* was numerically one. Suarez[6] held that numerical distinction was not repugnant to it; moreover, he also admitted that the Scotist rejection of absolute accidents that are more than modal could not be philosophically disproved. Add to this that the conception of *materia prima*, except in so far as it is synonymous with the occupation of space, is negative,[7] and we are led to the doctrine of Descartes that 'extension in length, breadth and depth constitutes the nature of corporeal substance.'[1] It is not an identification of matter with space, but of space with matter. Extension is the sole attribute of corporeal substance; and yet it is distinguished from it, not by a real distinction, such as exists between substances, nor by a merely modal one, but by a 'distinction of reason.' This does not mean that extension is anything distinct from bodies.

'I do not suppose,' says Descartes, 'any real qualities in nature which may be added to the substance as little souls to their bodies, and which could be separated from it by Divine power.'[2]

It follows from this necessary inherence of extension in matter that the universe is infinite. 'It involves a contradiction that the world should be finite or bounded.'[3] The crux of the Cartesian philosophy is the synthesis of thought and extension. This may be attempted either from the side of thought or from that of extension. The first way is that of Malebranche; the second that of Spinoza. According to Malebranche, there exists in the Divine Intelligence 'intelligible extension' —the archetype of matter.

'God includes within himself an ideal or infinite intelligible extension. For God knows extension, inasmuch as he has made it, and he can know it only in himself. . . . Intelligible extension is immovable even intelligibly. . . . But only by it are we able to see or imagine actually bodies in movement.'[4]

The difficulty in this conception is thus put by Kuno Fischer:

'The intelligible extension can belong neither to extension, for it is intelligible, nor to thought, for it is extension.'[5]

To have escaped this contradiction Malebranche should have placed in the Divine Reason, not extension, but its intelligibility.

The relation of the attributes, thought and extension, in the philosophy of Spinoza has received at least four different interpretations.[6] The Hegelian interpretation regards the attributes as something read into the substance by our minds —a view also maintained by Schwegler and Erdmann.[7] Only two interpretations concern us here—the mathematical and the dynamical. The former[8] emphasizes the unity of the attributes, and consequently brings the substance within each attribute according to Spinoza's own definition: 'An attribute I understand to be that which the intellect perceives as constituting the essence of a substance.' The latter, brilliantly advocated by Fischer, really separates the attributes. It places the substance outside them, as it were. They are forces proceeding from it. This agrees with Spinoza's definition of substance: 'I understand substance to be that which is in itself and is conceived through itself.' The definitions are inconsistent. Both interpretations are correct, and are the consequences of the inevitable dialectic which underlies our conception of space.

According to Leibniz, space is 'an order of coexistences.' It is 'a relation, an order, not only between things existing, but between possible things as if they existed.' According to Descartes, the sides of a hollow empty body would touch each other. Leibniz, on the other hand, says:

'I distinguish matter from extension, and I admit that, if there were a vacuum in a sphere, the opposite poles in the hollow space would not on that account touch. But I believe that this is a case which the divine perfection does not allow.'[9]

Space without body does not exist, and body has

[1] *Hist. of Mediæval Philosophy*, Eng. tr., London, 1909, p. 365.

[2] *Etudes sur la philosophie dans le Moyen Age*, Paris, 1840–42, iii. 57.

[3] Cardinal Mercier, *Cours de philosophie*, Louvain, 1892–99, ii. *Métaphysique générale*, pp. 78, 80; De Wulf, *Scholasticism Old and New*, tr. P. Coffey, Dublin, 1907, p. 108. See also on the general question J. B. Hauréau, *De la philosophie scolastique*, Paris, 1850, ii. 130–136; A. Stöckl, *Gesch. der Philosophie des Mittelalters*, Mayence, 1864–66, II. i. § 130; Ueberweg, *Hist. of Philosophy*, Eng. tr., London, 1874–75, i. 445 f.

[4] *Metaphysicæ Disputationes*, disp. xl. sect. iv. 15 ff., ed. Paris, 1619, ii. 378.

[5] *Metaphysica vera et ad mentem peripateticam*, Amsterdam, 1691, pt. i. § 4; *Opera Philosophica*, ed. J. P. N. Laird, 1892, ii. 222.

[6] *Metaph. Disp.* disp. xiii. sect. xi. 10 (ed. 1619, i. 304).

[7] Cf. Mansel, *Metaphysics*³, Edinburgh, 1875, p. 266.

[1] *Principia*, i. § 53.

[2] *Œuvres*, ed. V. Cousin, Paris, 1824–26, ix. 104.

[3] *Ib.* x. 241.

[4] *De la recherche de la vérité*, Paris, 1674–75, 10me éclaircissement, obj. iii.; cf. his *Entretiens sur la Métaphysique*, I. III.

[5] *Gesch. der neuern Philosophie*, Heidelberg, 1897-1901, ii. 71.

[6] Fischer, ii. 371–386, 560–562.

[7] *Hist. of Philosophy*, Eng. tr., London, 1889–90, ii. 72, note.

[8] Most clearly put by J. H. Stirling in his tr. of Schwegler's *Handbook of the Hist. of Philosophy*, Edinburgh, 1867.

[9] *Nouveaux Essais*, bk. ii. ch. 13.

extension and is in space by reason of its passive resistance or impenetrability.

'This primitive passive power or principle of resistance does not consist in extension but in an exigency of extension.'[1]

Leibniz in this language approaches very close to the aptitudinal extension of the Scholastics—an approach which becomes closer still in the *Systema Theologicum*.[2] Yet the difference is marked. To the Scholastic not the *materia prima*, but aptitudinal extension, is *extensionis exigentia*. To Leibniz the *materia prima* itself is this. The whole difference between Scholastic and modern philosophy lies in the change. The Leibnizian view is finally formulated by Wolf in the definition, 'Spatium est ordo simultaneorum, quatenus scilicet coexistunt.'[3]

A series of writers, mostly English, have put forward views affirming a direct relation between the Deity and space. Some, as Henry More,[4] have made it one of identity—a doctrine alluded to by Berkeley[5] and Leibniz[6] and also attributed to Jonathan Edwards. Newton[7] suggests that infinite space is the sensorium of the Deity. More definitely, in the general scholium at the end of the *Principia*, he says:

'The Deity is not eternity nor infinity, but He is eternal and infinite; He is not duration nor space, but He endures or is expanded. He endures always and is present everywhere; and by existing at all times and in all places, He makes duration and space, eternity and infinity to be.'

Clarke makes immensity, *i.e.* infinite space, 'a mode of an essence of substance incomprehensible to us.'[8] These speculations, if they mean anything, are important as asserting a direct relation between infinite intelligence and infinite space.

The main course of English philosophy is, however, concerned with the psychological question as to how we get our knowledge of space—a question still unsettled. To Hobbes space was the phantasm of an existing thing, as existing.[9] To Cudworth there is no actual infinity of space, only a potential infinity or indefinite increasableness of corporeal magnitude.[10] According to Locke, we get the idea of space through sight and touch. Pure space, which is capable neither of resistance nor of motion, he distinguishes from solidity.[11]

'The ideas of primary qualities of bodies are resemblances of them, and their patterns do really exist in the bodies themselves.'[12]

He distinguishes between the idea of the infinity of space and the idea of space infinite. The former is nothing but a supposed endless progression of the mind over what repeated ideas of space it pleases. The latter supposes the mind already passed over and actually to have a view of all those repeated ideas of space, which an endless repetition can never totally present to it, and carries in it a plain contradiction.[13] According to Berkeley, 'the ideas of space, outness, and things placed at a distance are not, strictly speaking, the object of sight.'[14]

'All place or extension exists only in the mind.'[15] 'Those qualities [extension and figure] are in the mind only as they are perceived by it;—that is not by way of *mode* or *attribute*, but only by way of *idea*.'[1]

According to Hume, 'the idea of extension is but a copy' of the 'impressions of colour'd points, dispos'd in a certain manner.' When the colours change, 'finding a resemblance in the disposition of colour'd points, of which they are compos'd, we omit the peculiarities of colour, as far as possible, and found an abstract idea merely on that disposition of points, or manner of appearance, in which they agree. Nay even when the resemblance is carry'd beyond the objects of one sense, and the impressions of touch are found to be similar to those of sight in the disposition of their parts; this does not hinder the abstract idea from representing both, upon account of their resemblance.'[2]

The remarkable point in this theory is that somehow out of mere qualitative differences of two senses, sight and touch, an idea of an order of disposition of points or, as Hume afterwards says, of co-existent parts is formed, which is the idea of extension or space.

The culmination of this whole subjective view of space is found in the theory of Brown, Bain, and J. S. Mill, by which, out of a series of muscular sensations, confessedly only occupying time, length of space, and with it longitudinal extension in every direction, is constructed, in such a way, however, that length in space is at bottom length in time. The difficulty in this theory has already been perceived by Hamilton.[3] It is briefly: How get length in space out of length in time? Mill in his reply very properly dwells on the fact that the notion of simultaneity must be supposed to have been already acquired; but his theory of the synthesis is not satisfactory.[4]

The chief contribution of Reid to the theory of our knowledge of space is his theory of natural signs, especially those of the third class.[5] This theory is highly suggestive, and resembles Lotze's theory of local signs, without the *petitio principii* involved in the very name of the latter. What is wanted is an analysis of these signs and an explanation of how it is that certain sensations of sight and touch should be able to act as such—what it is in them that constitutes the sign.

(*d*) *Kant.*—The most prominent theory of space in modern philosophy is that of Kant. According to Kant, space is not an empirical concept which has been derived from external experience. The reference outward of sensations and their representation as out of and near each other presuppose the representation of space: space is a necessary representation *a priori* lying at the basis of all external intuitions. It is not a discursive or general concept of the relations of things, but a pure intuition. Space is represented as an infinite given quantity; space does not represent any property of things in themselves, nor themselves in their relation to one another, *i.e.* no determinations of objects in themselves. Space is nothing else than the form of all phenomena of external sense.[6] Space is empirically real with regard to all possible external experience. It is transcendentally ideal as regards things in themselves. By means of this theory Kant undertakes to explain the *a priori* synthetical principles of geometry, and it is this claim that is contested at the present day. In a paper in *Mind*,[7] entitled 'Going Back to Kant,' the present writer pointed out that the synthesis involved in *a priori* knowledge is not explained by Kant; it is only assumed as already existing in the mind. In this respect the recent reaction against Kant's doctrine is

1 *Opera philosophica*, ed. J. E. Erdmann, 2 pts., Berlin, 1839–40, p. 436.
2 Tr. C. W. Russell, London, 1850, pp. 114–116.
3 *Philosophia prima sive Ontologia*, Frankfort and Leipzig, 1730–36, § 589.
4 *Enchiridion Metaphysicum*, London, 1671, ch. 6 ff.; cf. Cudworth, *The True Intellectual System of the Universe*, ed. J. Harrison, London, 1845, iii. 231.
5 *Works*², ed. A. C. Fraser, London, 1901, i. 323, *Siris*, § 270.
6 Third Paper to Samuel Clarke, in *A Collection of Papers which passed between the late learned Mr. Leibnitz and Dr. Clarke*, London, 1717, p. 57.
7 *Optics*, London, 1706, p. 20.
8 *Demonstration of the Being and Attributes of God*, London, 1705, p. 39.
9 *De Corpore*, pt. ii. ch. vii. § 2.
10 *The True Intellectual System of the Universe*, ed. J. Harrison, London, 1845, ii. 528.
11 *Essay*, bk. ii. ch. iv. 12 *Ib.* ch. viii. § 15.
13 *Ib.* ch. xvii. § 7. 14 *New Theory of Vision*, § 46.
15 *Principles of Human Knowledge*, § 67.

1 *Principles of Human Knowledge*, § 49.
2 *A Treatise of Human Nature*, bk. i. pt. ii. § iii.
3 *The Works of Thomas Reid*², ed. W. Hamilton, Edinburgh, 1849, p. 869.
4 J. S. Mill, *An Exam. of Sir W. Hamilton's Philosophy*, London, 1865, ch. xiii.; Bain, *The Senses and the Intellect*³, do. 1868, p. 375.
5 *Works of Reid*², p. 121 f.
6 *Critique of Pure Reason*, pt. i. 'Transcendental Æsthetic,' sect. i. 'Of Space,' §§ 2–4.
7 ix. [1884] 274 ff.

relatively justified; though the attempt to reduce mathematics to analytical truths cannot succeed, this synthetic reference must itself be explained.

In England Kant's doctrine of space was maintained by Hamilton and Mansel; but Hamilton also asserted an *a posteriori* perception of extension as distinct from the *a priori* form space.[1] This is the perception of a great truth. But, to make it such, it must be shown how the texture of *a priori* thought is interwoven with spatial reality.

In a one-sided form something like this is to be found in the deductions of space in post-Kantian idealism. The most remarkable is that of Fichte.[2] He here expresses verbally the principle which we have had in view throughout this article: 'No space, without construction of it, notwithstanding, not space, but only its consciousness is thereby to be produced [ideal relation]; no construction without presupposing it [real relation].' Further on he says we should never get space out of us if we had it not in us.

To Schelling, too, space is nothing but 'an action of the intelligence.' 'We can define space as arrested time, time as flowing space.'[3]

Precisely the same determinations are found in Hegel: 'This immediate unity of space and time is already the ground, through which they are; for the negation of space is time.' 'The past and future of time, as *being* in nature, is space.'

In other words, space, if it is the abstract out-of-itselfness of nature, is in constant process, a sort of ideal movement, like a vector in quaternions; but this movement is time. Conversely, this movement constantly deposits itself, as it were, in space. For the rest, Hegel, like Aristotle, Descartes, and Leibniz, regards space as always filled; nor can a space be shown that is distinguished from its filling.[4]

2. Laws of thought and the concept of space.—We have now surveyed the views of the great thinkers. Herbart and Lotze, Schopenhauer and Hartmann, really only repeat or modify previous philosophical standpoints. It remains that we sum the results of this history. It is not any intelligible or subjective space that stands over against or generates objective space, but intelligence or thought itself acting according to its own laws. What are those laws? They may be described as the well-known laws of Identity, Contradiction, and Excluded Middle. The elements in sensation out of which thought constructs space are its most abstract features—identity, difference, relation. But here a difficulty presents itself. Grassmann truly says:

'The concept of space can in no way be produced by thought, but always stands over against it as a given thing.' He adds: 'He who will maintain the opposite, must undertake the task of deducing the necessity of the three dimensions of space from the pure laws of thought—a task the solution of which presents itself as impossible.'[5]

We accept both these positions of Grassmann—that space must be given over against thought; that it cannot be got from the pure laws of thought alone. We go farther; we say that the pure laws of thought themselves cannot be got from thought alone; in other words, that the self-diremption of thought cannot take place apart from space and time. This means that abstract thought, space, and time are all correlative. This involves the apparent circle that, while space receives its determinate character from thought, the latter is again determined by the former. It has therefore to presuppose as prior to itself what itself has produced. But this is what this whole history has taught. This is Plato's 'bastard reasoning.' This is that aptitudinal extension which has to be presupposed as the basis of that actual extension which it is not, but which it produces. This is the source of that double interpretation, mathematical and dynamical, to which the attributes of Spinoza equally lend themselves. The psychological analysis of the English school—Locke, Berkeley, Hume, Brown, and Mill—acquires a new meaning when considered as the analysis not only of processes taking place in the individual mind, but also of universal relations of thought and being.

[1] *Lectures on Metaphysics and Logic*, Edinburgh, 1859-60, ii. 114.
[2] *Werke*, Berlin, 1845-46, ii. 90-94.
[3] *Werke*, Stuttgart, 1856-61, I. iii. 476.
[4] *Werke*, Berlin, 1832-40, VII. i. 44, 47, 57, 61.
[5] *Die Ausdehnungslehre v. 1844*[2], Leipzig, 1878, p. xxiii.

3. The three dimensions.—It remains to touch upon the problem of the three dimensions. Seeing that spaces of more than four dimensions, as well as non-Euclidean spaces generally, involve, as spaces, no internal contradictions—*i.e.*, the geometries based upon them are internally consistent—it is evident that we cannot derive the three dimensions from the mere principle of contradiction.

Leibniz[1] seeks to derive the three dimensions of space from the impossibility of more than three straight lines which cut in a point being perpendicular to each other. This has been objected to by Kant on the ground that it involves a circle. Kant himself conceived the possibility of two other proofs—one from the simplicity of the three first powers of numbers, which he rejects; another, and a highly interesting one, from the fact of substances in the existing world acting on each other in the inverse ratio of the square of the distance.[2] A proof with which he seems scarcely satisfied himself, and which seems at bottom not different from that of Leibniz, has been put forward by Lotze.[3] Hegel confines himself to saying that the necessity of three dimensions rests on the nature of the notion or concept.[4] Whewell[5] gives a proof from the fact that each portion of space has a boundary, and is extended both in the direction in which its boundary extends and also in a direction from its boundary. A derivation from the concept of motion similar to some of the foregoing has been put forward by Schmitz-Dumont.[6]

The fact that none of these attempts is satisfactory—all seem to involve *petitio principii*—should not preclude us from recognizing that they may be on the right track. The present writer believes that a proof may be derived from the imaginary symbol $\sqrt{-1}$ combined with the concept of order. A more satisfactory proof is the following. By far the most important and original contribution to our subject is the memoir by A. B. Kempe, 'On the Theory of Mathematical Form,' in the *Philosophical Transactions* of the Royal Society, for 1886,[7] with supplementary paper, 'The Subject-Matter of Exact Thought,' in *Nature*, December 18th, 1890. In the art. 'The Theory of Mathematical Inference' in the *American Mathematical Monthly* for Jan. 1900 the present writer said:

'Mr. Kempe has shown that between the mathematical theory of points and the logical theory of statements, a striking correspondence exists. Between the laws defining the form of a system of points, and those defining the form of a system of statements, perfect sameness exists with one exception. The former is subject to a law to which the latter is not subject. It is sufficient here to say that it is the law "which expresses the fact that two straight lines can only cut once."

From these conclusions we may draw the converse inference that the laws which govern geometrical theory can be deduced from logical or purely analytical principles, taken in conjunction with that law in which the form of a system of points differs from the form of a system of statements. We have now to ask, Is there anything omitted from the form of a system of statements as contemplated by Mr. Kempe, or by the ordinary logic (and there is complete agreement between them), which would account for the absence of the particular law which distinguishes geometrical theory? I think there is. Mr. Kempe in order to effect his assimilation of the logical to the geometrical theory, and in particular in explaining the processes of immediate inference, has introduced two constants which play the same part in the logical theory that the "absolute" does in geometry. He entitles them "truism" and "falsism" respectively. It is by relation to these that such logical relations as contrariety, sub-contrariety, sub-alternation, analogous to the metrical relations of points in geometry, are determined. He considers

[1] *Essais de théodicée*, Amsterdam, 1710, § 351; cf. § 196.
[2] *Werke*, ed. K. Rosenkranz and F. W. Schubert, Leipzig, 1838-42, v. 25, 27.
[3] *Metaph.* bk. ii. ch. ii. § 135.
[4] *Werke*, vii. 1, 48.
[5] *Hist. of Scientific Ideas*[3], London, 1858, i. 97.
[6] *Zeit und Raum*, Leipzig, 1875.
[7] Vol. clxxvii. p. 1.

"truisms" and "falsisms" as propositions or statements standing in the system of statements on the same footing with all other statements. In reality this is not so. The truism and falsism of Mr. Kempe are really the laws of Identity and Contradiction in disguise, and every synthetic statement or proposition expresses more than what these laws require. The principle that a real proposition refers to, or is a synthesis with, something more than itself, is as old as Aquinas, and is indeed the fundamental principle which makes our thinking dependent on experience. It is the non-recognition of this which prevents Mr. Kempe from evolving the relation of noncollinearity from the relation of a truism and falsism to each other, which ought to be capable of being done, if it were true that these propositions could rank *pari passu* with all other propositions. A truism is not as such a true proposition. Apart from the postulate of synthesis, no logical relation exists between the truism and falsism. Contradictories are in this case compatible, as Venn and Kant before him have pointed out.

If these views be true, I believe it ought to be possible to deduce the properties of Euclidean space, not from the analytical laws of thought, but from the pure postulate of synthesis, when subjected to conditions arising from these laws. The postulate can be shown to involve two things—(1) Infinity, (2) the necessary relation or connection of what Mr. Kempe styles truism and falsism equivalent to Boole's[1] $x(1-X)=0$.'

This pure postulate of synthesis is identical with that presupposition of the real existence of space which intelligence has to make as being prior to the very act by which it ideally determines space.

LITERATURE.—In addition to the references quoted in the art. see: T. K. Abbott, *Sight and Touch*, London, 1864; W. H. S. Monck, *Space and Vision*, do. 1872; J. H. Stirling, *Sir William Hamilton*, do. 1865; W. Wundt, *Grundzüge der physiologischen Psychologie*[4], Leipzig, 1893, ch. ii.; W. James, *Principles of Psychology*, 2 vols., London, 1891, ch. xx.; G. F. Stout, *A Manual of Psychology*[3], do. 1913, bk. ii. pt. ii.; B. Erdmann, *Die Axiome der Geometrie*, Leipzig, 1877; L. Couturat, *Les Principes des mathématiques*, Paris, 1905, 'Appendice sur la philosophie des mathématiques de Kant'; A. N. Whitehead, *An Enquiry concerning the Principles of Natural Knowledge*, Cambridge, 1919.

GEORGE J. STOKES.

SPENCER, HERBERT.—The philosophy of Herbert Spencer is eminently characteristic of the Victorian era. It is dominated by two fundamental principles: (1) the doctrine of evolution, which was defended by Spencer several years before Darwin's researches were published; (2) his conception of political and social freedom, which was so powerful a factor in political thought during the middle of the 19th century. It so happened, therefore, that the predominant interests of his mind were just those which most markedly captured public attention during his life. His intense conviction and high intellectual qualities naturally brought him to the front as the leading exponent of the progressive ideas of his time; and the change which subsequently overtook those ideas similarly involved a great decline in his influence. The natural growth of Spencer's mind was in close harmony with the spirit of the times in which he flourished. His philosophic principles luxuriated in a congenial soil and atmosphere; they drew to themselves the whole of the intellectual and emotional vigour of his mind; at an early age he began to *live* in his ideas; philosophy more and more absorbed his life; and the external movements and incidents of his career are of little interest. The real life which he lived was the subjective life, which is best recorded by a description of his philosophy.

1. Life.—Spencer was born at Derby on 27th April 1820, son of a school teacher of strong radical views in politics and Quaker tendencies in religion. The father, like the son, was characterized by extreme independence of thought and action, and Spencer's education was of an unusual character. He was taught little of the ordinary subjects of a school curriculum; but his natural powers of thought and observation were developed by his father's method of directing him in the way of self-education and of learning to find for himself the answers to the questions and problems set him. Thus at the age of thirteen he had received no instruction in English history or biography, or in the English language, and next to nothing in Latin or Greek. He had, however, some acquaintance with the rudiments of physics and chemistry, in which his father was specially interested; he had picked up some natural history; he was backward for his age in most subjects, except perhaps geometry, on which his father placed much reliance as an educational discipline. In short, his education was largely neglected; but such as he received was carried out on principles which in recent times have come into favour among the leading authorities on education. For a year or two he was subjected to a somewhat more intensive training at the hands of his uncle, Rev. Thomas Spencer, a well-known social reformer and temperance agitator of the time. But when his official education was concluded at the age of seventeen, the only subject in which he had attained an average standard was mathematics.

Spencer began life as an assistant schoolmaster at Derby; but after three months an opening occurred on the London and Birmingham Railway, and he determined to enter upon the career of a civil engineer. For three or four years he was employed upon the railways which were then being rapidly constructed. He developed a strong interest in mechanics, and, when in 1841 his engineering work temporarily came to an end, he turned joyfully to the prospect of living by mechanical inventions. But these for the most part met with no commercial success, and after a while he determined to seek his fortune in literature. In 1842 he wrote a series of letters to an advanced dissenting organ called *The Nonconformist*, maintaining the view that police administration and the preservation of order were the sole duties of the State, to the exclusion even of preparedness for war, which he then regarded as wrong both for offensive and for defensive purposes. After several years spent in casual political writing and in engineering, Spencer at length in 1848 became sub-editor of *The Economist* at a salary of 100 guineas a year, with free bedroom and attendance at its offices in the Strand. He became friendly with John Chapman, the publisher, at whose *soirées* he met George Henry Lewes and many more of his later friends, including George Eliot, with whom he was soon on terms of intimacy. About this time he also made the acquaintance of Huxley and Tyndall.

In 1850 Spencer began to win a literary reputation by the publication of his first book, *Social Statics*, the main doctrine of which was the same as he consistently maintained throughout his life—the limitation of the functions of government to the bare minimum of maintaining order at home and resisting aggression from abroad. Thereafter he found admittance to many of the leading reviews; one of his most interesting articles, which appeared in the *Leader* of 20th March 1852, dealt with 'The Development Hypothesis,' in which he advocated a theory of evolution, seven years before the publication of Darwin's *Origin of Species*. In 1853 Spencer resigned his position on *The Economist*, hoping to earn a sufficient livelihood through writing for reviews. In 1855 he published his first philosophical work, *The Principles of Psychology*, which was attacked in *The National Review* for its atheistic tendencies, but otherwise received little attention. During the writing of this work Spencer's health permanently broke down, and for the remainder of his life he was a victim of neurasthenia, which severely curtailed his hours of work; its chief symptom was an inveterate insomnia.

In 1858 Spencer drew up his scheme for 'A System of Philosophy'; and, to secure an income while writing it, he decided to issue it in quarterly instalments to subscribers at 2s. 6d. for each instalment of 80-96 pages. In England and America about 600 subscribers were obtained; but the work was carried on amid great financial difficulties, and was more than once threatened with stoppage. For many years Spencer's life is a mere record of ill-health, notwithstanding which volume after volume continued to appear. He lived mainly in boarding-houses in London till 1889, when he took a house with three maiden ladies in St. John's Wood. His most intimate friends were his fellow-members of the famous X Club, and he became a regular habitué of the Athenæum Club. The publication of the 'System of Philosophy' was concluded, after occupying 36 years, in 1896. Already for many years public recognition had been secured, and a chorus of public congratulation followed. In 1898 he removed to Brighton, where he died on 8th Dec. 1903. He was cremated at Golders Green without any religious ceremony, and his ashes were interred in Highgate Cemetery.

2. Works.—Spencer's writings as finally published are contained in 20 volumes, including the two volumes of *Autobiography*. In addition he published two small volumes of his father's—one a *System of Lucid Shorthand* (1893), the other an *Inventional Geometry* (1892) for the teaching of children. He published, moreover, during his lifetime eight folio volumes of *Descriptive Sociology* (1873-81), consisting of cuttings selected from numerous books of travel, describing the manners of primitive peoples. These served as a basis for the generalizations of his *Principles of Sociology*. Two further volumes have been published (1910) since his death, and also a posthumous pamphlet *Against the Metric System* (1904), an earlier edition of which he included in *Various Fragments* (1897, [2]1900). Some unimportant writings of Spencer are included in the authorized *Life and Letters* by David Duncan. Of Spencer's twenty

[1] George Boole, *An Investigation of the Laws of Thought*, London, 1854, p. 49.

volumes ten are devoted to his 'System of Synthetic Philosophy.' They are as follows:

(1) *First Principles.*[1]—This, the opening volume of the philosophy, is divided into two parts, of which pt. i., 'The Unknowable,' sets forth Spencer's religious and metaphysical views. He attempts to establish a reconciliation between science and religion, by accepting as the fundamental truth that factor which they both possess in common, viz. the belief in the existence of some ultimate cause of phenomena — some profound mystery which lies at the back of the universe and 'from which all things proceed.' This ultimate mystery he terms 'the Unknowable,' and he separates himself from religion in denying to it any attributes of personality, or immortality, or any moral bearing. Since it is unknowable, these qualities, he says, cannot be predicated of it. And yet, with strange inconsistency, he goes on to affirm that it is infinite and absolute, omitting to explain how that which is absolute can be the cause of (thus entering into relation with) the phenomena of the knowable. However that may be, Spencer presents this 'Inscrutable Existence' as his substitute for religion. He himself regarded it with reverence, and considered that the religion of the future would take the form of a passive contemplation of 'the Unknowable.' Needless to say, this reconciliation between science and religion has been accepted by neither party. Science moves in the sphere of matter and energy, and has no interest in ultimate metaphysical existences. Religion does not accept a logical formula as a substitute for a God — a formula barren of emotional content and with no moral colouring.

The second part of *First Principles* deals with 'the Knowable.' Spencer takes the two physical laws, Indestructibility of Matter and Conservation of Energy, combines them into one under the title 'Persistence of Force,' and formulates it as the widest generalization of Philosophy, from which all the minor laws of science may theoretically be deduced. He then proceeds to his doctrine of evolution—not organic evolution only, but universal evolution. He observes that all matter and energy is in a permanent state of change or flux; and he sets forth the laws according to which this flux everywhere proceeds—in the development of nebulæ to solar systems, the formation of the earth and geologic change generally, the evolution of animals and plants, the mind of man, the development of nations or societies, and all social institutions. This all-embracing law of universal evolution is stated in the last edition of *First Principles* as follows:

'Evolution is an integration of matter and concomitant dissipation of motion; during which the matter passes from a relatively indefinite, incoherent homogeneity to a relatively definite, coherent heterogeneity; and during which the retained motion undergoes a parallel transformation.'[2]

It is easy enough to perceive that such a formula does describe the main outlines of the course of change during the transformation of a nebula into a system of stars and planets; so also does it cover the naked-eye appearance of evolution from Amœba to man, and the development of the embryo in animals and plants. Even if, as Spencer endeavoured to prove, it is a correct statement of the course of all change in all spheres of human art and knowledge, the question still remains, How far is it significant? Has it the profound philosophical importance that he attributed to it? All that can be said at present is that, after more than half a century, it has proved to be heuristically barren. Spencer's case would perhaps have been stronger if he had left his formula as an inductive generalization. But, not content with this, he endeavoured to give it greater finality and deeper significance by deduction from the 'Persistence of Force.' In this attempt he certainly exceeded the range within which deduction is legitimate. The remaining sections of the philosophy are mainly and overtly the applications of the law of evolution to the various departments of human knowledge. He passed over astronomy and geology as being relatively simple, and proceeded at once to the organic realm.

(2) *The Principles of Biology.*[1]—The application of the law of evolution to living organisms brought Spencer into close connexion with the whole Darwinian movement. He was one of the very small minority who warmly believed in organic evolution and defended it in public, years before Darwin and Wallace announced their discovery of natural selection, to which Spencer in his *Principles of Biology* first gave the alternative name of 'survival of the fittest.' In the absence of this factor, Spencer imagined that inheritance of acquired characters was sufficient by itself to account for the whole phenomenon of organic evolution. He believed that the environment exerts direct and immediate action on individuals (which of course it does); he believed also that the use or disuse of its organs by any individual leads to the growth or reduction of those organs (which is equally undeniable); but he also held that these modifications of individual structure are passed on by heredity, and that their summation through many generations can thus account for the evolution of species. Of the latter doctrine there remains to the present day no evidence whatsoever. It must therefore be affirmed that Spencer, though right in his belief in organic evolution, was totally wrong in his conception of its method. On the discovery of natural selection, he immediately embraced the new theory, holding, however, that it was applicable chiefly to primitive forms of life. He consistently defended to the end of his life the doctrine that acquired characters are inherited, and that this is an adjuvant factor in evolution. In the nineties he carried on a long and vigorous controversy with Weismann on the subject.

Other features of *The Principles of Biology* were his definition of life as 'the continuous adjustment of internal relations to external relations'; a theory of heredity as being due to 'constitutional units,' larger than molecules, but smaller than cells, which, like the molecules of a crystal, were possessed of a fixed 'polarity' and tended to fall into an arrangement characteristic of the structure of the species; finally, a doctrine of the antagonism between individuation and reproduction. These theories still possess considerable interest and value.

(3) *The Principles of Psychology.*[2] — This is perhaps the most original and important of the philosophic series. It introduced into psychology for the first time the idea of evolution, which runs through the whole work, although first published four years before the *Origin of Species.* But it suffers again from the emphasis laid on inheritance of acquired characters as the main factor of mental evolution. Thus one of the most important theories of the work is that in which Spencer by the aid of this factor endeavoured to establish a compromise between the empirical and the transcendental schools. Locke affirmed that all intelligence was the product of experience by the individual. Kant, on the other hand, insisted that intelligence was an innate endowment. Spencer put forward the attractive theory that

[1] London, 1862, [6]1900; popular ed., 2 vols., 1910.
[2] ii. 321 (pop. ed.).

[1] London, 2 vols., 1864–67, rev. ed., 1898–99.
[2] The 1st ed., London, 1855, was in 1 vol.; 2nd ed. in 2 vols., 1870–72; [4]1899.

intelligence is in all cases originally based on experience, but that the experience may be inherited, so that individuals are in fact born with innate powers of intelligence. In other words, intelligence is *a priori* for the individual, but *a posteriori* for the race. Plausible as this theory first appeared, it has not stood the test of later knowledge. The theory now most widely held is, not that intelligence gradually becomes instinctive and automatic in the course of generations, but that it is formed out of automatic, reflex, and instinctive actions by increasing composition and complexity.

Spencer analyzed mind into 'feelings' and 'relations between feelings.' The fundamental process of thought is the recognition of similarity or dissimilarity between two successive states of consciousness. In this doctrine he closely approached the associationist school.

Coming to the question of realism *versus* idealism, Spencer began by inquiring what is the test of truth. He concluded that the ultimate test of the truth of any proposition lies in our inability to conceive its negation. This test he called 'the universal postulate,' which is involved in every link of a chain of argument or reasoning. Now the theory of idealism, he says, is based upon a chain of reasoning with many links, and therefore as many applications of the universal postulate. The theory of realism, on the other hand, being a direct deliverance of consciousness, involves but one application of the universal postulate; and realism is by so much the more probable theory than idealism. Spencer thus confessed himself a realist, though with the proviso that the only fundamental reality is 'the Unknowable,' of which all phenomena are but manifestations. In this amended form he called his doctrine 'transfigured realism.' Few persons in these days would accept it, and a doubt must be expressed whether Spencer, intent as he was on his own line of thought, ever really appreciated the arguments of Berkeley and Hume.

(4) *The Principles of Sociology.*[1]—This is the longest single division of the philosophy, the multitudinous facts contained in it being drawn from the tables of the *Descriptive Sociology*. The chief conclusions reached are that societies fall into two main categories, the militant and the industrial, which are in strong contrast to one another. The former type is characterized by compulsory co-operation, the latter by voluntary co-operation. In the militant type of society government ramifies through every branch of a citizen's activities, individual liberty is narrowly restricted, the lives and actions of men are severely controlled by the State. In the industrial type of society, on the other hand, individual liberty is highly developed, the functions of the State are limited within narrow boundaries, the régime of contract has superseded the régime of status. The militant type is adapted for war, and is found where wars are frequent; the industrial type is a product of peace. With the militant type Spencer finds associated many of the personal vices of mankind, whereas the virtues are associated with the industrial type. He further subdivides the militant type into that which is purely military and that which is socialistic. The fundamental resemblance between these two arises from the wide extension of governmental organization in each, by contrast with the individual liberty of the industrial type. He holds that the difference of purpose for which that organization exists in the two cases cannot obscure their fundamental similarity.

Of the other doctrines of *The Principles of Sociology* the most important perhaps are those contained in the 'Data' and in the 'Inductions,' which form pts. i. and ii. respectively of the work. In the former the origin of all forms of religious worship is traced to ancestor-worship. In the latter an analogy is drawn in extreme detail between the individual organism and the social organism.

(5) *The Principles of Ethics.*[1]—This work was regarded by Spencer as the flower of his whole philosophy. His ethical principles are based both on evolution and on hedonism. Moral conduct, he says, is that which conduces to the maintenance of life, whether of the individual or of the species, or of social life. A system of morals should therefore be founded on a true doctrine of the evolution of life. But the ends of life are in general furthered by happiness. The pursuit of happiness, with certain notable exceptions, is advantageous to survival; had it been otherwise, the species would long ago have become extinct. Hence an ethics of evolution is also an ethics of hedonism. The happiness to which Spencer refers is of course mainly that derived from the higher, and not the lower, emotions.

In 'The Ethics of Individual Life,' dealt with in pt. iii., Spencer emphasizes man's duty to himself as distinct from his duty to his neighbours. He should take sufficient rest, and attend to his health and amusements; dereliction from these duties is a breach of moral principle. Spencer opposed a life of undue self-denial, arguing that wholesome forms of enjoyment are demanded by ethical principles.

The culminating portion of the work, however, is in pt. iv., entitled 'Justice,' in which Spencer defined the duties of the State with respect to its component individuals. He starts from the theory of the survival of the fittest. In every society the most vigorous and strongest members will, if unimpeded, achieve most success, and will thus multiply and hand on their qualities to future generations. The weaker strains will fail and gradually die out. Society will thus be gradually purged of its weaklings, and the race will be carried on by the most efficient. The maintenance of this law was regarded by Spencer as of cardinal importance to the welfare of the species. In order that its effects might be most fully realized, therefore, he urged that individuals must be as far as possible emancipated from all interference by the State. They must be left to reap the natural rewards of their modes of life. Clearly, however, the doctrine of liberty cannot be rendered absolute; for then crime would be unrestrained, and the highest success might be attained by a career of robbery and fraud. The freedom of the individual must, therefore, be limited by the State just in so far as is necessary (and no more) to preserve the like freedom for every other individual. Spencer's formula is:

> 'Every man is free to do that which he wills, provided he infringes not the equal freedom of any other man.'[2]

The practical results deduced by Spencer from this formula are that the proper functions of the State are limited to two things only: (1) prevention of foreign aggression, for which purpose an army and navy must be maintained, and (2) prevention of crime at home, *i.e.* prevention of aggression by individuals on one another. He interprets the phrase 'individual aggression' with considerable latitude; thus loud street noises are to be regarded as an aggression which should be suppressed; so also keeping a house in an insanitary condition, to the danger or annoyance of neighbours. But, outside his formula, all other under-

[1] Vol. i., London, 1876, [3]1885; vol. ii., 1882; vol. iii., 1896.

[1] Two vols., London, 1892–93. 'The Data of Ethics,' forming pt. i. of vol. i., was originally published separately in 1879.

[2] *Principles of Ethics*, ii. 46.

takings—such as education, the post office, road-making—are regarded as outside the province of government. Spencer urges that, if the State had never embarked on these activities, they would have been carried on by corporations of private individuals, and for the most part far more efficiently than they are at present. Leaving aside Spencer's formula of justice, and the corollaries which he drew from it, the essence of his ethics is that individual freedom should be brought to the highest point consistent with social order. He recognized that all these conclusions may be abrogated in time of war, and he was an inveterate hater of all war. He held that peace was an inviolable condition of social prosperity and progress; that war, other than defensive war, was the most abominable of all crimes.

While thus reducing the functions of government to those of merely maintaining a social condition in which natural selection could work unhampered, Spencer was far from asserting that the severity of the process should not be tempered by philanthropic sentiment. Accordingly he concludes his *Principles of Ethics* with two sections devoted to 'Negative Beneficence' and 'Positive Beneficence,' in which he describes the various ways in which the business and social relations of men should be redeemed from the hardships of a crude struggle for existence. Poor relief, *e.g.*, though no business of the State, should be undertaken by private persons. The relations of employer and employed should be governed not only by economic pressure, but also by a proper infusion of humane and philanthropic sentiment. This, however, Spencer considers outside the province of law; and the injunctions of 'beneficence' are to be enforced only by public opinion.

This is the end of the 'Synthetic Philosophy.' It is sufficiently obvious without further comment why Spencer has now passed so much out of fashion. In the sphere of politics the dominating note has now become equality rather than liberty. It is very possible that liberty may once again become a political ideal, but hardly in the form in which Spencer preached it. The great and luminous conceptions which lie at the back of his ethics were worked out by him into formulæ too narrow and precise to contain them. Moreover, not unnaturally, the work itself is apt to be judged by its practical conclusions; these being rejected, the fundamental conceptions tend likewise to be consigned to oblivion. It is unfortunate that Spencer's fine conception of human freedom should be condemned wholesale, merely because he too often applied it in a dogmatic and unsatisfactory manner.

Besides the ten volumes of philosophy, Spencer published ten other volumes. Three of these contain his *Essays: Scientific, Political, and Speculative* (1857–74). Many of them were written while he was a young man; and their subject-matter is for the most part embodied in a more systematic form in the 'Philosophy.' They are written in a more vivacious and attractive style than occurs in Spencer's more formal works. *Social Statics* has been already alluded to. *Various Fragments* (1897, [2]1900) and *Facts and Comments* (1902) are two volumes of short essays on a great variety of subjects, written when Spencer was an old man. The *Autobiography* (1904) in two large volumes is the dullest of all Spencer's writings, and betrays the barrenness of his life, the current of which had been drawn away into his philosophical works. The two other volumes remaining to be mentioned achieved a far higher commercial success than any other of his publications. The *Study of Sociology* (1873) was written for the 'International Scientific Series' at the request of E. L. Youmans. It is concerned mainly with social science in general and the difficulties attending its study owing to the numerous different kinds of bias which intrude themselves at every point. Being comparatively short and intended for the popular market, it is the first book that should be read by a student of Spencer, and the only one of which perhaps it may be said that every well-read person ought to have read it. Finally, there is the *Education: Intellectual, Moral, and Physical* (1861), which has had the most profound influence on all modern educational theories. It extols science as by far the most important ingredient in a good education. It strongly insists, moreover, on non-coercive methods; it is in this sphere that Spencer's sentiments of liberty have found the widest acceptance.

LITERATURE.—The two main authorities on Spencer's life are *An Autobiography*, 2 vols., London, 1904; and David Duncan, *The Life and Letters of Herbert Spencer*, do. 1908. Apart from these, the only complete treatment of Spencer's life and works from the modern standpoint is the present writer's *Herbert Spencer*, in the series 'Makers of the Nineteenth Century,' London, 1917. In that volume will be found a complete bibliography, both of Spencer's own works and of the works by others who have dealt with him.

HUGH ELLIOT.

SPERONISTÆ.—This is the name by which the Cathari (see art. ALBIGENSES) were known in Italy in the 13th cent., and they are thus designated in a law of the emperor Frederick II., A.D. 1224 (Mansi, *Concilia*, Venice, 1759–98, xxiii. 590). Charles Schmidt is of opinion that it is probably derived from Sperone, an Italian town in Piedmont, whose bishop, Robert of Sperone, along with his followers, had embraced the dualistic theory of the Manichæans (*Hist. et doctrine de la secte des Cathares ou Albigeois*, Paris, 1849, ii. 281–282; see also J. C. L. Gieseler, *A Compendium of Ecclesiastical History*, Eng. tr., Edinburgh, 1853–65, iii. 446).

J. BASS MULLINGER.

SPHINX.—In the well-known Greek myth the composite monster, with the head and bosom of a woman, the body of a dog or a lion, the tail of a serpent, the wings of a bird, the paws of a lion, and a human voice, who propounded enigmas, destroying those who failed to solve them, and who perished, self-destroyed, when her riddle was solved by Œdipus, bore the name of Sphinx ('Strangler'). Greek travellers, coming into the Nile Valley, found there also a composite monster, or many varieties of such a creature, who recalled to them their own native tradition, and upon these they bestowed the name of the creature of the Greek myth. Apart from the name, however, and a superficial similarity in the fact that the Greek monster and the Egyptian (in some cases) were both human-headed and brute-bodied, there was really nothing in common between the two types or the conceptions which they represent.

The original idea of the Egyptian sphinx was that of an imaginary quadruped, human-headed, living in the desert, and assumed by the sun-god Ra as his incarnation, for the purpose of protecting his friends. Out of this conception grew the idea of the sphinx as the guardian of a temple, a deity, or a tomb; and Ra himself, the original guardian sphinx, is represented as being guarded by a sphinx in which is incarnate the god Aker, the watchman of the *duat*, 'under world,' and the special protector of Ra during the hours of darkness.

The former conception—that of Ra as guardian—is embodied in the greatest of all Egyptian sphinxes, that which crouches in front of the second pyramid at Gizeh. The date of this remarkable monument is uncertain. Its position in front of the Gizeh necropolis suggests that it was intended to guard the illustrious dead buried there against evil genii, and that, therefore, it may be roughly contemporary with the pyramids and tombs in its neighbourhood, *i.e.* of the period of the IVth dynasty. This date is so far countenanced by an inscription on the stele of Tahutmes IV., between the paws of the monster, which, though unfortunately mutilated at the point where its testimony would have been of most value, appears to mention Khafra, the builder of the second pyramid, as connected with the making of the statue of Tem-Heru-em-Khut, *i.e.* the sphinx. Maspero, however, prefers an even earlier date.

He regards this mention as 'the indication of an excavation of the Sphinx, executed under this prince [Khafra], consequently the almost certain proof that the Sphinx was already enveloped in sand in the time of Khéops and his predecessors.'[1] On the other hand, Petrie regards Tahutmes' mention of Khafra as entirely negligible.

'How much Tahutmes knew of Khafra, or cared to honour him, is shown by the material he selected for his tablet. It is carved on a grand door lintel of red granite, which almost certainly was robbed from the adjacent granite temple of Khafra.'[2]

Petrie suggests a date at all events later than the Old Kingdom, on the grounds that a tomb-shaft is found in the body of the image, that no tombs of earlier date than the IVth dynasty exist in this part of the necropolis, and that a tomb would hardly have been sunk in the rock of the statue after it had been carved to a divine form, and was generally venerated. The question of date, therefore, is in suspense.

The Great Sphinx is hewn out of the living rock, but has been patched and made up at various times with masonry. Human-headed and lion-bodied, it measures 150 ft. in length, and 70 in height, from the crown of the head to the base; the paws are 50 ft. long, the head is 30, and the face is 14 ft. wide. The Egyptian name for the Great Sphinx was Ḥu, and it represented Horus-on-the-Horizon, Heru-em-Khut, or Harmakhis. It is curious, if the early date for its existence be correct, that it is not mentioned in any early inscriptions, that no representations exist of so important a monument, and that no priests of the sphinx are recorded.

The stele of Tahutmes IV. already referred to was discovered by Caviglia in 1817. It stands between the outstretched paws of the figure, a granite tablet, 14 ft. in height. The inscription narrates how Tahutmes (1423–1414 B.C.), when hunting in the desert near Memphis, fell asleep under the shadow of the sphinx. Ra-Harmakhis appeared to him in a dream, and charged him to clear his image of the sand which had enveloped it on all sides, promising the king his favour if the task were executed. The inscription obviously fixes the lowest possible date for the existence of the sphinx, which must plainly have been of considerable antiquity in the time of Tahutmes IV.; beyond that it does not carry us with any certainty.

Apart from the Great Sphinx, there are few indications of the existence of sphinxes in the period of the Old Kingdom. It is only with the XIIth dynasty that the figure becomes popular, maintaining its popularity down to the time of the Ptolemys. The creature's function, as already indicated, is invariably to ward off evil genii from a tomb or a temple. Thus, in an inscription quoted by Bergmann,[3] we have the following:

'I protect the chapel of thy tomb. I guard thy sepulchral chamber. I ward off the intruding stranger. I cast down the foes to the ground, and their arms with them. I drive away the wicked one from the chapel of thy tomb. I destroy thine adversaries in their lurking place, blocking it that they come forth no more.'

To the period of the XIIth dynasty are now very generally assigned those sphinxes discovered at Tanis by Mariette in 1861, bearing heads of peculiar and strongly marked features, which were formerly held to be representations of a king of the usurping Hyksos dynasty. Golénischeff[4] has shown, by comparison of these with extant portraits of Amenemhat III. of the XIIth dynasty, that the Tanis sphinxes in all probability are portraits of that monarch.

The head of the sphinx, if human, was generally modelled on that of the Pharaoh in whose reign it was sculptured. It would therefore generally be the head of a king; but in the case of a temple founded by a queen the guardian sphinxes might be female, more particularly if they were also intended to represent a goddess. The sphinx, in fact, was not necessarily always a representation of an incarnation of Ra, but might represent other gods or goddesses. Thus Isis occasionally assumes the sphinx form, when she appears as the guardian of Osiris. From this fact arises the frequent representation of the sphinx with a head other than human. There are many instances of such images bearing the head of a jackal, a hawk, or, perhaps most common of all, a ram—the animal head being that of the particular god who was supposed to be incarnate in the sphinx in question.

From the time of the XVIIIth dynasty and onwards the sphinx becomes exceedingly popular—more, one may suspect, as a decorative adjunct to a temple than as bearing any special religious significance. Great numbers of these images are found in rows lining the approaches to the great temples—*e.g.*, the avenue of 122 sandstone sphinxes erected by Amenhotep III. before the temple of Khonsu, at Karnak, and similar avenues at Thebes. These were largely ram- and jackal-headed figures, often bearing between their fore-paws a small statue of the king who erected them. It may be questioned, however, whether these innumerable figures were actually meant to act as guardians of the temple or were not rather merely an architectural feature. Wiedemann's opinion is as follows:

'The stone rams, lions, etc., which we find as amulets, or which in many cases occupy the same position before Egyptian temples as the sphinxes, must by no means be confounded with the sphinxes; each was simply an image of the sacred animal of the god of the place, of the creature in which he took incarnate form, and each was therefore the equivalent of the statue of the god. There is no authority whatever for calling these objects by the name of sphinxes, and the mistaken nomenclature has arisen only from the fact that their office was the same, architecturally speaking.'[1]

The origin of the conception of the sphinx is obscure. Sayce is of opinion that it arose from a transference to Egypt of the Babylonian idea of guardian genii exemplified in the winged bulls and cherubim of Chaldæa.

'The curious similarity in the functions assigned to the images of composite animals both in Egypt and Babylonia raises the presumption that the composite forms themselves were ultimately derived from a Babylonian source. . . . It is only in Chaldæa that they find their explanation. . . . The sphinx of Giza still guards the desert of Giza because ages ago the flooding waves of the Persian Gulf made the Babylonians believe that the world had arisen out of a watery chaos peopled by unformed creatures of monstrous shape.'[2]

The inference, however, seems rather a wide one. The idea of the necessity of protecting the tomb against evil genii is of very early date in ancient Egypt, and is itself connected, in the Pyramid Texts, with the actual local flood—the inundation of the Nile; and it is difficult to see why it may not have arisen independently in Egypt under similar conditions to those which produced it in Babylonia. Moreover, the type of the sphinx which most closely resembles that of the Babylonian guardian genii, the winged type, is of later date than the normal Egyptian sphinx.

LITERATURE.—G. Maspero, *Hist. ancienne des peuples de l'Orient classique*, Paris, 1895–99, vol. i., 'Les Origines, Egypte et Chaldée,' *Egyptian Archæology*[5], Eng. tr., London, 1902; E. A. Wallis Budge, *A Hist. of Egypt*, do. 1902, vols. ii.–iv.; W. M. F. Petrie, *A Hist. of Egypt*, do. 1903–05, vol. i.; A. H. Sayce, *The Religion of Ancient Egypt*[2], Edinburgh, 1913; A. Wiedemann, *Religion of the Ancient Egyptians*, Eng. tr., London, 1897; M. Brodrick and A. A. Morton, *A Concise Dictionary of Egyptian Archæology*, do. 1902.

JAMES BAIKIE.

SPINOZA.—I. *LIFE.*—Baruch de Spinoza was born at Amsterdam on 24th Nov. 1632. He came of a tribe of Spanish Jews, who had found in Portugal a precarious refuge from the attentions

[1] *Hist. ancienne des peuples de l'Orient classique*, i. 366, note 1.
[2] *Hist. of Egypt*, i. 52 f.
[3] *ZÄ* xviii. [1880] 50.
[4] *RTr* xv. [1893] 131 ff.

[1] *Religion of the Ancient Egyptians*, Eng. tr., p. 199 f.
[2] *The Religion of Ancient Egypt*, p. 119 f.

of the Inquisition. His father, Michael de Spinoza, hearing that a securer home was to be found in the United Provinces, removed thither. Already, in 1593, a company of 'Marranos' had been received in Amsterdam, and had in 1598 formed the first synagogue in that city. Michael was chosen to fill several offices of trust in the fraternity. He was thrice married: by his first wife he had a daughter Rebekah; by his second a son Baruch and a daughter Miriam.

Spinoza was instructed in all the puerile wisdom of the Synagogue. Of Isaac de Fonseca it is enough to say that he was afterwards a victim of the impostures of the sham Messiah, Shabbathai Ṣebi. Rabbi Saul Morteira, though kindly, was intellectually hardly superior to Fonseca. In Manasseh ben Israel Spinoza might have found a more sympathetic adviser; but during the years of gradual alienation Manasseh was absent on that mission to the Republican Government of England which led to the return of the Jews to our island. For very few of the standard authors did Spinoza indulge any feeling but profound contempt. 'I have read,' he says, 'some of the Kabbalistic triflers, at whose follies I was astonished beyond description.'[1]

The Synagogue, moreover, was compelled to maintain a rigorous orthodoxy. Such toleration as was allowed to the Jews was watched with jealous eyes. In 1617 the Remonstrants, fretted by the limitations that hedged in their own worship, complained of the freedom accorded to the Synagogue; and the complaint, though it did the petitioners no good, did the Jews some harm. In 1640 the vagaries of Uriel da Costa had created an uneasiness totally out of proportion to their intrinsic importance; and it is small wonder, then, that the authorities watched anxiously the growth of heresy in Spinoza's mind.

Discontented with the Ḳabbālā, the young man turned to secular studies. He felt above all the need of Latin, then the language indispensable alike in diplomacy and in science. Its elements he studied under a master conjectured by Meinsma[2] to have been a German named Felbinger. From Felbinger he perhaps learned a tinge of Socinianism. His next teacher was Francis Van den Ende, a physician and schoolmaster, who was suspected, not without reason, of imparting much more than Latin to his pupils. He made Spinoza not only a classical scholar, but a master of all the physics and physiology then known. It is probable that through Van den Ende Spinoza became acquainted with Bacon, Descartes, Hobbes, Lord Herbert of Cherbury, and possibly Giordano Bruno. The subsequent history of Van den Ende is well known. In 1674 he engaged in the stupid conspiracy of Rohan and the Marquise de Villiers against Louis XIV., and suffered death along with his principals.

There were others with whom about this time Spinoza came into contact. We are told by Colerus that he became intimate with 'some learn'd Mennonites.' One of the members of this sect, Jarrig Jellis, appears among his correspondents; another, John Bredenberg, was the author of a so-called answer to the *Tractatus Theologico-Politicus*, which reveals more of the disciple than of the antagonist. Peter Serarius often visited Spinoza, and assisted him in his correspondence with Oldenburg. Peter Balling, Jan Rieuwertz, and others were also in his circle. The rumour indeed spread abroad that Spinoza was actually baptized.

All this could scarcely escape the eyes of Morteira and his colleagues. For some time they had been dissatisfied with the tone of their pupil; and matters came to a head when two of his companions stepped forward to accuse him of actual heresy. After a trial he was subjected to the 'lesser excommunication'; and Morteira is said to have made strong personal appeals to the young free-thinker. But all was in vain; and on 27th July 1656 the final sentence was pronounced. The text may be seen in Van Vloten or in Freudenthal;[1] it shows that the condemnation was less for speculative error than for some overt act. Much has been written in censure of the rabbis; their conduct will compare favourably with that of most other bodies on similar occasions. It is certain that Spinoza can have expected no milder treatment.

The heretic did not hear his sentence. Shortly before, according to a somewhat doubtful story, his life had been attempted by a fanatical Jew, and he removed to the house of a Remonstrant friend near Amsterdam. Thence he wrote his reply to the excommunication. This reply, which was in Spanish, is no longer extant; its substance is doubtless to be found in the *Tractatus Theologico-Politicus*. Thenceforward he was lost to his old associations, and perhaps, as some think, marked the severance by substituting for his Jewish name Baruch its Latin equivalent Benedict.

Following the Jewish custom, he had most probably already learnt the art of lens-polishing—an art which the rapid advance of science was then rendering daily more important. Through this he earned a modest livelihood; and through this he became acquainted with Huygens and, later, with Leibniz. Friends, indeed, he never lacked. His fellow-students under Van den Ende and his Mennonite acquaintances held by him. When, in 1660, he removed to Rynsburg, near Leyden, it was probably to be near the Remonstrants, Rynsburg being then their headquarters. In April 1663[2] he again removed, to Voorburg, a suburb of the Hague, remaining there six years.

From 1656 to 1660, or perhaps still earlier, he completed his study of the Cartesian philosophy, and developed at least the outlines of his own. It was his duty to teach Cartesianism to a certain private pupil; but he early became dissatisfied with many of the principles which he had to teach. His objections he submitted to a coterie of students in Amsterdam. These enthusiasts speedily formed a kind of Spinozistic school, discussed his papers, and communicated their difficulties to him. 'Spinoza's gifts as a teacher,' says Lucas,[3] 'were such that he insensibly converted all men to his views.' His influence over his little school, at any rate, was immense. Among the number were Simon de Vries, a wealthy medical student, John Bresser, apparently an older man, and Lodewijk Meyer, who afterwards edited more than one of his master's works. Other acquaintances, more or less intimate, rapidly gathered round him. Pontiaan van Hattem became the founder of a curious Spinozistic church. Niels Stensen turned Roman Catholic, and engaged in controversy with his former friend. The Huguenot St. Glain translated the *Tractatus* into French. Tydeman, Spinoza's Voorburg landlord, was accused of being the creature of the 'atheist and mocker.' John Casearius, a name unearthed by Meinsma,[4] became a botanist of eminence. To John Bouwmeester, an Amsterdam physician, Spinoza wrote the affectionate *Epistle* 37. Towards Adrian and John Koerbagh he cherished equally friendly feelings. The former was a physician of some skill, and, if we may trust Meinsma's conjecture[5] that to him *Epistle* 28 was addressed, prescribed for his friend more than once. Both Adrian and John came under ecclesiastical censure, and died in prison. Henry Oldenburg of Bremen, the famous first secretary of the Royal Society, met Spinoza in 1661. He was a man of insatiable curiosity, but of no philosophical depth, and constitutionally timid. At first his letters urge Spinoza to publish his speculations: but after the appearance of the *Tractatus* he never ceases to ingeminate caution.

Spinoza's adherence to Descartes, if ever complete, was shortlived. True, in 1663 he threw into geometrical form, for the benefit of Casearius, the first two parts of the *Principia*; but his own appendix, *Cogitata Metaphysica*, contains clear evidence of independent thinking. Still earlier, if we may trust internal evidence, had been written a treatise which shows yet more unmistakably how widely Spinoza had already diverged from Descartes. Before 1661 he had completed the *Korte Verhandeling van God, de Mensch, en deszelfs Welstand* ('Short Treatise on God, on Man, and his Well-being'), a work discovered only in 1852. Of this book two Dutch MSS exist. Both contain notes, some obviously written by disciples, a few perhaps by Spinoza himself. The original Latin has not been unearthed. Various strata of thought are to be detected in the work, from the early stage as represented in the curious dialogues to the mature appendix.

There is every reason also to believe that the *Ethics* was far advanced before Spinoza left Voorburg. We may fix its composition between 1661 and 1665, and the beginning of the *Tractatus Theologico-Politicus* in the latter year. The date of the unfinished treatise *de Intellectus Emendatione* is uncertain; but critics are practically unanimous in placing it before that of the *Ethics*. In addition to all this his correspondence also must have been voluminous; for the large amount preserved includes only those letters which have a philosophical or scientific interest. The letters to Oldenburg are valuable as illustrating the indirect intercourse between Spinoza and Boyle. The correspondence with Huygens is polite, but not very illuminating. That with Simon de Vries, on the other hand, is of great importance. That with Blyenbergh, a burgess of Dort, is interesting as showing how Spinoza could deal with tedious pretenders to learning. To Peter Balling (probably the 'P. B.' who translated the *Principia* into Dutch) and to Hugo Boxel of Gor-

[1] *Tractatus Theologico-Politicus*, ch. ix., tr. R. H. M. Elwes London, 1883, i. 140.
[2] *Spinoza en zijn kring*, p. 196.

[1] *Lebensgeschichte*, p. 115.
[2] Freudenthal, *Spinoza*, i. 120.
[3] See Freudenthal, *Lebensgeschichte*, p. 22, also *Spinoza, sein Leben und Seine Lehre*, p. 87.
[4] P. 182. [5] P. 246.

cum Spinoza writes with great sympathy and even with occasional flashes of humour, on the subject of ghostly manifestations.

In 1671 (or, as Pollock thinks, 1673) he received an epistle[1] now ascribed to Jacob Ostens, a Rotterdam surgeon. Ostens enclosed a document from Lambert Velthuysen of Utrecht, which contained a violent attack on the 'atheistic' and 'immoral' principles of the *Tractatus*. Spinoza's reply shows that he was unconscious of any irreligious tendency in his work. It is written in an unusually passionate tone. Strangely enough, at a later time he became friendly with Velthuysen, and even[2] urged him to publish his strictures.

With Albert Burgh, a scion of a rich Amsterdam family, once his disciple (indeed he was supposed till Meinsma's time to be the 'fellow-lodger' now known to have been Casearius), Spinoza had an interesting correspondence. In 1675 Burgh entered the Roman Church, and wrote to his old master a curious letter advising him for his good. Spinoza's answer is the most contemptuous of all his writings. Burgh's one argument, indeed—the continuity of the Church—was not likely to have weight with one who could trace his spiritual ancestry to Abraham.

Meanwhile, Spinoza entertained hopes of support from the de Witts; and they in return appear to have claimed such assistance as he could give. At what time he received the small pension which John de Witt settled on him we do not know; but as early as 1663[3] he was planning the open publication of his works, with the countenance of 'some holding the highest places in the State.' The Grand Pensionary must have known him even in the Rynsburg days. With de Witt's supporter, John Hudde, burgomaster of Amsterdam, we know[4] Spinoza to have been intimate; and contemporary squibs speak of the *Tractatus* as 'written in collaboration with the devil and published with the connivance of de Witt.' Spinoza did what he could for the Pensionary; and his hopes were centred in the success of the anti-ecclesiastical policy of the great statesman. De Witt, however, could not favour open heresy; and the publication of the *Ethics* was accordingly postponed. Excited perhaps by the appearance of a Dutch version of the *Leviathan* in 1667, Spinoza turned to other studies, and in 1670 the *Tractatus Theologico-Politicus*, a work of epoch-making importance, was published anonymously. Spinoza suppressed a projected Dutch translation;[5] but precautions were vain. On the rise of William of Orange to power, orthodoxy resumed its sway; and in 1674 the work was formally prohibited. The Church of Rome soon followed suit; and the *Tractatus* shares with the *Leviathan* the honour of figuring on the Index.

In 1670 Spinoza removed to the Hague, lodging at first in the Veerkay with a widow named Van der Werve. Thirty years later the Lutheran minister Colerus occupied the same room, and was thus able to make those inquiries the results of which appear in his biography. But Spinoza's stay was short. Within a year he removed to the house of a painter named Van der Spijck, on the Paviljoensgracht; and here he remained till his death. He might, it is true, have easily improved his financial position. Simon de Vries in vain offered him a donation of 2000 florins; and, when the same devoted pupil, feeling the approach of death, endeavoured to make Spinoza his heir, he refused to accept more than 300 florins per annum. He had already yielded up to his relatives the whole of his patrimonial inheritance except a single bed. In 1673[6] he declined the offer of the chair of philosophy at Heidelberg made by the Elector Palatine Karl Ludwig.[7]

During his remaining years he lived a life of extraordinary seclusion, staying within doors often for days together. Two episodes alone broke the monotony. In 1672 de Witt was brutally murdered by the populace. Spinoza's philosophic calm was for once disturbed. He burst into a passion of weeping, and was with difficulty prevented from affixing a placard, with the words 'Ultimi barbarorum' upon it, to the walls of the prison where the deed was done. Shortly afterwards he incurred an even greater risk. Condé's winter quarters were at Utrecht, and Spinoza visited the French general under safe-conduct. He there received marks of favour, and the offer of a pension from Louis XIV. Refusing the pension, he returned to the Hague, where he found himself in great danger of being torn to pieces as a spy. Van der Spijck indeed expected the house to be stormed by the mob; but Spinoza reassured him, saying that many of the chief men in the city knew the nature of his errand; if the worst came to the worst, he would go out alone and meet the fate of de Witt. The purpose of this strange excursion remains a mystery; but it seems most likely that the authorities deliberately chose him, as a man of European reputation but no diplomatist, to open up with the French informal negotiations which it would be easy to disavow.

Meanwhile his reputation continued to grow, and the circle of his acquaintance to widen. Chief among his new friends was Leibniz (*q.v.*), whose indebtedness to Spinoza, minimized by himself, has recently been made clear.[8] In 1670, having already read the *Tractatus*, Leibniz began to correspond on the neutral subject of optics. Spinoza received his advances with caution, refusing to show him the *Ethics*. But in 1676 Leibniz's aversion yielded to an admiration of which afterwards he endeavoured to make light. The introduction was brought about by George Schuller. At first the younger man was quite fascinated by the older; but there was a want of intellectual sincerity in Leibniz which rendered permanent confidence impossible. To Schuller was also due the acquaintance between Spinoza and Tschirnhausen. Correspondence began in 1675. Tschirnhausen was one of the select few to whom the *Ethics* was entrusted; and his criticisms were among the keenest that the author ever had to meet. Soon afterwards we find him in London, where he removed a misunderstanding that had clouded the relations of Boyle and Oldenburg with their friend. In later years Tschirnhausen drew largely, without acknowledgment, on Spinoza's *de Intellectus Emendatione* for his *Medicina Mentis*.

1 *Ep.* 42. 2 *Ep.* 69. 3 *Ep.* 13.
4 *Epp.* 34-36. 5 *Ep.* 43. 6 *Epp.* 47, 48.
7 See Freudenthal, *Lebensgeschichte*, p. 219.
8 L. Stein, *Leibniz und Spinoza*, Berlin, 1890.

Spinoza's mental activity during his later years, probably because of failing health, was slight in comparison with what it had been. It seems that he revised the *Ethics*, possibly adding the remarkable propositions that close the fifth part. In 1675 he endeavoured to publish the work; but the divines and the Cartesians again interfered.[1] Phthisis was congenital with Spinoza, and its advances were not retarded by the climate of the Hague. Early in Feb. 1677 Schuller wrote to Leibniz that the end was approaching. The *Tractatus Politicus* was laid aside for ever, and the design for a comprehensive scheme of natural philosophy was not even sketched out. Death came suddenly at the last, just in time, perhaps, to save him from the fate of Koerbagh. Feeling worse than usual, he had sent to Amsterdam for a medical friend, probably Schuller.[2] On Saturday, 20th Feb. 1677, he came downstairs and conversed with the Spijcks, smoked a pipe, and went early to bed. Next day he again came down. Schuller had now arrived, and ordered some broth, of which, on the return of the Spijcks from morning service, he partook quite heartily. There seemed no reason why they should not go to church again in the afternoon; but on their return they heard that Spinoza was dead. The physician returned at once to Amsterdam. Many apocryphal details have been added to this narrative by legend-mongers. There is no ground for the suspicion, entertained by Martineau among others,[3] that the physician and the philosopher had contrived a euthanasia—conduct condemned by Spinoza himself.[4] Spinoza's property fetched so little that his sister Rebekah did not claim the inheritance. The MSS of the *Opera Posthuma* were duly conveyed to Jan Rieuwertz. Meyer furnished the preface, and Schuller, as we now know, supervised the publication. In the next year the work was anathematized.

Spinoza was a man of middle height, with a distinctly Jewish countenance, the swarthy complexion of a Spaniard, and a forehead befitting a philosopher. He was abstemious almost to asceticism, rigidly careful to keep his expenditure within his means, but cheerful in his demeanour. He conversed on affable terms alike with the highest and the lowest. Such signs of impatience as we detect in his letters show merely that his serenity was not attained without an effort. A noble independence was perhaps the most marked feature in his character. His intellectual hardihood, almost unparalleled as it was, involved no intolerance of the views of others. Love of truth was his guiding principle. To children he showed himself tender, affectionate, and even playful. He is one of the very highest exponents of the philosophical and self-centred virtues; if we must find fault, it is to point out his lack of an active benevolence, of a passionate zeal like that of Paul for saving the world at large. He had not, in fact, a truly broad humanity. He has been charged with moral cowardice. It is asserted that there is a kind of *suppressio veri* in the *Tractatus*, and that theological terms are, in the *Ethics*, frequently used in a misleading sense. But this seems a harsh judgment. His learning has recently been shown to have been great.[5] The publication by Van Rovigens in 1889 of an inventory of his library proves the wide range of his acquirements. He was, unquestionably, weakest in the domain of the inductive sciences.

Of portraits of Spinoza the best is that at Wolfenbüttel, of which there is a copy at the Hague, and which is reproduced in Martineau. Some copies of the *Opera Posthuma* have a portrait, perhaps derived from the Wolfenbüttel painting. The miniature reproduced by Schaarschmidt[6] may be genuine. There is also a portrait in the German translation of Colerus.[7] Spinoza's drawing of himself as Masaniello was seen by Colerus, but has apparently perished.

The discovery of the *de Deo* in 1852, and the bicentury of his death in 1877, roused great interest. At the bicentenary Renan delivered his famous eulogium. In 1880 the bronze statue by Hexamer was unveiled at the Hague; while a tablet in the wall of the house that stands on the side of Spinoza's lodgings in the Paviljoensgracht marks the spot where he spent his last days.

II. *PHILOSOPHY.*—**I. Its aim.** — The speculations of Spinoza never forgot their practical end. It was his object to 'discover and attain something which would enable him to enjoy supreme, continuous, and permanent happiness.'[8] His philosophy aims at 'tranquillizing the mind of the individual, and elevating social life.'[9] But soon he discovered that well-being is not to be captured by a direct assault.[10] Hence Spinoza's doctrine is not primarily a metaphysic but an ethic; nay, more, it is not so much a philosophy as a religion.

1 *Ep.* 68. 2 Freudenthal, *Lebensgeschichte*, p. 296.
3 *Study of Spinoza*[3], p. 102 f.
4 *Eth.* iv. 18, schol.
5 See Leopold, *ap.* Freudenthal, p. 213.
6 *De Deo*, ed. C. Schaarschmidt, Amsterdam, 1869.
7 Pollock, *Spinoza: his Life and Philosophy*[2], pref.
8 *Int. Em.*, beginning. 9 *Eth.* ii. 49, cor. schol. *ad fin.*
10 Cf. *Int. Em.* i., ii.

'There is,' he says,[1] 'for sciences but one purpose, to which they should all be directed, namely, supreme human perfection.' And this perfection can be reached. 'Those who deny that men can ever attain virtue or truth, by that very denial prevent themselves from attaining it.'[2] But this virtue can be reached only through intellectual certainty. We may perhaps hazard a guess as to the process by which he was led to his deductions. His spiritual ancestry was theological; hence his first independent thought moved on theological lines. His life, again, had led him to attach a supreme importance to 'fortitude.' But a mere unreasoned fortitude was worse than useless. Spinoza was the last man to court unnecessary pain. Resolved to live his own life, he desired to practise that *animositas* by which 'a man strives to preserve his own being in accordance with the dictates of reason.'[3] Resolved, on the other hand, to be of use to his fellows, he desired also to practise that *generositas* whereby, solely under the dictates of reason, a man seeks to unite other men in friendship to himself. Virtue of any kind appeared to him impossible without 'adequate knowledge.'[4] Hence the necessity of a method for discovering the true.

2. Logic and doctrine of method.—Truth is its own ultimate guarantee; 'it is not necessary to know that we know.'[5] But by truth is not meant the correspondence with any physical fact. An architect's idea of a building is 'true,' even if the building is never erected, provided that the idea conforms to the rules of architecture.[6] On the other hand, a reckless assertion is none the less false because it may turn out accidentally 'true.' It is as well, therefore, to note how the true differs from the false.

Knowledge is of many kinds. It may arise from hearsay; from mere experience ('ab experientia vaga'—a phrase borrowed from Bacon); from inference ('ubi essentia rei ex alia re concluditur'). All these are 'inadequate' kinds of knowledge. True perception arises only when the thing is perceived solely through its essence or by the knowledge of its 'proximate cause.' Nor, when we employ this method, do we need another method to test it. Otherwise there would be a constant regress to infinity—which is as absurd as to say that, because tools are needed to make tools, therefore no tools can ever be made.[7] Falsity consists in mistaking accidents for essence.[8] Simple ideas then are necessarily true; inadequate ideas arise from the careless juxtaposition of two or more simple ideas. To attain truth, we have only to split ideas into their simple components.[9]

To exclude confusion, the following rules must be observed: (1) the definition of a thing should comprehend the proximate cause; and (2) all the properties of the thing must be capable of being deduced from it. Thus only shall we secure the two essentials of adequate knowledge—clearness and distinctness in our ideas. Spinoza illustrates his meaning by asserting that the ordinary definition of a circle merely defines one of its properties. It should be defined as the figure described by a line whereof one end is fixed and the other free.[10] To this assertion certain acute objections were made by Tschirnhausen; and Spinoza found some difficulty in answering them.[11] A further objection is of importance, as it brings us to the very centre of the Spinozistic philosophy. This idea of definition involves a confusion between the 'formal' law of cause and effect and the 'objective' law of

1 *Int. Em.* ii. note.
2 *De Deo*, ii. 8.
3 *Eth.* iii. 59, schol.
4 Cf. Camerer, *Die Lehre Spinoza's*, p. 254.
5 *Int. Em.* vi.
6 *Ib.* ix. 69.
7 *Ib.* vi.
8 *Ib.* ix. 72.
9 *Ib.* x.
10 *Ib.* xiii.
11 *Epp.* 82, 83.

logical deduction. 'The relation,' says Spinoza,[1] 'between the abscissæ and the ordinates of a curve *results from* the nature of the curve precisely as the essences of created things result from the nature of God.' But really this relation does not *result* at all; it only emerges later *in our minds* because of their incapacity to grasp many ideas at once. Nevertheless it is necessary to notice this essential feature of Spinoza's theory. An effect neither follows nor precedes its cause; the distinction between the two is merely, to him, one of logical convenience.[2]

So far, then, of the definitions of created things. But what of uncreated, and of the ultimate idea of all, that of God? If definition is nothing but the 'objective' (*i.e.* nearly what we now call the 'subjective') aspect of cause, what then of God the First Cause? The rules for defining an uncreated thing[3] lay it down that all idea of cause must be excluded, while no abstraction is permissible. It would seem therefore hard to define God; and yet all knowledge is conditioned by the knowledge of Him. Everything is either *in se* or *in alio*; if it is *in alio*, it must, as we have seen, be defined by the *aliud*; if *in se*, where is the definition to begin? If God is defined by His attributes, they must be His causes, and therefore (logically) prior to Him. Spinoza meets the difficulty by using the vulgar phrase ('ut vulgo dicitur'),[4] *Causa sui*. From this definition Spinoza imagined it possible to deduce properties.[5] Among these properties he regards existence as one: 'When the definition of the [uncreated] thing has been given, there must be no room for doubt as to whether it exists or not.'[6] Conceive a Being the very essence of which is existence. We *can* conceive such a Being: therefore it exists. This startling proposition is an extension of the Cartesian 'Cogito ergo sum.' Upon the idea of this Being all knowledge is based. 'That method is the most perfect which exhibits the standard of the idea of the most perfect Being.'[7] 'As soon as possible, we must inquire whether there is such a Being, which is the cause of all things as its "objective" essence is the cause of all our ideas.'[8]

What Spinoza meant by his 'perfect Being' is doubtful. But it is at any rate certain that it is not an *abstract* deity—so much so that Spinoza forbids us to deduce abstract essences from the idea of God. Such generalizations, formed by abstracting from a *number* of individuals, are nothing but negations. All things follow from the divine nature; but these 'things' are 'individuals';[9] and hence 'we must admit into our definitions as few abstract nouns as possible.'[10] Yet the first deducibles from God are not individual things; they are *res fixæ, æternæ*, and yet *singulares*. What then are these? They are present everywhere, the *genera* of the definitions of individual things, and the *causæ proximæ* of all things; but their real nature is obscure.

3. The geometrical method of the Ethics.—At this point the *Tractatus de Intellectus Emendatione* ('Treatise on the Improvement of the Understanding') breaks off; and we therefore turn to the *Ethics*. At the outset of this work we are struck by a change of method. The title-page speaks of 'Ethica *ordine geometrico* demonstrata.' Spinoza's motive for using axioms, postulates, and propositions is not quite clear. Causation being but logical deduction, he regarded things, which are implicit in the idea of God, as capable of being drawn out explicitly, precisely as from the definition of a circle its properties can be deduced. Con-

1 *Cog. Met.* i. 2.
2 Cf. here, *Ep.* 60.
3 *Int. Em.* xiii. 97.
4 *Ib.* xii. 92.
5 *Eth.* i. 16, dem., and *Ep.* 60.
6 *Int. Em.* xiii. 97.
7 *Ib.* vii. 38.
8 *Ib.* xiv.
9 *Ep.* 75.
10 *Int. Em.* xiv. 99.

fusing logical necessity with dynamic efficiency, he states in one place that God is the *cause* of all things;[1] in another, that God *is* all things. In i. 11 he tells us that everything must have a cause of its existence; but in the ordinary sense of the word 'cause' this is obviously false. What is necessary is a cause of its coming into existence. This confusion is the source of much difficulty in the interpretation of Spinoza. In any case the choice of the Euclidian method is the natural concomitant of this theory of causation. The example, it is true, had been set by Descartes; but Spinoza would have used it even if Descartes had not anticipated him. Not that he thought that the method excluded error. Already he had used it to exhibit the Cartesian system at a time when he did not believe in it. But he saw clearly that error is more easily brought to light by this means than by any other. Of course there are objections to its use. The cogency of Euclid is due to the fact that his primary assumptions are either self-evident or at least sufficiently near the truth for the purpose in hand; whereas it is precisely Spinoza's definitions and axioms that arouse controversy. Another objection was first brought forward by Tschirnhausen,[2] and has been developed by Joachim,[3] Busolt,[4] and others. From a geometrical definition we can deduce but one property. All others can be deduced only by bringing other definitions into relation with the first. Similarly, when Spinoza 'deduces' from the definition of God, he is really, though unconsciously, deducing from other definitions. His right to select one attribute as the defining property is the matter in dispute. And hence we are not surprised to find that he constantly, if tacitly, varies the definition. When 'Substance' fails him, he has recourse to 'Nature'; when 'Nature' gives way, he substitutes 'Reality'; when 'Reality' is not concrete enough, he falls back on 'God.' Thus Spinoza himself is often driven to drop the deductive method, and to allow himself the luxury of explanations, notes, and appendices. Occasionally he even calls in experience to confirm his theoretical propositions.

4. Metaphysical doctrine. — (*a*) *Substance.*—Spinoza's God is not the deity of any religious system. His conception may be expressed, provisionally at least, by the term 'Reality.' All things exist *in alio.* Retracing our course, we track the *aliud* to its conditioning somewhat; and finally we must arrive either at blank nonentity and scepticism or at certainty based on that ultimate Reality of which 'things' are expressions. The first alternative being impossible to Spinoza, he came to the second. He had already shown to his own satisfaction in the *de Deo* that God exists; and in the *Ethics*, though he gives certain formal definitions, he in fact takes Reality as a first postulate.

This Reality is not mere Being—not (to use Hegel's phrase) the night in which all cows are black. It is a concrete, pregnant, and living conception, positive in itself and capable of positive development. Spinoza makes desperate attempts to give it a higher position than that of the mere abstract home of attributes. The infinite is not less, but more, positive because it is indeterminate. Yet he cannot always rid himself of an abstract way of regarding Reality. As Caird well puts it,[5] the ultimate, with him, is reached not by reconciling opposing elements, but by abstracting from their difference. Still, Spinoza's intention was always to represent the real as concrete.

This idea appears under many different aspects. Tracing back the chain of causes, we reach at last the *Causa sui.* As cause, it is *Natura naturans,* that which underlies phenomena. As caused, it is *Natura naturata*; *i.e.*, it is identical, in a sense, with the phenomenal world. From another point of view, Reality is Substance, that which is in itself and is conceived through itself—a restriction of the use of the word which Spinoza had not always made.[1] Yet another word is 'Nature,' which[2] is *unum æternum, per se infinitum*; but the word expresses Reality rather as the productive source of things than as their underlying principle. Hence it is less frequently employed in the *Ethics* than elsewhere. Lastly, by the term 'God' is meant a Being absolutely infinite, that is 'Substance consisting of infinite attributes, whereof each expresses eternal and infinite essentiality.'[3] From this definition the idea of personality, often ascribed to God in the *de Deo* and in the *Cogitata Metaphysica,*[4] has been rigidly excluded. God is no longer good; He no longer has a will; He is 'perfect,' but not in the moral sense;[5] nor does He ever act for an end.

The first few propositions prove, or state, the identity of these various ideas. *Causa sui* must have necessary existence; hence it is Substance. Substance is necessarily infinite; therefore it is God. Thence we pass to the proof that there is but one Substance;[6] but, if God is infinite in infinite ways, this seems little more than a truism. Yet Spinoza was convinced[7] that he could deduce from his definitions less obvious conclusions than these. First, God is the most real (or perfect) entity. Secondly, He is one and whole. Thirdly, He is concrete, not abstract. He has infinite attributes, but not 'infinite' in a numerical sense; nor is He one in a numerical sense. He is in fact the unchanging Unity which underlies the fleeting manifestations of the many. Were there not this simplicity beneath the complexity of Nature, Nature could not possibly be conceived. Yet God is not the whole as including the parts;[8] for, if so, as parts, they would be independent of Him. To separate the whole into parts is to destroy it. By this we see that Spinoza means to assert that the Reality involves a reconciliation of all difference; but whether he is always consistent is another matter.

In what sense God is 'concrete' we have seen. He is 'infinite' not through negation, but because He admits of unlimited predicates being affirmed of Him. It is only the imperfection of language that compels us to use a negative term of a quality essentially positive.[9]

That God exists of necessity is shown both *a priori* and *a posteriori*;[10] but the real demonstration lies in the whole theory of which the proofs are a part, and this we may sum up as follows.

The notion of cause is reciprocal: everything that is involves God as its cause, just as much as God involves it. Now, things are perceived by us under the entangling notions of time, place, and the like. Such conceptions are mere phantoms. Nevertheless, the things are not altogether phantasmal; nay, they appear simply because they really are. 'Every idea of every existing thing necessarily involves the eternal and infinite essence.'[11] The tiniest entity implies infinitude. God, then, both is and is not identical with the many. He is identical with the many in so far as they are implicit in Him; He is different, inasmuch as He is not subject to the mutations of the many. He is not the sum of what appears; he is all that is. 'He is the immanent cause of all things, and not the transient.'[12] Spinoza will have no dualism. 'God *and* Nature'—the phrase of the earlier writings—gives place to 'God *or* Nature.' Nay, even space and thought must be united in one, which includes both. The idealists also allow but one; but that is done by subsuming space under thought. The materialists subsume thought under space. Spinoza's form of monism is peculiar to himself, and is exhibited in his remarkable doctrine of attributes.

(*b*) *Attributes.*—Substance can be, and is, known. 'I have,' says Spinoza, 'as clear an idea (if not as clear an *image*) of God as of a triangle.'[13] Experience shows that we can form two clear ideas of Substance—as extended and as thinking. Hence extension and thought are each co-extensive with Substance; nay, they are Substance, or, as Spinoza phrases it, they are attributes of Substance. 'It

[1] *Eth.* ii. 49, Cor. schol.
[2] *Ep.* 82.
[3] *A Study of the Ethics of Spinoza*, pp. 115–119.
[4] *Die Grundzüge der Erkenntnisstheorie und Metaphysik Spinoza's*, pp. 72–74.
[5] *Spinoza*, p. 146.

[1] See *Cog. Met.* ii. 12, where he speaks of 'created substances,' and *de Deo*, i. 2, where he calls extension a substance.
[2] *De Deo*, i. 2, dialogue, *ad init.*
[3] *Eth.* i. def. 6.
[4] See, however, the dialogue in *de Deo*, i. 2.
[5] Cf. *de Deo*, i. 2.
[6] *Eth.* i. 14.
[7] *Ep.* 83, to Tschirnhausen.
[8] *Eth.* i. 13.
[9] *Int. Em.* xi. 89.
[10] *Eth.* i. 11, and schol.
[11] *Eth.* ii. 45.
[12] *Ep.* 73.
[13] *Ib.* 56.

is essential to the nature of Substance that each of its attributes should be conceived *per se*. All the attributes have always been together in it, nor could one have been produced from another; but each expresses the reality of substance.'[1] Each of the two attributes that we know (and each of the others, did we know them) gives us a final account of ultimate Reality.

The two attributes were accepted from Descartes; but with startling differences. Descartes[2] denied that God is extended. Space is a creature of God, who gave it its 'primary' qualities of motion and rest, three dimensions, and the like. The 'secondary' qualities he regarded as not created by God, but due to the percipient mind. To Spinoza the whole idea of 'creation' is repugnant.

The attributes are independent of each other. Body cannot determine the mind to think, nor mind determine the body to move.[3] Ideas are due to God as *res cogitans* simply; motion and rest to Him as *res extensa* simply.[4] How, then, is the unity of God secured? There are infinite attributes, each pointing to an independent essence: how, then, is there but one Reality? Spinoza's proof[5] is curious. He says that, if twenty men exist, there must be a reason, over and above the cause of human existence in general, why *twenty* men should exist. But the definition of God, implying existence, yet contains no provision for several substances. Hence only one can exist. This ingenious argument occurs again; but it is hardly convincing. All that really is shown is that number is beside the question; and so Spinoza himself seems to recognize[6] when he says 'eum qui Deum unum vel unicum nuncupat, impropere de eo loqui.' God, then, is merely indivisible Reality. But, if there is no passage from extension to thought, how are we to account for the statement that extension and thought move in parallel lines—that for every affection of space there is a corresponding affection of mind?

The point is too abstruse to be discussed here in detail. Difficulties enough remain. If it is intelligence that perceives attribute, then thought, which is an attribute, seems made a judge of itself; indeed, as Tschirnhausen pointed out,[7] thought is conscious of extension also, and hence, in the forcible phrase of Martineau, elected as a consul, it soon poses as a dictator. In one of his most striking pages Pollock[8] asks what difference it would make if every attribute but thought were destroyed; and the answer is simply 'None.' Then why does Spinoza postulate other attributes? Above all, why demand an infinite number? We might ask other questions. Does thought correspond with *each* of them, so that we have a series of pairs of which thought is always one? Or is there another series of pairs, like extension and thought, but not the same, in each of which one, but not the other, can look over its neighbour's wall, and in which neither can see any farther? Spinoza[9] hints at answers to these questions, but gives no satisfactory solution.

Monism is neither good nor bad in itself. There is nothing, apart from good reasons, that makes monism better than dualism or than infinitism. What, then, is it beyond prejudice that compels us to posit any unifying principle of these infinite attributes, which are distinctly stated to have nothing in common? Spinoza's theory made him reduce the many to one. Experience showed him two. But you do not bridge the Channel by simply calling England a part of Europe.

As Martineau[10] has shown, there is an essential difference between extension and thought in their relations to their modes. Body is a limited fragment of extension; our minds are not limited fragments of the infinite mind-stuff. For, though all individual things are animate,[11] they do not think; they are only thought of. Nor does God Himself think; those who ascribe thought to Him are like those who should confuse the Dog-star with the animal that barks.[12] Intellect[13] belongs to *Natura naturata*, not to *Natura naturans*. Nay, to attribute thought to God would be to attribute to Him an imperfection.

There is difficulty enough, then, in the transition from substance to attribute. There is hardly less in that from attribute to mode.

1 *Eth.* i. 10, schol.
2 *Princ.* i. 23.
3 *Eth.* iii. 2.
4 *Ib.* ii. 5, 6.
5 *Ib.* i. 8, schol. 2, *Ep.* 34.
6 In *Ep.* 50.
7 *Ep.* 70.
8 *Spinoza*^{2}, p. 164.
9 *Ep.* 66.
10 *Study of Spinoza*^{3}, pp. 189–192, *Types of Eth. Theory*, i. 365.
11 *Eth.* ii. 13, schol.
12 *Ib.* i. 17, schol.
13 *Ep.* 9.

(*c*) *Modes, infinite.*—Mode is an affection of Substance, that which exists not *in se* but *in alio.*[1] It will thus partake of the twofold nature of Substance. As we have seen, 'things' are both extended and 'animata'; and modes are 'things' under the phenomenalizing influence of time. In coming under that influence they lose some of their reality. All things follow from the divine perfection, but all are not equally perfect—a doctrine of ethical import.[2] The First Cause alone is perfect; that which is directly produced by God is the nearest approach to perfection (it is 'infinite' in its own kind, and admits of the least negation). That which is produced mediately is imperfect in accordance with its degree of mediacy. Thus an infinite number of modes follows from God 'by the necessity of the divine nature.'[3] Mode, then, is a device for deducing the finite from the infinite. But the step is not made at once. We pass first to infinite modes. These are Substance in its totality considered as active. Extension is barren until touched to life by motion and rest; and these have an infinitely extended range. Similarly, Substance as thought, when its decks are cleared for action, appears as *intellectus absolute infinitus*. Yet both these, though infinite, are intelligible not *per se* but *per aliud*. They are therefore modes, not attributes—'sons of God' in the language of the *de Deo*.[4]

Each of these immediate infinite modes gives birth to 'mediate' infinite modes. Under motion and rest stands the *facies totius universi*,[5] which, though varying internally, is in total always the same. Spinoza's account is brief; but the doctrine seems to be derived from that of Descartes, that the quantity of motion in the universe is constant. By this Descartes meant momentum. Had Spinoza lived now, he would doubtless have expressed his 'mode' in terms of the Conservation of Energy. That there were other such 'mediate infinite modes' is likely enough; but conjecture may well be spared.

How intellect, which is a mode, can yet be absolutely infinite is hard to see. 'Our mind, so far as it understands, is an eternal mode of thinking, determined by another eternal mode, and this by another, and so on *in infinitum*; so that all together constitute God's eternal and infinite intellect.'[6] Thus 'God's intellect' is here used as equivalent to the sum-total of human intellects, including potential intellect as well as actual; and it deals not merely with extension, but with thought itself. Every thought is capable of being made the object of another thought, and so on *ad infinitum.* The absolutely infinite intellect is identical with the whole of these actual or potential series. Here for once Spinoza seems to use the term 'infinite' in the sense which he elsewhere rejects—that of indefinitely numerous.[7]

In the attribute of thought the mediate eternal mode, corresponding to the *facies* in extension, is not given by Spinoza. Did we know the other attributes, we should find each of them throwing off stems, first immediate and then mediate, in a series of similar pairs. But even so we have not bridged the chasm from the infinite to the finite. How is that to be done?

(*d*) *Modes, finite.*—Spinoza's answer is that finite things are themselves in a sense infinite. Their essences are eternal; their existence finite. In *Eth.* i. 17, schol., *e.g.*, we learn that a man is the cause of another man's existence, but not of his essence, for the latter is eternal.[8] Peopling the vast heaven of eternity are countless hosts of

1 *Eth.* i., def. 5.
2 *Ep.* 19.
3 *Eth.* i. 29.
4 i. 9.
5 *Ep.* 64.
6 *Eth.* v. 40, schol.
7 See Martineau, *Study of Spinoza*^{3}, pp. 198–200.
8 Cf. *Int. Em.* viii. 53.

eternal essences; they pass for a moment through the entangling atmosphere of existence, and flash into a transient light. Essence[1] is 'the manner in which created things are comprehended in God's attributes.' Hence the essences even of finite things are eternal. Thus the passage from the infinite to the essence of a finite thing is but a passage to the entirely finite. But whence comes the partial finitude?

Everything left to the play of its own essence would be eternal. Nothing can be destroyed,[2] except by a thing of the same kind, external to itself. The essence of a thing neither brings it into existence nor expels it thence. There cannot be a finite thing until there is another finite thing to determine it; and that other is itself determined by another finite thing; and so *ad infinitum*.[3] So also there is no particular thing than which there is not a more powerful one by which it may be destroyed.[4] But whence does the finite get its first impulse? This indefinite series is not true infinity.[5] Nay, finiteness, a mere negation, seems to have been unconsciously pressed into the domain of causality. As Martineau well puts it, finding the 'most capacious essences struck with sterility' in the domain of actual things, Spinoza invents a second kind of causality, the despised inductive.[6]

He has been defended on the ground that this second causality, being bound up with temporal existence, is a mere illusion. Spinoza's particular things, say some, have no real existence; and therefore the series of causes that leads to them, being illusory also, is of course irreconcilable with the eternal causality. Much in his language lends countenance to this theory. In *Ep.* 29, *e.g.*, he says that extended substance is not really divided, as we are so prone to divide it in imagination. Yet elsewhere he speaks of particular things as 'actually existing';[7] and this existence seems to have been objective (*formalis*). Else why does he tell us that the finite is only in part negative?[8] Admitting, then, to the full the illusoriness of the temporal existence of particular things, we are still unable to reconcile the two lines of causality into one. How they put on this illusory actuality is precisely the difficulty which Spinoza does not meet. He provides causes for the real and causes also for the phenomenal; but he says nothing as to how the real becomes phenomenal.

Assuming, however, this double causality, let us see how it works. The existence of each thing is a mediate infinite mode. If left to its essence, the thing would simply be. But it comes into a 'struggle for existence' with other essences.[9] Hence arise the ideas of contingency, possibility, and the like. If the circumstances of the temporal world forbid the appearance of the thing, we call its existence 'impossible'; should they not forbid it, we call it 'probable' or 'possible.' But in either case the contingency is merely a phrase for our ignorance.[10]

To sum up: a finite individual thing is a fusion of its eternal essence with the temporal chain of causality, which alone determines its duration. In both these senses the thing is called actual; but the actualities are of totally different kinds.[11] In the individuality of such a thing both attributes (and possibly even the infinite others also) must, in modal form, unite their forces. In a man, *e.g.*, must combine size, form, motion, etc., while external circumstances will, by their action upon him and upon themselves, decide the length of his terrestrial course. A man is a complex; and our knowledge both of his mind and of his body, as well as of his external conditions, must be fragmentary at best.[12]

(*e*) *Man as mode.*—Among all individuals man is highest. Not of course that he is the end of Nature, or that Nature in any sense aims at his welfare.[13] Nevertheless, as there are degrees of perfection, man, expressing the infinite both in mind and in body better than other finites, is the most perfect. Even in men there are degrees of perfection. The good man expresses God more

1 *Cog. Met.* i. 2.
2 *Eth.* iii. 4.
3 *Ib.* i. 28.
4 *Ib.* iv. ax.
5 *Ep.* 12, etc.
6 *Study of Spinoza*[3], p. 200, *Types of Eth. Theory*, i. 299.
7 *Eth.* ii. 11, 13, v. 29, schol., etc.
8 *Ib.* i. 8, schol.
9 *Ib.* iv. ax.
10 *Ib.* i. 33, schol. 1, iii. 4, 6, ii. 30, dem.
11 *Ib.* v. 29, schol.
12 *Ib.* ii. 16, 26 f., etc.
13 *De Deo*, ii. 24; *Tr. Pol.* ii. 8, and *passim*.

fully than the knave.[1] Ideas differ from one another in containing more or less reality.[2] Hence, by the doctrine of parallelism, the human body also is superior to other finite bodies. Not, of course, that there is any causal connexion between body and mind. The body and the idea of body (*i.e.* the mind) are the same individual conceived under different attributes.[3] The object of the idea constituting the human mind is the body and nothing else.[4] True, Spinoza probably began by regarding the body as the prior;[5] but in the *Ethics* this has been dropped, and the highly artificial doctrine which, for want of a better term, we have called 'parallelism' has been substituted. This doctrine involves the rejection of all belief in a real self in man, as is clearly seen in the series of propositions[6] in which the subject is discussed. There is no *faculty* of desiring, loving, understanding. All these are fictions, or metaphysical universals. To call them 'mind' is like explaining a stone by talking of lapidity.[7] 'The mind is a definite mode of thought, and not the free cause of its actions.'[8] The perceptions of the mind vary with the sensations of the body.[9] The idea which constitutes the actual being of mind is not simple, but compound.[10] The succession of thoughts *is* the mind. The human mind does not know the body to exist save through the ideas of the modifications whereby the body is affected; and[11] the idea of the human mind is referred to God (*i.e.* exists in the ordered sequence of the world) precisely as the idea of the human body. But how can the mind, which is nothing but a series of thoughts, be conceived by one link in that series? Spinoza answers[12] by propounding the theory of the mind not only as the idea of the body, but as *idea ideæ*, *i.e.* as conscious of ideas. Precisely as it sums up the sensations into one whole which we call the body, so these various ideas are summed up into one generalization and contemplated as a whole.[13] But the difference is obvious. An idea of an idea is caused by that idea, whereas the body is absolutely dissociated from the mind.

The ambiguity in the word 'idea' must already have struck the reader. When Spinoza tells us that all things are animate, or that the object of the idea constituting the mind is the body and nothing else, he does not mean by 'idea' what we now denote by 'concept,' but merely the parallel in thought to the body in extension. Thus the *idea corporis* is one kind of idea; the *idea ideæ* is another.

We may well ask how, if the mind is but a succession of ideas, it can form judgments. The answer is[14] that the judgment is in the idea itself, and not in the mind regarded as having the idea. The truth of an idea is its own standard; the mind does not judge its truth, but the idea asserts its own truth. A false idea, similarly, is negative in itself.[15] There is, as we have seen, no faculty of judgment; and the possibility of judgments is not explained, but simply referred dogmatically to the ultimate Substance. We shall find later that will, which is to Spinoza a judgment, is equally reduced to a mere point in a long line of points reaching back to infinity.

The purpose of the theory of *idea ideæ* was to reinstate after a fashion the 'self' which had been destroyed by the rejection of 'faculties.' But the self, lodged at the end of an infinite series, recedes like a will-o'-the-wisp the more it is pursued; and a mind which receives ideas passively *ab extra* has no claim to the character of a real mode of thought. Regarding man as finite, in fact,

1 *Ep.* 23.
2 *Eth.* ii. 13, schol.
3 *Ib.* ii. 21, schol.
4 *Ib.* ii. 13.
5 *De Deo*, suppl. p. 243, pt. ii., 'de Mente Humana,' 2.
6 *Eth.* ii. 11 ff.
7 *Ib.* ii. 48, schol.
8 *Ib.* ii. 48, dem.
9 *Ib.* ii. 14.
10 *Ib.* ii. 15.
11 *Ib.* ii. 20.
12 *Ib.* ii. 21.
13 *Ib.* ii. 21, schol.
14 *Ib.* ii. 43, schol.
15 *Ib.* ii. 35.

Spinoza seems to have *ipso facto* banished the self; for the essence of self is independent reality. There is in the mind much that we do not know, which yet may be postulated from considering the body; and *vice versa*. Hence to know the one thoroughly we must discuss the other; and Spinoza [1] proceeds to give us a few propositions (or 'lemmas') on body generally, into which we cannot here enter. The probability is (though Joachim and others dispute it) that a full knowledge of man would reveal body, mind, and an infinite number of other modes in the other attributes. When Spinoza says [2] that 'of things as they are in themselves God is the cause so far as he consists of infinite attributes,' he must surely mean that every individual thing, man included, is a fusion of modes of all the attributes.

5. **Theory of knowledge.**—At this point Spinoza resumes the thread of psychological analysis that was broken off in the *Tractatus de Intellectus Emendatione*. The test of truth is in the idea itself; the mind does not, strictly, *judge* its ideas. Nevertheless we need some method of comparing these ideas—and most of all in a system which regards the ideas *as* the mind. Spinoza accordingly gives us a classification. We find three classes: (1) ideas of the imagination, (2) ideas of reasoning, (3) ideas of intuition. In earlier times Spinoza seems to have regarded ideas as passive,[3] but in the *Ethics* he speaks otherwise: 'I call an idea a conception rather than a perception, because the latter word seems to imply that the mind is passive with respect to the object.'[4] An adequate idea, then, is one in which the intrinsic (or subjective) marks of truth are present, namely, clearness and distinctness; and to attain certainty we need only reduce ideas to simplicity. This is done directly by intuition, and mediately by reasoning; hence the only source of error is imagination.

(*a*) *Ideas of imagination.*—The question of the relation between mind and body was differently solved by Spinoza at different times. In the appendix to *de Deo* [5] he says, 'mens a corpore originem ducat.' In *Int. Em.*[6] the possibility of ideas arising from fortuitous motions of the body is admitted. To account for this influence he adopted Descartes's fantastic doctrine of animal spirits. This theory he utterly rejects in the *Ethics*.[7] Nevertheless a few traces of it seem to remain in the language which he uses to explain imagination.

We only know our body phenomenally, 'by the ideas of the affections of the body.'[8] Hence our knowledge of it is very imperfect. We know it not in its cause, but through ideas of its successive states, and these ideas are confused with those of other bodies.[9] This ill-blent conception is imagination. If we are affected by an external body, we regard that body as present;[10] and we tend to regard even absent external bodies as present also. This is explained [11] by a curious physiological doctrine, which we need not here examine. Anyhow, when the external body is really there, we 'perceive' it—*i.e.*, the mind forms an idea which is parallel to the contiguous body. This Spinoza calls the idea of the body—another instance of the ambiguity of the term 'idea.' Like Sir William Hamilton, he identifies the cause of a sensation with the object of a perception. Still more clear is this when we look at his account of representation—*i.e.* of the formation of pictures of external things that are not there. The external bodies have left a 'footprint' on the brain. Whenever that footprint is reproduced by internal causes, we invent the external cause. Modern psychologists would unanimously assert that we do not (as a rule) think *of* these states of the brain. The thought arises *from* them, doubtless; but an idea caused by a thing is not a knowledge of it. In any case, a knowledge of the body thus attained is inadequate; and the mind's knowledge of itself, being attendant on the ideas of bodily affections,[1] is equally inadequate.[2] We can often correct one imagination by another;[3] but full correction can come only from reasoning or intuition.

Should ideas be frequently given together, an association tends to be created by which the appearance of one idea arouses the others. Thus [4] from the word 'apple' we proceed to form the image of the fruit. (Spinoza does not distinguish this association from memory.) Should a large number of these images recur, the mind, retaining the *ratio patientis*,[5] and acting as a mere 'spiritual automaton,' selects those ideas that are alike in certain respects from those that are alike in others, and forms blurred images. This is the origin of those worthless 'universals' which, as we saw above (§ 2), are mere negations. To the universal we give an equally worthless class-name, which means one thing to one man and another to another.[6] Still more blurred are those abstract images which are represented by 'transcendental' terms like 'thing,' 'being,' 'somewhat.'[7] Such a fiction, so persistent that it hampers even philosophers, is that of time, which is 'nihil praeter modum cogitandi.'[8] This doctrine must not be confused with the Kantian 'forms of thought.' With Kant 'time is a necessary representation, lying at the foundation *of all our intuitions*.'[9] With Spinoza time is quite unessential to all rationally conceived ideas. So long as we confine ourselves to essences, we are in a region to which the notion of time is quite foreign. Time, in fact, is a form of contingency, which, as we saw above, is not in nature but in ourselves.

Equally illusory is the notion of freedom.[10] Not knowing the causes that impel us to action, we imagine ourselves free to do this or that. Even so a falling stone, if it could think, would fancy it fell of its own accord. Similar is that worst of all errors, the ascription to God of a purpose in His actions.[11] Intellect and will do not pertain to God; they are a mere *refugium ignorantiæ*.

(*b*) *Reasoning.*—If the imagination is prone to false generalizing, it does not follow that all generalizing is false. Without some form of generalization thought is impossible. In *Eth.* ii. 38 we learn what is the true form. 'Those things which are common to all, and which are equally in a part and in the whole, cannot be conceived except adequately.' Suppose our body to be acted on by an external thing. There must be something 'commune et proprium' to the two. Let the body be again acted on, this time by another external thing. There will again be something in common; and so on. The idea of this common element will be clear and distinct, *i.e.* adequate. Such a remaining common quality is weight. Our idea of weight, then, is adequate. Similarly with the yet wider idea of extension. Such *communes notiones*, unlike the false universals, are true; and the more the body has in

1 *Eth.* ii. 13.
2 *Ib.* ii. 7, schol.
3 *De Deo*, ii. 15: 'Tò intelligere puram esse passionem.'
4 ii. def. 3.
5 Pt. ii., 'de Mente Humana,' *ad init.*
6 xii. 91.
7 v. pref.
8 *Ib.* ii. 19.
9 *Ib.* ii. 16.
10 *Ib.* ii. 17.
11 *Ib.* ii. 17, schol.

1 *Eth.* ii. 23.
2 *Ib.* ii. 29.
3 *Ib.* ii. 17.
4 *Ib.* ii. 18, schol.
5 *Int. Em.* xi. 86.
6 *Eth.* ii. 40, schol. 1.
7 On these *entia ficta* see *Cog. Met.* i. 1, 6, etc.
8 *Cog. Met.* ii. 10, 5.
9 *Kritik der reinen Vernunft*, i. 2.
10 *Eth.* ii. 49.
11 *Ib.* i. appendix.

common with external bodies the more things can be adequately known.[1] These *communes notiones* may be made the basis of reasoning (*fundamenta rationis*), and will lead to other adequate ideas. Doubtless Spinoza had in his mind the fact that Euclid's axioms are called *communes notiones*; but he would have extended the phrase to include the fundamental ideas of physics, dynamics, and his own ethics. When once these foundations have been laid, accuracy in ratiocination will secure certainty.

Imagination regards things as contingent; reason regards them 'sub quadam aeternitatis specie.'[2] If a child sees Peter two or three times in the morning, he will associate the morning with Peter. If on occasion James should appear instead of Peter, the child's expectation will waver between the two. Reason, on the other hand, conceives things out of all relation to time. When considering a triangle, it does not consider whether the triangle is new, old, large, or small. Reason, in fact, views nature in an *ordo ad intellectum.*

But this phrase, 'sub specie aeternitatis,' is ultimately deposed in favour of another. To know the *communes notiones*, to know the 'essence' of an individual thing, to know a thing 'under the form of eternity,' are all reduced[3] to knowing a thing 'by reference to the eternal and infinite essence of God.' This is a sublime phrase, the full meaning of which will appear only as the whole philosophy is studied. At present a few words must suffice. All properties of matter are known with reference to extension. But extension is the infinite essence of God on one side. And therefore, as our knowledge of extension (the most ultimate of *communes notiones* in one attribute) is adequate, so our knowledge of any extended thing can be adequate only so far as it is referred to that ultimate attribute. Similarly with the other attribute of thought. Deductive reasoning is a safe way of attaining this adequacy—nay (apart from the obscure exception to which we now proceed), it is the only one.

(*c*) *Intuitive knowledge.*—Still higher than reason is *scientia intuitiva*, which is so darkly delineated that its features are only dimly discerned. We learn, however, the following points.

(α) It deals with the essences of singular things;[4] not, like *ratio*, with *communes notiones.* A word is here necessary on these essences. Spinoza is generally called a nominalist; and his rejection of 'universals' justifies us in so regarding him. But how, under a system of nominalism, essences can remain is a riddle. Retaining essences, we must mean by them the common properties of things; and so Spinoza does, when he calls the common properties of bodies the eternal essence of the human body—*i.e.* the essence of the human body is that which it shares with non-human bodies! But as a rule he speaks, as here, of the essences of individual things—a conception almost paradoxical. Yet some such conception seems necessary to explain that agreement between the idea and the *ideatum* which constitutes truth. In this agreement there is a kind of identity between the two, the 'formal' and the 'objective' being only aspects of the same thing; and that 'same thing' is the essence. This essence is not the product of the mind only —such a quasi-Berkeleian theory is utterly foreign to Spinoza; nor can it be in the body before the mind perceives it—else the body would be made prior to the mind. Such as it is, it is perceived by *scientia intuitiva.*

(β) It acts immediately and not deductively. The example given is as follows.[5]

Required a fourth proportional to three given numbers. Tradesmen arrive at the correct result either 'ab experientia vaga' or by remembering the rules of thumb learnt at school ('ex auditu'). The mathematician sees it 'sub specie aeternitatis,' having seen the laws of proportion and referred them to 'God'—*i.e.* to the controlling conceptions of space. But with very simple numbers there is no need of either process; in a single flash the correct answer is obtained; and this is intuition.[6]

Whether this intuition is due to long practice in *ratio*, or is a separate faculty, is not quite clear.[7] Spinoza confesses that the things he knows by this kind of knowledge are few;[8] but it is possible to attain it, for[1] 'we can form that kind of knowledge,' though we cannot form images of God as we do of bodies, and therefore fancy we have not as clear an idea of Him as of bodies.

(γ) A third hint as to the nature of intuition is given in *Eth.* v. 31. We there learn that it depends (1) on the mind, (2) on the mind as formal, (3) on the mind so far as the mind itself is eternal. On these enigmatical sentences much has been written. With hesitation we advance the following attempt at solution. 'The idea of every individual thing actually existing necessarily involves the eternal and infinite essence of God.'[2] If, *e.g.*, we wish to know any individual mode of extension, we must refer it to the attribute of extension in God. *Ratio* does in fact thus proceed. Beginning with space, it adds the differentiæ one by one, until it arrives at the definition required. This Spinoza would call 'acting as far as the mind is finite.' Intuition, on the other hand, beginning with the individual thing and acting by its 'eternal' powers, escapes all the intermediate stages, and grasps at once the relation of the thing to God. Seeing the unity of the individual thing as prior to its diversity, it proceeds at once to the unity of God whence that unity flows; whereas *ratio* sees the diversity first. Strictly, indeed, intuition does not *proceed* at all. Presented with a triangle, it would see at once what properties are general and what special, and would, by the eternity of the mind, refer the universal properties at once to the attribute of extension. Hence, as has often been pointed out, *scientia intuitiva* is really possible only for an infinite mind.

Scientia intuitiva ought, if it transcends reason, to carry us back to a principle that unifies alike the things among themselves and their differences from the perceiving mind. Spinoza has shut out this possibility by confining intuition to the perception of individual things. Nevertheless, he is not entirely unconscious of the obligation; for, when (as in *Eth.* v.) he speaks of the mind that has attained this knowledge, he is led on to speak of that mind as absorbed in the Reality which it grasps; as, in fact, one with God. 'To see God in all things, and all things in God'—Spinoza's ideal—is impossible save for God Himself; and even for Him impossible, since intellect does not belong to *Natura naturans.*

Ratio and intuition exhaust all possible instruments of knowledge. Intellect directed on either of these paths cannot err. To discern the true, all that is necessary is to resolve ideas into their simplest form. Nothing would induce Spinoza to give any other criterion of truth than truth itself; it is the rule both of itself and of the false.[3] When, in fact, we see the truth, we see it; and there is no more to be said.

6. Doctrine of the emotions.—*Scientia intuitiva* shows that, while all things depend on God, their individuality is not destroyed thereby. By a noble paradox it asserts that the aloneness of things is precisely the essence which they derive from God. From God they gain the power of existing (so to speak) apart from God. Once launched on the sea of life, they exert a power which is none the less their own that it is recognized to be God's. This doctrine Spinoza expresses in terms of the *conatus*; and it is here that we must seek the transition from knowing to doing, from metaphysic to ethic.

This theory is stated thus: 'Everything, as far as it *is* in itself, endeavours to continue in its being.'[4] That this 'endeavour' is a mere metaphor in many cases is at once seen. 'This *conatus* is nothing but the actual essence of the thing.' To some extent Spinoza had been anticipated by Descartes, who asserted the doctrine of *inertia*—*i.e.* that external causes alone can alter the state of a body. Other philosophers had already treated this *inertia* as a *vis*; and hence we are not surprised to find Spinoza speaking of this passive principle as a '*vis* qua res in existendo perseverat'; while in the *de Deo* it is called the *naturalis amor* of everything for the preservation of its body. In things generally the *conatus* is equivalent to their existence; in living things it is their life; but it belongs primarily to the mind-side of the thing,

[1] *Eth.* ii. 39, cor.
[2] *Ib.* ii. 44, cor. 2.
[3] *Ib.* ii. 45.
[4] *Ib.* v. 36, schol.
[5] *Ib.* ii. 40, schol. 2.
[6] See also *de Deo*, ii. 1.
[7] See Busolt, p. 62.
[8] *Int. Em.* iv. 22.

[1] *Eth.* ii. 47, schol.
[2] ii. 45.
[3] ii. 43, schol.
[4] *Ib.* iii. 6.

and in man[1] the mind is conscious of the *conatus*. The existence which we attempt to maintain is the temporal and phantasmal;[2] but the *conatus* follows from the eternal necessity of God's nature.[3] Referred solely to the mind, it is will; referred to body and mind in conjunction, it is appetite. Will, then, is simply 'appetite with consciousness thereof.'[4] This transformation of the mere essence of a man into the active principle of will is one of Spinoza's most astounding feats.

But observe that the will is, as we have seen, not 'free.'[5] God alone is free—and that in the sense that He works solely from the necessity of His own nature. Secondly, the will is not a faculty. *Voluntas* is only a general name for the sum of particular volitions, as the mind is the sum of particular ideas. Thirdly, *voluntas* is merely a judgment, not a desire. When I see a triangle and affirm that its angles are equal to two right angles, this affirmation is a *voluntas*. How far this identification, so strange to modern eyes, is absolute may be doubted. It has been well pointed out that the psychological classification of mind into will, feeling, and cognition was not known to Spinoza;[6] and possibly, as Pollock suggests,[7] Spinoza simply means to assert that the will is active as the understanding is active. In any case he excludes choice from will, and forbids us to pass what are ordinarily known as 'moral judgments' on any action whatever. Virtue thus reduces to an acquiescence in our fate. When we see that what happens both within us and without us is as 'necessary' as the properties of a triangle are necessary when once its essence is given, we shall endure our lot with even mind.[8]

Hence we do not desire a thing because it is good; we call it good because we desire it. Whatever satisfies the *conatus* in any degree is so far 'good'; whatever hinders it is so far 'bad.' The same series of deeds may be good or bad in different circumstances. Externally, the matricide of Orestes does not differ from that of Nero.[9]

Voluntas, or *appetitus*, being a judgment, may be either adequate or inadequate. From the former arise activities of the mind, from the latter passivities.[10] Whatever increases or diminishes the activity in the body, the 'idea' thereof increases or diminishes the power of thought in the mind.[11] Thus the mind can undergo change, and pass, like the body, to a greater or less 'perfection.' These states are called respectively pleasure (*lœtitia*) and pain (*tristitia*). The first active exercise of the *conatus* appears when the pleasure or pain has given rise to desire (conscious appetite).[12] Desire is mild or intense according to the intensity of the pleasure or pain in which it originates, and has as many varieties as there are varieties of that pleasure or pain. It is in fact 'the being of a man himself, so far as we conceive it as determined to a particular action by any given affection of it.'[13] Pleasure has one advantage over pain in that it increases the vitality to which it owes its origin;[14] hence desire arising from pleasure is, *ceteris paribus*, greater than that arising from pain. Desire, pleasure, and pain are to Spinoza the only primary emotions.

To develop his theory of the emotions, Spinoza relies largely upon association of ideas, which had already been applied to the same end, but with far less skill, by Hobbes. The result is universally regarded as Spinoza's masterpiece. His very success, however, makes it unnecessary for us to

1 *Eth.* iii. 9.
2 *Ib.* iii. 8.
3 *Ib.* ii. 45, schol.
4 *Ib.* iii. 9, schol.
5 *Ib.* ii. 48.
6 Joachim, p. 186.
7 P. 206.
8 *Eth.* ii. 49, Cor. schol.
9 *Ep.* 23.
10 *Eth.* iii. 3.
11 *Ib.* iii. 11.
12 *Ib.* iii. 9.
13 *Ib.* iii. Aff. def. 1.
14 *Ib.* iv. 18.

follow him in detail. A slight reference will be sufficient. Feelings are twofold: if based on inadequate ideas, they are passive; if on adequate, active. Subjection to the former is human bondage; subjection to the latter is only another word for the highest freedom.

Since we naturally endeavour to preserve our existence, we naturally endeavour to banish those images that lower our vitality, and to maintain those that heighten it. Hence arise the passive emotions of love (or liking) and hate (or dislike). By the law of association we soon come to like or dislike things in themselves indifferent to us;[1] and anything may, accidentally, be the cause of such an emotion.[2] Thus we explain avarice, regret, jealousy, and rivalry.[3] These emotions often, as in avarice, attain a power totally out of proportion to the pleasure or pain from which they spring.

By the very fact that we conceive a thing like ourselves to be affected with any emotion, we are ourselves subjected to a like emotion.[4] From this principle, applied in the fashion of Adam Smith, Spinoza works in order to trace many of our *affectus* to sympathy. It is this *imitatio affectuum* which, referred to pain, is called commiseration, and, referred to desire, is called emulation.[5] Thus we explain repentance, ambition, envy, or benevolence.

Contingency and freedom being illusions, we ought neither to regret our own (so-called) bad actions, nor to plume ourselves on our 'good' ones, nor to be angry with a man who injures us. 'Tout comprendre, c'est tout pardonner'; or, rather, to understand is to see that the very notions of approval and pardon are irrelevant. It is from such inadequate ideas that arise anger, remorse, self-approval, revenge.[6]

Such passive emotions, then, subjection to which is bondage, are defined generally as follows: 'Emotion which is called a passion of the soul is a confused idea whereby the mind affirms a greater or less force of existence in its body or some part thereof than it had before, on the occurrence of which the mind is determined to think of one thing more than of another.'[7]

Such emotions of course differ in different men,[8] or even in the same man. Spinoza would probably have allowed that the quality of a pleasure is to be taken into account as well as its quantity.[9]

We pass on now to active emotions, arising from adequate ideas. Some of these spring from *ratio*, others from *scientia intuitiva*. Where the mind conceives itself as active, it feels pleasure; hence the mind feels pleasure when it forms adequate ideas.[10] Desire also may arise from such ideas; but pain, by the very nature of the case, is excluded.[11] Spinoza has thus arrived at last at that *virtus* of the mind, *fortitudo*, which, as we saw, was the practical end he set before himself at the very commencement of his philosophy. *Fortitudo*, or strength of character, is merely the essence of the mind in its self-sustaining endeavour. The utmost that Spinoza can promise (on the other hand, the utmost that is worth having) is knowledge—knowledge more perfect in proportion to the greatness of the object that it covers. Fortitude is the courage to know—to get clear of the passive emotions, and to act from the *conatus* alone. As centred in ourselves, it is *animositas*, or valour; as directed towards others, it is *generositas*, or nobility. By the former is meant the desire whereby we strive to preserve our being in accordance with the dictates of reason; by the latter

1 *Eth.* iii. 14.
2 *Ib.* iii. 15.
3 *Ib.* iii. 35, 36, 56.
4 *Ib.* iii. 27.
5 *Ib.* iii. 27, schol. 1.
6 *Ib.* iii. 25, 40, 49, etc.
7 *Ib.* iii. Aff. def.
8 *Ib.* iii. 57.
9 See *ib.* iii. 57, schol.
10 *Ib.* iii. 58.
11 *Ib.* iii. 59.

the desire whereby we endeavour, solely under the dictates of reason, to aid others and be their friends. Temperance and presence of mind are varieties of the one; courtesy and mercy, of the other. A man of fortitude will never allow his desires to be excessive; he will not be disturbed even by the fear of death, for he will think of death less than of anything. All this is due to his possession of adequate knowledge.

Nor is even fortitude all that is possible to us. There are yet higher emotions, springing not from reason, but from intuition. These Spinoza does not yet consider, pausing to touch on our subjugation to the emotions.[1]

7. Human bondage, or the power of the emotions.—Though 'good' and 'bad' are relative terms, it is perhaps as well to retain them, provided we keep in mind the sense in which they are used, and Spinoza lays it down that he will use 'good' as the synonym of 'perfect.'[2] 'There is no individual thing in nature than which there is not a stronger thing that can destroy it.'[3] Hence the force whereby a man persists in existing is infinitely (*i.e.* indefinitely) surpassed by the power of external causes.[4] Passion, therefore, being due to these external causes, has enormous force, and can at times overcome all the rest of a man's activities.[5] A passion can be destroyed only by a contrary passion.[6] Reason may easily be overcome by emotion: knowledge can control the emotions only so far as it is itself one of them.[7] Desires may be controlled by other desires; and desire of future good is more easily controlled than desire of what is now agreeable.[8] Desire arising from pleasure we have seen to be stronger than that arising from pain.[9] Hence we might almost echo the despairing cry of the poet, 'Video meliora proboque: deteriora sequor'; but, says Spinoza, 'I have not written this to draw the conclusion that ignorance is better than knowledge, or that a wise man is no better than a fool. What reason *can* do in controlling the emotions I shall show later. At present I shall say that reason demands that every man should love himself, and should desire everything which really brings him to greater perfection.'[10]

Virtue is based on the self-maintaining impulse. Every man necessarily desires or shrinks from that which he deems to be 'good' or 'bad'—*i.e.* conducive to his self-conservation or the reverse. The more he endeavours to preserve his own being, the more virtuous he is; and only external causes can prevent his so endeavouring. No virtue can be conceived apart from the *conatus sese conservandi.* A man is not virtuous if he acts from inadequate ideas; for, 'acting' thus, he is really 'passive' and swayed by external causes. Virtue, then,[11] is intellect. In accordance with reason, we can endeavour nothing except to understand. Of these assertions, so Socratic in sound, it is certain that the proof would hardly have satisfied Socrates.

The following propositions (29-37) are even harder to follow. Nothing that has not something in common with our nature can do us good or harm (29)—an obvious truism. Yet we are told next (30) that a thing cannot be bad for us *through* that which it has in common with our nature. In so far as it is in harmony with our nature, it is necessarily good (31). The purpose of these three truisms is to lead up to positions of value in Spinoza's political system—viz. that men necessarily agree if they live in obedience to reason, and that apart from reason no truly social life is possible. A rational life is unfortunately rare; and yet, as Aristotle said, man cannot help being social. Duly to live the rational life, a complex organism is necessary. In Spinoza's Cartesian phraseology, 'Whatever disposes the human body so as to render it capable of being affected in a greater number of ways, or of affecting external bodies in a great number of ways, is useful to man,'[1] provided only this increased complexity is not purchased at the expense of stability of equilibrium. Such instability is always bad, even though it does not amount to what is usually called death.

To social life and a complex organism Spinoza proceeds to add[2] reasonable pleasure. Pleasure *per se* is good; pain *per se* is bad. Spinoza is no ascetic. Cheerfulness cannot be excessive, but is always good and an aid to perfection. It is the wise man's part to enjoy what comes in his way as much as possible—not, of course, to satiety, for that would not be enjoying it.

Hence we see what reason demands of man. He who lives by reason endeavours to render love for hatred, kindness for contempt.

'He who strives to conquer hatred with love, fights his battle in joy and confidence; he withstands many as easily as one, and has little need of fortune's aid. Those whom he vanquishes yield joyfully, not through failure but through increase in their powers.' . . . 'He who rightly realizes that all things follow from the necessity of the divine nature, will not find anything worthy of hatred, derision, or contempt; nor will he bestow pity on anything. He who is easily touched with compassion often does something which he afterwards regrets.' Yet 'he who is moved to help others neither by reason nor by compassion seems hardly a man at all.'[3]

Self-approval may arise from reason, and is indeed the highest object we can hope for. Humility, on the other hand, is no virtue, but a passion. Repentance, likewise, is no virtue; he who repents only makes himself miserable twice over—first by doing the bad action, and secondly by fretting about it. True, *as things are*, both humility and repentance do on the whole more good than harm; and, as 'sin' is inevitable, it is better to sin in the direction of repentance than in the opposite. It was natural, then, for the prophets, in an irrational age, to recommend so strenuously humility and repentance. Those who live under these emotions are not far from the kingdom of reason. But within that kingdom there is a better way.

Pride and dejection are both signs of weakness; but the latter, as a pain, is more easily cured. Dejection, says Spinoza very acutely, is indeed very near of kin to pride.

To all actions to which we are determined by emotion, we can be determined without emotion by reason.[4] Desire that springs from reason cannot be excessive; and the rational mind is affected equally whether the idea be of a thing future, past, or present;[5] hence, if our ideas were only adequate, we should desire a future thing as keenly as though it were present. But, having no adequate knowledge, we are reduced to reliance on the imagination, which prefers present things to future. We are often led by fear, and do good to escape evil, which is contrary to reason, and the lowest of superstitions. Under a reasonable desire we seek good directly and only accidentally shun evil.

The knowledge of evil is inadequate.[6] Spinoza's proof of this statement has been much criticized, and seems indeed to rest on a confusion between knowledge of a negation and a negation of knowledge. He is more correct when[7] he asserts that, as good and evil are relative terms, so a knowledge of either is incomplete without a knowledge of the other. If we possessed adequate knowledge, we should know neither. Precisely similarly,[8] Spinoza gets rid of sin by treating it as a mere negation.

As usual, the practical is not forgotten. Under the guidance of reason we must pursue the greater of two goods and the lesser of two evils; and the greater good in the future rather than the lesser in the present.[9] A reasonable man, living among the ignorant, will avoid receiving favours from them—but only as far as he can. Only 'free' men, however, are really 'grateful' to one another.[10] But a man is more truly 'free' in a society than in solitude; hence the reasonable man does not seek the fictitious freedom of a hermitage. In fact, he will acquiesce in things as they are, for, 'As far as we are intelligent we cannot desire anything save what is necessary, nor yield absolute acquiescence to anything save the true; hence the endeavour of the better part of ourselves is in harmony with the order of nature as a whole.'[11]

8. Human freedom, or the power of the understanding.—We now reach the most attractive, but at the same time the most enigmatical, part of the *Ethics.* Leaving the indicative mood, Spinoza passes on to the imperative; and, as we shall see, he ventures on daring flights.

'I shall treat,' he says, 'of the power of reason, showing how far the reason can control the emotions, and what is the nature of mental freedom or blessedness; we shall then be able to see how much more powerful the wise man is than the ignorant.'[12]

He leaves to logic the discussion of the means of perfecting the mind, and to medicine that of the means of perfectly adapting the body to its functions. The power of the mind over the emotions is not direct; it is defined by the understanding

[1] *Eth.* iv.
[2] *Ib.* iv. pref.
[3] *Ib.* iv. ax.
[4] *Ib.* iv. 3.
[5] *Ib.* iv. 6.
[6] *Ib.* iv. 7.
[7] *Ib.* iv. 14.
[8] *Ib.* iv. 16.
[9] *Ib.* iv. 18.
[10] *Ib.* iv. 17, schol.
[11] *Ib.* iv. 26-28.

[1] *Eth.* iv. 39, dem.
[2] *Ib.* iv. 41.
[3] *Ib.* iv. 46, schol., 50, schol.
[4] *Ib.* iv. 59.
[5] *Ib.* iv. 62.
[6] *Ib.* iv. 64.
[7] *Ib.* iv. 68.
[8] *Ep.* 19.
[9] *Eth.* iv. 65 f.
[10] *Ib.* iv. 71.
[11] *Ib.* iv. appendix, § 32.
[12] *Ib.* v. pref.

solely. In other words, the passions can be subdued only by knowing them.[1]

Then follows what has been called a 'great promise.' There is[2] no modification of the body whereof we cannot form some clear and distinct conception—*i.e.* we can reduce it to its proper place in the order of nature, and see it in its relation to the God of whom it is part. We have long learnt, by painful experience, that no scientific discovery is absolutely true. But to Spinoza, as to Bacon, it may well have seemed that a few generalizations, and the collection of a great but limited number of facts, would lay open the map of a known universe. Yet even Spinoza is doubtful, for he adds a scholium to the effect that every one has the power of knowing his emotions, if not absolutely, at least in part. The practical deduction is that we should try to form this clear and distinct notion of our passions. Thus we shall know their causes, and see them as necessary. Forthwith the inadequate idea, which is the emotion, passes into adequacy; the emotion fades; and in proportion as we understand things as necessary, in that proportion has the mind power over the emotions. No one, *e.g.*, pities a baby because it cannot walk. But, if most people were born full grown, and only here or there did babies appear, every one would pity babies, because infancy would not seem to be a necessary state.[3]

The strength of an emotion is in proportion to the number of simultaneous causes by which it is aroused.[4] So long as we are not assailed by emotions contrary to our nature, we have the power of arranging modifications of our body according to the intellectual order;[5] and here, practical as usual, Spinoza adds some directions for conduct so obvious and simple that they have often been ridiculed as childish. It is only, however, to plunge us almost at once into one of his most enigmatical utterances. 'The mind can bring it about that all bodily images of things may be referred to the idea of God';[6] and this clear and distinct understanding (which to us seems far more unattainable than it did to Spinoza) is henceforth to be known as the 'love of God.'[7] Precisely as rationality suddenly appeared in the emotional garb of *fortitudo*, so, equally suddenly, intuitive knowledge has donned the aspect of love. Some would explain this metamorphosis as due to a desire to accommodate philosophy to theology. Others assume that Spinoza still retained a rag of Jewish mysticism; others again that, like other philosophers, he had an esoteric and an exoteric speech—the one for the initiated, the other for the profane. Whatever the explanation, it is such passages as these that have given Spinoza his hold on men like Coleridge and Schleiermacher, and extorted the cry of Novalis that here was a 'God-intoxicated man.' In reality this 'love' is less emotional than it looks, amounting at most to an *acquiescentia* in our lot. God is without passions, nor is He affected by pleasure or pain; 'he who loves God cannot desire that God should love him in return.'[8] No one can hate God—a clear proof that this 'love of God' is not the opposite of hate, but something of a different order altogether. This love is fostered 'in proportion as we conceive a greater number of men to be bound to God by the same bond of love.'[9] In plain prose, a knowledge of the laws of Nature leads us to a sober acceptance of what befalls us, and to a readiness to do without what we cannot attain; and the discoveries of others, as we assimilate them, aid in the same soothing process.

To sum up: the mind's power over its emotions consists (1) in its knowledge of them; (2) in separating them from the thought of an indistinctly apprehended external cause; (3) in the fact that, with respect to time, the emotions referred to things we distinctly understand surpass those referred to things we conceive confusedly; (4) in the number of the causes which foster the affections having regard to God or to the common properties of things; (5) in the ability of the mind to re-arrange and associate its emotions one with another.

We have now reached the most tantalizing portion of Spinoza's work—a portion, indeed, which there is some reason to believe that he wished to mark off from the rest as not absolutely necessary to his theory, however fondly he might himself dwell upon it. At any rate, he says[1] that, even if the whole series of propositions through which we are now about to pass should be rejected, the virtue of *fortitudo* is none the less binding on us.[2]

So far there has been not the slightest trace of the meaning 'immortality' in Spinoza's use of the word 'eternal.' Eternal truth is simply necessary truth. Nor is there any reason to suppose that the word suddenly changes its meaning. When we read that something eternal remains of the mind after death,[3] there is nothing in the words to imply immortality. If, like Camerer, we hold such a view, we must defend it on other grounds. It is certain that Spinoza once maintained the actual immortality of the soul.[4] True, God, who made the soul, can destroy it; but it is tolerably sure that He never will. In the *de Deo* the position is more doubtful: some, with Sigwart, see in it still an assertion of immortality; to Martineau and others the opposite seems the case. 'If united with the body only, the soul must perish: if with something else that is unchangeable and abiding, then it cannot but be unchangeable and abiding also.'[5]

Adequate knowledge, then, is the only escape from death; even if it be a personal escape, it is open only to the philosopher. So far the *de Deo*; in the *Ethics* the word 'immortal' is dropped. But even from the *de Deo* we learn that (1) the presumed deathlessness of the soul must not interfere with the rigid parallelism of soul and body; (2) the deathlessness is a life to be enjoyed not hereafter, but here and now; (3) it is not open to all, but (in the strict sense) only to the possessor of adequate ideas; (4) the way to attain more of it is to increase our stock of such ideas.

Now the substitution of 'eternal' for 'immortal' would seem to imply the elimination of all idea of time from the conception of the mind.[6] But, while duration is no part of the definition of eternity, yet eternity must entail some kind of endless duration. Thus in *Eth.* v. 20, schol., the word 'duration' is applied to the mind's existence apart from the body. The arguments of Martineau and others against this are due to confounding duration with time (a confusion, indeed, from which Spinoza himself is not free).[7] While persistence is not necessity, that which does not persist cannot be necessary; and thus in *Ep.* 36 lack of duration is marked as an imperfection in extended things.

Again, nothing is eternal in its own right but God Himself. The essence of things is eternal, but not their existence.[8] The mind, then, as being produced by God, has no necessary existence; the existence of mind as such begins with that of the corresponding body.

1 *Eth.* v. 1–3. 2 *Ib.* v. 4. 3 *Ib.* v. 6, schol.
4 *Ib.* v. 8. 5 *Ib.* v. 10. 6 *Ib.* v. 14.
7 *Ib.* v. 15 f. 8 *Ib.* v. 19. 9 *Ib.* v. 20.

1 *Eth.* v. 41.
2 See Pollock, p. 263; and Taylor, in *Mind*, new ser., v. [1896] 243 ff.
3 *Eth.* v. 23. 4 *Cog. Met.* ii. 12.
5 *De Deo*, ii. 23. 6 *Eth.* ii. 44, cor. 2.
7 Joachim, p. 294. 8 *Eth.* i. 24.

We are now ready to deal with propositions 21 to 41 of pt. v. In spite of the arguments of Camerer,[1] conscious personal immortality is not implied in them; v. 21 shows that imagination and memory expire with the body; v. 34 that personal distinctions between man and man vanish at death; v. 22, an exceedingly obscure proposition, asserts that 'in God there is necessarily an idea, expressing under the category of eternity the essence of this or that human body'—*i.e.* that the human mind, considered as a necessary element in the thought-side of the universe, is so far eternal. But v. 23 adds more: it asserts duration, in some sense, of this eternal part of the mind. 'The human mind cannot be absolutely destroyed with the body, but something of it *remains* that is eternal.' Yet even this is not enough; v. 22 applies to the body as much as to the mind. How then does the eternity of the latter surpass that of the former? What is this *aliquid æternum* that survives? To the first question v. 23, schol., seems to supply the answer, viz. that the mind alone can know and enjoy its own deathlessness. To the second question Spinoza gives no explicit reply; but we may perhaps deduce it; v. 24, 25 show that the *aliquid* consists in knowledge of the third kind; but v. 27, asserting that this knowledge leads to *acquiescentia*, manifests also the essentially emotional character of this remnant. It is in fact not only intellectual, but an *amor*. Yet in v. 29 we learn that it arises from contemplating the essence of the body under the form of eternity—*i.e.* from using our own body as the type of extension, and then passing to adequate knowledge, first of extension generally, and thence of the mind also. An adequate knowledge of the body gives us, ultimately, a knowledge of God.[2] And this knowledge of God leads not only to acquiescence, but to the love of God—a love eternal,[3] and totally different from all other passions; for these disappear when the body dies.[4]

Thus this intellectual love of God endures after the death of the body. But it is no personal survival; for personality, by which memory is implied, perishes with the body.[5] But in proportion as our body is capable of more activities, in that proportion is our mind eternal,[6] for our mind will have more means of attaining knowledge, and thus will have more chance of attaining to the intellectual love of God. It is only a natural extension of this to assert that God loves Himself with an infinite intellectual love;[7] *i.e.* that the infinite Mind (made up into unity from all the finite minds) must have a complete knowledge of the universe in both its attributes, and must, with an infinite acquiescence, 'see that it is good.' This is not, as Martineau thinks, a mere tautology. The intellectual love of the mind towards God is part of the infinite love wherewith God loves Himself;[8] but the completeness of knowledge is to be attained only by the union in one of the infinite number of souls that people the universe. It is not, of course, the *Natura naturans* that loves itself; but neither is it the individual mind simply; it is that mind absorbed into the unity of infinite minds. In other words, only the adequate formulation of truth, itself possible only to the united mind of man, can persist unchanged.

To sum up in the words of Taylor:

> 'Those personal memories and affections which derive all their piquancy and poignancy from the personal reference, perish for ever, as such, at death. They depend for their very existence on just those differences which make the existence of one man separate from that of another; and it is for Spinoza only so far as men are indistinguishably one that they are immortal.'[9]

[1] P. 122. [2] *Eth.* v. 30. [3] *Ib.* v. 33.
[4] *Ib.* v. 34. [5] *Ib.* v. 34. [6] *Ib.* v. 39.
[7] *Ib.* v. 35. [8] *Ib.* v. 36
[9] *Mind*, new ser., v. 164.

Similarly with honest but defective scientific thought: the ideas of Ptolemy survive indeed, but metamorphosed beyond recognition. And all men are subject to this mortality; for[1] no man can make himself a mere home of adequate ideas. All men are subject to passion, and therefore mortal.[2] 'But an adequate idea, once thought, takes its place as a permanent addition to knowledge.'

To Spinoza, then, truth once discovered is absolute and lasting truth. 'Blessedness'—*i.e.* the intellectual acquiescence which springs from philosophic knowledge—is not the reward of virtue, but virtue itself. The pursuit of philosophy will, indeed, bring us nothing outside of itself; but it will bring us enough.

> 'The wise man is scarcely at all disturbed in spirit, but, being conscious of himself, and of God, and of things, always possesses true acquiescence. If the way is hard, yet it may be discovered. Needs must it be hard, since it is so seldom found. But all things excellent are as difficult as they are rare.'[3]

9. Attitude to religion and to theology.—Spinoza's enigmatical language has led to divergence of interpretation. He has been denounced as an atheist; on the other hand, he narrowly escaped being the eponymus of a Church. Pontiaan van Hattem, seizing upon some of his doctrines, and blending them with those of Christianity, produced a system which was in 1714 anathematized by the Dutch authorities. Another minister, Van Leeuhof, in a book called *Heaven and Earth*, endeavoured similarly to adapt Spinozism to orthodoxy. Herder, Schlegel, Schleiermacher, and Coleridge (the last by the most desperate methods of exegesis) also tried to enlist Spinoza on the side of ordinary theism. Even Goethe upheld this view against Jacobi: 'So möchte ich ihn Theissimum und Christianissimum nennen und preisen.'[4] Hegel, again, declared that he might rather be accused of acosmism than of atheism. By others he has been dubbed pantheist in all the meanings of that much-enduring word.

It is plain, then, that we must turn from the interpreters to Spinoza himself; and we believe that to those who do so, whatever the name they choose to describe him, the main lines of his thought will become clear.

God has neither intellect nor will.[5] God is 'free'—*i.e.*, He acts from the necessity of His own nature; but He has not the choice to make things other than they are. To deny this is really to deny God's omnipotence; it would imply that He can conceive things that He does not make. Things must have happened as they have happened;[6] to assert the contrary is to deny the perfection of God. Some would argue that there is no perfection or imperfection in things themselves, but that the perfection or imperfection is due to the will of God. But this would imply that God, who necessarily understands what He wills, could will that He should understand things otherwise than He does understand them.

God does not act to an end; nor is He a thinking thing in the sense of a self-conscious being. Intellect belongs only to *Natura naturata*; and even in *Natura naturata* the larger proportion of 'thinking things' do not really think. They are 'animate,' but not self-conscious. To Spinoza[7] thought was conceivable apart from ideas; hence, when he asserts[8] that there is in God an idea of His essence (a passage relied on by Busolt and others to prove the personality of God), we are not to assume more than we do when we assign an 'idea' to a stone. In *Eth.* ii. 11, cor., we are plainly told as much. 'When we say that God has an idea, not as merely constituting the human

[1] *Eth.* iv. 4. [2] *Ib.* v. 34. [3] *Ib.* v. 42, schol.
[4] Quoted by M. Grunwald, *Spinoza in Deutschland*, Berlin, 1897, vol. iii. p. 119, § 63.
[5] *Eth.* i. 17, schol. [6] *Ib.* i. 33. [7] *Ep.* ix.
[8] *Eth.* ii. 3.

mind, but as having along with the human mind also the idea of another thing, this is to say that the *human mind* perceives the thing inadequately.' Nothing is here referred to but *our* mind; and even when, as in v. 40, schol., we are told that finite thoughts together form the infinite intellect of God, it is in a sense we that supply the unifying principle.

All attempts, then, to save any remnant of personality to the Spinozian God are vain. There is no room even for such a 'teleology of the unconscious' as that afterwards developed by Schopenhauer (*q.v.*). Final causes are human figments.[1] Men persuade themselves that everything is created for their sake; they thus tend to consider what is useful to them as 'good,' what hinders them as 'bad.' Hence they are puzzled by seeing so many 'imperfections' in Nature, as if what does not suit them were imperfect. If we ask why God did not create all men so as to follow reason, Spinoza answers that the laws of His nature are so vast as to suffice for the production of every degree of perfection. This is not what even Goethe would call 'Christianissimum.'

Yet the whole argument of the *Tractatus Theologico-Politicus* goes to show that, whatever may do for philosophers, ordinary men need a religion of some sort; and we shall see later that Spinoza thought it desirable that the State should fix the religion for its subjects. No man is the worse for holding a practical rule of life, or for connecting it with a dogmatic system which satisfies his own mind, provided he does not interfere with others. 'All men can obey; there are few that can acquire a virtuous disposition by the guidance of reason'; hence the simple following of the Scriptures is sufficient for the vast majority of mankind.[2] 'Faith does not demand that doctrines should be true so much as that they should be pious.' Thus between faith and philosophy there is no connexion: the one looks for truth, the other for obedience. Faith therefore allows the greatest latitude in philosophic speculation, while it condemns those who teach opinions tending to obstinacy, hatred, and anger. It is indeed astonishing how far Spinoza, in the *Tractatus*, often carries his accommodation of philosophy to religion. God, *e.g.*, is sovereignly just and merciful, the exemplar of the true life, our equitable Judge. He does not act under compulsion, but by His absolute fiat and grace. He forgives the sins of those who repent.[3] It is needless to point out that this is not the language that Spinoza uses to the initiated.

Nevertheless the converse process was necessary; and the religion of the time required to be, to some extent, re-stated in philosophic language. While Spinoza wished the ordinary man to tolerate the philosopher, he also wished so to read the beliefs of the ordinary man as to make them not repugnant to the sage. It is here that, in the opinion of many, his chief glory lies; but he has suffered the usual fate of the pioneer. His results have been made the ladder for subsequent climbers, and have been unceremoniously kicked down when used.

Even he had his predecessors; but his work in the domain of Biblical criticism was amazingly original. He saw that the Bible is not one book, but a literature, produced at widely different dates, by men of widely different characters, and under the influence of widely different degrees of inspiration. On the other hand, he saw many miracles narrated in the Scriptures which the very slightest skill in exegesis would reduce to natural events; for it was his principle—at least ostensibly—that the Scriptures can teach nothing repugnant to our understanding. 'Truth,' he says, 'cannot be at variance with truth, or Scripture teach nonsense. Were we really to find in it what contradicts natural light, we should reject it as freely as we do the Koran or the Talmud. But'—and here there is surely some irony—'far be it from us to imagine that in the sacred writings there can be found any thing repugnant to the light of nature!'[1]

[1] *Eth.* i. appendix. [2] *Tract. Theol.-Pol.* xiv. [3] *Ib.* xiv.

From this principle flow two maxims. The Bible must agree with science. If they seem to disagree, either we must have interpreted the Bible wrongly or we must apply criticism to discover what the Bible really is — whether it claims inerrancy, whether particular passages are genuine, whether the author is confining himself to his proper sphere. Both these weapons Spinoza uses freely.

Thus prophecy[2] is an ordinary phenomenon. It is only the Jewish habit of omitting to take account of secondary causes that deludes us into imagining that the prophets derived their revelations directly from God. Those revelations were real when external to the mind of the prophet, imaginary when he was in a state likely to dispose him to fancy that he received them. The voice with which God revealed the law to Moses was real; that which called Samuel was imaginary. Similarly, the dreams in which God appeared to so many prophets seem to indicate imaginary colloquies. The prophets are fallible and self-contradictory.[3] The style of the prophecy varies with the prophet.[4] Ezekiel and Amos are less cultivated than Isaiah and Nahum. Even the visions vary in accordance with the character of the seer. Prophets are often ignorant: thus Joshua, or the man who wrote his history, fancied that the sun could stand still.

Similarly with other points. There is nothing special in the Jewish religion or history. The Hebrews had no monopoly in election, in prophecy, in oracles. Their long endurance as a nation is due largely to circumcision.

The masses are accustomed to call anything unusual a 'miracle,' imagining God to be generally asleep, and to wake in order to perform extraordinary deeds.[5] As a matter of fact Nature is immutable, and God's character is far better shown in ordinary events than in 'miracles.' By the 'will of God' Scripture means nothing but this immutable order; and many a so-called miracle is easily seen to be quite natural—*e.g.*, the call of Saul, the 'creation' of the rainbow, the raising of the Shunammite's son. Every event truly described in Scripture necessarily happened by immutable law. Many, however, are not related truly, but symbolically, fancifully, or in Oriental fashion. Such are the ascent of Elijah, the hardening of Pharaoh's heart, the cleaving of the rock in the desert. Scripture itself asserts unchanging law: 'Whatsoever God doeth, it shall be for ever.'[6] The Bible, it is true, being written in a dead language and in an Oriental style, is a specially difficult book; but it must nevertheless be interpreted by the same rules as apply to any other book.

Heresy being so dangerous, even Ben Ezra had been obliged to veil his meaning in a cloud of obscure phrases. Ben Ezra is the only predecessor to whom Spinoza acknowledges a debt; but he refers to Maimonides, and may have read the *Systema Theologicum* of La Peyrère (1655). Ben Ezra had already shown that Moses could not have written the Pentateuch; but Spinoza went farther, and pointed out that the book was based on earlier documents, and bears traces of an editorial hand. And that hand can be traced elsewhere, down even to 2 Kings. This compiler[7] may be presumed, in default of certain evidence, to have been Ezra. Whoever he was, some cause prevented him from giving his work complete consistency.

On the rest of the OT Spinoza is less full.[8] The books of Chronicles are of very late date, and of such low authority that we may well wonder how they got into a canon from which Wisdom was excluded. The Psalms and Proverbs were arranged about the time of the Second Temple. Jeremiah is a confused compilation, Ezekiel a fragment. It is remarkable that Spinoza does not seem to have detected the double authorship of Isaiah; but he saw much disorder in the prophecies as we have them. Job is possibly a translation from a Gentile poem; for 'the Satan' is not unlike the Greek Momus. Daniel is partly genuine, partly compiled from Chaldæan sources about the time of the Maccabees. Whoever the authors, there are many errors in the books. Those who try to reconcile contradictions are undertaking a futile task—'a pretty piety, forsooth, which accommodates the

[1] *Cogitata Metaphysica*, viii. 5; see also *Ep.* 21.
[2] *Tract. Theol.-Pol.* i.
[3] Cf. 1 S 15^{29} with 15^{35} and Jer 18^{10}.
[4] *Tract. Theol.-Pol.* ii. [5] *Ib.* vi.
[6] Ec 3^{14}. [7] *Tract. Theol.-Pol.* ix. [8] *Ib.* x.

clear passages to the obscure, the sound to the corrupt.' As to the authority of the canon of Scripture, what is it but that of the council of experts that made it? A fresh council might give a different decision.

Spinoza declines the task of applying criticism to the NT. He has not, he says—perhaps with a touch of irony—sufficient knowledge of Greek. He gives us, however,[1] some indications of his views. The apostles, like the prophets, told what they saw, and needed no supernatural gifts for what they did. Their epistles and sermons—those of Paul especially—reveal men of exceptional, but by no means miraculous, powers. Towards Christ the attitude of Spinoza is very remarkable.

'God can communicate immediately with man; still, a man who can by pure intuition comprehend ideas neither contained in nor deducible from the foundations of our natural knowledge must possess a mind far superior to those of his fellow-men: nor do I believe that any have been so endowed save Christ. To him the ordinances of God were revealed directly, without words or visions. The voice of Christ, like the voice which Moses heard, may be called the voice of God; and it may be said that the wisdom of God took upon itself in Christ human nature, and that he is the way of salvation.'[2]

To Christ God 'gave revelations unaccommodated to Christ's opinions,'[3] so that Christ's knowledge was adequate, and comprehended only *notiones communes et veras*. Yet the orthodox ideas of Christ were to Spinoza not only false but unintelligible. 'The eternal wisdom of God is shown in all things, but chiefly in the mind of man, and most of all in Christ. . . . But as for the proposition enounced by some churches, that God took on him the nature of man, it seems to me as if one should tell me that a triangle had assumed the nature of a square.'[4]

On the resurrection of Christ Spinoza's views are similar to those of some modern thinkers. He takes the death and burial literally, but the resurrection allegorically. 'I admit that the Evangelists believed it literally; but they might well be in error without prejudice to the Gospel doctrine. Paul, to whom also Christ appeared later, asserts that he knows Christ not after the flesh but after the spirit.'[5]

If, then, Spinoza is to be claimed as 'Theissimum et Christianissimum,' it must be on other grounds than his theological and philosophical views as recorded by himself; and, while his life was such that Christians may well own him as a brother, his belief was outside the most comprehensive Christian symbol.

10. Political philosophy.—Though it is likely that to Spinoza political speculation was more congenial than metaphysical, we need not examine his political writings at any length. In the first place, they can be understood with tolerable ease by the ordinary reader; in the second, they have exerted nothing like the same influence as his other works—partly, perhaps, because they were left unfinished. A brief summary, however, is desirable.

As might be expected, he treats men as they are, and not as philosophers or preachers would like them to be. Such writers, he says, have given us satires rather than systems of ethics, and have never produced political theories useful out of Utopia. It has been left for statesmen, with all their faults, to write serviceably on politics. Men are subject to passions; they pity the ill-off and envy the well-off. Those who fancy that men as a whole will follow reason are dreamers. 'And so I have laboured not to lament, mock, or execrate human actions, but to understand them; and to look on passions not as vices of human nature, but as properties as native to it as heat and cold to the atmosphere.'[6]

[1] *Tract. Theol.-Pol.* xi. [2] *Ib.* i.
[3] *Ib.* iv. [4] *Ep.* 73.
[5] *Ib.* 75. [6] *Tract. Pol.* i. 4.

Looking at facts, then, we find all men living in some kind of social order. Men have already tried all possible societies; all that remains for philosophy is to decide on the best ways of improving known types.[1]

There is no such thing as *jus naturæ*. Right is only another word for power. Every man has as much natural right as Nature allows him power. Man does, and can do, nothing not in accordance with the laws of Nature. Even in 'breaking' them we necessarily obey them; and the reasonable man is no more acting according to right of Nature than the fool. But men soon find that a right which belongs to everybody defeats itself. Hence arise commonwealths. Two men, though each has yielded up some of his power to the other, have more power (*i.e.* 'right') than one. One man may secure the dependence of another either by persuading his mind or by coercing his body;[2] and the same may be done by a combination of men. In a combination the power is proportioned to numbers; and this right or power is called 'dominion.' It is dominion that determines right and wrong, justice and injustice; for in 'Nature' everything belongs to anybody who can get it.

Under any dominion the State is 'civil'; the body under dominion is a 'commonwealth,' and the general business is 'affairs of State.' Whether the supreme authority be a monarch, an aristocracy, or a democracy, it has simple natural right, limited by the power of the multitude considered as one. Obviously, therefore, each single citizen's 'right' is less in proportion as the commonwealth exceeds him in power. Whatever it decrees, he must do; for, even if he knows it to be evil, it is a lesser evil than resistance. But[3] plainly those things to which no one can be induced by rewards or threats do not fall within the rights of the commonwealth. Nor are things within those rights which are abhorrent to the majority. Thus the external shows of religion are within, the inner emotions without, the purview of the State. One state is to another state as one man to another man; save only that a state can defend itself more easily than a man can defend himself. Two states are naturally enemies; and unfortunately one can make war, while it takes two to make peace. Two thus agreeing are called contracting powers; but contracts are binding only so long as the circumstances under which they were made remain unchanged. Every state can break its contract when its safety demands such action.[4] Spinoza sees the apparent immorality of this doctrine, and devotes a few lines to its defence.

The functions of the supreme authority[5] are to create 'rights' within the dominion, to make laws, to declare war and peace, to appoint executive officers, and the like. In so acting it may do foolishly, but it cannot (strictly) do 'wrong'; for it is itself the fountain of law. Civil jurisprudence depends on the mere will of the commonwealth, which is not bound to please any but itself.

Contracts by which the multitude transfers its right to one council or one man should without doubt be broken when general expediency demands. But to decide when it is thus expedient is within the right of him only who holds dominion. Nevertheless, if the breaking of them weakens the hold of the ruler upon the ruled, by that very fact the commonwealth is dissolved; civil law ceases, and war begins.[6] The sanction that constrains the ruler to keep the laws is simply this, that beyond a certain point he cannot go without destroying his position. All despotism is tempered by potential rebellion. It is futile to inveigh against the people for rebelling; people never rebel without a

[1] *Tract. Pol.* i. 3. [2] *Ib.* ii. 10. [3] *Ib.* iii. 8.
[4] *Ib.* iii. 14. [5] *Ib.* iv. [6] *Ib.* iv. 6.

cause. The end of all government is security.[1] Seditions and contempt of law are due not so much to the wickedness of the subjects as to the bad state of the dominion. For men are not born fit for citizenship; it is the business of the State to make them so. Men's passions are everywhere the same; if wickedness prevails more in one commonwealth than in another, it is because the one has not pursued the end of government so well as the other. Where licence is rare and virtue common, the rulers must receive the praise—as Hannibal is deservedly renowned because in his army there never arose a mutiny. Of course all this does not apply to a commonwealth that is held down by force or by the craft of a despot. Spinoza gives no counsel to such a despot; that has been done once for all by Machiavelli. Here Spinoza shows his acquaintance with the 'most ingenious' Florentine. 'If there is one writer,' says Duff, 'whom we may call Spinoza's master, it was Machiavelli';[2] and Goethe rightly declares that Spinozism is ultimately Machiavellism.

We next discuss in succession the three forms of government—monarchy,[3] aristocracy,[4] and democracy.

With a possible criticism of Hobbes, Spinoza asserts[5] that a really absolute monarchy cannot exist. The monarch has to seek coadjutors; and the 'monarchy' is thus really an aristocracy, but a concealed one, and thus the worst of aristocracies. Certain checks are therefore desirable. A parliament should be appointed by the king, and chosen from the various families in the State; it should advise the king, but the ultimate responsibility should be his. Smaller bodies should be chosen to form the executive and the council of judges; the latter should serve for only a year and vote by ballot. The army should be composed exclusively of citizens, and be paid only in time of war; the generals should be changed every year, and the officers receive no pay except plunder. By these means Spinoza hoped to prevent the usurpations of Cromwells and Sforzas. Certain laws are to be so firmly fixed that not even the king can abolish them—as Ulysses could not break the rule that he had laid down when about to pass the sirens. Under a monarchy no churches ought to be built at the public expense; nor ought laws to be made about opinions. Let such as are allowed the public exercise of their religion build a church at their own cost.

Under an aristocracy the factions in the governing body will be weaker the more there are to whom dominion is given. Hence that body should be large—a hundred good men at least; and, to ensure that number of good men, the total number ought to be at least five thousand. Thus we shall have enough men to provide ability, and too many to allow of the tyranny of a clique. To such a body absolute power may be trusted; for they could never be guided by one mind except for (at least apparently) honourable ends.[6] The polity most adapted to aristocracy is a confederation of cities,[7] but the seat of federal government should not be in one of the united cities. Under an aristocracy the governed are not citizens, but subjects; hence the army should be paid, and promotion should be possible, that *esprit de corps* may be secured. Aristocracies, indeed, by their very origin betray the fact that such *esprit de corps* is often wanting; for they have usually risen out of democracies.[8] Out of the council are selected syndics, men of some age, to watch and check the councillors. There shall also be chosen an executive senate, to inspect fortifications, pass laws, deal with other states, and so on. There should be an established religion, to which all patricians should conform, and State-provided churches. Freedom of worship is allowed, but only on condition that it 'goes softly.' Academies founded at the public expense are instituted to restrain men's natural abilities rather than to cultivate them. But in a free commonwealth arts and sciences will be best cultivated if every one that pleases is allowed to teach publicly, at his own risk.[1] The sanction of an aristocracy is the general perception that its destruction would be a great evil. Hence, if wise, it will take care to rule in accordance with the general desire, appealing to reason rather than to fear.

> 'A government which aims at nothing else than to guide men by fear will be rather free from defects than possessed of merit. Men are to be so guided that they may deem themselves not to be guided at all, but to live of their own free will.'[2]

Hence vexatious and trifling restrictions should be avoided; sumptuary laws should never be imposed;[3] and the common vices of peace are never to be forbidden directly, but by laying such foundations of dominion that the many may live—not wisely, for that is impossible, but under the guidance of passions useful to the commonwealth.[4] An aristocracy thus founded will be, internally, indestructible. Its fall, if fall there be, will come from without.[5]

Spinoza's definition of democracy deserves notice. In aristocracies citizenship is granted by the choice of the supreme council; in democracies it is allowed by law.[6] It might happen that the law gave this franchise to elder men only, or to first-born sons only, or to the wealthy only; it might be that the number of the enfranchised was far smaller in a democracy than in an aristocracy; but, as long as it is the law that fixes the franchise, a democracy it remains. It is obvious[7] that such a definition has a wide scope.[8] But Spinoza confines his attention to 'that in which all, without exception, who owe allegiance to the laws of the country only, and are independent and of respectable life, have the right of voting in the supreme council [he does not touch on representative government] and of filling the offices of the dominion.' He thus excludes aliens, slaves, and women. On the exclusion of women he has an interesting paragraph, with which the work breaks off unfinished.

> 'It may be asked whether women are under men's authority by nature or by convention. If we consult experience, we shall find the cause to be their weakness. There has never been a case of men and women reigning together; but, wherever men exist, men rule and women are ruled. If by nature women were equal to men, surely among nations so many and so different some would be found where both sexes rule alike, and others where men are ruled by women. And since this is not the case, one may assert that women have not by nature equal right with men.'

Elsewhere[9] Spinoza touches briefly on democracy, and seems to prefer it to other forms of government. But, under whatever form our lot is cast, our duty is to obey the commands of the dominion, and to recognize no right save that which sanctions.

LITERATURE.—The literature connected with Spinoza is enormous, and only a small selection can be given here. For further details the reader is referred to Pollock's first ed., to A. Van der Linde's *Benedictus Spinoza: Bibliographie* (The Hague, 1871), and to the British Museum Catalogue.

i. *LIFE.*—J. Colerus, *Leven van Spinoza*, Amsterdam, 1705, Fr. tr. (inaccurate), The Hague, 1706 (in *Opera*, ed. H. E. G. Paulus, 2 vols., Jena, 1802–03, and elsewhere); the Eng. tr. of the Fr. (London, 1706) is given in Pollock; Lucas, *La Vie de Spinoza* before 1688, reprinted, Amsterdam, 1719 (till recently Lucas was unknown, and this work was attributed to St. Glain and others; it is now established that Lucas is no pseudonym, and the work, once discredited, is now rehabilitated [Meinsma;

[1] *Tract. Pol.* v. 2.
[2] *Spinoza's Political and Ethical Philosophy*, p. 10.
[3] *Tract. Pol.* vi., vii.
[4] *Ib.* viii., ix., x.
[5] *Ib.* vi. 5.
[6] *Ib.* viii. 6.
[7] *Ib.* ix. 1.
[8] *Ib.* viii. 12.

[1] *Tract. Pol.* viii. 49.
[2] *Ib.* x. 8.
[3] *Ib.* x. 5.
[4] *Ib.* x. 6.
[5] *Ib.* x. 10.
[6] *Ib.* xi. 1.
[7] *Ib.* xi. 3.
[8] Pollock, p. 313.
[9] *Tract. Theol.-Pol.* xvi.

Freudenthal, p. 260 ff.]); **H. de Boulainvilliers**, a rehash of Colerus and Lucas, *Réfutation des erreurs de Benoît de Spinoza*, Brussels, 1731; other scattered notices are collected and, where necessary, translated by **J. Freudenthal**, *Die Lebensgesch. Spinozas in Quellenschriften*, Leipzig, 1899; **K. O. Meinsma**, *Spinoza en zijn kring*, The Hague, 1896 (admirable for all the newest information); **J. Freudenthal**, *Spinoza, sein Leben und seine Lehre*, i., Stuttgart, 1904 (a first-rate work; the second vol., on the philosophy, unfortunately never appeared). The English reader will consult **J. Martineau**, *A Study of Spinoza*[3], London, 1895; **F. Pollock**, *Spinoza: his Life and Philosophy*[2], do. 1899 (the 1st ed. [1880] is still accessible); **A. Wolf**, whose ed. of the *Short Treatise* contains a good brief Life (London, 1910).

ii. *THE WORKS.*—All other editions are superseded by **J. Van Vloten** and **J. P. N. Land**, 2 vols., The Hague, 1882–83, 2nd ed., 3 vols., do. 1895. The chief works have been translated by **R. H. M. Elwes**, 2 vols., London, 1883–84; the *Ethics* and *De Int. Em.* by **W. Hale White** ('Mark Rutherford'), revised by **Anna Hutchison Stirling**, London, 1894, 1895; *Short Treatise* ed. and tr. by Wolf, as above.

iii. *CRITICISMS OF THE PHILOSOPHY.*—**Martineau**, *A Study of Spinoza*[3], and *Types of Ethical Theory*, Oxford, 1885, i.; **Pollock**, as above; **T. Camerer**, *Die Lehre Spinoza's*, Stuttgart, 1877 (excellent and closely reasoned, limited chiefly to the *Ethics*); **I. Elbogen**, *Tract. de Int. Em.*, Breslau, 1898; **C. Sigwart**, *Spinoza's neuentdeckter Tractat* (the *de Deo*), Gotha, 1866; **R. Avenarius**, *Über die beiden ersten Phasen des spinozischen Pantheismus*, Leipzig, 1868; **J. Caird**, *Spinoza*, in Blackwood's Philosophical Classics, Edinburgh and London, 1888 (containing a brief account of Spinoza's predecessors; *Ethics* only); **H. H. Joachim**, *A Study of the Ethics of Spinoza*, Oxford, 1901 (difficult, but thorough and reliable); **G. Busolt**, *Die Grundzüge der Erkenntnisstheorie und Metaphysik Spinozas*, Berlin, 1875 (on its special subject admirable); **R. A. Duff**, *Spinoza's Political and Ethical Philosophy*, Glasgow, 1903 (a standard work on the Politics).

Of slighter works may be mentioned: **Matthew Arnold**, in *Essays in Criticism*, London, 1865; **J. A. Froude**, in *Short Studies on Great Subjects*, 1st ser., do. 1873; **E. Renan's** Bicentenary Address, *Spinoza: Conférence tenue à La Haye, le 21 février 1877*, The Hague, 1877, and *Nouvelles Etudes d'histoire religieuse*, Paris, 1884; **J. Iverach**, *Descartes, Spinoza and the New Philosophy*, Edinburgh, 1904; **T. H. Green**, *Lectures on the Principles of Political Obligation*, London, 1895, p. 49 ff., and *Works*[5], do. 1906, ii. 355 ff.; and, above all, the essay by **A. E. Taylor** in *Mind*, new ser., v. [1896] 243 ff. Those who wish to see a specimen of the early criticisms on Spinoza may find one in *The Living Temple* (London, 1675) of John Howe, the great Cromwellian preacher.

E. E. KELLETT.

SPIRIT (Holy), SPIRIT OF GOD.

SPIRIT (Holy), **SPIRIT OF GOD.**—The terms 'Spirit of God' and 'Holy Spirit' are common to several great speculative and religious systems. Zoroastrianism (*q.v.*) speaks of a Spenta Mainyu ('Holy Spirit'), which is variously represented: as a personified emanation of the Godhead, as a created being probably above the rank of angels, and even as identical with the Supreme Creator, Ahura Mazda. He possesses creative powers, ethical qualities, and teaching offices which closely resemble the Christian view.[1] The later Stoics spoke of a *spiritus sacer*=God, the *anima mundi*, who was conceived as a materialistic fiery breath, the intelligent permeating containing principle of the cosmos, resident in man and observant of his good and evil deeds.[2] In Greek mystery-religions we meet with 'Holy Spirit' (*τὸ πνεῦμα ἱερον, ἅγιον*), which comes from God into the initiate at the mysteries.[3] The Hebrews appear to have first grasped the concept of the Spirit of God, which in the OT faintly, and in Talmudical literature more clearly, approaches hypostatization. In Muhammadanism the Holy Spirit, probably under Jewish influence, was identified with the angel Gabriel.[4] Christianity, starting with the monotheistic doctrine of Judaism, included within its doctrine of God an inseparable distinction of agents—the Father, the Son, and the Holy Ghost—each possessing properties and characteristics which resemble, while they transcend, what is termed 'personality' in human beings.

The object of this article is to trace, in outline, the development of the doctrine of the Holy Spirit.

[1] Cf. *Yasna*, xxxi. 7, 9, 11, xxx. 3–5, xlv. 2, xxviii. 2, xlvii. 2, xxviii. 11, xliv. 7, and artt. AMESHA SPENTAS, DUALISM (Iranian).

[2] Cf. Diog. Laert. vii. 134; Stobæus, i. 322; Cicero, *de Nat. Deor.* ii. 7; Seneca, *Ep. Mor.* xli.

[3] Cf. R. Reitzenstein, *Die hellenistischen Mysterienreligionen*, Leipzig, 1910, p. 156 ff.

[4] Cf. *Qur'ān*, ii. 81, 254; cf. *DI*, artt. 'Gabriel,' 'Holy Spirit.'

By way of introduction we shall examine the Hebrew notions of 'spirit' amidst which the OT view of the Spirit of God (Jahweh) took its rise; then we shall mark the development of that conception in Biblical (OT canonical and extra-canonical) and subsequent rabbinical literature (Talmudic and post-Talmudic); and, finally, after examining the Biblical (NT) contributions, we shall trace the formulation of the doctrine of the Holy Spirit's person and work in the thought and life of the Christian Church.

I. *INTRODUCTION: HEBREW.*—Our limits, in this section, are the canonical books (OT), in which the characteristic Hebrew notions of spirit find expression. Towards the close of the canon, and in the apocryphal literature more notably, the term 'spirit' is extended, probably under Babylonian and Persian influences, to include angels and demons.[1] This extension we here lay aside. The term *rûaḥ* (רוּחַ), generally translated 'spirit' in English, comes from a Semitic root, *rûḥ*, which, in cognate languages, signifies 'to breathe,' 'to blow.' Kindred words in Heb. are *rêaḥ*, 'scent,' 'odour,' and the verb (only in Hiph.) *rûaḥ*, 'to smell,' 'to perceive odour.' With the verb the organs of breathing, the mouth and nostrils, are frequently mentioned. The primary signification of *rûaḥ* appears to be 'air in motion,' as wind or breath, and the general idea which is common to nearly all its usages is 'power in manifestation, or energy.' The various usages of *rûaḥ* (which occurs 378 times) may be roughly classified under four heads: (1) physically, (2) physiologically, (3) psychically, and (4) 'supernaturally.'

(1) *Physically* (131 times).—In this aspect *rûaḥ* is used of the air in motion, the wind in all its moods and phases, whether gentle or stormy, hot or cold. Then it serves to denote direction, the quarter from which the wind may blow (Gn 8[1], Ex 15[10], Gn 3[8], Jer 49[36]). In later writings it acquires the figurative sense of 'vanity,' 'emptiness' (Is 41[29], Job 7[7], Ec 1[14]).

(2) *Physiologically* (39 times).—This usage, which may be derived from the former by observation, denotes the breath in the bodies of men and animals. From the close connexion between the breath and the phenomena of life and energy, the *rûaḥ* came to be considered as the vehicle of life and even as the life itself. In sickness, exhaustion, or swoon the breath and corresponding vitality were reduced, and it was said that the *rûaḥ* had gone away; similarly, after food or under the stimulus of joy the *rûaḥ* returned and man revived (Gn 45[27], 1 S 30[12], Jg 15[19], 1 K 10[5]). When the *rûaḥ* left the body entirely, death took place (Ps 104[29f.]). The further induction that the *rûaḥ* was the immaterial life principle does not seem to have been common before the Exile; in Ezk (cf. ch. 37) it becomes prominent, and thenceforth *rûaḥ* is used, along with *neshāmāh* and *nephesh*, to denote the breath-soul in man. In the earlier literature *neshāmāh* is the usual term (Gn 2[7]) for the normal breathing, *rûaḥ* being reserved for the more violent breathing which marks exertion or emotional excitement. In the passage just referred to we have the first statement of the notion that man's breath-soul is derived immediately from God by spiration;[2] not until after the Exile does *rûaḥ* occur in that connexion (Is 42[5], Zec 12[1], Job 27[3], Ps 104[30]), and then it is applied to animals as well (Gn 6[17] 7[15] [P]). Yet a distinction is drawn between man and other animate beings. Both are formed out of the dust of the ground, but he becomes a living being by the direct inbreathing of Elohim, and at death his *rûaḥ* returns to God (Gn 2[7. 19], Ec 12[7], Ps 31[5]). Because man's *rûaḥ* comes from God, it is the

[1] See art. DEMONS AND SPIRITS (Hebrew), vol. iv. p. 598 f.

[2] For Babylonian parallel cf. *KAT*[3], p. 526.

object of His regard; He protects it and continues it in being, and so can be called 'the God of the spirits of all flesh' (Job 10^{12} 12^{10}, Nu 16^{22}). The Hebrew genius was not speculative, and the derivation of man's spirit from God probably expressed the popular opinion of animism, the wonderful power inherent in *rûaḥ* indicating the presence of deity in man. But the ideas of divine immanence or of the divine breath physically extended into man, as Stoicism fancied, cannot be in the Hebrew thought; they belong to later philosophical speculation, the first traces of which become apparent only in the extra-canonical literature (*e.g.*, Wisdom and Philo). Man's divine origin, however, lifts the Hebrew view above the Greek: he is no mere product of nature,[1] the dualism of Greek thought about man is avoided, and through the original connexion of man's *rûaḥ* with God the way was left open for those approaches of God to man which are the glory of Hebrew religious experience.[2]

(3) *Psychically* (74 times).—As the breath is often the visible index of man's stronger emotions, the term *rûaḥ* readily served to express his inner life in its emotional and mental aspects, and was used in parallelism along with the terms *nephesh* and *lēbh*. Anger, grief, and zeal were often exhibited with dilated nostrils and laboured breathing; hence we find *rûaḥ* as well as nostril (*'aph*) used as a synonym for anger, in both God and man (Mic 2^7 RVm 'impatient,' Jg 8^3, Job 4^9). In post-Exilic literature the term *rûaḥ* is extended to cover such emotions as sadness, trouble, bitterness, and longing, which are regarded as located 'in the *rûaḥ*' (1 K 21^5, Gn 41^{28} 26^{35} [P], Is 26^9, Job 7^{11}, 1 S 1^{15}). From Ezekiel's time onward the *rûaḥ* was regarded as the organ of knowledge (parallel to לֵב, *lēbh*, the usual term, Ezk 11^5 20^{32}, 1 Ch 28^{12}, Ps 77^6), and occasionally, though rarely, as the seat of volition (Ps $51^{12.\ 14\ [Heb.]}$, Ex 35^{21} [P] 'a willing spirit'), and, lastly, of it are predicated such ethical qualities as 'new,' 'guileless,' 'broken,' 'haughty,' etc. (Ezk 11^{19}, Ps 32^2 51^{17}, Is 57^{15}, Pr $16^{18f.}$).

Rûaḥ and nephesh.—At this point a word on the relation of these terms may fitly come in. It has been held that they express distinct substances or elements in man, which, along with *bāsār* ('flesh'), make up a trichotomy in human nature.[3] A comparison of passages where the terms occur together does not sustain this view (cf. 1 S 1^{15}, Is 26^9, Job 3^{20} 7^{11}). Both express the invisible immaterial element in man as contrasted with the flesh. *Rûaḥ* and *nephesh* are related together as animating principle and animated result: the former denotes the vital energy, which lies more basally in human nature than *nephesh*. From the point of view of experience, *nephesh* is the subject, the ego, whilst *rûaḥ* is less immediately under self-control, and is more moved from without. Hence it is that aspect of human nature more immediately in touch with the Divine Spirit. But it should be remembered that Hebrew thought does not work scientifically as it describes mental phenomena; it moves instinctively and intuitively, and deals with things, not abstractions. And, because *rûaḥ* had a physical quality and connoted power and energy, it was used to denote the causative principle in all actions, whether bodily or mental.

The connotation of power with *rûaḥ* explains its usage to denote the energy of the personality in particular manifestations. Some of these may be more settled—what we call character or disposition; to these the ethical predicates are applied (see above); less permanent manifestations, as humours, moods, whims, are frequently described in such phrases as 'spirit of wisdom,' of grace, of whoredoms, of deep sleep, etc. In so far as they are manifested in the human spirit, they may be grouped under the heading psychical, but by reason of the unusual force which they display, and in accord with primitive views of personality as liable to invasion by spirits from without, they fall rather to be considered under the next section.

(4) '*Supernaturally*' (134 times).—A stricter definition would be 'extra-human,' since Hebrew thought made no distinction between natural and supernatural, God being regarded as the cause of all that happens, whether good or evil. But for convenience' sake, and because the action of the Spirit of God falls under this head (though its detailed consideration is deferred to II.), the term may be allowed to stand. Under the heading 'supernatural' *rûaḥ* are included agencies operating upon man—only rarely upon inanimate nature—whose source is outside or above him. In the literature, as we now have it, they are all under God's control, but the literary phraseology suggests that in the pre-literary period they were not so viewed. These agencies appear to be 'survivals from the animistic past of Israel,'[1] in which sickness, insanity, abnormal powers of body or of mind, were accounted for as due to a subject becoming possessed by an extraneous spirit. Such were the evil spirit which rushed upon Saul and terrified him (1 S 16^{16} 18^{10}), the ill-will caused by an 'evil spirit' (Jg 9^{23}), the spirit of jealousy between man and wife (Nu 5^{14}), and the spirit of whoredom which makes Israel err and wander into idolatry (Hos 4^{12} 5^4). The over-mastering might of such beings is expressed by the vigorous verbs which describe their action. They 'rush upon,' 'fall upon,' 'come upon,' 'pass over upon' men; the action of the Spirit of Jahweh upon Elijah suggests storm-demons (1 K 18^{12}, 2 K 2^{16}). In one case a 'lying spirit' is distinctly hypostatized; it stands, speaks, receives commands, and departs (1 K 22^{19-26}).[2] This language had a marked influence upon the descriptions of the activity of the Spirit of God in both OT and NT. That Spirit is said to clothe (Jg 6^{34}; cf. Lk 24^{49}), come mightily upon, fall upon (Ezk 11^5, Ac 11^{15}), carry away (1 K 18^{12}, Ac 8^{39}), push or move (Jg 13^{25}, Mk 1^{12}, ἐκβάλλει) men. Another group of phrases, which first appears in the time of Isaiah, ascribes to *rûaḥ* material properties, as a kind of fluid element. Thus a 'spirit of perverseness' is 'mingled' by Jahweh in the midst of Egypt (Is 19^{14}), a 'spirit of deep sleep' is 'poured out' like a stupefying drug, producing effects like drunkenness (Is 29^{10}; cf. Ac 2^{13}). Such language is repeatedly used of the Spirit of God in the writing prophets (Is 32^{15} 44^3, Jl $2^{28ff.}$, Ezk 39^{29}, Zec 12^{10}). It relates itself with the idea of 'anointing' (*q.v.*), whereby is imparted the divinity that 'doth hedge a king' or prophet (1 S 10^1 16^{14}, Is 61^1). *Rûaḥ* can be put into a person (Is 63^{11}, Ezk 37^{14}, 2 K 19^7), so that he is 'filled' with it (Ex 31^3, Lk 1^{41}); it can be taken away (Ps $51^{13\ [Heb.]}$), and distributed upon others (Nu $11^{17.\ 25}$). It can be poured out with fertilizing effect upon inanimate nature as well as man (Is 32^{15} 44^3). As the 'demonic' *rûaḥ* suggested personal actions and so influenced NT terminology, so the fluid-like *rûaḥ* had a far-reaching influence, appearing in the NT conception of the Holy Spirit as a gift, and in the later theological speculations of the Greek Fathers as a kind of substance, which was imparted to believers in the sacraments. From this analysis it is clear that the term *rûaḥ* is a general one embracing, by syncretism, elements collected from various sources, and not derivable from one general principle. Herein lies the difficulty for the modern mind as it approaches the Hebrew idea of 'spirit.' For now spirit denotes, metaphysically, the immaterial as contrasted with the material; and the modern

[1] Cf. H. Siebeck, 'Die Entwicklung der Lehre vom Geist in der Wissenschaft des Altertums,' *Zeitschr. für Völkerpsych. und Sprachwissenschaft*, xii. [1880] 389 f.

[2] Cf. H. W. Robinson, *The Religious Ideas of the OT*, London, 1913, pp. 82, 110 f.

[3] Cf. F. Delitzsch, *A System of Biblical Psychology*, Eng. tr., Edinburgh, 1867, p. 113 ff.; R. H. Charles, *EBi*, col. 1342.

[1] Stade, *Biblische Theologie des alten Testaments*, Tübingen 1905, p. 99.

[2] See *ERE* iv. 595a.

mind finds it difficult to understand the materialistic view of spirit as an ethereal fluid substance, except in poetic metaphor. Again, the philosophical use of the term to denote a self-conscious subject possessing 'perdurable individuality' has little in common with the animistic meaning of *rûaḥ*, or the primitive psychology of the Semitic mind, which could identify mind with physical organs or physical breath. And yet there was an unconscious logic at work when popular fancies grouped such disparate elements under the term *rûaḥ*. The wind of heaven in its mighty, mysterious, quasi-personal activity is very similar to the action of 'spirits,' and both suggest the miraculous, supersensible power which streams through nature and into human life with such startling effects. Thus, unconsciously, *rûaḥ* expressed the metaphysical notion of causality, the principle of movement, energy, and life in the universe. But, in accord with the Hebrew genius, this principle was expressed, not in abstract static terms as in Greek—the Hebrew language was little fitted for that—but concretely, dynamically, picturesquely, realistically. And so *rûaḥ* was taken into the service of religion as the term whereby could be expressed the nature of the wind, the life of beasts and men, the deepest impulses in the breasts of saints and sages, and the modes of the manifold activities of God Himself.

LITERATURE.—The following may also be consulted: Lexicons, *s.v.* רוּחַ: Gesenius, *Hebrew and English Lex. of OT*, ed. Brown, Driver, and Briggs, Oxford, 1906; Siegfried-Stade, Leipzig, 1893; Gesenius-Kautzsch^{15}, do. 1910; artt. 'Spirit,' in *EBi*, *HDB*, *DCG*; 'Geist, heiliger,' in *PRE*^{3} (A. H. Cremer), *RGG* 'Geist u. Geistesgaben im AT' (Bertholet), 'Geist des Menschen' (Kalweit); works on Biblical theology by H. Schultz, R. Smend, B. Stade, A. B. Davidson; monographs: A. Sabatier, *Mémoire sur la notion hébraïque de l'esprit*, Paris, 1879; C. A. Briggs, in *JBL* xix. [1900] 132 ff.; P. Volz, *Der Geist Gottes*, Tübingen, 1910, pp. 6–53. There are discussions in works on Biblical anthropology. Good summaries of German discussions on the materiality (*Stofflichkeit*) of spirit will be found in J. Glöel, *Der heilige Geist in der Heilsverkündigung des Paulus*, Halle, 1888, p. 371 ff.; H. Gunkel, *Die Wirkungen des heiligen Geistes*^{2}, Göttingen, 1899, pp. 43-49. See H. W. Robinson, *The Christian Doctrine of Man*, Edinburgh, 1911; J. Köberle, 'Gottesgeist und Menschengeist im AT,' *NKZ*, Erlangen, 1902, pp. 321 ff., 403 ff. Cf. also artt. SOUL (Hebrew), LIFE AND DEATH (Hebrew).

II. *OLD TESTAMENT* (*CANONICAL AND EXTRA-CANONICAL*).—The sources readily fall into two main divisions, canonical and extra-canonical, each of which may be conveniently divided into two sections, viz. canonical: (1) pre-Exilic and (2) Exilic and post-Exilic; extra-canonical: (1) Palestinian and (2) Jewish-Alexandrian.

Our purpose is to trace historically the development of the conception of the Spirit of God, the various spheres of its working, and any hints of its hypostatization in this literature. Any development of the idea of God will be reflected in the doctrine of His Spirit.[1] The predominant designation in OT is 'the Spirit of JHWH,' less frequently 'Spirit of God' (רוּחַ אֱלֹהִים), sometimes with pronouns 'His,' 'thy,' 'my,' rarely absolutely as 'the Spirit,' and only thrice 'Holy Spirit,' and then with pronominal suffix, 'thy' or 'His' (Is $63^{10.\,11}$, Ps 51^{11}). The distinction between Spirit of Jahweh and Spirit of Elohim will be noted as it emerges in the literature.

What was said of *rûaḥ* in the previous section, as applied to man, is applicable to its use in connexion with God. The wind, in early poetry, was regarded as His breath (Ex $15^{8.\,10}$, Ps 18^{15}), and the storm, used frequently to describe theophanies, was the explosion of His wrath (Is 4^{7} $30^{27f.}$ 59^{19}, Job 4^{9}). In some cases there is ambiguity; *rûaḥ* may be viewed literally, as wind, or metaphorically (Ex 15^{10}, 1 K 18^{12}, Is 40^{7}, Hos 13^{15}). But, generally, it is used to denote the higher activities of the divine nature, which are, by anthropomorphism (*q.v.*), regarded as similar to the energies of thought and volition in man. Yet there is a striking difference. Only rarely (and that in late passages) is the spirit of man within his control as a subject (Ps 77^{6}, the earliest example); God's spirit, as befits perfect personality, is always at His command—not that it is thought of as another; the Spirit of God is God Himself. The nature of that Spirit is nowhere discussed; it is not presented metaphysically or statically: it is always an energy; the Spirit of God is God at work manifesting effective power. The various spheres of the Spirit's activity may be formulated as cosmical, intellectual, inspirational in the prophets and the Messiah, moral and religious in the 'pious'; but this belongs to dogmatics rather than to the scope of an Encyclopædia. The historical method here pursued, while surveying the entire field, has the added advantage of presenting the successive extensions of the Spirit's activity as they arose under a gradual revelation.[1]

1. Canonical. — i. PRE-EXILIC. — (*a*) *JE and kindred documents* (*9th–8th cent.* B.C.). — The earliest documents of the Pentateuch present the Spirit of Jahweh (or Elohim) in materialistic fashion. It is the divine essence which is common to Jahweh and the *bᵉnê-'elôhim*, as contrasted with flesh, the element proper to human beings (Gn 6^{3} J; cf. Is 31^{3}). By means of the illicit intercourse of the *bᵉnê-'elôhim* with the daughters of men, *rûaḥ* has passed into mankind, producing longevity, if not deathlessness, which Jahweh is resolved to abridge. The text is so confused that nothing can be deduced with certainty as to the action of *rûaḥ*.[2] Materially regarded is the spirit which is transferred from Moses to the seventy elders (Nu $11^{17.\,25}$ JE; cf. 2 K 2^{9}), producing a dual effect, viz. an outbreak of ecstatic transitory prophecy (v.^{15}) and the more abiding gift of rulership. The latter appears also in the case of Joseph (Gn 41^{38} E) and the early judges (Jg 3^{10} 11^{29}). What the outward phenomena of ecstatic prophecy are like is described more fully in the narratives about Balaam and in the earliest stories concerning Saul (Nu $24^{2ff.\,15f.}$ JE; 1 S $10^{1\text{-}13}$ 11^{6}). In language reminiscent of 'demonism' the Spirit of Elohim is said to rush upon Saul, producing amentia and excited utterances like ravings (*nb'* in Hithp.), so that he becomes another man, breaking out in warlike fury (1 S 11^{6}); a later passage states that he lay naked, unconscious, a day and a night (1 S $19^{18\text{-}24}$). In Balaam's case, he is thrown into a trance by the oncoming of the Spirit of Elohim, in which state he receives visions and messages. In such descriptions we have the onlooker's impressions: the unwonted abnormal excitation upon the person 'enthused' is ascribed to the 'spirit' which has taken possession of his faculties. The phenomena of prophet-bands in Saul's day, the use of music as a stimulus (cf. 2 K 3^{15}), and the passage of the 'spirit' by infection to others suggest that the earliest prophecy in Israel was akin to the mantic of heathendom (cf. 1 K 18^{29} of Baal-worship).[3] No messages are preserved (the Songs of Balaam are probably later); the deed alone interprets the Spirit's purpose, and so the patriotic fury of warriors, like Gideon and Saul, and the marvellous prowess of Samson are attributed to the Spirit, as in later days the phenomenal strength of Elijah was due to 'the hand of Jahweh' (1 K 18^{46}).

[1] For the idea of God and its development see art. GOD, vol. vi. p. 254.

[1] For classifications see H. B. Swete, in *HDB* ii. 402; A. B. Davidson, *The Theology of the OT*, Edinburgh, 1904, p. 120 ff.; more detailed in Irving F. Wood, *The Spirit of God in Biblical Literature*, London, 1904; E. W. Winstanley, *Spirit in the NT*, Cambridge, 1908, pp. 1–5.

[2] See Commentaries of Skinner, *ICC*, or Driver, *Westminster Comm.*, *ad loc.*

[3] See E. Rohde, *Psyche*^{2}, Freiburg i. B., 1898, ii. 9.

At this point we may observe some distinction in the use of the divine names. 'Spirit of Elohim' appears to denote the marvellous, the divinely-imparted power, in general; 'Spirit of Jahweh' the working might of Jahweh as it served to deliver Israel, Jahweh's covenant-people, in particular. Spirit of Elohim calls attention to the supersensible cause; Spirit of Jahweh, to the soteriological purpose. But how little of ethical content is conveyed can be seen when the homicidal mania of Saul is ascribed to the Spirit of Elohim (1 S 18^{10}). Yet ethical discrimination begins to appear. The evil spirit which induces the king's insanity is not Spirit *of*, but *from* (*me'eth*, 1 S 16^{15}) Elohim; the good spirit is Spirit of Jahweh.[1] The evil spirit is not so immediately in connexion with Jahweh as the good spirit, though originating causally with Him. The development of that discrimination to a separate hypostatic 'lying' spirit, and thence to a Satan as personal principle of evil (1 K $22^{21f.}$, Job 1^6, Zec 3^1), has a reflex action, beyond the OT limits, on the personality of the Holy Spirit.

(*b*) *Pre-Exilic writing prophets* (*8th cent.* B.C.).—The nature of 'spirit' is less physically viewed by proto-Isaiah; indeed, one passage is unique in presenting 'spirit' almost metaphysically, as the principle of the divine nature, dynamically viewed, and the equivalent of deity itself (Is 30^1 31^3). It is described as a 'subtle essence' poured forth from on high, and has a cosmical reference, in that it causes the amazing fertility of the land and ethical qualities in Israel, its people ($32^{15f.}$). But its special sphere is the national life, making Israel independent of foreign alliances, and invincible (31^3), but, if neglected, as it speaks through the prophet, the nation adds sin to sin (30^1). If this passage is a reference to the prophet's experience, it stands alone, and in the writing prophets such a reference is exceedingly rare. Hosea and Micah have but one such reference each (Hos 9^7, Mic 3^8, text suspect), while Jeremiah and the others, except Ezekiel, have none at all. This striking omission is probably due to the superior elevation of prophecy above the earlier ecstatic form, too closely associated with the term *rûaḥ*. Prophecy is now a clear-minded ethical communion with Jahweh, whilst the symptoms of popular prophecy, resembling drunkenness, and the fact that it could be artificially induced, along with the emphasis on the ecstatic form and not the ethical contents, may account for the preference for the phrase 'hand of Jahweh' (Is 8^{11}, Jer 15^{17}) to denote the force of the constraining prophetic impulse. Even Hosea's reference (9^7, 'the man of the spirit') may be only the popular language, cited by the prophet. The purpose of the Spirit's working is more ethically grasped, Micah receiving it as an aid in proclaiming to the nation its sin.

ii. EXILIC AND POST-EXILIC.—(*a*) *From the Exile to the Temple-rebuilding* (*590–520* B.C.).—The 6th cent. B.C. witnessed a universal impulse and advance to religion. Within this period two great religions, Confucianism and Buddhism, originated and spread; the genius of Greece blossomed in poetry, art, and philosophy, and prophecy reached its climax in Israel. The doctrine of the Spirit shared in this advance, as doubtless it prompted it. The Spirit of Jahweh is presented in manifold aspects as the principle of life and energy in God, the organ of His intelligence at work in creation, evolving order out of primeval chaos (Is 40^{13}, LXX νοῦς, Gn 1^2),[2] executing His purposes in history, even among the lower creatures (Is 34^{16}), the energizing cause of movement in the suprasensible sphere (Ezk $1^{12.\,20}$ 10^{17}), the principle of life which streams into a dead nation, revivifying it at Jahweh's bidding (Ezk 37^{5-9}; cf. Job 32^4), the immaterial principle and organ of mind in man (Ezk 20^{32}, Job 32^8), and the agent working ethical renewal within man (Ezk 11^{19} 18^{31} 36^{25}). Noteworthy is the fact that with the emergence of individualism in Ezekiel's teaching, and the recognition of spirit in man as an integral constituent of personality, the call is issued to man to co-operate with Jahweh in the making of a 'new spirit' into which Jahweh may pour His own (Ezk 18^{31}). And that new spirit is to be the possession not only of the prophet but also of the ideal Israel, as an 'abiding' endowment (Is 42^1), enabling it to carry religion (*mishpāt*) to other nations (cf. Is $44^{3ff.}$), and issuing in a moral life of unbroken fellowship with Jahweh (Ezk 39^{29}). Ezekiel's 'vision of the dry bones' (cf. 37^{1-14}) is the classic passage in all literature for its graphic portrayal of the might of the Spirit in quickening and regenerating a morally dead people, and marks the highest point reached in the OT doctrine of the work of the Spirit, anticipating the description of the Spirit in the NT and the Creeds, as τὸ ζωοποιοῦν (1 Co 15^{46}).

Within this period we mark the first hints of a hypostatization of the Spirit. The apostrophe to the *rûaḥ* in Ezekiel's vision is remarkable, indicating considerable independence (Ezk 37^9); still more so the passage in Deutero-Isaiah (48^{16}, but see Comm. on the text) where Jahweh's Spirit is sent as a working ally with the prophet. Similar traces meet us in the prophets of the Return. The Spirit is presented as 'standing in the midst' of the returned exiles, enabling them to complete the rebuilding of the Temple (Hag 2^5 RVm, Zec 4^6)—a task beyond ordinary human might. But the growing tendency to regard Jahweh as transcendent (cf. Ezk 43^6, the interpreting angel, Zec $1^{9.\,19}$) may account for these prophets making no claim to the possession of the Spirit: it is regarded as a medium whereby Jahweh's words were given to prophets of other and earlier days (Zec 7^{12}). The ebb-tide of prophecy has now begun.

(*b*) *From the Return to the close of the canon* (*520–c.150* B.C.).—In this period, when Israel had come under foreign dominion and legalism began to take the place of prophecy, references to the Spirit of God are confined, in the main, to the past history of Israel or its future glory under the Messiah. In these references the older terminology survives, like a literary tradition, but the 'demonic' might is associated with utterance, whether in song or in impassioned speech (1 Ch 12^{18}, 2 Ch 24^{20}), and the materialistic *rûaḥ* accounts for the superior skill of the craftsmen engaged upon the Temple vestments and furniture, whose 'filling' issues in wisdom, understanding, and knowledge (Ex 28^3 31^3 $25^{30ff.}$ P). This materialistic notion of 'spirit' appears again in the 'anointing' (*q.v.*) of the priest, the king, the prophet, and the Messiah (Ex 29^7 [Aaron], 1 S 10^1 [Saul] 16^{13} [David], Is 61^1 11^{2-4}), as in the ordination of Joshua (Nu 27^{23}). By means of the Spirit thus conveyed such persons became sacrosanct, and the vehicles through whom Jahweh ruled His people. But the emphasis is laid upon the heightened consciousness, as in the case of the Messiah, who is thereby equipped for all His functions, judicial, executive, and religious (Is 11^{2-4}; for date as post-Exilic cf. G. B. Gray, *ICC*, *ad loc.*). The inspiration is dynamic, an intensifying of the faculties, though, in the swan-song of David, the very words are said to be the utterance of the Spirit (2 S 23^2). We mark an increase in the use of personification as applied to the Spirit. He 'speaks' in David, was the instructor and leader of Israel in bygone days, will 'rest' upon the Messianic King, and was 'resisted,' 'rebelled against' and even 'vexed' by the stubborn, sinful nation (2 S 23^2, Neh 9^{20}, Is 63^{14} 11^2, Ps 106^{33}, Is 63^{11}). The last term was much used by the 4th cent. Greek Fathers to prove the personality of the Spirit, but, in view of the passage, a woman 'grieved in spirit' (Is 54^6), and the personification of the 'Word' and

[1] On texts cf. S. R. Driver, *Notes on the Heb. Text of the Books of Samuel*[2], Oxford, 1913, *ad loc.*

[2] Cf. art. COSMOGONY AND COSMOLOGY (Hebrew), vol. iv. p. 154^b, n. 1.

'Wisdom' (Is 55^{11}, Pr 1^{23}, where Wisdom has a 'spirit'), such language should not be unduly pressed. Further, ethical attributes are assigned to the Spirit; it is called 'good' (Neh 9^{20}, Ps 143^{10} RVm) and thrice 'holy' (Is $63^{10.\,11}$, Ps 51^{11}). 'Good,' however, may only indicate the results of its operation, and holy, in itself, does not necessarily carry an ethical connotation.[1] Etymologically the word probably means 'separation'; then it gathered about it the notions of the unapproachable—what, in comparative religions, is meant by the term 'tabu' (*q.v.*)—and acquired the signification of the divine as contrasted with the human, and is applied to things and places as belonging to God (cf. 'holy hill, arm,' etc.). Any ethical meaning that the term conveys depends upon how the Deity is conceived. From Proto-Isaiah onwards the prophets had conceived of God as ethical, and ethical requirements had been enjoined upon Israel, so that in fact, as well as in name, she should be God's 'holy people.' And it is precisely in connexion with Israel's refusal to accept the divine leading that the term is employed of the Spirit, and so the phrase 'His (thy) Holy Spirit' indicates 'a principle which is both pure and inviolable, which resents and draws back from the contact of human impurity and especially of wilful opposition.'[2] With this use of personal language we find an advance in the hypostatization of Jahweh's Holy Spirit when it is used in parallelism with the 'angel of the Presence,' as the medium of the divine guidance of Israel in the wilderness (Is $63^{9-11.\,14}$; but cf. LXX). 'The angel of His Presence' (*mal'akh pānâv*) appears to be a combination of *theologoumena* (cf. Ex $23^{20.\,22}$ *mal'akh*, 33^{14} *panâi*) which indicate how the transcendent Deity could yet temporarily descend to visibility, whilst 'Holy Spirit' presents His living energy at work in the people. This hypostatization, however, does not reach, though it prepares for, the doctrine of an inner distinction within the Godhead. In philosophical terms, the Spirit is the means whereby the Deity can be regarded as immanent and yet transcendent. Thus the term 'Spirit' could be used as synonymous with 'Divine Presence,' either as subjectively experienced by the penitent, whom it quickens with a poignant sense of sin (Ps 51^{11}), or, more objectively regarded, as omnipresent and omniscient (Ps 139^{7}). And so it was the bond uniting the worshipper with his God.

Such experiences in the OT were very rare, and eschatological hopes looked forward to the gift of the Spirit as a distinguishing feature of the day of the Lord, when it would be the perpetual possession of all Israel (Is 59^{21}), irrespective of sex or age (Jl 2^{28-30}), and there would be fulfilled the great wish of Moses, 'Would God that all the Lord's people were prophets, and that the Lord would put his spirit upon them!' (Nu 11^{29}).

2. Extra-canonical.—(*a*) *Palestinian.*—In this section, which extends to the end of the 2nd cent. A.D., the references to the Spirit of God are chiefly backward to canonical Scriptures or forward to Messianic hopes. The term 'Holy Spirit' is used more frequently, probably to indicate its ethical character and distinguish it from the crowd of spirits that fill the air, but it means little more than a pious disposition in individuals.[3] It is a *charisma*, giving skill in dream-interpretation, or pre-vision of the future, in the prophet or the blessings of the Patriarchs.[4] There is a marked emphasis on ethical qualities as the condition and result of its operation, and once it is said to be the creator of life, *i.e.* life after death.[1] Its vehicle in the future will be the Messiah, empowering Him for all various functions as ruler and judge by its abiding presence, and He in turn shall communicate it to men.[2] The hypostatization of the Spirit advances in this period to full personality. His mission at the creation is distinctly asserted,[3] He works independently of God,[4] and, in passages probably influenced by Christian ideas, the Spirit is the mother of Jesus,[5] a fellow-counsellor of Christ,[6] and stands in the place of God, as the object of worship,[7] though in angelic form.

(*b*) *Jewish-Alexandrian* (*Wisdom of Solomon, c. 150–50 B.C., Philo, 20 B.C.–A.D. 50*).—The outstanding feature in these authors is the attempt to combine Hebrew conceptions of spirit with those of Stoicism (*q.v.*). In Wisdom the term 'spirit' is bound up with wisdom, with which it is practically identified (1^{5-7} 9^{17}), and in which it is inherent (7^{22}; but cf. LXX A). This Spirit, whether of Wisdom or of the Lord, is presented as a material ductile essence, permeating and pervading the universe, of which it is the cohesive bond ($7^{22\text{ff.}}$ 1^{7} 12^{1}). Streaming into man by the divine inbreathing, it constitutes him an active soul and originates his spiritual nature (15^{11}, πνεῦμα ζωτικόν), and, in accord with the κοιναὶ ἔννοιαι of the Stoics, is the cause of his understanding of the phenomenal universe and the hidden counsel of God (7^{7} 9^{17} τὸ ἅγιόν σου πνεῦμα). It is an ethical principle, training men to virtue, fleeing from the wicked, and, since it is an extension of the divine Spirit into men, it is the medium whereby God is cognizant of their thoughts and deeds (1^{5-9}). The materialistic implications of 'spirit' check the tendency to hypostatize and personify it, and wisdom, which had been quasi-personalized in earlier literature (cf. Job 28, Pr 8^{22-31}, Sir 24^{3-12}), takes its place, and is more personally regarded, without, however, becoming fully a person or ceasing to be an attribute of God.[8]

In Philo both wisdom and Spirit are overshadowed by his doctrine of the Logos (*q.v.*). The Spirit of God (θεῖον πνεῦμα, πνεῦμα θεοῦ) is mentioned only (but cf. *de Migr. Abr.* ch. 7) when making citations from OT, and these are limited to man's creation and inspiration.

> 'The conception of πνεῦμα [in Philo] may be regarded as being closely analogous to the modern conception of "force," and especially to that form of the conception which makes no distinction of essence between "mind-force" and other kinds of force, such as light or electricity. It is analogous but not identical; for force is conceived to be immaterial, whereas πνεῦμα, however subtle, is still material.'[9]

The spirit which was imparted to man at his creation is the divine Spirit, which is 'a stamp and impress of the Divine power,'[10] a 'colony from that blessed nature,'[11] 'the image of the Divine and invisible,'[12] 'the basis (οὐσία) of our thinking reasonable nature.'[13] But it is not severed from its source, of which it is an extension, as a ray from the sun,[14] and this connexion explains how man is able to grasp God's thought,[15] for the πνεῦμα is 'the pure science of which every wise

1 See art. HOLINESS.

2 J. Skinner, *Isaiah*, Cambridge, 1896–98, ii. 201; see also Skinner, art. 'Holiness' in *HDB*, and A. B. Davidson, *Theology of the OT*, pp. 144 ff., 252 ff.

3 Sus 45; Theod. Jub. i. 22 f. citing Ps 51^{11}.

4 Dn 5^{12} 6^{4} LXX, $4^{5.\,6}$ Theod.; Sir 48^{24}; *Test. Pat.* Lev. 2^{8}; Jub 25^{14} 31^{12}.

1 *Apoc. Bar.* 23^{5}; cf. 4 Mac 7^{14}.

2 *Ps.-Sol.* 17^{42} 18^{8}; En. 49^{3} 62^{2} 67^{10}; *Test. Pat.* Lev. 18^{6}, Judah 24^{2}.

3 Judith 16^{14}.

4 *Sibyll.* 3^{701}.

5 Jerome, *Com. in Isaiam*, on Is 11^{2}, *Com. in Michæam*, on Mic 7^{6}, etc.

6 *Acts Thom.* 39^{50}.

7 *Ascension of Isaiah*, ed. R. H. Charles, London, 1900, p. l, Introd.

8 Wis 7^{26}; see, further, T. Rees, 'The Spirit of God as Wisdom,' in *Mansfield College Essays*, London, 1909, p. 289 ff.; *Apocrypha and Pseudepig. of OT*, Oxford, 1913, i. 528.

9 E. Hatch, *Essays in Biblical Greek*, Oxford, 1889, p. 126.

10 *Quod det. pot. insid.* 22.

11 *De Mund. opific.* 46.

12 *De Plant. Noe*, 5.

13 *De Concup.* 10.

14 *Quod det. pot. insid.* 24, *de Concup.* 11.

15 *Leg. Alleg.* i. 13, *Vit. Mos.* iii. 36.

man is a partaker.'[1] All men have visitations of the divine Spirit, but in men of pleasure, owing to the flesh, it makes no lasting stay, whilst its continuance with the prophet and philosopher requires that their normal faculties lie in abeyance, and, in ecstasy, they are played upon by the Spirit as the harpist strikes his harp.[2] Personal language is used to describe the mode of approach and the operations of the Spirit. It 'seeks men,' 'guides their feet to truth,' 'strengthens all and conquers all that is beneath'; it has distinctive properties as 'invisible,' 'all-wise,' 'divine,' 'indivisible,' etc.,[3] but such language, in view of the entire system of Philonic thought, does not denote personality. Whatever personalization and hypostatization of divine qualities take place must be looked for in connexion with the Logos.

LITERATURE.—In addition to works cited, the following may be consulted: E. Kautzsch, art. 'Religion of Israel,' in *HDB* v. 612 ff.; E. König, *Gesch. des AT Religion*, Gütersloh, 1912; H. W. Robinson, *The Religious Ideas of the OT*, London, 1913; H. B. Swete, art. 'Holy Spirit,' in *HDB* ii. 402–405.

III. *JEWISH* (*POST-BIBLICAL, TALMUDIC, AND POST-TALMUDIC*).—The Rabbinical teaching concerning the Spirit of God, or the Holy Spirit, belongs to the Haggādāh and shares the discursive, non-systematic character of that branch of instruction. The absence of doctrinal formularies from Talmudic Judaism[4] gave room for all shades of opinion, provided that they could in some way be connected with the letter of the OT Scriptures and did not contravene the doctrine of the *Shᵉmāʿ* (Dt 6^{4-6}). Hence no systematic or authoritative doctrine of the Holy Spirit can be deduced from the mass of traditions contained in the Gemara and the Midrashim, and the anonymous authorship of many sayings about the Holy Spirit makes the tracing of the historical development of doctrine well-nigh impossible. References to the Holy Spirit increase as we pass from the Mishnāh to the two Talmuds and the homilies in the Midrashim, but this increase is due mainly to the greater quantity of Haggādic materials contained in the latter sources. From the Targums, notwithstanding the fact that in their present form they are later than the Mishnāh (*c.* A.D. 200), we may roughly ascertain how the Holy Spirit was regarded in the early Synagogue. In the Talmuds we may see the opinions of the schools from the 2nd to the 6th cent. A.D., and the Midrashim, while containing early materials, bring us to the 11th cent. A.D.

The terms 'Spirit of God,' 'Spirit of Jahweh,' occur sparingly in Targums and Talmuds, owing to the desire to avoid the mention of the divine name, and the Holy Spirit (*rûaḥ haqqôdesh*, m., f. *qudshā'*) takes its place. The term 'holy' serves to denote that the Spirit belongs in some way to the sphere of the divine, and distinguishes it from the crowd of spirits which filled the air, according to Jewish belief. Sometimes the Targums translate 'Spirit of God,' 'Spirit of Jahweh,' by 'spirit of might' (*rûaḥ gᵉbûāh*), to interpret the 'demonic' working of the Spirit upon the early heroes, judges, and kings (Jg 13^{25} $14^{6.19}$ 15^{14}, 1 S 11^{6} 16^{14}, 1 Ch 12^{18}), but more frequently as 'spirit of prophecy' (*rûaḥ nᵉbû'āh*), to denote inspiration in its varied forms. The Holy Spirit is identified with the spirit of prophecy,[5] and the phrase 'my Spirit' is expanded into 'my Holy Spirit,' when used of God.[6] Once it is beautifully rendered 'spirit of compassions.'[7] In Is $63^{10ff.}$ we find 'the words of His holy prophets' for 'His ('thy') Holy Spirit,' and this paraphrase may be due to the desire to avoid early Christian applications of that passage to prove the hypostatization of the Holy Spirit. The relationship of *rûaḥ haqqôdesh* to God is expressed by the phrase *min qedhem*, lit. 'from before, or the presence of'—a phrase the significance of which is much disputed. According to modern Jewish writers, it is used merely to avoid anthropomorphic ideas concerning God, and the use of the divine name,[1] whereas others interpret it as distinctly hypostatizing the Holy Spirit, placing Him alongside of Meṭaṭron, Memra, and Shekinah, the beings who mediate the activities of God upon the world and mankind.[2] The controversy is part of the larger question whether the conception of God in rabbinic Judaism made Him so transcendent and absolute as to require these mediating agencies, and left no room for His immanence in the world and man. This view is valid if Judaism can be presented as a philosophical system, but it overlooks the testimony of religious experience, which felt, especially in prayer, that God was very near.[3] On the other hand, as W. O. E. Oesterley remarks,[4] 'it is significant how in modern handbooks on Judaism, this specifically Rabbinical doctrine of intermediate beings between God and man is passed over in silence.' The more recent attempt of Abelson[5] to extract a doctrine of divine immanence from Rabbinical literature is little else than a *tour de force*. Keeping strictly to the term *min qedhem*, it denotes, as applied to *rûaḥ haqqôdesh*, not so much 'the Spirit *of* God' as the 'Holy Spirit *near* God.'[6] As such there is hypostatization, but no clear emphasis upon 'personality.'

Along with Meṭaṭron and Shekinah, *rûaḥ haqqôdesh* occupies 'an intermediate position between personalities and abstract beings. While, on the one hand, they are represented as being so closely connected with God as to appear as parts of Him, or attributes, they are, on the other hand, so often spoken of as undertaking individual actions that they must be differentiated from God.'[7]

In the Talmud the Memra does not play the rôle which marks the Targums, possibly because it lay too near in thought to the Logos doctrine in early Christian discussions, and Shekinah is more frequently used than *rûaḥ haqqôdesh*. They appear to be used indiscriminately and interchangeably, and both are presented as the source of prophecy.[8] It is difficult to draw any distinction between the two terms, and yet in some passages some distinction seems intended.[9] Perhaps Shekinah mediates the presence of God more objectively in shining splendour, and *rûaḥ haqqôdesh* more subjectively to the human mind,[10] though *rûaḥ haqqôdesh* is regarded at times as manifest in forms of light and glory. There is a marked advance upon OT teaching in the use of language suggestive of hypostatization and personal activities in the Talmudic references to the Shekinah and *rûaḥ haqqôdesh*. In several passages *rûaḥ haqqôdesh* is clearly distinguished from God, as when He acts as mediator between Israel and God[11] and 'cries' to God.[12] Personal activities are described when He is said to speak, cry, rest upon, depart[13] from any one. He is said to weep,[14] to lead like a shepherd,[15] and even to love.[16] In this usage we find it used as a masc. substantive;[17] more usually, however, it denotes an impersonal power and is used as fem. substantive. A favourite term to describe its coming is *shārā'*, 'to settle upon,' whereby its action is presented as staccato and momentary, not as a permanent indwelling. It comes from heaven, or the Holy Place, but, in view of the rabbinical polemic against the presence of two powers in heaven,[18] we are not to think of any distinction within the Godhead. As in OT, so in Talmudic teaching, the nature of *rûaḥ haqqôdesh* is often put in materialistic and impersonal terms. It was one of the ten things created on the first day;[19] it can be drawn up, like water, from the wells of salvation;[20] it is likened to a weight which God measures out;[21] more frequently it is described as light and glory which glimmers and shines upon persons (cf. Pauline δόξα). It shone in the three court-houses of Shem, Samuel, and Solomon,[22] glimmered (נצוצה) upon Jacob, his sons, and Tamar;[23] when it shone upon Phinehas, his face glowed like a torch;[24] it shone on Moses, and passed from him to the seventy elders as a light from lamp to lamp.[25] In passages

[1] *De Gig.* 5, on Bezalel, Ex. 31^{3}; cf. E. Bréhier, *Les Idées philosophiques et religieuses de Philon*, Paris, 1908, p. 134 ff.

[2] *De Gig.* 5, *Quis rer. divin. heres.* 53, *de Mono.* 1, *ad fin.*, *de Spec. Legg.* iv. § 8; cf. Plato, *Timæus*, 71 D.

[3] *Somn.* ii. 252, *Plant. Noe*, 24, *Vit. Mos.* ii. 265, in L. Cohn and P. Wendland, *Philonis Alexandrini Opera*, 3 vols., Berlin, 1896–99.

[4] See art. CREEDS (Jewish).

[5] Targ. Jer. to Gn 41^{38}.

[6] Ps.-Jon. to Gn 6^{3}, Is 42^{1} 44^{3}, Ps 143^{10}.

[7] Ps.-Jon. Gn 1^{26}.

[1] Cf. *JE* vi. 6; J. Abelson, *The Immanence of God in Rabbinical Literature*, London, 1912, pp. 13, 37, 197, etc.

[2] Cf. F. W. Weber, *Jüd. Theol.*², Leipzig, 1897, § 40; P. Volz, *Der Geist Gottes*, Tübingen, 1910, p. 165.

[3] Cf. J. *Beraḥ*, 13*a*; *Debar. R.* 102*a*; and, in general, R. T. Herford, *Pharisaism: its Aim and Method*, London, 1912, pp. 250–262; C. G. Montefiore, *Liberal Judaism*, do. 1903, p. 55 f.

[4] *The Jewish Doct. of Mediation*, London, 1910, p. 197.

[5] *Op. cit.*

[6] Volz, p. 165.

[7] Oesterley, p. 197; cf. W. Bousset, *Die Rel. des Judenthums*², Berlin, 1906, p. 394 ff.

[8] Cf. B. *Sôṭāh*, 9*b*; J. *Ab. Zar.* 42*c*; B. *Bᵉrāk.* 31*b*; B. *Sanh.* 11*a*; B. *Bābhā Bathrā*, 134*a*, *b*; B. *Sôṭāh*, 13*a*; *Vajjik. R.* 8^{2}; *Meḥilta*, 44*a*, ed. M. Friedmann (Vienna, 1870), med. pag.; *Qoh. R.* 1^{2}; *Yalk. Sim.* to Jon. 1; Rashi on B. *Ḥag.* 13*b*; cf. Abelson, App. 1.

[9] Cf. B. *Yômā*, 21*b*; B. *Sanh.* 11*a*; *Meḥilta* to Ex 14^{12} (Friedmann, p. 28ᵇ), where Shekinah sends *rûaḥ haqqôdesh*.

[10] Weber, § 40.

[11] *Vajj. R.* 6^{1}; *Debar. R.* 3.

[12] *Cant. R.* 8^{12}; *Esther R.* 10^{4}; *Yalk. Sim.* to Est 5^{2}.

[13] *Gen. R.* 60^{3} 65^{4}: נטלה; נסתלקה.

[14] *Ex. R.* 15^{15}.

[15] *Pirqē de R. Eliezer*, 39.

[16] *Yalk. Sim.* to Jer 1^{5}.

[17] *Qoh. R.* 7^{29} (A.V. 28).

[18] Cf. B. *Ḥag.* 15*a*.

[19] B. *Ḥag.* 12*a*, *b*; cf. M. Friedländer's tr. of *Pirqē R. Eliezer*, ch. 3, pp. 12, 27.

[20] Is 12^{3}, J. *Sukk.* 55*a*; *Gen. R.* 70. 9; *Pesîqtā Rabbathi*, ed. Friedmann, 1ᵇ; *Ruth R.* 4^{12}; cf. Jn 7^{37-39}.

[21] *Vajj. R.* 16^{2} on Job 28^{25}.

[22] B. *Makk.* 23*b*, הופיע; *Qoh. R.* 10^{16}; *Gen. R.* 85^{12}.

[23] *Gen. R.* 74^{19} 84^{19} 91^{7} 85^{9}.

[24] *Vajj. R.* 1^{1}.

[25] *Ib.* 32^{4}; *Debar. R.* 13^{20}.

penetrating human nature,'[1] or death was necessary to liberate Christ's spirit from bodily and spatial limitations (Holtzmann, Loisy), is not expressly stated. Rather, the Spirit is withheld until the revelation which it is His office to explain and enforce is completed. The Spirit's relation to the Son is analogous to that of the Son to the Father. He comes not in His own name, to speak self-originated messages, but to testify to and glorify the Son, even as the Son did the Father. Within the Church the Spirit is the mode whereby the Risen Lord is yet present, and, as the 'other Paraclete,' the Spirit is a perpetual immanent teacher and exegete, a colleague in the Church's witness for Christ, convincing and convicting the world of its unbelief, wrongness, peril, and guilt ($14^{16f. 26}$ 15^{26} 16^{8-11}). His activity is so real and effective within the Church that all previous workings of the Spirit are, in comparison, as nothing (7^{39}), and 'from the Spirit' the individual gains the assurance that he abides in God and God abides in him (1 Jn 3^{24} 4^{13}).

LITERATURE.—The following may also be consulted: on the term 'Paraclete' ('Advocate'): J. C. Hare, *The Mission of the Comforter*^{3}, ed. E. H. Plumptre, London, 1876, note K; E. Hatch, *Essays in Biblical Greek*, Oxford, 1889, p. 82 f.; F. Field, *Notes on Translation of NT* (Otium Norvic. iii.), Cambridge, 1899, p. 102 f.; E. A. Abbott, *Johannine Vocabulary*, London, 1905, 1720 k., *Paradosis*, do. 1904, 1413 a.; B. F. Westcott, *Speaker's Comm.*, ii. [do. 1880] 211 f., add. Note to Jn 14^{16}; T. Zahn, *Das Evang. des Johannes*^{2}, Leipzig, 1909, p. 554.

More generally: F. J. A. Hort, *The Way, The Truth, The Life*, Cambridge and London, 1894; M. Goguel, *La Notion johannique de l'esprit*, Paris, 1902; E. F. Scott, *The Fourth Gospel*^{2}, Edinburgh, 1909; B. W. Bacon, *The Fourth Gospel in Research and Debate*, London, 1910; J. Moffatt, *The Theology of the Gospels*, do. 1912, ch. v.; artt. in *DCG* (J. Denney, W. R. Inge) on 'Holy Spirit,' and 'John, Gospel of,' give good bibliographies.

V. *CHURCH HISTORY AND DOCTRINE.*—Each of the great periods of Church history—the Patristic, mediæval, and Reformation—has been occupied with some aspect of this complex theme. In the first period (1st to 6th cent.) the Fathers drew the main lines of doctrine concerning the personality, deity, and procession of the Holy Spirit. That doctrine of the procession was, during the mediæval period, one of the causes which, unhappily, still sunder the Eastern and Western Churches. At the Reformation and during the modern period interest centred chiefly in the work of the Holy Spirit in redemption and sanctification, and the constitution and organization of the Christian Church. Such results as have attended these discussions are formulated in creeds, symbols, and confessions. There is, however, a striking disproportion between the place of the Holy Spirit in the formularies of the Church and in its religious experience. For the latter we must have recourse to the liturgies and hymns used in worship, to movements (Montanism, Mysticism, Quakerism) which have often been frowned upon, if not repressed, by ecclesiasticism, and religious biographies; and outside the Church philosophical discussions have modified the concepts of spirit and personality, so that there is a wide-spread conviction in the present age that the Patristic formulation in the Creeds of the doctrine of the Holy Spirit is inadequate and requires to be re-moulded and re-stated in terms of modern thought. These various aspects may be grouped thus, following, so far as possible, the chronological order: (1) to the formulation of the deity and personality of the Holy Spirit in the Nicæno-Constantinopolitan Creed (to A.D. 381–451); (2) the doctrine of the Procession to the Great Schism ('Filioque' controversy); (3) distinctive developments within Roman Catholicism (to Vatican Council, A.D. 1870); (4) Reformation and post-Reformation developments; (5) the Holy Spirit in liturgies and hymnology; (6) mysticism and the Holy Spirit; (7) modern philosophy and the Holy Spirit.

I. To the Nicæno-Constantinopolitan Creed (Chalcedon, A.D. 451).—The doctrine of the person of the Holy Spirit is part of the general Christian doctrine of God,[2] and the relations of the Holy

[1] W. Milligan, *The Ascension and Heavenly Priesthood of Our Lord*, London, 1891, pp. 209 ff., 213.
[2] See art. GOD, vol. vi. esp. pp. 259–263.

Spirit to the other Persons, and to the Son specifically, fall for fuller consideration under the art. TRINITY. The deliberate formulation of the doctrine does not begin until the middle of the 4th cent. and could not be attempted until the Church had settled the previous question as to the divinity of Christ. The result may be at once stated. The article in the Nicene Creed, *καὶ (πιστεύομεν δὲ) εἰς τὸ ἅγιον πνεῦμα*, is expanded in the so-called Nicæno-Constantinopolitan Creed to *καὶ (πιστεύομεν δὲ) εἰς τὸ πνεῦμα τὸ ἅγιον, τὸ κύριον, τὸ ζωοποιόν, τὸ ἐκ τοῦ πατρὸς ἐκπορευόμενον, τὸ σὺν πατρὶ καὶ υἱῷ συνπροσκυνούμενον καὶ συνδοξαζόμενον, τὸ λαλῆσαν διὰ τῶν προφητῶν.*[1]

We may take these two Creeds as landmarks for the historical stages of the discussion: (*a*) to A.D. 325; (*b*) 325–381 (?)

(*a*) *To A.D. 325.*—The apostolic age bequeathed to its successors four views of the Holy Spirit: (1) as an attribute of God without hypostatization; (2) as an impersonal energy or operation; (3) as a gift, expressed in impersonal terms; (4) as a Person with distinct hypostatization. The last was kept prominent before the Church by the baptismal formula,[2] the constant association of the Holy Spirit with the Father and the Son as the object of faith and worship, and the expositions of the faith such as meet us in the various early forms of the so-called Apostles' Creed.[3] The 2nd cent. apologists, in their polemic with heathendom, fell back upon the better-known philosophical terms, the Logos and Wisdom (*qq.v.*), to explain the creative providential operations of God in the world, and the inspiration of Scripture (OT), and, like Philo before them, found it difficult to keep the concept of Spirit distinct from that of the Logos.[4] In the early crude Christological speculations the Spirit, viewed as a divine essence, was frequently identified with the Son.[5] Gradually, however, the distinction between the Son (=pre-existent Logos) and the Spirit becomes clearer, Justin placing the Spirit third in order[6] in the divine name, Theophilus introducing the term 'Trinity' (*τριάς*) in a passage where Wisdom (=Spirit) is differentiated from the Logos;[7] and Athenagoras appears to have grasped the idea of the Spirit as the unifying bond of the divine life, and marks the unity and distinction of these united beings.[8] Yet he withholds the predicate *θεός* from the Spirit, when it is given to the Father and the Son;[9] Justin appears to rank Him with angels as objects of worship,[10] and Tatian subordinates Him to the Son as His 'minister.'[11] The same position is found in the Gnosticism (*q.v.*) of Basilides,[12] and the necessity of refuting the many Gnostic systems, by reflex action, directed attention to the inner relations within the Deity, though the Son rather than the Spirit was the main theme of consideration. Summaries of the traditional teaching of the Church were drawn up as Rules of Faith, and made the norm by which heretical doctrines were tested.[13] Irenæus, as against the

[1] H. Denzinger, *Enchiridion symbolorum, definitionum et declarationum*^{12}, Freiburg i. B., 1913, pp. 30, 38.
[2] Mt 28^{19}; cf. *Did.* vii. 1, 3; Justin Mart. *Apol.* i. $61^{3. 13}$.
[3] For Old Roman Symbol cf. art. CREEDS AND ARTICLES (Ecumenical), vol. iv. p. 237^{b}.
[4] Just. Mart. *Apol.* ii. 10; Theophilus of Antioch, *ad Autol.* i. 7, ii. 10, 15, 18, 23; Athenagoras, *Leg.* 5; cf. T. Rees, *The Holy Spirit*, London, 1915, p. 114 ff.
[5] Just. Mart. *Apol.* i. 33; Hermas, *Sim.* v. 5. 2, 6. 5, ix. 1. 1; Pseud-Clem., *ad Cor.* 9^{5} 14^{3}; cf. Iren. *adv. Hær.* v. 1, 2; Tatian, *Or. ad Græc.* 7; Tertull. *Apol.* 21, *adv. Marc.* iii. 16, 6, *de Car. Chr.* 18; see Lightfoot, *ad* Clem. Rom. ix. 4, and art. ADOPTIANISM, vol. i. p. 103^{b}.
[6] *Apol.* i. 13, *τάξις*.
[7] *Ad Autol.* ii. 15.
[8] *Leg.* 10. 4, 12. 2, 24.
[9] *Ib.* 10.
[10] *Apol.* i. 6.
[11] *Or. adv. Græc.* 13.
[12] Cf. vol. ii. p. 429.
[13] Cf. Iren. *adv. Hær.* i. 10. 1, iii. 3. 1, i. 9. 4; Tert. *de Præsc. Hær.* 13, *de Vel. Virg.* 1, *adv. Prax.* ii. 9 (ed. A. Souter, London, 1920), *adv. Marc.* i. 5, 21; Origen, *de Princ.*, præf.

emanation theory of Valentinus, who placed the Son and the Holy Spirit remotely and secondarily in a syzygy, unites them with God as 'His Hands' by which He created the world,[1] and Tertullian, unlike Irenæus, does not hesitate to borrow the Gnostic term προβολή (Lat. *emissio*) to describe the mode of issue of the Son and the Spirit from God, but he guards against the notion that it implies severance, and uses the illustrations of the root, the tree, and the fruit, the fountain, the river, and the stream, the sun, the ray, and the apex, to express the processions of the Son and the Spirit from, whilst yet continuing in union with, God.[2] Against the Monarchianism (*q.v.*) of Praxeas he asserted an economical Trinity, in which the Spirit had a hypostatic distinction, being third in order, 'the third name of divinity,' the 'vicar' of the Son, to whom He is subordinate, though He is divine, since He is 'of one substance' with the Father.[3] In Sabellianism (*q.v.*) the Holy Spirit receives more mention, but He and the Father and the Son are merely phases of the successive temporal manifestations of God, who is, in Stoic fashion, by a dialectic process, extended into a Trinity and contracts into a monad again, and thereby hypostatic distinction vanishes.[4] With Paul of Samosata (*c.* 269) the Logos and the Spirit are identical, and simply properties or attributes of God, and the Spirit wrought in Jesus as a mere power or influence, 'not essentially (οὐσιωδῶς) but as a quality' (ποιότητα). The two forms of Monarchianism, the modalistic and the dynamistic, found in Sabellius and Paul of Samosata their clearest utterance, and their standpoints also indicate the rival theories, representative of heathen pantheism and Jewish monotheism respectively, which confronted the Church. Origen (*c.* A.D. 185–254) rose above the materialistic Stoical view of Tertullian,[5] for to him the Holy Spirit was no mere influence, but 'an intellectual substance,' 'an energetic essence but not an energy,'[6] but in his freer speculations he regarded the Spirit, like Tertullian, as subordinate to the Son. Discussing the passage 'all things were made by Him' (*sc.* the Logos, Jn 1[3]), he throws out three possible views: (*a*) that the Spirit was made by the Logos; or (*b*) was 'ungenerate' (ἀγέννητον[7]), like the Father; or (*c*) has no proper essence (οὐσία) beyond the Father and the Son. He inclines to (*a*), allowing that the Spirit is in honour and rank above all other creatures, but younger than and inferior to the Son, whom He needs for both subsistence and attributes.[8] As Westcott observed, the temporal manifestation, and not the essential immanence, of the Trinity is in view.[9] Elsewhere Origen had pointed out that Scripture had nowhere clearly indicated whether the Spirit is to be regarded as born or (like the Father) 'ungenerate,' as also whether He was a Son or not.[10] But a different note is heard when he states that he found no passage in Scripture asserting that He is a creature, and that in the Rule of Faith the Spirit is associated with the Father and the Son in dignity and honour, and that there can be nothing greater or less within the Trinity.[11] Both these views came into collision in the next century, the subordinationism finding expression in Dionysius of Alexandria († A.D. 265)

1 *Adv. Hær.* iv. præf. 4; cf. *ib.* 7. 4.
2 *Adv. Prax.* 7, 8, 25.
3 *Ib.* 9, 30, *de Præsc. Hær.* 13, *adv. Prax.* 2 (ed. A. Souter, London, 1920); cf. *ERE* vi. 261[a].
4 Epiphanius, *Hær.* 62; Basil. *Epp.* 210. 5, 214. 5; Athanasius, *Or. c. Arian*, iv. 12, 25.
5 Cf. Tert. *de Anima*, 5-9.
6 *De Princ.* I. i. 3; frag. 37, ed. A. E. Brooke, *The Commentary of Origen on S. John's Gospel*, Cambridge, 1896, ii. 252.
7 For this term cf. art. EUNOMIANISM, vol. v. p. 575[a]; Suicer, *Thes.*, Amsterdam, 1682, pp. 49-53.
8 *In Joan.* ii. 10 [6].
9 *DCB* iv. 136[b].
10 *De Princ.*, præf.
11 *Ib.* I. iii. 7; præf., 4.

and Eusebius of Cæsarea (A.D. 264–340),[1] the other, based on Scripture and tradition, passing by way of Gregory of Neocæsarea († A.D. 270)—who spoke of the Spirit as 'having His subsistence from the Father'[2] and 'above creaturely state or servitude, co-eternal, equal in sovereignty, and ever with the Son'[3]—to Athanasius and thence to the great Cappadocians, Basil, Gregory of Nazianzus, and Gregory of Nyssa. Yet Origen prepared the way for the ultimate solution by his doctrine of the generation of the Son as an eternal immanent relation within the Godhead, which explained the consubstantiality of the Son and the Father, and then, by inference, of the Spirit with both.

(*b*) *To A.D. 325–381.*—Before dealing with that solution, we must briefly outline the outward history within this period. Although Arius in his *Thalia* regarded the Trinity as composed of persons whose glories and essences differed infinitely,[4] another generation passed before the question concerning the Spirit's place in the Godhead was definitely considered. The various Arian and semi-Arian synods held between 340 and 360 mentioned the Spirit in their creeds, but confined their attention to His work in the main, admitted His personal existence, anathematized those who regarded Him as a part of God, or, in Sabellian fashion, confused Him with the Father and the Son,[5] but went no further than affirming a unity of agreement between the 'Persons' of the Trinity, and hesitated about assigning the predicate of deity to the Spirit.[6] But about A.D. 358 in Egypt, and a few years later in Asia Minor, under the influence of a deposed bishop of Constantinople, Macedonius, and his follower, Marathonius, the doctrine was widely disseminated, reaching the West in a short time, that the Spirit 'was simply a creature, a servant of the Son, one of the ministering spirits, differing only in degree from the angels.'[7] They were variously styled Macedonians, Marathonians, 'Pneumatomachoi,' and, by Athanasius, the 'Tropicoi,' because they interpreted Scripture passages as τροποί, 'metaphors.' At once this view was assailed by synods, orations, and the pen. At Alexandria, in 362 and 363, it was anathematized, and the deity, consubstantiality,[8] and the duty of glorifying the Spirit with the Father and Son were enjoined.[9] In the West a series of councils were held in Rome (A.D. 369–380),[10] adopting the same course, and a letter from Pope Damasus expressing Western opinion was endorsed by no fewer than 146 Eastern bishops at Antioch in A.D. 378. Finally in 381, at Constantinople, a council (later recognized as the 2nd ecumenical) was held, at which the Nicene Creed was confirmed, the Macedonians anathematized, the worship of the Spirit as co-equal with the Father and the Son enjoined by imperial decree (and rigorously enforced by a subscription test two years later).[11] The decisions, however, rested on weightier support than the imperial fiat. Athanasius (*q.v.*), the great Cappadocian triumvirate,[12] Didymus the Blind, and Epiphanius had written treatises or produced orations refuting the Mace-

1 *de Ecc. Theol.* iii. 6.
2 *Expositio Fidei* (*PG* x. 985 f.).
3 *Ib.*, *ad fin.*
4 Athan. *de Syn.* 15.
5 Cf. Athan. *de Syn.* §§ 23–30; for creeds see Hahn-Harnack, *Bibliothek der Symbole*[3], Breslau, 1897, pp. 183–209.
6 Cf. 2nd Conf. of Antioch, A.D. 341, and the 'Macrostich,' A.D. 345.
7 Athan. *Ep. ad Serap.* i. 1; cf. art. MACEDONIANISM, vol. viii. p. 225.
8 So Soc. *HE* iii. 7.
9 Athan. *ad Jovian.* 4.
10 Cf. Hefele, *Conciliengesch.*[2], Freiburg i. B., 1873–90, i. 739–743.
11 For the question as to the validity of the Council and whether the creed which bears its name actually emanated from it cf. artt. COUNCILS AND SYNODS, vol. iv. p. 190[b], CREEDS AND ARTICLES (Ecumenical), vol. iv. p. 239 f.
12 See art. CAPPADOCIAN THEOLOGY.

donians and Eunomianism (*q.v.*), and worked out a doctrine of the Trinity. We summarize their conclusions so far as they bear upon the deity and personality of the Holy Spirit. That the Spirit is a living being is assumed because scarcely questioned. Yet Gregory of Nazianzus discusses every possible view. The Spirit either is a self-subsisting substance, or subsists in another as an accident, or in God. If an accident, He would be an activity of God, actuated but not active, and ceasing to be when the activity ceased. If a substance (*οὐσία*), He is either a creature of God or God. But Scripture says that He is active, 'working,' 'speaking,' 'separating,' etc., so He is more than an energy, an accident of God; and, since also we believe in Him and are perfected in Him, He is no creature, but is included in the idea of God. Therefore in substance He must be God, otherwise a creature *essentially* different from the divine would be intruded within the Trinity, and the unity of the Trinity would be disrupted. And it were blasphemous to worship a creature.[1] Further, the predicates of eternity and omnipresence ascribed by Scripture (Ac 5^{3}, 1 Co $2^{10f.}$ 3^{16} 12^{14}, 2 Co 3^{14-18} 13^{14}, 1 Jn 4^{13}, Mt 28^{19}, Gn 1^{2} most cited) to the Spirit, His glorious titles, His innate underived goodness and holiness, His operations in creation and redemption—*e.g.*, perfecting angels, quickening, liberating, sanctifying, 'deifying' men and uniting them to God—are properties and prerogatives of no creature but of God alone, and so the Spirit must be divine.[2] Again, since the working of the Spirit is similar to that of the Father and the Son, that similarity argues a community of essence.[3] Indeed the working of the Godhead is one, and, as the grace of the Father through the Son is completed in the Spirit, 'the Spirit is conjoined with and inseparable from the Father and Son in every operation.'[4] The Spirit is the perfecting cause in the united threefold divine working, and to reject the Spirit is to make faith in the Son impossible, to frustrate the blessings conveyed in baptism, to forfeit one's sonship.[5] That conjunction and co-operation imply coequality, and the numerical order of names in the baptismal formula implies connumeration, not subnumeration (*συναρίθμησις*, *ὑπαρίθμησις*) or subordination.[6] Further, since the Spirit is the Spirit of the Son, 'His very own,' He stands related to the Son as the Son to the Father, *i.e.* consubstantially and inseparably, and is in God by virtue of being in the Son, who is also in God.[7] Therefore the Holy Spirit is rightly included in the Godhead, and to be worshipped and glorified with the Father and the Son as divine.[8]

It is not within our province to discuss the Scriptural exegesis which supplies the material, and the Neo-Platonic metaphysics which furnishes the formal, principles of this argumentation. But, before proceeding to the next section, it is imperative to keep in mind that the 'personality' predicated of the Holy Spirit, as of the others in the Trinity, is not the modern concept of a self-conscious, self-determining ego. Rather, 'the three subjects ranked neither as separate persons, nor as attributes of the real divine being, but as three special bearers or independent *foci* of all attributes and activities of their common divinity, and also of a peculiar and characteristic property.'[9]

1 *The Five Theological Orations*, ed. A. J. Mason, Cambridge, 1899, v. 6; Athan. *ad Serap.* i. 17, 20, iii. 6; Gregory Naz. § 10.
2 Athan. *ad Serap.* i. 23 ff., iii. 3; Basil, *de Spir. Sanct.* chs. 9, 16, 19, 24; Gregory Naz. *Theol. Orat.* v. 14, 28, 33; Didymus, *de Trin.* ii.; cf. Niceta of Remesiana (A. E. Burn, Cambridge, 1905), *de Sp. S.* v.$^{5f.}$ xviii.
3 Basil, *Ep.* 189.
4 Athan. *ad Serap.* i. 14; Basil, *de Spir. Sanct.* 16 [38].
5 Basil, *de Spir. Sanct.* 10–12, 15.
6 *Ib.* 9, 18; cf. Greg. Naz. *Theol. Orat.* v. 19.
7 Athan. *ad Serap.* i. 27 f., 25 *ad fin.*, 27, iii. 5, iv. 3; Basil, *de Spir. Sanct.* 17 (43), 18 (45), *Ep.* 38^{4}.
8 See, further, artt. ATHANASIUS, vol. ii. p. 172; CAPPADOCIAN THEOLOGY, vol. iii. p. 212 f.; and TRINITY.
9 F. Nitzsch, *Evang. Dogm.*, Freiburg i. B., 1889–92, ii. 415; quoted by W. P. Paterson, *The Rule of Faith*^{2}, London, 1912, p. 218, n. 2.

2. The doctrine of the Procession (Filioque controversy). — We divide this section, which covers a thousand years, into two parts: (*a*) the divergence between the Eastern and Western Churches in doctrine, and (*b*) its conciliar expression.

(*a*) The Nicæno-Constantinopolitan Creed, after asserting in Scriptural phrases the consubstantiality of the Holy Spirit with the Father and the Son, formulated, in the clause *τὸ ἐκ τοῦ πατρὸς ἐκπορευόμενον*, that wherein He is differentiated from them. As 'ungeneracy' (*ἀγεννησία*) denotes the special characteristic of the Father as having the divine essence within and from Himself, so 'generation' (*γέννησις*) and 'procession' (*ἔκπεμψις*, *ἐκπόρευσις*) denote the special characteristic of the Son and the Holy Spirit respectively, as they eternally derive their being from the one fount of deity.[1] As against the Macedonians 'procession' implies that the Spirit is not a creature, and also evades the Eunomian dilemma that He is either 'ungenerate' or 'generate,' whilst the combination of Scriptural passages (Jn 15^{26}, 1 Co 2^{12})[2] in the formula removed the ground for complaint often urged against the unscriptural Nicene term *ὁμοούσιος*. The relation of the Spirit to the Son is not dealt with in the original form of this Symbol. The Greek Fathers of this period at times touch the matter. They appear to shrink from using the term 'procession' of the Spirit's timeless relation to the Son, sometimes using Jn 16^{14}, 'receiving from the Son,' in that connexion (so Athanasius and Epiphanius), at other times drawing a distinction between the egress of the Son and Spirit, the former being immediately, the latter mediately through the Son, from the Father. This distinction, shaped by Gregory of Nyssa,[3] became the typical Eastern formula.[4] And yet, in other passages, the Son and the Father appear as conjoined in the origination of the Holy Spirit[5] —a view which is never directly opposed for four centuries, except by Theodore of Mopsuestia († 429) and Theodoret († 458).[6]

In the West another direction was taken. Hilary (*c.* 360) had asked, without answering, the question whether the Spirit's receiving from the Son differed in meaning from the Spirit's proceeding from the Father (Jn 16^{14} 15^{26}), and Ambrose († 397) regarded the terms as parallel, though he did not teach the doctrine of an eternal procession from the Son.[7] It was Augustine, Ambrose's pupil, who laid down the doctrine of the dual procession, *i.e.* that the Spirit eternally proceeds from the Father and the Son, who together (and not, as in Greek theology, the Father solely) constitute the *principium* of the Spirit.

Not that they constitute two *principia*, as the Easterns later alleged, or that He proceeds from them as they are hypostatically distinct, but 'secundum hoc quod unum sunt . . . sicut Pater et Filius unus Deus et ad creaturam relative unus creator et unus Dominus, sic relative ad Spiritum sanctum unum principium.'[8]

He deduces the doctrine from Scripture, from the 'insufflation' in Jn 10^{22}.[9] Augustine had perceived that in the doctrine of the Trinity, as taught by the Greeks, subordination was not thoroughly excluded so long as the 'procession' of the Spirit was regarded as serial from the Father to and through the Son; so he reconstructed that

1 Greg. Naz. *Or.* xxxix. 12, xxv., *Theol. Orat.* v. 8; Greg. Nys. *adv. Eun.* 1; cf., on the term, Suicer, p. 1068 f.
2 See Hort, *Two Dissertations*, Cambridge, 1876, p. 86, n. 4.
3 See vol. iii. p. 214^{b}.
4 Cf. John Dam. *de Fide Orthod.* i. 12.
5 Greg. Naz. *Or.* xxxvii., τὸ ἐξ ἀμφοῖν συνημμένον; Did. Alex. *de Spir. Sanct.* §§ 34–37; Epiph. *Ancor.* ix. 69 f., παρ' ἀμφοτέρων, *ib.* 73, ἐκ, παρὰ πατρὸς καὶ υἱοῦ;
6 See art. ANTIOCHENE THEOLOGY, vol. i. p. 586.
7 *De Spir. Sanct.* ii. 11.
8 *De Trin.* v. 14.
9 *Ib.* iv. 29 (*PL* xlii. 908); *Tract. in Joann.* xcix. 7 ff.

doctrine and conceived of the Trinity as an eternal reciprocity of relations.

'Semper atque inseparabiliter, . . . simul in invicem, neuter solus, . . . quia unum sunt relative.'[1]

In that eternal mutual relation the spirit is the mutual love of both the Father and the Son, the harmony of their unity and equality, their communion, essential holiness, very nature and substance.[2] This doctrine of the dual procession permeated the Western Church and eventually found expression in the inserted clause 'Filioque' in Latin translations of the Nicæno-Constantinopolitan Creed.

(*b*) '*Filioque*' *Controversy* (*conciliar*).—This controversy strictly belongs to ecclesiastical history and not to the history of doctrine, but, for completeness, a brief outline is given. The first recorded mention of the insertion of the 'Filioque' clause appears in connexion with the Council at Toledo (A.D. 589) on the occasion of King Reccared's conversion from Arianism.[3] The interpolated creed was popular in Spain, France, and England, but not even Charlemagne could induce Leo III. to authorize its adoption in Rome (802). The innovation of this teaching was one of the counts of Photius's indictment against the Western Church in A.D. 866, which led to a rupture three years later. Not until A.D. 1017 did the interpolation receive official sanction at Rome, by Benedict VIII., and this was followed by the schism in 1054. At Bari, in 1099, Anselm of Canterbury produced his treatise on this theme; but not till the 2nd Council of Lyons (1274) did re-union appear practicable. An agreement was reached, explaining the dual procession as 'not from two *principia* but one *principium*, by one "spiration" and not two,' but attempts to enforce the agreement met with violent resistance in the Eastern Churches. Again at Ferrara-Florence, 1439,[4] a formula was reached in which the Greeks accepted *Filioque* as =*per Filium*. But synodal letters revoked the agreement in 1442 and 1453, and the following year the Eastern Church was under the rule of the Turk. At Bonn (1875) the Old Catholics attempted to heal the long-running sore, but the results reached lack official recognition.[5]

LITERATURE.—On the Patristic doctrine the best work in English is by H. B. Swete, art. 'Holy Ghost,' in *DCB* iii. 113 ff.; see also his *The Holy Spirit in the Ancient Church*, London, 1912. Good introductions and summaries may be found in A. Harnack, *Dogmengesch.*, Eng. tr., London, 1894–99, iv. 108–137; G. Thomasius, *Dogmengesch.*, Erlangen, 1874, i. 236–262; see also F. J. A. Hort, *Two Dissertations*, Cambridge, 1876; H. M. Gwatkin, *Studies of Arianism*², Cambridge, 1900; J. F. Bethune-Baker, *An Introd. to the Early Hist. of Christian Doctrine*, London, 1903, pp. 197–238.

On the history of the doctrine of the procession see the bibliography in *DCB* iii. 133. The standard works are: J. G. Walch, *Hist. Controversiæ Græcorum Latinorumque de Processione Spiritus Sancti*, Jena, 1751; H. B. Swete, *The Hist. of the Doctrine of the Procession of the Holy Spirit*, Cambridge, 1876.

3. Later Roman Catholic developments.—These developments, so far as they concern the doctrine of the Holy Spirit, bear upon His work in the inspiration of Scripture and tradition, and as guaranteeing the infallibility of the pope when pronouncing *ex cathedra* the doctrines implicit in the sources of revelation. The former was dealt with at the Tridentine Council (A.D. 1545–1563), the latter at the Vatican (A.D. 1870). Before narrating the developments, a brief résumé of the previous history of opinion may fitly be inserted here. The organ of the Holy Spirit's utterances was regarded by the sub-apostolic age as supremely the OT,[1] and until the disappearance of prophets towards the end of the 2nd cent. A.D. their presence within the Church visibly attested the Spirit's rule and guidance.[2] The excesses of ecstatic prophecy in Montanism (*q.v.*), and its protest against ecclesiastical laxity, provoked a reaction and strengthened episcopal organization, and henceforth the episcopacy was regarded as alone possessing a 'charism,' as the custodian of unwritten, apostolic tradition, and the bond of Church unity.[3] Against the heresies of the 2nd and 3rd centuries these traditions were used, along with and equal to NT Scriptures, as standards of doctrine; and the presence of bishops in general councils made possible the famous canon of tradition, as 'quod ubique, quod semper, quod ab omnibus creditum est.'[4] The general councils were held to be specially inspired by the Holy Spirit,[5] Gregory the Great († 604) even ranking the first four general councils as equal in authority to the four Gospels,[6] and with this the East was in accord.[7] One strong objection, indeed, of the Eastern Church to the interpolation of 'Filioque' was that it lacked ecumenical sanction. This is not the place to narrate the long struggles between East and West over papal supremacy, and between the Western Councils[8] and the popes as to the seat of authority. In sum, the papacy had become virtually an absolutism under the form of a constitutional monarchy, and the Reformers (see below) challenged the entire system. At Trent it was decreed that unwritten traditions were equal in authority with the written Scriptures, since they had come down in unbroken succession from the apostles, who had received them from the mouth of Christ Himself, or from the Holy Spirit's dictation; that the OT Apocrypha is canonical; that only the Holy Mother Church can authoritatively interpret and judge the true sense of Scripture, limited by the unanimous consent of the Fathers; that the Latin Vulgate is the authentic form of Scripture for preaching controversies, etc.[9] Although the Holy Spirit was supposed to preside at the sessions, only rarely is any decree made alluding to His prompting;[10] and the question whether the pope was the ultimate repository of tradition was adroitly evaded. Bellarmine, however († 1621), threw out the idea that the word of the Church, *i.e.* either of a Council or of the pope teaching *ex cathedra*, was no mere word of man, liable to error, but in some mode (*aliquo modo*) God's word, *i.e.* put forth by the assistance and governance of the Holy Spirit.[11] The papacy of Pius IX. (1846–78) marks the enactment of that view. His first encyclical (Nov. 1846) asserted infallibility, as also the declaration of the immaculate conception (1854);[12] he asserted that 'la tradizione sono io,' and the Vatican Council, while limiting the exposition of revelation or the deposit of faith so as not to declare new doctrines,[13] pronounced it as a 'divinely revealed dogma' that,

[1] Cf. *Ep.* 238¹²ff. (*PL* xxxiii. 1043), *de Trin.* vi. 9 *ib.* (xlii. 929).

[2] *De Trin.* v. 12 (*PL* xlii. 919), vi. 5 (*ib.* 927), xv. 27 (*ib.* 1080), *de Christ. Doct.* i. 5, *de Civ. Dei*, xi. 24; see, further, vol. vi. p. 262 f. and vol. iv. p. 240ᵇ.

[3] But cf. art. CREEDS AND ARTICLES (Ecumenical), vol. iv. p. 240ᵃ, and A. E. Burn, 'Some Spanish MSS. of the Constantinopolitan Creed,' in *JThSt* ix. [1908] 301 ff.

[4] Cf. vol. iv. p. 199.

[5] See, further, art. GREEK ORTHODOX CHURCH, vol. vi. pp. 426 f., 432 f.

[1] Clem. Rom. *ad Cor.* 45; Barnabas, etc.

[2] Cf. *Did.* xi.; Hermas, *Mand.* xi.; Barnabas, 16⁹; cf. Harnack, *TU* ii. 123 f.

[3] Iren. *adv. Hær.* III. iii. 18, iv. 26. 2; Cyprian, *de Unit. Eccl.* ch. 4.

[4] Vincent of Lerins (A.D. 434), *Common.* ch. 2.

[5] Cf. artt. COUNCILS AND SYNODS, vol. iv. p. 190 f., BIBLE IN THE CHURCH, vol. ii. p. 590.

[6] *Ep.* i. 24.

[7] Cf. John Dam. *de Fid. Orth.* i. 1, iv. 16 f.

[8] *E.g.*, of Constance, 1414–18; see artt. COUNCILS AND SYNODS, vol. iv. p. 198, GALLICANISM, vol. vi. p. 161ᵇ.

[9] Sess. iv. v.

[10] Cf., *e.g.*, sess. vi. pref., xxi. 1.

[11] *De Verb. Dei*, iii. 10.

[12] Cf. Lord Acton, *The Hist. of Freedom and other Essays*, London, 1907, p. 499; W. Ward, *The Life of John Henry Cardinal Newman*, ii. 295 ff.

[13] *De Eccl. Christi*, ch. iv.²

'when the Roman pontiff speaks *ex cathedra* . . . by the Divine assistance promised to him in the blessed Peter (Lk 22^{32} is usually meant), he possesses that power of infallibility with which the Divine Redeemer willed that His Church should be furnished in defining doctrine on faith or morals. . . .'[1] Thereby 'the infallible authority of the Council infallibly created the infallible authority of the Pope, and by that Act died,'[2] and the teaching office of the Spirit was confined to the pope, and, through him, the Roman hierarchy.

LITERATURE.—See art. COUNCILS AND SYNODS, vol. iv. p. 203, and add H. E. Manning, *The Temporal Mission of the Holy Ghost*[5], London, 1899; W. Ward, *The Life of John Henry Cardinal Newman*, 2 vols., do. 1912; G. P. Fisher, *Hist. of Christian Doctrine*[2], Edinburgh, 1897 (for good summary of Fessler's exposition of the dogma of infallibility); W. P. Paterson, *The Rule of Faith*[2], London, 1912, ch. i.

4. The Reformers and their successors.—With the Reformation the work of the Holy Spirit in the personal experience of believers was brought into the foreground. Both the formal and the material principles of the Reformation — the sufficiency of Scripture alone without the accretion of tradition, and justification by faith—were based upon the illuminating regenerating operations of the Spirit. Scripture had its authority, not from the Church, of which rather it was the norm and touchstone, but from the Holy Spirit, for, as Luther (1483–1546) said, it was 'the book, writing and word of the Holy Spirit,' and of that he was certain, because 'the Holy Ghost also writes it inwardly in the heart.'[3] Of that certainty,[4] both as to Scripture and as to the subjective assurance of election, Calvin (1509–64) was the chief exponent. It was a self-evident persuasion, wrought by the 'inward testimony of the Holy Spirit,' lifting the mind above doubts, hesitations, and scruples as to the truth of the Scripture; a persuasion superior to reason, needing no external arguments, for the Spirit that spoke in the prophets still speaks in the hearts of believers.[5] But against the Anabaptists (*q.v.*), who claimed the Spirit's inspiration for their visions, Calvin and the various confessions restricted the Spirit's operation to the Word of God, and thus prepared the way, in the absence of a reasoned theory of inspiration, for the later Protestant legalism,[6] which could assert that the consonants and vowel points of the Hebrew OT were inspired.[7] From this new Babylonian bondage to the letter deliverance came —to the heart, with the spread of Pietism (*q.v.*), under Spener († 1705) and Francke († 1727), who deeply influenced Moravianism, and thus the Evangelical Revival in England under Wesley, and to the mind, through the spread of Biblical criticism.[8] That the Quakers are in the line of the Reformers, notwithstanding the criticisms of John Owen and Richard Hooker, can be seen from George Fox's word in Lancaster court-house (1652):

> 'The Holy Scriptures were given forth by the Spirit of God, and all people must first come to the Spirit of God in themselves, by which they might know God and Christ, of whom the prophets and apostles learnt, and by the same Spirit know the Holy Scriptures; for as the Spirit of God was in them that gave forth the Scriptures, so the same Spirit of God must be in all them that come to understand the Scriptures.'[9]

All the various Protestant types agree as to the need for the Spirit's work in regeneration, but differ, owing to their anthropological views as to the extent of man's corruption, concerning the degree of this influence and the place of the human element in salvation. We cannot here go into the details distinguishing Lutherans, Calvinists, and Arminians.[1] Luther's beautiful language may be taken as typical:

> 'I believe that it is not of my own reason or by my own strength that I believe in Jesus Christ my Lord: it is the Holy Ghost that by the Gospel has called me, with His gifts has enlightened me, through genuine faith has sanctified and sustained me, just as He calls, gathers together, enlightens, sanctifies, and sustains by Jesus Christ, in true proper faith, all Christendom.'[2]

Both Luther and Calvin derive much from Augustine's doctrine of grace, for which Calvin preferred to use the term 'Spirit of God,' thus avoiding the nuance of quasi-physical force which clings to Augustine's thought and the mediæval sacramental theory of grace. He more closely connected the Holy Spirit with Jesus Christ:

> 'The Holy Spirit is the bond by which Christ efficaciously binds us to Himself,' it is the efficient cause of salvation creating faith 'by which he (*sc.* the believer) receives Christ,' and 'where the Spirit illumines to faith Christ inserts us within His body and we become partakers of all goods.'[3]

The instruments used by the Spirit are the Word of God, read or preached, and the sacraments, which are regarded as 'visible words, pictures of the word, signifying what the word proclaims.'[4] The retention of infant-baptism, however, scarcely accords with the condition of Church fellowship, which is 'principaliter societas fidei et Spiritus sancti in cordibus,'[5] and it was left to Anabaptists and Quakers to protest against this inconsistency.[6] The effect of the Spirit's working is faith, defined by Calvin as 'a certain and steady knowledge of the Divine benevolence towards us, revealed to our minds and sealed to our hearts by the Holy Spirit.'[7] Personal assurance as a part of saving faith, emphasized by early Reformers,[8] was ultimately dropped by their successors, though revived by the early Methodists.[9] Human co-operation with the Spirit in conversion was practically denied by the deterministic thought of Luther[10] and Calvin. Melanchthon, however, asserted three conjoint causes — the Word, the Holy Spirit, and man's will (the latter weakened by the Fall), and initiated the controversy over Synergism (*q.v.*); but later the human factor had freer play with ethical gain in the doctrines of Arminianism and Amyraldism (*qq.v.*).

As regards the person of the Holy Spirit, the traditional views were accepted by the Reformers, with the exception of the Socinians, who revived Arianism (*q.v.*), taking the ascriptions of personal activities in the NT as figures of speech, and the Spirit of God as a property of God without hypostatization.[11] Although Socinianism called forth a copious literature in opposition, the arguments for the Spirit's personality marked no advance upon Patristic discussions.[12]

Leaving the historical confessional formulation of the Spirit's person and work, we now turn to the presentation of the Holy Spirit as an experi-

1 Cf. T. Granderath, *Constitutiones Dogmaticæ Sacros. Œcum. Conc. Vat.*, Freiburg i. B., 1892, pars. 11, 'Const. de Eccl.' iv.[5]; the decree is given fully in vol. iv. p. 842[b].
2 A. Sabatier, p. 6.
3 J. Köstlin, *Luthers Theol.*[2], 2 vols., Stuttgart, 1901, ii. 7, Eng. tr., Philadelphia, 1897, ii. 226–253; Luther, *Sämmtliche Werke*, Erlangen, 1826–57, xxiii. 250.
4 See art. CERTAINTY (Religious), vol. iii. p. 325 f.
5 *Inst.* bk. i. ch. vii. §§ 2–5.
6 Cf. art BIBLIOLATRY, vol. ii. p. 616 (*f*).
7 *Cons. Helvet.*, 1675, art 2.
8 Cf. E. Reuss, *Hist. du canon des saints Ecritures*[2], Strassburg, 1864, chs. xvi.–xvii.; A. Sabatier, p. 204 f.
9 *The Journal of George Fox*, London, 1901, i. 138; see also R. Barclay, *Apology for the True Christian Religion*, London, 1678, prop. iii.

1 The various elements in their Confessions can be readily seen in J. G. B. Winer's *Doctrines and Confessions of Christendom*, ed. W. B. Pope, Edinburgh, 1873.
2 *Cat. Min.*, art. iii.; see also R. Otto, *Die Anschauung von dem heil. Geiste bei Luther*, Göttingen, 1898.
3 *Inst.* bk. III. ch. i. §§ 1, 4, ch. ii. § 35.
4 *Apol. Conf. Aug.* art. vii. § 5; *Inst.* IV. xiv. 10, 17, xvii. 10.
5 *Apol. Conf. Aug.* art. vi. § 5.
6 See art. BAPTISM, vol. ii. pp. 400–405, for a fuller discussion.
7 *Inst.* III. ii. 7.
8 Cf. Luther on Gal 2^{16}.
9 Cf. W. Cunningham, *The Reformers and the Theology of the Reformation*, Edinburgh, 1862, essay iii., and art. METHODISM.
10 Cf. R. Seeberg, *Dogmengesch.*, Leipzig, 1895–98, ii. 227.
11 F. Socinus, *Responsio ad libellum Jac. Vuieki*, cap. x.; *Cat. Racov.* cap. 6, qu. 12.
12 Cf. Pearson, *Exposition of the Creed*, London, 1659, art. viii., and notes in vol. ii. pp. 259–262, ed. E. Burton, Oxford, [3]1847.

ence. The remaining sections will treat that experience, normally as exhibited in liturgies and hymnology, distinctively and peculiarly as manifested in mysticism, and critically in the light of modern philosophical discussions of the concept of personality.

5. The Holy Spirit in liturgies and hymnology.—In the cultus of the Christian Church the Holy Spirit has been from the first an object of worship, with His appropriate festival of Pentecost,[1] special seasons (as baptism, the eucharist, anointing, confirmation, ordination [*qq.v.*]), when His presence and operation were invoked, and distinctive organs through whom He was mediated to the Church. In the apostolic age the eucharist was followed by what was practically the celebration of His 'real presence' within the Church.[2] His operation was represented in diverse fashion: as a sanctifying influence operating as a physical force upon the waters of baptism, and expelling the dragon therefrom,[3] as a magic power passing through the oil of unction into the body and soul of the anointed, imparting divine life, removing the traces of sin, charming away invisible evil spirits, producing gladness and making men 'christs.'[4] Or He comes as light, and the baptized become 'illuminati' and 'see things beyond man's ordinary vision,'[5] as a 'seal,' stamping the divine image upon the soul, giving it a 'character,' later regarded as indelible,[6] which served as a mark of identification for aiding angels on earth and the last Judgment in heaven, and as a potent amulet against the devil.[7] At the 'epiclesis' in the eucharist (*q.v.*) His coming shows forth (ἀποφήνῃ), changes, and sanctifies the elements,[8] and the prevailing Greek view was that thereby the holy food became 'the medicine of immortality.'[9] At the laying on of hands in confirmation and the ordination of bishops, presbyters, etc., the Holy Spirit came to be thought of as conveyed by physical contact.[10] Yet with all this materialistic and magical terminology, borrowed from the OT and mystery-religions, the religious instinct prevented the more spiritual view of the Holy Spirit as working in the mind and conscience of men from fading altogether away, and there were never wanting voices to assert that the Spirit was not tied to the sacraments, that faith and penitence were indispensable for the acquisition of the Spirit, that the agencies who conferred Him were not fontal but only ministerial, and that He was no impersonal gift but a living being. To these things the hymns of the Church universal give ample witness. Passing by the early doxologies, we may note the beautiful expression of the Spirit's influence in the recently discovered *Odes and Psalms of Solomon*:[11] near as the wings of a dove to its brood (28[1f.]), opening the soul as spring softens the hard clods (11), playing as a harpist upon the soul (6[1-4]), prompting praise and teaching His ways (36[1-4] 3[11f.]). Another Syrian singer, Ephraem of Edessa (*c.* 378), warns against too much scrutiny as to the Spirit's subsistence. 'Love the brooding of the Holy Spirit and approach not to pry into Him.'[1] The Latin hymn-writers, however, did not hesitate to set their doctrines to hymns, the dual procession, the Spirit as the bond of the Trinity, as the mutual love of the Godhead, finding frequent expression.[2] Impressive in its simple majesty is the solitary line of the *Te Deum*, 'Sanctum quoque Paraclitum Spiritum'; and, however the inclusion of the *Quicumque Vult* in the service-books of Western Churches, Roman Catholic and Protestant, is regarded, it at least kept in the foreground the personality and deity of the Spirit. Two noble hymns from the 9th and 11th centuries—the 'Veni Creator Spiritus' and 'Veni Sancte Spiritus'[3]—have served as models for most modern hymns dealing with the Spirit's work as experienced by devout believers. And, although Ritschl's criticism of Lutheran hymns for Pentecost, that little mention is made of the Spirit as the creator of a common consciousness and corporate fellowship within the Church[4] and 'a purely individual self-contemplation' is disproportionately emphasized, is applicable to most hymns, nevertheless the outburst of hymnody has created Churches, stimulated revivals, overflowed ecclesiastical boundaries, and, along with prayer, kept the Spirit's regenerating, renewing, consoling, teaching, guiding work before the Church, checked the crass materialism which ceremonialism undoubtedly fosters, as it has borne witness also that the Spirit ever indwells the Church.[5]

6. Mysticism and the Holy Spirit.—The mystics in their quest for an intense awareness of the Divine Presence meet with a response which they interpret as the direct action of the Spirit of God upon the human spirit. Various are the signs denoting the Spirit's activity—ecstasy,[6] glossolaly,[7] a fecundity of ideas which fall thick and fast as snowflakes on the mind,[8] emotional enthusiasm,[9] an inflow of divine love strengthening the will,[10] an accession of new vigour so that 'the operations of the soul entirely united to God, are all divine,'[11] and especially noble fortitude in martyrdom.[12] More generally the Spirit's coming is seen in the enhancement of the mental powers, purging 'the eye of the soul'[13] so that the hidden meaning of Scripture grows plain[14] and the mysteries of Christianity become clear. Thus Tertullian, the Montanist, claims that the Paraclete is the institutor of a new discipline, making the Catholic faith better known, clearing up obscurities and equivocations in Scripture, and reforming the intellect.[15] Origen

[1] See artt. Festivals and Fasts (Christian), vol. v. p. 847, 'Pentecost' in *DCA*, p. 1618 f.

[2] Cf. L. Duchesne, *Christian Worship: its Origin and Evolution*[4], Eng. tr., London, 1912, p. 48.

[3] Tertullian, *de Bapt.* v.; Cyril Jer. *Cat. Lect.* iii. 3.

[4] Cyr. Jer. xx. 3, xxi. 1 ff.; Methodius, *Con.* viii. 8.

[5] Justin Mart. *Apol.* i. 61; Cyr. Jer. xvi. 16.

[6] Augustine, *contra Ep. Parm.* ii. 13; Conc. Trid. sess. vii. 'de Sac. in genere,' can. ix.

[7] Cyr. Jer. xvii. 35, i. 2.

[8] *Apost. Const.* viii. 12, § 17; Cyr. Jer. xxiii. 7; *Liturg. Jacob.* xxxii.; *Liturg. Marc.* xvii.

[9] Ignatius, *Eph.* 20; Irenæus, iv. 38. 1; Greg. Nys. *Orat. Cat.* 37.

[10] Tertullian, *de Res. Carn.* 8; Cyprian, *Epp.* lxxiii. 7 f. (Oxford ed. lxxiv. 7 f.); pseudo-Cyprian, *de Aleat.* 3; Cyr. Jer. xvi. 26; *Apost. Const.* viii.; Augustine, *de Bapt. c. Donat.* iii. 16; *Catech. Rom.* pars. 11. ch. iii. qu. 24, ed. Florence, 1718; cf. Anglican Prayer Book at ordination of bishops.

[11] Ed. J. Rendel Harris[2], Cambridge, 1911.

[1] *Select Works*, tr. J. B. Morris, Oxford, 1847, p. 400 f.

[2] Cf. Paulinus of Nola, *Nat.* 9; Prudentius, *Cathem. Hy.* 5, v. 159; Adam of St. Victor, in H. A. Daniel, *Thesaurus Hymnologicus*, Leipzig, 1841–56, vol. ii. hy. 90[2].

[3] *Ap.* Daniel, i. 306, ii. 37.

[4] *Hist. of the Christian Doct. of Justification and Reconciliation*, Eng. tr., Edinburgh, 1872, p. 328.

[5] For the doctrine of the Holy Spirit in liturgies cf. A. J. Maclean, *The Ancient Church Orders*, Cambridge, 1910, ch. vii.; Swete, *The Holy Spirit in the Ancient Church*, p. 157 f.; for Anglican Prayer Book cf. art. 'Holy Spirit,' in *Prayer-Book Dictionary*, ed. G. Harford, etc., London, 1912; cf. art. 'Hymnody,' in *CE* vii. 596 f., where further literature is cited.

[6] Tertullian, *adv. Marc.* iv. 22; cf. Plotinus, *Enn.* vi. ix. 8 ff.; Bernard, *de Consid.* v. 11.

[7] Ignatius, *Phil.* 7; cf. exx. in G. N. Bonwetsch, *Gesch. des Montanismus*, Erlangen, 1881, p. 197 ff. for Montanism; and artt. Camisards, Irving and the Catholic Apostolic Church.

[8] Philo, *de Migr. Abr.* 7; Mme. Guyon, *Autobiography*, Eng. tr., Bristol, 1773, pt. ii. ch. 21.

[9] Cf. John of Ruysbroeck, *Vie et Gestes* (*Œuvres*, vol. i.), Paris, 1909, pp. 115, 119 ff., 123.

[10] Augustine, *de Spir. et Litt.* 49, on Ro 5^5; Richard of St. Victor, *de Contemp.* v. 5.

[11] John of the Cross, *Montée du Mt. Carmel*, French tr., Paris, 1866, iii. 1, Eng. tr., London, 1906, iii. 1, § 6.

[12] Cf. *Passio Perpetua et Felicitas*; Eusebius, *HE* v. 16 f.

[13] Cf. Clem. Alex. *Pæd.* i. 6. 28; Augustine, *Conf.* vii. 8, 10.

[14] Cf. art. Allegory.

[15] *De Monog.* 2, *adv. Prax.* 2, *de Res. Carn.* 63, *de Vel. Virg.* 1.

alleges that the Spirit enables men to acquire the gifts of learning, wisdom, and knowledge.[1] Cyril of Jerusalem points out that all intellectual beings, even the archangels, need the teaching and sanctifying influence of the Spirit,[2] and Gregory of Nazianzus claims that aid in the formulation of the doctrine of the Spirit.[3] Sometimes messages are received in the mystic state, by audition or vision, which are held to possess objective validity, and to continue, if not supersede, Scripture revelation. But a close scrutiny generally reveals that such messages have some basis in Scripture, or are the offspring of auto-suggestion, and the practical judgment of the Church has placed such communications or revelations in a place below canonical Scripture. A recurring feature is the view of the Spirit or Paraclete as marking the consummating age of revelation—the mature stage, the OT and NT being respectively the childhood and youth of religion. We meet it in Montanism as it protests against officialism within the Church;[4] in the Middle Ages in the protest against sacramentarianism of Amalric of Bena (*c.* 1204) and Joachim of Flore († 1202)—the latter the only prophet outside canonical Scripture mentioned by Dante[5]—who taught the supersession of the sacraments in the age of the Spirit; at the Reformation, when the thoroughgoing Reformers, the Anabaptists (*q.v.*), set the inward voice or word of the Spirit above the outward word of Scripture, and in Puritan England with the Quakers' protest against sacraments, orders clerical, and formal religion. Usually the mystic is found re-asserting some neglected or forgotten truth of religion or emphasizing a union with God so close as to verge on the absorption of the soul in God, as in pantheism (*q.v.*), and intensity of emotion is taken as the sign of the Spirit's presence. All movements of the soul are taken as the action of the Spirit, and consequently fanaticism and enthusiasm have been at a premium.[6] Yet, beyond question, springs of energy have been unsealed (cf. Catharine of Genoa, Mme. Guyon), an exhilaration of Spirit experienced, an inbreaking from the supersensible world apprehended and utilized, which have started revivals, lifted the Christian Church to higher levels of service and devotion, and prevented Christendom from accepting the world as a closed system into which new streams of blessing from God can find no entrance. The phenomena of revivals especially endorse the mystics' claims:

> 'The impulse of the Great Awakening (in America 18th cent.) was a theological conviction which took shape in (Jonathan) Edwards' [*q.v.*] mind, a belief in the immediate action of the Divine Spirit upon the human soul.'[7]

Of the Spirit's working the mystics have no doubt:

> 'Whoso hath felt the Spirit of the Highest
> Cannot confound nor doubt Him nor deny.'[8]

They are sure that they have reached the essence of essences, have touched the ultimate reality, God. But, when they are asked for further knowledge of the inner life of the Godhead, there is no fresh knowledge conveyed over and above the Christian revelation. The Trinity is still the dispensational Trinity, and, though Eckhart and John of Ruysbroeck may pass beyond that Trinity into the 'stillen Wüste' of Godhead, the secret of an immanent Trinity in the Godhead remains undisclosed. And orthodox mystics, as Sta. Teresa and St. John of the Cross,[1] fare no better. Behind all their musings we catch echoes of the Augustinian-Scholastic doctrine that the Son proceeds through the divine intellect and the Spirit through the divine will[2]—echoes which make clear that the human mind is not so bare and empty of earthly reasonings as was supposed. Still, the mystics of a speculative turn have served the race nobly by their scrutiny of the cognitive processes in mysticism. Eckhart's doctrine[3] of the *Fünkelein*—'the likest God within the soul,' 'the divine spark,' in which all other faculties of the soul meet—as the meeting-place of the temporal and eternal world, one with God in essence, is an advance on mediæval ideas of grace as a magical bestowal, lifts human nature above Augustinian doctrines of total depravity, prepares the way for the Quaker doctrine of the 'Inward Light,' for the modern view of divine immanence, and gives a ground for the working of God in other religions besides Christianity.[4] But the distinctive feature of Christian mysticism, as it bears on the Holy Spirit, is that the Spirit is the Spirit of Christ, the Eternal Son, who works within believers and brings them into the state of sonship to God, gives an assurance of salvation which no rationalism can shake, and to their 'wondering view reveals the secret love of God.'[5]

7. Modern philosophy and the Holy Spirit.—The Holy Spirit in the specific theological sense has been but little discussed in modern philosophy. Spinoza ([*q.v.*] 1632–77), it is true, examined the Biblical data in his *Tractatus Theologico-Politicus*,[6] but scarcely passed beyond the mediæval Jewish view of the Holy Spirit as the spirit of prophecy, reduced it to designate the contents of revelation or simply the ethical effects which He produces in men, and regarded the inner witness of the Spirit as pure presumption, a product of prejudice and passion, reason being really the light of the Spirit.[7] Hegel (*q.v.*) used the term 'Holy Spirit' to denote the spirit of logic, but the resemblance to the Christian doctrine is merely nominal. The God of Hegelianism is scarcely personal,[8] and the rôle of the Spirit as the synthesis of a dialectic process would make it the sole and supreme reality in the Trinity, and the Father and the Son inferior to, and mere abstractions from, its reality.[9] The *Geistesleben* of Rudolf Eucken's philosophy labours under the difficulty, common to idealistic systems, of showing how its manifold activities are explicable without a personal substrate or subject, and how 'an abstraction' can be 'of itself the most fruitful of realities,'[10] and, though God, as in speculative theism, is regarded as 'spirit,' the

1 *De Princ.* i. 1; cf. Basil, *de Spir. Sanct.* 9.
2 *Cat. Lect.* xvi. 23.
3 *Orat.* xli. 26; cf. John Smith, *Select Discourses*³, London, 1821, pp. 3 ff., 24.
4 Tertullian, *de Vel. Virg.* 1, *de Monog.* 14, *de Pudic.* 21; cf. Greg. Naz. *Or.* xli. ch. 11.
5 *Par.* xii. 139 ff.
6 Cf. art. ENTHUSIASTS (Religious).
7 A. V. G. Allen, *J. Edwards*, Boston, 1889; cf. J. Buchanan, *Office and Work of the Holy Spirit*⁵, Edinburgh, 1844, p. 402 f.
8 F. W. H. Myers, *Saint Paul*, London, 1867.

1 Cf. *The Interior Castle*, Eng. tr., London, 1906, viith Mansions, i. 9; *The Ascent of Mt. Carmel*, Eng. tr., London, 1906, bk. ii. ch. 29.
2 Cf. Augustine, *de Trin.* xv. 27; Thomas Aquinas, *Summa Theol.*, I. qu. xxvii.
3 Cf. W. R. Inge, *Christian Mysticism*² (*BL*), London, 1900, p. 157 f.; R. M. Jones, *Studies in Mystical Religion*, do. 1909, p. 231.
4 Cf. artt. INSPIRATION, POSSESSION.
5 See, further, artt. MYSTICISM; John Owen, *Works*, ed. W. H. Goold, Edinburgh, 1850–55, iv. 4–226; W. P. Paterson, *The Rule of Faith*², ch. iii.; F. von Hügel, *The Mystical Element of Religion*, 2 vols., London and New York, 1908; E. Herman, *The Meaning and Value of Mysticism*², London, 1916; on Eckhart see F. Pfeiffer, *Deutsche Mystiker des 14 Jahrhunderts*, Stuttgart, 1845–57, ii. 66, l. 2, 110, l. 26, 55, l. 22 f. Akin to the experience of the mystics is that of great poets and artists; cf. Dante, *Par.* i. 13–33; Milton's Invocation, *Par. Lost*, i. 17–26; Browning's *Cristina*, iii–iv; for a useful discussion cf. *The Spirit*, London, 1919, Essay vi. 'The Psychology of Inspiration' (C. W. Emmet); W. Macneile Dixon, 'Inspiration,' in *HJ* xii. [1914] 509 ff. See artt. POSSESSION.
6 Amsterdam, 1670.
7 Chs. i., xi., xv.
8 Cf. J. Ward, *The Realm of Ends*, Cambridge, 1911, pp. 160, 165, n. 1.
9 J. M. E. MacTaggart, *Studies in Hegelian Cosmology*, Cambridge, 1901, § 213 ff.
10 F. von Hügel, *HJ* x. [1912] 669.

Holy Spirit as an inner distinction within God is not discussed. The critical analysis of self-consciousness, which is distinctive of modern philosophy, has influenced the attitude of mind as it approaches this doctrine of the Spirit. The Kantian epistemology, with its limitation of the pure reason to the phenomenal, has restrained speculation on the transcendental factors experienced in religion, and fostered agnosticism in theology. This is apparent when Kant says, 'We can neither recognize a super-sensible object within our experience, nor exercise an influence upon it,' in his *Religion innerhalb der Grenzen der blossen Vernunft*,[1] in the Ritschlian theology with its exclusion of metaphysics from theology and the meagre attention given to the Holy Spirit's work, and in the 'religionsgeschichtliche' school (Gunkel, Weinel, Volz), who would evaluate the phenomena of the Spirit's working by parallelism with heathen views of demons, gods, and spirits.[2] The idealist reaction against Kant (Fichte, Schelling, Hegel), by examining the Ego in cognition and volition, has elucidated somewhat the meaning of personality. As a result the traditional interpretation of the Church, whereby personality is construed in terms of substance and accident,[3] is felt to be inferior to that in terms of self-conscious spirit. But personality (*q.v.*) as yet has been only partially explored, and the application of one mystery to another can hardly bring much light to the mind.[4] When applied to the Trinity, speculation can help us to conceive the timeless relation of the Father and the Son as mutually subject and object, but furnishes little explanation why a third is necessary, and the Augustinian interpretation of the Spirit as the mutual bond between the Father and the Son merely gives a relation, and a relation is not necessarily a person.[5] Even the analysis of the religious consciousness affords little help, for to practical experience the indwelling of Christ and the incoming of the Spirit cannot be differentiated.[6] In view of these facts, not to mention the divided state of Christendom, the stagnancy of thought in the Eastern Church, and the standardization of Aquinas's theology by the Roman Church, the likelihood of any ecclesiastical reformulation of the doctrine is very remote. The tendency of modern philosophy to postulate the metaphysical reality of spirit has also influenced theological thought on the doctrine of the Spirit. In this view, spirit is 'a substantial, yet immaterial, entity,'[7] a synonym of mind as the substrate of consciousness, whether in the individual or in a society. This usage is akin to that of the Logos in Greek philosophy, and meets us in the *Zeitgeist* of modern speech. It is of value in so far as it supposes consciousness as a quality of spirit, and points the inadequacy of representing mental phenomena in terms of matter and force. But, when it is applied to the Holy Spirit as the collective spirit (*Gemeingeist*) which animates the collective life of believers,[8] it does less than justice to the personal activities ascribed by Scripture to the Holy Spirit and repeats the Sabellian heresy. The religious instinct can

[1] Königsberg, 1793, tr. J. W. Semple, Edinburgh, 1838.

[2] Cf. K. F. Nösgen, *Der heilige Geist*, i. 25, n. 50.

[3] Cf. 'Athanasian' Creed; Basil, *Epp.* xxxvi. 6, xxxviii. 3; Thomas Aquinas, *Summa Theol.*, I. qu. xxix.

[4] Cf. W. Sanday, *Christologies, Ancient and Modern*, Oxford, 1910, p. 156 f., for the subliminal self as 'the sphere' where the Divine Spirit works; and cf. H. R. Mackintosh, in *ExpT* xxi. [1909–10] 553 ff. and art. CONSCIOUSNESS, vol. iv. p. 53 f.

[5] Cf. D. W. Forrest, *The Christ of History and of Experience*[7], Edinburgh, 1914, p. 210 f.

[6] Cf. J. Denney, *The Christian Doct. of Reconciliation*, London, 1917, pp. 308–312.

[7] J. Dewey, in *DPhP* ii. 308a.

[8] Schleiermacher, *Glaubenslehre*[4], Berlin, 1842, § 123; cf. Hegel, *Phil. of Religion*, Eng. tr., London, 1895, ii. 334, iii. 28; Ritschl, *The Christian Doctrine of Justification and Reconciliation*, Eng. tr., Edinburgh, 1900, 605 f.

acquiesce in no impersonal principle or transitory modality, and any interpretation of the Spirit which falls short of ascribing personal consciousness to Him makes Him cease to be an object of adoration and worship.[1] From the criticism of self-consciousness and the narratives of mystical experiences certain conclusions may be drawn—as that the Spirit is known only in His working, and not in Himself; that it is difficult to represent His personality to the mind, since He is manifested in the gifts which He confers without the medium of a physical body; that His presence is apprehended in the light that He brings rather than in what He is; that what lends precision to the idea of the Spirit is to be sought in the character and life of Jesus, God's Son, whose Spirit He is; that His individuality is suppressed in His mission to glorify the Son (Jn 16[14]); and that the organism He indwells, through which His operations are manifested, owing to the divided state of the Christian Church, is but dimly apprehended as the Body of Christ, 'the Temple, the Habitation of the Holy Ghost.'

On the whole question of the Spirit's personality and the difficulty of its expression we cannot better the language of Swete:

> 'The idea of the One Undivided Essence, subsisting eternally after a three-fold manner and in a three-fold relation, finds but very partial correspondencies in the nature of man or in any finite nature. When we try to express it in precise language, our terminology is necessarily at fault; the "hypostasis" of the philosophical East, the "persona" of the practical West, are alike inadequate; in the things of God we speak as children, and we shall continue to do so until "that which is perfect is come." Yet our imperfect terms represent eternal verities. The currency may be base, but it serves for the time to circulate amongst men the riches of God's revelation of Himself.'[2]

> 'Trasumanar significar *per verba* non si poria; però l' esemplo basti a cui esperienza grazia serba.'[3]

LITERATURE.—The following may be consulted: i. *GENERAL.*—Histories of Doctrine by G. P. Fisher[2], Edinburgh, 1897; K. R. Hagenbach, Eng. tr., do. 1880, i. 171–176, 365–371; F. Loofs, *Leitfaden*[4], Halle, 1906; R. Seeberg, *Lehrbuch*[2], 2 vols., Leipzig, 1908; M. Kähler, *Wissenschaft der christlichen Lehre*[3], do. 1905; B. H. Streeter and others, *The Spirit*, London, 1919.

ii. *PARTICULAR.*—G. Smeaton, *The Doctrine of the Holy Spirit*, Edinburgh, 1882; K. F. Nösgen, *Der heilige Geist, sein Wesen und die Art seines Wirkens*, 2 vols., Berlin, 1905–07; W. L. Walker, *The Spirit and the Incarnation*[2], Edinburgh, 1901, and *The Holy Spirit*, London, 1907; A. C. Downer, *The Mission and Administration of the Holy Spirit*, Edinburgh, 1909; F. B. Denio, *The Supreme Leader*, Boston, 1900; W. T. Davison, *The Indwelling Spirit*, London, 1911 (contains select bibliography); A. L. Humphries, *The Holy Spirit in Faith and Experience*, do. 1911; W. H. G. Thomas, *The Holy Spirit of God*, do. 1913; C. L. Slattery, *The Light Within*, do. 1915.

iii. *PHILOSOPHICAL.*—C. F. D'Arcy, *Idealism and Theology*, London, 1899, and art. 'Trinity' in *DCG*; W. Adams Brown, *The Trinity and Modern Thought*, n.p., 1906; J. Caird, *Fundamental Ideas of Christianity* (Gifford Lectures), 2 vols., Glasgow, 1899, lect. xix.; C. C. Everett, *Theism and the Christian Faith*, New York, 1909.

iv. *ON RITSCHLIANISM AND THE HOLY SPIRIT.*—A. E. Garvie, *Ritschlian Theology*[2], Edinburgh, 1902, ch. xi.; J. K. Mozley, *Ritschlianism*, London, 1909. See also artt. in *RGG*, *s.v.* 'Geist und Geistesgaben,' 'Trinität'; *CE* vii. 409 ff.; *DPhP*, *s.v.* 'Spirit (Spiritualism),' 'Pneuma.'

R. BIRCH HOYLE.

SPIRIT CHILDREN.—Different views may be accepted as to the nature of primitive religion, magic, and their relations to each other; but there is no doubt that among the lower races the subject-matter of magico-religious practices and ideas is largely taken from fundamental organic functions and crises of life. Food, matters of sex, economic activities on the one hand, birth, puberty, marriage, death on the other, are all associated with ritual

[1] Cf. Robert Hall's experience described in the memoir by Olinthus Gregory, prefixed to Hall's *Works*, London, 1846, i. 62.

[2] Church Congress, Exeter, London, and Derby, 1894, p. 694; see, further, art. PERSONALITY; A. E. Garvie, *The Christian Certainty and the Modern Perplexity*, London, 1910, ch. x.; W. P. Paterson, *Rule of Faith*[2], pp. 213–223; H. R. Mackintosh, *The Person of Jesus Christ*, London, 1912, pp. 508–526; C. C. J. Webb, *Problems in the Relations of God and Man*, do. 1911, p. 278 f.

[3] Dante, *Par.* i. 70–72.

and belief in the majority of native communities. Death is perhaps the most important fact among those with which primitive ritual and belief are concerned. The opposite gate of life is, on the other hand, probably the least prominent. Though there is no native community which does not speculate about what happens to a man after his death, only very few seem to have any ideas as to when and how life comes into existence. There is, however, a type of belief which deals with this problem and attempts to define the nature and condition of a person before birth. Using a term introduced by Spencer and Gillen and adopted by Frazer, we can apply the name 'spirit children' to such unborn beings waiting to come into this world.

As far as is at present known, the ethnographical area of this type of belief is restricted to portions of Australia and Melanesia. The ideas of the Central and Northern Australian tribes about spirit children are most definite and detailed, and we possess an excellent account of them in the works of Spencer, and of Spencer and Gillen.

1. **Arunta.**—The Arunta, who inhabit the Alice Springs district of Central Australia, are the tribe among whom this type of belief was first discovered by Spencer and Gillen. Their ideas may be described somewhat in detail as a typical example. The Arunta believe that in remote times their tribal hunting-grounds were peopled by half-human, half-animal beings, whom they call *alcheringa* (*q.v.*), and from whom the members of the present tribe are descended. These mythical ancestors were endowed with powers not possessed by their descendants. They roamed about the country in companies, whose members belonged to the same totem, and performed various deeds, mainly magical ceremonies. As a rule, in association with every important ceremony, they left traces in the form of natural features, such as water-holes, rocks, grottos, or creeks. Many of the tribal traditions are concerned with the manner in which the *alcheringa* ancestors came to be associated with definite localities, scattered over the tribal territory and marked by some striking feature. At some such places the ancestors simply performed a ceremony, and afterwards continued their wanderings; at others they passed underground, leaving behind their bodies or part of their bodies, or else they went down into the earth, spirit and body together. But at every such spot they left behind a number of spirit children (*erathipa* or *ratapa*). These spirit children live in the totemic centre, awaiting reincarnation.

Naturally many details of these beliefs are hazy and indefinite, varying according to the section of the tribe, the tribal status and intelligence of the individual native, and many other circumstances. It must be borne in mind that in this matter, as in every native belief, only the broad outline of the idea is fixed and definite. Within this a certain latitude is left to the individual mind, for, although ritual, custom, and myth cause the main points and many details of unwritten native tradition to become uniform and rigid, concerning other details there may be several currents of tradition.

Thus the relation of the *alcheringa* ancestor to the spirit child (*erathipa*) is not very clear. It seems that in some cases the ancestor is imagined by the natives to have been transformed into the spirit child; in other cases the latter is conceived by them as emanating from the *alcheringa* ancestor. In some instances it seems that a number of spirit children are descended from one mythical individual. Yet the main idea remains stable through every variation in belief, that every spirit child is definitely related to one individual *alcheringa*, and that the man into whom this spirit child will develop will inherit his totemic character from the *alcheringa* ancestor and be associated with the latter's bull-roarer.

The nature of the spirit children seems to be a point on which the opinions of the natives vary. Most generally they are regarded as fully developed babies, male or female, endowed with life. They are invisible to ordinary men, but can be seen by certain magicians.

There are also several opinions on record as to the manner in which the spirit child enters the body of a woman, who can become pregnant only if she passes near the totemic centre, the place of the *erathipa*. An *erathipa* may enter her womb through her flank, or an *alcheringa* ancestor associated with the totemic centre may throw a diminutive bull-roarer at the woman, which enters her body and becomes a child. The spirit child is probably associated or identified, in the ideas of the natives, with the bull-roarer. Again, the natives will affirm that in some cases the *alcheringa* ancestor himself enters the body of a woman and becomes a child. These cases are, as the natives affirm, very rare, and they can easily be diagnosed, since children conceived in this manner have fair hair and blue eyes.

Another point in which the Arunta seem to have no very detailed and definite views is the reincarnation of human beings. After an *alcheringa* ancestor has produced an *erathipa* which enters a woman and becomes a living individual, the question arises, Whither does his spirit or life principle go after death? Is it destroyed, or is it again changed into an *erathipa*? There is a belief among the Arunta, recorded by the missionary C. Strehlow, according to which the spirits of the dead go to an island, where they live a kind of replica of their earthly life and then are finally destroyed and return to this world no more. According to this belief, an individual sooner or later ceases to exist, and there is no reincarnation. Spencer and Gillen make no explicit statement as to the existence among the Arunta of beliefs in the reincarnation of human beings. On the other hand, these two authors found definite views concerning reincarnation among the tribes living all around the Arunta, and it seems more than plausible to assume that the belief in reincarnation does exist among this tribe. Here again it must be emphasized that the existence of variations in belief, of contradictions, or even of two mutually exclusive beliefs in the same tribe, is by no means an exceptional occurrence.

2. **Other Australian tribes.**—Only a few words need be said about the other Australian tribes among whom similar beliefs have been found by Spencer and by Spencer and Gillen. Thus the tribes living to the south of the Arunta believe in the existence of spirit children, derived from mythical totemic ancestors. These spirit children enter into women and become human beings. Again, each human individual returns after death to the state of a spirit child and reincarnates as a new earthly life. At each reincarnation the sex of the individual changes.

Among the Warramunga, a tribe living to the north of the Arunta, all the spirit children emanate from one ancestor. Human beings again become spirit children after death and reincarnate. Among some other tribes of that region similar beliefs exist, with the exception that women are not supposed to reincarnate, *i.e.* a woman's spirit ceases to exist after her death.

Among the tribes of the Northern Territory, investigated by Spencer, the same type of belief has been found in a definite form. These natives also affirm that companies of mythical ancestors roamed about the country and that a number of spirit children emanated from them. These spirit children, associated with totemic centres, enter the bodies of women and become human beings. Dead men become spirit children and are born again, the sex of the individual alternating at each rebirth. Every individual in the tribe can be traced to a particular totemic ancestor, and each man bears a name that indicates this relationship. In one of these tribes, the Kakadu, there is an interesting belief showing that the natives have the idea of a kind of spiritual continuity between the various reincarnations of the same individual ancestor.[1]

3. Melanesia.—The belief in spirit children, as known to exist in certain districts of Melanesia, is much less definite than among the Australian natives. W. H. R. Rivers has found among the natives of Banks Islands (Southern Melanesia) the belief that in some cases pregnancy is caused by an animal of supernatural character 'entering' the body of a woman. The natives consider this incarnation, not as a material, but as a spiritual act, and the 'supernatural animal' cannot be classed as a spirit child, unless we give this term a much broader meaning. Moreover, this form of conception is believed to take place only in exceptional cases, so that it cannot be considered a general theory of reproduction. It shows therefore very little resemblance to the Australian beliefs. The 'supernatural animal' stands in no relation to spirits of the dead, and consequently these natives cannot be said to believe in reincarnation.

A general theory of birth showing a distinct affinity to the Australian beliefs has been found among the Melanesians who inhabit the Trobriand archipelago off the north-east coast of New Guinea. These natives, who, like the Australian aborigines, are ignorant of physiological paternity, believe that pregnancy is caused by a spirit, who inserts an embryonic baby (*waiawaia*) into the womb of a woman. Each *waiawaia* is moreover a metamorphosis of an individual spirit. Every human being goes after death to the island of the spirits, where he lives through another existence, very much like that which he lived in this world. After a time he undergoes, of his own free will, a transformation; he shrinks into a *waiawaia*, which the natives imagine to be just like an embryo. Then another spirit—as a rule a female one—takes the spirit child and carries it to the village, where she inserts it into the body of one of her near relatives. All these individuals—the spirit child, the ministering spirit, and the prospective mother—are invariably of the same totemic clan; in fact they are always near relatives in the cognate line. There are several variants of this belief: thus some natives affirm that the spirit child is not an embryo, but a diminutive, invisible being of nondescript character, and that it is not inserted into a woman by another spirit, but floats amidst the foam of the sea and enters the girls while they are bathing in salt water. Again, some natives deny reincarnation: each spirit, after a prolonged existence in the nether world, finally dies. According to this version, the spirit children spontaneously come into being somewhere on Tuma, the island of the dead.

4. Summary.—Summing up the above data, we may conclude that the following ideas are characteristic of the belief in spirit children: (1) the spirits, or vital principles, of men to be born exist in a definite state before entering life; (2) they pass into life by entering or being inserted into the womb of a woman; the only cause of pregnancy is the entry of a spirit child into a woman's body; (3) sexual intercourse stands in no causal relation to pregnancy; (4) spirit children are a transformation of previous human or mythical beings, who thus become reincarnated. The belief in spirit children involves the ideas of reincarnation or of the continuity of life.

The beliefs in question are closely connected with the problem of totemism (*q.v.*), and they play an important part in J. G. Frazer's attempt to solve this problem. On the other hand, they are closely associated with the ignorance of physical fatherhood, which has left a distinct imprint on the folklore of primitive and civilized races.

LITERATURE.—The standard works by W. B. Spencer, and by W. B. Spencer and F. J. Gillen, are the most important sources for the Australian beliefs in question: Spencer-Gillen, *The Native Tribes of Central Australia*, London, 1899, ch. iv. p. 112 ff., esp. 119–127, *The Northern Tribes of Central Australia*, do. 1904, pp. 146–148, 156–158, 170; **W. B. Spencer**, *Native Tribes of the Northern Territory of Australia*, do. 1914, index, *s.v.* 'Spirit children.' The work of **C. Strehlow** (*Die Aranda- und Loritja-Stämme in Zentral-Australien*, so far pts. i.–iv., Frankfort, 1907–13) contains valuable additions in detail, but no new essential features. The claims of this author, who worked after Spencer and Gillen and had their achievements to guide him, to have corrected his predecessors' discoveries on certain vital points are evidently due to Strehlow's failure to grasp the intrinsic complexity of native beliefs.

The Melanesian sources are: **W. H. R. Rivers**, 'Totemism in Polynesia and Melanesia,' *JRAI* xxxix. [1909] 156 ff.; **B. Malinowski**, 'Baloma; the Spirits of the Dead in the Trobriand Islands,' *JRAI* xlvi. [1916] 353 ff.

J. G. Frazer, *Totemism and Exogamy*, 4 vols., London, 1910, and **E. S. Hartland**, *Primitive Paternity*, 2 vols., do. 1909, deal theoretically with this problem.

B. MALINOWSKI.

SPIRITISM.—Spiritism (or spiritualism) may be defined as the belief that it is possible to communicate with the 'spirits' of the dead so as to receive from them intelligent messages and proofs of their identity and survival, and as the study and practice of so doing. Thus defined, spiritism is of immemorial antiquity and universal distribution; it has always exercised an important influence on religions and philosophies, and has affected conduct, though not, apparently, to the extent which its theoretic importance would seem to warrant. Spiritism naturally has a strong attraction for those who have suffered bereavement, while their sense of loss is poignant; but the spirit-world is also a source of repulsions and an object of dread, and as a rule this view of it prevails over its attraction. So the religions hedge it round with powerful tabus, and endeavour to monopolize and regulate spiritistic practices so as to render them harmless or nugatory; the philosophies also mostly labour to show that there can be no scientific knowledge of the spirit-world. This contention is more or less justified by the fact that spiritism is much older than science; it embodies a large number of primitive ideas and superstitions, and concerns itself with a mass of obscure and elusive phenomena which science has neglected or put aside, because they did not seem capable of complete scientific explanation. They impress the popular mind, however, and spiritism has contrived to combine them in a more or less coherent interpretation. This interpretation is essentially prescientific, but it has nevertheless shown considerable capacity to develop in accordance with the ideas of the time.

The natural starting-point for this development is the world-wide notion of 'spirit' or soul—the 'breath' which animates the body and is its principle of life. This notion is easily suggested, not only by the apparently supernormal experiences to be mentioned, but by the familiar habits of sleeping and dreaming. Accordingly the spirit is conceived as detachable from the body and capable of wandering about at large while its owner is asleep or entranced. It is not, however, necessarily regarded as the real man. In the Homeric eschatology, *e.g.*, the real man (αὐτός) is the body, and is devoured by birds and dogs,[1] while the souls which descend into Hades are devoid of intelligence, until they are enabled to materialize themselves again by drinking the blood of Odysseus's sacrifice.[2] Being thus already independent of the body during life, the spirit naturally survives at death and becomes a 'ghost,' all the more formidable for being endowed with undefined powers,

[1] Spencer, *Native Tribes of the Northern Territory*, pp. 270–274.

[1] *Il.* i. 3 f. [2] *Od.* xi. 153.

and with a tendency to linger among its familiar haunts, especially if it is not 'laid' by proper burial rites. Their hankering to return to bodily existence renders 'spirits' capable of obsessions, *i.e.* of occupying and using, temporarily or permanently, any bodies into which they can find admission. The owner of a body so receptive of spirit influence then becomes a natural intermediary between this life and spirit-life, a 'medicine-man' or priest; in modern spiritist phraseology he is technically called a 'medium.' Moreover, whereas a spirit was originally supposed to produce effects in virtue of its own powers, the tendency in modern spiritism is towards a subtler theory which regards the presence of a medium as always necessary, even where it is not recognized. The rarity of mediumship and lack of mediumistic quality can then be used to explain why so few 'see ghosts' and have abnormal experiences, and why phenomena attributable to 'spirits' are on the whole rare everywhere.

The theory of mediumship and the idea of using a code of signals for spelling out communications are the two chief developments which characterize what is called 'modern spiritualism.' This arose in 1848 at Hydesville, New York State, in the family of John D. Fox, out of mysterious knockings, which appeared to be intelligent. One of the daughters suggested a code, three raps for yes, one for no, two for doubtful; and communication was established with what claimed to be a 'spirit.' The three Fox sisters became the first 'mediums,' and the practice of sitting in 'circles' (holding *séances*) for the purpose of communicating with 'spirits,' who answered by raps, tilts of the table, or other signals, rapidly spread over the whole world.

As time went on, the 'phenomena' of spiritism became very various. They are usually classified as (*a*) psychical and (*b*) physical. (*a*) Under psychical phenomena may be enumerated the various forms of automatism, of speech, of writing, of vision (*e.g.*, crystal-gazing [*q.v.*]), obsessions, impersonations, trances, apparitions, hallucinations, clairvoyance, clairaudience, hyperæsthesia, prophecy, and the like. Any supernormal knowledge elicited by any method of communication or in any of these states, or in 'veridical' dreaming, especially when yielding evidence of 'spirit-identity,' may also be claimed in favour of the spiritist interpretation. (*b*) As physical phenomena there are said to occur in *séances* inexplicable movements of bodies ('telekinesis'), sounds, lights, 'direct' spirit writing, the passage of solids through solids, as in the untying of knots, the 'materializations' of human and other forms, the bringing in of objects from a distance ('apports'), levitations, spirit photographs, immunity from the effects of handling fire, etc. In many cases, however, the question whether a phenomenon reported —*e.g.*, a spirit-light or an apparition—is 'physical' or 'psychical' (*i.e.* hallucinatory) may be the very point to be decided, and, if the evidence pointing to the occurrence of *collective* hallucinations is admitted, the ordinary criteria of physical reality rather break down. It should be remembered also that the convenient distinction between the physical and the psychical may not ultimately apply and that it may be unwise to take it too absolutely.

The examination of these phenomena, and in general the investigation of the subject, are beset with extreme difficulty. Nearly all the facts are in dispute, nearly all are susceptible of alternative interpretations. Nearly all the theories are vague and too ill-defined to be tested experimentally. Indeed, there is so little control of the phenomena that crucial experiments cannot be made. Those who interest themselves in the subject are commonly animated by strong prejudices and the most virulent forms of bias. The subject itself is essentially a 'borderland,' and it is not the business of any established science to concern itself with its systematic and persistent exploration. But for these very reasons it provides excellent material for those who are desirous of studying the making of a science.

Of the current interpretations the simplest is undoubtedly that of (1) fraud. It is certainly capable of disposing of much of the evidence, and no investigator can afford to disregard it so long as frauds of all sorts are possible and easy, as they must be so long as the phenomena are allowed to occur in the dark or in insufficient light, with little or no control of crude observation by apparatus, with mediums who are paid by results and are dependent for their livelihood on their success, or who resent ordinary precautions as imputations on their honesty. Still there is nothing genuine on earth that cannot be simulated, and the possibility of fraud is not always a proof of it. And it is fairly clear that ordinary fraud is not an adequate explanation of everything that is reported. The sitters often deceive themselves, and, *e.g.*, regard as supernormally acquired information which they have themselves inadvertently given to the mediums. The mediums, again, may be self-deceived, for their mental constitution is frequently abnormal, and, especially in the case of psychical phenomena, they are often in conditions of 'trance,' etc., in which they act out dreams, suggestions, and hallucinations, and are hardly responsible for their actions. Moreover, it has been shown experimentally[1] that many of the successful frauds are due, not to the ordinary methods of conjuring-tricks, but to a special source of error, viz. the impossibility of continuous observation, lapses of attention of which the observer is not himself aware.

When fraud has been sufficiently discounted, there still remains a choice of non-spiritistic interpretations which may or may not admit that the phenomena are in part supernormal. (2) Many of the 'psychical' phenomena—*e.g.*, impersonations, obsessions, premonitions, automatic writing, exhibitions of supernormal knowledge, etc.—appear to be genuine products of the subliminal, subconscious memory, multiple personality, and other imperfectly understood processes of the human mind, which can simulate spirit-communications to a surprising extent. It should be noted also that the phenomena appear spontaneously to assume a spiritistic form and that the communications regularly claim to come from 'spirits.'

The weakness of this method of explanation is that no definite limits are set to it. If even the faintest, and normally imperceptible, stimulus may impress the sense-organs, and if there can be submerged records of everything that ever has been, or might have been, noted, the feats of hyperæsthesia or of 'memory' may border on the miraculous. Consequently this explanation easily shades off into (3) the telepathic, which frankly admits that the phenomena transcend the limits of recognized human faculty, but refuses to ascribe them on this account to the spirits of the dead. This interpretation, though not incompatible with spiritism—for, if there can be telepathy between living minds, why not between the living and the dead?—is detrimental to it, because it renders it impossible to regard even the best evidence for spiritism as conclusive. It seems sufficient to suppose that knowledge may percolate from one living mind to another, supernormally but subliminally and unconsciously; for, if the supernormal knowledge is to be verifiable, it must have passed through some human mind. The existence of telepathy (*q.v.*), however, rests on a somewhat narrow experimental basis, while the principle itself is too negative to be a good explanation, and there is no evidence for it in the extended form,

[1] Cf. R. Hodgson and S. J. Davey, 'The Possibilities of Mal-Observation and Lapse of Memory,' in the *Proceedings of the Society for Psychical Research*, pt. xi. [1887] p. 381.

which assumes that any knowledge possessed by any mind may be reproduced in any other. Still even the spiritists are beginning to reckon with the possibility of telepathic percolation of knowledge from the mind of the sitter to that of the medium, and also to admit that the communications received from 'spirits' do not come directly from the nominal communicator, but are affected considerably by the mind of the medium, conscious and 'subliminal,' and by the 'control' of the medium in the 'spirit'-world, who forms a sort of second mediator. Communication thus becomes a highly complex process, and errors may be ascribed to failures of transmission, either from the communicator to the controlling spirit, or from the latter to the subliminal, or from the subliminal to the trance-consciousness of the medium, or lastly to the abnormality and lack of power of the medium.

(4) In addition to telepathy, some philosophers (*e.g.*, William James and Maeterlinck) have suggested, as a possible source of the supernormal knowledge, a sort of cosmic reservoir of knowledge which the medium's mind subconsciously taps.

(5) Lastly, many theologians, especially Roman Catholic, with some philosophic support,[1] still ascribe all the phenomena of spiritism to 'devils,' simulating the spirits of the dead.

To meet these alternatives, the supporters of the spiritistic interpretation have endeavoured to strengthen the evidence of spirit-identity with a certain amount of success. Experiments with sealed test-letters deposited by the departed have indeed hitherto failed, almost completely. Attempts have also been made to get what can be recognized as the same intelligence to manifest through a number of independent mediums. The difficulty of excluding telepathy in such cases has led on to the theory of 'cross correspondences,' as developed in the *Proceedings of the Society for Psychical Research* (from 1903), in which an often very complicated series of allusions is given, piecemeal, at different times, and through different automatists. Each allusion is unintelligible or nonsensical as it is given, but nevertheless, when the case is complete, they all dovetail together into a coherent and intelligible whole which is suggestive of the personality of a particular communicator. In this way it is claimed that the possibility of telepathy may be eliminated, since no living human mind knows the answer to the puzzle until it is given, and it is then also seen that an intelligence other than the medium's, and identical throughout, was at work all along, constructing the enigma. But of course chance coincidence can never quite be excluded, and the method of proof is too subtle to be popularly convincing. The chief exceptions taken to the character of the alleged spirit-communications have been ingeniously met: the triviality of the messages relied on to prove spirit-identity has been closely paralleled, in some experiments initiated by J. H. Hyslop, by the methods used among friends, (*a*) in determining the authorship of intentionally vague and general messages, and (*b*) in detecting impersonations. It was found that apparently quite inadequate clues were recognized as characteristic and led to correct identifications.[2] The objection that nothing of scientific novelty or value is ever imparted by spirits is met by pointing to the difficulty of verifying such information if it should be given; the frequent confusion and dreaminess of the messages is explained by the difficulties of communication 'with one asleep through one asleep.' To the objection that the 'spirits' do not behave in a dignified manner worthy of spiritual beings it is replied that there is no reason to think that the mere fact of death should entirely transform their character and outlook, and, besides, we know too little about their life to judge what behaviour would befit them. This reply has value if it acknowledges that at present the term 'spirit' is not much more than a name for our ignorance. Altogether, then, the evidence for the 'psychical' phenomena has to be left in a very ambiguous and unsatisfactory condition.

Nor is the situation any better as regards the 'physical' phenomena. They are of course far more improbable *per se* and very susceptible of explanation by fraud. Nevertheless, the evidence for their occurrence is quite copious, and by no means inferior in quality to that for the 'psychical' phenomena. Indeed, from first to last, from the mediumship of D. D. Home (1850) to that of Eusapia Paladino and Marthe Béraud (1914), some of the best and most elaborately recorded evidence has concerned 'physical' phenomena. Besides fraud and collective hallucination, the spiritist interpretation has here to reckon with the theory that the phenomena are due to some unknown force emanating from the medium, to which some of the observers have given the preference. In conclusion it may be said that, whatever view is taken of the phenomena as a whole, and even if they are destined to serve only to enlarge our conception of the possibility of fraud and self-deception, they are deserving of more, and more scientific, study than they have received.

LITERATURE.—The literature of the subject is immense, but much of it is of very little value. The year 1882 may be taken as the dividing point between the older and the later literature; for it is the date of the foundation of the Society for Psychical Research, by Henry Sidgwick, Edmund Gurney, Frederic Myers, W. F. Barrett, and others, with which may be said to have begun the continuous, systematic, and co-operative study of the phenomena alleged. The publications of this Society (*Proceedings* and *Journal*) are indispensable to the student, alike for their records and for their critical contents.

Among the works of the earlier period may be mentioned **E. W. Capron**, *Modern Spiritualism*, Boston, 1855; **J. W. Edmonds** and **G. T. Dexter**, *Spiritualism*, New York, 1853; **R. Hare**, *Experimental Investigations of the Spirit Manifestations*, do. 1856; **A. de Gasparin**, *Des Tables tournantes*, 2 vols., Paris, 1854; **M. Thury**, *Les Tables tournantes*, Geneva, 1855; **A. De Morgan** and **Mrs. S. E. De Morgan**, *From Matter to Spirit*, London, 1863; *Report of the Committee of the Dialectical Society*, do. 1871; **William Crookes**, *Researches in the Phenomena of Spiritualism*, do. 1874; **Alfred Russel Wallace**, *Miracles and Modern Spiritualism*, rev. ed. do. 1896; **D. D. Home**, *Lights and Shadows of Spiritualism*, do. 1877; **W. Stainton Moses** ('M.A.Oxon.'), *Spirit Identity*, do. 1879. Abroad **Allan Kardec** (M. H. D. L. Rivail), *Le Livre des esprits*, Paris, 1853, ^{13}1865, the chief of the reincarnationist spiritists, and the works (1852–67) of **K. von Reichenbach**, the discoverer of paraffin, on the (really subjective) manifestations of 'odic force' visible to his 'sensitives,' may be mentioned; also **J. K. F. Zöllner**, *Wissenschaftliche Abhandlungen*, 4 vols., Leipzig, 1878–81, tr. C. C. Massey, *Transcendental Physics*^{3}, London, 1885, in which spirits operating in a fourth dimension of space were invoked to explain the untying of knots.

Since 1882 the work of the S.P.R. group and their allies deserves special attention. Of these **E. Gurney**, **F. W. H. Myers**, and **F. Podmore**, *Phantasms of the Living*, 2 vols., London, 1886, was the first; **F. W. H. Myers**'s *magnum opus*, *Human Personality and its Survival of Bodily Death*, 2 vols., do. 1903, appeared posthumously. **F. Podmore**'s works, of a highly critical, not to say sceptical, character, include *Studies in Psychical Research*, do. 1897, *Modern Spiritualism*, 2 vols., do. 1902 (largely historical), and *The Newer Spiritualism*, do. 1910. The writings of **Richard Hodgson**, **Mrs. E. M. Sidgwick**, **J. G. Piddington**, **W. W. Baggally**, and **Mrs. Verrall** are confined to the publications of the S.P.R.; but those of **Andrew Lang** (*The Making of Religion*, London, 1898), **William James** (two brilliant essays in *The Will to Believe*, do. 1897, and *Memories and Studies*, do. 1911), **J. H. Hyslop**, Secretary of the American S.P.R. (*Psychical Research and Survival*, do. 1913), **Oliver Lodge** (*Raymond*, do. 1916), **W. F. Barrett** (*On the Threshold of the Unseen*, do. 1917), **J. A. Hill** (*Psychical Investigations*, do. 1917), **Hereward Carrington** (*The Physical Phenomena of Spiritualism*, Boston, 1907, *Eusapia Paladino and her Phenomena*, New York, 1909, *The Problems of Psychical Research*, London, 1914), and **F. C. S. Schiller** (two chapters in *Humanism*, do. 1903, on the psychological and philosophic aspects) are also available in book form.

[1] *E.g.*, F. H. Bradley, in *Essays on Truth and Reality*, Oxford, 1914, p. 440.

[2] Cf. *Pro. Soc. Psych. Res.*, pt. xli. [1901] p. 537 f.

In Switzerland T. Flournoy of Geneva maintains a scientific attitude very similar to that of the S.P.R.; his *Des Indes à la planète Mars*, Paris, 1900, with a supplement in *Archives de Psychologie de la Suisse romande*, no. 2 (1901), is a model study of an important case of somnambulic mediumship. Cf. also his *Esprits et médiums*, Paris, 1911. J. Maxwell, *Les Phénomènes psychiques*, do. 1903, Eng. tr. *Metaphysical Phenomena*, London, 1905; E. Morselli, *Psicologia e Spiritismo*, Turin, 1908; C. Lombroso, *After Death—What?*, Eng. tr., London, 1909; A. von Schrenck-Notzing, *Materialisations-Phänomene*, Munich, 1914; Mme. Alexandre Bisson, *Les Phénomènes dits de matérialisation*, Paris, 1914; and W. J. Crawford, *The Reality of Psychic Phenomena*, London, 1916, are mainly records of experiments. The *Report* (Philadelphia, 1887) of the Seybert Commission on spiritualism was negative, and enabled the testator's funds to be used to endow a chair of philosophy. Hostile criticism is also represented by A. Lehmann, *Aberglaube und Zauberei*, Stuttgart, 1898; A. E. Tanner, *Studies in Spiritism*, New York, 1910; and I. L. Tuckett, *The Evidence for the Supernatural*, London, 1911; and, as a specimen of dialectics, by F. H. Bradley's art. 'Evidences of Spiritualism,' in the *Fortnightly Rev.*, new ser., xxxviii. [1885] 811 ff.

Of periodicals there may be mentioned, in addition to the *Proceedings* and *Journals* (monthly) of the English and of the American S.P.R., *Light*, the official organ of English Spiritualism (weekly), *The Occult Review* (monthly), *Psychische Studien*, ed. A. Aksakow, and *Annales des sciences psychiques*.

F. C. S. SCHILLER.

SPIRITUALISM.—1. Spiritualism is a popular term for what is more correctly called Spiritism (*q.v.*).

2. In philosophy spiritualism is the opposite of materialism (*q.v.*), *i.e.* the doctrine that reality is ultimately spiritual in its nature. Of this doctrine there may evidently be two varieties, according as this is asserted of all reality or only of some; in the latter case spiritualism is compatible with a dualism which admits the reality also of material substance, as in Cartesianism.[1] In the former sense it is not easy to distinguish spiritualism from idealism (*q.v.*) (in some of the many senses of that term), and indeed the two notions are often used interchangeably. It may be said, however, more strictly that, whereas idealism renders all reality relative to and dependent upon mind, spiritualism regards it as consisting of 'spirits,' which are not wholly or chiefly minds, and so does not make the cognitive process essential to reality. It will follow from this distinction that the same philosophy may be both spiritualistic and idealistic; Berkeley's doctrine, *e.g.*, is idealism in that it denies the reality of material substance and conceives physical reality as existing only for minds and having for its *esse percipi*; but it is spiritualism in that it composes ultimate reality of spirits, whose *esse* is *percipere*.[2] F. C. S. SCHILLER.

SPIRITUALITY. — The term 'spirituality' has been used in a great variety of ways. The French have appropriated it as the name for the finer perceptions of life; by the American transcendentalists it is used as a special mark of superior intellects; it is often applied to those mediums through whom communications from departed spirits are said to reach common earth; Evangelical Christianity reserves the term to describe the warmer religious emotions; and it has its proper and peculiar application as the distinguishing quality of NT believers.

The substantive 'spirituality' does not occur in Scripture, but the adjective 'spiritual' (πνευματικός) is frequently employed to describe the character of the man who has entered the Kingdom of God. Such a man has the Holy Spirit as the vital, determining principle of his life. The NT usage does not permit us to apply the epithet to any one who has been moved in some vague way by holy impulses, for a definite and well-marked character is indicated by this description. Of spiritual persons Newman writes:

'He [the Holy Spirit] pervades us (if it may be so said) as light pervades a building, or as a sweet perfume the folds of some honourable robe; so that, in Scripture language, we are said to be in Him, and He in us.'[1]

Spirituality can best be understood by first considering the promises of Jesus and thereafter noting the experience of it in the early Church.

1. Spirituality the promise of Jesus. — The esoteric state called 'spirituality' is a legitimate outcome of the Christian life as it was conceived by its Founder. Our Lord went everywhere offering to men an effective holy life which would issue from union with Himself, but, as the days approached when He would be called upon to leave this earth, He began to promise another Presence, the Comforter, who would maintain this union. The life in Jesus would not dissipate itself as a tender memory on the rough sea of human history, but would communicate its virtues continuously to the faithful.

That spirituality was the chief feature of the life offered by Jesus is evident from His insistent demand, 'Ye must be born again' (Jn 3^7; cf. v.^{3}). Entrance into the Kingdom of God is possible only to that man who has undergone a distinct change in the character of his affections. The new birth[2] is further described as being 'born of water and of the Spirit' (Jn 3^5). After the manner of an inspiration, the heart is mysteriously moved towards the ideals of the Kingdom of Heaven, and the decisive moment in this change is an inward awakening to the presence, near a man, of a sphere of life infinitely more valuable, because more spiritual, than the natural life of mankind. In its mode of action the birth in the Spirit less resembles the heightening and deepening of moral instinct—common enough in human history — than the creation of a new kind of being. Mysterious in its origin, this new birth is not, however, dissociated from the ordinary workings of human faculty. It employs both the will and the heart; it works by convincing the one and softening the other.

The new life in the Kingdom was adequately described in the teaching and illustrated in the conduct of Jesus; and the promise of another Comforter was kept ever in strict agreement with that teaching and life.

The beneficial effects of the gracious operation of the Holy Spirit are three.

(1) When the Holy Spirit is come in His fullness, He will be present as an immediate and effective moral power in the heart: 'He . . . will convict the world in respect of sin, and of righteousness, and of judgment' (Jn 16^8). 'The idea of "conviction" is complex. It involves the conceptions of authoritative examination, of unquestionable proof, of decisive judgement, of punitive power.'[3] The result of the Holy Spirit's work will be to put believers in possession of clear moral ideals, so that they must be seen and acknowledged as true. The real nature of sin, the necessity of righteousness, and the inevitability of judgment will be alike recognized. In other words, the first effect of the Spirit's illumination is a clear insight into the moral relation of human action to the universe as that was conceived by Jesus. The conscience is at once enhanced in value and becomes more authoritative by the indwelling of the Holy Spirit.

(2) The second effect of the Spirit's presence will be a new possession of truth: 'He shall guide you into all the truth' (Jn 16^{13}). Truth was to Jesus, as to His Jewish contemporaries, that practical wisdom by which conduct was guided. The modern conception of truth as 'that which satisfies the intellect' was not in His mind. By 'truth' our Lord means a knowledge of that which is necessary for life in harmony with God. To those disciples who would obey Him Jesus promised a knowledge of the truth, and 'the truth shall make you free' (Jn 8^{32}). This was evidently a promise of practical freedom—freedom for action as well as for thought. It would, however, be a mistake to confine this understanding to practical truth alone, for in the gradual approximation to a complete knowledge of conduct the intellectual qualities would be brightened and a new point of view acquired. The spiritual mind may not only feel more warmly moved by the knowledge of moral truth; it may also act with greater intellectual prescience.

(3) The Holy Spirit will glorify Jesus; *i.e.*, He will reveal to

[1] See art. DESCARTES.
[2] See artt. BERKELEY, PERCEPTION.

[1] *Parochial and Plain Sermons*, new ed., London, 1868, ii. 222.
[2] See art. REGENERATION.
[3] B. F. Westcott, *The Gospel according to St. John*, London, 1908, ii. 219.

the heart of man the majesty and unspeakable beauty of the character and work of Jesus. Like a treasure of inexhaustible wealth, the Spirit will find Jesus an object adequate for all His blessed operations in the human soul (Jn 15^{26}). New aspects of the character, new satisfactions in the finished work, and new delights in the friendship of Jesus remain to be discovered to men by the Holy Ghost. In this, His most proper work, the Holy Spirit will be the witness of that divine love of which Jesus was the conspicuous agent.

In view of our Lord's promises, we may say that humanity and history, broadly conceived, will determine the limits of genuine spiritual experience; for, however mysterious in its origin, the new life in the Spirit identifies itself with the conscience and the heart of man; and the Spirit Himself lives more and more to exploit the perfect character of Jesus as that manifested itself in history. These two positions, clearly established in the Incarnation, must be the norm by which all spiritual pretensions are to be judged. Does any spiritual claim contradict an enlightened moral consciousness? Does it get ever quite out of touch with the historical Jesus? If so, it has thereby discredited itself in the Christian view of spirituality.

2. Spirituality the experience of the Church.—In striking agreement with the forecast of Jesus is the experience of the apostles, notably of St. Paul. For him the peculiar feature of the life in Christ is the presence of the living Saviour in the hearts of those who love Him. Love for God and man, efficient moral power, and the whole new life and hope of the gospel come from the indwelling Jesus, who more and more identifies Himself with the Christian—soul of his soul, heart of his heart, the life within his life. This blessed indwelling the apostle describes in other places as the indwelling of the Holy Spirit. For him, as for all the apostles, Pentecost was the birth-place of modern Christianity. What is noticeable in his Epistles is the growth of an experience which fully justifies the prophecies of Jesus about the Comforter.

The virtues foretold are precisely those which now appear in the experience of the Church.

(1) The presence of the Holy Spirit is a new principle of moral power. The Christian is free from the bondage of iniquity; the body is dead because of sin; and in the age-long struggle between the lower and the higher nature victory is now with the spirit (Ro 8, Gal 5). This domination of the Christian's conscience by the Holy Spirit extends to the farthest thought of the imagination which, with all other motions of the heart, is to be brought into subjection to Jesus (2 Co 10^{5}). So powerful is this influence that the body itself, the seat of so many imperfections, shall one day be quickened by the Spirit into an immortal existence (Ro 8^{11}). In one famous sentence St. Paul lets us understand his sense of the moral efficiency of the Holy Spirit in a Christian; 'where the Spirit of the Lord is, there is liberty' (2 Co 3^{17}). In this freedom, the summit of moral attainment, where the law becomes a habit of the soul, St. Paul recognizes the legitimate and inevitable effect of the indwelling of the all-powerful Holy Spirit.

(2) No less emphatically does the apostle describe the illuminating grace of the Holy Spirit. The Christian is an enlightened person, whose inner principle of intelligence is the infallible light of the Spirit of God (1 Co $2^{14\text{-}16}$). With full knowledge of the seriousness of the claim that he is making, the apostle proceeds to declare that in the light of the Holy Spirit a humble Christian is better informed than the princes of wisdom or the teachers of the schools (vv.$^{10\text{-}13}$). Here, as to his Lord, truth is for St. Paul practical wisdom—that which relates to conduct as it touches God and as it affects men. But St. Paul claims, without fear, for every spiritual man that he is so enlightened in those matters which most deeply influence human life that he may without presumption set himself up to judge all things (v.^{15}). The criterion of all practical truth is its conformity to that inner enlightenment which a believer enjoys in the Holy Spirit. Thus early did the Church claim those virtues promised by Jesus.

(3) The promise that the Spirit should testify of Jesus becomes so certain a maxim that St. Paul scarcely feels himself called upon to justify it. Only once, and that in an argument about the moral blindness of the Jews, does he declare that the Lord, *i.e.* the Christ, is the Spirit (2 Co 3^{17}). In all other places he allows himself to speak indifferently about the indwelling Christ and the indwelling Spirit. The total result of the Spirit's influence in the heart is that Christ is formed in us (Gal 4^{19}).

In this vital spiritual union with Jesus the virtues of Jesus are reproduced. The love of God is shed abroad in our hearts by the Holy Ghost (Ro 5^{5}); towards God the Christian attitude is the affectionate trust of a child (8^{15}); and in this loving experience joy rises to its crown, for therein Christians know themselves the children of God, assured of final salvation. In his relation to his neighbour the Christian is animated by the Spirit in tender affection. The apostle urges his converts not to grieve the Spirit by bitterness, wrath, and anger, but rather to please Him by being 'kind one to another, tenderhearted, forgiving each other' (Eph $4^{30\text{-}32}$). In the Epistle to the Galatians St. Paul consciously and definitely describes the conduct of the spiritual (πνευματικοί); they are to bear one another's burdens, to communicate their knowledge to the ignorant, and never to weary in well-doing (ch. 6). But it is in 1 Co 13 that the ardent apostle crowns love and sets it on the throne of Christian character. The conclusion of the whole matter is summed up in one sentence: the Spirit of God is a spirit of 'power and love and discipline' (2 Ti 1^{7}).

3. False spirituality.—This enlightened, holy, and loving life, the possession of all believers, is the mark of a true Christian and constitutes 'the spiritual man.' Such a lofty life runs the risk of all high things—it may be misunderstood. It is misunderstood by the formalists of all ages, who insist upon religion confining itself within strict rules or laws. This temper is always with us, but it was bravely faced and triumphantly defeated by St. Paul in his encounter with the Judaizing teachers. In the Epistle to the Galatians the supremacy of the Spirit and its inherent freedom are courageously expounded.

On the other hand, the promised gifts of the Spirit have led many to make extraordinary claims of spiritual enlightenment and independence. Mysticism (*q.v.*), so closely akin to the temper of the Indian *yogi*, the Buddhist *dhyana*, and the Muhammadan *ṣūfī*, has appeared in the Church from time to time, believing itself to be the natural development of the teaching of St. Paul. Numerous and sometimes moving attempts have been made to justify the mystic claim of 'immersion in the infinite ocean of God,' but these can be successfully dealt with only as St. Paul handled them. He adopted instinctively the norm which lies latent in Christ's promises. All pretended insight on the part of so-called 'spiritual' persons must be judged by one criterion: Does it testify of Jesus? To the Gnostic claims which began to make themselves felt in the church at Colossæ St. Paul opposes the history of Jesus. Do the Colossians believe themselves to be possessed of a wisdom (γνῶσις) superior to that of ordinary Christians? St. Paul replies that there is no need of any wisdom or help which could not be found in Christ (Col $2^{3.\,10}$). To the refined ideals of Gnosticism (*q.v.*), which shuddered at the thought of the contamination of the pure Deity in the creation of this material world, St. Paul simply cites Jesus, who so little considered matter evil that He was the medium of creation; and, so far from requiring some intermediate angelic agency, God had been pleased to make all fullness (πλήρωμα) dwell in Jesus (1^{19} 2^{9}). Spirituality is a character in closest touch at every moment with Jesus as He revealed Himself in history.

In the same way all practical results of spiritual possession must be tested by the moral standard of the gospel. Asceticism (*q.v.*), the cherished ideal of the Gnostics, is an error. 'Touch not, handle not' has a show of humility, but is not effective against the lusts of the flesh (Col 2^{23}). The true deliverance is in union with Jesus through the Spirit, whereby our affections are lifted to higher things (3^{5}). Even the earnest believer's desire for the supernatural gifts of the Spirit is not to be encouraged. There were, indeed, gifts of tongues, of prophecy, of faith, and such like; and without doubt some heightening of the natural qualities of man does follow the presence of the Holy Spirit in the heart, and may be beneficial for the extension of Christ's Kingdom; but the essential and particular characteristics of the spiritual man are these three things, enlightenment, love, and power. 'If I have the gift of prophecy, and know all mysteries and all knowledge; and if I have all faith, so as to remove mountains, but have not love, I am nothing' (1 Co 13²). The heightened powers of knowledge, of insight, and of superhuman gift are all, in the Holy Spirit, closely and intimately moral—after the morality of Jesus. From St. Paul's time to the present no better test has been found for the valuation of the spiritual phenomena of religion.

Spirituality is the essential temper of a Christian, and it consists in the possession of the individual by the Holy Spirit of Jesus, whose blessed presence is manifest in an increasing moral insight and conquest, a growing knowledge of the deep mysteries of God, and an ever more tender and sensitive love towards God and man; in a word, an ever closer approximation to the likeness of the Son of God as He lived among men. In the preservation and cultivation of this spiritual union the Christian finds the duty of his high calling. Kinship with Jesus through the Spirit has to be maintained by a life-long reaching unto consecration. In this task a ready and willing obedience is the surest means. Moral kinship grows with acts of morality, the kinship of loving hearts grows with acts of love, and the kinship of the Holy Spirit grows with acts of faith and spiritual conduct.

See also art. EXPERIENCE (Religious).

LITERATURE.—John Owen, Πνευματολογία; *or, A Discourse concerning the Holy Spirit*, London, 1674; H. C. G. Moule, *Veni Creator*, do. 1890; Maurice Goguel, *La Notion johannique de l'esprit et ses antécédents historiques*, Paris, 1902; Auguste Sabatier, *The Religions of Authority and the Religion of the Spirit*, Eng. tr., London, 1904, bk. iii., 'The Religion of the Spirit'; H. B. Swete, *The Holy Spirit in the New Testament*, do. 1909; Rudolf Eucken, *The Problem of Human Life*, Eng. tr., do. 1910, pt. ii. 'Christianity'; George Steven, *The Psychology of the Christian Soul*, do. 1911; Henri Joly, *The Psychology of the Saints*, Eng. tr., do. 1898.

DAVID FYFFE.

SPITTING.—See SALIVA.

SPONSORS.—1. Origin and meaning.—The word 'sponsors' was and is still applied to those who undertake certain spiritual responsibilities for the baptized, in some cases for infants who are unconscious of the vows of renunciation, faith, and obedience required before baptism, and in others for those who by strange circumstances have been placed in the same condition. St. Cyril of Alexandria[1] tells us that, when men were seized with extremity of sickness and it was thought proper on that account to baptize them, there were some appointed to make both the renunciation and confession of the same. For this reason they were also called *susceptores*. Directly the Church admitted the necessity of infant baptism, something of the kind was obviously necessary. To baptize children without demanding of them some profession of faith and obedience would be to abandon one of the most important parts of the rite and to lead to the opinion that baptism availed for salvation independently of the co-operation of the will of the baptized. If we believe that by baptism we put on Christ, as the seed may be said to put on the earth into which it is placed, then, just as the seed requires the care of the gardener, so the soul of the infant requires the care of the sponsor till it shoots up and is able, with the friendly help of the Sun of Righteousness and the dew of God's Holy Spirit, to take care of itself. The Church naturally shrank from placing a seed into the garden of the Lord unless there were some who by raking and weeding would give it the opportunity it needed.

2. Who may be sponsors.—In the first days the sponsors were ordinarily the parents of the child; they would be best fitted and naturally the most desirous so to train the child that it might realize and fulfil the promises and vows made in its name. And yet even then the Church was anxious to emphasize the truth of the spiritual birth of the child by making as little of the natural tie as possible. The natural parents became spiritual parents, representing the Mother Church whose children the infants became by baptism. Of course in many cases, especially during the days of persecution, there were no parents to stand for the child, and the Church would then provide deacons, deaconesses, or virgins, who would act in her name and make the profession demanded. So too in the large number of adult baptisms it must have often happened, as it does in the mission field, that the parents were heathen or so ignorant as to be unable to be responsible for the spiritual education of the candidates. Hence it became more and more exceptional to find parent sponsors, until at last parents were forbidden to take on themselves the office. It was doubtless felt that the new tie of god-parent, as the sponsor was called, was never very seriously recognized by those to whom the old tie was everything, and that there was a distinct gain in obtaining those outside the family to whom the spiritual tie was all important.

3. Sponsorial responsibilities.—It has sometimes been said that the pledges which the god-parents are asked to make are profoundly unreal. How can any one make a promise for some one else of whose character he knows nothing? And yet it has its analogy. Estates are held by trustees in behalf of children on special conditions, such as that they profess the Protestant religion or become Roman Catholics. These trustees pledge the children so far and do their best by providing them with suitable teachers to see that they fulfil the promises made in their name. And, as the children grow up, they are told that the property will not be theirs unless they accept the responsibility long ago made for them. So too the god-parents ought to see that their god-children realize the splendid inheritance which is to be theirs and the conditions on which alone they can hope to win it.

4. Number of sponsors.—The English Book of Common Prayer orders that there be three god-parents, two of the same sex as the baptized; but the Roman Church, in this more strictly in accord with primitive usage, requires only one, or at the most two. Bingham is very emphatic here:

> 'We never read of more than one in all the accounts of the ancients, and one of the same sex for adult persons. . . . Some rules forbid more than one, either in baptism or confirmation.'[1]

The number demanded by the English Church may be due to early stormy days when it was felt necessary to throw about the child as strong a bulwark of Christian friends as possible. They were, as is seen by the 29th canon, obliged to be communicants, and therefore naturally expected to be keenly interested in the spiritual training of the child. It was their duty to see that their god-children were taught to know the Creed, the Lord's Prayer, and the Ten Commandments, to learn their Catechism, and to be brought to the bishop to be confirmed by him.

5. Present practice.—It is to be feared that great laxity in practice is now to be found, partly through unwillingness to interfere with the rights

[1] *Comm. St. John*, xi. 26.

[1] *Antiquities of the Christian Church*, bk. xi. ch. viii. § 11.

of the parents, partly through the choice that is so often made, not of those who will be of spiritual help, but of those to whom the offer of the responsibility seems to be a compliment. And it is largely owing to this want of care in seeing that the baptized are spiritually educated that we find thousands of the baptized so ignorant of the most elementary principles of Christianity, in this particular offering a sad contrast to the intelligence and knowledge of catechumens in the mission field.

LITERATURE.—J. Bingham, *The Antiquities of the Christian Church*, bk. xi. ch. viii., *Works*, new ed., Oxford, 1855, iv. 143 ff.; *DCA* ii. 1923–1925; *The Prayer Book Dictionary*, ed. G. Harford and M. Stevenson, London, 1912, p. 371; F. Procter and W. H. Frere, *A new Hist. of the Book of Common Prayer*, do. 1901, p. 575n.; Darwell Stone, *Holy Baptism*³, do. 1901, p. 100 ff.

G. H. S. WALPOLE.

SPONTANEITY.—Spontaneity, in its most general meaning, denotes some form of internally initiated action. It is usually opposed to externally caused events, and probably arose in the defence of some sort of freedom as distinguished from determined or necessitated action. It is not exactly co-extensive with the idea of free action, as the latter implies reflexion and deliberation. Spontaneity seems to consist with unconscious action, though implying that it originates in the subject of it as distinguished from externally initiated actions.

In the physical world actions and motions connected with its natural order are supposed to be caused by some agency outside the subject in which the event takes place. Matter is supposed to be inert, which means that it will not change its present condition, whether of motion or of rest, without the interposition of external causes. Physical events do not take place of themselves—*i.e.*, they are not spontaneous. Hence we say that they are determined, and we mean by this that they are caused from without. But in living organisms we observe a type of actions that, whatever ultimate mechanical influences are supposed, seem to originate wholly within the subject of them. They apparently have no external causes. Consequently we have come to call them spontaneous. Plato called all such action 'self-motion.' This was his conception of free action. Later philosophic thought added self-consciousness and purposive mental states to the notion of freedom, and included spontaneity in it. This freedom implied the possibility of alternative choice as well as self-originative action, and the idea of spontaneity had either to be synonymous with this or to represent the unconscious but subjectively initiated actions of the lower organisms, which did not seem to be mechanically caused. It thus stood as a conception half-way between determined and free actions.

Thus spontaneity is a condition or element of freedom and responsibility, but does not constitute the whole of them. Responsibility implies conscious choice and the knowledge of the distinction between right and wrong, as well as subjective causation. Freedom may not imply more than conscious choice and self-caused actions, and so is not coterminous with responsibility. But spontaneity denotes nothing more than subjective causality, and may occur without conscious choice or the distinction between right and wrong. It is therefore the initial stage of development, or the point of transition, between mechanical and consciously determined actions.

LITERATURE.—G. F. Stout, *Analytical Psychology*, 2 vols., London, 1896–97, ch. vi.; A. Bain, *The Emotions and the Will*³, London and New York, 1880; J. H. Hyslop, *The Elements of Ethics*, New York, 1895, ch. iv.

JAMES H. HYSLOP.

SPRINGS AND WELLS. — See WATER, WATER-GODS.

STAFF.—A staff or wand carried in the hand has been put to many and various uses by man in the development of culture. The most obvious use for such an instrument is defence or attack. A piece of wood from two to four inches long is the constant companion of women in Australia and elsewhere; by its aid yams, fish, game, honey, and so forth are procured. By people to whom writing is unknown notched sticks are employed as helps to memory and as a means of carrying messages from one tribe to another. In this article, however, we shall confine our attention to the use of staves as instruments of magic or divination and as ensigns of dignity and authority.

1. The magico-religious use of staves.—In most parts of the uncivilized world wands carried in the hand are used for magico-religious purposes. Staves form part of the equipment of the medicine-man almost everywhere. These wands are regarded as endowed with supernatural power in various ways; sometimes it depends on an incantation sung over the instrument, as in the case of the pointing stick, at other times the magical virtue is inherent in the material itself, as, *e.g.*, the twigs of hazel or the mistletoe bough. Again, a rod may be possessed of magical power only on certain occasions (Midsummer Night, St. John's Day, etc.) or at particular places (*e.g.*, a tree grown on a grave).

The conception of sacredness in primitive society is generally allied to that of authority. It is therefore not surprising that the staff of office is often at one and the same time part of the insignia of rank and a magical instrument. The horse-staves of the Buriats may be quoted as an example of this class of wand. It is only in higher culture that the sceptre proper is found, usually having evolved out of an implement originally intended for defensive purposes.

The classification of the so-called *bâtons de commandement* is by no means easy, as their function is not yet clear. It seems almost certain from their ornamentation that they were used for ritual purposes, though their name suggests that they were wands of office. For the sake of convenience we shall consider them under the heading 'wands of office' (below, 3), although they seem to be more closely related in function to the Australian *churinga*.

2. Magic wands.—(*a*) *The pointing stick.*—One of the commonest forms of magic is the 'pointing' of a stick or bone at some individual with the object of injuring him. Among the Arunta tribe of Central Australia these pointing sticks are known under various names, such as *injilla*, *irna*, *ullinka*, etc. These may be taken as typical examples of a class of magical instruments of world-wide distribution. The *injilla* and *irna* are small bones about six inches long, at one end of which is a small lump of resin, and round this a few strands of human hair are wound. When a man (sometimes called *kurdaitcha*) goes forth to avenge the death of one who is supposed to have fallen a victim of evil magic, he equips himself with this instrument, and, after charging it with magical properties by muttering over it an incantation such as 'May your heart be rent asunder!', he points it in the direction of the foe. In due course the victim invariably dies, unless the evil magic can be removed by a medicine-man.[1] In the Malay form of *tuju*, or pointing, the sorcerer points a magic dagger or other weapon, repeating a similar curse, towards an enemy, who forthwith sickens and dies.[2]

The *irna* differs from the *injilla* by being rather longer, tapering to a point at one end, and not having a hair string

[1] Spencer-Gillen[a], p. 534 f.
[2] W. W. Skeat and C. O. Blagden, *Pagan Races of the Malay Peninsula*, London, 1906, ii. 199.

attached to it. The *ullinka* is a special form of *irna* with a hooked end instead of a lump of resin, and is supposed to be the charm used by the *iruntarinia*, or spirits, to annoy and often to kill men against whom they have some special grudge.[1]

Any stick, wand, or weapon which has been thus 'sung' is thought to be endowed with *mana* (*q.v.*) of a malignant nature—*arungquiltha*, as the Australian native would say. So strong is this belief that there are several cases on record of slight wounds from a charmed spear or boomerang proving fatal, by the power of suggestion.[2]

(*b*) *Churinga.*—When a man in Central Australia desires to use magic to help him to secure a wife from a distant group, he takes a small wooden *churinga* (sacred instrument of wood or stone), about six or eight inches long, called a *namatwinna*, and goes into the bush, accompanied by two or three friends. All night long the party keep up a low singing of songs and amorous phrases addressed to the woman. At daylight the man stands up and swings the *churinga*, causing it first to strike the ground as he whirls it round and round and makes it hum. The sound is supposed to reach the woman and stir up her affections towards the man.[3]

Special *churinga* may be used in various ways for particular magical purposes. Thus the *churinga unginia*, which has a lump of resin attached to one end and is painted with alternate stripes of red and black, is thought to promote the growth of the beard. Another is used to allay inflammatory affection of the eyes, consequent upon the bites of flies. Women, by procuring the spear-like seed of a long grass, and charming it by singing some magic chant over it, are able to injure a male enemy by pointing and throwing it towards him.[4]

(*c*) *Divining-rods.*—A tree that grows on a grave is regarded by the S. Slavonian peasant as sacred.

'Whoever breaks a twig from it hurts the soul of the dead, but gains thereby a magic wand, since the soul embodied in the twig will be at his service.'[5]

In Europe magical properties are attributed to certain flowers, seeds, and branches of trees gathered at midsummer.

Thus in Moravia, Mecklenburg, and apparently in England and Scotland, branches of hazel were cut down by night on Midsummer Eve, as mystic divining-rods, capable of revealing treasures buried in the ground, and also of detecting thieves and murderers. In the neighbourhood of Berlin it is said that 'every seventh year there grows a wonderful branch on a hazel bush, and that branch is the divining-rod.' This can be found only on the evening of St. John's Day, by 'an innocent child, born on a Sunday and nursed in the true faith.' If the rod is to discover gold, it is named Casper; if it is to reveal silver, it is called Balthasar; if it is to point out hidden springs of water, it is dubbed Melchior. In Sweden Midsummer Eve is also the usual time for procuring the divining-rod. Sometimes it is cut from a mistletoe bough, and sometimes from four different kinds of wood—mistletoe, mountain-ash, aspen, and another. When such a rod is laid on the ground directly over treasure, 'it will begin to hop about as if it were alive.'[6]

Plants like the mistletoe are frequently regarded as containing magical virtue—perhaps, as Frazer suggests, because they do not grow on the ground. Branches of these plants are often to be found attached to the ceiling of a house or over a stable door to prevent the ingress of witches. The famous golden bough that grew on a holm-oak in the Arician grove at Nemi is compared by Virgil to the mistletoe[7]—a view revived by Frazer in his immortal work which takes its title from the legend.[8] The mistletoe may well have been described as the 'golden bough' on account of the rich golden tinge which the plant assumes in withering. The yellow colour of the bough may have suggested its supposed property of discovering the spots where gold exists in the earth.[9]

Iron rods are used in rain-making among the Bari of Africa. One of these rods is provided with a hook, and another is a two-headed spear. With the hook the rain-maker hooks and attracts the rain-clouds; with the two-headed spear he attacks and drives them away. To make women fruitful, the rain-maker chief takes an iron rod with a hollow bulb at each end, in which are small stones. Grasping the rod by the middle, he shakes it over the would-be mother, rattling the stones and muttering an incantation.[1]

These are a few examples of sticks carried in the hand that are used as instruments of magic. Closely associated with the Australian *churinga* and pointing sticks are the various poles and posts erected in connexion with solemn magico-religious rites—*e.g.*, the *nurtunga*, the *kauaua*, the *ambilyeri-kirra*, the *waninga*, the *arachitta* poles used by the natives in their initiation ceremonies.[2]

3. Wands of office.—(*a*) *Bâtons de commandement.*—Before considering examples of staves used as insignia of office, a word must be said regarding the somewhat mysterious *bâtons de commandement* found in palæolithic caves. In their simplest form they are rods of reindeer horn, having one or more holes bored through them. Sometimes they are carved into a simple symmetrical form without ornamentation; at other times they are elaborately decorated with engravings of animals, especially the horse. One of these implements found by Lartet and Christy at La Madeleine is engraved on both sides with figures of horses following one another, four on one side and three on the other. Another staff from the same shelter has engravings of two fishes and a horse. In several cases the end is fashioned to represent the head of an animal. On a baton found in the cavern Mége Teyjat (Dordogne) appear the head of a hind, serpents, swans, a finely-engraved horse at a trot, and three curious anthropomorphic figures.[3]

Among the carvings on bones collected by M. Piette there are several skinned animal-heads, which surely can be explained only in terms of magic, since, as Salomon Reinach has pointed out, it is unthinkable that the pre-historic designer worked from a skinless model to improve his art.[4] What, then, is the significance of these elaborately decorated objects? De Mortillet called them *bâtons de commandement* because he imagined that they were sceptres, similar in type and purpose to the ivory wands ceremonially carried before persons of importance among the Eskimos, and to the clubs used in like manner by certain chiefs in N. America. Others have identified them with hooks for fastening garments—a rude kind of fibula.[5] It is not easy to believe, however, that a piece of bone about 18 inches in length would have been employed for this purpose, since the Magdalenians were quite capable of making more convenient fasteners. Moreover, there is not the slightest trace of similar objects used in this way by the Eskimos. Boyd Dawkins's view that they were arrow-straighteners is more plausible, though by no means convincing.[6] Sollas favours this explanation owing to the remarkable resemblance between the Magdalenian staff and the Eskimo's arrow-straightener,[7] but it has yet to be proved that Magdalenian man was acquainted with the bow. By other authors the *bâtons* have been identified as parts of reindeer harness, hunting trophies, tent-pegs, drum-sticks, and magic wands. That they have some magico-religious significance seems to be apparent from the elaborate ornamentation and their similarity to staves used for ritual purposes among modern people in a primitive state of culture. Bernardin compared the genealogical staves of the Maoris with the *bâtons de commandement*, interpreting the notches with which they are often marked as indicative of the chief's genealogy, and the drawing of an animal on one side as a tribal badge.[8] If they are taken in conjunction with the smooth pebbles painted on one side with dots and bands in red and black ochre, found by Piette at Mas d'Azil, it seems more than probable that these so-called staves of office were used ritually in 'pre-historic sanctuaries' as *churinga* or magic wands. In the present state of our knowledge it is not possible to affirm definitely that they were part of the ritual machinery of a palæolithic totemic cult, since the existence of the practice of totemism in this age is not con-

[1] Spencer-Gillen[a], p. 534 f.
[2] *Ib.* p. 537 f.
[3] *Ib.* p. 541.
[4] *Ib.* p. 545 ff.
[5] *GB*[3], pt. i., *The Magic Art*, London, 1911, ii. 33.
[6] *Ib.* pt. vii., *Balder the Beautiful*, London, 1913, ii. 67 ff.; cf. A. Lang, *Custom and Myth*, do. 1884, p. 191 ff.
[7] *Æn.* vi. 205 ff.
[8] *GB*[3], pt. vii., *Balder the Beautiful*, ii. 315 ff.
[9] *Ib.* p. 287.

[1] *GB*[3], pt. i., *The Magic Art*, i. 347.
[2] See art. POLES AND POSTS.
[3] *Rev. de l'Ecole d'Anthrop.* xix. [1909] 63.
[4] *Cultes, mythes, et religions*, Paris, 1905–12, iv. 36.
[5] *L'Anthropologie*, xii. [1901] 190.
[6] *Cave Hunting*, London, 1874, p. 355.
[7] *Ancient Hunters and their Modern Representatives*, London, 1915, p. 454.
[8] *Revue savoisienne*, Feb. 1876, p. 12; cf. *RA* ii. [1899] 478; *L'Anthrop.* xiv. [1903] 357.

clusively proved. It is not too much to say, however, that the gradually accumulating evidence is pointing to the latter conclusion.[1]

(*b*) *Horse-staves.*—Although we do not follow de Mortillet in his interpretation of the function of *bâtons de commandement*, yet there is abundant evidence that in all stages of culture a rod or staff has been regarded as a token of authority. The shamans among the Buriats of Baikal, in S. Siberia, are equipped with two horse-staves, made of wood or of iron, as part of the insignia of their office. When a novice is about to receive his first consecration, two planks are cut out of a birch-tree growing in the forest where the shamans are buried. This is done in such a manner that the tree does not die, as its death would be a bad omen for the shaman. From these planks the wooden horse-staves are made. The implement is 80 cm. long, having a horse's head carved at one end, and at the other the form of a hoof. Some distance from the lower end the knee-joints of the horse are cut out. Little bells, one of which is larger than the rest, are tied to the horse-staves, together with small conical weights of iron, blue, yellow, and red ribbons, and strips of ermine and squirrel fur. To add to the effect, miniature stirrups are also attached. The iron horse-staves, which the shaman does not receive till he is given the iron cap after the fifth ablution or consecration, resemble the wooden staves, and represent the horses on which he is supposed to ride to the upper and lower worlds.[2] The horse-staves, drums, and other ritual implements are kept in the *shiré*, a box 3½ ft. long and 1 ft. deep, standing on four legs. According to Klementz, the horse-staves take the place of the drum among the Buriats.[3]

(*c*) *Clubs and maces.*—The staves of office among people in higher states of culture have for the most part developed out of the wooden club, originally intended for defensive purposes. The simplest form of club is that made by cutting off the root ends of small trees to form a 'head,' the root-stumps making the weapon the more formidable and effective. The latter advantage has led to other clubs, not similarly provided with natural projections of this kind, being furnished with them artificially. In process of time these imitation root-stumps became conventionalized, especially when iron displaced wood in the manufacture of weapons.[4] An examination of mediæval maces and similar staves of office will reveal their lowly origin. In the ceremonial maces of the 17th cent. the clubbed end has become the handle, while the handle end has become the larger and more imposing by the addition of crowns and other ornamentation.

In America every tribe used clubs for defensive purposes, but after the adoption of more effectual weapons, as the bow and the lance, clubs in many cases were relegated to ceremonial functions. The chief man of the Mohave carried a potato-masher-shaped club in battle, similar to those found in the caves in S. Arizona. The Zuñi used in certain ceremonies huge batons made of agave flower-stalks, and in the new fire ceremonies of the Hopi a priest carries a club of the same material, shaped like a plumed serpent. Carved wooden batons were frequently carried by chiefs, shamans, and song-leaders on state occasions, as emblems of authority or rank, among the north-west tribes of America. In pre-historic times long stone knives, beautifully flaked, appear to have been frequently employed as ceremonial weapons, and their use still continues in parts of California. Among the Kwakiutl tribe club-shaped batons, carved to represent various animals, are used by the leaders in ceremonial dances.[1]

(*d*) *The scipio.*—In early classical times the sceptre was a long staff tipped with a metal ornament carried by persons in high official positions—kings, judges, consuls, priests, military leaders, etc. The sceptre of King Agamemnon was worshipped as a god at Chæronea; a man acted as priest of the sceptre for a year at a time, and sacrifices were offered to it daily.[2] Representations on the walls of the painted tombs of Etruria show that among the Etruscans sceptres of great magnificence were used by kings and priests. From these the Roman *scipio eburneus*, the ivory rod carried by the consul, was probably derived. On the medallions of the later Empire figures are represented holding rods tipped with an eagle (*sceptrum Augusti*).

(*e*) *The pastoral staff.*—With the advent of Christianity the *scipio* became an episcopal ornament.[3] Some writers regard the crozier as the survival of the *lituus*, or rod, used by the Roman augurs in their divinations, because this was curved at the top, recalling the shepherd's crook of the mediæval pastoral staff. But, since the crook did not appear till towards the end of the 9th cent., this suggestion seems to be highly improbable, if not altogether impossible. The only instance of a curve at the top of a pastoral staff before this time is in the sacramentary of Autun (*c.* 800),[4] but, as the date of the document is uncertain, the evidence is of little value. The early illustrations of croziers represent them as long rods held in the left hand and surmounted by a sphere.[5] This type persisted till the 10th century. The curve first appeared in the West as a right-angular band at the top of the staff resembling a modern walking-stick—*e.g.*, St. Fillan's staff at Edinburgh. This fact has led some to find the origin of the ornament in an ordinary walking-stick, but the more probable explanation seems to be that it was evolved out of the ancient staff of office carried by persons of rank as a symbol of jurisdiction. This view is supported by the fact that it has been customary from the Middle Ages for church officers to bear *ferules*, or wands, on certain occasions[6]—a custom that still survives in the wands carried in procession by churchwardens.

(*f*) *The beadle's staff.*—Just as the pastoral staff is the symbol of ecclesiastical jurisdiction, and the mace the outward sign of the corporation, so, as the movement towards local self-government developed, the authority exercised over the parish by the local officers was marked by the beadle's staff. Staves were borne by the parochial authorities from the time of Elizabeth and perhaps earlier. It was, however, after the Restoration that the beadle's staff came into general use. The creation of 50 new parishes in the City of London in Queen Anne's reign gave occasion for the making of a considerable number of staves, which accounts for the fact that very many in this district bear a date about that time. The numerous examples of staff-heads may be divided into: (1) plain pear-shaped knobs, (2) statuettes of saints and models of buildings such as Cripple Gate, the Tower of London,

1 Cf. art. SACRIFICE (Introductory and Primitive).

2 *JAI* xxiv. [1895] 86–90; cf. M. A. Czaplicka, *Aboriginal Siberia*, Oxford, 1914, p. 224.

3 Cf. art. BURIATS, vol. iii. p. 16.

4 H. Balfour, *The Evolution of Decorative Art*, London, 1893, p. 93 ff.

1 F. Boas, 'The Social Organisation and Secret Societies of the Kwakiutl Indians,' in *Rep. U.S. Nat. Mus. for 1895*, Washington, 1897, p. 311; A. P. Niblack, 'Coast Indians of S. Alaska and N. British Columbia,' *ib. for 1888*, do. 1890, p. 128.

2 Paus. IX. xl. 6.

3 *De eccles. Offic.* lib. ii. cap. v.

4 Léopold Delisle, 'Le Sacramentaire d'Autun,' *Gaz. Archéol.* [1884], p. 13, pl. 22.

5 O. M. Dalton, *Catalogue of Early Christian Antiquities in the British Museum*, London, 1901, p. 53; *The Benedictional of Archbishop Robert*, ed. H. A. Wilson, do. 1903, p. xi.

6 *Voyages liturgiques de France*, Paris, 1718, p. 29; *Archæologia*, lii. [1890] 277 ff.

etc., (3) medallions, mitres, crowns, crosses, etc.[1] The beadle in his official robes, staff in hand, is still to be seen in a few churches conducting the preacher from the priest's stall to the pulpit. The devout, however, will hardly regret that the quaint emblem of civil authority has, in most cases, given place to the symbol of redemption surmounting a tall wand of wood and metal, borne at the head of processions.

LITERATURE.—The literature has been given in the footnotes; cf. art. REGALIA.

E. O. JAMES.

STARS.—See SUN, MOON, AND STARS.

STATE.—1. Evidence.—The nature of the state is to be discovered by the observation of about forty contemporary organizations; each must be analysed and its value estimated both from the point of view of those (citizens or subjects) who belong to it and from the point of view of those who are not its citizens or subjects. But, since all states are results of growth, they must be understood by reference to the past. The number of states in existence is always changing: their organization is often entirely transformed and the relations of one to the other vary infinitely. Again, since there are many other forms of social organization (churches, clubs, trade unions, capitalist companies, etc.), the state must be understood by comparison with these, both as to past history and as to present circumstances. But underlying all organizations are the passions and ideas of men and women. These are to be seen not only in the actual structure of the forty or more states now existing, but also in the tendencies of government and law; for these point to a future which is somewhat different from the present. And, since the actual tendencies do not always indicate the intentions or ideals of men, such ideals should influence our judgment of the state; for an effective ideal sometimes corrects a tendency and sometimes illuminates actions which appear to be irrational.

An analysis of state structure at present should be derived less from philosophical treatises than from official reports and the unofficial comments on administration; for the philosopher is often unable to believe his eyes, even when he determines to use them. But the agent of the state and the practical man, on the other hand, seldom understand what they are doing, as the oarsman seldom understands mechanics. We must therefore interpret; and for this purpose we refer to philosophic writers, allowing always for their tendency to emphasize the obsolete and discounting the national or provincial limitations of all 'classical' authors.

From such evidence, from about forty specimens in contact one with the other and each with many different social organizations, from tendencies, ideals, reports, comments on administration, and philosophical opinions, we must discover the nature of the state. Every state to which we refer is independent of others in its internal administration and equal, at least in theory, to all others in its external rights; therefore it is called sovereign. Other uses of the word 'state' (*e.g.*, United States) we neglect, and we omit the discussion of part-sovereignty (*e.g.*, Oman). But, even if we limit the name to sovereign states, it must be recognized to be a name for a changing object and only for what is common to many different specimens.

2. General idea.—The state is at present the supreme organization of political life, and political life is that part of social life which is concerned with setting in order the various interests of man.[2] The state is not, therefore, necessarily concerned with religion as the Church is, nor with trade as the company or the trade union is, nor with art as the academy is, although the state must take account and adjust the claims of all these. In that sense politics is architectonic; but the state is not for that reason superior, as the policeman is not superior to the artist. There are, however, certain issues in which the state must take precedence, not only in authority, but also in affection, as, *e.g.*, when order or liberty is threatened. The precedence due to the state in purely political issues and in certain crises does not imply worship, since the state is a means to full social life and individuality and in no sense an end in itself.

It is implied in this conception of the state that social life takes shape in different forms of 'community,' if we understand by that word any unit of social grouping the 'frontiers' of which are sufficiently definite to be felt as dividing those who belong to the group from those who do not. Some of these communities are more permanent than others; some imply a more conscious common purpose among the members. A village community is more permanent than a committee; the members of a scientific society are more conscious of a common purpose than the members of a church. And among all the forms of community there are now distinct and co-ordinate communities or social organizations representing purposes or tendencies of men which are not normally confused or subjected one to the other: these are states, churches, labour organizations, capitalist companies, etc. The present distinctions of social organization are the result of a long development; for in earlier times only one form of social organization fulfilled vaguely all the functions now fulfilled separately by very many different 'communities.' That earlier form is sometimes called a state; but we shall not include that meaning in our use of the term. At present there is a distinct form of social organization through which administration, law, police, 'defence,' and other distinct social functions are fulfilled, and this alone we call a state. It is co-ordinate with religious or trade organizations; but its relations with these are not yet clear, either in theory or in practice. All that is obvious is that a church or religious society is not a part or a dependency of the state; nor is the state inferior to any church. Associations of those who have a common economic purpose are, also, not necessarily parts or dependencies of the state; nor is the state an economic unit. The state, however, must not be identified with 'the government.' It is the whole group of those who have, consciously or unconsciously, a common political purpose. We may, therefore, speak in metaphor of the soul of the state, as men used to speak of the soul of the Church. The members of a state, whether divided or not in religion, trade interests, or intellectual pursuits, are bound together by a sentiment, which is the expression of a vague purpose. On the other hand, this soul of the state is nothing without administration, which is the invariable sign of political life. Thus obedience to law is ultimately dependent upon enthusiasm for or acquiescence in a particular form of state life; but few men are 'politicals' in their inmost thoughts or for most of their lives, and perhaps very few men find in a state and its activities the highest and most permanent object of their enthusiasm, although many can be easily persuaded that all they hold valuable would be destroyed if the form of state life to which they are accustomed happened to disappear. In subordination to the state are all other forms of organization of the same social 'order' (*i.e.* the

[1] M. and C. Thorpe, *London Church Staves*, London, 1895.
[2] See art. POLITICS.

political order)—*e.g.*, municipal or provincial councils, systems of education and sanitation. As the activities directly connected with political organization tend to increase, the differentiation of subordinate state functions proceeds farther; but there is no likelihood of trade or religion or science or art being entirely absorbed by the state, although some would aim at such an artificial simplification of social organization. The tangled luxuriance of modern society annoys many; it is an object of perception, without emotion, for our present purpose. The state is the result of a relation between individuals, but all individuals are grouped in various ways, and the state may therefore be also the result of a relation between their groupings; that is to say, the 'members' of a state are not only individuals but also groups of individuals of the political order.

3. Internal structure.—The development of social life through which the state has reached its present form and position is dealt with in the art. POLITICS. Here we must analyse the present situation in political life; and for this purpose it is necessary to distinguish the inner structure of the state from its external contacts, although we must admit that neither would be what it is but for the other. Internal discord promotes external wars, and wars assist domestic tyranny. The internal structure of states is more highly developed, it has been given more thought, than the external contacts; for frontiers were once the limits of interest for the majority of citizens, subjects, or rulers.

(*a*) *Administration.*—The most important feature of internal structure is administration. The so-called executive is, therefore, the most general phenomenon of state life; the members of the executive are theoretically agents of the state group, and their action is state action. There is indeed a pious belief of philosophers that they express the 'real will' of the members (citizens or subjects) of the state; but the words imply too conscious a political life. In fact in most states most inhabitants acquiesce in the acts of an executive. This is an inherited attitude; and the forms of executive or administrative action are also in great part inherited. There are emperors, kings, and also presidents, and, more powerful in normal life than these, permanent officials generally belonging to a close social caste, with others of subordinate castes under them—secretaries, burgomasters, prefects, town clerks, inspectors, and policemen. In the administrative acts of these the state used to appear as repressive (a hindrance of hindrances), and now begins to appear as directive.

Internal structure differs in homogeneous (national) states and heterogeneous (non-national or imperial) states; for in the latter selected members of one (predominant) race administer the affairs of districts inhabited by other races. The subject races are necessarily not citizens, since that word implies a right to assist in choosing the form of administration. The frontiers of states therefore do not always mark distinctions of nationality; but in most states the administration is marked by the characteristics of one nationality, and unity of administration tends to eliminate the antagonisms of race, unless one race is oppressive to the other.

Local government is roughly of two kinds—regional, as in Great Britain and the United States, or centralized, as in France and Germany. In the regional type of government the inhabitants of small districts choose their own administrators for local interests (sanitation, housing, roads, etc.); in the centralized systems prefects or burgomasters are appointed by the central government, and the inhabitants of the district are allowed only advisory functions. The two systems tend to assimilate through an inspectorate in the regional and local patriotism in the centralized state.

As regards larger units of population (above about 5,000,000) administration is either unitary or federal. In the former nearly all provincial affairs are dealt with at one centre; in the federal system large powers (in education, taxation, etc.) are given to provincial (sometimes called 'state') groups under the general control of a federal council and executive. The growth in the size of states has led to an increase of federal government, sometimes proceeding by the 'devolution' of powers from a central executive to provincial or district administrations, sometimes by the organizing of close political dependence upon a central authority of groups hitherto independent.

All these differences of internal structure within one common character of all states show the desire to make administration effective over large areas, while allowing for divergent interests of different localities, nationalities, or political capacities. There is no universal method of distinguishing interests peculiar to small groups from those common to many groups or indeed to the whole human race, and all good methods of administration allow for a continual change in such interests.

(*b*) *Legislation.*—Administration is, as it were, the action of the state, but legislation is its mind or will. A permanent instrument of continuous legislation is, however, a comparatively recent development in the life of states; and, although the executive has always depended upon the mind, will, or opinion of the state group, there was for long no voice for such will or opinion. Even now in many states (France, Italy, etc.), by a device known as 'administrative law,' the members of the executive are given a legal position which divides them from the ordinary citizen. The state, acting by its appointed agents, is given special privileges (courts, etc.) as against the ordinary citizen. This system, although it is a development of the old autocratic government, is not simply primitive, and it does not tend to disappear. It seems to be a distinct line of development, and is contrasted with the 'rule of law,' under which the agents of the state itself can be tried in the common courts. The latter system is peculiarly English; but it has no hold in countries in which the strength of state administration is believed to be of the first importance.

The vitality of the state is generally concentrated in a representative body, parliament, or chamber, in which new needs are met by new enactments. But some states have fixed or rigid constitutions, or bodies of law within which the powers of the representative chamber are confined, while other states depend upon an undefined tradition which may be indefinitely modified by the legislature. Between these two extreme types are the majority of state systems. Where the unity of the state is not 'natural,' or where the sense of that unity is not innate in the citizens, the fixed or rigid constitution is strongest; but, where there is a long tradition of unity, what seems to be the very essence of the state can be changed by the legislature of the day. The judicature is often said to be a third function within the state, but it is hardly on a level with the two others. In most states those who decide the meaning of law or apply it to cases are subordinated either to the legislature or to the executive. The judicial system is, however, an expression of the will or mind of the state, intermediate between the legislative and the executive.

(*c*) *Parties.*—The life of the state in the legislature, and sometimes even in the executive, is shown in modern times by political parties, which with many variations in different lands seem in every state to conform roughly to two types—one devoted to the maintenance and development of established tradition, the other concerned with general principles of reform. Parties are also sometimes formed by social or economic classes for their own advantage; and sometimes the party is only the following of a strong person. It is usual to suppose that the parties in any state stand for differences which are subordinate to the common interest of all the citizens of that state; but this view is difficult to maintain in cases where the principles of the party refer to policy in general and not to specific local means to order and liberty. There is a tendency to underrate the value of parties in giving political consciousness, because of the abuses of party manipulation for trivial ends.

4. External contacts. — It is essential to the understanding of the state to note that every state is commonly regarded, by those who do not belong to it, as an armed band. The structure of every state and the attitude of its citizens are indeed greatly affected by the fact that every state is in contact with other states. The inherited contact may be described as suspicion tempered by diplomatic comity; but economic and cultural development has led to important beginnings of inter-state organization (the Universal Postal Union, etc.). There are administrative changes in the external structure of the state, and administration of this new kind tends to increase. It will undoubtedly change the common attitude towards 'other' states; and therefore it will affect the nature of the state. But the older non-administrative and quasi-legislative system of international law, together with its culminating expression in The Hague Conferences, has also considerably modified the nature of the state. Under such influences the state in its external contacts appears as one among many co-ordinate and equal political institutions; and state action, though not politically 'sanctioned,' is morally estimated by reference to a vague consensus of civilized opinion in all states. This section of state life is now developing rapidly, and therefore no conclusive or schematic view can be had of it.

In the external contacts of the state, where political organization has made no progress, crises occur which lead to a periodic atavism known as war. Preparations for this affect the structure and conduct of all states, and some states are so greatly affected that certain writers have thought war the highest function of state life. In war the external contacts of the belligerent states are reduced to force and fraud. There have been stages in state development when it seemed as if force and fraud would be delimited by distinguishing citizens from soldiers, neutrals from belligerents, and otherwise combining political and military conceptions; but it seems likely that such attempts will fail, because of the economic interdependence of groups and the more destructive mechanisms of modern times.

5. Tendencies.—The facts which we have so far analyzed are the result of about 2000 years of development, and the development has not ceased. In order to understand the state, therefore, we must look towards the future. The general tendencies are as follows.

(1) There has been an increase in the size (area and population), with a decrease in the number, of states. This decrease was most marked in the 19th cent. and has been due not only to conquest but also to political subordination following economic pressure. It is not clear whether, as some expect, the tendency will result in small states becoming mere satellites to empires; but already, in spite of the theory of international law, the 'Great Powers' arrange differences without consulting other states. The increase in the size of states involves that similar administration and similar laws are established among great numbers who inhabit vast spaces; and therefore the frontiers of political administration are fewer. If frontiers are regarded as sources of friction, the decrease in their number involves a decrease in the probabilities of war; and the greater size of states is, from this point of view, an advantage. But a larger state involves a greater number of officials and, what is more important, a greater separation between citizens and these officials, their agents. The result is that state action tends to become dehumanized, and no responsibility is felt by the general body of citizens for the acts done on their behalf. Thus the good effects of democratization are often counteracted by the evil effects of officialism. This obviously is not peculiar to political organization. The same causes have led to increase in the size and decrease in the numbers of businesses; and large financial companies tend to destroy the sense of moral responsibility among their members for the actions done in their interest.

(2) The second important tendency is the increasing frequency of contact between all states, even those far distant. Frontiers have become lines of contact as much as marks of division. Commercial treaties increase in number, and diplomacy is a continuous process, inter-relating all states. Here also the political world is like the economic; and, as in the economic sphere a world market is created by contact, so in the political sphere contact produces similarity of moral standards, of action, and even of administrative structure. If the trend of events in the 19th cent. continues, there will be much more common political ground for the whole human race, and this may possibly result in developing the League of Nations.

(3) On the other hand, there is a third tendency to variety of political structure. The monarchies of the 18th cent. were much more like one another than are the republics of the 20th. Political consciousness is more highly developed, and the result is a greater variety in the devices of administration; *e.g.*, new methods of local government are being tried in various states.

(4) Underlying the variety of structure there is a general tendency towards what may be called by the old name of democracy. The simple-minded faith of Rousseau, indeed, is not accepted without corrections; but there is undoubtedly an increasing control of government in most states by the ordinary citizen. This is no obstacle either in theory or in practice to the recognition of special ability. With this we may connect the increase of state action in favour of the greater number of the inhabitants of the territory of the state. The rights of the majority are being recognized even before their power is acquired. Wage-slavery, starvation, and premature death, now suffered by nine-tenths of the human race, may yet be regarded as of greater political importance than the 'rights of property' or the development of trade; but the nine-tenths of the race are politically powerless, and state-action—*e.g.*, to decrease infant mortality —will depend, not upon the number who have the vote, but upon the sense of responsibility among voters. In the new democracy the citizen thinks in new terms, not in the terms of family, trade, party, or frontier.

6. Interpretation. — Such tendencies as these indicate the ideals which fitfully illuminate political change. The intention of all those who are conscious of state life appears to be the attainment and maintenance of order and liberty—as much order as will allow all members of the state to develop their powers and as much liberty as will permit security of tenure or certainty of expectation. The kind of life desired, however, varies so much in different localities that what satisfies one group seems to another to be tyranny or licence. We are driven therefore to a philosophic interpretation of those human passions and ideas which result in ever-changing political organizations. A great part of the traditional interpretation is obsolete, and the inherited language is somewhat misleading. The state is not to be confused with society, and we must not identify individuality with citizenship. The problem of the citizen and the state is only one phase of the general problem of the individual and society. The 'real will' of the philosophers' creed is to be found in various social forms, not all in a hierarchy, but some co-ordinate. Any one civilized man is normally a meeting-place, occasionally a point of conflict, between different social allegiances which arise out of his different interests or emotions. He has special relations to others in accordance with their common dwelling-place, or language, or religion, or trade, or culture; and the state is that group of men, women, and children so related as to accept or to maintain a special method of obtaining order and liberty. Men so related are different from what they would be if, by an impossible hypothesis, they can be supposed to be separate atoms. There is no atomic individual. But, on the other hand, the state is not a new mind or soul. It is a reality of the social order, and metaphors drawn from the individual are misleading. The unity and fullness of state life are, however, often greater than those of a church or a trade union.

We have pointed out the signs of state life in administration and policy; but the State of which men sing, for which men die, is not the officialism of Washington or Whitehall. It may in metaphor be called a spirit or a soul, and it is expressed in myth as Britannia, La France, or Deutschland, although confused in such myth with the spirit of a nation. A nation, as distinct from a state, is usually held to be a group of those who speak the same language, are physically related, and accept the same moral tradition; and, where the boundaries of a state administration do not coincide with national distinctions, there are conflicts of allegiance. Other social groupings, such as churches, trading companies, and trade unions, also cause conflicts with state loyalty. The limit of allegiance is to be found by reference to the purpose for which state administration exists. No man is bound to support the action of a state official or even of the whole body of citizens in the sphere of fine art, for the state is not an institution for the purposes of artistry, nor is it supreme over art institutions. The precise delimitation of state functions may be difficult, but a limit does exist. In normal life, however, the conflict of claims is infrequent, and few are driven to decide a conflict of allegiance. The majority act impulsively on no consistent principles. It is therefore almost useless to define what we mean by the word 'state,' as it would be useless, except for purely legal purposes, to define what we mean by 'man.' State administration must be believed, by those who benefit directly, to exist for securing order and developing freedom. But every one of the institutions now called states is performing other functions besides this; and some such states appear to non-citizens to be obstructing that for which the state should exist. Again, every state is changing its nature under our very eyes; and it seems probable that the political and social life of the next century will create clearer distinctions between the different forms of organization within society and a rapid development of state activities.

LITERATURE.—B. Bosanquet, *The Philosophical Theory of the State*[2], London, 1910; J. K. Bluntschli, *Theory of the State*, Eng. tr., Oxford, 1885; A. V. Dicey, *Introd. to the Study of the Law of the Constitution*[7], London, 1908; J. N. Figgis, *Churches in the Modern State*, do. 1913; L. T. Hobhouse, *The Metaphysical Theory of the State*, do. 1918; G. Jellinek, *Das Recht des modernen Staates*[2], Berlin, 1905; A. L. Lowell, *Governments and Parties in Continental Europe*, 2 vols., London, 1896; R. M. Maciver, *Community*, do. 1917; H. Michel, *L'Idée de l'Etat*, Paris, 1896: H. Sidgwick, *The Elements of Politics*[2], London, 1897; R. K. Wilson, *The Province of the State*, do. 1911; L. S. Woolf, *International Government*, do. 1916.

C. DELISLE BURNS.

STATE OF THE DEAD.

STATE OF THE DEAD (Primitive and Savage).—**1. Introductory.**—No subject connected with his psychic life has so engrossed the mind of man as that of his condition after death. Savages in all regions of the world have generally very clear and vivid conceptions of the spirit-world—its life, its characteristics, its landscapes—and this suggests an intense preoccupation with the subject. The wide-spread fear of the dead points to a very primitive idea that their state was not one in which life had ended. Death had cut off energies; that was obvious enough; but were there not other energies at work, or were not those energies capable of manifestation in subtle, mysterious ways? Whether men at first believed in a spirit, soul, or ghost, separate from the body, or not, there seems every reason to believe that they regarded the dead as still carrying on some kind of existence, which rendered them objects of dread. Where burial was in use, perhaps the simplest idea was that the dead man lived on in the grave in bodily form. Such practices as binding the dead with cords, laying heavy stones or a mound of earth on the grave (doubtless to prevent their egress), or feeding the dead at the grave, or, again, the idea that the dead could come forth from the grave, not merely as spirits, but in the body—the root of the vampire superstition—all point in this direction. It is even confirmed by the fact that, where a separable spiritual essence is believed in, the spirit or ghost is invariably associated for a longer or shorter time with the grave, lingering round it for some days. The grave is the dead man's house—an idea surviving in the Scandinavian belief that the barrow is the abiding-place of the dead in bodily form. The idea of a subterranean world of the dead was probably of early origin, many graves together merging into one wide region underground, the individual grave or tumulus affording entrance to or egress from it. In the belief of many tribes the subterranean region is in the west, towards the setting sun. As the sun dies each day and sinks in the west, often to shine in the place of the dead, so man also goes in that direction. This idea of a western region of the dead is still found where an island spirit-world is believed in, or even, as with many prairie tribes of N. America, a distant paradise on the plains into which the sun seems to sink. Often, too, the idea of a return to the place whence the ancestors of the tribe first came, whether that was underground or not, is entertained. Again, where the spirit-land is on the surface of the earth, it is situated in distant mountains or valleys. Probably the conception of a spirit-world in heaven, or on the heavenly bodies, was not of primitive origin. As some think, it may have been suggested by the custom of cremation: as the smoke of the pyre rose upwards, so also did the soul.

The clear view of the other world found in many savage beliefs shows that men had thought much about it. Their fundamental idea of it was necessarily its likeness to this world: imagination then made it all that man could wish for; it was better, pleasanter, happier than this world. On the other hand, it might not be so good, but such an other world was usually for unworthy persons, and here retributive ideas, though not always on strictly ethical grounds, begin to dawn. The thoughts of men affected their dreams or trance-states. They believed that they saw the other world or that their spirits had been transported there. Dreams, trances, swoons, affected by the belief, reacted upon it in turn and gave greater detail to it.

Savages often assert that their knowledge of the state of the dead is derived from dreams. The Andaman Islanders, who think that no mortal has ever gone to the other world, assert that a medicine-man once had a dream about it.[1] The New Caledonians derive their knowledge from convulsionaries who have visited the land of the dead in trances—*i.e.* from their vivid dream experiences.[2] The Sia also have gained acquaintance with it from men who died for a time (passed into a swoon) and looked into the spirit-region, though they, like many other tribes, say that much knowledge was gained from the dead, who once returned bodily to enjoy a feast.[3] Medicine-men, who are very commonly believed to project their spirits into the other world, are also propagators of knowledge regarding it.[4]

The long journey to the other world, the obstacles encountered, the ordeals to be undergone, the spirits or demons to be met with, are often the subject of elaborate mythical accounts, and due preparation is made for the journey and its trials by the burying of objects with the dead, by the possession of necessary tatu marks, mutilations, and the like, or by acquaintance with what is likely to befall one. Where the sea has to be crossed, the boat is generally more or less magical. Constantly, too, we meet with the idea of a bridge over a river, ravine, or gulf. To cross this narrow log, serpent, or knife-edge

[1] E. H. Man, *JAI* xii. [1883] 161.
[2] J. J. Atkinson, *FL* xiv. [1903] 257.
[3] *11 RBEW* [1894], p. 143.
[4] See also art. DESCENT TO HADES (Ethnic), § I.

bridge is usually an ordeal.[1] The journey of souls to the other world is often the subject of detailed descriptive myths, affording knowledge to the soul of what it will encounter, just as in the Egyptian *Book of the Dead* and the Orphic-Pythagorean tablets buried with the corpse. In Fiji it forms the subject of a long poem,[2] and elsewhere it is almost equally elaborate, or may even be roughly mapped out.[3] To aid the dead man on the way, to give him light or warmth, fires are very commonly lit on the grave, and in order to satisfy his hunger food-offerings are placed there, or regular feasts for the dead are made from time to time,[4] while moccasins or (at higher levels) shoes may be supplied to the corpse as protection against the rough journey.[5] Having once reached the other world, the spirit, according to well-nigh universal belief, can return to earth, mostly to its old haunts, often invisibly, but sometimes manifesting itself in various ways.

The beliefs of most savage peoples regarding the state of the dead are seldom of one exclusive pattern. There are instances of this, but often different views are held, even of a contradictory kind. Where no fixed dogmatic creed is taught and believed, traditional belief will vary, and different beliefs, perhaps evolved by one people or taken over from other tribes, will be found in different sections of a tribe. A savage may entertain alternative or even contradictory beliefs without feeling their incompatibility. Such beliefs, however, become more reconcilable when they concern the fate of the various souls with which a human body is often supposed to be animated.

How soon man began to believe in a state of the dead cannot now be discovered. But, while skeletons unearthed belonging to the earlier stages of the palæolithic culture have not apparently been those of corpses carefully buried, this need not preclude the supposition that burial-rites were in use then.[6] In late Acheulean times evidence of these begins to be found. Then and in the Mousterian period the dead were buried in or laid out on the floors of grottos and caverns. Some of the skeletons are in a crouching position, and stone tools or bones of animals, possibly remains of food-offerings, are found with them.[7] In the next, or Aurignacian, period the evidence of ceremonial burial and the existence of grave-goods continues. Some skeletons are embedded in a mass of small shells, or the head rests on a stone, or has a necklet and a crown of shells. Others lie in a bed of red earth. Implements are also found with the skeleton, as well as remains of food. In some cases a number of skeletons are carefully interred together.[8] The Magdalenian age burials (*e.g.*, at Laugerie Basse and Chancelade) and those of the Azilian-Tardenoisian horizon (as at Ofnet, Mas d'Azil, and Fère-en-Tardenois) show equally and even more elaborate traces of ceremonial burial.[9] In all these cases the frequent connexion of tomb and hearth, the carefully prepared attitude of the body, its interment in a special layer of foreign material, the custom of collective burial, and the presence of grave-goods and food-offerings point to reverence for the dead, to some religious concep-

[1] See art. BRIDGE, vol. ii. p. 852 f., and later sections of this article.
[2] Art. FIJI, § II. 4; B. Thomson, *The Fijians*, London, 1908, p. 117 f.
[3] C. Hose and W. McDougall, *The Pagan Tribes of Borneo*, London, 1912, ii. 43.
[4] See art. DEATH AND DISPOSAL OF THE DEAD (Introductory), §§ X., XV.
[5] See art. SHOES AND SANDALS.
[6] A. Keith, *The Antiquity of Man*², London, 1915, p. 185, finds evidence in the Galley Hill remains of burial in the Chellean period.
[7] H. F. Osborn, *Men of the Old Stone Age*², London, 1916, pp. 24, 215 ff., 221; Keith, pp. 109, 116.
[8] R. Verneau, *Les Grottes de Grimaldi (Baoussé-Roussé)*, tome ii. fasc. 1 ('Anthropologie'), Monaco, 1908, *passim*; Osborn, p. 302 ff.; Keith, p. 119.
[9] Osborn, pp. 376, 475 f.; R. R. Schmidt, *Die diluviale Vorzeit Deutschlands*, Stuttgart, 1912, i. 41; J. Dechelette, *Manuel d'archéologie préhistorique, celtique et gallo-romaine*, i. ('Archéologie préhist.'), Paris, 1908, pp. 314 ff., 505 f.

tions, and to some belief in survival after death.[1] In the neolithic age the ritual of burial and the graves and sepulchral monuments are still more elaborate, the rites including discarniture, painting and adorning the body or skeleton, very complete deposition of grave-goods, and occasionally secondary burial. So, too, in the bronze age similar respect for the dead is found. Such careful attention to them argues fixed religious beliefs and some clear conception of a future life, and this is confirmed by the existence of similar burial customs among savage tribes known to possess elaborate beliefs regarding the state of the dead.[2]

For a comparative view of the subject, the various beliefs of different peoples may be classified and each described under a different heading, but always with the condition, noted above, regarding variety of beliefs among the same people. Often, too, those beliefs merge into each other. In most cases savages limit their conception of the other world to their own people, not troubling themselves about the fate of other tribes, except in some instances regarding souls of enemies as their slaves or allotting to them an evil destiny. How far an unending immortality is consciously believed in is seldom quite clear. In some instances the soul dies a second or even a third death, and there is an end of it. Probably in most cases savages do not trouble much about the condition of long-dead ancestors, unless these are famous enough to have their memory preserved for generations. As little do they trouble themselves about the duration of the future life. Ghosts are feared as long as they exist or have power to revisit the earth. The fear is greatest for those most recently dead; more distant dead persons are forgotten by degrees, hence not feared, and their existence is not a matter of inquiry. Frequently, according to Hertz, the fear is greatest as long as the process of decomposition lasts, and until the secondary funeral rites are accomplished.[3]

See further art. BLEST, ABODE OF THE (Primitive and Savage), § 1.

2. Extinction after death.—There are very few savage peoples who believe in utter extinction, and, where the belief exists, it arises perhaps as much from lack of interest in other-world conditions—an unusual attitude with the savage—as from a sceptical outlook. On the other hand, it is not uncommon to find that extinction or some very undesirable fate is expected for the common herd or for certain persons obnoxious to society.

Some American Indian tribes, or individual members of tribes who believe in a future life, are said to entertain no such beliefs; and among the natives of Kiwai on the Fly River, British New Guinea, while there is a definite belief in a future life, some think that there may be no such state.[4] Hyades and Deniker report of the Fuegians that they have no belief in a future life, yet some of them believe that the *walapatu*, who make strange noises at night and try to enter the huts and eat them, are spirits of the dead. Others, however, regard them as men of a neighbouring tribe.[5] The Abipones, again, are said to be ignorant of what becomes of the soul after death and not to think of inquiring. Yet they believe that spirits of the dead become visible at the call of the necromancer, and that certain small ducks which fly by night are souls. There is also some belief that ancestral spirits are in the Pleiades.[1]

3. Vague ideas of a future state.—The case of the Abipones just mentioned illustrates what is not uncommon among some savages, viz. a vague conception of the future life, joined with the view that there is no special region of the dead. They remain about the homestead or in some neighbouring part of the country, or haunt the grave, or wander aimlessly around.

The Aetas, a Negrito people of the Philippine Islands, believe that the spirits of the dead are all around, or that they enter one spirit inhabiting a large boulder.[2] Some of the Dravidian tribes of India are equally vague in their belief. The Kotis worship a stone into which the spirit of the dead man is supposed to have entered on the eleventh day after cremation.[3] Among the Coorgs of Mysore large forests, untrodden by human foot, are set apart as abodes of deified ancestors.[4] On the fifth day after a death the Gonds recall the soul, and, catching a fish or an insect, bring it to the house and place it among the sainted dead of the family, believing that the spirit has thus been brought back to the house. Sometimes the animal is eaten in the belief that the spirit will be reborn as a child. Ancestors are represented by pebbles kept in the sacred part of the house. Good souls are easily appeased, but bad souls and spirits of those dying a violent or unnatural death are mischievous.[5] The Nāgas of E. Assam are doubtful whether the spirit remains in the corpse or at the grave or goes to a far country. Some think that it dwells on a high hill to the west, others that it remains in stone monuments near the village, and others that it goes to an underground paradise, like this world, where it dies a second time and goes to a lower state. Dying there once more, it returns to earth as a butterfly or small house-fly and then perishes for ever.[6] The Khonds bring back souls to the house through the medium of a cock or a spider, and feed them twice a year with rice, but they also believe that souls are reborn in children. Spirits of men killed by tigers are believed to guide tigers in search of fresh victims.[7] Among the Veddas of Ceylon the *nae yaku*, or recently dead, are believed to attend on Kande Yaka, though there is no idea as to his whereabouts. Spirits of the dead are vaguely supposed to be all around or in hills, caves, and rocks. Spirits of wives of headmen haunt slopes or tops of hills, where they are sometimes jealous of people gathering honey. Certain *yaku*, probably those of the forgotten dead, are regarded as attached to forest glades, large trees or rocks, and hill-tops. In the last case they tend to take the name of the hill. A regular cult is offered to all these spirits.[8]

In Africa many Bantu tribes appear to have little or no idea of a future place of souls.

Of the southern Bantu Macdonald says that the spirit-world is very hazy and uncertain to their minds.[9] Sometimes, as with the Thonga, several ideas seem to be current. Thus these people think that spirits go to a great village under the earth where everything is white, and where they till and reap, and possess cattle and everything else in abundance. The funeral rites, however, suggest that the grave is the house of the dead, while a third belief places ancestral spirits in sacred woods,

[1] Cf. Dechelette, i. 301 f.

[2] Cf. Dechelette, i. 450 ff.; T. E. Peet, *The Stone and Bronze Ages in Italy and Sicily*, Oxford, 1909, p. 118 ff., 169 ff., and *passim*; B. C. A. Windle, *Remains of the Prehistoric Age in England*, London, 1904, p. 128 ff.; art. DEATH AND DISPOSAL OF THE DEAD (Europe, pre-historic), vol. iv. p. 465b.

[3] R. Hertz, *ASoc*, x. [1905–06] *passim*.

[4] *11 RBEW*, p. 484; G. Landtman, 'Wanderings of the Dead in the Folk-Lore of the Kiwai-speaking Papuans,' in *Festskrift tillägnad Edvard Westermarck*, Helsingfors, 1912, p. 71.

[5] *Mission scientifique du Cap Horn, 1882–83*, Paris, 1891, vii. 254 f., 257; J. Deniker, *The Races of Man*, London, 1900, p. 214 f.

[1] M. Dobrizhoffer, *An Account of the Abipones*, tr. S. Coleridge, London, 1822, ii. 74 f., 270; T. Waitz, *Anthropologie der Naturvölker*, Leipzig, 1859–72, iii. 501; see also art. MĀSAI, vol. viii. p. 481b.

[2] See *ERE* ix. 274a.

[3] *IGI*, Oxford, 1907–09, xv. 389.

[4] *Ib.* xi. 25.

[5] *Ib.* xii. 325.

[6] W. H. Furness, *JAI* xxxii. [1902] 463.

[7] *IGI* xv. 281 f.; *Census of India, 1911*, vol. xii., *Madras*, pt. i. p. 63.

[8] C. G. and B. Z. Seligmann, *The Veddas*, Cambridge, 1911, pp. 133, 140, 151.

[9] J. Macdonald, *JAI* xx. [1891] 120.

intrusion on which is tabu, and where they live a family life under human form, but appear to the living as snakes.[1] The Bageshu think that spirits remain about the house, making their wants known through dreams.[2] The Awemba speak vaguely of their friends as becoming good spirits in the other world, but nothing is said of its whereabouts. Souls of chiefs haunt the thickets in which they are buried, and sometimes appear as pythons.[3] The Ba-Huana think that man possesses two souls: one, the *bun*, disappears at death, none knows where, except that the *bun* of a man with many fetishes may enter a large animal; the other soul, the *doshi*, lingers in the air, visits its friends, and haunts enemies.[4] The Baganda believe that spirits had to appear before the god of death, Walumbe, to give an account of their deeds and to pay their respects to him. They do not appear to have been rewarded or punished, and after this audience they returned to the places where their bodies lay. Ghosts dwelt among the living and played at noon-tide in the gardens, but they were also attached to their jaw-bones, and those of kings were kept in special temples.[5] Ghosts of common people among the Ba-hima wander round the kraals, after having visited a distant land. Kings are believed to become lions, princes and princesses serpents.[6] The Ba-Mbala think that the soul wanders about, and, if the grave is neglected, it disturbs or causes the death of its relatives. If it is satisfied, it takes the form of some animal, the kind and size of which depend upon the position held by the deceased in life.[7]

Among the Wagogo of E. Africa, though souls are worshipped, little is known as to a spirit-land, but there may exist some belief in transmigration.[8] The A-Kamba and other E. African tribes think the *aiimu*, or spirits of ancestors, of which every one has several in his body, sit at death in trees, good and bad apart. Miniature huts are built for them, and the woods cannot be trespassed on with impunity. These spirits are controlled by the impersonal deity Mulunga and speak through mediums. Each wife of a mortal man has also a spirit-husband, on whom largely depends her fruitfulness.[9] The A-kikúyu think that spirits wander about and haunt the huts, while some pass into animals. Others, again, go to Mi-i-ri-nuja Mi-kon-go-i, a residence of the dead of former generations. The whole belief regarding the dead is vague.[10] The tribes of E. Central Africa—Angoni, Manganya, etc.—believe that the dead live on in the old place and see all that goes on there, but sometimes they appear as animals in order to play pranks.[11]

The Hottentots abandoned the village at a death, lest the dead should return and torment them; medicine-men had the power to exorcize the ghosts, whose presence was indicated by rattling noises, while they beat the living almost to death. Prayer was made at the grave, however, and water was thrown on it soon after burial, 'to cool the soul.' Souls were said to go to God, but where precisely their locality was is uncertain, though the belief that stars were souls or eyes of the deceased may indicate that they were somewhere in the sky. Criminals and slaves killed by their masters were left to be devoured by beasts and so annihilated.[12]

Unlike some other African Pygmies, those of the Congo region are said to have little or no belief in a life after death, though some of the dead are vaguely thought to live on as snakes or red bush-pigs, whose strange bristles attract the attention of these people by their bright colour.[13]

Apart from such Bantu tribes as have been noted above, most African races—Negroes, etc.—have more definite beliefs regarding the dead, which, indeed, other Bantu groups are known to possess.

While with most of the Papuo-Melanesian tribes in New Guinea the belief in the other world is full and clear, with some of them it is not so.

The natives in the Cape King William district regard the spirits of the dead as playing by day in open meadows and hiding at night in the forest. There is also a belief in transmigration, while some think that spirits go eastwards to Bukaua on Huon Gulf to spend a shadowy existence there.[1] The Papuans of Wakatimi (Dutch New Guinea) regard *niniki* (ghosts) as 'things which you could not see but are here and there in the air about you,' and when asked where souls have gone point vaguely to the horizon, repeating the word 'far.'[2]

Other sporadic instances of vague beliefs are found in S. America, where certain tribes in Colombia think that the ghosts wander round their earthly dwellings after death, or, in the belief of the Orinoco tribes, round their graves.[3] The Lenguas of Paraguay have similar beliefs and think that the spirits can be seen at night. There is also a belief in a gloomy under world.[4]

The Mafulu, a Negrito people modified by Papuan influence, think that the ghost at death goes to the mountains, where it becomes, if under 45 years of age, the shimmering light on the ground where the sun penetrates the forest, or, if older, a fungus. What precise meaning is attached to 'become' was not ascertained. Ghosts come down from the mountains to get ghostly food, but whether as shimmering light and fungus is not clear. If a ghost is dissatisfied with his mountain abode, he may return to the village, not apparently as light or fungus, and there he does harm. Natives avoid this shimmering light and fungus when on the mountains.'[5]

4. The state of the dead similar to earthly life.—Such a similarity is definitely asserted in the beliefs of many widely scattered peoples; of others it may be deduced from the available data. But it should be observed that occasionally the conditions of life in the other world may be slightly better than those here, though not enough so to mark these instances as distinctively apart. Less often, too, the state of the dead may be regarded as not so good as that which they enjoyed on earth. We shall consider here some instances of such a future state in which it is more or less clearly expressed that it is open to every one.

Where a definite future life is believed in by the Bantu tribes of Africa, it is usually conceived as being on the whole similar to this life. The Basutos conceive it as underground—*mosima*, 'the abyss'—with green valleys and villages like those of earth, where man's feelings, ideas, and doings are much the same as here. Others think that the shades are calm and silent, without joy and without grief.[6] Where the Zulu belief is definite, it also refers to an under world which men have visited from this world, but combined with this is the common idea that the dead re-appear as snakes—a general Bantu belief.[7] The Bondei belief is that souls go into a mountain (Mlinga) by a brass door, but they can also wander about on earth and cause dreams.[8] Among the western Bantu, while the future life is vaguely conceived, it is still a shadowy replica of this life. The spirit-world is regarded as being all around men, good and bad living together in Njambi's town, much as they do here, but free from the limitations of this life. The great, good, and rich remain in the spirit-world and form a class of spirits called *awiri*, who may

1 H. A. Junod, *The Life of a S. African Tribe*, Neuchâtel, 1912–13, p. 350 f.
2 J. Roscoe, *JRAI* xxxix. [1909] 188.
3 J. H. West Sheane, *JRAI* xxxvi. [1906] 152.
4 E. Torday and T. A. Joyce, *ib.* p. 291.
5 J. Roscoe, *The Baganda*, London, 1911, pp. 281 ff., 315.
6 Roscoe, *JRAI* xxxvii. [1907] 101 f.
7 Torday and Joyce, *JAI* xxxv. [1905] 417.
8 H. Cole, *JAI* xxxii. 328.
9 C. W. Hobley, *The Ethnology of A-Kamba and other E. African Tribes*, Cambridge, 1910, p. 85 f.
10 W. S. and K. Routledge, *With a Prehistoric People: the Akikúyu of British E. Africa*, London, 1910, p. 240.
11 Macdonald, *JAI* xxii. [1893] 114.
12 T. Hahn, *Tsuni-‖Goam, the Supreme Being of the Khoi-Khoi*, London, 1881, pp. 85, 109, 112 f.; G. Fritsch, *Die Eingeborenen Süd-Afrika's*, Breslau, 1872, p. 338; A. Le Roy, *La Religion des primitifs*, Paris, 1911, p. 374.
13 H. H. Johnston, *The Uganda Protectorate*, London, 1902, ii. 539, *George Grenfell and the Congo*, do. 1908, ii. 632.

1 R. Neuhauss, *Deutsch Neu-Guinea*, Berlin, 1911, ii. 245, 259.
2 A. F. R. Wollaston, *Pygmies and Papuans*, London, 1912, p. 132 f.
3 T. Koch, *Intern. AE*, xiii., suppl. [1900] p. 118; J. Gumilla, *Hist. naturelle, civile, et géographique de l'Orénoque*, Paris, 1758, p. 351.
4 S. H. C. Hawtrey, *JAI* xxxi. [1901] 288; see also art. PARAGUAY.
5 R. W. Williamson, *The Mafulu Mountain People of British New Guinea*, London, 1912, p. 266 f.
6 E. Casalis, *Les Bassoutos*, Paris, 1860, p. 261; *ERE* ii. 355b.
7 See art. SERPENT-WORSHIP (Introductory and Primitive), § 2.
8 G. Dale, *JAI* xxv. [1896] 232.

wander as ghosts, or take some visible form, or be born as children or as animals.[1] The Yaos think that the *lisoka*, or soul, leaves its earthly abode never to return, and goes to Mulungu (God, or the spirit-world, or the aggregate of all spirits). The spirit is there endowed with such powers as it never had on earth and is worshipped in the ancestral cult which predominates among the people.[2]

Several Negro tribes believe in different non-material parts of man, the fate of which after death is of a varied kind.

Among the Tshi- and Ewe-speaking peoples there is a clear belief in two non-material parts: (1) the *kra* (Tshi), *luwo* (Ewe), a sort of guardian, indwelling spirit, which existed before a man's birth and has already served many men; its connexion with an individual terminates at death, when it becomes a *sisa* (Tshi) or *ñoli* (Ewe). The *sisa* may be reborn at once or may remain with the corpse as a *kra*, but then must eventually become a *sisa* and retire to the land of the *insisa*, across the river Volta, where the *insisa* live and build houses. Thence it may return and annoy the living if their *kra* is absent—*e.g.*, in sickness or dreams. The *ñoli* lingers by the grave for a time and then enters a newly-born child or an animal, becoming a *luwo* again. Failing this, it wanders about, doing good or ill according to its disposition. (2) The *srahman* (Tshi) or *edsieto* (Ewe) is a ghostly counterpart of the man. If he dies before his time—*e.g.*, in battle or by accident—it lingers round his dwelling before setting out for Srahmanadzi, the land of ghosts. Srahmanadzi is a shadowy counterpart of this world, where chiefs are chiefs and slaves are slaves, but it is gloomier than life here. Houses, forests, and rivers there are all ghosts of those once existing on earth. Every one retains the age at which he died, as well as any bodily imperfections possessed in life. Edsie is the Ewe counterpart of Srahmanadzi; by the eastern Ewe it is called Kutome. There is no belief in immortality among the Ewe: their Dead Land is inhabited only by ghosts of the recently dead, who are cognizant of what goes on here and sometimes cause sickness when they desire the services of their descendants.[3]

The Kagoro of the Niger believe that all men have shadows or souls with the voice and form of the body. The soul must cross the stream which separates this world from the next by a bridge, and, if its body is not really dead, it is sent back. Ghosts or souls (*mobwoi*) lead the lives of men, fighting, eating, drinking, but without houses. Ghosts are always hungry and thirsty, and punish their living relatives if their wants are not attended to. A ghost has also the power of transmigrating into the body of a descendant, after which it is reborn.[4]

The Nandi identify the shadow with the soul and hold that all souls, whether of the good or of the bad, go underground and live there. The poor are still poor; the rich are still rich. This region has hills, rivers, plantations, and a sea, just as on earth.[5]

Several American Indian tribes regard the state of the dead as differing but little from that of men here, but the more general belief is that it is better, or, again, that there is a division between souls on various grounds.[6] To the Kiowa the other world is a shadowy counterpart of this, but they have also a vague idea of transmigration, owls being supposed to be animated by the souls of the dead.[7] The Seri believe that the dead return to the primordial under world where all things originated, but they are apt to come by night and work mischief among the living.[8] The Tewa Indians think that in their under world the sun shines at night, but is as pale as the moon. The human race lived there until they forced their way up to earth. The sun passes through a lake and enters it, but it is gloomy and dank. In it is the happy hunting-ground of the spirits, *wajima*, described as a *kiva*-like place.[9] The Mandans have a similar myth about their earliest home underground. Souls go there again after death by means of an underground lake, which the sins of the wicked are said to prevent them from crossing,

[1] R. H. Nassau, *Fetichism in W. Africa*, London, 1904, pp. 56, 77, 237.

[2] A. Hetherwick, *JAI* xxxii. 91 ff.; D. Macdonald, *Africana*, London, 1882, i. 66 f.

[3] A. B. Ellis, *The Tshi-speaking Peoples of the Gold Coast*, London, 1887, p. 149 f., *The Ewe-speaking Peoples of the Slave Coast*, do. 1890, p. 102 ff.; *L'Anthropologie*, xiv. [1903] 571.

[4] A. J. N. Tremearne, *JRAI* xlii. [1912] 158 f.

[5] A. C. Hollis, *The Nandi*, Oxford, 1909, p. 41.

[6] See below, §§ 5, 6.

[7] *17 RBEW*, pt. i. [1898] p. 237.

[8] *Ib.* p. 292*.

[9] *29 RBEW* [1916], p. 51.

but this is probably a reflexion of Christian belief.[1] The Seminoles know little about Po-ya-fi-tsa, the place where spirits go, but they call the dead 'the people of Po-ya-fi-tsa.' At burial the feet are placed to the east, so that, when the dead man rises to go to the skies on the fourth day, he may reach the sky-path at the place of the sun's rising. Otherwise he may be lost. Burnt wood is placed in the hand of the dead to protect them from evil birds on the skyward journey.[2] Similar beliefs regarding the shadowy likeness of the other world to this are found among the Carrier Indians, Chinooks, Cherokees, Chibchas, Hurons, and Hopi, as is shown in the artt. on these tribes.

The beliefs of the Papuans and the Melanesians and of those tribes which show a mixture of both races are very circumstantial regarding the other world. Among the Papuans of Dutch New Guinea the Noofoor think that it is under the earth or beneath the sea, and that everything there is as on earth, save that vegetation is more luxuriant. Every one goes there, but the dead still help the living, who pray to them and often revisit the earth. Souls, however, are also described as remaining in the grave with the corpse or residing in images which are made for them.[3] In the islands to the west souls also reside in images or miniature houses, but the mountain tribes of these islands locate the spirits among branches of trees, where food is placed for them.[4] The people of Windessi allot two spirits to every one. There is an under world where the dead dwell in a large house, where the two spirits of a woman are incarnate in a body and live idly. One of the spirits of a man also departs thither; the other is re-incarnated as a man or sometimes as a woman, who now becomes a medicine-man. Images of the dead are in vogue here also, and spirits can do mischief through them.[5] To the west of British New Guinea the people of Kiwai on the Fly River think that the spirits live in the ground beside their bodies, but easily come up to this world. This region in the ground, Adiri, was at first a dismal place, but was made fertile by Sido, the hero who first went there, as all do now.[6] In the island of Paho the region of spirits lies in the west and is very like this world. The dead appear to men in dreams, and offerings and prayers are made to them by the living.[7]

The Temi, a Melanesian people in New Guinea, think that men have two souls; one, which is long, appears at the moment of death to relatives at a distance and then goes to a village on the northern coast; the other, the short soul, after remaining for a time with the body, goes to Lamboam, an underground region, where the offerings made to it cause it to be well received. At first it is cold, but the friendly ghosts who meet it heat stones, by which it is soon warmed. It sometimes returns to earth. Lamboam is said to be a better place than earth, but life there continues the life here, and ghosts even die, after which they become ants or worms or mischievous wood-spirits.[8] The tribes about Wedau and Wamira say that a spirit goes to a valley in the mountains approached through a hole in the ground. Many questions are asked of it by the other spirits, after which it is admitted and lives feasting, dancing, and fighting. Should it be killed, that is the end of it.[9]

Outside New Guinea the Melanesians of Murua (Woodlark Island) place the region of spirits on the island of Watum, where good and bad live together under the rule of Paidogo.[10]

[1] *11 RBEW*, p. 512.

[2] *5 RBEW* [1887], p. 520.

[3] A. Goudswaard, *De Papoewa's van de Geelvinksbaai*, Schiedam, 1863, p. 77 f.; O. Finsch, *Neu-Guinea und seine Bewohner*, Bremen, 1865, p. 104 f.; M. Krieger, *Neu-Guinea*, Berlin, n.d. [1899], p. 400 f.

[4] F. S. A. de Clercq, *Tijdschrift van het koninklijk Nederlandsch Aardrijkskundig Genootschap*, 2nd ser., x. [1893] 198 f.

[5] J. L. D. van der Roest, *Tijdschrift voor Indische Taal-, Land-, en Volkenkunde*, xl. [1898] 164 f.

[6] Landtman, p. 59 f.

[7] *Ib.* p. 68 f.

[8] R. Neuhauss, *Deutsch Neu-Guinea*, Berlin, 1911, iii. 518.

[9] H. Newton, *In Far New Guinea*, London, 1914, p. 219.

[10] J. H. P. Murray, *Papua, or British New Guinea*, London, 1912, p. 129.

The general belief among the Melanesians is that a division is made between spirits, generally on ceremonial grounds.[1]

Among the Yakuts there is a belief that the region of the dead is beyond the eight grades of heaven to the west, where constant night reigns and winter prevails instead of summer, the sun there being turned upside down. Maidens never get husbands, and youths never get wives. Houses are of stone and iron, the top narrow, the bottom flattened out, and the centre bulging.[2]

Similar beliefs regarding one state for all, the conditions of which are similar to those of earth, are found among the Gilyaks, Lapps, Lithuanians, Ostyaks, to some extent in Indonesia, Indo-China, and among the Daphlās and Orāons in India.[3]

5. The state of the dead happier than earthly life.—In this section only such a state is described as is open to all, without any division being made between them.

Such a belief seems to have existed among the Tasmanians and among several Australian tribes, especially in the west and south and in New South Wales.[4]

Among the Melanesians the natives of the Hood Peninsula, New Guinea, think that the ghosts live in an underground region, which is better than this world, with good houses and gardens. Spirits have also access to the abodes of the living and harm those who displease them.[5] At Tube-tube the spirit-land is one of eternal youth, and all are changed into the prime of life. It is located on Bebweso, a wooded hill which the natives avoid. Death and sickness are unknown. Married people are reunited, and the unmarried marry; children are born; and the spirits of animals follow those of men thither. All things are plentiful; fighting and stealing are unknown.[6] Among the southern Massim of Bartle Bay the soul (*aru*) goes to Maraiya in the south-east, where the lord of the dead assigns it a place. After passing up the Uruam river to the mountains, it is met by waiting souls which have knowledge of its coming, and, after questioning it, lead it to its own friends, who take it to their village. The skin of the spirits is now white; there is plenty to eat, but no sickness or evil. Yet souls fight there, and, if one is killed, it dies for ever.[7]

The Monumbo in N.E. New Guinea believe that souls go to a region where there is no work or suffering, and where they engage in all the pleasant pursuits which they loved on earth. They can help or torment men and are seen flying through the air as shooting stars. When they grow old, they die and become plants or animals.[8] The Roro-speaking tribes distinguish between the shadow (*oriorema*) and the soul (*tsirama*). The latter haunts villages and sends bad luck if too many quarrels occur, or it steals away other souls. The abode of souls is Arizo in the bush, where a large garden is cultivated by them and all are happy. If a living man ventures there, he dies, and plants taken thence to mortal gardens are carried back or wither. A fiery spirit meets the soul and asks if its ears and nose are pierced, and by what death it died. According to the manner of death, the soul is sent by one of several roads all of which reach Arizo.[9]

The Papuan people of Rossel, south-east of Woodlark Island, believe that souls go to a mountain at the west of the island which, they say, is covered with beautiful gardens and houses, though to the eye there are only rocks and scrub.[10]

In New Caledonia the other world is under the mountain Mu and is like this world, but its fruits are finer and larger. Good men are welcomed, but quarrelsome and rancorous ghosts are beaten by dead chiefs, and ghostly monsters are said to devour souls. The dead also appear as lizards to the living. Lambert gives another account referring to the natives of the Belep group and the Isle of Pines. All souls go to a region under the sea, Tsiabiloum, where everything grows in profusion without cultivation. Souls are first caught in a net by a spirit called Kiemoua and beaten, after which they go to Tsiabiloum. Sickness, death, sorrow, sleep, and darkness are unknown there. In daytime on earth souls revisit their graves or the places where their souls are preserved, and where they receive worship.[11]

Melanesian beliefs are further considered in § 6.

Among the N. American Indians instances of a better state in the other world are found—*e.g.*, among some of the Pima, who think that souls go to the land of the dead in the east, where the sun rises, separated from the region of the living by 'earth crack,' a chasm. In this region there is rejoicing, gladness, feasting, and dancing. Others hold that souls live round their old places and play pranks on the living, causing sickness by showing themselves to these. Others, again, believe in transmigration into owls.[1] The Thompson River Indians think that the land of souls is underground, towards the sunset, reached by a long track, at the end of which is a great lodge with doors at its eastern and western sides and a double row of fires extending through its length. When the spirit reaches this, he hears his dead relatives, who have assembled there, laughing, talking, and singing. He is welcomed and, on entering, finds a beautiful region with plenty of grass, flowers, and fruit. Warmth, light, and a pleasant perfumed air characterize this country where the people are joyful and happy.[2] The future state, according to the adherents of the Sioux Ghost-dance religion, will be such that the whole Indian race, living and dead, will be reunited on a regenerated earth to live a life of unalloyed happiness, free from death, sickness, and misery. Each apostle of this religion has filled in the details according to his mental capacity and his ideas of happiness.[3] The Paiutes also believe that, when earth has grown old, it will be made new. All Indians will rise again or awake to immortality after a deep sleep.[4] The Porto Rico tribes believed that the dead go to a valley called Coaibai, where their ancestors lived, and where they will have many wives, and plenty to eat, as well as all kinds of pleasures.[5]

Other examples of such American Indian beliefs in a happy state for all are given in the artt. BLEST, ABODE OF THE (Primitive and Savage), § 6, ANCESTOR-WORSHIP (American), § 10, BEOTHUKS, § 5, CALIFORNIA, § 4, NATCHEZ, § 12, OJIBWA, § 4 (*c*).

The Indian tribes of the West India islands conceived the dwelling-place of the dead as situated within their own territory or, as some thought, among the valleys on the west side of Hayti. There in shady arbours they passed the time with beautiful women and in the enjoyment of delicious fruits.[6]

Similar beliefs exist among many S. American tribes. In Venezuela some of the tribes believe that the spirits go to certain lakes and are swallowed by great serpents, which carry them to paradise, where they enjoy a life of dancing and drinking.[7] The Boro, Witoto, and other tribes of the Issa-Japura district bury grave-goods with the dead and light fires upon the grave, round which (or in the house or the woods) the soul hovers for a time, and then departs to the happy hunting-grounds of the good spirit. There everything is on a pygmy scale, including the souls themselves. According to some tribes, this paradise is above the sky; in the opinion of others, it is in the far distance towards the setting sun. Evil things are excluded from it. Hunting is always successful, women are beautiful and obedient, and friends meet again. Souls are regarded as immortal, so long as they are remembered by the living or appear in dreams to them. This paradise is open to all tribesmen with whom the good spirit is not vexed, but enemies whose bodies have been mutilated or divorced from all their possessions wander in the forest or go down into holes in the earth. Medicine-men who have the power of assuming

1 See below, § 6.
2 W. G. Sumner, *JAI*, xxxi. 97 f.
3 *ERE* vi. 226a, vii. 797 f., viii. 115b, ix. 578, vii. 227 f., iv. 399b, ix. 505.
4 See art. BLEST, ABODE OF THE (Primitive and Savage), § 2, for details.
5 R. E. Guise, *JAI* xxviii. [1899] 216 f.
6 G. Brown, *Melanesians and Polynesians*, London, 1910, p. 443 f.
7 C. G. Seligmann, *The Melanesians of British New Guinea*, Cambridge, 1910, p. 657.
8 P. F. Vormann, *Anthropos*, v. [1910] 409 f.
9 Seligmann, p. 309.
10 Murray, p. 138.
11 J. J. Atkinson, *FL* xiv. 257 f.; Lambert, *Mœurs et superstitions des Néo-Calédoniens*, Nouméa, 1900, p. 13 f.; G. Turner, *Samoa, a Hundred Years Ago and Long Before*, London, 1884, p. 346, speaks of the spirits as departing to the forest.

1 H. B. Alexander, *North American Mythology* (=vol. x. of *The Mythology of All Races*), Boston, 1916, p. 147 f.
2 *26 RBEW* [1908], p. 252 f.
3 *14 RBEW*, pt. ii. [1896] p. 777.
4 *Ib.* p. 784 f.
5 *25 RBEW* [1907], p. 70.
6 Müller, p. 174.
7 W. E. Roth, *30 RBEW* [1915], p. 161.

tiger-shape in life may do so after death. The sun is said to be the abode of great priests, and stars are also thought to be souls of chiefs or great men.[1]

The Guarani revere Tamoi, who once dwelt among them, and, after having taught them agriculture, left them, promising to bring them at death to heaven, where they would have plenty of hunting and rejoin their friends and find their wives more youthful. When one of them dies, Tamoi raises him on a holy tree to heaven, and such a tree is always found near the dwellings as a perch for the departing souls.[2] The Tupinambas believe that all souls are immortal and dwell in beautiful regions watered by fine rivers and stored with many fruit-trees, where they pass their time in dancing.[3] The belief of the Warraus in rich hunting-grounds and luxuriant arable land in the other world is illustrated by a verse of the death-song: 'Bring him [the spirit of the dead man] to his friends whom thou hast robbed us of before, and may he find yams and cassava and hunt apes and ajuti.'[4] The Mokuschi think that they will dwell in another region of the earth, where their only occupation will be hunting, and hostile tribes will be their slaves.[5] The Chani Indians call the world of the dead Aguararenta, 'fox-village.' It is in the east, and there all the dead dwell, existing by day as foxes, rats, etc., but by night resuming human form and enjoying great drinking bouts. The dead sometimes appear to the living or take them on a visit to Aguararenta, and their death follows soon after.[6]

The anonymous 16th cent. author of *A Treatise of Brazil* speaks of the belief of the tribes (met with by him) in Elysian fields by the side of a fair river, with many fig-trees, where the spirits do nothing but dance.[7] This seems a wide-spread belief in S. America, as the instances cited have shown, together with those already referred to in art. BLEST, ABODE OF THE (Primitive and Savage), § 6, and in the artt. CHILE, § 9, PAMPEANS, § 3, and PATAGONIANS, § 4.

6. The state of the dead one of differing conditions upon various grounds.—While a division among the dead or a series of different fates based upon moral grounds is not uncommon even among savages, attention must be paid to what, in the savage moral code, constitutes good and bad, since 'goodness' may only mean bravery as opposed to cowardice, or the slaying and possibly the eating of many victims. No doubt bravery is a virtue, and sometimes the moral code goes beyond this. We have also to inquire whether Christian influences may not have been at work as regards savage retributive notions. But in other instances (and these by far the more numerous) the division may be based upon the nature of the death, the sort of burial, the character and amount of the funeral-offerings, the status of the deceased, or even upon his possession or non-possession of certain distinctive marks. Something approaching retribution may also be seen in the ordeals which the spirit has to undergo on his way to the other world, often at the hands of supernatural beings. These are to some extent judges of the dead, while sometimes ghosts themselves act as judges of a newcomer and decide whether he will be admitted to more blissful regions or not. Or again they may themselves punish an unworthy ghost. These ideas do not always occur with clear precision and often mingle with each other.

It is curious to observe that with many of the Pygmy (Negrillo and Negrito) races there is a certain idea of retribution, or of a division between good and bad, or of an ordeal to be undergone, the bad falling victims while undergoing this, but generally being released to the better world after a time. 'Good' and 'bad' must here be interpreted liberally, though by no means empty of moral content. We find this among the Andaman Islanders, and the Sakai, Semang, and Jakun of the Malay Peninsula.[1] The beliefs of the Pygmies of Central Africa have not yet been fully studied, but certain aspects of their beliefs regarding the dead are known. There is little or no cult of ghosts. The Ajongo tribe in the Gabun believe that the spirit or shade sinks into the ground, afterwards rising to the supreme god, who then rewards or punishes it. Punishment is meted out to such as have stolen the wives of others, to poisoners, and the like.[2] Judgment after death upon souls is ascribed to the supreme being Indagarra by the Wa-Twa of Urandi.[3]

Few Bantu tribes in Africa believe in a division between different classes or morally different persons in the other world, though, even where the state of the dead is vaguely conceived, some approach to this is found in the fact that translation into animal form is for chiefs only or is regulated according to the position of the spirit in this world. But the Bangala of the Upper Congo believe that a man who has been good according to the native code of morals remains in Longa, a subterranean region in which the conditions are the same as on earth. Men whose position in this world prevented their being punished for their crimes receive retribution in the other world, though by whom is not stated. Ghosts of the bad haunt the forest and river, where they do mischief to the living.[4] The Fan believe that the spirit dwells in a mysterious underground place, governed by a king who condemns to a second death those who conduct themselves badly there. They go to a terrible place, where they are unhappy and whence they never return. Men who were very bad in this life go there directly at death. This second death is the most terrible thing which can befall a man. Spirits of the dead have knowledge and power superior to the living. They regret their earthly life, however, and are hostile to those left behind. The spirit is also said to have the power of entering into any animal.[5]

With the Yoruba-speaking tribes of the Gold Coast, at the moment of death an invocation is said by the priest that the road may be open and good for the soul and that nothing evil may meet it. Similar invocations are said at the grave, where a goat is sacrificed and also a fowl, which is said to 'buy' or open a right of way for the ghost. The ghost goes to Ipo-oku, 'the land of the dead,' beneath the earth, but he does not reach it unless the prescribed ritual has been performed. If it is omitted, he wanders homeless or is cast by evil spirits into Orun-apadi, 'the unseen world of potsherds.'[6]

The retributive ideas of some Negro tribes have already been discussed, as well as their idea of goodness.[7] Some of the Dravidian tribes of India also make a division among the spirits of the dead. The Lushei Kuki clans think that the dead go to Mi-thi-kua, 'dead man's village,' beyond which is Pial-ral, an abode of bliss open only to those who have duly performed sacrificial rites, killed men and certain animals, and been successful in love affairs. Pupawla, the first man who died, shoots at all spirits except those of certain men whose prowess with women is specified. Those whom he hits cannot reach Pial-ral, but remain in Mi-thi-

[1] T. W. Whiffen, *The North-West Amazons*, London, 1915, pp. 55, 226, 234, *FL* xxiv. [1913] 54 f.
[2] A. D. d'Orbigny, *Voyage dans l'Amérique méridionale*, Paris, 1834–47, iv. 109.
[3] I. L. Gottfriedt, *Newe Welt und amerikanische Historien*, Frankfort, 1655, p. 143.
[4] R. Schomburgk, *Reisen in Britisch-Guiana*, Leipzig, 1847–48, ii. 446; Roth, *30 RBEW*, p. 160.
[5] Koch, p. 126.
[6] E. Nordenskiöld, *Indianerleben*, Leipzig, 1912, p. 255 f.
[7] *Hakluytus Posthumus or Purchas his Pilgrimes*, Hakluyt Soc. Ex. Ser., Glasgow, 1905–07, xvi. 419.

[1] See art. BLEST, ABODE OF THE (Primitive and Savage), § 2.
[2] A. Le Roy, *Les Pygmées*, Tours, 1905, p. 179.
[3] W. Schmidt, *Die Stellung der Pygmäenvölker*, Stuttgart, 1910, p. 234.
[4] J. H. Weeks, *JRAI* xl. [1910] 370, *FL* xii. [1901] 184.
[5] E. Allégret, *RHR* l. [1904] 219; A. L. Bennett, *JAI* xxix. [1899] 86.
[6] Ellis, *The Yoruba-speaking Peoples of the Slave Coast*, London, 1894, pp. 127, 137.
[7] BLEST, ABODE OF THE (Primitive and Savage), § 5.

kua, where life is troublesome and difficult, and everything is worse than on earth. Those who reach Pial-ral are called *thangchhuah*, and they enjoy there food and drink without labour. Women can pass there only if taken by their husbands. The spirits are sometimes re-incarnated as hornets, or as dew which, if it falls on a man, is born as his child.[1]

The place of the dead among the Todas is known as Amnodr, and it lies to the west, but below the surface of the earth, where it is lit by the sun as it sinks in that direction. Amnodr is presided over by the god Ön. The dead are known as the *amatol*, and it is believed that at one time the living could pay them a visit, returning again to earth, but that this was stopped by Ön because of the behaviour of one man. Life in Amnodr is like life on earth. There are buffaloes and dairies, just as the living Todas have, but no pigs or rats are permitted there because they would spoil the country by rooting it up. There are definite routes for the spirits, and at one point they knock on a stone and lose all affection for this world. Another stone causes them to be sound and vigorous. A ravine is crossed by a thread; the bad fall from it into a river and are bitten by leeches; they are then helped out by people on the banks, and remain with them for a time proportionate to their badness. Others cross the bridge easily. Bad people include the selfish, jealous, grudging, and all offenders against the sacred dairy. The prospect of this punishment has little effect on conduct, while the inhabitants of certain districts can cross the bridge, however wicked they are. As spirits walk about Amnodr, their feet and legs wear down; and, when they are worn to the knees, Ön sends them to this world to be reborn.[2]

The Nāga tribes of Manipur have various beliefs. Thus the Tangkhuls hold that spirits force their way into heaven by means of the spirit of a buffalo. There the deity judges them, and spirits are divided into two classes according as they acquired animals by stealing or by honest hunting. Thieves have now to take a road where they meet with dreadful things, honest men follow a pleasant road, but both finally arrive on the banks of a river, whence they go to the house of the deceased in the upper world. In Mao spirits are thought to strive with a deity. If they wound him, all is well; if not, they are enslaved for ever. A deity called Kechira is also said to sort out the dead according to merit (success in love) or the manner of death. Those dying in battle go to one place; those who have their ears split to another; those dying in childbirth to a third. There is also a pleasant place within the earth where the dead are said to go. In other cases the good and bad are thought to be divided, but what these words signify is uncertain. Some of the tribes also hold various theories of rebirth.[3]

The ideas of retribution current among American Indian tribes are frequently moral, though often bravery or status determines the place of the dead. The moral retribution has been in some cases coloured, if not more, by knowledge of Christian beliefs. To the instances already cited[4] may be added others.

The Omaha put the sign of the tabu with the dead, for recognition by friends in the other world—*e.g.*, moccasins of the skin of the male elk on the feet of him to whom the animal had been tabu. The Milky Way is the path of the spirits. Life in the other world is like life here, but free from sickness and want, and on the whole happier. There are seven spirit-worlds, each higher than the preceding, and progress is effected by the soul dying to each in succession. On the Milky Way sits an old man directing spirits of the good and peaceable by a short route to the region of souls. The contumacious have to take a longer way and wander wearily to it. Another account tells of a log over a chasm, whence the bad fall off and are lost. Murderers are thought to wander always without rest. The dead still take an interest in the affairs of earth and can revisit it.[5] The Hidatsa believe that each man has four souls which join together after death and are restored to the mansions of the ancestors underground, where life goes on as it does here. Ghosts of suicides, however, have a separate place in the Ghost Village. The idea of a narrow bridge over a river also occurs: brave warriors and good hunters easily cross it, but the worthless slip off into the stream and to oblivion.[6] The Sia of the Pueblos locate the region of the dead to the north, underground, in the place first occupied by their ancestors. The road thither is crowded with spirits of unborn infants coming to earth and with the spirits of the dead. These never return to earth, though they once did so and informed the living of the state of the other world, its fields, high mountains, lakes, and rivers. The spirits sleep by day and work by night—*i.e.*, when the sun reaches their world. The Sia wish to die when the body ceases to develop, so that they may gradually return to the conditions of infancy. At such a period a man does not die, but sleeps to awake as an infant in the other world. The spirit goes there four days after death and meets two guards, who ask for his credentials. If he has not got his *hä'chamoni*, he must roam about somewhere in the north. Others are shown their relatives and bidden to join them and be happy. The wicked are in no case allowed to enter, but are placed in a great fire. If theurgists have performed their duties with an unwilling heart, they must live apart in the spirit-world, without nourishment, for a time varying according to the amount of the purification required.[1]

The Assiniboin believe that the dead go to a land in the south where game is abundant and the rivers are full of fish, and where the good and brave find many women and buffaloes. But there is a region of perpetual snow and ice, or an island, where the wicked and cowardly are confined, deprived of all the pleasures of life. Ghosts of the dead may be seen, but more often heard, by the living, or may even become materialized and marry and live as ordinary human beings. Some Indians of this tribe, however, believe that there is nothing beyond this life.[2] To the Dakotans there is ascribed a belief in four spirits—one which dies with the body, one which always remains near it, a third, which goes to the other world in the south, and a fourth, which lingers with the dead man's hair kept by the relatives. This is thrown into an enemy country, where it roves to and fro causing disease and death. A fifth spirit is sometimes supposed to be reborn in an animal or a child.[3] An old woman sits on the road to the 'Many Lodges' and examines the spirits for tatu marks. Such as do not possess these are pushed over a cloud and fall to this world as wandering ghosts. A report of the New England tribes, dating from the 17th cent., states that souls of the great and good dwell with the gods; the bad are not allowed to join them, but wander without rest or home.[4]

The Tlingit Indians distinguish between the shadow and the ghost or spirit. The 'Ghosts' Home' is above the plane of this world, and some go to the sun, moon, or stars. If a person was unhappy in this world, a dead relative would bid him come to the spirit-world, and his death followed. A house there is called 'Sleep-house,' where the ghosts rest. This name was also given to the next higher region, to which those dying by violence go. It is reached by a ladder, guarded by a being in human shape. If a man dies unavenged, he cannot mount the ladder, but drifts about on the wind. Below the earth is a third region, for the drowned. The bad are said to go to the 'Raven's Home.' In the other world the spirits share the offerings made them by the living. The way there is difficult, and spirits are attacked by wolves and bears.[5] Two lower worlds are assigned to the dead in the belief of the Bellacoola Indians; and from the upper of these souls may be reborn into this world. This subterranean ghost-world is described as stretching along the banks of a sandy river. The ghosts walk head downwards and speak in a different tongue from that of the world above, while the seasons there are the contrary of those on the earth.[6]

According to Zuñi belief, the ghost hovers round the village for four nights after death and then starts for Ko'thluwaláwa ('dance village'), the abiding-place of the council of the gods, situated in the depths of a lake and containing the great ceremonial house of the gods. Then it proceeds to the undermost world, whence the Zuñi came, and whence the dead supply the earth with water. But the ghosts often return to Ko'thluwaláwa to join in the sacred dances. Ghosts of members of the Bow priesthood, however, join the Kúpishtaya, mighty warriors who control the lightning, and become lightning-makers.[7]

The Eskimo of Bering Strait think that there may be three forms of the spiritual essence or soul—one destined for a future life, one which takes flight into the air at death, and a third, which remains with the body and possesses evil powers.

[1] J. Shakespear, *The Lushei Kuki Clans*, London, 1912, p. 62; *IGI* xvi. 219.
[2] W. H. R. Rivers, *The Todas*, London, 1906, p. 397.
[3] T. C. Hodson, *The Nāga Tribes of Manipur*, London, 1911, p. 160 f., *JAI* xxxi. 307.
[4] Blest, Abode of the (Primitive and Savage), § 5.
[5] A. C. Fletcher and F. La Flesche, *27 RBEW* [1911], p. 588 ff.
[6] *11 RBEW*, p. 517.

[1] *11 RBEW*, pp. 68, 143 ff.
[2] *Ib.* p. 485.
[3] *Ib.* p. 484 ff.
[4] *14 RBEW*, pt. ii. p. 982 f.
[5] *26 RBEW*, p. 460 f.
[6] Alexander, *N. American Mythology*, p. 263.
[7] M. C. Stevenson, *23 RBEW* [1904], pp. 20, 65, 32, 307. For other American Indian beliefs regarding a division in the state of the dead see artt. Choctaws, § 4, Dénés (vol. iv. p. 640[a]), Hupa, § 2, Haida, § 16, and Blest, Abode of the (Primitive and Savage), § 5.

After lingering for a time at the grave, the first of these departs to the other world. Spirits of shamans and of those who die by accident, violence, or starvation go to a land of plenty in the sky, where there are light, food, and water. Their state becomes still better by the offerings of food made by relatives at the feasts of the dead. Those dying from natural causes and also shades of animals go to the underground world of the dead, where each kind of animal lives in a village of its own. Here their state entirely depends upon the aforesaid offerings. Thieves from fellow-villagers, witches and sorcerers, bad shamans, and people who practised forbidden ceremonies are unconscious after death, though they may return to haunt the living.[1] On the Lower Yukon the distinctions after death seem to be based entirely upon the offerings made. The shade sees nothing until it is placed in the grave-box, when it perceives other shades, who show it the way to the other world. On the way it subsists on the food buried with it, and in the spirit region it lives an aimless existence, dependent upon the offerings at the feasts on earth to which it is invited. It there temporarily enters the person chosen as its namesake or the next child born. Having eaten, it is then dismissed. If a person dies without any one to make a feast for him, he is forgotten and lives just as the poor and friendless do on earth. There appears also to be some idea of retribution for social offenders.[2]

The beliefs of the Central Eskimo differ from these. Their supreme being, Anguta, has a daughter Sedna, who is mistress of the land of Adlivun under the earth, living in a large house with a dog at the threshold. The dead are taken by Anguta and carried there. The dog just allows them to pass, and they remain for a year, pinched by Anguta. Some of the tribes know of a still lower region, Adliparmiut—a dark place where snowstorms rage and trouble abounds, and whence there is no return, according to Hall. He also says that a happy region in heaven is called Qudlivun or Qudliparmiut, or these are happy and light regions one above the other. They abound with deer which are easily caught, and there is neither ice nor snow, trouble nor weariness, and spirits there sing and play without end. The good—those who have been kind to the poor and who were happy on earth, also suicides, those killed by accident, starvation, or murder, and women dying in childbed—go to Qudlivun. The bad—the unkind and unhappy, and all who have killed men in anger—go to Adliparmiut and remain there.[3] But, according to Boas, all dying of diseases or infringing Sedna's orders go to Adlivun and remain there a year. Murderers and offenders against human laws never leave it. Other souls are taken to Adliparmiut, where they live comparatively at ease, though not so blessed as the 'Qudliparmiut.' They hunt whale and walrus, and are always troubled by ice and snow. These accounts vary, but the belief of the tribes is undoubtedly that all dying through accident or violence and women dying in childbirth go to the upper world. The general belief seems to be in a series of abodes of ascending or descending value.[4] Lyon, an earlier traveller, cites heaven as a delightful place, while four lower worlds exist through which the dead pass, the lowest being the best.[5] While the Iglulirmiut think that the soul leaves the body immediately and goes to Adliparmiut, the tribes of Davis Strait believe that it lingers for three days with the body. While it is in Adlivun, it is regarded as a malevolent spirit and frequently roams round the villages. Its touch kills a man; the sight of it causes sickness and mischief. When a soul passes to Adliparmiut, it is at rest and ceases to be feared.[6] The older writers on Greenland give varying accounts of the state of the dead, and probably the native accounts varied from tribe to tribe.

The Hudson Bay Eskimo hold that the place of spirits depends on their condition on earth, and especially on the manner of their death. The violent, starved, and women dying in childbirth go to the sky, where they lack many luxuries. They are called *kelugmyut*, from *keluk* ('sky'), the name of this region. Others go down into the earth (*nuna*) and are called *nunamyut*. The two classes can communicate with each other. All desire to go below and enjoy the pleasure of communion with those on earth—a pleasure denied to those in the sky-world. But, if a person dies from natural causes, his spirit dwells on earth and after four years rests in the grave.[7] This belief is the reverse of that of the Central Eskimo, though it agrees with that given by Rink, Crantz, and Nansen.[1]

Among the S. American tribes some allot a better fate in a cheerful paradise to chiefs, heroes, and wizards, especially such as have killed and eaten many enemies. They dwell in pleasant gardens behind the mountains, with clear streams, rich fruit-trees, and abundance of game, fish, and honey, and there they amuse themselves with songs, dances, and laughter.[2] Where a distinction exists, it is generally one between the great and the common people or between brave warriors and cowards. This is even expressed by the Isannas and Zaparo in transmigration doctrine: souls of brave men become birds of beautiful plumage and enjoy pleasant fruits, whereas others become reptiles or evil spirits.[3]

The Araucanians held that souls were invisible but corporeal. A long journey had to be made to Galicman, the spirit-land, and the sea had to be crossed. The island of Mocha was the starting-place, and a narrow path was followed where an evil old woman met the souls and demanded tribute. If it was refused and if she overcame them, she poked out an eye. Another old woman in the form of a whale carried them over the sea, or they were carried in canoes, according to the belief of the inland tribes. Evil spirits could not enter paradise, where the same castes existed as on earth. There was abundant feasting, drinking, and dancing, and men were waited on by their wives. Poor people, those robbed of their possessions, and public women went to a cold region where food was plentiful but of poor quality. The dead could return to earth, and generally appeared transformed and visible to the *pilli*. Another account says that souls were divided according as they died by drowning, in the forest, or in their huts.[4] The heaven to which the Bakairi go was once nearer the earth or part of it, and was the place where the first ancestors lived, and there all exists as is related in the old traditions. Heaven is richly endowed with fish and game. Worthless and evilly-disposed men continue their character in another place as malevolent ghosts wandering round and spreading fear and terror.[5] The Uaupes believe that they go to Jurupari, their ancestor, but, if they did not honour him in life, the way is difficult and they lose themselves. Women come to a shed of which the owner is Bichiú, an infernal spirit. It is full of various objects. If the women have seen the dance-masks and dresses or Jurupari on earth, they remain in the shed, which forms a kind of hell. If not, they go to the heaven of Jurupari and spend their time with the men in merriment and drinking. There is also an evil place, the locality of which is uncertain, where evil men arrive after having lost themselves on the way. There they live as on earth, but endure unhappiness and suffering.[6] In the province of Cumana the dead are believed to pass to the cave of Guacharo in the mountains on their way to the other world. If they are good, they go on immediately; if not, they must remain there for a longer or shorter period. The cries of birds heard from the cave are their groans and lamentations.[7] Lery gives an account of the Tupinambas different from that cited above.[8] Souls which have been virtuous, *i.e.* avenged them of their enemies and eaten many, fly beyond the mountains to join their ancestors, where they lead a joyous life in pleasant gardens. Souls of cowards, who did not care to defend their land, are violently carried away by Aygnan and live in torment with him.[9] Another idea of division is seen in the belief of the Bororo, who think that the sun is made up of dead *barih* (medicine-men), who rise daily with red-hot irons before their faces, after prowling about the earth at night. In the sun dwells also the head of all the *barihs*, who is intermediate between men and spirits. Less important *barihs* dwell in the moon. Stars are Bororo boys, or houses of dead children. Ancestors also dwell in the rocks in the form of parrots. Deer, jaguar, and vultures also contain souls of ancestors. Souls of the dead (*arué*) may appear in the world and be seen by relatives, but all become of one sex, female, at death.[10] Another method of distinction is found with the Otomacs, who think that souls go to the west and dwell there without trouble or toil. But on the way they are met by Tigtitig, a bird, which swallows all who are afraid to fight it.[11]

The belief in a species of fiery hell, entertained by some tribes, is probably of Christian origin, a

1 E. W. Nelson, *18 RBEW*, pt. i. [1899] p. 422.
2 *Ib.* pp. 424, 428.
3 C. F. Hall, *Life with the Esquimaux*, London, 1865, i. 524.
4 F. Boas, *6 RBEW* [1888], pp. 582 f., 590.
5 G. F. Lyon, *Private Journal*, London, 1824, p. 372.
6 Boas, p. 590.
7 L. M. Turner, *11 RBEW*, p. 192 f.

1 Blest, Abode of the (Primitive and Savage), § 2.
2 J. G. Müller, *Gesch. der amerikanischen Urreligionen*, Basel, 1855, p. 288.
3 C. F. P. von Martius, *Beiträge zur Ethnographie und Sprachenkunde Amerika's zumal Brasiliens*, Leipzig, 1867, i. 602.
4 Müller, p. 287.
5 K. von den Steinen, *Unter der Naturvölkern Zentral-Brasiliens*, Berlin, 1894, p. 349 f.
6 F. R. J. de Pons, *Travels in S. America, 1801-4*, Eng. tr., London, p. 129.
7 Roth, p. 161.
8 See above, § 5.
9 J. Lery, *Brasil*, in *Hakluytus Posthumus*, xvi. 550.
10 A. H. Savage Landor, *Across Unknown South America*, London, 1913, i. 242, 245, 256 f.
11 Roth, p. 161.

retributive doctrine tacked on to a simple belief in continuance of the soul in another region.

The Payaguas think that evil souls go to a place full of cauldrons and fire, but the good dwell under water-plants and are nourished on fish.[1] The Paressi believe that a fire which flickers up on the way to the other world destroys the wicked, but, should they survive it, a horrible monster tears out their eyes and kills them. Souls of the good dwell in heaven with ancestors as they did on earth and procreate many children.[2] The Maipures place the good in a pleasant region, but the evil go to a spring where a continual fire burns them.[3]

See also artt. BRAZIL, vol. ii. p. 863[a] (Arawaks), and BLEST, ABODE OF THE (Primitive and Savage), § 7.

Among the Massim of British New Guinea the abode of the dead with the tribes of Waga-Waga is a land called Hiyoyoa under the sea, where it is day when night comes on the earth. Tumudurere, a being who was never a man on earth, receives the ghosts and tells them where to make their gardens. But only those buried with their faces to the east are able to reach Hiyoyoa.[4]

In Tube-tube (Slade Island), S.E. New Guinea, the spirit rises from the grave the night after the burial, and a fire is therefore kindled to keep it warm on the journey to Bwebweso, which is a place of eternal youth. The spirits are in the prime of life, and there are no evil spirits, sickness, or death. There are reunions between husbands and wives, and the children born never grow older than maturity. Gardens yield plentifully, and spirits of useful animals abound. Fighting and stealing are unknown, and brotherhood prevails. The spirits, however, act as judges, and those who do not attain the right standard are kept in an outer circle whence Elysium is seen by them. The very wicked must wander up and down the earth for ever in great pain.[5]

The beliefs of the Eastern Melanesians from the Torres group to Fiji have already been considered,[6] but it is important to notice that ghosts are not eternal in the underground Panoi. They die a second death, or, as some believe, there are two regions called Panoi, one above the other, and, when ghosts die in the upper one, they live again as white ants' nests in the lower one.[7] The people of the Trobriand Islands think that at death the spirit splits up into two, or that there are two spirits—*kosi*, which remains near the village for a time playing tricks, and *baloma*, which goes to Tuma, an agreeable spirit-land on earth's surface, underground, or on an island. If to the last, it goes by a spirit-canoe. On the shore it bewails its fate along with spirits of kinsmen. At a well it washes its eyes and becomes invisible; then it knocks on two stones, and at the second knock all other *baloma* crowd round and welcome it. Now it meets Topileta, the headman of Tuma, who admits or rejects it according to the payment made of the *baloma* of things buried with it. According to the cause of death—by magic, by poison, or in war—the spirit traverses a different road to Tuma, that for spirits of men killed in war being the best, by poison not so good, and by magic the worst. Those unable to pay are banished to the sea and changed into mythical fish. Relatives now meet the *baloma*, and a house is built for it. It weeps much, but receives comfort, especially from female *baloma* with whom it forms connexion. After a time it dies, but is not annihilated. *Baloma* can revisit the earth from time to time, where they play tricks like the *kosi*. In Tuma they live the life of man, sleeping, eating, and love-making. According to one view, at the second death the spirit descends to a lower stage of Tuma, the underground view of its locality being the most general. *Baloma* may also be reborn on earth, according to a curious theory which connects all pregnancy with the act of a *baloma*.[8]

1 F. Azara, *Reise nach Süd-Amerika*, Berlin, 1890, p. 267.
2 Von den Steinen, p. 435. 3 Koch, p. 130.
4 Seligmann, pp. 610, 655.
5 J. T. Field, in G. Brown, *Melanesians and Polynesians* p. 442 f.
6 See art. BLEST, ABODE OF THE (Primitive and Savage), § 4.
7 R. H. Codrington, *The Melanesians*, Oxford, 1891, p. 273 ff.
8 B. Malinowski, *JRAI* xlvi. [1916] 354 ff.

At Maweo, in the New Hebrides, the ghost is thought to sit in trees mocking the relatives who are mourning over the dead body. It then departs to a ravine, over which it must leap, and, if it falls short, it returns to life again. Finally it reaches the shore, where the ghosts meet it. Those of men whom its owner has slain or killed by magic now avenge themselves on it. It is also thought that, if the ghost falls at a gully on the way to the other world, it is dashed to pieces. A fierce pig also meets ghosts and eats those who failed to plant pandanus trees on earth. In Panoi a ghost may not drink water if the ears were not pierced, or eat good food if he was not tatued.[1] In general over this area ghosts of men who possessed *mana* are worshipped, and they still work for the living. Ghosts are believed to be present and partake of the feasts, and are also associated with places or objects where their power is felt. Ghosts may also take up their abode in certain animals, which are accordingly held sacred. At Efate in the New Hebrides the soul passes through six stages of existence and finally is extinguished. The other world is in the west of Efate, and there the ghost meets Seritau, the cannibal executioner, and his assistants. If it cannot reply to his questions, it is handed to Maseasi, its tongue is cut out, its head split open, and then twisted round. But people of the Namtaku tribe and those with certain bodily markings pass those ordeals safely. In Malekula belief there are three stages of existence after death, the first 30 miles underground, and in these the soul becomes more and more ethereal and finally fades out. The ghosts rule the affairs of earth, and punish with death those on earth who transgress, especially in the matter of providing them with pigs.[2] In San Cristoval the soul may pass into an animal or be reborn as a child or exist as a ghost, going to Rotomana, the situation of which is variously described, but life there is like life here. A spirit at the entrance admits ghosts with ears and noses pierced and the proper marks under the right eye. Another belief is that of the continued life of the ghost in the village. Souls incarnated in animals still preserve human powers and may help the living.[3]

In north and east Melanesia the dead are believed to visit the earth from time to time, and they especially dwell about their skulls, which are duly preserved. There is a long journey to the other world, for which provision is made at the grave. Among the Sulka people who acted wrongly in life, or were murdered, or left few relatives, are not buried, and their ghosts perhaps do not enter the other world. Falling stars are ghosts descending to bathe in the sea, and the phosphorescence on the waves is caused by their movements there.[4] In New Britain the spirit-land, Matana nion, has no certain location, and it is said that, 'if our eyes were turned so that what is inside the head were now outside, we should see that Matana nion was very near to us.' Life there is like life in this world, but niggardly men are chastised, and breaches of custom—*e.g.*, theft—are also punished, after which the soul may enter an animal. There are also separate places for people who have died by sling or tomahawk and for those who have died of sickness or sorcery.[5] In the Gazelle Peninsula, New Britain, the natives believe that the island paradise is guarded by a being who asks the ghosts their names, their residence, and the amount of shell-money which they left behind. Rich ghosts are allowed to enter and enjoy the pleasures of paradise. Others are debarred from it and become wandering spirits, who avenge their fate on the living. But, if some one makes a feast and distributes shell-money on behalf of such a ghost, he can then enter into bliss.[6] On the mainland of New Britain there is a separate region for poor people and for those at whose burial no shell-money was offered.[7]

The beliefs of the Polynesians are considered in art. BLEST, ABODE OF THE (Primitive and Savage), § 3; see also art. HAWAII, vol. vi. p. 530[b]. For the Dayaks see *ERE* ii. 683[a] and vii. 245[b].

7. Rebirth and transmigration.[8]—The state of the dead is sometimes one of rebirth in human form or of transmigration into animal form or a

1 Codrington, p. 278 f.
2 B. T. Somerville, *JAI* xxiii. [1894] 10.
3 C. E. Fox and F. H. Drew, *JRAI* xlv. [1915] 161.
4 P. Roscher, *AA* xxix. [1904] 214 f.
5 G. Brown, *Melanesians and Polynesians*, p. 193 f.
6 P. A. Kleintitschen, *Die Küstenbewohner der Gazellehalbinsel*, Hiltrup bei Münster, n.d., p. 225.
7 Brown, p. 398.
8 Cf. artt. TRANSMIGRATION.

series of these. This belief is, however, sometimes associated with belief in another world, because of the inconsistency of savage ideas, because different strata of belief originating in different sources may exist, or because one of the non-corporeal parts of a man transmigrates, while the other goes to the spirit-world. Or the ghost may return from the other world and assume a new bodily form temporarily or permanently. Again, transmigration may be the fate of the wicked or of common people, others going to paradise, or, again, it may be the lot of the good. Some examples of such beliefs have already been recorded, but a few other typical instances may here be mentioned.

(*a*) Sometimes there is no belief in another world, but merely in transmigration. We find this with the Suk, who think that the spirit passes into a snake at death. It may enter the huts; and, if so, the ghost is hungry, and milk, meat, and tobacco are placed for it.[1] So, too, the people of Khé, E. Africa, hold that souls of ancestors inhabit the bodies of the colobus monkey, and under no circumstances will they kill that animal or allow it to be killed.[2] The Yaguas of S. America believe that the soul first mounts to God in heaven and then recommences life on earth.[3]

(*b*) Sometimes, along with belief in another world, we find women flocking to the death-bed of a tribesman in the belief that his soul will pass into their bodies and be reborn as a child, as among the Algonquians.[4] Other American Indian tribes bury their children by the roadside that their souls may enter women passing by, or medicine-men effect the transfer of soul to a relative, whose next child is animated by it, as among the Tacullis.[5] Many of the mountain and desert tribes believe in re-incarnation, though some of them limit it to the souls of children.[6] There are similar beliefs and customs in W. Africa, as in the Oil Rivers district, where re-incarnation is believed to be the common lot of human souls.[7]

(*c*) Transmigration is held with other beliefs—*e.g.*, among Australian tribes, where the return of the soul in animal shape or its rebirth as a white man may be believed in along with definite ideas of the other world.[8] So in Guiana this belief in the return of a native as a white man co-exists in some tribes with a belief in the continued presence of the spirit near the place where it lived or in a paradise of souls.[9] In New Guinea the Papuans of Sialum and Kwamkwam have various beliefs—*e.g.*, in a shadowy life in another region, in spirits hovering near the village, and in transmigration into animals.[10] In Melanesia it is also thought that ghosts may take up their abode in animal forms, the animals when known being then regarded as sacred, although the belief in another world is clear and vivid.[11]

(*d*) Again, while the rich, chiefs, and the like go to a better world, common people roam the earth as animals, as the Ahts believe.[12] In the Himalaya region spirits haunting mountains are believed to be those of people who have not

1 M. W. H. Beech, *The Suk*, Oxford, 1911, p. 20.
2 *JAI* xxi. [1892] 377.
3 F. de Castelnau, *Expédition dans les parties centrales de l'Amérique du Sud*, Paris, 1850–61, v. 25.
4 D. G. Brinton, *The Myths of the New World*³, Philadelphia, 1896, p. 293.
5 R. M. Dorman, *The Origin of Primitive Superstitions*, p. 35; T. Waitz, *Anthropologie der Naturvölker*, iii. 195.
6 Alexander, p. 146.
7 M. H. Kingsley, *West African Studies*, London, 1899, pp. 134 f., 144.
8 A. Lang, *JRAI* xxxv. 316.
9 E. F. im Thurn, *Among the Indians of Guiana*, London, 1883, p. 359 f.
10 Neuhauss, iii. 259.
11 Codrington, p. 178 ff.
12 Bancroft, *NR* iii. 521.

gone to heaven, and who assume animal forms temporarily and attack men.[1] Or, again, while the doctrine of transmigration is diffused among the American Indian tribes, it is sometimes regarded as the fate of the wicked, as among the Dogribs, who think that these become wolves.[2] This is also found among several S. American tribes.[3] Or it may take this form that, while nobles and warriors have pleasing animal forms after death, the common folk pass into unattractive or detested forms, as among the Tlascalans and also the Isannis of Brazil.[4] The idea of the Pankhas and Bunjogeos of India is, on the other hand, that, while all go to the hill whence men first emerged, none can return who led a bad life on earth, but Khozing, the patron god, sometimes sends back the good in a new body.[5]

(*e*) Re-incarnation may be merely a temporary matter for the spirits of the dead, as it was a privilege in ancient Egyptian belief. The general Bantu belief in souls as snakes and the like seems to be of this kind. The souls make themselves manifest to men in these animal forms, but pass a spirit life in another region, more or less vaguely conceived. In W. Africa belief in this occasional transmigration into an animal also occurs,[6] and we find it again among the Eskimo, with whom, *e.g.*, a woman would not eat walrus because her husband's soul had adopted it as a temporary habitation. The *angekok* announces to the woman the animal into which her husband's soul has entered.

(*f*) Among the Mohaves we find that the souls of the dead die a second death, now becoming owls. As owls they die a third time and become water-beetles, finally changing into air.[7] The Chiriguanos believe that souls go to Iguihoca, where they pass several years in enjoyment, and then become foxes or tigers.[8] On the other hand, the Bellacoola do not admit transmigration for souls which have died a second death and passed to the lowest under world.[9]

(*g*) The idea that stars are the souls of the dead is also met with, especially among S. American tribes. The Patagonians think that they are older members of the tribe, or that these hunt on the Milky Way, though the general belief is that souls return to the caverns where the gods live and where the Indians were created.[10] The Araucanians also think that their forefathers watch them from the sky as stars moving in the Milky Way,[11] and the Abipones place their ancestors in the Pleiades.

LITERATURE.—H. Berkusky, 'Totengeister und Ahnenkultus in Indonesien,' *ARW* xviii. [1918] 306 f.; W. Crooke, 'Primitive Rites of the Disposal of the Dead, with Special Reference to India,' *JAI* xxix. [1899] 271 ff., 'Death Rites among the Dravidian and other Non-Aryan Tribes of India,' *Anthropos*, iv. [1909]; R. M. Dorman, *The Origin of Primitive Superstitions*, Philadelphia, 1881; J. G. Frazer, *The Belief in the Immortality of the Soul and the Worship of the Dead*, i., London, 1913, 'On Certain Burial Customs illustrative of the Primitive Theory of the Soul,' *JAI* xv. [1886] 64 ff.; F. Grabowsky, 'Der Tod, das Begräbnis und Ideen über das Jenseits bei den Dajaken,' *Intern. AE* ii. [1889] 179 f.; R. Hertz, 'Contributions à une étude sur la représentation collective de la mort,' *ASoc* x. [1905–06] 48 f.; T. Koch, 'Zum Animismus der südamerikanischen Indianer,' supplement to *Intern. AE* xiii. [1900]; L. Marillier, *La Survivance de l'âme et l'idée de justice chez les peuples non-civilisés*, Paris, 1893; E. L. Moon Conard, 'Idées des Indiens algonquins relatives à la vie d'outre-tombe,'

1 A. H. Savage Landor, *In the Forbidden Land: Tibet*, London, 1898, i. 31 f.
2 Dorman, p. 35.
3 *Ib.*
4 Martius, *Beiträge*, i. 602.
5 T. H. Lewin, *Wild Races of S.E. India*, London, 1870, p. 244.
6 Nassau, p. 56.
7 J. G. Bourke, *JAFL* ii. [1889] 181.
8 Koch, p. 119.
9 Alexander, p. 281.
10 J. C. Prichard, *Researches into the Physical History of Mankind*, London, 1837–47, v. 490; cf. Waitz, iii. 501.
11 J. J. E. Reclus, *The Earth and its Inhabitants: the Universal Geography*, Eng. tr., London, 1878–94, iv. 442.

RHR xlii. [1900] 244 ff.; R. Parkinson, 'Ein Beitrag zur Ethnographie der Neu Guinea Küste,' *Intern. AE* xiii. [1900] 47 f.; R. Steinmetz, 'Continuität, oder Lohn und Strafe im Jenseits der Wilden,' *AA* xxiv. [1897] 577 f.; E. B. Tylor, *PC*4, 2 vols., London, 1904; J. Zemmerich, 'Toteninseln und verwandte geographischen Mythen,' *Intern. AE* iv. [1891] 217 f.

J. A. MacCulloch.

STATE OF THE DEAD (Babylonian).—The ideas of the Babylonians and Assyrians of the state of the dead must have varied greatly in different places and at different periods as religion developed, or at times suffered relapse, but our knowledge of the origin and composition of the religious or mythological literature is not sufficient to enable us to form any other picture of these eschatological beliefs than a general one, valid certainly at some one period, but of what origin and in what period we cannot say. Our knowledge in this case is therefore far below that attainable in the religion of Israel, since the application of criticism has permitted the approximate dating of the relevant parts of the religious literature. Yet that which is known is important in itself, for no picture of civilization in the great valley of the Tigris and Euphrates would be complete without the colour of religion, and in religious thought nothing touches man more intimately than his thought of the life after death. Besides this, the religious ideas of these peoples touched Israel so closely that, while light is reflected upon them from Palestine, there is also light from them upon the ideas of the Hebrews.

Our knowledge of Babylonian and Assyrian ideas concerning the state of the dead is primarily derived from three sources: (*a*) the epic of Gilgamesh, (*b*) the story of the Descent of Ishtar, and (*c*) the legend of Nergal and Ereshkigal. We do not know the date of the origin of any of the three, but the last-named has come to us in a form much earlier than the other two and may best be considered first.

Among the literary material in old Babylonian script found at Tell el-Amarna in Upper Egypt, in 1887, are two fragments of a legend concerning Nergal and Ereshkigal. They were deposited there during the reign of Amenophis IV. (Ikhnaton or Akh-n-Aten), king of Upper and Lower Egypt about 1360 B.C., and are therefore as old as or older than that time, but how much earlier the story was composed we do not know. So much literature is associated with the reign of Ḫammurapi, king of Babylon (2130–2087 B.C.), that there has grown up among Assyriologists a tendency to ascribe much else to that same period without positive evidence. This may be so old, but there is no proof of it, and to assign it to the period would be as uncritical as is the assigning to the Mosaic period of great pieces of Hebrew literature. Whatever its age or origin, it witnesses to a view of the world of the dead at about 1400 B.C., in Babylonia, and was considered of enough importance to have been carried into Egypt. This legend begins:

> 'When the gods prepared a feast
> To their sister Ereshkigal
> They sent a messenger:
> Even if we should descend to thee,
> Thou wouldst not come up to us,
> Therefore send (hither) and take thy portion [lit. 'food'].'

Here then we have a goddess in the nether world, among the dead, summoned to participate in a feast held among the gods above. She is called Ereshkigal ('ruler of the great place'), and the story represents her as an angry being, full of grim menace, easily provoked, fit indeed as a warder of the dead who might try to escape from hands more lenient. She is not married, for the place of the dead is not fit for the propagating of human kind—that belongs to the genial earth above. She has, however, a minister named Namtar, whom she sends to the feast of the gods above.

As the story runs, when Namtar entered the assembly of the gods, all but one rose to receive him, honouring him as the representative of Ereshkigal; the god Nergal kept his seat. When this was reported to Ereshkigal, she was furious and sent Namtar back to bring Nergal before her, threatening to kill him. To answer this summons, Nergal had to pass through fourteen doors, at each of which he stationed a demon whom his father Ea had sent with him as a body-guard. When at last he had reached the abode of Ereshkigal,

> 'Within the house he seized Ereshkigal,
> By the hair, bent her down from the throne
> To the ground, to cut off her head.'

Overcome by the god, her brother, Ereshkigal offered marriage to him, was accepted, and installed as the sovereign of the region.

The story is instructive. The abode of the dead was a prison-house indeed with a warder so severe as Ereshkigal, and now with a new master in the god Nergal, who was so much more severe than she that he could beat her into submission. In a kingdom of the dead, barred within no fewer than fourteen gates, these two ruled over their prisoners, of whose state nothing specific is told us.

For a little light upon that we must now turn to the story of Ishtar's Descent to Hades, the text of which is found on three tablets from Kuyunjik which probably belonged to the library of Ashurbanipal about 650 B.C.[1] The story appears to be a nature-myth in origin, in which Tammuz represents the spring vegetation which is parched by the summer heat and vanishes from earth during winter to be restored again by the goddess of fertility in the spring season. The cult of Tammuz spread widely, and appeared in Palestine (Ezk 8[14]), and in Greece in the story of Adonis and Aphrodite. The Babylonian story represents the goddess Ishtar as seeking entrance to the abode of the dead to search for her husband Tammuz. It begins thus:

> 'To the land of No-return, the region [. . .].
> Ishtar, the daughter of Sin, directed her thought,
> The daughter of Sin directed her thought,
> To the house of darkness, Irkalla's dwelling-place,
> To the house from which he who enters never returns,
> To the road whose path turns not back,
> To the house where he who enters is deprived of light,
> Where dust is their sustenance, their food clay,
> Light they see not, in darkness do they sit.'

Here then we have a picture of the miserable gloom in which the dead live, or rather maintain an existence of unending wretchedness. In this, as in the former legend, Ereshkigal is their warder, and now her estate is guarded by seven doors, instead of by fourteen, though there is no comfort to be taken from that, for the seven are quite as effective in holding the dead inside. As Ishtar comes to each of these doors, she is successively stripped of her ornaments and clothing until she comes at last nude into the presence of Ereshkigal and her prisoners. Not a ray of hope is there anywhere in it, until the god Ea determines to arrange a release for Ishtar, who is passed successively through the doors by which she had entered, receiving again each article of apparel or adornment. If Ishtar, having once entered this realm of the dead, could be released from it, faith might have taken wings and invented a hope that the dead also might find release in some fashion. We must next see whether there is any light upon this question in Babylonian eschatology.

The third source of Babylonian ideas of the state of the dead is the Gilgamesh epic found upon a series of tablets belonging to the Nineveh collec-

[1] The text is best published in *Cuneiform Texts from Babylonian Tablets, etc., in the British Museum*, xv. pls. 45–48; for tr. see Rogers, *Cuneiform Parallels*, pp. 121–131.

tions buried in the mound of Kuyunjik.[1] The hero of this epic is Gilgamesh, and the stories are woven about a historic character once king in Uruk (Erech), and are made the medium for the expression of the views and speculations of Babylonian priests, theologians, and philosophers concerning the mysteries of the universe. The only parts of the epic important for the present purpose are those in which Gilgamesh is associated with his friend Engidu and with the hero of the deluge whose name is read Ut-napishtim. Engidu has perished through the machinations of Ishtar, and Gilgamesh has good reason to fear that death will claim him also. He wanders in search of immortal life and, coming at last to the maiden Sabitu at the seashore, asks of her this great boon. He hopes to learn the great secret if he can find a way to reach Ut-napishtim amid the dead. Coming after much effort into his presence, he is surprised by his appearance.

'I consider thee, O Ut-napishtim,
Thy appearance is not changed, thou art like me,
Thou art not different, even as I am, thou art.'

Here then is a man who once lived among men, who is not in such a sorry plight as those of whom we have heard in the other stories. He has been exalted, and Gilgamesh would know why or how. This question opens the way to the telling of the story of the deluge and the great deliverance from it. After the story has been told, a way is made for Gilgamesh to return from his fruitless journey, for he has learned nothing. It would seem, as we survey the story from this great distance, that the stage was set for a larger hope, but it did not appear. If Ut-napishtim had found a life and not a mere existence after death, might not faith rise to grasp the idea that perhaps to another this might also happen, and, if to another, perhaps to many more? But Babylonian thought was unequal to so great a leap into the darkness. The utmost attained seems to be a hint that he who died in battle or in war (if this be really the meaning of a very obscure line) has a happier issue in the life to come.

'He who dies the iron death (?), saw you such an one? I saw,
Upon a bed of ease he rests, clear water he drinks.
He who dies in battle, saw you such an one? I saw,
His father and mother hold his head, and his wife bends over (?) him.'[2]

This is something, however vague, which is better than the state of the dead portrayed in the Descent of Ishtar. But it does not carry far, nor did it become general so as to be represented elsewhere in any literature yet recovered. Instead of rising into this and thence onward into a more spiritual belief, progress was apparently ended, and despair of any better future state drove man back into taking gain of this life. So it happens that in another and unhappily fragmentary text[3] we have Gilgamesh (herein called Gish) confronted with despairing advice:

'Gish, whither goest thou?
The Life, that thou dost seek, thou shalt not find.
When the gods humanity did make,
For humanity did death determine,
But life held in their own hands.'

What then is the conclusion of the whole matter? It is to make use of this life and abandon the hopeless search for immortality.

'Thou, Gish,—let thy body be filled,
Day and night be fraught with pleasure (?),
Daily make a feast of joy,
Day and night dance (?) and joy (?),
Clean be thy dress,
Thy head be washen, in water bathed,
Look joyously at the child that holds thy hand,
Hold thy wife in pleasureful embrace.'

Here is the end of it all. The centuries of thought and aspiration have ended in finding the be-all and end-all of hope in this, and not in the next, life. A study of the Hebrew ideas will show how much surer was the advance among them of thought from ideas quite as sombre as those of their great neighbours into a faith on which Jesus might later build a great assurance.

LITERATURE.—(*a*) *Texts and translations.*—Of the story of Nergal and Ereshkigal one piece is in the British Museum and is published by C. Bezold and E. A. W. Budge, *The Tell el-Amarna Tablets in the British Museum*, London, 1892, no. 82; the other is in the Berlin Museum and is published by H. Winckler and L. Abel, *Der Thontafelfund von El-Amarna*, Berlin, 1889, no. 240. It has been often translated, most recently in R. W. Rogers, *Cuneiform Parallels to the Old Testament*, New York, 1912, pp. 131–135, with further bibliography. The Descent of Ishtar is published in the original text in H. C. Rawlinson, *WAI* iv. [[2]1891] 31, and better in *Cuneiform Texts from Babylonian Tablets, etc., in the British Museum*, xv. [1901] pl. 45–48. It also has been frequently translated, last by Rogers, pp. 121–131, and by M. Jastrow, Jr., *The Civilization of Babylonia and Assyria*, Philadelphia and London, 1915, pp. 453–461, who also discusses its interpretation. The Gilgamesh epic is published in the original text by Paul Haupt, *Das babylonische Nimrod-Epos*, 2 vols., Leipzig, 1884–91, with supplements by the same in *Beiträge zur Assyriologie*, i. [1889] 49 ff., 97 ff. Parts of it have been much translated, especially the portion recounting the deluge. Certain portions are in Rogers, p. 80 ff., and in Jastrow, p. 443. But for a full treatment see A. Ungnad and H. Gressmann, *Das Gilgamesch-Epos*, Göttingen, 1911.

(*b*) *Discussions.*—A. S. Geden, *Studies in the Religions of the East*, London, 1913, p. 159 ff.; H. Schneider, *Kultur und Denken der Babylonier und Juden*, Leipzig, 1910, p. 152 ff.; M. Jastrow, Jr., *Aspects of Religious Belief and Practice in Babylonia and Assyria*, New York and London, 1911, p. 351 ff., *Hebrew and Babylonian Traditions*, London, 1914, p. 196 ff.; P. S. P. Handcock, *Mesopotamian Archæology*, do. 1912, pp. 399–405; S. H. Langdon, *Tammuz and Ishtar*, do. 1914.

ROBERT W. ROGERS.

STATE OF THE DEAD (Buddhist).

—Buddhism, like other religions, makes the distinction between the transitory world and the eternal, but except for the *arhat* death is merely the beginning of another life-course (*gati*) through this mutable universe. The individual may become an inhabitant of hell, an animal, a *preta*, a human being, or a god,[1] the three first being states of unhappiness (*apāya*). After *pretas* some schools place another unhappy state, that of *asura*, but the Hīnayāna refuses to recognize it as a separate *gati*.

1. Conditions of rebirth.—The kind of rebirth is determined by the individual's *karma* (*q.v.*). The view of R. C. Childers is often repeated, that at death the constituent elements (*khandhas*) of the individual perish, 'but by the force of his kamma a new set of khandhas instantly starts into existence, and a new being appears in another world.'[2] As pointed out in art. INCARNATION (Buddhist), the view that *karma* is the only link between two existences is unsupported by the texts. So also is the further inference that there is no real transmigration. There is of course no transmigration of an *ātman* in the sense of any permanent, stable, unchanging mind or consciousness. The link between two states of the individual, whether in one birth or in succeeding existences, is the causal relation between any one combination of elements forming the individual and the previous states. This combination is not a permanent *ātman*, nor is there any one element in it, such as consciousness, that forms a permanent basis.

The combination is '"a living continuous fluid complex," which does not remain quite the same for two consecutive moments, but which continues for an endless number of existences, bridging an endless number of births, without becoming completely different from itself.'[3]

---

1 The tablets are in the British Museum and have been published in the original text by Paul Haupt, *Das babylonische Nimrod-Epos*. It has been often translated; see Literature below.

2 *Gilgamesh Epic*, xii. 151–154.

3 The Meissner Fragment; see B. Meissner, 'Ein altbab. Fragment des Gilgamesepos,' *MVG* vii. [1902] pt. i.

1 *Majjhima*, i. 73.

2 *Dict. of the Pāli Language*, London, 1875, *s.v.* 'Khandho.'

3 L. de la Vallée Poussin, *The Way to Nirvāṇa* (*HL*), Cambridge, 1917, p. 35.

That the individual in this sense was previously a certain being, and that he may remember many previous existences, is not a mere accommodation to popular notions, but appears as a commonplace throughout the *Suttas*.

Rebirth in Kāmaloka, which includes the lower universe from the lowest hell up to and including the six sensual heavens, is in accordance with a man's moral or immoral acts. More than mere morality is required for rebirth in the higher realms. The four classes of the heavens of form, and the four stages of the formless world, correspond to the stages of trance, and are attained by the practice of the spiritual exercises.

2. The eight hot hells.—It is not clear that the Pāli Scriptures recognize one consistent system of hells (*niraya, naraka*). What is usually described as the Buddhist view is a system of eight hells. It is not found in the *Vinaya* or the *Suttas*, but occurs in the later books (*Jātaka* and *Abhidhamma*), and also forms the basis of the more developed Mahāyāna systems. These hells are below the earth, and their description in the commentary on *Jātaka* 530 (v. 270) is as follows:

(1) *Sañjīva*.—Beings are here cut to pieces by the keepers of hell, and come repeatedly to life to suffer the same punishment. Hence the name, which means 'resuscitation.'

(2) *Kālasutta*.—Beings are struck down with blazing weapons, and, while lying on the ground, are cut into eight or sixteen pieces with an instrument called *kālasutta* (Skr. *kālasūtra*).

(3) *Saṃghāta*.—Beings on burning mountains are crushed like sesamum seeds or sugar-cane by 'smiting' (*saṃghāta*).

(4) and (5) *Roruva*.—There are two hells of this name, Jālaroruva, 'Roruva of flame,' and Dhūmaroruva, 'Roruva of smoke,' where beings are correspondingly tortured. In Sanskrit works the names are Raurava and Mahāraurava, interpreted to mean 'wailing' and 'great wailing.' The Pāli form appears to be a derivative of the proper name Ruru.

(6) *Tapana*.—'Heating,' where beings are fixed on spikes the height of a palm-tree and burnt.

(7) *Pratāpana*.—'Great heating,' where beings are cast down from a blazing iron mountain, below which blazing stakes are set up.

(8) *Avīchi*.—Flames arise from each of the four walls, and from the top and bottom, and strike the opposite sides. The name, if divided *a-vīchi*, means 'without a wave,' but the commentaries, probably to get an intelligible meaning, make it signify 'without rest or cessation.' 'Here there is no interval of cessation either of the flames or of the pain of the beings.'[1] Kern has pointed out that it is probably from *avāch, avāchī*, 'downwards,' formed on the analogy of *udach, udīchī*, 'higher,' and means 'lowest point.'[2] This view is strengthened by the fact that it is the lowest point of the universe, and that in the Yoga system Avīchi is not a hell, but the lowest part of the universe, over which are placed the six hells of this system.[3]

3. Minor hells.—Besides these hells there are, according to the commentator, sixteen minor hells (*ussada*, 'excrescence') attached to each great hell, making 128 or, in all, 136. This account agrees essentially with the *Mahāvastu*, i. 4 ff. It is probably a systematizing of earlier and inconsistent accounts, as it contains details which do not harmonize, and of which the relation to the main features is not clear. The *Pañchagatidīpana*, a Pāli work known only from a Siamese source, gives four *ussadas* to each great hell: Mīlhakūpa, the hell of dung, where beings are pierced by worms; Kukkula, the hell of hot ashes; Asipattavana, the forest with leaves of swords; and Nadī (Vetaraṇī), the river of bitter water. The *Mahāvastu*, i. 7, has essentially the same, but Kuṇapa ('carrion') replaces Mīlhakūpa. It is usually taken for granted that these are the names of the four *ussadas* of each hell. This may be so, if we assume that the system is consistent, but, as will be seen, it is more probable that several systems are combined.

4. Earlier systems.—The *Suttas* know nothing of the eight hells, but have several passages in which hells are described. In *Aṅguttara*, i. 141, seven tortures are described.

[1] *Jātaka*, v. 271.
[2] *Geschiedenis van het Buddhisme*, i. 298.
[3] Vyāsa on *Yoga-sūtras*, iii. 25.

The king of hell, Yama, hands the culprit over to the keepers of hell, who torment their victim by thrusting an iron stake through each hand and foot, and breast (the 'five-fold bonds'); they chop him with axes; they set him upside down and chop him with adzes; they fix him to a chariot and move it backwards and forwards over the burning ground; they make him go up and down a mountain of burning coal; they put him head first into a blazing copper cauldron (*lohakumbhi*); they throw him into the great hell (Mahāniraya).

An evident modification of this occurs in the commentary on *Petavatthu*, iv. 1, 8, which speaks of the five-fold bonds, sprinkling with molten copper, ascending the mountain of coals, throwing into the copper cauldron, entering the forest with leaves of swords, crossing the Vetaraṇī, and throwing into the great hell. These are here called the seven *ussadas*, and, though the comment rests on a doubtful interpretation of *sattussada*, it illustrates the divergent conceptions and the attempt to harmonize them.

The above passage of the *Aṅguttara* recurs in the *Majjhima*, iii. 183, where it is followed by a description of the great hell (Mahāniraya), the great carrion hell (Gūtha), the great hot-ashes hell (Kukkula), the great silk-cotton tree forest (Simbalivana), the great sword-leaf forest (Asipattavana), and the great bitter-water river (Khārodaka). Here they are not *ussadas*, and there is no trace of the eight hells, but we find later the Mahāniraya (which is the proper name of a hell in the Hindu system) treated as the same as Avīchi, and the Gūtha and other hells termed *ussadas*.[1] With the absence of any mention of eight hells in the *Suttas*, and the existence of divergent descriptions, this probably implies the combination of two independent systems. The Mahāniraya is identified with Avīchi, and the Gūtha and other great hells are reduced to *ussadas* round the eight great hells. Both systems are no doubt in their main features pre-Buddhistic. Several of the names are identical with some in the system of the 21 Hindu hells[2] and the six of the Yoga system.[3]

There are still other unlocated hells, which appear to have developed out of the description of special kinds of tortures, Kākola, Khuradhāra, Sataporisa, Sattisūla, Sunakha.[4] In Sanskrit works we find as 'great hells' Śālmali (the Simbali forest of Pāli), Agnighaṭa, Andhakāla, Sitodaka (Sīt-?), Asichchheda, Sambara.[5]

In *Dīgha*, ii. 12, there is a reference to beings in the *Lokantarikā*, the space between every three adjacent universes, which is quite dark. It is described in the commentary[6] as a great hell, where sins of violence against relatives and virtuous ascetics are punished. In *Jātaka*, vi. 247, it is the penalty for heresy. The inhabitants have long nails, and like bats on trees they hang from the *chakkavāla* walls that encircle the world. Then, finding no food, they drop into the salt water below. They are classed as *pretas* in R. S. Hardy's Sinhalese sources,[7] but there is no indication of this in the Pāli.

A system which shows no relation to the eight hells is described in the *Suttanipāta*, iii. 10. Buddha is asked how long is the length of life in the Paduma hell. He answers that it is not easy to say how many years, but that it is possible to make a comparison. If a man were to take a single grain every century from a load of sesamum seed, the task would be finished in less time than the period of the Abbuda hell. Then follow nine other hells, the length of time in each of which is twenty times longer than the preceding: Nirabbuda, Ababa, Ahaha, Aṭaṭa, Kumuda, Sogandhika, Uppalaka, Puṇḍarīka, Paduma. This makes the length of the Paduma hell 512,000,000 times that of the Abbuda.

There is nothing to show that these are not

[1] *Mahāvastu*, i. 6–8.
[2] *Yājñavalkya*, iii. 222; *Manu*, iv. 88.
[3] Vyāsa on *Yoga-sūtras*, iii. 25.
[4] *Jātaka*, v. 143, 145, 247, 269, 274; cf. the tortures in *Suttanipāta*, 673–5.
[5] *Kāraṇḍavyūha*, 18, 50.
[6] *Dīgha Comm.*, Colombo, 1918, i. 289; cf. *Dialogues of the Buddha*, Oxford, 1899–1910, ii. 9.
[7] *Manual of Budhism*², pp. 48, 59.

distinct hells, as they are termed in the text. The commentator, however, says that they are not separate hells, but indicate the length of time in Avīchi. It is certain that the names do signify high numerals, but the identification with Avīchi is probably another case of harmonizing, as the punishments described in the verses following are not those of Avīchi. They are those of *Aṅguttara*, i. 141, and of what are called the 'seven *ussadas*' in the *Petavatthu* commentary. Although these verses may not be contemporary with the previous prose account of Abbuda, etc., there is nothing in either to suggest the system of eight hells. The commentator also shows that his view was not of unquestioned authority, as he states two other interpretations: (1) that the names Abbuda, etc., are due to the variety of pains and punishments in each, (2) that they are cold hells.

5. Cold hells.—It is as cold hells that eight of these ten hells appear in a modified form in Sanskrit works. The names in *Dharmasaṃgraha*, 122, are Arbuda, Nirarbuda, Aṭaṭa, Apapa, Hāhādhara, Utpala, Padma, Mahāpadma, the Pāli Kumuda, Sogandhika, and Puṇḍarīka being omitted, and Mahāpadma being added. The Pāli is more systematic, as the last five of this list are the names of the five kinds of lotuses. From the *Abhidharmakośa*[1] and Chinese sources we know that the names like Apapa and Aṭaṭa are interpreted as the sounds uttered by their inmates, and those named from the different kinds of lotuses (Utpala, Padma) are due to the frozen flesh of their victims exfoliating in the form of these flowers. There is no reason to think that this, any more than the whole system of cold hells, is anything but a development of scholastic exegesis, and the reduction to eight is probably due to a desire to make them conform with the hot hells.

6. Locality of hells.—The Scriptures imply that the hells are below the earth, apparently in descending order corresponding to the ascending heavens. Later writings give various inconsistent accounts, showing that they are merely the elaborations of commentators. Avīchi, according to *Abhidharmakośa*,[2] is 20,000 leagues (*yojanas*) below Jambūdvīpa. Other authorities put the hells 500 leagues down, and below the southern extremity of Jambūdvīpa. *Dharmasaṃgraha*, 123, makes Sañjīva and the other hells the lowest of the *pātālas*, or subterranean regions, with Avīchi consequently at the bottom of the universe. Accounts of the size are equally contradictory. The *Jātaka* commentator makes Avīchi 1800 leagues in diameter and 5400 in circumference, showing that he conceived it as circular.[3]

7. Crimes punished in each hell.—The criminals punished in the first hot hell are strikers, murderers, and those moved by covetousness and anger; in the second slanderers, liars, and those undutiful to father, mother, or friends; in the third those who kill rams, antelopes, and other living beings; in the fourth those who inflict torments on living beings; in the fifth those who destroy the property of the gods, of Brāhmans, of their *guru*, though charged to guard it; in the sixth those who burn forests and live animals; in the seventh the infidel (*natthika*) who reverses right and wrong; in the eighth those who kill disciples, father, mother, or *guru*. This is the arrangement of the *Pañchagatidīpana*, with which the *Mahāvastu* agrees in the main. It is naturally absent from the *Suttas*, which usually mention the traditional list of ten sins as leading to hell. The *Jātaka*, v. 267, puts parricides and slayers of ascetics in the first (Kālasutta), unrighteous kings in the sixth (Tapana).

The absence of certain notorious crimes is noticeable. These are punished in the minor hells—a fact which is not surprising, when we know that in the *Sutta* accounts they were not *ussadas*, but great hells. Violators of morality suffer in Mīlhakūpa; adulterers climb the thorny *simbali* trees; in the Asipattavana the destroyers of confidence are cut to pieces; robbers swallow hot balls of iron, and killers of fish are plunged into Vetaraṇī. In these *ussadas* the *Jātaka* also puts matricide, abortion, and adultery. The slaying of father or mother, slaying an *arhat*, shedding the blood of a Buddha, schism, and heresy are also said to be punished in Avīchi.[1]

8. Length of life in the hells.—There is no fixed duration of life for beings in states of punishment, according to *Abhidhammattha-saṃgaha*, v. 4. In *Itivuttaka*, 18, it is said that he who causes a schism suffers in hell for a *kappa*. Schism is punished in Avīchi according to later accounts, but there is no indication that the system of eight hells is recognized here. The passage became later a matter of controversy in different schools, especially as it was not agreed whether the *kappa* was a great æon, the period between two destructions of the universe, or a subdivision of this, an *antara-kappa*.[2] The account of the Paduma hell recognizes no definite period, since the unit of the ten periods is undetermined, and similarly in other parts of the *Suttas*, where the refrain occurs, 'and they die not until their evil karma is exhausted.'

An arrangement found in the *Abhidharmaśāstra* quoted by Feer makes the periods correspond to those of the heavens of Kāmaloka, *i.e.* in the Sañjīva hell 500 years, a day and night of which equal 50 human years. These periods are doubled for each succeeding hell, till we get for Avīchi 64,000 years, with a day and night of 6400 human years. The arrangement in Hardy's Sinhalese authorities[3] is apparently the same.

9. Animals.—Animals are classed as eaters of grass, of carrion, living in darkness (*i.e.* blind), in water, in filth. The foolish man, who formerly in this world has taken pleasure in these things and has done evil deeds, is born in one of these classes. As there is no morality and accumulation of merit in such existences, it is exceedingly difficult to escape from this state, and, if even after repeated animal births the individual reaches the state of man, he is born in a very low caste.[4] The *Pañchagatidīpana*, 45–50, makes animal birth correspond with the supposed characters of different kinds of animals. The licentious are born as geese and pigeons, the stupid as worms. Through anger they become serpents, and through pride and insolence asses and dogs. The envious and avaricious become monkeys, the meat-eaters tigers and other carnivorous animals.

In Mahāyāna the saving power of the *bodhisattvas* extends to all realms. Avalokiteśvara empties the hells and *preta*-world, he takes the form of a bee, and by humming his teaching to innumerable worms causes them to remember the Buddha, the Doctrine, and the Order, so that they are reborn as *bodhisattvas* in Sukhāvatī.[5]

10. Pretas.—A *preta* (Pāli *peta*) is properly one who has 'gone before,' a departed person. Hinduism developed a very characteristic form of worship of the dead.[6] Buddhism modified this by making *pretas* a special class, who have to expiate a certain kind of *karma* in the *preta*-realm (*petti-*

[1] L. de la Vallée Poussin, *Vasubandha et Yaçomitra. Troisième chapitre de l'Abhidharmakoça*, London, 1914–18, p. 80 ff.
[2] *Ib.* p. 78.
[3] Cf. art. COSMOGONY AND COSMOLOGY (Buddhist); and A. Rémusat, *Mélanges posthumes d'hist. et de littérature orientales*, Paris, 1843, p. 79.

[1] *Mahāvastu*, i. 26; other details are given in Feer (see Literature).
[2] *Kathāvatthu*, 476.
[3] *Manual of Budhism*[3], p. 28.
[4] *Majjhima*, iii. 167–169.
[5] *Karaṇḍavyūha*, p. 46.
[6] See art. ANCESTOR-WORSHIP AND CULT OF THE DEAD (Indian).

visaya). In the Buddhist view it is only the departed condemned to this realm that can benefit by offerings (*saddha, śrāddha*) made to them by their relatives and friends. In the other four courses the life of the departed person depends upon the means of support in the world to which he has gone.[1] The *Tirokuḍḍasutta*[2] describes the worship (*pūjā*) as consisting in actual offerings of food and drink set out for the departed.

'Those who are compassionate give to their relatives pure and excellent food and drink at the proper time, saying, "May this be for our relatives; may they be made happy." . . . The petas live on what is given from this world.'

The commentary explains that the offerings are made by giving alms to the Order, and the merit is assigned to the *pretas*, whereby they benefit. The monks performing the ceremony, in fact, take the place held in the Hindu rite by the Brāhman priests, who represent the deceased ancestors.[3]

11. Preta-realm.—The *pretas* are ghosts, which live at cross-roads and congregate outside the fences and at the doors of houses. They are described in the commentary as having long dishevelled hair and beard, lean, rough limbs, looking like burnt trees after a forest fire, some scorched with flames arising from their stomachs and issuing from their mouths through their burning hunger and thirst, some with bellies like mountains and their throats the size of a hole made by a needle. The effect of their *karma* is to make their relatives forget them, and then their only food is indescribable filth. Several kinds are mentioned: *kuppipāsika*, 'afflicted with hunger and thirst'; *vantāsa*, 'eating vomit'; *paradattūpajīvin*, 'living on what is given by others'; *nijjhāmataṇhika*, 'burning with thirst.'

12. Sins punished in the preta-realm. — The special sins leading to *preta* existence are niggardliness or refusing to give alms and envy of the blessings of others. Those who have dissuaded from giving become needle-mouthed, and those who, though intending to give, have afterwards regretted it become eaters of filth. This sin is put by *Saṃyutta*, i. 92, in the Mahāroruva hell. One who says unpleasant things in anger becomes a *preta* with fiery throat.[4]

In the *Kāraṇḍavyūha*[5] the city of *pretas* (*pretanagara*) is an abode adjoining Avīchi. It has door-keepers, and is mentioned in several passages along with various hells.

After *pretas* the *Pañchagatidīpana* groups several classes of superhuman beings, which, though strictly speaking divine, do not generally reside in heaven. They are chiefly beings whose *karma* is mixed: *kumbhaṇḍas*, demons attendant on Virūlhaka, one of the four great kings; *rākṣasas*, cannibal demons; *gandharvas*, divine musicians; *pisāchas*, *paṃsupisāchas*, mud-demons; *yakṣas*, demons, especially those attendant on Vessavaṇa, one of the four great kings; and *asuras*, gods expelled from the heaven of the Thirty-three, and forming a separate *gati* in some schools.[6] *Nāgas* and *garuḍas*, whose natural forms are serpents and birds respectively, are classed with the animals.

13. Man.—Rebirth as a man, whether from a previous higher or from a lower existence, implies that the individual has some good *karma* to his credit. The punishment of hell is monitory and retributory, not a purification as in the Christian purgatory; but, although a being in a state of punishment cannot acquire merit, he may be reborn as a man or god owing to the ripening of *karma* from a still earlier existence. Such *karma* may result in an individual being reborn as a man, who has done deeds that otherwise would have led to heaven or hell. If he has formerly been a shedder of blood, he will be short-lived; if an injurer and striker of living beings, he will be diseased; if of an angry and despairing nature, ugly; if eager for gain and honour, weak; if he is not a giver, poor; if proud and insolent, of low caste; if not an inquirer as to what is good and worthy, stupid. And the practice of the opposite virtues leads to long life and the other corresponding blessings.[1]

14. Heavens. — The arrangement of heavens, though peculiarly Buddhist as a system, is based upon Hindu conceptions, and the names of the lower heavens are often similar to or identical with those of the Yoga philosophy. There is little doubt that they are pre-Buddhistic, and hence it is not surprising that the original meaning of several of the names of different gods and heavens was apparently unknown to the Buddhists, who interpreted them in more than one way. The series of heavens as given in *Majjhima*, i. 289, is as follows:

A. THE SIX HEAVENS OF SENSUAL ENJOYMENT (Kāmaloka).—(1) *Chātummahārājika devas.*—This is the heaven of the four great kings, the gods of the four quarters, and protectors of each of the four continents. They are Dhataraṭṭha (Dhṛtarāṣṭra), king of the east; Virūlha (Virūḍhaka), of the south; Virūpakkha (Virūpākṣa), of the west; and Kuvera or Vessavaṇa (Vaiśravaṇa), of the north. Their attendants are respectively *gandharvas, kumbhaṇḍas, nāgas*, and *yakṣas*.[2] Their abode is half-way up Mount Meru, the centre of the world.

(2) *Tāvatiṃsa devas.*—The 33 gods, with Sakka at their head, dwell on the top of Mount Meru. The *asuras* are placed below or at the foot of Mount Meru, after being expelled from Tāvatiṃsa by Sakka. Other superhuman beings of general Hindu mythology (mentioned under *pretas*) properly belong to this region. Rebirth in the vegetable world is apparently absent from the Buddhist system, but trees and plants are really divine beings, *devatā*, and their life is that of the tree-spirit inhabiting them.

(3) *Yāma devas.*—This would naturally mean gods of the heaven of Yama, Yama being the Vedic king of the heaven of the fathers. In Buddhism, however, Yama has become king of hell and the *pretas*, and the commentaries interpret *yāma* in various ways—*e.g.*, 'the misery-freed gods'[3] or in the sense of a watch (period of three hours), as being the period by which these gods reckon time. Dhammapāla on *Therīgāthā*, 197, derives it from the root *yā*, in the sense of 'having attained divine pleasure.' Their king is Suyāma.

(4) *Tusita devas.*—These are the 'delighted or satisfied gods,' and their abode is the heaven from which the *bodhisattvas* descend to become Buddhas. The king is Santusita.

(5) *Nimmānarati devas.*—This means gods who delight in creation or transformation. The commentary on *Vimānavatthu*, 80, explains the name as those who take delight and sport by changing their forms at pleasure. *Dīgha*, iii. 218, interprets it as those who exercise their power over sensual desires created by themselves. Their king is Sunimmita.

(6) *Paranimmitavasavattī devas.* — According to *Dīgha*, iii. 218, these are gods who exercise their power over sensual pleasures created by others. Their king is Vasavattī, and as ruler of the highest of the Kāma heavens he is later identified with Māra.[4] As this and the previous heaven correspond to the Yoga Aparinirmitavaśavartin and Parinirmitavaśavartin, they are probably ancient terms, interpreted variously without reference to their original application. The Yoga terms show that *para-* may be a mistake for *pari-*, and the Buddhist interpretations consequently mere etymological illusions.

B. HEAVENS OF THE WORLD OF FORM (Rūpaloka).—The following list of 13 is that of *Majjhima*, i. 289. Other lists vary from 16 to 18, and have also minor differences in arrangement. The usual number of 16 is obtained by subdividing the first *dhyāna* into three, and adding the *asaññasattas* in the fourth *dhyāna*. The principle of division in all the lists is the classification of the heavens above Kāmaloka into eight planes, according to the four *dhyānas*, and the four higher 'attainments.'

(1) *First dhyāna.*—*Brahmakāyika devas*, gods of the troop of Brahmā, subdivided in *Vibhaṅga*, 424, into (*a*) *Brahmapārisajja devas*, gods of Brahmā's retinue, (*b*) *Brahmapurohita devas*, family priests of Brahmā, (*c*) *mahābrahmas*, great Brahmās. In the *Suttas* only one great Brahmā is at any given time supreme.

(2) *Second dhyāna.*—*Abha devas*, gods of brilliance, including (*a*) *parittābha devas*, gods of limited brilliance, (*b*) *appamāṇābha devas*, gods of unlimited brilliance, (*c*) *ābhassara devas*, radiant gods.

1 *Aṅguttara*, v. 269–271.
2 *Khuddakapāṭha*, vii.
3 W. Caland, *Altindischer Ahnencult*, Leyden, 1893, p. 154.
4 *Pañchagatidīpana*, 52–59.
5 Pp. 12, 35, 66.
6 Cf. *Kathāvatthu*, viii. 1.

1 *Majjhima*, iii. 202–206; *Pañchagatidīpana*, 70–102.
2 *Dīgha*, ii. 257.
3 S. Z. Aung and C. A. F. Rhys Davids, *Compendium of Philosophy*, London, 1910 (tr. of *Abhidhammattha-saṃgaha*), p. 138, n. 2.
4 *Jātaka*, i. 63.

(3) *Third dhyāna.*—*Subha devas*, gods of beauty or lustre, including (*a*) *parittasubha devas*, gods of limited lustre, (*b*) *appamāṇasubha devas*, gods of unlimited lustre, (*c*) *subhakiṇha devas*, gods of complete lustre.

(4) *Fourth dhyāna.*—(*a*) *Vehapphala devas*, gods of great fruit, (*b*) *aviha devas*, gods of non-increase (?), (*c*) *atappa devas*, gods of coolness, (*d*) *sudassa devas*, gods fair to see, (*e*) *sudassī devas*, well-seeing gods, (*f*) *akaniṭṭha devas*, gods among whom none is the youngest—a Vedic epithet of the *maruts*, but with no discernible reference to those gods.

In *Dīgha*, ii. 50, 52, the last five of this *dhyāna* are called the *suddhāvāsas*, 'gods of pure abode.' Another class of this *dhyāna* is that of the *asaññasuttas* or *asaṃjñisattvas*, beings of unconsciousness.[1] *Vibhaṅga*, 425, puts them first in this class. In Sanskrit lists are further found the *anabhrakas*, 'cloudless' gods, and the *puṇyaprasavas*, 'merit-producing' gods.

C. Heavens of the formless world (Arūpaloka).—The four divisions of this world correspond to the four attainments (*samāpattis*).

(1) *Ākāsānañchāyatanūpaga devas*, gods who have reached the stage in which the object of thought is space realized as infinite.

(2) *Viññāṇañchāyatanūpaga devas*, gods of the stage in which the object is cognition realized as infinite.

(3) *Akiñchaññāyatanūpaga devas*, gods of the stage in which the object is nothingness.

(4) *Nevasaññā-nāsaññāyatanūpaga devas*, gods of the stage in which the object is neither consciousness nor unconsciousness.

15. Life of the gods.—The *Vimānavatthu* commentary describes life in Kāmaloka as consisting of sensual pleasures like those on earth, but on a grander scale. The gods have each a palace of gold, ruby, etc., and retinues of nymphs. They move through space on flying couches, and sport in the Nandana grove, or in boats on the great lakes. The sun, moon, and other heavenly bodies are among the vehicles of such gods. Sakka has female attendants skilful in dancing and singing. They marry and intermarry with the gods of the four great kings and the *asuras*.

In Rūpaloka there is no sensual desire—*i.e.*, according to *Abhidhammattha-saṃgaha*, vi. 12, those groups of material qualities constituting smell, taste, body, sex, and those produced by food, are absent; and among the unconscious beings also the groups of seeing, hearing, mind, and voice. In Arūpaloka all the groups of material qualities are absent.

Birth in Rūpaloka and Arūpaloka is attained by the practice of the corresponding *dhyāna*, and birth in one of the three divisions of each of the first three *dhyānas* is in accordance with the limited, medium, and eminent exercise of each. *Vibhaṅga*, 425, includes in the fourth *dhyāna* also the four stages of Arūpaloka, and makes birth in the seven divisions from *asaññasattas* to *akaniṭṭhas* correspond to seven ways of practising this *dhyāna*. Birth in Arūpaloka is in accordance with the object of thought of each division. A somewhat different arrangement occurs in *Abhidhammattha-saṃgaha*, vi. 10.

16. Length of life in the heavens.—In the heaven of the four great kings a day and night equals 50 human years, and the length of life is 500 divine years—*i.e.* 9,000,000 human years. These figures are doubled for each of the following Kāma heavens, giving for the *paranimmitavasavattīs* a day and night equal to 1600 human years, and a life of 16,000 divine years.

The three divisions of the *brahmakāyikas* have a life of one-third, one-half, and a whole *kappa*; of the *parittābhas* it is two *kappas*, and, by successive doubling for each of the following, 64 *kappas* for the *subhakiṇhas*. *Asaññasattas* and *vehapphalas* both have 500 *kappas*, and the following to *akaniṭṭhas* successively double. In Arūpaloka the ages are 20,000, 40,000, 60,000, and 84,000 *kappas*.[2]

Further cosmological details will be found in art. Cosmogony and Cosmology (Buddhist), and an account of the paradises of Mahāyāna in art. Blest, Abode of the (Buddhist).

[1] *Dīgha*, iii. 263; *Kathāvatthu*, 260; *Dharmasaṃgraha*, 128.
[2] *Aṅguttara*, i. 213, 267; *Vibhaṅga*, 424–426. In *Compendium of Philosophy*, p. 142, the meaning of *kappa* in this connexion is discussed.

Literature.—L. Feer, 'L'Enfer indien,' *JA*, 8th ser., xx. [1892] 185 ff., 'Comment on devient preta,' *ib.* 8th ser., iii. [1884] 109 ff., 'Comment on devient deva,' *ib.* 8th ser., iii. 1 ff., 'Comment on devient arhati,' *ib.* 8th ser., i. [1883] 407 ff.; *Fragments extraits du Kandjour* (*AMG* v. [1883], containing translations of *Pañchagatidīpana*, and the Chinese *Lou-tao-tsi*, § 1, *Tien tao* ['Way to Heaven']); H. Kern, *Geschiedenis van het Buddhisme in Indië*, Haarlem, 1882, i. 287–299; R. S. Hardy, *A Manual of Budhism*[2], London, 1880.

Edward J. Thomas.

STATE OF THE DEAD (Christian).

1. General character of the Christian view.—The distinctive feature of the Christian doctrine of immortality, as distinguished from that of Greek philosophy, is its insistence upon the survival, not of a part only, but of the totality of human personality. The Greek view is sometimes spoken of as the doctrine of the immortality of the soul, but it is only of part of the soul that persistence is affirmed. If Plato at times, in accordance with popular ideas, speaks of friendship with the great and good as among the pleasures of the next world, thus implying the permanence of man's emotional and affective nature, his more usual view is cold and intellectual. In theoretic Platonism what survives is little more than the power of abstract thought, and eternal bliss consists mainly in the calm and unemotional contemplation of the eternal, unchanging 'Ideas.' In Aristotle this intellectualist tendency is still more pronounced. What survives at death is simply the divine principle of pure intelligence (νοῦς), which apparently is absorbed into the Divine Mind, so that it becomes a serious question, in spite of such passages as *Nic. Eth.* i. 11, whether Aristotle can rightly be regarded as a believer in individual immortality.

To the Jew the life of the affections, of the emotions, of the senses, and of active volition, seemed of more worth than the life of abstract thought. As soon as ever he conceived a blessed life beyond the grave as possible at all, he demanded that it should have all (and more than all) the warmth, the fullness, and the vivacity of earthly life. Eternal life, in his view, meant the enhancement and enrichment of life, not its impoverishment, and impoverished it would surely be, in his opinion, if it lost one single element which in the earthly life possesses artistic, moral, or emotional value. The Jew, then, stood for the survival of human personality in its entirety.

But this position, when logically thought out, seems to imply a life lived in a material environment, and even the survival (in some sense) of the human body. Sensation, *e.g.*, seems to require organs of sensation, emotion some sort of bodily organization, the recognition of friends some kind of visible form by which to distinguish them; furthermore, it seems impossible to understand how the artistic faculties can be exercised except upon sensible objects possessed of æsthetic charm. If, therefore, eternal life implies, as to a Jew it does, the most perfect and satisfying life imaginable, it must imply a life lived *in the body*, and *in a material universe*, both of which, however transfigured and glorified, must still be thought of under the category of matter.

This point of view, characteristic of the main stream of Jewish thought, as distinguished from the speculations of the Platonizing school of Philo, was that which commended itself to Christ and the first Christians. Hence their descriptions of the life to come are pictorial, vivid, almost sensuous, employing largely the current apocalyptic imagery. Such descriptions are undoubtedly symbolical, but they do not symbolize a purely spiritual existence. When we read of harpers with their harps, of the new song of the redeemed, of the new heavens and the new earth, of the new Jerusalem paved with gold, of its joyous inhabitants clothed in white and carrying palms, we are not meant to think of disembodied spirits existing *in vacuo*, but of visible human bodies gloriously arrayed, and of real sensible things corresponding in the heavenly sphere to what we should here call beautiful music, beautiful literature and poetry, beautiful architecture, and beautiful scenery.

But the Christian view of heaven, though containing an element which (in a good sense) may be called 'sensuous,' is not sensual. Christ was careful to guard from the first against those gross and carnal conceptions of future bliss which among His contemporaries tended to attach themselves to the doctrine of the resurrection of the body. According to His teaching, in the world to come man will have outgrown his lower animal propensities, such as the appetite of sex (Mt 22^{30}, Mk 12^{25}, Lk 20^{35}) and the desire of eating and drinking (Ro 14^{17}). Allusions to feasting in the next world are certainly to be understood symbolically, as is especially evident from Mt 26^{29}.

Occasionally, but very rarely, the same spiritual view of the resurrection life appears in rabbinical writings:

'In the world to come,' said Rabbi Rab, 'there is neither eating, nor drinking, nor sexual pleasure, nor strife, but the righteous with their crowns sit around the table of God, feeding on the splendour of His Majesty.'[1]

The risen Lord's eating with the disciples during the great 40 days is not inconsistent with this view. He ate, not as needing food, but in order to afford a convincing proof of His bodily resurrection (Lk $24^{36ff.}$, Ac 1^4 RVm, 10^{41}).

The resurrection bodies of the saints were conceived of not as natural, but as glorious and spiritual (Mt 22^{30}, 1 Co $15^{35ff.}$), like the bodies of the angels, whom the ancient Jews and the early Church (at least to the close of the 4th cent.) regarded not as strictly incorporeal, but as invested with spiritual bodies, it being the privilege of God alone to be purely incorporeal.[2] Although the identity of the resurrection body with the earthly body is often suggested, or even insisted on in the NT (see Mt $5^{29.30}$ 10^{28}, Ro $8^{11.23}$, 1 Co 15^{53}; cf. also Mt 27^{52}), the identity thought of was probably one of continuity, rather than of identical materials. The doctrine of the full material identity of the earthly with the resurrection body seems not to be part of the original tradition, and is probably inconsistent with the Pauline doctrine (see especially 1 Co 15). It cannot be proved by the analogy of the resurrection of Jesus Himself. That resurrection was indeed a type and figure of the resurrection of the saints, but it was also a convincing sign of the Lord's victory over death, and of the triumph of matter over spirit. Accordingly, for apologetic reasons the actual buried body rose, leaving the tomb empty, but at the moment of resurrection it was transformed into a glorious and spiritual body, belonging henceforth to the heavenly sphere, and perceptible to mortal senses only by virtue of a voluntary and temporary accommodation to earthly conditions. Such at least seems to have been the view of the first disciples, and it is still the belief of the majority of Christians.

2. The locality of heaven.—Undoubtedly heaven is a state rather than a place, but a religion which, like Christianity, teaches the resurrection of the body and the glorification not merely of the spiritual, but even of the material universe, cannot dispense altogether with the idea of locality in connexion with heaven. What appears to be the teaching of the NT is this. At present, owing to the imperfection of the universe, God's glory and majesty cannot be fully manifested in it. The boundaries of heaven (*i.e.* of the sphere in which the divine glory is fully manifested) are consequently restricted. But in the consummation and regeneration of the universe (παλινγενεσία, Mt 19^{28}; ἀποκατάστασις πάντων, Ac 3^{21}), which will accompany the resurrection, when the whole creation, which, being enslaved in the bondage of corruption, groaneth and travaileth in pain together (*or* together with man) until now, shall be delivered into the liberty of the glory of the children of God (Ro 8^{21}), then the glory of God, at present manifested within a limited heaven, will be manifested throughout the entire universe, and the boundaries of heaven and of creation will be conterminous (2 P $3^{10.13}$, Rev 21^1; cf. Is 65^{17} 66^{22}, Rev 11^{15}, etc.). The distinction between heaven and earth will then have no meaning. Wherever God's servants may be, on whatever employment, God will be with them, and they will see His face—in other words, they will be in heaven, just as at present the holy guardian angels, while performing their ministry on earth, never really leave heaven, because they always see God's face (Mt 18^{10}).

3. The essential bliss of heaven.—Since God is the object of a Christian's supreme love, to see Him face to face must be a Christian's supreme bliss. This unveiled vision of God, which is the unending joy of the angels (Mt 18^{10}), will also be the final reward of the pure in heart (Mt 5^8). Both St. John and St. Paul agree in this doctrine, but it is the author of the Apocalypse who works it out into the fullest detail.

'Beloved,' says St. John, 'now are we children of God, and it is not yet made manifest what we shall be. We know that, if he shall be manifested, we shall be like him; *for we shall see him even as he is.* And every one that hath this hope set on him purifieth himself, even as he is pure' (1 Jn $3^{2.3}$). 'For now,' says St. Paul, 'we see in a mirror, darkly [lit. 'in a riddle']; but then *face to face*: now I know in part; but then shall I know (ἐπιγνώσομαι) even as also I have been known' (1 Co 13^{12}).

This immediate contemplation of the Infinite Essence of God, which, as conferring the highest conceivable degree of bliss, is generally spoken of as the Beatific Vision, must be regarded as a strictly supernatural endowment of grace, not analogous to any faculty at present possessed by man. Here on earth even our own personality, in its full depth and reality, is mysteriously veiled from us. What the thinker is in distinction from his thought, what the self-identical soul is, as distinguished from its changing states, we have not the least idea. The more we try to fix our gaze inward upon our true selves, the more confused our vision becomes, and we have to abandon the task as hopeless. If, then, we cannot by nature know our own selves, how much less can we know the Absolute Spirit! Hence Christian thought has always recognized that in order to attain to the immediate vision of the Divine Essence, the human soul must be lifted above the natural order altogether, made to partake of the Divine Nature (2 P 1^4), and, so far as this is possible without complete absorption into the Godhead, even 'deified,' as the Greek Fathers did not hesitate to express it.

The richness, magnificence, fertility, and comprehensiveness of this doctrine must be admitted even by those who cannot share it. It sums up and includes all lesser ideals by transcending them. It satisfies the Platonic ideal, because God is Himself the ἰδέα τοῦ ἀγαθοῦ, and, in contemplating Him, the soul contemplates the Absolute Good. It satisfies also the Aristotelian ideal of perfect intellectual knowledge, because in God the soul sees the universe no longer in scattered fragments, but as a single whole, from which standpoint the cosmos appears to be what it really is, viz. an orderly rational system.

The need of satisfying the intellectual faculties

[1] *Ber.* 17*a*.

[2] See, for a full presentation of the evidence, 'Angélologie d'après les Pères,' in Vacant, *Dict. de Théol. cath.*

of man is not ignored by Christianity. It emphasizes the essential rationality and intelligibility of the universe by regarding creation as the work of the Logos, or Reason of God, which, having from the beginning been immanent in the world, was finally manifested in the person of Jesus Christ, and is the object of Christian worship. A religion which pays the homage of adoration to Reason cannot fairly be accused of neglecting the claims of intellect. Intellectual knowledge has always been one constituent in the Christian ideal of human blessedness. St. Paul longs for ἐπίγνωσις, which certainly includes intellectual knowledge; and Origen considers that the satisfaction of the thirst for knowledge, which God has implanted in the soul, will be among the greatest of the joys of heaven. According to him, the cultivation of philosophy, and even of natural science, will be among the principal occupations of the glorified saints of God.[1]

But Christianity does not fall into the mistake of ranking intellect above moral goodness. It is not mainly as the Supreme Reason, but as the All-Holy, that God is adored by angels and men (Is 6^{3}, Rev 4^{8}). Religion has always recognized that the true being of God is best expressed in terms of moral personality. Thus the ancient Jews regarded Him mainly as Monarch and Judge. Christianity, without rejecting these ideas, transfigured them by conceiving of God as Unbounded Love (Jn 3^{16}). God, then, for Christians, is primarily 'Our Father which art in heaven,' and from this point of view heaven is regarded in Scripture as *the home*, where God gathers His children round Him in the loving intercourse of family life. 'In my Father's house are many mansions; if it were not so, I would have told you; for I go to prepare a place for you' (Jn 14^{2}).

The most wonderful representation of God in this aspect is the parable of the Prodigal Son. Here the Infinite Creator appears as running (δραμών) to meet the repentant prodigal, falling on his neck and kissing him fondly (κατεφίλησε), bringing forth the best robe, putting a ring on his hand and shoes on his feet, and killing the fatted calf and making merry (Lk $15^{20ff.}$). In the same spirit, the author of the Apocalypse exhausts the resources of language and imagery in trying to describe God's tender and familiar intercourse with the saints in heaven (Rev 21^{3}).

As in the love of God Christianity finds the supreme satisfaction of the human affections, so in the worship of God it finds the chief satisfaction of human emotion. Of all the emotional states experienced on earth the profoundest and the most uplifting is the sense of boundless adoration, joined with abject self-abasement, which thrills through the devout soul as it contemplates the infinite perfections of God. In heaven this rapture of adoration will never cease. 'They have no rest day and night, saying, Holy, holy, holy, is the Lord God, the Almighty, which was and which is and which is to come' (Rev 4^{8}).

Worship is the emotional expression of man's consciousness of God's absolute transcendence, and of the infinite gulf which separates even the most exalted creature from the Infinite Creator. The Christian cannot feel towards His God like the pantheist, who knows no God higher than the universe of which he himself forms a part. The Christian's God is absolute, self-existing, self-sufficing, not dependent upon the universe in any way for His perfection and blessedness, but transcending it to an infinite extent, and therefore claiming a homage that is absolutely unbounded. The Incarnation, though it bridges the abyss, does not destroy it. Even as incarnate, immanent, and holding familiar intercourse with His creatures, the Creator still maintains His awe-inspiring and ineffable transcendence. Indeed, it is just this ever-present consciousness of His immeasurable elevation above all created being that lends to the idea of the incarnation of God its profound emotional value. Even before God incarnate the heavenly host falls down in boundless adoration (Ph 2^{10}).

[1] *De Principiis*, ii. 11, etc.

Heaven, therefore, both in the OT and still more in the NT, is represented as a glorious sanctuary in which God's servants worship Him unceasingly with inward purity of heart, and with the outward expression of a magnificent ritual. There will be no temple (*i.e.* no special temple) there (Rev 21^{22}), because the whole universe will become one vast temple of God; and the worship will be ceaseless, because every activity of whatever sort, having as its end the glory of God, will be an act of worship.

Chs. 4 and 5 of the Apocalypse give an ideal picture of the perfect worship of heaven. It is a worship in which all creation (nature as well as man) harmoniously joins. How precisely the writer thinks of nature is not quite clear. It is possible that he regards nature as offering its worship vicariously, through its king and high-priest, man. More probably, like most ancient thinkers and like St. Paul (Ro 8^{22}), he regards nature as animated, and thinks of a vast graduated hierarchy of nature-spirits, culminating in the soul of the physical universe regarded as created, joining with angels and men in the anthem of praise. The worship is paid not only to God, but also to God incarnate, 'the Lamb as it had been slain' (Rev $5^{6.\ 12}$, etc.; Ph 2^{10}, etc.).

4. Heaven as a perfect society.—Trinitarianism regards God not as a monad, but as a perfect society, and finds in the nature of the Godhead itself the heavenly archetype of the family and of the state. The idea of the Church and of the communion of saints is therefore of the essence of Christianity. Religion, from the Christian standpoint, is man's approach to God as a member of a brotherhood, a family of God, a holy Church, in whose fellowship his spiritual life is nourished and perfected. Christianity makes men members one of another, puts in their mouths a social prayer ('Our Father,' not 'My Father'), helps them on their way by social worship and social sacraments, and teaches them to regard the service of man as one with the service of God (see especially 1 Jn 3^{13-18} $4^{20.\ 21}$). Heaven, therefore, as realizing the social ideal, is continually represented in the NT as a perfect society, city, or state (He $12^{22ff.}$).

All war, violence, and danger from enemies external and internal will have ceased, and therefore the gates of the city 'shall in no wise be shut by day' (*i.e.* not shut at all), 'for there shall be no night there' (Rev 21^{25}). Heaven will be a sinless society, for 'there shall in no wise enter into it anything unclean, or he that maketh an abomination and a lie: but only they which are written in the Lamb's book of life' (21^{27}).

5. The activities of the heavenly citizens.—The unceasing worship of heaven is not to be taken as implying that there will be no other activity than worship there, but rather that all occupations of every sort, being undertaken for the glory of God and in His service, will partake of the nature of worship. Many NT passages imply that all worthy faculties of individuals and races will find due employment in heaven (Rev $21^{24.\ 26}$).

Thus, since heaven is a state or city, there will be a scope for faculties of government and administration there (cf. Lk 19^{17}, 'Have thou authority over ten cities'). Our Lord teaches both in the parable of the Talents (Mt $25^{14ff.}$) and in the parable of the Pounds (Lk $19^{12ff.}$) that all faculties worthily employed in this world will receive additional scope in the world to come. If the indications in the Apocalypse are to be trusted, there will be great scope for the artistic faculties. In heaven there will be beautiful architecture and craftsmanship (Rev 21^{12}), beautiful poetry (5^{9} 14^{3}

15^3), and beautiful music, both vocal and instrumental (14^2 18^{22}), or at least some higher reality corresponding to these. Of the cultivation of philosophy and science in heaven we have already spoken.

6. Relation to time.—Christianity took over from Greek philosophy, and to some extent developed independently, the profound and fruitful idea of the distinction between time and eternity, and between becoming and being. First clearly stated by Parmenides, *c.* 500 B.C. ('True Being never was and it never will be, since it is present all of it together, only in *the now*, one and indivisible'), it is worked out in considerable detail by Plato, *c.* 390 B.C., especially in his *Phædrus* and *Symposium*. Plato regards time, which is divisible into successive moments of which only one is actual at a time, as a half-unreal shadow of eternity, which latter cannot be divided into parts, is present whole and indivisible in the changeless now, and is the only true duration. Similarly he regards becoming (γένεσις), *i.e.* evolution or change, which takes place in time, as an imperfect shadow of true being (οὐσία), which is changeless and self-consistent, and exists only in eternity. This view is also found in the NT.[1]

The doctrine of eternity has an important practical bearing upon our conception of man's future beatitude. One of the greatest imperfections of our present thinking is its piecemeal character. Geometry, *e.g.*, must be painfully and imperfectly acquired as a series of successive propositions, each of which requires a separate demonstration. A perfect intelligence would grasp in one mental act all the possible spatial relations of bodies. For such an intelligence there would be no 'proofs,' for all geometrical truths in all their relations would be grasped in a single intuition. In this world all our thinking is of the same disjointed and unsatisfactory character. We think of God in church, but forget Him as soon as we leave, because we have other things to think about. When talking to one friend, we forget for the time all our others. We cannot think of history as a whole, but only of a succession of incidents, of which only one can be clearly grasped at a time. In all our attempts to take comprehensive views details drop out of sight; hence our best generalizations are unsubstantial and unsatisfying. Neither of God, nor of nature, nor of ourselves, nor of our neighbours, nor of our future destiny, can we form anything but fragmentary and inadequate views.

Christian theology teaches that one of the chief results of the Beatific Vision will be that the soul, seeing all things in God, will see them, as God sees them, 'sub specie aeternitatis,' *i.e.* entire and complete, in all their mutual relations, in one undivided and indivisible mental act. Partial knowledge will be replaced, not indeed by omniscience, but by complete and adequate knowledge of all things, at any rate, which come within the intellectual capacity of creatures. There will be a similar unification of the emotional and affective life, so that all the affections and emotions will be felt *at once*. This inner unification of our mental life, by virtue of which our total knowledge of ourselves, of God, of our friends, and of the universe, together with the whole of the affections, emotions, and volitions, which our relations to these will evoke, will be simultaneously present to the mind in one majestic harmony, will give to life lived in eternity a richness and a vivacity of which a life lived amid the distractions of time and change can give no conception whatever. It is this inner unification of life, and not its mere endlessness, that is signified when the life of heaven is spoken of as 'eternal' (αἰώνιος).

It does not, however, follow from what has been said that time will have no sort of existence in the world to come. It may be that the lower creation will still be subject to time and to some degree of change. But, for the redeemed (at any rate in the higher aspects of their life) time and all essential change will have ceased to be.

7. Heaven regarded as a state of progress.—Of late years the traditional view of heaven as a timeless and changeless state of perfection has been sharply challenged both from the standpoint of the evolution theory and from that of the philosophy of Bergson. Both these systems postulate unending change, and Bergsonism regards change, and its accompaniment time, as ultimate realities belonging to the very essence of true life. There is a certain tendency, therefore, among modern theologians to regard heaven not as a state of perfection, but as one of continuous progress towards perfection. Westcott[1] even claims NT support for this view, and interprets the heavenly μοναί of Jn 14^2, not as dwelling-places, but as temporary halting-places for the soul in its never-ending journey towards perfection.

To the present writer this view seems a serious impoverishment of the Christian ideal. If we admit that the essential life of God is eternal and not temporal, and that the Christian hope is to share it, then it seems natural to suppose that Christians will share in the eternity of that life. If they do not, the expression 'eternal life' is denuded of a large part of its meaning. Moreover, the modern theory seems to err by interpreting the higher in terms of the lower. If heaven is a state of the highest conceivable good, then it seems quite illegitimate to describe it in terms of analogies taken from the imperfect conditions of this fleeting world. Evolution and change are not good in themselves; on the contrary, they are signs of imperfection. They mark a struggle towards a goal, and, when the goal is attained, no place remains for them. Heaven, according to traditional ideas, means the attainment of the goal, the actual and abiding possession of the highest possible good that a creature can attain. That is surely a far more satisfying conception than unending progress towards a goal that is never reached.

8. The state of the lost.—The final condition of the lost is a problem of secondary importance. The possibility of final impenitence, and therefore of final perdition, seems necessarily involved in the accepted doctrines of the freedom of the will and the immortality of the soul; and Christ frequently warned His hearers against the danger of incurring final reprobation (Mt 25^{41-46} $5^{22.\,29}$ 8^{12} 10^{15} 11^{22} 12^{32}; cf. Mk 3^{29}, Mt $13^{42.\,50}$ 18^8 22^{13} $23^{15.\,33}$ 24^{51} 25^{30}, etc.). But it does not seem to follow from the possibility of this doom that any will actually incur it. It may be that the providence of God will find means to avert it, and that the solemn warnings of Christ are among these means. Even if we grant, as the general tenor of the NT seems to suggest, that some will remain hardened and impenitent to the end, yet assuredly these will be rare and exceptional cases. NT teaching, taken as a whole, suggests, not indeed universalism, but

1 See particularly Jn 8^{58}, 'Before Abraham was, I am,' where the γενέσθαι of Abraham is contrasted with the εἶναι of Jesus; Rev 10^6, χρόνος οὐκέτι ἔσται, where the RV, following all ancient authorities, correctly translates, 'there shall be time no longer'; 1^4, ἀπὸ ὁ ὢν καὶ ὁ ἦν καὶ ὁ ἐρχόμενος, where the absence of inflection shows that immutable duration, *i.e.* eternity, is meant; also αἰώνιος in such phrases as ζωὴ αἰώνιος, both in St. John's Gospel and in the Synoptics, means 'eternal' very much in the Platonic sense.

1 On Jn 14^2.

certainly the salvation of the great bulk of mankind.

God 'willeth that all men (πάντας ἀνθρώπους) should be saved, and come to the knowledge (ἐπίγνωσιν) of the truth' (1 Ti 2[4]). He 'is the Saviour of all men, specially of them that believe' (1 Ti 4[10]). The Son of God came to seek and to save that which was lost (Mt 18[11]), and to be the Saviour of the world (Jn 4[42], 1 Jn 4[14]). 'God sent not the Son into the world to judge [condemn] the world; but that the world should be saved through him' (Jn 3[17]).

Salvation, then, will be the rule, reprobation the rare exception. The process of reclamation may in some cases be difficult, the expiatory and cleansing discipline may be severe and prolonged, but in the end, after whatever perils and sufferings, the great majority of God's children will stand before Him, pardoned and sinless.[1]

With regard to the finally impenitent, our task here is not to investigate their probable fate as a question of pure philosophy, but to ascertain, as nearly as we can from the documents, what the original Christian view was. And, in the opinion of the present writer, an impartial criticism will in the end be driven to admit that Christ believed and taught that their doom will be eternal (Mt 25[41. 46] 18[8], Mk 3[29] 9[43-48], 2 Th 1[9], Jude[7]). Of the various expedients devised by modern criticism to avoid this conclusion the best is certainly that which interprets eternal death as annihilation (*q.v.*). Annihilation was an idea not altogether unfamiliar to our Lord's contemporaries. Not to mention apocalyptic writings,[2] Rabbi Hillel taught that, whereas hardened sinners will 'go down to Gehenna and be punished there for ages of ages,' sinners of lesser delinquency will be annihilated and cease altogether to exist at the judgment. According to Edersheim, annihilationism even became the favourite rabbinical doctrine in the 2nd century.[3]

Annihilationism has the indubitable advantages (1) of being possible historically; (2) of giving an adequate meaning to αἰώνιος (the wicked are destroyed for ever); (3) of providing for the final extinction of all evil, moral and physical; and (4) of thus establishing the absolute and unchallenged supremacy of good.[4] But, attractive as it is, it cannot be reconciled with the NT evidence taken as a whole. It may satisfy ὄλεθρος αἰώνιος, but not κόλασις αἰώνιος. Still less can it explain or satisfy such passages as Mk 9[46], 'Gehenna, where their worm dieth not'; and Mt 13[42. 50], 'the furnace of fire: there shall be the weeping and gnashing of teeth' (cf. 8[12] 22[13] 24[51] 25[30], Lk 13[28], etc.). The conscious existence of the lost is expressed or implied in so many NT passages that only a drastic and quite uncritical purging of the text can get rid of it.

The final question now arises: Is it possible to reconcile eternal punishment with the Divine benevolence and with the ultimate victory of good over evil? Probably it is. The general principle of the judgment will be the loss of faculties which have been abused (Mt 25[28], Lk 19[24]). Now, the faculty which, in the case of the finally impenitent, has been wholly and irremediably abused is that of free will, and, therefore, whatever else eternal loss may involve, it must involve the loss of this. But with the loss of free will disappears also the power of sinning, and of resisting God's will, and, therefore, at the judgment, moral evil will disappear, and the holy will of God will be supreme. The lost, deprived of all power of volition and choice, will sink to the rank of necessary agents, and will do the will of God, like the lower creation, by necessity. Thus all creation will be subject to its Creator, and God will be all in all (1 Co 15[28]).

[1] See below, § 9. [2] See art. ESCHATOLOGY.
[3] *The Life and Times of Jesus the Messiah*[4], London, 1889, ii. 791 ff.
[4] See art. CONDITIONAL IMMORTALITY.

It is not necessary to regard the condition of the lost as absolutely intolerable, though, in contrast with the bliss of the redeemed, it will appear most sad. Its sadness will consist mainly in regret for the loss of the Beatific Vision, and remorse for the criminal folly which has led to their degradation from the rank of responsible beings. On the other hand, their condition may admit of important alleviations. Thus they can sin no more, and will perform the will of God unerringly, which will surely be for their good. Moreover, their enjoyment of natural goods, though impaired, will not be destroyed. In fact it even seems possible to regard their condition as one of relative happiness of a purely natural kind. At any rate, we may be sure that their condition will be better than absolute non-existence, for we cannot imagine an omniscient and all-merciful God calling into being creatures whose final state will be worse than non-existence. The purely proverbial expression made use of, Mt 26[24], is not sufficient evidence to the contrary.

9. The intermediate state and purgatory.—The expectation that the final judgment would come within their own generation caused the doctrine of the intermediate state to appear relatively unimportant to the first Christians, and, as some think, even to Christ Himself. The references to it in the NT are accordingly not very numerous, and, were there a sufficient motive to do so, might possibly be explained away by the use of a little critical ingenuity. This has, in fact, been attempted even in so recent and judicial a work as Salmond's *Christian Doctrine of Immortality*[4]. But, inasmuch as the doctrine in question (in the most usual form of which the intermediate state was divided into two main compartments—a state of blissful expectancy in which the righteous awaited their reward, and a state of painful confinement in which the unrighteous expiated their crimes, and were in some cases cleansed from sin) had already attained considerable development before the Christian era, and is found in full possession of the field immediately after the apostolic age, there is nothing to prevent, but everything to suggest, our taking the relevant NT passages at their full face value.

The *locus classicus* is the parable of Dives and Lazarus (Lk 16[19ff.]), which embodies the Jewish conception entire, with only this difference, that the righteous are separated from the unrighteous by a great gulf, instead of by 'a hand's breadth' (the rabbinical view). Lazarus rests in Abraham's bosom—a common rabbinical designation of the intermediate abode of bliss—while Dives is in torments. That the torments of Dives are to be regarded as temporary is probably indicated by the use of ᾅδης instead of γέεννα, and by the softening of his hard and selfish nature indicated in v.[27ff.]

The purgatorial aspect of the punishments in Hades is still more clearly indicated in Mt 12[32], which seems to suggest that all sins, except one, may, under certain circumstances, find pardon in the world to come (a common Jewish expression for beyond the grave); also in Mt 5[26], which appears to imply that even grievous sinners may be released from their torments after adequately expiating their crimes. The possibility of the pardon of sin after death is also presupposed by 1 Peter (probably the work of the apostle himself), which represents Christ as preaching in Hades, not only to the righteous, but even to those sinners who rejected the preaching of Noah, and who, according to popular belief, were hopelessly lost (1 P 3[19] 4[6]). This, the natural and obvious sense of the passage, and that in which it was almost universally understood in ancient times, is now very generally recognized as the only tenable one.

The fact is that purgatorial ideas were well established in Judaism long before Christ, and that Christianity simply adopted them. Judas Maccabæus is represented as offering prayers and sacrifices for the sins of his soldiers fallen in battle, and thus making 'a reconciliation for the dead, that they might be delivered from sin' (2 Mac 12[39ff.]). Shammai taught that, whereas the sins of desperate sinners are punished for ever, others 'go down to Gehenna, and moan, and come up again.'[1] The early Church, while taking a very gloomy view of hell, took, on the whole, a hopeful view of Hades. Hades was regarded as a great mission-field for the evangelization of the heathen and of imperfect believers. As the Lord Himself had preached the gospel there, so, after their deaths, had the apostles. According to Hermas, they had even baptized there, thus rendering unnecessary the practice of vicarious baptism for the dead to which St. Paul alludes.[2] Clement of Alexandria says expressly that 'God's punishments in Hades are saving and disciplinary, leading to conversion, and choosing rather the repentance than the death of a sinner.'[3]

Along with the Jewish doctrine of Hades, Christianity took over the closely connected Jewish practice of offering prayers and oblations for the dead. This must have happened early in the apostolic age, since at a later period the mutual hostility of the Church and the Synagogue would have prevented it. It is true that the NT evidence is not demonstrative (though, if we accept the now widely prevalent view that the Kingdom of God preached by Christ is eschatological, it is difficult to exclude the dead from the petition, 'Thy kingdom come' in the Lord's Prayer; and the prayer for Onesiphorus, 1 Ti 1^{18}, is now almost universally regarded as a prayer for the dead;[4] cf. also 1 Co 15^{29}); but, at any rate, the practice was well established in the 2nd century. In the East there is the inscription on the tomb of Abercius (*c.* A.D. 175), inviting the Christian passer-by to pray for his soul, while in the West the incidental allusions of Tertullian (*c.* A.D. 200) point to an organized and long-established custom.

LITERATURE.—i. *GENERAL.*—W. R. Alger, *The Destiny of the Soul: a Critical Hist. of the Doctrine of a Future Life*[14], New York, 1889 (contains exhaustive bibliography by Ezra Abbott); S. D. F. Salmond, *The Christian Doctrine of Immortality*[4], Edinburgh, 1901; R. H. Charles, *Eschatology*[2], London, 1913; F. von Hügel, *Eternal Life*, Edinburgh, 1912; B. Bosanquet, *The Value and Destiny of the Individual*, London, 1913, and *The Principle of Individuality and Value*, do. 1912; J. Martineau, *A Study of Religion*[2], 2 vols., Oxford, 1889; J. Royce, *The World and the Individual*, 2 vols., New York, 1900–01; P. Kneib, *Der Beweis für die Unsterblichkeit der Seele*, Freiburg i. B., 1903; C. Piat, *Destinée de l'homme*[2], Paris, 1910; Thomas Aquinas, *c. Gentes*, ii. 79, 81, *Summa*, i. qq. 76, 90; H. Münsterberg, *The Eternal Values*, Boston and London, 1909; J. M. E. McTaggart, 'The Unreality of Time,' *Mind*, new ser., no. 68 [Oct. 1908], pp. 457–474, and 'The Relation of Time and Eternity,' *ib.* new ser., no. 71 [July, 1909], pp. 343–362; J. S. Mackenzie, 'Problem of Time,' *ib.* new ser., no. 83 [July, 1912], pp. 329–346; G. Fell, *The Immortality of the Human Soul Philosophically Explained*, Eng. tr., London and St. Louis, 1906; *Ingersoll Lectures* (especially those by W. James, *Human Immortality*, Boston, 1898; J. Royce, *Conception of Immortality*, do. 1900; J. Fiske, *Life Everlasting*, do. 1901; W. Osler, *Science and Immortality*, do. 1904; H. Münsterberg, *The Eternal Life*, do. 1905); S. C. Gayford, *Life after Death*, London, 1909; M. Maher, *Psychology*[6], New York and London, 1905; E. Fry, *Some Intimations of Immortality*, London, 1913; E. W. Winstanley, *Jesus and the Future*, Edinburgh, 1913; J. Fiske, *Man's Destiny in the Light of his Origin*, London, 1884; A. Schweitzer, *The Quest of the Historical Jesus*, Eng. tr., do. 1910, *Paul and his Interpreters*, Eng. tr., do. 1912; J. E. C. Welldon, *The Hope of Immortality*, do. 1898; E. Petavel [Olliff], *The Problem of Immortality*, Eng. tr., 1892.

ii. *DEALING WITH PSYCHICAL RESEARCH.*—F. W. H. Myers, *Human Personality and its Survival of Bodily Death*, 2 vols., London, 1903 (also abridged ed., do. 1907); O. Lodge, *The Survival of Man*, do. 1909; C. Lombroso, *After Death, What?*, Eng. tr., do. 1909; J. H. Hyslop, *Science and a Future Life*[4], New York and London, 1906; C. L. Tweedale, *Man's Survival after Death*, London, 1909; G. Delanne, *Evidence for a Future Life*, Eng. tr., New York and London, 1904; O. Lodge, *Raymond, or Life and Death*[8], do. 1917; B. H. Streeter, *Immortality, An Essay in Discovery co-ordinating Scientific, Psychical, and Biblical Research*, do. 1917.

iii. *DEVOTIONAL.*—R. Baxter, *The Saints' Everlasting Rest*, London, 1650; E. E. Holmes, *Immortality*, London and New York, 1908.

iv. *DEALING MAINLY WITH THE INTERMEDIATE STATE, PURGATORY, AND HELL.*—E. B. Pusey, *What is of Faith as to Everlasting Punishment?*[2], Oxford, 1880; R. Bellarmine, 'De Purgatorio,' in his *Disputationes de Controversiis Christianæ Fidei*, Cologne, 1628, ii. 390–416; A. J. Mason, *Purgatory*, London, 1901; E. H. Plumptre, *The Spirits in Prison*, do. 1884; H. M. Luckock, *After Death*[6], do. 1887, and *The Intermediate State*[2], do. 1891; H. C. Oxenham, *Catholic Eschatology and Universalism*[2], do. 1878; L. Billot, *Quæstiones de Novissimis*, Rome, 1903; J. Bautz, *Das Fegfeuer*, Mainz, 1883; *Is there a Hell? a Symposium by Leaders of Religious Thought*, London, 1913; St. G. Mivart, articles on 'Happiness in Hell,' in *Nineteenth Century*, Dec. 1902, Feb. and April, 1903; J. A. Beet, *The Last Things*, new ed., London, 1905; E. von Dobschütz, *The Eschatology of the Gospels*, do. 1910; W. O. E. Oesterley, *The Doctrine of the Last Things*, do. 1909; F. Boettcher, *De Inferis Rebusque post Mortem Futuris*, Dresden, 1845; J. Calvin, *Psychopannychia*, Paris, 1534.

See also Literature of art. ESCHATOLOGY.

C. HARRIS.

[1] *Rōsh Hashshānāh*, 16*b*.

[2] See 1 Co 15^{29}; Hermas, *Sim.* ix. 16; Clem. Alex. *Strom.* vi. 6.

[3] *Loc. cit.*

[4] Cf. art. PRAYER FOR THE DEPARTED (Christian).

STATE OF THE DEAD (Greek and Roman).

—I. **Greek.**—The spirits of the dead were regarded by the Greeks, all through their history, as still retaining a material vesture, but extremely attenuated. Their appearance to mortal eyes was shadowy and dreamlike. Homer[1] described them as ἀμενηνὰ κάρηνα, figures without vital strength (μένος), and especially bloodless. As is shown by the Νέκυια,[2] they are capable of feeding on the blood of sacrifice, which gives them temporary vitality; but without this reinforcement they seem to have neither speech nor memory. Ghosts were very commonly supposed by the Greeks to hover about the spot where their material remains were interred. Yet the conflicting idea that there is a common abode, vaguely named as 'the unseen' ('Αΐδης), in which all spirits normally dwell, became current in the earliest times. In the Homeric poems a few souls, by special favour of the gods, awarded apparently with no regard to moral merit, reach the home of bliss in the Elysian fields, and become in a sense divine. Such are Teiresias, Menelaus, Rhadamanthus, and Achilles. Homer presents also, very dimly, a picture of a region of woe beyond the grave to which are consigned a few abnormal sinners, such as Tityus, Tantalus, and Sisyphus; also the men who have taken an oath and forsworn themselves. From the earliest times the fate of the perjurer was conceived by the Greeks as especially dark. Later feeling about the dead was largely influenced by the mysteries and by philosophy. There floated about a conception that the origin of the soul was really divine, and that its imprisonment in earthly barriers was a punishment; that the body was in reality a tomb (σῶμα σῆμα). These ideas were largely spread by the Orphic and Pythagorean brotherhoods, in whose rituals was expressed the longing of the soul on earth to find its way back, after death, to the home of its origin. Empedocles described the soul in its earthly sojourn as 'an exile from the gods, and a wanderer' (φυγὰς θεόθεν καὶ ἀλητής). He held the doctrine of successive periods of existence, in which the soul is invested with different material forms, its fate in each period being determined by its conduct in previous stages. The best conditions are reserved for the ethically best, who become seers, poets, physicians, and princes. Sin-laden souls have to pass into the lower forms of life, and occupy the bodies of animals and even of plants. The persistently better spirits make their way back to the regions of the divine. These doctrines embody elements drawn from the East. They were accepted by Plato and elaborated by him with much mystic and poetic embroidery. In his writings the vision of life after death became vivid and pictorial. The teaching of transmigration (*q.v.*) was of course bound up with the idea of a judgment of souls after death. The judgment is conspicuous already in Pindar, but some of the details which were

[1] *Od.* x. 521, 536, xi. 29.

[2] *Od.* xi.

popularly accepted in later times—*e.g.*, the functions of the three judges, Minos, Æacus, and Rhadamanthus—appear first in Plato. In the *Gorgias* and *Phædo* the incurable souls enter on an eternity of misery. In Plato the references to pre-existence (*q.v.*) become explicit and detailed, and the process of recollection (ἀνάμνησις) becomes very prominent. By it the mind can recover memories of its primal happy state in possession of heavenly knowledge, which was obscured by its descent to earth. The means to this consummation was philosophic exercise. Later belief about the dead was influenced to a considerable extent by Stoicism. The Stoics believed in a periodic destruction and reconstruction of all created forms; therefore the departed spirit maintains its individuality only until the cataclysm that follows next after its death on earth. In later times a whole series of divinities came to be connected with the judgment and the governance of the dead, and notions of Elysium and Hades became more distinct. Hades was now conceived as a god and 'a discipliner of mortals' (εὔθυνος βροτῶν). Among the many gods to whom functions connected with the dead were assigned Hermes took a special place. He was the conductor of the spirits from earth to their place of abode in the other world, and obtained the title of 'conductor of souls' (ψυχόπομπος). In the great mysteries celebrated at Eleusis Demeter and her daughter Persephone were the grand figures, and it is well known that due participation in their ritual was deemed to ensure the happiness of the soul after death. Other mysteries served the same end, and pictured the journey of the soul from earth to the other world. Only in comparatively later times did Pluto (Πλούτων) come to occupy the infernal throne (first in the Attic poets of the 5th cent. B.C.). His name (connected with πλοῦτος, 'wealth') appears to be one of the numerous euphemistic titles bestowed on the powers of darkness. As in the case of the fairies among modern peoples, it was thought dangerous to assign to supernatural beings titles which implied evil, however truthfully. There were many spots in the Greek world at which there were popularly supposed to be gateways of the infernal abode, as at Cape Tænarus in Laconia. The same idea connected with Lake Avernus in Italy is doubtless of Greek origin.

In the late Greek age writers like Plutarch present a strange mixture of notions concerning the condition of the dead, and their abodes, and their migrations from form to form—a compound of popular Greek superstitions with elements drawn from mysteries and philosophy (especially Platonic and Stoic), and also from Oriental religions. The lore by which spirits might be invoked and compelled to disclose the future was greatly elaborated, and necromancy was one of its chief forms. It may be remarked that the Greek ghost did not often appear to mortals gratuitously—that is to say, without the compulsion which the sorcerer was able to lay upon him. The Homeric ghost is usually, like the Homeric god, seen by mortals in dreams; and in the whole age of Greek civilization the connexion of ghosts with dreams was very close. The modern 'ghost-story' has remarkably few counterparts in ancient literature, either Greek or Roman, although tales of haunted houses were not unknown, and such tales were made the theme of several Greek comedies, of which the authors are known, and doubtless of others of which there is no record. The Greek original of the *Mostellaria* of Plautus cannot be traced.

The belief in the dependence of the dead upon the offerings of the living for their comfort and consideration in the other world was universal in Greece, and was treated as rational by Aristotle; so was the belief that the dead spirits can powerfully affect the living, more for evil than for good. Among the Greeks the cult of ancestors did not occupy so prominent a place as it held among the Romans, who believed that the family had for its chief object the maintenance of this cult. The family *sacra* did not in Greece make nearly so deep an impression on religion and law and social usage as was the case among the Romans. And public ritual for the appeasement of the dead was not nearly so conspicuous in the area of Greek civilization as it was in the Roman area. In Athens and in a number of Ionic communities there was a ceremony called Anthesteria, celebrated in spring (February), when all life revives and the life of ghosts is unusually active, so that they come in numbers about the homes of the living. It was vitally necessary to protect the community against them. During the time of the ceremony many public and private activities were suspended. On the conclusion of the ritual the spirits were warned away by a cry which one of the ancient grammarians has preserved: θύραζε κῆρες, οὐκετ' ἀνθεστήρια ('Out, ye ghosts, the Anthesteria is over'). The word κήρ, which is here used of the ordinary ghosts, came to mean an avenging spirit, like the name Eumenides. There can have been originally no sharp dividing line between the non-human and the human avenging spirit. At the time of the Anthesteria the doors of houses were smeared with pitch, to keep the spectres aloof; this wears the appearance of a homœopathic remedy. Sulphur was also a prophylactic. The ceremony of Anthesteria probably derived its name from its occurrence in the season of spring flowers. Flowers were not conspicuous among offerings pleasing to the dead in the Greek ritual. They were far more prominent in later Roman civilization, when days were appropriated to the service of the spirits which bore the name of *dies rosæ* and *dies violæ*.

2. Roman.—It is clear that the Romans, from the remotest times, regarded the spirits of the dead as in some sense divine. All through their history the tomb was regarded as an altar, and it is often so described in inscriptions. Varro and other ancient scholars set forth the evidence relating to this matter. Servius, commenting on the expression *divi parentes*, put by Virgil into the mouth of Æneas[1] when he had accomplished the funeral ritual in honour of Anchises, quoted the expression *dei parentes* as commonly applied to deceased ancestors. But the word *divi* (properly used of deified mortals) better expresses the feeling of the classical age. In his ideal code of law in his *de Legibus* Cicero has: 'Leto datos divos habento.'[2] Certainly all through their history the Romans believed not merely that the living could influence the condition of the dead by assigning to them or withholding from them due honour and offerings, but also that the dead had great power to affect the fortunes of the living. Primarily, the duty of assuring to the dead their rights rested upon their living descendants. The Roman conception of the family regarded it as a perpetual corporation which included both the dead and the living. This sense of the perpetual unity and unbroken continuity of the family found expression in all the observances paid to the departed, beginning with the funeral procession, in which men walked, invested with the ancestral *imagines*, personating the dead to whom these belonged. 'Peace with the dead'[3] was important, not only to the separate families, but to the whole body of citizens collectively; it was hardly less

[1] *Æneid*, v. 47. [2] ii. 23.
[3] 'Pax mihi cum mortuis' in Plautus, *Mostellaria*, ii. 2, 89.

so, indeed, than the *pax deorum.* Therefore we find that, on the days in the calendar on which occurred ceremonies expressing the private reverence for the world of spirits, there were also celebrations ordained by the State and conducted by public religious and secular authorities.

The original Roman idea about the abode of the departed was that the soul of every deceased man whose funeral rites had been duly performed by the living dwelt in the tomb in which his body or his ashes had been deposited. Some ancient Roman scholars and many modern scholars have believed that in primitive times the bodies of the dead were actually buried within the family dwelling. But in the most distant pre-historic time to which research in Italy has enabled us to penetrate there were great cemeteries outside the bounds of the town-settlements. And in historic times burial within city limits was very unusual, except at the Greek city of Tarentum, where the intramural cemetery figures conspicuously in the stories of sieges and captures of the place. The life of the departed soul was envisaged as a continuance of his life before death. He has a 'house,' for *domus* is a common designation of the tomb.[1] Pre-historic funeral urns found in Latium are actually shaped like the huts in which the people lived at the time. In later Roman times phrases like *domus æterna* were quite common in inscriptions on tombs. The emperor Julian[2] speaks of *sepulcrum* as 'domus defunctorum.' The deceased was supposed to need in the other world everything that he required while on earth. Hence the multiplicity of articles which were buried with him (or burned with him, for material things seem to have been thought to have a ghostly survival) and the periodical offerings to him of food and drink—simple things in the earliest time, such as milk, honey, eggs and beans, and flowers to grace his repasts; later on wine occupied an important place. The ghost was thought of as a sort of 'breath' (*anima* or *spiritus*) and as bloodless. Hence his desire for blood to revive his strength. This was afforded by sacrifices at the tomb, the victims chosen being especially those of dark colour. The desire of the dead for blood is depicted in *Odyssey*, xi., where Odysseus lures the heroes slain at Troy to the upper world by the blood poured into a trench. The desire for blood is also attested by the history of the gladiatorial games, which, for some centuries after they were introduced from Etruria, were always ostensibly performed in honour of some particular deceased person. The chief form taken by the veneration of the dead was that of a meal celebrated at stated times at the tomb by the members of the family. Doubtless the deceased ancestors were imagined as present. The chief occasions were the anniversaries of the birth and death of the departed. Very often there were round about the tomb appurtenances for the convenience of these recurring observances—an assembly room (*schola*), a dining-room (*cenaculum*), a kitchen (*culina*), a garden. Many references to all these appear in inscriptions. Gifts to the dead man were *inferiæ* (a name obviously connected with *inferi*), whether given at regular times or irregularly.

In order that the deceased man might have rest in his tomb, it was necessary that the due ritual should have been gone through by the living (the *iusta*). Otherwise he had an evil influence on the survivors, and would hover about and torment them. It was the duty of every man who came across a corpse to throw earth upon it, in order that the spirit might have rest. Drowned men's souls flitted about above the water.[1] Even a priest, who was ordinarily deemed to be defiled by the presence of a corpse, was strictly held to the duty of appeasing the spirit by attending to the funeral rite. The only persons who had no claim to funeral honours were executed criminals, suicides, and men struck dead by lightning—a sign of divine wrath.

Departed spirits were most generally spoken of as *manes*, literally 'the good people.'[2] As some spirits were hostile to the living and others benevolent, the application of *manes* to all must be euphemistic, just as the phrase 'good people' is applied in Ireland to all the fairies, though not all are beneficent. The title *dis manibus* (often indicated by *D.M.* or *D.M.S.* [*dis manibus sacrum*]), which appears at the head of innumerable Roman tomb inscriptions, calls for some comment. This kind of titulature did not come into general use till the early imperial period. When the words are written in full, we find *diis* or *dis*, hardly ever *divis*.[3] In general, it is clear that the *di manes* are the family ancestors who are in amity with the living, and have been to some degree elevated to a superhuman level. The epithet *inferi* is often attached to them, as by Tacitus, *Annals*, xiii. 14: 'inferos Silanorum manes.' Passages such as that just quoted throw doubt on the idea which is often accepted, that, when *dis manibus* or *D.M.* is followed by the name, in the genitive, of the person to whom the tomb is dedicated, then the words indicate the spirit of that individual person.[4]

The conception of a general dwelling-place of departed spirits is much later than that of the tomb as the abode of the deceased members of the family, and may very possibly be not indigenous in Italy, but borrowed in very early times from the Greeks. In the prologue to the *Casina* of Plautus it is called *communis locus*, and quite early in Roman literature *plures* is a euphemistic phrase for the dead collectively, borrowed of course from the Greek πλείονες. But the mass of the people never abandoned the older idea, and the two views continued to exist side by side. There is no proper Latin name for this abode; it is generally designated by Greek names, such as Acheron. Some particular spots in Italy, especially Lake Avernus, came to be regarded as affording communication with the infernal world. There is practically no indigenous Italic mythology connected with this world; all the tales concerning it are borrowed from Greece. When, in his first book, Lucretius declaims against *superstitio*, his illustrative tales are those of Tantalus, Sisyphus, and the like. All definite Italian beliefs about judgments after death and rewards and punishments in the world beyond the grave seem to have been derived originally from the Greeks. Yet the notion of a general receptacle for departed souls, if not absolutely primitive among Romans, is involved in some practices which, as we shall see presently, are relatively early.

The ghosts were conceived as consisting of highly attenuated matter, and were generally denoted by the words *anima* and *spiritus*, both of which meant, originally, air or breath.[5] Their appearance was ugly; hence the epithet *deformes* was often applied. Sometimes the skeleton was supposed to be visible. Ghostly visions rarely appeared to waking men; the ghost is usually an accompani-

[1] So *casula* in H. Dessau, *Inscriptiones Latinæ selectæ*, Berlin, 1892–1906, no. 7519, and the curious phrase *domus Romula*, 'the grave of a Roman,' in inscriptions from Mauretania.

[2] *Cod. Just.* ix. 19. 4.

[1] Horace, *Odes*, i. 28.

[2] Cf. the opposite, *im-manis.*

[3] But cf. *divi parentum* in an ancient formula quoted by Festus, p. 230.

[4] Phrases like *patriis deis* (*CIL* iii. 3688) and *manes paterni* (Ovid, *Fasti*, v. 443) point in the same direction; rather the company of the family spirits is indicated.

[5] Virgil, *Æn.* v. 740, compares them to smoke.

ment of dreams. It will be remembered how important are these dream-visions in the explanation which Lucretius gives of the origin of the belief in immortality.[1]

The principal ceremonies for the appeasement of the dead took place on nine days in February (13th–21st); on the latter day the great State ceremony of the *Feralia* was performed. The other days were *dies parentales* as being sacred to the *di parentum*, the ancestors of the various families, and were days for private celebrations.[2] The day after the *Feralia* was called *Caristia* or *cara cognatio*, on which a kind of family reunion was held, embracing both the living members and the reconciled dead. The preceding ceremonies were supposed to have ensured perfect harmony between the upper and the nether worlds.[3]

The *lares* of the home were especially connected with this last celebration, and their relation to the *manes* is to be considered. Although the existing evidence shows the *lares* to have been pre-eminently protecting divinities of localities rather than of persons, they were so closely connected with the home that they presented themselves to the imagination of the living as the spirits of departed ancestors. While *manes* is a plural without any corresponding singular, the *lar familiaris* was the mythical ancestor who founded the family. He appears as a character in the *Trinummus* of Plautus. Another word applied to ghosts is *larvæ*. Those who bear the name are the unreconciled spirits who are malignant in their feeling towards the living. A madman was often called *larvatus*, *i.e.* one plagued by the *larvæ*, just as in Greece the madman was supposed to be harassed by the Furies. The word *furiæ* is indeed in Latin literature often used of the malignant ghost, as, *e.g.*, of the ghost of Clodius, who desired vengeance on Milo.[4] Another word applied to malevolent spirits is *lemures*. A very ancient ceremonial of reconciliation called Lemuria, originally public, but in a later time left in private hands, was performed on three days in February. In ancient literature *lemures* and *larvæ* are often synonymous terms. The object of this celebration was to expel the dark spirits from the house.[5] Black beans, thrown by the *paterfamilias* behind him, over his shoulder, were prominent in the ritual.

One other ceremony must be mentioned. There was a pit called *mundus*, which was the central spot in the old supposed Palatine 'city of Romulus.' This was closed by a great stone, called *lapis manalis*. On three days in the year this stone was lifted and a ritual was gone through which certainly had for its object the propitiation of the dead. It seems therefore that, whatever purpose this *mundus* primitively served (some scholars suppose that it originally contained reserve stores of provisions for the primitive community), it was assuredly regarded later as one of the openings to the infernal regions.

If the dead dwell together, it is natural to imagine them as having an ordered polity, governed by divinities, as in the upper world. To those of the lower regions the general term *di inferi* was applied, as opposed to *di superi*; but the circle of the *di inferi* is not easy to depict. The contrast between the two divine circles was very marked.[6] On days devoted to the veneration of the infernal powers the temples of the *di superi* were closed. In the classical age the supernal gods were figures borrowed from Greece; the Roman antiquarians, however, preserve the names of primitive Italic divine figures such as Mania, Dea Muta or Tacita, Furina, Laverna.

1 *De Rer. Nat.* iv.
2 W. Warde Fowler, *The Roman Festivals*, London, 1899, p. 307 ff.
3 Ovid, *Fasti*, vi. 621 ff.
4 Cicero, *pro Milone*, 91.
5 Nonius, p. 185, from Varro.
6 Cf. Virg. *Æn.* viii. 245: 'regna pallida dis invisa.'

When Greek philosophy gained influence over the education of the Romans of the upper classes, many conceptions of the condition of departed souls were borrowed, especially from Plato and the Academies and Stoics, who sometimes regarded souls as fragments of the divine element in the universe. Souls were deemed to have an affinity with fire, and after death good souls, which had not lost affinity with what is divine, were supposed to flee to the abode of fire in the upper circles of the sky, where they were in touch with the gods. This idea is often represented in the works of Cicero.[1] Traces of it are to be found in very early Latin literature, in the writings of Ennius and others. Some even went the length of supposing that the souls became stars.[2] The bad or common souls defiled by sin were still relegated to Tartarus. Sometimes the soul was identified with the man's *genius*, which was sent out from Juppiter at birth and returned to him at death.[3]

The monumental inscriptions of the imperial age oftenest represent death as eternal sleep, but many times it is intimated that this perfect rest is a boon dependent on a good life.

LITERATURE.—Information on this subject may be found in works on Greek and Roman religion, particularly in O. Gruppe, *Griechische Mythologie und Religionsgeschichte*, 2 vols., Munich, 1897–1906; G. Wissowa, *Religion und Kultus der Römer*, do. 1902, [2]1912; W. Warde Fowler, *The Roman Festivals*, London, 1899; also many artt. in Roscher, especially those by H. Steuding on 'Manes' and 'Inferi'; others in Daremberg-Saglio, especially that by J. A. Hild on 'Manes.' Greek and Roman ideas of the state of the dead are treated and compared with the ideas of other peoples in *GB*[3].

J. S. REID.

STATE OF THE DEAD (Hebrew).

—The early Hebrew ideas of the state of the dead are those common to all primitive peoples. Existence continues after death, but in a shadowy, dreamlike state which does not deserve the name of life. Most of these early ideas are illustrated in the story of the calling of Samuel by the witch of Endor (1 S 28). The dead are the replica of their living selves: Samuel appears as an old man covered with a cloak, but recognizable by Saul. They keep their personal characteristics: Samuel berates Saul as in life. They are divine beings (*elōhīm*) and foreknow the future, but are subject to the call of human spells. They are 'disquieted' by being brought back to earth, but are obliged to obey the summons of the necromancer.

The qualities of this existence were, so far as revealed by the literature, conceived mostly in a negative way. No one looked forward with pleasure to the life after death. A man to whom life has brought suffering may be pictured as longing for the refuge of death, but it is only as a place of rest from the unbearable tortures of life (Job $3^{3ff.\ 13f.\ 21f.}$, Ps $49^{11.\ 15}$). The term 'life' is not used of their existence. The dead are not living, for the spirit (*rūah*), which is the principle of life given by God, has been taken from them and returned to God (Ps $104^{29f.}$, Job $34^{14f.}$, Ec 12^{7}). They are not, then, souls, persons (*nephesh*) in any true sense. In the late codes H and P (Lv 19^{28} $21^{1.\ 11}$ 22^{4}, Nu 5^{2} 6^{11} $9^{6.\ 7.\ 10}$) and in Hag 2^{13} *nephesh* is used of the dead, but in most of the passages the reference is to the dead body which defiles the living person, not to the dead as existing in another realm. The early literature has no special name for the dead, but the Wisdom literature and other late passages use *reph'āīm* (Job 26^{5}, Is 14^{9} 26^{19}, Ps 88^{11}, Pr 2^{18} 9^{18} 21^{16}). The word is from a root meaning 'sunken,' 'flaccid,' 'powerless.' How early this name was used we cannot

1 As in *Somnium Scipionis*, 8, *Tusc. Disp.* i. 76.
2 Ovid, *Metam.* xv. 840 ff.
3 Macrobius, *Sat.* i. 10, 15.

say, but the idea which it connotes belongs to primitive thought and continued as long as the realm of the dead was a factor in Hebrew thought. The dead are weak, even kings having lost their power (Is 14^{9-17}). They are nowhere represented as able to bring harm to the living, though they may give useful information and presumably aid.

The early Hebrew writings give no detailed picture of the state after death to correspond with the pictures of Muhammadanism, Zoroastrianism, the religion of Egypt, or mediæval Christianity. The conceptions of Greece and Rome, which remained to the end remarkably primitive, are more vivid and pictorial than the Hebrew. The reason for this barrenness is not lack of imagination—there is no reason to suppose such lack of imagination—but rather the fact that the prophetic influence was against any emphasis on the life after death. Possibly, had the prophetic writers felt free to record all phases of the popular belief, the meagre outline of the picture might have been somewhat filled in. It is probable that the popular imagination was less barren than the literature would lead us to think. The place of the abode of the dead was called Sheol. The origin of the word is uncertain; it possibly means 'the hollow place,' 'the pit,' possibly 'the place of inquiry,' with reference to necromancy.[1] It is beneath the earth (Gn 37^{35}, Pr 15^{24}, Job 11^{8}, Is 14^{9}), and is called the pit (Is 14^{15}). Like most primitive races, the Hebrews attempted no sharp distinction between the realm of the dead and the grave. They brought to the grave offerings for the dead, whether for worship or for sustenance.[2] The dead dwell in the grave, but also in Sheol (Ezk $37^{12f.}$, Gn 37^{35}), while sometimes terms are used which imply that Sheol is the grave (Is 14^{11}). R. H. Charles holds that Sheol signifies 'all the graves of the tribe or nation . . . united in one.'[3] The meaning then expands to embrace the departed of all nations, and so Sheol comes to be the common home of the dead of all nations (Ezk $32^{21.27}$ 31^{15-17}). L. B. Paton[4] holds that the early idea of the dead was connected only with the tomb, and that Sheol was a Sumerian conception borrowed by the Canaanites, and from them by the Hebrews. However that may be, it is very common to find, in all early thought, the grave and the realm of the dead confused. Soon the grave loses its local and literal connotation, and is almost a synonym for the land of the dead. Even so, in Hebrew thought, to die is to be gathered to the fathers, even where, as in the case of Abraham, one is buried far from the ancestral tombs (Gn 25^{8}). When David says of his son, 'I shall go to him, but he shall not return to me,' he does not have the grave in mind (2 S 12^{23}).

The religious aspect of the state after death was determined by a singular belief: Jahweh had nothing to do with the dead. In Sheol no one praises Jahweh (Is 38^{18}). Jahweh is the God of the living, not of the dead. A psalmist reasons with Jahweh, 'Why will you kill me? If you do, I cannot praise you, and you will lose a worshipper' (Ps 6^{5}). It was one of the terrors of death to the devout worshipper of Jahweh that he would be deprived of the presence of God. In a late Psalm the writer feels so confident of the care of Jahweh that he says, 'If I make my bed in Sheol, behold, thou art there' (Ps 139^{8}); but this only expresses an extreme faith in the power of God and is a poetic rather than a creedal statement. Jahweh's blessing was concerned with this life. If He 'delivers from Sheol,' it is in the sense of keeping His people from death (Ps 30^{3} 49^{15} 86^{13}, Pr 23^{14}, Jon 2^{2}, Hos 13^{14}). With the growing conception of the power of Jahweh in the universe, it became more difficult to think of even Sheol as outside His vision and authority. Jahweh controlled all the world, and nothing lay beyond His ken. In the post-Exilic writing it became possible to say, without, however, carrying the statement to a logical conclusion, that Sheol lay open before Jahweh (Job 26^{6}, Pr 15^{11}). Even the early prophets had used such figures (Am 9^{2}). It is possible that in some of the passages the writer was using more than a figure, that his sense of the permanent relation of God to man pierced the veil of death with a venture of faith. It could not be that God would let go His hold for good or ill on the person of man. Some have seen this hope in Ps $16^{10f.}$ 17^{15}, but these passages are of doubtful import. It is more likely in Ps 49^{15}. Many suppose Job 19^{25-27} to represent such a mood of faith, but it may show only the confidence of a final vindication on earth. All these passages point the way to a religionizing of the ancient idea of Sheol. If the dead could be conceived as still standing in the presence of God, not cut off from Him, then this shadowy existence would be filled with life, and the dead might become living souls, whose destiny of happiness or unhappiness would be the result of good or evil in their life on earth. The growing emphasis on the universal power of God pointed the way to this result, but it never was attained. The deliberate suppression by the prophetic religion of attention to the state after death worked strongly in the opposite direction. Existence in Sheol became less and less real. The writer of Ecclesiastes leaves the impression that Sheol had come to be so negative that it was practically non-existent, and that death was thought to end all. Who can tell if man has a different future from the beasts (3^{21})? The dust returns to the earth as it was, and the spirit, the principle of life, returns to God who gave it (12^{7}). In Hebrew thought the primitive conception of a shadowy existence after death was slowly lost, pinched out by the richer, fuller value of a religion which had to do with life, not death.

Another primitive quality of Sheol was its non-moral character. It was not a place of punishment or reward. There were no compartments for good and bad, nor could the unsatisfying character of the existence after death be alleviated by any act of righteousness while alive. If Jahweh had no relation with Sheol, He would of course neither punish nor reward its inhabitants. His favour was shown by keeping the righteous from it, while allowing the wicked to be swept into it by death (Ps $49^{14f.}$). Rewards and punishments belong to this life. But what of those who do not receive their due rewards and punishments? It was this ethical problem that caused a new conception of the state after death to arise.

The tragedy of the problem of suffering in the book of Job lay in the belief that there was no life after death where God could do justice to the innocent sufferer. As Hebrew history went on, those faithful to Jahweh suffered and sometimes died for the preservation of the national faith. Would God give them no recompense? Would the triumphant wicked die in prosperity and God bring upon them no punishment? These ethical problems cried to heaven for solution, if the Hebrews were to keep faith in the justice of their God. Under this pressure a new factor, the resurrection, was added to the picture of the state after death. Two influences contributed to the rise of the belief in the resurrection. One was the hope of the renewed nation. The theory of the resurrection furnished the promise that the Jews who had laboured for their nation would be brought back to share in

1 See art. 'Sheol,' in *Hebrew and English Lexicon of the OT*, ed. F. Brown, S. R. Driver, and C. A. Briggs, Oxford, 1906.
2 See art. ANCESTOR-WORSHIP AND CULT OF THE DEAD (Hebrew).
3 *A Critical Hist. of the Doctrine of a Future Life*, London, 1899, p. 33.
4 'The Hebrew Idea of the Future Life,' in *BW* xxxv.

its future glory. The other was the Hebrew psychology. The Greeks thought of the soul as naturally immortal. This idea was borrowed by the Alexandrian-Jewish writers. It appears in Philo, in the Wisdom of Solomon (3^{1-9}), and also in Josephus: 'Souls have an immortal vigour in them.'[1] But most Jewish thought held consistently to the old Hebrew psychology. Man was a divinely given soul in a living body. Body and soul were both necessary to constitute life. Jewish thought had not yet arrived at Paul's subtlety of a spiritual body (1 Co 15^{23-49}). If God was to give life to men, He must restore them to earthly bodies. The earliest passage reflecting the thought of the resurrection belongs perhaps to the 4th cent. B.C.: 'Thy dead shall live; my dead bodies shall arise' (Is 26^{19}). So far as this passage shows, the thought of the resurrection was then limited to righteous Israelites, who will rise in Palestine and share in the glories of the renewed nation. The only other OT passage which offers a hope of resurrection is Dn 12^2, 'Many of them that sleep in the dust of the earth shall awake, some to everlasting life, and some to shame and everlasting contempt.' Since the time of the former passage the idea had grown. It had come to include the wicked as well as the righteous; but it was not yet universal. Those who had received due rewards and punishments in this life were not to be brought back from Sheol. The resurrection was a theory for satisfying the demand for justice. But the belief in resurrection did not grow up without protest. The writer of Ecclesiastes spoke for the conservative element which regarded this new speculation as an unproved hypothesis that might easily displace the sane balance of life. He insisted that no one could be sure of any reward after death. Existence after death was to him entirely negative (3^{19-22} 9^{2-6} 12^7). The Sadducees continued the conservative tradition, but all the other schools of Jewish thought accepted the new theory of the resurrection. In forming a picture of the state after death, there was some attempt to combine the new theory with the old belief in Sheol. In *Enoch*, 1–36, Sheol was said to contain four divisions: for the wicked who have received due punishment in this life and will not be raised; for the wicked who will be raised for punishment in the day of judgment; for the moderately righteous, who will be raised for their reward; and for the heroes of faith, who are waiting resurrection in a paradise of bliss. Gradually, however, the belief in resurrection became enlarged to include all the dead. Sheol in the old sense tended to disappear, and the state of the dead tended to become happiness for the righteous and misery for the wicked, while waiting for the resurrection.[2]

LITERATURE.—In addition to the works mentioned under art. ESCHATOLOGY, see C. F. Burney, *Israel's Hope of Immortality*, London, 1909; A. Lods, *La Croyance à la vie future et le culte des morts dans l'antiquité israélite*, Paris, 1906; L. B. Paton, 'The Hebrew Idea of the Future Life,' in *BW* xxxv. [1910] 8–20, 80–92, 159–171; H. Schultz, *Old Testament Theology*, Eng. tr.², Edinburgh, 1898, ii. 320–332; A. B. Davidson, *The Theology of the Old Testament*, do. 1904, pp. 402–532; H. W. Robinson, *The Religious Ideas of the Old Testament*, London and New York, 1913, pp. 91–101; H. P. Smith, *The Religion of Israel*, New York and Edinburgh, 1914, pp. 25–33, 289, 326–328; J. P. Peters, *The Religion of the Hebrews*, New York, 1914, pp. 446–463.

IRVING F. WOOD.

STATE OF THE DEAD (Hindu).—**I. Vedic.**—The chief source of our knowledge of the eschatology of the *Rigveda* is a short collection of funeral hymns in the late tenth book (xiv.–xviii.), composed to accompany the rite of burying or cremating the body of the dead. The latter rite was clearly becoming the normal form of disposal,

[1] *Ant.* XVIII. i. 3.

[2] For the resurrection and the Messianic time see artt. ESCHATOLOGY, § 10, BLEST, ABODE OF THE (Semitic).

but the fate of the soul had come to be regarded as independent of the mode of treatment of the body: those burned by fire and those not so burned are alike deemed to find their way to a heaven in the sky presided over by Yama, the first of mortals to die, and by the god Varuṇa. In this new abode the dead man retains his full personal identity; his spirit is united with a body, a sublimated form of his earthly frame; and the future life is a glorified edition of the life on earth. Yama, with the gods and the fathers, sits under a tree rich in foliage, while the flute sounds and songs are sung.[1] Soma places the worshipper in the heaven where there is light everlasting, where all desires are fulfilled, and every kind of pleasure abounds.[2] The spirits abiding in heaven are distinct from, but in the closest unity with, the gods; they come in thousands on Indra's car to share the offerings of men;[3] some drink the *soma*, others honey or melted butter.[4] But in addition to offerings the dead profit by their sacrifices and their gifts to the priests (*iṣṭāpūrta*) while on earth, for in some manner they are united with them in the new life.[5] Their descendants implore their favour, deprecate their anger for any sin committed against them, and entreat them to bestow boons, especially that of offspring—which may be a faint trace of a belief, long anterior to the doctrine of transmigration, that the ancestor is in some sense reborn in the infant which he is asked to bestow. As there are families in earth, so in the sky there are families—the Aṅgirases, the Vasiṣṭhas, Bhṛgus, Atharvans, Navagvas, Vairūpas, etc.

Those who attain to the heaven are specified in a late hymn;[6] they comprise the warriors who lose their life in battle, the bestowers of a thousand-fold largesse to the priests, the sages of a thousand songs and performers of penance—in other words, the warriors, the rich men of the clan, and the priests themselves, who naturally enough have depicted a heaven which is more in keeping with their vocations than with those of warriors. But there is no indication in the *Saṃhitā* of the mode in which the boon of heaven is allotted by the gods who are implored to accord it. Yama is not a judge of men's deeds; and, though he has two fierce dogs, with four eyes and wide nostrils, past whom the dead man has to go on his way to Yama's abode, their function seems to be that of messengers who bear to mortals the summons of death rather than of powers which discriminate the good and the evil. The grant of heaven must therefore be deemed an act of free grace bestowed by the gods on their worshippers rather than a reward adjudicated by a judge of souls. The fate of those who failed to achieve such a boon may then have been, as R. Roth[7] held, mere annihilation, with which would accord the stress laid by the *Rigveda* on length of life as the great aim of man. But we hear also[8] of a deep abyss made for those who are false, like women who are unfaithful to their husbands; a hymn[9] against demons consigns to an abode under the three earths the one who plots against the singer, and there are references to the wicked being consigned either to a pit (*karta*)[10] or to the lowest darkness,[11] which may be interpreted as allusions to a place of punishment.

Of other fates of the dead there is no direct proof in the *Rigveda*. It is a plausible conjecture that in the seers who guard the sun[12] we are to

[1] x. cxxxv. 1, 7. [2] ix. cxiii. 7 ff.
[3] x. xv. 10. [4] x. cliv. 1.
[5] x. xiv. 8. This is not to be interpreted in any mystic fashion; as the dead man is united with a body, so he needs the victims he sacrificed and the cows he bestowed on the priests in his life in the world to come.
[6] x. cliv. [7] *JAOS* iii. [1853] 345.
[8] IV. v. 5. [9] VI. civ.
[10] IX. lxxiii. 8. [11] x. clii. 4.
[12] x. cvii. 7, cliv. 5.

recognize an allusion to the idea that the stars are the souls of the holy dead—a conception natural enough when the sun, himself a god, is conceived as the home of the fathers. Of greater interest are those allusions which connect the dead more closely with the earth. We hear of the fathers as divided into the uppermost (those of the sky), the midmost (those of the air), and those who are among the abodes of men.[1] The distinction between the way of the fathers and that of the gods[2] may reflect a contrast between the fathers' abode on earth and that of the gods in the sky. The eye of the dead man is bidden to go to the sun and his breath to the wind, and he is invited to go to the sky, the earth, or the waters, and to enter into the plants with all his members.[3] In the ritual of burial the earth is conceived as according the dead a resting-place.[4] Yama, first of men to die, is described as proceeding along the mighty *pravataḥ*[5] — a term which suggests a journey to the limits of earth rather than an ascent to the sky. In these passages we may doubtless see relics of the older belief which tied the spirit closely to its former abode on earth, but the *Ṛigveda* throws no light on the ideals which promoted the setting in the sky of the abode of the dead. If it was an outcome of the practice of cremation, the connexion between the two ideas had disappeared in the Rigvedic period, which sets the dead in the heaven, whether cremated or not; and it is not impossible that the fathers were gradually elevated to the sky because of their assimilation with the gods in power and attributes, and that cremation was adopted after the belief in the heavenly abode of the soul had come into being as harmonizing well with that conception.

The later *Saṃhitās* and the *Brāhmaṇas* render more definite the description of heaven and hell. The *Atharvaveda* lays stress on the reunion of the dead with his wife and children,[6] and promises him abundance of sexual enjoyment,[7] as well as freedom from the exactions of temporal superiors.[8] The *Śatapatha Brāhmaṇa* explains that, in accordance with the nature of the sacrifices which a man offers on earth, in heaven he is freed from the necessity of eating: the mere offerer of the *agnihotra* must eat night and morning, but the piler of the fire-altar can exist for a hundred years of unalloyed bliss without nutriment.[9] The delights of heaven are a thousand times those of the happiest of mortal men.[10] Great stress is laid on rebirth in the next world with perfect members (*sarvatanūḥ sāṅgaḥ*), and for this the most careful collection of the bones of the dead man is necessary on earth, so that the theft of the bones is a most severe punishment.[11] Between men and the gods there is established the essential distinction that the former must lay aside their earthly bodies to attain immortality.[12] Immortality is essentially a second birth,[13] and its character is determined by man's deeds on earth,[14] and diverse ways of sifting the good and bad are laid down: after death the man must pass between two fires which consume the evil and permit the good to pass on, or he is weighed in a balance — perhaps a conception borrowed from the balance ordeal of ordinary life.[15] But the heaven which is attained is no longer necessarily the abode of Yama. A contrast is drawn between the world of heaven and that of the fathers, the entrance to the former being in

[1] x. xv. 1 f. [2] x. xviii. 1.
[3] x. xvi. 3. [4] x. xviii. 10 ff.
[5] x. xiv. 1. [6] xii. iii. 17.
[7] iv. xxiv. 2. [8] iii. xxix. 3.
[9] x. v. 1, 4. [10] xiv. vii. 1, 32.
[11] xi. vi. 3, 11, xiv. vi. 9, 28. [12] x. iv. 3, 9.
[13] xi. ii. 1, 1. [14] vi. ii. 2, 27.
[15] xi. ii. 7, 33; cf. art. ORDEAL (Hindu), vol. ix. p. 523 f.

the north-east, while that to the latter is in the south-east.[1] The due performance of rites leads to the performer attaining union and identity of world with the god in question, Agni, Āditya, Varuṇa, Indra, or Brahmā;[2] and in unequivocal terms the souls of the dead are declared to be stars.[3]

Hell now attains definite form: the oppressor of the Brāhman sits amid streams of blood chewing hair,[4] and the world of hell (*nārakaloka*) is definitely promised to the miscreant who refuses to give a priest the cow for which he asks.[5] The vision of Bhṛgu recorded in the *Śatapatha Brāhmaṇa*[6] preserves in a priestly form[7] a conception of hell as a place of retribution in which men are repaid by their victims the same tortures as they inflicted on them in life, and the *Kauṣītaki Brāhmaṇa* reinforces the same view.[8] But comparatively little prominence is given to hell in the *Brāhmaṇas*; there appears a more serious conception, that of repeated death in the next world, an idea of peculiar horror to the Vedic Indian, whose chief prayer was for length of days in this world and freedom from death (*amṛta*) in the world to come. But this conception, that of *punarmṛtyu*, appears only in the latest of the great *Brāhmaṇas*, the last book of the *Aitareya*, the *Śatapatha* and the *Kauṣītaki*, and it is not without importance that these are also the works which present hell as a place of retribution, rebirth and hell alike appearing as the penalty for ignorance of ritual, not as punishment for moral wrongdoing.

In the *Upaniṣads*, though not in the earliest portions of them, the decisive step is taken of transferring the rebirth to earth, which is foreshadowed in the *Śatapatha Brāhmaṇa*, and of making the fate of man depend on his metaphysical knowledge and his conduct. The new ideas necessitated a substantial revision of the old eschatology: the distinction between the way of the fathers and that of the gods was adopted, and the oldest text which adopts the full doctrine of transmigration, the *Bṛhadāraṇyaka Upaniṣad*,[9] distinguishes between the man who attains through true knowledge the way of the gods, to be merged ultimately in *Brahman*, the man whose good works entitle him to proceed on the way of the fathers to the moon, there to enjoy recompense for his works, and then to return to earth in a human form, and the wicked for whom the third place is reserved and who are fated to be reborn as inferior animals. An important change is made in the scheme by the *Chhāndogya Upaniṣad*,[10] which distinguishes between two classes of those who go to the moon—those of good conduct who are reborn as men, and those of abominable conduct who are reborn as dogs, pigs, or out-castes—but which illogically retains the third place, though the distinction between the two sets of those who go to the moon has robbed that category of its validity. The *Kauṣītaki Upaniṣad*, apparently in an effort at greater system, sends even those with the saving knowledge to the moon, whence they proceed after examination as to their knowledge to Brahmā, while the others return from the moon for rebirth according to their merits. The prominence of the moon in these views is remarkable, and is brought into combination with the clearly popular idea that the waxing and

[1] vi. vi. 2. 4, xiii. viii. 1. 5.
[2] ii. vi. 4. 8, xi. iv. 4. 2, v. 6, vi. 2. 2; *Aitareya Brāhmaṇa*, iii. 44; *Taittirīya Brāhmaṇa*, iii. x. 9, 11, 11. 6.
[3] *Śatapatha Brāhmaṇa*, vi. v. 4. 8; *Taittirīya Saṃhitā*, v. iv. 1. 3.
[4] *Atharvaveda*, v. xix.
[5] *Ib.* xii. iv. 36. *Nāraka* occurs also in *Jaiminīya Brāhmaṇa*, i. 325, where three heavens and three hells are alluded to.
[6] xi. vi. 1 ff.
[7] Cf. A. Weber, *ZDMG* ix. [1855] 237 ff.
[8] xi. 3. [9] vi. 2. [10] v. 10.

waning of the moon is connected with the movements of the souls, as they ascend to it or descend from it. But beside this complicated system, which endeavours to unite the popular belief in heaven and hell with the new faith of transmigration, there remains the simpler view that rebirth on earth is the fate of the soul, and occasionally there is enunciated the doctrine that for the possessor of true knowledge there is no rebirth, no reward in heaven or punishment in hell to face, but that by reason of this knowledge he is merged after death in the absolute spirit.

In the *Gṛhya-* and the *Dharma-Sūtras*, which deal with the domestic and legal rules prevailing at the end of the Vedic period, the new doctrine of transmigration appears side by side with, and united with, the simpler view of heaven and hell, while a new element appears in the conception that all creation, including heaven, is periodically destroyed. Thus Āpastamba[1] holds that the fathers exist in heaven until the end of a world-order, that after this destruction they exist again there as the cause of seed, that immortality consists in rebirth in the person of one's son, and that the wicked are extinguished. More important than these expressions of opinion as to the fate of the dead, which vary from *Sūtra* to *Sūtra*, are the ritual prescriptions for the tendance and worship of the dead, which in substance are doubtless older than the more elaborate ritual of the *Rigveda*. The dead are the recipients of many offerings, especially each month at the new moon, and these offerings are deposited in shallow pits, to which they are deemed to come in order to extract the heat from the food offered to them. After they have eaten, they are bidden to depart, and to return in a month's time bearing with them offspring.[2] But a clear distinction is made between the newly dead and those who have died before. The great-grandfather, grandfather, and father are normally alone invoked by name, but, for a period usually fixed at a year after death, a special offering is made to the dead man, and he is not included with his ancestors; at the end of this offering his spirit is not dismissed, but merely bidden to be at peace[3]—a clear indication that for this period the spirit was supposed to dwell in the neighbourhood of its former abode. Originally perhaps this belief may have stood in relation with the practice of a provisional followed by a final interment of the bones, but the connexion is not recognized by any Vedic text. To this view may be referred the allusion in the *Rigveda* to the fathers who are on earth: the *Taittirīya Saṃhitā*[4] threatens him who wounds a Brāhman with exclusion from the world of the fathers for as many years as the Brāhman's blood wets grains of sand; and, in contrast to the prevailing view of the fathers as dwelling in light, the *Śatapatha Brāhmaṇa*[5] and the *Kaṭha Upaniṣad*[6] see in the world of the fathers an abode of dreams. The same *Brāhmaṇa*[7] speaks of the fathers as creeping about the roots of the trees—apparently a relic of the belief that the soul of the dead clung to the tree under which its bones were buried or which served to supply its coffin.[8] Two *Sūtra* passages may be adduced for the view that the dead might pass into an animal form, apart from transmigration proper. When the bones were collected for final interment, if they could not be found, a garment might be spread out, and the dead invoked; if any animal then alighted on the garment, it was deemed to represent the dead;[1] and Baudhāyana[2] declares that the fathers go about in the semblance of birds.

1 II. ix. 23 f.
2 *Hiraṇyakeśi Gṛhya-Sūtra*, II. xiii. 2.
3 *Śāṅkhāyana Gṛhya-Sūtra*, IV. ii. 6.
4 II. vi. 10. 2. 5 XII. ix. 2. 2. 6 VI. 5.
7 XIII. viii. 1. 20.
8 The practice in the marriage ritual by which stepping on the threshold is avoided may be due to the belief that the spirits of the dead, once buried under the threshold, have their abode there (cf. M. Winternitz, *Das altindische Hochzeitsrituell*, Vienna, 1892, p. 72).

2. Post-Vedic.—In the post-Vedic literature, whether Brāhmanical, Buddhist, or Jain, none of which can in its present form be dated with any certainty or probability earlier than 200 B.C., the ideas regarding the state of the dead which are developed in the Vedic period are further elaborated, but without the addition of any conception of importance, and without any greater success in the effort to combine the older beliefs with the doctrine of transmigration. Nothing shows more convincingly the persistence of the popular belief in heaven than the dominant influence which it exercised on philosophical belief. The *Upaniṣads* tend on the whole to teach the doctrine of annihilation of personality for the possessor of true knowledge, but the *Vedānta-Sūtra*[3] clearly rejects this view in favour of the doctrine that the sage attains a future of unlimited power and bliss, inferior to the Lord only in not having the capacity of creating and maintaining the world, and this view, though rejected by Śaṅkara in his esoteric doctrine, is accepted as valid by Rāmānuja and by the sects of Vaiṣṇavas who follow the main lines of his philosophy; a similar view is held also by the Śaivas. Buddhism, which equally in its logical theory regards annihilation as the reward of enlightenment, admits for ordinary purposes the existence of heaven, and the Mahāyāna school exalts the attainment of heaven to the highest hope of man, depicting its joys in such works as the *Kāraṇḍavyūha* and the *Sukhāvatīvyūha* in the most exaggerated terms. Jainism similarly imagines in elaborate detail a complicated system of heavens for beings of diverse merits. The same tendency is seen in the epic: a scale of heavens is gradually evolved; the heaven of Brahmā is placed above the lower heavens, but even it is not a final abiding-place, and the heaven of Viṣṇu is superimposed upon it as the place where there is no change, and where the sage is exempt from the departure from the lower heavens entailed by the periodical destruction of existence.[4] The number of heavens is now unlimited, for each deity has his special world; many of them are described in the *Svargakhaṇḍa* of the *Padma Purāṇa*, and most *Purāṇas* contain some mention of them.

Parallel with the multiplication of heavens is the multiplication of hells. The *Mārkaṇḍeya Purāṇa* enumerates seven, and the Jains have also a list of that sacred Indian number. Multiples of seven are also known, 21 (which is given by Manu) being a special favourite, while there is preference with the Buddhists for eight and its multiples in reckoning hells, the number of which later is increased indefinitely. In the description of their horrors fancy runs riot, as in the long enumeration in the *Mārkaṇḍeya Purāṇa*,[5] and in the later art it is plain that the Indian conceptions were influenced by Christian legend and art. It is possible that an early example of such influence[6] is to be seen in the legend of the visit of King Vipaśchit to hell, which he refuses to leave until the pains of the inmates are removed, as recounted in that *Purāṇa*.[7] A somewhat similar tale is recounted also in the *Padma Purāṇa* of King Janaka and in the *Kāraṇḍavyūha* of Avalokiteśvara, and there is much earlier evidence of the existence of the legend of the visit of Christ to hell. With the development of the hell as a place of punishment, the necessity of providing some means of allocating

1 *Kauśika-Sūtra*, lxxxiii. 22 f.
2 *Dharma-Sūtra*, II. xiv. 9. 10. 3 IV. iv.
4 *Mahābhārata*, III. cclxi. 5 X. ff.
6 See F. B. Cowell, *JPh* vi. [1876] 222 ff. 7 XV.

heaven or hell to the soul is felt, and in the *Purāṇas* Chitragupta appears as the recorder of the deeds of men and Yama as a judge who sends them to heaven or hell according to their deserts.[1] But Yama tends to sink from his rank, and to become merely the lord of one of the hells, and the prevailing view is that heaven is essentially the result of divine grace, whether or not evoked by effort on the part of the recipient of the boon. Similarly, while the fate of the dead in theory depends on their own deeds, in practice it is regarded as dependent also on the actions of their descendants. An epic legend tells how Agastya saw his ancestors hanging head downwards in a hole called hell, because of his failure to beget sons, and the utmost stress is laid throughout the literature on the necessity of the due performance of the funeral rites, and of the offerings, generically entitled *śrāddhas*, requisite to secure the welfare of the departed soul. These offerings not only serve to provide the spirit, disembodied in the process of creation, with a celestial body, but also avail to raise him from one stage of existence to another; the *nārāyaṇabali* is especially commended in many texts as a means of securing the advancement of the dead to the Vaikuṇṭha heaven. The closeness of the dead to the living is seen in the daily offerings of food which are made to them; they are also fed specially at every occasion of family rejoicing, and with special solemnity before a marriage—a clear trace of their abiding concern with the continuance of the race.

Practically new in the literature of this period is the recognition of the spirit of the dead as a ghost appearing on earth in close contact with man. The absence of such accounts in the earlier texts may reasonably be ascribed to the character of the Vedic literature, for the distinction between the recently dead and the ancient fathers in the *Sūtras*, and the whole nature of the ritual, suggest clearly that there was nothing strange in the idea of the presence of the dead in the vicinity of human dwellings. The regularity of such presence is emphasized in the Buddhist *Peta-vatthu*, which reveals ghosts entering into conversation with men, lurking about houses and at cross-roads (a favourite place of burial and the resort of spirits), as wandering about unhappy, clothed only in their own hair, tormented by heat which neither wind, water, nor shadow can alleviate, unable to find anything to drink even in the midst of the Ganges, which turns to blood as they seek to swallow its water. The influence of the doctrine of transmigration is, however, obvious, as the dead often declare that they are fated to die again in a brief period and then to go to one hell or other. This belief in ghosts is universal in the later literature: the *Divyāvadāna*[2] tells of a ghost city, the *Jātaka*[3] of an island inhabited by female ghosts; and a famous scene in the *Mālatimādhava* of Bhavabhūti describes a common theme, the presence of countless ghosts at the place of the burning of the dead. A more poetic use of the same idea is seen in the *putradarśana* scene in the *Mahābhārata*,[4] where Vyāsa by his magic power summons up before the eyes of Dhṛtarāṣṭra and Gāndhārī the spirits of those who fought in the great battle. In modern tales stress is laid on untimely and violent death as a frequent source of the wandering of the restless spirit. Thus a legend in the late *Garuḍa Purāṇa* tells of a robber whom a tiger killed and who in consequence wandered about as a ghost until a crow dropped his bones in the Ganges, when the sanctifying power of its waters transferred his soul to heaven. The idea is doubtless primitive, though not expressly recorded in the earlier texts, save in so far as it may be inferred from the notice in Baudhāyana[1] that the spirit of an embryo becomes a blood-sucker, and from the bitterness against the slayer of embryos which is recorded as early as the *Saṃhitās* of the *Yajurveda* and may be ascribed to the resentment felt against a person who lets loose on the world so uneasy a spirit.

In the Vedic period very little stress is laid on the dangerous side of the dead. The *Rigveda* indeed deprecates the anger of the ancestors for sin committed against them;[2] the fathers are entreated to defeat the enemy of their descendants; and reference is made in the *Atharvaveda*[3] to fiends who creep in among the fathers, assuming the likeness of kinsmen, which may point to the spirits of the unfriendly dead. But, even if, as is possible, in the *rakṣasas* and *piśāchas* of the *Brāhmaṇas* and the later *Saṃhitās* we may see spirits of the hostile dead converted into demons, it is at least plain that the consciousness of such an origin was not normally present in the Vedic period. The later literature freely recognizes friendly spirits of the dead, which give good advice to men, and regards the ancestors as able and willing to aid, but it also lays stress on the malevolent tendencies of hostile spirits, and is especially prone to attribute to their agency the workings of disease, which, by perhaps an earlier stage of thought, are directly made personal powers in the *Atharvaveda*.

In this prominence of the idea of the hostility of the dead it is possible to see the result of the gradual Hinduization of the Indo-Aryan religion. The belief in the sending of diseases by spirits of the dead is widely present among aboriginal tribes,[4] but in itself it is too easily explainable as a natural development to be available as a proof of borrowing. Among the primitive tribes, apparently without Hindu influence, systems of belief as to the state of the dead have developed themselves which have often a somewhat striking similarity to those produced by Hinduism. The Khands have a god of judgment who dwells on a high rock surrounded by a black river, and the souls of the dead climb up the rock with much effort to await his decision. The good are accorded life in the sun, or are reborn in the tribe, the priests having the power to reveal in each case who is reincarnated in the newborn child, and the wicked are reborn as diseased and endure misfortune, or, if very wicked, suffer annihilation. The Oraons are less advanced, for they do not accept the belief in a life in heaven; unfortunate people survive death as unhappy ghosts; a man eaten by a tiger comes again to life as a tiger, but the ordinary man suffers annihilation. There are also traces of the belief that the spirit of the dead can pass directly into an animal—a belief which may have had a share in the development of the doctrine of transmigration.

LITERATURE.—For the Vedic period the most important works are J. Muir, *Original Sanskrit Texts*, v.[4], London, 1884; H. Zimmer, *Altindisches Leben*, Berlin, 1879; H. Oldenberg, *Die Religion des Veda*, do. 1894; W. Caland, *Altindischer Ahnencult*, Leyden, 1893, *Die altindischen Todten- und Bestattungsgebräuche*, Amsterdam, 1896; A. A. Macdonell, *Vedic Mythology* (=*GIAP* iii. 1a), Strassburg, 1897; A. Hillebrandt, *Vedische Mythologie*, 3 vols., Breslau, 1891-1902, *Vedische Opfer und Zauber* (=*GIAP* iii. 2), Strassburg, 1897; S. Lévi, *La Doctrine du sacrifice dans les Brâhmanas*, Paris, 1898; A. M. Boyer, *JA* IX. xviii. [1901] 451-490; M. Bloomfield, *The Religion of the Veda*, New York and London, 1908; P. Deussen, *The Philosophy of the Upanishads*, Eng. tr., Edinburgh, 1906. For Buddhism see H. Oldenberg, *Buddha*[5], Berlin, 1906; T. W. Rhys Davids, *Buddhism, its History and Literature*, New York and London, 1896; E. Windisch,

1 H. H. Wilson, *The Vishnu Purána*, ed. F. Hall, London, 1864-1877, ii. 216.
2 P. 7. 3 iv. 2. 4 xv. xxix.-xxxvi.

1 See A. Ludwig, *Der Rigveda*, Prague, 1876-88, v. 421.
2 x. xv. 6. 3 XVIII. ii. 28.
4 See J. M. Campbell, *IA* xxiii. [1894] 377 f., and art. DISEASE AND MEDICINE (Introductory and Primitive).

Buddha's Geburt, Leipzig, 1908; L. de la Vallée Poussin, *Bouddhisme: Opinions sur l'histoire de la dogmatique*, Paris, 1909; H. Hackmann, *Buddhism as a Religion*, London, 1910. For Jainism see J. G. Bühler, *On the Indian Sect of the Jainas*, London, 1903; Margaret S. Stevenson, *The Heart of Jainism*, do. 1915; Jagmanderlal Jaini, *Outlines of Jainism*, Cambridge, 1916. The epic material is treated fully by E. W. Hopkins, *Epic Mythology* (=*GIAP* iii. 1b), Strassburg, 1915, who deals with the whole subject in *The Religions of India*, London, 1896, as do also A. Barth, *Religions of India*, Eng. tr., do. 1882; A. B. Keith, *Indian Mythology* (=*Mythology of All Races*, vi.), Boston, 1917; L. Scherman, *Materialen zur Gesch. der indischen Visionslitteratur*, Leipzig, 1893. For Hinduism see M. Monier-Williams, *Brāhmanism and Hindūism*[4], London, 1891; P. Deussen, *Das System des Vedanta*[2], Leipzig, 1906, *Allgemeine Gesch. der Philosophie*, I. iii., do. 1908; G. Thibaut, *The Vedânta-Sûtras* (*SBE* xxxiv.), Oxford, 1890; R. G. Bhandarkar, *Vaiṣṇavism, Śaivism, and Minor Religious Systems* (=*GIAP* iii. 6), Strassburg, 1913. Of the innumerable accounts of the aboriginal tribes special value attaches to W. Crooke, *PR*, 2 vols., London, 1896; H. H. Risley, *The People of India*, do. 1915; E. Thurston and K. Rangachari, *Castes and Tribes of Southern India*, 7 vols., Madras, 1909.

A. BERRIEDALE KEITH.

STATE OF THE DEAD (Iranian). — The Mazdean doctrine of the state of men's souls after death is exceedingly simple and remarkably consistent through the whole range of literature from the *Gāthas* to the most recent Pahlavi treatises. It is summed up in the belief in a heaven and a hell for the virtuous man and the sinner respectively, each (at least in the *Gāthas*) apparently eternal in duration.

1. Heaven.—The celestial abode is designated in the *Gāthas* by the beautiful and poetical name of Garō-demāna, 'house of song'[1] (*i.e.* of hymns of praise), the dwelling-place of Ahura Mazda and his holy ones. It is also designated as the 'house or kingdom of Vohu Manah, the kingdom of blessing.' In the Later Avesta it assumes the form Garōnmāna, but also is styled Vahištā Anhuš, literally 'the best existence,' which has remained the ordinary term in subsequent epochs, down to the Modern Persian Bihišt. In Pahlavi literature it takes the form Garōtmān. Another term which seems to indicate the heavenly abode is Anagra Raochā, 'the everlasting lights.' Bartholomae, however, surmises that of all these terms Garō-demāna, in its various forms, may signify a kind of inner heaven, a 'holy of holies,' in paradise itself.[2] Dhalla writes:

> 'In contrast to the single heaven referred to in the Gathas, we meet with a fourfold division of heaven in the Avestan period. Garonmana, or the Abode of Praise, remains the highest heaven, the realm of bliss that is reached by traversing the three lower heavens, called Humata, or Good Thought, Hukhta, or Good Words, and Hvarshta, or Good Deeds, as beatific abodes for the soul.'[3]

The same writer also considers that, whilst Anagra Raochā in the Later Avesta designates Garōnmāna, the expression Vahištō Anhuš is a generic name for all four heavens. Söderblom, on the other hand, takes Vahišt as signifying the three inferior heavens, as opposed to the supreme Garōtmān, 'la félicité suprême auprès de Dieu,'[4] which seems less likely. The fourfold conception of heaven persists unchanged through the Pahlavi and subsequent periods. So does the presentment of heaven as a place of ineffable bliss, in company with Ahura and his celestial court, and of brilliant, dazzling light.

2. Hell.—In accordance with the Iranian love of symmetry, the place of the wicked after death is in all details the exact opposite of the heavenly abode. The Gāthic name of the Inferno is Drūjō-demāna, 'house of the *druj* (or of the lie)'—the later Pahlavi Drūzōtmān, or again Drūjī gereda, 'pit of the *druj*' (*i.e.* Angra Mainyuš). Similarly it is Achištā Anhuš, 'the worst existence'—in the Later Avesta *duz-ahū*. Dhalla also holds that there are in the Later Avesta, by contrast to the one hell of the *Gāthas*, four abodes of the damned—Dushmata ('evil thought'), Dushukhta ('evil word'), Dushvarshta ('evil deed'), and lastly the fourth or lowest hell, which has no specific name of its own in the Avesta, but is known as *anaghra temah* ('endless darkness').[1]

The miseries and tortures of the souls in hell are terrible indeed. Moulton sums them up in a striking passage.

> 'Hell is full of darkness, sad voices, stench, foul food, and cold. It would seem that the conception of it sprang from the privations of winter on the steppes during the migration southward, when the preciousness of the house-fire made Âtar the very symbol of all that was best for man.[2] For the Iranian, hell and the demons were always in the north. The idea of darkness is the distinguishing feature of the House of the Lie. It is worked out in the later fancy which conceives the damned so close together that they seemed an indistinguishable mass; yet in the darkness each ever wails, "I am alone!" The symbolism of Fire was kept out of this eschatology for obvious reasons.'[3]

3. Purgatory.—Thus Mazdeism had its Paradiso and Inferno; had it also a Purgatorio? Several scholars hold that such a state is indicated in *Yasna* xxxiii. 1, by the verb now read by Bartholomae[4] as *hememyāsaitē*, the whole sentence then reading:

> 'The Judge shall act most justly towards the wicked, the just, and him in whom the false and the right are commingled': ('bei dem sich [zu gleichen Teilen] mischen was falsch und was bei ihm recht ist').

Moulton[5] seems to consider that this 'discovery' of Bartholomae is in some sort of opposition to the view on the Pahlavi *hamīstakān*[6] expounded by E. W. West, C. de Harlez, and other writers. The difference, however, is one of etymology merely. If the above view of *Ys.* xxxiii. 1 is right, then we shall have the 'middle state' recognized in the Avesta itself: if not, it must be looked upon as a later Pahlavi development. But in either case there does not seem to be the idea of a place of *purgation* for souls after death.

4. Vision of Artā-ī Vīrāf.—As mediæval Christianity had its Dante who embodied the doctrine of the world beyond the grave in his immortal vision, so Sasanian Mazdeism had its famous prose legend of the somewhat similar vision, by an unknown writer, of the saintly Vīrāf, which very probably was based on much more ancient traditional material.

This short Pahlavi religious tractate known as the *Artā-ī Vīrāf Nāmak*, 'Book of Artā-ī Vīrāf,'[7] has for centuries been a favourite work with all classes of the Parsi community. It was sometimes read before large assemblies, with the effect thus described by its learned editor, Dastur Hoshangji:

> 'It speaks volumes both for the effective style of the Artâ Vîrâf Nâmak and for the implicit faith which the Parsis placed in what was written therein, that a few years ago, when the book used to be read before them, overpowered by consciousness of guilt, the punishment for which was so terrifically described, they, but especially the gentler sex, used to weep. It was a most affecting spectacle to witness the awakening conscience exhibiting itself in trickling tears.'

This popularity of the *Vision* is shown by the fact that, besides the original Pahlavi text, which exists in two or three considerably divergent recensions, translations into both Sanskrit and Gujarāti exist, besides several Persian versions, both in prose and in poetry. These poetical versions are quite modern and were composed respectively in A.D. 1530–31, 1532–33, and 1679.

In the very careful introductory essay prefixed to his edition, Haug comes to the conclusion that the author, whoever he may have been, must have

[1] Cf. Welsh, *Bôd alaw*, 'abode of music,' though of course not with the same signification.
[2] *Altiranisches Wörterbuch*, Strassburg, 1904, *s.v.*
[3] *Zoroastrian Theology*, p. 178.
[4] *La Vie future d'après le Mazdéisme*, p. 100.

[1] P. 179.
[2] Similarly it is recorded that the early Christian missionaries in the Scandinavian countries represented to their converts hell as a place of intense cold; the idea of fire would have suggested comfort rather than suffering.
[3] *Early Zoroastrianism*, p. 172 f.
[4] *S.v.* '*Myas*.' [5] P. 175. [6] See below, p. 848 f.
[7] As we might say, 'Saint Vīrāf.'

lived after the time of the celebrated Zoroastrian theologian, Ādarbād Māhraspand, the minister of Shāpūr II. (A.D. 309-379), but before the downfall of the Sasanian dynasty in the 7th cent., for the book undoubtedly belongs to Sasanian times, perhaps the 5th or 6th cent. A.D.

The general course of the *Artā-ī Vīrāf Nāmak*—the trance and vision of the Zoroastrian seer and his visit under the guidance of the spirits Srōsh and Ātaro, over the Chinvat Bridge, to the world beyond the tomb, first to the four heavens, thence by command of Aūharmazd through the horrors of the Inferno, finally back to the divine throne in Garōtmān—is too well known to need recapitulation here. It is, however, of interest to note that, whilst Dante is supposed to visit the world of spirits in his actual living body, so that it is noted by the spirits as a marvel that his body casts a shadow, Artā-ī Vīrāf's soul leaves his body whilst in the trance induced by *mang*, and thus disembodied makes the journey through heaven and hell. Here we have a striking analogy with the legend of Er, the son of Armenius, the Pamphylian, in Plato's *Republic*,[1] whose soul similarly leaves his body on the funeral-pyre and goes forth to view the spirit-world, but eventually (like that of Artā-ī Vīrāf) returns to his body still lying on the pyre.[2]

Both Artā-ī Vīrāf and Dante have the guidance of two celestial beings in their wonderful journeys. In the case of Dante the poet Vergil, and afterwards Beatrice, accompany and direct him through the spirit-world. With Artā-ī Vīrāf it is the archangel Srōsh (the Avestic Sraosha, the spirit of obedience, *i.e.* to the divine law) and the genius of fire, Ātaro, who together act as guides through the realms of heaven and hell. As they enter hell, Artā-ī Vīrāf remarks:

'Srôsh the Pious and Âtaro the angel took hold of my hand and I went thence onwards unhurt. In that manner I beheld cold and heat, drought and stench, to such a degree as I never saw nor heard of in the world. And when I went further, I also saw the greedy jaws of Hell, like the most frightful pit, descending in a very narrow and fearful place; in darkness so gloomy that it is necessary to hold by the hand; and in such stench that every one into whose nostrils that air ascends, will struggle and stagger and fall; and on account of such close confinement no man's existence is endurable.'[3]

The narrative continues:

'I came to a place and I saw a great river which was gloomy as dreadful Hell; on which river were many souls and fravashis; and some of them were not able to cross, and some crossed only with great difficulty, and some crossed easily, and I asked thus, "What river is this? and who are these people who stand so distressed?" Srôsh the Pious and Âtaro the angel said: "This river is the many tears which men shed from the eyes, for the departed. They shed those tears unlawfully, and they swell this river. Those who are not able to cross over are those for whom, after their departure, much lamentation and weeping were made; and those (who cross) more easily, are those for whom less was made. Speak forth to the world thus: 'When ye are in the world make no lamentation and weeping unlawfully, for so much harm and difficulty may come to the souls of your departed.'"'[4]

The crossing of a river as the means of entrance into the spirit-world is, of course, a commonplace of literature. We find it in Homer and Vergil, from whom Dante has borrowed his four infernal rivers, Acheron, Styx, Phlegethon, and Cocytus. It is also a commonplace of Iranian eschatology, as in the Avestic description of the adventures of the soul after death, which have been borrowed wholesale in the *Qur'ān*.

It may be observed how very large a proportion of Artā-ī Vīrāf's vision (no fewer than 83 out of the total 101 chapters) is devoted to the description of hell, whilst the description of heaven occupies only nine chapters. On the other hand, in the vision of heaven, as compared with that of hell, there is a certain orderly arrangement observable, whilst an entire want of order prevails in the long rôle of the various crimes and their punishments in the infernal regions — literally, 'Ubi nullus ordo sed sempiternus horror inhabitat.'

[1] x. 13. [2] x. 16. [3] xviii. 1-9. [4] xvi. 2-12.

It is a curious fact that all the sufferers in Artā-ī Vīrāf's hell are anonymous, with the single exception of the lazy man, whose name seems to have been Davānos, and who is punished like Dives, the rich man in the gospel, solely because of his laziness, since, when 'he was in the world, he never did any good work.' Yet, whilst his whole body was being gnawed by *khrafstras*, his right foot alone was untouched, 'for that he once with this right foot cast a bunch of grass before a ploughing ox,' so that his solitary good deed went not unrewarded.

Of the many and very miscellaneous kinds of sin and of their terrible and often grotesque chastisements enough has been said in the art. SIN (Iranian). But these punishments of the wicked in the *Artā-ī Vīrāf Nāmak* appear in no particular order, and, at least as regards hell, 'there is nowhere any system or plan perceptible.'[1]

Perhaps the most striking feature in the Inferno of both Vīrāf and Dante is the position assigned to the evil spirit, the arch-enemy of God and the dominant ruler of hell. The climax of Dante's Inferno is the vast figure of Lucifer frozen in the lowest depths of nether hell at the apex of the inverted cone in which it is formed. In the *Artā-ī Vīrāf Nāmak* Ahriman (Angra Mainyuš or Ganrāk Minōi) is similarly found in the darkest hell, which apparently is fixed in the very centre of the earth. Here the evil spirit ridicules and mocks the unfortunate sinners. And, just as, after beholding the horrors of Lucifer, Vergil leads Dante at once out to the southern hemisphere and the serener atmosphere of Purgatory, so Srōsh and Ātaro take hold of Artā-ī Vīrāf's hand at the same juncture and lead him forth 'from that dark, terrible, fearful place,' back to the eternal light of the presence of Aūharmazd—for it is a peculiarity of this *Vision* that it begins with the brief visit to the celestial court before the soul of the seer is led to the infernal regions.

The account of heaven is comparatively brief. Artā-ī Vīrāf's three first heavens are those of the stars, the moon, and the sun, whilst the fourth and last is the all-glorious Garōtmān, wherein is the throne of Aūharmazd. Brilliant light and glory are the characteristics of the heavens of both the Persian and the Italian seers, and adorn the blessed souls who inhabit them. Both Dante and Artā-ī Vīrāf behold in their respective paradises the soul of the first progenitor of the human race—Adam in the case of Dante, Gayōmard in the case of Artā-ī Vīrāf.

But what about the question of a purgatory? Certainly, immediately after the passage of the great river described above, Vīrāf says:

'I came to a place and saw the souls of several people who remained in the same position. And I asked the victorious Srôsh the Pious and Âtaro the angel: "Who are they? and why remain they here?" Srôsh the Pious and Âtaro the angel said: "They call this place Hamîstagân, and these souls remain in this place till the Resurrection; and they are the souls of those men whose good works and sins are equal, . . . for every one whose good works are three scruples more than his sins, goes to Heaven; they whose sin is in excess go to Hell; they in whom both are equal remain among these Hamîstagân till the Resurrection. Their punishment is cold or heat from the revolution of the atmosphere, and they have no other adversity!'[2]

This doctrine of the Hamīstagān is curiously like the Irish conception of Limbo in the 'Vision of Adamnan' (*Fis Adamnain*) as the place 'at the hither side of the lightless land for those whose good and evil have been equal.' Many writers, including J. J. Modi, see in the Hamīstagān the analogue of the Christian Purgatory. This is, however, scarcely tenable. It is true that, as in

[1] Haug, *Artā-ī Vīrāf Nāmak*, Introductory Essays, p. lxix.
[2] vi.

the Christian Purgatory, the sufferings of these souls will eventually come to an end, but there is no idea of purgation by suffering, as in Dante's Purgatorio. The Pahlavi name is a plural of the adjective *hamīstak*, meaning 'in equilibrium, or stationary,' and is no doubt derived from the idea of a balance in which the two scales are exactly balanced, and so stationary. These spirits, therefore, in the Iranian, the Irish, and the Italian visions, would seem more akin to those neutrals of whom Dante writes:

> 'Che visser senza infamia e senza lodo.'[1]

Even if we accept Bartholomae's reading and translation of the Avestan term in *Ys.* xxxiii. 1, already referred to, the etymology of *hamīstakān* (or *hamēstagān*, as sometimes written) remains obvious and certain.

We need not here enter into the question[2] as to the indebtedness of the Artā-ī Vīrāf legend to older Hebrew Vision literature of the same kind. That the central idea of describing the secrets of the other world under the allegorical form of a journey undertaken by a living man, guided by supernatural beings through the realms beyond the tomb, and even no inconsiderable part of the details of the description, may have been borrowed by a Persian writer from some Jewish original is by no means unlikely, especially when we remember that most characteristic tendency of the Iranian mind towards the adaptation and assimilation of outside theories and ideas which has been so marked through the whole course of its history. Nevertheless W. Bousset writes:

> 'Es scheint mir der Beweis erbracht, dass wir in der eranischen Religion die Heimat jener bunten Phantasien und jener ekstatischen Mystik zu suchen haben.'[3]

5. Duration.—For the *Gāthas* there is little doubt that the duration of both heaven and hell was conceived as eternal, as shown by the phrases *yavoi vīspāi*, 'in omne saeculum,' *ameretāitī*, 'eternity,' *utayūtā*, 'perpetuity,' applied to both the blessed and the damned. Later theology, however, seems to have modified this teaching, at least as regards the infernal regions. As has been remarked in art. SALVATION (Iranian), the great flood of molten metal at the end of time and the final resurrection and regeneration (*tanū-i pasīn*) is, according to some of the Pahlavi writers, to purify even hell and the wicked therein:

> 'Praise to Him, the merciful Lord, who . . . at the end shall deliver even the wicked from Hell and restore the whole Creation in purity.'[4]

LITERATURE.—J. H. Moulton, *Early Zoroastrianism (HL)*, London, 1913, esp. lect. v. 'The Last Things'; M. N. Dhalla, *Zoroastrian Theology from the Earliest Times to the Present Day*, New York, 1914, esp. chs. vii., viii., xix., xx., xxxi., xxxii.; N. Söderblom, *La Vie future d'après le Mazdéisme*, tr. from Swedish by J. de Coussanges, Paris, 1901, esp. chs. i. § 1, ii. § 1; L. C. Casartelli, *La Philosophie religieuse du Mazdéisme sous les Sassanides*, Louvain, 1884, ch. vii., Eng. tr. by Firoz Jamaspji Dastur, *The Philosophy of the Mazdayasnian Religion under the Sassanids*, Bombay, 1889. For the *Artā-ī Vīrāf Nāmak*, see the ed. of Hoshangji Jamaspji Asa, M. Haug, and E. W. West, *The Book of Ardā Vīrāf*, Bombay and London, 1872; Glossary and Index to same by West and Haug, Bombay, 1874; a French translation by A. Barthélemy, *Ardā Vīrāf-Namak, ou Livre d'Ardā Vīrāf*, Paris, 1887; a new ed. of the Pahlavi text, with Persian and Gujarāti trr. by Dastur Kaikhosru Jamaspji, Bombay, 1902; L. C. Casartelli, 'The Persian Dante,' in *The Dastur Hoshang Memorial Volume*, do. 1918.

L. C. CASARTELLI.

STATE OF THE DEAD (Muhammadan).—The *Qur'ān* abounds in pictures of the life after death. There is, however, a certain monotony in them, for they mostly present the same ideas, frequently repeated. They consist of three factors—(1) resurrection, (2) judgment, (3) heaven and hell—with occasional references to the state between death and the resurrection. Some of the passages reflect ideas which must have been current at the time:

> 'How will it be when the angels take their souls, smiting their faces and their backs?'[1]

This implies a contemporary belief in the angels who visit man in the grave and beat the wicked.[2] Abundant descriptions of heaven and hell are found, used for warning to disbelievers and encouragement to believers. As in Christian eschatology, the condition of souls in the intermediate state between death and the resurrection was not made clear in the early writings. Later speculation busied itself with the problem. Some held that the spirits of the faithful were taken up through the seven heavens into the presence of God, and then returned to the grave for the examination by the two angels, Munkir and Nakir. Martyrs were regarded, not as remaining in the graves, but as living in the presence of God, where 'there is no fear for them, and they shall not be grieved.'[3] The spirits of common believers stay near the graves, or, some hold, are in the lowest heaven with Adam. Infidels are beaten before and behind by the two examining angels, then crushed down into the earth and left to be bitten by great serpents. Their cries of pain may be heard by all, except men and *jinns*.

> Once the camel of Muhammad shied in passing a graveyard, and Muhammad said, 'Surely the infidels are punished in their graves, and, if I were not afraid you would leave off burying, verily I would call on God to let you hear what I now hear.'[4]

The infidel's own foul actions come to him as a devil with a hideous face, and taunt him,[5] as his evil deeds pursue and taunt the sinner in Zoroastrian eschatology. On the basis of *Qur'ān*, lxxxiii. 7–10, some say that the soul of the sinner awaits judgment in a pit in hell.

The general ideas of the resurrection are borrowed from Judaism and Christianity, with the addition of some details from Zoroastrianism. The resurrection will come at a time when evil is triumphant on the earth.

> God will say to the angels, 'Bring out those that shall be sent to hell.' They will say, 'How many are they?', and God will say, 'Nine hundred and ninety-nine out of a thousand.'[6]

The body of the resurrection will be a body of flesh, regenerated from the *os sacrum*, from which man was created.[7] The body will be created naked and uncircumcised, 'as at the first creation.' When Muhammad's wife, 'Ā'isha, objected that it was indecent, he replied, 'The business of the day will be too momentous to permit people looking at one another.'[8] God will judge from great books each as long as one can see. But a bit of paper with the Muslim confession on it will outweigh all the evil deeds of a man's life.[9] Muslims will ask Adam to intercede for them at the judgment, but he cannot, for he has sinned. Nor can Noah, Abraham, Moses, or Jesus, but Muhammad will do it. After the judgment men will pass over the bridge al-Aarāf. Muslims will go swiftly and easily, some in the twinkling of an eye, some like lightning, some like wind, some like birds, some like swift horses, some like camels. Of those who fall off, God will allow Muhammad to bring back all in whose heart there is any good. God will even bring into paradise a handful of men who have never done any good, and will purify them till they are pure as pearls.

Descriptions of the state of the good and of the evil in paradise and hell are almost entirely in

1 *Inferno*, iii. 36.
2 Ably discussed by M. Gaster in *JRAS*, 1893.
3 *ARW* iv. [1901] 169.
4 *Dinkart*, ed. P. B. Peshotan, Bombay, 1874–1917, vol. ii. ch. 81, § 6.

1 xlvii. 29.
2 See art. ESCHATOLOGY, § 9.
3 *Qur'ān*, iii. 164.
4 *Mishkat al-Masabih*, i. 39.
5 *Ib.* i. 40.
6 *Ib.* xxiii. 8; in ch. 10 Adam asks the same question and receives the same answer.
7 *Ib.* xxiii. 9.
8 *Ib.* xxiii. 10.
9 *Ib.* xxiii. 11.

terms of the senses. The life in paradise is described in terms of luxury, pleasure, and rest—which would naturally appeal to the Arab of the desert.

Paradise is better than anything in the world. It is a garden in which are rivers of water, flowing springs, branching trees with all kinds of fruit. There shall the saints recline on couches, on green cushions, and on beautiful carpets, bedecked with bracelets of gold and with pearls, wearing green robes of silk and brocade. Fruits shall be within reach, and whatever they call for shall be served them. Around them shall go eternal youths, with goblets, ewers, and a cup of flowing wine. No headache shall they feel therefrom, nor shall their wits be dimmed. They shall be served by large-eyed damsels of modest glance. They shall see the angels reclining about the throne, praising their Lord.[1]

In the traditions the same description is carried on. *Mishkat al-Masabih*, xxiii. 13, is devoted to a description of paradise.

It is made of gold and silver bricks, with musk for mortar; its gravel is pearls and rubies; its earth saffron. If a man from paradise were to appear and show the rings on his wrists, the splendour of them would hide the splendour of the sun. Everything is there which the senses can desire or which will delight the eye. A tree grows there under which one might ride for a year and come to no end. Every person will be pleased with his own place and not envy another. If a man wish to cultivate land, he may, and fruit will ripen and grow in a moment. No one will sleep there, for sleep is death's brother. All men and women are beautiful. The youth of men is renewed, and they enter paradise as beardless youths. In other places they are said to be in the prime of life at the age of thirty.

The *ḥūris*, the female companions of faithful men in paradise, are described in the *Qur'ān* as maidens, modest and beautiful, of equal age.[2]

Remembering the golden streets and gates of pearl in the book of Revelation, Christians have often asked if the sensuous descriptions of paradise in the *Qur'ān*, and still more in the traditions, were not to be understood as figurative expressions of spiritual ideas. Here and there a sect of Islām has so interpreted them. Mirza Ghulām Ahmād of Qadian, the leader of a sect of Indian Muslims, known as the Ahmadiyyah, argues[3] against the material interpretation of heaven. There are, he says, no cows and bees in heaven to make milk and honey. The goods of heaven are secrets from the earth,[4] so they cannot be material things. *Qur'ān*, ii. 23, 'they are provided with fruit,' has been misinterpreted. It means that they shall eat not fruits like those of the earth, but spiritual fruits.

'Heaven and hell, according to the Holy Quran, are images and representations of a man's own spiritual life in this world. They are not new material worlds which come from the outside. It is true that they shall be visible and palpable, call them material if you please, but they are only embodiments of the spiritual facts of this world. . . . Heaven and hell, according to Moslem belief, are the images of the actions which we perform here below.'[5]

This, however, has not been the general orthodox position of Islām. The literalness of interpretation in tradition is forcibly illustrated in *Mishkat al-Masabih*, xxiii. 13:

'Musselmen will be given strength and vigour in paradise to have connection with many women. It was said, "O messenger of God, will a man be able to connect himself with many women?" His Majesty said, "The powers of one hundred men will be given to one man."'

There are, however, elements of spiritual appreciation, both in the *Qur'ān* and in the traditions. *Qur'ān*, xlvii. 16 f., *e.g.*, couples among the goods of paradise all kinds of fruit and the forgiveness of the Lord. *Mishkat al-Masabih*, xxiii. 14, is headed 'On Seeing God.'

Muhammad said, 'Men shall see God as one sees this moon.' 'They will see God in paradise, and will love the sight of Him better than anything else.' Then he repeated *Qur'ān*, x. 27: 'To those who do what is good, goodness and increase! nor shall blackness or abasement cover their faces! these are the fellows of Paradise, they shall dwell therein for aye.'

Al-Ghazālī said:

'Nothing of the delights of paradise can be compared to the delight of meeting God; for the other bodily enjoyments of paradise dumb animals share with the believer, but this is reserved for him alone.'[1]

The suffering of the unbeliever, like the reward of the faithful, was conceived in material terms. The *Qur'ān* is rich in passages threatening tortures to the damned—'the companions of the fire,' as they are most often called.

They will live 'in hot blasts and boiling water and a shade of pitchy smoke.' They 'shall broil upon a burning fire, shall be given to drink from a boiling spring! no food shall they have save from the foul thorn, which shall not fatten nor avail against hunger.' They shall abide therein for ages. No cool thing shall they taste or drink. Nineteen angels are set over hell as its guardians. 'Whenever a troop of them [who disbelieve in their Lord] is thrown in, the keepers shall ask them, "Did not a warner come to you?" They shall say, "Yea, a warner came to us, and we called him a liar, and said, 'God has not sent down aught; ye are but in great error.'" And they shall say, "Had we but listened or had sense, we had not been amongst the fellows of the blaze!"' They will broil in the fire, and, 'whenever their skins are well done,' then other skins will be given them, 'that they may taste the torment.' Here in the hell of fire they will dwell for ever and ever.[2]

The traditions amplify, sometimes to grotesqueness, the physical tortures of disbelievers. *Mishkat al-Masabih*, xx. 15, is devoted to descriptions of 'The Fire and its People.'

The fire of hell shall be seventy times as hot as the fire of the world. God will make the bodies of the infidels large, so that they may suffer more. They will be given food infinitely loathsome, of which they will eat and still be hungry. They will be bitten by serpents as large as two hundred camels, and by scorpions as large as mules, and the bites shall give pain for forty years.

That the pains of hell are eternal is a tenet of Islām. When it is said that, since all things fleshy are temporal, the bodies of the unfaithful must at last be destroyed, answer is made that God is all-powerful and can do what He will, or that they will be re-created, after they have been burned, that their tortures may proceed.

The ultimate assignment to paradise or hell is on the basis of belief or disbelief in Muhammad's mission. In general, ethical considerations are not regarded in the assignment of a man's destiny. One passage in the *Qur'ān* has been made the basis for the theory of a Muslim purgatory:

'There is not one of you that will not go down to it,—that is settled and decided by the Lord.'[3]

Some hold that this refers only to the passage of all souls over the bridge al-Aarāf; some that all must pass through hell, but that to believers it will be cool and pleasant; and some that this text warrants the belief in a purgatory for such Muslims as need to be purified from sin, unless they have died in battle.

Muslim theology has divided both heaven and hell into regions. The *Qur'ān*, like the Jewish traditions, speaks of seven heavens,[4] but the abodes of the blest are reckoned as eight: Dāru'l-Qarār, 'the abode of rest,'[5] Dāru's-Salām, 'the abode of peace,'[6] Jannatu'l-Ḫuld, 'the garden of eternity,'[7] 'Illiyūn, 'the garden of the Most High,'[8] Jannatu'l-Firdāus, 'the garden of Paradise,'[9] Jannatu'l-Mā'wā, 'the garden of refuge,'[10] Jannatu'n-Na'īm, 'the garden of pleasure,'[11] Jannati 'Adin, 'the garden of Eden.'[12] These are doubtless synonymous terms in the *Qur'ān*, but tradition made them the names of different realms of bliss.

Likewise the different words used for hell have been taken to signify seven different realms of torture, as distributed among the adherents of the various religions, on the authority of a passage in the *Qur'ān*:[13]

'It has seven doors; at every door is there a separate party of them.'

1 See *Qur.* lv. 45 ff., lvi. 1–39, xlvii. 16 ff., xviii. 30 ff., xxxvii. 39 ff., xxii. 23 ff., x. 9, xxxviii. 50 ff., lxxvi. 12 ff., *et al.*
2 xxxviii. 52, lv. 56, *et al.*
3 In his *Teachings of Islam*, Eng. tr., London, 1910.
4 *Qur.* xxxii. 17. 5 P. 144 f.

1 Quoted in Klein, *Religion of Islām*, p. 96.
2 See *Qur.* lvi. 40 f., lxxxviii. 1–7, lxxviii. 21–30, lxvii. 6–12, iv. 58 f., lxx., lxxii. 24, lxxiv. 25–32, ci., *et al.*
3 xix. 72. 4 xxiii. 17. 5 xl. 42.
6 vi. 127. 7 xxv. 16. 8 lxxxiii. 18.
9 xviii. 107. 10 xxxii. 19. 11 v. 70.
12 ix. 73. 13 xv. 44.

Jahannam (Gehenna), the purgatorial fire, is for Muslims;[1] Laẓai, the flaming fire, for Christians;[2] al-Ḥuṭamah, the raging fire, for Jews;[3] Sa'īr, the blazing fire, for Sabæans;[4] Saqar, the scorching fire, for the Magi;[5] Al-Jahīm, the fierce fire, for idolaters;[6] Hāmiyeh, the abyss, for hypocrites.[7] There is no evidence that such classification of either the regions of reward or those of punishment was in Muhammad's thought.

If the paradise of Islām is almost lacking in spiritual satisfaction, its hell is entirely without spiritual torment. The torture of an accusing conscience, the absence from the vision of God, the sting of remorse, are nowhere expressed. Physical torture is magnified and multiplied, but no word is uttered of that greater suffering which the sensitive soul may endure through its own self-condemnation.

See also art. ESCHATOLOGY, § 9.

LITERATURE.—In addition to that mentioned under ESCHATOLOGY, the great collection of traditions in *Mishkat al-Maṣábíh* deals with this subject in bk. xxiii. (Eng. tr. by A. N. Matthews, 2 vols., Calcutta, 1809–10); Al-Ghazālī's tractate on eschatology, *Ad-Dourra al-Fâkhira*, tr. L. Gautier, *La Perle précieuse*, Geneva, 1878; M. Wolff, *Muhammedanische Eschatologie*, Leipzig, 1872, is a translation of a writing of recent date, author unknown; R. Leszynsky, *Mohammedanische Traditionen über das jüngste Gericht*, Berlin, 1909; E. Sell, *The Faith of Islám*², London, 1896; Stanley Lane-Poole, *Studies in a Mosque*², do. 1893; F. A. Klein, *Religion of Islám*, do. 1906.

IRVING F. WOOD.

STATE OF THE DEAD (Teutonic).—Our knowledge of early Teutonic ideas as to the state of the dead is entirely a matter of inference, as there are no extant sources from which direct information relating to that period can be obtained. For later times, coinciding in date with the introduction and establishment of Christianity in N. Europe, there is a considerable body of evidence, but mainly from one source—the early literature of Iceland. As this is not free from Christian and even classical influence, some care must be exercised in accepting the statements found there and in drawing conclusions from them; but there can be no doubt that with due precautions the evidence from this source is of the greatest value and that in the main it is of a very reliable character.

For the long pre-historic period which lies beyond these written records the only evidence of any kind is that furnished by the science of archæology. The great advances which this has made in recent times have established one fact which is of much significance as an indication of early Teutonic beliefs regarding the dead. From the earliest stone age down to the later iron age there can be traced the practice of depositing with the dead of either sex, whether simply buried or previously burned, not only articles of clothing and personal adornment, but weapons, utensils and implements of various kinds, and even articles of food and drink. While to a certain extent this might be accidental or at least not significant, all analogy and probability point to the conclusion that the practice was usually deliberate and full of meaning, and was based on the view that the deceased person still had some interest in, or some use for, such articles as accompanied his or her body in its final resting-place. Whatever the exact circumstances of the life after death might be, its requirements were obviously supposed to have some analogy with those of the living person and to require similar provision to be made for them. It is possible that this view may have undergone considerable modification in later times, and that latterly the depositing of such articles in the grave was rather a lingering convention than the result of a real belief in their necessity or usefulness: conventional survivals of the practice are in fact still widely existent in Teutonic as well as in other countries. From the Icelandic evidence, however, it appears most probable that on the whole the original belief which formed the basis of the custom remained in full vigour so long as the old religion survived. For those who held this belief the dead not only retained their personality, but had a definite abode in the grave in which they had been placed; in later times it is especially the grave-mound that figures as the actual home of the deceased, who is regarded as normally occupying it even at a time long after that in which he lived. As the dead had thus a fixed abode, it was natural that the surviving kinsfolk should regard it with respect, even for several generations, and that a certain cult of the dead should arise, which in special cases might develop into partial or complete worship. It is in this connexion that evidence on the subject first makes its appearance in written sources. Ecclesiastical regulations framed in Germany in the 8th and 9th centuries make reference to 'sacrificia mortuorum' (A.D. 742); 'sacrilegium ad sepulchra mortuorum,' and 'sacrilegium super defunctos, id est dadsisas' (*c.* 825), the meaning of the Old Saxon word *dadsisas* being doubtful. The prominence of the grave-mound as the place of burial is also shown by the enactment that the bodies of Christian Saxons are to be taken to the churchyard for interment, 'et non ad tumulos paganorum.' The same association of the mound with heathenism appears in phrases which survive quite late in Scandinavian documents (sometimes in forms which have become almost unintelligible, such as *frá heiðnum haugi*, 'from heathen mound,' as an expression for 'from ancient times.'

The bare suggestions conveyed by these brief phrases are quite in accordance with the details which can be gathered from the old Icelandic poems and sagas, in many of which there occur passages bearing directly upon the theme. In these records the grave-mound is as normally the abode of the stirring and conscious dead as the ordinary house is of the living person. There is practically no change except that the dweller in the mound (the *haugbúi*) no longer has his place among the living. Sometimes the mound is ancient and its occupant belongs to remote times—so remote that even his name has been forgotten—but he is still able to appear to the living and even to answer their inquiries as to his own identity.

So it was with King Ögvald of Rogaland in Norway, who gave answer as to the time at which he lived to one who was just setting out to settle in Iceland.[1] Another early king, Vatnar, appeared to a merchant who had told his story, while his ship lay beside the grave-mound, and rewarded him by instructions how to find treasure in the mound.[2]

In other tales the persons and incidents are still more legendary or unreal, as in those of Helgi and Sigrún, or of Hervör and Angantýr, in which the imagination of the poet has invested the belief with marvellous touches of pathos and terror. Such instances might have little value in themselves as evidence for any actual belief, but the practice of mound-burial remained in vogue so late in Iceland that various tales of the dead inhabitants have all the freshness of reality about them.

Thus *Landnámabók* tells of a certain Ásmund, one of the early settlers, who was laid in a ship with a thrall beside him. A woman who was passing the mound heard him recite a verse, in which he expressed his dislike at being burdened with such a companion; the mound was therefore opened and the thrall removed.[3]

The famous Gunnar of Hlíðarendi (killed in 990) was seen by moonlight in his open mound, in which four lights were also burning; he wore a joyous look and recited a verse about

[1] xix. 69, *et al.* [2] lxx. 15. [3] civ. 4. [4] iv. 11. [5] liv. 48. [6] ii. 113. [7] ci. 8.

[1] *Hálfs Saga*, 2.
[2] *Landnámabók*, Reykjavík, 1891, p. 231.
[3] *Landnámabók*, bk. ii. ch. 6.

himself in a voice which was audible at some distance off.[1] The poet Thorleif, who died about the same time, at a later date came out of his mound and helped a shepherd-lad to complete a verse in praise of himself; as the lad woke up from his vision, he saw the poet's back as he disappeared into the mound again.[2] Even a Christian like the colonist Ásólf, who died early in the 10th cent., was still interested in the state of his grave and the resting-place of his bones a full century later.[3]

So active were some of the dead, and so effective in the doing of harm to the living, that strong measures had to be taken to reduce them to a quieter state. Others, again, were formidable only when an attempt was made to enter the mound and rob them of their treasures. Tales of the performance of this perilous task are sometimes told of historical personages, but are more characteristic of the fictitious type of saga, in which the *haugbúi* becomes a stock character and is the subject of some grim narratives. Of those who leave the quiet of the mound in order to trouble the living there are some notable instances even in the more historical sagas, and many examples from the traditional lore of later times. The extensive ghost-literature of Iceland, indeed, both ancient and modern, affords one of the strongest proofs of the persistence of this belief in the individual survival of the dead among their old surroundings. Nor was their range confined to the immediate neighbourhood of the burial-place; they were, especially in the night or twilight, but exceptionally even in broad daylight, able to revisit the homestead and enter the houses, from which they sometimes even drove away the living occupants. The supreme example of this is the story of the hauntings at Fróðá on Snæfellsness in the year 1001, where the aggressive dead had finally to be expelled by a regular process of legal ejectment.[4]

When other means failed, the approved remedy was to open the mound and remove the body to some more distant place and, in the last resort, to burn it. It is thus clear that in the later days of the old religion the burning of the body was destructive of the real personality of the dead; whether this was so in earlier times when cremation was usual is a question which cannot be answered.

The attachment of the dead to the old home is also shown by certain instances in which the living person gives instructions as to his own burial.

Hrapp in Laxárdal (dying about 940) gave orders that he was to be buried in a standing posture under the doorway of his hall, so that he might continue to keep a watchful eye upon his household and homestead. His manner of doing so was so little appreciated that in the end his body was removed and subsequently burned, the ashes being disposed of at sea.[5] In a neighbouring district, at a slightly later date (988), Tungu-Odd requested his friends to take him up to Skáneyjarfell and bury him there, so that he might be able to look over all the neighbourhood; and his request was carried out.[6]

In place of the artificial grave-mound a natural hill or hillock was sometimes regarded as the abode to which members of a particular family retired on their departure from this life.

Thus the heathen kinsmen of an early Christian woman-settler in Iceland, Auðr or Uðr, had a religious respect for the hillocks on which she had raised crosses and performed her devotions; 'they believed that they died into the hillocks, and Thórð Gellir was led into them before he assumed the position of a chief.'[7] Another early settler, Thórólf, 'had so much reverence for the hill that stood on the ness, which he called Helgafell,' that he made it a place of sanctuary, 'and it was the belief of Thórólf and his kinsfolk that they all died into the hill.'[8] On the evening before Thórólf's son Thorstein was drowned his shepherd saw the hill opened up towards the north; within it large fires were burning, there was sound of revelry and drinking, and he could hear that greetings were given to Thorstein and his companions, and that to the former was assigned the seat of honour over against his father.[9]

Other instances of the same belief are found in

[1] *Njáls Saga*, 78.
[2] *Flateyjarbók*, i. 214.
[3] *Landnámabók*, ii. 16.
[4] *Eyrbyggja Saga*, 51–55.
[5] *Laxdæla Saga*, 17, 24.
[6] *Hœnsa-þóris Saga*, 20.
[7] *Landnámabók*, ii. 16.
[8] *Eyrbyggja Saga*, 4.
[9] *Ib.* 11.

Selthórir and his kinsmen, who died into Thórisberg, and Kráku-Hreiðar, who 'chose to die into Mælifell.'[1] The casual manner in which these are mentioned in the sources indicates that the idea was a familiar one which required no explanation or comment.

That the mound and its occupant were held in respect by the surviving relatives was natural and usual, and traces of this have survived to the present day in the Scandinavian countries. That such respect might also assume the character of actual worship of the dead is clearly indicated by the ecclesiastical prohibitions quoted above, though positive evidence for the practice is not common. Some of the early Swedish kings are recorded to have been honoured in this way. Grím Kamban, the first settler in the Færöes, 'was worshipped when dead on account of his popularity.'[2]

The scarcity of such instances may indicate that the practice was falling into disuse in the later centuries of heathenism, though it certainly survived in Germany at the close of the 10th cent. to such an extent that it was necessary for the Church to denounce the 'oblationes, quae in quibusdam locis ad sepulchra mortuorum fiunt.'[3] There are even apparent survivals of sacrifice to the dead in almost modern times, but it is doubtful how far these are of real importance as evidence for any continuation of the old belief. In the older Scandinavian period there is reason for believing that the name of 'elf' (*álf*) was one of the designations of the dead, and it is a natural inference from this that the ceremony known as *álfablót* was primarily intended either to honour or to propitiate the spirits of the departed. On the other hand, there is no evidence that the usual funeral feast had any such character, although the dead themselves might occasionally be present at it.

This is related to have happened among the other strange events at Fróðá, when the drowned Thórodd and his companions came into the hall in the evening in their wet clothes. The company were pleased at their appearance, 'for it was regarded as a truth that drowned men had a good reception from the goddess Rán, if they came to their own funeral feast.'[4]

Sometimes the appearance of the dead in company with each other was a token of coming death for others.

When Bárð in Eyjafirth (about 980) was leaving the house of his sister-in-law, his wife turned round to look after him and fell down in a faint. 'I saw dead men,' she explained, 'coming to meet Bárð, and he must be fey; we shall not meet again.'[5] The death of the foster-brothers of Ólafsdal by each other's hand (about 1025) was preceded by the appearance, close to the farm of Garpsdal, of Thorgeir Hávarsson and nine other men who had fallen along with him. They were all blood-stained, and they walked past the farm until they came to a stream near it, where they disappeared.[6]

The fore-warnings thus given by the voluntary appearance of the dead might also be attained by a deliberate process of interrogating them; but for this end it was necessary to 'wake up' the sleeping inmate of the grave, who might naturally be loath to be disturbed. Specific instances of this practice, however, belong rather to the realm of legend, as when Odin wakes up the sibyl to tell him the fate of Balder. The waking-up might also be performed for other reasons, as when Svipdag seeks the aid of his mother Gróa or when Hervör goes to demand the sword Tyrfing from her father Angantýr. In the story of Heðinn and Högni the dead men who have fallen in the battle are waked up again by Hild each night to resume the conflict; this nightly strife continued for nearly a century and a half before it was ended by a follower of Ólaf Tryggvason in the closing years of the 10th century.[7]

[1] *Landnámabók*, ii. 6, iii. 7.
[2] *Ib.* i. 6.
[3] Burchard von Worms, 'Decreta,' in J. Grimm, *Deutsche Mythologie*[4], Berlin, 1875 78, iii. 407.
[4] *Eyrbyggja Saga*, 54.
[5] *Víga-Glúms Saga*, 19.
[6] *Fóstbrœðra Saga*, 19.
[7] *Flateyjarbók*, i. 281–282.

From this shadowy and imperfect, though real and individual, existence there was one way by which the dead might escape—that of being born again. That the doctrine of rebirth was prevalent in older times is expressly stated by the unknown collector of the Edda poems.

'It was a belief in old times that persons were born again, but that is now called an old wife's delusion. Helgi and Sigrún are said to have been born again; he was then called Helgi, prince of the Haddings, and she Kára, daughter of Hálfdan.'[1]

In the mythical *Gautreks-saga* the berserks who wish to annoy Starkað call him a 'reborn giant.' In the historical period it was commonly believed that King Ólaf the Saint was a reincarnation of a remote ancestor, Ólaf of Geirstaðir, known as Geirstaðaálf.

Once, as the king rode past the grave-mound of this Ólaf, one of his followers ventured to say to him: 'Tell me, my lord, if you were buried here?' The king replied: 'My spirit never had two bodies, and has not now, nor will it have at the resurrection.' The retainer persisted: 'It has been said that when you came to this place before, you spoke thus: Here we were and here we walked.' The king flatly denied the assertion and rode away as quickly as possible.[2]

Even as late as the middle of the 13th cent. the belief in rebirth appears to have survived in Iceland.

A certain Thorgils, who at that time rose to distinction, was a source of great joy to the men of his district: 'It seemed to them that Kolbeinn was born again and come back to them, whom they had always longed for.'[3]

So long as the dead were regarded as intimately connected with the burial-place and the old homestead, it is obvious that any theory of a special place for the spirits of the departed was not urgently required. Such an idea, however, may actually have arisen at a very early period, and it is unnecessary to suppose that the two views would be felt to be mutually exclusive. At all periods when burning was the ordinary method of disposing of the dead, the idea must have been natural that body and spirit were separable, and that with the destruction of the body the spirit was free to go elsewhere. Even when simple burial was practised, such a separation was not unthinkable; the spirit might well have its usual abode apart from the body, though capable of returning to it at will.

In one of the Edda poems already cited[4] Helgi is buried in a mound, but departs to Valhall. One evening Sigrún's attendant sees him ride up to the mound 'with many men'; he says that leave to return has been granted to him. Sigrún then enters the opened mound, and there is talk of intense pathos between them; but towards morning Helgi has to depart again, so as to be back at Valhall before cockcrow. (Variations of the idea form the theme of many ghost-tales in different lands.)

Departure to another world after being consumed on the funeral pile comes out clearly in the story of Balder, whose horse was burned along with him, and who then rode off to the domain of the goddess Hel, and in that of Brynhild, who is represented as driving to the same place in the chariot in which she was laid and consumed. According to Snorri, the institution of burning was ascribed to Odin himself:

'He said that each man would come to Valhall with such treasures as he had on the funeral-pile.'[5] (A further point of the belief was that 'the higher the smoke rose into the air, the more exalted the person burned would be in heaven.')[6]

The departure to another world, however, might equally well take place when the body was left unburned.

King Harald Hilditönn, who was laid in a mound along with valuable rings and weapons, was provided with both a car and a horse, so that he might either drive or ride to Valhall.[7]

That these legendary instances have some foundation in actual custom is shown by the passage in *Gísla Saga* relating to events about 965.

In this, at the burial of Véstein, Thorgrim is made to say: 'It is the custom to bind hell-shoes on men, with which they shall go to Valhall, and I will do it for Véstein.' When he had done so, he said: 'I cannot bind hell-shoes, if these come loose.'[1]

Such accounts, however, belong to the Viking age, for which there is clear evidence of a developed theory of another life, with assignment of definite places for different classes of men. The earliest of these abodes of the dead was no doubt the realm of the goddess Hel, a world of shades similar to the Hades of the Greeks, in which the departed spirits appear to have had only a negative kind of existence, devoid of any occupation or interest.[2] At a later period, however, those who found their way to this region were only those who died of sickness or old age. Those who were drowned belonged to the goddess Rán, and those who fell in battle were divided between Odin and Freyja. There are also indications that some were supposed to fall to the lot of Thor, and that Freyja was the receiver of all women. Of the various conceptions arising from these views that which received most elaboration, if the extant evidence is to be relied on, was the life of the warriors who had gone to Odin in Valhall, of which a full account is given by Snorri in the first part of the Edda.[3] Whether any of the dead were supposed to remain loosely attached to earth itself, without having a definite place assigned to them, does not appear. There is no evidence that the ideas of the 'wild hunt' and similar companies of departed spirits, so prevalent in later tradition, go back to the early Teutonic period or reproduce any conceptions from that time.

It is only in Snorri's Edda (written about 1220), and in a few lines of the older poetry on which this is based, that any ethical idea appears in the allocation of the different abodes.

The highest god, All-father, 'created man and gave him a soul which shall live and never perish, even if the body decay to dust or be burned to ashes; and all men whose ways are right shall live and be with himself in the place called Gimlé; but wicked men go to Hel and thence into Niflhel, which is down in the ninth world.'[4]

When the world itself has been consumed by fire, the spirits of men will still subsist and have various abodes, many of them good and many bad. 'Then it will be best to be in Gimlé in heaven, where there will be abundance of good drink for those who enjoy that in the hall called Brimir. . . . That is also a good hall which stands on Niðafells, made of red gold; its name is Sindri. In these halls shall good and righteous men live.'[5]

On the other hand, all murderers and perjurers find a place of torment in a great hall on 'Corpse-strand,' the doors of which face northwards. The walls of this are wattled with snakes, whose heads are turned inwards; these spout out venom which flows through the hall in streams, and in these streams the wicked are doomed to wade.[6]

It is doubtful how much of this is genuine and how much is due to ordinary mediæval conceptions of heaven and hell. In any case the ideas are far removed from the more primitive beliefs which were still current in Snorri's time, and which, however much they may have been elaborated by the story-teller and the poet, clearly have their roots in the old Teutonic times of which no record has been preserved.

LITERATURE.—E. Mogk, *Mythologie*, in H. Paul, *Grundriss der german. Philologie*, Strassburg, 1891-93, iii. 249-266; E. Wadstein, *Kleinere altsächsische Sprachdenkmäler*, Norden, 1899, pp. 66, 142-144; H. Hildebrand, *Folkens Tro om sina Döda*, Stockholm, 1874; G. Storm, 'Vore Forfædres Tro paa Sjælevam-dring,' in *Arkiv för nordisk Filologi*, ix. [1893] 199-222; H. Schetelig, 'Folketro om Gravhauger,' in *Maal og Minne*, Christiania, 1911, pp. 206-212; H. Rosén, *Om dödsrike och dödsbruk i fornnordisk religion*, Lund, 1918.

W. A. CRAIGIE.

STATE OF THE DEAD (Tibetan). — The immediate ceremonies performed by Tibetans on a death, and their object, have already been de-

1 *Völsunga-kviða en forna, ad fin.*
2 *Flateyjarbók*, ii. 135.
3 *Sturlunga Saga*, ed. G. Vigfusson, Oxford, 1878, ii. 234.
4 *Völsunga-kviða en forna.*
5 *Ynglinga Saga*, 8.
6 *Ib.* 10.
7 *Sögubrot af Fornkonungum*, 9.

1 *Gísla Saga*, 14.
2 See *ERE* ii. 707 ff.
3 *Ib.* p. 707 f.
4 *Snorra Edda, Gylfaginning*, 3.
5 *Ib.* 52.
6 *Ib.*

scribed.[1] The Tibetan notions on the state into which the spirit or soul of a deceased person is supposed to pass after death are mainly of an animistic character, and derived from the aboriginal shamanist Bon cult (see art. TIBET), though veneered over more or less with the ritual of Indian Buddhism and 'celestial' Chinese cosmogony. The laity and most of the Lāmas believe that, at first at any rate, the spirits of all the dead tend to become malignant ghosts, which require propitiation by the surviving relatives, except in the case of a few great saints, like the Grand Lāmas, whose spirits are supposed to re-incarnate almost immediately. But, in the background, most Tibetans cherish the hope of attaining the western paradise of the blest, the everlasting solar paradise of 'the Buddha of Boundless Light' (Hod-dpag-med or Amitābha), the popular goal of Northern Buddhists generally, just as in Southern Buddhism, in Burma, Siam, and Ceylon, the popular goal is not a *nirvāṇa* of extinction, but Indra's paradise in the sky, whence, they are taught, Buddha Gautama descended to this world and which he frequently revisited. It is mainly with the object of gaining merit sufficient to reach this paradise that the Tibetans so assiduously tell their beads, mutter so incessantly the mystic *Om maṇi* formula, and ply their prayer-wheels, revolving the same printed sentence, which is believed to close the door of hell and be the passport to heaven. The idea of rebirth in human or other form is not a popular one; nearly all concentrate their hopes on reaching paradise. Even *nirvāṇa* is considered by most Lāmas to be not any extinction of existence, but a dreamy existence in a personal paradise outside the circle of rebirths and so infinitely remote that it is unknowable.

The prevalent belief that the spirit of the dead person becomes a malignant ghost at first is in practice generally assimilated to the Buddhist theory of hell, as a temporary purgatory of expiation for sin. The spirit is admonished by the priests, as soon after death as possible, to take the road pointed out to it leading to the tribunal of the Judge of the Dead, but it requires the assistance of the priests by masses at every stage throughout that journey to pilot it along. At the outset it is free for one or two weeks to wander about, and this is the period when it is likely to exercise a malignant influence on the survivors. The regions through which the soul is piloted by the priests are of the nature of outer hells beset by demons lying in wait for straying souls, and generally resemble those analogous regions through which the spirits of the deceased were supposed to pass as categorically described in the Egyptian *Book of the Dead* and reflected in Bunyan's *Pilgrim's Progress*. The masses prescribed by the priests of all sects of Lāmas for the protection of the soul of the deceased in this long journey are very elaborate, prolonged, and costly, and usually run the relatives into debt. The present writer has been told by Tibetan servants on more than one occasion that the priests had informed them that the masses already said and paid for had only helped the soul past such-and-such demons and regions, that it was now in such-and-such a distressful spot, and had such-and-such danger zones still to pass before reaching the judgment-seat, when the supreme effort of the priests would be necessary to procure 'rebirth' in paradise.

The hells offer the chief terror to the Tibetans, whom the priests have made familiar with the hideous tortures to be expected there by the harrowing scenes which they have painted in graphic gruesome detail on the walls of every temple, whilst the ubiquitous Wheel of Life fresco, which also depicts the hells and other spheres of orthodox Buddhist rebirth, displays in its upper compartment, in alluring contrast, the bliss and joys of paradise. A peculiarity of the Tibetan hells is the addition of a series of cold hells to the orthodox hells of the Buddhists.[1] It is easy to see how the idea of cold hells arose, on the extension of Buddhism from subtropical India to such totally different physical and ethnic conditions as exist in icy Tibet; the natives of the palæarctic region of Central Asia were accustomed to feel the bitter pain and misery of the arctic cold and to regard heat rather as a comfort and blessing. These cold hells are placed on the edge of the Buddhist universe in a subterranean region of darkness below its encircling wall (Chakravala). They are encircled by icy glacier mountains and have demon attendants of appalling aspect, as in the hot hells. They are eight in number, like the orthodox hot hells, and are thus described:

(1) *Ch'u-bur che'n-po* (Skr. Arbuda)='blistered or chapped.' The torture here is constant immersion of the naked body in icy glacier water, under which it becomes covered with chilblains (a torture which may be compared with the curse invented by a scribe in the reign of Athelstan for any one who should break the terms of his charters: 'May he be tortured by the bitter blasts of glaciers and the Pennine army of evil spirits').[2]

(2) *Ch'u-bur brol-wa* (Skr. Nirarbuda). The chilblains are rudely scarified by knives, producing open raw sores.

(3) *A-ch'u* (Skr. Aṭaṭa). 'Ach'u' and 'A-ṭa-ṭa' are explained as the exclamations of anguish beyond articulate expression, which resound through this hell.

(4) *Kyi-'ud* (Skr. Hahava). A worse degree of cold in which the tongue is paralyzed, and the exclamation of 'Kyi-u' or 'Ha-ha' is alone possible.

(5) *So-t'am-pa* (Skr. Ahaha). Here both jaws and teeth are spasmodically clenched through cold.

(6) *Ut-pal-ltar gas-pa* (Skr. Utpala). Livid sores develop which become everted like the petals of the blue Utpal lotus-flowers.

(7) *Padma-ltar gas-pa* (Skr. Padma). The sores become like the red lotus Padma flowers.

(8) *Padma-ch'en-po-ltar gas-pa* (Skr. Puṇḍarīka). Raw sores where the flesh falls away from the bones like the recurring petals of the great lotus, and which are continually pecked and gnawed by birds with iron beaks, as in Æschylus's Greek legend of *Prometheus Bound*.

The agonizing torments of these hells, so vividly pictured and described by the priests, no doubt act as a deterrent to evil-doers and have thus a certain ethical value, though this is largely discounted by the fear and loss of peace of mind inflicted on the surviving relatives by the harrowing stories of intermediate tortures requiring masses, invented by the self-interested rapacious priests.

The paradise of the blest, when once eventually reached, is considered to be everlasting, and thus is unlike Indra's heaven, the popular goal of Hindus and the Southern Buddhists, which, although more permanent than the earth, is finite, and its occupants subject inevitably to re-enter the cycle of ceaseless rebirths in a higher, but most often a lower, sphere of life, with, according to Buddhist teaching, its inveterate misery. The Tibetans thus look forward to a happier existence in the world beyond death than do the Hindus and Southern Buddhists.

LITERATURE.—E. Schlagintweit, *Buddhism in Tibet*, London, 1863, pp. 92 f., 134 f.; L. A. Waddell, *The Buddhism of Tibet*, do. 1895, pp. 76 ff., 127 f., *Lhasa and its Mysteries*, do. 1905, pp. 86 f., 222 f.

L. A. WADDELL.

STATIONS.—This word was used in Christian antiquity in more than one technical sense. We

[1] See art. DEATH AND DISPOSAL OF THE DEAD (Tibetan).

[1] See artt. STATE OF THE DEAD (Buddhist), COSMOGONY AND COSMOLOGY (Buddhist).

[2] Cited by D. W. Freshfield, in *Geog. Journal* [1894]. The cold hells figure in the N. European mythology as evidenced by this reference to them in the 10th cent. Anglo-Saxon tale 'Salomon and Saturn.' On the defeat of the rebel angels it said that 'for them, he [God] made Hell, a dwelling deadly cold, with Winter covered: Water he sent in and snake-dwellings, many a foul beast with horns of iron, bloody eagles and pale adders; thirst and hunger and fierce conflict, mighty terror, joylessness' (tr. J. M. Kemble, *Salomon and Saturn*, p. 173).

may first consider the word as used in the West in early times, the Latin *statio* being in question; and then 'stations of penitents,' and finally 'stations of the cross' will be dealt with.

1. Stations as fasts.—The first instance of this is in Hermas (early or middle 2nd cent.?), who, writing at Rome in Greek, transliterates *statio* into *σταττίων*. He says to the Shepherd, 'I am keeping a station' (*σταττίωνα ἔχω*). The Shepherd asks, 'What is a station?' Hermas replies that it is a fast, and that he is fasting according to his custom.[1] From the language used we may gather that 'station' was not a universally known name; and that it is not used in Hermas for a fast on any fixed day. Later, at the end of the 2nd cent. and early in the 3rd, Tertullian gives the name 'stations' to the half-fasts (*semijejunia*) of Wednesdays and Fridays,[2] which ordinarily ended at 3 p.m., but which the Montanists prolonged till the evening.[3] The 'Psychics' (Catholics) sometimes continued 'the station even over the sabbath (Saturday), a day never to be kept as a fast except at Pascha.'[4] In these half-fasts the 'Psychics' sometimes lived on bread and water, and they treated them as of voluntary observance rather than as matters of injunction, as the Montanists did.[5] The *de Jejuniis* was written after Tertullian became a Montanist. In another late work[6] he uses the word *statio* more generally, of Daniel's fast (Dn 10[2ff.]): 'in a station of three weeks aruit victu,' *i.e.* he practised xerophagy, a much restricted diet. In *de Jejun.* 13 Tertullian calls fasts held before the meetings of councils 'stations.' In an earlier work, written before he became a Montanist,[7] he speaks of the eucharist being celebrated on 'station days,' and of the scruples of some at communicating then, lest they should break their fast. He suggests (for the scrupulous) private reservation of the sacrament until the 'station' is over, but deprecates their absenting themselves from the eucharistic service: 'Will not thy station be more solemn if thou hast also stood (*steteris*) at the altar of God?' He goes on to explain that the word 'station' is derived from a military metaphor, 'for also we are God's soldiers' (*militia*; cf. 2 Co 10[4], 1 Ti 1[18], 2 Ti 4[7]). And this is doubtless the true origin of the name. In classical Latin *statio* is a military guard, and *stationarius* is a soldier on guard. Tertullian uses *stationes facere* ('to keep watch') both literally and figuratively of Christians on guard.[8] In the 4th cent. Augustine uses *stationarius* figuratively,[9] and Ambrose says that stations are encampments protecting us from the assaults of the devil; 'standing' in them, we repel the enemy.[10]

Tertullian uses *statio* also in other senses: as 'the resting place in believing' (*statio credendi*), a metaphor from a camp;[11] as a 'stage' of life (marriage as opposed to virginity);[12] and in a physiological sense, as the membrane round the heart (*statio sensuum*=*περικάρδιον*).[13]

It will be noticed that all the writers mentioned above were Westerns. Easterns, like the author of the *Didache*[14] and Clement of Alexandria,[15] speak of the Wednesday and Friday fasts, but do not use the word *statio*. An Eastern instance, however, of *statio* transliterated is the East Syrian (Nestorian) *isṭaṭyūnā*, used in the service-books for 'a doctrinal hymn.'[16]

[1] *Pastor*, *Sim.* v. 1.
[2] *De Jejun.* 2, 13 f.
[3] *Ib.* 1, 10.
[4] *Ib.* 14.
[5] *Ib.* 10, 13; in § 10 the *indignas*, 'unworthy,' of the MSS should probably be emended to *indictas*, 'enjoined.'
[6] *De Anima*, 48.
[7] *De Orat.* 19.
[8] *De Cor. Mil.* 11.
[9] *Enarr. in Ps.* xciii. Vulg. [xciv.], § 9.
[10] *Serm.* 25; ed. Paris, 1549, col. 716.
[11] *De Præscr.* 10.
[12] *De Exhort. Cast.* 9.
[13] *De Anima*, 48.
[14] § 8 (*c.* A.D. 130?).
[15] *Strom.* vii. 12 (*c.* A.D. 200).
[16] A. J. Maclean, *East Syrian Daily Offices*, London, 1894, p. 294.

2. Stations in churches and sacred places.—The name *statio* is also used for a public service (usually at Rome the eucharist), held in a previously arranged church or sacred place for the whole community; frequently there was a procession to the place, and the station may have been so called because the procession stopped there, though it has also been held that the name came from these public services being held on 'stated' days, or (originally) on 'station days,' Wednesday and Friday.[1] The name was also given to the church or place where the service was held, or to the processions themselves.[2] This use of the word is later than that described in the preceding section. But Cyprian in the 3rd cent. describes how the messengers of Novatus burst in 'in statione,' demanding that their accusations should be publicly investigated by Cyprian and the people; and 'in statione' can hardly mean here 'on a station day,' but must signify 'in a public assembly.'[3] Gregory of Nazianzus in the 4th cent. uses the cognate *στάσις* of an assembly in church.[4]

In the interesting *Pilgrimage of 'Etheria'* ('*Silvia*'), probably of the end of the 4th cent., stations at the holy places in and near Jerusalem are described in some detail, but they have no technical designation. The thing, but not the name, is there. We may gather that the Western (Spanish?) authoress did not know the name, or she could hardly have avoided using it. The place and time of the next station are publicly given out by the archdeacon just as in the *Ordines Romani* (below).[5]

At Rome we find both the name and the thing. Pope Gregory the Great (A.D. 590–604) is said[6] to have regulated the stations and to have fixed the churches in Rome where they should be held. The whole of the local Church took part in them, and hence in the *Ordo Romanus* of St. Amand, found in a 9th cent. MS, we read of a *statio catholica*.[7] Stations are frequently mentioned in the *Ordo Romanus Primus* (*c.* A.D. 770; founded on a similar document of the 6th cent.) and in the succeeding *Ordines*.[8] The eucharist was celebrated at the stational church with much solemnity by the pope. If a diocesan bishop said a stational mass in the absence of the pope, he did all as the pope would do; but, if a presbyter did so, then the 'Gloria in excelsis' was omitted, because it was said by a presbyter only 'in Pascha,' *i.e.* in Eastertide.[9] The archdeacon in the *Ord. Rom. Prim.* announces the next station,[10] but in *St. Amand* the deacon.[11] We read of a 'stational chalice,'[12] apparently a large one, and 'stational crosses,'[13] and a 'stational acolyte' (*unus ex acolythis stationarius*, or simply *stationarius*),[14] who goes before the pope on foot in the procession, with the chrism, a napkin (*mappula*) being wrapped round the *ampulla*, or vessel holding the chrism. It was at such solemn stations that ordinations were held in Rome, on the Saturday of Ember weeks.[15]

The *Gregorian Sacramentary*[16] gives masses for all the stations at the various churches in Rome.

3. Stations of penitents.—In the 4th cent., or possibly earlier, the penitential system was developed both in the East and in the West, but

[1] See above, § 1.
[2] Ducange, *Glossarium*, *s.v.* 'Statio,' § 1.
[3] *Ep.* xliv. [xl.], 'ad Cornelium.'
[4] *Orat. in Conc. Constant.*, near the end: *στάσεις πάννυχοι*.
[5] For the *Pilgrimage* see Duchesne, *Christian Worship*[4], Eng. tr., London, 1912, p. 490 ff.; esp. cf. p. 516.
[6] In his *Life* by John the Deacon, ii. 18.
[7] Duchesne, p. 473.
[8] E. G. C. F. Atchley, *Ord. Rom. Prim.*, London, 1905, p. 32, etc.; for the date see p. 7.
[9] *Ib.* p. 148.
[10] *Ib.* p. 142.
[11] Duchesne, p. 473.
[12] Atchley, p. 156.
[13] Duchesne, p. 474.
[14] Atchley, p. 118.
[15] *Ib.* p. 37; Duchesne, p. 353.
[16] Ed. H. A. Wilson, London, 1915 (Henry Bradshaw Society).

it is only in the East that the organized 'stations of penitents' are found, and even there not universally. There are differing grades of penitents, called *βαθμοί* or *βαθμοὶ ὡρισμένοι*, at the Council of Ancyra in N. Galatia (A.D. 314).[1] They were four in number: (*a*) 'mourners' (*flentes*, *προσκλαίοντες*), who might not enter the church (hence *πρόσκλαυσις* for the name of the station); perhaps also called at Ancyra[2] 'storm-driven' (*χειμαζόμενοι*), which usually means 'demoniacs,' as in the *Apostolic Constitutions*, viii. 12, 35, 38; (*b*) 'hearers' (*audientes*, *ἀκροώμενοι* [see below]), who stood within the church door or in the porch (hence *ἀκρόασις*, *ἀκροᾶσθαι*); (*c*) 'kneelers' (*substrati*, *ὑποπίπτοντες*), who might enter the church, but not pass the ambo (hence *ὑπόπτωσις*, *ὑποπεσεῖν*); (*d*) 'bystanders' (*consistentes*, *συνιστάμενοι* or *συνεστῶτες*), who might be present at the eucharist, but might not communicate or make an offering (hence *σύστασις*). The first three grades were dismissed before the *missa fidelium* began. In the second and third canonical epistles of Basil, bishop of Cæsarea in Cappadocia,[3] we find all four grades; thus a person in his first year would be 'expelled from prayer' and would 'weep at the church door' (=*a*), in his second he would be 'received to the sermon' (=*b*), in his third he would be 'admitted to penance' (=*c*; see below), in his fourth he would be allowed to 'stand with the people, while withheld from the oblation' (=*d*). In some cases[4] a station might be omitted, the penitent going straight from the first to the third station; in can. 81 of Basil, as in can. 7 of Ancyra, the last station is apparently omitted. This fourth station is also called 'joining only in prayer' or 'being without offering,' as at Ancyra[5] and Nicæa.[6] The third station seems to have been the most important, and Basil[7] calls it by the general name of 'penitence' (*μετάνοια*). The first mention of these four stations has been thought to occur in a passage of Gregory Thaumaturgus, bishop of Neocæsarea,[8] where all four are named; but this is probably an addition by a later writer,[9] and we cannot be certain of the existence of the four stations much before the 4th century. But they, or most of them, are mentioned at Ancyra,[10] at Nicæa,[11] at Neocæsarea in Pontus (A.D. 314 or later).[12] At the last a 'kneeler' is called *γόνυ κλίνων*.[13]

On the other hand, we do not find these grades of penitents in the Church Orders of the 4th (or 5th) cent.; thus in the *Apostolic Constitutions* (*c.* A.D. 375) the penitents are mentioned as being dismissed at the eucharist after the catechumens, but they are all called 'hearers,'[14] or, generally, 'those in penitence.'[15] In this work, then, we have no trace of stations of penitents, though *σύστασις* is several times used in it in other senses. And the same thing is true of the other Church Orders. It is equally true of Western and 'African' councils, such as those of Elvira in Spain (*c.* A.D. 305), Arles in Gaul (A.D. 314), Carthage II. (A.D. 387 or 390), Hippo in Africa (A.D. 393), Toledo in Spain (A.D. 400), Orange in Gaul (A.D. 441), Arles II. (A.D. 443 or 452), and others; these mention penitents, but have no stations. This is the case also with the Gallican *Statuta ecclesiæ antiqua* ('Gallican Statutes'; *c.* A.D. 500). In Tertullian the catechumens are the 'hearers' (*audientes* or *auditores*).[16]

[1] Can. 20 f., 23 f.
[2] Can. 17.
[3] *Epp.* cxcix., ccxvii., cans. 22, 56–83 (A.D. 375).
[4] As in can. 80.
[5] Cans. 4–6.
[6] Can. 13 (A.D. 325).
[7] Can. 22.
[8] *Ep. can.* 11 (*c.* A.D. 258).
[9] See *DCB* ii. 736b.
[10] Cans. 4–9, 16, 20–25, hearers, kneelers, bystanders.
[11] Cans. 11–14, the same.
[12] Can. 5, hearers, kneelers.
[13] For these stations see also J. M. Neale, *A Hist. of the Holy Eastern Church*, pt. i., *General Introduction*, London, 1850, i. 208 ff.
[14] viii. 6, 12.
[15] viii. 9.
[16] *De Pœn.* 6, where the meaning 'penitents' has been proposed, but is not really possible.

The name 'hearers,' whether used of penitents or of catechumens, comes from the fact that these classes heard the liturgical lessons (in some cases not the Gospel), though they were not allowed to be present at the more solemn part of the eucharist.

Even in the East the stations of penitents seem not to have been at all regularly organized. They are not mentioned in the *Apostolic Canons* (in their present form probably dating from *c.* A.D. 400), nor in the canons of Gangra in Paphlagonia (4th cent., date uncertain), or of Sardica, the modern Sofia in Bulgaria (A.D. 347; the genuineness of these canons is disputed), or of Antioch *in encœniis* (A.D. 341). These canons mention penitence, but not the grades or stations. At Laodicea in Phrygia (*c.* A.D. 386) 'hearers' may mean all penitents;[1] no other station is mentioned. The canons of the ecumenical councils of Constantinople (A.D. 381), Ephesus (A.D. 431), and Chalcedon (A.D. 451) do not deal with penitence. In Chrysostom's Constantinople writings there is no mention of the dismissal of the stations of penitents,[2] possibly because the office of penitentiary presbyter in that city had lately been abolished (*i.e.* A.D. 391).[3]

In the Churches of the farther East the stations of penitents, if they existed, apparently soon died out.[4] Jacob of Edessa, in his *Letter to Thomas the Presbyter*,[5] describing the liturgy as known to him (he died A.D. 708), speaks of the catechumens as 'hearers' and describes their expulsion in the liturgy before that of the 'energumens' and the 'penitents,' but says that it was in fact quite obsolete in his day. In the canons (8th or 9th cent.) of uncertain origin, perhaps Syrian Jacobite, given by H. Denzinger,[6] and in the Jacobite canons also given by him,[7] of a later date, there is just a trace of 'mourners' in the fact that some penitents are not allowed to enter the church, but are ordered to remain outside 'weeping for their sins,' usually for a year, but in some cases for a much longer period; after that they are allowed to enter the church, but are restrained from communion for a longer or shorter period; the penalty ordinarily provided is fasting, on a restricted diet, but in one case[8] a flogging, and in the latest set of canons a stated number of genuflexions and recitations of anthems (*sedrê*). In the Nestorian *Sunhadhus* (Book of Canon Law) there are no stations of penitents.

We must therefore conclude that stations of penitents were an Eastern, not a Western, organization, and that even in the East they were only partially recognized, and that but for a time. We find them, however, in the 'Trullan' (Constantinople) Council of A.D. 691 or 692.[9] This is a quotation from Basil, and speaks of all four stations of penitents, but does not name them.

4. 'Stations of the cross.'—This is a name given in post-Reformation days to a series of sculptures or pictures set up in many churches in the West, showing various events in the Passion of our Lord, for the devotion of worshippers who cannot go to the sacred places of the Holy Land, and who go round these stations, praying at each. The stations are fourteen in number, and do not all represent events explicitly mentioned in the Gospels. The name is apparently derived from the idea of a station described above in § **2**.

[1] Can. 5; ordinations were not to take place in their presence.
[2] J. H. Srawley, *The Early Hist. of the Liturgy*, Cambridge, 1913, p. 122.
[3] Socrates, *HE* v. 19; Sozomen, *HE* vii. 16.
[4] For a trace of them see Srawley, p. 123, n. 1.
[5] Eng. tr. in F. E. Brightman, *Liturgies Eastern and Western*, Oxford, 1896, i. 490.
[6] *Ritus Orientalium*, Würzburg, 1863–64, i. 474.
[7] i. 482–500.
[8] i. 484; can. 38.
[9] Can. 87.

LITERATURE.—This has been mentioned in the course of the article. Other meanings of *statio* and its derivatives may be seen *s.v.* in C. du F. Ducange, *Glossarium mediæ et infimæ Latinitatis*, Paris, 1840–50; new ed., Niort, 1883–87.

A. J. MACLEAN.

STEALING.—See CRIMES AND PUNISHMENTS.

STEDINGERS.—The crusade against the Stedingers was of the mixed political-religious type characteristic of all the later crusades. The Stedingers were a mixed race of herdsmen and fishermen who had colonized the lower Weser and the country north of Bremen. Disputes with the counts of Oldenburg from about 1187 were soon mixed up with questions of tithes. Some monks who urged the duty of payment were murdered, and a priest who had tricked a woman, by placing in her mouth a coin instead of the wafer, was slain by her husband. This led in 1206–07 to the attempt of Hartwig II., archbishop of Bremen († 3rd Nov. 1207), to reduce the Stedingers by force, but the first effort had little success. In 1229 a further attempt by Gerhard II. of Lippe, archbishop of Bremen, led on Christmas Day to the complete repulse of the crusades. Unfortunately the Stedingers, to celebrate their triumph, appointed mock popes, archbishops, and bishops, and this enabled the authorities to represent them as spiritual rebels. In 1230 the Stedingers were accordingly put under the ban at a synod in Bremen as the vilest of heretics, and on 3rd Feb. 1232 Gregory IX. ordered a crusade to be preached against them. They were described in the bull as heretics who worshipped demons, indulged in magic, and sometimes crucified priests. On 19th Jan. 1233 Gregory once more repeated his exhortations to the crusade in letters to the bishops of Westphalia.[1] An army was collected, but nothing was accomplished. As the crusaders melted away, Gregory, on 17th June 1233, ordered a new crusade.[2] He attributed past lack of success to the belief that the crusaders were not getting the same indulgences as those granted for the Holy Land. The bishops were ordered to make it clear that the indulgences were the same. The new crusade devastated the country; all the men captured were burned; but it was finally defeated, and its leader, Count Burchard of Oldenburg, was slain.

In 1234 a third crusade was preached by the Dominicans in Holland, Flanders, Westphalia, and the Rhinelands. On 27th May at Altenesch the Stedingers were broken up, chiefly by the force of Thierry, count of Cleves. To the memory of the 6000 Stedingers then slain a monument was dedicated on the field of battle on 27th May 1834. After the devastation of their land Gregory announced in Aug. 1236 that the rebellion was at an end, and that the survivors were to be reconciled to the Church.

LITERATURE.—The main authority is H. A. Schumacher, *Die Stedinger*, Bremen, 1865. There is a short abstract of this in H. C. Lea, *A Hist. of the Inquisition of the Middle Ages*, 3 vols., New York, 1887, iii. ch. iv. The primary sources will be found in the contemporary chronicles, especially Adam of Bremen, *Gesta Hammaburgensis Ecclesiæ Pontificum*, ch. 203, Albert of Stade, *Chronicon* and *Chron. Erfordiens.*, all in Pertz, *MGH*; see also O. Raynaldus, *Annal. Eccles.*, ed. J. D. Mansi, Lucca, 1747–56, *sub ann.* But the primary sources are very confused in their accounts.

H. B. WORKMAN.

STIGMATA.—Stigmata is the name specially applied to marks on the body which have a religious reference. Herodotus[3] relates, regarding a temple of Hercules in Egypt, that runaway slaves who took refuge in it were not liable to be re-captured if they had received on their bodies stigmata which signified their devotion to him. Such marks are alluded to by St. Paul in Gal 6[17], where he speaks of himself as bearing in his body 'the stigmata of the Lord Jesus'; and Pontius (3rd cent.) refers to Christian 'confessors whose foreheads were sealed with a (sacred) inscription.'[1]

1. From the 13th cent. (and perhaps earlier, although unrecorded) the word has been applied particularly to wounds resembling those of the crucified Jesus, and found on the person of a devout believer, especially after intent contemplation of our Lord's Passion. In over 100 cases one or more of the stigmata of the Cross—the wound on His forehead due to the crown of thorns, those on His hands and feet caused by the nails, and the wound in His side inflicted by the soldier's spear—are stated to have been reproduced in the persons of fervent Christians.[2] The earliest recorded and historically the most notable instance is that of St. Francis of Assisi, two years before his death; and in connexion with this reported stigmatization, chiefly, the question has been debated whether the alleged reproductions of Christ's stigmata really existed, and, if so, whether they were miraculously imparted, self-inflicted, or spontaneously formed as the outcome of abnormal yet not supernatural influence of soul over body.

2. The earliest detailed account of the stigmata of St. Francis is furnished by Thomas de Celano, whose first biography of the saint was composed, by order of Pope Gregory IX., at some date between 16th July 1228, when Francis was canonized (within two years after his death), and 25th Feb. 1229, when the biography received papal approval.[3] Celano relates how, in the autumn of 1224, the saint retired, along with a few companions,[4] for meditation and devotion to Mt. Verna, an isolated peak of the Apennines, over 4000 ft. in height. During their sojourn there the soul of Francis was filled with thoughts of our Lord's Passion. On one occasion, at the date of the Festival of the Elevation of the Holy Cross, 14th Sept.,[5] he saw in a vision a Man of God like a seraph, with six wings, standing above him, and nailed to a cross, with hands extended and feet joined together. Two wings were raised above the head; two were outstretched for flying; two covered his body. After Francis had experienced a brief rapture, the vision vanished; but its significance was soon revealed.

'In his own hands and feet there began to appear marks of the nails, just as, shortly before, he had seen those on the Holy Man crucified. His hands and feet appeared transfixed in the middle with nails; the heads of the nails appearing on the inner side of the hands, and on the upper side of the feet, while the points (*acumina*) of the nails were on the other side. Those marks were round on the inside of the hands, but oblong on the outside; and a fleshy excrescence (*caruncula*) appeared, projecting from the rest of the flesh, as if the tops of the nails were bent back and pierced through. The right side was as if transfixed by a spear, a scar being formed over the wound. This right side often emitted blood; so that his tunic and under-garments were frequently besprinkled. Ah! how few, while the crucified servant of the Lord was alive, had the privilege of beholding the sacred wound of the side! But Elias[6] was so fortunate as to be one who, while the saint lived, had the privilege of seeing both [blood and wound]. Happier still was Rufino who touched the precious wound. . . . For he [the saint] most anxiously concealed it from strangers; he concealed it most carefully even from his intimate friends; so that both the brethren who were moderately acquainted with him and also his most devoted followers were for long ignorant thereof. . . . It was his custom to reveal the precious secret to few or none (*raro aut nulli*). . . . After his death there remained on

1 A. Potthast, *Reg. Pont. Rom.*, Berlin, 1874–75, i. 778.
2 *Ib.* i. 790.
3 ii. 113.

1 *Vita et passio S. Cæcilii Cypriani*, ch. vii.
2 See Imbert-Gourbeyre, *Les Stigmatisées*, 1873. He enumerates 125 cases of women and 20 of men who were alleged to have stigmata—80 of them prior to A.D. 1700. A few may be deducted as barely relevant.
3 Celano, *Vita prima*, proleg. and note in the Paris MS.
4 *Vita prima*; *AS*, Oct. ii. 708 f. According to the *Fioretti* (14th cent., but believed to embody contemporary testimony), three of these were Leo, Masseo, and Angelo.
5 So the *Fioretti*; Celano does not indicate the exact date.
6 Vicar-general of the order, and successor of St. Francis. He was not in sympathy, however, with Francis' rule of absolute poverty, and was eventually superseded and disgraced.

him the appearance of the Passion; while he seemed as if he had been recently taken down from the Cross; having his hands and feet transfixed with nails, and his right side as if pierced with a spear. They beheld his flesh, which formerly had been dark, shining with exceeding brightness; they saw his face as it had been the face of an angel. . . . It was wonderful to see, in the middle of his hands and feet, not indeed the punctures of nails, but the nails themselves set in them with the black colour of fresh iron, and the right side reddened with blood. Brethren and sons ran to behold; weeping together they kissed the pious father's hands and feet, and also his right side.'

3. Several notable variations from this narrative are found in somewhat later records. (1) The writing attributed to 'Three Companions,' Leo, Angelo, and Rufino (in a part of it, however, which Sabatier[1] holds to be not of their authorship, yet very ancient) and also the biography of the saint composed by Bonaventura in 1260, represent as crucified not the seraph himself but a man borne by the seraph on his wings. (2) This narrative ascribed to the 'Three Companions' indicates that Francis could not prevent the stigmata from being manifest to his intimate friends;[2] and Bonaventura more emphatically declares that very many (*plurimi*) brethren saw the stigmata during the saint's life, including 'some cardinals owing to their intimacy with the holy man.'[3] (3) Matthew Paris, writing some time before 1259, ignores any appearance of stigmata until fifteen days before Francis' death, represents blood as 'continually flowing' from hands and feet, and refers to the wound in the side being 'open wide.'[4]

4. Celano does not profess to have beheld the stigmata; and, as already stated, he expressly names only two persons who had seen any of them. The narrative attributed to the 'Three Companions' is still less definite as to witnesses. From other sources, however, we have strong confirmation of the main testimony that, at some time or other, stigmata were seen on the person of St. Francis.

(1) Leo, one of his companions on the Verna, after authenticating the saint's autograph benediction (preserved at Assisi), adds the words which may still be read at the foot of the little document:

'The blessed Francis, two years before his death, kept Lent on the Verna, from the Festival of the Assumption of the Holy Virgin to the Festival of St. Michael in September; and the hand of God was laid upon him *per visionem et allocutionem seraphym et impressionem stigmatum Christi in corpore suo*.'[5]

(2) In the *Speculum Perfectionis*, substantially composed before 1247 by Leo, assisted by other 'companions,' there is a brief but distinct reference to the stigmata.

'In sacro monte Alvernae tempore quo recepit stigmata Domini in corpore.'[6]

(3) On the day of Francis' death his vicar-general Elias announced the fact of the stigmata to members of the order in France as follows:

'Not long (*non diu*) before his death our brother and father appeared crucified, bearing in his body five wounds which are truly stigmata of Christ: for his hands and feet bore as if marks (*puncturas*) of nails forming scars, and showing the blackness of nails; while his side appeared pierced with a spear and often exuded blood.'[7]

(4) Salimbeni, in his *Chronica* (1282–87), testifies that Leo, who was present when the corpse of Francis was washed, told him that the saint looked precisely like a crucified man taken down from the Cross.[1]

(5) In 1247, at an assembly of Franciscans in Genoa, Bonifacius, a member of the order, publicly and solemnly declared, in response to a question by John of Parma, general of the order:

'These sinful eyes beheld them [the stigmata]; these sinful hands touched them.'[2]

(6) In a bull of date 1237 Pope Gregory IX. (formerly Cardinal Ugolini), a personal friend of St. Francis, bears official testimony to the reality of the stigmata in hands, feet, and side, both during life and after death ('specie stigmatum divinitus extitit insignitus').[3]

(7) Bonaventura, in his *Legenda S. Francisci* (A.D. 1260), repeats substantially, although, as we have seen, with some variations, Celano's record on the authority of personal friends of the saint.

5. Notwithstanding these testimonies, the unreality of the stigmata (unless fraudulently inflicted by Elias on the night of Francis' death) has been maintained in modern times by Hase,[4] Renan, and others. This disbelief rests (1) on the alleged absence of direct testimony by any actual witness with the doubtful exception of Elias; but the statement of Leo in his *authentication* and the attested declaration of Bonifacius amount practically to such direct testimony; (2) on discrepancies as to details in the various primitive records—discrepancies, however, which do not affect the main points of the testimony; (3) on the admitted doubt or disbelief of the bishop of Olmütz and some other contemporaries, including certain Dominicans and secular clergy,[5] but these had not all the evidence before them, and they were affected by *a priori* considerations, such as the impropriety of representing any one except Christ as possessing the stigmata of the Holy Passion; (4) on suspicions connected with the obsequies of the saint, whose body was hastily coffined and entombed in the morning after the night of his death, while, on the occasion of its translation, the exact place of sepulture was concealed; but the hurried funeral (apart from the frequency of hasty burial in hot climates) was probably due to fear of relic-hunters tearing the body in pieces; and the subsequent concealment may have arisen from suspicion of the Perugians, who were believed to be anxious to possess the body; (5) on the absence of any reference to the stigmata in Gregory IX.'s bull of canonization. Gregory, however, as we have seen, testifies elsewhere to their reality.[6]

6. The testimonies adduced appear to prove, beyond reasonable doubt, that phenomena resembling the stigmata of Christ's Passion appeared in the person of St. Francis on Mt. Verna, and were also seen by numerous witnesses after his death. On the other hand, evidence that the stigmata were continuously on the saint's body during the two years between the Verna vision and his decease is inadequate and burdened with difficulty, while

[1] *Life of St. Francis*, Eng. tr., London, 1894, pp. 375–378. The original record was completed in 1246; but the existing document bears evidence (Sabatier maintains) of mutilation, and the latter part is apparently a summary by a different writer of the later portion of Francis' life.

[2] *AS*, Oct. ii. 741.

[3] *AS*, Oct. ii. 778. He specifies Pope Alexander IV. as having stated in his (Bonaventura's) hearing that he had seen the stigmata; but this pope in his bull *Benigna operatio* (A.D. 1255), while threatening with St. Peter's anger doubters of the miracle, rests his plea for the reality of the stigmata not on his own witness of them, but on the authority of his predecessor, Gregory IX. Bonaventura may have misunderstood Alexander.

[4] *Historia Major*, pp. 339–342.

[5] *Speculum Perfectionis*, ed. Sabatier, preface, p. lxviii.

[6] *Ib.* p. 194; Knox Little, in *Eng. Hist. Rev.* xvii.

[7] *AS*, Oct. ii. 669. Wadding, in his *Annales Minorum* (17th cent.), declares this letter to be a copy of an autograph preserved in a Belgian monastery (*AS*, Oct. ii. 648).

[1] Quoted by Sabatier, *Life of St. Francis*, Eng. tr., p. 438.

[2] Eccleston, *De adventu Fratrum Minorum in Angliam*, Coll. xii. in J. S. Brewer's *Monumenta Franciscana*, Rolls ser., IV. i. p. 51. Eccleston composed this work between 1250 and 1272. Bonifacius probably refers to what he saw and did after St. Francis' death; for during the saint's life he would not have been allowed to touch the wound in the side.

[3] *AS*, Oct. ii. 654. Bonaventura, indeed, in the preface to his Life of St. Francis (*Legenda Major*), states that at first Gregory doubted the reality of the stigmata; but the above testimony indicates that his doubts were dispelled after due investigation.

[4] *Franz von Assisi*, pp. 142–202 (1856 ed.). Hase, however, eventually adopted another view (see below).

[5] *AS*, Oct. ii. 654–658.

[6] See Sabatier, *Life of St. Francis*, Eng. tr., p. 438; and Knox Little, *Life of St. Francis*, pp. 315–317; both writers reply in detail to Hase's arguments.

the minute details given by Celano and others on reported testimony receive scant corroboration from eye-witnesses. For (1) no one actually declares that he had seen the stigmata during that interval; (2) only two persons, Elias and Rufino, are expressly stated to have seen or touched any of the wounds during Francis' life; (3) Elias testifies only to the appearance (or re-appearance) of the stigmata 'not long' before the saint's death, without either asserting or denying earlier stigmatization;[1] (4) Celano, indeed, as we have seen, states that Francis revealed the secret of the stigmata to few or none ('raro aut nulli'); yet, even supposing, as Bonaventura declares, that Francis, after the Verna vision, wore sandals and gloves for concealment, the wounds in his hands, if they continued to exist, could not have escaped fairly frequent observation. Accordingly, Bonaventura, perceiving doubtless this impossibility, yet believing in the continued existence of the stigmata, contradicts Celano and writes that *plurimi* saw them. (5) But, if very many saw them, how account for wide-spread early doubts arising after the saint's death as to the reality of the wounds, before adequate testimony to their existence was furnished[2]—doubts which were regarded as of sufficient importance to occasion two papal bulls denouncing doubters in 1237? (6) Elias, with every motive to magnify the miracle, writes, not, like Celano, of 'excrescences of flesh' and of 'heads and points of nails,' but simply of hands and feet having '*as if* the marks of nails' and 'shewing the blackness of nails.'

How much of the earliest records can we safely regard as true? We may accept (1) the main point of the narratives of Celano and others as to the saint's vision of a crucified seraph or man, in so far as that record is confirmed by Leo (who was with him) in his authentication of Francis' benediction; (2) the statement, also confirmed by Leo in that authentication, as well as by the *Speculum*, that on this occasion certain stigmata of the Passion appeared on the saint's person; (3) the testimony of Elias, of Pope Gregory IX., and probably of Bonifacius, that at the saint's death, and therefore presumably 'not long' before it, the stigmata were also visible. On the other hand, the continuance of the stigmata over two years, and several details in the narratives of Celano and Bonaventura, must be set aside as legendary accretions, occasionally inconsistent with each other, and the outcome of mere reported testimony in which fancy is mingled with fact.

7. Of the facts thus accepted three explanations have been offered.

(1) The stigmata were 'divine manifestations'—'in the true sense of the word miraculous'—given by God to St. Francis, in order to 'bear witness to his special sanctity' and spiritual likeness to Christ, as well as to vindicate the truth of his teaching. This was the view of his personal followers and of the great majority of his contemporaries; it is still upheld by most Roman Catholics and by some representatives of Reformed Churches.[3] This explanation harmonizes with the mediæval religious viewpoint and received general acceptance in mediæval Christendom. Yet the doubts of the contemporary bishop of Olmütz and others, grounded chiefly on dogmatic reasons, show that even in that age, and even when allowance is made for the prejudice and jealousy of secular clergy and rival orders, there were some to whom the alleged imprinting of stigmata by divine action appeared unbecoming. Most modern Protestants and probably many devout Roman Catholics realize as almost grotesque an alleged attestation of special holiness through infliction of bodily wounds.

(2) Another explanation is that Francis, during his vision on Verna, while in a state of ecstasy, and without distinct consciousness, inflicted on himself the stigmata, being moved thereto by an ecstatic desire to be 'crucified with Christ' and to become 'conformable unto His death.' This explanation is rendered tenable by the rejection of the details about 'fleshy excrescences' and about heads and points of nails under the flesh, as being inadequately attested, and by the limitation of the stigmata to what Elias calls '*as if* marks of nails' and 'scars in hands and feet,' along with 'a side which *appeared* as if pierced with a spear.'[1] One difficulty of accepting this view rests on the renewal of the stigmatization not long before Francis' death, when he may well have had a repetition of the vision, but when he may be assumed to have been too feeble for any considerable self-wounding such as would lead to a recognition of the stigmata of the Cross by his followers; and, even if we admit that enfeebled persons sometimes exert for a few moments in delirium præter-normal strength, could self-stigmatization, in such circumstances, have been effected by the saint without observation by others? The difficulty, however, of accounting, on this theory, for the later stigmata 'not long' before death would be removed, if we supposed (what Elias's real character, afterwards disclosed, renders conceivable) that Elias himself re-inflicted on the saint's corpse wound-marks which then no longer existed, but which Elias believed to have formerly existed in the living body for some time after the Verna vision. Francis died in the evening; Elias, as vicar-general, would be guardian of the body over night; and what is known of his ambition, worldliness, and intrigues, which eventually issued in his deposition, renders it not incredible that, for the great glory of the order, he should have conceived and carried out a scheme to relieve the former real stigmatization from such doubt as Francis' own habitual reticence had engendered.

(3) It is not necessary, however, to assume miraculous divine intervention, ecstatic self-infliction by the saint himself, or fraudulent production by another. The mutual influence of soul and body is a subject as yet only partially investigated. 'We have caught,' as Sabatier writes, 'but fleeting glimpses into the domain of mental pathology.'[2] The extraordinary is not to be identified with the miraculous; and we know enough not to be over-sceptical of the power of man's higher nature to impress itself, in certain cases, on the lower, and to cause the reproduction so far in the body of what is generated in the soul. The influence, *e.g.*, of a mother's thoughts on the person of her unborn child is widely accepted; the wonders of hypnotism and mesmerism are well known; and in numerous instances a man's character is observed gradually to mould his face. Granted, moreover, that in the great majority of alleged cases of stigmatism there is either some ground for suspecting imposture or at least the lack of adequate evidence of reality,

[1] Sabatier, indeed, inclines (Eng. tr., p. 436) to accept the reading *nam diu* for *non diu*; but there is no ancient authority for what is apparently a conjectural emendation grounded on what it was thought that Elias *ought* to have written.

[2] 'Multi de his (stigmatibus) per orbem dubitabant' (Eccleston, *loc. cit.*).

[3] Jörgensen, *Den helige Frans af Assisi*, French tr., pp. 434–448, Eng. tr., p. 291 ff.; Cuthbert, *Life of St. Francis*, p. 337; Knox Little (Anglican), *St. Francis of Assisi*, p. 319.

[1] Hausrath, *Die Arnoldisten*, p. 224; Bournet, *S. François d'Assise*; Hase, *Handbuch der prot. Polemik*, Leipzig, 1862, p. 492.

[2] Eng. tr., p. 434.

there remain some well-attested instances in which the sentiments of a soul, filled with thoughts of Christ's Passion, have been reproduced in bodily manifestations analogous to those recorded in the case of St. Francis.

8. We must leave out of consideration the celebrated case of St. Catherine of Siena, who testified before notable witnesses that after Holy Communion she felt in her body the stigmata of the Crucifixion, including those of nails in the middle of her hands; for the reality of such bodily stigmata is manifestly disputable without impugning Catherine's sincerity. But the following authenticated stigmatizations, recorded in modern times, render credible other instances less adequately attested.

(1) The case of Maria von Moerl of the Tyrol, in whose hands, feet, and side stigmata began to appear in 1834, after Holy Communion or meditation on the Passion; she survived until 1868. J. J. von Görres, who relates her experience, states that stigmata on her person were seen by thousands of observers. He himself saw her repeatedly in her ordinary condition as well as in her ecstasies, and clearly discerned the stigmata. He testifies also that there was in her case 'no previous learning of a part; the whole proceeds naturally from her inward self; nothing forced or exaggerated can be observed in the representation.'[1]

(2) Maria Dominica Lazzari of Capriana, about whom Dr. Leonard dei Cloche, director of the Civil and Military Hospital at Trent, testifies that he saw her repeatedly in a state of ecstasy in 1833–34. 'On the outside of her hands,' he declares, 'about the middle, rose a black spot, like the head of a thick nail, perfectly round. At the top of the right foot, about the centre, was a mark like those of the hands. Her mind appeared calm: her body was in a tremble. A wound in her side has been seen, only by stealth, by her mother and sisters. "I feel frightful pains," she said, "in every part of my body."'[2]

(3) Louise Lateau, of Bois d'Haine in Belgium, who bore an excellent character, was neither specially emotional nor exceptionally imaginative, was accustomed to hard work, and was one of the most helpful young women in her village. In 1868 she began to notice blood coming from her hands, feet, and side on Fridays after meditation on Christ's Passion. Dr. Ferdinand Lefebvre, Professor of Pathology in Louvain, devoted much attention to her case for six weeks, and took about 100 medical friends to examine the phenomena. She was put to various tests, to ascertain if the wounds were due to artificial causes. Thus Lefebvre called on a day when he had told her he would *not* come, and found her in an ecstasy, with blood newly exuded from her forehead and right hand. On another occasion, in the presence of two eminent physicians, he caused an artificial blister to be raised, similar to one which had appeared (so she declared) without her intervention. During her ecstasy the natural blister emitted blood, but the artificial one yielded none. The glove test was also applied. A leather glove, put on one hand, was tied and sealed at the wrist; when it was removed, on Good Friday, the blood flowed as before. It has been suggested that perforation with a needle may have taken place; but the hæmorrhage was preceded by the formation of a vesicle which became distended with serum, and spontaneously burst, after which blood flowed for several hours.[3]

Such cases appear to prove that stigmatization may result from extraordinary yet not supernatural intensification of that natural influence of soul over body which to some extent exists in all persons but is particularly potent in the case of intensely religious natures at times of special spiritual impression and ecstatic exaltation. This is substantially the view regarding the stigmata of St. Francis taken by Trench,[4] Sabatier,[5] and Doreau.[6]

LITERATURE.—i. *EARLY AUTHORITIES.*—De Celano, *Vita prima S. Francisci*, London, 1908; Bonaventura, *Legenda Major*, do. 1904; Autograph Benediction of St. Francis, with note by Leo (*AS*, Oct. ii. 666), preserved in the Church of St. Francis at Assisi; Letter of Elias (*AS*, Oct. ii. 668 f.); *Speculum Perfectionis*, ed. P. Sabatier, Paris, 1898, Eng. tr., London, 1898; *Legenda Trium Sociorum* (*AS*, Oct. ii.); *Fioretti di S. Francesco*, tr. T. W. Arnold, London, 1908; Thomas of Eccleston, *De adventu Fratrum Minorum in Angliam*, in *Monumenta Franciscana*, Rolls ser., IV. i. ii., ed. J. S. Brewer and R. Howlett, do. 1858–82; Salimbeni, *Chronica* (in *Analecta Franciscana*, iii., Quaracchi, 1885–1912); Matthew Paris, *Chronica majora*, ed. H. R. Luard (Rolls ser. LVII. i–vii), London, 1872–83.

ii. *LATER.*—L. Wadding, *Annales Minorum*, 8 vols., Lyons, 1625; K. Hase, *Franz von Assisi*, Leipzig, 1856, new ed., do. 1892; R. C. Trench, *Lectures on Medieval Church History*[2], London, 1879, ch. on 'Sects'; A. Bournet, *S. François d'Assise: Étude sociale et médicale*, Paris, 1893; P. Sabatier, *Vie de saint François d'Assise*, do. 1894, Eng. tr., London and New York, 1894; T. Cotelle, *Saint François d'Assise: Etude médicale*, Paris, 1895; P. Doreau, *Saint François d'Assise et son œuvre*, do. 1903; W. J. Knox Little, *St. Francis of Assisi; his Times, Life, and Work*, London, 1904, and art. in *English Hist. Rev.* xvii. [1902] 643 ff.; J. Jörgensen, *Den helige Frans af Assisi*, Copenhagen, 1907, French tr. T. de Wyzewa, Paris, 1909, Eng. tr. T. O'Connor Sloane, London, 1912; Father Cuthbert, *Life of St. Francis of Assisi*, London, 1912.

iii. *STIGMATIZATION.*—A. Tholuck, *Vermischte Schriften*, Hamburg, 1839, i.; L. Boré, *Les Stigmatisées du Tyrol*, Paris, 1847; (anon.), *Die Stigmatisierten des 19ten Jahrh.*, Regensburg, 1877; J. J. von Görres, *The Stigmata; a Hist. of Various Cases*, Eng. tr., London, 1883; A. Imbert-Gourbeyre, *Les Stigmatisées*, 2 vols., Paris, 1873, [2]1886, *La Stigmatisation, l'extase divine et les miracles de Lourdes*, 2 vols., do. 1894; A. Hausrath, *Die Arnoldisten*, Leipzig, 1895; O. Zöckler, *Askese und Mönchthum*, 2 vols., Frankfort, 1897; A. Macalister, art. 'Stigmatization,' in *EBr*[11] xxv. 917 ff.

H. COWAN.

STOICS.—The Stoics were the members of a philosophical school founded in Athens about 300 B.C., which in its developments became characteristic of the whole Hellenistic area and age. Rooted in the strong moral instincts of the Semites, it grew to embrace the scientific knowledge of the Greeks, and branched out in the logical and practical methods of Roman law and education. Its range in time extends over the three centuries before the Christian era and the first three centuries of that era; that is, it synchronizes with the history of the Roman Empire. Since that time its forces have been absorbed in the development of Christianity.

1. Origin and history.—The system was founded by Zeno, born at Citium in Cyprus in 336 B.C. His father was a merchant of purple, and as such a great traveller; the 'Socratic books' which he brought home from Athens were eagerly read by the young Zeno, and drew him to visit the Greek city. Whether Zeno himself was of Phoenician or of Greek descent concerns us little; that at Athens he was nicknamed 'the Phoenician' indicates that he brought with him to that city an atmosphere of Phoenician sentiment and morality. At Athens he attached himself to Crates of Thebes, then the representative of the Cynic school.[1] In Crates Zeno found the moral enthusiasm which seeks the good at however high a price, and which welcomes want and suffering as the discipline of individual character; but he also found a revolt against scientific knowledge and the ordered decencies of life from which he was soon eager to dissociate himself. He therefore became in turn a disciple of Stilpo the Megarian and Polemo the Academic. All these schools belonged to the Socratic succession; but, when Zeno turned his attention to the writings of Heraclitus (*q.v.*), he forged a link also with the Ionic philosophers.[2] About the year 300 B.C. he founded a school of his own, which (broadly considered) was based on the concretion of all these schools of thought, and the dogma of complete harmony (ὁμολογία, *convenientia*) in God, the universe, and man. Conversely, those of his followers in any period who failed to grasp his teaching in all its width are seen to fall back upon the more partial teaching of the constituent philosophies. The followers of Zeno were at first called Zenonians, but afterwards, from the 'picture porch' (στοὰ ποικιλή) where he delivered his lectures, Stoics. The first published work of Zeno was his Πολιτεία, or *Commonwealth*, written while he was still a member of the Cynic school. His picture of

[1] See his *Stigmata*, pp. 171–197, being a translation of part of his *Die christliche Mystik*, 4 vols., Regensburg, 1836–42.

[2] Von Görres (pp. 197–211), who quotes from a medical journal of Milan, embodying the description; L. Boré, *Les Stigmatisées du Tyrol*, Paris, 1847.

[3] Lefebvre, *Louise Lateau: sa vie, ses extases, ses stigmates: Etude médicale*, Louvain, 1870; G. E. Day, art. 'Louise Lateau,' in *Macmillan's Mag.*, xxiii. [1871] 488 ff.; *Brit. Med. Journal*, 6th and 20th May 1871.

[4] *Med. Ch. Hist.* p. 235.

[5] Eng. tr., pp. 433–443.

[6] *Saint François*, pp. 63–66.

[1] See art. CYNICS.

[2] See art. IONIC PHILOSOPHY.

a perfect state embraces the whole world, so that a man says, not 'I am a citizen of Athens,' but 'I am a citizen of the world.' The laws of this state must be prescribed by nature, not by convention. There must be no images or temples there, for these are unworthy of the deity; no sacrifices, because he is not to be appeased by gifts; no law-courts, for the citizens must not dispute; no statues, for the true adornment of a city is the virtue of its inhabitants; no gymnasia, for the youth must study virtue and not idle exercises. There must be no distinction of classes, for all must be wise men; no distinctive dress for the sexes, for their virtues and duties are the same; no delicate scruples as to the burning or burying of the dead, for souls, not bodies, are of importance. And in this state love must be master. Although the *Commonwealth* is, strictly speaking, a Cynic rather than a Stoic production, it represents the fundamental aims of the Stoic philosophy.

All the main doctrines of Stoicism are attributed to Zeno, but before describing these it may be well to give a short history of the chief teachers of the school, so that both deviations from Zeno's teaching and enrichments of it may be described under their proper headings.

Of the 'companions of Zeno' **Persaeus** of Citium pursued a political career, taking service with Antigonus Gonatas, king of Macedonia. **Aratus** of Soli was welcomed at the same court, and is known by his *Phaenomena*, an astronomical treatise translated by Cicero, largely used by Virgil in his *Georgics*, and containing the phrase 'for we are all his family' (τοῦ γὰρ καὶ γένος ἐσμὲν) quoted by St. Paul.[1] **Sphaerus** introduced the new philosophy at Alexandria. **Aristo** of Chios fell back on Cynic views; and **Dionysius** of Heraclea 'deserted' to Cyrenaicism. Zeno's successor was **Cleanthes** of Assos (331–232 B.C.), whose *Hymn to Zeus* is not only the prototype of Hellenistic hymnology, but also a fairly complete summary of Stoic theory as applied to religious worship. Cleanthes (*q.v.*) is the theologian of the Stoic school, and gives a special emphasis to that part of its doctrine which is derived from Heraclitus, including the theories of the 'universal fire,' of the Logos (λόγος), and of tone (τόνος, *intentio*). His hold upon the public seems to have been small, and it was reserved for his successor, **Chrysippus** (*q.v.*) of Soli (280–206 B.C.), to popularize the school and so become its second founder. His methods were illustration (for which the whole Greek poetry and especially the writings of Euripides were ransacked) and argument on the lines of the syllogism. His bias was towards the Academic element in Stoicism, and there is some weakening with regard to its first principles not only in his writings, but also in those of his successors, such as **Boethus** of Sidon, **Zeno** of Tarsus, **Diogenes** of Seleucia (238–150 B.C.), and **Antipater** of Tarsus (200–129 B.C.). In the 2nd cent. B.C. the Stoic teachers began definitely to measure their principles by comparison and conflict with the rival schools of the Academy, now flourishing under the guidance of Carneades and of Epicurus.[2]

At the end of that century we find Stoicism translated into the environment of the Roman nobility by **Panaetius** (189–109 B.C.), **Posidonius** (135–51 B.C.), and **Hecato**, all men of position and literary attainment in the island of Rhodes. None of these are philosophical teachers in the strictest sense; they were to a large extent men of letters and science owning a partial allegiance to a particular school of thought (*secta*). In particular, their respect for the writings of Plato led them to accept various doctrines which in fact harmonized better with the teaching of the Academic school. To the resultant teaching the name of the 'middle Stoa' has since been given. This name represents not a distinct philosophical system, but a partial failure to grasp the fundamentals of the system, which paved the way to the 'eclecticism' dominant at Rome in the time of Cicero, in which incongruous elements taken from all the philosophies were combined in ever-varying dishes to meet the ephemeral tastes of the debating-room and the dining-hall.

The more systematic teaching of Stoicism revived in the 1st cent. of the empire at Rome under a series of popular teachers, such as **Attalus, L. Annaeus Cornutus, Seneca, C. Musonius Rufus, Euphrates of Tyre,** and **Epictetus** (*q.v.*). Drawn from all nationalities and from every class, these teachers have it in common that they use such forms as the lecture, the poem, and the epistle, in which the fundamental doctrines of the system are assumed, but not taught. This method postulates a previous training in principles, though in practice such training must often have been as defective as the theological knowledge of the average listener to a modern sermon. All these teachers, as well as **Marcus Aurelius** (*q.v.*) the emperor, whose writings are addressed to himself, afford valuable illustrations of Stoic doctrine without giving us much help as to its real essence. Their teaching is usually orthodox, and therefore free from the vagaries of the 'middle Stoa'; but the more difficult theories tend to disappear, whilst the application to practice becomes all-important.

2. Teaching. — Reverting to the teaching of Zeno, we find that he took over the division of philosophy, generally accepted in his time, into the three sections of logic, physics, and ethics; but he held that these three were inseparable, since no one of them could be understood apart from the two others.

(*a*) *Logic.*—In logic Stoicism asserts the certainty of knowledge, as against the Academics, who deny this; and this assertion implies the existence of a 'criterion' (κριτήριον) by which the true can be distinguished from the false. Since a final and absolute criterion of truth is undiscoverable, we shall not expect to find that Zeno discovered it; such a criterion is necessarily an ideal towards which only an approximation can be made. Zeno and his successors were catholic in their investigations into the theory of knowledge, and, though we find a general sketch of their doctrine given in Cicero's *Academica*, we can hardly present it as a consistent system. Knowledge is attained by reason; but, since reason may fall, the aim is to keep reason upright. Men disagree; some therefore assert what is true, others what only seems to be true. Taking the knowledge that comes through the senses as the simplest type, we distinguish first the 'sensation,' which may be described as a pulsation which passes from an 'object' through the sense-organ to the mind, or *vice versa*; as a result there is impressed upon the soul an 'imprint' (φαντασία, *visum*). This imprint necessarily corresponds to the object if the intellect and the sense-organ are both healthy, the object really there, and the place and manner in accord; if these conditions are not fulfilled, the imprint corresponds to an imagined object only, *i.e.* to a 'phantasm.' The true imprint or mind-picture is distinguished from the false by its greater clearness (ἐνάργεια, *perspicuitas*). To determine whether the requisite clearness exists is the function of the will, which gives or refuses its assent (συγκατάθεσις). If this assent is given weakly or hastily, we attain 'opinion,' and not 'truth.' If it is rightly given, the truth so ascertained should be fixed in the mind by a firm grasp (κατάληψις, *comprehensio*), and retained there by memory.

Single truths when remembered can be compared, contrasted, and so forth, and thus the objects which they represent are subjected to 'reason's work of comparison' (*collatio rationis*). From comparison the reason develops general notions, which therefore have no real existence in themselves, but only a sort of existence in our minds. Yet these general notions could not be so developed unless they already existed in the mind, at any rate in a potential form. The doctrine of the *tabula rasa* is often attributed to the Stoics, but appears rather to be opposed to their system. It is true that we may trace the growth of ideas from the outside to the soul, but equally we are entitled to regard the soul as possessing all the ideas first in a rudimentary shape; they are stimulated and clarified, but not created, by contact with experience. The rudimentary or 'inborn' ideas are part of the soul's inheritance from that universal reason of which the soul is a fragment. The reconciliation and development of this theory is a most difficult matter, and so it was found by students of Stoicism, and increasingly in the intellectual decadence of the early Christian centuries. The question 'What is the Stoic criterion?' was probably a standing puzzle, which might be answered by the terms 'reason,' 'will,' 'clearness,' 'sensation,' and so forth, according to the bias of the individual. The practical application

---

[1] Ac 17[28].
[2] See artt. ACADEMY, ACADEMICS, EPICUREANS.

of the Stoic logic is easier to define. Believing truth to be attainable, the Stoic was in principle dogmatic; finding error to be common, he was no less critical. Careful observation, deliberation, memory, and other agencies must all be trained so as to reduce error; and the final issue gives assurance only if it records an agreement between individual observations and general theories, and between individual judgment and the 'common sense' or universal judgment of the race.

The study of definitions, syllogisms, paradoxes, and the like was all included in the Stoic logic, which also embraced the whole field of etymology, grammar, dialectic, and rhetoric.

(*b*) *Physics*.—Under the heading of physics are included all the problems of metaphysics, physics in the modern sense, astronomy, religion, anthropology, and psychology; in fact, we might briefly say that physics includes all subjects except logic and ethics. More definitely, physics is the study (1) of the universe, (2) of man. As regards the universe, the Stoics start from the 'four elements' of earth, air, fire, and water, which have remained over in common thought as a debris from the Ionic philosophies. These four elements are re-grouped in two classes as 'mind' and 'matter,' 'active' and 'passive,' 'soul' and 'body,' the first constituent of each of these pairs being more or less closely associated with 'fire,' and a distinction being made between the elemental or 'creative' fire and the destructive fire of the domestic hearth. But, although these various dualisms have a place in the Stoic system, they are all subject to a higher monism, that of the one elemental stuff or 'body' referred to in the paradox 'Soul is body.'

The history of the universe starts with the elemental or all-pervasive fire, which is also the Deity and the 'First Cause.' This fire is in turn pervaded by the Logos, or ordering force, which from one point of view is single and divine, and from another is made up of countless 'seed-powers' (σπερματικοὶ λόγοι) which are the germs of future individual existences. The primal fire, by processes of successive thickening and corresponding dilution of strain (τόνος), converts itself into the four elements, and these in turn into the various orders of living things. Of these gods and men constitute the highest class, dominated by the reasoning soul (νοῦς), which has its home in the ruling part (ἡγεμονικόν). Among gods are counted the sun and heavenly bodies, which are beings possessed of will and motion from within. Below the reasoning class come animals, which possess soul (ψυχή), but not reason; they also possess something corresponding to the reasoning powers, emotions, and inclinations of reasoning beings. Plants possess growth-power (φύσις), which is in turn a kind of soul; and even inanimate objects have cohesion (ἕξις), though without growth. Since all these powers are fragments of divine force, we may speak of 'God in the stone.' Thus the whole universe is pervaded by deity in a graded scale; and God is related to the universe as soul to body. It is, however, a paradox to say that 'God is the universe,' and the Stoic creed corresponds very imperfectly to modern pantheism.[1]

Body is combined with soul in its varying grades by the principle of pervasive mixture (κρᾶσις δι' ὅλων). Nowhere is there an absolute line of demarcation, and, as all beings have proceeded from God, so they will all be absorbed in deity at the general conflagration (ἐκπύρωσις) with which the history of the universe ends. Then God becomes 'all in all,' and from Him commences a new era of development.

During each stage the universe is controlled by the divine principle of order, which we may call the Divine Law or Destiny, but for which the most appropriate name is Providence. Providence is by its nature beneficent, chiefly in relation to reasoning beings; in this sense we may say that the whole universe is made for the good of man. The wickedness, suffering, and destruction everywhere seen in the world appear to contradict the belief in Providence, and the favourite subject of the Stoic sermon or essay is the surmounting of this contradiction.

Religion is the recognition by man of his relation to deity, and its essential features are not ceremony or sacrifice, but prayer, self-examination, and praise. Hence the early Stoics found themselves in conflict with conventional religion; later, and especially in Roman life, the Stoics reconciled themselves with it by the principles of interpretation and conformity. The work of Cornutus on the gods shows us this system in full play. Here the old gods of the Graeco-Roman mythology are interpreted as natural powers, and the legends concerning them are converted into parables conveying scientific truths. This method greatly aided the extension of Stoicism by making it a support of traditional customs and beliefs; at the same time its intensive power was weakened by the habit of compromise. In particular, the Stoics learnt to associate themselves with the practice of animal sacrifices just at the time when the general conscience was revolting against it as meaningless and cruel.

The most important chapter in the Stoic physics deals with the nature of man, who is the universe on a small scale, or a 'microcosm.' Each human soul is a fragment of the universal divine force, yet not completely sundered from its parent-stock. Thus, in the words of Aratus, 'we are all his family.' The soul is the ruling part (ἡγεμονικόν) of the man, and is possessed of reason; yet in its various parts or faculties it is spread throughout the whole man, and is found in all grades, even the lowest. Thus the 'five senses,' sight, hearing, smell, taste, and touch, are all functions of the soul, each working through its appropriate sense-organ, the eye, ear, nose, palate, and skin. These associate man with the outer world by way of knowledge; others, such as speech, motion (breathing, digestion), and procreation, by way of action. Thus human nature consists broadly in knowledge and action, and is guided by reason and will. The highest philosophy is to recognize that reason and will are ultimately one. Both are subject to disturbance, owing to the relaxation of the divine strain, or 'tone,' which gives men individuality and at the same time wilfulness or sin. The disturbances of the soul are diseased states (πάθη) or tempests (*emotiones*), but the discussion of them falls within the department of ethics.

The doctrine of the life of the soul after the death of the body was accepted in a general way, but without emphasis, by the Stoics; but in truth the Stoic system does not admit the existence of the body at all; for even the lowest parts of the body, the hair and the nails, possess φύσις, or vegetable growth. The embryo, according to the Stoics, is a vegetable; and apparently the Stoics vaguely conceived that at death the man was parted in two, the higher developments of soul finding their way to an ultimate reunion with the Deity, the lower sinking to vegetable and inorganic life and ultimately disappearing in the four elements ('earth to earth, ashes to ashes'). From either point of view the individuality is ultimately lost; and, as in the Roman period the hope of a future life was a passionate clinging to personality, the Stoic teachers meet this hope with an increasingly firm negation. In the earlier

[1] See art. PANTHEISM (Greek and Roman).

periods the whole question is left in the region of myth and fancy, most characteristically represented by Virgil's pictures of purgatory and Elysium.

(*c*) *Ethics*.—Ethics is built upon physics: what man ought is derived from what man is. This transition includes a logical contradiction which is unsurmountable. In physics the whole universe appears as 'good'; yet this 'good' is without colour, for it is contrasted with no evil. On the other hand, in ethics men are sharply divided into the 'good' and the 'bad.' The Cynics avoided this contradiction by ignoring physics and declaring the ethical standard to be self-illuminating or 'intuitive'; but to such a solution the Stoics were determinedly opposed. The starting-point of their own theory is to be found in the gradations of soul, by which a hierarchy of rank is established among living beings. Virtue for man is to maintain his rank as son and equal of God; vice is to fall to the level of the animals or the plants.

That 'virtue is the supreme good,' and the 'wise man' alone happy; that external circumstances, such as health, wealth, and good name, do not (as the Academics say) contribute to happiness even one atom; that a short and a long life may equally be complete—these and the like are paradoxes which Stoicism draws from its Cynic root. Its special contribution to philosophy is the elaborate analysis by which virtue is given a definite meaning, which in turn can be applied to all circumstances in life so as to guide and support the individual in his choice. This rule of life was at first summed up in the phrase 'to live consistently,' later 'to live consistently with nature.' With each successive teacher the formula was developed, the principle being best maintained by the phrase of Chrysippus, 'to live according to scientific knowledge of the phenomena of nature, doing nothing which the Universal Law forbids, which is the Right Reason which pervades all things, and is the same as Zeus, the Lord of the ordering of this world.' On the other hand, the practical applications follow more quickly from the phrase of Diogenes of Babylon, 'to take a reasonable course in choosing or refusing things in accordance with nature.' Nearly all modern writers on Stoicism assert, with Zeller, that the Stoics deliberately softened their original teaching so as to accommodate it to the practical needs of their hearers. This is a misapprehension: the Stoics from the first were occupied in interpreting their rule in a practical sense, and such deviations as occur are due to the influence (largely unconscious) of Academic teaching on Chrysippus and his successors of the 'middle Stoa.' That hearers also unconsciously influence their teachers is true of all schools of thought.

The general ethical teaching of the Stoics is made most clear to us in Cicero's *de Finibus*. All animals, we learn, as soon as they are born, seek to maintain their life and their bodily wholeness; thus self-preservation is the first law of nature. Later they seek to propagate their race, and at the same time feel an affection for their offspring; this is the second law. Man, however, is from the first a social animal, and is possessed of a love of knowledge; hence social and intellectual ends are specially characteristic of the human race; such is the third law. From such a group of natural laws we select certain objects, such as health, well-being, long life, which are set before us as aims to be attained, whereas their opposites are to be avoided. These are the προηγμένα and ἀποπροηγμένα of the Stoic system, and its critics are never weary of ridiculing these un-Greek terms borrowed from the hierarchies of Eastern courts. In our words, these ends are respectively 'desirable' and 'undesirable'; but none of them is 'good' or 'evil,' nor can we reach good by adding together any number of things desirable ('Bonum non fit accessione'). How, then, do we know the good? When a man has practised the attainment of the desirable, when he has learnt to prefer the higher to the lower amongst these, when he has disciplined his members and attuned his thoughts until without hesitation or slip he always attains the best in the individual case—when (*i.e.*) by training and self-discipline he has become possessed of true wisdom—then there will flash before his eyes at some one moment the 'vision of the good,' never afterwards to be lost to his view. This is the moment of 'conversion.' In modern terms we might perhaps say that 'virtue is defined by the intuition of the moral expert, or man of good life.' Logically this definition may leave much to be desired; its practical and educational value is attested by experience.

All virtue is one, yet it has many forms, such as the four virtues of popular philosophy—courage, wisdom, justice, and temperance. The practical workings of these are expounded in Cicero's *de Officiis*, in accordance with the teachings of Panaetius and Hecato; and, as we might expect, this ever-popular treatise is very largely Academic in its details. Opposed to the virtues are the four vices—fear, discontent, greed, and elation. These follow from weakness or ignorance; fear, *e.g.*, is derived from the error of seeing evils in the future when in truth only things undesirable are threatening. The later Stoics chiefly denounce anger as a vice. All the virtues and the vices are exhibited in social action, and the Stoic is before all things a man who lives in society, marries, and participates in the politics of his city: cloistered virtue ('vivere in umbra') is a form of cowardice.

The unbending gravity of the Stoic sage readily recommended itself as an ideal to the Roman nobility; but the later Stoics recognized the objection that the complete absence of the softer feelings implied an unattractive, if not repellent, character. Still rejecting all stormy states of the soul, they admitted that its surface should be like that of a sunny sea, not that of an ice-bound lake. Thus they came to find room for the 'good emotions,' now commonly called the 'affections.' These are identical in classification with the vices, but their play does not exceed the bounds of reason: 'caution' stops short of fear, and 'joy' of elation. Almost we admit that 'desipere in loco' may be virtuous.

The Stoic system of ethics thus developed was admirably suited for education, and is in fact the basis of all the traditional maxims which are today imparted to the young. Never does the Stoic teacher speak with a harsh voice, as his critics suggest, not knowing that rigid general principles must always be tempered in their practical application by consideration for person and place. If the soul of the 'wise man' is always tense, yet none knows better than the Stoic that 'relaxation' is needed by the young; if perfect action implies perfect knowledge, nevertheless it is quite practical to 'learn by doing.' Thus the youngest child may begin to 'get on,' *i.e.* to become a 'proficient,' and his well-wishers will not hurry him unduly to the stage of conversion. This practical application of Stoicism became, through Quintilian, the foundation of the modern theory of education.

3. Practical influence.—No system of philosophy, at any rate in the Western world, has borne fruit in practice to an extent comparable with that of Stoicism. Like all other great reforms, it was first ridiculed, then hated, and finally adopted. Ridicule of Stoicism is found in Cicero's speeches and in Horace, and through them is familiar to the modern literary world. Hatred of the system is most conspicuous in Lucretius.[1] Of its adoption Rhodes is the most typical example in the Greek-speaking world; but similar movements took place in all the great cities of Asia Minor and Egypt, and notably in Tarsus. In the West, Stoic principles are taken for granted in all Roman literature from the beginning of the Christian era. Of the greatest interest is perhaps the use of Stoicism by kings and governors. Among the successors to Alexander's empire many of the most eminent associated themselves with Stoic ministers. The Roman nobility adopted the system from Panaetius; the legislation of the Gracchi, the pure administration of men like Mucius Scaevola the *pontifex* and Rutilius Rufus, and the new spirit of Roman law embodied in the theories of the *ius gentium* and the *ius naturae* are all due to its influence. Under the early empire all good administrators were men imbued with Stoic principles; and it is not too

[1] See art. LUCRETIUS, §§ 8 and 9.

much to say that through Stoicism the Roman world-empire found itself a soul. The 'Stoic opposition' under Nero and his successors has become famous through the pages of Tacitus; but the passive resistance of such men as Thrasea has falsely suggested that Stoicism is in its essence individualistic and ethical. The examples of Seneca and Marcus Aurelius on the other side show its fuller development in social and political life.

4. Stoicism and Christianity.—Stoicism came early into contact with Christianity through the apostle Paul. The similarity in tone and content between parts of the Pauline epistles, the writings of Seneca, and the records of the teaching of Epictetus has long been familiar to students of Christian theology; the simple explanation is that Paul was brought up in Tarsus in a society permeated by Stoic thought.[1] Quite appropriately, he first appears in Christian history through his 'conversion,' in which he parted alike from Hebraism and from Stoicism. He realized that ethics can never be rooted in science, or the ideal in matter-of-fact; he therefore refused to give his allegiance to science or his admiration to the cosmos, and found himself in a higher region of 'spirit' in which 'faith' is the path-finder. The 'wise man' whom the Stoics could never find among their neighbours he recognized without hesitation in the Christ. But in the new religious belief the old foundations of the philosophy survive. Paul's use of the term 'body' is purely Stoic, and so are his whole analysis of 'bodies,' earthly, animal, celestial, and so forth, his analysis of human nature, and his conception of the functions of religion. His views of the divine birth of Jesus, and of His resurrection as the type of that of the Christian believer, are unintelligible except in terms of Stoicism.

Much controversy has arisen as to the origin of the terms 'the Word'[2] and 'the Holy Spirit' in Christian theology, and here we can only note that both terms were in familiar use in the Stoic school at the same epoch. They cannot, however, be claimed as distinctively Stoic. But the way of thinking according to which God is at the same time one and many belongs to the very core of Stoicism. Therefore, whilst the doctrine of the Trinity is somewhat dimly adumbrated by St. Paul, it has long ago been noted that its principle finds full expression in the earlier writings of Seneca: 'To whatever country we are banished, two things go with us, our part in the starry heavens above and the world around, our sole right in the moral instincts of our own hearts. Such is the gift to us of the supreme Power which shaped the Universe. That Power we sometimes call the "all-ruling God," sometimes the "incorporeal Wisdom" which is the creator of mighty works, sometimes the "divine Spirit" which spreads through things great and small with duly strung tone . . .'[1] The quotation is not complete, nor is it suggested that Seneca's theology would have satisfied an inquisitor. But, on the other hand, it may be fearlessly maintained that the Christian cult of 'the Holy Spirit' and the ecclesiastical dogma of the Trinity grew great in a soil enriched by Stoic speculation and experience.

From the 3rd cent. onwards Stoicism was rapidly absorbed in Christianity. A youth nurtured in Stoic principles rebelled against the continuance of animal sacrifices, and submitted gladly to the authority of a 'wise man' visible in the flesh. But the Stoic converts brought with them their scientific methods and even their school text-books; the *de Officiis* and the *Discourses of Epictetus* became for all practical purposes Christian manuals. It is greatly to be desired that modern theologians should be equipped with a better knowledge of the philosophy which more than any other was a nursing-mother to the Church.

LITERATURE.—The literature of Stoicism is voluminous and superficial. The early Christian writers were suspicious of a system which still maintained some independent vigour, and was associated in their minds with conformity to pagan cults. In and since the Middle Ages the respect paid to Plato and Aristotle has hindered the due recognition of the Hellenistic philosophies. Thus editions of the works of Cicero, Seneca, Epictetus, and Marcus Aurelius have appeared in rapid succession from the hands of editors, translators, and commentators who do not even claim to have studied the philosophy which these writers expound. Only in the last half-century has a real appreciation of the subject established itself.

The standard authority is E. Zeller, *Stoics, Epicureans, and Sceptics*, new ed., tr. O. J. Reichel, London, 1892. A shorter but sounder treatment is found in a study on 'Stoicism and the Last of the Stoics' by **G. H. Rendall**, prefixed to his tr. of *Marcus Aurelius Antoninus to Himself* (London, 1898). **W. L. Davidson**, *The Stoic Creed*, Edinburgh, 1907, and **R. D. Hicks**, *Stoic and Epicurean*, London, 1910, give good general sketches. **E. V. Arnold**, *Roman Stoicism*, London, 1911, is fuller in detail than other English books, and contains a bibliography of works ancient and modern on the subject. Of the original sources the ed. of *The Fragments of Zeno and Cleanthes* by **A. C. Pearson** (London, 1891) and **H. von Arnim**, *Stoicorum veterum fragmenta*, 3 vols., Leipzig, 1903–05, in addition to the classical authors already referred to and the *Anthologium* of J. Stobaeus (C. Wachsmuth and O. Hense, 5 vols., Berlin, 1884–1912), are the first necessaries for the student's equipment. Two treatises by **A. Bonhöffer**, *Epictet und die Stoa*, Stuttgart, 1890, and *Die Ethik des Stoikers Epictet*, do. 1894, give an admirable exposition of Stoicism in the form of a commentary on Epictetus, who would have been greatly pleased to learn that he knew his subject so well as this genial German writer suggests.

E. V. ARNOLD.

[1] See art. PAUL, § 2. [2] See art. LOGOS, § 1.

[1] Seneca, *Dial.* xii. 8. 3.

STONES.

STONES (Introductory and Primitive).—**1. Veneration of boulders and standing stones.**—As noted in art. STONE MONUMENTS, many of the menhirs in Europe and Asia Minor have probably been actually figures of deities. Rocks, boulders, and standing stones have been worshipped as gods or as inhabited by gods all over the world. Wherever men have been struck by the appearance or position of a rock or stone, they have regarded it with awe as uncanny, and in innumerable cases they have ultimately erected it into a divinity, brought offerings, and put up prayers before it. Instances need not be cited; they are found in every quarter of the globe. Among the natives of India the divinity frequently consists of, or is represented by, a group of comparatively small stones, which are usually painted red. Elsewhere, as among the Negroes of W. Africa, and occasionally in Europe by the pre-historic inhabitants, they have been roughly carved into a faint resemblance to human shape.[2] Many such stones are of great size; but others are quite small, and then, like the Indian *śālagrāmas*, almost indistinguishable from amulets. A *śālagrāma* is a water-worn concretion containing ammonites and other fossil shells, found in Nepāl, in the upper course of the river Gandakī, a northern tributary of the Ganges. It is looked upon as sacred, and is usually identified with the god Viṣṇu. As such it is the object of a cult by its possessor. Probably its veneration antedates the Aryan occupation, and it has been adroitly adapted to the Hindu religion in a manner not unknown in other aggressive religions.[3] Sometimes a tribe or clan claims to have issued from a rock: the Arab clan of Beni Saher ('sons of the rock') are said to have issued from a rock, still shown, in the land of

[2] C. Partridge, *Cross River Natives*, London, 1905, pp. 269, 271; *L'Anthropologie*, v. [1894] 22, 27 ff.

[3] *RHR* xliii. [1901] 325; A. M. T. Jackson, *Folk Lore Notes*, Bombay [1915], ii. 80.

Moab.[1] Tales of petrifaction of men and animals, of supernatural beings or monsters, or even other objects, are everywhere current accounting for rocks and great stones of suggestive shape, appearance, or position. Such a rock on the side of Mount Sipylos, in Lydia, doubtless gave rise to the ancient legend of Niobe. The transformation is said to be caused by offences of various kinds against the higher powers, by curses, by the infringement of a tabu, by mere caprice on the part of some divine being, or even to be without any assignable cause.[2] In many cases probably the boulder was the object of worship which has been forgotten, and the tale is the method of accounting for the awe and fear in which it has been held. Many stones to which worship has been accorded are, there can be little doubt, aerolites.[3] Such, *e.g.*, is the famous Ka'bah at Mecca. Among the Romans the Hermæ—stones carved with the head and trunk of human form, and representing the god Mercury—were boundary stones. Originally they were rough, unshapen stones. Such stones are still the object of veneration in Annam.[4] Their inviolability as boundary stones would naturally lead to more extended regard.

Another cause of reverence for rocks and stones has been a natural depression which has been interpreted as a footprint, or the impression of the hand, head, or knee of some supernatural personage—a god, saint, devil, or hero of old—or the hoof-prints of his horse. Such a mark is looked upon with awe, and, if attributed to a sacred person, usually becomes the object of devout observance, if not of an actual cult. Thus through the length and breadth of Europe the impress of the foot or of some other part of the body of the Virgin Mary or a saint is venerated, and various legends are told to account for it. So in India footprints of Viṣṇu and, where Buddhism reigns, footprints of Buddha are shown, many of which have been manipulated by art.[5] Both in Europe and in the East there are numerous depressions in rock attributed to mythical personages who have probably been displaced by the existing religion from the sacred position which they held, while the depressions now credited to the personages of the existing religion are generally taken over from a religion that has passed away. These are well known and need not be referred to in detail. Elsewhere, however, such impressions have excited the imagination and religious fervour.

'On the hills near Kachindamoto, on the south-west arm of Lake Nyasa, there is said to be a big flat stone on which are the footprints of man and all the animals, which emerged from a hole in the stone.'[6] On Vancouver Island the Kwakiutl show the footmarks of an ancient hero of their traditions.[7] According to the Lillooet, one of the ancient 'Transformers' stamped on a rock near a lake called Tsekalenal, and left the impress as a tribal boundary.[8] Similar marks on the Argentine shore of the Alta Paraná have been exploited by the Jesuit missionaries as the marks of the hands and feet of St. Thomas, the apostle of the Indies.[9] As in other parts of the world, impressions are identified by native tradition in America as those of different members of heroes or their mythical foes; and in some cases the colouring of strata of the rocks is thus accounted for.[10]

Stones pierced by a hole are frequently sacred. Persons desirous of being rid of sins or sickness creep, or are passed, through them for that purpose: the Mên-an-Tol near Penzance is a well-known example. Stones with smaller holes are utilized, by passing the hands through, to take an oath or enter into a solemn engagement.

'The Plichtin' Stane o' Lairg,' in Sutherlandshire, was built into a wall connected with the old parish church. It was famous as a medium for the making of bargains and the pledging of faith on all sorts of occasions, including the plighting of troth between young men and maidens. But some years ago the old church was pulled down to make way for improvements, and the stone passed into private hands. It was ultimately given by the then owner to the Archæological Museum at Toronto, where it is now exhibited.[1]

To many boulders and artificially-placed stones the belief attaches that they move at certain times. It is a jocular remark at Llandrindod that a certain stone goes to the brook to drink every time it hears the cock crow. Similarly, it is said of the Longstone on Minchinhampton Common, Gloucestershire, that it runs round the field when it hears the clock strike twelve.[2] But such a saying is merely a serious belief in decay. A large stone called 'the De'il's Cradle,' in Clackmannanshire, is believed 'by the superstitious in the vicinity' to be raised from its place every Hallowe'en to serve as a swing for the potentate whose name it bears.[3] In the Commune de Gardes in Charente, France, there is a block called 'the Mushroom,' which turns on Sunday at noon; the people of the neighbourhood have a certain veneration for it, and the old women are careful to protect themselves with the sign of the cross as they go by.[4]

Outside Europe there are similar beliefs. The 'moving stone,' which is believed by the natives of Borneo to be the waist-cloth of a hero called Simpurai, was hallowed by a ceremonial feast, as described by Bishop Chambers.[5] The Bribri Indians of Costa Rica say of certain stones on the mountain of Nemoie shaped like jaguars that they become alive and true jaguars when they are approached. They are the subject of a tradition relating to the ancient history of the people.[6] There is a boulder of reddish sandstone on the side of a steep hill on the north bank of the Marias river, in Montana, round which the soil is constantly worn away by wind and rain, and which consequently is moving slowly down the hill. The Blackfoot Indians believe it to be alive and make offerings to it.[7]

Rocking stones—boulders resting now only on a point of rock as a result of the disintegration of their supports—are capable of being moved. They are found in various places, the most famous being the Cornish Logan Stone. A legend frequently attaches to them; and sometimes, as at Vertolaye, in Auvergne, mothers take their children to the stone, that they may grow up healthy. At Pontivy such a stone is used by suspicious husbands for divination as to the virtue of their wives.[8]

A large number of erratic boulders and other single stones (sometimes heaps of stones) are attributed to supernatural beings who have thrown them in a contest, dropped them as they were being carried, generally with evil design, or emptied them from their shoes. In this way, too, rocks have been pierced or split, leaving a gaping chasm. These monuments of more than mortal power are not confined to the British Islands or even to Europe. They are found from the New Hebrides to the shores of the Arctic Ocean. And

[1] A. Jaussen, *Coutumes des Arabes au pays de Moab*, Paris, 1908, p. 107.
[2] E. S. Hartland, *LP* iii. 120. The stories are innumerable and a commonplace of tradition.
[3] W. Crooke, *FL* xi. [1900] 34.
[4] *Anthropos*, v. [1910] 522, 1156.
[5] W. Crooke, *PR* ii. 199, with plate.
[6] *JRAI* xl. [1910] 301.
[7] G. M. Dawson, *Proc. and Trans. Roy. Soc. Canada*, v. [1887] p. 20 (of offprint).
[8] *JAFL* xxv. [1912] 296.
[9] *Ib.* xvi. [1903] 58.
[10] *19 RBEW* [1900] pt. i. p. 480; J. Teit, *Traditions of the Thompson River Indians*, Boston, 1898, pp. 45, 96; F. Boas, *Indianische Sagen von der nord-pacifischen Küste Amerikas*, Berlin, 1895, pp. 202, 234; *Univ. California Pub.* x. [1914] 279; Dawson, *Proc. and Trans. Roy. Soc. Canada*, ix. [1891] p. 32 (of offprint); *RTP* xii. [1897] 357.

[1] *Ontario Archæological Rep.*, 1896–97, p. 64.
[2] *Archæologia Cambrensis*, 6th ser., xvii. [1917] 400; *FL* xxiii. [1912] 340.
[3] *County FL* vii. [1914] 309, quoting *The Scottish Journal of Topography*, etc., 1848.
[4] *L'Anthropologie*, x. [1899] 290.
[5] H. Ling Roth, *The Natives of Sarawak and British N. Borneo*, London, 1896, i. 353.
[6] *JAFL* xvi. 4.
[7] G. B. Grinnell, *Blackfoot Lodge Tales*, London, 1893, p. 262.
[8] L. J. B. Bérenger-Feraud, *Superstitions et survivances*, Paris, 1896, ii. 383.

they are of a sufficiently commonplace type to need no specification.

Sometimes stones are believed to grow out of the earth like a plant, as in Annam,[1] or to bring forth other stones, as in Mid-Celebes.[2] Even where they are not believed themselves to grow, they are frequently held to have power to cause organic life to increase.

On Mota, one of the Banks' Islands, a large stone with a number of small ones lying beneath it, like a litter of pigs, was held capable of bringing pigs to any one who offered money upon it;[3] in the Banks' Islands, indeed, no garden was planted without stones being buried in the ground to ensure a crop, and one shaped, as pieces of coral often are, like bread-fruit was of special virtue for ensuring a crop of bread-fruit.[4]

Finally, many of these rocks and stones are the objects, or at least the scenes, of magical or religious rites. Phallic rites at megalithic monuments have already been mentioned.[5] These are not the only rites performed at sacred rocks and stones. The mere sacredness renders them tabu, so that, as Sébillot notes in France, many peasants even at the present day are unwilling to pass them alone after nightfall or even in full daylight, their gestures showing the respect and hereditary fear which they inspire.[6] What is true of the French peasant is true of the folk everywhere, in Christian and pagan countries alike. Offerings of various kinds are made at such rocks and stones. The Mandans used to propitiate their oracular stone with knives, pipes, and cloth.[7] The Rāja of Dumrāon, who is the head of a sept of Panwārs, on succession, places upon a certain large stone for which they have a great reverence an offering of flowers, sweetmeats, and a few rupees.[8] Among the Chams of Annam any one finding a block of stone near his residence, among other rites, washes it, puts a cup of alcohol upon it, and calls upon the spirits to drink and to eat betel. To possess such a stone is to be well and to increase the number of one's children.[9] Near a certain Mordvin village lies an enormous stone, so sacred that at ordinary times no one dare approach it; but yearly, at a festival now identified with the Christian Trinity-day, a gathering is held there, a goose is sacrificed, and its head laid down beside the stone.[10] In Madagascar stones thought to be inhabited by spirits or possessed of power are smeared with grease, and sacrifices of domestic fowls are offered to them; the blood and feathers and the feet and head of the victim are smeared on, and placed about, them.[11] A very common rite in the offering of sacrifice to any object of worship is to sprinkle or smear the blood upon it. In India and adjacent countries (even as far away as the New Hebrides) blood is imitated with red powder or other colouring matter, and the mere rubbing of a stone with red constitutes it a sacred idol.[12] Among the A-Kamba of E. Africa there is a sacred rock called Kabubooni, where people go regularly to pray to the ancestral spirits for increase of worldly goods.

1 *Anthropos*, ii. [1907] 959.
2 A. C. Kruijt, *Het Animisme in den Indischen Archipel*, The Hague, 1906, p. 210.
3 R. H. Codrington, *The Melanesians*, Oxford, 1891, p. 181.
4 *Ib.* p. 183. For a similar custom in New Caledonia see *L'Anthropologie*, viii. [1897]; *FL* xiv. [1903] 256.
5 See art. PHALLISM, vol. ix. p. 825.
6 P. Sébillot, *Le Paganisme contemporain chez les peuples celto-latins*, Paris, 1908, p. 309.
7 *Papers of the Peabody Museum*, iii. [1906] 138.
8 W. Crooke, *Tribes and Castes of the N.W. Provinces and Oudh*, Calcutta, 1896, iv. 123.
9 A. Cabaton, *Nouvelles Recherches sur les Chams*, Paris, 1901, p. 158.
10 J. N. Smirnov, *Les Populations finnoises des bassins de la Volga et de la Kama* (French tr. by P. Boyer), Paris, 1898, i. 436.
11 *Antananarivo Annual*, 1892, p. 493; J. Sibree, *The Great African Island*, London, 1880, p. 305; G. Mondain, *Des Idées religieuses des Hovas*, Paris, 1904, pp. 12, 23.
12 L. K. Anantha Krishna, *The Cochin Tribes and Castes*, Madras, 1909-12, i. 12; *Census of India, 1911*, vol. vii., *Bombay*, pt. i. p. 67, do. vol. xvi., *Baroda*, pt. i. p. 68; Jackson, *FL Notes*, ii. 87; *Anthropos*, ii. 959; Codrington, p. 183.

A libation of mead is poured at the foot of the rock; a goat is killed, and its blood is allowed to run into the ground and mix with the mead.[1] The aborigines of the Canary Islands went in procession to certain sacred rocks in time of trouble, carrying libations of milk and butter; they danced round them, and from one of them warriors, it is said, threw themselves as expiatory sacrifices.[2]

Stones are set up, and ceremonies performed at both sacred rocks and stones, for various purposes. A very common object is to bring rain. The people of Hierro, in the Canary Islands, set free a pig at the rock with this object.[3] The A-Kamba, in the ceremony just cited, prayed for rain, that being necessary for the prosperity of their flocks and herds, their chief wealth. In Sumatra the Menangkabau of the Padang highlands have a stone at Kota Gadang in the form of a cat reputed to give rain, to which intent it is smeared with the blood of a chicken, and rubbed and incensed to the accompaniment of a magical formula.[4] To strike a stone much venerated by the Similkameen of British Columbia is sufficient to bring rain. About thirty years ago a Christian native made a bet with a heathen on the subject and struck the stone. The sky was then cloudless; but rain is said to have speedily gathered and poured down steadily for a week.[5]

In India a red painted stone is often set up to guard the fields.[6] In Annam a great unhewn or roughly-hewn stone is erected at the entrance of a village to arrest malign influences and evil spirits which might come that way to injure the inhabitants.[7] By every village on the island of Nias, at least on the east coast, a stone was erected, in order, it is said, that all the villagers should be of one mind. An offering was made at the erection of the stone, the stone was twisted round a little, and the priest addressed the people, warning them that, if any one would not follow the accepted customs, his neck should in like manner be twisted. Sacrifices were offered at the stone in case of adultery or theft. It was believed that to step over the stone was to lose the power of the limbs.[8]

The use of holed stones for the pledging of faith has already been mentioned. Such use is not confined to holed stones.

The stone at Shechem set up by Joshua as a witness to the Israelites' covenant is an example.[9] One of several sacred stones at Ambohimanga, the former capital of Imerina, Madagascar, was called 'the stone of oaths.' People were wont to resort to it for the taking of solemn oaths.[10] There is another stone at Ambohimanga, and a similar stone at Antananarivo, on which the monarch was required to stand at his installation, and where probably the oath of allegiance was taken.[11] The use of a special stone for this purpose is not unknown elsewhere: British readers will be reminded of the Coronation Stone in Westminster Abbey, previously at Scone and there used for the inauguration of the Scottish kings. The stone in such cases is probably sacred, and a portion of its sanctity is transmitted to the king thus ceremonially mounted upon it. The *Lia Fáil*, or 'stone of destiny,' at Tara, with which the Coronation Stone is claimed to be identical, was credited with divining power. 'It used,' we are told, 'to roar under the person who had the best right to obtain the sovereignty of Ireland at the time of the men of Ireland being in assembly at Tara to choose a king over them.'[12]

As might be anticipated, divination is often drawn from sacred rocks and stones. The rock already mentioned as venerated by the Mandans

1 C. W. Hobley, *The Ethnology of A-Kamba*, Cambridge, 1910, p. 167.
2 *American Anthropologist*, new ser., ii. [1900] 492.
3 *Ib.* p. 493.
4 Kruijt, p. 209.
5 *JAI* xxi. [1892] 314.
6 *Census of India, 1911*, vol. vii., *Bombay*, pt. i. p. 67; Jackson, *loc. cit.*
7 *Anthropos*, ii. 959.
8 Kruijt, *loc. cit.*
9 Jos 24[26].
10 *Antananarivo Annual*, *loc. cit.*
11 *Ib.* pp. 485, 492; A. van Gennep, *Tabou et totémisme à Madagascar*, Paris, 1904, p. 82.
12 G. Keating, *The History of Ireland*, tr. D. Comyn, London, 1902-08, i. 101; see E. S. Hartland, *Ritual and Belief*, do. 1914, p. 290 ff.

was consulted on going to war. Those who consulted it approached it weeping and groaning. After smoking they retired to a distance for the night. 'The next day they take down on parchment what the stone shows. The painted parchment is carried to the village, where the old men interpret it.' It is said that new figures are seen on the stone from time to time. The Minnetarees also had a stone which was consulted in 'practically the same way.'[1] In Borneo, 'in an interior Lundu house,' were the sacred objects of the tribe. Among these were several stones which 'turn black if the tribe is to be beaten in war, and red if to be victorious: any one touching them would be sure to die; if lost, the tribe would be ruined.'[2]

Rocks and stones are held valid for other purposes. Sunshine is believed to be produced in Melanesia by smearing a standing stone with red earth or winding a round stone, called a sun-stone, with red braid and sticking it with owl's feathers to represent rays, muttering a spell the while and hanging it on a tree.[3] Bontoc Igorot hunters hold a 'fire-feast for wild carabaos' at a certain rock, held to be a transformed spirit, with an incantation to the animals.[4] Below Paimut, on the Yukon, is a large block of stone, said to have been dropped there by the Raven Father after making the earth. He left instructions to the people, whenever fish became scarce, to tie an inflated bladder to the stone and fling both into the river. The story goes that the instructions were obeyed once, with the most satisfactory results.[5] In France standing stones and rocks are largely resorted to not only for phallic ceremonies, but also for the cure of various infantile and other disorders.[6] It is only necessary to refer to the numerous and complicated ceremonies performed at and with stones and rocks in the course of the *intichiuma* rites of the Central Australian aborigines, the object of which was the multiplication of the totem.[7] Simply to throw a stone on the top of a standing stone or rock, as on a rock in the Lutkoh River in the N.W. Frontier Province of India, is deemed auspicious;[8] and no passer-by omits to add to a heap of stones, whatever may be the original significance of the pile. These customs are universal.

2. Stones as amulets.—Stones as amulets have been already incidentally treated in artt. CHARMS AND AMULETS. But there are certain uses of such stones which may be here illustrated. In Scotland it was a common belief that distempers in cattle were to be cured by giving the ailing animals to drink water in which *lengan* (stones used for divination) had been dipped. The most celebrated of these stones is the Lee Penny, which gave the hint to Sir Walter Scott for the plot of *The Talisman*. It is an heirloom in the family of the Laird of Lee, whose ancestor, Sir Simon Lockhart, it is said, brought it back from Palestine, where he obtained it as part of the ransom of a Saracen chief. It is a triangular stone of a dark red colour set in a silver coin, which has been pronounced to be a groat of Edward IV. In addition to its virtue in curing cattle, it was believed to be powerful against hydrophobia, as was claimed to have been proved upon Lady Baird of Sauchtonhall near

[1] *Papers Peabody Museum, loc. cit.*
[2] Ling Roth, i. 232, quoting H. Keppel.
[3] Codrington, p. 184; cf. *JAI* xxxiv. [1904] 226.
[4] A. E. Jenks, *The Bontoc Igorot*, Manila, 1905, p. 82.
[5] *18 RBEW* [1899] pt. i. p. 426.
[6] P. Sébillot, *Amer. Anthr.*, new ser., iv. [1902] 78 ff.; see also the same writer's *Le Folk-lore de France*, 4 vols., Paris, 1904–07, *passim.*
[7] *Report on the Work of the Horn Expedition to Central Australia*, London and Melbourne, 1896, iv. 67; Spencer-Gillen[a], p. 167 ff.; Spencer-Gillen[b], p. 283 ff.
[8] *Census of India, 1911*, xiii., *N.W. Frontier Province*, p. 91.

Edinburgh about 1707. It has often been described and its cures narrated. It has been more than once the subject of complaint to the presbytery, and it has been exhibited to the Society of Antiquaries of Scotland.[1] Stones called curing-stones, used in a similar way, are known also in Ireland. To many of them a traditional history attaches, connecting them with the supernatural.[2] Other curing-stones are also found, the most noted of which are those of St. Fillan, pieces of quartzite preserved in a niche in the wall of the mill of Killin, Perthshire. These are said to be 'socket-stones in which the spindle of the upper millstone used to work before the introduction of the improved machinery.' M. Martin, in the *Description of the Western Islands of Scotland* (London, 1673), mentions a globe of stone of the size of a goose's egg, on the island of Arran, used to remove stitches from the sides of sick patients. The natives also swore decisive oaths upon it; and it was believed that, if it was cast in front of an enemy, he would lose courage and run away.[3] Curing-stones are known in many parts of the world. Many of them are pre-historic arrow-heads, called 'thunderbolts.' To this kind of stone must also be reckoned concretions like the bezoar-stone, ultimately of animal origin. They are used not only like the Lee Penny, but in various other ways.[4] In France and Belgium statues of saints, or stones looked upon as such, are rubbed with the body, or scraped and the resulting powder swallowed in water, for diseases, and especially by women for the cure of barrenness.[5] In the Fiji islands, where leprosy is not uncommon, there are stones, regarded with much awe as the shrines of ancestral spirits, which inflict the disease, and others which cause abdominal tumours and abdominal dropsy, but none, it seems, which are the means of healing.[6]

A curious use of what may perhaps be regarded as a kind of amulet is found in Ireland. Cup-markings in boulders and in rude stone monuments are well known and are by no means confined to these islands or to Europe. In Ireland such hollows in a stone or rock are called *bullàns*—a term also applied to the stone or rock itself. Their origin and purpose are to-day as much as ever the subject of puzzle and controversy. Many Irish examples have a small stone deposited in the basin. Such stones and similar ones lying on old altars of ruined churches, or on stones held to be altars, are regarded as endowed with extraordinary power. From their use they are often termed 'cursing-stones.' On the shore of Upper Lough Macnean, near the ancient ruined parish church of Killinagh, stands a *bullàn* stone containing ten cavities, each of them filled with a stone of suitable size. The *bullàn* is called St. Brigid's stone or altar. When any of the neighbours has a grudge against another and wishes him harm, he goes to the altar and there curses him, at the same time turning the stones deposited in the cavities.[7] So, among other places, at Croagh-Patrick, a mountain

[1] *Proc. Soc. Ant. Scotland*, xxvii. [1893] 494; C. Rogers, *Scotland, Social and Domestic*, London, 1869, p. 211; J. G. Dalyell, *The Darker Superstitions of Scotland*, Glasgow, 1835, pp. 157, 680; W. Henderson, *Notes on the Folk-lore of the Northern Counties of England*, London, 1879, p. 163.
[2] *Proc. Soc. Ant. Scotland*, xxvii. 444 n., 500; W. Gregor, *Notes on the Folk-lore of the North-East of Scotland*, London, 1881, p. 39; *Caledonian Medical Journal*, new ser., ii. [1896] 268.
[3] *Proc. Soc. Ant. Scotland*, xxvii. 447, 510, xlvi. [1912] 278.
[4] Authorities are numerous. Reference may be made to *Proc. Soc. Ant. Scotland*, xxvii. 503 ff.; Henderson, p. 165; *Journ. Roy. Soc. Ant. Ireland*, xliii. [1913] 267, *FL* ix. [1898] 86, xii. [1901] 272, xvi. [1905] 335; *Am Urquell*, vi. [1896] 161; G. Pitrè, *Biblioteca delle Tradizioni Popolari Siciliane*, xix. [Palermo and Turin, 1896] 294; *26 RBEW* [1908], p. 266.
[5] E. S. Hartland, *Primitive Paternity*, London, 1909, i. 63 f.; *RTP* xiii. [1898] 266.
[6] *FL* vii. [1896] 5.
[7] W. F. Wakeman, *Proc. Royal Irish Academy*, 3rd ser., i. 262.

in County Mayo and a place of pilgrimage, it is a custom that any of the pilgrims who have a quarrel with their neighbours will take up a certain flag from the sacred well on the mountain and turn it upside down in the name of St. Columkill, after which they return home and fast for fifteen days, taking nothing but bread and water once in twenty-four hours. The object of this is to honour the saint and induce him to put to death the person or persons against whom they have a grudge. If unsuccessful, they return to the well, there perform a 'station' backwards, and turn the flag upside down again.

'If stormy weather happen, either in spring or harvest, the whole country will say that it was because Columkill's stone was turned, and they will even watch in harvest to prevent the people from turning it.'

Pebbles are also carried home from another 'station' called 'Patrick's bed,' to prevent barrenness and to banish rats and mice.[1] On Caher Island, off the coast of Connaught, is a small church on the altar of which lies a stone called Leac na naomh ('flag of the saints'). It is said to be used to 'elicit the truth.' Any one on the west coast of the mainland or on the islands who is wronged, after praying and fasting at home, sails over to the Caher and turns the Leac. The weather then immediately becomes unfavourable, storms occur, and boats are often sunk, until the person who has turned the stone is vindicated.[2]

In Scotland, on the island of Fladda in Argyllshire, is a church dedicated to St. Columba. It has an altar at the west end, and on it a round blue stone which is always moist. Fishermen detained on the island by contrary winds used to wash this stone with water in the hope of procuring a favourable breeze.[3] On the island of Tiree in the Inner Hebrides is a stone almost buried in the ground. It is called Clach na stoirm ('the storm stone'). If taken out of the earth, cleaned, and set upright, it will cause a storm to arise.[4] The Roman geographer Mela tells of a stone or rock at the oracle of Ammon, in Cyrenaica, having similar powers. It was sacred to the south wind, and, whenever it was touched by the hand of man, a raging wind arose and drove the sands along like the waves of the sea.[5] In the Fiji islands there are stones which, if touched, cause a strong wind and a rising of the sea, more or less violent according to the force used against the stone.[6]

3. Crystals.—Among stones, crystals, commonly of quartz but also of other minerals, have everywhere attracted the attention of mankind. The use of crystals in what is known as scrying or crystal-gazing has been dealt with in art. CRYSTAL-GAZING. Scrying has been generally practised by both savages and people of the higher civilization[7] for the purposes of divination. But this is probably a special application of minerals already sacred, arising from their shape, lustre, refractions of light, transparency, and other striking properties, which have first caused them to be appropriated as amulets or reverenced. From pre-historic times in Europe they have been valued. In Anglo-Saxon graves in England balls and other pieces of rock-crystal, and in Frankish graves in Germany pieces of rock-crystal and milk-quartz, have been found. Balls of crystal have also been discovered in early graves in France, in Germany at Alzay, near Mainz, in Denmark near Aarslev in Fyen (the two last in women's graves), in a sepulchre at Mycenæ in Greece, and also at Rome. They were probably amulets, and certainly highly prized.[1] And the folk-tales of glass-mountains seem to be a distant echo of the uncanny properties attributed to crystals. Balls of rock-crystal mounted in silver are said to be not uncommon in Japan; but we have no information as to their use. Pieces of rock-crystal brought from a distant part of the island have been found in a pre-historic kitchen-midden in the south-west of the island of Trinidad.[2] There is scarcely a village in Yucatan without a quartz-crystal or other translucent stone called a *zaztun*, which is used for scrying by a diviner. It is first sanctified by burning before it gum-copal as an incense and by reciting certain magical formulas in an archaic dialect.[3] Numerous quartz-crystals have been found in the ruins at Casa Grande and elsewhere in Arizona, and in fetish-bags buried with the dead in various parts of the Pueblo country. The legends of the Pima and Pueblo traditions show that these crystals were employed in medical practice. The still living tribes of Arizona, particularly the Hopi, make use in their rites of a variety of stones, among which are 'rock-crystals, botryoidal stones employed in treating disease or by sun priests in rain ceremonies.'[4] The use of quartz-crystals in the Tusayan rites has been described by J. W. Fewkes,[5] and that of 'a crystal supposed to have been brought from the undermost world,' in the Zuñi rites, by Mrs. M. C. Stevenson.[6] A piece of rock-crystal was among the sacred objects seen by Charlevoix in a mausoleum of the chiefs of the now extinct Natchez of Louisiana.[7] Enormous crystals, sacred stones, endowed with power to kill or to protect, are mentioned in the traditions of the Luiseños of S. California; and rock-crystals are called 'the raven's arrows' and are regarded with superstitious fear, as is natural when they are connected with a bird so much feared.[8] Among the tribes of the North-West candidates for initiation into certain secret societies of the Nootka and of the Kwakiutl are supposed to be initiated by having a magical piece of quartz inserted into their bodies by supernatural beings, which has the effect of killing them. To restore the candidate to life the stone must be removed by shamans.[9] A piece of rock-crystal is mentioned in the legends of the Kwakiutl as given to or thrown at the hero by a supernatural being, and as conferring the power of flying.[10] And the neighbouring Catloltq tell of a double-headed snake that struck a hunter with a spear so that he fell as dead, afterwards giving him a transparent stone and leading his soul through all lands while his body lay where it fell until the soul returned.[11] So in S. America, among the Kobeua on the borders of Colombia and Brazil, in order to initiate a novice as a medicine-man, or *piaye*, an older *piaye* is said to fetch from a lofty mountain certain *dupa*, or magical white stones, which are voided by the great vulture. These stones he enchants 'through the novice's nose into his head; and there they eat up the whole brain and the eyes. Brain and eyes become and remain

1 P. D. Hardy, *Holy Wells of Ireland*, Dublin, 1836, pp. 30, 33.

2 C. R. Browne, *Proc. Royal Irish Academy*, 3rd ser., v. [1898] 69.

3 *FLJ* vii. [1889] 45.

4 J. G. Campbell, *Witchcraft and Second Sight in the Highlands and Islands of Scotland*, Glasgow, 1902, p. 93.

5 *De Situ Orbis*, i. 8.

6 *Anthropos*, vi. [1911] 724.

7 Cf. J. Wierus, *De Præstigiis Dæmonum*, Basel, 1577, bk. ii. ch. 4; J. Aubrey, *Miscellanies*⁴, London, 1857, p. 154; Reginald Scot, *Discoverie of Witchcraft* (reprint of 1st ed., 1584), ed. B. Nicolson, do. 1886, pp. 335, 344, 354, 360, 483.

1 *Proc. Soc. Ant. Scotland*, xxvii. 522; *Anthropos*, viii. [1913] 864.

2 *Amer. Anthr.*, new ser., xix. [1917] 477.

3 *FLJ* i. [1883] 245.

4 *28 RBEW* [1912] p. 130.

5 *Journ. Amer. Ethnol. and Archæol.* ii. [1892] 76, 123, 124.

6 *30 RBEW* [1915] 92.

7 *Bull. BE* xliii. [1911] 158, quoting P. F. X. de Charlevoix's *Journal of a Voyage to N. America*.

8 *Univ. California Pub. in Amer. Archæol. and Ethnol.* viii. [1908] 136, 147, 219.

9 F. Boas, *Rep. of 60th Meeting of Brit. Assoc.* [1890] p. 600; *Rep. U.S. Nat. Mus.*, 1897, p. 633.

10 Boas, *Indianische Sagen*, pp. 162, 165.

11 *Ib.* p. 82.

dupa.'[1] It is not expressly said that these stones are crystals. It is certain, however, that crystals play a large part in the magical practice of the tribes of the northern part of S. America. They are part of the stock-in-trade of the *piaye*; they are inserted in the calabash which forms his rattle; they are employed for charming, bewitching, or cursing others. Macusis and Wapisianas are described by R. Schomburgk as 'cutting each other's legs as a remedy for over-fatigue,' with a piece of rock-crystal, an instrument to which they ascribed particular virtue.[2] A more recent traveller describes the Andoke (also on the borders of Colombia and Brazil) as placing great faith in magical stones. When treating a patient, they lay stones on him.

'The medicine-man gazes on them abstractedly till a degree of self-induced trance is established. He will then break out into a frenzy, stamp, shout and brandish his rattle.' They 'are also used for magical rubbing.' The only ones which the traveller succeeded in seeing 'are of quartz, somewhat roughly made flat discs, worn smooth by continual use.'[3]

The Carib medicine-man is believed to send them into the body of any one whom he desires to render sick, and, if called on for aid, to eject them afterwards.[4]

In all parts of Australia the same virtues are ascribed to quartz-crystals and other shining stones. In New South Wales none of the medicine-man's possessions is more reverenced than quartz-crystals; they are held to possess marvellous powers.[5] They are sucked from the bodies of the sick, presumably first sent there by magical power.[6] They are used for rain-making.[7] In Queensland they are believed to be falling stars and are treasured by the natives with mysterious secrecy and used for incantation.[8] North and south, east and west, in the Australian continent quartz and rock-crystals are used for magical purposes; they are an essential part of the medicine-man's outfit, and they are buried with him.[9] They are made use of in the puberty ceremonies.[10] In Central Australia, and probably elsewhere, it is believed that at the initiation of a medicine-man the spirits implant in the body of the candidate a supply of these stones, upon which he is subsequently able to draw for the purposes of his craft.[11] Finally, in New South Wales, among the tribes of which the nearest approach to a belief in a divinity is found, these crystals are distinctly connected with Daramulun, Baiame, or whatever the chief personage of their mythology may be called. He it is who gives the crystals; and his own body in his camp on a high mountain or in the heavens, where he now presides, is itself partly a great crystal.[12]

Among the Melanesians of New Guinea pieces of quartz, both crystalline and vein-quartz, are used in sorcery for the purpose especially of causing death to an enemy; and they are part of a

[1] T. Koch-Grünberg, *Zwei Jahre unter den Indianern*, Berlin, 1910, ii. 155.
[2] *30 RBEW*, pp. 329 f., 352.
[3] T. Whiffen, *The North-West Amazons*, London, 1915, p. 184.
[4] *Ib.* p. 379.
[5] *Anthropos*, vi. 889; L. E. Threlkeld, *An Australian Language*, Sydney, 1892, p. 48, app. pp. 85, 93, 102.
[6] *JAI* xvi. [1887] 57.
[7] K. Langloh Parker, *The Euahlayi Tribe*, London, 1905, pp. 26, 35, 48, 74, 75, 80, 137.
[8] W. E. Roth, *N. Queensland Ethnog. Bull.* v. [1903] 8; E. M. Curr, *The Australian Race*, Melbourne, 1886–87, iii. 29.
[9] *JAI* vii. [1878] 248, 289, xiii. [1884] 130, 190, 194, 296, 299, 445, xvi. 26, 43, 48, xxviii. [1899] 20; R. Brough Smyth, *The Aborigines of Victoria*, Melbourne, 1878, i. 386, 464, 473; T. Worsnop, *The Prehistoric Arts etc. of the Aborigines of Australia*, Adelaide, 1897, p. 171; Howitt, pp. 357 f., 365, 400.
[10] Brough Smyth, ii. 272; *JAI* ii. [1873] 281, xiii. 296, 445, note 1.
[11] Spencer-Gillen[a], p. 525; Spencer-Gillen[b], p. 480; *JAI* vii. 289, xvi. 50.
[12] *JAI* xiii. 445 n., xvi. 51 f.; K. Langloh Parker, *More Australian Legendary Tales*, London, 1898, p. 80, *Euahlayi Tribe*, pp. 7, 76; R. H. Mathews, *Ethnol. Notes on the Aborig. Tribes of New South Wales and Victoria*, Sydney, 1905, p. 142.

sorcerer's outfit. Quartz pebbles are considered of deadly potency.[1] A tale reported from a Fijian source relates the gift by a supernatural being of a crystal which showed anything he wished to one who looked into it. The person to whom it had been given learned remedies for disease in this way and practised them with success; but he was eventually imprisoned when the Government heard of it.[2] The Dusuns of British N. Borneo carry quartz-crystals as amulets.[3] Among the Sea Dayaks of Sarawak every medicine-man possesses a piece of quartz-crystal, which, when called in to attend a sick man, he consults to ascertain where the escaped soul of the patient has hidden (scrying), so that he may fetch it back. But he does not appear to make any further use of it in his ceremonies.[4] Some at least of the S. African Bantu value a piece of crystallized feldspar and wear it round the neck as an amulet. They believe it to be brought down in the lightning and to be found when a flash strikes the earth.[5] A celebrated rain-doctor in Mashonaland owed his power to a small white stone, probably a piece of feldspar or quartz.[6] In Portuguese E. Africa the medicine-man uses hot pieces of quartz-crystal to heat the drink in the poison ordeal, doubtless because of their supposed magical effect.[7]

4. Stone money.—One of the most curious applications of stone is the use of large solid disks, or wheels of it, as money, or a medium of exchange, on the island of Yap, or Uap, a westerly outlier of the Caroline group in Micronesia.

These wheels consist of limestone or arragonite quarried and shaped in Babelthuap, one of the Pelew Islands, 400 miles to the southward. They vary in diameter from one foot to twelve feet, and each of them has in the centre a hole for the insertion of a pole sufficiently large and strong to bear the weight and facilitate transportation. They are known as *fei*. The limestone of which they are composed, to be of the highest value, must be fine, white, and of close grain. It is described as 'somewhat like quartz, but not so translucent, nor of so fine a grain.' They are cut as nearly circular as primitive resources permit. The hole in the centre is roughly about one-sixth of the total diameter. From their size and weight they are frequently not capable of being stored in the native houses; and, since they are not easily stolen, they are (perhaps more often than not) kept outside. Thus, as one traveller says, 'they are more for show and ornament than for use.' The houses of the richer men, and the *failu*, or *pabai*, the men's house where the men live and hold their councils and assemblies, in every village have their fronts adorned with *fei* that testify to the wealth of the inmates. The value depends not only on the size, but also on the quality of the material.

It need not be said that the islanders have also other currency, of smaller value but more portable, consisting of pearl-shells and sacred mats (called *umbul*) of banana fibre.[8]

LITERATURE.—This is mostly found in ethnographical works, as indicated in the foregoing pages. It may, however, be useful to refer to the classified list of rude stone monuments, in **S. Reinach**, *Cultes, mythes, et religions*, Paris, 1905–12, iii. 364. **Lord Avebury**, *Origin of Civilization*[5], London, 1889, pp. 307–316, gives a general account of stone-worship. A useful general account of the monuments themselves by **J. W. Fewkes** is given in *Great Stone Monuments in History and Geography* ('Smithsonian Misc. Collections,' vol. lxi. no. 6), Washington, 1913; a similar account of the rude stone monuments of India by **W. Crooke**, in *Proc. Cotteswold Field Club*, xv. [1905] 117 ff. See also, for those in the Nilgiri Hills, **W. H. R. Rivers**, *The Todas*, London, 1906, p. 438 ff. An account of stone cults in the Græco-Turkish area is given by **F. W. Hasluck** in *BSA* xxi. [1914–15].

E. SIDNEY HARTLAND.

STONES (Greek and Roman).

STONES (Greek and Roman).—The veneration of stones is one of the earliest forms taken by

[1] C. G. Seligmann, *The Melanesians of New Guinea*, Cambridge, 1910, pp. 284, 287, 290.
[2] *FL* xxiv. [1913] 233. [3] *JRAI* xlii. [1912] 393.
[4] E. H. Gomes, *Seventeen Years among the Sea Dyaks of Borneo*, London, 1911, p. 165.
[5] J. Chapman, *Travels in the Interior of S. Africa*, London, 1868, i. 262.
[6] *Journ. of the African Soc.* iv. [1905] 319.
[7] J. G. Frazer, *Folklore in the Old Testament*, London, 1918, iii. 376.
[8] W. H. Furness, *The Island of Stone Money*, Philadelphia and London, 1910, p. 93; F. W. Christian, *The Caroline Islands*, London, 1899, pp. 236, 256, 291.

magic and religion in all countries, and it is one of the most persistent. In the case of meteoric stones, which fall from the sky, veneration may well seem natural; but it is not confined to such. Stones of unusual colour or shape have frequently attracted veneration; and this has even been extended in modern Greece and Asia Minor to wrought stones from temples, or even marbles bearing inscriptions.

We may trace three stages in stone-worship in Greece. In the first the stone, in virtue of something strange about it—its colour, its shape, or some curious fact in regard to its appearance or history—is worshipped as a fetish. In the second it is regarded as the chosen seat of some divine power, some god or hero. In the third it is venerated in connexion with some interesting event in mythic history.

(1) In the pre-historic age of Greece stone pillars seem to have been objects of veneration. Several were discovered by Arthur Evans in the great pre-historic palace at Cnossus in Crete. They were usually dedicated, so to speak, by cutting on them the sacred sign of the double-axe, the symbol of the Cretan deity afterwards called Zeus. To this age must also belong, in the main, what we have called the first stage in the worship of stones, whether natural or rudely cut into conical shape. Such fetishism no doubt survived into the classical period on many sites, though, as is natural, the historians and poets of Greece make little mention of it; and later writers, such as Pausanias and Plutarch, are apt to interpret it through the medium of myth. Theophrastus, however, in the 4th cent. B.C., gives us, as a mark of the superstitious man (δεισιδαίμων), that he will pour oil on the already oily stones which stand at the cross-ways, and not pass on until he has prostrated himself and worshipped.[1] This rubbing or anointing with oil or with fat seems to have been the chief element of the ritual in regard to sacred stones.

Somewhat more elaborate was the cultus of a stone among the Ænianes of Thessaly. They made sacrifices to it, and placed on it the fat of the victims.[2] This is an extreme case; and the people told a mythical story to account for the custom.

Greek necklaces are extant in which wrought flints or small meteoric stones are enclosed in gold-work; and it has been supposed, with great probability, that they were regarded as bringing luck. We may perhaps have here the origin of the use of precious stones in jewellery.

(2) The second stage, in which a stone is regarded as the chosen seat and representative of a deity, was exemplified in many places in Asia Minor and Greece. One of the most noted of these primitive symbols occurs on the coins of Paphos in Cyprus. The place of honour in the temple of Aphrodite in that city was held by a conical stone, which stood for an image of the goddess. Similar conical stones may be found on the coins of Apollonia in Illyria and many other places. When Pausanias visited Greece, he found in many places, in the open air, stones which were called by the names of the deities.

At Pharæ in Achaia, he writes, 'in the market-place there stand about thirty squared stones: these the people of Pharæ revere, giving to each stone the name of a god.' 'In the olden time,' he adds, 'all the Greeks worshipped unwrought stones instead of images.'[3]

Many such stones, unwrought or rudely shaped, held their place in sacred shrines at a later time. In the old gymnasium at Megara[4] was a stone in the form of a small pyramid, which was called Apollo Carinus. A mere stone stood for Herakles at Hyettus; and in some of the most important temples of Greece stones retained their place of honour. Eros at Thespiæ was represented by an unwrought stone,[1] and the Graces at Orchomenus by stones which fell from the sky. In later Greece we have relics of the worship of the deities in such primitive forms in the representation of Apollo in the streets by mere columns and the frequent placing of the heads of Hermes and Dionysus on square pillars called 'Herms.'

Coins of the Roman age enable us to trace step by step the process by which these sacred stones were gradually transformed into the human image.[2] At Emesa in Syria the temple image was a mere conical stone, like the omphalos preserved at Delphi; at Perga in Pamphylia the head of a deity emerges from the top of a pyramidal stone; at Ephesus the figure of the goddess Artemis, 'the image which fell from heaven,' has articulate head and feet; but the body is not much more than a cone. At Samos, Aphrodisias, and Euromus we find on the coins primitive figures, articulate above, but ending below in a mere shapeless trunk. And, though such images, in the 5th and 4th centuries, were often removed to make way for the noble productions of the Greek chisel, they often returned to their place of honour some time before the Christian era.

(3) The third stage was reached when stones were no longer regarded as the dwelling-places of deities, but were held sacred in virtue of some mythological story connected with them; *e.g.*, a stone at Troezen, in Argolis, was said to have been the scene of the purification of Orestes after the murder of his mother. Another at Gytheium was the seat, sitting on which he had recovered from his madness.[3] Curiously, this stone was locally called Zeus Cappotas, or 'the Reliever,' whence it is clear that the story about Orestes is a later and rationalizing tale. Close to the altar of Apollo at Thebes was a stone, called 'the Chastener' (σωφρονιστήρ), which Athene had hurled at Herakles when he was mad, and attempting to slay his father Amphitryon.[4] Probably in all these cases the stone had been held sacred from early times, and the story was an invention of a later age.

The most noted sacred stone in Greece was the conical stone at Delphi, often figured on coins and vases as covered with woollen fillets. No doubt in early times it was held in honour as intrinsically sacred. But in later times the story told in regard to it was that it was the stone which Cronus had been induced to swallow in the place of the infant Zeus, whom his father wanted to make away with. This barbarous story was softened or superseded by the poets. Pindar attributes the sanctity of the stone to the belief that it was the exact centre of the earth, the γῆς ὀμφαλός.[5] Zeus, it was said, had let fly two eagles from the two ends of the earth, and they had met at Delphi. This statement, of course, from the scientific point of view has no basis. But the whole process of thought in regard to the stone, first magical, then mythological, and then pseudo-scientific, is very interesting and instructive. It is curious that close connexion between a stone and an oracle is found elsewhere. The chief oracle of the Mandan Indians of America was situated at a great stone, whither deputations resorted to seek divine guidance.[6]

Though the evidence is scanty, we cannot doubt that in Italy a similar range of ideas prevailed. Lucian[7] mentions a Roman, named Rutilianus, who furnishes a parallel to the superstitious man of Theophrastus. He was a gentleman and an official; but, whenever he saw a sacred stone anointed with oil or adorned with garlands, he would straightway fall on his knees, or, standing by it, utter prayers for various boons.

Two stones which were probably originally

1 *Characters*, ch. xvi.
2 Plutarch, *Quæst. Græc.* 13.
3 VII. xxii. 3.
4 Paus. I. xliv. 3.

1 Paus. IX. xxvii. 1.
2 P. Gardner, *Types of Greek Coins*, Cambridge, 1883, pl. xv.
3 Paus. II. xxxi. 4, III. xxii. 1.
4 *Ib.* IX. xi. 1.
5 *Pyth.* iv. 131; Strabo, ix. p. 419; cf. art. OMPHALOS.
6 J. G. Frazer, *Pausanias's Description of Greece*, London, 1898, iv. 155.
7 *Alexander*, 30.

fetishes play an important part in Roman history. In 204 B.C., during the war with Hannibal, the Romans, on the advice of the Sibylline books, imported from Pessinus in Asia Minor the stone which was there regarded as the dwelling-place of the mother-goddess Cybele. And Cybele brought with her to Rome an Oriental cultus and a train of priests. Again, in the 3rd cent. A.D., the emperor Elagabalus introduced at Rome the veneration of the sacred stone at Emesa which was regarded as the seat of the Oriental sun-god, and which appears in a chariot on the coins of the emperor.

Until the end of paganism there was in places apart from stir and progress a cult of stones. Arnobius, *e.g.*, who wrote in Africa about A.D. 300, says,[1] in regard to his pagan life, that, when he saw a sacred stone, he adored it, as if some virtue dwelt in it. And in fact such superstitions have not yet disappeared. In the *Annual of the British School at Athens* for 1914–16 F. W. Hasluck gives an account of the stones still held sacred in Greece and Turkey. Some of these may have kept their place from remote antiquity; but in some cases they are architectural fragments, or even marbles bearing inscriptions, which must have come to honour in comparatively recent times. The veneration of stones, in modern as in ancient times, is a matter not so much of date as of seclusion from the paths of education and progress. In Turkey, at the present day, the people often break up inscribed marbles in the hope of finding gold inside them; and, as this hope can scarcely be based on experience, it may well be a relic of the early veneration of stones.

LITERATURE.—F. Lenormant, art. 'Bætylia,' in Daremberg-Saglio; J. G. Frazer, *Pausanias's Description of Greece*, 6 vols., London, 1898, Index, *s.v.* 'Stone.'

P. GARDNER.

STONES (Indian). — **I. Stages in stone-worship.** —The worship of stones is widely spread throughout India, and assumes numerous and varied forms. In the first place, a distinction must be drawn between the pre-animistic and the animistic conception of sanctity in the stone. In the former the stone is regarded as sacred or tabu because it is vaguely conceived to possess some innate power which causes fear or reverence; in the latter the stone is believed to be the abode of some spirit. But in many cases it is not easy to separate these two forms of sanctity with any approach to precision.

'All the various functions of these stones, prophetic, kathartic, prophylactic, etc., are only various manifestations of its [the aerolitic stone's] supernatural power. In primitive days a sacred stone is a god of all work.'[2]

(*a*) *The pre-animistic stage.*—Here the stone is feared or reverenced mainly because its appearance is queer or uncanny, or because the circumstances of its discovery or erection suggest some tragical occurrence which continues to invest the place with a sense of awe or terror.

Thus, throughout India, we find 'the worship of a stone oddly shaped, of a jutting piece of rock, a huge boulder lying alone in the plain, a circle of stones, a peculiar mark on the hill-side or a hummock atop, an ancient carved pillar, a milestone unexpectedly set up where none was before, with strange hieroglyphics, a telegraph post, fossils with their shell marks; in fact, any object of the kind that catches attention as being out of the common way.'[3]

As instances of this class of belief, some curious fossils found near a Muhammadan shrine at Girar in the Wārdha district are supposed to be stock-in-trade of two Banjāra traders who mocked the saint, and their wares were turned into stone.[4] Some stones may be simply commemorative or used for some magical purpose.

1 *Adv. Gentes*, i. 39.
2 J. E. Harrison, *JHS* xix. [1899] 237.
3 A. C. Lyall, *Asiatic Studies*², London, 1897, i. 11 f.; cf. E. Westermarck, *MI*, London, 1906–08, ii. 592 f.
4 R. V. Russell, *Wardha Gazetteer*, Allahabad, 1906, i. 27 f.

Among the Bhīls, after a birth, the mother smears a spot outside her hut with cowdung marked with lines of turmeric. In the midst of the figure thus made she places five stones, corresponding to the number of days which have elapsed since the birth, and, laying round them pieces of coco-kernel, she sprinkles them with turmeric, millet, red powder, and spirits—possibly a magical charm to bring good luck on the child.[1] The Kurumbas, a forest tribe of S. India, place an ordinary stone in a cave; it is not a *liṅga*, and they call it Hiriadeva, 'great god.'[2]

Or, again, the appearance or position of a stone suggests a tragedy.

Such is the *baghaut*, or 'tiger cairn,' a pile of stones erected on the spot where a man has been killed by a tiger, to which every passer-by adds a stone.[3] Another case is that of Dāntan Deo, 'the deity with the teeth,' embodied in a projecting rock, which bears a rude resemblance to a hideous grinning skull, with enormous teeth.[4] In many instances curiously formed natural monoliths are supposed to represent a bride and bridegroom with their escort, as in the case of Dūlhā Deo.[5] In Bombay curiously cleft rocks or crags at Matherān and in the Poona district commemorate a similar tragedy, caused by the opening of the hill-side which engulfed the party.[6] In the Vizagapatam district some stones near a river pool represent a Banjāra (*q.v.*) and his pack bullock, turned into stone by the curse of the king of the fishes for killing and eating one of the sacred fish.[7] In the Himālaya a holy *faqīr* came to a mountain to worship and accomplished his pilgrimage. But he incurred the displeasure of the god by returning to ask some favour, and was turned into a rock, which now appears white at sunrise, red at midday, and green at sunset.[8]

Aerolites or meteoric stones, often found in India,[9] fall into the same class, it being 'probably easier, even for the naïve imagination of early men, to conceive of a stiff log-like idol descending thence than of a seated divinity shot from the sky, throne and all.'[10] In India some of these stones are worshipped as *liṅgas*; one in Bengal is called Adbhūtnātha, 'the miraculous god.'[11]

A famous stone, hung from an iron chain in the tomb of Maḥmūd at Bījāpur, was said to be a meteorite brought from Arabia, and was believed to protect the building from lightning; it has now been proved to be a piece of nephrite or jade.[12]

(*b*) *The animistic stage.*—In some of the instances already given we approach the animistic stage, where the stone is conceived to be the abode of a spirit. In the instances which follow this belief is clear.

In Burma some septs of the Karen tribe keep in their houses stones to which they make offerings of blood; as a member of the tribe explained, 'If they do not give it blood to eat, it will eat them.'

Some of these stones are supposed to give good crops of rice, others to be the embodiment of benevolent spirits, which, however, sometimes turn out to be malevolent; others are supposed to kill persons whom their owners dislike.[13] At a later stage these vague spirits become identified with special gods and receive definite names.

In the Deccan, at the full moon of Sept.–Oct., each Kunbī collects in his field six stones which he assumes to represent the five Pāṇḍava heroes of the *Mahābhārata* and their mother Kuntī; he smears them with lime and spots of red paint, breaks a coconut before them, and offers food.[14] The Shānārs, palm-tree tappers of Mysore, worship a male and a female deity, which, on holy days, are represented by two rude stones, taken up for the occasion; during the rite they are placed in a shed, but afterwards they are thrown away and neglected.[15]

1 *BG* xii. [1880] 87.
2 G. Oppert, *Original Inhabitants of Bharatavarṣa*, London, 1893, p. 235.
3 *PR*² i. 267 f. This mode of averting evil has been discussed by J. G. Frazer, *GB*³, pt. vi., *The Scapegoat*, London, 1913, p. 15 ff., who explains it as a means of purification, the evil being thought to be embodied in the missile which is thrown away (*ib.* p. 23 f.).
4 *PR*² i. 119.
5 *Ib.* i. 119 f.
6 *BG* xiv. [1882] 235, XVIII. iii. [1885] 141; for similar legends in Europe see J. Grimm, *Teutonic Mythology*, Eng. tr., London, 1880–88, iv. 1446 f.
7 E. Thurston, *Castes and Tribes of S. India*, Madras, 1909, i. 129.
8 *Census of India, 1901*, xvii., *Punjab*, pt. i. p. 127.
9 E. Balfour, *Cyclopædia of India*, London, 1885, i. 276, ii. 935.
10 *CGS* i. 335; cf. *JHS* xix. 236 f., xxi. [1901] 118 f.
11 *PR*² i. 82.
12 *BG* xxiii. [1884] 606.
13 *British Burma Gazetteer*, Rangoon, 1880, ii. 241.
14 *BG* xxi. [1884] 117.
15 F. Buchanan, *A Journey from Madras through . . . Mysore, Canara, and Malabar*, London, 1807, ii. 385, 415.

In a temple of Durgā at Manipur a rough black stone, apparently quite unworked, represents the goddess.[1] In Bengal, at the close of the festival which commemorates the end of the menstrual period of Mother Earth, a stone representing the goddess is placed erect on the ground; the top is painted with vermilion; it is purified by bathing, and decked with flowers, and offerings of milk and fruits are made to it.[2] The image of Āsāpūrṇā Mātā, 'she who fulfils desires,' at Madh in Cutch, is a red-painted rock, about 6 ft. high and 6 ft. broad at the base, narrowing to a point at the top, with some vague resemblance to the human form. People walk round it, and the chief annually sacrifices seven male buffaloes before it.[3] In Gujarāt many of the gods of the forest tribes are represented by stones. Vaitāl Dev, a hill-god, is a stone about 4 ft. high; Simādiā Dev, a red-coloured stone under a sacred tree, is worshipped at marriages.[4] In the Central Provinces, Bhaiṅsāsur, the buffalo-god, is a stone placed in every field, sometimes one or two for the whole village. It is worshipped when a cow runs dry or the milk goes bad. Muṭhiyā Deo, the divine watchman, is a stone smeared with vermilion at the meeting of the village cross-roads.[5] Ghaṭoiyā, 'lord of the crossing' (*ghāṭ*), is a round stone placed on a platform near fords, and Kheḍapati or Kheṛmātā, 'deity of the village site-mound' (*kheṛā*), is a stone worshipped at sowing-time and harvest.[6] In Kolhapur the local god, Jotibā, and his consort, Yamāī, dwell in rough stones.[7] All over N. India the collective gods of the hamlet are represented by a pile of stones of the most heterogeneous kind—water-worn pebbles, flint hammers, fragments of carved stone from ancient buildings, and the like—all arranged under the sacred tree of the hamlet.[8]

2. Stones used in orthodox Hindu worship.—Many stones are used in worship by Brāhmans and other high castes. Among the Hindus generally particular respect is paid to stones which appear spontaneously and bear no marks of human work. They are known as *svayambhu*, 'self-existent,' chiselling being regarded as disturbing and offensive to the indwelling spirit. Many of the most famous *liṅgas* and other holy stones are of this kind.[9]

The *śālagrāma*, a black ammonite, found in the Nepāl river Gaṇḍakī, from its curious interstices and other markings, is regarded as the abode of Viṣṇu.[10] Bairāgīs (*q.v.*) are specially careful about the *śālagrāma*; they will not eat without worshipping it, and, when so doing, they cover their heads with a piece of cloth upon which the name of Rāma is inscribed.[11] Smārta Brāhmans in S. India use five stones in their domestic worship—the *śāḷagrāma*, representing Viṣṇu; the *vāṇa-liṅga*, a white stone, Śiva; a piece of red jasper, Gaṇeṣa; a bit of metallic ore, Pārvatī, or a *liṅga-yoni*, Śiva-Pārvatī; a piece of pebble or crystal, the sun.[12]

3. Worship of special stones.—Worship of certain stones is specially important: the boundary-stone, the 'navel-' or village-stone, the death- and memorial-stone, the bride-stone, and the grindstone.

(*a*) *The boundary-stone.*—The best examples of this come from S. India. H. Whitehead[13] connects this cult with the totem sacrifice, the totem animal being slain that its blood may be shed and may thus secure the presence of the totem deity at a particular spot, which then becomes tabu. To prevent violation, the place is marked by a simple heap of stones, or by an upright stone-pillar, which would perhaps be sprinkled with the blood.

The boundary-stone, in India and elsewhere, marks the division between the cultivated area and the waste, a margin of separation between the sacred and the profane, within which the sacred processes of domestic life and husbandry might go on, undisturbed by dangers—human, spiritual, or what not—coming from the profane world beyond.[1] Throughout India the boundary-stone and its cults ensure the protection of the hamlet from foreign (and therefore hostile) spirits. Some tribes worship a god of boundaries, like Sundi Pennu of the Kandhs; others practise propitiation of foreign spirits at the boundary (*sīmānta pūjana*), when the party of the bridegroom arrives to fetch the bride.[2] In the Central Provinces there is a tree or stone worshipped as Miroī Deo, god of boundaries, to whom, in times of sickness, worship is done by hanging small flags on his shrine and by offering goats; in the Betul district, at the Dasahrā festival, the *bhūmkā*, or medicine-man, installs Dongar Deo, god of hills, on the boundary; he is believed to avert calamities for the coming year.[3] In Trichinopoly, at the propitiation of the boundary-goddess, the priest carries a pot full of boiled rice and the blood of a sacrificed lamb to the boundary-stone, walks round the stone three times, and at the third circuit smashes the pot on a second smaller stone at the foot of the boundary-stone.[4] In Mysore these stones are often adopted into the cults of the higher gods, by carving on them Śaiva or Vaiṣṇava symbols.[5] In Gujarāt Khetrpāl, 'tract-guardian,' the boundary-god, is represented by a stone on which is carved the figure of a horse.[6] In S. India such stones are held in great respect, are worshipped at the festivals of the village-goddesses, and may be known by their shortness and the oily incrustation caused by constant anointing; in Vizagapatam, when cholera appears, sacrifice is made at the stone, and crows' or peacocks' feathers are hung across the paths, or a broom is suspended to brush away all evil influences.[7]

(*b*) *Village-stones.*—In S. India such stones are known as 'navel'-stones. With these we may compare the omphalos (*q.v.*), or 'navel,' at Delphi, for which there are numerous parallels in many parts of the world.[8]

In the middle of the threshold of nearly all the gateways of ruined forts in the Bellary district there is a roughly cylindrical or conical stone, known as the 'navel' or 'middle' stone (*hoddu-rāyi*), planted there when the fort was built, and marking its limits. Before sowing, the village oxen are worshipped and driven past the stone to the sound of music; a mock combat follows between the owners of the cattle, each trying to drive his beast first through the gateway, and omens are taken from the colours of the animals: if a white ox wins, white crops, like cotton or white millet, will prosper in the coming year; if red, those with red grains, like red millet, will thrive.[9] In Mysore this cattle-stone is a rough slab, about 4 ft. high and 3 ft. broad, set upon a stone platform about 1½ ft. broad. When cattle suffer from sore feet, the owner pours curds over the stone for their recovery; charms against the evil eye and other dangers are engraved on stones, called 'amulet-stones' (*yantra-kallu*), which are often erected at the entrances of villages.[10]

[1] T. C. Hodson, *The Meitheis*, London, 1908, p. 102.
[2] *Census of India, 1901*, vi., *Bengal*, pt. i. p. 189.
[3] *BG* v. [1880] 233 f. [4] *Ib.* IX. i. [1901] 292.
[5] R. V. Russell, *Betul Gazetteer*, Allahabad, 1907, i. 54; *Chhindwara Gazetteer*, 1907, i. 446 f.
[6] Russell, *Damoh Gazetteer*, Allahabad, 1906, i. 36.
[7] *BG* xxiv. [1886] 300. [8] *PR*² i. 97.
[9] M. Monier-Williams, *Brāhmanism and Hindūism*⁴, London, 1891, p. 69; L. A. Waddell, *The Buddhism of Tibet*, do. 1895, p. 328.
[10] W. Ward, *View of the Hist., Lit., and Relig. of the Hindoos*², Serampore, 1815, ii. 221 ff.; V. Nagam Aiya, *Manual of Travancore*, Trivandrum, 1906, ii. 55 n.; M. A. Macauliffe, *The Sikh Religion*, Oxford, 1909, v. 78, n. 2.
[11] Thurston, i. 132. [12] *Ib.* i. 315.
[13] 'The Village Deities of India,' *Bull. Madras Museum*, v. [1907] 181 ff., *The Village Gods of S. India*, Oxford, 1916, p. 146 ff.

[1] W. W. Fowler, *Religious Experience of the Roman People*, London, 1911, p. 212, referring to Van Gennep, *Les Rites de passage*, Paris, 1909, ch. ii.; cf. Westermarck, *MI* ii. 67 ff., who regards the stone as an embodied curse.
[2] S. C. Macpherson, *Memorials of Service in India*, London, 1865, p. 366; J. M. Campbell, *Notes on the Spirit Basis of Belief and Custom*, Bombay, 1885, pp. 159, 217 f., 317.
[3] R. V. Russell, *Damoh Gazetteer*, i. 36, *Betul Gazetteer*, i. 56.
[4] Whitehead, *The Village Gods of S. India*, p. 104.
[5] B. L. Rice, *Mysore*², London, 1897, i. 508.
[6] *BG* IX. pt. i. [1901] 292.
[7] F. R. Hemingway, *Trichinopoly Gazetteer*, Madras, 1907, i. 81; W. Francis, *Vizagapatam Gazetteer*, do. 1907, i. 68.
[8] J. G. Frazer, *Pausanias's Description of Greece*, London, 1898, v. 314 ff.; J. E. Harrison, *Prolegomena to the Study of Greek Religion*, Cambridge, 1903, p. 557 ff.
[9] W. Francis, *Bellary Gazetteer*, Madras, 1904, i. 61; Thurston, i. 172 f.
[10] Whitehead, *Bull. Madras Museum*, v. [1907] 125; Rice, *Mysore*², i. 456 f.

In other parts of the country village-stones, embodying the luck of the community, are erected. The Garos erect sacrificial stones at the entrance of any large village. They are rough, unhewn stones, set up in the ground without any attempt at regularity, and seldom more than 3 ft. high. They are regarded with much reverence, and may never be removed. When a village site is changed, the stone remains, and the villagers return to the old stone for the annual ceremony. When the time of sacrifice arrives, the stones are decked with crowns made of bamboos, and sacrificial emblems are placed near them. Swords are brought out and planted, point upwards, in the hollow ends of a row of short bamboos. The priest slays the victim, and smears its blood on the stones. In some cases each stone appears to represent a particular guardian-spirit, and is given a name accordingly.[1] Among the Lushais, when the season for the jungle clearance (*jhūm*) begins, the Chiru clan kill a dog at a stone placed east of the village; as soon as it grows dark, men and women drink and dance round the stone.[2] The Pahāriyās of Chotā Nagpur sacrifice to their guardian stones and anoint them with red lead and oil.[3]

The worship of such stones is closely associated with the cult of sacred trees. The Skr. word *chaitya* (*q.v.*) means 'a funeral pile or grave, a monument or tombstone,' and also 'a sacred tree,' like the fig, 'growing in or near a village and held in veneration by the villagers, a place of sacrifice or religious worship, an altar.'[4] In some villages in S. India 'the deity is represented simply by a stone pillar standing in a field, or on a stone platform under a tree, or in a small enclosure surrounded by a stone wall.'[5] The Kurumbas worship a block of stone under a tree, by the name Gurunātha, 'lord teacher.'[6] In Mysore serpent-stones are set up on a platform facing the rising sun, under trees, one of which is invariably a sacred fig, which represents a female, and the other a margosa, a male.[7] Among the Garos near the stones erected by the tribe to commemorate a tragic death either a *mandal*-tree (*Erythrina suberosa*) or an Euphorbia cactus is planted.[8] The shrine of the village-deities in N. India always consists of a pile of stones collected under a sacred tree, usually a species of fig.

(*c*) *Death- and memorial-stones.*—In many cases the stone is designed to form a home for the spirits of the dead or to serve as a memorial of them.

In W. India the 'life-stone' (*jīv-khāḍā*) is used in the funeral rites. The Bhoīs of Bombay keep the stone with which, at the cremation, the water-jar is broken by the chief mourner in the house for the ten days of mourning. On the tenth day the chief mourner goes to the river with the 'life-stone,' offers grain and a copper coin to it or to the spirit immanent in it, and bathes it thrice. Then the Brāhman priest, muttering spells and prayers, flings the stone into the water, thus finally disposing of the spirit.[9] Among the Chodhrās, on the fourth day after a death, a spirit medium, accompanied by the friends of the dead man, sits in the *devāsthān*, a plot of ground set apart near each village for the spirits of their forefathers, in order that they may not wander through want of shelter and company. He kills a fowl, letting some of the blood fall upon the 'life-stone.' Then he offers grain and butter, paints the stone red, consecrates it to the spirit of the dead man, and in some cases covers it with a quaintly ornamented dome of clay. Near the stone the friends set a small clay cow or she-buffalo for a woman, and a horse for a man.[10]

1 A. Playfair, *The Garos*, London, 1909, p. 96 f.
2 J. Shakespear, *The Lushei Kuki Clans*, London, 1912, p. 168.
3 F. B. Bradley-Birt, *Story of an Indian Upland*, London, 1905, p. 295; cf. the custom of pouring blood on stones representing the great god, Marang Buru (*ib.* p. 258, with a photograph, p. 261).
4 M. Monier-Williams, *Skr.-Eng. Dictionary*, *s.v.*; cf. A. J. Evans, *JHS* xxi. 105 f., 126 ff.
5 Whitehead, p. 122.
6 Oppert, p. 235.
7 Rice, *Mysore*², i. 455; C. F. Oldham, *The Sun and the Serpent*, London, 1905, p. 152 f.
8 Playfair, p. 97.
9 *Eth. Surv. Bombay*, no. 115 [1908], p. 6.
10 *Ib.* no. 30 [1907], p. 3 f.

By an extension of the belief that the spirit immediately after death takes refuge for a time in the 'death-stone,' and may be disposed of if the survivors fling it into water, it is believed that the spirit may be embodied in a memorial-stone, raised on or near the grave, before which offerings are placed to propitiate the ghost.

The most typical case of such memorial-stones is found among the Khāsis.[1] The same custom prevails among other tribes on the frontier of Assam. Among the Lushais a big upright stone is erected in the centre of the memorial-platform, and on it 'various figures are roughly outlined, representing the deceased and sometimes his wives and children, and the various animals that he has killed.'[2] Among the Old Kukis the stone is erected in anticipation of death or at the funeral, and the corpse of a village officer is carried, from left to right, round his memorial-stone.[3] Among the Nāgas the custom of erecting such stones is closely connected with ancestor-worship. A man will erect a stone in the name of his father, from whom he believes he will receive help, should need arise. Hence the preservation of the stone is associated with the luck of the family, and a man erects a stone if he desires to found a family.[4] The Mikirs erect on the grave of a great man a tall upright stone, with a broad stone supported on short uprights; on the latter offerings for the spirit are placed.[5]

Among the Mūṇḍās of Bengal, at the death of a leading man, a great stone is dragged by several men to the burial-ground. Some wealthy men prepare the stone in anticipation of death. Near the stone a deep hole is dug for the reception of the cinerary urn. These massive gravestones mark all ancient villages.[6]

In W. India similar stones are erected by the forest tribes. The Nāiks of Gujarāt, a year after a death, with the help of a holy man (*bhagat*), bring a stone from a river-bed and set it up as a memorial. The *bhagat* or a member of the family smears the stone with red lead, kills a hen, and sprinkles its blood on the stone. The Mātā, the Mother-goddess, possesses the *bhagat*, who trembles all over, and says to the spirit of the dead man: 'See that you do not disturb this family!' After the rite the hen is roasted and eaten by the family. A similar offering is made annually at the Holī, or spring fire-festival.[7] The Bhīls, after a death, employ a mason to carve on a stone a figure of the deceased on horseback. The stone is washed, daubed with red powder, and taken to the village *devāsthān*, where a goat is killed, its blood sprinkled on the stone, and the flesh cooked and eaten with as much spirits as the party can afford to buy.[8] In almost every part of Kāṭhiāwār, near the entry to villages, are stones like tombstones, known as *pāliyā*, or 'guardians,' erected in memory of Chārans (*q.v.*), men and women who killed themselves to prevent the capture of the village cattle or to recover them from the predatory Kāṭhīs. The name of the Chāran, the date, and the object of the memorial are inscribed on the stone, while a rude sculpture shows the men on horseback killing themselves with sword or spear, and the women pressing daggers into their throats.[9]

In other parts of Bombay 'battle-stones' are found, carved on the top with a funeral urn, and an attendant on each side holding a fly-whisk. Below are panels representing battle-scenes and worship of the *liṅga*. These stones are known as the 'seven heroes,' and are much dreaded because their spirits are believed to scour the country at night.[10] Similar memorials of old border fighting are found in Rājputānā, and they easily develop into the ornamental *chhatrī*, or cenotaph, which is erected to the memory of distinguished men.[11] In the same class are the *satī* shrines, memorials of faithful wives who died with their lords.[12] In S. India these are known as *māstikal* (*mahā-satī-kal*, 'holy woman's stone'); they generally bear carvings of a pointed pillar or post, from which projects a woman's bent arm, holding a lime-fruit, which the *satī* always carried when going to her death.[13]

(*d*) *The bride-stone.*—During the marriage ceremony the bride is made to stand on a stone, which is in some places held sacred. According to the Vedic ritual, 'the rice, which had been put into a basket, is then taken up, and the stone is placed before the bride, who treads upon it with the point

1 See art. KHĀSIS; P. R. T. Gurdon, *The Khasis*, p. 144 ff.; E. T. Dalton, *Descriptive Ethnology of Bengal*, Calcutta, 1872, p. 55 f.
2 Shakespear, p. 85, with photographs of such stones, pp. 140, 147.
3 *Ib.* p. 165.
4 T. C. Hodson, *The Nāga Tribes of Manipur*, London, 1911, p. 138; Dalton, p. 43.
5 E. Stack, *The Mikirs*, London, 1908, p. 42.
6 Dalton, p. 202 f., with an illustration; Bradley-Birt, pp. 60 f., 101, with an illustration.
7 *BG* IX. pt. i. [1901] 325.
8 *Ib.* iii. [1879] 221.
9 *Ib.* viii. [1884] 136 f. n.
10 *Ib.* xi. [1883] 307 f., xiv. [1882] 57 f., 309 f., xxii. [1884] 716 f.
11 A. Adams, *Western Rajputana States*, London, 1900, p. 442, with photograph; F. S. Growse, *Mathura*³, do. 1883, pp. 150, 306; Oldham, p. 102.
12 *BG* IX. i. [1901] 358 ff.; *PR*² i. 185 ff.
13 B. L. Rice, *Mysore and Coorg from the Inscriptions*, London, 1909, p. 185.

of her right foot, while the groom recites the prayer: "Ascend this stone; be firm like this stone; distress my foes, and be not subservient to my enemies."'[1]

On the same principle, at initiation, a Brāhman boy is made to stand with his right foot on a stone, while the words are repeated: 'Tread on this stone; like a stone be firm.'[2] In the modern practice, at a Brāhman wedding, a stone (*aśman*) is kept near the marriage fire, and, at each turn, as the bride followed by the groom draws near the stone, she stops and stands on it until the priest finishes reciting a hymn.[3] The same custom is found among the forest tribes. At a Muāsī wedding seven little heaps of rice and turmeric are arranged on a curry-stone. At each turn, as the pair go round, the groom causes the bride to kick away one of the heaps, thus dispersing ill-luck; among the Mūṇḍās the bride stands on a curry-stone placed on a plough-shaft, supported on sheaves of grass and corn, emblems of fertility; among the Orāons the bridegroom stands on a curry-stone behind the bride and with his toes treads on her heels.[4]

(*e*) *The grindstone.*—This is used in birth and marriage rites as a symbol of fertility.

Among the Kunbīs of Kolābā, when a child is born, the grandmother or some elderly woman of the house places a grindstone in the lying-in room, and on it sets a small image of the tribal goddess made of rice-flour. She sprinkles red powder on the image, burns frankincense before it, offers fruit and flowers, and, wrapping the child in a cloth, presents it before the goddess, praying that she will accept the offerings, and be kind to the child.[5] The Rāmoshīs (*q.v.*) of Poona worship a grindstone on the fifth day after a birth.[6] The Govardhan Brāhmans, on the fifth day after a birth, place four stalks of millet on a grindstone, and keep a lamp burning all night to scare evil spirits.[7] At a Kunbī wedding a piece of cloth is steeped in turmeric, which scares evil spirits, and a root of tamarind, a holy tree, is placed on the cloth tied to the neck of the grindstone.[8]

4. Stones possessing magical powers.—Magical powers are attributed to many kinds of stones.

(*a*) *Holed stones.*—In many Indian dolmens there is a hole in the front slab. Many theories have been advanced—that it allows exit for the spirit of the dead man; that it permits offerings being passed into the inner chamber; that it allows an arm or other injured limb to be passed within the chamber, which possesses curative powers.[9] All holed stones possess magical powers, possibly because they afford entrance to a spirit which thus occupies the stone.[10] In the same class are the cup- and ring-markings found on many stones in India and elsewhere.[11] The meaning of these markings is obscure. In India a resemblance has been traced between them and the hemispherical depressions on village platforms, into which milk and Ganges water are poured to propitiate the malevolent dead.[12]

(*b*) *Creeping through or under sacred stones.*—The custom of creeping through the orifice of, or under, a sacred stone, as a mode of purification or as a test of purity, is common in India. At Dabhoī in Baroda, near a Musalmān tomb of some celebrity, there is an upright slab with a circular orifice, which discriminates between thieves and honest men. The stoutest man, unjustly charged with theft, can creep through it with ease, while the thinnest culprit will stick.[1] A stone with similar magical qualities is found at Bhaunagar, and is known as the 'window of Truth and Falsehood.'[2] At Śatrunjaya there is a holed stone, the hole being called Muktdwārā, 'door of bliss,' through which any one who can creep is sure of beatitude.[3] People creep through the hole in the Śrigunḍī stone at Malabar Point, in order to get rid of the ghost of men murdered by them. Śivajī performed this rite, probably to get rid of the clinging ghost of Afzul Khān, and Rahgunāthrāo Peshwa to escape that of his murdered nephew, Nārāyanrāo.[4]

(*c*) *Swearing on sacred stones.*—The common custom of swearing upon a sacred stone may be partly based on the belief that the strength and stability of the stone lend confirmation to the oath.[5]

The Tangkhul Nāgas of Manipur have in their village heaps of peculiarly-shaped stones on which they take oaths.[6] The Garos swear on a meteorite,[7] the oath sworn being: 'May Gōera (the god of lightning) kill me with one of these if I have told a lie!'; they also swear by the *śālagrāma* ammonite.[8] At Tirumala, in the N. Arcot district, the keys of the temple jewel-chest used to be placed on a stone, which was believed to guard the temple by moving round it at night; one night it killed a man who was accidentally locked in; people now take oaths before it, the witness, after bathing, moving round the stone in his wet clothing, touching the stone, and swearing.[9] At the shrine of a saint in Champāran, Bengal, there was once an inscribed stone by means of which thieves could be detected and stolen property recovered; Mahārājā Jang Bahādur is said to have carried it off to Nepāl.[10]

(*d*) *Stones which give strength and cure diseases.*—Some stones are believed to possess magical powers of giving strength and of curing disease.

In Manipur there is a 'war-stone,' which gives strength to warriors; heads taken in a raid were shown to it; no woman may look on the stone lest she destroy its powers.[11] In some of their hamlets the Kotas set up curiously carved stones believed to possess healing powers, if the member affected be rubbed against them.[12] In Bengal, during a cholera epidemic, a woman found a white, glittering stone in a tank. She took it home, and that night an old woman appeared to her in a dream and taught her how to expel the disease by worshipping the stone. She carried out the instructions, and the stone is now worshipped under the name of Dīdī Thakrūn.[13] In Central India stones known as Motī Mātā, 'pearl mother,' and Lālbāī Phūlbāī, 'dear flower lady,' are worshipped during epidemics of cholera. The *barwā*, or village medicine-man,

1 H. T. Colebrooke, *Essays on the Religion and Philosophy of the Hindus*², London, 1858, p. 135.
2 H. Oldenberg, *The Gṛihya Sūtras*, pt. ii., *SBE* xxx. [1892] 146.
3 *BG* xxii. [1884] 81.
4 Dalton, pp. 194, 234, 252.
5 *BG* xi. [1883] 56.
6 *Ib.* XVIII. i. [1885] 415.
7 *Ib.* p. 161.
8 *Ib.* p. 303.
9 For illustrations see J. Fergusson, *Rude Stone Monuments*, pp. 468, 469, 473; for similar holed dolmens in Europe and India, W. C. Borlase, *Dolmens of Ireland*, ii. 627 f., 708, iii. 723, 753, 758.
10 Campbell, *Notes on the Spirit Basis of Belief and Custom*, p. 164 f.; *PR*² ii. 64 f.; *Man*, iii. [1903] no. 8, p. 17 ff.; on promises made at holed stones, Scott, *The Pirate*, note BB.
11 J. H. Rivett-Carnac, *Arch. Notes on Ancient Sculpturings on Rocks in Kumaun, India*, Calcutta, 1883.
12 D. C. J. Ibbetson, *Outlines of Punjab Ethnography*, Calcutta, 1883, p. 116.

1 *BG* vii. [1883] 548.
2 A. K. Forbes, *Rās Mālā*, London, 1878, p. 574 f.
3 *Ib.* p. 576.
4 *BG* XXVI. iii. [1894] 607 f.; *Gazetteer of Bombay City and Island*, Bombay, 1909–10, ii. 360. Compare the creeping through the passage known as St. Wilfred's Needle at Ripon Cathedral (*NQ*, 8th ser., ii. [1892] 313, 398).
5 J. G. Frazer, *Lectures on the Early Hist. of the Kingship*, London, 1905, p. 73, *Pausanias's Description of Greece*, ii. 364.
6 Hodson, *Nāga Tribes of Manipur*, p. 110.
7 See § 1 (*a*).
8 Playfair, p. 75.
9 A. F. Cox and H. A. Stuart, *Manual of N. Arcot*, Madras, 1895, i. 329.
10 *Census of India, 1901*, vi., *Bengal*, pt. i. p. 178.
11 T. C. Hodson, *The Meitheis*, p. 102, *Nāga Tribes of Manipur*, p. 175; on similar tabus of menstruous women and of immorality see J. G. Frazer, *GB*³, pt. ii., *Taboo and the Perils of the Soul*, London, 1911, p. 145 ff.; Westermarck, *MI* ii. 417 ff.
12 Thurston, iv. 14.
13 *Census of India, 1901*, vi., *Bengal*, pt. i. p. 194.

slays a goat, the head of which, with lemons, copper coins, eggs, flowers, etc., is placed in a potsherd and offered to the stone; a small toy cart is placed near the stone, in which it is believed that the dreaded spirit may be induced to leave the place and take the disease with her.[1] The Burmese believe that a cabalistic figure engraved on a stone will make it float, and such a stone, if buried in a man's flesh, saves him from drowning. Certain stones, said to be found in the heads of birds, in trees, and in animals, are prized as amulets. They keep off sword-thrusts and evil spirits. When placed on a child's face or put into any one's blood, they introduce a spirit; the person so possessed falls into a trance, and may be questioned as to the doings of other evil spirits in the neighbourhood.[2] With such curative and magical stones may be compared the snake-stone and the jewel said to be found in the head of a snake.[3]

5. Pre-historic stones.—The pre-historic stone monuments of India include megalithic graves, known as dolmens and cistvaens, cairns, and standing monoliths.

An attempt has been made by G. Elliot Smith to assign the impulse for the erection of these monuments in Europe, Asia, and Africa to a single race starting from Egypt.[4] This view, as far as Europe is concerned, has not met with general acceptance.[5] In the case of India, it is difficult to attribute these monuments to a single race entering by the land route, because such monuments are rarely found in the Panjāb or along the routes which the so-called Aryans and other invaders from Central Asia followed. It seems more reasonable to suppose that the dolmen has for its antetype the hut, of which models, to provide for the repose of the spirit and for the supply of its food, were and are often erected.[6] If such monuments in certain areas assume the megalithic form, it is because stones suitable for the purpose are procurable there. So far as our present knowledge extends, the dolmens and other megalithic monuments of the Deccan and S. India appear to belong to the early Iron Age. Some of the three-sided open dolmens may have been used as ossuaries, like those of the Khāsis (*q.v.*). One difficulty in assigning a date to these erections is that they continue to be set up by some of the present tribes. Thus the Todas erect funeral-stones, at which buffaloes are slain at funerals; others mark the spot where the corpse is laid, or a mound is raised for the same purpose. But at present no sanctity is attributed to them, and there are no definite signs of veneration or worship.[7]

Among the Wās of Upper Burma are seen collections of boulders with pointed stones in the centre. In one village there is a large flat stone propped up on several others in dolmen fashion. These may have been graves, but they are now said to be the abode of the house-spirit—one belief not necessarily excluding the other.[8] The cairn is usually surrounded by a circle of monoliths, like the Vetālā circles in the Deccan. Here the circle encloses a stone, the god's house, the stones in the circle being called his watchmen. It has usually been assumed that such central stones or tumuli, surrounded by a circle of monoliths, passed into

1 *Census of India, 1901*, xiii., *Central Provinces*, pt. i. p. 78.
2 Shway Yoe [J. G. Scott], *The Burman*, London, 1882, ii. 128, i. 55.
3 H. Yule and A. C. Burnell, *Hobson-Jobson*², London, 1903, p. 847 ff.; *PR*² ii. 141 f., 143 f.
4 *The Ancient Egyptians and their Influence upon the Civilisation of Europe*, London, 1911, p. 176; *Man*, xiii. no. 105, p. 193 ff.
5 *ERE* iv. 468; J. W. Fewkes, *Great Stone Monuments in History and Geography* ('Smithsonian Misc. Coll.,' vol. lxi. no. 6), Washington, 1913.
6 See art. FOOD FOR THE DEAD, vol. vi. p. 66ᵇ.
7 W. H. R. Rivers, *The Todas*, London, 1906, p. 438 ff.
8 *Upper Burma Gazetteer*, Rangoon, 1900, I. i. 514, ii. 82.

Buddhism in the form of the *stūpa* (*q.v.*), with its elaborately carved railing; but V. A. Smith derives the domical *stūpa*, not from a tumulus, but from the curved roof of bamboos built over a primitive circular hut-shrine constructed of perishable materials.[1]

Cairns of mockery.—A curious variety of cairn in Bālūchistān is that known as the cairn of mockery or reproach.

'The stones of reproach in the Bugtī country . . . tell of some tribesman's black deed, incest may be, or flight from the field, or foul murder. Of these cairns there is no mistaking the meaning, for they are generally topped by a stone as black as the deed itself. And their size alone is enough to suggest that the larger cairns dotted about Baluchistan are memorials of some famous battle-field. In the Brāhūī country, . . . if a man is a miser, his neighbours vent their spleen by piling up a cairn against him; if a man flees from battle, a cairn will commemorate his cowardice; if a man brings down a fine head, there will be a cairn where he stood and another where the beast fell; if a man dies heirless, a cairn will be raised to his pitiful memory. Every little thing seems to prompt the Brāhūī to pile one stone upon another. . . . If dry cairns lie on the beaten track, they grow in height week by week; each passer-by will add his stone to the pile.'[2]

6. Flint implements.—Flint implements or celts, of both the Palæolithic and Neolithic types, are found in abundance in many parts of India.

Some hesitation has been expressed in accepting the fact that quartzite implements from the Indian laterite beds belong to the Palæolithic age; but it is now established that not only do the river-drift implements of W. Europe and those from the Indian laterite display the same general technique, but, what is of more importance, they evidently belong to the same geological horizon in both countries.[3]

According to Bruce Foote, 'the geological evidence afforded by the formations in which the chipped stone implements of Palæolithic type are found indicates—especially in the sections in Western India—that a great gap, historically speaking, exists between the date of deposition of such formations and of the beds in which, or on which, the earliest traces of neolithic man are met with. The geological evidence in Southern India, though less strikingly clear, points in the same direction.'[4]

No such break occurs between the Neolithic and the Iron Age. In fact, even at the present day, some tribes use implements made of stone. The Andamanese never made celts, but they use a quartz flake chipped off, never worked, for shaving and tatuing; these are now often replaced by flakes of glass obtained from the European settlements, and they still employ various stones for sundry domestic purposes.[5] Many of the jungle tribes still use, or have only recently abandoned, stone implements. The Keriyās of Chotā Nāgpur, up to the advent of the Hindus, from whom they obtained iron, used axes and grubbers of stone.[6] The Kādu of Mysore use bits of broken glass for razors.[7] In Bengal the umbilical cord is severed with a sharp-edged piece of bamboo or an oyster shell—an interesting survival of the time when metals were unknown.[8] Strabo[9] states that the Ichthiophagi of Bālūchistān possessed no iron.[10]

At the present day it is generally believed that celts are thunderbolts (κεραύνια).[11] Some Madras tribes believe them to be the thunderbolts of Viṣṇu.[12] The Khyens of Assam, when a tree is

1 *Hist. of Fine Art in India and Ceylon*, Oxford, 1911, p. 17.
2 *Census of India, 1911*, iv., *Baluchistan*, p. 64; cf. J. G. Frazer, *GB*³, pt. vi. *The Scapegoat*, p. 14.
3 A. C. Logan, *Old Chipped Stones of India*, Calcutta and London, 1906; *Man*, vii. [1907] no. 63, p. 110 f.
4 *Catalogue of the Prehistoric Antiquities in the Government Museum*, Madras, 1901, Introd. p. iv.
5 *Census of India, 1901*, vol. iii. p. 66; *JAI* vii. [1878] 446, xii. [1883] 379 f.
6 V. Ball, *Jungle Life in India*, London, 1880, p. 91.
7 Rice, *Mysore*², i. 213.
8 *Census of India, 1901*, vi., *Bengal*, pt. i. p. 480.
9 xv. ii. 2.
10 J. W. McCrindle, *Ancient India as described in Classical Literature*, London, 1901, p. 82.
11 Cf. *Man*, iii. [1903] no. 102, p. 182 f., viii. [1908] no. 54, p. 104 f.
12 Thurston, *Omens and Superstitions of S. India*, London, 1912, p. 178.

struck by lightning, search for the thunderbolt, and any likely stone is accepted as such, made over to the priest, held sacred, and sacrifice is made before it as to something sent from heaven.[1] V. Ball tells of a man finding a stone in a part of his field which had been struck by lightning during the preceding night.[2] The Malāyālīs of S. India place in their shrines celts and other stone implements; they do not understand what they are and reverence them accordingly; outside one of their villages was found a small stone shrine, capped with a stone slab, whereon were stacked several Neolithic celts, supposed to be thunderbolts sent from heaven.[3] Similar implements are often found at shrines in N. India.[4] The Nāgas believe that Neolithic celts found in their country fell from heaven, and the Shāns of Burma say that such stones fall in their country and are of three kinds —one like brass found only by lucky people, others which are living, and some which are dead and have lost their virtues.[5] Some of the wild tribes of Burma take oaths by drinking water in which a stone hatchet or celt (which they believe to be a thunderbolt) has been immersed, calling on the spirit immanent in the weapon to punish the man who commits perjury.[6] In Sikkim great faith is placed in the magical power of celts, or 'thunder-stones,' as they are called. The stone is washed with soap in a little warm water, and women are made to drink the water in order to ease the pains of delivery.[7]

LITERATURE.—There appears to be no comprehensive monograph on the sacred stones of India. References to some of the scattered literature are given in the article. For the Indian pre-historic stone monuments see W. C. Borlase, *The Dolmens of Ireland*, London, 1897, iii. 750 ff.; Meadows Taylor, 'Descriptions of the Cairns, Cromlechs, Kistvaens and other Celtic, Druidical or Scythian Monuments in the Dekhan,' *Trans. Royal Irish Academy*, xxiv. [1865] 329 ff.; J. W. Breeks, *An Account of the Primitive Tribes and Monuments of the Nilagiris*, London, 1873; W. Francis, *Gazetteer of the Nilgiris*, Madras, 1908, i. 94 ff.; J. Fergusson, *Rude Stone Monuments in all Countries, their Age and Uses*, London, 1872, p. 452 ff. Numerous papers on the subject will be found in *JAI*, vols. ii., vi., xiii., xvi. For the Khāsi monuments see P. R. T. Gurdon, *The Khasis*, London, 1907, p. 144 ff.

W. CROOKE.

STONES (Semitic).—**1. Ritual use of stone implements and stones.**—During the Stone Age religion developed among all the peoples of the world. In attempting to establish and perpetuate friendly relations with the gods and spirits, definite rituals were evolved, and the instruments employed in these rituals were naturally made of stone. Such is the conservatism of religious practice and of practices bordering on the religious, such as initiations, that stone implements and stones were used in these ceremonies long after the tools employed in everyday life were made of metal. Circumcision among the Semites began far back in the Stone Age, but as late as the Exodus from Egypt and the conquest of Palestine —a time on the borderland of the Iron Age—flint knives were still used in circumcision.

Zipporah is said to have circumcised the son of Moses with a flint (Ex 4[25]), and Joshua is said to have made flint knives on purpose to circumcise the Hebrews just before he undertook the conquest of Western Palestine (Jos 5[2f.]). Similarly, in an Egyptian tomb of the time of Teti,[8] the founder of the VIth dynasty about 2575 B.C., where we see the operation of circumcision being performed on two young men, the knife in the hand of the left-hand operator is clearly a flint; it is cone-shaped, with a sharp edge. The right-hand operator holds a square knife, which, so far as the form is concerned, might be of metal, but which Müller[9] thinks is a flint that has been shaped, and this is altogether probable.

1 Dalton, p. 115.
2 P. 473.
3 Thurston, *Castes and Tribes*, iv. 412, 421.
4 *PR*² i. 97.
5 *JAI* i. [1872], app. p. lxii.
6 C. J. F. Smith Forbes, *British Burma and its People*, London, 1878, p. 282.
7 *Census of India, 1901*, vi., *Bengal*, pt. i. p. 479.
8 See W. Max Müller, *Egyptological Researches*, i., Washington, 1906, pl. 106.
9 *Ib.* p. 61.

Closely connected with the ceremonial use of stones is their magical use.

In certain ancient Babylonian incantations a clay image of a witch was made, in the midst of which a stone from the mountain was put;[1] in another a stone was bound on to the son of a man.[2] In a fragmentary tablet which contains part of a ritual of a soothsayer directions are given for stringing a variety of precious stones, among which was lapis-lazuli, and hanging them on the neck.[3]

2. Sacred stones.—The ritual use of stones is connected with the fact that in many parts of the world certain stones have been considered sacred. The tradition that celts are 'thunder stones,' or stones that have fallen from heaven, probably arose from the fact that aerolites are found all over the world and, as stones that have fallen from heaven, are considered sacred.

Such a stone existed at ancient Ephesus, and is mentioned in Ac 19[35]. It is probable that the 'black stone' in the Ka'bah at Mecca is of this nature, and it has been conjectured that the Ark of Jahweh, carried from place to place by the Israelites in the wilderness, originally contained such a stone.[4]

Large stones and rocks, whether crags or boulders, have been considered sacred by the Semites.

Gideon offered food to an angel upon a rock, and the rock served as an altar (Jg 6[20]). Manoah did the same thing at Zorah, and the rock is definitely called an altar (13[19f.]).

Such sacred rocks, regarded as holy and serving as altars, have been found in various parts of Palestine. They are often over sacred caves.

One was discovered by Schumacher at Tell-el-Mutesellim,[5] another by Macalister at Gezer,[6] while under the dome of the Mosque of 'Umar in Jerusalem such a rock is still guarded as sacred by Muhammadans.[7] Those at Mutesellim and Gezer bore cup-marks, and all three show channels leading to openings through which sacrificial blood could flow to the sacred cave beneath. That at Gezer probably was over the sanctuary of the cave-dwelling people. On the rock at Jerusalem the Hebrews offered their sacrifices down to the destruction of the Temple by Titus.

In imitation of these natural rocks, or because of their influence, altars, and in one instance an entire high place, were hewn out of the solid rock. This was the case at Petra,[8] where the high place was of Nabatæan origin and probably does not greatly antedate the Christian era.

In Arabia a sacred rock became a god. The god al-Fals was a red projection of a somewhat human shape in the midst of the mountain Aga.[9] Indeed it is not too much to say that all over Palestine and Arabia sacred stones were abundant. In the Hauran saints are still believed to bless certain stones so that they have the power of healing. Vows are made, not to the stones, but to the saints.[10]

3. Heaps of stones.—In the trans-Jordanic part of Palestine heaps of stones, or cairns, were old in OT times. They were probably constructed by Neolithic men, and Hebrew tradition accounted for them as best it could.

Such a heap mentioned in Gn 31[48ff.] was believed to have been erected in patriarchal times as a witness of the agreement between Laban and Jacob. There is another such heap half-way up Mount Nebo, and another on its summit, where tradition has it that Moses died.[11]

1 K. L. Tallqvist, *Die assyrische Beschwörungsserie Maqlû*, Helsingfors, 1894, no. viii. 82.
2 *Ib.* no. vi. 48.
3 H. Zimmern, 'Ritualtafeln für den Wahrsager, Beschwörer, und Sänger,' no. 74, in *Beiträge zur Kenntnis der babylonischen Religion*, Leipzig, 1901.
4 Cf. G. A. Barton, *The Religion of Israel*, New York, 1918, p. 69.
5 G. Schumacher and C. Steuernagel, *Tell-el-Mutesellim*, Leipzig, 1908, p. 156 ff.; G. A. Barton, *Archæology and the Bible*, p. 168.
6 Cf. R. A. S. Macalister, *The Excavation of Gezer*, i. 102 ff., ii. 378 ff.; Barton, *Archæology*, p. 167.
7 Barton, *Archæology*, pp. 168 ff., 208.
8 Cf. R. E. Brünnow and A. von Domaszewski, *Provincia Arabia*, i. 239–245; G. Dalman, *Petra*, pp. 56–58; Barton, *Archæology*, p. 174 f.
9 J. Wellhausen, *Reste arabischen Heidentums*², p. 51 ff.
10 S. I. Curtiss, *Primitive Semitic Religion To-day*, p. 84 f.
11 For a picture of the last-mentioned see G. A. Barton, *A Year's Wandering in Bible Lands*, Philadelphia, 1904, opposite p. 143.

In Palestine and Arabia the *fellahin* accumulate heaps of stones at the point on a road where one first catches sight of a holy place or an important town. Each traveller casts his stone on one of the heaps, and the action is considered meritorious.

4. Monoliths.—The Semitic monoliths, or *maṣṣēbhāh*, are treated in a separate art. MAṢṢĒBHĀH, and those at the high places of Petra, Gezer, Taanach, Tell es-Safi, etc., are described in the art. HIGH PLACE. Such monoliths survive in places east of the Jordan and retain their sacred character in the estimation of the modern peasant.

At Ezra in the Hauran there are two pillars which, it is said, a bastard cannot pass.[1] At a village in the Druse mountains there are upright stones between which bridal couples must walk.[2] At Karyaten, the last outpost on the way to Palmyra, there is a prostrate pillar that is regarded as sacred to a certain saint. Near it is a mud hut about the size of a bee-hive, in which vessels containing oil to be burned are placed by those who pay vows to the saint.[3]

Sometimes stones are worshipped which have acquired sanctity during the historical period.

Thus near El-Merkez, in the Hauran, in front of a Muslim place of prayer is a rock 7 ft. high and about 4 ft. wide, called the Rock of Job. It is regarded as the dwelling-place of a *walī*. It is part of a monument of Ramses II. and bears a representation of his head and an inscription in hieroglyphs.[4]

According to Tacitus, one of those pillars stood in the temple of Astarte at Paphos in Cyprus. It was regarded as the statue of the goddess.[5] Similar pillars were employed as religious symbols in ancient Arabia, where they were called *anṣab* (sing. *noṣb*).[6] At Yeha and Aksum in Abyssinia monoliths of this character were connected with the ancient Semitic cult.[7] They were taller than the average of those found in Palestine, and had fire-hearths, or altar-hearths, at their bases. Perhaps it was such a pillar that Mesha, king of Moab in the 9th cent. B.C., calls an *ariel*, or fire-hearth.[8]

Pillars of this character stood before every Phœnician and Punic shrine. They are frequently pictured on the votive offerings which have been recovered in considerable numbers from those countries.[9] The tops of them are often carved into a pyramidal shape, suggesting the top of a phallus.

Egyptian obelisks were developed from such pillars. In tombs of the IVth dynasty obelisks 3 ft. in height have been found. That found in a Vth dynasty temple was about the height of some of those monoliths. It differed from them only in having its sides cut down to a square and the top shaped into the form of a pyramid.[10] In the time of the XIIth dynasty the main shaft was greatly elongated, thus making the obelisk with which travellers are familiar.[11]

LITERATURE.—C. R. Conder, *Survey of Eastern Palestine*, i., London, 1889; R. A. S. Macalister, *The Excavation of Gezer*, 3 vols., do. 1912; R. E. Brünnow and A. von Domaszewski, *Die Provincia Arabia*, 3 vols., Strassburg, 1904–09 (see index); G. Dalman, *Petra und seine Felsheiligtümer*, Leipzig, 1908 (see index); G. A. Barton, *Archæology and the Bible*, Philadelphia, 1917, pt. i. ch. xi.; J. Wellhausen, *Reste arabischen Heidentums*², Berlin, 1897, pp. 51–53, 118; W. R. Smith, *Lectures on the Religion of the Semites*², London, 1894 (see index); S. I. Curtiss, *Primitive Semitic Religion To-day*, New York and London, 1902, pp. 84–88.

G. A. BARTON.

STONE MONUMENTS (Rude).

1. Nomenclature and classification.—When monuments made of large undressed stone blocks first attracted the attention of the learned, in the 17th and 18th centuries, it was assumed that they were of 'Celtic,' or 'Druidic,' origin—an assumption which still remains enshrined in current terminology. Even in scientific writings several types are denoted by names derived from Celtic languages. This Celtic attribution is, however, certainly erroneous; such monuments are found in parts of the world where no Celts ever existed; and even in the Celtic regions of Europe they are to be attributed to races who preceded the Celts. The term 'megalithic,' to denote these structures, was formally adopted at the meeting of the Congress of Anthropology and Prehistoric Archæology in 1867. The monuments may be classified into two main divisions, which may be called non-constructional and constructional respectively. The first of these contains stones set on end, singly or in groups, not showing any greater architectural skill than is needed to erect a heavy monolith. The second contains all monuments in which heavy stones are built one over the other: these often indicate the possession of no small ingenuity on the part of the builders. In each of these divisions may be grouped three classes of monument: the non-constructional are *meini hirion*, or standing stones, alignments, and circles; the constructional are trilithons, dolmens, and cistvaens. There are several subordinate types in each class, some of which are noticed below.

2. General description of the different kinds of monuments.—(*a*) *Standing stones* (Welsh and Breton *maen hir*, *méan hir* [Anglicized 'menhir'], 'long stone,' plur. *meini hirion*; Irish *gallán*; sometimes, but now comparatively rarely, called by the Breton name *peûlvan* [*peûl-van*, 'stone figure']).—A standing stone is an undressed block of stone set up on end—the simplest form of stone monument. The height ranges from 2 or 3 ft. up to nearly 70, the height of an enormous menhir at Locmariaquer, Brittany (now fallen). The shape also is very various, some being quite irregular blocks, some being needles, with round, square, rectangular, or trapezoidal transverse section, others being flat slabs on edge, occasionally with the breadth nearly as great as the height. To some extent this depends on the nature of the stone available in the neighbourhood; but it is not the least remarkable fact about rude stone monuments that the builders often went far afield for the stones which they used, so that the monument belongs to a different formation from the country around it.

This is the case with the Locmariaquer menhir, which, though it weighs nearly 350 tons, must have been dragged a considerable distance before being set up. The blue stones at Stonehenge are likewise foreign to the district.[1] While in the prehistoric period of which we are speaking a menhir is essentially a rude undressed pillar, the tradition persists in the shapely form of Egyptian obelisks, or the column-like Pompey's Pillar; or else in masonry imitations of monolithic pillars like Trajan's Column at Rome or the Nelson Memorial in Trafalgar Square.

(*b*) *Alignments.*—These consist of standing stones arranged in straight lines. They may be of any number, from a single line of two stones up to the magnitude of the extraordinary monument at Carnac, Brittany. Here there are three groups of alignments, respectively 11, 10, and 13 in number, and containing when complete 1120 stones.

(*c*) *Circles.*—These consist of standing stones arranged in one or more rings, circular or oval. Single rings are by far the commonest, though double rings, more or less concentric, are also found, as at Avebury in Wiltshire. There is almost invariably an additional stone, either inside or (far more commonly) outside the circumference of the circle.

1 Curtiss, p. 84.
2 *Ib.* p. 84.
3 *Ib.* p. 85.
4 *Ib.* p. 86.
5 Tacitus, *Hist.* ii. 3.
6 Wellhausen², p. 118; W. R. Smith, *Religion of the Semites*², p. 201.
7 J. T. Bent, *The Sacred City of the Ethiopians*, London, 1892, pp. 180–185; J. Faïtlovitch, *Quer durch Abessinien*, Berlin, 1910, p. 35 f.
8 Barton, *Archæology*, p. 364.
9 Cf. *CIS*, *Tabulæ*, *passim*.
10 Cf. L. Borchardt, *Das Grabdenkmal des Königs Ne-User-Re'*, Leipzig, 1907, p. 184 and pl. 20; G. Maspero, *Art in Egypt*, Eng. tr., New York and London, 1912, p. 50.
11 Maspero, *Manual of Egyptian Archæology*⁵, Eng. tr., London, 1902, p. 105 f.

1 In such cases it is sometimes *possible* that the stones were ice-borne erratics, and actually found on the site.

The 'Friar's Heel' at Stonehenge, and 'Long Meg' in the group known as 'Long Meg and her Daughters' near Penrith, are good examples. Ship-shaped enclosures (*skeppssätningar*) are found in Scandinavia; the remarkable Deerpark monument in Co. Sligo, Ireland, may also be developed from the plan of a ship.

(*d*) *Trilithons.*—In these monuments two stones on end support a third, laid horizontally across their tops, after the fashion of the jambs and lintel of a doorway. Trilithons are rare as independent monuments; more frequently they enter into the composition of elaborate monuments, as at Stonehenge, and at the Deerpark in Co. Sligo. It is worth passing notice that the famous trilithons (so-called) of Tripoli are merely oil-presses of Roman date.

(*e*) *Dolmens.*—In a dolmen three or more stones on end support one or more large slabs (called the 'cap-stones') lying horizontally upon their tops, after the manner of a table. From this analogy the monument derives its name (Breton *taol-méan*, 'stone table').[1] The name *cromlech* (Breton *kroum-lec'h*, 'stone curve') is to be avoided, because it is not accurately descriptive, and, moreover, the word is more correctly used in French works to denote a quite different class of monuments, namely stone circles. This word is said to appear first in literature, in the Welsh Bible of Bishop Morgan (1588) at Is 2^{21}, to translate 'caverns.'

There are two principal varieties of dolmens: (1) dolmens proper, and (2) *allées couvertes.* In the dolmen proper the supporting stones are arranged more or less in a square, broad-oval, or circle, the two axes being approximately of the same length. In the *allée couverte* the supporting stones stand in two rows, parallel or slightly inclined to one another, and the enclosed space is roofed with a succession of slabs laid across them. The length of this class of monument is, therefore, much greater than the breadth. The rows are usually parallel, but Ireland has a number of examples of wedge-shaped *allées couvertes* in which the two lines expand from one end. In many cases, especially in dolmens with very heavy cap-stones, the supporting stones are absent from one side, so that the cap-stone rests partly upon the ground. A dolmen so constructed is sometimes called a *demi-dolmen.* A composite form is sometimes seen in which the cap-stone is partly supported, not on the ground but on a subordinate cap-stone. A good example of this not very common type exists at Trefignaeth near Holyhead, N. Wales.

(*f*) *Cistvaens* (Welsh *cist-faen*, 'stone coffer') are practically dolmens built of roughly squared slabs rather than of blocks of stone, fitting more closely together, so that the chamber within is much less open than in the ordinary dolmen. They are of a smaller size than the average dolmen.

A word may here be said of 'rocking stones,' which held a prominent place in the speculations of the pioneer archæologists. These are boulders so poised on a narrow part of their surface that a light pressure—even a child's hand—can make them oscillate, though a great force would be needed to dislodge them. In the early days of pre-historic research these were supposed to be 'Druidic oracles.' But it is now recognized that rocking stones are the accidental results of geological processes —ice transportation, denudation, and the like—and are of no archæological significance. It is by no means wildly improbable that stones so strangely balanced may have been used for the purpose suggested, but it is quite undemonstrable.

Many monuments combine the characteristics of several types.

Thus, to mention but a very few familiar examples, (i.) the great circle at Callernish, in the island of Lewis, has a large menhir at the centre, and is crossed by a single alignment running east and west, and by a double alignment running north and south. (ii.) Near Ronachan, Cantire, is an alignment of three stones ending in a dolmen. (iii.) Stonehenge, when complete, seems to have consisted of (1) an earthen mound enclosing an area about 300 ft. in diameter; (2) a circle of about 30 standing stones with a lintel across each pair, forming a continuous architrave, about 100 ft. in diameter; (3) the outer circle of 'blue stones' about 6 ft. high; (4) a series of five trilithons ranging in height from 16 to 21 ft., arranged in a horseshoe; (5) the inner circle of 'blue stones'; (6) the so-called 'altar-stone,' a recumbent block in the middle, about 16 ft. long; (7) an avenue running from the earthen ring to the north-east, with (8) the 'Friar's Heel,' a single stone standing at the end. The beautiful photographs of Stonehenge taken from a balloon[1] give an admirable idea of its plan and present appearance. (iv.) On the Meayll Hill, Isle of Man, is a circle of cists.

3. Method of erection.—The enormous weight of some of the stones used in these structures is one of the most surprising facts about them.

At Mount Browne near Carlow is a dolmen with a cap-stone weighing about 100 tons. This is exceptional—it is indeed the heaviest stone in a dolmen in Europe. But cap-stones of 40–70 tons are not uncommon; and to erect many of the single standing stones must have been a most formidable task. The stones were probably transported on rollers from their original sites, by the united labour of many men with or without the help of animals (cf. the Egyptian representations of the transportation of colossi). The standing stones, as well as the supporting stones of dolmens, were, most likely, erected by being run up sloping earth banks and tilted over the edge into the sockets prepared for them. In some excavations made at Furness, near Naas, Co. Kildare, a layer of made earth was found, overlying the natural soil,[2] round the foot of a great standing stone. This has been explained as the spread-out material of the inclined plane up which the stone had been rolled, to drop it into position. The same method was probably employed, when the upright stones of dolmens had been fixed in position, to raise the cap-stone to its place.[3]

However the difficulties of construction may have been overcome, the existence of these enormous monuments implies a considerable degree of social organization on the part of their builders. The co-operation of great numbers of men was necessary to transport and to deal with the blocks, and some compelling power must have existed to secure such co-operation—whether the external pressure of a despotic chief or medicine-man, or the more subtle influence of loyalty to common tribal interests. And in many cases there must have been the controlling power of a single mind superintending the work—an architect, with skill to assure himself that the supporting stones were properly spaced, and sufficiently firm to bear the weight of the cap-stone.

4. Purpose.—Rude stone monuments are either memorial or religious in their purpose; but these two explanations are supplementary, not mutually exclusive. For a memorial of a deceased chieftain is a shrine in honour of his ghost, and thus *ipso facto* acquires a religious significance.

The fact that interments have frequently been found at the foot of standing stones (as was the case at Furness, mentioned above) shows that such are often gravestones. Even down to the comparatively late date when writing was used by the Celtic-speaking inhabitants of Gaul, Britain, and Ireland this form of memorial was used; for undressed pillar-stones exist bearing inscriptions in Roman or Ogham letters, but otherwise not differing from the rude monuments of the pre-Celtic peoples. How far the chieftain's life was supposed to pass into the standing stone erected above his grave we cannot say. Such a transference of soul was certainly regarded as taking place in the case of a tree planted on the grave; and there is a curious idea still current among the Irish peasantry that stones, like trees, are capable of growth.[4] Thus it is by no means impossible that the connexion between the stone and the spirit of the buried chieftain was much closer than a mere relation of corpse and memorial, and that the stone was really a tangible recipient of honours offered to the departed.

But it is more than likely that many of the menhirs were actually figures of deities. Cæsar describes the Gauls as worshipping 'Mercury,' of whom they had many *simulacra.*[5] There are,

[1] In strict grammar the form with initial *d* should not be used except after the Breton definite article. *Taol* (also spelt *tôl*) is not a native Celtic word, but a loan-word from Latin *tabula.*

[1] *Archæologia*, vol. lx. pt. ii. [1907], plates 69, 70.

[2] *Proceedings Royal Irish Academy*, vol. xxx. sect. C [1912–13] p. 351 ff.

[3] See King Frederic VII.'s paper, 'Sur la Construction des salles dites des Géants,' in *Mémoires de la soc. royale des Antiquaires du Nord*, Copenhagen, 1850–60, p. 1.

[4] The present writer has been shown, by a not unintelligent farmer, a peculiar mark in the side of a pillar-stone which was explained as being due to the pressure of another stone while the first block was growing.

[5] *De Bell. Gall.* vi. 17.

actually, no images of gods in Gaul dating before the Roman period, if we except a few very rude representations of a female divinity.[1] The probability is that Cæsar was the spectator of rites round a menhir, which he took for a phallus, and, with the phallic associations of the Hermes figures in his mind, concluded that he was the spectator of a worship of Mercury. This probability is increased by an important passage in the 7th cent. life of St. Samson, bishop of Dol. Samson was a missionary from Britain, and, coming to Dol, was witness of a 'bacchic' adoration of a 'simulacrum abominabile,' which he proceeded to consecrate by cutting upon it the sign of the cross.[2] St. Patrick found at Magh Slecht, probably somewhere on the borders of counties Cavan and Leitrim in Ireland, the 'king-idol of Ireland,' whose name is variously given as Cromm Cruaich or Cenn Cruaich, with twelve attendant gods surrounding it; evidently a stone circle, with the additional stone above described, is intended. The saint destroyed it. The accounts of this monument and the adoration paid to it are obscure, thanks to the drastic editing that the surviving fragments of Irish literature have undergone at the hands of the monastic scribes to whom we owe their preservation; but it is not difficult to see evidence of human sacrifices and ceremonial mutilations in the expressions used.[3] Another idol of stone, called Cermand Cestach, is referred to in a gloss in the *Martyrology of Oengus*.[4] This stood close by the Cathedral of Clogher, Co. Tyrone, and was in some way consulted as an oracle. A stone alleged to be the idol in question stands on the place indicated, but its identity with the ancient stone is doubtful. A passage in one of the 'Brehon Law Tracts'[5] referring to the boundaries between adjacent properties enumerates among other forms of landmark 'a stone of adoration.' This indicates another use for rude stone monuments; but landmarks have at all times been under the protection of tutelary deities, so even here we cannot get away from a fundamental religious association in the monument. Slight traces of the conception of rude stone monuments as being, virtually, statues or embodiments of supernatural beings (gods or ghosts), survive in modern tradition—as in the name *fear breagach*, 'false man,' sometimes given to them, both in Ireland and in the Scottish Highlands; in alleged resemblances to human figures, which the local people sometimes point out, but which it requires the eye of faith on the part of a stranger to perceive; and in the crosses often cut or erected upon them, both in Ireland and in France, as though to drive the paganism out of them. On the other hand, the menhir of Kernuz, Finisterre, has had a figure of Mercury and some other figures sculptured upon it in Roman times.[6] In the neighbourhood of Confolens the dolmen of Saint-Germain-sur-Vienne has been turned into a chapel, by substituting moulded Gothic pillars for the supporting stones; and at Arrichinaga in Spain there is an example of a dolmen being turned into a baldacchino over the altar of a church. These remarkable cases of the Christianization of rude stone monuments will be found illustrated in Fergusson's work.[7]

The figure of Cromm Cruaich is said to have been of gold, or ornamented with gold. No standing stones bearing such ornaments are known—which is not to be wondered at. But a number are in existence which are ornamented with cups, spirals, or concentric circles; and generally it is a prominent stone of a group that is so decorated. 'Long Meg,' in the Penrith group, is a good example.[1]

A fine series of standing stones near Kilmartin, Argyllshire, shows a suggestive grouping: a tall slab ornamented with cups and rings on its western face, with a small enclosure immediately in front of it that has all the appearance of a sacrificial hearth, while two stones side by side some distance to the east, and a similar pair some distance to the west, appear to be the terminal gateways of an avenue (possibly once marked out with palisades) having the ornamented stone in the middle. The cups and rings are most probably religious (solar?) emblems.[2] A very similar group near Dingle, Co. Kerry, is known locally by the suggestive name 'the Gates of Glory.'[3]

Alignments are very probably avenues for ceremonial processions, but these are perhaps the most difficult of all rude stone monuments to explain. An alignment of two stones generally marks the head and foot of a grave. Circles likewise probably represent some form of procession or dance: the circle of sub-gods, exercising their evolutions around or in front of the chief god, may well be represented by these monuments. Traditional practices, such as the paying of 'rounds,' appear to indicate that some kind of circling procession was an important part of ancient ritual; such half-humorous survivals as the convention of passing wine sun-wise are reminiscences of the same order of observances. The tradition often preserved that stone circles are petrified men, who were turned into stone as a punishment for dancing improperly, or on the Sabbath, no doubt echoes dimly the original intention of the builders.

At Hollywood, Co. Wicklow, is a fine circle on a field known by the suggestive name of Aughgraney (*achadh gréine*, 'the field of the sun'); the circle is explained as the profane dancers, the outside stone as the piper. So in France stone circles are popularly called *les danses, la ronde des fées, le bal des dames*; in Germany *Steintanz*; and Geoffrey of Monmouth speaks of Stonehenge as *Chorea Gigantum*.

A circular enclosure is frequently marked out around a dolmen or a barrow by means of blocks of stone or stone pillars. Good examples are to be seen in Ireland at the *Leac na bhfian* (now called the 'kissing stone') at Carrowmore in Co. Sligo,[4] and at New Grange. In Denmark enclosures of this kind sometimes are square or rectangular. In such cases the circle is meant primarily to mark the enclosure sacred to the dead, either to protect it from trespass or to prevent the ghost from wandering at large among the living. Sometimes a stone circle has been found embedded in a tumulus, perhaps because the earth mound was raised higher than had been the original intention of the builders. Earthen mounds, however, often take the place of the stone ring in such cases.

The Semites were among the most assiduous raisers of 'pillars' in the ancient world, and perhaps it is among them that the subject can be most fully and instructively studied.[5] The erection of large stones as memorials is frequently referred to in the OT—more frequently as memorials of events than of individuals. But in many such cases the explanation is clearly traditional, associated with megalithic monuments of which the true origin had been forgotten.

Such was the stone circle which gave its name to Gilgal by the Jordan, explained as a memorial of the crossing of the Israelites (Jos 4[5]) and obscurely referred to in Jg 3[19] ('the graven images' in RVm). The 'pillar' over Rachel's grave was explained as a memorial of the dead (Gn 35[20]); such seem

[1] Illustrations in *L'Anthropologie*, v. [1894] 147 ff.
[2] *AS* (*Bolland.*), July, vol. vi. p. 584 D.
[3] See *The Tripartite Life of St. Patrick*, Rolls ser., LXXXIX. i., ii., ed. Whitley Stokes, London, 1887, i. 90-93; *RCel* xvi. [1895] 35, 163.
[4] Ed. Stokes, Henry Bradshaw Society, xxix., London, 1905, pp. 186, 187.
[5] *Ancient Laws of Ireland*, Dublin, 1865-1901, iv. 142, 143.
[6] See *RA*, ser. II. vol. xxxvii. [1879] plates 3-5; *Illustrated Archæologist*, ii. [1894] 16 ff.
[7] *Rude Stone Monuments*, pp. 337, 388.

[1] See J. Y. Simpson, *Archaic Sculpturings of Cups, Circles, etc.*, Edinburgh, 1867, plate vii.
[2] See *Proc. of Society of Antiquaries of Scotland*, xvi. [1881-82] 111.
[3] *Journal Royal Soc. of Antiquaries of Ireland*, 5th ser., viii. [1898] 161.
[4] W. C. Borlase, *Dolmens of Ireland*, i. 147.
[5] See artt. POLES AND POSTS, MAṢṢĒBHĀH, STONES (Semitic).

even to have been erected during the lifetime of the owner, as in the case of Absalom (2 S 18[18]), and a Phœnician inscription of one Abd-Asar in Cyprus, who says מצבת למבח״ ימנאת, 'I erected a *maṣṣēbhāh* [over my grave] in my lifetime.'[1] The 'stone of Bohan' (Jos 15[6]) seems to be some kind of landmark.

But it is as sacred stones—signs, representations, or habitations of deity—that pillars are of the most conspicuous importance among the Semites. A pillar, מצבת, of stone (or several pillars) was an essential part of a Canaanite high place (*q.v.*), and in the pre-Deuteronomic system an essential instrument of the Jahweh-worship of the Hebrews.

Jacob erected a pillar at Beth-el (Gn 28[18]); and, even so late as Isaiah, in an ideal picture of the extension of the cult of Jahweh over foreign countries, we read of an altar 'with a pillar at the border thereof' (19[19]). On the other hand, Hosea (10[1f.]) disapproves of the pillar-cultus, doubtless on account of the abuses that were inseparable from it, though it is straining the sense of 3[4] to consider that he regards pillars as prohibited. At last in the Deuteronomic legislation (Dt 16[22]) the erection of a pillar, as a thing hateful to Jahweh, is forbidden. A pillar was erected by Ahab in Samaria (2 K 3[2]) to the Tyrian Baal.

The alignment discovered at Gezer has enabled us to form a concrete picture of these groups of sacred stones.

Dolmens and the other constructional monuments are more specifically connected with burial than with religion, though no doubt these also were centres of funeral rites; and the emblems sometimes carved upon them (especially in Brittany and in Scandinavia) indicate at least a secondary religious purpose attaching to them.

Some dolmens were covered by earth, and thus became chambered tumuli, with or without an *allée couverte* leading to the central chamber. But it may be taken as certain that many of the dolmens that now stand free of earth were always intended to be so. An earth mound resists natural destructive causes to a surprising degree, and a human destroyer would not be likely to spare the stone structure at the centre if for any reason he took the trouble of disposing of the earth. It is impossible to explain what has happened to the earth if we are to suppose that dolmens were always covered in. Moreover, in many cases (as in the fine dolmen at Legananny,[2] Co. Down) the supporting stones are so far apart that they would not hold back the earth from running in under the cap-stone and filling the chamber which the stones were presumably intended to make. In several cases the dolmen is erected on the summit of a tumulus; here it must be considered as a mark or monument erected over the grave underneath. This must also be true of the numerous large dolmens, in which the chamber is too open to conceal a funeral deposit. Not improbably many dolmens are cenotaphs, erected to commemorate a warrior whose body could not be found, and whose ghost accordingly it was specially important to propitiate. Both in Bavaria and in Ireland excavation has shown that some of the most carefully built tumuli are cenotaphs.

Another use for standing stones is in ratifying contracts. The 'holed' stones—standing stones with a perforation through them—must have been especially used for this purpose, if we may trust the evidence of traditional customs existing till quite recently. At Stennis, *e.g.*, the most binding contract was that between two persons who clasped hands through a hole in one of the stones.

Herodotus tells us that 'the Arabians observe pledges as religiously as any people: and they make them as follows. When any wish to plight their faith, a third person standing between them makes a cut with a sharp stone in the palm of the hand, near the longest fingers, of the two contracting parties and then taking from the cloak of each a wool-flock, he smears seven stones lying between them with the blood, and doing so he calls upon Dionysus and Urania.'[3]

Holes are found in the stones of some dolmens, especially in India, but they are not uncommon nearer home, as in Cornwall, Brittany, etc. Probably the holes in dolmens are intended to allow egress to the ghost, or else for the deposit of offerings at the tomb.

[1] *CIS*, 46.
[2] Borlase, *Dolmens of Ireland*, i. 282.
[3] iii. 8.

Salomon Reinach, in an interesting article entitled 'Les Monuments de pierre brute dans le langage et les croyances populaires,'[1] has collected a number of names applied to stone monuments, which appear to enshrine vague recollections of their former purpose. Such names as *pierres du soleil*, *Sonnensteine*, suggest sun-worship; *pierre du serment*, *du feu*, *de la valse*, refer to oath-taking, fire ceremonials, or religious dances. *Pierres du sabbat* speaks of the Christianization of a district, after which the pagan monument would seem to the converts a resort of demons. Of a different order are names like 'Long Meg and her Daughters,' 'the Maidens of Lanyon,' *pierre de la justice*, which refer to family or assembly groups. Other names refer to ancient gods or fabulous beings, like 'Wayland Smith's cave' in Berkshire, or the numerous French structures called after the giant Gargantua. Others are called after dwarfs, sorcerers, mothers (=the groups of Gaulish and Germanic deities called *matres*), the devil; such heroes as King Arthur in England and Diarmait (with his lover Gráinne) in Ireland; the Druids; and historical persons like Cæsar, or certain saints. Other names such as 'Druids' altars,' and the like, are local attempts made to explain them. In many cases rude stone monuments are the subject of superstitious practices which have evidently a long ancestry behind them, designed to secure offspring, to cure diseases, to bring down curses on an enemy, to ratify contracts, etc. To others manifestations of life, talking, bowing at the Angelus, returning to their place if removed, etc., are ascribed. These will all be found analyzed in Reinach's paper. The conclusion at which he arrives is that the folk-lore of rude stone monuments is entirely pagan, and that, even when the Virgin, saints, the devil, and other conceptions due to Christian teaching are associated with them, these are merely secondary and have been substituted for beings of the earlier faiths.

5. Geographical distribution.—The geographical distribution of rude stone monuments extends, in the continental mass of the Old World, from the extreme west of Europe to the extreme east of Asia, and from Scandinavia to Central Africa; but the area over which they are found is not continuous. In spite of centuries of destruction, rude stone monuments of every type abound in the British and Irish Islands, and some of the most remarkable structures in Europe are found there.

In Ireland nearly 1000 dolmens have been recorded. In France they are also common—some 4000 dolmens are recorded as existing there. The peninsula of Brittany is especially rich in rude stone monuments of all kinds. The peninsula of Spain and Portugal contains some magnificent examples of dolmens, but circles seem to be less common there than in the other countries named above. In contrast to this comparative wealth in Spain rude stone structures are practically unknown in Italy (except at Otranto, in the 'heel' of the peninsula) and in Greece (except in one example in the north-east of the Morea). In Northern and Central Europe they occur in Belgium, Holland (in the province of Drenthe), and in Oldenburg, Brunswick, Mecklenburg—*i.e.* in the northern plain of Germany. They are common in Denmark and the Danish Islands, and also in S. Sweden. In Central Europe they are rare: a dolmen is reported at Chamblandes, Canton de Vaud.[2] The islands of the Mediterranean—the Balearic Islands, Corsica, Sardinia, Malta, and Gozo—possess many structures of this kind, in remarkable contrast to the barrenness of the adjacent mainland. They are found in S. Russia, in the Caucasus, and also in Bulgaria. Crossing to Africa, we find dolmens and circles abundant in the countries north of the Sahara, bordering on the Mediterranean. South of the Sahara no dolmens exist, but circles have been found in Gambia, and groups of standing stones in Nigeria and the Sudan. In Asia Palgrave describes a circle which he has seen in Arabia, and Doughty describes an alignment of stones; Western Palestine has yielded a few dolmens, but Eastern Palestine has large numbers. There is then a gap till we come to India, parts of which (especially the west coast) abound with dolmens and circles. In China they appear to be absent; but dolmens are frequent in Korea and Japan.[3]

This wide area, and the many gaps which it presents, make it impossible to accept the view that the rude stone monuments, wherever found, are to be assigned to a single race of dolmen-builders, and are to be taken as monuments of their wanderings. Given the large deposit of time on which we can draw, the theory that the trade and intercourse of the Stone and early Bronze Ages carried the knowledge of new religions and new arts from one people to another makes much less demand on our powers of credulity than that of one all-

[1] *RA* III. xxx. [1893] 195.
[2] *L'Anthropologie*, xii. [1901] 276.
[3] For references see the Literature.

pervading race, which manipulated and worshipped large blocks of stone, permeating the local races native to the different countries where these monuments are found, and existing side by side with them. Indeed, the theory of independent origin among different people and in different places is not more incredible. The present author is bound to admit, in spite of the many writings sustaining a contrary thesis, that he can see no difficulty in supposing that the spirals decorating a Maori chieftain's face and the spirals in the chamber at New Grange have had ancestries totally independent of each other, both being directly derived from natural forms (vine-tendrils or the like) observed independently in the geographical areas to which they severally belong. Nor can he see any difficulty in supposing that people in Peshawar and people in Spain should have hit independently on the same solution of the problem of how to bury their dead out of their sight, and how to commemorate and honour them.

6. Chronology.—The dolmens of Japan have to be treated separately in considering the chronology of rude stone monuments. These are comparatively late, being in many cases recognized as the tombs of emperors of known date. Gowland, the leading authority on the subject, dates the Japanese dolmens from 200 B.C. to A.D. 500 or 600. Certain Russian monuments built of large stones, being furnished with grave-goods of the late Bronze or early Iron Ages, are also comparatively recent. Apart from these groups, however, the origin of these monuments must be put back to a period of very considerable antiquity.

The date of such monuments as these can be determined (*a*) from objects to which a date can be assigned found in association with them, and (*b*) from ornamentation sculptured upon them. Much time and ingenuity has been wasted in endeavouring to solve the chronological problems by astronomical calculation, but too many arbitrary assumptions have to be made, and the results obtained carry no conviction.

Speaking generally, we may say (i.) that a single standing stone may belong to any age, from the Stone Age to the period of early Christianity, and that, unless datable objects be found in close connexion with any individual example, or unless it bears some datable inscription or ornament, it is impossible to say when it was erected; (ii.) that dolmens, on the whole, belong to the period of transition from the Stone to the Bronze Age; (iii.) that, to judge from the ornament sculptured on some examples, stone circles belong, on the whole, to the beginning of the Bronze Age, though some may belong to the end of the Stone Age. That stone implements were exclusively found in the excavation of Stonehenge does not vitiate this result; for stone implements would naturally be used instead of the comparatively soft and valuable bronze for such rough and coarse work as the quarrying and trimming of blocks of stone.

LITERATURE.—i. *GENERAL.*—G. de Bonstetten, *Essai sur les dolmens*, Geneva, 1865; J. Fergusson, *Rude Stone Monuments in All Countries*, London, 1872 (still useful as a topographical guide, with numerous cuts, but written to sustain an inadmissible hypothesis of their recent origin); S. Reinach, 'Terminologie des monuments mégalithiques,' *RA*, ser. III. vol. xxii. [1893] p. 34; Lord Avebury, *Prehistoric Times*[7], London, 1913; T. E. Peet, *Rough Stone Monuments and their Builders* (Harper's Library of Living Thought), do. 1912; G. Elliot Smith, 'The Evolution of the Rock-cut Tomb and the Dolmen,' in *Essays and Studies presented to William Ridgeway*, Cambridge, 1913, pp. 493–546 (with good bibliography).

ii. *LOCAL.*—(1) *Europe.*—ENGLAND AND WALES.—The Victoria County Histories, and the Reports of the English and Welsh Royal Commission on Ancient and Historical Monuments (in course of publication); W. J. Harrison, 'A Bibliography of the Great Stone Monuments of Wiltshire,' *Wilts. Arch. and Nat. Hist. Magazine*, vol. xxxii. p. 1 (Dec. 1901); B. C. A. Windle, *Remains of the Prehistoric Age in England*, London, 1904. SCOTLAND.—The Reports of the Scottish Royal Commission on Ancient and Historical Monuments (in course of publication); F. R. Coles, Papers on Scottish Stone Circles in the *Proceedings of the Society of Antiquaries of Scotland*, vols. xxxiv.–xlv. [Edinburgh, 1900–11]. IRELAND.—W. C. Borlase, *The Dolmens of Ireland*, 3 vols., London, 1897; W. G. Wood-Martin, *Rude Stone Monuments of Ireland*, Dublin, 1888. FRANCE.—E. Cartailhac, *La France préhistorique*, Paris, 1889; A. Bertrand, 'Les Monuments primitifs de la Gaule,' in *Archéologie celtique et gauloise*, do. 1889; J. Déchelette, *Manuel d'archéologie préhistorique, celtique et gallo-romaine*, do. 1908–14, i. (contains many valuable bibliographical references). GERMANY.—E. Krause and O. Schötensack, 'Die megalithischen Gräber (Steinkammergräber) Deutschlands,' *ZE* xxv. [1893] 105; E. Grabowsky, 'Die Lübbensteine bei Helmstedt,' *Beitr. zur Anthrop. Braunschweigs*, Brunswick, 1898. HOLLAND.—L. de Laigue, 'Les Monuments mégalithiques de la province de Drenthe (Pays-bas),' *L'Anthropologie*, x. [1899] 1, 179. BELGIUM.—A. de Loë, 'Etude sur les mégalithes . . . sur le territoire de la Belgique actuel,' *Fédération Hist. et Arch. de Belgique*, Brussels, 1888. SCANDINAVIA AND DENMARK.—O. Montelius, 'Sur les Tombeaux et la topographie de la Suède pendant l'âge de la pierre,' *Congrès d'archéologie préhistorique*, Stockholm, 1874, p. 152, and *Les Temps préhistoriques en Suède*, tr. S. Reinach, Paris, 1895, Eng. tr. F. H. Woods, London, 1888; N. H. Sjöborg, *Samlingar för Nordens Fornälskare*, Stockholm, 1822. SPAIN AND PORTUGAL.—Papers by different authors in various volumes of *Portugalia* and *O Archeologo português*; E. Cartailhac, *Les Ages préhistoriques de l'Espagne et du Portugal*, Paris, 1886. ITALY.—G. Nicolucchi, *Brevi note sui monumenti megalitici . . . di Terra d'Otranto*, Naples, 1893. BALEARIC ISLANDS.—L. C. Watelin, 'Contribution à l'étude des monuments primitifs des Iles Baléares,' *RA* IV. xiv. [1909] 333; E. Cartailhac, *Monuments primitifs des Iles Baléares*, Toulouse, 1892. MALTA.—A. Mayr, *Die vorgeschichtl. Denkmäler von Malta*, Munich, 1901, *Die Insel Malta im Altertum*, do. 1909; A. A. Caruana, *Report on the Phœnician and Roman Antiquities in the Group of the Islands of Malta*, Malta, 1882. SARDINIA.—L. C. Watelin, 'Les Nuraghes de Sardaigne,' *RA* IV. xvii. [1911] 6; E. Ardu-Onnis, 'La Sardeigna prehistorica,' *Atti d. società Romana di Anthrop.*, 1898, 1903. BULGARIA.—H. and K. Škorpil, *Pametnici iz Bulgarsko* ('Memorials of Bulgaria'), Sofia, 1888 (illustrated review and analysis in *Mittheilungen der anthrop. Gesellschaft in Wien*, xviii. [1888–89] 285). RUSSIA.—Joseph de Baye, *Au Nord de la chaîne du Caucase*, Paris, 1899, and 'Fouilles de Kourganes au Kouban,' *Mém. de la soc. nat. des antiq. de France*, lix. 43; E. Chantre, *Recherches anthropologiques dans le Caucase*, Paris, 1885–87, i.

(2) *Asia.*—SYRIA AND PALESTINE.—G. Schumacher, *Across the Jordan*, London, 1886; D. Mackenzie, 'The Megalithic Monuments of Rabbath Ammon at Ammân,' in *PEFAnnual*, i. [1911] 1. ARABIA.—W. G. Palgrave, *Personal Narrative of a Year's Journey through Central and Eastern Arabia*[2], London, 1868, ch. v.; C. M. Doughty, *Arabia Deserta*, Cambridge, 1888, i. 284, ii. 244, 304. TRANSCAUCASIA AND RUSSIAN ARMENIA.—E. Rösler, 'Neue Ausgrabungen . . . in Transkaukasien,' *ZE* xxx. [1898] 416; J. de Morgan, 'Note sur les Nécropoles préhistoriques de l'Arménie russe,' *RA* III. xvi [1890] 176. INDIA.—H. H. Wilson, *Ariana Antiqua*, London, 1841; W. Ross King, *The Aboriginal Tribes of the Nilgiri Hills*, do. 1870, p. 22 f.; Walter Elliot, 'On some Ancient Sepulchral Remains in Southern India,' *Prehistoric Congress*, Norwich Meeting, 1868, p. 240; J. D. Hooker, *Himalayan Journals*, London, 1854, ii. 319–321; H. H. Goodwin-Austen, 'On the Stone Monuments of the Khâsi Hill Tribes,' *JAI* i. [1872] 122, 'On the Rude Stone Monuments of Certain Naga Tribes,' *ib.* iv. [1875] 144, 'Further Notes on the Rude Stone Monuments of the Khâsi Hill Tribes,' *ib.* v. [1876] 37. KOREA.—W. Gowland, 'Notes on the Dolmens . . . of Korea,' *JAI* xxiv. [1895] 316; E. Baelz, 'Dolmen und alte Königsgräber in Korea,' *ZE* xlii. [1910] 776. JAPAN.—W. Gowland, 'The Burial Mounds and Dolmens of the early Emperors of Japan,' *JAI* xxxvii. [1910] 10, and 'The Dolmens of Japan,' *Archæologia*, lv. [1897] 439.

(3) *Africa.*—ALGERIA.—L. Levistre, 'Sur quelques Stations dolméniques de l'Algérie,' *Anthropos*, ii. [1907] 135; A. Lissauer, 'Archäologische und anthropologische Studien über die Kabylen,' *ZE* xl. [1908] 501. TUNIS.—Carton, 'Tunisie, les mégalithes de Bulla Regia,' etc., *L'Anthropologie*, II. [1891] 1. NIGERIA.—M. Desplagnes, 'Une Mission archéologique dans la vallée du Niger,' *Géographie*, xiii. [1906] 81. GAMBIA.—J. L. Todd, 'Note on Stone Circles in Gambia,' *Man*, iii. [1903] no. 93; Duchemin, 'Mégalithes de la Gambie,' *L'Anthropologie*, xvi. [1905] 633.

(4) *Oceania.*—W. J. Perry, *The Megalithic Culture of Indonesia*, Manchester, 1918. NEW CALEDONIA.—Archambault, 'Les Mégalithes néocalédoniens,' *L'Anthropologie*, xii. [1901] 257, xiii. [1902] 689. TONGA.—A. Bastian, 'Das Entdeckungsschiff im Neu-Seeland und die Dolmen von Tonga,' *ZE* xxvi. [1894] 163; W. Mariner, *An Account of the Natives of the Tonga Islands*, London, 1817, i. 153 (description of chieftains' burial-places).

(5) *America.*—Mounds take the place of stone monuments in America. For a rude circle in Peru see E. G. Squier, *Peru: Incidents of Travel and Exploration in the Land of the Incas*, London, 1877, p. 383. For the mounds see E. G. Squier and E. H. Davis, *Ancient Monuments of the Mississippi Valley* (vol. i. of the 'Smithsonian Contributions to Knowledge'), Washington, 1848.

R. A. S. MACALISTER.

STONING.—See CRIMES AND PUNISHMENTS (Jewish), ADULTERY (Jewish), (Muslim).

STORM, STORM-GODS.—**1. Introduction.** —The gods of cataclysms naturally held the first rank in the 'magic-religions' of the earliest types of human society. Some of them gradually became connected with the gods of abysses and especially with those of the earth and its depths. Others went to swell the army of the demons of darkness and of evil. The gods of hurricanes and tempests followed the same process, though more slowly.

They are the manifest product of naturism and personification; speculations on the composition and structure of the sky[1] deny them any rôle in the upper world; it is only by accident that they are sometimes connected with the activity, but not the personality, of the sky-god. By the same reasoning primitive man (or at any rate present-day uncivilized man) did not place the storm-gods on the physical plane inhabited by the gods of the air,[2] although sometimes, as the result of time and the confusion of myths, the maleficent storm-gods seem to become intermingled with the hierarchies of the air-gods. The general principle is that the storm-gods are personalities essentially distinct from the air-gods and having no logical connexion with them.

One of the clearest results of this is the frequent opposition between the air-gods, regarded as the regular and, on the whole, beneficent rulers of such-and-such a quarter of the atmosphere, and the storm-gods, naturally assimilated to maleficent principles. Another feature that separates the storm-gods from the air-gods is still more remarkable. As is shown in art. AIR AND GODS OF THE AIR, the air-gods usually dwell in the aerial regions. The search for the principle of causality, the observation of the relation of cause and effect, and, lastly, animism have on the contrary almost everywhere connected the storm-gods with the terrestrial plane, solid or liquid. Sometimes they are localized, and have as their habitat the summit or the peak of some high mountain, from which they are supposed to dart forth to cause their ravages; sometimes they are imagined as hidden in a grotto or cavern, or as wandering through the labyrinths of valleys and ravines, or ready to leap from the neck of a mountain or a pass or to spring from a precipice; or, again, they are the formidable gods of the desert who hide in great whirlwinds of sand, advancing in columns. Among peoples inhabiting the shores of large lakes or inland seas or the sea-coast the storm-gods seldom dwell at the bottom of those deep waters; they practically always leap from a cape, a point, or an isolated rock, to accomplish their work of destruction. At other times they come from a mysterious island, an islet remarkable for its strange shape, or a sea-grotto feared by fishermen; sometimes (more rarely) they are known to have their palace at the bottom of one of those gulfs, bays, or lagoons that are subject to sudden crashes of tempest. Their attack, both by sea and by land, is swift and unexpected; the poetry of Chaldæo-Assyrian cosmogony describing their tumultuous outbursts calls them 'wild horses born in the mountain.'

2. Diffusion.—In what regions do we find those gods? From the naturist point of view this question becomes theoretically a question of meteorological geography and practically a question of making an abstract of the evidence of ethnological geography. In Asia we find storm-gods in the labyrinths of passes of the Tibetan group, the formidable solitudes of the high summits of the Himālayas, the frozen tracks of the desert of Gobi; in Africa, in the mountainous group of the Cameroons, those of Ruwenzori and Kilima-njaro, the headlands of Lake Victoria-Nyanza and Lake Tanganyika, and the desert wastes of the Kalahari; in America, in the great passes and summits of the Andes, the islands of Lake Titicaca, and the volcanic peaks or the sierras of Mexico. Maritime regions also have their series of storm-gods: in the first rank naturally come the desolate countries of polar tempests, the ice-peaks of the 'gods of terror' in Greenland, those of the Eskimo regions, the frozen Arctic Ocean and Lapland with their 'tempest spirits,' and the Atlantic coast of Europe; in Africa it is mainly the more exposed west coasts; in the vast expanses of the Pacific two favourite regions are prominent at the two extremities: in the north between Japan and the Siberian coast, and particularly at the southern extremity of America towards Patagonia, Tierra del Fuego, and the Magellan Strait; in the Indian Ocean, and wherever typhoon holds sway, we find islands, gulfs, and rocks marking the sites of the kingdoms of the storm-gods; lastly, in the southern seas (Polynesia and Micronesia) cosmogonic mythology confirms the presumptions of geography by describing the eternal struggle of the gods of order, the allies of man, with the turbulent and destructive storm-gods.

Of course the parallelism between geography and mythology is not constant nowadays. Civilization first of all consigned a large number of the early storm-gods to the realm of allegory or dissolved them in syncretism. Then they passed away along with the oldest established polytheism, with which the advance of human speculation had connected them. Such was the case with the Chaldæan storm-god, the Egyptian Set, the sons of the Mediterranean Æolus, and the pre-historic storm-god who to the first sailors of our races personified the north wind (Boreas), the tramontane wind, and the tempest wind of the west Brittany coast. Traces of them recur in stories and throughout the deformations of classical folklore and mythology, and clearly enough to prove the correctness of the theoretically presupposed connexion between physical geography and religion; clearly enough too to show the connexion between their scattered traits and those of the storm-gods of the savage races of the present day, and to convince us that the work, characteristics, nature, and rôle of the storm-gods were uniformly identical in the first ages of all the religious groups.

The result is that the area of the diffusion of the storm-gods is entirely different from that of the air-gods. Not only is there nothing resembling the universality of the presence of the sky-god, but there are even complete religious zones from which the storm-god is absent.

3. Rôle. — The material characteristics and effects of the storm had the logical consequence of forcing the storm-gods into the army of evil, wherever men had arrived at the stage of disengaging the rudiments of dualistic classification from the apparently chaotic collision of the forces and beings of nature. Myth afterwards attempted to vindicate this classification. And, since by reason of their accidental character the harmful activities of the storm-gods fitted them only for a subordinate rôle in the great struggle, some of the myths aimed at explaining the times and circumstances of their appearances; and thus we see them figuring in the cosmogonic cycle. Since cosmogony is the putting in order and the 'stabilization' of the evil or incoherent energies of chaos, the rôle of the storm-gods, who are always the agents of confusion and destruction, necessarily places them among the conquered powers (*e.g.*, in Chaldæa). It is true that the dualistic struggle

[1] See art. SKY, SKY-GODS.
[2] See art. AIR AND GODS OF THE AIR.

persists in the majority of dualisms in order to explain the constant reappearance of evil, but in these also the storm-gods are always conquered in the end. They often call to their aid legions of malevolent phantoms and evil spirits who wander by night on the surface of the earth (*e.g.*, China, Korea). But this very alliance results in their gradually losing their personality and becoming merged in the huge army of secondary spirits in the service of the great maleficent deities.

Such were in primitive times the seven sons of Bel, the Chaldæan chiefs of the Annunaki, or Annunas, of the earth (here again we see the storm-gods connected with the terrestrial plane). They had 'grown up in the depth of the abyss'; they were 'the squall of wind which runs swiftly,' and the seventh one of them was 'the frightful whirlwind which smashes everything.'

Thus their human cult is very much reduced: they have neither sanctuaries nor priests; but here and there they have persons affiliated with them who control them by magical power and who can make them come and let loose their evil forces (*e.g.*, in Polynesia).

4. Cult.—The nearest approach to a cult of the storm-gods is among certain fishing peoples (in the Pacific—*e.g.*, Saghalien Island, etc.), who use propitiatory means to conciliate them when setting out on an expedition. But, though the Ainus may invoke or flatter Shi-Asha by offerings, the opposite process, viz. protection by the aid of a more powerful good spirit, seems to be the more frequent proceeding. The ancient Chaldæan poems say of them: 'they listen neither to prayer nor to supplication.'

In exceptional cases the storm-deity may not have a uniformly wicked character. Besides the very dangerous spirits of the icebergs and the scourges which they let loose by hurricanes, the Eskimos attribute to Arnaknagsak (or Sedna), mother of the tempests, an old woman who lives at the bottom of the sea, the power of procuring food for them. Cases of this kind (of which there are about half-a-score well authenticated) proceed as a rule from local observation of the consequences of a great storm, which are sometimes helpful to man. The Bretons of Ile de Sein attributed a beneficent character to the tempests of the south-west, because they brought shipwrecks to the coast.

In exceptional cases also the storm-god seems to be connected with the army of the sky-god. Thus among the Andamans the tempest is the result of the will of the famous Puluga. Such a fact tends to imply the evil character of the sky-god, and consequently is of great theoretical importance. On examination it appears that the confusion is caused by the presence in the tempests of those regions of a great number of meteorological phenomena, such as lightning, thunder, etc., whose management belongs by definition to the supreme god or the sky-god. In such cases the storm loses its personality; it becomes a manifestation of the sky-god and is interpreted as a punishment or revenge of the offended sky-god.

The same kind of mixture by confusion of myths or linking of exterior characteristics explains why certain peoples, such as those of Guiana or of Brazil (*e.g.*, the Botocudos) connect the storm-gods with the stellar deities or with the moon.

5. Representations.—The fetishistic representations of the storm-gods have so far received little study. Nevertheless they exist in large numbers in all the religious groups that have storm-gods and mainly in the groups in which fishing is the chief means of subsistence. These fetishes are inspired by the usual principles—supposed affinities, allusions to mythical episodes, attraction or repulsion (the same reasoning as for fetishes of diseases), amalgams of magical substances, etc. Some good specimens may be mentioned among the Ainus, and among the races of Polynesia, Micronesia, New Guinea (*e.g.*, in the Gazelle Peninsula), Vuatam Island, etc. Representations of an idolatrous but aniconic type have been studied still less. As is the rule in naturism, they are inspired at the outset either by the external appearance of the covering of the storm-god or by the usual principles of symbolico-magic (effect for cause, part for whole, etc.). The appearance of a tornado, of a water-spout, of the storm-clouds, of a whirlpool, of lightning, of typhoons, and the kinds of death and destruction caused by the storm-gods, have suggested a large number of abridged and distorted forms and secret magical forms. Nevertheless our ignorance of their real meanings and the reticence of the uncivilized render ethnological inquiry on this point very difficult.

When we pass to iconic reproductions, we find here also that the maleficent and dangerous character served as starting-point. The plastic expression by man of their material physiognomy offers at once a very great variety of material representation and extreme monotony of theoretical conception: fantastic ugliness (as terrifying as possible) has everywhere been used to express their wickedness, their fury, and the fear which they inspire. Naturally each local art borrowed from its special demonography and from local material elements its ugliest and most bizarre traits. Ethnographic collections show types borrowed from Polynesian religions, from the coast of W. Africa, and from pre-Columban America (the last especially in drawn and painted forms). The classical East has left us the distorted images of the south-west wind. Two details are common to all: (1) the use of composite traits, like the figures of nightmares—hideous mixtures of heads, members, and different parts of the body of the most repugnant and terrible animals; and (2) the almost complete absence of symbolic allusion to a mythical episode or a cosmogonic rôle of first rank. The Annunaki, sons of Bel, might have composite bodies of lions, serpents, or hideous animals, half-reptiles, and half-birds; but they were never anything but subordinates. It is purely literary licence when the poet calls them 'destroyers of the sky.'

6. Conclusion.—The evolution towards dualism has given only imperfect results. Nowhere has the storm-god succeeded in taking first rank in the army of evil, and the reason seems to be that such a place presupposes a continuous activity and a constant presence. The chthonian gods and the gods of darkness have made various storm-gods their subordinates, but not their equals. Where there has been organization of the original naturistic dualism, they have fallen to the rank of simple evil spirits or inferior demons. Among peoples who have attained to the redaction of stories of a properly mythological kind they are based on a number of episodes of a rather subordinate character — of which the religions of classical India and of Greece give us some satisfactory examples (cf. above). The purely allegorical and poetical myth marks the last visible shadow of their gradually disappearing traits.

LITERATURE.—There seems to be no monograph on the subject. Some of the classical literature will be found in the art. AIR AND GODS OF THE AIR. For literature on primitive races see artt. on the various peoples and their religions.

GEORGE FOUCART.

STRANGERS.—I. *PRIMITIVE USAGE IN REGARD TO THE FOREIGNER OR STRANGER.*—1. A survey of the evidence shows us that, among the peoples which occupy the lowest place in the scale of culture, the population lives scattered in small groups of the nature of families.[1] Among the Negritos of the Philippines the family group consists of from 30 to 40 persons,[2] in the case of the Yahgan of Cape Horn from two to five families are found in a single wigwam,[3] while, among the Central Australian tribes, members of the local group wander in small parties of one or two families over the land which they own.[4] These

[1] See W J McGee, 'The Siouan Indians,' in *15 RBEW* [1897], p. 200; and the instances in P. J. Hamilton-Grierson, *The Silent Trade: a Contribution to the Early Hist. of Human Intercourse*, Edinburgh, 1903, p. 6 and note 8.

[2] A. Schadenberg, 'Ueber die Negrittos der Philippinen,' *ZE* xii. [1880] 137.

[3] T. Bridges, *ap.* E. Westermarck, *The Hist. of Human Marriage*[2], London, 1894, p. 44.

[4] Spencer-Gillen[a], p. 16.

family groups are, in general, subdivisions of a larger unity. Thus the Negritos recognize the subsistence of social ties between a few families;[1] the Yahgan recognize clans which comprise many smaller divisions;[2] and the tribe of Central Australia is 'an entity . . . divided into a number of lesser groups. . . . These again are divided and subdivided until we reach the smallest group consisting of a few families or even only a single family.'[3] Further, as E. M. Curr[4] observes, every tribe has constant, and for the most part friendly, relations with other tribes.

At times these family groups join forces for the purposes of war or the chase; and at times they exchange visits, and, in some cases at all events, meet for the performance of ceremonies. As a general rule, however, such gatherings are occasional only and of short duration. They break up as soon as the purpose which brought them together is served; and of course they cannot outlast the food supply of the place at which they meet.

While, then, it is plain that the social feelings of the savage reach beyond the family groups to which he belongs, it is difficult or, rather, impossible to make a general statement as to the extent of their range. Bishop Stirling[5] says of the Yahgan that, beyond the family circle, the relation of man to man is doubtful, if not hostile. On the other hand, Spencer and Gillen[6] declare that permanent enmity between any two of the tribes with whom they are acquainted is a thing unknown. In short, the range of the social feelings is widely different in different cases. In some they reach beyond the clan or even the tribe; in others they hardly cross the limits of the family group. The statement of Spencer and Gillen as to the relations of the associated tribes of Central Australia suggests that these tribes have advanced no little way from the simplest stages of social life,[7] and that the Yahgan conception of the world beyond the family group (or little aggregate of family groups) as a hostile world may be taken as representing the 'primitive' conception.

In many instances this conception is held most strongly by that portion of a community which has no personal knowledge of the strangers whom it hates and fears.

Thus the Californian tribes which live at a distance from one another are in perpetual enmity;[8] and the Seri of Sonora, who never see their neighbours except on the frontier or in foray, kill them as a tribal duty, whenever opportunity offers.[9] Before the British settlement of the Andamans there existed extreme jealousy and distrust between adjacent tribes, and even between scattered communities of the same tribe; and it was often the case that tribes fifteen or twenty miles apart had no knowledge of one another.[10] So, too, those of the Yahgan who have never met with the Ona hate and fear them, while those who are their neighbours intermarry with them, with the result that both Yahgan and Ona learn one another's language and are, to some extent at all events, influenced by one another's manners and modes of life. In the same way the Yahgan dread the Alacaluf, believing them to be possessed of supernatural powers, until they have actually seen them, and have become familiar with their appearance.[11]

1 A. B. Meyer, 'Die Negrittos der Philippinen,' *Petermann's Mitth.* xx. [1874] 21.
2 Bridges, *ap.* Westermarck, p. 44.
3 A. W. Howitt, 'The Dieri and other Kindred Tribes of Central Australia,' *JAI* xx. [1891] 35.
4 *The Australian Race*, Melbourne and London, 1886–87, i. 63.
5 'Residence in Fuegia,' in *S. American Missionary Magazine*, iv. [1870] 11.
6 a p. 32, b p. 31.
7 Cf. A. Lang, *Social Origins*, London, 1903, p. 69.
8 J. Baegert, 'An Account of the Aboriginal Inhabitants of the Californian Peninsula,' tr. C. Rau, in *Annual Report of . . . the Smithson. Inst. . . . for the Year 1863*, Washington, 1864, p. 359.
9 W J McGee, 'The Seri Indians,' in *17 RBEW* [1899], pt. i. pp. 130, 132.
10 E. H. Man, *On the Aboriginal Inhabitants of the Andaman Islands*, London, 1883, p. xvii.
11 P. Hyades and J. Deniker, *Mission scientifique du Cap Horn*, Paris, 1885–91, vii. 15; see also the observations of Spencer-Gillen b, p. 31, regarding the prevalence of similar conceptions among some of the Australian tribes.

2. Whatever may be the proximate causes, whatever may be the precise degree of his fear and hatred, the fact remains that as a general rule the savage fears and hates the stranger, and looks upon him, certainly as an enemy, and, it may be, as a being brutish, monstrous, or devilish.

The Orang-Ot of Borneo, when they meet with strangers, turn their backs on them and squat on the ground, hiding their faces; and they explain this behaviour by saying that the sight of strangers makes them dizzy and affects their eyes like the sunlight.[1]

There are many instances of a people calling itself by a name which signifies nothing more than 'the men,' and thus distinguishing itself from the rest of mankind, whom it regards as belonging to a lower order of being. The designation 'Hos'—a branch of the Kols—means 'men' as contrasted with brutes;[2] and the Narrinyeri take great pride in their name, which means 'belonging to men.' 'We are men,' they say, while they call other natives 'wild black fellows.'[3]

Examples of like import are supplied by the Chingpaw, known as Kakhyen by the Burmese, the Tepecanos of Mexico, the Kurnai, the Wiimbaio, the Bakoba, the Yahgan, and the Arawaks and Caribs of Guiana, the Chiriguans, the Chippewas, the Wintūn, and other Californian tribes.[4]

3. The Tupi of Brazil call all men not of their race or speech 'Tapuya,' 'strangers' or 'enemies'[5]—a practice which Burton compares with the case of the 'Hebrew Goyi (Gentile), the Hindu Mlechchha (mixed or impure breed), the Greek βάρβαρος, the Latin Barbarus, and the Chinese Fan Kwei (foreign devil).'[6] Several of the Californian tribes are called 'Yuki.' The word in the Wintūn language means 'stranger,' and secondarily 'bad Indian,' 'thief,' and is applied in the same way as the Greek βάρβαρος.[7] In the language of the Pomo 'Chumaia' means 'stranger,' 'enemy,' and is used by them in speaking of their neighbours who are really Yuki.[8] The Chippewas, too, employ the word signifying 'stranger' in the sense of 'enemy';[9] and it may be noted, as showing the position which the stranger and the outcast occupied in early times, that a series of words which meant originally 'stranger,' 'outcast,' 'alien,' have come to mean 'miserable' or 'unfortunate.'[10]

4. In the Western Islands of Torres Straits it was regarded as meritorious to kill foreigners either in fair fight or by treachery, and honour and glory were attached to the bringing home of the skulls of the natives of other islands, slain in battle.[11]

J. J. Atkinson tells us that he had three servants, natives of New Caledonia, who had been with him for five years. Two of them belonged to one tribe, and the third, a boy, belonged to another. These tribes were neighbours. Atkinson gave the three a holiday, and landed them at the village of the two natives, with the result that the boy was killed and eaten by them the same night.[12]

1 C. A. L. M. Schwaner, *Borneo, Beschrijving van het Stroomgebied van den Barito*, Amsterdam, 1853, i. 229; P. J. Veth, *Borneo's Wester-Afdeeling*, Zalt-Bommel, 1854–56, ii. 392, gives the same account of the Poenans; and see also G. F. Lyon, *A Narr. of Travels in N. Africa*, London, 1821, p. 149; *Pilgrimage of Fa Hian*, from the French ed. of the *Foe Koue Ki* of Rémusat, Klaproth, and Landresse, Calcutta, 1848, p. 232.
2 E. T. Dalton, *Descriptive Ethnology of Bengal*, Calcutta, 1872, p. 178; cf. p. 35 as to the Dophlās.
3 G. Taplin, *ap.* J. D. Woods, *The Native Tribes of S. Australia*, Adelaide, 1879, p. 1.
4 Other instances will be found in A. H. Keane, *Man Past and Present*², Cambridge, 1899, 1920, *Ethnology*, do. 1896; and in Hamilton-Grierson, p. 30, note 2.
5 *The Captivity of Hans Stade of Hesse in A.D. 1547–1555 among the wild Tribes of E. Brazil*, ed. R. F. Burton, London, 1874 (Hakluyt Society), p. lxx.
6 *Ib.*
7 S. Powers, 'Tribes of California,' in *Contributions to N. American Ethnology*, Washington, 1877, iii. 125 f.
8 *Ib.* p. 136.
9 W. H. Keating, *Narr. of an Expedition to the Source of St. Peter's River*, London, 1825, i. 336.
10 O. Schrader, *Handelsgeschichte und Warenkunde*, Jena, 1886, p. 7; cf. J. Grimm, *Deutsche Rechtsalterthümer*³, Göttingen, 1881, p. 396 ff.
11 *Reports of the Cambridge Anthropological Expedition to Torres Straits*, Cambridge, 1901–12, v. 277 ff.
12 'The Natives of New Caledonia,' *FL* xiv. [1903] 250; cf.

The stranger in the Nissan Islands is regarded as an enemy, and is, if possible, killed and eaten.[1] We have a like account of the inhabitants of Mabuiag,[2] of the Massim of New Guinea,[3] and of the Battas. In the last case the inhabitants of the villages, which are cut off from one another by high grass and primeval forest, practise a system of mutual exclusion. To be a stranger is to be an enemy; and a native who enters the district of his neighbours runs the chance of being eaten.[4] So, too, Strabo[5] says of the Scythians on the Euxine that they sacrificed strangers, devoured their flesh, and used their skulls as drinking-cups. Among the Nāgas every tribe, almost every village, is at war with its neighbours; and he who leaves the territory of his tribe does so at the peril of his life.[6] The Wazaramo do not allow strangers to camp within their villages; and among the Wanyamwezi it is impossible for single individuals to move from one district to another. They are sure to be plundered, if not murdered.[7] The Bakete and Bakuba refuse all friendly advances by peoples in their vicinity, and the stranger who enters their territory is treated as an enemy.[8] The Akka look upon strangers as fair prey;[9] the Kabyles regard all who live beyond their frontiers as enemies;[10] and the Bakwiri villages are fences for protection, as they are continually at enmity with one another.[11] Schweinfurth[12] makes the general observation that in Africa there is an utter want of wholesome intercourse between race and race. For any member of a tribe which speaks one dialect to cross the border of a tribe which speaks another is to court destruction; and the effect of difference of language in intensifying the mutual discords between petty tribes has been remarked by A. von Humboldt[13] in the case of the American tribes between the equator and the eighth degree of north latitude. The Arab who meets an unknown wanderer in the desert acts in accordance with the saying, 'The stranger is for the wolf';[14] and it is a consequence of this desert law, which identifies the stranger with the enemy, that the *jinn* are regarded as hostile, as gods without worshippers, dwelling in haunts and not in sanctuaries.[15]

A stranger may not approach a Khond village,[16] unless invited; and, in speaking of Angamiland, G. Watt[17] says that it is no unusual state of affairs to find *khel* A of one village at war with *khel* B of another, while not at war with *khel* B of its own village. The *khels* are often completely separated by great walls, the people on either side living within a few yards of each other, yet having no dealings whatever.[18] Lyon tells us of two towns separated only by a wall. The inhabitants of the one town are at constant war with those of the other. They seldom see and are perfect strangers to one another.[1]

It is to be observed that in some countries the stranger, if he be of high repute for sanctity, may run the danger of being slain so that the blessing of his perpetual presence may rest on the land. Thus the Afghan Hazarehs kill and bury in their own country any foreigner who performs a miracle or shows any sign of divine favour;[2] and similar statements are made regarding the Wa[3] and the inhabitants of Yunnan.[4]

5. Among the Kabyles the foreigner is prohibited from performing any act which assures to him property or influence.[5] The Mairs will not tolerate the residence of any stranger among them;[6] and a similar policy was pursued by the tribes of which P. von Martius[7] speaks, and, at one time, by the Masai.[8] So too in Dahomey an alien may not establish himself in the country without the king's permission;[9] and J. H. van Linschoten[10] states that a similar regulation prevailed in China.[11] In the height of their prestige the Masai punished with death by beating any one of their people who returned after having gone to live with foreigners;[12] and the Wachaga formerly inflicted the death penalty on any woman of the tribe who married a stranger.[13] Among the Khonds marriage with a stranger adopted into the tribe is forbidden;[14] and, according to Ibn Batuta,[15] the women of Zebid will marry the stranger, but will not quit their country. Even in the burial of the dead the same conception prevailed. Thus the Choctaws thought it irreligious to bury their kinsman alongside of a stranger, much more to inter him in the tomb of an enemy.[16]

6. The stranger is regarded as a being without rights; for he is outside of the sphere within which alone they are recognized and enforced. This view prevails among many peoples.[17]

It is held, *e.g.*, by the Wakapomo,[18] the Wanyamwezi,[19] the Barea and Kunáma,[20] the Bogos,[21] the Pelew Islanders,[22] and certain Papuan tribes—the Yabim on the north coast of New Guinea, and the Tami Islanders.[23]

Except in so far as modified by treaty, by special protection, or by the institution of hospitality, the same conception ruled among the nations of classical antiquity.

'Cum alienigenis, cum barbaris, aeternum omnibus Graecis

V. de Rochas, *La Nouvelle-Calédonie*, Paris, 1862, p. 250; A. Bernard, *L'Archipel de la Nouvelle-Calédonie*, do. 1894, p. 292.

1 F. Sorge, 'Nissan-Inseln im Bismarck-Archipel,' *ap.* S. R. Steinmetz, *Rechtsverhältnisse von eingeborenen Völkern in Africa und Ozeanien*, Berlin, 1903, p. 414.

2 *Reports of the Cambridge Anthrop. Expedition*, v. 278.

3 C. G. Seligmann, *The Melanesians of British New Guinea*, Cambridge, 1910, p. 569.

4 F. Junghuhn, *Die Battaländer auf Sumatra*, Berlin, 1847, p. 109 f.

5 VII. iii. 6 f.

6 W. Crooke, *Natives of Northern India*, London, 1907, p. 43.

7 J. A. Grant, *A Walk across Africa*, Edinburgh, 1864, pp. 38, 102.

8 H. von Wissmann, L. Wolf, C. de François, and H. Mueller, *Im Innern Afrikas*, Leipzig, 1888, pp. 208, 227.

9 G. Burrows, *The Land of the Pigmies*, London, 1898, p. 195 f.

10 A. Hanoteau and A. Letourneux, *La Kabylie et les coutumes kabyles*, Paris, 1872–73, ii. 141.

11 Leuschner, *Die Bakwiri*, *ap.* Steinmetz, p. 21.

12 *The Heart of Africa*, tr. E. E. Frewer, London, 1873, i. 200.

13 *Personal Narr. of Travels to the Equinoctial Regions of the New Continent*, tr. H. M. Williams, London, 1814–29, v. 270.

14 C. M. Doughty, *Travels in Arabia Deserta*, Cambridge, 1888, i. 276; cf. p. 580.

15 W. Robertson Smith, *Lectures on the Religion of the Semites*², London, 1894, p. 119 ff.

16 H. B. Rowney, *The Wild Tribes of India*, London, 1882, p. 101.

17 'The Aboriginal Tribes of Manipur,' *JAI* xvi. [1887] 362.

18 See Keane, *Man Past and Present*, p. 189, as to the *khel*.

1 P. 162; for other instances see Hamilton-Grierson, p. 31.

2 R. F. Burton, *Sindh, and the Races which inhabit the Valley of the Indus*, London, 1851, p. 388; see also p. 86.

3 *Census of India, 1901*, i. Ethnographic Appendices, Calcutta, 1903, p. 217.

4 *The Book of Ser Marco Polo*, tr. H. Yule³, revised H. Cordier, London, 1903, ii. 79; W. Gill, *The River of Golden Sand*, do. 1880, i. 323.

5 Hanoteau-Letourneux, ii. 140.

6 Rowney, p. 54.

7 *Von dem Rechtszustande unter den Ureinwohnern Brasiliens*, Munich, 1832, p. 34.

8 S. L. and H. Hinde, *The Last of the Masai*, London, 1901, pp. 4, 105.

9 A. B. Ellis, *The Ewe-Speaking Peoples of the Slave Coast of W. Africa*, London, 1890, p. 227.

10 *Voyage to the East Indies*, London, 1885 (Hakluyt Society), i. 135.

11 See T. R. Jernigan, *China in Law and Commerce*, New York and London, 1905, p. 241.

12 Hinde, pp. 4, 76.

13 J. Kohler, 'Das Banturecht in Ostafrika,' *ZVRW* xv. [1902] 61.

14 S. C. Macpherson, *Memorials of Service in India*, ed. W. Macpherson, London, 1865, p. 69.

15 *Voyages d'Ibn-Batoutah*, tr. C. Defrémery and B. R. Sanguinetti, Paris, 1853–59, ii. 169.

16 J. Adair, *The Hist. of the American Indians*, London, 1775, p. 184.

17 See Hamilton-Grierson, p. 33.

18 A. Kraft, *Die Wakapomo*, *ap.* Steinmetz, p. 292.

19 Kohler, *ZVRW* xv. 46.

20 W. Munzinger, *Ostafrikanische Studien*, Schaffhausen, 1864, p. 477.

21 Munzinger, *Sitten und Recht der Bogos*, Winterthur, 1859, pp. 28, 48.

22 J. Kubary, 'Die Palau-Inseln in der Südsee,' *Journ. des Museum Godeffroy*, i. [Hamburg, 1874–75] 220, 238.

23 Kohler, 'Recht der Papuas,' *ZVRW* xiv. [1900] 388 f.

bellum est.'[1] 'No Greek,' says Cunningham, 'was ever at home in another Greek city than his own; he was liable to be sold in a city in which he had no rights and no status.'[2] In early Rome the citizen was regarded as the sole possessor of rights, the privileges conferred in later times on the *peregrinus* by the *jus gentium* being, in the main, a result of peaceful intercourse between the republic and the nations, introduced by an advancing commerce. Under the later emperors the merchant belonging to an independent country was subjected to numerous disabilities; and, on the breaking up of the empire, the old conception of the stranger's position immediately revived.[3] In the Middle Ages the foreigner was regarded as incapable of holding land; he was subjected to many disadvantages in matters of law and legal procedure; he was not permitted, or was permitted only upon making a payment (*gabella emigrationis*), to leave the country with the wealth which he had accumulated; on his death his property fell in whole or in part to the supreme authority; and it was confiscated on his banishment.[4] 'Peregrinum qui patronum non habebat vendebant Saxones.'[5]

It is worthy of remark by way of contrast that, in Babylonia, resident aliens became citizens and were under no disabilities.[6]

Again, the position of the alien was injuriously affected by the view, very generally held, that the family, the group, the community, or the district to which a criminal or a debtor belonged—his fellow-countryman or his fellow-townsman — was liable in the penalty which he had incurred or the obligation by which he was bound.[7] There are even cases in which a stranger is treated as bound to pay for what another stranger, with whom he is wholly unconnected, has taken without payment;[8] and in one case (Kunáma) the host whose guest is slain may slay the slayer's guest.[9]

7. The view that the stranger has no rights finds, among the Yabim, its most forcible expression in its application to shipwrecked persons.[10]

According to Herodotus,[11] the Tauri sacrificed all such unfortunates to the Virgin. They were plundered in New Zealand;[12] and, in Borneo, both wrecks and their crews belong to the district where the disaster occurs.[13] It was the custom at Malabar that everything obtained from a wreck fell to the fisc. Calicut formed the sole exception to this rule, which seems to have prevailed on all the Indian coasts.[14] The Fijians used to kill and eat even those of their own race who were cast ashore;[15] and, according to Wilkes,[16] they were accounted as an offering to the gods and sacrificed. Another authority, however, states that they were spared, because the gods would be angry if the gift which they had sent was rejected.[17] The Yahgan kill castaways;[18] and du Cange sums up the practice of the Middle Ages thus: 'Neque dumtaxat naves ipsae fractae et naufragium passae, resque in iis contentae dominorum erant: sed et homines ipsi, qui in iis vehebantur: adeo ut et per vim caperentur, et persoluto pretio a captivitate liberari cogerentur.'[19]

D'Arvieux[1] gives a similar account of the Arabs. A very different mode of treatment is found among the western islanders of Torres Straits, who adopt the stranger as a brother and give him a garden.[2]

The distinction between the position of a stranger and that of a fellow-tribesman is illustrated by the fact that among many peoples the thief is regarded as an offender only when he steals from a compatriot or fellow-tribesman or villager;[3] and that the goods of a foreign merchant become on his death the property of the king of the country in which he has died.[4] It was the custom, however, in India as well as in the Sudan not to interfere with the property of deceased strangers, but to hand it over to the persons entitled to it;[5] and, according to Tavernier,[6] a similar practice prevailed in Persia.

8. The position of the outlaw throws light upon that of the stranger.[7]

9. Another indication of the primitive view is to be found in the symbolic acts which are the necessary preliminaries to the stranger's reception —acts by which he makes clear that his intentions are friendly, or from which he ascertains that those whom he is approaching are well-disposed towards him.

Thus it is a common sign of friendliness to advance displaying green boughs,[8] or holding out grass, as among the Masai,[9] or waving white cloth.[10] Near Cape Hinchingbroke some of the natives stood up with their arms stretched out like a cross,[11] or held up a stick with the large feathers or wing of a bird tied to it,[12] or a leathern frock on the end of a pole,[13] or offered a white cock.[14] Among the Shoshones the stranger paints the women's cheeks with vermilion in token of peace;[15] and the red shield hoisted on the mast of a ship, or hung over the walls of a town, or swung over his head by a herald, was a sign of peace among the Scandinavians.[16] In New Guinea and the adjacent islands the natives broke their spears on their own heads to show their pacific intentions,[17] or dipped their hands in water and sprinkled it over their heads.[18] The last-mentioned practice

---

1 Livy, xxxi. 29; cf. G. Grote, *A Hist. of Greece*[4], London, 1872, ii. 162.

2 *An Essay on Western Civilisation in its Economic Aspects* (*Ancient Times*), Cambridge, 1898, p. 75.

3 R. von Ihering, *Geist des römischen Rechts*[4], Leipzig, 1878, i. 231 f.; W. Pappafava, *Über die bürgerliche Rechtstellung der Fremden*, tr. from Italian to Germ. by M. Leesberg, Pola, 1884, p. 4 ff.

4 L. Goldschmidt, *Handbuch des Handelsrechts*[3], Stuttgart, 1891, p. 120 ff.; see also W. J. Ashley, *An Introd. to English Economic History and Theory*, London, 1888–93, pt. ii. 'End of the Middle Ages,' p. 13 ff.; and below, § 7.

5 Maginardus, *Transl. S. Vitti*, ch. 13.

6 C. H. W. Johns, *Babylonian and Assyrian Laws, Contracts, and Letters*, Edinburgh, 1904, p. 113.

7 See Hamilton-Grierson, p. 16, note 2; G. Turner, *Samoa*, London, 1894, p. 92; G. Grey, *Journals of Two Expeditions of Discovery in N.W. and W. Australia*, London, 1841, ii. 239; J. Matthews, *A Voyage to the River Sierra-Leone*, do. 1791, p. 82; and cf. the curious customs noted at Hawaii by E. Dieffenbach, *Travels in New Zealand*, do. 1843, i. 199, and among the Abors by Dalton, p. 24; see also Jernigan, p. 74 f.

8 H. Capello and R. Ivens, *From Benguela to the Territory of Yacca*, tr. A. Elwes, London, 1882, ii. 242.

9 Munzinger, *Ostafrikanische Studien*, p. 477.

10 Kohler, *ZVRW* xiv. 388 f.

11 iv. 103.

12 J. S. Polack, *Manners and Customs of the New Zealanders*, London, 1840, ii. 68.

13 S. St. John, *Life in the Forests of the Far East*, London, 1862, ii. 292.

14 Ibn Batuta, iv. 97 f.; *Book of Ser Marco Polo*, ii. 386.

15 T. Williams and J. Calvert, *Fiji and the Fijians*[2], ed. G. S. Rowe, London, 1860, i. 210.

16 *Narr. of U.S. Exploring Expedition*, iii. 244, note.

17 G. Brown, *Melanesians and Polynesians*, London, 1910, p. 147.

18 T. Bridges, *Mœurs et Coutumes des Fuégiens*, tr. P. Hyades, *Bulletin de la Société d'Anthropologie de Paris*, ser. iii. vol. vii. [1884] p. 180.

19 *Glossarium mediæ et infimæ Latinitatis*, ed. L. Favre, Niort, 1883–87, *s.v.* 'Lagan.'

1 *Travels in Arabia, the Desart*[2], Eng. tr., London, 1723, p. 191 ff.; cf. p. 68 ff.

2 *Reports of Cambridge Anthrop. Expedition*, v. 278.

3 M. Elphinstone, *An Account of the Kingdom of Caubul*, new ed., London, 1839, i. 297 (Afghans); see authorities in Hamilton Grierson, p. 34.

4 Hamilton-Grierson, p. 35, note 4; and see A. L. von Schlözer, *Russische Annalen in ihrer slavonischen Grundsprache*, Göttingen, 1805, iii. 332; du Cange, *s.vv.* 'Albanagium,' 'Albani'; Goldschmidt, p. 121; and above, § 6.

5 Ibn Batuta, iv. 83, 42.

6 *The Six Voyages of J. B. Tavernier through Turkey into Persia and the East Indies*, made English by J. P., London, 1678, p. 103.

7 See art. OUTLAW.

8 Hamilton-Grierson, p. 70 and note 1; J. Cook, *A Voyage towards the South Pole and round the World, 1772–75*, London, 1777, i. 221 (Otaheite), ii. 35 (Mallicollo); K. Lehmann, 'Kauffriede und Friedensschild,' in *Germanistische Abhandlungen zum LXX. Geburtstag K. v. Maurer's*, Göttingen, 1893, p. 54 f. (Scandinavia); R. Taylor, *Te Ika a Maui*, London, 1855, p. 175 (New Zealand); J. Macgillivray, *Narr. of the Voyage of H.M.S. 'Rattlesnake,'* do. 1852, ii. 41 (islands of Torres Straits); 'Navigation Australe faite par J. Le Maire et W. C. Schouten . . . 1615–17,' *Recueil des Voyages . . . de la Compagnie des Indes Orientales*, Rouen, 1725, viii. 174 (New Guinea); O. Finsch, *Samoafahrten; Reisen in Kaiser Wilhelms-Land und Englisch-Neu-Guinea*, Leipzig, 1888, p. 295 (Kaiser Wilhelm's Land); B. Hall, *Account of a Voyage of Discovery to the West Coast of Corea and the Great Loo-Choo Island*, London, 1818, p. 145 (Loo-Choo Island); H. von Wissmann, *My Second Journey through Equatorial Africa*, Eng. tr., do. 1891, p. 143 (Baqua-Sekelai); C. A. Vincendon-Dumoulin and C. Desgraz, *Iles Marquises ou Nukahiva*, Paris, 1843, p. 13 (Marquesas).

9 C. H. Stigand, *To Abyssinia, through an Unknown Land*, London, 1910, p. 211 f.

10 Vincendon-Dumoulin and Desgraz, p. 13; U. Lisiansky, *A Voyage round the World, 1803–06*, London, 1814, p. 64 f. (Marquesas); 'Navigation Australe,' p. 174 (New Guinea); J. Cook, i. 83, 220 (New Zealand, Otaheite); J. Cook and J. King, *A Voyage of Discovery to the Pacific Ocean . . . 1777–80*, London, 1784, ii. 355 (near Cape Hinchingbroke); Lehmann, p. 54 f. (Scandinavia).

11 Cook-King, ii. 355; cf. p. 397.

12 *Ib.* p. 357.

13 *Ib.* p. 391.

14 Wilkes, iii. 279 (Fiji).

15 M. Lewis and W. Clark, *Travels to the Source of the Missouri River, 1804–1806*, new ed., London, 1815, ii. 86; cf. McGee, *17 RBEW*, pt. i. p. 168.

16 Lehmann, pp. 55–60.

17 'Navigation Australe,' p. 199.

18 *Journal of the Indian Archipelago and Eastern Gazette*, ed. J. R. Logan, iv. [Singapore, 1850] 8.

seems to be general among the Papuans.[1] It is found in Ceram[2] and at Ternate;[3] and a somewhat similar usage among the Wakikuju has been described by von Höhnel.[4] The Bushmen, to show their friendliness, lay down their arms and sandals while still at a distance,[5] or wave a jackal's tail attached to the end of a stick,[6] while the inhabitants of the island called 'Gente Hermosa' hold resinous sticks burning like torches for the same purpose, perhaps with the view of disenchanting the strangers, rather than with that of showing their friendliness.[7] An old Eskimo of the Isle of St. Lawrence held up a variety of articles, and then, extending his arms, rubbed and patted his breast—the usual Eskimo indication of friendship.[8] Thus savages, by displaying goods which they are ready to barter, show that they have come to trade;[9] and Livingstone says: 'The usual way of approaching an unknown people is to call out in a cheerful tone "Malonda," "Things for sale, or do you want to sell anything?"'[10]

In many places the rule is established that an approaching stranger must in some way give notice of his presence—*e.g.*, by sounding a trumpet,[11] by shouting or blowing a horn,[12] by coughing twice,[13] by uttering the cry peculiar to his tribe,[14] or by making a series of smokes.[15]

'If,' says an ancient law of the Javanese, 'any person enter a village at an improper hour, and is twice challenged without making any reply, he shall be considered a thief. A person skulking behind a door or fence, and refusing to answer, shall also be considered as a thief.'[16]

Sometimes an attempt is made to ascertain the real mind of the stranger by means of divination. Among the A-nyanja medicine is given to a goat or fowl for this purpose, and its death is regarded as of evil omen.[17] Dalton[18] speaks of a similar practice as existing among the Pádam.

10. The Ashango host smears himself with red as a mark of friendliness, and it is a favourable sign if he asks the stranger to do likewise.[19] The Ovambo welcome him by smearing his face and breast with butter,[20] while in New Guinea it is of good omen if the host presents betel-nut to the new-comer with the thick end towards him.[21] It is not improbable that the elaborate forms of salutation in use among many peoples[22] served originally to declare the intention of persons meeting for the first time.[1]

'The Tibu,' *e.g.*, 'is always distrustful; hence meeting a fellow-countryman in the desert, he is careful not to draw near without due precaution. At sight of each other both generally stop suddenly; then crouching and drawing the litham over the lower part of the face in Tuareg fashion, they grasp the inseparable spear in their right and . . . bill-hook in their left. After these preliminaries they begin to exchange compliments, inquiring after each other's health and family connection, receiving every answer with thanksgiving to Allah. These formalities usually last some minutes.'[2]

Doughty[3] tells us of the Arabs that, when a stranger enters the tent, his hosts 'observe an honourable silence, asking no untimely questions, (such is school and nurture of the desert) until he have eaten and drunken somewhat at the least, and by "the bread and salt" there is peace established between them, for a time.'[4] There are traces of a similar etiquette in the Homeric poems;[5] and it is found among the Omahas[6] and some of the Athapascan tribes of Alaska.[7]

With this form of politeness we may compare the solemn silence with which the Tupi[8] and the Caribs[9] receive the stranger on his first arrival. This abstention from speech with him may, it is thought, originate in their fear of him as not, it may be, inherently tabu, but as belonging to strange gods, as bringing with him strange supernatural influences.[10] Besides, it may be that the stranger is not a human being, but a spirit. Hence one must make some sound each time one draws in one's breath or be smitten with dumbness.[11] Among the N. American Indians it is a common notion that 'strangers, particularly white strangers, are oft-times accompanied by evil spirits. Of these they have great dread as creating and delighting in mischief.'[12] The Nāga, when entering or leaving a strange village, and especially when leaving after having enjoyed its hospitality, strikes his ears, forehead, and stomach with a sprig of wild indigo, which he then places in his kilt, in order to avert any evil consequences of his temerity;[13] and for the same reason the giver of hospitality is exposed to danger.[14] The Bakaïri believe that evil, sickness, and death come from the sorceries of strangers beyond their borders;[15] and similar views prevail among the Melangkaps of Borneo[16] and some of the Australian aborigines.[17] In mid-Borneo the stranger's presence at religious rites is feared, and is regarded as dangerous to

1 *Journ. of the Indian Archipelago and Eastern Gazette*, iv. 8.

2 S. Müller, *Reizen en Onderzoekeningen in den indischen Archipel*, Amsterdam, 1857, i. 55.

3 *Terra Australis Cognita, or Voyages to the S. Hemisphere, 16th–18th Centuries*, ed. J. Callander, Edinburgh, 1766–68, i. 260.

4 *Zum Rudolph-See und Stephanie-See*, Vienna, 1892, p. 315 f.; see also G. Forster, *A Voyage round the World in H.B.M. Sloop Resolution*, London, 1777, ii. 186, 235 (New Guinea, Mallicollo).

5 G. W. Stow, *The Native Races of S. Africa*, London, 1905, pp. 49, 142.

6 *Ib.* p. 49.

7 *The Voyages of P. Fernandes de Queiros, 1595–1606*, tr. and ed. Clements Markham, London, 1904 (Hakluyt Society), i. 427; see § 11 below.

8 F. W. Beechey, *Narr. of a Voyage to the Pacific and Beering's Strait*, London, 1831, i. 331.

9 O. von Kotzebue, *A Voyage of Discovery into the South Sea and Behring's Straits*, Eng. tr., London, 1821, i. 189.

10 D. and C. Livingstone, *Narr. of an Expedition to the Zambesi*, London, 1865, p. 434.

11 A. d'Orbigny, *Voyage dans l'Amérique méridionale*, Paris, 1839–44, iv. 164 (Yuracarès).

12 Grimm, *Deutsche Rechtsalterthümer*[3], p. 400; but see W. E. Wilda, *Das Strafrecht der Germanen*, Halle, 1842, p. 673, note 3 (old Germany).

13 P. Paulitschke, *Ethnographie Nordost-Afrikas; die materielle Cultur der Danâkil, Galla, und Somâl*, Berlin, 1893, p. 249 (Kafa); Lumholtz, *Unknown Mexico*, i. 258 f. (Tarahumares).

14 E. F. im Thurn, *Among the Indians of Guiana*, London, 1883, p. 321.

15 Spencer-Gillen[b], p. 569 (Australia).

16 J. Crawfurd, *Hist. of the Indian Archipelago*, Edinburgh, 1820, iii. 115.

17 H. H. Johnston, *British Central Africa*, London, 1897, p. 450; see D. and C. Livingstone, p. 109.

18 P. 25.

19 P. B. du Chaillu, *A Journey to Ashango-land*, London, 1867, p. 341.

20 C. J. Andersson, *Lake Ngami; or, Explorations and Discoveries, during Four Years' Wanderings in the Wilds of S.-W. Africa*, London, 1856, p. 184; cf. J. L. Burckhardt's account (*Notes on the Bedouins and Wahábys*, London, 1830, p. 102) of the Arabs of a tribe in Nejd.

21 J. Chalmers, *Pioneering in New Guinea*, London, 1887, p. 130.

22 See art. SALUTATIONS; R. Schomburgk, *Reisen in Britisch-Guiana*, Leipzig, 1847–48, i. 205, 361 f.; d'Orbigny, iv. 164 (Akawais, Arawaks, and Macusis); Duff Macdonald, *Africana*, London, 1882, i. 35 (Yaos); J. Lery, *Hist. Navigationis in Bresiliam*, chs. 17, 19, in T. de Bry, *Hist. Americæ*, pt. iii., Frankfort, 1590–1602 (natives of Brazil); H. Ling Roth, 'On Salutations,' *JAI* xix. [1890] 164 ff.

1 Hamilton-Grierson, p. 72.

2 E. Reclus, *The Earth and its Inhabitants*, Eng. tr., London [1878–94], xi. 430.

3 i. 228.

4 See below, § 18, and cf. H. C. Trumbull, *The Threshold Covenant*, New York and Edinburgh, 1896, p. 9.

5 E.g., *Od.* i. 120 ff., iv. 60 ff.

6 Edwin James, *Account of an Expedition from Pittsburgh to the Rocky Mountains . . . compiled from the notes of Major S. H. Long*, London, 1823, ii. 44.

7 Ivan Petroff, 'Report on the Population, Industries, and Resources of Alaska,' in *Compilation of Narratives of Explorations in Alaska*, Washington, 1900, p. 262.

8 Villegagnon's 'Voyage,' in *Terra Australis Cognita*, p. 269 f.

9 J. Gumilla, *Hist. naturelle, civile, et géographique de l'Orénoque*, French tr., Avignon, 1758, ii. 80–84; L. de Poincy and C. de Rochefort, *Hist. naturelle et morale des îles Antilles de l'Amérique*, Rotterdam, 1681, p. 514.

10 See F. B. Jevons, *An Introd. to the Hist. of Religion*[2], London, 1902, p. 71; R. R. Marett, 'Is Taboo a negative Magic?', in *Anthropological Essays presented to E. B. Tylor*, Oxford, 1907, p. 233. Marett adopts the view that the stranger is inherently tabu (*The Threshold of Religion*[2], London, 1914, p. 96).

11 V. Stefánsson, *My Life with the Eskimo*, London, 1913, p. 171.

12 R. I. Dodge, *Our Wild Indians*, Hertford, Conn., 1886, p. 119.

13 T. C. Hodson, *The Nāga Tribes of Manipur*, London, 1911, p. 135.

14 See art. GIFTS (Primitive and Savage), § 4 (1)

15 K. von den Steinen, *Unter den Naturvölkern Zentral-Brasiliens*, Berlin, 1894, p. 232 f.

16 J. Whitehead, *Exploration of Mount Kina Balu, North Borneo*, London, 1893, p. 193.

17 Curr, i. 50; cf. L. Fison and A. W. Howitt, *Kamilaroi and Kurnai*, Melbourne, 1880, p. 259.

young children.[1] In the eyes of the natives of India he is specially dangerous in relation to food;[2] and among some of the jungle tribes charmed circles are drawn to keep off 'spirits belonging to another settlement, which, being strangers, are presumably hostile.'[3]

If the stranger be thus possessed, he must be disenchanted.[4]

Among the Thonga tribes he must submit to a purifying ceremony;[5] and in Benin he was compelled to wash his feet before entering the country.[6] 'One of the duties of the medicine chief is to exorcise these spirits,'[7] and, when ambassadors visit the Tatars, 'they and their gifts must pass between two fires to be purified, lest peradventure they have practised some witchcraft, or have brought some poyson or other mischiefe with them.'[8]

It seems not unlikely that to present the stranger with a lighted cigar,[9] or with a bowl of liquor,[10] or with betel-nut,[11] or to offer him the firstfruits of the soil, and, on his accepting them, to entertain him with feast, dance, and song,[12] or to receive him with a sacrifice,[13] is to perform a symbolic act of which, in some cases at least, the original significance has been forgotten—to remove the tabu from him and admit him for a time within the circle of the group.[14]

In this practice is, we believe, to be found the explanation of two very curious modes of reception. When a stranger visits a Tupi camp, he goes to the hut of his chosen host and sits down without speaking. By and by the women come to him and weep over him, and commend him, and he, too, must weep. In the end the master of the hut addresses him, provides him with food, and slings a hammock for him; and he distributes small presents.[15] This weeping welcome has been observed in New Zealand,[16] Queensland,[17] Tahiti,[18] Ulietea,[19] in the Penrhyn Islands,[20] New Caledonia,[21] the Andaman Islands,[22] and among the Ainu of Yezo.[23] In the last three cases it appears that it is indulged in only at meetings of relatives, and to such the explanation offered by E. B. Tylor[24] (that it signifies grief for those who have died in the interval of separation) or that of H. Ling Roth[25] (that it is 'joy weeping') may apply. But neither explanation meets the case where the unknown stranger is wept over on his arrival.[26] In speaking of the natives of the island of Macassar, J. G. F. Riedel[27] says that men and women weep immediately on meeting.[28]

Another curious form is found among the Central Eskimo. The stranger is welcomed with a feast; and, as he slowly approaches, one of his hosts gives him a severe blow and awaits a blow in return, and an exchange of blows continues until one of the combatants yields.[1] At one time a similar custom prevailed in Greenland.[2] The explanation of this practice is apparently to be found in the account by Hall[3] of a similar ceremony in use among the Eskimo of Cumberland Inlet. There the combat is between the stranger and the sorcerer. After having exchanged blows, they kiss one another, and the stranger is hospitably received by all. The practice, in short, is a rite of aggregation.[4] Mariner[5] informs us that at Tonga visitors or persons who have been long absent may be challenged 'by any one, or every one of the island, so that in the end they are pretty certain of getting a thorough beating'; and we may note in this connexion the statement of St. John,[6] that the Koreans 'have no salutation except buffeting each other.'

In some cases the savage offers his blood to his own gods in order to gain their protection—a proceeding which has not infrequently been mistaken for a token of friendship;[7] or he takes the stranger to a temple and prays that any evil which the latter may have brought with him may be averted;[8] or, as among some of the nomadic Arabs of Morocco, he presents the stranger with drink, which, should the latter misbehave himself, 'would cause his knees to swell so that he could not escape. In other words, he has drunk a conditional curse.'[9]

11. Further, it is plain that the supernatural influences which accompany the stranger will be especially potent in his own country.

In some parts of Australia natives, in approaching a strange encampment, 'carry lighted bark or burning sticks in their hands, for the purpose, they say, of cleansing and purifying the air';[10] and Frazer[11] suggests that the fire borne at the head of the army in ancient Greece and among the Ovambo of S.W. Africa 'may have been intended to dissipate the evil influences, whether magical or spiritual, with which the air of the enemy's country might be conceived to teem.' In the country of the Brataua Lohan had his home; and they 'believed that he watched over them, and that he caused their country to be deadly to strangers. It was therefore to him that they attributed the taboo which protected them against the visits of other tribes.'[12]

The danger of trespassing upon tabued ground was, accordingly, very serious; and the dread of incurring it was formerly so powerful among the New Zealanders that, on going to a strange land, they performed certain ceremonies 'to make it *noa*, lest, perchance, it might have been previously *tapu*.'[13] In some cases the stranger seeks to render himself acceptable to the divine guardians of the place through which he must pass by throwing down on a heap a stone, a rag, a stick, or some grass;[14] and in this connexion we may mention the belief, current among the Bechuanas, that a stranger can ensure a friendly reception by spitting on a stone and adding it to a heap on the road.[15]

---

[1] A. W. Nieuwenhuis, *Quer durch Borneo*, Leyden, 1904–07, i. 74, 163.
[2] Crooke, *Natives of N. India*, p. 195.
[3] *Ib.* p. 259.
[4] See *GB*[3], pt. ii., *Taboo and the Perils of the Soul*, London, 1911, p. 102 ff.
[5] H. A. Junod, *The Life of a South African Tribe*, London, 1912–13, i. 153, 284.
[6] H. Ling Roth, *Great Benin*, Halifax, England, 1903, p. 123.
[7] Dodge, *loc. cit.*
[8] *The Texts and Versions of John Pian de Carpine and William de Rubruquis*, ed. C. R. Beazley (Hakluyt Society), London, 1903, p. 113; cf. p. 131. See § 11, below.
[9] Von Martius, p. 56 (natives of Brazil).
[10] Schomburgk, i. 197 (Indians of British Guiana); K. Weinhold, *Altnordisches Leben*, Berlin, 1856, p. 445 (old Scandinavia); cf. H. C. Trumbull, *Studies in Oriental Social Life*, London, 1895, p. 112 f.; and see C. H. Stigand, *To Abyssinia through an Unknown Land*, London, 1910, p. 211.
[11] Kohler, *ZVRW* xiv. 389; cf. Chalmers, p. 130 (Papuans).
[12] See A. van Gennep, *Tabou et totémisme à Madagascar*, Paris, 1904, pp. 44–46.
[13] Trumbull, *Threshold Covenant*, pp. 1–10, 58 f.
[14] See the mode of welcome at the island of Gente Hermosa (§ 9, above) and the practice of carrying fire noted in § 11, below.
[15] Villegagnon, p. 269 f.
[16] Taylor, p. 175; G. F. Angas, *Savage Life and Scenes in Australia and New Zealand*, London, 1847, ii. 107.
[17] C. Lumholtz, *Among Cannibals*, London, 1889, p. 224.
[18] W. Ellis, *Polynesian Researches*[2], London, 1831–36, ii. 337.
[19] J. Cook, i. 365.
[20] C. E. Meinicke, *Die Inseln des stillen Oceans*, Leipzig, 1875–76, ii. 264.
[21] C. Lambert, 'Mœurs et superstitions de la tribu Bélep (Nouvelle Calédonie),' in *Les Missions Catholiques*, xii. [Paris, 1880] 69.
[22] Man, pp. 73, 173.
[23] H. C. St. John, *Notes and Sketches from the Wild Coasts of Nippon*, Edinburgh, 1880, p. 245.
[24] *EBr*[9], *s.v.* 'Salutations.'
[25] *JAI* xix. 178 f.
[26] As to some of the Queensland tribes see Lumholtz, p. 224 f.
[27] *De sluik- en kroesharige rassen tusschen Selebes en Papua*, The Hague, 1886, p. 405.
[28] See also N. del Techo, 'The Hist. of the Provinces of Paraguay, Tucuman, Rio de Plata,' *ap.* A. Churchill, *Collection of Voyages and Travels*, London, 1704, iv. 718; A. F. R. Wollaston, *Pygmies and Papuans*, do. 1912, pp. 41, 56; *JRGS* xxxviii. [1911] 211.

[1] F. Boas, 'The Central Eskimo,' *6 RBEW* [1888], p. 609; cf. H. Rink, *Tales and Traditions of the Eskimo*, Eng. tr., Edinburgh and London, 1875, pp. 211, 240, 286.
[2] F. Boas, *loc. cit.*
[3] *Narr. of the Second Arctic Expedition*, ed. J. E. Nourse, Washington, 1879, cited in *GB*[3], pt. ii., *Taboo*, p. 108.
[4] See A. van Gennep, *Les Rites de passage*, Paris, 1909, pp. 55, 183, 236, 249.
[5] *An Account of the Natives of the Tonga Islands*[3], Edinburgh, 1827, i. 277.
[6] P. 245.
[7] Jevons[2], p. 71.
[8] G. Turner, *Samoa a Hundred Years Ago and Long Before*, London, 1884, p. 291.
[9] E. Westermarck, *MI* i. 590.
[10] R. Brough Smyth, *The Aborigines of Victoria*, Melbourne and London, 1878, i. 134.
[11] *GB*[3], pt. i., *The Magic Art and the Evolution of Kings*, London, 1911, ii. 264, pt. ii., *Taboo*, p. 111; see *The Voyages of P. Fernandes de Queiros*, tr. C. Markham (Hakluyt Soc. II. xiv. and xv.), London, 1904, i. 427; and *The Texts and Versions of John Pian de Carpine and William de Rubruquis* (Hakluyt Soc. Ex. Ser.), London, 1903, p. 113; cf. p. 131.
[12] Howitt, p. 485.
[13] E. Shortland, *Traditions and Superstitions of the New Zealanders*, London, 1854, p. 83.
[14] J. Thomson, *To the Central African Lakes and Back*, London, 1881, i. 228; see E. S. Hartland, *LP*, do. 1894–95, ii. 214 f.; and F. Liebrecht, *Zur Volkskunde*, Heilbronn, 1879, p. 267 ff.
[15] G. Fritsch, *Die Eingeborenen Süd-Afrika's*, Breslau, 1872, p. 200.

It is 'at the boundary of two districts, or where some dangerous tract of country commences,'[1] that the savage is most likely to regard any natural object which is strange or unusual as connected in some way with mysterious influences fraught with peril to himself. Nor is the reason far to seek; for the borderland is from its very nature the home of the mysterious and awe-inspiring. The line of division is marked sometimes by natural objects and sometimes artificially. These natural objects, such as mountains, rivers, forests, or jungles, are associated by the savage with demons or spirits or powers stronger than man and potent to work him good or evil;[2] and he regards with similar feelings the great tracts of waste lands which in many instances serve as boundary.

The Mangwangwana kings, *e.g.*, deliberately surrounded their country 'with an enormous starvation area, by ruthlessly destroying villages and whole races around them. The foodless belt was a greater protection to them than the great wall of China to the Chinese Emperors.'[3] J. B. Tavernier[4] attributes a similar policy to one of the Persian kings; and Cæsar says of the German tribes: 'Civitatibus maxima laus est, quam latissimas circum se vastatis finibus solicitudines habere.'[5] The Romans sometimes adopted this method of protection, and in Karolingian times the Spanish border was similarly secured.[6]

In other cases the boundary was marked by upright stones,[7] which, in Old Germany, *e.g.*, were not infrequently the gravestones of heroes.[8] In some parts of ancient Ireland pillar-stones were worshipped; and 'a stone of worship' is said by the Brehon laws to be one of the objects used for marking the limits of lands.[9] Hommel[10] observes that, 'in South Arabic inscriptions, *wathan* signifies "boundary pillar," and at the same time "statue of god," "idol."'[11] Grimm tells us that ordeals, especially ordeals by battle, generally took place in the border-land which lay between two districts. This spot—often a meadow or an island—was chosen because it was a holy place, sacred to powers whose presence ensured fair play to both combatants.[12] Sometimes the boundary is formally placed under the protection of the supernatural. P. B. du Chaillu gives an instructive account of the means taken to secure the Otando country against a plague of smallpox:

'To protect the village from the wizards who might enter it from the neighbouring villages . . . the doctor, accompanied by the whole of the people, went to the paths leading to Máyolo from other villages and planted sticks at intervals across them, connecting the sticks by strong woody creepers and hanging on the ropes leaves from the core of the crown of palm trees. It is recognized law among these people that no stranger can come within these lines.'[13]

So too Ellis[14] tells us that it was thought impossible for a hostile force to make its way into Elmina if the body of a human victim who had been sacrificed were cut up and distributed round the outskirts of the town so as to enclose it.[15] Among the aborigines of E. Brazil the *pajés* assist in laying down the tribal boundaries, by celebrating magical rites, and in some cases by hanging 'pieces of medicine' to the objects which mark the dividing-line.[16]

1 Thomson, *To the Central African Lakes*, i. 228.
2 Cf. Dalton, p. 38; W. R. Smith, *Religion of the Semites*², pp. 114, 120.
3 W. J. Ansorge, *Under the African Sun*, London, 1899, p. 42.
4 P. 9.
5 *De Bell. Gall.* vi. 23; cf. iv. 3.
6 H. Brunner, *Deutsche Rechtsgeschichte*, Leipzig, 1887–90, i. 115, note 3.
7 Hamilton-Grierson, p. 29.
8 J. Grimm, *Deutsche Grenzalterthümer* (*Kleinere Schriften*, Berlin, 1864–90), ii. 73.
9 P. W. Joyce, *A Social Hist. of Ancient Ireland*, London, 1903, i. 277; cf. ii. 266 ff.
10 Quoted by Trumbull, *Threshold Covenant*, p. 334.
11 Cf. *ib.* pp. 166 ff., 177 ff.
12 *Deutsche Grenzalterthümer*, p. 58 f.
13 P. 177.
14 *The Tshi-speaking Peoples of the Gold Coast of W. Africa*, London, 1887, p. 53.
15 Cf. Sall. *de Bell. Jugurth.* 78, where the story of the Philæni is told; see also Grimm, *Deutsche Grenzalterthümer*, ii. 73; R. M. Luther, *ap.* H. C. Trumbull, *The Blood Covenant*, London, 1887, p. 315; Hamilton-Grierson, p. 12 f. and note 4.
16 Von Martius, p. 34 f.; see Hamilton-Grierson, 'The Boundary Stone and the Market Cross,' *Scottish Historical Review*, xii. [1914] 24 ff.; and art. LANDMARKS AND BOUNDARIES.

II. *EXCEPTIONS TO, AND MODIFICATIONS OF, PRIMITIVE USAGE.*—**12.** The evidence which we have adduced makes it sufficiently clear that the limits of the primitive group constitute for its members the limits not only of their rights and duties, but also of the only life possible for them. Beyond those limits lies an unknown world peopled by hostile beings and pervaded by malevolent influences, and, therefore, of deadly danger to the stranger who crosses its boundary. Thus the phrase 'homo homini lupus' is apt to express the relation which normally subsists between group and alien group. Still, it is, as we shall see, susceptible of modifications in more ways than one. The stranger may be admitted to the membership of the group—*e.g.*, by adoption—or he may be so connected with it by marriage, friendship, or some such tie that he may, in virtue of that connexion, be permitted to share, to some extent at all events, in the rights of its members. Or he may remain outside of the group unconnected with it by any such tie, and yet be treated, in certain circumstances and subject to certain limitations, as a friend or, it may be, as a neutral.

A. Where the stranger is admitted to the membership of the group or is so connected with it by marriage, etc., that he is permitted to share in the rights of its members.—(*a*) *Persons who have 'made brothers.'* — See art. BROTHERHOOD (Artificial).

(*b*) *Captive and other persons adopted into the group.*—**13.** We find in the treatment of prisoners of war an example of the gradual mitigation of the rigour of primitive usage. In the earliest times the victor slaughtered not only the adult males, but the women and children of the vanquished. In some instances the slaughter of prisoners is due to the belief that, as worshippers of vanquished gods, they are an especially acceptable sacrifice to the gods of the victors.[1] A step in advance is taken when the victor, having grasped the fact that a living slave is worth more than a dead enemy, spares the conquered warrior.[2] When the Namaquas discovered that Damara prisoners made useful drudges, they ceased to kill them.[3] In New Zealand captives and their children were enslaved; and remnants of scattered tribes submitted to servitude in order to secure protection.[4] Among the tribes of Sierra Leone prisoners taken before the rice-crop were spared to cultivate the ground, while those taken afterwards were generally killed.[5] In the Marquesas prisoners are not always killed; they are sometimes adopted by chiefs and become members of the tribes or families which receive them. So close is this connexion that instances are cited in which an adopted captive has followed the chief who adopted him in a hostile expedition against the tribe of his birth.[6] A somewhat similar account is given by Rochas[7] of the natives of New Caledonia; and among the N. American Indians the custom of adopting prisoners of war to fill the places of dead persons is extensively practised. The adopted person becomes brother or sister, son or daughter, according to the position which the deceased occupied;[8] and, if he be assumed into the place of the head of the family, he exercises in regard to the dead man's wife and children the rights of husband and father.[9]

1 Ellis, *Tshi-speaking Peoples*, p. 170.
2 See R. von Ihering, *Der Zweck im Recht*³, Leipzig, 1893, i. 242.
3 Andersson, p. 288; see also the instances given by A. H. Post, *Grundriss der ethnologischen Jurisprudenz*, Oldenburg and Leipzig, 1894–95, i. 357.
4 Polack, ii. 52.
5 Matthews, p. 147.
6 Vincendon-Dumoulin and Desgraz, p. 258.
7 P. 252.
8 L. H. Morgan, *Ancient Society*, London, 1877, p. 341 f. He observes that adoption and torture were the alternative chances of the captive.
9 C. Colden, *The Hist. of the Five Indian Nations of Canada*³, London, 1755, i. 9 f.

It has been observed that, 'if prisoners thus admitted into families behave well, they have everything they want. But if they run away and are taken, their lives are in danger. . . . Even the nations to whom the runaways belong will not receive them, but treat them as ungrateful beings; they therefore turn out vagrants and infest the woods.'[1] Edwin James[2] adds that such persons become so identified with their adoptive nation that they regard the application to themselves of their name of origin as an insult.

(*c*) *Persons marrying into the group.*—**14.** In many cases a tribe ceases to regard or treat a stranger as an enemy if he has married into it. In Kreis Kita and among the Wachambala a stranger can enter into a family by marriage; and the practice has been observed among the Xarayes.[3] But intermarriage does not always produce peace,[4] for, in some instances, intertribal fights continue, and after the battle the women of the combatants visit each other and condole on the loss of their common relatives.[5] In the Marquesas a man who has married a woman of a neighbouring tribe may pass to and fro between it and his own tribe in time of war without fear of molestation.[6] In the Washington Islands men and women of different tribes betrothed on the conclusion of a peace are spared in time of war;[7] and among the tribes of the Nāga hills a native who has married a girl of another village and resides with her there is regarded as a neutral, and may safely go from her village to his own even during hostilities.[8] A similar account is given of the Asaba people of the Niger.[9] In Somaliland *abbans* are selected from men whose daughters are married to members of the tribe to be visited;[10] and within the borders of Sintang only those foreigners may exercise the calling of merchants who are married to women of the country.[11]

(*d*) *Persons introduced by a member of the group, mutual friend, etc.*—**15.** In many instances a friendly reception may be procured by means of an introduction. Among the Andaman Islanders a stranger may not enter a district without express permission, unless accompanied by a native of it. If he visit a camp for the first time, he will be welcomed if introduced by a mutual friend.[12] So, too, the Kurnai did not molest the Brajerak families which came into their country, because they regarded as brothers the Brabolung who had brought them in.[13] Again, Kolben[14] tells us that a traveller's best course among the Hottentots was to take a native with him. Then he was safe and was hospitably entertained. The same is true of the Western Eskimo;[15] Leo Africanus[16] says that in some parts of Morocco the stranger must have the escort of some saint or woman of the country; and among the Indians of the Goajira Peninsula

[1] G. H. Loskiel, *Hist. of the Mission of the United Brethren among the Indians in N. America*, tr. C. I. La Trobe, London, 1794, pt. i. p. 151; J. Carver, *Travels through the Interior Parts of N. America*, do. 1778, i. 346.

[2] ii. 20.

[3] J. Tellier, *Kreis Kita, Französischer Sudan, ap.* Steinmetz, p. 143; F. H. Lang, *Die Waschambala, ap.* Steinmetz, p. 221; L. L. Dominguez, *The Conquest of the River Plate* (Hakluyt Society, lxxxi.), London, 1891, p. 209 f.

[4] See H. B. Guppy, *The Solomon Islands and their Natives*, London, 1887, p. 18.

[5] Macpherson, *Memorials of Service in India*, p. 70.

[6] Vincendon-Dumoulin and Desgraz, p. 258.

[7] C. S. Stewart, *A Visit to the South Seas*, London, 1832, p. 230.

[8] R. G. Woodthorpe, 'Notes on the Wild Tribes inhabiting the so-called Naga Hills,' *JAI* xi. [1882] 67.

[9] J. Parkinson, 'Note on the Asaba People (Ibos) of the Niger,' *JAI* xxxvi. [1906] 316.

[10] F. L. James, *The Unknown Horn of Africa*², London, 1890, pp. 89–92.

[11] Schwaner, ii. 197. [12] Man, pp. 26, 46, 80.

[13] Fison-Howitt, p. 222; cf. Brough Smyth, i. 134.

[14] *The Present State of the Cape of Good Hope*, tr. G. Medley, London, 1731, p. 266.

[15] J. Simpson, 'Observations on the Western Eskimo,' in *Further Papers relating to the recent Arctic Expeditions, presented to both Houses of Parliament*, London, 1855, p. 926.

[16] *Hist. and Description of Africa*, tr. J. Pory, London, 1896 (Hakluyt Society), ii. 229, 326.

women are so much respected that a stranger protected by them may travel in perfect security.[1] The women of Konoma were occasionally hired as escort;[2] and the women of the Bhils protect the stranger against the cruelty or licence of the men.[3] Herman Melville[4] states that, although the hostilities between the tribes preclude any intercourse, yet a man who has formed a friendship with a member of a hostile tribe may, subject to certain restrictions, venture with impunity into its territory. 'The individual so protected is said to be "taboo," and his person, to a certain extent, is held as sacred.' In Fiji the stranger must be accompanied by a recognized herald or by a man specially appointed by a chief who is on friendly terms with the tribe to be visited;[5] and in the principalities of Ghazi-Kumuk and Kaidek he will be seized and sold unless he has a native with him or letters of recommendation to a prince, or knows or can name the prefect of the mosque whither he is bound.[6] In some cases the traveller depends on his engaging servants who assume the office of protectors;[7] and sometimes the host gives his staff[8] or his spear[9] to his guest as a passport, or makes certain marks upon him with white chalk, which serve the same purpose.[10] The gifts exchanged by kings and princes were used as tokens accrediting the persons who possessed them.[11] The σύμβολον of the Greeks, the *tessera hospitalis* of the Romans, and the *chirs aëlychoth* of the Carthaginians were similarly employed;[12] and we may perhaps compare with these practices that of the heathen Northmen, who frequently marked themselves with the cross in order more easily to enter into business relations with Christians.[13] Robertson Smith[14] mentions the case of an Arab patron, who stamped his client with his camel-brand; and the Narrinyeri *kalduke*[15] may be referred to in this connexion.

(*e*) *Persons connected by class and totem.*—**16.** The totem bond was very strong in some tribes.

Fison and Howitt say of tribes bound together by the great class divisions of Eaglehawk and Crow: 'It mattered not from how distant localities two men might be, their speech might be unintelligible to each other, their status of family and their customs might have marked variance, yet the common bond of class and "totem" was a brotherhood which they would not fail to acknowledge.'[16] In parts of New Guinea and in the western islands of Torres Straits 'a stranger from hostile tribes can visit in safety villages where the clan of his *nurumara* is strong, and visitors from other tribes are fed and lodged by the members of the *nurumara* to which they severally belong.'[17]

[1] F. A. A. Simons, 'An Exploration of the Goajira Peninsula, U.S. of Colombia,' *Proc. RGS*, new ser., vii. [1885] 792.

[2] Hodson, *Nāga Tribes of Manipur*, p. 115.

[3] Crooke, *Natives of N. India*, p. 43.

[4] *A Narr. of a Four Months' Residence among the Natives of a Valley of the Marquesas Islands*, London, 1846, p. 155.

[5] Fison-Howitt, pp. 192 f., 223, note.

[6] J. Reineggs and M. Bieberstein, *A General Hist. and Topographical Description of Mount Caucasus*, tr. C. Wilkinson, London, 1807, i. 95.

[7] L. Magyar, *Reisen in Süd-Afrika, 1849–57*, tr. J. Hunfalvy, Buda-Pest and Leipzig, 1859, i. 31 f.

[8] Munzinger, *Ostafrikanische Studien*, p. 384.

[9] Leo Africanus, ii. 327. [10] Magyar, i. 133.

[11] S. Laing and R. B. Anderson, *The Heimskringla or the Sagas of the Norse Kings*², from the Icelandic of Snorri Sturlason, London, 1889, i. 68; see also *The Story of Gísli the Outlaw*, from the Icelandic by G. W. Dasent, Edinburgh, 1896, p. 28; for the signet rings used as passes in Old Russia see von Schlözer, *Russische Annalen*, iv. 59; J. P. G. Ewers, *Das älteste Recht der Russen*, Dorpat and Hamburg, 1826, pp. 182–185, 193, note 43; for the 'scontrino' see K. von Scherzer, *Narr. of the Circumnavigation of the Globe by the Austrian Frigate 'Novara,'* Eng. tr., London, 1861–63, ii. 8, note.

[12] R. von Ihering, 'Die Gastfreundschaft im Alterthum,' in *Deutsche Rundschau*, li. [1887] 387 ff.; O. Schrader, *Reallexikon der indogermanischen Alterthumskunde*, Strassburg, 1901, p. 273.

[13] *The Story of Gísli*, p. 18 and note; G. Vigfusson and F. York Powell, *Origines Islandicæ*, Oxford, 1905, i. 329.

[14] *Religion of the Semites*², p. 148, note 2 (*ad fin.*).

[15] See art. BROTHERHOOD (Artificial), § 23.

[16] P. 233; cf. Howitt, *JAI* xx. 42; cf. pp. 74 (and note), 75.

[17] A. C. Haddon, *Head-Hunters, Black, White, and Brown*, London, 1901, pp. 103, 135; *Reports of Cambridge Anthrop. Exped.* v. 161.

And it was a fixed rule in battle that no man should attack or slay another bearing the same totemic crest as himself.[1] Seligmann observes,[2] however, that among some tribes totemism exerted no influence in the battle-field.[3] This branch of the subject receives elaborate treatment in Frazer's *Totemism and Exogamy*.

B. Where the stranger is not admitted to the membership of the group, and is not connected with it by marriage, etc., and yet is treated, in certain circumstances and subject to certain limitations, as a friend or neutral.—(*a*) *The trader*.—See artt. GIFTS (Primitive and Savage), MARKET, §§ 3, 8.

(*b*) *The guest protégé*.—**17.** Even the rudest savages are accustomed to pay visits to and receive them from their friends; and these visits are made the occasion of sports, dances, carousals, and distributions of gifts. The visitors are not merely entertained; they are secured, for the time being, against robbery and violence. And, when the need of holding intercourse of some sort with strangers arises, the hospitality exercised within the group supplies the form of the new relation, much as the earliest modes of trading with strangers seem to have been adaptations of the exchange of gifts in use among friends.[4] That the good treatment of the stranger was an innovation on the previous practice is shown by the fact that one word is in several languages used to express the conception of 'enemy' and that of 'guest.'[5]

18. It need hardly be said that the measure of the hospitality accorded differs widely among different peoples.[6]

19. Among many peoples the stranger is admitted during his stay to the marital privileges of his host, while in some cases the host's daughter, sister, or servant is offered.[7] To the desire to induce the stranger to bring his wares to market Heeren[8] ascribes certain Lydian and Babylonian regulations regarding the relations of foreigners with the women of the country; and we may assign to a like origin such customs as the temporary marriages of Central Asia and similar usages there and elsewhere.[9]

20. Buildings for the accommodation of wayfarers were provided by the nations of northern and classical antiquity;[10] and numerous instances of a like care are found among savage and barbarous peoples in cases where the burden of hospitality falls upon the king or the community.[11]

In ancient Ireland guest-houses or hospices were attached to the religious houses, and there were public hostels throughout the country, which disappeared, however, after the Anglo-Norman invasion.[12] The Incas built houses for travellers along the royal roads. But it is to be noted that the only travellers were those who bore the commands of the king or his officials.[1]

21. Frequently a parting gift to the guest[2]—it may be in the form of food for his journey[3]—or by the guest,[4] or an exchange of gifts,[5] accompanies or completes the exercise of hospitality.[6]

Among the Southern Slavs the guest is, in some districts, escorted to the limits of his host's possessions.[7] The practice is found in many other parts of the world—*e.g.*, in Circassia,[8] among the Moors,[9] in Egypt,[10] in Fiji,[11] and in the old North.[12]

22. In many instances the hospitable reception of the stranger is subject to certain restrictions—a fact which shows that, at all events in the early forms of the institution, the guest becomes a friend, and ceases to be an enemy, only for a limited time. Among the Arabs the peace established between the stranger and his hosts lasts for 'two nights and the day in the midst, whilst their food is in him';[13] and a similar period was the term of the guest's stay in old Germany[14] and among the Moors of Brakna on the Senegal.[15] In ancient Ireland the term was three days and three nights.[16] The Southern Slavs declare that 'a guest and a fish smell on the third day'; and the Anglo-Saxon saying ran, 'Two nights a guest, the third night one of the household,' *i.e.* a slave.[17] In New Zealand well-disposed strangers are hospitably treated during their stay, which, however, is not to be prolonged beyond the time required for the dispatch of their business.[18] In the Marquesas visitors who attend the festivals of hostile tribes leave on the evening of the third day, which seems to mark the limit of the security granted to them;[19] among the Wachambala the stranger receives food for a day, and, if he stays longer, must purchase his supplies, unless he has a protector.[20] In many cases hospitality and protection last only so long as the stranger resides with his host.

Thus, it is said of the Arab that 'he robs his enemies, his friends, and his neighbours, provided that they are not actually in his own tent, where their property is sacred.'[21] A similar account is given of the Fiji Islanders,[22] the Namaquas,[23] the Khonds[24] and Afghans,[25] the Kurds,[26] and the inhabitants of Ghazi-Kumuk and Kaidek.[27] If an enemy enters an Osage camp, and asks for protection, he is safe after he has eaten with his hosts, until he returns to his own home, when the privilege expires.[28] Among the Eskimo of Greenland the enemy was sheltered;[29] and in the old North not even the murderer of a

---

1 *Reports of Cambridge Anthrop. Exped.* v. 189; J. G. Frazer, *Totemism and Exogamy*, London, 1910, ii. 37; see Seligmann, *Melanesians*, p. 451.

2 P. 683 ff.

3 Cf. J. H. P. Murray, *Papua, or British New Guinea*, London, 1912, p. 122.

4 Hamilton-Grierson, pp. 16 f., 69; see art. GIFTS (Primitive and Savage), § 6.

5 See Hamilton-Grierson, p. 69, note 2.

6 See series of artt. HOSPITALITY.

7 Westermarck, *The Hist. of Human Marriage*2, pp. 73–75; *Book of Ser Marco Polo*, i. 210, 212, ii. 54, 56 f.; Post, *Grundriss der ethnologischen Jurisprudenz*, i. 28; P. Wilutzky, *Vorgesch. des Rechts*, Breslau, 1903, i. 45 ff.; see also Weinhold, p. 447.

8 *Historical Researches into the Politics, Intercourse, and Trade of the Principal Nations of Antiquity*, Eng. tr., Oxford, 1833, i. 105 f., ii. 199.

9 See *Book of Ser Marco Polo*, i. 193, 210, 212, ii. 44, 48, 54, 56 f.; M. A. Potter, *Sohrab and Rustem*, London, 1902, p. 145 ff.

10 Schrader, *Handelsgeschichte und Warenkunde*, pp. 28–31.

11 T. Bowrey, *A Geographical Account of the Countries round the Bay of Bengal, 1669–79*, London, 1905 (Hakluyt Society), p. 117, note 2 (Golcondah); Wilkes, ii. 149 (Samoa); Weinhold, p. 369 ff. (old North); H. O. Forbes, *A Naturalist's Wanderings in the Eastern Archipelago*, London, 1885, p. 140 f. (Sumatra); Ibn Batuta, i. 238 (Damascus); Hamilton-Grierson, p. 82, note 1.

12 Joyce, i. 330–333, ii. 171.

1 Garcilasso de la Vega, *First Part of the Royal Commentaries of the Yncas*, Eng. tr., London, 1869–71 (Hakluyt Society), ii. 29.

2 Steinmetz, p. 45 (Banaka and Bapuku); Hamilton-Grierson, p. 75, note 1 (Andaman Islands, Polynesia, Norse kingdoms).

3 C. Hager, *Kaiser Wilhelms-land und der Bismarck-Archipel*, Leipzig, n.d., p. 70 (natives of Kaiser Wilhelm's Land); W. N. Dall, *Alaska and its Resources*, Boston, 1870, p. 397 (Aleuts).

4 Nicole, *Die Diakité Sarrakolesen*, *ap.* Steinmetz, p. 123.

5 Hyades-Deniker, p. 373 (Yahgans); Man, pp. 26, 80, 172 (Andaman Islanders); J. Kohler, 'Das Recht der Marschall-Insulaner,' *ZVRW* xiv. 440 (Marshall Islanders); Tac. *Germ.* 21; Weinhold, p. 448 (old Germany); *Od.* xxiv. 272 ff. (Homeric world).

6 See Van Gennep, *Rites de passage*, p. 50 f.

7 F. S. Krauss, *Sitte und Brauch der Südslaven*, Vienna, 1885, pp. 646–650.

8 J. von Klaproth, *Travels in the Caucasus and Georgia in 1807–8*, tr. F. Shoberl, London, 1814, p. 336.

9 B. Meakin, *The Moors*, London, 1902, p. 294.

10 J. Petherick, *Egypt, the Soudan, and Central Africa*, London, 1861, p. 237.

11 Williams-Calvert, i. 155.

12 Weinhold, p. 447.

13 Doughty, i. 228; cf. ii. 94.

14 Grimm, *Deutsche Rechtsalterthümer*3, p. 400; Weinhold, p. 447.

15 R. Caillié, *Travels through Central Africa to Timbuctoo*, Eng. tr., London, 1830, i. 75.

16 Joyce, i. 331 f.

17 Westermarck, *MI* i. 595.

18 Cook-King, i. 139.

19 Vincendon-Dumoulin and Desgraz, p. 265.

20 F. H. Lang, *Die Waschambala*, *ap.* Steinmetz, p. 246.

21 Burckhardt, *Bedouins and Wahábys*, i. 158; Doughty, i. 30, 276, 377; W. J. Harding King, *A Search for the Masked Tawareks*, London, 1903, p. 61.

22 Wilkes, iii. 77.

23 Fritsch, p. 362.

24 Rowney, p. 101.

25 Elphinstone, i. 296 f.

26 C. von Hahn, 'Neues über die Kurden,' *Globus*, lxxxvi. [1904] 31.

27 Reineggs-Bieberstein, i. 96.

28 McGee, *15 RBEW*, p. 237.

29 F. Nansen, *Eskimo Life*, tr. W. Archer, London, 1893, p. 116.

brother could be turned away.[1] In Selangor a guest must stay three nights in the house, his departure on the first or second night being called 'insulting the night.' To avert the evil consequence of such an act, fumigation is resorted to.[2]

23. Among the tribes near Port Moresby the stranger stays with his specially good friend (*vasila*), no matter what his own group of descent may be;[3] the Kabyle stranger goes to a friend, or, if he has none in the village, to the *amin*, who provides for him according to his quality;[4] and, among the Wachambala, there is in every village an official who sees that a stranger receives food and lodging.[5] A like arrangement is found among the Ghiljies[6] and some of the Thonga tribes;[7] and in ancient Ireland a public hospitaller attended to the wants of the stranger.[8]

24. Among many peoples the stranger consults his safety best by choosing a protector. Among the Barea and Kunáma he must select a host, and, in the case of the latter people, if he leaves his host's house, he must be accompanied by a native.[9] The foreign settler in the country of the Bogos must take a protector from the Schmagilli, a class of nobles or, rather, freemen; and he and his descendants continue to be the dependents of the person chosen. The foreign merchant may, however, change his patron.[10] Among the Beni-Amer he must take a temporary guardian.[11]

Burton tells us that 'the Abban or protector of the Somali country is the Mogasa of the Gallas, the Akh of El Hejaz, the Ghafir of the Sinaitic Peninsula, and the Rabia of Eastern Arabia. . . . The Abban acts at once as broker, escort, agent, and interpreter, and the institution may be considered the earliest form of transit dues. In all cases he receives a certain percentage, his food and lodging are provided at the expense of his employer, and he not infrequently exacts small presents for his kindred. In return he is bound to arrange all differences, and even to fight the battle of his client against his fellow-countrymen. Should the Abban be slain his tribe is bound to take up the cause and to make good the losses of their protégé. . . . According to the laws of the country, the Abban is the master of the life and property of his client.'[12]

25. Ibn Batuta[13] informs us that at Magadoxo, when a vessel arrived, some of the young people of the place went on board, each bearing a covered dish containing food. This one of them presented to a merchant of the ship, crying, 'This is my guest'; and all the others acted in the same manner. The merchant left the vessel only to go to his host's house, unless he had visited the city often before, in which case he went where he pleased. The host sold for the merchant what he had brought with him, and made his bargains for him. A similar custom prevailed in the Maldives,[14] at Mindanao,[15] at Raiatea,[16] and at Rurutu;[17] and the Bachapin *maat* of the Klaarwater Hottentot not only supplies him with food and lodging, but assists him in making his purchases, and even collects articles to be ready for him on his next visit. When, on the other hand, the Bachapin visits his Hottentot *maat's* village, he lives there at free quarters.[1] In the time of Ibn Batuta[2] there existed among the Turkomans associations of bachelors, who made it their business to entertain strangers, whether merchants or merely travellers; and among the Eskimo of the Mackenzie river the stranger, by choosing a native as a protector, established with him a sort of relationship and a community of rights and duties.[3] According to Seligmann,[4] when a ship's crew arrives at the Papuan Gulf, each man chooses a friend; and the friends decorate each other with the personal ornaments which they have brought to barter.[5]

26. In Circassia there are fraternities the members of which are bound to defend and assist one another; and the stranger who has a member for his *konak*, or host, has a claim for protection and hospitality not upon him only, but upon all the members of his fraternity.[6] A similar account is given of the Turkomans,[7] while among the Ossetes the host is responsible for his guest's safety, even though he be an enemy.[8] Among the Pottawatomie, however, the laws of hospitality do not shield the enemy;[9] and among the Akikuyu they protect neither host nor guest.[10]

Every Kabyle village is a little isolated world. Were it not for the *anaya*, each would be at constant warfare with its neighbours. This institution secures a protection which is personal to the protégé, and the efficacy of which is measured by the influence and power of the protector.[11] The *anaya* may be accorded by an individual, a *sof*, a village, or a tribe. Breach of it is punished with death and confiscation;[12] and a Kabyle cannot refuse to grant it, even to a stranger, if he be in immediate danger.[13]

27. In many cases the most efficacious protection is that of the king of the country or chief of the village visited. Among the Battas the fugitive who trusts himself voluntarily to a petty rajah is absolutely safe.[14] In the country of the Kimbunda the king is the exclusive protector of strangers; and, while an injury to a guest is thought to draw down the wrath of the gods, his good treatment is due to the fact that the monarch, by using him well, is really serving his own interests.[15] It has been remarked that 'a chief is rather envied his good fortune in first securing foreigners in his town.'[16] In New Zealand a foreigner (*pakeha*) might obtain a chief's protection on the understanding that he gave him large presents for small, bought from him at the highest price, and kept him in tobacco.[17] Sometimes this protection was conferred in the form of a tabu.[18] When the stranger becomes the protégé of a ruler whose power is absolute, he may not as a general rule leave the country without the royal permission, or engage in trade with subject persons without the royal knowledge and approval. The king, in short, monopolizes commerce.[19] The blackmail which is

1 Weinhold, *Altnordisches Leben*, p. 442.
2 W. W. Skeat, *Malay Magic*, London, 1900, p. 351.
3 Seligmann, *Melanesians*, p. 68.
4 Hanoteau-Letourneux, ii. 45.
5 F. H. Lang, *Die Waschambala, ap.* Steinmetz, p. 246.
6 Elphinstone, ii. 155. 7 Junod, i. 323.
8 Joyce, ii. 168 ff.
9 Munzinger, *Ostafrikanische Studien*, p. 477.
10 Munzinger, *Sitten und Recht der Bogos*, pp. 43–46.
11 Munzinger, *Ostafrikanische Studien*, p. 314.
12 *First Footsteps in E. Africa*, London, 1856, p. 89; cf. Duff Macdonald, i. 117; and see J. Bruce, *Travels to discover the Source of the Nile*², Edinburgh, 1804, ii. 145 f. (*ghafir*); Doughty, i. 235, 360 (*rafīk*); L. W. C. van den Berg, *Le Hadhramout et les colonies arabes dans l'archipel indien*, Batavia and The Hague, 1887, p. 75 f. (*sayyir*); C. W. Isenberg and J. L. Krapf, *Journals detailing their Proceedings in the Kingdom of Shoa*, London, 1843, p. 256 (*mogasa*); and R. F. Burton, *The Lake Regions of Central Africa*, do. 1860, i. 253 (*balderabba* of the Abyssinians).
13 ii. 181 f. 14 *Ib.* iv. 119 f.
15 W. Dampier, *Voyage round the World, and other Voyages and Descriptions*, London, 1703, i. 328.
16 F. D. Bennett, *Narr. of a Whaling Voyage round the Globe*, London, 1840, i. 186 f.
17 Ellis, iii. 104 f.

1 W. J. Burchell, *Travels in the Interior of S. Africa*, London, 1822–24, ii. 555; Burton, *Lake Regions*, ii. 54.
2 ii. 261.
3 E. Petitot, *Les Grands Esquimaux*, Paris, 1887, pp. 138, 239.
4 *Melanesians*, p. 108.
5 See also B. Hagen, *Unter den Papua's*, Wiesbaden, 1899, p. 219; J. Pfeil, *Studien und Beobachtungen aus dem Südsee*, Brunswick, 1899, p. 124 f.
6 J. S. Bell, i. 84, 204; Klaproth, pp. 318, 336.
7 A. Vambéry, *Travels in Central Asia*, London, 1864, p. 49 f.
8 A. von Haxthausen, *Transcaucasia*, Eng. tr., London, 1854, p. 412.
9 Keating, *Expedition to the Source of St. Peter's River*, i. 98.
10 W. S. and K. Routledge, *With a Prehistoric People: the Akikuyu of British West Africa*, London, 1910, p. 247.
11 Hanoteau-Letourneux, iii. 70 ff.
12 *Ib.* iii. 61–63. 13 *Ib.* iii. 80.
14 Junghuhn, ii. 238.
15 Magyar, i. 224, 257, notes 11, 14.
16 D. and C. Livingstone, p. 224.
17 *Old New Zealand*, by a Pakeha Maori (F. E. Maning), London, 1863, pp. 165–168; cf. Polack, i. 44 f.
18 Angas, ii. 115; Cook-King, iii. 10, 163; Lisiansky, p. 104.
19 See A. G. Laing, *Travels in the Timannee, Kooranko, and Soolima Countries in W. Africa*, London, 1825, p. 356 f.; C. T. Wilson and R. W. Felkin, *Uganda and the Egyptian Soudan*, do. 1882, i. 209, ii. 17, 26; J. H. Speke, *Journal of the*

the price of the protection of many African potentates is not, in the opinion of Burton,[1] unjust. It forms the custom-dues of the government, and takes the place of the fees expected by the *abban*.[2] Until it is paid, the road is shut.[3] On payment of a similar impost the Tuareg nobles protect those who pass through their territories.[4]

The προξενία of the Greeks and the consulship of the Middle Ages supplied the stranger's need of a protector,[5] and were indeed offshoots of the institution of hospitality.[6]

28. The ἀνὴρ ξεινοδόκος commanded the respect and approval of the Homeric world;[7] and he is regarded with those feelings by many savage and barbarous peoples. 'Among the Arabs there is no better report of a man's life than to be called in his country *karîm*, a liberal soul; so nothing more hateful than the lean niggard's name, *bakhîl*.'[8] Among the Ahts,[9] the tribes south of the Yukon river,[10] and the Western Eskimo[11] reputation and rank are acquired by the exercise of liberality.[12] Among the Kukis a curious incentive to hospitality and bravery is found. 'All the enemies' that the tribesman 'has killed will be in attendance on him as slaves' in the next world, 'and the animals of all kinds he has eaten with his friends will live again as his farm-stock.'[13]

29. Some peoples treat the refusal of hospitality as a punishable offence.[14] Grimm[15] quotes a provision of the *Lex Burgundia* to the effect that 'quicumque hospiti venienti tectum aut focum negaverit, trium solidorum inlatione mulctetur'; and Bastian[16] tells us that, if a Slav refuses to receive a stranger, he is deprived of his property and his house is burnt down. Francis Fleming[17] observes that, if a Kafir rejects a request for hospitality, the headman of his kraal is fined in cattle, a portion of the fine being made over to the person aggrieved.

30. In the country of the Kimbunda an injury to a guest is thought to draw down the wrath of the gods;[18] and a similar view was held by the old Germans. They regarded it as a duty incumbent upon all to treat his person as sacred, and to lodge and maintain him.[19] In modern Arabia a protected stranger is called a *dakhîl*; in old Arabia he was called a *jār*. The relation was sometimes temporary, sometimes permanent, sometimes hereditary. The protection might be against a particular enemy, or against enemies in general. In some cases it was constituted by a solemn engagement at a sanctuary, and held good until renounced at the same place. Thus the god himself became the protector of the stranger's cause.[1]

According to the Hebrew lawgivers, the stranger had a sacred right to protection. He was regarded as poor and helpless, and was classed with the widow and the orphan as one not to be oppressed or afflicted; and, in this connexion, the law made no difference between native and foreigner.[2] In the world of the Homeric poems the normal relation of state to state was one of war. The stranger had no rights; and yet the degree of civilization to which a people had attained was estimated largely on a consideration of its attitude towards him. He was, as were the beggar and the suppliant, regarded as holy, and he enjoyed the special protection of Ζεὺς ξένιος. Moreover, the king must guard his guest against those of his subjects who would attack him, and must permit him to depart without let or hindrance. In some cases the relation between host and guest was hereditary.[3] The position of the stranger upon Italian soil seems to have been very similar. To slay the guest was to offend the gods of hospitality.[4] Mommsen[5] lays special emphasis on the legal nature of the compact of friendship. It rested, just as other consensual contracts rested, on the declared will of the parties, and it was recorded in duplicate on tablets—*tesseræ hospitales*.[6] Where it was entered into by private persons, the guest had a claim for maintenance and protection only on his host. It could be formed only between different communities or between members of different communities—a characteristic which also marked the relation of patron and client.

According to the Talmud and the Qur'ān, the exercise of hospitality is a religious duty;[7] and a similar view seems to have prevailed in ancient Egypt.[8] Among the Damaras a withering curse falls upon those who refuse to share their food with the stranger;[9] and a somewhat similar conception was held by the Masai.[10] But, according to Merker,[11] Masai hospitality was limited to Masai.

(*c*) *The fugitive and the suppliant.*—**31.** The practice of hospitality creates and fosters a disposition to be hospitable; and the protection enjoyed by the fugitive and the suppliant seems to be a natural extension of that accorded to the trader. In many instances where individual districts are united by no common bond the fugitive from one village flees to another, where he is maintained and protected;[12] and in some cases the privilege is granted by a chief from selfish motives—*e.g.*, to increase his following.[13] The security afforded may be limited to a fixed period. See art. ASYLUM.

(*d*) *The envoy.*—**32.** The duties of an envoy can frequently be performed only in a border-land; and in such cases the sanctity of his privilege is, in part at least, to be attributed to the sacred characteristics of the spot.[14] But the office and the privilege attached to it originate in the elementary needs of savage societies; and here, as in so many other instances, religion invests with its form and supports with its sanctions the institution which those needs have created. The envoy is regarded as inviolable in the Marquesas[15] and

Discovery of the Source of the Nile, Edinburgh, 1863, pp. 268, 304, 345, 373, 376; H. Low, *Sarawak*, London, 1848, p. 336; see also § 6 above.

1 *Lake Regions*, i. 253. 2 See above, § 24.

3 Speke, pp. 126, 131, 171; J. Thomson, *Through Masai Land*, London, 1885, p. 271.

4 Harding King, p. 263.

5 See P. Monceaux, *Les Proxénies grecques*, Paris, 1885, pp. 106–125; A. Schaube, 'Le Proxénie au moyen âge,' *Revue de Droit international et de Législation comparée*, xxviii. [1896] 525 ff.

6 See Schrader, *Handelsgeschichte und Warenkunde*, p. 12.

7 B. W. Leist, *Graeco-italische Rechtsgeschichte*, Jena, 1884, p. 213, referring to *Od.* iv. 33, viii. 545, xv. 54, xxiv. 272, *Il.* iii. 207, xviii. 387, 408.

8 Doughty, i. 430; cf. Burckhardt, i. 72.

9 G. M. Sproat, *Scenes and Studies of Savage Life*, London, 1868, p. 112 f.

10 Dall, p. 151.

11 H. Rink, *Eskimo Tribes*, London and Copenhagen, 1887, p. 28 f.

12 See also F. Boas, 'Second General Report on the Indians of British Columbia,' and H. Hale's 'Introduction,' in the *Report of the 60th Meeting of the British Association for the Advancement of Science*, London, 1891, pp. 557 ff., 588 ff., where the gift-festival ('potlatch') is described.

13 Dalton, p. 46.

14 G. Timkowski, *Travels of the Russian Mission through Mongolia to China*, London, 1827, ii. 345 (Mongols); Hanoteau-Letourneux, ii. 117 (Kabyles).

15 *Deutsche Rechtsalterthümer*³, p. 399.

16 *Der Mensch in der Geschichte*, Leipzig, 1860, iii. 231.

17 *Southern Africa*, London, 1856, p. 244.

18 Magyar, i. 224, 257, notes 11, 14.

19 Cæs. *de Bell. Gall.* vi. 23; Tac. *Germ.* 21.

1 Robertson Smith, *Kinship and Marriage*², p. 48 ff., *Religion of the Semites*², p. 75 f.

2 Ex $22^{21f.}$, Lv 19^{33}, Dt 10^{19}.

3 See L. Schmidt, *Die Ethik der alten Griechen*, ii. 276–286, 324 ff.; Leist, p. 213 ff.; A. G. Keller, *Homeric Society*, London, 1902, p. 299 ff., where the references to Homer are collected. See also Schrader, *Reallexikon*, p. 269 ff., and *Handelsgeschichte und Warenkunde*, p. 7 ff.

4 Livy, xxxix. 51; cf. i. 45.

5 *Römische Forschungen*², Berlin, 1864, i. 332 ff.

6 See above, § 15.

7 See Westermarck, *MI* i. 580.

8 E. A. W. Budge, *The Book of the Dead*, London, 1901, ii. 372.

9 Andersson, *Lake Ngami*, p. 147.

10 Frazer, *Totemism and Exogamy*, ii. 415.

11 *Die Masai*, p. 117.

12 A. Hellwig, *Das Asylrecht der Naturvölker*, Berlin, 1903, p. 15, citing *Das Ausland*, xxxviii. [1865] 731 (Samoa); see also Kubary, p. 218 (Pelew Islanders); A. H. Post, *Afrikanische Jurisprudenz*, Oldenburg and Leipzig, 1887, i. 190; Pauli, in *Peterm. Mitth.* xxxi. [1885] 21 (Bakwiri); M. Rautenen, *Die Ondonga*, *ap.* Steinmetz, p. 337 (Ondonga); Junghuhn, ii. 238 (Battas); see Macpherson, p. 66 (Khonds).

13 Fritsch, p. 93 (Amaxosa); T. Nauhaus, 'Regierungsform und Gerichtsbarkeit der Kaffern,' *ZE* xiii. [1881] 348.

14 See above, § 11; and cf. H. S. Maine, *Village Communities in the East and West*⁶, London, 1890, p. 193; Lord Avebury, *The Origin of Civilisation and the Primitive Condition of Man*⁶, do. 1902, p. 318 ff.

15 Vincendon-Dumoulin and Desgraz, p. 256.

among the Basutos;[1] and with all the Ewe-speaking tribes it is an unheard-of crime to molest an ambassador bearing the stick of office.[2] A like account is given of the ancient Irish,[3] of the Bushmen,[4] and of tribes in Guinea,[5] in Central Australia,[6] in New South Wales,[7] in Polynesia,[8] and in New Zealand; but, in the last instance, only if the envoy be related to the tribe to which he is sent.[9] Among the Bontoc Igorot of Luzon the life of the war messenger is secure, a near relative of the people challenged being, if possible, selected for the office.[10] Among the Brazilian aborigines foreign messengers are sometimes subjected to ill-treatment;[11] and authorities differ as to the practice of the N. American Indians in former times.[12] In New Caledonia a chief who wishes to sue for peace sends a woman with a man who has friends in the enemy's tribe to carry his proposals. They are safe, while other persons would be killed and eaten.[13] The Dieri send women as ambassadors or messengers.[14]

Among the Baris 'women are allowed to visit their relations in distant villages, and it is a recognised rule . . . that they should never be molested in any way. Thus, they are often able to act as ambassadors and peace-makers between contending tribes.'[15] The envoy was regarded as inviolable in Mexico and at Tezcuco;[16] and it is said of Muhammad that he spared the lives of certain persons on the ground that they were ambassadors and therefore privileged.[17] The messenger was sometimes accredited by a gift.[18]

(*e*) *Women, holy men, and other privileged persons*. — **33.** We have seen that in many instances women act as envoys to hostile tribes[19] without fear of molestation. It is not always easy to say whether they enjoy this privilege in virtue of the office with which they are entrusted, of the occupation in which they are employed, or of the sex to which they belong. Female captives are spared in many cases in which all the male captives are put to death;[20] and in some countries a traveller escorted by a woman[21] and an outcast who takes refuge with a woman[22] are treated as inviolable. In the last two cases, at all events, it seems as if it were the mysterious sanctity attributed universally by uncultured man to womankind that operates as a protective agency.[23]

In New Zealand women were permitted to go from camp to camp during war;[24] and the same is told of the Baris by Mounteney-Jephson,[25] of the natives of Engano by Bastian,[26] of the Nāga tribes of Manipur,[27] and of the Angemi and Kachu Nāgas by Dalton.[28] In the last case the statement holds true only of the tribe's intestine wars. When these same tribesmen are fighting with alien tribes, they spare neither age nor sex.

Among the Mandingoes there are four trades or professions, which rank in the following order: orators, minstrels, shoemakers, and blacksmiths. Their members can travel through the country unmolested, even in time of war; and strangers of African blood are safe under their protection.[1] A like inviolability and protective power are possessed by the Purrah men of the Timanee country,[2] and were possessed, according to Herodotus,[3] by the Argippæans; and certain tribesmen in Rājputana and Gujarāt, who are bards by profession, serve as the guardians of travellers in a country infested with robbers.[4] In the western islands of Torres Straits there were persons, to whom the name *paudagarka*, 'man of peace,' was applied, who were exempt from war and its consequences.[5] Among the Brazilian aborigines the property of the *pajés* is spared in time of war;[6] and, according to Bastian,[7] the hereditary priest of Christian Swanetia enjoys a like privilege. In Oromó wars merchants and priests are not molested;[8] and in Java the Badui are regarded as a sacred race, whose villages none may enter.[9] In some parts of Australia small parties of natives whose object is to procure red earth for colouring purposes are permitted to pass unharmed by the tribes through whose country their way lies.[10]

(*f*) *Frequenters of festivals and holy places*.— **34.** We have referred to the security enjoyed by the stranger during the celebration of festivals.[11] In the Marquesas, during certain festivities, of which the occasion is unexplained, hostile tribes come to share the pleasures of those with whom they fought yesterday and may fight to-morrow, and they are protected by a tabu, which, it seems, expires on the evening of the third day.[12] During the *nanga* rites at Viti Levu initiates belonging to hostile tribes may attend them in safety, provided that they reach the *nanga* unobserved.[13] In Australia hostile tribes meet in peace during the performance of certain initiation ceremonies;[14] and it is said of the Kisti and Ingush, once Christians, now Muslims, that they observe a feast at Easter at which the bitterest enemies refrain from violence.[15] During the fishing festival on the Barwan river the tribes occupy a common camping-ground, the neutrality of which is strictly preserved;[16] and Bastian[17] tells us that the temple of Cozumel in Yucatan was visited yearly by pilgrims, who passed thither through hostile territories without fear of molestation.

Among the Tuaregs[18] and in various parts of India[19] travellers encamping near such holy places as the shrines of saints are safe from spoliation.

W. R. Smith[20] observes that, in certain tracts of sacred land in upland Arabia, hostile tribes meet and drive their flocks together in peace, whereas on any other ground they would fly at one another's throats; and Catlin[21] says of Red Pipe Stone

---

1 E. Casalis, *The Basutos*, Eng. tr., London, 1861, p. 224.
2 Ellis, *The Ewe-Speaking Peoples*, p. 178.
3 Joyce, i. 135. 4 Stow, p. 221.
5 Waitz-Gerland, *Anthropologie der Naturvölker*, Leipzig, 1859–72, ii. 164; see also Matthews, p. 77.
6 Spencer-Gillen[b], p. 332, note 2; cf. p. 551.
7 Fison-Howitt, p. 283 f.; K. Langloh Parker, *The Euahlayi Tribe*, London, 1905, p. 63.
8 Cook-King, ii. 64, 66, 69. 9 Polack, ii. 20.
10 A. E. Jenks, *The Bontoc Igorot*, Manila, 1905, p. 177.
11 Von Martius, p. 47. 12 See Waitz-Gerland, iii. 154.
13 Lambert, in *Missions Catholiques*, xii. 176.
14 Howitt, *JAI* xx. 59 f., 72 f., *Native Tribes*, p. 682.
15 A. J. Mounteney-Jephson, *Emin Pasha and the Rebellion at the Equator*, London, 1890, p. 140.
16 A. de Herrera, *The General Hist. of . . . America*, tr. J. Stevens, London, 1725–26, ii. 248, iii. 317.
17 W. Muir, *The Life of Mahomet*, London, 1858–61, iv. 247.
18 Weinhold, p. 448; see above, § 15.
19 See above, §§ 14, 32.
20 G. Turner, *Nineteen Years in Polynesia*, London, 1861, p. 301 (Samoa); Paulitschke, p. 256 (Oromó); D. and C. Livingstone, p. 385 (Zulu); Junghuhn, ii. 158 (Batta); Crooke, p. 143 (Meos).
21 See above, § 15.
22 Grimm, *Deutsche Rechtsalterthümer*, p. 892; L. Fuld, 'Das Asylrecht im Alterthum und Mittelalter,' *ZVRW* vii. [1887] 150.
23 Seligmann, *Melanesians*, p. 640.
24 Turner, *Nineteen Years in Polynesia*, p. 334.
25 P. 140.
26 *Indonesien oder die Inseln des malayischen Archipel*, Berlin, 1884–94, Lief. iii. 51.
27 Hodson, *Nāga Tribes of Manipur*, p. 114.
28 P. 44.

1 A. G. Laing, p. 132.
2 *Ib.* p. 96. 3 iv. 23.
4 A. K. Forbes, *Râs Mâlâ*, new ed., London, 1878, p. 558, and H. Yule and A. C. Burnell, *Hobson-Jobson*, new ed., London, 1903, *s.v.* 'Bhāts'; Crooke, *Natives of N. India*, p. 108.
5 *Reports of Cambridge Anthrop. Exped.* v. 302.
6 Von Martius, p. 30.
7 *Der Mensch in der Geschichte*, iii. 369.
8 Paulitschke, p. 256. 9 H. O. Forbes, p. 102.
10 W. R. H. Jessop, *Flindersland and Sturtland*, London, 1862, ii. 211.
11 See above, § 22 f.
12 Vincendon-Dumoulin and Desgraz, p. 265; G. H. von Langsdorff, *Voyages and Travels in various Parts of the World, 1803–07*, London, 1813–14, i. 159 f.
13 B. C. Thomson, *The Fijians*, London, 1908, p. 147.
14 Angas, ii. 221.
15 Reineggs-Bieberstein, i. 51 f.
16 K. L. Parker, p. 8.
17 *Die Völker des östlichen Asien*, Leipzig and Jena, 1866–71, vi. 363 note, 364 note.
18 Harding King, p. 277. 19 Rowney, p. 126.
20 *Religion of the Semites*[2], p. 145.
21 *Letters and Notes on the Manners, Customs, and Conditions of the N. American Indians*[3], London, 1842, ii. 167.

Quarry, whither the tribes resorted to procure the red stone for the manufacture of their pipes, that it was a neutral ground 'to which the Indians came unarmed under the fear of the vengeance of the Great Spirit.'

III. *GENERAL OBSERVATIONS.*—35. We have seen that, to the savage, the world which lies beyond the community to which he belongs—*i.e.* beyond his group and the groups associated with it on terms which are friendly rather than hostile—is a world strange and mysterious, peopled by beings whom he hates and fears as his deadly foes. He thinks of them as belonging to an order other than his own, as less or, it may be, as more than human; and he looks upon them as absolutely rightless; for the sphere of rights is conterminous with the sphere within which he himself lives. As regards himself, life is possible for him only within the little circle of his community; with it he and his fellows must stand or fall; and, accordingly, its preservation is of vital importance to him and them. It would seem, then, that to secure the common safety must be the aim of each and all. And yet it is not to be supposed that the individual member has that aim consciously in view as the principle of his action. What he has in view is his own interest—in this case his own safety. But that can be secured only if the community be safe; and, accordingly, in seeking to serve his own interest, he contributes, although unconsciously, to the realization of the common aim. Custom makes obligatory the teachings of the group's experience. It compels performance of those actions which have been found to serve it, and abstention from those which have been found to disserve it. Custom, be it observed, not merely imposes a rule upon the individual from without, but provides an inward principle, which he accepts without reflexion, and upon which he acts as matter of course. It points out the way which all must take; and those to whom it speaks take that way, without question, as the only way possible. Thus custom is at once legal and moral; and it is also religious in the sense that any breach of it, whatever the specific character of that breach may be, will be punished with evils such as are associated with the mysterious and supernatural — disease, disaster, and death. Law, morality, and religion have not as yet secured separate domains. They co-exist undifferentiated as elements of custom, which forms, indeed, rather the atmosphere than the rule of life.[1]

36. Now, the safety of the community is menaced by the very existence of the stranger; and accordingly it is a duty imposed by custom on each of its members to hunt him down and put him to death, whenever opportunity offers. Still, many instances are to be found, even among the rudest peoples, in which the rigour of the early rule has been relaxed. The victors, *e.g.*, do not always seek to exterminate their opponents. Sometimes they marry the women, and sometimes they adopt the children, and even spare the adult males whom they have captured to serve as slaves, or, it may be, to be admitted to a full share in the rights and privileges which they themselves enjoy. Nor are the benefits of adoption confined to the captive. They are, in many cases, extended to the suppliant, the fugitive, and the stranger. Further, the group not infrequently admits to its membership the man who marries into it and the man who 'makes brothers' with some one of its members. In all these cases the stranger, by being incorporated into the group, acquires, to some extent at all events, the rights of a member. Again, there are instances in which the man who marries a woman of an alien group may pass to and fro between it and his own group, even in time of war, without fear of molestation. Here the privilege exists by reason not of incorporation, but of a personal bond. Sometimes the brotherhood which springs from community of class and totem asserts itself in the case of men whose groups are in open hostility. Here the member of a group is member of a larger unity to which his enemy also belongs. There is still another class of cases in which the stranger remains outside of the group, and yet is treated by its members as a being possessed of rights. The envoy, *e.g.*, is in general regarded as inviolable, even when he is a stranger to those to whom he bears his message. In some countries the women of groups engaged in war with one another may pass in safety from group to group; and priests, wizards, doctors, holy men, the members of certain classes and societies, persons engaged in certain religious and social observances, traders, and guests are treated as entitled to a like privilege. This privilege is not always strictly personal; sometimes, as in the case of *asyla* and places devoted to trade, it is attached to a certain spot, and sometimes it is effective only at a certain time, such as a market-day or day of festival.

[1] Hamilton-Grierson, pp. 38 f., 94.

37. To what cause, then, are we to attribute these modifications of the early rule—the rule that the stranger must die in the interests of the community? The answer seems to be plain. The rule is modified because experience has taught the community that its interests are better served by sparing and protecting than by killing him. The captive is allowed to live as soon as the captor discovers that a living slave is more useful than a dead enemy. The trader is maintained and protected as soon as those who wish to deal with him find that, in order to secure his presence, they must provide for the safety of his property and person.

It is, of course, an individual who initiates the change. Some one has an interest to serve, and, in order to serve it, he makes an experiment. If it turns out successful, it will be imitated by all who think that a like result would be beneficial to themselves. And, if experience shows that the practice thus formed is generally advantageous to the members of the community, it will gradually be adopted as a general practice, which, approved by public opinion, will, in its turn, become obligatory upon all, as part and parcel of the common custom.

38. In the early days of the change the old custom remains unaltered and unimpaired, except in so far as its operation is suspended in the common interest. In other words, the stranger is still regarded and treated as an enemy, except in a limited class of cases in which, in order to serve that interest, he is protected. The members of the community are, so far as it proscribes him, prohibited from extending to him their sympathy and generosity. It may be that some of them entertain such feelings towards him; but they may not act upon them, and they accept that prohibition as the rule of their conduct—a rule which, as befits a rule of custom, is at once legal, moral, and religious. In so far, however, as he is protected by the community, its members serve it best who give practical expression to such feelings in their dealings with him. And here again religion, law, and morality work, as it were, into one another's hands; for the command that the stranger shall be well treated is addressed to those who are disposed to treat him well. At the same time, it is to be observed that custom emphasizes now the religious, now the legal, now the moral, obligation which it imposes on its subjects, and thus initiates a process which results in the substitution of rules of law, morality, and religion for its own single rule.

39. Further, when custom gives free rein to kindly feeling, that kindliness reaches not only the stranger who is, in some sense or to some effect, useful to the community, but also the useless stranger—the beggar, the weakling, and the wanderer. Here morality takes possession of a field in the occupation of which law may or may not come to share. And, even if law be absent, morality may find itself supported by religion; for often the gods, who are the guardians of custom, take into their keeping those who have no claim to legal protection. As the stranger's position improves, his face becomes more familiar, his presence more welcome; and the better he is known and understood, the stronger grows the conviction that the restrictions, local, temporal, and personal, which hamper intercourse with him must be removed. Gradually the old order yields to the new, the duration of the movement and the character of its result being more or less determined by the disposition and circumstances of those who take part in it; and the stranger is at length secured, not by way of special privilege, nor by means of special institution, but by the public recognition that he is in himself the subject of rights.[1]

LITERATURE.—This is indicated in the footnotes.

P. J. HAMILTON-GRIERSON.

STRIKES.—A strike is a sudden and collective act of a body of workmen who decide to cease work on account of a dispute with their employers respecting wages or some matter affecting their employment. The men—to use their own expression—'down tools' and refrain from work until the cause of their complaint is adjusted. The act is one of social or economic warfare. A strike is a conflict between capital and labour, joint agents in the production of wealth. A lock-out is a corresponding act on the part of the employer, who refuses on the ground of some dispute to allow his employees to continue work. Strikes are much the more frequent; they generally involve a large number of workmen and may reduce an industry to stagnation for a considerable period, thereby causing both inconvenience and loss to the public.

A strike may be local, *i.e.* limited to one mine, mill, or district; or it may extend over a considerable area and affect the convenience and well-being of a large community, as in the case of a railway strike. Trade unions (*q.v.*), the organizations of men in the same industry, are frequent promoters or agencies of strikes.

This interruption of modern industry is one outcome of the large system of production which has grown up during the last century as a result of mechanical invention and the application of the forces of nature (steam power, electricity, etc.) on an enormous scale, the consequence being a vast aggregation of capital and labour in individual industries. These two agents in the production of wealth have thus been brought into very intimate and dependent relation, and have become joint sharers in the result of their co-partnership under the heads of wages and profits. This sharing of the joint earnings in the product gives rise to disputes, as do also the conditions under which the industries are carried on. These conflicts often precipitate strikes, causing the sudden suspension of industry.

Trade unions, the recognized organizations of workmen, perform various functions: they act as benefit societies for mutual help as well as combinations for collective bargaining as to rates of pay, hours of labour, and regulations touching the industry and its relations to other industries. The employees claim a right to a voice in the detailed methods of the industry to which they devote their lives and skill, corresponding to the rights of the owners, who have contributed their capital, business direction, and knowledge. Large production with its manifold benefits is thus made dependent upon the two factors—capital supplied by one group of agents and labour contributed by another. These factors in turn are dependent for their reward upon the product or service which they render to society; and they are in a certain degree opposed to one another in the division of the economic results of their combined action. The latter fact is the chief source of the conflicts which so often culminate in strikes. Strikes are not necessarily either immoral or illegal: they are ultimate appeals to force for a decision in cases of conflict where milder methods have failed; their ethical character depends upon the justice of the claims advanced and the manner in which the struggle is carried on.

In the early days of machine industry and large production, and before the economic relations of labour and capital on a large scale were understood, these disputes were often violent and accompanied by injurious acts. Strikes were then regarded as illegal and criminal, and were repressed by Conspiracy Laws and Acts for the protection of property. Since 1875 trade unions have been accepted as lawful institutions, and a large amount of legislation has been enacted concerning the relations of capital and labour—*e.g.*, the fixing of minimum wages in trades, the hours of labour, conditions affecting the safety and health of workmen, etc. With the vast growth of industry and the extension of the franchise trade unions have become powerful and have enlarged their field of action. They often exercise a kind of monopoly to prevent non-unionists from being employed in the same mine or factory; and they impose regulations on piece work, and create fine lines of demarcation between different classes of work, as, *e.g.*, between carpenters and joiners, bricklayers and masons. These rules tend to multiply the number of separate trades, and it is doubtful whether these refined subdivisions and classifications of labour are a benefit to society, whilst they have often led to disputes ending in strikes.

The effects of strikes upon the community are wholly injurious: they check supplies, raise prices, create inconvenience, and impede other dependent industries. Negotiation is the rational method for adjustment of differences, as it is generally practised in business affairs which involve competition; but strong feeling, ignorance, and the intervention of agitators all militate against negotiation. Both employers and employed need to realize that they are equally partners in production and mutually dependent. Since the product or service rendered must reward both classes, wisdom would dictate that their joint enterprise would succeed best when friction is reduced to a minimum. To this end economic knowledge of the principles of production and distribution is very necessary, while mutual confidence is also a desideratum. Opposed to these are the forces of ignorance, distrust, and selfishness, that lead to conflicts wasteful and destructive, which are an injury to both parties, while they also impose loss and inconvenience upon the community at large. Mutual confidence and a desire for equitable distribution is the object to be secured, and without conflict, *i.e.* by means of fair bargaining. In some trades standing committees of representatives of labour and capital have been established which meet at regular intervals to discuss difficulties; this method has been found very successful in avoiding friction and arriving at a common understanding.

In the early period of capitalistic production

[1] See Hamilton-Grierson, §§ 25, 52, 56–61.

strikes were very frequent owing to the ignorance and mutual distrust of employers and men. On the one side dictatorial methods, on the other measures for limiting production, hindrances to the use of machinery, and obstruction to improvements led to frequent suspensions of industry. Most of the large industries have at some period suffered from these modes of social warfare; the mining industries, the great railways, the building and textile trades, engineering, shipping, and even agriculture in which the organization of labour would seem almost impossible, have all suffered from strikes. In some cases the trade of the locality has been ruined; in all it has incurred waste, and great loss has fallen upon consumers through consequent scarcity and high prices.

Education, and more especially moral and economic instruction, is the most effective remedy for improving the relations between capital and labour, by teaching their mutual dependence and the importance of their joint efficiency. In recent years many trade union leaders have proved themselves wise administrators and have displayed much ability in the conduct of their unions; many have been elected to parliament, and some have filled high office, where they have demonstrated their capacity for legislation and have rendered valuable service as officials and even ministers. The position and public influence thus attained by these men effectually dispose of the charge of prejudice against labour, and prove that the interests of labour will be adequately secured as far as legislation can effect that object.

Many schemes for cementing the interests and activities of employers and employed have been devised with the object of avoiding the miseries of strikes. All such measures recognize and rest upon the principle of co-partnership between capital and labour and their joint interest in the productiveness of their industry.

Arbitration was an early method devised to terminate quarrels already begun, by calling in a competent judge or expert who should decide, after evidence and investigation, upon the merits of the case. This method succeeded in some instances where the arbitrators were men of large experience, sound judgment, and a reputation for sympathy with labour. In many cases, however, their decision was rejected when it was found to be unfavourable to the men. The utility of this method led in 1896 to the appointment of a Public Arbitrator, whose function was to investigate and offer mediation in cases where his intervention was accepted. Special qualities, however, are necessary for such a post, and the method cannot be regarded as a universal remedy. It suffers from the fact that it is applied only as an antidote, after the rupture has taken place and bitter feelings have been evoked. What is required is a means of prevention rather than a remedy.

Boards of Conciliation have also been devised with the object of avoiding strikes by smoothing over differences and removing causes of complaint. Representatives of employers and workmen meeting at regular intervals may constitute a Board of Conciliation and succeed in preventing conflict. Such methods conduce to mutual understanding and harmony; they lead to concessions and tend to consideration by making each side acquainted with the other's difficulties. Sometimes a sliding scale of wages has been adopted, but occasionally the union has rejected the scale when it has led to a fall in wages. That conciliation, however, cannot be a universal remedy is proved by the number and magnitude of strikes since first the system was adopted.

Profit-sharing and *co-partnership* are other schemes for securing the joint interest and friendly co-operation of capital and labour. They give a definite interest to the worker in the result of the enterprise; in effect he becomes a shareholder and a participator in the annual profit. This method has succeeded in special cases in maintaining good relations, but its scope and application are limited, and it is apt to fail in a year of no profits. Trade unions do not regard the system with favour, nor are employers generally willing to adopt it.

The South Metropolitan Gas Company is a well-known and remarkable instance of the success of this method. During many years its annual statement has shown a good division of profits, and it has maintained good relations between the company and the employees. This result was due mainly to the wise and sympathetic guidance of the manager, Sir George Livesey. About 120 such undertakings are reported as existing in the United Kingdom; these are due in a large degree to the sympathetic influence of individuals.

Defects in human nature—distrust, self-love, greed, idleness, and ignorance—are all antagonistic to economic peace and concord. But, if a whole nation can be captured by the passion of greed and lust for power to dominate the world, can we expect that groups of men engaged in industry will cease to succumb to motives of selfishness? When a higher morality has brought mankind to a nobler plane of justice and sympathy, universal peace may not be unattainable, and strikes, like other modes of warfare, may then disappear.

During the last two years the problem has been materially affected by the action of the Unions of the Coal Miners and the Railway-men, which have been captured by socialistic leaders and have adopted the projects of Nationalizing the Mines and the Railways in the interests of the 'workers.' So far the attempt has failed to do more than materially raise wages, and increase the cost of coal and railway traffic. Socialism and Syndicalism cannot be discussed under the title of this article. One can only point out that success would mean plundering the shareholders and consumers, and would threaten ruin to industry and the country.

LITERATURE.—G. Howell, *The Conflicts of Capital and Labour*², London, 1890; G. J. Holyoake, *The Hist. of Co-operation in England*, rev. ed., do. 1908; W. S. Jevons, *The State in Relation to Labour*⁴, do. 1910; L. L. F. R. Price, *Industrial Peace*, do. 1887; Sidney and Beatrice Webb, *Industrial Democracy*², do. 1902, *Hist. of Trade Unionism*³, do. 1911; D. F. Schloss, *Methods of Industrial Remuneration*³, do. 1907; and generally a section in every standard treatise on the Principles of Economics.

G. ARMITAGE-SMITH.

STRUGGLE FOR EXISTENCE.—This is a technical phrase used by Darwin to describe what occurs in Nature when living creatures respond by novel or intensified endeavours and reactions to the pressure of environing difficulties and limitations. The concept is wider and subtler than is suggested by the words taken literally.

'I should premise,' said Darwin, 'that I use this term in a large and metaphorical sense including dependence of one being on another, and including (which is more important) not only the life of the individual, but success in leaving progeny.' [1]

The struggle for existence is a fundamental idea in biology, but it is not so easily grasped as is usually supposed.

'Nothing is easier,' Darwin said, 'than to admit in words the truth of the universal struggle for life, or more difficult—at least I have found it so—than constantly to bear this conclusion in mind. Yet unless it be thoroughly engrained in the mind, the whole economy of nature, with every fact on distribution, rarity, abundance, extinction, and variation, will be dimly seen or quite misunderstood.' [2]

The central idea is that of a clash between the endeavours of living creatures on the one hand and environmental difficulties on the other.

1. Reasons for the struggle for existence.—The three chief difficulties that beset organisms are those involved in the tendency to over-population, in the nutritive dependence of one creature upon another, and in the changefulness—especially the

[1] *Origin of Species*⁶, p. 50. [2] *Ib.* p. 49.

irregular changefulness—of the environment. To these must be added the fact that it is in the very nature of organisms—of the typical majority, if not of all—to be aggressive or insurgent, ever seeking fuller self-expression and further mastery of their surroundings. This leads to 'struggle' in the widest sense.

2. Modes of the struggle for existence.—The struggle for existence is often spoken of as if it were confined to intraspecific competition.

Thus Weismann writes: 'The "struggle for existence," which Darwin regarded as taking the place of the human breeder in free nature, is not a direct struggle between carnivores and their prey, but is the assumed competition for survival between individuals of the same species, of which, on an average, only those survive to reproduce which have the greatest power of resistance, whilst the others, less favourably constituted, perish early.'[1]

But this restricted view is not Darwin's. 'Two canine animals, in a time of dearth, may be truly said to struggle with each other which shall get food and live. But a plant on the edge of a desert is said to struggle for life against the drought, though more properly it should be said to be dependent on the moisture. A plant which annually produces a thousand seeds, of which only one on an average comes to maturity, may be more truly said to struggle with the plants of the same and other kinds which already clothe the ground.'[2]

Similarly, he goes on to say that several seedling mistletoes may struggle with each other on the branch, while the mistletoe in its relation to birds may be said to struggle with other fruit-bearing plants. 'In these several senses, which pass into each other, I use for convenience' sake the general term of Struggle for Existence.'[3]

The fact is that the struggle takes place (*a*) between fellow-organisms of the same kith and kin, but (*b*) also between foes of entirely different natures, and (*c*) between living creatures and their inanimate surroundings. Furthermore, it may be for food, for foothold, for luxuries, for mates, and for the sake of the young. The essential idea is 'answering back' to environing limitations and difficulties; and in an outlook on animate Nature it is of real importance to be clear that the struggle for existence need not be directly competitive, need not be sanguinary, need not lead to elimination there and then, and that it may often be accurately described as an endeavour after well-being. It is very inaccurate to picture animate Nature as, in Huxley's phrase, 'a dismal cockpit.'

3. The breadth of the concept.—In face of difficulties and limitations one kind of organism may intensify competition, another may exhibit an elaboration of parental care, another may experiment in mutual aid, another may take to some form of parasitism, and another may change its habitat. These are some of the many 'answers back' which living creatures make to environing difficulties and limitations, and all are to be included in the concept of the struggle for existence. Instead of making an opposition between 'struggle for self' and 'struggle for others,' or between 'mutual struggle' and 'mutual aid,' it is scientifically clearer to recognize that the concept of struggle, as Darwin used it, includes all the fresh reactions and responses which individual organisms make in face of difficulties. As Spencer, Kessler, Geddes, Drummond, Kropotkin, Cresson, and others have shown, survival is often the reward of those organisms that give the best send-off to their offspring, or that vary most in the direction of self-subordination, or that experiment most successfully in sociality. But the important point is to get away from the nightmare idea that the struggle for existence is necessarily an internecine competition between kin at the margin of subsistence. Of this mode of the struggle there are not on record more than a few good illustrations; in any case, as Darwin emphasized, it is far from being the only mode.

As a technical term, 'the struggle for existence' is not applicable when organisms faced by difficulties and limitations do not 'answer back' to these. Thus it is not obviously applicable to such a case as that of the myriads of open-sea animals engulfed in the baleen whale's huge mouth; it is not obviously applicable to such a case as that of the grass on which the cattle browse. It is essential to the concept that there be an individual 'answer back.' Similarly, it may be argued that, when an adaptive response comes to be part of the constitution of a species, when all the members of a species are so hereditarily endowed that they meet a familiar difficulty with effectiveness, and with equal effectiveness, then the swirl of the struggle for existence has passed from that particular point to some other. These capacities of effective response have been wrought out in the course of ages of struggle; they are now engrained in the constitution of the species; they have, so to speak, passed beyond the scope of struggle, except in so far as their continued exercise is necessary for their continued efficiency. But it is very interesting to consider these securely established ways, for thus we realize how large a proportion of the energy and time at the disposal of living creatures is spent in activities which make not for self-increase, self-stability, or self-preservation, but for the welfare of the family, the kin, and the species. Survival has doubtless been in many cases the reward of the individualistic competitor—a fox, let us say—but not less frequently of those with a capacity for self-forgetfulness and other-regarding activities. An otter is a solitary predatory carnivore, but the preoccupation of the mother with the nurture and education of the cubs is surely a very important factor in the survival of the species. It may be said that neither naturalists nor philosophers have as yet adequately realized the extent to which there is throughout animate Nature a subordination of the individual to the species.[1]

4. Results of the struggle for existence.—The outcome of the struggle for existence varies with its conditions.

(*a*) When the 'answer back' which organisms give is uniformly ineffective, the result will be an indiscriminate reduction of numbers. This will doubtless relieve the pressure of population, but it will not directly make for progress. A diagrammatic illustration may be seen when great crowds of lemmings, whose numbers have outrun the means of subsistence, obey the instinct to pass on, and swim out to sea, where they are drowned.

(*b*) The 'answer back' which organisms give may be uniformly effective, as when large numbers succeed in finding a new habitat or in discovering a new mode of life. For animals, as for man, the exploration of new territory has been a frequently recurrent result of the struggle for existence, and one of the most important. It is very instructive also to notice how species nearly related keep out of one another's way by exploiting slightly different levels of the same crowded area. This is vividly illustrated on the seashore. This kind of outcome will not have any direct effect on the constitution of the race, but it may possibly be important in stimulating germinal and habitable variability. It should be noted that, when organisms survive difficulties in a struggle in virtue of individually acquired and non-heritable somatic modifications, or in virtue of individual and non-heritable plasticity of endeavour, there will not be any direct constitutional effect on the race.

(*c*) The result which has most evolutionary interest is discriminate elimination, where the sifting depends on the possession or non-possession of certain heritable variations. When different

[1] *Darwin and Modern Science*, ed. A. C. Seward, Cambridge, 1909, p. 20.

[2] *Origin of Species*[6], p. 50.

[3] *Ib.*

[1] See Kropotkin, *Mutual Aid*; and Cresson, *L'Espèce et son serviteur*.

members of the species 'answer back' in virtue of hereditary endowment with varied degrees of effectiveness, the struggle for existence will tend to bring about the elimination of the relatively less fit, and a variety may actually supplant the parent species. This does not necessarily mean internecine competition between the members of the species, for, when a microbe, *e.g.*, attacks a family, the resistive capacity of the survivors is not gained at the expense of the other members, nor does it hasten their elimination.[1]

It is often said that what the discriminative modes of struggle actually effect is elimination, rather than selection. This is true, but too much must not be made of it. What actually happens in natural selection is a change in the centre of gravity of variation by the removal or handicapping of the less adaptive variants, but the elimination of X is correlated with the survival of Y. Darwin showed his wonted shrewdness in giving to *The Origin of Species by means of Natural Selection* the alternative title *The Preservation of Favoured Races in the Struggle for Life*. The important point is to realize that the struggle for existence may result in a process of natural selection without there being any rapid killing off of the less fit. If the relatively less fit have a more difficult life and do not live so long as the relatively more fit, if they have smaller and less vigorous families, if the parents are harassed so that they cannot give their offspring the best available nurture, and so on, the process will, in the long run, work out to the same result as if the less fit had come to a rapid violent end. Another consideration, of great importance but rarely appreciated, is that the struggle for existence seems to the expert naturalist to operate in reference to an intricate web of life, or system of inter-relations, which has been gradually wrought out in increasing complexity. Steps of organismal progress become in some measure embodied in extra-organismal linkages, in a *systema Naturæ* which has been increasingly elaborated through the ages; and this is part of the explanation of the progressiveness of evolution. There has been an evolution of the environment—of the struggle, of the selection—as well as of the organisms. The sieve evolves as well as the material sifted.

5. General.—(*a*) It is a basal fact in the scheme of organic evolution that one type of organism depends on another for sustenance. On the whole, the lower feed the higher, though the tables are sometimes turned. The living material passes from one incarnation to another; and, while we may not be scientifically warranted in saying that the myriads of prolific crustaceans in the sea are there in order that fishes may be fed, the fact is that the existence and persistence of the teeming multitudes of small fry has made the great race of fishes possible. And the great multitude of fishes has made the livelihood of much higher organisms, such as ospreys, possible. This nutritive dependence of organism upon organism is one of the factors necessitating a struggle for existence; and there seems no good reason why in its general aspects it should grate on æsthetic or ethical susceptibilities. The tendency which many not very highly individuated organisms have to prolific multiplication sometimes leads to grim results, as when a sow has more offspring than she can feed; or when a marsupial mother has more offspring than her pouch has teats for, or when, as in the egg-capsules of some whelks, there is necessitated cannibalism in the cradle; but, in general, there is nothing incongruent with the rationality of animate Nature in the fact that, with heavy odds against life, there should be provision for a safe margin. It is very instructive to notice how reproductivity is economized, along many different lines, in proportion to the advance in instinctive or intelligent control of circumstances, or in effectiveness of parental care and nurture. It is true that the callous changefulness of the physical environment causes much misery among living creatures, but a much larger fact is the remarkable fitness of our earth to be a home of life.[1] Moreover, while the physical environment is often tyrannous in its changefulness, its importance as a stimulus to effort and possibly to variation must be borne in mind. Furthermore, against the callousness of the physical environment must be set the plasticity with which the animate environment adjusts itself in linkages or inter-relations to register, or organize, or systematize organismal advances in evolution. This is one of the largest facts of natural history, and must form part of the perspective of our picture of the struggle for existence.

(*b*) The currency of half-understood biological ideas has often proved mischievous. Thus a vindication of internecine competition and of warfare among men is sometimes sought in an appeal to the fact that there is universal struggle for existence in animate Nature. Can we improve upon Nature's régime?, it is asked—as if man had not been doing this (with clouded success, it may be admitted) since civilization began. In repelling this sophism, the following points may be noted. (1) The struggle for existence, as Darwin insisted, includes much more than internecine competition among nearly related kin. It includes many non-competitive forms of an endeavour after well-being. (2) Some non-competitive modes of struggle—*e.g.*, elaborations of mutual aid and improvements in co-operation—seem to have been factors in great steps of progress in Nature, and well deserve man's imitation, which indeed, consciously or unconsciously, they have always had. (3) The sifting that goes on in the struggle for existence does not in itself make for more than the survival of those relatively fittest to given conditions. This can be no criterion of human conduct, unless the given conditions include the highest values. To take a particular case, there is not in biological analogy any warrant for supposing that the result of war must needs be a survival of the fittest in any desirable sense. (4) There are many interesting analogies between animal and human societies, but the differences are greater than the resemblances, and there is apt to be fallacy in arguing from the former to the latter. This is made particularly clear in Chalmers Mitchell's *Evolution and the War*. (5) If, as the facts suggest, there has been in the realm of organisms an evolution not only of organisms but of modes of selection, this will hold *a fortiori* for mankind, where the gradual displacement of natural selection by rational and social selection, though fraught with great dangers, opens up great possibilities of amelioration. (6) Finally, it must be borne in mind that in mankind it is not enough to refer to biological criteria, for, while these are fundamental, social criteria are supreme. Thus, to look at the question of war from another point of view, a war which is, biologically regarded, a reversion to the crudest mode of the struggle for existence may be, socially regarded, an expression and discipline of many and high virtues in combatants and non-combatants alike.

LITERATURE.—Charles Darwin, *The Origin of Species*, London, 1859, [6]1872; Alfred Russel Wallace, *Darwinism*, do. 1889; T. H. Huxley, 'The Struggle for Existence in Human Society,' in *Collected Essays*, do. 1893–94, ix. 195 ff.; P. Geddes and J. Arthur Thomson, *Evolution*, do. 1911; J. Arthur

[1] For a critical discussion of the alleged keenness of competition among members of the same or nearly related species see P. Chalmers Mitchell, *Evolution and the War*.

[1] See L. J. Henderson, *The Fitness of the Environment*, London, 1913.

Thomson, *Darwinism and Human Life*, rev. ed., do. 1916, *The Study of Animal Life*, rev. ed., do. 1917; P. Chalmers Mitchell, *Evolution and the War*, do. 1915; P. Kropotkin, *Mutual Aid, a Factor of Evolution*, rev. ed., do. 1904; Henry Drummond, *The Ascent of Man*, do. 1894; A. Cresson, *L'Espèce et son serviteur*, Paris, 1913; C. C. Coe, *Nature versus Natural Selection*, London, 1895; A. Weismann, *The Evolution Theory*, Eng. tr., 2 vols., do. 1904; L. Plate, *Selektionsprinzip und Probleme der Artbildung : Handbuch des Darwinismus*[3], Leipzig, 1908. J. ARTHUR THOMSON.

STUDENT CHRISTIAN MOVEMENT.—

1. Origin, aim, and extent.—The Student Christian Movement is world-wide in scope and carries on work in some 2500 universities and colleges in forty lands. In 1920 the World's Student Christian Federation celebrated its 25th birthday. It federates national movements in the United States of America, Canada, Great Britain and Ireland, France, Italy, Switzerland, Germany, Holland, Russia, Scandinavia, S. Africa, China, India, Japan, and Australasia. Pioneer work, which will issue in further national movements, is in progress in S. America, Austria, Hungary, and the Balkans. Its membership, somewhat reduced by the war, is 176,000 students.

The Movement came into being as the result of several converging streams of influence. The beginnings in Great Britain may be traced to the evangelical revival of the middle of last century. Meetings held in Cambridge at the time of the Mission of Moody and Sankey in 1873, though not conducted by them, gave an impetus to already existing work there, and led to the formation of Christian Unions in Cambridge and Oxford. In 1877 an annual conference was instituted, attended by delegates from these two universities and from Edinburgh, Glasgow, Durham, and Dublin. The volunteering of the 'Cambridge Seven' for missionary work in China, followed by the visits to various colleges and universities of Stanley Smith and C. T. Studd in 1884 resulted among other things in the remarkable work carried on for ten years in Edinburgh under the leadership of Henry Drummond. To his influence, and to that of the student deputations from Edinburgh which visited other colleges, the Student Christian Movement both in America and in Great Britain is largely indebted. Meantime a similar movement was making progress in America, which took shape in 1886 in the Student Volunteer Missionary Union. Visits paid to this country by J. N. Forman and R. P. Wilder, two of the founders of that Union, led to the inauguration at a conference in Edinburgh in April 1892 of a similar Union for Great Britain. It is at this date that the Movement in an organized form may be said to begin.

These Unions were composed of men who had formed the purpose of becoming foreign missionaries, and the first aim of the founders was to appeal to the universities for volunteers for the mission field. Planted at first as a mustard-seed in some American Colleges, the Student Volunteer Missionary Union has grown to marvellous dimensions, and up to the year 1919 there were 9000 missionaries in the field whose names had been enrolled as Student Volunteers. The movement, therefore, from its origin has had as its horizon nothing less than the whole world.

It is impossible in a short article to trace the course of the Movement's growth throughout the world. The character and development of the national movements naturally vary in accordance with the differences characteristic of, say, America and Europe, East and West, Roman Catholic and Reformed countries. But there is enough in common to justify the taking of one national movement as illustrative of the rest. This article is therefore based on the writers' knowledge of the British Student Movement.

2. Development and methods.—The pioneers of the movement in 1892 were concerned to win men and women in the British colleges for service abroad. This simple beginning has led to a complex development. The search for volunteer missionaries revealed the religious needs of both men and women students in every kind of college. In the older universities Christianity was found to be institutionally represented. But even there, and still more in the newer universities, in national training colleges, in technical, medical, and other schools, great numbers of students were found to lie outside the embrace of organized Christianity. There are no 'enchantments of the Middle Ages' in the great majority of modern British colleges. They represent a growth of education which has been independent of the Churches. It fell therefore to the pioneers of the movement not only to appeal for 'student volunteers' from the colleges, but to cultivate in the colleges some oases of Christian life and conviction in their religious deserts. The S.V.M.U. thus gave rise to the General College Department, which is a federation of local Student Christian Unions. In 1892 only 20 colleges had religious organizations. In 1919 there were 126 Christian Unions in British colleges, with a total membership of about 6000 students. The missionary aim of the S.V.M.U. led not only to the formation of Christian Unions in secular colleges, but also to the creation of a Theological College Department, in which are associated 63 theological colleges, representative of all the Christian bodies other than Roman Catholic. This extension represented the desire to bring home to men preparing for the ministry both the missionary call of the hour and the religious needs and aspirations of their contemporaries about to enter other professions.

The College Christian Unions are self-governing. They are grouped in six intercollegiate Unions in Wales, Ireland, Scotland, North and South of England, and London, each with a representative Council. In Ireland, Scotland, and Wales especially the work has developed along characteristically national lines. The affairs of the Student Christian Movement as a whole are controlled by a General Committee elected annually and composed almost entirely of students still in college. This Committee employs, in 1920, thirty college men and women as Secretaries, most of them recent graduates, who act as links between the colleges, and help to bring to bear upon local problems the experience of the whole Movement. Methods of work vary with the college, but in nearly all there are lectures on the Bible, various aspects of Christian belief, the missionary enterprise and social questions, small groups of eight or a dozen meeting weekly for discussion of books published by the Movement for the purpose, prayer meetings and series of addresses designed to present the appeal of Christ to the entire body of students. These methods are supplemented by small Conferences in various parts of the college field for the more thorough study of the Bible, or missions or social problems under the guidance of experts. The Summer Conferences (held latterly at Swanwick, Derbyshire) are attended by students from all parts of the country. One of the most important departments of the Movement's work in recent years has been due to the presence in the colleges of increasing numbers (over 2000 in 1920) of students from other countries. It seeks to do all in its power to secure a friendly welcome for these men and women, whose presence provides a unique opportunity for the promotion of mutual understanding and international goodwill. Special secretaries have been set apart for this purpose. Several of these groups of foreign students have formed Christian Unions of their own. The Student Movement House in London provides premises for a Club which includes among its thousand members students of thirty-three nationalities.

The growth of the movement has therefore been in extension. It cuts a section through the length and breadth of the British adult education. It has also been in intension. The pursuit of the original and relatively simple missionary aim has laid bare a complexity of religious need and opportunity. The movement began with a certain evangelical *naïveté*. It was based on 'Bible Christian' assumptions and was not at first sensitive to the intellectual difficulties of students or to the relationship between foreign missionary enterprise and the reproach of the gospel constituted by social conditions at home. But with very great rapidity the movement was led to face the facts. It has set itself sympathetically to foster the quest of the younger generation after a fresh understanding of the gospel. It has boldly spread among students the positive and constructive results of Biblical study. At the same time it has recognized fully that the gospel has not only to be carried to the heathen but also to be applied to the Christianization of society everywhere. It has been foremost in the consciousness that the focus of Christianity according to the mind of the Master is something more than individual salvation. In other words, it has embraced the gospel of the Kingdom of God. This is of especial significance when the comprehensive character of the student field is taken into account. Every profession has its postulants in the colleges. The movement therefore has been stimulated to think out how Christianity applies to the life and work of men and women in every kind of secular profession. This complex development of the movement's activities is represented in the growth and character of its literature. Beginning with comparatively simple missionary and Biblical propaganda, it has expanded into something fairly representative of the relationship of Christ to the thought and life of the times.

At the same time the central and single loyalty of the founders of the movement has been continued: it is loyalty to Jesus Christ. Students have grown undoubtedly in an unwillingness merely to accept traditional beliefs about Him. The movement is now less possessed than formerly of a fixed and agreed message about Him. It is more of a quest after 'the truth as it is in Jesus.' But it has advanced in the conviction that the master-key to all the interwoven problems of the world lies with Him. It has therefore grown in a deepened and intensified loyalty to Him.

3. Doctrinal position and relation to the Churches.—For its faith and doctrinal position the movement has come to depend (in a way which what has been said will render intelligible) less upon any independent formulation of its own than upon the faith of the adult Churches. The movement after all is not a Church; it is the adolescent department of the Churches; it is the means of collecting and formulating to the elder Christian world the hopes, needs, and difficulties of the coming generation. It is also the channel through which the forces of the Christian Church may reach the student class, otherwise largely inaccessible. For teachers, writers, speakers, secretaries, it draws freely upon the ranks of organized Christianity. It has held consistently to the task of reinforcing the adult Church with the vigorous faith and service of the student whom it has helped to belief in Christ and to devotion to His cause.

Thus related to the Churches, the movement has been brought face to face with the problem of Christian unity. Yet its interest in the problem is not direct; it is incidental to the main work of winning students for Christ and His service. None the less the movement is doing formative work for the cause of Christian unity. It is not content with negations, but seeks to make to converge on the needs of students all the resources of the divided Body of Christ. The movement (and notably its conferences) is the meeting-place, under conditions of mutual need and adolescent candour, of men and women representative of the full width of Christian division. No one is asked to leave behind his denominational loyalty, but all bring it with them and make it their contribution to the common stock. Thus the movement, and notably its Theological College Department, has become the means of exchange of view and mutual understanding between representatives of Christian traditions as widely separated as the Friends on the one hand and Roman Catholicism on the other.

Such in outline is the British Student Christian Movement. Its significant features, missionary, social, intellectual, and ecclesiastical, deserve illustration and amplification from movements in other countries. There is no doubt, *e.g.*, that on the continent of Europe there is a far greater degree of alienation of the student class from organized Christianity than in Great Britain. Movements of intellectual and moral revolt have gone deeper. In fact, the World's Student Christian Federation by its touch with students is concerned with a whole world of deep spiritual, moral, and political unrest. Again, the movement in other lands has come to be quite clearly of opinion that, wherever liaison and co-operation with Catholic Christianity is feasible, it is the right policy, so that the streams of new life may be helped to flow down and purify the old channels. There are many Orthodox, Copt, Gregorian, and some Roman Catholic, students within the Federation. Everywhere the movement asks of students but two questions: whether they see in Jesus Christ the hope of the world; whether they will join with others in making Him King in their hearts and over the whole of life. To that common task it invites all to bring the treasures of their ecclesiastical inheritances wherewith to enrich the Student Christian fellowship.

It remains to add that the war but heightened the value and potentiality of the movement in all lands. The Student Federation held together despite all the ruptures of war, and on a general view has not lost ground despite all the losses of the war. In many parts of Europe, notably in the Balkans, Austria, Hungary, and Poland, movements of emancipation consequent on the war expose a deep need and opportunity for Student Movement enterprise. In some countries no doubt the movement is small and struggling, and faced by desperate difficulties. But everywhere, nevertheless, the true light already shineth. It is the light of Christ, in whom this movement trusts. He has greatly blessed it. The future, therefore, is bright with the hope of His using it afresh in His purposes of healing and reconciliation for the world.

LITERATURE.—W. H. T. Gairdner, *D. M. Thornton: A Study in Missionary Ideals and Methods*, London, 1908; George Adam Smith, *The Life of Henry Drummond*, do. 1899; Tissington Tatlow, *Martyn Trafford*, do. 1911; *The Student Movement* (the official organ of the British Student Christian Movement), and *The Student World* (organ of the World's Student Christian Federation). See also annual reports and pamphlets issued in connexion with the Movement.

N. S. TALBOT.
HUGH MARTIN.

STUNDISM.—See SECTS (Russian).

STŪPA.—*Stūpa* (Sanskrit), a Buddhist monument or mausoleum, generally called 'tope' (from Pāli *thūpa*) in India and adjacent countries, means 'mound' or 'tumulus,' and the term *chaitya* (*q.v.*) had originally the same meaning, though it afterwards came to denote any memorial or sacred spot or sanctuary of any shape, whereas *stūpas* were always built in the shape of towers, surmounted by a cupola and one or more *chattra* ('parasols'). King Aśoka, the Buddhistic Constantine (3rd cent. B.C.), is said to have erected, within the space of three years, 84,000 *stūpas* in different parts of India, to preserve the remains of Buddha.[1]

[1] There must have been *stūpas* long before the time of Aśoka, since he declared, in an inscription discovered by Führer in the Tarai, near the Nepālese village of Nigliva, that he increased or enlarged for the second time the *stūpa* of the Buddha Koṇākamana, a mythical predecessor of the historical Buddha, and since the ruined Piprāwā *stūpa* contains an inscription which is decidedly prior to the period of Aśoka.

Funeral tumuli are spread over the whole continent of Asia and Europe, and it may be taken for granted that the worship of *stūpas*, or mausoleums of distinguished personages, was handed down to the adherents of Buddha from a remote period. Thus the excavation, in 1905, of the curious earthen mounds north of the village of Lauriya, in the Bettiah subdivision, has revealed the interesting fact that these ancient conical structures contain deposits of bones as well as gold leaves and other ornaments. Aśoka erected one of his pillars near these old monuments, which had probably formed an object of worship long before his epoch, and may have contained the remains of royal persons. When dying, Buddha is said to have declared that, besides himself and his disciples, a monarch and a *pratyekabuddha* (*q.v.*) were worthy to be dignified with the erection of a *stūpa*. Nor were *stūpas* entirely confined to Buddhists in the historical period of India. There is a story of the Buddhist king Kaniṣka having by mistake paid homage to a heretical *stūpa*. *Stūpas* are mentioned in the sacred writings of the Jain sect, and an ancient Jain inscription discovered at Mathurā records the consecration of one or two statues at a certain ancient *stūpa*. A Brāhmanical hermitage, represented on the sculptures of Sānchī and Amarāvatī, shows the figure of a *stūpa*. All the *stūpas* actually discovered, however, seem to be of Buddhist origin, and we know for certain that it was an established usage of the Buddhist Church to raise memorials called *stūpas* on the ashes or relics of its teachers, and in those places which were hallowed by some remarkable event in the history of Buddha or of his followers. This accounts for the fact that *stūpas* are found not only in India itself, but also in all other countries where Buddhism is or has been in the ascendant.

1. Stūpas discovered outside of India.—Of these the ruins of a *stūpa* at Anurādhāpura (Ceylon), supposed to date from 161 B.C. to A.D. 137 or earlier, are perhaps the most ancient. The celebrated Javanese monument of Boro-Budur, in the central part of Java, which belongs to the 7th–9th cent. A.D., consists of eight terraces and contains no fewer than 73 *stūpas*, with sitting statues of Buddha. The temples of Ayuthia, the ruined ancient capital of Siam, exhibit a curious mixture of the *stūpa* style with other Indian elements. Other independent varieties of the *stūpa* have been developed in Burma, Nepāl, and Tibet. The Chinese *stūpas*, built since the 1st cent. A.D., have no cupola, but from seven to thirteen *chattras*. The dowager empress Hon of China is said to have built a *stūpa* of nine storeys, 900 ft. high, crowned by a mast of 100 ft. carrying 50 golden disks. In Ladakh Simpson discovered the reproduction of a *stūpa* with thirteen *chattras*. In Afghanistān some 60 *stūpas* were examined by Masson. They are remarkable for the fragments of one or two bones, evidently relics, which they generally contain in a small apartment in their centre, and to protect which they appear to have been erected. A certain *stūpa* near Kuchar in E. Turkestan was opened in 1889 by some natives of the place looking for treasure. What they actually found was not treasure, but a heap of very ancient Sanskrit MSS, which were afterwards deciphered by R. Hoernle in *The Bower Manuscript* (Calcutta, 1893 ff.). In the same country Stein discovered, in 1900, an enormous *stūpa*, situated in a rectangular courtyard, the walls of which were decorated with rilievos of the 4th century A.D.

2. Indian stūpas.—The rise and development of *stūpa* architecture may, however, best be studied in India, where it originated, especially in the ancient sculptural and pictorial representations of *stūpas*. A very ancient type of *stūpa*, which consists of a simple round tumulus surrounded by a balustrade, has been preserved in an old Sānchī sculpture. According to Rhys Davids, the first step in the development of the original cairn or mound into a *stūpa* consisted in building it more carefully than usual, with stones, and in covering the outside with fine *chunam* plaster to give a marble-like surface. The next step was to build the cairn of concentric layers of the huge bricks in use at the time and to surround the whole with a wooden railing. There can be no doubt that the railings and *toraṇas* (gates) were originally made of wood, like the wooden gates so common in the court-yards of Chinese and Japanese temples, which seem to have been derived from the Indian *toraṇas*, though the only preserved specimens of the latter—*e.g.*, the beautifully ornamented gate of the Sānchī tope—are made of stone. The *stūpa* itself was early placed on a circular terrace or plinth. A parasol (*chattra*) was added on the top, the sign of high station in the East. Between it and the cupola there was a quadrangular structure, fitly called the neck (*gala*) of the *stūpa*. Many *stūpas* contained quite a series of parasols, diminishing in diameter as they approached the top of the building. The height of the parasols was at least one-third of the whole height of the edifice (said to have been 632 ft. in the case of the famous sanctuary of Peshawār, as seen by a Chinese traveller). The miniature *stūpas*, which were used as objects of worship, containing small fragments of sacred texts, called *dharma-śarīra*, or religious relics, are only a few centimetres in height.

A Buddhist Sanskrit work, the *Divyāvadāna*, contains a description of the mode in which an elaborate *stūpa* was gradually erected by a rich Indian merchant. He began by having four staircases built on the four sides of the future *stūpa*. Then he built successively the three terraces or plinths which were to be reached from the staircases. They were surmounted by the dome or cupola, called 'egg' (*anda*), in which there was a hole for the pillar or flagstaff carrying the whole series of parasols (*chattrāvalī*). The cupola was crowned by a pavilion, or kiosk (*harmskā*), serving as a base for the pillar, which, rising from the dome, passed through the pavilion. A rain-water pot (*varṣa-sthāla*) is also mentioned, in which precious stones were deposited.

The *stūpas* of India may be conveniently divided into two classes, according as they were built as *dāgabas* (from Skr. *dhātugarbha*, 'receptacle for relics'), for the purpose of enshrining some sacred relic, or as memorials of some remarkable event in the life of a Buddha or other saint. A specimen of the latter kind is the famous *stūpa* of Sārnāth (*q.v.*), near Benares, situated in the Deer Park (*mṛgavana*), where Buddha took up his residence, with his five disciples, when commencing his mission as a teacher. The building now consists of a stone base 93 ft. in diameter, surmounted by a tower in brick-work, rising to a height of 110 ft. above the surrounding ruins, and 128 ft. above the plain. In his excavations Cunningham found, at the depth of 10½ ft. from the summit, a large stone inscribed with the Buddhist creed, but no relic.

Near Nagarahāra, in the Kabul valley, there were two *stūpas* intended to perpetuate the memory of the celebrated meeting of the future Buddha with his mythical predecessor, Dīpaṅkara. Many other such memorial *stūpas*, which have now disappeared, were seen and described by the devout Chinese Buddhist pilgrims who visited India between A.D. 400 and 800.

The *stūpas* of Bhīlsa (*q.v.*), in Central India, the most extensive group of topes in India, include the great memorial tope at Sānchī, supposed to have been built or commenced by King Aśoka (3rd cent. B.C.), a massive structure of brick and stones, 42 ft. high, rising on a stone plinth and surrounded by a stone railing containing four beautifully ornamented gates. *Stūpa* II. of Sānchī, on the other hand, is a relic shrine containing the remains of two contemporaries of King Aśoka, and *stūpa* III. has supplied two relic caskets bearing the names of two distinguished pupils of Buddha.

The great tope of Mānikyāla in the Panjāb, in its lowest deposit, which was discovered just below the centre, contains a brass cylindrical casket, with an old inscription and several coins of very ancient date. This tope is a hemisphere 127 ft. in diameter, the total height of the dome, as it now stands, being 92 feet. Four broad flights of steps facing the cardinal points lead to the top of the terrace for the use of pilgrims. In the Sonāla tope, near Mānikyāla, Cunningham discovered a crystal box containing the relic, which was a very small piece of bone wrapped in gold-leaf, along with a small silver coin, a copper ring, 24 small beads of pearl, turquoise, garnet, and quartz. These, with the gold-leaf wrappers, make up the seven *ratnas*, or jewels, which usually accompanied the relic deposits of the old Buddhists, and which are still placed in the *chortens* (*q.v.*) of the Buddhists of Tibet.

Near the ancient town of Sopārā, in the Thāna District of the Bombay Presidency, Indraji in 1881 opened a large dome-topped mound, the ruins of a brick Buddhist *stūpa*. In the centre of the dome, a little below the level of its base, he found a large circular stone coffer in which stood an egg-shaped copper casket surrounded by a circle of eight small seated copper images of Buddha, well-proportioned and gracefully formed. In the copper casket were enclosed, one within the other, four caskets, of silver, of stone, of crystal, and of gold. Between the silver casket and the copper casket were gold flowers of seven varieties, and a small image of Buddha, sitting cross-legged on a lotus, also 13 precious stones of seven kinds, apparently taking the place of the seven jewels, and 31 other drilled stones of various shapes, intended apparently as a necklace presented to the relics. Among the stones was a well-preserved unworn silver coin, with a legend referring to King Yajna Sātakarni (2nd cent. A.D. ?). The gold cup was found to contain 13 tiny pieces of earthenware; they were probably believed to be fragments of Buddha's begging bowl, which was held in great reverence by Buddhists. The idea of the builders of the *stūpa* seems to have been to enclose the relics in seven envelopes, each more valuable than the one below, the clay and brick of the mound being reckoned as the least valuable of all.

In the *stūpa* of Bhaṭṭiprolu in the Kistna District, Madras Presidency, several relic caskets were found by Rea in 1891, with interesting inscriptions, in ancient characters (of the 3rd cent. B.C. or so), declaring two of the caskets to be intended for relics of Buddha.

In the extreme north of India, near the Nepālese frontier, in the neighbourhood of the site of Kapilavastu (*q.v.*), Buddha's birthplace, W. C. Peppé, a landholder, excavated in Jan. 1898 the brick *stūpa* of Piprāwā. In its interior chamber he found a stone coffer containing several other vessels in which were preserved pieces of bone, quite recognizable as such. Round the rim of the lid of one steatite vase runs an inscription in ancient characters of the Maurya type, but without long vowels. This is the oldest inscription hitherto discovered in India, since it must belong to the 4th, or perhaps the 5th, century B.C. According to the interpretation given by Fleet, the record declares that 'this is a deposit of relics of the brethren of Buddha, together with their little sisters and with their children and wives,' and it commemorates the enshrining of relics of Buddha's kinsmen and of their families, probably after they had been massacred by the king of Kosala, as the Buddhist tradition has it. The vessels were found to contain, besides the bones, a vast number of various small ornaments and objects of art—*e.g.*, two small human figures in gold-leaf, jewels and articles made from them, coral and crystal beads, a coil of fine silver wire, a lion stamped on gold-leaf, an elephant, two birds of cornelian and metal, gold- and silver-leaf stars, etc. These were, according to Fleet's plausible conjecture, apparently the trinkets and household treasures of the women and the playthings of the children, entombed together with their bones by some unknown pious friend of the slaughtered people.[1]

3. Artistic value.—From an artistic point of view, the sculptures contained in the stone railings and huge gates of some *stūpas* are particularly interesting and important. Thus the sculptures of the eastern gate of the great Sānchī *stūpa* abound in life-like representations of the principal scenes of the romantic history of Buddha, of *stūpas* and their worshippers, of sacred trees and lotus-flowers, of elephants, camels, lions, and peacocks, of deities, kings, female dancers, etc. The style of these sculptures exhibits a strong Persian influence, notably in the bell-shaped capitals of pillars. The same style is visible in the splendid railings of Bhārhut (*q.v.*), the only remains of the great Bhārhut *stūpa*, which was situated about midway between Sānchī and Bodh Gayā, the place of Buddha's enlightenment, which is likewise marked by the remains of some interesting railings dating from the Aśoka period. The Bhārhut sculptures, now mostly in the Calcutta Indian Museum, belong to the same period as the Sānchī sculptures (*c.* 200 B.C.), and are particularly valuable for the old inscriptions explaining their meaning. The highly finished rilievos of the Amarāvati (*q.v.*) *stūpa*, on the other hand, which are now to be seen in London, are to some extent an offshoot of Gandhāra art, the Greek or Græco-Buddhist art of N.W. India having extended its influence as far southward as the course of the Kistna. The railings of Amarāvati, judging from the inscriptions, seem to belong to the end of the 2nd century B.C. The best preserved *stūpas* are those which form the innermost part of numerous cave temples in W. India. There is an open space round them for circumambulation, but there is nothing remarkable about them from an artistic point of view.

4. Worship of stūpas.—*Stūpas* were worshipped, not only by circumambulating them, with the right side turned towards the *stūpa*, but also by placing on them flowers, incense, cloth, parasols, flags, great banners, and ornaments, by offering them coins, by washing them with milk, etc. This worship has survived to the present day in Buddhist countries—*e.g.*, in Burma, where on festival occasions a thousand candles are burnt day after day before the great *stūpa* of Shwe-Dagon at Rangoon, which is devoutly believed to contain eight hairs of Buddha. The miniature *stūpas* of the Buddhists were manufactured in great numbers for devotional purposes and worshipped in the houses of the laymen. Buddhist monks used to make them with their own hands. Large *stūpas* were found in every Buddhist convent, and the sanctity attributed to them appears from the reply said to have been given by the then Buddhist community to King Puṣyamitra, the persecutor of Buddhism, when he asked which of their sanctuaries they would rather have destroyed, the *stūpas* or the monasteries, and they answered: 'The monasteries.' The relics recently dug out from some of the Indian *stūpas* have become an object of veneration to the Buddhists of other countries. When the splinters of Buddha's bowl

[1] See, however, art. KAPILAVASTU, vol. vii. p. 661[b].

had been excavated from the Sopārā *stūpa*, the Buddhist high-priest of Ceylon petitioned Government that a small portion of the bowl of the world-honoured Gautama might be given to him to deposit in the monastery of Adam's Peak—a petition which, we need hardly say, was readily granted. The relics contained in the Piprāwā *stūpa* were offered by the Indian Government to the king of Siam, who sent an envoy to India to receive the relics, and agreed to distribute portions of them among the Buddhists of Burma and Ceylon.

5. Who built the stūpas?—It may be confidently asserted that kings and princes were not the only builders of *stūpas*. The renowned King Harṣa (7th cent. A.D.) is reported to have erected several thousand *stūpas*, each about 100 ft. high, along the banks of the sacred Ganges. Merchants and traders, on the other hand, prevail among the donors referred to in the Sānchī and other inscriptions, and it seems that this class was the chief stronghold of Buddhism.

LITERATURE.—H. H. Wilson, *Ariana Antiqua*, London, 1841; A. Cunningham, *The Bhilsa Topes*, do. 1854, *Reports of the Archæological Survey of India*, i. ii. v. xiv., Calcutta, 1871–82, *The Stūpa of Bharhut*, London, 1879; Bhagvāntal Indraji, *Antiquarian Remains at Sopārā and Padana*, Bombay, 1882; J. Burgess, *Reports of the Amaravati and Jaggayyapeta Buddhist Stupas*, London, 1882, *The Ancient Monuments, Temples, and Sculptures of India*, do. 1897, *Buddhist Art in India* (tr. and enlarged from A. Grünwedel, *Buddhistische Kunst in Indien*, Berlin, 1893), do. 1901; A. Rea, *South Indian Buddhist Antiquities in the Krishna District*, Madras, 1894; A. Foucher, *Étude sur l'iconographie bouddhique de l'Inde*, 2 pts., Paris, 1899–1905, *L'Art gréco-bouddhique du Gandhâra*, do. 1905; C. M. Pleyte, *Die Buddha-Legende in den Skulpturen des Tempels von Bôrô-Budur*, Amsterdam, 1901; M. A. Stein, *Sand-buried Ruins of Khotan*, London, 1903; W. C. Peppé, 'The Piprahwâ Stûpa,' in *JRAS*, 1899; J. F. Fleet, 'The Inscription on the Piprāwā Vase,' *ib.* 1906; J. Fergusson, *Hist. of Indian and Eastern Architecture*, rev. ed., 2 vols., London, 1910.

J. JOLLY.

STYX.—The name clearly signifies, in respect of its derivation, the 'horror' or 'abomination.'[1] Homer describes the Thessalian Titaresius,[2] which flows into the Peneus but does not mix with it, as an effluent of the Styx, to which it owes its magical properties; for Styx is the most potent sanction of an oath, seeing that it was by the inviolable waters of the Styx that the immortals themselves swore.[3] The circumstances and consequences of the oath are detailed by Hesiod.[4] Zeus dispatches Iris to convey the magic water in a golden pitcher, and the defaulter is excluded from the Olympian community, and remains in a breathless trance for a period of nine years until the great cycle is complete. It may be said that the gods swear by Styx so as to invoke death, and that they issue a challenge involving the loss of their divinity in case of failure to fulfil the oath. But it was natural to ascribe to the gods a sanction which men themselves regarded as supremely holy. Thus even in the absence of direct evidence we should be ready to infer that the practice of swearing by Styx was current upon earth as well as in heaven. However, the fact is proved by the testimony of history. When Cleomenes in exile from Sparta tried to persuade the Arcadians to join him and march against his countrymen, he was eager to induce the chieftains to go with him to Nonacris and swear by the waters of the Styx that they would follow wherever he might lead.[5] The custom is explained by the belief in the deadly nature of the Arcadian spring, a draught of which was supposed to be instantly fatal.[6] Thus to invoke the waters of the magic stream, believing that they would kill the man who forswore himself, constituted an ordeal[1] like the drinking of bull's blood or the lifting of red-hot bars; and Styx is accordingly described as she who guards the right.[2] Generally, Stygian waters have a magic power either for harm or for weal. The Telchines sprinkled the fields of the island of Rhodes with Stygian water in order to make them unfruitful.[3] On the other hand, the vulnerability of Achilles' heel was said to be due to the fact that Thetis held him by the heel when she bathed him in the waters of the Styx to confer immortality upon him.[4] T. Bergk[5] quotes an Arcadian legend that whosoever drank of the waters of the Styx on a particular day of the year secured thereby immortality.

The name seems to have been appropriated generically to rivers which by the weirdness of their surroundings or the character of their waters were believed to possess a magic virtue. Besides the places already named, we read of a Styx in Egypt, in Arabia, in Ephesus, in Eubœa, and elsewhere. Hence it is not surprising that poetic imagination should have conceived of Styx as the chief river of the under world[6] and the source of Cocytus.[7] But the development of the idea that the Styx was a barrier shutting off the infernal regions which it encircled in a ninefold sinuosity,[8] and the fable of Charon in whose boat every shade must cross the river, are known to us from post-Homeric sources. The mythological connexions of Styx, as described in the *Theogony*, are of minor interest. She appears as daughter of Oceanus, spouse of Pallas, and mother of Zelos, Nike, Kratos, and Bia,[9] with whose support she assisted Zeus in his war with the Titans.[10]

A. C. PEARSON.

SUBCONSCIOUSNESS.—The question of the nature and existence of subconsciousness may be said to have begun with Leibniz, although it was much later before the term itself came into use. Locke, in attacking the Cartesian view that the mind thinks always, or is always conscious, had said that, since thinking is an operation, like motion in bodies, it must be intermittent; further, that we cannot think without being sensible of it, any more than we can be happy or miserable without being aware of it; and to say that we may be conscious at the moment of thinking, but forget it immediately, is to make a pure assumption; such fleeting impressions, 'characters drawn on dust, that the first breath of wind effaces,' would be of no value to the soul if they existed.[11] Leibniz's reply was that, as visible bodies and movements really depend on, and are made possible by, invisible or imperceptible bodies and movements, so there are numberless minute perceptions, not sufficiently distinct to be noticed or remembered, which yet can be inferred from their effects. Not only is there at any moment a multitude of impressions being made on the senses, only a very few of which can capture our attention, but also there is something remaining in the mind from every one of our past thoughts, none of which can ever be wholly effaced. In deep sleep, in a faint, perhaps even in death, when the unity of consciousness is broken, the mind splits up into an infinite number of minute confused sensations; perhaps this is also the natural condition of the waking mind of animals. Many of our actions, however impulsive and unmotived in appearance—habits, customs, passions—are determined by the pressure of these minute unobserved sensations. It is in-

1 See J. E. Harrison, *Themis*, Cambridge, 1912, p. 73.
2 *Il.* ii. 755.
3 Hom. *Il.* xiv. 271, *Od.* v. 185; Verg. *Æn.* vi. 324.
4 *Theog.* 784–805.
5 Herod. vi. 74.
6 Paus. VIII. xviii. 4, with Frazer's notes.

1 See art. ORDEAL (Greek).
2 Bacchyl. x. 9.
3 Nonnus, xiv. 46 ff.
4 Stat. *Achill.* i. 269.
5 *Kleine philolog. Schriften*, Halle, 1886, ii. 701.
6 Hom. *Il.* viii. 369.
7 *Od.* x. 514.
8 Verg. *Georg.* iv. 480.
9 Hes. *Theog.* 363 f.
10 *Ib.* 397.
11 Locke, *Essay concerning Human Understanding*, London, 1690, bk. ii. ch. i. § 15 (*Works*, ed. Bohn, do. 1876–77, i. 217).

teresting that the three features introduced by Leibniz—the unnoticed impressions of the moment, the traces representing past thoughts, the continuity and unity of the mind—have remained throughout the main elements in the problem of subconsciousness. It was on these 'petites perceptions' that Leibniz based his doctrine of the 'pre-established harmony' between soul and body, his law of continuity, his identity of indiscernibles;[1] his theory also of the summation of stimuli, the continued activity of the soul through the deepest sleep, the theory that sensations and perceptions are really sums of an infinite number of minute or infinitesimal sensations, etc. Kant followed Leibniz, connecting the idea of subconsciousness (1) with the differences of degree in the clearness and distinctness of ideas; (2) with the notion of a chart or field of consciousness, some parts of which are brightly, but much the greater part dimly, illumined; (3) with forgetfulness or dissociation, as in his argument that there can be no sleep without dreams, that those who suppose there is have only forgotten their dreams.[2]

In the discussion between Sir William Hamilton, W. B. Carpenter, and J. S. Mill, etc., as to the existence of *unconscious* mental modifications the question turned mainly upon what are now called *subconscious* ideas. Hamilton pointed out that Locke's assumption that consciousness and the recollection of consciousness are convertible is disproved by somnambulism and by many dreams, which can only be inferred, from actions carried out, to have taken place.[3] We are never suddenly awakened from a deep sleep without finding ourselves in the middle of a dream; the probability therefore is that we are always dreaming, or being conscious, in sleep, and that we forget these dreams because of the contrast and confusion between the two worlds of sleep and waking. It is as if the brightness of the real and sensory world dimmed the colours of the imaginary world. He accepts the conclusions of T. S. Jouffroy[4] that it is the body only that sleeps, the mind being constantly awake; that during sleep, while the senses, being bodily organs, are torpid on the whole, one or more of them may continue to send imperfect impressions through to the mind; that the mind, being awake, estimates the importance of these, and may, if it so decides, wake the body; a slight movement of the patient may wake the sick-nurse when the much greater sound of a passing wagon fails to do so; many persons can awake at a fixed hour, etc. Similar activities of the mind and similar modifications exist in waking life alongside of the fully conscious ideas. Hamilton details three degrees of these: (1) Our acquired habits of mind, the language or languages, the sciences we may have learned, and the like; they must have *some* sort of existence in the mind when they are not being actually put into operation. (2) There are systems and habits of which the mind is unconscious in its ordinary state, but which are revealed 'in certain extraordinary exaltations of the powers,'[5] such as madness, fever, etc. 'The evidence on this point shows that the mind frequently contains whole systems of knowledge, which, though in our normal state they have faded into absolute oblivion, may, in certain abnormal states, as madness, febrile delirium, somnambulism, catalepsy, etc., flash out into luminous consciousness, and even throw into the shade of unconsciousness those other systems by which they had, for a long period, been eclipsed and even extinguished.'[6] (3) The third group is those 'mental activities and passivities, of which we are unconscious, but which manifest their existence by effects of which we are conscious'[7] —the unconscious, or subconscious, as it would now be called, out of which the conscious is built up.

Hamilton's examples are partly those of Leibniz —perception through the senses, as the green of a distant forest is made up of the green of the separate trees and even leaves, which are not separately visible;[8] partly new instances, as the mediate association of ideas, where one idea suggests another through some hidden link, which may only afterwards and by special effort, if at all, be brought to full consciousness;[9] again, our acquired dexterities and habits, where, according to Hamilton, the mind exercises volition and so far a control over the whole series of acts (in speaking or writing, *e.g.*), but has no consciousness or deliberate volition in regard to each separate movement in the series. Yet the detailed movements must be somehow in the mind, before they are carried into execution. He proposes therefore to regard all such phenomena as implying 'latent modifications,' 'unconscious activities' of the mind.[1] J. S. Mill, in his *Examination of Sir William Hamilton's Philosophy*,[2] discusses the 'unconscious mental modifications' and points out that the acquired knowledge and skill, when not in use, are simply *capabilities*, not actions or passions at all, whether 'latent' or other:

'I have the power to walk across the room, though I am sitting on my chair; but we should hardly call this power a latent act of walking.'[3]

The second class of cases referred to by Hamilton, unconscious powers revealing themselves in abnormal circumstances, are not latent states of mind, but latent memory—'capabilities of being affected, not actual affections.' The really test case is therefore the third—present and actual mental modifications of which we are unaware—the elements of perception, etc. It is a pure assumption that, when an object is perceived, and therefore affects the mind, its parts as parts must also affect the mind:

'It is a supposition consistent with what we know of nature, that a certain *quantity* of a cause may be a necessary condition to the production of *any* of the effect.'[4]

With regard to the mediate associations and acts of dexterity, Mill rejects Hamilton's test of memory—that what we do not remember cannot have been in our consciousness at all; an evanescent consciousness may be followed by an evanescent memory; if the consciousness is too fleeting to fix the attention, *a fortiori* the remembrance of it must be so also.[5] In turning over the pages of a book which we are rapidly reading, we must form a conscious purpose to turn each page, but, 'the purpose having been instantly fulfilled, the attention was arrested in the process for too short a time to leave a more than momentary remembrance of it.'[6] The interest of the sensations or ideas is momentary; there is nothing to associate any one of them particularly with our permanent interests, and so they lapse immediately from the mind. On the other hand, Mill agrees with Hamilton that there *are* unconscious modifications, but they are of the *nerves*, not of the mind.

A wound is unnoticed in the heat of battle: 'The supposition which seems most probable is, that the nerves of the particular part were affected as they would have been by the same cause in any other circumstances, but that, the nervous centres being intensely occupied with other impressions, the affection of the local nerves did not reach them, and no sensation was excited.'[7]

So with mediate association: 'The chain of causation being continued only physically, by one organic state of the nerves succeeding another so rapidly that the state of mental consciousness appropriate to each is not produced.'[8] So in perception generally, and in feelings or emotions, where we appear to have a complex resultant of a multitude of simple impressions and feelings:

'The elementary feelings may then be said to be latently present, or to be present but not in consciousness. The truth, however, is that the feelings themselves are not present, consciously or latently, but that the nervous modifications which are their usual antecedents have been present, while the consequents have been frustrated, and another consequent has been produced instead.'[9]

This is W. B. Carpenter's well-known principle of 'unconscious cerebration'[10]—mental changes, of the results of which we subsequently become conscious, going on 'below the plane' of consciousness,

[1] See C. I. Gerhardt's Introd. in Leibniz, *New Essays concerning Human Understanding* (first published in his *Œuvres philosophiques*, Amsterdam and Leipzig, 1765), tr. A. G. Langley, London and New York, 1896, p. 11.
[2] Kant, *Anthropologie in pragmatischer Hinsicht*, Königsberg, 1798, ed. J. H. von Kirchmann, Leipzig, [3]1880, §§ 5, 35.
[3] *Lectures on Metaphysics*, Edinburgh, 1859, i. 319.
[4] *Mélanges philosophiques*, Paris, 1833, p. 318; [4]1866.
[5] P. 340. [6] *Ib.* [7] P. 347.
[8] P. 350. [9] P. 351.

[1] P. 361. [2] London, [3]1867, ch. xv.
[3] P. 329. [4] P. 332. [5] P. 337.
[6] *Ib.* [7] P. 341. [8] P. 341 f.
[9] P. 343.
[10] *Principles of Mental Physiology*, London, 1874, ch. xiii.

during deep sleep, or when the attention is wholly absorbed by other trains of thought; *e.g.*, we are trying to recollect something, a name or the like, and fail; later, when we are doing something quite different, the name may come suddenly into our mind, in O. W. Holmes's picturesque phrase, 'delivered like a prepaid parcel, laid at the door of consciousness like a foundling in a basket.'[1] The suggestion is that we voluntarily, or at least through our conscious efforts, set going certain processes in the brain, which continue while our consciousness is otherwise occupied, work out the result by themselves, and send it up into consciousness. Carpenter gives numerous instances of how the automatic motor apparatus, in speaking, writing, drawing, and many other forms, reveals thoughts, memories, new ideas, which are so strange to the individual that he cannot accept them as his own; in particular, many of the phenomena of spiritualism may be so explained—table-turning, planchette-writing, and other means of tapping the buried experiences and imaginings of the self. Mediate association he also explains by the 'doctrine of resultants,' and our complex perceptions in the same way as Mill. In rapid reading, calculating, etc., the individual letters or numbers are not separately noted, although in learning to read and to calculate it must have been so.

'An impression made by it [the individual number] upon the cerebrum, which does not produce any *conscious* recognition of its numerical value, comes to be adequate for the evolution of the result.'[2]

The development of thoughts, plans, inventions, compositions, in the mind of genius, and in ordinary mortals, both normally and also in abnormal, excited, absorbed states; the influence of moral character upon action, of intellectual character and experience upon decisions; the influence of prejudice, past experiences and associations, forgotten so far as the individual sources are concerned—all these are instances of the unconscious or rather the subconscious in mind, which Carpenter interprets in this physiological way. Practically the same explanation is adopted by G. H. Lewes in *Problems of Life and Mind*.[3] Meantime G. T. Fechner's *Elemente der Psychophysik*[4] brought about a return to Leibniz's views upon the nature of consciousness; consciousness in its kind and degree depends upon the 'psychophysical activity.'

'Essentially it is just the same principle that man's psychophysical activity must exceed a certain intensity, in order that *any* consciousness or waking shall take place, and that during waking life every special determination of this activity, whether excited by a stimulus or arising spontaneously, and which is capable of giving a special determination of consciousness, must exceed a certain intensity, in order really to be conscious.'[5]

He introduced the analogy of a wave, or curve, its height at any point indicating the intensity or other quantitative value of the impression represented at the corresponding point on the base. The height of the wave as a whole must somewhere exceed a given limit, in order that there shall be any consciousness; this is the main threshold, corresponding to the main or total wave. This wave in its turn is the resultant of an 'under wave,' and of a number of 'over waves,' each of which again has its threshold. Even those ideas of which the wave-crests are 'under-threshold' or 'subliminal' may contribute to the raising of the total wave over the threshold.

Thus 'every perception of things that we know vividly, a house, a person, draws through association a mass of other ideas with it, which remain in the unconscious, and yet, unconscious as they are, constitute for us the *meaning* of the house, of the person, which otherwise would count merely as a spot of colour for the eye.'[1]

All the systems and ideas in the mind of the individual are connected, or continuous, subliminally, while above the threshold they may be discrete, separate, whether simultaneously or successively; in the same way there is continuity between the minds of all living organisms, although the consciousness of one may normally have no touch with that of another. Different psychophysical conditions may raise or lower the general threshold, in the one case breaking up the continuous into discrete life (as in the splitting of personality), in the other case combining discrete individuals into a higher unity (as perhaps in the tribal consciousness or again in the unity of consciousness from the right and left halves of the human brain, or from the segments of radiate animals, etc.). It is also an important part of Fechner's theory that the intensity of consciousness varies with the amount of continuity or discontinuity; when the soul is split into two or more, the intensity of the consciousness in each is proportionately reduced.[2] In the case of the smaller or over-waves the same principle holds; they correspond to the variations of attention and discrimination in the individual's consciousness. The more widely the attention is spread or diffused, the less the intensity of each idea; the more concentrated or limited, the higher the intensity of the thoughts that are its object.[3] It is really the dissociation that explains the low intensity of subconscious states—not *vice versa*. Harald Höffding pointed out that in many of the instances given by Carpenter and others 'not conscious' means 'not self-conscious.'[4] We do not reflect upon such ideas sufficiently for their relation to the self or Ego to be brought out. On the other hand, it is impossible not to accept the law of continuity for the psychical as in the physical world, or to regard even the unconscious in mind as simply a lower degree, a 'continuation backwards of the series of degrees of consciousness.'[5]

William James[6] ridicules the notion of unconscious mental states as a 'sovereign means for believing what one likes in psychology, and of turning what might become a science into a tumbling-ground for whimsies.' In his detailed analysis and criticism of the supposed proofs he rests partly (1) on rapid and therefore easily forgotten consciousness, partly (2) on split-off consciousness, (3) on brain-tract stimulation without consciousness.

'There are all kinds of short-cuts in the brain; and processes not aroused strongly enough to give any "idea" distinct enough to be a premise may, nevertheless, help to determine just that resultant process of whose psychic accompaniment the said idea *would* be a premise, if the idea existed at all.'[7]

This would account for the supposed unconscious inferences in perception—*e.g.*, recognizing persons by their voices, where the determining fact may be the quality of the overtones in the voice, of which the percipient has no conscious knowledge. Learning and skill James regards as predispositions—not ideas, but particular collocations of molecules in certain tracts of the brain.[8] So instincts are mechanical actions of the nervous system; our rapid judgments of size, distance, etc., are simply cerebral associations, mechanisms either inborn or acquired by habit.[9] But the main criticism is (4) that the theory springs from a confusion between having an idea at a given moment and knowing about the idea afterwards—between a state of

1 Quoted in Carpenter, p. 520, from *Mechanism in Thought and Morals*, Boston, 1871, p. 41.
2 P. 530.
3 2nd ser., London, 1877, prob. iii., 'Animal Automatism,' ch. iv., 'Consciousness and Unconsciousness.'
4 Leipzig, 1859, 21889. 5 2ii. 454.

1 P. 461. 2 P. 537. 3 P. 541.
4 *Outlines of Psychology*, tr. Mary E. Lowndes, London, 1893, p. 72.
5 P. 82.
6 *The Principles of Psychology*, London, 1891, i. 162 f.
7 P. 167. 8 P. 168. 9 P. 169.

mind as a subjective fact and the objective thing it knows.[1] A given idea must be fully conscious, or it does not exist at all; something else is there which may be a substitute for the given idea, may take its place, but is not it. This may be a brain-process, or it may be another idea. The same idea is not sometimes less, sometimes more, clear and distinct; even obscure feelings *are* exactly as they are felt to be; attention or introspection does not alter elements that are already present; it may cause them to be replaced by others. The difference is that some ideas cognize the same object more fully, completely, adequately, than other ideas which refer to the same objects; but the latter are not in themselves vague or indistinct ideas. These are purely relative notions, relative to the way in which ideas represent objects. In the chapter on 'The Stream of Thought,' however, James seems to adopt the theory of the subconscious in a thorough-going form.[2]

The stream of thought is in very large degree constituted by feelings of tendency, the 'free water of consciousness,' in which 'every definite image is steeped and dyed.' With each such image there 'goes the sense of its relations, near and remote, the dying echo of whence it came to us, the dawning sense of whither it is to lead. The significance, the value, of the image, is all in this halo or penumbra that surrounds and escorts it,—or rather that is fused into one with it.'[3]

Differences in the shade of meaning with which the same common word may be used, lapses of speech or writing, etc., illustrate the existence of the 'psychic overtone, suffusion, or fringe.'[4] The fringe is caused by the stirring of faint brain processes, or rather it represents their influence upon our minds; but, as James protests,[5] this does not mean that the fringe is a kind of psychic material by which sensations are made to cohere; it is simply 'part of the object cognized,—substantive *qualities* and *things* appearing to the mind in a *fringe of relations.*' It is especially in reference to meanings that he makes use of this conception; as on p. 281, or again on p. 472:

'*The sense of our meaning is an entirely peculiar element of the thought.* It is one of those evanescent and "transitive" facts of mind which introspection cannot turn round upon, and isolate and hold up for examination. . . . In the (somewhat clumsy) terminology I have used, it pertains to the "fringe" of the subjective state, and is a "feeling of tendency," whose neural counterpart is undoubtedly a lot of dawning and dying processes too faint and complex to be traced.'

Thus 'subconsciousness,' like 'unconsciousness,' has come to mean a variety of different things to different psychologists; the simplest standpoint is that of Sully or Ward, that there are degrees in consciousness, and that the subconscious represents the lower degrees, short of unconsciousness.

'There are degrees of consciousness. In addition to the region of our distinct consciousness, there is a vast region of the subconscious or faintly conscious. This domain consists of all those psychical elements, which enter into and colour the conscious state of the time, but which are not discriminated or distinguished. . . . With this wide obscure region of the subconscious, there stands contrasted the narrow luminous region of the clearly conscious.'[6] In the theory of attention, Sully adds, we are confronted with the fact '*that psychical phenomena present themselves in unequal degrees of definiteness or distinctness*, or, to express the fact otherwise, that they may be more or less prominently present in consciousness, or may take up more or less of the conscious attitude. . . . At any moment we may become aware of the presence of such vague elements as bodily sensations, half-developed recollections, obscure and indefinable feelings. This dim twilight region may be marked off as that of the sub-conscious.'[7]

Two assumptions are made in these statements, which may be questioned: (1) that there are degrees of consciousness, and (2) that what we are conscious of is psychical—sensations, recollections, feelings. The existence of degrees of consciousness is also pressed in his most recent work by James Ward.[8]

[1] P. 172. [2] P. 224 ff. [3] P. 255.
[4] P. 258. [5] *Ib.* note 2.
[6] J. Sully, *Outlines of Psychology*[2], London, 1885, p. 74.
[7] *Ib.* revised ed., London, 1895, p. 78.
[8] *Psychological Principles*, Cambridge, 1918, p. 90 ff.

Since there is, above the threshold of consciousness, a gradual rise in the intensity of impressions, as attention is directed to them, we can hardly suppose that before this point 'their intensity changed instantly from zero to a finite quantity.' Rather 'there was an ultra-liminal or sub-liminal phase where too it only changed continuously. The latter alternative constitutes the hypothesis of subconsciousness.'[1] He adds that the hypothesis of subconsciousness is in the main nothing but 'the application to the facts of presentation of the law of continuity. Its introduction into psychology was in fact due to Leibniz, who first formulated that law.'[2]

But ideas as well as impressions rise and fall in consciousness; those ideas which are not for the moment in the mind, or not fully presented, cannot be said to be wholly outside of the mind, or non-existent; they are not mere possibilities; there is always a tendency towards their realization—*i.e.* a psychical disposition, which other dispositions, or actualities of thought, may hinder or may assist. To the range of this second form of sub-consciousness, that of mental dispositions or tendencies, there are no assignable limits.[3]

A third meaning of subconsciousness is the split-off consciousness, which may be illustrated by H. Bergson. Conscious states, as he has pointed out, have two quite distinct aspects, and much of the difficulty of such questions as that of subconsciousness arises from the confusion between them.

'Our perceptions, sensations, emotions and ideas occur under two aspects: the one clear and precise, but impersonal; the other confused, ever changing, and inexpressible.'[4] 'Sensations . . . seem to me to be *objects* as soon as I isolate and name them, and in the human soul there are only *processes.*'[5] 'States of consciousness [*i.e.* processes], even when successive, permeate one another, and in the simplest of them the whole soul can be reflected.'[6] 'It is only an inaccurate psychology, misled by language, which will show us the soul determined by sympathy, aversion, or hate as though by so many forces pressing upon it. These feelings, provided they go deep enough, each make up the whole soul, since the whole content of the soul is reflected in each of them.'[7]

But not every impression is incorporated into this mass of conscious states; the suggestions of hypnotism, the impulses of hereditary vice, the unfinished notions of a false education, tend to form secondary, parasitic selves, which continually encroach upon the main self, and restrict its freedom.[8] This is a different interpretation of subconsciousness; the secondary selves are subconscious to the main self, which may, however, at any time assert its strength.

'At the very minute when the act [suggested by the parasitic self] is going to be performed, *something* may revolt against it. It is the deep-seated self rushing to the surface. It is the outer crust bursting, suddenly giving way to an irresistible thrust.'[9]

So for Bergson the continuity of the past is guaranteed for the present self. Subconsciousness may refer either to the healthy and normal way in which the essential and valuable is picked out from the wealth of possible impressions and ideas which constitute the self; or again it may refer to the abnormal and unhealthy functioning, against the self, or at least independently of the self, on the part of groups and masses of the ideas of the past; or finally it may refer to the supernormal way in which thoughts, inspirations of genius, moral ideals, are elaborated in the subconscious workshop, throwing up into consciousness only their finished products. It is in the last two senses that the word is most frequently used in modern pathology and occultism. See art. UNCONSCIOUSNESS.

LITERATURE.—Besides the works mentioned in the footnotes, see Alois Höfler, *Psychologie*, Vienna, 1897, p. 270 ff.; J.

[1] P. 91. [2] P. 93. [3] P. 98.
[4] *Time and Free Will*, Eng. tr., London, 1912, p. 129.
[5] P. 131. [6] P. 98. [7] P. 165.
[8] P. 168.
[9] P. 169; so in *Matter and Memory*, tr. N. M. Paul and W. S. Palmer, London, 1911, p. 188, he describes our character as 'the actual synthesis of all our past states'; we use the whole of our lived experience; true we possess only a summary or digest of it, but at any moment it is the useful which consciousness picks out, rejecting the superfluous in this great mass of material which is potentially open to it.

Jastrow, *The Subconscious*, London, 1906; C. G. Jung, *Psychology of the Unconscious*, tr. Beatrice M. Hinkle, do. 1917, *Collected Papers on Analytical Psychology*[2], ed. Constance E. Long, do. 1917, esp. chs. xiv. and xv.; C. Lloyd Morgan, *An Introduction to Comparative Psychology*, do. 1894, chs. i. and ii.; F. W. H. Myers, *Human Personality*, 2 vols., do. 1903; E. B. Titchener, *Lectures on the Elementary Psychology of Feeling and Attention*, New York, 1908; A. M. Bodkin, 'The Subconscious Factors of Mental Process,' *Mind*, new ser., xvi. [1907]; 'Symposium on the Subconscious,' ed. Morton Prince, *Journal of Abnormal Psychology*, ii., New York, 1907; Guido Villa, *Contemporary Psychology*, tr. H. Manacorda, London, 1903, ch. vii., 'Consciousness.'

J. LEWIS McINTYRE.

SUBJECTIVISM and SUBJECTIVITY.—These are terms generally used to denote that type of philosophical and theological thought which makes the thinking and feeling subject the chief factor in experience. Though the terms are often regarded as interchangeable, they should be, and generally are, distinguished, subjectivism being confined to the various forms of philosophical theory, and subjectivity to the theological. For our present purpose it will be convenient to maintain this distinction.

Subjectivism may therefore be further defined as (1) that form of pure subjective idealism which would limit the mind to the consciousness of its own states and deny the possibility of objective knowledge of things in themselves; (2) that philosophical theory which lays chief stress on the function of the subjective factor in constituting experience, and asserts the subjective origin of forms of perception; (3) that type of ethical theory which finds in feeling, and especially in the feeling of happiness, the chief aim of morality.

1. Philosophical. — On the philosophical side subjectivism, or mentalism, as it is called by some modern writers, has a long and interesting history. It has been a powerful factor in every form of idealism. Idealistic systems indeed may be said to have varied mainly in the extent to which they have allowed prominence to the subjective element in knowledge. In modern philosophy Descartes's 'Cogito ergo sum' is the starting-point, but it is not until Berkeley that we find subjectivism carried to its logical conclusion. His position is that all knowledge is relative to the subject or perceiving mind, and therefore that the world of objects is no more than an inference from those subjective experiences which are the only immediate sources of knowledge. Though Berkeley's theory is crudely stated and one-sided, it marked a real advance in speculation and made the old forms of dogmatic dualism impossible. Its author was certainly not consistent, and, when he found that his formula '*esse=percipi*' did not cover the facts, he assumed the existence of a divine mind, or a number of minds like our own, to be the vehicles of ideas. Another type of subjective idealism is found in J. G. Fichte, whose epistemological point of departure is described as an absolute Ego—not to be identified with any individual subject—which sets up a non-Ego over against it. This so-called solipsism (*q.v.*), however, Fichte does not logically carry through, for he is compelled to find certain realities in the world of the non-Ego in order to give to the moral will some reasonable end or aim. A further development of subjectivism is seen in Leibniz's doctrine of self-determining monads, by which he sought to combat the prevalent materialism which would make thoughts the objects of sense-experience. Leibniz asserted the priority of spirit and maintained the rights of the thinking subject as over against the substance of Spinoza or the atoms of the empiricists. At the same time he admitted the necessity to thought of certain sense-given material. It was left to Kant to find a way out of these paradoxes and contradictions by a more searching critical process. He laid the foundation of all future idealism by carrying out a 'Copernican revolution' in the relations between mind and the universe, or subject and object.

'Suppose we try now,' he says, 'whether better success may not attend us in the problems of metaphysics if we assume objects to be under a necessity of adapting themselves to the nature of our cognition.'[1]

On this basis Kant proceeds to establish the place of the mind and its synthetic activity in the forming of experience, with a success which is now universally acknowledged. He argued that 'perception without conception is blind, conception without perception is empty.' At the same time he vindicated the place of the object in such a way as to show that the categories of the understanding are not valid for objects apart from experience. While it is true that 'understanding makes nature,' it makes it out of given material, viz. the phenomena or data of sensibility. His vindication of the subjective factor in knowledge underlies all the various forms of modern idealism, though they differ widely in the importance which they assign to it. While the priority of mind in the epistemological process is now generally conceded, the balance between subjective and objective must be maintained. It is recognized that they go together and that they represent an antithesis which is of quite gradual growth. Psychology points to a close parallelism in the origin and growth of the consciousness of the internal and external worlds, of the Ego and the non-Ego. Neither can exist without the other, and to exalt the one over the other is to give a one-sided presentation of the facts.

2. Ethical.—In ethics subjectivism is that form of moral philosophy which finds the end of moral action in a subjective state or feeling. This feeling is generally described as one of happiness, and conduct which tends to arouse and foster it is regarded as good, while conduct which defeats it or produces the opposite—pain—is bad. In the history of ethics subjectivism appears either as hedonism or as eudæmonism (*qq.v.*). As the former it lays chief stress on feelings of sensual gratification as the end to be sought, while the latter interprets feeling in the more intellectual, or even spiritual, sense as contentment or happiness resulting in well-being. In the former, too, the happiness of the individual is the chief end in view, but in eudæmonism it is generally the greatest happiness of the greatest number that is sought. Pure hedonism is practically confined to the Cyrenaics of the ancient world. They argued that the good of man consists in the sentient pleasure of the moment, and therefore to seek as much enjoyment as possible is the best and wisest course. Aristippus, *e.g.*, held the extreme subjectivist position that we know nothing of things save the impression they make on our senses. From this it was an easy inference that pleasure, or the 'smooth motion' of sense, is the only cognizable good, and that the part of wisdom is calmly and resolutely to pursue it.

Epicurus accepts this position in so far as he recognizes that pleasure is the chief good of man and pain the chief evil, but he is very far from confining pleasure to the gratification of the bodily senses. He regards the pleasures of the mind as more important, and more worth striving after, than those of the body, as they involve memory and anticipation as well as immediate enjoyment. The happiness at which he aims is thus a finer and more lasting thing than mere vulgar sensualism, though it is still dependent on sensation. It is this wider interpretation of happiness that underlies all the later forms of eudæmonistic ethics. Shaftesbury, *e.g.*, regards inner satisfaction as the end of morals; Lotze

[1] Preface to *Critique of Pure Reason*[2].

claims feeling as the only real and final standard of value; while the utilitarians find the goal of all moral action in the greatest happiness of the greatest number. There is no question that happiness, especially in the wider and deeper sense now generally given to it, is a legitimate end of human action. But, when it is claimed that it is the only end, the claim must be resisted. There are many ends which are entirely legitimate objects of pursuit, altogether independently of the feelings which they may excite. No system of ethics will satisfy which fails to take these into account.

3. Theological.—On the theological side of our inquiry subjectivity may be defined as that theory which finds the organ and criterion of religious truth in the intimations of the religious consciousness rather than in history or revelation. All mystical theology, *e.g.*, tends to exaggerate the subjective element, in so far as it rests on a direct, secret, and incommunicable knowledge of God, as opposed to that which is mediated through creatures or through revelation. Mystical experience, however, has this peculiarity, viz. that it implies a type of consciousness the end of which is to fuse subject and object into an undifferentiated one, or to absorb the individual in the whole. It involves union of the soul with God, though God is known only in and to the religious consciousness. It was Schleiermacher among theologians who first formulated this principle and so emphasized the function of the religious consciousness as to vindicate the independent reality of religion apart from knowledge and morality. He did so by insisting that religion belongs, not to the region of reason, conscience, or will, but to that of feeling—the feeling of absolute dependence. It is through this feeling, or consciousness, that God makes Himself known to man. The appeal, therefore, in the first instance, is not to history or Scripture, but to Christian experience. 'True religion is sense (*Sinn*) and taste for the Infinite.' Schleiermacher was by no means consistent in his subjective interpretation of religion, for he always regarded it as a historical phenomenon and held that it could not be rightly understood apart from history. He laid special stress on the importance of the historical person of Jesus Christ for Christianity and finds in the redemption wrought by Him the essence of His religion.

> At the same time, as Höffding says, 'He never abandoned the conviction that the innermost life of men must be lived in feeling, and that this, and this alone, can bring men into immediate relation to the Highest.'[1]

Schleiermacher's doctrine has had immense influence on all subsequent theology, especially in the importance that it assigned to religious experience. Ritschl is at one with him on this point, and finds the materials for Christian theology in the consciousness of redemption, though with him it is the consciousness of the community rather than of the individual that is concerned. But he differs from Schleiermacher in arguing that the whole basis of the Christian system is the definite historical revelation in the Person of Jesus Christ. At the same time he still further emphasizes the subjective element in theology in contending that religious beliefs are invariably judgments of value. By this he means that they are to be estimated by their worth or value for the percipient self, according to the pleasure or pain which they arouse. He says:

> 'Religious knowledge moves in independent value-judgments, which relate to man's attitude to the world, and call forth feelings of pleasure or pain, in which man either enjoys the dominion over the world vouchsafed to him by God, or feels grievously the lack of God's help to that end.'[2]

[1] Quoted in W. B. Selbie, *Schleiermacher: a Critical and Historical Study*, London, 1913, p. 136.

[2] *The Christian Doctrine of Justification and Reconciliation*, Eng. tr., Edinburgh, 1900, p. 205.

Largely under the influence of Ritschl and his followers there has arisen a marked tendency in modern theology to lay stress on the experimental process. To some extent this has been a reaction against the excessive objectivism of the older orthodoxy, which interpreted Christianity purely in terms of a supernatural revelation. Human nature was regarded as essentially alien to the divine, and needing some powerful influence or impression from without in order to arouse its latent spiritual capacities. In contrast to this, emphasis is now laid rather on the fact that religion is natural to man and is to be found in the development of his religious consciousness. Great importance is therefore attached to the study of this development both in the individual and in the race. This has given quite a new place to the psychology of religion, particularly in the adolescent stages of human development. There is no doubt as to the weight to be assigned to this subjective process, but the reaction in its favour goes too far when it is suggested that we can find here a complete explanation of religious phenomena. Experience can be truly gauged only when it is possible to give an answer to the question, Experience of what, or of whom? 'The immediate deliverances of the Christian consciousness' are really meaningless apart from the historic facts on which they rest and which have called them forth. Nor is man's proved capacity for religion a sufficient basis on which to build, apart from the action of objective forces without, which serve to elicit it and regulate the course of its action. In other words, God must be taken into account and something like revelation allowed for before the full story can be told. It is no doubt a great gain to have escaped from the old rigid supernaturalism, which seemed to impose religion on man as something from without, and essentially alien to his being; but it is an equally false view of the situation to regard religion as a mere emanation of man's consciousness without any objective reality to which it can correspond. The right solution of the problem is to be found in giving the proper emphasis to both the subjective and the objective elements, and not enhancing the one at the expense of the other.

LITERATURE.—i. *PHILOSOPHICAL*.—Histories of Philosophy, such as J. E. Erdmann, 2 vols., Berlin, [4]1895–96, Eng. tr., 3 vols., London and New York, 1890; W. Windelband, Freiburg, 1890–92, Eng. tr., London and New York, 1893; Berkeley, *Works*[2], ed. A. Campbell Fraser, 4 vols., Oxford, 1901; John Watson, *Kant and his English Critics*, Glasgow, 1881; W. Wallace, *Prolegomena to the Study of Hegel's Philosophy and Logic*[2], Oxford, 1894.

ii. *ETHICAL*.—E. Pfleiderer, *Eudämonismus und Egoismus*, Leipzig, 1880; J. Watson, *Hedonistic Theories, from Aristippus to Spencer*, Glasgow, 1895; H. Sidgwick, *Outlines of the History of Ethics*[3], London, 1892.

iii. *THEOLOGICAL*.—E. Caird, *The Evolution of Religion* (Gifford Lectures), 2 vols., London, 1894; L. F. Stearns, *The Evidence of Christian Experience*, New York and London, 1890; D. W. Forrest, *The Christ of History and of Experience*[3], Edinburgh, 1901; J. W. Oman, *Schleiermacher's Speeches on Religion*, London, 1893.

W. B. SELBIE.

SUBLAPSARIANISM.—Sublapsarianism is the name given to that milder form of Calvinistic predestinarian doctrine (called also infralapsarianism) in which the act of God, in decreeing to save some (election) and pass by others, is presumed to have in view mankind as already fallen, and sunk in corruption, in contrast with the supralapsarian form of the same doctrine, in which mankind are supposed to be regarded simply as creatures, not having done either good or evil. The distinction is not made by Calvin, but appears in the theologians who immediately succeeded him. By help of it the grace of God is thought to be enhanced to those that are saved, and His justice vindicated in the passing over of others, since, the whole race being already a *massa* *damnata*, not any have a claim on His mercy. It is the sublapsarian view that has commonly commended itself to Calvinists, and appears in their symbols. The canons of the Synod of Dort, *e.g.*, are sublapsarian.

See, more fully, artt. CALVINISM, SUPRALAPSARIANISM, where also consult literature.

JAMES ORR.

SUBORDINATION. — Subordination (*subordinatio*, ὑποταγὴ τάξεως) is a technical term used in Christian theology to describe a relationship existing between the Son and the Father, and more rarely a relationship of the Spirit to the Father and the Son.

The doctrine of subordination was, as Dorner affirms, 'an auxiliary doctrine,'[1] and assumed various forms before a satisfactory theological formulation of it was achieved by the Nicene theologians. The Nicene doctrine is thus defined by R. L. Ottley:

> 'The Father (ὁ θεός, αὐτόθεος) is the fountain-head or root of Deity (πηγή or ῥίζα τῆς θεότητος). The Son and the Spirit, though co-eternal and co-equal, are subordinate in rank, because the Divine essence in them is derived from the Father. So in the language of Nicene theologians, the Father alone is ἀγέννητος, the Son is γεννητός: the Father αἴτιος, the Son αἰτιατός: the Father is ὁ θεός: the Son is of Divine essence (θεός). . . . As the original source of the Son's Deity, the Father may be termed "greater" than the Son. . . . The subordination is a τάξις not of time, but involved in the relationship of cause and effect. Such subordination is entirely compatible with equality of essence and majesty. So far the Nicene theology recognises the subordinationist views which had prevailed and had been carried to excess in third century writers.'[2]

Episcopius (the 17th cent. Arminian theologian) has briefly summarized it thus:

> 'Generatio divina est fundamentum subordinationis inter P. et F. Plus est esse a nullo quam esse ab alio, generare quam generari.'[3]

Although the dogmatic theologians have been inclined to base their doctrine on metaphysical grounds and to find it in the notion of generation or derivation, its basis is primarily Scriptural. Apart from the numerous passages in the Synoptic Gospels which set forth the Son as obedient to the Father in His incarnate life and as living on earth only to accomplish His Father's will, there are many other passages which set forth this filial subordination as being a feature of the eternal (not merely of the temporal and mundane) relations of the Son to the Father. NT writers who are in no sense Adoptianist,[4] but hold the Logos Christology and believe in an eternal and pre-existent Christ, are explicit teachers of this subordination. Thus the author of the Fourth Gospel cites Jesus as saying, 'I and the Father are one' (10^{30}; cf. 1^1 17^5) and also 'The Father is greater than I' (14^{28}). St. Paul, although in Ph 2^6 he writes of the Son that He was originally 'in the form of God'[5] and is 'before all things' (Col 1^{17}), yet affirms that at the conclusion of His redemptive mission 'shall the Son also himself be subjected unto him that did subject all things unto him, that God may be all in all' (1 Co 15^{28}). The writer of the Hebrews, while affirming, on the one hand, that the Son is the effulgence (ἀπαύγασμα) of His Father's glory and the very image of His substance (χαρακτὴρ τῆς ὑποστάσεως) (1^3), yet asserts, on the other hand, that he, 'though he was a Son, yet learned obedience by the things which he suffered' (5^8; cf. $2^{10f.}$). Thus, although the text of Scripture plainly taught the subordination, subjection, or obedience of the Son to the Father, yet it was a belief never held strongly without some danger to Christian orthodoxy, as is evident from a study of the Fathers of the 2nd and 3rd centuries. This was due to the tendency to interpret the obedience of the Son as denoting some inferiority in the divine nature of the Son. This was a note of Arian teaching, and it was able to claim not a few of the orthodox writers of the 3rd cent. as giving some support to its contention—*e.g.*, Tertullian, Hippolytus, Origen. This Arian emphasis on subordination produced a natural reaction in orthodox circles, especially in the West, the Western orthodox tendency being to interpret the Son's subordination as having reference only to His manhood. Hence the *Quicunque Vult* affirms that the Son is 'equal to the Father as touching His Godhead, but inferior to the Father as touching His manhood,'[1] and that 'in this Trinity there is nothing before or after, nothing greater or less, but the whole three Persons are co-eternal and co-equal.'[2] Herein it goes farther than the great Nicene theologians of the East would have ventured to go, and is perilously near eliminating the Nicene doctrine of subordination altogether. That this is not a misinterpretation of the Western orthodox tendency as exhibited in the *Quicunque* is proved by the rise of the doctrine of the double procession of the Holy Spirit a little later in the same theological circles.

The history of the doctrine indicates that there is danger in regarding subordination as possessing a metaphysical significance. The metaphysical inferiority of the Son may not properly be deduced from it. Orthodoxy affirms that the substance, essence, and nature of Father and Son are identical (ὁμοούσιος). The subordination of the Son ought not to be regarded metaphysically. It is entirely moral. Although identical in substance and equal in nature, the will of the Son is subject to the will of the Father, and this subjection is a voluntary subjection.

In the world of mundane standards obedience and subordination may seem to denote inferiority; in the realm of divine ideas there is no necessary connexion between the two. The Son is obedient to the Father for no such metaphysical reason as that the Father is the πηγὴ τῆς θεότητος, or *fons et principium divinitatis*, and generates the Son eternally (*i.e.* above and outside time). The Son is obedient because of the moral perfection of the Father. The will of the Father is that which the Son, with every moral and rational being, is morally bound to obey, not because the Father is ingenerate, but because His will is supremely good. Subordination in the form of voluntary and rational obedience, so far from being a mark of inferiority of nature, is the mark of identity with the divine nature. Christ exhibited this identity by the perfection of His obedience. In the case of men who are potentially sons of God, subordination becomes increasingly the dominant note of their nature as they grow into the divine likeness. The notion that subordination denotes inferiority of nature is essentially unchristian and subversive of the whole ideal of Christian ethics. 'He that is greatest among you let him be your servant.' On the other hand, the denial of subordination can be maintained only in the face of all the significant NT utterances on this point, and such denial tends to break up the μοναρχία by making it merely a metaphysical and not a moral unity.

The μοναρχία (or unity of the divine nature in the three Persons of the Trinity) is preserved on its metaphysical side by the doctrine of the identity of substance (ὁμοούσιος) of the three divine Persons, but on its moral side it is preserved by the doctrine of the subordination of the will of the Son to the

1 *Doctrine of the Person of Christ*, div. i., vol. ii., p. 110.
2 *The Doctrine of the Incarnation*[2], London, 1902, p. 579 f.
3 Cited by Dorner, div. ii., vol. ii., p. 349, n. 3.
4 See art. ADOPTIANISM.
5 See Lightfoot, *ad loc.*

1 'Aequalis Patri secundum divinitatem, minor Patri secundum humanitatem'; cf. the Orleans, Stavelot, Troyes, and Fortunatus commentaries in A. E. Burn, *The Athanasian Creed and its Early Commentaries* (*TS* iv. 1), Cambridge, 1896, pp. 7–40.
2 'Nihil prius aut posterius, nihil maius aut minus.'

will of the Father, and the will of the Spirit to that of the Father and the Son.

Origen's doctrine of the eternal generation of the Son, when combined with the doctrine of the Son's moral subordination to the Father, seems to provide that way of regarding the hypostasis of the Son and His relation to the Father which satisfies both the Christian intellect and the Christian conscience.

It would save confusion if the term 'subordination' were always limited in Christian dogmatics to the Nicene doctrine, and 'subordinationism' used of its heretical travesty or exaggeration.

LITERATURE.—K. R. Hagenbach, *A Hist. of Christian Doctrines*[5], Eng. tr., Edinburgh, 1880–81, i. 178–183, gives a number of pertinent Patristic quotations and also references to modern theologians. For further references see A. Harnack, *Hist. of Dogma*[3], Eng. tr., London, 1894–99, iii. 134 f., iv. 21, 23, 65 f., 72, 75, 87, 124, 129; J. F. Bethune-Baker, *An Introd. to the Early Hist. of Christian Doctrine*, do. 1903, pp. 148 f., 151, 161, 163, 177, 180; I. A. Dorner, *Hist. of the Development of the Doctrine of the Person of Christ*, Eng. tr., Edinburgh, 1892, A. i. 274, ii. 17 f., 77 ff., 80, 87, 117, 144, 175 f., 194, 228, B. ii. 160 ff., 349 f., 357, iii. 21.

H. D. A. MAJOR.

SUBSTANCE.—There have been many attempts in modern philosophy to interpret experience intelligibly without the aid of the category of substance, but, even when it has been denied in words, it has not been possible to deny it in thought. Those who rid themselves of it in particular forms or meanings to which exception could be taken are mistaken in supposing that they have thereby got away from the category itself. For the notion of substance as 'a sort of Kantian *Ding-an-sich*' is one from which we simply cannot get away. It will suffice at present to recall the position of Leibniz, that a correct view of substance is the key to philosophy, and the view of Kant that substance is the supreme and first principle of nature, which alone secures unity of experience.

1. Definition and rise.—The presupposition of the real is being. The principle of being gives rise to the distinction of substance and attribute. The attribute exists only in and through the substance in which it inheres. The notion of substance arises in experience as that of something which has being, or exists in itself (οὐσία, *ens in se subsistens*). It is viewed as distinct from phenomenon. But there is the further notion of substance as a support or subject (ὑποκείμενον, *substantia*) of accidents, as the old logicians called them. Ontologically, the former is clearly that which has the greater fundamental importance. Existing in itself is an absolute perfection of substance; supporting accidents or temporary modes is but a relative perfection.

Greek philosophy 'is dominated from beginning to end by the problem of reality (τὸ ὄν).'[1] True reality or being is accordingly our theme, as the notion of such substance has been developed from Aristotle onwards. An ever-identical substance, immutable and homogeneous throughout, was sought, no doubt, by the Eleatics, but such an inactive, changeless substance, though supposed to be psychically animated, could not give an absolute substance. For its general ground of pure being was such as to negate the very essentials of substance, which must be a unitary substrate of manifold modes or accidents. What the view, therefore, gained in logical consistency it lacked in philosophical value, and the Eleatics were driven to the denial of the phenomenal world.

The interest largely centres in the discussions of the Scholastic philosophers, and these were based on Aristotle. We have seen that substance is *per se*, accident is *in altero*. The relation of the accidents proved very troublesome to the Scholastics. Of these we shall now mention only two, in addition to Aquinas: Gilbert de la Porrée and Albertus Magnus. The position of Aquinas (*q.v.*) amounted to this, that a substance is a thing whose nature is not to exist in another, while an accident is a thing whose nature is to exist in another. But the notion of substance, taken as inclusive of existing in itself and also of supporting accidents, is very abstract and generic in character, and must not be simply transferred or applied to the real order of things. Indeed, the being denoted by substance is essential, and not merely existential, being. For all that, it was in respect of finite or created being that the substance category was applied by the Scholastic philosophers. Substance, or being, may be thought of as a regulative notion in the mind, whose content, as objectively affirmed, is determined only in the course of speculation. This is not to say that the corporeal world, and our experience of it, have not to do with the way in which we gain our hold on the concept of substance; nor is it to suggest in any way that substance is not a category of the real. The world of positive phenomena is the foundation of the world of metaphysics, but the force postulated by metaphysics is not to be identified, for all that, with physical forces. Metaphysics deals with being in itself—not in its empirical suchness. It is only in and through form that substance is intelligible; and form disappears with substance. Substance is, in fact, the persistent value which we find subsisting throughout all the transformations of phenomena, and it is often regarded as the most important of the categories. But where, or how, is this substance to be found? A substantial entity which shall meet the case is what philosophy has sought from its earliest beginnings up to the present—in vain. No existent has been found in nature, or within the whole range of human knowledge, that could really remain identical with itself while undergoing changes and transformations. It thus becomes evident how the substance concept took its rise. It was abstracted from cause, was in origin psychological, and is in character anthropomorphic. The law of causality could not suffice; some basis in eternal fact still remained necessary; but no act of perception could give such necessary or eternal fact as was required. It could only be embodied in some entity that deserved to be called a substance; it could only be witnessed to by reason itself. Philosophers who believed in a single substance called it God; those who preferred a plurality of substances still made God the supreme substance, and treated other existences as substantial only in a secondary or derivative sense. Thus it was that the doctrine of substance came to be the keystone of Continental rationalism, and we shall presently glance at the way in which the doctrine worked.

Thought was further driven to find the source of the substance concept at last in the notion of the self-identical Ego or subject, whose varying states are but attributes of this self-identical Ego. In the unity of this self or subject, amid its changing states, has been found the substance so long sought for by philosophy, unique and incomparable as it is among the substances of the world. Aristotle had already placed the primal ground in pure self-activity, *actus purus*, although this in itself could be no final resting-place for thought. His doctrine of substance as a self-active principle is fundamental in our cognitive experience. It is an intellectual intuition. It springs up in experience every time my self-activity is inhibited by anything whatsoever. It is but the inevitable making real of that which I must so interpret in terms of my real self. Substance is thus an ultimate in experience, beyond or behind which we cannot go.

Descartes viewed substance as existing *per se*, but his inveterate dualism led to two disparate

[1] J. Burnet, *Greek Philosophy*, pt. i., London, 1914, p. 11.

hypothetical substances, each of which he wrongly conceived as essentially inert. His 'thinking substance' (*res cogitans*) was being whose essence is thought; in thinking, the spirit passively received ideas; its manifestations were accidents of a non-extended substance, which was the matrix of intensive or psychical modes. Then his 'extended substance' (*res extensa*) was matter extended in three dimensions and conceived as inert; it was the substratum of physical modes; and its manifestations were accidents of an unconscious space-filling substance. It was evidently hopeless for Descartes and his followers rationally to account for the connexion or intercommunication that appeared to subsist between those two disparate substances. They overlooked that such material extension, and the modes of motion found therein, are, in our actual awareness, psychical manifestations—part of conscious content, as Berkeley was not slow to perceive. Berkeley himself, however, gave no satisfactory account—no self-consistent one—of his two substances, the finite and the infinite Spirit. The other substance of Descartes, the psychical form, was attacked by Hume, who argued that our conscious awareness is only of psychical states or particulars, and these of purely experiential origin; from all which it is clear that we cannot conclude to a permanent psychical or thinking substance. But Hume's view overlooked that our conscious states are transient, and lacking in power, agency, and enduring consistency. Such a thoroughgoing phenomenalism as that of Hume is really out of the question, and would render an intelligible theory of things impossible. The fact is that, whatever he may have done with the notion of an unknowable substratum—and substance in this sense he roundly denied—Hume did not do away with substance in the sense of something which exists in itself. He says:

> 'We may well ask, *What causes induce us to believe in the existence of body?* but 'tis vain to ask, *Whether there be body or not?* That is a point, which we must take for granted in all our reasonings.'[1]

Not only so, but he goes on in the same work to assume the extraordinary position of substantializing the accidents.

As for Locke, he no more denied substances than did Descartes, but he held that all our ideas of substances come short of exact correspondence to their objects. Substance meant for him only a supposed, but unknown, support for accidents, for a proper definition of substance he never reached. Substances were for him supposed to carry with them the supposition of some real being, and substances and modes alike were constructs (see below).

At this point some notice must be taken of Spinoza's position. Spinoza tried to prove that the two substances of Descartes, the thinking and the extended, were but attributes of one and the same substance—a substantial One-and-All.

All things and individuals he merged in this universal substance. Descartes had defined substance in an ambiguous manner, though he doubtless meant it in the Scholastic sense of that which exists *of* itself. His definition is: 'By substance, I mean that which is in itself, and is conceived through itself: in other words, that of which a conception can be formed independently of any other conception.'[2] This meant necessary being, or what the Scholastics called *ens a se*. To him God alone was substance, all was in God, and moved by Him. In Spinoza attributes are those necessary attributes which express essence. Of course the Spinozan transition from the two passive and opposed substances of Descartes to one absolute, timeless, ever-identical substance was intelligible enough. But his consistency was doubtful enough when he postulated for it a power of self-determination whereby it became (logically or not) differentiated into attributes and modes, with whatever result to its ever-identical perfection. Says Spinoza, in a formula of not very explicable character, after all the discussion expended upon it: 'By attribute, I mean that which the intellect perceives as constituting the essence of substance.'[3]

[1] *A Treatise of Human Nature*, London, 1739, bk. i. pt. iv. sect. ii.

[2] *Ethics*, bk. i. def. iii. [3] *Ib.* bk. i. def. iv.

Spinoza might, no doubt, get substance, as one and indivisible and containing an endless multiplicity, in this way, but there was a great deal to be said against his turning the term 'substance' aside from the meaning that it had borne. Spinoza also misused the category of causation, wherein cause is an essentially relative and temporal term, to style his absolute substance 'self-caused' (*causa sui*). In this way is set up his absolute substance or God-Nature (*Deus sive Natura*), but in a manner obviously open to criticism. Then, having so gained his absolute substance, he treats it, in his artificial system, as the *ratio* or logical ground of all reality.

Leibniz made substance not one, but many. He took self-acting force or power to be substance, made substance indestructible and immaterial, and broke up the one thinking substance into a multiplicity of individuated thinking atoms. These simple and unextended substances were his windowless monads, impenetrable and indestructible. They constituted essentially active entities. Activity was his basal note. But he left his self-acting force unexplained; and his monads, with no real interaction between them, were not satisfactorily accounted for either. Logical contradiction there may not be, but his supposed harmony without real interaction breaks down in the actual universe. From Leibniz, however, the individualistic character of substance—its essential character, in the concrete sense, as individuality—may be said really to date. Of course, Aristotle had regarded as the pure form not substance, applied to actual things, but individual substance—the concrete individual. But Leibniz took the conception away from its Cartesian domination by the idea of space. To him each monad is a microcosm—a mirror of the universe. Rational monads are, in the hierarchy of substances, God's agents, while sub-rational monads are His instruments. Activity, as an ideal-spiritual function, was, for him, of the essence of substantial being. But there are inherent difficulties in his theory of the relation of individual substances to the Supreme Monad, which he has left unresolved. By his dynamical conceptions, however, he had prepared the way for Kant.

2. Kantian and post-Kantian developments.—The substance notion began in Kant to shape itself in the form of a subject-activity; that is to say, imperfectly or unconsciously the substance notion was passing away from the idea of mere dead substrate into the conception of a living subject. Substance was, for Kant, that which may be conceived as subject, without itself being predicate of anything else. He had got so far beyond the substance concept as to make it a category. Kant laid an epistemological basis for the substance doctrine, which cannot be discussed here; he showed how metaphysically unfruitful was the tendency to treat thing and property in independence; he tried—and it was a new thing—to make substance one of the constitutive elements of experience. Even if he carried his work only half through, he merits gratitude for doing as much for experience as he did.

In opposing Berkeley's identification of being and the perceptions of being, Kant treated substance as merely the permanence (*Beharrlichkeit*) of the thing in the form of time. The protensive character of substance was thus emphasized. Kant viewed this persistent or permanent background as a necessary demand of thought, whereby change or alteration could be understood. Upon this permanent the notion of change rests, and the paradoxical position of Kant accordingly was that only the permanent is subject to change. But it is doubtful whether our conception of substance and quality is so much a matter of pure thought as Kant supposed, for substance is objectively real in all being as perceived and known by reason. The element of permanence, however important for philosophy, must not be regarded, in the case of specific substances, as being so much of the essence of substance as it has been by Kant, Green, and others. Substance as subject, and substance as the permanent—Kant but ill connects these two. The primary and essential idea or notion of substance is that of subsistence—that which has a proper being of its own. It was essentially by the help of the substance category that Kant thought his thing-in-itself. It is not in accord with Kant's teaching that a recent philosopher[1] has treated substance and the unconditioned as identical, in Spinozan style. Kant held that substance belongs to the category of relation, although it has been ably argued that he ought to have held more firmly to pure substance (not being put together out of parts) as pure intuition (*Anschauung*, not *Begriff*), and ought not to have made it belong to his doctrine of the categories. The substance conception, it is urged, first makes experience possible, and cannot be got from experience, which at most yields its *Vorstellung*. Against these positions it may be remarked that substance is being, and that a *Begriff* of substance is therefore possible, even if we call it an abstraction, and challenge its place in the Kantian categories.

Hegel held substance to be the absolute form-category. Metaphysics had, for him, no higher category than that of actuality: the actual is the system of phenomena; this actual is a concrete universal; it is a self-subsistent unity, like the substance of rationalistic philosophers. But the march of Hegel's thought is from substance to subject, a thought-unity which breaks itself up into its own particulars. Thought, his self-actualizing universal, became constituted through its own immanent dialectic, but with a one-sided neglect of *Erfahrung*. When it came to the absolute spirit, however, Hegel had the merit to make it a person (*einer*), not a substance (*eines*). In the infinite positiveness of the substantial this living substance, which is the eternal, is immanent and present, in his view, within the appearances of the temporal and transitory.

Schopenhauer rested the fact of change upon substance as its unchangeable substratum. To him the law of causality held only for phenomena, not for substances themselves. The world is my presentation, he says, and the ground or reason is Will. Universal, all-pervading Will is the true ground or reason of all phenomena; this, as blind and unconscious, is obviously not without affinities to the one universal substance of Spinoza.

Lotze makes substance matter of experience, and emphasizes the aspect of the self as subject in our knowledge of substance—a term which is rather ill-defined in his treatment. He has a good deal to say of an infinite substance, which encloses all things, and in which every event has its ground. His monism is resolute, but not thought out to the end. His infinite substance is conceived as in constant change: he conceives it as world-idea or animating soul of world-culture. His attempt to set out the spirituality of the infinite substance left it in too indeterminate a form. His basal insistence, however, was that the world is a unity, with one soul Being conditioning and enclosing all other being. His conception is too abstract, the inner essence of the unity not being defined. It does not seem that those who have ascribed a substantialized concept of the soul to Lotze are really right, for the substance was to him a *Schein*, and the soul was no thing.

Hartmann took substance, in the metaphysical sphere, to be pure subject of activity, and the metaphysical subject of such activity was to him, before all things, a substantial unity. The necessity for a permanent, unchangeable, non-spatial, supra-temporal substance Hartmann founds upon the fact of change. Substance for him subsists in itself and for itself, and is therefore of itself and through itself. It seems, indeed, on his full account, to be the last miracle of all. A concrete, substantial monism is what he postulates, and the modes are the changing accidents of the one concrete substance. His stress on the dynamic theory of matter led him to emphasize intensity instead of extension, as Spinoza had done. But it was on very inadequate grounds that he sought to raise the Unconscious to the position of the Absolute, or a thoroughgoing world principle. Renouvier, in the final phase of his thought, used the term 'substance' for the monad. But this spiritual substance is for him only a sign or symbol to mark the co-ordination of phenomena co-existent and successive—the continuity of memory and revolvings in time having their place. There is obviously nothing of the old term 'substance' here except the name; no absolute unity excluding every multiplicity of distinct facts, nothing but just the soul as the theory of actuality thinks of it. To the critical realism of Wundt substance is the concept which springs from the attribute of permanence. The underlying substratum of things is being, unchanging and absolute. But the concept has no great metaphysical justice from Wundt; he does not allow it to be an original concept, but takes it as ground of experience, and of purely logical import. He fails to do justice to the part played by the activity of the object, and he objects to the substance concept being applied to inner experience. Wundt and Paulsen apply it only to the corporeal world, where the atoms are the absolutely permanent substratum of all corporeal reality.

3. Conclusion.—In our discussion it has been shown that extension and motion are, in our actual awareness, of purely psychical significance. This is an important result for substance, from the metaphysical point of view. Of course, the permanence of substance amid all changes is, nevertheless, taken by science as a postulate, for it is an axiom with which the scientific mind cannot dispense. Hence Haeckel finds the last unity in substance, but his substance is too much a play of pluralistic-mechanistic elements to be a real monism. The law of substance is for him, however, fundamental, and in the idea of substance he finds matter and energy inseparably bound together. But he unsatisfactorily confounds matter and energy with matter and spirit or mind. It is, however, clear that the notion of an ultimate material substance is as completely discarded by modern science as Berkeley could have wished. In metaphysics the substance category has survived every metaphysical attack in a way which proves the term to meet something ineradicably planted in our cognitive being or experience. The fact is here, so to speak, its own ground: mere 'groundedness' is absent; the character of *essentiality* makes the concept of substance. Substance, in its most generic concept, is to be taken as real, although substance has always, in metaphysics, been non-perceptible. We can, by metaphysical abstraction, reach a notion of substance that appears, in a sense, accordant with that which is fundamentally present in modern physics, as reducible to persistent forms of energy. But Ostwald substantializes energy, holds it for substance because existing in space and time, and claims his logically over-weighted energy concept to be the most universal in science. Hartmann allows energy to be a real, objective appearance, as much as matter. But Riehl urges against Ostwald that energy is an abstraction, and that the forms of energy are concrete, so far as known to sense, and bound to spatial things. He objects to energy as a single magnitude, because every form of energy is, in his view, a product of two magnitudes, both of them real—a factor of capacity and a factor of intensity. The metaphysical implications of his energy concept have not been worked out by Ostwald in any satisfactory way.[1] It must suffice to say that experi-

[1] A. Spir, *Denken und Wirklichkeit*[4] (=*Gesammelte Werke*, i.), Leipzig, 1908-09.

[1] See J. Lindsay, *Fundamental Problems of Metaphysics*, p. 24 f., and *A Philosophical System of Theistic Idealism*, pp. 280-282, 341 f.

ence shows that, in analyzing any empirical substance, we are dealing with something that occurs in our consciousness, and has its factors there, so that our view of the world is modified by this metaphysical reflexion. One notion of substance is that it is due to the activity of an object given us in sense-perception—an activity independent and causal in its working. This self-asserting individuality of substance has been emphasized by realistic philosophers.

From the standpoint of the realist, 'the relation of mind and object is comparable to that between table and floor, and the cognitive relation—if you abstract, as you may, from the distinctive character of the mental term—is merely the simplest and most universal relation between finite things in the universe.' 'Hence such errors as that we impute substance or causality to things on the analogy of mind, instead of actually finding them there.'[1]

Substantiality is then an objective implication of our experience—in this connexion, our object-subject experience. Hence the claim of science to have established an objective synthesis of cosmical relations, whose existence does not depend simply on human perception. Nevertheless, substance must be sought, not only in the changing *continuum* of sense, but also in the self, which attests itself as substantial being behind all its activities. The transcendent substance which we seek must be found in the subject, whose consciousness of the object is so exhausted in knowledge of the object itself as not to know that it knows its object. But this knowing subject, this highest unity of transcendental apperception, is itself substance, and the support of all being, as we know it. In other words, what we are yields the fullest consciousness of substance that we have, in virtue of its self-identical Ego amid changing states or manifestations. That Ego or consciousness already carries within itself, in virtue of its own rational intuition, the whole idea of being, apprehended as substance and quality. Even Locke did not fail to incorporate the idea of the self in his views on substance, albeit in a scattered and unsystematic fashion, which deprived his philosophy of the full unity which it might have possessed.

Of course, the whole system of objects, whether persons or things, must be related substantially, or grounded in real being. Such is the basis of knowledge—the basis of science and philosophy, which are thereby made possible to us. This objectivism has need to be kept in view from the metaphysical side itself, with its deep demand for a problematic substance. For insistence is sometimes made on the permanence, singularity, and activity of substance, as attributes of substance due simply to man's projection of his own perduring, unified, and active self. In other words, the substance concept is accused of being really anthropomorphic. But an unconditioned knowledge is certainly impossible, and the world known by us may still be an honest world. Our knowledge is of the objective—the real; and knowledge is always of that which transcends what is given in mere sense-perception.[2] Knowledge of the objectively real can never be satisfactory so long as it is regarded merely as a multiplicity of parts, without being taken up into the unity of the subject. Knowledge of substance we have seen to be through its attributes or predicable qualities: there is for us no knowing substance without knowing quality; the substance so known is that which underlies or binds substance and attributes together. Our knowledge of substance is thus not of substance *per se*, as contrasted with its attributes. But, if we make substance merely a unity of the qualities, we get only a bare abstract unity, which cannot help us in any concrete fashion. Hence the real must be held, as Hegel insisted, to be the individual—the self-fulfilling subject in the manner already shown. It is scarcely necessary to refer to the peculiar use of the substance category by J. E. McTaggart, who makes minds or spirits find their metaphysical satisfaction in substance, not in self-consciousness. To him the self is substance existing in its own right, and spirits have their self-identity in their substance and its persistence. The theory is not one that is likely to appeal to many minds.

In view of all that has been advanced, the concept of substance is here taken to be that of an absolute form-concept—the absolute self-determining activity, in fact, and foundational in importance for metaphysics. We cannot get along metaphysically without this concept of substance, in some form or other, be it as matter, or energy, or soul. The substance category has yielded to that of spirit; the substance conception has been replaced by that of subject, for the substance concept has been shown to be no adequate or exhaustive one for our ultimate consciousness of what we are; and there is opened up the discovery of a real Absolute, whom, as externalized, we know as existential counterpart of the unity of experience. The way to a spiritualistic monism is thus reached, on which no more need now be said.

LITERATURE.—i. *HISTORICAL.*—The leading Histories of Philosophy; J. Lindsay, *Studies in European Philosophy*, Edinburgh, 1909, ch. ii.; J. Royce, 'Latin and Scholastic Terminology,' in *DPhP* i. [1901] 628 ff.; R. Eucken, *Gesch. der philosophischen Terminologie*, Leipzig, 1879; K. Heidmann, *Der Substanz-Begriff von Abälard bis Spinoza*, Berlin, 1890; A. Leschbrand, *Der Substanz-Begriff in der neueren Philosophie von Cartesius bis Kant*, Rostock, 1895; P. H. Ritter, *Schets eener critische Geschiedenis van het Substantiebegrip in de nieuwere Wijsbegeerte*, Leyden, 1906; A. Drews, *Die deutsche Spekulation seit Kant*², 2 vols., Berlin, 1895; J. T. Merz, *A Hist. of European Thought in the 19th Century*, Edinburgh, 1896–1914, vol. ii.; L. Lévy-Bruhl, *Hist. of Modern Philosophy in France*, London, 1899; E. Laas, *Kants Analogien der Erfahrung*, Berlin, 1876; A. Rosmini, *The Origin of Ideas*, Eng. tr., 3 vols., London, 1883–86; and the numerous monographs on individual thinkers who treat of substance; also the works of J. Burnet, and A. Spir, mentioned in the article.

ii. *SYSTEMATIC.*—T. Harper, *Metaphysics of the School*, 3 vols., London and New York, 1879–84; G. T. Ladd, *A Theory of Reality*, New York, 1899; J. Lindsay, *A Philosophical System of Theistic Idealism*, Edinburgh, 1917, *The Fundamental Problems of Metaphysics*, do. 1910, ch. ii.; C. Read, *The Metaphysics of Nature*², London, 1908; A. Riehl, *Introd. to the Theory of Science and Metaphysics*, tr. A. Fairbanks, London and New York, 1894; J. Rickaby, *General Metaphysics*, London, 1890; O. Külpe, *Einleitung in die Philosophie*², Leipzig, 1898, Eng. tr. of 1st ed., London, 1897; H. Lotze, *Metaphysic*, Eng. tr., Oxford, 1884; J. H. Stirling, *The Categories*, Edinburgh, 1903; P. Coffey, *Ontology or The Theory of Being*, London, 1914; F. E. Abbot, *The Syllogistic Philosophy or Prolegomena to Science*, 2 vols., Boston, 1906; B. Boedder, *Natural Theology*², London, 1896; W. E. Hocking, *The Meaning of God in Human Experience*, New Haven and London, 1912; A. T. Ormond, *Foundations of Knowledge*, London, 1900; G. Thiele, *Die Philosophie des Selbstbewusstseins*, Berlin, 1895; J. Laird, *Problems of the Self*, London, 1917. Among works bearing on substance from the scientific side may be mentioned: E. Haeckel, *The Riddle of the Universe*, tr. J. McCabe, London, 1902; H. Bergson, *Creative Evolution*, tr. A. Mitchell, do. 1911; H. Driesch, *The Hist. and Theory of Vitalism*, tr. C. K. Ogden, do. 1914; E. Montgomery, *Philosophical Problems in the Light of Vital Organization*, New York, 1906; J. Johnstone, *The Philosophy of Biology*, Cambridge, 1914; F. W. Westaway, *Scientific Method: its Philosophy and Practice*, London, 1912, with some relevant works on physics mentioned therein.

JAMES LINDSAY.

ŚŪDRA.

ŚŪDRA.—Śūdras are the fourth, or servile, class in ancient Hindu society, as contrasted with Brāhmans, or priests, Kṣatriyas, or warriors, and Vaiśyas, the common folk.

1. Name.—The derivation of the term is uncertain. Native writers derive it from Skr. *such*, 'to be afflicted.' It has been supposed that it was originally the name of a tribe living near the Indus, and it has been compared with that of the town Σύδρος on the lower Indus and of the Σύδροι tribe in N.

[1] S. Alexander, *The Basis of Realism*, London, 1914, pp. 10, 29.

[2] See art. EPISTEMOLOGY.

Arakhosia.[1] They have also been identified with the Abhīras and Nishādhas, a black, long-haired race of aborigines, not originally a component part of the Aryan race, but brought under its influence by conquest; and it has been supposed that, the Śūdras being thus the first tribe reduced to servitude by the Aryans, on the further occupation of India by the Aryans the name was extended to all the servile classes. The name Dasyu or Mlechchha was then applied to the unsubdued foreign tribes, who did not speak Sanskrit and had not been influenced by Aryan culture.[2] Zimmer identifies them with the Brāhūī of Baluchistān. The latest view is that the term was probably applied by the Vedic Indians to the nations opposing them who ranked as slaves, and also to various classes of humble position who supplied the needs of the village communities, and it included Aryans who, on account of some offence against tribal discipline or for other reasons, were excluded from the Aryan community.[3] Fustel de Coulanges[4] compares the position of the Roman plebeians with that of the Śūdras, as the former had no *sacra* or ancestors, and did not belong to a family or gens.

2. Legendary accounts.—The uncertainty felt regarding the meaning of the name is reflected in the contradictory legends accounting for their origin.

In the hymn known as the *Puruṣa Sūktā*,[5] when the primal male, Puruṣa, was cut into pieces, 'the Brāhman was his mouth; the Rājanya was made his arms; that which was the Vaiśya was his thighs; the Śūdra sprang from his feet.' The same story is told in the *Bhāgavata Purāṇa*, ii. 5. 37. The *Bṛhad Āraṇyaka Upaniṣad* states that Brahmā created the caste of the Śūdras 'as the nourisher. The earth is the nourisher.'[6] The *Taittirīya Brāhmaṇa* says: 'The Brāhman is a caste derived from the gods; the Śūdra is one derived from the Asuras,' or demons.[7] According to Manu, 'for the sake of the prosperity of the worlds, he [the Creator] caused the Brāhmaṇa, the Kṣatriya, the Vaiśya and the Śūdra to proceed from his mouth, his arms, his thighs, and his feet.'[8] In a later passage, however, he says that 'elephants, horses, Śūdras, and despicable barbarians, lions, tigers and boars are the middling states, caused by the quality of darkness (*tāmasi*).'[9] Again, in the *Vāyu Purāṇa* we are told that 'those who were cleansers (?), and ran about on service, and had little vigour or strength, he [Brahmā] called Śūdras . . . he assigned the practice of the mechanical arts and service to the Śūdras.'[10] According to the *Harivaṃśa*, the Śūdras were formed 'from a modification of smoke . . . the Śūdras spread over the earth are unserviceable owing to their birth with all its circumstances, to their want of initiatory rites, and the ceremonies ordained by the Vedas.'[11] Finally, in the *Mahābhārata*[12] another theory is suggested: 'Those red-limbed Brāhmans [twice-born] who were fond of sensual pleasure, fiery, irascible, prone to daring, and who had forsaken their duties, fell into the condition of Kṣatriyas. The yellow Brāhmans [twice-born] who derived their livelihood from cows and agriculture, and did not practise their duties, fell into the state of Vaiśyas. The Brāhmans [twice-born] who were addicted to violence and lying, who were covetous, and subsisted by all kinds of work, fell into the position of Śūdras. . . . He who is unclean, is addicted constantly to all kinds of food, performs all kinds of work, has abandoned the Veda, and is destitute of pure observance, is called a Śūdra.'[13]

One point seems to be clear from this medley of priestly legend—that the Śūdras, from the fact of their creation, though it was from the feet of Brahmā, and in spite of the contempt with which they were regarded, were acknowledged to be members of the Hindu polity, in contrast to the outer non-Aryan barbarians, the Dasyus or Mlechchhas.[14]

3. Position of Śūdras in the law literature.—While theoretically the Śūdras were included in the Aryan society, it became the leading principle of their overlords to reduce them to a condition of degraded servitude. This was probably due to two leading motives: (1) the desire to preserve the purity of the dominant whiter race, and thus prevent as far as possible *connubium* between the two peoples, by inflicting degrading punishments for violation of the laws of marriage, and by reducing the offspring of such unions to a condition of humiliation; (2) as in the case of the Helots of Sparta, the desire to guard the ruling race from the danger of insurrection on the part of their slaves, who were numerically superior to their rulers, and thus constituted a perpetual source of danger. The position of the Śūdras under Brāhman legislators is clearly stated in the law-books—the *Laws of Manu*,[1] and the *Sacred Laws of the Āryas* as taught in the schools of Āpastamba, Gautama, Vāsiṣṭha, and Baudhāyana.[2]

'A Śūdra, whether bought or unbought, a Brāhmaṇa may compel to do servile work; for he was created by the Self-existent (Svayambhū) to be the slave of a Brāhmaṇa. A Śūdra, though emancipated by his master, is not released from servitude; since that is innate in him, who can set him free from it?'[3] 'A low-caste man who tries to place himself on the same seat with a man of high caste, shall be branded on his hip and be banished, or the king shall cause his buttock to be gashed.'[4] If a Śūdra has intercourse with a woman of the twice-born class, if she was unguarded, he shall be mutilated; if she was guarded, he shall lose his life.[5] If a Śūdra intentionally listens to a recitation of the Veda, his ears shall be filled with molten tin or lac; if he recites Vedic texts, his tongue shall be cut out; if he remembers them, his body shall be split in twain.[6] The slaying of a Śūdra by a Brāhman is a minor offence, causing loss of caste (*upapātaka*).[7] The penalty for killing a Śūdra is the same as that for killing a flamingo, a crow, an owl, a musk-rat, or a dog.[8] Another text fixes the penalty for slaying a Vaiśya at one hundred, and a Śūdra at ten cows.[9] Eating with a Śūdra is strictly forbidden; if a Brāhman dies with the food of a Śūdra in his stomach, he will become a village pig in his next birth, or be born in the family of that Śūdra.[10] Food which has been brought by an impure Śūdra, whether he has or has not touched it, must not be eaten.[11] If a Śūdra touches a Brāhman, the latter shall cease eating.[12]

Among other disabilities of the Śūdra the following may be mentioned.

He cannot be initiated,[13] be a judge,[14] receive leavings at the mind-rite for the dead (*śrāddha*),[15] receive spiritual advice from a Brāhman,[16] sacrifice,[17] or travel with a *snātaka* (a Brāhman who has completed his studentship).[18] According to the same authority, his duties are to serve meekly the other three castes,[19] but he may not carry out a dead Brāhman, if men of the same caste are at hand, for the burnt-offering which is defiled by a Śūdra's touch hinders the passage of the deceased to heaven.[20] A Brāhman who gains his subsistence from Śūdras ranks with a breeder of dogs, a falconer, one who defiles maidens, and him who delights in injuring living creatures.[21] But, with his habitual inconsistency, the lawgiver rules that, among Śūdras, a Brāhman may eat the food of his friend, cow-herd, farm-labourer, slave, or barber.[22] A Brāhman may confidently seize the goods of his Śūdra slave, for that slave can possess no property.[23] While intercourse of a Śūdra with a Brāhman woman is sternly forbidden, a Brāhman may have a Śūdra wife, and her son receives a share of the inheritance.[24]

4. The Śūdra in modern times.—The position of the Śūdra in N. India differs from that in the South.

In Bengal a distinction is drawn between what are known as 'clean' and 'unclean' Śūdras. This is explained by Jogendra Nath Bhattacharya thus:

'To form an idea of the exact status of these [the artisan castes] and other clean Sudras, the reader should bear in mind the following rules of the Hindu caste system:—1. A man of any of the superior castes may drink such water as is fetched or touched by a clean Sudra, whether the water be of the river

1 Ptolemy, vi. 20.
2 R. Caldwell, *Comparative Grammar of the Dravidian or S. Indian Family of Languages*², London, 1875, p. 112; J. Wilson, *Indian Caste*, Bombay, 1877, i. 111 ff.
3 A. A. Macdonell and A. B. Keith, *Vedic Index of Names and Subjects*, London, 1912, ii. 265, 388, 391 f.
4 *La Cité antique*³, Paris, 1870, p. 279 ff.
5 *Rigveda*, x. xc. 12.
6 J. Muir, *Orig. Sanskrit Texts*, i. [1858] 13.
7 *Ib.* i. 14.
8 *Laws*, i. 31.
9 *Ib.* xii. 43.
10 Muir, i. 31.
11 *Ib.* i. 35.
12 *Śānti Parva*, 188 f.
13 Muir, i. 38 f.
14 See art. CASTE.

1 *SBE* xxv. [1886].
2 *Ib.* ii. [²1897], xiv. [1882].
3 Manu, viii. 413 f.
4 *Ib.* viii. 281; Gautama, xii. 7; Āpastamba, II. xxvii. 15.
5 Manu, viii. 374; Āpastamba, II. xxvi. 20, xxvii. 9.
6 Gautama, xii. 4–6.
7 Manu, xi. 67.
8 Baudhāyana, I. x. 19. 6.
9 *Ib.* I. x. 19. 2.
10 Vasiṣṭha, vi. 27.
11 Āpastamba, I. v. 16. 22.
12 *Ib.* I. v. 17. 1.
13 Manu, x. 4.
14 *Ib.* viii. 20 f.
15 *Ib.* iii. 249.
16 *Ib.* iv. 80 f.
17 *Ib.* iii. 178.
18 *Ib.* iv. 140.
19 *Ib.* i. 91.
20 *Ib.* v. 104.
21 *Ib.* iii. 164.
22 *Ib.* iv. 253.
23 *Ib.* viii. 417, xi. 13.
24 *Ib.* ix. 154; for further details of the legal position of the Śūdra see J. Wilson, *Indian Caste*, i. 46 f.

Ganges, or from any other source. 2. The water of the river Ganges, though fetched by an unclean Sudra, is not thereby rendered unfit for the high caste Hindu's drinking purposes. But every other kind of water is polluted by the touch of an unclean Sudra. 3. Even the water of the sacred Ganges is rendered useless to a Hindu by the touch of a non-Hindu. 4. The touch of non-Hindus and unclean Sudras being contaminating, it is only the clean Sudras that can render the necessary personal service to the high caste Hindus like the Brahmans, Rajputs, Vaidyas, and Kayasthas. 5. The twice-born castes cannot, without rendering themselves liable to expiation, eat any cooked food touched by a Sudra. The result of this rule is that a Sudra menial, whether clean or unclean, can be of no use to a high caste Hindu for the actual cooking of his food, or the serving of it. In fact, in the absence of his Brahman cook, the high caste Hindu has himself to cook the food of his servant. For the actual cuisine work, the clean and the unclean Sudra stand on the same footing. But while the clean Sudra can assist in the process in various ways, the unclean Sudra is not allowed even to enter the cook-room. It is for this reason that the clean Sudras alone are usually appointed menials in Hindu households. Another important difference between the clean and the unclean Sudras lies in the fact, that while a Brahman can minister to the former without losing his Brahmanism, he cannot show such honour to the latter without being degraded for ever. Further, though the Shastras forbid the acceptance of the Sudra's gifts without any reference to his status, yet in practice the best Brahmans do not hesitate to accept the bounty of the Nava Sayakas [or clean Sudras], when the amount offered is a large one.'[1]

The author seems to be unconscious of the strange picture which he draws of the caste system in Bengal at the present day. It attempts to adhere to the primitive four-group system of Vedic times; but this has become gradually broken down when certain of the so-called menial groups secure a position of wealth and authority. They retain the name of Śūdra, but they become 'clean,' as contrasted with their humbler brethren who accept a position of servitude. As he points out, the greed of the Brāhman priests is tending, by the acceptance of gifts from classes which they hold to be impure, to render the archaic system, under modern conditions, unworkable.

In S. India, on the other hand, especially by Brāhmans and by those Europeans who take their caste nomenclature from Brāhmans, the term Śūdra is applied to the mass of the Dravidian population, including many castes which claim a high social position and enforce rigid precautions to secure personal purity, such as an exaggerated fear of pollution not merely by the touch but even from the immediate neighbourhood of out-castes.[1]

'Whilst it is evident that the entire mass of the Dravidians were regarded by Manu and the authors of the Mahābhārata and the Purāṇas as Kshatriyas by birth, it is remarkable that the Brāhmans who settled among the Dravidians and formed them into castes, in imitation of the castes of the North, seem never at any time to have given the Dravidians—with the exception perhaps of the royal houses—a higher title than that of Śūdra. They might have styled the agricultural classes Vaiśyas, and reserved the name of Śūdra for the village servants and the unenslaved low castes; but acting apparently on the principle that none ought to be called either Kshatriyas or Vaiśyas but Aryans, and that the Dravidians were not Aryans, they seem always to have called them Śūdras, however respectable their position. In consequence of this the title Śūdra conveys a higher meaning in Southern than in Northern India. . . . In Southern India it was upon the middle and higher classes of the Dravidians that the title Śūdra was conferred. . . . The Brāhmans, "who came in peaceably and obtained the kingdom by flatteries," may probably have persuaded the Dravidians that in calling them Śūdra they were conferring upon them a title of honour. If so, this policy was perfectly successful; for the title of Śūdra has never been resisted by the Dravidian castes; and hence while in Northern India the Śūdra is supposed to be a low-caste man, in Southern India he generally ranks next to the Brāhman. The term Śūdra, however, is really as inappropriate to any class of Dravidians as the term Kshatriya or Vaiśya. It is better to designate each Dravidian caste simply by its own name.'[2]

In deference, however, to popular sentiment, at the Madras census of 1901 the use of the term 'Śūdra' by enumerators was forbidden. The difficulty arising from the use of the term is shown by the necessity of dividing the ill-organized Nāyar group into high, intermediate, and low-caste Śūdras.[3]

LITERATURE.—The chief authorities have been quoted in the course of the article. For the Bengal Śūdras see H. H. Risley, *Tribes and Castes of Bengal*, 2 vols., Calcutta, 1891; and for S. India E. Thurston, *Castes and Tribes of S. India*, 7 vols., Madras, 1909; G. Oppert, *On the Original Inhabitants of Bharatavarṣa or India*, Westminster and Leipzig, 1893.

W. CROOKE.

[1] *Hindu Castes and Sects*, Calcutta, 1896, p. 225.

[1] See art. OUT-CASTES.

[2] Caldwell, p. 116 f.; cf. V. Kanakasabhai, *The Tamils Eighteen Hundred Years Ago*, Madras, 1904, pp. 113, 116.

[3] L. K. Anantha Krishna Iyer, *Cochin Tribes and Castes*, Madras, 1909, i. 18.

THE END OF VOL. XI.

Printed by MORRISON & GIBB LIMITED, *Edinburgh*